1987 Britannica Book of the Year

Encyclopædia Britannica, Inc.
Chicago
Auckland/Geneva/London/Manila/Paris/Rome
Seoul/Sydney/Tokyo/Toronto

Library of Congress Catalog Card Number: 38-12082
International Standard Book Number: 0-85229-466-2
International Standard Serial Number: 0068-1156

THE UNIVERSITY OF CHICAGO
The Britannica Book of the Year is published with the editorial advice of the faculties of the University of Chicago.

CONTENTS

CALENDAR 1987

JANUARY

1 New Year's Day
6 575th anniversary of the probable birthday of Joan of Arc (1412)
12 250th anniversary of the birth of John Hancock, the first person to sign the U.S. Declaration of Independence
19 U.S. federal holiday honouring the Rev. Martin Luther King, Jr.
26 Australia Day, commemoration of the first British settlement (1788)
27 20th anniversary of the Apollo 1 tragedy; three U.S. astronauts were killed by fire during a launch rehearsal at Cape Kennedy, Florida
29 Chinese New Year, ushering in the Year of the Hare

FEBRUARY

6 Waitangi Day in New Zealand
7 175th anniversary of the birth of Charles Dickens, British novelist
8 400th anniversary of the execution in England of Mary Queen of Scots
10 75th anniversary of the death of Joseph Lister, British surgeon and father of antiseptic medicine
11 Japan's National Foundation Day
14 Valentine's Day
16 Observance of George Washington's birthday (Feb. 22, 1732)
18 20th anniversary of the death of J. Robert Oppenheimer, U.S. theoretical physicist who directed the Los Alamos, N.M., laboratory during the development of the atomic bomb

MARCH

3 Mardi Gras, also called Shrove Tuesday and other names; an occasion for gala celebration on the eve of Ash Wednesday
6 World Day of Prayer
9 125th anniversary of the U.S. Civil War battle between the *Monitor* and *Merrimack;* it was the first duel between two ironclad warships
17 St. Patrick's Day
21 Earth Day, dedicated to fostering environmental awareness and conserving the Earth's resources
29 75th anniversary of the day British naval officer Robert Falcon Scott presumably died while returning from the South Pole

APRIL

8 In Japan, birthday of the Buddha
12 75th anniversary of the death of Clara Barton, founder of the U.S. Red Cross
14 Passover, the Jewish Festival of Unleavened Bread
15 75th anniversary of the early morning sinking of the British passenger liner *Titanic* on its maiden voyage
19 Easter in both the Western and Eastern Orthodox churches
30 Projected first day of the Islamic month of Ramadan, during which time Muslims fast from sunrise to sunset
30 150th anniversary of the founding of the University of London

MAY

1 May Day, celebrated as International Labour Day in many countries
6 50th anniversary of the explosion of the dirigible *Hindenburg* as it arrived at Lakehurst, N.J.
10 Mother's Day in the U.S.
18 Victoria Day in Canada
21 60th anniversary of Charles Lindbergh's solo transatlantic flight
25 Observance of U.S. Memorial Day
27 50th anniversary of the opening of San Francisco's Golden Gate Bridge
29 Id al-Fitr, end of the month-long fast of Ramadan observed by Muslims
31 Chinese Dragon Boat Festival, observed by boat races and the eating of rice cakes wrapped in leaves

JUNE

2 Republic Day in Italy (1946)
3 50th anniversary of the marriage of the duke of Windsor, former king of England as Edward VIII, and Wallis Warfield Simpson, an American divorcée
10 20th anniversary of the end of the Six-Day War between Israel and Arab nations of the Middle East
13 Official celebration of the birthday of Queen Elizabeth II of Britain
18 175th anniversary of U.S. Pres. James Madison's declaration of war against Britain. The war ended inconclusively on Dec. 24, 1814, but it instilled in Americans a new sense of nationhood

JULY

1 Canada Day
2 50th anniversary of the disappearance of Amelia Earhart and her copilot on a flight across the Pacific Ocean
4 Independence Day in the U.S.
11 50th anniversary of the death of George Gershwin, U.S. composer
14 Bastille Day in France
20 50th anniversary of the death of Guglielmo Marconi, Italian inventor and Nobel laureate in physics (1909)
21 National holiday in Belgium marking the establishment of the kingdom (1831)
30 75th anniversary of the death of the Meiji emperor of Japan

AUGUST

6 Peace Festival in Hiroshima, Japan
6 350th anniversary of the death of Ben Jonson, English dramatist and poet
12 175th anniversary of the victory of the USS *Constitution* ("Old Ironsides") over the British frigate *Guerrière* during the War of 1812
16 Tenth anniversary of the death of pop singer Elvis Presley
23 60th anniversary of the executions of Nicola Sacco and Bartolomeo Vanzetti after a sensational seven-year trial in Massachusetts. The two Italian anarchists were convicted of murdering the paymaster of a shoe factory and a guard during a robbery

SEPTEMBER

7 Labor Day in the U.S. and Canada
11 Coptic Orthodox New Year
12 Tenth anniversary of Stephen Biko's death. The founder of South Africa's Black Consciousness movement died of head injuries while in police custody
12 300th anniversary of the death of John Alden, last male survivor of the Mayflower Company
17 200th anniversary of the signing of the U.S. Constitution
24 Rosh Hashana, Jewish New Year
26 900th anniversary of the coronation of King William II of England, son of William the Conqueror
28 Birthday of Confucius (551 BC)

OCTOBER

2 800th anniversary of the capture of Jerusalem by Saladin, the most famous of Muslim military heroes
4 30th anniversary of the Space Age. It began with the successful launching of Sputnik by the U.S.S.R.
9 540th anniversary of the proclamation of the Korean alphabet (*han'gul*) by King Sejong
11 25th anniversary of the opening of the second Vatican Council
12 Columbus Day
12 Thanksgiving Day in Canada
24 United Nations Day
24 450th anniversary of the death, at age 28, of Jane Seymour, third wife of King Henry VIII of England

NOVEMBER

7 70th anniversary of the Bolshevik Revolution in Russia
7 25th anniversary of the death of Eleanor Roosevelt, humanitarian, political activist, and wife of U.S. Pres. Franklin D. Roosevelt
11 Veterans Day in the U.S.
15 200th anniversary of the death of Christoph Gluck, German composer
19 Tenth anniversary of Egyptian Pres. Anwar as-Sadat's historic visit to Israel to initiate Mideast peace talks
20 40th anniversary of the marriage of Queen Elizabeth II and Prince Philip
25 30th anniversary of the death of Diego Rivera, Mexican muralist
26 Thanksgiving Day in the U.S.

DECEMBER

1 70th anniversary of the founding of Boys Town, Neb.
3 20th anniversary of the first human heart transplant; the surgery was performed by Christiaan Barnard in Cape Town, South Africa
16 First day of Hanukka, Jewish festival also called the Festival of Lights
25 Christmas Day
25 Tenth anniversary of the death of Charlie Chaplin, British-born comedian of international renown
26 15th anniversary of the death of Harry Truman, 33rd U.S. president
30 40th anniversary of the death of Alfred North Whitehead, British philosopher and mathematician

The Philippines
Is Democracy Restored?

BY ALBERT AND MARJORIE RAVENHOLT

Modern revolutions have a cruel way of cannibalizing both their leaders and the ideals that originally generated them. As 1986 drew to a close, it was not yet clear whether this would be the fate of the extraordinary popular revolt that had elevated a once housewifely widow, Corazon Aquino (*see* BIOGRAPHIES), to the presidency of the Philippines. With an almost fiesta-like mobilization of "people power," the Filipinos deposed a dictatorship that had robbed the now 40-year-old republic of its zestful political life and plundered its economy. This nation of 7,100 islands, guarding the Pacific approaches to Southeast Asia, had paid dearly for the years of tyranny. Two-thirds of its 56 million citizens were impoverished, many had suffered in prisons, some had been murdered, and others had fled into exile.

In February 1986, as the lunar new year inaugurated the year of the tiger, hundreds of thousands of students, nuns, and entire families of ordinary people, armed only with prayers, flowers, and food, turned back the tanks of the despot who aimed to steal his reelection as president. In a demonstration of nonviolence that sent ripples of hope throughout the lands where dictators ruled, Filipinos displayed a depth of commitment to democracy that surprised even themselves. For those who value human liberty and champion the rights of the individual, it was one of the most positive and stirring events of modern times.

It was not, however, a universally popular upheaval. Over the past 15 years, thousands of students and other dissatisfied or fearful young people had taken to the hills. Joining the New People's Army (NPA), which operates under the outlawed Communist Party of the Philippines (CPP), they established a growing alternative authority. By 1986 these insurgent forces ruled between one-third and one-half of all Philippine territory. Even on the outskirts of Greater Manila, it was a rare fishpond owner who did not pay tax to this rival government. Ambushing Philippine Army patrols, enforcing vigilante justice in the countryside, and indoctrinating recruits with teach-ins, the insurgents continued to extend their reach. In December 1986 their open organization, the National Democratic Front (NDF), negotiated a cease-fire with the new national government.

The leaders of the insurgents are doctrinaire Marxists, as they define their ideology. They boycotted the February 7 election in which incumbent Pres. Ferdinand E. Marcos and his vice-presidential candidate, Arturo Tolentino, were defeated by a united opposition led by Corazon Aquino and now Vice-Pres. Salvador P. Laurel. The Marxists had refused to join the protests triggered by the assassination of former senator Benigno Aquino on Aug. 21, 1983. They were absent from the almost religious massing of "people power" that brought Marcos's rule to an end. Only belatedly did the Communists and their ideological allies acknowledge that they had made a tactical blunder. They now seek credit for initiating popular resistance to the Marcos regime. Meanwhile, insurgent Muslim Moros in Mindanao and the Sulu Archipelago and Kalinga and Apayao tribesmen of the northern Luzon cordillera have agreed to a cease-fire that could lead to a political settlement of their grievances.

Many besides the Filipinos have a stake in the outcome of this drama. Neighbouring countries—Indonesia, Malaysia, Singapore, Thailand, Taiwan, Japan, South Korea, even China—all look with nervous concern at what is happening in the Philippines. For these neighbours, peace in the region is a prerequisite for their own internal progress. Nor do they want an expansion of the Soviet military presence into the Philippine Archipelago. For Americans the quandary is particularly acute. For nearly half a century, beginning in 1898, the Philippines was under the American flag. There the U.S. made its most sustained effort to foster democracy among another people. The two largest U.S. military bases outside North America, Clark Air Force Base and Subic Bay Naval Base, are both on Luzon. On a more human level, an almost familial relationship has evolved between Filipinos and Americans, who shared combat against the Japanese in World War II and grew to be comrades in many of life's important arenas. It is not within the range of realistic options for the United States to walk away and leave the Filipinos to a hostile fate.

Fate of a Nation. Countries and peoples, much like families, experience life in cycles; periods of setback and discouragement alternate with times of exhilaration and hope. It was exhilaration and hope that marked the "time of Magsaysay," as ordinary Filipinos call the events of 30-odd years ago. Then the country had a larger-than-

Albert and Marjorie Ravenholt have made Manila their base since soon after World War II, he as a foreign correspondent and associate of the American Universities Field Staff International, and she as an area consultant on the Philippines and Southeast Asia. Albert Ravenholt wrote the feature article "The Philippine Republic: A Decade of Independence" in the 1957 Britannica Book of the Year *and a subsequent book,* The Philippines: A Young Republic on the Move.

A soldier of the New People's Army (left) collects taxes from a local mayor in Albay Province on the island of Luzon. By 1986 the insurgent NPA forces held stern authority—rival to the national government—in more than one-third of the Philippine lands.

MARYANN DE LEO—SIPA/SPECIAL FEATURES

life president of boundless energy, scrupulous honesty, and a compelling faith in the common man. A former World War II guerrilla chieftain, Ramón Magsaysay used his shrewd judgment of men to cleanse government of corruption and restore faith in the electoral process. Picking up the tasks barely begun by the first two presidents of the republic, Manuel Roxas and Elpidio Quirino, he proceeded to rebuild the society from the chaos left by the Japanese military occupation in World War II.

Yet new nations are especially vulnerable to the unexpected. Magsaysay was killed on the night of March 17, 1957, when his airplane crashed on a mountain in the central island of Cebu. Leadership of the Philippine republic passed to the incumbent vice-president, Carlos P. Garcia. A product of provincial politics, Garcia, who was reelected in November 1957 on the Nacionalista Party ticket, declared a "Filipino First" policy that started the nation on the path of manufacturing for import substitution rather than building an agricultural and industrial system that could compete in the world market. Self-styled Filipino nationalists, profiting at the expense of consumers, jealously campaigned against the foreign commercial participation that might have forced them to become efficient. Despite its great advantages—privileged access to the U.S. market; English as the language of education and government; a corps of highly educated technocrats; vast natural resources—the Philippines fell far behind such less favoured neighbours as Taiwan, South Korea, Hong Kong, and Thailand.

Diosdado Macapagal, elected president on the Liberal Party ticket in 1961, abolished most foreign exchange controls and attempted to open up the economy, despite stubborn resistance within the Congress. The most notable accomplishment of his administration, however, was enactment of the Land Reform Code, which benefited tenants cultivating rice and corn. In every congressional district or province proclaimed a "land reform area," all tenant farmers—who usually had been sharecroppers dividing the net harvest after the cost of threshing 50–50 with the landowners—were entitled to shift to leasehold with the start of the next agricultural year. For former tenant farmers this Land Reform Code proved a boon, though not all of them have taken advantage of the purchase option, and the procedures for securing titles are complex. However landless labourers, who were not provided for in the code, have suffered; the new owner-farmers usually have proved less generous to rural labourers than the paternalistic, semifeudal *hacenderos* who preceded them.

Enactment of the Land Reform Code set in motion critical political changes, especially in central Luzon. This region had spawned pre-World War II socialist and Communist movements that joined forces against the Japanese occupiers as the Hukbalahap guerrillas. After Japan's defeat, the "Huks" were denied recognition, back pay, and veterans' benefits by the U.S. Army board sitting in Manila. Bitter and ripe for Communist propaganda, the Huks rose in revolt in 1948 against the often oppressive Philippine government forces. It was only after Magsaysay, who became secretary of defense in 1950, began disciplining the Philippine armed forces while offering land to guerrillas who surrendered that the Huks were defeated and their *supremo,* Luis Taruc, turned himself in.

As tenant farmers became owners, the Huk organizers who had retained their roots in central Luzon turned to new ventures. Beginning in 1964, escalation of the conflict in Vietnam resulted in vastly expanded activities and personnel at the Clark and Subic bases. The former Huk organization became a mafia-type operation, smuggling, dealing drugs, selling protection, and controlling filling stations, taxis, bars, and a huge gambling casino patronized by U.S. servicemen. In reaction against this profiteering, the more idealistic revolutionaries broke away and founded the NPA with its own Maoist-oriented CPP. Virtually forsaking central Luzon, they followed the early Chinese Red Army pattern of moving into inaccessible mountainous regions, like the Sierra Madre of Luzon, the hinterland of Samar, and the vast interior of Mindanao.

After Ferdinand Marcos was elected president in November 1965, some Filipinos who worked intimately with him felt that he showed great promise, though older politicians recalled that, while still a law student, he had been convicted of murdering his father's political opponent, Julio Nalundasan (the Supreme Court later reversed the decision). There also was controversy concerning Marcos's claim to be a much-decorated wartime hero, which U.S. Army records failed to substantiate. As chief executive, Marcos emphasized building infrastructure. During his first administration and after his reelection in November 1969, new roads were built and neglected ones surfaced, long-stalled bridge construction was completed, rural electrification was extended, harbours were improved, and irrigation systems were expanded. However, technocrats working with the Marcos administration soon discovered that the project proposals most readily endorsed for action were those promising lucrative contracts for the president's cronies.

Martial Law. The social dynamite that still threatens to tear the Philippines apart was planted with Marcos's proclamation of martial law, effective at midnight on Sept. 21, 1972. Announced justifications included what he subsequently acknowledged was a faked ambush of then Secretary of Defense Juan Ponce Enrile (*see* BIOGRAPHIES); insurgent moves by the NPA, then numbering only a few hundred; and deteriorating peace and order. The real reasons lay deeper, however. A new political movement, Statehood USA, threatened old-line politicians in the elections scheduled for November 1973. A constitutional convention presided over by former president Macapagal had introduced a resolution that would prohibit any previous president from being reelected. Marcos saw to it that 12 of the elected convention delegates were imprisoned, along with hundreds of opposition politicians and journalists from closed newspapers, and most of the remaining delegates were so intimidated that by early 1973 they produced a constitution that allowed Marcos to remain in office with enlarged powers. The Congress was disbanded, and portions of the chambers where the Senate and House of Representatives had met since 1916 were converted into a museum.

With the proclamation of martial law and the 1973 constitution, which was approved by a casual "show of hands" plebiscite, Marcos ensured that he could remain in Malacañang Palace. He subsequently amended this constitution twice: in 1976 to provide for a prime minister and in 1981 to accord the presidency enhanced powers, somewhat after the French model. An interim Batasang Pambansa (National Assembly) was chosen in 1978 and given limited legislative functions. At the outset some aspects of martial law were popular with many Filipinos. A reported one-fourth of Manila's adult male population had carried weapons or hired private bodyguards, and their vendettas were often settled in public places; now many of their weapons were confiscated by the military, as were the weapons of private armies linked to provincial political dynasties. Much of the press had become irresponsible and corrupt, and a significant number of the members of Congress had become champions of special interest groups often linked to their own families. Businessmen were relieved to have strikes ended (though they learned later that Marcos could mandate successive cost-of-living allowances and in time would force them to pay into a fund purportedly established to provide housing for urban employees). Marcos gained support in the countryside by proclaiming the entire Philippines subject to land reform on annually tenanted rice and corn lands. He created a Ministry of Information and asserted control of the media. The armed forces were given greatly augmented powers and expanded rapidly.

Opposition to martial law first developed among middle-class Filipinos. As the courts were politicized to serve the interests of the fraternity of power holders around the president and his prominent wife, Imelda Romualdez Marcos, that faith in the legal process so essential to fair government dwindled. The extension of Mrs. Marcos's authority as governor of Metro Manila and concurrently as minister of human settlements, her frequent foreign excursions as ambassador extraordinary and plenipotentiary, and her blatant spending at home and abroad intensified the discontent.

PHOTOGRAPHS, UPI/BETTMANN NEWSPHOTOS

Beloved former president Ramón Magsaysay (left) purged the Philippine government and began rebuilding the economy. Killed in a plane crash in March 1957, he was replaced by Carlos P. Garcia (far right), whose isolationist policies strangled the newborn hope for international market strength.

Perhaps inevitably, unrestrained power in the hands of a political cabal and the military had led to growing abuses. Surveillance of persons opposing the regime became routine, and recourse to legal protection was not available. Some who were only suspected of opposition were hustled off to prison. Torture became frequent, partly the vicious product of according unsupervised power to enforcers at all levels. "Salvaging" became the euphemism for the murder—by the military, police, or hired goons—of someone who had been arrested and never brought to trial. Military sweeps in the countryside became the occasion for soldiers to help themselves to chickens, pigs, and sometimes the daughters of rural families. There were some officers who maintained strict discipline and were viewed by the people as protectors. Unfortunately, they were rarely rewarded by their superiors.

A Traumatized Society. In the social pressure cooker created by martial law, every feature of the economy and of daily life was affected. Traditionally, three-fourths of the people relied on farming and fishing. As the population grew to its current total of 56 million—eight times what it was in 1900—pressure on resources became acute. Formerly, most farming was carried on in the lowlands, but now at least half of all rural households are on slopelands, where leaching of soil nutrients and erosion are exacerbated by intense rainfall during the southwest monsoon. Subsistence fishing declined as dynamiting and poisoning to trap fish destroyed breeding waters. Seventy percent of the population, urban and rural, is officially classed as living below the poverty level of a monthly income equivalent to $110 for a family of six, and just over half the population suffers from minor to severe malnutrition.

Rice is the basic staple of Filipinos, except for a corn-eating minority in the central Visayan islands. The Philippines imported rice throughout the early part of the 20th century. Except for Thailand, Burma, and southern Vietnam, which have extensive well-watered alluvial soils, the other countries of Southeast Asia also have been rice importers in modern times. These shortages began to diminish after the establishment of the International Rice Research Institute (IRRI) by the Rockefeller and Ford foundations in 1962. Located on land adjoining the University of the Philippines College of Agriculture at Los Baños, some 65 km (40 mi) southeast of Manila, IRRI has developed numerous new varieties of high-yield rice and greatly improved methods of cultivation. The Philippine government's "Masagana 99" program of the early and mid-1970s encouraged adoption of the improved technology by assuring rice farmers of adequate credit. Credit was occasionally misused by agents who had to approve loans, and rural banks have yet to collect some of the payments. Yet the results were so successful that in normal years the Philippines is more than self-sufficient in rice and the problem is to keep prices from dropping so low as to discourage farmers. As elsewhere throughout Asia, there is a constant tug-of-war between city dwellers who want cheap rice—and government officials sensitive to their demands—and the farmers.

Sugar production has been an important sector of Philippine agriculture since the Chinese first introduced cultivation of the sweet cane in the 14th century. During and after World War I, U.S. technical and financial interests helped create a modern sugar industry. When the U.S. Congress began regulating the sugar industry in 1934 by assigning quotas to producing areas, the Philippines was accorded its share, and this market share was protected in the independence legislation. By the 1960s the islands were supplying between 11 and 12% of all sugar consumed by Americans, at prices usually above those of the world market. After the Marcos administration took office, the Philippines encountered difficulty in meeting its U.S. sugar quota, now augmented by part of the unfilled Cuban and Puerto Rican quotas. Against the advice of its National Economic Development Agency, the Philippine government sanctioned construction of 18 new sugar mills and 3 new refineries.

The failure of the U.S. Congress in 1973 to renew the Sugar Act that had stabilized the industry for 40 years was a disastrous blow to the Philippine economy, though initially the undependability of an open market was masked by a rise in world prices caused by poor growing weather in several producing areas. The Marcos administration concentrated all sugar trading for export in the Philippine Sugar Exchange, a subsidiary of the Philippine National Bank, and later in the Philippine Sugar Commission and the National Sugar Trading Agency headed by Marcos's former classmate Roberto Benedicto. For a time these monopolies profited at the expense of growers and millers, but as world sugar prices plunged from almost 40 U.S. cents per pound in 1980 to less than 5 cents in 1984, attempts at support fell short. Mills and *hacenderos,* accustomed to living on credit, went bankrupt. Bacolod City, the capital of Negros Occidental once noted for its high living, became a depressed community.

Directly or indirectly, the sugar industry had supported some five million Filipinos, or nearly 10% of the population. Now the monocrop haciendas became scenes of destitution as starving workers marched into the cane fields and took over plots to plant sweet potatoes and other food crops. Insurgent agitators and compassionate priests joined in demanding a new social order. But crop diversification and a change in the semifeudal economy can come only haltingly; even able planters are reluctant to believe the new government of President Aquino when it tells them large-scale sugar production has no real future in a world where corn sweeteners and other substitutes are taking over the market.

Coconuts traditionally have been the main source of livelihood for nearly one-third of the Philippine population, and the archipelago has supplied more than 60% of the coconut products moving in world commerce. But despite the vital role of coconuts in its agriculture and export earnings, the Philippines has not pursued scientific research on cultivation, production, and utilization of this "tree of life." Meanwhile, coconuts have been losing out to other sources of vegetable oil; only coconuts for direct consumption or for specialty export items have maintained their market share.

The Marcos administration initiated a program for the coconut industry that may have begun with positive intentions but degenerated into a racket that impoverished small growers throughout the country. Eduardo Cojuangco, one of the wealthiest of Marcos's cronies and a first cousin of Corazon Aquino, had traded part of his agricultural landholdings in central Luzon for control of Bugsug Island off the eastern coast of Palawan. There he started large-scale production of hybrid seed coconuts. To finance farmers' purchases of these seed nuts, an export levy was imposed on all copra, and the funds were deposited in the United Coconut Planters Bank, which Cojuangco and his group (including Enrile) controlled. To further clinch their monopoly, this group and its allies bought or otherwise gained control of the mills that processed copra and exported oil and copra meal pellets for livestock feed. The hybrid coconut seed was an inferior type, but even so the monopoly reaped huge profits. Emmanuel Pelaez, former vice-president and now ambassador to the U.S., was shot by goons for speaking out on behalf of coconut farmers. At the same time, the price of vegetable oils in world markets was declining drastically, and poverty spread through the coconut-growing regions.

The situation was made to order for Communist organizers. They did not usually discuss Karl Marx or even Mao Tse-tung. Instead, they talked about the low prices farmers received for their coconuts compared with the world price, and the implication that greedy officials were stealing the difference caught on. The NPA has grown strong in the coconut-growing communities, where their alternative government operates openly. Similarly, in the Muslim-dominated regions of Mindanao and the Sulu Archipelago, where coconuts are also the main cash crop, the machinations of the so-called Coco Bank group have contributed to discontent and rebellion.

Timber, including the renowned Philippine mahogany, is another once-valuable source of foreign exchange in decline. In the 1950s and 1960s fortunes were made exploiting easily available stands close to water, but only a few companies made a conscientious effort to preserve the forests for sustained yield. Corrupt senior officials of the Bureau of Forestry allowed clear-cutting without reforestation, and during martial law timber concessions were allotted to relatives and other favourites of the Marcos clan with scant regard for forest protection. Mrs. Marcos ordered 25-year forest concession leases canceled on trumped-up charges, and these areas sometimes became grab bags for local politicians, who sent their tenants to become slash-and-burn squatter farmers. As a result, this may be the last generation of Filipinos to see a virgin tropical rain forest.

Quandary of the Young. While the nation's economy deteriorated, problems of employment were compounded. At least one-fifth of the employable adults are jobless, and another two-fifths are underemployed. Roughly half of the population is under 21 years of age, and of these 28 million young people, 10 million to 12 million are out-of-school youths who cannot afford to attend high school or college, even if they qualify. They rarely have steady employment, so there is scant opportunity for them to learn skills. The result is apathy and, sometimes, anger.

The Spanish made little progress in encouraging education during the 300-odd years that they controlled the islands, but the Americans instituted a radical change. They brought in teachers who quickly trained more teachers to staff the public schools that were established throughout the country. Once Filipinos saw that those who learned English and earned a diploma were given the jobs in government and business, they avidly took to education. The tradition of education as the largest government enterprise was reinforced after the commonwealth was established in 1935 and has continued since independence.

As of 1985, over nine million students were enrolled in public elementary schools and some 490,000 in the much more expensive private schools. Government secondary schools had just under 2 million, while private secondary school students numbered about 1.3 million. There were 319 government-supported colleges and universities—headed by the University of the Philippines system with nine campuses—with a total enrollment of about 230,000. Private colleges and universities numbered 838 with a total enrollment of 1,274,000, and the best private universities, often managed by religious orders, are comparable to the better schools abroad.

Despite this enormous educational industry, only two-thirds of the population, at best, is functionally literate. The new constitution to be submitted to a plebiscite in 1987 mandates the development of Filipino as a national language, but neither it nor any of the eight major regional languages offers significant access to technical, scientific, or historical knowledge. It is a rare individual who can get ahead without mastery of English. In reality, the Philippines is a two-class society divided between those who do and those who do not possess effective command of spoken and written English.

As the economy deteriorated and opportunities for employment shrank, an ever greater number of Filipinos began to seek opportunities elsewhere. Those with suitable skills sought to participate in the boom in the oil-producing countries. Employment agencies mushroomed in Manila as an estimated 750,000 Filipinos went to the Middle East. Another 165,000 or so are seamen. While British immigration laws allowed, Filipinas were in demand as domestic help in London, where about 10,000 are still employed, and Filipinas also found work as amahs, cooks, and housemaids in Hong Kong and Singapore, where the Chinese now preferred to work in factories or shops. Filipino technicians and hotel staff could be found throughout the region, from Sabah in East Malaysia to Guam and the Pacific island states. The remittances from these migrants became the country's largest single source of foreign exchange, bringing an estimated equivalent of $1.5 billion annually.

In the minds of Filipinos, however, the great land of opportunity has remained the United States. In 1985 alone, some 47,000 received U.S. immigrant visas, and the total since the proclamation of martial law is 480,000 legally admitted immigrants. Well over a million Filipinos are officially present in the U.S., and at least another 500,000 are probably there illegally. Filipinos are now the second largest Asian component of the U.S. population, after the Chinese, and another 500,000 are registered on the computers at the U.S. consulate general in Manila awaiting their turn to enter. Some 16,000 Filipino doctors were practicing in the U.S. at last count, and several thousand Filipino nurses go to the U.S. each year.

In contrast, no regular annual immigrant visas are issued for the Philippines, and the quota for foreign nationals seeking permanent residence is 50 per country per year; nonquota residence admissions are available to those who marry Filipinos. Under the Marcos regime foreigners were forbidden to be executives or to work in any enterprise involving mining, fishing, forestry, agriculture, or other natural resources, and they were excluded from numerous other forms of employment, except as consultants specifically allowed by presidential order. The new draft constitution prohibits foreigners from practicing any profession. A foreigner is not allowed to acquire land, even a house lot. After the proclamation of martial law, the Marcos-dominated Supreme Court ruled that any property acquired by Americans in the Philippines during the 27 years after July 4, 1946, had been acquired illegally, thus negating land titles issued under a 1946 constitutional amendment allowing Americans to own land. Most severely hurt were thousands of Filipinos who had become U.S. citizens through military service or residence and who now lost property they had saved to buy in their ancestral home. Later Marcos gave special exemption to Filipino-Americans and to Americans resident for at least 15 years, but by then most owners had disposed of their properties at bargain prices. This attitude toward foreign land ownership has put the Philippines at a disadvantage in attracting foreign investment.

For those who remain at home but lack influential connections, the struggle to make a living is intense. With roughly one-fourth of Greater Manila's eight million inhabitants living in shantytowns or slums, it is common to find teams of youngsters sorting through garbage containers, trash piles, and dumps throughout the city. In desperation, unemployed youths enter a life of crime. Syndicates of purse snatchers are often in league with collectors of *lagay,* the squeeze money jitney drivers and many others pay. After the Marcos regime fell, the extortion money extracted in return for issuing licenses to taxi and other professional drivers was reduced, but the gangs of racketeers that dominate Manila's harbour have yet to be eliminated.

An intriguing new underground industry that has emerged during the past decade and now involves between 450,000 and 500,000 Filipinos is panning and digging for gold, using the crudest methods and frequently without any legal claim. The Philippines was a major gold producer before World War II, but the mines were wrecked during the Japanese invasion. By the war's end both knowledge and men had been lost, although old-timers still told tales of rich, lost veins. This began to change after 1973, when the U.S. halted gold sales at $35 per ounce. As the price

(LEFT) ANDY HERNANDEZ—SYGMA; (RIGHT) TOSHI MATSUMOTO—SYGMA

Lean-to shacks made of rotting wood, cardboard, and tin huddle in stark contrast to nearby homes of the wealthy in Manila. Thousands of poor residents in the Tondo district make "careers" of garbage picking, reaping their livelihood from the scraps and castoffs of their rich neighbours.

skyrocketed, the lure of gold reached into remote barrios, holding out an opportunity for the unemployed. Today gold panning is a major activity in at least 20 localities. Conservatively the free-lance panners and miners recover one-half to one gram of gold a day, worth $6 to $12, and in the jungles of eastern Mindanao the occasional schoolboy becomes a peso millionaire. The best estimates are that over $1 billion in gold annually is extracted and smuggled out of the Philippines, where government regulations prohibit private trading in the metal.

Surreptitious export of gold is not new to the islands. During the two decades when Marcos was chief of state, a major effort was made to locate the gold and other valuables buried by the Japanese when they were facing defeat in 1945. A special recovery unit of the military focused on this search, and a mint that smelted and refined gold was established in Quezon City. Estimates vary as to how much of this gold Marcos and his associates removed from the country, but some who have done considerable research calculate that its present value would be worth more than the nation's foreign debt.

Benigno ("Ninoy") Aquino. The decision of former senator Benigno Aquino, known popularly as Ninoy, to return to the Philippines from the U.S. on Aug. 21, 1983, was to prove fatal to him and, in time, to the Marcos dictatorship. By fateful coincidence, it was 12 years to the day since Aquino had escaped assassination when he was delayed in arriving at a Liberal Party rally at the Plaza Miranda, where grenades tossed on the platform killed and wounded a number of candidates. The son of a prominent family in central Luzon and possessed of notable energy and wit, he had been the youngest correspondent to cover the Korean War. He had married Corazon Cojuangco, the attractive and well-educated daughter of one of the richest men in the Philippines. Like him, she was from Tarlac, where both families held sugar and rice lands. In the pattern of young, politically ambitious Filipinos, he was elected, in succession, mayor of his hometown, governor, and senator.

Throughout his career as a provincial politician, Aquino had played the rough-and-tumble role that survival demanded. He used his own armed guards and made deals for support with local power brokers, who in some Tarlac municipalities included former Huks. This was part of the charge brought against him when, under martial law, he was tried by a military court, refused to defend himself on the grounds that the court lacked civil jurisdiction, and was convicted of murder and treason and sentenced to death. Imprisoned for seven years, Aquino became a changed man, reading and thinking, evolving ideas on nonviolence based on the writings of Gandhi and others. For 40 days he went on a hunger strike. When he suffered cardiac problems, Marcos authorized his leave to go to the U.S. for surgery. He spent three years with his family near Boston, studied at Harvard, lectured, and visited abroad, including the Middle East.

Reports that Marcos was critically ill prompted Aquino's supporters to urge him to return. Although strenuous efforts were made to disguise the president's illness and his American physicians have been reluctant to talk, it appears that Marcos had a kidney transplant early in August 1983 and that it was less than successful. In mid-August members of the Cabinet reportedly said Mrs. Marcos had told them to prepare for the succession. In that time of acute political tensions, the Philippine chief of staff (and an old Marcos associate), Gen. Fabian Ver, took extraordinary security precautions. Military men met the China Airlines flight bringing Aquino from Taiwan, and he was separated from accompanying newsmen, led down an outside service stairway, and shot in the head from behind before he reached the tarmac. Rolando Galman, a small-time gangster, was shot at about the same time, before or after he was pushed from a nearby waiting van. In subsequent hearings and at a staged trial, the government tried to make the case that Galman was a Communist agent sent to murder Aquino, but this farce was so crudely managed that it only reinforced the belief that Aquino's murder had been ordered by the highest authority. A new trial was ordered after Corazon Aquino took power but, meanwhile, some of the original 26 defendants, including General Ver, had left the country.

Radio Veritas, the Roman Catholic broadcasting station, made its reputation on August 21. While the Marcos-intimidated media tried to ignore the assassination, Radio Veritas was giving an eyewitness account. Ten days later nearly two million mourners followed Aquino's funeral cortege through Greater Manila. Shocked and angered by the flagrant murder of Marcos's most outspoken political opponent, who had become an idol to many young people, the nation at last began to stir.

The Price of Abusing Power. Officially Marcos had abolished martial law in January 1981, but he had retained powers to issue commitment and preventive detention orders, and he kept in force the presidential decrees and letters of instruction through which he had controlled the society. Relatives and cronies continued to receive favours, and opponents were targets of the military. At one stage "secret marshals" were authorized to kill on sight—supposedly they were after gangsters, but innocents also suffered. Claudio Teehankee, appointed chief justice by Mrs. Aquino and one of the few jurists who had defied Marcos, said later in a public address:

> During those 14 years [1972–86], we were a nation lost in the woods of history. In place of truth reigned falsehood, disinformation, outright deception and fraud. Justice, freedom, equality became mere words used to cover crime against human dignity and basic human decency. Public office lost all concept of public trust and public accountability—lost was the distinction between what belonged to the state and what belonged to the servants of the state. They behaved as though they had received the mandate of heaven to rule, rather than to serve, and no individual rights, freedom or liberty was large enough or precious enough not to be cast into the sacrificial flames of the most capricious of

TOSHI MATSUMOTO—SYGMA

Benigno Aquino (right) meets with media people aboard a China Airlines jet returning him to his homeland on August 21, 1983, after three years of exile that had included study and lecturing. He was assassinated as he left the plane at Manila International Airport.

(Left) Presidential incumbent Ferdinand Marcos and wife, Imelda, campaign for reelection at a rally in Manila in January. (Right) In the same month, Corazon Aquino, riding with running mate Salvador Laurel in Cebu, strengthens her bid for the office.
PHOTOGRAPHS, ANDY HERNANDEZ—SYGMA

all authoritarian gods—that of national security. Every excess and abuse of power—every disregard of the sacredness of human life and liberty—every suppression of free expression—was premised on national security, even though it involved nothing more than the ruler's perpetuation in office and the security of relatives and some officials in high positions and their protection from public exposure in the press of their acts of venality and deception in government.

These were years of systematic undermining of the national will . . . of systematic looting and plunder of the economy. And it seemed to matter little which came first, the bankrupting of the national treasury or of public morality, we ended up bankrupt in both.

In an effort to give credibility to his government, Marcos called elections for mid-May 1984 to replace the interim legislative body with a full-fledged National Assembly. Every device was used to ensure that Marcos's Kilusang Bagong Lipunan (KBL; New Society Movement) would win; candidates were given lavish funds, public works were manipulated to their advantage, and in some districts newly emerged private armies were employed to register voters and to see that they got to the polls and cast properly marked ballots. Fortunately, the National Movement for Free Elections (Namfrel) was allowed to function, mobilizing volunteers across the country as private poll watchers who also participated in the tabulation of results. The opposition won one-third of the 182 members elected to the assembly, although Marcos had the power to name another 30. While the election left the KBL in control of the legislature, the opposition learned that the elective process, scarred by fraud and violence though it was, could be used to gain an independent voice in national affairs.

In November 1984 Marcos survived another health crisis and began recovering some of his earlier vitality; he may have had a second kidney transplant, although the nature of his illness has been carefully concealed. Meanwhile, the mismanagement of government and abuses of power were coming home to roost. There was a massive flight of capital out of the country as, one after another, the crony companies went bankrupt and the owners moved both their wealth and themselves abroad. As a result, the government institutions, like the Government Service Insurance System into which civil servants pay their retirement funds, no longer could provide savings for capital investment. Having borrowed recklessly abroad, the Philippines was now compelled to adopt the austerity program set by the International Monetary Fund before foreign private lenders would agree to roll over loans. The political circus was ending.

Marcos remained intransigent. He refused to retire General Ver as chief of staff, despite the popular conviction that Ver was involved in the Aquino assassination. The general, who used military intelligence funds casually for political and personal purposes on behalf of the Marcos family, seemed to have become the president's "security blanket." An indication of Marcos's fear of elimination was his stubborn refusal to have a vice-president. At this juncture the Roman Catholic Church and the U.S. government asserted themselves. The church, which claims slightly over two-thirds of Filipinos as communicants, was prompted to open criticism of the Marcos regime both by the outraged consciences of its leaders and by pressure from within. As for the U.S., the Aquino assassination had focused American attention on the calamitous drift in Philippine affairs. Particularly disturbing to the U.S was the deterioration in the armed forces.

The U.S. loss of confidence became evident with the visit of Sen. Paul Laxalt (Rep., Nev.) to Manila in October 1985. Laxalt was not a specialist on the Philippines, but he was a close personal friend of Pres. Ronald Reagan, and when he told Marcos that the old political shell game had ended, no one in Malacañang could doubt his word. About two weeks later, on November 3, Marcos announced that he was calling a "snap" election for president and vice-president on Feb. 7, 1986. He seems to have calculated that he could neutralize domestic and U.S. pressure to clean up his government by staging his own reelection. Apparently he assumed that enough votes could be bought to ensure his victory.

Commitment to Democracy. Marcos had underestimated the determination of Filipinos to win their freedom. Reluctantly, Corazon Aquino, the widow of the slain senator, agreed to stand for president provided a million

Locked ballot boxes are carried through crowds in Makati, a suburb of Manila. Several such boxes were impounded during the presidential elections held on February 7 when officials detected voting fraud at the polls. Other irregularities included vote-buying and intimidation.
ALAIN EVRARD—SIPA/SPECIAL FEATURES

Filipinos signed a petition requesting her candidacy. Her supporters reasoned that she would attract sympathy and, as a female, she was less likely than a man to be murdered. Two cousins, Joaquin ("Chino") Roces, a former publisher, and Jesus Marcos ("Tuting") Roces, former vice-mayor of Manila, took the lead in organizing the Cory Aquino for President Movement, with the former serving as the first chairman. Within a few weeks they and their covolunteers had collected 1.3 million signatures. Salvador Laurel, the scion of a prominent political family, also wanted to be a presidential candidate, but after intense jockeying and the intervention of Manila's archbishop, Jaime Cardinal Sin, a Unido PDP-Laban coalition was formed with Laurel as Mrs. Aquino's vice-presidential running mate and yellow as its colour. Unido (United Democratic Organization) was Laurel's party and the only one in the coalition registered with the Commission on Elections (Comelec) and therefore authorized to have watchers in polling booths. PDP (Pilipino Democratic Party) was headed by Aquilino Pimentel, a Mindanao politician, and Laban (Lakas ng Bayan or Strength of the Nation), established by Benigno Aquino, was the umbrella for several groups of varying strength and ideology.

It was an extraordinary campaign. On one side was the professional political machine of President Marcos, his vice-presidential candidate, Arturo Tolentino, and the KBL party organization. They were never short of money, and they dominated the electronic and print media. However, their campaign was handicapped by Marcos's lack of vitality. Marcos also was burdened by nearly two decades of promises that he had failed to keep, while his family and cronies conspicuously enriched themselves. The contrast with the Cory Aquino campaign was startling. She was the first woman ever to seek the Philippine presidency. Initially shy, this mother of five children soon gained support with her engaging simplicity. When Marcos denigrated her competence, she challenged him to come out and "stand up like a woman" to debate. Her organization, managed by leading independent businessmen and committed priests, depended on volunteers who gave their labour and paid their own way to the immense rallies that filled Manila's historic Luneta Park, facing Manila Bay. Equally vital was the performance of Namfrel, led by modern-minded businessman José Concepcion and banker Vicente Jayme. With roughly 500,000 volunteers, Namfrel belatedly won from Comelec the role of representing the public with poll watchers in some 90,000 precincts. Still, the old political machines manipulated registration, and many voters in opposition strongholds were disenfranchised.

Election day, February 7, was tense. By law the police and military are required to keep their distance from the polling booths. In many communities violence erupted as hoodlums tried to upset peaceful polling; most strong-arm tactics were on the KBL side, although the opposition occasionally tried to retaliate. Women and young Filipinos, many of whom had never known a real election, struggled to protect the balloting. The turnout among an estimated 27 million eligible voters approached 90%, but not all of them succeeded in casting a ballot. Media coverage was exceptional; nearly 900 foreign journalists and cameramen joined the domestic press to provide graphic accounts from major cities and a few rural areas. Marcos had specifically invited a U.S. congressional delegation to observe the voting, and a larger international contingent of observers joined in visiting provincial voting precincts.

As an older Filipino politician explained: "There are two ways you cheat on elections. One is when the votes are cast and the other is when they are counted. Marcos is depending mostly on the latter." After votes were tabulated in view of the poll watchers, including representatives of both political parties and Namfrel, the ballot boxes were taken to the municipal and city treasurers. Canvassing of the total vote was done at the provincial and chartered city level, and returns were transmitted to Comelec. This cumbersome process took days to complete, and Comelec, which was packed with Marcos appointees, used the opportunity to tamper with the final tally. On the basis of that tally, the National Assembly proclaimed Marcos and Tolentino as winners, to the consternation of most Filipinos and much of the world. Namfrel, meanwhile, had been tabulating results based on reports from its watchers around the country, and Father James Reuter and his associates in the Catholic Broadcasters Association were sending tabulated voting returns to Namfrel from their nationwide network of radio stations and mobile transmitters. Both tallies showed that massive manipulation had not prevented Aquino and Laurel from garnering over 58% of the votes.

People Power. Faced with the National Assembly's proclamation of Marcos's reelection, Aquino and Laurel led a prayer rally at the Luneta and adjoining Rizal Park on February 16, where some two million people massed in protest. They then traveled to the southern islands to mobilize passive resistance, including a boycott of companies controlled by the Marcos cronies. The Catholic bishops' conference issued a blunt denunciation of terror and cheating aimed at thwarting the people's will.

Meanwhile, a drama was being played out within the Philippine military. Months earlier several groups with a shared aversion to the corruption and favouritism of the Marcos-Ver regime had been preparing secretly for

In a display of unarmed "people power," supporters of Juan Ponce Enrile and Fidel Ramos—who withdrew their loyalty from Marcos—block government tanks outside the Ministry of Defense. The results of such ardour are blared in headlines displayed by a crowd at Malacañang Palace.

PHOTOGRAPHS, TOSHI MATSUMOTO—SYGMA

a change. One was led by Minister of National Defense Enrile and his younger associates, who had grouped men and weapons in the Cagayan Valley of northeastern Luzon. Another was RAM, the Reformed Armed Forces Movement, composed primarily of younger officers. A third consisted of retired generals and colonels who wanted to restore professionalism to the armed forces and end the Communist-led insurgency. These groups and others had been quietly planning a coup. The announcement of the election led them to postpone their moves, but when they saw that Marcos intended to remain in power, they prepared for action.

One plan was to cross the Pasig River in assault boats with the help of collaborators in the Presidential Security Command, kidnap President and Mrs. Marcos, General Ver, and their immediate associates, and proclaim a new, predominantly civilian government. Only hours before this plan was to be initiated, Col. Gregorio Honasan, Enrile's chief of security, learned that a double agent in the Presidential Security Command had betrayed the plot to General Ver's son, and a trap had been arranged. As Marcos's people and Ver prepared to mobilize troops to capture the defense headquarters at Camp Aguinaldo, Enrile invited Gen. Fidel Ramos, the vice-chief of staff, commander of the Philippine Constabulary, and a West Point graduate, to join him in support of the truly elected government. Enrile and Ramos later moved across the highway to the constabulary headquarters at Camp Crame, where, with some 400 soldiers, they made their stand.

For a time it seemed that the Marcos-Ver forces would succeed in destroying the defectors—the telephone lines remained open between Marcos and Enrile. Then Cardinal Sin appealed over Radio Veritas for the people to protect Camp Crame, and they came by the hundreds of thousands, blocked the tanks, prayed for the soldiers to join their peaceful revolution, and kept vigil through three nights. As a steady stream of army, air force, and navy units joined General Ramos—a count he reported regularly on Radio Veritas—Ver became a general with few troops to command. An untold story was the role played by commanding officers' wives, who in several critical instances persuaded their husbands to ignore the orders to move their troops against the revolution. In this confused period, Marcos's followers succeeded in wrecking the transmission towers of Radio Veritas, forcing it to broadcast on a weak signal from a borrowed station. The revolutionary forces soon recouped by capturing, with limited bloodshed, the government's Channel 4 and the crony-owned Channel 9, leaving the Marcos forces without television coverage.

Aquino was in Cebu City as the struggle was coming to a head in Greater Manila. She flew back to Manila, and it was decided that she would take her oath of office. At the Club Filipino in a Greater Manila suburb, she was duly and simply sworn in as the seventh president of the Philippines on Feb. 25, 1986, with Laurel, Enrile, Ramos, and other supporters at her side. A few hours later, with his popular following melting away, Marcos proceeded with his own inauguration at Malacañang Palace, guarded by troops from the mobs that threatened to storm in. It was a sad final gesture by a man who could have had an honoured place in his country's history. Instead he desperately sought any face-saving opportunity to stay and avoid mob vengeance. In a transpacific telephone call to Senator Laxalt in Washington, D.C., Marcos got the final word to "cut and cut clean."

Late on February 25 Marcos telephoned Enrile and requested him to ask the U.S. ambassador, Stephen Bosworth, for help in leaving. That night the Americans arranged for four helicopters to carry Marcos, his family, servants, and close cronies to Clark Air Force Base, but they had such mountains of luggage that some of them had to travel by road. President Reagan had offered asylum in the U.S., and early the next morning the escapees and tons of their personal effects were loaded on two U.S. Air Force planes for the flight to Guam and, after a layover, to Hawaii. In arranging their departure, the U.S. government undoubtedly saved the lives of Marcos and his wife, for the crowds that broke into the palace grounds that night were lusting for blood. The action also helped minimize the cost in life and property, which inevitably would have risen if the power struggle had been prolonged. Marcos later suggested that the Americans kidnapped him and that all he had wanted was to go home to his native province of Ilocos, but in fact he knew where he was going on each leg of the journey.

A New Era. The Aquino-Laurel government is avowedly revolutionary. The National Assembly was disbanded, governors and mayors were replaced with appointed officers, and Marcos's 1973 constitution was replaced by a Freedom Constitution incorporating selected elements of previous statutes. Some of Marcos's presidential decrees remain in force. Meanwhile, President Aquino also rules by decree, though with comparative restraint. The judiciary is being revamped and cleaned up, and new institutions include a Human Rights Commission to investigate past misdeeds of police and security agencies (but not the NPA). A board of respected retired generals is screening the military for those who have abused their positions or illegally enriched themselves. Most of the generals Marcos kept on past retirement age have been retired, and nearly two dozen younger officers have been promoted to general rank. A Presidential Commission on Good Government under former senator Jovito Salonga is screening the business empires accumulated by the Marcos clan and cronies and sequestering some of the properties. The PCGG has only begun to recover small portions of the immense wealth the former ruler, his family, and his favourites shipped abroad, often under covert identities.

In a plebiscite scheduled for Feb. 2, 1987, Filipinos are to decide whether to adopt the new constitution drafted by a 47-member Constitutional Commission appointed by President Aquino. In its essentials, this draft constitution contains many of the provisions of the 1935 constitution. One change is that presidents are limited to a single six-year term. There is a distinct separation of powers between the executive, the judicial, and the legislative branches, and the latter will again be composed of two houses, a 24-member Senate and a 250-member House of Representatives. Senators can serve a maximum of two six-year terms, and representatives will be limited to three consecutive three-year terms. A comprehensive Bill of Rights seeks to guard against future repetitions of the abuses perpetrated by the Marcos dictatorship. Capital punishment is abolished, and no person may be imprisoned for debt or nonpayment of poll tax. Independent commissions are provided for the civil service, elections, and audit. Two autonomous geographic regions are created—for the minority tribes of the northern Luzon cordillera and for Muslim areas of Mindanao and the Sulu Archipelago—each to be governed according to an organic act passed by the new congress. That congress is to be elected on the second Monday in May 1987.

The Aquino government has made an encouraging beginning, but it confronts enormous problems. The Cabinet is less than unified; most ministers had not worked together before and joined the coalition chiefly to defeat Marcos. Several Cabinet members have already set their sights on campaigning for the 24 at-large Senate seats to be filled in May 1987, and some have presidential ambitions. The New Armed Forces of the Philippines are upgrading their organizations professionally. At year's end Rafael Ileto became the new minister of defense; this low-key retired former vice-chief of staff, who served as ambassador to Iran and Thailand, is a graduate of West Point, fought with the U.S. Army in World War II, and transferred only in 1950 to the Philippine Army, where he organized the rangers. Gradually factionalism among the military is being reduced and deficiencies are being corrected, but there are differences between the military and some civilian Cabinet ministers on tactical deployment.

Moro soldiers of the southwestern islands are being paid 1,500 pesos (approximately $75) upon enlistment and given uniforms, weapons, training, and other compensations, apparently with funding from Islamic sources abroad. The NPA in some areas has done even better; in addition to the same 1,500 pesos paid to the enlistee, an extra 1,000 pesos is given for goodwill to neighbours who will be deprived of the new recruit's assistance. Official estimates of 23,500 to 26,000 hard-core armed NPA troops understate reality. Armed insurgents have been operating virtually where they choose, capitalizing on frustration among the young and offering a Communist vision of Utopia. Through the NDF, which serves as their political umbrella, the NPA and CPP negotiated a cease-fire with the government early in December 1986. The insurgents' demands for a coalition government, integration of their troops into the national armed forces, and removal of U.S. military bases were rejected. Instead, the insurgents were urged to seek their goals through the parliamentary process, raising the issue of legalizing the Communist Party. The government has not provided meaningful opportunities for those who surrender, and regional Communist commanders ruthlessly block followers who want to return to the government side. The Communists have recouped their fortunes and expanded their power since their low point, when they boycotted the elections and the "people power" revolution of February 1986, and they now use flamboyant public relations to further improve their image. Within the government, leaders have disagreed on how to cope with this growing insurgent challenge that commands both guns and votes. Now that political negotiations are beginning, they must resolve their differences.

It was unrealistic to expect that Corazon Aquino could fulfill all the popular expectations that her victory generated. Nevertheless, many Filipinos feel let down. Few recognize that the civil service had become so demoralized and mired in bad habits that long, sustained effort will be required to make it effective. Corruption has been curbed only in some ministries and government agencies. Dramatic gestures of public redress, such as President Magsaysay's Presidential Complaints and Action Commission at Malacañang Palace, through which any citizen could appeal to him, have not been implemented. The Tanodbayan, designed to function as an ombudsman, is itself bogged down in bureaucracy and busy with the new trial of those accused in the slaying of Benigno Aquino. Government banks are just beginning to turn over foreclosed properties for distribution to the landless. The desperate desire of at least two-thirds of all Filipino families to own a home with a lot where they can grow some food has yet to be met, although housing construction could be a major source of jobs.

The challenge confronting President Aquino and her administration in dealing with the Philippines' pressing needs and raising funds, chiefly abroad, demands inspired leadership. This first woman president of the republic is surrounded by a trusted inner circle that, observers report, sometimes shields her from realistic awareness of the fundamental problems of rural Filipinos. She cannot do everything. Like other national leaders, she must pick and choose among the innumerable demands for her attention. Neither is wisdom easily attained by equally hard-pressed Cabinet ministers who have little time to think beyond the immediate future. Like most governments in the less developed world, that of the Philippines was not designed for development; it is primarily an administrative structure. Filipinos who care about their country are challenged as never before. Passionately concerned civilians joined with like-minded military to make the February revolution. The task ahead is less dramatic yet tougher. How Filipinos cope with the tortuous problems of their society will decide whether their mustering of popular action to topple a truculent dictatorship was a transient, though glorious, historical episode or a major step in the building of a prosperous and genuine democracy.

Two Bicentennials: An Introduction

Two of the world's leading constitutional democracies will be celebrating 200-year anniversaries in the years 1987–88. In 1987 the United States commemorates the creation of its Constitution by the convention that met at Philadelphia from May through September 1787. Australia's celebration is of a different sort. While delegates from most of the 13 American states were arriving in Philadelphia, a fleet of 11 ships departed England for Australia carrying about 1,500 persons. These individuals would become the first colonists of a new nation when they arrived at their destination in January 1788.

These two bicentennials are obviously quite different in their focus. Australia's festivities look back to the country's very origins. As such, it is an anniversary more comparable to remembering the first English settlements in the United States, at Jamestown or Plymouth, in 1607 and 1620, respectively.

The United States, on the other hand, was already in place as a settled, well-populated country in 1787. The 13 former colonies had declared their independence from Great Britain in 1776 (occasion for yet another bicentennial celebration in 1976). In 1787 they were about to take the fateful step of forming themselves into one nation, instead of a weak confederation of 13 quarreling and mutually suspicious states. A similar federation of states would not come into being in Australia until 1901, when the act creating the federation came into effect.

If the two bicentennials are quite different in what they celebrate, there are, nevertheless, historical undercurrents that connect the two nations. There were, in each case, similar patterns of colonization. Both were colonized largely by immigrants from the British Isles. When they arrived at their destinations, whether North America or Australia, they claimed to find an empty continent waiting for settlement. In reality, of course, the continents were only said to be empty. Each had its native populations: North America its hundreds of Indian tribes and Australia its Aborigines. Each of these populations, in time, became a disadvantaged minority. They lost much of their land and became underclasses virtually subject to the increasingly more numerous white colonists.

A more positive assessment of the two bicentennials can be made by regarding the constitutional traditions of each country. Both nations were rooted in English constitutionalism, as it had developed since Magna Carta in 1215. These very issues of constitutionalism, or representative government, and of the rights of Englishmen first became paramount in the North American colonies and divided the colonies from the mother country.

What happened in North America cast a long shadow on the later development of the Commonwealth of Nations. After the American Revolution, no other British colony found it necessary to declare its independence unilaterally until Rhodesia did so in 1965 (but for quite different reasons). Britain assessed the damage of 1776 and moved more cautiously with the remaining colonies.

Another positive consideration is the impact the Constitution of 1787 has had around the world. In the year the new Constitution began functioning, France launched its revolution. Within two decades the Spanish colonies of Central and South America would pattern their revolutions (although not necessarily their governments) on what had happened in the United States. The experiment of 1787, giving rise to what is now the oldest government with a written constitution, also served to inspire the future independent members of the Commonwealth. The forms of government are not precisely the same: Australia has a parliamentary, Cabinet system, in contrast to the separation of powers in the federal government of the United States. But the persistent development of political democracy, inaugurated in England and carried forward in the United States, has been emulated in Australia's historical progress.

In the following pages the two bicentennials are examined in the context of historical significance and current relevance.

Mortimer J. Adler, philosopher, author, and chairman of the Board of Editors of Encyclopædia Britannica, reflects on the role played by the United States Constitution in creating a nation and a sense of nationhood.

Kenneth Inglis, professor of history at the Australian National University and a scholar of Australian and American government, explores the bicentennial celebration about to start in his continent-country, with occasional asides on the American experience.

The Real American Bicentennial

BY MORTIMER J. ADLER

The bicentennial celebrated by the United States of America in 1976 was the 200th anniversary of its Declaration of Independence, but assuredly not of the establishment of the nation the world knows by that name today.

To be sure, that Declaration spoke for "the United States of America," but in fact the 13 rebellious colonies that there proclaimed themselves states were united only in their resolution to fight for independence from the British crown. Indeed they reached that agreement only after more than a year of actual warfare. The only link between the states was a Continental Congress, which did not even have the power to levy taxes but had to raise by persuasion funds to support the Continental—not U.S.—Army.

In 1781 the Continental Congress managed to work out a compact to connect the 13 sovereign states in some kind of formal structure. And that pact, the "Articles of Confederation and perpetual Union between the States," quickly proved incapable of perpetuating union, or even of preserving the hard-won peace.

In order to conduct foreign and even interstate trade, to settle boundary quarrels, indeed to coexist, the states were obliged to negotiate with one another. The peacetime union proved to be as shaky as that of the wartime days before the Articles of Confederation. At last, out of a series of meetings among a few of the states over navigation and fishing rights grew the momentous convention at Philadelphia in the summer of 1787.

From united states to United States. Although the delegations of the 12 states[1] that attended the Philadelphia convention were not authorized by their legislatures to do so, once there a majority of them recognized the need "to form a more perfect Union," and consciously set about creating a "Constitution for the United States of America."

The document framing and formulating that more perfect union was properly called a "constitution" for, once ratified, it did two things a constitution should do.

Both were things the Articles of Confederation did not do and could never do, for the Articles had merely established an alliance of sovereign states, and no more created an organic union than does the Charter of the United Nations.

In the first place, the great document of 1787 *constituted* a single, sovereign state out of the 13 formerly independent states.

In the second place, the Constitution of the United States established a government, outlined its purposes, limited its scope, identified by name and function the several branches of that government, and defined the offices of each branch, specifying how they should be filled and how the authority and power vested in each should be related one to another.

While they were engaged in their war for independence, the former colonies might properly have referred to themselves as "the united states of America," but not until the adoption of the Constitution could they be styled "the United States of America" as the world now understands that term.

At Gettysburg in 1863, Abraham Lincoln said, "Four score and seven years ago [1776] our fathers brought forth on this continent a new nation. . . ." How are we to interpret that? Clearly, Lincoln meant by it a new *people,* for the term nation that he used originated in the Latin word *nascor,* "to be born"; the use of "nation" in the sense of nation-state is a 20th-century development. And a new people was indeed brought forth by the Declaration, but it remained for the Constitution to fashion that people into a single nation-state out of 13 formerly sovereign states.

Strictly speaking in contemporary terms, it remained for the adoption and implementation of the Constitution to make a nation of the American people. Put another way, the Constitution forged the American nation into a state. It created the first federal republic in history.

The phrase "United States" appears twice in the Preamble to the Constitution:

> We the People of the United States, in Order to form a more perfect Union, establish Justice, insure domestic Tranquility, provide for the common defence, promote the general Welfare, and secure the Blessings of Liberty to ourselves and our Posterity, do ordain and establish this Constitution for the United States of America.

In its first appearance in the Preamble, the phrase should have been written "united states," as it should have appeared in the Declaration, for when the Constitution was promulgated by the 1787 convention the 13 quarrelsome, independent states were still linked only by the Articles of Confederation.

LIBRARY OF CONGRESS

The Preamble to the Constitution defines in brief the encompassing purpose of the document. The "more perfect Union" intended for the 13 states was to become the first federal republic in history.

A painting depicts George Washington presiding at the 1787 Constitutional Convention in Philadelphia. The date of the gathering may be considered the conception date of the United States of America because the delegates were the first to adopt the Constitution. Not until 1789 was the charter implemented.
THE GRANGER COLLECTION, NEW YORK

In its second appearance in the Preamble, the capital initial letters in United States are appropriate, because that phrase should be interpreted as prospective. It refers to the nation or national state that will come into existence only when the document of 1787 has been ratified and implemented.

For ratification, two-thirds of the 13 states had to adopt the proposed Constitution, and that did not come to pass until June of 1788, with the other states falling into line somewhat later. Not until 1789 was the new charter actually implemented, with the United States Congress supplanting the Continental Congress, and with the inauguration of George Washington to the new office of president of the United States.

In political as well as biologic life there is a period of gestation between conception and birth. In American history we may think of 1789 as the birth of the United States of America, and the adoption of the Constitution by the Philadelphia convention in August of 1787 as its conception. The months of turbulent debate over ratification that went on between those dates were its period of gestation.

In some human cultures, age is counted from conception, rather than from birth. In these terms 1987 is the bicentennial of the United States. That bicentennial can also be appropriately seen as a three-year celebration to conclude on April 30, 1989 (the bicentenary of Washington's first inauguration as president). But whatever date or dates we select, the great accomplishment of 1787 is well worth celebrating. Indeed much of the world has celebrated it for many of its 200 years, not infrequently by imitation.

The Birth of Constitutional Government. The idea of constitutional government, as radically contrasted with royal or despotic regimes, is as old as ancient Greece. We are told that among Aristotle's political works was a treatise on Greek constitutions in which he described and discussed more than 100 of them, although his account of only one—that of Athens—has survived.

Plato distinguished legitimate governments from illegitimate ones by the supremacy of laws instead of the supremacy of men. Following Plato, Aristotle defined a constitution as the fundamental law that conferred rightful authority, and in one remarkable passage he described those who first founded a state as the greatest of benefactors. Although we do not know, it is reasonable to conjecture that he had in mind Solon and Lycurgus, who framed constitutions, respectively, for Athens and Sparta.

In earlier societies, the people living under the rule of Egyptian pharaohs or Persian kings were subjects or slaves, not citizens. That kind of government—absolute, royal, or despotic—is appropriate for families, Aristotle said, but not for states. States do not come into existence until governments are constituted—until constitutions come into existence. It was the invention of constitutions by the ancient Greeks that introduced the state and, with it, the concept of citizenship.

While it was manifestly not the first ever created, it is true that the Constitution of the United States was the first national constitution ever deliberately drafted by a group of men meeting for that purpose in what they themselves called a constitutional convention. And with ratification of the Constitution by the ninth state, constitutional government began in the United States at one fell swoop.

This was not at all the case with the oldest constitutional government in the modern world, that which began in England with Magna Carta in 1215. Magna Carta was only the first step in a long series of enactments that limited the power of English kings, increased the power of representative parliaments, and made those who voted for members of parliament self-governing citizens as well as subjects of the king.

It is worth noting that although we speak of the British constitution as an unwritten one, all of the enactments that cumulatively comprise British constitutional law are in fact written. They simply are not gathered into a single document. The fact that the U.S. Constitution as promulgated in 1787 and ratified in 1788 is a single instrument is one of its unique qualities.

Toward a More Perfect Union. In their Preamble to the Constitution, the American founding fathers declared their intention "to form a more perfect Union." The greater perfection they sought, and attained, lies in a single fact. Under the Articles of Confederation, each of the 13 states retained its individual sovereignty, not diminished one whit or in any respect by its confederacy with the other 12 states. But under the Constitution each of the 13 states surrendered all of its external sovereignty, both in relation to the other American states and in relation to foreign states in the arena of international affairs.

Yet the 13 retained a significant measure of internal sovereignty. Each state remained sovereign in relation to the U.S. citizens living within that particular state. The Constitution introduced the novel concept of dual sovereignty: each state sovereign within its own boundaries and in the governance of its internal affairs; and it made the federal union of states sovereign in war and peace, in international trade and commerce, in foreign relations, and in all other international affairs.

Part and parcel of the notion of dual sovereignty was that of dual citizenship: the citizen of each individual state was at the same time a citizen of the United States.

Under the Articles of Confederation, citizenship was unitary; a citizen of Virginia had no special standing in New York. Sovereignty was unitary, too. While the states retained their external sovereignty, as they did under the Articles of Confederation, they were free to make treaties and alliances with one another, and ultimately to make war with one another. Although actual military action between states never quite came to pass under the Confederation, disputes over trade, access to seaports, navigation and fishing rights in shared bodies of water, and other such problems demonstrated to the wise men in all the states the perils and shortcomings embedded in the Articles of Confederation and ultimately led them to Philadelphia in 1787.

The very same concerns were repeatedly invoked in the campaign for ratification. Particularly in the first nine of *The Federalist Papers,* Alexander Hamilton, James Madison, and John Jay called attention to the intermittent but incessant warfare among the separate unfederated sovereign states of Europe. What could prevent the same thing from befalling the unfederated American states? Nothing, they answered, except the more perfect union offered by the federal constitution and the surrender by the states of their external sovereignty in relation to one another as well as in relation to other states abroad.

For all their participation in United States citizenship, most Americans continued to think of themselves first as citizens of their particular states. This remained the case throughout the country until well after the Civil War, and in the seceding states for many decades after that. Gradually, however, and especially since the turn of the 19th century, the Americans' sense of U.S. citizenship as primary has spread to the point where it is almost universal.

The Slavery Issue. The fact that that kind of popular perception of federal citizenship as primary was so long in coming to pass reflects another important truth about the Constitution. Its framers sought a *more perfect* union; they did not promise a *perfect* one. Many differences between states and regions were worked out in the Philadelphia convention, but the fundamental division between North and South over the issue of slavery was beyond resolution and so was compromised in the convention in Article I Sections 2 and 9, and in Article V.

The former section, dealing with apportionment of the House of Representatives, counted

> the whole Number of free Persons, including those bound to Service for a Term of Years, and excluding Indians not taxed, three fifths of all other Persons.

The "other persons" were slaves. Slavery was thus acknowledged by the Constitution, and the sparsely populated southern, slaveholding states were allowed to count slaves toward their congressional apportionment—but only at a reduced rate (three-fifths) so as not to inflate their share of representatives enough to threaten the numerical superiority of the northern states.

Article I Section 9 provided, in its first paragraph, that this unnatural condition had to prevail for at least 20 years:

> The Migration or Importation of such Persons as any of the States now existing shall think proper to admit, shall not be prohibited by the Congress prior to the Year one thousand eight hundred and eight, . . .

Thus antislavery delegates traded tacit acceptance of slavery *now* for congressional freedom to outlaw it 20 years hence.

Article V provided for amending the Constitution, and its penultimate clause protected the 20-year inviolability of slavery written into Article I Section 9:

> provided that no Amendment which may be made prior to the Year One thousand eight hundred and eight shall in any Manner affect the first and fourth Clauses in the Ninth Section of the First Article; . . .

(The fourth clause prohibited a head tax on the "importation of certain persons.")

Thus from the language of the Constitution it is evident that the charter established only a *more perfect,* and not a *perfect,* Union.

But the founders, in the very Article V partially quoted above, created a mechanism for the process of perfecting

PROJECT '87 OF THE AMERICAN HISTORICAL ASSOC. AND THE AMERICAN POLITICAL SCIENCE ASSOC.

The 1787 Assembly Room of the Old State House in Philadelphia is the subject of one of 12 commemorative posters by Project '87 for the exhibit "The Blessings of Liberty."

The U.S. Constitution and Declaration of Independence are displayed at the National Archives in Washington, D.C. Helium-filled, sealed cases protect them from what would be normal deterioration.
NATIONAL ARCHIVES; PHOTOGRAPH, HUGH TALMAN

to continue, giving to the Congress or to the legislatures of the states the means to propose amendments, always "provided that no State, without its Consent, shall be deprived of its equal Suffrage in the Senate."

The tensions over slavery that existed within the Philadelphia Convention and that were compromised there, ultimately by postponement, of course continued, and worsened, and fed the approaching Civil War—not a civil war like Oliver Cromwell's against King Charles I, but a war of secession that sought to dissolve the federal union.

Had the amendments (XIII, XIV, and XV[2]) to the Constitution that followed the victory of the northern states been an integral part of the Constitution itself, the Civil War might have been prevented, but scholars of the Convention of 1787 are virtually unanimous that a serious attempt to force those provisions on the Constitution would have disrupted the convention and prevented it from finishing the work.

The fullness of time, however, brought to pass those amendments that could not have been part of the original document. Slavery was outlawed, not 20 but almost 80 years after the Constitution was adopted. Equality was an idea on which the founders could not agree in 1787.

Ideas of the Constitution. A number of ideas were to be found in the Preamble to the Constitution, some of them foreshadowed in the words of the Declaration. They are the ideas of

Justice
Domestic Tranquility (or Civil Peace)
The Common Defense (or National Security)
The General Welfare
The Blessings of Liberty

All of these ideas are also ideals. They were ideals in the 18th century at the inception of the Constitution. Some of them, especially justice and liberty, along with the ideals of equality and of democracy, were realized more in successive amendments than in the Constitution itself. This is especially true of the first ten amendments, known collectively as the Bill of Rights, but also of the Thirteenth, Fourteenth, Fifteenth, Nineteenth, and Twenty-Fourth amendments, all of which gradually moved the federal republic more and more in the direction of democracy, by extending suffrage and removing obstacles to it. In these amendments we find such phrases as "equal protection of the laws" and "due process of law" that evoke the idea—and the ideal—of a government of laws.

It is worthy of note that the substance of many future amendments, and particularly of the Bill of Rights, was discussed at great length in the Convention of 1787. George Mason, one of the most influential of the founders, opposed ratification of the Constitution to which he contributed so much because it did not include a Bill of Rights. The first Congress under the Constitution proposed 12 such amendments, of which the 10 comprising the Bill of Rights were promptly adopted by the states.

In this light, the text of Article V, the article that enabled the Constitution to correct itself as mandated by future experience, may be a fit subject for special notice in the celebration of the real American bicentennial:

> The Congress, whenever two thirds of both Houses shall deem it necessary, shall propose Amendments to this Constitution, or, on the Application of the Legislatures of two thirds of the several States, shall call a Convention for proposing Amendments, which, in either Case, shall be valid to all Intents and Purposes, as Part of this Constitution, when ratified by the Legislatures of three fourths of the several States, or by Conventions in three fourths thereof, as the one or the other Mode of Ratification may be proposed by the Congress; Provided that no Amendment which may be made prior to the Year One thousand eight hundred and eight shall in any Manner affect the first and fourth Clauses in the Ninth Section of the first Article; and that no State, without its Consent, shall be deprived of its equal Suffrage in the Senate.

This essay is in part a paraphrase of and in part excerpts from the opening chapters of a book written by Mortimer Adler, entitled *We Hold These Truths: Understanding the Ideas and Ideals of the Constitution,* to be published by Macmillan in the bicentennial year of 1987.

[1]Rhode Island did not participate but did ratify the resulting Constitution in 1790.

[2]Amendment XIII abolished slavery; Amendment XIV made all persons born or naturalized in the United States citizens of the United States and of the state where they reside and extended due process of law and equal protection under the law to all; Amendment XV provided that the right to vote "shall not be denied or abridged . . . on account of race, color, or previous condition of servitude."

Australia's Bicentennial Year

BY K. S. INGLIS

1988 will be celebrated as Australia's bicentennial year. The United States bicentennial celebration of 1976 was fresh in memory when the planning began, and Australians, as usual these days, looked across the Pacific to learn how such things are done. There were limits to what they could learn, not only because the disasters of Watergate and Vietnam still hung in the American air in 1976, darkening festivity, but because the events commemorated in the two countries were so different.

Bicentennial of What? Every American knew that the 1976 bicentennial was about the Declaration of Independence on July 4, 1776. All ceremonial oratory could begin with the words, noble and familiar, of the document itself. But the Americans' revolution had made it virtually certain that no white British colonists elsewhere in the world would have to win independence by force of arms. In Australia the imperial power yielded to, sometimes even encouraged, expressions of national consciousness, giving colonial subjects no powerful cause for either complaint or celebration. Each colony was granted a large measure of self-government in the later 19th century; an act of the imperial Parliament federated the colonies into states of the Commonwealth of Australia in 1900; the Statute of Westminster gave formal recognition in 1931 to the uncontested fact that Australia and the other dominions (Canada, Newfoundland, New Zealand, South Africa, and Ireland) were autonomous members of the British Commonwealth of Nations. When Queen Elizabeth II assented in March 1986 to an act of her Australian ministers removing the last vestiges of the imperial connection, the newspapers had to explain exactly what those vestiges had been; hardly anybody remembered. No stage on the road from dependency to full formal sovereignty yielded a historic date, unless it was the opening of the first federal Parliament on May 9, 1901. That was recalled when the politicians, having met in Melbourne until the national capital was built, moved into Canberra's new Parliament House on May 9, 1927. There was a plan to use this day again for ceremony in 1988.

What happened in 1788 was an imperial beginning, not a national achievement. In 1770 James Cook had charted and named the coast of New South Wales, on the east of what the Dutch had called New Holland, and recommended the place be named Botany Bay for British settlement. On Jan. 26, 1788, Gov. Arthur Phillip ordered the British flag raised at Sydney Cove in Port Jackson after his 11 ships had spent more than eight months crossing the world to found a penal colony. (He had landed first at Botany Bay, just to the south, but preferred Port Jackson.) The 50th anniversary of that event was celebrated in Sydney on Jan. 26, 1838, as the Australian Jubilee, with fireworks, boat races, and speeches dwelling on the transformation of the colony from a receptacle for outcasts into a proud home for free men and women. Half a century later, when leaders from other Australian colonies were guests at centennial celebrations in Sydney, there was among them a faint sense of contamination by association with a colony of such squalid origins—and a stronger feeling of irritation over the project of politicians in New South Wales, on the eve of the festive year, to annex the name "Australia" for their colony. By 1938 there was still no solid sentiment outside the senior state of the federation to share in commemoration of its nativity, and the "sesquicentennial" celebrations that ran from January 26 to April 25 were largely confined to New South Wales. In the Pageant of Nationhood through the streets of Sydney on January 26, convicts were not represented.

January 26, Australia Day, is a public holiday throughout Australia, but commemoration is notoriously tepid. Among its traditions are editorials deploring the defective sense of nationality revealed on the anniversary and interviews in news columns reporting what citizens know and think of the day; some people confuse Phillip with Cook, 1788 with 1770. In the last few years, editorial writers have looked ahead to 1988. "We are now only two years from the Bicentenary," said the national daily *Australian* on Australia Day 1986. "It is to be hoped that in those two years the interest of the people of this nation in the history, the traditions, and, most importantly, the future of Australia will continue to grow. . . ." Anniversary rhetoric has also been enlivened by debate about whether January 26 is the best date to recall. February 7, when Phillip's commission as governor was read to the convicts and their guards, has its champions, and the historian Geoffrey Blainey has proposed January 18, the day the fleet reached Botany Bay at the end of its great voyage. What the debate shows is that, after two centuries, Jan. 26, 1788, has not attained the sacred character in Australian minds that July 4, 1776, has for Americans, July 14, 1789, for the French, or Nov. 7, 1917, for Russians. Only one day in Australian history glows with nationality as those dates do, and that is April 25, 1915, when Australian soldiers went to war on the beaches of Gallipoli, in Turkey. On early anniversaries of that landing—Anzac Day (for Australia and New Zealand Army Corps)—people at home began to say, for the first time with conviction, that Australia was truly a nation. That is why the planners of sesquicentennial festivity in 1938 had it begin on January 26 and end on April 25. Among the heap of criticisms collected by bicentennial planners, one is that they appear to be neglecting Anzac Day.

Laying Plans. This time the occasion is to be thoroughly national. It happens that three of the six states—Western Australia, Victoria, and South Australia—have lately had sesquicentennial celebrations, and in federal Australia it makes for amity if a national enterprise has the air of complementing, rather than usurping, local initiative. Seen from a distance, "Canberra," like "Washington," can easily appear an ogre. It was shrewd of the Australian Bicentennial Authority (ABA) to make its headquarters not in Canberra but in Sydney—in the oldest part of the oldest city, with post office box number AUS 1988.

The conservative Liberal and National parties coalition government under Malcolm Fraser created the ABA early in 1980 with agreement of all the states. Its constitution was imaginative. The ABA was incorporated as a company whose shareholders were Commonwealth, state, and Northern Territory ministers and leaders of the opposition. The board was composed of the politicians' nominees and the ABA's appointed chairman, and each state and territory had its own council. It thus represented all major political parties and all partners in the federal compact. As a company, the ABA created its own bureaucracy. A well-known businessman, John Reid, was made chairman, and the board chose as chief executive officer David Armstrong, director of a college of advanced education.

The ABA's plans were unveiled in a series of quarterly newsletters with a blue-and-gold masthead, "Bicentenary '88" ("Bicentenary" as a noun, "Bicentennial" as an adjective, an early issue explained). A variety of books were to be commissioned, among them a short history of Australia by the university historian John Molony; *Generations: Daughters, Mothers and Grandmothers in Australia* by the anthropologist Diane Bell; and a novel by Elizabeth Jolley. A National Science Centre was to be built in Canberra. A dramatic performance based on episodes from the six volumes of *A History of Australia* by the most eminent of Australian historians, Manning Clark, would go on tour. The Australian Exhibition was to travel the country by truck, rolling into town like a circus and pitching huge tents. It would cost $30 million: $19 million from the ABA, $5 million from entrance fees, and $6 million from BHP (for Broken Hill Proprietary), Australia's largest company. Committees were appointed to inquire into the state of Australian studies in schools and tertiary institutions.

Each state had enterprises of its own, most of them modest, like the 200-km (124-mi) walking track from Sydney to Hunter Valley, but some grander, especially in New South Wales and Queensland. The premier of New South Wales, Neville Wran, declared in 1981 that his state—"the Premier State" as it was now called on vehicle license plates—would put on the biggest celebrations. His government committed itself to redeveloping down-at-the-heels Darling Harbour, one bay farther than Phillip had gone in 1788 when he chose Sydney Cove, as a centre for conferences, exhibitions, and other sorts of conviviality.

AUSTRALIAN BICENTENNIAL AUTHORITY

An Australian official and local Aborigines discuss plans for a new community centre in Townsville, one of several projects awarded grants in June as part of the National Aboriginal and Torres Strait Islander Program serving the Aboriginal population.

Queensland, with ABA support, put a successful proposal to the Bureau of International Expositions. Brisbane's Expo 88 was being promoted by the proudly provincial government of Sir Johannes Bjelke-Petersen as "the greatest celebration ever held in Australia, the headline event of the Bicentenary." It might well be. The theme would be Leisure in the Age of Technology, and the entertainment director was Ric Birch, the Australian who designed the opening ceremony of Brisbane's Commonwealth Games in 1982 and, on the strength of that essay in razzmatazz, won the same job at the Los Angeles Olympic Games. His model for Expo 88, Birch said, was Disneyland. Homelier activities were being planned in the Bicentennial Communities Programme, described by the ABA in 1981 as "involving every one of Australia's 850 local government areas." Many historical societies were benefiting from small grants made by the ABA and state councils.

Endorsed Activities. The ABA also was granting "endorsement" to projects generated outside the official network. Though the ABA had never actually said so, anybody running a project offering anything for sale *without* its consent and using "Bicentenary," "Bicentennial," "200 Years," or any other words on a list of "prescribed expressions" in conjunction with two or more of the figures 1788, 1988, and '88 would be guilty of an offense under the Australian Bicentennial Authority Act of 1980. Benefits of endorsement, the ABA pointed out, included publicity and enhanced opportunities for sponsorship. Possibly the most ambitious enterprise given "endorsement" was an 11-volume history series called *Australians: A Historical Library,* a collaborative work by several hundred people, financed mainly by the Australian National University, the University of New South Wales, the Australian Research Grants Scheme, and advance royalties from the publishers, Fairfax, Syme & Weldon Associates. The Australian Academy of the Humanities was mounting an international conference on the theme "Terra Australis to Australia," which the U.S.-owned oil company Esso underwrote once it had ABA endorsement.

The Australian and New Zealand Association for the Advancement of Science, which first met in 1888, had endorsement for its own centennial conference. Among scores of other endorsed gatherings were a world Scout jamboree, a bicentennial dog show, the first international congress on corrections (which would have on its agenda the punishment of those first convicts), and a festival of left-handed golfers. Australia Post had endorsement for a philatelic collection that had been advertising the bicentenary superbly since the first stamps were issued in 1984. The boldest of all endorsed projects, which the organizers had hoped would get more material support from the ABA, would reenact the voyage of the first fleet, the 11 square-rigged sailing ships leaving Portsmouth, England, as Phillip's did, and taking the same time to reach their destination.

The ABA itself was sponsoring a different maritime project, the "Tall Ships," intended to bring some of the last windjammers still afloat to an Australia Day Parade of Sail in Sydney Harbour on Jan. 26, 1988. Water police might be busy directing traffic if the Tall Ships and the fleet from Portsmouth both arrived that day. Most of the Tall Ships were used as naval training vessels, and this project depended on cooperation from other governments. The British government was making a gift of a schooner, to be sailed out by a young crew. There were negotiations for an international naval regatta. France proposed to create a museum at Botany Bay dedicated to the navigator La Pérouse, who arrived there on Jan. 26, 1788, just as the British were leaving for Port Jackson. Ireland was sending out, on microfiche, the records of all convicts transported from Irish ports. In 1888 or 1938 such a gift, even if technically possible, would have been diplomatically unthinkable; today, say the authors of the serialized publication *Two Hundred Years* ("A week by week historical countdown to Australia's Bicentennial"), "those with convict origins are the bluebloods of Australia." As this publication was owned by the newspaper magnate Rupert Murdoch, who had exchanged Australian for U.S. citizenship in 1985, it could be counted among American offerings to the bicentenary.

Of all foreign countries the U.S. was likely to contribute the most. When Bob Hawke visited Washington as prime minister in April 1986, Congress resolved that the U.S. government "help Australia observe its Bicentennial year with appropriate activities and ceremonies." The American-Australian Bicentennial Foundation, based in Washington, had on its board businessmen with Australian interests and former U.S. ambassadors. It was devising a program of sport, science, culture, and education, with the help of an advisory committee that included Edsel Ford II, the TV personality Art Linkletter, and the golfer Jack Nicklaus. Government-initiated committees were also at work in Japan, West Germany, and The Netherlands.

The Politics of Celebration. A change of government in March 1983, from the coalition under Malcolm Fraser to Labor under Bob Hawke, made no immediate difficulties for the ABA. The blue in its newsletter and logo had to be replaced by green in 1984, when the federal government deemed green and gold to be Australia's official colours. As a statement of the bicentennial theme, Hawke and his colleagues preferred "Living Together" to "The Australian Achievement," which the Fraser government had insisted on against the ABA's own preference. To the ears of ABA executives, "The Australian Achievement" was old-fashioned drum banging. They preferred the gentler, harmonious sound of "Living Together" (despite its possibly signaling also the practice of de facto marriage). They wanted the bicentennial program to register the fact that post-World War II migration had turned an almost wholly British population into one in which perhaps a quarter were now of other origins. It became an official ABA objective to "recognise the multicultural nature of modern Australia." The largest publication commissioned by the ABA would be a million-word *Encyclopedia of the Australian People,* modeled on the *Harvard Encyclopedia of American Ethnic Groups.*

Some commentators on the political right were unhappy with the emphases revealed in ABA planning. Ken Baker, a research fellow with the conservative Institute of Public Affairs, observed in the institute's *Review* that in ABA imagery Australia was "a nation of varied cultures and origins, but one without a unifying core." He noticed that its National Programme of projects and events nowhere acknowledged the British origin of Australian institutions, or the American alliance, or Christian values, or the spirit of Anzac, or the family. He detected a hidden agenda: to enact a subtle rewriting of Australia's history. "The Bicentennial celebrations," he declared, "ought to encourage us to value our traditions and achievements, not expunge them." The Hawke government appeared to be no more worried by such criticism than by the derision of the *Canberra Times*'s columnist Ian Warden at the ABA's endorsing a project for the development of a new azalea, a flower that seemed to him "as Australian as, say, the kimono or the giraffe" and likely to reveal in Australians "a slowness to come to terms with and to feel a real fondness for the funny continent in which they find themselves."

What provoked Hawke's intervention was an apprehension that the ABA was spending a lot of money—more than $A 20 million by mid-1985—to not much purpose. A Gallup Poll discovered that most people had not heard of plans to celebrate the bicentenary. Nearly half the nation's local government areas had still not taken up the Communities Programme. The Victorian government's representative on the board resigned on July 10, 1985, alleging waste and mismanagement and inadequate accountability of staff to the board. Hawke decided that the charges were valid, and the chairman, John Reid, obtained the resignation of David Armstrong as chief executive on August 22. When it was revealed that Armstrong's agreement to go had been encouraged by a golden handshake of about $A 500,000, the prime minister and the chairman gave contradictory accounts of Armstrong's departure, and on September 26 Hawke got Reid himself to resign.

A Gallup Poll at that moment would have shown a huge increase in national awareness of the bicentenary; the bad news about the ABA was on the front page of every paper and in every television and radio bulletin. Within government, it was being said that never again would a publicly funded enterprise be constituted as an autonomous company. For the time being Hawke himself took charge of the ABA as political opponents accused him of bullying, dishonesty, and incompetence. Officers of the prime minister's department kept a close eye on the ABA, and in November, after a long search, another businessman, Jim Kirk, agreed to come in as both chairman and chief executive, having just retired from both those jobs at Esso.

However frugally and responsibly the ABA was run from then on, its new controllers had to live with controversy. The criticisms Ken Baker had aired in the *Institute of Public Affairs Review* were developed in the same journal by the historian Geoffrey Blainey, who warned that the celebrations would be a national farce if the majority of Australians were given too little to celebrate. The leader of the federal opposition, John Howard, spoke similarly in an address for Australia Day 1986, expressing concern that the ABA was expecting everybody to reflect too much on what had gone wrong with the country, rather than on what had gone right. On the other hand, people in what Blainey called "the multicultural lobby" were bound to deplore what seemed to them any dilution of the ABA's commitment to ethnic communities, as happened in May 1986 when a planned program of multicultural events was withdrawn and all such activities were assigned to a new Multicultural Foundation. Non-Anglo-Saxon Australians, said the journal *Ethnos,* published by the New South Wales Ethnic Affairs Commission, were in danger of being excluded from the bicentenary.

The First Australians. Aborigines threatened to exclude themselves. In 1888 nobody thought to put survivors from pre-European Australia on the centennial stage, for whatever their past, they were generally assumed to have no future. On Jan. 26, 1938, a few were given walk-on parts—or rather walk-off parts, since they impersonated their ancestors withdrawing before a boatload of actors playing Governor Phillip and his men. Other Aborigines designated Jan. 26, 1938, as a Day of Mourning, and about a hundred of them gathered to make a statement of "protest against the callous treatment of our people by the whiteman during the past 150 years" and an appeal for

A model shows the new Parliament House that is being constructed in Canberra as a monument to Australia's bicentenary. The distinctively curved walls of the low structure outline the separate elements of Parliament. Garden areas and tennis courts help to blend the building with the rest of the city. Completion is set for May 9, 1988, the anniversary of Parliament's first meeting in 1901.
PROMOTION AUSTRALIA

"a new policy which will raise our people to full citizen status and equality within the community."

Full citizenship in the Commonwealth was granted to Aborigines in 1967, though some state laws still imposed measures of discriminatory protection. Social equality was another matter; every measure of welfare, from child mortality to employment, showed Aborigines much worse off than whites. Their numbers were increasing—by almost 50% between the censuses of 1971 and 1981—though that probably had as much to do with changes in self-identification by people of mixed ancestry as with improved health. They remained few—around 159,000 by 1985, in a population of 15.7 million—but that 1% now made much more than 1% of the news, as a result of heightened group consciousness among Aborigines and an increasing, though perhaps not durable, sense of obligation among whites to make up for the "callous treatment" deplored by the pioneer protesters of 1938. "What have Aborigines got to celebrate in 1988?" a group of them asked on national television in 1985.

When the ABA was formed, some white Australians had just begun a campaign for a treaty, called in the language of one Northern Territory people a *makarrata,* that would recognize that a wrong had been done in 1788 when the newcomers, blind to the culture of hunter-gatherers, declared the land unoccupied. The treaty would acknowledge the sovereignty of Aborigines in 1788, recognize the land rights of those still living in traditional ways, and make other amends to the rest. What if the treaty could be signed at a healing ceremony in 1988? The idea appealed to David Armstrong at the ABA, and he and his colleagues explored it with prominent Aborigines. As one Aboriginal participant, Eric Wilmott, reported a meeting: "They said 'Say the 11 ships sail into Sydney Harbour and a bunch of Aborigines are standing on the shore symbolically dressed and the boats land and a man walks out and he is Phillip and governor general and the Aborigines race down to the beach and hand him a *makarrata* on which is written the land rights legislation, which he then signs.' I said, 'You pull that off and you've got a deal.'"

Aboriginal activists pursued the notion of a deal. "Land Rights now will give Aborigines a reason to celebrate too," said full-page advertisements in 1984. "Support Land Rights and let's Celebrate 1988 together." But the *makarrata* movement came to a halt, largely for want of Aboriginal involvement, and in March 1986 the Hawke government abandoned legislation for land rights, blaming hostile public opinion. The ABA, under both old and new managements, did its best to win Aboriginal involvement or at least tolerance. *After Two Hundred Years,* a book from the Australian Institute of Aboriginal Studies, would be a "landmark title" in the ABA's publication program. An "Aboriginal assessment panel" was appointed to advise the ABA how to spend the $A 8 million allocated for its Aboriginal program—and also, though this was not said, to persuade recipients to take it, in the face of Aboriginal declarations that ABA funds were "blood money."

The federal government's backing down on land rights was bad news for the ABA. The Northern Land Council, the most representative Aboriginal body in the Northern Territory, responded by withdrawing all support for bicentennial activities. Into Box AUS 1988 in Sydney came a pile of cards marked "Boycott the bicentenary," and Aborigines demonstrated outside the ABA's offices. In July 1986 three Aborigines lodged a writ in the High Court challenging the constitutional validity of the part of the ABA Act of 1980 that would prevent them from using certain bicentennial symbols without the ABA's permission. Were they serious? Custodians of the British-Australian judicial system had to assume so, and whatever happened, the initiative would provide an entertaining countertheatre. There would surely be more. The 1938 Day of Mourning was stored in Aboriginal folk memory, and so was the "Aboriginal Embassy," tents pitched on the grass outside Parliament House in Canberra on Jan. 26, 1972, which stayed there for months, television cameras peering whenever policemen were sent in to remove the national embarrassment of dark people appearing as alien petitioners in their own country.

If Aborigines did boycott, or deride, or otherwise dissent from bicentennial activities, they could count on sympathy from ministers of religion. The Australian Council of Churches, representing nearly all major denominations except the Roman Catholics, wanted Christian participation in 1988 to be contingent on the granting of land rights, and that approach might well prevail in the Catholic Commission for Justice and Peace as well. It would divide congregations, some of whose members complained that they had not been consulted.

Symbols of Nationhood. The fate of Aborigines was mentioned when Australians debated the erecting of monuments in 1988. "What government department, authority or citizen body," asked a correspondent in the *Sydney Morning Herald,* "has the courage and honesty to promote or undertake the erection of a memorial to the Aboriginal people subsequently wiped out in the conquest, and how should that monument be designed?"

The questions remained unanswered, though one architect, invoking England's Stonehenge, sensed that, given "an ages-old Aboriginal culture deeply rooted in the signs and symbols of nature, there should be a distinct possibility of achieving a uniquely Australian expression of what the Bicentennial monument might be." A giant kangaroo? Or, expressing the new culture rather than the old, a colossal "digger" (Australians' name for the soldier)? Both were proposed. In New South Wales the government held a competition for a monument to be placed in Centennial Park, which itself was Sydney's finest memorial of 1888, and when a postmodernist rotunda looking rather like a Roman temple was chosen, critics said that it would be anachronistic before it was finished.

The one material monument sure to be created in 1988 was a new Parliament House in Canberra. Like royal visits, public anniversaries can provide deadlines for jobs that should have been done sooner. For 1988 the federal government launched, for example, a measles-eradication campaign and a national road-development program for highways around the continent. Signs on road works proclaiming this program were possibly the most widely seen advertisements for the bicentenary. And on Canberra's Capital Hill the government committed itself to finishing by 1988 a structure that would replace the "provisional" Parliament House, opened in 1927, which was supposed to last for only 50 years. The American planner of Canberra, Walter Burley Griffin, did not want the legislators to sit as high above the people as the location on Capital Hill would make them, but the politicians, after decades of indecision, chose that site, and the architects, as if in deference to Griffin's wish, designed a building that hugs, even burrows into, the ground. (The architects are Mitchell/Giurgola Architects of New York, and the building appears to be the joint inspiration of Romaldo Giurgola and Richard Thorp, an Australian who works for the firm, in proportions unknown outside the office.) Barring acts of God or militant unionists, or a severe depression, the building would be opened on May 9, 1988, the anniversary of the Parliament's first meeting in 1901.

A huge flag would fly high over its roof. If the campaigners of "Ausflag 1988" had their way, it would not be the one flown for the Commonwealth since 1901, combining the British flag, the stars of the Southern Cross, and a federal star. Ausflag 1988 was an initiative of people not otherwise radical. Their founding president, Sir James Hardy, was a rich yachtsman who became irritated, flying the Australian flag during races off Florida and The Bahamas, to be asked again and again what part of Britain he was from. But the proposal for a new emblem provoked vigorous opposition, centred on the Returned Services League (RSL), custodians of the Anzac tradition, who created an Australian National Flag Association to defend the old emblem. To the argument that the British element in the flag meant nothing to immigrants from other countries, one RSL leader retorted that if the Union Jack in the corner offended them, "they can nick off right back to where they came from." Another said that changing the flag would be like burning all the history books.

To the delight of the old soldiers who often feared they were guardians of a dying cause, more than 60% of people surveyed said they were content with the flag they had. Sir James Hardy resigned and would have to go on being mistaken in yachting waters for a Briton. The executive director of Ausflag 1988 complained that Kirk, the head of the ABA, would not see him. Kirk assured audiences that the flag would not be changed by 1988. If, as generally expected, Queen Elizabeth II opened the new Parliament House as monarch of Australia, she would see overhead and below, up through the glazed ceiling of the central hall and down in a reflecting pool, a flag still one-quarter English.

The Beacons of '88. Malcolm Fraser had expected to open the Parliament House and to preside over the bicentennial celebrations his government had authorized, but the election of 1983 decided otherwise. Bob Hawke's Labor government won another election at the end of 1984. Under the Australian system of governments chosen by triennially elected parliaments, Hawke would have to go to the polls by early 1988. He could defer voting day beyond January 26 but not until May 9. In the sumptuous new chambers of the Senate and the House of Representatives, the ministerial benches would be occupied by a reelected Labor government or by its opponents.

Observers of federal politics used to think that being in office for 1988 would be an advantage. Who wants to be nasty to the host at a birthday party? But the ructions over the ABA in 1985 did Hawke no good. Controversy over Aboriginal participation and multicultural activities do not make "Living Together" seem right as a theme. (The ABA, taking advice from advertising agents, moved late in 1986 to "Celebration of a Nation," with the plaintive additions "Let's Make It Great in '88" and "Give Us a Hand to Make It Grand.")

Worst of all, Australia's external debt rose to dangerous heights during 1986, and the exchange value of the Australian dollar kept falling. In March Kirk was forecasting a rise in what the bicentennial year would cost the federal government, but after the budget in August he was having to administer cuts in ABA programs, and the builders on Capital Hill were instructed to save $A 30 million on the new Parliament House while still having it ready to open on May 9, 1988. Bicentennial prophecies turned bleak. Maximilian Walsh, most respected of economic journalists, predicted that 1988 could "see control of our economy handed over to the International Monetary Fund." "All in all," declared Noel Butlin, doyen of Australian economic historians, "the bicentenary year does not look like being a good one." The dominant public mood could well be one not so much of celebration as of meditation, on the consequences for the nation of being unable any longer to prosper on its traditionally linked policies of induced population growth and protection of manufacturing industry.

However sombre the year might be for the Australian economy, there was a good chance that the continent would be lit up on the night of June 18, in the Southern Hemisphere midwinter, by a blaze of beacons beginning—as 1788 did—at Botany Bay and covering the nation as people see the neighbours' bonfire and ignite their own. The idea came biculturally from an Australian-born historian and a Chilean-born sociologist, Geoffrey Blainey and Claudio Veliz. Fire, Blainey argued in his *Triumph of the Nomads: A History of Ancient Australia,* was used by Aborigines for many millennia as a device to manage the environment. The campfire is central to white Australian legend. The ABA approves the plan as imaginative, symbolic of national unity, and requiring no subsidy. In England a century earlier, bonfires were lit on every hill one night in 1887 in honour of Queen Victoria's jubilee and were long remembered as flares marking the end of an age. The beacons of 1988 could burn similarly in Australian memories.

Britannica Awards for 1987, honouring exceptional excellence in the dissemination of learning, were presented to a British naturalist and television broadcaster, a U.S. physicist and science writer, a U.S. author and professor of management, a Polish jurist, and a Japanese economist and educator.

Although many medals and prizes mark original contributions to the world's sum of knowledge, the Britannica Awards, presented for the first time in 1986, celebrate both exceptional skills in imparting learning to others and a passion for its dissemination. The persons singled out to receive the awards have demonstrated these skills in the media of broadcast and print journalism, lecturing, and books, and in doing so they have made fields of highly specialized knowledge intelligible and accessible to a wide general audience.

The Britannica Awards embrace the whole spectrum of knowledge. Candidates for the award are nominated by members of Britannica's Board of Editors and its Editorial Advisory Committees drawn from the faculties of great universities in the United States, Canada, Japan, Australia, the United Kingdom, and continental Europe. Final selections are made by a committee consisting of the chairman of the corporation's Board of Directors, the chairman of its Board of Editors, its president, and its editor in chief.

The award consists of a gold medal, $15,000 in cash, and an allowance for the expenses of attending the presentation and subsequent lectures. The awards were to be presented on Feb. 16, 1987, at a celebratory banquet at the United Nations Delegates' Dining Room in New York City. Each recipient would deliver a Britannica Award Lecture in his own country and another elsewhere in the world.

Attenborough, Sir David

David Attenborough was at the top of his profession when he decided to quit the British Broadcasting Corporation (BBC), where he was director of television programming and a member of the Management Board, to become a free-lance filmmaker and author. He had long since harnessed the enormous potential of television for popular education in both natural history and human culture.

He was born David Frederick Attenborough on May 8, 1926, in London and grew up in Leicester, where his father was principal of University College. Many of his forebears were educators, and both his son and daughter became teachers. But the classroom was not David's métier. From childhood he was a passionate inquirer into the ways of nature. He attended Wyggeston Grammar School for Boys and went on to Clare College, Cambridge, where he earned an M.A. in zoology and geology in 1947. He finished two years in the Royal Navy as a lieutenant and in 1949 got a job as an editorial assistant in an educational publishing house.

In 1952, after completing a training program at the BBC, he became a producer and quickly found his niche. One of his early shows featured reptiles brought from the London Zoo by a curator, Jack Lester, with whom he soon dreamed up a series to show animals both in the wild on film and live in the studio. The idea won approval from both the BBC and the zoo and resulted in a joint venture that led to a landmark series called "Zoo Quest" that was a hit for ten years.

AP/WIDE WORLD

Early in the "Zoo Quest" series Jack Lester, who had been the presenter or narrator, became ill and died, and Attenborough, a bit tentative about the idea, went before the cameras in his stead. He proved to be a natural and continued his backstage role as well. He also wrote a series of "Zoo Quest" books telling the story of the globe-girdling expeditions to film the TV programs. Then in 1963 he gave up television to study anthropology in graduate school.

In 1965 the BBC persuaded him to return as controller of its new second television channel, BBC-2. His innovative programming quickly expanded its audience, and he helped launch such dramatic productions as "The Forsyte Saga" and cultural-educational series such as Jacob Bronowski's "The Ascent of Man" and Kenneth Clark's "Civilisation."

This track record moved the BBC to give Attenborough the programming helm of both of its television networks, but the joys of management soon palled, and in 1972 he quit to free-lance. He was not idle; he resumed writing and producing seminal TV series of the general sort that had made his reputation, including "The Tribal Eye" (1975), "Life on Earth" (1978), and "The Living Planet" (1984). All won large audiences, and he turned all of them into successful books.

Attenborough was knighted in 1985. His brother is Sir Richard Attenborough, the distinguished actor and director.

Bernstein, Jeremy

There is little interglobal conversation among other occupants of the three worlds in which Jeremy Bernstein operates. He is a major channel of communication among them: the worlds of the physicist, the mountaineer, and the interpreter of science for the intelligent nonprofessional reader. He has won distinction in all three. In the last, he has been celebrated for two decades for the clarity of his writing about the major issues of modern physics.

Bernstein was born Dec. 31, 1929, in Rochester, N.Y. He was educated at Harvard University, where he earned B.A. (1951) and M.A. (1953) degrees in mathematics and a Ph.D. in physics in 1955. After working as a research associate in physics at Harvard's Cyclotron Laboratory, he was appointed to the Institute of Advanced Studies at Princeton, N.J. In 1960 he went to the Brookhaven National Laboratory in New York and while he was there won (1961) a position on the staff of *The New Yorker.*

Mountain climbing was a major avocational interest for Bernstein, and he was able to arrange his dual career so that he could spend three months every year climbing—usually in Switzerland or France. In 1962 he became associate professor of physics at New York University, and in 1967 he was named professor of physics at Stevens Institute of Technology at Hoboken, N.J. He also became an adjunct professor at Rockefeller University in New York City. At various times he has held a National Science Foundation fellowship and concurrent appointments at the University of Oxford; CERN (Conseil Européen pour la Recherche Nucléaire), near Geneva; the University of Islamabad, Pak.; France's École Polytechnique, Paris;

ARTHUR KRASINSKY—KPI, NY

Columbia University, New York City; and, twice, as Ferris professor of journalism, at Princeton University. He writes for his peers as well as for nonscientists and is the author of some 50 technical papers.

In interpreting science to the general public, usually initially through the pages of *The New Yorker* and then through books into which the articles evolved, Bernstein has shed light on topics ranging from cosmology to the origins of the computer. He has published a dozen books addressing such diverse topics, and he also writes a biennial column, "Out of My Mind," for *The American Scholar.* His science writing for the general reader has brought him many honours, including the American Physical Society-U.S. Steel Award (twice) and the American Association for the Advancement of Science-Westinghouse Award. His autobiographical memoir, *The Life It Brings,* was published in 1986.

Drucker, Peter F.

He is a famous economist, teacher, and author, one of the most influential management consultants and professors in the world, a thoughtful philosopher of modern organization, and recognized as the man who developed the concept of professional management.

Peter Ferdinand Drucker was born Nov. 19, 1909, in Vienna, the son of a senior civil servant and lawyer. He was educated at Gymnasium in Vienna and graduated in 1927. After matriculating at the University of Hamburg, Germany, he went on to study law at the University of Frankfurt, Germany, earning an LL.D. in 1931.

As a student he had become a reporter with a Frankfurt daily newspaper, the *General-Anzeiger,* and after graduation he stayed on as foreign and financial editor for two years. However, the emergence of Hitler and the Nazis prompted him to leave Germany, a step he took as soon as Hitler won the chancellorship in 1933. Drucker went to London, where he found work as an economist in an international banking house. In 1937 he immigrated to the United States, where he busied himself as a U.S. adviser to British banks and a U.S. correspondent for British newspapers. He also published a book of reflections on totalitarian and democratic systems and a number of articles in such journals as *Harper's* and *The New Republic* on Germany under the Nazis. Drucker's writings brought him a growing audience among business and industrial leaders, and he gradually developed a thriving management consulting practice. In 1942 he accepted an appointment at Bennington (Vt.) College as professor of philosophy and politics and taught there until 1949. He became a U.S. citizen in 1943.

In 1950 Drucker began a 22-year tenure at New York University as professor of management. In 1971 he moved to California to take the Clarke chair in social science at the Claremont Graduate School of the Claremont Colleges while continuing his NYU relationship as distinguished university lecturer. During extensive travels in the Orient, Drucker had become a collector of and authority on Japanese art, and in 1979, while still continuing to teach at the graduate school, he became a professor in the art history department at Pomona College, another of the Claremont Colleges.

In his teaching, as in his consulting work and his writings, Drucker has consistently and lucidly advocated common sense and a generalist's-eye view for solving (or forestalling) management problems. He has been much honoured by business schools and business associations.

Lachs, Manfred

A Polish writer, educator, diplomat, and jurist who has profoundly influenced the postwar development of international law, Manfred Lachs is unique among the important figures in the Communist states because of the respect with which he is viewed by scholars and jurists in the West and the third world as well as in the socialist sphere. He is a member of the International Court of Justice and is serving his third nine-year term as one of its judges. He was president of the court in 1973–76 and has long been chairman of its committee on revising court procedures.

Manfred Lachs was born April 21, 1914, at Stanislawow, Poland. He was educated at Jagiellonian University of Krakow, where he earned LL.M. and Dr. Juris. degrees, and did graduate work at the Con-

sular Academy of Vienna and the London School of Economics before the outbreak of World War II.

Lachs is a linguist of considerable ability, fluent (in writing as well as in speech) in English, French, German, and Russian in addition to Polish. Indeed, his first public notice in the West came in 1945 with the publication in London of his first book: *War Crimes: An Attempt to Define the Issues.* His latest, *The Teacher in International Law (Teachings and Teaching),* received the 1984 annual award of the American Society for International Law.

When Poland's postwar provisional Government of National Unity was established, Lachs was made a delegate to both the Paris Peace Conference and the first UN General Assembly (1946). The following year he was appointed director of the Legal and Treaties Department of the Foreign Ministry, a post he held until 1960. In that year he became legal adviser to Foreign Minister Adam Rapacki, with the rank at first of minister plenipotentiary and later of ambassador. Lachs played a central role in the development of the Rapacki Plan for making Central Europe a nuclear-free zone.

His command of international law and his amicable working relationships with his colleagues brought him considerable prominence in the UN, where he was a Polish delegate to most General Assembly sessions through 1966. In that year Lachs was elected a judge of the World Court, formally the International Court of Justice, at The Hague, Neth. The esteem with which he is held in the West is reflected by the fact that he was nominated jointly by the United States, Canada, the United Kingdom, and other Western nations. Throughout his political and legal careers Lachs has continued to teach and has lectured around the world.

Okita, Saburo

Saburo Okita is a man of many careers, through most of which runs prominently the common thread of an uncommon command of the English language. This has enabled the sometime engineer, economist, government official, and foreign minister to become one of the foremost interpreters of his country to the world.

Okita was born Nov. 3, 1914, and was educated at Tokyo University, graduating as an electrical engineer in 1937. Upon his graduation he entered government service as an engineer in the Ministry of Posts and Communications. After the end of World War II, he was transferred to the Economic Stabilization Board as chief of its research section.

He served during 1952–53 in the UN's Economic Commission for Asia and the Far East and then returned to the Japanese government in 1953 as chief of the Economic Planning Agency (EPA) economic cooperation unit. In 1957 he was made director general of the EPA's Planning Bureau, where he was placed in charge of preparing the "income-doubling" plan of Prime Minister Ikeda Hayato (1960) that set off Japan's economic miracle. In the meantime, he had begun repeated efforts to persuade his government to establish a Japanese version of the Marshall Plan for Asia.

These efforts did much to interpret Japan's interests and concerns to the outside world. After leaving government service in 1963, he became president of the Japan Economic Research Center, and he was named its chairman in 1973. He also was president (1973–77) of his country's Overseas Economic Cooperation Fund for financial aid to less developed nations.

AP/WIDE WORLD

He was named minister for foreign affairs (1979–80) by Prime Minister Masayoshi Ohira. Then, following service as government representative for external economic relations, he became chairman of the Institute for Domestic and International Policy Studies and president of the International University of Japan, both of which posts he continues to hold. His fluency in English and his abundant contacts with foreign economists and other scholars have made him a two-way channel for the exchange of ideas and understanding between Japan and the outside world. Okita has written extensively for scholarly journals in Japan and abroad. Among his books are three that were written in English, *Japan and the World Economy* (1977), *Developing Economies and Japan—Lessons in Growth* (1980), and *Japan's Challenging Years—Reflections on My Lifetime* (1983).

(BRUCE L. FELKNOR)

Major Revisions from the 1987 *Macropædia*

The purpose of this section is to introduce to continuing *Book of the Year* subscribers selected *Macropædia* articles or portions of them that have been completely revised or written anew. It is intended to update the *Macropædia* in ways that cannot be accomplished fully by reviewing the year's events or by revising statistics annually, because the *Macropædia* texts themselves—written from a longer perspective than any yearly revision—supply authoritative interpretation and analysis as well as narrative and description.

Three wholly new articles have been chosen from the 1987 printing: The ISLĀMIC WORLD and POPULATION, printed here in part, and a biography of the philosopher Friedrich NIETZSCHE. Each is the work of a distinguished scholar, and each represents the continuing dedication of the *Encyclopædia Britannica* to bringing such works to the general reader. New bibliographies accompany the articles as well for readers who wish to pursue certain topics. A more general bibliographical updating of the *Macropædia* begins on page 50.

The Islāmic World

Adherence to Islām is a global phenomenon: Muslims predominate in some 30 to 40 countries, from the Atlantic to the Pacific and along a belt that stretches across northern Africa to the southern borders of the Soviet Union and the northern regions of the Indian subcontinent. Arabs account for fewer than one-fifth of all Muslims, more than half of whom live east of Karāchi, Pak. Despite the absence of large-scale Islāmic political entities, the Islāmic faith continues to expand, by some estimates faster than any other major religion.

A very broad perspective is required to explain the history of today's Islāmic world. This approach must enlarge upon conventional political or dynastic divisions to draw a comprehensive picture of the stages by which successive Muslim communities, throughout Islām's 14 centuries, encountered and incorporated new peoples so as to produce an international religion and civilization.

In general, events in this article are dated according to the Gregorian calendar and eras are designated BCE (before the Common Era or Christian Era) and CE (Common Era or Christian Era), equivalent to BC (before Christ) and AD (Latin anno Domini). In some cases the Muslim reckoning of the Islāmic era is used, indicated by AH (Latin anno Hegirae). The Islāmic era begins with the date of Muḥammad's emigration (*hijrah*) to Medina, which corresponds to July 16, 622, in the Gregorian calendar. The term Islāmic refers to Islām as a religion. The term Islāmicate refers to the social and cultural complex historically associated with Islām and the Muslims, even when found among non-Muslims. Islāmdom refers to that complex of societies in which the Muslims and their faith have been prevalent and socially dominant.

The article is divided into the following sections:

Prehistory (c. 3000 BCE–CE 500)

The prehistory of Islāmdom is the history of central Afro-Eurasia from Hammurabi of Babylon to the Achaemenid Cyrus II in Persia to Alexander the Great to the Sāsānian emperor Nūshīrvān to Muḥammad in Arabia; or, in a Muslim view, from Adam to Noah to Abraham to Moses to Jesus to Muḥammad. The potential for Muslim empire building was established with the rise of the earliest civilizations in western Asia. It was refined with the emergence and spread of what have been called the region's Axial Age religions—Abrahamic, centred on the Hebrew patriarch Abraham, and Mazdean, focused on the Iranian deity Ahura Mazdāh—and their later relative, Christianity. It was facilitated by the expansion of trade from eastern Asia to the Mediterranean, and by the political changes thus effected. The Muslims were heirs to the ancient Egyptians, Babylonians, Persians, Hebrews, even the Greeks and Indians; the societies they created bridged time and space, from ancient to modern and from east to west.

THE RISE OF AGRARIAN-BASED CITIED SOCIETIES

In the 7th century CE a coalition of Arab groups, some sedentary and some migratory, inside and outside the Arabian Peninsula, seized political and fiscal control in western Asia, specifically of the lands between the Nile and Oxus (Amu Darya) rivers—territory formerly controlled by the Byzantines in the west and the Sāsānians in the east. The factors that surrounded and directed their accomplishment had begun to coalesce long before, with the emergence of agrarian-based citied societies in western Asia in the 4th millennium BCE. The rise of complex agrarian-based societies, such as Sumer, out of a subsistence agricultural and pastoralist environment, involved the founding of cities, the extension of citied power over surrounding villages, and the interaction of both with pastoralists. . . .

CULTURAL CORE AREAS OF THE SETTLED WORLD

By the middle of the 1st millennium BCE the settled world had crystallized into four cultural core areas: Mediterranean, Nile-to-Oxus, Indic, and East Asian. The Nile-to-Oxus, the future core of Islāmdom, was the least cohesive and the most complicated. Whereas each of the other regions developed a single language of high culture—Greek, Sanskrit, and Chinese, respectively—the Nile-to-Oxus region was a linguistic palimpsest of Irano-Semitic languages of several sorts: Aramaic, Syriac (eastern or Iranian Aramaic), and Middle Persian (the language of eastern Iran).

The Nile-to-Oxus region. The Nile-to-Oxus region differed in climate and ecology, too. It lay at the centre of a vast arid zone stretching across Afro-Eurasia from the Sahara to the Gobi; it favoured those who could deal with aridity—not only states that could control flooding (as in Egypt), or maintain irrigation (as in Mesopotamia), but also pastoralists and oasis dwellers. Although its agricultural potential was severely limited, its commercial possibilities were virtually unlimited. Located at the crossroads of the trans-Asian trade and blessed with numerous natural transit points, the region offered special social and economic prominence to its merchants.

The period from 800 to 200 BCE has been called the Axial Age because of its pivotal importance for the history of religion and culture. The world's first religions of salvation developed in the four core areas. From these traditions, for example, Judaism, Mazdeism, Buddhism, and Confucianism, derived all later forms of high religion, including Christianity and Islām. Unlike the religions that surrounded their formation, the Axial Age religions concentrated transcendent power into one locus, be it symbolized theistically or nontheistically. Their radically dualistic cosmology posited another realm, totally unlike the earthly realm and capable of challenging and replacing ordinary earthly values. The individual was challenged to adopt the right relationship with that "other" realm, so as to transcend mortality by earning a final resting place, or to escape the immortality guaranteed by rebirth by achieving annihilation of earthly attachment.

In the Nile-to-Oxus region two major traditions arose during the Axial Age: the Abrahamic in the west and the Mazdean in the east. Because they required exclusive allegiance through an individual confession of faith in a just and judging deity, they are called confessional religions. The god of these religions was a unique all-powerful creator who remained active in history; and each event in the life of every individual was meaningful in terms of the judgment of God at the end of time. The universally applicable truth of these new religions was expressed in sacred writings. The traditions reflected the mercantile environment in which they were formed in their special concern for fairness, honesty, covenant keeping, moderation, law and order, accountability, and the rights of ordinary human beings. These values were always potentially incompatible with the elitism and absolutism of courtly circles. Most often, as for example in the case of the Achaemenid Empire, the conflict was expressed in rebellion against the crown or was adjudicated by viewing kingship as the guarantor of divine justice.

The Abrahamic and Mazdean traditions

Although modern Western historiography has projected an East–West dichotomy onto ancient times, Afro-Eurasian continuities and interactions were well established by the Axial Age and persisted throughout premodern times. The history of Islāmdom cannot be understood without reference to them. Through Alexander's conquests in the 4th century BCE in three of the four core areas, the Irano-Semitic cultures of the Nile-to-Oxus region were permanently overlaid with Hellenistic elements, and a link was forged between the Indian subcontinent and Iran. By the 3rd century CE, crosscutting movements like Gnosticism and Manichaeism integrated individuals from disparate cultures. Similarly organized large, land-based empires with official religions existed in all parts of the settled world. The Christian Roman Empire was locked in conflict with its counterpart to the east, the Zoroastrian–Mazdean Sāsānian Empire. Another Christian empire in East Africa, the Abyssinian, was involved alternately with each of the others. In the context of these regional interrelationships inhabitants of Arabia made their fateful entrance into international political, religious, and economic life.

The Arabian Peninsula. The Arabian Peninsula consists of a large central arid zone punctuated by oases, wells, and small seasonal streams and bounded in the south by well-watered lands that are generally thin, sometimes mountainous coastal strips. To the north of the peninsula are the irrigated agricultural areas of Syria and Iraq, the site of large-scale states from the 4th millennium BCE. As early as the beginning of the 1st millennium BCE the southwest corner of Arabia, the Yemen, also was divided into settled kingdoms. Their language was a South Arabian Semitic dialect and their culture bore some affinity to Semitic societies in the Fertile Crescent. By the beginning of the Common Era (the 1st century AD in the Christian calendar) the major occupants of the habitable parts of the arid centre were known as Arabs. They were Semitic-speaking tribes of settled, semi-settled, and fully migratory peoples who drew their name and apparently their identity from what the camel-herding Bedouin pastoralists among them called themselves: *ʿarab*.

The Arab tribes

Until the beginning of the 3rd century of the Common Era the greatest economic and political power in the peninsula rested in the relatively independent kingdoms of the Yemen. The Yemenis, with a knowledge of the monsoon winds, had evolved an exceptionally long and profitable trade route from East Africa across the Red Sea and from India across the Indian Ocean up through the peninsula into Iraq and Syria, where it joined older Phoenician routes across the Mediterranean and into the Iberian Peninsula. Their power depended on their ability to protect islands discovered in the Indian Ocean and to control the straits of Hormuz and Aden as well as the Bedouin caravanners who guided and protected the caravans that carried the trade northward to Arab entrepôts like Petra and Palmyra. Participation in this trade was in turn an important source of power for tribal Arabs, whose livelihood otherwise depended on a combination of intergroup raiding, agriculture, and animal husbandry.

By the 3rd century, however, external developments began to impinge. In 226 Ardashīr I founded the Sāsānian Empire in Fars; within 70 years the Sāsānian state was at war with Rome, a conflict that was to last up to Islāmic times. The reorganization of the Roman Empire under Constantine the Great, with the adoption of a new faith, Christianity, and a new capital, Constantinople, exacerbated the competition with the Sāsānian Empire and resulted in the spreading of Christianity into Egypt and Abyssinia and the encouraging of missionizing in Arabia itself. There Christians encountered Jews who had been settling since the 1st century, as well as Arabs who had converted to Judaism. By the beginning of the 4th century the rulers of Abyssinia and Ptolemaic Egypt were interfering in the Red Sea area and carrying their aggression into the Yemen proper. In the first quarter of the 6th century the proselytizing efforts of a Jewish Yemeni ruler resulted in a massacre of Christians in the major Christian centre of Najrān. This event invited Abyssinian Christian reprisal and occupation, which put a virtual end to indigenous control of the Yemen. In conflict with the Byzantines, the Zoroastrian–Mazdean Sāsānians invaded Yemen toward the end of the 6th century, further expanding the religious and cultural horizons of Arabia, where membership in a religious community could not be apolitical and could even have international ramifications. The connection between communal affiliation and political orientations would be expressed in the early Muslim community and in fact has continued to function to the present day.

The long-term result of Arabia's entry into international politics was paradoxical: it enhanced the power of the tribal Arabs at the expense of the "superpowers." Living in an ecological environment that favoured tribal independence and small-group loyalties, the Arabs had never established lasting large-scale states, only transient tribal confederations. By the 5th century, however, the settled powers needed their hinterlands enough to foster client states: the Byzantines oversaw the Ghassānid kingdom; the Persians oversaw the Lakhmid; and the Yemenis (prior to the Abyssinian invasion) had Kindah. These relationships increased Arab awareness of other cultures and religions; and the awareness seems to have stimulated internal Arab cultural activity, especially the classical Arabic, or *muḍarī,* poetry, for which the pre-Islāmic Arabs are so famous. In the north, Arabic speakers were drawn into the imperial administrations of the Romans and Sāsānians; soon certain settled and semi-settled Arabs spoke and wrote Aramaic or Persian as well as Arabic, and some Persian or Aramaic speakers could speak and write Arabic. The prosperity of the 5th and 6th centuries, as well as the intensification of imperial rivalries in the late 6th century, seems to have brought the Arabs of the interior permanently into the wider network of communication that fostered the rise of the Muslim community at Mecca and Medina.

Formation and orientation (c. 500–634)

THE CITY OF MECCA: CENTRE OF TRADE AND RELIGION

Although the 6th-century client states were the largest Arab polities of their day, it was not from them that a permanently significant Arab state arose. Rather, it emerged among independent Arabs living in Mecca (Makkah) at the junction of major north–south and west–east routes, in one of the less naturally favoured Arab settlements of the Hejaz (al-Ḥijāz). The development of a trading town into a city-state was not unusual; but unlike many other western Arabian settlements, Mecca was not centred on an oasis or located in the hinterland of any non-Arab power. Although it had enough well water and springwater to provide for large numbers of camels, it did not have enough for agriculture; its economy depended on long-distance as well as short-distance trade.

Mecca under the Quraysh clans. Around the year 400 CE Mecca had come under the control of a group of Arabs who were in the process of becoming sedentary; they were known as Quraysh and were led by a man remembered as Quṣayy. During the generations before Muḥammad's birth in about 570, the several clans of the Quraysh fostered a development in Mecca that seems to have been occurring in a few other Arab towns as well. They used their trading connections and their relationships with their Bedouin cousins to make their town a regional centre whose influence radiated in many directions. They designated Mecca as a quarterly *ḥaram,* a safe haven from the intertribal warfare and raiding that was endemic among the Bedouin. Thus Mecca became an attractive site for large trade fairs that coincided with pilgrimage (*ḥajj*) to a local shrine, the Kaʿbah. The Kaʿbah housed the deities of visitors as well as the Meccans' supra-tribal creator and covenant-guaranteeing deity, called Allāh. Most Arabs probably viewed this deity as one among many, possessing powers not specific to a particular tribe; others may have identified this figure with the God of the Jews and Christians. . . .

Quarterly haven at Mecca

The Meccan link between shrine and market has a broader significance in the history of religion. It is reminiscent of changes that had taken place with the emergence of complex societies across the settled world several millennia earlier. Much of the religious life of the tribal Arabs had the characteristics of small-group, or "primitive," religion, including the sacralization of group-specific natural objects and phenomena and the multifarious presence of spirit beings, known among the Arabs as *jinn.* Where more complex settlement patterns had developed, however, widely shared deities had already emerged, such as the "trinity" of Allāh's "daughters" known as al-Lāt, Manāt, and al-ʿUzzāh. Such qualified simplification and inclusivity, wherever they have occurred in human history, seem to have been associated with other fundamental changes—increased settlement, extension and intensification of trade, and the emergence of lingua francas and other cultural commonalties, all of which had been occurring in central Arabia for several centuries.

Changes in religion: the sharing of deities

New social patterns among the Meccans and their neighbours. The sedentation of the Quraysh and their efforts to create an expanding network of cooperative Arabs generated social stresses that demanded new patterns of behaviour. The ability of the Quraysh to solve their problems was affected by an ambiguous relationship between sedentary and migratory Arabs. Tribal Arabs could go in and out of sedentation easily, and kinship ties often transcended life-styles. The sedentation of the Quraysh did not involve the destruction of their ties with the Bedouin or their idealization of Bedouin life. Thus, for example, did wealthy Meccans, thinking Mecca unhealthy, often send their infants to Bedouin foster mothers. Yet the settling of the Quraysh at Mecca was no ordinary instance of sedentation. Their commercial success produced a society unlike that of the Bedouin and unlike that of many other sedentary Arabs. Whereas stratification was minimal among the Bedouin, a hierarchy based on wealth appeared among the Quraysh. Although a Bedouin group might include a small number of outsiders, such as prisoners of war, Meccan society was markedly diverse, including non-Arabs as well as Arabs, slave as well as free. Among the Bedouin, lines of protection for in-group members were clearly drawn; in Mecca, sedentation and socioeconomic stratification had begun to blur family responsibilities and foster the growth of an oligarchy whose economic objectives could easily supersede other motivations and values. Whereas the Bedouin acted in and through groups, and even regularized intergroup raiding and warfare as a way of life, Meccans needed to act in their own interest and to minimize conflict by institutionalizing new, broader social alliances and interrelationships. The market–shrine complex encouraged surrounding tribes to put aside their conflicts periodically and to visit and worship the deities of the Kaʿbah; but such worship, as in most complex societies, could not replace either the particularistic worship of small groups or the competing religious practices of other regional centres, such as aṭ-Ṭāʾif.

Very little in the Arabian environment favoured the formation of stable, large-scale states. Therefore, Meccan efforts at centralization and unification might well have been transient, especially because they were not reinforced by any stronger power and because they depended almost entirely on the prosperity of a trade route that had been formerly controlled at its southern terminus and could be controlled elsewhere in the future, or exclude Mecca entirely. The rise of the Meccan system also coincided with the spread of the confessional religions, through immigration, missionization, conversion, and foreign interference. Alongside members of the confessional religions, unaffiliated monotheists, known as *ḥanīfs*, distanced themselves from the Meccan religious system by repudiating the old gods but embracing neither Judaism nor Christianity. Eventually in Mecca and elsewhere a few individuals came to envision the possibility of effecting supra-tribal association through a leadership role common to the confessional religions, that is, prophethood or messengership. The only such individual who succeeded in effecting broad social changes was a member of the Hāshim (Hāshem) clan of Quraysh named Muḥammad ibn ʿAbd Allāh ibn ʿAbd al-Muṭṭalib. One of their own, he accomplished what the Quraysh had started, first by working against them, later by working with them. When he was born, around 570, the potential for pan-Arab unification seemed nil; but after he died, in 632, the first generation of his followers were able not only to maintain pan-Arab unification but to expand far beyond the peninsula.

Concept of social unity through shared deity

THE PROPHET MUḤAMMAD

Muḥammad's years in Mecca. *Spiritual awakening.* Any explanation of such an unprecedented development must include an analysis not only of Muḥammad's individual genius but also of his ability to articulate an ideology capable of appealing to multiple constituencies. His approach to the role of prophet allowed a variety of groups to conceptualize and form a single community. Muḥammad was, according to many students of social behaviour, particularly well placed to lead such a social movement; in both ascribed and acquired characteristics he was unusual. Although he was a member of a high-status tribe, he belonged to one of its less well-placed clans. He was fatherless at birth; his mother and grandfather died when he was young, leaving him under the protection of an uncle. Although he possessed certain admirable personality traits to an unusual degree, his commercial success derived not from his own status but from his marriage to a much older woman, a wealthy widow named Khadījah. During the years of his marriage, his personal habits grew increasingly atypical; he began to absent himself in the hills outside Mecca to engage in the solitary spiritual activity of the *ḥanīfs*. At age 40, while on retreat, he saw a figure, whom he later identified as the angel Gabriel, who forced him to repeat these words: "Recite: In the name of God, the Merciful and Compassionate. Recite: And your Lord is Most Generous. He teaches by the pen, teaches man what he knew not." Although a few individuals, including his wife Khadījah, recognized his experience as that of a messenger of God, the contemporary religious life of most of the Meccans and the surrounding Arabs did not prepare them to share in this recognition easily.

Muḥammad's first recitation

Arabs did recognize several other types of intermediaries with the sacred. Some of the kings of the Yemen are said to have had priestly functions; and tribal leaders, *shaykhs*, in protecting their tribes' hallowed custom (*sunnah*), had a spiritual dimension. Tribal Arabs also had their *kāhins*, religious specialists who delivered oracles in ecstatic rhymed prose (*sajʿ*) and read omens. They also had their *shāʿirs*, professionally trained oral poets who defended the group's honour, expressed its identity, and engaged in verbal duels with the poets of other groups. The power of the recited word was well established; the poets' words were even likened to arrows that could wound the unprotected enemy. Because Muḥammad's utterances seemed similar, at least in form, to those of the *kāhins*, many of his hearers naturally assumed that he was one of the figures with whom they were more familiar. Indeed, Muḥammad might not even have attracted attention had he not sounded like other holy men; but by eschewing any source other than the one supreme being, whom he identified as Allāh ("the god") and whose message he regarded as cosmically significant and binding, he was gradually able to distinguish himself from all other intermediaries. Like many successful leaders Muḥammad broke through existing restraints by what might be called transformative conservatism. By combining familiar leadership roles with a less familiar one, he expanded his authority; by giving existing practices a new history, he reoriented them; by assigning a new cause to existing problems, he resolved them. His personal characteristics fit his historical circumstances perfectly.

Public recitations. Muḥammad's first vision was followed by a brief lull, after which he began to hear messages frequently, entering a special physical state to receive them and returning to normalcy to deliver them orally. Soon he began publicly to recite warnings of an imminent reckoning by Allāh that disturbed the Meccan leaders. Muḥammad was one of their own, a man respected for his personal qualities. Yet weakening kinship ties and increasing social diversity were helping him attract followers from many different clans and also from among tribeless persons, giving all of them a new and potentially disruptive affiliation. The fundamentals of his message, delivered often in the vicinity of the Kaʿbah itself, questioned the very reasons for which so many people gathered there. If visitors to the Kaʿbah assumed, as so many Arabs did, that the deities represented by its idols were all useful and accessible in that place, Muḥammad spoke, as had Axial Age figures before, of a placeless and timeless deity that not only had created human beings, making them dependent on him, but would also bring them to account at an apocalypse of his own making. In place of time or chance, which the Arabs assumed to govern their destiny, Muḥammad installed a final reward or punishment based on individual actions. Such individual accountability to an unseen power that took no account whatsoever of kin relationships and operated beyond the Meccan system could, if taken seriously, undermine any authority the Quraysh had acquired. Muḥammad's insistence on the protection of the weak, which echoed Bedouin values, threatened the unbridled amassing of wealth so important to the Meccan oligarchy.

Early reactions to Muḥammad's preachings

Efforts to reform Meccan society. Yet Muḥammad also appealed to the town dweller by describing the human being as a member of a polis (city-state) and by suggesting ways to overcome the inequities that such an environment breeds. By insisting that an event of cosmic significance was occurring in Mecca, he made the town the rival of all the greater cities with which the Meccans traded. To Meccans who believed that what went on in their town and at their shrine was hallowed by tribal custom, *sunnah,* Muḥammad replied that their activities in fact were a corrupt form of a practice that had a very long history with the god of whom he spoke. In Muḥammad's view, the Kaʿbah had been dedicated to the aniconic worship of the one God (Allāh) by Abraham, who fathered the ancestor of the Israelites, Isḥāq (Isaac), as well as the ancestor of the Arabs, Ismāʿīl (Ishmael). Muḥammad asked his hearers not to embrace something new, but to abandon the traditional in favour of the original. He appealed to his fellow Quraysh not to reject the *sunnah* of their ancestors, but rather to appreciate and fulfill its true nature. God should be worshiped not through offerings but through prayer and recitation of his messages, and his house should be emptied of its useless idols.

In their initial rejection of his appeal, Muḥammad's Meccan opponents took the first step toward accepting the new idea: they attacked it. For it was their rejection of him, as well as his subsequent rejection by many Jews and Christians, that helped to forge Muḥammad's followers into a community with an identity of its own and capable of ultimately incorporating its opponents. Muḥammad's disparate following was exceptionally vulnerable, bound together not by kinship ties but by a "generic" monotheism that involved being faithful (*muʾmin*) to the message God was sending through their leader. Their vulnerability was mitigated by the absence of formal municipal discipline; but their opponents within Quraysh could apply informal pressures ranging from harassment and violence against the weakest to a boycott against Muḥammad's clan, who were persuaded by his uncle Ṭālib to remain loyal even though most of them were not his followers. Meanwhile Muḥammad and his closest associates were thinking about reconstituting themselves as a separate community in a less hostile environment. In about 612 some 80 of his followers made an emigration (*hijrah*) to Abyssinia, perhaps assuming that they would be welcome in a place that had a history of hostility to the Meccan oligarchy and that worshiped the same god who had sent Muḥammad to them; but they eventually returned without establishing a permanent community. During the next decade, continued rejection intensified the group's identity and its search for another home. Although the boycott against Muḥammad's clan began to disintegrate, the deaths of his wife and his uncle, in about 619, removed an important source of psychological and social support. Muḥammad had already begun to preach and attract followers at market gatherings outside Mecca; now he intensified his search for a more hospitable environment. In 620 he met with a delegation of followers from Yathrib, an oasis about 200 miles to the northeast; in the next two years their support grew into an offer of protection.

Muḥammad's emigration to Yathrib (Medina). Like Mecca, Yathrib was experiencing demographic problems: several tribal groups coexisted, descendants of its Arab Jewish founders as well as a number of pagan Arab immigrants divided into two tribes, the Aws and the Khazraj. Unable to resolve their conflicts, the Yathribis invited Muḥammad to perform the well-established role of neutral outside arbiter (*ḥakam*). In 622, having sent his followers ahead, he and one companion, Abū Bakr, completed the community's second and final emigration, barely avoiding Quraysh attempts to prevent his departure by force. By the time of the emigration a new label had begun to appear in Muḥammad's recitations to describe his followers; in addition to being described in terms of their faithfulness (*īmān*) to God and his messenger, they were also described in terms of their undivided attention, that is, as *muslims*, individuals who assumed the right relationship to God by surrendering (*islām*) to his will. Although the label *muslim,* derived from *islām,* eventually became a proper name for a specific historical community, at this point it appears to have expressed commonalty with other monotheists: like the others, *muslims* faced Jerusalem to pray; Muḥammad was believed to have been transported from Jerusalem to the heavens to talk with God; and Abraham, Noah, Moses, David, and Jesus, as well as Muḥammad, all were considered to be prophets (*nabīs*) and messengers of the same God. In Yathrib, however, conflicts between other monotheists and the *muslims* sharpened their distinctiveness.

Use of the terms *islām* and *muslim*

The forging of Muḥammad's community. As an autonomous community *muslims* might have become a tribal unit like those with whom they had affiliated, especially because the terms of their immigration gave them no special status. Yet under Muḥammad's leadership they developed a social organization that could absorb or challenge everyone around them. They became Muḥammad's *ummah* ("community") because they had recognized and supported God's emissary (*rasūl Allāh*). The *ummah*'s members differed from one another not by wealth or genealogical superiority but by the degree of their faith and piety; and membership in the community was itself an expression of faith. Anyone could join, regardless of origin, by following Muḥammad's lead, and the nature of members' support could vary. In the concept of *ummah,* Muḥammad supplied the missing ingredient in the Meccan system: a powerful abstract principle for defining, justifying, and stimulating membership in a single community.

Muḥammad made the concept of *ummah* work by expanding his role as arbiter so as to become the sole spokesman for all residents of Yathrib, also known as Medina. Even though the agreement under which Muḥammad had emigrated did not obligate non-Muslims to follow him except in his arbitration, they necessarily became involved in the fortunes of his community. By protecting him from his Meccan enemies, the residents of Medina identified with his fate. Those who supported him as Muslims received special designations: the Medinans were called *anṣār* ("helpers"), and his fellow emigrants were distinguished as *muhājirūn* ("emigrants"). He was often able to use revelation to arbitrate. Because the terms of his emigration did not provide adequate financial support, he began to provide for his community through caravan raiding, a tactic familiar to tribal Arabs. By thus inviting hostility, he required all the Medinans to take sides. Initial failure was followed by success, first at Nakhlah, where the Muslims defied Meccan custom by violating one of the truce months so essential to Meccan prosperity and prestige. Their most memorable victory occurred in 624 at Badr, against a large Meccan force; they continued to succeed, with only one serious setback, at Uḥud in 625. From that time on, "conversion" to Islām involved joining an established polity, the successes of which were tied to its proper spiritual orientation, regardless of whether the convert shared that orientation completely. During the early years in Medina a major motif of Islāmic history emerged: the connection between material success and divine favour, which had also been prominent in the history of the Israelites.

The relation of material success to divine favour

The ummah's allies and enemies. During these years, Muḥammad used his outstanding knowledge of tribal relations to act as a great tribal leader, or *shaykh,* further expanding his authority beyond the role that the Medinans had given him. He developed a network of alliances between his *ummah* and neighbouring tribes, and so competed with the Meccans at their own game. He managed and distributed the booty from raiding, keeping one-fifth for the *ummah*'s overall needs and distributing the rest among its members. In return, members gave a portion of their wealth as *zakat,* to help the needy and to demonstrate their awareness of their dependence on God for all of their material benefits. Like other *shaykhs*, Muḥammad contracted numerous, often strategically motivated, marriage alliances. He was also more able to harass and discipline Medinans, Muslim and non-Muslim alike, who did not support his activities fully; he agitated in particular against the Jews, one of whose clans, the Banū Qaynuqa, he expelled.

Increasingly estranged from nonresponsive Jews and Christians, he reoriented his followers' direction of prayer from Jerusalem to Mecca. He formally instituted the *ḥajj* to Mecca and fasting during the month of Ramaḍān as distinctive cultic acts, in recognition of the fact that *islām,* a generic act of surrender to God, had become Islām, a proper-name identity distinguished not only from paganism but from other forms of monotheism as well. As more and more of Medina was absorbed into the Muslim community, and as the Meccans weakened, Muḥammad's authority expanded. He continued to lead a three-pronged campaign, against nonsupporters in Medina, against the Quraysh in Mecca, and against surrounding tribes; he even ordered raids into southern Syria. Eventually, Muḥammad became powerful enough to punish nonsupporters severely, especially those who leaned toward Mecca. For example, he had the men of the Qurayẓah clan of Jews in Medina executed after they failed to help him against the Meccan forces at the Battle of the Ditch in 627. But he also used force and diplomacy to bring in other Jewish and Christian groups. Because they were seen, unlike pagans, to have formed *ummahs* of their own around a revelation from God, Jews and Christians were entitled to pay for protection (*dhimmah*). Muḥammad thus set a precedent for another major characteristic of Islāmicate civilization, that of qualified religious pluralism under Muslim authority.

Muḥammad's later recitations. During these years of warfare and consolidation, Muḥammad continued to transmit revealed recitations, though their nature began to change. Some commented on Muḥammad's situation, consoled and encouraged his community, explained the continuing resistance of the Meccans, and urged appropriate responses. Some told stories about figures familiar to Jews and Christians, cast in an Islāmic framework. Though still delivered in the form of God's direct speech, the messages became longer and less ecstatic, less urgent in their warnings if more earnest in their guidance. Eventually they focused on interpersonal regulations in areas of particular importance for a new community, such as sexuality, marriage, divorce, and inheritance. By this time certain Muslims had begun to write down what Muḥammad uttered or to recite passages for cultic worship (*ṣalāt*) and private devotion. The recited word, so important among the Arab tribes, had found a greatly enlarged significance. A competitor for Muḥammad's sta-

The importance of the recited word

tus as God's messenger even declared himself among a nonmember tribe; he was Maslamah of Yamāmah, who claimed to convey revelations from God. He managed to attract numerous Bedouin Arabs but failed to speak as successfully as Muḥammad to the various available constituencies.

Activism in the name of God, nonmilitary as well as military, would become a permanent strand in Muslim piety. Given the environment in which Muḥammad operated, his *ummah* was unlikely to survive without it; to compete as leader of a community he had to exhibit military prowess. (Like most successful leaders, however, Muḥammad was a moderate and a compromiser; some of his followers were more militant and aggressive than he, and some were less so.) Circumstantial necessity had ideological ramifications, too. Because Muḥammad as messenger was also, by divine providence, leader of an established community, he could easily define the whole realm of social action as an expression of faith. Thus Muslims were able to identify messengership with worldly leadership to an extent almost unparalleled in the history of religion. There had been activist prophets before Muḥammad, and there were activist prophets after him, but in no other religious tradition does the image of the activist prophet, and by extension the activist follower, have such a comprehensive and coherent justification in the formative period.

ISLĀM AT MUḤAMMAD'S DEATH

Muḥammad's continuing success gradually impinged on the Quraysh in Mecca. Some defected and joined his community. His marriage to a Quraysh woman provided him with a useful go-between. In 628 he and his followers tried to make an Islāmized *ḥajj* but were forestalled by the Meccans. At al-Ḥudaybiyah, outside Mecca, Muḥammad granted a 10-year truce on the condition that the Meccans would allow a Muslim pilgrimage the next year. Even at this point, however, Muḥammad's control over his followers had its limits; his more zealous followers agreed to the pact only after much persuasion. As in all instances of charismatic leadership, persisting loyalty was correlated with continuing success. In the next year the Meccans allowed a Muslim *ḥajj;* and in the next, 630, the Muslims occupied Mecca without a struggle. Muḥammad began to receive deputations from many parts of Arabia. By his death in 632 he was ruler of virtually all of it.

The Meccan Quraysh were allowed to become Muslims without shame. In fact, they quickly became assimilated to the actual *muhājirūn,* even though they had not emigrated to Yathrib themselves. Ironically, in defeat they had accomplished much more than they would have in victory: the centralization of all of Arabia around their polity and their shrine, the Kaʿbah, which had been emptied of its idols to be filled with an infinitely greater invisible power.

Because intergroup conflict was banned to all members of the *ummah* on the basis of their shared loyalty to the emissary of a single higher authority, the limitations of the Meccan concept of *ḥaram,* according to which the city quarterly became a safe haven, could be overcome. The broader solidarity that Muḥammad had begun to build was stabilized only after his death; and this was achieved, paradoxically, by some of the same people who had initially opposed him. In the next two years one of his most significant legacies became apparent: the willingness and ability of his closest supporters to sustain the ideal and the reality of one Muslim community under one leader, even in the face of significant opposition. When Muḥammad died, two vital sources of his authority ended—ongoing revelation and his unique ability to exemplify his messages on a daily basis. A leader capable of keeping revelation alive might have had the best chance of inheriting his movement; but no Muslim claimed messengership, nor had Muḥammad unequivocally designated any other type of successor. The *anṣār,* his early supporters in Medina, moved to elect their own leader, leaving the *muhājirūn* to choose theirs; but a small number of *muhājirūn* managed to impose one of their own over the whole. That man was Abū Bakr, one of Muḥammad's earliest followers and the father of his favourite wife, ʿĀʾishah. The title Abū Bakr took, *khalīfah* (caliph), meaning deputy or successor, echoed revealed references to those who assist major leaders and even God himself. To *khalīfah* he appended *rasūl Allāh,* so that his authority was based on his assistance to Muḥammad as messenger of God.

ABŪ BAKR'S SUCCESSION

Abū Bakr soon confronted two new threats: the secession of many of the tribes that had joined the *ummah* after 630 and the appearance among them of other prophet figures who claimed continuing guidance from God. In withdrawing, the tribes appear to have been able to distinguish loyalty to Muḥammad from full acceptance of the uniqueness and permanence of his message. The appearance of other prophets illustrates a general phenomenon in the history of religion: the volatility of revelation as a source of authority. When successfully claimed, it has almost no competitor; once opened, it is difficult to close; and, if it cannot be contained and focused at the appropriate moment, its power disperses. Jews and Christians had responded to this dilemma in their own ways; now it was the turn of the Muslims, whose future was dramatically affected by Abū Bakr's response. He put an end to revelation with a combination of military force and coherent rhetoric. He defined withdrawal from Muḥammad's coalition as ingratitude to or denial of God (the concept of *kufr*); thus he gave secession (*riddah*) cosmic significance as an act of apostasy punishable, according to God's revealed messages to Muḥammad, by death. He declared that the secessionists had become Muslims, and thus servants of God, by joining Muḥammad; they were not free *not* to be Muslims, nor could they be Muslims, and thus loyal to God, under any leader whose legitimacy did not derive from Muḥammad. Finally, he declared Muḥammad to be the last prophet God would send, relying on a reference to Muḥammad in one of the revealed messages as *khatm al-anbiyāʾ* ("Seal of the Prophets"). In his ability to interpret the events of his reign from the perspective of Islām, Abū Bakr demonstrated the power of the new conceptual vocabulary Muḥammad had introduced.

Ban on revelation and secession

Had Abū Bakr not asserted the independence and uniqueness of Islām, the movement he had inherited could have been splintered or absorbed by other monotheistic communities or by new Islām-like movements led by other tribal figures. Moreover, had he not quickly made the ban on secession and intergroup conflict yield material success, his chances for survival would have been very slim, because Arabia's resources could not support his state. To provide an adequate fiscal base, Abū Bakr enlarged impulses present in pre-Islāmic Mecca and in the *ummah.* At his death he was beginning to turn his followers to raiding non-Muslims in the only direction where that was possible, the north. Migration into Syria and Iraq already had a long history; and Arabs, both migratory and settled, were already present there. Indeed some of them were already launching raids when ʿUmar I, Abū Bakr's acknowledged successor, assumed the caliphate in 634. The ability of the Medinan state to absorb random action into a relatively centralized movement of expansion testifies to the strength of the new ideological and administrative patterns inherent in the concept of *ummah.*

The fusion of two once separable phenomena, membership in Muḥammad's community and faith in Islām—the mundane and the spiritual—would become one of Islām's most distinctive features. Becoming and being Muslim always involved *doing* more than it involved *believing.* On balance, Muslims have always favoured orthopraxy (correctness of practice) over orthodoxy (correctness of doctrine). Being Muslim has always meant making a commitment to a set of behavioral patterns because they reflect the right orientation to God. Where choices were later posed, they were posed not in terms of religion and politics, or church and state, but between living in the world the right way or the wrong way. Just as classical Islāmicate languages developed no equivalents for the words *religion* and *politics,* modern European languages have developed no adequate terms to capture the choices as Muslims have posed them.

Fusion of community and faith

Conversion and crystallization (634–870)

SOCIAL AND CULTURAL TRANSFORMATIONS

The Arab conquests are often viewed as a discrete period. The end of the conquests appears to be a convenient dividing line because it coincides with a conventional watershed, the overthrow of the Umayyad caliphs by the ʿAbbāsids. To illustrate their role in broader social and cultural change, however, the military conquests should be included in a period more than twice as long, during which the conquest of the hearts and minds of the majority of the subject population also occurred. Between 634 and 870 Islām was transformed from the badge of a small Arab ruling class to the dominant faith of a vast empire that stretched from the western Mediterranean into Central Asia. As a result of this long and gradual period of conversion, Arab cultures intermingled with the indigenous cultures of the conquered peoples to produce Islām's fundamental orientations and identities. The Arabic language became a vehicle for the transmission of high culture, even though the Arabs remained a minority; for the first time in the history of the Nile-to-Oxus region, a new language of high culture, carrying a great cultural florescence, replaced all previous languages of high culture. Trade and taxation replaced booty as the fiscal basis of the Muslim state; a nontribal army replaced a tribal one; and a centralized empire became a nominal confederation, with all of the social dislocation and rivalries those changes imply. Yet despite continuous internal dissension, virtually no Muslim raised the possibility of there being more than one legitimate leader. Furthermore, the impulse toward solidarity, inherited from Muḥammad and Abū Bakr, may have actually been encouraged by persisting minority status. While Muslims were a minority, they naturally formed a conception of Islāmic dominance as territorial rather than religious; and of unconverted non-Muslim communities as secondary members. In one important respect the Islāmic faith differed from all other major religious traditions: the formative period of the faith coincided with its political domination of a rich complex of old cultures. Thus, during the formative period of their civilization, the Muslims could both introduce new elements and reorient old ones in creative ways. . . .

Arabic as a language of high culture

ʿUMAR I'S SUCCESSION

The spirit of conquest under ʿUmar I. Abū Bakr's successor in Medina, ʿUmar I (ruled 634–644), had not so much to stimulate conquest as to organize and channel it. As leaders he chose skillful managers experienced in trade and commerce as well as warfare and imbued with an ideology that provided their activities with a cosmic significance. The total numbers involved in the initial conquests may have been relatively small, perhaps less than 50,000, divided into numerous shifting groups. Yet few actions took place without any sanction from the Medinan government or one of its appointed commanders. The fighters, or *muqātilah,* could generally accomplish much more with Medina's support than without. ʿUmar, one of Muḥammad's earliest and staunchest supporters, had quickly developed an administrative system of manifestly superior effectiveness. He defined the *ummah* as a continually expansive polity managed by a new ruling elite, which included successful military commanders like Khālid ibn al-Walīd. Even after the conquests ended, this sense of expansiveness continued to be expressed in the way Muslims divided the world into their own zone, the Dār al-Islām, and the zone into which they could and should expand, the Dār al-Ḥarb, the abode of war. The norms of ʿUmar's new elite were supplied by Islām as it was then understood. Taken together, Muḥammad's revelations from God and his *sunnah* (precedent-setting example) defined the cultic and personal practices that distinguished Muslims from others: prayer, fasting, pilgrimage, charity, avoidance of pork and intoxicants, membership in one community centred at Mecca, and activism (*jihād*) in the community's behalf.

ʿUmar I, successor to Abū Bakr

Forging the link of activism with faithfulness. ʿUmar symbolized this conception of the *ummah* in two ways. He assumed an additional title, *amīr al-muʾminīn* ("commander of the faithful"), which linked organized activism with faithfulness (*īmān*), the earliest defining feature of the Muslim. He also adopted a lunar calendar that began with the emigration (*hijrah*), the moment at which a group of individual followers of Muḥammad had become an active social presence. Because booty was the *ummah*'s major resource, ʿUmar concentrated on ways to distribute and sustain it. He established a *dīwān,* or register, to pay all members of the ruling elite and the conquering forces, from Muḥammad's family on down, in order of entry into the *ummah.* The immovable booty was kept for the state. After the government's fifth-share of the movable booty was reserved, the rest was distributed according to the *dīwān.* The *muqātilah* he stationed as an occupying army in garrisons (*amṣār*) constructed in locations strategic to further conquest: al-Fusṭāṭ in Egypt, Damascus in Syria, Kūfah and Basra in Iraq. The garrisons attracted indigenous population and initiated significant demographic changes, such as a population shift from northern to southern Iraq. They also inaugurated the rudiments of an "Islāmic" daily life; each garrison was commanded by a caliphal appointee, responsible for setting aside an area for prayer, a mosque (*masjid*), named for the prostrations (*sujūd*) that had become a characteristic element in the five daily worship sessions (*ṣalāt*s). There the fighters could hear God's revelations to Muḥammad recited by men trained in that emerging art. The most pious might commit the whole to memory. There, too, the Friday midday *ṣalāt* could be performed communally, accompanied by an important educational device, the sermon (*khuṭbah*), through which the fighters could be instructed in the principles of the faith. The mosque fused the practical and the spiritual in a special way: because the Friday prayer included an expression of loyalty to the ruler, it could also provide an opportunity to declare rebellion.

Distribution of booty among the *ummah*

Origin of the garrison mosque

The series of ongoing conquests that fueled this system had their most extensive phase under ʿUmar and his successor ʿUthmān ibn ʿAffān (ruled 644–656). Within 25 years, Muslim Arab forces created the first empire permanently to link western Asia with the Mediterranean. Within another century, Muslim conquerors surpassed the achievement of Alexander the Great, not only in the durability of their accomplishment but in its scope as well, reaching from the Iberian Peninsula to Central Asia. Resistance was generally slight and nondestructive, and conquest through capitulation was preferred to conquest by force. After Sāsānian al-Ḥīrah fell in 633, a large Byzantine force was defeated in Syria, opening the way to the final conquest of Damascus in 636. The next year, further gains were made in Sāsānian territory, especially at the Battle of al-Qādisīyah; in the next, the focus returned to Syria and the taking of Jerusalem. By 640, Roman control in Syria was over; by 641, the Sāsānians had lost all of their territory west of Zagros. During the years 642 to 646 Egypt was taken under the leadership of ʿAmr ibn al-ʿĀṣ, who soon began raids into what the Muslims called the Maghrib, the lands west of Egypt. Shortly thereafter, in the east, Persepolis fell; in 651 the defeat and assassination of the last Sāsānian emperor, Yazdegerd III, marked the end of the 400-year-old Sāsānian Empire.

ʿUTHMĀN'S SUCCESSION AND POLICIES

Discontent in ʿUthmān's reign. This phase of conquest ended under ʿUthmān and ramified widely. ʿUthmān may even have sent an emissary to China in 651; by the end of the 7th century Arab Muslims were trading there. The fiscal strain of such expansion and the growing independence of local Arabs outside the peninsula underlay the persisting discontents that surfaced toward the end of ʿUthmān's reign. The very way in which he was made caliph had already signaled the potential for competition over leadership and resources. Perceived as pliable and docile, he was the choice of the small committee charged by the dying ʿUmar with selecting one of their own number. Once in office, however, ʿUthmān acted to establish the power of Medina over and against some of the powerful Quraysh families at Mecca and local notables outside Arabia. He was accused of nepotism for relying on his own family, the Banū Umayyah, whose talents ʿUmar had already recognized. Among his many other "objectionable" acts was his call for the production of a single standard collection of Muḥammad's messages from God, which was known simply as the Qur'ān ("Recitation" or "Recitations"). Simultaneously he ordered the destruction of any other collections. Although they might have differed only in minor respects, they represented the independence of local communities. Above all, ʿUthmān was the natural target of anyone dissatisfied with the distribution of the conquest's wealth, since he represented and defended a system that defined all income as Medina's to distribute.

ʿUthmān's standardization of the Qur'ān

The difficulties of ʿUthmān's reign took more than a century to resolve. They were the inevitable result not just of the actions of individuals but of the whole process initiated by Muḥammad's achievements. His coalition had been fragile. He had disturbed existing social arrangements without being able to reconstruct and stabilize new ones quickly. Into a society organized along family lines, he had introduced the supremacy of trans-kinship ties. Yet he had been forced to make use of kinship ties himself; and, despite his egalitarian message, he had introduced new inequities by granting privileges to the earliest and most intensely devoted followers of his cause. Furthermore, personal rivalries were stimulated by his charisma; individuals like his wife ʿĀ'ishah, his daughter Fāṭimah, and her husband ʿAlī frequently vied for his affection. ʿUmar's *dīwān* had, then, reinforced old inequities by extending privileges to wealthy high-placed Meccans, and it had introduced new tensions by assigning a lower status to those, indigenous or immigrant to the provinces, who joined the cause later (but who felt themselves to be making an equivalent or greater contribution). Other tensions resulted from conditions in the conquered lands: the initial isolation of Arab Muslims, and even Arab Christians who fought with them, from the indigenous non-Arab population; the discouragement of non-Arab converts, except as clients (*mawālī*) of Arab tribes; the administrative dependence of peninsular Arabs on local Arabs and non-Arabs; and the development of a tax system that discriminated against non-Muslims.

Intra-Muslim conflicts. The ensuing conflicts were played out in a series of intra-Muslim disputes that began with ʿUthmān's assassination and continued to the end of the period under discussion. The importance of kinship ties persisted, but they were gradually replaced by the identities of a new social order. These new identities resulted from Muslim responses to anti-Muslim activity as well as from Muslim participation in a series of controversies focused on the issue of leadership. Because the *ummah,* unified under one leader, was seen as an earthly expression of God's favour, and because God was seen as the controller of all aspects of human existence, the identities formed in the course of the *ummah*'s early history could fuse dimensions that secular modern observers are able to distinguish—religious, social, political, and economic. Furthermore, intra-Muslim rivalries changed during the conversion period; the meaningfulness of the new identities expanded as non-Muslims contributed to Islām's formation, through opposition or through conversion, and the key issues broadened as the participating constituencies enlarged. At first the disputes were coterminous with intra-Arab, indeed even intra-Quraysh, rivalries; only later did they involve persons of other backgrounds. Thus the faith of Islām was formed in conjunction with the crises that attended the establishment of rule by Muslims. Muslims might have produced an extremely localized and exclusivistic religion; but in spite of, and perhaps because of, their willingness to engage in continuing internal conflicts, they produced one of the most unified religious traditions in human history. . . .

Unifying of the Muslim tradition

Reform, dependency, and recovery (1683 to the present)

The history of the Muslims in modern times has often been explained in terms of the impact of "the West." From this perspective, the 18th century was a period of degeneration and a prelude to European domination, symbolized by Napoleon's conquest of Egypt in 1798. Given the events of the 1980s, however, it is possible to argue that the period of Western domination was an interlude in the ongoing development of indigenous styles of modernization. In order to examine that hypothesis, it is necessary to begin the "modern" period with the 18th century, when activism and revival were present throughout Islāmdom. The three major Muslim empires did experience a decline during the 18th century, as compared to their own earlier power and to the rising powers in Europe; but most Muslims were not yet aware that Europe was partly to blame. Similar decline had occurred many times before, a product of the inevitable weaknesses of the military conquest state turned into centralized absolutism, overdependence on continuous expansion, weakening of training for rule, the difficulty of maintaining efficiency and loyalty in a large, complex royal household and army, and the difficulty of maintaining sufficient revenues for an increasingly lavish court life. Furthermore, population increased, as it did almost everywhere in the 18th-century world, just as inflation and expensive reform reduced income to central governments. Given the insights of Ibn Khaldūn, however, one might have expected a new group with a fresh sense of cohesiveness to restore political strength.

Had Muslims remained on a par with all other societies, they might have revived. But by the 18th century one particular set of societies in western Europe had developed an economic and social system capable of transcending the 5,000-year-old limitations of the agrarian-based settled world as defined by the Greeks (who called it Oikoumene). Unlike most of the lands of Islāmdom, those societies were rich in natural resources (especially the fossil fuels that could supplement human and animal power) and poor in space for expansion. Cut off by Muslims from controlling land routes from the East, European explorers had built on and surpassed Muslim seafaring technology to compete in the southern seas and discover new sea routes—and, accidentally, a new source of wealth in the Americas. In Europe, centralized absolutism, though an ideal, had not been the success it was in Islāmdom. Emerging from the landed classes rather than from the cities, it had benefited from and been constrained by independent urban commercial classes. In Islāmdom, the power of merchants had been inhibited by imperial overtaxation of local private enterprise, appropriation of the benefits of trade, and the privileging of foreign traders through agreements known as the Capitulations.

Economic and social strengths in western Europe

In Europe independent financial and social resources promoted an unusual freedom for technological experimentation and, consequently, the technicalization of other areas of society as well. Unlike previous innovations in the Oikoumene, Europe's technology could not easily be diffused to societies that had not undergone the prerequisite fundamental social and economic changes. Outside of Europe, gradual assimilation of the "new," which had characterized change and cultural diffusion for 5,000 years, had to be replaced by hurried imitation, which proved enormously disorienting. This combination of innovation and imitation produced an unprecedented and persisting imbalance among various parts of the Oikoumene. Muslims' responses paralleled those of other "non-Western" peoples but were often filtered through and expressed in peculiarly Islāmic or Islāmicate symbols and motifs. The power of Islām as a source of public values had already waxed and waned many times; it intensified in the 18th and 19th centuries, receded in the early 20th century, and surged again after the mid-20th century. Thus European colonizers appeared in the midst of an ongoing process that they greatly affected but did not completely transform.

PRE-COLONIAL REFORM AND EXPERIMENTATION (1683–1818)

From the mid-17th century through the 18th and early 19th centuries certain Muslims expressed an awareness of internal weakness. In some areas, Muslims were largely unaware of the rise of Europe; in others, such as India, Sumatra, and Java, the 18th century actually brought European control. Responses to decline, sometimes official and sometimes unofficial, sometimes Islāmizing, sometimes Europeanizing, fell into two categories, as the following examples demonstrate.

In some areas, leaders attempted to revive existing political systems. In Iran, for example, attempts at restoration combined military and religious reform. Around 1730 a Turk from Khorāsān named Nāder Qolī Beg reorganized the Ṣafavid army in the name of the Ṣafavid shah, whom he replaced with himself in 1736. Nāder Shāh extended the borders of the Ṣafavid state further than ever; he even defeated the Ottomans and may have been aspiring to be the leader of all Muslims. To this end he made overtures to neighbouring rulers, seeking their recognition by trying to represent Iranian Shīʿism as a *madhhab* alongside the Sunnite *madhhab*s. After he was killed in 1747, however, his reforms did not survive and his house disintegrated. Karīm Khān Zand, a general from Shīrāz, ruled in the name of the Ṣafavids but did not restore real power to the shah. By the time the Qājārs (1779–1925) managed to resecure Iran's borders, reviving Ṣafavid legitimacy was impossible.

Restoration in the Ottoman Empire

In the Ottoman Empire, restoration involved selective imitation of things European. Its first phase, from 1718 to 1730, is known as the Tulip Period, because of the cultivation by the wealthy of a Perso-Turkish flower then popular in Europe. Experimentation with European manners and tastes was matched by experimentation with European military technology. Restoration depended on reinvigorating the military, the key to earlier Ottoman success, and Christian Europeans were hired for the task. After Nāder Shāh's defeat of the Ottoman army, this first phase of absolutist restoration ended, but the pursuit of European fashion had become a permanent element in Ottoman life. Meanwhile, central power continued to weaken, especially in the area of international commerce. The certificates of protection that had accompanied the Capitulations arrangements for foreign nationals were extended to non-Muslim Ottoman subjects, who gradually oriented themselves toward their foreign associates. The integration of such groups into the Ottoman state was further weakened by the recognition, in the disastrous Treaty of Küçük Kaynarca (1774), of the Russian tsar as protector of the Ottoman's Greek Orthodox *millet*. A second stage of absolutist restoration occurred under Selim III, who became sultan in the first year of the French Revolution and ruled until 1807. His military and political reforms, referred to as the New Order (Nizam-ı Cedid), went beyond the Tulip Period in making use of things European; for example, the enlightened monarch, as exemplified by Napoleon himself, became an Ottoman ideal. Here, as in Egypt under Muḥammad ʿAlī (reigned 1805–48), the famed core of Janissaries that had been a source of Ottoman strength was destroyed and replaced with European-trained troops.

In other areas, leaders envisioned or created new social orders that were self-consciously Islāmic. The growing popularity of westernization and a decreasing reliance on Islām as a source of public values was counterbalanced in many parts of Islāmdom by all sorts of Islāmic activism, ranging from educational reform to *jihād*. "Islāmic" politics often were marked by an oppositional quality that drew on long-standing traditions of skepticism about government. Ṣūfism could play very different roles. In the form of renovated *ṭarīqah*s it could support reform and stimulate pan-Islāmic awareness. Ṣūfīs often encouraged the study of *ḥadīth* so as to establish the Prophet Muḥammad as a model for spiritual and moral reconstruction and to invalidate many unacceptable traditional or customary Islāmic practices. Ṣūfī *ṭarīqah*s provided interregional communication and contact and an indigenous form of social organization that could even lead to the founding of a dynasty, as in the case of the Libyan monarchy.

Ṣūfism could also be condemned as a source of degeneracy. The most famous and influential militant anti-Ṣūfī movement arose in the Arabian Peninsula and called itself al-Muwaḥḥidūn ("the Monotheists"); but it came to be known as Wahhābīyah, after its founder, Muḥammad ibn ʿAbd al-Wahhāb (1703–92). Inspired by Ibn Taymīyah (see above *Migration and renewal (1041–1405)*), Ibn al-Wahhāb argued that the Qurʾān and *sunnah* could provide the basis for a reconstruction of Islāmic society out of the degenerate form in which it had come to be practiced. Islām itself was not an inhibiting force; "traditional" Islām was. Far from advocating the traditional, the Wahhābīs argued that what had become traditional had strayed very far from the fundamental, which can always be found in the Qurʾān and *sunnah*. The traditional they associated with blind imitation (*taqlīd*); reform, with making the pious personal effort (*ijtihād*) necessary to understand the fundamentals. Within an Islāmic context, this type of movement was not conservative, because it sought not to conserve what had been passed down but to renew what had been abandoned. The Wahhābī movement attracted the support of a tribe in the Najd led by Muḥammad ibn Saʿūd. Although the first state produced by this alliance did not last, it laid the foundations for the existing Saudi state in Arabia and inspired similar activism elsewhere down to the present day.

Islāmic activism in West Africa

In West Africa a series of activist movements appeared from the 18th century into the 19th. There as in Arabia, Islāmic activism was directed less at non-Muslims than at Muslims who had gone astray. As in many of Islāmdom's outlying areas, emergent groups of indigenous educated, observant Muslims, such as the Tukulor, were finding the casual, syncretistic, opportunistic nature of official Islām to be increasingly intolerable. Such Muslims were inspired by reformist scholars from numerous times and places—al-Ghazālī, as-Suyūṭī, Maghili; by a theory of *jihād* comparable to that of the Wahhābīs; and by expectations of a *mujaddid* as the Islāmic century turned in AH 1200 (AD 1785). In what is now northern Nigeria, the discontent of the 1780s and '90s erupted in 1804, when Usman dan Fodio declared a *jihād* against the Hausa rulers. Others followed, among them Muhammad al-Jaylani in Aïr, Shehuh Ahmadu Lobbo in Macina, al-Ḥajj ʿUmar Tal (a member of the reformist Tijānī *ṭarīqah*) in Fouta Djallon, and Samory in the Malinke (Mandingo) states. *Jihād* activity continued for a century; it again became millennial near the turn of the next Muslim century in AH 1300 (AD 1882), as the need to resist against European occupation became more urgent. For example, Muḥammad Aḥmad declared himself to be the *mahdī* in the Sudan in 1881.

In the Indian Ocean area, Islāmic activism was more often intellectual and educational. Its best exemplar was Shāh Walī Allāh of Delhi (1702–62), the spiritual ancestor of many later Indian Muslim reform movements. During his lifetime the collapse of Muslim political power was painfully evident. He tried to unite the Muslims of India, not around Ṣūfism as Akbar had tried to do, but around the Sharīʿah. Like Ibn Taymīyah, he understood the Sharīʿah to be based on firm sources—Qurʾān and *sunnah*—that could with pious effort be applied to present circumstances. Once again, the study of *ḥadīth* provided a rich array of precedents and inspired a positive spirit of social reconstruction akin to that of the Prophet Muḥammad.

DEPENDENCY (1818–1962)

The many efforts to revive and resist were largely unsuccessful. By 1818, British hegemony over India was complete; and many other colonies and mandates followed between then and the aftermath of World War I. Not all Muslim territories were colonized, but nearly all experienced some kind of dependency, be it psychological, political, technological, cultural, or economic. Perhaps only the Saudi regime in the central parts of the Arabian Peninsula could be said to have escaped any kind of dependency; but even there oil exploration, begun in the 1930s, brought European interference. In the 19th century westernization and Islāmic activism coexisted and competed. By the turn of the 20th century secular ethnic nationalism had become the most common mode of protest in Islāmdom; but the spirit of Islāmic reconstruction was also kept alive, either in conjunction with secular nationalism or in opposition to it.

In the 19th-century Ottoman Empire, selective westernization coexisted with a reconsideration of Islām. The program of reform known as the Tanzimat, which was in effect from 1839 to 1876, aimed to emulate European law and administration by giving all Ottoman subjects, regardless of religious confession, equal legal standing and by limiting the powers of the monarch. In the 1860s a group known as the Young Ottomans tried to identify the basic principles of European liberalism and even love of nation with Islām itself. In Iran, the Qājār shahs brought in a special "Cossack Brigade," trained and led by Russians, while at the same time the Shīʿite *mujtahids* viewed the decisions of their spiritual leader as binding on all Iranian Shīʿites and declared themselves to be independent of the shah. (One Shīʿite revolt, that of the Bāb [died 1850], led to a whole new religion, Bahāʾī.) Like the Young Ottomans, Shīʿite religious leaders came to identify with constitutionalism in opposition to the ruler.

Reaction against Europeans and westernization

Islāmic protest often took the form of *jihād* against the Europeans: by Southeast Asians against the Dutch; by the Sanūsī *ṭarīqah* over Italian control in Libya; by the Mahdist movement in the Sudan; or by the Ṣaliḥī *ṭarīqah* in Somalia, led by Sayyid Muḥammad ibn ʿAbd Allāh Ḥasan, who was tellingly nicknamed the Mad Mullah by Europeans. Sometimes religious leaders, like those of the Shīʿites in Iran, took part in constitutional revolutions (1905–11). Underlying much of this activity was a pan-Islāmic sentiment that drew on very old conceptions of the *ummah* as the ultimate solidarity group for Muslims. Three of the most prominent Islāmic reconstructionists were Jamāl ad-Dīn al-Afghānī, his Egyptian disciple Muḥammad ʿAbduh, and the Indian poet Sir Muḥammad Iqbāl. All warned against blind pursuit of Westernization, arguing that the blame for the weaknesses of Muslims lay not with Islām, but rather with Muslims themselves, because they had lost touch with the progressive spirit of social, moral, and intellectual reconstruction that had made early Islāmicate civilization one of the greatest in human history. Although al-Afghānī, who taught and preached in many parts of Islāmdom, acknowledged that organization by nationality might be necessary, he viewed it as inferior to Muslim identity. He further argued that Western technology could advance Muslims only if they retained and cultivated their own spiritual and cultural heritage. He pointed out that at one time Muslims had been intellectual and scientific leaders in the world, identifying a Golden Age under the ʿAbbāsid caliphate and pointing to the many contributions Muslims had made to "the West." Like al-Afghānī, Iqbāl assumed that without Islām Muslims could never regain the strength they had possessed when they were a vital force in the world, united in a single international community and unaffected by differences of language or ethnos. This aggressive recovery of the past became a permanent theme of Islāmic reconstruction. In many regions of Islāmdom the movement known as Salafīyah also identified with an ideal time in history, that of the "pious ancestors" (*salaf*) in the early Muslim state of Muḥammad and his companions, and advocated past-oriented change to bring present-day Muslims up to the progressive standards of an earlier ideal. In addition to clearly Islāmic thinkers, there were others, such as the Egyptian Muṣṭafā Kāmil, whose nationalism was not simply secular. Kāmil saw Egypt as simultaneously European, Ottoman, and Muslim. The Young Turk Revolution of 1908 was followed by a period in which similarly complex views of national identity were discussed in the Ottoman Empire.

RECOVERY (1922 TO THE PRESENT)

Progress of secular nationalism. Despite the ideological appeal of such positions, the need to throw off European control promoted the fortunes of secular nationalism and other narrower forms of loyalty. Especially after Japan's defeat of Russia in 1905, nationalist fervour increased. Sometimes it was associated with related ideologies, such as pan-Arabism, Pan-Turkism, or Arab socialism. Many nationalists enthusiastically admired things European despite the fact that they were committed to resisting or removing European control. Often accepting European assessments of traditional religion as a barrier to modernization, many nationalists sought an identity in the pre-Islāmic past. Kemal Atatürk looked to the Turkic past in Central Asia and Anatolia to transform Ottomanism into a Turkish identity not dependent on Islām. "Islāmic" dress was discouraged. Muslim males, who prayed with covered heads, were now asked to replace the fez, which could be kept on during prayer, with the brimmed hat, which could not. Arabic script, too closely associated with Islām, was replaced with the Roman, after the Cyrillic (the alphabet of Central Asian Turks) had been considered and rejected. In Iran, Reza Shah Pahlavi argued that the Islāmic period was but an accidental interlude in the continuous history, since Achaemenid times, of Iran as a unified entity. The Egyptian Taha Hussein connected his country's national identity with Pharaonic times and with Mediterranean–European culture; and therefore it could easily partake of modern Western civilization. Christians were thus as much Egyptians as were Muslims; the accompanying development of a standard literary Arabic, *fuṣḥā,* emphasized the unity of all Arabs, regardless of confession. These approaches allowed, indeed required, all religious communities to partake of a single legal and societal system, at the price of denying the public relevance of a primary loyalty for the majority of the population.

Opposition to nationalism

Other nationalists made more of Islām. In Saudi Arabia and Pakistan, for example, Islām played a primary role in the formation of a national identity. In Pakistan it provided, according to the statesman Mohammed Ali Jinnah, an alternative for Muslims who would otherwise have to share in an identity defined by a Hindu majority. In many Arab countries, especially in the Maghrib, secular nationalism's downgrading of Islām was muted by a qualified acceptance of Islām as one, but not the only, important source of loyalty. At the same time there were Muslims who opposed nationalism altogether. In India, Mawlanā Abu'l-ʿAlā' Mawdūdī, who was the founder of the Jamāʿat-i Islāmī, opposed both secular and religious nationalism and argued for the Islāmization of society and an Islāmic alternative to nationalism. In Egypt, Sayyid Quṭb and Ḥasan al-Bannā', who were the mentors of the Muslim Brotherhood, fought for the educational, moral, and social reform of an Islāmic Egypt and indeed of all Islāmdom.

Creating national identities. Only a few existing states where Muslims predominate, such as Turkey and Saudi Arabia, had no colonial interval; most became independent after World War II. An even larger number of countries have Muslim minorities. Like the citizens of many new nations, Muslims have not found the creation of national identities to be easy, especially considering the pace at which it has had to occur. More than two-thirds of the world's nations have come into existence since the end of World War II; foreign dependency is a living memory for many of their citizens, or at least for the parents and grandparents of their citizens. Many of them are not nation-states—that is, states established by a group of people who decided that they belonged together and therefore went about acquiring sovereignty over a territory—but rather are state-nations, composed of groups of people who acquired or were given sovereignty over a territory and then had to develop a sense of nationality. The most obvious state-nations are Syria, Iraq, Lebanon, and Jordan. All resulted from the interaction of intra-European rivalry and diplomacy with the aspirations of a prominent Ottoman-Hāshimite sharifian family in Mecca to create a single Arab state in the East. Instead of a single state, however, three monarchies emerged: the kingdom of Ḥusayn ibn ʿAlī in the Hejaz (to be replaced by the Saudis), the kingdom of Fayṣal I in Iraq (because he had to be compensated for being ousted from Syria), and the kingdom of Abdullah in Transjordan. Lebanon was carved from French Syria with borders that would establish a bare Christian majority loyal to the French. In Ottoman Palestine, Jewish nationalists clashed with Arab nationalists, at a time when both groups felt betrayed by the British. In subsequent armed clashes, Zionist groups defended a set of boundaries as artificial as many others, creating a state that has remained a target for anti-imperialist sentiment. Eventually, Jewish nationalism spawned another nationalism, that of the Palestinians, inchoate before the founding of Israel but crystallized by the failure of any party to the conflict—Arab states, foreign powers, Palestinian leaders, or Israel itself—to make a place for most of the former Arab residents of Palestine.

Many Muslim countries were united by negative nationalism, aimed at ejecting a common enemy; but turning negative into positive has been difficult. Rarely have the groups that achieved independence survived. Often, as in Libya or Iraq or Egypt, further revolutions have occurred, in many cases led by the military, whose role as a vehicle for modernization cannot be underestimated. Subsequent governments have had to deal with the social and economic problems that plague all developing countries, as well as with regional rivalries and conflicts. Almost nowhere did the colonizers leave an infrastructure sufficient to support the growth of population that European medicine and hygiene had produced.

Relation of religion and nationality. Given the multicommunal structure of premodern Muslim societies, the relation between religion and nationality has been another major problem. Nationalism has frequently led to competition and rivalry among a new nation's religious communities. As they became independent, citizens of the nations of Islāmdom could draw on no direct equivalent of national identity. The broadest identity was provided by membership in a pan-territorial community like the *ummah* of all Muslims, or the Greek Orthodox Church, or the Turkic tribes; the narrowest, family or neighbourhood. In the middle of the spectrum was membership in a local confessional community, with all its implications of status, occupation, manners, and customs. Citizens of the new nations would theoretically have to find an identity that could subsume and supersede all others; and the rulers of new nations would have to take the unprecedented step of declaring all citizens subject to the same law, rather than members of quasi-autonomous, self-governing religious communities with their own legal systems. Yet the significance of being a member of a religious community could not easily be undone or replaced.

Rivalry among religious communities

Many countries inherited a relatively simple form of this problem: the people within their borders were primarily of one faith, Islām, and of one form of that faith. That majority adherence could in some way be associated with or bolster the national identity, while discomfiting only a small number of people. Turkey, Iran, Jordan, Indonesia, the Yemens, and all the states of North Africa and the Arabian Peninsula fall into this category. Even so, religious minorities in these countries (such as the Armenians) suffered and shrank; for Jews communal lines were hardened by the emergence of the state of Israel, the hostility it evoked from most Arab states, and its aggressive efforts at ingathering. The self-consciously Islāmic government in Iran has also introduced a religious intolerance that, while it is discouraged by the Sharīʿah, is encouraged by local sentiment as well as by the staunch nationalism Iran shares with secular states. In reaction to the Pahlavi state they overthrew, in which trying to restore Zoroastrianism had not been unthinkable, the leaders of the Islāmic Republic of Iran have associated being Iranian with being Muslim.

Farther from the centre of Islāmdom, Islām plays various roles as a minority religion. Among Turks in the southern republics of the Soviet Union, for example, Islām is an important source of identity. Muslims living in western Europe and the Americas are generally able to form communities and practice their religion as they will: in Canada, for example, Ismāʿīlī Muslims, under the guidance of Aga Khan IV, form a cohesive group that promotes the economic and cultural development of its members. In the United States, tenets of Islām were embraced by the founders of the American Muslim Mission (originally called Nation of Islam) in the early 1930s. As the community has developed, its leaders have increasingly emphasized the Qur'ān and Muḥammad's example as sources of authority.

Survival of Islāmic activism. Although Islāmic activism never disappeared during the years in which Muslim countries were becoming independent, other ideological orientations seemed more important between the end of World War II and the declaration of the Islāmic Republic of Iran in 1979. Many Westerners or westernized Muslims expected religion to recede as modernization progressed. Already in the 1950s, however, the Muslim Brotherhood in Egypt called for an exclusively Islāmic state in place of the secular multi-communal state that Gamal Abdel Nasser had founded. In the early 1960s new circumstances were beginning to foster increased self-consciously Islāmic activity, some popular, some supported by official institutions. In these years critics of Mohammad Reza Shah Pahlavi began to rally around the exiled ayatollah Ruhollah Khomeini; the writings of ʿAli Shariʿati began to influence Muslims inside and outside Iran; and two great pan-Islāmic organizations were formed, the Muslim World League (1962) and the Organization of the Islāmic Conference (1971). Although Westerners have become most familiar with activism's violent forms, its educational, cultural, pietistic, and political dimensions have been more extensive. All these developments occurred in the wake of the formation of the Organization of Petroleum Exporting Countries in 1961 and culminated in Egypt's success in its war with Israel in 1973. The resurgence of economic and military power was not the only factor that could foster those who had maintained an interest in Islām all along. In a few parts of the Muslim world, petroleum-based prosperity promoted increased international influence and pride; elsewhere modernization was producing widespread educational and economic cleavages and populations with very low median ages. As dissatisfaction with the material failures of secular modernization grew, so did disenchantment with the Western ideologies that had undergirded it. While these other ideologies were being tried and discredited, Islām had remained relatively peripheral to public policy, and thus unassailable. All the while, citizens of Muslim countries were echoing the anti-imperialist rhetoric that was increasing throughout the developing world.

Pan-Islāmic organizations

Situation of Muslim women. For women, modernization is especially problematic. Urged on the one hand to be liberated from Islām and thereby become modern, they are told by others to be liberated from being Western through being self-consciously Muslim. There is little information on the situation of ordinary women in premodern Islāmdom, but evidence from the modern period underscores the enormous variety of settings in which Muslim women live and work, as well as the inability of the stereotype of meek, submissive, veiled passivity to reflect the quality of their lives. As always, Muslim women live in cities, towns, villages, and among migratory pastoral tribes; some work outside the home, some inside, some not at all; some wear concealing clothing in public, most do not; for some, movement outside the home is restricted, for most not; and, for many, public modesty is common, as it is for many Muslim men. For many, the private home and the public bath continue to be the centres of social interaction; for others, the world of employment and city life is an option. As always, few live in polygamous families. Strict adherence to the Sharīʿah's provision for women to hold their property in their own right has produced Muslim women of great wealth, in the past as well as today. Clearly, any simple description of the lives of Muslim women is misleading.

Modern Islām's unifying forces. Modern Islāmdom can appear so diverse as to defy description, yet it is also held together by stronger centripetal forces than almost any other pan-national solidarity group. The *ḥajj* attracts more than 1,000,000 Muslims annually; and, despite significant religious cleavages, Islām remains one of the least sectarian of world religions. Most Muslims live in societies in which the force of tradition is very strong and in which modernization has also penetrated to some extent. The majority of Muslims remain, as they have always been, agricultural. A very small minority are migratory pastoralists; a larger minority are village, town, and city dwellers. In all settings tradition, including religious tradition, is being drawn upon as a source of change and modernization, with the consequence that the Western equation of modernization and secularization has been severely tested and even undermined.

Yet the role of tradition varies. Some Islāmic activists rely on a kind of secularized "cultural" Islām, somewhat like cultural Judaism, that depends very little on personal piety or the observance of Islāmic law or the many customs that have come to be associated with being Muslim, while others cling to the customs associated with Islām with little awareness of Islām's more learned side. Labels such as Shī'ite, which always carried an oppositional quality, may be formerly nonessential attributes that have become salient in the wake of the success of the ayatollah Khomeini in Iran. When disadvantaged persons who happen to be Shī'ites find an opening for communal protest, or when those for whom Shī'ite theology means little find its vision of justice and radical revolution appropriate to their specific circumstances, an old label acquires a new valence.

Like any other explanatory system, Islām has always had to provide a way of talking about the world, of establishing identity in the world, and of managing the world's affairs. In performing these functions, Islām has from its inception been forced to compete with other explanatory systems for the "mental space" of its adherents and simultaneously to define its stance toward preexisting and ongoing extra-Islāmic influences. Islām continues to compete, aided unwittingly by the weaknesses of its competitors, spurred on by the freshness of its own demands for public attention, and fueled by the remarkable ability of many of its adherents to respond to the connection between the mundane and spiritual that has been the hallmark of all religious life.

BIBLIOGRAPHY

Surveys: The most visionary general work on Islāmic history is MARSHALL G.S. HODGSON, *The Venture of Islam: Conscience and History in a World Civilization,* 3 vol. (1974), which sets Islām into a world historical context. A similar but shorter work, sumptuously illustrated, is FRANCIS ROBINSON, *Atlas of the Islamic World Since 1500* (1982).

Regions of Islāmdom: PETER B. CLARKE, *West Africa and Islam: A Study of Religious Development from the 8th to the 20th Centuries* (1982); JAMIL M. ABUN-NASR, *A History of the Maghrib,* 2nd ed. (1975); CLIFFORD GEERTZ, *Islam Observed: Religious Development in Morocco and Indonesia* (1968, reissued 1971); S.M. IKRAM, *Muslim Rule in India and Pakistan, 711–1858 A.C.,* rev. ed. (1966); RAPHAEL ISRAELI, *Muslims in China: A Study in Cultural Confrontation* (1980); and NEHEMIA LEVTZION (ed.), *Conversion to Islam* (1979).

Periods and aspects of Islāmicate history: On premodern Islāmicate social structure, see ROY P. MOTTAHEDEH, *Loyalty and Leadership in an Early Islamic Society* (1980); IRA LAPIDUS, *Muslim Cities in the Later Middle Ages* (1967); and S.D. GOITEIN, *A Mediterranean Society: The Jewish Communities of the Arab World as Portrayed in the Documents of the Cairo Geniza,* 4 vol. (1967–83). HAMILTON A.R. GIBB, *Studies on the Civilization of Islam* (1962, reissued 1982), is a collection of interpretive articles on history, historiography, literature, and philology. RENÉ GROUSSET, *The Empire of the Steppes: A History of Central Asia* (1970; originally published in French, 1939); and JOHN J. SAUNDERS, *The History of the Mongol Conquests* (1971), deal with the Mongol conquests. JOHN J. SAUNDERS (ed.), *The Muslim World on the Eve of Europe's Expansion* (1966), combines primary sources on the last three great empires; and the most comprehensive account of modern Islām, with an especially fine treatment of the 18th century, is JOHN OBERT VOLL, *Islam, Continuity and Change in the Modern World* (1982). On Muslim women, see, for example, LOIS BECK and NIKKI KEDDIE (eds.), *Women in the Muslim World* (1978); ELIZABETH WARNOCK FERNEA and BASIMA QATTAN BEZIRGAN (eds.), *Middle Eastern Muslim Women Speak* (1977, reprinted 1984); and JANE I. SMITH (ed.), *Women in Contemporary Muslim Societies* (1980).

Collections of primary sources in English translation: ERIC SCHROEDER, *Muhammad's People* (1955); ARTHUR JEFFERY (ed.), *A Reader of Islam* (1962, reprinted 1980); JOHN ALDEN WILLIAMS (ed.), *Islam* (1961, reissued 1967), and *Themes of Islamic Civilization* (1971, reprinted 1982); WILLIAM H. MCNEILL and MARILYN ROBINSON WALDMAN, *The Islâmic World* (1973, reprinted 1983); JAMES KRITZECK, *Anthology of Islamic Literature* (1964, reissued 1975); and BERNARD LEWIS (ed.), *Islam: From the Prophet Muhammad to the Capture of Constantinople,* 2 vol. (1974, reissued 1976).

Major reference works: The Encyclopaedia of Islam, 5 vol. (1913–36), and a new edition, of which 5 vol. appeared from 1960 to 1986; *The Shorter Encyclopaedia of Islam* (1953, reprinted 1974), with articles culled from the *Encyclopaedia of Islam; The Cambridge History of Islam,* 2 vol. (1970, reprinted in 4 vol., 1980); JEAN SAUVAGET, *Jean Sauvaget's Introduction to the History of the Muslim East: A Bibliographical Guide* (1965, reprinted 1982; originally published in French, 2nd ed., 1961), a dated but still useful annotated bibliographic guide; and CLIFFORD EDMUND BOSWORTH, *The Islamic Dynasties: A Chronological and Genealogical Handbook,* rev. ed. (1980). JEAN JACQUES WAARDENBURG, *L'Islam dans le miroir de l'Occident,* 3rd rev. ed. (1970); and EDWARD W. SAID, *Orientalism* (1978, reissued 1979), are critiques of Western approaches to Islām.

(MARILYN R. WALDMAN)

Population

Few aspects of human societies are as fundamental as the size, composition, and rate of change of their populations. Such factors affect economic prosperity, health, education, family structure, crime patterns, language, culture—indeed, virtually every aspect of human society is touched upon by population trends.

The study of human populations is called demography—a discipline with intellectual origins stretching back to the 18th century, when it was first recognized that human mortality could be examined as a phenomenon with statistical regularities. Demography casts a multidisciplinary net, drawing insights from economics, sociology, statistics, medicine, biology, anthropology, and history. Its chronological sweep is lengthy: limited demographic evidence for many centuries into the past, and reliable data for several hundred years are available for many regions. The present understanding of demography makes it possible to project (with caution) population changes several decades into the future.

This article is divided into the following sections:

THE BASIC COMPONENTS OF POPULATION CHANGE

At its most basic level, the components of population change are few indeed. A closed population (that is, one in which immigration and emigration do not occur) can change according to the following simple equation: the population (closed) at the end of an interval equals the population at the beginning of the interval, plus births during the interval, minus deaths during the interval. In

Closed and open populations

other words, only addition by births and reduction by deaths can change a closed population. The notion of a closed population is not an abstraction; unless one believes that there has been substantial migration to and from this planet, the world population as a whole is closed.

Populations of nations, regions, continents, islands, or cities, however, are rarely closed in the same way. If the assumption of a closed population is relaxed, in- and out-migration can increase and decrease population size in the same way as do births and deaths; thus, the population (open) at the end of an interval equals the population at the beginning of the interval, plus births during the interval, minus deaths, plus in-migrants, minus out-migrants. Hence the study of demographic change requires knowledge of fertility (births), mortality (deaths), and migration. These, in turn, affect not only population size and growth rates but also the composition of the population in terms of such attributes as sex, age, ethnic or racial composition, and geographic distribution.

Fertility. Demographers distinguish between fecundity, the underlying biological potential for reproduction, and fertility, the actual level of achieved reproduction. (Confusingly, these English terms have opposite meanings from their parallel terms in French, where *fertilité* is the potential and *fécondité* is the realized; similarly ambiguous usages also prevail in the biological sciences, thereby increasing the chance of misunderstanding.) The difference between biological potential and realized fertility is determined by several intervening factors, including the following: (1) most women do not begin reproducing immediately upon the onset of puberty, which itself does not occur at a fixed age; (2) some women with the potential to reproduce never do so; (3) some women become widowed and do not remarry; (4) various elements of social behaviour restrain fertility; and (5) many human couples choose consciously to restrict their fertility by means of sexual abstinence, contraception, abortion, or sterilization.

Potential and realized fertility

The magnitude of the gap between potential and realized fertility can be illustrated by comparing the highest known fertilities with those of typical European and North American women in the late 20th century. A well-studied high-fertility group is the Hutterites of North America, a religious sect that views fertility regulation as sinful and high fertility as a blessing. Hutterite women who married between 1921 and 1930 are known to have averaged 10 children per woman. Meanwhile, women in much of Europe and North America averaged about two children per woman during the 1970s and 1980s—a number 80 percent less than that achieved by the Hutterites. Even the highly fertile populations of developing countries in Africa, Asia, and Latin America produce children at rates far below that of the Hutterites.

The general message from such evidence is clear enough: in much of the world, human fertility is considerably lower than the biological potential. It is strongly constrained by cultural regulations, especially those concerning marriage and sexuality, and by conscious efforts on the part of married couples to limit their childbearing.

Dependable evidence on historical fertility patterns in Europe is available back to the 18th century, and estimates have been made for several earlier centuries. Such data for non-European societies and for earlier human populations are much more fragmentary. The European data indicate that even in the absence of widespread deliberate regulation there were significant variations in fertility among different societies. These differences were heavily affected by socially determined behaviours such as those concerning marriage patterns. Beginning in France and Hungary in the 18th century, a dramatic decline in fertility took shape in the more developed societies of Europe and North America, and in the ensuing two centuries fertility declines of fully 50 percent took place in nearly all of these countries. Since the 1960s fertility has been intentionally diminished in many developing countries, and remarkably rapid reductions have occurred in the most populous, the People's Republic of China.

There is no dispute as to the fact and magnitudes of such declines, but theoretical explanation of the phenomena has proved elusive. (See below *Population theories.*)

Biological factors affecting human fertility. Reproduction is a quintessentially biological process, and hence all fertility analyses must consider the effects of biology. Such factors, in rough chronological order, include:

- the age of onset of potential fertility (or fecundability in demographic terminology);
- the degree of fecundability—*i.e.,* the monthly probability of conceiving in the absence of contraception;
- the incidence of spontaneous abortion and stillbirth;
- the duration of temporary infecundability following the birth of a child; and
- the age of onset of permanent sterility.

The age at which women become fecund apparently declined significantly during the 20th century; as measured by the age of menarche (onset of menstruation), British data suggest a decline from 16–18 years in the mid-19th century to less than 13 years in the late 20th century. This decline is thought to be related to improving standards of nutrition and health. Since the average age of marriage in western Europe has long been far higher than the age of menarche, and since most children are born to married couples, this biological lengthening of the reproductive period is unlikely to have had major effects upon realized fertility in Europe. In settings where early marriage prevails, however, declining age at menarche could increase lifetime fertility.

Variations in fecundability

Fecundability also varies among women past menarche. The monthly probabilities of conception among newlyweds are commonly in the range of 0.15 to 0.25; that is, there is a 15–25-percent chance of conception each month. This fact is understandable when account is taken of the short interval (about two days) within each menstrual cycle during which fertilization can take place. Moreover, there appear to be cycles during which ovulation does not occur. Finally, perhaps one-third or more of fertilized ova fail to implant in the uterus or, even if they do implant, spontaneously abort during the ensuing two weeks, before pregnancy would be recognized. As a result of such factors, women of reproductive age who are not using contraceptive methods can expect to conceive within five to 10 months of becoming sexually active. As is true of all biological phenomena, there is surely a distribution of fecundability around average levels, with some women experiencing conception more readily than others.

Spontaneous abortion of recognized pregnancies and stillbirth also are fairly common, but their incidence is difficult to quantify. Perhaps 20 percent of recognized pregnancies fail spontaneously, most in the earlier months of gestation.

Following the birth of a child, most women experience a period of temporary infecundability, or biological inability to conceive. The length of this period seems to be affected substantially by breast-feeding. In the absence of breast-feeding, the interruption lasts less than two months. With lengthy, frequent breast-feeding it can last one or two years. This effect is thought to be caused by a complex of neural and hormonal factors stimulated by suckling.

A woman's fecundability typically peaks in her 20s and declines during her 30s; by their early 40s as many as 50 percent of women are affected by their own or their husbands' sterility. After menopause, essentially all women are sterile. The average age at menopause is in the late 40s, although some women experience it before reaching 40 and others not until nearly 60.

Contraception. Contraceptive practices affect fertility by reducing the probability of conception. Contraceptive methods vary considerably in their theoretical effectiveness and in their actual effectiveness in use ("use-effectiveness"). Modern methods such as oral pills and intrauterine devices (IUDs) have use-effectiveness rates of more than 95 percent. Older methods such as the condom and diaphragm can be more than 90-percent effective when used regularly and correctly, but their average use-effectiveness is lower because of irregular or incorrect use.

The effect upon fertility of contraceptive measures can be dramatic: if fecundability is 0.20 (a 20-percent chance of pregnancy per month of exposure), then a 95-percent effective method will reduce this to 0.01 (a 1-percent chance).

Abortion. Induced abortion reduces fertility not by affecting fecundability but by terminating pregnancy. Abortion has long been practiced in human societies and is quite common in some settings. The officially registered fraction of pregnancies terminated by abortion exceeds one-third in some countries, and significant numbers of unregistered abortions probably occur even in countries reporting very low rates.

Sterilization. Complete elimination of fecundability can be brought about by sterilization. The surgical procedures of tubal ligation and vasectomy have become common in diverse nations and cultures. In the United States, for example, voluntary sterilization has become the most prevalent single means of terminating fertility, typically adopted by couples who have achieved their desired family size. In India, sterilization has been encouraged on occasion by various government incentive programs and, for a short period during the 1970s, by quasi-coercive measures.

Mortality. As noted above, the science of demography has its intellectual roots in the realization that human mortality, while consisting of unpredictable individual events, has a statistical regularity when aggregated across a large group. This recognition formed the basis of a wholly new industry—that of life assurance, or insurance. The basis of this industry is the life table, or mortality table, which summarizes the distribution of longevity—observed over a period of years—among members of a population. This statistical device allows the calculation of premiums—the prices to be charged the members of a group of living subscribers with specified characteristics, who by pooling their resources in this statistical sense provide their heirs with financial benefits.

Life table

Overall human mortality levels can best be compared by using the life-table measure life expectancy at birth (often abbreviated simply as life expectancy), the number of years of life expected of a newborn baby on the basis of current mortality levels for persons of all ages. Life expectancies of premodern populations, with their poor knowledge of sanitation and health care, may have been as low as 25–30 years. The largest toll of death was that exacted in infancy and childhood: perhaps 20 percent of newborn children died in their first 12 months of life and another 30 percent before they reached five years of age.

In the developing countries by the 1980s, average life expectancy lay in the range of 55 to 60 years, with the highest levels in Latin America and the lowest in Africa. In the same period, life expectancy in the developed countries of western Europe and North America approached 75 years, and fewer than 1 percent of newborn children died in their first 12 months.

Greater longevity of females

For reasons that are not well understood, life expectancy of females usually exceeds that of males, and this female advantage has grown as overall life expectancy has increased. In the late 20th century this female advantage was seven years (78 years versus 71 years) in the industrial market economies (comprising western Europe, North America, Japan, Australia, and New Zealand). It was eight years (74 years versus 66 years) in the nonmarket economies of eastern Europe.

The epidemiologic transition. The epidemiologic transition is that process by which the pattern of mortality and disease is transformed from one of high mortality among infants and children and episodic famine and epidemic affecting all age groups to one of degenerative and manmade diseases (such as those attributed to smoking) affecting principally the elderly. It is generally believed that the epidemiologic transitions prior to the 20th century (*i.e.,* those in today's industrialized countries) were closely associated with rising standards of living, nutrition, and sanitation. In contrast, those occurring in developing countries have been more or less independent of such internal socioeconomic development and more closely tied to organized health care and disease control programs developed and financed internationally. There is no doubt that 20th-century declines in mortality in developing countries have been far more rapid than those that occurred in the 19th century in what are now the industrialized countries.

Infant mortality. Infant mortality is conventionally measured as the number of deaths in the first year of life per 1,000 live births during the same year. Roughly speaking, by this measure worldwide infant mortality approximates 80 per 1,000; that is, about 8 percent of newborn babies die within the first year of life.

Variations in infant mortality

This global average disguises great differences. In certain countries of Asia and Africa, infant mortality rates exceed 150 and sometimes approach 200 per 1,000 (that is, 15 or 20 percent of children die before reaching the age of one year). Meanwhile, in other countries, such as Japan and Sweden, the rates are well below 10 per 1,000, or 1 percent. Generally, infant mortality is somewhat higher among males than among females.

In developing countries substantial declines in infant mortality have been credited to improved sanitation and nutrition, increased access to modern health care, and improved birth spacing through the use of contraception. In industrialized countries in which infant mortality rates were already low the increased availability of advanced medical technology for newborn—in particular, prematurely born—infants provides a partial explanation.

Infanticide. The deliberate killing of newborn infants has long been practiced in human societies. It seems to have been common in the ancient cultures of Greece, Rome, and China, and it was practiced in Europe until the 19th century. In Europe, infanticide included the practice of "overlaying" (smothering) an infant sharing a bed with its parents and the abandonment of unwanted infants to the custody of foundling hospitals, in which one-third to four-fifths of incumbents failed to survive.

In many societies practicing infanticide, infants were not deemed to be fully human until they underwent a rite of initiation that took place from a few days to several years after birth, and therefore killing before such initiation was socially acceptable. The purposes of infanticide were various: child spacing or fertility control in the absence of effective contraception; elimination of illegitimate, deformed, orphaned, or twin children; or sex preferences.

With the development and spread of the means of effective fertility regulation, infanticide has come to be strongly disapproved in most societies, though it continues to be practiced in some isolated traditional cultures.

Mortality among the elderly. During the 1970s and 1980s in industrialized countries there were unexpectedly large declines in mortality among the elderly, resulting in larger-than-projected numbers of the very old. In the United States, for example, the so-called frail elderly group aged 85 years and older increased nearly fourfold between 1950 and 1980, from 590,000 to 2,461,000. Given the high incidence of health problems among the very old, such increases have important implications for the organization and financing of health care.

Marriage. One of the main factors affecting fertility, and an important contributor to the fertility differences among societies in which conscious fertility control is uncommon, is defined by the patterns of marriage and marital disruption. In many societies in Asia and Africa, for example, marriage occurs soon after the sexual maturation of the woman, around age 17. In contrast, delayed marriage has long been common in Europe, and in some European countries the average age of first marriage approaches 25 years. Another aspect of historical marriage patterns in Europe is the high incidence of permanent celibacy: as many as 10 percent of women never marry. In contrast, nearly all women marry in most traditional developing countries of Asia and Africa.

Disruption of marriage

In the 20th century dramatic changes have taken place in the patterns of marital dissolution caused by widowhood and divorce. Widowhood has long been common in all societies, but the declines of mortality (as discussed above) have sharply reduced the effects of this source of marital dissolution on fertility. Meanwhile, divorce has been transformed from an uncommon exception to an experience terminating a large proportion (sometimes more than a third) of marriages in some countries. Taken together, these components of marriage patterns can account for the elimination of as little as 20 percent to as much as 50 percent of the potential reproductive years.

Many Western countries have experienced significant increases in the numbers of cohabiting unmarried couples.

In the 1970s some 12 percent of all Swedish couples living together aged 16 to 70 were unmarried. When in the United States in 1976 the number of such arrangements approached 1,000,000, the Bureau of the Census formulated a new statistical category—POSSLQ—denoting persons of the opposite sex sharing living quarters. Extramarital fertility as a percentage of overall fertility accordingly has risen in many Western countries, accounting for one in five births in the United States, one in five in Denmark, and one in three in Sweden.

Migration. Since any population that is not closed can be augmented or depleted by in-migration or out-migration, migration patterns must be considered carefully in analyzing population change. The common definition of human migration limits the term to permanent change of residence (conventionally, for at least one year), so as to distinguish it from commuting and other more frequent but temporary movements.

Human migrations have been fundamental to the broad sweep of human history and have themselves changed in basic ways over the epochs. Many of these historical migrations have by no means been the morally uplifting experiences depicted in mythologies of heroic conquerors, explorers, and pioneers; rather they frequently have been characterized by violence, destruction, bondage, mass mortality, and genocide—in other words, by human suffering of profound magnitudes.

Early human migrations. Early humans were almost surely hunters and gatherers who moved continually in search of food supplies. The superior technologies (tools, clothes, language, disciplined cooperation) of these hunting bands allowed them to spread farther and faster than had any other dominant species; humans are thought to have occupied all the continents except Antarctica within a span of about 50,000 years. As the species spread away from the tropical parasites and diseases of its African origins, mortality rates declined and population increased. This increase occurred at microscopically small rates by the standards of the past several centuries, but over thousands of years it resulted in a large absolute growth to a total that could no longer be supported by finding new hunting grounds. There ensued a transition from migratory hunting and gathering to migratory slash-and-burn agriculture. The consequence was the rapid geographical spread of crops, with wheat and barley moving east and west from the Middle East across the whole of Eurasia within only 5,000 years.

Growth of migratory populations

About 10,000 years ago a new and more productive way of life, involving sedentary agriculture, became predominant. This allowed greater investment of labour and technology in crop production, resulting in a more substantial and securer food source, but sporadic migrations persisted.

The next pulse of migration, beginning around 4000 to 3000 BC, was stimulated by the development of seagoing sailing vessels and of pastoral nomadry. The Mediterranean Basin was the centre of the maritime culture, which involved the settlement of offshore islands and led to the development of deep-sea fishing and long-distance trade. Other favoured regions were those of the Indian Ocean and South China Sea. Meanwhile, pastoral nomadry involved biological adaptations both in humans (allowing them to digest milk) and in species of birds and mammals that were domesticated. Once completed, these adaptations allowed humans to consume the meat of most male newborn animals and the maternal milk thereby made available.

Both seafarers and pastoralists were intrinsically migratory. The former were able to colonize previously uninhabited lands or to impose their rule by force over less mobile populations. The pastoralists were able to populate the extensive grassland of the Eurasian Steppe and the African and Middle Eastern savannas, and their superior nutrition and mobility gave them clear military advantages over the sedentary agriculturalists with whom they came into contact. Even as agriculture continued to improve with innovations such as the plow, these mobile elements persisted and provided important networks by which technological innovations could be spread widely and rapidly.

That complex of human organization and behaviour commonly termed Western civilization arose out of such developments. Around 4000 BC seafaring migrants from the south overwhelmed the local inhabitants of the Tigris–Euphrates floodplain and began to develop a social organization based upon the division of labour into highly skilled occupations, technologies such as irrigation, bronze metallurgy, and wheeled vehicles, and the growth of cities of 20,000–50,000 persons. Political differentiation into ruling classes and ruled masses provided a basis for imposition of taxes and rents that financed the development of professional soldiers and artisans, whose specialized skills far surpassed those of pastoralists and agriculturalists. The military and economic superiority that accompanied such skills allowed advanced communities to expand both by direct conquest and by the adoption of this social form by neighbouring peoples. Thus migration patterns played an important role in creating the early empires and cultures of the ancient world.

Urban cultures

By about 2000 BC such specialized human civilizations occupied much of the then-known world—the Middle East, the eastern Mediterranean, South Asia, and the Far East. Under these circumstances human migration was transformed from unstructured movements across unoccupied territories by nomads and seafarers into quite new forms of interaction among the settled civilizations. . . .

Natural increase and population growth. *Natural increase.* Put simply, natural increase is the difference between the numbers of births and deaths in a population; the rate of natural increase is the difference between the birthrate and the death rate. Given the fertility and mortality characteristics of the human species (excluding incidents of catastrophic mortality), the range of possible rates of natural increase is rather narrow. For a nation, it has rarely exceeded 4 percent per year; the highest known rate for a national population—arising from the conjunction of a very high birthrate and a quite low death rate—is that experienced in Kenya during the 1980s, in which the natural increase of the population approximated 4.1 percent per annum. Rates of natural increase in other developing countries generally are lower; these countries averaged about 2.5 percent per annum during the same period. Meanwhile the rates of natural increase in industrialized countries are very low: the highest is approximately 1 percent, most are in the neighbourhood of several tenths of 1 percent, and some are slightly negative (that is, their populations are slowly decreasing).

Population growth. The rate of population growth is the rate of natural increase combined with the effects of migration. Thus a high rate of natural increase can be offset by a large net out-migration, and a low rate of natural increase can be countered by a high level of net in-migration. Generally speaking, however, these migration effects on population growth rates are far smaller than the effects of changes in fertility and mortality.

Population "momentum." An important and often misunderstood characteristic of human populations is the tendency of a highly fertile population that has been increasing rapidly in size to continue to do so for decades after the onset of even a substantial decline in fertility. This results from the youthful age structure of such a population, as discussed below. These populations contain large numbers of children who have still to grow into adulthood and the years of reproduction. Thus even a dramatic decline in fertility, which affects only the numbers at age zero, cannot prevent the continuing growth of the number of adults of childbearing age for at least two or three decades.

Eventually, of course, as these large groups pass through the childbearing years to middle and older age, the smaller numbers of children resulting from the fertility decline lead to a moderation in the rate of population growth. But the delays are lengthy, allowing very substantial additional population growth after fertility has declined. This phenomenon gives rise to the term population momentum, which is of great significance to developing countries with rapid population growth and limited natural resources. The nature of population growth means that the metaphor of a "population bomb" used by some lay analysts of population trends in the 1960s was really quite inaccurate. Bombs explode with tremendous force, but such force is rapidly spent. A more appropriate metaphor for rapid population growth is that of a glacier, since a glacier moves at a slow pace but with enormous effects wherever it goes and with a long-term momentum that is unstoppable.

POPULATION COMPOSITION

The most important characteristics of a population—in addition to its size and the rate at which it is expanding or contracting—are the ways in which its members are distributed according to age, sex, ethnic or racial category, and residential status (urban or rural).

Age distribution. Perhaps the most fundamental of these characteristics is the age distribution of a population. Demographers commonly use population pyramids to describe both age and sex distributions of populations. A population pyramid is a bar chart or graph in which the length of each horizontal bar represents the number (or percentage) of persons in an age group; for example, the base of such a chart consists of a bar representing the youngest segment of the population, those persons less than, say, five years old. Each bar is divided into segments corresponding to the numbers (or proportions) of males and females. In most populations the proportion of older persons is much smaller than that of the younger, so the chart narrows toward the top and is more or less triangular, like the cross section of a pyramid; hence the name. Youthful populations are represented by pyramids with a broad base of young children and a narrow apex of older people, while older populations are characterized by more uniform numbers of people in the age categories. . . .

Population pyramids

Contrary to a common belief, the principal factor tending to change the age distribution of a population—and, hence, the general shape of the corresponding pyramid—is not the death or mortality rates, but rather the rate of fertility. A rise or decline in mortality generally affects all age groups in some measure, and hence has only limited effects on the proportion in each age group. A change in fertility, however, affects the number of people in only a single age group—the group of age zero, the newly born. Hence a decline or increase in fertility has a highly concentrated effect at one end of the age distribution and thereby can have a major influence on the overall age structure. This means that youthful age structures correspond to highly fertile populations, typical of developing countries. The older age structures are those of low-fertility populations, such as are common in the industrialized world.

Sex ratio. A second important structural aspect of populations is the relative numbers of males and females who compose it. Generally, slightly more males are born than females (a typical ratio would be 105 or 106 males for every 100 females). On the other hand, it is quite common for males to experience higher mortality at virtually all ages after birth. This difference is apparently of biological origin. Exceptions occur in countries such as India, where the mortality of females may be higher than that of males in childhood and at the ages of childbearing because of unequal allocation of resources within the family and the poor quality of maternal health care.

Sex differences in natality and mortality

The general rules that more males are born but that females experience lower mortality mean that during childhood males outnumber females of the same age, the difference decreases as the age increases, at some point in the adult life span the numbers of males and females become equal, and as higher ages are reached the number of females becomes disproportionately large. For example, in Europe and North America, among persons more than 70 years of age in 1985, the number of males for every 100 females was only about 61 to 63. (According to the Population Division of the United Nations, the figure for the Soviet Union was only 40, which may be attributable to high male mortality during World War II as well as to possible increases in male mortality during the 1980s.)

The sex ratio within a population has significant implications for marriage patterns. A scarcity of males of a given age depresses the marriage rates of females in the same age group or usually those somewhat younger, and this in turn is likely to reduce their fertility. In many countries, social convention dictates a pattern in which males at marriage are slightly older than their spouses. Thus if there is a dramatic rise in fertility, such as that called the "baby boom" in the period following World War II, a "marriage squeeze" can eventually result; that is, the number of males of the socially correct age for marriage is insufficient for the number of somewhat younger females. This may lead to deferment of marriage of these women, a contraction of the age differential of marrying couples, or both. Similarly, a dramatic fertility decline in such a society is likely to lead eventually to an insufficiency of eligible females for marriage, which may lead to earlier marriage of these women, an expansion of the age gap at marriage, or both. All of these effects are slow to develop; it takes at least 20 to 25 years for even a dramatic fall or rise in fertility to affect marriage patterns in this way.

Ethnic or racial composition. The populations of all nations of the world are more or less diverse with respect to ethnicity or race. (Ethnicity here includes national, cultural, religious, linguistic, or other attributes that are perceived as characteristic of distinct groups.) Such divisions in populations often are regarded as socially important, and statistics by race and ethnic group are therefore commonly available. The categories used for such groups differ from nation to nation, however; for example, a person of Pakistani origin is considered "black" or "coloured" in the United Kingdom but would probably be classified as "white" or "Asian" in the United States. For this reason, international comparisons of ethnic and racial groups are imprecise, and this component of population structure is far less objective as a measure than are the categories of age and sex discussed above.

Geographical distribution and urbanization. It goes without saying that populations are scattered across space. The typical measure of population in relation to land area, that of population density, is often a meaningless one, since different areas vary considerably in their value for agricultural or other human purposes. Moreover, a high population density in an agrarian society, dependent upon agriculture for its sustenance, is likely to be a severer constraint upon human welfare than would the same density in a highly industrialized society, in which the bulk of national product is not of agricultural origin.

Also of significance in terms of geographical distribution is the division between rural and urban areas. For many decades there has been a nearly universal flow of populations from rural into urban areas. While definitions of urban areas differ from country to country and region to region, the most highly urbanized societies in the world are those of western and northern Europe, Australia, New Zealand, temperate South America, and North America; in all of these the fraction of the population living in urban areas exceeds 75 percent, and it has reached 85 percent in West Germany. An intermediate stage of urbanization exists in the countries making up much of tropical Latin America, where 50 to 65 percent of the population lives in cities. Finally, in many of the developing countries of Asia and Africa the urbanization process has only recently begun, and it is not uncommon to find less than one-third of the population living in urban areas.

The rapidity of urbanization in some countries is quite astonishing. The population of Mexico City in 1960 was around 5,000,000; it was estimated to be about 17,000,000 in 1985 and was projected to reach 26,000,000 to 31,000,000 by 2000. A rule of thumb for much of the developing world is that the rate of growth of urban areas is twice that of the population as a whole. Thus in a population growing 3 percent annually (doubling in about 23.1 years), it is likely that the urban growth rate is at least 6 percent annually (doubling in about 11.6 years).

Growth of cities

POPULATION THEORIES

Population size and change play such a fundamental role in human societies that they have been the subject of theorizing for millennia. Most religious traditions have had something to say on these matters, as did many of the leading figures of the ancient world.

In modern times the subject of demographic change has played a central role in the development of the politico-economic theory of mercantilism; the classical economics of Adam Smith, David Ricardo, and others; the cornucopian images of utopians such as the Marquis de Condorcet; the contrasting views of Malthus as to the natural limits imposed on human population; the sociopolitical theories of Marx, Engels, and their followers; the scientific revolutions engendered by Darwin and his followers; and so on through the pantheon of human thought. Most of these theoretical viewpoints have incorporated demographic components as elements of far grander schemes. Only in a few cases have demographic concepts played a central role, as in the case of the theory of the demographic transition that evolved during the 1930s as a counter to biological explanations of fertility declines that were then current.

Population theories in antiquity. The survival of ancient human societies despite high and unpredictable mortality implies that all societies that persisted were successful in maintaining high fertility. They did so in part by stressing the duties of marriage and procreation and by stigmatizing persons who failed to produce children. Many of these pronatalist motives were incorporated into religious dogma and mythology, as in the biblical injunction to "be fruitful and multiply, and populate the earth," the Hindu laws of Manu, and the writings of Zoroaster.

Greek and Roman views

The ancient Greeks were interested in population size, and Plato's *Republic* incorporated the concept of an optimal population size of 5,040 citizens, among whom fertility was restrained by conscious birth control. The leaders of imperial Rome, however, advocated maximizing population size in the interest of power, and explicitly pronatalist laws were adopted during the reign of Augustus to encourage marriage and fertility.

The traditions of Christianity on this topic are mixed. The pronatalism of the Old Testament and the Roman Empire was embraced with some ambivalence by a church that sanctified celibacy among the priesthood. Later, during the time of Thomas Aquinas, the church moved toward more forceful support of high fertility and opposition to birth control.

Islāmic writings on fertility were equally mixed. The 14th-century Arab historian Ibn Khaldūn incorporated demographic factors into his grand theory of the rise and fall of empires. According to his analysis, the decline of an empire's population necessitates the importation of foreign mercenaries to administer and defend its territories, resulting in rising taxes, political intrigue, and general decadence. The hold of the empire on its hinterland and on its own populace weakens, making it a tempting target for a vigorous challenger. Thus Ibn Khaldūn saw the growth of dense human populations as generally favourable to the maintenance and increase of imperial power.

On the other hand, contraception was acceptable practice in Islām from the days of the Prophet, and extensive attention was given to contraceptive methods by the great physicians of the Islāmic world during the Middle Ages. Moreover, under Islāmic law the fetus is not considered a human being until its form is distinctly human, and hence early abortion was not forbidden.

Mercantilism and the idea of progress. The wholesale mortality caused by the Black Death during the 14th century contributed in fundamental ways to the development of mercantilism, the school of thought that dominated Europe from the 16th through the 18th century. Mercantilists and the absolute rulers who dominated many states of Europe saw each nation's population as a form of national wealth: the larger the population, the richer the nation. Large populations provided a larger labour supply, larger markets, and larger (and hence more powerful) armies for defense and for foreign expansion. Moreover, since growth in the number of wage earners tended to depress wages, the wealth of the monarch could be increased by capturing this surplus. In the words of Frederick II the Great of Prussia, "the number of the people makes the wealth of states." Similar views were held by mercantilists in Germany, France, Italy, and Spain. For the mercantilists, accelerating the growth of the population by encouraging fertility and discouraging emigration was consistent with increasing the power of the nation or the king. Most mercantilists, confident that any number of people would be able to produce their own subsistence, had no worries about harmful effects of population growth. (To this day similar optimism continues to be expressed by diverse schools of thought, from traditional Marxists on the left to "cornucopians" on the right.)

Physiocrats and the origins of demography. By the 18th century the Physiocrats were challenging the intensive state intervention that characterized the mercantilist system, urging instead the policy of laissez-faire. Their targets included the pronatalist strategies of governments; Physiocrats such as François Quesnay argued that human multiplication should not be encouraged to a point beyond that sustainable without widespread poverty. For the Physiocrats, economic surplus was attributable to land, and population growth could therefore not increase wealth. In their analysis of this subject matter the Physiocrats drew upon the techniques developed in England by John Graunt, Edmond Halley, Sir William Petty, and Gregory King, which for the first time made possible the quantitative assessment of population size, the rate of growth, and rates of mortality.

Laissez-faire economics

The Physiocrats had broad and important effects upon the thinking of the classical economists such as Adam Smith, especially with respect to the role of free markets unregulated by the state. As a group, however, the classical economists expressed little interest in the issue of population growth, and when they did they tended to see it as an effect rather than as a cause of economic prosperity.

Utopian views. In another 18th-century development, the optimism of mercantilists was incorporated into a very different set of ideas, those of the so-called utopians. Their views, based upon the idea of human progress and perfectibility, led to the conclusion that once perfected, mankind would have no need of coercive institutions such as police, criminal law, property ownership, and the family. In a properly organized society, in their view, progress was consistent with any level of population, since population size was the principal factor determining the amount of resources. Such resources should be held in common by all persons, and if there were any limits on population growth, they would be established automatically by the normal functioning of the perfected human society. Principal proponents of such views included Condorcet, William Godwin, and Daniel Malthus, the father of the Reverend Thomas Robert Malthus. Through his father the younger Malthus was introduced to such ideas relating human welfare to population dynamics, which stimulated him to undertake his own collection and analysis of data; these eventually made him the central figure in the population debates of the 19th and 20th centuries.

Malthus and his successors. In 1798 Malthus published *An Essay on the Principle of Population as It Affects the Future Improvement of Society, with Remarks on the Speculations of Mr. Godwin, M. Condorcet, and Other Writers.* This hastily written pamphlet had as its principal object the refutation of the views of the utopians. In Malthus' view, the perfection of a human society free of coercive restraints was a mirage, because the capacity for the threat of population growth would always be present. In this, Malthus echoed the much earlier arguments of Robert Wallace in his *Various Prospects of Mankind, Nature, and Providence* (1761), which posited that the perfection of society carried with it the seeds of its own destruction, in the stimulation of population growth such that "the earth would at last be overstocked, and become unable to support its numerous inhabitants."

Critics of Malthus

Not many copies of Malthus' essay, his first, were published, but it nonetheless became the subject of discussion and attack. The essay was cryptic and poorly supported by empirical evidence. Malthus' arguments were easy to misrepresent, and his critics did so routinely.

The criticism had the salutary effect of stimulating Malthus to pursue the data and other evidence lacking in his first essay. He collected information on one country that had plentiful land (the United States) and estimated that its population was doubling in less than 25 years. He attributed the far lower rates of European population growth to "preventive checks," giving special emphasis to the characteristic late marriage pattern of western Europe, which he called "moral restraint." The other preventive checks to which he alluded were birth control, abortion, adultery, and homosexuality, all of which as an Anglican minister he considered immoral.

In one sense, Malthus reversed the arguments of the mercantilists that the number of people determined the nation's resources, adopting the contrary argument of the Physiocrats that the resource base determined the numbers of people. From this he derived an entire theory of society and human history, leading inevitably to a set of provocative prescriptions for public policy. Those societies that ignored the imperative for moral restraint—delayed marriage and celibacy for adults until they were economically able to support their children—would suffer the deplorable "positive checks" of war, famine, and epidemic, the avoidance of which should be every society's goal. From this humane concern about the sufferings from positive checks arose Malthus' admonition that poor laws (*i.e.,* legal measures that provided relief to the poor) and charity must not cause their beneficiaries to relax their moral restraint or increase their fertility, lest such humanitarian gestures become perversely counterproductive.

Having stated his position, Malthus was denounced as a reactionary, although he favoured free medical assistance for the poor, universal education at a time that this was a radical idea, and democratic institutions at a time of elitist alarums about the French Revolution. Malthus was accused of blasphemy by the conventionally religious. The strongest denunciations of all came from Marx and his followers (see below). Meanwhile, the ideas of Malthus had important effects upon public policy (such as reforms in the English Poor Laws) and upon the ideas of the classical and neoclassical economists, demographers, and evolutionary biologists, led by Charles Darwin. Moreover, the evidence and analyses produced by Malthus dominated scientific discussion of population during his lifetime; indeed, he was the invited author of the article "Population" for the supplement (1824) to the fourth, fifth, and sixth editions of the *Encyclopædia Britannica.* Though many of Malthus' gloomy predictions have proved to be misdirected, that article introduced analytical methods that clearly anticipated demographic techniques developed more than 100 years later.

Neo-Malthusians

The latter-day followers of Malthusian analysis deviated significantly from the prescriptions offered by Malthus. While these "neo-Malthusians" accepted Malthus' core propositions regarding the links between unrestrained fertility and poverty, they rejected his advocacy of delayed marriage and his opposition to birth control. Moreover, leading neo-Malthusians such as Charles Bradlaugh and Annie Besant could hardly be described as reactionary defenders of the established church and social order. To the contrary, they were political and religious radicals who saw the extension of knowledge of birth control to the lower classes as an important instrument favouring social equality. Their efforts were opposed by the full force of the establishment, and both spent considerable time on trial and in jail for their efforts to publish materials—condemned as obscene—about contraception.

Marx, Lenin, and their followers. While both Karl Marx and Malthus accepted many of the views of the classical economists, Marx was harshly and implacably critical of Malthus and his ideas. The vehemence of the assault was remarkable. Marx reviled Malthus as a "miserable parson" guilty of spreading a "vile and infamous doctrine, this repulsive blasphemy against man and nature." For Marx, only under capitalism does Malthus' dilemma of resource limits arise. Though differing in many respects from the utopians who had provoked Malthus' rejoinder, Marx shared with them the view that any number of people could be supported by a properly organized society. Under the socialism favoured by Marx, the surplus product of labour, previously appropriated by the capitalists, would be returned to its rightful owners, the workers, thereby eliminating the cause of poverty. Thus Malthus and Marx shared a strong concern about the plight of the poor, but they differed sharply as to how it should be improved. For Malthus the solution was individual responsibility as to marriage and childbearing; for Marx the solution was a revolutionary assault upon the organization of society, leading to a collective structure called socialism.

The strident nature of Marx's attack upon Malthus' ideas may have arisen from his realization that they constituted a potentially fatal critique of his own analysis. "If [Malthus'] theory of population is correct," Marx wrote in 1875 in his *Critique of the Gotha Programme* (published by Engels in 1891), "then I can*not* abolish this [iron law of wages] even if I abolish wage-labor a hundred times, because this law is not only paramount over the system of wage-labor but also over every social system."

The anti-Malthusian views of Marx were continued and extended by Marxians who followed him. For example, although in 1920 Lenin legalized abortion in the revolutionary Soviet Union as the right of every woman "to control her own body," he opposed the practice of contraception or abortion for purposes of regulating population growth. Lenin's successor, Joseph Stalin, adopted a pronatalist argument verging on the mercantilist, in which population growth was seen as a stimulant to economic progress. As the threat of war intensified in Europe in the 1930s, Stalin promulgated coercive measures to increase Soviet population growth, including the banning of abortion despite its status as a woman's basic right. Although contraception is now accepted and practiced widely in most Marxist-Leninist states, some traditional ideologists continue to characterize its encouragement in Third-World countries as shabby Malthusianism.

Stalin's pronatalism

The Darwinian tradition. Charles Darwin, whose scientific insights revolutionized 19th-century biology, acknowledged an important intellectual debt to Malthus in the development of his theory of natural selection. Darwin himself was not much involved in debates about human populations, but many who followed in his name as "social Darwinists" and "eugenicists" expressed a passionate if narrowly defined interest in the subject.

In Darwinian theory the engine of evolution is differential reproduction of different genetic stocks. The concern of many social Darwinists and eugenicists was that fertility among those they considered the superior human stocks was far lower than among the poorer—and, in their view, biologically inferior—groups, resulting in a gradual but inexorable decline in the quality of the overall population. While some attributed this lower fertility to deliberate efforts of people who needed to be informed of the dysgenic effects of their behaviour, others saw the fertility decline itself as evidence of biological deterioration of the superior stocks. Such simplistic biological explanations attracted attention to the socioeconomic and cultural factors that might explain the phenomenon and contributed to the development of the theory of the demographic transition.

Theory of the demographic transition. The classic explanation of European fertility declines arose in the period following World War I and came to be known as demographic transition theory. (Formally, transition theory is a historical generalization and not truly a scientific theory offering predictive and testable hypotheses.) The theory arose in part as a reaction to crude biological explanations of fertility declines; it rationalized them in solely socioeconomic terms, as consequences of widespread desire for fewer children caused by industrialization, urbanization, increased literacy, and declining infant mortality.

Changing role of the family

The factory system and urbanization led to a diminution in the role of the family in industrial production and a reduction of the economic value of children. Meanwhile, the costs of raising children rose, especially in urban settings, and universal primary education postponed their entry into the work force. Finally, the lessening of infant mortality reduced the number of births needed to achieve a given family size. In some versions of transition theory, a fertility decline is triggered when one or more of these socioeconomic factors reach certain threshold values.

Until the 1970s transition theory was widely accepted as an explanation of European fertility declines, although conclusions based on it had never been tested empirically. More recently careful research on the European historical experience has forced reappraisal and refinement of demographic transition theory. In particular, distinctions based upon cultural attributes such as language and religion, coupled with the spread of ideas such as those of the nuclear family and the social acceptability of deliberate fertility control, appear to have played more important roles than were recognized by transition theorists.

TRENDS IN WORLD POPULATION

Before considering modern population trends separately for developing and industrialized countries, it is useful to present an overview of older trends. It is generally agreed that only 5,000,000–10,000,000 humans (*i.e.*, one one-thousandth of the present world population) were supportable before the agricultural revolution of about 10,000 years ago. By the beginning of the Christian era, 8,000 years later, the human population approximated 300,000,000, and there was apparently little increase in the ensuing millennium up to the year AD 1000. Subsequent population growth was slow and fitful, especially given the plague epidemics and other catastrophes of the Middle Ages. By 1750, conventionally the beginning of the Industrial Revolution in Britain, world population may have been as high as 800,000,000. This means that in the 750 years from 1000 to 1750, the annual population growth rate averaged only about one-tenth of 1 percent.

The reasons for such slow growth are well known. In the absence of what is now considered basic knowledge of sanitation and health (the role of bacteria in disease, for example, was unknown until the 19th century), mortality rates were very high, especially for infants and children. Only about half of newborn babies survived to the age of five years. Fertility was also very high, as it had to be to sustain the existence of any population under such conditions of mortality. Modest population growth might occur for a time in these circumstances, but recurring famines, epidemics, and wars kept long-term growth close to zero.

Modern increase in world population

From 1750 onward population growth accelerated. In some measure this was a consequence of rising standards of living, coupled with improved transport and communication, which mitigated the effects of localized crop failures that previously would have resulted in catastrophic mortality. Occasional famines did occur, however, and it was not until the 19th century that a sustained decline in mortality took place, stimulated by the improving economic conditions of the Industrial Revolution and the growing understanding of the need for sanitation and public health measures.

The world population, which did not reach its first 1,000,000,000 until about 1800, added another 1,000,000,000 persons by 1930. (To anticipate further discussion below, the third was added by 1960, the fourth by 1974, and the fifth before 1990.) The most rapid growth in the 19th century occurred in Europe and North America, which experienced gradual but eventually dramatic declines in mortality. Meanwhile, mortality and fertility remained high in Asia, Africa, and Latin America.

Beginning in the 1930s and accelerating rapidly after World War II, mortality went into decline in much of Asia and Latin America, giving rise to a new spurt of population growth that reached rates far higher than any previously experienced in Europe. The rapidity of this growth, which some described as the "population explosion," was due to the sharpness in the falls in mortality that in turn were the result of improvements in public health, sanitation, and nutrition that were mostly imported from the developed countries. The external origins and the speed of the declines in mortality meant that there was little chance that they would be accompanied by the onset of a decline in fertility. In addition, the marriage patterns of Asia and Latin America were (and continue to be) quite different from those of Europe; marriage in Asia and Latin America is early and nearly universal, while that in Europe is usually late and significant percentages of people never marry.

These high growth rates occurred in populations already of very large size, meaning that global population growth became very rapid both in absolute and in relative terms. The peak rate of increase was reached in the early 1960s, when each year the world population grew by about 2 percent, or about 68,000,000 people. Since that time both mortality and fertility rates have decreased, and the annual growth rate has fallen moderately, to about 1.7 percent. But even this lower rate, because it applies to a larger population base, means that the number of people added each year has risen from about 68,000,000 to 80,000,000.

The developing countries since 1950. After World War II there was a rapid decline in mortality in much of the developing world. In part this resulted from wartime efforts to maintain the health of armed forces from industrialized countries fighting in tropical areas. Since all people and governments welcome proven techniques to reduce the incidence of disease and death, these efforts were readily accepted in much of the developing world, but they were not accompanied by the kinds of social and cultural changes that had occurred earlier and had led to fertility declines in industrialized countries.

The reduction in mortality, unaccompanied by a reduction in fertility, had a simple and predictable outcome: accelerating population growth. By 1960 many developing countries had rates of increase as high as 3 percent a year, exceeding by two- or threefold the highest rates ever experienced by European populations. Since a population increasing at this rate will double in only 23 years, the populations of such countries expanded dramatically. In the 25 years between 1950 and 1975, the population of Mexico increased from 27,000,000 to 60,000,000; Iran from 14,000,000 to 33,000,000; Brazil from 53,000,000 to 108,000,000; and China from 554,000,000 to 933,000,000.

The greatest population growth rates were reached in Latin America and in Asia during the mid- to late 1960s. Since then, these regions have experienced variable but sometimes substantial fertility declines along with continuing mortality declines, resulting in usually moderate and occasionally large declines in population growth. The most dramatic declines have been those of the People's Republic of China, where the growth rate was estimated to have declined from well over 2 percent per year in the 1960s to about half that in the 1980s, following official adoption of a concerted policy to delay marriage and limit childbearing within marriage. The predominance of the Chinese population in East Asia means that this region has experienced the most dramatic declines in population growth of any of the developing regions.

Population control in China

Over the same period population growth rates have declined only modestly, and in some cases have actually risen, in other developing regions. In South Asia the rate has declined only from 2.4 to 2.0 percent; in Latin America, from about 2.7 to about 2.3 percent. Meanwhile, in Africa population growth has accelerated from 2.6 percent to more than 3 percent over the same period, following belated significant declines in mortality not accompanied by similar reductions in fertility.

The industrialized countries since 1950. For many industrialized countries, the period after World War II was marked by a "baby boom." One group of four countries in particular—the United States, Canada, Australia, and New Zealand—experienced sustained and substantial rises in fertility from the depressed levels of the prewar period. In the United States, for example, fertility rose by two-thirds, reaching levels in the 1950s not seen since 1910.

A second group of industrialized countries, including most of western Europe and some eastern European countries (notably Czechoslovakia and what is now East Germany), experienced what might be termed "baby boomlets." For a few years after the war, fertility increased as a result of marriages and births deferred during wartime. These increases were modest and relatively short-lived, however, when compared to those of the true baby-boom countries mentioned above. In many of these European countries fertility had been very low in the 1930s; their postwar baby boomlets appeared as three- to four-year "spikes" in the graph of their fertility rates, followed by two full decades of stable fertility levels. Beginning in the mid-1960s, fertility levels in these countries began to move lower again and, in many cases, fell to levels comparable to or lower than those of the 1930s.

A third group of industrialized countries, consisting of most of eastern Europe along with Japan, showed quite different fertility patterns. Most did not register low fertility in the 1930s but underwent substantial declines in the 1950s after a short-lived baby boomlet. In many of these countries the decline persisted into the 1960s, but in some it was reversed in response to governmental incentives.

By the 1980s the fertility levels in most industrialized countries were very low, at or below those needed to maintain stable populations. There are two reasons for this phenomenon: the postponement of marriage and childbearing by many younger women who entered the labour force, and a reduction in the numbers of children born to married women.

POPULATION PROJECTIONS

Demographic change is inherently a long-term phenomenon. Unlike populations of insects, human populations have rarely been subject to "explosion" or "collapse" in numbers. Moreover, the powerful long-term momentum that is built into the human age structure means that the effects of fertility changes become apparent only in the far future. For these and other reasons, it is by now conventional practice to employ the technology of population projection as a means of better understanding the implications of trends.

Population projections represent simply the playing out into the future of a set of assumptions about future fertility, mortality, and migration rates. It cannot be stated too strongly that such projections are not predictions, though they are misinterpreted as such frequently enough. A projection is a "what-if" exercise based on explicit assumptions that may or may not themselves be correct. As long as the arithmetic of a projection is done correctly, its utility is determined by the plausibility of its central assumptions. If the assumptions embody plausible future trends, then the projection's outputs may be plausible and useful. If the assumptions are implausible, then so is the projection. Because the course of demographic trends is hard to anticipate very far into the future, most demographers calculate a set of alternative projections that, taken together, are expected to define a range of plausible futures, rather than to predict or forecast any single future. Because demographic trends sometimes change in unexpected ways, it is important that all demographic projections be updated on a regular basis to incorporate new trends and newly developed data.

A standard set of projections for the world and for its constituent countries is prepared every two years by the Population Division of the United Nations. These projections include a low, medium, and high variant for each country and region. . . .

BIBLIOGRAPHY

General works: ROLAND PRESSAT, *The Dictionary of Demography* (1985; originally published in French, 1979); JOHN A. ROSS (ed.), *International Encyclopedia of Population,* 2 vol. (1982), a comprehensive reference work that contains articles on topics ranging from classic demography to current problems and that provides coverage of world regions and countries as well as organizations and agencies active in the field; PETER R. COX, *Demography,* 5th ed. (1976), an examination of methods used in the study of population; DENNIS H. WRONG, *Population and Society,* 4th ed. (1977), an introduction to the main aspects of the population dilemma; and WARREN S. THOMPSON and DAVID T. LEWIS, *Population Problems,* 5th ed. (1965), a comprehensive sociological study.

Population change: ARTHUR A. CAMPBELL, *Manual of Fertility Analysis* (1983), a methodological study: GERRY E. HENDERSHOT and PAUL J. PLACEK (eds.), *Predicting Fertility: Demographic Studies of Birth Expectations* (1981), a survey of the concepts, knowledge, and methods of fertility; NORMAN E. HIMES, *Medical History of Contraception* (1936, reissued 1970), a classic historical treatise; JOHN BONGAARTS and ROBERT G. POTTER, *Fertility, Biology, and Behavior: An Analysis of the Proximate Determinants* (1983), a scholarly examination of such aspects of the population problem as family planning, family size, birth intervals, and fertility; ANSLEY J. COALE and SUSAN COTTS WATKINS (eds.), *The Decline of Fertility in Europe* (1985), a summary of studies of fertility transition in Europe during the 1970s; MICHAEL S. TEITELBAUM and JAY M. WINTER, *The Fear of Population Decline* (1985), the history and bases of past and current concerns about low fertility, with special emphasis on major Western countries; PRANAY GUPTE, *The Crowded Earth: People and the Politics of Population* (1984), a study of the effects of Western development programs on overpopulation; SAMUEL H. PRESTON, *Mortality Patterns in National Populations: With Special Reference to Recorded Causes of Death* (1976), a discussion of the determinants and consequences of national mortality patterns, with attention to the role of standards of living, sex differences, and major causes of death; ALAN A. BROWN and EGON NEUBERGER (eds.), *Internal Migration: A Comparative Perspective* (1977), a collection of scholarly articles; *International Migration Policies and Programmes: A World Survey* (1982), a study of immigration and refugee programs, one of the series of population studies conducted by the United Nations; DAVID GRIGG, *Population Growth and Agrarian Change: An Historical Perspective* (1980), a study of the relationship between demography and economics; ELI S. MARKS, WILLIAM SELTZER, and KAROL J. KRÓTKI, *Population Growth Estimation: A Handbook of Vital Statistics Measurement* (1974), an examination of methods for demographic estimates; and NATHAN KEYFITZ, *Population Change and Social Policy* (1982), a compendium of insightful essays. The 1984 issue of the annual *World Development Report* of the World Bank focuses on population changes in underdeveloped countries.

Population composition: COLIN MCEVEDY and RICHARD JONES, *Atlas of World Population History* (1978), comparisons of population statistics; NATHAN KEYFITZ and WILHELM FLIEGER, *World Population: An Analysis of Vital Data* (1968), a statistical analysis of demographic data for different countries; NATHAN KEYFITZ (ed.), *Population and Biology: Bridge Between Disciplines* (1984), a collection of papers on biological aspects of demography; DOROTHY L. NORTMAN, *Population and Family Planning Programs: Compendium of Data Through 1983,* 12th ed. (1985), including an analysis of demographic and social characteristics; DAVID M. HEER, *Society and Population,* 2nd ed. (1975), a brief study of the population of nation-states; PHILIP M. HAUSER *et al.*, *Population and the Urban Future* (1982), which examines various demographic topics, including the quality of life of urbanized populations; RAYMOND F. DASMANN, *Environmental Conservation,* 5th ed. (1984), a study of the human influence on nature and its consequences for human population; and COLIN CLARK, *Population Growth and Land Use,* 2nd ed. (1977), an analysis of specific problems.

Population theories: RONALD FREEDMAN (ed.), *Population: The Vital Revolution* (1964), is a collection of authoritative essays on major aspects of contemporary demographic analysis. The history of population theory is presented in CHARLES EMIL STANGELAND, *Pre-Malthusian Doctrines of Population: A Study in the History of Economic Theory* (1904, reprinted 1967); JOSEPH J. SPENGLER, *French Predecessors of Malthus: A Study in Eighteenth-Century Wage and Population Theory* (1942, reprinted 1980); WILLIAM PETERSEN, *Malthus* (1979); PATRICIA JAMES, *Population Malthus, His Life and Times* (1979); E.P. HUTCHINSON, *The Population Debate: The Development of Conflicting Theories up to 1900* (1967); and J. DUPÂQUIER, A. FAUVE-CHAMOUX, and E. GREBENIK (eds.), *Malthus Past and Present* (1983). Other works include ALFRED SAUVY, *General Theory of Population* (1969; originally published in French, 1952–54), a study of the relationship between the demographic-biological characteristics of societies and their economic and social circumstances; PHILIP M. HAUSER (ed.), *The Population Dilemma,* 2nd rev. ed. (1969), a collection of papers by leading theoreticians; GARRETT HARDIN, *Population, Evolution, and Birth Control: A Collage of Controversial Ideas,* 2nd ed. (1969), a survey of the history of views and opinions; JONAS SALK and JONATHAN SALK, *World Population and Human Values: A New Reality* (1981), which traces changes in attitudes to developments in population; and JULIAN L. SIMON, *The Ultimate Resource* (1981), an optimistic perspective for the world's population.

Development trends: The spatial distribution of population characteristics is studied in GLENN T. TREWARTHA, *The Less Developed Realm: A Geography of Its Population* (1972), and GLENN T. TREWARTHA (ed.), *The More Developed Realm: A Geography of Its Population* (1978). ALFRED SAUVY, *Fertility and Survival: Population Problems from Malthus to Mao Tse-Tung* (1961; originally published in French, 1959), presents an analysis of problems and proposes solutions. Other works include *The Determinants and Consequences of Population Trends: New Summary of Findings of Interaction of Demographic, Economic, and Social Factors,* 2 vol. (1973–78), a monumental compendium of theory and evidence on population trends compiled by the United Nations; the *Demographic Yearbook,* published by the Statistical Office of the United Nations, a basic source for more than 200 countries and territories; and BERNARD BERELSON (ed.), *Family Planning Programs: An International Survey* (1969), and *Family Planning and Population Programs: A Review of World Developments* (1966), comprehensive assessments of data. Later sources on trends in population development include ESTER BOSERUP, *Population and Technological Change* (1981); GAVIN W. JONES, *Popula-*

tion Growth and Educational Planning in Developing Nations (1975); JOHN CLELAND and JOHN HOBCRAFT (eds.), *Reproductive Change in Developing Countries: Insights from the World Fertility Survey* (1985); GAVIN W. JONES (ed.), *Demographic Transition in Asia* (1984); C. ALISON MCINTOSH, *Population Policy in Western Europe: Responses to Low Fertility in France, Sweden, and West Germany* (1983); DONALD J. BOGUE, *The Population of the United States: Historical Trends and Future Projections* (1985); JOHN L. ANDRIOT (ed.), *Population Abstracts of the United States* (1980); RICHARD L. RUBENSTEIN, *The Age of Triage: Fear and Hope in an Overcrowded World* (1983); JANE MENKEN (ed.), *World Population & U.S. Policy: The Choices Ahead* (1986), papers by leading experts prepared for the second American Assembly on population issues; and NATIONAL RESEARCH COUNCIL, COMMITTEE ON POPULATION, *Population Growth and Economic Development: Policy Questions* (1986).

Population projections: World Population Prospects: Estimates and Projections as Assessed in 1982 (1985), and *Patterns of Urban and Rural Population Growth* (1980), are publications of the United Nations Department of International Economic and Social Affairs. See also JUST FAALAND (ed.), *Population and the World Economy in the 21st Century* (1982), a collection of papers with economic and demographic forecasts; and MICHAEL D. BAYLES, *Morality and Population Policy* (1980), and *Reproductive Ethics* (1984), which discuss the moral aspects of long-term population policies.

For current discussions of relevant topics and reports of recent research the following periodicals may be recommended: *Contraception* (monthly); *Demography* (quarterly); *Economic Development and Cultural Change* (quarterly); *Economic History Review* (quarterly); *Family Planning Perspectives* (bimonthly); *Human Biology* (quarterly); *International Labour Review* (bimonthly); *International Migration Review* (quarterly); *Journal of Biosocial Science* (quarterly); *Journal of Economic History* (quarterly); *Journal of Interdisciplinary History* (quarterly); *Monthly Labor Review; Population and Development Review* (quarterly); *Population Bulletin* (quarterly); *Population Index* (quarterly); *Population Studies* (three times a year); *Science* (weekly); and *Social Biology* (quarterly). Many non-English periodicals in the field appear with systematic summaries in English: *Annales: Économies, Sociétés, Civilisations* (France, bimonthly); *Demografia* (Hungary, quarterly); *Demografía y economía* (Mexico, quarterly); *Demografie* (Czechoslovakia, quarterly); *Genus* (Italy, weekly); *Journal of Population Problems* (Japan, quarterly); and *Population* (France, bimonthly).

(MICHAEL S. TEITELBAUM)

Nietzsche

Friedrich Nietzsche, a 19th-century German philosopher and writer, was one of the most influential modern thinkers. His attempts to unmask the root motives that underlie traditional Western religion, morality, and philosophy deeply affected generations of theologians, philosophers, psychologists, poets, novelists, and playwrights. He thought through the consequences of the triumph of the Enlightenment's secularism, expressed in his observation that "God is dead," in a way that determined the agenda for many of Europe's most celebrated intellectuals after his death in 1900. Although he was an ardent foe of nationalism, anti-Semitism, and power politics, his name was later invoked by Fascists to advance the very things he loathed.

The early years. Nietzsche was born on Oct. 15, 1844, in Röcken, a village in Prussian Saxony. His home was a stronghold of Lutheran piety. His paternal grandfather had published books defending Protestantism and had achieved the ecclesiastical position of superintendent; his maternal grandfather was a country parson; his father, Carl Ludwig Nietzsche, was appointed pastor at Röcken by order of King Friedrich Wilhelm IV of Prussia, after whom Friedrich Nietzsche was named. His father died in 1849, before Nietzsche's fifth birthday, and he spent most of his early life in a household consisting of five women: his mother Franziska, his younger sister Elisabeth, his maternal grandmother, and two maiden aunts.

In 1850 the family moved to Naumburg on the Saale River, where Nietzsche attended a private preparatory school, the Domgymnasium. In 1858 he earned a scholarship to Schulpforta, Germany's leading Protestant boarding school. He excelled academically at Pforta, received an outstanding classical education there, and, having graduated in 1864, went to the University of Bonn to study theology and classical philology. Despite efforts to take part in the university's social life, the two semesters at Bonn were a failure, owing chiefly to acrimonious quarrels between his two leading classics professors, Otto Jahn and Friedrich Wilhelm Ritschl. Nietzsche sought refuge in music, writing a number of compositions strongly influenced by Robert Schumann, the German Romantic composer. In 1865 he transferred to the University of Leipzig, joining Ritschl, who had accepted an appointment there.

University years

Nietzsche prospered under Ritschl's tutelage in Leipzig. He became the only student ever to publish in Ritschl's journal, *Rheinisches Museum* ("Rhenish Museum"). He began military service in October 1867 in the cavalry company of an artillery regiment, sustained a serious chest injury while mounting a horse in March 1868, and resumed his studies in Leipzig in October 1868 while on extended sick leave from the military. During the years in Leipzig, Nietzsche discovered Arthur Schopenhauer's philosophy, met the great operatic composer Richard Wagner, and began his lifelong friendship with fellow classicist Erwin Rohde (author of *Psyche*).

The Basel years (1869–79). When a professorship in classical philology fell vacant in 1869 in Basel, Switz., Ritschl recommended Nietzsche with unparalleled praise. He had completed neither his doctoral thesis nor the additional dissertation required for a German degree; yet Ritschl assured the University of Basel that he had never seen anyone like Nietzsche in 40 years of teaching and that his talents were limitless. In 1869 the University of Leipzig conferred the doctorate without examination or dissertation on the strength of his published writings, and the University of Basel appointed him extraordinary professor of classical philology. The following year Nietzsche became a Swiss citizen and was promoted to ordinary professor.

Nietzsche obtained a leave to serve as a volunteer medical orderly in August 1870, after the outbreak of the Franco-Prussian War. Within a month, while accompanying a transport of wounded, he contracted dysentery and diphtheria, which ruined his health permanently. He returned to Basel in October to resume a heavy teaching load, but as early as 1871 ill health prompted him to seek relief from the stultifying chores of a professor of classical philology; he applied for the vacant chair of philosophy and proposed Rohde as his successor, all to no avail.

During these early Basel years Nietzsche's ambivalent friendship with Wagner ripened, and he seized every opportunity to visit Richard and his wife, Cosima. Wagner appreciated Nietzsche as a brilliant professorial apostle, but Wagner's increasing exploitation of Christian motifs, as in *Parsifal*, coupled with his chauvinism and anti-Semitism proved to be more than Nietzsche could bear. By 1878 the breach between the two men had become final.

Nietzsche's break with Wagner

Nietzsche's first book, *Die Geburt der Tragödie aus dem Geiste der Musik* (1872; *The Birth of Tragedy from the Spirit of Music*), marked his emancipation from the trappings of classical scholarship. A speculative rather than exegetical work, it argued that Greek tragedy arose out of the fusion of what he termed Apollonian and Dionysian elements—the former representing measure, restraint, harmony, and the latter representing unbridled passion—and that Socratic rationalism and optimism spelled the death of Greek tragedy. The final 10 sections of the book are a rhapsody about the rebirth of tragedy from the spirit of Wagner's music. Greeted by stony silence at first, it became the object of heated controversy on the part of those who mistook it for a conventional work of classical scholarship. It was undoubtedly "a work of profound imaginative insight, which left the scholarship of a generation toiling in the rear," as the British classicist F.M. Cornford wrote in 1912. It remains a classic in the history of aesthetics to this day.

By October 1876 Nietzsche requested and received a year's sick leave. In 1877 he set up house with his sister and Peter Gast, and in 1878 his aphoristic *Menschliches, Allzumenschliches* (*Human, All-Too-Human*) appeared. Because his health deteriorated steadily he resigned his professorial chair on June 14, 1879, and was granted a pension of 3,000 Swiss francs per year for six years.

Decade of isolation and creativity (1879–89). Apart from the books Nietzsche wrote between 1879 and 1889, it is doubtful that his life held any intrinsic interest. Seriously ill, half-blind, in virtually unrelenting pain, he lived in boarding houses in Switzerland, the French Riviera, and Italy, with only limited human contact. His friendship with Paul Rée was undermined by 1882 by their mutual if unacknowledged affection for Lou Salomé, author, later the wife of the Orientalist F.C. Andreas, mistress of the poet Rainer Maria Rilke, and confidant of Sigmund Freud, as well as by Elisabeth Nietzsche's jealous meddling.

Nietzsche's acknowledged literary and philosophical masterpiece in biblical narrative form, *Also sprach Zarathustra* (*Thus Spoke Zarathustra*), was published between 1883 and 1885 in four parts, the last part a private printing at his own expense. As with most of his works it received little attention. His attempts to set forth his philosophy in more direct prose, in the publications in 1886 of *Jenseits von Gut und Böse* (*Beyond Good and Evil*) and in 1887 of *Zur Genealogie der Moral* (*On the Genealogy of Morals*), also failed to win a proper audience.

Nietzsche's final lucid year, 1888, was a period of supreme productivity. He wrote and published *Der Fall Wagner* (*The Case of Wagner*) and wrote a synopsis of his philosophy, *Die Götzen-Dämmerung* (*Twilight of the Idols*), *Der Antichrist* (*The Antichrist*), *Nietzsche contra Wagner* (Eng. trans., *Nietzsche contra Wagner*), and *Ecce Homo* (Eng. trans., *Ecce Homo*), a reflection on his own works and significance. *Twilight of the Idols* appeared in 1889, *Der Antichrist* and *Nietzsche contra Wagner* were not published until 1895, the former mistakenly as book one of *The Will to Power*, and *Ecce Homo* was withheld from publication until 1908, 20 years after its composition.

Collapse and misuse. Nietzsche collapsed in the streets of Turin, Italy, in January 1889, having lost control of his mental faculties completely. Bizarre but meaningful notes he sent immediately after his collapse brought Franz Overbeck to Italy to return Nietzsche to Basel. Nietzsche spent the last 11 years of his life in total mental darkness, first in a Basel asylum, then in Naumburg under his mother's care and, after her death in 1897, in Weimar in his sister's care. He died on Aug. 25, 1900. Informed opinion favours a diagnosis of atypical general paralysis caused by dormant tertiary syphilis.

Years of mental darkness

The association of Nietzsche's name with Adolf Hitler and Fascism owes much to the use made of his works by his sister Elisabeth. She had married a leading chauvinist and anti-Semite, Bernhard Förster, and after his suicide in 1889 she worked diligently to refashion Nietzsche in Förster's image. Elisabeth maintained ruthless control over Nietzsche's literary estate and, dominated by greed, produced collections of his "works" consisting of discarded notes, such as *Der Wille zur Macht* (1901; *The Will to Power*). She also committed petty forgeries. Generations of commentators were misled. Equally important, her enthusiasm for Hitler linked Nietzsche's name with that of the dictator in the public mind.

Nietzsche's sister's misuse of his literary estate

Nietzsche's mature philosophy. Nietzsche's writings fall into three well-defined periods. The early works, *The Birth of Tragedy* and the four *Unzeitgemässe Betrachtungen* (1873; *Untimely Meditations*), are dominated by a Romantic perspective influenced by Schopenhauer and Wagner. The middle period, from *Human, All-Too-Human* up to *The Gay Science*, reflects the tradition of French aphorists. It extols reason and science, experiments with literary genres, and expresses Nietzsche's emancipation from his earlier Romanticism and from Schopenhauer and Wagner. Nietzsche's mature philosophy emerged after *The Gay Science*.

In his mature writings Nietzsche was preoccupied by the origin and function of values in human life. If, as he believed, life neither possesses nor lacks intrinsic value and yet is always being evaluated, then such evaluations can usefully be read as symptoms of the condition of the evaluator. He was especially interested, therefore, in a probing analysis and evaluation of the fundamental cultural values of Western philosophy, religion, and morality, which he characterized as expressions of the ascetic ideal.

The ascetic ideal is born when suffering becomes endowed with ultimate significance. According to Nietzsche the Judeo-Christian tradition, for example, made suffering tolerable by interpreting it as God's intention and as an occasion for atonement. Christianity, accordingly, owed its triumph to the flattering doctrine of personal immortality, that is, to the conceit that each individual's life and death have cosmic significance. Similarly, traditional philosophy expressed the ascetic ideal when it privileged soul over body, mind over senses, duty over desire, reality over appearance, the timeless over the temporal. While Christianity promised salvation for the sinner who repents, philosophy held out hope for salvation, albeit secular, for its sages. Common to traditional religion and philosophy was the unstated but powerful motivating assumption that existence requires explanation, justification, or expiation. Both denigrated experience in favour of some other, "true" world. Both may be read as symptoms of a declining life, or life in distress.

Nietzsche's critique of traditional morality centred on the typology of "master" and "slave" morality. By examining the etymology of the German words *gut* ("good"), *schlecht* ("bad"), and *böse* ("evil"), Nietzsche maintained that the distinction between good and bad was originally descriptive, that is, a nonmoral reference to those who were privileged, the masters, as opposed to those who were base, the slaves. The good/evil contrast arose when slaves avenged themselves by converting attributes of mastery into vices. If the favoured, the "good," were powerful, it was said that the meek would inherit the earth. Pride became sin. Charity, humility, and obedience replaced competition, pride, and autonomy. Crucial to the triumph of slave morality was its claim to being the only true morality. This insistence on absoluteness is as essential to philosophical as to religious ethics. Although Nietzsche gave a historical genealogy of master and slave morality, he maintained that it was an ahistorical typology of traits present in everyone.

Nietzsche's etymological approach to the interpretation of morality

"Nihilism" was the term Nietzsche used to describe the devaluation of the highest values posited by the ascetic ideal. He thought of the age in which he lived as one of passive nihilism, that is, as an age that was not yet aware that religious and philosophical absolutes had dissolved in the emergence of 19th-century Positivism. With the collapse of metaphysical and theological foundations and sanctions for traditional morality only a pervasive sense of purposelessness and meaninglessness would remain. And the triumph of meaninglessness is the triumph of nihilism: "God is dead." Nietzsche thought, however, that most men could not accept the eclipse of the ascetic ideal and the intrinsic meaninglessness of existence but would seek supplanting absolutes to invest life with meaning. He thought the emerging nationalism of his day represented one such ominous surrogate god, in which the nation-state would be invested with transcendent value and purpose. And just as absoluteness of doctrine had found expression in philosophy and religion, Nietzsche thought that absoluteness would become attached to the nation-state with missionary fervour and zeal. The slaughter of rivals and the conquest of the earth would proceed, self-deceptively, under banners of universal brotherhood, democracy, and socialism. Nietzsche's prescience here was particularly poignant, and the use later made of him especially repellent. For example, two books were standard issue for the rucksacks of German soldiers during World War I, *Thus*

God is dead

Spoke Zarathustra and *The Gospel According to St. John.* It is difficult to say which author was more compromised by this gesture.

Nietzsche often thought of his writings as struggles with nihilism, and apart from his critiques of religion, philosophy, and morality he developed original theses that have commanded attention, especially perspectivism, will to power, eternal recurrence, and the superman.

Perspectivism is a concept which holds that knowledge is always perspectival, that there are no immaculate perceptions, and that knowledge from no point of view is as incoherent a notion as seeing from no particular vantage point. Perspectivism also denies the possibility of an all-inclusive perspective, which could contain all others and, hence, make reality available as it is in itself. The concept of such an all-inclusive perspective is as incoherent as the concept of seeing an object from every possible vantage point simultaneously.

Nietzsche's perspectivism has sometimes been mistakenly identified with relativism and skepticism. Nonetheless, it raises the question of how one is to understand Nietzsche's own theses, for example, that the dominant values of the common heritage have been underwritten by an ascetic ideal. Is this thesis true absolutely or only from a certain perspective? It may also be asked whether perspectivism can be asserted consistently without self-contradiction, since perspectivism must presumably be true in an absolute, that is a nonperspectival sense. Concerns such as these have generated much fruitful Nietzsche commentary as well as useful work in the theory of knowledge.

Critical responses to Nietzsche's concept of perspectivism

Nietzsche often identified life itself with "will to power," that is, with an instinct for growth and durability. This concept provides yet another way of interpreting the ascetic ideal, since it is Nietzsche's contention "that all the supreme values of mankind *lack* this will—that values which are symptomatic of decline, *nihilistic* values, are lording it under the holiest names." Thus, traditional philosophy, religion, and morality have been so many masks a deficient will to power wears. The sustaining values of Western civilization have been sublimated products of decadence in that the ascetic ideal endorses existence as pain and suffering. Some commentators have attempted to extend Nietzsche's concept of the will to power from human life to the organic and inorganic realms, ascribing a metaphysics of will to power to him. Such interpretations, however, cannot be sustained by reference to his published works.

The doctrine of eternal recurrence, the basic conception of *Thus Spoke Zarathustra,* asks the question "How well disposed would a person have to become to himself and to life to crave nothing more fervently than the infinite repetition, without alteration, of each and every moment?" Presumably most men would, or should, find such a thought shattering because they should always find it possible to prefer the eternal repetition of their lives in an edited version rather than to crave nothing more fervently than the eternal recurrence of each of its horrors. The person who could accept recurrence without self-deception or evasion would be a superhuman being (*Übermensch*), a superman whose distance from the ordinary man is greater than the distance between man and ape, Nietzsche says. Commentators still disagree whether there are specific character traits that define the person who embraces eternal recurrence.

Nietzsche's influence. Nietzsche once wrote that some men are born posthumously, and this is certainly true in his case. The history of 20th-century philosophy, theology, and psychology are unintelligible without him. The German philosophers Max Scheler, Karl Jaspers, and Martin Heidegger laboured in his debt, for example, as did the French philosophers Albert Camus, Jacques Derrida, and Michel Foucault. Existentialism and deconstructionism, a movement in philosophy and literary criticism, owe much to him. The theologians Paul Tillich and Lev Shestov acknowledged their debt as did the "God is dead" theologian Thomas J.J. Altizer; Martin Buber, Judaism's greatest 20th-century thinker, counted Nietzsche among the three most important influences in his life and translated the first part of *Zarathustra* into Polish. The psychologists Alfred Adler and Carl Jung were deeply influenced, as was Sigmund Freud, who said of Nietzsche that he had a more penetrating understanding of himself than any man who ever lived or was ever likely to live. Novelists like Thomas Mann, Hermann Hesse, André Malraux, André Gide, and John Gardner were inspired by him and wrote about him, as did the poets and playwrights George Bernard Shaw, Rainer Maria Rilke, Stefan George, and William Butler Yeats, among others. Nietzsche is certainly one of the most influential philosophers who ever lived; and this is due not only to his originality but also to the fact that he was the German language's most brilliant prose writer.

MAJOR WORKS

Definitive editions of Nietzsche's collected works have been edited by Giorgio Colli and Mazzino Montinari, *Werke: Kritische Gesamtausgabe* (1967–), projected for 30 vol., of which 21 had been published by 1984, and *Sämtliche Werke: Kritische Studienausgabe,* 15 vol. (1980). These strictly chronological editions render all earlier collections obsolete. All books authorized for publication by Nietzsche exist in English translations, the most reliable of which are by Walter Kaufmann. The original works in the following list have been translated and edited by Walter Kaufmann unless noted otherwise: *Die Geburt der Tragödie* (1872; *The Birth of Tragedy*); *Unzeitgemässe Betrachtungen,* 4 vol. (1873–76; *Untimely Meditations,* trans. by R.J. Hollingdale); *Menschliches, Allzumenschliches* (1878; *Human, All-Too-Human,* trans. by Marion Faber and Stephen Lehmann); *Morgenröte* (1881; *Daybreak,* trans. by R.J. Hollingdale); *Die fröhliche Wissenschaft* (1882), new ed. augmented by book 5 and *Lieder des Prinzen Vogelfrei* (1887; *The Gay Science*); *Also sprach Zarathustra,* parts 1–3 (1883–84) and part 4 (1885; *Thus Spoke Zarathustra*); *Jenseits von Gut und Böse* (1886; *Beyond Good and Evil*); *Zur Genealogie der Moral* (1887; *On the Genealogy of Morals*); *Der Fall Wagner* (1888; *The Case of Wagner*); *Götzen-Dämmerung* (1889; *Twilight of the Idols*); *Der Antichrist* (1895; *The Antichrist*); *Nietzsche contra Wagner* (1895); *Ecce Homo* (1908). A selection from Nietzsche's notes never intended for publication appeared as *Der Wille zur Macht* (1901; *The Will to Power,* trans. by Walter Kaufmann and R.J. Hollingdale). An important translation and selection of Nietzsche's early unpublished writings is *Philosophy and Truth* (1979), ed. and trans. by Daniel Breazeale. The fundamental chronological edition of Nietzsche's letters by Giorgio Colli and Mazzino Montinari, *Briefwechsel: Kritische Gesamtausgabe* (1975–), is planned for 20 vol., of which 17 had appeared by 1984, containing the correspondence of 1850–89. A fine selection in English is *Selected Letters of Friedrich Nietzsche* (1969), ed. and trans. by Christopher Middleton.

BIBLIOGRAPHY. The *International Nietzsche Bibliography,* ed. by HERBERT W. REICHERT and KARL SCHLECHTA, rev. and expanded ed. (1968), lists more than 4,500 studies in 27 languages. Especially noteworthy English-language studies are WALTER KAUFMANN, *Nietzsche: Philosopher, Psychologist, Antichrist,* 4th ed. (1974), a work that exposed many myths about Nietzsche; R.J. HOLLINGDALE, *Nietzsche: The Man and His Philosophy* (1965), an intellectual biography; and ARTHUR C. DANTO, *Nietzsche as Philosopher* (1965, reissued 1980), a treatment through the eyes of Analytic philosophy. See also RONALD HAYMAN, *Nietzsche: A Critical Life* (1980), an excellent biography for the general reader in English; BERND MAGNUS, *Nietzsche's Existential Imperative* (1978), a comprehensive discussion of Nietzsche's doctrine of eternal recurrence; RICHARD SCHACHT, *Nietzsche* (1983), a comprehensive interpretation that makes extensive use of *The Will to Power;* and ALEXANDER NEHAMAS, *Nietzsche: Life as Literature* (1985), a treatment of Nietzsche's philosophy on the analogy of the interpretation of a literary text.

(BERND MAGNUS)

Bibliography: Recent Books

The following list encompasses some 170 recent books that have been judged significant contributions to learning and understanding in their respective fields. Each citation includes a few lines of commentary to indicate the general tenor of the work. The citations are organized by subject area, using the ten parts of the *Propædia* as an outline.

Matter and Energy

Nick Herbert, *Quantum Reality: Beyond the New Physics* (1985), a stimulating survey of various scientific views on the physics of elementary particles.

Alastair I. M. Rae, *Quantum Physics, Illusion or Reality?* (1986), a lucid introduction to concepts of quantum mechanics.

Lewis H. Ryder, *Quantum Field Theory* (1985), a readable, well-organized reference work.

Richard P. Feynman, *QED: The Strange Theory of Light and Matter* (1985), an exposition of the theory of quantum electrodynamics.

Joel F. Liebman and Arthur Greenberg (eds.), *Chemical Bonding Models* (1986) and *Studies of Organic Molecules* (1986), informative collections of writings by authorities in the field.

Anthony J. Pearson, *Metallo-Organic Chemistry* (1985), an important survey of organo-transition-metal compounds and their applications.

Jean Audouze and Guy Israel (eds.), *The Cambridge Atlas of Astronomy* (1985; originally published in French, 1983), a comprehensive atlas of the universe, illustrated with recent photographs.

Iain Nicolson and Patrick Moore, *The Universe* (1985), a brief, accurate, well-illustrated reference work of broad scope.

Ronald Greeley, *Planetary Landscapes* (1985), an illustrated description of geologic characteristics of planetary bodies that have solid surfaces.

David Malin and Paul Murdin, *Colours of the Stars* (1984), a beautifully presented and explained collection of astronomical photography, with a survey of the history and techniques of the process.

Robert T. Little, *Astrophotography: A Step-by-Step Approach* (1986), an informative and well-illustrated guide to equipment and techniques.

Hubert Reeves, *Atoms of Silence: An Exploration of Cosmic Evolution* (1984; originally published in French, 1981), a historico-philosophical study of the structure of the universe.

Simon Mitton and Jacqueline Mitton, *Invitation to Astronomy* (1986), an enthusiastic introduction to the profession of an astronomer.

The Earth

Richard Fifield (ed.), *The Making of the Earth* (1985), a collection of articles on developments in all aspects of earth sciences.

Henry G. Houghton, *Physical Meteorology* (1985), an exposition of the fundamentals of meteorology, based on the direct application of the laws of physics.

Peter O'Neill, *Environmental Chemistry* (1985), a sound introduction to the broad subject of chemical processes in the environment.

Joel S. Levine (ed.), *The Photochemistry of Atmospheres: Earth, the Other Planets, and Comets* (1985), a comprehensive survey with detailed study of all layers of atmosphere.

K. O. Emery and Elazar Uchupi, *The Geology of the Atlantic Ocean* (1984), a detailed treatise accompanied by a set of maps in a separate volume.

D. L. Dineley, *Aspects of a Stratigraphic System: The Devonian* (1984), a well-illustrated analysis of a critical period in the geologic record.

Kiyoo Mogi, *Earthquake Prediction*, trans. from the Japanese (1985), an authoritative review of contemporary research in seismology.

Tjeerd H. van Andel, *New Views on an Old Planet: Continental Drift and the History of Earth* (1985), a historical survey of geology, climatology, oceanology, and geography and their relation to the development of life on Earth.

Peter Cattermole and Patrick Moore, *The Story of the Earth* (1985), a brief, well-illustrated, multidisciplinary outline of the Earth's history.

Organisation for Economic Co-operation and Development, *The State of the Environment, 1985* (1985), an informative account of the conditions of the environment and natural resources and of the prospects for improvement.

John J. Berger, *Restoring the Earth: How Americans Are Working to Renew Our Damaged Environment* (1985), a journalist's report on several restoration projects undertaken as part of a popular ecological renewal movement.

Life on Earth

Steven M. Stanley, *Earth and Life Through Time* (1986), a comprehensive historical introduction to biologic and geologic aspects of evolution.

Mae-Wan Ho and Peter T. Saunders (eds.), *Beyond Neo-Darwinism: An Introduction to the New Evolutionary Paradigm* (1984), a cross-disciplinary survey of views on evolutionary theory.

Adrian Friday and David S. Ingram (eds.), *The Cambridge Encyclopedia of Life Sciences* (1985), a well-organized and well-illustrated summary of zoology and botany, with a backdrop of geology and earth sciences.

Vaclav Smil, *Carbon, Nitrogen, Sulfur: Human Interference in Grand Biospheric Cycles* (1985), a thorough survey of research into the major biogeochemical cycles.

Lynn Margulis and Dorion Sagan, *The Origins of Sex: Three Billion Years of Genetic Recombination* (1986), a study of reproductive processes and sexuality in living organisms.

Bettyann Kevles, *Females of the Species: Sex and Survival in the Animal Kingdom* (1986), a sociobiological interpretation of animal sex and reproduction.

W. B. Schofield, *Introduction to Bryology* (1985), a systematic description of mosses and lichens.

J. Derek Bewley and Michael Black, *Seeds: Physiology of Development and Germination* (1985), a comprehensive discussion of seed biology.

Ghillean Tolmie Prance, *Leaves: The Formation, Characteristics, and Uses of Hundreds of Leaves Found in All Parts of the World* (1985), an informative and richly illustrated book.

Christopher M. Perrins and Alex L. A. Middleton (eds.), *The Encyclopedia of Birds* (1985), a comprehensive, detailed reference work, arranged in taxonomic order.

Sally Tongren, *To Keep Them Alive: Wild Animal Breeding* (1985), a well-organized account of methods and techniques used to preserve endangered animal species.

Jacques G. Richardson (ed.), *Managing the Ocean: Resources, Research, Law* (1985), an informative survey of marine resources and perspectives of aquaculture.

Karl D. Kryter, *Physiological, Psychological, and Social Effects of Noise* (1984), an authoritative study, profusely illustrated and accompanied by an exhaustive bibliography.

Leon Kass, *Toward a More Natural Science: Biology and Human Affairs* (1985), an analysis of ethics of biologic technology.

Human Life

Eric Delson (ed.), *Ancestors, the Hard Evidence* (1985), a collection of essays on the current status of research in human physical evolution.

Gyles Brandreth, *Your Vital Statistics: The Ultimate Book About the Average Human Being* (1986), a compendium of entertaining information about the human body.

Richard F. Thompson, *The Brain: An Introduction to Neuroscience* (1985), a basic introduction to the workings of the nervous system.

Harlan Lane, *When the Mind Hears: A History of the Deaf* (1984), a scholarly though partisan history of education for the deaf.

Joseph A. Califano, Jr., *America's Health Care Revolution: Who Lives? Who Dies? Who Pays?* (1986), a graphic analysis of the American health care system and its problems.

Alan L. Sorkin, *Health Care and the Changing Economic Environment* (1986), a study of the economics of the health care industry, especially its recent trends.

Earl E. Shelp, *Born to Die?: Deciding the Fate of Critically Ill Newborns* (1986), a comprehensive and provocative study of the decision making on a vital contemporary issue.

Derek Humphry and Ann Wickett, *The Right to Die: Understanding Euthanasia* (1986), a historical study of the legal, religious, and ethical aspects of euthanasia, with an analysis of modern developments.

Harvey B. Milkman and Howard J. Shaffer (eds.), *The Addictions: Multidisciplinary Perspectives and Treatments* (1985), a collection of interpretative papers on causes and treatment of addictive behaviour.

Dennis Altman, *AIDS in the Mind of America* (1986), a critical analysis of the social and political impact of the disease.

Richard Bergland, *The Fabric of the Mind* (1986), a comprehensive history of mankind's understanding of the brain.

Michael S. Gazzaniga, *The Social Brain: Discovering the Networks of the Mind* (1985), an account of important contemporary research into the global organization of the brain.

Allen W. Gottfried and Catherine Caldwell Brown (eds.), *Play Interactions: The Contribution of Play Materials and Parental Involvement to Children's Development* (1986), a comprehensive, well-documented collection of articles on the developmental role of children's play.

Alan Garnham, *Psycholinguistics: Central Topics* (1985), an analysis of the major issues in the cognitive sciences.

Nicholas Humphrey, *The Inner Eye* (1986), a short psychological study of the uniqueness of human social consciousness.

Susie Orbach, *Hunger Strike: An Anorectic's Struggle as a Metaphor for Our Age* (1986), a sociological and psychological analysis of this widespread problem.

Human Society

Dean Peabody, *National Characteristics* (1985), an authoritative discussion of nationalities, based on ratings of both descriptive and evaluative factors.

Kingsley Davis (ed.), *Contemporary Marriage: Comparative Perspectives on a Changing Institution* (1986), a survey of approaches to this important issue.

Robert L. Simon, *Sports and Social Values* (1985), a well-documented study of moral and ethical issues in sports.

Michael G. Wade (ed.), *Constraints on Leisure* (1985), an anthology of studies on leisure and recreation as social phenomena.

Joseph P. Forgas (ed.), *Language and Social Situations* (1985), a study of the influence of social context upon both linguistic and psychological aspects of language use.

J. G. Kyle and B. Woll, *Sign Language: The Study of Deaf People and Their Language* (1985), a clear analysis of the linguistic, historical, cognitive, and social aspects of sign language.

Patricia A. McBroom, *The Third Sex: The New Professional Woman* (1986), a study of compromises for the sake of adapting to the professional and business environment.

Joni Lovenduski, *Women and European Politics: Contemporary Feminism and Public Policy* (1986), a comparative history of women's movements in Europe.

Ruth Sidel, *Women and Children Last: The Plight of Poor Women in Affluent America* (1986), a study of the economic and social trends of the modern society that push women into poverty.

John A. Krout, *The Aged in Rural America* (1986), an informative overview of sociological and demographic research on the problems of the elderly.

James Rachels, *The End of Life: Euthanasia and Morality* (1986), a persuasive philosophical exploration of the problem, clearly in favour of voluntary euthanasia.

Kenneth Fox, *Metropolitan America: Urban Life and Urban Policy in the United States, 1940–1980* (1986), a cross-disciplinary historical study of urban society.

Michael Poole, *Industrial Relations: Origins and Patterns of National Diversity* (1986), a comparative exposition of theoretical guidelines, covering the economies of selected countries.

F. Gerard Adams and Susan M. Wachter (eds.), *Savings and Capital Formation: The Policy Options* (1986), an analysis of savings policies and the role of savings in economic growth.

Paul N. Bloom and Ruth Belk Smith (eds.), *The Future of Consumerism* (1986), a study of the developments in this expanding field.

Stephen M. Hills (ed.), *The Changing Labor Market: A Longitudinal Study of Young Men* (1986), a collection of essays exploring the socioeconomic factors influencing the employment characteristics of the younger population.

Colin Gill, *Work, Unemployment, and the New Technology* (1985), an overview of contemporary research in the social aspects of industrial technology.

Beverly May Carl, *Economic Integration Among Developing Nations: Law and Policy* (1986), a discussion of the principles and systems of economic integration.

Henry J. Aaron and Harvey Galper, *Assessing Tax Reform* (1985), an analysis of the principles of taxation, the current economic debate, and existing options.

Keith B. Payne, *Strategic Defense: "Star Wars" in Perspective* (1986), an informed though partisan study of the Strategic Defense Initiative.

Neil C. Livingstone and Terrell E. Arnold (eds.), *Fighting Back: Winning the War Against Terrorism* (1986), a collection of essays expounding the use of force in the struggle against terrorism.

John Keegan and Andrew Wheatcroft, *Zones of Conflict: An Atlas of Future Wars* (1986), a military history and a forecast of potential conflicts based on the present international situation.

Earl W. Foell and Richard A. Nenneman (eds.), *How Peace Came to the World* (1986), a summary of entries in the *Christian Science Monitor*'s Peace 2010 contest, explaining how people expect world peace to be achieved.

Jack Donnelly, *The Concept of Human Rights* (1985), a philosophical analysis of human rights as natural rights.

Jeffrie G. Murphy and Jules L. Coleman, *The Philosophy of Law: An Introduction to Jurisprudence* (1984), a comprehensive though brief treatment of historical, theoretical, and economic uses of the law.

Valerie P. Hans and Neil Vidmar, *Judging the Jury* (1986), an authoritative discussion of the functions, duties, competence, and effectiveness of a jury.

James A. Banks and James Lynch (eds.), *Multicultural Education in Western Societies* (1986), a critical discussion of intercultural education and its social significance.

Mark Bray, Peter B. Clarke, and David Stephens, *Education and Society in Africa* (1986), a study of the sociological aspects of education in mostly English-speaking countries of the sub-Saharan region.

Art

H. W. Janson, *History of Art: A Survey of the Major Visual Arts from the Dawn of History to the Present Day*, 3rd ed., edited by Anthony F. Janson (1986), a newly revised and expanded authoritative standard history.

Jacques Maquet, *The Aesthetic Experience: An Anthropologist Looks at the Visual Arts* (1986), a well-illustrated, cross-cultural, sociological analysis of aesthetic creativity.

Peter Selz, *Art in a Turbulent Era* (1985), an interpretative and informative survey of modern art.

Richard M. Ludwig and Clifford A. Nault, Jr. (eds.), *Annals of American Literature, 1602–1983* (1986), a detailed chronology of American writings.

Philip Edwards, *Shakespeare: A Writer's Progress* (1986), a concise but comprehensive overview of Shakespeare's work.

Bernard Bergonzi, *The Myth of Modernism and Twentieth Century Literature* (1986), a collection of literary reviews of major modernist writings.

Miller Williams, *Patterns of Poetry: An Encyclopedia of Forms* (1986), an introductory treatise on the poetic forms, and a guide to versification.

Glynne Wickham, *A History of the Theatre* (1985), a historical overview of the ties between theatre and society, covering the period from preclassical Greece to the 1980s.

Austin E. Quigley, *The Modern Stage and Other Worlds* (1985), a pluralistic analysis of the form of 19th- and 20th-century European drama.

George M. Wilson, *Narration in Light: Studies in Cinematic Point of View* (1986), a philosophical study of the narrative, story-telling aspect of modern film, illustrated, with analyses of several well-known movies.

George Slusser and Eric S. Rabkin (eds.), *Shadows of the Magic Lamp: Fantasy and Science Fiction in Film* (1985), a collection of studies on the genre and its tradition in the 20th century.

John Edward Hasse, *Ragtime: Its History, Composers, and Music* (1985), an anthology of writings on the history, philosophy, and practitioners of the style.

Paul A. Robinson, *Opera & Ideas: From Mozart to Strauss* (1985), a study of the interplay of philosophical, social, and political ideas in the history of music.

Robert Coe, *Dance in America* (1985), a history of contemporary dance and a survey of major dance companies.

Michael Forsyth, *Buildings for Music: The Architect, the Musician, and the Listener from the Seventeenth Century to the Present Day* (1985), a well-illustrated historical description of architecturally prominent concert halls and opera houses.

Spiro Kostof, *A History of Architecture: Settings and Rituals* (1985), a comprehensive, beautifully illustrated introduction to architecture as an embodiment of the culture of the time.

Bernard S. Myers and Trewin Copplestone (eds.), *The History of Art: Architecture, Painting, Sculpture,* rev. and updated ed. (1985), an encyclopaedic survey of Western art.

David Bindman and Nigel Morgan (eds.), *The Thames and Hudson Encyclopaedia of British Art* (1985), a useful compendium of most current information available on a broad range of relevant subjects.

William L. Broecker (ed.), *The International Center of Photography Encyclopedia of Photography* (1984), a comprehensive reference source.

Technology

Thomas R. DeGregori, *A Theory of Technology: Continuity and Change in Human Development* (1985), an exploration of the interdependence of technological progress and social change.

Neil Longley York, *Mechanical Metamorphosis: Technological Change in Revolutionary America* (1985), an analysis of specific features of the development of technology in America as compared with the Old World.

Langdon Winner, *The Whale and the Reactor: A Search for Limits in an Age of High Technology* (1986), a study of the serious concerns raised by the ambiguous effect of high technology on the natural environment.

Hubert Schmitz, *Technology and Employment Practices in Developing Countries* (1985), a well-documented study of the impact of technological innovations on labour supply.

Robert W. Kates, Christoph Hohenemser, and Jeanne X. Kasperson (eds.), *Perilous Progress: Managing the Hazards of Technology* (1985), a study of technological risk and its control by contemporary society.

John W. Twidell and Anthony D. Weir, *Renewable Energy Resources* (1986), an up-to-date discussion of modern developments.

I. J. Higgins, D. J. Best, and J. Jones (eds.), *Biotechnology: Principles and Applications* (1985), a well-organized, comprehensive overview of the field.

John Elkington, *The Gene Factory: Inside the Genetic and Biotechnology Business Revolution* (1985), an analysis of the business aspects of the biotechnology industry.

Sonny Kleinfield, *A Machine Called Indomitable* (1985), a factual account of an important stage in the development of medical technology.

Richard D. Yoakam and Charles F. Cremer, *ENG, Television News and the New Technology* (1985), an analysis of the role of new technology in the media.

Edward M. Spiers, *Chemical Warfare* (1986), a historical survey of the uses of chemical weapons and an analysis of the threat of the high-technology arms race.

Christopher Lee, *War in Space* (1986), an informative study of military applications in space.

Wallace Tucker and Karen Tucker, *The Cosmic Inquirers: Modern Telescopes and Their Makers* (1986), an instructive book about the development of sophisticated telescopes, the technology of astronomy, and astronomers.

Religion

John Polkinghorne, *One World: The Interaction of Science and Theology* (1986), an analysis of relations between Christian doctrine and science by an author who is both a clergyman and a noted physicist.

Ronald B. Flowers, *Religion in Strange Times: The 1960s and 1970s* (1984), an informative study of contemporary theological and religious movements.

William H. Gentz (ed.), *The Dictionary of Bible and Religion* (1986), a comprehensive ecumenical reference source.

Gordon Stein (ed.), *The Encyclopedia of Unbelief,* 2 vol. (1985), a comprehensive reference source on the concepts and proponents of religious unbelief.

J. G. Davies (ed.), *A New Dictionary of Liturgy & Worship* (1986), a wealth of information on the history of religions and forms of worship.

John B. Gabel and Charles B. Wheeler, *The Bible as Literature* (1986), a useful basic sourcebook and reference guide.

J. N. D. Kelly, *The Oxford Dictionary of Popes* (1986), a comprehensive, concise reference work, arranged chronologically and supplied with an index and cross-references.

Hans Küng *et al., Christianity and the World Religions: Paths of Dialogue with Islam, Hinduism, and Buddhism* (1986; originally published in German, 1984), an informative scholarly discussion of important issues in these four major religions.

Nolan Pliny Jacobson, *Understanding Buddhism* (1986), an introduction to Buddhist philosophy and practices, intended for the Western reader.

Arthur Green (ed.), *Jewish Spirituality* (1986), a collection of scholarly essays on the spiritual values of the Jewish faith.

Roderick Strange, *The Catholic Faith* (1986), a sensitive introduction to Catholicism, touching on current problems.

Roger Haight, *An Alternative Vision: An Interpretation of Liberation Theology* (1985), an overview of liberation philosophy in Christian theology.

Renny Golden and Michael McConnell, *Sanctuary: The New Underground Railroad* (1986), an analysis of the Sanctuary Movement and its social repercussions.

Michael P. Carroll, *The Cult of the Virgin Mary: Psychological Origins* (1986), a study of popular devotion and the differences between Roman Catholicism and Protestantism.

Kim Knott, *My Sweet Lord: The Hare Krishna Movement* (1986), an informative introduction to the movement and its influence in the West.

The History of Mankind

Christian Habicht, *Pausanias' Guide to Ancient Greece* (1985), recent research on the ancient description of Greece and grecisms.

Alasdair Whittle, *Neolithic Europe* (1985), an overview of the history of both the subject and the archaeological research.

J. Maxwell Miller and John H. Hayes, *A History of Ancient Israel and Judah* (1986), an accurate, conservative history of biblical events.

P. M. Holt, *The Age of the Crusades: The Near East from the Eleventh Century to 1517* (1986), a concise but comprehensive historical account.

Robert Irwin, *The Middle East in the Middle Ages: The Early Mamluk Sultanate, 1250–1382* (1986), an analytical outline of the early period of the Mamluk rule.

Ralph A. Griffiths and Roger S. Thomas, *The Making of the Tudor Dynasty* (1985), a scholarly examination of the late medieval period in England.

J. R. Hale, *War and Society in Renaissance Europe, 1450–1620* (1985), a broad sociological outline of the period.

Geoffrey Treasure, *The Making of Modern Europe, 1648–1780* (1985), an overview of the political, social, economic, and cultural history of early modern Europe.

Robert Muchembled, *Popular Culture and Elite Culture in France, 1400–1750* (1985; originally published in French, 1977), an analysis of the transformation of France's culture in the late medieval and succeeding periods under the impact of growing church influence and the centralization of the monarchy.

Geoffrey Alderman, *Modern Britain, 1700–1983: A Domestic History* (1986), a treatment of the development of modern British society and the changes of political atmosphere.

Peter Gatrell, *The Tsarist Economy, 1850–1917* (1986), a survey of both Western and Eastern European research on the prerevolutionary economic history of Russia.

David Lane (ed.), *Labour and Employment in the U.S.S.R.* (1986), a collection of articles surveying the historical, economic, social, and legal aspects of full employment.

Geoffrey Hosking, *The First Socialist Society: A History of the Soviet Union from Within* (1985), a detailed chronological study of the domestic history.

Alan P. L. Liu, *How China Is Ruled* (1986), a realistic analysis of the country's political power and its evolution.

Judith M. Brown, *Modern India: The Origins of an Asian Democracy* (1985), a study of the complex political development with emphasis on the first half of the 20th century.

P. J. Vatikiotis, *The History of Egypt*, 3rd ed. (1986), a careful modern history including the post-Anwar as-Sadat years.

Conor Cruise O'Brien, *The Siege: The Saga of Israel and Zionism* (1986), a history focusing on the 20th-century development of the Zionist movement.

Michael R. Marrus, *The Unwanted: European Refugees in the Twentieth Century* (1985), an introduction to the special subject in the history of international relations and population movements.

Lloyd Timberlake, *Africa in Crisis: The Causes, the Cures of Environmental Bankruptcy* (1985), an exploration of the policies and politics that resulted in the mismanagement of natural and human resources.

Robert W. Shenton, *The Development of Capitalism in Northern Nigeria* (1986), a history of the economics of the area in the first half of the 20th century.

Lloyd G. Reynolds, *Economic Growth in the Third World, 1850–1980* (1985), an informative study of 41 major African, Asian, and Latin-American countries.

Saadet Deger, *Military Expenditure in Third World Countries: The Economic Effects* (1986), a documented analysis of the detrimental effects of defense spending on the economic development of Brazil, South Korea, India, and Indonesia.

Kenneth M. Coleman and George C. Herring (eds.), *The Central American Crisis: Sources of Conflict and the Failure of U.S. Policy* (1985), a collection of essays advocating nonintervention in the region and criticizing U.S. policies.

Sandor Halebsky and John M. Kirk (eds.), *Cuba—Twenty-Five Years of Revolution, 1959–1984* (1985), a compendium of informative writings by political scientists.

John Fitzmaurice, *Québec and Canada: Past, Present, and Future* (1985), a comprehensive study of the multitude of factors related to the separatist movement.

The Branches of Knowledge

A. E. A. Almaini, *Electronic Logic Systems* (1986), an analysis of the principles of design for logic systems.

Kiyosi Itô, *Introduction to Probability Theory*, trans. from the Japanese (1984), a clear introductory exposition of the theory, by a noted scientist.

Laurie Buxton, *Mathematics for Everyone* (1985), an informal exploration of mathematics as a method of research.

William R. Arnold and John S. Bowie, *Artificial Intelligence: A Personal, Commonsense Journey* (1986), an introductory discussion of current developments in the field.

Claire L. Parkinson, *Breakthroughs: A Chronology of Great Achievements in Science and Mathematics, 1200–1930* (1985), an encyclopaedic description of events in the major scientific disciplines, well-organized and supplied with indexes.

P. B. Medawar, *The Limits of Science* (1984), an insightful philosophical evaluation of the role of science, by a Nobel laureate.

William W. Lowrance, *Modern Science and Human Values* (1985), a pluralistic study of the social aspects of scientific and technical progress.

Wesley C. Salmon, *Scientific Explanation and the Causal Structure of the World* (1984), an accessible examination of the methodology of science.

Euan Squires, *To Acknowledge the Wonder: The Story of Fundamental Physics* (1985), a history of ideas, including an account of the experimental research of the 1980s.

Verne Grant, *The Evolutionary Process: A Critical Review of Evolutionary Theory* (1985), a discussion of classical approaches to the theory.

John Walton *et al.* (eds.), *The Oxford Companion to Medicine*, 2 vol. (1986), a broad encyclopaedic reference source presenting authoritative historical scholarship.

Roger Trigg, *Understanding Social Science: A Philosophical Introduction to the Social Sciences* (1985), an introductory analysis of the theory of the subject.

Howard Gardner, *The Mind's New Science: A History of the Cognitive Revolution* (1985), a historical study of the methodology of research in psychology and especially in theories of cognition.

Alden Whitman (ed.), *American Reformers: An H. W. Wilson Biographical Dictionary* (1985), a collection of valuable information on more than 500 notable figures, covering the period from the 17th to the mid-20th century.

Tom McArthur, *Worlds of Reference: Lexicography, Learning, and Language from the Clay Tablet to the Computer* (1986), a history of reference sources and the development of information storage.

David Lowenthal, *The Past Is a Foreign Country* (1985), an imaginative analysis of the past as part of the present by an author who is a historian, geographer, and political scientist.

Anthony Giddens, *The Constitution of Society: Outline of the Theory of Structuration* (1984), an original work of social theory.

James P. Scanlan, *Marxism in the U.S.S.R.: A Critical Survey of Current Soviet Thought* (1985), a scholarly examination of the philosophy of Marxism-Leninism and its developments.

Barry Stroud, *The Significance of Philosophical Scepticism* (1984), a careful explanatory investigation within the framework of the theory of knowledge.

Charles Taylor, *Philosophy and the Human Sciences* (1985), an exploration of the central themes of modern philosophy and sociology.

(Overleaf) Photograph, Dr. Robert Gale—Sygma

THE YEAR IN REVIEW

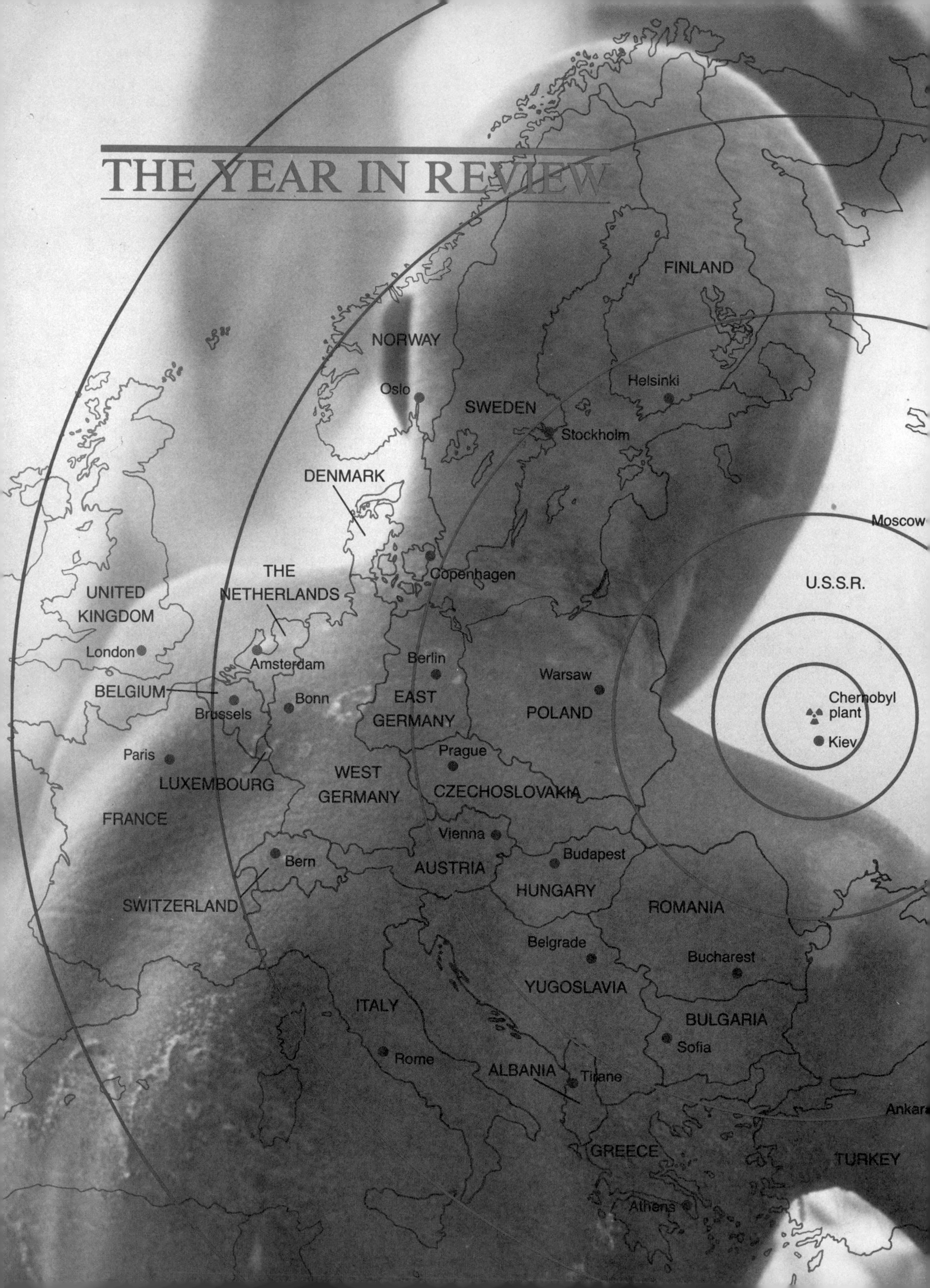

Chronology of 1986

JANUARY

1 **Common Market expands.** After years of negotiations Spain and Portugal became the 11th and 12th members of the European Communities. Spanish Prime Minister Felipe Gonzáles Márquez marked the occasion by telling his television audience that the nation now shared "a common destiny with the rest of Europe." The group, which currently represented some 320 million consumers, was originally formed in 1957 by Belgium, France, Italy, Luxembourg, The Netherlands, and West Germany.

6 **U.S. and Vietnam discuss MIAs.** A high-level U.S. delegation arrived in Hanoi for two days of talks aimed exclusively at resolving the issue of 1,797 Americans still unaccounted for some ten years after the end of the Vietnam war. The Vietnamese wish for broader discussions was flatly rejected by the U.S. representatives. In July 1985 Vietnam had returned the remains of 26 Americans, and the following November it had permitted a team of Americans to examine the site of a downed B-52. There was, therefore, guarded optimism that the current businesslike talks would prove to be another positive step toward a final resolution of the issue.

Liberia gets civilian rule. Gen. Samuel K. Doe, Liberian head of state since he seized power in 1980, was sworn in as president of a new civilian government. Shortly thereafter he ordered the release from prison of 18 politicians and journalists. Doe became president-elect in October 1985 after a successful campaign that was criticized because opposition groups had been openly harassed and certain politicians banned from political activities. A month after the election rebel troops shelled the Executive Mansion, but the attempt to take over the government was foiled by Doe's supporters.

8 **U.S. freezes Libyan assets.** U.S. Pres. Ronald Reagan signed an executive order freezing all Libyan government assets in the U.S. and in U.S. banks overseas. The action was described as retaliation for Libya's role in promoting international terrorism. Reagan's appeal to U.S. allies to join in imposing sanctions against Libya was widely ignored; Canada, however, was a notable exception. Many leaders contended that past experience had shown that such measures seldom produce their desired effect. Members of the Islamic Conference Organization, including such U.S. allies as Pakistan and Turkey, went on record as supporting Libyan leader Mu'ammar al-Qadhdhafi. On January 16 U.S. Secretary of State George Shultz publicly declared that when the U.S. could identify the source of terrorism, it had to "go after it." He mentioned Qadhdhafi as a clearly identified terrorist. U.S. Secretary of Defense Caspar Weinberger, by contrast, suggested that caution was more important than "instant gratification."

Report issued on acid rain. Canada and the U.S. issued a joint report on acid rain, a problem that Canada felt the U.S. had brushed aside for too long a time. The report recommended that, above all else, the U.S. government financially assist industry in developing methods to burn coal more cleanly. Other approaches to the problem were, for a variety of reasons, deemed less feasible. Acid rain originates with sulfur and nitrogen compounds that are generated, for the most part, by motor vehicles and industrial plants. After undergoing chemical changes, these airborne pollutants fall to the Earth and cause extensive damage to wildlife, vegetation, and buildings.

11 **Solidarity leader arrested.** Polish officials announced that police had captured Bogdan Borusewicz, the long-sought leader of an underground movement that supported Solidarity and produced a steady stream of publications in support of the outlawed federation of trade unions. Borusewicz became a political activist in 1968 while still in high school and, it was said, persuaded Lech Walesa to lead a strike of fellow workers at the Gdansk shipyards; that action inspired the formation of Solidarity.

14 **Cerezo assumes presidency.** Marco Vinicio Cerezo Arévalo was sworn in as president of Guatemala. In his inaugural address Cerezo noted that the national treasury was empty and warned that the country faced a period of great austerity and suffering. The country had been dominated by the military for more than 30 years, even during the tenure of Julio César Méndez Montenegro, who held office as a civilian from 1966 to 1970.

15 **Philippine election heats up.** With opposition candidate Corazon Aquino drawing large crowds in her campaign to unseat Pres. Ferdinand Marcos in the February 7 election, emotions reached new intensity when a local politician who supported Aquino was murdered. The same day, a U.S. congressional subcommittee said it had evidence that Marcos had acquired U.S. property worth hundreds of millions of dollars. The implication was that the money used for the purchases was tainted with corruption. On January 19 a grenade was thrown into a crowd attending a pro-Aquino rally in Zamboanga City. On January 21 the election committee announced that foreigners invited by Marcos to observe the fairness of the election would be imprisoned and deported if they approached closer than 45 m (150 ft) to any polling place. On January 22 the *New York Times* published an article claiming that Marcos's record as a guerrilla war hero had been declared "fraudulent" and "absurd" by the U.S. Army. On January 25 the Philippine government reported that there had been 13 political murders so far during the campaign.

17 **Spain recognizes Israel.** Spain formally established diplomatic relations with Israel during an unannounced meeting of foreign ministry officials in The Hague, Neth. Spain, newly admitted to membership in the European Communities, had been the only Western European nation that had not formally recognized Israel. Spain indicated that its new relationship with Israel would not alter its opposition to Israeli occupation of West Jerusalem, the West Bank, and other territories seized from the Arabs during the 1967 war. On January 19 the prime ministers of Spain and Israel met in The Hague to conclude the diplomatic formalities.

19 **South Yemen rebels seize power.** Forces loyal to 'Abd al-Fattah Ismail, a hard-line Communist and former president of South Yemen, proclaimed victory after a fierce six-day battle for control of the small Arab nation. Pres. Ali Nasir Muhammad Husani, also an avowed Marxist, was reported to have fled to Ethiopia the previous night. On January 13 the Husani government had announced that an attempt to overthrow and assassinate the president had failed. The first deputy prime minister and a former president, according to one report, were charged with complicity in the alleged plot and then executed. Few details of the revolt, however, could be confirmed by independent sources.

20 **Lesotho leader overthrown.** Chief Leabua Jonathan, prime minister of Lesotho since it gained independence from Britain in 1966, was overthrown in a military coup. The government was taken over by a military

The billowing cloud from the tragic explosion of the U.S. space shuttle *Challenger* obliterates even a glimpse of the ill-fated spacecraft.

SISSON—SIPA/SPECIAL FEATURES

council headed by Gen. Justin Lekhanya. South Africa, which totally surrounds Lesotho, had been blockading the small African nation since the beginning of the year because Jonathan was providing asylum to members of the African National Congress, which was seeking to force an end to apartheid in South Africa. Jonathan had also encouraged the Communist governments of China, North Korea, and the Soviet Union to open embassies in Lesotho.

21 **U.S. crime figures convicted.** Five men, considered prime figures in U.S. organized crime, were convicted by a federal grand jury in Kansas City, Mo., of conspiring to divert several million dollars in untaxed proceeds from gambling casinos in Las Vegas, Nev. After a four-month trial, the jurors deliberated for 30 hours before finding the defendants guilty of all eight charges against them. Among those convicted were Joseph J. Aiuppa, the alleged head of organized crime in Chicago, and John P. Cerone, his chief lieutenant. Similar trials against other reputed crime figures were being conducted simultaneously in New York City and Boston.

23 **Tribal clashes in South Africa resume.** At least 30 more persons were reported killed south of Durban, South Africa, as Zulus and Pondos renewed their tribal warfare. Hundreds of shanty homes were destroyed by fire during the fighting, which involved hand-to-hand combat with spears, clubs, knives, and homemade guns. The most recent outbreak of violence appeared to have been sparked by disputes over water rights and jobs. During similar fighting some weeks earlier, about 60 persons had lost their lives.

Italy issues warrant for Abu Nidal. Italy issued an international arrest warrant for Abu Nidal, a Palestinian terrorist whose real name was given as Sabry al-Banna. The government believed it now had evidence that Abu Nidal had masterminded the attack on the Rome airport on Dec. 27, 1985, that took the lives of 16 people. Italian officials also suspected that Abu Nidal was behind other terrorist attacks that had taken place on Italian soil.

24 **Voyager 2 probes Uranus.** The Voyager 2 spacecraft continued to transmit a stream of photographs and scientific data as it sped past Uranus some 3,220,000,000 km (2,000,000,000 mi) from Earth. Flight-control engineers at the Jet Propulsion Laboratory in Pasadena, Calif., said that Voyager 2, which was launched in 1977, came within 82,100 km (51,000 mi) of the clouds of Uranus, the third largest planet in the solar system. Though scientists expected to spend years analyzing the data, the probe had already provided evidence that the Uranian system was unlike any other known to exist in the solar system. Geologists were also puzzled and astonished to learn that one of the moons orbiting Uranus appeared to be a "bizarre hybrid" of terrains.

26 **Hussein confers with Arafat.** Two days after King Hussein of Jordan reportedly assured Israel that he intended to pursue a Middle East peace settlement with or without the cooperation of Syria and the Palestine Liberation Organization (PLO), the king began new discussions with Yasir Arafat, chairman of the PLO. Chief obstacles to a settlement continued to be the PLO's refusal to formally recognize Israel and its right to secure borders and Israel's refusal to sanction the establishment of an independent Palestinian state. On January 31 the Reagan administration yielded to pressure from Congress and indefinitely postponed efforts to win approval of Jordan's request to purchase $1.9 billion in air defense equipment. Congress was demanding more concrete evidence of Jordan's contributions to a Middle East peace settlement.

27 **Honduras gets new president.** José Azcona Hoyo took the oath of office as president of Honduras. The country was beset by many problems. Most observers expected Azcona to continue many of the basic policies of former president Roberto Suazo Córdova. These included close relations with the U.S., heavy reliance on the military, and tolerance of Nicaraguan guerrilla forces on Honduran soil.

28 **U.S. space shuttle explodes.** A horrendous explosion totally destroyed the U.S. space shuttle *Challenger* about 73 seconds after it was launched from Cape Canaveral, Fla. All seven persons aboard were presumed to have died instantly. The flight was the 25th space shuttle mission and the worst accident in the history of the U.S. space program. The dead included Gregory B. Jarvis, a civilian engineer; Sharon Christa McAuliffe, a high school teacher and the first private citizen to fly in the shuttle; Ronald E. McNair, a physicist; Lieut. Col. Ellison S. Onizuka of the Air Force, an engineer; Judith A. Resnick, a civilian engineer; Francis R. ("Dick") Scobee, a veteran test pilot and commander of the ill-fated flight; and Comdr. Michael J. Smith of the Navy, pilot of the space shuttle. NASA officials said the cause of the accident would not be known until the widely scattered debris was recovered from the ocean floor and all available data were carefully analyzed.

29 **Ugandan president ousted.** Yoweri Museveni, leader of the National Resistance Army (NRA), took the oath of office as president of Uganda. He replaced Gen. Tito Okello, who became chairman of a Military Council that ruled the African nation after the overthrow of Pres. Milton Obote in July 1985. Museveni, who promised to restore democracy and respect individual rights, had been fighting the central government for five years. On January 26, five weeks after Okello and Museveni had signed a peace accord in Kenya, the NRA declared that it had captured Kampala, the capital, and that total control of the country was thus assured.

Savimbi visits U.S. Jonas Savimbi, the anti-Communist leader of rebel forces in Angola, arrived in the U.S. seeking support for his cause. U.S. Secretary of Defense Caspar Weinberger expressed hope that Congress would provide the rebels with "appropriate" assistance that would facilitate a diplomatic solution to the conflict and the departure of Cuban troops from the country. President Reagan, during his meeting with Savimbi, cautiously remarked that the U.S. wanted to find the best way to be helpful to the rebel cause. The Marxist government of Pres. José Eduardo dos Santos had the support of the Soviet Union and Savimbi the support of South Africa.

W. CAMPBELL—SYGMA

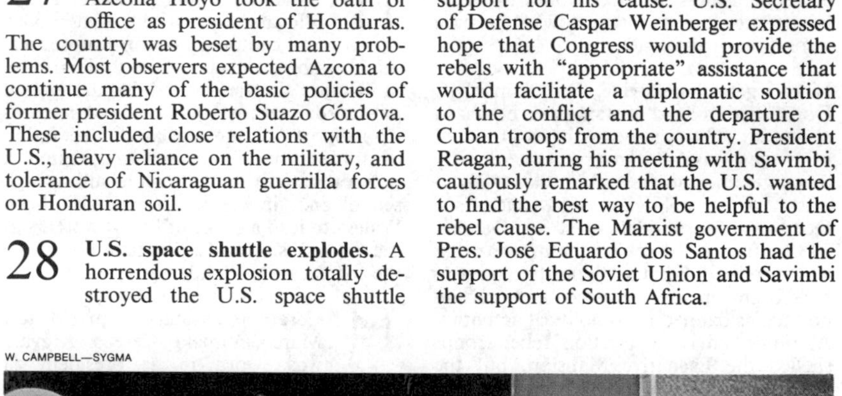

Yoweri Museveni, self-proclaimed new president of Uganda, flanked by officials and supporters, takes the oath of office on January 29.

FEBRUARY

2 **Costa Rica holds election.** Oscar Arias Sánchez, the 44-year-old candidate of Costa Rica's Partido de Liberación Nacional, defeated Rafael Angel Calderón Fournier of the Partido Unidad Social Cristiana in a contest for the presidency. The fact that both candidates campaigned on similar platforms reflected the homogeneity of the population and the common concerns of the voters. These included corruption in government, the faltering economy, an antipathy toward the Sandinista government in neighbouring Nicaragua, and a determination to remain neutral in regional conflicts. Toward that end Costa Rica had abolished its armed forces in 1948.

Dalai Lama meets pope in India. The Dalai Lama, the exiled spiritual leader of the Yellow Hat Sect of Tibetan Buddhists, met with Pope John Paul II in New Delhi on the second day of the Roman Catholic pontiff's ten-day visit to India. It was the third time the two men had arranged such a meeting. Two weeks earlier the pope had suggested that all the world's spiritual leaders meet together for a period of reflection, but it was too soon to know what kind of response the invitation would receive. Although huge crowds greeted the pope at some of his stops, he encountered opposition in other quarters, notably from fundamentalist Hindus, who resented the notion that they should be subjects of religious conversion.

4 **Oil prices continue to fall.** Crude oil prices continued their fall, approaching $15 a barrel on world markets after a committee representing the Organization of Petroleum Exporting Countries (OPEC) ended a two-day meeting in Vienna without affirming that OPEC intended to solve the worldwide surplus in oil by curbing production. With the world demand for oil fixed at about 15.5 million bbl a day, OPEC itself was producing an estimated 18 million bbl a day. As a consequence the price of oil had dropped from about $30 per barrel as recently as November 1985 to its lowest level in about seven years.

7 **Haitians overthrow Duvalier.** After years of oppressive and insensitive rule, Haitian Pres. Jean-Claude Duvalier was forced to flee into exile. The anger and frustration of the Haitian populace reached unprecedented intensity early in the year after demonstrators began anew to openly defy the government. On January 8 all schools were closed in the aftermath of a student boycott of classes on January 7. With more than half of Haiti's work force unemployed, the country was ranked as the poorest in the Western Hemisphere. Even so, the Duvaliers lived lives of ostentatious luxury. On January 30 U.S. officials announced that $26.6 million in military and economic aid would be blocked because of the government's disregard for human rights. The next day Duvalier declared a state of siege. As violence became more uncontrollable and the death toll mounted, the 34-year-old Duvalier agreed to board a U.S. Air Force C-141 and fly to France with his wife, children, and entourage. French Pres. Francois Mitterrand, however, made it clear that Duvalier's record on human rights excluded him from permanent residence in France.

Philippine election creates chaos. Hopes that the Philippine presidential election would restore calm to the nation quickly evaporated when reports spread that Pres. Ferdinand Marcos's loyalists were stuffing and stealing ballot boxes, buying votes, threatening Corazon Aquino's supporters, destroying voter lists in Aquino strongholds, and engaging in a host of other election irregularities. Some instances of such conduct were documented on film and shown on television around the world. Once the vote count started, it was clear that Marcos could lose the election. On February 9 some 30 computer operators from the Commission on Elections walked off their jobs because, they told reporters, the vote count was being rigged in Marcos's favour. It came as no surprise, therefore, that the National Assembly officially certified on February 15 that Marcos had been reelected. Aquino, assured by her own independent vote counters that she had unquestionably won the election, refused to accept defeat and urged her followers to organize nonviolent strikes and boycotts to prevent the Marcos government from stealing the election. With neither side appearing willing to yield, there were genuine fears that uncontrollable chaos might engulf the nation.

11 **Shcharansky freed by Soviets.** Anatoly Shcharansky, a 38-year-old human rights activist, was set free in West Berlin after spending eight years in Soviet labour camps and in prison. Several hours later he arrived in Frankfurt, West Germany, where he met his wife. The two had not been together since their wedding in 1974. Shcharansky and three others, all charged with spying for NATO, were exchanged for five persons, all from Warsaw Pact nations, who had been charged with espionage. The exchange was arranged during several months of secret negotiations.

12 **U.K. helicopter fracas ends.** A minor dispute over investments in a British helicopter company was finally settled after the matter had escalated into a political crisis that threatened the leadership of Prime Minister Margaret Thatcher. Shareholders in Westland, Britain's only helicopter manufacturer, voted by a 2–1 margin to allow the Sikorsky division of United Technologies, a U.S. company, and Fiat, an Italian firm, to purchase about 25% of the company's shares for more than $55 million. The money would permit Westland, which had lost more than $137 million the previous year, to restructure its financing. The minister of defense, Michael Heseltine, had quit the Cabinet after accusing Thatcher of using underhanded means to nullify a bid by a European consortium that included two British companies. Two weeks later Leon Brittan, the trade and industry secretary, who opposed Heseltine in Cabinet discussions, was forced to resign by fellow Conservatives. By that time the matter had become a major policy issue, namely, choosing between European industrial allies and U.S. "colonial" multinationals.

14 **South Korea curbs student activists.** Some 2,500 South Korean police armed with warrants began to search 129 college campuses around the country and confiscated tens of thousands of items that were deemed subversive. The list reportedly included five firebombs, gasoline, clubs, and a huge mass of printed material apparently meant for distribution during rallies and demonstrations. A few days earlier the Supreme Prosecutor's Office had issued guidelines for the arrest and punishment of anyone, including students and politicians, who was involved in a petition drive to obtain signatures calling for a revision of the constitution. The campaign to pressure the government into allowing direct popular election of the next president had already gathered momentum. The government, however, insisted that ordinary citizens had no right to involve themselves in a matter

NEVEU—GAMMA/LIAISON

Philippine Defense Minister Juan Ponce Enrile (left) and Deputy Chief of Staff Fidel V. Ramos announce their decision to quit the government of Ferdinand Marcos, accusing the president of 20 years of fraudulent manipulation in the February elections. Their bold step soon led to Marcos's exile from the country.

that by law was reserved to members of the National Assembly. On February 24 Pres. Chun Doo Hwan told leaders of opposition parties that he was in favour of a change in the constitution but only after the 1988 Olympic Games had been staged in Seoul and the next president elected. There was no indication that the opposition was willing to accept this timetable.

16 **Soares wins Portuguese election.** Mário Soares, a Socialist, was elected president of Portugal in a close runoff election against Diogo Freitas Amaral, a Christian Democrat. Soares, who had been prime minister three times, was the people's choice to resurrect the civilian presidency, which had died in 1926 when the military seized power. Although Marcelo Caetano, the last of the military dictators, was overthrown in 1974, his place had been taken by António dos Santos Ramalho Eanes, who served two successive five-year terms but was constitutionally prohibited from running for the office again.

Radical Sikhs defy local authorities. Radical Sikhs continued to defy the moderate Sikh authorities in the Indian state of Punjab by refusing to vacate the Golden Temple at Amritsar. More than 100,000 Sikhs gathered in Anandpur to demand that the government force the armed fundamentalists to leave Sikhism's holiest shrine, part of which had already been deliberately destroyed. Many of those attending the meeting carried rifles, submachine guns, spears, or swords—an ominous sign that fratricidal violence was not improbable. The Sikh fundamentalists had repeatedly charged that the moderates were undermining sacred Sikh traditions by condoning such things as smoking, drinking, and the cutting of hair.

French troops return to Chad. Some 200 French troops reestablished a French presence in Chad after an interval of 15 months and destroyed an airstrip in the northern part of the country that was allegedly being used by Libya to supply rebel forces trying to overthrow Pres. Hissen Habré. The following day a Soviet-made Libyan plane dropped a bomb on the airport in N'Djamena, the capital. The French defense minister then announced he would dispatch a squadron of military aircraft to serve as a deterrent force in France's former colony.

19 **U.S. ratifies UN convention.** The U.S. Senate approved the United Nations Convention on the Prevention and Punishment of the Crime of Genocide. The vote (83–11) came 37 years after it was first submitted to the Senate by Pres. Harry Truman. The document stigmatized genocide as an international crime and obliged the signatories to punish anyone found guilty of genocide. Though the UN General Assembly adopted the convention in 1948, the U.S. Senate had been content to let the matter slide because certain legislators feared the document might infringe on U.S. sovereignty. Those fears were allayed to the satisfaction of most senators when the Foreign Relations Committee added certain provisos, one of which denied World Court jurisdiction in cases brought against the U.S. unless the U.S. gave its consent.

A crowd watches as smoke billows from one of several luxury hotels set ablaze in Egypt by rioting military police. The mutiny of thousands resulted in 36 deaths and hundreds of injuries.
M. ELKOUSSY—SYGMA

22 **Military leaders desert Marcos.** Philippine Defense Minister Juan Ponce Enrile and Deputy Chief of Staff Fidel V. Ramos brought the nation's political crisis to a head when they moved into the headquarters of the Defense Ministry and announced that they were deserting Pres. Ferdinand Marcos because he had abused his power for years and had achieved victory in the February 7 presidential election through massive fraud. The two men then said they were backing Corazon Aquino as the new legitimately elected president of the Philippines. When news of this event spread through Manila, thousands of ordinary citizens raced to the encampment to form a human shield around the rebels; in effect, the people dared the government troops to attack. Others heeded the suggestion of Jaime Cardinal Sin and began carrying food and other supplies to those holed up inside the camp. Each hour brought new evidence that support for Marcos was crumbling on nearly every front. On February 25, after futile appeals to the U.S. for backing, Marcos reluctantly agreed to abandon Malacanang Palace and fly by U.S. helicopter to Clark Air Force Base with his wife, children, and a sizable group of faithful friends and relatives. Marcos later contended that he had been told he could return to his native province in northern Luzon. Instead, he and his entourage were flown to Guam and then on to Hawaii, where U.S. customs officials impounded huge sums of currency and other valuables carried by the exiles. The Aquino government quickly laid claim to the money and to billions of other dollars Marcos was said to have stolen from the government or otherwise acquired illegally and deposited in banks or invested in property around the world.

25 **Military police riot in Egypt.** Several thousand Egyptian military police raced into four luxury hotels near the Pyramids of Giza and terrified guests by setting fires and looting. Two hotels were reportedly destroyed. The violence was allegedly touched off by rumours that the men's tour of duty was to be extended from three to four years, but the root causes of the unrest were apparently much more serious. They involved social, political, economic, and even religious problems that the government of Pres. Hosni Mubarak recognized but was unable to solve in the foreseeable future. Mubarak viewed the affair as yet another attack against the government itself. Although government troops were able to quell the riots in the Cairo area and contain similar outbursts in other parts of the country, many feared that widespread dissatisfaction among the general populace would kindle new violence in the months ahead.

28 **Swedish prime minister slain.** Olof Palme, prime minister of Sweden, was shot and killed shortly after he left a Stockholm film theatre with his wife. The 59-year-old leader of the ruling Social Democratic Party had dismissed his bodyguards earlier in the day. Palme was the first European head of government to be assassinated since Armand Calinescu, the prime minister of Romania, was killed in 1939. On March 12 the Swedish Riksdag chose Ingvar Carlsson as Palme's successor. That same day police picked up a 32-year-old male suspect, and on March 17 they charged him with involvement in the crime. Two days later he was released because, police said, the evidence against him would not stand up in court.

MARCH

2 **Brazil's debt restructured.** A group of international bankers, satisfied that Brazil was making a sincere effort to solve its financial problems, announced lower interest rates on about one-third of the country's $104 billion foreign debt. The decision to refinance $31 billion in loans was a positive response to Pres. José Sarney's recently announced program to rein in rampant inflation at whatever cost and revitalize the economy. Most agreed that the president had placed his political career in jeopardy when he froze wages and prices on February 28 and introduced a new currency. Certain economists doubted that these and other measures under consideration would produce their desired effects.

4 **Geneva arms talks recessed.** The U.S.-U.S.S.R. arms control talks that began in Geneva in mid-January were recessed with no sign that significant progress had been made. The Reagan administration reportedly felt that negotiations on medium-range missiles had the best prospect for eventual success. The two other areas under discussion were intercontinental weapons and defense and space arms.

6 **Soviets end party congress.** The Communist Party of the Soviet Union ended its nine-day congress in Moscow after scores of persons were officially named to the Central Committee and to other influential posts. Anatoly Dobrynin, the longtime ambassador to the U.S., was one of five persons appointed national party secretaries. In an early speech to the delegates, Premier Nikolay Ryzhkov declared that the economy was being undermined by such things as red tape, cost overruns, and outmoded thinking. Party General Secretary Mikhail Gorbachev, in his final address to the congress, said all Soviet citizens had to be prepared for a "radical transformation of all spheres of life."

7 **U.S. orders Soviet UN staff cuts.** The U.S. government ordered the Soviet, Ukrainian, and Byelorussian missions to the United Nations to reduce their staffs in the U.S. from 275 to 170 by April 1, 1988. The cuts, which would take place in four steps, were directly related to alleged espionage activities. The Soviet missions, which were larger than the combined staffs of the two next largest UN missions, were, the U.S. contended, not only not warranted by the need to conduct official UN business but posed a threat to U.S. national security. The U.S. maintained a staff of 126 and China, 116.

Kashmir's chief minister removed. Indian Prime Minister Rajiv Gandhi authorized Congress Party (I) representatives in Kashmir to withdraw from the governing coalition in the state assembly, thereby forcing the resignation of Ghulam Muhammad Shah, the state's chief minister. Kashmir, which had a special status in the Indian constitution and was officially called the state of Jammu and Kashmir, was predominantly Muslim. Neighbouring Pakistan, an Islamic state, had therefore laid claim to part of the territory as a logical extension of its present borders. China had also claimed sovereignty over territory in the northern part of the state.

South Africa ends emergency. South Africa ended the state of emergency that had been proclaimed on July 20, 1985, because, Pres. P. W. Botha explained, political violence had abated. During the previous year and a half more than 1,150 people had been killed. Botha's action, welcome as it was, did not substantially alter the state of affairs. It merely meant that ordinary procedures would once again have to be followed before police could search premises or detain anyone without filing charges. On March 26 at least 30 blacks were reported killed in confrontations with police in various parts of the country.

9 **Colombians choose legislators.** Colombians gave the Liberal Party 49% of the votes cast in elections to the National Assembly and only 38% to the ruling Conservative Party headed by Pres. Belisario Betancur. The rest of the votes went to lesser parties. The results boded well for Virgilio Barco Vargas, leader of the Liberal Party, as he prepared for the presidential election in May. Since Betancur was prohibited by law from seeking reelection, the Conservatives had chosen Alvaro Gómez Hurtado as their candidate.

12 **Spain to remain in NATO.** After a heated campaign, Spanish voters heeded the pleas of Prime Minister Felipe Gonzáles and approved continued membership in NATO. It was the first time any of the 16 members of the military alliance had held such a referendum. Support for the referendum was made easier by the inclusion of three provisos: Spain would continue to ban nuclear weapons from its territory; Spanish troops would remain outside NATO's command structure; and the U.S. would withdraw some of the 12,500 troops it had stationed in Spain.

14 **Giotto probes Halley's Comet.** The Giotto spacecraft, launched by the European Space Agency in July 1985, sent back remarkable photographs and other valuable data as it passed within 540 km (335 mi) of the nucleus of Halley's Comet. Scientists were fascinated to learn that the comet's nucleus was "the darkest dark you can imagine." They concluded that the "dirty snowball" contained far more dark dust than had been suspected. Just two seconds before Giotto made its closest approach to Halley's nucleus, bombarding particles of dust knocked the probe's antenna askew and interrupted transmissions for more than half an hour.

15 **Medical council issues guidelines on care of comatose patients.** The judicial council of the American Medical Association, during a meeting on ethics and medicine, declared that it would be ethical for doctors to withhold all means of life-prolonging medical treatment, including food and water, from any patient who was beyond doubt in an irreversible coma. Adequate steps, however, would first have to be taken to confirm the accuracy of the diagnosis. Doctors were neither obliged to follow the guidelines in their practice nor protected from lawsuits that might be brought because they had followed them. At most, they could cite the council's opinion in their own defense if they were taken to court.

JASMIN—GAMMA/LIAISON

Members of the Communist Party of the Soviet Union listen to one of several speakers in the Kremlin's spacious Palace of Congresses as part of the nine-day 27th congress.

16 **French Socialists lose election.** French Pres. Francois Mitterrand's Socialist Party lost control of the National Assembly when it received fewer than 38% of the votes cast in the general election. The defeat would have been much worse had Mitterrand not decided in March 1985 to increase the size of the Assembly from 491 to 577 seats and introduce proportional representation. The Socialists actually received more support than any other individual party, but two allied conservative parties won 41% of the vote and 277 seats. With the addition of 14 seats held by small right-wing groups, the conservatives would control 291 seats, a majority of 2. The neo-Gaullist Rassemblement pour la République was led by Jacques Chirac, the mayor of Paris and a former prime minister; the Union pour la Démocratie Francaise was organized under the leadership of Jean Lecanuet. The far-right National Front headed by Jean-Marie le Pen captured 9.7% of the vote and 35 seats. Its representatives, however, had been forewarned they would not be welcome as partners in a conservative government if they succeeded in winning parliamentary representation for the first time. The Communists, once a potent force in French politics, continued to lose favour, winning only 9.8% of the vote and 35 seats. Most important of all, the election created a potential constitutional crisis because the new National Assembly was certain to repudiate many of Mitterrand's Socialist programs. The president still had the right to appoint a new prime minister, but the National Assembly could approve or reject the nominee. Consequently, on March 20 Mitterrand named Chirac prime minister, and the government began a period of "cohabitation." With both the president and prime minister looking toward the presidential election in 1988, neither appeared anxious to upset the unique arrangement.

Swiss reject UN membership. Swiss voters overwhelmingly rejected a government proposal to seek membership in the United Nations. The measure, which was defeated in all of the country's 26 cantons, was endorsed by fewer than 25% of the voters. Most Swiss appeared to view the UN as merely a forum for highly partisan politicking. They also seemed to feel that the nation's long tradition of neutrality would be compromised if the country became involved in UN peacekeeping missions. Switzerland would continue to belong to various UN specialized agencies.

17 **Japanese yen hits new high.** The Japanese yen reached its highest value since the end of World War II, trading at about 174.50 yen to the U.S. dollar. The decline of the dollar was expected to help ease the U.S. balance of trade deficit because Japanese cars, electronic equipment, and other items would rise in price and thus become less attractive buys in U.S. markets. The decline of the dollar was deliberately engineered by the Group of Five: France, Great Britain, Japan, the U.S., and West Germany.

24 **U.S. and Libyan forces clash.** U.S. and Libyan military forces faced a showdown in North Africa after U.S. aircraft deliberately entered airspace over the Gulf of Sidra. Libyan leader Col. Mu'ammar al-Qadhdhafi had warned that blood would flow if the U.S. dared to cross the "line of death" he had drawn across the gulf at 32° 30′. The U.S. contended that the waters were international, that they had been navigated by U.S. vessels eight times since 1981, and that Qadhdhafi had no right to arbitrarily claim them as part of Libya. After Libya was reported to have fired six surface-to-air missiles at U.S. aircraft, U.S. Navy planes attacked and damaged two Libyan patrol boats in the gulf and a missile site at Sidra.

Thai general forced to retire. Gen. Arthit Kamlang-ek, head of Thailand's armed forces, was ordered to retire from military service by Prime Minister Prem Tinsulanond. Arthit, who was opposing Thailand's gradual transition from military to civilian rule, had requested that the date of his retirement be extended for a second time. Although no charges were ever brought against him in connection with a failed military coup on Sept. 9, 1985, some suspected he was involved in some capacity, even though he was out of the country at that time.

30 **Koreans hold rally in Kwangju.** More than 50,000 South Koreans attended a peaceful rally in the city of Kwangju to press demands that the nation's next president be chosen by popular vote and not, as the constitution provided, by members of the electoral college. Kim Young Sam, a prominent political activist, assured the crowd that "the war for democracy has started." He and others compared conditions in South Korea with those in the Philippines before Pres. Ferdinand Marcos was overthrown. Kim Dae Jung, perhaps Pres. Chun Doo Hwan's most vocal critic, was not permitted to leave Seoul to attend the rally.

APRIL

2 **Bomb explodes aboard TWA plane.** An explosion aboard a Trans World Airlines commercial jet flying from Rome to Athens caused four persons, one of them an infant, to be swept through a gaping hole in the fuselage and plunge to their deaths on the ground. A group calling itself the Arab Revolutionary Cells claimed it had planted a bomb to retaliate for U.S. attacks on Libya in the Gulf of Sidra. Although the pilot was able to land the damaged aircraft at the Athens airport, a spokesman for the International Air Line Pilots Association said a move was under way to boycott countries found responsible for such terrorist acts. On April 17 plastic explosives were found in the purse of a woman about to board an Israeli El Al flight at London's Heathrow Airport. After interrogating the woman, Scotland Yard arrested the woman's Arab fiancé on suspicion of concealing the explosives in the woman's purse without her knowledge.

6 **France devalues franc.** During a meeting in Ootmarsum, Neth., the eight member nations of the European Monetary System agreed to devalue the French franc by an average 4.9% against other European currencies. The move was designed to encourage lower interest rates in France and make French goods less expensive in other countries. The new conservative administration of Prime Minister Jacques Chirac was also in the process of cutting government spending and removing the price and currency controls imposed by Socialist Pres. François Mitterrand. The French finance minister declared that France, through these and related measures, had embraced "a new economic policy."

7 **Violence continues in Lebanon.** A contingent of Druze Muslim militiamen killed a reported 17 Sunni Muslims in the mountain village of Bsaba, southeast of Beirut. Some 50 houses were also burned during the most violent inter-Muslim conflict ever reported from that region of Lebanon. The next day a car bomb killed at least 11 persons and wounded about 100 others when it exploded in Juniyah, the largest Christian community in the country. In addition, about 100 parked cars and several buildings were badly damaged by fire. Most of the 60 or so Christians who had lost their lives in such acts of violence since the beginning of the year had been killed in Beirut. On April 17 the bodies of two Britons and one American were found near Beirut. Many foreigners, fearful for their own safety, were reportedly preparing to leave the country.

Contadora meeting fails. After three days of futile and often heated debate, negotiators for the Contadora Group (Colombia, Mexico, Panama, and Venezuela) and the supporting countries of Argentina, Brazil, Peru, and Uruguay left Panama without signing an agreement aimed at ending the fighting in Central America. Costa Rica, El Salvador, and Honduras accused Nicaragua of deliberately sabotaging the peace effort by continuing to insist that it would sign no regional accord until the U.S. withdrew support from the *contras* fighting Nicaragua's government.

12 **China concludes People's Congress.** The fourth session of China's sixth National People's Congress ended in Beijing (Peking) with formal approval of Premier Zhao Ziyang's (Chao Tzu-yang's) report on the country's just completed five-year plan and of the State Council's new five-year plan for the economic and social development of the country. Special importance was attached to the adoption of principles governing

Residents survey the destruction in Tripoli caused by the April 14 U.S. bombing raid, a response to terrorism reportedly backed by Libya.
ERIC BOUVET—GAMMA/LIAISON

the civil code and to laws regarding compulsory education and enterprises wholly owned by foreigners.

13 **Pope visits Rome synagogue.** Pope John Paul II, during a historic and probably unprecedented papal visit to the central synagogue in Rome, was warmly welcomed by Chief Rabbi Elio Toaff and the Jewish congregation. The pope, quoting from a declaration of the second Vatican Council, declared that the church "deplores the hatred, persecutions, and displays of anti-Semitism directed against the Jews at any time and by anyone." Both the pope and his audience were well aware that in 1555 Pope Paul IV had issued a decree consigning Roman Jews to a ghetto. John Paul said his visit to the synagogue was intended "to make a decisive contribution to the consolidation of the good relations between our two communities."

Marcos backers stage rally. An estimated 15,000–20,000 supporters of Ferdinand Marcos held a rally in Manila to demand that the former president be allowed to return to the Philippines and resume the presidency. The following day members of Marcos's political party attempted to convene a session of the National Assembly, even though it had been dissolved by newly elected Pres. Corazon Aquino. The government, meanwhile, was taking legal steps to recover money and property that Marcos had allegedly acquired illegally. The Swiss government, in an unusual move, agreed to freeze all accounts reportedly linked to the Marcos family. Some estimates of the amount of money involved were in excess of $1 billion.

14 **U.S. planes bomb Libya.** President Reagan announced to the nation that U.S. Air Force and Navy planes had bombed five sites in Libya. He claimed that Libyan leader Col. Mu'ammar al-Qadhdhafi had earlier been warned that the U.S. would retaliate if there was clear evidence that Libya was involved in further terrorist attacks against U.S. citizens. Reagan, justifying the U.S. air strikes, contended that irrefutable evidence linked Libya to the bombing of La Belle discotheque in West Berlin on April 5; one U.S. serviceman and one Turkish woman were instantly killed and hundreds of others wounded, including about 50 U.S. military personnel. U.S. targets in the Tripoli area included the military section of the airport, the Sidi Bilal port facility, where Libyan commandos reportedly trained, and the Bab el-Azziziya military barracks. The Benina air base and the Jamahiriya barracks, both near Benghazi, were attacked by navy A-6 and A-7 aircraft from the *Coral Sea* and *America* early on the morning of April 15. Because France had refused to allow the British-based F-111 bombers to pass over its territory, the aircraft traveled over open waters and entered the Mediterranean through the Strait of Gibraltar. Reaction to the bombings ranged from outrage, especially among Arab nations, to unqualified support from such countries as Great Britain and Israel.

18 **Pretoria rescinds pass laws.** In a speech to the South African Parliament, Pres. P. W. Botha announced that the country's pass laws would no longer be enforced and that those imprisoned or awaiting trial for violations of the laws would be released immediately. More than 200,000 blacks a year had been arrested for not carrying their passbook identifications or for being in white areas without proper authorization. Although the nation's blacks welcomed the news that the hated pass laws had been rescinded, they noted that apartheid—the government policy of racial separation—was still the law of the land.

20 **Sudanese elect Assembly.** After nearly two weeks of balloting, Sudanese voters appeared to have given the Umma Party a plurality of seats in the new People's Assembly. It was the country's first multiparty election in 18 years. The Umma Party, which expected its leader, Sadiq al-Mahdi, to become the new prime minister, would face strong opposition from the fundamentalist National Islamic Front, which pledged to fight any attempt to repeal the nation's Islamic legal system. Pres. Gaafar Nimeiry, who had been overthrown in a bloodless military coup in April 1985, had made Islam the law of the land in 1983. Although voting had been postponed in 37 of the country's 68 southern districts, supporters of the insurgent Sudan People's Liberation Army and the people in general were known to oppose islamization because it was alien to their Christian and animist beliefs. After elections were held in all the southern districts, the Assembly would set to work writing a new constitution.

24 **Waldheim's past scrutinized.** The director of the Office of Special Investigations within the U.S. Department of Justice recommended that Kurt Waldheim, the secretary-general of the United Nations from 1972 to 1981, be barred from entering the United States because of alleged complicity in Nazi war crimes. Waldheim, who vehemently insisted that his accusers had misread or misinterpreted his war record, had been an officer in the Balkans during brutal Nazi campaigns against Yugoslav partisans and the deportation to death camps of Jews living in Greece. Waldheim's commander at the time was Gen. Alexander Löhr, who was subsequently convicted of war crimes and hanged in 1947.

25 **Car bomb kills five in Madrid.** A car bomb, detonated by remote control during the early-morning rush hour, blasted two holes in the maternity wing of the Nuestra Señora del Rosario Hospital in central Madrid. Two operating rooms were destroyed, but no babies were killed. Five civilian sentries, however, lost their lives as they drove past the hospital after guard duty at the Italian embassy. Authorities believed the terrorist attack, the worst in Spain in two years, was the work of ETA (Basque Homeland and Liberty), a Basque separatist guerrilla organization.

28 **Nuclear accident hits Chernobyl.** The Soviet Union reported that "an accident" had occurred at its Chernobyl nuclear power plant, about 130 km (80 mi) north of Kiev, capital of the Ukrainian S.S.R. The public announcement came only after Sweden, Finland, and Denmark had detected abnormally high levels of radioactivity in their respective atmospheres. The U.S.S.R. then asked Sweden and West Germany for help in fighting a fire in the core of one badly damaged reactor. While scientists around the world waited for an explanation of what had happened, the Soviet government was evacuating people from the area, organizing emergency medical treatment for those in need of immediate care, and taking steps to prevent additional radiation from escaping into the atmosphere. Only two persons were reported killed, but it seemed certain that many more would eventually die from radiation poisoning. Food, water, and livestock in the area had also been dangerously contaminated.

29 **Indonesia bars Australian reporters.** President Reagan arrived in Bali, Indon., where he planned to meet with the foreign ministers of the Association of Southeast Asian Nations (ASEAN). His schedule would next take him to Tokyo, where leaders of seven industrialized democracies were to hold their annual economic summit. The

ASEAN meeting was overshadowed by Indonesia's refusal to permit two journalists to cover the Reagan visit. They had arrived from Washington, D.C., on the White House press plane and represented the Australian Broadcasting Corporation. Both were ordered to leave Indonesia after being accused of writing derogatory reports on President Suharto's personal wealth.

30 **Police raid Golden Temple.** Paramilitary police in India's state of Punjab seized control of the Golden Temple in Amritsar, the holiest shrine of Sikhism. About 200 militant Sikhs who had occupied the temple for some three months put up no resistance when they were arrested. A similar raid by the Indian Army in June 1984 had resulted in hundreds of deaths and provoked two Sikh bodyguards to assassinate Prime Minister Indira Gandhi the following October. In yet another attempt to control violence between Sikhs and Hindus in the region, Prime Minister Rajiv Gandhi had reorganized the police on April 6. The previous day six policemen had been killed when armed Sikhs invaded a courthouse and succeeded in freeing three persons charged with killing a Hindu editor.

MAY

1 **Smugglers of aliens convicted.** A Presbyterian minister, a Roman Catholic priest and a nun, and three lay workers were convicted by a federal jury in Tucson, Ariz., of conspiring to smuggle Salvadorans and Guatemalans into the United States. Two of five other defendants were found guilty of lesser charges. All 11 were associated with a movement to provide church sanctuary to illegal aliens from Central American countries torn by violence. Sentencing was set for July 1. The Sanctuary Movement, which began in Tucson in 1982, was publicly supported by about 300 churches, some 20 U.S. cities, and the state of New Mexico.

Salvadorans protest Duarte rule. An estimated 20,000 Salvadoran workers marched in San Salvador to express disappointment in Pres. José Napoleón Duarte and opposition to his policies. The demonstration tended to confirm the general belief that labour union support for Duarte had dissipated during his two years in office. For one thing, Duarte had not been able to keep the promise he had made to end the civil war; in addition, he had felt compelled by economic realities to impose austerity measures that did not sit well with many workers. Among the marchers were undetermined numbers of university students, teachers, public employees, and masked leftist guerrillas. Some of those who addressed the crowd condemned the United States along with Duarte.

Thai Parliament dissolved. Gen. Prem Tinsulanond, the prime minister of Thailand, dissolved Parliament and called for general elections on July 27. Prem, who had survived two attempted military coups since coming to power in 1980, headed a coalition civilian government. The government fell when Prem's deputy prime minister and other members of the coalition failed to support the prime minister when votes were cast on the relatively unimportant issue of raising taxes on certain types of vehicles.

3 **Sri Lankan jet bombed.** A bomb, believed to have been hidden inside a cargo of vegetables, exploded in the rear section of an Air Lanka Lockheed Tristar jet that would have been in the air had it taken off from the Colombo airport on schedule. Sri Lankan authorities presumed the bomb, which killed 15, was the work of Tamil guerrillas, the most militant of whom had long demanded that "their area" of the country be granted independence from the rest of the island nation, which was by and large inhabited by ethnic Sinhalese. On May 7 the Central Telegraph Office in Colombo was bombed; at least 11 persons were killed and more than 115 wounded, some critically. Tamil guerrillas were also suspected of killing 20 Sinhalese, half of them children, in the jungle hamlet of Siripura on May 25. Two days earlier similar atrocities had been inflicted on nearby villages. Both attacks occurred on major Buddhist festivals widely observed by the Sinhalese.

Benazir Bhutto rallies supporters. Benazir Bhutto, the 32-year-old leader of the Pakistan People's Party, told some 50,000 cheering supporters in Karachi that Gen. Mohammad Zia-ul-Haq, the president of Pakistan, "must go and he must go now." The next election was not scheduled to take place until 1990. Bhutto, who returned from self-imposed exile in Europe on April 10, was the daughter of Zulfikar Ali Bhutto, who had been overthrown by Zia in 1977 and hanged in 1979 after being declared guilty of conspiring to murder a political opponent.

4 **Economic summit held in Tokyo.** Japanese Prime Minister Yasuhiro Nakasone officially welcomed the leaders of six industrial democracies to an economic summit in Tokyo. Among the guests were Prime Ministers Margaret Thatcher of Britain, Brian Mulroney of Canada, and Bettino Craxi of Italy. Others who attended were U.S. Pres. Ronald Reagan, French Pres. François Mitterrand, French Prime Minister Jacques Chirac, and West German Chancellor Helmut Kohl. Ruud Lubbers, president of the European Council, and Jacques Delors, president of the European Commission, were also invited. During the welcoming reception unidentified radicals operating from an apartment building managed to launch five homemade rockets in the general direction of the guest house, but no one was injured. Before parting company the seven heads of state and government strongly condemned persons and governments that sponsor or support international terrorism. Their official statement, which clearly pleased the U.S. delegates, singled out Libya as a sponsor of such terrorist activities. The world leaders also expressed sympathy for the victims of the Chernobyl nuclear disaster and promised to provide whatever assistance was requested. They also underscored the responsibility of each nation to make sure all its nuclear facilities were made as safe as possible. Calling attention to the ever

SANDRO TUCCI—GAMMA/LIAISON

Shattered remains of a Sri Lankan jet lie strewn at the Colombo airport after a bomb that was probably hidden amid cargo exploded in early May, killing 15 people.

increasing interdependence of nations and to the progress that had been made through economic cooperation in recent years, the industrialized democracies pledged afresh "to fight against hunger, disease and poverty, so that developing nations can also play a full part in building a common, bright future."

Afghan leader resigns. The Soviet press agency TASS reported that Babrak Karmal had resigned as general secretary of the People's Democratic (Communist) Party of Afghanistan and would be replaced by Najibullah, a former head of the Afghan secret police. Karmal, who was rumoured to be in ill health, retained his position in the Politburo and remained president of the Revolutionary Council, a position equivalent to head of state.

7 **Bangladesh holds elections.** The Jatiya Party of Lieut. Gen. Hossain Mohammad Ershad, president of the martial-law government that had ruled Bangladesh since a successful coup in March 1982, won more than half of the 300 contested seats in elections to Parliament. The opposition Awami League captured 75 seats and its allies an additional 21. The Bangladesh Nationalist Party led a seven-party boycott of what was the first national election in seven years. Voting was disrupted by widespread violence that reportedly claimed at least two dozen lives. Antigovernment groups characterized the election results as blatantly fraudulent.

8 **Arias assumes presidency.** Oscar Arias Sánchez was sworn in as president of Costa Rica during a ceremony held in the national stadium in San José. In his inaugural address the new president extolled democratic government and emphasized the importance of revitalizing the economies of Latin America. He also pledged to keep Costa Rica out of the armed conflicts that were brutalizing Central America even though he would endeavour through diplomatic and political means "to prevent Central American brothers from killing each other."

9 **Brundtland to lead Norway again.** Gro Harlem Brundtland, leader of the Labour Party, once again became prime minister of Norway. She succeeded Kåre Isaachsen Willoch, who had resigned on April 30 after his coalition government was narrowly defeated (79–78) in a parliamentary vote of confidence on the budget. After her appointment Brundtland warned her compatriots that "austerity is an inadequate term for the vast economic restructuring that must take place."

16 **Balaguer returned to office.** Joaquín Balaguer, the 78-year-old former president of the Dominican Republic, regained the presidency with a narrow victory over 51-year-old Jacobo Majluta Azar, president of the Senate. Juan Bosch, also a former president, finished a distant third. The Central Electoral Board was not expected to announce the official results until a formal recount of the ballots was completed toward the end of the month.

Leaders and delegates of seven industrialized nations met in Tokyo for an economic summit in May. The heads of the European Council and European Commission also attended.
SIMMONS—SIPA/SPECIAL FEATURES

19 **China and Taiwan hold talks.** Representatives of the Civil Aviation Administration of China and others representing the China Air Lines in Taiwan reached agreement in Hong Kong on the return of a cargo jet that had been flown to Canton on May 3 by a pilot who defected to the mainland because he wanted to be reunited with his elderly father in Sichuan (Szechwan) Province. China agreed to fly the plane to Hong Kong and return the other two members of the crew. Although Taipei and Beijing (Peking) acknowledged that the negotiations involved only airlines, not governments, it was the first time since 1949 that officials from the two parts of divided China had held face-to-face discussions.

21 **Dutch voters back government.** Voters in The Netherlands surprised political pundits by increasing the parliamentary representation of Prime Minister Ruud Lubbers's Christian Democrats from 45 to 54 in the 150-seat lower house. This guaranteed that the coalition of Christian Democrats and Liberals (who won 27 seats) would remain in power. The shift away from the Labour Party, which in November 1985 had lost its long battle to prevent the deployment of cruise missiles on Dutch soil, meant that the Labour Party no longer had the largest representation in Parliament. Lubbers was expected to continue to pursue the goals he had already established for himself and the nation; these included lower expenditures for welfare and stimulation of the economy.

23 **Lebanese casualties mount.** The three-day death toll from vindictive bombings in Lebanon rose to 64 when a car bomb explosion killed 11 persons in Christian East Beirut. More than 80 persons were wounded, and about a dozen buildings were destroyed or set ablaze by the explosives. It was the tenth car bomb detonated in that area since the beginning of the year. Many of the most recent casualties were victims of artillery and rocket attacks launched by rival groups, notably across the Green Line separating Muslim West Beirut from Christian East Beirut. Intense fighting, however, also occurred in other parts of Lebanon and, for the first time since the civil war began in 1975, it reached Shi'ah Muslim villages near the Syrian border.

24 **Thatcher visits Israel.** British Prime Minister Margaret Thatcher was greeted by Israeli Prime Minister Shimon Peres and his entire Cabinet when she arrived at Ben-Gurion Airport outside Tel Aviv. The visit had special significance inasmuch as Thatcher was the first British head of government ever to visit the country. Thatcher remarked: "I have been to your Arab neighbours as a friend. I come to Israel as a friend—indeed as an old friend. I want to help [bring about a Middle East peace settlement] if I can."

25 **Barco wins Colombian election.** Virgilio Barco Vargas, the 64-year-old candidate of the opposition Liberal Party, was elected president of Colombia. He overwhelmed his principal rival, Alvaro Gómez Hurtado, nominee of the Conservative Party, by capturing 58.3% of the popular vote to Gómez's 35.9%. Even though the Liberal Party would be in control of both houses of Congress when Barco assumed office in August, the new government would be hard pressed to find solutions to such intractable national problems as armed insurgency, unemployment, drug trafficking, land reform, and human rights abuses.

Aquino establishes commission. Philippine Pres. Corazon Aquino named 45 persons with diverse religious and political backgrounds to a commission that would be entrusted with the responsibility of writing a new constitution. The next day five additional seats set aside for "the opposition" were filled by Blas Ople, who had held the post of labour minister in Ferdinand Marcos's Cabinet, and four of his associates. Ople was one of the first members of the National Assembly to pledge loyalty to the new government after Marcos fled the country in February.

26 **Japan to hold double elections.** Leaders of Japan's ruling Liberal-Democratic Party (LDP) reached agreement to hold an extraordinary session of the Diet (parliament), a prerequisite for calling unusual simultaneous elections for both houses of the Diet. Prime Minister Yasuhiro Nakasone managed to convince fellow politicians that the Diet could be convened to discuss, among other things, the rise in the value of the yen, a hot political issue that Nakasone's critics had been using against him. Most LDP politicians gradually came to view summer elections as an opportunity to expand their own political influence and strengthen the party as a whole.

29 **Barbados changes leaders.** The ruling Barbados Labour Party was soundly defeated in national elections when the Democratic Labour Party, headed by former prime minister Errol Barrow, captured 24 of 27 constituencies. Barrow then succeeded Bernard St. John, who had become head of government in March 1985 following the unexpected death of J. M. G. ("Tom") Adams.

31 **Solidarity fugitive arrested.** The Polish Interior Ministry was quoted as saying that 31-year-old Zbigniew Bujak, leader of the Solidarity underground, had been captured. No details of the arrest were made public, however. Bujak had gone into hiding in December 1981 when martial law was declared and thousands of members of the Solidarity labour federation were rounded up by police. Since that time Bujak had used clandestine radio broadcasts and the underground press to issue statements and directives. Lech Walesa, the founder of Solidarity, responded to the news report by remarking that Polish authorities throughout the nation's history had often arrested the country's most patriotic sons and charged them with betrayal. He then personally thanked Bujak for all that he had done.

JUNE

1 **UN drafts African plan.** The General Assembly of the United Nations approved a Program of Action for African Economic Recovery and Development, 1986–1990. It was the first time the UN had ever taken the initiative to solve economic problems in a specific region of the world. The Assembly was optimistic because many black African leaders had expressed a willingness to change long-established policies that would, it was believed, have impeded effective implementation of the program. The UN blueprint, moreover, was expected to have positive results because donor nations, all of whom would participate voluntarily, would have common goals in dealing with such things as food emergencies, desertification, transportation, communications, trade, finances, and education relevant to the continent's special needs.

Voters challenge Ecuador's leader. Early election returns indicated that Ecuadoran Pres. León Febres Cordero's supporters had won only 17 of the 59 district seats in the 71-seat National Chamber of Representatives. The 12 other representatives, selected on a nationwide basis, had been elected in 1984 at the same time as the president. With the leftist opposition controlling a solid majority in the unicameral legislature, Febres Cordero would have a formidable task trying to carry out his programs. The president suffered an additional loss of prestige when voters overwhelmingly rejected a referendum that would have permitted candidates with no party affiliations to run for office as independents.

2 **India arrests protesters.** Indian authorities reported that about 1,000 Sikh militants had been arrested in the Punjab for holding a protest to commemorate the day, two years earlier, that the Indian Army raided the Golden Temple in Amritsar. On June 7 nine more persons were killed in the area, presumably by Sikh extremists, thereby raising the death toll to 16 for the week and to more than 400 since the beginning of the year. On June 16 some 13,000 Hindus, marching to demand that the Army put an end to Sikh terrorism in the Punjab, were taken by police to a sports stadium, where they were briefly confined for flouting a ban on public gatherings.

7 **Bhutto campaigns in hometown.** Benazir Bhutto, daughter of Pakistan's former prime minister, urged an exuberant crowd of some 100,000 in her hometown of Larkana to help pressure Pres. Mohammad Zia-ul-Haq out of office and prepare for new elections in the autumn. After her return from voluntary exile in Europe in April, Bhutto had assumed the role of Zia's most severe critic and began to campaign for his ouster. She represented the first vigorous opposition to Zia's regime since he overthrew Zulfikar Ali Bhutto in 1977.

8 **Waldheim elected president.** Kurt Waldheim, the 67-year-old former secretary-general of the United Nations and the candidate of the People's Party, was elected president of Austria with 53.9% of the popular vote. In the runoff election he faced Kurt Steyrer, a Socialist. Waldheim's victory, larger than many politicians had expected, was apparently bolstered by an upsurge of patriotism among those who resented recent accusations by non-Austrians that Waldheim had been involved in Nazi war crimes while serving as a lieutenant in the German Army.

GAMMA/LIAISON

Kurt Waldheim, candidate of Austria's People's Party, campaigns in Vienna before the June presidential election, which he won.

9 **Report on *Challenger* issued.** A U.S. presidential commission issued its report on the *Challenger* space shuttle disaster that occurred in January. The 13-member group concluded that the failure of a joint seal between segments of a solid-fuel booster rocket was the sole physical cause of the explosion that took the lives of all seven persons aboard the spacecraft. The report also listed a long series of avoidable engineering and managerial mistakes that had virtually assured that a tragedy would happen sooner or later. In addition, the commission made 11 broad recommendations for improving the design of the rockets and the management of NASA's manned-spaceflight program.

Koreans debate constitution. South Korea's National Assembly began formal discussions on revising parts of the nation's constitution. There was general agreement that changes were in order, but on several basic issues the perspective of the ruling Democratic Justice Party (DJP) differed sharply from that of the New Korea Democratic Party (NKDP) and other members of the opposition. The DJP and certain scholars, for instance, appeared to favour a parliamentary form of government because, among other things, it would permit political power to be shared more equitably. The NKDP, on the other hand, generally preferred direct elections of a president who would have ample authority to keep the military out of politics.

11 **Chirac pushes new legislation.** The new conservative government of Prime Minister Jacques Chirac began to study two new controversial bills, the first dealing with immigration policy, the second with television stations. Both changes were opposed by Pres. François Mitterrand. If revised as proposed, the immigration laws would give local authorities broader powers to expel foreigners without proper visas. Resentment against illegal residents had been building in France for some time, especially against Arabs from North Africa. The proposal to sell one of the three government-owned television stations was already being hotly debated in the press and on the streets.

Many objected to the sale on the grounds that private ownership would deprive the French people of part of their national cultural heritage and could erode objective reporting on local political issues.

12 **Pretoria declares emergency.** South Africa declared a nationwide state of emergency and took into custody at least 1,000 black activists. The government appeared to be especially anxious to abort expected demonstrations on June 16, the tenth anniversary of the Soweto township uprisings. The emergency decree, among other things, gave all types of security forces personnel the right to arrest without warrant anyone judged to be a "threat to public order." These detainees would have no access to outsiders, not even to legal counsel, before, during, or after being interrogated. The decree also banned unauthorized television, radio, and photographic coverage of any "subversive activity." On June 16 millions of blacks defied the government by refusing to report to work. The next day the government reported that 11 blacks had been killed during what was described as a day of silent protest.

Ulster assembly dissolved. British Prime Minister Margaret Thatcher informed the House of Commons that a decision had been taken to dissolve the Northern Ireland Assembly because for four years Roman Catholics and Protestants had failed to use the forum to discuss their political and religious differences. The Assembly had been created in the hope that an honest exchange of views would make both sides realize that the sectarian violence, which had taken such a tragic toll in Ulster, would not end until both sides accepted a compromise.

15 **Secular Israelis attack Orthodox.** Bitter resentment against militant Orthodox Jews reached new heights in Israel when secular Jews vandalized two religious schools and painted swastikas on the walls of the Great Synagogue in Tel Aviv. They also ripped apart prayer shawls, phylacteries, and prayer books and smashed the holy ark that contained the Torah scrolls. Similar events were reported in other parts of the country. Militant Orthodox had provided an excuse for acts of retaliation by burning or defacing more than 100 bus shelters carrying advertisements that offended their religious sensibilities. The mayor of Tel Aviv blamed the latest outburst on "the crazies" on both sides. Many felt that the problem would continue, and perhaps get worse, unless police and politicians alike insisted on punishing anyone found guilty of breaking the law.

Chernobyl bosses dismissed. *Pravda,* the official daily newspaper of the Central Committee of the Communist Party of the Soviet Union, reported that the director and chief engineer at the Chernobyl nuclear facility had been dismissed from their jobs and that other top officials had failed in their duties or even fled the scene of the nuclear explosion and fire on April 26. Two weeks earlier a tunnel to the reactor had been completed so that cement could be poured through pipes to envelop the reactor completely and permanently. It would take centuries for the radioactive fuel to lose its lethal potency through natural decay.

22 **Socialists win in Spain.** The Spanish Socialist Workers' Party (PSOE), led by Prime Minister Felipe González, retained control of the Cortes (parliament) by winning 184 of the 350 seats in the Congress of Deputies. The margin of victory was smaller than that in 1982, but it guaranteed that González would remain head of government. The PSOE also won 124 of 208 contested seats in the 253-seat Senate. González had called elections four months early after voters agreed in a March referendum to keep Spain in the North Atlantic Treaty Organization.

25 **Philippines gets U.S. aid.** The U.S. signed an agreement to give the new Philippine government of Pres. Corazon Aquino $200 million in aid to help meet the country's severe financial needs. Congress had authorized the money while Ferdinand Marcos was still president, but the money had never been transferred because of a dispute over how the money was to be spent.

27 **Irish uphold ban on divorce.** In a direct referendum Irish voters decided by a 3–2 margin not to change the law that prohibited divorce. It was a victory for the Roman Catholic hierarchy and, indirectly, for the political opponents of Prime Minister Garret FitzGerald. The prime minister had urged his compatriots to demonstrate that Ireland was willing to view itself as a pluralistic society where secular rights were respected. The negative vote, some believed, could adversely affect efforts to reach a political accommodation with Northern Ireland, where Protestants constituted a majority of the population.

U.S. and New Zealand at odds. During a meeting in Manila, U.S. Secretary of State George Shultz informed New Zealand's prime minister, David Lange, that the U.S. no longer felt bound to abide by the ANZUS (Australia, New Zealand, U.S.) Pact commitments it had made in 1951 regarding the defense of New Zealand. The falling out of the old allies was the result of Lange's determination to ban visits to New Zealand by nuclear-powered or nuclear-armed naval vessels.

28 **Yugoslavia replaces old leaders.** During a national convention of Yugoslavia's Communist Party, 127 new members were elected to the Central Committee and only 38 retained. The members of the new committee then announced that 17 of the 23 members of the presidium had been replaced. The new leaders faced the difficult task of trying to revitalize the nation's economy, which was at its lowest level in 40 years. Many attributed the economic crisis to a lack of strong central government. After the death of Tito in 1980, those who successively shared power had generally been unable to implement policies that were opposed by one or more of Yugoslavia's six constituent republics and two autonomous provinces.

30 **Supreme Court rules on homosexuality.** The U.S. Supreme Court ruled 5–4 that a Georgia law prohibiting anal and oral intercourse did not violate the constitutional right to privacy. In effect, the court ruled that the Constitution did not protect homosexual relations between consenting adults, even in the privacy of their homes. Earlier in the month, the court had struck down the "Baby Doe" regulations promulgated by the Reagan administration. It ruled that there was no evidence that hospitals had been acting improperly and therefore no basis for the federal government to require hospitals to undertake life-prolonging medical treatment for newborn infants with severe handicaps. Two days later, on June 11, the court overturned a Pennsylvania law that was designed in part to deter women from having abortions. The law had also required doctors to place in jeopardy the health of pregnant women if this was necessary to save their fetuses.

JULY

2 **Court backs minority quotas.** The U.S. Supreme Court, in two separate cases, ruled that in certain circumstances minority hiring quotas and racial preferences in work opportunities could be required to rectify past social discrimination, even though the persons involved had not been victims of such discrimination. One case involved a New York City sheet metal workers' union; the other involved firefighters in Cleveland, Ohio. Civil rights leaders viewed the court's pronouncements on affirmative action programs as landmark victories.

General strike called in Chile. In Chile a scheduled two-day strike began that left eight people dead. The strike was organized by the National Assembly of Civil Society, a protest coalition that included workers, students, professionals, and others. The coalition demanded that the country's military leaders begin serious discussions about ending the nearly 13-year-old regime of Pres. Augusto Pinochet Ugarte. On July 11 Pinochet reiterated his determination to remain head of the Chilean government and said he was certain the people would support his election to a new eight-year term in 1989.

3 **Polish Communists reorganize.** Poland's Communist Party ended a five-day congress in Warsaw after Gen. Wojciech Jaruzelski was reappointed to the top post of first secretary.

A car bomb, triggered by remote control, exploded in Madrid on July 14, killing 10 Civil Guards and injuring over 50 other people.
ZETA—SIPA/SPECIAL FEATURES

In a drastic reorganization of the Central Committee, all but 57 of the 214 members were replaced. After three generals were appointed to the policy-setting Politburo, there were more high-ranking military personnel in the Polish Politburo than in any other in the Soviet bloc.

Kuwait assembly dissolved. The emir of Kuwait, who narrowly escaped assassination in May 1985, dissolved the National Assembly in the face of a "fierce foreign conspiracy which threatened lives and almost destroyed the wealth of the homeland." Two weeks earlier an attempt had been made to bomb Kuwait's oil pipelines. It was believed that those responsible were members of an underground Iraqi organization that sought revenge for Kuwait's support of Iran in its protracted war with Iraq. Kuwait's assembly had been the only freely elected Arab representative body in the region.

5 **Turkish Cypriot rebuffs UN.** Rauf Denktash, the leader of the so-called Turkish Republic of Northern Cyprus, rejected a United Nations request for an urgent meeting to discuss reopening the border that since 1983 had unofficially separated the northern section of the island nation from the southern section. Denktash said his decision to seal the border was a direct response to those who had criticized Turkish Prime Minister Turgut Ozal for visiting northern Cyprus. Denktash remarked that Ozal's visit had proved "that this second republic exists . . . and the Greek Cypriots [in the southern part of the island] have no say over it." Turkey was the only country that recognized northern Cyprus as an independent nation.

6 **Japan holds Diet elections.** Japan's ruling Liberal-Democratic Party (LDP) scored a stunning victory in national elections, capturing 304 of the 512 seats in the House of Representatives and 72 of the 126 contested seats in the House of Councillors. The unusual simultaneous election to both houses of the Diet (parliament) had been engineered by Prime Minister Yasuhiro Nakasone, who gambled his political future on the outcome. The Socialist Party, which had been the government's strongest political opponent, was badly damaged when it won only 85 seats in the lower house—27 fewer than it had captured in 1983. It also secured 20 seats in the upper house. Komeito remained Japan's third most popular party, winning 56 seats in the lower house and 10 in the House of Councillors. Because the LDP victory was so impressive, it appeared likely that the party would disregard a long-standing tradition and extend Nakasone's tenure as party president and prime minister after his second two-year term expired in October.

Pro-Marcos group seizes hotel. About 300 armed soldiers loyal to deposed Philippine president Ferdinand Marcos seized control of the Manila Hotel after 75-year-old Arturo Tolentino declared himself acting president. During the February presidential election, Tolentino had been Marcos's vice-presidential running mate. The attempted coup was doomed to fail when Defense Minister Juan Ponce Enrile and armed forces Chief of Staff Fidel Ramos both reaffirmed their allegiance to Pres. Corazon Aquino. On July 9 Aquino announced that the rebels would be shown clemency but that rallies and demonstrations that were "not truly an exercise in freedom of speech and assembly but are designed to further the rebel cause" would be banned. On July 29 all members of the armed forces were required to take an oath of allegiance to the Aquino government.

7 **Jordan closes al-Fatah offices.** Jordan's information minister announced that all 25 al-Fatah offices were being closed for reasons of national security. Al-Fatah, the main faction of the bitterly divided Palestine Liberation Organization (PLO), was headed by Yasir Arafat, who in February had refused to back King Hussein's plan for achieving a Middle East peace settlement with Israel. The PLO, which Arafat represented as chairman, maintained its headquarters in Tunis, Tunisia.

Malaysia hangs two Australians. Two 28-year-old Australians were hanged in Kuala Lumpur, Malaysia, after being convicted of trafficking in heroin. In 1983 Malaysia, which already had stringent narcotics laws, had imposed a mandatory death sentence in cases involving more than 15 g (0.5 oz) of heroin. The two men were carrying nearly 180 g (6.4 oz) when they were seized at the airport before they could leave the country. Australian Prime Minister Bob Hawke and British Prime Minister Margaret Thatcher had pleaded in vain for the death penalty to be set aside for humanitarian reasons.

9 **Paris hit by terrorists.** A bomb demolished the fifth and sixth floors of the Paris police headquarters annex, killing a police inspector and wounding more than 20 other persons, some seriously. A group called Action Directe claimed responsibility for the daring attack, the third such bombing in Paris since July 6. Police speculated that Action Directe was out to prove that it was still to be feared even though police had disrupted some of the organization's operations.

14 **Bomb explodes in Madrid.** Ten Civil Guards were killed and over 50 other persons injured when a car bomb was detonated by remote control in a residential section of Madrid. The government believed that the attack was carried out by Basque political extremists, who had already been accused of some 20 other bombings during the year, including one on April 25 that killed five Civil Guards. On July 21 a powerful car bomb exploded outside the Defense Ministry just minutes after 12 antitank rockets had been fired at the building. Nine persons were reported wounded.

Former FBI agent sentenced. Richard W. Miller, the first FBI agent ever convicted of espionage, was sentenced by a federal judge in Los Angeles to two life sentences and to 50 years in prison, all to be served concurrently, for spying for the Soviet Union. Miller, who was 49 years old, would not be eligible for parole for 16 years and 8 months. On July 24 Jerry Whitworth, a former U.S. Navy radioman, was convicted by a federal jury in San Francisco on seven counts of spying for the Soviet Union and five counts of tax fraud.

Israeli agency to be probed. The attorney general of Israel announced that the police would investigate Shin Bet, the nation's domestic intelligence agency, which had reportedly been involved in the murders of two Palestinian bus hijackers and in a subsequent cover-up of the crime. After heated debate, a majority of the Cabinet had voted not to appoint a group of senior judges to a commission of inquiry that, by its very nature, would have been largely independent of government influence. The central figure in the investigation would be Avraham Shalom, the head of Shin Bet, who had already gone on record as saying that everything he did had been approved by his superior at the time, Yitzhak Shamir. Shamir was scheduled to relinquish his position as foreign minister to Shimon Peres in October and replace him as prime minister.

17 **U.S. approves extradition treaty.** The U.S. Senate, by a vote of 87–10, approved an extradition treaty with Great Britain that would facilitate the deportation of accused terrorists who had sought refuge in the United States. Although the United States would con-

tinue to recognize the right of political dissidents to seek asylum in the U.S., the new treaty stipulated that a request for extradition should be honoured unless a federal judge concluded that those accused of terrorist acts would not receive a fair trial in Britain because of their race, religion, nationality, or political opinions. The British were seeking the extradition of certain Irish Republican Army members who claimed that the crimes of terrorism they had been charged with were simply expressions of political dissent.

23 **Shimon Peres visits Morocco.** Israeli Prime Minister Shimon Peres and King Hassan II of Morocco ended two days of talks with a pledge to continue working together to establish peace in the Middle East. There were no new agreements, and no noteworthy changes were made in either leader's previous positions. The Peres visit began in secrecy, but news of the Israeli leader's arrival in Morocco quickly reached the capitals of other nations. On July 22 Syria severed diplomatic relations with Morocco, and other hard-line Arab nations denounced King Hassan for "betraying the Arab cause." Egyptian Pres. Hosni Mubarak, however, expressed hope that the meeting would advance the cause of peace. On July 27 Hassan, reacting to severe criticism of his meeting with Peres by other Arab leaders, resigned as conference chairman of the Arab League.

China expels *New York Times* reporter. John F. Burns, a British subject employed by the *New York Times* as its bureau chief in Beijing (Peking), was expelled from China after being accused of breaking into a restricted military zone and photographing classified objects. In an official statement, China said that such conduct "obviously constitutes an act of spying and intelligence gathering which will not be tolerated by any sovereign state." Burns and his two companions had been detained by local authorities for two days in Shaanxi (Shensi) Province in early July while on an extensive tour of the area. The trio were allowed to return to Beijing on July 7, but Burns was arrested on July 17 when he and his family were preparing to board a plane for a vacation outside the country.

A southeastern U.S. farmer resorts to feeding his cattle hay—normally needed only in winter—in midsummer because the severe drought had turned pastures into singed wastelands.
LAURA SIKES—SYGMA

25 **Drought devastates U.S. states.** U.S. farm experts estimated that a severe drought in eight mid-Atlantic and southern states would result in the loss of about $2 billion in crops and livestock—roughly 15% of farmers' gross earnings of 1985. Officials at the Department of Agriculture said the lack of rain and the searing temperatures had created the worst farm crisis in 50 years. While the federal government took steps to accelerate the processing of applications for emergency assistance, farmers in other parts of the country began shipping hay to stricken areas so that starving animals would not have to be slaughtered.

27 **Thais elect Parliament.** Record voter turnout and sporadic violence marked an election in which the Democratic Party, under the leadership of Deputy Prime Minister Bhichai Rattakul, won 100 of the 347 seats in Thailand's House of Representatives, nearly double its former total. The Thai Nation Party, which led those opposing the ruling coalition government, won 63 seats. The Social Action Party captured 51, the newly formed United Democratic Party 38, and the Thai Citizens' Party 24. The remaining seats were shared by 11 other parties. Because Bhichai was not considered acceptable to the Army, which played a prominent role in Thai politics, Prime Minister Prem Tinsulanond, a retired general with no party affiliation, was expected to be asked to form another coalition government.

29 **Italy's political crisis ends.** The leaders of five of Italy's political parties ended a month-long government crisis by agreeing to let Bettino Craxi continue on as prime minister with a new coalition Cabinet. Craxi had resigned on June 27 after the loss of a key parliamentary vote. Craxi, a Socialist who had served as prime minister for nearly three years, had given Italy one of its most enduring governments in the post-World War II period.

Football lawsuit settled. After 31 hours of deliberation, six federal jurors in New York City found the National Football League (NFL) guilty of damaging the rival, and relatively new, United States Football League (USFL) because it controlled television coverage of professional football. The jury, however, concluded that the NFL's de facto monopoly had already evolved before the USFL appeared on the scene and was not the direct result of improper or illegal practices. As a consequence the USFL was awarded just one dollar in token damages. The jury's verdict appeared to signal the demise of the USFL because the owners of the financially troubled league had already lost millions of dollars and had hoped to guarantee the league's future by winning as much as $1,690,000,000 in the antitrust suit.

AUGUST

5 **Commonwealth at odds over sanctions.** British Prime Minister Margaret Thatcher and the leaders of six other Commonwealth nations ended a meeting in London still in sharp disagreement over the effectiveness and advisability of imposing meaningful sanctions against South Africa to bring about an end to apartheid. When Australia, The Bahamas, Canada, India, Zambia, and Zimbabwe realized they could not induce Britain to take a firmer stance against South Africa, the six leaders reaffirmed the sanctions they had already adopted in the Nassau accord of 1985 and then added others. Thatcher endorsed only certain voluntary sanctions, but she indicated Britain would enforce any economic sanctions related to the importation of South African coal, iron, steel, or gold coins if such sanctions were adopted by the European Communities.

6 **Israeli court upholds pardons.** The Israeli Supreme Court ruled that presidential pardons granted to the head of Shin Bet, the nation's domestic intelligence agency, and to three subordinate agents were legal and binding. All had been implicated in the murders of two Palestinian hijackers and in a subsequent cover-up of the alleged crime, but none had been formally charged. The decision of the court in effect precluded any further investigation of the allegations and would probably encourage others who had also been implicated in the case to seek similar pardons.

14 **Bhutto arrested as unrest spreads.** Benazir Bhutto, leader of a movement to oust Pakistani Pres. Mohammad Zia-ul-Haq from power, was jailed after a rally held in defiance of a ban against public gatherings. At least four persons were reported killed during the day as antigovernment protesters clashed with Lahore police; hundreds of others were injured during demonstrations in various parts of the country. About 20 more persons were killed before the vio-

Displaced Sudanese children are fed from scanty rations in the country's rebel-controlled south. Rebel forces had forbidden all air traffic, including shipments of food, to enter their territory.
WILLIAM CAMPBELL—SYGMA

lence burned itself out several days later. Bhutto's arrest in Karachi occurred while Zia was on a pilgrimage to Mecca, Saudi Arabia, and Prime Minister Mohammad Khan Junejo was entrusted with keeping antigovernment forces under control. Bhutto, who had organized the Pakistan People's Party "to restore democracy" through new elections, was released from jail on September 8.

U.S. drug agent tortured. The FBI and the U.S. Drug Enforcement Administration began an investigation of the reported kidnapping and torture of a U.S. narcotics agent by Jalisco state police in Mexico. U.S. officials claimed that Victor Cortez, Jr., who had been working in Guadalajara, was abducted on August 13 and severely tortured before being released the following morning. The incident immediately brought to mind the case of Enrique Camarena Salazar, another U.S. narcotics agent, who in February 1985 was brutally beaten and killed, along with his Mexican pilot, by drug traffickers and police in Guadalajara.

16 **Rebels down Sudanese plane.** The Sudan People's Liberation Army, which had the support of neighbouring Ethiopia, shot down a Sudan Airways plane that was flying over the southern part of the country. The rebels had earlier warned that they would shoot down any aircraft flying over rebel-controlled areas. All 60 persons aboard the aircraft were killed. A spokesman for the rebels said the blame for the deaths of "innocent citizens" rested on the shoulders of the Khartoum government because they had failed to heed the rebels' initial warning. The rebels had been fighting since 1983 to gain autonomy for the south. Because most southerners were Christians or animists and spoke their own tribal languages, they felt little identity with the Arabic-speaking Muslims in the north and resented having to live under Islamic law. Both the International Red Cross and the United Nations had to halt food shipments, and officials expressed fears that huge numbers of displaced Sudanese would die of starvation if planes were not allowed to fly food into the war area.

18 **Israelis and Soviets meet in Finland.** Representatives of Israel and the Soviet Union met in Helsinki, Fin., for their first official discussions since the Arab-Israeli war of 1967. The talks, which reportedly were to continue for two days, ended after only 90 minutes. There were indications, however, that future talks might be held to discuss "consular matters." The Soviets had expressed a desire to inspect Soviet-owned property in Israel, presumably buildings belonging to the Russian Orthodox Church. Israel was believed to have made a counter request to visit Moscow. Both sides appeared to be weighing the prospects of eventually normalizing relations.

19 **Bomb explodes in Tehran.** A car bomb exploded in one of the most crowded areas of Tehran, the capital of Iran, killing 20 people and injuring some 75 others. Three days earlier 13 persons had been reported killed and more than 100 injured in a similar bombing in Qom. A total of seven such attacks were said to have occurred since the beginning of the year.

21 **Toxic gases kill Cameroonians.** An estimated 1,700 sleeping villagers in a remote area of northwest Cameroon were killed by toxic gases that erupted from a crater lake. When news of the tragedy reached the capital, Pres. Paul Biya issued a call for international assistance. Rescue teams found the landscape littered with human remains and dead livestock. The top priority became the treatment and evacuation of survivors to safe areas.

22 **African nations cautious in face of South Africa's economic threats.** The leaders of nine black African nations, after a meeting in Angola, issued a communiqué condemning South Africa's policy of apartheid. The document praised Zambia and Zimbabwe, two of the six so-called frontline nations, for imposing sanctions against South Africa, but Angola, Botswana, Mozambique, and Tanzania decided that for the present South Africa's threats of economic retaliation prevented them from taking similar action.

23 **U.S. seizes Soviet diplomat as spy.** The FBI announced that a Soviet diplomat accredited to the United Nations had been arrested in New York City and charged with espionage. He had been taken into custody while accepting classified documents provided by a defense contractor employee cooperating with the FBI. Gennady F. Zakharov had been assigned to the Center for Science and Technology for Development, an agency of the United Nations Secretariat. Zakharov's diplomatic status did not provide immunity from prosecution in the case of espionage.

27 **Bonn to slow flood of refugees.** West German Chancellor Helmut Kohl, responding to public demands, announced that new measures would be taken to restrict the record number of refugees who had been pouring into the country. Many believed that a majority of the 100,000 persons who were expected to request political asylum during the current year were in fact "economic" rather than political refugees. West Germany's liberal asylum laws, which had been passed mainly for the benefit of refugees from Communist countries, had prompted thousands of people from Africa, Asia, the Middle East, and other parts of the world to make West Germany their home. The new restrictions would centre on such things as work permits and penalties against airlines that carried people without proper visas to West Berlin or other West German cities.

28 **Bolivia under state of siege.** Víctor Paz Estenssoro, who became president of Bolivia for the fourth time in August 1985, attempted to contain labour unrest by declaring a national state of siege. Thousands of soldiers were dispatched to the Andean highlands to prevent tin miners from marching on the capital. The workers were protesting not only the closing down of unprofitable mines and the consequent loss of some 7,000 jobs but also government plans to lay off 8,000 of the 20,000 miners who were still at work.

Whitworth gets long sentence. A federal district court judge in San Francisco sentenced 47-year-old Jerry Whitworth to 365 years in prison and fined him $410,000 for actively participating in a Soviet spy ring. The former U.S. Navy radioman, who had been convicted on July 24, would not be eligible for parole for 60 years.

30 **Soviets arrest U.S. reporter.** Nicholas Daniloff, a correspondent for *U.S. News & World Report* magazine, was arrested in Moscow just moments after a Soviet acquaintance handed him a packet containing two maps marked "top secret." U.S. officials were openly angry that the Soviets had apparently decided to frame Daniloff after one of their United Nations diplomats was arrested in New York City and charged with espionage. Emotions were running so high that some diplomats feared the Daniloff affair would seriously harm U.S.-Soviet relations if the reporter were not set free in the very near future.

SEPTEMBER

1 **Nonaligned meet in Zimbabwe.** Robert Mugabe, the newly named chairman of the Nonaligned Movement, opened a meeting in Zimbabwe with a call for selective sanctions against South Africa as a way to help bring about an end to apartheid. Mugabe was aware that South Africa was in a position to inflict significant hardships on black African nations that seriously challenged it. He therefore urged the delegates to supplement their efforts by persuading such nations as Great Britain, Japan, the U.S., and West Germany to use their far more considerable economic power to back the antiapartheid cause.

5 **Pan Am jet seized in Karachi.** A Pan Am Boeing 747, on a flight from Bombay to New York City, was seized by four Arabic-speaking terrorists during an early morning stopover in Karachi, Pak. The gunmen, dressed in security guard uniforms, fired automatic weapons as they raced for the steps that led to the plane's cabin. Sixteen hours later, while the terrorists' demand that they be flown to Cyprus was still being negotiated, the cabin lights dimmed as a power generator ran low on fuel. When the lights failed completely, the terrorists began to fire wildly and hurl hand grenades. Amid great confusion, most of the passengers managed to escape through emergency exits. The hijackers were captured, but 21 persons lost their lives. Pres. Mohammad Zia-ul-Haq promised that the terrorists, whom he identified as Palestinians with no known ties to any government, would be severely punished if they were convicted of hijacking.

6 **Jews massacred in Turkey.** Two Arabic-speaking terrorists entered the Neve Shalom synagogue in Istanbul, sealed the doors with iron bars, then began firing submachine guns and hurling hand grenades as the Sabbath worshipers scurried for cover. Seven rabbis and 14 other members of the congregation were killed. Both gunmen also died. Up to that time Istanbul's tiny Jewish population had lived in relative peace with its Muslim neighbours. Turkish Prime Minister Turgut Ozal, after a special session with his Cabinet, condemned the attack and joined the call for international cooperation to combat terrorism. He called the murders especially heinous because they had occurred in a house of worship. From its headquarters in Tunisia, the Palestine Liberation Organization also condemned "the massacre of innocents, even if it concerns Jews." Because several groups claimed responsibility for having committed the crime, the affiliation of the terrorists remained in doubt.

Woman to lead Japan's Socialists. Takako Doi, a member of the Japanese Diet (parliament) since 1969, became the first woman ever to head any of the nation's major political parties when fellow Socialists overwhelmingly elected her leader of their party. Although Doi was determined to rebuild the Socialist Party (SP) after its disastrous defeat in the July national elections, some politicians felt the SP had permanently lost its appeal as a credible alternative to the long-ruling Liberal-Democratic Party led by Prime Minister Yasuhiro Nakasone.

7 **Pinochet survives ambush.** Chilean Pres. Augusto Pinochet Ugarte narrowly escaped assassination when gunmen attacked his motorcade as it crossed a bridge outside Santiago. Five members of the president's armed escort were killed and 11 wounded. In a statement sent to the Reuters news agency, the Manuel Rodríguez Patriotic Front took responsibility for the attack and pledged that the next attempt on Pinochet's life would not fail. Francisco Javier Cuadra, the government's secretary general, said four vehicles were destroyed when the motorcade was assaulted by explosives, rockets, and sniper fire. Within hours Pinochet declared a state of siege. New restrictions were placed on civil liberties; six magazines were forbidden to publish; the Reuters operation was suspended; and a number of Pinochet's "opponents" were arrested.

11 **Nakasone's term extended.** During a party caucus before the opening of a new session of the Diet (parliament), Japan's ruling Liberal-Democrats (LDP) voted unanimously to retain Yasuhiro Nakasone as party president for another year. This departure from party rules meant that Nakasone would remain prime minister for another year after his second consecutive two-year term expired at the end of October. In effect, the LDP acknowledged both Nakasone's contribution to the party's landslide victory in the July national elections and the right of other party leaders to seek the prime ministership.

12 **Court dismisses acquittals in Aquino murder trial.** The Philippine Supreme Court voted 8–0, with 3 abstentions, to overturn the December 1985 acquittals of the 26 men who had been on trial for the political assassination of Benigno Aquino, Jr., in August 1983. In a 50-page statement the justices called the verdict a travesty of justice and ordered a new trial. They also declared that Ferdinand Marcos had used his presidential powers to "corrupt and make a mockery of the judicial process." On September 22 the last of the 24 original defendants still in the Philippines surrendered to authorities. Two others, Gen. Fabian Ver, the former chief of staff of the armed forces, and an air force captain, Felipe Valerio, were believed to be in the U.S.

14 **Bomb kills five in Seoul.** Five persons were killed and more than 30 injured when a powerful bomb exploded in the arrivals hall of South Korea's Kimpo International Airport in Seoul. The afternoon blast occurred after athletes had begun to arrive for the Asian Games, which were scheduled to begin on September 20. The director of the national police claimed that the terrorists were either North Koreans or "impure elements directed by the northern Communists." Additional security forces had already been assigned to the airport because the Seoul government feared that North Korea, which was boycotting the Games, might try to sabotage them.

16 **EC imposes mild sanctions on South Africa.** The foreign ministers of the 12 European Communities (EC) countries reached agreement in Brussels to impose mild new economic sanctions on South Africa because it had failed to take steps to abolish apartheid.

BOUVET/SOLA—GAMMA/LIAISON

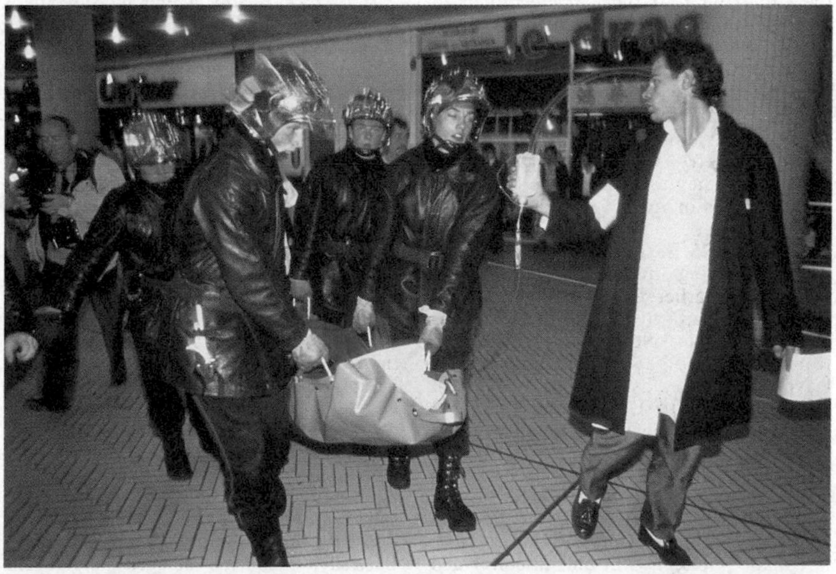

Rescuers assist one of the 53 persons injured in a Paris department store bomb blast, which killed 5 others, on September 17. It was the fifth terrorist bombing in the city in ten days.

Convicted Soviet spy Gennady Zakharov waves farewell after his release from U.S. custody. One day earlier U.S. reporter Nicholas Daniloff had been freed from Soviet detention. Official reports, however, denied a direct link between the two cases.

A. TANNENBAUM—SYGMA

The EC pledged not to import South African iron, steel, or gold coins and to prohibit new investments in South Africa. West Germany strongly opposed a ban on imports of South African coal, saying it would impose too severe a hardship on black miners. The ministers, however, agreed to discuss the matter again at a later meeting because coal was by far South Africa's most important export item.

17 **Terrorists hit Paris again.** Unidentified terrorists carried out their fifth successful bombing in Paris in ten days. In the latest attack, 5 persons were reported killed and 53 wounded outside Tati, a department store on the Rue de Rennes. On September 15 one person was reported killed and 51 injured when a bomb exploded in the driver's license section of the Paris police headquarters. On September 14 one person was reported killed and two injured by a bomb that exploded beneath the Pub Renault on the Champs Élysées. Two days earlier 41 persons had been injured when a bomb went off in a cafeteria at La Défense. The first bombing in the most recent series occurred on September 8. One person was reported killed and 15 wounded at the City Hall post office. Determined to end the terror, Prime Minister Jacques Chirac, who was also mayor of Paris, sent hundreds of police and military personnel into the streets with authority to examine packages that might contain explosives. France also announced that all visitors to the country would have to obtain visas unless they came from the European Communities or from Switzerland.

U.S. expels 25 Soviets. The U.S. government, following up on a demand made six months earlier that the Soviet Union reduce its staff at the United Nations headquarters in New York City, gave Moscow a list of 25 persons who had to leave the country by October 1. The list was also given to UN Secretary-General Javier Pérez de Cuéllar, who questioned the legitimacy of the order, even though it was officially described as necessary to bring the size of the Soviet UN mission into line with those of other nations. Although the names of individuals were not made public, a U.S. official confirmed that the head of the Soviet Committee for State Security (KGB) in the U.S. and the head of the Soviet military intelligence agency (GRU) were among those being expelled.

18 **Aquino explains her views.** Philippine Pres. Corazon Aquino, in a 25-minute address to a joint session of the U.S. Congress, said she felt she must first "explore the path of peace to the utmost" so that a moral basis could be established before "taking up the sword of war" against Communist insurgents who refused to accept her overtures of peace. Aquino had been criticized both at home and abroad for being too soft on the rebels. In a speech before the UN General Assembly on September 22, Aquino pointed out that her compatriots had freed themselves from the oppression and corruption of the Marcos regime without any help from outsiders. Then, speaking to the victims of apartheid, she served warning that the blacks of South Africa should not expect to secure freedom and dignity except through their own efforts and determination. "Do not waver," she said; "look only to your own strength in determination."

20 **GATT meeting adjourns.** Ministers of the General Agreement on Tariffs and Trade (GATT), after a week-long conference in Punta del Este, Uruguay, endorsed new multilateral negotiations aimed at further liberalizing and expanding world trade, especially for the benefit of less developed nations. The ministers also emphasized the need to provide greater access to world markets by reducing and eliminating tariffs, by removing quotas, and by doing away with other obstacles to free trade. For the first time, the GATT ministers agreed to include services as well as goods in future multilateral negotiations so that banks and other institutions would be following the same guidelines in their international operations.

21 **Stockholm talks called success.** Representatives of NATO and the Warsaw Pact nations reached agreement in Stockholm on several points that were viewed as key elements in lessening the possibility of war in Europe. Basically, each side pledged to give the other advance notice of all significant military exercises and the right of inspection to guarantee that neither was preparing a surprise attack. The inclusion of on-site inspection was especially welcomed by the West because it was a critical element in other arms control negotiations. Soviet leader Mikhail Gorbachev called the Stockholm accord a victory for common sense and a major step in reducing international tensions.

25 **French troops to help Togo.** France's Defense Ministry announced that, in response to a request from Pres. Gnassingbe Eyadema, it was sending planes and troops to the West African nation of Togo following an attempted coup on September 23. France had signed an agreement in 1963 to send military aid to its former colony if it were threatened by a foreign power. Eyadema claimed that the insurgents had come from another country, but he declined to be more specific.

26 **Rehnquist becomes chief justice.** William H. Rehnquist, a conservative nominated by President Reagan, took the oath of office as the 16th chief justice of the United States. He replaced Warren E. Burger, who had announced in June that he would retire. Members of the Senate Judiciary Committee, who had earlier questioned Rehnquist at great length about his past and current views on race and other topics, never reached agreement on his suitability to serve as chief justice. The Senate, however, approved the controversial nomination by a vote of 65–33. Antonin Scalia, a federal appeals court judge who replaced Rehnquist as an associate justice on the court, was also sworn in. The Senate had approved his appointment 98–0.

29 **Daniloff and Zakharov are freed.** The Soviet Union allowed Nicholas Daniloff, a U.S. reporter assigned to Moscow, to leave the country without standing trial on charges of espionage. He had been detained on August 30 just moments after a Soviet acquaintance handed him classified documents. Just one week earlier FBI agents in New York City had picked up Gennady Zakharov, a Soviet diplomat assigned to the United Nations, and charged him with spying. Although the release of the two men had been worked out after long and tedious negotiations, the U.S. repeatedly insisted that the two cases were not related because Zakharov was indeed a spy and Daniloff a legitimate reporter who had been framed. To bolster its contention that there was no direct link between the two cases, the U.S. noted that Daniloff had been freed one day before Zakharov; that Zakharov, unlike Daniloff, had been convicted of spying after pleading no contest in court; and that the Soviets had agreed to allow dissident Yury Orlov and his wife, Irina Valitova, to leave the Soviet Union by October 7. Despite such explanations, many continued to believe that the Reagan administration had in fact negotiated a swap. The news that both Daniloff and Zakharov were being released was followed by the totally unexpected announcement that President Reagan and Soviet leader Mikhail Gorbachev had agreed to meet in Iceland on October 11.

OCTOBER

2 **U.S. acts against apartheid.** The U.S. Senate voted 78–21 to override President Reagan's veto of sanctions against South Africa because it had steadfastly refused to abandon apartheid, the government's policy of racial separation. On September 29 the U.S. House of Representatives had been even more emphatic in condemning South Africa; it voted 313–83 to override the president's veto of sanctions. The legislation, which became law after the Senate vote, banned all new investments in South African businesses by U.S. citizens. It also prohibited the importation of such items as South African steel, coal, uranium, textiles, and agricultural products. In addition, it canceled the right of South African airlines to land at U.S. airports. Some of the provisions took effect immediately, while others would be introduced gradually and would come into effect by the end of the year. Reagan had argued that sanctions would prove to be ineffective and would undermine U.S. efforts to bring about change through persuasion.

6 **Soviet nuclear sub sinks.** The U.S. Defense Department reported that a 20-year-old Soviet nuclear submarine, which had been crippled by an explosion and fire on October 3, had sunk in the Atlantic about 970 km (600 mi) east of Bermuda. Although the 9,400-ton vessel reportedly carried 16 ballistic missiles, each armed with two nuclear warheads, there was no evidence of a radioactive leak. After the accident, which claimed the lives of at least 3 members of the 120-man crew, the submarine tried unsuccessfully to operate under its own power. It was under tow from a Soviet merchant ship when it began to sink.

7 **Nicaragua captures U.S. pilot.** Nicaraguan officials called a news conference so reporters could see Eugene Hasenfus, a U.S. pilot, whose cargo plane had been downed by a surface-to-air missile on October 5. Hasenfus was reportedly transporting supplies from El Salvador to Nicaraguan *contras* fighting the Sandinista government. During the news conference two other U.S. citizens who were said to have died in the crash were also identified. The Reagan administration was quick to assert that Hasenfus had no connection with any U.S. government agency and apparently worked for a private organization headed by retired general John K. Singlaub. Nonetheless, Nicaragua issued a formal diplomatic protest to U.S. Secretary of State George Shultz, accusing the U.S. of sponsoring the supply lift. During a trial in Managua, Hasenfus was convicted of violating a public security law that forbade "actions aimed at subjecting the nation totally or partially to foreign domination, or infringing on its independence or integrity." He was then sentenced to 30 years in prison.

10 **Pérez de Cuéllar reelected.** The United Nations Security Council and the General Assembly unanimously approved a second five-year term for Javier Pérez de Cuéllar as secretary-general of the international organization. The voting was uneventful compared with what had happened in 1981. On that occasion, the Security Council, whose responsibility it was to nominate the secretary-general, became deadlocked. China repeatedly vetoed the reappointment of Kurt Waldheim, and the U.S. adamantly refused to back Salim A. Salim, the foreign minister of Tanzania who had the support of the Organization of African Unity. When it became evident that the balloting was leading nowhere, both candidates withdrew from consideration. Pérez de Cuéllar was then elected as a compromise candidate. Although he could not point to any stellar successes during his first term in office, the 66-year-old Peruvian said he had decided to accept a second term because the UN was in the midst of a financial and organizational crisis.

12 **Gorbachev and Reagan end meeting in Iceland.** Soviet leader Mikhail Gorbachev and President Reagan ended their quickly arranged "pre-summit" meeting in Reykjavík, Iceland. At one point it appeared to hold promise of a historic breakthrough on arms control, but it ended with no significant progress. Although media reports of what each side actually offered during the negotiations differed substantially, there was general agreement that at one stage the two leaders had virtually concurred on some of the most sweeping arms reductions in decades. The final sticking point, however, proved to be Reagan's refusal to abandon his Strategic Defense Initiative, popularly called "Star Wars," and Soviet insistence that efforts to develop and test such a system had to be sacrificed or there would be no accord. The meeting, which began on October 11, ended in disappointment and bitterness and virtually ensured that Gorbachev would not visit the U.S. before the end of the year as he had tentatively planned.

15 **Hossain Ershad wins election.** Pres. Hossain M. Ershad of Bangladesh, having resigned as army chief of staff, was elected to a five-year term as the civilian candidate of his newly created National Party. With the opposition coalition boycotting the election, Ershad faced only token challenges from 11 minor candidates. Even so, there were reports of widespread vote fraud. Ershad came to power in 1982 by overthrowing Pres. Abdus Sattar in a bloodless coup. He then suspended the constitution and declared martial law. Hasina Wajad, the daughter of Sheikh Mujibur Rahman, the country's first president, was one of two women openly challenging Ershad's claim to power. In the May elections, her followers won 76 of the 300 directly elected seats in Parliament; Ershad's party won 153. Wajad, however, had refused to participate in parliamentary debates as long as martial law remained in effect. When Ershad removed martial law on November 10, there were violent protests because the government had also passed a law that was intended to formally legitimate Ershad's martial law regime and thereby protect it from future prosecutions.

17 **U.S. changes immigration laws.** The U.S. Senate voted 63–24 in favour of the same compromise immigration bill that the House of Representatives had approved two days earlier by a vote of 238–173. The new legislation, called the Immigration Reform and Control Act of 1986, would introduce a historic change in U.S. immigration policy. For the first time, employers who knowingly hired illegal aliens would be subject to civil fines ranging from $250 to $10,000 for each illegal alien hired. Another landmark feature of the bill would grant legal status to millions of illegal aliens who had resided continuously in the U.S. (except for "brief, casual or innocent absences") since before Jan. 1, 1982. Aliens who qualified for legal residence would, however, have to prove that they had been in the U.S. during the required period of time. Immigration officials, consequently, expected to be hard pressed to determine which rent receipts, paycheck stubs, income tax forms, birth certificates, and the like were genuine and which were bogus. Some observers

G. GIANSANTI—SYGMA

Religious leaders from around the world gather for prayer in Assisi, Italy, in a summit called by Pope John Paul II to focus on peace. More than 150 high clerics attended.

U.S. Pres. Ronald Reagan (left) and Soviet leader Mikhail Gorbachev share a relaxed moment in Reykjavík, Iceland, where they met for a minisummit that ended without substantive results.
PHILIPPE LEDRU—SYGMA

noted that many eligible aliens might not be able to provide the documentation necessary to support their applications. On November 6 President Reagan signed the bill into law.

19 **Crash kills Mozambique leader.** Pres. Samora Machel, the 53-year-old leader of the eastern African nation of Mozambique from the time it won independence from Portugal in 1975, was killed in a plane crash in South Africa. Machel, an influential and uncompromising critic of apartheid in South Africa, was returning home from Zambia after talks with the leaders of Angola, Zaire, and Zambia. South Africa, anxious to stifle rumours that it might have had something to do with the crash, invited foreign aviation experts to join Mozambicans in their investigation. Thirty-four persons lost their lives when the Soviet-built Tupolev-134A went down. On November 3, six days after Machel's funeral, 47-year-old Joachím Chissanó was named president. He had served as foreign minister since 1975 and was a member of the Mozambique Liberation Front (Frelimo), a professed Marxist organization that was the only legal political party in the country.

20 **Shamir and Peres exchange posts.** Yitzhak Shamir was sworn in for a 25-month term as prime minister of Israel, replacing Shimon Peres, who took over Shamir's responsibilities as foreign minister. The exchange of jobs had been agreed to in 1984 when Shamir's Likud bloc and Peres's Labour Party found themselves with almost equal electoral strength after national elections. When neither side was able to form an acceptable coalition, the two entered into the unusual arrangement, which would last, provided the coalition did not break up, until new elections were held in 1988. Shamir's Cabinet was not expected to differ markedly from the one that served Peres, although Shamir was likely to be somewhat more hawkish in dealing with Israel's Arab adversaries.

22 **U.S. reforms tax code.** President Reagan signed into law a revolutionary tax-reform bill that he described as "the best antipoverty bill, the best pro-family measure and the best job-creation program ever to come out of the Congress of the United States." For years new tax laws had been demanded by virtually all segments of the nation, but every attempt to formulate new legislation was met with hostility from one group or another. Under the new law, corporate taxes were expected to increase by $120 billion over a five-year period and the taxes paid by individuals to be reduced by an equal amount. About six million people with low incomes would pay no taxes; about 15% would pay more; and the rest would pay about the same as they did in former years. The old multiple tax brackets would be reduced to five in 1987 and to just two thereafter (15% and 28%). Capital gains would be taxed as income. Personal exemptions would increase in stages from $1,080 to $2,000 in 1989. Interest payments on home mortgages and certain other expenses would still be deductible by taxpayers who itemized their tax returns, but many individuals would no longer be able to deduct up to $2,000 put into Individual Retirement Accounts. All in all, most citizens seemed to feel that the new tax laws, despite their complexity, introduced a new element of fairness into the tax code.

24 **Britain breaks ties to Syria.** Great Britain announced that it was severing diplomatic relations with Syria because it had "conclusive evidence" that Syrian diplomats and agents had been directly involved in an attempt to plant a bomb aboard an Israeli commercial airliner in April before it left London's Heathrow Airport. The announcement was made after Nezar Hindawi, a Jordanian, was convicted of concealing the bomb in a piece of carry-on luggage and giving it to his unsuspecting fiancée. Hindawi was sentenced to 45 years in prison. The U.S. and Canada called their ambassadors home from Damascus. On November 10 all of Britain's partners in the European Communities except Greece agreed to ban new arms sales to Syria.

27 **Religious leaders pray for peace.** Prominent leaders of 12 different religious groups joined Pope John Paul II in Assisi, Italy, for a World Day of Prayer for Peace. The pope had suggested such a meeting in February. Amerindian religions, the Baha'i faith, Buddhism, Christianity, Jainism, Judaism, Hinduism, Islam, Shintoism, Sikhism, traditional African religions, and Zoroastrianism were all represented. Each group prayed separately, an indication that even though all major religions advocated world peace, religion itself contributed to divisiveness.

30 **Yamani removed as oil minister.** The official Saudi Arabian news agency released a royal decree removing Sheikh Ahmed Zaki Yamani as the nation's minister of petroleum and mineral resources. He had held the post for almost 25 years and had been a leading force in establishing the Organization of Petroleum Exporting Countries in 1961. In the same decree, King Fahd named Hisham Nazer to the vacant post. There was no official explanation for the change.

31 **Seoul police end student sit-in.** After a violent battle with students holed up in five buildings at Konkuk University in Seoul, South Korea, police ended the 66-hour sit-in with the arrests of hundreds of student activists. Of the 1,525 originally taken into custody, about 200 were judged to have been victims of circumstance because they were trapped inside the buildings when the protest started. Although the government was expected to show leniency toward most of the others because they had no previous record of antigovernment activities, 22 students were charged with violating the severe National Security Law and could receive lengthy prison terms.

SYGMA

The shattered remains of a Soviet-built Tupolev-134A airplane are searched after its crash in South Africa killed Mozambique's Pres. Samora Machel and 33 others aboard.

NOVEMBER

4 Democrats to control U.S. Senate. The Democratic Party won control of the 100-seat U.S. Senate by increasing its representation from 47 to 55 seats in national elections. The victory would give the Democrats control over both houses of Congress during the two remaining years of President Reagan's administration. The Democrats also moderately increased their majority in the House of Representatives. The fact that Republicans had a net gain of 8 governorships (24 of 50) suggested that voters were concerned less about party affiliations than about the qualifications of individual candidates.

7 Abdullah renamed chief minister. Indian Prime Minister Rajiv Gandhi, with the consent of his Congress (I) party, named Farooq Abdullah chief minister of the Muslim-dominated Indian state of Jammu and Kashmir. Some Hindu leaders, however, openly questioned Abdullah's loyalty to the central government, especially after Indira Gandhi had felt it necessary to remove him as chief minister two years earlier for unacceptable expressions of attachment to neighbouring Pakistan, a Muslim nation that laid claim to part of the Indian state. Rajiv's appointment was seen as an attempt to restore the state to a semblance of normality.

9 Egypt gets new prime minister. Egyptian Pres. Hosni Mubarak removed Prime Minister Ali Lutfi from office and named Atef Sedki as his successor. Sedki was given orders to formulate a firm plan to control the prices of essential commodities. He would also be immediately involved in arranging a $1 billion emergency loan from the International Monetary Fund, which was critical if Egypt was to renegotiate $38.6 billion in foreign debts.

10 Chemical spill pollutes Rhine. Environmental experts in France, The Netherlands, West Germany, and Switzerland declared that the tons of chemicals that had accidentally spilled into the Rhine River in Schweizerhalle, near Basel, Switz., threatened to destroy all life in the vital waterway. The four countries through which the Rhine flows had already closed down all plants processing Rhine water for household use. The toxic chemicals, which included mercury, had entered the river nine days earlier after a fire at a chemical storage warehouse. On November 12 Switzerland said it would compensate countries that had been affected by the pollutants.

13 U.S. violates Iran arms boycott. President Reagan went on national television to confirm and explain the astonishing revelation some days earlier that the U.S. had secretly supplied Iran with military equipment at the very time it was urging its allies not to do so. After the story first broke, government officials began openly to contradict one another to such an extent that it appeared not even the president was fully aware of everything that had taken place. Reaction to the news of the arms deal ranged from disbelief and outrage to a grim determination to subpoena witnesses, if necessary, so that Congress and the American people would learn the entire story.

U.S. bishops issue statement on nation's economic policies. The National Conference of (Roman) Catholic Bishops ended a four-day meeting in Washington, D.C., after approving by a vote of 225–9 the third and final version of a 115-page statement containing their views on economics in the United States. The pastoral letter, entitled "Economic Justice for All: Catholic Social Teaching and the U.S. Economy," declared that the level of poverty in the U.S. was "a social and moral scandal." The bishops called for such changes as less military spending, an increase in the minimum wage, and an expansion of federal welfare programs. It also criticized policies of the World Bank, the International Monetary Fund, and multinational corporations.

14 Taiwan bars dissidents. The Chinese Nationalist government in Taiwan refused to admit four of seven members of the newly formed Democratic Progressive Party who had arrived at the international airport near Taipei without valid visas. A ruckus ensued when the group tried to force its way past airport officials. On November 30 a more violent confrontation occurred when several thousand people battled with police while trying to reach the airport to welcome home Hsü Hsin-liang, a leading dissident charged with treason. After spending seven years in the U.S., Hsü declared that he was returning to Taiwan, but he was not allowed to board a Taipei-bound plane during his stopover in Tokyo.

Boesky penalized $100 million. A U.S. government official announced that Ivan F. Boesky, a well-known speculator who had been accused of using illegal insider information to amass a personal fortune on Wall Street, had agreed to pay a $50 million civil penalty in addition to the $50 million he had accrued in ill-gotten gains. In addition, Boesky agreed to plead guilty to one criminal charge and would be barred for life from the U.S. securities industry. Boesky had obtained his illegal information from Dennis B. Levine, a merger specialist, who had agreed to cooperate with government investigators after his illegal activities were uncovered.

20 Chile gets World Bank loan. The World Bank approved a $250 million loan to Chile despite accusations that the government of Pres. Augusto Pinochet Ugarte was still flagrantly and repeatedly violating human rights. Italy opposed the loan, while France, Spain, and the U.S. abstained during the voting. In an unusual manifestation of discord among members of the World Bank, only 53% of the weighted vote was in favour of bolstering the Pinochet government's efforts to foster growth by increasing the country's exports, savings, and employment.

23 Aquino fires defense minister. After several weeks of persistent rumours of an impending coup and no convincing evidence that the leftist guerrillas were prepared to accept an offer of peace, Philippine Pres. Corazon Aquino took a decisive step by demanding the resignations of her entire Cabinet. She then dismissed Defense Minister Juan Ponce Enrile, one of her most vocal critics, and named Rafael Ileto, a retired general, as his successor. Enrile was widely believed to be the key figure in any attempt to oust Aquino, but the president had the firm backing of Gen. Fidel Ramos, chief of staff of the armed forces. The president also announced that she would give the rebels until the end of the month to accept her final offer of a truce. On November 24 Ileto said he would reassign rebellious officers with known ties to Enrile. On November 28 Aquino dismissed two more Cabinet ministers and said other changes were under consideration.

25 Gorbachev visits India. Indian Prime Minister Rajiv Gandhi welcomed Mikhail Gorbachev to New Delhi as the Soviet leader began a four-day visit to the subcontinent. Gorbachev was expected to offer India greater military and economic assistance. Indian officials said that new Soviet credits would be used to modernize steel plants and finance other industrial projects.

JACQUES GARDIN—SYGMA

A warehouse for storing drums of toxic chemicals at Basel, Switzerland, stands damaged by a fire that led to a chemical spill, seriously polluting the nearby Rhine River.

Negotiators for the Philippine government of Pres. Corazon Aquino and the insurgent Communist-led forces of the New People's Army rejoice at the signing of a 60-day truce in late November.
SYGMA

26 **Philippine rebels accept truce.** Leaders of the Philippine Communist insurgents and Pres. Corazon Aquino's administration formally agreed to a 60-day cease-fire commencing December 10. It would be the first formal cessation of hostilities in nearly 18 years of guerrilla warfare. The rebels, who had an estimated armed force in excess of 20,000 men, said the peace talks would have to satisfy their demand for the removal of U.S. military bases from the country. They also intended to raise such topics as human rights, land reform, foreign investments in the country, and the nation's participation in international economic institutions.

27 **French students protest.** Several hundred thousand high school and university students marched to the National Assembly in Paris and in about 50 other French cities to protest the government's plan to make the 70-odd state-run universities slightly more expensive and somewhat more selective in accepting applicants. The demonstrators, who hoped to influence the National Assembly debate, were peaceful as they denounced "the American system of elitism and inequality." With the exception of a few highly specialized schools, high school graduates had come to expect that they would automatically be admitted to whatever university they chose.

28 **U.S. exceeds 1979 arms accord.** The U.S. exceeded the limits of the strategic arms accord it had reached with the Soviet Union in 1979 when it dispatched a B-52 bomber, newly fitted to carry cruise missiles, to Carswell Air Force Base in Texas to become part of the Strategic Air Command arsenal. The accord, which had never been ratified by the U.S. Senate, had stipulated an overall ceiling of 1,320 nuclear weapons. These were defined as either bombers carrying cruise missiles or ballistic missiles with multiple warheads. Although the U.S. could revert to the former level by dismantling other long-range weapons, such as an old Poseidon missile-carrying submarine, the White House said it had no such intention.

29 **Police block Seoul protest.** Tens of thousands of South Korean police, many armed with riot gear and tear gas, disrupted a planned political demonstration in the nation's capital. The police, ordered to prevent large groups from forming, cut off segments of the downtown area from one another by blocking intersections, subway entrances, and access to major buildings. For several months members of the opposition, notably the leaders of the New Korea Democratic Party, had demanded during negotiations that the constitution be changed so that Pres. Chun Doo Hwan's successor could be chosen by popular vote. When the government could not persuade opposition leaders to accept a later date for revising the constitution, it tried in vain to dissuade them from holding the massive and potentially explosive rally they had planned. When the showdown occurred, the government's strong show of force demonstrated its determination to talk to, but not yield to, the opposition and to retain firm control over the schedule of events leading up to greater democratization of the country.

DECEMBER

6 **Taiwan voters back new party.** The Democratic Progressive Party (DPP), which had been in existence for only two months, won 12 seats in elections to Taiwan's legislative council (*yüan*) and 11 seats in the National Assembly, which every six years elected the nation's president and vice-president. Although the DPP won an unexpectedly high 23% of the popular vote, the ruling Kuomintang (Nationalist Party) captured 63% of the vote and retained firm control of all branches of government. The remaining 14% of the vote went to independents and members of two minor parties. The most popular candidate turned out to be Hsü Jung-shu, the wife of an imprisoned dissident and a member of the DPP. The next two most popular candidates were also DPP members. Hsü Kuo-tai finished in fourth place. He too was a member of the opposition and the brother of Hsü Hsin-liang, a dissident who had tried unsuccessfully to return to Taiwan in November.

8 **Chirac drops school plan.** Jacques Chirac, prime minister of France and mayor of Paris, announced he would no longer press for legislation that would increase slightly the personal cost of higher education and somewhat restrict the right of students to attend, with a few exceptions, any university of their choice. In effect, Chirac acknowledged his inability to cope with uncompromising student demonstrations even though they had been peaceful until a few individuals, suspected provocateurs, became violent.

11 **Pretoria intensifies crackdown.** The government of South Africa expanded the provisions of its June 12 emergency decree so that virtually every news report dealing directly or indirectly with apartheid first had to be approved by the government. Pretoria apparently felt that such news reports served to fuel international criticism of its racial separation policy and the measures it was taking to stifle black demands for change. The new restrictions, moreover, were so broad that virtually every type of gathering or nonconformist act could be construed as subversive and could not, therefore, be reported in any medium without government approval. Those found guilty of violating the decree would be subject to heavy fines or long imprisonment.

FREDERIQUE HIBON—SYGMA

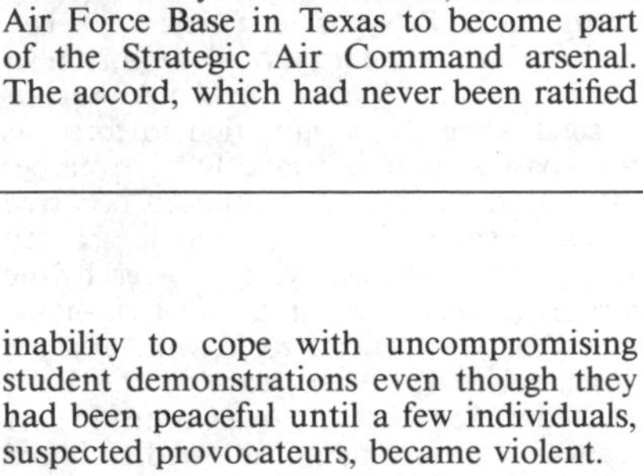

Nobel Prize-winning Soviet physicist Andrey Sakharov and his wife, Yelena Bonner, returned to Moscow after internal exile.

14 **Pakistan torn by riots.** At least 54 persons were killed and hundreds injured when ethnic Pathans attacked mostly Urdu-speaking Mohajir residents of Orangi Town, a suburb of Karachi. One social worker described the beating, stabbing, and burning of women and children, as well as men, and the random torching of homes, shops, and cars as the worst acts of barbarism he had ever witnessed. The immediate cause of the Pathans' anger appeared to be resentment over a house-to-house government search for illegal arms and drugs a few days earlier. The Mohajirs were presumed to have acted as government informers. On December 15 the death toll reached 125 as the violence spread to new areas and police and military personnel fought to bring the situation under control. With a curfew rigorously in force, the rioting subsided on December 16 after more than 150 persons had been killed. On December 30 Prime Minister Mohammad Khan Junejo's entire Cabinet resigned after a far-ranging discussion of what had happened.

15 **Trinidad and Tobago elects new leader.** General elections were held in the Caribbean nation of Trinidad and Tobago. The Elections Commission released preliminary tallies the following day showing that the ruling People's National Movement (PNM) party under Prime Minister George Chambers had been soundly defeated by the opposition National Alliance for Reconstruction (NAR) party in parliamentary elections. The NAR had so decisive a victory that it captured 33 of the 36 seats in the House of Representatives and even took away Chambers's seat in the legislature. The PNM had held power in the former British colony since 1956. After A. N. R. Robinson assumed office as Chambers's successor, he was expected to reaffirm the country's firm ties to the West.

17 **Hasenfus granted freedom.** U.S. mercenary Eugene Hasenfus was pardoned by Nicaragua's Sandinista government after being convicted on November 15 of criminal association, terrorism, and violating public order and security. He had been sentenced to 30 years in prison. Hasenfus, whose three flight companions were killed when their weapons-laden plane was shot down over southern Nicaragua on October 5, was released into the custody of Sen. Christopher Dodd (Dem., Conn.). During his trial Hasenfus testified that he had agreed to ferry arms to the Nicaraguan rebels simply because he was well paid for doing so. His release was seen in some quarters as enhancing the prestige of the Sandinistas and undermining the Reagan administration's policy in Central America.

Vietnamese leaders resign. Vietnam announced that three of its top leaders had resigned during the third Communist Party congress being held in Hanoi. Truong Chinh, the 79-year-old general secretary of the Communist Party, Pham Van Dong, who as president of the Council of Ministers held a position equivalent to that of prime minister, and Le Duc Tho, a leading member of the Politburo, all stepped aside as Vietnam prepared to attack anew its severe economic problems and wide dissatisfaction among the general populace. Nguyen Van Linh replaced Truong as head of the Communist Party, but other appointments were not made public, and might not even have been made, before the congress adjourned.

19 **Walsh to probe Iranian arms deal.** A three-judge panel in Washington, D.C., named Lawrence E. Walsh, a former federal judge, special prosecutor in charge of investigating secret U.S. arms sales to Iran, the alleged transfer of money from those sales to Nicaraguan rebels, and the role Iran was said to have played in the release of U.S. hostages held in Lebanon. After the first details of the bizarre story were published in a Lebanese magazine on November 3, there was an avalanche of revelations, conjectures, accusations, denials, refusals to comment, lapses of memory, and categorical statements by certain top U.S. officials that were in direct conflict with statements made by still other officials. Such diverse countries as Switzerland, Canada, Brunei, Panama, Israel, Saudi Arabia, and Italy were all said to have been involved, one way or another, in the incredibly complex affair. Two figures, however, appeared to possess information perhaps known to no others: Vice-Adm. John Poindexter, national security adviser to the president before he resigned on November 25, and Poindexter's aide, Lieut. Col. Oliver North, who was relieved of his duties the same day. When called to testify before the Senate Intelligence Committee behind closed doors, both men invoked their Fifth Amendment right to remain silent in order to avoid self-incrimination. Daniel Inouye (Dem., Hawaii) had already been named head of an 11-member Senate committee that would undertake its own independent investigation of the Iranian arms deal. The following day, December 17, a similar, 15-member investigative committee was set up in the House of Representatives with Lee Hamilton (Dem., Ind.) as chairman.

Sakharov granted freedom. Soviet leader Mikhail Gorbachev notified Andrey Sakharov by phone that he was free to leave his internal exile in Gorky and return to his home in Moscow. The world-renowned physicist, who had been awarded the Nobel Peace Prize in 1975 for his defense of human rights, had been banished to Gorky without trial in January 1980. The Soviet government, which had been widely criticized for its treatment of Sakharov and other dissidents, simultaneously pardoned Yelena Bonner, Sakharov's wife, who had been convicted of anti-Soviet activities in 1984.

23 **Voyager flies nonstop around the world.** Dick Rutan and Jeana Yeager made aviation history when they landed their *Voyager* aircraft at Edwards Air Force Base in California. The two U.S. pilots had just flown a total of 40,269 km (25,012 mi) at an average speed of 186.4 km/h (115.8 mph) during a nine-day nonstop flight around the world. Most remarkable of all, they made the entire voyage without refueling either on the ground or in the air. The lightweight experimental plane had been so severely battered by storms—especially as it crossed the South China Sea, Africa, and the Atlantic—that Rutan and Yeager were badly bruised and several times considered aborting the mission. When they finally arrived home, physically and mentally exhausted, they were greeted by some 40,000 cheering spectators. The plane, which took off with 454 dekalitres (1,200 gal) of gasoline, had been designed by Burt Rutan, the pilot's brother.

The experimental plane *Voyager* is checked for damage by its designer, Burt Rutan, from a twin-engine chase plane following a scrape on the runway that occurred during takeoff.

JEFFREY VOCK—VISIONS

26 **Beijing responds to protests.** City officials in Beijing (Peking), following the lead of their counterparts in Shanghai, banned further unsanctioned demonstrations by university students who for several weeks had taken to the streets to demand greater freedom. Though they articulated few demands beyond a spirited call for democracy, they complained about inflation, the way local elections were run, and the poor living conditions at the universities. Caught off guard by the discontent China's young elite had shown, government officials initially reacted with considerable restraint. They conceded that such protests were a constitutional right, but when demands for change appeared to be gathering momentum and spreading to other cities, government officials vigorously condemned "bourgeois liberalism" and warned against repeating the violence and chaos that had marked the heyday of the Red Guards during the Cultural Revolution (1966–76). Conservative officials, moreover, who had long opposed the pace and even the notion of opening China to Western influences, had been quick to warn that matters were getting out of hand. On December 27 Beijing voters were told they would be given a choice of candidates in the upcoming municipal elections. Three days later the central government ruled out price increases for a number of basic commodities. Apparently choosing to minimize the importance of such concessions, various student groups declared they would continue to press their demands by defying the government's ban on unauthorized marches. In such circumstances, a severe crackdown seemed inevitable.

People of 1986

BIOGRAPHIES

Aquino, Corazon

In the male-dominated Philippines of 1986, Corazon Aquino became more than just a household word. The mother of five and widow of opposition leader Benigno Aquino, Jr., she stepped out from behind her husband's ghost to replace dictator Ferdinand Marcos as president on February 25. Just weeks before, she had apparently lost to Marcos in voting marred by fraud and violence. But Aquino led peaceful demonstrations that—bolstered by the military rebellion of Defense Minister Juan Ponce Enrile (*q.v.*)—toppled Marcos, who had ruled the nation for two decades. The petite (1.6-m [5-ft 2-in]) new president then faced another difficult challenge: how to tackle the nation's problems without taking her eye off ambitious allies such as Enrile, who coveted her job.

Corazon Cojuangco was born Jan. 25, 1933, in Tarlac Province, into a family of bankers, landowners, and politicians. Her background enabled her to attend elite primary schools in Manila and Catholic secondary schools in the U.S. After earning a degree in mathematics and French at Mount St. Vincent College in New York, she began studying law in Manila but soon quit to marry Benigno Aquino.

During most of their marriage, she confined herself to being a housewife while he concentrated on being elected mayor, governor, and senator. According to Aquino, when her husband and his cronies talked politics, "I would never say anything . . . or contradict any of them. As far as I was concerned, I was supposed to just listen." But her role began to change in 1972, when Marcos declared martial law and imprisoned Benigno. For the next eight years, Aquino trained in Philippine politics by shuttling messages between her jailed husband and the outside world—mainly the press and his supporters. Later, living with her exiled husband in Newton, a suburb of Boston, she happily resumed her role as housewife. In August 1983, however, Benigno returned to the Philippines and was assassinated, an act that unexpectedly caused a second casualty: Mrs. Aquino's passive nature.

Buoyed by the support of more than a million petition signatures, Aquino in December 1985 entered the race against Marcos, whom she called a prime suspect in Benigno's murder. She roused the public with emotional, moralistic appeals and thus became something more than just a symbol of her slain husband. Meanwhile, Marcos played hardball, complaining that his opponent fell far short of the ideal woman "who does not challenge a man, but who keeps her criticism to herself and teaches her husband only in the bedroom." Soon afterward, Aquino's revolution rudely awakened him to 20th-century woman.

(MICHAEL AMEDEO)

ANDY HERNANDEZ—SYGMA

Arias Sánchez, Oscar

When Oscar Arias Sánchez became Costa Rica's president-elect on Feb. 2, 1986, he claimed that voters had faced a choice between bread and guns; the people, he triumphantly declared, had chosen bread. The election campaign was dominated by the issue of Costa Rica's proclaimed neutrality in Central American affairs, a policy to which Arias was strongly committed. He was not a supporter of the Communist government in neighbouring Nicaragua, but his pledge to curb the activities of anti-Sandinista *contra* forces in Costa Rica proved more appealing to the electorate than the virulently anti-Communist proclamations of his principal election rival, Rafael Angel Calderón Fournier.

The election was hard fought, with an acrimonious campaign. Arias scored an unexpectedly easy victory for the ruling centre-left National Liberation Party (PLN), taking 53% of the vote, compared with 45% for Calderón, the candidate of the Partido Unidad Social Cristiana. He was sworn into office on May 8, 1986, becoming only the second Costa Rican president in the previous 40 years to have retained power for the incumbent party. At age 44 he was the youngest president in the country's long history of stable democracy. He represented a new generation of national politicians who were pulling away from the PLN's traditional conservatism, and his choices of Cabinet and vice-ministers reflected this. One of his vice-presidents, for example, was the first woman to reach such high office.

Oscar Arias Sánchez was born in the capital, San José, on Sept. 13, 1941, into one of the country's richest coffee-elite families. He studied at the London School of Economics and in 1972 was awarded a doctorate in political economy by the University of Essex, Colchester, England. Prior to becoming president he held directorships at Costa Rica's National University, central bank, and Technological Institute. In 1972 he was appointed minister of national planning and economic policy, and in 1978 he became secretary-general of the PLN, a post that he resigned in 1981 in order to organize the successful presidential campaign of his predecessor in office, Luis Alberto Monge Álvarez. Arias faced the difficult problem of fulfilling his high-spending election promises—including a major house-building program—without antagonizing Costa Rica's international creditors.

(JANET KRENGEL)

Azcona Hoyo, José Simón

In elections held on Nov. 24, 1985, José Azcona Hoyo was elected president of Honduras for the period 1986–90. Born on Jan. 26, 1927, in the port of La Ceiba on the northern coast of Honduras, Azcona was a civil engineer by training. He graduated from the Honduran National Autonomous University and also studied at the Technological Institute for Superior Studies in Monterrey, Mexico. He held several important posts as a student and subsequently served as director of the Liberal Action Front from 1962 to 1974. He was a candidate for Congress in the department of Francisco Morazán for the planned October 1963 general elections, which were canceled because of a military coup.

In 1973 Azcona became the coordinator of the Liberal Engineers of the Rodista Liberal Movement (MLR), a faction of the Liberal Party, and in 1975 he was chosen as secretary of organization and publicity for the Central Directorate of the faction. Two years later he became a member of the Central Executive Committee of the Liberal Party as secretary for political training, rising to the committee's presidency in 1983. From 1973 to 1982 he was also general manager of the Honduran Federation of Housing Cooperatives Ltd., prior to which he had worked in industrial engineering and on roads and electrical engineering in the public sector.

Azcona was responsible for the organization and publicity of the Central Executive Committee in the Liberal Party's successful campaign in the National Constituent Assembly elections of 1980. After the Liberal Party won the 1981 general elections, he became general secretary of the Central Directorate of the MLR. He was chosen as coordinator of the commission supporting Roberto Suazo Córdova's successful candidacy for the 1982–86 presidency, and Azcona himself won a seat in the National Congress. During the period 1982–83 he held two ministerial posts—of communications and public works and transportation—before resigning because of President Suazo's attempts to centralize the Liberal Party.

In his own presidential campaign Azcona was supported by the MLR and the Popular Liberal Alliance, a separate Liberal faction. In the November 1985 elections the Liberal Party won a majority of the votes and Azcona the highest number of votes among Liberal candidates. He was officially confirmed as president on Dec. 24, 1985, and sworn in on Jan. 27, 1986.

(BEN BOX)

Baker, Kenneth Wilfred

Within less than a year of his promotion to the British Cabinet, the talk was of Kenneth Baker as a possible Conservative prime minister in succession to Margaret Thatcher. He came into the Cabinet as secretary of state for the environment in the reshuffle of September 1985, and in May 1986 he was promoted to succeed Sir Keith Joseph as education secretary. The move assured that his name would remain in the headlines.

At the Department of the Environment his chief task had been to carry through the abolition of the Greater London Council (GLC) in the face of an inspired, and expensive, antiabolition publicity campaign conducted by GLC Labour leader Ken Livingstone. The task enabled Baker to demonstrate his talents as a presenter of policy, an ability Thatcher had come to rate highly as the government lurched through its midterm troubles. Baker was also handed the controversial issue of household rates (property tax) reform and found himself with the task of defending nuclear safety following the disaster at the Chernobyl nuclear power plant in the U.S.S.R.

His successful handling of these assignments made him an obvious choice to succeed Joseph, who had presided over what had become a crisis in the secondary school system. Baker's first task on his appointment in May was to defuse the issue of education as a potential vote-loser for the government at the coming general elections (due before mid-1988). This meant settling the long-running dispute over teachers' pay. He extracted a substantial fund from the Treasury and then threatened to impose, if necessary, a pay deal structured toward the improvement of teaching standards. His own contribution toward this end was to give poetry lessons during his ministerial visits to schools; he had published a slim volume of poems himself.

Born Nov. 3, 1934, at Newport, Wales, Baker was educated at Magdalen College, University of Oxford. He won election to the House of Commons at a by-election in 1968. His rapid promotion in 1985–86 contrasted with his treatment during the early part of the Thatcher administration. As parliamentary private secretary to Edward Heath when he was deposed as leader of the Conservative Party by Thatcher (1975), Baker was not—as she would say—"one of us." Excluded from her first government, he wrote her a letter urging the importance of information technology, with the result that, in 1981, she made him responsible for it.

(PETER JENKINS)

Barco Vargas, Virgilio

Following the biggest landslide victory in the country's electoral history, Virgilio Barco Vargas became president of Colombia on Aug. 7, 1986, for a four-year term. Born in Cúcuta, Norte de Santander Department, on Sept. 17, 1921, Barco completed his undergraduate training in engineering at the National University of Colombia and qualified as a civil engineer at the Massachusetts Institute of Technology. He obtained a master's degree in social sciences from Boston University in 1952.

Barco began his professional career as secretary of public works and of finance in Norte de Santander in 1943. Two years later he became secretary of the Ministry of Communications and entered politics as councillor and president of the Council of Durania. He subsequently held other councillor positions, including that of Bogotá in 1970–72 and 1976–78. He was also

UPI/BETTMANN NEWSPHOTOS

twice elected a member of the House of Representatives and twice a senator between 1949 and 1978. He held Cabinet positions as minister of public works during 1958–61 and minister of agriculture in 1962–64. Besides undertaking several special ambassadorial missions, he was ambassador to the U.K. in 1961–62 and to the U.S. in 1977–80. Barco was an executive director for the World Bank from 1968 until 1974, when he became a member of Colombia's Foreign Relations Advisory Committee for four years. It was the way in which he performed his duties as mayor of Bogotá during 1966–69, however, that earned Barco his reputation as a hard worker and an excellent administrator. In August 1985 the national convention named him presidential candidate and national director of the Liberal Party.

In the May presidential elections, Barco obtained 58% of the vote. This strong mandate, together with a Liberal-dominated Congress, prompted him to end nearly three decades of power sharing between Liberals and Conservatives and to form a totally Liberal government. His policies were based on a social market economy with an efficient state to guide market forces toward improved welfare. Eradication of poverty and job creation were the stated priorities of his administration.

(ALEXANDER JOHNS CAMPBELL)

Barrow, Errol Walton

A sweeping election victory for the Democratic Labour Party (DLP) returned Errol Barrow to power as prime minister of Barbados on May 28, 1986, ending ten years of rule by the rival Barbados Labour Party (BLP). For Barrow, who had served three terms as premier and prime minister between 1961 and 1976, it was a triumphant return from the low point of the mid-1970s, when the BLP, under the leadership of J. M. G. ("Tom") Adams, had capitalized on economic discontent to win power.

Barrow was first elected to Parliament as a BLP member in 1951, but he became disillusioned with the party's conservatism and in 1955 helped found the DLP. His administration took Barbados into independence in 1966 and remained in power until 1976, when he lost popularity as a result of the deterioration in the economy that followed the oil price rise of the early 1970s. Barrow's moves to increase the government's influence on judicial appointments also proved damaging, and the BLP won 17 out of 24 seats in the 1976 election.

Born on Jan. 21, 1920, Barrow was educated in Barbados. His studies were cut short by the outbreak of World War II; he joined the Royal Air Force and piloted more than 50 missions over Western Europe. After the war he qualified as a barrister at Lincoln's Inn and then obtained an economics degree at the London School of Economics. He returned to Barbados in 1950 and entered politics a year later.

An energetic advocate of regional integration, Barrow was influential in the foundation of the Caribbean Free Trade Association, which later became the Caribbean Community and Common Market (Caricom). Following his election in 1986 he made efforts to resolve difficulties within Caricom, notably those with Trinidad and Tobago. Together with Prime Minister James Mitchell of St. Vincent and the Grenadines, he strongly opposed upgrading of the Regional Security System, particularly by means of a formal treaty, and he was also against any increase in U.S. influence over Barbados and the region as a whole. Barrow appeared intent on strengthening intraregional economic links and on diversifying Barbadian trade and financial relations, singling out Asia as a likely source of investment. (ROD PRINCE)

Bhutto, Benazir

The return to Pakistan in 1986 of Benazir Bhutto, the elder daughter of Pakistan's former prime minister Zulfikar Ali Bhutto, was marked by both jubilation and the worst violence the country had witnessed in many years. Since the death of her father in 1979, Benazir Bhutto had become the titular head of the Pakistan People's Party (PPP), but her political commitment had frequently been the cause of severe social unrest, and much of her life had been spent under house arrest or in exile in Europe. She was recognized as the only real threat to the government, but at the same time the PPP lacked solidarity and there were doubts as to whether she had sufficient political support to keep the country united.

Born in Karachi on June 21, 1953, Benazir was educated at Harvard University (1969–73) and subsequently at Oxford. After graduating from the latter with a degree in philosophy, politics, and economics in 1976, she became the first Asian woman president of the Oxford Union in 1977.

She returned to Pakistan in mid-1977, but within days of her arrival a military coup ousted her father from power. Bhutto was imprisoned in September 1977 and executed in 1979 on the grounds that he had conspired to murder a party

ANDY HERNANDEZ—SYGMA

colleague. From the time of her father's first imprisonment until 1984 when she was allowed to leave the country, Benazir was often under house arrest. She returned from exile in London in April 1986, free once again to take up the political challenge. Martial law in Pakistan had been lifted at the end of 1985, and political freedom was restored simultaneously. Benazir received a rapturous welcome, but her challenge to Pres. Zia-ul-Haq to hold elections later that year went unheeded. To her supporters she pledged revolution, the handover of power to the people, and a reversal of the Islamic policies that had been introduced by Zia's government.

The jubilation was short-lived, however. By June there were major splits in the PPP, and Benazir's own commitment to freedom and a mixed economy was being doubted. The lack of response to her call for a "Black Day" to mark the ninth anniversary of the overthrow of her father reflected growing disillusion. Fears of repression and instability were being expressed, and political rallies more and more resulted in violence. Increasing confrontation between Benazir and the government culminated, following her address to a banned Independence Day rally on August 14, in the worst violence in several years. She was arrested and served most of a 30-day sentence before being released under a general amnesty. (JANET H. CLARK)

Binnig, Gerd

For developing the scanning tunneling microscope (STM), two scientists at the IBM Zürich Research Laboratory, Gerd Binnig of West Germany and Heinrich Rohrer (*q.v.*) of Switzerland, divided half of the Nobel Prize for Physics in 1986. (Ernst Ruska [*q.v.*] of West Germany won the other half of the prize for inventing the electron microscope.) The STM produces images of the surfaces of conducting or semiconducting materials in such fine detail that individual atoms and even smaller features can be clearly identified.

Binnig, the youngest among the Nobel Prize winners of 1986, was born on July 20, 1947, in Frankfurt, West Germany. He graduated from the Johann Wolfgang Goethe University in Frankfurt, earned a Ph.D. in physics from the University of Frankfurt in 1978, and then joined the IBM Zürich Research Laboratory, where he and Rohrer designed and built the first STM.

During the operation of the STM an electric current passes between the surface being studied and a tungsten probe that is moved in a path covering a selected area. The strength of this current depends on the distance of the probe from the surface, and this distance is kept constant by measuring the current and using it to control the position of the probe. To form an image sharp enough to reveal single atoms, the tip of the probe itself must consist of a single atom, and its elevation above the surface must be monitored with a precision of a few hundredths of an angstrom (the diameter of an atom is about one angstrom, or a ten-billionth of a metre). The probe is steered through its invisible motions by minutely altering the lengths of the legs of a supporting tripod; these legs are made of a piezoelectric material that changes its dimensions under the influence of an electric field. An elaborate suspension system is required to protect the STM from the disastrous consequences of even the slightest vibrations.

(JOHN V. KILLHEFFER)

Black, Barbara Aronstein
When Barbara Aronstein Black assumed her post in February 1986 as the new dean of Columbia Law School, she was making history as the first woman to head a major private American law school. An authority on law in colonial America, legal historian and scholar, mother of three, and one of Columbia's most popular professors, she defined herself as a woman "who took on the traditional duties and obligations and joys of the woman's role, who traveled a terribly circuitous path back to the job that she had always wanted, whose work was not of the quantity that the more direct male path would have produced. . . . I really do believe that where I am today has *everything* to do with the years that I spent hanging on to a career by my fingernails." Black succeeded Benno C. Schmidt, Jr., who was named president of Yale University.

Barbara Aronstein was born May 6, 1933, in Brooklyn, N.Y. She earned her B.A. from Brooklyn College in 1953 and was one of the few women (15% of the class) in Columbia's law school class of 1955. Married in 1954 to Charles L. Black, Jr., then a Columbia law professor, she spent the nine years following graduation from Columbia raising their children. In 1965 she began work on a doctorate at Yale but remained intent on balancing family with career goals. After receiving her doctorate in history, she became an assistant professor of history at Yale in 1976, joined the law faculty in 1979 as an associate professor, returned to Columbia as a visiting professor in the spring of 1984, and by fall had been made a full professor. At the time of her appointment as dean, she was working on a book on contract theory, a constitutional history of 17th-century Massachusetts, and a two-volume edition of the Massachusetts General Court judicial proceedings from 1634 to 1696.

An avid baseball fan and ballet buff, Black described her initial goals for the elite, thriving law school she now headed as modest. She found few flaws with the way Columbia had been operating but acknowledged the need for some changes in curriculum and faculty appointments. She believed a law school's strength was its faculty and considered the venerated Ivy League institution ideal for teaching law. Yet another personal goal emerged for Dean Barbara Black as she began her stewardship: "Now I would like to help persuade society that it should not be as difficult as it is for women to succeed at home and work both."

(BONNIE OBERMAN)

Bourassa, Robert
Four days after his Liberal Party lost the 1976 Quebec election to the Parti Quebecois, Premier Robert Bourassa abruptly quit politics. On Dec. 12, 1985, he was again sworn in as premier of Quebec, culminating a long campaign to recapture his former position. In 1980 Bourassa had returned from his self-imposed exile to campaign against independence for Quebec in the referendum on that issue. After regaining the leadership of the Quebec Liberals on Oct. 15, 1983, he worked at rebuilding the party before winning a seat in the Quebec National Assembly in June 1985. He lost that seat in the December 1985 election but returned to the Assembly after winning a by-election in January 1986.

Born on July 14, 1933, in Montreal, Bourassa received his degree in law from the University of Montreal, winning the Governor General's Medal for standing first in the class of 1956. He received his M.A. in political economy from the University of Oxford (1959) and his LL.M. in corporate and tax law from Harvard (1960). Returning to Canada, Bourassa became a fiscal adviser to the Canadian government (1960–63) and then secretary and research director of the Bélanger Commission on Taxation (1963–65).

First elected to the Quebec National Assembly in 1966, Bourassa became the leader of the Quebec Liberal Party and the youngest premier in Quebec history in 1970. The greatest monument of his years as premier (1970–76) was the massive James Bay hydroelectric project, built to supply electricity to Quebec and the northeastern U.S. Soon after he assumed office, however, radical terrorism caused the imposition of martial law in the province, and in 1971 he refused to sign a constitutional agreement with the other provincial premiers, leading to a weakening of Quebec's position in the Canadian confederation. Perceived by the voters as a weak leader and a lacklustre federalist at a time of emerging Quebec nationalism, Bourassa lost the 1976 election to the Parti Quebecois and its platform of independence for Quebec.

After leaving politics in 1976, Bourassa accepted several university lectureships in Europe, the U.S., and Canada. By 1983, when he regained the Liberal leadership, he had dispelled his image as a weak leader. His 1985 election platform was almost the same as his 1970 election platform: implementing measures to produce economic recovery for the province and gaining concessions from the Canadian federal government before signing the Canadian constitution on Quebec's behalf.

(DIANE LOIS WAY)

Bradley, Pat
When Pat Bradley broke the career-earnings record for women golfers in 1986, it was as if she had sneaked up on it unnoticed. For 13 professional seasons she had been overlooked as merely a performer in an era that favoured personalities.

The consistency and concentration that carried Bradley to success also kept her off centre stage. She marched straight to the top with her head down. She did not sell shampoo or sex appeal. She was not comfortable joking with galleries. She just played golf as well as any woman and better than most.

"I'm a very private person," Bradley said. "I do not go out of my way to get my name into papers. I'm very serious on and off the course. I want to be the top player in women's golf."

Golf never was supposed to be as easy as Bradley made it look. She conquered a course as routinely as mowing the lawn. She drove down the middle of the fairway and putted into the hole without a ripple of outward emotion. "If I could steal something from Pat, I'd swipe her concentration," said Muffin Spencer-Devlin, another competitor on the Ladies Professional Golf Association (LPGA) tour.

Bradley established a standard of consistency that included nine straight $100,000 years in earnings, another LPGA record. In 365 events she finished 206 in the top ten, 147 in the top five, 42 in second place, and 21 as champion, including six majors. She missed only three 36-hole cuts in ten years.

But she was never neck-turning spectacular until 1986, when her five tournament victories included three of the four majors, tying a 36-year-old record. Besides raising her career earnings to $2,286,218, she won a record $492,021 for the year. She won a $125,000 bonus for leading the points standings, helped by five victories and six second-place finishes in 27 events, and her 71.1 strokes per 18 holes also led the tour. She also won her first player of the year award.

Bradley was born March 24, 1951, in Westford, Mass. She was Westford Academy's best player in field hockey, softball, and basketball and showed world-class promise in skiing before deciding at 17 to concentrate on golf. After making all-America as Florida International University's only woman golfer, Bradley won the qualifying tournament for the LPGA tour in 1974.

(KEVIN M. LAMB)

Branson, Richard
Richard Branson was one of the U.K.'s business stars. His entrepreneurial flair and enterprise had produced an almost unbroken record of successful business ventures for almost half of his 36-year lifetime. His achievements and flamboyant style made him increasingly the focus of media attention. Born July 18, 1950, in Surrey, England, where in Shamley Green, near Guildford, he spent his early life, Branson was educated at Stowe School. It was there that he was inspired to launch a national newspaper, and he spent much of his time while still at school finding contributors and selling advertising. On leaving school at age 15, he had already secured more than £3,000 in advertising revenue, and in 1968 the first issue of *Student* appeared. It sold 50,000 copies.

Student gave Branson the grounding and experience in business that was to contribute to his phenomenal success. It also gave birth to what was to become a multibillion-pound enterprise—Virgin—when an advertisement for inexpensive records brought such a response that it quickly generated a mail-order business in discount records. The business mushroomed until 1970, when it was threatened by a postal strike. To avert a possible financial collapse, Branson moved quickly into direct retailing, and on Jan. 1, 1971, he opened his first shop. The success of the central London outlet led to the opening of such shops all over the U.K. In 1972 Branson's next Virgin endeavour, a recording company, had its first release.

When business conditions deteriorated in the mid-1970s, Branson engaged the Sex Pistols rock group to revitalize the market. Business again boomed, and Virgin shops were opened in some 20 countries. In 1984 he diversified notably from the Virgin Group's mainstream activities of records, videos, and retailing when he launched the airline Virgin Atlantic. When in November 1986 Branson's Virgin Group was floated on the U.K. stock exchange, the annual turnover had reached £325 million (1985) and the group was employing 2,500 people. Earlier in 1986 Branson was put in charge of a government project to clean up Britain, and in June he captained his *Virgin Atlantic Challenger II* powerboat when it broke the record for crossing the Atlantic. As the year drew to a close, he took up yet another challenge when Virgin, together with the Granada Group, Pearson Group, Amstrad Consumer Electronics, and Anglia Television, formed British Satellite Broadcasting, which in December was awarded a 15-year franchise to operate a direct broadcasting satellite—the first in the world to be privately financed. The consortium planned to begin transmissions in 1990.

(JANET H. CLARK)

Brundtland, Gro Harlem
Gro Harlem Brundtland, leader of the Labour Party, started her second stint as Norway's prime minister in May 1986, following the resignation of the Conservative-led minority coalition. She had made history in February 1981 when she became Norway's first woman prime minister and the first woman to lead its largest political party. Her first spell in office was brief. She replaced Odvar Nordli, forced to retire by ill health, at a time when Labour was split on many issues, its fortunes fading, and parliamentary elections only seven months away. Under her firm leadership, party unity improved, but there was too much ground to be made up in the opinion polls, and in the September 1981 elections Labour lost office.

In 1986, as in 1981, Brundtland faced serious problems on taking office. This time, however, they concerned the country as a whole. The collapse of world petroleum prices had removed the main support of Norway's prosperity, with disastrous consequences for both government

UPI/BETTMANN NEWSPHOTOS

revenues and the balance of trade. She warned that austerity was "an inadequate term for the vast economic restructuring" that the country needed. Labour, she added, would have to discard the program of expansion on which it had campaigned half a year earlier, before the oil price slide.

The Cabinet she appointed was radical in only two respects—it contained a record number of women (8 out of 18), and its members had an average age of only 46.5 years. Otherwise, the ministers chosen belonged mostly to Labour's centre or right wing, like Brundtland herself. She represented the growing faction of middle-class academics in the party leadership, as opposed to the working-class, self-educated trade union officials who had previously held the reins. Brundtland believed keenly in the need for women to play a greater role in politics, where "women's values" were badly needed. Another of her major interests was in the environment.

Born in Oslo on April 20, 1939, the daughter of a former Labour government minister, Gro Harlem married Arne Olav Brundtland in 1960, while at medical school in Oslo. She left medicine for politics in September 1974, when she was invited to become environment minister in the Labour government. In October 1979 she left that job to become deputy chairman of Labour's parliamentary group and chairman of the important Foreign Affairs Committee of the Storting (parliament). (FAY GJESTER)

Buchanan, James M.

Cited for developing new methods for the analysis of economic and political decision making, especially those involving "public choice theory" pertaining to government spending, James M. Buchanan of George Mason University in Fairfax, Va., was the 14th American in 17 years to be awarded the Nobel Memorial Prize in Economic Science. Public choice theory, which applies economic method to the problems of political science, was regarded as a major influence on the 1986 U.S. tax reform. Sometimes viewed as outside the mainstream of economic theory, Buchanan strove to explain how governments make economic policy decisions—much as traditional economists evaluate consumer and business attitudes. He was, in fact, so deeply involved in tying together economics and politics that his selection as winner of the $290,000 Economics Prize surprised several of his colleagues.

Buchanan was involved with such issues as rewards or costs to politicians and/or voters for particular changes in public expenditures and the need for long-range planning involving broad-based interests rather than piecemeal political compromises. He believed there was no reason to assume that government intervention is beneficial economically—a small-government view with obvious appeal to conservatives. He also believed that huge budget deficits can cause enormous damage, and his ideas contributed to the campaign for a constitutional amendment mandating a balanced U.S. federal budget.

James Buchanan was born in 1919 in Tennessee, where his grandfather had been governor from 1891 to 1893. He studied at Middle Tennessee State University and the University of Tennessee and then, after five years in the Navy, went on to the University of Chicago to receive his doctorate. His interest in combining economic and political analyses began in 1956 when he was a professor at the University of Virginia in Charlottesville. For 12 years he directed the university's centre for studies in political economy and social philosophy. After a brief time at UCLA, he became a professor at the Virginia Polytechnic Institute and a founder of the Center for Study of Public Choice. In 1982 the centre, and Buchanan, moved to George Mason University. He was the author of numerous book reviews and articles as well as some 20 monographs and books, the best known being *The Calculus of Consent* (with Gordon Tullock; 1962). (BONNIE OBERMAN)

Bujak, Zbigniew

On May 31, 1986, the speaker of Warsaw Television announced triumphantly that Zbigniew Bujak, the 31-year-old "enemy of the Polish People's Republic," had finally been caught. He had been the highest ranking official of the banned trade-union movement Solidarnosc (Solidarity) to evade capture. While the secret police celebrated the exploit, many Poles heard the news with chagrin. "Zbyszek"—as he was generally called—had escaped the authorities for 4 years and 132 days; the facility with which he had been able to secure refuge during that period, and the fact that he was never betrayed, were a measure of his popularity. On September 12 he was freed together with 225 other political prisoners.

Born Nov. 29, 1954, at Lopuszno, a village in Kielce Province, Bujak was the 13th child of a peasant family. When he was three years old, his father sold his farm and moved with the family to Ursus, near Warsaw, where a tractor factory was being enlarged. Both father and son were practicing Roman Catholics, and both declined to join the Communist Party. The young Bujak was called to military service in 1976; healthy and athletic, he was enlisted in a parachute regiment. As his commanding officers noticed his ability to command and to organize, they encouraged him to choose a military career. He told them that he had already chosen to be a mechanical engineer.

Immediately on his return to Ursus, Bujak joined the KOR (Committee for the Defense of Workers), founded in 1976 by a group of Polish intellectuals. When Solidarity was born in August 1980, its charismatic leader, Lech Walesa, appointed the 26-year-old Bujak to organize the region of Mazowsze, of which Warsaw was the chief town. At the first meeting of the region's delegates in September 1981, Bujak was elected president by 80% of the vote. In the meantime, the authorities were preparing to crush Solidarity. The following month Gen. Wojciech Jaruzelski was elected first secretary of the Polish United Workers' (Communist) Party, and two months later he proclaimed martial law. When the authorities occupied all Solidarity's offices and arrested over 5,000 leaders and officials, a few dozen—Bujak among them—escaped internment. A week later he organized the underground Provisional Commission of Coordination, the main task of which was to keep alive the Solidarity network. (K. M. SMOGORZEWSKI)

Burns, George

If the Americans, like the Japanese, designated certain citizens as national treasures, George Burns would surely have attained that status. The popular comedian, who marked his 90th birthday on Jan. 20, 1986, had entertained vaudeville, motion-picture, radio, and television audiences for some 80 years. About 30 of those were spent as half of the Burns and Allen comedy team, in which Gracie Allen played the scatterbrained female who charmed with her senselessness, and George (her husband in real life) was her exasperated "straight man."

George Burns was born Nathan Birnbaum in New York City on Jan. 20, 1896. He had 11 siblings, and after their father died, he left school at age 13 to help support the family. He organized a group of child singers (who passed the hat for remuneration) and then began appearing in vaudeville. Burns met Gracie Allen in the early 1920s, when she was already a vaudeville performer in her own right. She joined Burns's act, and he, recognizing her natural abilities as a comedienne, changed his own role to complement her "dizzy dame" character. They were married in 1926 and soon afterward signed a six-year contract that led to performances in both the U.S. and Europe. In 1930 they joined Eddie Cantor, George Jessel, and other stars in a nine-week vaudeville celebration in New York. A year later they signed a contract with Paramount Pictures, beginning a long motion-picture career with *The Big Broadcast* (1932). The pair's extraordinarily successful radio career got under way the same year, and during its 20-year span their show attracted an estimated 45 million-plus listeners.

KIP RANO—GAMMA/LIAISON

With the advent of television, Burns and Allen successfully transferred to the new medium with a biweekly CBS series called "The George Burns and Gracie Allen Show" that began in November 1950. After Gracie retired in 1958 (she died in 1964), Burns began his own TV series entitled "The George Burns Show," and he made sporadic appearances throughout the '60s. But it was in 1975 that his second career took off, when his portrayal of an aging vaudeville performer in the movie *The Sunshine Boys* won him an Academy Award for best supporting actor. Two years later he had another hit, playing a harried God in *Oh, God!* Other movies followed, including *Sergeant Pepper's Lonely Hearts Club Band* (1978) and the latest in what had become the "Oh, God!" series, *Oh, God! You Devil* (1984). Suddenly the octogenarian with the trademark cigar had become a hot property. "I'm going to stay in show business," he said, "until I'm the only one left." (BONNIE OBERMAN)

Burrows, Eva

On May 2, 1986, the High Council of the Salvation Army elected Eva Burrows to become general and world leader. She succeeded Gen. Jarl Wahlström in the office on July 9. As general, she commanded the worldwide forces of the Salvation Army, giving spiritual and administrative oversight and direction to the movement. She was the 13th and youngest general and only the second woman to hold this responsibility. Her positive style in organization was matched by her forthright proclamation of the gospel, her motto for the years ahead being "Christ for the World."

Born Sept. 17, 1929, in Newcastle, Australia, to Salvation Army parents, Burrows committed her life to God for service as a Salvation Army officer while studying at the University of Queensland. She entered the William Booth Memorial Training College in London in 1950 and was commissioned an officer in 1951. Within months of receiving her commission she was appointed to Rhodesia (now Zimbabwe) as an educator, serving for 17 years at the Salvation Army's Howard Institute. She took a particular interest in the training of black teachers and later undertook a course at the University of Sydney for the degree of master of education, presenting her thesis on the training of African teachers from Zimbabwe. Upon her return to that country, she became a consultant to the government Education Department.

In 1970 Burrows was appointed to London, where she spent five years at the International College for Officers, first as vice-principal and then as principal. There she gained a deep insight into the internationality of the Salvation Army. In 1975 she became leader of the Women's Social Services in Great Britain and Ireland. Burrows looked back on that particular appointment as having given her "a sensitivity to the lost and lonely, the disadvantaged and deprived of the great crowded cities of Britain."

In January 1977 there began for Burrows a period of territorial command that culminated in her election as general. As territorial commander she was both the spiritual and administrative leader of the Salvation Army's forces. Her first command, in Sri Lanka, was followed by three years in Scotland and four years in the Southern Territory of her native Australia. The establishment of "Employment 2000," an imaginative program for unemployed youth, was one example of the significant and innovative initiatives that characterized her leadership style during that period. (ROB GARRAD)

Carlsson, Ingvar Gösta

The man who took over as prime minister of Sweden following the assassination of Olof Palme on Feb. 28, 1986, was a calm and cautious individual, possessed of neither charisma nor great powers of oratory, in marked contrast to his predecessor. Before his formal swearing-in on March 12, Ingvar Carlsson had always chosen to remain very much in the background, deputy to Palme and almost totally obscured by the giant shadow he cast.

While Palme was from an upper-class, privileged family, Carlsson's origins were pure working class. His father, Olof, and his mother, Ida, were factory workers. His great love was soccer, which he continued to play. Born Nov. 9, 1934, in the town of Borås, Carlsson attended commercial high school and then went on to take a degree in political science at the University of Lund in 1958. During the period 1958–60 he was, like Palme, one of "Erlander's boys," part of the group of bright young men working with Prime Minister Tage Erlander. After spending a year studying in the U.S. in 1961, Carlsson returned to Sweden to become chairman of the Social Democratic Youth Movement.

CAMERA PRESS LTD.

At the age of 31 he was elected to the Riksdag (parliament), and three years later he graduated to the post of undersecretary in the Cabinet Office. In 1969, the year Palme took over the party leadership and the premiership, Carlsson was appointed minister of education. In 1973 he was made minister of housing. In 1976, when the Social Democrats lost power after 44 years in office, Palme gave Carlsson the job of orchestrating the party's return to power, coupled with the task of preparing a master plan to put the economy on a sounder footing.

When the party returned to power in 1982, Carlsson received his reward. He became deputy prime minister and, as Palme's personal troubleshooter, occupied himself with a study of possible future strategies for the Social Democrats. When the party won again in 1985, he was appointed minister of the environment. After taking over the premiership, he pursued a predictably cautious path, his biggest triumph being victory over public-sector labour union militancy in late 1986. (CHRIS MOSEY)

Carr, Shirley

On May 1, 1986, Shirley Carr was elected president of the Canadian Labour Congress, a national union federation with a membership of almost 100 Canadian trade unions representing over two million workers. Carr was the first woman and the first public-sector unionist to head the Congress. Dedicated and forceful, she would find her diplomatic skills of use in achieving her first goal as president: returning unity to the Canadian labour movement.

A politician at heart, Carr was once a candidate for a seat in the Ontario legislature (1971). However, she devoted most of her career to the labour movement. In 1960, while employed as a social worker in Niagara Falls, Ont., Carr joined the Canadian Union of Public Employees (CUPE). She was instrumental in forming a local to represent the municipal employees of her area and was the first president of that local (1970–74). Carr was first elected to the Ontario executive and national executive of CUPE in 1967, and by 1974 she had risen to president of the Ontario division. Shirley Carr was the first woman elected to the 38-member executive of the Canadian Labour Congress (1974). From her first position as executive vice-president for research and legislation, economics, and government employees, she rose to be secretary-treasurer of the Congress before being elected president.

Born in May 1929 in Niagara Falls, Ont., Shirley Geraldine Edwina Carr was never one to allow someone else to speak for her, but she felt a commitment to work for those people who could not look out for themselves. She worked in the welfare department in Niagara Falls as a field investigator and welfare caseworker and in 1984 served on a Canadian government Advisory Committee on Prison Inmate Employment. For her contribution to vocational/technical education, she received the Centennial Medal of the Canadian Organization for Rehabilitation Through Training.

In 1974 Carr was made a delegate to the American regional conference of the International Labour Organization (ILO), a UN organization with representatives of governments, workers' organizations, and employers. From 1980 to 1985 she was a member of the ILO's Governing Body—its first female voting member. She was chairman of the workers' group on the Committee on Discrimination and the workers' spokesman on the Committee on Apartheid. In 1980 the Canadian government made her an Officer of the Order of Canada.

(DIANE LOIS WAY)

Cerezo Arévalo, Marco Vinicio

On Jan. 14, 1986, Marco Vinicio Cerezo Arévalo of the Christian Democrats (DCG) became Guatemala's first freely elected civilian president since 1970 and only the second since 1954. Presidential and congressional elections held on Nov. 3, 1985, showed Cerezo to be the most popular candidate, although he failed to gain the 50% majority required to secure the presidency; a second round on December 8 proved conclusive when he won 68% of the vote.

The son of a member of Guatemala's Supreme Court, Vinicio Cerezo was born in Guatemala City on Dec. 26, 1942. Like his father he studied law, beginning his own rise to political prominence in the DCG while still a student at the University of San Carlos, Guatemala City. He eventually became his party's national organization secretary, traveling extensively throughout the country. For several generations Cerezo's family had actively opposed military dictatorship, and his determination to see his country restored to stable democratic rule was fired at the age of 11, when he witnessed the coup aided by the U.S. Central Intelligence Agency in 1954.

While Cerezo described himself as an independently minded liberal not bound by party orthodoxy, his right-wing opponents perceived him as a leftist. Since 1980 three attempts on his life had been made by the notorious death squads—a reminder of the power wielded by Guatemala's military and paramilitary.

The most notable achievements of this witty and debonair president were in the field of international and regional relations. On a trip to Washington in December 1985, Cerezo won the respect of the U.S. administration, ensuring the resumption of U.S. economic assistance, and a tour of Western European countries late in 1986 was equally successful. The formation of a Central American parliament, aimed at resolving regional conflict, was the result of a Cerezo initiative, and in May he was host to a preliminary summit of regional leaders. The major challenges facing him in his five-year term of office were to reverse Guatemala's economic decline and to improve living standards for the landless peasantry without incurring the wrath, and political might, of the large landowners.

(JANET KRENGEL)

Channon, (Henry) Paul Guinness

As a general rule, Old Etonians had not flown high in the Conservative Party government of Prime Minister Margaret Thatcher, and Paul Channon was no exception. Passed over in 1983 when Norman Tebbit succeeded Cecil Parkinson as secretary of state for trade and industry and again when Leon Brittan was demoted to that post from the Home Office in the 1985 reshuffle, Channon seemed destined to remain number two. He finally entered the Cabinet in January 1986 when Brittan suddenly left it, a casualty of the crisis over the future of a helicopter company that had become known as the "Westland affair." Channon had some experience in taking over at short notice and in difficult circumstances, for he had run this huge conglomerate department while Tebbit recovered from the injuries he received when the Irish Republican Army bombed a hotel in Brighton during the Conservative Party conference in October 1984.

Within days of his taking over in 1986, a great parliamentary row broke over the plans of his predecessor—of which Channon allegedly knew little—to sell the constituent parts of the nationalized British Leyland motor company to U.S. companies, including its much-loved Land Rover division to General Motors. Channon's unabrasive, gentlemanly manners were appropriate to the task of conducting the undignified retreat from his predecessor's policies that subsequently took place.

Born Oct. 9, 1935, in London and educated at Christ Church, University of Oxford, Channon entered Parliament at the age of 23, virtually inheriting his Southend-on-Sea (Essex) constituency from his father, Sir Henry ("Chips") Channon, a brilliant gossip and socialite who had married into the Guinness family. Not only did this make Paul Channon (who also married a Guinness) a millionaire, it also—he joked—gave him a certain immunity while serving as minister of state in the Northern Ireland Office (1972). "The Irish will never shoot a Guinness," he said. In his early career he acted as parliamentary private secretary (1960–62) to R. A. Butler when he was home secretary, and in successive administrations he held various junior appointments. By the end of 1986 it was impossible to say whether he would make his mark at Cabinet level. It had been rumoured that he would be demoted once the Westland crisis had passed, but he survived what was, very probably, the final reshuffle before the next general elections. (PETER JENKINS)

Chiang Ching-kuo

In 1986 important changes took place in Taiwan under the leadership of Chiang Ching-kuo, president of the Republic of China and chairman of the ruling Nationalist Party, the Kuomintang (KMT). Declaring his determination to bar military rule and any of his family members from succeeding him as president, he announced in October that martial law and the ban on organized political opposition would soon be lifted. Reversing a downward trend in economic development, Chiang took steps that restored Taiwan's economic prosperity and its huge trade surplus. An opposition group, the Democratic Progressive Party, was allowed to come into existence in September and compete with the KMT in the December parliamentary elections. The balloting, believed to have been generally honest, went a long way toward establishing a multiparty democratic system in Taiwan. The winds of change finally began blowing in Nationalist China.

Born into the family of Chiang Kai-shek on March 18, 1910, in Fenghua County, Chekiang, Chiang studied in the Soviet Union (1925–37) before working for five years in southern Kiangsi as a regional commissioner. After World War II he attempted without success to carry out sweeping economic and financial reforms by curbing hyperinflation, speculation, and black markets. After the Nationalist government moved to Taiwan Province in 1949, he was involved with political training in the Army and with security and intelligence operations. Elected to the KMT's Standing Committee in 1952, he established a youth corps, developed veterans' rehabilitation programs, and became premier in 1972. After his father's death in 1975, he became chairman of the KMT's Central Committee and was elected president in 1978; he was elected to a second term in 1984. Chiang's credits included sweeping social, political, and economic reforms and a major economic development program called "Ten Major Construction Projects." The latter laid a solid foundation for Taiwan's modernization and economic prosperity and helped Taiwan win a major place in world trade. Chiang's position was strengthened by economic advances and by his encouragement of more Chinese natives of Taiwan Province to join the KMT and his administration. (WINSTON L. Y. YANG)

Chirac, Jacques René

On March 18, 1986, the conservative Jacques Chirac agreed to become prime minister in "cohabitation" with France's left-wing Pres. François Mitterrand. The two leaders thus became the architects of a process of political change that was to transform France, and Chirac returned to the Hôtel Matignon, the residence of France's prime minister, ten years after he had resigned from the office.

Born Nov. 29, 1932, in Paris, Chirac was the grandson of schoolmasters from the Corrèze, the département in central France he was to

RICHARD MILDENHALL—CAMERA PRESS LTD.

represent in the National Assembly. His father was a manager at the Potez aircraft company. Chirac was educated at schools in Paris and at the École Nationale d'Administration (1957–59), the leading postgraduate institute in France, where for a short time he was involved in Communist politics.

Following military service in Algeria, he joined the Cour des Comptes (the government audit office). There he caught the attention of Gaullist Prime Minister (later President) Georges Pompidou, who in 1962 appointed him to his private office at the Hôtel Matignon. The young protégé advanced quickly. He was first elected to the National Assembly in 1967, and in the same year he was appointed to a junior government post. He went on to hold a number of Cabinet posts, including minister of agriculture and rural development (1972–74) and minister of the interior (1974).

When Pompidou died in 1974, Chirac took advantage of a new opportunity to further his career by supporting Valéry Giscard d'Estaing's candidacy for the presidency, rather than the official Gaullist candidate, Jacques Chaban-Delmas of the Union des Démocrates pour la République (UDR). Chirac was rewarded by the successful Giscard with the appointment of prime minister in May 1974. There were profound policy disagreements between Giscard and Chirac, however, and on Aug. 26, 1976, the latter resigned, claiming that he was unable to govern effectively. In December of that year Chirac formed the Rassemblement pour la République (RPR), which replaced the UDR. The new Gaullist movement gathered momentum when Chirac was elected mayor of Paris in March 1977.

With Mitterrand's election to the presidency in 1981, Chirac began a period in the political wilderness. The RPR, however, spearheaded the victory of the right wing over the Communists and Socialists in France's March 1986 legislative elections, and consequently Chirac was called upon by Mitterrand to take over as prime minister. By establishing himself as unchallenged leader of the right wing, Chirac also made a significant step toward his next goal, the presidency, elections for which were due in 1988. (JEAN KNECHT)

Chissanó, Joaquim

On Nov. 3, 1986, Joaquim Chissanó was chosen as Mozambique's president to succeed Samora Moises Machel (*see* OBITUARIES). He shared the political views of Machel, with whom he had worked closely since the formation of the ruling party, the Mozambique Liberation Front (Frente de Libertação de Moçambique; Frelimo), in 1962. Although a professed Marxist, Chissanó interpreted the doctrine pragmatically and told visiting U.S. congressmen that Mozambicans had learned that "Marxism doesn't always work." He was willing to deemphasize Marxism to improve relations with the West, which he had done much to foster since 1975, when he became foreign minister. He had earlier served as prime minister during the transition period leading up to Mozambique's independence in 1975.

Chissanó was born in Chibuto, a village in the southern province of Gaza, on Oct. 22, 1939, and was one of the first black students admitted to the Portuguese high school in Lourenço Marques (subsequently Maputo). He abandoned his medical studies in Lisbon, for which he had won a scholarship, to devote more time to the anti-Portuguese liberation movement. Because of his political activities he was forced to leave Portugal and went to Paris, where he represented the first leader of Frelimo, the late Eduardo Mondlane. Chissanó became an active guerrilla fighter, and when Mozambique became independent in 1975, he was given the rank of major general. While in France he became fluent in French and English as well as in Portuguese, the language in which he was educated.

By temperament Chissanó was a diplomat rather than a militarist. Quiet-spoken and modest, he played a key role in reconciling the hard-line Marxists with the more moderate pragmatists in the internal struggle within Frelimo after Mondlane's death. He supported Machel's flexible foreign policies, which enabled Frelimo to retain its good relations with China and develop closer ties with both the U.S.S.R. and Western nations. As president, Chissanó announced that he would abide by the March 1984 Nkomati accord, the nonaggression agreement with South Africa, and committed his government to fighting the rebel Mozambique National Resistance (MNR), stating, "We will continue the war in order to finish the war." (COLIN LEGUM)

Clemens, Roger

Eight months before Roger Clemens struck out 20 Seattle Mariners on April 29, he had undergone shoulder surgery on his right, pitching arm. "We're all going to have our arms operated on," marveled fellow Boston Red Sox pitcher Bob Stanley after the Seattle game. But that was not Clemens's secret. His pitches combined 153-km/h (95-mph) speed with pinpoint accuracy. As teammate Marty Barrett said, "Lots of people throw hard, but Roger puts it where he wants." His 20-strikeout game was all the more remarkable because he walked nobody.

It was the first sign of a special season that climaxed with the first American League most valuable player award for a starting pitcher in 15 years. Clemens also was MVP of the All-Star game and the third unanimous selection for the

AP/WIDE WORLD

American League's Cy Young award for pitcher of the year. In his first full major-league season he led the league in victories and winning percentage (.857) with a 24–4 record and in earned run average (ERA) with 2.48. He won his first 14 decisions. He helped the Red Sox gain their first pennant since 1975 by winning 14 games after Red Sox defeats, including 2 on a 3–10 western trip that might otherwise have ruined the season.

William Roger Clemens was born Aug. 4, 1962, in Dayton, Ohio, where his older brother, Randy, arranged for him to play on older youth teams. "Control has never been a problem because mechanics have never been a problem," said Clemens, who was so obsessed with his pitching motion that he practiced it every day in front of a mirror. He finished high school in Houston, Texas, where he became a devoted fan of Nolan Ryan, baseball's all-time strikeout leader.

Like most fastball pitchers, Clemens was a late bloomer. He went to San Jacinto Junior College before he was accepted at the University of Texas. Even after he struck out the last six batters in Texas's 1983 College World Series championship, Clemens was only the 19th player drafted. But he finished his first pro season with a 9–2 record, a 1.19 ERA, and 108 strikeouts and 14 walks in 98 innings.

He joined the Red Sox in May 1984 only to have his first two seasons cut short by a pulled forearm muscle and then loose cartilage around his rotator cuff. With his career in jeopardy before it really started, Clemens attacked his rehabilitation workouts as zealously as he attacked the corners of home plate. "Not everyone works as hard at it as Roger," teammate Dwight Evans said. (KEVIN M. LAMB)

Cohen, Stanley

Stanley Cohen, a biochemist on the faculty of Vanderbilt University School of Medicine, Nashville, Tenn., was awarded the Nobel Prize for Physiology or Medicine and the Albert Lasker Award for Basic Medical Research in 1986. He shared both prizes with Rita Levi-Montalcini (*q.v.*), who discovered nerve growth factor (NGF). Cohen purified NGF, proved that it is a protein, and, while studying it further, found a related substance—epidermal growth factor (EGF). Cohen established the molecular structure of EGF, identified the site at which it becomes attached to cell surfaces, and demonstrated the process by which it passes through the wall of a cell into its interior.

Cohen's search for EGF was stimulated by finding that when crude tissue extracts containing NGF were injected into newborn mice, their eyes opened and their teeth emerged from their gums several days sooner than those of mice not given the extract. These events, not related to development of nerve tissue, indicated to Cohen that a second growth factor must be present. EGF was later shown to accelerate the growth of several kinds of tissue in the body; clinical trials of its value in speeding up the healing of wounds in human patients were already in progress.

Cohen was born on Nov. 17, 1922, in Brooklyn, N.Y. After graduating from Brooklyn College in 1943, he continued his education at Oberlin (Ohio) College and the University of Michigan, receiving a Ph.D. from the latter in 1948. He engaged in pediatric research at the University of Colorado until 1952, then joined Levi-Montalcini as a member of Viktor Hamburger's research group at Washington University, St. Louis, Mo. He moved to Vanderbilt in 1959, becoming professor of biochemistry in 1967 and American Cancer Society research professor in 1976. (JOHN V. KILLHEFFER)

Collins, Phil

Phil Collins was one of the world's most unlikely superstars. A stocky, short, and balding Englishman, he was the unquestioned star of the Live Aid shows on July 13, 1985, achieving the remarkable feat of performing at both the British and the U.S. concerts. After his performance at Wembley Stadium, London, he flew by Concorde to New York City and arrived in Philadelphia in time to appear there. Both performances were watched by a television audience of more than a million around the world.

This extraordinary piece of showmanship was typical of Collins's style and career. He might look completely wrong for the part, but he had succeeded first as a drummer with the massively popular rock band Genesis before branching out to achieve even greater success as a soloist. In 1986, after collecting three Grammy awards for his best-selling single, "Take Me Home," and album, *No Jacket Required,* he was soon back in the charts with the Genesis album *Invisible Touch.* He succeeded partly because of his undoubted musical skill, his songwriting ability, and his strong, relaxed voice and partly because of his easygoing, apparently totally honest personality. In a business full of would-be macho men, pretty boys, and sex symbols, Collins succeeded remarkably well by seeming rather ordinary.

Born in London on Jan. 30, 1951, Philip Collins had been involved in show business all his life. He worked as a child actor in the London West End production of *Oliver* in the 1960s. His real interest was music, however, and in 1970 he joined Genesis, exponents of a theatrical brand of "art rock," mixing swirling, complex melodies with a visual display provided largely by lead singer Peter Gabriel. When Gabriel quit in 1975, Collins took over as lead singer. Many people thought the band's success was over, but to the amazement of the music industry it became even more popular. Collins continued to play, tour, and record with Genesis. In 1981 he launched his parallel and even more successful solo career, singing both ballads and black American-influenced dance, soul, and funk material. (ROBIN DENSELOW)

Conable, Barber Benjamin, Jr.

On March 13, 1986, Ronald Reagan, president of the United States, nominated Barber Conable for a five-year term—beginning July 1, 1986—as president of the International Bank for Reconstruction and Development, the most important corporation in the group known as the World Bank. It was customary for the bank's executive directors to elect as president the nominee of the U.S., the largest subscriber among the bank's member nations. Although he had never been a banker, Conable had gained respect for his financial knowledge as a member of the Ways and Means Committee of the U.S. House of Representatives. He was also considered a competent negotiator.

Conable took office at the bank after a bitter argument over the salaries of bank officials. Subscribing nations had opposed officials' demands for a raise. Conable's cautious, affable approach helped to heal wounds. At the bank's annual meeting, held September 24–October 3, Conable requested additional loans and suggested that the bank increase its emphasis on improving the status of women and stabilizing the world's population.

Barber Conable was born in Warsaw, N.Y., on Nov. 2, 1922. He received a B.A. from Cornell University, Ithaca, N.Y., in 1942 and served in the U.S. Marine Corps from 1942 to 1946, rising from private to lieutenant. He received an LL.B. from Cornell in 1948 and practiced law in Buffalo, N.Y., from 1948 to 1950. After serving in the Marine Corps again from 1950 to 1951, in 1952 he entered law practice with his father in Batavia, N.Y., where he became active in Republican politics. In 1962 he was elected to the state Senate and in 1964 to the first of ten terms in the U.S. House of Representatives. His district, reapportioned slightly during his tenure, included northwestern Rochester as well as suburban and rural territory.

Conable became a member of the powerful Committee on Ways and Means in 1967 and ranking member of the committee's Republican minority in 1977. Considered a fiscal conservative but not a believer in Reaganomics, he sponsored the Reagan administration's bill for reducing taxes in 1981, although he doubted that the reductions alone would cause economic recovery. Conable did not seek reelection to the House in 1984. From 1985 to 1986 he was professor of political science at the University of Rochester. (CHARLES JOHNSON TAGGART)

Dean, Brenda

One of the few female labour union leaders in Britain, Brenda Dean was a central figure in the industrial dispute that troubled the country's newspaper industry during 1986. As general secretary of the Society of Graphic and Allied Trades (SOGAT) 82, the union to which many printing workers belonged, Dean found herself confronting the aggressive management tactics of Rupert Murdoch's News International group and the challenge posed to her union's members by the rapid introduction of new technology into their traditionally labour-intensive industry.

Brenda Dean was born on April 29, 1943, in Salford, Lancashire, the daughter of a railroad inspector. After attending school in Eccles and Stretford, she went to work in Salford as a secretary but quickly decided that union work was more stimulating. She gained her first post within SOGAT in 1959 and became a national executive council member in 1977. Her presidency of the union (1983–85) was followed by her selection as its general secretary, and effective head, in 1985.

UNIVERSAL PICTORIAL PRESS & AGENCY LTD.

Her shrewdness, calmness under negotiating pressure, and personal charm were at once put to the test by the News International dispute, involving some of Britain's leading national newspapers (*The Times, Sunday Times, Sun,* and *News of the World*). Murdoch was intent on shaking out excess labour, bringing in new technology (which involved journalists taking on tasks formerly the exclusive province of printing workers) and moving to new plants, away from the newspapers' traditional bastions of Fleet Street and Gray's Inn Road in London. As part of this strategy Murdoch dismissed SOGAT members, offering compensation and, at one stage, the use of the *Times*'s old premises for a left-of-centre newspaper enterprise. Electricians were hired to replace the printing workers on the new production system.

The dispute caused interunion discord and tested Dean's mettle. Aware that much of her personal support within the union came from members working outside London, she stressed that she was anxious to obtain a solution beneficial to all printing workers and not merely to the Fleet Street "elite." Though Murdoch's compensation offer was rejected, many observers believed that Dean's pragmatic leadership tended toward a realistic settlement rather than the war of attrition favoured by the more militant workers. (BRIAN WILLIAMS)

Deaver, Michael K.
Former White House deputy chief of staff Michael Deaver was under investigation in 1986 for possible unethical lobbying activities. In May 1985 he had quit his post to form a Washington, D.C., public relations firm. Under the Ethics in Government Act Deaver was barred for one year from lobbying the White House and for two years from representing clients on issues with which he had been involved while he was a government employee. Within a year of his resignation, however, his firm, Michael K. Deaver & Associates, had several million dollars in contracts that raised questions about Deaver's use of his connections inside Pres. Ronald Reagan's administration.

Possibly the most serious of the accusations concerned Deaver's dealings with the Canadian and South Korean governments. In early 1985 Deaver was said to have attended meetings on the president's upcoming talks with Canada about acid rain. Some critics speculated that he was approached then by the Canadians to help foster their cleanup plans. In any case, four months after leaving office he signed a contract for an annual $105,000 to do just that. The South Korean government reportedly paid him $1.2 million for a three-year contract to help improve their relations with the United States. Other deals with Saudi Arabia, Puerto Rico, and private firms such as Rockwell International (the U.S. manufacturer of the controversial B-1 bomber) also raised questions.

Deaver, who had been allowed to keep his White House pass as a courtesy and had continued to receive a daily copy of Reagan's schedule, denied all wrongdoing, but he returned the pass and cooperated with several separate investigations. Deaver's supporters said that he was being singled out because of growing concern in Washington about "influence peddling" as more and more former government officials and ex-members of Congress became highly paid lobbyists and consultants.

Deaver was born April 11, 1938, and attended San Jose (Calif.) State University. He worked briefly in business, but after Reagan's election as governor of California, Deaver joined his staff as a political aide in 1967. He became a close personal friend and confidante of Reagan and of his wife, Nancy. Deaver's lack of political ideology and his loyalty made him invaluable, and for the next 18 years he stage-managed everything about Reagan's daily life and public image. He limited real access to the president by the press while arranging photo opportunities, organized Reagan's daily schedule, offered the president personal advice on nonpolicy issues, and devised the low-key advertising campaign used in Reagan's 1984 bid for reelection.

(MELINDA SHEPHERD)

Doi, Takako
With the support of every faction of the Japan Socialist Party (JSP), Takako Doi won 83% of the votes in early September party elections and thereby became the first Japanese woman ever chosen to lead a major political party. Her victory followed the resignation of Masashi Ishibashi, who felt obliged to step aside as chairman of the central executive committee after the JSP suffered a disastrous defeat in national elections to the Diet (parliament) two months earlier. The Socialists had long represented the strongest political alternative to the ruling Liberal-Democratic Party (LDP), but in July they lost 25 of their 111 seats in the lower house and had an approval rating of only about 10%.

Doi, who was first elected to the Diet in 1969 after serving as vice-chairman of the JSP for three years, assumed her new responsibilities determined to rebuild her party and avoid, for the present, such potentially divisive issues as Japan's Self-Defense Forces, the U.S.-Japan security treaty, the use of nuclear power, and the recognition of South Korea. She promised, however, to formulate policies on all important matters before the party held its next convention in December 1987. For the present Doi would address less controversial topics such as

REUTERS/BETTMANN NEWSPHOTOS

care for the elderly and taxation, which she referred to as "politics of the heart."

Doi, who was dubbed "the people's politician," was born in Hyogo Prefecture on Nov. 30, 1928. A constitutional lawyer who never married, she once taught at Doshisha University in Kyoto and made protection and implementation of the peace constitution one of her abiding concerns. Doi faced a formidable challenge as she tried to rejuvenate the JSP. For one thing, membership in the LDP exceeded three million, while that in the JSP now numbered only 85,000. Doi, moreover, had always been something of an outsider in intraparty debates that had most often been dominated by aging males backed by labour unions. Doi quickly launched a vigorous campaign to recruit new members, especially women, and hoped to strengthen the JSP's local political organizations. Her engaging personality would help, but only time would tell if the JSP would be able to present a serious challenge to the LDP when the next Diet elections were held in 1990. (GERD LARSSON)

Drapeau, Jean
Eight terms in office spanning 32 years made Jean Drapeau of Montreal the longest-serving mayor of any major North American municipality and the longest-serving politician in Canada at any level. Drapeau's great ambition was to make Montreal the world's premier city by 1990, and to that end he created a series of expensive and splendid projects for his city: underground shopping plazas, a subway system, an art centre, and the Olympic Stadium. In 1969 he brought major league baseball to Montreal with the Montreal Expos, but his two most grandiose achievements were the 1967 world's fair, Expo 67, and the 1976 Summer Olympics. For his efforts, Drapeau received an award from the trade and industry departments of the Canadian provinces for contributing most to industrial development in Canada (1965). In 1967 he was made a Companion of the Order of Canada, and in 1984, a Commander of the French Legion of Honour.

Born Feb. 18, 1916, near Montreal, Jean Drapeau received his B.A. (1938) and law degree (1941) from the University of Montreal. After running unsuccessfully for the Canadian Parliament and the Quebec National Assembly, he found his niche in Montreal civic politics. He acted as the prosecutor for the Caron Inquiry into Montreal civic corruption (1949–50) and in 1954 was elected mayor. Defeated in the 1957 election, he formed the Parti Civique de Montréal to serve as his political vehicle, and in 1960 he was returned to office.

Drapeau was known as a showman, a master of circumlocution and charm, and he managed Montreal's civic affairs with iron determination. He believed that the populace drafted a leader and entrusted the fate of the city to him. His Parti Civique admitted no members besides its city councillors and never had a stated platform. All major plans for Montreal were made by the mayor in consultation with six members of the City Council executive committee and presented to the council for rubber-stamp approval. When *Monsieur le maire* announced that he would not run for a ninth term in 1986, he made it clear that this was not his choice but a concession to his health problems. In his departure speech, Drapeau said his reward was the feeling that he had contributed to cleansing the city's public affairs and transforming Montreal from the city Montrealers loved into one they loved even more. (DIANE LOIS WAY)

Eastwood, Clint
In April 1986 actor Clint Eastwood gave a sneak preview of his latest role. Playing against his usual type, Eastwood became a bureaucrat—the newly elected mayor of Carmel-by-the-Sea, a California village of 4,700 people. At his victory news conference he vowed to "bring the whole community together" by reversing the antibusiness policies of previous mayors. The new mayor looked and sounded familiar; his steel-edged squint, spare but decisive gestures, and soft and low, almost menacing, tone of voice were vintage, big-screen Eastwood. The only thing missing was the cool cynicism of his screen characters, the "come on punk, make my day" attitude that had made him one of the world's most popular actors.

Eastwood first made a name for himself in television when he played a lead role in the

J. COOLEN—GAMMA/LIAISON

series "Rawhide" from 1959 to 1966. He first gained attention in the movies when he starred as The Man With No Name in *A Fistful of Dollars* (1964), a grimly humorous western filmed in Italy. Eastwood's brutal, crafty, almost mute drifter was a hero in Europe, where the film and its two sequels broke box-office records. Though those films also fared well in the U.S., Eastwood's first American hit did not come until 1971 with *Dirty Harry.* As laconic and self-assured detective Harry Callahan, Eastwood calmly wages a private war against San Francisco's most vicious criminals, thus defying the weak-willed bureaucrats who—in the name of the Constitution—appease and protect them. Eastwood excited the U.S. public—who made him the top money-making star in 1972 and 1973—but outraged the media. *The New Yorker* said he stood "for nothing but violence," a "hero of a totally nihilistic dream world."

By the 1980s Eastwood had converted the critics. He won praise for playing relatively gentle characters in *Bronco Billy* (1980) and *Honkytonk Man* (1982), both of which he directed. Moreover, in a U.S. increasingly concerned about law and order, critics suddenly warmed to Dirty Harry, whom director Eastwood again portrayed in *Sudden Impact* (1983), a box-office hit. In Harry's behaviour, the *New York Times* saw the message that surrendering to violent crime "is as morally reprehensible as creating it."

Eastwood was born in Oakland, Calif., on May 31, 1931, to a family struggling to survive the Depression. But 55 years later reporters covering his mayoral campaign were less interested in where he came from than in where he was going; they wanted to know whether the one-time Man With No Name would next ride after the biggest role of all: the U.S. presidency.

(MICHAEL AMEDEO)

Enrile, Juan Ponce

On Feb. 22, 1986, Juan Ponce Enrile left the people of the Philippines rubbing their eyes and doing double takes. The man they had known as a conservative defense minister barricaded himself and his military supporters inside defense headquarters and announced he was abandoning the government of Ferdinand Marcos to support Corazon Aquino (*q.v.*), who, just weeks before, had lost to Marcos in an apparently rigged election. By February 25 Enrile's rebellion and Aquino-inspired street demonstrations had broken Marcos's 20-year stranglehold on the presidency. In explaining his defection, the 62-year-old Enrile said, "I was affected by a moral dilemma: my loyalty to a man, and my loyalty to my country. I chose to serve my country."

Some doubted his sincerity, and with good reason: he had served Marcos, rather than the country, for two decades. Enrile joined the government in the mid-1960s as commissioner of customs, later becoming minister of justice and, in 1970, minister of defense. In the defense post, he administered martial law between 1972 and 1981. At the same time, he, like other Marcos ministers, accumulated great wealth, gaining a coconut monopoly through presidential decree and increasing the value of his logging interests through the alleged use of his martial-law powers. Enrile's ambition grew, but before he could become a competitor for the presidency, Marcos reduced his power.

Enrile was more complicated than the average politician in authoritarian government. Although he had presided over the 1972 arrest and eight-year detention of opposition leader Benigno Aquino, Jr., Corazon's husband, Enrile reportedly cried upon seeing the assassinated man's body in August 1983. Among the Marcos inner circle, Enrile was the only one who tried to attend Aquino's funeral.

Born to a poor village girl in Ilocos Norte Province, Enrile became an overachiever. He was graduated at the top of his class from the University of the Philippines law school, and in 1955 he earned a master's degree in law from Harvard. A successful law practice in Manila kept him busy until the Marcos years. Retained as defense minister by new president Corazon Aquino, Enrile continued to surprise, even bewilder, the nation. Just weeks after helping her come to power, he began scorning her policies, particularly that of negotiating with the country's Communist insurgents. By late 1986 Manila was buzzing with rumours of an impending, Enrile-led coup, but it was not Aquino who blinked. On November 23 she reshuffled her Cabinet, and when she finished, Enrile was among the missing. (MICHAEL AMEDEO)

Fletcher, James Chipman

On May 12, 1986, James Fletcher began his second tenure as administrator of the U.S. National Aeronautics and Space Administration (NASA), which had been governed by an acting administrator since December 1985 and which was trying to recover from the aftermath of the deaths of seven astronauts in the explosion of the space shuttle *Challenger* on Jan. 28, 1986. The U.S. Senate, by a vote of 89–9 on May 6, had approved U.S. Pres. Ronald Reagan's nomination of Fletcher, who had faced sharp questioning before a committee of the Senate about his own possible responsibility for events leading up to the explosion of the *Challenger*. The *New York Times* on April 23 had published an article accusing NASA, under Fletcher and his successors, of saving money by disregarding safety. First appointed administrator in 1971 at the end of the Apollo program, Fletcher had made the decision to develop the Space Transportation System, including the shuttle.

As administrator, Fletcher approved a long-term plan for a space station and promised that no shuttles would be launched again without a careful review of safety precautions. Fletcher was not singled out for criticism in the report of a presidential commission on the *Challenger*, received by President Reagan on June 9. Morale at NASA rose when a Delta rocket was launched successfully from Cape Canaveral in Florida on September 5. On October 3 NASA released an ambitious plan for launching space shuttles, beginning in February 1988.

James Chipman Fletcher was born in Millburn, N.J., on June 5, 1919. He received a B.A. from Columbia University, New York City (some of his credits being from Brigham Young University, Provo, Utah), in 1940. He did scientific research for the U.S. Department of the Navy in 1940–41 and for Harvard University in 1941–42 and then served as an instructor at Princeton University from 1942 to 1945. In 1945 he began teaching and studying at California Institute of Technology, from which he received a Ph.D. in 1948. Fletcher taught at UCLA from 1948 to 1950. During those same years he was a laboratory director at Hughes Aircraft Co., and from 1954 to 1958 he served as a laboratory director at Ramo-Woodridge Corp. In 1958 he founded the Space Electronics Corp. in Glendale, Calif., with himself as president, to make electronic equipment suitable for space vehicles. After Space Electronics merged with Aerojet-General Corp. in 1960, Fletcher served as an executive in the new corporation. He was president of the University of Utah from 1964 to 1971 and administrator of NASA under Pres. Richard Nixon and Pres. Gerald Ford from 1971 to 1977. From 1977 to 1986 he taught at the University of Pittsburgh, Pa., and ran a consulting engineering business in McLean, Va. (CHARLES JOHNSON TAGGART)

Fluck, Peter, and Law, Roger

Every decade or so a new comedy form emerges on British television. The 1960s brought "That Was the Week That Was" and the 1970s "Monty Python's Flying Circus." In the 1980s the innovator was "Spitting Image"—a television series with not a single live celebrity to be seen. Instead the satirical comedy relied on the most savage, unforgiving caricatures of politicians, pop stars, and actors, brilliantly fashioned from foam rubber and plastic and operated with almost lifelike precision by a team of puppeteers.

Sparing neither U.S. Pres. Ronald Reagan, Queen Elizabeth II, nor Pope John Paul II, the models were the inspired creations of Peter Fluck (born April 7, 1941, in Cambridge) and Roger Law (born Sept. 6, 1941, in Littleport, Ely, Cambridgeshire). The two men left school at 16 with unpromising futures and met at the Cambridge School of Art—one of the few places where their love of drawing and lack of other qualifications were no obstacle. The political cartoons and later caricature models of Fluck and Law first appeared in a variety of political and satirical magazines as well as in Britain's two major Sunday newspapers, *The Sunday Times* and *The Observer*. In 1976 the two formed a formal partnership and soon coined the professional identity "Luck and Flaw."

It was only a matter of time before a television company plucked up the nerve to invite them to work for television. The break came when John Lloyd, producer of the British Broadcasting Corporation's successful satire "Not the Nine O'Clock News," teamed up with Fluck and Law to present the "Spitting Image" project to Central Television, the Independent Television (ITV) company operating the broadcasting franchise in the English Midlands. Central commissioned the project, and the "Spitting Image" team began making puppets in Limehouse Studios, London, from where they were transported to Birmingham for recording sessions. The first show was broadcast in February 1984.

Initially the shows were coolly received, mainly because the early scripts failed dismally to match the humour and brilliance of Fluck and Law's extraordinary caricatures. As the writing team grew in confidence, however, the shows improved to the point that "Spitting Image" became ITV's entry in the 1985 Golden Rose of Montreux competition, where it won the silver award. By now without question the satirical torchbearer of the 1980s, it nevertheless failed to elicit complaint from the politicians it so effectively lambasted; indeed, almost the only outcry since the program began concerned the one person in Britain apparently universally considered to be above parody and reproach—Queen Elizabeth, the Queen Mother.

(PATRICK STODDART)

Gale, Robert Peter

Californian Robert Gale was catapulted to international attention in 1986 when he became the first Western physician invited by the Soviet Union to help in a disaster—in this case, history's worst nuclear accident, the April 25 explosion of reactor 4 at the Chernobyl nuclear power plant in the Ukraine. (*See* ENERGY: *Sidebar*.) Six days later Gale, who chaired the advisory committee of the International Bone Marrow Transplant Registry, was on his way to Moscow to meet with Soviet doctors at the request of the Soviet government.

Some 300 victims were in Moscow's Hospital Number 6 when Gale arrived, and hundreds more were hospitalized in Kiev. Within a week an international team of bone marrow transplant specialists had begun transplants on ten patients who had suffered radiation damage as a result of the Chernobyl accident. According to Gale, there had never been so many seriously contaminated patients requiring bone marrow transplants at the same time. By mid-May all the transplants that could be done were completed, and Gale, now a celebrity, returned to Los Angeles. He flew back to Moscow on May 25 bearing medicine and gifts. By the end of September, the death toll stood at 31, and thousands who had lived near the plant were facing long-term health problems of unknown severity. The transplants were not a panacea for those who had sustained serious damage. At the beginning of July, only 5 of the 13 victims who had received transplants were still alive.

Robert Peter Gale, the head of the bone marrow transplant unit at the UCLA medical centre, was born Oct. 11, 1945, in New York City and attended Hobart College in Geneva, N.Y., before going on to medical school. His career as an extremely successful physician could not prepare him for the devastation at Chernobyl or the damage to its victims. On his second trip, he visited Chernobyl and Kiev. As his helicopter circled Pripyat, the now deserted workers' town some three kilometres (about two miles) from the reactor, the physician was overwhelmed by the sight: "This is it—this is what we've been afraid of all these years: a city devoid of human life because of radiation." Shortly thereafter, Gale and the director of the Soviet Union's Central Institute for Advanced Medical Studies signed an agreement to monitor 100,000 people who lived in what scientists refer to as the danger zone. (BONNIE OBERMAN)

Garang de Mabior, John

The imposition of Shari'ah (Islamic law) in The Sudan by Pres. Gaafar Nimeiry in September 1983 proved the focus of major discontent in the non-Muslim south of the country. Shortly afterward Col. John Garang formed the Sudan People's Liberation Movement (SPLM) in opposition to Nimeiry's rule and to the introduction of Shari'ah in particular. The SPLM manifesto declared its opposition to all forms of military rule and its support of democratic parliamentary government. The movement did not call for secession of the south but favoured a unified country with a nonmilitary government and sought the support of both Muslims and Christians in the war against Nimeiry. The Sudan People's Liberation Army (SPLA), the military wing of the SPLM, was welcomed by two of Nimeiry's most hostile neighbours, Libya and Ethiopia, which gave it arms and allowed SPLA bases on their territories.

When Nimeiry was overthrown in 1985, however, Garang refused to end his fight and join the interim government because of its military involvement. For the same reason, he refused to allow the SPLM to participate in the 1986 elections for a new civilian government. He insisted on the abolition of Shari'ah as a prerequisite for a cease-fire. Although he made an agreement with the northern political leaders to end the fighting and to participate in the drafting of a new democratic constitution, the agreement was not honoured because, he stated, the terms were not met—Shari'ah had been suspended but not abrogated. Meanwhile, his forces gathered strength throughout the south, and the new civilian government of Prime Minister Sadiq al-Mahdi (*q.v.*), appointed in May, faced continuing aggression.

Garang was born in 1943 into a poor Dinka family in Jongley Province of The Sudan on the banks of the Nile River. The family moved to Tanzania, where Garang received his early education. He won a scholarship to Grinnell (Iowa) College, from which he graduated in 1969. He returned to The Sudan and joined the Anya Nya rebellion, which had been started by the non-Muslim southerners at the time of Sudanese independence in 1956. They sought the secession of the non-Islamic southern provinces from the Islamic north. After the fighting ended in 1972, Garang joined the national Army but soon afterward returned to the U.S., where he received a doctorate in agricultural economics at Iowa State University. He then resumed his military career and was soon promoted to chief of the Military Research Center with the rank of lieutenant colonel. (COLIN LEGUM)

Giamatti, A(ngelo) Bartlett
As baseball's World Series began in October 1986, one duty of the National League's incoming president was to root for the league champion New York Mets. For that, his two sons called him a traitor.

The Mets were playing the Boston Red Sox, and Angelo Bartlett Giamatti had been a Red Sox fan almost since his birth, April 4, 1938, in Boston. He grew up in Hadley, Mass., with dreams of becoming the next Bobby Doerr, the star second baseman of the Red Sox. As an athlete, Giamatti reached his peak keeping statistics and carrying equipment for the South Hadley High School team. But as a fan he was second to none, for years delighting the Yale University community with the incongruity of a bearded Renaissance scholar wearing a Red Sox cap.

"There still is always a place in my heart for the Red Sox," Giamatti said as the Series began. "You never forget the first girl you fall in love with." But his true love was baseball, not the team that introduced him to it. "Baseball becomes not simply a team, but a way of life," he said.

Giamatti assumed his new office Dec. 12, 1986, with a reverence for baseball's traditions. He had written contemptuously of the players' interruption of the game for their 1981 strike and of the owners' shortsighted quest for television income at the cost of the game's control. He was an opponent of artificial turf, which was more abundant in the National League, and the designated hitter, a refinement confined to the American League.

Tradition was endemic to an academic career of lectures on Dante, Machiavelli, and "Myths and Mythography in Renaissance Cultures." Giamatti's father, Valentine, was a professor of Romance languages and Italian literature at Mount Holyoke College in South Hadley. Giamatti received his doctorate in comparative literature at Yale in 1964 and became a professor of literature there two years later, after teaching earlier at New York University and Princeton University.

In 1977, to sidetrack a premature announcement that he was becoming Yale's youngest president in more than 200 years, Giamatti said, "The only thing I want to be president of is the American League." While serving as Yale's president, Giamatti was seriously considered for the baseball commissioner's job that went to Peter Ueberroth in 1984, and the owners remembered him when Charles ("Chub") Feeney retired after 17 seasons as NL president.
(KEVIN M. LAMB)

Glass, Philip
The phenomenal success of Philip Glass's album *Songs from Liquid Days* in 1986 defied conventional wisdom by demonstrating that an avant-garde composer could penetrate the commercial mainstream. Glass, who cited both rock and jazz as major influences on his compositions, saw the culmination of many years of work as his album climbed to the number one spot on the classical charts and as popular audiences acclaimed his music. The seal on his arrival as a popular personality was his invitation to appear on two of America's most heavily watched television shows, "Saturday Night Live" and the "Today" show.

Glass was born Jan. 31, 1937, in Baltimore, Md. His father owned a record store where the boy developed a fondness for chamber music. Extremely precocious academically as well as musically, Glass entered the University of Chicago at age 15 and graduated with degrees in mathematics and philosophy. Meanwhile, he studied music intensively, taught himself the 12-tone system, and graduated from New York's Juilliard School in 1962. His next stop was Paris, where he studied with Nadia Boulanger.

Glass's dramatic instincts allowed him to create highly theatrical music. The new wave in opera was exemplified by his *Einstein on the Beach* (with designer Robert Wilson), which was performed before a sold-out house at the Metropolitan Opera in 1976—the year Glass considered that he, a supposedly fiery rebel, was discovered by the general public. The second score in what would become an operatic trilogy dealing with science, politics (the story of Gandhi's nonviolence), and religion, respectively, was *Satyagraha,* originally written in Sanskrit and performed in 1980. The third work, *Akhnaten,* originally written in ancient Egyptian, was completed in 1984.

But the operas, while successful, could not compete with the commercial appeal or the hype surrounding *Songs from Liquid Days.* The CBS Masterworks album contains music composed around lyrics by Paul Simon, David Byrne, Laurie Anderson, and Suzanne Vega, sung by Linda Rondstadt and the Roches, among others. Highly advertised in rock magazines, it had sold more than 150,000 copies by April. Glass also composed scores for films, including *Koyaanisqatsi,* a 1983 Godfrey Reggio film, and Paul Schrader's *Mishima,* and he was collaborating on works with choreographer Twyla Tharp and novelist Doris Lessing. Said Glass: "There may be people out there who still don't like my music, but I don't think they can ignore it any longer." (BONNIE OBERMAN)

González Márquez, Felipe
Prime Minister Felipe González of Spain won two major personal victories in 1986: he persuaded the Spanish electorate to vote positively in a referendum to keep Spain in the North Atlantic Treaty Organization (NATO), and then in general elections he received overwhelming support as the unchallenged leader of the government. Nevertheless, he began to show the strain of leading the government since 1982.

There were signs that the electorate was becoming disillusioned with the González style of government, and this was reflected in declines in voter turnout rates. His Spanish Socialist Workers' Party (PSOE) was seen as becoming complacent, given its secure majority in both houses of the Cortes (parliament) and the ineffective and divided opposition. He appeared to be leaving the day-to-day running of his country to his second in command or to his ministers, especially when issues were controversial and when unpopular decisions had to be made. In October 1986 González publicly admitted that the PSOE was beginning to show "oligarchical tendencies, intolerance toward dissent, and an abusive overidentification of party matters with those of the government." This trend had distanced the PSOE from the people, thereby, according to González, destroying much of its impetus.

González's search for the political middle ground, while at the same time trying to satisfy the more militant party members, led to what appeared to be policy contradictions. In line with his 1982 election pledge he urged the U.K. to negotiate on the reintegration of Gibraltar into Spanish territory, but at the same time he curtailed the rights of Muslims in Spain's African enclaves of Ceuta and Melilla and threatened the forced repatriation of unemployed Muslims to their "homelands." His support of Argentina's claims of sovereignty over the Falkland Islands/Islas Malvinas (unrecognized by treaty) and that of Spain over Gibraltar (recognized) was construed as political strategy to appease South American and Spanish nationalistic sentiments and not as part of a long-term solution to the problems. Despite the fact that Spain was to remain a member of NATO, González was committed to reforming the armed forces, as a result of which the role of the military was declining.

As 1987 approached, González, who was born in Seville, Andalusía, on March 5, 1942, and was Europe's youngest leader when he was elected prime minister in 1982, faced many challenges. Not least among them was how to reduce the levels of unemployment and high wage awards, in both of which Spain was leading Europe.
(MICHAEL WOOLLER)

Hadlee, Richard John
For most of the 110 years that test-match cricket had been played, Australia and England had been the leading countries; in 1985–86, however, they were sent to the bottom of the unofficial league of test-playing nations, largely through the exploits of New Zealander Richard Hadlee. His fast-medium bowling enabled New Zealand to beat Australia in series both at home and away and to defeat England away—all feats that New Zealand, traditionally the weakest team in test cricket, had never before achieved.

Born July 3, 1951, in Christchurch, Richard John Hadlee was the son of Walter Hadlee, an accountant and former captain of the New Zealand cricket team, and the younger brother of two other cricketers who also represented their country. In both spheres the father might be said to have had an influence, for Richard Hadlee became the most calculating and economical of contemporary cricketers. He constantly set himself batting and bowling targets and often surpassed them. In 1984, playing for Nottinghamshire in the English county championship, he became the first all-rounder since 1967 to score 1,000 runs and take 100 wickets in a season. He was the only New Zealander to have achieved this "double" in test cricket as well, and the only one to have taken 200, let alone 300, test wickets.

In his nine test matches against Australia and England in 1985–86, Hadlee took 68 wickets, which gained third place among the test-wicket takers of all time, behind Ian Botham (England) and Dennis Lillee (Australia). Hadlee set a new world record by taking 5 wickets in a test innings for the 26th time, but his finest achievement was to take 15 wickets against Australia at Brisbane, including 9 wickets for 52 runs in one innings. Both set new records for his country, as did his 33 wickets in a three-test series.

Close to nervous exhaustion, Hadlee almost suffered a breakdown after the test matches. But he recovered and returned to his hard-earned place as the leading bowler in cricket—including the all-out speed bowlers from the West Indies—at the relatively senior age of 35.

(SCYLD I. BERRY)

Hassan II

On March 3, 1986, King Hassan II of Morocco celebrated the 25th anniversary of his accession to the throne. The celebrations were a testimony to the monarch's considerable political talents and to his success in restoring stability to Morocco's political institutions after the vicissitudes of the early years of his reign.

Hassan was born on July 9, 1929, into the Alawite dynasty and was educated under both Muslim and European systems, including studies at the University of Bordeaux, France. Despite the role he played alongside his father, Mohammed V, in Morocco's struggle for independence, he had never enjoyed the same degree of prestige as his father. Shortly after ascending the throne, Hassan led his nation in an inconclusive war with neighbouring Algeria over a dispute relating to their common border. The decline in royal prestige manifested itself in two plots against the monarchy in the early 1970s. In 1973 there was an unsuccessful rural rebellion, combined with urban bombings.

In an attempt to unite the nation behind the monarchy, King Hassan launched a campaign to recover the Western Sahara in 1974. That campaign escalated into a war against the Popular Front for the Liberation of Saguia el Hamra and Río de Oro (the Polisario Front) and its backer, Algeria. Nonetheless, the king maintained popular support for the issue inside Morocco. At the same time, he was able to use this consensus to create a limited party democracy in Morocco, to restore the prestige of the regime, and to push through radical reforms of the economy designed to stimulate the private sector. He also made considerable efforts to convince the West of Morocco's strategic importance.

Despite Western anger over its treaty of union with Libya in August 1984, Morocco was able to establish itself as a mediator in the Arab-Israeli conflict. This was, perhaps, Hassan's greatest political gamble. He was instrumental in early contacts between Egypt and Israel that led to the Camp David accords and later flouted Arab disapproval by allowing Israelis to attend Jewish events in Morocco in 1984 and by meeting Israeli Prime Minister Shimon Peres to discuss the Arab-Israeli conflict in 1986. Despite the disapproval of Arab radicals, he enjoyed the tacit approval of Arab moderates and was regarded by them as one of the most accomplished political tacticians in the Middle East and North Africa.

(GEORGE JOFFÉ)

REUTERS/BETTMANN NEWSPHOTOS

Herschbach, Dudley Robert

One of the three recipients of the Nobel Prize for Chemistry for 1986 was the U.S. chemist Dudley R. Herschbach. Yuan T. Lee of the United States and John C. Polanyi of Canada (*qq.v.*) shared the award, which recognized the contributions of the three scientists in reaction dynamics, the study of time-dependent details of chemical processes.

Herschbach was one of the first scientists to adopt the technique of molecular beams for chemical research purposes. Since the early 20th century, physicists had used narrow streams of particles moving at known speeds to study properties of matter that could not be conveniently observed otherwise. In 1959 Herschbach built an apparatus in which two beams, each consisting of particles of a single substance, could be made to intersect. When atoms and molecules of different species collided, they reacted with one another, and molecules of newly formed substances would fly away from the site at which the beams crossed. In certain reactions the final products were not the immediate result of the collision but formed indirectly, by the disintegration of intermediate species that persisted for unexpectedly long intervals. Using a variety of particle detectors, Herschbach was able to determine the energy of the reaction products and how this energy was distributed among the different possible forms, such as translation (motion of the molecule as a whole), vibration (internal oscillations of the parts of the molecule), and rotation (tumbling or spinning).

Herschbach was born in San Jose, Calif., on June 18, 1932. He earned a B.S. in mathematics (1954) and an M.S. in chemistry (1955) at Stanford University and a Ph.D. in chemical physics at Harvard in 1958. He joined the faculty of the University of California at Berkeley in 1959 and then moved to Harvard as professor of chemistry in 1963. During the period 1961–68, Lee—first as a doctoral candidate, then as a postdoctoral fellow—was one of Herschbach's collaborators.

(JOHN V. KILLHEFFER)

Honda, Soichiro

In 1986 the Honda Motor Co. produced about 1.5 million cars and twice as many motorcycles, with total sales in excess of two trillion yen. Those figures demonstrated what Soichiro Honda, the company's founder, had long believed: success, even in highly educated and tradition-bound Japan, is possible for those with only a modest education if they harbour dreams. After World War II the newly established Honda Technical Research Institute began fitting 50-cc army surplus engines onto bicycles. In 1949 the first Honda motorcycle went on the market; it was called Dream. As his company grew, Honda ignored Japanese managerial traditions by placing unprecedented responsibilities on the shoulders of his employees to fulfill their dreams by tapping their creativity. Honda continued to spend time on the shop floor tinkering with machines. To employees he became known as *Oyaji* ("Pop"), but when an employee committed the same mistake twice, *Oyaji* turned into *Kaminari-oyaji* ("Mr. Thunder").

Honda, the son of a village blacksmith, was born in Shizuoka Prefecture on Nov. 17, 1906. Though he had scant formal education, he had a passion for motors and was a demon race driver in his early years. When he went into business for himself, his mind was ever playing with new ideas. Innovations were so much a part of his thinking that in time he personally held more than 100 patents. Despite Honda's near total absorption with cars and motorcycles, he never allowed himself to view the company he founded as his personal possession. When he retired at age 66, he turned over the presidency to a company engineer. Neither Honda nor any members of his family kept any managerial posts or held major blocks of stock in the Honda enterprise. Although Honda accepted the title supreme adviser, he never offered advice on running the company. His son ran a component company that occasionally did business with the Honda Motor Co.; his married daughter lived in Australia.

In 1977 Honda used his own funds to set up a foundation to support studies in ecotechnology. He also lent support to various international groups studying traffic systems and promoting safe driving. During his leisure hours he enjoyed golf, having been persuaded in his late 70s to give up hang gliding and piloting.

(GERD LARSSON)

Hopper, Grace Murray

In August 1986 Rear Adm. Grace Murray Hopper, the oldest officer on active U.S. naval duty, retired—again. The occasion, held on board the USS *Constitution,* marked the end of a long and influential career as one of the nation's first computer programmers.

Hopper was born in New York City on Dec. 9, 1906. She obtained a degree in mathematics and physics from Vassar College, Poughkeepsie, N.Y., in 1928 and did graduate work in mathematics at Yale University (M.A., 1930; Ph.D., 1934). She taught mathematics at Vassar from 1931 but felt the need to do more and, after two more years of study at New York University, she joined the Naval Reserve in 1943, attending midshipman's school in Northampton, Mass. The next year she was assigned to the Bureau of Ordnance's Computation Project

UPI/BETTMANN NEWSPHOTOS

under Howard Aiken at Harvard University. There she worked on Mark I, the first large-scale automatic calculator. In 1946 she sought active duty in the regular Navy, but she was rejected as "too old." She resigned from the Vassar faculty and remained at Harvard as a civilian research fellow.

In 1949 Hopper moved to the emerging computer industry at Eckert-Mauchly Corp., where the first commercial electronic computer, Univac I, was under construction. There she combined her military experience with a desire to design an improved compiler (a high-level computer language that enables programmers to write instructions in simpler, more easily accessible language). Hopper remained with the company when it was taken over by Remington Rand in 1951 and by Sperry Corp. in 1955, rising to the position of staff scientist in 1961. In 1957 her division completed the first English-language data-processing compiler. Known as Flow-Matic, it was a major forerunner of Cobol (computer business oriented language), the first high-level language devoted to business needs. In 1969 the Data Processing Management Association designated her its first computer science Man of the Year. When Hopper retired from the Univac division of Sperry in 1971, the company founded the annual Grace Murray Hopper Award, to be given to a promising young programmer.

Throughout her years in industry Hopper remained in the Naval Reserve until she retired

in 1966 as a commander. Her retirement was short-lived, however; the Navy recalled her to active service only a year later to develop naval applications of Cobol. From 1967 she served as special adviser to the Naval Data Automation Command at the Pentagon. Nineteen years later, four months short of her 80th birthday, Rear Admiral Hopper retired for the last time.
(MELINDA SHEPHERD)

Hunt Brothers

When Texas oil wildcatter H. L. Hunt died in 1974, he left 14 children by three marriages (one of them bigamous) and an estate valued at about $4 billion. The six children by his first wife inherited little of the estate, but their own substantial holdings (including trust funds set up in the 1930s) already rivaled their father's. Nelson Bunker (b. 1926) was an oil and commodities speculator who made millions in Libyan oil until his company was nationalized in 1973. William Herbert (b. 1929) collected a fortune in ancient bronzes and handled daily operations of several joint ventures. Lamar (b. 1933), a nonactive financial partner, was owner of the Kansas City Chiefs and cofounder of the modern National Football League. At the centre of the brothers' fortune, however, were the jointly owned Placid Oil Co., one of the country's largest independent oil companies, and Penrod Drilling Co., the nation's largest privately owned oil-drilling contractor.

Financial problems began for the Hunts in the late 1970s when Bunker and Herbert, together with several Arab investors, acquired as much as 120 million oz of silver bullion and futures contracts and drove the price up to more than $52 per ounce. Their alleged attempt to corner the silver market backfired in March 1980 when the Chicago Board of Trade and the New York Commodities Exchange restricted trading in silver and increased margin cash requirements, thus forcing the price down. The Hunts had to come up with more cash in a falling market and lost about $900 million. Placid borrowed $1.1 billion to cover the loss, and later that year Penrod borrowed another $850 million. The Hunts were philosophical about their losses. "A billion dollars isn't what it used to be," said Bunker.

Throughout the 1980s the Hunts continued to lose money on other investments, including a sugar-beet-refining business and a questionable deal on soybean futures. Placid and Penrod were able to renegotiate their debts on the basis of increasing oil revenues. By March 1986, however, falling oil prices had left both companies strapped for cash. Placid missed a $30.6 million payment on March 27, and Penrod missed an $8.5 million payment in May. The 23 banks involved rejected all further attempts to refinance, claiming that the Hunts had spent more than $100 million that should have been used for debt repayment on risky drilling operations in the Gulf of Mexico. The brothers insisted that the drilling was the only way to recoup their losses. On June 24 the Hunts filed suit against the banks, asserting that they had not bargained in good faith. Later the Hunts filed another suit charging conspiracy by the banks, and the banks countersued. On August 29 Placid filed Chapter 11 bankruptcy in New Orleans, La., despite a court ruling that the firm could file only in Texas. Penrod avoided similar action only when Herbert filed bankruptcy on his trust fund.
(MELINDA SHEPHERD)

Hussey, Marmaduke James

The death on Aug. 29, 1986, of Stuart Young (*see* OBITUARIES), chairman of the board of governors of the British Broadcasting Corporation (BBC), left a vacancy to be filled by government appointment at a time of particularly sensitive relations between the corporation and the Conservative Party. The chairman of the party, Norman Tebbit, a close adviser to Prime Minister Margaret Thatcher, was engaged in a prolonged campaign against what he claimed was lack of professionalism (widely interpreted as meaning "antigovernment bias") in the BBC's television news coverage. The appointment of

CAMERA PRESS LTD.

a chairman, nominally made by Queen Elizabeth II, was in fact made by the home secretary with the prime minister's knowledge, and there was widespread speculation that Thatcher wanted a "strong man" who would "put the BBC in order." The appointment on October 1 of Marmaduke ("Duke") Hussey was a widely welcomed surprise. One of Hussey's first public acts, after taking up his chair in November, was to reject Tebbit's latest assault in a sharply worded statement.

Born Aug. 29, 1923, in Worplesdon, Surrey, Hussey was at 2 m (6 ft 7 in) tall a figure of formidable stature, not diminished by the severe war wounds to his legs. Educated at Rugby School and at the University of Oxford, he completed his establishment pedigree by marrying Lady Susan Hussey, a lady-in-waiting to the queen and sister of Environment Minister William Waldegrave. By profession Hussey was a newspaper manager. He joined Associated Newspapers in 1949, advanced to the board of directors in 1964, and became managing director of a subsidiary (1967–70) before moving to the Thomson Organization as chief executive and managing director of Times Newspapers in 1971.

In this role he achieved his greatest public prominence. Following the failure of his attempt to lead a joint effort of national newspaper managements and print unions to agree on the introduction of new technology, he was at the centre of the 1978–79 confrontation in which the Thomson Organization suspended publication of *The Times* and *The Sunday Times* in a bid to force the unions to end disruption and agree on new terms. The dispute was long and increasingly bitter, but there was general agreement that Hussey himself was the victim of management uncertainty higher in the Thomson hierarchy. He was one of the few senior executives to stay with the newspapers after their takeover (1981) by Rupert Murdoch, and he remained on the board of Times Newspapers Ltd. until his appointment to the BBC.
(PETER FIDDICK)

Karolyi, Bela

When he defected from Romania on March 30, 1981, Bela Karolyi did not know any English. He had only enough money to fly his family from New York City to Los Angeles, where he found work loading ships and washing dishes.

What Karolyi knew best was gymnastics. He had coached Romania's national team for more than a decade, and he had set the standard for developing young gymnasts. His first star pupil, Nadia Comaneci, became the first woman to score a perfect 10 in the Olympic Games, in which she won three gold medals in 1976. When the Romanian team won the 1979 world championship, it was the first time the Soviets had lost it. The Romanians were touring the United States, hours away from departure, when Karolyi decided at 3 AM to stay in the U.S.

University of Oklahoma coach Paul Ziert soon involved him in U.S. gymnastics. One year after Karolyi took charge of a gymnastics club in Houston, Texas, he started his continuing four-year streak of coaching America's Cup champions with Mary Lou Retton. She became the all-around gold medalist in the 1984 Olympics and the first woman to reach all four Olympic event finals.

In 1986 Karolyi coached the top four U.S. junior women. Kristie Phillips, at 1.45 m (4 ft 9 in) and 35.4 kg (78 lb), won her second U.S. junior championship and dominated U.S. gymnastics. Phillips and second-ranked Phoebe Mills scored high enough to finish 1-2 in the senior nationals, although each was only 13 years old when the year began.

When Karolyi began coaching in 1962, his youngest student was 12. Gymnastics was considered an activity for cute, little dancing girls. "At the time," Karolyi said later, "nobody had even thought of turning them into little bombs. Into animals. Killers." He changed gymnastics by putting preadolescent girls on world-class training paths and by emphasizing strength and teamwork. He earned his protégées' loyalty by his enthusiastic support and motivation. When Retton won the gold medal, she said, "We did it!" Karolyi had produced 23 Olympians, 7 Olympic champions, 14 world champions, and 12 European champions.

He was born Sept. 13, 1942, in Cluj, Rom. He went to the 1956 Olympics in his first sport, the hammer throw. Karolyi's lust for team spirit led him to the national team handball squad that won world championships in 1958 and 1962. He discovered gymnastics at the University of Bucharest, where he earned his Ph.D. in physical education in 1963.
(KEVIN M. LAMB)

Kristiansen, Ingrid

When she ran the 5,000 m in 14 min 37.33 sec in Stockholm on Aug. 5, 1986, Ingrid Kristiansen regained not only the world record from South African-born athlete Zola Budd but also the distinction, which she had had for a month in 1985, of being the only athlete—man or woman—to hold world-best times simultaneously at 5,000 m, 10,000 m, and the marathon. A month earlier, at the Bislett Games in Oslo, she ran 10,000 m in 30 min 13.74 sec, taking an amazing 45.68 sec off her own world record. She set the marathon record of 2 hr 21 min 6 sec in London in 1985. In 1986 she also won her first gold medal in a major championship, winning the European 10,000-m title by about half a lap.

Born Ingrid Christensen on March 21, 1956, at Trondheim, Norway, she began running competitively early in life. As a tiny 15-year-old she was knocked to the track in the heats of the European 1,500 m. Her first successes came not on the track but at cross-country skiing, in which she competed in the 1976 Olympic Games and in the 1978 world championships, finishing 15th. She continued to use skiing training during the cold Norwegian winters, running indoors on a treadmill; she declared that "after that, to run against a watch is a laugh." She won bronze medals in the 3,000 m at the 1980 world championships and the European marathon in 1982. Following the birth of her son Gaute in August 1983, she was running again after ten days and, astonishingly, ran her fastest marathon ever to win at Houston, Texas, just five months later. In early 1984 she became the first Norwegian woman in 14 years to beat Grete Waitz, and she followed that with a marathon win in London and the first sub-15-min 5,000 m by a woman. She was, however, disappointed by finishing fourth in the 1984 Olympic Games marathon.

The superiority Kristiansen had attained in distance running by 1986 was unparalleled since the days of Emil Zatopek of Czechoslovakia in the early 1950s. Like Zatopek, she appeared to run in agonized distress, with a hunched style, but also like him, she had a sparkling, happy personality. She ascribed her frowning while running to the fact that she could not see very well and her hunched shoulders to "too much knitting." (PETER J. MATTHEWS)

LaRouche, Lyndon Hermyle, Jr.
United States voters who lived in fear of the drug lobby, the Israeli Mafia, a Swiss-controlled grain cartel, and Soviet agents spreading AIDS found their man in Lyndon LaRouche. In March 1986 two followers of the conspiracy-obsessed presidential aspirant won Democratic Party primary races for secretary of state and lieutenant governor of Illinois. (Since under Illinois law the candidates for governor and lieutenant governor must run as a team, the gubernatorial candidate quit the Democratic slate and formed a third party.) Although the "LaRouchies" failed in the general election in November, startled Democrats nationwide feared that xenophobia, anti-Semitism, and panic peddling had found acceptance among their voters. Other pols noted that the LaRouchies won through voter ignorance, running in contests that the party had ignored because the winners were certain to lose to Republican incumbents.

LaRouche habitually began his own campaigns by accusing groups as disparate as the

UPI/BETTMANN NEWSPHOTOS

International Monetary Fund, the queen of England, and the Rockefeller family of conspiring to bring the world to economic ruin and total war through such evils as drug running, weakening currency values, and dismantling nuclear-power programs. People who contributed to LaRouche-affiliated organizations such as the Fusion Energy Foundation, or who subscribed to his weekly *Executive Intelligence Review,* found themselves hounded by campaign workers to give more money to his cause. Such methods were said to ignore legal niceties. In October 1986 ten of LaRouche's associates were indicted for defrauding a thousand contributors of more than $1 million by obtaining their credit card account numbers and then billing them for extra purchases and contributions.

Lyndon Hermyle LaRouche, Jr., was born Sept. 8, 1922, in Rochester, N.H. He attended Northeastern University in Boston and served as an army medic from 1944 to 1946. In 1948 LaRouche began an association with the leftist Socialist Workers Party that lasted until the 1960s; he and a group of followers later formed the United States Labor Party. Under this party's banner, LaRouche ran for president in 1976, receiving 40,043 votes out of more than 80 million cast. In 1980, having formed the National Democratic Policy Committee, he ran in ten Democratic primaries, collecting 177,784 votes. In 1984 he took 121,276 votes in the primary and then ran as an independent in November, winning 78,807 votes (0.1% of the total). Undaunted by these low figures, LaRouche predicted that in the 1988 presidential election he would change history. (ROBERT CURLEY)

Law, Roger
See FLUCK, PETER

Lee, Yuan Tseh
As one of the creators of the scientific specialty called chemical reaction dynamics, Yuan T. Lee shared the Nobel Prize for Chemistry in 1986 with Dudley R. Herschbach of the United States and John C. Polanyi of Canada (*qq.v.*).

Lee was born at Hsin-chu, Taiwan, on Nov. 29, 1936. He earned a bachelor's degree from the National Taiwan University, Taipei, in 1959 and a master's from the National Tsing Hua University, Hsin-chu, in 1961. He then moved to the University of California at Berkeley, where—under the supervision of Herschbach—he earned a Ph.D. in chemistry in 1965. He continued his research with Herschbach as a postdoctoral fellow until 1968, when he joined the faculty of the University of Chicago. In 1974 he returned to the Berkeley campus as professor of chemistry; in the same year, he was naturalized as a citizen of the United States.

Lee expanded Herschbach's application of colliding molecular beams for investigating the details of chemical reactions of gaseous substances, introducing mass spectrometry for the identification of the products resulting from the reactions of oxygen and fluorine atoms with complex organic compounds. The results he obtained in studying the reactions of oxygen attracted particular interest in connection with combustion processes, which are notoriously difficult to analyze because they are so rapid and complicated. These reactions also have a bearing on chemical events that occur in the Earth's atmosphere, such as those in which airborne pollutants interact with ozone. Lee also employed lasers to alter the distribution of energy within the molecules of one beam before they collide with those of the other. This technique permitted him to analyze further details of the relative motion of the atomic nuclei within the compounds as they undergo chemical change. (JOHN V. KILLHEFFER)

Lee Teng-hui
Lee Teng-hui, who became vice-president of the Republic of China in Taiwan in 1984, attracted increased attention in 1986 as Pres. Chiang Ching-kuo's health became more worrisome. Though given more responsibilities by Chiang, he continued to keep a low profile. A native of Taiwan Province and an ardent supporter of democracy, Lee was acceptable to most factions of the ruling Nationalist Party (Kuomintang or KMT) and was expected to play a vital role in Nationalist China's political future as Chiang's constitutional successor, even though he lacked a strong political base within the KMT.

Born into a farm family near Tamsui, Taiwan, on Jan. 15, 1923, Lee attended colleges in Japan and Taiwan and received his Ph.D. in agricultural economics from Cornell University, Ithaca, N.Y., in 1968. While teaching at National Taiwan University (1958–78), he contributed much to Taiwan's economic growth and development as a member of the Joint Commission on Rural Reconstruction. He was a major force in establishing farmers' associations and irrigation systems. He also promoted agricultural mechanization and helped enact the Agricultural Development Act, which spurred Taiwan's balanced agricultural growth along with industrial development. Lee joined the Cabinet in 1972 and carried out, as mayor of Taipei (1978–81), such projects as the construction of freeways and reservoirs and the modernization of sewage disposal. As governor of Taiwan (1981–84) he introduced regional planning and agricultural reforms and contributed to the renovation of rural villages and the construction of irrigation systems.

Modest, pleasant, and a devout Christian, Lee appeared destined to play a major role in the political and economic future of Taiwan. The lifting of martial law and the sanctioning of opposition parties, both major political developments announced by President Chiang in October 1986, would further strengthen Lee's role as a bridge between the Chinese who migrated from provinces on the mainland and those who were natives of the island province of Taiwan. (WINSTON L. Y. YANG)

Lekhanya, Justin
On Jan. 20, 1986, Maj. Gen. Justin Lekhanya ousted Prime Minister Leabua Jonathan of Lesotho, who had held power since 1965. His action, which received popular support, was prompted by the prime minister's statement that he might turn to the Eastern bloc for arms that he would use against South Africa.

Prior to the coup, relations between Lesotho and South Africa had deteriorated, and the latter had imposed border restrictions on Lesotho because of Jonathan's refusal to hand over insurgents belonging to the banned African National Congress (ANC), who were alleged to be operating in Lesotho. Jonathan denounced the actions of South Africa, and on January 17 Lekhanya flew to Pretoria as one of a seven-man delegation to persuade the South African government to lift the restrictions. It was suggested that the coup was planned while he was in Pretoria.

Born in Thaba-Tseke, Lesotho, on April 7, 1938, Lekhanya was commander of Lesotho's Army when he seized power; until that time he had maintained a low profile, and little was known about him. Following the coup he announced that in the future all executive and legislative power would be vested in King Moshoeshoe II—whose powers had been curbed since 1967—who would select a six-man Military Council, chaired by Lekhanya, that would advise him. Additionally Lekhanya would head a Council of Ministers and retain control of defense; both councils were sworn in by the end of January. All political activity was banned, and a policy of national reconciliation was declared.

Lekhanya's main objective was to restore good relations with South Africa, and by January 25 the latter had lifted the restrictions on border traffic that had been crippling Lesotho's economy. Lekhanya did not, however, accede to the request of the South African government to hand over 57 South African refugees who had been living in Lesotho but instead arranged for them to go to Zambia. He did expel 19 North Korean technicians who were believed to be connected with Jonathan's Youth League and reestablished diplomatic relations with South Korea, suspended since June 1983. On March 26 Lekhanya also reached an agreement with South Africa on mutual security. It prohibited the use of either country's territory for planning acts of aggression toward the other. As the year progressed, relations with South Africa continued to improve. (GUY ARNOLD)

Lendl, Ivan
Finishing second in tournaments bothered Ivan Lendl even more than the catcalls he received. He knew only one solution; "I've always had to work harder than anyone else," he said.

Lendl's work was rewarded in 1986 with the highest earnings ever in men's tennis for the second straight year. His $1,987,537 included an $800,000 bonus for his number one world ranking and brought his career earnings to a record $10,302,109. In 15 tournaments in 1986 Lendl won nine singles championships and finished second three times, including his best performance ever at Wimbledon. He won two of the other three Grand Slam tournaments, the French and U.S. opens, for the second time each. In the U.S. Open, climaxed with a 6–4, 6–2, 6–0 rout of Miloslav Mecir in the finals, Lendl lost only one set and 60 games in 22 sets.

The 1985 U.S. Open was Lendl's breakthrough. He defeated John McEnroe in the final match and then went on to win 54 of 56 matches. Lendl had not ranked below third in the world since 1980, but he had won only one of seven championship matches in Grand

Slam events. He had lost finals in three straight U.S. Opens.

For his success Lendl gave partial credit to his coach, Tony Roche, a former Australian star player. He also credited the low-fat, high-carbohydrate diet that relieved the recurring energy losses he had suffered through 1984. Lendl finished 1985 with 11 singles championships in 17 tournaments and his first number one ranking.

It had been a long climb from Ostrava, Czech., 16 km (10 mi) from the Polish border, where Lendl was born March 7, 1960, the only child of Olga and Jiri Lendl. His father was a government lawyer, chess master, and tennis player who had ranked as high as 15th nationally. But it was his mother, once the number two Czechoslovak woman tennis player, who pushed and browbeat Ivan to tennis skill and success. Lendl had his first racket at 6, began traveling to tournaments at 9, and won his first national age-group championship at 12.

He had other interests. He played chess and golf. He learned six languages. His flair for math and physics led him to computers. But it was tennis that so consumed Lendl that he stamped all weaknesses out of his game. Fellow professional Mats Wilander called Lendl "one of the few players who can play a perfect game."

(KEVIN M. LAMB)

Levi-Montalcini, Rita

A long and productive career in medicine, embryology, and neurology was crowned in 1986 by the awarding of two highly esteemed prizes to Rita Levi-Montalcini, a citizen of both the United States and Italy. She received the Albert Lasker Award for Basic Research and the Nobel Prize for Physiology or Medicine in recognition of her discovery of a natural substance that promotes the growth of nerve cells. (Her former collaborator, Stanley Cohen [*q.v.*] of the United States, was similarly honoured.)

Levi-Montalcini, who was born in Turin, Italy, on April 23, 1909, graduated from the medical school of the University of Turin in 1936. She stayed at the university until 1939, when she was forced out by Mussolini's anti-Semitic policies. While she continued her research on chick embryos in an improvised laboratory in her family home, she also provided clandestine medical care to residents of the poor neighbourhoods of Turin. When the Germans occupied Italy in 1943, Levi-Montalcini went into hiding in Florence. After the war she recovered her academic position in Turin, leaving in 1947 to accept a post at Washington University, St. Louis, Mo., with Viktor Hamburger, a zoologist who was using chick embryos in studies of the development of nerve tissue.

In 1948 it had been found that if a fragment of sarcoma 180, a tumour of mice, was implanted in a chick embryo, nerve fibres from the embryo rapidly invaded it. In 1952 Levi-Montalcini extended this experiment and proved that the nerve growth was caused by a soluble substance released by the tumour. In 1953 she showed that sarcoma 180 caused the same growth in nerve tissue kept alive in a culture medium after removal from the embryo. The use of cultures greatly simplified further research—in many laboratories—on the nerve growth factor. Levi-Montalcini remained active in this field, working at Washington University until 1961 and subsequently at the Institute of Cell Biology in Rome. (JOHN V. KILLHEFFER)

Liu Binyan

After months of silence and rumours about being forced to withdraw from literary circles, Liu Binyan (Liu Pin-yen) emerged again in 1986 to reveal in ruthless terms his vision of the dark side of China. In late December, however, he was denounced and purged for his advocacy of "bourgeois liberalization" by the Communist Party, which blamed Liu and other liberal intellectuals for encouraging national student demonstrations against the party and the government. In the interval, his reports and stories, including "China on the 37th Floor," had renewed his powerful attacks on Chinese corruption, decadence, and selfishness. Taking advantage of China's new but limited artistic freedom, Liu had forcefully opened Chinese literature to the winds of free inquiry and contributed much to open discussions about Chinese society's shortcomings and difficulties.

Born in 1925 into the family of a railroad worker in Chang-chun, Jilin (Kirin) Province, Liu Binyan received little formal education but managed to acquire a reading knowledge of Japanese and Russian. After the Communists came to power in 1949, he became a journalist and an editor of *Youth Daily.* His 1956 feature story "At the Bridge Site" attracted national attention for its revelation of complex forces contributing to conservatism, which he felt indicated a decaying Communist bureaucracy. This and later writings were read as exposés baring some of the deep-rooted political problems in China. Liu thus became one of the first few Chinese writers to openly criticize the Communist authorities.

Denounced as a "rightist" in 1957, Liu remained in obscurity until his rehabilitation in 1979. After being elected vice-chairman of the Chinese Writers Association in 1983, he became even more relentless in attacking Communist institutions and bureaucrats in such works as "Between Men and Phantoms," "The Unfinished Burial," and "The Second Type of Loyalty." Respected in some quarters for daring to challenge the Communist establishment, Liu held a unique place in contemporary Chinese literature. (WINSTON L. Y. YANG)

Mahathir bin Mohamad, Datuk Seri

In 1986 Datuk Seri Mahathir bin Mohamad faced his toughest tests since he became prime minister of Malaysia five years earlier. His influential partner in government, Deputy Prime Minister Musa Hitam, created a stir by dramatically resigning his post in February. Between March and May Mahathir worked closely with his top ministers to defuse political tensions in the East Malaysian state of Sabah, which had boiled over into street violence. And throughout the year pressure mounted on the government as the nation, used to fast economic growth, remained in the grip of a severe recession. Politically, however, Mahathir weathered the crisis when his party, the United Malays National Organization (UMNO), spearheaded an overwhelming victory for the ruling National Front in general elections in August. As a result, the prime minister emerged with his authority strengthened.

The break with Musa was a particularly disenchanting experience at a personal level for Mahathir. The two men had been close friends since the late 1960s. When they took over the running of Malaysia in 1981, the duo provided a model of effective teamwork and were popularly dubbed the "2 Ms" by their compatriots. But rumours of a rift had surfaced by 1984. They were confirmed in late February 1986 when Musa submitted a letter of resignation in which he referred to certain government policies he had "questioned" and said the prime minister had unfairly blamed him for "playing politics" and trying to "unseat" Mahathir from the top job. Some thought Musa was playing for sympathy within UMNO and would bide his time before making a political challenge. Mahathir appointed UMNO veteran Ghafar Baba as his new deputy. The results of the general elections provided a great boost for the prime minister, who was able to reform his Cabinet as he wanted. He removed Musa's allies from powerful posts while boosting the positions of his own.

Mahathir was born on Dec. 20, 1925, in Alor Star, Kedah State. In 1953 he received a degree in medicine at the University of Malaya in Singapore. Initiated into politics in the mid-1940s, Mahathir was elected to Parliament in 1964 and 1974. He was appointed a senator in 1973 and minister of education the following year. Mahathir became deputy prime minister in 1976 under Prime Minister Hussein bin Onn.

(THOMAS HON WING POLIN)

Mahdi, Sadiq al-

On May 6, 1986, Sadiq al-Mahdi became prime minister of The Sudan for the second time in his career when the country returned to civilian rule after a quarter of a century of military government. Beginning in July 1966, he had served for just under a year as prime minister when he was leader of the Umma, the party of the Ansar, the dominant Islamic sect of which he was the titular religious head. Al-Mahdi's great-grandfather was the famous al-Mahdi (Muhammad Ahmad ibn as-Sayyid 'Abd Allah), who led the revolt against Egyptian domination of the Sudan that culminated in the capture of Khartoum in 1885, after a siege that had lasted more than ten months.

Al-Mahdi was a devout Muslim but at the same time bitterly opposed Shari'ah (Islamic law), which had been introduced by former president Gaafar Nimeiry; he believed that Shari'ah was a corruption of the Qur'an and should not be imposed on the non-Muslim communities of The Sudan. His defiance of Nimeiry caused him to be exiled for two periods in the 1970s. Al-Mahdi was completely modern in his outlook and strongly opposed the fundamentalist Muslim Brotherhood, which was led by one of his brothers-in-law.

DAVID CHANNER—CAMERA PRESS LTD.

While the Umma Party was the largest in the country, it was nevertheless a minority in al-Mahdi's coalition government. To maintain the uneasy coalition he brought tolerance and a flair for conciliation; his manner was dignified, courteous, and charming. Al-Mahdi was born in 1936 in The Sudan. He was educated at the University of Oxford, where he later returned to undertake postgraduate studies at St. Anthony's College. His interest in politics began at an early age, and in the early 1960s he helped his father, the late Imam Siddiq, organize the National Opposition Front against an earlier military regime.

Al-Mahdi's skills as a politician stood him in good stead in mediating the conflicts within the Ansar sect, where an interfamily quarrel at first prevented his succession as the Mahdi after the death of his father. He believed strongly in Arab unity and, though pro-Western in his orientation, carried a commitment to his country's role as a nonaligned nation. (COLIN LEGUM)

Mandela, Winnie

During the 24 years that her husband, Nelson Mandela, had spent in a South African prison, Winnie Mandela had emerged as a formidable political figure in her own right. Notwithstanding imprisonments and banishment to a remote town in the Orange Free State, she had maintained a relentless campaign against apartheid and for the release of her husband, who remained the acknowledged leader of the banned

African National Congress (ANC). Her defiance and refusal to obey the conditions of her banishment orders finally led the authorities to yield to her demand that she be allowed to live in the family home in Soweto, the black metropolis near Johannesburg.

Born Nkosikazi Nobandle Nomzamo Madikizela in 1934 at Bizana, Transkei, she fully lived up to her Xhosa name Nomzamo ("she who strives"). The daughter of a teacher, she was trained as a medical social worker in Johannesburg. She married Nelson Mandela, then a lawyer, in 1958. Within two months of her husband's conviction in 1962, she was served with her first banning order, which forbade her to leave Johannesburg and restricted her participation at public and private meetings. Stricter banning orders forbidding her to leave Soweto and to have more than one visitor at a time were later imposed. In 1974–75 she served a six-month prison sentence for banning-order violations. When the house where she lived after her exile in 1977 was burned down by vigilantes in 1985, she moved to Soweto and resisted eviction attempts.

Subsequently she was left undisturbed by the police, even though she ignored the banning order that forbade her to speak at public meetings. Whenever she appeared at such meetings or at the funerals of those killed in police shootings, she attracted crowds of up to 40,000 people. Mandela supported violent resistance to the South African regime, was in favour of the imposition of sanctions, and urged strike action by black workers. She aroused considerable controversy in early 1986 when she appeared to condone "necklacing"—the practice of killing "collaborators" by hanging a burning tire around their necks. She later disavowed the statement. In December there were reports that she had evoked the wrath of her fellow blacks by supporting a convicted murderess.

(COLIN LEGUM)

Maradona, Diego Armando

On June 29, 1986, Argentina defeated West Germany 3–2 in the final of the soccer World Cup, played in the Aztec Stadium, Mexico City. Diego Maradona, captain of the Argentine team, was the outstanding individual player of the tournament. His brilliance in the midfield allowed him to dominate play to such an extent that some commentators suggested, during the earlier rounds of the competition, that the Argentine team would be an insignificant force without him. At the same time, he was a prolific scorer. Although he failed to score in the final game, he tallied five goals during the competition, finishing second to Gary Lineker (England) as top marksman overall.

These talents combined to make Maradona one of the most gifted all-rounders in the history of the game. Soccer fans throughout the world delighted in his strong, fluid running and tight ball control, by which he achieved astonishing penetration of an opposing team's defense.

Born Oct. 30, 1960, in Lanes, Buenos Aires, one of a family of eight children, Maradona acquired his soccer skills in the back streets of Villa Fiorito, a poor suburb of the capital. His outstanding ability was soon recognized, and he was invited to join the Argentinos Juniors club, where he remained until he transferred, for a record $8 million fee, to Boca Juniors in 1981. When Boca defaulted on payment of the fee, Maradona returned briefly to Argentinos Juniors before being signed to play for the Spanish team Barcelona. During the two seasons he spent with Barcelona, he played with distinction, though he was plagued by injury and illness. In 1984 he moved to Italy when the Napoli club paid a $9 million fee for his services.

At the age of 16 Maradona had made his international debut when, playing as a substitute, he took part in Argentina's defeat of Hungary in Buenos Aires in 1977. After that he was always in the reckoning for a place on the national team. One notable exception to his selection occurred in 1978, when Argentina's team manager, Cesar Menotti, considered him too young to be included in the team that went on to win the World Cup in Buenos Aires. When the competition took place four years later in Spain, Menotti had no such qualms; by then, however, Maradona was a member of an otherwise aging team that was defeated in the second round of the competition.

(TREVOR WILLIAMSON)

Mikulic, Branko

In May 1986 Branko Mikulic succeeded Milka Planinc as premier of Yugoslavia for a four-year term. His appointment was made under the unique collective system of leadership that had existed since the death of President-for-Life Tito in 1980. Mikulic was proposed by the Collective Presidency and was supported by the country's six republics and two autonomous provinces. The premier is responsible mainly for Yugoslavia's financial affairs, foreign policy, defense, and regional funds; political matters are handled almost entirely by the Central Committee Presidium (CCP) of the Yugoslav League of Communists (Communist Party). When Mikulic was elected, however, there were hopes that because he had been a member of the CCP, he would also be able to influence it when necessary to enable him to bring about badly needed economic and political reforms.

Mikulic was born in 1928 at Gornji Vakuf in Bosnia and Hercegovina, although he was a Croatian by nationality. After studying economics he joined Tito's National Liberation Army in 1943 and in 1945 became a member of the League of Communists, for which he served on many committees in subsequent years. In 1964 he was secretary of the Central Committee in Bosnia and Hercegovina, which he served as president in 1969–74. From 1969 to 1978 he was a member of the Presidium of the League of Communists. As chairman of the Organizing Committee of the XIV Olympic Winter Games, "Sarajevo-84," held in the republic of Bosnia and Hercegovina, he demonstrated strong organizational skills and acquired a reputation for being a tough and interventionist manager. In the same year, he was made a member of the CCP.

Mikulic faced many problems, not least of which was to keep Yugoslavia united, given the wide range of religious, cultural, and linguistic differences that were constant causes of friction. Social tensions were being exacerbated by the country's poor economy, with prices in 1986 nearly double those of the previous year and the already high rate of unemployment increasing. Solving economic problems was difficult because the constituent republics, with their often "nationalistic" leaders, had so much power. At the same time, Mikulic faced the dilemma that constantly confronted socialist economies—how to reconcile socialist principles with the need to create market forces. It was becoming apparent by year's end that he lacked the power and perhaps the will to carry out the reforms that he stated in his inaugural speech were necessary.

(K. M. SMOGORZEWSKI)

Moses, Edwin Corley

His childhood dream was to become a physician. Running track was just a diversion. Even after he won his first major international race, earning a 1976 Olympic gold medal with his world-record 47.63 sec in the 400-m hurdles, Edwin Moses worried that training had detracted from his studies.

There was no hint then that he would revolutionize his event in the next ten years. Through 1986 he won 118 consecutive races, usually by wide margins. "I never thought I'd be in track and field this long," he said.

Growing up, Moses was a better student than athlete. His parents made that the priority. He was the second of three sons of Irving and Gladys Moses, both school administrators in Dayton, Ohio, where Edwin Corley Moses was born Aug. 31, 1955. When he went to Morehouse College in Atlanta, Ga., it was on an academic scholarship at a school without its own track.

Moses did not waste his B.S. degree in physics and engineering. "I used what I learned in terms of dynamics and mechanics to help me with technique, to break down the motion of my body," said Moses, 188 cm (6 ft 2 in) and 75 kg (165 lb). He kept computer records of all his workouts. His training regimen ran the gamut from ice baths to proprioceptive neuromuscular facilitation, which uses the muscles' own neural receptors to coordinate and strengthen them.

Unlike most of his competitors, Moses took only 13 strides between each of the ten 91.4-cm (36-in) hurdles, a pace few could match. His last defeat was Aug. 26, 1977, to West German Harald Schmid in West Berlin. By the end of 1986 Moses had set four world records, the latest 47.02 sec on Aug. 31, 1983. He ranked first in the world in 9 of 11 years, missing the entire season in 1982 because of pneumonia and in 1985 because of a knee injury. Moses's 1986 comeback added nine victories to his streak, which included 103 in event finals.

In both 1983 and 1984 Moses won the Sullivan Award as the top amateur athlete in the U.S. He was chosen to deliver the athletes' oath at the opening of the 1984 Olympics at Los Angeles. He was one of his sport's most eloquent and respected spokesmen against drug use and outdated amateur restrictions, and he served as a member of U.S. track and field's Athletics Advisory Council.

(KEVIN M. LAMB)

Mswati III

The coronation of King Mswati III of Swaziland was held on April 25, 1986. He succeeded his father, King Sobhuza II, who died in 1982 after a reign of more than 60 years. Mswati was, at 18 years old, the world's youngest head of state. His accession had been expected to take place when he reached the age of 21, but the political uncertainty resulting from the lack of a monarch was thought to have caused the coronation to be held earlier.

The new king was born in Swaziland in 1968, one of more than 60 sons of Sobhuza; according to some estimates, Sobhuza had had 112 wives and as many as 600 children. Reported to be the second youngest son of Sobhuza, Prince Makhosetive had the necessary qualifications to succeed him—he had no full brother and was left-handed—and as soon as he was chosen, he was sent to be schooled in the U.K., where, at Sherborne School in Dorset, he resumed his education following his coronation.

Leaders representing 37 countries from many parts of the world traveled to Mbabane for the ceremony, which included a series of rich displays of Swazi culture: traditional dances, a choir of 400 performing a special song composed for the occasion, and Swazi poets reciting coronation poems. No invitations were issued for the royal dinner, to which all were welcome. Hundreds of thousands of Swazis attended the ceremonies, and every Swazi household contributed about £1.50 toward the costs.

The highlight of the ceremony was the wedding of the king to his chosen bride. A Swazi king may take any number of wives. King Mswati married the girl he was courting, and his attitude toward polygamy was unknown.

The king of Swaziland serves as head of state and exercises power through a Cabinet headed by a prime minister. Despite his youth, King Mswati was quick to consolidate his power. In May he dissolved the Liqoqo (council of elders), which was the king's traditional advisory body but which had become the most powerful body in Swaziland during the three years without a monarch and thus posed a potential threat to his power base. In October he appointed Sotsha Dlamini as prime minister and reshuffled his Cabinet, putting two of his brothers in key positions. This was in line with his coronation pledge to work with people who would help him make Swaziland peaceful and prosperous. King Mswati faced many problems, not least of which were the country's economic difficulties and the problems posed by the disturbances in South Africa, with which it had close trade and financial links.

(GUY ARNOLD)

Museveni, Yoweri Kaguta
On Jan. 29, 1986, Yoweri Museveni was sworn in as president of Uganda after his National Resistance Army (NRA) captured the capital, Kampala, and routed the government forces of Gen. Tito Okello. Museveni had launched his armed struggle in December 1980 after alleging that the election that had given victory to Milton Obote's Uganda People's Congress had been rigged. In that election his own party, the Uganda Patriotic Movement (UPM), which had fielded 44 candidates, managed to win only one seat; Museveni himself had lost in his home constituency, where he was defeated not by Obote's party but by the opposition Democratic Party. While that party, which had won a substantial number of seats, decided to oppose Obote by constitutional means, Museveni took his supporters into the bush to wage an

CAMERA PRESS LTD.

armed struggle. The decision led to a conflict that lasted five years.

Born at Ntungamo in southwestern Uganda in 1944, Museveni was the son of refugees who had fled from Rwanda. He attended school in Mbarara and then studied political science and economics at University College, Dar es Salaam, Tanzania (1966–70). During this period he spent time with the Mozambique Liberation Front (Frelimo) guerrilla group, which subsequently won power in Mozambique and provided Museveni's forces with training facilities. He returned to Uganda, where he worked for a short time in the office of Obote during his first term as president until he was overthrown by Idi Amin in 1971. Museveni then fled to Tanzania.

In 1972 Museveni and Obote joined forces and invaded Uganda but were decisively defeated, causing a split between the two leaders. After the defeat Museveni returned to Tanzania, where he formed the Front for National Salvation. It participated in the 1979 invasion that overthrew Amin. After Amin's downfall, Museveni was made defense minister in Pres. Yusufu Lule's transitional government in 1979, but he soon quarreled with many of his colleagues. He then set up the UPM to campaign in the 1980 elections.

After taking power in January 1986, Museveni adopted a pro-West policy and sought friendship in particular with the U.K., to which he made an official visit in November; the U.K. minister of state at the Foreign Office made a return visit the following month. Museveni's reputation as a Marxist gradually diminished during the year, particularly given his choice of a politically broad-based Cabinet. Apart from serious economic problems he faced continuing civil war, with parts of the north of the country completely controlled by rebel forces.

(COLIN LEGUM)

Najibullah, Mohammad
On Dec. 23, 1986, Maj. Gen. Mohammad Najibullah officially took over control of Afghanistan when he was elected president by the country's top decision-making body, the Revolutionary Council Presidium. He succeeded Babrak Karmal, who resigned as president on November 20, ostensibly for health reasons, after seven years in office. Najibullah in reality took power on May 4, when he was made general secretary of the People's Democratic Party of Afghanistan (PDPA), leaving Karmal with the powerless title of president. This demotion of Karmal had led to an increase in fighting between supporters of the two men, and Najibullah was reported to be angered by the pro-Karmal demonstrations that had been taking place in Kabul, the capital.

The PDPA was divided into two factions: the Kahlq ("masses"), made up of mostly rural Pushtun tribes, which formed the largest ethnic grouping and traditionally provided Afghanistan's rulers, and the more urban Parcham ("flag") faction, which had dominated the Karmal regime. The Parcham faction was broadly based, and Karmal's rule had given the Soviet-imposed government the credibility it sought. However, Karmal was too nationalistic, and the choice of Najibullah to succeed him was not surprising. He gained the confidence of the Soviets, an accomplishment that was reflected in the timing of his first elevation (May), just one day before UN-sponsored Afghanistan peace talks were held in Geneva. Previous talks led by Karmal had been inconclusive, but those scheduled for May 5 were considered to be crucial. Najibullah showed total commitment to the U.S.S.R.

Born in 1947 in Kabul, Najibullah was educated at the Habibia Lycée before studying medicine at Kabul University. He joined the PDPA when he was still a student in 1965 and was twice imprisoned for political activities before serving as ambassador to Iran, from which posting he was fired for allegedly plotting the overthrow of the regime of Hafizullah Amin. His rise to power largely stemmed from his appointment as head of Afghanistan's secret police—the widely feared KHAD—from 1979 until November 1985, when he was promoted to secretary of the party Central Committee with responsibility for security. As head of KHAD, Najibullah reportedly recruited a large number of spies to operate in the resistance movement and bribed tribal leaders to fight guerrillas. At the same time, he won support for his assistance to the cause of Islam, which endeared him to religious leaders. It remained to be seen whether the Soviets would feel confident enough in Najibullah to withdraw their forces from Afghanistan, but the chances for this were greater than when Karmal was ruling.

(DILIP GANGULY)

Nakano, Koichi
No one expected Koichi Nakano to win his tenth consecutive world professional cycling sprint championship at Colorado Springs, Colo., on Sept. 1, 1986. Expectations were low because Nakano, while training, had broken five ribs in May and a collarbone in July. The crowd of 6,000, consequently, rose en masse when Nakano covered the 200 m in 11.08 and 10.67 sec. It was a thrilling spectacle for Nakano's parents, who had made their first trip outside Japan to watch their 30-year-old son race for the world championship. After his spectacular victory, Nakano remarked that the time to retire might have arrived.

Born in Kurume, Fukuoka Prefecture, on Nov. 14, 1955, Nakano as a primary school student was ashamed to fill out forms identifying the profession of his father, Mitsuyoshi, as *keirin* ("professional bicycle racer"); he wrote instead *jiyu-gyo* ("free work"). Later he came to realize that even a sport involving gambling required fortitude and a clear conscience. His father had built an apartment house with honest earnings; following in his father's footsteps, he would do even better and build a mansion.

After graduating from Yame Industrial High School, Nakano entered the Japan Bicycle Racing School in Shuzenji, Shizuoka Prefecture, where he trained 13½ hours daily for ten months before making his debut as a pro cyclist in May 1970. He had already developed strong thighs by riding a bicycle up and down the mountain roads behind Kora-san Shrine outside Kurume and, he recalled, by dashing across rice paddies as a boy to avoid barking dogs that frightened him. Although Nakano stood 1.72 m (5 ft 7 in) tall and weighed a husky 80 kg (176 lb), he claimed that part of his strength also came from *zeni* ("money"). Since turning pro he had won 470 of 775 races and earned 838 million yen ($5.8 million). His greatest thrills were being invited to the emperor's annual autumn garden party in 1984 and being honoured with the Prime Minister's Award on Oct. 17, 1986. When he proposed marriage to 22-year-old Naomi Kokubo, a former pop singer, he asked with a straight face: "Will you wash my cycling trunks?" She blushed and said: "It will be an honour."

(KAY K. TATEISHI)

Nakasone, Yasuhiro
When Yasuhiro Nakasone was elected president of Japan's ruling Liberal-Democratic Party (LDP) in November 1982, he was also guaranteed the prime ministership. Six weeks after becoming head of government, he began a series of overseas trips to cement ties with Japan's allies and enhance his nation's reputation as one of the world's leading economic powers. Nakasone had been elected to the lower house of the Diet (parliament) for the first of 15 terms in April 1947 and thereby became the youngest person ever to hold a seat in that body. Twelve years later he earned his first Cabinet portfolio, but in 1976 he resigned as party secretary-general and embarked on a grass roots tour of the country. At one time Nakasone was labeled *kazami-dori* ("weather vane") for allegedly shifting political allegiances and policies to advance his career. Later he gained notoriety for his outspoken opinions and was even compelled to issue a public apology for remarking that the level of education in the U.S. was lower than that of Japan because the U.S. had such a large minority population.

Nakasone was born on May 27, 1918, in Takasaki, Gumma Prefecture, the son of a lumber dealer. He graduated from Tokyo University in March 1941 and served in the Imperial Navy during World War II. His decision to enter politics was partly influenced by the terrible destruction that had been inflicted on Japan during the war. Nakasone's patriotism had always been one of his most distinguishing characteristics. He was always immaculately dressed, spoke English, and had a fair command of French,

CAMERA PRESS LTD.

German, and Chinese. Although he was known as a workaholic, he kept fit by playing tennis and golf and by swimming. He was also a good amateur painter, wrote several books, and composed haiku, classical poems consisting of 17 syllables. His love of music extended from Bach to old Japanese tunes and modern pop hits.

Nakasone's apparent disregard for tradition took on an added dimension in July. After leading the LDP to a spectacular victory in the national elections—the LDP won 304 seats in the 512-seat lower house—Nakasone made political history by having his tenure as prime minister extended. (KAY K. TATEISHI)

Namphy, Henri

A modest and self-effacing man, Lieut. Gen. Henri Namphy in February 1986 became at 53 president of Haiti's interim governing council, made up of six civilian and military members. His appointment followed the fall of the government headed by President-for-Life Jean-Claude Duvalier, who fled the country with his family on Feb. 7, 1986. Duvalier had assumed the presidency in 1971 after the death of his father, François, who had been head of state since 1957.

Namphy's selection as president was not surprising. He was widely liked and respected and had a reputation for being honest and apolitical. His early weeks in power were traumatic as Haitians ceased their jubilant celebrations over the departure of Duvalier and started rioting and looting. In March, as violence swept the capital, Port-au-Prince, the most popular member of the council resigned as justice minister and Namphy dismissed three other members who had had close ties with the Duvalier regime. The new council had two other members apart from Namphy himself. By April the strain was beginning to tell, and for a short period Namphy was treated in the hospital for exhaustion. The governing council had difficulty in exerting its authority throughout 1986 because of frequent strikes and demonstrations. Observers at home and abroad regarded Namphy and his interim government as ineffective. At the same time, there was no alternative, and an election held in October for a constituent assembly to prepare a draft constitution reflected a lack of public interest in determining the country's political future.

Namphy was unusual in his lack of political ambition. From the start of his presidency he made it clear that he would hand over power to an elected president. (Elections were scheduled for November 1987, with the swearing in of the new government in February 1988.) His lack of political dynamism possibly explained why support for him was waning. The electorate demanded the removal of all associates of Duvalier from Namphy's administration, while at the same time he faced opposition from supporters of Duvalier who had lost the privileges they enjoyed during the latter's rule. Against this, Namphy maintained the support of church leaders and, since some 80% of the island's population were Roman Catholics, this was a strong unifying factor. Toward the year's end his popularity was boosted when he returned from a visit to the U.S. after having obtained $10 million worth of new aid, and by December the island was relatively peaceful.

(ROBIN CHAPMAN)

REUTERS/BETTMANN NEWSPHOTOS

O'Malley, Desmond Joseph

When Desmond O'Malley launched the Progressive Democrats Party in December 1985, the instantaneous and overwhelming reaction from the people of Ireland was one of strong support. Much of this was a personal vote for O'Malley, whose proven ability as a politician, coupled with his right-wing views on the economy, appealed to the business sector and the hard-pressed taxpayers. But support also came from all across the political spectrum for a party that was seen to be attempting to break the mold of "civil-war" politics that prevailed within Ireland's two traditional parties, Fine Gael and Fianna Fail.

O'Malley's entry into politics was controversial. Born Feb. 2, 1939, in Limerick, County Limerick, he studied law at University College, Dublin, and then practiced as a solicitor in his father's firm in Limerick. When his uncle, Minister for Education Donough O'Malley, died, his nephew decided to contest the by-election despite the intention of his uncle's widow to seek the nomination. He won the seat and entered the Dail (parliament) in 1968 as a member of Fianna Fail. His ability was quickly recognized, and in less than a year he became parliamentary secretary to Jack Lynch, the then taoiseach (prime minister).

In 1970 O'Malley was appointed minister for justice, where his tough, abrasive style won him grudging admiration. In 1977 he became what was later described as the most capable minister for industry and commerce that Ireland had known. Considered by many members of Fianna Fail to be the natural heir to Lynch, he suffered a turn for the worse in his career when Charles Haughey took over the party leadership in 1979. O'Malley subsequently was involved in three unsuccessful attempts to remove Haughey. His final break with the party came when he criticized his leader's interpretation of the report of the New Ireland Forum. O'Malley was expelled in May 1985 for "conduct unbecoming," a phrase that was to become famous in Irish politics.

A small, gritty, abrasive man who seldom smiled and whose chief relaxation was attending horse races, O'Malley was married and had six children. Opinion polls in 1986 indicated that his party could take about eight seats in general elections and thus hold the balance of power.

(MAVIS ARNOLD)

Pattison, James Allen

Vancouver's Expo 86, the last world's fair planned for North America in the 20th century, was the largest such event in Canada since Montreal's Expo 67. The person chosen by the British Columbia government to head this gigantic transportation and communications fair was an aggressive, energetic, and successful Vancouver businessman named Jim Pattison. He began as chairman of the board of directors of Expo 86, but in June 1985 he fired the president of the exposition for making extravagant use of his expense account. Taking complete charge, he managed the fair as though it were one of his companies. For all this, Pattison was paid one dollar a year. Known as a great booster of the city of Vancouver, he was also made chairman of B.C. Place, a provincial government corporation formed to develop the fair site as a huge urban renewal project after the exposition closed.

Born Oct. 1, 1928, in Saskatoon, Sask., James Allen Pattison grew up in Vancouver. He began his career as an entrepreneur by selling garden seeds to people in his neighbourhood. Pattison financed his studies toward a commerce degree at the University of British Columbia by selling used cars. In 1951 he became the manager of a large General Motors dealership in Vancouver; in 1961 he bought the dealership; and he eventually became Canada's largest auto dealer. By 1986 he was president and chief executive officer of the Jim Pattison Group, Canada's largest solely owned conglomerate, consisting of more than 30 companies and doing business in transportation, real estate, food and beverages, communications, and financial services. Pattison was also the owner of the Vancouver Canadians, a minor league baseball team.

A staunch free-enterprise businessman, Pattison worked hard, took few vacations, and expected his top managers to do the same. As an auto dealer, he fired the salesman with the lowest production each month. In the Jim Pattison Group, each corporation ran its own operations, but Pattison kept careful check on them, spending much of his time visiting and consulting with the managers. He learned from his Japanese suppliers and colleagues the importance of quality and teamwork. His annual management conference was called "Partners in Pride," and his corporate symbol stood for "people utilizing capital to create a product or service for the marketplace." (DIANE LOIS WAY)

Polanyi, John Charles

The Canadian chemist John C. Polanyi shared—with Yuan T. Lee and Dudley R. Herschbach (*qq.v.*) of the United States—the Nobel Prize for Chemistry in 1986. Polanyi was cited for his investigations of infrared chemiluminescence, the emission of radiation by molecules when their rotations and internal vibrations slow down. Analysis of this radiation provides detailed information about the distribution of energy within chemical species and the relation of this distribution to the details of the sequences of events occurring during reactions. Polanyi's technique is a complement to the molecular-beam approach developed by Herschbach and Lee.

Polanyi was born on Jan. 23, 1929, in Berlin. In 1952 he received a Ph.D. in chemistry from the University of Manchester, where his father, the late Michael Polanyi, a noted physical chemist, had been a professor until 1948. He undertook postdoctoral research at the National Research Council of Canada in Ottawa and at Princeton University and then joined the faculty at the University of Toronto in 1956.

Earlier chemists had shown that many reactions of simple compounds are quite complicated. For example, the reaction between hydrogen and chlorine, forming hydrogen chloride and releasing considerable energy, occurs at a rate best explained by proposing that a series of several steps, instead of simple two-body collisions, must take place. This account, however, leaves open the question of the precise origin of the heat. Studying one of the proposed steps, Polanyi found that when hydrogen atoms and chlorine molecules collide at 77 K (−321° F), the newly formed hydrogen chloride molecules have vibrational kinetic energies corresponding to a temperature of about 3,000 K (4,940° F). That is, the energy must first appear in the form of vigorous vibration, rather than the alternative forms of abnormally fast rotation or rapid motion of the molecule through space.

(JOHN V. KILLHEFFER)

Puttnam, David Terence

In September 1986, shortly after his production *The Mission* won the Grand Prize of the Cannes Film Festival, David Puttnam took up his appointment as chairman and chief executive of Columbia Pictures Industries Inc., which had recently been incorporated into the giant Coca-Cola Corp. The move to Hollywood startled the general public, which, since the success of *Chariots of Fire* (1981), had seen Puttnam as the saviour and champion of the British film

GEMMA LEVINE—CAMERA PRESS LTD.

industry. Those who knew him better, however, were already aware of his disillusionment with British cinema; he complained that there had never been a national film tradition, and he had always criticized the lack of government support. He had spoken of leaving films to return to advertising and of accepting a Harvard University fellowship to study philosophy. Instead, he announced that in Coca-Cola he had at last found the truly international organization for which, as a filmmaker, he had always yearned.

Puttnam's career had moved far and fast. The son of a Fleet Street agency photographer, he was born Feb. 25, 1941, in Southgate, north London. At 16 he left his local grammar school to join an agency as a messenger boy. Within four years he was handling accounts. In 1966 he started his own photographic agency, to which he rapidly attracted some of the best talents in the business. Two years later, with Sandy Lieberson, he formed his first film production company. In the years that followed, which included a brief period in Hollywood, he had as many failures (including three films directed by Ken Russell) as successes, but the successes—*That'll Be the Day* (1974), *Bugsy Malone* (1976), *Midnight Express* (1978), *Local Hero* (1983), *The Killing Fields* (1984), and, above all, *Chariots of Fire*—erased the memory of the rest.

Puttnam was one of the rare producers whose name counted for more on a film than that of the director. In part this derived from his preference for newcomer directors, who were likely to accept more comfortably his strong creative contribution. He was inspired by the U.S. films of his boyhood—"films that were deeply thematic, but easily accessible to the audience"—and felt that movies should "show what is best in society, or what can be so, given the exceptional man or woman with vision and willpower." He was also confident that his taste as "the absolutely quintessential middle-class person" coincided with that of a large, important audience. He had never underestimated this audience's intellect, but neither had he strained it too far. (DAVID ROBINSON)

Ratzinger, Joseph Alois Cardinal
Appointed to the office of prefect of the Sacred Congregation for the Doctrine of the Faith (formerly the Holy Office) in November 1981, West German theologian Joseph Cardinal Ratzinger arrived in Rome to take up his appointment in early 1982. Though Pope Paul VI (1963–78) had attempted to change its role to that of "encouraging sound theology," during the era of Pope John Paul II the function of the Congregation had reverted to the task of denouncing alleged errors and ousting unorthodox theologians. The shift in emphasis was well exemplified by events in 1986. In August the Rev. Charles E. Curran lost his license to teach as a Roman Catholic theologian at the Catholic University of America, Washington, D.C., or at any other Roman Catholic school. In September the Rev. Edward Schillebeeckx of The Netherlands was informed that his views on "apostolic succession" and ordination were not in agreement with a Ratzinger declaration of 1983. South American liberation theologians also came under the scrutiny of Ratzinger in the course of 1986, although in April the order of silence placed on Brazilian priest Leonardo Boff a year earlier was removed.

The cardinal explained his thinking in *The Ratzinger Report* (1985). He believed that liberal theologians had become too "secular" in their outlook and opened themselves indiscriminately to the modern world. He maintained that there was need of a "restoration"—a term Ratzinger defined not as some impossible turning back of the clock but as "the quest for a new equilibrium." But however defined, it came across as a distinctly conservative attitude. The fact was all the more surprising in that at the Second Vatican Council (1962–65) Ratzinger had been justifiably regarded as one of the more open-minded theologians. Indeed, he had helped launch an attack on iniquitous methods employed by the office that he subsequently headed. His swing to the right could, however, be traced back in his career; as long ago as 1968 he was alarmed by the spread of neo-Marxist ideas among West German theology students, and he broke with the ultraprogressive theologians associated with *Concilium*, a multilanguage theological review. Ratzinger claimed to have been thoroughly consistent: "I have not changed—the others have."

Ratzinger was born April 16, 1927, at Marklt, Bavaria, the son of a policeman. He was a brilliant student and held chairs of theology successively at the Universities of Freising (1951), Bonn (1958), Münster (1963), Tübingen (1966), and Regensburg (1969). He was made archbishop of Munich-Freising and a cardinal in the same year, 1977. In Munich he had to struggle with the consequences of what he believed to be the "secularization" of a once deeply Catholic region. (PETER HEBBLETHWAITE)

Reagan, Ronald Wilson
On Jan. 1, 1986, Soviet television broadcast, unedited, a taped, five-minute speech by Ronald Reagan, president of the United States. The same day, most television stations in the U.S. broadcast a similar speech by Mikhail Sergeyevich Gorbachev, general secretary of the Communist Party of the Soviet Union. However, the widespread assumption that Gorbachev would visit the U.S. in 1986 came to nothing, despite frequent correspondence—and an unproductive meeting—between the two leaders. The fate of the proposed summit was, perhaps, symbolic of the president's year, which careened from highs—the spectacular celebration of the Statue of Liberty's centennial, with Reagan presiding; more substantively, passage of the long-promised tax reform—to laws: the abortive meeting with Gorbachev; the loss of GOP control of the Senate despite Reagan's vigorous campaigning; the scandal of U.S. arms shipments to Iran that threatened, at last, to touch the man journalists had nicknamed the "Teflon president."

The start of the year was shadowed by the explosion of the space shuttle, forcing the president to delay his state of the union message. But in mid-February a warmly received visit to Grenada recalled how the U.S. had "stood tall" by sending military help to the troubled island in 1983, and if the April air raid on Libya—in retaliation for alleged terrorist acts—troubled the country's allies, it seemed popular with most Americans. At the summit of seven leading industrialized nations in Tokyo in May, the final communiqué appeared to reflect Reagan's views on free markets and terrorism. A June Gallup Poll gave the president a 68% approval rating.

Slippage began with the "presummit" meeting with Gorbachev at Reykjavík, Iceland, October 11–12, suggested by the general secretary and accepted by Reagan, despite the reservations of some foreign policy experts over the lack of preparation. From all reports, the two leaders came close to an unprecedented agreement on nuclear disarmament, but the meeting broke up over Gorbachev's insistence that the U.S. forgo testing of a major Reagan defense program, the Strategic Defense Initiative antiballistic missile system.

The White House insisted the meeting was an overall success, but it was not so easy to explain away news that the U.S. had sold arms to Iran, although the president had branded it a terrorist state, and that some of the money had been used to help the Nicaraguan *contras*, possibly in violation of U.S. law. (*See* WORLD AFFAIRS [North America]: *United States*.) Though all the facts were not known at year's end, it seemed that, at best, Reagan had not kept tight control of his own administration. Still, there was a reservoir of goodwill toward the president, and it was strengthened by news that he faced prostate surgery early in 1987. As the year drew to a close, the future of the Reagan presidency was an open question.

Ronald Reagan was born in Tampico, Ill., on Feb. 6, 1911. In 1937 he became an actor under contract to Warner Brothers, and he served as president of the Screen Actors Guild from 1947 to 1952 and 1959 to 1960. He was governor of California from 1967 to 1975 and began his first presidential term in 1981.

(CHARLES JOHNSON TAGGART)

Rehnquist, William Hubbs
On Sept. 17, 1986, the U.S. Senate confirmed, by a vote of 65–33, Pres. Ronald Reagan's nomination of Justice William Rehnquist to be chief justice of the United States. Never before had so many senators voted against a nominee for the Supreme Court who was not rejected. Rehnquist was regarded, even by his harshest critics, as highly intelligent and as eloquent—if often sharp—in advocating a very limited role for the courts in blocking the actions of federal and state officials. He was sworn in as chief justice on September 26.

William Hubbs Rehnquist was born on Oct. 1, 1924, in Milwaukee, Wis. He served in the U.S. Army Air Corps from 1943 to 1946 and received both a B.A. and an M.A. from Stanford University in 1948 and another M.A. from Harvard University in 1949. He received an LL.B. from Stanford in 1952, graduating first in his class. He served as law clerk to Robert H. Jackson, a justice of the U.S. Supreme Court,

AP/WIDE WORLD

from 1952 to 1953. Controversy surrounded Rehnquist's memorandum to Jackson affirming states' authority to enforce racial segregation; Rehnquist said that the memorandum reflected Jackson's opinion.

In 1953, attracted by economic growth in the area, Rehnquist went to work for a law firm in Phoenix, Ariz. He was a full partner in succeeding firms after 1956. Active in Republican politics, he was outspokenly opposed to governmental restrictions on property owners. As a Republican poll watcher in 1962, he challenged black and Hispanic voters on the grounds of illiteracy; one witness accused him of harassment.

In 1969 U.S. Pres. Richard Nixon appointed Rehnquist assistant attorney general for the Office of Legal Counsel. He frequently defended, before congressional committees and before the press, the administration's surveillance and prosecution of persons who protested against U.S. military policies. Though offensive to civil libertarians, his speeches were considered eloquent and learned.

Rehnquist was appointed a justice of the Supreme Court by President Nixon in 1971; 26 senators voted against his nomination. In 1972 he was criticized for not disqualifying himself in *Laird* v. *Tatum,* in which he voted to uphold the legality of a plan for military surveillance of civilians though he had been a member of the administration that had devised the plan. His decisions generally adhered to precedents but interpreted them to favour actions by legislatures and by police officers. He interpreted the rights of criminal defendants and prison inmates narrowly, affirmed states' authority to forbid abortion, and suggested that the government might favour religion over irreligion.

(CHARLES JOHNSON TAGGART)

Robertson, The Rev. Pat

In his blend of old-time religion and modern communications technology, the Rev. Pat Robertson may have found a potent political formula. In the summer of 1986 the "televangelist" ran thousands of candidates in the Republican precinct-delegate elections in Michigan, a first step toward selecting state delegates for the party's national convention in 1988. Although the final tally remained in dispute, Robertson followed closely enough behind GOP favourites Vice-Pres. George Bush and New York Rep. Jack Kemp to raise the prospect that he might become a power broker during the presidential primaries. Then in September he declared that he would run for president himself if, within a year, voters contributed three million signatures and $3 million to his campaign for moral and spiritual revival. As head of the Christian Broadcasting Network (CBN), reported to reach more than 25 million viewers per month and bring in almost $200 million per year, Robertson was not expected to have much trouble reaching that goal.

UPI/BETTMANN NEWSPHOTOS

Marion Gordon Robertson was born in Lexington, Va., on March 22, 1930, the son of a U.S. senator. He attended Washington and Lee University in Lexington (B.A. 1950), and during the Korean War he was an officer in the Marine Corps. He graduated from Yale University Law School in 1955 but, after failing the New York State bar exam, he began a career in business. At the age of 26 he experienced a Christian rebirth, whereupon he entered the New York Theological Seminary (M.Div., 1959) and was ordained into the Southern Baptist Church. He then moved to Portsmouth, Va., where in 1960, using borrowed and donated money, he set up the nation's first Christian television station. During the next quarter of a century Robertson, using the innovations of satellite and cable transmission, built his tiny station into CBN, which in 1986 was reported to be one of the four largest cable networks in the United States.

CBN offered old films and network reruns as well as its own news programs, made-for-TV movies, and even a Christian soap opera. The mainstay of the network was the religious talk show "The 700 Club," with Robertson as a host. Judging by the response of the viewers, whose donations provided the bulk of CBN's income, this program of gospel and wholesome entertainment was well received. As a political candidate, Robertson found a more skeptical audience. In October 1986 he filed suit against detractors who claimed that he had used his father's influence to avoid combat duty in Korea. Criticism also grew around his use of CBN for free campaign publicity.

(ROBERT CURLEY)

Robinson, Peter David

Ever since 1966, when he heard Northern Irish politician Ian Paisley rouse a great political rally at the Ulster Hall in Belfast, Peter Robinson had followed in Paisley's footsteps. A 17-year-old schoolboy at the time, he immediately committed himself to the Protestant fundamentalist and militant Loyalist movement. When Paisley was elected to the U.K. Parliament in 1970, Robinson went with him as his political secretary, and he was a founder member of the Democratic Unionist Party (DUP)—Paisley's response to moderate tendencies within the Unionist Party (later the Official Unionist Party [OUP])—at its launch in 1972.

Born on Dec. 29, 1948, in Belfast and educated at Northern Ireland's Annadale Grammar School and Castlereagh Further Education College, Robinson rose quickly within the DUP. He became party secretary in 1973 and its full-time general secretary in 1975. He moved the party headquarters to East Belfast, a strongly working-class district, where he proceeded to establish a political base of his own; in 1979 he won the parliamentary seat there. The DUP began to flourish under Robinson as his organizational skills proved complementary to the charismatic appeal of Paisley, who had his base in the Free Presbyterian Church of Ulster, of which he remained moderator. While the latter expounded religion, Robinson used computer technology to help project the DUP into working-class areas at the expense of the OUP.

After the 1979 general elections the DUP lost some of its momentum until 1985, when the U.K. government of Prime Minister Margaret Thatcher entered into a new relationship with the government of the Republic of Ireland. The Anglo-Irish agreement signed at Hillsborough in November of that year at once fanned the fires of Protestant extremism and revived the fortunes of the DUP. Paisley, who in 1986 reached the age of 60, had lost some of his appeal. Robinson, meanwhile, was reputed to have closer contacts with the "hard men" of the Ulster Defence Association, the principal Loyalist paramilitary organization. In August 1986 he led a group of Protestants across the border into County Monaghan in the Republic, ostensibly to demonstrate the inadequacy of cross-border security measures. During an attack on the police station in the village of Clontibret, Robinson was arrested and held for 40 hours. He was due to stand trial in Dublin in mid-January 1987 on charges connected with the incident. The affair established Robinson as a hero in the eyes of many Protestants and confirmed his position as heir apparent to Paisley.

(PETER JENKINS)

Rohrer, Heinrich

As one of the principal developers of the scanning tunneling microscope (STM), the Swiss physicist Heinrich Rohrer shared, with Gerd Binnig (*q.v.*) of West Germany, half of the Nobel Prize for Physics in 1986. (Ernst Ruska [*q.v.*] of West Germany won the rest of the prize.)

Atoms are about 1 Å (one angstrom, a ten-billionth of a metre) in diameter. Since the 19th century, physicists have sought devices for producing images of them. Optical microscopes cannot resolve objects less than about 2,500 Å across; electron microscopes, invented by Ruska in the early 1930s, lowered this limit to 5 or 10 Å.

In the STM the tip of a tungsten probe is brought within 5–10 Å of the surface of a conducting or semiconducting material. When the electric potential of the tip, itself only an atom or two wide, is made to differ by a few volts from that of the surface, a measurable current crosses the gap. This current is explained by the quantum mechanical phenomenon called tunneling, in which the wavelike properties of electrons and other minute particles make it possible for them to appear in places that, under the rules of classical physics, they could not reach. The strength of this current is extremely sensitive to the distance between the probe and the surface. As the tip scans the surface, it can be kept a fixed distance away by raising and lowering it so as to hold the current constant. A record of the elevation of the probe is a topographical map of the surface, on which the contour intervals are so small that the individual atoms are clearly recognizable.

Rohrer was born in Switzerland on June 6, 1933, and educated at the Swiss Federal Institute of Technology in Zürich, receiving a Ph.D. in 1960. He held a two-year postdoctoral fellowship at the State University of Rutgers, New Brunswick, N.J., before returning to Switzerland to join the IBM Zürich Research Laboratory.

(JOHN V. KILLHEFFER)

Ruska, Ernst August Friedrich

Until the 1930s the examination of tiny objects relied on optical microscopes, in which glass lenses focus a beam of light to illuminate the specimen. In the course of about five centuries of development, the various defects of these lenses had been corrected, and the magnifying power of optical microscopes had been pushed close to the theoretical limit fixed by the wavelengths of visible light. These microscopes can produce useful images about 2,000 times larger than the object and can distinguish features that are about eight millionths of an inch apart. To study objects smaller than this, another technique is needed.

During the 1930s it was shown that electrons have the properties of waves much shorter than those of light. If electrons could be focused as sharply as light, magnifications 100,000 times greater than those of optical microscopes should be possible. Glass lenses are useless for this purpose, but in 1931 Ernst Ruska built the first electron lens, an electromagnet that created a specially shaped field. By 1933 his electron microscope gave greater magnification than the best optical microscopes. Electron lenses suffer all the image distortions of light lenses, but it has not been possible to correct them fully. Even so, commercial electron microscopes now produce magnifications about 1,000 times greater than the optical analogues. For his achievements, Ruska was awarded half the Nobel Prize for Physics in 1986. (The other half was shared by Gerd Binnig and Heinrich Rohrer [*qq.v.*].)

Ernst August Friedrich Ruska was born in Heidelberg, Germany, on Dec. 25, 1906. He began his higher education at the Technical University of Munich but transferred to the Technical University of Berlin, which awarded him a doctor's degree in engineering in 1934. He held industrial research positions from 1933 until 1955. Then—until his retirement in 1972—he was director of the Institute of Electron Microscopy of the Fritz Haber Institute of the Max Planck Society. For many years he combined his research career with teaching positions at the Technical University and the Free University of Berlin. (JOHN V. KILLHEFFER)

Savimbi, Jonas Malheiro
Jonas Savimbi won a substantial victory in January 1986 when the U.S. administration agreed to supply his National Union for the Total Independence of Angola (UNITA) with economic and military aid. Because the Angolan regime was strongly supported by the U.S.S.R. and Cuba, Savimbi, its challenger, had become a favourite of the conservative caucus in Washington, which had lobbied hard on his behalf. Savimbi had waged a military struggle against the regime of the Popular Movement for the Liberation of Angola (MPLA) ever since independence in 1975.

Savimbi was born Aug. 3, 1934, in Munhango, Ovimbundu territory. His father, the first black stationmaster under Portuguese colonial rule, was determined that his son should receive a good education to enable him to participate in the struggle for Angolan independence. After completing his secondary education in mission schools, Savimbi received a scholarship to train as a doctor at Coimbra University in Portugal. He soon fell foul of the Portuguese security police, however, and in 1960 escaped to Switzerland, where he enrolled at Lausanne University and gained a doctorate in political science, even though his studies were constantly interrupted by his political activities as a member of the Union of the Angolan Peoples, rival to the MPLA. He broke with its leader, Holden Roberto, and in 1966 formed UNITA, which was given military support by China. Savimbi, who returned to Angola in the mid-1960s, was the only guerrilla leader who remained inside the country until 1975, when Portuguese colonial rule ended. The Alvor agreement, under which the three liberation movements were to form a coalition government at independence, was not honoured; instead, the rival movements fought for power, with the Soviets and Cubans supporting the MPLA and the South African Army supporting UNITA.

JAN KOPEC—CAMERA PRESS LTD.

Although strongly opposed to apartheid, Savimbi maintained that it was necessary to accept help from any source for the sake of survival. His connection with the Pretoria regime had turned many, though not all, African governments against him. Relying on the support of the Ovimbundu, the largest tribal group in the country, Savimbi built up an army estimated at 80,000. While he acknowledged that neither side could win the military struggle, he believed that a military stalemate would inevitably lead to the creation of a coalition government and the end of civil strife. (COLIN LEGUM)

Scalia, Antonin
In nominating Antonin Scalia to the U.S. Supreme Court in June 1986, Pres. Ronald Reagan delivered a political and judicial masterstroke. The president reasoned that Scalia, a youth at age 50 compared with Justices William Brennan (80), Lewis Powell (78), Harry Blackmun (77), and Thurgood Marshall (77), would be a conservative voice on the court for years to come. Even liberal judges had to admit that their eloquent, scholarly, and congenial colleague would be a formidable opponent of "judicial activism," the courts' practice of using their powers of legal review to mandate social programs without passing legislation. Republican strategists were pleased that Scalia, the son of an Italian immigrant, came from a largely Democratic ethnic group whose traditional values the GOP had long hoped to translate into conservative votes.

These advantages swept the nominee to unanimous confirmation by the Senate—in contrast to William Rehnquist (*q.v.*), whose seat on the bench Scalia was taking and whose own confirmation as chief justice came only after grave misgivings had been voiced by many senators.

Antonin Scalia was born March 11, 1936, in Trenton, N.J. After a Roman Catholic high-school education in New York City, he was graduated in 1957 at the top of his class from Georgetown University, Washington, D.C. He went to law school at Harvard, editing the *Law Review* and graduating in 1960. From 1961 to 1967 he worked for a law firm in Cleveland, Ohio. He taught law at the University of Virginia from 1967 to 1974, also serving as a counsel in the White House Office of Telecommunications Policy (1971–72). From 1974 to 1977 he was an assistant attorney general in the Office of Legal Counsel at the U.S. Department of Justice.

Returning to academia full-time, Scalia taught law at the University of Chicago from 1977 until Reagan appointed him to the U.S. Court of Appeals, District of Columbia Circuit, in 1982. He served there until sworn in as associate justice of the Supreme Court on Sept. 26, 1986.

As an advocate of "judicial restraint," Scalia insisted that the court had no business granting the right to abortion before society could decide, through the democratic process, whether such a right existed. In affirmative action cases, he believed that plaintiffs must present specific evidence that employers were motivated by bias in denying them jobs. (ROBERT CURLEY)

Shah, Eddie
Though its launch on March 4, 1986, was overshadowed by the dispute between printworkers and management at Rupert Murdoch's News International, Eddie Shah's daily newspaper, *Today,* sent shock waves through Britain's traditionally conservative national press. Being a pioneer was risky, however, and by August Shah had lost control of his paper. Yet its impact was unquestionable.

Born Selim Jehan Shah in Cambridge, England, on Jan. 20, 1944, he was the son of Anglo-Iranian parents. After schooling, which included a spell at Gordonstoun (the private school in Scotland later chosen for the prince of Wales), he tried his hand at the theatre and television before taking a job selling advertisement space in the Manchester area. The boom in free papers, given away and wholly funded by advertising, was opening up opportunities for entrepreneurs ready to take advantage of the old-fashioned attitudes and creaking technology prevalent in much of Britain's press. By 1974 Shah was owner of the *Sale and Altrincham Messenger,* and subsequently he built up a business empire based on free papers using new technology.

By the 1980s, ready to move on to the national stage, he announced his plans for a new national daily paper, *Today,* an all-colour tabloid that would employ direct news input by journalists (bypassing the printworkers who had traditionally handled composition). In 1983 Shah had confronted the print unions head-on during a violent dispute with the National Graphical Association over a closed-shop policy operated by the union at Shah's Warrington plant. Alerted by Shah's challenge, other newspaper managements had begun modernizing their plants by the time *Today* first appeared.

The long-awaited tabloid failed, however, to make inroads on its rivals, and its circulation sagged within weeks. Critics were unimpressed by its poor colour reproduction, patchy distribution, and tardy news coverage—Shah himself admitted these failings. In June the Lonrho group mounted a rescue bid, and by August Shah had relinquished his stake and his role in the ailing paper. He remained chairman in name only. He returned to his base in northwest England and promptly bought the *Warrington Guardian* newspaper group, a rival to his *Messenger* chain. Undaunted, Shah envisioned further innovations, including laser printing and desktop production. (BRIAN WILLIAMS)

Shamir, Yitzhak
The first tenure of Yitzhak Shamir as Israel's prime minister in 1983–84, following the resignation of Menachem Begin, was traumatic. He was attacked, criticized, and denigrated not only by the opposition but also by colleagues—and rivals for office—in his own party, Likud. They believed he lacked stature, charisma, and experience and, in the face of serious economic and political difficulties, his position looked extremely vulnerable. But the calibre of Shamir was underestimated.

Shamir spent his early life in Poland, where he was born in 1915. He studied law at Warsaw University and continued his studies at Israel's Hebrew University. During World War II he was arrested by the British while he was fighting with the Freedom Fighters of Israel. Following periods of imprisonment and political asylum in France, he returned to Israel in 1948. He resumed his political activities in 1955 and for ten years was involved in intelligence work. First elected to the Knesset (parliament) in 1973, he served as foreign minister (1980–83).

When his premiership was challenged in 1983, Shamir had no difficulty in demonstrating his authority, and after the general election

AP/WIDE WORLD

of 1984, which produced a political stalemate, he responded positively to Pres. Chaim Herzog's suggestion that a government of national unity be formed in which power would be shared equally between Likud and Labour. The national unity government was based on an agreement whereby Labour leader Shimon Peres would serve for two years as prime minister with Shamir as foreign minister, after which their roles would be reversed. Few Israelis believed the arrangement would or could work. It did, however, and on Oct. 20, 1986, Shamir became prime minister and presented a virtually unchanged government.

For Israel it had been a revolutionary and startling experience, which had allowed the sound and fury of party and sometimes of partisan politics without threatening cohesion. The original unity agreement was framed so that the rotation of roles depended on Peres and Shamir remaining as the leaders of their parties. A successful challenge to Shamir's leadership would have involved a breakup of the coalition and new elections, which neither Likud nor Labour wanted. It was for Shamir—and Peres—the most potent sanction against restless party rivals.

Shamir maintained a noncontroversial profile as foreign minister during Peres's premiership. He concentrated on strengthening his leadership of Likud and maintaining a highly competent and professional staff at the Foreign Ministry to handle foreign policy. (JON KIMCHE)

Shcharansky, (Anatoly) Natan

On Feb. 11, 1986, long-time Soviet dissident and human rights activist Anatoly Shcharansky and three men accused of being NATO spies were exchanged for five people from Warsaw Pact countries on the Glienicke Bridge on the outskirts of West Berlin. Thus ended eight years of incarceration in prisons and labour camps for Shcharansky, an ardent campaigner for the right of Soviet Jews to emigrate. Defiant to the end, when a KGB agent on the bridge instructed Shcharansky to walk straight ahead to a waiting car, he walked in a zigzag fashion instead.

Within hours of his snowy walk across the bridge to freedom, an overjoyed Shcharansky was reunited with his wife, Avital, whom he had not seen since 1974, and they were on their way to Israel. In a welcoming speech, Israeli Prime Minister Shimon Peres, announcing that Shcharansky was adopting the Hebrew name Natan (which means "gift of God"), said, "We receive here a great and heroic man, made of unbreakable material, unbreakable spirit."

Anatoly Borisovich Shcharansky was born Jan. 20, 1948, in the Ukraine. He was trained at the Moscow Physical-Technical Institute, where he became a computer specialist, and after graduation in 1972 was employed as a programmer

MICHAEL BLACKMAN—CAMERA PRESS LTD.

at the Oil and Gas Research Institute. The job supposedly exposed him to state secrets and became the official reason for denying his request for an exit visa. Shcharansky became involved in the dissident movement in Moscow, where he met Avital. In the summer of 1974, soon after they were married, she left for Israel thinking he would follow shortly.

Shcharansky was arrested in March 1977 and sentenced on July 14, 1978, to 13 years' imprisonment for treason, espionage, and anti-Soviet agitation. In his closing remarks to courtroom spectators, Shcharansky reiterated his commitment to emigration for himself and thousands of others: "I say, turning to my people, my Avital: 'Next year in Jerusalem.' Now I turn to you, the court . . . To you, I have nothing to say."

In his first press conference in Jerusalem following his release, Shcharansky described his life in Soviet jails: the physical hardships, the psychological burden of isolation, both in a cell and from his family, and the constant pressure to inform on others or confess fictitiously. However, those who knew the man before his arrest said he was little changed, his wit and humour intact and his passion for truth unabated. On August 25 he was reunited in Vienna with his mother and brother, who had refused to apply for exit visas until Anatoly was released. In November a child was born to Avital and Natan. (BONNIE OBERMAN)

Shepherd, Cybill, and Willis, Bruce

Television viewers who tuned in late to ABC's detective series "Moonlighting" one night during its first season probably thought their colour sets were broken. The entire episode was shot in black and white in the style of 1940s *film noir.* On another night the leading characters answered fan mail at the opening of the show. Still other episodes featured the "Moonlighting" versions of the Christmas classic *It's a Wonderful Life* and Shakespeare's *The Taming of the Shrew,* the latter in iambic pentameter. After its first episode aired on March 3, 1985, "Moonlighting" inched its way upward in the ratings to a regular place in the top ten, and in its first season it received 16 Emmy nominations. One of the reasons for its success was undoubtedly its high production values; at an estimated $1.6 million per episode, it was one of the most expensive hour-long series on TV, and shooting each episode took at least four more days than the usual time allotted for such shows. But the main attractions were the partners in the Blue Moon detective agency: the cool, glamorous Maddie Hayes, played by Cybill Shepherd, and her impudent wise-guy cohort, David Addison, played by Bruce Willis. As *Newsweek* magazine put it, they had "a sexual chemistry potent enough to curl plexiglass," and week after week they teased their audience with it, leaving everyone to wonder when they would finally get together.

Shepherd was born Feb. 18, 1950, in Memphis, Tenn. She was Miss Teenage Memphis, a contestant in the 1966 Miss Teenage America pageant, and a successful model before her critically acclaimed film debut in *The Last Picture Show* in 1971. Despite her performances in such movies as *The Heartbreak Kid* (1973) and *Taxi Driver* (1976), her career went into retreat. She returned to Memphis, married, and had a child. After her marriage ended in divorce, she moved back to Hollywood to resume her career. She starred in the TV series "The Yellow Rose" in 1983, and critics singled her out for praise. When Glenn Caron, executive producer of "Moonlighting," was writing the pilot, he realized he had Shepherd in mind for Maddie.

Casting the part of David was not as easy. About 3,000 men tried out for the part, among them Willis, who sported a punk hairstyle, army fatigues, and earrings. Caron spotted Willis's potential, however, and a screen test proved him right—the special chemistry was there. Willis was born March 19, 1955, in West Germany and grew up in New Jersey. He moved to New York City in 1978 and appeared in a number of off-off-Broadway and off-Broadway plays before starring in Sam Shepard's *Fool for Love* for four months in 1984. He also appeared on TV in episodes of "Miami Vice" and "The Twilight Zone." His first lead in a feature film was in Blake Edwards's *Blind Date,* due for release in 1987. Both Shepherd and Willis had record albums planned for 1987, but their public just wanted to know what Maddie and David were planning. (BARBARA WHITNEY)

Soares, Mário Alberto Nobre Lopes

The election in 1986 of lifelong Socialist Mário Alberto Nobre Lopes Soares as president of Portugal marked the culmination of 12 years of active political life in the country since democracy was restored in 1974. Soares won 51.3% of the votes despite the formidable challenge posed by the popular conservative Diogo Freitas do Amaral. His victory was remarkable, given the decisive defeat of his Socialist Party (PSP) in general elections just three months earlier, when he was succeeded as prime minister by the right-wing Aníbal Cavaço Silva.

Born Dec. 7, 1924, in Lisbon, Soares completed his studies at the Sorbonne in Paris, where he graduated in law. He began his political activities at a young age and was a member of the Central Executive of the United Democratic Youth Movement in 1946–48. Subsequently he was imprisoned 13 times and exiled in France for his political activities against the dictatorship. After a military coup in 1974, he returned to Portugal and served as foreign minister until the 1976 general elections, when he was chosen to lead a minority Socialist government until 1978. In 1983–85 he was elected prime minister for a second term.

Soares was quick to recognize the need for a diplomatic president, and within days of being elected he renounced his leadership of the PSP, the party he had helped to found in 1973, and emphasized that in the future he would be a leader of all people, regardless of their political views. Although he was no friend of the Communists, they had voted for him as "the lesser of two evils," and he expressed his commitment to having a compatible relationship with right-wing Prime Minister Cavaço and his minority government; this was in contrast to his own often tempestuous relationship as prime minister (1983–85) with Pres. António dos Santos Ramalho Eanes. To broaden his base of support, Soares spent his 1986 summer holiday at the royal palace at Guimarães in the north of the country, where he was least popular, instead of his usual beach holiday spent with family and staunch PSP members in the south.

Soares assumed an international role as the country's most experienced elder statesman and could claim credit for having successfully negotiated Portugal's Jan. 1, 1986, entry into the European Communities (EC), a move that was already providing benefits, particularly in the farm sector. He enjoyed considerable international status as a member of the Socialist International and, despite his political views, had a good relationship with U.S. Pres. Ronald Reagan. His first foreign presidential visit was to the U.K. in May. (MICHAEL WOOLLER)

Soyinka, Wole

The first African writer to win the coveted Nobel Prize for Literature was Nigerian playwright and poet Wole Soyinka, for over 20 years an outspoken critic of his country's military rulers. Learning of his selection, Soyinka was quick to voice the hope that he had not received the award for his political convictions. Nor did he deem the $290,000 prize a personal one: "I don't for a minute consider that the prize is just for me. It's for what I represent. I'm a part of the whole literary tradition of Africa."

The son of a school inspector belonging to the Yoruba tribe, Akinwande Oluwole Soyinka was born at Abeokuta near Ibadan in the British colony of Nigeria on July 13, 1934. After studying at University College in Ibadan (now the University of Ibadan), he left Nigeria in 1954 to continue his education at the University of Leeds, England, where he received his degree in English. He then worked at the Royal Court Theatre in London from 1958 to 1959. Returning to Nigeria in 1960 with a Rockefeller grant, he formed the Masks drama company, which produced his play *A Dance of the Forests,* a skeptical view of Africa's supposedly glorious past.

All of Soyinka's subsequent plays and poems dealt with Africa's vast political jungle. In 1965 Soyinka was arrested for allegedly forcing some radio station technicians at gunpoint to replace a minister's broadcast with a protest against vote fraud. Two years later, while visiting the Biafran rebels, he was jailed again, this time for 22 months. In prison he wrote extensively—on sheets of toilet paper—works that eventually were published with the title *A Shuttle in the Crypt.* During the 1970s Soyinka's reputation began to spread beyond Nigeria. His poetry is in the language of his Yoruba tribe, but his dramatic works are written in English, the better to reach his people. Nigerians speak several languages, but English, the language of the former colonial masters, is also the common language of road signs, newspapers, and the courts.

Much of Soyinka's work focuses on Africa's cultural and political failures. His serious dramas discuss the meaning of self-sacrifice and death and loyalty. Among them are *Death and the King's Horseman, The Strong Breed, The Trials of Brother Jero, The Road,* a BBC-produced radio play, "Camwood on the Leaves," and, most recently, *A Play of Giants* (1984) and *Requiem for a Futurologist* (1985). Two novels, published in 1965 and 1973, respectively, are *The Interpreters* and *Season of Anomy.* A collection of essays especially cited by the Swedish Academy is entitled *Myth, Literature, and the African World.* (BONNIE OBERMAN)

Sugar, Alan Michael

Even before Alan Michael Sugar launched his Amstrad PC1512 in September 1986, the international electronics industry was living in fear of what he would launch next. His Amstrad Consumer Electronics PLC., headquartered in Brentwood, Essex, England, had for several years been the focus of international attention as it moved quickly and successfully into developing new and innovative products for retailing at sharply competitive prices. Sugar's talent derived from his desire to sell to—and ability to identify the demand in—the mass market. By 1986 he had a firm grip on the European market for electronics equipment, and as the year drew to a close, he was testing his strength in the U.S.

There was little reason to suppose from his inauspicious start in life that Sugar would become one of the U.K.'s most dynamic industrialists. Born in Hackney, east London, on March 24, 1947, one of four children, he left school at the age of 16. He started several jobs in both government service and the private sector, all of which he tired of in only a few months, and decided to start his own business. This he did—selling car aerials from his own van—and from humble beginnings he developed his strong entrepreneurial skills. His contribution to British business was widely recognized, and in 1984 he received *The Guardian*'s Young Businessman of the Year award.

Although Amstrad had become a household name throughout Europe, it was Sugar, the man behind the company, whose name was by far the more important "label." His style of management was perhaps unique—always in control at the top but never afraid to delegate—and he ran his business like his products, without pretentious frills. He formed Amstrad in 1968 to find gaps in the consumer market and fill them. By exploiting state-of-the-art technology, he cut out unnecessary components and by 1980 had developed a successful business—mainly in audio and TV products. A major breakthrough took place in September 1985 when Sugar introduced onto the market a complete and versatile word-processing system to retail at the incredibly low price of £399. It was a phenomenal success, and sales reached £23 million within three months of its introduction; it also won the *Sunday Times* 1985 award for the Best Home/Small Business Computer. In September 1986 the computer world was shaken by the appearance of Sugar's latest IBM-compatible computer, modeled on the standard IBM personal computer but priced at a third of the latter's cost. It remained to be seen whether Sugar would erode IBM's estimated 40-45% share of the personal computer business and, more importantly, whether he would successfully break into the U.S. market. (JANET H. CLARK)

Taylor, Lawrence

Ever since Lawrence Taylor broke into professional football in 1981, he had been a prototype for linebackers. Coaches begged scouts to get them a Lawrence Taylor as though it was as simple as shopping for a Cadillac.

But there was only one. He was 1.9 m (6 ft 3 in) and 110.2 kg (243 lb), with halfback speed, 40 yd in 4.5 seconds. Taylor could rush the passer and then turn after the ball was thrown and catch the receiver downfield. He was strong enough to toss 122.5-kg (270-lb) linemen aside like bales of hay. He inspired the one-back offense because teams needed an extra lineman to block him.

AP/WIDE WORLD

Taylor was still improving in 1986, when he led the New York Giants to a 17–2 record and the Super Bowl championship. He became the second defensive player to win the National Football League's most valuable player award. His best season followed two off-season developments. In March he went through a rehabilitation program for substance abuse. In the spring he undertook his first serious weight-lifting program to prepare for an assignment change that would make him a pass rusher 85% of the time, up from 42%. He increased his quarterback sacks from 13½ to 20½ and started in his sixth consecutive all-star Pro Bowl.

"A sack is like a touchdown for the defense," Taylor said. "It turns the momentum toward the defense and forces the offense to try to hit the big play." He liked any kind of hard hit, though, often asking coaches to rerun film so that he could savour the sight of football's most violent collisions.

Taylor was born Feb. 4, 1959, the second of three sons in a middle-class family in Williamsburg, Va. He starred at baseball and basketball, but as an 83.9-kg (185-lb) high school senior he was not widely recruited for college football. He did not become a star as a North Carolina defensive end until his senior year. After growing ten centimetres (four inches) and gaining 9 kg (20 lb) between seasons, he was Atlantic Coast Conference player of the year with 16 sacks.

As a rookie in 1981 Taylor was named the defensive player of the year in the National Conference, an award he repeated in 1982 and 1986. He led the Giants' resurgence from 4–12 in 1980 to 9–7 and a play-off berth in 1981. When they slipped below .500 the next two years, he became so frustrated that in 1983 he volunteered to cover kicks and play tight end, ideas the coach rejected. "I want to be part of a winning team," Taylor said. He backed that desire up after the 1986 regular season by helping the Giants win the Super Bowl, after which he issued a warning to other teams. "You can always play better," Taylor said.

(KEVIN M. LAMB)

Thatcher, Margaret Hilda

In 1986, which marked the beginning of her eighth year in power, U.K. Conservative Prime Minister Margaret Thatcher approached the edge of disaster for the second time in her career. The first occasion had been on that April day in 1982 when the news came through of the Argentine invasion of the Falkland Islands/Islas Malvinas, and she had realized that unless she could recover them her government would fall. In 1986 the threat came from the equally improbable source of an ailing helicopter company, Westland, based in Yeovil, Somerset; such was the imbroglio into which Thatcher and her Cabinet got themselves that, for a brief moment at least, it seemed possible that she might be destroyed. (*See* WORLD AFFAIRS [Western Europe]: *United Kingdom.*) Indestructability was, however, an aspect of her resilient style, and she was soon behaving as if nothing had happened and—some of her critics said—as if she had learned nothing.

If she won a third term in general elections (due by mid-1988 and likely to take place in 1987), she would break all modern records. She might also succeed in her bid to change the landscape of British politics and save her country from socialism, which she regarded—and she made no secret of it—as a fate worse than death. Whether she would also succeed in arresting and reversing the path of economic deterioration on which Britain seemed firmly set when she first came to power in 1979 would prove a question less easily, and less quickly, answered. Certainly in 1986 she found herself presiding over policies that were a far cry from the rhetoric that accompanied her first coming to power: public expenditure planned to increase, monetary targets abolished, and a consumer boom stimulated by relatively high wage agreements.

Nevertheless, as she progressed from strength to strength—or from "banana skin" to strength—it became more widely accepted, by foe and friend, that she had accomplished a revolution of a kind. The past was being written, the present defined, and the future devised around Thatcher and "Thatcherism." It was a

GEMMA LEVINE—CAMERA PRESS LTD.

remarkable dominance for a girl born over a grocer's shop in Grantham, Lincolnshire, on Oct. 13, 1925. Her combination of hard work and bold opportunism had taken her to the top and, in 1986, kept her there. (PETER JENKINS)

Tisch, Laurence Alan
On Sept. 10, 1986, William Paley, the founder and retired chairman of CBS Inc., joined with board member Laurence Tisch in a power struggle to take control of the communications giant. When the dust settled, Paley had been reinstated as chairman, and Tisch, chairman and chief executive officer (CEO) of Loews Corp., was the acting president and acting CEO of CBS.

From early 1985 CBS had experienced a series of hostile takeover attempts, including one by U.S. Sen. Jesse Helms (Rep., N.C.) and another by Atlanta businessman Ted Turner, as well as internal strife in the television news division. Tisch began buying CBS stock in mid-1985. By October Loews had become the largest stockholder, with 12%, and the beleaguered firm asked Tisch to join the board of directors as a "white knight" to scare off other corporate raiders. Loews continued to acquire CBS stock in 1986 until Tisch controlled 24.9%. Many board members, particularly CBS president and CEO Thomas Wyman, expressed concern when Tisch refused to sign an agreement not to purchase more than 25%, although Tisch repeatedly denied plans to buy more.

When the CBS board met in September 1986, Wyman announced negotiations for a buyout of the firm by Coca-Cola Corp. This sudden reversal of policy triggered mass defections by Wyman's supporters, and the board ousted Wyman from office in favour of Paley and Tisch. Tisch took immediate action to streamline what he considered inefficient management, reestablish control of CBS News with a new president, and sell off book- and music-publishing operations to relieve CBS's heavy debt load.

Laurence Tisch was born on March 15, 1923, in Brooklyn, N.Y. He was graduated from New York University in banking and finance at the age of 19 and received his M.B.A. from the Wharton business school at the University of Pennsylvania two years later. After serving in the Army in World War II, Tisch briefly attended Harvard Law School. He and his younger brother, Preston Robert, then bought a New Jersey resort hotel. It was the beginning of the hotel chain Tisch Hotels, Inc., and a lifelong business partnership. While Robert Tisch usually handled daily management of the company, Laurence sought out undervalued investments and built corporate assets. In 1959 the brothers took control of Loews Theaters, Inc., and merged the two companies into Loews Corp.

UPI/BETTMANN NEWSPHOTOS

In the 1960s and '70s Loews took over several other companies, diversifying into real estate, watch manufacturing, tobacco, and insurance. (MELINDA SHEPHERD)

Waldheim, Kurt
On June 8, 1986, Kurt Waldheim was elected president of Austria, defeating his Socialist Party of Austria (SPÖ) rival, Kurt Steyrer. A first ballot in May failed to produce a decisive result, and Waldheim narrowly missed his 50% target. Two candidates withdrew from the June poll in which Waldheim won 53.9% of the vote, compared with 46.1% for Steyrer. Although officially an independent candidate, Waldheim was strongly supported by the conservative opposition People's Party, and the result was a severe setback for the SPÖ, which had held the office of president since World War II.

Waldheim was born Dec. 21, 1918, in Sankt Andrä-Wördern, Austria, the son of a school inspector. After voluntary military service in 1936, he studied law in Vienna and registered

CAMERA PRESS LTD.

at the Consular Academy. During World War II he served in the German armed forces on the Eastern Front. After gaining his doctorate of law in 1944, he entered the diplomatic service. In 1948 he moved to Paris to take up the post of first secretary at the Austrian embassy, where he stayed until 1951, returning to Vienna to work in the head office of the Foreign Ministry. He became an observer at the UN in New York and was later appointed Austrian ambassador in Canada. In 1960–64 he was political director of the Foreign Ministry and then became a permanent representative at the UN. He was foreign minister (1968–70) in a conservative Cabinet. Following his unsuccessful stand for the presidency in 1971, Waldheim returned to the UN and in the same year was elected secretary-general. He was reelected for a second term five years later and was prepared to stand for a third term, but he was unsuccessful because of opposition from the Chinese.

Waldheim became a controversial candidate for the presidency after the World Jewish Congress claimed that he had lied about his wartime activities and had even been implicated in the Final Solution. These accusations were widely resented in Austria and led to a revival of anti-Semitism and xenophobia. Waldheim protested that he had only done his duty as a soldier and that he had joined Nazi associations to further a career in the diplomatic service. He had previously omitted references to his wartime service in the Balkans because, he claimed, it would have been too boring. Waldheim denied all knowledge of the deportation of Jews from the Balkans to the concentration camps or the shooting of Yugoslav partisans. Despite international pressure, he refused to withdraw from the campaign. (MELANIE ANN SULLY)

Weaver, Sigourney
In 1986 superwoman—that modern phenomenon who heroically juggles career and family—had nothing on Sigourney Weaver: as astronaut Ripley in the film *Aliens,* Weaver became a warrior and mother, a thinking woman's Rambo who uses guns, wits, and love to save a little girl from hordes of overgrown, acid-drooling insects. The 1.8-m (5-ft 10½-in) Weaver—whom *Time* once called "intimidatingly beautiful"—played her androgynous character with a verve and conviction that made *Aliens* a hit with critics and paying customers alike.

Born Susan Weaver in New York City on Oct. 8, 1949, she was raised on show business. Her father, Sylvester ("Pat") Weaver, headed NBC during the early 1950s and created the talk-show format for "Today" and "The Tonight Show." Her mother was Elizabeth Inglis, a British stage actress and a contract player for Warner Brothers.

Despite her genes, Weaver had to struggle to achieve acting success. In summer stock during her high-school years, directors told her she was too tall and clumsy for any role; in drama school at Yale University teachers relegated her to the campus cabaret, insisting she had little talent for serious acting. Even after touring with Ingrid Bergman in *The Constant Wife* (1974), appearing off-Broadway in Christopher Durang's *Titanic* (1976), and teaming with Durang to write and perform improvisational comedies, Weaver still found many dressing-room doors closed to her. Movie producers felt that her Stanford University and Yale education made her too intellectual for mainstream roles.

Weaver's big break in movies came in 1979, when she accepted a part originally written for a man. Playing spaceship officer Ripley in *Alien,* the predecessor of *Aliens,* Weaver blended toughness and intelligence with vulnerability and sex appeal. Her performance convinced Hollywood that she was perfectly cast as a strong, independent woman; offers to portray a determined newswoman in *Eyewitness* (1981), a mysterious diplomat in *The Year of Living Dangerously* (1983), and a haunted musician in *Ghostbusters* (1984) soon followed. The new star, whose Broadway debut in *Hurlyburly* earned her critical acclaim, said of her ability to be simultaneously tough and tender: "Maybe I'm acting for the women in men—the feminine side of men." (MICHAEL AMEDEO)

Wiesel, Elie
"Elie Wiesel has emerged as one of the most important spiritual leaders and guides in an age when violence, repression, and racism continue to characterize the world." Thus began the announcement of the award to Wiesel of the 1986 Nobel Peace Prize. It continued: "Wiesel is a messenger to mankind. . . . His message is based on his own personal experience of total humiliation and of the utter contempt for humanity shown in Hitler's death camps." Indeed, Wiesel, the sensitive and compassionate author of over 25 books about the Holocaust, was recognized more as a witness, a reminder, a force for keeping alive the most painful issues of history's recent past with the intent of changing the future.

Eliezer Wiesel was born in Sighet, Rom., near the Hungarian border, on Sept. 30, 1928, to Hasidic parents. He studied both Torah and Talmud (Jewish law and tradition) at an early age. When he was 15, in 1944, the Germans ordered Sighet's 15,000 Jews deported to Auschwitz, where Wiesel saw his mother and one of his sisters die. Later, at Buchenwald, he watched his father beaten to death. The deep despair he experienced as a teenager recurs; the scars of course are permanent. "But," he says, "we have to go into the despair and go beyond it, by working and doing for somebody else, by using it for something else."

Liberated by the Allied forces at age 16, Wiesel went to Paris. He studied philosophy at the Sorbonne and after 1949 became the chief foreign correspondent for the Israeli newspaper *Yedioth Ahronot.* In 1958 his first book, "*La*

AP/WIDE WORLD

Nuit" ("Night"), describing existence in Nazi death camps, was published. Wiesel continued to write and lecture about the Holocaust and human rights, seeking to establish his theme at a universal level. The Nobel Committee statement declared: "Wiesel's commitment, which originated in the sufferings of the Jewish people, has been widened to embrace all oppressed peoples and races."

From 1976 Wiesel had been a professor of humanities at Boston University. He still wrote in French, and his Viennese-born wife of 17 years, Marion, translated his work into English. His books include *The Jews of Silence* (1966), *A Beggar in Jerusalem* (1970), and *Souls on Fire* (1972). On the day Wiesel received the Nobel Prize, he summarized his mission: "I decided to devote my life to telling the story because I felt that having survived I owe something to the dead. That was their obsession to be remembered, and anyone who does not remember betrays them again." (BONNIE OBERMAN)

Willis, Bruce
See SHEPHERD, CYBILL

Winnie the Pooh

In 1986 teddies around the world were still recuperating from the parties, parades, and tributes that commemorated the "1985 Year of the Teddy Bear" when they received an invitation to celebrate Winnie the Pooh's birthday. When the beguiling tawny bear, who has delighted children for generations with his whimsical antics, blew out the candles on his birthday cake, he had turned 60 years old.

FROM *WINNIE-THE-POOH* BY A. A. MILNE, ILLUSTRATION BY ERNEST SHEPARD; E. P. DUTTON, N.Y., 1954

Pooh, a British bear, was born on Oct. 14, 1926, on the pages of the classic children's book *Winnie-the-Pooh* (1926; the hyphens were later dropped). His characteristics were likened to a bear belonging to Christopher Robin, the son of *Punch* contributor and playwright A. A. Milne. After penning Pooh's adventures, he commissioned Ernest H. Shepard to provide the sketches featuring Pooh and his unique assortment of friends, including Piglet, Rabbit, Eeyore (a donkey with a loose tail), Kanga and Roo, Owl, Tigger, and, of course, Christopher Robin. Pooh, "a bear of little brain," is also more formally known as Edward Bear. He lives in a house in the forest with a sign over the door to his den that reads, "Mr. Sanders." He captured the hearts of both young and old as he romped in such books as *Now We Are Six* (1927), *The House at Pooh Corner* (1928), and *The Christopher Robin Birthday Book* (1930). After the death of Milne in 1956, Pooh starred in a series of three animated cartoons produced by Walt Disney; *Winnie the Pooh and the Honey Tree* (1965), *Winnie the Pooh and the Blustery Day* (1968), which won an Academy Award, and *Winnie the Pooh and Tigger Too* (1974).

Pooh, who has continued to endear himself to readers, also has his own line of children's clothing and stuffed look-alikes that are immensely popular.

While Pooh's friends offered him their warmest wishes at his surprise birthday party in Rabbit's burrow, they also cautioned him on eating too much birthday cake and reminded him of the week he spent trying to lose enough weight to be pulled out of Rabbit's front door after he ate too much honey and drank too much milk. (KAREN JUSTIN)

Wyeth, Andrew Newell

In 1986 the usually reclusive, publicity-shy artist Andrew Wyeth found himself the subject of questions and speculation. In a 1985 interview published in *Art & Antiques* magazine, he had revealed the existence of a previously secret series of 246 works executed over a period of 15 years. Wyeth had sold three of them to collectors in recent years and had given one to his wife, Betsy. He gave her two more and decided to try to find a single buyer for the rest of the collection. When the sale to Pennsylvania publisher Leonard E. B. Andrews came to light in August, the art world was abuzz. The subject of almost all of the works was a woman at first identified only as Helga. Who was she? Why had the collection been kept secret? When Betsy was asked what the works were all about, she answered simply, "Love," a reply that inspired more speculation, even after Helga turned out to be Helga Testorf, a fellow resident of Chadds Ford, Pa. To one art professional the use of the word love meant Wyeth's "love of creating and being an artist . . . his self-esteem and his need to break new ground." Some people suggested that it meant Wyeth was as skilled at creating publicity as he was at creating art.

Wyeth was born July 12, 1917, in Chadds Ford. His father, the well-known illustrator N. C. Wyeth, was his only teacher. Wyeth painted, in a realistic manner, the people and places he knew best, those of the areas where he grew up—Chadds Ford, his hometown, and Cushing, Maine, where he spent his summers. His first one-man show was held in New York City in 1937 and sold out on the first day. In 1948 his landscape "Christina's World" brought him further renown; it remained his best-known work. In 1967 his exhibition broke attendance records at the Whitney Museum in New York City. Among his awards and honours were the first Presidential Freedom Award to a painter (1963), the first election of a U.S. artist to the French Académie des Beaux Arts since John Singer Sargent (1977), and the first election of a living U.S. artist to Britain's Royal Academy (1980). As 1986 ended, the art world awaited the first public showing of the "Helga" series. (BARBARA WHITNEY)

York, Duke and Duchess of

On July 23, 1986, Prince Andrew Albert Christian Edward, second son of Queen Elizabeth II, married Sarah Ferguson, whom he had known since childhood but who had made a late and relatively unobserved appearance as a prospective wife for the man fourth in line to the British throne. The wedding of "Andy" and "Fergie" was enacted with traditional pomp and circumstance in London's historic Westminster Abbey. Another chapter in the story of royal romances had been concluded.

Sarah Margaret Ferguson was born on Oct. 15, 1959, in London and grew up in the village of Sunninghill, near Ascot, Berkshire. Though a commoner, she was very much a member of the British royal social circle. Diana, princess of Wales, a longtime friend, was reported to have encouraged the love match. Sarah's father, Maj. Ronald Ferguson, was polo manager to Charles, prince of Wales. Her parents were divorced and had both remarried—her mother, Susan, to Argentine polo player Hector Barrantes. An unexceptional upbringing in the country, private school, a job with a London publisher: in these the future duchess of York presented a rather sedate image, compared with some of the girlfriends claimed in the past by Fleet Street newshounds as candidates for Prince Andrew's hand. On being thrust into the public eye, she revealed a bouncy personality and an apparent tolerance of the rigours of public life that made her immediately popular with many British royalty-watchers.

IAN SWIFT—CAMERA PRESS LTD.

Born on Feb. 19, 1960, at Buckingham Palace, London, Prince Andrew was educated at Gordonstoun school in Scotland and subsequently attended the Royal Naval College, Dartmouth (Devon). Joining the Royal Navy, he served as a helicopter pilot aboard HMS *Invincible* during the 1982 Falkland Islands/Islas Malvinas conflict between the U.K. and Argentina. Immediately after the Falklands campaign, reports that he had gone to relax in the Caribbean with movie actress Koo Stark attracted media interest and (it was suggested) a maternal reprimand. Being fourth in line to the throne meant that Andrew faced less obvious pressures than his elder brother, Charles. However, his commitment to a naval career seemed to have settled the question that historically had perplexed monarchs' younger sons: what to do.

Public response to the wedding confirmed the enduring appeal of the monarchy to most Britons. The newlyweds received an additional wedding gift from the queen: the titles of duke and duchess of York. The dukedom of York, traditionally given to the sovereign's second son, was last held by the queen's father, later King George VI. Prince Andrew was the 13th holder of the title. (BRIAN WILLIAMS)

OBITUARIES

Alessandri Rodríguez, Jorge, Chilean politician and businessman (b. May 19, 1896, Santiago, Chile—d. Aug. 31, 1986, Santiago), served (1958–64) as president of Chile and was the son of Arturo Alessandri Palma, who twice served (1920–25 and 1932–38) as president of the country. After graduating (1919) from the University of Chile with a degree in civil engineering, Alessandri held various posts in government and business before founding Chile's largest paper and cardboard manufacturing company. In 1947 he was appointed minister of finance and in this post was responsible for balancing the national budget while avoiding unemployment, eliminating the deficit, and accumulating the first budgetary surplus in 20 years. In 1957 Alessandri was elected to the Senate, representing Santiago, and the following year he entered the presidential race as an independent. He won the election and took office on Nov. 3, 1958, pledging an austerity budget to return the country to financial stability. Alessandri was a reserved and austere man, who shunned the presidential palace in favour of his apartment. When his term of office expired, he was succeeded by Eduardo Frei Montalva, a Christian Democrat. Alessandri again ran for the presidency in 1970 but was narrowly defeated by Socialist Salvador Allende Gossens. A right-wing conservative, Alessandri initially supported the 1973 military coup that toppled President Allende, but in 1980 he withdrew from political life when he could not reach agreement with the military government on a timetable for a return to democracy.

Arland, Marcel, French writer (b. July 5, 1899, Varennes-sur-Amance, Haute-Marne, France—d. Jan. 12, 1986, Brinville, Seine-et-Marne, France), first achieved wide literary recognition in 1929 when his novel *L'Ordre* gained him the prestigious Prix Goncourt. In the early 1920s Arland and André Maurois were partners in the launching of two literary reviews, *Aventures* and *Dés,* and in 1925 Arland began a long association with the *Nouvelle Revue Française* (*NRF*). For many years before and after World War II, Arland shared direction of the *NRF* with Jean Paulhan. After Paulhan died (1968) Arland served as sole director until 1977. Arland's wide-ranging output includes such *récits* as *Terres étrangères* (1923) and *Zélie dans le désert* (1944); such short stories as "L'Eau et le feu" (1956) and "À perdre haleine" (1960); and numerous collections of essays and critical studies; among the latter are *Marivaux* (1949) and *La Grâce d'écrire* (1955). *Lumière du soir* (1983) was the last of several volumes of memoirs. Arland was elected to the Académie Française in 1968.

Arlen, Harold (HYMAN ARLUCK), U.S. composer (b. Feb. 15, 1905, Buffalo, N.Y.—d. April 23, 1986, New York, N.Y.), was the prolific songwriter of such enduring popular tunes as "Get Happy," "Stormy Weather," "That Old Black Magic," "Blues in the Night," and "Over the Rainbow," the wistful song from the 1939 motion picture *The Wizard of Oz* that won him an Academy Award and became Judy Garland's signature. Arlen, a serious student of piano, dropped out of high school to form the Snappy Trio; he also performed with the Southbound Shufflers and the Buffalodians before embarking on a songwriting career. His first songs, "My Gal, My Pal" and "I Never Knew What Love Could Do," were never published, but he scored a hit on Broadway with "Get Happy" for the *9:15 Revue* (1930). From 1930 to 1934 he collaborated with lyricist Ted Koehler to produce eight editions of the Harlem revue *Cotton Club Parade,* a stint that established him as one of the great songwriters of all time. He also wrote the scores for such Broadway musicals as *Life Begins at 8:40* and *Earl Carroll's Vanities* before moving to Hollywood in 1935. During Hollywood's golden age of musicals he composed songs for such films as *The Wizard of Oz* (1939), *Cabin in the Sky* (1943), *A Star Is Born* (1954), and *The Country Girl* (1954). His more than 500 compositions, a distinctive blend of black jazz and blues idioms, include at least 35 songs that are considered "standards," such all-time favourites as "I Love a Parade," "I've Got the World on a String," "I Gotta Right to Sing the Blues," "Between the Devil and the Deep Blue Sea," "It's Only a Paper Moon," "Let's Fall in Love," and "Come Rain or Come Shine." In 1955 he returned to New York City to once again compose for theatre.

Arnaz, Desi (DESIDERIO ALBERTO ARNAZ Y DE ACHA III), U.S. actor and producer (b. March 2, 1917, Santiago, Cuba—d. Dec. 2, 1986, Del Mar, Calif.), became an American institution as the conga-playing offscreen and television husband of the redheaded comedienne Lucille Ball, costarring with her in "I Love Lucy" (1951–57), one of television's best loved and longest running situation comedies. Arnaz and Ball founded (1951) the Desilu Production Co., which produced "I Love Lucy," featuring Arnaz and Ball as Ricky and Lucy Ricardo. Their television landlords and best friends, Fred and Ethel Mertz (portrayed by William Frawley and Vivian Vance, respectively), also became embroiled in the couple's domestic tribulations and appeared variously with one or both of them in later series as well. Arnaz, who was a Latin bandleader before making his motion-picture debut in 1940 in *Too Many Girls,* married Ball, the star of the film, in the same year. A shrewd businessman, Arnaz purchased RKO studios in 1957 and amassed a fortune as a producer and executive of Desilu. He was credited with pioneering the three-camera filming technique, in which film from three cameras operating simultaneously from different angles was edited together to produce a final program. Arnaz also appeared with Ball in such films as *The Long, Long Trailer* (1954) and *Forever Darling* (1956) before they divorced in 1960. After selling his interest in Desilu to Ball in 1963, he created a number of comedy-series pilots.

Baddeley, Hermione, British actress (b. Nov. 13, 1906, Broseley, Shropshire, England—d. Aug. 19, 1986, Los Angeles, Calif.), enjoyed a 60-year career, as comedienne and dramatic actress, in the theatre, in motion pictures, and on television and earned an Academy Award nomination for her performance in the film *Room at the Top* (1958). During the 1930s Baddeley achieved remarkable success in the theatre. She studied dancing, made her stage debut at the age of 11, and triumphed in *The Likes of Her* (1923) and *The Punch Bowl* (1924). For the next 20 years she specialized in theatrical revue, interpreting and often embroidering on scripts by Herbert Farjeon. Besides appearing with her sister Angela, she also shared billings with Hermione Gingold and Henry Kendall before scoring her final revue success in *At the Lyric* (1953; revised as *Going to Town,* 1954). Meanwhile her screen career, which had started in 1928, flourished with parts in such notable films as *Brighton Rock* (1947), *Passport to Pimlico* (1949), and *Scrooge* (1951). After her New York stage debut in *A Taste of Honey* (1961), she lived mainly in the U.S., appearing in such Broadway productions as *The Milk Train Doesn't Stop Here Anymore* (1963) and *Whodunnit* (1982). She played the housekeeper in the film *Mary Poppins* (1964) and frequently appeared on television, notably (and again as a housekeeper) in "Maude." Her autobiography, *The Unsinkable Hermione Baddeley,* was published in 1984.

Bayar, Mahmud Celal, Turkish politician (b. 1883, Umerbey, near Bursa, Ottoman Empire [now Turkey]—d. Aug. 21, 1986, Istanbul, Turkey), was president of the Turkish Republic from 1950 to 1960. The son of a schoolteacher, Bayar was taught at home until he studied finance and economics at a French school in Bursa. His first job was with the Deutsche Orient Bank, where he gained much of his banking expertise. His political life began in 1907 when he joined the Union and Progress Party. In 1908 he was promoted to secretary of the party's Smyrna branch. In 1920 Bayar was elected to the last Ottoman Parliament. When the Ottoman Empire collapsed, at the end of World War I, he escaped to Ankara, where he held several ministerial posts in the government of the Grand National Assembly, which was the foundation of modern Turkey. He was economy minister (1921–22) and minister of reconstruction and settlement (1922–24). In 1924 he returned to banking to head the Is (Work) Bank, which became one of the largest in Turkey. After returning to politics as minister of national economy, in 1932, he became a leading exponent of a state-operated economy. He introduced five-year development plans and helped to revitalize the economy through industrialization. In 1937 he became prime minister but resigned in January 1939 following the death of Kemal Ataturk, first president of modern Turkey. After World War II he resigned from the Republican People's Party, which Ataturk had founded, to help found and lead the opposition Democrat Party, which flourished under Bayar's leadership. The party had a landslide victory in the 1950 general elections, and Bayar was made president; he was reelected in 1954 and 1957. His economic policy gave priority to private enterprise, with the state acting as coordinator and regulator. Bayar placed great emphasis on developing foreign relations, and it was possibly this preoccupation that allowed conditions at home to deteriorate. Following the military coup d'état in May 1960, Bayar was tried, along with other leaders of the Democrat Party, on dubious charges of crimes against the state and was sentenced to death. In his case the sentence was subsequently commuted to life imprisonment; in 1964 he was released because of sickness and old age. His civil rights were restored in 1974, but he refused to take his rightful seat in the Senate.

Beauvoir, Simone de, French writer (b. Jan. 9, 1908, Paris, France—d. April 14, 1986, Paris), was internationally acclaimed as the pioneer of post-World War II feminism with her study *Le Deuxième sexe* (1949; *The Second Sex,* 1953) and established herself as an influential intellectual figure with her essays, novels, and memoirs. The daughter of a lawyer, she was brought up

AGIP/PICTORIAL PARADE

in a traditional middle-class family, which discouraged her interest in philosophy. Beauvoir obtained her *licence* at the Sorbonne and in 1929 the prestigious *agrégation,* being placed second to Jean-Paul Sartre in the competitive examination. Attracted to Sartre's intellectual brilliance and nonconformism, she became his lover, and their relationship endured until Sartre's death. Their liaison was the most creative literary partnership of the century and a model union outside the "bourgeois" institution of marriage. For a long time her work was overshadowed by his and she was viewed as a worthy, if not an equal, companion; it was not until the 1970s that the importance of her work was recognized and some began to suggest that it was Beauvoir rather than Sartre who was the more original thinker. Separated by Sartre's mobilization and imprisonment at the start of the World War II, they were reunited in 1941. She lost her teaching post in 1943, the year in which she published her novel *L'Invitée.* Beauvoir worked in radio and wrote plays and novels, causing a scandal with *Le Deuxième sexe* and achieving literary success when *Les Mandarins* (1954) won the Prix Goncourt. Actively engaged in politics and polemical journalism during the 1950s, Beauvoir and Sartre became celebrated figures of the political left and she published essays on their visits to China and the Soviet Union. Her memoirs, starting with *Mémoires d'une jeune fille rangée* (1958), were an unflinchingly truthful account of her upbringing, her early years with Sartre, and their aspirations, struggles, and mistakes. In *La Cérémonie des adieux* (1981), she recounted Sartre's later years and shocked some of his admirers by refusing to disguise his physical degeneration. In her best-written work, *Une Mort très douce* (1964), she applied the same courageous objectivity to her record of her mother's death. After Sartre died on April 15, 1980, she published his letters to her, continued to edit and review *Les Temps modernes,* which they founded in 1945, and obstinately defended her left-wing and feminist beliefs. From 1974 she was president of the Ligue du Droit des Femmes.

Bennett, Donald Clifford Tyndall, Australian-born aviator (b. Sept. 14, 1910, Queensland, Australia—d. Sept. 14, 1986, Denham, Buckinghamshire, England), as the youngest air vice-marshal in the Royal Air Force during World War II, led the Pathfinder Force, a vital contingent in the saturation bombing of German cities by Bomber Command. As a child, Bennett was inspired by the Wright brothers' demonstration of their aircraft in Australia. He later became an air cadet and in 1931 joined the RAF in Britain. Bennett transferred to civil aviation in 1935 as a pilot and test pilot and pioneered several air routes. In 1938 he was awarded the Johnston Memorial Trophy. Recommissioned in the RAF, he won the Distinguished Service Order for his part in the attack on the German battleship *Tirpitz.* Though he was shot down over Norway during the operation, he escaped to England through Sweden and was rapidly promoted before retiring in 1945. He then joined British South American Airways as chief executive but was dismissed after he continued to support the use of the Tudor aircraft following a 1948 disaster. He then formed his own company, Airflight Ltd., and flew Tudor aircraft in the Berlin airlift. He was briefly (in 1945) a Liberal member of Parliament and remained a Liberal until the early 1960s, though his sympathies were well to the right. In 1967 he stood as a National Party candidate and later helped to found fringe right-wing groups. Bennett wrote a standard manual on air navigation and a volume of war memoirs, *Pathfinder* (1958). He was made a Commander of the Order of the British Empire (1943) and was awarded the Soviet Order of Alexander Nevsky (1944).

Bergner, Elisabeth, Austrian-born actress (b. Aug. 22, 1900, Vienna, Austria—d. May 12, 1986, London, England), established her name in the German theatre and cinema during the 1920s before fleeing to England to escape the Nazi regime. She trained in Vienna and made her debut in Zürich, Switz., playing Ophelia in *Hamlet* and Rosalind in *As You Like It.* Bergner's greatest success came, however, in Berlin where Max Reinhardt directed her in George Bernard Shaw's *Saint Joan* in 1924. She also appeared in silent films, including Paul Czinner's *Nju* (1924) and Jean Giraudoux's *Amphitryon 38.* After moving to London she and Czinner were married. In 1933 she played Gemma Jones in Margaret Kennedy's *Escape Me Never,* a part that was written expressly for her—it was deemed her most outstanding performance. In 1936 she appeared as David in Sir James Barrie's last play, *The Boy David*—also written especially for her. Though Bergner was criticized for her decision to remain in the U.S. during World War II, she scored a success on Broadway in *The Two Mrs. Carrolls* (1943–44). During the 1950s she returned to the German theatre in a production of Terence Rattigan's *The Deep Blue Sea.* Bergner's autobiography describes the fluctuations in her career and her friendships with many of the leading artistic figures of her time.

Beuys, Joseph, West German artist and sculptor (b. May 12, 1921, Krefeld, North Rhine-Westphalia, Germany—d. Jan. 23, 1986, Düsseldorf-Oberkassel, West Germany), was an idiosyncratic avant-gardist whose creations defied comparison with those of any of his contemporaries; he was internationally known as a protagonist of "action art." A conceptualist who believed that the artist's mission was to communicate ideas and not merely to create aesthetic objects, he invariably caused controversy among critics and the public with his action-art "events" or "happenings." His works included objects constructed from such materials as fat, felt (Beuys always sported a felt fedora and was known as "the man with the hat"), wood and metal junk, old newspapers, or anything else at hand and might feature a piano filled with detergent, a live coyote, or a dead rabbit. In 1940, soon after leaving school, Beuys was conscripted into the Luftwaffe and became a bomber pilot. He was shot down over the snow-covered Crimea in 1943 but was saved from freezing to death by Tatar tribesmen who wrapped him in layers of fat and felt—whence his later addiction to those materials as creative mediums. After the war he studied at Düsseldorf's Staatliche Kunstakademie (1947–52). Nine years later he was appointed professor of sculpture there, but his tenure was marked by conflict with his more conservative academic colleagues, especially after he founded an "Organization for Direct Democracy." Beuys's alignment with student protest led to his dismissal in 1972, but six years later he was reinstated. The political involvement that underlaid Beuys's artistic activity was reflected in his founder-membership in the West German Green Party. One-man exhibitions of his drawings, sculptures, and "happenings" were mounted throughout Europe and the U.S., notably at the 1976 Venice Biennale and at the Guggenheim Museum, New York City, in 1979.

Björnstrand, (Knut) Gunnar, Swedish actor (b. Nov. 13, 1909, Stockholm, Sweden—d. May 24, 1986, Stockholm), was a leading figure on the Swedish stage and appeared in more than 100 films but was best remembered for his work with the director Ingmar Bergman. Their association began with *Frenzy* (1944), which Bergman scripted for Alf Sjöberg, and ended with *Fanny and Alexander* (1982). Björnstrand also turned in exceptionally fine performances in many other Bergman productions; he was notable as the squire to Max von Sydow's knight in *The Seventh Seal* (1956–57) and as the priest in *Winter Light* (1962). Björnstrand studied at the Royal Dramatic Theatre in Stockholm and made his stage debut in Finland at the Vasa City Theatre in 1933. He continued to make regular appearances on the stage throughout his life. His film career was launched in a French version of *The False Millionaire* (1931). He also appeared in films directed by Sjöberg, Arne Mattsson, and Erik ("Hampe") Faustman and later in films by Vilgot Sjöman, Jan Troell, and Mai Zetterling. In Bergman's films he often portrayed withdrawn, inhibited, or nostalgic characters, as in the films *Wild Strawberries* (1957) and *Autumn Sonata* (1978). In later years Björnstrand also became a physiotherapist. As a confirmed Roman Catholic and a committed socialist, he held that his religious and political beliefs justified his dual career.

Bollardière, Jacques Marie Roch André Paris de, French army officer (b. Dec. 16, 1907, Châteaubriant, Loire-Atlantique, France—d. Feb. 21, 1986, Guidel, Morbihan, France), played a leading role in the French Resistance during World War II and in the preparation for the Normandy landings. He then served in Indochina and Algeria and became an advocate of nuclear disarmament, taking an active part in protests against the testing of nuclear weapons on Mururoa Atoll (French Polynesia). Bollardière studied at the military academy of Saint-Cyr and was an officer with the Foreign Legion at the time of his escape to England in 1940. He took part in operations in Africa, Italy, and the Middle East before being parachuted into the Ardennes in 1944 to take charge of the local maquis. In 1957 he publicly protested against the use of torture by French forces in Algeria and was disciplined by being confined to his quarters for two months. By the 1960s he was a convinced advocate of nonviolence, and in 1973 he joined an expedition to Mururoa in an attempt to prevent the nuclear tests on the island. Interned and removed from the reserve, he continued to campaign, standing unsuccessfully as an ecologist candidate in the 1984 elections to the European Parliament. As well as holding the British Distinguished Service Order, Bollardière was a Grand Officer of the Legion of Honour, though he returned the distinction to Pres. Georges Pompidou in 1973 in protest against his forced retirement from the army reserve.

Boothby, Robert John Graham Boothby, BARON, British politician (b. Feb. 12, 1900, Edinburgh, Scotland—d. July 16, 1986, London, England), played a colourful role in British public life for over 60 years but never achieved the high office for which his great talents qualified him. He was educated at Eton College and at Magdalen College, University of Oxford, and was elected Unionist member of Parliament for East Aberdeenshire in 1924, holding the seat until created life peer in 1958. He was parliamentary private secretary (1926–29) to Winston Churchill, then chancellor of the Exchequer. During the decade preceding World War II, Boothby, like Churchill, was in the political wilderness; he shared Churchill's alarm over the growth of Hitler's power and urged rearmament. After Churchill became prime minister in 1940, Boothby was appointed parliamentary secretary to the Ministry of Food. Although he maintained he was innocent, he resigned the post in January 1941 after a parliamentary select committee found him guilty of offering political services in return for financial gain. A strong supporter of the Western European alliance, he became a delegate to the Consultative Assembly of the Council of Europe (1949–57). Boothby wrote a number of books of personal and political commentary, including *Boothby: Recollections of a Rebel* (1978). A convivial companion and a popular television personality, he wished to be remembered as "a man who loved life—and lived it."

Borges, Jorge Luis, Argentine poet, essayist, and short story writer (b. Aug. 24, 1899, Buenos Aires, Arg.—d. June 14, 1986, Geneva, Switz.), was a literary giant in the Spanish-speaking world and gained international renown after some of his works were translated into French and then into English—most notably, his masterpiece, *Ficciones 1935–1944* (1944; Eng. trans.,

1962). Borges, who learned to read and write English before he learned Spanish, was educated at home until the age of nine, when he entered a private school. Under the tutelage of his father, Borges devoured the classics and at the age of six launched his literary career. His mother, a teacher who lived into her 90s, was also a translator and helped him in his literary endeavours as blindness encroached on him. As a youth he lived in Palermo, a suburb of Buenos Aires, but in 1914, on the eve of World War I, the family went to Geneva, where he learned French and German and received his B.A. from the Collège de Genève. In 1919 they moved to Majorca and in 1920 to Spain, where he became a disciple of the Ultraists, a group of avant-garde Spanish poets who believed that all poetry was metaphor and thus avoided traditional form and content. After returning to Argentina in 1921, he was credited with establishing the Ultraist movement in South America. During this period he penned volumes of free verse and essays and founded three literary journals. He ended this phase of his career with the biography *Evaristo Carriego* (1930). Later he renounced the Ultraists and scorned his early works.

In the early 1930s Borges began developing his unique style of fiction. With the publication of a book of sketches, *Historia universal de la infamia* (*A Universal History of Infamy*), a collection of hoaxes and pseudoessays, he launched a new phase in his career. A master storyteller who fused illusion and reality in his dreamlike fables, Borges adopted the short story as his favourite genre. His works, usually no longer than 20 pages, were characterized by the recurrent image of a labyrinth of myth and imagination. In 1938 Borges joined the staff of a Buenos Aires library but continued to write during his nine unhappy years there. In the same year, his father died, and Borges suffered a severe head wound and subsequent blood poisoning, which left him near death. The illness seemed to unleash some of his most creative forces, and he produced some of his most imaginative and celebrated works during this period, including "Pierre Menard, Author of the Quixote," *El jardín de senderos que se bifurcan,* and *Ficciones.*

After the dictator Juan Perón became president of Argentina, Borges was demoted to inspector of poultry and rabbits in the public market. He resigned the post. After Perón was ousted in 1955, Borges was appointed director of the national library in Buenos Aires. Unfortunately, a rare hereditary condition rendered him totally blind, and Borges, who was an avid reader, noted the irony: "I, who imagined Paradise in the shape of a library."

The total loss of his sight, however, sharpened his imaginative skills, and he created such works as *Dreamtigers* and *The Book of Imaginary Beings.* Unlike his earlier fictions, which were identified by brevity, humour, and dependence on such devices as mazes, mirrors, and odd beasts, his works in 1970 began to exhibit a realistic or straightforward approach, as witnessed in *El informe de Brodie* (1970; "Doctor Brodie's Report") and *El libro de arena* (1955; "The Book of Sand"). In 1961 Argentina's man of letters shared the prestigious Formentor Prize with Samuel Beckett, and in 1980 he won the Cervantes Prize, Spain's highest literary award. Though he was often cited as a leading candidate for a Nobel Prize, the award eluded him.

UPI/BETTMANN NEWSPHOTOS

Bowles, Chester Bliss, U.S. advertising entrepreneur and public official (b. April 5, 1901, Springfield, Mass.—d. May 25, 1986, Essex, Conn.), became a millionaire as cofounder (1929) with William Benton of the Benton and Bowles advertising agency but sold his interest in the company in 1941 to serve in the Connecticut wartime rationing administration under the governor. A Yale graduate (1924), Bowles worked as a reporter and then as an advertising copywriter before making his fortune. Ten days after the Japanese attack on Pearl Harbor (Dec. 7, 1941), Bowles became director of Connecticut's Office of Price Administration, in charge of rationing scarce commodities. In 1943 he was appointed federal price administrator by Pres. Franklin D. Roosevelt. After World War II Pres. Harry S. Truman urged Bowles, a liberal Democrat, to accept the position of director of the newly created Office of Economic Stabilization, a post he held from February to July 1946. In the same year, he was defeated in his quest to gain the Democratic nomination for governor of Connecticut. Bowles then served (1947–48) as a special consultant to the UN secretary-general and as international chairman of fund-raising efforts for the Appeal for Children. He was elected governor of Connecticut in 1948 and established the first state commission on civil rights; he lost his reelection bid in 1950. The following year he fulfilled a lifetime ambition when President Truman appointed him ambassador to India and Nepal; he served until 1953, when he was elected to the House of Representatives from Connecticut. After three terms in the House, Bowles was named (1961) under secretary of state by Pres. John F. Kennedy. Later in the same year, he was appointed special representative and adviser to the president on African, Asian, and Latin-American affairs. He was a staunch opponent of American involvement in Cuba and Vietnam. In 1963 he was reappointed ambassador to India and held the post until 1969, when he retired from public life. Bowles was the author of 11 books, including *The New Dimensions of Peace* (1955), *The Coming Political Breakthrough* (1959), *The Conscience of a Liberal* (1962), and *Promises to Keep: My Years in Public Life* (1971).

Braine, John Gerard, British author (b. April 13, 1922, Bradford, Yorkshire, England—d. Oct. 28, 1986, London, England), achieved instant fame with his first novel, *Room at the Top* (1957), and became associated with such writers as Kingsley Amis and John Osborne, who became popularly known as the "angry young men" because of their disenchantment with the British class system. Although none of Braine's later books won such critical acclaim, he was among the 20 or so most widely read novelists in Britain in the 1980s. Though he left grammar school without qualifications, Braine held various casual jobs and then worked as a librarian fairly continuously from 1940 to 1957, taking some time off to pursue his writing. During World War II he served in the Navy (1942–43) but was discharged when he contracted tuberculosis. His novels *Room at the Top* and its sequel, *Life at the Top* (1962), chronicled the career of a working-class youth entering upper-middle-class society. They were filmed (1958, 1965) and also serialized for television under the title "Man at the Top" (1970, 1972). Braine, who claimed to have no "message," also produced *The Jealous God* (1964), a chilling study of the effects of Catholicism on those raised in that faith. His novel *Stay with Me till Morning* (1970) charted marital disharmony, and such books as *One and Last Love* (1981) and *These Golden Days* (1985) reflected his experience as a middle-aged Yorkshire writer. Braine also wrote two spy stories, a biography of J. B. Priestley (1979), and a textbook, *Writing a Novel* (1974).

Bruhn, Erik (Belton Evers), Danish ballet dancer (b. Oct. 3, 1928, Copenhagen, Den.—d. April 1, 1986, Toronto, Ont.), served as director of ballet at the Royal Swedish Opera House (1967–72) and of the National Ballet of Canada from 1982 and ranked among the most outstanding dancers of the century. He was noted especially for his brilliant classical technique, shown in such ballets as *La Sylphide* and *Giselle.* He was enrolled in the school of the Royal Danish Ballet (1937), where he was trained on the principles laid down by August Bournonville. He began dancing with the Royal Danish Ballet (1946), becoming a permanent member (1947) and a principal dancer (1949). His first major role was that of Adonis in Harald Lander's production of *Thorvaldsen.* Thereafter, although again dancing with the Royal Danish Ballet (1953, 1958–61), he quickly moved onto the international stage, working as guest artist with the London Metropolitan Ballet (1949), the American National Ballet Theatre (1949, 1951, 1953), the New York City Ballet (1959), the American Ballet (1960), the Bolshoi Ballet (1961), and the Royal Ballet, London (1962). He was a permanent member of the American National Ballet Theatre (1953–58). He had choreographed *Concertette* (1953) and *Festa* (1957). Illness caused Bruhn to give up dancing in 1972, but he returned briefly to dance in *Epilogue* and *Miss Julie.* He had an important influence on Rudolf Nureyev, and with Lillian Moore he wrote *Bournonville and Ballet Technique* (1961).

Bubbles, John (John William Sublett), U.S. dancer (b. Feb. 19, 1902, Louisville, Ky.—d. May 18, 1986, Baldwin Hills, Calif.), was a tap dancing vaudevillian who pioneered rhythm tap dancing, in which both the heels and the toes are used to create a syncopated sound. Bubbles was probably best known as the original Sportin' Life in George Gershwin's opera *Porgy and Bess* (1935). Bubbles, who broke into vaudeville in 1919 appearing with his partner, Ford Lee ("Buck") Washington, in the Buck and Bubbles act, transcended the colour barrier when he appeared at the Radio City Music Hall. He also appeared on Broadway in *Blackbirds of 1930, The Dance of Death* (1932), and *Carmen Jones* (1945) and brought his talents to the silver screen in such films as *Varsity Show, Cabin in the Sky,* and *Eight Pathé Shorts.* In 1967 Bubbles went into semiretirement when a stroke left him partially paralyzed. However, in 1980 he appeared in *Black Broadway,* a salute to the black musicals of the first half of the 20th century.

Byam Shaw, Glen(cairn) Alexander, British stage director (b. Dec. 13, 1904, London, England—d. April 29, 1986, Goring-on-Thames, England), as codirector with Anthony Quayle (1952–56) and sole director (1956–59) of the Shakespeare Memorial Theatre, Stratford-upon-Avon, was instrumental in reviving the theatre company that in 1961 became the Royal Shakespeare Company. His Shakespeare productions showed classical good taste and fidelity to the original text. He later became director of productions at Sadler's Wells Opera (1962–68) and at the London Coliseum. A son of the artist John Byam Shaw, he was educated at Westminster School and became an actor. He was for a time a member of J. B. Fagan's company at the Oxford Playhouse and was with John Gielgud in his 1937–38 season at London's Queen's Theatre. He collaborated with Dodie Smith in the production of her play *Dear Octopus* (1938). During World War II he served with the Royal Scots in Burma and there planned the production of *Antony and Cleopatra* (1946) that was staged at the Piccadilly Theatre. At Stratford his successes included *Macbeth* (1955) and *Hamlet* (1958). Among his London West End productions were Terence Rattigan's *Ross* (1960) and *You Never Can Tell* (1965). At Sadler's Wells he was responsible for performances of *Così fan tutte* (1963), *Faust* (1964), and *Orpheus and Eurydice* (1967); in the 1970s at the Coliseum, he directed a number of Wagner operas. Byam Shaw was married to the actress Angela Baddeley, who died in 1976.

Cagney, James Francis, U.S. actor (b. July 17, 1899, New York, N.Y.—d. March 30, 1986, Stanfordville, N.Y.), in scores of films portrayed the fast-talking, hot-tempered, machine-gunning gangster; his hunch-shouldered shrug became a widely imitated trademark of his tough guy persona. His most rewarding role, however, was as the patriotic songwriter George M. Cohan in *Yankee Doodle Dandy* (1942), a role that earned him the Academy Award for best actor. Cagney launched his career in show business dancing in a vaudeville act. He starred on Broadway in *Penny Arcade* (1930) with Joan Blondell, and the two were propelled to Hollywood to star in the screen version, *Sinner's Holiday* (1930). He costarred in three other films before gaining immortality as the thug who squashed a grapefruit into Mae Clarke's face in *The Public Enemy* (1931). As a hoodlum he had an energy that

AP/WIDE WORLD

was defined by the excitement and suspense he created by poising on the balls of his feet ready to spring into action. He denied, however, ever uttering the line "you dirty rat," a phrase that was universally mimicked. Some of his classic roles as a gangster included *Angels with Dirty Faces* (1938), *The Roaring Twenties* (1939), and *White Heat* (1949). Cagney, nevertheless, always considered himself a song-and-dance man and showcased his fancy footwork in such films as *Footlight Parade* (1933), *The Strawberry Blonde* (1941), and *The Seven Little Foys* (1955). He further exhibited his versatility by playing Bottom in *A Midsummer Night's Dream* (1935), a prison governor in *The Mayor of Hell* (1933), a cocky race car driver in *The Crowd Roars* (1932), an airline pilot in *Ceiling Zero* (1936), the racketeer boyfriend of Doris Day in *Love Me or Leave Me* (1955), a World War II cargo ship captain in *Mr. Roberts* (1955), the silent movie actor Lon Chaney in *Man of a Thousand Faces* (1957), and a crusty Coca-Cola executive in Billy Wilder's *One, Two, Three* (1961), his last film before announcing his retirement. He returned to the screen in 1981, however, to play a cameo role, that of police commissioner Waldo, in *Ragtime*. In 1983 he made a movie for television, "Terrible Joe Moran," which was broadcast in 1984. He was also nominated for an Academy Award for his roles in *Angels with Dirty Faces*, *Love Me or Leave Me*, and *Ragtime*. In 1974 he received the life achievement award of the American Film Institute.

Canning, Victor, British popular novelist (b. June 16, 1911, Plymouth, England—d. Feb. 21, 1986, Ewen, Gloucestershire, England), was the prolific author of novels in a variety of genres but was best known for such thrillers as *The Golden Salamander* (1949) and *Venetian Bird* (1951). His first novel, *Mr. Finchley Discovers His England* (1934), written when he was an office worker, was a best-seller, and he followed it with other humorous stories. During World War II he served with the Royal Artillery, which sparked his interest in espionage, the background for his most successful postwar books. Canning also published animal stories: *The Runaways* (1972), about a cheetah, and *The Doomsday Carrier* (1976), about a chimpanzee that escapes when infected with a deadly disease. His last novels, starting with *The Crimson Chalice* (1976), were based on Arthurian legend or historical themes.

Cassou, Jean, French writer (b. July 9, 1897, Deusto, near Bilbao, Spain—d. Jan. 16, 1986, Paris, France), was a poet, novelist, and art critic who set up the Musée National d'Art Moderne in Paris after World War II. As the museum's chief curator (1945–65), he organized important exhibitions of contemporary art and acquired paintings, including a gift of 11 canvasses by his friend Picasso. Cassou's difficult childhood and youth were described in a semiautobiographical novel, *De l'Etoile au Jardin des Plantes* (1935), and he developed his theories of history in a study of the revolution of 1848, *Quarante-huit* (1939). After joining the Resistance at the start of the German occupation of France during World War II, he was arrested and imprisoned. His war poetry, published clandestinely under the name Jean Noir, expressed a faith in liberty and the individual that was central to his otherwise pessimistic view of the modern world. As well as novels, among them *Légion* (1939) and *Le Centre du monde* (1945), he wrote important critical studies of El Greco, Picasso, the Impressionists, and other artists. Grand Officer of the Légion d'Honneur, he was awarded the Grand Prix National des Lettres in 1971, and in 1983 the Société des Gens de Lettres presented him its award in recognition of the entire body of his work.

Cecil, Lord (Edward Christian) David Gascoyne, British man of letters (b. April 9, 1902, London, England—d. Jan. 1, 1986, Cranborne, Dorset, England), was best known for his biographies of literary figures, notably neglected authors or those out of favour with the literary establishment. Cecil served as Goldsmith's professor of English literature at the University of Oxford (1948–69). The younger son of the 4th marquess of Salisbury, he was educated at Eton and at Christ Church College, Oxford, where he studied history. While he was a fellow at Wadham College, Oxford (1924–30), his interests shifted from history to literature. During the 1930s he left academic life in order to concentrate on his writing, but he returned to Oxford to take up a fellowship at New College in 1939 and was later elected to the newly formed Goldsmith's professorship. Cecil brought to his teaching a vitality and lack of dogmatism that also characterized his writings. His biographies include *The Stricken Deer* (1929), a study of William Cowper; *Jane Austen* (1935); *The Young Melbourne* (1939) and its sequel, *Lord M* (1954); *Hardy, the Novelist* (1943); and *Max* (1964), a life of Max Beerbohm. Cecil also wrote a family history, *The Cecils of Hatfield House* (1973), and published collections of his lectures. He was appointed a Companion of Honour in 1949.

Chase, Lucia, U.S. ballerina and dance patron (b. March 24, 1897, Waterbury, Conn.—d. Jan. 9, 1986, New York, N.Y.), as cofounder (1940) and codirector (1945–80) of the Ballet Theatre (from 1957, American Ballet Theatre [ABT]), selflessly donated her talent, boundless energy, and a large portion of her personal fortune to sustain the company and helped build it into one of the premier companies in the world. Chase, who studied ballet with Fokine, Nijinska, and Mordkin, was a ballerina (1938–39) with the Mordkin Ballet, which became the nucleus of Ballet Theatre. With American Ballet Theatre she created such dramatic roles as the nurse in Tudor's *Romeo and Juliet*, the oldest sister in *Pillar of Fire*, and the stepmother in *Fall River Legend*. As codirector of Ballet Theatre with Oliver Smith, she helped incorporate European dance traditions into ABT while maintaining an eclectic repertory with works by such American choreographers as Jerome Robbins, Michael Kidd, and Agnes de Mille; the Russian dancers and choreographers David Lichine and Léonid Massine; and the British choreographer Antony Tudor. Through the years ABT also boasted a star-studded array of dancers including, among many others, Ivan Nagy, Erik Bruhn (*q.v.*), Alicia Alonso, Igor Youskevitch, Nora Kaye, Maria Tallchief, Cynthia Gregory, Natalia Makarova, and Mikhail Baryshnikov. Chase, who danced until well into her 70s, retired as codirector of ABT in 1980, when Baryshnikov took over sole directorship. In the same year, Chase was awarded the Presidential Medal of Freedom.

Chen Yonggui (Ch'en Yung-kuei), Chinese politician (b. 1913, Xiyang [Hsi-yang], Shanxi [Shansi] Province—d. March 26, 1986, Beijing [Peking], China), was the leader and chief propagandist (1963–73) of the infamous Dazhai (Ta-chai) commune, an agricultural community that purportedly reaped record harvests through hard work, self-reliance, and cooperative living. Mao Zedong (Mao Tse-tung) made Dazhai a national symbol, and the slogan "In agriculture, learn from Dazhai!" was emblazoned on walls throughout the country in an effort to stimulate workers into emulating the commune. Chen reportedly mobilized 83 families to carve granite slabs out of the hillsides and to construct terraces and reservoirs. After the entire operation was exposed as a sham in 1978, it was revealed that battalions of army labourers had terraced the hills and dug irrigation ditches and that grain output had actually decreased year after year, with peasants going hungry. Chen, a peasant who learned to read and write when he was in his 40s, worked as a poor land labourer before the Communists came to power in 1949. The following year he set up the Dazhai agricultural commune and gained national prominence by touting its accomplishments, by receiving delegations of admirers, and by traveling to other communes to promote Dazhai work methods. In 1973 he was elected a member of the Politburo of the Chinese Communist Party, and in 1975 he was appointed vice-premier. He also headed friendship delegations to Mexico (1975) and Cambodia (1977) and was elected (1978) deputy for Shanxi Province. In 1978 Deng Xiaoping (Teng Hsiao-p'ing) scrapped Mao's system of agricultural communes, and though Chen remained in the Politburo and the Central Committee until 1982, he was later posted to the Dongjiao (Tung-chiao) farm and was not heard from again until his death.

Ciardi, John Anthony, U.S. poet, critic, translator, and author (b. June 24, 1916, Boston, Mass.—d. March 30, 1986, Edison, N.J.), wrote some 40 books including verse, children's poems, criticism, and etymological works but was most widely hailed for his 1960 textbook *How Does a Poem Mean?* (rev. ed., with Miller Williams, 1975) and for his brilliant translation of Dante's *Divine Comedy* (*The Inferno*, 1954; *The Purgatorio*, 1961; *The Paradiso*, 1970), which became a standard college text. His translation of the latter from Italian to English was a monumental undertaking; he masterfully captured the feeling of the original text even though he chose a modern verse idiom for the translation rather than the original rhyme scheme. Ciardi's poetry was enjoyed by both adults and children, who appreciated his witty, often deeply moving, and notably accessible verses; critics were often divided in their views. Ciardi earned an M.A. from the University of Michigan in 1939 and the following year published his first book of poetry, *Homeward to America.* He supplemented his income by working as an instructor (1940–42) at the University of Kansas City, Mo., before serving in the Army Air Corps during World War II. After a brief return to his Kansas City position in 1946, he taught at Harvard University (1946–53), then joined (1953) the faculty at Rutgers, the State University of New Jersey, where he remained until his retirement in 1961. As poetry editor (1956–72) of *Saturday Review,* Ciardi was noted for his controversial, often brutally honest reviews. He was widely upbraided for his harsh review of Anne Morrow Lindbergh's *The Unicorn* (1956). His children's books, including *The Reason for the Pelican* (1959), *Scrappy the Pup* (1960), *The Man Who Sang the Sillies* (1961), and *The Wish Tree* (1962), were popular partly because they were not restricted to the saccharin sentiments evident in most other children's poetry. His poetry for adults, which explores the commonplaces of everyday life, includes such volumes as *Live Another Day* (1949), *I Marry You* (1958), *The Little That Is All* (1974), and *Selected Poems* (1984). Later nonpoetic works include two books written with Isaac Asimov, *Limericks, Too Gross* (1978) and *A Grossery of Limericks* (1981), and *A Browser's Dictionary, and Native's Guide to the Unknown American Language* (1980).

Clegg, Sir Alec (ALEXANDER BRADSHAW CLEGG), British educationist (b. June 13, 1909, Sawley, Derbyshire, England—d. Jan. 20, 1986, York, England), as chief education officer (1945–74) for the (then) West Riding of Yorkshire County Council, was a pioneer of freer teaching methods in primary schools and later promoted programs that would extend the emphasis on children's creativity and project work into middle schools. An opponent of elitism in education, he favoured setting up comprehensive schools and helped tailor the Certificate of Secondary Education examinations to suit those children whose gifts were practical rather than academic. He was educated at Long Eaton Grammar School and at the Quaker-run Bootham School at York; after studying modern languages at Clare College, Cambridge, he took a diploma in education at the University of London. Clegg was an assistant master (1932–36) at St. Clement Danes School, West London, before becoming an administrator. He was an administrative assistant (1936–39) to Birmingham's Education Committee, assistant education officer for the Cheshire County Council (1939–42), and deputy education officer for the Worcester County Council (1942–45). In West Yorkshire he set up (1952) Woolley Hall, Britain's first in-service teacher-training centre. After his retirement he was chairman of the governors (1976–79) of the Centre for Information and Advice on Educational Disadvantage. Clegg's special sympathies were reflected in such books as *Children in Distress* (with B. Megson, 1968), *The Changing Primary School* (1972), and *About Our Schools* (1981). He was knighted in 1965.

Cohn, Roy Marcus, U.S. lawyer (b. Feb. 20, 1927, New York, N.Y.—d. Aug. 2, 1986, New York), was best remembered as the notorious yet brilliant grand inquisitor during U.S. Sen. Joseph McCarthy's 1950s "witch hunt" for purported members of or sympathizers with the Communist Party. McCarthy and Cohn successfully destroyed the reputations and careers of a large group of people in government service and the entertainment industry. Cohn, who graduated from Columbia Law School at the age of 20, had to wait until he was 21 before he could be admitted to the bar. He then secured a position on the staff of the U.S. Attorney's Office in Manhattan and was touted as a "boy wonder," specializing in uncovering subversive activities. Described as arrogant and ruthless, Cohn helped prosecute the atomic espionage case that sent Julius and Ethel Rosenberg to the electric chair. He left the Justice Department in 1953 to join McCarthy's permanent investigations subcommittee as chief counsel. Cohn became involved in another imbroglio when he failed to secure special army privileges for his friend Gerald David Schine and threatened to "wreck the Army" with an investigation. The ensuing Army-McCarthy hearings of 1954, however, ruined McCarthy's reputation, and he receded from the limelight. In 1954 Cohn left Washington to begin a lucrative private practice, representing such clients as Mafia boss Carmine Galante, jet-setter Bianca Jagger, real-estate mogul Donald Trump, fashion designer Calvin Klein, and pop-culture figure Andy Warhol. Cohn courted the rich and famous and was valued for his loyalty by such friends as FBI Director J. Edgar Hoover, Terence Cardinal Cooke, right-wing journalist William F. Buckley, and television journalist Barbara Walters. His legal dealings led to several indictments on charges that included extortion, bribery, and mail fraud, but he was never convicted. Though he amassed a fortune, he reportedly owed some $3 million to the Internal Revenue Service, which had audited his tax returns for more than 20 years. In June 1986 Cohn was disbarred by the New York State Supreme Court's Appellate Division for dishonesty, deceit, fraud, and misrepresentation.

Coluche (MICHEL GÉRARD JOSEPH COLUCCI), French comedian (b. Oct. 28, 1944, Paris, France—d. June 19, 1986, near Grasse, Alpes-Maritimes, France), was known for the vulgarity and irreverence of his humour. His most celebrated joke, the announcement of his candidacy in the 1981 presidential election on a platform of sex, drugs, and rock and roll, made a sizable mark on the opinion polls and caused panic among the more orthodox candidates before he withdrew. In the six months before his death (in a motorcycle accident), he had won less grudging respect from the French establishment with his *restaurants du coeur,* offering free meals to the poor. The operation boasted 500 restaurants and provided up to 60,000 meals per day. Coluche came from a working-class family, began work in a factory at the age of 14, and spent many years in poverty, scraping together a living in various jobs before becoming a café entertainer. Wearing the blue dungarees and cloth cap of the ordinary worker, Coluche entertained audiences on stage, on radio, and on television with anecdotes and sketches satirizing the attitudes of politicians and the French middle and lower middle classes. He also made films, notably *Tchao Pantin* (1984), for which he won an award. He became, with his restaurants, his contributions to appeals for Ethiopia, and his activities in an antiracist organization, almost respectable; after his death it was announced that a school in Val-de-Rueil (Eure) was to be named after him.

Confalonieri, Carlo Cardinal, Italian ecclesiastic (b. July 25, 1893, Seveso, Italy—d. Aug. 1, 1986, Rome, Italy), served as dean of the Sacred College of Cardinals from 1977, was private secretary to Pope Pius XI (1922–39), and was prefect of the Sacred Consistorial Congregation (later the Congregation for Bishops) from 1961. Educated in the Milanese diocesan seminary and at the Gregorian University, Rome, he continued his studies while serving (1914–19) in the Italian Army during World War I. He was ordained priest while on leave in 1916. He worked as a parish priest in the diocese of Milan (1919–21) and was taken to Rome in January 1922 by Ambrogio Cardinal Ratti, then archbishop of Milan, for the conclave at which Ratti was elected Pope Pius XI. Confalonieri was also secretary (1939–41) to Pope Pius XII. While archbishop of L'Aquila (1941–50), he persuaded the German forces not to destroy the city during their retreat through Italy in World War II. After Confalonieri served as secretary of the Sacred Congregation of Seminaries and Universities (1950–58), Pope John XXIII created him a cardinal in 1958. Thereafter he was a dominant and influential figure who served on the Congregations for the Doctrine of the Faith, for Catholic Education, for the Clergy, for the Eastern Churches, and for the Evangelization of the World. He wrote a book on Pius XI in 1957 and one on his pastoral work at L'Aquila in 1967.

Cooper, David Graham, South African-born psychiatrist (b. Feb. 11, 1931, Cape Town, South Africa—d. July 29, 1986, Paris, France), was, with R. D. Laing, a proponent in the 1960s of "antipsychiatry"; later he claimed that the age of "nonpsychiatry" was coming into being. A Marxist, he came to regard psychiatry as a tool of capitalism and maintained that "all delusion is political statement," the individual's protest against bourgeois conformism. "Antipsychiatry" (later rejected by Laing) was represented as the struggle against medical manipulation. In the 1970s, convinced that capitalism was already in its death throes, Cooper asserted that with "nonpsychiatry" disturbed behaviour would be channeled as a source of social creativity. Cooper studied medicine at the University of Cape Town before going to England, where he held a series of posts in London hospitals. He became director of Villa 21, an experimental unit for young schizophrenics. He and Laing founded the Philadelphia Association, which established such therapeutic communities as Kingsley Hall in London's East End (1965–70). Cooper became an "antidirector" of the so-called Institute of Phenomenological Studies and in 1967 organized a Congress on the Dialectics of Liberation. From 1974 he lived mainly in Paris, lecturing in psychopathology at the University of Vincennes (University of Paris VIII), having abandoned all psychiatric practice. He traveled extensively, visiting the U.S., South America, Mexico, Japan, Belgium, and Italy. His books include *Psychiatry and Anti-Psychiatry* (1967), *The Death of the Family* (1971), and *The Language of Madness* (1978).

Cooper, Lady Diana (DIANA, VISCOUNTESS NORWICH), British socialite and actress (b. Aug. 29, 1892, London, England—d. June 16, 1986, London), attracted a brilliant and influential circle of friends with her aristocratic charm and wit. Her reputation as an actress was based on some silent films, including a performance as Queen Elizabeth I, and her role in Max Reinhardt's stage pageant *The Miracle,* which she performed (1923) in New York before touring the U.S. and Europe. Some measure of her personality could be ascertained from her autobiographical writings, starting with *The Rainbow Comes and Goes* (1958), and from her fictional appearances in works by Evelyn Waugh, D. H. Lawrence, and Nancy Mitford, which celebrated her eccentricities. Officially daughter of the 8th duke of Rutland, although her natural father was probably the poet Harry Cust, she was educated by governesses and was already a glittering figure before World War I, during which she served as a nurse. In 1919, against parental opposition, she married Alfred Duff Cooper, a diplomat, politician, and writer who was British ambassador in Paris from 1944 until 1947; she abandoned the theatre to support his political career. During the 1930s she was a friend of the prince of Wales and Wallis Simpson (*q.v.*), accompanying them on a notorious cruise after he became King Edward VIII. She showed less predictable qualities when she successfully devoted herself to farming her estates during World War II. Her husband died less than two years after being made Viscount Norwich in 1952.

Cooper, Martin Du Pré, British music critic (b. Jan. 17, 1910, Winchester, England—d. March 15, 1986, Richmond, Surrey, England), as a music editor of the London *Daily Telegraph* (1954–76) was widely respected by both musicians and the concertgoing public. Educated at Winchester College and at the University of Oxford, Cooper studied music under the composer and musicologist Egon Wellesz at the University of Vienna (1932–34). After returning to England, he became assistant editor (1935–36) of the *Royal Geographical Society Journal* and also music critic (1934–39) of the *London Mercury*. He was critic for the *Daily Herald* from 1945 until 1950, when he joined the *Daily Telegraph* as assistant to Richard Capell. During 1953–56 Cooper also edited the *Musical Times*. He was the author of several books, including *Gluck* (1935), *Bizet* (1938), *French Music from the Death of Berlioz to the Death of Fauré* (1951), *Russian Opera* (1951), *Ideas and Music* (1966), and *Beethoven—the Last Decade* (1970); he contributed the articles on Georges Bizet and César Franck to *Encyclopædia Britannica*. A talented linguist, Cooper also translated works from German, French, and Russian. He was president (1959–60) of the Critics' Circle and in 1976 was elected to fellowship of the Royal Academy of Music.

Cousins, Frank, British labour unionist (b. Sept. 8, 1904, Bulwell, Nottinghamshire, England—d. June 11, 1986, Chesterfield, Derbyshire, England), was general secretary of the Transport and General Workers' Union (TGWU) and a member of the general council of the Trades Union Congress from 1956 until 1969. During 1964–66 he was seconded as minister of technology in the Labour government headed by Harold Wilson (later Lord Wilson of Rievaulx). Cousins, who left school at age 14 and worked first as a coal miner and then as a truck driver, became a TGWU organizer in 1938. He progressed through the union hierarchy to the position of assistant general secretary in 1955. As general secretary from the following year, he became a powerful figure in the union movement and a leading opponent of Labour's wage restraint policy. His appointment in October 1964 to head the newly created Ministry of Technology was seen as an attempt by Wilson to defuse this opposition. However, in July 1966 Cousins resigned in protest against the Prices and Incomes Bill introduced by the government; five months later he also resigned his parliamentary seat as Labour member for Nuneaton, which he had won in a January 1965 by-election. Back in his TGWU post, he resumed his criticism of Labour's economic policies. He then served as chairman (1968–70) of the Community Relations Commission. Although standing to the left of the union movement, Cousins was nevertheless strongly anti-Communist. He was also a notable supporter of the Campaign for Nuclear Disarmament.

Crawford, (William) Broderick, U.S. actor (b. Dec. 9, 1911, Philadelphia, Pa.—d. April 26, 1986, Rancho Mirage, Calif.), specialized in portraying fast-talking, hard-boiled gangsters and in 1949 garnered the Academy Award for best actor for his brilliant depiction of the ruthless politician Willie Stark in *All the King's Men,* but he would probably be best remembered as the no-nonsense chief Dan Matthews on the television series "Highway Patrol" (1955–58). Crawford, the son of famed comedienne Helen Broderick, worked as a stevedore and merchant seaman between stints on stage. He made his official stage debut in London in *She Loves Me Not* (1934) and first appeared on Broadway in *Point Valaine* (1935) before making his Hollywood debut in *Woman Chases Man* (1937). He achieved critical acclaim on Broadway for his sensitive portrayal of the half-wit Lennie in *Of Mice and Men* (1937), but Crawford reached the pinnacle of his career in his first starring role, that of Willie Stark in *All the King's Men,* which was based on Robert Penn Warren's fictionalized account of the rise and fall of Louisiana kingpin Huey Long. The beefy, gravelly voiced Crawford scored another success when he played junk merchant Harry Brock, who bullied dumb blonde Judy Holliday in *Born Yesterday* (1950). His weakness for liquor hampered his career, however, and after starring in *The Mob* (1951) and *Not as a Stranger* (1955), he was relegated almost exclusively to supporting roles. Besides "Highway Patrol," he appeared on television in "King of Diamonds" (1961) and "The Interns" (1970). Some of his other screen credits include *Human Desire* (1954), *New York Confidential* (1955), *Il Bidone* (*The Swindle;* 1955), *The Private Files of J. Edgar Hoover* (1978), and *Liar's Moon* (1982).

Crawford, Cheryl, U.S. theatrical producer (b. Sept. 24, 1902, Akron, Ohio—d. Oct. 7, 1986, New York, N.Y.), was an influential figure in American theatre as a founder of the Group Theater (1931; with Harold Clurman and Lee Strasberg), the American Repertory Theater (1945; with Eva Le Gallienne and Margaret Webster), and the Actors' Studio (1947; with Elia Kazan and Robert Lewis). Crawford, who began staging plays while attending Smith College, Northampton, Mass., began her professional theatrical career in 1923 when she appeared as an actress with the Theatre Guild. In 1937 she left the Group Theater and, with *All the Living* (1938), became an independent producer. Some of her other productions included *Porgy and Bess* (1942), *Brigadoon* (1947), *The Rose Tattoo* (1951), *Camino Real* (1953), *Sweet Bird of Youth* (1959), *Mother Courage and Her Children* (1963), and *Colette* (1970). Crawford also served (from 1950) as one of the directors of the ANTA play series produced annually by the American National Theatre and Academy. Her final credits included *So Long on Lonely Street* (1985) and *Legends* (1986).

Crowley, James H. ("Sleepy Jim"), U.S. football player and coach (b. Sept. 10, 1902, Chicago, Ill.—d. Jan. 15, 1986, Scranton, Pa.), was the legendary 72.6-kg (160-lb) Notre Dame halfback who, with backfield teammates Harry Stuhldreher, Don Miller, and Elmer Layden, was immortalized by sportswriter Grantland Rice when he wrote, "Outlined against a blue-gray October sky, the Four Horsemen rode again. In dramatic lore they are known as Famine, Pestilence, Destruction and Death. These are only aliases." The colourful account described Notre Dame's 13–7 victory over Army in 1924. During the 1923–24 season the "Four Horsemen" led Notre Dame to a 19–1 record and the 1924 national championship. Their coach, football giant Knute Rockne, nicknamed Crowley "Sleepy Jim" because of his stooped shoulders, short steps, and relaxed motion; Rockne remarked, "You look like a tester in an alarm clock factory." In 1922 Crowley was Notre Dame's leading rusher, and he was leading passer in 1922 and 1923. He ended his playing career with 1,841 yd on 294 carries, for a 6.3-yd average. After graduation he began his coaching career as backfield assistant at the University of Georgia, then moved to Michigan State University as head coach (1929–32); he reached the pinnacle of his career at Fordham University (1933–41), where he coached the 1936 "Rocks" and the impregnable "Seven Blocks of Granite," who did not allow a touchdown in 1937. After serving as a navy commander during World War II, he became commissioner of the All America Football Conference and then part-owner and coach of the Chicago Rockets. He later became a successful businessman, and he served as chairman of the Pennsylvania Athletic Commission until his retirement in 1972. The witty Crowley, who was famous for his tongue-in-cheek humour, never had a losing season as a college coach and was a member of the National Football Hall of Fame.

Dassault, Marcel, French industrialist (b. Jan. 22, 1892, Paris, France—d. April 18, 1986, Paris), created the company that, after World War II, built the most successful European military aircraft, including the Mystère, Mirage, and Étendard series of fighters and fighter-bombers. His other interests included publishing and politics; he was a deputy in the National Assembly from 1951 to 1955, a senator from 1957 to 1958, and a deputy again from 1958 until his death. Born Marcel Bloch (he changed his name in 1949), he was an enthusiast for technological marvels from his early youth. After obtaining degrees in aeronautical design and electrical engineering, he started his career as a designer with the French Air Force during World War I. With his partner, Henri Potez, Dassault manufactured the Éclair propeller and a monoplane, the SEA4. After the war he ran a successful property business before returning to aircraft manufacture in the 1930s, first with the notorious Bloch 210, then with the 220. His company was nationalized in 1936. However, Dassault remained in charge and, because he refused to work with the Germans during the World War II occupation, he was interned, then sent to Buchenwald. After Dassault was released, he led the revival of the French aircraft industry with the Générale Aéronautique Marcel Dassault. The first Mystère flew in 1951, and a later model became the first European supersonic aircraft. The Mirage III achieved Mach 2 in 1956, and the Mirage IV bomber set an international speed record in 1959. The Dassault enterprise remained in the forefront of aircraft and missile technology, a vital component of Gen. Charles de Gaulle's policy of military, political, and economic independence. By the 1980s the company was the eighth largest in its field in the world, with a work force of 15,000 and over 70% of its output sold abroad. In 1981, after the election of the Socialist government, the state took a controlling interest in the company. Dassault held the Grand-Croix de la Légion d'honneur, the Croix de Guerre 1939–45, and the Médaille de l'Aéronautique.

Defferre, Gaston, French politician (b. Sept. 14, 1910, Marsillargues, Hérault, France—d. May 7, 1986, Marseille, France), as mayor of Marseille from 1953 until his death, helped to shape and implement important legislative measures; he combined the beliefs of a liberal social-democrat with the influence of a feudal landlord to rule France's second-largest city. Trained as a lawyer, Defferre fought as a member of the Resistance to the German occupation during World War II and served briefly as mayor of Marseille in 1944–45. He was a deputy to the National Assembly for Marseille almost continuously from 1945 until his death. As minister for overseas territories under the Fourth Republic, he pushed through a bill giving greater autonomy to France's former colonies, preparing their way for independence. He attracted attention as an opponent of the government's Algerian policy and resigned his ministerial post in 1957. After Gen. Charles de Gaulle came to power in the following year, Defferre lost his parliamentary seat until 1962, when he began to rally the Socialist opposition to de Gaulle's presidency. Defferre was hostile, however, to the Communist Party, the other main element on the left. Standing as the Socialist presidential candidate in 1969, Defferre received only 5% of the vote, in part because of his rivalry with other Socialist figures. A combative politician, he fought a fencing duel with a Gaullist deputy in 1967. From the 1970s Defferre supported François Mitterrand's candidacy and, despite his doubts about Communist participation, the Union of the Left. As the president's closest colleague and as interior minister, Defferre was responsible for the 1982 decentralization measures that were the most significant administrative reforms of the Socialist government under Mitterrand's presidency. But his most formidable power base was in the town hall at Marseille, where for 33 years he managed to hold off the challenge from the right—including the National Front—and presided over the creation of a modern city, built up its social and cultural amenities, and overcame problems of finance, housing, and an influx of emigrants from Algeria in 1962. His last political battle came on the eve of his death when he collapsed following his defeat at a stormy meeting of the local Socialist federation.

Dillon, James Mathew, Irish politician (b. Sept. 26, 1902, Dublin, Ireland—d. Feb. 10, 1986, Ballaghadeerreen, County Mayo, Ireland), was a firm but nonfanatical nationalist and served as minister of agriculture (1948–51 and 1954–57) and leader of Fine Gael and of the opposition in the Dail (parliament; 1959–65). His family was distinguished in the cause of Irish independence; his grandfather John Blake Dillon had been a member of the Young Ireland movement in the 1840s, and his father, John Dillon, a nationalist member of the Westminster Parliament (1880–83 and 1885–1918). Educated at Mount St. Benedict School, Gorey, and at University College, Dublin, he studied business in London and Chicago before being called to the bar at the Dublin King's Inns (1931). Dillon served in the Dail as member for County Donegal (1932–37) and for County Monaghan (1937–69). He early became deputy leader of Fine Gael, the main opposition to Eamon De Valera's party, Fianna Fail, but in 1942 he resigned because of Fine Gael's support for Irish neutrality during World War II. Dillon's first tenure of the post of minister of agriculture was as an independent, but he rejoined Fine Gael (1951), succeeding John Costello as party leader (1959). Dillon improved his party's standing in the 1961 general election by opposing a proposal for the compulsory use of Gaelic in school and public service examinations. He refused nomination as president in 1966.

Ding Ling (Ting Ling) (JIANG WEIZHI [CHIANG WEI-CHIH]), Chinese writer (b. 1904, Changde, Hunan Province, China—d. March 4, 1986, Beijing [Peking], China), was one of 20th-century China's most important writers and a champion of women's rights who produced about 300 novels, short stories, plays, and essays. As a young woman Ding Ling studied for a time at Shanghai and Peking universities. She began writing short stories in 1927 and, in 1930, joined the League of Left-Wing Writers, where she edited the organ *The Great Dipper.* In 1931 she joined the Chinese Communist Party (CCP), and her work began to focus on the effects of the Communist revolution on the lives of Chinese peasant women. Her novel *Flood* (1931) was acclaimed as a model of Socialist-Realist fiction in China. Ding Ling was abducted by agents of the Nationalist Party in 1933 and imprisoned until 1936, when she escaped disguised as a soldier. From 1934 to 1949 her works were banned by Chiang Kai-shek's Nationalist government. Ding's most famous work was the proletarian novel *The Sun Shines over the Sangkan River*

AP/WIDE WORLD

(1949), a vivid account of the land-reform program taking place at that time in Manchuria. The book won the Stalin Prize for Literature in 1951, the first Chinese novel so honoured. In other writings she created heroines who rebelled against the constraints of a patriarchal society in order to gain independence and equality. After the Communists took power in 1949, Ding Ling held a number of prestigious literary posts. However, despite her literary achievements, her criticism of the party's treatment of women angered Chairman Mao Zedong (Mao Tse-tung), and in 1957 she was officially censured and expelled from the CCP as a rightist. Her works were again banned from 1958 until 1978, and she was imprisoned for five years (1970–75) during the 1966–76 Cultural Revolution. In 1979 her party membership was restored, and she produced such works as *A Hell of Demons and Monsters* and *A World in Wind and Snow.*

Doisy, Edward Adelbert, U.S. biochemist (b. Nov. 13, 1893, Hume, Ill.—d. Oct. 23, 1986, St. Louis, Mo.), won the 1943 Nobel Prize for Physiology or Medicine for the discovery of vitamin K. Doisy shared the prize with Henrik Dam, who independently isolated the vitamin in 1939. After earning A.B. and M.S. degrees from the University of Illinois, Doisy received (1920) his Ph.D. from Harvard University and then joined the faculty of Washington University School of Medicine, St. Louis. Doisy, working with embryologist Edgar Allen, isolated a variant form of vitamin K, vitamin K_2, and such sex hormones as estron (theelin, 1929), the first estrogen to be crystallized; estriol (theelol, 1930); and estradiol (dihydrotheelin, 1935). After helping to establish the biochemistry department at Washington University, Doisy was named chairman of the department in 1924. His accomplishments were recognized in 1955 when the university's department of biochemistry was named for him. Doisy retired in 1965. Some of his scientific writings include *Sex Hormones* (1936) and *Sex and Internal Secretions* (1939), with Allen amd Charles H. Danforth.

Douglas, Thomas Clement ("TOMMY"), Scottish-born Canadian politician (b. Oct. 20, 1904, Falkirk, Scotland—d. Feb. 24, 1986, Ottawa, Ont.), was the head of the socialist Cooperative Commonwealth Federation (CCF) who was elected premier of Saskatchewan and led the first socialist government in North America. Douglas was born in Scotland and, with

UPI/BETTMANN NEWSPHOTOS

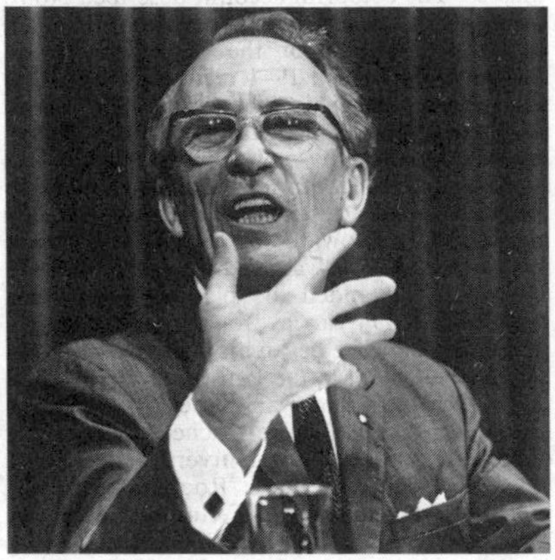

his family, settled in Canada at the age of six. In 1930 he was ordained a Baptist minister. Elected to the Canadian House of Commons in 1935, he served there until 1944, when he was elected premier of Saskatchewan. During his tenure as premier, his innovative administration introduced government-financed health care (which became the model for Canada's socialized health-insurance scheme), public-sector collective bargaining, trade union laws, rural electrification, and government-sponsored automobile insurance. His provincial government also organized an excellent educational system and formed government-owned corporations. He resigned as premier in 1961 to serve as the first federal leader of Canada's New Democratic Party, the successor to the CCF as the country's primary socialist party. In 1971 Douglas retired as party leader, but he continued to sit in the House of Commons until 1979.

Dumézil, Georges Edmond Raoul, French academic (b. March 4, 1898, Paris, France—d. Oct. 11, 1986, Paris), made a fundamental contribution to the understanding of Indo-European culture and civilization. His work on mythology, grounded in his knowledge of more than 20 languages, showed underlying affinities among Indo-European religions, including Greco-Roman, Hindu, and Nordic mythology. Following service in World War I, he lectured at the University of Warsaw before becoming professor of the history of religions at the University of Istanbul (1925–31). He then was a reader at the University of Uppsala, Sweden (1931–33), before returning (1933) to France, where he served (1935–68) as director of studies at the École Pratique des Hautes Études. From 1949 he concurrently held the chair of Indo-European civilization at the Collège de France. Dumézil's work rested on the discovery of similar patterns in Hindu, Roman, and Nordic mythologies, including a triad of deities corresponding to a social division between three classes—priests, warriors, and peasants. His thesis on comparative religion, *Le Festin d'immortalité,* was published in 1924 and was followed by numerous other major studies, including a three-volume study of Roman mythology (1942–47) and the three-volume *Mythe et épopée* (1968–73). Although some of his theories were misused to support anti-Semitism and aspects of Nazism, he never subscribed to these interpretations. Dumézil was elected to the Académie des Sciences et des Belles-Lettres in 1970 and to the Académie Française in 1978.

Eastland, James Oliver, U.S. politician (b. Nov. 28, 1904, Doddsville, Miss.—d. Feb. 19, 1986, Greenwood, Miss.), was the longtime (1941–78) Democratic senator from Mississippi, was notable for his staunch opposition to desegregation, and became one of the most powerful men on Capitol Hill as chairman of the Judiciary Committee for 22 years, a position he used in killing 127 civil rights bills. Eastland, a lawyer and cotton plantation owner, was a member (1928–32) of the state House of Representatives but entered national politics when he was appointed (1941) to fill a vacant Senate seat after the death of Sen. Pat Harrison. He won election to the seat in 1942. During his long tenure as senator, he served on the Agriculture and Forestry Committee, chaired the Immigration and Naturalization Subcommittee, was adviser to the Senate Appropriations Committee, and in 1972 was elected president pro tempore of the Senate. A staunch anti-Communist, Eastland maintained that Communists had infiltrated civil rights organizations, and he was ardently in favour of U.S. involvement in Vietnam to "rattle the teeth of the Reds." When it became apparent that he could not rally the black vote for his reelection to the Senate, Eastland retired in 1978.

Edrich, Bill (WILLIAM JOHN EDRICH), British cricketer (b. March 26, 1916, Lingwood, Norfolk, England—d. April 24, 1986, Chesham, Buckinghamshire, England), was a fine bowler, a remarkable fielder, and an outstanding batsman whose partnership with Denis Compton in the immediate post-World War II years was one of the most memorable in English cricket. But in the years immediately before the war, his first test appearances had been a disappointment. His career batting average in first-class cricket was 42, including 86 centuries, and as a fast bowler, then an off-spinner, he took 479 wickets. He held a record among his contemporaries of 522 catches. Edrich came from a cricket family and made his mark in 1937, scoring 2,000 runs in the season and another 1,000 before the end of May in the following year. The 1938 test matches against Australia were a disaster for him, however. During the war he served with the Royal Air Force, winning the Distinguished Flying Cross, and in the 1946–47 season he and Compton produced a record-breaking partnership. They made 370 against South Africa at Lords; Edrich averaged 110 and took 16 wickets as a bowler in four test matches. The partnership helped England to victory again in 1953. From 1951 to 1957 Edrich was captain of Middlesex, for the first year jointly with Compton, and he continued to play for Norfolk until 1971.

Eliade, Mircea, U.S. religious scholar (b. March 9, 1907, Bucharest, Rom.—d. April 22, 1986, Chicago, Ill.), gained worldwide fame for his studies of religious beliefs and practices and for his attempts to relate them to primordial myths. Eliade, who earned (1928) an M.A. in philosophy from the University of Bucharest, studied (1928–31) Sanskrit and Indian philosophy at the University of Calcutta before writing his Ph.D. dissertation on yoga. From 1933 to 1939 he taught the history of religions and Indian philosophy at his alma mater in Bucharest, and from 1945 until 1956 he served as a visiting professor at the École des Hautes Études of the Sorbonne. He joined the faculty at the University of Chicago in 1956 and remained there until his retirement in 1985. There he was named (1962) Sewell Avery distinguished service professor in the divinity school and the committee on social thought and headed the department of religion. In 1961 he founded the international journal *History of Religions* and set forth his religious ideas in three volumes, *From the Stone Age to the Eleusinian Mysteries, From Gautama Buddha to the Triumph of Christianity,* and *From Muhammad to the Age of Reform,* published by the University of Chicago (1978–85). Eliade, who spoke six languages and wrote fluently in three, was the author of more than 50 books, notably such novels as *The Forbidden Forest* and *The Old Man and the Bureaucrats* and collections of essays, including *The Quest: History and Meaning in Religion* (1969) and *Occultism, Witchcraft, and Cultural Fashion: Essays in Comparative Religion* (1976).

Fairley, Barker, Canadian painter and man of letters (b. May 21, 1887, Barnsley, England—d. Oct. 11, 1986, Toronto, Ont.), was considered one of the century's foremost scholars in the field of Germanic studies and an authority on Goethe, as was illustrated by his *Goethe as Revealed in His Poetry* (1932) and *A Study of Goethe* (1947). Fairley studied at the University of Leeds, England, and at the University of Jena, Germany, where he lectured while earning a Ph.D. (1910). From 1910 until 1915 he taught at the University of Alberta, and from 1915 to 1932 and from 1936 until his retirement in 1957 he was on the faculty of the University of Toronto. Earlier, in 1920, together with C. B. Sissons and F. H. Underhill, Fairley had cofounded *The Canadian Forum*, an independent monthly journal of opinion and the arts. Fairley's columns extolled Canadian art and focused especially on the Group of Seven, like-minded painters who found inspiration in northern Ontario landscapes. After his retirement, Fairley devoted much of his time to painting; his works were widely exhibited. His one year of poetic efforts was published as *Poems of 1922 or Not Long After* (1972), and his book *Portraits* appeared in 1981.

Farr, Tommy, British boxer (b. March 12, 1914, Tonypandy, South Wales—d. March 1, 1986, Shoreham, Sussex, England), became British and Empire heavyweight champion in 1937 and in the same year narrowly failed to take the world heavyweight title from U.S. boxer Joe Louis. His career epitomized the struggle to escape from the bleak prospects of South Wales during the Depression years. Farr started work as a miner, supporting his brother and sisters and supplementing his income with fights in fairground booths. Helped by his mentor, "Joby" Churchill, he moved to Slough and began boxing seriously. He fought in London, and in 1934 he won the Welsh light-heavyweight title, adding the Welsh heavyweight title two years later when he knocked out Jimmy Wilde. In 1937 he defeated Joe Zeeman of the U.S. before taking the British and Empire titles from the South African Ben Foord. In April of that year he confounded expectations with a decisive win over the German Max Baer, and two months later he knocked out Walter Neusel, to the disgust of Hermann Göring, who was watching the contest. Smaller than most of his opponents, he attacked them with courage, skill, and quick wit, winning a huge following among British fans. On Aug. 30, 1937, he challenged Louis in the "Brown Bomber's" first defense of his world title and became one of only three contenders to survive 15 rounds with the champion. Many considered that Farr had won, though he later acknowledged Louis's superior strength and skill. He stayed another two years in the U.S., losing all his matches, including one with Baer, who avenged his earlier defeat. During World War II Farr served with the Royal Air Force. In 1950 he made a comeback; he was stopped by Don Cockell in an elimination bout for the British title in 1953. He retired to become director of a paint firm.

Feinstein, Moses, U.S. religious leader (b. March 5, 1895, Uzda, Russia—d. March 23, 1986, New York, N.Y.), was an influential and widely respected Jewish Orthodox rabbi who drew upon his vast knowledge of the Talmud to solve contemporary religious problems for Orthodox Jews throughout the world. Feinstein studied at the yeshivas of Slutzk and Schklov and served as his hometown rabbi from 1916 to 1918. From 1921 to 1937 he was rabbi of Luban, a town near Minsk, before immigrating to the U.S. in 1937. As rosh yeshiva of New York's Mesivta Tiferet Jerusalem, he helped it become one of the leading U.S. yeshivas. Feinstein was an acknowledged scholar of Halakha (Jewish law), and his wide-ranging opinions on contemporary society and modern science and technology in the light of Halakha guided the lives of millions of Orthodox Jews and rabbis who embraced his authoritative decisions on the practical application of age-old Jewish principles to modern life. Feinstein published his rulings in such books as *Orah Hayyim* (1959), *Yoreh De'ah* (1959), *Even ha-Ezer* (1961), and *Hoshen Mishpot* (1963). From 1966 until 1976 he served as president of the Union of Orthodox Rabbis in America and Canada, and at the time of his death he was chairman of the Council of Sages of Agudath Israel of America.

Fernández, Emilio, Mexican film director (b. March 26, 1904, El Seco, Coahuila, Mexico—d. Aug. 6, 1986, Mexico City, Mexico), made important contributions to the Mexican film industry directing films that dealt with nationalistic themes and explored the plight of the Mexican Indian. Fernández, known as "El Indio," fought in the Mexican Revolution on the side of Adolfo de la Huerta, was captured, and was sentenced to 20 years' imprisonment. In 1923 he escaped to the U.S., where he appeared in films in bit parts. He returned to Mexico in 1933, after an amnesty was declared, and began acting in Mexican films, notably *Janitzio* (1934). During the 1940s and '50s he established a reputation as a gifted director, and his film *María Candelaria* won first prize as best film at the 1946 Cannes Film Festival. Of the 42 films he directed, 16 won international prizes. Some of his other notable motion pictures include *Pepita Jiménez; La perla* (*The Pearl*; 1945), *Enamorada* (*In Love*; 1946), which was remade in English under the title *The Torch* (1950), and *Río Escondido* (*Hidden River*; 1947). In 1958 Fernández returned to acting. With his stocky frame and big, drooping mustache, he was a natural for supporting roles in such films as *The Wild Bunch* (1969), *Bring Me the Head of Alfredo Garcia* (1974), and *Under the Volcano* (1984). In 1976 he was sentenced to four and a half years in prison after he killed a farm labourer, allegedly in self-defense, while scouting locations in northern Mexico, but he was paroled six months later.

Fichte, Hubert, West German writer (b. March 21, 1935, Perleberg, Brandenberg, Germany—d. March 8, 1986, Hamburg, West Germany), established his reputation with the novel *Das Waisenhaus* (1965) and its sequel, *Die Palette* (1968), the latter of which attracted particular critical attention with an experimental form that combined fictional and documentary elements. A member of Gruppe 47, Fichte worked at various jobs in Sweden, West Germany, and France before winning a grant after the publication of *Der Aufbruch nach Turku* (1963), a collection of stories. *Das Waisenhaus* gained the 1965 Herman Hesse International Prize, and Fichte was recognized as a leading exponent of realism in the German novel. He later devoted himself to the study of anthropology and published a book on Afro-American religions.

Fleming, Lady Amalia, Greek politician (b. 1912?, Constantinople, Ottoman Empire [now Istanbul, Turkey]—d. Feb. 26, 1986, Athens, Greece), was a bacteriologist and a humanitarian and activist known for her courageous opposition to the military junta that ruled Greece from 1967 until 1974. On the outbreak of World War I her father, Harikios Coutsouris, a physician, took his family to Athens, where Amalia later studied medicine. During World War II she was a member of the Greek underground and resistance movement, providing supplies and information to British and Greek fighters and helping Greek Jews to escape. She was arrested by the Italians and imprisoned until the British liberated Greece in 1944. She received a British Council scholarship (1946) and worked (1946–51) at St. Mary's Hospital in London as research assistant for Sir Alexander Fleming, the discoverer of penicillin. They were married in 1953. After his death (1955) she remained in England until 1967, when she returned to Greece and became involved in human rights work. In 1971 she was arrested and accused of involvement in the abortive prison escape of Alexandros Panaghoulis, a soldier connected with an attempt in 1968 on the life of Prime Minister Georgios Papadopoulos. Stripped of her Greek citizenship, she was deported to Britain, but returned to Greece after the junta fell (1974). A supporter of Andreas Papandreou's opposition Panhellenic Socialist Movement (Pasok), she was elected to the Greek Parliament (1977) and became deputy for Athens when Pasok won power in 1981. Lady Fleming was a member of the European Rights Commission and also an active member of the European Parliament.

Fournier, Pierre Léon Marie, French cellist (b. June 24, 1906, Paris, France—d. Jan. 8, 1986, Geneva, Switz.), established a reputation as a musician of restraint and warmth and became internationally known after World War II as one of the world's leading cello soloists. He studied under Paul Bazelaire and André Hekking at the Paris Conservatoire, where he later taught. After making his Paris debut in 1928, he appeared as a soloist with leading orchestras and in 1943 replaced Pablo Casals as cellist in a renowned trio with Jacques Thibaud and Alfred Cortot. Besides appearing with other chamber ensembles, Fournier made recordings of Dvorak, Strauss, and Beethoven and gave the first performances of a concerto by Albert Roussel as well as of works written for him by Honegger, Poulenc, and Martinu. Fournier, who lived in Geneva from 1956, was honoured in 1981 in Zürich at a concert organized by Mstislav Rostropovich, who recognized the exceptional stylistic quality of his playing. His last concert, in 1985, was at the Aldeburgh Festival in Britain, where he enjoyed considerable popularity.

Fulton, John Scott Fulton, Baron, British university administrator (b. May 27, 1902, Dundee, Scotland—d. March 14, 1986, Thornton Dale, North Yorkshire, England), was an innovative vice-chancellor of the University of Sussex from its foundation in 1959 until 1967. He chaired a committee on the civil service which, when the Fulton Report was published in 1968, strongly appealed for greater professionalism and for the opening of the higher civil service to a wider range of talent. Fulton studied at Saint Andrews University and at Balliol College, University of Oxford, before teaching politics and philosophy at the London School of Economics and Political Science and at Balliol. After World War II he was principal of University College, Swansea, and vice-chancellor of the University of Wales before his appointment to the new University of Sussex. There he initiated a policy of rapid growth, showing his exceptional administrative talents and setting the model for the new universities of the 1960s. Though Prime Minister Harold Wilson accepted Fulton's 1968 report, its proposals for abandoning Whitehall's "cult of the generalist" and enrolling more specialist scientific and managerial staff remained largely unimplemented. Fulton was also vice-chairman of the British Broadcasting Corporation and chairman of the University Council for Higher Education Overseas. Knighted in 1964, he became a life peer in 1966.

Galili, Yisrael, Israeli politician (b. May 1911, Brailov, Ukraine, Russia—d. Feb. 8, 1986, Kibbutz Na'an, Israel), was political commander of the Haganah, Israel's pre-independence underground army. He later became founder of the left-wing Ahdut ha-'Avoda party and served in government as minister of information and as the man chiefly responsible for Labour Party policy in the occupied territories. Galili went to Palestine at the age of four and was active in the Self-Defense Forces and as an organizer of the youth movement of the Histadrut (labour organization) when barely in his teens. In 1930 he founded Kibbutz Na'an, which served as an armory for the Haganah. He resigned from the Haganah high command in 1948 and ran his party until it merged with the Labour Party in 1963. His policy toward the territories occupied after the 1967 war allowed for the return of some areas in a peace agreement, as well as settlement of others. Galili left politics in 1980 and devoted his time to educational programs on his kibbutz.

Gardner, Dame Helen (Louise), British academic and literary critic (b. Feb. 13, 1908, London, England—d. June 4, 1986, Bicester, Oxfordshire, England), was Merton professor of English literature at the University of Oxford (1966–75) but was best known to the general public as editor and compiler of *The New Oxford Book of English Verse 1250–1950* (1972). Among fellow academics she made her name as a specialist writer and lecturer on the Metaphysical poets of the 17th century. She was educated at the North London Collegiate School and at St. Hilda's College, Oxford, where she studied English language and literature. After a year as research scholar at St. Hilda's (1929–30), she taught for two terms at the University of Birmingham before serving as assistant lecturer at Royal Holloway College, University of London (1931–34). She returned, first to Birmingham as a lecturer (1934–41), and then to St. Hilda's as college tutor in English literature (1941–54). She held the post of university reader in Renaissance English literature from 1954 to 1966. In 1959 Gardner became the first woman to be appointed a delegate to the Oxford University Press. In 1961 she was appointed by Prime Minister Harold Macmillan as a member of the Robbins Committee on Higher Education. Her books include *The Art of T. S. Eliot* (1949), *The Divine Poems of John Donne* (1952), *The Business of Criticism* (1960), *Religion and Literature* (1971), and *In Defence of the Imagination* (1982). Gardner was made a Commander (1962) and a Dame Commander (1967) of the Order of the British Empire.

Genet, Jean, French writer (b. Dec. 19, 1910, Paris, France—d. April 15, 1986, Paris), shocked and at the same time fascinated society with a fundamental repudiation of all its values, creating in his poems, novels, and plays an inverted morality through images of criminality, blasphemy, eroticism, desertion, and betrayal. On the evidence of a passage in Genet's *Journal du voleur* (1949), the writer Jean-Paul Sartre declared that Genet, illegitimate, abandoned by his mother, and branded a thief at the age of ten, was determined to live out the role society had chosen for him. He spent much of his adolescence in a reformatory, escaping from it to join—and immediately desert from—the Foreign Legion and graduating ultimately to terms in a number of prisons in France and Spain, with interludes as a beggar and homosexual prostitute in various European cities. *Notre-Dame-des-Fleurs* (1944), his first novel, was written in prison at Fresnes and, like his poetry and other fictional writings, was an extraordinary mixture of lyricism and obscenity. The early works came to the attention of the poet-artist Jean Cocteau, who, with Sartre, became one of Genet's most influential protectors. In fact, these men, joined by many other notable French writers, succeeded in securing his reprieve from a sentence of life imprisonment in 1948. His other novels of this period—*Miracle de la rose* (1945–46), *Querelle de Brest* (1947), and *Pompes funèbres* (1947)—continued to portray a dark beauty in the loves and betrayals of prison life, expressed with a complete commitment to the author's relentless nihilism. His "canonization" in Sartre's *Saint Genêt, comédien et martyr* (1952), an existential analysis of his work and personality, profoundly affected Genet, and he nearly stopped writing. But he did continue to write the dramas that proved to be his greatest contributions, finding a natural outlet in the theatre. In his plays, including *Les Bonnes* (1947), *Les Nègres* (1958), and *Le Balcon* (1956), Genet found the rituals of absurd drama ideally suited to expressing the nature of a world in which black was white, servants were mistresses, and the clientele of a brothel, dressing up as judges or bishops, gave an authentic picture of social identities. All his plays caused scandal, notably *Les Paravents* (1961), with its condemnation of the French Army in Algeria. From that time he wrote little, but his last work, in 1977, was a characteristic article in *Le Monde* defending the Baader-Meinhof terrorists and praising Soviet Communism. Personally mild-mannered and reclusive, he was honoured by literary society, which compared him to Villon, Rimbaud, and Sade. It was, however, an effort to classify the unclassifiable.

© JERRY BAUER

Gerstenmaier, Eugen Karl Albrecht, West German politician and theologian (b. Aug. 25, 1906, Kirchheim unter Teck, near Stuttgart, Germany—d. March 13, 1986, Bonn, West Germany), as president of the Bundestag (parliament) from 1954 to 1969 and a supporter of Chancellor Konrad Adenauer, was at one time considered a possible contender for the chancellorship. He studied theology and philosophy at Tübingen University and was teaching at Berlin University when he lost his post because of his opposition to the Nazi regime. Gerstenmaier went to work for the foreign section of the Evangelical Church. Involved in a resistance group, he was imprisoned following the attempt on Hitler's life in 1944. Following the war he headed the relief work of the Evangelical Church in Germany, known as Evangelisches Hilfswerk; he was German delegate at the Ecumenical Council of Churches and to the Council of Europe. A prominent member of the Christian Democratic Union, he was elected to the Bundestag in 1949 and in 1954 became its first elected president. Gerstenmaier was a strong advocate of European post-World War II reconciliation and unity. In 1969 he was criticized for accepting money to compensate for loss of salary under the Nazis and, though he had not been accused of any legal offense, he resigned from the Bundestag. He remained a respected figure in public life and in 1981 published his memoirs.

Glubb, Sir John Bagot, British army officer (b. April 16, 1897, Preston, Lancashire, England—d. March 17, 1986, Mayfield, Sussex, England), was commander of the Arab Legion (a force raised in 1921 by the British in their Transjordanian protectorate) and, until his dismissal by King Hussein of Jordan in 1956, one of the most influential figures in Middle Eastern politics. Universally known as Glubb Pasha, he created a legend that, in the Arab world, outstripped that of Lawrence of Arabia. He claimed to have been one of the chief architects of the kingdom of Jordan as well as the last of a great line of British soldiers in the Arab world. Glubb studied at the Royal Military Academy, Woolwich, before serving with the Royal Engineers during World War I, winning the Military Cross and suffering a jaw wound, which became a distinguishing feature. After the war he volunteered for service in Iraq and worked for the Royal Air Force intelligence. In 1926 he resigned his commission to join the Mandatory administration in Iraq. Already his travels and exploits were becoming legendary, and in 1930 he went to Transjordan, where he set about creating a local police and defense force, the Desert Patrol, to police the Bedouin. In 1939 he was appointed to command the Arab Legion and with them took part in operations in Iraq and Syria with notable success. By 1945 the Legion had grown to a force of 8,000 and was deeply involved in the Palestine issue and, after the creation of the state of Israel, in policing the Jordanian border. The rise of Arab nationalism and the assassination of King Abdullah in 1951 greatly weakened Glubb's position, and he found the young King Hussein difficult to deal with. Seen as a representative of British imperialism, Glubb became increasingly unpopular, and in March 1956 he was ordered to leave the country within two hours. He dissuaded the Bedouin regiments from rising in his favour and remained friendly toward Jordan and loyal to the Arab cause. He returned to England nearly penniless and was obliged to support himself by writing and lecturing. He wrote many books, including *War in the Desert* (1960), and lectured extensively in the U.S. He was knighted in 1956.

Gmeiner, Hermann, Austrian social administrator (b. June 23, 1919, Alberschwende, Vorarlberg, Austria—d. April 26, 1986, Innsbruck, Austria), was the founder of SOS Children's Villages (SOS Kinderdorf Verein), the international charity that provides homes for many thousands of orphaned and abandoned children. The seventh of eight children, Gmeiner was brought up by his father and eldest sister after his mother died when he was four. While serving in the German Army on the Eastern Front during World War II, he was deeply affected by the suffering of children rendered homeless by the war. In 1949 he established the first SOS Village at Imst, Austria, and soon abandoned his medical studies at the University of Innsbruck in order to concentrate on raising money for the project. The movement spread across Europe and later to other parts of the world. By 1985, when Gmeiner retired from the organization, there were 223 SOS villages in over 80 countries on five continents. The aim of the organization was to provide a family-style environment for small groups of children living together under the care of a house mother and a patriarchal village manager. Gmeiner, who was twice nominated for the Nobel Peace Prize, received many honours during his lifetime, including the Austrian Silver Order of Merit.

Goldie, Grace Wyndham, British television producer (b. March 26, 1900, Arisaig, Inverness-shire [now Highland region], Scotland—d. June 3, 1986, London, England), was largely responsible for establishing the form and tone of British current affairs programs during the post-World War II era. The daughter of a civil engineer, Grace Murrell Nisbet was educated at Cheltenham Ladies' College, at the University of Bristol, and at Somerville College, University of Oxford. In 1934 Goldie moved to London, where she served (1934–41) as dramatic and entertainment critic for *The Listener,* the weekly magazine of the British Broadcasting Corporation (BBC). After two years at the Board of Trade during World War II, she was appointed BBC talks producer in 1944 and presided over the broadcasting of programs on a number of vital subjects, such as the use of atomic energy. After joining BBC Television in 1948, she became assistant head of talks in 1954 and head of talks and current affairs in 1962. Her achievements included instituting the now standard practice of televised coverage for general elections; enlisting talented colleagues, such as Huw Wheldon (*q.v.*) and Alasdair Milne; and launching such successful and long-running current affairs programs as "Panorama" and "Tonight." Her definitive views on the independent and neutral role necessary in all broadcasting were forcefully put forth in her book *Facing the Nation: Television and Politics, 1936–76* (1977).

Goodman, Benny (BENJAMIN DAVID GOODMAN), U.S. clarinetist and orchestra leader (b. May 30, 1909, Chicago, Ill.—d. June 13, 1986, New York, N.Y.), was the legendary virtuoso clarinetist who was dubbed the King of Swing after popularizing that jazz style and ushering in a new era in American popular music. Swing was typified by a solid, driving, rhythmic beat accompanied by riffs (repeated phrases), which generated an electrifying yet controlled excitement. Goodman, who joined the band at Jane Addams' Hull House in 1920, made his professional debut the following year at Central Park Theater in Chicago. He joined Ben Pollack's band in Los Angeles as a soloist in 1925 and moved with the band to New York in 1928. The following year he became a freelance musician; he continued free-lancing until 1934, when he founded his own 12-piece band. The group became an instant smash when, at the Palomar Ballroom in Los Angeles, they performed a series of arrangements written by Fletcher Henderson—the event was often cited as the birth of swing. Goodman's celebrated trio (1935–36; himself, drummer Gene Krupa, and pianist Teddy Wilson [*q.v.*]) was followed by a quartet (1936–39) that added vibraphonist Lionel Hampton. With the inclusion of Wilson and Hampton, Goodman's band became the first racially mixed popular jazz band. On Jan. 16, 1938, Goodman and his orchestra made history when they performed in Carnegie Hall; it was the first jazz concert ever held there. He recounted the experience in his autobiography, *The Kingdom of Swing* (1939). Goodman's all-star band served as a springboard to fame for such musicians as Hampton, Wilson, Krupa, trumpeters Bunny Berigan, Harry James, and Ziggy Elman, pianist Jess Stacy, and singer Peggy Lee. The band became so popular that it had a prominent role in such motion pictures as *Big Broadcast of 1937* (1936), *Hollywood Hotel* (1938), *Stage Door Canteen* (1943), and *Sweet and Lowdown* (1944). During the early 1940s the orchestra changed its sound with arrangements by Eddie Sauter and frequent changes in sidemen, but its high level of musicianship was never altered. The tall, bespectacled, apple-cheeked bandleader, who was affectionately known as "the professor" to his band, was an exacting master. In 1938 he launched a second career as a classical clarinet player and displayed his technical genius performing Mozart's "Quintet for Clarinet and Strings" with the Budapest String Quartet. He also commissioned Bela Bartok's "Contrasts" and Aaron Copland's "Clarinet Concerto." Goodman was a leading instrumentalist of his era, and according to one authority he was the most recorded solo instrumentalist in history. Some of the all-time favourite numbers performed by his band included "King Porter Stomp," "Sing, Sing, Sing," "Seven Come Eleven," "Let's Dance," the orchestra's theme song, and "Goodbye," their closing signature. After the decline of the big band era, Goodman dismantled his band but reorganized groups for special engagements, notably for a historic 1962 trip to the U.S.S.R., where American jazz was introduced. In 1955 Goodman recorded the soundtrack for a film biography, *The Benny Goodman Story. B.G. on the Record,* a discography by D. Russell Connor and Warren W. Hicks, was published in 1969.

Grant, Cary (ARCHIBALD ALEXANDER LEACH), British-born U.S. actor (b. Jan. 18, 1904, Bristol, Gloucestershire, England—d. Nov. 29, 1986, Davenport, Iowa), was a suave and dapper leading man whose irresistible charm and mastery of the art of light, sophisticated comedy was showcased in such films as *Topper* (1937), *The Awful Truth* (1937), *Bringing Up Baby* (1938), *His Girl Friday* (1940), *My Favorite Wife* (1940), and *The Philadelphia Story* (1941). Although perhaps his most challenging roles were in such Alfred Hitchcock suspense thrillers as *Suspicion* (1941), *Notorious* (1946), *To Catch a Thief* (1955), and *North by Northwest* (1959), his only two Academy Award nominations were for accomplished but uncharacteristically serious roles in *Penny Serenade* (1941) and *None but the Lonely Heart* (1944). Grant, the product of an impoverished childhood, ran away from home at the age of 13 to join a traveling troupe of acrobatic dancers and pantomimists. In 1920 he arrived in New York City and worked at various odd jobs while still performing with the troupe. Three years later he returned to England, where he appeared in musical comedies. There he was discovered by Arthur Hammerstein, who took Grant back to New York, where he scored successes on Broadway before embarking on a Hollywood motion-picture career. His performance opposite Marlene Dietrich in *Blonde Venus* (1932) was so impressive that Mae West chose him as her costar in *She Done Him Wrong* (1933). But it was his superb gift for comic economy and impeccable timing and his magnetic screen persona that made him a star. Grant, who was married five times (to Virginia Cherrill, Barbara Hutton, Betsy Drake, Dyan Cannon, and Barbara Harris), never lost his classic good looks, his elegance, or his wit. He appeared in more than 70 films during a 35-year motion-picture career and retired in 1966 after starring in *Walk, Don't Run.* He then became an executive for, among other businesses, the Fabergé cosmetics firm. His acting skills, which to many appeared effortless, were recognized in 1970 when he received a special Academy Award for his cumulative contribution to film.

SYNDICATION INTERNATIONAL/PHOTO TRENDS

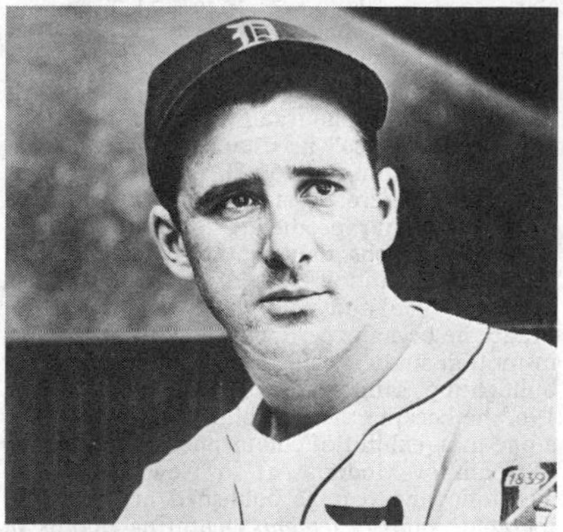

NATIONAL BASEBALL LIBRARY, COOPERSTOWN, N.Y.

Greenberg, Hank (HENRY BENJAMIN GREENBERG), U.S. baseball player (b. Jan. 1, 1911, New York, N.Y.—d. Sept. 4, 1986, Beverly Hills, Calif.), as first baseman and left fielder for the Detroit Tigers (1930, 1933–41, and 1945–46), was a powerhouse hitter who earned the nickname "Hammerin' Hank" for his slugging prowess. Greenberg excited baseball fans in 1938 when by slamming 58 home runs he challenged Babe Ruth's home run record of 60; he also had 146 runs batted in that year. During his career Greenberg had a lifetime batting average of .313 and accumulated 331 home runs. He was named the American League's most valuable player in 1935 and 1940 and four times led the league in home runs and runs batted in. While playing in four World Series for the Tigers (1934, 1935, 1940, and 1945), Greenberg hit five home runs and drove in 22 runs in 23 games; the team won the World Series in 1935 and 1945. After a lacklustre season with the Pittsburgh Pirates in 1947, Greenberg retired as a player. He later became part-owner and general manager of the Cleveland Indians and then vice-president and general manager of the Chicago White Sox before retiring from baseball in 1965. Greenberg was inducted into the Baseball Hall of Fame in 1956.

Grumiaux, Arthur, BARON, Belgian violinist (b. March 21, 1921, Villers-Perwin, near Charleroi, Belgium—d. Oct. 16, 1986, Brussels, Belgium), was a child prodigy who gained an international reputation as a virtuoso violinist. Grumiaux, who combined feeling with exceptional technique and precision, first performed in public at the age of five. He studied at the Charleroi Conservatoire and then, from the age of 12, at the Royal Conservatoire, Brussels, under Alfred Dubois. Grumiaux made his debut with the Brussels Philharmonic in 1940, and during the German occupation of Belgium in World War II he was a member of the Artis String Quartet. After the war ended, he made an early debut in the U.K. and then performed throughout Europe and (from 1952) in the U.S. In 1949 he succeeded Dubois as violin professor at Brussels, and in 1960 he formed the Grumiaux Trio, with Georges Janzer and Eva Czako. In addition to his appearances on the concert stage, he made many recordings, notably of Mozart, Bach, Paganini, and Brahms, with the trio and with various orchestras. He garnered a Golden Disc for the success of his recording of Paganini's Fourth Violin Concerto. Belgium awarded him a barony in 1973.

Haas, Ernst, Austrian-born photojournalist (b. March 2, 1921, Vienna, Austria—d. Sept. 12, 1986, New York, N.Y.), caught the essence of abstract art and reporting in his eloquent colour photo essays, which graced the pages of such magazines as *National Geographic, Heute, Look, Time,* and, notably, *Life,* for which he created the 1953 colour photo essay "New York," an innovative spread that covered an unprecedented 24 pages. Haas, who was dubbed "the father of colour photography," scored his first commercial success in Vienna in 1949 with his photo story "Returning War Prisoners." These studies prompted Robert Capa to invite Haas to join the influential Magnum Photos, a prestigious international photojournalist agency. With "The Miracle of Greece" he established an international reputation. In 1950 Haas moved to New York City, where he started his experimental work with colour, producing, for example, stunning photographs that captured reflections in puddles and windows. He also produced essays on Paris (1955) and Venice (1956), and while in France he began experimenting with his colour-in-motion studies, using slow shutter speeds, of bullfighting, sailing, rodeos, and car racing. In 1962 he became the first photographer to have a one-man exhibit of colour photographs at the Museum of Modern Art in New York City. The following year he published his first photographic book, *Elements*, featuring photos of natural forms presented in an abstract manner. In 1971 he published *The Creation*, his interpretation of the book of Genesis, which was followed by *In America* (1975), *In Germany* (1977), and *Himalayan Pilgrimage* (1978). At the time of his death, Haas was working on a photographic essay of Japan and on a series of videotapes in which he compared the rhythms in poetry to those found in photography.

Halleck, Charles Abraham, U.S. politician (b. Aug. 22, 1900, Jasper County, Ind.—d. March 3, 1986, Lafayette, Ind.), was a conservative Republican from Indiana who served (1935–68) in the U.S. House of Representatives as both the minority and the majority leader. After earning (1924) a law degree from Indiana University, he practiced law for a decade before being sent to the House in a special election in 1935. An ambitious party leader who aspired to a vice-presidential nomination, Halleck was disappointed in this quest but remained a powerful figure because of his expertise in leading successful floor fights in the House. He was known to millions of television viewers as a participant in the press conferences that became known as the "Ev and Charlie Show," featuring Halleck and Everett Dirksen of Illinois, the Republican leader in the Senate. The two regularly lambasted the Democrats and their programs. Halleck was an isolationist until Pearl Harbor; later he voted for aid to such countries as Greece and Turkey and endorsed the Marshall Plan. His voting record was a conservative one; he opposed the Fair Labor Standards Act, the military draft, school aid, omnibus housing measures, and a 1962 farm bill. He retired in 1968.

Harriman, W(illiam) Averell, U.S. statesman (b. Nov. 15, 1891, New York, N.Y.—d. July 26, 1986, Yorktown Heights, N.Y.), served with distinction under five U.S. presidents during pivotal periods in history but was most effective as the leading U.S. diplomat in relations with the Soviet Union during the cold war era following World War II. The son of railroad tycoon E. H. Harriman, who instructed him that "great wealth is an obligation," W. Averell Harriman was elected to the board of the Union Pacific Railroad Co. while he was a senior at Yale University. At the age of 28 he founded his own investment firm, and he made trips to the Soviet Union in the 1920s to negotiate mining rights. Aware of this experience, Pres. Franklin D. Roosevelt sent Harriman on a diplomatic mission to Britain and the Soviet Union to expedite U.S. lend-lease aid. Harriman served as U.S. ambassador to the Soviet Union (1943–46), ambassador to Great Britain (1946), and secretary of commerce (1947–48). He was credited with helping to maintain the uneasy alliance between Winston Churchill and Joseph Stalin during World War II. He served Pres. Harry S. Truman as European administrator of the Marshall Plan, a U.S.-sponsored program designed to revitalize the economies of post-World War II European nations. Harriman then served as governor of New York (1955–58) but lost a reelection bid to the more charismatic Nelson Rockefeller. In 1963 he became Pres. John F. Kennedy's chief representative in negotiating the Nuclear Test-Ban Treaty, which was signed by the U.S., Great Britain, and the Soviet Union. Under Pres. Lyndon B. Johnson, Harriman served as ambassador at the Paris peace talks between the U.S. and North Vietnam (1968–69). Harriman was called on again in 1976 by presidential candidate Jimmy Carter, who sent him to Moscow to reassure Soviet leader Leonid Brezhnev on arms control. During his long diplomatic career he had more experience dealing with the Soviet Union than any other American, and at the age of 91 Harriman traveled there again at the invitation of Soviet leader Yury Andropov. His negotiating technique, described as "water torture," was deliberately tedious and plodding and designed to eventually wear down his opponent. Harriman recounted his diplomatic career in such volumes as *America and Russia in a Changing World* (1971) and *Special Envoy to Churchill and Stalin, 1941–1946* (with Elie Abel; 1975).

Haughton, William ("BILLY"), U.S. harness-racing driver and trainer (b. Nov. 2, 1923, Gloversville, N.Y.—d. July 15, 1986, Valhalla, N.Y.), was for more than 30 years one of the sport's leading competitors. During his long career he won 4,910 races and $40.2 million in purses, placing him fourth among harness drivers in both categories. In 1968 he was inducted into the Hall of Fame of the Trotter. Haughton won almost every major stakes race in harness racing, including four Hambletonians, five Little Brown Jugs, and seven Messengers. Among the outstanding horses that he drove were Green Speed, Handle With Care, Keystone Pioneer, Rum Customer, Trenton Time, and Burgomeister. He died of head injuries suffered in an accident during a race at the Yonkers (N.Y.) Raceway on July 5, 1986.

Head, Bessie (BESSIE AMELIA EMERY), South African-born novelist (b. July 6, 1937, Pietermaritzburg, Natal, South Africa—d. April 17, 1986, Serowe, Botswana), was a powerful writer whose work provided illuminating accounts of African life and social problems. The themes of her books were determined by her personal circumstances, and she sensitively and positively explored the position of outcasts and underdogs. The child of a Zulu stable boy and of his wealthy employer's daughter, she was born in the mental asylum in which her mother was confined. She was educated in a mission orphanage and worked as a primary school teacher and later as a journalist on the liberal magazine *Drum*. She was briefly married (1961–64) to the journalist Harold Head and at that time joined the African National Congress. She then moved with her son to Bechuanaland (now Botswana). Her first novel, *When Rain Clouds Gather* (1969), published both in New York and in London, explored the difficulties encountered by a black political refugee trying to adapt to life in a traditional village society; a similar experience of exclusion was charted in her book *Maru* (1971), about the social ostracism of a Bushman woman. *A Question of Power* (1973) was based on the mental breakdown that she herself suffered in 1971. Head was associated with South African rebel Patrick van Rensburg's Swaneng Hill project in community farming and education at Serowe; she explored themes dealing with communal development in her short-story volume *The Collector of Treasures* (1977) and in *Serowe, Village of the Rainwind* (1981).

Helpmann, Sir Robert Murray, Australian ballet dancer and choreographer (b. April 9, 1909, Mount Gambier, South Australia—d. Sept. 28, 1986, Sydney, Australia), partnered Alicia Markova and Margot Fonteyn in the Vic-Wells (later Sadler's Wells) Ballet and served as director of the Australian Ballet (1965–76). He also achieved success as choreographer, actor, and director; acting was his first choice of profession before he joined Anna Pavlova's ballet company as a student during its 1926 Australian tour. Helpmann, who possessed a vivid sense of theatre and an extraordinary ability as a mime, partnered Fonteyn for 15 years and contributed to the success of ballet in Britain both as a dancer and as a choreographer after World War II. His productions of *Hamlet* and *Miracle in the Gorbals,* in which he also danced the leading roles, were memorable achievements. From 1950 he devoted much of his time to acting and directing stage plays in Britain and Australia, including *Murder in the Cathedral* and *Antony and Cleopatra.* As choreographer he created *Elektra* for the Royal Ballet in 1963 and later produced it with the Australian Ballet. Helpmann excelled in comic roles, notably when he and Sir Frederick Ashton danced as the Ugly Stepsisters in *Cinderella.* He also appeared in over a dozen motion pictures, including *One of Our Aircraft Is Missing* (1942), *Henry V* (1944), and *Patrick* (1978). Helpmann, who was knighted in 1968, danced in *Checkmate* just six weeks before he died.

Henderson, Loy Wesley, U.S. diplomat (b. June 28, 1892, near Rogers, Ark.—d. March 24, 1986, Bethesda, Md.), was a master troubleshooter who for three decades skillfully conducted negotiations to neutralize potentially volatile situations, notably while serving as minister to Iraq (1943–45), ambassador to India and minister to Nepal (1948–51), and ambassador to Iran (1951–55). His expertise in diplomacy earned him the nickname "Mr. Foreign Service." Henderson, who studied at the University of Denver, Colo., law school, intended to form a partnership with his twin brother, who was attending Harvard University, but when his twin died, he decided to pursue a career in the Foreign Service. During World War I he joined the Red Cross after being rejected by the military because of a stiffness in one of his arms. He passed the civil service examination in 1922 and became vice-consul in Dublin. After being transferred to Washington, he was promoted (1925) to consul, and in 1927 he was named a secretary in the diplomatic service. In 1934 he was appointed to the Moscow embassy, where he held the ranks of second secretary (1934–36), first secretary (1936), and chargé d'affaires ad interim (1936–38). In 1938 he returned to Washington as assistant chief of the Division of European Affairs; from 1942 to 1943 he served in the U.S.S.R. as counselor of the Moscow embassy. As minister to Iraq he successfully dealt with most of the oil-producing Middle Eastern states, but he was recalled to Washington to head the Division of Near Eastern and African Affairs of the State Department. While serving as ambassador to Iran, he was instrumental in settling the dispute between Iran and the international oil companies over the attempt to nationalize the oil fields, and as deputy undersecretary of state for administration (1955–61), he played a leading role as an adviser on Mideast policy in the Eisenhower administration. In 1956 he helped defuse the Suez Canal crisis as a member of an international body formed to restore canal service following the French-British-Israeli Sinai campaign against Egypt. After his retirement as a career diplomat, he taught for many years at American University, Washington, D.C.

Herbert, Frank Patrick, U.S. science-fiction writer (b. Oct. 8, 1920, Tacoma, Wash.—d. Feb. 11, 1986, Madison, Wis.), was the object of a cultlike following as the best-selling author of the "Dune" series of futuristic novels; he produced carefully researched, highly complex works that explored such themes as ecology, human evolution, the consequences of genetic manipulation, and mystical and psychic possibilities. Herbert's fiction, which reflected present-day political and social realities rather than escapist fantasy, included the epic *Dune* (1965), which was translated into 14 languages and sold more than 12 million copies, and its sequels *Dune Messiah* (1969), *Children of Dune* (1976), *God-Emperor of Dune* (1981), and *Chapterhouse: Dune* (1985). Though Herbert worked for several newspapers, including the *San Fran-*

cisco Examiner and the *Seattle* (Wash.) *Post-Intelligencer*, he left journalism in 1972 in order to devote all his time to writing. Included among his more than two dozen novels were the highly acclaimed *Dragon in the Sea*, *The Green Brain*, *The God Makers*, *The Santaroga Barrier*, *The Heaven Makers*, *The Dosadi Experiment*, and *The Jesus Incident*. At the time of his death, Herbert was working on the next novel in the "Dune" series.

Hijikata, Tatsumi, Japanese dancer and teacher (b. March 9, 1928, Akita Prefecture, Japan—d. Jan. 21, 1986, Tokyo, Japan), originated the avant-garde dance Butoh, a Japanese theatre-dance form that combines expressionistic and folk-dance movements to create unique and sometimes disturbing works. The language of Butoh grew out of the hardships of Hijikata's childhood; his first dances were often grotesque, rough, and sad. Later works, usually performed to the beat of Western music, also poked fun at Japanese traditions. Hijikata and his disciple Kazuo Ohno gave their first performances of Butoh in 1959, but the erotic dance form first caused a stir in the U.S. when it was introduced by the Dai Rukuda Kan company at the 1982 American Dance Festival. Butoh was later adopted by the Sankai Juku company, which toured the U.S. in 1985. The troupe made headlines when, as they were performing the "Jomon Sho" (Homage to Prehistory) at an outdoor performance in Seattle, Wash., one of four dancers hanging upside down and being slowly lowered from the roof of the Mutual Life Building fell six stories to his death. Though Hijikata had not performed since the mid-1970s, he continued to teach and choreograph.

Hill, Abram, U.S. theatre founder, director, and playwright (b. Jan. 20, 1910, Atlanta, Ga.—d. Oct. 6, 1986, New York, N.Y.), established (1940) the American Negro Theater (ANT) in Harlem, which became a training ground for such gifted black performers as Harry Belafonte, Alice Childress, Ruby Dee, and Sidney Poitier. Hill studied at the City College of New York and at Lincoln University in Pennsylvania, where he majored in theatre arts. After graduation he joined the Federal Theatre Project and wrote such works as *Liberty Deferred* (1936), *Hell's Half Acre* (1937), and *On Striver's Row*, the ANT's first production. He also adapted for the theatre group such plays as Phoebe and Henry Ephron's *Three's a Family* (1943) and Philip Yordan's *Anna Lucasta* (1944), a major success that enjoyed 900 Broadway performances. After leaving the ANT in 1948, Hill directed (1951–55) dramatics at Lincoln University and taught English in New York City schools from 1957 until his retirement in 1980.

Hobson, Laura Zametkin, U.S. author (b. June 19, 1900, New York, N.Y.—d. Feb. 28, 1986, New York), was best remembered for her scathing novel on anti-Semitism, *Gentleman's Agreement* (1947), the story of a Gentile magazine writer who poses as a Jew in order to gain authentic material for an article he is preparing. The best-selling book was later translated into more than a dozen languages, sold more than 1.6 million copies, and was made into a motion picture starring Gregory Peck that won the 1947 Academy Award for best picture. After graduating from Cornell University, Ithaca, N.Y., Hobson collaborated with her husband in writing western novels and worked as an advertising copywriter until 1934, when she became a promotion writer for *Time, Life,* and *Fortune* magazines. In 1940 she quit her job as promotion director for *Time* in order to devote all her time to creative writing. Hobson, the author of nine novels, also wrote *The Other Father* (1950), *First Papers* (1964), and *Consenting Adult* (1975), a quasi-autobiographical story of the relationship between a mother and her homosexual son. At the time of her death, she was working on the second volume of her autobiography—the first, *Laura Z: A Life,* appeared in 1983.

Hubbard, L(afayette) Ron(ald), U.S. author and religionist (b. March 13, 1911, Tilden, Neb.—d. Jan. 24, 1986, San Luis Obispo, Calif.), was the charismatic founder (1954) of the embattled Church of Scientology, a movement based on his 1950 best-selling book, *Dianetics: The Modern Science of Mental Health.* Hubbard, who proclaimed himself a World War II hero and nuclear physicist, gained an enormous following in the late 1960s when he declared that Scientology was a "new religion," not based on the worship of God. Hubbard's Dianetics philosophy contended that each experience is recorded as a mental image and that painful experiences (engrams) are not totally available to the conscious mind and thus cause emotional problems and psychosomatic illnesses if they are not confronted. Therapy included one-on-one work with a church counselor in "auditing" (monitoring a client's responses to questions by using an electrical device on the client's skin) in order to "clear," or free, the mind of engrams. Scientology also adhered to beliefs in reincarnation and in the occult. During the 1970s Hubbard's wealthy church boasted as many as six million members worldwide (though detractors estimated that the number was closer to two million), and elite members of the organization conducted an intelligence operation by infiltrating some 100 U.S. government agencies. In 1979 Hubbard's wife, Mary Sue, and ten other Scientologists were convicted of burglarizing and wiretapping government agencies. In 1984 the church's tax-exempt status was revoked, and Hubbard, who was accused of embezzling church revenues to build his own business empire, retreated into seclusion. He apparently died of a stroke; in accordance with his religious preference, no autopsy was performed.

Hynek, J(osef) Allen, U.S. astrophysicist (b. May 1, 1910, Chicago, Ill.—d. April 27, 1986, Scottsdale, Ariz.), was instrumental in obtaining a measure of respectability for the study of unidentified flying objects (UFOs) by neither discounting nor sensationalizing the possibility of their existence. The "Galileo of UFOlogy" earned a Ph.D. (1935) from the University of Chicago and taught astronomy (1935–41 and 1946–56) at Ohio State University. In 1948 he became scientific consultant on UFOs to the U.S. Air Force, and his levelheaded and open-minded approach gained him respect in the scientific community. Though Hynek felt that most "flying saucers" could be explained as meteors, weather balloons, aircraft, hallucinations, or hoaxes, he claimed to have studied more than 10,000 sightings and concluded that at least 500 were unexplained. In 1966, when an unusually high number of sightings occurred in Michigan, Hynek was summoned to investigate; he discovered that the strange celestial lights probably were caused by luminous marsh gas. In 1956 he joined the Smithsonian Astrophysical Observatory as associate director to Fred L. Whipple. In preparation for the 1957–58 International Geophysical Year, and the orbiting of artificial satellites to gather data, Hynek was placed in charge of predicting the satellite orbits and supervising optical tracking of the satellites by 12 observatories strategically placed throughout the world. The project became known as Operation Moonwatch. From 1960 until his retirement in 1978, Hynek was chairman of the department of astronomy at Northwestern University, Evanston, Ill., and director of its Dearborn Observatory. He was the author of *Challenge of the Universe* (1962) and *The UFO Experience* (1972), in which he coined the phrase "close encounters of the third kind" to describe contact with a UFO or an alien being. For many years he published a monthly newsletter, *International UFO Reporter,* and in 1973 he established the Center for UFO Studies in Evanston, which he relocated in Scottsdale when he moved there in 1985.

Inman, Florence Elsie, Canadian politician (b. Dec. 5, 1890, West River, Prince Edward Island—d. May 31, 1986, Ottawa), was a longtime (1955–86) liberal senator who was named (July 28, 1955) to her seat by Prime Minister Louis St. Laurent at a time when such an appointment carried a lifetime tenure. Inman, who at the time of her death was the Senate's oldest member, was prominent in Prince Edward Island politics for many years, notably as chair (1949–55) of the Mother's Allowance Commission of P.E.I., in charge of administering a financial-aid program for needy mothers. As a senator she prided herself on her independence and was one of nine senators who voted against adopting the 1982 Canadian constitution, which severed all remnants of legal dependence on Britain. She remained active in her senatorial duties until she became ill in the winter of 1985.

Isherwood, Christopher (CHRISTOPHER WILLIAM BRADSHAW-ISHERWOOD), British-born U.S. novelist and playwright (b. Aug. 26, 1904, High Lane, Cheshire, England—d. Jan. 4, 1986, Santa Monica, Calif.), was the renowned author of more than 20 books but was best remembered for his quasi-autobiographical *Goodbye to Berlin* (1939), a collection of short stories that served as the basis for the play *I Am a Camera* (1951; film, 1955) and the hit Broadway musical *Cabaret* (1966; film, 1972). While attending St. Edmund's School in Surrey, England, Isherwood established a lifelong friendship with the poet W. H. Auden. During the 1930s the two collaborated on three verse dramas and *Journey to a War* (1939), a travel book of their 1938 trip to China. But it was earlier, when he went (1929) to Berlin and made a detached analysis of the simultaneous decay of the Weimar Republic and the rise of Nazism, that he established a reputation as an important writer with *Mr. Norris Changes Trains* (1935; U.S. title, *The Last of Mr. Norris*). Other themes that were prevalent in Isherwood's works included homosexuality and Vedanta, the Hindu philosophy advocated by Swami Prabhavananda; books dealing with homosexuality included *A Single Man* (1964) and *Christopher and His Kind* (1976), which was heavily autobiographical. *A Meeting by the River* (1967) dealt with Hinduism and homosexuality, and *My Guru and His Disciple* (1980) explored Isherwood's relationship with Prabhavananda and his own conversion to Vedanta. Isherwood also wrote a memoir about his parents, *Kathleen and Frank* (1971). Both Isherwood and his longtime companion, Don Bachardy, were involved in the homosexual rights movement.

Jameson, (Margaret) Storm, British novelist (b. Jan. 8, 1891, Whitby, Yorkshire, England—d. Sept. 30, 1986, Cambridge, England), was a prolific writer, best known in the 1930s, 1940s, and 1950s. She was president (1938–44) of the English section of the international writers' association PEN and did much to help continental colleagues escape from Nazi persecution. Jameson was a determined advocate of women's rights. Her first marriage did not survive her commitment to putting her work before all else; her second marriage, in 1926, was to the historian Guy Chapman. Born into a ship-owning and seafaring family, she was educated at home and at the University of Leeds (1909–12), where she was the first woman to earn a degree in English. She later held research fellowships there and at King's College, London. Jameson worked as a copywriter, then as editor of the magazine *New Commonwealth,* and was London agent for the U.S. publishers Alfred Knopf. In 1920 she published her first novel, *Happy Highways.* From 1930 on she produced a novel almost annually. Of her more than 50 novels, *The Green Man* (1952) was a best-seller, and *Cousin Honoré* (1940), a study set in Alsace between the wars, was, and remained, highly regarded. She also wrote a two-volume autobiography, *Journey from the North* (1969–70) and *Parthian Words* (1970).

Javits, Jacob Koppel, U.S. politician (b. May 18, 1904, New York, N.Y.—d. March 7, 1986, Palm Beach, Fla.), was widely admired as the quick-witted, committed, liberal Republican senator from New York (1957–80) and was especially lauded as a champion of civil liberties and a friend of the performing arts. Born in a New York City tenement, Javits worked his way through Columbia University, New York City, and New York University School of Law before joining his brother's law firm. He served four terms (1947–55) in the U.S. House of Representatives before winning election (1954) as New York attorney general, upsetting Franklin D. Roosevelt, Jr. Setting his sights on the Senate, the ambitious Javits defeated another powerful Democrat, Robert Wagner, the mayor of New York City. Javits, a perennial favourite of New York's liberal Jewish community, consistently fended off challenges to his Senate seat by such formidable opponents as James B. Donovan, Paul O'Dwyer, and Ramsey Clark; his only election loss came in 1980, when voters became wary of his age and failing health (he suffered from amyotrophic lateral sclerosis, also known as Lou Gehrig's disease). As a senator he helped shape such important legislation as the War Powers Act, which limits the president's power to commit acts of war without congressional approval, and the Employment Retirement Income Security Act, which tried to secure and guarantee private pensions. He also helped create the National Endowment for the Arts to provide government subsidies for cultural projects. Even after his formal retirement from the Senate, where he was the ranking Republican on the Foreign Relations Committee, he continued to conduct business from his wheelchair. He quipped, "Life does not stop with terminal illness. Only the patient stops if he doesn't have the will to go forward with life until death overtakes him." His last book, *Javits: The Autobiography of a Public Man,* appeared in 1981.

Jolly, Hugh Reginald, British pediatrician (b. May 5, 1918, Douglas, Isle of Man—d. March 4, 1986, Kingston, Surrey, England), was physician in charge of the pediatrics department of the Charing Cross Hospital, London (1965–84). He was internationally known for his widely translated *Book of Child Care* (1975) and was largely responsible for the current, more relaxed attitudes toward all aspects of child rearing. He encouraged the presence of fathers at their children's births and promoted breast-feeding on a system he called "ask feeding." Jolly was also a pioneer in allowing unrestricted parental visits with children in the hospital. Educated at Marlborough College and at Sidney Sussex College, University of Cambridge, he completed his medical studies at the London Hospital, qualifying in 1942. Following service as a captain in the Royal Army Medical Corps (1944–47), he worked at the Hospital for Sick Children, Great Ormond Street, London, before spending the 1950s as consultant pediatrician at Plymouth. Jolly was also professor of pediatrics, University College, Ibadan, Nigeria (1961–62), and visiting professor of child health at Ghana Medical School (1965–67). Although his contributions to psychoanalysis are not explicit, Jolly felt that the problems of children are often really those of their parents. He stressed the psychological necessity of mourning and encouraged maternity staff to treat the parents of stillborn babies with greater understanding. Jolly was renowned in Britain as a medical journalist in both broadcast and print media, as well as for such books as *Sexual Precocity* (1955) and *Diseases of Children* (1964).

Kaldor, Nicholas Kaldor, BARON, British economist (b. May 12, 1908, Budapest, Austria-Hungary—d. Sept. 30, 1986, near Cambridge, England), served as professor of economics at the University of Cambridge and was adviser in economics to British Labour Party chancellors of the Exchequer (1964–68, 1974–76) and to Labour opposition leader Neil Kinnock in the 1980s. A post-Keynesian economist, he vigorously opposed Conservative Prime Minister Margaret Thatcher's monetarist policies, which he castigated in a number of books, including *The Scourge of Monetarism* (1982). The son of a prosperous lawyer, Kaldor was educated in Budapest and at the London School of Economics, where he taught (1932–47). He was part-time research assistant at the National Institute of Economic and Social Research (1943–45) and in 1945 was chief of the economic planning staff for the U.S. Bombing Survey's British unit, assessing the damage done to German industry by Allied bombing. He was at Geneva (1947–49) as director of the Research and Planning Division of the Economic Commission for Europe. Kaldor was appointed a fellow of King's College, Cambridge, and a university lecturer in economics in 1949, becoming a reader three years later. In 1966 a personal chair in economics was created for him. A member of the Radcliffe Royal Commission for Taxation (1951–55), he helped shape many of the Labour Party's economic policies. During the 1950s and 1960s he was special economic adviser to such countries as India (1956) and Iran (1966). His books include *An Expenditure Tax* (1955) and *Economics Without Equilibrium* (1985). He was created a life peer in 1974.

Kanellopoulos, Panayotis, Greek politician (b. Dec. 13, 1902, Patrai, Greece—d. Sept. 11, 1986, Athens, Greece), held ministerial office in a number of governments and was twice (November 1945 and April 1967) prime minister, for periods of less than one month. On the latter occasion he was overthrown by the military junta that then held power until 1974. A member of Athens Academy from 1959 and author of several books, including the two-volume *History of the European Spirit* (1941–47), he was a distinguished scholar who had studied law and sociology at the Universities of Athens, Heidelberg, and Munich. Kanellopoulos was chair of sociology at Athens University from the late 1920s but soon entered politics. A convinced republican, he founded the National Unionist Party in 1935 and was exiled (1936–40) during the dictatorship of Ioannis Metaxas. During World War II he fought on the Albanian front, organized a resistance group, and in 1942 joined the government in exile in the Middle East. He returned to Greece in 1944, and during the ensuing chaos his brief government was one of many. Elected member of Parliament for Patrai in 1946, he served in a succession of centrist governments as minister of air (1947), of war (1949–50), and of national defense (1952–55). He was deputy prime minister in 1950, 1954–55, and 1959–63. Kanellopoulos became leader of the National Radical Union in 1963 and prime minister in 1967 when his party withdrew its support from the caretaker government of Ioannis Paraskevopoulos. He returned to Parliament in 1974 but retired from politics following his unsuccessful candidacy for the presidency the following year.

Kantorovich, Leonid Vitalyevich, Soviet economist (b. Jan. 19, 1912, St. Petersburg, Russia—d. April 7, 1986, Moscow, U.S.S.R.), was in 1975 joint winner (with Tjalling Koopmans) of the Nobel Memorial Prize in Economic Science for his application of the analytical technique of linear programming in order to improve economic planning. Working in mathematical terms, Kantorovich was primarily concerned with the best use of scarce resources. Educated at Leningrad University, he became an instructor at the Leningrad Institute of Industrial Construction Engineering (1930–32) and at Leningrad University (1932–34), where he then was professor (1934–60). He was head of the department of mathematics and economics in the Siberian branch of the U.S.S.R. Academy of Sciences (1961–71), head of the research laboratory at Moscow's Institute of National Economy Control (1971–76), and thereafter on the staff of the Scientific Institute of System Research. His theory of linear programming, put forward in his paper *Mathematical Methods of Organizing and Planning Production* (1939), was at first not taken seriously, a circumstance perhaps fortunate since unorthodox thinking was at that time often punished. In *Economical Calculation of the Best Use of Resources* (1959; Eng. trans. 1965), he demonstrated the importance of pricing policies and put forward a plan for subsidizing enterprises in work-starved areas, advocating the training of seasonal workers in other skills. His other works included three books on functional analysis and *On Optimal Planning* (1976). Kantorovich was appointed a full member of the Soviet Academy of Sciences in 1964 and the following year was awarded the Lenin Prize.

Katayev, Valentin Petrovich, Soviet novelist and playwright (b. Jan. 28, 1897, Odessa, Russia—d. April 12, 1986, Moscow, U.S.S.R.), as one of the earliest writers of the postrevolutionary period, followed the requisite party line but nevertheless introduced into his novels and plays a vein of redeeming satire. After serving as a volunteer soldier (1915–17) in World War I, he took part in the subsequent fighting in the Ukraine. In the 1920s he settled in Moscow as one of a group of young writers there. His early novel *Rastratchiki* (1926; *The Embezzlers,* 1929) was an entertaining story of two crooks living it up on misappropriated funds. *Vremya, Vperyod* (1932; *Time, Forward!,* 1933), one of many novels written to celebrate the first five-year plan, told the story of a brigade of concrete mixers. In *Beleyet parus odinoky* (1936; *Lonely White Sail,* or *A White Sail Gleams,* 1937) he dealt with two boys' experiences in Odessa during the Revolution of 1905 when the crew of the battleship *Potemkin* mutinied. One of Katayev's plays, *Kvadratura kruga* (1928; *Squaring the Circle,* 1934), concerned the trials of two newlywed couples forced to share a basement room. Later plays receiving English translation included *The Blue Handkerchief* (1944) and *The Magic Flower* (1947). Katayev was editor (1955–61) of *Yunost,* a monthly magazine in which young talent was given expression. His last novel was *The Diamond Crown* (1977). He later joined in attacking dissident writers.

Kawamata, Katsuji, Japanese business executive (b. March 1, 1905, Mito, Ibaraki Prefecture, Japan—d. March 29, 1986, Tokyo, Japan), as the dynamic president (1957–73) and chairman (1973–85) of Nissan Motor Co., implemented innovative mass-production techniques that established the company as the second largest automobile manufacturer in the country and thus helped to secure Japan's position as a giant in the worldwide automobile industry. After graduating (1929) from Tokyo University of Commerce, he worked for 18 years with the Industrial Bank of Japan before becoming (1947) a member of the board at Nissan. He was instrumental in helping to rebuild the company after World War II, and under his guidance a 10,000-unit-a-month automobile factory was erected (1959) in Oppama, the nation's first full-scale automobile plant. Kawamata also served as president (1962–72) of the Japan Automobile Manufacturers' Association until he was named vice-chairman of the Federation of Economic Organizations, Japan's leading business group. He retired from Nissan in 1985 but continued to serve in an advisory capacity.

Kekkonen, Urho Kaleva, Finnish politician (b. Sept. 3, 1900, Pielavesi, Fin.—d. Aug. 31, 1986, Helsinki, Fin.), was president of Finland from 1956 until 1981, when he resigned because of ill health. At the age of 17 Kekkonen fought against the Bolsheviks in Finland's war of independence. After the war he worked as a journalist. A keen athlete, he twice held the Finnish high-jump championship and in 1923 set the national 100-m record of 11.1 sec, which stood until 1959. Kekkonen studied law at the University of Helsinki, and in 1936, after obtaining his Ph.D., he was elected to Parliament. He was made minister of justice and in 1937 became minister of the interior. In his formative years Kekkonen held right-wing views, but in the early 1930s he recognized the threat posed to democracy by Nazism. He was a devout nationalist and took responsibility for the resettlement in Finland of 300,000 Karelians ejected from the U.S.S.R. during the Winter War of 1939–40. His opposition to the Soviet peace terms that followed caused his withdrawal from politics. Kekkonen later renounced his idealistic political views and adopted a more realistic stance. In 1944 he returned to politics in the government of Prime Minister Juho Paasikivi and was a key negotiator in the controversial trials of war criminals. From 1950 to 1956 he served as prime minister and foreign affairs minister in several coalitions and in 1956 was elected president. The Kekkonen presidency lasted 25 years—one of the most crucial periods in Finnish history. His leadership qualities were equaled by the diplomatic skills he used to develop relations with Kremlin leaders. His fierce determination to preserve Finland's independence from the U.S.S.R. meant that his leadership was marked by controversy and acts of brinkmanship. Postwar Soviet trust in Finland was at a low ebb following an attempt to recover territory ceded to the U.S.S.R. after the 1939–40 war. Restoration of confidence was a top priority. President Paasikivi had begun the effort, but it was Kekkonen who made real progress. The relationship also involved some loss of sovereignty: Finland pledged to remain neutral and never to allow foreign troops on its soil. When the 1958 Finnish election produced an administration that the U.S.S.R. did not endorse, diplomatic relations broke down. These were not restored until the Finnish government resigned and was replaced by another that the U.S.S.R. favoured and that Kekkonen had recommended previously.

Koch, Erich, German Nazi administrator (b. June 19, 1896, Prussia—d. Nov. 12, 1986, Barczewo, Poland), was convicted in 1959 of complicity in the killing of over 300,000 Polish people, two-thirds of them Jewish, during World War II. The death sentence passed on him was commuted to life imprisonment through the exercise of a Polish law preventing execution of the sick, and he spent the remainder of his life in Barczewo Prison, within the territory he had once administered. Koch joined the Nazi Party in the early 1920s, and shortly after Hitler came to power in Germany in 1933, he was appointed party leader and governor of East Prussia. Following the Nazi invasion of the U.S.S.R., he was appointed Reich commissioner of the Ukraine. At the end of the war he avoided capture by fleeing first to Denmark and later to the British zone of occupied Germany, where he lived near Hamburg under an assumed name. After his true identity was discovered in 1949, Koch was extradited to Poland by the British authorities the following year; he came to trial in Warsaw in 1958. He was said to have attempted to starve himself to death in the intervening period. Apart from the war crimes for which he was convicted, Koch was held responsible for the deaths of some four million people in the Ukraine and the deportation to Nazi labour camps of some two million others.

Krishnamurti, Jiddu, Indian spiritual philosopher (b. May 22, 1895, Madanapalle, India—d. Feb. 17, 1986, Ojai, Calif.), rejected the messianic role for which he had been groomed by theosophist leader Annie Besant and instead enjoined a more personal spirituality, teaching that truth is a "pathless land" and refusing to set himself up as any sort of prophet. In 1909 his father, a Brahman and a long-convinced theosophist, took his family to the international headquarters of the Theosophical Society at Adyar, Madras. There Krishnamurti was singled out by Charles Leadbeater, one of Besant's colleagues and a self-styled clairvoyant, as the "vehicle" of a new incarnation of the Lord Maitreya, or "World Teacher." Besant founded (1911) the World Order of the Star in the East, placing Krishnamurti at its head; she then sent him to England, where he was privately educated at her expense. He returned to India (1921) and began a series of world tours.

AP/WIDE WORLD

His unwillingness to assert spiritual authority gradually disappointed members of the order, which he dissolved in 1929, totally rejecting the persona that had been attributed to him. Despite his sustained modesty, simple life-style, and continued refusal to pontificate, he became regarded as a major spiritual teacher. The nonprofit Krishnamurti Foundation, with offices in California, Great Britain, and India, was set up to administer funds contributed to run the schools he founded and promote his teachings. His many books on philosophy and religion include *The First and Last Freedom* (1954), *Truth and Actuality* (1977), and a series of *Commentaries on Living* (1956, 1958, 1960). Mary Lutyens's *Krishnamurti: The Years of Awakening* (1975) chronicles the decisive earlier phases of his life; her biography of him continued with *Krishnamurti: The Years of Fulfillment* (1983), which follows his life until 1980.

Laker, Jim (JAMES CHARLES LAKER), British cricketer (b. Feb. 9, 1922—d. April 23, 1986, London, England), was one of the great off-spin bowlers of all time and held the probably unbeatable score of 19 wickets for 90 runs against the Australians in two innings at Old Trafford in 1956. Although not an outstanding batsman or fielder, he bowled a devastating eight wickets for two runs during a test trial in Bradford in 1950. Laker was to have played for Yorkshire before World War II, but on his return from service with the Army in North Africa, he joined the Surrey team and helped them to their series of victories during the 1950s. From 1956 he was a regular member of the English national team until his retirement in 1964. His omission from the 1954–55 national team, considered incomprehensible by cricket fans and commentators, was probably due to his outspoken manner and his autobiography, which upset some figures in the game. Laker left Surrey in 1959 and moved to Essex in 1962. After retirement he became a member of the Surrey committee and the Marylebone Cricket Club. He continued to be remembered as one of England's most effective bowlers, with his 1956 test record of 46 wickets for the year.

Lancaster, Sir Osbert, British cartoonist and writer (b. Aug. 4, 1908, London, England—d. July 27, 1986, London), encapsulated the society of his time in the "pocket cartoons" that he contributed to the *Daily Express* from 1939 until 1981. These witty miniatures captured the fashions, features, and foibles of the British upper-middle class, exposing them accurately but without malice. Lancaster was educated at Charterhouse (Godalming) and at Lincoln College, University of Oxford, but achieved no particular distinction at either place. He could have been a figure from his own cartoons, with his handlebar mustache and tweed suit, but this bluff appearance concealed a perceptive wit and a considerable intelligence. After leaving Oxford he went on to study at the Slade School of Art (London) and during the 1930s worked as a book illustrator and a journalist with *The Architectural Review.* Lancaster had an abiding enthusiasm for architecture, and his books *Pillar to Post* (1938), *Classical Landscape with Figures* (1947), *Drayneflete Revealed* (1949), and *Sailing to Byzantium* (1969) were original and serious works, celebrating the classical styles that he loved and deploring what he saw as a decline in architectural standards. For a spell during and after World War II, Lancaster worked for the Foreign Office in London and for the British embassy in Athens. Following his return from Athens in 1946, he achieved considerable success as a designer for opera and ballet with the Old Vic, Sadler's Wells, the Royal Ballet, Glyndebourne Opera, and the Bulgarian National Opera. He published two books of autobiography, *All Done from Memory* (1953) and *With an Eye to the Future* (1967), and a collection of his pocket cartoons was published in 1961. He was made a Commander of the Order of the British Empire in 1953 and was knighted in 1975.

Lanchester, Elsa (ELIZABETH SULLIVAN), British-born U.S. actress (b. Oct. 28, 1902, London, England—d. Dec. 26, 1986, Woodland Hills, Calif.), scored her best-known film success in a dual role: she portrayed the author Mary Shelley and the bride of the monster in the 1935 classic horror film *Bride of Frankenstein.* A versatile character actress who excelled in eccentric and comic roles, Lanchester performed on the London stage before arriving in the U.S. in 1931. She married the actor Charles Laughton in 1929 and thereafter often appeared with him; for example, in such films as *The Private Life of Henry VIII* (1933), *Rembrandt* (1936), *The Vessel of Wrath* (1938), and *The Big Clock* (1948). Besides earning two Academy Award nominations for best supporting actress in the films *Come to the Stable* (1949) and *Witness for the Prosecution* (1958), she received critical acclaim for her performances in *David Copperfield* (1935), *The Spiral Staircase* (1946), and *The Inspector General* (1949). After Laughton's death in 1962 she appeared in *Mary Poppins* (1964), *That Darn Cat* (1965), *Willard* (1971), and her last, *Murder by Death* (1976).

Lartigue, Jacques-Henri-Charles-Auguste, French photographer (b. June 13, 1894, Courbevoie, near Paris, France—d. Sept. 12, 1986, Nice, France), with his photographs, supplemented by his diaries and his paintings, compiled a unique portrait of life in the French middle classes, which he observed with both sympathy and detached humour. Lartigue possessed a camera from the age of seven, when he began to record the pursuits of his family and friends. A determined amateur who cared little for technical perfection, he excelled from the beginning in snapping his subjects at unguarded moments and was noted for his ability to capture a sense of movement in his photographs. His depiction of the era before World War I, in images centred on the tennis courts, beaches, and promenades of seaside resorts, captured a special innocence and evoked a poignancy that led to his "rediscovery" at the 1963 exhibition at the Museum of Modern Art, New York City. Lartigue was never attracted to gloomy subjects. His awareness of the ephemeral nature of everything that he recorded and his innate sense of composition, however, raised his snapshots above the level of mere sociological document and ensured their survival. In 1979 he donated his entire work to the French state, and a permanent exhibition of his photographs was on show at the Grand Palais in Paris. He published several collections of his work, including *Diary of a Century* (1970). Lartigue was a Chevalier of the Légion d'Honneur.

Layne, Bobby, U.S. football player (b. Dec. 19, 1926, Santa Anna, Texas—d. Dec. 1, 1986, Lubbock, Texas), was a phenomenal, flamboyant, and durable professional football quarterback who played for the Chicago Bears (1948), the

New York Bulldogs (1949), the Detroit Lions (1950–58), and the Pittsburgh Steelers (1958–62). Layne, who had a remarkable 15-year career, completed 1,814 of 3,700 passes for 26,768 yd and 196 touchdowns. The beer-drinking quarterback, who never learned to throw a spiral pass, was the last professional football player to eschew wearing a face mask and refused to wear rib pads or extra protection for his thighs, hips, or knees. He was an artist in the two-minute offense at the end of a half or a game and a skilled leader. His most spectacular seasons were with the Detroit Lions, whom he led to consecutive National Football League titles in 1952 and 1953. Layne accomplished his best work playing for coach Buddy Parker, who recognized that Layne needed latitude both on and off the field. He allowed Layne to call his own plays and ignored Layne's curfew the night before a game. Layne was inducted into the Professional Football Hall of Fame in 1967.

Le Duan, Vietnamese politician (b. April 7, 1908, Quang Tri Province [now Binh Tri Thien Province], Vietnam—d. July 10, 1986, Hanoi, Vietnam), became leader of North Vietnam after the death of Ho Chi Minh in 1969 and oversaw the final victory of the Communist forces in the Vietnam war and the subsequent reunification of North and South Vietnam. He adopted pragmatic economic policies and advocated collective political leadership. Le Duan did not succeed Ho as president of North Vietnam but continued to serve as first secretary (later secretary-general) of the Communist Party, a post he had held since 1959. Under his direction Vietnam moved toward achieving self-sufficiency in agriculture, but the economy was seriously weakened and the country was unable to maintain its policy of neutrality between the U.S.S.R. and China. The son of a carpenter, Le Duan worked as a railway clerk in Hanoi before joining the Indochinese Communist Party (forerunner of the Vietnamese Communist Party) on its foundation in 1930. He spent 10 of the next 15 years imprisoned by the French authorities and, on his release, became Viet Minh political commissar in the south of the country. He moved north after the division of Vietnam in 1954 and rose to become one of the major strategists of the war. Following the Communist victory in 1975, he opposed party hardliners by introducing economic reforms and attempting to maintain a balanced alliance with both Moscow and Beijing (Peking). The signing of a friendship treaty with the U.S.S.R. in 1978 signaled the failure of the latter policy and, as a result, Le Duan faced opposition from pro-Chinese elements in the country and in exile. Vietnam's occupation of Kampuchea in 1979 further isolated the country diplomatically. The growing economic crisis, as well as Le Duan's ill health, apparently led to the postponement of the Communist party congress, scheduled for early 1986, until December.

Le Luron, Thierry Jean-Gilles, French comedian (b. April 2, 1952, Paris, France—d. Nov. 13, 1986, Paris), had an extraordinary talent for savagely impersonating his country's leading political figures and for caricaturing their personalities. During the presidency of Valéry Giscard d'Estaing, one of his favourite targets, le Luron presented up to four shows a day in different theatres and even in different cities and developed a combination of political satire and spectacle that reached its height during the "affair of the diamonds." When Giscard was accused of accepting a gift of diamonds from Emperor Jean Bédel Bokassa of the then Central African Empire, le Luron swept on stage covered from head to foot with cut glass. He later turned his attention to Giscard's successor, Pres. François Mitterrand, Communist Party leader Georges Marchais, and National Front leader Jean-Marie le Pen. Even the man in the street, was not spared. "Adolphe-Benito Glandu" was his epitome of the average provincial Frenchman, nostalgic for the days of Marshal Henri Pétain. Le Luron and his fellow comedian Coluche (*q.v.*), who died a few months before him, introduced new boundaries of acceptability in French humour and language.

Lekai, Laszlo Cardinal, primate of the Roman Catholic Church in Hungary (b. March 12, 1910, Zalalovo, Austria-Hungary—d. June 30, 1986, Esztergom, Hung.), adopted a policy of cautious cooperation with the Communist authorities, thereby achieving a modus vivendi for the Catholic Church in Hungary. Lekai was ordained a priest in 1934. From 1944 he was in close contact with Jozsef (afterward Cardinal) Mindszenty, then his diocesan bishop, and with him was imprisoned by the Nazis (1944–45). He did not share Mindszenty's total opposition to Communism, however, and he remained an active parish priest during Mindszenty's later period of imprisonment (1948–56) and subsequent self-imposed exile. Lekai was appointed bishop of Veszprem in 1972 and was nominated apostolic administrator of the archdiocese of Esztergom in 1974, when Pope Paul VI declared the archbishopric vacant by reason of Mindszenty's departure. Lekai was thus archbishop in all but name and succeeded to the full title, becoming ipso facto primate of Hungary, when Mindszenty died the following year. In 1976 he was made a cardinal. Working in association with Archbishop Agostino Casaroli, the Vatican's "foreign minister," he arranged the meeting in Rome in 1977 between Pope Paul VI and Janos Kadar, general secretary of Hungary's Communist Party.

Lerner, Alan Jay, U.S. lyricist (b. Aug. 31, 1918, New York, N.Y.—d. June 14, 1986, New York), was an extraordinary librettist and musical comedy writer who collaborated with composer Frederick Loewe to create such magical and enduring Broadway hits as *Brigadoon* (1947), *Paint Your Wagon* (1951), *My Fair Lady* (1956), and *Camelot* (1960) and the motion picture *Gigi* (1958). Lerner, the son of the founder and president of Lerner Stores, was educated at Bedales School in England, and later he attended Harvard University, where he worked on several Hasty Pudding shows. In New York City he began writing advertising copy and radio scripts; he was involved in writing sketches and lyrics for the annual spring "Gambols" show at The Lambs theatrical club when he met Loewe. The two launched their partnership in the unsuccessful Broadway production *What's Up?* (1943). *The Day Before Spring* (1945) was successful, but they scored their first solid hit in 1947 with the charming, romantic *Brigadoon*. During their nearly 20-year collaboration, the two produced such memorable songs as "They Call the Wind Maria," "I Could Have Danced All Night," "Almost like Being in Love," "The Rain in Spain," "Gigi," "Wouldn't It Be Loverly?," and "On the Street Where You Live." Their biggest success, *My Fair Lady*, was faithfully adapted from George Bernard Shaw's *Pygmalion* and enjoyed 2,717 performances on Broadway. The musical was mounted in more than 20 countries, was translated into 11 languages, and set a record for the longest original run of any musical production in London or New York. The original Broadway cast recording sold more than five million copies, and the 1964 motion picture garnered eight Academy Awards. Such sentimental favourites as *Brigadoon* (1954), *Camelot* (1967), and *Paint Your Wagon* (1969) were also successfully adapted to the screen. Loewe retired after the Broadway production of *Camelot,* and Lerner collaborated with Burton Lane (*On a Clear Day You Can See Forever* [1965] and *Carmelina* [1979]) and with the composers André Previn (*Coco* [1969]) and Leonard Bernstein (*1600 Pennsylvania Avenue* [1976]), but he never recaptured the enchantment of the Lerner-Loewe combination. Lerner also collaborated with Kurt Weill on the innovative 1948 musical *Love Life* and wrote the screenplays for *Royal Wedding* and *An American in Paris,* both in 1951; he won an Academy Award for his script for the latter. His memoir, *On the Street Where I Live*, appeared in 1978. In 1985 Lerner and Loewe were honoured at the Kennedy Center in Washington for their contributions to American culture.

Lifar, Serge, Russian-born ballet dancer (b. April 2, 1905, Kiev, Russia—d. Dec. 16, 1986, Lausanne, Switz.), was ballet master with the Paris Opéra from 1929 to 1958 and the last of the great male dancers in Sergey Diaghilev's Ballets Russes. Celebrated for his good looks and driving ambition, he established himself more through force of personality than technique but went on to create some memorable roles and to exercise a beneficial influence on the Paris Opéra. He trained with Bronislava Nijinska, and when she left to join Diaghilev in the West, Lifar followed her, though he had not been included on her shortlist of favoured pupils. Diaghilev recognized his potential and helped him to improve his technique. From 1925 Lifar took leading roles, culminating in the Balanchine ballets *Apollon Musagète* (1928) and *The Prodigal Son* (1929). He was appointed principal dancer at the Paris Opéra in 1929 and ballet master shortly thereafter. He continued to dance under the German occupation during World War II but was afterward censured and dismissed. However, Lifar was cleared of collaboration, was recalled, and continued to dance until his final performance, in *Giselle* in 1956. He retired in 1958. His personality attracted controversy; he once fought a duel with the marquis de Cuevas, and he was sometimes accused of being unscrupulous in furthering his personal ambition. He wrote several works on ballet and an autobiography, *Ma Vie* ("My Life"). Lifar was a member of the Académie des Beaux-Arts and Chevalier of the Légion d'Honneur.

Lipinski, Edward, Polish economist (b. Oct. 18, 1888, Nowe Miasto, Poland—d. July 13, 1986, Warsaw, Poland), served as director of the Institute of National Economy and president of the National Economic Bank immediately following World War II and at the age of nearly 90 became one of the country's most outspoken dissidents. Lipinski had the authority of a lifelong socialist, having been a political activist since the age of 16 and imprisoned in 1906 for his opposition to czarist rule. In the 1930s he was professor at the Warsaw Higher School of Commerce, editor of the country's leading economic journal, and founder of the Institute for the Study of Economic Trends and Prices. After World War II, during which he continued to run clandestine university courses, he was appointed to positions of national influence by the new Communist regime. By the end of the 1940s, however, he had fallen out of favour with the government, and in 1950 he returned to academic life as professor at the University of Warsaw. Following the 1956 uprising he once again served briefly as economic adviser to the government, advocating reformist policies. In later years his opposition to government policies intensified, and in 1975 he handed in his party card. He was a founder of the Workers' Defense Committee (KOR), established in 1976, and became an adviser to the trade union movement Solidarnosc (Solidarity)—both organizations outlawed by the authorities. A formidable public speaker, protected by his reputation as much as by his age, Lipinski continued to demand the freeing of political prisoners and to denounce the errors of the regime.

Lipmann, Fritz Albert, German-born U.S. biochemist (b. June 12, 1899, Königsberg, Germany—d. July 24, 1986, Poughkeepsie, N.Y.), was the corecipient (with Sir Hans Krebs) of the 1953 Nobel Prize for Physiology or Medicine for the discovery of coenzyme A, an important substance in cellular metabolism. Lipmann earned his M.D. (1924) and his Ph.D. in chemistry (1927) from the University of Berlin. He conducted research at the Kaiser Wilhelm Institute of Biology, Berlin and Heidelberg (1927–30), and at the Biological Institute of the Carlsberg Foundation, Copenhagen (1932–39), before immigrating to the U.S., where he joined the staff of the Cornell Medical School, New York City (1939–41). He then moved to Massachusetts General Hospital, Boston (1941–57), where he was director of the Biochemistry Research Department, and to Harvard Medical School (1949–57), where he was professor of biological chemistry. Lipmann first discovered the enzyme in 1945 and identified it as an important factor in providing physical energy for the human body. While conducting research on pigeon liver extracts, Lipmann found a catalytically active, heat-stable factor that aids in converting fatty acids, steroids, amino acids, and hemoglobins into energy. He subsequently isolated, named, and then determined the molecular structure of this factor—coenzyme A. In 1957 Lipmann joined the Rockefeller Institute (now Rockefeller University), New York City, and served as professor until 1970, when he became professor emeritus. He continued to operate a laboratory and to conduct research there until shortly before his death. In addition to his Nobel Prize, in 1966 Lipmann received the National Medal of Science, the highest award for scientific achievement in the U.S. His autobiography, *Wanderings of a Biochemist,* was published in 1971.

Loewy, Raymond Fernand, French-born U.S. industrial designer (b. Nov. 5, 1893, Paris, France—d. July 14, 1986, Monte Carlo, Monaco), created streamlined designs for automobiles, railroad cars, buses, airplanes, and even spacecraft. Loewy also changed the appearance of such everyday items as electric shavers, office machines, soft-drink dispensing machines, radios, and refrigerators, thereby establishing industrial design as a profession. After graduating from the University of Paris in 1910, he studied advanced engineering at the École de Lanneau but interrupted his education to serve in the French Army during World War I. Loewy earned his degree in 1918 and the following year immigrated to the U.S., where he launched a career as a fashion illustrator for such magazines as *Vogue* and *Harper's Bazaar.* In 1929 he started his own design firm; he scored a major success in 1934 when he designed the Coldspot for Sears, Roebuck and Co. The nonrusting, aluminum-shelved refrigerator was a commercial triumph, and it won first prize at the Paris International Exposition of 1937. Loewy, the first to introduce functional styling to industrial products, formed Raymond Loewy Associates in 1945 with five partners. The firm produced designs for a myriad of products, including lipsticks, electric shavers, automatic pencils, and labels and packaging for soaps, toothpastes, and cigarettes. Loewy was responsible for a dramatic increase in sales of Lucky Strike cigarettes during World War II when he eliminated the green from the packaging and declared, "Lucky Strike green has gone to war." Loewy's sleek designs transformed the U.S. landscape and reinforced his artistic credo, "Good design keeps the user happy, the manufacturer in the black, and the aesthete unoffended." He was responsible for designing Studebaker automobiles, locomotives and passenger cars for the Pennsylvania Railroad, buses for Greyhound, and Air Force One for Pres. John F. Kennedy. Loewy later designed the stamp commemorating the assassinated president. From 1967 to 1973 he worked for the U.S. National Aeronautics and Space Administration, producing spacecraft designs for the Apollo and Skylab projects. His writings include *The Locomotive* (1937), *Never Leave Well Enough Alone* (1951), and *Industrial Design* (1979).

London, Artur, Czech politician (b. Feb. 1, 1915, Ostrava, Moravia [now Czechoslovakia]—d. Nov. 7–8, 1986, Paris, France), as undersecretary for foreign affairs (1949–51) was one of the 14 defendants accused of treason, spying, and sabotage in the notorious political trial of November 1952. Later, in his book *L'Aveu* (1969; *The Confession* [1970]), he described the brutality and systematic brainwashing used to ensure that the accused pleaded guilty. A film version of the book, *The Confession,* directed by Costa-Gavras, was made in 1970. London was of Jewish origin. He joined the Communist Party in 1929 and went to Moscow in 1934. After fighting in the International Brigades during the Spanish Civil War (1936–39), he entered France clandestinely, later working with the Resistance against the Nazis. He was arrested in 1942 and sent to Mauthausen concentration camp. After World War II, he returned to Czechoslovakia, where the Communists had seized power (1948). Arrested in January 1951, he was held in solitary confinement; following his trial he was sentenced to life imprisonment, but he was released in 1956. London settled in France in 1963 but kept in close touch with Czechoslovak affairs. He was president of the Committee for the Defense of Czech Liberties and supported the dissident Charter 77 movement. During the era of the liberal Communist leader Alexander Dubcek, he was invested with the Order of the Czechoslovak Republic, but after that regime's collapse, and as a result of the publication of his book, he was deprived of his Czechoslovak citizenship in 1970.

MacDonald, John Dann, U.S. mystery writer (b. July 24, 1916, Sharon, Pa.—d. Dec. 28, 1986, Milwaukee, Wis.), created one of the most popular detectives in fiction, Travis McGee, the unconventional private eye whose exciting adventures feature beautiful women and plenty of money and whose interests in the environment and economics mirror those of his creator. MacDonald was graduated from Syracuse (N.Y.) University (1938) and earned an M.B.A. from Harvard (1939) but was dismissed from his early jobs in business for his outspokenness. While serving in the Army in World War II, he wrote his first short story. MacDonald wrote more than 70 books in all, including 21 Travis McGee mysteries. He published his first book, *The Brass Cupcake,* in 1950, and his publications garnered wide critical acclaim as well as great popular success. He introduced the Travis McGee series (all the titles include a colour) with *The Deep Blue Goodby* (1964) and followed it with *Nightmare in Pink* (1964), *A Purple Place for Dying* (1964), *Dress Her in Indigo* (1969), and *The Green Ripper* (1979), which won the American Book Award for mystery fiction in 1980. MacDonald also wrote under the pseudonyms John Wade Farrell, Robert Henry, John Lane, Scott O'Hara, Peter Reed, and Henry Rieser. Many of his works were adapted for film and television. Other books include *Murder for the Bride* (1951), *A Bullet for Cinderella* (1955), and *Cry Hard, Cry Fast* (1955). In 1972 the Mystery Writers of America presented him with its Edgar Grand Master Award, their highest honour.

Machel, Samora Moisès, Mozambican politician (b. Sept. 29, 1933, Xilembena, Gaza Province, Mozambique—d. Oct. 19, 1986, near Nkomati, Natal, South Africa), served as his country's president from its independence (1975) until he was killed in a plane crash while returning to Maputo from Lusaka, Zambia. Many of his political adherents believed the South African government was responsible for the crash (Pretoria strongly denied the accusation). An avowed Marxist and one of southern Africa's most charismatic leaders, he had proved a pragmatist in office, taking aid for his impoverished country from the West and from South Africa as well as from the Communist bloc. Ironically, his death occurred close to the town where, in March 1984, he had concluded the controversial Nkomati accord with Pres. P. W. Botha of South Africa, in which each leader agreed to cease harbouring the other's dissident guerrillas. Educated first in a Protestant mission institution and later in a Roman Catholic mission school, Machel rejected the higher education that was offered only if he entered a seminary. Instead, for ten years he worked as a nurse. Machel went to Tanzania in 1962 to join the newly founded Mozambique Liberation Front (Frelimo) and received military training in Algeria. He was made responsible for a sector of Frelimo's guerrilla operations (1964) and became its commander in chief (1968). Eduardo Mondlane, Frelimo's founder and leader, was assassinated in 1969, and Machel succeeded him as leader the following year. After independence his attempts to establish a fully socialist state were hindered by popular apathy and by the incursions of the dissident Mozambique National Resistance (MNR). In southern African politics he preferred conciliation to confrontation and was a moderating influence on Prime Minister Robert Mugabe of Zimbabwe. Machel retained the image of a military leader, however, and was prepared for major operations against the MNR.

MICHAEL KAHN—CAMERA PRESS LTD.

McKenna, Siobhan, Irish actress (b. May 24, 1923?, Belfast, Northern Ireland—d. Nov. 16, 1986, Dublin, Ireland), scored her greatest triumph in 1954 at the Arts Theatre in London in the title role of Bernard Shaw's *Saint Joan.* Her performance was spellbinding; a slight figure, with a soft Irish voice capable of extraordinary power at moments of dramatic intensity, she gave what was immediately recognized as a definitive interpretation of Shaw's heroine. A native Gaelic speaker, she studied at University College, Galway, and made her debut in 1940 at the Gaelic-language An Taibhdhearc Theatre, Galway, where she also starred in the leading role in her own translation of *Saint Joan.* She later performed at the Abbey Theatre, Dublin (1943–46). McKenna first appeared on the London stage in 1947, and from 1955 to 1960 she divided her time between Britain and North America, acting in Shakespearean and modern roles. She was outstanding in J. M. Synge's *The Playboy of the Western World* (1960) and also appeared in the film version of the play two years later, but she remained primarily a figure on the Irish stage. During the 1970s her work included an often-revived one-woman anthology of Irish literary portraits of women, *Here Are Ladies.* McKenna was appointed to the Council of State of the Republic of Ireland in 1975.

Macmillan, (Maurice) Harold, 1st Earl of Stockton, Viscount Macmillan of Ovenden: *see* Stockton, (Maurice) Harold Macmillan, 1st Earl.

Malamud, Bernard, U.S. author (b. April 26, 1914, Brooklyn, N.Y.—d. March 18, 1986, New York, N.Y.), was the prolific and award-winning author of dramatic short stories and novels that explored Jewish themes, but he was also anxious to be recognized as an American writer of universal appeal. His novels, which were a combination of realism and symbolism, featured characters who experienced hardship and suffering before earning redemption. Malamud, the son of Russian-Jewish immigrants who operated a grocery, earned an M.A. from Columbia University, New York City, in 1942. He taught English in night high school (1940–49) before joining Oregon State University in

1949. At that time his books began receiving critical praise. Except for two years at Harvard, 1966–68, from 1961 until his death he served on the faculty of Bennington College in Bennington, Vt. Malamud's first novel, *The Natural* (1952), a realistic fable that recounted the comeback of an aging baseball star after endless travails, was made into a 1984 motion picture starring Robert Redford. His second novel, *The Assistant* (1957), chronicled the life of a hard-working Jewish grocer and established Malamud as a major writer. His short-story collection *The Magic Barrel* (1958) earned him his first National Book Award and was followed by such other collections as *Idiots First* (1963), *Pictures of Fidelman* (1969), and *Rembrandt's Hat* (1973). His critically acclaimed novel *The Fixer* (1966), dealing with anti-Semitism in tsarist Russia, won him a second National Book Award and the Pulitzer Prize. Some of his other works include *The Tenants* (1971), *Dubin's Lives* (1979), and *God's Grace* (1982).

Malone, Dumas, U.S. historian (b. Jan. 10, 1892, Coldwater, Miss.—d. Dec. 27, 1986, Charlottesville, Va.), spent the greater part of his career composing his scholarly masterwork *Jefferson and His Time,* a comprehensive six-volume biography of Thomas Jefferson, which in its unfinished state garnered the Pulitzer Prize for history in 1975. The volumes include *Jefferson the Virginian* (1948), *Jefferson and the Rights of Man* (1951), *Jefferson and the Ordeal of Liberty* (1962), *Jefferson the President: First Term, 1801–1805* (1970), *Jefferson the President: Second Term, 1805–1809* (1974), and *The Sage of Monticello* (1981). After earning a Ph.D. from Yale University in 1923, he taught at the University of Virginia before serving (1945–59) as professor of history at Columbia University, New York City, but he returned to Virginia to become Thomas Jefferson Foundation professor of history. Among his other accomplishments, Malone edited the *Dictionary of American Biography* (1929–31) and served as its editor in chief (1931–36). He also was director of the Harvard University Press for seven years. Some of his other books include *The Public Life of Thomas Cooper* (1926), *Saints in Action* (1939), and *Empire for Liberty,* 2 vol. (1960, with Basil Rauch).

Marchenko, Anatoly, Soviet dissident (b. Jan. 23, 1938, Barabinsk, western Siberia, U.S.S.R.—d. Dec. 8, 1986, Chistopol, U.S.S.R.), was one of the most courageous members of the Public Group to Promote the Fulfillment of the Helsinki Accords of 1975, spent 20 years in prison or internal exile. In *My Testimony,* secretly circulated (Eng. trans., 1969), he provided a graphic account of life in a Soviet labour camp. The son of a railway worker, he became a construction labourer on a hydroelectric project in Siberia. Involved in a brawl (1957), he was convicted of hooliganism and sent to a labour camp near Karaganda in Kazakhstan. He escaped (1959) and attempted to reach Iran but was recaptured when he was almost within sight of freedom. After another escape attempt, he was sent to Moscow's notorious Vladimir Prison. His health rapidly deteriorated, and he became almost totally deaf. After his release in 1966, he worked as a labourer near Moscow and became involved with other dissidents, who persuaded him to write of his experiences. He was again arrested (1968) for writing an open letter warning the Czechoslovaks of the danger of a Soviet invasion and was sent to a labour camp in the northern Urals. He was released to internal exile in the Siberian town of Chuna in 1971 and subsequently married Larisa Bogoraz, also under sentence for pro-Czechoslovak agitation. A victim of cat-and-mouse policies, Marchenko was again sent to a labour camp (1981) and transferred to Chistopol Prison (1985) for alleged violation of camp rules. He reportedly began a hunger strike in August 1986 to protest brutal treatment of prisoners, and although his wife was assured in November that he was in good health, in mid-December she received a telegram reporting his death from heart and lung failure.

Marjolin, Robert Ernest, French economist (b. July 27, 1911, Paris, France—d. April 15, 1986, Paris), was first secretary-general (1948–55) of the Organization for European Economic Cooperation (replaced by the Organization for Economic Cooperation and Development in 1961) and a leading architect of French and European economic planning. He was instrumental in negotiating the 1957 Treaty of Rome and became a vice-president of the Commission of the European Economic Community set up under that treaty the following year. After studying economics at the University of Paris, Marjolin worked in the faculty of law under Charles Rist from 1934 to 1939. In 1941 he went to London where he met economist Jean Monnet, the "father of Europe." Marjolin helped to formulate France's first post-World War II economic plan, involving consultations with different sides of industry and the civil service. After leaving the Commission in 1967, he became financial adviser to various international firms, stood unsuccessfully for Parliament, and taught in Nancy and Paris. He wrote books on the economic crisis, on U.S.-European economic relations, and (in collaboration) a study of European institutions.

Markham, Beryl, British pilot (b. Oct. 26, 1902, Melton Mowbray, Leicestershire, England—d. Aug. 3, 1986, Nairobi, Kenya), became the first woman to fly solo westward across the Atlantic on Sept. 4, 1936. Taking off from Abingdon, Berkshire, England, she crossed in 21 hr 25 min, flying a single-engine Percival Vega Gull VP-KCC, without radio and in terrible weather conditions. She landed in a swamp at Beleene Cove, Cape Breton Island, Nova Scotia. The account of her flight, *West with the Night* (1942), little noticed at the time, was highly successful when reissued in 1983 after it became known that Ernest Hemingway had described it in a letter as "bloody wonderful." Beryl Clutterbuck was taken to Kenya in 1906 by her father, who farmed and trained racehorses. She received little formal education, and at age 17 she began training racehorses, winning the Kenya St. Leger in 1920. She learned to fly and pioneered the aerial scouting of elephants for hunters. Her marriage in 1927 to Mansfield Markham, son of an English coal magnate, was her second. Her striking looks, reminding some of Greta Garbo, attracted many men, including the professional hunter Denys Finch Hatton and Henry, duke of Gloucester. She and Markham soon separated and were divorced in 1942. After her flight she lived in California and was married (1942–47) to Raoul Schumacher, who ghostwrote her book. She returned to Kenya in the early 1950s, resumed training horses, and won the Kenya Derby on six occasions.

Maybray-King, Horace Maybray Maybray-King, Baron, British politician (b. May 25, 1901, near Middlesbrough, Yorkshire [now Cleveland], England—d. Sept. 3, 1986, Southampton, England), was speaker of the House of Commons (1965–70), the first Labour Party member of Parliament to hold that office. The son of a steelworker, he was educated at Stockton and at King's College, University of London. He held a number of teaching posts and was headmaster (1947–50) of a Southampton secondary school. For some years he served as a Labour councillor on Hampshire County Council and as an alderman of Southampton. In 1950 he was elected to Parliament as member for the Test Division of Southampton, and he went on to represent Southampton's other constituency, Itchen (1955–70). He was elected deputy speaker in 1964 and speaker the following year. Maybray-King was created a life peer in 1971 and appointed a deputy speaker of the House of Lords. He was author of a number of books on Parliament and edited selections from the works of Homer and Macaulay. Like his father he was a local Methodist preacher.

Michel, Henri Jules, French historian (b. April 28, 1907, Vidauban, Var, France—d. June 5, 1986, Paris, France), was president (1970–85) of the International Committee on the History of the Second World War and a specialist on the history of the French Resistance during that conflict. Founder and editor of the *Revue d'histoire de la seconde guerre mondiale,* he was remarkable both for his individual contributions to the history of the period and as the creator and leader of a research team that worked throughout France. Michel studied history and taught in Toulon up to and after the outbreak of war, narrowly avoiding arrest for his intelligence work on behalf of the Resistance. In 1947 he was appointed secretary-general to the Commission on the History of the Occupation and Liberation of France and soon realized that, given the wealth of living testimony on the period, writing its history must be a collective as well as an individual task. He created a network of departmental correspondents, organized seminars and conferences, and supervised the writing of theses. His own, on the philosophy of the Resistance, was completed in 1962, and in 1968-69 he published the two-volume *La Seconde guerre mondiale* (*The Second World War*). He also advised Alain Resnais on the making of the film *Nuit et brouillard* (1955). Some of his other works include *La guerre de l'ombre* (1970; *The Shadow War*), as well as studies of wartime Vichy and Paris and a biography of Jean Moulin. At the time of his death he was working on a biography of Adm. François Darlan.

Milland, Ray (Reginald Truscott-Jones), U.S. actor (b. Jan. 3, 1905, Neath, West Glamorgan, Wales—d. March 10, 1986, Torrance, Calif.), portrayed a self-assured leading man in films during the 1930s, turned to a more sinister character in the 1940s and 1950s, and later successfully promoted himself in a string of science-fiction thrillers. He reached the pinnacle of his career as the pitiable alcoholic in *The Lost Weekend* (1945), a role that won him the Academy Award for best actor. The debonair actor made his British film debut in 1929 under the name Spike Milland but in the following year set out for Hollywood. In 1934 he went under contract with Paramount Pictures; he costarred in such films as *The Gilded Lily* (1935; with Claudette Colbert), *The Jungle Princess* (1936; with Dorothy Lamour), and, notably, *Dial M for Murder* (1954) as the superficially charming though murderous husband of Grace Kelly. Some of his other memorable roles were one of the noble brothers in *Beau Geste* (1939), a ship salvager who battles a monstrous squid in the ocean epic *Reap the Wild Wind* (1942), a man falsely accused of murder in *The Big Clock* (1948), a self-destructive surgeon in *X—The Man with X-Ray Eyes* (1963), and Ryan O'Neal's curmudgeonly father in both *Love Story* (1970) and *Oliver's Story* (1978). After his contract with Paramount ended, Milland did free-lance work in B films and in his own productions, notably *The Safecracker* (1958). Among his other screen credits were *Escape to Witch Mountain* (1975) and *The Attic* (1980). Milland also appeared on television in "The Ray Milland Show" (1953–55), "Markham," a detective story (1959–60), and the made-for-television movies "The Dead Don't Die" (1975) and "Look What's Happened to Rosemary's Baby" (1976).

Minnelli, Vincente, U.S. motion picture director (b. Feb. 28, 1910, Chicago, Ill.—d. July 25, 1986, Los Angeles, Calif.), was a stylistic genius who brilliantly integrated theme, music, and vibrant colour to produce sophisticated lyricism in dazzling Hollywood musicals, notably *Cabin in the Sky* (1943), *Meet Me in St. Louis* (1944), *The Pirate* (1948), *An American in Paris* (1951), *The Band Wagon* (1953), and *Gigi* (1958), which won nine Academy Awards, including one for best director. The versatile Minnelli, who also applied his technique to comedy and drama, was celebrated as one of Hollywood's consummate auteurs, a director who so totally dominated the making of a motion picture that he was considered to be its author. The son of theatrical parents, Minnelli performed in their traveling tent show before working as a stage designer in Chicago and as a costume designer in New York. After serving as chief costume designer at Radio City Music Hall (1935), he made his directorial debut (1936) on Broadway with *At Home Abroad;* that was followed by *The Show Is On, Ziegfeld Follies,* and *Very Warm for May.* In Hollywood he signed with Metro-Goldwyn-Mayer (MGM) studios, and from 1942 to 1962 Minnelli directed 29 films. In 1945 he directed Judy Garland in the drama *The Clock,* and they married the same year. The following year their daughter, Liza, was born; she became an accomplished actress in her own right. The couple divorced in 1951. Minnelli's successful comedies included *Father of the Bride* (1950) and *The Long, Long Trailer* (1954). His dramas *The Bad and the Beautiful* (1952) and *Lust for Life* (1956) were followed by such stylized melodramas as *Some Came Running* (1959), *Home from the Hill* (1960), and *The Four Horsemen of the Apocalypse* (1962). Minnelli's last film, *A Matter of Time* (1976), starred his daughter, Liza. He published his memoirs, *I Remember It Well,* in 1974.

Moczar, Mieczyslaw, Polish politician (b. Dec. 25, 1913, Lodz, Poland—d. Nov. 1, 1986, Warsaw, Poland), as a member of the Politburo of the Polish United Workers' (Communist) Party (PUWP; 1970–71 and 1980–81), was at times in his career a serious contender for leadership of the party. Born Mikolaj Demko, he took his name from the Communist guerrilla group—Moczary ("swamps")—which he commanded

CAF/EASTFOTO

during World War II. The postwar regime in Poland was dominated by those Communists who had spent the war years in Moscow. After Wladyslaw Gomulka assumed the PUWP leadership in 1956, however, Moczar's political career advanced rapidly. As interior minister (1964–68) he was a key figure in a campaign launched in 1967 against "revisionists" and "Zionists." His own bid to succeed Gomulka was unsuccessful, and shortly after Edward Gierek became party leader in December 1970, Moczar was dropped from both the PUWP Central Committee and the Politburo, apparently at the insistence of Moscow. He staged a dramatic but brief comeback in 1980 when the emergence of the Solidarnosc (Solidarity) trade-union movement plunged the PUWP leadership into crisis. By March 1983 he had resigned from his last major post, that of chairman of the Supreme Chamber of Control.

Molotov, Vyacheslav Mikhaylovich (Vyacheslav Mikhaylovich Skryabin), Soviet statesman and diplomat (b. March 9, 1890, Nolinsk, Russia—d. Nov. 8, 1986, near Moscow, U.S.S.R.), as commissar (later minister) for

EB INC.

foreign affairs (1939–49), was a major representative of Soviet foreign policy during and immediately after World War II. The last of the "old Bolsheviks," he was one of Joseph Stalin's most self-effacing collaborators from the early 1920s until shortly before Stalin's death in 1953. Born into a bourgeois family, he joined the Bolsheviks in 1906 and became a full-time organizer for the party while studying at the Polytechnic Institute in St. Petersburg (now Leningrad). Arrested several times for political activities before the 1917 Revolution, he subsequently held several posts in provincial Communist Party organizations before becoming a candidate member of the Politburo in 1921. Five years later he became a full member. As head of the Moscow party organization (1928–30) he directed a purge of anti-Stalinist elements. From 1930 to 1941, as chairman of the Council of People's Commissars (later Council of Ministers), he was head of government.

Immediately after Molotov was put in charge of foreign affairs by Stalin in May 1939, he negotiated the nonaggression agreement with Nazi Germany that was known as the Molotov-Ribbentrop Pact. After Germany invaded the U.S.S.R., he negotiated the Soviet alliances with both the U.K. and the U.S. and subsequently attended the major Allied conferences at Tehran (1943), Yalta (1945), and Potsdam (1945). An important element in Molotov's fall from favour in the late 1940s was apparently Stalin's distrust of his Jewish wife, Paulina Zhemchuzhina, who was arrested in 1948 and remained in internal exile until after Stalin's death. Molotov left the Foreign Ministry in 1949. He returned to the post when Nikita Khrushchev became party leader in 1953, but political disagreements soon surfaced; Molotov lost the foreign affairs portfolio in June 1956 and all other important party and state positions the following year. In 1964 it was revealed that he had been expelled from the Communist Party. He retired to his home near Moscow and for two decades was not active in political life. His readmittance to party membership in 1984 was apparently on the advice of Andrey Gromyko, foreign minister at the time. Although Molotov's funeral took place at the exclusive Novodevichii cemetery in Moscow, the ceremony was notable for the absence of Politburo members.

Moore, Henry, British sculptor (b. July 30, 1898, Castleford, Yorkshire, England—d. Aug. 31, 1986, Perry Green, Much Hadham, Hertfordshire, England), was a towering figure in 20th-century art and one of the few to achieve international fame and invite comparison with great masters of the past. Moore, whose best-known work was probably his series of reclining female nudes, was reviled early in his career for what was considered abstract extremism, but after World War II he achieved almost universal critical acclaim. Moore was the son of a coal miner. He served in the British Army in World War I, subsequently obtained a grant to study at Leeds School of Art, and then won (1921) a scholarship to the Royal College of Art, London. Besides studying contemporary European sculpture, he discovered in the museums of London and, later, France and Italy the archaic and primitive beauty in Egyptian, Etruscan, pre-Colombian, and African sculpture. He held his first one-man exhibition in 1928 and obtained his first major sculpture commission for the London Transport Board headquarters. During the 1930s Moore drifted from the human figure to explore abstract shapes, sometimes combining the two. In 1932 he founded the sculpture department at the Chelsea School of Art, but when the school was evacuated from London, he stopped teaching, moved briefly to Kent, then returned to London, working in a studio in Hampstead. When this was damaged by bombing in 1940, he moved to Much Hadham, which became his permanent home. During this period he made the drawings of Londoners sheltering in the Underground that became his most celebrated work in a medium other than sculpture. His later drawings included a series on Stonehenge, an elephant's skull, and sheep. In 1943 Moore created a "Madonna and Child"; a 1944 commission, for a family group, marked a dramatic change in style to a more naturalistic approach. With this work he achieved popular appeal, and the dozens of clay and terra-cotta studies for these 1943 and 1945 works he cast in bronze and issued in editions of seven to nine copies each, thus making his works available to museums and collectors throughout the

© GISELE FREUND

world. His humanistic approach secured his international reputation; a retrospective of his work was mounted at the Museum of Modern Art in New York City in 1946, and in 1948 he was awarded the sculpture prize at the Venice Biennale. Financial freedom enabled Moore to work on a monumental scale, and some of his commissions included family groups for the new towns of Stevenage, Hertfordshire, in 1948 and Harlow, Essex, in 1954–55; "Three Draped Standing Figures" in stone (1947–48) for Battersea Park, London; a "Madonna" for St. Peter's Church in Claydon, Suffolk, in 1949; and a large "Reclining Figure" for the 1951 Festival of Britain. The 1950s signaled a period of renewed experimentation, and his postwar work tended to be predominantly in bronze and, in the 1960s, marble, though he never abandoned carving in stone. Moore, credited with the revival of sculpture in Britain, became a Companion of Honour in 1955 and gained the Order of Merit in 1963. He established the Henry Moore Foundation in 1977.

Motte, Claire Renée Eliane, French ballerina (b. Dec. 21, 1937, Belfort, France—d. July 15, 1986, Paris, France), as a star of the Paris Opéra Ballet from 1960 to 1979, was described by Serge Lifar (*q.v.*), who created many roles for her, as "the Callas of dance." She joined the

Opéra Ballet school at the age of 14 and made her debut as a leading dancer (*danseuse étoile*) in *Swan Lake* when she was 23. She went on to dance all the major classical roles. Greatly admired for her technical skill, she took part in many international tours and reached a wider public through television productions of *Phèdre* and *The Firebird.* After retiring as a performer, she ran a ballet school, and in 1983 she was invited by Rudolf Nureyev to return to the Opéra Ballet as ballet mistress.

Mulliken, Robert Sanderson, U.S. chemist and physicist (b. June 7, 1896, Newburyport, Mass.—d. Oct. 31, 1986, Arlington, Va.), was awarded the 1966 Nobel Prize for Chemistry for "his fundamental work concerning chemical bonds and the electronic structure of molecules." Mulliken graduated from the Massachusetts Institute of Technology in 1917 and earned a Ph.D. from the University of Chicago in 1921. After conducting research on war gases for the Army during World War I, he began studying (1923) molecular spectra and molecular structure. In 1928 he joined the faculty of the University of Chicago, and he subsequently held chairs in both physics and chemistry. Mulliken, who was dubbed "Mr. Molecule" by his colleagues, was the creator of the molecular orbital theory, which postulates that when atoms combine to form a molecule their electrons no longer orbit the original nuclei but form new orbital configurations around groups of nuclei to create bonds that hold the molecule together. His work, which laid the foundation of molecular science, was so original yet so technical that he never attempted to explain it for the layman. It was not until high-powered computers became available that he was able to accurately describe the orbitals for important molecules. During World War II Mulliken worked on the development of the atomic bomb. In 1965 he joined the Institute of Molecular Biophysics at Florida State University but also retained his position at the University of Chicago, where he conducted research until 1985.

Murphy, Lionel Keith, Australian judge (b. Aug. 31, 1922, Sydney, Australia—d. Oct. 21, 1986, Canberra, Australia), was a colourful and controversial figure who, as federal attorney general in the Australian Labor Party (ALP) government of 1972–75, had been responsible for a number of liberalizing laws. He made divorce easier, restricted monopolies, and improved legal aid. Murphy introduced legislation to protect the environment, drastically curtailed the trade in Australian fauna, and sued the French government in the International Court of Justice for its nuclear testing in the Pacific region. He was from 1975 a justice of the High Court of Australia. Murphy was educated at Sydney Boys' High School and at the University of Sydney, where he studied science and law. Called to the bar in 1947 and appointed a queen's counsel in 1960, he specialized in trade union law. He was elected to the federal Parliament as a senator for New South Wales (1962), and he later led the ALP group in the Senate in opposition (1967–72) and in government (1972–75). As attorney general he aroused controversy in 1973 when he headed a police raid on the headquarters of the Security and Intelligence Organization, which he suspected of withholding files from him. In July 1985 Murphy was found guilty of attempting to pervert the course of justice in committal proceedings concerning an acquaintance. Sentenced to 18 months' imprisonment, he was given bail pending appeal. Although Murphy was found not guilty in the Appeal Court (April 1986), the allegations continued and an investigative committee was appointed; the matter was dropped, however, when it became known that he was terminally ill with cancer.

Myrdal, Alva Reimer, Swedish sociologist and diplomat (b. Jan. 31, 1902, Uppsala, Sweden—d. Feb. 1, 1986, Stockholm, Sweden), was the corecipient of the 1982 Nobel Prize for Peace (with Mexican diplomat Alfonso García Robles) for her dedicated advocacy of nuclear disarmament. She was also well known as a pioneer in family welfare issues, and her writings on education and child care, some coauthored by her husband, economist Gunnar Myrdal (a 1974 Nobel laureate in economics), laid the foundation for Sweden's welfare policies. After studying psychology at Stockholm University, she received her B.A. in 1924, the same year she married Myrdal. She continued her studies in the U.S., where she traveled as a Rockefeller fellow, and in Geneva before earning her M.A. at Uppsala University in 1934. In 1936 she founded a training college for nursery school teachers and served as its first director (1936–48). Myrdal was principal director (1949–50) of the UN Department of Social Affairs before becoming director (1951–55) of Unesco's Department of Social Sciences. After serving as minister and then as ambassador to India, Burma, and Ceylon (1955–61), she was elected to the Swedish Senate (1962–70). From 1962 to 1973 she led her country's delegations to meetings of the 18-nation Geneva Disarmament Conference. Her books, many of which were translated into English, include *Postwar Planning* (1944), *Women's Two Roles* (1956; with Viola Klein), and *The Game of Disarmament* (1976). She was also awarded several peace prizes, including the West German Peace Prize, which she received with her husband.

Neagle, Dame Anna (FLORENCE MARJORIE ROBERTSON WILCOX), British actress (b. Oct. 20, 1904, London, England—d. June 3, 1986, Surrey, England), projected an image of essentially English gentility and "niceness" but also exhibited a tough determination that allowed her to pursue successfully a professional career of more than 60 years and to survive private misfortunes in later years. During the 1930s she was among Britain's biggest box-office attractions, portraying romantic or historical heroines in motion pictures. One of her most successful roles was that of Queen Victoria in *Victoria the Great* (1937), directed by Herbert Wilcox, who guided her career and was to become her husband in 1943. Neagle studied dancing as a child and during the 1920s appeared in revues on the London stage. Her film career began in 1930 in *Should a Doctor Tell?,* and her star quality was confirmed by *Goodnight Vienna* a year later, but she continued to appear on stage in parts ranging from musical comedy to Shakespeare. She moved to Hollywood in 1939 to play the title role in *Nurse Edith Cavell* and to star in three fondly remembered musicals (*Irene, No, No, Nanette* [both 1940], and *Sunny* [1941]) before returning to England in 1941 for the part of Amy Johnson in *They Flew Alone.* Immediately after World War II she acted with Michael Wilding in a series of light romantic films in a London setting, including *Spring in Park Lane* (1948) and *Maytime in Mayfair* (1949), which precisely suited the postwar mood. Her talent in more demanding roles was demonstrated in *Odette* (1950) and *The Lady with a Lamp* (1951), in which she played Florence Nightingale. Neagle exhibited her versatility by playing Nell Gwyn, Queen Victoria, and two other parts in the stage musical *The Glorious Days* in 1952–53, making it almost a review of her career. Some ten years later, under the stress of her husband's illness and financial disaster, she showed considerable strength of character and achieved a popular stage success with *Charlie Girl* (1965–71). During the 1970s she wrote an autobiography, *There's Always Tomorrow,* and was in *No, No, Nanette, The Dame of Sark, My Fair Lady,* and the Silver Jubilee show *Most Gracious Lady.* She was made a Commander (1952) and Dame (1969) of the Order of the British Empire.

O'Keeffe, Georgia, U.S. painter (b. Nov. 15, 1887, near Sun Prairie, Wis.—d. March 6, 1986, Santa Fe, N.M.), during a 60-year career established herself as one of the most original and significant American painters of the century, creating bold, semiabstract, vibrant paintings of bleached animal bones, enlarged flowers, clouds, mountains, rocks, and landscapes of Manhattan and New Mexico. O'Keeffe studied at the Art Institute of Chicago (1904–05), the Art Students League of New York (1907–08), the University of Virginia (1912), and Columbia University, New York City (1914–16), also working as a commercial artist and art teacher. In 1916, unbeknownst to O'Keeffe, a friend showed a sample of her pictures to the famous photographer Alfred Stieglitz, and he displayed them in his avant-garde gallery, "291." When she later demanded that he return her works, he persuaded her to let them remain. Stieglitz became her mentor and, in 1924, her husband. He took more than 500 highly acclaimed photographs of her and showcased her works in numerous one-woman shows before his death in 1946. Together, O'Keeffe and Stieglitz ushered in a crucial phase in American modernism, establishing a creative partnership that would carve for each of them a unique niche in the history of art. Early in her career O'Keeffe became known for her scenes of New York, notably "Radiator Building—Night New York" (1927). She became restless there, however, and, while visiting (1929) a friend in New Mexico, became so intrigued by the architectural forms and the seemingly endless tawny spaces that she gradually adopted the state as her home, moving there permanently after Stieglitz's death. The desert became her inspiration, and she painted mountains and animal bones, notably "Black Iris" (1926) and "Cow's Skull, Red, White and Blue" (1931). Her powerfully individualistic style was devoid of European influences; when she traveled abroad in 1959, for instance, the artistic results of her transatlantic flight were exquisite paintings of clouds. Though some of her works, especially her flower paintings, have been interpreted as erotic, she vehemently denied any such intent. The genius of the doyenne of American painting was recognized with many awards and honours, including election to the National Institute of Arts and Letters and receipt of the 1977 Presidential Medal of Freedom. A major retrospective of her work was held at the Whitney Museum of American Art, New York City, in 1970, and she published her autobiography, *Georgia O'Keeffe,* in 1976. Failing eyesight and ill health afflicted her final years, but O'Keeffe's artistic vision remains immutable testimony to her stature in the history of American art.

AP/WIDE WORLD

Palme, (Sven) Olof Joachim, Swedish politician (b. Jan. 30, 1927, Stockholm, Sweden—d. Feb. 28, 1986, Stockholm), served as chairman of the Social Democratic Party from 1969 and prime minister of Sweden from 1969 to 1976 and again from 1982 to 1986, when he was assassinated by an unknown gunman while walking home from a cinema. Born into a wealthy Swedish family, Palme was educated at a private boarding school before graduating from Kenyon College, Gambier, Ohio (1948), and Stockholm University (1951), where he received a degree in law. There he joined the National Swedish Union of Students and became politically committed to the left. He strongly opposed the 1948 Communist coup in Czechoslovakia, and in 1949 he married (but later divorced, in accordance with their agreement) a Czech girl to help her emigrate. After working at the Ministry of Defense in Stockholm, he became personal secretary (1954–63) to the prime minister, Tage Erlander. After Palme entered the Cabinet as minister without portfolio (1963), he served as minister of communications (1965) and minister of education and religious affairs (1967). A critic of continued American involvement in the Vietnam war, he achieved some notoriety

SVENSKT/PICTORIAL PARADE

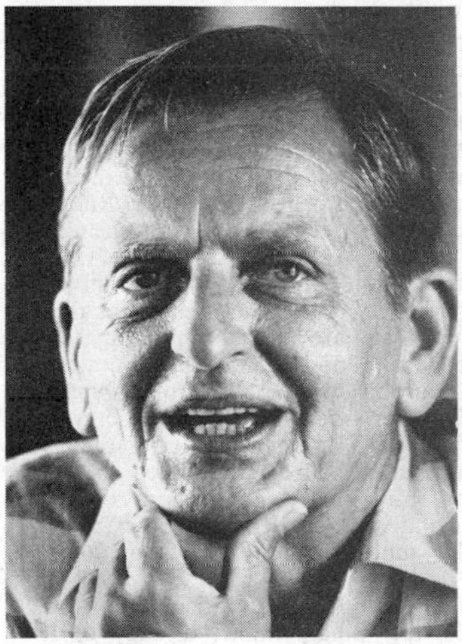

when, in 1968, he marched in protest outside the U.S. embassy in Stockholm. He also condemned the Soviet invasion of Czechoslovakia that same year. When Erlander retired (1969), Palme was unanimously elected chairman of the Social Democratic Party and thus became prime minister. He led a fact-finding delegation to southern Africa (1977) on behalf of the Independent Commission on International Development Issues (the Brandt Commission) and acted as a UN special envoy to mediate in the war between Iran and Iraq. Palme chaired the Independent Commission on Disarmament and Security, advocating the establishment of a nuclear-free zone in Europe. Although he was criticized for domestic economic policies and for inadequate protests against Soviet submarine intrusion into Swedish waters, Palme was returned to power in the general election of September 1985.

Palmer, Lilli (LILLIE MARIE PEISER), German-born actress (b. May 24, 1914, Posen, Germany [now Poland]—d. Jan. 27, 1986, Los Angeles, Calif.), brought elegance and sophistication to a wide range of roles on both stage and screen. The daughter of an actress, she grew up in Berlin, where she studied drama. She and her sister were sent to Paris in 1933 after the Nazis came to power in Germany. The two sisters performed as a duo in cabaret. Shortly after moving to Britain in 1935, Palmer won a film contract. In 1945, two years after her marriage (later dissolved) to Rex Harrison, she accompanied him to Hollywood. The couple starred together in *The Rake's Progress* (1945; U.S. title, *Notorious Gentleman*). Palmer, who was apparently motivated by a desire to promote a spirit of reconciliation among wartime enemies, accepted an invitation to make a film in Germany in the early 1950s; from then on she often worked in Europe. Among Palmer's films were *Good Morning Boys* (1937), *Thunder Rock* (1942), *The Gentle Sex* (1943), *The Pleasure of His Company* (1961), *Lotte in Weimar* (1975), and *The Boys from Brazil* (1978). Her stage appearances included roles in *Caesar and Cleopatra* (1949), *Bell, Book and Candle* (1950), and *The Love of Four Colonels* (1953). Palmer's autobiography, *Change Lobsters, and Dance* (1975), became a best-seller, and she also wrote several novels.

GUIDO MANGOLD—CAMERA PRESS LTD.

Pears, Sir Peter Neville Luard, British tenor (b. June 22, 1910, Farnham, Surrey, England—d. April 3, 1986, Aldeburgh, Suffolk, England), was the most outstanding male singer of his time in Britain and had an immense influence on musical development in the country, most notably through his relationship with the composer Benjamin Britten. Most of Britten's works were scored with Pears's voice in mind. Their successful partnership included many song recitals, not only of Britten's work and arrangements but of the lieder of Schubert and Schumann. With Eric Crozier they founded (1947) the Aldeburgh Festival. The Britten/Pears Library and School at Aldeburgh also became important. Though Pears's voice was not strong, it had a peculiarly compelling and enchanting quality, and he was a master of musical technique. Educated at Lancing College, Pears held an organ scholarship (1928) at Hertford College, Oxford, before returning to his preparatory school at Crowborough, Sussex, as director of music (1929–33). He won a scholarship to the Royal College of Music (1933) but stayed only two terms. During the 1930s he sang with the BBC Singers, the New English Singers, and in the chorus at the Glyndebourne Opera House. He and Britten first began to give regular recitals together in 1938, and after their visit to the U.S. (1939–42) Pears joined the Sadler's Wells Opera. It was there that he sang the name part in Britten's new opera *Peter Grimes* (1945). He had lead roles in virtually all of Britten's other works, notably those of Captain Vere in *Billy Budd* (1951) and Aschenbach in *Death in Venice* (1973). When Britten (a temperamental character for whom Pears often acted as informal public relations officer) no longer wished to accompany his singing, Pears began to give recitals with the pianist Murray Perahia and the harpist Osian Ellis. He also sang in oratorios. His wide knowledge of music and literature helped not only Britten but other musicians; he contributed to the libretto of Britten's opera *A Midsummer Night's Dream* (1960) and was responsible for the idea of Sir William Walton's comic opera *The Bear* (1967). After suffering a stroke in 1980, Pears ceased to sing in public. He was knighted in 1977.

Penhaligon, David Charles, British politician (b. June 6, 1944, Truro, Cornwall, England—d. Dec. 22, 1986, near Probus, Cornwall, England), as Liberal member of Parliament for Truro from October 1974, was, apart from its leaders, one of the very few members of the Liberal-Social Democratic Party Alliance to be known nationwide. A down-to-earth Cornishman, he nevertheless became one of his party's most successful communicators, speaking frequently on television and radio. Penhaligon was educated at Truro School and at Cornwall Technical College, becoming a precision engineer. He joined the Liberal Party in 1964 and unsuccessfully contested Totnes in South Devon (1970). He failed to win Truro in February 1974 but took the seat by 464 votes eight months later and at every subsequent election increased his majority; in 1983 it reached 10,480 and was larger than that of any other Alliance member. He was Liberal spokesman on employment (1976–81, 1983–85), on industry (1981–83), and on the Treasury (from 1985) and was president of the Liberal Party (1985–86). Unlike some Liberals, he favoured the retention of Britain's nuclear deterrent and wholeheartedly supported the Alliance. Hardworking in his constituency, he fought hard for Cornish miners when the tin industry collapsed. He met his death while driving on icy roads to give Christmas greetings to postal workers.

Perkins, (Richard) Marlin, U.S. zoologist and television personality (b. March 28, 1905, Carthage, Mo.—d. June 14, 1986, St. Louis, Mo.), delighted millions of television viewers as the genial and unflappable narrator of "Zoo Parade" (1949–58) and as the host of "Mutual of Omaha's Wild Kingdom" (1963–85), two programs that extolled the importance of preserving endangered species. While growing up on the family farm, Perkins became fascinated with animals. He studied zoology for two years before joining (1926) the St. Louis Zoo as a labourer. His talents were soon recognized, and he became reptile curator, a post he held until 1938, when he became director of the Buffalo (N.Y.) Zoo. In 1945 he became director of the Lincoln Park Zoo in Chicago, and in 1949 he launched "Zoo Parade," a behind-the-scenes glimpse at animals in the zoo. The show went on network television the following year. In 1962 Perkins returned to the St. Louis Zoo as director, and the following year he also assumed duties as the host of "Wild Kingdom." The safari-format program, which was lauded for its unique footage, won four Emmy awards and was seen on 200 stations in North America and in more than 40 countries worldwide. Perkins, who appeared unperturbed after being charged by an irate bull seal, sprayed by a baby elephant, and bitten by a cottonmouth moccasin and a rattlesnake, helped dispel superstitions about feared animals by keeping his composure on camera. He dedicated his career to the preservation of wildlife and was the author of four books: *Animal Faces, Marlin Perkins' Zoo Parade, I Saw You from Afar,* and his 1982 autobiography, *My Wild Kingdom.*

Phoenix, Pat (PATRICIA PILKINGTON), British actress (b. Nov. 26, 1923, County Galway, Ireland—d. Sept. 17, 1986, Manchester, England), achieved fame playing the part of Elsie Tanner in Granada Television's long-running soap opera "Coronation Street." With only a break of three years in the 1970s, she appeared from the first episode in 1960 until 1984; in 1983 she had asked to be written out of the series. Phoenix captured the hearts of viewers as the warm-hearted and impetuous Elsie, whose personality and turbulent life-style reflected something of the actress herself. At its peak the program attracted 20 million viewers. Phoenix's success in the part came after a long apprenticeship in the theatre and as a child actress on radio, in "Children's Hour." She appeared in motion pictures, including *The L-Shaped Room* (1962), and on the provincial stage. But it was as Elsie Tanner that the public saw her and the press pursued her, reporting the failure of her brief first marriage; her separation from her second husband, actor Alan Browning (who also played Elsie's husband on "Coronation Street"), and his subsequent death from alcoholism; and her deathbed marriage to actor Anthony Booth after she had been told she was dying of cancer.

Her two volumes of autobiography included *All My Burning Bridges* (1974) and *Love, Curiosity, Freckles and Doubt* (1983).

Plante, Jacques, Canadian hockey player (b. Jan. 17, 1929, Shawinigan Falls, Que.—d. Feb. 26, 1986, Geneva, Switz.), graced the ice for 19 years as an innovative goaltender who popularized wearing a face mask and roamed daringly from the net to clear pucks from opposing forwards. Plante, who played for five National Hockey League (NHL) teams, was best known as the star goalie for the Montreal Canadiens during the 1950s, when the team captured five consecutive Stanley Cup championships. Plante adopted a face mask in 1959 during a game in which a hard slap shot required him to receive 21 facial stitches; because he was the only goalie on the team, he resumed play wearing the face mask for protection. His superb skating and defensive skills earned him numerous honours and the moniker "Jake the Snake." Plante was an all-star goalie seven times, won the Vezina Trophy a record seven times (as the goaltender allowing the fewest goals), and for the 1961–62 season was presented the Hart Trophy as the league's most valuable player. During his career he compiled an impressive record: 82 shutouts in 837 games and a goals-against average of 2.37. Plante, who also played for the New York Rangers, the St. Louis Blues, the Toronto Maple Leafs, the Boston Bruins, and the Edmonton Oilers of the World Hockey Association, retired in 1975 and was inducted into the Hockey Hall of Fame in 1978.

Pollard, Fritz (FREDERICK DOUGLAS POLLARD), U.S. football coach and player (b. Jan. 27, 1894, Chicago, Ill.—d. May 11, 1986, Silver Spring, Md.), was the lightning-swift Brown University All-American halfback (1916) who paved the way for blacks in the sport by playing in the first professional football league and by becoming the first black head coach of a National Football League (NFL) team. Pollard, who played (1919–21 and 1925–26) with the Akron Pros, took over most of the team's coaching duties, but his contributions were never publicly acknowledged. He claimed to have been head coach of the NFL's Milwaukee Badgers in 1922 but was not recognized as a head coach until he coached the Hammond Pros of Indiana (1923–25). He later played (1926) for the Providence Steamrollers before leaving the NFL to coach college football, at Lincoln (Pa.) University, and to organize the first black all-star football team, the Brown Bombers. He also enjoyed a business career, launching the first black American investment firm and becoming the first black assistant producer of all-black films. Pollard was a member of the National Football Foundation Hall of Fame for college players.

Prebisch, Raúl, Argentine economist (b. April 17, 1901, Tucumán, Arg.—d. April 29, 1986, Santiago, Chile), as the leading spokesman for less developed nations during the 1950s and '60s, advocated the creation of a "global strategy of development" that relied heavily on establishing new patterns of international trade. This strategy included promoting trade among the less developed countries themselves and between less developed countries and Communist countries, as well as initiating trade concessions for third world countries in their relations with industrial nations. Prebisch was adamantly in favour of Latin-American countries reducing imports by using their own raw materials to manufacture goods. He felt that exporting all natural resources without producing finished goods could lead to economic disaster. After graduating from the University of Buenos Aires in 1923, he taught (1925–48) at the university and served in a succession of government posts, including deputy director (1925–27) of the Argentine Department of Statistics, director of economic research (1927–30) at the National Bank of Argentina, under secretary (1930–32) at the Ministry of Finance, and director general (1935–43) of the Central Bank of the Argentine Republic. From 1950 to 1963 he was executive secretary of the UN Economic Commission for Latin America, and in 1963 he was elected secretary-general of the United Nations Conference on Trade and Development (UNCTAD), a post he held until 1969, when he retired to serve as director general for the Latin American Institute for Economic and Social Planning, in Santiago.

Preminger, Otto Ludwig, U.S. motion-picture director (b. Dec. 5, 1905, Vienna, Austria—d. April 23, 1986, New York, N.Y.), was the autocratic, shiny-domed filmmaker whose provocative independent productions, including *The Moon Is Blue* (1953), *Anatomy of a Murder* (1959), and *The Man with the Golden Arm* (1955), were instrumental in helping to dismantle the motion-picture industry's own censorship bans by using forbidden words ("virgin," "pregnant," and "contraceptive") and by exploring such then taboo subjects as rape and drug addiction. Preminger enjoyed a career in Europe as an actor and assistant to the famed director Max Reinhardt before fleeing Austria in 1935 and moving to the United States. The following year he directed his first U.S. film, *Under Your Spell.* He also continued to act, often portraying Nazis, as in the Broadway production of *Margin for Error* (1939) and in the film *Stalag 17* (1953). Preminger's predilection for bullying subordinates and terrorizing actors earned him the enmity of his contemporaries, who dubbed him "Otto the Terrible." The innovative director was widely acclaimed for his taut crime films, including *Where the Sidewalk Ends* (1950) and *Anatomy of a Murder* (1959), and he was especially hailed for the haunting *Laura* (1944), which was considered his masterpiece. Such glossy projects as *Saint Joan* (1957), *Exodus* (1960), and *The Cardinal* (1963) were less warmly received. Some of his other credits include *Forever Amber* (1947), *Carmen Jones* (1954), *The Court Martial of Billy Mitchell* (1955), *Advise and Consent* (1962), and *The Human Factor* (1980). Preminger received Academy Award nominations as best director for *Laura* and *The Cardinal* but won neither.

Pritzker, Abram Nicholas, U.S. hotelier and philanthropist (b. Jan. 6, 1896, Chicago, Ill.—d. Feb. 8, 1986, Chicago), was the savvy proprietor of the worldwide chain of 120 Hyatt hotels and the patriarch of the family-owned Marmon Group, which boasted more than 250 companies and subsidiaries including *McCall's* magazine, Braniff Airlines, and gambling casinos in Nevada and New Jersey. A graduate (1920) of Harvard Law School, Pritzker worked in his father's law firm before launching his business career. He purchased the Hyatt House in Los Angeles in 1957 and parlayed his investment into an empire. Dismissing the advice of lawyers and financial experts, who favoured public sales of stock to increase capital, Pritzker prided himself on his own judgment and accumulated one of the country's largest private fortunes, estimated to be worth $1.5 billion. He also administered much of the family fortune and generously endowed educational and medical organizations. Though Pritzker turned over control of most of the business to his sons in 1980, he continued to monitor his interests from an office in a Chicago bank building.

Putrament, Jerzy, Polish writer and politician (b. Nov. 14, 1910, Minsk, Russia—d. June 23, 1986, Warsaw, Poland), was a distinguished poet, novelist, and journalist and an active figure in Polish political life. He studied at the Stefan Batory University, Wilno, Poland (now Vilnius, U.S.S.R.), and was working in literary journalism during the 1930s when he was arrested and tried as a Communist. During World War II he escaped to the Soviet Union, where he jointly founded the Union of Polish Patriots. His first novel, *Reality* (1947), drew on the experiences of his trial and was followed by some 50 fictional works. His novel *Boldyn* (1969) was set during wartime, as was his documentary prose work *September* (1952). A member of the Polish United Workers' (Communist) Party from 1944, he was a Central Committee member during 1964–81, served as Polish ambassador to Switzerland (1945–47) and France (1948–50), and was a member of the Sejm (parliament) from 1953 to 1961. As editor of *Literature Monthly* and then of *Literature,* he exercised considerable influence on cultural policy from the 1960s onward. His other works include his memoirs, published as *Half a Century* (1969).

Rainwater, (Leo) James, U.S. physicist (b. Dec. 9, 1917, Council, Idaho—d. May 31, 1986, Yonkers, N.Y.), together with Danish physicists Aage N. Bohr and Ben Roy Mottelson, shared the 1975 Nobel Prize for Physics for "the discovery of the connection between collective motion and particle motion in atomic nuclei and the development of the theory of the structure of the atomic nucleus based on this connection." Work on the theory began in 1949. The shape of the atomic nucleus had been accepted as spherical, but in his research Rainwater theorized that some atomic nuclei took different asymmetrical shapes because of the velocity of movement in the particles that shape the inner and outer nucleus. His colleagues in Denmark experimented and proved his theory. Rainwater earned a physics degree (1939) from the California Institute of Technology and an M.A. (1941) and Ph.D. (1946) from Columbia University, New York City, where he then spent the rest of his professional career teaching physics. He twice served (1951–54 and 1957–61) as director of Columbia's Nevis Cyclotron Laboratories in Irvington, N.Y., and in 1983 he was appointed Michael I. Pupin professor of physics at Columbia. He also participated in Atomic Energy Commission (AEC) and naval research projects and was awarded the AEC's Ernest Orlando Lawrence Prize for Physics in 1963.

Ram, Jagjivan, Indian politician (b. April 5, 1908, Arrah, Bihar, India—d. July 6, 1986, New Delhi, India), held senior Cabinet posts almost consecutively from 1946 to 1979 and was an unchallenged leader in his home state of Bihar and among the scheduled castes (former untouchables). Born into a family of Untouchables, he nevertheless received schooling and later attended Banaras Hindu University and the University of Calcutta. Ram became involved in social work, seeking to improve the condition of the untouchables; he also inaugurated the Agricultural Labour Movement in Bihar. He was parliamentary secretary to the government of Bihar (1937–39) and vice-president of the Bihar branch of the All-India Trade Union Congress (1940–46). Ram also became a member of the All-India Congress Committee and during World War II was twice imprisoned by the British (1940 and 1942–43). After independence he held a number of ministerial posts, with responsibility for labour affairs, agriculture, and communications, but was perhaps most effective as minister of defense (1970–74 and 1977–79). Deploring Prime Minister Indira Gandhi's seizure of emergency power in 1975, he formed (1977) the Congress for Democracy, which, in alliance with the Janata Party, defeated Gandhi in the 1977 general elections. Ram became deputy prime minister in 1979. After Gandhi's return to power in 1980, he was for a short time leader of the opposition but later rejoined the Congress.

Reed, Donna (DONNA BELLE MULLENGER), U.S. actress (b. Jan. 27, 1921, Denison, Iowa—d. Jan. 14, 1986, Beverly Hills, Calif.), capitalized on her wholesome farm girl image during a long television and motion picture career but, ironically, won an Academy Award as best supporting actress for her portrayal of a prostitute in *From Here to Eternity* (1953). After being named campus queen at Los Angeles City College (1940), Reed was pursued by talent scouts, whom she held at bay until the following year, when she made her motion picture debut in *The Get-Away.* She played a succession of "nice girls" in *Shadow of the Thin Man* (1941), *The Courtship of Andy Hardy* (1942), and *The Picture of Dorian Gray* (1945) before her first major role, as Jimmy Stewart's wife, Mary, in the film classic *It's a Wonderful Life* (1946). She appeared in more than 30 motion pictures before abandoning the wide screen for television in 1958. She was probably best remembered as the apron-clad devoted wife and mother on the television comedy "The Donna Reed Show" (1958–66). In 1984, after a long absence from television, Reed joined the cast of "Dallas" as Miss Ellie after actress Barbara Bel Geddes became ill. When the latter was reinstated in the role for the 1985–86 season, Reed, who had had a three-year contract, filed a $7.5 million lawsuit but accepted a $1 million settlement. She died of cancer of the pancreas.

Richards, Sir Gordon, British jockey (b. May 5, 1904, Oakengates, Shropshire, England—d. Nov. 10, 1986, Kintbury, Berkshire, England), was Britain's champion jockey in 26 seasons and at one time held the world record with 4,870 winning rides. He received a knighthood—he was the only jockey to have been so honoured—in 1953, the year in which he won the Derby on Sir Victor Sassoon's Pinza. He won 13 other classic races: the Oaks twice, the St. Leger five times, and the 2,000 and 1,000 Guineas three times each. One of 12 children of a former miner who kept ponies for hire, Richards left school at 13 and worked in a pit store warehouse until 1919, when he went to work as a stable boy for trainer Martin Hartigan at Foxhill, near Swindon, Wiltshire. He was unplaced in his first ride, at Lingfield (1920), but won the Apprentice Plate at Leicester (April 1921). He moved to Darling's stables at Beckhampton, Wiltshire, in 1930 and rode for many famous owners, including King George VI. In the 1933 season he rode 259 winners, beating the record held by Fred Archer (champion jockey 1874–86); in 1947 Richards achieved 269. After a nasty fall in 1954 he retired and took up training (1955–70). In this, although he loved the venture and found the challenge more exhilarating than that of racing, he was only moderately successful. In 1970 he became a racing manager and was active until his sudden death.

Rickover, Hyman George, U.S. naval officer (b. Jan. 27, 1900, Makov, Russia—d. July 8, 1986, Arlington, Va.), was a no-nonsense military dynamo who attacked naval bureaucracy, ignored red tape, cajoled subordinates, and defied protocol in his single-minded effort to launch the U.S. Navy into the nuclear submarine age, a feat he accomplished by designing and producing the world's first nuclear-powered engines and by developing the USS *Nautilus*, the world's first nuclear-propelled submarine. Rickover, who graduated from the U.S. Naval Academy at Annapolis, Md., in 1922, served as an ensign aboard the USS *Lavallette* and the USS *Nevada*, before returning to Annapolis to study electrical engineering. He later earned (1929) an M.S. in this field from Columbia University, New York City. After serving on submarine duty, Rickover was given command of the USS *Finch*, a minesweeper; in 1937 he reported for duty at a navy yard in the Philippines. He was later assigned (1939) to the Bureau of Ships of the Navy Department and served as head of its electrical section during World War II. For his wartime effort in mobilizing men and equipment to produce the Navy's electric power and lighting equipment, he was awarded the Legion of Merit. In 1946 he joined the Atomic Energy Commission's Manhattan Project at Oak Ridge, Tenn., where research was being conducted on atomic reactors. Rickover, who was convinced of the need to outfit submarines with nuclear power, persuaded Adm. Chester Nimitz, chief of naval operations, that his plan was feasible. In 1947 Rickover returned to the Bureau of Ships in charge of the Navy's nuclear propulsion program and inspired his handpicked team of specialists to deliver the *Nautilus*, whose keel was laid in June 1952 and which was launched on Jan. 21, 1954. Rickover was also responsible for the development of the first U.S. full-scale experimental nuclear power plant, at Shippingport, Pa. (1956–57). The fact that his promotion from captain to rear admiral was blocked twice would have forced his retirement, but his record was reevaluated, and he was promoted to rear admiral (1953), vice-admiral (1959), and admiral (1973) and was awarded a gold medal for his achievements. The "father of the nuclear navy" retired in 1982, at which time he voiced his misgivings about nuclear weapons. He was the author of *Education and Freedom* (1959), *American Education, a National Failure* (1963), and *How the Battleship Maine Was Destroyed* (1976).

Rous, Sir Stanley Ford, British sports administrator (b. April 25, 1895, Mutford, near Lowestoft, England—d. July 18, 1986, London, England), was secretary of England's Football Association from 1934 to 1961, president of the governing body of world football (soccer), the Fédération Internationale de Football Associations (FIFA), from 1961 to 1974, and finally honorary life president of FIFA. He redrafted many soccer rules and introduced the "diagonal" system under which referees move along an imaginary diagonal instead of pursuing play on all parts of the field. Following army service in World War I, he was sports master at Watford Grammar School until 1934; he achieved international status as a referee. During World War II he organized sports events to raise funds for the Red Cross, and in 1948 he served on the organizing committee for the London Olympic Games. He continued to be an active member of the British Olympic Committee, but his most enduring influence was on football, at both the national and international level. He influenced the British football associations to rejoin FIFA in 1947, thus ending a 20-year rift, introduced an international youth tournament, and encouraged exchanges of referees. In England he also helped to bring the game to unprecedented status as a national sport. Rous was made a Commander of the Order of the British Empire in 1943 and was knighted in 1949.

Rubbra, Edmund, British composer (b. May 23, 1901, Northampton, Northamptonshire, England—d. Feb. 14, 1986, Chalfont St. Peter, Buckinghamshire, England), was a prolific composer of 11 symphonies, four string quartets, and large quantities of church music and was recognized as one of the leading English exponents of the symphony in the mid-20th century. As a boy he was taught piano by his mother and gained musical exposure at his uncle's small music shop. At the age of 14 he left school to work as an office boy but was composing music as well. At the age of 16 he organized a concert devoted to the works of Cyril Scott, and as a result of this Rubbra became Scott's student. At the age of 19 Rubbra won a composition scholarship to the University of Reading, and the following year he was awarded an open scholarship to the Royal College of Music in London, where he studied composition with Gustav Holst and harmony and counterpoint with R. O. Morris. After leaving the college in 1925, he taught music and wrote critical reviews. His first symphony appeared in 1937, and his reputation grew rapidly with his second (1937) and third (1939) symphonies. He was soon widely regarded as one of the major English composers of his time. During World War II he served as an antiaircraft gunner before playing in a trio in the Army Music Unit; the group, formed with Erich Gruenberg and William Pleeth, continued performing after the war. Rubbra later served as a senior lecturer in music (1947–68) at the University of Oxford and professor of composition (1961–74) at London's Guildhall School of Music. He wrote *Holst: A Monograph* (1947) and *Counterpoint: A Survey* (1960).

Ruffing, Red (CHARLES HERBERT RUFFING), U.S. baseball player (b. May 3, 1904, Granville, Ill.—d. Feb. 17, 1986, Mayfield, Ohio), as the phenomenal right-handed pitcher for the New York Yankees (1930–46) and a powerhouse hitter besides, helped the Yankees capture seven pennants and six World Series championships during the 1930s and '40s. Ruffing, who had an unspectacular pitching career (1924–30) with the Boston Red Sox, winning only 39 and losing 96 games, reached his stride with the Yankees and in his first season with them posted a 15–5 record. During his 15 years with the team, he recorded only one losing season, in 1933. His 22-year career record included 273 wins and 225 losses and a lifetime batting average of .269. After the 1946 season Ruffing was traded to the Chicago White Sox. He retired as a player the following year but continued to manage minor league teams. He was inducted into the Baseball Hall of Fame in 1967.

Rulfo, Juan Pérez, Mexican writer (b. May 16, 1918, Sayula, Mexico—d. Jan. 7, 1986, Mexico City, Mexico), was an important and influential Latin-American author who was credited with being one of the founders of the "magic realism" school of writing, the techniques of which—such as flashbacks, interior monologues and dialogues, stream of consciousness, and atemporal structure—he used to create a unique

AP/WIDE WORLD

blend of realism and fantasy. He came from a family of prosperous landowners who lost their fortune in the brutal Cristero uprisings of 1926–29 and moved to Mexico City. Many of the short stories that were published in *El llano en llamas* (1953; *The Burning Plain*) portray the violence of Mexican village life and the bleak lives of the villagers. His highly regarded *Pedro Páramo* (1955) depicts the hardships inflicted on the villagers by the autocratic *cacique* (boss) and landowner Páramo, who eventually starves the people to death. Halfway through the novel it is revealed that all of the characters are dead. Rulfo, who never published a third book, counseled young writers at the Centro Mexicano de Escritores (Centre for Mexican Authors) and was awarded Mexico's National Prize of Letters in 1970 and Spain's Príncipe de Austurias in 1983.

Russell, Dora Winifred, British feminist and pacifist (b. April 3, 1894, Thornton Heath, Essex, England—d. May 31, 1986, Porthcurno, Cornwall, England), was a pioneer of women's rights and throughout her long life was a forceful and ebullient campaigner for peace. She was born Dora Black, the daughter of an eminent civil servant. She had wished to go on the stage but went instead to Girton College, University of Cambridge, where she gained a first-class degree in modern languages in 1915. She visited Russia in 1920 and accompanied the philosopher Bertrand Russell (whom she had met in 1919) to China. They married in 1921 and lived in

London before starting their progressive school, Beacon Hill, West Sussex, in 1927. Following their separation in 1932 (they were divorced three years later), she ran the school until the outbreak of World War II, when she worked for the Ministry of Information. She promoted friendship with the U.S.S.R. in her writings for the paper *British Ally.* In the 1950s and 1960s, appalled at the development of the cold war, she traveled through Europe, the U.S., the U.S.S.R., China, and India with the Women's Peace Caravan. She was a founder member of the National Council for Civil Liberties (1934) and of the Campaign for Nuclear Disarmament (1958). Her books include *Hypatia; or, Woman and Knowledge* (1925), *The Right to Be Happy* (1927), and *In Defence of Children* (1932). Her three volumes of autobiography, *The Tamarisk Tree* (1975–85), were partly responsible for her "rediscovery" by contemporary feminists.

Ryder, Robert Edward Dudley, British naval officer (b. Feb. 16, 1908—d. June 29, 1986, at sea), led the successful raid on the German-occupied French port of Saint-Nazaire in March 1942 and was among five members of the attacking force to win the Victoria Cross. Educated at Cheltenham College, he joined the Royal Navy in 1927 and had an adventurous career before the outbreak of World War II. He was a member of the Graham Land expedition, for which he won the Polar Medal. Torpedoed in June 1940, he clung to wreckage for four days before being rescued. In 1942 he was chosen to lead the Saint-Nazaire raid, designed to destroy the port's docks and prevent their use by the German battleship *Tirpitz* as a base for attacks on shipping in the Atlantic. The plan, code-named Operation Chariot, involved a force of 611 men, a destroyer, and several small vessels; the destroyer, *Campbeltown,* was to be packed with explosives and rammed into the dock gates. Despite heavy gunfire from the shore, this was done, and the *Campbeltown* exploded, destroying the dock gates and killing some 400 Germans. More than one-third of the raiding party were captured, and 169 died. Ryder described the operation in his book *The Attack on St. Nazaire* (1947). From 1950 to 1955 he was Conservative member of Parliament for Merton and Morden. Ryder died while on board a yacht in the English Channel.

Saifuddin Sa'adul Khairi Waddin, Sir Omar Ali, 28th sultan of Brunei (b. Sept. 23, 1916, Bandar Seri Begawan, Brunei—d. Sept. 7, 1986, Bandar Seri Begawan), was ruler of the then British-protected state from 1950 until his abdication in 1967. He remained politically influential, however, and was thought to have been responsible for the demand that Brunei should retain the services of a British Army Gurkha battalion after independence in 1984. In the same year, he became minister of defense. Educated at Malay College, Kuala Kangsar, Perak, Malaya, he worked in various government departments in Brunei before becoming grand vizier (first minister) and member of the State Council (1947–50) during the sultanate of his elder brother. As sultan himself, he was less anxious than some of his subjects, and even than the British, that his country should move toward independence. However, he produced a written constitution in 1959, when the British relinquished control of Brunei's internal affairs. During a revolt that year, Saifuddin had no hesitation in calling in British troops to quell it. He refused to take Brunei into the Federation of Malaysia, which was formed in 1963. A poet, a keen sportsman, and an Anglophile, he traveled frequently to Britain and Europe, once to North America, and twice on pilgrimage to Mecca.

Seifert, Jaroslav, Czech poet (b. Sept. 23, 1901, Prague, Austria-Hungary—d. Jan. 10, 1986, Prague, Czech.), in 1984 became the first Czech to be awarded the Nobel Prize for Literature. Before he received the prize, he was little known outside his native country, though he was greatly admired within Czechoslovakia, where he was named poet of the nation in 1966. Seifert, who after finishing his education worked as a journalist until 1950, published his first volume of poetry, *Mesto v slzach* ("City in Tears"), in 1920. At the time, his poems, reflecting his enthusiasm for Communism, were written in the proletarian mode. Following a visit to the U.S.S.R. in 1925, however, he became disenchanted with the revolutionary example afforded by that country. His impressions were expressed in *Slavik zpiva spatne* (1926; "The Nightingale Sings Poorly"). In 1929 he left the Communist Party to join the Social Democratic Party. While his work continued to be concerned with political developments within Czechoslovakia, his style became more lyrical. The German occupation of his country during World War II prompted *Svetlena odena* (1940; "Clothed in Light"), about Prague, which became one of his best known collections. After the Communists came to power in 1948, Seifert's work became less overtly political. He was, however, one of the Czech writers who spoke out against the Soviet intervention in 1968, and he later signed the "Charter 77" human rights document. When Seifert was awarded the Nobel Prize, the Czechoslovak authorities made no reference to his post-1968 work. During his lifetime Seifert published some 30 volumes of poetry, including *Na vlnach T.S.F.* (1925; "On Wireless Waves"), *Jablko z klina* (1933; "An Apple from the Lap"), *Zhasnete svetla* (1938; "Switch Off the Lights"), *Morovy sloup* (1977; "The Plague Column"), and *Destnik z Piccadilly* (1979; "Umbrella from Piccadilly"). Seifert was president of the Czechoslovak Writers' Union from 1969 until its dissolution the following year.

Semenov, Nikolay Nikolayevich, Soviet scientist (b. April 15, 1896, Saratov, Russia—d. Sept. 25, 1986, Moscow?, U.S.S.R.), was joint winner of the 1956 Nobel Prize for Chemistry and the first Soviet citizen to be thus honoured. He shared the prize with the English scientist Sir Cyril Hinshelwood. Both men conducted research on the mechanism of chemical chain reactions and their significance in relation to explosions. Semenov was the first to show that chain reaction is the norm in chemical transformation of matter; his discoveries had important implications for the refining of petroleum and natural gases, and this work also led him into the field of nuclear fission. Educated at the University of St. Petersburg (later Leningrad), Semenov graduated in 1917 and became a lecturer at the University of Tomsk in western Siberia. In 1920 he returned to Leningrad as assistant director and laboratory manager at the Physico-Technical Institute, where he became a professor in 1928. He was founder of and leading researcher (1931) at the Institute of Chemical Physics, becoming its director in 1939. After the institute moved from Leningrad to Moscow in 1943, he also became (1944) a professor at the Moscow State University. A corresponding member of the Soviet Academy of Sciences from 1929, he became a full member in 1932. He joined the Communist Party in 1947 and was a deputy to the U.S.S.R. Supreme Soviet. Semenov won the Stalin Prize (1941) and nine Orders of Lenin.

Shariat-Madari, Sayyed Mohammad Kazem, Iranian Islamic clergyman (b. 1905, Tabriz, Azerbaijan, Persia—d. April 3, 1986, Tehran, Iran), as one of the five Shi'ah grand ayatollahs, or "sources of imitation," was the leading representative of the clergy during the final years of Shah Mohammad Reza Pahlavi's reign. An early associate of Ayatollah Ruhollah Khomeini, he held more liberal views, and the two men fell out after the establishment of the Islamic republic. He remained an influential figure but was unable to use his influence to steer the country toward more moderate policies. He studied in Najaf, Iraq, and then in Qom, Iran, where he met Khomeini and with him began energetic campaigns to set up theological schools and support charities. Both men opposed the land reforms of the 1960s, and Shariat-Madari protected Khomeini when he was accused of involvement in antigovernment riots. Khomeini was exiled, and Shariat-Madari remained to lead the country's Muslim clergy. On Khomeini's return, Shariat-Madari opposed the 1979 constitution and was placed under house arrest. He was supported by the Muslim People's Republican Party but dissociated himself from the party's revolt in Tabriz, which was savagely put down, losing perhaps his last opportunity to present a serious challenge to the Khomeini regime. In 1982 he was accused of complicity in a plot against Khomeini's life. He denied this but remained in official disgrace.

Shinwell, Emanuel Shinwell, BARON, British politician and centenarian (b. Oct. 18, 1884, London, England—d. May 8, 1986, London), was an ebullient and outspoken member of the Labour Party who for over 60 years aroused controversy and won affection among his fellow parliamentarians. "Manny" Shinwell was the son of Jewish-Polish clothing manufacturers in London's East End; the family later moved to Glasgow, where, at the age of 11, Shinwell was apprenticed to a tailor. He joined a trade union in 1901, later organized striking Clydeside seamen, and after a demonstration in 1919 was imprisoned for incitement to riot. He was Labour member of Parliament for Linlithgow (1922–24 and 1928–31), serving as parliamentary secretary to the Department of Mines (1924 and 1930–31) and as financial secretary to the War Office (1929–30). He lost his seat in 1931 but four years later was elected for the Seaham division of Durham, defeating his former leader, Ramsay MacDonald, who had deserted Labour in 1931 to form the National Government. Although staunchly patriotic, Shinwell stayed outside the World War II coalition government. When Labour gained power, he was appointed minister of fuel and power (1945–47) and carried through the nationalization of the mines. Severely criticized for coal shortages during the bitter winter of 1946–47, he lost his seat in the Cabinet until appointed minister of defense in 1950. He sat in the House of Commons as member for the Easington division of Durham (1950–70), but he lost his seat on Labour's National Executive in 1951 and four years later left the shadow cabinet. Chairman of the Parliamentary Labour Party for the period 1964–67, he resigned after strongly opposing an attempt to join the European Communities. He went to the House of Lords as a life peer in 1970. Concern over the growth of militant left-wing influence in the Labour Party caused him to resign the post of party whip in 1982. His 100th birthday was enthusiastically celebrated by politicians of all persuasions; although a hard-hitting speaker, he had always been generous to individuals and was much loved. Shinwell's autobiographical books include *Conflict Without Malice* (1955) and *My First Ninety-Six Years* (1981); *The Labour Story* (1963) and *Lead with the Left* (1981) proclaim his political message.

Smith, Kate (KATHRYN ELIZABETH SMITH), U.S. singer (b. May 1, 1909, Greenville, Va.—d. June 17, 1986, Raleigh, N.C.), became a beloved symbol of patriotism with her stirring rendition of Irving Berlin's "God Bless America," which served as an inspiration for the nation during World War II. She was only a teenager when she decided on a career in show business, and in 1926 she landed a role in the Broadway musical *Honeymoon Lane.* She was a smashing success in a string of Broadway comedies in which cast members poked fun at her weight, but they were roles she despised. In 1930 she met Columbia Records executive Ted Collins, who became her manager and showcased her untrained, yet robust contralto singing voice in a record long-running engagement at the Palace Theatre in New York City. The following year she made her radio debut on "Kate Smith Sings" (1931–47) and became familiar to thousands of listeners with such songs as "The Music Goes Round and Round," "The Last Time I Saw Paris," and her theme song, "When the Moon Comes over the Mountain." It was in 1938, however, when she gained exclusive rights to sing "God Bless America," which became the nation's unofficial anthem, that she won the hearts of the public. During World War II she sold a phenomenal $600 million worth of war bonds and entertained troops throughout the country with her traveling show. Her popularity was so universal that when Pres. Franklin D. Roosevelt introduced her to King George VI in 1939, he said simply, "This is Kate Smith—this is America." In the 1940s she was dubbed the "first lady of radio," and in 1943 she appeared in the motion picture *This Is the Army.* During her career she recorded nearly 3,000 songs, and some 600 of them made the hit parade. In 1950 she branched into television with "The Kate Smith Hour," which was broadcast until 1955, and in 1960 she briefly returned to the medium with a new variety show, but it was canceled within six months. She later appeared as a guest on many television variety shows, and during the 1970s her rendition of "God Bless America" rallied the struggling Philadelphia Flyers hockey team to a winning streak. After a stroke in 1976 she made few public appearances. In 1982 she was awarded the Presidential Medal of Freedom by Pres. Ronald Reagan. Smith also published two autobiographies, *Living in a Great Big Way* (1938) and *Upon My Lips a Song* (1960).

Spinelli, Altiero, Italian politician (b. Aug. 31, 1907, Rome, Italy—d. May 23, 1986, Rome), founded the European Federalist Movement in 1943 and continued to work throughout his life for its cause. As a student he became a Communist and in 1927 Mussolini sentenced him for antifascist activities to ten years' imprisonment and six years' exile on the island of Ventotene. He left the Communist Party in 1937, and in 1941, while in exile, he joined Ernesto Rossi and Eugenio Colorni in writing "The Ventotene Manifesto" in support of European federalism. After his release in 1943, he continued to campaign for European federalism, as secretary-general of the Italian Action Party (1943–62), as founder and director of the Institute of International Affairs in Rome (1967–70), and as a member of the Executive Commission of the European Communities (1970–76). He was then elected to the Italian and European parliaments, and in 1984 he succeeded in pushing through the Treaty of European Unity, which called for the eventual transfer of political power in the European Communities to the European Parliament. Spinelli was the author of a number of books on European federalism, notably *The European Adventure* (1972).

Stockton, (Maurice) Harold Macmillan, 1st Earl, British statesman (b. Feb. 10, 1894, London, England—d. Dec. 29, 1986, Chelwood Gate, West Sussex, England), was prime minister from January 1957 to October 1964 and recently the proud old man of British politics. He succeeded unexpectedly to the prime ministership following the illness and resignation of Sir Anthony Eden. Macmillan emerged as more likely to restore Conservative morale after the Suez crisis (1956) than the better known but enigmatic R. A. Butler. The main goals of his administration were friendship with the U.S., a (frustrated) desire to join the European Economic Community, and an accelerated but dignified retreat from empire. He initiated a thaw in East-West relations and with U.S. Pres. John F. Kennedy negotiated a nuclear test ban treaty with the U.S.S.R. (1963). A Conservative of the Disraeli "one nation" school, he sought at home to increase living standards for all, and he pursued reflationary policies in a determination to avoid unemployment. Macmillan came to power when postwar austerities seemed at last forgotten, and his (much misquoted) statement "most of our people have never had it so good" expressed his and the country's mood. His popularity ratings long remained high, and the nickname "Supermac," ironically employed by the cartoonist Vicky, stuck and came to be

PAMELA CHANDLER—CAMERA PRESS/PHOTO TRENDS

used with admiration. Decisive and a skillful delegator, he maintained a facade of "unflappability," but in private he described himself as "a strange, buttoned-up person."

Great-grandson of a Scottish crofter, Macmillan belonged to the family that founded and owned the well-known publishing house. Educated at Eton College and at Balliol College, Oxford, he fought in France during World War I and was three times wounded. He was aide-de-camp (1919–20) to the governor-general of Canada, the 9th duke of Devonshire, whose daughter, Lady Dorothy Cavendish, he married (1920). His firsthand experience of the horrors of the Depression led him, as MP for Stockton-on-Tees (1924–29, 1931–45), to advocate Keynesian policies then unpopular in his party; he was also out of step in opposing appeasement of Hitler and Mussolini. During World War II, as minister resident at Allied Headquarters in North Africa (1942–45), he established an excellent accord with Gen. Dwight Eisenhower, and he later played a major role during the Allied occupation of Italy and the British intervention in Greece. Losing his Stockton seat in the Labour landslide of 1945, he became MP for Bromley, Kent (1945–64). As minister of housing and local government (1951–54), he triumphantly fulfilled a Conservative pledge to build 300,000 new houses a year. He then served successively as minister of defense (1954–55), foreign secretary (April–December 1955), and chancellor of the Exchequer (1955–57). As prime minister he toured Africa and made, in Cape Town (1960), his famous "wind of change" speech, which predicted the rise of African nationalism and criticized the policy of apartheid. By 1962 support for Macmillan was beginning to decline; after a number of by-election disasters he dismissed seven senior ministers (July 1962) in the so-called "night of the long knives." A series of political scandals (1962–63) followed. Then (October 1963) Macmillan fell ill and resigned while hospitalized. After his retirement he wrote his memoirs (six volumes, 1966–73), helped to run the Macmillan publishing business, and took an active role in his duties as chancellor of the University of Oxford. He received the Order of Merit in 1976 and was created earl in 1984.

Streatfeild, (Mary) Noel, British novelist (b. Dec. 24, 1895, Amberley, Sussex, England—d. Sept. 11, 1986, London, England), made her name as a writer of children's books, and her much acclaimed *Ballet Shoes* (1936) popularized "career novels." A rebellious younger daughter in a strict clerical household, she decided at the age of 12 to become an actress. She attended the Academy of Dramatic Art in London and toured in Australia and southern Africa. Streatfeild turned to writing in 1929 to enable her to live with her widowed mother. Her first novel, *Whicharts* (1931), and its immediate successors were for adults, but she was advised to turn to children's books. Another of her career novels, *The Circus Is Coming* (1938), won the 1938 Library Association's Carnegie Medal. She cleverly exploited topical themes by writing on British evacuees in *Children of Primrose Lane* (1941) and by producing *The Boy Pharaoh* (1972) at the time of the London Tutankhamen exhibition. *The Bell Family* (1954), *New Town* (1960), *The Growing Summer* (1966), and *Thursday's Child* (1970) all became television serials. Streatfeild wrote three autobiographical volumes, *A Vicarage Family* (1963), *Away from the Vicarage* (1965), and *Beyond the Vicarage* (1971), and a perceptive study of the children's writer E. Nesbit, *Magic and the Magician* (1958).

Szent-Gyorgyi, Albert, Hungarian biochemist (b. Sept. 16, 1893, Budapest, Austria-Hungary—d. Oct. 22, 1986, Woods Hole, Mass.), was awarded the 1937 Nobel Prize for Physiology or Medicine for his work on biologic combustion and specifically for isolating vitamin C; he also conducted important research on the physiology of muscles. After earning (1917) his M.D. from the University of Budapest, Szent-Gyorgyi received (1927) a Ph.D. in physiology from the University of Cambridge. While working there, and at the Mayo Clinic, Rochester, Minn., Szent-Gyorgyi discovered and isolated (1928) an organic compound, which he named hexuronic acid (later renamed ascorbic acid), from plant juice and adrenal gland extracts. Four years later, while serving on the faculty of the University of Szeged, Hung., he began conducting tests on paprika and found that it yielded substantial amounts of the acid. He identified the acid as identical to the antiscurvy vitamin C, discovered by Axel Holst and Alfred Frölich in 1907. As the first Hungarian to be awarded a Nobel Prize, he became a national hero. He stayed in his native country during World War II, but he went into hiding when his anti-Nazi activities became known. After the country was liberated (1945) by the Soviet Army, he was offered the presidency of Hungary, but he declined. Two years later, disillusioned with the Soviet domination of his country, he immigrated to the U.S. and took up residence in Woods Hole, where he was immediately appointed director of the Institute for Muscle Research. Szent-Gyorgyi isolated two kinds of muscle protein from the substance myosin. He named the rod-shaped particles myosin and the minute globular beads actin. He called the compound actomyosin. In his research on the physiology of muscles, he identifed actomyosin as the compound that causes muscles to contract and discovered that the compound adenosine triphosphate (ATP) is the immediate source of energy necessary for contraction. His research helped provide a better understanding of such diseases as muscular dystrophy. In 1954 he was awarded the prestigious Albert Lasker Award for his work on the physiology of muscle contraction. His work on muscles also led to research into the causes of cell division and the causes of cancer. A fierce opponent of U.S. involvement in Vietnam, he wrote *The Crazy Ape* (1970). His scientific books include *On Oxidation, Fermentation, Vitamins, Health, and Disease* (1940), *Chemical Physiology of Contraction in Body and Heart Muscle* (1953), and *Introduction to a Submolecular Biology* (1960).

Tarkovsky, Andrey Arsenyevich, Soviet film director (b. April 4, 1932, Moscow, U.S.S.R.—d. Dec. 29, 1986, Paris, France), was internationally acclaimed for his film *Andrey Rublyov,* which won the Critics' Prize at the 1969 Cannes Film Festival. Its religious theme and complex structure bore resemblance to the career of the director himself, who had puzzled the Soviet authorities with whom he was frequently in conflict, not least because he was a Christian. Though for most of his career he was allowed the facilities to make films in his own country, his films were given a much wider showing abroad. The son of the poet Arseny Tarkovsky, he studied music and painting before going to the State Film School. His diploma work, *The Steamroller and the Violin* (1960), won a prize at the New York Film Festival, and his first full-length film, *Ivan's Childhood*, was awarded the Golden Lion in Venice in 1962. Though the three-hour-long *Andrey Rublyov* was an intellectually demanding work, it gained immediate acceptance with Western audiences and was eventually hailed in the Soviet Union. Two science-fiction films, *Solaris* (1972) and *Stalker* (1978), employed few special effects but pursued Tarkovsky's central spiritual themes, while *Mirror* (1975) was a fragmented reflection of the director's own childhood. His last two major works, *Nostalgia* (1983) and *The Sacrifice* (1986), were made after he had settled in Western Europe. His 1984 decision not to return to the U.S.S.R. resulted in the revocation of his citizenship. Tarkovsky also staged an opera, *Boris Godunov*, in London in 1983, and his book, *Sculpting in Time* (1986), explored his concept of the central role of the director in the art of cinema.

Taussig, Helen Brooke, U.S. cardiologist (b. May 24, 1898, Cambridge, Mass.—d. May 20, 1986, West Chester, Pa.), achieved international recognition as codeveloper (1944; with Alfred Blalock) of an operation to treat congenital heart defects in "blue babies," infants with a blue colouring because of the lack of oxygen in their blood. The Blalock-Taussig surgical procedure involved devising an artificial ductus arteriosus for children dying of anoxemia; it saved thousands of lives. Taussig attended Radcliffe College, Cambridge, Mass., and the University of California before studying medicine at Harvard University as a special student (women were not admitted to the regular session at that time). She then attended Boston University but earned her M.D. from Johns Hopkins University, Baltimore, Md., in 1927. She served (1928–30) her internship in pediatrics there and then was appointed head of the Children's Heart Clinic of the Harriet Lane Home, the pediatrics division of Johns Hopkins Hospital, where she remained until her retirement in 1963. After years of research on congenital malformations of the heart, she discovered that blue babies could be saved by an operation on their constricted arteries. Taussig and Blalock experimented on some 200 dogs before they performed their first human surgery in 1944. The "first lady" of pediatric cardiology also conducted a first-hand investigation of the epidemic of birth defects in West Germany attributed to their mothers having taken the tranquilizer thalidomide. When she returned to the U.S., she warned physicians about the dangers of the drug and recommended to the U.S. Food and Drug Administration that thalidomide be barred from the market. In recognition of her contributions, she was awarded the Presidential Medal of Freedom in 1964, and in 1965 she became the first woman president of the American Heart Association. In later years she researched and studied deformed hearts in birds.

AP/WIDE WORLD

Tenzing Norgay (Namgyal Wangdi), Sherpa mountaineer (b. 1914, Tami, Solo Khumbu, Nepal—d. May 9, 1986, Darjeeling, India), accompanied the New Zealander Edmund Hillary on the first ascent to the summit of Mt. Everest, on May 29, 1953. Tenzing himself was unsure of the exact date of his birth. The son of a herdsman, he tended his father's yaks before going to Darjeeling in 1932 to work as an expedition porter. He was taken on the British Everest expeditions of 1935 and 1936 and in H. W. Tilman's expedition of 1938 carried loads to 8,296 m (27,200 ft), thereby earning the Tiger Medal of the Himalayan Club. During World War II he served as a guide with the Chitral Scouts and as a ski instructor to the Indian Army. He was on expeditions to the Hindu Kush in 1945 and the Karakoram Range in 1950. As sirdar (organizer of porters) he accompanied two Swiss Everest expeditions in 1952 and, climbing with Raymond Lambert, came very close to the summit. Tenzing was again chosen as sirdar of John Hunt's 1953 British expedition. Following the failure of the first attempt on the summit, he and Hillary formed the second, successful, assault team. Tenzing received Britain's George Medal, the Star of Nepal, and the U.S. National Geographic Society's Hubbard Medal for his success. He was field director of training at the Himalayan Mountain Institute from its foundation by the Indian government in 1954 until 1976. Tenzing continued to participate in major expeditions and traveled widely, to North America, the U.S.S.R., Europe, Japan, New Zealand, and Antarctica.

Tierno Galván, Enrique, Spanish politician (b. Feb. 8, 1918, Madrid, Spain—d. Jan. 19, 1986, Madrid), founded a small clandestine socialist group in 1954 (later the Popular Socialist Party), which later merged with the Spanish Socialist Workers' Party, and in 1979 was elected mayor of Madrid. Tierno, who exhibited a studious and erudite manner, was reelected in 1983 and gained immense popularity for his opposition to urban property speculation, promotion of conservation, and support for a cultural revival. He served (1953–65) as professor of political science at the University of Salamanca until he was dismissed by the Franco government for joining with students in antigovernment demonstrations. In 1962 he founded a university reform movement. Tierno became a mediating figure between the older Socialist leaders exiled in France and those newer leaders who had remained in Spain, but in 1965 he was expelled from the grouping by the leaders in France. During periods of self-imposed exile, Tierno taught at Princeton University, Bryn Mawr (Pa.) College, and the University of Puerto Rico. Following the death of Franco in 1976, he regained his chair at the University of Salamanca. But his party failed to win much support during the elections, and it merged with its sometime rival, the Socialist Workers' Party, in 1978. More a scholar than a man of action, Tierno was a natural loner whom the people of Madrid ultimately took to their hearts as "the old professor."

Trevelyan, John, British film censor (b. July 11, 1903, Beckenham, Kent, England—d. Aug. 15, 1986, London, England), was secretary of the British Board of Film Censors (BBFC; later the British Board of Film Classification) from 1958 to 1971. Trevelyan, who once stated that, in theory, he did not believe in censorship, nonetheless insisted that safeguards were necessary to shield impressionable children. He guided the British film industry during a transitional period in which public taste became less puritanical and more permissive. Trevelyan studied history at Trinity College, Cambridge, before teaching in Africa and then served as an educational administrator in Britain and in Germany, where he set up schools for the children of Allied soldiers. After writing an article attacking the film censors for not heeding the effects that films have on children, Trevelyan was invited to join the BBFC as an examiner in the early 1950s; eight years later he was appointed secretary. He took a keen interest in the industry and won the respect and confidence of filmmakers by consulting with them about scripts even before production started. He favoured liberalization of the rules but was aware of the possibility that a reaction against "permissiveness" could exploit the laws against obscene publications. He attempted to prevent police seizure of the Andy Warhol film *Flesh* (1971), and on other occasions he exploited the law himself to encourage limited local exhibition of films generally refused a certificate by the BBFC. Trevelyan published his views in *What the Censor Saw* (1973). He was made a Commander of the Order of the British Empire in 1971.

Vaidya, Arun Shridhar, Indian army officer (b. Jan. 27, 1926, Bombay, India—d. Aug. 10, 1986, Pune, Maharashtra), as chief of staff from August 1983 until January 1986, was responsible for mounting the military attack ordered by Prime Minister Indira Gandhi in June 1984 on the Golden Temple at Amritsar, Punjab, which was being used as an arsenal by Sikh extremists. When infantry assault proved unsuccessful, tanks were sent in, and as a result the temple, the Sikhs' holiest shrine, was severely damaged. Though Vaidya subsequently allowed the reinstatement of some Sikh army mutineers, he was not safe from Sikh revenge; he was the object of numerous death threats, and his assassination, like that of Indira Gandhi in October 1984, was a direct result of the assault on the temple. Born of a Brahman family, Vaidya was commissioned in the Deccan Horse in 1945 and served briefly as a tank officer when the British Army was driving the Japanese from Burma. He was an infantry commander in the Ladakh area of Kashmir during the Chinese invasion of 1962 and again in the Indo-Pakistan wars of 1965 and 1971, commanding a brigade of the Deccan Horse in 1965 and an armoured division that won a notable victory in 1971. He twice received the Mahavir Chakra, one of the Indian Army's highest awards.

Vallee, Rudy (Hubert Prior Vallee), U.S. singer (b. July 28, 1901, Island Pond, Vt.—d. July 3, 1986, Hollywood, Calif.), enjoyed mass adulation during the 1920s and '30s and made female audiences swoon with his collegiate good looks and twangy baritone crooning through a hand-held megaphone. Vallee, who played his saxophone at dances to earn tuition for the University of Maine and then Yale University, interrupted his education in 1924 to perform at the Savoy Hotel in London. While there he adopted his theme song, "My Time Is Your Time," and a suave continental manner that made him especially appealing when he returned to the U.S. After earning a B.A. in philosophy at Yale in 1927, he formed his band, the Yale Collegians (later renamed the Connecticut Yankees), and secured an engagement in New York City at the Heigh-Ho Club, the inspiration for his trademark greeting, "Heigh-ho, everybody!" He became a singing idol and enthralled his fans with his renditions of such songs as "When It's Springtime in the Rockies," the University of Maine "Stein Song," "Cheerful Little Earful," and "I'm Just a Vagabond Lover." In 1928 his 16-piece ensemble began broadcasting from the Heigh-Ho Club; they enjoyed a ten-year stint on "The Fleischmann Variety Hour" radio program. His screen debut in the 1929 motion picture *The Vagabond Lover* was followed by starring roles in a string of light romantic comedies, including *Sweet Music*, *Gold Diggers in Paris*, *Second Fiddle*, and *The Palm Beach Story*. After serving in the Coast Guard during

World War II, Vallee returned to radio in 1944 and performed in films and clubs; he did not make the transition to television in the 1950s. In later years he portrayed eccentric millionaires on stage and screen. He was especially lauded for his Broadway (1961–64) and film (1967) portrayal of tycoon J. B. Biggley in *How to Succeed in Business Without Really Trying.* Vallee also wrote three autobiographies, *Vagabond Dreams Come True* (1930), *My Time Is Your Time* (1962), and *Let the Chips Fall* (1975).

Veeck, Bill (William Louis Veeck), U.S. sports executive (b. Feb. 9, 1914, Hinsdale, Ill.—d. Jan. 2, 1986, Chicago, Ill.), as the maverick baseball owner of the minor league Milwaukee Brewers (1941) and three major league teams, including the Cleveland Indians (1946–49), the St. Louis Browns (1951–53), and the Chicago White Sox (1958–61 and 1975–81), was beloved by baseball fans and reviled by fellow owners for his flamboyant contributions to the game, including the first exploding scoreboard and the appearance (Aug. 19, 1951) of a midget as a pinch hitter. Veeck, the son of a sportswriter who later served for 24 years as president of the Chicago Cubs professional baseball team, developed an abiding love for baseball as a youth. His fondest dream was to be remembered as one of the boys who planted the legendary ivy at Wrigley Field. After the death of his father in 1933, Veeck joined the Cubs as an office boy but continued his education by attending night school at the Chicago campus of Northwestern University. After an injury during World War II forced the amputation of his right leg below the knee, the spunky Veeck sported a peg leg. During his heyday Veeck was responsible for breaking the American League's colour barrier by signing Larry Doby and pitcher Satchel Paige, who helped spur the Cleveland Indians to their first pennant in 28 years. In 1975 he acquired the White Sox a second time to save them from being moved to Seattle. A supreme showman who had a keen knowledge of the game and a deep devotion to its fans, Veeck was often referred to as the "P. T. Barnum of baseball." He placed players' names on the backs of their uniforms, gave orchids to female fans, tucked gift certificates under stadium seats, and sent circus clowns to the coaching lines. He wrote such books as *Veeck, as in Wreck* (1962) and *The Hustler's Handbook* (1965).

Wallis, Hal B. (Harold Brent Wallis), U.S. motion-picture producer (b. Sept. 14, 1898, Chicago, Ill.—d. Oct. 5, 1986, Rancho Mirage, Calif.), was an eclectic filmmaker whose credits included such classics as *Little Caesar* (1930), *The Maltese Falcon* (1941), *Casablanca* (1942), and *The Rainmaker* (1956). Wallis, who left school at the age of 14 to help support his family, worked as an office boy and later as a traveling salesman before going (1922) to Los Angeles, where he secured a job as manager of a movie palace. The following year he was invited to join Warner Brothers as a member of the publicity staff, and by 1930 he had been made a producer. In 1933 he succeeded Darryl F. Zanuck as executive producer. At Warner Brothers he turned out such films as *Captain Blood* (1935), *The Charge of the Light Brigade* (1936), *Jezebel* (1938), *Dark Victory* (1939), and *Yankee Doodle Dandy* (1942). In 1944 he left Warner Brothers to form Hal Wallis Productions, and he became the highly successful independent producer of *Come Back, Little Sheba* (1952); such Elvis Presley films as *Loving You* (1957) and *G.I. Blues* (1960); vehicles for Dean Martin and Jerry Lewis including *My Friend Irma* (1949) and *Living It Up* (1954); lavish costume dramas such as *Becket* (1964) and *Anne of a Thousand Days* (1969); and westerns including *Gunfight at the O.K. Corral* (1957), *True Grit* (1969), and *Rooster Cogburn* (1975). His pictures were released through an independent arrangement with Paramount and then with Universal Studios. He was also credited with discovering such stars as Shirley MacLaine, Errol Flynn, Burt Lancaster, and Kirk Douglas. During his long career Wallis produced or oversaw some 400 feature-length films; they received 121 Academy Award nominations and garnered 32 Oscars. Wallis received the Academy of Motion Picture Arts and Sciences Irving G. Thalberg Award for outstanding producers in 1938 and 1943. In 1970 the Museum of Modern Art launched a retrospective of some of his works, and in 1980 Wallis published *Starmaker: The Autobiography of Hal Wallis.*

Warner, Rex Ernest, British author (b. March 9, 1905, Birmingham, Warwickshire, England—d. June 24, 1986, Wallingford, Oxfordshire, England), enjoyed wide popularity with his translations from Greek, versions of classical mythology, and historical novels but was probably best remembered for his experimental, politically allegorical novels. The first of these, *The Wild Goose Chase* (1937), was written while he was teaching in Egypt and was heavily influenced by the work of Franz Kafka. Warner studied at Wadham College, University of Oxford, where he was a contemporary and friend of such leading writers as W. H. Auden and Stephen Spender. *The Wild Goose Chase* was followed by *The Professor* (1938) and *The Aerodrome* (1941), both suggesting a decline in human values in confrontation with totalitarianism and nihilism. His liberal and Christian beliefs were expressed in such works as *The Cult of Power* (1946) and his translation of the *Confessions* of St. Augustine (1963). After serving as a member of the Allied Control Commission in Berlin and then for two years as director of the British Institute in Athens, Warner continued his academic career, including ten years, from 1964, at the University of Connecticut. His historical novels include *The Young Caesar* (1958) and *Imperial Caesar* (1960), the latter of which won the 1961 James Tait Black Memorial Prize.

Wedel, Cynthia Clark, U.S. religious leader (b. Aug. 26, 1908, Dearborn, Mich—d. Aug. 24, 1986, Alexandria, Va.), as a prominent ecumenicist was the first woman elected president (1969–72) of the National Council of Churches of Christ in the U.S.A.; she also served as president (1975–83) of the World Council of Churches. Wedel was a vigorous Episcopal churchwoman who volunteered her services to the Red Cross, the Girl Scouts, and the Public Welfare Advisory Committee of the District of Columbia. She earned a Ph.D. in psychology at George Washington University, Washington, D.C., in 1957. In 1954 she became a member of the board of directors of the National Council of Churches and wrote several discussion and study guides, including *Citizenship, Our Christian Concern* (1952), *What of the Women?* (1953), and *Women in the Church* (1955). Wedel became assistant general secretary of the National Council in 1962 and held that post until 1965, when she assumed the position of associate general secretary. On Dec. 4, 1969, in the first contested election in the organization's history, Wedel was chosen president of the National Council of Churches, receiving 387 of the 480 votes cast and defeating the Rev. Albert B. Cleague, pastor of the Shrine of the Black Madonna in Detroit. Some black church leaders asked for her withdrawal, charging that Wedel was a compromise choice intended to prevent a black from acceding to the presidency. She refused their request and countered that women were also victims of discrimination and that her election was a "belated recognition of their importance in the church."

Wheldon, Sir Huw Pyrs, British television manager and presenter (b. May 7, 1916, Prestatyn, Flintshire [now Clwyd], Wales—d. March 14, 1986, London, England), as managing director (1968–75) of BBC Television, was probably best known to the viewing public as the suave commentator who described the palaces and art treasures of the British royal family for the series "Royal Heritage" (1977). Of a Welsh-speaking family, he was educated at Friars School, Bangor, and at the London School of Economics. During World War II he was commissioned in the Royal Welsh Fusiliers and served in the Middle East and northwestern Europe, winning the Military Cross. He was Arts Council director for Wales (1946–48) and from 1949 was involved in the planning for the Festival of Britain in 1951. Wheldon joined the BBC's publicity department in 1952 and soon switched to programs, first appearing as a children's interviewer for "All Your Own." He became head of documentary programs (1962) and also head of music (1963) before being made controller of programs in 1965. Wheldon also ran the successful arts magazine program "Monitor" (1958–64). His notable television series included the controversial "Yesterday's Men" (1971), on Labour Party leaders, "The British Empire" (1972), and "Destination D-Day" (1984). Wheldon was knighted in 1976 and received the gold and silver medals of the Royal Television Society, of which he was president (1979–85), and an International Emmy (1981).

White, Theodore Harold, U.S. author (b. May 6, 1915, Boston, Mass.—d. May 15, 1986, New York, N.Y.), was a master storyteller who captured the imagination of his readers with his four-book *Making of the President* series, which conveyed the behind-the-scenes excitement of the U.S. electoral process. His innovative approach, using novelistic techniques to chronicle history, was elevated to an art form, and he was awarded the 1962 Pulitzer Prize for general nonfiction for *The Making of the President, 1960.* In later years White had reservations about his pioneering microscopic examination of political candidates; he felt that too many journalists had adopted his technique, thus making "behind-the-scenes" coverage impossible. Though White's father was a lawyer, he collected rents for slumlords to maintain the family during the Depression, and White as a boy hawked newspapers on streetcars before dawn. After graduating from Boston Latin School in 1932, he entered Harvard University on a scholarship awarded to newsboys and earned (1938) a B.A. summa cum laude in history. In the same year, he embarked on world travels that took him to China, where his reporting skill soon gained him assignment as *Time* magazine's Far Eastern correspondent and head of its China bureau from 1939 to 1945. His departure from *Time* was followed immediately by the publication of his first book, *Thunder out of China* (1946; with Annalee Jacoby), a controversial study critical of the Nationalist Chinese, based on White's years in that turbulent country. He served as European correspondent for the Overseas News Agency (1948–50) and for *The Reporter* (1950–53). White worked for *Collier's* magazine until it folded in 1956 and then began writing novels, including *The Mountain Road* (1958) and *The View from the Fortieth Floor* (1960); but it was for his *Making of the President* books (covering the elections of 1960, 1964, 1968, and 1972) that he gained renown. Some of his other works included *Fire in the Ashes* (1953), *Breach of Faith: The Fall of Richard Nixon* (1975), *In Search of History: A Personal Adventure* (1978), and *America in Search of Itself: The Making of the President, 1956–80* (1982). The witty raconteur, who was affectionately known as "Teddy," was also a member (1971–86) of the Encyclopædia Britannica board of directors.

Wilson, Teddy (Theodore Wilson), U.S. jazz pianist (b. Nov. 24, 1912, Austin, Texas—d. July 31, 1986, New Britain, Conn.), was a superb technician whose subtle and elegant piano playing was ideally suited to the singing of Billie Holiday and to the sound of Benny Goodman's (*q.v.*) trio (with drummer Gene Krupa) and quartet (with vibraphonist Lionel Hampton). He was instrumental in breaking the colour barrier in popular music when in 1936 he joined Goodman's previously all-white band, making it one of the first integrated groups ever to perform in public. Wilson, who spent a year studying music at Talladega (Ala.) College, secured his first professional work in Detroit in 1929 with

Speed Webb. He then settled in Chicago and performed with several bands before playing with Louis Armstrong's band in 1933. Wilson's unique piano style, influenced by Earl Hines, Fats Waller, and Art Tatum, was a streamlined and lightened approach to the two-fisted style of the 1920s; he used his right hand to spin gliding melodies while his left hand delineated the harmonies at a leisurely tempo. After serving as an important anchor in the Goodman bands (1936–39), Wilson formed his own big band in 1939, but it lasted only a year. He led a highly successful sextet from 1940 until 1944, when he rejoined Goodman. During his more than 50-year career, he accompanied such singers as Ella Fitzgerald, Sarah Vaughan, and Mildred Bailey, made numerous recordings with Goodman and other artists, and toured extensively with Goodman for "reunions" and concerts, notably their 1962 trip to the U.S.S.R. Wilson also appeared with Goodman in such films as *Make Mine Music* and *The Benny Goodman Story.* He made frequent solo tours of Europe. In 1985 Wilson excited audiences at Carnegie Hall when he evoked the magic of his stunning improvisations and delicate touch at a concert featuring his music.

Windsor, Duchess of (Wallis Warfield Simpson), U.S.-born wife of Prince Edward, duke of Windsor (b. June 19, 1896, Blue Ridge Summit, Pa.—d. April 24, 1986, Paris, France), was a complex and intriguing woman who captured the attention of the world when on Dec. 11, 1936, King Edward VIII announced that he was abdicating the British throne for "the woman I love." Their romance, one of the great love stories of the century, aroused controversy because Simpson, a twice-divorced commoner, could not be accepted as queen. In spite of opposition from Prime Minister Stanley Baldwin, his ministers, the royal family, and the Church of England, Edward persisted in his decision to marry Simpson. After her second divorce was finalized, the couple married on June 3, 1937, in a Church of England ceremony at Monts, France.

Bessie Wallis Warfield was an only child whose father died when she was five months old. She and her mother lived in genteel poverty, but Bessie was educated in private schools by her wealthy bachelor uncle, Solomon Davies Warfield. At the age of 20 she married (1916) navy pilot Earl Winfield Spencer, but they were divorced in 1927. The following year she married shipping broker Ernest Simpson in London. She first met Edward (then prince of Wales) in 1930, and in 1932 the Simpsons received the first of many invitations to Fort Belvedere, his country home. In Ernest's absence on business, Wallis accompanied the prince's party to Biarritz (August 1934), and she often acted as his hostess. Meanwhile, she separated from Ernest, and her preliminary divorce decree was granted on Oct. 27, 1936. In November Edward told Baldwin that he would marry Wallis and was "prepared to go," and in December the British press broke its long silence and the king abdicated, even though Wallis had offered to withdraw and had already left England for Cannes. Edward, then created duke of Windsor by his brother, King George VI, lived in Austria until Wallis's divorce was final. After their marriage they lived in France (1937–40) and in the Bahamas (1940–45), where Edward held the post of governor. They then returned to France. After the duke's death in 1972, the duchess lived in seclusion and was severely incapacitated for a number of years before her death. A degree of reconciliation was later effected by the royal family that allowed the duchess to be buried beside her husband at Frogmore on the grounds of Windsor Castle. In 1956 Wallis published her memoirs, *The Heart Has Its Reasons,* and in 1986 the couple's intimate correspondence, *Wallis and Edward: Letters 1931–1937,* was published, according to her wishes, posthumously.

AP/WIDE WORLD

Yamasaki, Minoru, U.S. architect (b. Dec. 1, 1912, Seattle, Wash.—d. Feb. 6, 1986, Detroit, Mich.), was the renowned designer of New York City's $350 million twin-towered World Trade Center (1974), the world's second tallest building; his works, which departed from the modernistic trends of the 1950s and early 1960s, were characterized by such decorative embellishments as neogothic arches and lacy grillwork, intended to exude Asian qualities of serenity, surprise, and grace. Yamasaki, who graduated from the architectural school at the University of Washington, arrived in New York City in 1934 with only $40 and no prospects. He eventually found work as a draftsman and engineer, and in 1945 he became chief designer for the large architectural firm of Smith, Hinchman and Grylls in Detroit. He later (1949) became a partner with George Hellmuth and Joseph Leinweber and collaborated with the firm of Emery Roth & Sons before establishing his own partnership, Minoru Yamasaki & Associates. Though Yamasaki had a decided preference for ornamentation, in the latter years of his career and after extensive travels, he began to consider the functional aspects of building design as important as the aesthetic environment. Some of his architectural accomplishments included the Lambert-St. Louis (Mo.) Municipal Airport Terminal (1956), the U.S. Consulate-General Office Building and Staff Headquarters, Kobe, Japan (1957), the U.S. Pavilion, Agriculture and Trade Fair, New Delhi, India (1959), the Civil Air Terminal, Dhahran, Saudi Arabia (1961), Century 21 (World's Fair) Buildings, Seattle (1962), Century Plaza Hotel, Century City, Los Angeles (1966), Eastern Air Lines Terminal, Logan International Airport, Boston (1969), and the 40-story Rainier Square Bank Tower, Seattle (1977). His book, *A Life in Architecture,* appeared in 1979.

Ye Jianying (Yeh Chien-ying), Chinese military and politicial leader (b. 1896, Mei-xian [Mei-hsien], Guangdong [Kuangtung] Province, China—d. Oct. 22, 1986, Beijing [Peking], China), dramatically influenced the course of Chinese history as one of the prime leaders of the epochal 10,000-km (6,000-mi) Long March (1934–35), as chief of staff of the renowned Eighth Route Army during the Sino-Japanese War (1937–45), and as a powerful political figure who engineered the downfall of the notorious "gang of four," which was led by Mao Zedong's (Mao Tse-tung's) widow, Jiang Qing (Chiang Ch'ing). After graduating from the Yunnan Military Academy in 1919, Ye formed a friendship with Zhou Enlai (Chou En-lai) while both were on the faculty of the prestigious Huangpu (Whampoa) Military Academy. In 1929 he and Zhou went to Moscow for advanced military training. After distinguished service in the Sino-Japanese War, Ye was sent to Chongqing (Chungking) during World War II as a liaison officer with the U.S. forces. When the Communists came to power in 1949, Ye was named mayor of Beijing, then mayor of Guangzhou (Canton) and commander of the Guangdong Military District and of the South China Military Region. He held a succession of high-level posts and in 1955 was promoted to marshal, China's highest military rank. Ye rose to power in 1971 when he replaced Lin Biao (Lin Piao) as defense minister, although he was not officially appointed to the post until 1975. From 1976 to 1977 he served as the Communist Party's deputy chairman, but in 1978 he was forced to step down as defense minister because of ill health. He assumed the less demanding role of chief of state and held the formal title of chairman of the Standing Committee of the National People's Congress. In 1985 Ye, greatly enfeebled, was forced to retire.

Youde, Sir Edward, British diplomat (b. June 19, 1924, Penarth, Glamorgan, Wales—d. Dec. 4, 1986, Beijing [Peking], China), as governor of Hong Kong from May 1982 played an important part in the negotiations that led to the 1984 Sino-British agreement, designed to return the British crown colony to China in 1997. He was deeply versed in the culture and politics of China, having held a series of diplomatic posts there (1948–51, 1953–56, 1960–62, and 1974–78). Youde worked tirelessly to promote the existing prosperity and future special status of Hong Kong. The son of a company secretary, he was educated at Penarth County Secondary School. After a short period at the School of Oriental and African Studies, University of London, he served with the Royal Navy (1943–46) and entered the diplomatic service in 1947. He served at home in the Foreign Office (1951–53 and 1962–65), was first secretary at Washington (1956–59), and was counsellor and head of chancery to the U.K.'s mission at the UN (1965–69). He became head of personnel services at the Foreign and Commonwealth Office (1971–73), assistant under secretary of state (1973–74), deputy under secretary (1978–80), and under secretary (1980–82) as "chief clerk" responsible for the administration of Britain's diplomatic service worldwide. As ambassador at Beijing (1974–78) he gradually established a more cordial relationship with the Chinese after the death (1976) of Mao Zedong (Mao Tse-tung) and the disgrace of the "gang of four." Youde was knighted in 1977.

Young, Stuart, British businessman (b. April 23, 1934, London, England—d. Aug. 29, 1986, London), was best remembered as chairman (1983–86) of the board of governors of the British Broadcasting Corporation (BBC); he was the youngest chairman ever appointed to the post. Young left school at age 16 and in 1956 became a fellow of the Institute of Chartered Accountants. He was widely recognized for his expertise in corporate finance and built up his own successful partnership, Hacker Young. His reputation was enhanced by the directorships he held with several companies, including Caledonian Aviation Group (1973–86), Tesco Stores (1982–86), Bank Leumi (U.K.; 1975–83), and Jewish Chronicle Newspapers (1982–83). Young's association with the BBC began in 1980 when he was involved in a consortium bidding for the new breakfast television franchise. The bid failed, but his interest in the BBC led to his being invited to become a governor; he accepted and two years later became chairman. His chairmanship came under pressure in July 1985 when the board of governors decided that a documentary film on Northern Ireland should not be shown in its existing form. The controversy centred on accusations of government censorship and led to a protest strike by the BBC's World Service. Young's integrity, however, was never questioned and, in addition, his resistance to earlier pressures to introduce advertising, as a means of financing the BBC, was widely admired. Young also devoted much of his time to the Jewish community and was chairman of the Central Council of Jewish Social Services.

Events of 1986

Agriculture and Food Supplies

Many agricultural commodities continued to be in oversupply in much of the world in 1986, resulting in depressed international prices. Out-of-control modern nuclear technology endangered agriculture in the Soviet Union, while an age-old threat to farming reappeared in force in Africa. The effects of the 1985 U.S. farm bill began to be felt strongly in international agricultural trade. The enlargement of the European Communities (EC) engendered a dangerous agricultural trade dispute between it and the U.S. just as major international trade negotiations prominently featuring agriculture got under way.

African Food Situation. An unusual two consecutive years of good weather in sub-Saharan Africa resulted in bumper food crops in many countries and a buildup of excessive stocks of corn and sorghum that created storage problems in some. A variety of higher market or government support prices, guaranteed government purchases, and delayed arrivals of food aid contributed to the surpluses. They were largest in Zimbabwe, Kenya, and The Sudan.

The surpluses created interest in trilateral food-aid transactions under which aid donors provide wheat or rice to the surplus countries in exchange for shipping corn or sorghum to needy neighbouring countries. The United Nations Food and Agriculture Organization (FAO) estimated (mid-September) that aid donors had supported local purchases or triangular transactions involving about 600,000 tons of food in 1985–86. The EC and its member countries made the greatest use of this method.

Not all African countries had yet recovered from the food emergencies of 1984. FAO cited Angola, Botswana, Cape Verde, Ethiopia, Lesotho, Mozambique, and The Sudan as still facing abnormal food shortages. Localized food shortages also continued in several other nations, partly reflecting military disorders and logistic problems.

In The Sudan crop production recovered, thanks to good weather and exceptional efforts to provide farmers with seeds. The recovery resulted primarily from a large expansion of planted area in the east by a small group of farmers who operated large mechanized farms and had the resources to pay for labour and such inputs as fertilizers. However, an estimated four million small farmers and nomads in the west and north were too destitute to purchase eastern grains. That situation, along with warfare in parts of the country, increasing numbers of refugees in

Table I. Selected Indexes of World Agricultural and Food Production

(1976–78 average = 100)

Region or country	Total agricultural production						Total food production						Per capita food production					
	1981	1982	1983	1984	1985	1986[1]	1981	1982	1983	1984	1985	1986[1]	1981	1982	1983	1984	1985	1986[1]
Developed countries	108	110	102	112	113	111	108	110	103	113	114	112	105	106	99	107	108	105
United States	113	113	92	109	115	109	113	114	94	110	117	111	108	108	88	102	107	101
Canada	113	118	113	110	120	131	113	119	113	110	120	132	108	112	105	101	109	119
Western Europe	110	113	111	119	116	114	110	113	111	119	116	114	108	111	109	117	114	111
EC	110	114	111	120	116	115	111	114	111	120	117	115	109	112	109	118	114	112
Japan	92	94	94	100	100	99	92	94	94	100	101	100	89	90	90	95	95	93
Oceania	106	98	115	114	116	114	105	95	116	113	112	110	100	89	108	104	102	99
South Africa	119	107	94	102	109	110	121	107	93	102	109	110	109	94	80	85	89	88
Centrally planned economies	103	110	114	119	118	119	102	109	113	118	116	118	98	103	107	110	108	109
U.S.S.R.	92	98	102	102	101	105	91	98	102	102	101	102	87	93	96	96	94	94
Eastern Europe	95	101	103	105	104	105	102	105	104	112	108	109	100	102	101	108	103	104
China[2]	126	139	150	164	162	165	124	136	146	156	157	161	118	127	135	143	143	145
Less developed countries	112	113	115	120	125	126	112	114	116	121	125	128	102	101	101	102	104	103
East Asia	117	119	124	129	132	135	117	120	124	130	133	136	108	108	109	112	112	113
Indonesia	131	129	140	148	154	157	133	131	140	150	155	159	120	116	122	127	129	129
South Korea	98	102	104	107	109	109	100	102	105	109	110	111	93	94	95	98	98	97
Malaysia	121	130	125	131	142	154	132	145	136	147	164	181	120	129	118	125	135	147
Philippines	115	114	112	111	114	119	115	113	109	109	113	118	103	99	94	92	93	95
Thailand	118	120	132	136	135	133	118	118	132	137	134	131	109	106	116	119	114	110
Vietnam	118	126	132	140	137	142	118	126	132	139	137	142	108	112	115	118	113	115
South Asia	111	109	120	123	125	127	111	108	122	123	124	127	102	97	107	105	104	104
Bangladesh	110	114	117	117	123	123	112	116	119	120	124	126	99	100	99	97	99	97
India	111	108	122	125	126	128	110	107	123	124	125	128	101	96	108	107	105	105
Pakistan	122	124	120	128	133	143	119	118	123	118	118	133	105	101	102	95	93	101
West Asia	103	111	113	115	120	130	105	114	114	118	123	134	94	99	97	97	99	104
Iran	89	96	95	94	104	113	89	97	96	95	106	115	79	83	80	76	83	87
Turkey	108	114	114	115	112	121	112	117	116	118	116	126	102	105	101	101	97	103
Sub-Saharan Africa	111	112	106	111	117	120	111	113	107	110	117	119	99	98	89	90	93	92
Ethiopia	108	119	109	100	104	118	108	123	111	102	106	115	102	113	99	89	93	97
Nigeria	113	115	101	113	116	119	114	115	101	114	117	120	100	98	84	93	93	93
Sudan, The	110	99	102	94	121	114	119	98	97	86	119	113	103	82	78	67	88	84
North Africa	105	114	113	116	125	130	104	115	114	117	127	133	92	99	96	95	101	103
Morocco	86	111	106	107	111	130	86	111	106	107	112	131	78	98	91	90	92	105
Egypt	112	115	117	118	124	128	111	116	119	122	126	133	98	99	99	98	99	101
Latin America	116	116	114	121	126	123	115	117	114	121	127	125	105	104	99	103	105	101
Argentina	103	112	107	118	116	120	106	114	109	121	119	123	99	105	99	107	104	106
Brazil	124	120	120	129	144	129	117	121	115	126	138	131	106	106	98	105	112	104
Colombia	123	121	120	122	122	126	122	121	120	123	126	128	113	110	106	106	107	107
Mexico	120	114	119	117	118	121	122	117	122	120	122	125	110	103	104	99	99	99
Venezuela	110	118	117	120	129	133	110	120	117	123	131	135	96	102	97	99	103	103
World	108	111	110	117	118	118	107	111	110	117	118	119	100	102	100	104	104	102

[1]Preliminary. [2]Represents about two-thirds of all field crops (includes all major field crops) but excludes livestock products.
Source: USDA, Economic Research Service, International Economic Division, December 1986.

the capital, and the government's poor financial condition, continued to make external food aid necessary.

The return of rains in 1985 following three years of drought stimulated the rapid multiplication and migration of grasshoppers and locusts, which threatened food supplies in some 30 African countries. Both national governments and foreign aid donors responded quickly with measures including both ground and large-scale aerial spraying of insecticides to protect crops. The FAO, which coordinated the national and international efforts, estimated (in October) that external assistance to the campaign had totaled the equivalent of $35 million. These efforts were successful in avoiding catastrophic crop losses, but the FAO warned that further efforts would be required in 1987 to bring the pests under control.

Chernobyl Nuclear Accident. The Soviet government at first responded to an accident on April 26 at its nuclear power plant at Chernobyl in the northern Ukraine by abandoning agricultural activity within a 30.5-km (19-mi) radius of the reactor. The people living in the zone around Chernobyl were said to have been evacuated, while reports conflicted about whether livestock in the area were slaughtered or evacuated. Farming activities were later discontinued to a radius of 59.6 km (37 mi), and decontamination of soil was said to have begun.

Cesium isotopes were the radioactive material with the longest radioactive life that were carried downwind in large volume from the immediate vicinity of the reactor. The persistence of their radioactivity—half is lost in 30 years—rather than the intensity was the primary concern. Western scientists said that techniques for decontamination available to the Soviets included plowing contaminated soil under to reduce direct radiation and adding clay or potassium fertilizer to the soil in order to reduce the amount of cesium absorbed by plants eaten by either animals or humans.

Surface winds the first five days blew mainly northwest toward the Baltic; they then turned toward the southwest or south in the early days of May. Leafy vegetables and milk were most susceptible to radiation absorption outside

A farmer in Van Buren, Arkansas, drains a storage tank of milk unacceptable for sale because his cows were fed grain treated with heptachlor, a carcinogenic pesticide. The chemical, though banned since 1983, was found to contaminate milk in almost 100 dairies.
MICHAEL WYKE/THE NEW YORK TIMES

the 30.5-km zone, but few details were released by Soviet officials. Raised radiation levels were reported in Eastern and Western Europe. The EC in early May banned most imports of fresh foods from the Soviet Union and Eastern European countries within 1,030 km (640 mi) of Chernobyl. The ban was replaced at the end of May by measures taken by individual countries to monitor radiation levels in imports from all sources.

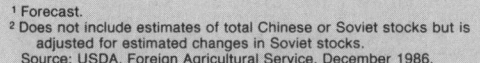

Table II. World Cereal Supply and Distribution
In 000,000 metric tons

	1983–84	1984–85	1985–86	1986–87[1]
Production				
Wheat	490	512	500	522
Coarse grains	688	814	844	837
Rice, milled	308	319	320	318
Total	1,485	1,644	1,663	1,676
Utilization				
Wheat	482	495	488	505
Coarse grains	762	784	772	786
Rice, milled	308	314	318	321
Total	1,553	1,593	1,578	1,611
Exports				
Wheat	102	107	85	85
Coarse grains	92	100	84	80
Rice, milled	13	12	13	12
Total	206	219	181	176
Ending stocks[2]				
Wheat	110	126	138	154
Coarse grains	77	108	180	231
Rice, milled	17	22	24	22
Total	204	257	342	407
Stocks as % of utilization				
Wheat	22.7%	25.5%	28.2%	30.6%
Coarse grains	10.1%	13.8%	23.3%	29.3%
Rice, milled	5.6%	7.1%	7.6%	6.7%
Total	13.1%	16.1%	21.7%	25.2%
Stocks held by U.S. in % of world total				
Wheat	34.8%	30.8%	37.6%	33.3%
Coarse grains	51.7%	53.6%	70.6%	75.4%
Rice	8.7%	9.0%	10.3%	9.3%
Total	39.0%	38.5%	53.0%	55.9%

[1] Forecast.
[2] Does not include estimates of total Chinese or Soviet stocks but is adjusted for estimated changes in Soviet stocks.
Source: USDA, Foreign Agricultural Service, December 1986.

Production. Total world agricultural and food production in 1986 increased very little from the previous year, according to preliminary estimates by the U.S. Department of Agriculture's Economic Research Service. Among the developed countries the U.S. and Western Europe experienced the largest declines, but smaller harvests did little to alleviate large commodity surpluses in those regions. Both the centrally planned and the less developed countries recorded modest overall gains.

Grains. The expansion of world grain production in 1986–87 was expected (in December) to be slightly less than the 1% recorded during the previous year. A strong increase in wheat production was likely to more than offset small declines for coarse grains and rice. Total grain use declined in 1985–86, largely as the result of reduced demand for livestock feed in the industrialized countries. Trade in wheat and coarse grains contracted even more sharply than grain use despite the continuing steep decline in international grain prices. Trade could decline even further in 1986–87 because recent increases in grain production had tended to be concentrated in major grain-importing countries. Grain stocks increased by one-third during 1985–86 and were expected to expand further in 1986–87 for the fourth year in a row.

World production of wheat increased in 1986–87 and surpassed total wheat consumption for the sixth consecutive year. Wheat stocks at the beginning of the season were equivalent to more than 30% of total annual wheat consumption, the highest since the late 1960s, when the ratio reached 38%. The U.S. Gulf ports price (f.o.b.) for No. 2 hard winter wheat provided a rough indicator of how expanding excess supplies had resulted in a steady decline in world trade prices for wheat. It averaged $176 per ton in 1981 and 1982, fell to $137 in 1985, and was selling at about $105 in late 1986.

Although low prices for wheat in several countries seemed likely to stimulate a strong increase in wheat consumption, including more feeding of lower quality wheat to animals, world trade in wheat was expected to continue at the depressed level of 1985–86. Most of the wheat production increases in 1986 were in countries that imported wheat. Such increases, especially those in the Soviet Union, acted to reduce import demand substantially. Wheat production fell in the U.S. for the second straight year but increased significantly in the competing exporting countries of Canada and Australia.

Soviet imports of U.S. wheat in 1984–85 fell 1.1 million tons short of the annual four million-ton minimum specified in the U.S.-Soviet Long Term Grain Agreement. The Soviets claimed in justification that U.S. priccs were not internationally competitive and objected to being excluded from the Export Enhancement Program (EEP). They also suggested that their purchase of 15.7 million tons of corn (agreement minimum of 4 million to 6 million) compensated for the shortfall. Soviet foreign exchange shortages resulting from a sharp decline in petroleum export revenues and complaints about the quality of U.S. grain may also have been factors. The U.S.S.R. again reneged in 1985–86 when its purchases of U.S. wheat were less than 200,000 tons. The Soviets refused a U.S. offer to sell four million tons of wheat released from government stocks under the EEP.

Table III. World Production of Oilseeds and Products
In 000,000 metric tons

	1984–85	1985–86[1]	1986–87[2]
Production of oilseeds	191.1	195.7	196.5
Soybeans	93.0	96.3	98.8
U.S.	50.6	57.1	54.7
China	9.7	10.5	11.0
Argentina	6.8	7.3	7.7
Brazil	18.3	13.4	16.2
Cottonseed	33.6	30.4	27.4
U.S.	4.7	4.8	3.5
U.S.S.R.	4.8	4.8	4.5
China	10.6	7.1	6.4
Peanuts	19.8	20.4	20.7
U.S.	2.0	1.9	1.6
China	4.8	6.7	6.1
India	6.5	5.2	5.9
Sunflower seed	17.8	19.6	18.9
U.S.	1.7	1.4	1.1
U.S.S.R.	4.5	5.2	4.6
Argentina	3.4	4.1	3.5
Rapeseed	16.7	19.0	20.1
Canada	3.4	3.5	3.9
China	4.2	5.6	5.9
India	2.9	3.0	3.3
Flaxseed	2.3	2.4	2.7
Copra	4.8	5.2	5.3
Palm kernel	2.3	2.6	2.7
Crushings of oilseeds	151.1	154.9	155.7
Soybeans	73.8	76.4	78.9
Ending stocks of oilseeds	21.2	26.0	29.7
Soybeans	17.6	22.5	25.2
World production[3]			
Total fats and oils	58.2	61.3	61.3
Edible vegetable oils	44.3	47.4	47.6
Soybean oil	13.3	13.7	14.1
Palm cil	7.0	8.1	8.3
Animal fats	11.9	11.9	11.7
Industrial and marine oils	2.0	2.0	2.0
High-protein meals[4]	97.7	99.9	101.2

[1] Preliminary.
[2] Forecast.
[3] Processing potential from crops in year indicated.
[4] Converted, based on product's protein content, to weight equivalent to soybeans of 44% protein content.
Source: USDA, Foreign Agricultural Service, June and December 1986.

The volume and market share of U.S. wheat exports continued their steady decline from their peak of 48 million tons and 48%, respectively, in 1981–82 to 25 million tons and 30% in 1985–86. By the beginning of 1986–87 U.S. stocks were almost the equivalent of one year of domestic wheat consumption and exports. Among the other major wheat exporters, stocks were declining except in Canada, where they could increase sharply by the end of 1986–87, and in the EC, where they had stabilized at a relatively high level since 1984–85.

A new Wheat Trade Convention (WTC), part of the International Wheat Agreement, began operation in July 1986. It was to run for five years, with provision for successive two-year extensions. Like the expiring WTC it contained no economic provisions but strengthened provisions that called for consultations and exchange of information. It also extended coverage of the convention to other grains, such as barley, corn (maize), sorghum, and rice.

Total world rice production had varied little since 1982. Consumption had slowly risen, and stocks had edged downward.

World output of coarse grains was expected to be a little smaller in 1986–87 than in 1985–86, although production was expected to exceed consumption for the fourth year in a row. Among exporters, U.S. corn (maize) production fell 24 million tons to 251 million. Most of the other major coarse-grain exporters, except for Canada and China, also experienced smaller harvests. Production increases were concentrated in those countries that had usually imported coarse grains, especially the Soviet Union and Eastern Europe.

World stocks of coarse grains, which grew by two-thirds in 1985–86, were expected to increase another two-fifths in 1986–87. The U.S. was expected to account for at least 90% of the increase in both years. The rapid rise in stocks was accompanied by an equally rapid decline in world trade prices for coarse grains. The U.S. Gulf ports price for No. 3 yellow corn averaged about $138 per ton in 1983 and 1984, fell to $114 in 1985, and had dropped to $67 by the fall of 1986.

Oilseeds. World oilseed production was estimated (in December) to have risen very little in 1986–87, reflecting a small increase in area planted to oilseeds. Some large reductions in plantings and output in the U.S. were offset by increases in other countries. The increase in production of oilseed meal was expected to slow to about 1% after increasing 2.3% in 1985–86.

The demand for protein meals strengthened relative to that for edible oils in 1985–86, as was evidenced by their relative price movements. The price of soybean meal (c.i.f., Rotterdam) bottomed out at an average of $155 per ton in 1984–85, recovered to $183 in 1985–86, and remained near that level at the beginning of 1986–87. The price of soybean oil, which averaged $625 per ton (f.o.b., Rotterdam) in 1984–85, averaged $377 in 1985–86, fell as low as $271 in August 1986, and recovered to about $320 at the beginning of the 1986–87 season.

The more rapid growth of poultry production throughout the world relative to other livestock favoured increased consumption of protein meals because poultry rations contain a higher percentage of meal than do those of other livestock. East Asia, North Africa, and the Middle East continued to demonstrate the strongest growth in consumption and imports of oilseed meals, particularly soybean meal. Those countries were expanding their poultry production rapidly and had little domestic oilseed production.

A 17% expansion in Malaysian output of palm oil was a major factor in the strong growth in production of vegetable oils in 1985–86. The resulting buildup of stocks of vegetable oils, mediocre demand prospects, and expectations of larger crushings of oilseeds in 1986–87 seemed likely to prevent a substantial recovery in international prices for vegetable oils.

Meat. World meat production was estimated to have grown 1% in 1986, with most of the growth taking place in poultry and pork. Production of beef and veal declined, reflecting the second straight year of reduced cattle numbers. Cattle herds were smaller in almost all of the major beef-exporting countries, although rebuilding appeared to be under way in Australia. Government measures designed to reduce dairy surpluses in both the EC and the U.S. contributed to the reduction and led to sales of beef abroad by both at below-normal trade prices. The loss of certain tax deductions for feeding cattle might be contributing to the reduction in U.S. cattle herds.

The EC had little success in reducing government-held stocks of beef, which totaled 1.2 million tons (carcass weight equivalent) at the beginning of 1986. The EC Commission released a study recommending that the EC purchase price for beef be allowed to fall by 15% in order to discourage excess production. The EC announced a ban on the use of growth hormones in meat production, to be effective in January 1987, and the ban was to apply to imported meat in January 1988. Argentina continued to reduce cattle herds because of financial pressures on farmers caused by high interest rates, low crop prices, and heavy taxation. Cattlemen in Brazil withheld their livestock from the market to protest a government retail price freeze, and the government responded by suspending beef exports, importing beef, and confiscating the animals of some producers.

Low feed-grain prices in several countries stimulated pork and poultry production in 1986. Both hog inventories and pork production grew overall in the major pork-producing nations, but output increased only a little more than 1% after expanding 4.7% in 1985. U.S. pork production fell 5%, while that in China (the world's largest pork producer) slowed to 3% after increasing 14% in 1985. After expanding rapidly in the 1970s, world trade in pork had stagnated at about 1.7 million tons (excluding intra-EC trade). China and Taiwan were becoming increasingly important exporters of pork.

World poultry production continued its rapid expansion in 1986, about matching the 3.8% rate of growth achieved in 1985. Poultry, because of the shorter growth cycle and greater yield of meat per unit of feed relative to cattle and hogs, provided several less developed countries with a quick and economic way of increasing domestic meat consumption. Much of the expansion was in Middle Eastern countries, which had begun to import substantial quantities of poultry meat during the years when their petroleum export revenues started to expand. Many sought to achieve self-sufficiency in poultry production by subsidizing feed and other production inputs, although import demand continued to be strong, thanks in part to low prices for frozen poultry.

For several years U.S. poultry consumption had increased much faster than that of other meats, possibly indicating a major shift in consumer preference in its favour. A major contributing factor was the widening price spread in recent years between red meat (especially beef) and the lower priced poultry. Others included the promotion of poultry meat as a convenience food and the attractiveness to some health-conscious consumers of skinned poultry meat because of its lower saturated fat content.

New Zealand, which accounted for more than one-half of the approximately one million tons of world trade in lamb and mutton in 1986, began experimenting with possible year-round production of lamb. The country hoped to develop markets for such processed lamb products as frozen steakettes, burgers, boneless roasts, and frozen dinners, as well as exporting more fresh-chilled (not frozen) lamb.

Dairy Products. The production of milk from cows increased about 1% in 1986 for the second straight year, led by increases in the U.S., EC, and Soviet Union. Output rose despite government plans in both the U.S. and EC to reduce dairy herds. The U.S. dairy herd shrank an estimated 4% in 1986 and was to become even smaller in 1987 because of government inducements to dairymen to go out of business. These inducements took the form of herd buyouts authorized by the 1985 farm bill. However, low feed prices and gains from genetic improvements and other management practices continued to generate increased U.S. milk production. Output was expected to decline in 1987, but there was a continued possibility in the U.S. of annual increases of 3–4% in milk output per cow over the next five years.

The resulting increased production of butter and nonfat dry milk (NFDM) led to substantial increases in stocks of those products. Nearly all the increase in butter and NFDM stocks occurred in the EC, which controlled three-fourths of world butter stocks. In order to avoid paying domestic producers the full intervention (support) price of the equivalent of $3,163 a ton and $400 a ton annual storage costs, the EC offered an export subsidy of $2,363 a ton for butter traded at $800–$1,100 per ton on world markets. Despite such subsidies the EC's butter exports declined a little in 1986. The EC's large stocks of NFDM caused it somewhat less distress because more opportunities existed for disposing of them through subsidized feeding of pigs and poultry. The EC Commission estimated in a November report that the EC was producing a 9.5 million-ton annual surplus

Table IV. Livestock Numbers and Meat Production in Major Producing Countries

In 000,000 head and 000,000 metric tons (carcass weight)

Region and country	1985	1986[1]	1985	1986[1]
	Cattle		Beef and veal	
World total	958.2	952.0	42.87	42.65
Canada	10.6	10.3	1.04	1.02
United States	105.5	101.8	11.00	11.08
Mexico	33.7	34.2	1.34	1.25
Argentina	57.6	56.5	2.74	2.70
Brazil	95.2	96.0	2.40	2.20
Uruguay	10.0	10.4	.34	.31
Western Europe	91.5	90.2	8.52	8.40
Eastern Europe	36.8	36.7	2.55	2.40
U.S.S.R.	120.8	122.0	7.40	7.60
Australia	23.2	23.3	1.34	1.38
India	275.3	273.6	.34	.36
	Hogs		Pork	
World total	728.9	740.1	54.07	54.74
Canada	10.7	10.9	.90	.88
United States	52.3	50.0	6.72	6.39
Mexico	13.1	13.1	.87	.92
Western Europe	122.0	123.7	12.38	12.67
U.S.S.R.	77.6	77.5	5.85	5.85
Japan	11.1	11.2	1.53	1.50
China	331.5	343.3	16.50	17.00
	Poultry		Poultry meat	
World total	...	...	25.17	26.10
United States	...	...	7.87	8.35
Brazil	...	...	1.53	1.65
EC	...	...	5.31	5.42
U.S.S.R.	...	...	2.70	2.75
Japan	...	...	1.40	1.40
	Sheep		Sheep, goat meat	
World total	692.1	703.9	4.82	4.71
			All meat	
Total	...	...	126.91	128.19

[1] Preliminary livestock numbers at year's end. Consists of 47 countries for beef and veal, 38 for pork, 42 for poultry meat, and 30 for sheep and goat meat; roughly the same coverage for animal numbers. Includes nearly all European producers, the most significant in the Western Hemisphere, and scattered coverage elsewhere.
Source: USDA, Foreign Agricultural Service, September 1986.

A Chianina represents one of several exotic crossbreeds that are intended to yield very lean beef for diet-conscious U.S. consumers. Other animals raised to provide beef with less fat and fewer calories include Brae, beefalo, and zebu.

GRANT HEILMAN

of milk, in part because of loopholes in production control measures introduced in 1984. The 1986–87 program to pay farmers to permanently quit dairying compensated them less than the 1985 program and was not producing the desired reduction in milk deliveries.

Exports of butter, nonfat dry milk, and casein declined in 1986 as import demand remained weak, while the quantity of cheese exported was unchanged. International prices for butter, butter oil, and cheese declined further in 1986, while those for NFDM and casein remained stable. U.S. exports of NFDM grew, thanks to larger food aid shipments and direct government sales from surplus stocks.

Sugar. World stocks of sugar failed to contract during 1985–86 despite a 2% smaller sugar harvest. The price (International Sugar Agreement world price) for freely traded sugar, which had averaged 5.2 cents a pound in 1984, was driven down to 3 cents in the second quarter of 1985 by the large buildup in stocks during 1984–85. The smaller 1985–86 crop caused a small recovery in 1985 prices, which averaged 4.1 cents overall. They reached 8.3 cents in April 1986 and then drifted into the 4.5–5.5-cent range in the fall. The forecast (in November) of a 1% increase in sugar output during 1986–87 gave no immediate prospect of a reduction in these price-depressing stocks. They were estimated to have equaled about 47% of annual sugar consumption at the end of 1985–86.

Sugar consumption was increasing most rapidly in parts of the Middle East and Asia, particularly in China. In many other less developed countries the domestic demand for sugar was being retarded by slow economic growth in recent years or by a shortage of foreign exchange with which to finance sugar imports. Demand was dampened in many developed countries by competition from low-calorie sugar substitutes or from other caloric sweeteners. In the U.S. consumption of lower priced corn sweeteners probably exceeded that for sugar for the first time in 1985. U.S. sugar price supports, backed by import controls, held the domestic wholesale price of sugar at 22 cents per pound during 1986, while high-fructose corn sugar traded in the 12–14-cent range.

Total world imports of sugar in 1985–86, at 27.5 million metric tons (raw value), were slightly smaller than a year earlier mainly because of reduced U.S. imports. The U.S., the second largest importer of sugar after the U.S.S.R., in December announced a drastic reduction in its sugar import quota for 1987. The new 1 million short ton quota represented the smallest net imports of sugar since 1888. The first full fiscal year in which the quota was operational was 1982–83, when quota imports totaled 2,980,000 tons. The large reduction was considered necessary to comply with a provision of the 1985 U.S. farm bill that required the U.S. sugar price support program to be administered at no cost to the federal government "by preventing the accumulation of sugar acquired by the [U.S. government's] Commodity Credit Corporation." Smaller supplies of sugar were expected to keep U.S. market prices for sugar in the 20–22-cent-per-pound price range needed to discourage producers from surrendering their sugar in return for government price support payments. The U.S. said that it would offer $179.6 million in surplus agricultural commodities to a group of less developed countries to help mitigate the effects of the reduction.

Coffee. The most serious drought in 40 years led to an estimated 58% decline in coffee production in 1986–87 by Brazil, the world's largest coffee producer. Total world output of coffee was estimated (in December) to have been 15% smaller than in 1985–86. News of the damage began to emerge late in 1985. By February 1986 the composite indicator price of the International Coffee Agreement (ICA) had exceeded $1.50 per pound sufficiently long to trigger suspension of the ICA's export quotas. The price had peaked at $2 in January, fell to $1.43 in July, recovered to $1.80 in October, and then fell to the neighbourhood of $1.45 in December. The ICA called for export quotas to be reinstalled when the price fell to $1.35. However, before they could be reimposed, those countries that produce and consume coffee would have to agree among themselves on quota reallocations.

Even more serious issues could arise, judging by statements issued by two groups of Latin-American and African coffee producers that each was considering coordinated measures to prevent a further decline in coffee prices. If actually implemented, such measures could well be considered by importing countries to be serious violations of the ICA. It was only in April 1986 that the U.S. withdrew a threat to quit the ICA in protest against what it considered the nonfulfillment of export quotas by some members, especially those exporting to non-ICA members. The legislation authorizing U.S. implementation of the ICA expired in September, but the government's April 1986 request for extension contained in the Senate trade bill was abandoned because of failure to agree on more controversial issues. The legislation, which would authorize limitations on coffee imports from nonmember countries, was expected to be reintroduced in February 1987.

Cocoa. World production of cocoa beans was estimated (in October) to have increased marginally in 1986–87, after declining 6% the previous year. Cocoa grindings were estimated at 1,810,000 metric tons in 1985–86, down 1% from 1984–85, but grindings were not expected to increase sufficiently in 1986–87 to prevent a third year of buildup of cocoa bean stocks. Cocoa prices (New York futures, nearest three-month average), which averaged $1.06 per pound in

Cauliflower is dumped from a truck in Colmar, Alsace, France, as part of efforts to dispose of produce tainted by the fallout from the Chernobyl nuclear plant disaster in the U.S.S.R. Radiation was detected over wide areas and protective measures were taken throughout Europe.
LAMBERT—GAMMA/LIAISON

1984, slipped to 99 cents in 1985 and fluctuated between 81 cents and $1.01 in 1986.

Agreement was reached in July 1986 on a new International Cocoa Agreement (ICCA) to replace the old ICCA that expired on Sept. 30, 1986. The Côte d'Ivoire, the world's largest cocoa producer, became a new member, while the largest importer, the U.S., refused membership, as it had in the 1980–86 agreement. The agreement was to run for three years, with the possibility of a two-year extension.

The old ICCA attempted to maintain market prices within a $1.06–$1.45-per-pound price band, primarily by the management of an international buffer stock. Prices, however, remained below $1.06 during almost its entire life. The management of a 250,000-ton-capacity buffer stock financed by levies on exports and imports provided the new agreement's major operating tool. The stock started with 100,000 tons of cocoa carried over from the old ICCA.

The new agreement shifted the price band downward and brought more flexibility to the system by introducing a semiautomatic price adjustment system based on periodic price reviews. The new mechanism combined mandatory buying and selling triggers for the buffer stock with intermediate optional transactions and introduced the concept of a "median price." These price points of the new agreement were denominated in International Monetary Fund Special Drawing Rights to allow for currency fluctuations. They are expressed below, per pound, in October 1986 U.S. currency equivalents:

Upper intervention price (must sell)	$1.21
Upper optional price (may sell)	$1.18
Median price	$1.03
Lower optional price (may buy)	$0.88
Lower intervention price (must buy)	$0.85

Should prices remain outside the above intervention price band for a specified period and certain buffer stock transactions occur, the ICCA would provide for automatically shifting the entire price band up or down by up to six cents centred on a new median price band calculated from the previous 12-month average price. A special supplementary scheme would also permit the buffer stock manager to authorize countries to withhold specified quantitites of cocoa from the export market when prices fell to, or below, the lower intervention level for a specified period. Such cocoa would be released for export after the indicator price had risen to at least the median price for a sufficient time.

Cotton. World stocks of cotton continued to increase during 1985–86, reaching 65% of annual cotton use despite smaller output and accelerating use of the fibre. The 1986 cotton harvest was estimated (in December) to have been smaller for the second year in a row, as U.S. production declined 27%. China continued to decrease planted area and output in order to reduce its stocks of cotton, which represented 43% of the world supply at the beginning of 1986–87. Australia, Brazil, and Mexico were other major producers that cut back planted area.

The large stocks depressed cotton prices, which averaged about 49 cents per pound (Northern Europe Outlook "A" Index) in 1985–86, compared with about 69 cents the previous year, and slipped to nearly 36 cents in July 1986 before climbing back to 53 cents in November. The lower prices promoted increased substitution of cotton for synthetic fibres, the prices of which had also been falling but had stabilized well above those for cotton. This contributed to a 7% increase in world use of cotton to 74.6 million bales (480 lb each) in 1985–86. Total cotton use appeared to be slowing in 1986–87, although trade seemed to be picking up after several years of decline or stagnation.

Trade and Food Policy. The 1985 U.S. farm bill (Food Security Act of 1985) began to have a major impact on world commodity prices and trade as its provisions began to be applied to U.S. crops harvested in the fall of 1986. The bill's reduction of the loan rates that establish the effective U.S. support prices for most commodities increased the ability of U.S. farmers to compete aggressively with other exporters for sales of such commodities as wheat and corn. This action lowered the price "umbrella" that had sheltered U.S. competitors by permitting them to price their commodities just a little under the levels at which U.S. farmers found it more profitable to "sell" their commodities to the U.S. government than to foreign buyers. For rice and cotton special marketing loans made U.S. exports competitive in those cases where loan rates were still too high. The EEP provided surplus government commodities, particularly wheat, at reduced costs to U.S. exporters whose sales were targeted at markets where competitors, most especially the EC, were deemed to be unfairly subsidizing their exports. Provisions applying to the U.S. sugar program led to sales of the government's surplus sugar and increased restrictions on imports, thereby increasing the availability of sugar in world markets.

Most of these actions tended to depress international agricultural commodity prices and, together with depreciation of the U.S. dollar, to enhance U.S. chances of regaining its earlier share of world markets. They also met with strong objections in some quarters, both in the U.S. and abroad. The EC was disturbed by the U.S.'s publicly avowed aim of forcing it to cut back on agricultural subsidies and engage in negotiations on agricultural trade issues. More important, the export subsidies needed to relieve the surpluses created by the EC's common agricultural policy (CAP) were increasing, because of both depressed agricultural trade prices and competitive requirements in targeted markets. The development was particularly unwelcome because the EC already faced a large budget deficit for which the CAP was primarily responsible. Other export competitors that had not heavily subsidized their agricultural sectors, such as Australia, claimed that they were caught in the middle of a subsidy war between the U.S. and the EC. They said that it was caused by inappropriate domestic agricultural policies in both regions that were driving down world prices to the detriment of everyone.

Agriculture and EC Enlargement. The entrance of Spain and Portugal into the EC on Jan. 1, 1986, made the Community the world's largest agricultural export market. It also marked both the initial application of the CAP to those countries and the beginning of another serious agricultural trade dispute between the EC and the U.S. By the year's end the dispute threatened to degenerate into a full-scale trade war.

The transition to full application of the CAP was expected to take seven to ten years, during which time import tariffs among Spain and Portugal and the ten older members of the EC would gradually be eliminated. A common external tariff would eventually be applied, including the variable import levy that was the cornerstone of the CAP system for insulating the EC's domestic agriculture market from external competition. Movement of the two countries behind the CAP barriers increased the opportunity for trade among them and the old members, sometimes at the expense of non-EC exporters such as the U.S. Both Spain and Portugal were net importers of grains, meat and milk products, sugar, and potatoes, while the other EC members generated large surpluses of those products. Also, the two new member nations exported fruits and vegetables, of which the EC had been net importers. Prices for most agricultural commodities were lower in Spain than in the EC but tended to be equal or higher in Portugal.

Enlargement added 3 million Spanish and Portuguese farms to the 6.8 million in the old EC. Some 2.9 million persons were added to the 8 million already employed in agriculture. In comparison with the other EC countries, farms in Spain and Portugal were generally smaller, farm incomes were lower, and unemployment was higher. Farm productivity tended to be low in both countries, and the scheduled gradual adjustment of their prices to those maintained under the CAP was likely to stimulate higher yields and production for many commodities.

The U.S. dispute with the EC originated in disagreement over what constituted adequate "compensation" for a potential loss in U.S. exports of agricultural commodities to the EC resulting from the latter's enlargement. Article XXIV:6 of the General Agreement on Tariffs and Trade (GATT) obligates a customs union to negotiate compensation with another country for exports lost by the latter because enlargement of the customs union leads to the application of higher import barriers than it had previously fixed or "bound" by formal agreement. Compensation may be in the form of agreed-upon reductions of barriers to that country's other exports. The U.S. claimed that its exports were hurt because: (1) the new variable levy on Spanish corn imports was higher than its old bound

Table V. World Production and Stocks of Dairy Products[1]

Region and country	1984	1985	1986[2]
	Production of cow's milk		
	In 000,000 metric tons		
North America	76.9	80.0	81.7
United States	61.4	65.2	65.8
South America	19.1	19.5	19.4
Brazil	10.8	10.4	9.8
Western Europe	132.8	131.0	131.5
EC	116.2	114.6	115.4
France	27.6	26.8	27.1
West Germany	26.2	25.7	26.2
Italy	10.2	10.2	10.1
Netherlands, The	12.8	12.6	12.8
United Kingdom	16.6	16.3	16.4
Other Western Europe	16.6	16.4	16.1
Eastern Europe	43.7	43.5	42.6
Poland	16.8	16.6	15.7
U.S.S.R.	97.9	98.6	101.0
China	2.2	2.5	2.8
India	17.1	19.0	20.1
Australia/New Zealand[3]	13.7	14.1	14.4
Japan/South Africa	9.6	9.7	9.7
Total	413.0	417.9	423.2

Product/Region	Production 1985	Production 1986[2]	Year-end stocks 1985	Year-end stocks 1986[2]
	In 000 metric tons			
Butter	6,756	6,871	1,768	2,059
EC	2,013	2,147	1,313	1,596
U.S.	585	540	98	85
Cheese	9,444	9,708	1,534	1,472
EC	3,962	3,991	718	752
U.S.	2,279	2,365	428	335
Nonfat dry milk	4,041	4,142	1,369	1,554
EC	1,946	2,162	611	1,002
U.S.	631	585	459	280

[1]Based on 37 major producing countries. Those not shown individually include (North America) Canada and Mexico; (South America) Argentina, Brazil, Chile, Peru, and Venezuela; (EC) Belgium-Luxembourg, Denmark, Greece, Ireland, Portugal, and Spain; (Other Western Europe) Austria, Finland, Norway, Sweden, and Switzerland; and (Eastern Europe) Czechoslovakia, East Germany, and Yugoslavia.
[2]Preliminary.
[3]Year ending June 30 for Australia and May 31 for New Zealand.
Source: USDA, Foreign Agricultural Service, November 1986.

Table VI. World Production of Centrifugal (Freed from Liquid) Sugar

In 000,000 metric tons raw value

Region and country	1984–85	1985–86	1986–87[1]
North America	8.8	9.2	9.6
United States	5.3	5.5	5.8
Mexico	3.4	3.6	3.7
Caribbean	9.7	8.5	9.0
Cuba	8.1	7.1	7.6
Central America	1.8	1.8	1.8
South America	14.6	13.2	14.2
Argentina	1.5	1.2	1.1
Brazil	9.3	8.2	9.1
Europe	21.2	21.0	20.4
Western Europe	15.5	15.5	15.0
EC	14.4	14.4	14.1
France	4.3	4.3	3.6
West Germany	3.1	3.4	3.5
Eastern Europe	5.6	5.5	5.4
Poland	1.9	1.8	1.7
U.S.S.R.	8.6	8.3	7.7
Africa and Middle East	10.2	10.0	10.4
South Africa	2.5	2.2	2.3
Turkey	1.7	1.4	1.6
Asia	21.2	22.4	23.4
China	4.6	5.5	5.5
India	7.1	8.0	8.7
Indonesia	1.7	1.7	1.8
Philippines	1.8	1.4	1.5
Thailand	2.5	2.6	2.5
Oceania	4.0	3.7	3.8
Australia	3.5	3.4	3.3
Total production	100.2	98.1	100.1
Total consumption	96.7	97.7	99.7
Total ending stocks	46.0	46.4	46.8

[1]Preliminary.
Source: USDA, Foreign Agricultural Service, November 1986.

duty, permitting the substitution of other grain imports by Spain's livestock industry; (2) the reservation of 15.5% of Portuguese grain imports for other EC suppliers, in effect, established an import quota for non-EC suppliers that was contrary to GATT; and (3) new Portuguese restrictions on domestic sales of vegetable oils produced from imported oilseeds would, in effect, limit the importation of soybeans for which the EC long ago negotiated a zero-rate tariff binding with the U.S.

Agriculture and the MTN. The intensification of trade disputes among major agricultural exporters and importers in recent years caused agriculture to become a major topic for negotiation in a new round of multilateral trade negotiations (MTN) that was launched in September 1986. The negotiations were beginning amid growing recognition that mutual reductions of agricultural trade barriers were unlikely to be achieved without important modifications of domestic agricultural policies in many of the countries concerned. The negotiations, conducted under the auspices of GATT, were scheduled to be completed in four years. GATT, created in 1947, was designed to be the primary international institution for conducting trade negotiations and establishing international trading rules.

The broad objectives of this "Uruguay Round" were to liberalize world trade, strengthen GATT trade rules and widen their coverage, improve the world trading system while taking account of difficulties in commodity markets, and foster more cooperative interaction among the trade, monetary, and economic policies of governments as they affected world economic growth. Under a "standstill" agreement new trade restrictions were not to be created as bargaining "chips." Topics to be negotiated, other than agriculture, included trade in services, trade-related investments, intellectual property rights, tropical and natural-resource-based products, and textiles. Several subjects were relevant to both agricultural and nonagricultural trade sectors. They included a "rollback" of measures inconsistent with GATT, subsidies and countervailing measures, dispute settlement procedures, tariffs, nontariff measures, safeguards, and the articles that govern GATT.

The agreed-upon negotiating ground rules for agriculture in the MTN called for "improving the competitive environment by increasing the discipline on the use of all direct and indirect subsidies and other measures affecting directly or indirectly agricultural trade, including the phased reduction of their negative effects and dealing with their causes." This language gave explicit recognition to the relationship between agricultural trade policies and domestic agricultural policies and made the latter, for the first time, a legitimate subject for negotiation. The agricultural negotiations would also attempt to improve market access by reducing import barriers and minimizing the adverse trade effects of various sanitary regulations.

Some progress had been made by members of GATT in reducing agricultural tariffs during past MTNs, but the agreement had not been very effective in eliminating the major barriers to agricultural trade. One reason was that countries had tended to adopt nontariff trade barriers as tariffs were lowered. GATT negotiating procedures lent themselves better to bargaining over tariff barriers than over such measures as quotas and variable levies.

A more important reason was that the GATT membership had explicitly exempted agriculture in many important instances from the application of GATT rules. The principal example was GATT Article XVI, which contains a general prohibition of export subsidies but which in Paragraph 3 exempts "primary products," including unprocessed agricultural products. The U.S. was among those countries that originally insisted on this exemption in 1957. Under it, a nation could subsidize the exportation of such products if it did not gain more than an "equitable share of world export trade in that product" as a result of the subsidy. GATT so far had not been able to arrive at a very precise definition of what constituted "equitable."

The GATT membership also waived application of the rules to agriculture for particular countries in certain cases. For example, the 1955 so-called Section 22 waiver legitimated the use of import quotas (authorized by Section 22 of the U.S. Agricultural Adjustment Act of 1933) to prevent the undermining of U.S. domestic price support programs designed to limit agricultural output. Another prominent exemption was one that permitted the EC to use its variable levy to restrict agricultural imports in order to keep domestic agricultural prices above support levels as part of its CAP.

Even in cases where GATT rules were generally agreed to apply, its proceedings often had an indecisive character, with some disputes seeming never to reach final resolution. In forming GATT its members were unwilling to surrender national sovereignty to the degree necessary to make GATT judgments automatically legally binding and enforceable. Legal considerations aside, the establishment of a broad consensus (often, unanimity) was the practical requirement for most successful GATT actions. Nations often blocked consensus when they believed their vital interests to be threatened. The acceptance of GATT obligations and commitments in specific cases to a large extent depended on recognition of countries' mutual interests in fulfilling them. One of those interests involved uncertainty and fear about the consequences of a complete breakdown in international trading rules and the disastrous

Table VII. World Green Coffee Production

In 000 60-kg bags

Region and country	1984–85	1985–86[1]	1986–87[2]
North America	16,710	14,921	16,925
Costa Rica	2,516	1,514	2,200
El Salvador	2,680	2,225	2,375
Guatemala	2,703	2,640	2,950
Honduras	1,400	1,088	1,600
Mexico	4,250	4,480	4,660
South America	42,258	49,676	31,212
Brazil	27,000	33,000	13,900
Colombia	11,000	12,000	12,400
Ecuador	1,500	1,997	2,100
Africa	20,048	20,513	21,331
Cameroon	2,316	1,602	2,025
Ethiopia	2,600	3,100	3,150
Côte d'Ivoire	4,609	4,333	4,700
Kenya	1,493	2,087	2,000
Uganda	2,800	2,700	3,000
Zaire	1,540	1,800	1,620
Asia and Oceania	11,558	10,719	11,494
India	3,250	2,033	2,700
Indonesia	5,600	5,800	5,800
Total	90,574	95,829	80,962

[1]Preliminary.
[2]Forecast.
Source: USDA, Foreign Agricultural Service, December 1986.

Table VIII. World Cocoa Bean Production

In 000 metric tons

Region and country	1984–85	1985–86	1986–87[1]
North and Central America	102	100	106
South America	608	563	569
Brazil	415	395	400
Ecuador	128	100	100
Africa	1,077	1,089	1,065
Cameroon	120	117	120
Ghana	175	215	240
Côte d'Ivoire[2]	565	570	525
Nigeria[3]	170	135	125
Asia and Oceania	177	212	234
Malaysia	100	130	150
Total	1,963	1,964	1,974

[1]Forecast.
[2]Includes some cocoa marketed from Ghana.
[3]Includes cocoa marketed through Benin.
Source: USDA, Foreign Agricultural Service, October 1986.

A South Carolina farmer walks among stunted soybeans in a drought-stricken field. Nearly a month of dry days with temperatures above 32° C (90° F)—ten days above 38° C (100° F)—in the southeastern U.S. devastated crops, caused cattle to starve, contributed to more than 430 forest fires, and left ten people dead.
AP/WIDE WORLD

consequences such an occurrence could have for the international economy, as evidenced by the trade wars of the 1930s and their contribution to the Great Depression.

The question remained as to whether a consensus was obtainable on agricultural issues in the MTN. The answer would likely depend on how willing the principal participants were to modify the highly visible and sensitive domestic agricultural policies that their agricultural trade measures were designed to protect. Their willingness, in turn, would depend on the political dynamics and balance of interests existing in each country.

Food Security. The 1986 Food Aid Convention (FAC), part of the International Wheat Agreement (IWA), entered into force on July 1, 1986. It replaced the 1980 convention and would have a life of three years, with provision for successive two-year extensions should the Wheat Trade Convention, also part of the IWA, remain in force. The new FAC was closely patterned after the old, which contained pledges by member nations of the minimum quantities of food aid that they obligated themselves to provide annually. The total committed, in the form of grain or cash, was expected to match approximately the old FAC's 7.6 million tons.

The easing of the African food crisis led to a reduction in the shipment of food aid in cereals in 1985–86 from the previous year's record 12.5 million tons, but the amount provided still exceeded the internationally accepted ten million-ton target for the second year in a row. The continuation of more than ample grain supplies in the grain-exporting countries made it likely that 1986–87 commitments would about match those in 1985–86.

Pledges to the International Emergency Food Reserve (IEFR) administered by the World Food Program (WFP) in 1986 totaled 539,663 tons of cereals and 20,994 tons of other food as of October 17. The WFP, as of the same date, had in 1986 conducted 42 emergency operations (21 in Africa, 11 in Asia, 2 in the Middle East, and 8 in Latin America). The $131 million in aid, financed by the IEFR and a WFP emergency allocation, helped refugees (74%) and victims of drought (23%) and other natural disasters (3%).

Food aid pledges to the WFP by 58 countries for the 1987–88 biennium as of October totaled $623 million ($250 million by the U.S.), against a $1.4 billion WFP pledging target. The pledges for 1985–86 equaled $1,070,000,000, 79% of that biennium's target. James Ingram of Australia was reappointed jointly by the FAO director general and the UN secretary-general in October to a second five-year term as executive director of the WFP beginning in April 1987. (RICHARD M. KENNEDY)

See also Gardening.

This article updates the *Macropædia* article The History of AGRICULTURE.

Table IX. World Cotton Production
In 000,000 480-lb bales

Region and country	1984–85	1985–86	1986–87
Western Hemisphere	22.1	20.9	16.4
United States	13.0	13.4	9.8
Mexico	1.2	1.0	0.7
Brazil	4.4	3.8	3.4
Europe	1.0	1.2	1.1
U.S.S.R.	11.9	12.1	11.2
Africa	5.9	5.7	6.0
Egypt	1.8	2.0	2.0
The Sudan	1.0	1.0	0.1
Asia and Oceania[1]	57.3	39.0	35.7
China	28.7	19.0	17.2
India	7.9	8.4	7.8
Pakistan	4.6	5.7	5.5
Turkey	2.7	2.4	2.1
Total	88.1	78.9	70.4

[1]Includes Middle East.
Source: USDA, Foreign Agricultural Service, December 1986

Table X. Shipments of Food Aid in Cereals
In 000 metric ton grain equivalent

	Average 1981–82, 1983–84	1984–85	1985–86[1]	1986–87[1]
Australia	431	466	400	400
Canada	753	943	900	900
EC	1,705	2,504	1,600	1,600
By members	801	1,245	...	...
By organization	904	1,259	...	...
Japan	490	280	280	300
Sweden	96	88	87	80
United States	5,457	7,536	7,200	7,200
Others[2]	458	646	529	362
Total	9,390	12,463	10,996	10,842
Percentage to low-income food-deficit countries[3]	81%	85%	85%	86%

[1]Partly estimated.
[2]Includes Argentina, Austria, China, Finland, India, Norway, OPEC Special Fund, Saudi Arabia, Spain, Switzerland, Turkey, and World Food Program, but not necessarily for all years.
[3]Per capita incomes under U.S.$790 in 1984.
Source: FAO, *Food Outlook*, November 1986.

FISHERIES

Two major influences on fisheries emerged in 1986—*surimi* and superships—and the two were closely linked. The prophets of 1985 had confidently predicted a small-boat bonanza as Europe and the U.S. prepared to exploit their now more exclusive coastal waters. Instead, there was a boom in big processing trawlers with new orders being placed—Irish interests purchased two trawlers reported to be worth £6 million and £11 million, respectively. In the U.S. processing and factory trawlers were suddenly viable propositions, and an old trawler, *Seafreeze Atlantic,* was refurbished and given a new name.

In The Netherlands big trawlers continued to come off the slipways, led by the 90-m (295-ft)-long *Geertruid Margreta,* with 2,950 cu m (104,000 cu ft) of refrigerated carrying capacity. The Dutch supertrawlers were designed to serve as refrigerated carriers and to operate in distant waters under joint-venture agreements. There were more big ships for Norway, the Faeroe Islands, and Greenland. Norway had a new shrimp trawler that was 56 m (184 ft) long and could process and freeze 56 metric tons of shrimp in 24 hours, while scallop dredgers were reaching equally large proportions. A Norwegian yard built the 65-m (213-ft) *Arctic Challenge* for Ireland, with another to follow, and Norway was delivering ships to the Faeroese and Greenland fleets that were capable of working in pack ice and freezing shrimps on board. There was investment in big scallop vessels in Iceland as well. An important factor relating to shrimp and scallop vessels was that they needed to be large enough to fish offshore in rough waters and to process on board to ensure quality and extended trips.

The Irish and U.S. investment resulted from the phenomenal success in the 1980s of *surimi* (crab sticks), which were being imported in vast quantities by the U.S. from Japan. *Surimi* had heralded a completely new role for fish that was almost entirely complementary to the existing market for fish products. *Surimi* are made from minced, processed, and extruded fish, preferably bland fish such as Alaska pollack, with flavour and colour added to create a product resembling, for example, crab, prawn, or scallop. U.S. processors were quick to realize that buying Japanese *surimi* made of Alaska pollack fished from U.S. waters was a waste of foreign exchange, and their decision to catch and process for themselves led to the refurbishing of old trawlers. The scheme escalated, and it was announced that a 100-m (328-ft) former navy vessel was to be converted to a *surimi* factory with Norwegian funding. Other ship conversions were to follow, and output of 225,000 metric tons of *surimi* yearly by 1990 was forecast.

AP/WIDE WORLD

Workers position imitation scallops, spreading them out for freezing, at a processing plant in Redmond, Washington. Imitation scallops, prawns, and crab are among fish products made from *surimi*—minced, processed, and flavoured flesh of low-value fish.

In Europe the *surimi* revolution began when food technologists discovered that low-value abundant species such as blue whiting, Norway pout, and even sand eels could be processed into *surimi,* and that the product had wide applications. This necessitated giant trawlers, capable of taking 400 metric tons of such fish in a single tow and chilling it. The risk factor was negligible, given that production could always be switched to fish meal. Japan was quick to recognize the market potential, and its Kibun Group had built a *surimi*-product factory in Scotland.

The advent of *surimi* had implications for conservation since it would reduce the strong demand for traditionally accepted species. Scientists estimated that the oceans contained many millions of tons of small edible pelagic fish. It was possible, however, that the *surimi* market could have implications for the fish meal industry. Increased investment in Ireland was not only prompted by *surimi;* Norwegian shipbuilders were offering a highly competitive grant and loan package to foreign buyers that could not be matched by Irish or British yards.

In the European Communities (EC) 1986 was marked by the entry of Spain and Portugal. Although EC fishermen had seen Spanish entry as a threat to fish stocks because of the large Spanish fleet, their fears proved unfounded. Some Spanish trawlers earned a bad reputation, however, by breaking EC rules in the Irish Sea. The EC common fisheries policy continued to work reasonably well. Regulations were more rigidly enforced, and there were moves toward less reliance on catch quotas and more on licensing systems.

Spain and Portugal were quick to take advantage of EC grants to support their fleet-renewal programs. Portugal had announced a £37 million fleet-restructuring program that was mainly directed at the coastal and inshore sector, but because of its previous reliance on overseas fisheries, Portugal's data on domestic fish stocks were inadequate. Under Spain's new director of fisheries planning, Rafael Jaen Vergara, there was to be a major increase in the size of the fisheries inspectorate and more money was to be invested in fish farming and in stock enhancement by "re-seeding" the sea. Spain remained a major importer of fish and shellfish, though EC markets were seen as providing an opportunity to increase exports of processed, fish-based products, both canned and frozen. In 1986 most foreign joint-venture agreements of Spanish fishing companies became due for renegotiation under EC rules. Favourable terms were expected because of the combination of Spanish expertise and the greater bargaining power that the EC could command because of the potential market it represented.

France had a number of problems, including the closing of several shipyards and the decline of the port of Boulogne. Boulogne's activities were based originally on the herring and mackerel trade, and it was suffering because of its failure to meet consumer demand for more variety—the rival port of Lorient offered no less than 60 types of fish. Boulogne also suffered from poor infrastructure and bad industrial relations. It was hoped that a development plan would reverse the trend, which had already cost Boulogne six large trawlers. Like the U.S., France suffered from the low price of tuna. The cost of shipping it to Boulogne

Ship and crew are bade farewell as they leave Yokohama Port for Japan's last commercial whaling mission—for the present. Japan would abide by a conservation decree of the International Whaling Commission that, as of 1986, banned all but subsistence whaling.
AP/WIDE WORLD

had become excessive, with the result that greater emphasis was being placed on the West African canning plants. While the U.S. had sought new tuna grounds in the South Pacific, France had moved its ships to the Indian Ocean. A new price-support scheme was announced by the EC in October.

U.S. tuna-based canneries had been having a difficult time, and several plants were closed. Low prices had also affected Mexican plans to build up a tuna industry. One Star-Kist plant in Canada had to shut down following allegations of tainted tuna; the decision of the fisheries minister to release the tuna for sale had forced his resignation in September 1985. Later, 5,000 metric tons of good Star-Kist tuna was sold to France. In October 1986 an agreement was reached between the U.S. and the 13-nation South Pacific Forum (SPF) that would give the U.S. tuna-fishing rights in zones claimed by the South Pacific countries. In return, the SPF would receive license fees and a generous aid package.

The Falkland Islands remained in the news as massive catches of loligo squid by Poland, the U.S.S.R., and Spain depressed the world squid market. A British fishing company chartered 50 Japanese squid boats and planned to double that number within a year. In 1986 the first small consignment of processed crabmeat arrived in the U.K. from the Falklands. Problems with Argentina persisted, however. The Argentine 200-mi limit overlapped the U.K.'s 150-mi security zone, which Argentina did not recognize. Three foreign fishing vessels came under fire from Argentine vessels, once with loss of life.

Krill fishing proved less lucrative than had been hoped. Although easy to catch, krill were so delicate that only small amounts could be brought aboard, and processing proved difficult and costly. Only Polish, Soviet, and Japanese vessels were fishing krill in any quantity. Marketing was difficult, although frozen krill had proved ideal for feeding farmed salmon. Significantly, the optimum catch was revised downward to only 50,000 metric tons, well below the 125,000 metric tons currently being fished and the 150 million metric tons that had been widely predicted. There were fears that to catch krill at all might upset the delicate balance of the Antarctic food chain. The Falklands fishery was being blamed for a new, high mortality among penguins resulting from malnutrition.

More positively, Japan and Norway agreed to phase out whale catching, but Iceland flouted the whale ban by catching for "research purposes," which provided quite a large quota. It also provided a problem, since under International Whaling Commission rules meat and by-products from these whales could not be exported, and Iceland would have difficulty consuming the entire catch. (*See* WORLD AFFAIRS [Western Europe]: *Iceland.*)

The U.S.S.R. tried to stimulate domestic fish consumption to 18 kg (40 lb) a head yearly; at the same time, it called for improved technology and for more emphasis on quality rather than quantity. Poland was building new vessels, including 94-m (308-ft) factory ships to join its 81 factory trawlers, 465 cutters, and 2 mother ships. A Finnish shipyard announced it was building three 179-m (587-ft) crab- and fish-processing ships with a daily capacity of 40,000 cans and 60,000 kg (130,000 lb) of fish or crab for the U.S.S.R.

Members of the EC were also eager to adopt more high technology, and the "Halios" project was launched to produce designs for the "trawler of the 1990s." Finance was provided by the participating countries, chiefly France and Spain. China increased its contacts with the West in an effort to improve its technology, held a fisheries exhibition, and passed new laws promoting fishing and aquaculture. Output in 1986 was about 4.1 million metric tons from the sea and 1.4 million metric tons from inland fisheries, while the fleet was estimated at 39,000 boats. In Southeast Asia rapid expansion of fisheries and aquaculture led to

Table XI. World Fisheries, 1984[1]
In 000 metric tons

Country	Catch		Trade	
	Total	Inland	Imports	Exports
Japan	12,021.2	202.7	1,296.8	887.8
U.S.S.R.	10,592.9	881.5	371.2	497.0
China	5,926.8	2,249.7	—	105.8
U.S.	4,814.3	74.6	1,140.2	459.9
Chile	4,499.3	0.4	—	951.3
Peru	2,997.0	24.5	—	516.5
India	2,858.9	1,081.9	—	84.7
South Korea	2,477.1	50.1	88.9	376.9
Norway	2,456.0	0.3	57.6	760.0
Thailand	2,249.8	150.0	94.6	403.9
Indonesia	2,217.2	538.0	50.5	65.4
Philippines	1,935.4	600.0	6.1	51.9
Denmark	1,846.6	22.7	307.7	757.8
North Korea	1,650.0	100.0	—	26.5
Iceland	1,534.8	0.4	3.2	483.4
Spain	1,267.6	24.0	293.7	205.0
Canada	1,220.6	46.0	117.3	492.3
Mexico	1,103.6	116.9	21.4	54.6
Brazil	946.0	201.0	41.5	43.4
Ecuador	867.5	—	—	155.6
United Kingdom	815.3	10.1	770.2	295.1
Vietnam	765.0	220.0	—	16.1
Bangladesh	758.0	586.0	—	16.8
France	738.8	...	532.7	163.6
Poland	719.2	34.5	140.7	124.9
Burma	612.8	140.0	—	5.7
South Africa	598.8	0.8	105.6	94.0
Turkey	566.9	46.5	0.3	27.0
Italy	495.0	43.8	421.2	113.1
Morocco	467.5	1.3	0.3	162.5
The Netherlands	462.4	3.9	452.1	481.5
Pakistan	378.7	70.6	—	33.2
Nigeria	373.8	183.5	138.0	—
West Germany	326.8	22.8	961.6	372.4
Faeroe Islands	320.8	—	2.8	128.9
Argentina	314.2	9.3	12.3	126.2
Portugal	285.2	...	108.2	59.9
Sweden	279.0	10.0	221.5	137.6
Venezuela	265.0	21.1	2.6	28.0
Tanzania	262.8	231.6	—	—
Ghana	238.4	40.0	—	—
Romania	232.2	55.8	42.0	—
East Germany	223.3	18.1	27.2	—
Senegal	222.6	...	17.1	90.1
Other	6,113.2	1,601.8	2,910.4	1,514.3
World	82,769.8	9,716.2	10,757.5	11,370.6

[1]Excludes whaling.
Source: United Nations Food and Agriculture Organization, *Yearbook of Fishery Statistics*, vol. 58 and 59.

expectations that the region would shortly surpass Europe's export performance. India planned an additional 100 or more deep-sea trawlers.

Further advances were made in communications with the promise of a $5,000 satellite system for smaller vessels, while the eventual phaseout of the Loran C navigation system in favour of the new Global Positioning System was predicted. Fish finders could now search for fish in all directions simultaneously. Expected in the near future were a three-dimensional sonar display and a "spiral scan" of the water column. (H. S. NOEL)

This article updates the *Macropædia* article Commercial Fishing and Marine Products.

FOOD PROCESSING

The physical effects of the nuclear power station disaster at Chernobyl, U.S.S.R., in April 1986 on food-processing operations in Western Europe were still evident several months after the event. (*See* ENERGY: *Sidebar*.) Dairy products were most vulnerable to radioactive contamination, and certain brands were withdrawn from the market. Meanwhile, food processors were cautious about importing canned fruit and vegetables from Eastern Europe for use in food manufacturing.

Irradiation. The psychological effects of the disaster persisted throughout the year and led to questioning of an official report, published in Britain just before the accident, on irradiated foods. The report stated that such foods were safe and wholesome and recommended that legislation be enacted to permit the use of irradiation as a preservative technique. Issued by the U.K. government's Advisory Committee on Irradiated and Novel Foods (ACINF), it was the culmination of several years' study, in which the Leatherhead Food Research Association played a major part. This establishment, which was rapidly becoming the world's leading authority on irradiation for preservation, attracted considerable international attention.

Irradiation was being used in a number of countries, including the U.S. (where it was permitted in 1985 for pork and vegetable seasonings), France, The Netherlands, Bangladesh, Brazil, Chile, and South Africa. It was reported that an irradiation plant was under construction in Paraguay. There was also considerable interest in the Far East, and a plant for irradiating prawns was to be built in Thailand. In Europe, France led the field in the application of irradiation to food, with four plants in commercial operation and about a dozen more planned. In Canada a committee of consumers and food industry representatives recommended special labeling of irradiated foods, with wholly irradiated foods and food containing irradiated ingredients being clearly distinguished.

Consumer Campaigns. While Chernobyl prompted attacks against the use of irradiation to preserve foods, these assaults were only part of a much wider and rapidly escalating campaign against modern food-processing techniques in general and food additives in particular. In Britain the antiadditive campaign coincided with the reorganization of the food industry's trade body, which on January 1 became the Food and Drink Federation (FDF). The FDF resulted from the merger of two separate bodies, the Food Manufacturers' Federation and the Food and Drink Industries Council, and their many affiliates. It gave the U.K. food industry a single representative voice, and as soon as it was formed the FDF announced that its first priority would be to counter what was seen as organized propaganda against the food industry emanating from the media.

Independently of the FDF, sections of the U.K. food industry and individual companies acted to defend their products. Thus, for example, the sugar industry, through its trade association, the Sugar Bureau, held seminars to reassure consumers that sugar has no causal links with heart disease, diabetes, obesity, or other scourges of society. The attitude of some other segments of the food industry was more pragmatic and ambivalent. Throughout the Western world food companies responded positively to the growing antagonism toward additives and the increased awareness of the importance of good diet. Increasingly products were advertised as being free from artificial colourings, flavourings, and other contentious ingredients. At the same time, suppliers of ingredients were directing their research efforts toward developing natural and nature-identical counterparts of hitherto widely used substances now being stigmatized as artificial.

Health Foods. The health food industry, in particular, benefited from these trends, and many health food products were developed by food manufacturers large and small.

AGRICULTURAL RESEARCH SERVICE, USDA; PHOTOGRAPH, BARRY FITZGERALD

Mangoes are irradiated in tests at the USDA Subtropical Horticultural Research Station in Miami, Florida. The process was approved as an alternative to chemical pesticides for fruits, vegetables, and fresh pork.

The market was burgeoning in all the Western industrialized countries, led by the U.S. and West Germany. The success of new food products depended on added value, convenience, and a suggestion of health benefit. In the U.S. fitness foods became the fastest growing sector of the industry. No longer restricted to health fanatics and the elderly in California and New York City, these foods had captured more than 10% of the $300 billion-a-year retail food market in the U.S. Sales were growing by more than 6% annually, compared with less than 1% for the rest of the food industry.

Fitness foods included high-fibre, low-sodium, reduced-fat, low-cholesterol, reduced-calorie foods and beverages and low-caffeine drinks. They produced huge sales and profits, and most major U.S. manufacturers had at least one fitness version of their conventional products. Many of the largest food processors failed to find substitute ingredients for sugar, sodium, or fat, however, so they simply reduced the sugar and salt content of their existing brands to produce what marketing people called "flankers"—healthier versions of existing products.

New Products. Snack foods had become big business and an established part of the U.S. and European diet. The European market for snack foods was growing at three times the rate of the food industry as a whole. Europeans were following the U.S. practice of "grazing"—eating on the move whenever they felt hungry. Previously restricted to young people, snacks were also becoming popular among the elderly who, finding three meals a day unnecessary, replaced one with a snack that combined ease of preparation with small portion size. Reflecting the concern over fitness, snacks were becoming more nutritious and satisfying, with much of the increased nutrition coming from processed proteins. New products in this category that had been tried on the U.S. market included a meatless sausage made from *surimi* (fish protein), a high-fibre, high-protein powdered drink made from *surimi* and cottonseed protein, and cheese analogues in which the butterfat was replaced by vegetable fat. (See *Fisheries,* above.)

The microwave oven had become a standard appliance in the U.S., and in the U.K. domestic penetration was expected to reach 20% of households by the end of 1986. The boom affected manufacturers of food products and of packaging materials. Increasingly, consumers and retailers asked that more products be developed for microwave cooking and that microwave instructions be put on such products as prepared meals.

Packaging Developments. Apprehensive manufacturers of food and packaging materials worldwide paid increased attention to the problem of product tampering, which until recently had been confined to the U.S. In 1982 seven people in the Chicago area had died from taking cyanide-laced capsules of the over-the-counter painkiller Tylenol, and in 1986 a New York woman died from the same cause. Poisonous substances were found in or warnings were received about a wide variety of food products, including orange juice, yogurt, packaged cakes and biscuits, hotdogs, sauces, and other products in packages that were simple to open. The food industry was a particularly vulnerable target for terrorism and extortion of this kind since most food outlets were self-service stores where products lay unattended. The logical deduction was that the poisoned products had been bought, taken away for impregnation, and then surreptitiously put back on the supermarket shelves.

Because packaging materials, heat-sealing machines, and vacuum formers for making small plastic parts were easily obtainable, plastic closings and seals could be reapplied to packages after the original materials had been removed. The packaging industry was attempting to fight back by developing closings with a higher degree of tamper evidence—that is, closings that would clearly show when the seal had been broken. One example was a screw cap for a vacuum container with a flexible blister in the centre; the blister remained flat until the pack was opened, but when the vacuum seal was broken, it stood up in relief. An effective technique was to incorporate a hologram, of the type used on credit cards, in the packaging material. The holograms were virtually impossible to forge, but they were expensive to produce and would raise packaging costs to an unacceptable level.

The Austrian wine scandal of 1985 was followed by the Italian scandal of 1986, when a number of persons died from poisoning by methyl alcohol. Only one type of Italian red wine was implicated. Several wine merchants suspected of adding methyl alcohol to increase the alcohol content, and hence the value of the wine, were arrested.

The use of plastic bottles and jars for food and drink continued to grow, and several manufacturers of packaging materials announced plans to boost output, particularly of polyethylene terephthalate (PET). The world's fastest growing packaging material, PET was already widely used for soft-drink bottles and was increasingly being used for alcoholic drinks and general food products. Eastman Kodak, the world's largest producer of PET, was building two plants, one in the U.S. and the other in the U.K. Imperial Chemical Industries, Europe's biggest PET supplier, was also building new plant capacity. Plysu, a U.K. plastic-container manufacturer, opened a factory in Bedfordshire specifically for the production of plastic milk and fruit-juice bottles.

Company Developments. Some noteworthy new food plants were opened or announced during the year. The Kibin Group, a Japanese leader in food technology and processing, invested nearly £3 million in a factory near Glasgow, Scotland, to produce a line of high-quality frozen seafood-style products from *surimi.* Opened in mid-1986, the plant was the first of its kind in Europe. The Coca-Cola Co. announced plans to establish a citrus project in Belize over the next 7–15 years. If successful, the project would convert 10,000 ha (24,700 ac) of timber forest into an alternative source of citrus concentrate for the company. The value of the project was believed to be around $120 million. The 100th anniversary of the invention of Coca-Cola by an obscure pharmacist in Atlanta, Ga., was celebrated in May by the company and its subsidiaries throughout the world.

Legislation. On July 25 the Council of Ministers of the European Communities (EC) adopted a directive on liability for defective products, which the U.K.'s FDF considered discriminatory against food manufacturers. Under the terms of the directive, producers would be strictly liable, without proof of fault, for any damage or injury caused by a defective product, and consumers would no longer have to prove negligence on the part of manufacturers. Because the directive exempted primary agricultural products, food and drink processors using such products could find themselves liable for an inherent defect in a raw material over which they had no control. The FDF was pressing the EC Commission for an interpretation that would treat processors more favourably. The Council of Ministers also announced a total ban on the use of growth-promoting hormones in the rearing of livestock, which should reduce the EC meat surplus. (ANTHONY WOOLLEN)

See also Environment; Health and Disease; Industrial Review: *Beverages; Textiles; Tobacco.*

This article updates the *Macropædia* article FOOD PROCESSING.

Anthropology

New primate fossils were found during the last two years, particularly in China and Africa, but advances in the study of human evolution relied less on new finds than on new ways of analyzing the existing data. More paleontologists and geologists were joining anthropologists and anatomists in the study of hominoid and hominid evolution. Environmental reconstruction was playing a greater role in interpretation of the fossil record, while high-tech microscopy imaging was making microanatomical investigations feasible on fossil bones and teeth. The 60th anniversary of the discovery of the first australopithecine gave rise to extensive published symposia.

New Asian fossil primates included a jaw fragment of *Amphipithecus,* an Eocene gibbon-sized primate previously known only from the type specimen. The new find made possible the reconstruction of most of the lower left jaw. As had been previously proposed, *Amphipithecus* was an anthropoid. This again raised the possibility that the origin of the monkey-ape-human ancestry could have been in southern Asia. Other fossil finds were the products of the active research of Chinese paleontologists. The Lufeng site produced a large collection of *Ramapithecus* and *Sivapithecus* bones and teeth, and eight locations in north and south China yielded additional specimens of *Homo erectus* representing a time span of 800,000 years. From a site in North Vietnam came evidence that *H. erectus* and *Gigantopithecus* coexisted in one locality.

Continuing analysis of the Buluk site (early Miocene of Kenya) resulted in a fossil, dated older than 17.2 million years, that was identified as a *Sivapithecus.* This was the earliest date for this genus, which also existed in India, Turkey, and Greece, as well as in Pakistan and China, where it dates as recently as 8 million years ago. It was possible that the 17.2 million-year-old fossil belonged to the genus *Kenyapithecus,* a middle Miocene group now considered separate from the Ramapithecines but close to the ape-human divergence. There was general agreement that all the pongids, or great apes, diverged from an ancestral stock in the middle Miocene, and that the hominid split-off presumably occurred in the late Miocene. The paucity of fossil evidence in Africa at this time was particularly unfortunate, since this was where the last common ancestor of the African pongids and humans should be found. At least this would be consistent with both the morphological and molecular indications.

Announcement of a *Sivapithecus*-like hominid fossil dated at 4,150,000 years would seem to close the gap somewhat. It was found west of Lake Baringo in Kenya at a location called Tabarin. Older by one million years than the material from Laetoli, Tanzania, or the Afar area of Ethiopia, it resembles the smaller hominid fossils at those sites. Little more could be said because to date the Tabarin fossil consisted of only a fragment of mandible, the first and second molar, and a piece of a premolar.

A find from the newly explored western shore of Lake Turkana in Kenya, dated at 1.6 million years, was a young male *Homo erectus* with much of the whole skeleton intact. The approximately 12-year-old boy was about 1.6 m (5 ft 5 in) tall and would have reached 1.8 m (6 ft) as an adult—certainly taller than most, if not all, of the earlier hominids. The postcranial skeleton is quite modern, although with a somewhat distinct femoral joint.

Another fossil from the western shore, WT 17000, was dated at 2.5 million years and consisted of part of a skull lacking most of the teeth. Alan Walker and Richard Leakey assigned the fossil to *Australopithecus boisei,* making it substantially the oldest of the robust australopithecines. *A. boisei* had been considered the end of the lineage that may have begun with *A. afarensis* (represented by "Lucy," the 40% complete skeleton discovered at Hadar); now it appeared almost at the beginning. This caused some investigators to revise the two-pronged diagram that had the australopithecines evolving in one direction after *A. afarensis* and the *Homo* line going in a different but somewhat parallel direction. Instead, the new model called for a trifurcation, with the new line being that of *A. boisei.* Not everyone agreed, however. WT 17000 shares a number of primitive features with *A. afarensis* and with the chimpanzee and gorilla and thus may have evolved parallel to a Lucy-type primate instead of being its descendant. Or perhaps WT 17000 represents the "other" kinds of fossils at Hadar that coexisted with Lucy but are thought by some experts to be of a different species. Others would deny that WT 17000 is an *A. boisei* at all.

"Archaic *Homo sapiens*" is a term used to refer to those populations that are presumably morphologically transitional between *Homo erectus* and modern *Homo sapiens.* That this is a piece of ongoing evolution is generally accepted. While most research had been devoted to divergence of the human from the ape lineage, increasing research was now directed to the origin of the modern *H. sapiens* species. The questions involved the extent to which there was a radiation outward from a centre of modern types, or whether most local populations of *H. erectus* gradually evolved, in situ, into *H. sapiens.* Both processes seemed to have been operating.

Nevertheless, an African origin for the first fully modern humans was proposed because of the modern morphology of fossils from Ethiopia, Kenya, The Sudan, Morocco, and, particularly, from the Middle Stone Age deposits at the South African site of Klasies, dated at 100,000 years ago. While there was some doubt about the evolution of anatomically modern humans from western European "classic" Neanderthal populations, continuous evolutions of such populations in central Europe and the Middle East may have occurred. As for Asia, some investigators proposed a "multiregional evolution theory," postulating that regional distinctiveness first appears at the edges of the range of polytypic human species and by gene flow continually shares with populations situated closer to the middle. David Pilbeam suggested that archaic human morphology showed great stability and that the transition to modern human morphology was long and slow, beginning about 100,000 to 300,000 years ago and gradually picking up speed until the final, very rapid change to fully modern *H. sapiens.*

In general, the change everywhere was from a robust morphology to a gracile one, with the extreme of robustness represented by the classical Neanderthals of western Europe. The evolutionary reasons for the change are not at all clear. Cultural change, including an increasingly effective tool kit, does not coincide well chronologically with morphological change, nor is it clear whether there was sufficient time for a cultural change to exert selective pressure leading toward the rather dramatic "gracilization" of worldwide human populations. Continuing detailed study of Neanderthal morphology, particularly of the postcranial skeleton, revealed not only a rugged anatomy but one that in some parts differs considerably from modern *H. sapiens.* For example, Neanderthal pubic bones provided for a birth canal 15–25% larger than in modern humans. Did this result in a longer gestational period? Were Neanderthal babies more neurologically mature at birth? A new find in

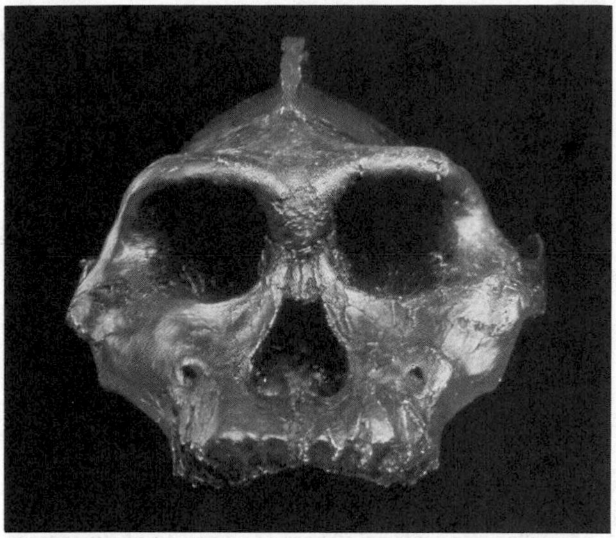

Fossil WT 17000, dated at 2.5 million years, is the oldest discovered *Australopithecus boisei*. Since the skull's age nearly equals that of a species formerly considered a precursor of *A. boisei*, the find led some researchers to revise a current evolution model.

JOHN BOWDEN/DISCOVER MAGAZINE © 1986 TIME INC.

the Devil's Tower Cave in England yielded a Neanderthal child who died at age three but whose brain size was 95% that of an adult. In modern humans this stage of maturity is not achieved until at least age six.

There was new research on the evolution of the size and complexity of the brain based on detailed examination of the interior of fossil skulls. Some of these investigations were greatly aided by new radiographic imaging techniques. Evidence from brain vascularization and the patterns of the sulci, the shallow grooves on the brain surface, seemed to indicate that the hominid brain enlarged before it increased in complexity. The humanlike brain might not have existed until the *H. habilis* stage of evolution was reached about two million years ago.

(HERMANN K. BLEIBTREU)

See also ARCHAEOLOGY.

This article updates the *Macropædia* article Human Evolution.

Archaeology

Eastern Hemisphere. Judging from what had been reported by year's end, there seemed to have been no particularly remarkable archaeological find made in the Old World during 1986. For obvious political reasons, little excavation was possible in many of the Old World areas critical for the recovery of culture-historical data. These included Iran and Iraq, where the war between those two countries dragged on, and Lebanon, still torn by factional strife. The political situation also had its effect in other ways. The large and elaborately planned world archaeological congress of the International Union of Prehistoric and Protohistoric Sciences, scheduled to be held in Southampton, England, in September 1986, was canceled following a dispute over whether colleagues from South Africa would be allowed to attend. The *New York Times* reported that the Israel Museum in Jerusalem was the centre of a controversy regarding the exhibition of the large private collection that the late Moshe Dayan had obtained through questionable means. The *Times* also gave the background for the two-year delay in an exhibition, at the Metropolitan Museum of Art in New York City, of a large collection of antiquities from Israel. The delay was caused by Arab claims against Israel's right to many of these objects.

Among other archaeological news items of the year might be included the marked increase in field "schools" that accept paying amateur volunteers and the buildup of attention, pro and con, over the question of whether there has ever been unequivocal evidence of cannibalism. A University of Colorado team, working in southeastern France, reported the recovery of human bones from which the flesh had been stripped with stone tools. The February issue of the journal *World Archaeology* contained an excellent series of articles on current understandings of the beginnings of writing, including Egyptian, Mesopotamian, Hittite, Cretan, Indian, and Chinese. Interest in the return of Halley's Comet prompted searches for evidence of earlier sightings. Both the 11th-century Bayeux Tapestry and Babylonian cuneiform tablets of 380–40 BC indicate knowledge of the comet.

Several highly respected archaeological colleagues died during the year. Harvard lost a brilliant young prehistorian, Glynn Isaac, and a revered classical scholar, George Hanfmann. Richard Barnett, a British Museum specialist on Near Eastern art, and the distinguished French prehistorian André Leroi Gourhan also died.

Pleistocene Prehistory. As usual, the claims for the earliest traces of human activity (in this case, simple quartz tools of 2 million to 2.5 million years ago) came from Africa, at sites along the Semliki River in Zaire. Claims of basal Pleistocene occupations were made for both Israel and European Turkey. In the latter case, a cave called Yarimburgaz just west of Istanbul yielded pebble tools of the early African Olduvan type, geologically sealed in a very early deposit. If further evidence substantiated the find, Yarimburgaz might well provide the earliest trace of hominid occupation in Europe proper. From Jersey (once a peninsula of western Europe), traces of a mammoth stampede trap of *c.* 200,000 years ago were reported. The Arago cave in the French Pyrenees, *c.* 120,000 BC, continued to yield good evidence of the *Homo erectus* form itself, an impressive stone industry, and both animal remains and environmental data. Its excavator, Henry de Lumley, believed that Arago shows the earliest convincing evidence of hunting by humans. It had been generally believed that the earliest hominids were simple collectors and scavengers.

Marek Zvelebil of the University of Sheffield, England, provided (in *Scientific American,* May 1986) a useful summary of the evidence for postglacial foragers in the early forests of northern and western Europe. In the Languedoc region of France, four "mesolithic" sites yielded bones believed to be of domesticated sheep, and there were large quantities of legumes (lentils, peas, chick-peas) as well as wild fruits and nuts. It was announced that the tree-ring chronology for western Europe, linking the Irish and West German sequences, was now firm back to 7,277 years ago. There were hopes for an earlier reach backward once a broken span of tree rings was filled in. In Denmark a major find was reported as coming from the remains of a 6,000-year-old fishing settlement on the island of Fyn.

Middle East. The claim for an "important" and "new" Egyptian tomb near Sakkara appeared to be much overstated. However, "stalactites and stalagmites of salt" in the tomb stimulated new studies of how moisture leaches into Egyptian tombs. No other detailed reports on archaeological activity in Egypt had come through by year's end, although archaeologists from many different countries were active there. Of particular interest was a study, by a Smithsonian Institution team, of long cores drilled from

Noel T. Boaz (left) and John W. K. Harris record data from stone tools at least two million years old. They discovered nearly 300 such tools in eastern Zaire. The finds argue for further study of human evolution in the largely unexplored area of Africa in which they were found.

WILLIAM DEKAY © 1986 NATIONAL GEOGRAPHIC SOCIETY

the sediments of the Nile Delta. They included volcanic ash, evidently from the violent eruption of the Santorini volcano in the Aegean about 3,500 years ago. This ash could account for the biblical "thick darkness in all the land of Egypt, three days" of the Moses story.

Archaeologists, both domestic and foreign, were active in Israel during the year. A reconsideration of the claim that Jericho was already a fortified town over 9,000 years ago was made by Hebrew University professor Ofar Bar-Yosef, whose study indicated that the "wall" was part of a flood-control system. The location of a rich tomb in a First Temple context in Jerusalem was taken to mean that the city was then both larger and grander than had heretofore been supposed. Owing to an unusually low water level in the Sea of Galilee, a wrecked wooden boat of the 1st century BC was recovered (and dubbed by the media the "Jesus boat").

There were teams from most of the Western European countries and from Australia, Canada, and the U.S. at work in Jordan. A new American Schools of Oriental Research institute building was completed in Amman. Among other sites, there were notable results from many years' work on both the settlement area and the cemetery at Bab-ed-Drha (one of the "Cities of the Plain"), dating back toward 3000 BC.

Nothing of archaeological interest happened in Lebanon or Iran, and little had been reported from Iraq and Syria, where most efforts had dealt with salvage excavations on sites in areas soon to be flooded behind dams. The salvage work along the upper reaches of the Euphrates in Turkey was about to end as the waters rose behind two major dams. The most remarkable event of the year in Turkey, in the ancient Hittite capital city of Bogazkoy, was the recovery of a fine large inscribed bronze tablet with the complete text of a heretofore incomplete inscription.

The Greco-Roman World. In Greece and Italy the long-continuing field programs of the various national "schools" had not yet been reported. There was concern among the French, who for many years had been working in ancient Delphi, that a proposed bauxite-processing plant nearby would pollute the buildings on the site. The harmful effects of air pollution on the monuments of the Athenian Acropolis were well known. On Crete a Royal Ontario Museum team continued digging in both Minoan and protogeometric Greek levels at Komos. At the site of Murio in Tuscany, Italy, a U.S. team had recovered much new information on Etruscan culture. At Bova Marina, on the very toe of the Italian "boot," what might well be the earliest Jewish synagogue in Europe was being cleared. The floor plan of a sumptuous Roman house was encountered during the construction of a parking lot in Aix-en-Provence, France.

Eastern Asia. In the U.S.S.R. east of the Urals, a site described as the "Troy of Siberia" was under excavation. It was said to have been the capital of the Khakasses, destroyed in the Mongol invasion, as described in the poem "Iskander Name." In Tadzhikistan a site called Takhti Sanguine was yielding an interesting collection of Bactrian and Hellenistic material. There appeared to be an increasing amount of archaeological activity in China, much of it pointed toward the clearance of tombs. In one case, the tomb of a nobleman of *c.* 2,500 years ago near Xian (Sian), the tomb itself was completely bare save for the "gambling implements" of tomb robbers of much later times. An "archaeological boom" was also reported from Japan, particularly near the city of Nara where artifacts and inscriptions of the Asuka period (AD 552–645) were being recovered. (ROBERT J. BRAIDWOOD)

Western Hemisphere. Noteworthy developments in archaeology during 1986 included the emergence of hotly debated positions concerning legislation and policy decisions on antiquities smuggling and disputes over Native American rights concerning the reburial of precontact human remains, as well as significant new discoveries.

In heated debates that reflected deep divisions within agencies, universities, and the archaeological profession, archaeologists and physical anthropologists were forced to confront a clash between scientific and cultural values over the issue of long-term storage and study of bones versus Native American demands for the respectful treatment and reburial of ancestral remains. While some in the scientific community upheld the scientific benefits of unrestricted access to human skeletal material for studies of past pathology and physical characteristics, others argued that long-term storage is unnecessary and that the scientific techniques for proper analysis can better address the sensitivities of both Native Americans and Europeans concerned about ancestral remains. In New York the site of a projected $20 million sewage-treatment plant was found to contain the well-preserved remains of an early Iroquois settlement and six human burials. After intense negotiations between traditional Iroquois leaders and federal and state officials, the burials were temporarily removed, briefly studied in coordination with an Indian spiritual leader, and ceremonially reburied according to traditional procedures.

Of concern to Native Americans and archaeologists throughout the U.S. was the burgeoning growth of black-market trade in pillaged artifacts from prehistoric sites. As recently as the 1970s, the problem appeared to be centred in Latin America, where whole culture areas were being ravaged. However, it was now becoming a focus of concern in the U.S. as well. A *New York Times Magazine* article highlighted the limited response by the authorities as compared with the high profits for the looters. Single specimens of ancient Pueblo pots were selling for an average of $15,000, a ceremonial Hopi basket for as much as $120,000, and the financial harvest from a single site could reach $1 million. In Virginia treasure hunters were sentenced to a year in jail after they were caught using sophisticated detection devices to plunder Civil War artifacts from the Richmond National Battlefield Park. In the Southwest, where federal officials estimated that 80 to 90% of all sites had been disturbed or destroyed, one treasure hunter found with $2 million worth of stolen artifacts received only a suspended sentence.

It was noteworthy that a rising number of archaeological discoveries resulted from legally mandated environmental impact studies, and that many of these field investigations were conducted by private archaeological enterprises rather than universities or museums, the traditional sponsors of field survey and excavation teams. During a government-sponsored archaeological survey in California's Sierra Nevadas, a team led by Ann Peak of Peak and Associates found what might represent the oldest human dwelling in North America. A radiocarbon age determination of at least 9,700 years from charcoal in a hearth located within an oval packed-earth house floor suggested that Native Americans were living in more sedentary, permanent settlements 2,000 to 3,000 years earlier than had previously been documented.

One important line of evidence used to document the early presence of man in the Americas beyond 12,000 years ago was refuted in 1986 by new age determinations. In 1966 animal bone was found eroding out of a deep gorge of the Old Crow River in the Yukon Territory, Canada, which included several fragments of bison and mammoth and a sharpened caribou bone tool or "hide scraper." Initially it yielded a series of radiocarbon dates of between 25,000 and 32,000 years ago, suggesting the presence of early man 20,000 years before the time that many archaeologists believe man first ventured onto the North American continent. Suspecting contamination from modern carbon sources, D. Earl Nelson of Simon Fraser University, Burnaby, B.C., used minute samples from previously untested protein-containing tissues of the bones to test the radioactive age in a nuclear accelerator. The new dates were almost 30,000 years younger. Although the bone artifacts were ancient, they were manufactured several hundred years before the time of Christ.

In several localities in North America where conditions had favoured exceptional preservation, unexpected discoveries were brought to light, including a fleet of 2,000-year-old wooden canoes in North Carolina and preserved cloth associated with a 7,500-year-old cemetery in Florida. Stephen R. Claggart of the North Carolina Division of Archives was directing a project to salvage the remains of at least 21 cypress wood canoes, which were exposed by falling water levels in Lake Phelps in Pettigrew State Park. The decline was caused by drought and the use of lake waters to fight forest fires. The boats, one of which was some 8.5 m (28 ft.) in length, appeared to have been abandoned by ancient inhabitants whose artifacts and stone tools provided the first clues to the discovery as the modern shoreline began to recede.

In another case of exceptional preservation, David Dickel and Glen Doran, codirectors of the three-year-old Florida State University excavation of a cemetery dating to 5500 BC, discovered the body of a seven–eight-year-old female child covered by a cloth that represents the earliest known example of one complex weaving technique. Around her neck was a bead necklace. Both finds, like the ancient house floor in California, suggest that archaeological reconstructions concerning the supposed "hunter-gatherer" lifestyle of these early Indian peoples might have to be revised. The discoveries point to a more "leisure and production"-oriented way of life and the presence of social status differences thousands of years earlier than had been projected by many archaeologists.

A major trend in recent South American archaeological research was the increasing shift to a concern for past environmental conditions, food patterns, and non-Western agricultural and animal-domestication practices through time. Excavations in Peru by Sheila and Thomas Pazorski of the University of Denver, Colo., added new evidence indicating the existence of a diversified coastal agricultural complex, based on native potato-like tubers, beans, peanuts, and native fruits such as peppers and lucuma, that was well established as early as the 2nd millennium BC. The Pazorskis' tabulations of the differing plant foods through time showed that corn (maize), the main staple of ancient Mexican cultures, did not even make its appearance on the coast of Peru until 900 BC. Many scholars had assumed that the coastal peoples were primarily dependent on fish and marine resources, but the research supports the existence, as early as 2000 BC, of a distinctive coastal agricultural system that differed from both the Mexican maize-based economy and the native grain and camelid economies of the Andean highlands.

A parallel study of changing animal bone ratios through time, from excavations of the southern highlands of Junin in Peru by Katherine Moore of the University of Michigan, documented the fundamental shift to a mixed hunting economy and the potential domestication of camelids as early as the 4th millennium BC. These plant and animal

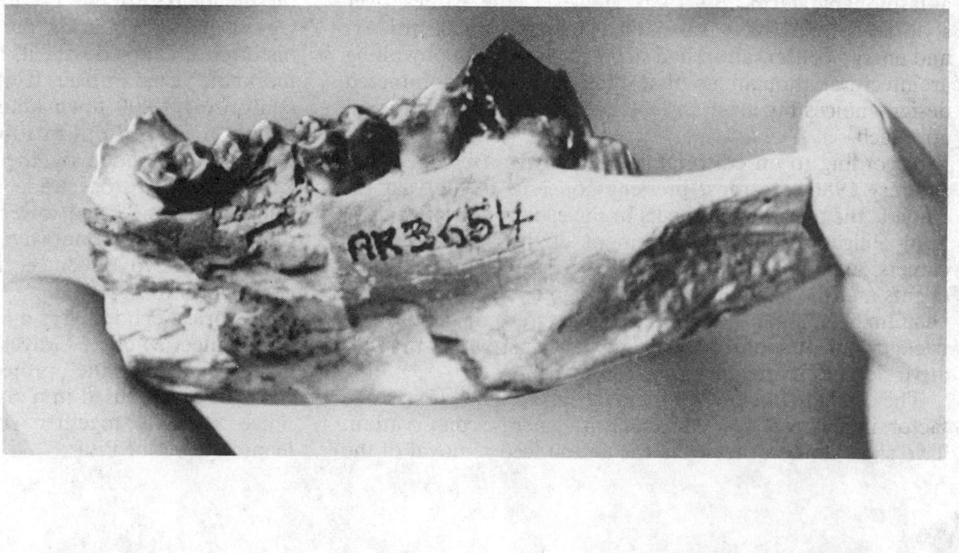

AP/WIDE WORLD

The jawbone of a Propleopus, a small kangaroolike animal, was among several discoveries of remnants of previously unknown species millions of years old in Riversleigh, Australia.

studies together added new evidence for the clear presence of indigenous economic patterns early in Andean culture history, long before the establishment of the Pre-Inca and Inca empires in coastal and highland Peru.

In the former Inca territory of Mendoza Province in west-central Argentina, Juan Schobinger of the National University of Cuyo announced the discovery of an Inca child mummy found at over 4,575 m (15,000 ft.) elevation. The remains of the well-preserved eight–nine-year-old child were found in a stone cairn, wrapped in a feather-covered textile and associated with small stone llama and human figurines covered with gold and spondylus shell from coastal Ecuador.

Controversial new lines of evidence relating to the antiquity and date of entry of early man into the New World also surfaced in Chile. Thomas Dillehay of the University of Kentucky, working at the well-publicized early man site of Monte Verde in south-central Chile, reported the discovery of early houses and living floors dating 13,000 years ago. This date attribution was viewed with caution by many scholars because it was several thousand years before the date range of 10,000–12,000 years ago generally accepted for man's immigration into North America. Subsequently, however, Dillehay gathered new data from excavations into an even deeper occupation level, two metres (six feet) below the 13,000-year-old site. These excavations yielded a small hearth together with broken and split cobbles, and radiocarbon determinations suggested human habitation as early as 33,000 years ago. While the stratigraphic sequence was well documented, a number of archaeologists were withholding acceptance until the materials had been subjected to the same level of reexamination and new dating techniques as the Old Crow River finds.

(JOEL W. GROSSMAN)

See also Anthropology.

Architecture

It became apparent in 1986 that changes in architectural thought had taken place. During the 1970s, when there had been a struggle for form and style, the design ethic known as "postmodernism" was born and flourished. Also at that time new concerns with conservation and preservation emerged and influenced architectural style. Conservation of energy and resources dictated some facets of design, while a renewed interest in history and cultural heritage led to new creativity in restoration, reuse, and harmony of new with old. Contextualism—or how a new building fits into its visual, social, and historical context—became a fashionable term. By 1986, however, the battles over style seemed to have subsided. Concerns about context and energy conservation had been absorbed into prevailing architectural thought so that they no longer dominated design choices but were instead part of an inclusive design approach.

According to an editorial in *Progressive Architecture* in January 1986, the most pressing concerns of the year included "the place of architects in the economic world, their legal obligations, the management of their practices and careers, and the relationships of the design professions to clients and the general public." Design could not exist in a vacuum. The most successful practices created a favourable background of sound management against which the creative side of architecture might flourish.

The dramatic slump in oil prices during the year was one factor in the reduced concern with energy conservation. Two signs of the times were the announced removal of the solar collectors that had been installed in the White House during the administration of Pres. Jimmy Carter and the abolition by the American Institute of Architects (AIA) of its Energy Committee.

The importance of an integrated architectural approach that would satisfy planning criteria was especially noticeable in regard to new large-scale developments. This was true whether such developments were commercial, mixed-use, or cultural. For example, developer Peter Palumbo's plans for the Mansion House Square site in the City of London, the subject of a long and bitterly fought battle over a design for a glass tower by the late Ludwig Mies van der Rohe, continued to attract controversy and criticism from conservation bodies even after the tower was rejected in 1985. Following rejection of the Mies design by the planning authority, Palumbo announced the selection of James Stirling as architect for the site. In June 1986 plans for two possible alternative developments were unveiled, only one of which would demand the demolition of the Victorian Mappin and Webb building. However, the new design for a trimmer tower attracted complaints from English Heritage, which felt that it would block significant views of St. Paul's Cathedral and the church of St. Mary-le-Bow.

A proposed development in London's dockland, known as Canary Wharf, also met opposition from planners. The scheme, proposed by a consortium of U.S. banks and designed by Skidmore, Owings & Merrill of Chicago with I. M. Pei & Partners of New York City and the English firm of YRM, would cover 28 ha (70 ac) on the Isle of Dogs and provide a financial centre of approximately 930,000 sq m (10 million sq ft). The most controversial features were three 240-m (790-ft) towers, which, according to opposing conservationists, would spoil the view and overpower the surrounding landscape. A proposed new plan for Charing Cross station, London, unveiled by the Terry Farrell Partnership in March, would provide more than 37,000 sq m (400,000 sq ft) of commercial space by using the air rights over the railway tracks. This scheme would also depend upon approval by the planning authority.

Political rather than planning factors threatened the future of the new Opéra Complex at the Place de la Bastille in Paris. There was speculation that the project, designed by Carlos Ott, might be reduced, modified, or even eliminated following the March 1986 French general elections. The complex was originally conceived by the former Socialist government and was scheduled to be opened in July 1989, the 200th anniversary of the French Revolution.

PortAmerica, designed by architects Philip Johnson and John Burgee, was to be a $1 billion mixed-use project on the banks of the Potomac River in Prince George's County, Md., adjoining the Capital Beltway. Its amazing historicism coupled with its staggering scale promised a remarkable visual impact. It was to include a residential area comprising 1,200 town houses and condominiums (some bow-fronted) laid out in rows clustered around a series of parks and intended by the designers to evoke Georgian England. A 52-story trade centre would be housed in a reflective glass-faceted tower surrounded by five Italianate office buildings. Waterways and the river frontage were designed to evoke Venice. The project was scheduled for completion in 1996.

Historical echoes were a feature of a mixed-use complex by architect Michael Graves in the foothills of San Diego, Calif. "The Aventine" project included a 400-room hotel, a health club housed in a classical rotunda, and a six-story office "palazzo" together with a tower that resembled the leaning tower of Pisa.

New York City developer Donald Trump faced opposition to his massive Television City project, which would require zoning changes. The design, by architect Helmut Jahn, featured the world's tallest tower, a 150-story, 509-m (1,670-ft) triangular monolith topped by a spire that would bring the overall height to 580 m (1,900 ft). The site for the project, the former railroad yards of the Penn Central, covered 40 ha (100 ac) and extended from 59th to 72nd Street along the Hudson River. Also planned were six 76-story towers, one 65-story block, and a 15-story television centre. Included in the 1.7 million sq m (18.5 million sq ft) of the project were 8,000 new residential units. The project would affect three subway stations, and its critics claimed that it would have a vast impact on the neighbourhood, bringing in a projected 20,000 new residents and 40,000 office workers.

Three major trade centres in China would have a prominent effect on the skylines of Beijing (Peking), Shanghai, and Guangzhou (Canton). Each was designed by a Western architect in a mode familiar in Houston, Texas, or Atlanta, Ga. Doubts were expressed about the appropriateness of such projects and designs for a very different culture. Each centre was intended mainly for foreign use. The largest was the China World Trade Centre in Beijing, by architects Sobel/Roth of the U.S. Due for completion in 1988, it included two hotels, apartments, and a 40-story office tower that would be the tallest in the city. The Shanghai Centre, by John Portman & Associates of Atlanta, would include a 48-story tower, with projected completion in 1988. Henry Hwang & Partners and 3D International, Houston, were architects for the Trade Tower Complex to be located on the trade fair grounds in Guangzhou. At 62 stories, the tower would be China's tallest building.

Vancouver's Expo 86 did not provide the showcase for architectural expression achieved by previous world's fairs because the organizers insisted that visiting nations use standard pavilions. The modular structures, designed by architect Bruno Freschi, were black boxes with heavy tubular steel exterior skeletons. Each nation could personalize its pavilion: the Hong Kong box featured white bamboo scaffolding, while others painted on facades. The Canadian pavilions were individually designed by more than 30 architectural firms, mostly based in Vancouver. The British Columbian complex, by Waisman, Dewar, Grout, Carter of Canada, featured two three-story wings, a detached pavilion, and a large open space partially roofed by a decorative space frame. (*See* WORLD AFFAIRS [North America]: *Canada:* Special Report.)

Educational and Cultural Buildings. The trustees of the National Gallery in London selected Robert Venturi of Venturi Rauch & Scott-Brown, Philadelphia, to be the architect of the gallery's proposed extension. Venturi's appointment ended a long period of uncertainty for this project, which had been controversial since British architects Ahrends Burton & Koralek won a competition in 1982. Their winning design was criticized by Prince Charles, who likened it to "a monstrous carbuncle on the face of a much-loved friend." Following a public inquiry, the project, which combined gallery and office space, failed to obtain planning permission, and the developers pulled out. In April 1985 the Sainsbury brothers offered to fund a new building to be used solely by the gallery. The planned extension was to include permanent picture galleries to house the early Renaissance collection.

Two museum projects in New York City attracted a lively debate. The Whitney Museum withdrew the previously published design for an extension by Michael Graves for further reduction, review, and consideration following opposition from the public and conservationists. The Guggenheim Museum also faced fierce criticism and opposition to Gwathmey Siegel & Associates' proposed extension and alteration to Frank Lloyd Wright's landmark. The Metropolitan Museum of Art announced a further addition, this time for a $35 million wing to be designed by Kevin Roche to house the European sculpture and decorative arts collection.

The central atrium of the Lloyd's of London steel-and-glass skyscraper, probably the world's tallest room, reaches up 73.5 metres (241 feet). Richard Rogers designed the spacious, innovative building with its barrel-vaulted glass roof. It cost about $245 million.
THE GUARDIAN

The Arthur M. Sackler Museum, an addition to Harvard University's Fogg Art Museum, was dedicated in October 1985 and likened to a "turkey club sandwich" and a "fascist nursing home," among other images. Architects James Stirling and Michael Wilford and Associates with Perry, Dean, Rogers, & Partners preferred a car battery analogy. Distinguished by alternating bands of red and blue brick, the dense, complex structure housed offices and classrooms as well as a museum. The museum facade was a monumental brick elevation with a neo-Mycenaean entrance, distinguishing it from the classroom and office component. A random window pattern on the latter element occurred because each room had a window in its centre, thereby giving priority to interior window placement. The regular and monotonous striping of the brick tamed this feature and seemed to strap the building together.

A cultural centre for the Faeroe Islands was designed by architects Ola Steen with Kolbrun Ragnasdottir and featured steel struts reminiscent of a Viking ship to secure the roof against intense gales. The centre provided space for concerts, theatre, dancing, films, exhibitions, and conferences within its 800-sq m (8,600-sq ft) black box. The turf-covered roof enabled the building to blend into the natural landscape.

The British firm Colquhoun and Miller won a competition for a new biological sciences faculty building at the University of Cambridge on the old Addenbrookes Hospital site. The structure was to be built in two stages at an estimated total cost of £5 million. British architects YRM completed the Sultan Qabus University, Oman, in 1986. The £225 million complex provided 570 staff houses, 13 residence halls, 5 major colleges, and a mosque. The King Fahd International Stadium, a tentlike fabric structure, neared completion in Riyadh, Saudi Arabia. The Olympic-size stadium, by architects Ian Fraser, John Roberts and Partners, was the largest free-span, cable-tensioned, and Teflon-coated fibreglass fabric structure in the world.

Public Buildings. A number of new diplomatic buildings were worthy of note. A project for a new U.S. embassy in Muscat, Oman, by James Stewart Polshek & Partners was to be situated in a diplomatic compound, and the overriding need for security was a major design criterion. The design was reminiscent of the repetitive forms of mosque architecture and featured a courtyard with a perimeter wall. The building would be of concrete clad with stone or tile.

Antiterrorist features, including a 30-m (100-ft) setback from the property line, a heavily reinforced concrete structure, and small windows set 1.8 m (6 ft) above floor level to minimize danger from shattering glass, were incorporated into a design for the new U.S. embassy in Damascus, Syria, by Gatje Papachristou Smith. The courtyard was to be of pink and tan stone with round towers reminiscent of mosque minarets. A new complex for the French embassy in New Delhi, India, was completed by Paris-based architects Paul Chemetov and Borja Huidobro, who had won a government-sponsored competition in 1980. The formal design with its axial symmetry made little use of local materials. For security as well as symbolic reasons, the only entrance was the main one set behind a protective porte cochere.

TIMOTHY HURSLEY

The Arthur M. Sackler Museum, with alternating layers of coloured brick, is an addition to Harvard University's Fogg Art Museum. Windowed space in the L-shaped structure is for offices and classrooms; galleries are in inner chambers.

The Queen Elizabeth II Conference Centre in Westminster was one of the largest government buildings erected in central London for many years and was claimed to be the most important modern government building ever built in London. Set between the Foreign Office and Treasury buildings and the domed Central Hall, near the Abbey and Palace of Westminster, it certainly was one of the most prominent. Though modern, the building formed a harmonious counterpart to its Edwardian Baroque neighbours. Lines, materials, roof pitch, and setback all contributed to the building's looking "right" in context, with its lead-clad curtain walls and prominent cantilevered concrete structure. The centre thus illustrated a successful solution to the problem of "contextuality." Architects were Powell Moya & Partners.

A major development for a derelict site in Gibraltar was the subject of a government-sponsored competition won by the architects department of Taylor Woodrow. The design featured a landscaped piazza surrounded by a covered cloister that would provide tourist shopping facilities, offices, and residential accommodations. The project, begun late in 1986, was scheduled for completion in early 1988.

Mitchell/Giurgola Architects won a nationwide competition in the U.S. for a new courthouse complex for Suffolk County, N.Y. The complex, housing 80 courtrooms, was praised for its appropriateness to the landscape. A diagonal wall across the site would separate traffic and a parking area from the courtrooms. The project, to be built in three stages and completed in 2020, included a park with a lake. In Oceanside, Calif., plans were unveiled for a new $20 million civic centre following a national competition won by Charles Moore and the Urban Innovations Group.

Commercial Buildings. Procter & Gamble's new headquarters in Cincinnati, Ohio, opened late in 1985. Designed by Kohn Pedersen Fox of New York City, it was inevitably dubbed the "Ivory Tower" after the company's most famous product. Twin 17-story towers, clad partly in Indiana limestone with flat marble pilasters above and capped by stainless steel pyramids, formed a gateway to the original 1956 headquarters building, which was retained. Grandly scaled and classical in feeling, the design used sumptuous materials, art deco-style detail, and straight lines to emphasize the horizontal and vertical. The new offices totaled approximately 74,000 sq m (800,000 sq ft).

Charlotte, N.C., was soon to possess its first postmodern skyscraper, the 34-story Two First Union Center by JPJ Architects. The design featured a setback facade clad in bands of silver reflective glass and red granite and capped with a glassed-in vault. Completion was scheduled for mid-1987. The Republic Bank Center, a traditional-looking granite-clad 60-story tower in downtown Dallas, Texas, would be the tallest concrete-core/steel-framed structure in the U.S. when completed. Chicago architects Skidmore, Owings & Merrill were designers.

In mid-1986 ground was broken for Richard Meier's first high-rise building, the 15-story People's Bank in Bridgeport, Conn., on a site adjacent to the Connecticut Turnpike. The building was to be shielded from the turnpike by an arc-shaped parking structure. Michael Graves's first residential project in New York City was announced. It would be part of a 31-story mixed-use development designed for Sotheby's auction house to utilize the air rights over their existing four-story structure on York Avenue and 72nd

Street in Manhattan. The design included renovation and redesign of the existing building to form a base visually for the residential units above.

Awards. The AIA Gold Medal for 1986 was presented to Arthur Erickson of Vancouver, B.C. The 1986 Architectural Firm Award of the AIA went to Esherick Homsey Dodge & Davis of San Francisco, a firm best known for its Cannery building in San Francisco and for the new Monterey Bay Aquarium in California. *Progressive Architecture* named Norman Foster's Hong Kong Bank, widely featured in architectural journals, as its building of the year. The Royal Institute of British Architects awarded its Gold Medal for 1986 to Japanese architect Arata Isozaki, while the prestigious Pritzker Prize went to Gottfried Böhm of West Germany.

In reporting on the AIA Honor Awards, *Progressive Architecture* sensed a new emphasis on small-scale architecture. Of the 14 awards, 5 went to single-family houses and only one to a commercial building, a low-rise suburban complex. The absence of urban commercial architecture, such as the KPF Procter & Gamble headquarters, was notable. Winning houses included a steel and glass house in Chicago by Krueck & Olsen Architects, the Bergren Residence in Venice, Calif., by Mayne & Rotondi Architects, and a house in Dallas by Edward Larrabee Barnes Associates. The only high rise to receive an award was 500 Park Tower in New York City, by James Stewart Polshek & Partners with Schuman, Lichenstein, Claman & Efron, Associated Architects. I. M. Pei & Partners' IBM corporate office building in Purchase, N.Y., was the only commercial winner. Educational buildings honoured were the Loyola Law School in Los Angeles, by Frank O. Gehry & Associates with Brooks/Collier, and Herring Hall at Rice University in Houston, by Cesar Pelli & Associates.

The design world mourned the deaths of architect Minoru Yamasaki and industrial designer Raymond Loewy (*see* OBITUARIES). (SANDRA MILLIKIN)

See also Engineering Projects; Historic Preservation; Industrial Review: *Building and Construction.*

This article updates the *Macropædia* article The History of Western ARCHITECTURE.

Art Exhibitions and Art Sales

The year 1986 marked the 600th anniversary of the birth of Donatello, Italy's greatest sculptor of the early Renaissance. To mark the occasion several important exhibitions were organized and shown, including a major show by the Detroit Institute of Arts. With the addition of some material, it was later seen at the Palazzo Vecchio in Donatello's home city of Florence, Italy, and at the Kimbell Art Museum, Fort Worth, Texas. Called "Sculpture in the Time of Donatello," the show included 100 items lent from collections in Europe and the U.S. An intelligent, well-chosen, and manageable exhibition, it illustrated Donatello's range of talent and his influence on contemporaries and followers through many works of the highest quality.

Many of Donatello's finest portable works were taken to Detroit. Perhaps the most remarkable was the bronze reliquary bust of San Rossore from Pisa, a little-known piece which demonstrated that Donatello "invented" the modern portrait bust. Inevitably, however, a trip to Italy was the only way to see Donatello's major monumental pieces of sculpture. In Florence the Donatello celebrations were further marked by a show of Italian drawings at the Uffizi Gallery consisting of 167 sheets from the great sculptor's time.

The Donatello show in Detroit, which cost over $1 million, was made possible by commercial sponsorship. As was the case with many large exhibitions in recent years, the cost was partly underwritten. In the 1970s major loan exhibitions became economically impossible as rising art values were reflected in rising insurance costs. Lending increased risk, and insurance premiums for major pieces were prohibitive. Since the recent growth in sponsorship, the trend had been reversed, and in the 1980s loan exhibitions were being mounted on a scale not seen for over a decade.

Sculpture was the subject of several other important exhibitions in 1986. The work of the Victorian sculptor Alfred Gilbert, best known for the Shaftesbury Memorial (also known as "Eros") in Piccadilly Circus, London, was shown at the Royal Academy in London in the spring. Many of Gilbert's massive marbles and bronzes could not be taken to the gallery and were represented by models, sections, and photographs. A separate part of the exhibition focused on Gilbert's applied and decorative art metalwork, including exquisite jewelry and spoons and, on a grander scale, the epergne and the Rosewater ewer and dish lent by the royal collection. In Paris the first major show since 1975 to be devoted entirely to French sculpture was mounted at the Grand Palais and entitled "La Sculpture Française au XIXe Siècle." It was displayed in a controversial architectural setting especially installed for the sculpture show. Included were a group of paintings depicting sculptors in their studios, a popular 19th-century French genre, as well as many small "statuettes," a modish 19th-century type, by artists such as Jules Dalou.

Nineteenth-century sculpture was also the subject of a show devoted to the work of Augustus Saint-Gaudens, one of the most notable sculptors working in the U.S. in that period. It was organized by the Metropolitan Museum of Art, New York City, and shown there and later at the Museum of Fine Arts, Boston. Saint-Gaudens was particularly well known for his monuments. Many of his portrait reliefs and busts were included in the show. "The Painter-Sculptor in the 20th Century" was a small exhibition at the Whitechapel Art Gallery, London, which focused on artists who worked in both the two-dimensional and the three-dimensional. Artists represented included Picasso, Matisse, and Giacometti, as well as more recent names such as de Kooning and Lichtenstein.

Several of the year's outstanding art exhibitions were devoted to non-Western art. Perhaps the grandest was "The Great Eastern Temple: Treasures of Japanese Buddhist Art from Todai-ji," which was at the Art Institute of Chicago throughout the summer. The exhibition, which was shown only in Chicago, consisted of 149 works never before seen outside Japan, and it was the first time such a large number of ancient Buddhist treasures had been allowed to leave that country. Todai-ji is the Buddhist temple in Nara, the holy city of Japanese Buddhism where Japan's emperors are crowned. The temple was said to be the world's largest wooden structure, and the works shown were among the world's greatest. National treasures sent to Chicago included bronzes, masks, scrolls, and wooden sculptures, among them a poignant 13th-century portrait sculpture of the monk Chogen in extreme old age.

An enormous show devoted to 18th-century Chinese paintings and organized by the Phoenix (Ariz.) Art Museum was shown at Santa Barbara, Calif., and in New York at the Metropolitan Museum of Art. After its New York showing it was to travel to Hong Kong. "The Elegant Brush:

An intricately realistic wood statue of the monk Chogen, a Japanese national treasure, was part of a summer exhibit at the Art Institute of Chicago. The 149 works in "The Great Eastern Temple: Treasures of Japanese Buddhist Art" had never before been shown outside Japan.
TODAI-JI (THE GREAT EASTERN TEMPLE), NARA, JAPAN

Chinese Painting Under the Quianlong Emperor, 1735–95" included a silk scroll showing inauguration portraits of the emperor and his 11 imperial consorts. The Quianlong (Ch'ien-lung) emperor was a prolific prose writer and poet and a great patron of the arts who had a painted record of his reign made by his court academy.

In the spring there was a preview showing at the Los Angeles County Museum of Art of "Masterpieces of the Shin-enkan Collection: Japanese Painting of the Edo Period." The exhibition comprised 75 of the 300 paintings in the museum's collection. The entire collection was to be installed in the museum's new Pavilion for Japanese Art in 1987. The collection was formed by Joe D. Price, who named it "The House of the Far Away Heart" after the studio of the painter Ito Jakuchu. It was especially strong in paintings dating from the period 1750–1850 and included many fine screens. Also in Los Angeles, "Tokyo: Form and Spirit" was shown at the Museum of Contemporary Art in the autumn. This major traveling exhibition contrasted traditional and contemporary Japanese works of architecture and design, including painted screens, ceramics, lacquerware, costumes, and prints from the Edo period and modern three-dimensional environments.

An ambitious show that presented a new interpretation of Mayan civilization was organized for the Kimbell Art Museum in Fort Worth and was also seen in Cleveland, Ohio. "The Blood of Kings: A New Interpretation of Maya Art" focused on 1,800 years of Mayan civilization primarily by exhibiting sculpture, including remarkable examples of portraiture. A number of items were lent by the British Museum. "Ancient Eskimo Ivories of the Bering Strait" was exhibited at the Anchorage (Alaska) Museum of History and Art and circulated by the American Federation of Arts. Included in the exhibition were some of the finest ancient Arctic works ever made, with pieces dating from the 3rd century BC to about AD 1100. Some objects were ritualistic carvings of human figures, while others were ornamented utilitarian pieces such as harpoon heads.

Decorative arts were the subject of a major group of shows in 1986. The Walters Art Gallery in Baltimore, Md., showed "Silver Treasure from Ancient Byzantium." All the pieces in the exhibition were thought to be part of a vast treasure dug up in northern Syria in 1908 and fed to the art market gradually to avoid depressing prices. It was reassembled for the first time at Baltimore. Included were the 25 pieces of the Hama Treasure bought by Henry Walters in the 1920s, the Riha Treasure from Dumbarton Oaks, Washington, D.C., the Stuma Treasure from Istanbul, and the Antioch Treasure from the Metropolitan Museum of Art, New York. An exhibition in September at the Royal Palace, Turin, Italy, showed over 1,000 pieces of porcelain and silver belonging to the House of Savoy, mostly dating from the 18th century, though there was also some fine silver from the period 1820–49. The porcelain included Chinese, Japanese, and European examples, and the show gave an interesting insight into the history of collecting.

A major show at the Musée de Luxembourg, Paris, was devoted to the art nouveau artist, glassmaker, and furniture designer Émile Gallé. His pottery and furniture were given the same prominence as his better-known glass objects. Oriental influence was apparent in many of Gallé's pieces, and 60 of his working drawings provided an insight into his methods and creativity. On display were 90 pieces of glass, including the famous Orpheus vase and some of his rare glass orchids. The Corcoran Gallery of Art in Washington, D.C., selected 70 examples of Italian Renaissance majolica from its own collection to form a traveling exhibition. The Corcoran's majolica collection was one of the finest in the U.S. The show would tour for two years, returning in 1988 after visiting nine cities in the U.S. and Canada.

Because drawings are often more easily assembled than paintings, and because many collections contain a wealth of fine examples that are rarely seen, drawings were again shown widely. One exhibition of drawings during the year was "Master Drawings in the Royal Collection" at the Queen's Gallery, Buckingham Palace, London, which comprised masterpieces from the 15th to the 18th century drawn from the Royal Library at Windsor Palace. Some more modest drawings dating from the 19th and 20th centuries were also shown. The latter group included portraits of Queen Adelaide (the wife of William IV of England), the composer Sir Edward Elgar, and the novelist Henry James. Among the 18th-century drawings exhibited were five chalk drawings by Piazetta and five fine Canalettos. The depth of the royal collection was made evident by the inclusion of examples from most major Italian, French, Dutch, and German artists, with the notable exception of Rembrandt. Leonardo, Michelangelo, and Raphael were all represented, and this remarkable assembly of highest quality works was to be on view until early 1987.

The Art Gallery of Ontario in Toronto organized "Italian Drawings from the Collection of Duke Roberto Ferretti," which was shown in New York City at the Pierpont Morgan Library and included 80 drawings from the 16th to the 18th century, all collected over the previous ten years. "Italian XVIIth-Century Drawings from the Uffizi" at the Montreal Museum of Fine Arts was the largest group of drawings ever lent by that premier Florentine museum and included works by Guido Reni, the Carracci family, and Guercino.

An exquisite selection of drawings by a master draftsman was shown in New York City at the Frick Collection. "J. A. D. Ingres: Fifty Life Drawings from the Musée Ingres at Montauban" was organized by the Museum of Fine Arts, Houston, Texas, and complemented an earlier show, "Ingres and the Contesse d'Haussonville," held at the Frick in the winter. It provided an unrivaled opportunity to study and enjoy a representative selection of the artist's finely detailed and blunt characterizations not usually seen together in such quantity by art lovers in the U.S. Not all were portraits; there were also drawings of costumes, landscapes, animals, and architectural designs. The portrait pencil drawings by Ingres were among the most beautiful ever made.

The Louvre in Paris celebrated completion of the museum's comprehensive catalog of its collection of pastels by staging an exhibition of a selection of 19th-century pastels at the Pavillion de Flore. Included were works by the greatest artists of the era: Manet, Renoir, Delacroix, and others. There was an exceptional group of works by Degas, including some superb examples of ballet dancers.

Impressionist paintings were also shown in an exhibition that assembled canvases from each of the eight founding Impressionist exhibitions. "The New Painting: Impressionism 1874–1886" comprised 135 works, 47 of which were borrowed from French collections, including 20 from the Musée d'Orsay. While some works were familiar, many were not, and the show conveyed a good idea of how Impressionism appeared to the art world when it was first introduced. Organized by the Fine Arts Museums of San Francisco, it was seen in that city and at the National Gallery of Art, Washington, D.C. A fine show of 82 Impressionist drawings organized by the Arts Council of Great Britain was shown in Oxford and Manchester. This gem of an exhibition, which showed what a wide range "drawing" could encompass, included pastels, pencils, and even watercolour sketches by Cézanne, Manet, Degas, Picasso, Renoir, and others. The show was limited to works borrowed from public and private collections in Britain.

The Tate Gallery in London mounted "Forty Years of Modern Art 1945–85," its biggest show ever, which afforded the British public the chance to reassess the achievement of painters and sculptors of that period. The show also marked the retirement of Ronald Alley, for 20 years keeper of the Tate's modern collection. The exhibition was a reflection of the history of the museum's acquisition policy and taste and of the general state of the art market over the period. Entire rooms were devoted to Dubuffet, Rothko, and Giacometti. The Tate marked the centenary of the birth of Oskar Kokoschka with a large retrospective in the summer. It was the first time in 24 years that a full-scale exhibition of his work had been mounted in London. There were more than 150 oils, watercolours, and drawings covering the artist's full range. Included was a 1909 portrait of the Viennese architect Adolf Loos, done when Kokoschka was only 23 years of age.

Canada's leading 19th-century painter, James Wilson Morrice, was the subject of an exhibition at the Montreal Museum of Fine Arts that later traveled to New Brunswick. The museum, which celebrated its 125th anniversary in 1986, possessed 800 works by Morrice, who spent much of his life in Europe, where his work was better known than in his native Canada. A major show devoted to the work of Marie Laurencin, in which 40 of her paintings were exhibited, was held in Paris at the Galerie Daniel Malingue. It was the first such show in Europe or the U.S. since her death in 1956. During the 1970s and '80s she had attracted extensive interest in Japan, where a private museum devoted to her work opened in 1983 and where many exhibitions had been mounted. She was a prolific portrayer of a luminous fairy-tale world.

The first major show in a generation devoted to the work of Sir Joshua Reynolds was mounted at the Royal Academy in London in the winter. The vast exhibition, the largest ever devoted to Reynolds, included 121 oils as well as some drawings and sketches, but inevitably some major portraits were not lent. Many works were borrowed from private collections in the U.K. and abroad, and two of the artist's self-portraits—one early and one late—were especially notable. The show also included a small selection of pictures by contemporaries of Reynolds, as well as some

COURTESY OF THE ART INSTITUTE OF CHICAGO

Gustave Caillebotte's 1877 painting of a street on a rainy day in Paris was one of more than 150 works exhibited in "The New Painting: Impressionism 1874–1886," a show that was at the National Gallery of Art in Washington, D.C., and then at the Fine Arts Museums of San Francisco.

furniture and personal items to set his work in context. An exhibition devoted to the English landscape artist John Constable toured Japan in 1986. It was the first time his work had been seen there. Many items in the show were from the extensive collection held by the Victoria and Albert Museum in London. The show included 82 paintings, watercolours, drawings, and prints.

The death in March at age 99 of the U.S. artist Georgia O'Keeffe (*see* OBITUARIES) coincided with a retrospective of her work at the Hirschl and Adler Galleries in New York City. It was the first commercial gallery show ever held of works by O'Keeffe, who was surely among the most important woman painters.

A major art exchange of 150 treasures from the Thyssen-Bornemisza collection in Lugano in return for treasures from Leningrad was arranged between the Swiss and Soviet cities. Among the treasures exchanged was a jeweled and enameled 17th-century chalice from the workshops of the Kremlin, while the Swiss collector sent jewels, items by Fabergé, and a tureen from the dinner service made for Catherine the Great.

A winter show at the Grand Palais in Paris comprised 240 works of art acquired by the French government between 1981 and 1985. Most of the works were donated in part payment of inheritance taxes. Vermeer's "The Astrologist," Cezanne's portrait of his wife, and a small painting by Lorenzo Lotto were among the fine examples displayed.

"Henry Matisse: The Early Years in Nice 1916–1930," which opened at the National Gallery, Washington, in the autumn, included 171 paintings from this somewhat misunderstood period of the artist's career. At the Whitney Museum, New York City, a John Singer Sargent retrospective revived interest in the great portraitist of Edwardian society, who for many years had been dismissed as superficial and outmoded. The exhibition would move to the Art Institute of Chicago in the spring of 1987.

(SANDRA MILLIKIN)

ART SALES

Market Trends. The 1985–86 auction season began on a muted note, though there were no exceptional problems in late 1985. The U.S. bombing raid on Libya in April 1986 and the fear of reprisals drastically reduced the number of U.S. tourists traveling to Europe, and the art market suffered greatly as a result. Sales in March, April, and May in Europe recorded a very high proportion of unsold lots. The New York City sales did not do particularly well either. For no apparent reason there was a major return of confidence in mid-1986. Sotheby's sale of Impressionists in New York in May signaled the turn in the market. Seven paintings sold at over $1 million and only 7% remained unsold, one of the lowest figures ever recorded in this very expensive field.

Christie's continued to struggle with sensational court cases in the U.S. A claim for damages resulting from bad advice on a sale of Impressionist paintings in 1981 was reinstated on appeal in May 1986. In another suit, Christie's was accused of falsely cataloging a Fabergé Easter egg as made for the Russian imperial family. New York City's Department of Consumer Affairs spent the year discussing new auction regulations, and there was speculation that strict regulations might send much auction business back to London.

Something of a sensation was created in the art world in August when it was revealed that a series of 240 hitherto unknown works by the American artist Andrew Wyeth (*see* BIOGRAPHIES) had been purchased by a Pennsylvania collector, Leonard E. B. Andrews. The price was not revealed, but there was speculation that it might have exceeded $10 million. All but one of the works, which Wyeth had kept secret for 15 years, featured a model called Helga, later identified as a neighbour of the Wyeth family in Chadds Ford, Pa.

Works of Art. The most important painting scheduled for sale during the year was Goya's portrait of "La Marquesa de Santa Cruz." Christie's was to sell it in London on April 11 on behalf of Lord Wimborne's family trusts. The Spanish government, however, claimed that it had left Spain with an improper export license. On April 9, after a legal battle, the painting was sold to the Spanish authorities for $6 million, with Lord Wimborne taking a loss. Sotheby's claimed to have set a new auction price record for Goya with the "Flight of Witches," sold in Madrid for 78.4 million pesetas. The price would have been far higher if there had been a chance of obtaining an export license.

The top Old Masters of the year tended to present problems. In Paris in December 1985 Georges de La Tour's "Souffleur a la pipe" was expected to fetch several million dollars, but at the last minute word came from the Louvre that the painting was probably the work of a pupil or follower of La Tour, and the picture was left unsold. In contrast, a hitherto unknown Mantegna, "The Holy Family," was sold by Sotheby's in Monaco for F 17,760,000, although many people considered it the work of a Mantegna follower. Significant private sales included a reputed $3 million for Lorenzo Lotto's "Venus and Cupid," bought by the Metropolitan Museum of Art, New York City, and something over £1 million paid by the National Gallery, London, for Caravaggio's "Boy Bitten by a Lizard."

Further down the price scale, decorative Dutch and Flemish paintings were in demand. Collectors descended on Sotheby's in London from all over the world to pay £2.8 million for 17 paintings by Pieter Brueghel the Younger from the collection of Charles de Pauw. American paintings continued to climb in price with the National Gallery, Washington, paying a new auction price record of $4,070,000 for Rembrandt Peale's "Rubens Peale with a Geranium." Sotheby's May 1986 sale set 23 auction records for individual artists, including $1,485,000 for John Singer Sargent's "Mrs. Cecil Wade."

Several remarkable collections came on the market. In November 1985 the Hans E. Bühler Gericault collection made £4.9 million at Christie's. Some 300 Old Master prints from the Chatsworth collection sent for sale by the duke of Devonshire made £3.6 million at Christie's, with a Rembrandt etching at £561,600, a Castiglione monotype at £345,600, and a Mantegna at £275,400. German Expressionists from the famous collection formed by Morton D. May of St. Louis, Mo., set a new level of prices at Christie's in June 1986 with a Max Pechstein at £162,000 and a Heinrich Campendonk at £129,600. In the same sale, the Otto Dix "Der Salon I" became the most expensive 20th-century German painting at £561,700.

The sensation of the year was Christie's dispersal of the cargo of the *Geldermalsen,* a Dutch East Indiaman which sank in 1752. The sale, held in Amsterdam in May, brought in 37,372,919 Dutch guilders. Including over 160,000 items of porcelain and 125 gold bars, the cargo had been salvaged from the South China Sea by Capt. Michael Hatcher and a team of divers. The romance went to buyers' heads, multiplying normal market values by anything from 2 to 20. The lively market between dealers and retailers after the sale multiplied prices several times more.

Other exceptional prices included £105,000 for a 1787 bottle of Château Lafite bearing the initials of Thomas Jefferson. An ormolu-mounted ebony clock made by Thomas

Britain's Lord Wimborne displays "La Marquesa de Santa Cruz," his Goya masterpiece, for sale at Christie's in London in April. A legal dispute over the work's export from Spain led to its sale to Spanish authorities for $6 million (£4.1 million), far less than would have been expected otherwise.
AP/WIDE WORLD

Tompion for King William III of England as a gift to the grand duke of Tuscany made £248,400. An enameled gold pocket watch of around 1650 set with diamonds, made by Jehan Cremfdorff of Paris, secured Sw F 1,870,000.

Books. The book market held steady, though the attention given to glossy catalogs and marketing by the auction rooms made for erratic differences in price between much-publicized and little-publicized sales. Illuminated manuscripts were attracting the attention of both the J. Paul Getty Museum in Malibu, Calif., and J. Paul Getty II, reclusive son of the museum's founder. The museum sent its emissary to Paris in November 1985 to pay F 8 million for a French illuminated manuscript of the Gospels dated to around 1515. In June 1986 John Paul Getty II paid £1,375,000 to acquire four leaves belonging to a 13th-century illustrated life of St. Thomas à Becket. Other outstanding manuscripts on the market included a 9th-century Gospel book written and illuminated at the Abbey of St. Amand in Flanders, sold by Sotheby's for £1,430,000, and a 12th-century French Psalter sold in Avranches for F 7.8 million.

In the field of 19th-century and modern illustrated books, the U.S. millionaire Fred Koch was an important influence. He was capable of buying up to 30% of the lots in a single sale as well as bidding heavily on outstanding items. While he would not confirm purchases, he was believed to have been the buyer of Edward Lear's autograph *Book of Nonsense* at £143,000 in June, the manuscript of A. A. Milne's *When We Were Very Young* at £132,000 in July, and a two-page letter from Charlotte Brontë to her publishers that had accompanied the manuscript of *Jane Eyre* at £27,500 in December 1985. There was also said to be a big American buyer in the music manuscript market, which again scored some sensational prices. Wagner's first draft of the libretto of *Lohengrin* made £187,000 at Sotheby's in November 1985 and Schubert's overture to the opera *Fierabras,* £165,000 in May 1986.

The sensation of the year in the natural history field was the eight volumes of original watercolour illustrations by Pierre-Joseph Redouté for *Les Liliacés.* In the hope of preventing the set from being broken up, Sotheby's offered them as one lot with a low reserve with the intention that the plates would be sold individually if the reserve was not met. An investment consortium organized by Graham Arader III bought them as a single lot for a modest $5.5 million, but with the intention of splitting them up—which defeated the whole exercise. In October 1985 a copy of Audubon's *Birds of America* was split up and sold for $1,761,842.

Several major collections were sold en bloc during the year. The Smithsonian Institution in Washington spent $7 million to acquire the collection of Oriental manuscripts and miniatures formed by Henri Vever (1854–1943). The collection of early English printed books and manuscripts from the Carl and Lily Pforzheimer Foundation was acquired for around $15 million by the electronics millionaire H. Ross Perot on behalf of the University of Texas. The library of Sir Richard Burton, Victorian traveler and writer, was bought for $500,000 by the Christensen Fund of California and placed on indefinite loan at the Huntington Library, San Marino, Calif. (GERALDINE NORMAN)

This article updates the *Macropædia* articles The History of Western PAINTING; The History of Western SCULPTURE.

Astronomy

In many ways 1986 was to have been the most spectacular year ever for U.S. spacecraft-based astronomy. Among space instruments to have been launched were the ASTRO-1 satellite, to observe Halley's Comet at ultraviolet wavelengths; the Ulysses solar polar flyby; the Galileo Jupiter orbiter and probe mission; and the most ambitious scientific satellite ever, the Hubble Space Telescope, an Earth-orbiting optical observatory. The disastrous end of the space shuttle *Challenger* in January, however, put these major astronomical missions on hold. On the plus side, the year did include the triumphs of the Voyager 2 encounter with the planet Uranus in January and the bevy of ground-based and spacecraft observations of Halley's Comet. (*See* Special Report.) In addition, a wide variety of other exciting astronomical discoveries and insights were made during the year.

Sun. The origin of the Sun's energy has long been a scientific mystery. In 1938 U.S. theoretical physicist Hans Bethe proposed a theory of nuclear reactions in the Sun that has come to be one of the mainstays of all astrophysics. The theory correctly treats the Sun's energetic output and many other problems concerning its structure, size, mass, and composition. Nevertheless, one major and embarassing difficulty has remained. Along with the light that is seen leaving the Sun's exterior surface, the Sun should be emitting neutrinos from deep within its interior. These elusive particles have no charge and interact only very weakly with matter. Unlike sunlight, which percolates extremely slowly from the solar interior to the surface, neutrinos should be streaming to Earth directly from the

(continued on page 153)

Special Report: Astronomy

Encounters with Halley and Uranus

BY KENNETH BRECHER

In early 1986 a handful of space probes far from home sped past their targets, dutifully observing, measuring, and relaying their results to eager scientists back on Earth. All but one were contributing to a common mission: an unprecedented look at the world's most famous comet. The last machine, already in space for almost a decade, had a rendezvous with remote Uranus, the seventh planet from the Sun. What these missions discovered vastly changed scientists' ideas about the solar system.

Halley's Comet. For more than two millennia the return of Halley's Comet every 76 years or so has been observed and recorded on Earth. Its 1985–86 visit, however, marked the first time that humans took a close look at its mysterious nucleus. Five spacecraft from Europe, Japan, and the Soviet Union flew past the comet, one of which approached within hundreds of kilometres of the nucleus; several more viewed the comet from a distance. Hundreds of scientists from dozens of countries spent thousands of man-years preparing for those encounters, as well as for studying the comet with more conventional Earth-based instruments. They found major surprises. In a nutshell, the comet that came in was thought to be a "dirty snowball," spherical in shape, perhaps a few kilometres in diameter, and highly reflecting. The comet that went out was known to be peanut-shaped, perhaps 15 km long and 10 km across, and as black as any material ever seen (one kilometre is about 0.62 mi).

The spacecraft launched specifically to observe the comet included two Japanese missions, Sakigake and Suisei, the former sent to probe the comet's outer coma, the latter to approach the cometary nucleus; two Soviet probes, Vega 1 and Vega 2, each of which came within 10,000 km of the nucleus on March 6 and March 9, respectively; and, most spectacularly, the European Space Agency's Giotto space probe, which passed within 600 km of Halley on March 14. The U.S. International Ultraviolet Explorer satellite, in orbit about the Earth, and the Pioneer Venus Orbiter, circling the planet Venus since late 1978, also observed the comet, though from comparatively great distances.

Until 1986 astronomers had observed only from far away the tails of comets. The tail consists of the gases and dust boiled off the comet as it is heated by the Sun. The new observations showed that water molecules freed from the comet leave its surface, spread out, and then dissociate into hydrogen, oxygen, and the hydroxyl radical (OH^-). Pioneer Venus found that this cloud spread out over a region some 20 million km across, 15 times larger than the Sun. Various spacecraft measured the outflow of gas and dust, finding that at the time of encounter Halley was giving off about 25 tons of gas and perhaps 5 tons of dust every second. In other words, the comet was losing roughly ten metres (33 ft) of material from its surface each orbit, suggesting a lifetime of only about 1,000 orbits—less than 100,000 years. Measurements also found that about 80% of the ejected gas originates as water and most of the rest as carbon dioxide and carbon monoxide. The bulk of the dust consists of atoms of hydrogen, carbon, nitrogen, and oxygen, with smaller amounts of sulfur, sodium, magnesium, silicon, calcium, and iron—a composition similar to that of the so-called carbonaceous chrondrites, a rare type of stony meteorite rich in carbon-based organic materials.

As the Japanese craft approached the comet, they noticed a "breathing," a regular variation in the intensity of the gas being detected. This was thought to be due to the comet's rotation, which showed a period of about 52 hours (2.2 days). Scientists had long suspected that comets rotate, but this was the first direct observation of the effect. The spacecraft found by direct photographic observation that the comet sheds its mass in jets, rather than uniformly from all over the surface as had been generally thought, and that the jets emanate from only the sunlit side. As the jets are carried around to the dark side by the comet's rotation, they "turn off," while new jets appear on the sunward side. The surface temperature on the sunlit side turned out to be about 300 K (27° C, or 81° F), only about 100 K higher than the temperature needed to vaporize material from the surface, and much cooler than had been predicted. This finding implies that heat is conducted from the surface to the icy interior, giving rise to the subsurface heating that forms the jets.

Most spectacular of all are the photographs of Halley's nucleus returned by the Giotto mission. The body has

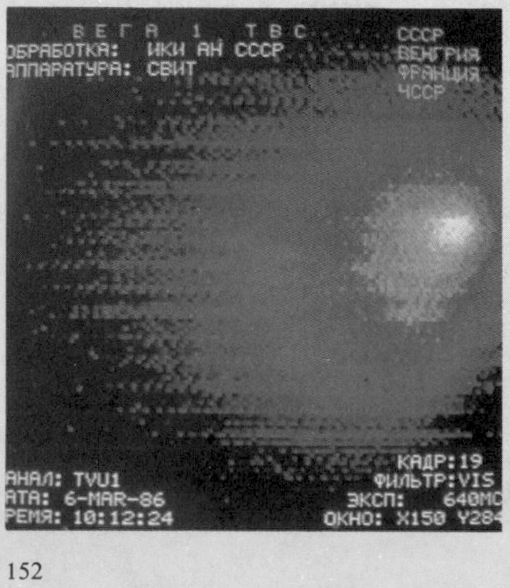

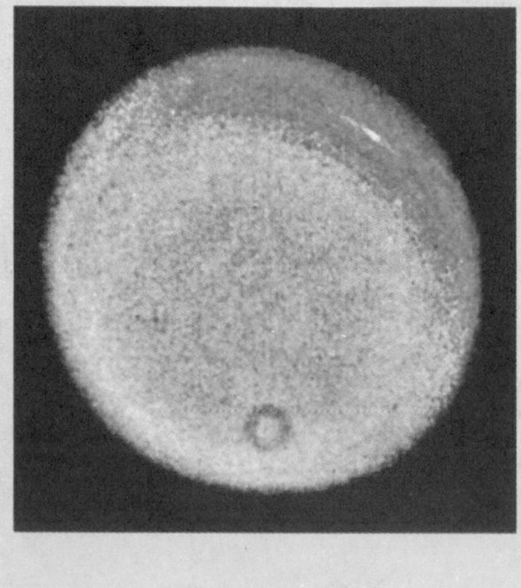

(LEFT) SIPA/SPECIAL FEATURES; (RIGHT) JPL

A computer-processed false-colour view of Uranus (left) is one of a series provided by Voyager 2 that for the first time revealed to scientists cloud formations rotating with the planet. A colour-enhanced view of Halley's Comet (far left) came from Vega 1.

not only an irregular shape but also an exceedingly black surface, darker than black velvet, that reflects only about 4% of the sunlight hitting it. Though the data from Halley will continue to be analyzed for years, the scientific view of comets has already been greatly enhanced by this first direct encounter.

Uranus. Uranus was discovered by William Herschel in 1781, the first planet found in modern times. During the past two centuries, owing primarily to its great distance, little had been learned about it other than such basic details as mass and diameter. It was known to have only five large moons. In 1977 a system of rings somewhat like Saturn's was discovered around it. Then, on Jan. 24, 1986, within a few hours, the Voyager 2 spacecraft flew by Uranus, passing within 82,000 km of its visible surface, and dramatically changed scientists' conception of it.

For the first time, the rotation period of the planet was directly measured; it turned out to be about 17.2 hours. Instruments aboard Voyager determined the composition of Uranus's atmosphere, which proved to be 88% hydrogen and 12% helium, almost the same as the overall composition of the Sun and the other giant planets Saturn and Jupiter. Unlike other planetary atmospheres in the solar system, the Uranian atmosphere rotates in the same direction as the planet, exhibiting winds of about 200 km/hr (125 mph). The spacecraft also detected a new type of atmospheric emission, tentatively called electroglow. The glow appears only on the day side of Uranus and seems to be quite distinct from either the Earth's aurora or its airglow, both of which arise from the interaction of solar particles and radiation with the atmosphere.

The magnetic field of the planet was found to be about 0.25 gauss at the surface, similar in strength to the Earth's surface magnetic field. The field appears to be mostly dipolar in shape, like the Earth's, but also has a significant component with more complex (multipole) structure. Most remarkably, the axis of the magnetic field is tilted by about 55° from the spin axis (which itself lies in the plane of Uranus's orbit about the Sun). Why both the spin and magnetic field axes are tilted the way they are remains a total mystery.

Perhaps equally exciting were discoveries concerning the rings and moons of Uranus. As Voyager approached, it found a tenth major ring circling the planet and as many as 100 less distinct rings interspersed within the main rings. Prior to the encounter the only known Uranian moons were Miranda, Ariel, Umbriel, Titania, and Oberon, ranging from about 500 to 1,600 km in diameter. Voyager found ten more satellites having diameters of 40 to 80 km and all lying within the orbit of the closest large satellite, Miranda. The major moons themselves proved surprisingly variable in appearance. Oberon has a mountain protruding at least 20 km above its surface. Umbriel displays a much darker surface than the others, suggesting the presence of rocky material overlying the otherwise ice-rich satellite. Ariel has many valleys, cliffs, and other scars. Perhaps strangest of all is Miranda, which displays among other features three large closed patterns of light and dark bands, scarps and ridges, that are 100–300 km wide.

Voyager 2, launched in 1977, has now successfully visited Jupiter, Saturn, and Uranus, vastly increasing knowledge of each of these systems of planets, moons, and rings. In 1989 Voyager is scheduled to fly past Neptune, the last of the giant gas planets, and document its mysteries before leaving the solar system forever.

Kenneth Brecher is professor of astronomy and physics at Boston University.

(continued from page 151)

nuclear reaction region. In the late 1960s Raymond Davis, Jr., then of Brookhaven (N.Y.) National Laboratory, set up a tank containing some 100 tons of carbon tetrachloride deep underground in the Homestake Gold Mine near Lead, S.D., to detect solar neutrinos. Over the space of a month a few neutrinos would interact with chlorine atoms in the tank, turning them into argon atoms, which subsequently could be removed from the chlorine and counted. As the years have gone by, no more than one-third the predicted number of neutrinos have been detected. The missing neutrinos could be taken as evidence that the theory of nuclear reactions in the Sun is wrong or must be modified.

In 1986, nearly 50 years after his original Nobel Prize-winning theory, Bethe offered a novel solution to the so-called solar neutrino puzzle. It was based on the fact that the solar neutrinos being detected in Davis's tank are only of the type called electron neutrinos. A second type, muon neutrinos, also exist, and there may be a third type, tau neutrinos. If on the way to Earth from their place of formation in the Sun, electron neutrinos are turning into the second or third type, the shortage of predicted neutrinos could be understood. Bethe, starting from a suggestion made by two Soviet scientists, S. P. Mikheyev and A. Yu. Smirnov of the Institute for Nuclear Research in Moscow, proposed and then calculated the way in which the electron neutrinos might transform as they move out through the dense solar interior. If the theory is correct, it implies that the neutrino, which had generally been considered a massless particle, has a very small mass, perhaps a billionth (10^{-9}) that of an electron, the lightest particle known. The theory would be subject to testing in future experiments, under construction in 1986, that used gallium instead of chlorine as the target material. Within a few years scientists expected to establish with certainty whether the current theory of the origin of the Sun's energy is correct after all.

Stars. Although people have witnessed supernovas—the violent explosive death of stars—for thousands of years, the first direct observation of star birth was reported only during the year by astronomers from the University of Arizona, including Charles Lada, Philip Maloney, Christopher Walker, and Erick Young, along with Bruce Wilking of the University of Missouri at St. Louis. The difficulty in witnessing the birth of a star arises because regions of star formation are enshrouded in the gas and dust out of which stars form. The dust makes it virtually impossible to see the event at optical wavelengths. Infrared and radio radiation, however, can penetrate these dusty regions.

The purported embryonic star was first detected in 1983 by the Infrared Astronomical Satellite (IRAS) and was designated IRAS 16293-2422. It lies in an interstellar cloud some 500 light-years from the Earth. The astronomers then studied the star at radio wavelengths using the 12-m radio telescope at the National Radio Astronomy Observatory at Kitt Peak, Arizona. The radio observations allowed them to determine that the infrared source is in fact collapsing inward. Presently the condensing cloud is some 650,000,000,000 km (400,000,000,000 mi) in diameter and contains about one-tenth the mass of the Sun. According to theoretical models this protostar is only 30,000 years old and will take another 100,000 years before its collapse and further mass accumulation is halted by the onset of nuclear reactions, at which time it will become a normal nuclear burning star.

When stars die, they can leave behind a stellar remnant in the form of a white dwarf, neutron star, or possibly a black hole. New observations of the first two of these objects were reported during the year.

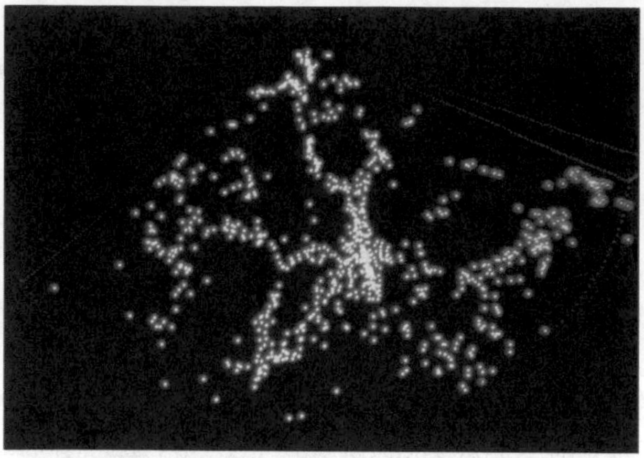

A new computer-generated sky chart plots the positions of 1,061 galaxies in a way that the researchers who developed it claimed shows that galaxies form on the periphery of giant "bubble voids," vast empty parts of space. This challenged accepted views.
MICHAEL KURTZ AND MATHEW SCHNEPS, SMITHSONIAN ASTROPHYSICAL OBSERVATORY

In the mid-1980s more than 100 white dwarfs were known. These objects typically have Sun-sized masses but only a hundredth the diameter; consequently, their densities may be more than a million times higher. Many, if not all, stars also generate magnetic fields. The Sun's average surface magnetic field is about one gauss, about the same as the strength of the Earth's field at the surface. In the case of perhaps two dozen white dwarfs, magnetic fields were thought to be as much as a million gauss. In 1986 a group of astronomers including Gary D. Schmidt of the University of Arizona, Steven C. West and James Liebert of Steward Observatory at the University of Arizona, Richard F. Green of Kitt Peak, and H. S. Stockman of the Space Telescope Science Institute, Baltimore, Md., reported a white dwarf having a magnetic field measured in some areas at as much as 700 million gauss. The object, designated PG 1031+234, was studied by use of the Palomar Mountain 5-m telescope, the Steward Observatory 2.3-m telescope, and the International Ultraviolet Explorer Observatory satellite. Unlike most white dwarfs, which rotate quite slowly, this object was found to rotate in only 3 hours 24 minutes (which can be compared with an average rotation period of 28 days for the Sun). Because of the observed rapid rotation, the structure of the field also was determined. It has not only a dipole configuration (similar to the Earth's) but also a very intense "spot" or region of enhanced field, somewhat like the magnetic regions (sunspots) on the solar surface.

Neutron stars were first identified in the late 1960s. Since then several hundred have been found. Some are single stars; others exist as members of binary star systems. Like white dwarfs, neutron stars have masses comparable to that of the Sun, but their diameters are about 100,000 times smaller. They were first discovered as pulsars, objects that produce flashes of radio waves typically every second or so. These pulses are interpreted as radiation emitted in a beaconlike beam by a rapidly rotating, highly magnetized (typically a trillion gauss) neutron star. In 1982 a pulsar was discovered that pulsed some 642 times per second, implying a rotation period of only 1.6 milliseconds (ms). The origin of such a high spin for a single star was difficult to explain. A year later a second millisecond pulsar, this time with a six-millisecond period, was discovered. The second object was found to be a member of a binary system. Could this characteristic somehow be linked to the rapid spin?

In 1986 David Segelstein, Joseph H. Taylor, Daniel Stinebring, and Lloyd Rawley of Princeton University described a third millisecond pulsar, this time with a period of 5.4 ms. It, too, is in a binary star system. It could be that all of these fast pulsars are or have been members of binary systems in which mass transfer from one star to the other—or some other process—has "spun up" the pulsars to their current spectacular rotation rates. It also seemed strange that all three millisecond pulsars have about the same magnetic field strengths, some 300 million gauss. This not only is much less than is typical for hundreds of other known pulsars but also is less than that of the white dwarf discussed above.

Galaxies and Cosmology. During the year distance records for galaxies and quasars were extended once again. While galaxies, like our own Milky Way, were known to be made primarily of stars, gas, and dust, the exact nature of quasars remained a mystery. When the latter objects were discovered in the early 1960s, they appeared "quasi-stellar" in optical photographs, hence their name. They have high redshifts, indicating that they are moving away from the Earth at enormous speeds. Such speeds are generally taken to mean that quasars are very far from the Earth and receding still farther as part of the general expansion of the universe.

In mid-1986 astronomers reported a new record redshift for a quasar, 3.8, implying that the object is receding at more than 90% the speed of light and that it lies between 10,000,000,000 and 20,000,000,000 light-years from the Earth. By year's end Stephen Warren and Paul Hewitt of the University of Cambridge had found yet a new record holder having a redshift of 4.01. This quasar, lying in the direction of the constellation Sculptor, is receding at about 93% the speed of light.

The search for distant quasars also led to discovery of the most distant galaxy found to date. A group headed by Stanislav Djorgovski of the University of California at Berkeley reported a galaxy having a redshift of 3.218, which places it some 10,000,000,000 to 15,000,000,000 light-years from Earth and in the realm where quasars are generally found. The find implied that galaxies were formed early in the history of the universe, since the farther out in space one looks, the earlier is the time being observed. If more such galaxies could be found, they might help in determining the large-scale structure of the universe.

Finally, scientists at the Harvard-Smithsonian Center for

Earth Perihelion and Aphelion, 1987

Jan. 4	Perihelion, 147,104,000 km (91,406,000 mi) from the Sun
July 4	Aphelion, 152,102,000 km (94,511,000 mi) from the Sun

Equinoxes and Solstices, 1987

March 21	Vernal equinox, 03:52[1]
June 21	Summer solstice, 22:11[1]
Sept. 23	Autumnal equinox, 13:45[1]
Dec. 22	Winter solstice, 09:46[1]

Eclipses, 1987

March 29	Sun, total (begins 10:03[1]), visible in southern South America, South Atlantic Ocean, part of Antarctica, Africa except extreme northwest, southeast Europe, southwest Asia.
April 14	Moon, total (begins 00:20[1]), visible in North America except Alaska, Central and South America, Africa, Europe, eastern half of Asia, and Antarctica.
Sept. 23	Sun, partial (begins 00:15[1]), visible in eastern Asia except extreme northeast, Japan, eastern Indonesia, Philippine Islands, New Guinea, northeast Australia, and New Zealand except extreme south.
Oct. 7	Moon, total (begins 01:53[1]), visible in North, Central, and South America; Greenland; Europe; Africa; eastern Asia; and Antarctica toward South America.

[1]Universal time.
Source: *The Astronomical Almanac for the Year 1987* (1986).

Astrophysics presented evidence for what might be called a soap-bubble or cosmic-foam view of the distribution of galaxies in the universe. Margaret Geller, John Huchra, and Valérie de Lapparent surveyed about 1,100 galaxies lying within a region of the sky measuring some 117° by 6°. The survey was a systematic collection within that region of all redshifts of galaxies having magnitudes greater than 15.5. By plotting out the spatial distribution of the galaxies, the investigators found what appeared to be circular chains of galaxies surrounding vast open spaces. Since the plot is two-dimensional, it appears to represent a cut through a section of space that in fact contains galaxies arrayed over the surfaces of vast bubble-shaped regions that enclose galaxy-poor voids as large as 150 million light-years across. The survey extends out to a distance of perhaps 450 million light-years, fairly modest by cosmic standards. Nonetheless, if the surveyed region was representative of the universe, it presented cosmologists with a view of the universe that differed radically from the smooth, uniform galactic distribution usually assumed to describe the cosmos.

(KENNETH BRECHER)

See also Space Exploration; Space Exploration: *Special Report.*
This article updates the *Macropædia* articles The COSMOS; EXPLORATION: *Space Exploration*; GALAXIES; The PHYSICAL SCIENCES: *Astronomy and Astrophysics*; The SOLAR SYSTEM; STARS AND STAR CLUSTERS.

Botanical Gardens and Zoos

Botanical Gardens. During November 1985 delegates from botanical gardens in 39 countries met in Las Palmas, Gran Canaria (Spain), for a conference arranged by the International Union for Conservation of Nature and Natural Resources (IUCN) with the theme "Botanic Gardens and the World Conservation Strategy." The meeting followed publication of the IUCN World Conservation Strategy document, which was commissioned by the United Nations Environment Program (UNEP) and the World Wildlife Fund (WWF). In his introduction to the conference, Kenton R. Miller, director general of IUCN, spoke of botanical gardens developing into a new global force for conservation, with a need to link their conservation activities through an organization that might be coordinated under IUCN.

Four days of deliberation revolved around a draft document on strategy that drew heavily on the results of an extensive questionnaire, previously circulated to all botanical gardens throughout the world. In light of the comments made at the conference, the draft was to be reviewed so that a definitive policy document could be published to provide guidelines for the future. One of the most significant of the 13 conference recommendations requested IUCN to set up a secretariat to coordinate implementation of the strategy. It was agreed that sponsorship would have to be obtained, since the botanical gardens were unlikely to generate enough funds. Following the conference, sufficient funds were forthcoming to make establishment of the secretariat likely in the near future.

The latest figures published by IUCN indicated that as many as 50,000 plant species could become extinct by the year 2050 if present trends continued. This meant that one in four to one in five of all the world's plants were under threat. While forests of the western Amazon region of Brazil, the interior of the Guianas, and central Africa might remain relatively undisturbed, it appeared that all other tropical and subtropical forests would be destroyed or severely disturbed within 30 years. This made it increasingly important for botanical gardens to coordinate their activities and to support gardens in the tropical and subtropical areas.

The Göteborg (Sweden) Botanical Garden celebrated the reopening of its restored Palm House in May 1986 by holding a conference, with the support of the Royal Swedish Academy of Sciences and the World Wildlife Fund, Sweden. Again, the theme was conservation and plant utilization, with particular emphasis on the promotion of research and education. On the international level, both the U.S.S.R. and China were well represented at international meetings. However, central control of botanical gardens in those countries made it difficult for delegates from individual botanical gardens to contribute to policy discussions.

The annual meeting of the American Association of Botanical Gardens and Arboreta, held in Honolulu in June, was attended by 150 delegates from botanical gardens across the U.S. and overseas. The delegates discussed the dual themes of in situ conservation of endangered plants and how to coordinate common activities. Closely linked to these themes was the work of 18 botanical gardens and horticultural institutes in the U.S. that were attempting to bring into cultivation some 3,000 species of threatened vascular plants native to the country. The Center for Plant Conservation, based at the Arnold Arboretum at Harvard University, was coordinating and providing financial support for the project. The aims were to establish a living gene bank for research, evaluate the potential usefulness of the plants to humans, develop a seed bank, and protect wild populations from unnecessary collecting.

(REGINALD IAN BEYER)

Zoos. Prominent among the subjects discussed at a meeting of the International Union of Directors of Zoological Gardens in Poland in September 1986 was the need to continue increasing the level of national and international cooperation in the management, exchange, and breeding of zoo animals. The theme had been emphasized at a meeting of the Captive Breeding Specialist Group in Cologne, West Germany, the previous month. A wide range of items on captive propagation and conservation was considered, and many good examples of cooperation were cited. The major concerns of the meeting included up-to-date information, appraisal, and recommendations where necessary on studbooks (there were 71 international studbooks in existence in 1986); Arabian oryx reintroduction plans; the Global Tiger Propagation Plan; and primate conservation and captive breeding, especially for gorillas, chimpanzees, and lemurs.

Among species eliciting particular concern, the possible reintroduction of the Przewalski horse (*Equus caballus przewalskii*) into Mongolia was discussed. A number of golden-headed lion tamarins (*Leontopithecus r. rosalia*) that had been illegally exported were returned to Brazil; five zoos agreed to take part in an international management program with Brazil, and one birth was reported by the National Zoological Park in Washington, D.C., in August. Although the protracted legal bickering among conservationists, biologists, and government officers continued, the U.S. Court of Appeals ruled in June that the U.S. Fish and Wildlife Service could take into captivity the last three California condors (*Gymnogyps californianus*) that were left in the wild.

An estimated 500–1,000 individuals of the Sumatran rhinoceros (*Didermocerus sumatrensis*) remained in the wild in Sumatra (Indonesia), Malaysia, and Thailand, but rapid deforestation would quickly reduce this small and scattered population. An agreement was signed between the

A rare red panda sleeps contentedly at the new one-hectare (2.5-acre) Himalayan Highlands habitat in New York City's Bronx Zoo. The habitat took two years to plan and construct and cost about $700,000. It attempts to reproduce the terrain of northern India, Nepal, and Tibet.

FRANK C. DOUGHERTY/THE NEW YORK TIMES

Indonesian government and the Howletts and Port Lympe Foundation in the U.K. allowing up to four pairs to be taken from a forest scheduled for clearance. By November 1986 seven animals were in captivity. The plight of the two African species of rhino was highlighted at a meeting convened in Cincinnati, Ohio, in October and attended by zoo authorities, field authorities, field biologists, and other research workers. The situation of the black rhino (*Diceros bicornis)* was particularly critical. An estimated population of only 3,800 remained, compared with around 20,000 in Kenya less than 20 years earlier. The meeting agreed that the 180–190 black rhino in captivity urgently required an international management plan to maximize the breeding potential. A herd of 40 Père David's deer (*Elaphurus davidianus*), now extinct in the wild, was sent to a protected area in China from a consortium of British zoos.

Notable breedings included: yellow-headed blackbirds (*Ageliaus icterocephalus*) at the National Aquarium, Baltimore, Md.; Jambu fruit doves (*Ptilinopus jambus*) at the Memphis (Tenn.) Zoo; false killer whale (*Pseudorca crassidens*) at Sea Life Park, Honolulu; killer whale (*Orcinus orca*) at Sea World of Florida, Orlando (in 1985), and at Sea World, San Diego, Calif.; giant panda (*Ailuropoda melanoleuca*) at Ueno Zoo, Tokyo; and golden monkey (*Pygathrix roxellana*)—on loan from China and later returned there—at Washington Park Zoo, Portland, Ore.

New exhibits, the majority of which incorporated naturalistic elements, included a new carnivore house at the Cincinnati Zoo; "Treehouse" at the Philadelphia Zoo; Seaquarium at Willemstad, Curaçao, Netherlands Antilles; Aquaticus at the Oklahoma City (Okla.) Zoo; the Max Bell Marine Mammal Centre at the Vancouver (B.C.) Aquarium; Jungle of the Apes at the St. Louis (Mo.) Zoo; Mountain Habitat at the Arizona-Sonora Desert Museum; and the African Veldt exhibit at the Phoenix (Ariz.) Zoo. The Chinese Association of Zoological Gardens was formally established on Oct. 24, 1985, in Beijing (Peking).

(P. J. OLNEY)

See also Environment; Gardening.

Chemistry

Organic Chemistry. Activation of carbon-hydrogen bonds in simple, saturated hydrocarbons continued to attract interest during 1986. These compounds, of which the simplest is methane, the major component of natural gas, burn in air to give carbon dioxide and water. Chemists would prefer to have them react with oxygen or other elements in a way that leads to useful intermediates like methanol.

Kotaro Ogura and Kenji Takamagari of Yamaguchi (Japan) University found that methane can be converted directly to methanol and chloromethanes at room temperature by the combined action of electricity and light. They introduced methane into a transparent cell fitted with a platinum electrode partially immersed in aqueous potassium chloride and passed current through the system. At the same time, the cell was illuminated with ultraviolet light. The products varied with the electrolysis potential but consisted primarily of methanol, chloromethane, and dichloromethane.

A different approach to alkane activation was explored by Craig L. Hill and Roman Renneke of Emory University, Atlanta, Ga. They used a heteropolytungstic acid, a compound whose anion comprises 12 hexavalent tungsten atoms and 40 oxygen atoms around a single phosphorus atom, as a homogeneous catalyst. On irradiation with blue or near-ultraviolet light, this catalyst goes into an excited state that oxidizes organic molecules. The coincident reduction of the catalyst is reversed by the presence of platinum. Carried out in acetonitrile solvent, the reaction converted alkanes to alkenes, ketones, and acetamides, according to the conditions and nature of the starting materials (*see* 1).

Living organisms continued to provide chemists with novel organic substances, among them a toxic dipeptide produced by Colorado potato beetles and diterpenes produced by corals. The dipeptide, identified by D. Daloze, J. C. Braekman, and J. M. Pasteels of the Free University of Brussels, is the major compound in the beetles' defensive secretions. It is unusual in that one of its two constituent amino acids is 2-amino-3(*Z*),5-hexadienoic acid. This amino acid, which is not used in building proteins, had never before been found in insects but proved to be related to unsaturated amino acids found in some fungal compounds that act as enzyme inhibitors. At the Duke University marine laboratory in North Carolina, John D. Costlow and colleagues isolated diterpenes with molecular weights of 450–500 daltons from coral. These compounds, which were identified by Kenneth L. Rinehart, Jr., and Paul A. Kiefer of the University of Illinois, prevent barnacle larvae from attaching to the coral and thus could lead to new antifouling compounds for treating ships' hulls.

The ability to make peptides and proteins in the laboratory has grown dramatically since Bruce Merrifield introduced automated protein synthesis in the 1960s (for which he received the Nobel Prize for Chemistry in 1984). During the year researchers from the California Institute of Technology and the Walter and Eliza Hall Institute of Medical Research, Melbourne, Australia, synthesized the 140-amino-acid protein interleukin-3 and showed that the synthetic version had a growth factor activity similar to that of the natural material. The advantage of such syntheses is that the natural structure can be modified comparatively easily. In this case, by means of selective modifications the researchers were able to show that full activity depends on the tertiary structure of the complete molecule.

A synthetic peptide based on two fragments from the coat protein of the foot-and-mouth disease virus was shown

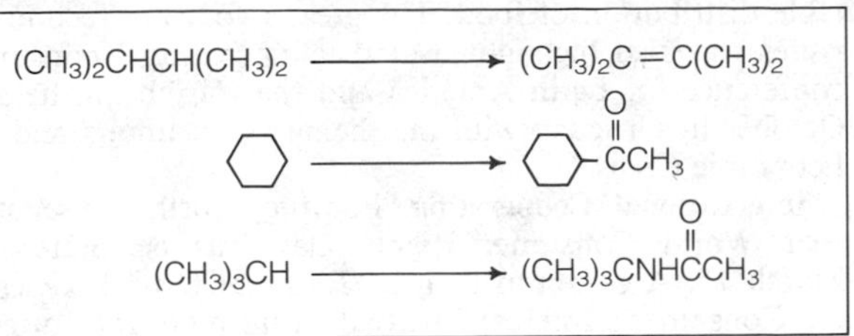

1

to produce an antibody response under the same conditions used to test conventional vaccines made from living or killed organisms. Scientists from Eli Lilly's research laboratories in the U.S. and the U.K. and from the Animal Virus Research Institute in the U.K. made two short peptides of known immunogenicity and linked them together with a spacer molecule intended to impart a secondary structure to the synthetic peptide to enhance its activity.

Physical Chemistry. Physical chemistry shared the spotlight with the recipients of the 1986 Nobel Prize for Chemistry. The prize was divided among Dudley Herschbach of Harvard University, Yuan T. Lee of the University of California at Berkeley, and John Polanyi of the University of Toronto (*see* BIOGRAPHIES) for the development of sophisticated methods for studying the way in which chemical reactions take place. Herschbach and Lee pioneered the use of colliding beams of molecules at low pressure for studying the interactions that produce a chemical reaction, while Polanyi developed a technique for measuring infrared radiation given off as a new molecule forms from its precursors, thereby providing detailed information about the energy pathways taken by reactions.

In recent years physical chemistry has made major contributions to the understanding of atmospheric processes. This upsurge was triggered by concern in the 1970s about the effects of supersonic aircraft and of aerosol sprays on the ozone layer high in the atmosphere that protects the Earth's surface from much of the Sun's ultraviolet rays. During the 1980s acid rain became a topic of major concern.

As rain falls, it scavenges gaseous pollutants such as sulfur dioxide from the atmosphere to form acid solutions. Stephen Adams and colleagues from the University of Auckland, N.Z., devised an instrument that measures the size of natural raindrops and used it to plot the change in acidity with raindrop size. They found marked differences; the scavenging ability of a fine drizzle is not the same as that of a shower of large drops. Not only were these results expected to open up prospects for additional physicochemical studies on transport of atmospheric gases, they also warned against the overly simple hypotheses that frequently dog environmental controversies in their early stages.

Inorganic Chemistry. Fluorine is the most electronegative element in the periodic table and, consequently, one of the most reactive. It was first isolated in elemental form in 1886 by the French chemist Henri Moissan, although its existence had been known for nearly three-quarters of a century before that. Moissan made fluorine by electrolyzing cooled hydrogen fluoride, and the element has been made by electrochemical means ever since. In 1986 Karl O. Christie of Rockwell International, Canoga Park, Calif., succeeded in producing elemental fluorine by a purely chemical reaction for the first time.

Christie's starting materials were derived from hydrogen fluoride, not the element itself, so the synthesis was a genuine one. It involved heating potassium manganese hexafluoride (K_2MnF_6) with antimony pentafluoride (SbF_5). Christie reasoned that the potassium ions would preferentially link with the antimony ions, leaving an unstable manganese tetrafluoride to decompose into manganese trifluoride and free fluorine. At 150° C (300° F), he found that the reaction occurred as predicted with a yield of 40%.

Understanding of the chemistry of silicon has expanded rapidly since the discovery of the first silicon-silicon double bond in 1981. Alexander Sax and Rudolf Janoschek of Graz (Austria) University calculated that the most stable form of the silicon analog of benzene (Si_6H_6) would have a prismlike structure (2) rather than the hexagonal structure found in benzene. The prismane form of benzene is much less energetically favoured than the hexagonal form because of the preference for sp^2 hybridization in carbon atoms, a preference absent in silicon.

In 1985 the first silicon-nitrogen triple bond was reported. During 1986 Akira Sekiguchi, Steven S. Zigler, and Robert West of the University of Wisconsin suggested that dimethyldisilyne, a compound containing a silicon-silicon triple bond, may be an intermediate in their synthesis of (3).

Otto J. Scherer and colleagues from the University of Kaiserslautern, West Germany, reported the first synthesis of a compound containing the phosphorus analog of the cyclopentadienyl ligand. This double-decker sandwich compound (4) has a central five-membered phosphorus ring linked to two chromium atoms that, in turn, are linked to pentamethylcyclopentadienyl ligands.

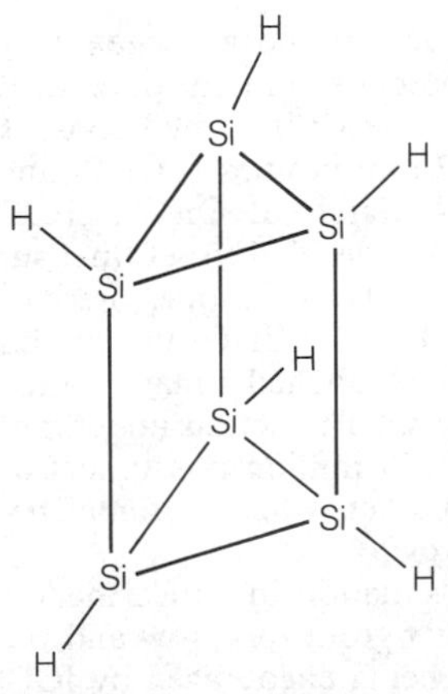

2

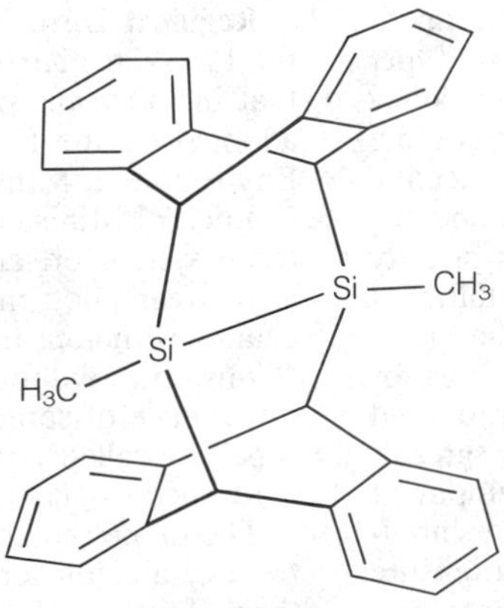

3

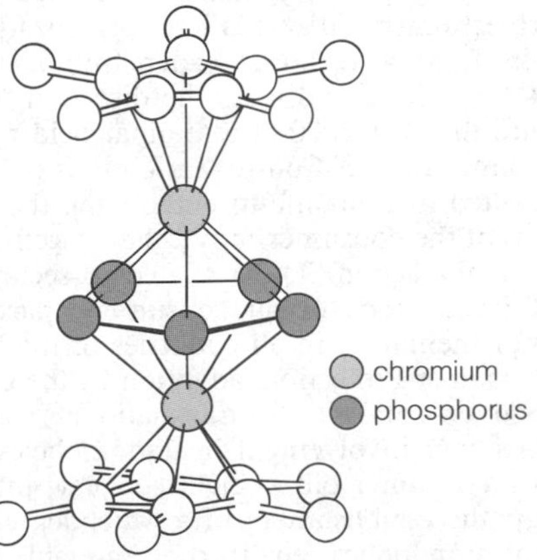

4

Analytical Chemistry. Chemists have worked for many years to detect and identify the trace constituents of wines, the combination and concentration of which differentiate fine wine from vin ordinaire. Because these volatile components usually make up less than 0.1% of a wine's volume, analysis is difficult and, until the past year, had not been very successful. A new method, described by R. H. Tomlinson of McMaster University, Hamilton, Ont., and J. Boison of the University of Saskatchewan, used chlorofluorocarbon solvent (Freon) to extract the flavour components of wine more effectively than previous methods. Special treatment of the extract concentrated it so that it could be analyzed by combined techniques of gas chromatography and mass spectrometry. Using this method the researchers found 0.02 parts per billion of 2-methoxy-3-isobutylpyrazine in a good-quality cabernet sauvignon. This compound had been thought for some time to be a key flavour component in wines made from this grape but had never been identified in a wine by chemical analysis. In all, Tomlinson and Boison detected 260 trace components in the cabernet sauvignon, 34 more than had been noted previously.

Study of the carbon- and nitrogen-isotope ratios in bone collagen can provide clues to the diets of historic and prehistoric populations, according to Stanley H. Ambrose and Michael J. DeNiro of the University of California at Los Angeles. Carbon-isotope ratios can distinguish between plants that use different metabolic pathways, while nitrogen-isotope ratios can differentiate marine from terrestrial plants. As materials move up the food chain, isotopic ratios vary from those found at the bottom; consequently, herbivores and carnivores may be told apart by isotopic analyses. Ambrose and DeNiro tested these hypotheses on collagen obtained from human bones in African museum collections. In most cases their results accorded with dietary pictures constructed from archaeological and ethnographic evidence. Further research, they believed, could throw new light on the significance to human evolution of hunting versus gathering. (MARTIN A. SHERWOOD)

This article updates the *Macropædia* articles Physical and Chemical ANALYSIS AND MEASUREMENT; CHEMICAL COMPOUNDS; CHEMICAL ELEMENTS; CHEMICAL REACTIONS; IMMUNITY; Principles, Methods, and Instruments of MEASUREMENT AND OBSERVATION; MOLECULES; The PHYSICAL SCIENCES: *Chemistry.*

Consumer Affairs

The trend in the consumer movement toward greater concentration on economic issues was confirmed in 1986. Consumer groups became more vocal on such issues as protectionism, deregulation, privatization, and competition. In May consumer leaders from all over the world met in New York to discuss the direction of consumer policy until the year 2000 at a seminar held by the International Organization of Consumers Unions (IOCU). The meeting resulted in a manifesto embodying the principles and beliefs of the consumer movement, together with ten priority areas for action. These related to securing the fulfillment of basic needs of all consumers, particularly the poor; implementation in all countries of the UN Guidelines for Consumer Protection; adoption by the UN of the proposed code of conduct on transnational corporations; greater consumer involvement in trade policies; the development of a consumer bill of rights on new information technology; the establishment of a watchdog capability to ensure that monopolies remained accountable to consumers; and elimination of economic practices that inhibit the equitable distribution of food. The greater focus on economic issues was also highlighted at the first regional consumer conference for Latin America and the Caribbean, held in October in Uruguay with the theme "Consumers and the Economic Crisis."

International Cooperation. For the fourth consecutive year World Consumer Rights Day was celebrated on March 15. A common theme, "Rational Drug Policies in the Consumer's Interest," was taken up by dozens of consumer groups. Renewed interest in educating consumers led to the launching of a network for that purpose serviced by IOCU. In 1986 IOCU was officially recognized as a nongovernmental organization (NGO) by the World Health Organization (WHO) and participated at the 39th World Health Assembly (WHA) in May in Geneva. The assembly unanimously approved the WHO revised drugs strategy and adopted the report of the Nairobi, Kenya, conference on the rational use of drugs held in late 1985. Health Action International (HAI) and International Baby Food Action Network (IBFAN) produced an NGO newspaper entitled *Health Now* for delegates at the WHA. Two charts based on a survey by IBFAN showed that, five years after the adoption of the international code of marketing for breast-milk substitutes, the stated marketing policies of companies belied their actual practice.

The Action Groups to Halt Advertising and Sponsorship of Tobacco (AGHAST) network, which aimed to end all promotion and advertising by the tobacco industry, published a report on the smoking situation in nine Asian countries. AGHAST lobbied successfully for the adoption of a resolution by the WHA to make control of cigarette smoking its major public health project for the next decade. Pesticide Action Network's (PAN's) 1985 "Dirty Dozen Campaign" resulted in the banning of several blacklisted pesticides in Ecuador, Colombia, and Costa Rica and a tightening of safety standards in Indonesia and Malaysia.

The Bhopal Syndrome, published by IOCU in June, studied the 1984 disaster at Bhopal, India, when more than 1,700 people were killed by toxic gas leaking from a Union Carbide plant. It concluded that one of the lessons to be learned from the tragedy was that a similar catastrophe was not only possible but probable, given that many potentially hazardous industrial plants were known to be operating under conditions resembling those at Bhopal. New interest was shown in the subject of irradiation as a method of food preservation. Views among consumer groups varied, but there was general agreement that benefits for consumers had not been proved and that an effective system of monitoring, testing, regulating, and enforcing the strictest standards of food safety would have to be developed before irradiation was introduced.

Regional Developments. In Europe an amendment to the 1984 directive on transborder shipments of toxic wastes that included the principle of prior informed consent was adopted by the European Communities (EC) Council of Environment Ministers on March 6. On April 22 the Council of Ministers of the EC decided to set up a surveillance system on home accidents in Europe, preceded by a five-year pilot phase. On July 1 BEUC (the EC bureau dealing with consumer affairs) launched a major campaign, "Consumers without frontiers." The action underlined the impatience of some of the 320 million consumers in Europe's so-called common market, where national borders continued to play a strong role.

The depressed economic situation in Africa made it extremely difficult for consumer groups to grow and prosper there. Existing NGOs were being encouraged by IOCU to become interested in consumer protection and educational

A woman checks the label of a calcium supplement. Women are particularly prone to osteoporosis, a degenerative bone disease. It is widely believed but has not been conclusively proved that increased calcium consumption helps avoid the malady.

JACQUES M. CHENET/NEWSWEEK

work. Following a 15-month campaign by the Association de Consommateurs de l'Île Maurice, the Mauritius government announced it would adopt the list of essential drugs by generic names. The government of Zaire was expected to decide on new legislation dealing with advertising. An Action for Rational Drugs in Asia campaign was launched on March 26. In July consumer groups from six Asian countries held a workshop to discuss a campaign against the indiscriminate use of monosodium glutamate (MSG) in the region. A "No MSG Please" action network was formed, and a declaration of demands included a ban on the use of MSG in foods meant for infants and young children.

The Australian Federation of Consumer Groups discussed its policies and priorities for action for the next two years at its biennial meeting in November 1985. At the top of the list was the establishment of a national consumer product safety commission. A first national consumer protection meeting took place in Uruguay in April, and the Brazilian consumer groups held their seventh annual national meeting in September to discuss their response to the economic and financial reforms in that country. Ecuador set up a Directorate for Consumer Protection.

(RUTH VERMEER)

A study by the Technical Assistance Research Program Institute for the U.S. Office of Consumer Affairs in 1986 concluded that satisfying complaining customers could lead to greater profits for companies with complaint-handling strategies. For complaints on products and services that involved less than $5, a company could gain 34% more repeat business if the complaint was not ignored; when the purchase price was $100 or more, 54% of customers would repurchase the product if the problem was resolved.

In April a U.S. District Court judge in Boston ruled that warnings on cigarette packages do not protect tobacco companies from claims that they failed to give consumers adequate warning that cigarettes are dangerous. In the ruling, Liggett & Myers Tobacco Co. was denied its request for dismissal of a suit brought against it by the family of a smoker who died of cancer, allegedly caused by smoking. Liggett planned to appeal the decision to the Supreme Court. A rash of product-tampering incidents involving over-the-counter drugs and food products such as soup and baby foods forced companies to step up their efforts to provide tamper-proof packaging. Manufacturers believed that improving product safety outweighed any possible adverse reaction to "tamper-evident" packaging, the industry term for safety seals and jar tops that show whether they have been broken or opened.

During the year more than 80 proposals were introduced in 35 states to regulate manufacturers and distributors who sell products and services over the telephone. The proposals involved regulating who may be called, the hours that telemarketing may be conducted, and the method of calling, such as computer dialing or using recording devices. In addition, 115 bills dealing with consumer privacy, harassment, eavesdropping, wiretapping, and other aspects of telemarketing were being considered by state legislatures. "Asterisk bills" prohibiting calls to consumers who request not to be solicited were being considered in 11 states, including California, New York, and Michigan.

Increasing costs of liability insurance caused many companies to raise the prices of certain products and to stop manufacturing and distributing others. For example, Lederle Laboratories, a unit of American Cyanamid hit with 109 vaccine lawsuits in 1985, stopped distributing DPT (diphtheria, pertussis, tetanus) vaccines because it could not obtain insurance. This caused vaccine prices to rise from $5.43 for 15 doses in 1981 to $65 in 1986. The annual insurance premium for obstetricians in the New York City area was nearly $85,000, and small accounting firms experienced premium increases of 200 to 400%. (*See* INDUSTRIAL REVIEW: *Special Report.*) Fourteen states passed legislation requiring insurers to underwrite high-risk lines of business through state-run insurance pools. In Minnesota commercial insurers had to take part in state pools if they wished to continue to do business in the state.

Over 2,000 bills were introduced in state legislatures in 1986 to reform tort law, the state statutes and court decisions that govern product and personal liability suits, and 19 states enacted laws. In June Californians voted for Proposition 51, which limited awards for noneconomic damages such as pain and suffering. The new law lessened the significance of the "deep-pockets doctrine," which often requires a wealthy codefendant in a personal injury suit, such as a manufacturer or local government, to pay all of the victim's damages even if another party was to blame. Trial lawyers, who spent $5 million to prevent the proposition from passing, were joined in opposing it by consumer advocate Ralph Nader. In April the state of Washington passed legislation that limited the "deep-pockets doctrine" by capping awards for noneconomic damages and banning payments in cases where the plaintiff's intoxication was the primary cause of the accident.

(EDWARD MARK MAZZE)

See also Economic Affairs: *World Economy;* Industrial Review: *Advertising.*

Crime, Law Enforcement, and Penology

Violent Crime. *Terrorism.* "Barbarians of the modern age" was the label French Prime Minister Jacques Chirac gave to terrorists who during a ten-day period in September 1986 set off five bomb blasts in Paris, turning the French capital into a city of fear. The bombings, which left 10 people dead and more than 160 wounded, were among a frightening series of attacks committed by terrorists during the year, prompting target nations to begin instituting tough new antiterrorist measures.

In March a U.S. task force on terrorism, headed by Vice-Pres. George Bush, suggested that military action could be a useful deterrent to future terrorist acts. This philosophy was put to the test on April 15, when U.S. military planes attacked Libyan targets. (*See* WORLD AFFAIRS [Middle East and North Africa]: *Libya.*) The raid, ordered by U.S. Pres. Ronald Reagan, came in response to several terrorist incidents believed to have been sponsored by Libyan leader Col. Mu'ammar al-Qadhdhafi. Among them was the April 5 bombing of a West Berlin discotheque that resulted in the deaths of a U.S. serviceman and a Turkish woman and injuries to more than 200 people.

Within hours of the raid, William J. Calkins, an officer at the U.S. embassy in Khartoum, The Sudan, was shot and seriously wounded by a gunman suspected of being a member of the Libyan- and Syrian-backed Abu Nidal terrorist faction, while in Lebanon a previously unknown terrorist group calling itself the Arab Commando Cell claimed responsibility for executing two British teachers and an American librarian, whose bodies were found near Beirut on April 17. On that same day an attempt to smuggle a bomb aboard a fully loaded El Al jumbo jet at London's Heathrow Airport was foiled by alert security guards. In October Nezar Hindawi, a Jordanian, was convicted and sentenced by a British court to 45 years in prison for his role in the plot, which involved planting a bomb in the bag of his pregnant Irish fiancée before she boarded the Israeli plane. Britain subsequently broke diplomatic relations with Syria, which it accused of masterminding the affair.

After a lull over the summer, a renewed surge of terrorist incidents began in September. Avoiding heavily guarded airports in Europe, four Palestinian hijackers posing as security officers seized Pan Am Flight 73 on September 5 as it boarded passengers in Karachi, Pak. For 16 hours the hijackers held nearly 400 passengers and crew members aboard the 747 while authorities negotiated for their release. Then an apparent mechanical failure cut off lighting in the aircraft cabin, prompting the jittery hijackers to open fire and throw grenades at their hostages. A bloodbath ensued as Pakistani security forces unsuccessfully attempted a rescue operation. Twenty-one persons died and more than 120 were injured. The hijackers, who survived, were taken into custody.

On September 6 two men posing as tourists entered a synagogue in Istanbul and turned machine guns and grenades on the worshipers, killing 21 and injuring 4 before they were blown up by one of their own grenades. Turkish authorities said the two terrorists, who were thought to be Arabs, left no clues as to where they came from or what organization they represented. Responsibility for the bomb explosions in Paris in September was claimed by a group calling itself the Committee for Solidarity with Arab and Middle Eastern Political Prisoners. The group, which was thought to be receiving support from Syria, demanded the release from a French prison of Georges Ibrahim Abdallah, leader of a left-wing Maronite Christian terrorist faction, and two others. An ultraleftist French terrorist organization, Action Directe, was believed to be linked to the group. Action Directe claimed responsibility for killing Georges Besse, the president of Renault, on November 17.

In October a report of a judicial inquiry into the crash of an Air-India Boeing 747 jet off the Irish coast on June 23, 1985, was introduced in the Indian Parliament. The inquiry concluded that the crash, which killed all 329 passengers and crew, was caused by a bomb explosion aboard

Police at London's Heathrow Airport were armed with submachine guns. Terrorism had forced a change from the traditional unarmed bobby that had become one of the symbols of England.
REUTERS/BETTMANN NEWSPHOTOS

the aircraft. The bombing was said to have been part of a plot to destroy two Air-India jets on the same day, but a second bomb exploded prematurely in a suitcase at Tokyo's Narita Airport, killing two baggage handlers. The plot was believed to have originated in Canada among members of a fundamentalist Sikh group fighting for a separate Sikh nation in northern India. On Aug. 10, 1986, Sikh terrorists assassinated India's former chief of staff, Gen. Arun Vaidya, who had helped to plan the 1984 military assault on the Golden Temple at Amritsar, the Sikhs' most holy shrine. On October 2 Prime Minister Rajiv Gandhi escaped unharmed when a lone gunman, thought to be a Sikh, fired shots at him during a prayer service at a memorial to Mahatma Gandhi in New Delhi.

The assassination of Sweden's Prime Minister Olof Palme stunned that nation earlier in the year. On February 28 Palme and his wife were walking home from the movies in central Stockholm when an unidentified gunman shot the prime minister at point-blank range. It was the first political assassination in Sweden for almost two centuries. The assassin had not been identified at year's end.

Murder and Other Violence. There was conflicting information concerning trends in serious crime in the U.S. in 1986. A survey by the U.S. Bureau of Justice Statistics showed that the number of crimes committed against individuals and households in the preceding year had fallen to the lowest level since the government began collecting such information in 1973. In 1985, 34.9 million crimes occurred, compared with 35.6 million at the start of the survey. However, the FBI's Crime Index, based on information provided by 16,000 law-enforcement agencies, indicated that serious crime increased by 5% in 1985 over 1984. Preliminary FBI Crime Index figures for the first six months of 1986 showed this upward trend continuing. In Canada the number of serious offenses reported to the police showed a slight increase of about 1% in 1985, but the overall rate of crime remained far below that of the

U.S. The homicide rate in Canada, for example, was 2.9 offenses per 100,000 population in 1985, compared with 7.9 in the U.S.

Yves ("Apache") Trudeau achieved a certain notoriety during the year by becoming the most prolific known murderer in Canadian history. Trudeau, a Hell's Angels motorcycle gang leader, was permitted to plead guilty in Montreal in February to 43 reduced counts of manslaughter in exchange for information and testimony relating to other Hell's Angels killings. Quebec police said Trudeau, whose victims were mainly fellow bikers, had already helped to solve about 40 additional murders. A joint task force of 45 FBI, state, county, and city police continued a lengthy and expensive search in the U.S. Pacific Northwest for the Green River serial killer, who was believed to have murdered as many as 46 young women in the Seattle, Wash., area between 1982 and 1984. Local officials complained that the task force, established in January 1984, was preempting law-enforcement personnel needed to investigate other crimes.

Police in the U.S. were equally frustrated in their search for the person or persons responsible for a renewed outbreak of product-tampering cases. On February 8 a young woman in Yonkers, N.Y., died after taking Tylenol capsules laced with cyanide, and two more poisoned bottles of the popular painkiller were found in the same area five days later. The incident was similar to the still-unsolved poisonings that had resulted in the deaths of seven Chicago-area residents in 1982. Throughout the year food and drug products were pulled from store shelves in response to letters warning that some packages had been poisoned. In May Edward Marks of Los Angeles, a former brokerage clerk, was arrested and charged with poisoning drugs manufactured by the SmithKline Beckman Corp. in the hope of profiting by trading in SmithKline stock.

On August 20 Patrick Sherrill, a U.S. postal employee threatened with dismissal, entered a post office in Edmond, Okla., with three guns and opened fire, killing 14 people and injuring 7 before taking his own life. It was the worst such attack in the U.S. since a shooting rampage at a McDonald's restaurant in San Ysidro, Calif., in 1984 left 21 people dead and 18 injured. The New York State Court of Appeals reinstated charges of attempted murder and assault against Bernhard H. Goetz, the so-called subway vigilante, who shot four black youths on a Manhattan subway in 1984 allegedly because he feared they would rob him. Goetz's case had given rise to worldwide debate over the question of when a citizen is justified in using lethal force in self-defense.

J. PAVLOVSKY—SYGMA

Mourners carry the coffin of one of the more than 20 victims of two men who entered a synagogue in Istanbul, drew machine guns and hand grenades, and attacked worshipers. The terrorists accidentally blew themselves up with one of their own grenades.

The tragic consequences of drug abuse were dramatically illustrated by a number of cases during the year. At Oxford University Olivia Channon, daughter of a British Cabinet minister, died of a drug overdose on June 11 after a party. Among those charged in connection with her death were two university colleagues and an heir to the Guinness brewing fortune. In Los Angeles in September Cathy Evelyn Smith, a Canadian singer who had injected comedian John Belushi with a fatal mixture of heroin and cocaine in 1982, was sentenced to three years in prison after pleading no contest to involuntary manslaughter and other charges. U.S. public opinion was most aroused, however, when two prominent athletes, University of Maryland basketball player Len Bias and Don Rogers of the Cleveland Browns football team, died of cocaine overdoses within a few days of each other in June. President Reagan and his wife, Nancy, launched a major antidrug campaign, and Congress passed a legislative package that included stiffened penalties for drug offenses and $1.7 billion for law-enforcement and drug-abuse programs. At the same time, the growing practice of testing for drug use, especially as it involved persons not in occupations directly affecting public safety, led to debate over possible threats to civil liberties.

In the Soviet Union drug abuse was also acknowledged to be a problem. The Soviet news agency TASS reported that on September 20 two "drug addicted" gunmen tried to seize a Soviet plane in the Ural Mountains city of Ufa. Two police officials and two passengers in the plane were slain before security forces overpowered and killed the hijackers.

Nonviolent Crime. *Political Crime.* Relations between the U.S. and Mexico were strained by allegations that massive corruption associated with drug trafficking to the U.S. existed within the Mexican government. The allegations were heatedly denied by Mexican officials, but Pres. Miguel de la Madrid, who took office in 1982 with promises of a "moral renovation," seemed to have made little headway against the corruption claimed to exist at virtually all levels of government. Rampant fraud and corruption under the regime of former Philippines president Ferdinand Marcos came to light following his removal from office in February. (*See* WORLD AFFAIRS [Southeast Asia]: *Philippines.*) In an unprecedented move the Swiss government, at the request of the new Filipino government of Pres. Corazon Aquino, froze all bank deposits of the Marcos family in Switzerland. This action appeared likely to influence the future financial planning of dictators, drug traffickers, and swindlers who had long viewed Swiss banks as the ultimate secret haven for their funds.

White Collar Crime and Theft. The largest insider stock-trading scandal in Wall Street history began in May when the Securities and Exchange Commission (SEC) filed criminal charges against Dennis Levine, a senior executive of Drexel Burnham Lambert Inc., one of New York City's leading investment banking firms. The SEC claimed that over five years Levine had illegally used advance knowl-

A specially constructed courtroom in Palermo, Italy, was the site of a massive trial of hundreds of people alleged to be members of the Mafia. Thirty cells that line the back of the room accommodate defendants.
ALAIN NOGUES—SYGMA

edge to earn $12.6 million from trading stocks and options. Agreeing to cooperate with the government, Levine pleaded guilty in June to charges of income tax evasion, securities fraud, and perjury while turning over $11.5 million in illegal profits to federal authorities. Levine, in turn, led the SEC to Ivan Boesky, a speculator who specialized in corporate takeover stocks. On November 14 the SEC announced that Boesky had agreed to pay $100 million in fines and returned illegal profits. Boesky was said to be cooperating with the authorities, and at year's end Wall Street nervously awaited further revelations.

The massive sums at stake in the international black market in weapons were highlighted in April when the U.S. Customs Service accused 17 defendants of a $2 billion conspiracy to sell sophisticated war planes, tanks, and missiles to Iran, despite a U.S boycott. Late in the year, however, it was revealed that the U.S. government had apparently violated its own boycott by selling arms to Iran and that some of the money was diverted to aid the Nicaraguan *contras,* although such aid was forbidden by law. Several investigations of the affair were being launched at year's end. (*See* WORLD AFFAIRS [North America]: *United States.*) In August 155 Sri Lankan Tamils were found floating in two lifeboats off the foggy coast of Newfoundland. A Royal Canadian Mounted Police investigation revealed that the Tamils, who sought political refugee status in Canada, had paid as much as Can$500,000 to be taken to that country from West Germany aboard a Honduran-registered vessel. Three West Germans were charged in connection with the elaborate plot, but they remained outside the country.

Operation Falcon, an undercover operation conducted by U.S. and Canadian police and wildlife officials, reportedly caught 100 people during the past four years who were involved in smuggling live wild falcons or falcon eggs to Middle Eastern countries. There the falcons were sold as hunting birds to wealthy Arabs for as much as $100,000 each. In Zimbabwe government officials expressed deep concern about a highly organized poaching operation that was denuding the nation's wildlife reserves of elephants and rare black rhinoceros. The poachers were seeking elephant ivory and rhinoceros horn, thought to be an aphrodisiac. Antipoaching units reported in July that over 18 months they had arrested 6 poachers and killed 12.

Law Enforcement. In Italy and the U.S. there were some signs of success in the long struggle between law-enforcement agencies and the Mafia. In February the trial of 474 alleged mafiosi (later reduced to 467) on charges ranging from drug trafficking to murder began in Palermo, Sicily. It was expected to take more than a year and to cost $100 million. Testimony was given by several prominent *pentiti* (repentant) members of the Mafia, including Tommaso (Don Masino) Buscetta. In April Buscetta gave a chilling account of a gang war among rival Mafia families for control of the lucrative U.S. heroin trade. In the course of the struggle, about 200 murders a year were said to have taken place between 1980 and 1982.

In the U.S. the Presidential Commission on Organized Crime issued a report confirming that the Mafia's dominance over organized crime was declining. The commission estimated the Mafia's current strength in the U.S. at 24 families with about 1,700 members, less than half the number estimated in the 1960s. Between 1981 and 1985 federal prosecutors had brought 1,025 indictments against 2,554 mafiosi and convicted 809 Mafia members or their associates. In the fall this series of prosecutions continued in New York City. Eight defendants, representing four of New York City's most powerful Mafia families, were convicted on racketeering charges in Manhattan, and seven members of the powerful Gambino family faced similar charges in Brooklyn. Despite these encouraging developments, the commission warned that other organized criminal groups were already filling the gaps left by the disruption of Mafia operations.

In July Richard W. Miller, the first FBI agent ever to be convicted of espionage, was sentenced in Los Angeles to two concurrent terms of life imprisonment and one concurrent 50-year term on four counts of spying for the Soviet Union and two counts of bribery. The FBI was further embarrassed in August when a notorious fugitive from U.S. justice, Edward Lee Howard, turned up in Moscow. Lee, a former CIA employee suspected of being a double agent for the Soviets, had slipped through an FBI surveillance net in Santa Fe, N.M., in September 1985.

The dangers of law-enforcement work were demonstrated in April in Miami, Fla., when a gun battle between FBI agents and bank robbers left two agents and two robbers dead and five agents wounded. The shoot-out, one of the bloodiest in FBI history, prompted debate over whether the weapons issued to U.S. police were outmoded. Law-enforcement officials reported that police were encountering growing numbers of automatic weapons, including machine guns.

Corruption scandals rocked police departments in a number of U.S. jurisdictions in 1986. In Boston a grand jury indicted ten police officers on charges of stealing police promotion exams and rigging the results. The grand jury said the scheme was part of a conspiracy to conceal other crimes committed by the defendants, including a bank robbery and cocaine trafficking. In New York City 13 officers were suspended from a Brooklyn precinct after allegedly being involved in mugging addicts and drug dealers for cash and drugs. The officers were snared by the police department's own internal affairs unit. Nine current and former Philadelphia police officers were among those indicted in October for running illegal lotteries.

(DUNCAN CHAPPELL)

Prisons and Penology. Hard-line punitivism continued to dominate penological debate and practice throughout the world in 1986. Opinion polls in the U.S. showed 75% supporting the death penalty for murder, while a similar proportion favoured more severe punishment for criminals generally. President Reagan's appointment of conservative Supreme Court justices and other federal judges presaged a more severe judiciary. The president of the Supreme Court of China claimed the harsh penal policy introduced in August 1983 was a continuing success. Rates of murder, rape, robbery, and theft, as well as "economic crime," had fallen. In the U.S.S.R. General Secretary Mikhail Gorbachev's determination to eliminate black marketeering and corruption bore results. Four senior officials received 15-year prison sentences in June 1986 for accepting bribes, and in September Vakhobzan Usmanov, a former minister for the cotton industry in Uzbekistan, was sentenced to death for falsifying production figures, helping embezzlers, and taking bribes. In many Islamic countries public floggings and hangings for breaches of the Shari'ah (Islamic law) continued.

Conservative MPs in the U.K. campaigned for mandatory sentences for violent crimes and for giving the prosecution the right to appeal overly lenient sentences. (Under the proposed provision, the penalty suffered by the defendant in the case under appeal would not be affected, but the appellate court would have the opportunity of declaring, for the guidance of future sentencers, that the punishment should have been more severe.) The British government expressed interest in removing the right to trial by jury for certain minor offenses to help relieve congestion in the courts. It also proposed extending the power to strip criminals of their assets, allowed for drug traffickers under an act of 1986, to all forms of profitable crime.

Liberal penal reformers in the U.K., meanwhile, expressed concern over the disparities in the sentences passed by magistrates' courts, suspected discrimination against black people, and wrongful convictions. Some disturbing examples of the last, originally proved by JUSTICE, the British section of the International Commission of Jurists, led to the quashing of a number of convictions on appeal, often after years of wrongful imprisonment. These cases all involved life sentences for murder or long prison terms for armed robbery, suggesting that many innocent people may have been convicted of lesser crimes as well.

Capital Punishment. Amnesty International reported some 1,100 officially documented executions worldwide in 1985, 20% fewer than in 1984. It stated, however, that these figures did not reflect the true situation, because "many governments fail to announce, or deliberately hide, executions." Many more civilians were believed to have died at the hands of the police, army, other security forces, or government-approved "death squads" than by formal execution. In June, when Peruvian security forces killed 124 inmates of Lurigancho prison near Lima and more than 125 prisoners in two other prisons, they insisted that only the force needed to quell a mutiny had been used. However, Pres. Alan García Pérez said that at least 100 prisoners suspected of left-wing guerrilla activities had been deliberately murdered. (*See* WORLD AFFAIRS [Latin America and the Caribbean]: *Peru.*) Even in relatively peaceful Britain, some criminologists believed the abolition of hanging in 1965 had led to an increase in the number of fatal police shootings.

Ten years after the reinstatement of capital punishment in the U.S., more than 2,600 people had been sentenced to death, over 65 had actually been executed, and about 1,700 awaited execution—and public protests were subsiding. Up to 20,000 people had been executed in China, usually in public by firing squad, since the government's anticrime campaign began in 1983. British Prime Minister Margaret Thatcher refused a request by MPs for a referendum on hanging but reiterated her support for the death penalty "for hideous crimes." In France Jean-Marie le Pen, leader of the right-wing National Front, attracted widespread support when he demanded a return of the guillotine, abolished in 1981.

The hanging in Malaysia in July of two Australians for possessing drugs attracted worldwide publicity and protest, including requests for clemency from both the British and Australian prime ministers. However, little attention had been paid to previous executions in Kuala Lumpur of 36 Asians for similar offenses.

Prisons. In most countries generally rising crime rates and harsher sentencing policies produced growing prison populations, more overcrowding, and deteriorating conditions for prisoners and their guards. The U.S. prison population rose by 5% to nearly 530,000. British and Spanish jails were disrupted by prison personnel engaging in industrial action to protest unacceptable working conditions. There was a general reluctance to increase funds.

In the U.S. and U.K. the rising number of babies born in and received into women's prisons and the rapidly growing number of AIDS (acquired immune deficiency syndrome) victims in men's prisons aroused special concern. The British Prison Officers' Association demanded that AIDS sufferers be segregated. Overcrowding was blamed for occurrences such as the torture by fellow inmates of two youths charged with sexual offenses in England and a record 27 murders in Texas jails. Two spectacular prison escapes in 1986 were those of Charles Sobhraj from the maximum security prison in New Delhi, India, after giving his guards birthday cake laced with drugs and of Michel

SIPA/SPECIAL FEATURES

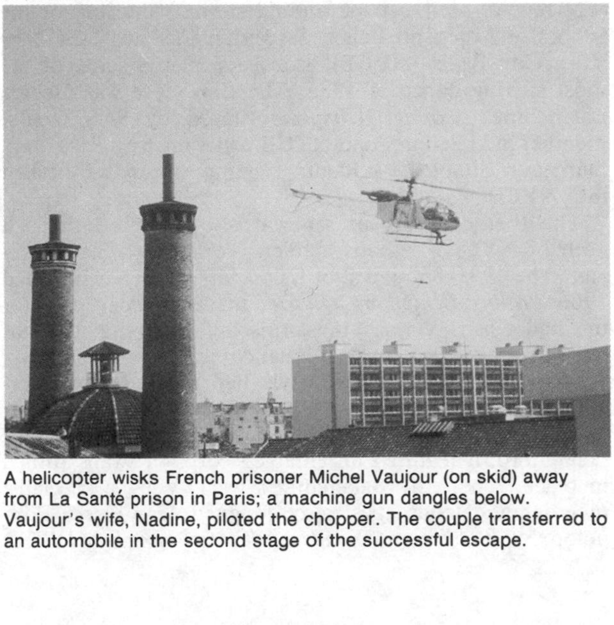

A helicopter wisks French prisoner Michel Vaujour (on skid) away from La Santé prison in Paris; a machine gun dangles below. Vaujour's wife, Nadine, piloted the chopper. The couple transferred to an automobile in the second stage of the successful escape.

Vaujour from La Santé prison in Paris in a helicopter piloted by his wife.

The debate about privatization of prisons continued. By June more than 12 private corporations were building or running prisons in the U.S. at an estimated cost saving of 15–20% (the Correctional Corporation of America charged $21 per inmate per day, as against an average of $25 in state-run facilities). At the same time, they claimed to offer a better service to prisoners, their families, and the courts and improved working conditions for staff. French Minister of Justice Albin Chalandon said his government would have to consider the economic advantages of privatization. Although the U.K. government had ruled out privatization in late 1985, it was reconsidering the possibility, and a party of officials planned to inspect privatized jails in the U.S.

In the U.S. "house arrest" had been used by state and local judges since 1980 and by federal judges starting in 1986 as a means of saving money, easing overcrowding, and reducing human suffering. Low-risk offenders were sentenced to remain at home except when going to work, receiving counseling or medical treatment, or going out for any other purpose specified by the court. Surveillance could be used, and the sanction for default was removal to jail. Judge Nicholas Calabella of New York thought house arrest appropriate where probation was too lenient.

Life in a U.S. prison, however, was not uncongenial to one British convict, who declined repatriation under the new Council of Europe Convention on the Transfer of Sentenced Prisoners. He appreciated the cooking, his job, rate of pay, and the athletic facilities in a Kentucky jail. Luxurious conditions were enjoyed by an alleged drug trafficker in a Mexico City jail, with carpeted cell, private bathroom, television, videorecorder, cassette player, refrigerator, stove, manservant, and unrestricted visits by his wife and other women. "Stone walls do not a prison make," he quoted, adding that, "Even a Mexican prison isn't really so bad, so long as you've got money."

(C. R. M. DAVIES)

See also Law.
This article updates the *Macropædia* articles CRIME AND PUNISHMENT; POLICE.

Dance

North America. Now and then, the art of dance unexpectedly renews itself. At the annual spring workshop of the School of American Ballet (SAB), affiliated with the New York City Ballet (NYCB), teenagers offered some of the most stirring dance of 1986. The showpiece was George Balanchine's *Cortège Hongrois,* staged by SAB faculty member Suki Schorer and NYCB ballet mistress Rosemary Dunleavy. Six of the students, a bumper crop, were taken into NYCB.

The theme of urgent renewal also throbbed through both of NYCB's seasons at New York City's State Theater. The 1985–86 revival of Balanchine's often deprecated 1966 *Brahms-Schönberg Quartet* made a strong case for the ballet as a vintage masterpiece. The spring brought translucent performances of Balanchine's *Divertimento No. 15*—a ballet whose limpid style had seemed unrecoverable in recent years—and a new, bracing production of his one-act *Swan Lake,* designed by Alain Vaes. Set in a polar fjord, it featured an enlarged corps of swans tutued in black, reportedly Balanchine's wish. Vaes, a specialist in enigmatic landscapes, also designed Jean-Pierre Bonnefoux's *Shadows* and *Songs of the Auvergne* by NYCB's

Dancers Ricardo Bustamante (left), Leslie Browne, and Mikhail Baryshnikov, against a backdrop painted by David Salle, perform in the American Ballet Theatre's production of *The Mollino Room*, a modern work by Karole Armitage.
CAROL ROSEGG—MARTHA SWOPE

co-ballet master in chief, Peter Martins. Jerome Robbins, NYCB's other co-chief, crafted two small-scale but lively works, *Quiet City* and *Piccolo Balletto.* Both starred new NYCB principal Robert La Fosse, recently of American Ballet Theatre (ABT).

Many stylists and scholars celebrated the past. In honour of the centenary of Mary Wigman's birth, the Dance History Scholars devoted part of their annual conference to seminars and films about the German expressionist choreographer, and one of her students, dancer Susanne Linke, made a well-regarded U.S. debut as part of the 1985–86 Next Wave series at the Brooklyn Academy of Music (BAM).

Vienna: Lusthaus, a dance-theatre piece about pre-World War I Vienna by former Pilobolite Martha Clarke, packed in New York audiences. A conference on "Jews and Judaism in Dance" ranged from the Renaissance Guglielmo Ebreo to Meredith Monk. The company of recently deceased choreographer Charles Moore performed *Traces,* a panorama of black American dance, and a number of well-known modern dancers organized *Roots,* a gala of early American modern dance. Kasyan Goleizovsky, the constructivist choreographer whose work deeply impressed Balanchine in the '20s, was the subject of a public seminar by the Dance Critics Association.

Festivals, conferences, and anniversaries also pointed up contemporary artists. For the 60th anniversary of her company, Martha Graham choreographed two works (*Tangled Night, Temptations of the Moon*). The highlights of her New York season, however, were the brilliant revivals of *Heretic* (1929) and *Every Soul Is a Circus* (1939). Celebrating its 30th anniversary, the Joffrey Ballet offered a company premiere of Sir Frederick Ashton's *La Fille mal gardée* and commissioned works from young U.S. and Canadian choreographers. Joffrey codirector Gerald Arpino, observing his 25th year as a choreographer, made

Birthday Variations for the company. Longtime principal Denise Jackson retired with a farewell gala. Paul Taylor, observing his 26th year of collaboration with the painter Alex Katz, revived the Taylor-Katz-Bach ballet *Junction* (1966) and made a new satirical piece with Katz to P. D. Q. Bach, *Ab Ovo Usque Ad Mala (From Soup to Nuts).* Taylor's other new work was *A Musical Offering.*

In Los Angeles gala performances marked the 20th anniversary of the Lewitzky Dance Company. For its 20th anniversary, the Repertory Dance Theatre of Salt Lake City, Utah, commissioned a new work by Bill T. Jones and Arnie Zane. The Bucket Dance Theater of Rochester, N.Y., trained by director-choreographer Garth Fagan to a hair-raising virtuosity, thrilled New York audiences and critics in its 15th anniversary season. The Japanese-born dance-mimes Eiko and Koma, celebrating their tenth year in the U.S., gave a gala at New York City's Asia Society. They also set *Broken Dreams* on New York's CoDanceCo, their first work for other performers. "Fascinating Rhythms: A Jazz Tap Celebration" brought such tap stars as Charles ("Honi") Coles, Eddie Brown, and Steve Condos to Boulder, Colo., for classes and performances.

Modern dancers continued to infiltrate the ballet. Prominent in 1986 was the 30-year-old Seattle (Wash.)-based prodigy Mark Morris, who fulfilled commissions for the Joffrey (*Esteemed Guests*) and Boston (*Mort Subite*) ballets and for the Seattle Opera's *Salome.* Laura Dean also fulfilled a Joffrey commission with *Force Field.* (*Impact,* her 1986 collaboration with Steve Reich for her own company, won a Bessie award.) Molissa Fenley made *Feral* for Ohio, and Lucinda Childs made her second piece for Pacific Northwest Ballet, *Clarion.*

At ABT three of the year's five new works were by moderns: David Parsons (*Walk This Way*), Karole Armitage (*The Mollino Room*), and David Gordon (*Murder*). ABT's well-attended and provocative spring season at the Metropolitan Opera House in New York City was dedicated to Lucia Chase (*see* OBITUARIES), longtime company leader, who died in January. Current artistic director Mikhail Baryshnikov was dancing with great confidence. His most affecting performance was the season's last, a *Giselle* with Alessandra Ferri on July 5, one day after he had become a U.S. citizen. The Met season also honoured ABT's choreographer emeritus Antony Tudor, 1986 winner of the Capezio Award: *Dark Elegies* was revived and an all-Tudor gala produced. The season's surprise was the sudden return to the stage of Natalia Makarova for four performances after a self-imposed retirement.

Handsome and charming but with a scrambled classical technique, the Paris Opéra Ballet made its first U.S. visit in nearly 40 years. The Sadler's Wells Royal Ballet brought its *Sleeping Beauty* and an evening of David Bintley's work to BAM. The Central Ballet of China and post-modernists Michael Clark of England and Anne Teresa de Keersmaeker of Belgium were all first-time visitors. The Moiseyev and Kirov companies from the Soviet Union made U.S. minitours, with the Kirov enjoying a national telecast of its *Swan Lake.* Audiences were particularly struck by the leonine majesty of the young ballerina Altinay Asylmuratova.

U.S. dance was supposedly declining, yet 1986 was the year of some very ambitious productions. In ballet it brought new *Sleeping Beauty*s (Ballet West, Indianapolis [Ind.] Dance Theatre) and a full *Swan Lake* (Dallas [Texas] Ballet). In modern dance there were Lucinda Childs's evening-length *Portraits in Reflection,* David Gordon's spatially aggressive *Transparent Means for Travelling Light,* Erick Hawkins's all-male tragedy, *Ahab* (35 years in the making), Douglas Dunn's evening-length *Dances for Men, Women, and Moving Door,* Phyllis Lamhut's evening-length *Die Bewegung,* and Sally Silvers's fecund and sprawling *Swaps Ego Says So. Roaratorio: An Irish Circus on Finnegans Wake,* the 1983 John Cage-Merce Cunningham extravaganza, was given its long-delayed U.S. premiere. Cunningham presented the childhood memoir *Grange Eve* and, with Cage, received a Bessie for special achievement.

Company bases expanded. The Cleveland Ballet became the San Jose (Calif.) Cleveland Ballet, and the Alvin Ailey American Dance Theater had an extended "second city" residency in Kansas City, Mo. The Kansas City Ballet grew to the State Ballet of Missouri (Todd Bolender, director). The brand-new Miami (Fla.) City Ballet, directed by Edward Villella, also performed in Fort Lauderdale. Notable deaths included John Bubbles (*see* OBITUARIES), genius inventor of rhythm tap; NYCB principal Joseph Duell; dancer-choreographer William Dollar; dance photographer Kenn Duncan; lighting designer Ronald Bates; and the monthly periodical *Ballet News* (1979–86).

Among the prizes, the $25,000 Scripps went to Katherine Dunham, the Tony for choreography to Bob Fosse (*Big Deal*). Because of the death of publisher Jean Gordon, *Dancemagazine* withheld awards. In the third USA International Ballet Competition in Jackson, Miss., Nina Ananiashvili and Andris Liepa of the Soviet Union won the first-ever Jackson Grand Prix.

PAUL KOLNIK
The classical corps de ballet from the School of American Ballet performs in Balanchine's *Cortège Hongrois*, staged by Suki Schorer and Rosemary Dunleavy.

In Canada the overwhelming news was the death of Erik Bruhn (*see* OBITUARIES), artistic director of the National Ballet of Canada (NBC) and one of the world's great classical dancers. Bruhn had encouraged new Canadian choreography, and commissions for 1986 included Danny Grossman's *Hot House: Thriving on a Riff,* Glen Tetley's *Alice,* and Constantine Patsalas's *Lost in Twilight.* (NBC brought the three to the Met in July—the company's first appearance there without a guest star.) Bruhn's assistants Valerie Wilder and Lynn Wallis would assume NBC management as associate artistic directors. Principals Vanessa Harwood, Mary Jago, and Nadia Potts retired from NBC; principal Jerilyn Dana left Les Grands Ballets Canadiens (GBC); and artistic director Brydon Paige left the Alberta Ballet.

Among the choreographers, James Kudelka, resident at GBC, created *The Heart of the Matter* for the Joffrey, and Edouard Lock of La La La Human Steps received a Bessie for choreography (*Human Sex*). At Expo 86 in Vancouver, B.C., a juried program of Canadian modern dance choreographers was performed, and Ginette Laurin (*Chevy Dream*) received the year's Chalmers Award. Two new, competing companies had sprung up in British Columbia: Ballet B.C. (directed by Annette av Paul) and the Goh Ballet (directed by Chiat Goh, brother of the Washington [D.C.] Ballet's Choo San Goh). Danse Montréal, that city's first modern dance repertory company—primarily for the work of Canadian choreographers—was being codirected by the avant-garde choreographer Paul-André Fortier and GBC veteran Daniel Jackson. (MINDY ALOFF)

Europe. The nuclear-reactor disaster at Chernobyl, U.S.S.R., in April 1986 had consequences for dance in the form of the eve-of-departure cancellation of a three-city tour by London Festival Ballet, which would have been the first British ballet company in the U.S.S.R. in 25 years. A reciprocal tour by Moscow's Bolshoi Ballet two months later went ahead as planned, opening in Dublin and including appearances in London (the first since 1974), Manchester, and Birmingham in the U.K. and in Paris. During the London season the company appeared at the Royal Opera House, Covent Garden, for three weeks of full-length ballets and then in a 4,000-seat tented theatre set up in Battersea Park for eight performances of excerpts and divertissements. While in the U.K. the visitors were accorded media coverage on a scale usually reserved for major sporting events, but critical opinion indicated modified rapture.

AP/WIDE WORLD

Members of Leningrad's Kirov Ballet are poised in a scene from *Swan Lake*, part of the influential company's repertoire for its first North American tour since 1964. The itinerary included several cities in both the United States and Canada.

International events impinged again when fear of terrorist attack led Sadler's Wells Royal Ballet dancers at first to refuse a tour to Israel. They later reversed their decision after security assurances were given, and the tour took place without incident. While some dancers from the U.S. abandoned plans to travel to Europe, others, including the companies of Martha Graham, Merce Cunningham, and Dance Theatre of Harlem, were not dissuaded. Alvin Ailey's American Dance Theater undertook 41 performances in Greece, Denmark, Switzerland, Norway, and France. Exchange visits with the Far East became more frequent, bringing a first London season by the Central Ballet of China and a second for the Tokyo Ballet from Japan, both performing in Western technique but with some works on Oriental themes. In return, Switzerland's Basel Ballet went to China, West Germany's Hamburg Ballet to Japan, and the Scottish Ballet to Hong Kong and on to Australia, where Netherlands Dance Theatre also made an extended tour.

Britain's Ballet Rambert celebrated its 60th anniversary—40 years as a classical ballet company and the subsequent 20 years as a modern-dance ensemble. New and recent repertory works were given in a special anniversary season at Sadler's Wells Theatre, in the wake of internal policy conflicts that brought the abrupt resignation of Robert North as artistic director. He was replaced by resident choreographer Richard Alston. Former principal dancer Anthony Dowell became director of Britain's Royal Ballet at Covent Garden in succession to Norman Morrice, who had held the post for nine years. In an interview Dowell placed greater priority on standards than on repertory and expressed a continuing allegiance to foundation classics. He was to direct a new staging of *Swan Lake* as his own first contribution, and while he would still dance occasionally he was to give up major roles. Sir Kenneth MacMillan extended his contract as principal choreographer at the Royal Ballet for another three years.

Other directorial changes brought the resignation of British-born Ronald Hynd midway through his second four-year term at the Bavarian State Opera, Munich, West Germany. He claimed that the ballet received inadequate resources and production time compared with the opera company. His departure followed the premiere of his ballet, *Ludwig—Fragments from a Mystery,* commissioned to mark the 100th anniversary of the death of King Ludwig II of Bavaria, the patron of Wagner, some of whose music was quoted in the new score for the ballet by British composer Douglas Young. In Italy similar difficulties attended the Soviet-born former ballerina Violetta Elvin at Naples, where she resigned the ballet directorship after one year. The U.S. dancer Patricia Neary took charge at La Scala, Milan, instead of Vassily Vassiliev, named as incoming director in earlier reports. Egon Madsen left the Royal Swedish Ballet to become director at Florence and was replaced at Stockholm by Nils-Ake Häggbom. The unanimous vote of all dancers at the Rome Opera brought another American, William Carter, to succeed Maya Plisetskaya as ballet director there. Carter inherited a major new development with the opening in Rome on October 16 of the renovated Teatro Branaccio, which, by providing a venue especially for dance productions, brought the

The Central Ballet of China featured Jiang Zuhui's (Chiang Tsu-hui's) *The New Year's Sacrifice* in its New York debut, part of an 11-city U.S. tour. The troupe intends to artistically combine ballet with Chinese dance and to present Western classical ballet in pure form, both new directions for Chinese performers.
TOM CARAVAGLIA

promise of longer seasons and a wider repertory. The New Music Theatre at Amsterdam opened on September 23 with a double bill of ballet and opera, signifying its intended purpose as the shared home of the Dutch National Ballet and the Netherlands Opera.

In a comment on the dance situation in West Germany at the time of Hynd's resignation, Horst Koegler, a leading dance writer, observed: "Ballet has to fight for its very existence now, not only in Munich, but everywhere in West Germany, where it is under the constant and heavy attack of the Wuppertal-led cohorts of the dance-theatre movement." His reference was to the innovative Wuppertal Dance Theatre directed by Pina Bausch, which since its formation in 1973 had gained increasing international acclaim for a performance style nearer to theatre revue, including speech and song, than dance. The theatre's work was one of numerous directions concerning which the *Times* of London commented: "The practitioners of 'New Dance' have a self-inflicted obligation to do something different, and nowadays there are so many of them that finding a suitable difference becomes a major operation." Another direction was exemplified at the Vienna State Opera with a new and bleak version of *Orpheus,* choreographed by Ruth Berghaus in her return to dance after more than 20 years directing drama and opera, to music by Hans Werner Henze.

The production followed the third Vienna Dance Biennale in early 1986, where 88 performances were given in eight weeks by 18 companies from Europe, the U.S., and the U.S.S.R. Concentrations of this kind represented an attempt to relate ends to means as costs continued to spiral upward. Other comparable events included an international dance biennale at Lyon, France, in September–October and Britain's Dance Umbrella, devoted entirely to modern and new dance, involving 70 performances in London and six other centres in October-November.

In Britain the most visible exponent of "New Dance" was Michael Clark, who started out under the Dance Umbrella and became widely touted as "the post-punk superstar of dance." He staged a new program with his company at Sadler's Wells Theatre in September under the title *No Fire Escape in Hell.* Intended for touring internationally, it mixed sexual provocation with rock music and revue-like theatricality but nevertheless used Clark's classical ballet training as the basis for its performance style.

Classical ballet continued to adhere to literary sources, especially for full-length works. Examples in 1986 included Bintley's *The Snow Queen* (Hans Christian Andersen), music compounded from Mussorgsky (Sadler's Wells Royal Ballet); Vassiliev's *Aniuta* (Anton Chekov), music by Valery Gavrilin (San Carlo, Naples); Andŕe Prokovsky's *Victoria* (Knut Hamsun), music by Ragnar Söderlind (Norwegian National Ballet); and Pierre Lacotte's *24 Hours in the Life of a Woman* (Stefan Zweig), music by Hervé Niquet (Ballets de Monte Carlo). The Ballets de Monte Carlo was a new company under the direction of Ghislaine Thesmar and Pierre Lacotte, endorsed by Prince Rainier III of Monaco and his daughter Princess Caroline.

At the Paris Opéra a dispute developed between incumbent director Rudolf Nureyev and Maurice Béjart and Roland Petit, the French directors of other companies, over the promotion of two dancers to *étoile* (an official rank meaning "star") without managerial or directorial agreement. Makarova danced her official preretirement farewell, as Tatiana in John Cranko's *Onegin,* with London Festival Ballet in London on July 16. London Festival Ballet acquired its first president in former ballerina and cofounder Dame Alicia Markova. Other honours were accorded to Royal Ballet ballerina Merle Park, also director of the Royal Ballet School, who was appointed Dame Commander of the Order of the British Empire, and to Paolo Bortoluzzi, directing the Ballet of the Deutsche Oper am Rhein, Düsseldorf-Düisburg, who was created Chevalier (Knight) in the French Ordre des Arts et Lettres.

Deaths during the year included Sir Robert Helpmann (*see* OBITUARIES), Australian-born leading dancer of Sadler's Wells Ballet until 1950 and later director of the Australian Ballet; Claire Motte (*see* OBITUARIES), ballet mistress and former *étoile* of the Paris Opéra Ballet; and Yuri Zhdanov, former leading dancer of Moscow's Bolshoi Ballet and from 1971 director of the Moscow Classical Ballet. (NOËL GOODWIN)

This article updates the *Macropædia* article The History of Western DANCE.

Disasters

The loss of life and property from disasters in 1986 included the following:

Aviation

January 18, Santa Elena, Guatemala. A twin-engine jet used to transport tourists to the Santa Elena airport, some 40 km (25 mi) from Tikal, one of the largest of the Mayan cities, crashed in the jungle while approaching the airport; all 93 persons aboard perished.

January 29, Near Los Mochis, Mexico. A DC-3 passenger plane carrying 21 persons slammed into a hill and burst into flames while trying to land at an abandoned airstrip because the fog-enshrouded airport was closed; all 21 persons aboard perished.

February 10, Off the coast of Corsica. A French Navy helicopter carrying 14 persons crashed during a blinding snowstorm; all aboard were feared dead.

February 16, Taiwan. A Boeing 737 carrying 13 persons was missing on a routine 40-minute flight from Taipei to the offshore island of Penghu; all aboard were feared dead.

March 27, Bangui, Central African Republic. A French Air Force fighter plane experienced mechanical problems on a routine training flight and slammed into an Islamic school; 35 persons were killed.

March 31, Pemba, Mozambique. A Mozambican Air Force plane crashed on takeoff and burst into flames on impact; 44 of the 49 persons aboard lost their lives.

March 31, Near San Miguel el Alto, Mexico. A Boeing 727 Mexicana Airlines jet, carrying 166 persons, crashed into the side of a mountain after the pilot radioed ground controllers that he had an emergency aboard and wished to return to Mexico City; in May investigators blamed a tire blowout in the landing gear, which ruptured fuel, hydraulic, and electrical lines and ignited a fire, as the cause of the crash.

April 2, New Mexico. A U.S. Air Force rescue plane carrying 11 persons crashed after takeoff from Kirkland Air Force Base; there were no survivors.

May 1, Near Ilopango, El Salvador. A DC-6 military transport plane crashed moments after takeoff owing to mechanical problems; all 37 soldiers aboard perished.

May 3, Colombo, Sri Lanka. A bomb, concealed in a vegetable basket in the cargo of an Air Lanka jet, exploded near the tail of the plane while passengers were boarding; 16 persons died as a result of the blast.

May 3, Tai Hsi, Taiwan. Two military helicopters crashed into a rice paddy after one of five helicopters flying in formation during a drill caught fire and smashed into another; unconfirmed reports of casualties placed the death toll at 22.

May 18, Djibouti. A French reconnaissance plane carrying 20 persons crashed in heavy rain; all aboard were killed.

June 10, Cairo, Egypt. A twin-engine airliner, returning to the airport because of sandstorms, crashed into the courtyard of a construction company and burst into flames; 20 of the 25 persons aboard perished.

June 18, Grand Canyon, Arizona. A twin-engine sight-seeing plane collided with a helicopter and both plunged into a deep gorge in flames; all 25 persons aboard the two aircraft were killed in the collision, which investigators believed occurred when the airplane, flying above the helicopter, skidded on top of the chopper.

July 19, Northeastern Nicaragua. An air force transport helicopter carrying 22 persons developed mechanical problems shortly after takeoff and plunged into the Río Grande de Matagalpa; there were no survivors.

August 3, Off the coast of St. Vincent. A small commercial plane carrying 13 persons apparently crashed into the Caribbean Sea after attempting three landings at an airport near Kingstown during a driving rainstorm; searchers were unable to locate the plane.

August 14, Eastern Honduras. A Hercules C-130 plane flying from Tegucigalpa to Durzuna crashed in the jungle; all 52 military personnel and civilians aboard were killed.

August 16, Near Malakal, The Sudan. A Sudan Airways plane carrying 60 persons was shot down by Sudanese rebels using a heat-seeking missile; all aboard perished.

August 31, Cerritos, Calif. A small plane collided with an Aeromexico DC-9 jetliner, presumably moments after the pilot of the small plane suffered a heart attack; all 67 persons aboard the two aircraft were killed when the planes plummeted into a residential area, where at least 15 persons on the ground were feared dead.

September 2, Roatan, Honduras. A twin-engine plane crashed moments after lifting off the runway; all 10 persons aboard were killed.

October 23, Near Peshawar, Pak. A Pakistan International Airlines passenger plane slammed into an empty field some eight kilometres (five miles) from the Peshawar airport, where it was scheduled to land; of the 54 persons on board, 13 died, 26 were injured, and 15 were unaccounted for.

AP/WIDE WORLD

Damage and debris mar Cerritos, California, after a small plane collided with a DC-9 on August 31. The small plane severed the key horizontal stabilizer of the DC-9, and both planes plummeted into the residential area below.

October 30, Nicaragua. An air force helicopter crashed and 21 soldiers were killed; the Nicaragua government claimed the incident was an accident, but in Honduras the *contras* claimed they shot down the aircraft a few kilometres from the Honduran border.

November 2, Near Zahidan, Iran. An Iranian military transport plane, carrying 103 persons, slammed into a mountain after its altimeter malfunctioned; all aboard were killed.

November 6, Off the coast of Sumburgh Head, Shetland Islands. A Chinook helicopter, ferrying 47 persons from a North Sea oil field, plunged into the North Sea moments before its final landing approach; there were 2 survivors in the worst civilian helicopter disaster to date.

December 12, Near East Berlin. A Soviet twin-engine TU-134 jetliner crashed in a wooded area in dense fog while attempting to make an approach to Schönefeld Airport; of the 82 persons aboard, only 12 were rescued from the fiery wreckage.

December 19, Northern Nicaragua. A Soviet-built AN-2-TP, carrying 11 Sandinista soldiers, crashed in the mountains during bad weather; all aboard were killed.

December 25, Arar, Saudi Arabia. An Iraqi airliner carrying 107 persons crash-landed and exploded into flames after hijackers aboard the aircraft hurled hand grenades into the cockpit and other areas of the aircraft, causing at least two explosions; 62 persons were reported dead.

December 27, Nadi, Fiji. A light airplane on a routine 240-km (150-mi) flight from Savusavu to Nadi crashed while attempting to land there; 11 persons were killed and 3 others were injured, 2 of them critically.

Fires and Explosions

January 23, New Delhi, India. A fire swept through the lower floors of the Siddharth Continental Hotel; 38 persons lost their lives.

January 25, Near Iquique, Chile. An explosion, followed by a chain of secondary blasts, rocked the Cardoen arms factory where cluster bombs were being assembled; some 25 to 30 persons were feared dead and 11 others were injured.

February 11, Atagawa, Japan. An early morning fire raced through a wooden seaside hotel annex and reduced the structure to ashes; 24 persons were feared dead in the blaze.

February 17, Rio de Janeiro. A fire in a 13-story office building forced some workers to flee to outside window ledges in order to escape the advancing flames; 23 persons were killed, including 3 persons who jumped to their deaths.

March 3, Caracas, Venezuela. A fire, which erupted in a 14-story office building that housed the Chilean embassy offices, claimed the lives of at least 12 persons including the Chilean ambassador.

April 5, Bocaue, Phil. Triple explosions leveled an illegal fireworks factory and killed 11 workers.

April 5, Osan, South Korea. A jet fuel storage tank at the U.S. Air Force base exploded and precipitated a raging fire that took several hours to bring under control; 15 Koreans and a U.S. Air Force sergeant were killed in the blast.

April 7, South Korea. Forest fires, fanned by strong winds, claimed the lives of at least 20 persons and injured 17 others.

April 20, Near Dhaka, Bangladesh. A fire in a refugee camp destroyed some 200 huts and killed 32 persons; about 20,000 were left homeless.

April 26, Chernobyl, U.S.S.R. An explosion at the Chernobyl nuclear power plant resulted in a raging fire and the release of a cloud of deadly radioactive dust after the roof of the plant was blown off; 2 persons were killed immediately, more than 200 others were hospitalized, and by year's end at least 29 persons had died of radiation exposure.

June 14, Agueda, Port. A raging forest fire threatened the town as more than 350 firefighters formed a human circle to subdue the out-of-control blaze; 15 persons lost their lives, 13 of them firemen, some of whom were believed

A helicopter rescues survivors from the roof of a high-rise luxury hotel in San Juan, Puerto Rico, as a fast-climbing blaze rises from the ballroom and casino below. The New Year's Eve inferno, believed to have been the result of arson, left at least 96 dead.
AP/WIDE WORLD

trapped in five firefighting vehicles incinerated by flames.

September 5, Kristiansand, Norway. An early-morning fire, which apparently started in the hotel lobby, raged through the premises and cut off exit routes to some of the 135 hotel patrons; 14 persons died in the blaze and more than 50 others were injured.

September 6, Fujian (Fukien) Province, China. A firecracker explosion aboard a bus traveling from Ganzhou (Kan-chou) to Xiamen (Amoy) killed 20 persons and badly burned 22 others.

October 22, Southern Taiwan. A fire in an unlicensed hotel located above a barbershop claimed the lives of 14 persons and injured 6.

November 1, Near Varna, Bulg. An explosion at a chemical plant occurred apparently when a pipe, used for chemicals, ruptured; 17 persons were killed and 19 others injured.

November 9, Butuan City, Mindanao Island, Phil. A predawn fire in a department store, also used to provide sleeping quarters for some employees, claimed the lives of 21 slumbering persons.

December 31, San Juan, P.R. An apparent explosion in the Dupont Plaza Hotel, followed by a fire that gutted the ballroom and the casino and sent flames and toxic fumes through the high-rise luxury hotel, claimed the lives of at least 96 New Year's Eve revelers; investigators believed that arson was the cause of the fire, and they were exploring an employee labour dispute as a possible motive for the blaze.

Marine

February 16, Near Dhaka, Bangladesh. A bus attempting to board a ferry plunged into the Buriganga River; at least 11 persons were killed.

February 16, Near Khulna, Bangladesh. A motor launch sank after colliding with another vessel; 200 persons were missing and feared dead.

February 21, Off the coast of Outer Hebrides. A year-old French trawler sank in the North Atlantic in moderate to rough seas; 16 seamen were killed, including one man from a rescue vessel.

Early April, Central China. A ferry flipped over on the Yellow River after being buffeted by a large wave; some 100 persons were missing and feared dead.

April 1, Near Kaligani, Bangladesh. A river steamer struck a rock and capsized; 20 persons were killed and 40 others were missing.

April 11, Guinea Bissau. A canoe transporting passengers across the Rio Cacheu estuary capsized; 18 persons drowned and 3 others were injured.

April 20, Near Munshiganj, Bangladesh. A double-decker ferry carrying some 1,500 passengers sank in the Dhaleswari River during a storm; 168 persons were known dead and 300 others were missing and feared dead.

April 24, Off the coast of Leyte Island, Phil. An interisland passenger ship, which was apparently taking on water before it left the wharf in Isabela, capsized and sank in the Visayan Sea; of more than 400 passengers and crew, 29 persons were known dead and 170 others were missing and feared drowned.

May 25, Meghna River, Bangladesh. The double-decker river ferry *Shamia,* carrying 1,000 persons, capsized and sank during a raging storm; 80 persons were known dead and 500 others were missing and feared dead after being caught in the current and swept downstream.

August 31, Black Sea, off the coast of Novorossiysk, U.S.S.R. A Soviet freighter rammed into and sank a Soviet passenger ship carrying 888 passengers and 346 crew members apparently after ignoring warnings from the passenger ship that the two vessels were on a collision course; 398 persons were presumed drowned.

September 7, Off the coast of Port Harcourt, Nigeria. Two passenger ships carrying some 700 persons collided in the Atlantic Ocean, apparently after both vessels tried to avoid what was thought to be an abandoned oil-rig platform; 100 persons drowned and 5 others were missing and presumed dead.

November 11, Off the coast of La Gonâve, Haiti. An overcrowded ferry, carrying more than twice its safe capacity of passengers, sank in the bay of Port-au-Prince; nearly 200 persons were feared dead and only 20 were rescued.

December 22, Off the coast of Puerto Rico. A boat carrying 48 illegal aliens from the Dominican Republic capsized in rough waters; at least 14 persons were known dead and 18 others were missing and feared drowned.

December 26, Off the east coast of Iceland. A British cargo ship sank in the North Atlantic after crashing into Skrudur Rock, a 162-m (531-ft) outcrop at the mouth of the Faskrudsfjordur; all 12 crewmen aboard the vessel lost their lives.

Mining

February 18, Southern Hungary. Collapsed mine shafts caused cave-ins that killed at least six miners; six others, still trapped underground, could not be found by rescuers.

June 25, Bytom, Poland. A cave-in at a coal mine trapped ten men working underground; two miners were killed, one was injured, and seven others were trapped in the tunnel and feared dead.

July 16, Brisbane, Australia. An explosion caused a cave-in at a coal mine and 12 miners lost their lives after being trapped in an area that had only an hour's supply of air.

September 16, South Africa. A fire erupted in the Kinross gold mine when an acetylene bottle used in the welding process ignited; noxious fumes, emitted from "polyurethane-type foam" used to help seal structural bracings in the tunnels, claimed the lives of 177 miners, injured 235, and left 5 others missing. It was the country's worst gold mine disaster to date.

December 24, Near Donetsk, U.S.S.R. A methane-gas buildup caused an explosion and a fire at the Yasinovskaya-Glubokaya coal mine; reports indicated that there were heavy casualties.

Miscellaneous

January 12, Cairo, Egypt. A five-story apartment building collapsed causing four adjoining tenements to cave in; 12 persons were feared dead.

January 28, Seventy-three seconds after launch from Cape Canaveral, Florida. The space shuttle *Challenger* exploded in an orange-and-white fireball some 14¼ km (9 mi) above the Atlantic Ocean; all seven crew members, including civilian schoolteacher Christa McAuliffe, were killed.

February 21, Jiangsu (Kiangsu) Province, China. When a crowd of some 100,000 people surged forward for a better view of a lantern festival, 21 persons were trampled to death.

March 15, Singapore. A 15-year-old, six-story hotel collapsed, trapping some 50 persons under piles of concrete rubble; 33 persons were killed but 17 were rescued.

Mid-March, Bauchi State, Nigeria. An outbreak of cerebrospinal meningitis claimed the lives of 70 persons.

Mid-March, New Delhi, India. Meningitis affected some 600 persons and killed at least 55 of them.

March–April, Italy. Wine, tainted with wood alcohol, poisoned at least 24 persons who died after drinking the contaminated beverage.

April 14, Hardwar, India. A sunrise stampede on a narrow bridge spanning the Ganges River claimed the lives of at least 46 Hindu pilgrims who were trampled when huge crowds surged forward to make their way to the sacred bathing area during the Kumbha Mela religious festival.

April 20, Eastern Sri Lanka. A dam, which burst at the 800-year-old Kantalai Reservoir, was sabotaged by a Tamil guerrilla group, which claimed responsibility for the disaster; thousands of people were left homeless, at least 14 persons were killed and several others were missing and presumed dead.

Late April, Somalia. A cholera epidemic claimed the lives of more than 1,000 persons during a four-month period.

Early August, Hong Kong. The colony was declared cholera-infected after ten persons succumbed to the disease.

Early August, West Sumatra, Indonesia. A cholera outbreak claimed the lives of 59 persons during a three-month period and affected more than 700 others.

August, Chamonix, France. Eleven mountain climbers lost their lives during the month while attempting to ascend Mont Blanc, Europe's highest mountain.

August, Kaunas, Lithuanian Soviet Socialist Republic. The ingestion of antifreeze killed 15 persons who thought they were consuming concentrated alcohol.

September 12, Dazheng (Ta-cheng), Henan (Honan) Province, China. A school collapsed after officials apparently ignored reports that the building had serious structural defects; 11 children were killed and 35 others were injured.

September 20, Latvian Soviet Socialist Republic. A 40-year-old highway bridge collapsed while 14 gravel-laden vehicles and their drivers were stationed on the roadway during a test of strength; ten persons were killed when a 76-m (250-ft) span gave way and dropped the conveyances into the river below.

October 2, Pará State, Brazil. A high wall collapsed at the Serra Pelada goldfield in northern Brazil; ten prospectors were killed and eight others were injured.

November 9, Ajodha, India. A stampede at the entrance to the temple of Lord Rama, the main Hindu deity, occurred when a barrier rope gave way; 32 persons were trampled to death and scores of others were injured at the major pilgrimage site.

Late November, Eastern Nigeria. A yellow fever epidemic claimed the lives of more than 500 persons; some 3,000 persons were treated for yellow fever and associated diseases.

Natural

January, Sri Lanka. Floods and landslides killed 43 persons during the month, affected 12,000 families, and damaged thousands of homes.

January 3, Capilluchari, Peru. A landslide buried a farmhouse, resulting in the deaths of at least 13 Indian peasants inside the dwelling.

Mid-January, Indonesia. A spate of landslides and floods, following heavy monsoon rains, claimed the lives of 19 persons.

January 27, Niigata Prefecture, Japan. A snowy avalanche buried 13 persons in their homes in the mountain town of Nohmachi; 23 others were rescued from their houses.

Early February, Italy, France, Spain, Austria. Winter storms caused avalanches, flooding, and widespread power outages; 39 deaths were attributed to the severe weather.

February 13–14, California, Nevada, Colorado, Idaho, Utah, and Canada. Waves of brutal and punishing Pacific storms lashed the affected areas producing flooding, mud slides, high winds, avalanches, and at least 17 deaths; hardest hit was northern California where 12,335 houses and 927 businesses were damaged or destroyed.

Mid-February, Maharashtra State, India. A week of severe rains accompanied by hailstorms killed at least 11 persons.

March 5, Narvik, Norway. An avalanche felled 31 members of a Norwegian Army ski patrol on NATO maneuvers; 17 were feared dead, and 14 others survived but were injured.

March 9, Northern Peru. An avalanche, touched off by heavy rains, buried parts of two villages in northern Peru; 40 persons were missing and presumed dead and more than 350 were left homeless.

Mid-March, Peru. Severe flooding resulted after Lake Titicaca overflowed its banks and inundated the city of Puno; the advancing floodwaters left thousands of persons homeless and claimed the lives of at least 12 persons and possibly 28 others who were reported missing.

Workers sift through the rubble of a three-story building in a suburb of Taipei, Taiwan, where some 60 people who lived on the upper floors were trapped. Two major earthquakes, measuring 6.8 and 6.3 on the Richter scale, struck the area on November 15.

AFP PHOTO

March 17, Madagascar. Cyclone Honorinnia destroyed 80% of the port of Toamasina and left some 20,000 persons homeless; at least 32 persons were known dead, several others were missing, and buildings and crops were severely damaged.

March 24, Western Europe. Some of the worst storms in 50 years, packing hurricane-force winds, led to the deaths of at least 17 persons and 19 others were missing; several ships sank off the coasts of Spain, France, and Sweden.

March 24, Tokyo, Japan. A snowstorm that dumped up to 500 mm (20 in) of precipitation led to the deaths of at least 13 persons, 7 of them lost at sea and presumed dead.

April 5, Peru. A strong earthquake measuring 5 on the Richter scale ruptured water lines, caused avalanches that may have damaged the ancient Inca ruins, and destroyed nearly 700 homes; more than 15 persons were killed and 30 others were injured.

April 14, Bangladesh. An ice and wind storm producing giant hailstones lashed Gopalganj, Barhmanbaria, and Dhaka; hundreds of homes were flattened, some 700 windshields were shattered, at least 92 persons were killed, and some 3,000 others were injured.

May 5, Malatya Province, Turkey. A strong earthquake measuring 5.8 on the Richter scale destroyed at least 400 homes, claimed the lives of 15 persons, and injured 100 others.

CHUCK NACKE—PICTURE GROUP

Floodwaters in a northern California town leave streets hidden and animals stranded after ten days of Pacific storms in February doused several western U.S. states and Canada. Mud slides and avalanches destroyed thousands of homes and businesses, and at least 17 lives were lost.

May 12, Colombia. Another in a series of landslides, triggered by heavy rains, claimed 8 lives; this brought to 26 the number of persons killed in landslides within a month.

May 16, Rajasthan State, India. A fierce cyclone claimed the lives of at least 11 persons; more than 100 others were injured.

May 19, Solomon Islands. Typhoon Namu annihilated the archipelago's crops, left one-third of the population homeless, and stripped the country of its lush woods; over 100 people were killed and some 90,000 were left homeless in the worst storm to hit the Solomon Islands to date.

May 25, Near Chushan, Taiwan. A landslide thundered down on some 120 tourists in a scenic gorge, killed 14 of them, and injured 28 others; 25 persons were buried and rescue workers were attemping to free them.

May 30, Etna, Pa. Severe thunderstorms triggered mudslides and flash floods when Pine Creek and Little Pine Creek, tributaries of the Allegheny River, overflowed their banks; eight persons were known dead and several others were missing and feared dead.

May 31, Karachi, Pak. A blinding dust storm reduced visibility to near zero and blew down flimsy wood and bamboo shanties; 11 persons were killed, most of them when their homes collapsed, and 250 others were treated for injuries resulting from flying debris.

Mid-June, Central Chile. Widespread flooding killed 10 persons and left some 35,000 others homeless; Santiago's fresh water supply was cut off for two days.

June 21, Near Las Monas, Colombia. A roaring landslide of mud and rocks killed 20 persons and probably buried 15 others alive; the slide occurred as bus passengers were changing vehicles to continue their journey after a landslide two days earlier had blocked the road.

June 22, Taloja, India. A textile factory collapsed during monsoon rains, causing workers inside to be trapped in debris: 11 workers were known dead and 6 others were feared lost in the ruins.

July 9, Northern Philippines. Typhoon Peggy battered the country's northern provinces, causing severe flooding, landslides, and extensive property damage; more than 70 persons were known dead.

July 11, Southeastern China. Rampaging floodwaters, triggered by the torrential rains of Typhoon Peggy, claimed more than 170 lives and injured at least 1,250 persons; the typhoon destroyed more than 250,000 homes.

Late July, Uttar Pradesh, India. Heavy monsoon rains had claimed the lives of at least 71 persons during the month.

August 21, Northwest Cameroon. A deadly cloud of volcanic gas burst forth from Lake Nyos and enshrouded the sleeping inhabitants of nearby villages; at least 1,700 persons succumbed to the lethal vapours, and hundreds were buried in mass graves by national army units, fearing an epidemic; more than 400 others were hospitalized with first- and second-degree burns, pulmonary complications, and swellings on the face and legs.

August 22, Central Taiwan. A typhoon that packed powerful winds and unleashed torrential rains struck the country, killing at least 22 persons and injuring more than 110 others; 9 persons were also reported missing and feared dead.

August 25, British Isles. The tail of Hurricane Charley lashed Ireland, England, Scotland, and Wales with heavy rains accompanied by gale-force winds; at least 11 deaths were attributed to the violent storm.

Late August, Andhra Pradesh, India. Heavy monsoon rains precipitated severe flooding that killed more than 200 persons and affected nearly 100,000 others; many homes were swept away in the floodwaters.

September 4, Vietnam. A typhoon ravaged the country's northern coastal villages, destroyed rice fields, and sank fishing boats; the storm killed 400 persons and injured at least 2,500 others.

September 13, Kalamai, Greece. A powerful earthquake that measured 6.2 on the Richter scale was followed two days later by strong aftershocks; at least 20 persons were known dead, many of them killed when their apartment buildings collapsed, and some 300 others were injured.

September 19, Taiwan. Typhoon Abby roared through the country causing some $80 million in damages; 13 persons lost their lives in the storm.

October 6, Manila. Heavy rains inundated the capital city and surrounding provinces, causing severe flooding that claimed the lives of at least 14 persons and forced nearly 60,000 others from their homes.

October 10, San Salvador, El Salvador. A major earthquake, measuring 7.5 on the Richter scale, followed by several aftershocks and tremors, rocked the capital city and reduced downtown buildings to rubble; more than 1,000 persons lost their lives, more than 8,000 others were injured, and some 200,000 people were left homeless.

November 14, Kashmir State, India. A thick blanketing of snow on the Zoji La Pass was responsible for the deaths of 60 persons.

November 15, Taiwan. Successive earthquakes, measuring 6.8 and 6.3 on the Richter scale, shook the country and claimed at least 14 lives; hardest hit were Hua-lien and Chung-ho, where the collapse of a three-story building caused numerous casualties.

November 17, Northern India. A blinding snowstorm trapped some 300 persons, including 50 Indian soldiers, in a mountainous region above Srinagar; 60 persons, many of them truck drivers or labourers, were killed in the storm.

Railroad

February 8, Near Hinton, Alta. A 118-unit freight train collided head-on with a passenger train, causing diesel fuel to explode in a fireball; 26 persons were killed and dozens of others were injured.

February 17, Near Limache, Chile. A head-on collision between two passenger trains claimed the lives of 62 persons and injured 464 others; the crash was the country's worst rail disaster to date.

February 28, Near Tellicherry, Kerala State, India. An express train mowed down 27 persons who had fled to the railroad tracks to escape stray fireworks being shot off during a religious festival; 100 others were also injured.

May 5, Póvoa de Santa Iria, Port. A passenger train slammed into a crowded commuter train that was stopped at the station; 14 persons died as a result of the crash and 80 others were injured.

Railroad cars, twisted and burned, lie zigzag across the landscape following the head-on collision of a passenger train and a freight train on February 8 in western Alberta.
AP/WIDE WORLD

July 26, Near Lockington, England. A passenger train traveling from Bridlington to Hull hit a truck at a railroad crossing and then the first three cars jumped the tracks; at least 9 persons were killed, 42 were injured, and others were believed dead in the wreckage.

August 6, Eastern Bihar State, India. A passenger train plunged off a bridge and plummeted into a monsoon-swollen river after slamming into several freight cars that had uncoupled from a train during the night without the engineer's knowledge; 52 persons were known dead and 150 others were feared drowned as rescue workers frantically struggled to free them during a blinding rainstorm.

September 2, Near Mianwali, Pak. A train struck an overcrowded bus that was attempting to drive across the tracks at an unguarded railroad crossing; 31 persons lost their lives in the crash and about 40 were injured.

Traffic

January 10, Karbala, Iraq. A bus collided with a truck; 29 persons were killed and 10 others were injured.

January 17, Near Bombay, India. A bus fell off a mountain road and plunged down a slope; 41 persons were killed and 8 others were injured.

February 19, Serunuwara, Sri Lanka. Two buses and a truck were blown up after tripping a land mine planted by Tamil separatists; 36 persons were killed and 20 others were injured.

March 15, Parachinar, Pak. Two pickup trucks carrying Afghan refugees to a wedding were blown up after setting off an antitank mine on the road; 19 persons lost their lives in the blast and 8 were injured.

March 29, Irapuato, Mexico. A truck carrying more than 50 teenagers to Easter religious services was struck by a train engine when it attempted to cross the railroad tracks ahead of the train; 30 teens were killed and 27 were injured.

May 11, Near San Salvador, El Salvador. An open truck collided with a bus some 48 km (30 mi) from the capital; 31 persons were killed and 9 others were injured.

May 19, Saraburi Province, Thailand. A bus burst into flames when the driver attempted to start the engine while the vehicle was being filled with gasoline; 13 persons were burned to death and 12 others were injured in the incident, which occurred some 108 km (67 mi) north of Bangkok.

May 30, Andhra Pradesh State, India. A truck overturned after swerving to avoid a man sleeping in the middle of the road; 16 persons riding on top of the truck's load of logs were killed and 37 were injured.

May 30, Near Walker, Calif. A tour bus, transporting residents from a retirement home back to Santa Monica after a four-day junket in Lake Tahoe, Nev., fell, at high speed, off a twisting mountain road and plunged into a racing icy river; 20 persons were killed and 5 were hospitalized in serious condition.

June 17, Peru. A bus carrying 35 children rolled down a steep gorge after a group of playing children apparently fell into the driver, who lost control of the vehicle; 20 children lost their lives in the crash and 15 others were seriously injured.

June 23, Near London, England. A van carrying music fans back from a rock festival barreled through a barrier and slammed into a station wagon; two other cars plowed into the wreckage, and 13 persons lost their lives.

August 1, Near Badrinath, India. A bus toppled into a ditch, killing 30 Hindus; 12 others were seriously injured.

August 10, Bendel State, Nigeria. Two buses collided between Benin City and Agbor; 72 persons were killed and 30 others were seriously injured.

September 19, Guangdong (Kwangtung) Province, China. A bus carrying 64 persons plunged off a mountain road in Gaozhou (Kaochou) County and plummeted down an embankment; 27 persons died in the crash and dozens of others were seriously injured.

September 26, Northern Tanzania. A bus fell into a river near Mt. Kilimanjaro; 16 persons lost their lives in the crash and 45 others were injured.

Early October, Taiwan. A tour bus traveling on the country's east-west Cross Island Highway swerved to avoid an oncoming truck and then plunged off the roadway; 39 persons were killed and 6 others were seriously injured.

October 9, Uttar Pradesh, India. A bus traveling to Rae Bareli plunged off the bridge leading to the town and fell into the Ganges River; 30 passengers were feared dead and some 45 others were hospitalized.

October 11, Punjab, India. A bus veered off a road into a ditch in the village of Dhar Kalan; 11 persons died and more than 20 were injured.

December 6, Near Chengalpattu, Madras, India. A collision involving a bus and a truck claimed the lives of 16 persons and injured 20 others.

December 20, Shimla, Himachal Pradesh, India. A bus being operated by a drunken driver plunged into a remote mountain gorge; 47 of the 48 persons aboard lost their lives in the crash.

Earth Sciences

GEOLOGY AND GEOCHEMISTRY

The successes of the long-term, international Deep Sea Drilling Project and the Ocean Drilling Program and of the Soviet Union's 13-km superdeep well on the Kola Peninsula were helping to stimulate programs for deep drilling through the Earth's continental crust. (A kilometre is about 0.62 mi.) In West Germany possible sites for a superdeep hole were narrowed to two by 1986. In the U.S. study of the first deep hole of the new Continental Scientific Drilling Program of the National Science Foundation began during the year and was scheduled to continue into 1988. The site, a two-kilometre-deep former oil well that was to be extended to five kilometres, is near the San Andreas Fault at Cajon Pass in California. A principal scientific objective was a test of the relationship between stress and heat generation associated with this major fault. Other results should lead to improved understanding of the regional geology, tectonics, and geochemistry of the southwestern U.S.

Even superdeep drill holes sample only the skin of the Earth, whereas geologic processes are driven by events occurring in the Earth's mantle below the crust. The conditions and processes at depth are calibrated by laboratory experiments at high pressures and temperatures. For 20 years or so two different approaches to high-pressure experiments have been followed. In the U.S. apparatus using opposed anvils made of small diamonds has been developed. In Japan industrial and academic research has concentrated on the use of very large presses squeezing together various arrays of multiple anvils composed of tungsten carbide or sintered diamond.

Both approaches were rewarded by significant results in 1986. Improvements in design of diamond-anvil equipment extended the pressure range from one megabar (about a million atmospheres) to about five megabars, a pressure greater than that at the Earth's centre. Japanese researchers reported achieving pressures of 250 kilobars, corresponding to a depth of about 700 km in the Earth. Eiichi Takahashi of Okayama University published detailed melting relations of a peridotite for pressures as high as 200 kilobars. Peridotite is the main candidate for material composing the upper mantle to a depth of about 650 km. The experiments confirmed that perovskite becomes the dominant mineral at depths greater than 650 km. The solidus curve for the beginning of melting in the Earth provides a most important constraint for models of mantle convection and of magma generation. Before these new experiments, its position was known only to depths of 180 km.

The 650-km depth in the Earth's mantle is a level of fundamental change, attributed by some to the formation of perovskite in a phase transition and by others to a change in chemistry. What happens at this depth is related directly to the geology and geochemistry of near-surface rocks. Evidence from the distribution of deep-focus earthquakes had indicated that subducted oceanic crust reaches 650 km but no deeper. This was consistent with the argument, based on the geochemistry of lavas, that mantle rocks flow in two layers, one shallower and one deeper than 650 km. During the year, however, T. H. Jordan of the Massachusetts Institute of Technology presented seismic evidence that the subducted slab may actually penetrate 350–550 km below the 650-km level. This finding supported the alternative view that there is only one, mantlewide convection layer in the Earth. A third interpretation, offered by D. L. Anderson of the California Institute of Technology, required a change in chemistry, with a 400-km-thick layer rich in garnet and pyroxene immediately above the 650-km level. At the Fourth International Kimberlite Conference in Perth, Australia, A. E. Ringwood of the Australian National University presented a fourth model, in which the subducted oceanic plates accumulate in large masses at 650 km, balanced by their density. He proposed that the oceanic plate material eventually spreads at this level to form a continuous layer about 200 km thick between the upper and lower convecting layers of the mantle. Thus, by the end of the year earth scientists had a choice of four mantle models for interpreting the geochemistry of basalts from various environments such as ocean ridges, oceanic islands, and continents.

The First International Kimberlite Conference was held in 1973 in South Africa, the home of localities for kimberlites, then the only known source rock for diamonds. The Fourth Conference was concerned not only with kimberlite but with the recent discovery in Australia of significant diamond concentrations in a different rock called lamproite. The explosive volcanic materials that brought diamonds into the crust must have risen rapidly from a depth of at least 150 km, and these eruptions transported, in addition to diamonds, fragments of the mantle rocks through which they passed. At the 1986 conference, in addition to discussions of the origin of kimberlite and lamproite and of their diamond and mantle-rock inclusions, attention focused on the migration of melts and fluids through the mantle and their effects on mantle rocks and their state of oxidation. The degree of oxidation at depths greater than 150–200 km must be low enough for carbon to exist as diamond and for gases to be dominated by methane, yet the melts rising from these depths normally contain oxidized carbon, such as carbon dioxide, and water as they pass through the continental crust. S. E. Haggerty of the University of Massachusetts described the formation of titanates of rare earth elements in metasomatized (chemically changed) rocks carried up from a layer between about 90 and 70 km in depth, where rocks were more oxidized than the deeper source rocks. The variation in oxidation as a function of depth and the question of whether this variation is controlled by the minerals present or by fluids passing through them was of significance not only for the origin of kimberlites and basalts but also for the nature of gases escaping from the deep Earth and for the proposal, championed by Thomas Gold of Cornell University, Ithaca, N.Y., that methane from the mantle may represent a significant source of natural gas deposits trapped in the Earth's crust.

Fluids and gases emerge not only from continents but also from the ocean floor. L. D. Kulm of Oregon State University and associates published in 1986 the first detailed report of the colonies of clams and tube worms, together with mineral precipitates, that are associated with the venting of cool fluids at ocean depths of about 2,000 m in the subduction zone where the Pacific Plate is sinking below Oregon. (One metre is about 3.3 ft.) It appeared that compressive stresses expel methane and other potential nutrients from buried sediments. Evidence suggested that the organisms use methane as an energy and food source. Similar biologic communities were described recently at a depth of 3,900 m along the continental slope of Peru.

The hydrothermal vent systems associated with the oceanic ridges differ from those of subduction complexes. In hydrothermal systems seawater circulates through the oceanic crust, where it picks up heat and dissolved minerals from the hot basalt through which it passes. The hot, mineral-laden water then returns to the ocean as clear, white, or black "smokers" that precipitate minerals (rich

The waters of Lake Nyos in Cameroon, once clear, have become an ominous brown after a deadly cloud of gases was released from the lake bottom. The gases wafted down the mountain slope, killing more than 1,700 villagers and thousands of animals.
THIERRY ORBAN—SYGMA

in metallic sulfides), building chimneys as high as five metres. A newly discovered field of hydrothermal vents on the Axial Caldera of the Juan de Fuca Ridge off the coast of Oregon and Washington was found to include every type of venting system so far discovered in the Pacific and Atlantic oceans, with some fluid temperatures exceeding 330° C (630° F). Scientists in the Canadian submersible vessel *Pisces IV* reported a variety of tube worms, shelled animals, and mats of white bacteria. The site could prove ideal for long-term studies of the effect of fluid circulation and venting on the chemistry of the oceans.

The ocean-ridge and subduction-zone environments on Earth are the surface expression of extensional and compressional stresses on a global scale. Evidence was presented at the 17th Lunar and Planetary Science Conference in 1986 that Venus has also experienced global tectonics. The graphic evidence included radar images having a resolution of 1–2 km that were obtained by the Soviet Venera 15 and 16 spacecraft orbiting Venus. The images also revealed strike-slip deformation and topography of possible volcanic origin. The features are relatively young, according to analysis of impact-crater frequencies, and it appeared that some major resurfacing process operates on the planet.

In a closer and more localized environment, the Sahara Desert has been resurfaced by windblown sand over the last several hundred thousand years. In 1981 signals sent from an imaging radar system aboard an orbiting U.S. space shuttle penetrated several metres of sand and were reflected from the bedrock to yield pictures of the buried topography. According to a recent analysis by researchers at the U.S. Geological Survey in Flagstaff, Ariz., the radar images revealed an ancient drainage system in northeastern Africa quite different from the present system. Formerly the major rivers with headwaters between Egypt and The Sudan flowed southwestward across Africa and into the Atlantic Ocean near the present Niger delta. Doming and intracontinental volcanism beginning about 15 million years ago disrupted this drainage system, with the northward-flowing Nile becoming the dominant river of the region. The ancient drainage system failed when the climate began to turn arid about two million years ago; eventually desert sands covered the old streambeds. (PETER JOHN WYLLIE)

GEOPHYSICS

Clear, blue Lake Nyos nestled like a jewel in the verdant crater of a long dormant volcano in northwestern Cameroon. Known locally as the "good lake," on Aug. 21, 1986, it proved otherwise, producing the worst geophysical disaster of the year. Late that evening the lake disgorged a vast cloud of noxious gases, mainly carbon dioxide with lesser amounts of carbon monoxide and hydrogen sulfide, accompanied by a low rumble. Although the latter two gases are poisonous, in this instance the more deadly effects came from the nontoxic carbon dioxide. This gas is heavier than air and displaces it near the ground. When it accumulates in sufficient amount, as in this case, it causes death by asphyxiation.

The cloud spilled out of the crater, and as it rolled down the slopes of the volcano, it caught most of the inhabitants of the surrounding villages in their beds; even those who were still awake struggled in vain to escape the deadly miasma. The exact toll might never be known, but 1,746 of the dead were officially accounted for. Of the 20,000 inhabitants of the 26 sq km (10 sq mi) blanketed by the cloud, thousands were injured and nearly all of their livestock perished.

Investigators differed as to the mechanism by which the gases were released. One theory supposed that a subterranean volcanic or tectonic disturbance vented them from a subsurface reservoir. Another, more widely accepted explanation was that the gases seeped slowly from cracks or vents in the floor of the crater, gradually accumulating in the lake-bottom sediments where they remained trapped until turbulence and vertical currents caused by an underwater landslide released them to the surface. The latter theory was used to explain a similar event that occurred in 1984 at nearby Lake Monoun, killing 37.

On the whole, seismic activity was moderate. The largest earthquake of the year, on May 7, registered 7.7 on the Richter scale. Centred in the Andreanof Islands of the Aleutian Islands chain, it caused minor damage on Adak and Atka. The shock generated a tsunami (seismic sea wave) that was recorded as far away as New Zealand and Chile. At Adak, near the epicentre, the wave reached a height of 175 cm (68.9 in).

Although several other large earthquakes ranging in magnitude from 7.0 to 7.4 occurred, casualites and damage were low. Indeed, the most disastrous shock had a magnitude of only 5.4. It struck on October 10 about 16 km (10 mi) northwest of San Salvador, the capital city of El Salvador, and left as many as 1,000 dead, thousands more injured, and perhaps 30,000 homeless. More than 900 aftershocks were recorded in the following three days.

Many of the world's volcanoes were highly active, producing clouds of ash, pyroclastic flows, fissures, and minor lava flows but experiencing no major eruptions. Among the more active were Piton de la Fournaise on Réunion Island in the Indian Ocean; Mount Etna, Sicily; Ambrym

A small new island forms in the Pacific Ocean near Iwo Jima, a result of the eruption of an underwater volcano. The volcano, which had been dormant since 1914, shot lava 300 metres (1,000 feet) into the air and belched smoke higher than 4,000 metres (13,000 feet).
AP/WIDE WORLD

volcano on Vanuatu Island in the South Pacific; Mt. St. Helens, Washington; Nevado del Ruiz, Colombia, scene of the previous year's catastrophic eruption that killed 25,000; and Kilauea, Hawaii, which had experienced more than 50 eruptive episodes since January 1983. The volcano on Augustine Island, which juts out of Cook Inlet about 280 km (175 mi) southwest of Anchorage, Alaska, began a series of ash and gas eruptions March 27 that ended ten years of dormancy.

A sudden advance of the Hubbard Glacier in southeastern Alaska in early June dammed off the mouth of Russell Fjord from Disenchantment Bay, turning the 55-km (34-mi)-long saltwater body into a lake and trapping numerous species of marine life. The newly created Russell Lake quickly began rising from an inflow of precipitation and glacial meltwater. Fears that a spillover within two years would flood the nearby Situk River, damaging an important salmon and steelhead fishery, brought together experts from federal, state, local, and Indian agencies to discuss ways of dealing with the glacier's effects. In October the ice dam burst, reconnecting the fjord with the open sea, but glaciologists expected the surging glacier to block the fjord again.

The Joint Oceanographic Institutions for Deep Earth Sampling (JOIDES) launched its new ocean drilling ship, the *JOIDES Resolution*, and a new Ocean Drilling Program (ODP) in early 1985. By the end of that year, Legs 100 through 106 had been completed. After a shakedown cruise (Leg 100), exploration began on the carbonate banks in The Bahamas (Leg 101), continued on to the Bermuda Rise (Leg 102), across the Atlantic to the Gallicia continental margin northwest of the Iberian Peninsula (Leg 103), north to the Norwegian Greenland Sea and the edge of the Voring Plateau off the coast of Norway (Leg 104), back to the straits between Greenland and Baffin Island to the most northern site ever drilled (Leg 105), and then to the Mid-Atlantic Ridge (Leg 106), where a new technique for drilling into bare seafloor rock was initiated. Previous attempts to drill into bare rock had failed because the stabilizing sleeve usually provided by sediments was missing. Accordingly, a 20-ton, block-shaped drill guide was lowered to the bottom, where it rested on pillow lava in 3,344 m (10,968 ft) of water. It was secured in place by an additional 50 tons of cement pumped into bags attached to the underside of the base. A cone to catch and guide the descending drill string was mounted on gimbals in the centre of the block. The first experimental hole was drilled to a depth of 33 m (108 ft) without problem.

The 1986 odyssey of the *JOIDES Resolution* began in the Tyrrhenian Sea southwest of Italy (Leg 107), shifted to the continental margin off Morocco (Leg 108), then returned to the Mid-Atlantic (Leg 109) to reoccupy the bare rock hole drilled on Leg 106. After a successful reentry and further drilling, the ship sailed to the Barbados Ridge and then through the Panama Canal to the East Pacific Rise southwest of Mexico to drill another hole in bare rock with the new technique. (RUTLAGE J. BRAZEE)

HYDROLOGY

Surface-water resources continued to come under increasing strain during 1986 to meet the demand for public water supply, irrigation, industry, recreation, fish and wildlife habitats, and energy needs. In the U.S. the problem was emphasized in a report, *National Water Summary 1985—Hydrologic Events and Surface Water Resources,* published in October by the U.S. Geological Survey. The report focused on surface-water resources and included state summaries on the occurrence, use, and management of surface water in the U.S. Nearly 80% of that nation's daily water consumption drew from surface-water sources, although percentages by state ranged widely—from 15% in Kansas to 100% in the District of Columbia. One possible way to ease the strain was coordinated water-supply management, which could help increase water availability. The report also gave a review of hydrologic conditions including descriptions of the drought in the Delaware River basin, record-high water levels in the Great Lakes, and the August 1985 flood in Cheyenne, Wyo.

In 1986 below-normal streamflow occurred in most parts of the southeastern U.S. and in many smaller areas scattered throughout southern Canada. In sharp contrast, streamflow was above normal in most of the Great Lakes region, the upper Mississippi River region, the Red River of the North, and streams in the Great Basin. The combined flow of the Mississippi, St. Lawrence, and Columbia rivers from October 1985 to September 1986 averaged 1,111,860 cu ft per second, which was well above normal but still below the record high of 1,439,000 cu ft per second set in 1973 (one cubic foot is about 0.028 cu m).

It was estimated that 2,500 waste sites in the U.S. posed a risk to public health. Groundwater contamination was recognized in every state, and the number of reported cases was increasing each year. In response many state and federal programs were established to protect groundwater resources from contamination and to clean up contaminated sites. During the year the 99th Congress worked to protect groundwater by amending the Safe Drinking Water Act, reauthorizing and expanding the Superfund program for cleaning up toxic-waste dumps, and attempting to extend the Clean Water Act. Changes to the Safe Drinking Water Act required the Environmental Protection Agency over the next three years to set standards for 83 more contaminants, including benzine, cyanide, and radioactive substances. States would be provided funds to map vulnerable aquifers and establish aquifer protection programs.

The expanded Superfund Act authorized $8.5 billion for a cleanup program over five years, three times the previous level of spending, and included $500 million for cleaning up leaking underground fuel tanks that were contaminating groundwater. Extension of the Clean Water Act was to provide $18 billion through 1994 for construction of sewage-treatment plants and other projects to reduce pollution of lakes and streams. In November, however, U.S. Pres. Ronald Reagan refused to sign the bill because of its high cost.

For two years the U.S. Department of Defense (DOD) had been expanding its Installation Restoration Program (IRP) to evaluate and clean up groundwater contamination at military installations. Hazardous-waste disposal practices at many DOD bases had polluted groundwater, in some places beyond the boundaries of the base. The IRP program, the DOD's equivalent of Superfund, included more than 450 bases with an estimated 800 hazardous-waste sites. The DOD planned to spend $380 million for cleanup in 1986 and $400 million in 1987.

The ever shifting weather patterns of regions affected by drought and floods continued to be evident in the return of beneficial rains to East and West Africa. Parts of The Sudan experienced flooding late in 1985. In India failure of monsoon rains to appear caused widespread crop losses and attendant misery. Drought problems also affected such diverse areas as Australia, Israel, and Italy. Floods plagued parts of Bangladesh, southern India, eastern Australia, and the central Philippines in 1986.

The inevitable recurrence of these devastating events brought renewed emphasis on disaster mitigation and prevention as an essential element of integrated water development policy. This awareness was being demonstrated by the HydroNiger Project, a flood-prediction system intended for the multinational waters of the Niger River basin in eight West African countries. French-designed, the project received support from the World Meteorological Organization.

According to a report issued by the United Nations Environment Program (UNEP), many tropical and subtropical areas of the world would face critical water shortages by the middle of the next century. The report pointed out the need for long-term soil conservation projects because of the increasing demands on water resources. It also called attention to the continuing loss of potable water in Africa and Asia due to deforestation, desertification, and the pollution of rivers, lakes, and groundwater.

The accident on April 26 at the Chernobyl nuclear power station in the Soviet Ukraine aroused worldwide concern for the effects of the spread of radioactivity into the environment. Although drinking water supplies were at risk, effects apparently were confined to a limited area (a 29-km, or 18-mi, zone) near the accident site and to the Pripyat River and reservoir systems downstream from the plant. Cesium-137 and other radioactive contaminants were released to plants, soil, surface water, and groundwater. For a time there was great concern that the reactor core would melt down into the aquifer beneath the power station. (JOHN E. MOORE)

METEOROLOGY

Prolonged dryness affected various parts of the world during 1986. Regions of Brazil, Paraguay, Bolivia, and Argentina experienced subnormal rainfall early in the year, while in southeastern Europe drought conditions spread northward from Bulgaria into Romania and the Ukrainian S.S.R. The important agricultural region of the Volga River Valley sustained prolonged rainfall deficits, and some sections of eastern China suffered drought conditions. Part of eastern Australia, especially southeastern Queensland and northeastern New South Wales, was afflicted by abnormal dryness during the first half of the year.

A prolonged drought that began in the southeastern U.S. in late 1985 persisted through the better part of 1986. Eventually it covered all or parts of states from southern New Jersey, Maryland, and Delaware southward through Virginia, the Carolinas, and Georgia to northern Florida and westward into Alabama, Tennessee, and Kentucky. For most of those states it was the worst drought in more than a century, and it contributed to an outbreak of spring forest fires in North Carolina, Tennessee, and Virginia. Not until August did some sections receive above-normal rainfall. Comparatively heavy rains in October finally brought a measure of relief, but large rainfall deficits remained. The severe dryness, which damaged crops and reduced water supplies, was exacerbated by record high temperatures over most of the stricken area during June and July.

In contrast to the drought in the Southeast, heavy rains deluged the central states in September and early October as a stagnant weather situation developed in the region.

AP/WIDE WORLD

High but dry, cattle in Fort Scott, Kansas, calmly survey their predicament of being stranded by receding floodwaters.

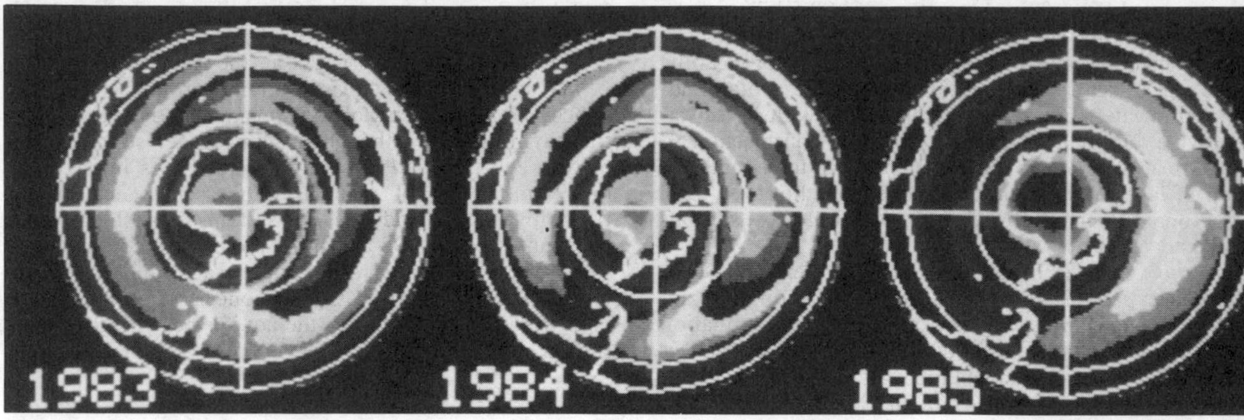

Computer image derived from satellite measurements reveals the progressive thinning of the ozone layer over the Antarctic. Variations in the annual concentration levels near the centre "hole" are shown as ring-shaped zones of differing shades.
GODDARD SPACE FLIGHT CENTER/NASA

The result was widespread flooding from northern Texas northward to the northern plains and westward to the Great Lakes region. The worst flooding in Oklahoma's history followed 2½ weeks of heavy rains in September and October, during which more than 50 cm (20 in) of rain fell in a five-day period in parts of the state. Michigan suffered its worst flooding in modern times during September after several weeks of rain. Parts of Illinois, Kansas, Iowa, Montana, Missouri, Minnesota, and Ohio were also hard hit. Thousands were forced from their homes, and damage was estimated in the hundreds of millions of dollars. Water levels on the Great Lakes approached or exceeded record highs.

The hurricane season, so active in 1985, was abnormally quiet in 1986, bringing only five named storms. Three became minimal hurricanes and two made landfall in the U.S. Hurricane Bonnie formed in the Gulf of Mexico and crossed the coast between Galveston Island and Port Arthur, Texas, on June 26. Hurricane Charley came in at North Carolina on August 17, continued along the coast off the Maryland shoreline, and then moved out to sea. The hurricane caused little damage, and its rains helped alleviate the drought conditions in parts of the Carolinas, Virginia, and Maryland. The year was also the fifth consecutive one without a hurricane in the Caribbean—a very rare occurrence.

The 1986 tornado season, while producing about the normal number of tornadoes, brought the lowest U.S. death toll in record history. Fourteen persons lost their lives, compared with the previous low of 24 deaths in 1981. In the past 30 years the number of deaths from tornadoes had declined to an annual average of 87, compared with an average of 191 deaths for the previous 30 years. The decrease was attributed to improvements in forecasting and warning, community involvement in the warning process, and steady advances in public education and awareness.

Worldwide debate continued among atmospheric scientists over the causes of a "hole" over Antarctica in the stratospheric ozone layer that screens out biologically harmful ultraviolet light from the Sun. The transient thinning of the layer, which occurs at the end of the Antarctic winter, had been the subject of intense research since its discovery in 1985. Some scientists believed that global pollutants were changing the chemistry of the stratosphere in such a way that ozone was being destroyed more quickly than it could be generated by solar ultraviolet radiation. Other scientists thought the effect to be a natural fluctuation, one possibly connected with the solar cycle. The preliminary findings of a late-year Antarctic expedition of U.S. researchers favoured the former view, although it was acknowledged that a much clearer picture of the meteorology and chemistry of the Antarctic stratosphere would be needed in order to understand the significance of the ozone hole. (RICHARD E. HALLGREN)

This article updates the *Macropædia* article CLIMATE AND WEATHER.

OCEANOGRAPHY

The Strait of Gibraltar, between Morocco and Spain, is less than 400 m deep at its shallowest point (a metre is about 3.3 ft). It is the only connection through which water flows between the Atlantic Ocean and the Mediterranean Sea. Because evaporation in the Mediterranean is higher than in the adjoining Atlantic (about 1.5 metres/year, compared with about one metre/year), Atlantic water flows through the strait into the Mediterranean at the surface, whereas Mediterranean water made salty by the excess evaporation flows along the bottom of the strait out into the Atlantic. In 1986 scientists completed a major study of flow through the strait. Temperature and salinity of water in and around the strait were mapped in a series of expeditions whose cumulative duration at sea was many months. During and between these expeditions, moored current meters were maintained at various locations and at a number of levels in the water column. Bottom-mounted instruments recorded temperature, salinity, and seafloor pressure continuously during the study. Acoustic measurements from shipboard were used to track the vertical motion of small marine organisms—and hence of the water itself—in the strait.

Analysis of the observations were only beginning in late 1986, but some results were clear. The outflow of deep Mediterranean water can actually reverse during the daily cycle of tides (although the average daily deep flow is almost always outward into the Atlantic). As the deep flow over the shallowest sill floods westward into the Atlantic, the interface between the inward and outward flowing water is deformed into a corrugated pattern that remains fixed relative to the seafloor and whose corrugations may displace the interface by more than 100 m. When the deep current slacks and then floods eastward into the Mediterranean, this corrugated pattern propagates eastward as a packet of waves along the interface. These waves are the mechanism by which flow conditions in the strait influence those on the Mediterranean side of the strait. The fact that they cannot move against the deep current when it is flowing outward into the Atlantic was thought to mean that the amount of fluid flowing out through the strait over the shallowest sill is controlled directly by conditions there but not farther toward the Atlantic. Additional study of the data would test this idea.

The electrical conductivity of the materials beneath the ocean is influenced by their water content and temperature as well as their composition. Knowledge of the conductivity can thus reveal much about the materials present. Earlier studies had estimated seafloor conductivity by observing its effects on naturally occurring electromagnetic fluctuations in the sea, those associated with magnetic storms and auroral events or with the motion of the water through the Earth's magnetic field. During the year a new method for measuring seafloor conductivity was described, and first results for the seafloor west of California were presented. A 600-m-long insulated cable, equipped with voltmeters to record the potential difference across its ends, was laid out along the seafloor. This detector received signals from a man-made electrical source—a section of insulated cable whose bared ends were in contact with the seafloor and through which power from a ship's generators was driven—as the source was dragged from one place to another by the ship. The signal could be detected as far as 65 km from the source. It reflected electrical conductivity in the upper 40 km of material below the ocean, with its highest frequency components telling the most about conductivity nearest the surface. Conductivity of the three-to-seven-kilometre-thick crust just below the much thinner sediment layer was sufficiently large that seawater had probably penetrated much of this material through cracks and fissures. But below about five kilometres conductivity was so low that hardly any seawater could have leaked to this level.

Water in crustal material can have important effects on its mechanical properties and its motion. In 1986 the Ocean Drilling Program, a continuing program of seafloor drilling around the world, worked sites in the eastern Caribbean Sea in order to clarify the way in which the motion of the Atlantic crust as it descends below the Carribean Plate there is influenced by water in the crustal material. This water was evidently trapped in sediments overlying the Atlantic crust as they were deposited. Some of the sedimentary material then was subducted along with the crustal material and the water subsequently squeezed out by the pressure of overlying rock. Some of this water, now rich in minerals and warmed during its descent, may feed seafloor hot-water springs. Its presence just above the descending Atlantic crust may reduce friction between the two crustal plates and thus facilitate subduction.

Scientists discovered during the year that the small clam *Solemya reidi* commonly found near sewage outfalls and pulpmill effluent sites along the coast can derive energy directly from sulfide compounds normally poisonous to animals. Chemosynthetic bacteria that extract energy from hydrogen sulfide had been found previously in the vicinity of hydrothermal vents (mineral-rich hot-water springs occurring in regions of seafloor spreading), and it had also been discovered previously that some animals harbour symbiotic bacteria that use sulfide compounds and that may then provide the host animal with nutrients. *S. reidi,* however, was the first known example of an animal that uses sulfide compounds directly as an energy source.

(MYRL C. HENDERSHOTT)

See also Disasters; Energy; Life Sciences; Mining; Space Exploration; Sports and Games: *Spelunking.*

This article updates the *Macropædia* articles ATMOSPHERE; The EARTH; EARTHQUAKES; The EARTH SCIENCES; GEOCHRONOLOGY; Principles, Methods, and Instruments of MEASUREMENT AND OBSERVATION; OCEANS; PLATE TECTONICS; RIVERS; VOLCANISM.

Economic Affairs

During 1986 the principal features of the world economy were a satisfactory, if unexciting, rate of growth based on relatively strong consumer and investment demand, a spectacular deceleration in inflation largely as a result of falling oil and commodity prices, falling interest rates, the continuation of major international payments imbalances coupled with renewed problems for the larger debtor countries, a realignment of exchange rates, and only a modest improvement in the level of unemployment. As is usually the case, the situation varied greatly between the developed and the less developed countries. Thus, members of the Organization for Economic Cooperation and Development (OECD), consisting of most of the non-Communist industrialized countries, did reasonably well, while other, economically less developed nations faced serious problems of low export prices and weak foreign exchange performance.

OECD growth during 1986 was estimated at just under 3%, similar to the gain recorded in the previous year. This figure, however, disguised considerable variations in performance; while the U.K. and Japan each experienced a deceleration in growth (from 3.8 to 2.5% and 4.5 to 2.5%, respectively), the U.S. economy maintained its expansion

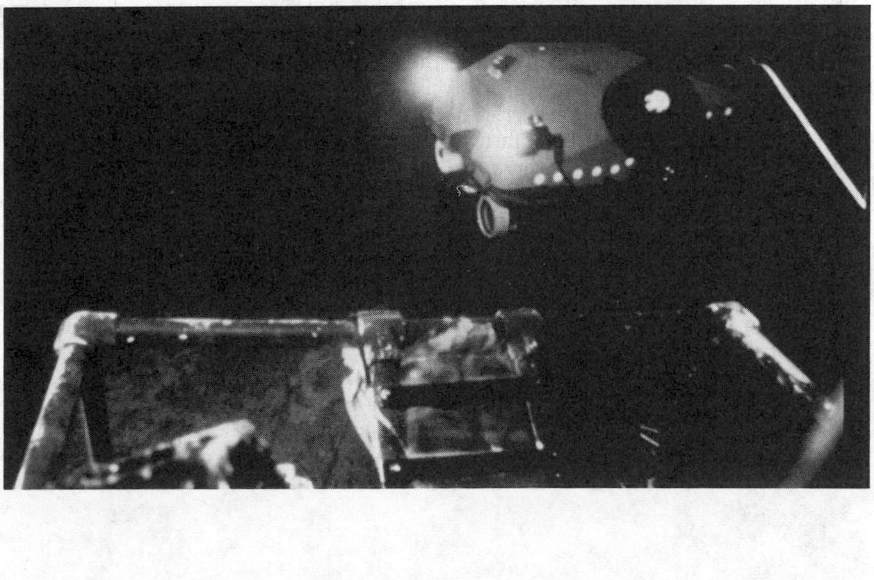

AP/WIDE WORLD

A tethered undersea robot called Jason Jr. is guided by remote control through the dark, deep waters of the Atlantic to photograph the sunken *Titanic*. In a 12-day mission in July, the robot's cameras scrutinized, inside and out, the "unsinkable" luxury liner, which sank in 1912 after a collision with an iceberg.

at just under 3% and both West Germany and France achieved significant acceleration. As in 1985 the mainstay of OECD growth was the strength of consumer expenditure. This was stimulated by a significant slowdown in inflation, which not only boosted real purchasing power but also enabled governments to pursue more relaxed monetary policies that further strengthened the individual's propensity to consume. All the major countries shared in this trend; in the U.K., for example, the volume of consumer expenditure rose faster than at any other time since 1978, while in Japan the latest estimates pointed to a growth that was about one-third faster than in 1985.

Another fairly buoyant component of demand was investment. In general terms this benefited from less restrictive monetary policies; a rapid fall in interest rates; a strengthening of profitability, partly as a result of lower oil and commodity prices; and widespread expectations of continued economic growth in the medium term. All in all, the volume of fixed investment in OECD countries was estimated to have grown by about 5%, with most countries—with the possible exception of Japan, where buoyant housing construction was offset by weak plant and equipment investments—registering an increase in excess of that achieved in the previous year.

During 1986 the volume of world trade was estimated to have grown by just under 4%, somewhat faster than the 3% gain achieved in 1985 but not as fast as the 4–4.5% advance originally expected. Among the reasons for this relatively disappointing outcome was the poor trade performance of the less developed countries. Although economic growth in the OECD area led to an increase in demand for oil and other commodities, this was not sufficient to offset the drop in the price of those products. Consequently, the less developed countries faced a decline in their export earnings that forced them to adopt fairly cautious policies toward imports. Partly as a result of this, OECD exports did not do very well. In volume terms they were estimated to have risen by about 2.5%, as against a 4.5% increase in 1985. The volume of OECD imports, however, grew at about 7%, largely because of the demand-boosting effects of low commodity prices coupled with buoyant consumption expenditures.

The performances of individual countries varied widely. Export volumes were thought to have increased less rapidly than in 1985 in Japan and West Germany, largely because of the appreciation in the external value of their currencies, and in the U.K. and France because, despite weak exchange rates, international competitiveness was adversely affected by an increase in unit labour costs. By contrast, U.S. export performance improved significantly—heading for a 1–2% gain, compared with a decline of a similar magnitude in 1985—mostly because of the steady fall in the external value of the dollar for most of the year.

The trend of imports, however, pointed in the same direction in most countries. The fastest growth took place in West Germany and Japan, where the effects of the consumer boom were reinforced by the import price effects of currency appreciation. In the U.S. the weaker dollar tended to make imports more expensive, with the result that in volume terms they grew by 8%, as against 8.7% in 1985. In the U.K. the movement of exchange rates exerted its influence in the same way, but import volumes still grew marginally faster than in the previous year.

Thus, although the relative movement in volume exports and imports was broadly consistent with a reduction in the trade and payments imbalances between individual OECD countries, in terms of value the discrepancies became more pronounced. This was mainly the result of changes in international currency values. Thus, the two major surplus countries saw a large increase in their dollar-denominated current account balances, from $50 billion to $80 billion in the case of Japan and from $13 billion to some $26 billion in West Germany. By the opposite token, the U.S. current account deficit was estimated to have risen from $118 billion to $138 billion, while in the U.K. the 1985 surplus of £3,500 million was turned into a deficit of about £1,000 million. All in all, however, the current account of the OECD area improved significantly; in late 1986 the total deficit for the year was estimated at about $10 billion, compared with $57 billion in 1985. This was, unfortunately, achieved largely at the expense of the less developed countries. Oil-exporting nations, faced with falling prices, were believed to have recorded a deficit of $50 billion (as against $7 billion in 1985), while the non-oil bloc recorded an actual improvement of $5 billion–$10 billion from the 1985 deficit of $27 billion.

Table I. Real Gross Domestic Products of Selected OECD Countries

% annual change

Country	1983	1984	1985	1986*
United States†	3.4	6.6	2.2	3.0
Japan†	3.2	5.1	4.6	3.2
West Germany†	1.5	3.0	2.4	3.5
France	0.8	1.5	1.2	2.5
United Kingdom	3.3	2.8	3.2	3.0
Canada†	3.3	5.0	4.5	3.8
Italy†	−0.2	2.8	2.3	2.8
Total major countries	2.8	5.1	2.7	3.0
Australia	1.5	6.8	4.7	3.5
New Zealand	5.3	4.8	0.8	−1.0
Austria	2.0	2.0	2.9	2.8
Belgium	−0.1	1.3	1.1	1.8
Denmark	2.1	3.5	3.1	2.5
Finland	2.9	3.0	2.8	1.5
Greece	0.3	2.6	1.7	0
Iceland†	−5.7	2.5	2.8	3.0
Ireland†	−1.8	2.3	−0.7	3.0
Luxembourg	2.8	4.9	1.9	2.0
Netherlands, The	0.9	1.8	2.0	1.5
Norway	4.5	5.6	4.4	4.2
Portugal	−0.9	−1.5	2.8	3.8
Spain	2.0	2.2	2.1	3.0
Sweden	2.4	3.4	2.3	2.0
Switzerland	0.7	2.1	3.8	2.8
Turkey†	3.3	5.9	4.9	4.8

*OECD projection. †GNP.
Source: OECD *Economic Outlook*, May 1986.

The continued presence of large payments imbalances caused considerable friction between individual OECD countries as well as between the less developed and developed worlds with regard to national economic policies. Within the OECD the U.S. argued that countries with surpluses in their foreign accounts should do more to boost their domestic economies and imports, but those nations countered with demands for more prudent fiscal policies in order to cut the large U.S. budget and trade deficits. Nevertheless, despite these pressures the "Plaza" understanding reached in September 1985 between the U.S., Japan, the U.K., West Germany, and France on the need to reduce the value of the dollar survived more or less intact. As a result, the value of the dollar fell steadily against the Deutsche Mark and the yen, with the result that its average trade-weighted value declined by some 13% between January and late November. In terms of sterling, however, the dollar saw some appreciation, as did most other currencies, leading to a fall of about 13% in sterling's trade-weighted value. The French franc was also weak; as part of a realignment within the European Monetary System (EMS) it was devalued by nearly 6% against the Deutsche Mark and the other stronger European currencies.

A rapid fall in world interest rates took place in 1986, reflecting more relaxed monetary policies and the easing of inflationary pressures. Rates fell quite sharply in most countries, with the U.S. federal discount rate moving steadily from 7 to 5.5% and the Bank of Japan's discount rate dropping from 5 to 3% in the first 11 months of the year. There were smaller reductions in other countries; in West Germany—despite strong pressure from the U.S.—the authorities refused to cut the discount rate by more than 0.5 percentage point, to 3.5%, while in the U.K. a rapid fall in the bank rate gave way to a one-percentage-point rise to 11% in October, a move forced on the authorities by the weakness of sterling.

The trend of interest rates provided some much-needed relief to the countries that were facing large debt-servicing obligations. However, this was more than offset by the effects of the decline in world commodity prices (estimated at 40% for oil and 5% for metals and minerals), which had an adverse effect on the foreign exchange earnings of the countries that produced those goods. Partly for this reason, the problem of world debt did not show any improvement during the year.

Thanks to the weakness of commodity prices, inflation lost considerable momentum in most countries. In the OECD area as a whole, consumer prices rose by some 2.7%, compared with an increase of 4.5% in 1985. As usual, West Germany and Japan performed best in this area; Japanese consumer prices were only about 1% higher than a year earlier, while those in West Germany did not increase at all. Inflation rates in other large OECD countries fluctuated within one percentage point of the area's average, although Italy was still heading for a rise of about 6% in the wake of the 9.2% hike in 1985.

Unemployment continued to be a major problem although—expressed as a percentage of the labour force—it probably declined modestly for the entire OECD from 8.1 to about 7.9% in 1986. Much of the improvement occurred in the U.S., where the rate was thought to have fallen from 7.2 to 6.9% between 1985 and 1986, and in West Germany, where the acceleration in economic growth brought about a decline from 9.3 to 8.8%. Rather untypically, Japanese unemployment was believed to have risen, but even so the rate was still only about 3%. There was some evidence of an improvement in the U.K. The rate of unemployment there trended downward for most of the year, and by October it stood at 11.3%, as against 12.2% in January.

Inflation Rate
(Average percentage change from preceding year)

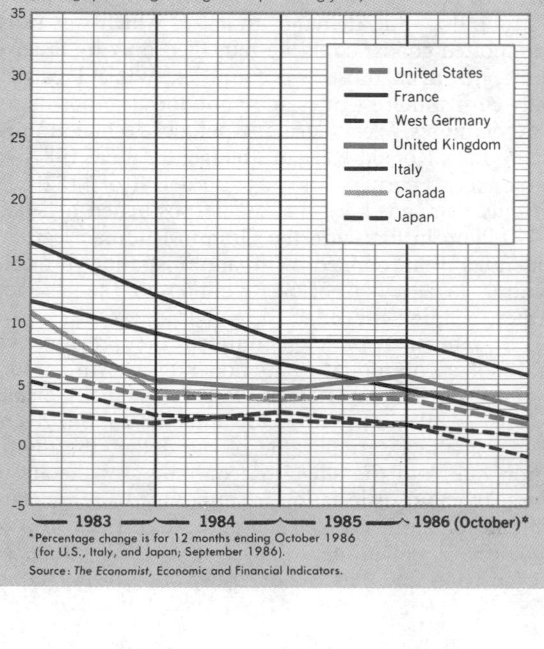

*Percentage change is for 12 months ending October 1986 (for U.S., Italy, and Japan; September 1986).
Source: *The Economist*, Economic and Financial Indicators.

NATIONAL ECONOMIC POLICIES

Developed Market Economies. *United States.* The U.S. economy during 1986 enjoyed its fourth successive year of economic expansion. Yet there was broad agreement among most economists that the fundamental economic situation was far from satisfactory on account of the sluggish growth rate and the widening budget and trade deficits.

The 1985 pattern of overall sluggish annual growth rate in the gross national product (GNP), around 2.5%, coupled with sharp quarter-to-quarter fluctuations, continued during 1986. The opening quarter registered an encouraging 3.5% annualized growth rate after the disappointing 0.7% in the closing quarter of 1985. True to form, growth fizzled out in the second quarter, with GNP expanding by only 0.5%. However, it rebounded in the third quarter with a respectable 2.9% annual growth, raising hopes that the final quarter would expand at a similar rate; this would result in a GNP growth rate for the year as a whole of 2.7%—the same as during the previous year.

Robust personal consumption, the main driving force behind the growth rate since 1983, once again grew strongly during 1986. Real incomes, boosted by continued employment growth, lower oil prices, and gently falling interest rates, enabled consumers to step up their spending by an estimated 3.3%. Retail sales, housing, and automobile markets were the major beneficiaries. Yet U.S. industrialists were unable to take advantage of buoyant consumer demand. Industrial production throughout the year was largely flat as higher demand was met by supplies from other countries. Because it typically takes 9–12 months for the effects of the lower dollar to have a beneficial impact, it was not surprising that manufacturers' new orders did not begin to rise until the final quarter.

Unemployment continued its downward trend, firmly established since 1983, despite a temporary setback in February caused by layoffs in the oil and gas industry. Thus, the unemployment rate, having started the year at 6.7%, rose sharply to 7.3% in February before edging down steadily thereafter. By November it stood at 6.8% and was still pointing downward. Despite the overall downward trend, job losses continued in the manufacturing and energy sectors, but new jobs created in the service and construction industries more than offset them.

Fixed capital formation was mixed during 1986. Nonresidential investment fell by an annualized rate of 8% during the first half of the year, reflecting the cutbacks in oil and gas investment in response to lower oil prices. The weak energy sector coupled with excess capacity in manufacturing caused nonresidential fixed investment to remain flat. Residential construction, by contrast, was very strong early in 1986, and despite a leveling out in the summer and the autumn, it expanded by about 6% for the year as a whole.

The other favourable economic indicator during the year was the trend of consumer price inflation. In the opening months of 1986 the rate of inflation declined, thanks to lower oil prices. However, the benefits arising from the oil price collapse were less pronounced in the U.S. than in other developed economies; the latter benefited twice—first from lower oil prices and second from exchange rate appreciation against the dollar. Thus, at the end of April consumer prices were 1.6% higher than a year earlier, and they remained largely unchanged until August–September, when oil prices rose significantly. In spite of a marked upturn in the inflation rate during the final quarter, at 3–3.5%, the average level of consumer prices in 1986 was estimated to have been only 2.2% higher than in 1985. This was the lowest annual increase in more than two decades.

Six of the world leaders who met in Tokyo in May at the annual economic summit include (left to right) U.S. Pres. Ronald Reagan, U.K. Prime Minister Margaret Thatcher, Canadian Prime Minister Brian Mulroney, Japanese Prime Minister Yasuhiro Nakasone, French Pres. François Mitterrand, and West German Chancellor Helmut Kohl.

BISSON—SYGMA

For the second consecutive year the economy was shackled by a large trade deficit. Lower oil prices and the depreciating dollar had little beneficial impact on the deficit during the first half of the year. This was due to a higher volume of oil imports coupled with greater imports from those countries whose currencies had not experienced a large appreciation against the dollar (such as South Korea and Taiwan). Exports, on the other hand, responded sluggishly to the competitive advantage offered by the currency movements. Part of the explanation lay in problems experienced by the U.S. in selling its agricultural surplus in depressed world markets. A cumulative deficit of $79.5 billion registered during the first half continued to rise, although more slowly, in the second half and was estimated to have reached $165 billion for the year as a whole, 11% over the previous year.

Against the backdrop of adverse currency movements, the current account deficit continued to widen and was expected to reach $130 billion, an increase of $13 billion over the previous year's total. Without the benefit of high interest rates and a strong dollar, as in 1985, capital inflows were weaker and the financing of the deficit at times was precarious. The weakening of the dollar and progress made in negotiations with Japan, South Korea, and the European Communities (EC) helped to contain the protectionist pressures in the Congress.

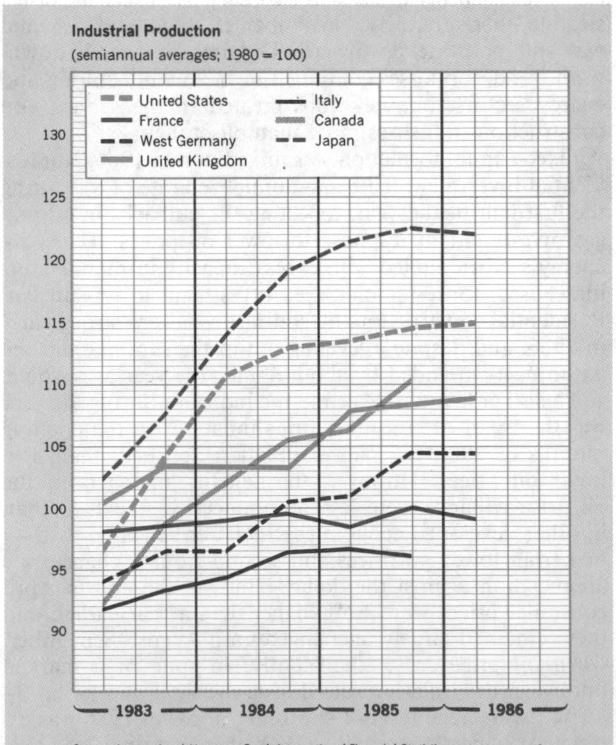

Source: International Monetary Fund, *International Financial Statistics.*

The stance of fiscal policy during 1986 was moderately expansionary, and the budget deficit for fiscal 1986 (ended September 30) was $220.7 billion, easily topping the previous year's $211.9 billion. The budget, following cuts imposed by the Congress, intended a deficit of $175 billion, but it became clear at the midyear review in February that it was going to be larger. The first step of the Gramm-Rudman cuts, which envisaged the elimination of the deficit by 1991, was effectively sidestepped (the Gramm-Rudman-Hollings deficit-reduction act was declared unconstitutional by the Supreme Court in July).

The sluggish economic growth and underestimation of inflation reduced revenue inflows, while expenditure, led by defense spending, was ahead of schedule. The sustained weakness of the economy—particularly in the first half—worried the U.S. economic policymakers and led to a barrage of criticism aimed at Japan and West Germany. The U.S. believed that its unhealthy economic situation of strong domestic demand, much of which was satisfied by imported goods, could be remedied only by faster economic growth in those two countries. While Japan eventually cut its interest rates and announced minor increases in expenditures, West Germany politely declined to oblige.

U.S. Pres. Ronald Reagan's budget for fiscal 1987, when presented in February, envisaged a deficit of $182 billion, but cuts demanded by the Senate postulated a deficit of $144 billion in line with the Gramm-Rudman legislation. The fiscal year opened with administration projections pointing to a deficit of $170 billion in the absence of further spending cuts enacted by the Congress.

U.S. monetary policy continued the previous year's stance of accommodating a moderate growth in money supply. The Federal Reserve Board (the Fed) displayed considerable flexibility in policy implementation, given the decline in the external value of the dollar, the lower inflation rate, and the sluggish economic growth rate. In a period of rapid disinflation, it interpreted the increase in demand for money as normal and decided not to accommodate it as deflationary. Therefore, in the spring, when M1 (currency and demand deposits) was growing far above the target range, the Fed cut the discount rate from 7 to 6.5%, enabling the commercial banks to reduce their lending rates by a similar amount. Two more cuts followed in July and August, bringing the discount rate to 5.5%. These cuts were interpreted by some observers as a message to other major developed economies that if they failed to adopt more stimulatory policies, the U.S. would take all necessary steps to invigorate its industrial performance, even if this meant a still lower dollar. The risk of higher inflation was judged to be minimal. At year's end the vice-chairman of the Fed was talking about a possible further cut in the discount rate early in the new year.

Japan. A marked slowdown in the growth of the Japanese economy took place in 1986. As the year drew to a close, it was estimated that the volume of gross domestic product (GDP) would register a gain of only 2–2.5%, compared with the government's official growth target of 4% and an increase of 4.5% in 1985. The two principal reasons for this rather disappointing performance were the strong rise in the foreign exchange value of the yen and the failure of the authorities to provide any significant boost to domestic economic activity until late in the year. Yet the signs were there for all to see early in 1986. National income figures for the January–March period recorded an annualized real decrease of 2.1%, the first quarterly drop in 11 years. This was largely due to a spectacular slump in the volume of exports, which lost much competitiveness as a result of the steady appreciation of the yen after September 1985. This in turn had an adverse effect on industrial output and confidence that led to a cutback in inventories and a substantially reduced rate of growth in private capital investment activities.

Despite calls for reflationary measures from both Japan's trading partners and its business community, the government did not respond, arguing that the cut in the discount rate from 5 to 3.5% in three successive reductions between January and April would provide the necessary stimulus. However, although this helped to underpin the already fairly buoyant trend of private housing expenditure, it had little effect on private plant and equipment investments.

Nevertheless, economic growth accelerated in the second quarter; although inventory and plant/equipment demand remained weak, consumer expenditure and residential investment grew faster, and the volume of exports also increased modestly. However, the quarter's annualized GNP gain of 3.6% was clearly not sufficient to provide even a faint hope of reaching the government's original target of an advance of 4% for the year as a whole. Furthermore, by the time the April–June GNP figures were released, several leading indicators were pointing to a renewed weakening in business activities in the second half of the year. The Economic Planning Agency's diffusion index, used to forecast economic growth in the months ahead, fell below the 50 mark in September, indicating a substantial slowdown, while the trend of machinery orders and of investment intentions also reflected a loss of confidence. Foreign trade returns suggested a drop in the volume of exports combined with an increase in that of imports, giving rise to expectations of a serious cutback in net overseas demand.

Reflecting these trends, the index of industrial production recorded a drop of about 1% between the second and third quarters, with the utilization ratio of manufacturing capacity registering a large fall of 2.7 points to 95 in August. In the meantime, the external value of the yen continued to appreciate, holding out the prospect of an additional loss of competitiveness of Japanese products.

The strength of the yen was partly due to the stance of the U.S. Arguing that Japan should do more to underpin domestic economic growth, Washington adopted a strategy of talking down the value of the dollar (and, therefore, boosting that of the yen) in order to improve its own export competitiveness and to create a bargaining counter with which to encourage a more expansionary Japanese domestic economic policy.

Faced with these pressures, the Tokyo government was finally forced at the end of September to introduce a series of measures to encourage business. According to official calculations, these provided for an additional expenditure of 3,636,000,000,000 yen (approximately $23 billion) in the form of extra public works projects, housing, and other loans as well as increased capital investments by public utilities. Following this, the Bank of Japan announced a reduction of 0.5 percentage point in the discount rate to 3% at the end of October, and in return the U.S. agreed to stabilize the yen–dollar exchange rate at its then-current level of about 160 yen. Although there was widespread welcome for the September and October measures, it was generally believed that their effects on the 1986 growth rate would be limited. Initial calculations suggested that, at best, they would add 0.5 percentage point to the advance in GNP, bringing it to about 2.5%.

Thus, in 1986 Japan lost its usual position as the fastest growing of the developed countries; in fact, several countries, including Canada and West Germany, were heading for an increase in excess of 2.5%. However, Japan had reinforced its reputation for controlling inflation. As a result of the fall in oil prices, the effect of the appreciating yen on the cost of other imported products, productivity

Table II. Percentage Changes in Consumer Prices in Selected OECD Countries

Country	1981	1982	1983	1984	1985	1986*
United States	10.4	6.1	3.2	4.3	3.5	1.8
Japan	4.9	2.7	1.9	2.2	2.1	0.2
West Germany	6.3	5.3	3.3	2.4	2.2	−0.4
France	13.4	11.8	9.6	7.4	5.8	2.3
United Kingdom	11.9	8.6	4.6	5.0	6.1	3.0
Italy	17.8	16.6	14.6	10.8	9.2	5.5
Canada	12.5	10.8	5.9	4.3	4.0	4.1
Austria	6.8	5.4	3.3	5.6	3.2	1.7
Belgium	7.6	8.7	7.7	6.3	4.9	0.9
Denmark	11.7	10.1	6.9	6.3	4.7	4.6
Finland	12.0	9.6	8.3	7.1	5.9	3.2
Greece	24.5	21.0	20.2	18.5	19.3	22.7
Iceland	51.6	49.1	86.5	30.9	31.9	17.4
Ireland	20.4	17.1	10.5	8.6	5.4	3.1
Luxembourg	8.1	9.4	8.7	5.6	3.1	−0.3
Netherlands, The	6.7	6.0	2.8	3.3	2.3	−0.6
Norway	13.6	11.3	8.4	6.2	5.7	8.6
Portugal	20.0	22.4	25.5	29.3	19.2	11.5
Spain	14.6	14.4	12.2	11.3	8.8	9.5
Sweden	12.1	8.6	8.9	8.0	7.4	4.4
Switzerland	6.5	5.6	3.0	3.0	3.4	0.6
Turkey	37.6	32.7	28.8	45.6	45.0	34.1
Australia	9.6	11.1	10.1	3.9	6.8	8.9
New Zealand	10.5	7.8	7.4	6.2	15.4	11.0

*Twelve-month rate of change (not directly comparable with annual changes).
Sources: OECD, *Economic Outlook*, May 1986; OECD, *Main Economic Indicators*, November 1986.

Table III. Standardized Unemployment Rates in Selected OECD Countries

% of total labour force, seasonally adjusted

Country	1981	1982	1983	1984	1985	1986*
Canada	7.5	10.9	11.8	11.2	10.4	9.4
United States	7.5	9.5	9.5	7.4	7.1	6.9
Japan	2.2	2.1	2.6	2.7	2.6	2.8
Australia	5.7	7.1	9.9	8.9	8.2	7.5
France	7.3	8.1	8.3	9.7	10.1	10.1
West Germany	4.4	6.1	8.0	8.5	8.6	8.3
Italy	8.3	9.0	9.8	10.2	10.5	10.9
Sweden	2.5	3.1	3.5	3.1	2.8	2.8
United Kingdom	9.9	11.4	12.6	13.0	13.2	13.3

*Partially estimated.
Source: OECD, *Economic Outlook*, May 1986.

improvements, and a relatively small raise in wages, there was a sharp fall in the rate of inflation. Thus, wholesale prices recorded an actual drop from the previous year; by September the appropriate index was nearly 12 percentage points below its level of 12 months earlier. The downward trend appeared to have continued in the closing months of 1986 with the result that the average for the year was expected to register a decrease of about 10%, as against a decline of only 1% for 1985. The trend of consumer prices also took a turn for the better, but progress in this area was far from spectacular. Despite the large fall in the wholesale price index, consumer prices recorded small (but decelerating) increases every month. In late 1986 the year-on-year gain was down to about 0.5%, with the annual average heading for a rise of some 1%. This was better than the authorities' original expectations and the lowest inflationary increase among OECD members except for West Germany.

The level of unemployment also remained extremely low in an international context. However, by Japanese standards there was a significant increase, from 2.6% in 1985 to about 3%. Other relevant indicators, such as the amount of overtime worked and the job offer–seeker ratio, also pointed to a weakening in the labour market. On the basis of nine months' figures it was estimated that the index of industrial production would fall marginally from the 1985 average.

In the field of foreign trade and payments, the year was dominated by the rapid rise in the international value of the yen and a further significant increase in the country's already large trade and balance of payments surpluses. At the start of the year the dollar was worth approximately 200 yen, but partly because of the policies to weaken the dollar set forth by the major OECD countries in September 1985, and also because of the strong Japanese overseas payments position, a sustained upward trend took place during the next nine months. By late September the dollar had fallen to 160 yen, but—following the U.S.-Japanese agreement (*see* above)—the rate stabilized at about that level for the last few months of 1986.

Although, as already pointed out, the rise in the value of the currency slowed down the volume growth of exports and speeded up that of imports, these changes were not large enough to offset the effects of the stronger currency on foreign trade values. Thus, during the first nine months of the year, the dollar value of imports fell by 3.1%, while that of exports rose by just over 22%. The result was a spectacular increase in the trade surplus to $65 billion, compared with $30 billion in the same period of 1985. As the year drew to a close, there were no signs of a change in the underlying trend despite the relative stability of the exchange rate against the dollar, and it was estimated that the current account surplus for the whole of 1986 would reach $80 billion, compared with $50 billion for 1985.

United Kingdom. During 1986 the U.K. economy was characterized by a satisfactory rate of growth, a fall in the external value of sterling, a deterioration in the balance of payments, a deceleration in the rate of inflation, a modest decline in interest rates, and a little progress on the unemployment front. Coupled with this not unsatisfactory performance, however, was a strong degree of uncertainty about the underlying trend of the economy, a concern caused by fairly sharp short-term fluctuations in the key indicators as well as a series of reforms in the country's financial sector. There were also some signs of a change in the authorities' economic stance as the government began to prepare for general elections, widely predicted for the first half of 1987.

On the basis of figures for the first three quarters, GDP was estimated to have risen by just under 2.5% in constant prices. Although this represented a significant slowdown from the 3.8% gain recorded for the previous year, it was broadly in line with OECD growth, which was estimated to have been in the region of 2.8%. As in 1985, most principal components of demand contributed to the improvement, with consumer expenditure providing the major stimulus. Wages rose by about 7.5%, against an inflation rate of some 3.5%, leading to a highly beneficial effect on the level of real personal disposable income. This was further enhanced by the liberalization of the financial sector, one effect of which was the adoption of more aggressive credit marketing policies by banks, building societies, and similar institutions. As a result, the volume of consumer expenditure was believed to have recorded a gain of approximately 5%, nearly twice as large as that experienced in the previous year and larger than at any other time since 1978.

There was an acceleration in the growth of investment expenditures; largely because of strong profits and expectations of sustained economic growth, these were estimated to have risen by about 2%, as against just under 1.5% in 1985. Stock building also contributed to the buoyancy of demand, although not as strongly as in the previous year, while government expenditure seemed to have sustained its 1985 growth rate of about 1% throughout most of 1986.

Exports were subject to two conflicting influences. On the one hand, unit labour costs rose sharply because the rise in productivity was well below that of wages. Thus, in a year when West German unit labour costs advanced by 1% and those in Japan fell by 1.5%, the comparable U.K. index recorded an increase of approximately 5%. In terms of overseas competitiveness, some of this was offset by the fall in the external value of sterling. However, the effect on export prices appeared to have been limited, as manufacturers took advantage of the weak exchange rate to boost profits rather than pass on the benefit of devaluation to overseas customers. Partly because of this, the volume of exports of goods and services rose by only about 1%,

Table IV. Changes in Output in the Less Developed Countries, 1980–85

In %

Area	Annual average 1968–77	Change from preceding year 1981	1982	1983	1984	1985
All less developed countries	6.2	2.2	1.6	1.3	4.1	3.2
Oil-exporting countries	8.4	0.9	−0.1	−1.8	1.2	−0.1
Non-oil less developed countries	5.4	2.7	2.5	3.0	5.5	4.8
Africa	5.3	1.7	0.8	−1.5	1.6	1.6
Asia	5.4	5.5	5.0	7.4	7.9	6.1
Europe	6.0	2.3	2.4	1.0	3.5	2.5
Middle East	9.2	−1.8	−0.2	0.1	0.7	−1.6
Western Hemisphere	6.0	0.9	−0.9	−3.1	3.1	3.8

Source: International Monetary Fund, *World Economic Outlook*, 1986.

Table V. Changes in Consumer Prices in the Less Developed Countries, 1980–85

In %

Area	Annual average 1968–77	Change from preceding year 1981	1982	1983	1984	1985
Less developed countries	15.2	26.0	24.5	32.7	37.4	39.3
Oil-exporting countries	10.7	16.2	17.7	24.7	19.3	14.7
Non-oil less developed countries	17.1	30.7	28.0	37.1	47.6	53.0
Africa	10.0	21.3	12.7	18.6	19.8	13.6
Asia	8.8	10.6	6.2	6.6	7.1	6.7
Europe	9.9	24.1	23.7	23.1	27.9	27.9
Middle East	9.8	15.3	12.7	12.1	13.9	13.8
Western Hemisphere	27.9	59.1	66.3	102.4	122.6	144.0

Source: International Monetary Fund, *World Economic Outlook*, 1986.

as against an increase of over 6% in the preceding year. By contrast, imports were more buoyant than in 1985. Although the weakness of the currency had the result of increasing import prices, import demand—fueled by the consumer boom—remained strong. In consequence, the volume of imports of goods and services rose by an estimated 6%, compared with a gain of just over 3% in 1985.

Not surprisingly, these developments led to a significant deterioration in the country's external payments position. A further adverse factor was the weakness of oil prices, which depressed the level of oil earnings. All in all, the balance of trade was estimated to have been in deficit to the tune of £9,000 million, as against £2,500 million in the previous year. Approximately £3,000 million of the £6,500 million deterioration was attributed to movements in non-oil trade, with the remainder accounted for by lower oil prices. However, a significant part of the oil-related deterioration in the visible trade account was recouped in invisible transactions in the form of lower dividends, profits, and interest paid to foreign oil companies. Invisible trade also benefited from higher overseas earnings by British companies, more than offsetting lower net receipts from tourism, which was adversely affected by concern about terrorist action in the wake of the U.S. bombing of Libya. Thus, the surplus on invisible transactions rose from £5,500 million in 1985 to £86,000 million, leaving a current account deficit of approximately £1,000 million, compared with a surplus of £3,500 million in 1985.

Apart from a comparatively buoyant period in the spring, the external value of sterling was on a downward trend. The principal reasons for this were the weakness of oil prices, the deterioration in the nation's external payments position, and the apparent lack of any clear government policy toward sterling. Rates against the stronger currencies, such as the Deutsche Mark and the Japanese yen, were already falling at the start of the year, although sterling actually gained some ground in the spring and early summer. The underlying trend, however, was firmly downward, and by the second quarter of 1986 sterling's trade-weighted average rate was some 5% lower than in the last three months of 1985. During the third quarter there was an additional decline of 5%, and in October, with the fall threatening to gain further momentum, the chancellor of the Exchequer was forced to raise the bank rate by 1 percentage point to 11%. This had a generally stabilizing effect, especially on the sterling–dollar rate. Nevertheless, in late November, sterling (at about $1.43) was no stronger against the dollar than at the start of the year, while the depreciation in terms of the Deutsche Mark and the yen was 19 and 20%, respectively.

The trend was also downward in terms of most other currencies, with the result that sterling's trade-weighted value declined 13% to 68 in early January. Interest rates were falling throughout the spring. The bank rate was cut by 0.5 percentage point on four separate occasions up to May, but half of the decrease was recouped in the attempt to shore up the defenses of sterling in October. During the last few months of the year, there was some evidence that the government was becoming determined to support sterling, even at the cost of a further rise in interest rates. However, despite considerable pressure from both European and U.K. commentators, it refused to take part in the European Monetary System (EMS). EMS members undertook to pursue economic policies consistent with the aim of limiting fluctuations in their currencies within a relatively narrow band, but the U.K. authorities seemed reluctant to assume such obligations.

Table VI. Balances of Payments on Current Account, 1980–85

In $000,000,000

Area	1981	1982	1983	1984	1985
All less developed countries	−49.2	−90.9	−58.9	−35.1	−34.1
Oil-exporting countries	31.0	−25.6	−14.8	−8.6	−6.5
Non-oil less developed countries	−80.2	−65.3	−44.1	−26.5	−27.6
Africa	−21.9	−21.3	−11.6	−6.7	−1.4
Asia	−20.7	−17.3	−14.3	−4.8	−15.4
Europe	−9.9	−6.1	−4.2	−1.9	−2.3
Middle East	45.8	−5.1	−18.5	−18.5	−10.7
Western Hemisphere	−42.6	−41.1	−10.3	−3.6	−4.3

Source: International Monetary Fund, *World Economic Outlook*, 1986.

The rate of unemployment decreased somewhat but was still comparatively high as the year drew to a close. In October 1986 the seasonally adjusted number on the unemployed register expressed as a percentage of the labour force stood at 11.3%, as against 12.2% at the start of the year. Although the government claimed (as it had done several times before) that this was the beginning of a new trend, there was some evidence that much of the apparent decline was the result of various schemes designed to provide temporary training/employment for the young and the long-term unemployed. Such schemes, it was argued, did not create real long-term jobs and were promoted by the government mainly in order to provide some temporary relief for the politically sensitive unemployment statistics. Against this view, officials pointed to the steady growth in the number of those who were employed and to the substantial increase in the number of unfilled vacancies (up by 2.2% between the third quarters of 1985 and 1986) as evidence of an underlying improvement on the employment front.

As for inflation, there was an undoubted improvement. In 1985 retail prices rose by 6.1%, but the increase for 1986 was estimated at only 3.5%. The main reason for this was the large decline in world commodity prices, which more than offset the adverse price effects of weak sterling and which was reflected in a reduction of about 8% in the price index of materials used by industry.

The deceleration in inflation came about in spite of a faster than expected increase in money supply. This raised questions about the role of monetary aggregates as a major determinant of inflation; even the chancellor of the Exchequer appeared to have become a skeptic and suggested that this indicator would play a relatively unimportant role in future policy-making. The official reason given was that, owing to widespread reforms to the financial system of the country, money supply had become difficult to measure effectively. In broad terms, the aim of these changes (collectively often referred to as the Big Bang) was to allow a much greater degree of competition among various financial institutions such as banks, building societies, stockbrokers, and investment managers. These, together with the continuation of the government's efforts to divest itself of large state-owned companies (which culminated in the £5,600 million sale of British Gas to the public in November–December), led to an increasing interest in savings, investment, and stock ownership. Another important policy change by the government was the decision to revise its public spending plans upward for 1987 and beyond, providing more evidence that it intended to seek another five-year term from the electorate sometime during that year.

France. Following the election in the spring of a new government, headed by Jacques Chirac, the pace of economic activity accelerated. This led to an estimated real growth in GDP of 2.2%. Unspectacular as this might have been, it was significantly higher than the growth rate achieved in any other year since 1980. Two major weaknesses remained, however: a stubbornly high unemployment rate and a weak trade balance.

The major contributors to economic growth during 1985 were private consumption and corporate-sector fixed investment. Consumer expenditure and retail sales were strong because of a rise in disposable income; this, in turn, was stimulated by fiscal measures taken by the previous government, headed by Laurent Fabius. The sharp decline in oil prices also boosted consumers' disposable income by virtue of the fact that energy products account for a sizable proportion of household budgets. As the year drew to a close, consumer demand strengthened further and was estimated to have expanded by 3% in volume terms, compared with 2.4% in 1985. This was accompanied by a strong upturn in gross fixed investment. Improved corporate profitability, due to the decline in input prices (fuel and raw materials) and relaxation of price controls in April, coupled with better export prospects in the wake of the devaluation of the franc against the Deutsche Mark, was the major factor that induced many firms to modernize and expand. Based on partial data, it was estimated that growth of fixed investment in 1986 was of the order of 3.5%, slightly higher than in the previous year.

Despite the fall in oil prices, France's trade balance deteriorated disquietingly during 1986. The strong domestic demand led to an upsurge in the volume of imports, while exports were hampered by flagging competitiveness in manufactured goods. Thus, foreign trade, for the second year in a row, exerted a negative influence on growth during the period under review.

Despite stronger domestic demand and higher industrial output, unemployment deteriorated slightly during 1986. The average number of unemployed (seasonally adjusted) in the second quarter stood at 2,444,000, compared with 2,378,000 in the previous quarter. In October the number of unemployed stood at 2.4 million, or 10.8% of the work force. In the absence of various employment support programs, the situation would have been worse.

The reduction in the inflation rate, which had gathered steam in the second half of 1985, continued into 1986, resulting in an estimated average rate of 2.8%. This was less than half the 1985 average and compared favourably with the 1981–85 average of nearly 10%. Unlike 1985, when disinflation owed much to a price and incomes policy reinforced by tight monetary and fiscal measures, the fight against inflation during 1986 was greatly assisted by the collapse in oil prices. Thus, the authorities were able to give a mild stimulus to domestic demand without seriously prejudicing their inflation targets. However, faced with the prospect of overshooting its own inflation target, the new government postponed the freeing of prices in the services sector, despite its electoral promises.

The economic policy of the Chirac government as presented to the National Assembly on April 9 was to increase employment, reduce the inflation rate, cut the burden of taxation, and eliminate the budget deficit within three years. Employment creation was linked with the regaining of dynamism by business firms, a goal that required economic reforms. Thus, a bill introduced in the spring emphasized three areas: measures for liberalizing the market economy, plans for promoting youth employment, and, finally, privatization schemes. Two early steps taken to promote those goals were, first, a devaluation of the French currency against that of West Germany by 5.8%—the maximum allowed within the EMS exchange rate mechanism—and second, extension of the wage and salary restrictions that were designed to freeze the real level of increases.

There was also a declaration that the growth of money supply in 1986 would be held to below 5%. This represented a modest relaxation of the monetary policy of the previous administration and paved the way for interest rate reductions. By the end of 1986 the Banque de France's key intervention rate was down by 0.75 percentage point to 7.25%, while the commercial bank base rates fell by 1% to 9.5%.

The thrust of fiscal policy until the autumn was largely neutral with respect to the budget the new government inherited, which stipulated a deficit of F 145.3 billion. A supplementary budget introduced in April provided for F 22.5 billion of savings, but these were lost through an increased expenditure of F 20.1 billion. The budget for 1987, approved in September, showed a remarkable degree of continuity with the fairly restrictive fiscal policy in force since 1984. Additional defense and employment-promotion expenditures were balanced by lower government expenditures. Despite a reduction in the corporation tax rate to 45%, announced in the spring, accompanied by a similar reduction in personal income tax, a slight (11%) reduction in the overall budget deficit was postulated.

West Germany. The West German economy entered 1985 with high hopes of a rebound. The strong growth rate in the second half of 1985, coupled with the massive impetus from the collapse of oil prices, led to expectations of 3.5% growth in 1986. As it happened, the first quarter registered a 1.6% fall in GNP from the previous quarter—caused by destocking triggered by the sharp disinflation—but GNP bounced back in the second quarter. A strong level of economic activity for the remainder of the year led to an estimated growth rate of 3% in 1986. While this was higher than the previous year's growth rate, it was no more than a return to the rate achieved in 1984.

As in the previous year, the major contributors to economic growth were fixed capital investment and private consumption rather than exports. Consumer expenditures and retail sales were buoyant—even during the otherwise depressed opening quarter—owing to a rise in disposable income. With negligible inflation, real earnings surged

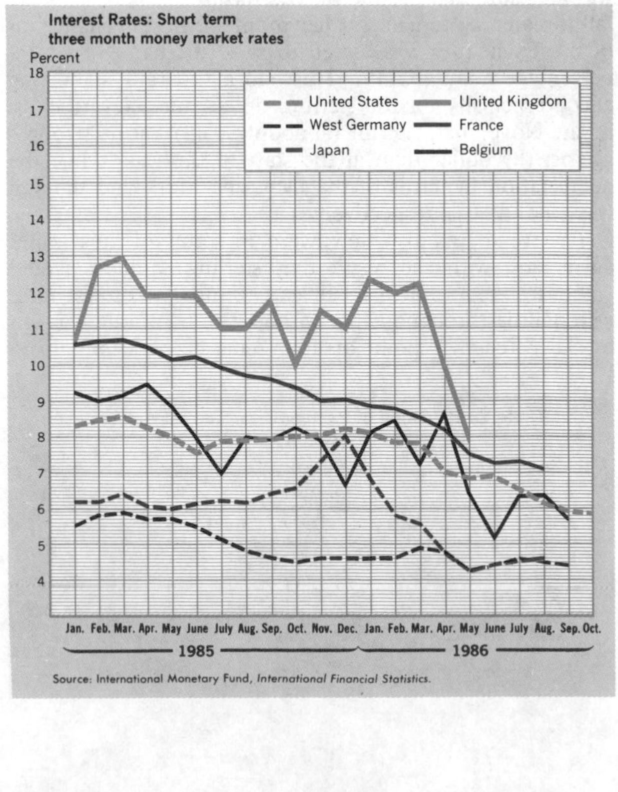

ahead and were given a further boost by the sharp decline in oil prices. Consumer demand remained strong throughout the year and, based on incomplete data, real consumer spending was estimated to have expanded by 4%, a five-year high. Sales of consumer durables such as automobiles led the way with an estimated 10% real increase.

Capital investment also performed exceptionally well during 1986, with the available data suggesting a growth rate in the 9–10% range. During previous years expenditure in this area had been largely confined to replacement and efforts to increase efficiency. Arguably, West Germany fell behind its competitors in investment in new technology. During 1986 there was a definite upsurge in investment, this time biased toward new technology, stimulated by the prospects of stable and reasonably high corporate profitability. Even the construction industry embarked on a long-overdue recovery.

Differentiating 1986's encouraging economic growth rate from rates of previous years was the absence of export impetus and the deterioration in the real foreign balance. While the trade surplus continued to surge ahead—estimated at DM 100 billion, compared with DM 75 billion the year before—the underlying increase in the volume of exports slowed appreciably to 4% (7% in 1985 and 10% in 1984) at the same time that imports in real terms accelerated to more than 7% (approximately 5% in the previous two years). Apart from the appreciation in the value of the Deutsche Mark against other major currencies, principally the dollar, sluggish import demand in OECD countries and a further setback to demand from the Middle East as a result of falling oil revenues were the main factors. Despite the adverse trend of the real foreign balance, the current account, which includes service transactions and transfer payments, registered another large surplus. The total during the first half was DM 32.6 billion, compared with DM 14.4 billion in the same period of the previous year. A similar trend continued into the autumn, leading to expectations of a surplus of at least DM 60 billion.

With import prices having plummeted as a result of the appreciation of the West German currency and the fall in oil prices, it was not surprising that disinflation became the norm during most of the year. West German consumer prices stopped rising as early as the summer of 1985 and, following a marginal uplift in the winter, fell steadily thereafter. It was widely expected that the average inflation rate during 1986 would be zero, but there was an outside chance of a small negative figure. Excluding energy costs, however, inflation was expected to rise by about 1.5% in 1986, indicating that it was not quite totally out of the system but was too small to be of any significance.

After a series of false dawns, unemployment in West Germany achieved a sustained decline, albeit one of undramatic proportions. The monthly jobless total during the first quarter was 0.6% below that of the previous year, and as the year progressed, a sharper decline in unemployment doubled the gap. Job vacancies had accelerated meanwhile and in the autumn were nearly 50% ahead of the previous year. Nevertheless, just under 2 million (8.7%) people remained unemployed (2.2 million seasonally adjusted), while an acute shortage of skilled labour existed in electrical engineering and information technology.

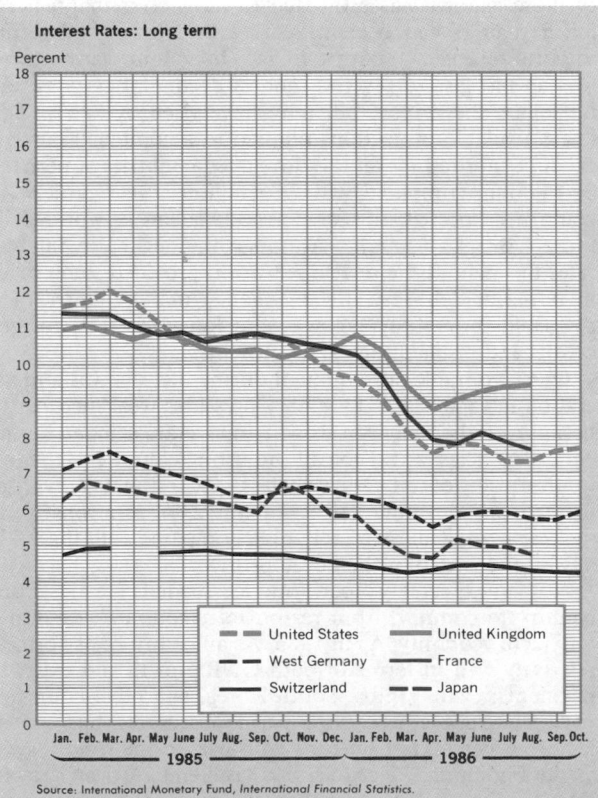

Monetary conditions were slightly easier during 1986, continuing the trend established in the second half of 1985. In December 1985 the Bundesbank raised the monetary growth target 0.5 percentage point to 3.5–5.5%. During the first quarter, when the money supply vastly overshot the target, the authorities—mindful of the sluggish economic performance—did not take steps to reduce it. More significantly, in early March the discount rate was reduced by 0.5 percentage point to 3.5% as part of a general round of interest cuts in the major economies. Although West Germany came under increased international pressure in the summer and early autumn to cut interest rates in order to aid world economic recovery, it steadfastly refused to do so. Worries about the domestic component of inflation and high utilization of capacity in many industrial sectors were cited as reasons for not bowing to this outside pressure. However, prime lending rates at 7% were unmistakably high in real terms and concerned the business community.

After four years of restrictive budgets, the stance of fiscal policy was more accommodating during 1986. The first phase of tax cuts, announced in December 1984, became effective in January 1986, but the overall decline in the government deficit was projected to continue, though at a slower pace. The 1986 budget was framed on the basis of assumptions of 3% real GNP growth and 2% inflation, leading to a deficit of DM 23.7 billion, or 1.2% of anticipated GNP. In view of the early sluggishness of the economy in 1986 and the better-than-anticipated inflation rate, government revenues suffered more than the savings on expenditure. Based on incomplete data, the deficit was forecast at DM 24.3 billion, higher than the target in absolute terms but slightly down as a percentage of GNP.

Despite international pressure on West Germany to reflate further, the budget for 1987 envisaged a modest tightening of fiscal policy to produce a lower budget deficit than 1986's anticipated DM 24.3 billion. It was said that this strategy would make room for tax cuts early in 1987 should the economy start to run out of steam.

Less Developed Countries. The evidence available at the end of 1986 pointed to fairly sluggish economic growth for the less developed countries. Owing to the lack of up-to-date information, a precise estimate of their overall growth rate could not be made, but there were widespread fears that progress might have fallen below even the previous

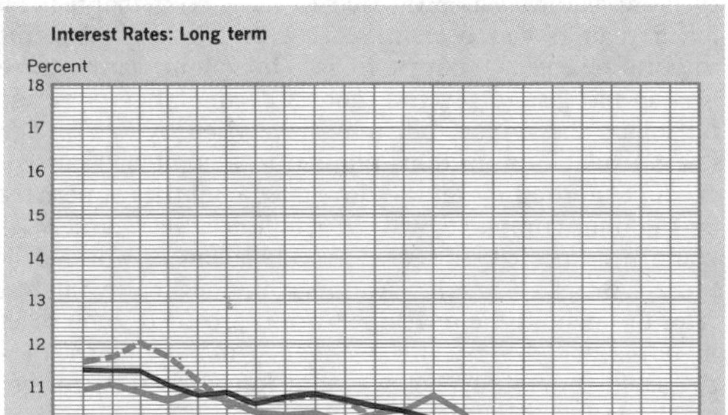

year's unsatisfactory performance. In 1985 the GNP of the less developed world rose 3.2%, a significant slowdown compared with the rise of 4.1% in 1984. This was largely due to the weakness of commodity prices, which led to balance of payments difficulties—difficulties that in turn forced many of these countries to put the brake on domestic demand. An important contributory factor was the spectacular slowdown in the industrialized world's growth (from 4.7% in 1984 to 2.8% in 1985), which inevitably had an adverse effect on the less developed economies. Although growth in the developed world was not such a problem in 1986, the adverse trends in commodity prices continued more or less unabated.

During 1986 oil prices were estimated to have declined by some 40%. There was also some weakness in the prices of agricultural materials, although there were one or two notable exceptions such as coffee, the price of which was forced up by frost in Brazil. At the same time, prices of manufactured goods, which accounted for a significant proportion of the imports of less developed countries, recorded some increase. The result was that, just as in 1985, the terms of trade moved strongly against the less developed world, which led to a serious deterioration in their external payments situation. Faced with large international debts, many less developed countries had no choice but to introduce fiscal and other policies to curb demand with a view to limiting their external imbalances. This had an adverse effect on their growth, and it was feared that the final figures for 1986 could register a 0.5-percentage-point drop compared with the rise in GNP in 1985.

The extent of the problem could readily be seen from the trend of the less developed countries' trade and export earnings. Partial statistics suggested that—largely because of the moderate economic growth in the industrialized world—the volume of the less developed countries' exports may have risen by 3–4%, as against 0.5% in 1985. However, because of the adverse trend of prices, the value of those exports was estimated to have been about 4–5% lower than it had been a year earlier. In general terms imports reflected a mirror image. In volume terms there was no increase (or even a modest decline), but expressed in dollars the import bill may have risen by 2–3%. The latest available projections pointed to a combined current account shortfall for all less developed countries of perhaps $70 billion, compared with $35 billion a year earlier. As could be expected, this made the problem of world debt more difficult to handle. Although the decline in interest rates throughout the developed world provided some relief in terms of debt-servicing payments, many countries (as discussed more fully below) were forced to seek further credits and rescheduling arrangements.

One favourable development during the year was a moderation in inflation. Inflationary pressures weakened partly because of the sluggish growth in overall demand, price control policies, and—for oil-importing countries—the fall in the price of oil. Nevertheless, the estimated average increase in consumer prices—about 23%, as against 39% in 1985—was still extremely high compared with the 2.7% advance recorded in the developed world.

Not unexpectedly, performance varied greatly from country to country, from region to region, and according to type of economy. As in 1985, Asian countries performed relatively well in terms of both GNP growth and external payments; China, India, South Korea, and other countries with relatively large exports of manufactures made satisfactory progress, but one or two others in the region, such as the Philippines, faced serious problems. African growth rates tended to be weaker than the average, but there was some evidence that growth might have accelerated slightly between 1985 and 1986. Latin America experienced a loss of economic momentum and a slowdown in inflation; although Brazil produced a satisfactory performance, Mexico, dependent on oil for a large part of its overseas earnings, was seriously affected by the fall in oil prices. The same influence was also at work in the Middle East, which did particularly poorly in terms of growth and the balance of payments.

In fact, the sharpest contrast in performance was between oil exporters and the non-oil less developed countries. This latter group suffered from the weakness of primary commodity prices but, along with the developed countries,

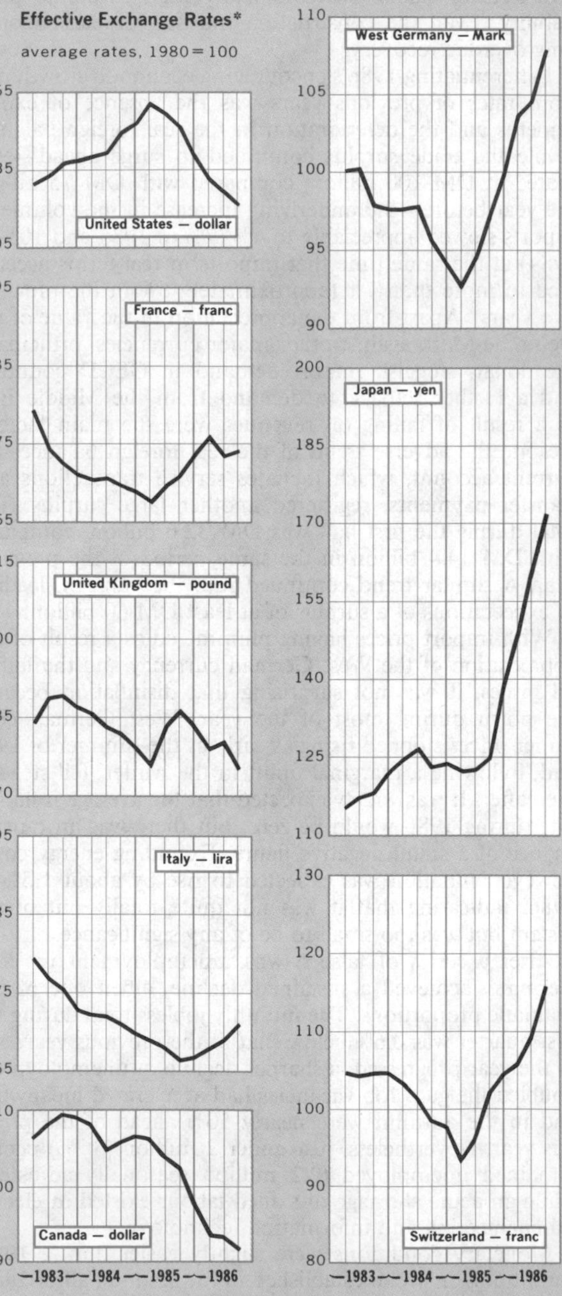

*Measure of a currency's value relative to a weighted average of the values of the currencies of the country's principal trading partners.

Source: International Monetary Fund, *International Financial Statistics.*

gained considerable benefit from low oil prices. These had a beneficial effect on costs and on the balance of payments, which enabled such nations to maintain growth at a relatively high level. In fact, the latest available indicators suggested that despite a somewhat disappointing start their overall growth might have exceeded the 4.8% registered in 1985 and that the current account deficit of $27 billion recorded in 1985 might have been cut by $5 billion–$10 billion.

In contrast, GDP in oil-exporting countries seemed to be heading for a volume decrease of 0.5–1%, compared with a largely static position in 1985 and a growth of about 1% in the preceding year. There was also a spectacular deterioration in their trade balance, which—together with a possible worsening in the balance of their invisible transactions—was estimated to have brought their combined current account deficit to about $50 billion, as against one of some $7 billion a year earlier.

Centrally Planned Economies. The 42nd session of the Council for Mutual Economic Assistance (Comecon) was held in Bucharest, the capital of Romania, during Nov. 3–5, 1986. The session was attended by leaders of all the member states: the heads of government of Bulgaria, Czechoslovakia, East Germany, Hungary, Mongolia, Poland, Romania, and the Soviet Union; the vice-president of Cuba; and the deputy premier of Vietnam. The Yugoslav vice-president also attended, as did observers from Angola, Afghanistan, Yemen (Aden), Laos, Nicaragua, and Ethiopia. The head of the Romanian delegation, Prime Minister Constantin Dascalescu, chaired the session.

It was noted that the national income produced by the member countries as a whole increased by 3.6% in 1985 over that of the previous year. Over the same period industrial production rose by 3.9% and foreign trade by 3.2%.

The delegates discussed a report presented by the Executive Committee that dealt with Comecon activity between the 40th and the 42nd sessions of the Council. The main topic of discussion was the implementation of the Comecon countries' "Comprehensive Program for Scientific and Technical Progress" for the year 2000. The program had been sanctioned at the extraordinary 41st session of Comecon held on Dec. 17–18, 1985, in Moscow. The delegates stressed the importance of adopting new methods of production to increase output and that these should reflect scientific and technical developments. Special emphasis was put on the use of advanced technology that would meet the highest international standards, especially in such sectors as fuel, energy, robots, raw materials, and automated planning systems.

Delegates decided that the nuclear power capacity in their countries should be increased. At the same time, additional measures to conserve energy and raw materials were to be adopted. The session approved the program for the construction of nuclear power stations and nuclear energy supplies up to the year 2000.

Sessions dealt in detail with new forms of cooperation such as the creation of more direct links between economic enterprises and the scientific institutes of the Comecon countries. Vietnam, Cuba, and Mongolia were encouraged to increase their participation in the international socialist division of labour. Nicaragua, Mozambique, Mexico, and Iraq were to be given the opportunity to develop links with the Comecon countries. Cooperation agreements were ratified with Angola, Ethiopia, and Yemen (Aden).

The 42nd session expressed approval of the recent progress that had been made in establishing official relations between Comecon and the EC and between individual countries of Eastern and Western Europe. The session noted that implementation of a number of large-scale multilateral agreements would have to be accelerated. These included the construction of a gas pipeline from Hamburg, West Germany, to the Soviet border. The natural gas was to provide transport fuel.

Soviet Premier Nikolay I. Ryzhkov in his speech criticized other member countries for failing to increase economic activity. He complained that although the U.S.S.R. was supplying Eastern European countries with adequate fuel and raw material, the industrial goods that the Soviet Union was importing from them did not come up to the expected standards. Ryzhkov said that traditional forms

AP/WIDE WORLD

An electric board shows 152.90 yen against the U.S. dollar at a Tokyo foreign exchange on August 20. The dollar's nosedive reached 152.55 yen that day and closed at 153.05 yen, the lowest dollar-yen closing since the late 1940s.

of trade should be progressively abandoned and replaced by new forms of "interaction in production." By this he meant an increase in cooperation between enterprises that shared resources and expertise. He told the delegates that the purpose of such economic reforms was to make cooperation easier by reducing the role of economic ministries and foreign trade organizations.

Not for the first time, Romania openly criticized the Comecon cooperation plans. Romanian Pres. Nicolae Ceausescu in the speech he delivered said that the current Comecon five-year plan did not assist his country with its problems. Ceausescu stated that those problems should be discussed at a summit meeting of the party leaders of the Comecon countries that ought to be called shortly. Romania wanted more fuel, energy, and raw materials from the Soviet Union, as well as a larger share of Comecon markets for its industrial products. Romania was the only member country that did not sign the agreements relating to the implementation of the Comecon long-term program sanctioned at the 41st session.

In spite of the criticism, from Romania in particular, the agreements reached at the 41st extraordinary session of the Council in 1985 seemed destined to be of considerable importance in the future development of the Comecon joint economic policy. A key factor was to be the implementation of the "Joint Program for the Development of Science and Technology." Establishing direct links between economic enterprises and scientific institutions of various Comecon countries would depend, however, on the progress of economic reforms that were currently being undertaken in the Soviet Union and some other member countries. Although these were well advanced in Hungary and East Germany, they were only in the early stages in the Soviet Union. Moreover, some countries, including Czechoslovakia and Romania, were strongly opposed to any reforms that had as their objective the decentralization of power and that aimed at releasing some market forces into the planned economy. The Soviet Union was likely to cut out the bureaucratic obstacles that would prevent the setting up of direct links between enterprises of various countries. The Soviet authorities also accepted the idea that the monopoly of state enterprises that existed over given markets did not facilitate competition and, therefore, did not promote the introduction of more advanced technology and products of better quality.

Many Eastern European economists, however, thought that much more fundamental problems needed to be solved if profitable and efficient links were to be established between enterprises. These would involve the setting up of a common pricing system, the introduction of convertible currency, and much freer competition between economic enterprises than was currently possible. Such changes implied a reform of the entire economic system. This in turn would lead to a considerable weakening in the power of central authority and in the overall control of economic life that was being exercised by the Communist parties. There was no doubt, however, that the Soviet Union was beginning to set the pace of reform in Eastern Europe and that the planned cooperation with Comecon reflected the more dynamic and pragmatic approach of Soviet leader Mikhail Gorbachev.

INTERNATIONAL TRADE

Evidence available at the end of 1986 suggested that the volume of world trade would grow by just under 4% during the year. Although this was somewhat better than the gain of 3% achieved in 1985, when set against earlier expectations of a 4.5–5% increase it was seen as a disappointment. The key factors behind the comparatively poor performance were the failure of the developed economies to respond as strongly as expected to the reduction of oil prices, the fall in the external value of the dollar, and the adverse movement in the terms of trade of less developed countries. Thus, economic growth in the OECD area was estimated to have been just under 3%, representing no improvement over the previous year's advance.

As in 1985, the volume of international trade grew faster in the developed world than in the less developed countries. The volume of OECD exports rose by about 2.5%, nearly two percentage points less than the gain in 1985. This was due partly to a slowdown in the growth of U.S. imports that resulted from the depreciation of the dollar and also to the fall in overseas purchases by less developed countries brought about by a shortage of foreign exchange. The volume of OECD imports, however, grew a little faster (around 7%); one of the important reasons for this was the low price of oil, which—together with earlier reductions in stockpiles—led to higher purchases of petroleum products. With the exception of the U.S. and Canada, most major OECD members experienced a slower growth in volume exports than in the previous year, while in the case of imports most countries fared better. This was particularly true of Japan and West Germany, where the rapid appreciation of their currencies made imports significantly cheaper; the principal exception was the U.S., where the weakening currency had the opposite effect.

In the less developed world the oil producers did rather well in terms of export volumes with an estimated growth of 7%, as against a decline of 10% in 1985. Non-oil less developed countries, however, turned in a fairly gloomy performance. Despite the weakness of commodity prices, the level of demand did not expand significantly in the developed world; this resulted in a volume gain of only 4% in their exports, as against 5% a year earlier. Import volumes, constrained by the slow growth of exports and adverse price movements, grew by only 3% (as against 4% in 1985) in the non-oil less developed economies, while imports by oil exporters were estimated to have fallen by 8–10% as weaker oil prices lowered oil export revenues despite an increase in the quantities shipped.

Table VII. Output of Basic Industrial Products in Eastern Europe, 1985

In 000 metric tons unless otherwise stated

Country	Anthracite (hard coal)	Lignite (brown coal)	Natural gas (000,000 cu m)	Crude petroleum	Electric power (000,000 kw-hr)	Steel	Sulfuric acid	Cement
Bulgaria	228	30,636	...	...	41,616	2,928	810	5,220
Czechoslovakia	26,220	102,312	24,300	120	80,628	15,036	1,281.6	10,164
East Germany		312,156	...	2,016	113,832	7,848	882	11,604
Hungary	2,640	21,408	267,984	...	26,712	3,648	520.8	3,684
Poland	191,640	54,144	199,920	...	137,712	16,128	2,863.2	14,988
Romania	...	...	...	...	...	...	...	...
U.S.S.R.	491,760	155,280	22,257,444	594,996	1,545,000	...	...	...

Source: UN, *Monthly Bulletin of Statistics.*

As indicated above, the terms of trade moved against the less developed countries (and in favour of the developed economies) for the second year in succession. Full figures were not available at the end of 1986, but it was clear that for most of the year there was sustained weakness in both oil and non-oil commodity prices. At the same time, there was a strengthening in the price of manufactured goods. These developments had a highly adverse effect on the import/export values of the less developed world, which in turn created a serious shortage of foreign exchange and further difficulties in servicing their large outstanding debts. (See *International Exchange and Payments,* below.) Although toward the end of the year there were some signs of a modest recovery in oil prices, in late November these were still some 35% lower than at the end of 1985. Metal and mineral prices were heading for an average annual decline of some 5%; prices of agricultural raw materials remained largely static, although the prices of food exports appeared to have recorded a 10% increase.

The main beneficiary of the above trends was the developed world; according to OECD estimates the combined terms of trade of its members might have improved by as much as 5–6% during 1986. Combined with the relatively favourable trend in OECD trade volumes, the result was a significant improvement in the area's trade surplus. Thus, it was estimated that the value of imports rose by about 17% to $1,600,000,000,000, while exports advanced by a massive 30% to approximately $1,645,000,000,000. The combined trade surplus for the developed world was, therefore, some $45 billion, as against a deficit of nearly $110 billion in 1985.

The two largest surpluses were recorded in Japan and West Germany. Although the volume of imports grew faster in those countries than that of exports, the rapid appreciation of their currencies boosted the dollar value of their overseas sales but depressed the value of their purchases abroad. As a result, Japan was heading for a massive trade surplus of $65 billion, as against $56 billion in 1985. At the same time, West Germany was estimated to have accumulated a positive trade balance of about $100 billion, nearly 25% higher than in the previous year.

Most other OECD members experienced an improvement in their trade balances. France turned an earlier deficit into a modest surplus, and Italy recorded a shortfall of $7 billion, compared with $13 billion a year earlier. The two principal exceptions to the rule were the U.S. and the U.K. Despite a slowdown in the growth of imports and an acceleration in that of exports, the change in the value of the dollar led to a trade deficit in the U.S. of about $145 billion (substantially the same as in 1985), nearly offsetting the combined surpluses of West Germany and Japan. In the U.K. the excess of imports over exports rose from $2.5 billion in 1985 to a staggering $9 billion in 1986. Unlike the situation in the U.S., however, this resulted largely from a slowdown in the volume growth of exports from 6 to only 1% and an acceleration in import growth from 3 to 6%, fueled by buoyant domestic consumption.

In contrast to the OECD performance, the trade balances of other countries suffered heavily. Early returns during 1986 suggested that the principal oil exporters, faced with weak oil prices and only a modest growth in world oil usage, might not have recorded more than a $10 billion surplus, as against $48 billion a year earlier. Non-oil less developed countries, many of which cut imports, were thought to have turned in a trade deficit of $15 billion–$20 billion, as against $27 billion in 1985. Agricultural exports from the U.S.S.R. and Eastern Europe were seriously affected by contamination of farm products following the disaster at the Chernobyl nuclear power plant near Kiev; partly for this reason their trade activities probably produced a surplus well below the $9 billion recorded in 1985.

Not surprisingly, the widespread trade imbalances gave rise to much argument among nations and groups of nations about their partners' trade and economic policies. On the one hand, the less developed countries felt that the economic policies of the developed nations discriminated against them in matters such as agricultural trade, commodity prices, and assistance for their exports of manufactures. At the same time, within the developed world itself the argument continued between the surplus and deficit countries. Japan in particular faced considerable pressure from the U.S. and the EC to boost its economy, remove nontariff barriers to imports, and exercise more "voluntary" restraint on exports.

The major issues affecting world trade were put into sharp focus at the meeting of 74 of the 92 members of the General Agreement on Tariffs and Trade (GATT) held at Punta del Este, Uruguay, at the end of September. The meeting, the culmination of six months of preparatory work in Geneva, was to agree on a broad agenda for the eighth round of GATT negotiations aimed at eliminating or reducing many of the principal obstacles to the free flow of goods and services between member countries. As the meeting took place, however, it confounded the earlier, somewhat pessimistic, expectations. Representatives of the 74 countries agreed to a remarkably broad agenda, probably broader than on any other similar occasion in the past. They also set a relatively ambitious target of no more than four years for the conclusion of the detailed negotiations; some past exercises of this nature had lasted for more than six years. In addition, they agreed not to introduce new restrictive trade measures offending against GATT rules and to dismantle existing restrictions during the negotiating period.

The principal items on the agenda for the coming years included world trade in agriculture, the trade-distorting effects of barriers to foreign investment, the question of bringing trade in services within the framework of GATT rules, the protection of intellectual property rights, and a further reduction, or the elimination, of tariff and nontariff trade barriers. The inclusion of trade in agricultural products was regarded as a major step forward as well as a considerable victory for agricultural exporters. Despite the differing interpretations of the scope of the negotiations

Table VIII. Soviet Trade with Eastern European Countries

In 000,000 rubles, current prices

	Exports			Imports		
Country	1983	1984	1985	1983	1984	1985
Bulgaria	5,510.8	6,124.4	6,434.7	5,053.3	5,608.0	6,040.0
Czechoslovakia	5,871.6	6,590.8	6,813.3	5,420.4	6,016.5	6,587.3
East Germany	6,797.8	7,481.4	7,651.7	6,595.7	7,367.2	7,553.0
Hungary	4,058.0	4,320.8	4,560.0	4,007.0	4,434.4	4,850.1
Poland	5,274.3	6,069.2	6,516.7	4,786.7	5,296.8	5,525.0
Romania	1,639.6	1,807.2	1,948.8	1,665.3	1,755.2	2.276.5

Source: U.S.S.R. Foreign Trade Statistics/Moscow.

Table IX. Soviet Crude Petroleum and Products Supplied to Eastern Europe

In 000 rubles

Country	1983	1984	1985
Bulgaria	1,784,757	2,020,887	2,211,090
Czechoslovakia	2,433,526	2,746,953	2,924,466
East Germany	2,740,140	3,124,839	3,106,406
Hungary	1,156,062	1,396,398	1,476,068
Poland	2,185,268	2,520,403	2,653,655
Romania	185,201	283,596	388,533

Source: U.S.S.R. Foreign Trade Statistics/Moscow.

envisaged on this topic, it was generally expected that the question of farm subsidies and other protective measures that formed the cornerstone of EC and U.S. farm policies would be on the agenda for negotiation.

The question of trade in services—banking, telecommunications, construction, etc.—became part of the agenda at the insistence of the U.S. and in the face of opposition from a number of less developed countries. They believed that competition from the more developed countries could prejudice the profitable growth of their service sector. There was some optimism over the acceptance of the need to eliminate trade restrictions not compatible with GATT rules during the negotiating period, although there were differing views as to whether this would encompass such arrangements as multilateral export restraint schemes, most of which were against the letter of the GATT rules.

A few months after the Uruguay statement, detailed negotiations began in Geneva. They were widely expected to be prolonged and difficult, with many of the parties attempting to restrict or redefine the scope of the agreed-upon outline agenda to suit their interests. Nevertheless, most observers believed that GATT members took a large step forward in accepting that the principles of, and framework for, free trade needed to be strengthened and enlarged in a structural way in place of the previous tinkering with the rules.

INTERNATIONAL EXCHANGE AND PAYMENTS

During 1986 the international financial scene was characterized by little or no improvement in the problem of world debt, a failure to reduce the large international payment imbalances, and a sharp divergence of views among the major financial powers on the best way of dealing with these and related difficulties. On the positive side, however, there was sufficient international cooperation to manage the problem of world debt and prevent any major debt-related upheavals for the principal debtor countries and the world financial system. Thus, protectionist sentiments in the U.S. did not strengthen significantly, and the larger advanced countries moved a little closer to a greater degree of multilateral surveillance of their economies with a view to providing advance indications of developments that could lead to stresses and strains for the world financial system.

Despite the strong—and at times even acrimonious—disagreements on the most appropriate national and international measures to deal with the question of imbalances, a pronounced fall in interest rates as well as an orderly realignment of exchange rates in the right direction took place during the year. As a result, there was—toward the end of the year—widespread, if cautious, hope of some improvement in the situation during 1987 and beyond.

As in 1985, the centrepiece of the imbalance in international payments was the huge deficit built up by the U.S. and the large, and rapidly increasing, surpluses accumulated by Japan and West Germany. During the year the external value of the dollar underwent a significant depreciation, especially in terms of the Deutsche Mark and the Japanese yen. Although this exerted a modest positive influence on the volume of U.S. net exports (exports less imports), the change was not sufficiently large to offset the adverse effect of the weaker U.S. currency on the dollar value of exports and imports.

As a result, the U.S. current account deficit rose even further; by the end of the year it was forecast to reach a total of some $130 billion, some 10% more than in 1985. Since exchange-rate adjustments rarely produced the desired effect on the balance of payments without a considerable time lag, this was not regarded as unduly disappointing, although U.S. policymakers argued that the surplus countries—principally Japan and West Germany—should have done more to promote economic growth and thereby increase their propensity to import. Although the Tokyo government announced some timid business-boosting measures in early November, partial figures suggested that for 1986 as a whole Japanese economic growth would be considerably weaker than in the preceding year and that the increase in net volume imports would be fairly limited. Given the stronger yen, which had the effect of inflating the dollar value of the trade surplus, Japan's current account surplus rose from $50 billion in 1985 to an estimated $80 billion. West Germany experienced a similar scenario; despite a modest acceleration in economic growth, its current account surplus was heading for a twofold increase to approximately $26 billion.

Except for a few countries, including the U.K. and Canada, most other OECD countries improved their balance of payments positions. In fact, the OECD area as a whole was thought to have reduced its 1985 current account deficit of $57 billion to about $10 billion in 1986. In part this was a reflection of the worsening performance of the less developed countries. This was in line with the trend for 1985, but in 1986 the weakness of world trade was not

© STEVEN TURTIL—ROTHCO

among the factors responsible. In fact, growth in the volume of world trade accelerated from 3 to around 4%, but any benefits from this were offset by a further deterioration in the terms of trade for less developed countries. Oil-exporting countries suffered most; in the face of a fall of about 40% in the price of oil, their current account deficit rose from $7 billion in 1985 to an estimated $50 billion. In contrast, the position of non-oil-producing countries improved modestly from a deficit of $27 billion to about $20 billion.

In regard to exchange rates, the most important development was the weakening in the external value of the dollar. The U.S. currency was already falling in value in 1985, and the agreement (in September of that year) among the U.S., the U.K., Japan, West Germany, and France to accelerate this process ensured a sustained downward trend to late 1986. Thus, by late November the average trade-weighted value of the dollar was 13% lower than it had been in early January. The biggest falls were recorded against the Japanese yen and the Deutsche Mark. Thus, the yen–dollar rate stood at 202.6 yen per $1 at the beginning of the year, but by November it was down to 164 yen, representing a depreciation of the dollar of nearly 20%. During the same period, the dollar–Deutsche Mark rate fell by about 19%, but—following a period of weakness during the first half of the year—the rate against sterling recovered and by early November was marginally above that recorded at the start of the year.

Despite a sustained weakness against the yen and the Deutsche Mark, the average trade-weighted value of sterling dropped only modestly in the early months of 1986 and then recovered quite sharply during the spring. However, largely because of a deteriorating balance of payments performance, accompanied by growing concern about the effect of the sluggish oil prices on the trend of foreign exchange receipts, sterling came under considerable pressure from mid-1986 onward. This led to a rapid fall in its overseas value, although the downward trend was arrested in mid-October as a result of heavy support operations by the Bank of England and an increase of one percentage point in the bank rate. At about this time sterling also received some assistance from the efforts of the Organization of Petroleum Exporting Countries (OPEC) to underpin oil prices. Nevertheless, in comparison with the start of the year, the currency remained weak, with its trade-weighted value some 12% below that recorded in early January.

As was normally the case, currencies within the EMS were relatively stable. However, a wide-ranging realignment took place in April, with a 3% devaluation of the French franc accompanied by a revaluation of 3% for the Deutsche Mark and the Dutch guilder and one of 1% for the Danish and Belgian currencies. The Italian lira, which had been devalued by 6% in June 1985, and the Irish punt were not affected on that occasion, but in August the Irish government was forced to implement a downward adjustment of 8%. From the middle of the year onward, the EMS came under considerable pressure, largely because of the strength of the Deutsche Mark against the dollar, which necessitated large-scale intervention by European central banks to defend the central parities of the weaker European currencies. Even so, at times the French franc traded below its central rate against the Deutsche Mark. Britain was pressed strongly by its European partners to join the EMS, but—although there were signs of some weakening in the U.K.'s opposition to membership—there were no indications of an early change in existing policy.

As discussed above, despite the fall in the external value of the dollar, the U.S. trade and current account deficit did not improve during 1986. Even allowing for the inevitable time lag between exchange rate and balance of payments adjustments, this was regarded as somewhat disappointing and led to serious disagreements between the U.S. and the principal surplus countries. On the one hand, the U.S. argued that the lack of sufficient progress in cutting back its external deficit was partly due to the slow growth in the Japanese and West German economies, resulting in weak import demand. For their part, the Japanese and West German governments argued that the lack of progress was due to structural problems in the U.S. economy and the failure of the U.S. administration to live up to earlier undertakings to implement a significant cut in the nation's large budget deficit. Faced with Japanese and West German unwillingness to boost their economies, the U.S. declared its intention to push down the value of the dollar even further. This caused considerable concern in Europe, partly because of the effect of such a move on its export competitiveness and because it was feared that this could lead to an uncontrolled fall in the value of the U.S. currency with potentially harmful effects for the U.S. and the world economies.

These disagreements, which created an underlying feeling of uncertainty in world financial markets for much of the year, dominated the deliberations of the annual meetings of the World Bank and the International Monetary Fund (IMF) in late September. However, unlike a year earlier, when the G5 group (U.S., U.K., Japan, West Germany, and France) agreed to work for an orderly depreciation of the dollar, no clear agreement on the fundamental policy issues emerged, although there was some meeting of minds on the need to play down the differences between the U.S. and the surplus countries. Following this, Japan and the U.S. reached a bilateral accord involving a 0.5-percentage-point reduction in the Bank of Japan's discount rate (regarded as a modest gesture toward providing some stimulus to the sluggish Japanese economy) and an agreement by the U.S. not to encourage a further fall in the dollar. As a result, the dollar strengthened marginally, reaching 163 yen in early November, as against 154 yen three weeks earlier.

At the same time, the IMF also attempted to pour oil on troubled waters. In a relatively optimistic annual report, it spoke encouragingly of the positive effects of joint monitoring of economic developments in member countries agreed to at the summer economic summit held in Tokyo and argued that the existing pattern of exchange rates was broadly sustainable. The report also expressed optimism about the strengthening of world economic growth during the second half of 1986 and hinted at closer collaboration with the World Bank in dealing with the problems of debtor countries.

World interest rates during 1986 were on a steady downward trend. This was the consequence of an absence of serious inflationary pressures, which made a more relaxed monetary policy possible, as well as some concern about the possible slowdown in economic growth—especially during the first half of the year—which made interest rate cuts highly desirable. The trend was broadly similar in OECD members, although the timing, the extent, and the reasons for the rate reductions varied widely from country to country. The first nation to cut its official discount rate was Japan; a reduction there of 0.5 percentage point to 4.5% in January was followed—partly in response to sluggish domestic demand and U.S. pressure—by further downward adjustments that brought the rate to 3% by late October. The U.S. Federal Reserve Bank followed suit with a reduction from 7.5 to 7% in March; concern about the tempo of economic growth and the desire to accelerate the depreciation of the dollar gave rise to a quick succession of subsequent cuts, bringing the discount rate to 5% by October. West Germany also started well and implemented a reduction from 4 to 3.5% in April but—despite strong U.S. and European pressure—proved unwilling to go further. In contrast, a rapid fall in the bank rate from 12.5 to 10% took place in the U.K. between January and August, but—faced with strong pressure on sterling in subsequent months—the Bank of England reluctantly raised the rate to 11% in October. Rates were also falling in other European countries; the principal exception was France, where exchange-rate worries kept the official discount rate at 9.5%.

Falling interest rates provided some relief for countries with large foreign debts. However, in spite of this and the various international efforts and plans to reschedule debts and provide additional credit, the underlying problem of world indebtedness remained as serious as ever. The 1985 Baker Plan (after U.S. Secretary of the Treasury James Baker), aimed at providing large amounts of additional credit, did not find adequate support among world bankers. The weakness of oil prices hit oil-producing debtors, while a generally indifferent trade and payments performance created serious difficulties for other less developed countries. The only mildly satisfactory feature of the year was that governments and financial institutions were successful in averting any major debt-related upheavals in the economies of debtor countries and the international banking system. The principal achievement was the new support scheme negotiated for Mexico, which suffered a spectacular deterioration of its foreign earnings because of weak oil prices. The scheme stretched out some $44 billion of previously rescheduled debts to 20 years, free of interest for the first 7 years. It also provided new credits of $12 billion—$6 billion from the IMF and other official sources and $6 billion from the world banking system at a comparatively low interest rate, less than one percentage point above the London Interbank Offered Rate (LIBOR). In a departure from usual practice, the agreement also provided for additional help to cushion Mexico against adverse economic developments; there would be a further credit of $1.2 billion if the oil price fell below $9 per barrel for three months and one of up to $500 million if the country's official growth targets were not met.

While the Mexican agreement was praised for its ingenuity, it also generated considerable concern. During the year more and more debtor countries had been hardening their approach to debt, repayments, and new lines of credit, and it was believed that the deal with Mexico would encourage this trend. Peru, which refused to meet its obligations in 1985, continued to take a hard line in 1986 and was declared ineligible for further funds by the IMF. Argentina had also begun to press for lower interest rates on its foreign debt, while Brazil, which had a relatively strong foreign exchange position, was pressing for a limitation of debt-service payments to 2.5% of GDP.

In commercial banking circles it was widely believed that the relatively "soft" (and, from the bankers' point of view, none too attractive) provisions of the Mexico package would encourage debtor militancy, putting increasing pressure on creditors to extend additional loans just to ensure that interest payments were maintained, rather than bringing about an improvement in the underlying situation. It was, therefore, widely predicted that commercial banks, many of which already had large loan exposures, would become increasingly reluctant to take part in rescue packages, putting an increasing share of this burden on creditor governments and official banks. (IEIS)

This article updates the *Macropædia* articles BANKS AND BANKING; ECONOMIC GROWTH AND PLANNING; GOVERNMENT FINANCE; INTERNATIONAL TRADE.

STOCK EXCHANGES

Stock exchanges throughout the world generally experienced broad-based gains in 1986, while international commodity price indexes were generally lower. Sixteen of the world's 18 major stock price indexes were higher at the end of 1986 than at the end of 1985 (TABLE X). In markets for individual commodities, plunging oil prices and sharply higher quotations for platinum and gold held the spotlight.

Stock prices on average moved higher during the first half of 1986 in the expectation that the worldwide economic recovery would gather speed. The impressive advance came in response to a convergence of a number of factors, all of which were widely regarded as extremely favourable for financial markets. Relatively low inflation, high real interest rates, expansionary monetary policy, and excess capacity and supply together created an extremely favourable environment for financial assets. While falling inflation and declining interest rates prevailed for the better part of 1986, the pace of economic growth expanded at a moderate rate. As a result, the real inflation-adjusted rate of return on fixed-income securities, that is, the interest rate minus the inflation rate, remained at relatively high levels, and the outlook on corporate profits and dividends was extremely positive. Moreover, low interest rates tend to sustain economic expansion by reducing corporate borrowing costs, thereby promoting capital investment. In addition, governments of the industrial West continued to favour free-market solutions to economic problems, including encouraging their citizens to invest in equity securities by privatizing state-owned companies. In such an environment equity securities are much more attractive than alternative investments.

However, the rise in stock prices stalled when investors realized that national disparities among the major industrialized countries would postpone higher real growth rates and lower interest rates. The reluctance of West Germany or Japan to serve as the world's locomotive for faster economic growth meant that the initially envisioned gains in corporate profits and dividends would not materialize and that equity securities, as a result of their impressive appreciation, were no longer at bargain levels. Moreover, the persistence of slow worldwide economic growth, the lack of a solid response to falling interest rates, and the sharp decline in the value of the U.S. dollar versus the Deutsche Mark and the Japanese yen raised investor fears that the drop in interest rates would not produce real investment in new plant and business equipment as much as it would stimulate the refinancing of old investments at more favourable rates. Fears were also expressed that the currency shifts in the yen and the Deutsche Mark relative to the dollar slowed real growth of GDP in the affected countries, while growth was accelerating in other countries where there had been little, if any, changes in exchange rates relative to the dollar.

In short, trends in international capital markets toward the end of 1986 seemed predicated on the belief that the rising values in equity securities had created enormous liquidity to finance an eventual upturn in real economic activity and that the new creditor nations of Europe and the Far East could assume the international responsibility that went with their growing trade surpluses. Investors also seemed confident that ways would be found to overcome the problems associated with the growing threat of protectionism and the international debt-service burdens of the

In Beijing (Peking) the New York Stock Exchange vice-chairman, Richard Shinn, and the People's Bank of China vice-governor, Liu Hongru (Liu Hung-ju), shake hands after signing an agreement for the exchange of experts for educational and training purposes.
AP/WIDE WORLD

less developed countries. At the same time, the basic ingredients that had created the favourable environment for financial assets since the end of world recession in 1982 were still very much in place, offering the prospect that the worldwide bull market in equity securities would continue into 1987. (ROBERT H. TRIGG)

United States. The bull market, which began in August 1982, continued into 1986 with an almost uninterrupted rise in stock prices during the first half of the year. The second half was marked by considerable uncertainty due to insider-trading scandals, continuing economic sluggishness, and poor corporate earnings. The Dow Jones Industrial Average finished the year up 22.58%, at 1,895.95. This was its fifth year-to-year gain in as many years. The major price increases occurred largely in blue-chip issues, while second-tier stocks, which did well in the first half of 1986, fell off the pace later in the year. The DJIA scored its biggest one-day gain for the year on March 11 with a climb of 43.10 points. The index set a record for a one-day loss when it dropped 86.61 points on September 11. The market slowly recovered from the historic plunge despite year-end selling by investors trying to lock in gains prior to the capital gains tax increase scheduled for 1987. Bonds did well despite the dark cloud cast on the "junk bond" market by the Ivan Boesky scandal. High-grade corporate and government issues were buoyed by good inflation reports and the apparent progress in reducing budget deficits. The municipal bond sector fared relatively poorly, as new issues fell 28% to $143.5 billion from the 1985 figure.

Investors were optimistic despite a sluggish economy and disappointing corporate profits. They focused on plunging interest rates, all but nonexistent inflation, and the still falling U.S. dollar, which seemed to promise a strengthening of the competitive posture of many U.S. businesses both overseas and at home. There were concerns about the new tax law, which would raise capital gains rates, and there was uncertainty about how the changing tax environment would affect corporate earnings. At the year's end there were concerns about the surge in oil prices, the dollar's continued slump in foreign-exchange markets, and inflation. Net foreign purchases of U.S. securities rose sharply during 1986. Purchases of U.S. government securities rose to $68.4 billion in 1986, up from $24.8 billion in 1985, while foreign investments in equities jumped from $5 billion in 1985 to $20 billion in 1986, a 300% increase.

Major stock-market developments included record merger, acquisition, buy-out, and divestiture activity; the expansion of mortgage-backed securities volume; increased program trading; insider trading scandals; the entry by banks into the securities field; and major foreign investments in U.S. securities. A record $267 billion in securities were issued to finance mergers, acquisitions, and leveraged buy-outs in 1986, compared with $235 billion the year before. The year's biggest deals were the acquisition of RCA by General Electric for $6.4 billion, of Beatrice by Kohlberg Kravis Roberts for $6.2 billion, and of Safeway Stores by Kohlberg Kravis Roberts for $5.3 billion. The volume of issues backed by mortgages and other assets in 1986 reached $69.6 billion, three times the corresponding figure for 1985. Most of the obligations backed by mortgages were so-called arbitrage issues, in which investment bankers purchase mortgages, package them into securities, and then issue the securities themselves, through subsidiaries. Twelve of the 30 largest debt offerings in 1986 were backed by mortgage loans.

Sophisticated computerized program trading by large institutions resulted in automatic "sell" signals periodically during 1986. This exacerbated the instability of the market and was partly to blame for triggering the DJIA's record one-day decline in September.

During May Dennis Levine, a managing director of Drexel Burnham Lambert, Inc., the dominant firm in the junk bond field with a 45% market share, was charged with using private information to reap at least $12.6 million in profits. It was the largest insider trading action ever brought by the SEC to that time. In November Ivan Boesky, a prominent arbitrageur and merger stock speculator, admitted to offering bribes for secret stock tips and touched off the largest insider trading inquiry in history. (*See* WORLD AFFAIRS [North America]: *United States.*)

The federal courts recognized the rights of banks to sell commercial paper and some classes of securities through subsidiaries during 1986, and a number of major banks teamed with mutual fund groups to market a broader spectrum of financial products. During the year the dollar lost 21% of its value against the West German and Japanese currencies. Against this background foreign investors bought more than $13.4 billion worth of U.S. stocks in the first half of the year, dwarfing the record of $5,810,000,000 in

(continued on page 195)

Privatization—An Emerging Force

BY JOHN ANDREWS

The selling of state assets had become a subject of constant debate by 1986. Over 50 governments around the world had become practitioners of "privatization," ranging from the U.K., selling utilities such as the gas monopoly, to Malaysia, selling shares in its airline. Even Communist China and Cuba were selling public housing units to their tenants. But the popularity of privatization did little to still the controversy that surrounded it. Proponents of privatization argue that it creates economic efficiency and dynamism by freeing market forces from the "dead hand" of government. In that spirit, U.S. Pres. Ronald Reagan claimed: "In the equation of real world economics, individual initiative rises as rigid government control declines." On the other side, opponents of privatization, mainly trade unionists, argue that it transfers the wealth of the people as a whole to the ownership of a shareholding minority—and does so at a price that can never compensate for the loss of the asset. Cynics believe the practice to be a shortsighted device of governments to raise easy money for their current spending.

Two factors confuse any evaluation of privatization. One is timing: if state assets are sold during a period of economic recession, they will inevitably perform well during a subsequent economic recovery; accordingly, any proper test of their performance in the private sector will have to await another downturn of the economic cycle. The second factor concerns definition: in the U.K. privatization means the transfer of at least 50% of a state asset—and thereby its control—to the private sector; elsewhere it may mean any divestment, however small, of the state's holdings.

The British Experience. Regardless of the academic debate, privatization in the first half of the 1980s led to the greatest ever peacetime transfer of resources between governments and their private citizens. In the lead was Prime Minister Margaret Thatcher's Conservative government in the U.K. In the belief that state industries had a natural tendency to soak up subsidies, the Conservatives used state asset sales to cut the role of government in the economy. The state industries' share of gross domestic product—10% when Thatcher came to power in 1979—had almost halved by late 1986.

Beginning in February 1981, when 51.6% of British Aerospace was sold for £48 million, the state by the end of 1986 had progressively surrendered its controlling presence in aerospace, telecommunications, and energy. With the sale of British Gas in November–December 1986 raising nearly £5,600 million, the British Treasury would have amassed some £25,000 million from asset sales, including public housing to tenants. Planned sales of other assets such as British Airways and the Rolls-Royce aero-engine company, the possible sale of the water industry, and the potential to sell off minority state holdings in companies already privatized could, in theory, add another £19,000 million to the Treasury's receipts.

The Trend Away from Nationalization. Such arithmetic intrigued treasuries throughout the world. In Western industrialized countries nationalization carried out in the years after World War II had been generally discredited by the 1970s. Rather than increasing industrial efficiency by eliminating wasteful competition, nationalization had facilitated the survival of inefficient monopolies through increased state subsidies. In 1979–80, for example, subsidies to the U.K.'s rail, coal, and steel industries amounted to £1,800 million, representing a threefold increase over a decade. Various attempts to extract greater efficiency from state industries, with or without competition, all failed. State-owned automobile companies in the U.K. and France suffered enormous losses—but to match the efficiency of their private-sector competitors would have involved shedding labour or closing factories at a rate deemed to be politically or socially unacceptable.

Much the same held true for poorer countries, where the state tended to play a greater role. The net losses of Turkey's public enterprises equaled 3.9% of the country's gross domestic product (GDP) in 1977–79. The current and capital account deficits of Thailand's state enterprises amounted to approximately 3.5% of GDP in 1986, and their foreign borrowings took up about two-thirds of the country's public external debt.

The solution looks simple: a government sells its state assets, cuts public spending with its inflationary tendencies, and sheds the burden of subsidizing inefficiencies. But asset sales tend to finance rather than cut public spending—and the potential for a government to spend beyond its means remains. Furthermore, it may be difficult to find buyers. It is also noteworthy that in many less developed countries assets were nationalized originally to stop unscrupulous exploitation by their private-sector owners—privatization could lead to a resumption of this practice.

Nevertheless, by 1986 privatization had become fashionable. There were two reasons: even in the richest countries increasing subsidies to state enterprises could not be sustained; and in the poor countries, aid from the developed world was being tied to privatization to help stimulate economies and make them less dependent on aid.

Obstacles to Privatization. To conclude a satisfactory sale, certain conditions must exist, and these are more prevalent in some countries than in others. At one level, this is simply a question of having the right kind of expertise; an array of merchant banking and accounting skills is needed to prepare an honest and comprehensive sales prospectus, and these skills are much more available in the City of London or on New York City's Wall Street than in Barbados or Zambia.

These skills may be imported, but a more basic requirement is the capital, and it is this that sets Western Europe, Japan, and North America apart from the rest of the non-Communist world. Stock markets in less developed countries are tiny and cannot afford a reasonable price for an international airline or a brand-new steel plant. Wider share ownership involving individuals is a key argument for privatization, but what happens if the individuals have insufficient money?

Disparities in market capitalization inevitably influence the scale of a privatization. Even in Western Europe most exchanges are puny; France's stock market capitalization is only about 13% of its GDP, compared with 50% or more

John Andrews, a journalist specializing in privatization, is Southeast Asia bureau chief for The Economist, *London.*

in the U.S. and Japan. At the end of October 1986 Japan announced plans to sell half its telecommunications giant, Nippon Telegraph & Telephone (NTT), over four years, beginning late in 1986. The sale valued NTT at a massive $116 billion—still only about 5% of the capitalization of the Tokyo Stock Exchange. Despite the enormous sums involved in selling off NTT and in the planned sales of the state airline, railway company, and tobacco monopoly, there was no doubt that Japanese investors had the funds to purchase.

By contrast, Malaysia's government, which began to "privatize" the Malaysian Airline System (MAS) in December 1985, still retained 55% of the airline after a second share offering in October 1986. And that offering, because of the shallowness of the local market, was placed entirely with foreign investors in London, Tokyo, New York, Hong Kong, and Brunei. Even in Singapore, with a relatively well-developed stock market, the state retained 63% in Singapore Airlines. Although Singapore's plans involved heavy privatization, the government recognized that the transfer of the state's holdings in some 57 corporations had to be phased to prevent a crash in the stock market.

Lack of funds is only one obstacle to privatization in the third world. Others are nationalism, incompetence, and corruption. In the Philippines the government identified for privatization 396 state-owned companies with a book value of $7 billion—equal to roughly one-quarter of the country's foreign debt. Yet virtually no progress was made in 1986 as interested buyers, both foreign and Filipino, found it almost impossible even to get a price quoted to them. Bangladesh's program of denationalizing jute mills was similarly marred by corruption.

Such imperfections should not, however, obscure the genuine benefits of privatization. Early evidence from the U.K. showed that the very prospect encouraged managements—and work forces—to perform better. This was true of British Airways, the National Freight Consortium, and Jaguar cars. Influenced by the U.K. experience, the French government of Prime Minister Jacques Chirac in 1986 announced the denationalization of some 65 insurance companies, banks, and industrial enterprises, beginning with the Paribas banking group, the Saint-Gobain glass company, and the Assurances Générales de France insurance group.

Finally, any judgment of privatization must rest on a pragmatic view of corporate balance sheets. This is not just because practice is the only proof worth having but also because the theorists of privatization in the year or so up to 1986 gave ground to political expediency. Early dogma on privatization held that it should be used to foster competition, which implied that any public-sector monopoly ought to be broken up into competing parts, or otherwise provided with competition, before privatization. But investors will pay more for a share in a monopoly, and governments faced with the choice of competition or more money favour the latter. This was demonstrated by the U.K. government's sale of British Gas. The defense is that some monopolies such as gas distribution are "natural," in that competition would prevent economies of scale at cost to the consumer. It is further argued that an independently regulated private-sector monopoly is less likely to exploit consumers than a state-owned monopoly vulnerable to political whims.

The fact that the arguments persist, and that most "privatizations" around the world still involve heavy state control of the assets, suggests that there is no certain trend in the longer term.

(continued from page 193)

1981. Salomon Brothers, Inc., was the leading underwriter for U.S corporations in 1986 for the fourth straight year. The firm was lead manager for $53.6 billion of offerings for U.S issuers.

There were a number of disappointments in the economy during 1986 that resulted in downward pressure on interest rates. Real GNP grew at a low rate; international trade balances were negative; and the 1986 U.S. budget deficit at $221 billion was the highest in history. Interest rates declined fairly steadily throughout the year. The Federal Funds rate fell from a peak of nearly 9% in January 1986 to a low of 5.5% by the year's end. The Federal Reserve cut the discount rate four times during 1986 to a low of 5.5% in August, the lowest level in nine years. Treasury bill rates continued to decline during the year from about 7 to 6.5%; government bond yields likewise declined from about 9 to 7%. The prime rate dropped from 9.5% in January to 7.5% by the end of the year. From February to mid-April bond prices rallied sharply, fueled by an unexpected drop in oil prices. This was followed by $8\frac{1}{2}$ months of seesawing, with Treasury bond yields locked in a trading range of 7.125 to 8%.

Trading volume on the New York Stock Exchange set new daily records in 1986, with a turnover on December 19 of 244.7 million shares. For the year turnover was 35,680,016,341 shares, up 29.6% from the corresponding figure of 27,510,706,353 in 1985. The most heavily traded share issues were AT&T, 528,686,700; USX, 435,055,-

New York Stock Exchange Common Stock Index Closing Prices
Stock prices (Dec. 31, 1965 = 50)

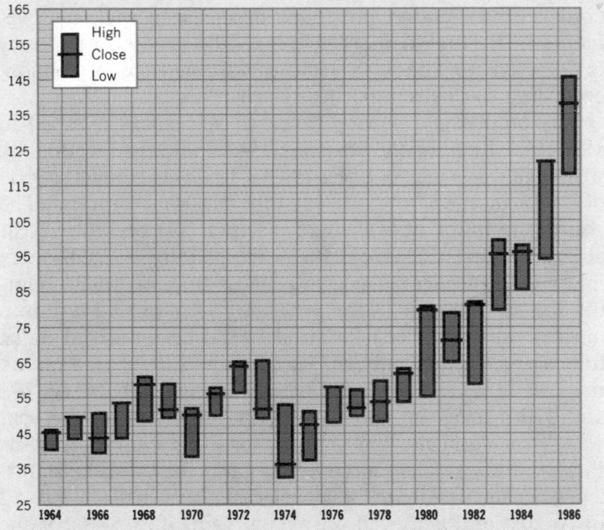

Number of shares sold
In millions of shares

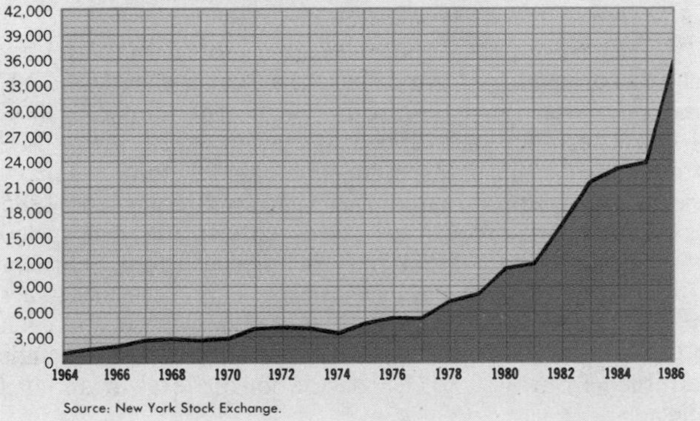

Source: New York Stock Exchange.

300; IBM, 407,602,900; Mobil, 262,651,800; and Exxon, 241,345,800. There were 1,597 advances, 699 declines, 22 unchanged, and 2,318 issues traded on the NYSE in 1986. Bond volume was $10,475,399,000 in 1986, up 15.7% from the 1985 level of $9,046,452,000. A seat on the New York Stock Exchange sold for a record price of $600,000 in December 1986. Seats were being quoted at $530,000 bid and $750,000 offered at the year's end.

On the American Stock Exchange stock turnover was 2,978,540,000, up 41.7% from the 1985 figure of 2,100,-860,000. There were 556 advances, 380 declines, 18 stocks unchanged, and 954 issues traded in 1986. The Amex Index gained 6.96% in 1986, compared with the performance of the NYSE Composite Index, which rose by 13.98%. Bond sales on the Amex were $810,264,000, up 25.5% from 1985. Trading in the over-the-counter markets rose sharply in 1986, with more than 70,000,000,000 shares traded, compared with about 50,000,000,000 in 1985. Nasdaq volume totaled 26,658,897,000 shares, compared with 19,281,412,800 the previous year, a gain of 38.2%. The Nasdaq OTC composite index was up 7.36% for the year. Blue chip stocks generally did better in 1986 than did the second-tier offerings.

Sales of stock, bond, and income mutual funds nearly doubled in 1986, reaching an estimated $211 billion. This compared with a record $114 billion in sales in 1985. Among all funds sales of international funds showed the sharpest increase, rising about 300% to an estimated $7.6 billion from $1.9 billion in 1985. Total net assets of all funds were $732 billion by the end of the year, compared with $495 billion at the start of 1986. Among the fastest growing bond market investment vehicles in 1986 were "index funds," bond portfolios designed to match movements in the broad market index. The amount of money in indexed portfolios in 1986 quadrupled to $50 billion, according to one report.

The Standard & Poor's Index of 500 stocks climbed in 1986. The high for the year was 254.00 and the low 203.49, with a gain for the year of 14.62%. This was below the gain of 26.3% in 1985 but continued the bull-market trend. The composite index of 500 shares (TABLE XI) began the year at 208.19, up 21.3% from the corresponding 1985 January figure, and rose irregularly to peak in June at 245.30. During the second half of the year the index moved within a narrow range between 237 and 245. The industrial index followed a similar pattern, rising from 230.37 in January to peak at 274.55 in June before seesawing between 263 and 270 during the rest of the year. The high for the year was 282.77 and the low 224.88, for a net gain of 15.08%. Public utility stocks scored better gains than did the industrials. From a January level of 92.06 they rose to 118.53 in August and achieved an overall gain of 20.52% for the year. Railroad stocks were laggards. At 142.49 in January, well above the 111.65 level of a year earlier, they peaked in March at 156.43 before trending downward.

U.S. government bond yields in 1986 (TABLE XII) declined consistently from 1985. At a January level of 9.51, the index was down 15% from the corresponding month of 1985. The index had dipped to 7.59 by April, down 34% from April 1985. This index fluctuated within a narrow range during the remainder of 1986, well below the 1985 levels. A sharp drop in oil prices early in the year fueled the biggest bond market rally in history. From February 10 to April 16, some actively traded U.S. Treasury issues soared more than 26 points, more than $260 for each $1,000 face amount. The yield on 30-year Treasury bonds tumbled from 9.29 to 7.11%, the lowest level in about a decade.

U.S. corporate bond yields (TABLE XIII) also were at lower levels during 1986 in comparison with 1985. In January the index was at 10.05, compared with 12.08 the year before. The yield dipped to 8.79 by April before rising in June and then moving in an irregular pattern below 9% during the remainder of the year.

The options markets were confronted with off-board trading, the development of new contracts, and movement toward round-the-clock operations during 1986. The industry was also concerned with addressing the stock price volatility problem caused by the "triple witching hour," the simultaneous quarterly expiration of stock index futures, options, and individual stock options. The Chicago Mercantile Exchange proposed moving the expiration to the opening of trading, rather than the close, on quarterly witching hour days. Total futures trading volume was estimated at 155 million contracts in 1985 and 170 million in 1986. These figures included interest rate, foreign currency, and stock index futures.

Canada. Canadian stock markets performed well in 1986 despite a decline in issues related to energy. Gains were particularly strong for stocks concerned with paper and forest products, gold, consumer products, and real estate and construction companies. Oil and gas, metals and minerals, and most bank stocks declined.

The Toronto Stock Exchange's composite index, which was dominated by mining and energy stocks, rose only 5.7% in 1986. From a level of 2,870 in January the index dipped to a low of 2,750 in February and then climbed steeply to a high of 3,125 in April before embarking on a zigzag course to end the year at 3,066.18. Volume on the TSE rose 53.1% during the year to 4,900,000,000 shares with a value of $63.6 billion, up 52.2%. The paper and forest products index led other industry sectors, rising 56% as pulp and lumber price increases drove up industry earn-

New York Stock Exchange Composite Index, 1986
Stock prices (Dec. 31, 1965 = 50)

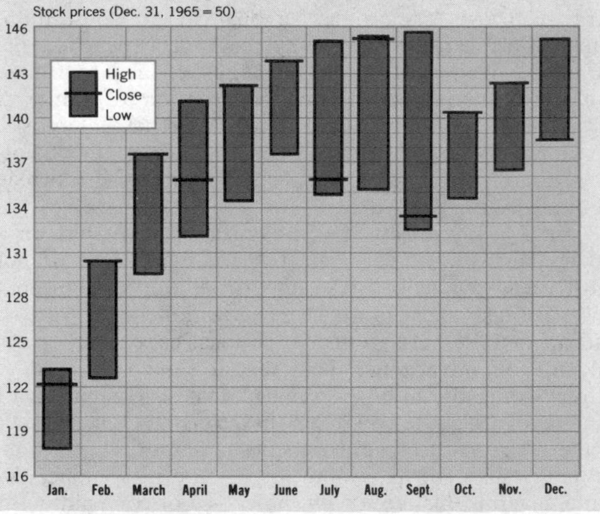

Average daily share volume
In thousands of shares

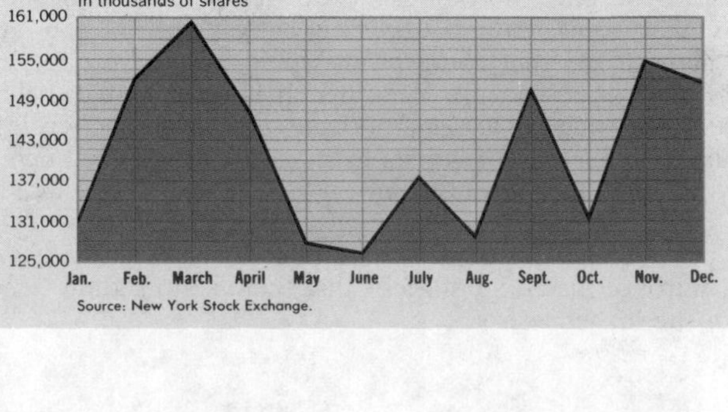

Source: New York Stock Exchange.

ings. The real estate and construction industry index had a record year, rising 37% on a surge in housing sales, particularly in Ontario. Activity on the Montreal Stock Exchange also set records. Volume rose 63% to 1,100,000,000 shares, and the value of shares traded increased 51% to $16 billion. But Montreal's Market Portfolio Index, at 1,533.45, was up only 3.5% from the end of 1985. The Vancouver Stock Exchange index rose 5.5% to 1,353.63 as new records were set in both trading volume and value.

Canadian investor expectations during the year were affected by disappointments that included weak economic growth, a growing deficit on current account, and a major budget deficit. There was no improvement in the rate of inflation, with the consumer price index at 4.4% in October 1986, the same as in December 1985.

Interest rates did not conform to the U.S. pattern. The Canadian prime rate began 1986 at 10% but climbed sharply during the first quarter of the year to a high of 13% before drifting down to end the year just below 10% once more. The T-bill rate climbed in the early months of the year from 9 to 11.5% in February and then fell steadily to lower levels by May.

Canadian companies followed those in the U.S. by engaging in greater takeover activity in 1986, triggering disputes over rights of voting and nonvoting shareholders. The internationalization of the securities markets was recognized with Ontario planning to enhance Toronto's role in international markets by allowing foreign firms to own up to 100% of a Canadian securities firm over time.

(IRVING PFEFFER)

Western Europe. Stock markets in Europe were generally strong during 1986. The five largest industrialized countries—Great Britain, West Germany, France, Italy, and Spain—all experienced higher prices. Among the smaller countries Austria, Sweden, and Belgium enjoyed extremely bullish markets, while more modest plus signs prevailed in The Netherlands. On the bearish side Switzerland was able to post only a fractional gain over the year, while lower stock prices were recorded in Denmark and Norway.

For the seventh year in a row the broad trend of stock prices in Great Britain was bullish. The *Financial Times* index of 30 industrial issues traded on the London Stock Exchange was up 16%. The index reached an all-time high on April 3, while the year's low was recorded January 14.

A major event during the year was the celebrated "Big Bang," which deregulated the London securities markets to allow new competition and new technology. Fixed brokerage commissions were eliminated; prohibitions on foreign competition were lifted; and a new regulatory system for the protection of the investing public was being installed.

Weakness in stock prices began early in January as the sharp drop in oil prices raised concerns that the resulting decline in the British pound would force the Bank of England to lift interest rates to defend the currency. However, the decline in the U.S. dollar overshadowed the pound's oil-related problems and focused investor attention instead on the increased prospects for worldwide economic growth that could be expected from the fall in oil prices and interest rates.

At the beginning of April the *Financial Times* industrial share index closed above 1,400 for the first time. The subsequent decline, which lasted until early August and cut equity values nearly 13%, was largely a result of the realization that the nation's economic growth in 1986 would not reach 2.5% and that the benefits from the decline in oil prices would not come until the following year. Moreover, a shortfall of government revenues related to the decline in oil prices raised the risk that Britain's public-sector borrowing requirement would be exceeded, placing upward pressure on interest rates. A relatively mild technical rally followed through early September, but stocks then entered a new consolidation phase that carried the share price index to a level only slightly above the summer lows.

In mid-October concerns about the nation's substantial current account deficit and the threat of rising inflation led the British government to endorse a 1% increase in the base lending rate of commercial banks to 11%. In addition

Table X. Selected Major World Stock Price Indexes*

Country	1986 range† High	1986 range† Low	Year-end close 1985	Year-end close 1986	Percent change
Australia	1,473	1,011	1,002	1,473	+ 47.0
Austria	267	227	120	232	+ 93.3
Belgium	4,132	2,767	2,943	4,096	+ 39.2
Denmark	251	186	237	192	− 19.0
France	414	268	266	398	+ 49.6
West Germany	2,279	1,762	1,952	2,046	+ 4.8
Hong Kong	2,568	1,560	1,752	2,568	+ 46.6
Italy	908	455	457	723	+ 58.2
Japan	18,936	12,981	13,083	18,821	+ 43.9
Mexico	10,132	2,568	2,686	10,132	+277.2
Netherlands, The	304	234	243	273	+ 12.3
Norway	403	332	393	358	8.9
Singapore	941	563	620	891	+ 43.7
South Africa	1,420	1,019	1,165	1,416	+ 21.5
Spain	209	101	100	208	+108.0
Sweden	2,673	1,730	1,738	2,459	+ 41.5
Switzerland	626	497	588	589	+ 0.2
United Kingdom	1,426	1,094	1,131	1,314	+ 16.2

*Index numbers are rounded and limited to countries for which at least 11 months' data were available on a weekly basis.
†Based on daily closing price.
Sources: *The Economist, Financial Times, Barron's.*

Table XI. U.S. Stock Market Prices

Month	Railroads (6 stocks) 1986	Railroads (6 stocks) 1985	Industrials (400 stocks) 1986	Industrials (400 stocks) 1985	Public utilities (40 stocks) 1986	Public utilities (40 stocks) 1985	Composite (500 stocks) 1986	Composite (500 stocks) 1985
January	142.49	111.65	230.37	191.64	92.06	75.83	208.83	171.61
February	150.10	120.18	241.91	202.13	97.13	78.14	219.37	180.88
March	156.43	114.15	256.25	200.42	102.01	78.89	232.33	179.42
April	148.69	113.56	263.89	201.13	103.78	81.25	237.98	180.62
May	142.02	117.19	266.38	204.83	102.39	83.60	238.40	184.90
June	144.23	121.48	274.55	208.50	106.65	86.90	245.30	188.89
July	134.52	130.00	266.17	212.90	112.13	87.22	240.18	192.54
August	131.50	125.85	270.23	209.40	118.53	83.21	245.00	188.31
September	133.04	123.58	263.62	205.15	113.11	81.46	238.27	184.06
October	135.51	126.58	263.09	207.65	124.01	81.49	237.36	186.18
November	. . .	133.46	. . .	219.44	. . .	86.80	. . .	197.45
December	. . .	140.41	. . .	230.29	. . .	90.83	. . .	207.26

Sources: U.S. Department of Commerce, *Survey of Current Business;* Board of Governors of the Federal Reserve System, *Federal Reserve Bulletin.* Prices are Standard & Poor's monthly averages of daily closing prices, with 1941–43 = 10.

Table XII. U.S. Government Long-Term Bond Yields

Month	Yield (%) 1986	Yield (%) 1985	Month	Yield (%) 1986	Yield (%) 1985
January	9.51	11.15	July	7.86	10.51
February	9.07	11.35	August	7.72	10.59
March	8.13	11.78	September	8.08	10.67
April	7.59	11.42	October	8.04	10.56
May	8.02	10.96	November	. . .	10.08
June	8.23	10.36	December	. . .	9.60

Source: U.S. Department of Commerce, *Survey of Current Business.* Yields are for U.S. Treasury bonds that are taxable and due or callable in ten years or more.

Table XIII. U.S. Corporate Bond Yields

Month	Yield (%) 1986	Yield (%) 1985	Month	Yield (%) 1986	Yield (%) 1985
January	10.05	12.08	July	8.88	10.97
February	9.67	12.13	August	8.72	11.05
March	9.00	12.56	September	8.89	11.07
April	8.79	12.23	October	8.86	11.02
May	9.09	11.72	November	. . .	10.55
June	9.13	10.94	December	. . .	10.16

Source: U.S. Department of Commerce, *Survey of Current Business.* Yields are based on Moody's Aaa domestic corporate bond index.

to the increase in short-term interest rates, the market was hurt by the government's investigation of possible insider trading prior to corporate merger announcements. Offsetting these concerns were the success of the government's plans to sell state-owned industries and the ample liquidity that was fueling the home-building and related sectors. Consequently, considerable uncertainty prevailed among investors as to whether the long bull market would continue into 1987.

In West Germany the pace of real growth of the GDP was about 3.5%, while inflation fell to about zero for the first time since 1954. Capital spending was a major growth element, and construction contributed to real GDP growth for the first time in almost five years, thanks to lower interest rates. However, the value of the Deutsche Mark against the U.S. dollar increased approximately 21%, which acted unfavourably on West Germany's export-oriented industries. The dollar's decline relative to the Deutsche Mark was heightened by continental speculators who purchased Deutsche Marks and sold British pounds, French francs, and Italian lire, further weakening the dollar against the Deutsche Mark and increasing expectations of realignment in the EMS. As a result, stock market gains were limited by the lack of stability in foreign exchange rates, the prospect of renewed inflation, and fears that the inept political image of Chancellor Helmut Kohl's pro-business coalition government might prove fatal in the upcoming January 1987 general election. During 1986 the Commerzbank index of 60 issues traded on the Frankfurt Stock Exchange recorded a new all-time high and finished the year with a net gain of 5%.

The influence of slow, noninflationary economic recovery and the restructuring of both private and state-owned companies were especially apparent in the French stock market. Average share prices on the Paris Bourse increased nearly 50% from the end of 1985 to the end of 1986. The sharp decline in oil prices was especially beneficial to the French economy. Between the end of 1985 and mid-March, stock prices registered a gain of 22%. Prices continued to rise following the appointment of Jacques Chirac as prime minister and the unveiling of the new conservative government's economic measures to encourage growth, fight unemployment, and begin denationalizing state assets. As a result, stock prices reached a level in early May some 53% above the 1985 close.

SRJDA DJUKANOVIC—CAMERA PRESS LTD.

The BZW (Barclays de Zoete Wedd) equity floor, designed to handle business after the deregulation of the London Stock Exchange in October, is alive with people, paper, and computers. Only a year before the area was an open-air automobile parking lot.

Ivan Boesky, one of the most successful stock-market speculators in the United States, was caught in an insider-trading probe that set Wall Street abuzz. He agreed to pay $100 million in penalties and illicit profits and to give up professional stock trading.

ROBERT A. CUMINS—BLACK STAR

During the ensuing months the market dropped almost 16% owing to profit taking, poor trade deficit figures, and investor concerns that Chirac would be unable to avoid conflicts with Socialist Pres. François Mitterrand. After an announcement in September regarding the first three state-owned companies to be privatized, stock prices recovered and eventually regained all of the earlier loss. The market reached a record high on December 15 and finished the year about 4% below its all-time peak.

In Italy stock prices turned in a strong performance in 1986. After a period of hesitation the price index of shares traded on the Milan Stock Exchange rose throughout most of the year. From the end of 1985 to the end of 1986, stock prices on the average jumped 58%. This gain followed a near doubling of the index in 1985.

The stock market in Spain in 1986 was higher for the fourth consecutive year. The price index of shares traded on the Madrid Stock Exchange more than doubled during the year. Despite official unemployment of 20%, the highest in continental Europe, Prime Minister Felipe González Márquez's Socialist government was able to continue its program to modernize the fifth largest economy in Western Europe and promote job creation through industrial investment. Foreign companies, for example, increased their investment in Spanish subsidiaries by more than 100% in the first nine months of 1986.

In Belgium stock prices also followed a bullish pattern. From the end of 1985 to the end of 1986, prices on the Brussels Bourse increased 39%. Investor sentiment revealed a high degree of confidence in the ability of Prime Minister Wilfried Martens's centre-right government to bring down the huge Belgian budget deficit and establish the basis for renewed real growth.

Bourses in the Nordic nations recorded mixed results in 1986. Sweden was a star performer as average share prices rose more than 41% after rising 28% in 1985. Real GDP was expected to grow 3% in 1986, and the rate of inflation was likely to be half of what it was in 1984. As a result, interest rates plunged below 10% for the first time since 1978. In contrast, lower stock prices prevailed in Denmark (−19%) and Norway (−9%). To cope with faltering economies both nations introduced tough austerity programs, which included devaluation of their currencies and tightening credit to control fast-rising consumption.

Contrasting trends prevailed in The Netherlands and Switzerland, both of which belong to the Deutsch Mark bloc countries. The Dutch stock market in 1986 enjoyed a 15% increase in equity values. Supporting the bullish environment were relatively modest real economic growth (+2.8%), with near zero retail price inflation, and the unexpected election victory of the centre-right government, which displaced the socialist Labour Party as the nation's strongest political force.

The Swiss stock market was plagued by currency unrest in 1986. The increase in the value of the Swiss franc relative to the U.S. dollar hurt Swiss multinational stocks, which are important factors in the popular price index of the Zuřich Stock Exchange. As a result, stock prices were able to post only a fractional gain for the year as a whole.

Other Countries. For the second year in a row the stock market in Mexico enjoyed the largest increase (+277%) among the world's major indexes. In 1986 the Mexican economy was battered by plunging oil prices and soaring inflation that was expected to exceed 100%, surpassing the 98.8% of 1982. To protect themselves against declines in purchasing power and eroding asset values, Mexicans had no choice but to invest their savings in, and add to holdings of, securities traded on the Bolsa Stock Exchange.

Stock prices in Japan rose 44% in 1986, continuing the bull market that had begun near the end of 1977. The Nikkei Dow Jones average of leading industrial shares surpassed the 18,000 level in August. From its peak on August 20 the Nikkei index of shares traded on the Tokyo Stock Exchange fell nearly 15% before rebounding during the week of October 24. The depreciation of the U.S. dollar against the Japanese yen reached a record low after having completed a five-year climb to record highs early in the previous year. The gain in the value of the yen against the dollar amounted to almost 25%, on top of the 25% rise in 1985 that came after the Group of Five meeting in September of that year at which the decision was made to drive down the value of the dollar. The ensuing rally in stock prices, which recovered most of the loss, reflected investor expectations that the U.S. dollar's revaluation against the Japanese yen was completed and that the economic stimulative measures announced in September, along with the tax-reform package approved by the ruling Liberal-Democratic Party in December, would boost domestic industrial activity and reduce the nation's trade surplus with the United States and Western Europe.

Other Pacific Basin countries also experienced stock market gains about the size of Japan's. In Australia prices on the Sydney Stock Exchange gained 47% in 1986. This was the same performance as the Hang Seng index (+47%), which measures 33 stocks traded on the Hong Kong Exchange, and slightly ahead of Singapore (+44%). The pegging of currencies of the newly industrialized countries of Asia, which included Hong Kong and Singapore as well as South Korea, Taiwan, Thailand, and Malaysia, to the U.S. dollar produced strong economic growth and big gains in their competitive positions versus Japanese and European competition.

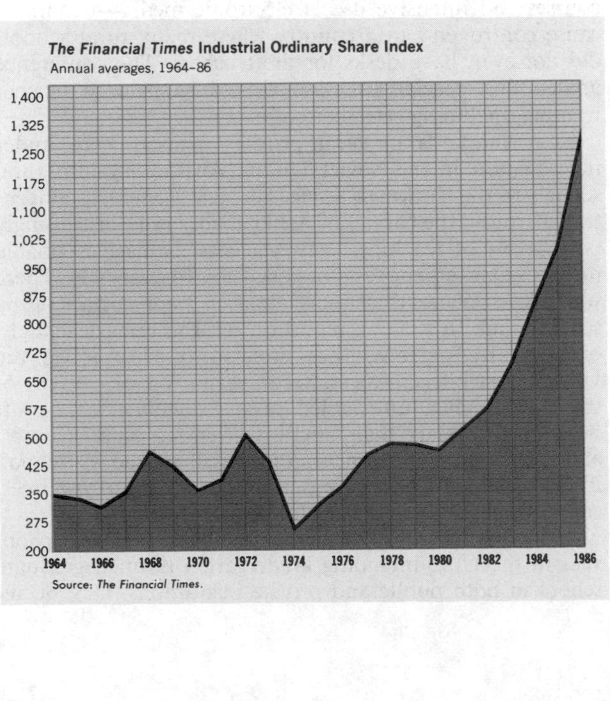

Commodity Markets. The broad trend of world commodity price indexes was generally lower in 1986, although many individual commodities experienced widely fluctuating prices. *The Economist*'s commodity price index, which measures spot prices in U.S. dollars for 28 internationally traded foodstuffs, nonfood agricultural products, and metals, fell nearly 5% from the end of 1985 to near the end of 1986.

The price of crude oil, which was not included in *The Economist*'s index, was particularly volatile. During 1986 the spot price of North Sea Brent, the barometer of European prices, fluctuated as high as $28 and as low as $9 per barrel. From the end of 1985 to the end of 1986, the cost of a barrel of European oil from the North Sea fell nearly 37%. In July oil prices reached their lowest level in 15 years. However, prices in the spot market recovered when the Organization of Petroleum Exporting Countries acted to curb production. In a series of agreements in August and December, OPEC oil ministers agreed to reduce output and return to a fixed price of $18 per barrel. Thus, as 1986 came to a close, the spot price of North Sea Brent reached $17.55 per barrel, nearly double the July low.

The two major sectors of *The Economist*'s index of dollar commodity prices experienced divergent patterns. The average 1986 price level of the food index fell 16%, while that of industrial raw materials gained nearly 6%. Within the industrial raw materials component, nonfood agricultural prices rose 14% and metals remained essentially unchanged. Nearly all of the decline in the price index of foodstuffs was experienced during the first six months of the year.

Gold experienced a breathtaking ride in 1986. In early January news that crude oil prices had tumbled to their lowest level in five years bolstered gold prices as investors' concerns about inflation were eclipsed by worries about the possibility of instability in the worldwide banking system caused by defaults on energy loans. The purchase of gold by nervous investors seeking refuge drove the price from the $325-per-ounce level at the end of 1985 to $350, but by mid-June the price had drifted back below $335. After closing above $400 per ounce in September for the first time in three years, the price of gold climbed to $439 on October 8. Much of the buying was attributed to disenchantment by non-U.S. investors with declining interest rates and weaknesses in the U.S. dollar, which made U.S. investments, especially bonds, less attractive.

However, once gold fell below the psychologically important $400-per-ounce level in mid-November, investors took money out of the metal and switched to stocks and bonds. With all the signs pointing to relatively low inflation and no evidence of a banking system collapse, there was no pressing need to hold gold as a hedge against depreciating currencies and international turmoil. Overall, the price of gold ended 1986 with a net gain of 20%, some 55% below its peak of $875 per ounce set in January 1980.

(ROBERT H. TRIGG)

This article updates the *Macropædia* article MARKETS.

Education

Contraction of the education system in some countries, expansion in others, and financial constraint everywhere marked 1986. Since the biggest single element in education spending is the cost of teachers, there was no lack of collision between teachers' unions and governments over pay. Great Britain witnessed the longest such dispute since World War II. The Conservative government was determined to tighten conditions of service—for example, by lengthening the school year five days—in return for concessions over pay. The teachers argued that their salary levels had declined by more than 30% in real terms over the previous seven years, and by the end of 1986 increases on the order of 15 to 20% had been wrung from the government.

In Peru, Sutep, the teachers' union, argued that teachers' pay should be more than doubled to bring it up to the general level of salaries. Some 90% of Peru's 180,000 teachers struck in May, and there were violent clashes in Lima. In Denmark, where teachers were well paid by European standards, they pointed out that 15 years previously primary school teachers had earned 50% more than skilled workers, but by 1986 the two groups were paid about the same. The result, argued the union, was a shortage of good applicants. Men seemed to find teaching particularly unattractive, and the Danish teaching force had become 70% female.

In West Germany, where teacher unemployment—mainly through failure to hire newly qualified teachers—was unusually high, the principal teachers' union, the Gewerkschaft Erziehung und Wissenschaft (GEW), accused the government of underestimating staff needs. The GEW forecast an annual need for 17,000 new teachers over 20 years from the early 1990s, simply to maintain existing teacher-pupil ratios. The government argued that there were likely to be enough qualified teachers to make up any shortfall, but the union called for an immediate end to the reduction of teacher-training courses and for a long-term policy of recruiting 10,000 new teachers a year. Meanwhile, several of the Länder education ministers urged school-leavers not to opt for teaching, and the education minister for Baden-Württemberg, Gerhard Mayer-Vorfleder, said young people opting for teacher training were "qualifying themselves out of work."

Two reports issued in the U.S. suggested far-reaching changes in the training and compensation of teachers. The report of the Carnegie Forum on Education and the Economy called for the creation of a nation of thinkers to revitalize U.S. education and prepare the nation to compete with other economic powers. Teaching should be converted into a full-fledged profession, according to the report, *A Nation Prepared: Teachers for the 21st Century.* Its recommendations included replacement of four-year teacher-preparation programs with four years of liberal arts and a fifth year of graduate work in pedagogy; creation of a new national certifying body largely composed of teachers; creation of salary structures in which $35,000 would be typical and $72,000 possible; permitting parents and students to select which schools the children would attend; transfer of considerable power from administrators to teachers; and bonuses for schools whose students excel. The cost of the reforms was estimated at $50 billion over a ten-year period. Many of the recommendations were endorsed by the two major teachers' unions, the National Education Association and the American Federation of Teachers.

Another report, that of the Holmes Group, also recommended moving teacher education from the undergraduate to the graduate level. The group, originally composed of administrators from 40 major research universities, urged improvement of liberal arts courses taken by teachers, ranking of teachers based on preparation, creation of professional schools modeled after teaching hospitals, and requirements for teaching competence as well as course work.

In France the new right-wing government was accused by teachers' unions of deliberately attacking them. It had been the practice in France for teachers, at the beginning of the school year, to give children proposal forms for their own insurance company (Mutuelle Accident Élève). Some six million pupils normally filled these in, netting F 120 million per year for the union. The new minister for education, René Monory, prohibited this practice—a serious blow to union funds. A crisis of a different kind (and of many years' standing) continued to afflict the Roman Catholic teaching orders—the dramatic decline in the number of religious. This was especially notable in Ireland, where the Roman Catholic Church effectively dominated primary education. An internal report published by the Conference of Major Religious Superiors highlighted the crisis. In 1985 there were 1,527 religious working full-time in Ireland's primary schools, but only 107 were under the age of 36. At the same time, nearly 19,000 laymen and women were teaching in the primary schools. In the secondary schools the picture was much the same, with just under 1,800 nuns, brothers, and priests, fewer than 200 of whom were under 36, and 10,000 lay teachers. As a result, some previously unthinkable changes seemed likely to occur, including lay principals of Catholic secondary schools, boards of management with parent and teacher representation, coeducational schools, and amalgamations with local education authority schools.

Primary and Secondary Education. A draft policy on education endorsed by the Indian Parliament had, as its main objective, universal elementary education by 1990 and a massive adult education program to end illiteracy in the 15–40 age group. Vocational education would be introduced for 10% of the student population by 1990 and for 25% by 1995. In a meeting organized by the Indian National Institute for Educational Planning and Administration in New Delhi in the summer and inaugurated by Prime Minister Rajiv Gandhi, it was agreed that the formal system at all levels had reached its limits. Accordingly, the emphasis was on nonformal modes such as correspondence courses and intensive use of electronic media—certain to cause controversy in a country where many rural schools did not even have desks for the teachers. The conference argued that special attention should be paid to teacher training, including refresher courses.

Low standards in rural primary schools were under investigation in the Soviet Union. An inquiry into rural schools in the Turkmen Soviet Socialist Republic, concentrated around the capital of Ashkhabad, found disturbingly poor levels of teaching, with teachers themselves unable to pass achievement tests designed for 14-year-olds. There was also evidence that many children were not attending school at all. In Wales a report on rural secondary schools, organized by Roger Webster, professor of education in the University College, Aberystwyth, dismissed the "myth of the cozy, idyllic, untroubled rural secondary school." It went on to declare that "small is often far from beautiful and a 10% drop in numbers in a small secondary school, if accompanied by a corresponding decrease in resources, can have devastating results for curricular provision."

A total of 57,422,000 students began the 1986–87 school year in the U.S., including kindergarten through graduate school in both public and private institutions. U.S. Secretary of Education William J. Bennett noted that one of every four Americans was in school. Of the total, 40 million were in public schools: 27.2 million in the grades (up slightly from 1985–86) and 12.3 million in high schools (a small decline). Private school enrollment held steady at 5.7 million. Some $14 million was spent on private schooling, while public schooling for kindergarten through 12th grade cost $170 billion. The average cost per public school student was $4,263, an increase of 5.2% (adjusted for inflation). Teachers' salaries rose by 7.3% in a time of 3.2% inflation, and strikes involved a few thousand teachers and some 110,000 students in eight states. Less than half the education dollars were spent on teachers' salaries. One percent of the federal budget went to education.

Education was the main agenda item at the annual meeting of U.S. governors. The conference released a report entitled *Time for Results,* which called for an increased state role in improving education. Secretary Bennett termed the report the single most important development in the field of education in five years. A highly controversial section of the report called for more choice in the selection of schools by parents and students. The Reagan administration advocated federal support of parent-student school choice, but Congress had not acted on the proposal. The governors also recommended state control of school districts that fail to meet state standards. If a troubled school did not improve after receiving state help in planning and finances, the state would take direct control and reorganize the district. Major changes were already taking place in a number of states as the result of various reform movements. Twenty states raised teacher salaries, 42 now required competency examinations for working and prospective teachers, and 41 increased the number and the nature of subjects required for high school graduation.

Nursery and kindergarten enrollments in the U.S. reached 6.3 million in 1985, reflecting the increase in births. Nursery enrollments had risen 25% since 1980. Currently, about 39% of children aged three–four were enrolled in a preschool program, three times as many as in 1965. Missouri became the first state to require school districts to employ child development specialists to collaborate with parents of newborn children and toddlers. New York City announced that it would provide classes for all its four-year-olds by 1989.

Emphasis on vocational and technical education at the secondary level continued to grow in 1986. In China a national conference on technical and vocational education was held in August. Since 1979 China had been giving prominence to the technical and vocational side of education, and by 1986 there were more than 14,000 technical and vocational middle schools with more than four million students. Even so, fewer than 10% of secondary students received systematic technical and vocational education, representing only about 50% of the country's technical manpower requirements. Granted a large measure of autonomy by the reforms of May 1985, most provinces seemed to have given funds chiefly to senior middle schools and institutions of higher learning.

The main instrument for encouraging a technical and vocational bias in secondary schools in Britain was the Technical and Vocational Education Initiative. This was extended in 1986 to all schools in the country. In addition, the minister of education announced in October that some 20 "city technical schools" would be established in inner city areas. They would not be run by local authorities but would receive grants from the central government. In Japan there was evidence that more parents were opting to send children to technical schools, sometimes in preference to universities. The private technical training schools, or *senshu galeko,* which attracted 2.6% of 18-year-olds in 1976, had increased their share to 11.2% by 1986.

Pres. Ronald Reagan greets Guy Doud, the 1986 National Teacher of the Year, as Secretary of Education William Bennett looks on. Doud is from Brainerd, Minnesota. The award is sponsored by the Encyclopædia Britannica Companies, *Good Housekeeping* magazine, and the Council of Chief State School Officers.

AP/WIDE WORLD

In general, however, it was difficult to convince parents that technical and vocational education had the same prestige as academic courses. In France, for example, a third of 15-year-olds attended *lycées d'enseignement professionelle,* which provided specialized courses for specific jobs—for example, bricklayers and plumbers—and prepared students for the *brevet* examination, taken at age 15. In 1986 as many as half of those who took the examination failed, and some teachers described these schools as educational dustbins. In the main *lycées,* however, the percentage of students passing the *baccalauréat* (taken at 18 or 19) increased to 68.5%.

In Britain, 1986 was designated Industry Year, and vigorous attempts were made to impress on schools the importance of industrial and commercial activity. Early in the year the minister of education made a special point of encouraging "economic awareness" in secondary school curricula. But perhaps the most conspicuous result of Industry Year was seen in the efforts of a network of committees, set up some 15 years earlier, called Science and Technology Regional Organizations. These committees, organized by science teachers, had encouraged projects in which secondary schools went to industrial firms and produced curricular material as a result of their experiences. These ranged from a computer simulation of the organization of inventories at Rolls-Royce to the production of an in-house factory newspaper.

Perhaps the most arresting curricular proposals came from Scotland, which was beginning to emerge as a leader in curriculum reform in Europe. The Robertson Report (David Robertson was director of education in Tayside, a Scottish local authority) called for better balance in the curriculum, with more time given to aesthetic and practical/technological subjects for the 10–14 age group. The report criticized the amount of time devoted to English, mathematics, and modern languages and recommended that subjects like English and mathematics be taught across the curriculum.

With her husband behind her, Vicki Frost of Church Hill, Tennessee, exhibits some of the books she objects to having in classrooms. Frost and others won a court ruling allowing them to teach their children at home in order to avoid exposing them to the books.

ROB NELSON—PICTURE GROUP

In Norway curriculum proposals entitled "Monsterplan 85" were challenged by the main teachers' union, which accused the government of trying to introduce a "crude emphasis on basic skills and Christian beliefs" and excluding humanistic elements. Partly as a reaction to the growing crisis over apartheid, the newly formed National Education Crisis Committee put forward proposals for a new curriculum for black schools in South Africa. It sought the recasting of much of the current syllabus, notably history, to "reflect people's history" and urged concentration on "relevant" aspects of poetry, drama, and English literature.

Controversies over sex education flared in several jurisdictions. In the U.K. the government accused one or two local education authorities of including teaching on homosexuality in lessons to secondary-school children and, in a new Education Bill, made sex education in schools subject to control by boards of governors on which parents would have a large representation. Ireland's Health Education Bureau was criticized by a visitor from the U.S., Onalee McGraw of Pres. Ronald Reagan's National Council for Educational Research, who denounced the bureau's "secular humanist" approach. In rebuttal, Bishop Brendan Comiskey, president of the Roman Catholic Communications Institute, spoke up against the "extremes" of a purely biologic approach on the one hand and the view that any sex education is a threat to faith and morals on the other. In a report on AIDS (acquired immune deficiency syndrome), the U.S. surgeon general, C. Everett Koop, urged that children be given explicit instruction about the disease "at the lowest grade possible" as a way of helping to head off a possibly catastrophic epidemic. Since AIDS is transmitted primarily by sexual contact, the proposal sparked immediate opposition from adversaries of sex education in the schools.

Under the sponsorship of the Carnegie Corporation, a group of scientists, lawyers, educators, and others were undertaking a study of troubled teenagers, with the aim of helping to prevent the "casualties of adolescence." Data on teenage pregnancy and drug abuse reinforced the group's goal. According to a study by the *Ladies' Home Journal,* there were approximately one million teenage pregnancies in the U.S. each year, and about half the girls kept their babies. Many of them dropped out of school and became trapped in poverty, but there was sharp controversy over how to deal with the problem. In Chicago, for example, two clinics in inner city high schools that dispensed contraceptives were denounced by some as condoning immorality and praised by others for helping girls, who would be sexually active in any case, remain in school. Less acrimony surrounded antidrug education. As part of the administration's drive against drug abuse, the Department of Education prepared and distributed one million copies of the booklet *Schools Without Drugs,* setting out a 12-point program for combating use of drugs among students.

Standards of educational attainment continued to worry industrialists and politicians, but in most advanced countries where adequate measurement was attempted, there was little evidence that standards were falling. In England, where perhaps the most careful assessment of standards was going on, the Assessment of Performance Unit of the Department of Education and Science published reports of changing standards in English and mathematics at the age of 11 and 15. In the case of English, they found that the majority of pupils at both 11 and 15 could produce "interesting and legible work—only a small minority were in great difficulty with writing." As for mathematics, English children seemed to have considerable difficulty with decimals. About one-fifth of 15-year-olds and two-thirds of 11-year-olds appeared to ignore the points in decimal numbers.

Elementary school achievement scores in the U.S. reached their highest levels in three decades, according to a study by the Congressional Budget Office, but high school test scores were close to those of the 1970s. Although there were continuing disparities, black and Hispanic students tested closer to their white counterparts than in earlier years. The average score on the American College Testing Program's college admission test edged upward for the third consecutive year, while scores on the Scholastic Aptitude Test remained the same as in 1985. Authorities noted that the averages remained stable even though the number of persons taking the test increased, a factor that usually causes a downward trend in scores. On the debit side, the National Assessment of Education Progress said that students' writing skills were no better in 1984 than in 1974. The Census Bureau estimated that 13% of U.S. adults were illiterate in English, with a much higher figure for those having a different native language. Disagreement continued over the efficacy of bilingual programs, and there were movements in some states to have English declared the official language. A referendum to that effect was passed by voters in California.

The Supreme Court continued to uphold affirmative action as a remedy for overcoming blatant past discrimination when other remedies failed. The administration had argued that numerical hiring and promotion goals are immoral and perpetuate discrimination. At the same time, the court and the Justice Department tended to accept dismantling of desegregation plans once segregation had been eliminated. Proponents of continuing court-ordered plans said that without them schools could become resegregated. In a case that received wide publicity, a federal court in Atlanta, Ga., ruled that alternative instruction would have to be provided to the children of fundamentalist Christians who claimed the standard texts were tainted with secular humanism, supernaturalism, male-female reversal, and other philosophies they found objectionable. The school board, which had argued that allowing children to opt out of part of the curriculum would make a mockery of education, filed an appeal.

Higher Education. The demand for higher education continued to grow in 1986, but the capacity of countries to meet that demand did not. This was especially true in the case of demand for purely academic courses. At the post-secondary as at the secondary level, vocational courses were often shunned. In India a drive for "vocationalization" was started, and a moratorium was introduced on further development of higher education except in such fields as agriculture, home economics, forestry, and transport management. The Indian university system had grown from 27 institutions with 362,000 students in 1950 to 144 institutions with 3.5 million students in 1986. In Malaysia there was a 6% increase in university places, and the declared aim, in line with the industrialization of the country, was to double the size of six universities. The prime minister of Singapore promised an additional £16,000 million for the national university and the polytechnics, in addition to the new campus for the Nanyang Technological Institute. Expansion also continued in China, but there was a revealing decision to tighten up the allocation of jobs for graduates. In the previous year students had been allowed to "negotiate their careers" but in 1986, 10% would be sent to remote areas such as Tibet and Manchuria. The Ministry of Education emphasized, however, that all graduates would be guaranteed a job.

Soviet leader Mikhail Gorbachev's new broom was applied to higher education. The Communist Party announced plans for a "major retuning" that promised more investment, better pay for teachers, more integration of higher education with production, fewer formal lectures, and more seminars. Italy's minister of education, Franca Falcucci, faced with chronic overcrowding in the nation's universities, tried to curb the number of first-year registrations in Rome's main university, La Sapienza. Similar efforts were made in the University of Naples, but the fixed-quota policy aroused considerable criticism. The Finnish government increased the outlay on universities (including research) for 1987 by 13%. This compared with an 8% growth in other branches of public expenditure and a 2.5% inflation rate. In Hong Kong, which was to become a "special administrative region" of China in 1997, China had agreed to allow education to remain unchanged for 50 years. Plans were being made for a third university that would open in 1994 and have 7,000 students by the year 2000. It was estimated that Hong Kong would need 250 additional university staff per year for the next ten years.

The average cost of attending a public college in the U.S. in 1986 rose to $5,604 for those living on campus and $4,467 for commuters. The increases averaged 6%. At private colleges students paid an average of $10,199 if they lived on campus and $8,809 if they commuted.

In France the worst student uprising since 1968 forced the government to withdraw a proposed measure to overhaul the country's university system. Among other things, the legislation would have increased fees, allowed universities to be more selective in their admissions, and given universities the right to issue their own diplomas in place of the state diploma that did not mention any specific institution. The students attacked the proposals as elitist, and after three weeks of escalating disorders, Prime Minister Jacques Chirac announced on December 8 that the plan was being abandoned.

(JOEL L. BURDIN; TUDOR DAVID)

See also Libraries; Motion Pictures.

This article updates the *Macropædia* articles History of EDUCATION; TEACHING.

What Makes a Good Primary School?

London, one of the biggest urban educational authorities in the world, carried out a study of its primary schools in 1986 in order to find out what makes an effective school. Some of the answers were obvious—good physical amenities, more classes with fewer than 24 pupils, and stability in school staffing. None of these, however, are entirely within the control of the school itself. The survey identified 12 key factors that are *within the control of the school:*

1. Purposeful leadership of the staff by the head teacher.
2. Involvement of the deputy head.
3. Getting teachers themselves involved in planning the curriculum and making decisions on spending.
4. Getting teachers to be consistent in their approach throughout the school.
5. A structured school day for the pupils.
6. Teaching that is intellectually challenging.
7. Less emphasis on routine matters in teaching and more in talking about the content of work with pupils.
8. Limiting the focus of learning within teaching sessions.
9. Maximizing contact between teachers and pupils.
10. Sound record-keeping, including pupils' personal and social development as part of the records.
11. Involving parents both through helping in classrooms and attending meetings with teachers, as well as working with children at home.
12. Encouraging a positive climate with more emphasis on reward than punishment and an interest in the children as individuals, not just as pupils.

(TUDOR DAVID)

"Son, you're all grown up now. You owe me two hundred and fourteen thousand dollars."

Energy

Two historic events dominated the energy scene in 1986. The first was the collapse of the international crude oil market. The Organization of Petroleum Exporting Countries (OPEC) had announced late in 1985 that it was abandoning its policy of attempting to maintain an official pricing structure by restricting production. Under its new policy it would henceforth sell at whatever price was necessary in order to obtain what it regarded as its rightful market share.

OPEC began following this new policy in December 1985, and during January 1986 prices fell rapidly. OPEC met early in February to deal with the situation but failed to reach any agreement. To oil traders this signaled the total loss of market control by OPEC, and the price slide intensified, approaching $15 a barrel, compared with a level of $27 in the preceding November. A second OPEC meeting in March was equally futile, and prices continued to fall, plunging below $10 a barrel.

In April Sheikh Ahmad Zaki Yamani, the Saudi oil minister, announced that the price decline could not be stopped without the cooperation of non-OPEC exporters. Mexico and Norway stated their willingness to consider such cooperation. Another OPEC meeting in June ended in disarray, but in August a conference was finally able to achieve unanimous agreement. The members pledged to abide by previously established production quotas during September and October and to set up machinery to monitor compliance. In a totally unexpected move Iran agreed to maintain its current production level, hampered as it was by Iraqi attacks on shipping facilities, while allowing the Iraqis to produce more than their quota.

While the world waited during August to see whether the plan would work, Mexico, Norway, and the Soviet Union all announced that they would cooperate with OPEC by cutting back their production. Buyers, deciding that the bottom had probably been reached, began buying again, and the market firmed. As September and October passed, the OPEC plan worked, to the surprise of many. OPEC production was actually less than the total of quotas. Prices stabilized in the range of $13–$14 per barrel. In October, after meeting 17 days (the longest in the organization's history), OPEC members extended the August agreement through the end of the year.

OPEC met again at Geneva in December in an effort to achieve a world price for oil of $18 per barrel. A major stumbling block in the negotiations was the refusal of Iraq to join in any plan to cut production; still embroiled in their war with Iran, the Iraqis did not want their production quota set at less than that of Iran. On December 20, after more than a week of sometimes acrimonious talks, the

Chernobyl: The Sequence of Events

The accident at the Chernobyl nuclear power plant resulted from the combination of a reactor design with inherent control problems and the reckless and deliberate disregard of established safety procedures by the plant operators. The series of events leading to the explosion began with the initiation of a test to see how long the steam turbines would run (and thus provide power for emergency safety systems) while coasting to a stop when the reactor was suddenly shut off.

At 1 AM on April 25, 1986, reactor operation was reduced to 50% of full power as the first step in setting up test conditions. Thirteen hours later, at 2 PM, the emergency core cooling system was disconnected, at which time further preparations were postponed because power from the reactor was needed for the grid. The reactor operated in this condition for the next nine hours, when test preparations were resumed. The power level was further reduced, and computer control of some of the automatic control rods was switched off. At low power levels, however, the operators had trouble maintaining a stable output from the reactor (in part because of the previous prolonged operation at low power), and it took almost two hours to get the power output to the desired level. At this point almost all the safety features of the reactor had been disconnected or turned off.

Shortly after 1 AM on April 26 the operators turned on additional water circulation pumps to begin the final steps in setting up the test. At the 7% power level at which the reactor was operating, this action dropped the steam pressure and the water level in the steam separation drums below emergency levels, but the operators blocked the signals to the emergency reactor protection system.

At 1:19 AM the operators attempted to build up the water level by introducing additional water into the steam system. This led to further control problems, but at 1:23 AM the operators decided conditions were satisfactory for the actual test to begin. Blocking off further emergency protection signals so that the test could be repeated, the operators shut off the flow of steam to the turbine, which began to coast down to a stop. As a result, the circulation pumps also slowed, and the flow of coolant to the reactor declined. This led to a sharp temperature rise in the fuel channels of the reactor. Because of the reactor design this meant that the reactor was out of control.

Realizing an emergency was at hand, the supervisor ordered a "scram," the term used in the nuclear power industry for the rapid insertion of all control rods to shut the reactor down. The reactor was already so overheated, however, that most of the control rods could not go in all the way. At 1:24 AM there were two explosions.

The details of the explosions will never be known in full, but apparently there was a runaway nuclear reaction. Within three seconds the power output of the reactor rose from 7 to 50% of full power. This caused the fuel elements to burst apart, placing the superheated fuel particles in direct contact with the cooling water, which immediately flashed to steam. There was an almost instantaneous pressure shock that blew off the top of the reactor vessel, blew the roof off the building, and caused the servicing crane to come crashing down on the reactor.

The rupture of the fuel elements and cooling tubes also brought steam in direct contact with the zirconium coating on the fuel elements and with the graphite blocks surrounding the cooling tubes. Both zirconium and graphite react with steam at high temperatures to produce hydrogen. With the reactor exposed to the atmosphere, the hydrogen ignited and caused fires that burned out of control for almost four hours.

(BRUCE C. NETSCHERT)

members agreed to reduce the cartel's oil production to no more than 15.8 million bbl per day for the first six months of 1987; this represented an approximately 7% reduction from recent levels. Iraq refused to sign the agreement. Oil prices quickly rose in response to the agreement, and at the year's end some key U.S. and British grades were nearing the OPEC target of $18 per barrel.

The collapse of a market for such a basic commodity as oil naturally had far-reaching effects. The New York stock market suffered a decline in response to the initial price drop in January. Consumers basked in the comfort of low product prices. The effect on the world oil industry was disastrous. Oil companies sharply reduced staffs and slashed spending on exploration and development. In the U.S. the number of active drilling rigs dropped to a point that had not been approached in over 40 years; thousands of marginal wells were shut in, and hundreds were permanently abandoned. Oil imports, which had been declining for several years, rose again. (*See* Special Report.)

The second historic event was the explosion on April 26 at the Chernobyl nuclear power plant near Pripyat, 130 km (80 mi) north of Kiev. (*See* Sidebar.) This was the first accident at an operating nuclear plant anywhere in the world that involved direct fatalities and a significant release of radioactivity. Two days after the accident Swedish authorities detected abnormal radioactivity levels in the atmosphere and asked the Soviets if there had been an accident. The Soviets at first denied it but then announced the location and nature of the accident. As the days passed, the true scope of the disaster became apparent. The radioactive particles injected into the atmosphere by the explosion and fires were carried by the winds over much of Scandinavia and central and eastern Europe. Milk, meat, and crops from the affected countries were embargoed, and large quantities of foodstuffs and livestock (including the Lapland annual reindeer crop) were destroyed.

In the Soviet Union the consequences of the explosion were severe. Their full extent was revealed at an international conference in August at which the Soviets gave the details of the accident, described its local effects, and recounted the measures they had taken to deal with it. There were 2 deaths from the explosion and 29 from radiation sickness. More than 200 people were treated for radiation sickness or burns. Evacuation of the 780-sq km (300-sq mi) area around the plant involved 135,000 people. Although none of the other three reactors at the Chernobyl plant was directly damaged in the accident, high radiation levels and cleanup activity prevented their operation. It was not until the end of September that any of the undamaged reactors produced power again. The total cost of the disaster was several billion dollars.

The accident also had an adverse effect on nuclear power programs throughout the world. Opponents seized the opportunity to press their case for no new nuclear plants and the progressive abandonment of existing ones. Several countries adopted such policies. One beneficial result of Chernobyl was the establishment of new mechanisms for the international sharing of information on all future incidents and for cooperating in dealing with them.

Ironically, April was also the month in which the Superphénix, the French prototype industrial-size breeder reactor near Lyon, was brought up to its full power of 1,200 MW. It became the third such reactor, joining two already in operation in the Soviet Union. Widespread use of breeder reactors for power generation would have the effect of multiplying the potential nuclear fuel resources of the world hundreds of times. There were hopes that similar reactors would be developed outside Europe.

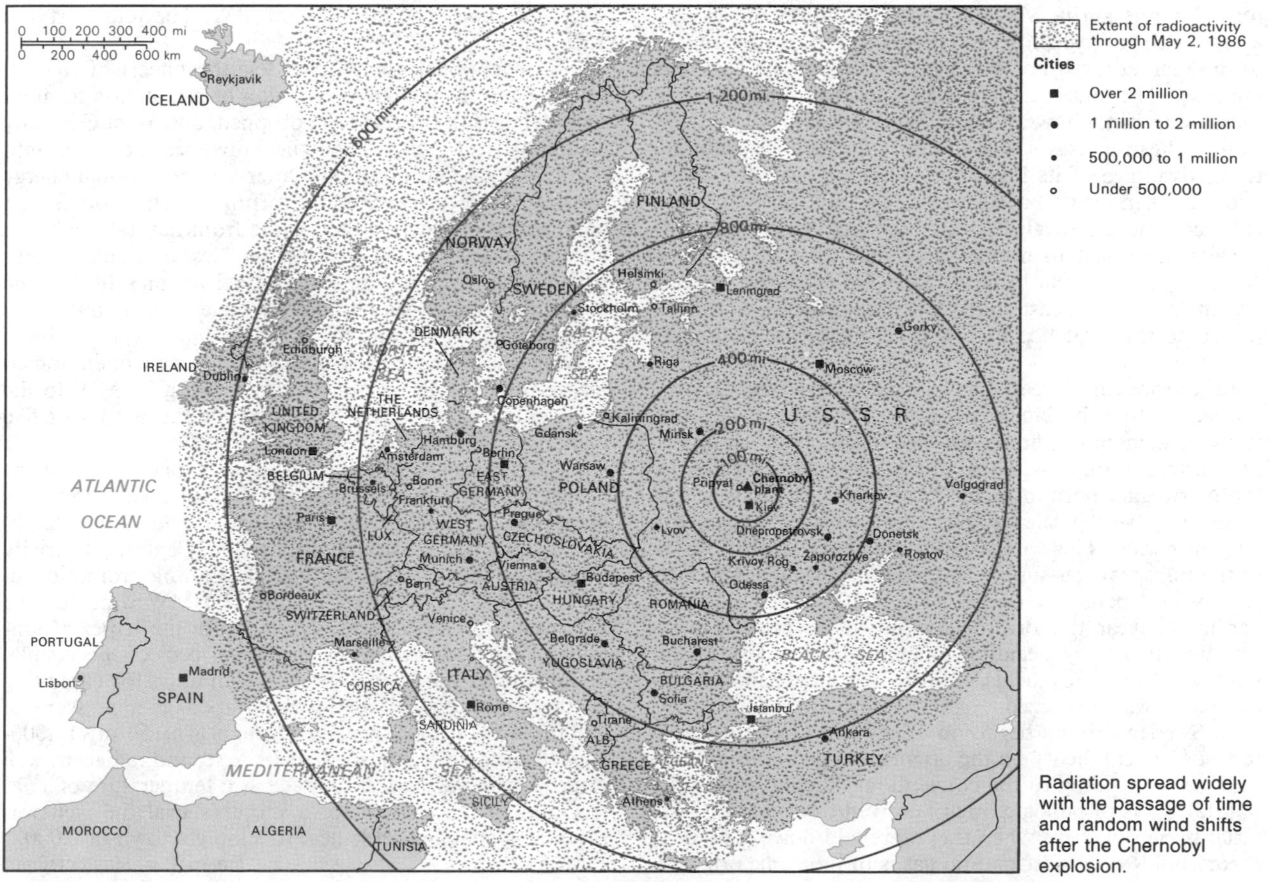

Radiation spread widely with the passage of time and random wind shifts after the Chernobyl explosion.

Low gasoline (petrol) prices cheered consumers in 1986 but worried producers. A Saudi Arabian move to abandon the Organization of Petroleum Exporting Countries' price bases for crude oil allowed the market value of the resource to drop by nearly 50%.

PHIL HUBER—BLACK STAR

In gas matters, as part of its continuing process of decontrolling natural gas prices, the U.S. Federal Energy Regulatory Commission in May permitted the wellhead price of all gas with controlled prices less than market price to rise to the market level. For some gas this meant a severalfold increase. The market price was, however, under severe pressure from the low oil prices, since gas and oil compete in most heating uses. Users of heavy fuel oil, for example, took advantage of its low price to switch away from gas, and the gas industry, burdened with "sticky" prices in long-term contracts, struggled to maintain its market share. A California project to import large quantities of gas from Alaska and Indonesia in liquid form for regasification and use in the West Coast market was abandoned, as was a project to ship liquefied natural gas from British Columbia to Japan.

In Europe the largest gas sale in history was accomplished in June by Norway. After 18 months of negotiations, agreement was finally reached to supply the countries of Western Europe with gas from huge fields located in the Norwegian portion of the North Sea. The transaction would involve the sale of $64 billion worth of gas over a 27-year period. This would constitute between 10 and 25% of the European gas supply and would substantially reduce European dependence on gas from the Soviet Union. Earlier in the year the British government reversed a long-standing policy by deciding to permit the export of gas from its North Sea fields. British Gas, the national gas company, was privatized.

In Sweden drilling began on a 7,500-m (24,750-ft) well to test a radical theory on the origin and occurrence of natural gas. According to the conventional theory, almost all natural gas is of biologic origin, derived from organic material buried in rocks when they were laid down. The new theory holds that most natural gas is of inorganic origin, a residue of the creation of the Earth. Thus, any well drilled deep enough almost anywhere on Earth should encounter gas. The site of the project was an ancient asteroid impact crater. According to the new theory, this created conditions favourable for the accumulation of gas at a comparatively shallow depth. Confirmation of the theory would mean that the total quantity of gas potentially available far exceeds all other energy resources. (See *Natural Gas,* below.)

The world coal industry also suffered from low oil prices as large users switched from coal to oil. In the U.S. coal producers glumly lowered prices and tried to forestall further increases in the excess capacity that had already existed. Britain and France, with subsidized coal industries, also cut prices, the latter for the first time since World War II. In the Soviet Union, as part of a continuing expansion in coal use, the first "supertrain" for coal haulage was put into service. Consisting of 438 cars and 14 electric locomotives, the train carried coal from the Ekibastuz fields in Kazakhstan to power stations near the Urals.

July heat waves in the South and along the east coast of the U.S. resulted in record-breaking electricity consumption in many states. For some systems demand was close to generating capacity. In May the Federal Energy Regulatory Commission, in a precedent-setting decision, gave permission for the establishment of the first broker/marketer of wholesale electric power. The decision opened the way for brokers, owning neither generation nor transmission facilities, to buy power from generating utilities, "wheel" it over utilities' transmission lines, and sell it in competition with the utilities themselves.

In Venezuela the Guri hydropower project, on the Caroní River in the province of Guiana, was finally completed after 23 years of work. The first stage, finished in 1968, had given the project the title of the world's largest, with 10,000 MW of capacity. With the addition of the second stage, the project boasted 17,000 MW. The total cost was $5.2 billion.

Unconventional energy also felt the effects of low oil prices. Plans for the large expansion of production from oil sand deposits in Alberta were dropped, and West Germany abandoned all projects for the conversion of coal into liquid and gaseous products. Other unconventional energy projects, however, were more fortunate. The world's first commercial production of gasoline from natural gas began at a plant near New Plymouth on New Zealand's North Island. The plant was designed to deliver one-third of the country's gasoline supply and produce as a by-product a petrochemical that was the basis for new types of high-duty plastics. The largest solar plant began operation at Daggett, in southern California, delivering 30 MW to the local utility. Contracts were signed for the output of five additional units of similar size.

In Japan the world's first full-scale plant for the recovery of uranium from seawater started production. The plant had a capacity to produce ten kilograms (22 lb) of uranium per year. In Britain the Central Electricity Generating Board, as part of its continuing promotion of alternative energy sources, ordered a 1-MW wind turbine for installation at Richborough, Kent. In the Jemez Mountains of New Mexico an experimental project successfully demonstrated the "hot dry rock" technique for exploiting geothermal energy. Water was pumped at a pressure of 7,000 psi (476 atmospheres) through a 5,150-m (17,000-ft) well to fracture the solid rock. A second, adjacent well returned the water to the surface at a temperature of 177° C (350° F). At the end of a month's trial the well was producing enough usable heat to supply a town of 2,000.

(BRUCE C. NETSCHERT)

COAL

Despite some anxieties in 1985 about prospects for the coal industry during that year, world production of hard coal amounted to 3,234,000,000 metric tons according to the UN. This was an increase of 5.7% over output in 1984. The ten largest producers yielded 93.2% of the global output, and China alone accounted for over a quarter, with the U.S. contributing 22.9% and the U.S.S.R. 17.6%. China's production was estimated to have increased by more than 10%, compared with the previous year, while U.S. output fell by 1.1%.

The overall increase nearly matched the rise in consumption, which was nearly 5% in 1985. An analysis by the UN Economic Commission for Europe (ECE) revealed a sharp rise of 11% in coal consumed within the European Communities (EC) as supplies to the market were renewed following the end in March 1985 of the year-long miners' strike in the U.K. For the U.S. the corresponding increase was 2.4%; in the U.S.S.R. there was a small decline, but the rest of Eastern Europe showed growth of 4.2% in consumption. It was notable that in all these areas the use of nuclear power grew more rapidly.

World production of brown coal (including lignite) reached 1,173,000,000 metric tons, an increase of 3.7%. As in earlier years, the largest producer by far was East Germany (26.6%), followed by the U.S.S.R. (13.4%). Brown coal output continued to be dominated by the ten largest producers, which between them accounted for 89.4% of world production. Apart from the major differences in quality between hard coal and brown coal, there are differences in quality within each of these categories. These differences are eliminated by the conversion of the various types of coal to metric tons of coal equivalent (tce), which takes into account the different calorific values, moisture content, and mineral structure. On this standardized basis, the UN estimated that 1985 output of hard coal was 2,658,000,000 tce, while that of brown coal was only 443,000,000 tce. Total output was 3,101,000,000 tce, 5.2% more than in 1984.

The ECE noted that increasingly coal was being traded interregionally, resulting in prices becoming more uniform on a world scale. During 1985 there was an 8.4% increase in global trade in hard coal, so that well over one-tenth of output was being traded internationally. There were increases in exports from Australia, the U.S., South Africa, Canada, the U.S.S.R., China, and the U.K. Coal prices declined. There was a continuing reduction of coal stocks in Western Europe. There was also a large percentage increase in trade in brown coal, but it had little significance since the absolute quantity amounted to only 0.36% of world brown coal production.

Assessment of prospects for coal remained difficult. Its major uses were for generating energy, particularly electrical energy, and to fuel the iron and steel industry. It had to compete with oil, natural gas, and nuclear power. Oil prices had declined to their lowest levels in 12 years by mid-1986, after which there was only a weak recovery. Government support of coal industries in such a situation was badly frustrated, given the reaction of industry to volatile prices, which in this case was to switch to oil. The main threat to coal continued to be from electricity, and supplies of this were being stimulated by the increasing use of nuclear power stations. To some extent this threat was reduced during 1986, on the one hand by the collapse of oil prices, which made other forms of energy less competitive, and on the other by the Chernobyl nuclear power station accident in the U.S.S.R. The severe contamination caused by the Chernobyl disaster gave rise to fears about the general safety of nuclear plants, although there were few signs of nuclear programs being scaled down.

Environment. The International Coal Development Institute (ICDI), a trade association of commercial companies that produced a total of around 450 million metric tons of hard coal a year, in its second year of existence picked out as a major theme the need "to address—in common with other fuels—environmental problems such as air pollution." This response to an area of growing public concern was also reflected in an acknowledgment by the Coal Research Service of the International Energy Agency (IEA) of "the prevailing pressure that coal use should conform to stricter environmental standards."

Once again the IEA research topics reflected this pressure. They reviewed oxidation of sulfur dioxide emissions in the atmosphere, which produced sulfate aerosols that were transported over long distances. Models were used to predict these movements over regions the size of Europe or eastern North America. Among the effects on health, materials, and the atmosphere itself was reduced visibility in some areas. It was noted that this led to pressure for reducing sulfur dioxide emissions in areas with high atmospheric clarity such as the southwestern states of the U.S. Because of this IEA examined the flue gas desulfurization (FGD) technologies that were available. FGD systems were found to be routinely capable of operating at the efficiencies of sulfur dioxide removal claimed by their designers. IEA was publishing an index of 100 FGD systems commercially available, with brief descriptions of their characteristics.

Response by governments to information on environmental damage was patchy. In December 1983 the European Commission had submitted a draft council directive for combustion plants of 50 MW (thermal) and over. This required target reductions of at least 60% of sulfur dioxide, 40% of dust, and 40% for oxides of nitrogen by 1995, compared with the annual mean level of emissions in 1980. But as of October 1986 the EC had not agreed to adopt the directive, even though the 12 member states were estimated to be discharging into the air 18 million metric tons of sulfur dioxide and 10 million metric tons of oxides of nitrogen a year. Some interim decisions, however, were made by the EC. From July 1987 all new industrial plants had to be equipped with "the best technology available to reduce emissions into the atmosphere." And a second directive made assessments of the environmental impact of defined public and private projects compulsory. A (nongovernmental) European parliamentary conference held in Stockholm in September 1986 forcefully urged all European governments to cooperate in preventing transboundary air pollution. Sixteen northern and central European nations united in their call for tighter controls, an enlarged European monitoring program, and more research.

Coal-Liquid Mixtures. Developments in both production and use of coal slurry mixtures achieved technical success but were generally not put into effect because of the fall in oil prices. Development had always been directed toward the conversion of coal to a form that could be transported and fired in oil-handling equipment. In recent years emphasis had shifted from mixing coal with oil to mixing it with water, yielding a more manageable liquid fuel. John Beer of the Massachusetts Institute of Technology reported on impressive demonstrations in which these fuels were burned in a 12-MW industrial boiler at the Chatham power station in Canada. According to a Babcock-Hitachi spokesman, one plant in Japan was producing nearly one million metric tons of coal-oil fuel for use in electricity generation, while at Nakoso power station 15 metric tons an hour of coal-water fuel were prepared and burned. Other large demonstration projects were reported in China and South Korea, while the Italian group Snamprogetti was to build a five million-metric-tons-a-year coal-water fuel plant in Siberia.

The main development relating to the chemical conversion of coal was a major project announced in Sweden in November 1985. There a consortium of industrial groups signed an agreement to build the world's largest coal-gasification plant at Nynäshamn, south of Stockholm. Costing $440 million and scheduled to go into production in late 1989, the plant was to produce 450,000 metric tons of ammonia a year, excess heat for district heating, and fuel gas. (ISRAEL BERKOVITCH)

ELECTRICITY

Against a background of continued improvement in the world economy in 1985 and 1986, the use of electricity rose. The general economic climate was an important factor influencing the use of all energy—the recession that followed the second oil crisis in 1979 had produced a change in attitude not only to oil but to energy use generally. Alternatives to oil were being sought throughout the non-oil-producing world, and conservation was constraining growth.

Despite the complexity of the energy situation and the factors that affected it, not least of which were the fluctuating oil prices that had an influence on all other sources of energy, electricity supplies and consumption in 1985 and 1986 remained approximately in line with the medium- and long-term plans of various governments. In most countries the level of electricity generated and consumed tended to rise. This was true of both industrialized and less developed countries. Growth in consumption in the industrialized countries was quite buoyant at 2.2% in the U.S., 3% in Japan, 2.7% average in the 12 countries of the EC, 3.5% in the U.S.S.R., and 5% in Canada. In some of the less developed countries growth was faster, reflecting the high level of development. Notable was India, which used 8% more electricity in 1985 than in 1984, bringing the increase since 1979 to 59%. China also stepped up

Electrical Power Production of Selected Countries, 1985
By source

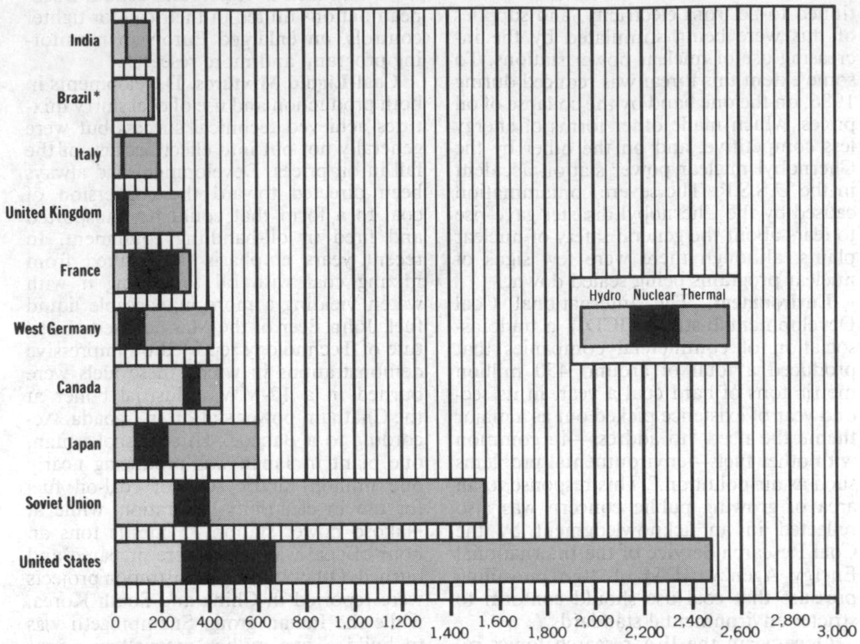

000,000,000 kilowatt-hours
*1984.
Sources: U.S. Department of Energy, *1985 International Energy Annual;* United Nations, *Monthly Bulletin of Statistics.*

its consumption, with comparable growth rates of 8.7 and 44%.

The U.S. continued to be the world's leading consumer of electricity, and this was reflected in its 1985 output of 2,500,000,000,000 kw-hr. Output in the EC countries (1,572,000,000,000 kw-hr) moved ahead of the U.S.S.R. (1,545,000,000,000 kw-hr). Japan (600,000,000,000 kw-hr) was in fourth place, followed by Canada (450,000,000,000 kw-hr) and China (405,000,000,000 kw-hr). Although output was increasing rapidly in some of the less developed countries—in Pakistan it more than doubled between 1979 and 1985—there were still enormous differences in their consumption compared with that in the industrialized countries. For example, although the populations of Japan and Pakistan were similar, Japan's consumption was 25 times greater. The U.S. and the U.S.S.R. between them accounted for about half the world's electricity consumption, although they had only 10% of the population. If Canada, Europe, and Japan, representing 20% of the world's population, were added, the proportion of world electricity consumed by this group of countries rose to 80%. By comparison, use in Africa accounted for only 2.4%, and about half of that was consumed in South Africa.

Total electricity generated in 1985 was about 9,500,000,000,000 kw-hr. It derived from three main sources: water (hydro), nuclear, and fossil fuels such as coal, natural gas, and oil. In 1985 some 21% of the total was generated by hydro (1,993,000,000,000 kw-hr), while nuclear increased its share to 15.6% (1,486,000,000,000 kw-hr). The remaining 63.4% was generated from primary sources, of which coal and lignite were the most important.

There continued to be a strong dependence on fossils fuels to generate electricity in the main consuming countries. In the U.S. the proportion was about 67%, the U.K. 77%, West Germany 57%, Denmark 98%, and the U.S.S.R. 64%.

The pattern of electricity generation changed markedly after the 1973 and 1979 oil crises. Most governments or electricity-generating authorities reassessed their means of generation and made changes. The objectives were threefold. First, they wanted to reduce their dependence on, and vulnerability to, fluctuations in the hydrocarbons market; the rise in oil and gas prices had had devastating effects. Second, they wanted the power to control costs. Third, they wanted to increase their national independence in energy; this was particularly true in France, Japan, Switzerland, and Belgium, where there was a lack of indigenous energy sources.

The result of the restructuring that took place was remarkable. It was particularly noteworthy in France, where in 1973 oil had contributed 39% toward electricity generation; by 1986, however, this share had fallen to below 1%, having been supplanted by nuclear sources. Nuclear energy contributed 8% of electricity generated in France in 1973; by 1986 this had increased to 70%.

In other countries, particularly in Western Europe, electricity industries were restructured according to various local factors, particularly the state of coal reserves in West Germany and the U.K. Other countries that greatly increased the share of electricity generated in nuclear power plants included Belgium with nearly 60%, Taiwan 53%, Sweden 42%, Switzerland 40%, West Germany 31%, and Japan nearly 25%. The U.S.S.R. was the third largest generator of nuclear-fired electricity—in 1985 this totaled 152,000,000,000 kw-hr—but because of its huge overall output of electricity, the nuclear share was below a quarter. In general, more effort was made to reduce the share of hydrocarbons in generating electricity in order to reduce costs in the longer term and preserve oil and natural gas reserves.

Nuclear development. The switch from oil to other means of producing electricity tended to favour nuclear generation for a number of reasons. Coal and lignite—the latter has a lower calorific value—remained an attractive means of generating electricity, as did hydro. As far as coal and other fossil fuels were concerned, however, apart from the constraints of use imposed by the proximity of resources—which many countries lacked—and the often high cost of exploitation, the detrimental effect on the environment was increasingly being seen as unacceptable. Because of this a growing number of requirements for environmental protection were imposed. It became necessary to install highly sophisticated desulfurization and denitrification systems in new power stations and, increasingly, in old ones as well. Such requirements increased the capital investment costs for the power stations, canceling out some of the cost advantage that could be gained from having on-the-spot fossil fuel supplies, as was the case in the U.K., West Germany, Japan, the U.S., and Belgium. This was even true where there were relatively cheap supplies of lignite.

Total nuclear capacity on Jan. 1, 1986, was 258,671 MW, and there were 381 nuclear generating units in 26 countries. Many more power stations were under construction and planned, however, and by 1992 a phenomenal increase of 55% of capacity to 400,000 MW was expected. By that time 32 countries would be using nuclear energy, which would account for one-quarter of all the electricity being generated. Most of the capacity was in five countries, led by the U.S. with 77,804 MW and followed by France with 37,533 MW, the U.S.S.R. with 27,756 MW, Japan with 23,665 MW, and West Germany with 16,413 MW. France was heavily dependent on nuclear sources in terms of total electric generation, a 65% share, compared with only 15% for the U.S. In the U.S.S.R. and other Eastern-bloc countries, many nuclear plants were being built. In Czechoslovakia more than three times the capacity that existed in 1985 was under construction, bringing the number of units to 16 from 5; in East Germany six units under construction would more than triple capacity; and in Bulgaria capacity was being more than doubled. The biggest expansion programs were being undertaken in the U.S.S.R., with 31,816 MW under construction, followed by the U.S. (29,258 MW) and France (25,017 MW).

While there were a number of developments in the nuclear field, the year was most memorable for the first civil nuclear catastrophe. On April 26 reactor No. 4 of the Chernobyl nuclear power station, 130 km (80 mi) north of Kiev in the U.S.S.R., suffered a rapid and uncontrolled power surge leading to two massive explosions. (*See* Introduction; Sidebar.)

In spite of the accident, the U.S.S.R., which supplied electric power to many of the Eastern-bloc countries, declared an acceleration in its ambitious construction program. More reactors were to be built on the edges of towns to maximize their potential for domestic use. In Bulgaria, however, concern about the lack of safety standards led to the erection of steel-reinforced containment structures around new reactors (such structures were obligatory in the West) to prevent radiation leaks.

(GEORGES F. LUCENET)

NATURAL GAS

The growth in the world's estimated proven reserves of natural gas slowed down in 1985 and 1986. The fall in oil prices hindered exploration activity and affected the economic feasibility of developing some known gas reserves. Even so, the estimate of world proven reserves as of Jan. 1, 1986, was a record 97,749,000,000,000 cu m (97,749 billion cu m or bcm). This was only 1.6% higher than the 1985 estimate, but it reflected a growth of 26% over the estimated reserves five years earlier and was equivalent to 55 years of production at the 1986 rate of consumption.

World commercial gas production in 1985 totaled 1,770 bcm, an increase of 4% over 1984, which set another record. In addition, some 170 bcm were reinjected, either as a conservation measure, rather than flaring unwanted gas, or as a means of increasing oil recovery. The increasing emphasis on conservation helped to reduce the amount of gas flared to only 4% of gross production.

There was little change in the location of reserves. The U.S.S.R. continued to have by far the largest of these. At 38,500 bcm they constituted 39% of the world total; not surprisingly the U.S.S.R. had the highest production in 1985 at 643 bcm as well as being the leading gas exporter. Iran had the second highest reserves at 13,860 bcm but produced only 17 bcm, all of which was destined for domestic use; Iran, however, was increasingly interested in resuming gas exports. The U.S. had reserves of 5,300 bcm and produced 468 bcm. Canada, the third largest producer, produced 84 bcm, of which 26 bcm were exported to the U.S. Other major producers included The Netherlands (81 bcm, of which 45 bcm were exported), the U.K. (43 bcm), and Algeria (38 bcm).

The volume of international gas trade continued to rise, reaching 234 bcm in 1985. Of this total 70 bcm came from the U.S.S.R. Soviet exports to Western Europe rose, as did those from Algeria, both as liquefied natural gas (LNG) and through the pipeline to Italy. Japan's imports of LNG from Indonesia and Malaysia also increased. Declining oil prices may have had an adverse effect on the prospects for new LNG deals as oil became more competitive, but some major contracts revealed that there was still a demand for pipeline gas, provided the price reflected the competitive situation.

The most important event in the international gas trade in 1986 was the provisional agreement on exports from Norway's Troll and Sleipner fields. In 1985 the British government had vetoed imports of gas from Sleipner, which left Norway without any immediate prospect of selling gas to Britain in the 1990s. But several other European countries were interested in importing Norwegian gas, and in June 1986 Norway agreed to sell some 20 bcm a year from 1993 to 2020 to a consortium involving French, Dutch, Belgian, and West German companies.

The unusual aspect of this huge deal, which was estimated to be worth some $60 billion, was that Norway did not commit the output of a particular field to a single contract. The gas was to come initially from Sleipner, but later it would be from the huge Troll field. Large as the contract was, it would account for perhaps only a quarter of Troll's reserves, which could amount to 1,200 bcm. Other countries, including Italy, Austria, and Spain, were also interested in Norway's gas, and in the longer term Britain too might want access to Troll gas. A new pipeline running the length of the North Sea was to be built to deliver gas to Zeebrugge, Belgium. This would bring Norwegian gas within easy reach of the east coast of England.

The future of Britain's gas supplies was expected to be made clear following privatization of British Gas. The Gas Act passed in July 1986 established a new regulatory framework and permitted authorization of other would-be competitor gas suppliers. The government sold all the shares in British Gas in November–December 1986, and the private company that emerged might have greater freedom to make decisions about the need for imported gas.

The gas market in North America continued to react to deregulation of prices in Canada and the U.S. Not only did gas prices fall, but the established structure of long-term contracts between producers, pipeline companies, and utilities was being replaced increasingly by spot market deals and a more competitive market. This was aided by regulations that provided freer access to the pipeline system, allowing utilities to deal directly with producers.

Elsewhere gas prices tended to decline, either as a result of contract terms being linked to oil prices and thus falling automatically with the drop in oil prices or because producers were forced to renegotiate terms in order to remain competitive. Algeria, for example, agreed on new contract terms with France and Spain. LNG export prices were no longer to be linked to artificially high official crude oil prices but would be linked to actual market prices of oil. Falling prices hit several projects, such as development of offshore Canadian reserves and the planned gas-to-methanol plant in Trinidad and Tobago.

These short-term developments would pale into insignificance if a Swedish drilling project provided conclusive proof of the theory put forward by Thomas Gold of Cornell University, Ithaca, N.Y. For several years he had been claiming that natural gas, which is mainly methane, might not always originate, as conventional theories assumed, from decomposition of biologic material in sedimentary strata. Instead, he claimed, vast quantities of methane might have been trapped deep inside the Earth very early in its history; this "nonbiogenic" methane migrated upward and could be trapped in areas where biogenic natural gas could not exist. In Sweden drilling of an exploration well up to 7,500 metres deep in an area of nonsedimentary rocks began. The well was an interesting test of Gold's theory; if successful, it would open the way to new gas resources in previously unexpected areas. (RICHARD J. CASSIDY)

PETROLEUM

Once again in 1986 OPEC dominated oil industry activities as it attempted to preserve its market share and at the same time maintain prices. This proved to be impossible and resulted in one of the most precipitous price declines in recent oil history. From nearly $28 per barrel in January the average OPEC crude oil price fell to below $10 in July, after which it recovered and in November was fluctuating around $15.

During the first half of 1986 OPEC output rose 16% over the same 1985 period, while total world production increased only 5%. Saudi Arabia's output rose 39.3% to 4.7 million bbl a day—the rise reflecting its failure to be the active swing producer (adjust its output in response to market conditions) that had caused it to cut back its output dramatically in 1985. Nearly everywhere else in the Middle East the rises were almost as high; the exception was Iran, where output stagnated. Increases in Western Europe, China, and the Soviet Union were only 2–2.4%, but Indonesia's production rose 10%. Total OPEC production during the first quarter of 1986 averaged 17.5 million bbl a day, and it reached 18.7 million bbl a day in the second quarter. In June it climbed to 19.7 million bbl a day and in July to more than 20 million bbl a day, compared with an average of 17,225,000 bbl a day in 1985.

Oil market conditions had deteriorated since 1980, when OPEC output peaked at 26.8 million bbl a day. In 1982 an overall quota of 17.5 million bbl a day was set, and in October 1984 this was reduced to 16 million bbl a day, a total that was maintained only because Saudi Arabia played the role of swing producer. In December 1985 the Saudis were no longer prepared to support the rest of OPEC and adopted a "market shares" policy that allowed them to raise their production. As a result, supplies to the market increased, and prices started to nosedive.

Divisions within OPEC proved too difficult to reconcile. A meeting in Geneva in late March totally failed in its attempt to restore order to the market. There was a deep split within OPEC between those nations—Iran, Algeria, and Libya—that wanted the lowest possible output ceiling (14 million bbl a day) in order to restore the price level to at least $28 per barrel, and those led by Saudi Arabia, which sought a reasonable and rational expansion in collaboration or sensible competition with non-OPEC producers to stimulate demand and revive prices. At a second meeting in Geneva in April, the majority of members supported Saudi Arabia's strategy, leaving Iran, Algeria, and Libya in a minority. Subsequent meetings failed to reach agreement, and at the end of June prices plummeted. Another Geneva meeting in early August produced enough tentative agreement on production schedules to stimulate prices and restore some producer confidence. Attitudes were moderating, but the replacement of Saudi Arabia's oil minister Sheikh Ahmad Zaki Yamani at the end of October by Hisham Nazer signified a stronger pricing policy by Saudi Arabia. Its actions remained crucial to the oil market. In December the OPEC oil ministers again met in Geneva. After more than a week of negotiations, all members except

An auctioneer in Odessa, Texas, sells oil-drilling equipment to less than eager buyers. With the price of a barrel of crude down worldwide and demand for active drilling rigs at a 30-year low in the U.S., equipment sold for one-fifth its worth.

KATZ—BLACK STAR

Iraq agreed that for the first six months of 1987 production would be cut 7% from recent levels.

Reserves. During 1985 total commercial proven reserves increased to 707,600,000,000 bbl. Western Hemisphere reserves at 127,300,000,000 bbl increased slightly, but the share remained unchanged, at 17.9%, as did Latin America's at 11.9%. Reserves in the Middle East were little changed at 397,500,000,000 bbl (56.3%), with a reserves/production (r/p) ratio of over 100 years (meaning that the reserves will last over 100 years at the current rate of production). Africa's share was little changed from 1984 at 56,200,000,000 bbl (8.1%), while that of Western Europe was marginally up at 26,400,000,000 bbl (3.7%); of that the U.K. had half. The U.S.S.R.'s share at 61,000,000,000 bbl (8.6%) reflected a further decline, as did China's at 18,400,000,000 bbl (2.6%). Reserves in the U.S. rose slightly to 35,600,000,000 bbl (5%). Saudi Arabia remained the largest single source of reserves with 168,800,000,000 bbl, 23.8% of the total.

Production. World oil production decreased by 1.8% in 1985 to 57,340,000 bbl a day, with OPEC output down 7.2% to 17,225,000 bbl a day. Middle East output fell to 10,870,000 bbl a day; the region's share thus became 19.2%, its lowest since 1967. Qatar suffered the biggest output decline, by 28.2% to 310,000 bbl a day, followed by Saudi Arabia by 25% to 3.6 million bbl a day. Kuwait production fell 8.1% to 910,000 bbl a day. Several countries in the region recorded increased output: Iraq by 16.8% to 1,435,000 bbl a day (2.5% of the total); Iran by 1% to 2,225,000 bbl a day (4%); and Oman by an impressive 20.7% to 505,000 bbl a day. Dubai's output rose 6.8% to reach a record 390,000 bbl a day.

Despite a 3% decline in production to 12,140,000 bbl a day, the U.S.S.R. remained the largest producer. China's output (2.5 million bbl a day) rose 8.9%, and U.S. production reached a record 10,540,000 bbl a day, giving it 17.9% of the total. Latin-American output fell marginally to 6,655,000 bbl a day, but the region kept its 11.9% share of the total. The decline in Venezuela continued by a further 7.4% to 1,745,000 bbl a day, only half the 1971 volume (3.2% of the world total). Mexico's output was unchanged, while Brazil, Colombia, and Ecuador all achieved record production; however, that of Argentina declined 4.3%.

Western Europe again achieved the largest regional rise, at 3.8% to 3,940,000 bbl a day (6.8% of the total), stimulated by record output in the U.K. (2,640,000 bbl a day) and Norway (840,000 bbl a day), which rose 1.3 and 10.2%, respectively. African production increased slightly to 5,285,000 bbl a day (9.1% of the total), led by Nigeria with 1,475,000 bbl a day (up 6.1%), followed by Libya (1,090,000 bbl a day) and Algeria (1,040,000 bbl a day), both of which suffered small falls.

In Asia and Australasia output rose 1.3% to a record 3,280,000 bbl a day (5.7% of the world total), still dominated by Indonesia despite its 7.8% decline in output to 1,310,000 bbl a day. Australasia's production rose to 650,000 bbl a day, and there was an 8.5% rise in South Asia's output, which had doubled since 1981 to 665,000 bbl a day.

Consumption. Between 1980 and 1985 there was little change in total world consumption or in the pattern of regional demand. In 1985 total consumption dropped marginally to 58,465,000 bbl a day. North American consumption accounted for 28.2% of the total at 16,640,000 bbl a day, with the U.S. share at 15,170,000 bbl a day, 0.4% down from 1984. The U.S.S.R. consumed 1.6% more and 15.9% of the total (9,060,000 bbl a day), followed by Japan with 4,320,000 bbl a day, its lowest since 1971. By contrast, China's consumption was a record 1,760,000 bbl a day (3.1%), almost tripling since 1970.

Western European consumption was 20.2% of the total but fell 1.5% to 11,915,000 bbl a day. West Germany remained the largest consumer at 2,410,000 bbl a day, followed by France and Italy, consuming 1,785,000 and 1,745,000 bbl a day, respectively. Use in the U.K. declined by 13.2% to 1,635,000 bbl a day because of the settlement of the coal strike. Consumption in Turkey rose strongly by 11.6% to a record 390,000 bbl a day.

Australasian consumption fell 5% to the 1983 level of 670,000 bbl a day, but there was little change in Latin America (4,430,000 bbl a day) and the Middle East (1,980,000 bbl a day). Africa (1,715,000 bbl a day) and South Asia (1,095,000 bbl a day) both increased their usage, by 2.8 and 6%, respectively.

Refining. World refining capacity declined for the fifth consecutive year in 1985, reaching 73,275,000 bbl a day, its lowest in a decade. This brought refinery capacity and throughput into better balance than at any other time since the late 1960s and early 1970s; refinery throughput was 56,465,000 bbl a day—a negligible decline from 1984. The U.S. still had the largest (20.7%) capacity at 15,180,000 bbl a day (down 3%). Canada increased its capacity by 2.6%. Latin America, with 9.8% of the total, declined 10% to 7,140,000 bbl a day, over half of this attributable to the Caribbean. Trinidad's capacity fell 18.8% to a 25-year low at 260,000 bbl a day. Only in Venezuela was there a marginal increase, to 1,230,000 bbl a day. In Western Europe there was no change in overall capacity. The largest fall (17.1%) took place in West Germany, to 1,750,000 bbl a day. Capacity in Italy (2,585,000 bbl a day) and France (2,175,000 bbl a day) fell 5.9 and 3%, respectively. Middle East capacity rose 5.5% to 3,710,000 bbl a day, giving it 4.9% of the total. There was no change in Bahrain, Iran, and Iraq, but Saudi Arabia added 28.9% more capacity to bring its total to 1,115,000 bbl a day. Africa was little changed, with 2,545,000 bbl a day.

In Asia and Australasia overall capacity changed little at 10,775,000 bbl a day, but in South Asia it rose 15.7% to 1,150,000 bbl a day, and in Australasia it declined 10.4% to 705,000 bbl a day. Capacity in Japan, Indonesia, and Singapore was unchanged, as also was the case in the U.S.S.R. (12 million bbl a day) and China (2,150,000 bbl a day).

Tankers. The world tanker fleet continued its steady decline from its 1977 peak of 332.5 million tons deadweight (dw) to 246.8 million tons dw, down 8.5% from 1984. The greatest reduction (15%) was in tankers of 200,000–320,000 tons dw, though they continued to be the single largest class at 94.9 million tons dw. Tanker tonnage scrapped was a record 26.5 million tons dw, a 45.3% increase over 1984. Nearly half of the tanker fleet in 1985 was constructed between 1971 and 1975, and new orders totaled 11.6 million tons dw. The leading tanker owner by flag continued to be Liberia, followed by Japan, Greece, Panama, and the U.S. In 1985 some 24.1 million bbl a day were transported by tanker, a drop of 2.6% from 1984. Tanker movements were dominated by imports into Western Europe and the U.S., and the Middle East remained the largest source (38.7%). (R. W. FERRIER)

See also Engineering Projects; Industrial Review; Mining and Metallurgy; Transportation.

This article updates the *Macropædia* articles ENERGY CONVERSION; FOSSIL FUELS.

Special Report: Energy

After the Oil Price Collapse

BY PETER R. ODELL

In January 1986 the average price of internationally traded oil was $28.33 per barrel. By late July it had fallen below $10 per barrel. An agreement by the Organization of Petroleum Exporting Countries (OPEC) in early August to reduce production brought a recovery of a few dollars but, in the absence of a major escalation of the Gulf War between Iran and Iraq, the price of oil was not expected to exceed $18 per barrel. After more than 12 years during which oil had been sold far above its competitive long-run supply price (that is, the price at which it provides an acceptable profit to the highest-cost supplier to the market), oil once again became cheap.

The Oil Price Shock. The collapse in the oil price surprised most Western energy policymakers. They had believed the price would go on rising, even beyond the high of almost $40 per barrel that it reached in the early 1980s, because supplies were insufficient to meet future demand. Those who argued that the price of oil was temporarily high because of short-term political controls over supply were thought to be unrealistic. In this context the reaction of the West to the events of 1986 in the world of oil was full of paradoxes. There was praise for the way market forces had worked to undermine the OPEC cartel, but this reaction was accompanied by fears about the impact of low oil prices on demand. The likely acceleration of economic growth was welcomed; at the same time there were fears about the losses that would be sustained by producers of competitive energy sources. The advantages of cost savings for oil-importing countries were offset by concern about the effect on Western institutions of the deterioration in the economies of oil-exporting countries.

Policymakers could not accept the premise that these paradoxes would be resolved without intervention. Although lip service was paid to market forces, controls were being used to cut back consumption of oil, particularly OPEC oil, in order not to undermine the expansion of nuclear power, coal, gas, and alternative energies.

Central to these policies was the perception that it was either impossible or undesirable to negotiate with OPEC countries to ensure an adequate supply of low-cost oil. Thus, oil demand restraints, together with the expansion of alternative energy sources, now threaten to exacerbate economic problems such as imbalance in international trade and high inflation rates (partly caused by high oil prices during 1972–85) even though oil prices have fallen to lower levels. The world's oil problem—usually portrayed as arising from resource scarcity—has been revealed by the events of 1986 to be more complex.

Problems for Oil Producers. With the impact of high oil prices, conservation, and the encouragement of alternatives on the demand for oil—in 1985 it was 14% less than in 1979 and even 2.5% less than in 1973—the oil exporters' difficulties were brought into sharp focus as prices fell. It became obvious that there would be no shortage of world oil supplies for many years to come. This problem for the OPEC countries was compounded by the fact that non-OPEC oil supplies had been, and still could be, expanded rapidly.

Between 1973 and 1986 oil production in the Communist world expanded by over 65%, putting the U.S.S.R. ahead of the U.S. as the world's largest producer. Soviet oil output declined in 1985, but in 1986 it again increased at a time when oil use at home and in Eastern Europe was being supplanted by plentiful supplies of Soviet natural gas. Thus Soviet oil exports to the non-Communist world were set to increase. This prospect was of major economic significance for the U.S.S.R., given its heavy dependence on hard currency earned by exporting oil to pay for imported goods and services. The situation was similar in China, where oil production and exports had been increasing rapidly.

Meanwhile, non-OPEC countries in the non-Communist world had also developed their oil production under the stimulus of high prices in order to reduce their dependence on OPEC supplies. Output in 1986 was over 50% above 1973 and, if the U.S. (where output was little changed from 1973) was excluded, 1986 output was 2.5 times the 1973 level. The new Western oil producers had benefited enormously from the recent development of their oil resources. Many of these governments still wanted to increase production further in order to help offset the loss of revenues caused by the fall in price. Non-OPEC, non-Communist world supply would therefore continue to expand.

Nevertheless, for both Communist and non-Communist countries the lower price of oil, and the more competitive market conditions created by OPEC attempts to win back part of the 50% of the market that it had lost since 1973, meant that oil would make a smaller contribution to their economies in the future. This was true of rich industrial countries, such as the U.K. and Norway, as well as many countries in the third world—notably Mexico but also Egypt, Malaysia, Angola, Oman, India, and Brazil, among others—where oil revenue had been used primarily to fund economic development.

For the OPEC countries the situation and outlook were even worse, given their heavy economic dependence on oil. The erosion of their oil markets since 1973 had been more than compensated in financial terms by the higher value of oil sold until 1985. They had been able to achieve high rates of economic growth and large rises in per capita incomes and/or to invest in large-scale infrastructural and industrial projects. The collapse of oil prices in early 1986 brought this period to an end. Venezuela, Nigeria, and Indonesia (among the most populous OPEC countries) were confronted by debt-repayment problems as well as difficulties in maintaining living standards. Even some of the wealthiest OPEC countries such as Saudi Arabia, Kuwait, and the United Arab Emirates, which had large oil industries and small populations, were forced to sell foreign assets and/or to cancel orders for capital and consumer goods.

If oil remained cheap, all OPEC members would suffer deteriorating economic conditions that could lead to social and political unrest. The Western world's political and economic interest would be best served by ensuring that such problems did not arise. This implied that they should keep up—or even increase—their purchases of OPEC oil and even cooperate to prevent the price of oil from being brought under more pressure. By the end of 1986, however, there was no sign that the need for policies aimed at achieving these goals had been recognized.

Oil Importers Face Difficulties. Given that high oil prices were blamed for the earlier economic problems of the oil-importing countries, it should follow logically that such countries would be well placed to enjoy the benefits flowing from much cheaper oil. While it was true that import costs would reduce balance of payments problems and that savings might stimulate economic development, there were several negative factors to be considered. First, for some significant oil-importing countries, notably Japan and West Germany, the fall in the oil price served to strengthen their currencies. Because their governments were unwilling to reflate—for fear of pushing up prices—these economies would not be able to expand sufficiently to make up for the fall in demand from the oil-exporting countries. Second, for many third world oil importers the high oil price was only one of several adverse elements affecting their economic performance. Oil savings alone would not lead to any dramatic improvement in their prospects.

Third, in most oil-importing countries the savings on oil were not wholly—or even partly—passed on to consumers, a move that would have stimulated demand. Instead, governments increased taxes on oil and use as prices fell, either to raise revenue or to inhibit low-cost oil's ability to compete against alternative energy sources. During the period of high oil prices most countries deliberately stimulated the development of alternative energy, often at high cost. Projects included the expansion of deep-mined coal production in some Western European countries; exploitation of solar, wind, wave, and water power in favourable locations around the world; and the establishment of biomass energy production, of which Brazil's use of alcohol from sugarcane as a substitute for gasoline (petrol) was the best known. In terms of the investment involved and the energy contributions expected, however, the post-1973 commitment to nuclear power was of greatest importance.

Nearly all investments in alternative energies had been made on the assumption that oil would reach $60 or even $100 per barrel during the lifetime of the projects. With oil prices at $15 a barrel and most alternatives to oil costing $20 or $25 per barrel equivalent, investment in most non-oil projects became unprofitable. Thus, even for many oil-importing countries cheap oil was not proving to be an unmitigated blessing; in cases such as France, where massive investments had been made in nuclear power, the oil price collapse might even lead to economic difficulties.

In conclusion, the arrival of cheap oil in 1986, following the lengthy period of adjustment to expensive oil, was not universally welcomed. The fact that so many countries perceived their interests to be best served by relatively high oil prices suggested that oil would not remain at $12 or less per barrel for long. Equally, the market would not sustain a price double that amount or more (as in 1979–85). The post-1986 challenge was for technical, economic, and political efforts to be directed toward ensuring a slowly increasing supply of and demand for oil at $15–$18 per barrel. At that level, producer countries could satisfy their economic aspirations, while importing countries and consumers would be able to buy the energy they required at a price that did not inhibit development.

Peter R. Odell is director of the Centre for International Energy Studies at Erasmus University, Rotterdam. His numerous papers and books on energy resources include Oil and World Power; Energy, Needs and Resources; The Western European Energy Economy: The Case for Self-Sufficiency, 1980–2000; *and* The Pressures of Oil.

Engineering Projects

Bridges. By the end of 1986 the Paraná Bridge joining Paraguay to Argentina, a total distance of 2,690 m (1 m = 3.3 ft), was nearing completion. With a main span of 330 m and two anchor spans of 170 m, it was one of the world's largest concrete cable-stayed girder bridges. The two towers of the bridge were A-frames, from the top of which 26 pairs of stay cables splayed out to anchor points along the outside edges of the trapezoidal-shaped deck girder; the girder was built up from ten-metre-long hollow boxes that weighed 250 metric tons each. The boxes were taken to the site on pontoons and lifted into place by pairs of twin-boom derricks. The two derricks started work at the Argentine tower, one derrick lifting the first box in the main span and the other derrick the first box in the anchor span; the derricks were then moved onto the erected boxes and lifted the second boxes into position; the process was repeated until 16 boxes were in place in each span, with support for the cantilevers being provided by the stay cables. The derricks were then moved to the Paraguayan tower and the whole process repeated until single closing boxes were put into place to complete the spans. The bridge joining the two countries was expected to be open to traffic near the end of 1987.

Over the Bosporus Straits in Turkey a suspension bridge with a main span of 1,090 m was taking shape. Both towers were complete, and the temporary walkways and main cable "spinning" equipment were in position. Thus, bridge construction was back on schedule for completion late in 1988. The bridge would carry eight traffic lanes across the straits and provide a fixed link between Asia and Europe south of the Black Sea for long-distance traffic, leaving the first Bosporus bridge, which had opened in 1973, to carry local traffic within the Istanbul area.

In Vancouver, B.C., the longest stayed-cable girder bridge in the world was completed. With a main span of 465 m, it provided a crossing with six lanes from Annacis Island over the southern arm of the Fraser River to Delta on the south shore. The shallow deck system consisted of steel floor beams topped by precast concrete panels with a thin cast-in-place top surface. The bridge had twin H-frame towers, and each of the 192 stay cables was 237 m long and weighed up to 25 metric tons. The cables were sheathed in black polyethylene to provide protection and minimize the risk of corrosion. In India, near Calcutta, work was continuing, though much more slowly, on a big steel cable-stayed bridge over the Hooghly River. It was to have a main span of 475 m.

The most impressive bridge construction continued to be in Japan, where rapid progress was being made on the Kojima-Sokaide road-and-rail bridge chain, the central one of the three crossings between the islands of Honshu and Shikoku. One set of bridges in the chain comprised six major structures, all large: three suspension bridges with main spans of 940 m, 990 m, and 1,110 m; two cable-stayed bridges, each with a main span of 420 m; and a continuous truss bridge. Together with the approach and linking viaducts, the full length of the chain was 12 km (7.5 mi). The suspension bridge with a main span of 1,100 m, the Mimami Bisan Seto Bridge, would have the fifth-longest span in the world and would be by far the longest carrying a railway. Throughout the length of the chain, the bridges had twin decks, one carrying rail and the other road traffic. Construction started in 1978 and was scheduled for completion in early 1988.

During 1986 the Honshu Shikoku Bridge Authority

(HSBA) announced that it soon was going to invite bids from selected companies, both Japanese and foreign, for the construction of the massive Akashi Kaikyo Bridge in the most northerly of the three links between the two islands. At the same time, HSBA changed its plans for this section to road only rather than road and rail. The elimination of the railway enabled HSBA to consider increasing the main span of the bridge to 1,980 m and thus avoid placing both tower foundations in very deep and fast-flowing waters. The changes also meant that construction time could be reduced from 13 to 10 years. At 1,980 m the bridge would be the longest single bridge span in the world, exceeding the second-place Humber Bridge in England by nearly 600 m.

Eventually to be the longest bridge in the world was that planned to link Messina in Sicily with Calabria on Italy's mainland. In early 1986 approval was given for a single-span suspension bridge of 3,320 m to cross the Strait of Messina at a height of 80 m above the water. Work was due to begin in 1989. (DAVID FISHER)

Buildings. In April 1986 the newly completed headquarters building for the Hong Kong and Shanghai Banking Corp. in Hong Kong was officially opened; it had been under construction since 1981. The building was of outstanding engineering and architectural interest; it stood 180 m high, measured 70 m by 55 m on each floor, and rose 47 stories supported on two rows of four steel masts each. Each mast comprised four tubular steel columns interconnected at each story by rectangular beams. The floors themselves were not supported directly on the masts but hung in groups of seven stories from two-story-deep suspension trusses at five levels. This structural arrangement facilitated a large column-free zone at the ground-floor level. The banking hall was housed in a 13-story atrium illuminated by a novel arrangement of sun scoops that reflected light into the building.

The new Lloyd's redevelopment in London became operational in 1986. The remarkable building was some 100 m high with a central atrium extending the whole height. The main floor areas, known as galleries, were column-free areas surrounding the atrium. Vertical circulation and environmental-services distribution zones were confined to six towers around the perimeter of the main structure. Different parts of the galleries had varying numbers of stories so that the glazed atrium walls were exposed in some areas, rising to a crowning barrel vault roof. The main floors themselves were of novel construction; their main beams had an 18-m span and were constructed of prestressed-concrete inverted U beams. The floor itself was set on a 1.8-m-square grid of rectangular beams with stub columns at the nodes that supported a 100-mm (4-in)-

PHOTOGRAPHS, IAN LAMBOT—FOSTER ASSOCIATES

The futuristic silver-gray tower of the new headquarters for the Hong Kong and Shanghai Banking Corp. rises 180 metres high over Hong Kong. Two rows of steel masts serve as the building's inner spine, but suspension trusses carry the actual weight of the open floors.

thick concrete slab. Each story had high- and low-level services zones; the high-level zone, located below the slab, contained lighting, return air ducts, smoke detectors, and sprinklers. The lower zone was above the slab and below a raised floor containing supply air ducting, chilled water, electric power, and communications cabling.

A notable large-span roof covered the new King Fahd International Stadium near Riyadh, Saudi Arabia. The amphitheatre substructure was relatively conventional and large enough for 66,000 spectators to be seated around an Olympic-size running track and international-size football (soccer) playing field. The roof above the spectators was made of a white Teflon-coated fibreglass fabric with 24 peaks supported on hollow, steel-cabled, stayed columns. A feature of the stadium was the five-story Royal Pavilion, which contained conference rooms, dining facilities, bedrooms, and administrative facilities. The electrical systems included a television scoreboard, repeater (replay) screens, and international communications links.

On a lesser scale, but of significant technical interest, was a demountable enclosure for the New York Church of all Nations for use in various countries in Africa. An original "tent" supplied in 1980 was ripped apart by strong winds in 1983 and had to be redesigned using as much of the old structure as possible. By testing in a wind tunnel models of the original profile and one with an aerodynamically improved profile, a modified shape that resulted in a 35% reduction in peak wind pressures was developed. The 12 lattice-steel supporting masts were reused in a slightly different configuration, and a new fabric envelope of polyester coated with polyvinyl chloride was made. Fabric roofs of this type were commonly made with fibreglass-based cloth, but they deteriorated when folded and so were not ideally suited for the demountable type of application.

Under construction in 1986 in New Delhi, India, was the largest of seven houses of worship for the Baha'i faith. The building was to take the form of a giant lotus flower with two layers of nine unfolding petals constructed in marble-clad reinforced-concrete shells. Within the main petals was a steel and glass roof.

An architectural landmark was achieved in 1986 with the completion of the Theatre Essen (West Germany). It was designed by Alvar Aalto 27 years earlier, when it won the architectural competition for a new opera house for Essen. Detailed design of the theatre continued intermittently but because of lack of funds did not get under way seriously until 1981, by which time Aalto had died. The design was developed, however, with few alterations and was likely to be the last of his works to be completed. With 11 floors, the building was impressive in scale, and the exterior walls were entirely clad in gray granite.

(GEOFFREY M. PINFOLD)

Dams. Dam building continued to be faced with many obstacles in 1986, including financial difficulties, environmental objections, and structural failures. However, these were not enough to deter new construction, as the need for water remained paramount.

Countries large and small continued to clamour for more and faster construction of dams, for many reasons. Nepal, having sampled the benefits of the completed Kulekhani Dam with its small hydroelectric plant, was pushing forward with its Marsyangdi Dam. With a generating capacity of 70 MW, it would be the largest hydroelectric plant in the country.

Malaysia's Kenyir Dam, a 150-m-high rockfill type with a 400-MW power plant, was nearing completion. Also in Malaysia the Bakun Dam was involved in bitter controversy over the impact it would have on the lives of the people living nearby. Approximately 4,000 of them faced resettlement. Compensation for this relocation was claimed to be inadequate. Indonesia was moving ahead with its Mrica Dam on the Serayu River; it was designed to provide 180 MW for use in central Java.

Kenya decided to proceed with its 100-m-high Turkwell Gorge Dam to develop 105 MW of power. It would also irrigate 12,000 ha (30,000 ac) of fertile land that was lacking water. Cameroon began construction of a storage dam on the Mape River to provide water to nearby cities and produce 265 MW of power for their industries.

In Algeria two dams were completed. The Sidi Yakoub

THE NEW YORK TIMES

An artist's drawing gives some idea of the size of the Three Gorges Dam, proposed for China's Chang Jiang (Yangtze River). Proponents say the dam would supply immense energy for the populous country and serve to control floods. Its backed-up waters, however, would fill famous scenic gorges and displace about one million people.

Dam on Wadi el Ardjem was designed to store 280 million cu m (9,900,000,000 cu ft) of water to irrigate 9,000 ha (22,200 ac) and supply water for 30,000 people. The Duerdeur Dam on Wadi Herresa would store 7.5 million cu m (265 million cu ft) of water and supply the needs of the town of Sanyat at Had.

A slowdown in dam construction for various reasons was also in evidence during the year. India's Narmada Sagar Dam might have to be reduced in height to satisfy environmentalists and local people, who objected to the inundation of jungle areas and relocation of several villages. Enthusiasm for the Three Gorges project in China was dampened, and the planners were restudying the impact the dam would have when one million people needed to be resettled. Construction of the Kumgangsan Dam on the Han River in North Korea caused South Korea to charge that the dam posed a security threat because a natural or man-made disaster to the structure would flood South Korea's agricultural heartland. Late in the year South Korea decided to build a dam on the Pukhangang River to counter the threat from North Korea. Austria decided to revoke its plans to develop the Hainsburg project on the Danube because of environmental pressures and instead would develop a wildlife preserve in the area.

Research was being intensified to find cheaper ways to build spillways, a major element in dam safety. Experiments were being conducted with spillways surfaced with grass, reinforced grids, fabric mats, and roller-compacted concrete.

The Kantalai Dam in Sri Lanka failed, with 135 deaths reported and 2,500 people missing. The original dam was constructed in the 7th century and was periodically rehabilitated and repaired. The dam was 15 m high and provided irrigation for 10,000 ha (25,000 ac) and water supply to several villages. The storm surge barrier in The Netherlands was inaugurated and declared ready to provide protection from flooding by high tides and wave surges. The bold scheme cost more than $2 billion and took ten years to complete. (T. W. MERMEL)

Roads. Rehabilitation and maintenance projects were expected to be the primary road-related concerns of less developed nations during the next decade. Because of the lack of effective maintenance programs, coupled with rapidly increasing traffic volumes and axle loads, more than half

Major World Dams Under Construction in 1986[1]

Name of dam	River	Country	Type[2]	Height (m)	Length of crest (m)	Volume content (000 cu m)	Gross reservoir capacity (000 cu m)
Altinkaya	Kizilirmak	Turkey	E,R	195	604	2,600	5,763,000
Ataturk	Euphrates	Turkey	E,R	184	746	85,000	48,700,000
Bakun	Rajang	Malaysia	R	210	900	29,400	43,800,000
Boruca	Terraba	Costa Rica	E,R	267	700	43,000	14,960,000
Bureya	Bureya	U.S.S.R.	G	139	810	3,561	20,900,000
Casa de Piedra	Rio Colorado	Argentina	E	56	10,000	16,500	4,000,000
Chapeton	Paraná	Argentina	E,G	35	224,000	296,200	60,600,000
Cipasang	Cimanuk	Indonesia	E,R	200	1,860	90,000	860,000
Corpus Posadas	Paraná	Argentina/Paraguay	E,G	65	8,474	18,200	13,000,000
Dabaklamm	Dorferbach	Austria	A	220	332	1,000	235,000
Dongfeng	Yachi He	China	A	166	263	860	970,000
Dongjiang	Laishui	China	A	157	438	940	9,150,000
Dorna	Lerez	Spain	G	151	163	68	27,500
Gallito Ciego	Jequetepeque	Peru	E,R	112	750	15,000	400,000
Garabi	Uruguay	Argentina/Brazil	E,G	60	3,960	18,740	10,974,000
Guavio	Guavio	Colombia	E,R	243	390	17,755	1,020,000
Hrusov-Dunakiliti	Dunaj	Czechoslovakia	E,G	29	31,500	18,340	199,000
Ilha Grande	Paraná	Brazil	E,G	29	7,060	11,573	30,000,000
Ingapata	Paute	Ecuador	G	166	430	1,600	413,000
Kayraktepe	Goksu	Turkey	E,R	199	580	17,000	4,800,000
Kishau	Tons	India	E,R	253	360	18,400	2,400,000
Kouilou	Kouilou	Congo	A	137	345	390	35,000,000
La Vueltosa	Caparo	Venezuela	E	118	1,200	15,000	5,300,000
Lhakwar	Yamuna	India	G	192	440	2,000	580,000
Lower Tunguska	Lower Tunguska	U.S.S.R.	E,G	210	6,200	23,000	45,000,000
Lower Usuma	Usuma	Nigeria	E	49	1,350	93,000	100,000
Maqarin	Yarmuk	Jordan	E,R	164	700	21,000	486,000
Menzelet	Ceyhan	Turkey	E,R	151	425	8,000	19,500,000
Michihuao	Limay	Argentina	E	70	6,700	29,840	5,860,000
Nan Choan	Quae Yai	Thailand	R	187	430	12,400	5,950,000
Pati	Paraná	Argentina	E,G	36	174,900	230,180	38,000,000
Paute	Mazar	Ecuador	G	180	400	1,650	500,000
Piedra del Aquila	Limay	Argentina	G	174	795	2,764	12,800,000
Planicie Banderita	Neuquen	Argentina	E	35	350	1,194	43,000,000
Potrerillos	Mendoza	Argentina	E	146	550	17,120	860,000
Rocandor	Uruguay	Brazil/Argentina	E,R	78	1,598	9,940	33,580,000
Rogun	Vakhsh	U.S.S.R.	E,R	335	602	85,000	13,300,000
San Roque	Agno	Philippines	E	210	1,130	43,150	990,000
Sardar Sarovar	Narmada	India	G	163	1,199	7,472	9,500,000
Tehri	Bhagirathi	India	E,R	261	570	22,750	3,539,000
Thein Dam Ranjit	Ravi	India	E,R	160	565	16,187	3,280,000
Upper Wainganga	Wainganga	India	E	43	181	6,290	50,700,000
Urra II	Sinu	Colombia	R	170	275	23,500	34,300,000
Yacyreta-Apipe	Paraná	Paraguay/Argentina	E,G	42	82,000	61,200	21,000,000
Major World Dams Completed in 1985 and 1986[1]							
El M'Jara	Ouergha	Morocco	E	87	1,600	25,000	4,000,000
Grand Maison	Eau d'Oile	France	E,R	160	550	12,500	140,000
Guri (Raúl Leoni)	Caroni	Venezuela	E,R,G	162	11,409	77,971	138,000,000
Kara Kaya	Euphrates	Turkey	A	173	462	2,000	9,580,000
Kenyir	Trengganu	Malaysia	E,R	150	800	16,800	13,500,000
Khudoni	Inguri	U.S.S.R.	A	201	545	1,475	365,000
Longyangxia	Huang He	China	A,G	175	375	1,750	24,700,000
Naramata	Naramata	Japan	E,R	158	520	12,500	90,000
Oosterschelde	Vense Gat Oosterschelde	The Netherlands	E,R	50	9,000	50,000	2,780,000
Porto Primavera	Paraná	Brazil	E,G	38	11,385	8,441	18,500,000
São Felix	Tocantins	Brazil	E,R	160	1,950	34,000	55,200,000
Tres Irmaos	Tiete	Brazil	E,G	67	3,700	15,000	3,450,000
Warna	Warna	India	E,G	91	1,580	15,310	964,000
Zillergründl	Ziller	Austria	A	186	506	1,355	90,000

[1] Having a height exceeding 150 m (492 ft); or having a volume content exceeding 15 million cu m (19.6 million cu yd); or forming a reservoir exceeding 14,800 × 10^6 cu m of capacity (12 million ac-ft).

[2] Type of dam: E = earth; R = rockfill; A = arch; G = gravity.

(T. W. MERMEL)

of all paved roads in the 85 less developed countries were estimated to be in need of major repairs. About one-quarter of all paved roads in those nations, a total of some 270,000 km (1 km = 0.62 mi), would require anything from partial to complete reconstruction.

In the United States the 68,500-km Interstate System celebrated its 30th birthday and was showing signs of old age. Eight percent of the network was in poor condition, and more than 34% was in only fair condition. Current estimates for repairing the roads amounted to $64.3 billion. Only 2.8% of the Interstate System remained to be completed, including the $1.6 billion Century Freeway in Los Angeles, the most expensive highway in California's history. In action mirroring increased trends toward new methods of highway financing, the state of Pennsylvania approved construction of 400 km of toll roads in the state at a cost of between $3 billion and $5 billion.

In Canada the federal government planned to spend $20 million on improving and maintaining the Yukon section of the Alaska Highway, the largest road project in the nation. Canada was cooperating closely with the U.S. on the $150 million, five-year Strategic Highway Research Program, which was investigating methods of preserving deteriorating highways and bridges.

Mexico planned to add some 300 km of trunk roads to its road network during 1986, while in Panama a multilane highway was under consideration that would speed traffic between the Atlantic and Pacific coasts in less than 30 minutes. More than 600 km of Chile's North-South Highway had been rebuilt under a long-term rehabilitation program.

Hong Kong was building a major road crossing into China at Lok Ma Chau in the New Territories. In Japan the last 75 km of the 300-km Kanetsu Expressway were completed in 1986, and construction of the Joban, Kinki, and Sanyo expressways was being accelerated, aiming at a total national expressway network of 4,302 km.

Thailand, which had spent $330 million on its road program by the end of 1986, was constructing a largely elevated expressway system to relieve congestion in Bangkok and save an estimated $400,000 in fuel costs each day. Australia's Stuart Highway, a 925-km road linking Port Augusta on the Spencer Gulf with Kulgera in the Northern Territory, was completed in 1986.

Kenya and Nigeria completed their segments of the 6,399-km Mombasa-Lagos Trans-African Highway, which also crossed Uganda, Cameroon, the Central African Republic, and Zaire. A 520-km road connecting Cairo with the port of Nuwebah on the Red Sea and with Jordan and other Arab countries was under construction.

In Britain the 193-km M25 ring road around London was completed, even while traffic congestion made it necessary to add a fourth lane to an existing segment of the motorway. The last link in the N2 expressway in Switzerland, between Biasca-Giustizia and Bellinzone-Nord, was opened in May 1986. A new segment of the M1 expressway linking Budapest, Hung., with the Austrian border was opened between Herceghalom and Bicske.

CHANNEL TUNNEL (CHUNNEL)

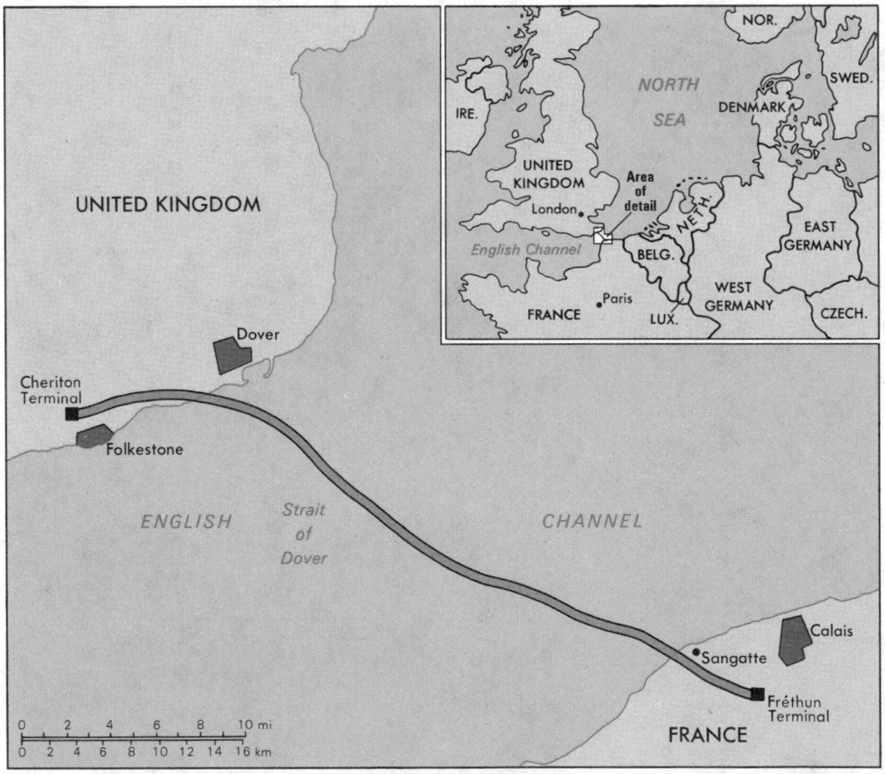

The English Channel Tunnel, or "Chunnel," was to be an alternative to ferry transport between England and France. The official go-ahead was given for the chosen design of twin rail tunnels—and a service tunnel—bored 40 metres (130 feet) beneath the Channel bed. Shuttle trains would carry road vehicles and their passengers. The closest rival design was a similar tunnel with a drive-through expressway for cars and trains. In the Euroroute option road vehicles passed into a tunnel through offshore man-made islands with spiral ramps, and a second tunnel carried rail traffic. Also rejected was the Eurobridge plan, a tubular suspension bridge that would contain a multilevel road, all built over the Channel waters. This plan also included a separate railway tunnel underground.

PROPOSED CROSS-CHANNEL OPTIONS
In Cross Section

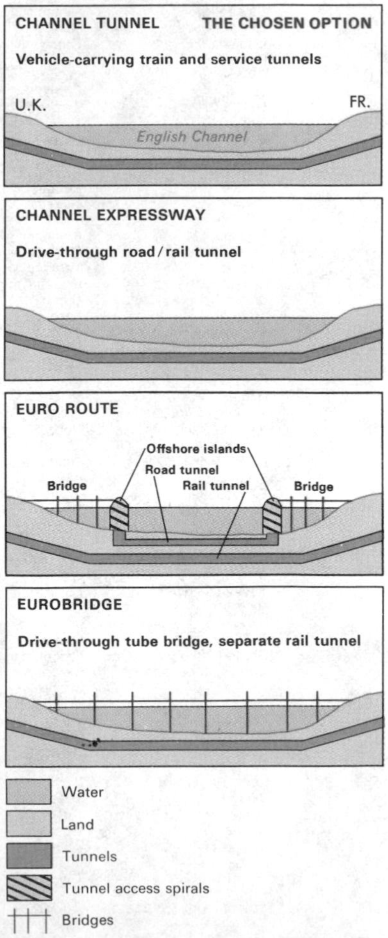

Source: *The Times* (November 1, 1985), p. 28

A new expressway network connecting Sweden's major population centres at an estimated cost of $1,650,000,000 was under study. The recent entry of Spain and Portugal into the European Communities resulted in plans for a major new highway and tunnel through the Pyrenees Mountains at a possible cost of $1 billion.

(HUGH M. GILLESPIE)

Tunnels. In Western Europe the most important event of 1986 was the selection of a proposal by the British and French governments for a tunnel under the English Channel. (*See* Sidebar.) With a cost of almost $3.8 billion, this project dwarfed most others in money terms, but it was surpassed when the U.S. government announced that it was considering spending $4 billion on the world's largest physics machine, a superconducting super collider (SSC) similar to the large electron positron (LEP) collider that was under construction near Geneva. The SSC would require 9.6 km of circumferential tunnels to house the test machinery.

In Japan a major construction venture was a combined tunnel and bridge to be built between Kawasaki and Kisarazu across Tokyo Bay. The cost, projected at $6 billion, included financing 9.6 km of four-lane highway in the tunnel. Construction work was expected to take eight years, and geologic difficulties were expected.

Continuing a trend that began in 1980, construction was under way on many urban mass transit systems. The success of this form of transport was demonstrated by the number of cities that decided to expand their existing facilities as well as those planning or already constructing mass transit railways (MTR). Singapore's MTR system was to be 67 km long with 21 km of tunnels and was due to open in 1988. In the U.K. London's Heathrow Airport expanded, adding a fourth terminal by constructing twin tunnels under the runways and airfield perimeter. Mexico City's tunnels survived a devastating earthquake in September 1985 and were operational again within hours. The city planned to add a further 100 km to its network. In Caracas, Venezuela, construction work was under way on the subway system to extend its track length with eight kilometres of tunnel and eight stations by 1989.

Intense tunneling activity in Montreal was directed toward easing the pollution of the St. Lawrence and Prairie rivers. Since 1975 the city had built approximately 100 km of tunnels and associated works. A formidable collection of tunnel boring machines (TBM) were employed in Montreal, and contractors from North America and Europe participated and brought with them state-of-the-art expertise. Other cities spending heavily to fight pollution and meet the transport needs of growing populations were Istanbul, Turkey; Milwaukee, Wis.; Cairo, Egypt; Bilbao, Spain; and Hamburg, West Germany.

Overseas activities by designers and contractors from all the traditional tunneling nations reached record levels in 1986. As developments in their own countries neared completion, there was an increase in the export of skills and knowledge to less developed countries that lacked the necessary skills. (GEOFFREY J. NOBLETT)

This article updates the *Macropædia* articles BUILDING CONSTRUCTION; PUBLIC WORKS.

The Channel Tunnel: A Positive View

On Jan. 20, 1986, the British and French governments announced their decision that the fixed link across the English Channel would take the form of a tunnel railway system handling road and rail traffic, passengers, and freight between Cheriton near Folkestone, England, and Fréthun near Calais, France. After a year of competition between opposing groups offering a variety of projects involving tunnels, bridges, or combinations of the two, the award went to the Anglo-French construction and banking group that became known as Eurotunnel, at a construction cost of about £2,500 million (almost $3.8 billion).

In contrast to more adventurous and futuristic proposals, Eurotunnel offered an updated version of the South Eastern Railway project started in 1874 and abandoned in 1883, the Fox-Sartiaux proposals of 1907–13, and the Anglo-French government-sponsored plan of the early 1970s that was canceled for economic reasons. A factor working in favour of a tunnel was undoubtedly the suitability of the existing chalk-marl soil composition for tunnel construction. Together with the use of proven technology, this was to be a vital factor in raising the project capital. Uniquely for a venture of this size, there was to be no government investment by either country.

British membership in the European Communities (EC) had progressively increased the volume of traffic and trade across the Channel to the extent that by 1984 British exports to the EC accounted for 60% of the U.K.'s total (non-oil) exports. The expansion made the case for a fixed link a pressing one. At the same time, governments were wary of being totally dependent on one form of transport. The proposed system was to coexist with other cross-Channel operations that it was never intended to replace. Traffic movements were expected to double by the year 2000, providing a healthy commercial market for a variety of services. The link could also provide up to 8,000 permanent jobs, with another 10,000 employed during its construction in France and the U.K. The manufacturing and provision of equipment and materials for the project would also generate badly needed employment in many areas outside the immediate construction regions.

Although the Channel Tunnel would be Europe's biggest construction project of the 20th century, because of favourable geologic factors it was unlikely to provide the technical challenges and difficulties of the great Alpine tunnels or the Japanese Seikan Tunnel. The greatest challenge was logistic. The twin rail tunnels and their service tunnel would total some 150 km (93 mi), and as many as seven mechanical boring machines would have to operate simultaneously. The amount of waste to be removed would approach eight million cubic metres, and more than 1.8 million metric tons of concrete and iron tunnel linings would have to be installed.

Opening to rail traffic in 1993, the link would eventually carry up to 4,000 vehicles an hour in each direction by means of shuttle trains built especially for the 30-minute journey. Conventional train services were to share the tunnels, thus directly connecting the U.K. passenger and freight networks with the European system. (GEOFFREY J. NOBLETT)

Environment

Most of the important environmental issues of 1986 concerned the generation of electricity, and they led to contradictory solutions. The catastrophic explosion of a nuclear reactor at Chernobyl, U.S.S.R., early on the morning of April 26 caused extensive, though minor, radioactive contamination across much of northern Europe. The incident dominated environmental discussions for much of the year and led to demands for the abandonment of nuclear power programs in several countries. Coal-burning power stations were blamed by some for the "acid rain" phenomenon, though disagreements over causes and cures continued. The implications of a global climatic warming due to the "greenhouse effect" suggested that the world should reduce its dependence on all carbon-based fuels. Continuing controversy over plans to dam the Danube in central Europe seemed to suggest limits to the use that could be made of hydroelectric power.

INTERNATIONAL COOPERATION

UN Environment Program. On Nov. 10, 1985, UNEP Executive Director Mostafa Tolba announced a plan to rehabilitate land in Africa that had suffered from poor environmental management. The scheme was developed by UNEP, the UN Economic Commission for Africa, the Organization of African Unity, and other agencies and was endorsed by ministers from 46 African countries at a meeting in Cairo on December 16–18. It was to be based on 30 pasture areas and 150 village projects in 50 countries. Governments were asked to contribute about $50 million for five years to cover foreign currency costs and to meet local costs themselves.

UN Food and Agriculture Organization. At its biennial conference held in Rome in November 1985, the FAO adopted an international code of conduct on the distribution and use of pesticides. The code called for child-proof packaging that was difficult to reuse, labeling in local languages that also took levels of literacy into account, the marketing of products in ready-to-use forms, and the use of less toxic products.

European Communities. Environment ministers agreed in March 1986 to extend the ban on discharges into Community waters to three substances—DDT, pentachlorophenol disinfectant, and carbon tetrachloride solvent. In April the European Commission called for a program to investigate the presence of persistent compounds in human milk and body tissues.

International Council of Scientific Unions. An International Geosphere-Biosphere Program was launched at an ICSU meeting in Berne, Switz., in September. The aim was to collect enough information within ten years to permit events in critical environmental areas to be predicted a century or so in advance.

The "Greenhouse Effect." At a closed meeting of scientists from about 30 countries held in Villach, Austria, in October 1985, it was agreed that within the next century there could be a global increase in temperature of 1.5° to 4.5° C (2.7° to 8.1° F) and a rise in sea level of 20 to 140 cm (8 to 55 in). Held under the auspices of the World Meteorological Organization, UNEP, and the ICSU, the meeting was told that the atmospheric concentration of carbon dioxide, nitrogen oxide, methane, ozone, and chlorofluorocarbons (CFCs) was increasing because of human activities, mainly the burning of fossil fuels and the clearing of tropical forests. The scientists agreed that the climatic consequences called for urgent consideration.

Similar warnings were repeated throughout the year. In November 1985 the results of another study were discussed at UNEP headquarters in Nairobi, Kenya, where particular attention was paid to the risks of CFC-induced depletion of the ozone layer. The study warned that temperatures could rise by 4.5° C within 80 years. A rise of 1° to 5° C (1.8° to 9° F) by 2050, continuing well into the 22nd century, was predicted in January 1986 by scientists at the U.S. National Center for Atmospheric Research, and in April scientists in Europe produced evidence of a warming. British workers at the Climatic Research Unit, University of East Anglia, said they had detected a warming in both hemispheres, and

(LEFT) AP/WIDE WORLD; (RIGHT) KATHARINE S. THOMAS—TAURUS PHOTOS

Canadian Prime Minister Brian Mulroney and U.S. Pres. Ronald Reagan exchange documents after signing an agreement toward reducing acid rain. Proposed measures emphasized cleaner coal burning by industries. Sulfur oxides, chiefly from coal smoke, drifting through the air—sometimes across country borders—returned to Earth as vegetation-killing acids. A thinned North Carolina forest (right) is evidence of the damage.

climatologists at the University of Utrecht, Neth., reported a worldwide glacial retreat, starting in the 1830s and linked to accumulating carbon dioxide. Scientists from the British Meteorological Office reported a rise in ocean temperatures and changes in wind patterns in low latitudes that suggested that rising levels of carbon dioxide might have contributed to droughts in the Sahel region of Africa.

In May the U.S. Department of Energy published four reports on the effects of accumulating carbon dioxide. Agreeing with other scientists that sea levels were rising at 10 to 25 cm (4 to 10 in) a century and that an overall climatic warming was taking place, the reports warned that the effects could accelerate suddenly and that by 2100 temperatures could have reached levels not experienced for at least 100,000 years, with major changes in sea levels. In September, at an informal meeting of the signatories of the Vienna Convention on the Protection of the Ozone Layer in Leesburg, Va., delegates proposed controls on emissions of CFCs, especially CFC-11 and CFC-12, which might set a precedent for controls on other "greenhouse" gases.

NATIONAL DEVELOPMENTS

Acid Rain. British forests showed little acid rain damage and appeared healthier than they were a year earlier, according to the report of a survey given by Roger Bradley, Forestry Commission commissioner for private forestry and development, speaking at a conference on "The State of the Nation's Trees" on April 15. This impression was confirmed at the end of June, when the Forestry Commission published the results of its 1985 surveys of conifers and beech trees.

Central Electricity Generating Board (CEGB) scientists pointed out several times during the year that the link between acid rain damage and power station emissions was far from clear. In January CEGB scientists warned that reducing nitrogen oxide emissions from vehicles might increase ozone pollution, since ozone is broken down by nitrogen oxide. A videotape issued by the CEGB suggesting that British power stations contributed little to Norway's acid rain led the Norwegian Ministry of the Environment to hold a press conference in London in December 1985 to protest, and in January 1986 the U.K. Department of the Environment dissociated itself from the film. In March U.K. Minister of State for the Environment William Waldegrave agreed with Norwegian Environment Minister Rakel Surlien that sulfur dioxide from Britain contributed significantly to the damage suffered by Norwegian lakes. Both ministers agreed that damage to trees is caused mainly by nitrogen oxides from vehicle exhaust. Although Britain was still not prepared to join "the 30% club," in fact it would achieve a 30% reduction in its sulfur dioxide emissions between 1980 and 1993.

A new coal-fired boiler came into operation at Fiddler's Ferry power station, near Widnes, Cheshire, in November 1985. Part of a CEGB research program into acid rain, the boiler was designed to emit 40% less nitrogen oxides than other boilers; by separating the flow of air and coal, and thus reducing the amount of oxygen during combustion, it released gaseous nitrogen rather than nitrogen oxides. In May 1986 the Drax B power station opened in Yorkshire amid protests from environmental groups because it had no pollution-control equipment and would release 150,000 metric tons of sulfur dioxide a year. U.K. Secretary of State for the Environment Nicholas Ridley announced on September 11 that the existing Drax B, Fiddler's Ferry, and West Burton coal-fired power stations, along with all new coal-fired installations, would be fitted with flue-gas desulfurization equipment, to be in operation by 1997.

In November 1985 Karel Nutil, deputy chairman of the Czechoslovak State Commission for Scientific and Technical Development, announced a 15-year program for environmental improvement to deal mainly with acid disposition. The most seriously affected areas were around the industrial centres of northern Bohemia, Prague, Bratislava, and Ostrava-Karvina. An emergency survey of forests in the Kanto plain around Tokyo was announced by Japan's Environment Agency in February 1986. It followed the publication of two research reports, from the Gumma Prefectural Health and Pollution Research Centre and Chiba University, giving evidence of extensive air pollution damage to trees. At a September meeting of the Nordic Council in Stockholm, the Swedish government recommended a reduction of up to 90% in sulfur dioxide and 75% in nitrogen oxide emissions, with reductions in hydrocarbon emissions to decrease pollution by ozone. The proposal, which urged that the two specified reductions be achieved by 1993 and 1995, respectively, was supported by environmental groups and by experts from the UN Economic Commission for Europe.

The Swiss Forestry Office reported in January that acid rain damage had affected 43% of the trees in the central Alpine region, as well as 10% of the "barrier forests," which hold back snow and help prevent avalanches. Fearing that some mountain passes might become too dangerous to use, in September the government proposed measures aimed at reducing air pollution to its 1950 levels by 1990. Opponents of the move, and of the earlier imposition of speed limits and the compulsory introduction of catalytic converters on automobiles from 1987, raised a petition calling for a referendum on the issue.

In January William Davis, former premier of Ontario, and Drew Lewis, former U.S. secretary of transportation, presented U.S. Pres. Ronald Reagan and Canadian Prime Minister Brian Mulroney with the results of their negotiations on reducing acid deposition. Admitting that U.S. emissions caused damage in Canada, they recommended that $5 billion be spent by the U.S. government and industry over a five-year period to reduce sulfur emissions and to develop cleaner technologies for burning coal. President Reagan welcomed the report but made no promise to increase the $1.5 billion already set aside by Congress for research in those two areas. While Reagan and Mulroney were meeting in March, the U.S. National Academy of Sciences published *Acid Deposition: Long-Term Trends,* which found a link between sulfur dioxide emissions, the presence in the air of sulfate aerosols, reduced visibility, and wet sulfate deposition, leading to the acidification of lakes and dwindling fish populations.

There was a small deterioration in the condition of West German forests, according to the 1985 Forest Damage Inventory published at the end of 1985. New damage occurred mainly at high altitudes and in the south, and there was some recovery in lowland areas.

Air Pollution. A study of the health of residents in Armadale and Bathgate near Edinburgh, Scotland, reported in the *British Journal of Industrial Medicine* in January, showed high incidences of cancer, apparently linked to ore boiling at the steelworks in each town. Armadale was said to have the highest overall death rate from all causes of any town in Scotland and especially high rates of cancers of the esophagus and stomach. In Bathgate the incidence of lung cancer was double the British average. Scotland had the highest incidence of lung cancer in the world.

The number of smog-damaged trees in U.S. national parks in California doubled between 1982 and 1986, according to James Bennett, a National Park Service ecologist

A banner that translates as "Requiem for the Rhine" indicates the attitude of 300 music academy students who demonstrated in Basel, Switzerland, in reaction to the pollution of the Rhine River. The pollution, caused by chemicals washed into the river with water used to fight a fire in a chemical warehouse, killed fish and other life forms and generated odours in shoreline communities.

DPA/AFP PHOTO

based in Colorado. He said in August that smog from Los Angeles and the San Joaquin Valley had affected more than half the trees in Yosemite Park and almost 90% of pines and oaks in the Sequoia and Kings Canyon parks.

Freshwater Pollution. Farms were revealed as a major source of river pollution in several reports published in the U.K. during the year. In June the Southwest Water Authority stated that in five years farm effluent had halved the total length of unpolluted rivers in its area. The Northwest Water Authority said there had been a 30% increase in the length of rivers in which no fish could live. Effluent from manufacturing industry was the most serious source of pollution, but discharges from farms had reduced by 200 km (124 mi) the overall length of clean or only slightly polluted rivers. On July 24 the Water Authorities Association and the Ministry of Agriculture, Fisheries, and Food published *Water Pollution from Farm Waste: 1985,* showing that in 1985 the number of pollution incidents increased by 25% to 3,500, caused mainly by leakage of silage liquor and livestock slurry, and the number of prosecutions increased by 45% to 159, with farm wastes accounting for half.

In Shanghai, where industrial effluent caused severe pollution in the Huangpu (Huang-p'u) River and Suzhou (Suchow) Creek, a $1 billion scheme to rebuild the sewerage system was under consideration. In September it was reported that the city hoped to obtain a $145 million loan from the World Bank to help buy equipment. The plan was to build a 40-km (25-mi) tunnel to carry the waste to the estuary of the Changjiang (Yangtze River), where it would be flushed away by the tides.

In Woburn, Mass., two companies, Beatrice Cos. and W. R. Grace and Co., were sued for polluting water with chemicals blamed for causing cancer and other illnesses. A drycleaning company that had also been implicated, Unifirst, agreed out of court to pay $1 million to families of the alleged victims. The companies were accused of discharging 200 parts per billion (ppb) of trichloroethylene, 20 ppb of tetrachloroethylene, and traces of (1,1,1)-trichloroethane, (1,2)-*trans* dichloroethylene, and chloroform found in local wells. The trial jury cleared Beatrice but found that Grace had "substantially contributed" to the pollution. Further court proceedings were scheduled, but before they got under way, Grace agreed to pay more than $9 million to nine families and an unspecified amount to five others.

President Reagan killed reauthorization of the Clean Water Act in November by a pocket veto (failure to sign a law within ten days when Congress is adjourned) because of the high cost. Supporters of the bill said they intended to reintroduce it in the next session of Congress.

Vladimir Denisov, an inspector from the Soviet Ministry of Water Resources, warned on Radio Moscow in early September that the saline Balkuduk Lake, in the Kazakh Republic, had received 80 million cu m (105 million cu yd) of waste water from the industrial area around the town of Pavlodar and was so overburdened that a severe storm might burst its banks and cause flooding. If that happened, the resort of Muyaldy would be engulfed, and the polluted water would flow into the Irtysh River, the main source of water for Kazakhstan and western Siberia.

Land Conservation. In January Australia's minister for primary industries, John Kerin, authorized logging in 25 areas of Tasmania, including four unique rain forests, to supply nearly three million metric tons of timber a year for 15 years. The Australian Heritage Commission advised against the scheme. Conservation groups opposed it, as well as plans for logging in East Gippsland, Victoria, and near Eden, New South Wales.

Financing of the Danube hydroelectric scheme at Nagymaros, Hung., was taken over by Austria in December 1985. Austrian Finance Minister Franz Vranitzky said the 8 billion schilling ($450 million) cost would be provided by a consortium of Austrian banks, to be repaid over 20 years from electricity sales. Besides supplying power, the Nagymaros dam would accommodate surges from the storage reservoir at Dunakitili, below Bratislava, serving the Gabcikovo generating station. The scheme was opposed by environmentalists in Austria and Hungary because it could destroy wetlands and pollute the Budapest water supply.

In the U.S. representatives of the oil industry, environmental groups, local fishermen, and Alaskan communities reached an agreement on oil drilling off the Alaskan coast and were brought together in May by the actor Robert Redford to urge Secretary of the Interior Donald Hodel to ratify it. When existing licenses expired at the end of 1986, the agreement would prevent drilling in 96 million ha (240 million ac) designated as environmentally sensitive but would permit it in four areas of the Bering Sea.

Following outspoken academic opposition, Soviet schemes to divert Siberian rivers southward were not included in the 1986–90 five-year plan adopted in March.

The objectors argued that the ecological and social consequences had not been considered fully and the scheme would be uneconomic. On August 15 TASS reported that the Politburo had dropped the schemes.

Radioactive Wastes. The most serious accident in the history of the nuclear power industry occurred on April 26 at Chernobyl, about 130 km (80 mi) north of Kiev in the Ukraine. One of four identical 1,000-MW RMBK (water-cooled, graphite-moderated) reactors caught fire, leading to a series of explosions that severely damaged the building housing it and releasing a large amount of radioactive material, most of which fell within a 40- to 100-km (25- to 60-mi) radius of the plant. Two workers were killed at once, and by the end of September the death toll had risen to 31. More than 135,000 people were evacuated from the Pripyat, Kiev, and Gomel (Belorussia) areas.

The explosions released an estimated total of 10^{16} becquerels (the becquerel is the standard international unit of radioactive activity), about half of which rose to at least 6,000 m (20,000 ft) and drifted eastward. The remainder was emitted as a second cloud and drifted northwestward at low altitude, crossing northern Poland (where iodine tablets were issued to counteract the radioactivity), Scandinavia, and northern Britain. Above-average radioactivity was detected as far away as Israel, Japan, and North America. Nowhere in Western Europe did contamination approach international safety limits, although some governments banned or issued warnings against the sale of fresh milk and leafy vegetables. The movement and slaughter of sheep was restricted in parts of northern England and North Wales on June 20 and southern Scotland later when cesium-134 and cesium-137 radiation exceeded an "action level" of 1,000 becquerels per kilogram of meat.

The reactor was sealed with sand, lead, and boron dropped from helicopters, and liquid nitrogen was used to cool its base. It was declared safe on May 11, and the installation was finally encased in concrete. The official Soviet report of the incident was issued in August to delegates attending a meeting of the International Atomic Energy Agency in Vienna. The RMBK design had been considered by Western nuclear industry experts but rejected in the 1970s as unsafe. (*See* ENERGY: *Sidebar*.)

There were several more leaks of radioactive material from the Sellafield nuclear reprocessing plant in Cumbria, England, and controversy continued to surround the complex and its managers, British Nuclear Fuels Ltd. (BNFL). On January 23 there was a discharge of uranium into the Irish Sea, and on February 5 about 50 microcuries of plutonium were released into the outside air when a valve failed in a 20-year-old chemical separation plant handling spent Magnox fuel. BNFL said two workers were contaminated in the incident, but a preliminary assessment by the Nuclear Installations Inspectorate revealed that 11 had been affected. On February 19, following a third release the day before, the Isle of Man government expressed its concern about safety at Sellafield, and on the same day Irish Prime Minister Garret FitzGerald raised the matter with U.K. Prime Minister Margaret Thatcher. The environmentalist groups Greenpeace and Cumbrians Opposed to a Radioactive Environment accused BNFL of lying about the number and severity of leakages, and although the company denied these charges, the government was under increasing pressure to open the plant to inspection by officials of Euratom. A House of Commons Select Committee on the Environment report was highly critical of the Sellafield management.

Four sites for the shallow burial of low- and medium-level waste were named on February 25: Bradwell, Essex; South Killingholme, Humbershire; Fulbeck, Lincolnshire; and Elstow, Bedfordshire. Supported by their MPs, local residents began to form protest groups, and when attempts were made in August and September to start test drilling, they were delayed by protesters. The public inquiry into the proposal to build a nuclear-fuel reprocessing plant at Dounreay, Caithness, Scotland, opened in Thurso on April 7. It was boycotted by the main antinuclear groups because the plant was not yet designed and, therefore, there was no way to assess its safety or environmental impact.

In August the U.S. Environmental Protection Agency (EPA) set safety standards for radioactive radon gas in residences. The colourless, odourless gas occurs naturally as a decay product of uranium. Depending on the local geologic formation, it can seep into houses, and prolonged exposure can cause lung cancer. The EPA estimated that about eight million homes in the U.S. may have unacceptable levels of radon. It stated, however, that the primary responsibility for testing and remedial measures would rest with the state governments.

Toxic Chemical Wastes. Western Europe's most serious environmental crisis in many years began Nov. 1, 1986, when water used to extinguish a fire in a Sandoz AG chemical company warehouse in Schweizerhalle, near Basel, Switz., washed millions of litres of highly toxic chemicals, including mercury compounds, into the Rhine River. The damage was compounded by a smaller spill of poisonous herbicide from the Ciba-Geigy chemical plant in Basel, which had occurred on October 31 but was reported several days later. Hundreds of thousands of fish and eels died as a result, and it was feared that the entire ecosystem of the river had been damaged, wiping out years of work to restore the Rhine's wildlife. The water supplies of towns along the river were also endangered.

On November 12 scientists assessing the situation said that the Rhine from Basel to Mainz, West Germany, had suffered severe damage, but below Mainz the effect would be minor. At an emergency meeting in Zürich, Switz., of environment ministers of countries bordering the Rhine, the Swiss government was severely criticized for not alerting other countries in time to take preventive measures. Switzerland accepted responsibility for the accident and agreed to pay compensation. The Swiss also said they would consider bringing their antipollution regulations into line with the stricter rules adopted by the EC after poisonous gas leaked from a plant at Seveso, Italy, in 1976.

Legal arguments arising from the accident at Bhopal, India, in December 1984 continued throughout 1986. The Indian government argued that claims of persons injured by the poisonous gas leak from a Union Carbide Corp. plant should be heard in U.S. courts, but on May 12 Federal District Judge John Keenan, sitting in New York, ruled against this. The cases were transferred to New Delhi, where they opened on October 6, only to be adjourned, amid rumours of an out-of-court settlement, because Union Carbide was not represented. In March Union Carbide had reached a $350 million tentative settlement with victims, but the government sought compensation of about $1 billion.

The report of the official Indian investigation into the accident published at the end of December 1985 agreed with the Union Carbide finding that about 500 kg (1,100 lb) of water had entered a tank containing methyl isocyanate, but it maintained that the tank was contaminated by metal ions that catalyzed the reaction. This apparently ruled out the claim of sabotage advanced by a corporate director of Union Carbide. More than 2,000 people were arrested at Bhopal on September 29 when demonstrators demanded more aid for survivors, many of whom were said to be still

A West Berlin worker in protective clothing dumps vegetables near a sign indicating radiation danger. Local authorities ordered the action against food contaminated by fallout from the April nuclear power plant explosions in Chernobyl, U.S.S.R.

AP/WIDE WORLD

suffering from mental disorders and respiratory difficulties. Infant mortality and the incidence of miscarriages and low birth weight were also high.

Union Carbide was fined more than $1.3 million on April 1 for 221 violations of 55 federal safety and health regulations at its Institute, W.Va., plant where a leak of aldicarb oxime gas injured workers and local residents in August 1985. This was the largest enforcement action ever brought by the U.S. Occupational Safety and Health Administration.

A study of the health effects of exposure to dioxins, in particular the 2,3,7,8-TCDD that contaminated the defoliant Agent Orange, based on studies of U.S. veterans exposed during the Vietnam war, was suspended in April 1986 because of difficulties in establishing adequate exposure criteria and in correctly classifying degree of exposure. Chloracne was the only clear-cut health problem established, despite studies implicating liver disease, cancer, and birth defects. Another study, presented to the American Chemical Society in April, suggested that, although dioxins might persist in the soil for long periods, they did not travel readily through food chains.

The Superfund to clean up hazardous wastes in the U.S. was extended for five years when President Reagan, after threatening a veto because of the cost, yielded to congressional urging and signed the authorization bill on October 17. The cost of the program was set at $8.5 billion, most of which was to be raised from various taxes including a new broad-based tax on business. The legislation set strict standards for cleaning up waste sites and mandated the EPA to begin work on the 375 worst sites within five years. A rider attached to the bill authorized $500 million to clean up old gasoline (petrol) storage tanks that were leaking into groundwater.

The U.K. Health and Safety Executive (HSE) was reported in March to be compiling a list of 34,000 factories, chemical stores, and other places where more than 25 metric tons of a range of toxic and explosive substances were stored. Details of 200 of the most dangerous sites were released, and the HSE said that the full register would be available for public inspection. British imports of hazardous wastes rose from 3,786 metric tons in 1981 to 24,548 metric tons in 1985, according to *Hazardous Waste Management,* the annual report of the Hazardous Waste Inspectorate, published in July 1986. The Major Hazard Incident Data Service was launched in London on September 9. Established by the HSE and the Safety and Reliability Directorate of the U.K. Atomic Energy Authority, the service planned to record details of incidents and make information concerning them available throughout the world. Environment Secretary Ridley announced on August 7 that an Inspectorate of Pollution was to be formed. It would begin work on April 1, 1987, and would incorporate the Industrial Air Pollution Inspectorate, the HSE, the Hazardous Waste Inspectorate, and the Radiochemical Inspectorate.

In October 1985, during a hearing in the Irish High Court, Merck, Sharp and Dohme (Ireland) admitted that for 40 to 50% of the time between 1978 and 1982, a chemical waste incinerator owned by the company had been operating at a temperature too low to destroy toxic components in the waste and that emissions from it had not been monitored until 1982. The company was defending itself against allegations by a farmer, John Hanrahan, that pollution from the incinerator was responsible for illness among local people, the deaths of some 200 farm animals, and stillbirths or birth deformities in other livestock. The court decided that, although the farm had suffered unusual damage, there was no proof that the incinerator was responsible.

Asbestos. In the U.S. the EPA proposed in January to ban immediately the use of asbestos roofing felts, asbestos flooring felts, vinyl asbestos floor tile, asbestos cement pipe and fittings, and asbestos clothing; mining, importing, and all other uses of asbestos would be phased out within ten years. The ban would not affect asbestos already in place. Under legislation signed by President Reagan in October, schools would be required to protect children and school employees from asbestos hazards. It was estimated that some 35,000 schools would be affected.

Lead. In the U.K. the permitted amount of lead in petrol was reduced from 0.4 to 0.15 grams per litre as of Jan. 1, 1986. The first totally unleaded petrol appeared at some U.K. filling stations in late June, following the announcement by Environment Minister Waldegrave that unleaded petrol would be on sale by October 1987 and would be widely available by October 1989. It was introduced early mainly because of complaints from tourists who could buy it in their own countries and preferred it. It was expected that half of all petrol bought in West Germany would be unleaded by year's end.

A report issued by the EPA suggested that the danger to the U.S. public from lead in drinking water might be greater than previously thought. According to the new estimates, at least 38.1 million people were being exposed to unacceptable levels of lead in their water supplies, usually as a result of corrosion of old lead pipes. New rules on permissible levels of lead were being considered by the EPA. Meanwhile, officials of some water systems cited in the report denied that lead was a problem.

Pesticides. In the U.K. the Working Party on Pesticide Residues reported on March 4 that between 1982 and 1985 organochlorine residues were found in less than 1% of home-grown and about 2% of imported fruit and vegetables and in some freshwater fish and wild birds. Some residues had been found in meat products imported from China, and talks were being held to find ways of reducing them. The Advisory Committee on Pesticides published its first annual report on April 11, recommending the continued use of 2,4,5-T and giving qualified commercial clearance to 13 compounds. New statutory controls on the use of pesticides were presented to Parliament for approval on July 3 and came into force on October 6.

Lake Mashu, Japan, formed 7,000 years ago in a caldera and fed only by rain and drainage through surrounding rocks, was said by the Environment Agency in April to be contaminated by benzene hexachloride (BHC). Banned in Japan, the BHC was believed to have been carried from Korea and China.

"Green" Politics. In Britain the Green Party fielded 1,000 candidates in the May local government elections. At its annual conference in September the party reaffirmed its opposition to nuclear power and decided to increase the number of parliamentary candidates by 50% to 150 in the next general election, concentrating its campaigns in areas where new nuclear facilities were planned. The party had 6,000 members and three district councillors.

In Switzerland the Action Committee Against Nuclear Plants said on May 19 that it would collect the 100,000 signatures needed for the Socialist Party of Austria to force the government to hold a national referendum on nuclear power. This would be the third referendum on the matter.

Following the formation of a coalition government between the Green Party and the Social Democratic Party (SPD) in the West German state of Hesse in October 1985, Josef ("Joschka") Fischer of the Greens was sworn in as the state environment minister on December 12. He issued his first regulations early in March 1986, ordering the Farbwerke Hoechst chemical factory to make a fourfold reduction in its daily discharges of mercury and cadmium and to reduce its total acid discharges from 150 to 10 metric tons a day. The company said it would comply.

Opposition to nuclear power remained the main item in the Green manifesto, and at a party congress in Hanover on May 16–19 party leaders called for a campaign to force the government to change its policy on the matter. An opinion poll conducted soon after the Chernobyl accident gave the Greens 9% of the national vote, and another in June gave them 12%, but on June 15 the results of elections in Lower Saxony, the first to be held after Chernobyl, showed they had increased their support only from 6.5% in 1982 to 7.1%. "Fundamentalists" and "realists" within the party continued to disagree over collaboration with the SPD in the event that they held the balance of power following a federal election. Collaboration would require them to make compromises. In late September, following an eight-hour debate at the preelection conference in Nürnberg, collaboration was accepted by 230 votes to 190. Following the vote Johannes Rau, SPD candidate for chancellor, reiterated his view that the policies of the two parties on energy, nuclear power, and defense were irreconcilable and that he would not form a coalition with the Greens.

(MICHAEL ALLABY)

WILDLIFE CONSERVATION

A number of whaling nations defied the moratorium on commercial whaling imposed by the International Whaling Commission (IWC), which started in October 1985. Iceland, South Korea, Norway, Japan, and the U.S.S.R. all took whales during 1986. Although the U.S. was required by law to impose sanctions on nations that "diminish the effectiveness" of the IWC, the U.S. Supreme Court ruled on June 30 that the U.S. administration had discretion in applying sanctions, overturning the decisions of two lower courts. As a result the U.S. would not cut Japan's fishing rights in U.S. waters, and Japan notified the IWC that it was withdrawing its objection to the moratorium and would end commercial whaling in 1988. Japan announced its intention, however, of continuing whaling under the guise of scientific research. The enormous loophole in IWC rules whereby nations could issue an unlimited number of permits for taking whales for scientific research threatened the moratorium. Norway announced that it would halt commercial whaling by 1988 but would continue scientific whaling. Iceland also intended to continue scientific whaling, and in November two of its whaling ships were scuttled and a whale-oil plant in Reykjavik was sabotaged. An international environment group, the Sea Shepherd Conservation Society, claimed responsibility. (*See* WORLD AFFAIRS [Western Europe]: *Iceland.*)

The accident at Chernobyl was likely to have far-reaching consequences for wildlife in the region. It was estimated that 180,000 reindeer in Scandinavian Lapland would have to be destroyed because of abnormally high levels of radioactive cesium. The total evacuation zone around Chernobyl included part of a reserve, the Dneprovsko-Terevskoe Nature Hunting Reserve, listed by the Commission on National Parks and Protected Areas of the International Union for Conservation of Nature and Natural Resources (IUCN) as a threatened protected area.

Between February and May hundreds of dead penguins were found in the Falkland Islands and in Argentina. Suspected causes were food shortages resulting from overfishing, the seabird disease puffinosis, and lead contamination, but investigations revealed no conclusive evidence.

In the U.K. National Bat Year was launched on January 29, and a great deal of publicity was given to the need to conserve the country's declining bat populations. One species, the mouse-eared bat (*Myotis myotis*), had declined to such an extent that only one was believed to be left. Meanwhile, Israeli conservationists were trying to end the annual fumigation of bat caves carried out because fruit bats were mistakenly regarded as pests by fruit growers. In fact, the bats eat only fruit that is too ripe for commercial harvesting.

It was the Chinese year of the tiger, but concern was expressed at the International Symposium on Tigers in April that the Chinese tiger (*Panthera tigris amoyensis*) had been reduced to 50–80 scattered individuals and could become extinct if no action was taken. Laos, Kampuchea, and Vietnam agreed to cooperate in an effort to save the world's most endangered bovine, the kouprey (*Bos sauveli*); only about 200 remained, living in the war-torn border areas of these countries and in Thailand. Conservationists in the U.S. had captured what were believed to be the world's last 6 black-footed ferrets (*Mustela nigripes*), but 12 more were found in their last-known site in Wyoming. Four were taken to join the six already held in captivity for breeding purposes. The plight of koalas caused concern in Australia. It was discovered that several maladies that had been affecting the animals were all caused by the widespread bacterium *Chlamydia psittaci,* but it was not known why the organism had become so virulent. According to one theory, human pressure had forced the koalas into less favourable and overcrowded habitats so that their resistance was lowered.

Ten living individuals of a gazelle species, *Gazella bilkis,* were discovered in a private collection in Qatar. The species had previously been known only from museum skins and skulls collected in North Yemen in the 1950s. Preliminary tests on a Mexican cat, the onza, shot in January 1986 suggested that it was a new species. Photographs of a thylacine (*Thylacinus cynocephalus*), published on April 24 in the *New Scientist,* opened up the possibility that the animal was not extinct after all. They had been taken in 1985 in dense forest in Western Australia. At least two ivory-billed woodpeckers, thought to be extinct, were sighted in Cuba.

Five pairs of scimitar-horned oryx (*Oryx dammah*) bred in British zoos were reintroduced into Bou Hedma National Park, Tunisia. They had disappeared from the country in 1935. In August 40 Père David's deer (*Elaphurus davidianus*) were flown to China from British zoos and released into a specially created reserve 250 km (155 mi) north of Shanghai. The deer had become extinct in China by the beginning of the century, and the reintroduced animals were descended from individuals sent to the Zoological Society of London in 1869. It was reported that the brush-tailed bettong (*Bettongia penicillata*) had been successfully introduced onto four islands in South Australia. Once widespread, it was now extinct in the wild except in parts of Western Australia and Queensland.

Some plants were brought back from the brink of extinction. A Canary Island endemic, *Senecio hadrosomus,* with ten individuals left, had been selected as one of the 12 most endangered plant species in the world by the IUCN General Assembly in 1984. It was successfully propagated by tissue culture, and it was hoped that 1,000 plants would be growing by the end of 1986. An outstanding array of plants from the foggy coastal ridges of Chile's Atacama Desert were protected when the Pan de Azucar National Park was established in May.

The most endangered of southeastern Brazil's primates, the golden lion tamarin (*Leontopithecus chrysopygus*), was the focus of a rescue attempt. It was restricted to two reserves in the state of São Paulo, and since a large part of one of them, the Morro do Diablo, was to be submerged when the Rosano hydroelectric dam was completed in late 1986, a number of organizations cooperated to rescue and translocate the lion tamarins and other primates to nearby protected forests. Also in Brazil, in August, an international team set out to rescue hundreds of Amazon River dolphins (*Inia geoffrensis*) trapped in irrigation channels in a plantation in Araguaia. Fishermen had been killing them for their eyes and genital organs, which were sold as lucky charms.

The larger mammals of Africa continued to suffer from poachers, although there were some gains in a few areas. Poaching in the Garamba National Park, Zaire, was brought more under control, and the remnant white rhino (*Ceratotherium simum cottoni*) population there increased to 17. A number of Kenya's scattered black rhinos were rounded up and moved into a safer area in Lake Nakuru National Park. Poaching for the illegal trade in ivory was apparently the main cause of the continuing decline in many African elephant populations. Much of the poaching was carried out using automatic weapons, but in southern Tanzania and in Mozambique there were reports of poachers baiting paths with poisoned pumpkins. In the biggest haul of illegal ivory ever made outside Africa, Belgian customs officers in Antwerp confiscated 1,889 elephant tusks on January 15. The tusks, believed to have been taken from Tanzania, were en route to Dubai.

Illegal trade continued to threaten the world's wildlife. The U.S. was the world's largest importer of wildlife, and an estimated 25% of declared imports were illegal. In Malaysia a campaign was launched to try to end the thriving illegal trade supplying restaurants, which served up many endangered species as specialty dishes. In Greece an investigation revealed an abundance of furs from endangered species for sale. The traders were either ignorant of the illegality of their trade or were prepared to issue false documents to enable tourists to import the furs into their home countries. The World Wildlife Fund set up two new offices in Europe, one in Italy and one in Austria, to help strengthen trade controls within the European Communities. Austria was a major conduit for illegal trade in endangered species entering Europe, and Italy had no framework to enforce the Convention on International Trade in Endangered Species of Wild Flora and Fauna. Ninety-one countries were parties to the convention by March 1986.

(JACQUI M. MORRIS)

See also Agriculture and Food Supplies; Botanical Gardens and Zoos; Energy; Historic Preservation; Life Sciences; Transportation.

This article updates the *Macropædia* article CONSERVATION OF NATURAL RESOURCES.

MARILYN ACHIRON—NEWSWEEK

Rangers in search of poachers in Zimbabwe inspect the carcass of a rhinoceros that was killed for its valuable horn.

Fashion and Dress

What was fashion made of in 1986? Curves, ripples, and ruffles, together with gathers and draped effects. No longer out to conquer but anxious to charm, the woman of 1986, progressively renouncing the aggressive approach, threw out the androgynous look and with it the loose garments still popular early in the year. Even the Japanese discovered the female figure. Body beautiful was back in the summer and well established by the autumn.

Rippling peplums on closely fitted suit jackets with arched shoulder lines were discreet reminders of the Dior "New Look," which had rocked the fashion world in 1947. This time they were worn with skinny skirts instead of full ones. The 1986 flavour was reinforced by Azzedine Alaïa, the Paris-established Tunisian couturier, who frequently canceled the skirt altogether in favour of stovepipe trousers or body-hugging stockings. Azzedine was influential in bringing back curves. His knee-high jersey dresses with zip fastenings whizzing here and there were a smash hit in Paris.

Jersey, plain or with narrow ribbing, was by far the most effective fabric for side-draped dresses, with gathers, horizontal shirring, and low sashes hugging the hips. Jersey was ideal for shaping the body and cupping the derriere—as, for example, on a long, black evening sheath with a V neck cut to the waist or a plunging cowl neckline at the back. For the young and trendy, hemlines during the summer were down to just above the ankles or at mid-thigh with a centre split at the hem, back or front. A zip fastening in the seam controlled the height of the slit. Fashion was more low-key in the establishment group, where skirts hovered around the kneecap.

Another perennial that went through a beauty treatment was blue denim. During the summer it was chosen for loose, long coats, blousons, jackets, and, particularly, short and skimpy skirts up to mid-thigh with a low slit in front or back at the hemline. The new treatment and well-pressed look were emphasized by the choice of accessories and the association of blue denim with silk scarves, earrings, bracelets, and pearl necklaces. The denim story unfurled in the following winter with the addition of velvet collars, fur linings, quilted satin linings, more masses of jewelry, and even gloves!— much favoured by the London Sloane Ranger, the Paris BCBG (*bon chic bon genre*), and the preppie group in the U.S. Preppie style was stimulated in the U.S. by designer Ralph Lauren, who succeeded in spreading his style to Paris, where he opened a boutique.

The summer street look was a two-piece story. The top—in cotton jersey, cropped and loose, hovering above the waistline and revealing skin—had a rounded neckline and no sleeves. The top could be reduced to a brassière with a high turtleneck or it could be a long-sleeved shirt, plain white or striped like a man's, worn with free, flying tails, dipping at the back, or with tails negligently knotted in front. The skirt was either full and swinging to the ankles or narrow, neat, and ending anywhere from knee to mid-thigh. Navy and white nautical stripes also fitted into the two-piece story. Low-heeled cyclist shoes or spiky-heeled sandals completed the look.

Along the Mediterranean coast the Italian influence was evident in tiered and ruffled petticoats and skirts, a myriad of butterfly bows in the hair, and a spray of sequins on accessories, from skullcaps, belts, and gloves to shoes and handbags. On the beaches it was a choice between a flashback to the 1950s, with a two-piece swimsuit composed of a strapless top and matching abbreviated ruffled skirt

A full skirt and scooped neckline combine with a balanced-brim hat in one example of the return of femininity to women's fashion that all but did away with the recent androgynous look.

DON HOGAN CHARLES/THE NEW YORK TIMES

instead of trunks, and today's draped or ruffled cover-up. But the newest style was the all-in-one princess cut with a tiny flaring skirt, like a skating skirt, and a low-slit top with a plunging neckline in front. Even on the beaches bareness seemed to be out; fashion apart, there was a new awareness of the dangers of overexposing the skin to the sun.

The influence of the 1950s was also apparent in lingerie, as in the *guêpiée* and the all-in-one "body" with lace inserts—black on white was favoured—trimming the tiny ruffled culottes. Silk, principally satin, was predominant. Garter belts (suspender belts) or garters and sheer black stockings gained over tights for evening. For daytime, when colour played an important role, tights were preferred. Opaque and plain or with a narrow rib, they matched the knee-high jersey ensembles in scarlet red, blue, green, or plain black.

Fake furs made a big impact in the autumn. The jungle look was not only for the adventurous. Tiger stripes, leopard spots, and giraffe and zebra patterns were more fun than mink. Among coats, hooded jackets, waistcoats, skirts, trousers, hats, shoes, belts, and handbags, the choice was vast. Greater still were the possibilities in printed copies of fakes used for sweaters, blouses, dresses, scarves, underpants, tights, and gloves. Jungle prints in silk satin for brief skirts or short jackets were paired with black jersey in the Saint Laurent Rive Gauche boutique. Even costume jewelry embraced the jungle look.

The daytime silhouette of broad-shouldered sweater slimming at mid-thigh into a hip-hugging band, in black-and-white jacquard patterns featuring flashes of lightning or horizontal stripes, appeared somewhat top-heavy over a tiny skirt. Nor was the long-legged look of the body stocking for everyone. But everyone fell for the bright colours that started off the autumn season. With a tiny black skirt one could match a scarlet, double-breasted, fitted jacket worn without a blouse; or a fuchsia pink coat flaring from shoulders to knees; or an indigo blue ankle-length coat ready to cover up anything. There was always the camel-hair coat, long and slim, or the plain cashmere and wool one, usually dark navy or black. The classic double-breasted Chesterfield, like the one borrowed from Papa the previous winter but now cut to size, was the main mannish element in the season, along with basic slacks and sturdy shoes.

In the way of hats, there were lots of berets, more or less puffed up and trimmed with bows or with fancy pins and brooches featuring crouching tigers and leopards. Little skullcaps matching the coat colour and pull-on felts were also featured. Accessories displayed considerable dash. With costume jewelry becoming more and more imaginative and closer to the real thing (only larger in size), there was no limit to its scope: a slab or two of sapphire blue, emerald green, or ruby red pinned to a lapel; heavy metal chains and pearls combined in double or triple rows around the neck; wide and chunky bracelets, or narrow ones worn in dozens on both wrists. When worn alone, the silver chain prevailed over the gold. Earrings—metal or coloured plastic hoops for daytime wear and sparkling diamond chandeliers for evening—were essential from morning till night.

Chignons and all kinds of pinned-up hairstyles were in fashion: Moulin Rouge fringes brushing the eyebrows, little twisted buns placed in front or slightly off-centre in the spirit of the '50s, pony tails neatly brushed back and stylishly tied with a satin bow. Coloured side combs, or a huge laundry clip in some bright shade of plastic, were different ways of showing imagination and expressing the personality.

A lot of work went into makeup. Skin was prepared like a painter's canvas. New products were applied under the usual base for translucent and opaline effects, aiming at Japanese whiteness. Fuchsia to gardenia pink was one range; brick to chocolate was another, for the jungle look. For eyeshadow, three colours such as yellow, purple, and orange, or shades from black to light gray, were blended together. Lipstick came in two shades, one for the upper lip, one for the lower. (THELMA SWEETINBURGH)

Men's Fashions. At least two new exhibitions were added to an already full program of national fashion presentations and international trade fairs in Europe in 1986: one in Britain and one in Spain. Both were held in September. The Designer Menswear Show was held in London, and the Gaudi Hombre Menswear Fair in Barcelona established itself as the voice of fashion for Spanish men. The Salon International de l'Habillement Masculin in Paris, also in September, was attended by 722 exhibitors from 20 countries. The signs here and at other major trade fairs during the year—Men's Fashion Week in Cologne, West Germany, Modam in Amsterdam, and the IMBEX 86 and Menswear Association of Britain International exhibitions in London—pointed to traditional but updated styling for 1987 and to a series of supporting fashions variously described as Yuppie ("young urban professional"), Street Scene, Out of Africa, Colonial, and the updated Ivy League campus styles from the U.S.

The year 1986 witnessed the revival of the blazer, usually double-breasted and often in striped materials—cotton or linen for summer and pure new wool or blends

Striped fashions in wool or wool blends by Jean Charles Castelbajac exemplify a style that was popular as the casual look of loose-fitting jackets and trousers for men continued.
TREVIRA/LINDNER

of wool with a man-made fibre for autumn and winter. Denim, more black than blue, continued to be fashionable for trousers, jackets, and jeans. There was a return to popularity of safari jackets, inspired by the clothes worn by Robert Redford in the award-winning motion picture *Out of Africa.* To a lesser extent, shorts, in styles shorter than the Bermuda length, were seen in places other than holiday resorts. Increased television coverage of sporting events, both outdoor and indoor, brought an upsurge in sales of sportswear. The track suit was now established as a garment to change into after work, as well as being the uniform for active sportsmen.

The traditional suit for town and business wear underwent some subtle changes during the year, not so much in the styling as in the suitings. The more colourful check patterns for country wear were bigger and bolder and sometimes combined with a windowpane overcheck. The business suit, on the other hand, was shown in smaller, neater patterns. Stripes were discreet, and there were more double-breasted styles than usual.

Like business suits, traditional knitwear underwent few changes in styling. Materials and patterns provided the main interest. Lightweight cotton and linen sports shirts were worn during the summer, while the heavier wool and acrylic garments provided warmth in winter. There was a marked contrast between the soft pastel shades of summer knitwear and the darker, richer colours shown for winter. (STANLEY H. COSTIN)

See also Industrial Review: *Furs.*

This article updates the *Macropædia* article DRESS AND ADORNMENT.

Gardening

The big news in the U.S. in 1986 was the official naming of the rose as the national flower. A voice vote taken in the House of Representatives on September 23 confirmed what the Senate had done the year before. Hopes of those who championed a native plant such as the marigold, corn tassel, dogwood, or mountain laurel were dashed. The U.S. joined Britain and Iran, which also considered the rose a national emblem. A second boost from the nation's capital was the designation of April 13–19 as National Garden Week. The legislation was introduced by Sen. Mark Hatfield (Rep., Ore.), an avid gardener.

Gardening continued to be the nation's number one pastime. More than 60% of the population grew some food plants, and 25% gardened for pleasure. Market analysts noted a decline in backyard fruit growing, however. Sales of the larger fruit trees had tapered off over the past three years, although dwarf and miniature trees were still popular for planting in patio tubs. Gardening in the U.S. was a $15.2 billion business that included professional lawn care, landscaping, and supplies for both outdoor and indoor gardeners. "How-to" videocassettes for gardeners appeared, with offerings designed for both beginning and experienced growers.

The value of the garden market in the U.K. also increased. Annual sales of seed packets rose by 9%, although within that total there was a slight drop in sales of vegetable seed packets. Retail sales of nursery stock were worth £125 million and of potted plants, £150 million, the latter divided equally between flowering and foliage plants. *Ficus elastica,* the rubber plant, was the top-selling plant at the Netherlands auctions for the second year in succession. The value of potted plant sales in Britain had doubled over five years, mainly as a result of sales through nontraditional outlets such as supermarkets.

Interest in visiting gardens continued to grow in the U.K. There was a 9% increase in garden visitors in England and Wales during 1985, outstripping the increase in visitors to historic houses and other sights. The garden-visiting habit was much better established in the U.K. than in the rest of Europe. Britain's second national garden festival was held in 1986 at Stoke-on-Trent, near the centre of the country, on a 32-ha (80-ac) site that had been reclaimed from derelict industrial land. The festival was open for six months, but there were fewer visitors than had been expected. The promoters had not yet found a formula that would attract gardeners from a distance as well as local visitors. In the neighbourhood of the festival site, a remarkable but neglected 19th-century garden, Biddulph Grange, was taken over by the National Trust and would be restored over the next few years.

The National Centre for Organic Gardening was opened at Ryton near Coventry in England. It was being developed mainly as a demonstration garden for nonchemical methods of cultivation and for compost making. Britain was behind the rest of Europe in "biological" gardening. For example, ecological principles had been invoked in West Germany in the use of herbaceous perennials. Unimproved or wild species were placed in environments similar to their natural habitats so they required less maintenance than the traditional herbaceous border. The idea was first demonstrated in public at the Munich International Garden Festival in 1983, and three years later the borders remaining from the festival illustrated the practicality of the idea. In the U.S. as well, there was a marked trend toward less lawn and lower-maintenance gardening using native plants and ornamental grasses. U.S. homeowners were beginning to show a preference for ready-to-use pesticides that could be consumed in one season, eliminating storage and disposal problems.

Among awards made during the year in the U.K., Fleuroselect chose *Impatiens walleriana* Starbright, with bicoloured flowers in orange, violet, rose, and red shades and a white star. The flowers of this strain had stable colouring; earlier introductions had shown variability in colour at low temperatures. No gold medals were awarded to roses by the Royal National Rose Society, but an interesting new cultivar raised in The Netherlands was Pink Torch, a shrub rose that drops its petals after flowering.

September 20 was named as the third annual Flowerbulb Day in the U.S., promoted by the Netherlands Flowerbulb Information Center in New York City. The promotion had increased sales of hardy Dutch bulbs by 55%. An estimated 630 million bulbs were shipped to the U.S. during 1985 for planting in private gardens and public parks. According to the Flowerbulb Center, the tulip was the most popular of the hardy bulbs, representing 44% of the U.S. market. Gardeners who were surveyed on the subject of bulb planting indicated that they usually placed bulbs next to fences, near walls, or along walks or driveways. Nearly half of the respondents said they thought bulb planting was one of the easiest of garden chores.

With the price of homes continuing to rise, many suburban dwellers in the U.S. were finding it was cheaper to enlarge or renovate an existing home than to buy a new one. One result was that nurseries were experiencing an upsurge in the business of revitalizing older landscapes.

(JOAN LEE FAUST; ELSPETH NAPIER)

See also Agriculture and Food Supplies; Botanical Gardens and Zoos; Environment; Life Sciences.

This article updates the *Macropædia* article GARDENING AND HORTICULTURE.

PAUL HOSEFROS/THE NEW YORK TIMES

Two U.S. representatives "stop to smell the roses" along Pennsylvania Avenue in Washington, D.C. A September vote of the House of Representatives declared the rose the U.S. national flower. The Senate had passed the motion in 1985.

Health and Disease

Acquired immune deficiency syndrome (AIDS) provoked growing concern during 1986 as health authorities began to realize the full implications and international dimensions of the disease. The potential global consequences of the AIDS epidemic were officially recognized by the World Health Organization (WHO) in November in an announcement that described the disease as "a health disaster of pandemic proportions." Admitting that WHO officials had, until then, underestimated the seriousness of the deadly disease, agency head Halfdan Mahler said his organization would begin to mount a campaign against AIDS similar in magnitude to its successful earlier effort to eradicate smallpox.

Although the rate of increase in the number of cases among homosexual men in the U.S. declined slightly, a far greater danger became apparent in parts of tropical Africa, where the AIDS virus was apparently being transmitted through heterosexual activity. A survey published in February showed that the organism had spread extensively among prostitutes in the city of Nairobi, Kenya. In parts of Central Africa the proportion of male and female patients was equal, and about 15% of pregnant women were infected with the virus. Epidemiological data from Zaire, Rwanda, and other countries in west and central Africa led some experts to believe that the disease could eventually pose problems on as large a scale as the famines that had affected those regions in recent years.

The prospect that heterosexual transmission might become predominant outside of Africa could not be dismissed by U.S. public health officials. In a report issued in October, Surgeon General C. Everett Koop warned of the potential spread of AIDS beyond the already identified high-risk groups to the population at large. The report, unprecedented in its explicit language, advocated elementary-school-level sex education—dealing with both heterosexual and homosexual relations—cautioned against having sex with prostitutes, and advised drug addicts to use only sterile needles. Equally urgent in tone was the report of a special panel of health experts from the Institute of Medicine and the National Academy of Sciences (IOM/NAS). The IOM/NAS team concluded that the AIDS epidemic could result in a public health catastrophe in the U.S. The panel criticized the administration of Pres. Ronald Reagan for failing to take a more active part in the effort to halt the spread of the disease.

There was some concern among epidemiologists that a few governments, anxious not to publicize their plight, were reluctant to adopt appropriately vigorous measures to chart the movement of AIDS virus and if possible arrest its spread. But the political dimension was altered significantly in September by a study suggesting that AIDS did not, as had been previously supposed, originate in Africa, subsequently spreading to the West Coast of the U.S. A survey of more than 6,000 Africans showed that antibodies against AIDS virus—and thus infection with the disease itself—were extremely rare in that continent before 1985. In Britain, nonetheless, there were suggestions that African students should be screened and excluded if they were found to be carrying AIDS.

Although U.S. blood banks had, in the spring of 1985, begun routinely testing all donated blood for antibodies to the AIDS virus, the nation's blood supply was not as safe as had been hoped. In July 1986 researchers reported that the tests used to screen donor blood for the presence of AIDS antibody apparently failed to identify some people who were in the earliest stages of infection. The test used by the American Red Cross, for example, missed 17 out of 30 specimens from newly infected AIDS patients. In 1986 at least two people in the U.S. contracted the disease after receiving transfusions with blood that had passed AIDS screening tests yet was contaminated with the virus. A study of two groups of hemophiliacs, one known to have been exposed to the AIDS virus through a contaminated lot of commercial blood-clotting factor, demonstrated no difference in the prevalence of AIDS antibodies among the groups. A five-year follow-up study would monitor both groups for the development of full-blown disease.

As a result of the uncertainties about screened blood, blood banking experts advised people considering elective surgery to donate their own blood in advance of their operations so as to alleviate the need for transfusions with donor blood. Federal health officials also cautioned that any man who had had sexual relations with another man at any time since 1977 should not give blood. Later, in a further step to safeguard the blood supply, the U.S. Food

AP/WIDE WORLD

Distraught with grief, a brother of basketball player Len Bias is comforted by his father (third from right) at the funeral. The 22-year-old University of Maryland superstar fell victim to a cocaine overdose, leaving behind his dream—a career in the National Basketball Association.

and Drug Administration (FDA), responding to growing concern over heterosexual transmission of AIDS, recommended that prostitutes and their customers voluntarily refrain from donating blood.

In September 1986 a clinical trial of an anti-AIDS drug was concluded early because the drug appeared so promising that wider use seemed warranted. The drug, known as azidothymidine (AZT), does not kill the virus but does stop it from replicating. The study of AZT began in February 1986. Two hundred eighty-two AIDS patients at 12 clinical centres across the U.S. were divided at random into two groups. Members of one group received AZT, and the members of the other received a placebo. The trial was a double blind study; neither the patients nor their doctors knew which treatment each subject was receiving. The survival rates of the AZT-treated patients were significantly better than the survival rates of those taking placebo. In addition, the AZT patients tended to gain weight and developed fewer life-threatening infections. The drug's manufacturer, the Burroughs Wellcome Co., applied to the FDA for approval to market the drug. In the meantime, Burroughs was to begin distributing AZT to doctors who had some expertise in treating AIDS patients so that it could be given to those whose key symptom was pneumocystis pneumonia, because it was this subgroup of patients that was the focus of the clinical trial. Anthony Fauci, director of the National Institute of Allergy and Infectious Diseases, estimated that 6,000 to 7,500 AIDS patients would soon be eligible to receive the drug.

Although this was an important category of AIDS sufferers (comprising some 60% of the victims in the U.S. at the time), the much less pronounced effect of AZT in other AIDS patients indicated the need for caution and continued research. The apparent limitations in the effectiveness of AZT, along with an acute shortage of thymidine, the material from which the drug is synthesized, led researchers and administrators to encourage other pharmaceutical companies to continue with independent approaches and not abandon their work in light of Burroughs Wellcome's widely publicized success.

Efforts to evolve an AIDS vaccine continued, despite the inherent conundrum of how to trigger the body's immune system against a disease that manifests itself by destroying that system. One distinguished immunologist, N. Avrion Mitchison from University College, London, suggested that the horrendous nature of AIDS would justify a small trial using killed AIDS virus as a vaccine, as was done decades earlier with yellow fever. But the possible hazards in this strategy and the attendant legal risks were sufficient to ensure that researchers pursued more cautious approaches. One route leading to significant success was based on the idea of incorporating parts of the AIDS virus into that of vaccinia (cowpox), the organism once used as a vaccine against smallpox. In September scientists from two companies based in Seattle, Wash., Oncogen and Genetic Systems Corp., reported that they had tested such a vaccine in macaques. Made by inserting into vaccinia the genes coding for proteins in the AIDS virus envelope, it induced the monkeys to make antibodies against the proteins *and* to generate defensive lymphocytes of the sort that are impaired by AIDS itself.

Adding to the complications involved in creating a vaccine—and compounding the problem of screening donor blood—was the discovery that AIDS, like polio, may be caused by several different viruses. During the course of 1986 three research teams reported finding previously unknown AIDS viruses, one of which apparently causes no disease in humans. The newest AIDS virus, identified by Swedish researchers working with West African patients, was found to be structurally quite different from the virus first believed to be the sole cause of the disease.

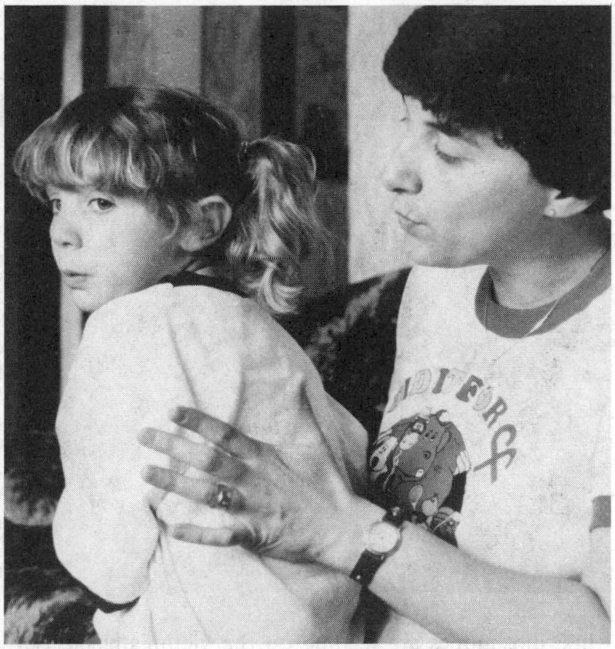

A young cystic fibrosis patient is clapped on the back by her mother as part of essential daily therapy to clear her lungs. A discovery in DNA gene mapping now allows prenatal diagnosis of CF victims and soon may allow accurate detection of carriers.

SUDHIR—PICTURE GROUP

Immunology. Novel methods of immunization against several other infections were announced during the year. Scientists at the University of Rochester (N.Y.) School of Medicine and Dentistry and Scripps Clinic and Research Foundation, La Jolla, Calif., reported success with an entirely man-made vaccine against enteritis-causing strains of the normally harmless bacterium *Escherichia coli.* The new vaccine contained chemically synthesized versions of the toxins responsible for diarrhea, triggering the manufacture of antibodies but without producing disease. In Bangladesh a trial organized by WHO and the International Centre for Diarrhoeal Disease Research established that a vaccine containing killed cells of the cholera bacterium plus a subunit of its toxin dramatically reduced the incidence of cholera.

In the U.S., a new vaccine against hepatitis B, the first agent of its kind to be produced through genetic engineering techniques, was approved by the FDA, marking the beginning of what health officials heralded as a "new era" in vaccine production. Unlike the old hepatitis B vaccine, which was made from the blood serum of people who had serological evidence of infection with the hepatitis B virus, the laboratory-synthesized version carries no risk of transmitting disease.

There was encouraging progress toward immunization against malaria, a major cause of death among young children in tropical Africa. Scientists at the Naval Medical Research Institute, Bethesda, Md., and other U.S. centres reported evidence that antibodies against part of the initial sporozoite stage of the malarial parasite are important in reducing the prevalance of the disease with increasing age among people in areas where malaria is endemic. This finding suggested the possibility of preventing malaria by using a vaccine targeted at sporozoites—the stages in the parasite's life cycle that are injected into the bloodstream

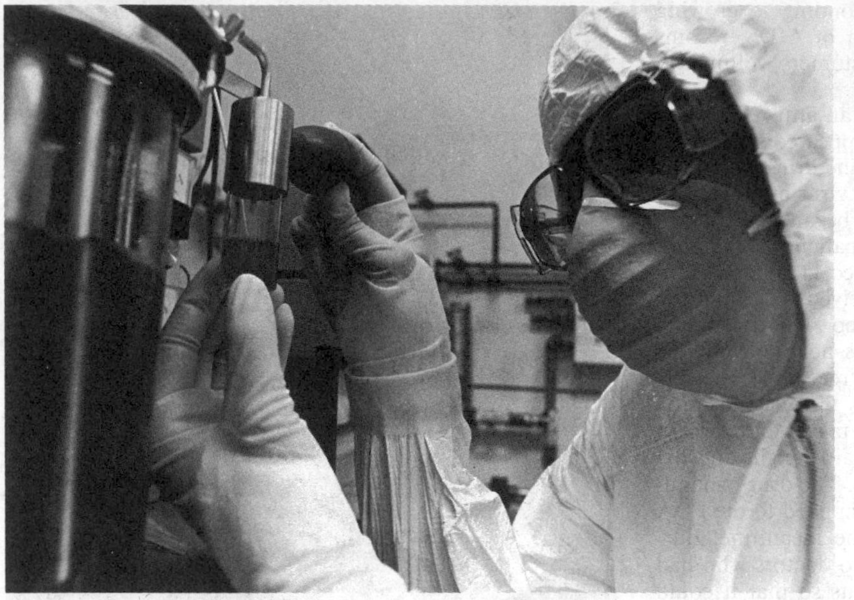

A scientist draws a sample from a fermentation unit used in the development of the first genetically engineered human vaccine. The vaccine protects against infection by the hepatitis B virus, which causes liver disease and is a predisposing factor for liver cancer.
MERCK SHARP & DOHME

while mosquitoes are feeding on the victim's blood. Several such vaccines were being developed and should be tested in humans in the next few years, though competition between them and vaccines against other stages in the malarial parasite's development made it uncertain which would eventually prove most effective.

Progress in protection against rabies came on two fronts. Collaboration between teams in France, England, and Thailand led to the introduction of a vaccine that was highly effective when given to individuals bitten by rabid animals. The new vaccine, prepared by growing the virus in tissue culture, was expected to be considerably cheaper than a similar agent introduced a few years previously and considerably safer than the version prepared in animal brains and still given to some 90% of patients. A parallel approach, pioneered by French and Belgian researchers, was to produce a vaccine with which to immunize the wild fox population in countries where those animals carried the infection. A genetically engineered version of vaccinia, like that being used in AIDS research, was developed, but in this case it carried rabies virus genes. The animal vaccine elicited high antibody levels when given by mouth to foxes. The long-term aim was to make the wild animals immune to, and thus free from, rabies by distributing the vaccine in chicken heads or other bait.

New Blood Test. In late summer of 1986, U.S. blood banks began testing all donor blood for the type of hepatitis known as non-A, non-B hepatitis. Although the test should make blood safer, the cost was great, and blood could become more scarce as a result of the test. Non-A, non-B hepatitis was discovered in the 1960s and was later recognized to be caused by an unidentified infectious agent—probably a virus—and to be transmitted through blood. According to a spokesman for the U.S. National Institutes of Health, anyone who received more than three units of blood had a 5–6% risk of developing the disease. There was no treatment for non-A, non-B hepatitis and, although some patients would get better on their own, others would go on to develop cirrhosis and might eventually die of liver failure.

The test for non-A, non-B hepatitis was, unfortunately, far from ideal. It detected a liver enzyme that is elevated when the liver is inflamed and, separately, it detected a protein from hepatitis A. Neither of these indicators was proof of non-A, non-B infection. Researchers suspected that those who have been exposed to hepatitis B are more likely to also have been exposed to non-A, non-B. Because of the limitations of the new test, a large proportion of the results—as many as 60 to 70%—would be false positives (*i.e.,* individuals who test positive but do not have the disease). And the test was expected to detect only 30 to 40% of donors who could transmit the disease. Even so, this testing was expected to prevent as many as 50,000 cases of non-A, non-B hepatitis each year.

The Common Cold. Interferon, whose early promise as an antiviral drug had been bedeviled by evidence of toxicity and conflicting evidence about its potency, reemerged as a potentially valuable weapon against respiratory infections. Work at the University of Adelaide, South Australia, established that a genetically engineered version of alpha-2 interferon, taken as a nasal spray, protected many test subjects exposed to common cold through household contact. These findings were independently corroborated by similar studies at the University of Virginia School of Medicine. Although both research groups reported nasal bleeding in 10% of those using interferon spray, they considered the high level of protection sufficient to outweigh this minor side effect.

Genetic Disorders. The year 1986 saw important advances accruing from another range of techniques made possible by genetic engineering—the prenatal diagnosis of inherited diseases by means of gene "probes" capable of identifying malfunctioning pieces of fetal DNA or by related methods of interpreting the genetic code. In 1985 researchers announced the discovery of the approximate location of the gene responsible for Duchenne muscular dystrophy. This accomplishment paved the way for the development of a gene probe that can be used to detect affected children before they are born and determine whether women carry the deadly gene that causes the illness. Duchenne muscular dystrophy afflicts males almost exclusively, and in a large majority of cases, it is the mother who carries and transmits the disease-causing gene (a few cases are caused by new mutations). Victims of this progressive muscle-wasting disease usually are confined to wheelchairs by age 12 and frequently die in their early 20s. Women who carry the gene are not affected, but if they give birth to a boy, there is a 50% chance that he will have the disease. Their daughters each have a 50% chance of being carriers. The first applications of the new screening technique were carried out at Children's Hospital in Boston and at the University of Pennsylvania.

In other advances in prenatal diagnosis, researchers in London and Brussels demonstrated that cystic fibrosis could be diagnosed using such probes during the first trimester of pregnancy. Collaboration between institutions in Oxford, England, and Heidelberg and Bonn, West Germany, confirmed the presence of polycystic kidney disease in a nine-week-old fetus at risk of this condition. From London and Oxford there was a report of the diagnosis of the hemoglobin disorder beta-thalassemia major during the first trimester of pregnancy in 80% of 280 "at risk" families. Research in Houston, Texas, and Toronto showed that a similar technique could be used prenatally to diagnose $alpha_1$-antitrypsin deficiency, a condition that can cause severe early-onset emphysema and fatal cirrhosis of the liver. Biologists in Denmark and the U.S. introduced an improved prenatal test for phenylketonuria, a metabolic disorder. Finally, Canadian-American collaboration provided the basis for predicting which people at risk of developing the inherited form of the eye tumour retinoblastoma will actually manifest the cancer; this was the first successful attempt to identify a gene associated with an inherited predisposition to a type of cancer.

Alongside these advances, however, was growing concern about the ethical, personal, and psychological problems some tests of this sort may generate. Particular anxiety centred on Huntington's disease, an untreatable condition that produces progressive neurological deterioration and eventually death. All those who carry the gene eventually develop the disease. However, the first manifestations of the disease generally do not appear until middle age, usually *after* the victim has had children. People with one affected parent must wait until late middle age before they can be fairly sure that they are unlikely to develop the condition themselves. A DNA probe capable of identifying those who carry the gene—and who will, therefore, develop the disease—would thus be valuable, and one recently became available. But then a difficult question arose: Should individuals be offered the opportunity of knowing that they are certain to succumb to a harrowing and fatal disease some years in the future? Ethical guidelines for this and many similar questions likely to flow from emerging methods of early diagnosis were being urgently sought.

HEMSEY—GAMMA/LIAISON

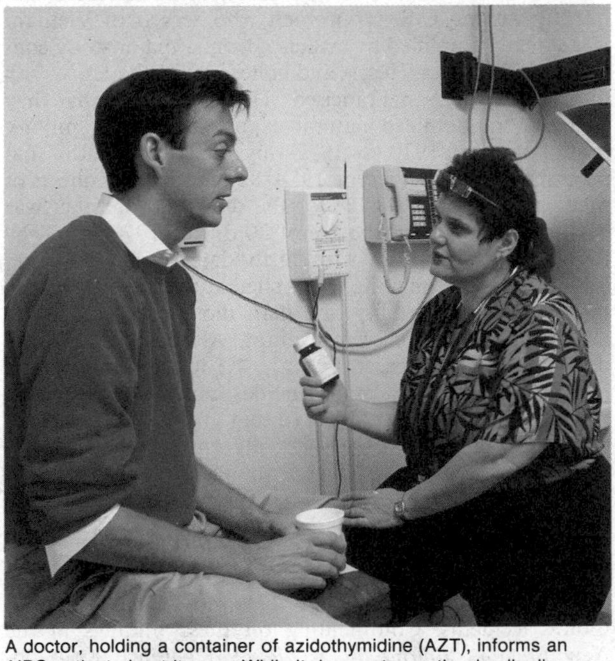

A doctor, holding a container of azidothymidine (AZT), informs an AIDS patient about its use. While it does not cure the deadly disease and it can have serious side effects, the experimental drug offered some hope to AIDS victims.

Ethical Guidelines for Reproductive Technology. In September 1986 the American Fertility Society released a set of proposed ethical guidelines for new reproductive technologies, including artifical insemination, in vitro fertilization, and surrogate motherhood. The committee said that certain procedures, such as surrogate motherhood, are ethically questionable and should be undertaken only at institutions with ethics review boards. Other procedures, including in vitro fertilization, are ethically acceptable, but infertile couples have a right to know the success rate of the clinic providing the service. In vitro fertilization could cost as much as $6,000 per attempt yet, even at the best clinics, there was only a 25% chance that an attempt would succeed. Some clinics charging the full amount had yet to achieve a successful pregnancy.

Cancer. In December 1985 Steven Rosenberg of the U.S. National Cancer Institute (NCI) reported that an experimental therapy with a drug called interleukin-2 (IL-2) had proved to be highly effective against cancer, turning ordinary white blood cells into powerful lymphokine-activated killer (LAK) cells. The cancer institute immediately began experimental studies of the drug's effects on cancer patients at six U.S. medical centres. In 1986 Rosenberg and his colleagues reported further success using IL-2 alone and in combination with LAK cells. Although the results of the most recent study met with tremendous public enthusiasm, some in the medical community had serious reservations. An editorial in the *Journal of the American Medical Association* was critical of the study design itself, the therapeutic benefits claimed, and the NCI's characterizing of the new treatment as a "breakthrough," thus spurring the hopes of thousands of critically ill people.

Two U.S. statisticians, John Bailar of the Harvard School of Public Health and Elaine M. Smith of the University of Iowa Medical Center, claimed in 1986 that the war on cancer was, at best, a stalemate. The NCI had said its goal was to reduce age-adjusted cancer mortality by 50% by the year 2000. Bailar and Smith argued that this goal was unreasonable. They pointed out that in the U.S. age-adjusted mortality rates actually increased during the 20-year period from 1962 to 1982 (the most recent year for which data were available). Although there were remarkable success stories in the treatments of rare cancers such as childhood leukemias and Hodgkin's disease, those successes were almost canceled out in the statistics, according to Bailar and Smith, because they represented such a small proportion of cancers. However, a spokesman for the American Cancer Society pointed out that most cancer deaths were from just a few kinds of cancer, particularly lung cancer, which accounted for a significant percentage of cancer deaths and was still on the increase.

Heart Disease and Atherosclerosis. There was increasing evidence in 1986 of both the benefits of measures designed to prevent coronary heart disease and the extensive dangers attributable to smoking. A European study of more than 60,000 men in Belgium, Italy, Poland, and the U.K. revealed a 10% reduction in heart disease among the men who were given advice about overweight, exercise, and a cholesterol-lowering diet. In Finland, where the rate of coronary heart disease was formerly the highest in Europe, similar health education measures initiated around 1960 led to a decline in mortality of 63% among males and 68% among females age 64 years or less over the following 12-year period. The importance of initiating preventive measures early in life was emphasized by the Bogalusa Heart Study in Louisiana, which provided evidence that atherosclerosis begins in childhood. However, physicians continued to debate the merits of cholesterol restriction in the diets of infants and children. The year 1986 also saw several advances in treatment—including the use in bypass surgery of the mammary artery rather than veins from the leg, producing a longer-lasting graft, and the adminstration of beta blockers soon after the onset of a heart attack to improve long-term survival. But the swing in medical thinking toward prevention was accentuated by the reported success of preventive measures and the accumulating evidence that such measures might be made even more effective if the people at greatest risk could be identified through genetic screening for possible hereditary predisposition to developing heart disease.

Health Risks of Smoking. Studies at the University of Auckland, N.Z., established that cigarette smoking was associated with a 3-fold increase in the risk of stroke—and a 20-fold increase for individuals who both smoked and had high blood pressure. Similar research among male smokers of Japanese ancestry in the Honolulu Heart Program indicated a risk level for stroke four to six times higher than that among nonsmokers. There was evidence from Sweden of a 50% increase in the risk of childhood cancer among the offspring of women who smoked heavily during pregnancy. The results of an investigation in Denmark confirmed that passive smoking by the developing fetus is related to decreased birth weight and showed for the first time that even smoking by household members other than the mother has a measurable effect. Such statistics, reinforcing well-established data about lung cancer and coronary heart disease, led medical institutions to indulge in much stronger invectives against tobacco advertising and sales. Litigation against tobacco companies was becoming increasingly common, with cases pending in Australia, the U.S., and the U.K.

Chernobyl: Radiation Exposure. A tragic and unanticipated opportunity for advancing medical understanding of the effects of radiation arose following an accident at the Chernobyl nuclear power plant in the Soviet Union on April 26. According to an account given four months later at a conference organized in Vienna by the International Atomic Energy Agency, the first 29 casualties, many contaminated with radioactive substances, were attended on site within an hour. After two hours, 108 patients had been admitted to local hospitals, followed by a further 24 later in the day. Within two days, 129 patients had been sent to specialist facilities in Moscow, and 72 with acute radiation sickness were admitted to a hospital in Kiev. Although no local residents apparently received sufficient radiation to cause acute radiation sickness, the 45,000 inhabitants of the nearby town of Pripyat were advised to remain indoors with their windows closed; they were subsequently evacuated. Ten days after the accident the remaining 90,000 residents in an area 30 km (18.6 mi) around the plant had all been evacuated and medically examined.

Of the patients with acute radiation injury, most developed skin burns (in some cases affecting 90% of the body surface) from beta irradiation. Four months later 31 of them had died from these injuries and/or damage to the blood-producing cells in the bone marrow. Although there was considerable publicity in Western news media about the use of bone marrow grafts, the Vienna conference reported that these measures had been almost totally unsuccessful. Marrow transplants even contributed to two deaths when they reacted against some patients' own tissues. But the incident did provide new evidence of the efficacy of the antiviral drug acyclovir, which combated the severe herpes infections that occurred as a result of patients' immune defenses being depressed.

Deaths of Heart Patients. William J. Schroeder, the longest-surviving artificial heart recipient, died on Aug. 6, 1986, having lived 620 days after the implantation of his Jarvik-7 heart. At the time of his death, Schroeder was the only survivor of the five patients who had received permanent Jarvik-7 hearts; Murray P. Haydon, who lived 16 months and 2 days after implant surgery, had died two months earlier. The first woman to receive an artificial heart, Mary Lund, died in October, nine months after the device had been replaced by a human donor heart.

(BERNARD DIXON; GINA KOLATA)

MENTAL HEALTH

As indicated by a case study report from The Bahamas, a problem whose horrendous potential became apparent during 1986 was posed by the increasing availability of "crack," a smokable form of freebase cocaine that is considerably more addictive than powdered cocaine hydrochloride and causes severe psychological and medical problems. The Bahamian episode came to light as a result of a sharp increase in the number of new cases of cocaine abuse seen at the only psychiatric hospital and the primary outpatient psychiatric clinic in The Bahamas. Admissions rose from none in 1982 to 69 in 1983 and 523 in 1984. Describing the Bahamian cocaine epidemic in *The Lancet,* James Jekel and colleagues concluded that as freebasing became more popular and crack more widely available, there would be an unprecedented influx of drug addicts into emergency rooms, psychiatric facilities, and drug treatment programs. In fact, this prediction had already begun to come true in the United States, where treatment facilities were being overwhelmed by large numbers of coke addicts, many of them victims of the long-held misapprehension that cocaine is not an addictive drug.

Previous suggestions of high levels of psychosocial difficulties among U.S. servicemen who served in Vietnam were greatly amplified by evidence from a major study conducted by Norman Hearst and colleagues at the University of California at San Francisco. They exploited what they called a "randomized natural experiment"—the military draft lottery of 1970 to 1972—by analyzing deaths that occurred during the decade 1974–83 among two cohorts of men, one that was eligible for the draft and one that was exempt, who reached the age of 20 during 1970–72. They found that individuals with birth dates (and, therefore, lottery numbers) making them eligible for the draft had a higher average mortality rate than those who had higher lottery numbers and were exempt. Although the overall death rate was increased by only 4% in the draft-eligible men, there were 13% more suicides and 8% more deaths from motor vehicle accidents in that group. But only 26% of those eligible for service actually entered the military. Taking service as the risk factor, the researchers found that for veterans the figures had to be raised to 86% and 53%, respectively, for the increased risk of suicide and death from road accidents.

Compared with nonveterans, veterans were 65% more likely to die from suicide and 49% more likely to die in motor accidents. Commenting on these findings in the *New England Journal of Medicine*, Lawrence Kolb observed that the majority of former combatants who seek medical help for anxiety or depression suffer from chronic and delayed forms of posttraumatic stress disorder. Warning fellow physicians that the lessons learned in treating neuropsychiatric casualties of World Wars I and II and the Korean War had been forgotten, Kolb called for wider recognition of ongoing stress disorders in America's Vietnam combatants.

In Britain there was growing recognition of a civilian parallel to the Vietnam experience—apparently heightened rates of illness and death among the country's population of unemployed persons. One study by the Social Statistics Research Unit at City University, London, extended an earlier survey for the period 1971–81 that revealed a 20–30% "excess mortality" and a strikingly high suicide rate among men seeking work in 1971, compared with rates in a matched group of employed individuals. There was also an excess mortality of about 20% among the wives of the job seekers, and the differences in the death rates had persisted for both groups over the decade. The new analysis established that these disparities could not be accounted for, as some had suggested, on the basis of preexisting ill health or disadvantaged socioeconomic status. A consensus was emerging among physicians that unemployment itself was responsible, directly or indirectly, for the heightened risk of death. While factors such as physical inactivity and poor diet might play a part, many psychiatrists had begun to believe, from the prevalence of suicide among the unemployed, that psychological disturbance is a crucial influence.

Public and political concern in Britain also centred on a study conducted by staff at the Institute of Psychiatry, London, on mental disorders among women admitted to jail. They screened a random sample of 708 women in Holloway Prison and found that 195 of them had a history of self-harm, some 125 had a history of psychiatric illness, 99 were opiate-dependent, and 89 took psychotropic drugs regularly. These findings suggested a need for psychiatric units in women's prisons, investigators Trevor Turner and David Tofler concluded. They also urged that changes be made in the admissions policies of psychiatric hospitals.

(BERNARD DIXON)

This article updates the *Macropædia* article MENTAL DISORDERS and Their Treatment.

DENTISTRY

During 1986 the American Dental Association (ADA) joined other leading health organizations in launching a broad-based attack against smokeless tobacco products. Recognizing the popularity of such products among teens and young adults, the ADA, along with the American Cancer Society and other concerned groups, conducted a massive—and ultimately successful—campaign to require warning labels, similar to those on cigarette packages, on all snuff, chewing tobacco, and related products sold in the United States.

Lasers could prove to be a valuable and safe tool in root canal therapy, according to University of Alberta dental researchers. In traditional root canal procedure, the nerve-containing pulp in the centre of the tooth was scraped out and replaced with a rubbery material. But sometimes the small opening at the base of the tooth where the nerve exits was not completely sealed off and bacteria congregated in that area. This could cause an abscess, triggering painful inflammation. In experiments on extracted human teeth, high-power carbon dioxide lasers were used to fuse enamel plugs at the base of the tooth. Short bursts of laser energy were then applied to sterilize and glaze the walls of the reamed-out canal. The primary advantage of laser therapy over conventional root canal treatment was that it prevented recurrence of abscess in teeth that were already infected. A crucial step in developing the process for practical use would be to design a small laser generator and a beam-directing device that could fit in the mouth.

In 1986 scientists at the National Institute of Dental Research (NIDR) reported the development of a new method for administering drugs directly to the site of periodontal, or gum, disease. They developed a small pellet that could be placed in the mouth to produce a continuous release of tetracycline for one week. The "intra-oral controlled release delivery system" for tetracycline could supplement or replace the current mode of therapy, in which patients take the antibiotic in capsule form. Tetracycline released from the pellets inhibited the growth of harmful bacteria just as tetracycline from a capsule did, but more of the medication reached the site of the infection.

W. H. DOUGLAS, UNIVERSITY OF MINNESOTA, SCHOOL OF DENTISTRY

An artificial mouth should help reduce the time and cost of testing dental materials. It simulates chewing as hydraulic pistons move artificial and recently extracted teeth that are mounted on a flexible base. The mouth is suspended in synthetic saliva.

New scientific information about nerve channels connecting the teeth and brain was raising questions about the brain's sensitivity to events affecting the nerves outside the brain. In animal experiments researchers at the University of Washington School of Medicine found that the area of the brain stem that receives sensory messages from the teeth is much larger than was previously believed. This might be a factor in the nerve degeneration that occurs in the brain stem when teeth are lost, whether shed naturally or taken by injury or surgery. The finest branches of nerve network from the missing tooth disintegrate, but the network reconnects eventually, depending on the person's age and the number of missing teeth. The same researchers were investigating whether this phenomenon was linked to facial sensory problems experienced by some older people who had lost most or all of their teeth. (LOU JOSEPH)

VETERINARY MEDICINE

Consumer pressure against the use of hormonal-type growth promoters in cattle was so strong that the European Communities (EC) banned all such substances from use, effective as of the end of 1987. The scientific evidence commissioned on the subject was ignored; this evidence showed that, correctly used, the growth promoters left no residues in meat and, by improving productivity, kept the cost of food down.

Fear of residues was not, however, the motivation behind U.S. opposition to a new type of growth promoter, a bovine growth hormone (BGH), produced by genetic engineering techniques. The product, approved for use in dairy cows, was expected to increase milk yields by as much as 40%. Farmers objected because such an increase in output could have a serious effect on the farming economy, already suffering from overproduction. It was feared that more than 25% of dairy farms might be forced out of business. Furthermore, because high-level yields would make significant changes in the quantity and type of feed required, environmentalists argued that it would change land use unacceptably; the animal welfare advocates opposed BGH because they believed its use would increase the risk of stress-induced diseases in dairy cows, including mastitis and metabolic disorders.

ARTHUR SHAY

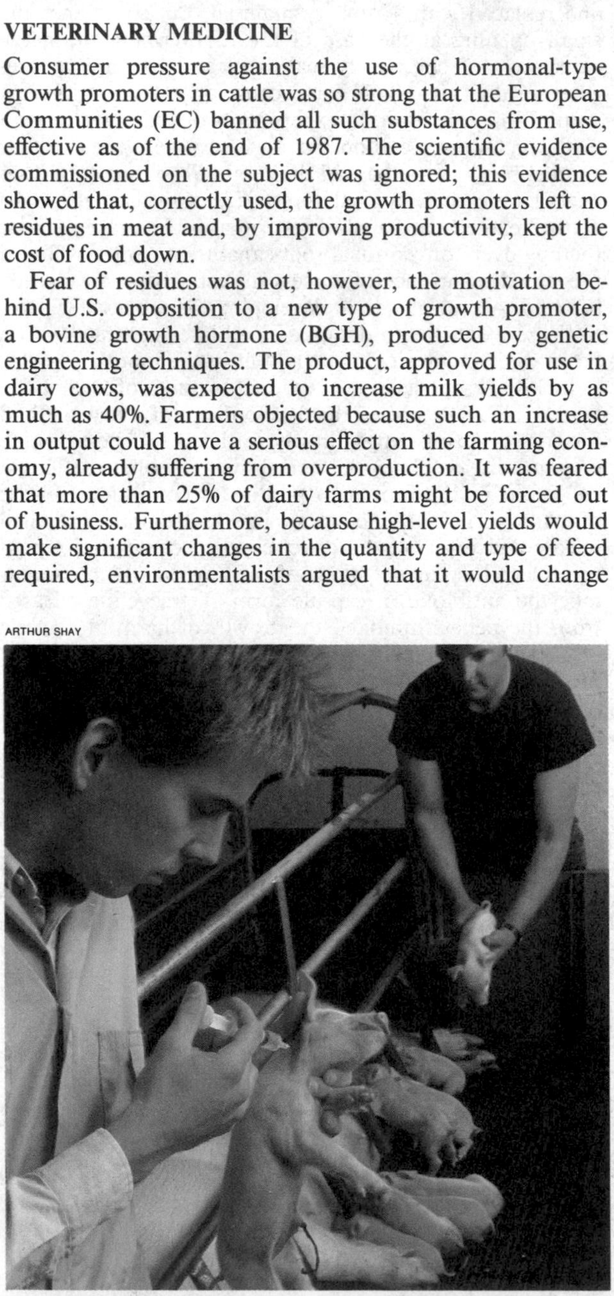

A veterinarian injects a piglet with Omnivac-PRV, a genetically engineered vaccine that protects against deadly pseudorabies. The vaccine was taken off the market after a complaint that federal guidelines for the release of such drugs had not been followed.

The veterinarian has a unique position relative to the use of laboratory animals. His professional skill and status make him the guardian of the health and welfare of all animals, including those subjected to experiments in scientific research essential to developing lifesaving medicines. In recent years not everyone had seen these two concerns as compatible, and a number of eminent veterinary scientists had been subject to attacks from animal-rights activists. In 1986 concerted efforts by welfare, veterinary, scientific, and governmental bodies were being made to codify procedures to ensure that laboratory animals were properly cared for and humanely treated. In the U.K. the Animals (Scientific Procedures) Act was passed, detailing the conditions to be observed before animals could be used experimentally and setting out the limitations on procedures. It also ensured that all laboratory animals would be under the care of a registered veterinarian. Similar legislation was being drafted by the EC, and in the U.S. the American Veterinary Medical Association was working in liaison with the National Academy of Sciences in a comprehensive study on the use of animals in research.

Greater importance was being attached to a type of animal therapy that was increasingly used in various kinds of institutions, including hospitals, nursing homes, and prisons. An international conference organized by the Delta Society, held in Boston in August, studied beneficial aspects of the relationship between humans and animals. Children with psychological or developmental difficulties improved in their ability to communicate as a result of interaction with pets. By helping to combat depression, confusion, and loneliness in nursing-home patients, the presence of animals actually reduced the pressure on nursing staff. The introduction of pets in prisons improved relations between prisoners and guards. A pervasive theme at the conference was the growing role of animals in providing assistance to people with physical disabilities.

Developments in medical treatment included the use of infrared lasers to relieve such conditions as swelling and inflammation associated with soft-tissue injuries in horses. The treatment produced changes in the levels of hormones associated with pain control, swelling, and tissue healing.

(EDWARD BODEN)

See also Life Sciences; Nobel Prizes; Populations and Population Movements; Social Security and Welfare Services.

This article updates the *Macropædia* articles DISEASE; MEDICINE.

Historic Preservation

As of November 1986, 91 countries had ratified or accepted the International Convention Concerning the Protection of the World Cultural and Natural Heritage (1972). The latest adherents were Maldives, China, the Philippines, and Saint Christopher and Nevis. At the tenth session of the World Heritage Committee, held at Unesco headquarters on Nov. 24–28, 1986, 22 new cultural properties were added to the World Heritage List, bringing the total of cultural and natural properties to 247 in 59 countries.

Among the cultural heritage additions to the list were the Roman monuments, cathedral, and Church of Our Lady in Trier, West Germany; the Roman ruins of Trier date from the 2nd through the 4th century AD, while the later Christian monuments were built on and in the ruins from the 11th through the 17th century. The Temple of Apollo Epicurius at Bassae, Greece, built in the second half of the 5th century BC, belongs to the first generation of post-Parthenon edifices. The churches and convents of Goa, Daman, and Diu, India, greatly influenced the development of architecture, sculpture, and painting wherever Roman Catholic missions were established in Asia from the 16th to the 18th century.

The Khajuraho group of monuments in Madhya Pradesh, India, include the surviving Hindu and Jain temples dating from the 10th and 11th centuries AD, notable for their highly original architecture and decorative sculpture. Also in India are the monuments at Hampi, Karnataka, the last capital of the great kingdoms of south India, and Fatehpur Sikri, Uttar Pradesh, the "City of Victory" which was, briefly, the capital of the Mughal Empire. The individual red sandstone monuments of Fatehpur Sikri have designs based on Hindu, Persian, and Indo-Muslim artistic traditions.

The old town of Ghadamis, Libya, is a unique pre-Saharan oasis town. Chan Chan, Peru, was the capital of the Chimu Kingdom, which reached its zenith in the 15th century AD, shortly before being conquered by the Incas. The structures of the historic centre of Évora, Port., within the Vauban-style walls (built in the 17th century from plans of Nicolas de Langres, a French engineer) date from the 12th through the 18th century. Four monuments of Mudejar architecture in Teruel, Spain, comprise an ensemble that was included on the World Heritage List: the Church of San Pedro, the cathedral, and the Churches of San Salvador and San Martin. Mudejar, meaning literally "allowed to remain," refers to Muslims who lived under Spanish Christian kings from the 11th through the 15th century, and their art and architecture is an amalgam of both western medieval and eastern Islamic traditions. Other Spanish sites added to the list were the city of Toledo, in its entirety, and the old town of Cáceres. In the Near East, Hattusas, near the modern village of Bogazkoy, Turkey, was the capital of the Hittite Empire in the 2nd millennium BC. The site of Hattusas was discovered in 1834 and excavated primarily after 1906.

A number of British sites were included, among them Durham Cathedral (1093–1133) and Castle, located on a rocky butte overlooking a bend in the River Wear. Ironbridge Gorge, Shropshire, was the first industrial archaeological site to be included on the World Heritage List. At the Coalbrookdale blast furnace Abraham Darby I successfully used coke to smelt iron ore in 1709, the first step in the Industrial Revolution. The Ironbridge itself, the first known metal bridge, was completed in 1779 by Abraham Darby III from drawings by the architect Thomas Farnolls Pritchard. Studley Royal Park and the ruins of Fountains Abbey, North Yorkshire, include the largest medieval ruins in the U.K., the Cistercian abbey built between the 12th and 16th century. Stonehenge, Avebury, and associated sites in Wiltshire are unquestionably the best known of the hundreds of circular megalithic ensembles that were characteristic of neolithic civilization in Britain. The castles and town walls of Edward I in Gwynedd, north Wales, are among the finest surviving examples of late 13th- and early 14th-century military architecture in Europe.

Rounding out the list, the old city of San'a', North Yemen, has existed as a densely packed urban complex for 2,000 years, although most of its multistoried earthen structures with their distinctive exterior painted decorations date from the Islamic period. Studenica Monastery, Serbia, Yugos., dating primarily from the 12th to the 14th century, is preeminent both because of the quality of its architecture and because of its association with Serbian history and culture. Great Zimbabwe National Monument, the ruins of the 11th–15th-century-AD Shona city of Zimbabwe, has become identified symbolically with the new nation of that name. Also in Zimbabwe, the Khami Ruins National Monument, Matabeleland, is similar to the later period of Great Zimbabwe.

The Statue of Liberty receives extensive cosmetic cleanup as well as structural stabilizing in preparation for a onetime grand birthday celebration and a long future of continuing to welcome immigrants to her nation's shores.

DAN CORNISH—ESTO

The International Council of Museums (ICOM), a Unesco nongovernmental organization of museum professionals, held its 14th General Conference and 15th General Assembly in Buenos Aires, Arg., from Oct. 26 to Nov. 4, 1986. Some 1,300 professionals from 70 countries gathered to assess developments in the museum field worldwide and to vote a program of goals and activities. An ICOM Code of Professional Ethics was adopted unanimously.

The restoration of the Statue of Liberty in New York Harbor was successfully completed in time for the 1986 celebration of Independence Day and the centennial of its original unveiling. (*See* WORLD AFFAIRS [North America]: *United States:* Sidebar.) (JOHN POPPELIERS)

See also Architecture; Environment; Museums.

Human Rights

Human rights are rights to life, liberty, and sociopolitical equality. Ideally, their observance should be examined positively, by scrutinizing the extent to which people living within different political systems enjoy these rights. Yet the nature of reporting on human rights forces the observer to be concerned primarily with denials of rights rather than with their observance—a circumstance that necessarily skews understanding of the world.

Denials of human rights should be considered on several levels of quantitative or qualitative impact. Distinctions must be made among those denials that stem from (1) massive struggles between whole nations and peoples; (2) violent struggles of governments or quasi-governments with their peoples or important segments of their populations; (3) the normal functioning of those political systems that do not acknowledge basic human rights; and (4) exceptional situations in generally nonrepressive systems. Denials of human rights on any level are most commonly ascribed to governments, and governments are blameworthy to the extent that they fail to take actions to guarantee that human rights are observed. In that they have become almost customary, denials of rights on the third level are likely to be the least painful and newsworthy; yet in any year the most continuous and widespread violations will occur on this level.

On the first level the outstanding problem in 1986 was the ongoing war between Iran and Iraq. Thousands continued to be conscripted in each country and sent off to death or injury. The Iran-Iraq war exceeded even World War I in senselessness in that for several years the battlefront had remained essentially the prewar boundary of the two states. Also on the first level was the continued Soviet attempt to destroy the resistance of the Afghan tribesmen. In this struggle, the killing, maiming, and starvation of thousands had been accompanied by the forced emigration of millions of Afghans. The responsibility rested with the U.S.S.R. and its clients, since the Afghan resistance leaders had not ignited the conflict and did not have a readily available way to end it. During 1986 Vietnam also continued its military effort in Kampuchea, though this involved much less death and destruction; further, Vietnam's rescue of the country from even worse evils under Kampuchea's previous regime lessened abhorrence of the occupation. However, Vietnam's quieter occupation of Laos did not have this justification.

In recent years human rights violations have been much more common on the second level of violent struggles within countries, including the struggle of governments against their own peoples. In Central America only Costa Rica and Belize were free of such struggles. However, the level of killing and torture in Panama and Honduras remained quite low. In Guatemala killing and torture continued at a reduced level in 1986, without the complicity of the newly elected civilian government. Active warfare continued in El Salvador and Nicaragua. Respect for liberty and political equality had improved considerably in El Salvador following the establishment of a functioning and competitive political process, but the country still lacked an adequate legal system, convincing civilian control of the military, and adequate outlets for the full spectrum of opinion. In Nicaragua the freedom evident in the early years of Sandinista rule had declined owing to increasing pressure on the government from the war with the *contras.* The Roman Catholic Church and opposition party and business leaders were outspoken critics of the government's tougher stance. The government's efforts to control Nicaragua led to oppression of the country's Indian population, while the war with the *contras* produced atrocities on both sides.

Broadly, the human rights situation in South America showed significant institutional improvement in 1986. Guerrilla warfare continued on a diminished scale in Colombia after the principal guerrilla organization decided to take part in the civilian political process. However, atrocities by the guerrillas and the Colombian Army in rural areas were reported. In Peru the more violent Sendero Luminoso (Shining Path) guerrillas had caused great loss of life, directly and through military counteractions. The killing of a large number of unarmed guerrilla prisoners after a prison mutiny further tarnished Peru's human rights record, though the new government's admission that excessive force had been used and the action taken against many of those responsible contrasted with the reactions of governments in Central America. (*See* CRIME, LAW ENFORCEMENT, AND PENOLOGY: *Prisons and Penology.*) A welcome growth in respect for rights could be read in the willingness of the Argentine government to sentence high-ranking generals for their part in the secret torture and killing of thousands of citizens during the 1970s.

In Europe struggles of governments against portions of their people were generally muted or, as with the Roman Catholics in Ulster, the Basques in northern Spain, and the Albanians in Yugoslavia, tragedies of history for which

AP/WIDE WORLD

Workers wait with tons of Operation Rainbow food supplies at the Khartoum airport. It was hoped that the international aid would be airlifted to southern Sudan where starvation had been used as a weapon in the country's ethnic conflicts.

Anatoly Shcharansky and his wife, Avital, answer questions at a press conference in Jerusalem after his release by the Soviet Union. Accused of being a spy, he had spent nine years in Soviet labour camps and prisons.
MILNER—SYGMA

blame was difficult to apportion. All the countries of Eastern Europe continued to deny basic rights and freedoms to their peoples, but only in Poland was there resistance on a massive scale. During the year the violence of the Polish government's relatively mild repression declined still further. By late 1986 all political prisoners had been released, and a quasi-legal opposition seemed to be accepted.

In Asia denials of rights in struggles between central governments and minority groups were common. During the year the most publicized struggles were those of the Indian government with Sikh militants and a variety of minority peoples in the borderlands. The Indian government's continuing attempt to overcome these problems achieved some success among Sikhs in the Punjab, while in the northwest the Mizo rebellion was successfully concluded, at least for the moment, by a compromise respecting the interests of both state and people. China maintained its more enlightened policy toward its marginal peoples, but the same could not be said for Burma, which continued to conduct a determined and bloody war against a variety of ethnic groups. The effort of the Iranian theocrats to impose their ideals on the country's entire population again led to the harsh punishment and even execution of those, such as the Baha'is, who were ruled unacceptable.

In the Middle East the worst denials of human rights stemmed from the fratricidal struggles of Lebanon's religious groups and subgroups. In this case, much of the responsibility rested with outside governments, such as Libya, Syria, Iran, and Israel. But it was in Africa that governments were most commonly and violently at war with their own peoples. While the scale of internal struggle declined in Uganda, massive killings continued in many other countries. In Ethiopia and The Sudan ethnic wars had been particularly destructive, with starvation a major weapon of the contenders. In neither case had an adequate attempt been made to meet the claims of the rebellious minorities, although conceivably the new elected government in The Sudan might find a way. Marxist-Leninist regimes in Angola and Mozambique continued to struggle against rebel movements. Here, as elsewhere, outside interference on both sides served to exacerbate the destructiveness of war.

The struggle of the white South African government to maintain its hegemony over a majority black population received more publicity during 1986 than any other human rights situation. The state of affairs there was hardly new, but it had been brought to world attention by the growing militance of black organizations and the increasing use of force against them by the South African security system. Thousands were imprisoned, at least briefly, while many were treated brutally, injured, or killed. Censorship and other controls over news gathering and dissemination were greatly strengthened under emergency regulations. The increase in the violence of the struggle, and the attendant denial of associated human rights, came at a time when many aspects of apartheid, inherently antithetical to many human rights, were being discarded or at least softened. Large black unions came into existence; South African citizenship was extended to many blacks who previously had been denied it; and the infamous pass laws used to regulate the movements of blacks and maintain residential segregation were set aside.

Events in South Africa, and the reaction to them, strengthened the realization that all peoples—and thus all governments—have a responsibility to strive for the elimination of human rights violations wherever they occur. The belated efforts of the U.S. to support changes in oppressive regimes in the Philippines and Haiti, as well as the hemisphere-wide pressure against the continuation of the autocratic regime in Chile, were other examples. In part, this was due to increasing activity on the human rights front, from the U.S. State Department's annual reports to Congress to the efforts of a variety of human rights organizations.

But for all the publicity surrounding many of these events and situations, most human rights violations in the world in 1986 went largely unrecorded, for they represented the quiet, third-level denials of basic rights to political and civil freedoms that continued to circumscribe the lives of two-thirds of humanity. China, the home of one-fourth of the world's people, had greatly improved its human rights performance in recent years, but it remained an authoritarian state ruled from the top. Where the oppressive system was shaky, as in South Korea, Pakistan, and Chile, demonstrations and their repression produced expressions of concern in the West, but the continuing oppression of ordinary citizens—in the Soviet Union, North Korea, Malawi, Saudi Arabia, Indonesia, Zaire, and many other countries—elicited little more than silence.

(RAYMOND DUNCAN GASTIL)

See also Race Relations.
This article updates the *Macropædia* article HUMAN RIGHTS.

Industrial Review

Manufacturing activity in the Western world continued to advance in 1985 but did not reach the spectacular 7% growth rate achieved in the previous year. The increase, about 4%, was the combined result of the comparatively moderate rise in manufacturing output in the developed industrial countries—about 3%, compared with 7% in 1984—and the fairly high 7.5% increase in the less developed countries, where the rate of growth was only marginally below that of 1984. In the centrally planned economies production grew by 4.5%, also fractionally less than in 1984.

In the industrial areas there was a marked slowdown in North America, particularly in the U.S., and also in Japan, while in Western Europe growth continued at the rather moderate rate of the previous year. It was not only the rates of progress in the three main Western centres of manufacturing that approached each other within a narrow range but the pattern of development as well; most growth in 1985 was achieved in the first half of the year, after which almost all industrial countries experienced stagnation. Preliminary indicators pointed to the continuation of this trend into the first half of 1986, and it appeared that manufacturing production changed very little in the 12 months to mid-1986.

Apart from weaker internal demand, an important factor contributing to the slowdown of growth in the manufacturing industries was the relatively sluggish development in 1985 of world trade in manufactured goods. The rapid rise of world trade in 1984, about 10% by volume, was followed by an increase of only 3.5% in 1985. The stagnating or falling export incomes of the Organization of Petroleum Exporting Countries (OPEC) as well as of less developed nations—a result of sharply falling prices of their primary products—significantly contributed to this slowdown in trade.

The metal products industries showed the fastest growth in output in both the market economies and the centrally planned countries; the production of base metals (such as iron and steel) grew much more slowly. This trend was most marked in developed countries, where the output of base metals rose in 1985 by 0.1% while that of metal products increased by 5%. The diverging trend reflected

(continued on page 240)

Table I. Index Numbers of Production, Employment, and Productivity in Manufacturing Industries

1980 = 100

Area	Relative importance[1] 1980	Relative importance[1] 1985	Production 1984	Production 1985	Employment 1984	Employment 1985	Productivity[2] 1984	Productivity[2] 1985
World[3]	1,000	1,000	107	111	...	...	...	...
Industrial countries	861	845	105	109	...	...	...	...
Less industrialized countries	139	155	116	124	...	...	...	...
North America[4]	282	289	110	113	...	...	...	...
Canada	22	21	102	107	93	93	110	115
United States	260	268	114	117	96	95	119	123
Latin America[5]	79	71	96	99	...	...	...	...
Argentina	12	9	93	83	...	...	...	...
Brazil	26	20	80	84	...	...	...	...
Mexico	18	18	101	108	96	...	111	...
Asia[6]	183	215	122	130	...	...	...	...
India	11	13	122	130	106	...	115	...
Japan	131	145	117	122	107	109	109	112
South Korea	6	9	160	167	121	...	132	...
Europe[7]	422	395	100	103	...	...	...	...
Austria	9	9	104	109	89	90	117	121
Belgium	13	12	102	104	...	...	...	...
Denmark	5	6	117	122	97	102	121	120
Finland	6	7	112	118	96	95	118	124
France	75	65	98	95	91	...	108	...
West Germany	114	108	99	104	89	90	111	116
Greece	4	4	95	97	101	99	94	98
Ireland	2	2	125	128	86	84	145	152
Italy	54	47	95	96	89	...	107	...
Netherlands, The	14	14	105	107	85	86	123	124
Norway	5	5	100	103	92	89	109	116
Portugal	3	3	105	110	...	...	...	...
Spain	23	21	100	102	84	...	119	...
Sweden	13	13	109	110	90	90	121	122
Switzerland	13	12	97	103	93	93	104	111
United Kingdom	58	55	100	104	79	79	127	132
Yugoslavia	10	11	112	114	113	...	99	...
Rest of the world[8]	34	30	...	...	...	...	...	...
Oceania	15	13	96	97	...	...	...	...
Australia	13	11	95	97	99	99	96	98
South Africa	8	7	100	94	99	95	101	99
Centrally planned economies[9]	...	...	115	120	...	...	...	...

[1] The 1980 weights are those applied by the UN Statistical Office; those for 1985 were estimated on the basis of the changes in manufacturing output since 1980 in the various countries.
[2] This is 100 times the production index divided by the employment index, giving a rough indication of changes in output per person employed.
[3] Excluding Albania, Bulgaria, China, Czechoslovakia, East Germany, Hungary, Mongolia, North Korea, Poland, Romania, the U.S.S.R., and Vietnam.
[4] Canada and the United States.
[5] South and Central America (including Mexico) and the Caribbean islands.
[6] Asian Middle East and East and Southeast Asia; including Japan, Israel, and Turkey.
[7] Excluding Albania, Bulgaria, Czechoslovakia, East Germany, Hungary, Poland, Romania, and the U.S.S.R.
[8] Africa and Oceania.
[9] These are not included in the above world total and consist of the European countries listed in note 7 above.

Table II. Pattern of Output, 1982–85

Percent change from previous year

	World[1] 1982	World[1] 1983	World[1] 1984	World[1] 1985	Developed countries 1982	Developed countries 1983	Developed countries 1984	Developed countries 1985	Less developed countries 1982	Less developed countries 1983	Less developed countries 1984	Less developed countries 1985	Centrally planned economies[2] 1982	Centrally planned economies[2] 1983	Centrally planned economies[2] 1984	Centrally planned economies[2] 1985
All manufacturing	−3	3	7	4	−4	3	7	3	2	3	8	7	3	5	5	4
Heavy industries	−5	3	9	4	−5	3	9	4	1	2	10	8	4	5	6	5
Base metals	−13	2	9	0.5	−15	3	9	0.1	2	0.2	12	3	0.5	4	3	3
Metal products	−4	3	10	6	−4	3	10	5	−2	2	13	11	4	6	7	6
Building materials, etc.	−5	2	4	0.4	−6	3	3	−0.4	0.5	−1	6	4	2	4	3	4
Chemicals	−2	5	7	4	−4	6	6	3	4	5	9	7	3	4	5	4
Light industries	−1	3	4	3	−2	3	4	1	2	4	6	7	2	4	4	3
Food, drink, tobacco	2	2	3	3	0	1	2	2	6	3	5	6	3	5	4	4
Textiles	−3	3	2	1	−4	2	1	0.8	−0.4	4	2	3	−0.7	2	1	0.8
Clothing, footwear	−2	0.3	3	0.4	−3	−0.3	1	−0.9	0.1	2	8	5	0.5	2	3	2
Wood products	−5	7	4	1	−6	7	4	−0.1	0.5	7	3	8	3	5	4	4
Paper, printing	−0.4	5	7	2	−0.7	5	7	2	2	2	6	4	3	5	4	4

[1] Excluding centrally planned economies. [2]Excluding China.
Source: UN, *Monthly Bulletin of Statistics.*

Special Report: Industrial Review

The Liability Insurance Crisis

BY DAVID C. BECKWITH

In Georgia hundreds of doctors marched on the state capitol to protest rising medical malpractice insurance premiums. The famous Coney Island Cyclone roller coaster was temporarily shut down because of excessive insurance costs. The Bully Hill winery in Hammondsport, N.Y., sharply curtailed its free wine tasting because its insurance premiums rose fivefold in a year. Blue Lake, Calif., shut its skating rink, parks, and tennis court when insurance costs became prohibitively expensive.

These incidents were but small pieces of a new national crisis that intensified across the U.S. in 1986, affecting everything from the price of ski lift tickets to the pace of oil exploration to the availability of day care for children. The main symptoms of the crisis were skyrocketing insurance costs and canceled insurance policies, but the underlying causes were varied and complex. Several powerful and persuasive segments of society affected by the problem—consumers, insurance executives, lawyers, manufacturers, politicians—assessed blame for the embroglio in vastly different ways. "We have not been able to get past the finger-pointing stage," summarized South Dakota Sen. Larry Pressler.

Passing the Buck. Consumer activists objected to allegations that more lawsuits and soaring judgments were the root cause; they said the main problem was overreaction and greed on the part of the insurance industry. Insurers agreed with greed as a motivation, but they pointed to lawyers who, they said, twisted the law and softhearted jurors into providing a windfall for themselves and their clients. The lawyers, in turn, blamed manufacturers and businessmen for alleged negligence; only by the threat of a major damage case, they claimed, could victims be compensated and businesses coerced into producing safe products. For their part, businessmen bemoaned changing public attitudes. Individual acceptance of risk and responsibility had been replaced, they said, by the attitude that every accident should generate a lawsuit.

The debate was badly clouded by the use of misleading statistics—particularly on numbers of court cases filed and costs of judgments—by virtually all parties. Still, the difficulty remained that all of the explanations for the crisis contained a substantial element of truth.

The number of malpractice and product liability suits filed in U.S. courts, while not rising as rapidly as some insurance and manufacturing representatives claimed, was clearly growing, and the process was becoming more expensive. Million-dollar verdicts, a rarity only a decade earlier, were now commonplace. Further, there was substantial inefficiency in the U.S. court system. A congressional committee was told in July that the U.S. tort system soaked up $68 billion in national resources in 1985, a 40-fold increase since 1950, with only one-quarter of that sum going to compensate victims for actual economic loss.

Financial dealings of liability insurance companies were also complicating the problem. In the early 1980s, when interest rates soared to over 20%, insurers wrote policies liberally, based on the belief that they could earn large profits on invested premiums for years until claims wound their way through the legal process and had to be paid. As interest rates fell, however, the insurance industry adopted what one critic called a "manic-depressive" response, canceling risky policyholders and raising rates by geometric progression on others.

And, as legal experts pointed out, the trend was being accelerated by the willingness of courts and legislatures to expand the definition of who can be sued and on what grounds. Governments, once largely immune from suit, could now be hauled into court in many cases, and accident victims were increasingly able to collect even when they were partially responsible themselves for their own misfortune. In addition, so-called deep pocket defendants were being hit under two expanding legal doctrines: joint and several liability, which holds even minor defendants liable for an entire judgment if others at fault cannot or will not pay; and strict liability, which holds a manufacturer responsible for any injury that arises from use of his product.

Widening Circles. The trends combined to produce some far-reaching results that touched virtually every American. In one highly publicized case, a two-year-old

ROB NELSON—PICTURE GROUP

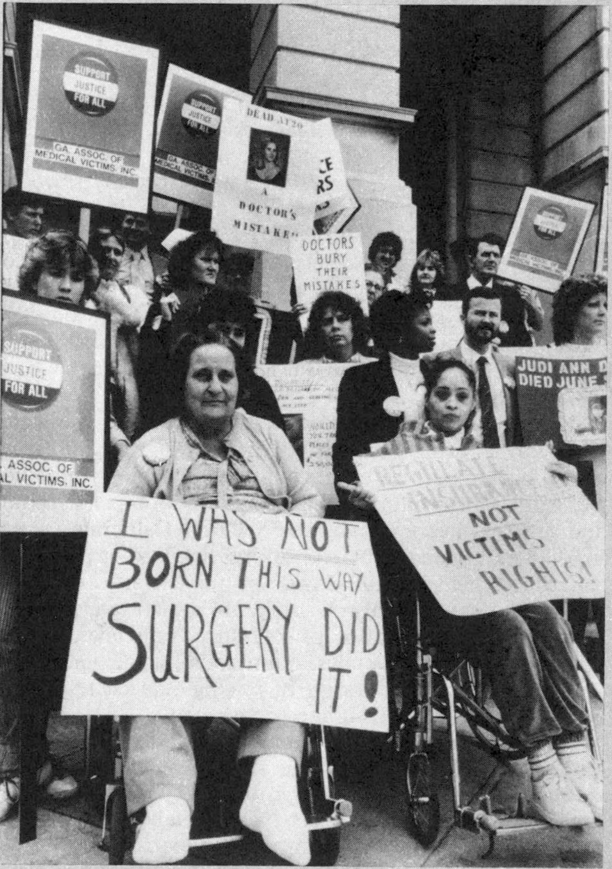

Victims of probable malpractice and those supporting their cause demonstrate against laws that might limit the right to sue doctors for large amounts of money. Huge awards in such cases have driven the cost of malpractice insurance to dizzying heights.

David C. Beckwith is a national correspondent for Time *magazine in Washington, D.C.*

boy fell through an opening in an 11-ft (3.4-m) Chicago playground slide designed for older children, suffering injuries that resulted in paralysis and permanent brain damage. Although park district officials contended the boy's mother was largely at fault for lax supervision, its liability insurers settled the boy's lawsuit for $1.5 million. They also slashed the park district's liability coverage and boosted the premium. In the end, gun-shy over other suits, park officials dismantled and removed every slide and jungle gym over 6½ ft (2 m) in height from the city's more than 500 playgrounds.

Other developments raised costs and reached far into the social fabric. The American College of Obstetricians and Gynecologists estimated that 73% of its 24,500 members had been sued at least once for malpractice, and some 3,000 had quit the specialty because of soaring malpractice insurance costs. Beech Aircraft contended that liability insurance added $80,000 to the cost of each plane it manufactured, helping to devastate the owner-pilot market. An estimated 2,000 local governments, unable or unwilling to pay escalating insurance premiums, went without coverage ("went bare"), exposing taxpayers to the full risk of future suits.

Elusive Remedies. What could be done to correct the disturbing trend? The answer was clearly not as simple as cracking down on greedy lawyers or greedy insurers. Before real reform could begin, some academics contended, the country would have to decide whether it wanted a purely compensatory system for accident victims or a fault-based liability system that required only culpable defendants to pay and restored to victims some of the risks of being alive. According to Gustave Shubert, director of the Institute for Civil Justice: "We are experiencing the disadvantages of trying to operate both systems in tandem, the worst of both worlds."

A decision on that basic choice appeared nowhere in sight, however, and both state and federal governments continued to struggle with a wide variety of patchwork solutions. In Washington progress was especially slow. A bill setting uniform national standards in product liability cases had languished in Congress for a decade, with heavy lobbying by manufacturers and insurers unable to overcome similarly ferocious arm-twisting by consumer groups, unions, and trial lawyers. Suggestions that Congress repeal the antitrust exemption granted to insurers, the better to foster competition in the insurance industry, had gone nowhere.

More than 1,400 bills were introduced in 50 state legislatures during 1985–86 to deal with the insurance crisis, but trends were difficult to spot. Maryland and Missouri limited damages that could be awarded for pain and suffering in some cases to $350,000. California voters in 1986 eliminated joint and several liability for pain and suffering. Michigan cut down on the use of expensive expert witnesses in trials. An alternate route in state action involved tighter regulation of insurance companies, a duty left by law to the 50 states. Numerous jurisdictions were strengthening state oversight of pricing, cancellation, and payment policies by insurance companies.

These piecemeal reform attempts promised only a slow and costly recovery from the immediate crisis and no solution at all to the basic problem. The U.S., once a nation of rugged individualists, had now taken on a no-risk mentality that dictated, when an accident or misfortune occurred, that somebody should pay. As jury awards and insurance rates rose throughout the nation, sometimes without apparent connection to economic reality, that somebody was turning out to be everybody.

(continued from page 238)
technological changes such as the switch to lighter products, the replacement of metals by such materials as plastics and ceramics for some products, and the growing importance of products based on microelectronics (computers and telecommunications equipment). The production of building materials, together with associated nonmetallic mineral products, grew most slowly in 1985 because of the weak investment in new civil engineering projects and other (particularly residential) buildings in the developed countries.

The progress of the light industries lagged behind that of the heavy industries everywhere, most remarkably in developed countries, where production in some consumer industries, for example, clothing and footwear, actually fell. It was evident that the shift of some consumer goods industries to the less developed countries—particularly to the newly industrializing ones such as South Korea, Taiwan, and Singapore—was continuing.

Among the six main industrial countries productivity per hour in manufacturing rose the most rapidly, by about 5%, in West Germany and the United States. In the others progress was slower—3–5.5% in Japan and the United Kingdom and 2.5–3% in France and Italy. Much of the improvement in labour productivity generally resulted from the dissemination of new technologies, generally based on microelectronics.

Manufacturing production in the centrally planned economies of the U.S.S.R. and Eastern Europe (excluding China) grew about 4.5% in 1985, apparently outpacing the developed market economics. The faster growth reflected the much less developed base from which the centrally planned economies started. Progress in the Eastern-bloc countries was fairly uniform with the exception of Hungary, where output stagnated. (G. F. RAY)

Table III. Annual Average Rates of Growth of Manufacturing Output, 1973–85

Percent

Area	1973–78	1978–81	1982	1983	1984	1985
World[1]: market economies	2.2	1.4	−3.4	3.2	7.1	3.7
Industrial countries	1.7	1.0	−4.4	3.2	6.9	3.1
Less industrialized countries	5.8	3.6	1.7	3.2	8.3	7.5
Centrally planned economies[1]	7.6	3.2	2.7	4.7	4.7	4.4

[1] For definition *see* Table I.
Source: UN, *Monthly Bulletin of Statistics.*

Table IV. Output per Hour Worked in Manufacturing

1980 = 100

Country	1981	1982	1983	1984	1985
France	101	105	110	116	119
West Germany	102	103	110	113	119
Italy	104	104	105	112	115
Japan	100	100	103	112	116
U.K.	105	110	117	122	126
U.S.	104	107	114	118	124

Source: National Institute, *Economic Review.*

Table V. Manufacturing Production in the U.S.S.R. and Eastern Europe[1]

1980 = 100

Country	1981	1982	1983	1984	1985
Bulgaria[2]	105	110	115	120	124
Czechoslovakia	102	104	107	111	115
East Germany[2]	105	108	113	117	122
Hungary	103	106	107	110	110
Poland	86	84	89	94	98
U.S.S.R.	103	106	111	116	...

[1] Romania not available.
[2] All industries.
Source: UN, *Monthly Bulletin of Statistics.*

ADVERTISING

A U.S. Supreme Court ruling in 1986 broadened government power to restrict advertising. The case concerned the right of the Puerto Rican legislature to prevent casinos from advertising locally. In a 5–4 ruling, the court declared that it was up to state and federal legislatures, not the courts, to decide how best to regulate legal but potentially harmful businesses such as gambling, liquor, and tobacco. This was the first time the court had upheld a ban on truthful, accurate advertising for a product. In entering the ruling, the court relied on the four-part test established in *Central Hudson Gas & Electric Corporation* v. *Public Service Commission of New York* (1980), which upheld advertising regulation if the commercial speech was not truthful advertising for a legal product. The test allowed regulation of truthful advertising for legal products if the government interest was substantial, if the proposed regulation directly advanced that government interest, and if the regulation was not more extensive than necessary. The 1986 ruling gave constitutional support to legislative proposals that would forbid all tobacco advertising in magazines and newspapers and on billboards.

A. C. Nielsen Co., a Chicago marketing research firm, introduced the Cable Audience Profile (CAP) to measure cable network viewing on a system-by-system basis. CAP used Nielsen's Station Index Diaries, placed in the homes of selected viewers, to calculate viewership and demographic information for 500 cable systems during four sweep periods. (Sweep periods are used to determine advertising rates for the year.) The top 50 multiple-cable systems accounted for approximately $119 million in local advertising sales in 1985. The CAP report would enable advertisers to pinpoint specific demographics within systems and relate them to viewing levels for each cable network in those systems.

According to *Advertising Age,* the 100 largest national advertisers in the U.S. increased their spending in 1985 to $26,670,000,000, up 2.7% from the revised figure of $25,970,000,000 in 1984. The small increase was blamed on a stagnant economy and restructuring of product lines to make them less cyclical. Network television spending dropped to $6,340,000,000, a decline of 2.6% from 1984. Spot television made the greatest gain in dollar volume (up 9.5% from 1984 to $3,070,000,000), but network radio showed the greatest percentage increase, rising 77.3% to $272 million. The five leading national advertisers in the U.S. in 1985 were Procter & Gamble, Philip Morris Cos., RJR/Nabisco, Sears, Roebuck & Co., and General Motors. Procter & Gamble spent $1.6 billion, 9.6% more than in 1984. Philip Morris spent $1.4 billion.

In 1986 the three major television networks experienced ownership or management changes that could affect future programming. (*See* TELEVISION AND RADIO.) "The Cosby Show" was the highest priced show in the U.S. during the year, commanding an average of $375,000 for 30 seconds of television time. Because of the high cost of TV time, advertisers stepped up pressure on television networks to sell 15-second commercial time slots. CBS sold 15-second spots alone, but the other networks resisted the practice because they would have to sell twice as many spots and would be unable to separate commercials for competing products.

The Saatchi brothers of Great Britain created the world's largest advertising agency holding company in 1986 with the purchase of Ted Bates Worldwide for $400 million. The new agency would have annual billings of $7.6 billion and 150 offices. The new agency surpassed Omnicom Group, with annual billings of some $5 billion, which had become the world's largest when it was formed, in April, by a merger of BBDO International, Doyle Dane Bernbach Group, and Needham Harper Worldwide, the 6th, 12th, and 16th largest U.S. agencies, respectively. Such massive mergers raised problems for competing companies that found they were now clients of the same agency.

The raising of private funds to restore the Statue of Liberty caused a stir in the advertising community when the federal government granted certain companies exclusive rights to use a logo of "Miss Liberty" in their advertising. Sixteen companies pledging a total of $60 million began to use an image of the statue in advertising for such products as Oscar Mayer wieners, Kellogg's corn flakes, and Stroh's beer. Criticism was leveled at the commercialization of a national symbol.

Advertising spending in Western Europe in 1986 rose 28% over 1985, with the largest increase taking place in television advertising. Traditionally, television advertising in most European countries had been closely regulated, but in 1986 new commercial time was added in Great Britain, Italy, and Belgium. Denmark, one of the last holdouts against commercial television, dropped its ban on television advertising during the year. The decision was tied to the start-up of a second national Danish television channel, scheduled for 1988. An independent state-run company was established to sell advertising time on this new station, with advertisers having to buy time one year in advance. Commercials would be limited to three five-minute blocks a day, with ten minutes shown during national programming and five minutes during regional programs. Advertising for tobacco and alcohol including beer, medicine, banks, and political parties would be prohibited.

A study by the Television Bureau of Advertising in October 1986 reported that the U.S. financial services industry spent 30% more on television advertising in the first half of 1986 than in the corresponding period of 1985. Increased competition resulting from deregulation was pinpointed as the cause of the increase. The study projected that the financial services industry would spend more than $900 million in 1986. This would make it the fifth largest advertiser on commercial television, exceeded only by food and food products, the automotive industry, toiletries, and restaurants and drive-ins. Among financial services advertisers, Sears, Roebuck was the biggest spender in 1986.

(EDWARD MARK MAZZE)

AP/WIDE WORLD

A pop-up ad for Transamerica in the September 8 issue of *Time* magazine features the insurance company's headquarters towering over the San Francisco skyline. Other advertisers also tried three-dimensional ads aimed at grabbing readers' attention by surprise.

AEROSPACE

The air transport industry in 1986 was characterized by continuing financial losses, more takeovers and mergers in the U.S., growing restiveness with the lack of competition in Europe, which resulted in artificially high fares, and continued reequipment. In October the chairman of the airlines' regulatory body, the International Air Transport Association, predicted losses of up to $800 million for 1986. He stated that terrorism was a major factor constraining the industry's growth and called for new measures to deal with the problem. The North Atlantic route had been badly affected after the U.S. bombing raid on Libya in April, several hijackings,

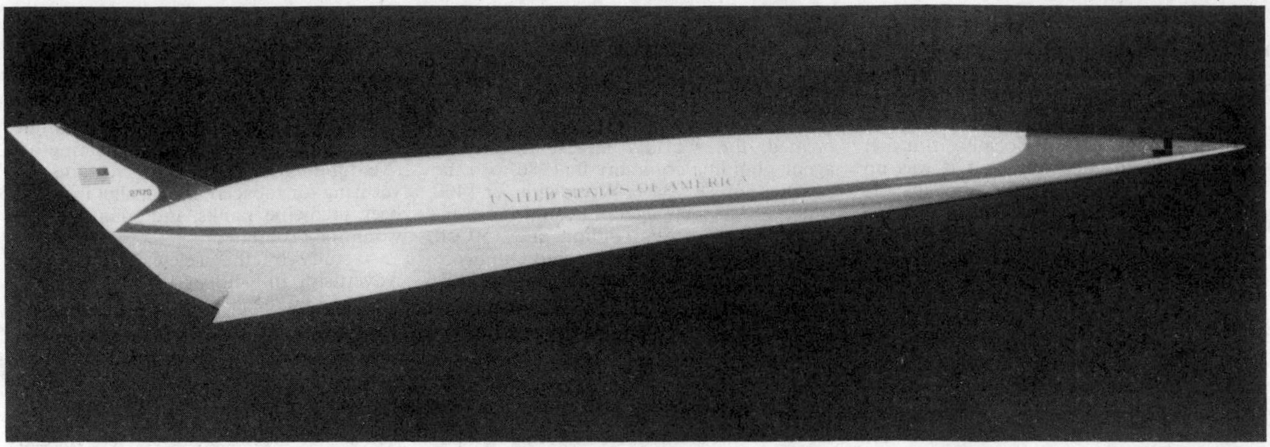

An artist's conception shows the proposed Orient Express, a hypersonic U.S. commercial jet intended to exit Earth's atmosphere, enter low orbit, and return with ease. Its speed would be up to 25 times that of sound, trimming travel time between Washington, D.C., and Tokyo from 15 hours to 2 hours. The jet might not be completed until the 21st century.
NASA

and a spate of bombings in Paris; the number of U.S. tourists visiting Europe fell dramatically.

The brisk activity in airline mergers in the U.S. reached new levels. Despite protests by labour unions and other pressure groups and some senior airline staff, the U.S. Department of Transportation generally favoured the trend as a way of increasing efficiency within the industry following deregulation. Opposition to the high fare structure on European routes continued to grow, fostered by consumer bodies, the European Commission, the European Council of Transport Ministers, and the British government, which notably wanted fewer regulations. The airlines—all the large ones were state-owned, though British Airways was due for privatization in January 1987—protested that there was already adequate competition and that, in many cases, the traffic volume would not sustain additional services. The airlines were due to make their case by early 1987, failing which the Commission was threatening action before the European Court.

In late 1985 Boeing launched its long-awaited 747-400—the world's largest airliner. By the end of 1986 there were 70 of those $115 million airplanes on order, and the company was planning a 747-500, which some airlines complained would be too big for their terminals. Like the supersonic transport Concorde, the 747 remained unique some two decades after its launch, although nearly 800 had been sold, compared with fewer than 20 Concordes. McDonnell Douglas (MD), which a few years earlier was being written off in the airliner market by industry observers, returned to the market with new versions of the MD-80 modeled on the long-serving and popular DC-9. MD's airline business was heavily supported by production of the KC-10 tanker version of the DC-10, which went to war for the first time during the U.S. raid on Libya. By year's end MD appeared set to reopen the DC-10 production line with the MD-11.

Airbus Industrie was remarkably successful in obtaining an order from the U.S. operator Northwest Orient for 100 Airbus A320s worth $3.2 billion. By the end of the year Airbus Industrie was completing plans to build a four-engine, 250–270-seat airliner, the A340, for launch in March 1987.

The 1986 Farnborough (England) Air Show was used by engine manufacturers to promote a revival of the propeller under a host of names as new as the devices themselves: the General Electric Co.'s Unducted Fan, Pratt & Whitney's Advanced Ducted Prop and Countra-rotating Integrated Shrouded Propfan, Rolls-Royce's Contrafan, International Aero Engines' SuperFan, and a similarly named propulsor by Allison. All were aimed at exploiting the superior propulsive efficiency of propeller-type devices over high-bypass fans as a means of reducing fuel costs, but much more research was needed before they were adopted; also, there were doubts about whether they would prove competitive, compared with the existing generation of proven turbofans and given the decline in the price of oil.

The General Electric Co. engine made its first flight aboard a modified Boeing 727 in August, and the same engine was to be flown in a DC-9, while Allison was to fit its propfan to a Gulfstream business jet for airborne tests. Boeing was proposing a twin-engine 150-seat airliner, the 7J7, to compete with the Airbus A320 (which was to have conventional fan engines). MD was also testing the market with a similar project, a derivative of the MD-80 known as the MD-91X.

In January the Anglo-French Concorde supersonic transport completed a decade of service. While its scheduled routes dwindled to four (London and Paris to New York City and occasionally Washington, D.C.), its image remained glamorous, and there was great demand for charter work.

Airships became increasingly popular. The U.K. company Airship Industries was collaborating with the U.S. company Westinghouse to design a lightweight craft for the U.S. Navy's surveillance airship program against competition from Boeing and Goodyear. The last-named firm produced the "blimps" long used by the U.S. Navy but phased out in 1963 with the advent of new and highly capable fixed-wing aircraft.

The U.S. Air Force's Rockwell B-1B became operational many years after its original launch, having survived a four-year suspension initiated by former president Jimmy Carter in 1977. Debate continued about whether production of the B-1B should cease after 100 aircraft, as planned, in favour of the highly secret Northrop Advanced Technology Bomber (ATB). The July crash of a U.S. Air Force "stealth" fighter in California was much publicized, and there was speculation that as many as 50 of these advanced aircraft were being flight-tested in Nevada by night to avoid observation.

In Europe two new fighters made inaugural flights and gave impressive displays at Farnborough. They were France's Rafale A by Dassault-Breguet and the British Aerospace Experimental Aircraft Program (EAP); the latter was designed to test the technology for the 1990s Eurofighter to be built by the U.K., West Germany, Italy, and Spain. Rafale A was to pave the way for the all-French Rafale B. Prototypes of two more fighters, Sweden's JAS 39 Gripen and Israel's Lavi, were being prepared for first flights. All four craft had tail-first configurations to exploit the maneuverability and other benefits made possible by advanced digital flight-control systems. Plans for the U.S. Air Force's Advanced Tactical Fighter (ATF) moved a step forward when seven top U.S. companies made bids in July; in October Northrup and Lockheed were selected to build prototypes for competitive evaluation.

The U.S. strike against five Libyan targets on April 14–15 proved to be an operational test of the first magnitude, involving F-111 fighter-bombers from U.S. bases in the U.K. synchronized with A-6 and A-7 bombers and F-14 and F-A-18 fighters from a two-carrier U.S. task force in the Mediterranean Sea. The refusal by France and Spain to allow overflying greatly lengthened the F-111's journey, and a massive air-refueling operation supported the mission. (MICHAEL WILSON)

AUTOMOBILES

Essentially 1985 was a year of progress in the automobile industry, with no major changes in company ownership, takeovers, or mergers. The strong grew stronger. The state-owned companies became an even bigger burden on their countries' taxpayers. It was a year of rapid technical innovation with the promise of even better products in the near future. At the same time, there were growing worries about 1986, particularly for Japan, where marked changes in world currency values were threatening the price competitiveness of its vehicles.

World production of passenger and commercial vehicles reached a new peak in 1985 of 43,761,000 units. This eclipsed the previous record of 41,892,000 in 1978 and marked a strong 6% advance over 1984. The three leading producers—Japan with 12,271,000 vehicles, the U.S. with 11,652,000, and West Germany with 4,446,000—accounted for 44.3% of total world output. Both Japan and West Germany recorded their highest production ever, while the U.S. figure was the best since 1981. Spain, Canada, and Sweden also set new records in 1985.

In the seven European Communities (EC) vehicle-manufacturing countries (including Spain for the first time), production rose 5% to a record 12,067,000, although France and Italy suffered small downturns. In the U.K. car output rose from 909,000 in 1984 to 1,048,000, and commercial vehicle production was up from 225,000 to 266,000. In South America, Brazil's car output slumped from 538,000 in 1984 (600,700 in 1980) to 445,000, but commercial vehicle output rose strongly from 328,000 to 522,000, the highest level since 1980. In Argentina the general weakness of the economy was reflected: car output dropped from 142,000 to 118,000 (228,000 in 1980), and commercial vehicle production declined from 25,400 to 19,700. Australia boosted its annual car production from 370,000 to a new peak of 384,000, although its commercial vehicle output declined from 28,700 to 27,600.

As in 1984, South Korea recorded the largest year-on-year gain with its 67% jump in car output to 264,500 units and 9% rise in commercial vehicle production to 118,700 units. South Korea's output of cars had more than quadrupled and that of commercial vehicles had almost doubled since 1980. The U.S. continued to dominate world car production with 8,185,000 units, followed by Japan with 7,647,000 and West Germany with 4,167,000. The other significant producers were France, 2,632,000; the U.S.S.R., 1,805,000; Italy, 1,389,000; Spain, 1,230,000; Canada, 1,078,000; the U.K., 1,048,000; and Brazil, 445,000.

The world's top 12 automobile producers for 1985 were General Motors Corp. (8,468,000, 2.6% up from 1984); Ford Motor Co. (5,550,000, down 0.6%); Toyota (3,545,000, up 3.3%); Nissan (2.5 million, up 0.7%); Volkswagen/Audi (2,389,000, up 11.2%); Chrysler Corp. (1,926,000, up 2.1%); Renault (1,675,000, down 29%); Fiat (1,631,000, up 15.8%); Peugeot-Citroen (1,626,000, up 0.5%); Honda (1,363,000, up 4.4%); Mazda (1,330,000, down 0.4%); and Mitsubishi (1,236,000, up 6%).

Europe and Australia. Some of the smaller European companies experienced excellent sales and production gains in 1985, particularly those with strong exports to North America. In West Germany Mercedes-Benz car output rose from 463,000 to 538,000, BMW from 412,000 to 431,000, and Porsche from 44,000 to 54,000. In the U.K. the Rover Group increased output from 383,000 to 465,000 (without any substantial North American market); Jaguar rose from 33,000 to 38,000; and Rolls-Royce rose from 2,200 to 2,590. In Sweden Volvo's output rose from 248,000 to 289,000, and Saab's production rose from 102,000 to 111,000.

The year was one of relative industrial calm, steady sales growth, and profitability, with the continuing notable exceptions of state-owned Renault in France, Italy's Alfa Romeo, and the Rover Group in the U.K. Despite a record Australian car and commercial vehicle market, General Motors' Australian subsidiary, General Motors-Holden's Ltd., suffered a financial loss.

The move to unleaded gasoline (petrol) in Europe by about 1990 was presaged by the introduction in West Germany of several models using unleaded fuel for the domestic market. The Australian market enjoyed a miniboom, partly as a result of buyers acquiring the last leaded-gasoline cars prior to the mandatory use of unleaded gasoline for new cars from 1986.

(JOHN R. WEINTHAL)

AP/WIDE WORLD

Hundreds of new, low-cost Excel subcompact cars bound for the U.S. await loading at Ulsan, South Korea. Such cars broadened the international nature of the U.S. market and served to warn others of tough competition ahead.

United States. The U.S. auto industry in 1986 resorted to discount financing programs that offered new car loans with interest rates as low as 0% to entice buyers into the market. But despite these incentives—and the tax reform that would eliminate the income tax deduction for sales taxes and consumer credit—the automakers were able to sell only 8,050,000 new cars in the model year ended Sept. 30, 1986, a 3.8% decline from the 8,380,000 sold in the 1985 model year. Imports, meanwhile, led by the Japanese producers, sold a record 3.1 million cars in model year 1986. This topped the previous high of 2.6 million sold in model year 1985.

Because of the strength of the imports, combined domestic and foreign car sales of 11.1 million units topped the 11 million cars sold in the U.S. during the previous year. It was the second highest combined total in industry history, trailing only the 11.8 million sold in 1973. The pickup truck market was strong, with a record 4.8 million units sold in the U.S., passing the old record of 4.5 million sold in 1985. The total number of all vehicles sold, imported and domestic combined, reached a record 16 million units, up from the old record of 15.6 million in 1985.

General Motors, plagued by bulging inventories of unsold cars throughout the year (based for the most part on consumer complaints that the styling of its car lines was so similar that buyers could not tell the difference between an Oldsmobile and a Cadillac), sold 4.5 million cars in 1986, down from 4.7 million in 1985. Ford sold 1.9 million cars, down from 2.1 million the previous year. The drop in Ford's sales was attributed to a slow production startup of its new line of family-size front-wheel-drive cars, the Ford Taurus and Mercury Sable. For the entire model year Ford had more orders for the cars than it could produce. Chrysler sold 1,148,000 cars, a slight increase from the 1,144,000 sold the previous year and its highest total since the record 1,180,000 sold in 1977. Honda, based on sales of its compact Accord built in Ohio, retained its spot as fourth largest domestic producer for the second consecutive year. Honda sold 183,629 cars, up from 147,674 the year before.

American Motors Corp. sold 82,292 cars, down sharply from 137,493 the previous year; it was the first time since 1982 that AMC had fallen below the 100,000 mark. Volkswagen sold 76,410 U.S.-made cars, up from 71,884 a year earlier, and Nissan, in its second year of building cars in Tennessee, sold 49,325 cars, up from 21,077 in 1985.

Among the major imports, Toyota again was the top selling producer, with sales of 617,010 units. Nissan followed with 511,559. The best-selling individual vehicle in the industry was the F-series Ford pickup truck, with sales of 544,191 units. The Chevrolet C/K pickup was second at 442,580.

Among cars, the top make was the subcompact Ford Escort at 415,521, followed by the midsize Chevrolet Celebrity at 395,860, subcompact Chevrolet Cavalier at 386,258, midsize Oldsmobile Cutlass Ciera at 330,572, compact Honda Accord at 295,593, compact Ford Tempo at 251,-

618, full-size Oldsmobile 88 at 241,417, midsize Buick Century at 239,278, full-size Chevrolet Caprice at 228,706, and subcompact Honda Civic at 228,506.

The strength shown by the Japanese imports surprised many industry observers because the value of the Japanese yen against the U.S. dollar rose by about 30% during the year and was responsible for price increases on Japanese makes amounting to more than $1,000 on average. Then, too, the Japanese did not offer financing incentive programs as their U.S. rivals did. But Japanese automakers either firmed up existing plans or mapped new ventures to build cars in the U.S. to avoid future problems with either the yen or protectionist retaliation by the U.S. Congress. (See *Japan,* below.)

GM and Volvo formed a joint venture to produce trucks in the U.S. It was GM's second joint European venture as custom body builder Pininfarina of Italy began making the bodies for Cadillac's new luxury two-seater $50,000 Allante. Pininfarina assembled the bodies in Italy and then flew them to Detroit, where Cadillac added engines, transmissions, and other parts.

Chrysler entered into an agreement, an industry first, with AMC whereby the latter agreed to build the full-size, rear-wheel-drive Chrysler Fifth Avenue, Plymouth Gran Fury, and Dodge Diplomat at the Kenosha, Wis., assembly plant where it built the subcompact Renault Alliance. Chrysler moved those cars out of its St. Louis assembly plant to make room for added output of its highly successful minivans. But since the big Chrysler cars were still selling well, it found a way to keep producing them, albeit by a competitor. Because of the poor sales of the Alliance, AMC had ample capacity.

Though not specifically citing money problems resulting from sagging new car sales, costly incentive programs, and expensive acquisitions, GM said that its initial target for its much heralded Saturn car would be to build 200,000 cars annually and employ 3,000 workers at the new Spring Hill, Tenn., plant. And while it at first had said that Saturn would be a small car to compete with imports, GM later announced that the first Saturn model in mid-1990 would be "larger."

Early in November GM announced that over the next three years it would shut down 11 of its plants in the U.S. Many of the 29,000 workers in those plants would be laid off, though others would be transferred and retrained. GM estimated that the closings would cut its fixed costs by $500 million per year. Months of infighting among GM's top executives ended December 1, when Texas billionaire H. Ross Perot was removed from the board of directors.

With the 1986 model year behind them, the automakers rolled out some new entries for the 1987 model year, which began Oct. 1, 1986. Among the notable additions at Cadillac were the Allante and a Sixty Special DeVille sedan that was 12.5 cm (5 in) longer than the existing front-wheel-drive sedan—an effort to quiet complaints that the cars were now too small.

Chevrolet brought out the compact Corsica sedan and Beretta coupe, its first compacts since dropping the Citation after 1985. Pontiac introduced its own version of the Oldsmobile 88 and Buick LeSabre full-size, front-wheel-drive, H-body cars called the Bonneville. As an indication that fuel economy had become less important to drivers, GM dropped the 2.5-litre four-cylinder engine in its Chevolet Camaro and Pontiac Firebird lines and added the 5.7-litre V-8 engine from the Chevrolet Corvette in those cars—as well as putting a 145-mph speedometer in the dashboard.

Ford came out with a four-wheel-drive version of its compact Tempo and Mercury Topaz and also added rear-wheel antilock brakes to its F-series pickup truck and its Ford Bronco full-size and Bronco II compact-size utility vehicles. With antilock brakes, computers control wheel spin to avoid skidding in a panic braking situation.

Chrysler had the most new entries among the U.S. manufacturers with a stretched version of its mini Dodge Caravan and Plymouth Voyager vans that was 37 cm (15 in) longer, a sporty front-wheel-drive coupe and convertible rival to the Camaro and Firebird called LeBaron, and new front-wheel-drive subcompacts called Dodge Shadow and Plymouth Sundance. Chrysler also brought out the Dakota, a midsize pickup truck.

GM and Ford asked the U.S. government to relax federal mileage standards once again so that the requirement calling for each producer to obtain 27.5 miles per gallon from its fleet of cars in the 1987 model year would be lowered to 26 mpg. The government, which had agreed to the same request by relaxing the 1986 standard to 26 mpg, again agreed to the request and also set the 1988 law at 26 mpg. The automakers said that to meet the 27.5-mpg requirement they would have to close plants making large cars.

The mini Chevrolet Sprint captured the title as most fuel-efficient model on the U.S. market for the second consecutive year with a 54-mpg city mileage rating. While carrying a U.S. name, Sprint also carried a one-litre, three-cylinder engine produced by Suzuki of Japan. If mileage was high, so too were prices as the U.S. automakers imposed increases of from 1.6 to 2.6% in the fall at the outset of the new model year. (JAMES L. MATEJA)

Japan. The Automobile Industry Association of Japan reported a record high total output of 6,240,437 units during the first half of the 1986 calendar year, a 2% improvement over the corresponding period a year earlier. The units sold in the domestic market amounted to 2,928,183, including imported cars, again a record and representing a 4.1% increase. Exports rose by a strong 5%, although the rate of increase slowed considerably in the second quarter of 1986.

Many Japanese economists and trade problems observers asserted that the biggest problem facing Japan in 1986 was how to cope with the adverse effects of the increased value of the yen against the U.S. dollar. After September 1985, when a convention of finance ministers from five developed countries was held, the value of the yen rose from 240 to 150 against the dollar. This compelled Japanese automakers to raise the selling prices of their cars in the U.S. four times in one year.

In the four rounds of price hikes, Toyota raised its prices $1,358 in the aggregate (14.1% increase), Nissan $1,339 (12.5% increase), Honda $1,199 (14.5% increase), and Mazda $1,408 (15.6% increase). Despite these higher prices the automakers could not offset the losses they suffered from the abrupt appreciation of the yen, and their profits in the 1985–86 fiscal year appeared to have been considerably reduced from a year earlier.

The high value of the yen prompted those manufacturers to construct new plants in the U.S. As of mid-1986 Japanese corporations manufacturing passenger cars in North America included Honda, Nissan (both independently), and Toyota (through a joint venture with GM). Those deciding to manufacture in the U.S. in the future included Mazda (independently), Mitsubishi (through a joint concern with Chrysler), Toyota (independently), Fuji Heavy Industries and Isuzu Motor (through a joint venture between the two), and Suzuki Motor (through a joint venture with GM). This meant that out of nine Japanese passenger car manufacturers, eight had already begun or would begin production in North America.

As a result, some industry observers were worried that the domestic Japanese auto industry might become "hollow," an industry in name only, and company executives were trying to work out countermeasures. However, such a situation would be more or less unavoidable as long as the carmakers continued with large-scale production projects in the U.S.

It remained an indisputable fact that the high value of the yen had a greater impact on Japan's auto export trade to the U.S. than did the two oil crises. The Japanese auto industry, under "voluntary restraints" on exports to the U.S., was supposed to fulfill a quota of 2.3 million units of cars to the U.S. for the 1986 fiscal year. Some economists predicted, however, that the industry might find it difficult to fill the quota.

Under those circumstances manufacturers were showing more interest in European markets. European countries were also implementing various quota systems on imports of cars from Japan, but by taking case-by-case countermeasures, Japanese auto manufacturers were successful in selling their cars throughout Europe. Among the most noteworthy events were Nissan's opening of a new plant in Britain and Honda's development of a passenger car for delivery to the Austin Rover Group.

Demand for passenger cars in Japan remained steady, mainly owing to an increased sales volume of new models that gained popularity among users from 20 to 30 years old. Based on these rapidly selling new models, two quite opposite trends of specialization in car design could be seen: high-priced, high-performance models and low-priced, low-fuel-consumption, subcompact cars for business use, both of which were selling "explosively."

(NOBUYOSHI YOSHIDA)

BEVERAGES

Beer. World beer production in 1985 totaled an estimated 972.4 million hectolitres (1 hl = 26.4 U.S. gal), a 2.3% increase over 1984. Of the established brewing nations in Europe, North America, and Australasia, only West Germany, Spain, Italy, and The Netherlands increased their output. Production increased most in third world countries, particularly in Mexico, Brazil, Colombia, and Peru. There was accelerated interest and investment in brewing in China, where beer consumption was growing rapidly.

The world's crop of hops was 2.4 million zentners (1 zentner = 50 kg [110 lb]), 2% down from 1985 but still in excess of demand. Crops declined in all the major growing countries except Czechoslovakia. The leading producer remained the U.S., followed by Czechoslovakia and the U.S.S.R.

Leading brewing nations continued to export technology and technical expertise to China. The China Council for the Promotion of International Trade sponsored a visit by British brewers to advise on minibreweries. Pabst Blue Ribbon brewing plants in Vancouver, B.C., and Newark, N.J., were dismantled and shipped to Zhoaqing (Chao-ch'ing) in Guangdong (Kwangtung) Province, where the first U.S. beer was being brewed. Czechoslovakia's state-owned Technoexpert Corporation won a $22 million contract to build the Mwanza Brewery in Tanzania.

International agreements to brew under license proliferated. Budweiser, the main beer of the U.S. giant Anheuser-Busch, which was already brewed in the U.K. and Japan, stated its intention to produce at Smithwick's Brewery, Kilkenny, Ireland, in 1987. Australia's Foster's Lager of Carlton United Breweries agreed with Carling O'Keefe to brew under license in Canada.

U.K. beer exports reached an all-time record, the main customers being the U.S., Belgium, and Italy. Over 3,000 breweries worldwide were invited to compete for the 1987 Brewing Industry International Awards, held in England. The awards dated back more than 100 years, and the current holders included the Guernsey Brewery in the Channel Islands for bottled ale and the Lion Brewery of Wellington, N.Z., for bottled lager. (MICHAEL D. RIPLEY)

Spirits. The continuing trend toward lighter spirits and stricter controls on alcohol advertising made 1986 another difficult year for the spirits market worldwide. Traditional spirits came under intense pressure from table wines, coolers, and lower-strength liqueurs, reflecting the increased emphasis on healthier living. Since 1976, ten European countries had introduced major changes in laws governing alcohol advertising, and tougher restrictions were being considered in France, Greece, Italy, and The Netherlands. Discouraging messages such as "Alcohol ruins the family" were being placed on spirit bottles in parts of India, and new controls in Australia prohibited drinks advertising between 5 AM and 8:30 PM. The U.S. Congress ordered a study of the effect of warning labels on alcoholic beverage containers.

A clerk removes Italian wines from shelves in the U.S. after methanol-tainted wines were linked to 18 deaths in Italy. Contaminated Italian wine was found in West Germany, Denmark, and Switzerland.
AP/WIDE WORLD

The steady decline in sales of traditional dark spirits such as whisky and brandy showed little sign of halting, although single malt Scotch whisky became a dynamic growth area, with sales doubling between 1979 and 1985. Sales of white spirits such as vodka and gin held steady, but the underlying trend was toward lower-strength liqueurs. The resurgence in Japan of the traditional white spirit *shochu* continued to devastate whisky sales there. In 1986 *shochu* was being marketed in four different strengths, reflecting the increasing demand for lower-alcohol drinks. Similarly, in the U.K. Greenall Whitley decided to test-launch a low-strength vodka.

Major takeovers in 1986 included Allied-Lyons's $1,860,000,000 purchase of the wine and spirit assets of Hiram Walker Resources (Canada); the long-running Guinness and Argyll Group battle for Distillers, which was finally won by Guinness; and the successful Elders-IXL bid for the Courage beer, wine, and spirits empire.

(ANTONY C. WARNER)

Wine. Wine consumption was declining in the major producing countries in 1986, whereas in other countries it was rising as consumers developed a taste for new products. Nevertheless, the imbalance between supply and demand was growing, and wine surpluses were causing problems. Despite a fall in acreage devoted to wine production, output continued to rise, reflecting better yields, from an average 326,646,000 hl in 1976–80 to 330,816,600 in 1981–85.

In the industrialized countries it was the high-quality wines that generated profits. Meanwhile, in the newly emerging consumer countries, wines were being made not from grapes but from other ingredients such as rice. Modern technologies were being used to produce new types of wine-based drink to suit the demands of the young and fashion conscious, including cocktails, semisparkling light wines, and "coolers." Producers of such drinks took advantage of the latest production methods

Table VI. Estimated Consumption of Beer in Selected Countries

In litres[1] per capita

Country	1983	1984	1985
West Germany	148.7	144.4	145.5
East Germany	146.7	. . .	141.6
Czechoslovakia	147.8	140.1	130.8
Denmark	133.97	129.74	121.26
Belgium	128.0	126.3	121.0
Luxembourg	121.8	120.6	120.0
Australia[2]	117.8	115.0	115.6
New Zealand	114.1	115.3	115.2
Austria	109.4	107.7	111.6
United Kingdom	110.5	110.1	108.9
Ireland	121.0	120.0	100.0
Hungary	88.8	87.0	92.4
United States	92.0	90.7	90.3
Netherlands, The	87.53	83.43	84.5
Canada[3]	83.5	83.1	. . .
Switzerland	70.3	68.6	69.2
Bulgaria	61.2	60.0	60.0
Venezuela	71.8	. . .	59.5
Finland	57.37	56.65	59.02
Colombia	45.0	45.0	55.2
Yugoslavia	50.0	. . .	50.0
Spain	58.4	59.0	48.0
Norway	45.32	46.82	47.52
Sweden	44.7	44.5	46.8
Romania	45.0	. . .	. . .

[1] One litre = 1.0567 U.S. quart = 0.8799 imperial quart.
[2] Years ending June 30.
[3] Years ending March 31.

Table VII. Estimated Consumption of Spirits in Selected Countries

In litres[1] per capita

Country	1983	1984	1985
Hungary	4.80	5.10	5.4
East Germany	4.8	. . .	4.8
Poland	4.1	4.2	4.6
Czechoslovakia	3.32	3.28	3.36
U.S.S.R.	3.3	3.3	3.1
Bulgaria	3,04	3.0	3.0
Spain	3.0	2.8	3.0
Canada[2]	3.06	2.79	. . .
Finland	2.83	2.87	2.76
United States	2.86	2.81	2.72
Luxembourg	8.0	6.75	2.5
Japan	2.16	2.1	2.4
West Germany	2.46	2.32	2.37
France[3]	2.38	2.22	2.3
Iceland	2.10	2.21	2.26
Netherlands, The	2.63	2.36	2.24
Switzerland	2.15	2.11	2.18
Belgium	2.17	1.91	2.12
Cyprus	2.3	2.3	2.1
Sweden	2.26	2.10	2.05
Yugoslavia	2.3	. . .	2.0
Romania	2.0	2.0	. . .
United Kingdom	1.63	1.61	1.72
New Zealand	1.69	1.72	1.71
Denmark	1.55	1.50	1.61

[1] One litre = 1.0567 U.S. quart = 0.8799 imperial quart.
[2] Years ending March 31.
[3] Including aperitifs.

Table VIII. Estimated Consumption of Wine in Selected Countries

In litres[1] per capita

Country	1983	1984	1985
Portugal	89.1	84.2	87.0
Italy	91.4	90.5	84.8
France	85.0	82.0	80.0
Argentina	71.1	66.3	60.1
Luxembourg	53.6	62.5	57.3
Switzerland	48.3	49.9	49.6
Spain	57.0	45.0	48.0
Greece	44.1	43.9	42.5
Chile	39.1	35	40.0
Austria[2]	37.4	36.4	34.3
Romania	29.0	. . .	. . .
Uruguay	30.0	. . .	28.0
Yugoslavia	30.0	. . .	26.5
West Germany	26.5	25.7	25.6
Hungary	29.6	30.7	24.8
Belgium	21.7	22.9	22.7
Bulgaria	22.6	22.5	22.5
Australia[2]	20.4	21.3	21.3
Denmark	18.86	18.86	20.71
Czechoslovakia	14.6	15.6	15.8
Netherlands, The	13.87	15.22	14.96
New Zealand	12.8	13.9	14.5
Cyprus	11.1	11.9	11.9
Sweden	10,80	11.61	11.7
U.S.S.R.	12.9	12.7	11.6

[1] One litre = 1.0567 U.S. quart = 0.8799 imperial quart.
[2] Years ending June 30.

Source: Produktschap voor Gedistilleerde Dranken, *Hoeveel alcoholhoudende dranken worden er in de wereld gedronken?*

and made maximum use of new marketing techniques. Spain, Italy, Australia, California, South Africa, and Argentina were all involved in the new viticulture.

In 1986 the provisional wine output of EC member countries was estimated at 200 million hl. For France, with 72.1 million hl, 1986 was the "vintage of the century." Italy reported 71 million hl, Spain 36.2 million hl, West Germany 10 million hl, and Portugal 9.5 million hl. Total European production was estimated at 260 million hl. Elsewhere, output was estimated at 80 million hl, 60 million hl of which was in the U.S. (with the Californian vintage being of very high quality), 14 million hl in Africa, 3 million hl in Asia, and 4 million hl in Oceania. This brought the world total to over 340 million hl.

World consumption had declined by 17 million hl since 1980. Contributory factors included taxation, antialcohol campaigns, the tarnished image of wine following cases of adulteration, and the increased popularity of other drinks. Portugal led in annual average consumption with 87 litres, followed by Italy (85 l) and France (80 l). Among the countries with low consumption, the U.S.S.R. average was only 12 l, but the authorities were trying to encourage wine consumption as an alternative to strong spirits. (MARIE-JOSE DESHAYES)

Soft Drinks. Greater than expected growth of the soft drink market, which some had called "stagnant" and "mature" at the outset of the decade, continued to surprise even soft drink executives and beverage industry analysts. For the fourth consecutive year soft drink sales grew at 5% or more. As in the previous year, much of the growth in 1986 came from new products and categories. Marketing again played an important role in stimulating sales.

Juice-added soft drinks, introduced by several companies in 1984, represented one of the fastest-growing beverage categories. Another category—vitamin-enriched soft drinks—was not new, but in the fitness-conscious climate of the 1980s it attracted a greater degree of consumer interest than before. Two soft drink companies were quick to offer versions of this revitalized category, adding such nutrients as calcium, vitamin C, and the B vitamins.

The size of the diet soft drink market continued its steady climb, approaching one-quarter of total soft drink sales in the U.S. Most packaged diet soft drinks were sweetened with 100% aspartame (NutraSweet), a sweetener approved for use in soft drinks by the U.S. Food and Drug Administration in 1983, while saccharin or aspartame-saccharin blends were used in fountain-dispensed beverages. The industry looked forward to several new alternative sweeteners still in the development stage.

Soft drink franchise companies were involved in a flurry of merger and acquisition activity. Several companies and divisions were bought by others in 1986. Two major franchise companies bought a number of large bottlers in moves that consolidated more than 30% of their production under franchise ownership. In one case the franchise company spun off most of its bottling operations to form a new publicly owned corporation. A major European concern became the third largest soft drink company in the world through its purchase of a multibrand U.S. soft drink operation.

(FREDERICK L. WEBBER)

BUILDING AND CONSTRUCTION

Dollar outlays for new construction put in place in the U.S. were at record or near-record levels during each month in the first three quarters of 1986. For the entire year it was estimated that building and construction outlays would exceed $375 billion. In 1986, as in prior years, a high proportion of construction in the U.S. was carried out in the private sector. Fifty-three percent of private construction was for residential buildings, 31% for nonresidential, and 15% for public utilities and farm buildings. Dollar outlays for public construction were also at record levels, and it was estimated that for the year they would be in excess of $72 billion, compared with $62,342,000,000 in 1985.

In July 1986 the Composite Construction Cost Index of the U.S. Department of Commerce reached 112.9 (1982 = 100); in 1985 the index had averaged 109.4. Producer price indexes of materials used in building construction remained stable during the year. Average interest rates on conventional mortgage loans had declined in 1985, and this trend continued in 1986. In 1982 the average effective interest rate had been 15.33%, in 1985 it was 11.71%, and by Novmber 1986 it was 9.3%. While interest rates were coming down, the median price of new homes sold in the U.S. continued to rise, reaching $95,500 in November 1986. However, the lower interest rates—and the resulting lower monthly mortgage payments—stimulated the purchase of both new and existing housing.

In Canada housing investment rose 13% and business investment 2.7% in the third quarter of 1985, but housing starts fell more than 30% in the first quarter of 1986. A rise in the value of building permits issued in the second quarter indicated that construction would recover later in the year.

In Great Britain the upswing in private fixed investment had lost its momentum. However, there had been a rise in real personal income in 1985 and 1986, and the expectation was for small increases in private industrial investment and residential construction. The forecast for private investment in housing in 1986, based on 1980 constant pounds, was £6,754 million, compared with £6,553 million in 1985. Public outlays were expected to be less than one-third that amount. In France gross domestic product (GDP) was expected to rise about 2% in 1986 after a disappointing first quarter in which there was essentially no increase in industrial production. However, there were indications that the depressed housing and construction industries would benefit from the lower rate of inflation and the more favourable outlook for consumer spending.

The upturn in economic activity and industrial growth in West Germany that began in 1983 continued into 1986. However, fixed capital investment had remained at about the same level in real terms, and private housing investment had declined. The outlook improved during 1986 as higher consumer expenditures were expected to stimulate the housing industry while government incentives, lower interest rates, and higher profit margins increased industrial investment. In Italy the rapid increase in production in 1986 was expected to stimulate investment in plant and equipment. Interest rates continued to fall, holding out hope for the severely depressed housing industry.

In 1986 Japan experienced its first quarterly fall in GDP in over a decade. Compared with an increase in GDP of 4.6% in 1985, the forecast for 1986 was 3.2%. A survey by the Economic Planning Agency revealed that capital spending intentions in 1986 were substantially below those in 1985. Some expansion in public works investment was forecast, and the growth in residential construction that had occurred in 1985 was expected to resume under the stimulus of stable prices for construction materials and lower mortgage rates.

(CARTER C. OSTERBIND)

CERAMICS

U.S. ceramic industry sales in 1985 were again influenced primarily by a strong U.S. dollar and worldwide competition for common consumer markets. At about $28 billion, they were close to the total for 1984. The overall breakdown by categories was also similar to that for 1984. Glass retained its dominant share with 64% of all ceramic sales, while advanced ceramics accounted for 14%, porcelain enamels followed at 13%, and whitewares trailed at 9%.

Within the U.S. glass industry a few applications accounted for the majority of all sales. Glass containers totaled 24% of sales, flat glass 23%, fibreglass 23%, and lighting glass 17%. The remainder consisted of consumer glassware at 6%, television and cathode-ray tube glass at 4%, and a variety of smaller categories at 3%.

Sanitary ware again represented 48% of all U.S. whiteware sales, but many U.S. producers discontinued production of vitreous china bathroom fixtures because of increasing competition from imports. U.S. producers still making such goods were expected to concentrate on the luxury segment of the market. Within the next largest category, floor and wall tile at 23% of whiteware sales, modernization of production facilities was an important factor in increased 1985 sales. Sales of dinnerware and fine china improved substantially, but sales of artware and products for institutional food service were down.

U.S. porcelain enamel sales declined 7.5% to about $3.8 billion. The vast majority of those sales, 92%, were in appliances, with intense competition among the major companies still in the field. Porcelain enamel sanitary ware, at 7% of enamel sales, made up most of the rest of that sector of the ceramic industry.

U.S. sales of advanced ceramics, at about $3.9 billion, increased only slightly from 1984. The electrical and electronic segment accounted for 53% of all advanced ceramic sales. Sales of capacitors and substrates were disappointing as a result of sluggishness throughout the electronics industry, particularly in the computer area, but sales of optical fibres continued their spectacular rise. Some U.S. suppliers doubled their optical fibre production over 1984 levels. Low-voltage electrical porcelain, primarily in the form of automotive spark plugs, accounted for 24% of all U.S.

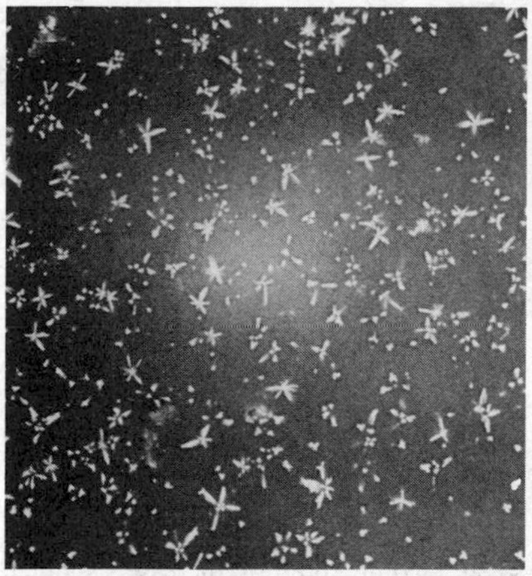

Zirconia crystals, on the surface of a glass-ceramic, and a single crystal are seen through a scanning electron microscope, greatly magnified for study. Scientists found that crystalline zirconia added to glass-ceramics increased their strength and toughness.
PHOTOGRAPHS, SANDIA NATIONAL LABORATORIES

advanced ceramic sales. The engineering ceramic sector of the advanced ceramics category, including ceramics for heat engines, cutting tools, wear applications, and bioceramics, accounted for only 18% of the total. Japanese sales of advanced ceramics were almost as large as U.S. sales, but European sales were much smaller.

A new development in optical fibres that promised to spur continued rapid growth in the area was the increasing likelihood that they would compete favourably for parts of the telecommunications market previously dominated by satellite links. This had already begun on high-capacity trunk routes between large population centres. By 1986 there was a possibility that recent progress in optical fibre hardware might make optical fibre circuits competitive with satellites as feeder links from local telephone switching stations to large office buildings and even to private homes. The substitution of light-emitting diodes for lasers as light sources into single-mode fibres was a key development in this regard. Major producers of fibres for telecommunications applications included AT&T Technologies, Corning Glass Works, and Spectran Corp. in the U.S. and Sumitomo in Japan.

Worldwide sales of high-performance structural ceramics increased but more slowly than many had expected. Nissan Motor Co. introduced ceramic turbocharger rotors into some of its Fairlady Z models for domestic Japanese sales; Mazda Motor Corp. edged closer to production of ceramic combustion chamber parts for some of its diesel engines and was looking at the extensive use of ceramics in prototype rotary engines; and a consortium of 30 engine and engine-component manufacturers was formed in the U.K. to explore opportunities for their entry into the market. However, there were also some serious expressions of caution and concern. Higher engine temperatures were found to have harmful as well as helpful effects on engine design; falling oil prices postponed some of the emphasis on fuel economy; and ceramic producers still faced the challenge of producing reliable and long-lived parts at a price acceptable to the automotive market.

Nevertheless, some studies were predicting increases in high-performance advanced ceramic sales on the order of 15% per year over at least the next few years. Growth was expected to occur primarily in gas and humidity sensors, structural ceramics other than those for engine applications, and cutting tools.

(NORMAN M. TALLAN)

CHEMICALS

The chemical industries of the major chemical-producing countries of the world experienced moderate growth in 1985, and managers in those industries were expecting similar progress in 1986. Chemical sales in the three major chemical-manufacturing areas, the U.S., Western Europe, and Japan, totaled an estimated $514 billion in 1984. Those sales rose by 2.7% to an estimated $528 billion in 1985.

In the U.S. the value of shipments of chemicals and allied products, as compiled by the Department of Commerce, rose by only 1.2%, from $211.8 billion in 1984 to $214.3 billion in 1985. Part of the reason for the modest increase in the dollar value of shipments was lower chemical prices, which, in turn, were at least a partial result of lower oil prices. Reduced costs of oil and other hydrocarbons meant that the petrochemical industry, an important sector of the chemical industry, was paying less for its feedstocks. It also meant that the entire chemical industry was paying less to satisfy its enormous appetite for energy.

One dark cloud for the U.S. chemical industry was the continued strength of the dollar relative to the currencies of the country's major trading partners, a strength that contributed to the shrinking of the favourable trade balance in chemicals. As recently as 1982, the U.S. trade surplus in chemicals had exceeded $10 billion. In 1984 the Commerce Department reported that the surplus had declined to $8.6 billion. In 1985 it fell to $7.2 billion as exports dropped by 2.6% to $21,760,000,000 and imports increased by 6.1% to $14,530,000,000.

Figures for the first months of 1986 indicated little change in the overall trends of the U.S. chemical industry. The Federal Reserve Board's index of chemical production in the first four months of 1986 averaged 131.1, an increase of 3.1% over the average for 1985. The U.S. Department of Labor's index of chemical prices declined steadily to 298.6 in May. Despite a fall in the value of the dollar, the chemical trade surplus in the first quarter of 1986 was $1.7 billion, equivalent to $6.8 billion on an annual basis.

In Japan chemical executives were concerned about the strength of the yen, which had appreciated 40% against the U.S. dollar between September 1985 and June 1986. Japan, despite its overall strength in trade, had experienced a trade deficit in chemicals through 1983. In 1984 chemical exports and imports were approximately in balance, and figures compiled by the Japan Chemical Exporters' Association and the Japan Chemical Importers' Association indicated that for the full year 1985 the country registered a chemical trade surplus of $2.6 billion. Early in 1986 the same two organizations estimated that for 1986 the surplus would drop to $2 billion on exports of $11.7 billion and imports of $9.7 billion.

In most respects the Japanese chemical industry was in good health. Sales rose by 4% in 1985, topping $100 billion for the first time. According to the country's Ministry of International Trade and Industry, the index of chemical production rose by 3.2% to 121.7 (1980 = 100). In the first quarter of 1986, however, the index declined by 3.9% to 117.

But the longer term worry for Japanese chemical makers was increased competition for some of their export markets. Producers of synthetic fibres reported that they were feeling the impact of low-cost apparel-grade fibres from such countries as Taiwan and South Korea and of cotton from China. Chemical producers in Japan were also concerned about the large-scale production of important chemicals in Saudi Arabia and other less developed countries having cheap hydrocarbon feedstocks. They believed that although European countries were the most logical immediate targets of such production, some material would eventually be shipped into Japan and into traditional Japanese export markets, including China and Southeast Asia.

The strong currencies that were hurting the chemical industries in the U.S. and in Japan were helping their counterparts in Western Europe. In its annual report for 1985, the European Council of Chemical Manufacturers' Federations (CEFIC) reported that sales of the chemical industries in Western Europe increased by 7.6% in 1985 from 246.8 billion European Currency Units (ECU) to ECU 265.4 billion. At the average exchange rates (ECU 1 = $0.7956 in 1985 and ECU 1 = $0.777 in 1984), that translated to 1984 sales of $516.1 billion, increasing by 2.4% to $528.3 billion in 1985. Nine members of the EC, West Germany, the United Kingdom, France, Italy, Belgium/Luxembourg, The Netherlands, Denmark, and Ireland, increased their sales by 5.1% ($8.2 billion) to $170 billion in 1985.

In the West German chemical industry, optimism was tempered with caution, mainly about the strengthening of the Deutsche Mark against the dollar. CEFIC's figures indicated 1985 chemical sales in the country at $51.9 billion, a 3.4% increase over 1984 sales. Exports accounted for nearly half of those sales, but in 1986 chemical makers were bracing for the impact of the declining dollar against the Deutsche Mark. In the spring of 1985 the U.S. dollar was worth DM 3.10; by early 1986 it was down to DM 2.50.

In recognition of the dangers of too heavy a reliance on exports, the West German chemical makers had been increasing their presence in other countries, particularly in the U.S. In 1986 they were facing some difficulties in their home markets—higher wages as well as environmental and political problems. Still, with a strong industry and a zero inflation rate at home, they were allocating $3 billion for investment, 7% more than they spent in 1985.

Unlike other large chemical-producing countries, the U.K. was not benefiting from the lower oil prices. The reason was that although the lower prices reduced the feedstock costs, the national economy was so closely tied to the production of North Sea oil that the lower oil price was exerting a downward pressure on economic growth and, therefore, on demand for chemicals.

CEFIC reported that U.K. chemical sales rose by 6.3% in 1985 to $27 billion, and the Chemical Industries Association (CIA) reported that exports climbed 7% in the same year. CIA early in 1986 was expecting a 1% increase in output for the year. Later it revised that to 3% because of the prospects of higher demand following the oil price decrease. But the demand did not materialize, and by the end of the second quarter, CIA had dropped its estimate back to 1%. (DONALD P. BURKE)

ELECTRICAL

Two problems preoccupied corporate policymakers in the world's major electrical companies in 1986: the high cost of research and development (R and D) needed to keep up with competition from other technologies, and the blow dealt to prospects of a new round of nuclear power station orders by the world's worst civil nuclear accident at the Chernobyl power station in the U.S.S.R. in April. (*See* ENERGY: *Sidebar*.)

All the major electrical equipment manufacturers in the industrialized countries suffered a continuing fall in orders and profits in traditional equipment markets. New and innovative products were needed, but development of high-technology systems required massive financial resources. Siemens AG of West Germany had increased R and D expenditure heavily in 1984–85 to DM 4,799,000 (a rise of 26% from 1983–84); over half went into the new technologies for factory automation, the electronic office, communications, and components. Corporate policy was to maintain this level of R and D to match market expansion, but in some areas costs were so high that cooperative ventures, or acquisitions, were necessary.

To stay ahead in the technology race, Siemens joined Philips of The Netherlands in bidding for the leading U.S. programmable controller manufacturer, Allen-Bradley Co., when it was put on the market in 1985; however, Allen-Bradley eventually was sold to Rockwell International Corp. for $1,650,000,000. When it was sold, Allen-Bradley had an annual turnover of $950 million and a 20% profitability. This meant that Rockwell paid 18 times earnings for the firm, justified on the assumption that the Allen-Bradley strategy to become a leading global automation supplier would work out.

Siemens, with total sales of DM 54,616,000,000 in the year to Sept. 30, 1985, up 19% from 1983–84, and net profits up 43% to DM 1,528,000,000, was in the same league as the U.S. firm General Electric Co. (GE). In the heavy power plant market, Siemens, through its Kraftwerk Union AG (KWU) subsidiary, saw little prospect of domestic nuclear power station orders, and export orders for all types of power plant were fiercely competitive. So KWU diversified into environmental technology, waste pyrolysis, and reactor life extension and decommissioning. Siemens confidently expected that this would help to support KWU's engineering skills so that it could meet any resurgence of nuclear orders.

Corporate policy at GE was similar. In the five-year period 1980–85, GE invested $7.8 billion in R and D plus $3.6 billion in plant and equipment for its advanced high-technology business. This compared with $2 billion invested in the firm's traditional core businesses, which included power generation, large domestic appliances, motors, transportation equipment, and construction equipment. In 1980 GE's earnings were derived equally from these core businesses and from services plus advanced technology (factory automation, medical electronics, aerospace, aircraft engines, and materials). By 1985 services plus advanced technology were responsible for 70% of earnings. In 1985 the high-technology factory automation business became profitable for the first time, but earnings from heavy electrical generating plant and nuclear plant fell again, in line with the long-term downward trend in the domestic market for such equipment.

GE's total earnings in 1985 were $2,336,000,000, an increase of 2% over 1984, on total sales of $28,285,000,000, 1% up from 1984. In 1985 R and D by GE was $1,065,000,000, compared with $1,038,000,000 in 1984, but capital expenditure on plant and equipment fell from the record $2.5 billion in 1984 to $2 billion in 1985. Like Siemens, GE was interested in acquisition, and its top priority was the acquisition, through merger, of RCA Corp. The agreement, which was approved by RCA shareholders in February 1986, cost GE $6.3 billion.

In December 1985 General Electric Co. (GEC) of the U.K. bid £1,180 million for Plessey, a high-technology electronics company. The bid was referred to the government's Monopolies and Mergers Commission, and the takeover was finally blocked in August 1986 because the combined group would have been the largest supplier to the U.K. Ministry of Defence. After that GEC looked overseas to acquire an electronics manufacturer. GEC's total sales in the year ended March 30, 1986, were £5,250 million, an increase of 0.5% over the previous year, but profits dropped 3.3% to £701 million. More impressive were the sales of $10,700,200,000 by Westinghouse Electric Corp. in 1985, a 4% rise from 1984, and an operating profit of $742.1 million, an increase of 22%. Company-sponsored R and D expenditure totaled $246 million, $176 million of which went to energy and advanced technology.

The Swedish electrical equipment manufacturer ASEA AB paid an undisclosed cash sum for its Finnish rival, Strömberg. A major reason for the purchase was to increase the Scandinavian market for ASEA. (T. C. J. COGLE)

FURNITURE

Retail household furniture sales in the U.S. climbed to a projected $24.8 billion in 1986, the highest in three years, according to the American Furniture Manufacturers Association. This was 8.2% above 1985 (5.8% adjusted for inflation) and represented a respectable but disappointing increase. Analysts attributed the rise to a surge in housing sales, stimulated by lower mortgage interest rates. However, it was less than projected because disposable personal income did not increase as much as had been forecast. Consumer finances were still tight, although this was expected to change early in 1987.

Manufacturers were particularly disappointed because domestic production of wood, upholstery, and metal furniture remained about the same as in 1985, totaling approximately $15 billion at wholesale. More important, furniture imports began leveling off as compared with the last few years, but they were still about 20% higher than in 1985, according to Communications/Today Inc., an industry source. At

MICHAEL ARNAUD/THE NEW YORK TIMES

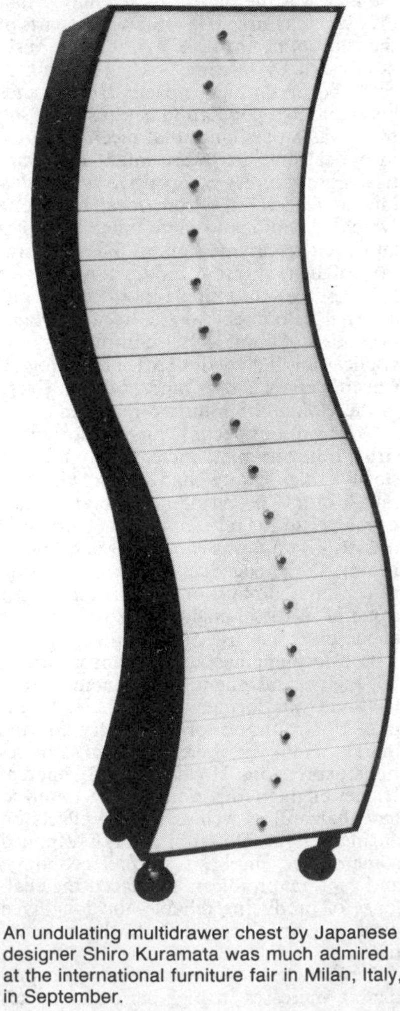

An undulating multidrawer chest by Japanese designer Shiro Kuramata was much admired at the international furniture fair in Milan, Italy, in September.

midyear this group projected year-end totals above $3 billion.

Prompted by unimpressive earnings and reacting to the threat of imports, the industry underwent some drastic and probably long overdue changes. Traditionally, the furniture industry had been a collection of small, fiercely independent, often family-owned companies. This changed dramatically in 1986 as closings, mergers, buyouts, and consolidations restructured both the manufacturing and retailing segments. By year's end more than two dozen major acquisitions, affecting about 50 of the largest manufacturing companies and more than 10% of the volume of shipments, had taken place, and more were expected in the battle for market share. At retail, along with some mergers, there were two notable changes. For the first time ever, the major retailers' organization, the National Home Furnishings Association, developed a national credit card for use by smaller stores. Also, the "gallery" concept—"stores within stores" featuring one manufacturer—was expanded as manufacturers and dealers solidified cooperative marketing.

One of the biggest trends of 1985, RTA, or ready to assemble, furniture, hit a rough spot with the failure of its trade association and difficulty in marketing the concept. Nevertheless, RTA continued to grow, and more sophisticated designs were being developed. In terms of style, what was old was new. After the previous year's love affair with name designers and trendy merchandise, 18th-century traditional reproductions and adaptations dominated the market. Second in popularity was the more informal Country style, which was exhibiting some Shaker and Amish influences.

In motion seating, recliners and incliners could now be operated electronically, at the push of a button—a real boon for the elderly. Another highly successful category turned out to be entertainment cabinetry. Optimists predicted that within five years 95% of all households would have furniture to house their electronic equipment. In large part, this expectation was prompted by the phenomenal popularity of videocassette recorders (VCRs). According to the Electronic Industries Association, sales of VCRs had almost doubled since 1984, with 13.8 million units sold in 1986.

In the long-term, ongoing battle to avoid government regulation, the industry won a major victory when the U.S. Consumer Product Safety Commission issued a release acknowledging the value of UFAC (Upholstered Furniture Action Council) upholstery. UFAC was a national, industry-supported, voluntary program developed to reduce fires in upholstery.

(ABBY CHAPPLE)

FURS

Sales of fur apparel continued to expand in 1986, with many retailers recording their best business ever. Although the U.S. reinforced its number one position with sales of close to $2 billion, the Japanese market grew some 25% to an estimated $1.5 billion. Fur garments were relatively new to Japan, having become popular as part of the post-World War II trend toward more westernized dressing. Sales of furs in West Germany revived in 1986 following five years of decline. The gain coincided with the strong turnaround of the Deutsch Mark, which advanced some 33% against the dollar compared with 1985. Because the dollar is the standard for most international trade in furs, this made the commodity much more accessible to the German market.

World production of ranched mink reached a new high of 34 million pelts in the 1986–87 crop year. However, this was less than the total supply of 37 million available in 1986; that figure reflected a carryover of 5 million, all of which was consumed. Scandinavia produced nearly 15 million pelts. The Soviet Union was thought to produce close to that amount, but it put only about 25% of its crop on the open market. U.S. mink production was steady at about 4.5 million. China, a new producer, had already passed the 3 million mark.

Pelt prices, which had dropped sharply in 1985, rebounded strongly as demand picked up. Although the largest price gains were in mink, almost all furs scored major gains. Sable prices advanced as much as 50% from an already high level. This fur was produced only in the Soviet Union, which maintained rigid control and had limited production to 150,000 pelts annually—enough for about 3,000 coats and jackets for the entire world.

Fur apparel manufacturing continued to shift to third world countries because of the availability of good labour at lower rates. Principal gainers were Hong Kong, South Korea, Taiwan, the Dominican Republic, and some Eastern European countries. The U.S. was still the largest producer, but manufacturing there had been declining, mainly because of natural attrition. Imports accounted for about 50% of total U.S. retail sales in 1985 but leveled off in 1986 as the dollar weakened.

Activity by antifur groups continued in 1986, mostly in northern Europe. Vandalism and violence by some groups in England created a backlash that worked against the antifur forces there. The U.S. industry established a "Fur Is for Life" public relations and advertising campaign to combat antifur appeals.

(SANDY PARKER)

GAMES AND TOYS

In 1986 there was a proliferation of talking toys on world markets. This followed in the wake of basic toys, particularly dolls and plush items such as Tonka's Pound Puppies, which had returned to favour in 1985. The U.S. company Worlds of Wonder Inc. claimed the distinction of introducing animation and speech to the traditional favourite, the teddy bear. Its product, given the name of Teddy Ruxpin and distributed by Mattel Inc., achieved sales amounting to more than $68 million in the U.S. in its first nine months. The manufacturers claimed that this exceeded the achievement of the highly successful Cabbage Patch dolls in 1983. Variations on the same theme were quick to follow from rival U.S. and Far East manufacturers.

The talking toys were comparatively highly priced, and some leading toymakers did not produce them, foreseeing rapid obsolescence as competing refinements were added. Teddy Ruxpin was operated by a cassette player that enabled the toy's nose, eyes, and mouth to move in synchronization with the sound track. This original concept was quickly followed by the development of noncassette talkers that used microchip circuitry to facilitate response to nearby voices. Lewis Galoob Toys, Inc., introduced this method in a soft toy, Smarty Bear, and a doll, Baby Talk.

Action figures remained popular, especially Thundercats by L.J.N. Toys Ltd., Rambo by Coleco Industries, Inc., and Hasbro Bradley's long-lasting G.I. Joe. The major development of the year in regard to games was their adaptation to videocassette recorders. Such favourites as Clue, Candyland, and Chutes and Ladders were taped to be played on VCRs.

Erno Rubik's new brainteaser, Rubik's Magic, was launched at the 1986 Budapest Trade Fair. Like Rubik's Cube, more than 150 million of which were sold, the challenge of Magic was to manipulate shapes from chaos into a pattern. Eight flat plastic plates decorated with brightly coloured arcs were joined by movable hinges that created 45 angles. The objective was to

The Heart Family New Arrival set by Mattel features a father and pregnant mother and includes a newborn baby (not shown).

AP/WIDE WORLD

form an interlocking pattern of rings by moving the hinged plates through a seemingly infinite combination.

European toy markets, particularly those in the U.K., West Germany, and France, continued to be penetrated by imported products. The biggest penetration in 1985 was experienced by West Germany, which yielded 64.5% of its market to imports. For France the figure was 62% and for the U.K., 60%. West Germany, however, remained the dominant toy-exporting country in Europe with 62% of its output in 1985 going to foreign markets. The U.K. achieved 38.8% and France, 24.2%.

U.S.-owned multinational companies continued to make inroads into Europe. Hasbro Bradley Inc. and Mattel were successful in the U.K. and France, the former company achieving 12% of the U.K. market and 7% of the French market in 1984. Because the population of Europe was 50% larger than that of the U.S., a good European network was a strong attraction to multinationals.

In September 1986 Hasbro Bradley acquired Sindy, the fashion doll, from the British company Pedigree Dolls & Toys. The doll and its accessories had been successful in the U.K. and some other European countries for many years and provided strong competition to Mattel's well-known Barbie doll.

In the toy retailing sector, the U.S. company Toys "Я" Us estimated that its market share in the U.S. had risen to 15.5%. The company opened 40 new stores in the U.S. in 1985, and 10 internationally. Three new stores were opened in the U.K. in 1986. The company's move into the West German market was not as rapid as expected, and it was committed to only one store there in 1987.

The 12th annual meeting of the International Committee of Toy Industries (ICTI), held in Scottsdale, Ariz., in May 1986, was attended by 25 delegates representing 12 countries. Almost without exception delegates expressed concern about the continued practice of counterfeiting. Some progress in curtailing this was reported by Far East producers as a result of the committee's lengthy debate on counterfeiting at the 1985 meeting. The Hong Kong trademarks law was being amended to enable owners to take civil action and the government to proceed under criminal law. The Taiwan delegate reported his trade association's efforts to combat the problem and the setting up of an Intellectual Property Association that was proving to be effective. Product safety, including developments on a worldwide basis, was a major focus of the meeting. ICTI's toy safety standard was being reviewed, and final revisions were expected to be approved in 1987. (THEODORE V. THOMAS)

GEMSTONES

The gemstone market was uneventful in 1986 until October, when a sale of diamond jewelry by Sotheby's of London realized the highest prices in six years—a diamond sautoir that had been expected to fetch £25,000 to £30,000 was sold for £94,600. Art Deco jewelry continued to be popular, and there was a strong demand for aquamarines, tourmalines, and garnets, which were used to make imitations.

Emeralds were abundant on the European market. Rubies appeared on the London market periodically, but probably with colour enhanced. A fine Burmese-ruby and diamond ring was sold for £110,000, more than double the amount expected, at Sotheby's. The weight of the stone was 5.94 carats, thus proving that a fine ruby will fetch more than an outstanding diamond, weight for weight.

There were no major developments in the diamond market in 1986. Political difficulties in South Africa did not affect the diamond mines, and the West continued to import diamonds from that country. On the other hand, the increased movement of diamonds via the De Beers sights (viewings by prospective buyers) in 1986 presumably reduced the stockpile.

Donations to gemstone collections in major U.S. museums fell sharply, presumably because inflated values had been attached to some of them for tax purposes, and as a result they were being subjected to increased scrutiny by the tax authorities. There were fears that collections could be adversely affected by the clampdown. Exhibitions of work by young jewelers remained a prominent feature of the London scene, and in this respect London continued to dominate the world.

Although government-sponsored gem-mining enterprises continued to exist in Pakistan, Burma, and Sri Lanka, among other countries, the lack of buoyancy in the world economy had reduced the level of prospecting, particularly in the less accessible sites. Political troubles hindered development of the Sri Lanka gem industry, though the established sites were not affected. Indications that there was more activity in Burma were not borne out by evidence at the annual gem auction, but much of the trade in gems continued to be unofficial, and smuggling was an enormous problem. In general, market conditions in 1986 were more stable than in the earlier years when there had been overproduction and heavy advertising.

(MICHAEL O'DONOGHUE)

GLASS

In 1986 there were definite signs of a worldwide recovery in the profitability of glass manufacture. At the same time, there was growing confidence in the industry's future potential, which was reflected in continuing investment in long-term research and modern production facilities. The U.S. glass industry, the world leader in size, reported improved sales volumes and profit margins in all sectors except household products, and the benefits of the streamlining measures taken in recent years began to show. The major growth areas were in telecommunications (optical fibres), fibreglass for the construction industry, flat glass for the housing and automobile markets, and reinforcement fibres for motor bodies and combustion. The poor performance of the domestic glassware sector reflected the lack of competitiveness of the industry compared with that of countries with lower production costs.

A significant development in 1986 was the strong interest shown by China in making contracts with other nations to enable it to modernize its glass production methods and expand its industry. PPG Industries and Corning Glass Works of the U.S., Coutinho Glass Engineering from West Germany, and King Taudevin and Gregson of the U.K. all concluded agreements in 1986 to supply technology, production equipment, and expertise to China.

New technical developments in 1986 showed that glass had many surprising new applications that could be adopted by innovative sectors of industry. A new dental technique used glass inserts in composite fillings to improve durability and reduce shrinkage of fillings during the hardening process. It was believed that this technique would facilitate production of a low-cost, mass-produced filling material for many dental applications where appearance was important. In the U.K. Pilkington Space Technology (of the Pilkington Group) received a Queen's Award for Technological Achievement for a special glass to protect solar cells on satellites. This glass—CMX—could be as fine as a human hair and offered substantial payload savings in space flight. In the U.S., Dlubak Studios developed Decoglass. This was a lamination of fabric between two layers of glass that could be cut by a water jet—itself another development in glass-cutting techniques—and was suitable for many decorative uses where durability and control of light and sounds were required.

In the wake of the 1985 International Partners in Glass Research project, which aimed to develop a container glass ten times stronger and half the weight of that currently used, eight U.S. glassware manufacturers in the flat glass, fibreglass containers, pharmaceuticals, scientific glassware, and tableware sectors pledged nearly $1 million to support an Industry-University Centre for Glass Research at the New York State College of Ceramics at Alfred (N.Y.) University. In a project that was to last at least three years, AFG Industries, Corning Glass Works, Ford Motor Co., Manville Building Materials Corp., Owens-Corning Fiberglas, Owens-Illinois, PPG Industries, and Speciality Products Co. aimed to develop glass science and engineering as subjects for university study, to provide graduates in those subjects, and to increase fundamental knowledge for the benefit of the glass industry in the 21st century.

(ALLEN F. BROBYN)

INSURANCE

Private insurance sales in 1986 showed strong global growth, with sharp premium increases in liability, aviation, and some other types of coverage. New markets appeared in several countries as governments reduced their involvement in providing and regulating insurance protection. France announced its intention to "privatize" state-owned insurers, which accounted for one-third of the premium income there. South Korea opened its doors to foreign companies writing fire and automobile insurance, and Taiwan discussed a similar relaxation of restrictions. In China the government insurer, the People's Insurance Company, forged links with overseas insurers in order to meet rapidly expanding insurance needs.

The destruction of the U.S. space shuttle *Challenger* intensified insurance problems for future launchings. Rates rose by 25% or more, and some insurers discontinued this coverage.

British insurance companies, with worldwide premiums exceeding £15,000 million in general insurance and £17,000 million in long-term (principally life) insurance, scrambled to reduce heavy underwriting losses in automobile and liability lines by raising rates. Lloyd's of London imposed expulsions, suspensions, and fines—including one for £1 million—in response to misappropriations of funds by several members. To increase its financial strength, Lloyd's recruited almost 3,100 new underwriting members, bringing total membership to 28,600, and 9,000 existing members increased their underwriting capacity by 25%. On Lloyd's three-year accounting system, the 1983 account was closed with underwriting profits on all classes of business except general liability, which lost £285 million. Total profit was £36 million on £2,600 million of premiums.

For the U.K. market as a whole, liability insurance was the most stricken area. As some important reinsurers withdrew from the professional liability market, insurance for high limits was difficult to obtain in many professions. Seven large international accountants set up a captive insurer, and a quasi-insurance scheme increased charges to medical practitioners by 70%. In life insurance, some indexed social security pensions were restricted, and individuals would have to set up personal pension funds with insurers, banks, or building societies.

In the U.S. new life insurance premium volume topped $10 billion, although the 10% annual growth rate was less than in recent years. Replacements decreased slightly from 45 to 40%, with more than half the new premiums purchasing the increasingly popular universal, current assumption, and variable life contracts. Most observers predicted that the Tax Reform Act of 1986 would benefit future sales of cash value life insurance and single-premium annuities because tax-favoured treatment of policyholders was retained. Insurers, however, faced higher taxes under the new law. New restrictions were placed on pension and retirement plans, including lower maximum benefits for early retirement, increased withdrawal penalties, and limits on 401(k) payroll deduction savings plans and individual retirement accounts. Many large financial institutions continued to position themselves to provide comprehensive financial services. The Travelers insurance company's purchase of a major investment banking firm, Dillon Read & Co., was an example.

Health insurance was one of the most competitive U.S. markets in 1986. In most urban areas, traditional health insurers experienced sharp competition from new health maintenance organizations (HMOs) and preferred provider organizations (PPOs), which offered comprehensive benefits including preventive medical care. A federal law effective July 1, 1986, mandated continued group health insurance coverage for up to three years for many terminated employees and their dependents. Health care cost containment measures helped slow some insurance increases. Property-liability insurance results during the first half of 1986 showed significant improvement. By midyear written premiums were up 25% to $85 billion, and net income soared to nearly $6 billion, two-thirds of which was accounted for by realized capital gains on investments. Underwriting losses fell to $8 billion.

Insurers and risk managers struggled with the introduction of new "claims-made" forms for commercial general liability contracts. With high rates and a much smaller London market, many new insurers and self-insurance pools appeared, particularly for excess liability insurance and hard-to-place liability lines. The Risk Retention Amendments of 1986 permitted more pooling by purchasing groups for some insurance buyers. Tort and civil justice reform laws aimed at reducing liability claims costs were passed in approximately 30 states, but the changes varied greatly. (*See* Special Report.) Other insurance reforms accompanied many of the laws, including requirements for more detailed statistical reporting by insurers and tighter regulation of loss reserves.

(DAVID L. BICKELHAUPT)

IRON AND STEEL

In 1985 the recovery in steel production that had characterized the previous two years slowed down. The 717 million metric tons of crude steel produced throughout the world was only 1% higher than in 1984 and still some 4% below the record annual level achieved in 1979. Within this total picture the situation in different countries varied. Japan and the European Coal and Steel Community (ECSC) maintained much the same levels of production in 1985 as in 1984, whereas in the U.S. there was a decline of 6%, equivalent to a reduction of some five million metric tons of crude steel. Some other countries, however, achieved large increases, often associated with a larger share of foreign trade in steel. Brazil, with an increase of two million metric tons, was the most notable example.

Table IX. World Production of Crude Steel

In 000 metric tons

Country	1981	1982	1983	1984	1985	1986 Year to date	1986 No. of months	1986 Percent change 1986/85
World	707,660	644,870	663,200	710,320	717,410			
U.S.S.R.	148,520	147,150	152,510	154,200	154,500	38,300*	3	+3.0
U.S.	109,590	67,640	76,760	84,500	79.240	51,560	8	−4.1
Japan	101,680	99,550	97,170	105,580	105,280	66,020	8	−7.0
West Germany	41,610	35,880	35,730	39,390	40,500	25,510	8	−6.3
China	35,600	37,120	40,020	43,360	46,700	†		
Italy	24,780	24,010	21,810	24,060	23,870	15,270	8	−3.4
France	21,260	18,400	17,580	19,000	18,820	11,800	8	−6.4
Poland	15,720	14,790	16,240	16,530	15,800	4,320	3	+19.2
U.K.	15,570	13,700	14,990	15,120	15,722	9,300	8	−12.0
Czechoslovakia	15,270	14,990	15,020	14,830	14,960	3,883	3	+1.5
Canada	14,810	11,870	12,830	14,700	14,650	9,580	8	−0.5
Brazil	13,230	13,000	14,670	18,390	20,450	13,760	8	+3.8
Romania	13,030	13,060	12,590	14,440	13,760	†		
Spain	12,900	13,180	13,010	13,500	14,230	8,200	8	−9.9
Belgium	12,380	9,990	10,150	11,300	10,680	6,550	8	−7.9
India	10,780	11,000	10,240	10,550	11,140	7,740	8	+4.3
South Korea	10,750	11,760	11,920	13,030	13,540	9,610	8	+8.1
South Africa	9,010	8,280	7,180	7,730	8,510	5,920	8	+7.2
Mexico	7,660	7,060	6,920	7,480	7,260	5,020	8	+7.3
Australia	7,640	6,370	5,680	6,300	6,410	4,270	8	+3.1
East Germany	7,470	7,170	7,220	7,573	7,840	1,999	3	+2.8
North Korea	5,500	5,800	6,100	6,500	8,400*	†		
Netherlands, The	5,470	4,350	4,480	5,740	5,520	3,550	8	−4.3
Austria	4,660	4,260	4,410	4,870	4,660	2,960	8	−4.7
Yugoslavia	3,980	3,840	4,130	4,290	4,470	3,470	8	+16.2
Luxembourg	3,790	3,510	3,290	3,990	3,945	2,480	8	−5.5
Sweden	3,770	3,900	4,210	4,705	4,810	2,980	8	−3.1
Hungary	3,650	3,700	3,620	3,750	3,620	938	3	+6.7
Taiwan	3,160	4,150	5,030	5,010	5,090	3,490	8	+4.0
Argentina	2,530	2,910	2,940	2,650	2,940	2,031	8	+12.5
Bulgaria	2,480	2,590	2,830	2,870	2,880	721	3	+12.0
Turkey	2,430	3,180	3,830	4,330	4,950	3,976	8	+29.2
Finland	2,430	2,410	2,420	2,640	2,520	1,683	8	+2.7
Venezuela	2,030	2,278	2,320	2,770	3,055	2,143	8	+3.2
Iran	1,200*	1,200*	1,200*	1,200*	1,200*	†		
Switzerland	930	840	840	980	990	†		
Greece	910	930	870	900	990	638	7	+14.3
Norway	850	780	900	920	940	528	8	−12.7

*Estimated. †1986 figures not yet available.
Sources: International Iron and Steel Institute; United Nations.

Table X. World Production of Pig Iron

In 000 metric tons

Country	1981	1982	1983	1984	1985
World	497,290	452,350	457,830	489,740	493,060
U.S.S.R.	107,770	106,720	110,450	110,800	111,000*
Japan	80,050	77,660	72,940	80,400	80,570
U.S.	66,740	39,281	44,210	47,090	45,280
China	34,170	35,510	37,380	40,000	41,000
West Germany	31,880	27,620	26,600	30,200	31,530
France	16,960	14,720	13,500	14,710	15,070
Italy	12,260	11,540	10,310	11,630	11,660
Brazil	10,790	10,830	12,950	17,220	15,130
Czechoslovakia	9,900	9,530	9,470	9,560	9,600
Belgium	9,810	7,830	8,070	9,010	8,750
Canada	9,740	8,000	8,570	9,640	9,640*
India	9,470	9,640	9,160	9,460	9,840
U.K.	9,470	8,330	9,480	9,490	10,380
Poland	8,870	8,110	9,470	9,540	9,250*
Romania	8,860	8,640	8,180	9,560	9,500*
South Korea	7,930	8,440	8,020	8,760	8,830
South Africa	7,370	6,760	5,220	5,530	5,010*
Australia	6,740	5,950	5,060	5,330	5,610
Spain	6,260	6,000	5,420	5,340	5,480
North Korea	5,000	5,250	5,500	5,750	7,750*
Netherlands, The	4,600	3,620	3,750	4,930	4,820
Mexico	3,770	3,600	3,540	3,870	3,530
Austria	3,480	3,120	3,320	3,745	3,700
Luxembourg	2,890	2,590	2,320	2,770	2,750
Yugoslavia	2,820	2,700	2,840	2,850	3,110
East Germany	2,430	2,150	2,210	2,360	2,500*
Hungary	2,210	2,200	2,060	2,100	2,000
Turkey	2,050	2,170	2,720	2,900	3,190
Finland	1,970	1,940	1,900	2,030	1,900
Sweden	1,770	1,780	2,010	2,210	2,420
Taiwan	1,610	2,700	3,420	3,290	3,430
Bulgaria	1,520	1,560	1,630	1,580	1,600*
Argentina	920	1,020	910	920	1,310
Egypt	920	1,070	990	940	950*
Algeria	900	1,100	1,100	1,100	1,100*
Zimbabwe	640	480	580	400	800*
Chile	590	450	540	590	580
Norway	570	480	600	550	610
Venezuela	420	200	170	330	440

*Estimated.
Source: International Iron and Steel Institute.

At the beginning of 1986 the reduction in oil prices and the weakening of the U.S. dollar against other major currencies began to make a major impact on the world's steel industries. The low oil prices did not immediately produce increased activity in steel-using sectors, as had been hoped, but there was an immediate reduction in demand from the oil exploration and recovery industry. This adversely affected those steel producers that were involved in the manufacture of oil-well pipes and pipelines. In addition, traditional importers of steel in countries that depended heavily on oil and gas exports for their foreign exchange considerably reduced their purchases. Total steel production levels in 1986, however, were sustained to some extent by continuing strong demand for consumer goods in many industrialized countries, which kept demand for sheet steel products at a relatively high level.

The realignment of exchange rates increasingly affected patterns of world steel trade as 1986 progressed. The strong yen hindered Japanese exports in its important Far East markets but gave a boost to other producers, including South Korea and Brazil, where currencies had not appreciated to the same extent against the U.S. dollar. The ECSC was also affected by an increase in imports as stronger currencies caused prices on their markets to become more attractive to exporters. There was an even greater impact on exports from ECSC countries. During the first six months of 1986 these declined 25% from the previous year.

In the U.S. a reduction of 15% in imported quantities of steel reflected the effect of the voluntary export restraint agreements that had been negotiated with 27 exporting countries during 1984 and 1985 as much as it did the depreciation of the dollar. At the end of 1986 the U.S. was still trying to extend its negotiated import restrictions to Sweden and Taiwan, and steel imports from Canada were being strongly criticized by U.S. producers for being exempted from any formal restraint agreement. But during 1986 the dispute with the ECSC over trade in semifinished steel was resolved when the ECSC agreed to limit exports to the U.S.; as a result, the U.S. lifted its unilaterally imposed restrictions, and the ECSC in turn removed its retaliatory import controls on a number of nonsteel products.

The major restructuring of the steel industries in industrial countries continued through 1986, and this factor, as well as market conditions, was reflected in financial results. Within the ECSC large steel producers in West Germany, Luxembourg, and the U.K. made profits in 1985 following several years of losses. Large losses persisted in some French and Italian companies, but significant improvements were forecast for the following year or two as modernization measures took effect.

In Japan the steel industry suffered from the realignment of currencies. Fears that imports would take a significant share of the Japanese market were realized, and exports suffered in terms of price and quantity. Japan's exports of manufactured goods made of steel were also adversely affected. Some major Japanese steel producers, as a result, suffered financial losses.

In the U.S. restructuring and modernization continued to gather pace. Steel consumption remained at a low level, blamed largely on an increasing adverse balance of trade in steel-using goods, and most producers registered heavy financial losses in 1986. Two of the major producers sought legal protection from their creditors under Chapter 11 of U.S. bankruptcy legislation while they undertook financial and physical restructuring. A number of other producers negotiated contracts with the unions in such a way as to reduce labour costs and thus help to improve their competitiveness. In the case of the steel division of USX (formerly U.S. Steel Corp.), the largest U.S. steel producer, this led to a long strike that began in early August. After three months, however, other U.S. producers had maintained adequate supplies to the home market, and the U.S. government had not found it necessary to relax negotiated import restrictions.

In a number of newly industrialized countries such as Brazil, South Korea, Taiwan, China, and Turkey, internal demand increased. This encouraged those nations to use their recently acquired steelmaking skills to supply most of their own requirements. (IAN D. MATTHEWS)

MACHINERY AND MACHINE TOOLS

Worldwide production of machine tools, those power-driven machines not portable by hand that are used to shape or form metal by cutting, impact, pressure, electrical techniques, or a combination of those processes, totaled $21.8 billion in 1985, the latest year for which figures were available. This included metal-cutting machine tools valued at $16.9 billion and metal-forming machines worth $4.9 billion. The major producers included Japan, with total production worth $5.3 billion; West Germany, $3.2 billion; the Soviet Union, $3 billion; and the U.S., $2.7 billion. Based on data from the first six months of 1986, it appeared that machine tool production in the U.S. in all of 1986 would increase about 5% compared with 1985.

The leading machine tool consuming nations (those installing newly produced machines having the greatest total value) were the Soviet Union, which reportedly installed machines worth $4.1 billion; the U.S., $3.9 billion; Japan, $3.4 billion; and West Germany, $1.8 billion. Data from the first six months of 1986 indicated that total consumption of machine tools in the U.S. for all of 1986 would rise about 11% from the 1985 level.

Since 1978 the U.S. had been a net importer of machine tools. In 1985 imports were valued at $1.7 billion and exports at $450 million. Those countries that were major exporters of machine tools to the U.S. included Japan, with shipments to the U.S. valued at $850 million; West Germany, $250 million; and Taiwan, $130 million. Based on data for the first six months of 1986, machine tool imports to the U.S. were expected to rise in 1986 to $2.1 billion, and Italy would displace Taiwan as the third most significant exporter.

Machine tools built in the U.S. were exported primarily to Canada; shipments to that country in 1985 were valued at $82 million; Mexico, $64 million; Japan, $36 million; United Kingdom, $31 million; China, $27 million; Brazil, $25 million; and West Germany, $23 million. Total exports of machine tools from the U.S. were expected to rise 12% in 1986 from 1985 levels and reach $500 million.

The most current available data indicated that the U.S. had more than 2.2 million machine tools installed in various plants and factories; West Germany had more than 1.3 million, and Japan more than 1 million. Approximately one-third of the machine tools installed worldwide were under 10 years old; one-third were 10 to 20 years old; and one-third were over 20 years old. These statistics pointed out that many manufacturers had not yet taken full advantage of the improved flexibility and productivity of most of the newer machines. (JOHN B. DEAM)

MICROELECTRONICS

In economic terms 1986 opened with considerable promise for the microelectronics industry; growth was projected to be 14%. But by the year's end it was apparent that the promise would go unfulfilled. Instead, the growth rate reached only 7%. In dollars, industry sales totaled $26.5 billion. In technological terms, however, the year was a ringing success, with significant gains being made in the areas of logic and memory.

One of the most important factors in preventing the market from performing as expected was the continued slump in the computer industry. Indeed, the computer industry consumed 41% of the world's semiconductor production.

Another important factor was the severe price erosion for electronic parts, memories in particular. Many parts—such as 64-kilobit dynamic random-access memories (DRAMs)—were bought on the basis of price alone. The prices of Japanese memories fell so low that three major U.S. semiconductor makers filed charges against the Japanese companies, alleging that they were dumping. Dumping, an illegal practice in the U.S., is the selling of products below the cost of making them.

Before the suit was finally settled, an agreement with the U.S. Department of Commerce was reached in which a complex formula called the "foreign market value" was put into effect. The result was a significant increase in prices. This further reduced consumption as computer companies and other semiconductor consumers sought out new lines of supply.

A third reason for the slow growth rate was new inventory-management techniques, such as just-in-time delivery. Semiconductor users were reducing their inventories of chips from a 1984 high of about 12 weeks to as few as 4 and in some cases none. In spite of these factors, however, semiconductor analysts were predicting a 20% rise in sales for 1987.

In 1986 three U.S. chip makers started selling microprocessors whose raw processing power of five million instructions per second matched that of low-end mainframe computers. But the year belonged to the special-purpose signal processor. Exceedingly fast digital signal processors were introduced by all of the major companies competing in that arena, both U.S. and Japanese. Digital signal processors perform the multiplication and accumulation required in such applications as speech synthesis and computer imaging.

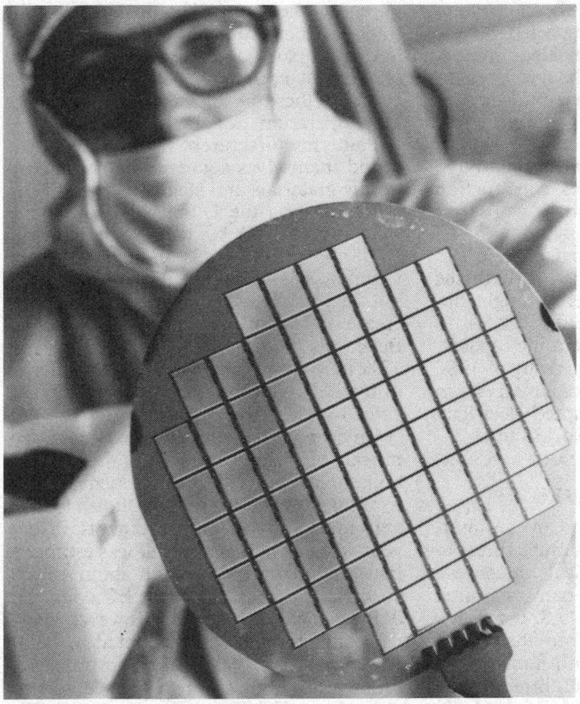

New solid-state sensors by Eastman Kodak, held on a wafer, boost information-gathering capabilities sixfold compared with other advanced sensors in use.

AP/WIDE WORLD

A new type of signal processor called a vector signal processor emerged. Vector processors operate on blocks of data, called vectors, instead of on one data input at a time, as do scalar processors.

A number of semiconductor companies brought out processor chips that specialize in graphics and text handling. These chips would greatly reduce the number of components needed by computer makers building graphics systems.

On the memory side, one-megabit DRAMs—chips that can store one million bits of information—were being sold, though in limited quantities. Designers began working on four-megabit DRAMs.

Static RAMs (SRAMs) with 256-kilobit densities became available in limited quantities. They were expected to be in great demand in the years to come because of their advantages over DRAMs. SRAMs are typically faster and are easier to design into a system because they do not need to be constantly refreshed by the microprocessor.

Work in the research laboratories continued, with several firms developing new circuit-design techniques. One company applied complementary metal-oxide semiconductor (CMOS) cell characteristics to bipolar chips to reduce power consumption and chip size without giving up the bipolar chip's inherent speed advantage.

(STEPHEN M. ZOLLO)

NUCLEAR INDUSTRY

The world's worst nuclear power disaster, at Chernobyl in the Soviet Union on April 26, was expected to have little effect on the future design of nuclear power stations outside the Soviet Union. By contrast, the Three Mile Island Unit 2 (TMI 2) accident in the United States in March 1979, which was safely contained and had no measurable radiological consequences, resulted in extensive reappraisal of basic designs, control room layout, operator training, regulatory procedures, and many other aspects of the industry's activities on a worldwide basis.

The accident in the Ukraine was not confined by an engineered containment, and radioactive releases continued during an extended period with serious potential consequences for human health and safety. In the surrounding population of about 140,000, a total of 2,000 excess fatal cancers may have been caused (about 30,000 cancer deaths would normally be expected in a population sample of this size).

Soviet engineers gave a full and frank account of the accident and its aftermath to industry representatives from all over the world at a special International Atomic Energy Agency (IAEA) meeting in August. Fundamental changes would be made to the water-cooled graphite-moderated (RBMK) series of reactors to ensure inherent stability of the nuclear chain reaction as required in Western designs. This requires permanent neutron absorbers in the reactor core and increased fuel enrichment, which raises operating costs. (*See* ENERGY: *Sidebar*.)

Recovery in the Soviet Union was rapid; at the end of September the first of the three undamaged Chernobyl reactors was restarted, almost five months to the day after the accident. (Compare this with six and a half years before Three Mile Island Unit 1 was restarted after the TMI 2 accident.) The urgency to bring the Soviet plant back on line was due to the early arrival of winter weather following a dry season that reduced normal hydroelectric capacity. There were nine power stations in the Soviet Union operating RBMK-type reactors (28 units) with 7 units under construction and 8 more planned.

A number of proposals were advanced by another Soviet delegation to the IAEA later in the year, most of which were concerned with international communication, mutual assistance, and third-party liability measures. It was also proposed that the IAEA should set and enforce world standards on siting, design and construction, operation and decommissioning, and radioactive waste treatment, to be adopted by all nations using nuclear power.

Immediately after the Soviet accident, Pres. Corazon Aquino of the Philippines announced the cancellation of a nuclear power project started under the previous regime, stating concern over safety as the reason. However, in the Philippines, as in such countries as Taiwan, Egypt, and Brazil, national economic difficulties were the dominant reasons for delays in new or existing nuclear power programs.

A local magistrate blocked the restart of Angra 1 in Brazil when it suffered a minor leak in a valve. Angra had been shut down for repairs early in the year. Because of Chernobyl it was claimed that insufficient attention had been given to emergency evacuation plans. This provoked renewed calls from antinuclear politicians that Brazil's nuclear power program should be halted. Lack of finance for completion of the Angra 2 and 3 units under construction led to the resignation of a director of the Brazilian state holding company, Nuclebras. The reactors were being built by the West German manufacturer Kraftwerk Union (KWU), and the delays in the program led to the loss of about one-quarter of the 160 West German specialists on the project.

Chernobyl also finally sealed the fate of the mothballed Zwentendorf plant in Austria. Though completed in 1978, the station never went into operation after the Austrians voted against nuclear power. The Austrian electrical utility decided no future change of policy could be expected. The plant was, therefore, being dismantled and, if possible, would be sold piece by piece by the U.S. engineering company Bechtel.

Austrian protests over the Wackersdorf reprocessing plant, under construction across the border in Bavaria, caused Austrian Pres. Kurt Waldheim to ask West Germany to "reconsider" plans for the plant. Violence in West Germany escalated in demonstrations against this and other plants, including 69 cases of attempted arson and 3 cases where explosives were used. Karl-Heinz Beckurts, research and technology director of Siemens, the parent company of KWU, died when a bomb was remotely detonated beside his car as it passed by. The start-up of the SNR-300 fast breeder reactor at Kalkar, due early in 1987, became a political issue, and its fate awaited the outcome of the January 1987 elections. Meanwhile, the high temperature gas-cooled reactor (HTGR) at Uentrop, claimed to be one of the safest reactor designs, began its first year of commercial operation. But both Japan and the U.S. announced that expenditures on HTGR development were being cut.

In Britain, where early maneuvering for the next general election had begun, the principal opposition parties adopted stands against nuclear power, saying they would cancel the Sizewell pressurized-water reactor (PWR) project if the Conservatives decided to go ahead after receiving the long-delayed report of the inspector, Sir Frank Layfield, from the 1983–84 public inquiry. Political pressure to phase out nuclear power increased because of unfavourable public opinion after Chernobyl, the availability of 2,000 MW of low-cost (mostly nuclear generated) power from France via a new cross-Channel cable link, and the dramatic drop in the costs of oil and coal. But Britain's national power utility, the Central Electricity Generating Board, declared that, whereas the main argument for the new PWR plant at the time of the inquiry was its lower generating costs, the subsequent delays and increasing power consumption now required the power station to be operational as soon as possible to meet projected demand.

The Korea Electric Power Co. awarded "first rights of negotiation" (the first steps in the long negotiations toward an order) for South Korea's 10th and 11th nuclear power reactors to Combustion Engineering of the U.S. This was the first new plant order won by a U.S. vendor since 1978 and the first order for a reactor won from overseas by Combustion Engineering. The turbine generators for the plant were to be made by the U.S. firm General Electric.

The protracted negotiations with China on the Daya Bay power station in Guandong (Kwangtung) Province finally reached the signing of contracts for the two 900-MW PWRs, with Framatome of France and General Electric Co. of the U.K. and, for engineering/design, with Électricité de France. The plant was to be a joint venture with Hong Kong, which would take 25% of the output from the station. But the Sunan project, which KWU had been confidently expecting to come its way, and that in Liaoning Province were dropped.

In the U.S. further delays were announced in the restart of the Tennessee Valley Authority's five nuclear units, shut down in 1985 because of training and administrative inadequacies. The first of these, Sequoyah 2, was delayed until at least January 1987.

In Ontario the new Liberal government's select committee reported on the future of the Darlington nuclear station, where four 881-MW Candu-type pressurized heavy water reactors were under construction near Toronto. Compiled well after the Chernobyl accident, the report called for the completion of the plant but a halt to further nuclear power construction in Ontario and a complete review of safety procedures and emergency plans.

According to International Atomic Energy Agency figures published early in the year, 32 power reactors were brought online during 1985, adding 30,057 MW to the total world nuclear generating capacity of 248,577 MW. At the beginning of 1986 there were 374 power reactors in service in 26 countries. Nuclear-generated electricity accounted for 15% of the world's total.

(RICHARD A. KNOX)

PAINTS AND VARNISHES

There was a major upheaval in the international ranking of paint manufacturers in 1986. ICI (Imperial Chemical Industries), long the leading U.K. company, acquired Glidden, the third-ranking U.S. company, for $580 million and shot to the top of the international league with annual output of 720 million litres (1 litre = 0.26 gal). The former leader, PPG of the U.S., fell back to second with 450 million litres, followed by BASF (Bayerische Anilin-und-Soda Fabric) of West Germany with 440 million litres.

Glidden was bought from the U.K. Hanson Trust, which had acquired it in early 1986 as part of the U.S. conglomerate SCM. Hanson retained the business in titanium dioxide, the main white pigment, which was currently very profitable. Further restructuring occurred in the U.K. industry when Akzo acquired the leading trade supplier Blundell-Permoglaze and the Snowcem paint operation of the Blue Circle cement company. Akzo proceeded to combine these businesses with its existing U.K. operation, Sikkens.

Paint manufacturers in most countries found themselves squeezed by rising costs of raw materials and stagnant demand. An exception was the U.S., where shipments were running 7% by volume and 10% in value above 1985 levels. In Europe, French industry sales changed little from 1985, but higher prices brought a revenue increase of 7%. Strong export growth helped Belgium's industry to increase its sales by 13% in volume and value terms, whereas in the U.K. volume rose by only 2.5% and value by 8%.

Environmental pressures led to the removal of lead compounds from U.K. household paints. ICI developed a prize-winning water-based metallic finish for cars and made further improvements in solvent-free powder coatings. It was estimated that the latter were used on about 10% of all metal surfaces coated in EC countries, double the U.S. figure. However, powder coatings were being adopted in North America at twice the European rate, and soon both regions were expected to produce about 90,000 metric tons a year. The penalties of failure to reduce pollution fast enough were illustrated by a case involving Austin Rover, the leading U.K. car manufacturer. People living near its Oxford assembly plant had complained that paint fallout was damaging their homes, gardens, and cars. Although Austin Rover had spent about £1 million on new filters and baffles, it was prosecuted and found guilty because it had not complied with an abatement notice. Legal costs reached £76,000, and civil actions were still to be heard.

(LIONEL BILEFIELD)

PHARMACEUTICALS

The struggle between brand-name drug manufacturers and their newly invigorated generic competitors seemed to become even more heated in 1986 as more drugs went "off patent," thus becoming fair prey for registration by the generic segment. Nevertheless, there were signs that the surge in U.S. Food and Drug Administration (FDA) approvals of these "me too" drugs was beginning to slow as fewer important drugs neared the end of their patent life.

Frank McKim, publisher of a newsletter that tracked drug developments, predicted that generic sales would continue to grow at a rate of 20 to 25% per year—twice the rate of the pharmaceutical industry as a whole—for the rest of the decade. Not all this additional business would be at the expense of brand-name manufacturers, however. Several of those companies were already important in the generic segment of the business, and others planned to follow suit, either by buying generic firms or by embarking on joint ventures with them.

Since generic drugs were disparaged by brand-name manufacturers for decades, this movement represented a profound change in strategy, spurred by recognition of changed attitudes toward generics throughout the health care establishment. Cost-containment pressures on hospitals, nursing homes, and other institutions had opened the door to generic drug sales,

TASS/SYGMA

An inspector checks radiation levels near components at a Chernobyl power unit following the nuclear power disaster there in April that released dangerously high amounts of radiation.

A culture of genetically engineered bacteria that produce interleukin-2 is aerated to help them work. The new substance offers a glimmer of hope to cancer and AIDS victims.
ZEVA OELBAUM

and physicians had become more aware of how important generic prescription-writing could be, especially for older patients. Meanwhile, signs of strain surfaced as generic manufacturers scrambled to catch up with demand.

The long-cultivated relationship of the drug industry with pharmacists was mildly threatened by the growing trend for physicians to sell drugs directly to their patients. The National Association of Pre-Packaged Drug Distributors estimated that $20 million worth of drugs would be repackaged for distribution by doctors and clinics in 1986. Since the prescription drug market in the U.S. amounted to about $20 billion, this was a far larger slice of the total market than most industry sources had been expecting.

Earlier in the decade it had been forecast that biogenetically produced drugs would comprise a substantial portion of the prescription drug market by 1987, but problems in working up to production quantities, getting the drugs clinically tested and FDA-approved, and ironing out the respective roles of the pharmaceutical manufacturer and the biogenetic research firms held back development of all but interferon and insulin. At least two biogenetic research firms indicated they were preparing to get into drug production themselves, and a major drug firm sold off its share in a research firm. Interest in biogenetically based or produced drugs continued, however, and there were indications that drugs made in this manner would be among the first used to treat several forms of cancer and AIDS (acquired immune deficiency syndrome).

Extra-Strength Tylenol had made a remarkable comeback since 1982, when seven persons died after taking cyanide-laced capsules of the popular over-the-counter painkiller in a product-tampering case that was still unsolved. When a woman died under similar circumstances in 1986, however, Johnson & Johnson, the manufacturer, announced that it would stop making Tylenol in capsule form and would substitute "caplets," tablets—which are more resistant to tampering than capsules—coated to make swallowing easier.

(DONALD A. DAVIS)

PLASTICS

The fortunes of the plastics industry in 1986 were heavily influenced by the fall in crude oil prices that took place early in the year. This resulted in a comparable reduction in the cost of petrochemical feedstocks, which stimulated demand for the major commodity plastics and enabled manufacturers to regain some profitability. Another important effect was to reduce the competitiveness of new producers, notably those in Saudi Arabia who had been expected to benefit from operations based on abundant local supplies of petroleum-associated gas. The price differential between the latter and naphtha, the traditional feedstock for making ethylene, narrowed dramatically. This gave welcome relief to European manufacturers of low-density polyethylene, which, with its linear variant, had been the main Saudi Arabian product. The first polyvinyl chloride plant in the area started up in the autumn, but it did not represent a threat to producers outside the Middle East because local demand for output, mainly of pipe, was strong.

The commodity plastics market was thus more buoyant in 1986 than had been expected. Nevertheless, although polypropylene again did well, growth in that sector (which accounted for about 30 million metric tons a year, or around two-thirds of the world total) amounted to only a few percentage points at best. Because of the sheer size of the business, however, commodity plastics continued to have the largest increase in volume. Oil companies, which dominated the marketplace, reaffirmed their faith in the viability of commodities following the modernization of previous years.

In the U.S. output of plastics increased 5.5% in the first half of 1986 as compared with the same period in 1985. The comparable figure for West Germany was 2.2%, which was probably typical of Europe as a whole. The U.S. and West Germany, the world's leading producers, had manufactured about 21 million metric tons and 8 million metric tons of material, respectively, in 1985.

As in previous years, the more specialized plastics did better than the commodities. These were generally known as engineering plastics, but by 1986 a further subdivision of "performance plastics" had emerged. The former were regarded as including the medium-priced thermoplastics that industrial designers found invaluable for all kinds of demanding molded components, such as those in cars. World demand for the principal engineering plastics exceeded one million metric tons in 1986, reflecting an increase of 7–9% per year.

The performance plastics were even more specialized and more expensive. Overall consumption was probably no more than 20,000 metric tons in 1986, but the market was growing by 15–20% annually. Each year a number of new candidates emerged from the laboratory; some soon disappeared, but others were destined to meet a particular high-technology need in a specialist area such as aerospace. The large chemical manufacturers saw such high added-value materials as offering good opportunities for diversification, and in several cases they established separate operations to handle them. Examples were British Petroleum (BP) Performance Poly-

GENERAL ELECTRIC RESEARCH AND DEVELOPMENT CENTER

Richard T. Rische (left) and Joe M. Watson created a computer program based on Rische's 15 years of troubleshooting plastic injection-molding problems. The resulting software should allow the solution of 75 to 85% of such problems in the plant, without outside help.

mers Inc. and Imperial Chemical Industries (ICI) Advanced Materials. The term performance related to advantages in such properties as heat resistance and strength that thermoplastics had not been able to attain previously.

An important event in 1986 was the Chinaplas exhibition held in Beijing (Peking). With its accelerating development and vast population, China was the last and greatest undeveloped world market for plastics.

(ROBIN C. PENFOLD)

PRINTING

Developments in the printing industry in 1986 led to significant changes in production costs, methods of printing, and working practices. Prices of colour-page composition came down. Japanese and European manufacturers, as well as Israel's Scitex Corp., introduced compact colour pagination and scanning systems. The addition of typesetting and page makeup facilities became feasible.

Dainippon Printing of Japan developed a compact page-generation method designed for a wide market. Previously, most of the big systems had catered to the requirements of large users. Flatbed electronic scanning came to be seen as the industry's future method of integrated picture and text composition. At Dr.-Ing Rudolf Hell in West Germany, fine arts and electronics were merged when the company's annual report was produced with illustrations "painted" by artists directly onto the electronic screen of the Chromacom.

In the field of typesetting, desktop publishing arrived in earnest. Even complicated pagination, colour graphics, and book and magazine production became possible on low-cost personal computer (PC) systems. Large manufacturers were quick to recognize the potential of desktop publishing. Monotype took an interest in Chelgraph Compac. Compugraphic, part of Agfa-Gevaert, and Linotype were among the first to see that laser printing offered fine typeface reproduction and resolution that would eventually replace photographic film materials in the graphic arts. Nebilo reestablished itself in larger sheetfed offset.

Printing machine designs improved to provide more rapid rates of production. In sheetfed offset, full-format printing accelerated to 13,000 sheets an hour. At the Drupa exhibition in early 1986, M.A.N.-Roland presented the fastest ever commercial web offset press. Also interesting was the trend among manufacturers to offer complete press systems packages with in-line facilities. Albert and M.A.N.-Roland, both of West Germany, were most prominent in this field.

Flexo and anilox newspaper printing made headway. After extensive trials in the U.S., two British national newspaper groups ordered major press lines for flexo presses from Koenig & Bauer of West Germany, which had shipped the first Courierflex press to the *Providence* (R.I.) *Journal* in the U.S. Rockwell International's graphic systems division Goss announced a flexo newspress speed of 70,000 revolutions per hour.

(W. PINCUS JASPERT)

RUBBER

Much of the news in the rubber industry in 1986 centred on corporate maneuvers, many caused by the actions of corporate raiders who targeted firms in the rubber industry as hostile-takeover targets. Goodyear, the world's largest rubber company, was targeted by Sir James Goldsmith of Great Britain in a move that caught not only the company but industry analysts by surprise. By late 1986 Goldsmith had accumulated nearly 12% of Goodyear's stock with intentions of gaining majority interest.

Goodyear had worldwide sales of $9.9 billion in 1985 and was the top synthetic rubber producer as well as the world's largest tire manufacturer. To help fight the takeover attempt, the company closed its Windsor, Vt., shoe products manufacturing plant and was considering other restructuring moves. Goldsmith stated that upon completion of the takeover, he would sell off Goodyear's non-core-item units, which would include the Goodyear Aerospace division and the recently acquired Celeron oil and gas subsidiary. Goodyear announced that it was looking for a buyer for Celeron, hoping that its sale would help thwart the attempted takeover.

Corporate raiders also had a hand in the formation of a new tire company as Uniroyal and B.F. Goodrich merged their tire operations. Uniroyal was the target of another hostile takeover attempt, which resulted in the company's top management purchasing Uniroyal through a leveraged buy-out. To do this they were forced to sell the chemical division to help pay off the debt incurred. Avery Inc. acquired the chemical business for $720 million, buying all trade names for the company's rubber chemicals, elastomers, and polyurethanes; three manufacturing plants in the U.S.; and plants in Italy, the U.K., Brazil, Mexico, and Taiwan. Uniroyal also sold its power transmission business to Gates Rubber. The new Uniroyal Goodrich Tire Co., combining the ninth and tenth largest tire companies worldwide, was expected to rank fifth in tire sales with close to $2 billion, accounting for 7% of the market.

The rubber industry also faced problems outside the boardrooms. Production overcapacity in many areas still was evident even after the large number of plant closings that had occurred in the last ten years. Since September 1985 five tire manufacturing facilities in the U.S. had been closed with little effect on capacity because production was shifted to other plants. Firestone announced that three of its facilities were given distress notices, usually the first step toward closure. The plants that were closed were B. F. Goodrich's Miami, Okla., and Oaks, Pa., plants; Firestone's Albany, Ga., plant; General Tire's Waco, Texas, plant; and Armstrong Rubber's Natchez, Miss., facility. The three Firestone plants that were labeled as distressed were its Oklahoma City, Okla., Des Moines, Iowa, and Bloomington, Ill., tire-manufacturing facilities.

Overcapacity also affected the European industry, with consolidations taking place in several countries. Michelin, the largest tire manufacturer in Europe and second biggest worldwide, acquired majority interest in Kléber and its three manufacturing plants, and Italy's Pirelli S.p.A. took over one CEAT plant and had a contract for the majority of production of CEAT's other facility. Plants were closed by Michelin and Dunlop in Ireland. Dunlop, which in 1985 sold its European operations to Sumitomo Rubber Industries, transferred its world tire organization to Japan from Europe. Sumitomo gained majority interest in Dunlop Tire Corp., which operated in North America.

Worldwide consumption of rubber in 1986 rose slightly from 1985, with most geographic regions posting increases. Apparent consumption of new rubber was up less than 0.5% in the U.S. through July 1986, countering predictions of a decline in consumption in that market. Consumption of natural rubber in the U.S. declined 3.5%, while that of synthetic rubber was running 2.3% ahead of the 1985 figures.

The International Institute of Synthetic Rubber Producers estimated that 1986 rubber consumption for North America would be in the range of 2.9 million metric tons, with the synthetic product accounting for a little more than 2 million tons. Other regional estimates by the IISRP revealed that Asia and Latin America were experiencing the largest increases in rubber consumption. Consumption for Asia and Oceania was estimated at 2.7 million tons, an increase of almost 100,000 tons. Synthetic rubber accounted for 1.4 million tons of that figure. Consumption in Latin America was expected to increase 5% to 733,000 metric tons, with 521,000 tons of synthetic consumed. Consumption estimates for Western Europe, Africa, and the Middle East were pegged at 1,030,000 tons, with synthetics accounting for 600,000 tons. Estimates for the centrally planned economies of Eastern Europe showed consumption at 3.4 million tons, 2.9 million tons of which were synthetic.

(DONALD SMITH)

SHIPBUILDING

The world recession in shipbuilding gathered more momentum in 1986. Its severity and length began to take their toll, and in Sweden all the remaining major shipyards were scheduled to be closed. In several other countries, including West Germany, the U.K., France, Norway, The Netherlands, and Spain, major yards closed. In Finland, France, and Denmark yards were saved by mergers, and elsewhere there were government subsidies to ease difficulties temporarily. The tonnage of merchant ships on order had almost steadily declined by one million tons gross per quarter over the previous five years, and total world orders fell to 39.1 million tons deadweight (dw), reflecting a decline of almost one-third since the record year of 1976.

Despite reports to the contrary, the "big six" shipbuilders—Japan, South Korea, China, Brazil, Yugoslavia, and Taiwan—lost some of their market share, which declined by 2.8% to 75.5%. Japan remained the world leader with 15.5 million tons dw on order, followed by South Korea with 7.5 million tons dw. Chinese shipyards moved into third place with orders of 2.1 million tons dw, followed by Brazil with 1.9 million tons dw. In seventh place behind Yugoslavia (1.3 million tons dw) and Taiwan (1,150,000 million tons dw) was Poland (983,000 tons dw), which was the only major builder to increase its orders, largely because of orders from the U.S.S.R. Romania, Yugoslavia, and India managed small increases, as did the U.K. Large-scale streamlining of the Italian shipbuild-

The 205-metre (671-foot) *Sgt. William R. Button*, the last ship to be built at the General Dynamics shipyard in Quincy, Massachusetts, heads out toward sea for two days of seaworthiness trials in May. The shipyard closed in June, a casualty of the industry's worldwide decline.
AP/WIDE WORLD

ing industry kept that country in eighth place, but this was believed to have resulted from substantial financial subsidies; nevertheless, with orders into 1988, Italy's shipbuilding industry was stronger than many others.

The only European government that decided actively to preserve its industry was Italy. The Swedish government decided on the almost complete shutdown of its shipbuilding industry because of its lack of price competitiveness. In West Germany the overall position of the shipyards worsened during the year. Because of the West German federal system of government, certain yards received financial help, but several yards faced closure.

Efforts by ministers of the EC to agree on a uniform European shipbuilding policy failed completely because of the great differences in national political-economic positions. The situation was not helped by the general lack of national shipbuilding policies. The failure of Western European shipbuilders to agree on a policy involving a controlled level of subsidies indicated that EC members would continue to fall lower on the world shipbuilding table.

The decline in the number of general-purpose cargo ships that began in early 1984 was halted during the year, mainly because China placed a substantial order in Romania for 12 vessels of 4,870 tons dw each, and Dutch shipowners ordered 13 coasters, ranging from 2,650 to 2,800 tons dw, from Dutch yards. Excluding containerships, orders for dry-cargo ships during the year totaled 341 vessels with an aggregate of nearly three million tons dw. Containership orders totaled 131 with an aggregate of 2.8 million tons dw. Orders for bulk carriers and combination carriers topped the list, with 298 vessels amounting to total tonnage of 19 million tons dw, compared with 25.7 million tons dw a year earlier. Tanker orders rose slightly from 284 vessels of 12.9 million tons dw in 1985 to 255 ships with an aggregate of 14.3 million tons dw in 1986. Most of the orders went to South Korea and Yugoslavia, with very few going to Japan following the heavy appreciation of the yen.

By flag ownership, Japanese shipowners had the greatest tonnage on order, with a total of 7.5 million tons dw, including 106 dry-cargo ships, tankers, and bulk carriers. Liberian flag owners were in second place with 92 ships totaling 6.8 million tons dw, and Panama followed with 103 ships that, because of their smaller size, accounted for only 3.2 million tons dw. These three flags accounted for nearly half of the total on order. Prices remained low during 1986, and with banks reluctant to advance loans, owners were discouraged from buying more ships and increasing the serious overcapacity in the world freight markets.

(W. D. EWART)

TELECOMMUNICATIONS

The recognition by telephone companies throughout the world that the merging of computers and communications was providing significant advantages to consumers expedited the conversion of telephone central offices to "digital switches." They were rapidly replacing central offices that employed electromechanical switches and relays, and even central offices that used analog electronic systems.

With digital equipment a voice is sampled many times a second, and the result of each sample is converted to a coded character. It is then transmitted, for a long-distance call, from one central office to another and finally decoded for transmission to the distant telephone.

This procedure sounds simple, but the cost of developing such a system is enormous—on the order of $1 billion. Therefore, it was no suprise that those companies with developed and operational digital switching systems were making every effort to sell them everywhere in the world. Since the U.S. in 1986 represented a large part of the worldwide market, and because the seven regional holding companies (those operating companies formed as a result of the breakup of the Bell System in 1984) controlled 80% of the U.S. market, a tremendous selling effort was being expended in that direction.

Telephone companies throughout the world in 1986 continued to spend millions of dollars on fibre optics and its associated electronics. As many as 8,000 telephone conversations could simultaneously be carried on a single pair of glass fibres, and this number could be doubled by applying a technology called wavelength division multiplexing.

U.S. Sprint Communications, a joint venture of GTE and United Telecommunications, planned to have 37,800 km (23,000 mi) of fibre in operation by the end of 1987, and construction was proceeding at a rapid rate. The price tag of the undertaking approached $2 billion. MCI, long dependent on microwave (indeed, that is what the "M" in the name originally stood for), was rapidly converting to glass fibres, aiming at 11,300 km (7,000 mi) before the end of 1987. And AT&T Communications, the long-distance arm of AT&T, pegged 16,400 km (10,200 mi) as its near-term goal. Others, including the National Telecommunications Network, a joint venture of seven companies, and various regional networks, brought the total to more than 96,500 km (60,000 mi).

During this expansion, fibre technology continued to improve, and its capabilities reached unimagined levels. In past years multimode fibres (glass strands about as thick as a human hair) were most often used. But during recent months the move to single-mode fibre (one-tenth the thickness of a human hair) received most of the world's attention. Such a fibre allows only one "ray" of light to pass through it, and this in turn permits transmission over much longer distances before the signal being transmitted needs to be amplified and regenerated.

By 1986 users of such fibres were not limited to transmission of a single modulated light beam. By multiplexing (mixing) light beams of different frequencies (different colours) on the same strand of glass and then separating those beams at the receiving end, engineers greatly expanded the capacity of the system.

Until recently the long-distance telephone market was responsible for most of the fibre sales. However, industry observers believed that the "local loop" market (that segment of the telephone plant that extends from the central office toward the subscriber) would soon take the lead.

A new entrant to the field of high technology in telecommunications was the pay telephone. In past years this phone depended on a collection of levers and switches for its operation except when other than a local call was being placed, in which case there was a live operator at a distant office. But coin boxes often filled to overflowing before a coin collector made his rounds. An even more serious problem was the vandalizing of phones—and the inability of the telephone company to do anything about it.

Technicians in the Atlanta, Georgia, monitoring centre for the long-distance telephone company U.S. Sprint keep watch over a multitude of signals from fibre-optic lines. The efficiency of fibre optics in handling information attracted many communications companies.
ROGER ALLEN GRIGG/TIME

All this changed with the introduction of the "smart" pay phone called a COCOT (customer-owned coin-operated telephone). It includes electronic devices that store a table of charges to all parts of the country, taking into account day of week and time of day. These devices control other devices that generate a synthesized voice. Therefore, a user who places a long-distance call to some other part of the country is "told" exactly how much money should be deposited. The COCOTs also measure and store a running total of the money collected and transmit this information to a maintenance centre when interrogated. Finally, a number of sensitive points are automatically monitored to protect against vandalism and, if an improper action is noted, a telephone call is automatically placed to the proper authorities. (ROBERT E. STOFFELS)

TEXTILES

The trend in manufacturing in 1986 was to eliminate people and craft skills where possible but to combine automation with versatility. Reducing labour in most parts of textile manufacturing was not difficult, but in garment making the big reductions in labour were yet to come. The cutting itself was becoming very automated—the pieces could even be adjusted for different sizes by computer—but people still had to cut out components of garments and assemble them for sewing. Japan and the U.S. were investing heavily in research and development on possible systems for assembling and sewing pieces together automatically, but Europe showed little interest.

Rotor spinning continued to encroach on the traditional preserves of short-staple ring spinning in industrialized countries, although the U.S. market appeared to be reaching the saturation point. Ring spinning, however, was likely to be given new impetus because of technical developments that reduced the labour requirement and made it possible to produce large bobbins of knotless yarn instantly ready for either weaving or knitting. The move to shuttleless looms continued. In 1985 there were some 2,500,000,000 looms worldwide, 10.7% of which were shuttleless. More significantly, only 22% of looms shipped in 1985 had shuttles.

An important trend that was often overlooked was the rapid annual growth in the output of fabrics that were neither woven nor knitted, including disposable materials for medical purposes. Much of this growth was in areas with no tradition of textile use. (PETER LENNOX-KERR)

Wool. During 1986 the demand for wool continued to be dominated by the highly volatile currency situation. The weaker Australian dollar made wool cheaper to buy for all the major users. It also meant that Australia was favoured for much of the year as a relatively cheap source. The Australian Wool Corporation raised its reserve price by only 1.6% overall at the end of June, but a few weeks later it announced that it would operate its floor price "flexibly"—in effect, a little above the stated level.

In Australia and other primary markets, the selling season started hesitantly, but demand picked up later and brought firmer prices. Total world wool supplies in the 1986–87 season were estimated at 1,851,000 metric tons, 1% more than in 1985–86. Production in the 1986–87 season was expected to be virtually unchanged at 1,659,000 metric tons (clean basis), while carryover stocks in grower countries were up 12% at an estimated 192,000 metric tons. The supply situation set against consumption trends indicated that prices overall would remain steady through early 1987.

Virgin wool used as a fibre in the wool textile sector of the industry gained market share from other fibres in 1985. According to the Commonwealth Secretariat, virgin wool accounted for 30.2% of all fibres used, compared with 29.8% in 1984 and 29.2% in 1983. Virgin wool consumption in nine leading countries totaled 571,000 metric tons, 1% above 1984. A cyclical downturn in wool-textile manufacturing activity, which became evident in the final quarter of 1985, tended to develop in 1986. (H. M. F. MALLETT)

Cotton. There was a fall of over 7% in world cotton production in the 1986–87 season to 15,798,924 metric tons (estimate). Drought in the U.S. Cotton Belt was largely responsible, but there were also sizable declines in Australia (66%), India (an estimated 17%), Turkey (7%), and Israel (about 22%). Surprisingly, output rose in much of Africa, although there were reductions in Cameroon, Egypt, Mali, Nigeria, Tanzania, Burkina Faso, and Zaire. Many countries carried over substantial stocks of raw cotton, and world consumption was estimated at 16,266,661 metric tons in 1986, about 4% more than in 1985. Consumption of cotton declined in many of the poorer countries. It also fell in Hong Kong, where use was determined by export demand.

A major problem in cotton processing continued to be the sticky elements often found in the cotton bolls, which tend to clog processing equipment. Israel made progress toward combating the problem, but it was far from being solved. There was no prospect of finer strains of cotton being developed in the near future. Production of the high-quality long-staple cottons for which Egypt and The Sudan are known continued to rise in Israel, India, and the U.S.

An emerging problem was the demand for cotton to blend with the increasingly fine man-made fibres being developed. This, in turn, required the development of textile processes capable of handling finer material, but the consumer would benefit eventually by having more comfortable garments. (PETER LENNOX-KERR)

Silk. During 1985–86 silk continued to enjoy good worldwide demand, stemming from the return to more formal dressing and the general swing back to natural fibres. Another factor was increasing prosperity, especially in the silk-producing countries of China and India. The main beneficiary was China. The decline in the value of the U.S. dollar, on which both

China and Brazil now based their export prices, stimulated confidence and demand. The U.S. remained a large customer, despite the weaker dollar, while Hong Kong continued to increase in importance as a consumer of both raw silk for its growing industry and silk fabric for garments. Statistics reported by the European Commission for the Promotion of Silk showed increasing demand in the main European countries.

Fashion swung away from spun silk and blends just as the supply of silk waste for this trade increased; prices declined and demand was sluggish. On the technological front, research continued into devising a reliable system of testing silk electronically. Work was also being done in developing finishes to make silk more attractive to the modern consumer.

In Japan the government-held stock of raw silk at last showed signs of declining. On Jan. 1, 1984, it totaled 10,475 metric tons and a year later, 10,762 tons, but on Jan. 1, 1986, it stood at 9,319 tons, largely as the result of reduced domestic production. During 1984 world production of raw silk totaled 56,128 metric tons, with China producing 28,140 tons and Japan, 10,800 tons. (ANTHONY H. GADDUM)

Man-Made Fibres. Growth in man-made fibre capacity in 1986 continued to be concentrated in the Far East, excluding Japan, which, in common with most industrialized countries, had overcapacity. The U.S. fibre maker Du Pont planned to dismantle a surplus nylon tire cord factory and ship it to Turkey, where it would supply the Turkish market and manufacturers in the Mediterranean area. Great emphasis was placed on the fact that world synthetic fibre capacity was unaffected. Most Western European fibre capacity had already contracted, but in the U.K. ICI Fibres announced its gradual withdrawal from the polyester trade. Courtaulds of the U.K. acquired a Spanish company and was reportedly looking for others.

Two major commercial developments indicated that high-performance polyolefin fibres, often comparable with aramids, could be produced much more cheaply. Thus it was possible that much of the aramid trade could be replaced by less costly substitutes. Because of their low specific gravity, the new fibres floated in water, making them particularly suitable for marine use, and their resistance to ultraviolet light and abrasion was believed to be greater than that of aramids.

The technologically advanced fibre makers were looking at new fibre types such as PEEK (polyetheretherketone) and silica for use in high-performance composites and stable circuit boards and for aerospace applications. Italy's Snia Fibre Co. created a flexible sound-absorbent composite sheet using lead fibres. Of much greater market potential was the pending arrival of "solvent spinning" of cellulosic fibres of the rayon family. When fully developed, the process was expected to create a new generation of fibres that could be made from much lower-grade raw materials than were currently required.

(PETER LENNOX-KERR)

TOBACCO

Despite a growing awareness of the health hazard posed by smoking, in 1986 world sales of cigarettes (still the most favoured form of tobacco consumption) rose about 1.5%. The main increases were in China, other less developed countries, and Eastern Europe but, despite every discouragement, most of the EC countries smoked more in 1986, and the consumption decline in the U.S. and Japan was only slight. Authoritative projections estimated that world cigarette consumption in 1990 would be about 10% more than in 1986.

Advanced countries, whose social attitudes were widely, though often unconsciously, adopted in the rest of the world, had sharpened their opposition to tobacco every year since the smoking and health debate started in the U.S. in 1964. The cumulative effect of 22 years of propaganda was becoming visible in forecasts by the tobacco industry for reduced sales in mature markets. Taxation authorities in many countries raised rates on cigarettes; smoking was being more widely and boldly banned; and ever more insistent health education messages were being directed toward young people.

Manufacturers in advanced countries were becoming reconciled to a more persecuted future. Those that had no export trade—the majority—saw consumption in mature markets leveling off, if it had not already done so, and then declining. The general response to such conditions was to try to increase profitability by audacious pricing in weak or sliding markets and to cut operating costs, principally labour, by concentrating manufacture in fewer, highly efficient factories. One generation previously, the newest machinery had an hourly output of 2,000 cigarettes; machines in 1986 had no more operators but produced three to five times more per hour.

The industry's biggest anxiety was that in the U.S. or Europe the courts might rule against a major tobacco business in one of the product liability suits popular among ex-smoker litigants and their heirs. Were that to happen, the subsequent cost of a rush of similar claims and negative publicity would be grave, if not mortal, to the business involved.

Such concerns were remote from the world's tobacco growers, who in 1985 harvested an estimated 6,556,000 metric tons of tobacco—enough to meet all current demands while leaving in stock a near-record of about 7,450,000 metric tons of maturing leaf (almost enough for 15 months of manufacture). (MICHAEL F. BARFORD)

TOURISM

World tourism maintained its underlying strength in 1986. Global international arrivals rose from 333 million to 350 million, an increase of 5%. Receipts from foreign travel were estimated to have risen by about 10% from $109,566,000,000 in 1985. The world's biggest spender on foreign travel was West Germany, whose residents bought travel services exceeding $20 billion. Second place was taken by the U.S., whose citizens, however, traveled comparatively long distances abroad.

The decline in the international value of the U.S. dollar, fear of reprisals after U.S. raids on Libya, and anxiety about visiting countries affected by radiation following the accident at the Chernobyl nuclear power plant in the U.S.S.R. exerted a profound effect on travel patterns in 1986. Following 1985, an exceptionally good year for hotel profits, European tour operators were optimistic about future prospects. In fact, however, there was a marked decline in international arrivals in Europe in the spring and summer. Those sectors of the industry dependent on affluent U.S. travelers were especially hard hit. Airlines too were beset by excess capacity, especially on the North Atlantic. Most travel industry sectors sought to counteract the decline by means of market inducements and discounting.

The deterioration in the U.S. market was felt by most European countries. Typical declines in arrivals were: Austria −50%, West Germany −25%, Hungary −38%, Italy −33%, Poland −36%, Portugal −35%, Spain −29%, and Switzerland −43%. However, most countries also reported that tourism from North America was increasing in late 1986.

Other markets for Europe, including intraregional tourism (such as travel by Europeans within Europe), showed a mixed trend. There were some significant gains

JONATHAN PLAYER/THE NEW YORK TIMES

Yeoman warders stand near the Tower of London, all but deserted by tourists. The number of U.S. tourists in Great Britain was down 40% in the spring but gradually increased to near normal in winter.

in total international arrivals, including Cyprus 13%, Hungary 8%, Malta 11%, Spain 10%, and Portugal 5%. Other countries, such as Austria and Yugoslavia, marked time. However, anxiety about terrorism affected Italy (−11%); the strong Swiss currency proved too much for visitors (−7%); and U.K. dependence on the U.S. market led to a 7% falloff despite the boost provided in July by the wedding of Prince Andrew and Sarah Ferguson.

Asia showed considerable strength in 1986. This was partly due to self-generated demand attributable to the growing economic prosperity of the region and partly to the quest of North Americans for destinations perceived as less troubled. The six countries of the Association of Southeast Asian Nations (ASEAN) exceeded ten million international arrivals for the first time. Arrivals in Malaysia grew 7% and those in Singapore (experiencing a hotel glut), 4%, while Thailand registered an 11% increase in arrivals. This especially good performance was attributed to the increase in nonstop air services to Bangkok and to preparations for celebrations marking the Thai king's 60th birthday in 1987. In the Philippines the "people power" revolution led to a 4% drop in arrivals, though Australian travelers surveyed after the "coup" claimed that they would be more likely to visit the Philippines following the toppling of the Marcos regime.

Hong Kong reported 8% more visitors and South Korea, 13%. India enjoyed greater popularity among Canadian, Japanese, and U.K. visitors. Sri Lanka succeeded in containing losses to only 4% despite adverse publicity resulting from Tamil United Liberation Movement activities. However, the rising value of the yen appeared to have discouraged holiday travel to Japan, which experienced a 14% decline in international visitors.

Table XI. Major Tourism Spenders and Earners in 1985

Major spenders	Expenditure
United States	$17,043,000,000
West Germany	14,607,000,000
United Kingdom	7,047,000,000
Japan	4,814,000,000
France	4,557,000,000
Canada	4,125,000,000
Austria	3,333,000,000
Netherlands, The	3,118,000,000
Switzerland	2,399,000,000
Italy	2,283,000,000
Sweden	2,270,000,000
Mexico	2,262,000,000
Belgium	2,048,000,000
Kuwait	1,988,000,000
Norway	1,925,000,000
Australia	1,873,000,000
Denmark	1,410,000,000
Major earners	**Receipts**
United States	$14,144,000,000
Italy	8,758,000,000
Spain	8,150,000,000
France	7,942,000,000
United Kingdom	7,877,000,000
Austria	6,041,000,000
West Germany	5,899,000,000
Switzerland	3,145,000,000
Canada	3,056,000,000
Mexico	2,900,000,000
Singapore	2,310,000,000
Belgium	1,960,000,000
Hong Kong	1,831,000,000
Brazil	1,740,000,000
Netherlands, The	1,503,000,000
Turkey	1,482,000,000
Greece	1,428,000,000
Sweden	1,332,000,000

Source: World Tourism Organization, 1986.

North America showed some useful gains in 1986. These resulted both from European demand and from travel internally generated in the U.S. Canada was host to 27% more visitors. The five-month-long Expo 86 held in Vancouver, B.C., was visited by more than 22 million people. Mexico recovered well from the earthquake that had destroyed many Mexico City and resort hotels in 1985. Arrivals there were up 5%, as were those in the U.S. Caribbean nations were optimistic that the 1986–87 winter season would confirm their success in tapping the U.S. market.

Visitor counts in 1986 were somewhat lower in Africa and the Middle East. Arrivals in Egypt and Israel each declined 17%. In Morocco arrivals were down 2%, but overnight stays grew by 4%. Tunisia recorded a 5% decline in overnight stays.

China expanded hotel capacity to meet growing international tourist demand. American Express claimed that 22% more packages to the Orient and China were sold by its outlets in 1986 compared with 1985.

France imposed a visa requirement on most non-European Communities nationals (including U.S.) in an attempt to curb the international terrorist threat. Among travel "taxes," a $5 U.S. immigration user fee went into effect in December 1986.

Canada became the 109th nation to join the World Tourism Organization (WTO) when it acceded to the world body in the fall of 1986. World Tourism Day, Sept. 27, 1986, was celebrated on the theme "Tourism—a vital force for world peace."

After 32 years, WTO secretary-general Robert C. Lonati (France) died on his last day of office, Dec. 31, 1985. He was succeeded by Willibald P. Pahr (Austria), who had been unanimously elected head of the intergovernmental tourism body in September 1985 by the sixth WTO General Assembly. (PETER SHACKLEFORD)

WOOD PRODUCTS

Hardwood. The world hardwood market in 1986 was heavily influenced by poor supplies of two major commercial species: Philippines lauan and Brazilian mahogany. In the Philippines efforts to reduce corruption in the forestry industry led to the suspension of many logging and production licenses, which cut production of lauan lumber dramatically; output was also affected by a particularly wet monsoon season. Although a huge volume of contract business was not fulfilled in the first half of the year, by midyear Philippine exporters were transacting new business at higher prices and neglecting the earlier contracts. Importers in Europe were left short and were reluctant to place new orders. The short supplies of lauan put pressure on mills in Indonesia and Sabah and even peninsular Malaysian meranti/seraya mills, which again could not fulfill their orders.

Brazilian mahogany mills were short of logs all year. Because of bad weather and poor prices early in the year, most mills restricted purchases and reduced output. Consequently, lumber prices rose, and mills moved back into the market only to find logs scarce and costly. By September there was little high-grade mahogany for export as producers caught up with orders.

West African sipo/utile producers benefited from stronger demand as importers tried to meet the shortfall in Brazilian supplies. Ghana was well placed to take more orders following huge investments by the World Bank and European governments in its timber industry. Japanese oak exports declined, with U.S. white oak taking a larger share. Most other hardwoods enjoyed a steady demand.

Softwood. Most softwood producers enjoyed stable markets in 1986. Improved demand in Europe helped counter a slump in the Middle East and North Africa. Countervailing duty continued to be an issue, with the U.S. maintaining that Canadian imports were cheaper than U.S. production because of high subsidies by the Canadian government. A duty of 35% was imposed on U.S. imports of Canadian shakes and shingles, which provoked retaliatory tariffs from Canada, and a 15% tariff was imposed on Canadian lumber later in the year.

The main concern in Europe was what would happen to the ten million cubic metres of softwood that the U.S. usually bought from Canada. There were fears that large sales by Canada to other countries would cause prices to nosedive. From mid-July, however, a fierce labour dispute halted production in most of Canada's West Coast mills for more than four months, and the resulting shortages pushed up prices. Oversupply in Sweden and Finland persisted and caused major production cutbacks by industry leaders. Producers tried to diversify from bulk lumber production in order to add value to exports.

Prices held firm for most of 1986. Significant increases were expected for the fourth quarter, but in spite of limited supplies of joinery-quality whitewood and redwood, suppliers lacked confidence, and by September some had taken orders into the first half of 1987 at prices only slightly above those of the third quarter of 1986. Far Eastern plywood prices, however, moved into 1987 on a very firm basis. Indonesia's quotas and pricing policy led to price increases of up to 10% in the last quarter. Producers were given strong incentives to sell into "developing markets" such as Japan and China. Strong demand from Singapore and other Pacific Rim countries helped strengthen prices.

While wood products consumption levels remained stable in the U.S. and Europe and dipped in the Middle East and North Africa, China continued to increase its timber imports. India, too, proved an insatiable market for hardwoods. Similar trends were expected for 1987.

(JEAN CLARK CAMERON KLOOS)

See also Agriculture and Food Supplies; Consumer Affairs; Economic Affairs; Energy; Information Processing and Information Systems; Labour-Management Relations; Mining; Photography; Television and Radio; Transportation.

This article updates the *Macropædia* articles BEVERAGE PRODUCTION; ELECTRONICS; ENERGY CONVERSION; FORESTRY AND WOOD PRODUCTION; FURS, LEATHERS, AND HIDES; INDUSTRIAL GLASS AND CERAMICS; Chemical Process INDUSTRIES; Extraction and Processing INDUSTRIES; Manufacturing INDUSTRIES; Textile INDUSTRIES; INSURANCE; MARKETING AND MERCHANDISING; PRINTING, TYPOGRAPHY, AND PHOTOENGRAVING; TELECOMMUNICATIONS SYSTEMS; TOOLS.

Information Processing and Information Systems

The slump that struck the U.S. computer industry in 1985 exacted its toll in 1986 as two industry giants merged and another reported its worst losses ever. Even industry leader IBM suffered, reporting meagre profitability in the first quarter and equally gloomy results throughout the year.

Despite the hard times, 1986 was also a year of risk taking as several vendors ventured into new markets or introduced products using new technologies. And, as befits a maturing industry, the year was also marked by signs of greater sophistication on the part of business computer users and an increased presence of the federal government in the industry.

For most, though, 1986 would be remembered as the year of Burroughs Corp.'s $4.8 billion purchase of Sperry Corp. The two firms, both longtime sellers of minicomputers and mainframes, would together comprise a company with annual sales of $10 billion, a total second only to that of IBM. The merger was the first major shake-up in the U.S. computer industry since Xerox Corp. sold its mainframe division to Honeywell Inc. ten years earlier; it came after weeks of behind-the-scenes negotiations in which Sperry had spurned Burroughs's offers. Sperry, which had sought a price of $80 per share, accepted Burroughs's final offer of $76.50 per share in late May. Burroughs said that the new company would save approximately $15 million a year by combining operations and that it would continue to maintain and improve existing Sperry products.

All told, between 250 and 300 mergers—a record number—occurred in the U.S. computer industry in the first nine months of 1986, according to Broadview Associates, a New Jersey firm that managed software industry mergers. The mergers were spawned by the one-year-old sales slump that dogged the industry throughout 1986, a time when the economy as a whole showed robust health. One study, which compared the performance of computer industry stocks against the Standard & Poor's Index of 500 stocks, found that, while most stocks increased 40% in value, computer stocks were selling at about the same price as in 1985. The reason for this was that most computer manufacturers were reporting flat growth or actual declines in profitability in 1986. Among those hardest hit was Control Data Corp., which in February reported a $567.5 million loss, the worst in its history. Minicomputer vendor Data General Corp., meanwhile, responded to a revenue downturn by laying off 900 employees. Even IBM took a beating; its first-quarter report showed profits up a modest 3.1%, while sales showed a slight decline.

Not every computer company suffered in 1986. Digital Equipment Corp. (DEC), in fact, registered dramatic increases in profits and sales. The number two U.S. computer company attributed its success to the fact that its VAX minicomputers could be easily interconnected and all operated the same software, a feature not offered by IBM minicomputers. During 1986 DEC expanded its VAX line and introduced an IBM-compatible personal computer designed for office networks.

DEC's success came largely at IBM's expense, and in 1986 IBM retaliated, replacing several of its minicomputers with more powerful and more easily connected machines. In an even bolder move, IBM later introduced the 9370 line, a series of mainframes as compact and almost as cheap as DEC minicomputers. Nonetheless, the mainframe market, IBM's forte, remained depressed in 1986.

Despite the atmosphere of fiscal gloom, 1986 was also marked by innovation. For example, IBM and Hewlett-Packard Co. each made a daring commitment to the Reduced Instruction Set Computer (Risc) architecture, which ran programs adapted to the architecture far faster than a standard computer. Hewlett-Packard said that all of its future computers would be based on the technology, though it did not ship the first product in its Risc-based line until late in the year. IBM's Risc machine, an engineering workstation called the RT PC, gained limited initial sales because few programs were available for it and because its price and speed were still comparable to that of non-Risc machines from other vendors. Later in 1986 IBM enhanced the RT with greater storage and memory, but observers said that sales were still below expectations.

In the personal computer business, where the IBM PC had become the standard, IBM introduced a lap-size PC called the Convertible. It also experienced limited sales, largely because of complaints about the readability of its liquid crystal display screen and because its internal modem, used for data communications, varied from the industry's modem standard.

While most personal computer vendors avoided new markets until IBM had set a standard, Compaq Computer Corp. in late 1986 beat IBM to the punch by becoming the first maker of personal computers to introduce a machine based on the Intel Corp. 80386 microprocessor, a high-speeed 32-bit chip. Because the 80386 was a direct descendant of the Intel 80286 and 8088 chips, which powered the IBM PC family, the Compaq Deskpro 386 could operate all of the software for the PC line but at speeds up to three times as fast.

IBM got an additional dose of bad news in 1986 when the personal computer market became awash in a flood of low-cost machines similar to the IBM PC, many of which were being produced in Asia. Before the end of the year, analysts estimated that machines such as the Leading Edge Model D had collectively reduced IBM's share of the U.S. personal computer market to less than 40%.

In software 1986 was the year of desktop publishing, a task in which a personal computer and a laser printer were used to create a reproducible document that combined pictures and text. Desktop publishing, of everything from newsletters to annual reports, became the vogue in 1986, and Aldus Corp.'s Page Maker desktop publishing program for the Apple Macintosh became a top seller. By the year's end Aldus had announced a version of Page Maker for the IBM PC.

In 1986 the top users of computers, U.S. corporations, continued to decentralize their computing, often by putting minicomputers in regional offices or departments. Yet they also continued to centralize control over the use and acquisition of personal computers. In the area of PC software, corporate buyers flexed their muscles most, forcing many major vendors to abandon copy protection for their software—since copy-protected software is difficult to use on a personal computer's hard disk—and also requiring those sellers to offer bulk-purchase discount plans.

Business computer users also began to demand that their computers be able to talk to each other, in both the factory and the office. Heeding that call, many computer vendors said they would incorporate General Motors Corp.'s Manufacturing Automation Protocol into their factory automation computers, and approximately 60 vendors began joint research on the Open Systems Interconnection model, a standard for communication among office computers.

The federal government also took on an increasingly important role in the U.S. computer industry in 1986,

CD-ROM: The Possibilities Grow

"Books" that come alive with sound and animated pictures. Pocket-size players to "read" them on. Maps you can explore down to the street level. Storage for thousands of photos. These are but a few of the possibilities for a technology called compact disc-read only memory (CD-ROM).

Like the compact disc audio recordings that gained great popularity in 1986, CD-ROM is a technology in which a laser beam is used to record information on a plastic disc 12.06 cm (4.75 in) in diameter. CD-ROM discs are played back into a personal computer (PC) instead of into a sound system, but their capabilities are no less striking. One CD-ROM disc, for example, can store all of the data contained on approximately 1,200 single-sided floppy disks or 270,000 pages of printed information. To play a CD-ROM disc, however, requires a personal computer, a special player, and software. Interest in CD-ROM in 1986 was, therefore, confined largely to businesses that needed to process or manipulate information. Nonetheless, annual sales of CD-ROM players were predicted by one market research firm to soar from a total of about 6,180 in 1986 to 534,700 in 1990.

With a PC and a CD-ROM player, a financial analyst can search a data base containing descriptions and financial data on 1,300 U.S. corporations. A medical researcher can use a CD-ROM disc to browse through the research abstracts of the National Library of Medicine. While both the analyst and the researcher could have found their information in a public library, the search would probably have been considerably more difficult.

An important advantage of CD-ROMs is that software has been developed for use with them that allows a CD-ROM data base to be searched on the basis of a key word. By entering the word cancer, for instance, a medical researcher can get a list of all of the articles that contain the word cancer in a CD-ROM article data base of enormous size. The CD-ROM disc, which itself costs about $60, is also cheaper and easier to distribute and store than a printed publication containing as much information.

But there are drawbacks to CD-ROM. Perhaps the biggest is that it cannot be written upon by the personal computer user. So it is useful only where "frozen" data are acceptable. A second disadvantage is that there is no dominant standard for CD-ROMs as there is for audio discs. As a result, only about 60 data bases and other software products have been introduced on CD-ROM.

Word in the industry is that both these problems could be solved in the next few years because high-tech firms are competing less and working together more than they did in the past. They feel there is ultimately going to be enough profit for everybody to share. The key to all that profit is probably the development of CD-I, or compact disc interactive. This turns the CD-ROM disc into one that not only stores sound and pictures as well as text but also allows quick and easy movement from one to the other. Some giants in the electronics industry are betting heavily that, together with small players already in development, CD-I will totally change the way information of all kinds is stored and retrieved. (EDWARD S. WARNER)

both as a customer and as a regulator. As a customer, the government found itself buying more personal computers than ever before. According to a 1986 report from the General Services Administration, the government bought 67,502 personal computers in 1985, 50% more than it had the year before. In 1986 the Internal Revenue Service signed a contract with Zenith Data Systems for 15,000 lap-top portable personal computers, as many as the biggest lap-top computer vendor had sold in all of 1985, and the federal PC-buying spree showed no signs of abating.

The federal government also rode to the rescue of the U.S. semiconductor industry in 1986 by convincing the Japanese government to monitor the production costs of Japanese-made semiconductors so that the U.S. could more easily determine when Japanese computer chips were being sold below cost on the U.S. market. U.S. semiconductor makers had demanded government action after low-cost Japanese chips had drastically reduced the sales of U.S. manufacturers.

Lest the government seem totally enamoured of computing and its technology, the Congressional Office of Technology Assessment warned in a 1986 report that increasing the use of computer networking and microcomputers might imperil a citizen's right to privacy. Data networks make it possible for one agency to access the confidential information stored on another agency's computers, the report warned, noting that IRS tax records were being used to track down welfare cheaters. Microcomputers, meanwhile, might allow agencies to keep secret dossiers that could not be legally kept on mainframe computers.

(EDWARD S. WARNER)

The output of computers and their peripheral equipment in Japan rose by some 14.1% during 1985, reaching a total value of 3,332,700,000,000 yen. Of this total, computer mainframes accounted for 1,363,100,000,000 yen, a significant gain of 23.3% from the previous year. Production of peripheral equipment accounted for 1,308,200,000,000 yen, about an 11.3% rise, and of terminal equipment, 521 billion yen, a marginal increase of 1.6%.

The substantial increase in the output of mainframes in 1985 was attributed to the fact that the introduction in February of the new general-purpose computer 3090 by IBM Corp. of the U.S. inspired NEC and Hitachi to start full-scale production of their ACOS 1500 series and M-68 X series, respectively.

Production of personal computers reached 1,920,000 units, totaling 335.8 billion yen, a considerable gain of 25.8%. This increase was, however, somewhat smaller than the 30% annual rise achieved in the past few years, mainly because of a leveling off of exports to the U.S.

The output of small-business computers recorded a moderate gain of some 11.5%, amounting to 141.6 billion yen. This modest rise reflected the fact that such machines had been significantly overshadowed by rapidly improved personal computers.

In terms of market share by type of computer, IBM Corp. of Japan ranked first in the general-purpose type, holding a share of some 26.7% of the Japanese market (on the basis of the number of computers sold and still in use). Fujitsu was second with 22%, and Hitachi was third with 17%. In the personal-computer sector, NEC held an overwhelming share of about 47%, thereby opening up a big lead over Fujitsu (19%) and IBM Japan (7%). In the small-business computer sales race, NEC and Fujitsu were neck and neck, each taking some 22% of the market.

(TAKUZO NIWA)

This article updates the *Macropædia* article INFORMATION PROCESSING AND INFORMATION SYSTEMS.

Labour-Management Relations

In the labour field generally, the climate, at least in the advanced industrialized market economies, was strongly affected in 1986 by continuing high levels of unemployment. Associated factors were the drive to remain competitive, leading enterprises to seek to reduce their labour costs; the onset of technological change; and the continuing decline of many old-established manufacturing and mining industries. Pressure on public expenditure continued to constrain the numbers and pay of public-service employees. The stress on competitiveness focused attention on obstacles to flexibility in the labour market, leading, among other things, to a review of restrictions that had been placed on work since World War II.

United Kingdom. The biggest story in industrial relations during the year concerned British newspaper production, which for decades had suffered from high costs and low productivity. Every effort at improvement had been thwarted by powerful trade unions, and little use had been made of new technology. In January, however, confronted with yet another dispute, News International, the company responsible for *The Times,* the *Sunday Times,* the *Sun,* and the *News of the World,* switched production overnight to a completely new plant in Wapping, East London, using modern technology and a mainly new, reduced labour force. Some 5,000 striking printing workers were dismissed. The Wapping plant was picketed, and there were ugly demonstrations, but the newspapers continued to appear. Negotiations between the employers and the print unions were carried on during the year, but though a substantial monetary offer was made to the dismissed workers, it was rejected by the unions. The employers then made its terms available to individual employees.

The Wages Act received the royal assent in July. It made several changes relating to wages councils and removed the statutory right of manual workers to be paid in cash, while protecting them from unlawful deductions from pay. It also restricted payment of the state subsidy for statutory redundancy (severance) pay to companies with fewer than ten employees. Under discussion were proposals to link workers' pay more closely to employers' profits.

AP/WIDE WORLD

About 5,000 union members gather at Trafalgar Square in the rain to support printing workers fired when News International moved its printing to a technologically advanced plant in Wapping, East London.

United States. In the U.S. many employers continued to seek concessions from trade unions in collective bargaining. There were several disputes in the airlines industry as the carriers attempted to cut operating costs to meet the severe competition that followed deregulation. Strikes generally appeared to be on the increase.

After 30 years of industry-wide bargaining, the financially weak steel industry started company-level bargaining. The United Steelworkers of America (USW) accepted significant wage and benefit cuts, though it often secured arrangements for stock or profit sharing and some provisions concerning subcontracting, overtime work, and employment security. The leader of the industry, however, the steel-manufacturing division of USX (formerly U.S. Steel), did not open negotiations early, and no agreement had been reached when the contract ran out in July. The company declined a union offer to continue under the old contract, and 22,000 steelworkers stopped work on August 1 in what the company called a strike and the union a lockout; attempts in November to negotiate a settlement failed. The second biggest steelmaker, LTV, settled its contract with the USW in April, when the union accepted substantial cuts because of the company's difficult financial position. In July LTV filed for bankruptcy protection, and in September it moved to renegotiate the April agreement.

A bitter yearlong strike by 1,500 workers aimed at restoring a wage cut and improving working conditions at the Austin, Minn., works of the Hormel meat-processing company ended when 500 returned to work and the company hired 600 new employees. The United Food and Commercial Workers International headquarters was not satisfied with the way Local P-9 handled the dispute, and it was put under trusteeship. A new contract agreed to in August covered both the Austin and other Hormel plants. It provided for restoration of earlier wage levels, the phasing out of a two-tier wage structure, and preferential hiring for strikers who had lost their jobs. The International Typographical Union, the oldest continuous union in the U.S., merged with the Communications Workers of America.

Continental Western Europe. In West Germany a heated dispute arose concerning the provisions of Section 116 of the Promotion of Work Act, which dealt with short-time pay and unemployment benefit for workers unable to work normally because of a labour dispute elsewhere. Such payments had become an issue in the metalworkers' strike of 1984. Government proposals to restrict workers' entitlements in the case of a dispute in another region were strongly opposed by the unions, but to no avail. New legislation excluded from benefit nonstrikers working in the sector and region involved in a dispute, as well as workers in the same sector but not the same region if they stood to gain from the outcome of the dispute.

The change of government in France in March had implications for labour relations. New legislation prior to the election made it possible for industries and trade unions to negotiate a measure of flexibility in the arrangement of work time, subject to a preagreed ceiling and weekly average. The new government wanted greater flexibility, however, including provision for settlements at the corporate level. The details were left to be worked out by employers and unions, and an important agreement was made by the metal employers' federation and two trade union organizations in July. In addition to more flexibility in weekly hours, the agreement dealt with the extension of shift work, night shift work for women, overtime, and compensatory time off.

There was considerable argument about the new government's determination to abolish the extensive and cumbersome arrangements concerning administrative authorization before dismissals could be effected. A law of July 3 provided immediate relief from some of the administrative procedures. Further relaxation was scheduled for Jan. 1, 1987, but another law was envisaged on procedures for informing and consulting workers' representatives and on the establishment of plans to deal with the social effects of dismissals in enterprises where they were expected. A central employer-union agreement, reached in October 1986, provided procedures for dealing with different levels of redundancy. A decree of August 8 eased restrictions in the Labour Code relating to irregular work. Certain restrictions on the use of fixed-term and temporary contracts were lifted, and the use of part-time and intermittent contracts was facilitated. The same measure introduced new arrangements permitting certain workers to work half-time for a period preceding full retirement. Two further decrees adopted October 21 sprang from the long-standing interest of the right-wingers in workers' participation. One extended existing profit-sharing and share-ownership arrangements, and the other facilitated the appointment of employee representatives to company boards.

The Belgian government secured special powers to introduce economic reform. The normal increase in wages resulting from indexation to the cost of living was to be reduced by 2% for 1986, with the savings used to create jobs. An austerity program that included substantial cuts in public expenditure was not well received, and there were widespread strikes against it, mainly in the public sector, in May. On April 23 the National Labour Council produced a draft agreement providing extensive flexibility in working hours. The draft implied legislative changes, and agreement had to be reached at the industry or company level before the new working patterns could be introduced. If implemented, the changes would necessitate job creation. A major central agreement reached on September 11 provided a framework for the private sector for purchasing power, employment and training, and work time over the years 1987–88. It was the first agreement of its kind in more than ten years.

At a time when industrial conflict in most of the industrialized world had been declining, there was increased militancy in the traditionally peaceful Nordic countries, notably in the public sector. In Sweden it had seemed likely that bargaining in the private sector would be decentralized, but after the death of Prime Minister Olof Palme, central negotiations proved possible. Two-year agreements were reached—though not without some difficulty—for both white-collar and blue-collar workers. Negotiations in the public sector proved exceptionally difficult and were accompanied by widespread strikes in several public services until agreement was reached on October 30.

A number of industries in Norway were involved in disputes in April. Apart from pay, the principal issues were work time and the employers' desire to renegotiate the guarantee establishing a floor for industrial workers' earnings at 85% of the average industrial wage. After strikes and a lockout involving over 100,000 workers, an agreement was reached that included a reduction of working hours to 37½ a week with effect from Jan. 1, 1987. The offshore oil and gas industry also experienced a major strike and lockout in April, originating in a claim by catering workers for wage parity with oil-rig workers. In May there was a strike of public-sector employees.

Finland was also afflicted by unrest. A claim by blue-collar workers led to a stoppage in March by some 250,000 workers that lasted between two and three days. A strike by public-sector employees lasted five weeks—seven in the Helsinki area. White-collar workers generally were restive, feeling that their pay had fallen behind that of blue-collar workers. In the private sector separate agreements provided for phased reductions in working time to 1988 for white-collar workers and to 1990 for blue-collar workers.

Australia. The 1983 national pay and prices accord that had facilitated economic and employment growth without a wages explosion came under strong pressure in 1986 as world prices for many major exports fell. Continued wage restraint was crucial if industry was to remain competitive, but unions were becoming dissatisfied with the accord. It was replaced in June by a National Wage Decision that established a revised set of principles to govern wages for the next two years. It stressed the importance of national economic considerations and introduced an "incapacity to pay" principle to help employers who could not afford to pay increases that were awarded. (R. O. CLARKE)

The views expressed in this article are the author's and should not be attributed to any organization with which he may be connected.

See also Economic Affairs: *World Economy;* Industrial Review.
This article updates the *Macropædia* article WORK AND EMPLOYMENT.

Law

Court Decisions. In 1986 the various judicial tribunals throughout the world decided a number of important cases, most of which involved civil rights, government affairs, and business matters, particularly banking.

Civil Rights. In *Thornburgh* v. *American College of Obstetricians and Gynecologists,* the U.S. Supreme Court, in a 5–4 decision, held a Pennsylvania statute unconstitutional on the grounds that it required the delivery of information designed to influence a woman's informed choice between abortion and childbirth. In 1973 the court ruled in *Roe* v. *Wade* that a woman has an absolute right to an abortion under certain circumstances, but the decision recognized that the state has "an important and legitimate interest in preserving and protecting the health of the pregnant woman." Pennsylvania passed a statute that required any doctor to obtain the informed consent of the woman before performing an abortion for her. The statute specified the information that must be delivered to the woman at least 24 hours before her consent is given: (1) the name of the physician who will perform the abortion; (2) the fact that there may be detrimental physical and psychological effects that are not accurately foreseeable; (3) the particular medical risks associated with the particular abortion procedure to be employed; (4) the probable gestational age of the fetus; and (5) the medical risks associated with carrying the child to term. In addition, the statute required that the woman be told that medical assistance benefits may be available to her for prenatal and neonatal care and that the father is liable to assist in the child's support.

The majority of the court found that much of this information was designed not to inform the woman's consent but to persuade her to withhold it altogether. Moreover, the requirement that the information be given in every case, irrespective of the particular needs of the patient, intrudes upon the discretion of the pregnant woman's physician. For these reasons the court struck down the statute. The case was considered significant because of the defection of Chief Justice Warren Burger from the pro-abortion position he advanced in *Roe* v. *Wade*, reducing the court's majority on abortion questions to 5–4 from 6–3. Subsequently, however, Burger resigned from the court. He was succeeded as chief justice by Justice William Rehnquist (*see* BIOGRAPHIES), and the vacancy was filled by Antonin Scalia (*see* BIOGRAPHIES), who had been an outspoken opponent of abortion as a lower court judge.

In another case that attracted considerable attention, the Supreme Court, in *Bowers* v. *Hardwick,* sustained the constitutionality of a Georgia statute criminalizing consensual sodomy. The court held that the fact that homosexual conduct occurred in the privacy of the home did not make it legal, and it firmly rejected the principle that any kind of private sexual conduct between consenting adults is constitutionally protected. In this regard, it stated that there should be great resistance to the expansion of the due process clauses of the U.S. Constitution to cover new, allegedly fundamental rights, because such an expansion, if unchecked, could lead to the judiciary taking upon itself the power to govern the country. In a strong dissent, Justice Harry Blackmun said it was incorrect to characterize the case in terms of a fundamental right to engage in homosexual activity; rather, he opined, in the words of the late Justice Louis Brandeis, the case was about " 'the most comprehensive of rights and the right most valued by civilized men,' namely 'the right to be let alone.' "

Four other U.S. Supreme Court cases in the area of civil rights were also noteworthy. *Ford* v. *Wainwright* held that the Constitution prohibits a state from inflicting the death penalty on one who is insane. In *Batson* v. *Kentucky,* the court held that the state's privilege to dismiss potential jurors in criminal prosecutions through peremptory challenges is subject to the limitations of the equal protection clause. Both the state and the defendant may strike any potential juror for cause, and prior to *Batson* they also had certain peremptory challenges that could be used to eliminate particular jurors without any reason being given. *Batson* held, however, that peremptory challenges cannot be exercised to exclude potential jurors on account of their race. The decision did not make clear whether this limitation applies only to the prosecution or to both prosecution and defense.

Goldman v. *Weinberger* held that the First Amendment right of freedom of religion does not prevent the military from strictly enforcing uniform dress requirements. A serviceman, an Orthodox Jew and an ordained rabbi, claimed that a U.S. Air Force regulation prohibiting the wearing of headgear indoors prevented him from wearing his yarmulke and thus infringed his freedom to exercise his religious beliefs. The decision was predicated on the principle that the military must foster instinctive obedience, unity, commitment, and esprit de corps, objects requiring subordination of the individual's desires and interests to the needs of the service. Three dissenting opinions stressed that no proof had been offered to show that discipline in the armed forces would be subverted if Orthodox Jews were allowed to wear yarmulkes, and even the military must have a reasoned basis for denying members of the service their basic rights.

In *Wygant* v. *Jackson Board of Education,* the Supreme Court drew some important lines restricting the use of affirmative action in some fields. The case involved the validity of portions of a collective bargaining agreement between a local board of education and a teachers' union that gave preference to minority personnel if it became necessary to lay off teachers. Subsequently, layoffs became necessary, and nonminority teachers who were fired ahead of minority teachers complained that they had suffered discrimination on account of their race. The Supreme Court agreed and held the collective bargaining agreement illegal. It stated that, in the context of affirmative action, racial classifications must be justified by a compelling state purpose and that societal discrimination alone is insufficient to justify a racial classification. Rather, there must be convincing evidence of prior discrimination by the governmental unit involved. The court also rejected the contention that reverse discrimination was necessary in this educational context because "role models" were needed for minority schoolchildren.

At least two important civil rights cases were handed down by the courts of other nations. The Supreme Court of India set aside a sentence of public hanging, stating that everyone has a right to die with dignity. The decision embraced the U.S. constitutional principle that there should be no cruel or unusual punishment and thus had a potential impact broader than the facts of the particular case. In Switzerland the Federal Court of Cassation held a policeman criminally liable for firing at a fleeing motorist suspected of an offense against property, as opposed to an offense against a person. The court said that the activities of the police must square with the principle of proportionality.

Government Affairs. Major political news was made in the U.S. during the year when the Supreme Court declared the Balanced Budget and Emergency Deficit Control (Gramm-Rudman-Hollings) Act of 1985 unconstitutional. This act established the maximum federal deficit for each of the fiscal years 1986 through 1991, and if the budget for a fiscal year exceeded the prescribed maximum, across-the-board cuts were mandated. Under the procedure set forth in the act, Congress would report its deficit estimates and program-by-program budget-reduction calculations to the comptroller general, who, after reviewing them, would report his conclusions to the president. The president, in turn, would mandate the cuts as specified by the comptroller, and his order would become effective unless, within a specified time, Congress legislated its own reductions. In *Bowsher* v. *Synar,* the Supreme Court declared this approach unconstitutional because of the authority vested in the comptroller general to execute the law. The Office of Comptroller was created by Congress, and the comptroller is an arm of the Congress. The court said that by giving executive power to the comptroller, Gramm-Rudman violated the constitutional command that Congress play no role in the execution of the laws. Although the decision made headline news, legal scholars found it a rather routine and pedestrian exposition of the firmly established constitutional doctrine of separation of powers.

The Federal Court of Switzerland refused to permit a Thai family to attach the bank accounts of the U.S.S.R. in Geneva for damages caused by the death of a family member when a Soviet military plane shot down a South Korean commercial airliner in 1983. The court held that the Soviet accounts were protected by the doctrine of sovereign immunity.

Business and Banking. In *FDIC* v. *Philadelphia Gear Corp.,* the U.S. Supreme Court held that standby letters of credit are not insured by federal deposit insurance, even though the statute establishing the Federal Deposit Insurance Corporation specifically lists "letters of credit" as one kind of item covered. The court found that this language was intended to give coverage to "documentary letters of credit" but not to standby letters of credit, pointing out that documentary letters were the only kind known when Congress enacted the statute in 1933. The case had major implications in the U.S., where over $200 billion of standby letters had been issued by banks.

In another important decision affecting banks and business in the U.S., the Supreme Court held in *Board of Governors* v. *Dimension Financial Corp.* that the Federal Reserve Board had no authority to promulgate a regulation that would limit the activities of so-called nonbank banks. For some purposes, Congress defined a "bank" as an institution that accepts demand deposits and makes commercial loans. Because of the way the law is phrased, enterprises may conduct either of these activities without being subject to bank regulations, as long as they do not engage in both. The Federal Reserve Board tried to curtail the growth and power of these nonbank banks by redefining "bank" so as to include them, but the court held that the board had acted beyond the scope of its statutory authority.

In Great Britain the government's plan to denationalize its banks was aided by a decision from its highest court, the House of Lords, that the assets of a bank do not belong to its depositors. A creditor-debtor relationship exists between a bank and those who deposit money in it. Since the bank becomes the owner of deposited money, the ownership of the bank can be transferred without the consent of its depositors. (WILLIAM D. HAWKLAND)

International Law. *International Violence.* Of the two major wars being carried on in 1986, the Soviet intervention in Afghanistan did not give rise to any new legal issues. The Iran-Iraq war, however, continued to cause concern over the laws of neutrality and the use of poison gas. Although many neutral vessels in the Gulf of Sidra were correctly stopped by Iranian warships and searched for contraband, there were also many instances of direct air attack on such ships in international waters without a request to stop and be searched. Neutral states themselves, however, showed little inclination to observe the rules of neutrality in their trading policies. It seemed that states, and scholars, had lost their familiarity with the laws of war generally and that the rules were being kept alive only in naval tradition and practice.

Claims that Iraq was using mustard and nerve gas against Iranian troops increased; the supporting evidence became conclusive and led to a condemnation of Iraq by the UN Security Council. As a step toward improving control generally, the Canadian government submitted to the UN secretary-general a *Handbook for the Investigation of Allegations of the Use of Chemical or Biological Weapons.* Many countries imposed bans on the export of chemicals used in making such weapons, and a "warning list" of "dual use" chemicals was drawn up and introduced in 18 Organization for Economic Cooperation and Development countries, the European Communities (EC), the U.S., Canada, Japan, Australia, and New Zealand. The U.S.S.R. put forward proposals at the UN Disarmament Conference, in line with previous U.S. proposals, for a new treaty to supplement the 1925 Geneva Protocol on chemical warfare. However, extensive production of chemical weapons in the U.S. and proposals for their future deployment led to concern within NATO.

The treatment of prisoners of war was described by the president of the International Committee of the Red Cross as having deteriorated over the previous five years. The Geneva Conventions were not being observed in Iraq, Iran, Lebanon, Western Sahara (where a wall built by Morocco to keep out Polisario guerrillas had brought the ten-year war into stalemate), Chad, Ethiopia, Somalia, Angola, Kampuchea, Afghanistan, and other parts of the world.

Unlawful state violence persisted. South African troops made raids into Angola, Swaziland, Lesotho, Botswana, Zimbabwe, and Zambia. Nicaraguan troops made incursions into Honduras, and troops from Zaire entered Uganda. Israeli aircraft seized a Libyan civilian plane in international airspace east of Cyprus and forced it to land in Israel for inspection. The UN Interim Force in Lebanon (UNIFIL) came under increasing attack, and some French and Irish soldiers were killed. This led to renewed questioning, particularly in French circles, of the function of UNIFIL and the way it was being deployed.

The aftermath of an earlier example of state violence, the French attack on the Greenpeace environmental organization's ship *Rainbow Warrior* in New Zealand's Auckland Harbour in 1985, reached a conclusion in July 1986. France made a formal admission of responsibility and a public apology and paid New Zealand $7 million in damages. In return, the two French agents convicted by the New Zealand courts in connection with the incident were released into French custody (and detention on a French Pacific island for three years).

The most dramatic examples of state violence during the year were the air and sea battle in March in the disputed Gulf of Sidra between U.S. and Libyan forces and the controversial air raid on Tripoli and Benghazi by U.S. planes the following month. (*See* WORLD AFFAIRS [Middle East and North Africa]: *Libya.*) The raid was justified by the U.S. on the basis of Article 51 of the UN Charter as self-defense against state terrorism emanating from Libya and involving danger to and murder of U.S. citizens in Europe.

International Adjudication. In June the International Court of Justice delivered its judgment on Nicaragua's suit against the U.S., finding that the U.S. had breached customary international law and the U.S.-Nicaragua Treaty of Friendship by directly attacking Nicaraguan territory in 1983–84, by training, arming, and supplying the rebel *contra* forces, and by laying mines in Nicaraguan waters. The U.S. declared that it was not bound by the judgment and would ignore it; a Nicaraguan motion in the UN Security Council to enforce the judgment was vetoed by the U.S.

The International Court of Justice delivered a further judgment in the Tunisia-Libya continental shelf dispute in December 1985, holding that Tunisia's request for revision

AP/WIDE WORLD

Nicaragua's legal counsel, Alain Pellet (left) and Ian Brownlie, await the verdict of the International Court of Justice in the 26-month-old case *Nicaragua* v. *United States*. The outcome favoured Nicaragua on most counts against U.S. aid for Nicaraguan rebels.

of the court's 1982 judgment was inadmissible; but it interpreted that judgment, on points of detailed mapping, in favour of Libya and reiterated that the parties were obliged to negotiate a treaty themselves to settle the boundary definitively. Nicaragua introduced two actions before the International Court—against Honduras and Costa Rica—alleging intervention in its internal civil war, and the court called upon Burkina Faso and Mali to withdraw their troops from disputed border territory. El Salvador and Honduras, unable to agree on parts of their border and sovereignty over the island of Meanguera, signed a formal agreement to submit their dispute to the court.

The U.S.-Iran Claims Tribunal continued to produce decisions. Its interlocutory award in *Sedco Inc.* v. *National Iranian Oil Co.* contained a lengthy analysis of the customary international law standard for compensation in case of expropriation. The previous year the English High Court, in *Dallal* v. *Bank Mellat,* had recognized the jurisdiction of the tribunal and refused to allow an unsuccessful U.S. claimant to relitigate his claim in the U.K. Egypt and Israel agreed on the terms of arbitration over the disputed Taba region at the head of the Gulf of Aqaba.

Territory. Territorial adjustments and sovereignty featured prominently in the year's events. The Marshall Islands, the Federated States of Micronesia, and the Northern Marianas, administered for 39 years by the U.S. as a UN trust territory, were given semi-independence with the U.S. recognizing their sovereignty but retaining responsibility for defense. (*See* WORLD AFFAIRS: *Dependent States.*) Border delimitation treaties were signed or ratified between Sweden and Finland, France and Italy, and Norway and the U.S.S.R., but disputes between China and India and Guatemala and Belize continued under discussion. Cross-border damage on a large scale was caused by the nuclear power plant explosion at Chernobyl in the Ukraine, U.S.S.R., which polluted the air and grass of most of Europe, and the chemical plant fire in Basel, Switz., which seriously contaminated the Rhine. State liability for compensation in both cases was mooted but remained uncertain.

At sea, territorial sovereignty continued to be infringed by Soviet submarines in Swedish waters and by unidentified submarines in Norwegian fjords. The problem of busy covert submarine traffic through international waters in the Irish Sea causing damage to fishing vessels was raised by Ireland in the International Maritime Organization. Norwegian authorities claimed that civilian vessels required advance permission to enter territorial waters, and the Greenpeace ship *Moby Dick* was prosecuted for entering without a permit. On the other hand, the U.S. asserted (against Soviet protests) that its warships had the right of innocent passage through Soviet territorial waters in the Black Sea, and it used armed force to deny Libyan claims to exclusive use of the Gulf of Sidra as territorial waters. Canada formally reasserted its claim to full sovereignty over the Canadian Arctic Archipelago and over the archipelagic waters, including the Northwest Passage, as internal waters.

Chile claimed a 350-mi continental shelf around Easter Island and the islands of Sala y Gomez. Mexico passed an act on its maritime boundaries laying down a territorial sea of 12 mi measured from a combination of natural and straight baselines, a contiguous zone of an additional 12 mi, an economic zone out to 200 mi, and a continental shelf of the same extent or up to the continental terrace, whichever was farther. Belgium announced its intention to increase its territorial waters to 12 mi and was preparing to negotiate on its continental shelf limits on the basis of the 1982 Law of the Sea Convention. France altered its economic zone law to forbid any marine research within the 200-mi limit except with a permit. Sweden's continuing dispute with the U.S.S.R. over the continental shelf boundary east of Gotland gave rise to a number of incidents but little progress. The U.K. established a 150-mi fishery protection zone around the Falkland Islands/Islas Malvinas, over protests from Argentina, which had signed fishing treaties with the U.S.S.R. and Bulgaria covering the disputed waters. In the Pacific the U.S. concluded a treaty with the 16 member states of the South Pacific Forum to allow U.S. tuna fishing within the latter's 200-mi fishing limits. (*See* WORLD AFFAIRS [Oceania]: *Oceanian Affairs.*) The U.S. hoped to prevent fishery agreements from being concluded or renewed with the U.S.S.R. Piracy continued off Thailand and the Philippines. Pirates attacked a freighter in Freetown Harbour, Sierra Leone, and Polisario Front guerrillas attacked a Spanish merchant ship en route for the Canaries, killing one crew member.

Diplomatic Immunity. Abuse of diplomatic immunity continued to cause concern, particularly in connection with the growing phenomenon of "state terrorism." The scanning of diplomatic bags by metal detectors was introduced by Italy, the first country to do so. The use of the French diplomatic bag to carry circulars from French trade unions was queried in the French Senate, but assurances were given that no abuse of the facility would be allowed. The perennial problem of diplomatic parking offenses improved in the U.K., with only 33,904 unpaid parking fines for the year, compared with 92,285 for the previous period; however, use of wheel-clamping devices on diplomatic vehicles was regarded as contrary to the Vienna Convention and was not done. Under a new policy of notifying persistent nonpayers that they were jeopardizing their diplomatic status, 57 letters were sent by the U.K. government requesting the repatriation of offenders unless their parking fines were paid.

During the first nine months of 1986, 13 diplomats were removed from the U.K., accused of serious offenses. In November a large number of bugging devices were found in the Swedish embassy in Moscow, and a strong protest was made to the Soviet government against such a flagrant breach of the Vienna Convention. In Chile a Dutch embassy car driven by the cultural attaché was attacked by armed police, the diplomats were threatened, and four Chilean students were forcibly removed; a strong protest was made by The Netherlands to the Chilean government. The status of missions accredited to the UN in New York was the subject of a careful statement by the U.S. legal counsel in connection with a request by the U.S. for a reduction in the size of the Soviet mission.

(NEVILLE MARCH HUNNINGS)

See also Crime, Law Enforcement, and Penology; World Affairs: *United Nations.*

This article updates the *Macropædia* articles CONSTITUTIONAL LAW; INTERNATIONAL LAW.

Libraries

Public libraries in 1986 continued to be under considerable financial pressure. In the less developed countries, particularly in Africa, there was a lack of funds being allocated for the purchase of books or journals. As a result, scholars and scientists, administrators, and educators became more isolated from their fields of study. In the developed industrialized countries libraries were suffering for two reasons. In the educational and scientific spheres, they were vulnerable to financial cutbacks because of their status as a general service rather than a central administrative service that had its own administrative cadre to maintain payrolls, buildings, and so forth. Second, the efficiency of public libraries was rarely a high priority for the electorate, so library deficiencies did not evoke voters' reactions in the same way that a lack of fire-fighting services, water, or sewerage services would.

Because of this, in the U.K. the British Library produced a strategic plan that aimed to eliminate duplication and waste and produce a better service at lower cost. To this end it organized itself into two principal units—Humanities and Social Sciences and Science and Technology. In Belgium the Royal Library was in dire financial straits; the bulletin boards that announced recent acquisitions were bare; offices were empty because staff had not been replaced; and many periodical subscriptions had been discontinued because of the lack of financial resources.

All libraries, however, were not in such a poor state, and the resources made available continued to depend very often on local interest and attitudes as well as on the ability of the library director to persuade governing bodies (university councils, government departments, local government authorities, research institutes) to allocate funds for staff, acquisitions, and modernization. In spite of financial restrictions, libraries in many countries had funds allocated for computerization.

In addition to their becoming more aware of the difficulties of funding acquisitions, librarians became increasingly aware of the importance of conserving their materials, and preservation became one of the ongoing programs of the International Federation of Library Associations and Institutions (IFLA). It was noteworthy that the British Library in recent months had been spending more on preservation than on acquisition. Preservation was no longer seen as appropriate only for the rare printed books of the 15th to the 17th century—though they maintained their importance. An even bigger problem in terms of volume concerned books of the previous 150 years, which were printed on acid chemical paper and therefore were likely to disintegrate in the near future. This stock of books constituted the major portion of the world's active library stocks. The British Library Association devoted its major conference in 1986 to conservation, thus underlining the importance of the topic to all kinds of libraries. The Ratcliffe Report in Britain exposed the vast problem that faced libraries, and the British Library set up a National Preservation Office.

In spite of the constraints imposed on them, public libraries continued to develop special services—for commerce and industry, ethnic minorities, the disadvantaged, the specialist research worker, the educator, and the student—and were becoming increasingly innovative. They were also facing absorption into the wider area of information—international data bases, information specialists of numerous kinds—and competition in the supply of services from information brokers and consultants in the private sector. (P. HAVARD-WILLIAMS)

Attracted by the enormous data-storage capacity of new laser optical media, libraries in the U.S. began using compact disc-read only memory (CD-ROM) publications as tools for reference services as well as for bibliographic management. (*See* INFORMATION PROCESSING: *Sidebar.*) Of all CD-ROM publications available in June, some 25% were for library applications. By the year's end Pennsylvanians could search from among 653,000 titles in a hundred library locations by inserting one disk in a local personal computer. A Minnesota project was under way to link the collections of 450 school libraries through CD-ROM technology.

Smoke billows from the Los Angeles Public Library on April 29 in one of the worst library fires in the history of the U.S. There was another fire at the same library on September 3.

AP/WIDE WORLD

Academic library users kept up with high-tech catalogs and on-line data bases through ambitious "information literacy" training programs such as that pioneered at Cornell University's Mann Library, Ithaca, N.Y. A new communications network at Lehigh University, Bethlehem, Pa., linked every office, laboratory, classroom, and student resident room to the library's on-line catalog. Cooperative programs among public libraries helped U.S. circulation rise 1.8% to approximately 1,150,000,000; operating expenditures increased 9.7% to some $2,760,000,000.

A grave loss of about 400,000 books and damage to a million more resulted from one of the nation's worst library fires, April 29 at the Los Angeles Public Library, and a second fire there September 3. The historic Central Library survived the two arson fires and was to be restored as planned in a major redevelopment project. Other library woes included severe funding cutbacks in oil-producing states and illegal sit-ins at the Library of Congress in protest against reduced public hours. That library's collections were enriched, however, by 20,000 early television programs donated by NBC.

New York State's $74 million allocation was the nation's highest state aid to libraries. The Boston Public Library announced a $50 million fund-raising campaign, and the New York Public Library began a five-year, $307 million campaign; both libraries, as in Atlanta (Ga.) in 1985, won landmark 1986 funding as well for major improvements. The San Jose (Calif.) Public Library opened its Silicon Valley Information Center, an innovative venture to serve the community's industrial interests.

During the year the U.S. Department of Education announced that in 1985–86 an estimated 93% of the nation's public elementary and secondary schools reported having library media centres, up from 85% in 1978. In the annual American Association of School Librarians/Britannica Companies competition, honours for the best school library media program in the U.S. went to School District 108 of Highland Park, Ill. (ARTHUR PLOTNIK)

This article updates the *Macropædia* article LIBRARIES AND LIBRARY SCIENCE.

Life Sciences

The Reagan administration in June 1986 announced a broad, complex program for overseeing U.S. genetic engineering research and biotechnology that could influence future biotechnology regulation policies throughout much of the world. Under the program, which comprised a coordinated framework of definitions, rules, and guidelines, biotechnology companies would be asked to submit most of their products—including drugs, vaccines, and pesticides—to one or more federal agencies for review, while scientists wishing to test engineered bacteria, plants, or other organisms in the environment would need federal approval. The new regulations expanded and consolidated a patchwork of rules and interim policies that had been instituted since the mid-1970s in attempts to keep pace with the country's rapidly maturing biotechnology industry. Responsibility for reviewing new biotechnology products went to the Food and Drug Administration, the Department of Agriculture, the Environmental Protection Agency, and the Occupational Safety and Health Administration, whereas the task of overseeing genetic engineering research fell to the National Institutes of Health, the National Science Foundation, and the Department of Agriculture.

Reaction of scientists, legislators, and public interest groups to the announcement was mixed. Some doubted the program's ability to protect the environment; others felt that certain potentially harmful organisms could escape adequate review. The biotechnology industry expressed some relief in getting a clearer picture of the regulatory approval process but was concerned about the program's vagueness in assigning agency jurisdiction and about its interpretation of such terms as pathogen, environmental release, and containment. (CHARLES M. CEGIELSKI)

ZOOLOGY

Zoologists used modern technology and field observations during 1986 to understand the behavioural, ecological, and physiological relationships of animal species. Biochemical genetics, fossil findings, and field investigations provided insight into the animal kingdom.

Fascinating information about the sensory capabilities of animals was revealed for a diverse array of species. Katharine Payne of Cornell University, Ithaca, N.Y., and associates discovered that various members of an elephant herd commonly produce low-frequency sounds (14–24 hertz) that may function in social communication. The sounds are inaudible to humans, whose detection range normally does not extend below 30 hertz. Communication by sound may also occur on a regular basis among American alligators. Observations in the Okefenokee Swamp in Florida by Howard Hunt of the Atlanta (Ga.) Zoo showed that many sounds other than the often-heard distress signals of young alligators and the bellows of the males are uttered by all sizes of both sexes. These gregarious reptiles apparently have a more complex social structure than originally believed, and the sounds are presumably used for information exchange among individuals. From experiments with eastern red-spotted newts, John B. Phillips of Cornell found that these migratory salamanders are capable of using the Earth's magnetic field to orient on long treks. Although local landmarks and other cues may also be employed, the salamanders rely on magnetic guidance, as do certain migratory birds.

The first report of the ability of a mammal to detect low-level electric fields came from Henning Scheich of the Technical University, Darmstadt, West Germany, and colleagues in experiments with duckbill platypuses. When active, low-voltage, dry-cell batteries were placed in underwater locations in a laboratory pool, the platypuses sought them out, preferring them to either dead batteries or pieces of shrimp tail. A foraging platypus presumably can detect low-level electrical emissions from the muscles of aquatic crustaceans and small vertebrates, its primary foods. Praying mantises, originally believed to have no sense of hearing, were found able to detect ultrasonic sounds. Cornell investigators David D. Yager and Ronald R. Hoy discovered a structure on the insect's underside that is used for hearing high-frequency sounds, especially those made by flying bats, major predators of some mantises.

A topic in evolutionary ecology was addressed by Richard Shine of the University of Sydney through field research on the file snake, a heavy-bodied species of tropical Australia. File snakes display sexual dimorphism in that females are much larger than males. Charles Darwin theorized that in species that show sexual dimorphism a process known as sexual selection operates on traits that give individuals a competitive reproductive advantage. By contrast, some modern investigators consider that sexual dimorphism results primarily from natural selection operating on behavioural or ecological differences between the sexes. In file snakes larger females have more young and therefore a reproductive advantage, supporting the hypothesis that sexual selection favors large females and consequently results in larger females than males. On the other hand, differences between the two sexes in head size and choice of prey support the hypothesis that sexual dimorphism in some traits is unrelated to reproduction and can be explained by ecological differences between the sexes. One interpretation of the study is that sexual selection is responsible for the initial differentiation in a trait but that, once the sexes of a species have diverged, natural selection operates on traits independently in the two sexes in a manner unrelated to reproduction.

Zoologists of the world continued efforts to determine the phylogenetic relationships and origins of species. The use of modern genetic approaches may have provided an answer for pandas. Stephen J. O'Brien and colleagues from the National Cancer Institute in Maryland and the National Zoological Park, Washington, D.C., examined molecular and genetic evidence from lesser and giant pandas and resolved that the Chinese mammals are less closely related than originally suspected. According to the research team's findings, raccoons and bears branched into two lineages more than 30 million years ago. The lesser panda split from the raccoon line at some later time, and about 20 million years ago the giant panda diverged from the bears as a separate lineage. Thus, lesser pandas are more closely related to raccoons, whereas giant pandas' closest relatives are the bears. Another Chinese mammal, the takin, a hoofed animal of mountain forests, drew recent attention because of its rarity and little-known biology. Field observations of this endangered species by George B. Schaller of the New York Zoological Society revealed that several thousand animals, often in herds, live in the panda preserves of northern Sichuan (Szechwan). Their closest relatives were believed to be musk oxen.

A previously unknown echinoderm—a member of the phylum that includes starfish, sea urchins, and sea cucumbers—was discovered in a piece of sunken driftwood on the seafloor off the New Zealand coast by Alan Baker and Helen Clark of the National Museum of New Zealand and Francis Rowe of the Australian Museum in Sydney. This marine invertebrate, christened a sea daisy, measured no more than nine millimetres (a third of an inch) across

The lesser panda (left) and giant panda had their ancestry clarified. A study of genes and proteins from pandas, raccoons, and bears showed the two animals to be less closely related than scientists had thought they were.

NATIONAL ZOOLOGICAL PARK; PHOTOGRAPHS, JESSIE COHEN

its fringed, disk-shaped body but appeared so specialized anatomically that an entirely new class was devised for it.

Opportunities to define phylogenetic relationships of certain major groups came from fossil discoveries. A fossil lower jaw reported from 100 million-year-old Early Cretaceous rocks in Utah by Jeffrey Eaton of the University of Colorado and Richard Cifelli of the Museum of Northern Arizona could represent the oldest marsupial known. South American marsupial fossils were several million years younger, and those from Australia were even more recent. Michael Archer of the University of New South Wales and colleagues found the oldest known fossil of a monotreme—a member of the group to which duck-bill platypuses belong—in Early Cretaceous sediments in Australia. The discoveries should provide insight into the phylogenetic relationships among marsupials, monotremes, and placental mammals. Fossil finds from the Middle Cambrian (more than 500 million years ago) in British Columbia by Desmond H. Collins of the Royal Ontario Museum, Toronto, and in Utah by Richard A. Robison of the University of Kansas confirmed that most invertebrate animal groups were present in Cambrian seas. The discoveries, which included numerous species of both known and previously unknown groups of invertebrates, allowed a unique look into the early evolution of higher life on Earth.

Endangered and threatened species continued to be of great interest to zoologists. Because only three adult California condors were alive in the wild at the beginning of the year, the U.S. Fish and Wildlife Service was given legal authorization to capture them for a captive breeding program. An egg removed from the last known natural nest of North America's largest bird was hatched in captivity in early summer. Biologic evidence suggested that many of the wild condors had died from consuming lead shot in the dead animals that they normally feed on. Nevertheless, prospects looked bright for the captive rearing of condors and their eventual release into the wild.

An attempt at replacing lost habitat for a threatened species, the wood stork, appeared to have succeeded in the southeastern U.S. Malcolm Coulter and Bill McCort of the Savannah River Ecology Laboratory, Aiken, S.C., reported that a wetland foraging habitat was created at Kathwood Lake (Silver Bluff Plantation Sanctuary, Jackson, S.C.) in the vicinity of the most northern and inland colony of wood storks. Loss of foraging habitat was considered the major cause of decline in wood stork numbers because of their requirement for shallow, productive waters to obtain fish and other aquatic prey. By regulating water levels and concentrating fish at Kathwood Lake, researchers attracted a large portion of the birds from the colony to the newly created foraging site. This success gave impetus to the concept of environmental mitigation as an approach to saving declining populations of some species.

Research on sea turtles, a group endangered or threatened throughout most of the world, led to a better understanding of their life history and ecology. Most sea turtle information had been obtained from adult females that come ashore for nesting and from the eggs they lay. Studies by Nat Frazer of Mercer University, Macon, Ga., on longevity and growth of loggerhead turtles confirmed the expected long life span (60 years or more) and slow growth to maturity (12–30 years) of these marine reptiles and provided evidence that as few as one egg in a thousand laid survives to become an adult turtle. Such information was needed to develop proper management and protection plans for species whose biology was poorly known.

(J. WHITFIELD GIBBONS)

Entomology. During the year an expedition of beekeepers from Canada, the U.S., and Mexico, led by Orley Taylor of the University of Kansas, investigated the spread of the Africanized honeybee north of Panama. Beekeepers were justifiably sensitive about references to "killer bees," which also amused residents of countries where the original African bees were endemic, and resented being blamed for the problems that had arisen in the Americas since a few swarms of African bees had been accidentally released from an experimental breeding program in Brazil in 1957. Since then, however, the honey industry in the Americas had been seriously affected wherever the bees had spread. A commission set up when the bees were first observed in the Canal Zone in 1982 destroyed over 5,000 swarms, but its work did not prevent the spread of the bees into Central America.

Africanized bees work poor sources of nectar on which the European honeybee cannot survive without food supplementation, but they also rob the hives of the European bee, which can be found starving next to thriving Africanized bee colonies. Africanized bees are more difficult to work because of their violent reaction to interference and their ability to follow and sting victims for nearly a kilometer (half a mile). The Africanized bee stores less honey than its European counterpart, produces more brood, and is more ready to swarm. Breeding experiments to date had not produced a hybrid between the Africanized and European bees that combined their favourable characteristics and an ability to compete with feral Africanized bees. From Panama to Costa Rica, wherever the bees had become established, beekeeping and honey production had fallen dramatically.

Those beekeepers who were determined to meet the challenge learned to handle the bees, however, and even to exploit their working and rearing characteristics by selling pollen and royal jelly (a substance fed to future queens) to supplement reduced income from honey production. North American beekeepers concluded that further spread of the Africanized bee was inevitable. Both the public and the honey industry would be best served if resources were concentrated on training a body of professional apiarists who could manage the bees and on furthering genetic research through which to tame and harness the invaders.

Onchocerciasis (river blindness) is one of the insect-borne scourges of tropical Africa. Minute embryonic forms, called microfilariae, breed from nematodes (roundworms) transmitted to humans by *Simulium damnosum,* a blackfly, the larvae of which live in running water. The worms invade eye tissues, where their effects are cumulative; in some areas of West Africa, more than 5% of the population eventually become blind as a result. Since the heyday of insecticidal campaigns against malarial mosquitoes in the 1950s, programs for the control or eradication of insect pests in third world countries had achieved scant success, but the program against *Simulium,* started in 1970, was at last proving effective. The Onchocerciasis Control Program embraced the countries of the Volta River basin and had its headquarters at Ouagadougou, Burkina Faso. According to the Gambian physician who directed the program, success was due to spraying rivers and streams with an especially effective strain of the insecticidal bacterium *Bacillus thuringiensis,* to treatment of patients with a semisynthetic filaricide developed from a soil organism, *Streptomyces avermitilis,* and above all to the military precision with which survey and treatment teams coordinated and performed their work.

Copidosomopsis tanytmemus is a small parasitic wasp that lays its eggs in those of the European flour moth. The wasp eggs remain dormant until the moth caterpillar hatches. Thereafter, in a process known as polyembryony that is confined to a few such parasites, the embryo splits into a ball of cells, each of which develops into a separate larva. What makes *C. tanytmemus* and a few related species even more remarkable, however, is that some of these larvae grow a precociously developed head and jaws and are unusually mobile, although they are so poorly developed in other respects that they cannot survive long. In the past they had been considered nonfunctional genetic aberrations.

This is not so, according to Y. P. Cruz of the University of California at Berkeley, who discovered such larvae in the act of attacking parasites of other families of wasps when multiparasitism of the flour moth caterpillar had occurred. This was not the only example of what Cruz called "ultimate altruism" in the insect world. Shigeyuki Aoki of Hokkaido University, Japan, had some years previously described species of colonial aphids that produce warrior, first-stage larvae unable to develop further and apparently devoted to protecting their fellows from predators. Whereas there was at least a possibility of genetic diversity in the aphid colonies to account for the separate development of warrior larvae, none seemed possible in the cloned, polyembryonic wasp larvae. Thus, how such "soldiers" are determined remained unexplained, but Cruz thought that the reason for their existence was related to the protection of a shared genome (set of genes). (PETER W. MILES)

WHO; PHOTOGRAPH, W. IMBER

A helicopter lays a swath of insecticide spray over a potential blackfly breeding site in an attempt to control onchocerciasis, known as river blindness. The disease, a scourge of tropical Africa, is caused by nematode worms transmitted to humans by blackfly bites.

This article updates the *Macropædia* article INSECTS.

Ornithology. The 19th International Ornithological Congress, held in Ottawa in 1986, proved to be the best attended ornithological meeting in history, with no fewer than 1,200 bird scientists present. The president, Klaus Immelmann of West Germany, discussed ornithology as an interdisciplinary science. Another of the five plenary speakers, Peter Berthold, also of West Germany, held the rapt attention of his audience with an exposition of the mechanisms that control the migration of European warblers. The start of preparation for migration (for example, molt and putting on fat as fuel) is triggered genetically; the actual time of departure is triggered by changes in day length acting through the eye on the brain; and the knowledge of directions to take and of resting places to be used is under endogenous control.

Just how stay-at-home bird species like titmice, which are about the size of warblers, cope with winter weather was reported by Randi Reinertsen of Norway. The smaller a bird is, the more difficulty it has in withstanding the cold. The willow tit, the smallest bird to winter north of the Arctic Circle, has a multifaceted survival kit for coping with the long, cold boreal nights in particular. First, it finds a tree cavity (a close relative in Siberia digs a snow hole). Second, because heat escapes faster through "horn" than through feathers, it tucks its beak in its shoulder feathers and squats in order to cover its legs with its body feathers; in this way it traps a thicker layer of warm air next to its body. Third and most remarkable of all, the bird actually lowers its body temperature so that it requires less heat.

In the same way that the tit puts on fat for the winter, so does the ptarmigan, a snow grouse that spends the winter farther north than any other bird—for example, on the Svalbard archipelago (Spitsbergen), north of Norway. These birds put on an extra 35% above normal weight to help them through a particularly difficult period centred around December 21, when even at midday there is barely enough light by which to feed. The birds are so close to the North Pole that at this time the Moon's light may be more important than the negligible amount of sunlight reflected from the sky.

English gardeners had long noticed that some holly trees keep their berries throughout the winter while others lose their fruit early on. New research showed that mistle thrush commandeer a holly in autumn, defend it as a larder all winter, and even feed their young on any remaining berries in the spring. Ivy and mistletoe might be similarly defended, but not as frequently as holly. To be suitable for defense, a holly tree must be freestanding and of manageable size. It is worthwhile for the thrush to establish and maintain ownership of a holly tree because the fruits last almost unaltered for nearly nine months, neither shriveling nor rotting. In severe weather a mistle thrush sometimes exhausts itself trying to defend its food supply against flocks of Eurasian redwings and eventually loses control of the tree.

Migrating birds were known to employ more than one direction-finding method, including orientation by the Sun by day and by the stars at night. Some scientists believed that odours also help birds to orient. During the year the case for birds' use of the Earth's magnetic field as a kind of

An artist's reconstruction of *Protoavis* is based on two fossil skeletons found in western Texas. The bird could prove to be the oldest known.

DRAWING BY MICHAEL W. NICKELL

map was strengthened when workers at the State University of New York at Geneseo found deposits of magnetite, an iron oxide sensitive to magnetism, in the cranium of the bobolink; the most likely reason for its presence seemed to be for use in way finding.

Three species thought to be extinct were rediscovered during 1986. The long-lost Jerdon's courser, last recorded in 1900, was found in Andhra Pradesh, India. In Thailand, Gurney's pitta, a member of the attractive family of jewelthrushes, was seen for the first time in 34 years. The ivory-billed woodpecker, apparently not seen since 1974, was found in a pine forest in Cuba.

The discovery of a brand-new old bird was also announced during the year. Two fragmentary fossil skeletons found in the arid badlands of western Texas were christened *Protoavis* because the birdlike animal they represent appeared to have lived 70 million years before *Archaeopteryx.* The species was believed to have been contemporaneous with the earliest dinosaurs. If its discoverer's claims stood the test of time, *Protoavis* could replace *Archaeopteryx* as the best known forerunner of the birds. But *Archaeopteryx,* while it might eventually be supplanted, was unlikely to be discarded altogether, despite claims made in the past two years that the feather impressions of the specimen in the British Museum had been faked by pressing bird feathers into a limestone paste around a genuine reptilian fossil. Responding to the charges, a team of paleontologists from the British Museum undertook a careful analysis of the fossil using microscopy and ultraviolet photography, from which they concluded that *Archaeopteryx* is completely authentic. (JEFFERY BOSWALL)

This article updates the *Macropædia* article BIRDS.

MARINE BIOLOGY

The newly established international Ecology Institute awarded its first prizes in 1986. They went to Tom Fenchel of Denmark for his studies of the "microbial loop" in marine ecosystems, which opened up a new research field, and to Colleen Cavanaugh of the U.S., who was the first to show that the nutrition of marine animals near hydrothermal vents and other sulfide-rich habitats depended upon symbiotic, chemoautotrophic, sulfur bacteria.

At diving stations in the Baltic Sea, the lower depth limit of the brown alga *Fucus vesiculosus* was shown to be 8.5 m (27.9 ft) in 1984, compared with 11.5 m (37.7 ft) in 1944. Deepest specimens at 8.5 m in 1984 had the same dwarfed appearance as those at 11.5 m in 1944, when growth at 8.5 m was luxuriant. Changes were attributed to decreased water transparency following man's increased nutrient input. The abundance of dog whelks (snails of the genus *Nucella*) near centres of boating and shipping in the U.K. was found to have declined markedly since the early 1970s; tributyltin, a popular pesticide in antifouling paints, was implicated. Eelgrass (*Zostera*) in the Great Bay estuary of the U.S. decreased dramatically between 1981 and 1984. Isolated from eelgrass tissue was *Labyrinthula,* a slime mold associated with *Zostera* wasting disease, which had devastated populations on both sides of the Atlantic in the 1930s.

Shipboard and satellite data were combined during the year in synoptic studies of marine birds and mammals. Seabirds showed a strong preference for particular water masses associated with frontal eddies in the Gulf Stream, and cetaceans were more abundant in chlorophyll-rich waters off California. Close-range photographs of humpback whales were taken in the central and eastern North Pacific from 1977 to 1983. The stock was found to be organized into several geographically isolated feeding herds that intermingle on wintering grounds near Hawaii and Mexico but show strong preference for localized feeding areas off Alaska or central California.

Earlier hydrographic research had revealed a marked layering in the Black Sea, with fresher water at the surface and stagnant, more saline water containing hydrogen sulfide at depth. Recent Soviet studies conducted from the manned submersible *Argus* showed that optimal conditions for marine plankton were correspondingly sharply constrained. Dense concentrations of the ctenophore (comb jelly) *Pleurobrachia pileus,* the copepod crustacean *Calanus helgolandicus,* and the chaetognath (arrowworm) *Sagitta setosa* occurred in separate, narrow layers at middle depths. Studies of vertical migration of larvae of the crab *Rhithropanopeus* suggested a combination of two alternative hypotheses explaining such migration in plankton. At sunrise and throughout the day, larvae were associated with an isolume, a boundary defined by points of equal light intensity, with high light levels acting as a barrier to upward movement; at sunset the rate and direction of change of light intensity initiated upward movement.

Simultaneous studies of corals over extensive areas of the Great Barrier Reef off Queensland, Australia, demonstrated synchronous spawning by many species of widely different coral types, a phenomenon apparently unique in marine communities. In the deepwater coral *Leptoseris,* pigments were found that emitted a reddish fluorescent glow under natural lighting conditions. The pigments possibly transform violet light into longer wavelengths, thus increasing the photosynthetic efficiency of the coral's symbiotic microorganisms, the zooxanthellae, at depth. On Caribbean coral reefs gorgonian octocorals (sea whips) are preyed upon by the ovulid gastropod (egg-shell snail) *Cyphoma,* the distribution of which is markedly clumped. Gregariousness of the snail was shown to be achieved by mucus-trail following and probably serves to deter predatory fish, which would more quickly learn to avoid the unpalatable flesh of the snails if they moved in groups.

(ERNEST NAYLOR)

This article updates the *Macropædia* articles CRUSTACEANS; FISHES; MOLLUSKS; etc.

BOTANY

One of the more intriguing aspects of biology is the coevolution of insects that pollinate flowers and of the flowers that attract the insects. Many interesting and often bizarre interactions occur between the orchids, the most highly evolved monocotyledonous plants, and such insects as wasps and bees. The mechanisms by which the insects are attracted to the flowers, the dusting of the insect with pollen, and the subsequent deposition of the pollen on an appropriate stigma have long attracted the interest of ecologists and evolutionary biologists.

During the year studies of a genus of orchids (*Catase-*

tum) that have structurally distinct male and female flowers showed that a unique competition exists among the more abundant male flowers to improve the chances of pollen from a particular flower being deposited in a female flower by a particular pollinator, euglossine bees. When such a bee enters a male flower in search of its chemical perfume, the flower attaches its pollen to the bee with a forceful blow, causing the insect to avoid other male flowers. This aversion does not extend to female flowers, which have a different appearance, and thus increases the chance that the bee will deposit the pollen on the stigma of a female flower. The orchid's unusual pollination method may account for the widespread difference in appearance between sexes that exists in the genus.

In addition to their photosynthetic response to light, plants are able to detect and respond to both the quality and quantity of light and to make developmental adjustments accordingly. The most dramatic example of the latter ability is etiolation, a combination of developmental characteristics including stem lengthening, lack of chlorophyll synthesis, and lack of leaf expansion, all of which occur in seedlings grown in the dark. Subsequent exposure of the seedlings to appropriate wavelengths and light intensities changes the developmental program of the plant to a normal pattern. Other such photomorphogenic responses, including the induction of flowers in short-day and long-day plants by appropriate light schemes, have been thoroughly documented. By 1986 it was known that these environmental cues are received by the pigment phytochrome and possibly other light receptors. It was not understood just how the change in pigment conformation that results from the absorption of light is then used to switch genes on or off, the protein products of which must ultimately control development.

Monoclonal antibodies and other tools and techniques of molecular biology were making it possible to study some of the proteins that are inducible by light and to begin to compare the specific nucleotide sequences of plant DNA that are somehow influenced by phytochrome. Although much work remained to be done, the recent discovery of specific regions of DNA that code for light-induced proteins and the initiation of comparative studies of these regions were encouraging.

Plants produce a variety of chemical products unique in biology. While the metabolic pathways by which many of these substances are produced were known, the roles that these substances play in the development and life history of the plants that produce them were proving more difficult to determine. Such naturally occurring substances are often called secondary plant products or, more generically, natural products. Included in this group are substances called phenols, which were implicated as regulators of developmental events in plants.

It was shown recently that seven plant-produced phenols can activate genes for virulence in the bacterium *Agrobacterium tumefaciens*, which is responsible for the plant-tumour disease known as crown gall. The bacterium is able to infect a wide range of host plants that have sustained tissue injury. The studies suggested that increased levels of phenolic compounds produced by the injured host plant may be the stimulus that activates the virulence genes in the bacterium and so allows infection to begin. These compounds form a diverse group, which may account for the wide range of host plants that *A. tumefaciens* can infect.

Both aquatic and terrestrial organisms that contain chloroplasts generally have been considered autotrophs (organisms that synthesize their required organic nutrients from such simple inorganic substances as carbon dioxide and nitrogen) since they convert light energy into the chemical bonds of organic molecules. That their distinction from heterotrophs (organisms that ingest and break down organic matter for nutrients) is not always clear-cut was emphasized by reports that certain lake algae supplement their carbon supply by taking up organic carbon. A recent study of algae belonging to the genus *Dinobryon* in Lac Cromwell, Quebec, indicated that these photosynthetically capable organisms ingest bacteria at rates similar to those measured for some nonphotosynthetic microorganisms, thus obtaining a substantial fraction of their energy and nutrients by ingestion rather than photosynthesis.

(PHILIP D. REID)

MOLECULAR BIOLOGY

Cancer and Blood Vessel Growth. Diffusion is a slow process, particularly over macroscopic distances. For this reason the solid tissues of the human body are penetrated by small, closely spaced blood vessels, which facilitate removal of metabolic waste products and allow a steady inflow of nutrients and oxygen. Without such vascularization no solid tissue can grow beyond the size of a small pea. Indeed, when tumour cells are cultured in soft nutrient agar, they at first grow and divide rapidly but, once having formed small spherules, they cease growing. This so-called dormant state can be maintained for months, provided that fresh medium is supplied at intervals. Microscopic examination reveals that cells at the surface of these small tumours continue to grow and divide, while those in the interior die and necrose, presumably because their needs for nutrients and waste removal cannot be met by simple diffusion. The outgrowth at the periphery balances the necrosis at the core, leading to the apparent dormancy.

Exactly the same restraints apply in the body. How then do tumour cells in solid tissues manage to grow to palpable size? If a small mass of tumour cells is transplanted, for example, into the cornea of a rabbit eye, its growth can be watched. The tumour expands to a diameter of one to two millimeters; growth then pauses while small blood vessels grow from the host tissue into the tumour. Once angiogenesis—the invasion of the tumour by a microvasculature from the host—has occurred, the tumour resumes unrestrained growth. It is clear that tumour cells secrete a diffusible factor that stimulates the ingrowth of small blood vessels.

This substance has been called tumour angiogenesis factor, endothelial cell growth factor, or, most recently, angiogenin by the different groups of scientists investigating it. Its identity, which was finally reported in late 1985, had been vigorously pursued for at least a decade. It undoubtedly deserved this effort because without angiogenesis there can be no significant tumour growth; knowing what angiogenin is and how it works could lead to means of preventing its action and thus of halting tumour growth and spread. Moreover, the existence of an angiogenic factor could mean the existence of an antiangiogenic factor, which inhibits blood-vessel outgrowth. This conclusion follows from the steady state observed in normal adult tissues, in which no net growth of capillaries occurs until healing of a wound requires it.

Those attempting to isolate angiogenin faced difficult obstacles. The substance is released by tumour cells only in small amounts, and its activity is difficult to measure quantitatively. When it was finally isolated, by Bert Vallee and colleagues of Harvard Medical School, the culture medium from which it was extracted yielded only 0.5 microgram of angiogenin per liter—equivalent to 17 billionths (17×10^{-9}) of an ounce per quart. To produce enough angiogenin for study, the Harvard researchers undertook the large-scale culture of cells derived from a human colon cancer. The culture medium containing the angiogenin was then collected, concentrated, freed of small molecules by dialysis, and freeze-dried. The pure material proved to be astoundingly active in stimulating an angiogenic response.

Angiogenin is a small protein having a molecular weight of 14,400 daltons and comprising a linear chain of 123 amino acids. When Vallee's team determined the identities and sequence of the amino acids and compared them with those of known proteins, they found angiogenin to be related to ribonuclease A.

Ribonuclease A is a digestive enzyme, secreted by the pancreas, that catalyzes the breakdown of ribonucleic acid (RNA) into small fragments. The similarities between angiogenin and ribonuclease are impressive; 35% of the amino acid sequence in these two proteins (both of human origin) is identical, and another 33% represents conservative replacement of one amino acid by another that is similar to it. Moreover, those amino acids known to be involved in catalysis at the active site of ribonuclease are all conserved in angiogenin. This led the investigators to test angiogenin against a variety of RNAs. They found that angiogenin, unlike ribonuclease A, did not act upon a wide variety of RNAs but that it did act with great selectivity upon two large RNAs. These molecules turned out to be components of the subcellular organelles called ribosomes that play a key role in the synthesis of proteins within cells. This raised the possibility that the biologic activity of angiogenin involves very specific cleavages of RNA.

During the biosynthesis of any protein, each amino acid is dictated by a specific sequence of three ribonucleotides in the messenger RNA, which is specified in turn by a specific sequence of three deoxyribonucleotides (DNA) in the corresponding gene. Since the genetic code is known and since small fragments of genes can be synthesized, it was possible, given the sequence of amino acids in angiogenin, to synthesize a bit of the corresponding DNA. This fragment was prepared with a radioactive label and was used, in turn, to select the angiogenin gene from among the tens of thousands of human genes. This selection depended upon the ability of any strand of DNA to hybridize, or bind, very specifically with any other strand whose sequence of constituent nucleotides is complementary. Of the four nucleotides—adenine (A), guanine (G), thymine (T), and cytosine (C)—that make up DNA, adenine on one strand will bind only with thymine on the other, while guanine on the one will bind only with cytosine on the other. Two strands are complementary when every nucleotide in the sequence of one strand lies opposite, and can bind with, its corresponding nucleotide on the other strand. An example is shown in the figure. When the gene that bound the synthesized fragment of angiogenin DNA was analyzed, its sequence of nucleotides corresponded exactly with the sequence of amino acids in the angiogenin protein.

Since angiogenin is secreted from tumour cells, like other proteins destined for secretion it was expected to be made with a special "signal" peptide (a short amino acid chain) at one end that would allow it to pass through intracellular membranes. The angiogenin gene does indeed code for a

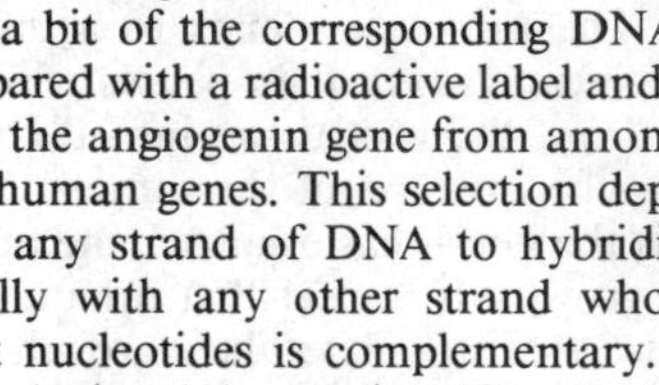

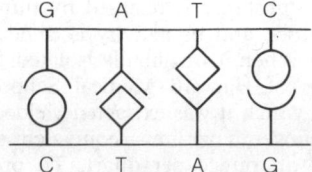

signal peptide about 24 amino acids long, which immediately precedes the 123 amino acids of angiogenin. It may well be that any tissue, be it normal or cancerous, that is starved for nutrients and oxygen or is being poisoned by its waste products will commence secretion of angiogenin. This would have the effect of assuring adequate vascularization of any growing tissue. Such a possibility remained to be explored.

Finding angiogenin was an important step in the fight against cancer. A next step would be to find a means of opposing the action of angiogenin. Because most protein growth factors bind to heparin, which is a sulfated polysaccharide (complex sugar) found in many tissues, the interactions of angiogenin and heparin were examined. Heparin, an anticoagulant, was found to moderately increase the effectiveness of angiogenin. Surprisingly, heparin plus cortisone, a steroid hormone made in the adrenal gland, opposed the effect of angiogenin and thus inhibited angiogenesis. Cortisone alone had no effect. The amount of heparin that can safely be given a cancer patient is limited by its anticoagulant action, which can cause hemorrhaging. This problem was circumvented by the finding that part of the heparin molecule, a six-sugar fragment that is devoid of anticoagulant activity, is nevertheless still active in preventing angiogenesis in the presence of cortisone. Administration of this heparin fragment plus cortisone caused regression of tumours in mice. This dramatic effect was not understood and demanded further study.

Another approach to the inhibition of angiogenesis exploits the similarity between ribonuclease A and angiogenin and the effort already devoted to studying the basis of the catalytic activity of ribonuclease A. Compounds are known that bind with high affinity to the active site of ribonuclease A and, in so doing, block its catalytic effect. These compounds may also bind to the structurally similar region of angiogenin and block its activity.

(IRWIN FRIDOVICH)

Toward Understanding Cancer. Every year millions of people worldwide learn that they have cancer, and every day thousands of its victims die. Although cancer continues to rank as one of the most frequent causes of death, in the past several years much has been learned about its causes and potential cures. It is known, for instance, that most cancers arise as families of cells descended from single "abnormal" precursor cells. It is also known that most compounds (or their metabolic derivatives) that cause cancer in humans raise the frequency of mutation events (changes in genetic material) in bacteria. Moreover, it is known that the incidence of cancer rises steeply with age. Statistical analysis suggests that for some forms of cancer at least three to six independent and heritable random mutations must accumulate within a single cell line for it to become cancerous. The combined weight of these and other data strongly indicates that cancerous cells can arise from "normal" cells in the body via a process of cumulative mutation. On the other hand, cancer can arise when a normal cell is infected with a tumour virus, suggesting that whatever is achieved during the course of collective mutations can be mimicked by the activity of specific viral genes in the otherwise normal cell. How can these observations be explained? Furthermore, how can they be used to elucidate the underlying mechanisms ultimately responsible for cancer?

Using techniques of gene transfer and recombinant DNA manipulation, researchers in many laboratories, perhaps most notably that of Robert A. Weinberg at the Massachusetts Institute of Technology, were beginning the process of determining exactly which genes in cells or in tumour viruses "cause" cancer. Several dozen such genes, called oncogenes, were known by 1986. This ever growing collection was large enough for scientists to begin studying the protein products encoded by these genes and the way they interfere with the normal workings of a cell.

In order to pursue the issue of mechanism, one must first determine exactly how a cancer cell differs from a normal cell. Although the observed differences are numerous and complex, they can be listed roughly under two broad headings: mortal versus immortal, and controlled growth versus uncontrolled growth. Interestingly enough, the collection of known oncogenes can also be so grouped; some bestow immortality upon otherwise normal, mortal cell lines, while others uncouple cell proliferation from its normal means of control.

Highly correlated with the apparent abilities of various oncogene products is the location of those proteins in the cell. Gene products capable of immortalizing a cell line are found in the nucleus, while those capable of uncoupling growth control are found in the cytoplasm, on the cell surface, or in both locations. As more of these proteins were being isolated and studied, patterns were emerging. For example, oncogenes that promote cellular immortalization also greatly stimulate the transcription of other cellular genes into messenger RNA. Whether these two functions are causally related was not yet known.

The weight of data amassed about cytoplasmic oncogene products suggests that they act to uncouple regulation of growth control at any one of the several levels thus far uncovered. Normal animal cells require the presence of specific growth factors (for example, epidermal growth factor and nerve growth factor) to continue growing and dividing. One of the fundamental traits of tumour cells is their decreased dependence on externally aided growth factors. This apparent independence can be explained in several ways. The first mechanism, termed autocrine growth, was proposed in 1980 by Michael B. Sporn and George J. Todaro, then of the U.S. National Cancer Institute. It depends on the ability of a tumour cell to manufacture and respond to its own growth factors. In fact, cultured cells transformed by certain cytoplasmic-acting oncogenes do release growth-stimulating factors into their culture medium. Interestingly, some of these oncogenes do not themselves encode the growth factors but stimulate the expression of those factors from other normal genes in the cell.

A more direct autocrine route involves the mutation of a normal growth factor gene such that it escapes regulation and becomes effectively oncogenic. The oncogene called *sis,* for example, was found in 1983 to be a mutated form of the normal gene that encodes platelet-derived growth factor (PDGF). Alternatively, an oncogene may code for a mutated form of a growth factor receptor. Located on the cell surface, these receptor molecules are normally responsible for recognizing the presence of growth factors outside the cell and transmitting appropriate signals to the inside. Were a receptor to transmit signals aberrantly, it could trigger unregulated proliferation. Several examples of this scenario were known.

A more indirect but equally effective means of uncoupling growth control would involve mimicking or bypassing the transmission of signals from the growth factor receptors to intracellular targets farther downstream in the signaling pathway. A number of good candidates for this mechanism of action had been identified by 1986. One such protein, encoded by an oncogene called *ras,* appeared to be a mutated form of an otherwise normal protein involved in signal transmission. The normal protein becomes activated, transmits its signal, and then quickly shuts down until it receives another signal. By contrast, the oncogenic form of the protein, although able to receive and transmit signals, can no longer efficiently shut itself off.

Given that many oncogenes have been shown to be closely related to normal cellular genes coding for growth factors, receptors, and the like, the question arises as to how potential oncogenes become actual oncogenes. The data thus far suggest two alternatives. Chromosomal rearrangements may cause a gene that codes for an otherwise normal protein to express that protein overabundantly or at the wrong times. In addition to this, or in place of it, the gene coding for a protein may be mutated so that the protein no longer responds to normal forms of control designed to regulate its function. Examples of both mechanisms were documented.

If cancer can arise from any of a number of events leading to the deregulation of otherwise tightly regulated normal cellular processes, how can it be treated or cured? Although early detection and selective treatment are obvious avenues of attack, they rely upon the ability to distinguish between normal and cancerous cells, and the differences can be elusively subtle. Chemotherapy in the 1980s often involved such drugs as methotrexate, which kills rapidly growing cells and thus can be quite effective against cancer. Unfortunately, many normal cells in the body that also grow rapidly (*e.g.,* hair-follicle cells, bone-marrow cells, and cells in the lining of the gut) suffer under the drug treatment.

The development of monoclonal antibody technology could help change this. It was possible to make large amounts of identical antibody molecules that are able to distinguish very small differences between otherwise similar proteins. Given the collected information on known oncogenes, it was possible to generate antibodies that can recognize the presence of oncogenic proteins even against the overwhelming background of normal proteins. Similarly, many tumours have been shown to exhibit surface molecules, called antigens, that might allow specific antibodies to differentiate them from normal cells. Antibodies generated against common oncogenic products and tumour surface antigens could prove to be a very powerful weapon in the battle against cancer, a rifle instead of a shotgun.

The first obvious application of such antibodies would be as an early warning system. Assuming that bits of cancer cells break off and travel through the bloodstream (as is the case for normal cells), specific antibodies could be used to detect the presence of tiny amounts of cancer-specific products in the blood. In theory, if not in practice, this simple blood test should be able to detect cancer formation earlier than current diagnostic techniques. Some versions of this test were undergoing clinical trials. Were cancer-specific products detected in an individual, tagged antibodies could be injected and traced to help locate the tumour.

A second application of cancer-specific antibodies would be in actually fighting an established cancer. The appropriate antibodies could be linked to drugs designed to kill only those cells specifically recognized by the antibodies. Better yet, molecular markers recognized by the patient's immune system could be linked to the cancer cells by use of specific antibodies. In that way the cancerous cells would be destroyed by the body's natural defenses.

(JUDITH L. FRIDOVICH-KEIL)

See also Earth Sciences; Environment.

This article updates the *Macropædia* articles BACTERIA; Animal BEHAVIOUR; BIOCHEMICAL COMPONENTS OF ORGANISMS; The BIOLOGICAL SCIENCES; CANCER; ECHINODERMS; ECOSYSTEMS; The Principles of GENETICS AND HEREDITY; Biological GROWTH AND DEVELOPMENT; PROTOPHYTES; REPRODUCTION AND REPRODUCTIVE SYSTEMS; SENSORY RECEPTION.

Literature

The awarding of the 1986 Nobel Prize for Literature to the Nigerian writer Wole Soyinka (*see* BIOGRAPHIES) was a popular decision, for Soyinka had enthusiastic admirers in many countries. A Yoruba writing in English, this versatile and prolific writer was praised for his plays and poems, his essays and novels, his achievements as an actor and film actor, and for his bold and principled political stance. It was supposed that his memoir, *Aké,* had endeared him to the Swedish jury, as a previous Nobel Prize winner, Elias Canetti, had won human sympathy through the publication of his reminiscences. Canetti's stature became more evident during the year as his German writings were translated in the U.S. and slowly arrived in Britain.

Several commentators took Soyinka's prize as a compliment to African literature and complained that African writing was insufficiently regarded in the West. Two other West African novelists attracted admiration. One of them was Ben Okri, a young Nigerian of Soyinka's school, with his darkly magical stories of Africa and London, *Incidents at the Shrine.* The other was a Ghanaian, B. Kojo Laing, with his exuberant and experimental novel about politics and religion in Accra, *Search Sweet Country.* Both writers exhibited some of Soyinka's characteristics: the bold and accomplished handling of English, the political concern, and the feeling for the numinous, revealed in West African concepts of religion.

It was noted in *The Economist* that book prizes in the U.S. attracted less attention and had less effect on readership than such European awards as the Booker Prize in Britain or the Prix Goncourt in France. There were protests in Paris when the Goncourt went to a writer published by Grasset, since it was held that the prize was awarded too frequently to France's biggest publishers—Grasset, Seuil, and Gallimard.

THOMAS VICTOR

Margaret Atwood

Those concerned with publishers rather than writers observed that the Prix Renaudot went to a Gallimard author, Christian Giudicelli, for *Station balnéaire,* a novel first offered to Seuil. However, Goncourt winner Michel Host was genuinely admired for his successful novel *Valet de nuit,* a sombre story of Parisian family life, using the Homeric story of Ulysses' son in the manner of James Joyce's *Ulysses.* The literary world's richest prize, the $50,000 Ritz Paris Hemingway Award, went to 1984 Goncourt winner Marguerite Duras for her novel *L'Amant.*

Among the international offerings of particular note were three original novels from Asia and Africa. One was *Maps,* an informative and experimental study of the Somalis of Mogadishu by Nuruddin Farah. *Stones of the Wall* was a lively and thoughtful Chinese novel about the aftermath of the Cultural Revolution, by Dai Houying (Tai Hou-ying). Most cosmopolitan of all was *The Golden Gate,* a novel in verse about California, written in English, using Pushkin's stanza form, by Indian-born Vikram Seth.

ENGLISH

United Kingdom. The year was marked by a spirit of businesslike laissez-faire and an unwillingness to subsidize writers with public money. This reluctance was candidly expressed in the ambiguously titled *Giving It Away,* a memoir by Charles Osborne, former literature director of the Arts Council of Great Britain. Osborne vividly expressed his hostility to providing writers with money, particularly in the form of travel grants, though he was less averse to subsidizing reputable journals like the *New Review,* the *London Magazine,* and the *London Review of Books.* He depicted both writers and readers in a scornful manner, justifying the subtitle of his book—"Memoirs of an Uncivil Servant."

At long last the final volume of the *Supplement to the Oxford English Dictionary* made its first appearance. The editor, Robert Burchfield, had introduced the first volume in 1972, after 15 years of work, confidently predicting that it would be complete, in three volumes, by 1978. In the event, it required four volumes, and the last of these was published in 1986. The dictionary was generally admired for its command of learned and demotic usages in all parts of the world where English is spoken. Similarly weighty and authoritative was the latest volume of the *Dictionary of National Biography: 1971–1980.* Edited by Lord Blake and C. S. Nicholls, this compilation recorded and discussed the lives of eminent men and women who died in the 1970s.

Literary attention was drawn backward, as so often in Britain, to the heroic Victorian ancestors (with studies of their sex lives and their journalism), to Shakespearean studies (with new additions and unconvincing attributions), and to World Wars I and II. Jeanne Mackenzie, an accomplished biographer, distinguished herself further with *The Children of the Souls: A Tragedy of the First World War,* the story of eight young soldiers of high promise, all killed during the conflict.

A more embarrassing history was *The Unknown Army: Mutinies in the British Army in World War One,* by Gloden Dallas and Douglas Gill. One of these mutinies, at the Étaples base camp, attracted more attention and some political anger when it was presented in fictional form as a television drama series, "The Monocled Mutineer," by Alan Bleasdale, adapting a book of the same title by William Allison and John Fairley. The furious reaction provoked by this BBC offering indicated the strength of feeling still evoked by literary treatments of World War I.

Fiction. On the whole, British fiction had a wan, despondent air in 1986. Kingsley Amis won the Booker Prize with *The Old Devils,* a bleak comedy about the sorrows of old age, like his earlier novel, *Ending Up.* This was a cheering success, for in latter years Amis's novels had not been considered respectable enough for prizes.

The other contenders in the shortlist for the Booker Prize were mostly of overseas extraction. *An Artist of the Floating World* was offered by Kazuo Ishiguro, of Japanese origin; it was the story of a Japanese artist who strongly supported his government's war effort in the 1940s and felt worried, in peacetime, that his old enthusiasm might damage his daughter's chances of finding a husband. Timothy Mo, another British-educated Asian, presented *An Insular Possession,* a historical romance about the British occupation of Hong Kong in the 19th century.

Then there were two Canadians. The veteran Robertson Davies, educated at the University of Oxford, presented *What's Bred in the Bone,* an elegant tale of an Oxford-educated Canadian who becomes rich after a life of espionage and forgery. *The Handmaid's Tale* was a futuristic, dystopian story by Margaret Atwood, imagining North America controlled by fascists, breeding women in pens, like chickens. The only British native in the shortlist, apart from Amis, was Paul Bailey with *Gabriel's Lament,* a lugubriously jaunty tale of bed-wetting and class prejudice.

There was a public dispute between the male judge and the female judges about a novel by Julian Barnes, *Staring at the Sun,* the story of the long life of an uninteresting woman, beginning in 1942 (before Barnes was born) and concluding in the 21st century; it was rejected from the shortlist by the female judges. Another of the younger, backward-looking novelists, A. N. Wilson, produced *Love Unknown,* the title taken from an Anglican hymn; it was largely concerned with bourgeois adultery and sneers at women, but its basic concern was with the value and efficacy of the Church of England.

From the Roman Catholic side, Anthony Burgess proffered a clever, frivolous little comedy, *The Pianoplayers,* about a piano accompanist in public houses, cinemas, and concert parties (a man resembling Burgess's own father), the struggles of his life, and the resemblance between piano playing and sexual intercourse, from a male point of view. The octogenarian Anthony Powell was sincerely applauded for *The Fisher King,* a mythological novel presenting as its title character a monstrously powerful photographer, adored by subservient women but disabled by war wounds. An energetic expression of despair was David Caute's *News from Nowhere,* a historical romance about the left-wingers of the 1960s and the transformation of

Anthony Powell
FAY GODWIN

Rhodesia into Zimbabwe; the novel offered a world-weary examination of left-wing ambitions and failures, contrasted with an almost parodied account of sincere, simple heroes and villains—presented as not quite real, sometimes aware that they are merely characters in a novel.

Lives, Letters. Recollections of famous statesmen predominated. The 30th anniversary of the Suez conflict of 1956 drew attention to two new books. One was *Anthony Eden,* a biography of the British prime minister whose downfall coincided with the failure of the Suez operation. The book, by Robert Rhodes James, a Conservative member of Parliament, was sympathetically received, with some reviewers still expressing support for the military action against Egypt. Lord Home of the Hirsel, another former Conservative prime minister, affirmed that the result of the Suez action was "an infinitely sad ending to the career of a brave man—a peacemaker and one who set himself the task of fostering harmony and cooperation among the nations."

The subject was treated in a different, less lapidary style through *Descent to Suez: Diaries 1951–56,* the diaries of a civil servant, Sir Evelyn Shuckburgh, one of Eden's recalcitrant subordinates in 1956. Rhodes James felt that Shuckburgh ought not to have published his diaries—and it was observed that Rhodes James "was born clutching his lapels." It was also alleged that Shuckburgh had expressed the "Arabist" prejudices of the Foreign Office. The "pro-secrecy" element in British life made its feelings clear not only over Shuckburgh's diaries but over the memoirs of another civil servant, Peter White, a former member of the British secret service who had settled in Australia. The head of the British civil service was sent to Australia to try to persuade the courts to prevent the book, provisionally entitled "Spycatcher," from being published there.

Former Labour prime minister Lord Wilson of Rievaulx proffered a third volume of his memoirs, reverting to his earliest years, 1916–64. Paul Foot, a persistent left-wing critic, saw Wilson's career as one of failure and affirmed that the seeds of that failure were apparent from the very beginning in Wilson's admitted "pragmatism," his empiricism and distrust of political theory. One of Wilson's colleagues, Jack Jones, published his memoirs under the title *Union Man.* He had been general secretary of the Transport and General Workers Union, an important position during Labour's days in power; his book was well liked but, in the political climate of 1986, his attempts to save dockworkers' jobs and his refusal to support British membership in the European Communities found little support in the press.

Roy Jenkins, another of Wilson's old colleagues before he became a leader of the Liberal-Social Democratic Party Alliance, maintained his reputation as a biographer with a new study of U.S. Pres. Harry S. Truman. Norman St. John-Stevas completed the 15th and final volume of his edition of *The Collected Works of Walter Bagehot,* which he had begun in 1960. Bagehot, the politician's favourite Victorian, was persuasive and down-to-earth in his pragmatic explanations of economic forces and British political institutions; his faith in progress, remarked St. John-Stevas, was "remarkably confident," and his Victorian religion was not exuberant enough to alienate the modern reader.

Two admired Roman Catholics received new, long biographies. Michael Ffinch's life of G. K. Chesterton affirmed that his religion was closely connected with his devotion to liberty, though it might "come as a surprise that in religion Chesterton should have moved away from the Liberal Unitarianism of his childhood towards Catholicism." This seeming paradox was the source of all the other paradoxes and parallelisms of Chesterton's writing, according to Ffinch. The life of Evelyn Waugh was recorded again by Martin Stannard in a two-volume project, beginning with "The Early Years 1903–1939." He presented Waugh (in Lord Quinton's summary) as a man with "a sense of civilization as an endangered inheritance from Rome, sustained by the Roman Church against the destructive tides of humanist antinomianism."

Among the more reckless Lives were those of *The Lamberts: George, Constant, and Kit,* Andrew Motion's study of composer Constant Lambert with his father, an Edwardian portrait painter, and his son, Kit, the manager and creator of a rock-music group. Both the father and the grandfather were careless, irresponsible parents, and the line died out with Kit's destruction by drug addiction. *The Orton Diaries,* edited by John Lahr, were the unashamed confessions of Joe Orton, a rather brilliant young playwright, brightly recording his pederastic adventures in the months before he was murdered by his lover.

Poetry. Hard feelings were stimulated by *The Faber Book of Political Verse,* with the editor, Tom Paulin, in public dispute with his publisher, Craig Raine, himself an influential poet. Enoch Powell, Ulster Unionist MP for South Down, Northern Ireland, remarked that Paulin had "over-Irished his introduction" and that his prose suffered from "the preciosity which lecturers in English" at modern universities "seem obliged to affect." When Raine's new book was published, it was described as "a further strand in his continuing argument with Tom Paulin." Raine's book was a libretto, designed to be set to music, and entitled *The Electrification of the Soviet Union.* It was explained by Blake Morrison as an interpretation of a novella by Boris Pasternak about Russians in 1916.

Raine's influence was apparent in several younger poets. R. S. Thomas published a book of verses aptly entitled *Experimenting with an Amen,* since they consisted of arguments with himself about the validity of religious experience. Several early and characteristically difficult poems by the late William Empson were discovered and published in *The Royal Beasts.*

Jenny Joseph used both prose and verse in *Persephone,* a modern retelling of the Greek myth of Demeter, the earth mother, and her search for her daughter, the Spring, stolen away by the king of the underworld; this version was seen and welcomed, uneasily, as a feminist statement of the maternal sort. Geoffrey Hill startled everyone by refusing the U.K. and Europe regional award in the British Airways Commonwealth Poetry Prize—which he had unwittingly won; acceptance necessitated a five-day "reading tour," reciting to poetry lovers, and this Hill could not bear to do. The regional award went instead to Ian Crichton-Smith, and the overall prize was divided between Vikram Seth and the Nigerian Niyi Osundare. (D. A. N. JONES)

United States. *Fiction.* Among the uncompleted work left by Ernest Hemingway at his death in 1961 was the large, untidy manuscript of a novel, *The Garden of Eden,* which he had begun in 1946 and worked on intermittently during the last 15 years of his life. Appearing in 1986 as the ninth of its author's posthumously published works, *The Garden of Eden* proved to be a very odd, if interesting, addition to the Hemingway canon. The novel also quickly became a best-seller, though that was probably due less to the author's literary reputation than to the public's interest in the book's un-Hemingway-like scenes of androgyny and bisexuality. These involved a young couple variously identified as the author and his second wife, Pauline, and Scott and Zelda Fitzgerald. But sensationalism and literary parlour games aside, the critics generally liked the novel, seeing *The Garden of Eden* as significant, if flawed and minor, Hemingway.

There was no question about the autobiographical basis of another posthumously published novel, *Stillness,* by John Gardner, who was killed in a motorcycle accident in 1982. A tortured portrait of a "famous novelist [and] professor of classical and medieval literature," Gardner's novel, unlike Hemingway's, was more valuable for its autobiographical revelations than as fiction. According to Nicholas Delbanco, Gardner's literary executor and editor of the novel, *Stillness* was hastily written in the early 1970s—partly as an act of therapy—and then shelved.

Perhaps the most universally praised fiction to appear during 1986 was *Kate Vaiden,* by Reynolds Price, which the critics hailed as the finest novel in a distinguished writing career that began in 1962 with *A Long and Happy Life.* Written in the form of a memoir by the title character,

Reynolds Price

THOMAS VICTOR

a woman in late middle age from Price's usual North Carolina up-country, *Kate Vaiden* powerfully and authentically creates a voice and a landscape. The renewed interest in an earlier luminary of the Southern Renaissance that was generated by the appearance in 1985 of Peter Taylor's *The Old Forest and Other Stories* (which won the PEN/Faulkner Award) was furthered by the publication of Taylor's new novel, *A Summons to Memphis.* Only the second novel in his long literary career, Taylor's new book was another masterly picture of the world of his Tennessee gentry.

In *World's Fair* E. L. Doctorow recreated with vivid precision the details of his Bronx childhood in the late 1930s. Combining, as Edmund White said in his review, elements of oral history, memoir, and novel, Doctorow's story reaches a brilliant climax in the young narrator's visit to the 1939 World's Fair. Richard Yates's *Cold Spring Harbor,* a bleak account of a doomed marriage, presented family life as largely the tyranny of the weak. While well crafted and often displaying the brilliant characterization that is Yates's great strength, *Cold Spring Harbor* was a slighter, less interesting novel than its predecessor, *Young Hearts Crying.*

Although littered with lengthy hunks of cosmology and biology and computer science, *Roger's Version* by John Updike seemed clearly intended as a comedy of manners rather than a novel of ideas. Updike's narrator, a dry, middle-aged theologian, presents his account of the eccentric project of a devout, ingenuous graduate student to demonstrate the existence of God by using a computer. Clever and complex and marked by Updike's customary brilliant writing, *Roger's Version* was less successful simply as a story. Filtered through its narrator's dyspeptic consciousness and larded with learning, Updike's story palled before its close.

Though there was some critical uncertainty about the nature of Updike's satirical purpose in *Roger's Version,* there could be none about that of black writer Ishmael Reed, whose seventh novel, *Reckless Eyeballing,* created controversy by the explicitness and nastiness of its satirical portraits, novelist Alice Walker among them. *Masters of Atlantis* by Charles Portis, author of *True Grit* and *Dog of the South,* was far more amiable in its farcical account of the strange muddle of personalities drawn to occultism—dreamers and con men, milquetoasts and sensualists.

The reputation established in 1984 by Louise Erdrich's prizewinning first novel, *Love Medicine,* was amply confirmed by her second, *The Beet Queen.* The second of a projected quartet of novels set in the same region of the Upper Midwest and dealing with the same group of related characters and events, *The Beet Queen* once again effectively employed the technique of multiple narrators used in the earlier book. David Leavitt's second book, *The Lost Language of Cranes,* explored graphically and at novel length the theme of homosexual identity that had appeared in a number of the short stories in his highly praised collection, *Family Dancing,* which appeared in 1985. Poet Tess Gallagher published her first book of fiction, *The Lover of Horses and Other Stories,* a generally successful collection of stories dealing with small-town women.

Notable debuts were made by two short-story writers, Deborah Eisenberg, author of *Transactions in a Foreign Currency,* and Tama Janowitz, author of *Slaves of New York.* Both collections were marked by sharp-eyed observations of the Manhattan social scene in the era of Ronald Reagan, approaching the dilemmas of their heroines with what critic Carol Anshaw saw as "a chilling sort of acceptance that seems best described as post-feminist."

Literary journalist James Atlas, author of a biography of Delmore Schwartz that was nominated for a National Book Award when it appeared in 1977, published his first novel, *The Great Pretender,* a largely autobiographical account of a bookish young man growing up in a Chicago suburb in the 1950s and 1960s. If somewhat derivative, Atlas's story of his self-absorbed, literature-intoxicated hero was often amusing, notably in a very thinly disguised, very funny portrait of the late Robert Lowell. Growing up in Chicago was also the subject of Alex Hancock's eloquent, moving first novel, *Into the Light,* which skillfully employed a chorus of narrators composed of the members of three generations of a doomed working-class family. The American movies of the 1940s and 1950s contribute to the texture of *Into the Light* as literary allusion does to *The Great Pretender,* and one of Hancock's achievements was to translate brilliantly into his fiction the "continuous play of doubt and shadows" that his film-intoxicated young hero relishes in old detective movies.

THOMAS VICTOR

Arthur M. Schlesinger, Jr.

Tess Gallagher

THOMAS VICTOR

Certainly the most widely noted literary debut of the year was that of Sue Miller, whose first novel, *The Good Mother,* received a rhapsodic response from the critics and reached the best-seller list. Miller skillfully employed a soap-opera plot and great psychological insight to explore several complex and highly contemporary moral dilemmas.

History, Biography, and Belles Lettres. Kenneth T. Jackson's *Crabgrass Frontier: The Suburbanization of the United States,* which was the first comprehensive account of the decentralization of America's population from the early 19th century to the present day, won both the Bancroft Prize, given by Columbia University to the year's best work of history, and the Francis Parkman Prize, awarded by the Society of American Historians. In *The Cycles of American History,* Arthur M. Schlesinger, Jr., brilliantly traced the competition of what he sees as two deeply rooted but conflicting views of the nature of American democracy—a rationalistic view that regards the U.S. as a great experiment in government and a messianic vision of America as a divinely ordained society, a "city on a hill." The messianic impulse in modern American life was part of the subject of Frances Fitzgerald's *Cities on a Hill: A Journey Through Contemporary American Cultures.* Interesting in its details if not always persuasive in its conclusions, Fitzgerald's book examined four recent communities she believed were characteristic of the American impulse to transform society: the Castro, the San Francisco homosexual district; Jerry Falwell's Liberty Baptist Church; the Florida retirement community of Sun City; and the now-disbanded Oregon commune of the Indian guru Bhagwan Shree Rajneesh.

Certainly the year's most interesting debut in historical writing was that of David Eisenhower, who produced a vivid, balanced account of his grandfather's years as Allied Supreme Commander. *Eisenhower: At War 1943–1945* was the first of a three-volume series Eisenhower planned to write about his grandfather's career. Far less flattering was *Truman: The Rise to Power* by Richard Lawrence Miller, a revisionist account of Truman's prepresidential years. Miller exhaustively details the future president's business and political dealings in attacking, as one reviewer put it, "the popular portrayal of Truman as a man of integrity who rose unsullied from his political roots in Boss Pendergast's Kansas City Democratic Machine."

A number of richly detailed and well-written biographies of various icons of recent American journalism were published during the year. A. M. Sperber's monumental *Murrow: His Life and Times* admirably avoided hagiography in presenting the heroic life of the most famous newsman in the history of broadcasting. Vicki Goldberg's *Margaret Bourke-White* was less critical in dealing with the rather unattractive human side of the great photojournalist. Ira Berkow's *Red: A Biography of Red Smith* was a skillful account that focused on the professional life of the legendary sportswriter.

Perhaps the most interesting experiment in biography to appear during 1986 was Theodore Rosengarten's *Tombee: Portrait of a Cotton Planter*. Rosengarten, who won the National Book Award in 1974 for his brilliant portrait of a black sharecropper, *All God's Dangers: The Life of Nate Shaw*, combined a well-written biography of Thomas B. Chaplin, a slave-owning planter from the South Carolina low country, with Chaplin's own journal, kept between 1845 and 1861, which was

THOMAS VICTOR

Robert Penn Warren

carefully edited and annotated. Another brilliant piece of historical recovery work was *George Washington Williams* by John Hope Franklin. Franklin's book was a masterful study of the life and times of the pioneering 19th-century black historian.

Arctic Dreams: Imagination and Desire in a Northern Landscape by Barry Lopez effectively combined lyricism and scientific data in its record of four years of travel and thought about "the High Arctic," the beautiful, barren regions on the rim of the frozen polar sea. Oliver Sacks, author of *Awakenings*, brought a similar combination of poetic insight and technical knowledge to the fascinating studies of brain-disordered patients contained in *The Man Who Mistook His Wife for a Hat and Other Clinical Tales*. Frank Gonzalez-Crussi, professor of pathology and author of *Notes of an Anatomist*, once again combined literary grace and gruesome subject matter in his new collection of essays, *Three Forms of Sudden Death: And Other Reflections on the Grandeur and Misery of the Body*.

Poetry. Robert Bly's *Selected Poems* was arranged to illustrate his artistic development during a career that began in 1962 with *Silence in the Snowy Fields*. Raymond Carver, one of the most admired of contemporary U.S. short-story writers, published his fourth book of poetry, *Where Water Comes Together with Other Water*. It deals with the battered lives of ordinary people, the chief subject of his fiction. Adrienne Rich, who in 1986 became the first recipient of the $25,000 Ruth Lilly Poetry Prize, the largest award offered to poets in the U.S., published *Your Native Land, Your Life*. It marked something of a departure from the exclusive concern with radical feminism that had characterized her recent books.

Literary Awards. Pulitzer Prizes were awarded in 1986 for work published in 1985. The winners included: fiction—Larry McMurtry, *Lonesome Dove;* history—Walter A. McDougall, . . . *the Heavens and the Earth: A Political History of the Space Age;* biography—Elizabeth Frank, *Louise Bogan: A Portrait;* general nonfiction—Joseph Lelyveld, *Move Your Shadow: South Africa Black and White;* and J. Anthony Lukas, *Common Ground: A Turbulent Decade in the Lives of Three American Families;* poetry—Henry Taylor, *The Flying Change*. No Pulitzer Prize for drama was awarded in 1986, the 13th time this had occurred in the 70-year history of the awards. On February 26 Robert Penn Warren was designated the first official poet laureate of the United States. The post had been created in 1985 when Congress authorized adding the title of poet laureate to the position of consultant in poetry to the Library of Congress. Warren was selected by Daniel Boorstin, the librarian of Congress. Chris Llewellyn was the winner of the 1986 Walt Whitman Award of the Academy of American Poets for her first book of poetry, *Fragments from the Fire*, a narrative poem about the Triangle Shirtwaist Co. fire in 1911, in which 146 garment workers were killed.

(FITZGERALD HIGGINS)

Canada. If anyone had been entertaining the notion that Canadian literature is solely concerned with the Canadian psyche alone in the Canadian wilderness, the publications of 1986 would quickly disabuse them. True, there were novels set in Saskatchewan—*Dust-Ship Glory*, for example, in which Andreas Schroeder's fanatical mechanical-genius-hero-slob labours to build an oceangoing ship 1,027 mi from the sea; or *The Gates of the Sun*, Sharon Butala's mocking yet moving tribute to an old rogue for whom, after horses, women, and booze have failed him, only the prairie itself has meaning. But there were also many books set in the world at large, such as Josef Skvorecky's *Dvorak in Love*, celebrating the composer's passion for black American music and the Bohemian Countess Josephine; Judith Ann Terry's *Miss Abigail's Part: Or Version and Diversion*, revealing the reverse side of Jane Austen's *Mansfield Park* in the turbulent world below stairs; Matt Cohen's *Nadine*, whose heroine, born almost under the walls of a concentration camp in Germany, realizes who and what she is during a terrorist attack in Jerusalem 40 years later; Timothy Findley's first detective story, *The Telling of Lies*, in which a crew of eccentric characters attempts to save a famous old Maine hotel from the wrecker's ball; and Scott Symon's *Helmet of Flesh*, in which the hero struts and frets his hours among the misfits of Morocco.

Other Canadian characters were on the move, as in Paulette Jile's *Sitting in the Club Car Drinking Rum and Karma-Cola: A Manual of Etiquette for Ladies Crossing Canada by Train*, a sardonic takeoff on detective fiction; and Aritha van Herk's *No Fixed Address: An Amorous Journey*, the tale of a female rogue who unabashedly demonstrates that a woman can dehumanize her lovers as effectively as any man. There were also journeys through time, as in Heather Robertson's *Lily: A Rhapsody in Red*, the second in her trilogy of the Mackenzie King years in which the fictional heroine trips through the actualities of the '20s and '30s, adroitly foiling the real prime minister; and Hugh Hood's *The Motor Boys in Ottawa*, in which the Goderich family embarks on a tour de force through the '60s and '70s.

THOMAS VICTOR

Alice Munro

Short-story collections continued to be popular, including Alice Munro's *The Progress of Love,* tales so finely etched they created a hyperrealism, a supersolution of character and emotion crystallizing into truth at the touch of exactly the right word; Audrey Thomas's *Good-Bye Harold, Good Luck,* provocative evocations of loneliness and regret; Elizabeth Spencer's *The Light in the Piazza,* exploring the intimate connections between people and places; and H. R. Percy's *A Model Lover,* the dissection of the miserable innards of losers, lowlifers, and other social outcasts.

Among many books of poetry by well-known authors were Dorothy Livesay's *The Self-Completing Tree,* the author's favourite works from all periods of her writing life; Irving Layton's *Dance with Desire,* love poems selected from the adventures of an amorous mind over 20 years; Margaret Atwood's *Selected Poems II,* covering the years 1976–86; Al Purdy's *Collected Poems, 1956–1986,* all the poems he wished to retain from a prolific career; and Anne Szumigalski's *Dogstones: Selected and New Poems.*

John Newlove was back with *The Night the Dog Smiled,* in which irony and understatement underpin a reckless assault on mind and sense, and Ray Souster returned with *It Takes All Kinds,* short, deceptively simple lyrics packing a powerful punch. Penny Kemp was *Travelling Light* in her tenth collection, exploring the bewildering byways of interpersonal relations, while Anne Michaels presented her first book, the enigmatic and ambitious *The Weight of Oranges.* In *Whiskey Jack,* the late Milton Acorn expresses his never-ending, innocent wonder at the habits of birds of all feathers, while in *Immune to Gravity,* Mary di Michele speaks eloquently for and about women who attempt to fly against the odds.

Among anthologies were *Sp/Elles: Poetry by Canadian Women,* edited by Judith Fitzgerald; two books inspired by Vancouver's centenary, *Vancouver Poetry,* edited by Alan Safarik, and *Vancouver: Soul of a City,* edited by Gary Geddes; along with bill bissett's *The Last Blewointment Anthology,* presenting writings and graphics from the 20 years of the press's existence.

(ELIZABETH WOODS)

FRENCH

France. "I could no longer speak in poetry, which is my way of speaking," Jacques Roubaud wrote in *Quelque chose noir,* after a silence that had lasted since the death of his young wife in 1983. Refusing to sublimate grief in elegy, he grimly stated the limitations of his art: "A poem is always potentially dialogue. . . . This poem is addressed to you and will encounter nothing." Paradoxically, this painful assertion of the inadequacy of literature was Roubaud's most moving and accessible work, and it confirmed his status as the outstanding poet of his generation.

There was a decline in the number of first novels published in 1986, with publishers preferring to gamble on established writers. Women novelists were especially hard hit, though one exception was Anne Garreta's highly praised first novel, *Sphinx.* Overall, the situation in publishing was quite healthy, with good sales for the winners of the major prizes and for established names. The 1986 Prix Goncourt, the leading award for fiction, went to Michel Host's *Valet de nuit.*

Michel Host
J. RENÉ JACQUES GRASSET

History and biography continued to attract readers; Jean Orieux published *Catherine de Médicis,* and Jean Lacouture continued his biography of Charles de Gaulle. *L'Identité de la France* was the last work by the eminent historian Fernand Braudel (d. 1985). Every period attracted attention, from the Middle Ages (Jacques Le Goff's *L'Imaginaire Médiéval)* through the Revolution (François Furet's *Marx et la Révolution française*) to the Algerian war (with Ali Haroun's study of the Algerian Front de Libération Nationale campaign inside France, *Le Septième Wilaya*). Jean Delay concluded a fascinating piece of social and family history with the final volume of *Avant-mémoire.*

Historical fiction was less prominent than previously, though the period between World Wars I and II and during the German occupation provided the setting for Michel Mohrt's *La Guerre civile.* Jorge Semprun gave a portrait of modern Europe through the interlocking lives of the three central characters of *La Montagne blanche,* while Pierre Moutiers's *Un Aristocrate à la lanterne,* the story of the last days of Philippe Egalité, illustrated the main problem of the genre when dealing with earlier times in its failure to settle on an appropriate language for the 18th-century prince.

Bernard Cazes, in *L'Histoire des futurs,* examined futurology from ancient times to the modern period. Despite having one of the pioneers of science fiction in Jules Verne, modern French literature was not notable for its contribution to this field, though Richard Canal's *La Malédiction de l'éphémère* was one attempt to extend its range in the conventional context of a postnuclear world. *La Vie d'un bébé,* François Weyergans's prenatal narrative, was an example of a type of fantasy, outside the conventions of science fiction, that more often appealed to French writers.

In politics it was the year of "cohabitation" between right and left, and Maurice Duverger offered a timely guide, *Le Bréviaire de la cohabitation.* It was also a disastrous year for the Communist Party, the subject of studies by Michel Cardoze (*Voyage à l'intérieur du Parti communiste français*) and Jean-Pierre Gaudard (*Les Orphelins de Parti communiste*). The novelty of developments on the political scene also explained the success of Frédéric Bon and Michel-Antoine Brunier's satirical *Que le meilleur perde.* Pascal Ory and Jean-François Sirinelli contributed a profile of *Les Intellectuels en France.*

While at the extremes there was still a marked distinction between "popular" and "serious" literature, some of the boundaries were eroded by the sales guaranteed to the main prizewinners and the assured success of writers like Michel Tournier (*La Goutte d'or*). Tie-ins with the cinema only partially explained the critical and popular success accorded to Philippe Djian (*Maudit manège*). Danièle Sallenave achieved something of a tour de force in her novel *La Vie fantôme,* a love story that did not pretend that its characters or their situation were anything but commonplace, while Christian Giudicelli's *Station balnéaire* took a rather pathetic couple and gave their brief escapade a tragic dimension. It won the Prix Renaudot.

In a novel remarkably similar in theme, as well as in title, to Jean Bloch-Michel's *L'Évanouie,* which appeared in late 1985, Jean-Denis Bredin (*L'Absence*) described a middle-aged man abandoning the habits of a lifetime to accompany his dying mother to Venice and then vanishing as if, by this departure from character, he had ceased to exist for the novelist. Patrick Modiano, in *Dimanches d'août,* seemed at times to be recalling not the real circumstances of the occupation but the atmosphere of mystery, betrayal, and decadence of his earlier novels with a wartime setting.

A fragmentary text by Henry de Montherlant, *Moustique,* was published 14 years after his death, and there was a collection of stories by Pierre MacOrlan, *Manon la Souricière,* most of which had been unobtainable since they first appeared in periodicals. There were studies of André Gide (by Auguste Anglès) and Communist influence in French literature during the 1920s (*Le Roman insupportable* by Jean-Pierre Morel), as well as several works on Michel Foucault—not all of them favourable. Among writers who died in 1986 was Jean Genet (*see* OBITUARIES), whose record of visits to Palestinian camps, *Un Captif amoureux,* was published during the year.

(ROBIN BUSS)

Canada. André Roy won the Governor General's Award for his collection of poems *Action Writing* (this was the "French" title—just as French as the one given by René-Daniel Dubois to his successful play *Being at Home with Claude*). Published in December 1985, *Action Writing* offered a selection of Roy's poetry and prose written between 1973 and 1984. A sort of sampler of trends in Québécois poetry during the last decade, it goes from rather harsh formalism to greater accessibility and even, in some cases, to straightforward narration. Another noteworthy book of poetry, *Dans l'après-midi cardiaque* by Patrice Desbiens, is striking for the way down-to-earth situations and banal/trivial expressions are transformed into unpredictable images expressed in a modern idiom unique in French-Canadian poetry.

If some readers of Antonine Maillet were worried lest the author of *Pélagie-la-Charrette* should be unable to renew her themes and style, Maillet's latest work proved to be reassuring. The novel *Le Huitième Jour* is a 300-page tale depicting four larger-than-life characters whose adventure-filled journey through time and space is linked to a symbolic process of growth and maturation.

If ever a book raised "great expectations," it was René Lévesque's *Attendez que je me rappelle,* published simultaneously in French and English. The style of these memoirs of Quebec's former premier and founder of the Parti Québécois is as lively and colourful as the man himself. As is often the case with books of this type, *Attendez que je me rappelle* begins as an autobiography and ends as memoirs when Lévesque presents the role he played in the events that radically changed Quebec society from 1960 to 1985. In all cases, the former broadcaster turned politician knows how to manipulate an audience through humour, irony, and well-measured doses of emotion.

Pierre Perrault, better known for his films than for his writing, also knows his audience well, and *De la parole aux actes,* collected essays dating from 1967 to the early '80s, serves as an interesting complement to Lévesque's memoirs. Perrault's style, however, is definitely that of the essay: rhetorical and persuasive, rejecting abstractions. Above all, it is a call to action.

(PIERRE HÉBERT)

GERMAN

West Germany, Austria, Switzerland. Perhaps the major publication of 1986 was Günter Wallraff's *Ganz unten,* which described the author's experiences disguised as a foreign worker and sold two million copies in four months. German-language fiction was also thriving, despite those who moaned that it was irrelevant. A new novel by Günter Grass was a major event. *Die Rättin* was an apocalyptic work that broached such themes as ecological collapse, women's rights, and the "false" 1950s. It contained some outstanding images and visions, notably the theme of the rat, man's eternal companion, which because it lives on his refuse will survive him. Grass's preoccupations were shared by others. Uwe Timm's *Der Schlangenbaum* concerned European technological exploitation of South America. In the more conventional domain of science fiction, Michael Springer's *Leonardos Dilemma* discussed the possibilities and perils of biotechnology.

Aging and dying and art's attempts to forestall them were important themes. Martin Walser's *Brandung* was a brilliant satire on U.S. university campus life, but it was also about the vanity of attempts to deny one's age. Thomas Bernhard's "comedy" *Alte Meister,* another of its author's diatribes against Austria, was also a novel on the vanity of art's search for immortality. In Erica Pedretti's *Valerie,* the story of a woman dying of cancer, the narrator herself gradually becomes the subject of the narration. The death of a mentally retarded brother was the occasion of Roswitha Quadflieg's meditations in *Der Tod meines Bruders,* while in Daniela Castner's *Preussisches Familienglück* the protracted dying of a father causes a daughter to remember incidents from the past.

Male-female relationships formed the subject of a number of works, especially by women. In *Die liebe Angst,* Liliane Dirks, like Castner, described a childhood under the domination of a father. By contrast, Ludwig Harig's *Ordnung ist das ganze Leben* was a man's affectionate account of the life and times of his father, an overcozy hymn to petty-bourgeois philistinism. Angelika Mechtel's occasionally surreal satires *Das Mädchen und der Pinguin* concerned, in part, the cynical discrimination practiced against women. Lilian Faschinger's *Die neue Scheherazade* was a series of episodes fantasizing relationships with various male archetypes, including Clint Eastwood, Tom Waits, and Roman Polanski. More demanding, both in content and in narrative style, was Elfriede Jelinek's *Oh Wildnis, oh Schutz vor ihr,* also a satire on the current romantic mode. Gerd-Peter Eigner's *Brandig* was another complex novel, set in the aftermath of West German terrorism, in which the sexual relationships are almost exclusively erotic male fantasies.

Unexpected in a time of fast food and instant literature was the appearance of two novels of monstrous proportions, Stefan Schütz's 900-page *Medusa* and Marianne Fritz's 3,000-page *Dessen Sprache du nicht verstehst.* The former, grotesque in its dimensions, language, and images, was a critique of patriarchal society, reflecting in part its author's origins in East Germany. Fritz's fantasy epic appeared to be emulating J. R. R. Tolkien, but the fact that she dispensed with the conventions of sentence construction made the title of her novel ("incomprehensible") somewhat unfortunate. Gerhard Köpf's *Die Strecke,* another large-scale novel, impressively encapsulated 19th-century optimism, contemporary decline, social comment, and personal biography in the metaphor of its title: the life of an elderly railway worker unfolds as he walks along a line that is about to be closed.

Elisabeth Borchers received the Hölderlin Poetry Prize for *Wer lebt.* Other important collections of poetry included Ulla Hahn's highly acclaimed *Freudenfeuer,* Peter Hamm's *Die verschwindende Welt,* Michael Krüger's *Die Dronte,* and Wolf Wondratschek's *Carmen.*

THOMAS VICTOR

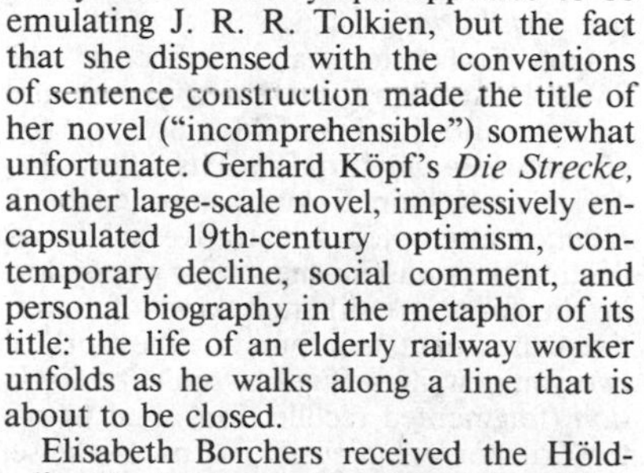

Günter Grass

East Germany. The past was the dominant time mode in the literature of 1986. Christoph Hein confirmed his stature with his first novel, *Horns Ende.* Told by several "voices," the story stresses the importance of remembering, in this case the early years of East Germany when, contrary to official assumptions, the mentality and behaviour of Germans had not changed overnight from Fascist to socialist. Heinrich Ehlers's *Die letzten Jahreszeiten* looked back to the end of World War II but was also alarmed at the possibility of a future apocalypse. Walter Baumert's biographical novel *Das Ermittlungsverfahren* contributed to the iconography of the murdered Communist leader Ernst Thälmann, while Gerhard Holtz-Baumert's *Die pucklige Verwandtschaft* described the author's childhood and adolescence between 1933 and 1945.

Karl der Grosse was an impressive debut by Andreas Montag, a part-existential, part-satirical account of a marriage that has gone stale. For other accounts of the contemporary scene one had to turn to shorter prose works such as Hermann Kant's satirical *Bronzezeit;* Christine Lamprecht's *Männerbekanntschaften,* in which 12 men of various ages and professions describe their lives and loves; or the controversial *Das siebente Brennesselhemd* of Ingrid Johannis, which broached the problem of alcoholism for the first time.

(J. H. REID)

SCANDINAVIAN

Denmark. Per Hultberg's *Requiem* (1985) caused a stir in reviewers' circles: 600 pages long, but scarcely a novel properly speaking, it gave in 537 sections glimpses of that number of human situations and personalities, often reflecting aggressiveness and brutality in the human makeup. Another literary sensation was Helle Stangerup's *Christine* (1985), about King Christian II's daughter, who spent her life vainly intriguing throughout Europe to regain the Denmark her father had lost. Henrik Stangerup also published a historical novel in 1985; *Det er svært at dø i Dieppe* was also about an exile, but there the similarity ended. Stangerup's book was a study in expressionistic vein of the 19th-century critic P. L. Møller, a man obsessed and doomed to debauched failure.

In *Springet,* Tage Skou-Hansen returned to Denmark under the Nazi occupation, juxtaposing the attitudes of some of those affected with their attitudes 40 years later. The occupation and the psychology of a cross section of the population at the time were at the centre of Anders Bodelsen's *Revision* (1985). The veteran Faeroese William Heinesen's latest novel, *Laterna magica*—really a series of loosely connected short stories—looked further back, to the turn of the century. Set in Tórshavn, capital of the Faeroe Islands, it offered a rich variety of tragedy and comedy.

The 1980s had seen a profusion of poetry in Denmark. Henrik Nordbrandt's *Håndens skælven i november* continued a process of ever greater concentration, its 91 short poems clearly reflecting Nordbrandt's linguistic invention and his ability to create new, pregnant images. *Hvid feber* by the young but highly respected Pia Tafdrup continued the motifs of her earlier work, not least as seen in *Springfloden* (1985). With *Porten til jorden,* Bo Green Jensen completed the cycle of seven volumes portraying a growing understanding of life and the consequent feeling of angst. Other well-established poets made their contributions in abundance: Jørgen Gustava Brandt with *Emanation* and *Harlekinade* (both 1985), Benny Andersen with *Tiden og storken* (1985), and Erik Knudsen with *Ord fra Humlebæk.*

The young Faeroese poet Roi Patursson was awarded the Nordic Council Prize for Literature, while a former winner of that and many other prizes, Villy Sørensen, received the Swedish Karl Ragnar Gierow Prize for Literature. (W. GLYN JONES)

Norway. Outstanding by any yardstick was Rolf Jacobsen's 12th collection of poems, *Nattåpent,* combining universal with deeply personal themes and achieving record sales figures. Distinguished storytelling, masterly use of language, profound psychological insight, and unfaltering command of rural cultural history characterized the second volume, *I syndefallets teikn,* in an outstanding series of novels by Johannes Heggland entitled "Seglet og vinden," devoted to the life of Syllfest, a fisherman and farmer in western Norway in the latter half of the 19th century. The historical novel was also well served by Vera Henriksen, whose *Runekorset* took the reader back to 11th-century Norway, Iceland, Greenland, and the North American continent at a time when the Old Norse pagan religion clashed with the new Christian belief; and by Carl Fredrik Engelstad, whose storyteller, Philippe de Laval, looked back in *De levendes land* on events in 15th-century France.

The subtle inner tension in Finn Carling's novel *Lille Orlando* made this strange masterpiece of psychological insight one of the outstanding works of the year. Calumny and jealousy were brought into play within a claustrophobically tight-knit rural Norwegian setting in Anne Karin Elstad's novel *—for dagene er onde.* Two short-story debuts, Jostein Gaarder's *Diagnosen* and Mette Elisabeth Nergård's *Frosne roser,* were uneven but contained some excellent material. The "white niggers" of Ingvar Ambjørnsen's novel *Hvite niggere* were youngsters living on the fringes of Norwegian society in a world of alcohol, drugs, and sex. Even more depraved was the world of sex and prostitution depicted in Arild Kolstad's *Alf Hansens hjemkomst.* A fictitious small town in western Norway was the setting for Rolf Sagen's bizarre but amusing novel *Springfart ved fjorden.* Ketil Bjørnstad's semidocumentary novel about Edvard Grieg, *G-moll-balladen,* was an example of fascinating material largely wasted.

Stein Mehren, in his collection of poems *Corona. Formørkelsen og dens lys,* was at his best in a number of computer-inspired aphorisms. For the first time, Henrik Ibsen's complete poems were published in English, in translations by the Ibsen scholar John Northam. *Den fremmede passasjer* was a collection of essays by Ingar Hauge on Ibsen's plays from *Peer Gynt* to *The Lady from the Sea.*

(TORBJØRN STØVERUD)

Sweden. Swedish literature had moved away from social realism and prescriptive left-wing political commitment toward free fiction with an admixture of magical realism. In *Lustarnas herre,* Theodor Kallifatides presented a portrait of the Athenian Alcibiades, a friend of Plato and Socrates. Vibeke Olsson concluded her tetralogy about the life and death of a former slave girl finally married to a Roman officer; *Sabina och Alexander* represented a sombre and imaginative feat. By contrast, the poet-philosopher Lars Gustafsson, now living in Texas, published *Bernard Foys tredje rockad,* about a young rabbi (except that he was not) caught up in international skulduggery.

Göran Tunström had affinities with Dostoyevsky and the Swede Lars Ahlin by virtue of his compassion and ability to present the dark sides of human nature in a prose of remarkable vitality, periodically erupting into absurd humour; in his richly imaginative novel *Tjuvan,* sin (cruelty and selfishness) and grace were the dimensions in which the characters had their being. In *Legender,* Torgny Lindgren—deeply religious and totally undogmatic—told fresh and subversive legends of his own invention. Ann-Charlotte Alverfors had a similar gift for appealing directly to her readers' hearts and imaginations: her fairytale-like novel *Stjärneklok,* about the tyranny of a mother over her middle-aged son, functioned as a parable of hope against the odds. The same sad yet essentially humane imaginative power was found in Stewe Claeson's collection *Stenhuggaren som gick barfota.*

Lars Gyllensten, a member of the Swedish Academy, presented seven tales of love and its manifold guises in *Sju vise mästare om kärleken.* His fellow academician Kerstin Ekman's unusual book *Hunden* attempted a narrative solely reflecting the consciousness of a puppy lost in the forest. A different kind of narrative experiment was found in the work of two young writers: Stig Larsson's *Introduktion* (fragmented recollections) and Christer Eriksson's *Luften är full av S* (dense, poetic, concerned with human communication).

Several young poets published good collections; among them were Ulf Eriksson's *Färjefärd,* Ylva Eggehorn's *Ett brev till min älskade,* Eva Runefelt's *Längs ett oavslutat ögonblick,* and Ernst Brunner's lively *Separator.* Academician Lars Forssell chose the sonnet form for his *Sånger.*

(KARIN PETHERICK)

ITALIAN

When Italo Calvino died in 1985, he left unfinished a book that was to have included five stories, one for each sense, and to be entitled accordingly: "I cinque sensi." Published posthumously, *Sotto il sole giaguaro* included only three of the projected pieces, those devoted to smell, taste, and hearing. In all three Calvino combined his remarkable originality with a sharp and witty language. Particularly memorable was the title story, in which eating replaced all forms of contact between the male and female protagonists as well as between them and Mexico, the country they were visiting and slowly coming to know through all the foods they ate or read about.

Two established writers published collections of short stories: *Zita dei fiori* by Mario Tobino, set in Tuscany during World War II, and the more popular *Il capostazione di Casalino* by Piero Chiara, tales of contemporary life in the best tradition of Italian narrative. Among distinguished novels, *Rinascimento privato* by Maria Bellonci was perhaps the most successful book of the year; a biography of the famous Renaissance figure Isabella d'Este, it was a sensitive mix of history and fantasy.

The aftermath of World War I provided the background for *L'anno della vittoria* by Mario Rigoni Stern, the story of a community returned to a peaceful way of life and patiently trying to rebuild and restore all that "victory" had torn apart or destroyed. A strong historical sense of outrage underlay *Gli sposi di via Rossetti* by Fulvio Tomizza, a tragic love story set among the Istrian minority in Trieste under Nazi occupation. Contemporary themes were imaginatively treated by Giovanni Arpino in *Passo d'addio,* a serious thriller focusing on euthanasia, and by Ferdinando Camon in *La donna dei fili,* which narrated the life of a woman through the device of analysis sessions. Stefano D'Arrigo's *Cima delle nobildonne,* a novel in three temporal and spatial settings, each centring on the human placenta, was remarkable for boldness of invention and stylistic lucidity.

Among young writers, Daniele Del Giudice, Roberto Pazzi, and Aldo Busi, all three on their second novels, largely fulfilled the expectations aroused by their debuts. Del Giudice's *Atlante occidentale* was an intriguing novel almost without a story: a meeting of minds between an old writer and a young physicist confronted by dissolving matter. The author's terse and self-conscious narrative was often felt to be reminiscent of Calvino's style, though it lacked, perhaps, his wit and warmth. Pazzi's *La principessa e il drago* was, like his first novel, a psychological portrayal of a Russian prince, this time George Romanov, brother of Tsar Nicholas II, who died of consumption in 1899. The novel convincingly portrayed the character as he lived out the inevitable waning of tsarist power. The writer's attempt to incorporate his own views on the history and future of absolute power was less successful; these ideas seemed inert and confused, in contrast to the compelling picture of the dreaming and dying prince.

Busi's *Vita standard di un venditore provvisòrio di collant* (1985) was probably the most engaging of the three. Its protagonist was a middle-aged, uncouth industrialist from Lombardy, a thoroughly odious yet vital character in whom, perhaps, the narrator meant to sum up and satirize the prototype of the successful businessman in economically booming northern Italy. Busi displayed an impressive ability to combine—in an outrageous style—irony, sarcasm, lyricism, comic and grotesque elements, and a pained yet outspoken denunciation of a decaying social environment.

Marta Morazzoni, a newcomer, deservedly attracted much critical praise with her book *La ragazza col turbante.* It included five short stories, uneventful yet full of suspense, set in the 16th to the early 20th centuries and in various locations, from The Netherlands and Spain to Venice and Vienna. Settings and characters—some historical, like Mozart, Da Ponte, and Charles V—were all submerged in a distant, almost transparent atmosphere and enveloped in a mystery that gradually became haunting. Morazzoni's language was unassuming, yet fully mature and perfectly under control. It was seen to confirm the general trend among recent serious writers toward a clear and simple style of classical harmony and composure, without the syntactical complexities and elaborate preciosities of conventional Italian prose.

The continuing vitality of poetry was revealed, despite a dwindling readership, by the quantity and quality of verse collections published. Among the most notable were: Giovanni Caproni, *Il conte di Kevenüller;* Giovanni Testori, *Diadèmata;* Maria Luisa Spaziani, *La stella del libero arbitrio;* Andrea Zanzotto, *Idioma;* Giovanni Giudici, *Salutz;* Paolo Volponi, *Con testo a fronte;* and Giovanni Raboni, *Canzonette mortali.*

The novelists Maria Bellonci and Goffredo Parise died during the year.

(LINO PERTILE)

SPANISH

Spain. In three slim volumes, Camilo José Cela's *Nuevo viaje a la Alcarria* retraced the famous itinerary of his first *Viaje a la Alcarria* (1948). The landscapes seen by the foot traveler four decades earlier were viewed this time through the tinted windows of Cela's chauffeured Rolls-Royce, but the master prose stylist succeeded in transforming the media event into a fascinating literary commemoration. Gonzalo Torrente Ballester, whose vast and varied production also spanned 40 years, received the highest of Hispanic literary awards, the Miguel de Cervantes Prize, late in 1985; new editions of several of Torrente's earliest novels, suppressed or altered by postwar censors and long out of print, such as *Javier Mariño* (1943), received fresh critical scrutiny and popular acclaim. The Planeta Prize went to Terenci Moix's novel *Nunca digas que fue un sueño,* a playfully pseudo-historical account of what "really" happened between Antony and Cleopatra.

In *Un parado en el top-less,* which won the rich Plaza & Janés International Novel Prize, Cristóbal Zaragoza gave his unemployed, fervently Catholic protagonist a job in a sleazy Valencian nightclub, then led him from temptation to moral triumph. Julián Ríos extended the dazzling (multi)linguistic pyrotechnics of his *Larva* cycle through its second volume, *Poundemonium: Homenaje a Ezra Pound;* and a pseudonymous character from Luis Goytisolo's reader-focused metafictional novel, *La cólera de Aquiles* (1979), reappeared as a writer-protagonist in *Investigaciones y conjeturas de Claudio Mendoza* (1985). Soledad Puértolas was recognized as a gifted emerging talent with her second novel, *Burdeos,* a triptych in traditional narrative style, hinging on the theme of solitude in contemporary life.

An unusually large number of historical studies, occasioned by the 50th anniversary of the beginning of the Civil War (1936–39), dominated best-seller lists throughout the year. For the nation's literature, perhaps the single most catastrophic consequence of that conflict was the assassination, by Falangists, of Federico García Lorca (1898–1936); the life and works of Spain's most universally appreciated modern poet and dramatist were the subjects of countless new studies, exhibitions, and performances, both in Spain and abroad.

Readers unfamiliar with Benito Pérez Galdós's grand four-volume masterpiece, *Fortunata y Jacinta* (1886–87), were treated to a magnificent English translation, nearly 20 years in the making, by Agnes Moncy Gullon. (ROGER L. UTT)

Latin America. The major writers to publish books during the year were the Colombian Nobel laureate Gabriel García Márquez, the Peruvian Mario Vargas Llosa, the Mexican José Agustín, the Argentine Julio Cortázar, and the Chilean Jorge Edwards. The second novel by the Chilean Isabel Allende, *De amor y de sombra* (originally published in 1985), was still a best-seller in some urban centres of Latin America.

García Márquez's love story *El amor en los tiempos del cólera* was the most widely acclaimed and consistent best-seller in Latin America. Set in 19th-century Colombia, it is a straightforward account of an aging couple's passionate love affair. The brief *¿Quién mató a Palomino Molero?,* in the detective-novel genre and one of Vargas Llosa's minor novels, was also amply read in Latin America. José Agustín's *Cerca del fuego,* among his most accomplished books, relates the serious yet humorous consequences surrounding the protagonist's return to Mexico City after six years of amnesia. It is a devastating portrayal of the problems of Mexico's capital. *El examen,* Cortázar's posthumous novel, was written during the early 1950s in an experimental prose. Edwards published *La mujer imaginaria.*

The two most important novels to appear in Mexico, besides Agustín's *Cerca del fuego,* were Héctor Aguilar Camín's *Morir en el golfo* and Homero Aridjis's *4092, Vida y tiempos de Juan Cabezón de Castilla.* In *Morir en el golfo,* the narrator-journalist pens a story of crime involving the petroleum industry in the state of Veracruz. Aridjis's well-constructed historical novel is set in 15th-century Spain and told in a picaresque mode. Other noteworthy Mexican novels were *Donde las cosas vuelan* by Ethel Krause, a short work about a love affair between a journalist and a sociologist; Jaime del Palacio's *Mitad de la vida,* dealing with interpersonal relationships in contemporary Mexico; and Mónica de Neymet's *Las horas vivas,* concerning middle-class Mexican women.

UPI/BETTMANN NEWSPHOTOS

Gabriel García Márquez

Mario Vargas Llosa

THOMAS VICTOR

Gustavo Álvarez Gardeazábal scandalized Colombian readers with his ninth book of fiction, *El divino.* The five female narrators in this novel tell the story of a Colombian drug king. It was among the most widely read novels in Colombia during the year. One of Colombia's best young writers, Jorge Eliécer Pardo, brought out a volume of stories, *La octava puerta* (late 1985), and his second novel, *Irene,* a love story portraying a woman and her daily life in a fashion unlike the frequent stereotypes of the Colombian woman. Julio Olaciregui also published a novel concerning a woman in Colombia, *Los domingos de Charito,* the young author's second book. Mario Escobar Velásquez, an established author of two novels with vigorous plots, published a third along similar lines, *Toda esa gente.* The Fundación Guberek in Colombia continued to publish a series of books of little commercial value but considerable literary merit: Rafael del Castillo's *Canción desnuda* (poetry), M. García Herreros's *Lejos del mar* and *Asaltos* (fiction), Carlos Lleras Restrepo's *De ciertas damas* (essays), Daniel Samper's *Balón y pedal* (fiction), Nicolás Suescún's *3 a.m.* (fiction), and Darío Jaramillo's *Poemas de amor* (poetry).

Literary activity continued to flourish in Argentina under the democratic government. Two of the most noteworthy books published there were Tomás Eloy Martínez's best-selling novel *La novela de Perón* and Héctor Libertella's experimental *¡Cavernícolas!* Martínez made good use of a documentary impulse to create a semibiographical account of the former head of state Juan Perón. *¡Cavernícolas!* consists of three stories that consistently have as their subject language rather than plot. Juan Carlos Martini's *El fantasma imperfecto,* the second novel of a trilogy, does have a vague plot but is also a self-conscious treatment of language. One of Argentina's best authors of short fiction, Isidoro Blaisten, published a volume of stories, *Carroza y reina.* Other important books of fiction published in Argentina were Carlos Catania's *El pintadedos,* Rodolfo Enrique Fogwill's *Pájaros de la cabeza,* Gudiño Kieffer's *Magia blanca,* and Abelardo Castillo's *El que tiene sed.*

The Argentine Fernando López won the Casa de las Américas novel prize with *Arde aún sobre los años.* Jorge Luis Borges (*see* OBITUARIES), the venerable author of fiction and poetry and father figure for several generations of Latin-American writers, died at the age of 86. The year began with the death of Juan Rulfo (*see* OBITUARIES), the author of two classic Mexican books, the stories *El llano en llamas* (1953) and the novel *Pedro Páramo* (1955).

(RAYMOND LESLIE WILLIAMS)

PORTUGUESE

Portugal. Fiction continued to flourish in Portugal, and the success it had gained at home appeared to be winning it some recognition outside the country, as evidenced by the translation into English of *Ballad of Dogs' Beach* by José Cardoso Pires and *The Wondrous Physician* by Jorge de Sena.

Fiction writers were still deeply committed to experimentalism, but at the same time they showed great concern over the choice of theme and subject. Mário Cláudio, a prizewinning author and one of the most distinguished avant-garde writers of the 1960s, had the idea of using biography as the flesh and bone of the novel. By centring his narrative on the lives of artists born in northern Portugal, he succeeded in capturing the spirit and mood of the period, as it was seen in the work or artistic performance of his subjects. After *Amadeo,* the life story of a great modernist painter, Mário Cláudio produced *Guilhermina*—an account of the life of Guilhermina Suggia, the brilliant cellist who became an international star in the 1920s. The most impressive quality of this work was the musical pattern of its composition. The author's approach to the main theme of his story—the pursuit of happiness—varied frequently, and these constant shifts of angle imparted a melodic quality to his descriptions. The pursuit of happiness posed the problem of the relation between art and life.

Lobo Antunes had written a powerful novel of the colonial wars up to and immediately after the April 1974 revolution in *Fado Alexandrino,* in which war memories haunted officers and soldiers who, having returned to Portugal, felt unable to adjust to ordinary life. The novel paved the way for *Auto dos Danados,* in which the characters were the landowners of southern Portugal in the heady days of the revolution, when starving farm workers occupied the estates of their former employers. It was a complex story of personal despair, betrayed love, and self-deception. The novel was awarded a prize for fiction by the Association of Portuguese Authors.

(L. S. REBELO)

Brazil. Translations of foreign literature and thought dominated the Brazilian bestseller list throughout 1986. With the exception of Rubem Fonseca's latest novel, the sensational detective thriller *Bufo & Spallanzani,* the few Brazilian national bestsellers were by literary figures working in other scholarly areas. For example, *Olga* by Fernando Morais is a rather astonishing biography of Olga Benário Prestes, wife of the head of the Brazilian Communist Party. *Fidel e a Religião* by the Dominican Frei Betto, the record of his interview with Cuban Pres. Fidel Castro (at the latter's request), was a raging success throughout Latin America. The anthropologist and novelist Darcy Ribeiro published *Brasil: Aos Trancos e Barrancos,* a vivid year-by-year "replay" of the highlights and low depths of Brazilian life since 1900. Its message is a call for popular unity.

The centenary of the poet Manuel Bandeira's birth was celebrated with many new editions of his works, conferences, and important critical studies, including those by Giovanni Pontiero and Candace Slater, whose volume includes new English translations of some poems. The poet Henriqueta Lisboa died in late 1985, just as her *Complete Works* began to appear. José Paulo Paes published his complete poems, *Um por Todos,* while Ferreira Gullar issued a collection of poems written in the 1950s. Oliam José published a new collection of introspective verse, *O Efêmero e o Eterno.*

Rachel de Queiroz's latest novel, *O Galo de Ouro,* is set in Rio's Ilha de Governador. In late 1985 Rubem Mauro Machado published *A Idade da Paixao,* a semiautobiographical tale of coming of age in Brazil during the early 1960s. There were a number of new novels by "*gaúchos,*" southern Brazilian writers. José Clemente Pozenato's *O Quatrilho* is set in the nascent Italo-Brazilian community of the early 20th century; Patricia Bins's *Janela do Sonho* is a psychological study of a woman; and Charles Kieffer published *Valsa para Bruno Stein.* Sérgio Sant' Anna's *Amazona* narrates a love triangle set in Rio. New short stories by Domingos Pellegrini, Jr., Márcia Denser, José Louzeiro, and Jefferson de Andrade also appeared during the year.

Marisa Lajolo and Regina Zilberman coauthored a significant new history of Brazilian children's literature. New studies of poetry by João Cabral de Melo Neto and Murilo Mendes, as well as Lygia Fagundes Telles's fiction, appeared. Stella Rodrigues published the "true story" of her brother, the sportswriter and dramatist Nelson Rodrigues. Two important novels by the eminent Clarice Lispector appeared in English translations by Giovanni Pontiero.

(IRWIN STERN)

RUSSIAN

Soviet Literature. The eighth congress of Soviet writers, held in 1986, sharply criticized elements of stagnation and negative trends in the development of Soviet literature. Books on petty themes, timeserving and antihistorical, were severely denounced. The delegates stressed that a truthful portrayal of life in all its complexity and the dramatic struggle of the new with the old and outdated should be the decisive criteria in assessing works of fiction.

As in 1985, the attention of critics and readers was drawn to books with a social message. Notable among them were Viktor Astafiev's novel *A Sad Detective Story,* published in the magazine *Oktyabr;* Chinghiz Aitmatov's novel *The Scaffold,* which appeared in *Novy Mir* magazine; and Andrey Voznesensky's poem "The Trench," printed in *Yunost* magazine. Equally successful books by writers less familiar to the foreign reader were Chinghiz Guseinov's *Family Secrets,* Anatoly Kurchatkin's *Evening Light,* Mikhail Shukshin's *A Name for My Son,* and Yury Arakcheyev's *Rostov Elegy.*

Writers of essays linked issues of public and personal ethics with topical problems. They included Ivan Vasiliev (whose latest books were awarded the 1986 Lenin Prize), Yury Chernichenko, Anatoly Strelyany, Gennady Lisichkin, Simon Soloveichik, Vasily Selyunin, Yury Galkin, and Olga Chaikovskaya.

Books about the Great Patriotic War (World War II) continued to appear; Vasil Bykov's short novel *The Quarry* was distinguished by a tense plot. Among books examining the psychology of contemporaries were novels by Georgy Semyonov (*Jasmine in the Shade of the Fence* and *The Intelligence of the Fox*), Mikolas Slutskis (*Tree of Light*), Ruslan Kireyev (*Stuck*), and Viktor Kanetsky (*Again I Can't Think of a Title*). The most outstanding recent works of lyric poetry were David Samoilov's *Voices Beyond the Hills* and Gennady Rusakov's *Time of the Bird.* Poetry lovers were again attracted to the experiments of the group of young poets that included, among others, Aleksandr Yeremenko, Alexey Parschikov, Sergey Soloviev, and Tatyana Scherbina.

The tendency to bring the nation's forgotten and semiforgotten literary heritage to the mass Soviet reader continued. Thus the weeklies *Literaturnaya Rossia* and *Ogonyok* published some of Nikolay Gumelyev's poems in honour of the centennial of his birth. Andrey Platonov's short novel *Juvenile Sea* was published in the magazine *Znamya.* The appearance of two volumes by Boris Pasternak was a notable event in literature. Additional volumes in the complete works and corre-

P. NOSOV—TASS/SOVFOTO

Andrey Voznesensky

spondence of Nikolay Nekrasov and Fyodor Dostoyevsky appeared, and the works of Aleksandr Pushkin (in three volumes) and Vladimir Mayakovsky (in two volumes) were published.

(SERGEY CHUPRININ)

Expatriate Russian Literature. Several interesting works by writers both in the Soviet Union and in exile were published in the West. Leonid Borodin's latest novel, *Rules of the Game,* came out in the Russian émigré journal *Grani,* published in Frankfurt, West Germany. The author was sentenced in 1983 to ten years in a labour camp and five in internal exile. Vladimir Voinovich published an extract from his novel *Moscow—2042* in another émigré journal appearing in West Germany, *Kontinent.*

Vladimir Maximov's novel about the White Russian leader Adm. A. V. Kolchak, *Before the Abyss,* was brought out by YMCA Publishers in Paris. Hermitage in New Jersey published *A Miraculous Sortie* by Lev Losev, a collection of verse bringing together four of the author's volumes. Losev had immigrated to the U.S. in 1976. *The Same Sea in Us All,* a collection of verse by the Estonian poet Jaan Kaplinski (translated by the author and Sam Hamill), was published in Portland, Ore. Another Estonian poet, Kalju Lepik, had his 11th collection published by Eesti Kirjanike Kooperatiiv, an Estonian-language publisher in Sweden, where Lepik had been living since 1944. A new émigré publishing venture, Russian Roulette Press, was launched in London by two exiled writers, Igor Pomerantsev and Zinovy Zinik, with the intention of providing an outlet for new literary work of quality. In their first year they published Pomerantsev's collection of short stories *Aubades and Serenades* and Zinik's novel *Rousseauphobe and Fungophile.*

The poet Irina Ratushinskaya, sentenced to 12 years of imprisonment and internal exile in March 1983, was released in October following a vigorous campaign on her behalf in Britain and elsewhere. In December she and her husband were permitted to seek medical treatment in Britain, where they announced plans to remain in the West. An English collection of her work, *No, I'm Not Afraid,* was published in Britain earlier in the year, and in June the Rotterdam (Neth.) Arts Council awarded her the Persecuted Poet Prize at its annual International Poetry Festival.

Anatoly Marchenko, the author of *My Testimony,* one of the most important books to come out of the Soviet Union in the last 20 years, died in prison at the age of 48 (*see* OBITUARIES). Ironically, news of his death came on the eve of International Human Rights Day, December 10. Having spent most of his adult life in prison or labour camp, Marchenko was serving a sentence of ten years' imprisonment, imposed in 1981, to be followed by five years of internal exile. Marchenko was the first truly working-class person to gain prominence in the human rights movement, and *My Testimony* was the first book by a Soviet political prisoner, writing under his own name, to describe the horrendous conditions in the labour camps of the post-Stalin era. It was smuggled out and published in London in 1969.

(GEORGE THEINER)

EASTERN EUROPEAN LITERATURE

The literary scene in the Soviet-dominated countries of Central and Eastern Europe presented something of a paradox: while in Czechoslovakia little of real interest could be discovered, the official publishing houses in Romania (where Pres. Nicolae Ceausescu ran a more brutal regime than the one in Prague) and Poland (still virtually under military rule despite the lifting of martial law) often put out books of quality. On the other hand, Romania had no *samizdat,* whereas both Czechoslovakia and Poland continued to produce a vast quantity of underground literature.

An interesting novel by Norman Manea, *The Black Envelope,* came out in Bucharest, and the same author was one of 33 Romanian writers represented in a German anthology of short stories called *Erkundungen II* ("Reconnaissances"), published in 1985 in East Berlin. Two books by the exiled Romanian author Emile Cioran came out in Paris: a novel, *Des Larmes et des saints* ("Tears and Saints"), written when Cioran was still living in Romania in the late 1920s, and *Exercise d'admiration* ("An Exercise in Admiration"), a collection of essays on Beckett, Borges, and others. Also in Paris, the dissident poet Dumitru Tsepeneag brought out his first novel in French, *Roman de gare.* In February the American PEN Centre sent a petition containing 240 signatures to President Ceausescu, demanding an investigation of the suspicious deaths of writers Gheorghe Ursu and Arpad Visky.

In Warsaw an official publishing house produced the ten-volume *Complete Works* of the late Witold Gombrowicz—a commendable venture somewhat marred by the excisions of the censor. Other books of note published officially in Poland were a "Dictionary of Myths, Traditions, and Cultures" by Wladyslaw Kopalinski, which became a best-seller, and a collection of verse by the eminent poet Wislawa Szymborska. Unofficial and émigré output included *Dishonour at Home* by Jacek Trznadel, a series of interviews with Polish writers who had subscribed to the Communist faith in the 1950s, and Stefan Kiszelewski's new novel, *Everything's Different,* published by PULS, London. This émigré publisher also launched a poetry series with volumes by Jan Polkowski and Bronislaw Maj, both living in Poland, and Stanislaw Baranczak, now resident in the U.S. Two noteworthy volumes from the large underground output in Poland were a collection of short stories by Marek Nowakowski and the translation of Aleksandr Nekrich and Mikhail Heller's history of the U.S.S.R., *Utopia in Power.*

With only a few exceptions (Bohumil Hrabal, Ladislav Fuks, and two or three others), the best Czechoslovak writers could only be published abroad or in *samizdat.* In London Alexander Tomsky's "Rozmluvy" (Conversations) series included Ivan Klima's major novel *Judge on Trial,* the two-volume *Collected Works* of the Catholic poet Bohuslav Rejnek, who died in the early 1970s, Ivan Divis's collection of verse, *Psalms,* and *Václav Havel, a Long-Distance Interrogation,* the text of Karel Hvizdala's interview with the famous dissident Czech playwright. *Václav Havel, or Living in Truth,* edited by the poet Jan Vladislav, came out in English in November on the occasion of the Erasmus Prize being awarded to Havel.

In Toronto, 68 Publishers, an émigré firm run by the writers Josef Skvorecky and Zdena Salivarova, brought out, among other works, Josef Hirsal's experimental *Song of Youth; Twilight; A Time of Coupling,* an anthology of work by women writers both in Prague *samizdat* and in exile; Minka Rybakova's science-fiction novel *Malicious Earthlings;* and *Miss Rosie from Chicago,* letters written by a Czech servant girl in the U.S. in the late 19th century. The 72-year-old author Bohumil Hrabal was put under police surveillance after the appearance of his latest book, *Proluky* ("Empty Spaces"), in Prague *samizdat.*

Readers International in London published *Flight of Ashes* by Monika Maron, a novel about the tribulations of an investigative journalist in East Germany that obviously drew on personal experience.

In Hungary the comparatively benevolent attitude shown toward *samizdat* publishers prior to and during the International Cultural Forum in Budapest the previous year came to an end with police raids on the homes of writers and publishers.

(GEORGE THEINER)

JEWISH

Hebrew. Three works of fiction were especially acclaimed in 1986: *Ayen Erekh: Ahava* by David Grossman, a novel that grapples emotionally with the ghostly presence of the Holocaust; *Arabeskot,* by the Arab-Israeli Anton Shamas; and *Epikorus Be'al Korho* by Yehoshua Bar-Yosef, appreciated mainly for its racy portrayals of sin within Jerusalem's religious community. Other noteworthy novels included David Shahar's *Yom haRefa'im,* the fifth in his *Hekhal* series; Moshe Shamir's moralistic *Yaldei haSha'ashu'im;* David Melamed's apocalyptic *haHalom haRevi'i;* Aharon Appelfeld's *Be'et Uve'ona Ahat;* and the absurdist work *Zelig Mintz Vega'agu'av al haMavet* by Itamar Levy. Amos Oz and Yitshak Orpaz shared the Bialik Prize, and A. B. Yehoshua won the Alterman Prize for fiction.

Yossel Birstein published his fifth short-story collection, while the playwright Hanoch Levin issued a volume of his collected stories. Yoram Kaniuk issued two collections, including *Sipurei Sofshavu'a.* An intriguing book was Shabtai Levy's *Beseter Ohalei Sinai,* mainly about Bedouin family life, and Ada Amiral-Yeivin published her prizewinning collection, *Hupat Avelim.* Poetry books included the fourth volume of Natan Alterman's notebooks, Yehuda Amichai's *Me'adam Ata ve'el Adam Tashuv,* T. Carmi's *Ahat Hi Li,* Meir Wieseltier's *Mikhtavim,* and Aharon Shabtai's *Begin.* The posthumous volume *Mofa* by Yona Wollach also appeared. Ya'ir Hurvitz was awarded the Alterman Prize for poetry. The poet Dan Pagis was deeply mourned.

Among works of criticism were Dan Miron's study of H. N. Bialik's first decade of poetry, Yitshak Bakon's work on Y. H. Brenner and U. N. Gnessin as dual-language writers, Avraham Balaban's essays on Amos Oz, and Uzi Shavit's analysis of Haskalah poetry. Gershon Shaked was awarded the Bialik Prize for criticism, honouring his multivolume history of modern Hebrew fiction. The critic Israel Cohen died at the age of 81. Other publications included what was apparently the final issue, owing to financial difficulties, of the renowned scientific literary journal *haSifrut*. (WARREN BARGAD)

Yiddish. The year's major event in poetry was Avrom Sutskever's volume *Twin Brother,* poems of the decade 1974–85. *Across Sutskever's Poetic Landscape* by Dovid Volpe examined the poet's work from a variety of aspects.

July 1986 marked the 25th anniversary of *Sovetish Heymland,* the only Yiddish literary journal in Eastern Europe. Earlier in the year, the first volume of a literary annual, *Year by Year,* made its appearance, reprinting notable materials from the monthly. Its editor, Arn Vergelis, also published *Magic,* a volume of poetry. Dovid Bergelson's rapportage about World War II, *At the House of Testing,* was brought out in Moscow.

The Holocaust remained a perennial category in Yiddish letters. Zami Feder's *Through the 12 Fires of Hell* traced the Nazi movement from its rise through the establishment of the death camps. Simkha Poliakevitsh's *At the Burned-Out Stake* is a powerful first-person recounting of the Nazi occupation of Poland. Mordkhe Tsanin's *Verdict* continued his cycle of novels about the end of the Warsaw Ghetto. Life in a Polish city during the period between World Wars I and II is captured in Yehuda Elberg's *In Clay Houses.*

The poet Y. Kh. Biletski presented his poetic and philosophical credo in the imaginative poetry-album *Forty Balloons.* M. M. Shaffir brought imaginative power to bear on his lapidary verse in the collection *I Thank You.* Avrom Beker's free translations of Esther, Ruth, Ecclesiastes, and Lamentations give the reader a fresh appreciation of these biblical books. Blume Lempl makes a melancholy pilgrimage through her life in the collection of stories *A Ballad of Dreams. The Street* is a cameo masterpiece by a neglected master, Israel Rabon; Khone Shmeruk contributed a valuable introduction. In *Between Yes and No,* Arye Leyb Pilovski assembled a significant chronicle of the fate of Yiddish in Palestine and Israel between 1907 and 1948. Shloyme Vorzoger's *As Follows* is an important collection of reflective essays on literary themes.

Literary critic Elias Schulman was awarded the prestigious Manger Prize but died in Israel on June 19 before receiving it. (THOMAS E. BIRD)

CHINESE

China. During 1986 there were mixed signals on literary freedom emanating from China. While liberal writers and artists continued to attack restrictions on artistic freedom and a return to tight ideological control, even stressing the need for expressing the self in art and literature, the pro-Communist literary establishment continued to advocate the official line that art and literature should serve China's modernization drive and upgrade "socialist morality." Despite their support for more liberal policies and "democratic pluralism," Zhu Houze (Chu Hou-tse), the Communist Party's propaganda chief, and Wang Meng, the minister of culture, stressed the social responsibility of writers and artists and the need for proper self-restraint. Early in the year three Cabinet ministries were given the power to confiscate the books or magazines of persons who failed to register with the government. The forced reorganization of the literary magazine *China* was a clear setback for those who opposed restraints. Toward the end of December, nationwide student demonstrations advocating democracy and political reforms led to attacks on several leading intellectuals and writers.

Thus, Liu Binyan (Liu Pin-yen; *see* BIOGRAPHIES), a leading writer who ruthlessly exposed the dark side of China, was denounced and purged for his advocacy of "bourgeois liberalism" and Western values. His "China on the 37th Floor," though it praised China's "open-door" policy, revealed the magnitude of the problems confronting the Chinese reformers. Ke Yunlu's (Ko Yün-lu's) novel *Night and Daytime* launched a powerful attack on corruption and loss of purpose on the part of Communist officials.

The highly personal and ambiguous poetry of Yang Lian (Yang Lien) attracted attention. The affirmation of the self became an important theme in the fiction and prose of such writers as Dai Houyin (Tai Houyin) and Ba Jin (Pa Chin). Wang Meng's story "Men with Changeable Shapes" stimulated great interest with its subtle psychological analysis. The search for cultural and ethnic roots became a popular theme for the works of Jia Pingyao (Chia Píng-yao) and others. Wei Minglun's (Wei Minglun's) Sichuanese (Szechwanese) opera *Pan Jinlien* was an instant success.

Taiwan. While such major political developments as the lifting of martial law and the ban on opposition parties were taking place in Taiwan, few major literary works were published. An increasing number of writers devoted themselves to political or social movements. Nevertheless, Lung Ying-t'ai and Sung Tse-lai created great controversies on the state of Taiwan's culture and literature. "Taiwan consciousness" became a popular concern among many native Taiwanese writers. Wang T'o's novel *The Story of Niu-tu Harbor* and Wang Chen-ho's story "Life and the Singer King" were among the best examples.

After several years of silence, Pai Hsien-yung published "Ashes from Cremation," a sentimental but powerful tale of the history and tragedies of modern China as seen through the eyes of two dying old men. Equally powerful were Huang Fan's tales on politics and Sung Tse-lai's novel *Ruined Taiwan in 2010,* which portrays the island as destroyed by disastrous accidents created by nuclear energy plants. Hu Chin-Ch'üan's innovative work "The Butterfly Dream" became a popular stage play. (WINSTON L. Y. YANG)

JAPANESE

The most remarkable book of the year was an impressive biography of the ex-admiral *Seibi Inoue* by the novelist Hiroyuki Agawa. Admiral Inoue was one of the few Japanese who openly opposed the idea of war against the U.S. His career as a naval commander was far from brilliant, and his 4th Fleet was the first in the Japanese Navy to suffer defeat in the Great Pacific War

Hiroyuki Agawa
SHINCHOSHA

(World War II). Considered by his fellow naval officers as weak and incompetent, he was an intelligent, perceptive man but more antihero than hero. Having opposed the war and predicted Japan's defeat, he could have glorified himself as a prophet in postwar Japan. Instead, he chose to live as a hermit in a crude cottage in the Miura Peninsula, tutoring neighbourhood boys and girls in English for a livelihood and refusing to speak in public or give interviews until late in life. Agawa succeeds in making him the subject of an absorbing, vivid biography, exposing his failures and weaknesses but gradually revealing his true stature.

Another remarkable book was an autobiographical novel by Takeshi Kaiko in two volumes, *Broken Coons* and *Night and the Shimmer of the Air,* subtitled "Story of the Era." The author attempted to create a new type of autobiography, concentrating on his auditory experiences throughout his career. The style is both colloquial and poetic, and the impulsive but sensitive responses of the narrator-hero are richly evocative.

The Women Writer's Prize for the year was awarded to *Land of Dirt, Glorified* by Sonoko Sugimoto, whose main theme was the cultural shock created by Buddhism in 8th-century Japan. Yumiko Kurahashi's *Travel to Amanon Country* was a witty, satirical tour de force dealing with imaginary visits to the Feminist Utopia, which turns out to be a nightmarish cul-de-sac.

In literary criticism, Akira Abe's *Homage to the Short Story* was both readable and stimulating, stressing the subtle charms of this neglected genre. Toru Haga's *The Little World of Yosa Buson* successfully evoked the delicate artistic balance of the 18th-century Edo culture, and Koichi Isoda's *Vicissitude of Leftist Writers in Japan* was an effective analysis of the leftist cult. (SHOICHI SAEKI)

See also Art Exhibitions and Art Sales: *Art Sales;* Libraries; Publishing.

This article updates the *Macropædia* article The History of Western LITERATURE and articles on the literatures of the various languages.

Mathematics

The Fields Medals are the mathematician's equivalent of the Nobel Prizes. A small number (two to four) have been awarded at each quadrennial International Congress of Mathematicians since 1936—by tradition, to mathematicians under the age of 40. In 1986 the medals were given to Gerd Faltings of West Germany, Michael Freedman of the U.S., and Simon Donaldson of Great Britain.

The medal to Faltings was for his proof of the Mordell conjecture, a result in algebraic geometry that has interesting consequences in number theory. In the 17th century Pierre de Fermat claimed (although never set down a proof) that the equation $x^n + y^n = z^n$ has no solutions in nonzero integers when the integer n is greater than 2. (When $n = 2$, there are infinitely many solutions, termed Pythagorean triples, corresponding to the sides of right triangles.) Although this claim, usually called Fermat's last theorem, is known to be true for some values of n, it is still unknown for most values.

If Fermat's theorem is false and there is a solution (x,y,z) for some value of n, then one can find a family of solutions of the form (kx,ky,kz) for any integer k. A primitive solution is a solution (x,y,z) such that no integer greater than 1 divides all three numbers. Primitive solutions are the smallest solutions in a family; all other solutions in the family are multiples of it.

A consequence of Falting's work on the Mordell conjecture is that for any value of n there can be only a finite number of primitive solutions of the Fermat equation. Thus, if Fermat's theorem is false, it is just barely false. Of course, most mathematicians believe that there are *no* primitive solutions to the Fermat equation; for example, it is known that there are none for n less than 125,000. Falting's result, however, may provide a crucial step in settling a question that has vexed mathematicians for more than 300 years.

Freedman and Donaldson received their medals for independent work in topology, specifically for their new results about four-dimensional manifolds. One consequence of their work startled the mathematical world: Euclidean space of dimension four is much more complicated than anyone had previously suspected.

Topology studies spaces and continuous maps between them. One familiar example of a space is the real number line, $\mathbb{R}$. A continuous map from $\mathbb{R}$ to $\mathbb{R}$ is a rule that assigns to each real number another number so that numbers close to one another are assigned to other numbers close to one another—in other words, there is no ripping or tearing, only stretching and shifting. A smooth map is a continuous map that has no sharp bends or wrinkles.

Another example of a space can be made from the number line. By considering pairs of numbers, one gets the Euclidean plane, $\mathbb{R}^2$, a flat, infinite surface. In the same way, one can consider n-tuples of real numbers to get Euclidean space of dimension n, denoted by $\mathbb{R}^n$.

The Euclidean spaces of dimension one, two, and three are familiar, corresponding to points on the line, the plane, or the space around us. Euclidean space of dimension four is harder to visualize, but mathematicians reason by analogy: A two-dimensional being who lives on a plane might know about Euclidean three-dimensional space without actually experiencing it.

Of course, there is often more than one way to describe the same space. For example, $\mathbb{R}^2$ can be described both as pairs of numbers and as points in the plane. Two spaces are considered to be topologically the same (homeomorphic) if their points can be identified, one for one, by continuous maps from one space to the other. If the maps used are smooth, then the spaces are said to be smoothly the same (diffeomorphic).

Can two spaces be homeomorphic without being diffeomorphic? (Such spaces would be identified with one another, but not without bending and wrinkling.) It had long been known that, for the number line, the answer is no. Any two spaces that are topologically the same as the number line are smoothly the same: There is only one number line. The same had been proved for Euclidean spaces of all dimensions except in dimension four. Whether there actually is more than one $\mathbb{R}^4$ remained an open question, although most mathematicians believed that Euclidean space was too simple to allow more than one.

The work of Freedman and Donaldson startled everyone. Not only are there two spaces that are topologically the same as $\mathbb{R}^4$ without being smoothly the same but, as other mathematicians soon showed, there are infinitely many different such spaces. Euclidean four-dimensional space is extremely complicated. It is convincing evidence that dimension four, the dimension of space-time used in Einstein's theories of relativity, is strikingly different from all other dimensions. (JOHN EWING)

This article updates the *Macropædia* articles GEOMETRY and NUMBER THEORY.

Military Affairs

Two events that occurred late in 1986 overshadowed the more substantive defense trends of the year. The first was the October "presummit" meeting between U.S. Pres. Ronald Reagan and Soviet leader Mikhail Gorbachev in Reykjavík, Iceland. The second was the revelation that the U.S. had been selling arms to Iran for use in its war against Iraq in what appeared to be an attempt to secure the release of U.S. hostages held by Shi'ah Muslim factions in Lebanon.

At Reykjavík the two superpowers discussed far-reaching, if imprecise, measures of nuclear disarmament, including halving the number of strategic nuclear warheads in the first five years of a ten-year agreement. These proposals went much further than those made in the 14-year-old Strategic Arms Limitation/Reduction Talks (SALT/START) and were, indeed, so sweeping that they seemed designed largely for propaganda purposes. The Soviet charge that President Reagan had blocked an agreement by refusing to abandon the Strategic Defense Initiative (SDI) thus seemed disingenuous. The U.S. was quick to point out that the Soviets had a much larger space-based missile defense program and were constructing the basis for a nationwide antiballistic missile (ABM) system in violation of the 1972 ABM Treaty.

However, Reykjavík seemed to have shifted the superpowers' arms-control talks in the direction of sweeping—even utopian—proposals that captured the public's imagination. It would be difficult to reach agreement on such proposals, yet difficult to return to talks about more limited measures. Even these measures had proved difficult to agree on and of minimal effect, as was shown by the Soviet announcement that the U.S.S.R. would resume nuclear tests early in 1987, and President Reagan's decision to cease observing the unratified SALT II treaty. (See *Arms Control and Disarmament,* below.)

The revelation of U.S. arms sales to Iran led to the resignation of Vice-Adm. John Poindexter, President Reagan's special adviser on national security affairs. Under

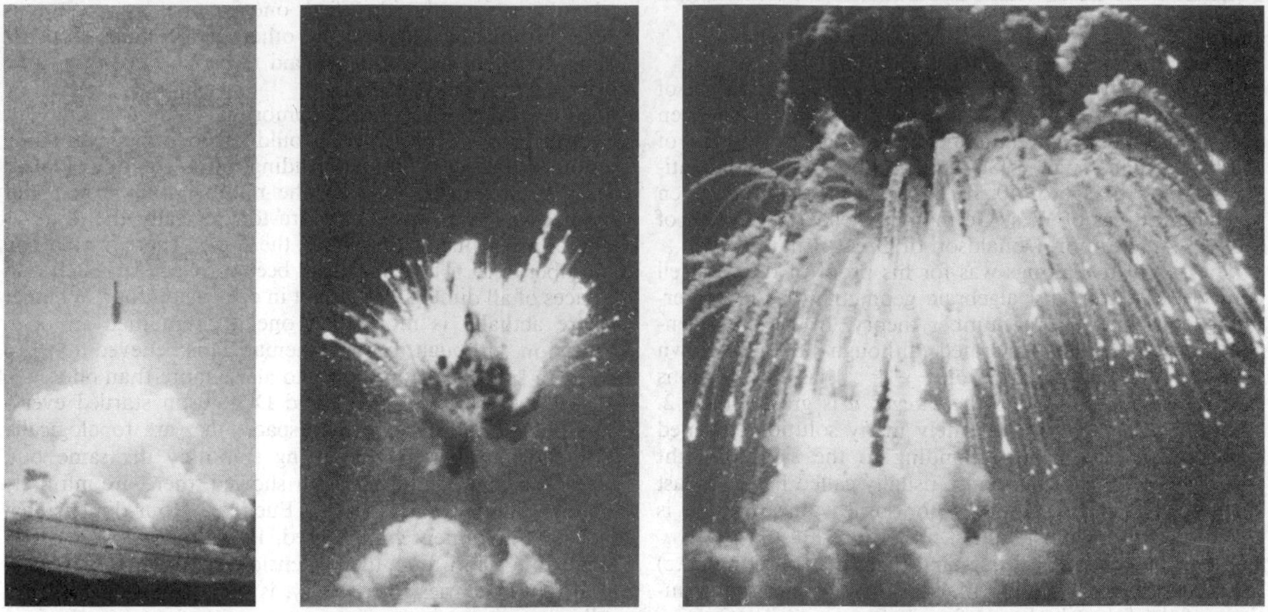

A Titan 34D rocket lifts off, explodes, and showers debris over Vandenberg Air Force Base in California on April 18. The secret military payload is said to have included a reconnaissance satellite intended to monitor the Soviet military. Titan rockets had had a history of problems, creating concern among aerospace and military experts.

AP/WIDE WORLD

Poindexter's direction and that of his predecessor, Robert C. McFarlane, the National Security Council (NSC), set up as an advisory and policy-coordinating group, had become improperly involved in operational issues. This was a major problem with the section headed by Marine Corps Lieut. Col. Oliver North, who was fired from the NSC when Poindexter resigned.

At year's end the details of the Iranian arms sales remained unclear, but intensive investigations were being mounted by the Senate, the House of Representatives, and a newly appointed special prosecutor, among others. It was clear that significant arms sales had taken place and that the U.S. had attempted to negotiate with so-called Iranian moderates. There was evidence that some of the profits from these sales had been used to aid the *contra* forces fighting the Soviet-backed Sandinista government of Nicaragua, although Congress had banned such aid at the time. It was unclear how much President Reagan had known of the details of these operations.

The hostile public reaction to the affair stemmed largely from opposition to helping the Ayatollah Ruhollah Khomeini's regime, which had held U.S. embassy personnel in Tehran hostage for 444 days in 1979–81. The public also appeared to feel that this was not the kind of foreign and defense policy President Reagan had been elected to carry out. It remained to be seen whether the Reagan administration could recover and conduct a coherent defense policy in its last two years. (*See* WORLD AFFAIRS [North America]: *United States*.)

Yet despite the attention focused on Reykjavík and the Iranian arms sales, neither event seemed likely to alter the basic defense issues facing the U.S. In 1986 the three main issues were Gorbachev's expansionist policies, third world wars, and increased terrorism. These developments were interrelated.

The U.S. had hoped that the new Soviet leadership would move away from confrontational cold war policies. Instead Gorbachev, like his predecessors, sought to expand the areas under direct and indirect Soviet control with the objective of eventually gaining control of one or more of three world power centres not under Soviet domination—Western Europe, Japan, and China. Also like his predecessors, President Reagan aimed to contain the Soviets within the areas they already controlled, including Eastern Europe, while maintaining the independence of the three other major power centres. However, the competition between the two superpowers was still constrained by their possession of nuclear weapons and by the emergence of a stable balance of nuclear deterrence. Although the U.S.S.R. had acquired superior nuclear as well as conventional forces in the 1970s, Soviet leaders continued to believe that the potential costs of a nuclear war outweighed the potential gains. The balance of nuclear deterrence between the U.S.S.R. and the three smaller nuclear powers—Britain, France, and China—also remained stable.

In military terms, the international system was divided between the balances of nuclear deterrence and the balances of conventional deterrence. Within the nuclear balances, nations were deterred by the threat of nuclear war from using force, nuclear or conventional, directly against one another. However, the emergence of the Soviet Union as a global military power added a superpower dimension to existing regional conflicts, most notably in the Middle East. This increased the danger that such conflicts could escalate, dragging the superpowers into a confrontation neither had intended or wanted. Adding to the danger were the spread of nuclear weapons to other countries, now thought to include Israel, South Africa, India, and Pakistan, and the proliferation of chemical and biological weapons (CBW), brought to world attention by their use in the continuing Iran-Iraq war.

Outside the nuclear balances, in the third world, states could wage wars in the traditional Clausewitzian manner to achieve political objectives, but with the spread of advanced conventional weapons, these conflicts were becoming increasingly destructive. While the Soviets attempted to make gains in these trouble spots, especially through the use of proxy forces such as the Cubans and Vietnamese, the U.S. increased its support for opposition groups, notably the Nicaraguan *contras* and the National Union for the

Total Independence of Angola (UNITA) forces of Jonas Savimbi (*see* BIOGRAPHIES) in Angola. The April 14–15 U.S. air strike against Libya underlined U.S. determination to oppose state-sponsored terrorism. Such actions by themselves were unlikely to reverse the gains the Soviets had made in the last decade. Nonetheless, these events seemed to set the pattern for the rest of the decade: limited superpower proxy wars and regional conflicts; continued terrorist actions and reprisals on a worldwide scale.

UNITED STATES

U.S. all-volunteer armed forces in 1985 totaled 2,143,955 personnel (202,700 women). Retention rates remained high, as did personnel quality. The defense budget for fiscal 1987 was $292.5 billion, some 6.4% of 1984 gross domestic product (GDP) and about 28% of the federal budget.

The U.S. defense debate centred on the size of the defense budget and the types of force it purchased. Congress felt the Reagan defense buildup had gone far enough and held the 1986–87 budget to zero real growth. This also went some way toward meeting the targets of the Gramm-Rudman-Hollings deficit-reduction act. However, U.S. defense spending as a percentage of GDP was much less than the 1954–64 average of 10%, suggesting that the U.S. could spend more on defense if necessary.

Secretary of Defense Caspar W. Weinberger argued that the U.S. needed to spend more to obtain forces adequate to meet its political commitments. In his view the existing mix of air, land, and sea forces, with high-tech weapons offsetting the Soviets' massive quantitative superiority, was about right, but the total was too small. Despite well-publicized horror stories of cost overruns, the procurement process was working well. On the other hand, critics in the influential military reform movement argued that the U.S. was spending too much for ineffective forces, that weapons were too complicated to work properly, that the procurement process was inflating costs, and that the services, including the Joint Chiefs of Staff, were not organized to maximize their combat potential. Although appealing, the reform arguments were weakened by the lack of specific, workable alternatives. Nevertheless, the administration was unlikely to get increases in defense spending from Congress larger than those needed to offset inflation, while the crucial question of whether U.S. forces were adequate remained unresolved.

Modernization of U.S. strategic and intermediate-range nuclear forces continued. In the Strategic Air Command (SAC), the first squadron of Rockwell B-1B strategic bombers was operational. The aging B-52 bomber force was further reduced to 151 B-52Gs and 90 B-52Hs (first deployed in 1959 and 1962, respectively). Of the B-52Gs, 90 carried 12 AGM-86B air-launched cruise missiles (ALCM) each, while 61 were equipped with the Harpoon air-to-surface missile (ASM) and used in a nonnuclear antishipping role. SAC also had 55 FB-111A medium-range nuclear bombers. Development of the advanced technology (stealth) bomber and the advanced cruise missile continued.

No remedy had been found for the vulnerability of the land-based fixed-silo intercontinental ballistic missile (ICBM) force. At the end of 1986 this force comprised 1,000 silos containing Minuteman II and III ICBM. Only the 550 Minuteman IIIs were modernized missiles, each carrying three multiple independently targetable reentry vehicles (MIRV). The 450 Minuteman II missiles were nearly 20 years old. The ten remaining Titan II missiles were scheduled to be retired. Production of 50 MX Peacekeeper ICBM had been approved, and deployment was to be completed by 1988. These large missiles weighed about 88,000 kg (195,000 lb) each and carried ten MIRV. Tests of the MX Peacekeeper in 1986 were highly successful. However, the Peacekeepers were to be deployed in existing Minuteman silos, which were vulnerable to Soviet attack. Development of the small, single-warhead Midgetman ICBM (about 11,350 kg [25,000 lb]) continued. Under consideration was a land-mobile version carried in armoured vehicles.

The ballistic missile nuclear submarine (SSBN) force totaled 36, carrying 640 submarine-launched ballistic missiles (SLBM). The eight new Ohio-class SSBN each carried 24 Trident I/C-4s, to be replaced by the Trident II/D-5 SLBM in 1988–89. Older SSBN included 12 Franklin class (96 Trident I/C-4s, 96 Poseidon C-3s) and 16 Madison and Lafayette class (96 Trident I/C-4s and 160 Poseidon C-3s). Deployment of submarine-launched nuclear cruise missiles continued, with five nuclear cruise-missile submarines (SSGN) so equipped. Plans called for a total of 700 BGM-109A Tomahawk sea-launched cruise missiles (SLCM). In addition, 2,300 conventionally armed Tomahawk SLCM were being deployed to give each vessel a mix of nuclear and conventionally armed missiles. Dispersing the nuclear SLCM would enhance their survivability.

The minimally equipped North American Aerospace Defense Command had only 76 U.S. F-15 Eagle and 38 Canadian CF—18D (F-18) Hornet modern interceptors. To balance the Soviet antisatellite (ASAT) system, the U.S. was developing an ASAT system carried by F-15 Eagles. Development of SDI components continued. Despite its nickname of "Star Wars," SDI would be only partially space-based.

Still building toward its 600-ship goal, the U.S. Navy had 222 major surface combatants, 93 nuclear-attack submarines (SSN), and 570,973 personnel. These provided 14 carrier battle groups (to rise to 15), each with an attack wing of some 86 aircraft plus escorting surface vessels and SSN. Of the 12 modern (post-1955) aircraft carriers, 4 were nuclear powered and 8 were conventionally powered. Modern aircraft included 300 F-14A Tomcat interceptors, 350 A-6 Intruder and 196 F/A-18A Hornet strike planes, and 64 E-2C electronic warfare/airborne electronic warning aircraft. A third World War II battleship, the *Missouri,* was being recommissioned with Tomahawk SLCM. The 9 nuclear and 22 conventionally powered guided weapons (GW) cruisers included four new Ticonderoga-class ships

AP/WIDE WORLD

As part of Star Wars research, the second stage of a Delta 180/SDI rocket is positioned on a pylon as a prop target in radar cross-section testing at the McDonnell Douglas facility near Palmdale, California.

Table I. U.S./NATO–Soviet Strategic and Intermediate Nuclear Force Balance, July 1986

Weapons systems	Range (km)	Payload[1] (000 lb)	Warheads, yield[2]	CEP[3]	Speed (Mach)	Number deployed
UNITED STATES Strategic Forces						
Intercontinental ballistic missiles (ICBM)						1,000
Minuteman II	11,300	1.6	1 × 1.2 mt	370	...	450
Minuteman III Mod 1	14,800	2.2	3 × 170 kt	350	...	250
Mod 2	12,900	2.4	3 × 335 kt	220	...	300
M-X Peacekeeper	11,000	7	10 × 335 kt	100	...	...
Submarine-launched ballistic missiles (SLBM; in 36 nuclear submarines)						640
Poseidon C-3	4,600	3.3	10 × 50 kt or 14 × 100 kt	450	...	256
Trident I/C-4	7,400	3.0+	8 × 100 kt	450	...	384
Manned bombers and air-launched cruise missiles (ALCM)						
B-52G	12,000	70	20	...	0.95	90
B-52H	16,000	70	8	...	0.95	90
FB-111A	4,700	37.5	6	...	1.5	55
B-1B	12,000	64	32	...	1.25	19
AGM-86B ALCM	2,400	0.60	200 kt	...	0.7	1,380
U.S./NATO Intermediate Nuclear Forces[4] (Total: 702 weapons, 342 delivery systems)						
Intermediate-range ballistic missiles (IRBM)						
U.S. Pershing II	1,800	3	5–50+ kt	45	...	96
Manned bombers and ground-launched cruise missiles (GLCM)						
U.S. F-111 E/F	4,700	28	3	...	1.5	250[5]
U.S. Tomahawk GLCM	2,500	0.27	10–50 kt	20	0.7	128
BRITAIN (Strategic and INF)[6]						
Submarine-launched ballistic missiles (SLBM; in 4 nuclear submarines)						
Polaris A-3	4,600	1.5	3 × 200 kt	900	...	64
Strike aircraft						
Tornado	2,800	16	2	...	1.5	170
FRANCE (Strategic and INF)[6]						
Submarine-launched ballistic missiles (SLBM; in 5 nuclear submarines)						
MSBS M-20/TN 60	3,000	...	1 × 1 mt	...	...	80
MSBS M-4/TN 70	4,400+	...	6 × 150 kt	...	...	16
Intermediate-range ballistic missiles (IRBM)						
SSBS S-3D/TN 61	3,500	...	1 × 1 mt	...	...	18
Strike aircraft						
Mirage IVA	3,200	22	1 × 60–150 kt	...	1.0	22
Mirage IIIE	2,400	18	2 × 15 kt	...	1.8	30
Super Etendard	1,500	10	2 × 15 kt	...	1.0	36
SOVIET UNION Strategic Forces						
Intercontinental ballistic missiles (ICBM)						c. 1,500+
SS-11 Mod 1	1,500	2	1 × 1 mt	1,400	...	} 448
Mod 2/3	13,000	2.5	3 × 100–300 kt	1,100		}
SS-16	9–10,000	...	3 × 150 kt	...	...	c. 100[7]
SS-17 Mod 3	10,000	...	4 × 500 kt	...	...	150
SS-18 Mod 4	11,000	16.7	10 × 500 kt	250	...	308
SS-19 Mod 3	10,000	8	6 × 550 kt	300	...	360
SS-24	10,000	8	8–10 × 100 kt	200	...	} 080
SS-25	10,500	1.6	1 × 550 kt	200		}
Submarine-launched ballistic missiles (in 63 nuclear plus 14 diesel submarines)						c. 1,000
SS-N-5 Serb	1,400	...	1 × 1–2 mt	2,800	...	39
SS-N-6 Mod 1,2	2,400	1.5	1 × 1 mt	1,300	...	} 304
Mod 3	3,000	1.5	2 × 500 kt	1,300	...	}
SS-N-8 Mod 1	7,800	1.5	1 × 1 mt	1,500	...	} 292
Mod 2	9,100	...	1 × 800 kt	900		}
SS-N-17	3,900	2.5	1 × 1 mt	1,500	...	12
SS-N-18 Mod 1	6,500	5	3 × 500 kt	1,400	...	}
Mod 2	8,000	3.6	1 × 450 kt	600	...	} 224
Mod 3	6,500	...	5 × 500 kt	600	...	}
SS-N-20	8,300	...	9–12 × 200 kt	...	...	80
SS-N-23	8,300	...	...	900	...	32
Manned bombers and air-launched cruise missiles (ALCM)						c. 420
Tu-95 Bear B/C/H	12,800	40	5–9	...	0.78	140
Mya-4 Bison	11,200	20	4	...	0.87	20
Tu-26 Backfire B	11,000	17.5	4	...	1.9	260
AS-15 ALCM	1,800	...	250 kt	...	0.6	c. 240
Soviet INF (Total: c. 4,823 warheads, c. 1,423 delivery systems)						
Variable/intermediate/medium-range ballistic missiles (V/I/MRBM)[8]						
SS-4 Sandal	2,000	3	1 × 1 mt	2,300	...	112
SS-20 Mod 1	5,000	1.2	1 × 1.5 mt	...	...	}
Mod 2	5,000	...	3 × 150 kt	c. 400	...	} c. 1,423
Mod 3	7,400	...	1 × 50 kt	...	...	}
Medium/short-range ballistic missiles and ground/sea-launched cruise missiles[9]						
SS-22 MRBM	c. 1,000	...	1 × 500 kt	300	...	c. 130
SS-N-12 G/SLCM	1,000	2.2	1 × 350 kt	...	...	c. 200
Manned bombers[10]						745
Tu-16 Badger	4,800	20	2	...	0.8	480
Tu-22 Blinder	4,000	12	2	...	1.5	165

[1] Payload refers to a missile's throw weight or a bomber's weapons load.
[2] For MIRV and MRV the figure to the left of the multiplication sign gives the number of warheads and the figure to the right is the yield per warhead. For bombers, weapons per bomber are given.
[3] Circular Error Probable: the radius (in metres) of a circle within which at least half of the missile warheads aimed at a specific target will fall.
[4] INF systems are missiles with ranges or aircraft with unrefueled combat radii of 1,000–5,499 km; combat radii are about one-third or less of the range.
[5] Total deployed worldwide; 150 is the inventory normally based in Europe, or within striking range of Europe.
[6] British nuclear forces are under national control but may be assigned to NATO. French nuclear forces are controlled and targeted independently of NATO.
[7] Mobile SS-16 ICBM reported deployed, based on SS-20 V/IRBM.
[8] Total deployed against both NATO and China theatres; two-thirds are thought to be deployed against NATO. Three missiles per launcher for SS-20. Includes 39 non-SALT counted SS-N-5 theatre missiles in 13 diesel submarines.
[9] Although not always classified as Soviet INF, Soviet M/SRBM and G/SLCM could hit targets in Western Europe and are therefore shown for illustrative purposes.
[10] Total deployed worldwide. Of these, about half are allocated to Soviet Naval Aviation (some 240 Tu-16, 35 Tu-22, and 120 Tu-26). Two-thirds of the remaining strike bombers and ASM carriers are considered deployed against NATO. Tu-26 Backfire is now counted as strategic.

Sources: International Institute for Strategic Studies, *The Military Balance 1986–1987;* and *Aviation Week and Space Technology.* Figures for Soviet forces, especially INF, can only be estimates.

The Bradley mechanized infantry combat vehicle, an armoured troop carrier with antitank missiles, is put through its paces at Fort Hood, Texas. The demonstration was for the media in hopes it would help convince the public and Congress of a need for the vehicle.
AP/WIDE WORLD

equipped with the Aegis fleet air defense missile/radar system. Other major surface combatants included 38 GW and 30 gun/antisubmarine warfare (ASW) Spruance-class destroyers and 53 GW and 53 gun frigates.

The Marine Corps, with 196,273 personnel, was—together with the Navy—the main U.S. power-projection force. The Corps was organized in three divisions, each with its air wing. Modern aircraft included 60 F/A-18 Hornet interceptor/strike aircraft, 86 A-6 Intruder strike aircraft, and 77 AV-8A/C Harrier vertical/short takeoff and landing (V/STOL) interceptor strike aircraft. Amphibious warfare ships included five Tarawa- and seven Iwo Jima-class helicopter/Harrier/troop carriers.

The 605,800-strong Air Force had approximately 7,358 combat aircraft. Among modern types were 757 F-15 Eagle interceptors, 977 F-16 Falcon fighter-bombers, and 34 E-3A Sentry airborne warning and control systems (AWACS). Older types included 1,212 F-4 Phantom fighter-bombers/reconnaissance, 280 F-111A/D/E/F medium bombers, and 565 A-10A Thunderbolt ground-support aircraft.

The Army, with 770,904 personnel, formed 18 divisions (18,500 men each): 4 armoured, 6 mechanized, 2 infantry, 4 light infantry, 1 air assault, and 1 airborne. The light infantry divisions were smaller (about 10,200 men each) and easier to transport. They were intended as part of the Rapid Deployment Force for use outside NATO-Europe.

Armour included 4,798 M-1 Abrams tanks and 3,492 M-2/3 Bradley mechanized infantry combat vehicles (MICV), plus some 7,000 M-60A1, M-60A2, and M-60A3 Patton tanks and 12,700 M-113 armoured personnel carriers (APC). Among new missile systems were multiple-launch rocket systems and Patriot surface-to-air missiles (SAM). The Army manned the two new intermediate-range nuclear forces (INF) systems, the Pershing II intermediate-range ballistic missile (IRBM; range 1,800 km [1,100 mi]) and the BGM-109-A Tomahawk ground-launched cruise missile (GLCM; range 2,500 km [1,550 mi]). A total of 150 Pershing IIs and 128 GLCM were operational.

U.S.S.R.

The Soviet military machine was still the world's most powerful, with some 5.1 million personnel (including 1.5 million command and general support personnel) plus 25 million in the reserves. Defense spending remained high at about $295 billion. These figures showed that the post-

Brezhnev leadership was continuing to concentrate Soviet resources on military power. The CIA and U.S. defense intelligence agencies, with rare unanimity, agreed that Soviet defense spending had risen to 12–17% of GDP and could rise to 20%. As Table II shows, 20% was a level exceeded only by Israel, Saudi Arabia, Oman, and Iraq. No other major 20th-century power had spent at such levels except in wartime. The West continually expected Soviet defense spending to fall; instead, it rose even higher.

In part this was because the Soviets' dependence on military forces to sustain their superpower status was becoming irreversible. Fear of Soviet military power had created the NATO alliance of the U.S. and Western Europe and the U.S. alliances with Japan and South Korea. It had helped to turn China from a Soviet ally into an opponent. After more than 40 years of hegemony in Eastern Europe, the Soviets could not rely on the loyalty of their own satellites. Having thus helped to create the hostile world they saw around them, the Soviets could find no solution other than to increase their military power still further. And because they defined their security in absolute terms, their forces were always too few rather than too many. Hence their drive for increased quantity and quality—at increased cost. Similar increases were being made in the forces of their military proxies, such as Cuba, and in their arms shipments to regional allies, including Iraq and Syria.

Observers who hoped the Soviet Union was becoming less secretive and repressive were disabused by its first reaction to the explosion and fire at the Chernobyl nuclear power plant in the Ukraine, when—despite the possible health hazards—no information was given out until neighbouring countries had gathered incontrovertible evidence of radioactivity drifting from the U.S.S.R. The unresolved question was how long the Soviet Union could remain a first-rate military power and a second- or third-rate power in other respects, most notably, in terms of its economy. The answer was probably at least until the end of the century, barring major, unexpected setbacks. But as Chernobyl showed, setbacks could occur in the Soviet system. Given the Soviet reliance on military assets, they were particularly likely in the defense field.

The Strategic Nuclear Forces had 300,000 troops and continued to increase their superiority over U.S. and NATO strategic and intermediate-range nuclear forces in missile and warhead numbers and in warhead yields and accuracy. As of 1986 the Soviets had a first-strike capability that the U.S. would not match before the end of the century. The figures shown in Table I underestimate the Soviet advantage because the U.S.S.R. also deployed 1,000–3,000 reload missiles for their ICBM, IRBM, and SLBM launchers. New systems being tested and deployed included two ICBM, the SS-24 and SS-25 (both mobile); five long-range cruise missiles, three of which were similar to the U.S. Tomahawk, the SS-NX-21 SLCM, SSC-X-4 GLCM, and AS-X-15 ALCM (all in the 3,000-km [1,860-mi] range), plus two long-range G/SLCM; and the SS-N-23 SLBM. The four Typhoon-class SSBN, each carrying 20 SS-N-20 MIRVed SLBM, were the world's largest, displacing 23,000 tons.

The strategic aviation force comprised the new Blackjack A, larger than the U.S. B-1B; 160 older Bears and Bisons (production of the Bear H, as an ALCM launcher, was being resumed); and 140 Tu-22M Backfire B/Cs. Additional medium-range bombers included 130 Tu-22 Blinder A/Bs, 240 obsolete Tu-16 Badgers, and 450 Su-24 strike aircraft. Soviet strategic defensive forces were also large. The Soviet National Air Defense Troops (VPVO) formed a separate service with some 371,000 personnel, 1,300 interceptors, and 9,300 SAM launchers at 1,200 fixed sites. The latest SAM, the SA-12, had a tactical antiballistic missile capability. Soviet upgrading of the ABM system around Moscow, together with construction of other ABM radars, would enable the U.S.S.R. to field a nationwide ABM system.

The two million-strong Army was organized into 51 tank, 142 motor rifle (mechanized), 16 artillery, and 7 airborne divisions (10,500–12,500 men each). Equipment—at much higher levels than for the U.S., its NATO allies, or China—included 53,000 tanks (modern types comprised 9,900 T-72/-80s and 9,300 T-64s, plus 33,600 older T-54/-55/-62s); 63,000 armoured fighting vehicles (AFV); and 29,000 artillery pieces, including new self-propelled 203-mm, 152-mm, and 122-mm guns.

Soviet Army forces continued to be deployed roughly two-thirds against NATO-Europe and one-third against China. There were three Strategic Theatre Commands (GTVD) and a central strategic reserve military district with 16 divisions. The Western GTVD controlled 26 Soviet divisions (14 tank, 12 motor rifle) and 45 non-Soviet divisions in Central and Eastern Europe, plus 63 divisions (31 tank, 30 motor rifle, 2 airborne) in the European U.S.S.R. The Southern GTVD controlled 30 divisions, mainly motor rifle, including some 118,000 troops occupying Afghanistan. The Far Eastern GTVD controlled 53 divisions (7 tank, 45 motor rifle, 1 airborne). There were large overseas deployments in Syria (4,000), Vietnam (7,000), and Cuba (8,000) and smaller ones of 500–2,500 troops each in Algeria, Angola, Ethiopia, Iraq, Laos, Libya, and North Yemen.

WARSAW PACT

In Eastern Europe political uncertainties remained about the degree of non-Soviet Warsaw Pact support for a possible Soviet invasion of Western Europe. Some modernization of forces appeared to be taking place. Soviet forces stationed in the area included 20 divisions in East Germany, 2 in Poland, 5 in Czechoslovakia, and 4 in Hungary. Poland maintained the largest military forces of the Eastern European nations, totaling 402,000 personnel and including a 295,000-strong Army with 3,470 T-54/55/-72 main battle tanks (MBT) and an 88,000-strong Air Force with 675 combat aircraft (400 MiG-21/-21U/-23 interceptors). Czechoslovakia's 201,000-strong forces, the second largest, comprised an Army of 145,000 with 3,500 T-54/-55/-72 tanks and an Air Force of 56,000 with 444 combat aircraft (275 MiG-21/21U/-23 interceptors).

East Germany's armed forces totaled 179,000, including an Army of 123,000 with 1,800 T-54/-55/-62-72 tanks (plus 1,000 in storage) and an Air Force of 40,000 with 337 combat aircraft, including 270 MiG-21F/MF/PF/U/-23 interceptors. Hungary's armed forces, with 105,000 personnel, included an Army of 83,000 with about 1,200 T-54/-55/-72 tanks and an Air Force of 22,000 with 130 MiG-21/-23 interceptors. All four countries allocated much lower proportions of their gross national products (GNPs) to defense than did the U.S.S.R.; 1984 figures were 7.7% for East Germany, 4% for Czechoslovakia, 3.7% for Poland, and 3.9% for Hungary.

NATO

The long crisis caused by NATO's 1979 decision to deploy 572 new INF (108 Pershing II IRBM and 464 GLCM) had finally been resolved when Belgium and The Netherlands agreed to permit deployment on their soil. Britain, Italy and West Germany continued deployment, and protests against the missiles had become negligible. Nevertheless, the effects of the crisis seemed likely to weaken the alliance

Art work depicts two Soviet SU-27 Flanker fighters. The new fighter is capable of combating low-flying aircraft and cruise missiles.
AP/WIDE WORLD

for many years to come. The idea of INF deployment had originated with NATO-Europe, particularly Britain and West Germany, to alleviate fears that the U.S. was decoupling its defense from that of Western Europe. The U.S. had agreed to build and man these INF and then found itself fighting an uphill battle to get their deployment approved by the NATO-Europe countries that had requested them in the first place. Soviet propaganda had played on Western European fears of nuclear weapons, helping to create popular movements against deployment and to suggest that the real threat to European security came from the U.S.

In the aftermath, NATO-Europe governments would be reluctant to take any major initiatives in defense that could trigger similar protest movements. The Netherlands had withdrawn from two nuclear roles in return for accepting cruise missiles, and the unilateral reduction of NATO theatre nuclear forces continued. At the same time, these European developments were generating a reluctance on the part of the U.S. to increase or maintain its NATO-Europe forces. The U.S. made modernization of its obsolete chemical weapons (CW) stockpile conditional on NATO acceptance of these new weapons. This was given, but it was so highly qualified that U.S. production might not go ahead. There was thus an increased questioning, on both sides of the Atlantic, of both the basis for the alliance and its continuation in the form that had emerged by the 1950s, with major U.S. conventional and nuclear force deployments in NATO-Europe for deterrence and defense. These general questions about the future of NATO were sharpened by specific issues facing the alliance.

One such issue was participation of NATO members in the SDI program. Opponents of SDI argued that it was potentially destabilizing and threatened to leave NATO-Europe exposed to Soviet nuclear weapons while the U.S. was sheltered behind its strategic shield. Supporters, on the other hand, argued that SDI would promote stability because it would balance Soviet strategic defenses and that it would provide a shield for NATO-Europe as well as the U.S. The U.S. agreements with Britain and West Germany on their participation in SDI constituted a major advance in alliance cooperation. Canada, Denmark, and Norway had decided that their governments would not participate, although private firms could do so.

As had been the case for some years, however, the major problem facing the alliance was its lack of political will to fund the emerging conventional weapons technologies needed to offset the buildup of Soviet/Warsaw Pact forces. On the crucial Northern/Central Front, stretching from Norway to West Germany, the balance of forces, in terms of total war-mobilized divisions (or their equivalent), was, for NATO, 58 divisions (17 tank, 21⅔ mechanized, and 19⅓ other) with 9,000 MBT; and, for the Warsaw Pact, 106⅔ divisions (75 Soviet) comprising 43 tank, 56 mechanized, and 7⅔ other with 29,500 MBT. This gave the Soviet/Warsaw Pact forces an advantage of about 2 to 1 in divisions and more than 3 to 1 in MBT. The military imbalance was accentuated by the imbalance in the sharing of military expenses. As Table II shows, U.S. defense spending as a percentage of 1984 GDP was, at 6.4%, approximately twice that of France and West Germany (4.1% and 3.3%) and about three times that of Canada, Denmark, and Italy. Britain's defense spending, at 5.5% of GDP, was comparable to that of the U.S.

UNITED KINGDOM

Defense expenditure for 1985–86 totaled $24,879,000,000 (5.5% of 1984 GDP). The all-volunteer forces were efficient but relatively small and short of modern equipment. The Army of 162,000 had 250 new Challenger and 900 Chieftain MBT plus 2,338 MICV/APC. The Royal Air Force (RAF), with 93,400 personnel, had about 600 combat aircraft. Some 204 of the new Tornado GR-1 multirole combat aircraft were being deployed in fighter, ground-attack, and reconnaissance models, replacing 150 Phantom fighters. Other modern aircraft included 52 Harrier GR-3/T-4 V/STOL, 75 Jaguar GR-1 ground-attack/reconnaissance planes, and 34 Nimrod MR-1/-1A/-2 maritime reconnaissance aircraft. During the year the U.K. government decided to scrap its Nimrod program in favour of the U.S. AWACS. The Royal Navy was third largest naval force in the world with 68,300 personnel, 29 attack submarines (14 nuclear), 59 major surface combatants including 3 ASW carriers with Sea Harriers, 15 GW destroyers, and 39 general-purpose frigates. Royal Marine personnel totaled some 7,600.

Britain's major overseas deployment was the British Army of the Rhine with 56,000 army and 10,600 RAF personnel. An additional 2,000 personnel manned the Falkland Islands base. Modernization of Britain's national nuclear forces continued with the construction of four SSBN carrying 64 U.S. Trident II SLBM with U.K. nuclear warheads.

FRANCE

Defense spending in 1986 was estimated at $22,342,000,000. Modernization of France's national nuclear forces continued, with five SSBN operational, one being refitted, and one under construction. The M-20 SLBM was being replaced with the M-4. Medium-range and tactical nuclear forces were also being increased, including the ASMP nuclear air-to-surface missile (ASM).

Military personnel totaled 557,500 (300,000 in the Army) but were to be reduced by 37,500 by 1988. Equipment included 1,300 AMX-30 MBT (248 new AMX-30B2), 780 AMX-10P/PC Milan MICV, and about 3,000 APC. These were organized in six armoured, two light armoured, and two motor rifle divisions, plus a Rapid Action Force for overseas intervention consisting of one parachute, one air portable marine, one light armoured, one alpine, and one air mobile division (mostly with 8,000 personnel each). The Air Force of some 96,000 personnel had 555 combat aircraft, the newer models including 170 Mirage F-1C and 40 Mirage 2000C interceptors plus 30 Mirage 5F and some 138 Jaguar A ground-attack fighters. The 66,345-strong Navy's 46 major surface combatants included 2 light and 1 helicopter carrier, 17 destroyers, and 25 frigates; the Navy also had 17 attack submarines (2 SSN). Approximately 33,500 personnel from all services were deployed overseas, with an additional 50,000 in West Germany. French nuclear tests in the Pacific continued, including tests of French neutron (enhanced-radiation) weapons.

WEST GERMANY

West Germany's defense budget amounted to $22,487,000,000 in 1986. Standing armed forces totaled 486,000, more than half of them volunteers, rising to 1,256,000 on mobilization, plus 20,000 paramilitary forces. The 340,800-strong Army included 12 divisions organized in 5,000-man brigades, 70 of which were tank, 64 armoured infantry, 33 armoured artillery, 12 parachute, and 4 mountain. Armour included 1,513 new Leopard 2 and 2,437 Leopard 1 MBT, plus about 2,136 MICV and 3,436 APC. Large numbers of artillery, antiaircraft guns and missiles, antitank guns, and guided weapons were also deployed.

The Air Force had 108,700 personnel with 525 combat aircraft. These included 143 new Tornados, 186 older F-4 Phantoms, and 90 obsolete F-104G and 173 Alpha Jet ground-attack fighters. The 36,300-strong Navy, designed for coastal warfare in the Baltic Sea, had 40 fast-attack craft equipped with guided missiles, 7 GW destroyers, 6 GW frigates, and 24 coastal submarines. The naval air arm consisted of 105 combat aircraft, including 46 Tornados and 40 F-104 attack/reconnaissance planes.

ARMS CONTROL AND DISARMAMENT

President Reagan's controversial decision to deploy the 131st B-52 bomber with ALCM put the U.S. over the limits of the unratified 1979 SALT II treaty. In explaining the action, the U.S. pointed out that the treaty had expired on Dec. 31, 1985, and while the U.S. had observed its limits, the Soviets had not. Cited as a particularly blatant violation by the Soviets was their testing of two new ICBMs instead of the one permitted. Soviet violations had been detailed in the U.S. Defense Department's November 1985 report.

Critics argued that the Soviet violations were not militarily significant, that the administration was jeopardizing the chances of reaching a replacement agreement, and that terminating SALT II while proceeding with SDI threatened the 1972 ABM Treaty, the last major agreement of the 1970s still in force. The ABM Treaty was due for review in 1987, but Soviet violations, particularly the continued construction of an ABM radar at Krasnoyarsk, made it doubtful that the treaty could last indefinitely, as had been intended. The president also insisted he would not sacrifice SDI. (See *Introduction,* above.)

In light of these developments, the continued U.S.-U.S.S.R. negotiations in the talks covering strategic offensive forces (START), weapons in space, and INF were not expected to produce effective results. The proposals put forward by both sides, particularly the various Soviet offers of major reductions in strategic forces, seemed designed for propaganda purposes. In Stockholm the Conference on Confidence- and Security-Building Measures and Disarmament in Europe adopted a major arms-control accord that dealt with advance notice and verification of military exercises and other conventional force activities, but no progress was made in the other arms-control negotiations, including the Vienna talks on mutual and balanced force reductions.

Overall, the arms-control record since the 1972 SALT I agreements had proved disappointing. The U.S. had had high hopes of achieving a series of agreements that would place balanced, effective, and verifiable limits on nuclear, conventional, and chemical and biological weapons, but the limits agreed on had imposed little real restraint on weapons programs and had been violated by the U.S.S.R. and other countries. Expectations for arms control in the late 1980s had been lowered accordingly.

MIDDLE EAST

The Middle East remained the most militarily unstable area in the world. Its sharp divisions over economic, political, racial, and religious issues were reflected in the high relative levels of defense spending and large military forces of the major regional powers. These divisions created overlapping balances of military forces.

In the Israeli-Arab military balance, Syria had emerged as the greatest threat to Israel, defeating the Israelis in the conflict for control over Lebanon north of the Awali River. Nevertheless, Syrian conventional forces were inadequate for attacking Israel unaided. Jordan's King Hussein was unwilling to combine his forces with Syria's since this would risk losing Jordanian territory to either Israel or Syria. Egypt had been an uneasy ally of Israel since the 1978 Camp David agreements. The U.S. was committed to supporting Israel for moral and domestic political as well as strategic reasons and thus also supported Jordan and Egypt. Syria and Iraq, both hard-line states in the confrontation with Israel, received assistance from the Soviets.

The second military balance, that of conservative versus radical Arab states, was reflected in the Iran-Iraq war, which entered its seventh year. This had produced unlikely alliances, with the generally anti-Soviet conservative states, notably Saudi Arabia and the other Persian Gulf oil producers, joining with the U.S.S.R. to support Iraq. Iraq's opponent, the fundamentalist Shi'ah regime in Iran, was supported by the radical states, notably Libya, as well as by Israel, which wanted Iraq's forces tied down. Israel appeared to have played a crucial role in the secret U.S. arms sales to Iran. China and France sold arms to both combatants.

The third military balance was between the main factions of the Palestinian movement and their supporters. All were opposed to Israeli control of the West Bank, but Syria supported only those factions prepared to accept its

Table II. Approximate Strengths of Regular Armed Forces of the World

Country	Military personnel in 000s: Army	Navy	Air Force	Warships[1]: Aircraft carriers/ cruisers	Submarines[2]	Destroyers/ frigates	Jet aircraft[3]: Bombers and fighter-bombers	Fighters/ reconnaissance	Tanks[4]	Defense expenditure as % of 1984 GNP[5]
I. NATO										
Belgium	67.4	4.5	19.5	—	—	4 FFG	124 FB	72, 20 R	334	3.2
Canada[6]	21.0	5.5	15.3	—	3	4 DDG, 19 FF	105 FB, 18 MR	—	114	2.1
Denmark	15.6	6.9	7.0	—	4	5 FFG, 5 FF	64 FB	16,16 R	208	2.3
France[7]	296.5	66.3	96.0	2 CV, 1 CVH, 1 CG	15, 2 SSN, 5 SSBN	17 DDG, 25 FFG	30 B, 288 FB	186, 53 R, 42 MR	1,300	4.1
Germany, West	340.8	36.3	108.7	—	24	7 DDG, 6 FFG, 3 FF	534 FB	60, 87 R, 14 MR	4,895	3.3
Greece	165.5	19.5	24.0	—	10	14 DD, 2 FFG, 5 FF	167 FB	100, 35 R, 16 MR	1,776	7.2
Italy	270.0	47.2	70.6	2 CVH, 2 CAH	9	4 DDG, 12 FFG, 4 FF	306 FB	29 R, 14 MR	1,770	2.7
Luxembourg	0.7	—	—	—	—	—	—	—	—	1.1
Netherlands, The	66.2	17.0	17.9	—	5	17 FFG	190 FB	18 R, 15 MR	1,146	3.2
Norway	20.0	7.6	9.4	—	14	5 FFG	98 FB	7 MR	122	2.8
Portugal	40.0	14.4	13.8	—	3	17 FF	48 FB	—	60	3.2
Spain	230.0	62.5[(8)]	33.0	1 CVH	8	11 DD, 11 FFG	43 FB	114, 17 R, 6 MR	883	2.8
Turkey	542.0	55.0	57.3	—	17	13 DD, 4 FF	308 FB	32, 35 R	3,700	4.4
United Kingdom	162.0	68.3[8]	93.4	3 CVH	15, 14 SSN, 4 SSBN	15 DDG, 39 FFG	461 FB	70, 27 R, 28 MR	1,050	5.5
United States	770.9	767.1[8]	605.8	3 BBG, 5 CVN, 10 CV, 9 CGN, 22 CG, 5 LHA, 7 LPH, 13 LPD, 28 LSD/T	86 SSN, 36 SSBN, 5 SSGN,	38 DDG, 30 DD, 53 FFG, 53 FF	260 SB, 230 B, 2,110 FB	2,330, 270 R, 380 MR/ASW	14,296	6.4
II. WARSAW PACT										
Bulgaria	148.5	8.5	35.0	—	3	2 FFG	100 FB	150, 30 R	1,950	3.9
Czechoslovakia	145.0	—	56.0	—	—	—	132 FB	275, 37 R	3,500	4.0
Germany, East	123.0	16.0	40.0	—	—	3 FFG	49 FB	270, 18 R	2,800	7.7
Hungary	83.0	—	22.0	—	—	—	15 FB	130	1,260	3.9
Poland	295.0	19.0	88.0	—	3	—	240 FB	400, 35 R, 10 MR	3,470	3.7
Romania	150.0	7.7	32.0	—	—	—	120 FB	240, 18 R	1,380	1.4
U.S.S.R.	3,276.9	451.0[8]	1,086.0[9]	4 CV, 2 CVH, 2 CGN, 27 CG, 8 CA	130, 70 SSN, 63 SSBN, 14 SSB, 48 SSGN, 17 SSG	45 DDG, 16 DD, 32 FFG, 35 FF	420 SB, 615 B, 2,940 FB	3,560, 660 R, 135 MR	53,000	12–17
III. OTHER EUROPEAN										
Albania	31.5	3.3	7.2	—	2	—	—	100	190	5.5
Austria	50.0	—	4.7	—	—	—	32 FB	—	170	1.2
Finland	30.0	2.0	2.9	—	—	—	—	61	*c.* 100	1.6
Ireland	12.3	1.0	0.9	—	—	—	—	—	—	1.6
Sweden[10]	47.0/800.0	9.6	8.0	—	12	—	120 FB	180, 54 R	670	3.0
Switzerland[10]	20.0/1,100.0	—	3.0/45.0	—	—	—	139 FB	128, 18 R	970	2.1
Yugoslavia	161.5	12.5	36.0	—	6	3 FFG	200 FB	140, 45 R	1,020	3.8
IV. MIDDLE EAST AND MEDITERRANEAN; SUB-SAHARAN AFRICA; LATIN AMERICA[11]										
Algeria	150.0	7.0	12.0	—	2	3 FF	170 FB	140, 6 R	890	2.0
Egypt	320.0	20.0	105.0	—	12	1 DDG, 4 FFG	90 FB	169, 31 R	2,250	9.6
Iran[12]	305.0	14.5	35.0	—	—	3 DDG, 4 FFG	50 FB	10 F, 7 R	1,000	12.3
Iraq[12]	800.0	5.0	40.0	—	—	—	15 B, 181 FB	270	4,500	51.1
Israel[10]	112.0/606.0	9.0/19.0	28.0/78.0	—	3	—	532 FB	13 R	3,660	24.4
Jordan	62.7	0.3	7.2	—	—	—	67 FB	34	790	13.4
Kuwait	10.0	1.1	2.0	—	—	—	34 FB	34	240	7.6
Lebanon[13]	...	...	...	—	—	—	—	...	...	...
Libya[14]	55.0	6.5	10.0	—	6	1 FFG	7 B, 176 FB	272, 2 R	2,360	...
Morocco	150.0	7.0	13.0	—	—	1 FFG	68 FB	—	110	5.0
Oman	16.5	2.0	3.0	—	—	—	40 FB	—	39	24.2
Qatar	5.0	0.7	0.3	—	—	—	23 FB	—	24	...
Saudi Arabia	40.0	3.5	14.0	—	—	4 FFG	65 FB	45, 10 R	450	20.9
Sudan, The	53.0	0.7	3.0	—	—	—	32 FB	—	140	...
Syria	320.0	2.5	130.0	—	—	2 FF	193 FB	280, 10 R	4,200	15.1
Tunisia	30.0	3.5	3.5	—	—	1 FF	14 FB	—	68	5.4
United Arab Emirates	40.0	1.5	1.5	—	—	—	3 FB	30	136	8.3
Yemen, North	35.0	0.6	1.0	—	—	—	—	91	659	17.8
Yemen, South	24.0	1.0	2.5	—	—	—	77 FB	36	470	16.3
Angola[15]	36.0	1.5	2.0	—	—	—	98 FB	38	470	...
Ethiopia[16]	220.0	3.0	4.0	—	—	—	145 FB	—	1,000	11.4

direction and opposed the more independent, ultraradical groups. Egypt opposed both Libyan- and Iranian-supported radical Islamic organizations.

The fourth military balance was in the Persian Gulf, where Saudi Arabia, Kuwait, and the other members of the Gulf Cooperation Council were trying to defend their vast oil fields with forces that—despite major efforts—were too small for the task. U.S., British, and French assistance to the conservative oil-rich states was useful but modest.

Overall, the Middle East was the most dangerous of the third world regions. There were too many conflicts at too many levels, and too much was at stake, most notably the poorly protected oil reserves. The conflicts covered the spectrum from terrorist acts carried out by shadowy groups to full-scale conventional warfare (including the use of chemical weapons) in the conflict between Iraq and Iran. In the background were Israel's nuclear forces, officially denied but generally believed to exist and to be increasing.

Assisted by massive Soviet aid, Syria's Pres. Hafez al-Assad remained the regional strongman. Syrian armed forces personnel totaled 392,500, with an Army of 320,000 comprising five armoured and three mechanized divisions. Equipment included 1,100 new T-72 and 3,100 T-54/-55/-62 MBT and 2,600 BMP/BTR-series MICV/APC. The separate Air Defense Command had 60,000 personnel manning 87 batteries with Soviet SA-2/-3/-5/-6 SAM. The 70,000-strong Air Force had some 480 combat aircraft, including 30 MiG-25 Foxbat E, 70 MiG-23 Flogger E, and 180 MiG-21 PF/MF interceptors and 50 MiG-23 Flogger F and 40 Su-20 fighter-bombers. Defense spending totaled $3,623,000,000 in 1986.

Israel remained the region's strongest military power, especially in the quality of its weapons. Its defense spending burden, which reached $5,378,000,000 for 1986–87,

Country	Military personnel in 000s			Warships[1]			Jet aircraft[3]			
	Army	Navy	Air Force	Aircraft carriers/ cruisers	Submarines[2]	Destroyers/ frigates	Bombers and fighter-bombers	Fighters/ recon-naissance	Tanks[4]	Defense expenditure as % of 1984 GNP[5]
Kenya	13.0	0.6	—	—	—	—	11 FB	—	76	4.1
Madagascar	20.0	0.6	0.5	—	—	—	12 FB	—	—	2.3
Mozambique[17]	28.0	0.8	1.0	—	—	—	53 FB	—	250	8.4
Nigeria	80.0	5.0	9.0	—	—	1 FFG	51 FB	—	112	1.9
Somalia	40.0	0.7	2.0	—	—	—	21 FB	36	211	11.3
South Africa[10]	76.4/404.5	9.0	13.0	—	3	—	14 B, 112 FB	37	250	4.1
Tanzania	40.3	0.85	1.0	—	—	—	—	29	30	2.5
Zaire	22.0	0.9	2.5	—	—	—	—	8	50	2.0
Zimbabwe	41.0	—	1.0	—	—	—	5 B, 14 FB	—	42	4.8
Argentina	40.0	18.0[8]	15.0	1 CV	4	6 DDG	7 B, 106 FB	13 MR	260	3.3
Brazil	183.0	49.8[8]	50.7	1 CVH	7	10 DD, 6 FFG	35 FB	17, 32 MR	—	0.5
Chile	57.0	29.0	15.0	—	4	4 DDG, 2 DD, 2 FFG	58 FB	24, 6 MR	91	8.5
Colombia	53.0	9.0	4.2	—	2	4 FFG	13 FB	—	12	1.1
Cuba	130.0	13.5	18.5	—	3	—	51 FB	289	1,000	7.9
El Salvador	38.6	1.3	2.7	—	—	—	8 FB	—	—	4.5
Mexico	105.0	28.0[8]	6.5	—	—	2 DD, 5 FF	—	11 F, 11 MR	—	0.3
Nicaragua	69.0	1.0	2.0	—	—	—	...	...	120	11.7
Peru	85.0	27.0[8]	15.0	2 CA	12	8 DD, 3 FFG	20 B, 60 FB	13 MR	280	7.8
Venezuela	34.0	10.0	5.0	—	2	6 FFG	20 B, 13 FB	57	81	2.2
				V. FAR EAST AND OCEANIA[11]						
Afghanistan[18]	45.0	—	5.0	—	—	—	18 B, 95 FB	—	450	6.9
Australia	32.0	15.5	22.7	—	6	3 DDG, 10 FFG	23 B	56, 20 MR	103	2.8
Bangladesh	82.0	6.5	3.0	—	—	3 FF	18 FB	12	50	1.8
Burma	170.0	7.0	9.0	—	—	—	—	—	24	3.9
China	2,110.0	350.0[8]	490.0	—	112, 3 SSGN, 2 SSBN	15 DDG, 26 FFG, 5 FF	800 B, 500 FB	4,600, 300 R	11,450	1.6–7.0
India	1,100.0	47.0	113.0	1 CV	8	3 DDG, 10 FFG, 10 FF	188 FB	376, 20 R, 8 MR	2,790	3.9
Indonesia	216.0	38.0[8]	27.0	—	2	4 FFG, 9 FF	32 FB	15	—	3.0
Japan	155.0	44.0	44.0	—	15	31 DDG, 3 DD, 3 FFG, 15 FF	50 FB	223, 16 R, 94 MR	1,070	1.0
Korea, North	750.0	35.0	55.0	—	20	2 FF	80 B, 410 FB	270	3,275	10.2
Korea, South	520.0	48.0[8]	33.0	—	—	7 DDG, 2 DD, 2 FFG	260 FB	65, 10R	1,300	5.4
Laos	50.0	1.0	2.0	—	—	—	20 FB	—	30	...
Malaysia	90.0	9.0	11.0	—	—	2 FFG, 2 FF	58 FB	3 MR	—	5.9
Mongolia	22.0	—	3.5	—	—	—	—	17	650	11.5
New Zealand	5.8	2.6	4.1	—	—	4 FFG	22 FB	6 MR	—	1.8
Pakistan	450.0	13.0	17.6	—	6	7 DDG	108 FB	200, 13 R, 3 MR	1,600	7.1
Philippines	70.0	26.0[8]	17.0	—	—	7 FF	20 FB	18	—	1.5
Singapore	45.0	4.5	6.0	—	—	—	68 FB	26, 13 R	—	5.8
Taiwan	309.0[8]	38.0	77.0	—	2	23 DD, 9 FF	377 FB	15, 8 R, 29 MR	309	5.9
Thailand	166.0	42.0[8]	48.0	—	—	6 FF	13 FB	39, 10 R, 9 MR	365	4.2
Vietnam	1,000.0	40.0[8]	15.0	—	—	6 FF	83 FB	200	1,600	...

Note: Data exclude paramilitary, security, and irregular forces. Naval data exclude vessels of less than 100 tons standard displacement. Figures are for July 1986.

[1]Aircraft carrier (CV); aircraft carrier, nuclear (CVN); helicopter carrier (CVH); general purpose amphibious assault ship (LHA); amphibious transport dock (LPD); amphibious assault ship (helicopter) (LPH); dock/tank landing ship (LSD/T); battleship (BBG); heavy cruiser (CA); guided missile cruiser (CG); guided missile cruiser, nuclear (CGN); helicopter cruiser (CAH); destroyer (DD); guided missile destroyer (DDG); frigate (FF); guided missile frigate (FFG); N denotes nuclear powered.

[2]Nuclear-powered attack submarine (SSN); ballistic missile submarine (SSB); guided (cruise) missile submarine (SSG); coastal (C); N denotes nuclear powered.

[3]Bombers (B), fighter-bombers (FB), strategic bombers (SB), reconnaissance fighters (R); maritime reconnaissance (MR). Data include jet combat aircraft from all services including naval and air defense. MR also includes propeller drive ASW and ECM aircraft; data exclude light strike/counter-insurgency (COIN) aircraft.

[4]Main battle tanks (MBT), medium and heavy, 31 tons and over.

[5]Figures for NATO members and Israel are for GDP.

[6]Of Canada's other military personnel, approximately 41,200 are not identified by service.

[7]French forces were withdrawn from NATO command structure in 1966, but France remains a member of NATO.

[8]Includes marines.

[9]Figure includes the Strategic Rocket Forces (298,000) and the Air Defense Force (335,000), both separate services.

[10]Second figure is fully mobilized strength.

[11]Sections IV and V list only those states with significant military forces.

[12]Losses in Iran-Iraq war made remaining force estimates uncertain.

[13]Lebanon's civil war and division mean that there are no longer any truly national forces, only militias.

[14]Some advanced Libyan aircraft are maintained and manned by Soviet/Warsaw Pact crews.

[15]Plus 30–35,000 Cubans and 500 East Germans serving with Angolan forces.

[16]Ethiopia also has 7,000 Soviet, Cuban plus other Soviet bloc troops, and a 150,000-strong People's Militia.

[17]Plus Cuban, Warsaw Pact, and Chinese advisers and technicians.

[18]Figures approximate, given Soviet occupation of Afghanistan. Excludes about 118,000 Soviet occupation troops, plus 5,000 Cubans/Czechs.

Sources: International Institute for Strategic Studies, 23 Tavistock Street, London, *The Military Balance 1986–1987, Strategic Survey 1985–86.*

was becoming increasingly difficult to support, even with massive U.S. aid. Defense had consumed 24.4% of GDP in 1984. With a population of only 4.4 million, Israel raised standing armed forces of 149,000 that would increase to 703,000 on mobilization. The Army of 112,000 formed 11 armoured divisions and 9 mechanized infantry, 7 parachute, and 15 artillery brigades. These forces had some 3,660 MBT and 6,300 MICV/APC. The 28,000-strong Air Force had 629 combat aircraft, including 50 U.S. F/TF-15 Eagles, 67 U.S. F-16A/B Falcons, 150 Israeli Kfir C1/C2/C7s, and 131 U.S. F-4E Phantom interceptor/fighter-bombers.

Egypt's armed forces totaled 445,000 personnel; defense spending was estimated at $5,215,000,000 in 1986–87. The nation's conversion from Soviet to Western equipment was continuing, with most of the Soviet equipment in reserve. The Army of 320,000 had 753 U.S. M-60A3 and 500 effective Soviet T-54/-55/-62 MBT. Effective aircraft for the 25,000-strong Air Force comprised 33 F-4E Phantoms and 54 Mirage 5SDE2 fighter-bombers plus 35 F-16A and 100 MiG-21 interceptors. Jordan's small but effective Army (70,200 personnel) had 794 MBT, and the Air Force (7,200) had 67 F-5E/F and 34 Mirage F-1CJ/EJ fighter-bombers.

The Iran-Iraq war continued as a World War I-type conflict of attrition between entrenched infantry, supported by artillery and limited quantities of armour. Casualties were heavy, and much equipment was destroyed; the figures in Table II are rough estimates. Iraq continued its air strikes on oil tankers in the Persian Gulf in an effort to limit Iranian earnings from oil exports. However, the small strike forces available to Iran and Iraq kept damage to shipping to tolerable levels. Strikes against cities, halted in 1985, showed signs of being resumed at year's end. (*See* WORLD

A fire-damaged Soviet nuclear submarine surfaces about 970 kilometres (600 miles) east of Bermuda. Soviet leader Mikhail Gorbachev sent a message to U.S. Pres. Ronald Reagan assuring him that the circumstances posed no danger of nuclear explosion or missile launching.
AP/WIDE WORLD

AFFAIRS [Middle East and North Africa]: *Middle Eastern and North African Affairs.*) Libya's forces remained large, totaling 71,500 personnel with 2,360 MBT and 489 combat aircraft. Libyan forces were actively engaged in northern Chad.

SOUTH, EAST, AND SOUTHEAST ASIA

The Soviet occupation of Afghanistan continued, but the Soviet forces were still unable to gain complete control of the country. The U.S.S.R. announced the withdrawal of some troops, though the U.S. claimed the move was merely normal troop rotation. (*See* WORLD AFFAIRS [South Asia]: *Afghanistan.*) Border incidents between Afghanistan and Pakistan and the possibility of Soviet military strikes into the Baluchistan area of Pakistan remained a potential danger. Despite increased U.S. military aid, Pakistan's armed forces totaled only 480,600 personnel, mainly an Army of 450,000 with 1,600 MBT (mostly Type-59). The Air Force comprised 17,600 personnel and 373 combat aircraft, including 30 F-16 Falcon and 50 Mirage 5PA3 fighter-bombers. The defense budget in 1985–86 totaled $2,067,000,000.

India's armed forces in 1986 totaled some 1,260,000 personnel. The 1.1 million-strong Army had some 2,800 MBT, including 350 new T-72s. The Air Force of 113,000 had 728 combat aircraft, including 72 MiG-23 Flogger H and 50 Jaguar GR-1 fighter-bombers. Defense spending in 1986–87 amounted to $6,956,000,000.

China's forces remained strong in manpower (2.9 million) but weak in modern equipment. Its defense expenditure was estimated at about 7% of GNP. However, its military modernization program was of major long-term significance. The nominally conscript forces were effectively volunteers, with high standards of professionalism. These assets were combined with existing equipment in a distinctively Chinese mix to produce units of considerable combat effectiveness. The moderate, affordable modernization now under way could produce significant increases in this effectiveness. Accordingly, China appeared certain to play an increasingly important role in the military balance vis-à-vis the U.S.S.R. and elsewhere in Asia.

China's nuclear stockpile was small, with limited numbers of comparatively old, vulnerable delivery systems. These included about 6 ICBM (DF-4/-5), 60 DF-3 IRBM, and 50 DF-2 medium-range ballistic missiles, along with 120 H-6 (Tu-16) medium bombers. Two Xia-class SSBN with 12 CSS-NX-4 SLBM (modified DF-3s) were operational. The Army's 2,110,000 personnel was to be reduced. Equipment included only 11,450 MBT (mostly T-59/-69), while the 490,000-strong Air Force's 5,300 combat aircraft were modifications of old Soviet models, including 3,000 J-6/MiG-19 fighters.

Vietnam remained the largest active military power in Southeast Asia, with armed forces, mostly Army, totaling 1,155,000. The Army had about 1,600 MBT, and the 15,000-strong Air Force had approximately 290 combat aircraft. Deployment of occupation forces abroad included 140,000 in Kampuchea and 50,000 in Laos. Evidence of illegal Vietnamese use of Soviet-supplied chemical and biological weapons, especially against the Hmong people of Laos, continued to be put forward.

Although North Korea's forces were larger than those of South Korea, they were not sufficient to launch an invasion of the South. The balance was 840,000 personnel, 3,275 MBT, 1,400 APC, and 854 combat aircraft (mostly older types) for the North versus 601,000 personnel, 1,300 MBT, 860 APC, and 462 combat aircraft (mostly modern types) for the South.

The government of Japanese Prime Minister Yasuhiro Nakasone decided that it would break the long-standing tradition of spending no more than 1% of GNP on defense. Japan's 1986–87 defense expenditure was $20,129,000,000. Armed forces personnel totaled 243,000, including an Army of 155,000 with 1,070 MBT. The Air Force and Navy had 44,000 personnel each. Equipment included 50 Japanese-made F-1 fighter-bombers, 83 F-15J/JD Eagle and 110 F-EJ Phantom fighter-bombers, 34 destroyers (18 GW), 18 frigates, and 15 submarines. Taiwan's armed forces, totaling 424,000 personnel, continued to provide a credible defense against China. The Army, with 270,000 personnel, had 309 MBT, and the 77,000-strong Air Force had 562 combat aircraft, including 255 F-5E/F fighter-bombers. Defense spending in 1986–87 was $4.2 billion.

In the Philippines the transfer of power from the regime

of Pres. Ferdinand Marcos to that of Corazon Aquino was assisted by the U.S. The existing U.S. lease on the irreplaceable Clark and Subic Bay military bases would expire in 1990, but the attitude of the new government toward renewal of the lease had not been made clear.

AFRICA SOUTH OF THE SAHARA

Conflicts between South Africa and Angola and between the white and nonwhite populations within South Africa continued to overshadow other events in sub-Saharan Africa. South Africa was the dominant military power in the region, with armed forces totaling 106,400 (rising to 423,500 on mobilization). Equipment included 250 MBT, 1,500 Ratel MICV, and 372 combat aircraft. These were extremely effective forces with considerable combat experience. Defense spending was estimated at $2,270,000,000 for 1985–86.

South Africa's conflict with Mozambique had been partly settled by negotiation in 1984, but the fate of the settlement was uncertain in the wake of Mozambican Pres. Samora Machel's death in a plane crash—blamed by some on the South African government. Meanwhile, the conflict with Angola continued. The latter's armed forces, of poor quality, totaled 50,000, assisted by 35,000 Cubans (27,000 troops) and some 1,000 Soviet advisers. South Africa and Angola were both trying to ensure the presence of a friendly government in South West Africa/Namibia when and if that territory became independent. At the same time, South Africa was supporting UNITA in its attempt to overthrow the Angolan government. Most of the military activity consisted of low-level guerrilla operations, but occasionally division-sized units (15,000 troops) were involved.

LATIN AMERICA

In August the U.S. Senate approved military as well as humanitarian aid to the *contra* rebels fighting the Sandinista government of Nicaragua, reflecting a bipartisan consensus in both the House and Senate that Nicaragua threatened the security of its Central American neighbours. The situation in Central America demonstrated the vulnerability of Latin America to the forces of instability, both internal and external. Depressed economic and social conditions encouraged revolutionary movements, and the increased Soviet willingness to aid such movements directly and indirectly, through Cuba, was a destabilizing factor. Latin America's armed forces, primarily internal-security infantry troops with little equipment, were poorly paid and often poorly led. They were also small relative to the size and population of their countries, as is apparent from Table II.

Because these armed forces were at such low levels, Cuba, with Soviet aid, was able to become a major regional military power. Cuba's armed forces totaled 162,000 personnel, including significant overseas deployments in Angola (27,000), Ethiopia (4,000), and Nicaragua (3,500). Well trained and effectively led, with Soviet and Warsaw Pact personnel in key positions, these forces wielded an influence out of proportion to their size. The Cuban example helped to explain U.S. and Central American concern over the rapid expansion of Nicaragua's armed forces to a total of 72,000 in a population of nearly 3.2 million. Nicaragua received more Soviet armour, armed helicopters, antiaircraft guns, and missiles during the year. While the Sandinista government claimed that this aid was needed to defeat the antigovernment guerrillas, it would also increase Nicaragua's ability to intervene in its neighbours' affairs.

Nicaragua was already intervening in El Salvador, where the government of Pres. José Napoleón Duarte was facing approximately 10,000 rebel guerrillas, aided by Nicaragua and Cuba and with Soviet-supplied weapons. Against these, President Duarte had armed forces totaling 42,640, mostly Army. Even with U.S. economic and military assistance, the Army was only partially successful in gaining ground against the rebels, and the situation remained highly unstable and potentially dangerous. There were also a number of incidents on the Nicaragua-Honduras border as Nicaraguan troops pursued *contras* based on the Honduran side. The U.S. maintained a military presence in Honduras, and in at least one instance U.S. helicopters ferried Honduran soldiers to the border area where fighting was in progress.

(ROBIN RANGER)

See also Space Exploration.

This article updates the *Macropædia* article The Technology of WAR.

AP/WIDE WORLD

A Canadian Forces Chinook transport helicopter from Quebec City is unloaded from a hired Panamanian cargo ship at the port of Bogen, Norway. The transfer, part of a NATO exercise, was the biggest since World War II for the Canadian Forces, requiring four chartered ships.

Mining

Some hopeful signs for the mineral industries appeared during 1985 and 1986. The painful refinancings, reorganizations, and retrenchments that had marked the mining industry's efforts to accommodate itself to the hard new world of high energy prices, reduced demand for most commodities, and inadequate research and marketing to assure future markets began to give way to some optimism as the effects of those economies began to bear fruit and, at the beginning of 1986, energy prices broke. No one imagined that the halcyon days prior to the 1973 Israeli-Arab conflict, which probably marked the beginning of the end of cheap energy, would return, but mine operators and workers could at least look forward to a period during which economic constraints would not simultaneously become tighter in every aspect of operations.

New problems, of course, existed. Chief of these was probably that of capital, as most new mine developments required substantial investments and time before extraction began to return profits, and world capital markets were hesitant to initiate new loans in the already debt-ridden countries where this capital was most needed. After capital, marketing of mineral commodities was often identified by commentators as a significant need, both to establish new markets for the products and to place the products in existing markets where the commodities might have become economically competitive.

Exploration. The fundamental importance of exploration both as a safeguard against depletion of existing reserves and as a means of developing new options for the maintenance of continued economic progress was underscored during 1986 for both developed and less developed countries. Czechoslovakia, which possessed one of the oldest mining industries in the world, had for five years conducted an extensive survey of its national territory. The outcome included both coal and natural gas prospects, the former around the borders of existing coal fields and the latter in new terrain. New deposits were discovered of high-quality porcelain and refractory clays; new prospects were identified for base metals, tungsten, and gold.

Among the most active zones of exploration were the shallow gold deposits of the southwest Pacific, which had been encountered in a variety of localities from Papua New Guinea eastward. Other areas that attracted the interest of prospectors were Saudi Arabia, where both new and previously worked areas of the Arabian shield were the object of reconnaissance; the Peloponnese, where the Greek Institute of Geological and Mineral Research conducted several productive surveys (lead, zinc, gold) in the Molai area; and the Kola Peninsula, where the U.S.S.R. and a Swedish consortium were negotiating barter arrangements of technological assistance from the West in return for Kola minerals.

Mine Operations. Mining management's right to manage became an issue in September, when the Western Australian (state) Supreme Court upheld a ruling by the state industrial relations commission that Peko-Wallsend, Ltd. had to reinstate 1,160 fired workers at its Robe River operations in the Pilbara region. Peko had acquired a majority interest in the operation in 1985 and in its initial survey of operations had found what it viewed as restrictive work practices enjoyed by members of seven labour unions, who had achieved those conditions over a number of years by means of various labour actions. When Peko rejected an initial ruling by the commission that it should negotiate the end of these practices, it closed the mine site, fired the workers, and appealed the ruling.

In the United States the periodic renewal of labour agreements, especially in the copper and aluminum industries, had in the past led to labour stoppages, diminished supplies, and rising prices. Renewals during 1985 and 1986, however, contained such extensive wage cuts and givebacks conceded by labour to preserve jobs that employers were themselves moved to restore portions of the wage cuts or to indicate that they might do so when business conditions permitted, despite the terms of the contracts.

Safety. The safety record of the South African mining industry again became an issue in September, when a fire at the Kinross gold mine near Evander caused 177 miners to die of asphyxiation; fumes were probably generated by burning polyurethane foam used as a water sealant to line portions of the shaft in which the men were working. The accident came only days after the best mine safety report in the history of the South African industry, a January to

©1987 JEFFREY MUIR HAMILTON

A new solvent-extraction process for producing copper lowers costs, giving new hope to a U.S. industry suffering because of inexpensive imports.

Indexes of Production, Mining and Mineral Commodities

(1980 = 100)

	1981	1982	1983	1984	1985	1986 I	1986 II
Mining (total)							
World[1]	92.1	85.3	84.5	87.0	89.5	98.6	...
Centrally planned economies[2]	99.5	102.3	104.7	106.9	108.6	114.4	109.7
Developed market economies[3]	103.1	98.2	97.3	100.7	102.2	105.1	98.7
Less developed market economies[4]	83.9	74.4	73.0	75.0	78.4	91.9	...
Coal							
World[1]	100.3	102.0	101.5	100.1	105.4	110.1	...
Centrally planned economies[2]	98.4	102.4	104.6	107.0	108.9	113.5	108.6
Developed market economies[3]	101.0	100.8	97.7	92.4	100.1	103.7	101.3
Less developed market economies[4]	109.2	112.3	115.5	124.6	131.9	149.6	...
Petroleum							
World[1]	89.0	80.5	78.9	81.5	83.9	95.7	...
Centrally planned economies[2]	102.1	104.5	105.8	107.3	108.0	112.0	109.1
Developed market economies[3]	105.7	100.9	99.2	104.4	104.9	110.6	96.4
Less developed market economies[4]	81.9	71.5	69.8	71.4	74.6	89.3	...
Metals							
World[1]	99.7	93.7	94.6	99.0	100.4	102.6	...
Centrally planned economies[2]	88.7	89.9	92.9	93.2	95.5	99.3	100.9
Developed market economies[3]	100.0	90.4	92.6	98.6	98.1	100.1	101.8
Less developed market economies[4]	101.4	99.9	98.1	100.7	105.1	107.2	...
Manufacturing (total)	100.6	98.5	101.9	108.7	113.7	117.1	...

[1] Excluding Albania, China, North Korea, and Vietnam.
[2] Bulgaria, Czechoslovakia, East Germany, Hungary, Poland, Romania, and the U.S.S.R.
[3] North America, Europe (except centrally planned and Yugoslavia), Australia, Israel, Japan, New Zealand, and South Africa.
[4] Caribbean, Central and South America, Africa (except South Africa), Asian Middle East, East and Southeast Asia (except Israel and Japan), and Yugoslavia.
Source: UN, *Monthly Bulletin of Statistics* (November 1986).

June count of 234 fatalities in smaller accidents. The black National Union of Mineworkers protested strongly against conditions in the mines. The South African industry was, however, by no means unrepresentative of the world industry's standards; a similar report for the first six months of 1986 for the much smaller mine sector of South Korea indicated 99 fatalities during the period. The industry of South Korea, however, was based much more on small operations, which usually lacked the safety equipment and programs that larger operations could afford.

More subtle threats to miners' health and safety existed, however, and in 1986 the World Health Organization published a technical report on recommended limits for occupational exposure to certain mineral dusts (silica and coal). Although miners had long tended to be fatalistic about dangers that were not immediate, many labour unions and workers' groups were becoming increasingly militant about such issues; an example was a strike early in the year by some 200 miners at the Ranger uranium mine in Australia's Northern Territory in protest against exposure to sulfuric acid in the mine.

Business and Markets. A 1986 report by the Congressional Research Service, "The Competitiveness of American Metal Mining and Processing," represented a major departure from the usual indifference to and disregard of the mining industry by almost all elements of U.S. national government except the military. The report identified several fundamental changes that had affected the domestic industry, including ready import availability of concentrated or fabricated raw materials (eliminating the advantage of nearness to markets) and the government-owned or government-influenced character of many overseas competitors, for whom subsidies were readily available and for whom full employment might represent a higher priority than profit. More imponderable but equally compelling factors included the value of the U.S. dollar in international transactions and the high-quality ores of many newly opened overseas operations.

Internationally, one of the most significant changes in the business and marketing arena took place on the London Metal Exchange (LME) as a result in part of the October 1985 default of the International Tin Council (ITC). Not all of the change apparent in 1986 was, in fact, connected with the ITC. The United Kingdom's general planned restructuring of financial markets would affect LME as it would the London Stock Exchange, since both were to be subject to regulation by either statutory or self-regulatory organs. The former would involve the Securities and Investment Board (SIB) and the latter, an approved self-regulatory organization (SRO). Discussions between the SIB and LME had, through late 1986, focused on three issues: "price transparency" (the customer's assurance of being quoted the going rate); "audit trail" (the ability to determine after the fact that a trade or transaction has taken place at market-level prices); and aggregation of accounts (the broker's past practice of lumping all client accounts and laying off only net risk).

Whatever form external regulation finally took, the LME had already (in March) announced that it would reorganize internally, utilizing a new clearinghouse system that would protect members from the default of other members and would protect private investors as well. It was expected to come into existence in March 1987. Recommendations were also made for a new supervisory and governing board and council and for changes in the way that transactions were handled and governed. A number of these reforms would have taken place without the impetus of the ITC default.

Technology. Among the significant developments at scientific- and research-oriented meetings concerned with the mining field was the growing recognition that, as world reserves were depleted during the next decades, economic survival would be based on each company's or country's successful record of locating, analyzing, and exploiting efficiently the highest quality minerals. To this end airborne and satellite exploration systems were employing a variety of electromagnetic survey instruments and data processing equipment.

Sophistication in mine operations advanced with the announcement of a new integrated mine-monitoring system produced for the Xin Long Zhuang (Hsin Lung Chuang) coal mine in China by the West German firm of Funke and Huster. The system gathers data concerned with environment (gas concentrations and temperatures), water drainage, product flow, and power distribution. Ore processing also benefited from recent scientific advances with additions to the process engineer's tool kit in such areas as airjet autogenous milling (in which the product grinds itself in jets of compressed air and thereby avoids contamination by milling apparatus), mobile separation plants (for

Miners from the Kinross gold mine join thousands of other miners in singing freedom songs during a rally commemorating the 177 workers killed in September in South Africa's worst mining disaster. Winnie Mandela spoke at the rally.

REUTERS/BETTMANN NEWSPHOTOS

such applications as diamond prospecting), and bacterial leaching of ores at the mining site.

Production. An extensive revision of the UN overall indexes of mining production for the period 1981–85 and the first two quarters of 1986 (*see* Table) revealed substantial changes in the production levels achieved by all groups. This was especially true for the less developed market countries, where data for metals and petroleum for the years 1983 through 1985 revealed final outputs as much as 20% higher than originally calculated. Interestingly, metals output for those countries apparently maintained base year 1980 levels throughout 1981–85 instead of declining after 1982 by the previously reported 10% or more, while petroleum production, which had been reported to have declined to 60% or less of 1980 levels, maintained itself at closer to 70% levels. These revisions had the apparent effect of raising world output levels for 1983–85 by as much as 6%.

In the U.S. mining in 1985 reported a total value of $23,718,000,000, comprising subtotals of $5,633,000,000 for metals and $18,085,000,000 for nonmetals. The overall total represented a 2.5% gain in current prices over 1984, nonmetals showing a 5.3% rise, while metals fell by 5.8%. After processing, these mineral commodities were valued at an estimated $244 billion, a decline from 1984 when the total approximated $253 billion.

Mining Magazine's 19th annual survey of mining activity in the Western world revealed some 1,232 mines handling more than 150,000 tons of ore per year. This total included metals and nonmetal commodities but excluded energy-related operations (coal mines and oil tar and shale operations), which numbered an additional 1,250.

Aluminum. Preliminary U.S. Bureau of Mines (USBM) estimates for 1985 indicated a drop of almost 10% in world production of bauxite, the principal ore of aluminum. Total output fell from 84,664,000 metric tons in 1984 to about 76.3 million tons in 1985. Most of the losses occurred among the four leading countries: Australia (off some 2.3 millon tons to about 27 million tons—40% of world output); Guinea (off 1,160,000 tons to about 12 million tons); Brazil, despite a 38% decline, retaining third place (at 6,430,000 tons); and Jamaica (off 29%, or 2,522,000 tons, to 6,119,000 tons). These events reflected reduced demand in the industries using alumina (a concentrated intermediate product) and aluminum metal, where weak prices, excess stocks, idle production capacity, and reduced consumption dimmed short-term prospects though the long-term outlook remained good. World aluminum metal production, at some 15 million tons in 1985, was off by only about 3.3% from the previous year. In the U.S., Europe, and Japan high energy and labour costs were more likely to lead to increased recovery from scrap and recycling activity than to increased demand for primary stocks of bauxite or alumina.

Antimony. World mine output of antimony in 1985 declined slightly from the previous year to about 53,160 metric tons. The major Western producer was Bolivia, although its output continued to drop along with that nation's tin mining production; output was approximately 8,925 metric tons, off 5% from the previous year. China, the leading producer worldwide, probably mined nearly twice as much as Bolivia but published no data on output; Soviet production was estimated to be similar to but probably slightly higher than that of Bolivia. South Africa was fourth at about 7,390 tons. Reduced demand for electronic applications weakened sales in the short term, but prospects for the longer term remained good, with exploration and development activity continuing at and near existing mines.

Cement. China surpassed the U.S.S.R. as the leading producer of cement in 1985, reaching more than 142 million metric tons (up 17.5% over 1984); the U.S.S.R. showed a slight 2% gain to about 135 million tons. The two countries together accounted for about 28% of world production. Japan and the U.S. continued to comprise the second rank of producers, at 72,847,000 (off 7.6%) and 71,540,000 tons, respectively. Demand in the U.S. increased for the third year in a row as a result of a stable private housing market and a growing civil engineering sector.

Chromium. South Africa in 1985 remained the world's leading producer of chromite, the principal ore of chromium, with 3,340,000 metric tons, just over one-third of the world total of 9.6 million tons. It widened its lead over the second-leading producer, the U.S.S.R., which appeared to be declining as both a producer and a supplier; Soviet output, recently thought to approximate 2.9 million–3 million tons a year, seemed more likely to be about 2.5 million tons. The circumstances of both Soviet and South African operations seemed markedly alike in that both near- and medium-term projections made ferrochrome (crude alloys with iron) operations healthier in outlook than the purely chromium-producing operations. Lesser producers such as Albania (about 920,000 tons), Turkey (724,000 tons), India (550,000 tons), and Zimbabwe (526,000 tons) maintained or gained in output, although Zimbabwe had not yet regained production levels of the mid-1970s, when it was (officially, at least) the object of trade sanctions.

Copper. World mine output of copper in 1985 was estimated by the USBM at 7,805,000 metric tons, within 0.5% of production in 1984. Chile and the U.S., the two main suppliers, both registered increases; Chile, with 1,360,000 tons in 1985 (up 5%), retained its primacy, while the U.S., recovering slowly from the doldrums of the early 1980s, topped the 1.1 million-ton mark for the first time since 1981. Canada also showed a modest increase, rising to 730,347 tons. In the U.S. efficiencies imposed or mandated by foreign competition and the strong U.S. dollar, and achieved through sales and closings of mines and refineries, improved technology, and labour concessions or buyouts, caused several copper-mining operations—notably Inspiration and Cyprus Mineral—to report profits for 1985; others, including Phelps Dodge and Newmont, reported increased income in the first half of 1986 compared with the same period in 1985. Some 1985 company profit reports were the first since 1981. A coalition of brass companies and labour unions filed antidumping and countervailing-duty petitions with the U.S. International

Trade Commission in March against seven countries (Brazil, Canada, France, Italy, South Korea, Sweden, and West Germany), claiming that they were selling their goods more cheaply in the U.S. than at home.

Gemstones. World mine production of diamonds, both gem and industrial, declined slightly in 1985 according to preliminary USBM estimates. Output of gem diamonds amounted to some 25 million carats, off about 2.5% from the previous year; production of industrial diamonds declined only about 1%, totaling some 37.8 million carats. Worldwide demand in 1986 was so strong that the year's projected output of both gem and industrial diamonds was estimated at some 89 million carats, up more than a third over 1985 and in volume nearly twice the world total of only five years earlier. South Africa, once preeminent, by 1986 ranked no higher than fifth in anticipated total output, at 10 million carats, trailing Australia (29 million carats), Zaire (20 million), Botswana (12.9 million), and the U.S.S.R. (12 million). Patterns of consumption, particularly of gem diamonds, were changing almost as radically during the mid-1980s, as it became apparent that India had surpassed both Israel and Belgium as a trader and, notably, as a cutter, especially of low-grade stones formerly destined for industrial use.

Gold. World mine output of gold increased 5.5% during 1985, attaining an estimated 1,543 metric tons. South Africa accounted for more than 43% of the world total (about 673 tons), although most of the recent growth worldwide was among smaller producers. The U.S.S.R. was thought to be the second most productive country, at some 270 tons, followed by Canada (86 tons), the U.S. (79 tons), Brazil (63 tons), China (59 tons), and Australia (57 tons). Despite labour unrest in South African mines and a decline in the grade of ore being milled, output there remained largely unchanged, off only 1.5% in 1985. While demand in 1985 showed few significant changes aside from a dropoff in the minting of official coins, 1986 appeared to hold out more promise as gold prices rose above $400 per ounce, generating increased exploration and development activity in mine properties. It appeared also that central banks had begun to expand their gold reserves during 1985 and were continuing to do so in 1986, although perhaps the strongest area of growth during 1986–87 would be in gold coinage, as Japan, Czechoslovakia, the U.S., Brazil, Australia, and Luxembourg all planned to mint gold coins; the Japanese issue was to be commemorative in nature (honouring Hirohito's 60th anniversary as emperor) and would be sold well above the gold value of the coin.

Iron. Production of iron ore rose substantially in 1985, amounting to perhaps 900 million metric tons. The major producer was the U.S.S.R., at 248 million tons (28% of world output and up slightly from 1984). China showed strong growth again (8.7% in 1985), reaching a total of 132,492,000 tons; Brazil followed with 123 million tons, also up strongly from 111 million tons in 1984. A weak fourth quarter kept Australia from achieving 100 million tons, but a national record was nevertheless set at 97,373,000 tons. The U.S. and Canada followed these leaders more distantly, at 48,751,000 and 40,348,000 tons, respectively. All these producers, especially Brazil with its high-grade Carajás ores, competed strongly with one another in the world market and also had to contend with newer producers, such as India. Attempting to maintain market position, Australian companies planned substantial new investments (up to $A 200 million for individual projects) for the late 1980s to develop the deposits of the Pilbara Range for Asian markets. Depletion of the Soviet Union's high-grade resources over the last decade reduced or eliminated its exports to customers in Japan, the Comecon countries of Eastern Europe, and the European Communities (EC).

Lead. Preliminary USBM estimates of lead production in 1985 indicated approximately 4.7% growth and a total output of about 3,350,000 metric tons. Australia, with about one-seventh of this total, widened its margin as the major producer with 491,000 tons, a 10% increase over 1984. The U.S. improved its output by more than 28% to 414,000, but this was largely due to restoration of capacity that existed prior to labour strikes in 1984. In the second rank of producers Canada led with 264,000 tons (same as 1984), followed by Peru, with 210,000 tons (up slightly), and Mexico, with 206,000 tons (up 5%). U.S. mine output during the first six months of 1986 declined almost 50,000 tons, compared with the same period in 1985, as a result of mine closings in Idaho in April and Missouri in June.

Magnesium. Production of magnesium worldwide was virtually unchanged in 1985 at approximately 325,000 metric tons. The U.S. output of 126,660 tons represented about 40% of this total, a decline of about 12% from 1984. Norway, the second largest producer, had not issued any figures on output since 1983 but remained active as Norsk Hydro A.S. formally approved plans to construct a 65,000-ton-per-year facility at Becancour, Que., beginning early in 1987. AMAX's Rowley, Utah, facility, consisting of solar brine evaporating ponds, was damaged in June 1986 when the rising waters of the Great Salt Lake breached dikes that separated AMAX's ponds from the lake and thus diluted the brines. The facility continued operations with available (and, later, purchased) stocks, but by September AMAX officials had apparently decided not to reclaim the ponds but rather to establish new evaporation facilities in the western part of Utah.

Manganese. World mine production of manganese was estimated by the USBM to have risen by about 2% during 1985 to some 23.4 million metric tons. The U.S.S.R., the principal source, was believed to have produced about 10 million tons. The major Western supplier, South Africa, showed a strong 7% gain during 1985, reaching 3.6 million tons. The middle rank of producers comprised Brazil (about 2.3 millon tons), Gabon (2,159,000 tons, up slightly), and Australia (1,988,000 tons, up 6%). The strategic significance of South African manganese was among the subjects of a 1986 USBM study on the impact of various interruptions of supply on the U.S. The study determined that there existed alternative, non-Communist (especially Brazilian and Gabonese) supplies of manganese that could be expanded.

Mercury. Mercury showed a strong 7.7% gain in production in 1985, based on preliminary USBM data. World mine output reached an estimated 188,000 34.5-kg (76-lb) flasks, compared with 174,488 the previous year. The U.S.S.R., at about 64,000 flasks, accounted for more than one-third of the world total; Spain, at about 44,000 flasks, ranked second. The USBM estimated that Algeria had more than doubled its output in 1985 to some 23,000 flasks, relegating the U.S. to fourth place at 16,530 flasks. Minas de Almadén, the Spanish mercury producer, was forced to suspend production temporarily in 1986 because of low-priced Soviet exports to the EC, Almadén's chief market.

Molybdenum. World mine output of molybdenum was estimated to have risen about 0.5% during 1985; the U.S. accounted for 49,174 metric tons, approximately half of the world total of 95,030 tons. U.S. output showed a moderate 4.6% gain for the year. Chilean output increased substantially, up 8.4% to 18,390 tons, but Canadian output dropped by more than one-third from 11,557 tons to only 7,569 tons.

Nickel. Nickel output worldwide increased slightly in 1985 according to preliminary USBM data, rising to approximately 745,000 metric tons. The U.S.S.R. and Canada were the two major producing countries, with Soviet output estimated in the 175,000–180,000-ton range and Canadian output recorded as 175,570 tons, up slightly from the previous year. Australia, the third largest producer, registered a moderate 2.7% increase, reaching 85,450 tons. Nickel production in the U.S. dropped precipitously in 1985, falling by 60.6% to 6,127 tons (shipments) both as a result of cutbacks in response to low prices throughout the world and in order to add technological improvements to existing facilities (as at M. A. Hanna's Riddle, Ore., mine and smelter facility). The strategy proved only a delaying tactic, however, as continued low prices forced Hanna to close again in August 1986; at the termination of operations it was the only operating U.S. nickel mine and smelter. Cuba, at 33,400 tons the sixth largest producer, wanted to improve nickel's current 10% share of export earnings by expanding output to the 100,000-ton-per-year range by the 1990s but in 1985–86 was experiencing difficulties starting up the first new refinery called for by that program, at Punta Gorda.

Phosphate Rock. Rock phosphate, used primarily in fertilizers and chemical operations, demonstrated a relatively strong gain in 1985 of 4.9% to some 159 million metric tons, despite long-standing perceptions of oversupply in the world market. As production continued unabated for most producers, it had to be assumed that markets were found. The U.S., representing about 32% of the world total, gained slightly to 50,835,000 tons; about 10% of this was exported. The U.S.S.R., at about 33 million tons, was thought to be the second largest producer, followed by Morocco (20,737,000 tons, off slightly from the previous year) and China (about 13 million, although actual production levels were uncertain).

Platinum-Group Metals. World mine production of the platinum-group metals (platinum, iridium, palladium, osmium, rhodium, and ruthenium) revealed a 4.2% gain during 1985, reaching approximately 230 metric tons of output. The U.S.S.R. probably was the major producer, at about 115 metric tons. The leading Western producer, South Africa, accounted for almost all the world gain, with a strong 10% improvement to almost 100 tons, about 72 tons of which were platinum alone. Details from the three major producing companies in South Africa were lacking, but output from one of them, Western, accounted for 13.1 tons of platinum, 9.1 tons of ruthenium, 7.9 tons of palladium, 1.5 tons of iridium, and 1 ton of rhodium during fiscal 1984–85. Demand remained strong in 1986, especially in the automobile-exhaust catalyst, investment (bars and coins), and jewelry markets. Canada improved its output slightly, to 10.425 tons.

Silver. Mexico and Peru continued to lead the world in silver production in 1985, and both showed growth at the year's end, indicating that the USBM's initial estimate of a slight decline based on their early results was probably incorrect. World output amounted to some 12,250 metric tons; of this Mexico accounted for 2,160 (up 8.7%) and Peru for 1,895 (up 7.8%). The U.S.S.R. probably ranked third, at about 1,460 tons, followed by the U.S. and Canada at 1,224 and 1,209 tons, respectively. Prices, consumption, and supplies all remained relatively constant during 1985, although consumption dropped off somewhat during 1986, as did prices, silver reaching a 1986 low on May 20 of $4.85 per troy ounce. Although it later recovered slightly, it gave no sign of regaining even the $5.80–$6 level of 1985.

Tin. Mine production of tin remained fairly stable through 1985, off only about 3.8% to an estimated 201,000 metric tons. Malaysia and the U.S.S.R. led in production, at 36,884 (off 10.7%) and 35,000 tons, respectively. Output in other countries also fell. Indonesian production declined 5.8% to 21,864 tons, and Thai output dropped to 16,596 tons (off 23%); Bolivian exports fell 19% to 16,140 tons. Brazilian production, on the other hand, rose by nearly one-third to a new high of 26,520 tons. Historic low prices, substantial oversupply in the world market, and continuing debt and marketing difficulties beset the older tin producers, particularly the members of the ITC. The collapse of the ITC on Oct. 24, 1985, set the scene for ITC's 1986 negotiations with the LME, the ITC's creditors, and ITC members among themselves in hopes of establishing export and production controls to regain control of their markets. Until late in the year these negotiations led only to individual programs by such relatively low-cost producers as Indonesia and Brazil to preserve their markets. In November, however, members of the Association of Tin Producing Countries agreed in principle, though not in quantities, to cut production in 1987 in order to reduce stocks. The LME terminated tin trading altogether on March 7, announcing a fixed price for ITC creditors and setting in motion legal moves by a group called TinCo Realizations, comprising 11 LME brokers, to test ITC's claim that as an intergovernmental organization it had sovereign immunity to legal actions against it as operator of the International Tin Agreement.

Titanium. World output of titanium sponge (unconsolidated refined metal) fell about 8% in 1985, according to USBM estimates, to approximately 90,000 tons. Japan established itself as the major Western producer with a 42% increase in sponge output, reaching a total of 21,897 tons; this slightly outpaced the 21,100 tons produced by the U.S. Together the two accounted for nearly half of world output. The U.S.S.R.'s output about equaled those two together. Australia continued as the major supplier of ilmenite and rutile, the two principal mineral bases for the extraction of titanium metal; output reached 1,314,000 and 208,000 tons, respectively. Brazil in 1986 announced plans for the construction of a $150 million titanium-recovery plant in the Tapira region of the state of Minas Gerais. It would be based on the use of anatase, rather than the more common ilmenite or rutile. Output would be oxide, rather than metal.

Tungsten. Production of tungsten worldwide was estimated by USBM to have remained approximately steady during 1985, rising only slightly to about 45,100 metric tons. China was believed to be the world leader at an estimated 13,500 tons, unchanged from the previous year. The U.S.S.R. was probably second at about 9,100 tons. The major Western suppliers were Canada, at 4,002 tons (off 4.6%); South Korea, 3,250 tons; Bolivia, 2,240 tons; and Australia, 1,912 tons. Prices for wolframite (the principal tungsten mineral ore) had declined by 1986 to two-thirds of the 1977 levels of $180 per metric ton as a consequence of overexpansion of mining capacity and of recycling and substitution in industrial applications, according to a study in March 1986 by Charles River Associates. Long-term forecasts were not attempted, but substantial volatility in trade flows and prices in the contemporary market was noted, attributable, it was thought, to a combination of Chinese export marketing practices, Soviet demand, and Western (especially U.S.) stockpiling and consumption patterns.

Zinc. Zinc enjoyed a relatively good year for a base metal, gaining 2.2% to an estimated total of 6,650,000 tons. Canada, at 1,038,504 metric tons (down about 2% from the previous year), accounted for nearly one-sixth of world output. Other principal producers included Australia, 727,000 tons (up 11.1%); Peru, 594,000 tons (up 6%); Mexico, 275,000 tons; and the U.S., 218,000 tons. The 1985 total represented a new high of 5,140,000 tons for the Western market (non-Communist) countries, despite declining prices. The drop in prices eventually forced some mine closings in early 1986, and the additional complication of labour strikes in Peru and Australia during the year lowered expected output to 4,850,000 tons. (WILLIAM A. CLEVELAND)

See also Earth Sciences; Energy; Industrial Review: *Gemstones; Iron and Steel.*

This article updates the *Macropædia* article Extraction and Processing INDUSTRIES.

Motion Pictures

The year 1986 was not a memorable one in cinema history. Throughout the world, it seemed, commercial producers were trying to emulate U.S. styles with films about delinquent or manic youth, horror, and crime. The single most remarkable phenomenon was the continuing rapid growth of the Cannon Corp., which by 1986 had been transformed by two Israeli cousins, Yoram Globus and Menahem Golan, into the largest industrial empire in the history of cinema. By year's end, however, there were signs that Cannon might have expanded too far, too fast. During the year the highly successful British independent producer David Puttnam (*see* BIOGRAPHIES) moved to Hollywood as chairman of Columbia Picture Industries Inc.

English-Speaking Cinema. *United States.* The capitulation of Hollywood to the teenage audience seemed practically complete in 1986. A new generation of teenage stars (or those who could pass for teenage) came to the fore and were quickly dubbed "the brat pack." Some of them—Matt Dillon, Rob Lowe, Matthew Broderick, Michael J. Fox, and Ralph Macchio—demonstrated creditable professional standards. One of the most commercially successful of these 1986 teen movies, John Hughes's *Ferris Bueller's Day Off,* epitomized the mood of anarchy, rejection of

Tom Cruise, with costar Kelly McGillis, plays Maverick, a macho, tough, daredevil naval fighter pilot in *Top Gun*, a movie that had audiences breathless and at the edge of their seats during its dramatically filmed sequences of state-of-the-art aerial combat.
AP/WIDE WORLD

adult rules and values, and boredom. A successful sequel was John Avildsen's *The Karate Kid Part II.*

Among the top box-office successes of the year, one designed to appeal to the taste for spectacularly staged future-world fantasies was James Cameron's *Aliens,* taking up the story of Ridley Scott's original *Alien* (1979) and again starring Sigourney Weaver (*see* BIOGRAPHIES). John Carpenter's *Big Trouble in Little China* used San Francisco's Chinatown as the setting for supernatural magic. *Star Trek IV: The Voyage Home,* directed by Leonard Nimoy, successfully continued the saga of the crew of the starship *Enterprise,* bringing them back in time to 20th-century San Francisco to obtain some humpback whales. Notable for its special effects and a strong lead performance by Jeff Goldblum was David Cronenberg's *The Fly.*

Another major hit of 1986 was *Top Gun,* a panegyric to the U.S. school for crack naval fighter pilots, directed by Englishman Tony Scott. John Badham's *Short Circuit* was a charming fantasy about a robot who runs amok, absorbs humanist culture, and decides he does not want to be a war machine after all. Barbara Margolis made a fine documentary on U.S. attitudes in the cold war, *Are We Winning, Mommy?—America and the Cold War.*

Among the year's notable comedies were *Ruthless People,* codirected by Jim Abrahams and David and Jerry Zucker, about kidnappers whose "victim" (Bette Midler) proves so unmanageable that they would gladly pay to have her taken off their hands, and Paul Mazursky's *Down and Out in Beverly Hills,* also with Midler, about the transformation of a wealthy family by a bum.

Other films of individuality were Eugene Corr's *Desert Bloom,* a sensitive and intelligent family drama set against the backdrop of the first atom bomb tests; Martin Scorsese's *The Color of Money,* a sequel to Robert Rossen's *The Hustler* (1961), observing the techniques, psychology, and relationships of professional gamblers; Mike Nichols's comedy of manners in modern marriage, *Heartburn,* adapted from her own novel by Nora Ephron; and Jonathan Demme's quirky, intelligent road film about the corruption of an innocent, *Something Wild.* Blake Edwards revealed a more serious vein with *That's Life,* a deeply personal reflection on the pain of growing old and facing the approach of death.

Francis Coppola returned to form with *Peggy Sue Got Married,* which used the styles and methods of contemporary juvenile film with mature wit and intelligence; Kathleen Turner played a young woman transported back through time to relive the relationships of her youth with the knowledge of middle age. The most distinguished film of the year came from Woody Allen; *Hannah and Her Sisters* marked a new peak in the work of the U.S.'s outstanding clown commentator on the human condition. It surveys two years in the lives of three sisters caught up in the throes of various aspects of romantic love.

Among the noteworthy films released late in the year were David Lynch's darkly satirical *Blue Velvet;* Peter Weir's *The Mosquito Coast,* adapted from a novel by Paul Theroux; Clint Eastwood's *Heartbreak Ridge,* about the U.S. invasion of Grenada, with the director as star; Frank Oz's *The Little Shop of Horrors,* based on a 1960 comic horror film that was later transformed into an off-Broadway musical; Randa Haines's love story about a teacher of the deaf and one of his students, *Children of a Lesser God,* from a play by Mark Medoff; Oliver Stone's *Platoon,* an enlisted man's view of the war in Vietnam; and Michael Ritchie's adventure comedy *The Golden Child.*

Among independent productions Bill Sherwood's *Parting Glances*—a delicate study of relationships of a "yuppie" social circle, at the centre of which are a pleasant, bored homosexual couple and their friend, dying of AIDS (acquired immune deficiency syndrome)—marked a notable debut. Spike Lee's *She's Gotta Have It* was a promising if flawed picture about an independent young black woman juggling three men and other admirers.

At the annual awards ceremony of the Academy of Motion Picture Arts and Sciences in Hollywood in March, Sydney Pollack's *Out of Africa* took seven awards, including best picture, best director, best screenplay adaptation (Kurt Luedtke), best cinematography (David Watkin), best art direction, and best original score (John Barry). The Oscars for best actor and actress went to William Hurt (*Kiss of the Spider Woman*) and Geraldine Page (*The Trip to Bountiful*). Best supporting players were Don Ameche (*Cocoon*) and Anjelica Huston (*Prizzi's Honor*). The best foreign-language film was adjudged the Argentine production *The Official Story.*

Great Britain. One of the most costly British films in history, the $18 million *Sky Bandits,* a comedy adventure set among World War I fliers, proved a major disappointment. There were several other big-budget disasters during the year: Hugh Hudson's ill-scripted story of the American Revolution, *Revolution;* Julian Temple's *Absolute Beginners,* a pop video travesty of Colin MacInnes's 1950s novel; and Russell Mulcahy's muddled time-slip story *Highlander.*

Another costly effort, Roland Joffé's *The Mission,* though lacking any strong centre, had the advantages of a literate script by Robert Bolt, magnificent location photography by Chris Menges, and the Cannes Festival Palme d'Or award. The outstanding success of the year, however, was James Ivory's more modest but generally faultless adaptation of E. M. Forster's *A Room with a View.* Visual flair and economy of means also distinguished Derek Jarman's imaginative re-creation of the life of *Caravaggio.* Comedy seemed in eclipse, although Christopher Morahan's *Clockwise,* the story of a pedantic and meticulous man subjected to a day of accidents, had some success.

Generally the successes of the year were medium-budget films. Bill Douglas's long-awaited story of the Tolpuddle Martyrs, *Comrades,* revealed an inspired visual sense but lacked discipline in script and structure. Lowlife of one sort or another proved creatively rewarding; Neil Jordan's *Mona Lisa* was an eccentric romantic thriller about a small-time crook who falls under the domination of a high-class black prostitute, and Alex Cox's *Sid and Nancy* was an unsparing account of the bizarre relationship and deaths of the punk singer Sid Vicious and the U.S. rock groupie Nancy Spungen.

Australia. In *Cactus* Paul Cox related a complex love story between a French woman threatened with the loss of her sight and a man blind from birth. Tim Burstall courageously and with moderate success tackled D. H. Lawrence's autobiographical novel *Kangaroo.*

BRIAN HAMILL—PHOTOREPORTERS

Title stars of Woody Allen's *Hannah and Her Sisters* (left to right), Mia Farrow, Barbara Hershey, and Dianne Wiest, portray pieces of a family puzzle that includes Allen himself as Hannah's ex-husband.

Jeremy Irons, as Father Gabriel in *The Mission*, takes on the role of Jesuit missionary to South American Indians. The British film, written by Robert Bolt and directed by Roland Joffé, took the Cannes Festival's prestigious Palme d'Or award.

Three directors adopted different approaches to relationships between white and Aboriginal society: Bruce Beresford's *The Fringe Dwellers* was a somewhat superficial account of life in the ghettoes of the city edges; Bill Bennett's *Backlash* was a drama of relationships between an Aboriginal woman accused of murder and the police escorting her across the outback; and George Ogilvie's *Short Changed* dealt with a child custody dispute between a white mother and an Aboriginal father. *Crocodile Dundee,* directed by Peter Faiman and starring Paul Hogan as a rugged man of the outback encountering urban civilization for the first time in New York City, broke all box-office records in Australia. Taken to the U.S. in September, it was also a major hit there.

Canada. Some of the best work was in documentaries. Donald Brittain's *The Champions Part 3—The Final Battle* was a brilliant analysis of Canadian politics at the time that Pierre Trudeau and René Levesque opposed each other late in their careers; and Fernand Bélanger and Dagmar Gueissaz Teufel's *Passiflora* was a sardonic account of the day when both Pope John Paul II and Michael Jackson appeared, at different hours, in the Olympic Stadium in Montreal. John N. Smith's drama-documentary *Sitting in Limbo* exposed the problems of young English-speaking blacks in French-speaking Montreal.

Western Europe. *France.* The biggest box-office successes of the year included Jean-Jacques Beineix's *Betty Blue,* a tale of passionate love; Claude Miller's *L'Effrontée,* a charming portrait of an awkward, affectionate early adolescent; and Claude Berri's two-part adaptation of Marcel Pagnol's *Jean de Florette* and *Manon des sources*—reckoned the most costly French film in history. Alain Resnais's *Melo* was a filmed play (from Henri Bernstein's much-filmed 1929 success). Eric Rohmer's *Le Rayon vert,* fifth in his series of "Comedies et Proverbes," managed to command sympathy for an essentially irritating heroine desperate to break out of her loneliness but always rejecting other people's advances. Claude Chabrol continued in his own set path with a quirky mystery story, *Inspecteur Lavardin.* Alain Cavalier's austere and exquisite *Thérèse,* based on the life and journals of Saint Thérèse of Lisieux, won the Jury Prize at Cannes.

There were a number of modest but promising debuts: Frederic Andrei and Sebastian Frall with lively crime thrillers, *Paris minuit* and *La femme secrète,* respectively; Thomas Gilou with *Black Mic-Mac,* a charming and hilarious comedy about a group of Africans confronted with Parisian bureaucracy; and Regis Wargnier with a psychological drama about a man's struggle to conquer alcoholism, *La Femme de ma vie.*

West Germany. The two most conspicuous successes of the year were achieved by women. Margarethe von Trotta's *Rosa Luxemburg,* a somewhat literal and turgid biographical study, benefited from audiences' curiosity about this outstanding figure of early European socialism. In contrast, the former actress Doris Dorrie scored a major hit with *Men . . .,* a crisp, simple comedy about a man who wins back his straying wife by reforming his hippie rival into the kind of boring executive that he had formerly been himself.

The award of the main prize of the Berlin Film Festival to Reinhard Hauff's *Stammheim* aroused official disapproval, though the film's dramatic re-creation of the Baader-Meinhof trial was intended as a future warning rather than an incitement to fresh terrorism. *Die Reise,* a Swiss-German coproduction directed by Markus Imhoof of Switzerland, treated the same subject, dramatizing the autobiography of one of the Baader-Meinhof group. Other notable productions included *Daheim Sterben die Leut,* a story of corruption in rural Bavaria, and Jorg Gfrorer's *Ganz Unten,* a clandestinely filmed documentary about the mistreatment of workers in the Thyssen steel mills.

Italy. Many veteran directors were active. Federico Fellini's *Ginger e Fred* was a study in nostalgia, declaring an old man's undisguised distaste for a brash and careless modern society. Mario Monicelli made an attractive psychological

Maggie Smith (left) plays Charlotte Bartlett, chaperone to Lucy Honeychurch, played by Helena Bonham Carter, on a holiday trip to Florence, Italy, in *A Room with a View*. The film turns gossip and meddling into rapiers used to duel playfully with views of propriety.

comedy, *Speriamó che sia femmina,* about the life of an all-female family. Mario Bolognini's *La venexiana* was an elegant adaptation of a 16th-century erotic comedy. Francesco Maselli returned after a long absence from feature films with *Storia d'amore,* a story of the hopes and frustrations of the underprivileged young in contemporary society.

Among more recently established directors, Franco Zeffirelli directed his own very independent interpretation of Verdi's *Otello;* Pupi Avati made a taut and fascinating drama concentrated on one night of gambling at cards, *Regalo di natale;* and the director-star Nanni Moretti created an intelligent comedy about the trials of a young priest, once a 1960s radical, in *La messa e finita.*

Scandinavia. Perhaps the most outstanding Scandinavian film of the year was a Swedish production by expatriate Soviet director Andrey Tarkovsky (*see* OBITUARIES); charged with religious conviction and emotion, *The Sacrifice* tells of one man's reaction to the ultimate, nuclear catastrophe. Among other Swedish films of note were *Amorosa,* Mai Zetterling's impressionistic biography of the writer Agnes von Krusenstjarna; Lasse Hallstrom's *My Life as a Dog,* an exquisite portrayal of an orphan childhood in rural Sweden; and Carsten Barnd's adaptation of Lars Norea's play about domestic hells, *Demons.*

The most ambitious Danish film of the year was Henning Carlsen's biographical study of Gauguin, *The Wolf at the Door.* In Finland Jaakko Pakkasvirta made a handsome and ambitious adaptation of Kafka's *The Castle.* Norwegian Odvar Einarson made a striking debut with *X,* which told with great mastery the love story of a gangly 19-year-old artist and a runaway 14-year-old girl.

Spain. Spanish filmmakers continued to be fascinated by the history of Gen. Francisco Franco's era. Jaime Camino's low-budget *Dragon rapide* re-created, in neodocumentary style, the story of Franco's movements in the two weeks leading up to the Spanish Civil War. Vivente Aranda adapted Martin Santos's novel *Tiempo de silencio,* set in the late 1940s, while Benito Rabal's *El hermano bastardo de Dios* followed a now-familiar Spanish convention of a child's-eye view of the war. Carlos Saura continued his series of ballet films with *El amor brujo,* performed by Antonio Gades. Agustin Villaronga's *Tras el cristal* was a brilliant but horrifying film about a sex murderer. Perhaps the outstanding film of the year, Fernando Fernan Gómez's *Viaje a ninguna parte,* was a comic-pathetic tale of a group of touring actors in the 1950s.

Greece. Theo Angelopoulos, Greece's most distinguished director, directed *The Beekeeper,* a film of masterly visual style, tracing the peregrinations of a bitter and confused man (Marcello Mastroianni) spending his last days wandering through the haunts of his earlier life.

Eastern Europe. *U.S.S.R.* More liberal attitudes to culture were reflected in the number of films that were released after long periods on the shelf. Among them was an extraordinary Estonian black comedy, *Madness* (1968), with the improbable theme of the Nazi extermination program. *The Swimmer* (1981), an anarchic Georgian comedy previously released only in a cut version, was an absurdist view of history through the eyes of three generations of a family of champion swimmers. In *Trial on the Road* (1971) Andrey German reversed the stereotype by making the hero a temporary collaborator with the Nazis.

From Georgia, Georgy Shengelaya's *Journey of a Young Composer* was the story of a naive young man becoming embroiled in political activities following the 1905 revolution. From Estonia, Piter Sim's *Ideal Landscape* was a comedy about a young Komsomol organizer's problems in a backward village in the 1950s, and Marina Sheptunova's *Keep Smiling, Baby* was a compassionate film about the inmates of an orphanage. While Soviet political dramas were less aggressive than their U.S. counterparts, the U.S. figured as the villain in two such films, Sergey Mikaelyan's *Flight 222,* a suspense story about Soviet defectors, and *The Detached Mission,* directed by Mikhail Tumanishvily, about a U.S. plot to start World War III.

The Swedish film *The Sacrifice*, written and directed by Soviet expatriate Andrey Tarkovsky, takes place during a family party and explores the reaction of a despairing intellectual to an impending nuclear disaster.

Hungary. The best film premiered in 1986 was Zoltan Varkonyi's *The Bitter Truth,* made in 1956, when its tale about corruption and hypocrisy in the lower ranks of the Communist Party was unacceptable to the authorities. Among new films the best was Ferenc Andras's *The Great Generation,* the story of a group of friends from 1968 meeting in contemporary times in various states of disillusion. Two films made good use of a raw, documentary style and improvisational acting: Pal Zolnay's *Embryos* dealt with the problems of a gynecologist who has to deal with her own unwanted pregnancy, and Pal Erdoss's *Countdown* showed the perils of private enterprise (now officially permitted) through the misfortunes of a young man who sets up his own one-man trucking business.

Yugoslavia. The prize of the Pula Festival for the best Yugoslav film of the year went to Stole Popov's *Happy New Year 1949,* a drama showing the effects on private individuals of the troubled times of Yugoslavia's split from the U.S.S.R. Recent history also inspired Veljko Bulajic's *The Promised Land,* which dealt with the plight of resettled peasants. Two witty sex comedies, Zivko Nikolic's *The Beauty of Vice* and Rajko Grlic's *Three's Happiness,* offered shrewd reflections on contemporary Yugoslav morals and manners.

Czechoslovakia. A debut film by Zdenek Zaoral, *The Cobweb,* was an innovation in Eastern European cinema with its frank treatment of the drug problem among teenagers. Contemporary teenagers, with dreams that exceed their possibilities, were also the subject of Eva Stefankova's *Salty Sweets.* More comic views of contemporary living appeared in Jiri Menzel's *My Sweet Little Village* and Vit Olmer's *Like Poison,* the latter recalling Czech cinema of the 1960s in its treatment of an architect's mid-life crisis and office romance.

East Germany. Konrad Wolf's *Sonnensucher* (1958), released in East and West Germany in 1972 and then generally in 1986, had been held back because of its depiction of Soviet uranium mining during the cold war. Coincidentally, *Das Haus am Fluss,* a tragic war novel by Konrad Wolf's father, Friedrich, that contained a strong metaphorical statement on German guilt, was filmed during 1986 by Roland Graf.

Middle East and North Africa. Youssef Chahine continued his partly autobiographical series on Egypt in the 1940s with *The Sixth Day,* a story of the loves and dreams of a group of movie-struck friends. Tunisian Nouri Bouzid's *Man of Ashes* was a skillful and assured first film about a young man's sexual maturing in a society of rigid moral and family standards. In Algeria Mohamed Lakhdar made *La Dernière Image,* a reminiscence of a youth in 1940 and the colonial period. Among the ambitious Israeli films of the year was Amos Gitai's *Esther,* a rather stolid biblical pageant that endeavoured to draw modern political parallels. Shimon Dotan's humane *The Smile of the Lamb* showed Arab-Israeli confrontation at an intimate personal level. Eli Cohen made a remarkable debut with *Ricochets;* originally intended as a military instruction film, it had a disabused and philosophical view of war that earned it commercial distribution.

Latin America. *Argentina.* In a year of flourishing and distinguished production, the era of the "dirty war" preoccupied filmmakers. Miguel Pérez's *La república perdida* was an outstanding documentary on the history of the period 1976–83. Héctor Olivera's *The Night of the Peaches* dramatized the kidnapping, torture, and ultimate killing of six high-school youths in 1976. Two Argentine films gained outstanding success at the Venice Film Festival in August. After *Camila,* María Luisa Bemberg's talent was confirmed with *Miss Mary,* a shrewd account of the adventures of an English governess (Julie Christie) in a rich Argentine family. Carlos Sorin made a remarkable debut with *La pelicula del rey,* the story of a director making a film about a 19th-century megalomaniac who declared himself king of Arauconia and Patagonia.

Cuba. Two major documentary productions dealt fiercely with Chile under Gen. Augusto Pinochet Ugarte's regime—Manuel Littin's clandestinely filmed *Acta general de Chile* and Juan Andres Racz's *Dulce patria.* Jesús Díaz's well-crafted *The Parting of the Ways* was the story of a Cuban mother returning from exile in Miami, Fla., to be reunited with her son who has grown up with the Revolution.

Brazil. Ruy Guerra, the country's leading director, made the first Latin-American musical in some years, *Opera de malandro,* an uncredited transference of *The Threepenny Opera* to Brazil. Lauro Escorel Filho's *Endless Dream* was a picaresque tale based on the life of a stuntman who became a pioneer of Brazilian film production, while David Neves's *Fulaninha* was a charming comedy about a group of Bohemians. Sergio Rezende's *The Man with the Black Coat* was a fine, if eulogistic, film biography of contemporary Brazilian Tenorio Cavalcanti.

Asia. *Japan.* Japanese directors appeared to be tackling more offbeat themes than in recent years. One of the biggest successes was Masanori Hata's *The Adventures of Chatran,* relating the life and encounters of a characterful male cat. Yutaka Osawa's *Bokuchan's Battlefield* was a moving account of the experiences of a small, frail, but brave little boy sent to a youth camp during World War II. One of the most distinguished and unusual films of the year, Yoshishige Yoshida's *Promise,* was a tragedy centring on an old man's mercy killing of his beloved wife.

In a more traditional vein, Masahiro Shinoda's *Gonza the Spearman* was an elegant classical adaptation of a Monzaemon Chikamatsu play about honour and adultery. Another highly accomplished adaptation was Yoshimitsu Morita's *And Then,* from the novel by Soseke Natsume. The newer wave of directors was represented by Yojiro Takita, whose *Comic Magazine* was a satire about a reporter's quest for self-respect in a society obsessed with gossip and scandal, and by Juzo Itami's *Tampopo* ("Dandelion"), an eccentric comedy based on gastronomic obsessions.

China. The Chinese film was undergoing a remarkable renascence, with the emergence of outstanding new talents and a more liberal approach. Zhang Luanxin (Chang Luan-hsin), a woman director, made *Sacrifice of Youth,* which described the reactions of a young woman rigidly trained under the Cultural Revolution to the apolitical peasants with whom she is sent to work. Yan Xueshu's (Yen Hsüeh-shu's) *Wild Mountains* told a story of wife-swapping among country people confused by social changes. Zhong Huangjian's (Chung Huang-chien's) *A Girl of Good Family* was also set in the remote countryside, where in 1949 the new order had not yet affected age-old custom; an 18-year-old woman is forced into an arranged marriage with a 6-year-old husband. A more directly critical film, Zhang Zeming's (Chang Tse-ming's) *Swan Song,* satirized the current rush to consumerism as well as the Cultural Revolution.

India. A handful of films stood out among the vast bulk of Indian production. Shyam Benegal's *Trikal—Past, Present and Future* was a family saga that looked with humour and sentiment at the changes that came with the end of the Portuguese empire in Goa. Ramesh Sharma's *New Delhi Times* was a controversial drama about corruption in high places. Uptalendu Chakraborty's *The Child God* was a fable in a rural setting about a confidence trickster who represents a deformed child as a deity, with tragic outcome. Pradip Krishan made a promising debut with *Massey Sahib,* the story of the rise and fall of a good-natured, exasperating social climber, exposing the irreconcilable differences between Indians and the British Raj.

(DAVID ROBINSON)

Nontheatrical Motion Pictures. Based on the number of awards, a student film, *Heroes,* earned top honours in 1986 among nontheatrical motion pictures. The short depicts one step in an eight-year-old girl's process of growing up. Produced by a group of University of Southern California cinema students headed by Camille Thomasson, it won three grand prizes (in Spain, Austria, and France) plus a gold medal in Belgium and a Golden Eagle in the U.S.

Almost as impressive were the prizes captured by a Canadian short feature, part of the miniseries *Anne of Green Gables.* Part Two, *A Bend in the Road,* was the winner. It was chosen for the coveted Emily Award at the American Film Festival plus top honours at Columbus, Ohio, San Francisco, and New York City.

In the International Industrial Film and Video Congress held in 1986 at Zürich, Switz., West Germany walked off with the grand prize plus two firsts and two special awards. *Ikarus 2000,* sponsored by the chemical giant BASF and produced by Gesellschaft für Bildende Filme, was designed to stimulate interest in engineering by comparing modern achievements to nature. (THOMAS W. HOPE)

See also Photography; Television and Radio.
This article updates the *Macropædia* article MOTION PICTURES.

Museums

In late 1985 two studies on the nature and functions of museums were published. *The Origins of Museums,* edited by Oliver Impey and Arthur MacGregor, published the proceedings of a symposium that marked the 300th anniversary of the Ashmolean Museum, Oxford. The symposium focused on the evolution of educational collections for the advancement of knowledge from the 16th and 17th centuries to the present. *Museums: Two Contributions to the Debate* by Sir Roy Strong, director of the Victoria and Albert Museum in London, considered the problems posed by a policy of continuing acquisitions.

Funding remained a prime concern in 1986. Traditional sources of museum funding—private endowment and donations and government revenue—were frequently inadequate, and recourse to different sources of revenue had become widespread in the previous 20 years. Most controversial was the introduction of entrance charges. In 1985 the Victoria and Albert Museum had introduced a voluntary donation scheme, and in late 1986 it was announced that as a result the museum would be able to return to a seven-day schedule. Voluntary donations had raised over £400,000, although attendance had dropped by more than 40%. Earlier in the year Strong told members of Parliament that recent accidents to exhibits at the Victoria and Albert would have been prevented if the government had provided enough funds to maintain the Victorian fabric of the building. In March flooding in the basement caused damage estimated at £250,000.

An imaginative revenue-raising scheme was to use the pictures themselves to earn money. Dulwich College Art Gallery and the Courtauld Institute Galleries, both in London, sent pictures abroad and benefited from funds raised from fees, openings, and special events. Dulwich was negotiating with Japan to send about 30 pictures to that country for a flat fee of over £100,000. Among major gifts the Art Institute of Chicago was awarded $3.8 million by the MacArthur Foundation, the first large grant of its type ever given to fund special exhibitions. The New Museum in New York City received $1.5 million from the Henry Luce Foundation, and the Lannan Museum in Lake Worth, Fla., was given $80 million by the estate of its founder, J. Patrick Lannan. The entire collection of Henry P. McIlhenny, valued at more than $100 million, was bequeathed to the Philadelphia Museum of Art. The earthwork "Double Negative, 1969" by Michael Heizer, a

The Paris Fashion Museum

Paris, renowned as the mecca of high fashion, had been devoid of a fashion museum until the omission was remedied in 1986 with the foundation of the Musée des Arts de la Mode. The museum was officially inaugurated on Jan. 28, 1986, by Pres. François Mitterrand of France. The location was highly prestigious: within the building of the Louvre, the great art museum, next door to the department of the Louvre assigned to the decorative arts.

Professionals from the fashion and textile worlds had contributed over the years to the archives, documents, and costumes owned by the Union des Arts Décoratifs. The new museum housed this collection, together with one assembled over the previous 25 years by Yvonne Deslandres for the Union Française des Arts du Costume. In all, some 9,000 costumes were collected, most of them dating from the 18th century to the present, as well as 1,200 hats, 800 fans, 500 pairs of stockings, 700 pairs of shoes, 300 handbags, and over 100 parasols.

Eleven floors with a total surface area of over 4,000 sq m (44,000 sq ft), were given over to the museum. The five upper floors were devoted to public exhibitions. The four lower floors contained the library and conference rooms. Costumes not on show were stored in the basement. On inauguration day 18th-century clothes were on show on the ninth floor, 19th-century clothes on the eighth floor, and clothes of the 20th century up to 1940 on the seventh floor. Mannequins were placed in settings designed to produce picturesque effects. Reproductions of railway carriages belonging to the Orient Express served as props for beaded and embroidered dresses dating from 1925. Dresses by Madeleine Vionnet, Gabrielle "Coco" Chanel, and Jeanne Lanvin evoked the fluid lines of the 1930s. Elsa Schiaparelli's costumes, placed in a gilt cage, were typical of her circus period.

Besides glamorous shows for the public, theme exhibitions for guidance and research on the history of clothes were planned, as were exhibitions oriented toward contemporary creativity in the economic and technological arenas. Within the museum there were facilities for meetings and debates. Stylists, fashion reporters, students, and professionals were encouraged to consider the museum building as a place of work and for the exchange of ideas. An Institute of Fashion was established to provide training for young fashion designers.

Special events gave an indication of the range of interests to which the museum catered. In midyear a vast showing was dedicated to Yves Saint Laurent, spanning the 28 years of his career. A later show celebrated Manuel Canovas, a designer of interior fabrics, while a Christian Dior show was planned for early 1987.

(THELMA SWEETINBURGH)

D. SIMON—GAMMA/LIAISON

Exhibits by the thousands dazzled visitors to the Musée des Arts de la Mode, Paris's new fashion museum.

455-m (1,500-ft)-long groove cut into rock and set on 24 ha (60 ac) of Nevada desert, was donated to the Museum of Contemporary Art in Los Angeles by the former art dealer Virginia Dwan.

The fourth and largest branch of the Whitney Museum of American Art, New York City, opened in the Manhattan building of the Equitable Life Assurance Society. While the corporation would fund the Whitney's activities there, the museum would advise on corporate art purchases. The Whitney's branches within corporate premises had produced a new category of museum. Another new museum type was the so-called personal museum established to house the collection of one individual. However, the California businessman and architect Edward Broida abandoned his well-publicized plans to open a museum in New York City, and the U.S. collector Fred Koch, who had planned to establish a gallery and study centre devoted to 19th-century art in St. John's Lodge, Regents Park, London, abandoned the project after lengthy battles over planning. In Koch's case, problems had arisen over details of the proposed conversion of St. John's Lodge, a listed building with fine Victorian features. It was hoped that Britain might still benefit from the Koch collection if a new home could be found.

Controversy surrounded the appointment of a new director for the National Gallery of Art in London in mid-1986. First choice of the trustees was American Edmund Pillsbury, director of the Kimbell Art Museum in Fort Worth, Texas, but he declined the offer. In the event, the appointment went to Neil MacGregor, editor of the *Burlington Magazine,* who had never worked in a museum. Feminist arguments were aroused by continued planning for a 1987 opening of the National Museum of Women in the Arts in a refurbished, early 20th-century building in Washington, D.C. In Stockbridge, Mass., the Norman Rockwell Museum began a $5.5 million campaign for a new building despite the objections of local residents that it would change the character of the community.

The Huntington Library Art Gallery in San Marino, Calif., reopened after a year of renovation. In 1985 the art gallery had suffered extensive smoke damage in a fire, and the most famous canvases—"Pinkie" and "Blue Boy"—had been temporarily housed in the gallery of the library. At the National Gallery, London, restoration of the Barry rooms, designed by E. M. Barry and originally opened in 1876, was completed, thanks to substantial support from the J. Paul Getty Jr. Endowment Fund. The new Arthur M. Sackler Museum at Harvard University increased storage and display facilities for the overstretched Fogg Art Museum, where previously less than 10% of the collection had been visible. (*See* ARCHITECTURE.)

The Los Angeles County Museum of Art opened the Robert O. Anderson Building for modern and contemporary art and temporary exhibitions. In New York City, the Metropolitan Museum of Art completed its $26 million Lila Acheson Wallace Wing for the display of 20th-century art; with 5,200 sq m (56,000 sq ft) of gallery space, the wing would be the second largest modern art museum in New York, after the Museum of Modern Art. In Paris the Musée d'Orsay, housed in a converted railroad station and devoted to the arts of the second half of the 19th and the early 20th century, opened in December.

The New Orleans (La.) Museum of Art celebrated its 75th anniversary. The Portland Art Museum changed its name to the Oregon Art Institute and began a five-year, $3.5 million drive for a structure that was to include a video and computer graphics laboratory.

(JOSHUA B. KIND; SANDRA MILLIKEN)

See also Art Exhibitions and Art Sales.

TED THAI/TIME MAGAZINE

The sweeping atrium stairway and surrounding area of the new, permanent quarters of the American Craft Museum in New York City are typical of its sleek and spacious interior. The museum had for decades moved from one temporary home to another.

Music

Classical. Many were the reasons offered for the change in the music of the 1980s: radical conservatism, the hand of the "moral majority" reflected in the arts; a return, as many Britons saw it, to "Victorian" values; outright revisionism; or merely a tiredness with the few remaining vestiges of what U.S. composer Philip Glass (*see* BIOGRAPHIES) in 1986 dubbed the "creepy" music of wholesale serialism. But by 1986 one thing had become clear: for all practical purposes, serial methods of composition, as preached by Arnold Schoenberg and the Second Viennese School and stretched to their limits, theoretical and practical, by such figures as France's Pierre Boulez, were dead. Be it the predominantly gentle, pastel-shaded *ostinati* of minimalist composers such as John Adams, Glass, or Steve Reich or the sinewy atmospherics of Witold Lutoslawski, Peter Maxwell Davies, or Sir Michael Tippett, "traditional" techniques had found their feet again. Melody, albeit of a uniquely 20th-century kind, had reasserted itself.

Centenaries celebrated during 1986 included that of conductor Wilhelm Furtwängler, the high priest of German romanticism. The anniversary of his birth was marked by numerous disc reissues. British composer Eric Coates was also honoured on the 100th anniversary of his birth with a range of disc reissues, republication of his long out-of-print memoirs *Suite in Four Movements,* and a new critical study by Geoffrey Self, *In Town Tonight.*

Notable prizewinners of 1986 included Barry Douglas of Northern Ireland, who took first laurels at the Moscow piano competition and so became the first Briton to win the prize outright in the contest's long and prestigious history. At 19 years of age Soviet pianist Stanislav Bunin won first prize at the Warsaw piano competition, while Canadian-born, London-domiciled Angela Hewitt, winner of the first prize at the 1985 International Bach piano competition in

Toronto, launched an international career and cut her first record. Russian-born master pianist Vladimir Horowitz, Hewitt's senior by some 58 years, returned to his homeland and the Moscow Conservatory for the first time in more than half a century to give a series of tumultuously received recitals.

Losses to the world of music in 1986 included those of cellist Pierre Fournier, critic-scholar Martin Cooper, composer Edmund Rubbra, lyricist Alan J. Lerner, tenor Sir Peter Pears, violinist Arthur Grumiaux (*see* OBITUARIES), critic-scholar Denis Arnold, composer-conductor Nelson Riddle, record producer Rainer Brock, tenors Donald Grobe and Rudolf Schock, pianists Magda Tagliafero and Lili Kraus, soprano Elisabeth Grümmer, and conductor Maurice Handford.

Symphonic and Instrumental Music. Noteworthy premieres during 1986 included no fewer than two from 73-year-old Polish-born composer Lutoslawski, whose Violin Concerto received its first performance in West Berlin at the talented hands of rising star Anne-Sophie Mutter and whose substantial Third Symphony, similarly premiered in Berlin, received the unheard-of accolade of being recorded commercially twice (by Columbia-CBS and Philips) in the year of its creation. Meanwhile, violinist Isaac Stern traveled from his New York City base to premiere Peter Maxwell Davies's new and demanding Violin Concerto at a music festival held at St. Magnus Cathedral on the island of Pomona in the Orkney Islands, Scotland. The concerto was subsequently recorded by Stern (for Columbia-CBS) with André Previn and London's Royal Philharmonic.

Other important first performances included that of *Pentode,* by veteran U.S. composer Elliott Carter, one of a number of avant-garde compositions with which Boulez and the Paris-based Intercontemporary Ensemble toured the U.S. The first-ever performance in Paris (at the city's Salle Pleyel) of Dmitry Shostakovich's sombrely forbidding 13th (*Babiy Yar*) Symphony took place almost a quarter century after its premiere in Moscow and subsequent hasty withdrawal at the behest of the Soviet authorities.

By way of a foretaste of celebrations to mark Leonard Bernstein's upcoming 70th birthday, the multigifted maestro's current recording company, West Germany's prestigious Deutsche Grammophon, announced that Bernstein's ongoing, peripatetic cycle of Mahler symphony performances would be taped live and issued on disc; a New York Philharmonic Seventh and Amsterdam Concertgebouw Ninth were first off the presses. At the U.K.'s London-based Bernstein Festival, sponsored by the London Symphony Orchestra, Bernstein went so far as to declare that in British conductor Bramwell Tovey he had found "a new hero." Tovey had been called in unprepared, at 36 hours' notice, to replace the ailing Lukas Foss at an all-Bernstein program that included the technically demanding *On the Waterfront* suite.

In the U.S. André Previn replaced Carlo Maria Giulini as principal at the Los Angeles Philharmonic; Maxim Shostakovich, stripped of his Soviet citizenship following his defection to the West, was appointed conductor in chief of the New Orleans (La.) Symphony; Edo de Waart stepped into Sir Neville Marriner's shoes as head of the Minnesota Orchestra; rising star Semyon Bychkov became chief conductor of the Buffalo (N.Y.) Philharmonic; and Sir John Pritchard, outgoing head conductor at the British Broadcasting Corporation (BBC) Symphony Orchestra in London, was appointed first-ever music director of the San Francisco Opera.

Elsewhere, Italian-born Riccardo Chailly, conductor of West Berlin's RIAS Radio Orchestra, was named to succeed Bernard Haitink at the Amsterdam Concertgebouw Orchestra, while composer-conductor Colin Davis was a welcome surprise choice as assistant conductor of the Sir Thomas Beecham-founded London Philharmonic. Libor Pesek doubled the role of chief conductor of Prague's Czech Philharmonic with that of principal conductor of and artistic adviser to the U.K.'s Royal Liverpool Philharmonic; Sir Charles Mackerras succeeded Richard Armstrong at the Welsh National Opera, Cardiff; and composer Peter Maxwell Davies was named associate conductor of the Scottish Chamber Orchestra, Edinburgh, for which a Fourth Symphony was, as a result, promised for the 1989–90 concert season. Also in Edinburgh, Norway's visiting Oslo Philharmonic and its Soviet-born conductor, Mariss Jansons, scored a particular success at the city's annual International Arts Festival.

A prime area of controversy in the U.K. during 1986 centred on an Arts Council report that favoured the creation of a British "super orchestra" in the same league as the Berlin and Vienna Philharmonics. It would use the highly regarded City of Birmingham Symphony as its base.

La Scala Opera House, Milan, Italy, staged a spring festival of works by Claude Debussy that showcased such rarities as the composer's unfinished opera *The Fall of the House of Usher,* after Edgar Allan Poe, and the ballet *Khamma.* The Beaubourg (Pompidou Centre) in Paris was host to the British Arditti Quartet in a unique, first-ever cycle of works for string quartet by the reclusive Italian composer Giacinto Scelsi. A curiosity in the musicological community occurred with the completion, by Australian-born British musicologist-pianist Leslie Howard, of an unfinished string quartet (Köchel catalog number 464) by Mozart. Premiered by the Endellion Quartet, it proved entirely convincing.

Opera. The operatic premiere of the year took place in London, where the English National Opera (ENO) mounted the first staging of Harrison Birtwistle's difficult if rewarding *Mask of Orpheus.* At the same time, ENO maintained its fine reputation as the country's most imaginative and resourceful house with its annual run of *Madama Butterfly* and *Rigoletto,* punctuated by such novelties as the first U.K. staging of Ferruccio Busoni's deeply philosophical *Doktor Faust* and new productions of *Moses* (Rossini) and *Parsifal* (Wagner). Highlights of the Royal Opera House at Covent Garden (London) season were a rare staging of Alexander von Zemlinsky's *The Birthday of the Infanta* and a controversial production from ex-Welsh National Opera star Mike Ashman of Wagner's *The Flying Dutchman* that featured leading U.S. bass Simon Estes.

The Glyndebourne Opera Festival (U.K.) offered memorable stagings of Gershwin's *Porgy and Bess* and Benjamin Britten's uniquely English-provincial opera, after Maupassant, *Albert Herring.* The hallowed portals of the Bayreuth Wagner Festival (West Germany) rocked to the passionate comings and goings of the season's *Tristan and Isolde,* performed by Peter Hofmann and Janine Altmeyer and conducted by Daniel Barenboim. Soviet emigré Yury Lyubimov's thoroughly controversial production of Mussorgsky's unfinished *Salammbo* at the Nice Opéra (France) traveled to Paris and the Palais Garnier. Also in Paris, operagoers found much to enjoy during the 1986 season, from the massively gesticulating pyrotechnics of Prokofiev's *War and Peace* to the antiquities of Jean-Baptiste Lully's *Atys* and the high Gallic fun of Offenbach's frothy *Robinson Crusoe.*

A major event of the season at the Metropolitan Opera in New York City was the new production of *Die Walküre,* the first of four planned new stagings of Wagner's Ring cy-

Vladimir Horowitz acknowledges the applause of the audience that packed Leningrad's Great Hall of the Philharmonic to hear him play during his first trip back to the Soviet Union after an absence of more than 60 years.
AP/WIDE WORLD

cle. Otto Schenk and Gunther Schneider-Siemsen as directors and designers skillfully used modern stage technology so that a 19th-century production was suggested while its cliches were avoided or muted beyond recognition. Outstanding performances at the Met were given by Dame Joan Sutherland in Bellini's *I Puritani* and, in her debut at the company, by Eva Marton in Puccini's *Tosca.* Among the season's other noteworthy productions were Mozart's *The Marriage of Figaro* by the New York City Opera and *Parsifal* by the Lyric Opera of Chicago.

Everywhere, refreshing performances awaited the jaded palate, from Riccardo Zandonai's hugely recherché *Francesca da Rimini* at Karlsrühe, West Germany; André-Ernest Grétry's *Zémire et Azor* and Jules Massenet's *The Cid* at the Liége (Belgium) Opera; and Rimsky-Korsakov's *The Tsar's Bride* at Monte-Carlo, Monaco; to a strikingly successful staging of Stravinsky's evergreen tale of vice condemned, *The Rake's Progress,* at Lille, France. Opera had never seemed more alive.

Albums. In the year that marked the 100th anniversary of the death of composer-pianist Franz (Ferenc) Liszt, much recording space was devoted to the work of this extraordinary Hungarian-born virtuoso, not least by Hungary's thriving state-owned record company, Hungaroton. Of particular value were first-ever recordings of works still unpublished, among them the one-act operetta *Don Sancho* and a series of late, near-impressionist piano pieces. Notable among prizewinning albums from overseas selected by Budapest's Ferenc Liszt Society during 1986 was a two-disc Angel-EMI set that showcased the talents of U.S.-Hungarian pianist and Bernstein protégé André Watts.

As far as replay technology was concerned, 1986 witnessed the continued ascendancy of the digital-audio compact disc (CD). Penetration into certain of the smaller national markets still fell below the percentage level regarded as essential to ensure long-term commercial viability of this technology, but elsewhere, especially in the U.S., Japan, and Western Europe, the "silver disc" swept all before it. (*See* INFORMATION PROCESSING: *Sidebar.*)

A potential rival technology to CD, digital audio tape (DAT), was launched at the annual consumer electronics show in Tokyo, but licensing difficulties—Philips, coinventors with the Sony Corp. of CD, had refused DAT reproduction rights for any of its products—together with an expected degree of market confusion, did not bode well for the immediate commercial success of DAT. But if CD had sounded the death knell for the vinyl long-playing record (LP), DAT seemed similarly set to wipe away a quarter century's accumulated analog cassette tape technology.

Noteworthy album releases (both CD and LP) of 1986 included first recordings of Alexis de Castillon's Piano Concerto and *Symphonic Sketches* and Guy Ropartz's Third Symphony (Angel-EMI France); Ernest Chausson's unfinished opera *King Arthur,* César Franck's *The Beatitudes,* and Handel's *Tamerlano* (RCA-Erato); Handel's *Athalia* (London-Decca); Charles Koechlin's *The Jungle Book* (Cybelia); Giovanni Paisiello's *The Barber of Seville* and Antonio Salieri's *Falstaff* (Hungaroton); Rossini's *The Voyage to Reims* (Deutsche Grammophon); and two early, previously unknown string quartets by Sibelius (Finlandia).

A strong list of remastered historical material was headed by a third, massive 13-disc volume in Angel-EMI's epoch-making *The Record of Singing* series; the collected disc recordings of piano virtuosi Ignaz Friedman (Danacord) and Simon Barere (Archive Piano Recordings); and numerous archive recordings from Angel-EMI France, presenting the artistry of such celebrated figures of the past as Guido Cantelli, Alfred Cortot, Walter Gieseking, the youthful Vladimir Horowitz, and the infant Yehudi Menuhin.

(NICHOLAS HARPER)

Jazz. In 1986 the major record companies rediscovered jazz. RCA introduced a new label, Novus, and reactivated its Bluebird reissue series; MCA revived the Impulse label as a vehicle for new jazz artists; and Atlantic began to record jazz again. Much of this activity was spurred by the growing market for compact discs. There was also a notable trend in the jazz reissue field toward large and lavish boxed sets; outstanding among these were PolyGram's *The Complete Keynote Collection,* a 21-record box tracing the history of a significant 1940s label, and Fantasy's *Thelonious Monk: The Complete Riverside Recordings,* weighing in at 23 discs. Both these sets were produced in Japan.

Jazz made its mark on film as well. *Round Midnight,* a French-American production starring Dexter Gordon in a role based on a composite of Bud Powell and Lester Young, received critical accolades and revived the career of the 63-year-old tenor saxophonist. A number of other well-known musicians were featured in cameo roles, including Bobby Hutcherson, Wayne Shorter, and Herbie Hancock, the film's musical director. *Bring On the Night,* a well-made documentary featuring the rock star Sting and many jazz performers, boosted the career of saxophonist Bran-ford Marsalis, who later toured and recorded with his new quartet.

Another notable instance of crossover between rock and jazz was the big (32 pieces) band formed by Rolling Stones drummer Charlie Watts, which included the cream of Britain's jazz players. It was originally organized for the filming of a videocassette but created sufficient response for successful tours in Britain and the U.S. Both Watts and Sting, like so many British rockers, spent their formative years playing jazz. A somewhat different case of crossbreeding was the unexpected partnership between alto saxophonist Ornette Coleman, a veteran of the jazz avant-garde, and Pat Metheny, one of the bright young stars of fusion jazz. In a group that also featured longtime Coleman associate Charlie Haden on bass and Coleman's son, Denardo, on drums, the alto saxophonist and the guitarist created excellent, uncategorizable music. Their album, *Song X* (Geffen), was one of the most interesting of the year.

Woody Herman celebrated his 50th anniversary as a big-band leader, a record of longevity matched only by Duke Ellington. For big-band fans the joy of this milestone was somewhat dimmed by the death of Benny Goodman, who had begun to become active again as a performer in 1985 and had been making plans for further concert and recording engagements. Within six weeks of Goodman's passing came the death of Teddy Wilson, the brilliant pianist who (in 1936) became the first black musician to perform as a member of an otherwise white group when he joined the Goodman Trio. (*See* OBITUARIES.) Also affecting the fortunes of big bands was the death of the greatly gifted trumpeter-composer-arranger Thad Jones, who in 1985 had taken the helm of the Count Basie Orchestra; he resigned from that position when illness struck and was replaced by his erstwhile Basie colleague Frank Foster, also a gifted arranger and composer, whose instrument was the tenor saxophone.

In a venture supported by New York City's Cooper Union, the jazz critic Gary Giddins formed the American Jazz Orchestra (AJO), an ensemble dedicated to keeping alive the full panoply of the jazz repertory. With the greatly respected John Lewis as musical director, the AJO made its debut with a concert featuring works from the Duke Ellington, Count Basie, and Jimmie Lunceford canons and a newly commissioned work by Slide Hampton celebrating the music of Dizzy Gillespie. This was followed by a tribute to Benny Goodman, highlighted by a new work composed by Bob Brookmeyer. This noted trombonist-composer-arranger also made major contributions to the continued artistic success of the Mel Lewis Jazz Orchestra, which celebrated its 20th birthday in 1986 with a week's stand at its permanent home, New York City's Village Vanguard, and the release of its first album in five years, on the Atlantic label.

After six years of sponsorship by a tobacco company, New York City's major jazz festival, produced by George Wein, received underwriting from a leading Japanese electronics firm, thus becoming the JVC rather than the Kool Jazz Festival. Among its biggest draws were two concerts by Miles Davis. The trumpeter also made news in 1986 by switching his allegiance from Columbia, his record label for 30 years, to Warner Brothers. His first album under the new contract was the most pop-oriented of his career.

The jazz comeback story of the year belonged to alto saxophonist Frank Morgan. After making a well-received debut album in 1955, Morgan vanished from the jazz scene, his career apparently destroyed by drug addiction and scrapes with the law. But he emerged in late 1985 with an impressive new record, which was followed by club and festival appearances; a second, even better record in 1986 and his New York debut at the Village Vanguard brought him wide acclaim as one of the most gifted inheritors of the Charlie Parker tradition. (DAN M. MORGENSTERN)

Popular. In 1986 the pop music industry looked back on the 1985 Live Aid shows, congratulated itself on what appeared to be a newfound power and idealism, and put its effort behind a whole new range of social and political causes. During the year the man behind Live Aid, singer Bob Geldof, continued to harangue governments about aid problems, addressed the UN, and organized a new project, Sport Aid. He was awarded an honorary knighthood in Britain and was nominated, though unsuccessfully, for the Nobel Peace Prize.

The most prominent musical "good cause" of 1986 was the Conspiracy of Hope benefit tour for Amnesty International, the human rights group, which celebrated its 25th anniversary during the year. The event was marked by a large-scale fund-raising tour in the U.S., involving such artists as Sting, Peter Gabriel, U2, Jackson Browne, and veteran folksinger and activist Joan Baez. Browne also released his most political album to date, *Lives in the Balance,* which included songs strongly critical of U.S. policy in Central America.

In the U.K. Red Wedge, a left-wing group set up to encourage young people to become more involved in politics and to win support for the Labour Party, arranged an unusual and rousing series of concerts, in which speeches were mixed with music from best-selling artists such as the Style Council, the Communards, and soloist Billy Bragg. Bragg also appeared at a massive free show at the end of March marking the last day in existence of the Greater London Council, abolished by the Conservative Party government.

The Live Aid spirit even crossed behind the iron curtain. Following the disaster at the Soviet nuclear power station at Chernobyl in the Ukraine, a benefit concert was held in the U.S.S.R. There was a further sign of Western pop music infiltrating the Communist world when the British band Queen performed in a sports stadium in Budapest, Hung., at the largest rock show ever held in Eastern Europe.

Granted the new political mood, and events in South Africa, it was inevitable that musicians would also become increasingly involved in antiapartheid campaigns. In the U.K. Artists Against Apartheid (AAA) was formed by Jerry Dammers, former leader of The Specials and composer of "Free Nelson Mandela," and Dali Tambo, son of African National Congress leader Oliver Tambo. AAA hoped to encourage musicians to join the UN-approved Cultural Boycott against South Africa by refusing to play in that country or to allow their records to be released there. A large festival organized by AAA in a London park attracted surely the best lineup seen on any British stage all year; it included Sting, Boy George (making his last appearance before a widely publicized drug charge), Peter Gabriel, Sade, and Hugh Masekela, veteran South African trumpeter enjoying renewed popularity.

The spirit of international solidarity was somewhat dampened by a musically superb album, *Graceland,* by Paul Simon, which was partly recorded in South Africa and used some of the country's finest black musicians. This led to a furious row between those who claimed that Simon had broken the boycott and those who argued that the boycott was nonsense if it meant that black musicians were penalized. Nevertheless, the album became Simon's biggest seller in years.

The fusion of Western and African music in Simon's work was indicative of one of the year's musical trends—

a renewed interest among Western musicians in different types of music from the third world, including black South Africa. In San Francisco a new movement known as Worldbeat, headed by such musicians as Dan Del Santo and The Looters, set out to fuse different global styles from Africa to the Caribbean. The new mood seemed likely to help musicians such as Fela Kuti of Nigeria and David Rudder of Trinidad.

Elsewhere, the most interesting developments were in black American music. Rap, the rhythmic talk-over style that originated in the ghetto areas of the Bronx, New York City, became popular with white as well as black audiences, as was proved by the success of the duo Run-DMC. They reached a wide, mainstream audience with their hit "Walk This Way," in which they joined forces with the white heavy-metal band Aerosmith in one of the most unlikely collaborations of the year.

In purely commercial terms the most successful black performer of the year was Whitney Houston, niece of pop singer Dionne Warwick. Her self-titled first album sold more than six million copies. Madonna remained one of the most successful white singers in the U.S., although it seemed her career might suffer through poor reviews of her British-made film, *Shanghai Surprise.* A far happier marriage of pop music and cinema was achieved by David Byrne of the Talking Heads. He made his debut as director with the surreal, wildly imaginative *True Stories,* a bizarre story of "everyday life" in an imaginary Texas town. The band's album of the same name was also one of the high points of the year.

Veteran groups and stars enjoyed renewed success during the year. Boston recorded its first album in eight years, *Third Stage,* which topped the charts soon after it was introduced. Steve Winwood's *Back in the Highlife,* his first album since 1982, also gained great popularity. One of the major events of the year was *Bruce Springsteen & the E Street Band Live/1975–1985,* which achieved the rare feat of rising to first on the sales charts in its first week.

The U.S. Grammy awards ceremony in February 1986 was dominated by British musicians, most notably Phil Collins (*see* BIOGRAPHIES). Away from the U.S., a Norwegian trio, A-ha, enjoyed commercial success. Even when pop music was taking itself seriously, a well-marketed bunch of good-looking young men could still sell records by the million. (ROBIN DENSELOW)

See also Dance; Motion Pictures; Television and Radio; Theatre.

This article updates the *Macropædia* article The History of Western MUSIC.

BILL ALLER/THE NEW YORK TIMES

D.J. Run and D.M.C. of Run-DMC became a major force in spreading rap music with their single "Walk This Way" and album "Raising Hell." Such successes moved rap out of the inner city and into communities everywhere, with an assist from disc jockeys and MTV.

Philately and Numismatics

Stamps. Despite the considerable efforts of leading philatelic organizations and the British Post Office, interest in systematic stamp collecting among children under 16 years of age remained below the hoped-for level. The top end of the market was lively in 1986, and auction prices for rare stamps and postal history set new records. Examples included £80,000 for an unused block of 12 Great Britain 1840 1*d* black, Plate 1b, and £3,520 for the 1841 1*d* red, Plate 77, with the check letter "A" omitted. The "Pegasus" collection of airmail stamps realized £311,515. One of the last big general collections, formed by the late Gordon Woods of Sydney, Australia, realized £150,227, with the best single stamp, the 1867 Great Britain £5 orange, fine unused, fetching £1,760. Two very high auction prices were £2,240 for a complete Fournier Forgery Collection (no. 422), assembled by the Union Philatélique de Genève in 1929 for sale at 60 Swiss francs (equivalent to £3 at that time), and £2,750 for a postal forgery of the 1899 20-sen Japanese stamp on a registered cover.

In May William Raife Wellsted, curator of the (British) National Postal Museum, was arrested and formally charged with stealing stamps worth £38,000 and obtaining £1,500 from the Post Office by deception. He pleaded not guilty and was released on £10,000 bail. Later he was dismissed from his position on unrelated disciplinary charges. The case was to be heard early in 1987. In January Robert C. Wurdeman, Barry J. Reiger, and Alan Kaplan pleaded guilty in New York to charges concerning the forging of Philatelic Foundation Expert Committee certificates. A foundation employee, John Peters, who was also charged, elected to be tried by jury and was acquitted.

During the year the Fédération Internationale de Philatélie (FIP) sponsored international exhibitions in Chicago and Stockholm. The major awards at Ameripex '86 in Chicago were: FIP Championship Class (formerly FIP Grand Prix d'Honneur), Enrique Martin de Bustamente (Spain) for a collection of Venezuela; Grand Prix National (for U.S. stamps), Ryoehei Ishikawa (Japan) for U.S. issues of 1847–69; Grand Prix International (for non-U.S. material), Rae Mader (U.S.) for British Guiana. The Stockholmia '86 awards included: FIP Championship Class, John Foxbridge (U.S.) for an entry of British North America; Grand Prix National (for Swedish stamps), Hugo Josefsson (Sweden) for Swedish issues of 1855–82; Grand Prix International (for non-Swedish material), Christian Sundman (Finland) for Finland 1637–1885. A special prize for non-European stamps went to Joseph Hackmey of Israel for a collection of early issues of Ceylon.

Deaths in 1986 included those of William Bogg (U.S.), postal historian; Cyril H. C. Harmer (U.K.), president of philatelic auctioneers Harmers; and Miroslaw Arthur Bojanowicz (Polish-born naturalized British subject), an expert on Central European philately.

In June John H. Levett, a London stockbroker, was elected president of the Royal Philatelic Society, London,

The American eagle, the first U.S. gold bullion coin, features a striding Lady Liberty and an eagle returning to its nested mate. Issued in October, the coin was an immediate success with the public and dealers. Its four versions had face values of $50, $25, $10, and $5 and sold at prices determined by the weight of the gold they contained.
PHOTOGRAPHS, TOM SOBOLIK—BLACK STAR

in succession to John B. Marriott. At the British Philatelic Federation congress held in Norwich in September, there were three new signatories to the Roll of Distinguished Philatelists: John A. L. Fosbery (U.K.), a specialist in the philately of Latin America; F. Burton Sellers (U.S.), president of the 50,000-strong American Philatelic Society; and Paolo Vollmeier (Switzerland), a postal historian specializing in the former Italian kingdoms and states.

(KENNETH F. CHAPMAN)

Coins and Paper Money. Sales of South African Krugerrands, once the world's most widely traded gold coin, continued to decline during 1986. A new U.S. law—passed by the Congress over Pres. Ronald Reagan's veto—made permanent economic sanctions imposed on the South African government in 1985, including a ban on the importation of Krugerrands. The United Kingdom and some other countries also limited or prohibited Krugerrand imports during the year to protest South African racial policies.

A few nations, most notably the U.S., began making their own gold coins in an attempt to capture the market share lost by South Africa. On Sept. 8, 1986, the U.S. Mint began producing four types of "American eagles"—the first gold bullion coins in U.S. history—for sale through coin dealers and financial institutions. Later in the year U.S. officials introduced yet another type of bullion coin, a .999-fine silver dollar. The Treasury expected to sell about 2.2 million troy ounces of gold by the end of the program's first year; if so, the American eagle could become the world's dominant gold coin. Australia and Switzerland, among other countries, also turned out new bullion items during 1986, while gold-coin issues of Canada and China remained popular. The Canadian maple leaf captured nearly two-thirds of the international gold-coin market in 1985 with sales of 1,878,000 troy ounces.

Throughout the year the U.S. Mint sold noncirculating coins commemorating the 1986 centennial of the Statue of Liberty. Although final sales figures would not be compiled until 1987, experts predicted that the project might raise as much as $75 million to help pay for repairs to the statue and to the old immigration facilities on nearby Ellis Island in New York Harbor. Japan launched its biggest-ever commemorative coin program, producing millions of gold, silver, and base-metal pieces honouring the 60th year of the reign of Emperor Hirohito. Canada released four more in a series of ten sterling silver coins marking the 1988 Winter Olympics in Calgary, Alta.

Several countries issued new types of coins or paper money in 1986 for use as legal tender, especially those nations experiencing high inflation. For example, a new monetary unit in Brazil, the cruzado, was worth 1,000 of the badly inflated cruzeiros. Meanwhile, the U.S. Treasury trimmed production of circulating coinage further during 1986, the result of reduced demand for "hard money" from banks and businesses. During the first six months of 1986, federal mints made 20% fewer coins than in the same period of 1985. The decline in coinage demand might be attributable in part to the increased use of credit cards and to the 1982 conversion to copper-plated zinc cents, which could have reduced hoarding of one-cent pieces.

The Bank of Canada issued new $2 and $5 banknotes that featured special counterfeiting deterrents, including multidirectional fine-line patterns, which should make the currency more difficult to duplicate on improved photocopying machines. The U.S. Treasury announced in March that it would make two subtle changes on Federal Reserve notes in an effort to thwart would-be counterfeiters using new colour copiers.

Rare-coin prices increased 7.2% in the 12 months ended June 1, 1986, according to a Wall Street securities firm, putting coins seventh on a list of 14 investment vehicles. Nonetheless, the values of many rare items remained far below the highs set earlier in the decade. For example, one of 15 known U.S. silver dollars dated 1804 fetched $187,000 at a June 1986 auction; the same coin sold for $400,000 in 1980. (ROGER BOYE)

This article updates the *Macropædia* article COINS AND COINAGE.

Photography

Camera designers in 1986 continued to emphasize autofocus systems for interchangeable-lens, single-lens-reflex (SLR) 35-mm cameras. Several prototype all-electronic still cameras and systems were demonstrated, pointing the way to photography's future growth, while conventional silver-halide photography was enriched by the introduction of improved films in colour and black-and-white. Culturally 1986 was an active year with important exhibitions, international convocations, and institutional changes.

Photo Equipment. Minolta's introduction during the previous year of its line of Maxxum autofocus 35-mm SLR cameras proved highly successful and stimulated responses from other camera makers in 1986. Most important was the Nikon N2020 AF, an SLR with advanced features that included an autofocusing system built into the camera body. Because the camera maintained the Nikon bayonet mount, it accepted nearly all the lenses in the huge Nikon system, although only some could be focused automatically. Nikon also introduced a new line of AF Nikkor lenses that connected to the camera's focusing motor and provided automatic focusing in two modes: "continuous" for follow-focusing of subjects in motion and "single servo," which locked onto the focused subject when the shutter release button was partly depressed, thus allowing the photographer to recompose if desired. More than 30 existing AI Nikkor or Nikon Series E lenses could be adapted to autofocus use by means of an AF Teleconverter TC-16A, which also increased the focal length of the lens. All other Nikkor lenses could be used with manual focusing on the N2020; those with apertures of *f*/4.5 or greater activated a visual focusing aid in the viewfinder (two red arrows and a green dot).

The N2020 had a built-in motor drive, a top shutter speed of 1/2000 second, and a choice of programmed exposure modes including P, for average subjects; P Hi, favouring faster shutter speeds for action subjects or when using a long-focal-length lens; and P Dual, which automatically chose either P or P Hi depending on the focal length of the Nikkor AF or A1-S lens used. An accessory SB-20 Speedlight using infrared light enabled the N2020 to focus automatically even in total darkness.

Another new autofocus SLR was the Olympus OM-77AF, a highly automated but very compact 35-mm design. When set for "single" autofocus it locked in on a centred subject as the shutter release was pressed halfway; for follow-focusing of moving objects there was a "continuous" AF mode. Also provided was the option of two-speed power manual focusing. For the autofocus to function, one of a new series of Olympus AF lenses was required. In dim light an LED (light-emitting-diode) illuminator automatically provided sufficient light for focusing.

The OM-77AF, with a top shutter speed of 1/2000 second, was programmed to automatically select a mode (aperture or shutter-speed preferred) depending on the focal length of the lens being used and to automatically shift programs with changes in focal length of zoom lenses. It was the first autofocusing SLR to provide a built-in flash, hidden in the handgrip, but it also could be used with the Full-Synchro Flash F280, which was capable of fully synchronized flash photography at shutter speeds to 1/2000 second.

During the year a number of prototype video still cameras (VSCs) were shown. Although most of these filmless picture-making systems were not likely to be in production

AP/WIDE WORLD; PHOTOGRAPH, CAROL GUZY

A photo of a 13-year-old Colombian girl hopelessly trapped after the Nevado del Ruiz volcanic eruption of Nov. 13, 1985, was one in the collection that won for Carol Guzy and Michel duCille of the *Miami Herald* the Pulitzer Prize for spot news photography.

for two years or so, and then only at a high price, they did dramatically point the way toward photography's future growth. All the VSC equipment shown in 1986 placed as many as 50 colour images on a video floppy disk. These images could be played back over a TV set or monitor, transmitted by telephone line or satellite, or used to produce colour prints. Then, if one wished, the disk could be wiped clean and used again. None of the cameras, whose light-sensing chips contained anywhere from about 250,000 to 400,000 light-gathering elements, could produce images comparable in sharpness and quality to those of conventional silver-halide photography.

Canon, which had successfully used a VSC prototype model to send colour images of the 1984 Summer Olympics from Los Angeles to Japan, led the way in 1986 with a market-ready modification, the Canon Still Video Camera RC-701, backed up by a system that included a recorder, a transceiver (for telephone transmission of images), and a four-colour, eight-dye ink-jet printer that made snapshot-size prints in three to four minutes.

Among new and improved silver-halide materials, Kodak introduced a Kodachrome 200 professional film that promised traditional Kodachrome sharpness and rich colour at about triple the speed previously available. For the colour print film market Kodak brought forth Kodacolor VR-G 100, 200, and 400, with improved colour saturation, finer grain, and enhanced sharpness. Fuji significantly improved its line of colour print films with Fujicolor Super HR 100, 200, 400, and 1600. For the first time, Kodachrome 64 was made available in 120 roll-film format. Konishiroku introduced Konica Color SR-V3200, a colour print film with the record-breaking exposure index of ISO 3200. New black-and-white films included a Neopan 400 professional film from Fuji that delivered a fine-grain, high-quality image despite its comparatively fast exposure index of 400. Kodak introduced T-Max 100 and T-Max 400 films, claiming that in terms of grain and sharpness the new ISO 100 film would surpass ISO 32 Panatomic-X, while the ISO 400 version would be superior to ISO 125 Plus-X.

Polaroid introduced its new Spectra instant film and camera system. The camera itself was a compact non-SLR design having automatic exposure, dual (infrared and sonar) autofocus, and built-in, rapid-recycling flash. The new Spectra film, supplied in a ten-shot pack including a six-volt battery, showed improvement in colour saturation and sharpness over the existing 600-series film.

Cultural Trends. The International Museum of Photography at George Eastman House in Rochester, N.Y., announced a multimillion-dollar fund-raising campaign principally to construct a new archives building to house its extensive photographic technology, still image, and motion picture collections. In recent years the museum had been experiencing financial difficulties and faced the possibility of its collections being dismantled and moved to another institution. Local institutions and individuals, however, rallied to keep the museum intact, and the Eastman Kodak Co. provided a major endowment.

The Friends of Photography, a nonprofit educational institution dedicated to excellence in photography, announced its intention to leave its home in Carmel, Calif., for new and larger quarters in a proposed Ansel Adams Center in San Francisco. The late Adams was long a supporter of the Friends and provided a substantial bequest for establishing the new facility, which would include 100 of his prints as well as considerably increased gallery and study space.

The photographic community lost some of its most dis-

A shot showing a kind gesture toward a homeless man is part of a photo essay entitled "The Street People—How They Survive," by Tom Gralish of the *Philadelphia Inquirer*, which took the Pulitzer Prize for feature photography.
AP/WIDE WORLD; PHOTOGRAPH, TOM GRALISH

tinguished practitioners during the year, including Ernst Haas, Jacques-Henri Lartigue (see OBITUARIES), and Ralph Steiner. Haas, a native of Austria, went to the U.S. after World War II. Establishing himself as a black-and-white photojournalist, and long associated with Magnum Photos, a noted photojournalists' agency, he later turned to colour photography, evolving a poetic, impressionistic style that received wide acclaim. Lartigue, a Frenchman, became interested in photography as a young boy before World War I. His delightful photographs of his family, early automobiles, and flying machines were brought to public attention only late in his life, when they were hailed as brilliant early examples of the spontaneous snapshot aesthetic. Steiner began his career as an advertising and magazine photographer in 1920, then also became involved in filmmaking. In 1936 with Paul Strand he documented the Wyoming dust bowl in *The Plow That Broke the Plains,* and in 1939 with Willard Van Dyke he produced *The City* for the New York World's Fair.

Photographer Alfred Eisenstaedt, 88, celebrated his 50th anniversary with *Life* magazine, being the only surviving member of its original four-person photographic staff. A major retrospective exhibition of his work was shown at the International Center of Photography in New York City. Another important retrospective, "Robert Frank: New York and Nova Scotia," opened at Houston's Museum of Fine Arts in conjunction with the publication of five books. The main cultural exhibition at Photokina '86 in Cologne, West Germany, was an ambitious survey of 50 years of colour photography.

In Japan photographers took an increased interest in Tokyo as a photographic subject. One book, *Map of Tokyo 1945,* by Akihiko Hirashima with text by Kazuo Nishi, successfully evoked the now largely vanished city of four decades earlier. The history of Japanese photography benefited from Kotaro Iizawa's diligent study of *The Age of Artistic Photographs,* which gave a full account of the "pictorialism" that had prevailed in Japan at the beginning of the 20th century.

The 1986 Pulitzer Prize for spot news photography went to Carol Guzy and Michel duCille, both of the *Miami* (Fla.) *Herald,* for their coverage of the catastrophic volcanic eruption in Colombia in 1985. The Pulitzer for feature photography was presented to Tom Gralish of the *Philadelphia Inquirer* for a photographic essay on local homeless people. The World Press Photo of the Year Award went to French photographer Frank Fournier of Contact Press Images.

At the 43rd Pictures of the Year competition sponsored by the National Press Photographers Association and the University of Missouri School of Journalism, the Newspaper Photographer of the Year Award went to Steve Ringman of the *San Francisco Chronicle,* the Magazine Photographer of the Year Award was shared by Harry Benson of *Life* and James Stanfield of *National Geographic,* and the Canon Photo Essayist Award went to David C. Turnley of the *Detroit Free Press* for his picture essay "Images of Apartheid." South Africa's Peter Magubane won the Robert Capa Gold Medal from the Overseas Press Club of New York, while Belgian photojournalist John Vink took the W. Eugene Smith Grant in Humanistic Photography for his ongoing coverage of the African drought.

(ARTHUR GOLDSMITH)

See also Motion Pictures.
This article updates the *Macropædia* article PHOTOGRAPHY.

Physics

The familiar laboratory microscope is more accurately called an optical microscope because it uses light, or visible photons, to produce a magnified image of the object being studied. The reason for specifying "optical" is that by 1986 many alternate forms of energy were being applied to methods for picturing the microscopic world. They include short-wavelength photons in the X-ray region of the spectrum, electrons, ions, and high-frequency sound waves.

X-ray Microscope. The X-ray microscope has long been a goal of crystallographers, materials scientists, and life scientists, among others. For the first two groups its attractiveness lies in the possibilities it would open up for visualizing the structure of materials deep below the surface. Because X-ray wavelengths are considerably shorter and more highly penetrating than those of visible radiation, an X-ray microscope would have higher resolution than an optical microscope and would be able to image the interior of the material rather than just the surface. Life scientists for their part have long sought a microscope that would image biologic samples in their natural state as close to molecular resolution as possible.

For many applications the ideal source of radiation for X-ray microscopy would be an X-ray laser, which would supply a coherent, intense source of highly penetrating, short-wavelength photons. Although progress was being made in this direction, in 1986 the most useful sources of X-rays were synchrotron radiation facilities, where radiation is generated by electrons propelled near the speed of light along curved paths in synchrotron storage rings. Synchrotron sources produce "soft" (comparatively long-wavelength) X-rays that can be tuned to particular wavelengths. Their monochromatic, high-brilliance beams were proving applicable to a range of imaging tasks. One exciting possibility was X-ray holography, which would allow reconstruction of a three-dimensional view of a biologic

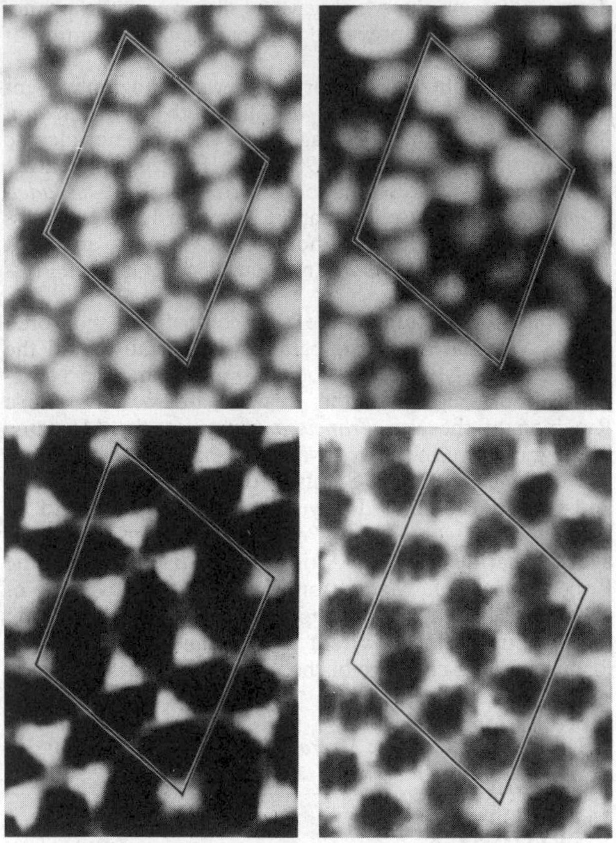

Views with the scanning tunneling microscope move into a silicon crystal, revealing both its atoms and their bonds. In the first picture (top left) the bright spots are surface atoms. In the second (top right) they are bonds from these atoms. In the third (above left) they are bonds from the second layer of atoms. In the fourth they are bonds that reach out sideways from the atoms of the second layer.
IBM CORPORATION

or metallurgical sample as well as a moving view within the sample. By 1986 X-ray microscopy had achieved resolutions of better than 1000 angstroms (an angstrom is one hundred-millionth of a centimetre). Although not adequate for the solid-state physicist who wanted to visualize the three-to-five-angstrom spacing between atoms in solids, this resolution was welcomed by biologists who desired to image, in real time, the living cell.

Acoustic Microscope. Acoustic microscopy uses ultrasonic waves rather than electromagnetic radiation to create a magnified image. Because visible light generally is quite strongly reflected or absorbed by most solid surfaces, the optical microscope provides only a surface image of any opaque sample studied. By contrast, acoustic waves pass through most interfaces; only a portion of their energy is reflected to the observer. The returning energy, which has been affected by its interaction with the sample's structure at or below the surface, can be used to construct a picture of these regions. This principle was being exploited by the semiconductor industry to make images of integrated circuits. Such circuits consist of several metal and semiconductor layers one on top of the other. The acoustic microscope is well suited to adjusting its focus from one layer to the next and can build up an image of the circuit that contains far more information than an optical image and at a resolution perhaps ten times better.

Simple in design, the acoustic microscope consists of a transducer that both generates the acoustic pulse in response to electrical stimulation and detects the return echoes, which it converts back into electrical signals for computer processing. Zinc oxide is widely used as the transducer material because of its performance at very high frequencies (as high as five gigahertz, or 5×10^9 cycles per second) and its efficient conversion of electrical to acoustic energy (about 50%). The zinc oxide is deposited as a thin film onto the flat face of a two-sided sapphire lens; the opposite face of the lens is concave. When the device is placed under water and stimulated electrically, the acoustic pulse launched by the zinc oxide is focused to a point. Water serves to carry the ultrasound between the sapphire lens and the sample. In addition, because water conducts sound more slowly than does sapphire, it focuses the pulse by refraction in much the same way that light is refracted when passing between air and glass. Liquids with an even lower velocity of sound than water provide higher resolution; liquid helium maintained at a temperature near absolute zero was being used for that purpose.

The microscope can be operated two different ways. The first relies simply on reflection of the ultrasound from the various surface and subsurface features of the sample. Acoustic pulses are focused on the surface of the sample by suitably positioning the lens and then are scanned across the surface while the amplitude (strength) of the return signals are recorded. This process is repeated for various depths in the sample by lowering the lens and hence its focal point. The image from each level can then be assigned a different colour and assembled into a composite colour image by computer.

The second mode of operation involves interference effects that can occur only when the lens is not sharply focused but, rather, deliberately defocused. Interference then can take place between the ultrasonic wave reflected from the sample and a second wave that has traveled a more complicated path. This second wave starts as a normal compressional ultrasonic wave, but on reaching the surface it is converted into a surface wave, which skims along the interface between water and sample, scattering from irregularities in its path. After a short distance energy from the wave leaks back into the water, forming a compressional wave that returns to the lens and interferes with the direct reflection.

Since the surface wave carries information on the portion of the surface it traversed, the interference pattern contains the same information. As a result, the contrast on the final image of the sample can be greatly enhanced. Enhanced contrast is one of the overriding advantages of the acoustic microscope and is evident for objects as different as glass-reinforced polymer, individual bacteria, grain structure in metals, and the all-important electronic circuit. These areas of application guaranteed the acoustic microscope a prosperous commercial future.

Scanning Tunneling Microscope. Perhaps the most exciting recent development in microscopy was the scanning tunneling microscope (STM), which won for its developers, Gerd Binnig and Heinrich Rohrer (*see* BIOGRAPHIES) of the IBM Research Laboratory, Zürich, Switz., a share in the 1986 Nobel Prize for Physics. Although the basic idea was born in the early 1980s, it became recognized during the year as the method most suited to image the arrays of atoms in a solid surface. This ability was particularly important in view of the recent development of interest in monoatomic layers (layers one atom thick), heterostructures (layered single-crystal films of different materials), and superlattices (numerous alternating heterostructure layers). The STM can provide topographic pictures of surfaces on an atomic scale, each atom rising out of the imaged surface like a raisin on a cake.

The basic technique is straightforward and consists of scanning a very sharp metal tip a few angstroms over the surface of the sample while both tip and sample are kept under ultrahigh vacuum. If a small voltage is maintained between tip and sample, then surface electrons will cross the gap by means of a quantum physics process called tunneling. This flow of electrons, or tunneling current, varies with the size of the gap. The STM scans the tip across the surface, monitoring tunneling current by continually adjusting the gap between sample and tip to maintain a constant current at a constant tunneling voltage. The gap is kept adjusted by having the tip attached to a piezoelectric element that changes its length as a voltage is applied. Tip movement of two angstroms per volt applied to the piezoelectric element is readily achievable.

If a homogeneous sample is being scanned, the in-and-out movement of the tip required to maintain constant tunneling current and voltage provides a qualitative image of the regular undulations of the surface. A sample of different material will possess a different "work function" for the tunneling electrons and will effect a change in the relationship between surface undulation and tip movement. As a result, a contamination or impurity in an otherwise pure, homogeneous surface will appear in the STM image as a hump or hollow (depending on the work function of the impurity) even though the impurity actually may be level with the rest of the surface.

Developments during the year indicated that scanning tunneling microscopy could be done in air at atmospheric pressure or even in a liquid environment—vital for biologic studies. Other work produced an STM able to image insulators as well as conductors and a refinement that yields images of the electron bonds holding the atoms in place on a silicon surface. In the future the STM could have a unique role not only as an observing system on the atomic scale but also as a manipulator. The scanning tip might be able to write atomic-sized patterns as well as read them, finally realizing the idea of the Bible engraved on a pinhead. (S. B. PALMER)

This article updates the *Macropædia* articles MATTER: *Solid State;* Principles, Methods, and Instruments of MEASUREMENT AND OBSERVATION; The PHYSICAL SCIENCES: *Physics.*

Populations and Population Movements

DEMOGRAPHY

World population reached 5,000,000,000 on July 7, 1986, according to a widely publicized estimate of the private Population Institute of Washington, D.C. The latest UN "medium" projections suggested that this milestone would not be reached until March 1987, but demographic experts agreed that the earlier date was plausible, given the uncertainty of data for some large less developed countries, such as Nigeria. According to the latest UN medium estimates, world population passed the 4,000,000,000 mark in 1974 and would reach 6,000,000,000 in 1999. The annual growth rate of world population about 1986 was 1.63%, down from the peak of 2.04% in 1965–70, and the annual number added was 83 million, which would grow to a peak of 89 million a year in 1990–95 before declining. In 1986, 76% of the world's population lived in the less developed countries of Africa, Asia (except Japan), and Latin America. Natural increase (births minus deaths) averaged 2% a year in these countries, compared with 0.6% in the more developed countries.

The proportion of population living in urban areas in 1986 was estimated at 43% for the world as a whole. Although this proportion was still only 34% in less developed countries (compared with 72% in more developed countries), the UN Fund for Population Activities declared in its "State of World Population 1986" report that the rapid growth of urban population in these countries was causing particular problems. By 2000 close to 50% of their populations would live in urban areas, and of the six cities projected to have over 15 million people, four would be in less developed countries (Mexico City; São Paulo, Brazil; and Calcutta and Greater Bombay, India).

Based on U.S. Census Bureau estimates, the U.S. population (including armed forces overseas) was 241,489,000 on July 1, 1986, an increase of 2,206,000 over a year earlier. About 1.7 million of this was due to natural increase and the remainder to the combined effect of legal and illegal immigration into the country and emigration from it. For its estimates, the Census Bureau calculated annual net illegal immigration into the U.S. at 200,000. In 1986 the urban proportion of the U.S. population was about 75%.

Birth Statistics. Provisional estimates of the National Center for Health Statistics put the number of births in the U.S. at 3,749,000 in 1985, 2% more than the 3,669,141 births registered in 1984 and the highest number since 1965. The estimated birthrate was 15.7 births per 1,000 population, and the fertility rate was 66.1 births per 1,000 women aged 15–44, both 1% higher than the rates for 1984. The increase in numbers of births continued into 1986. For the 12-month period ended in May, there were 1% more births than in the same period a year earlier. However, the birthrate and fertility rate remained unchanged, because the total population and the number of women of childbearing age increased between the two periods. Detailed data showed a continuing trend of declining birthrates for women under 30 and increasing rates for women over 30. In 1984 the birthrate for women aged 15–19 was the lowest since 1940, and the proportion of all births occurring to teenaged women, 13%, was the lowest since 1957.

The total fertility rate, which indicates the average number of lifetime births per woman if current fertility rates were to continue, was 1.8 for U.S. women as a whole in 1984, 14% below the "replacement" level of 2.1 births

(continued on page 319)

World's 25 Most Populous Urban Areas[1]

Rank	City and Country	City proper Population	City proper Year	Metropolitan area Population	Metropolitan area Year
1	Tokyo, Japan	8,353,674	1985 cen.	29,002,000	1981 est.
2	New York City, U.S.	7,164,742	1984 est.	17,807,100	1984 est.
3	Mexico City, Mexico	9,931,413	1985 est.	17,321,800	1985 est.
4	Osaka, Japan	2,636,260	1985 cen.	16,224,000	1983 est.
5	São Paulo, Brazil	10,099,086	1985 est.	15,280,375	1985 est.
6	Los Angeles, U.S.	3,096,721	1984 est.	12,372,600	1984 est.
7	London, England	6,767,500	1985 est.	12,231,200	1983 est.
8	Shanghai, China	6,725,700	1985 est.	12,050,000	1985 est.
9	Cairo, Egypt	6,205,000	1985 est.	12,001,000	1983 est.
10	Rhine-Ruhr, W.Ger.	[2]	[2]	10,984,000	1982 est.
11	Rio de Janeiro, Brazil	5,615,149	1985 est.	10,217,269	1985 est.
12	Paris, France	2,140,000	1985 est.	10,210,059	1982 cen.
13	Buenos Aires, Arg.	2,924,000	1985 est.	9,677,200	1981 est.
14	Seoul, South Korea	[3]	[3]	9,645,932	1985 cen.
15	Beijing, China	4,983,000	1985 est.	9,470,000	1985 est.
16	Calcutta, India	3,305,006	1981 cen.	9,194,018	1981 cen.
17	Moscow, U.S.S.R.	8,408,000	1985 est.	8,642,000	1985 est.
18	Bombay, India	[3]	[3]	8,243,405	1981 cen.
19	Chicago, U.S.	2,992,472	1984 est.	8,035,000	1984 est.
20	Tianjin, China	4,123,800	1985 est.	7,990,000	1985 est.
21	Nagoya, Japan	2,116,350	1985 cen.	7,968,000	1981 est.
22	Jakarta, Indonesia	[3]	[3]	7,585,000	1985 est.
23	Manila, Philippines	1,725,500	1983 est.	6,914,581	1985 est.
24	Tehran, Iran	[3]	[3]	6,093,900	1984 est.
25	Istanbul, Turkey	5,494,916	1985 cen.	5,858,558	1985 cen.

[1]Ranked by population of metropolitan area.
[2]An industrial conurbation within which no single central city is defined.
[3]Administrative unit within which a separate city proper is not distinguished.

Special Report: Populations

Domesday Book

BY ANN WILLIAMS

In 1986 exhibitions were held in London and Winchester, Hampshire, to celebrate the 900th anniversary of Domesday Book, the survey ordered by William the Conqueror that is the first public record in England.

The Making of Domesday. At Christmas 1085 William the Conqueror, the first Norman king of the English (1066–87), ordered a survey made of his kingdom to discover, in the words of a contemporary chronicler, "how it was peopled and with what sorts of men." The investigations took place in the spring and summer of 1086, and the written results were gathered at Winchester, where one of the royal scribes edited them into a single volume, soon to be called Domesday Book. His labours lasted a year and were never, in fact, completed. King William died in September 1087, and the last returns, relating to East Anglia, were not entered in Domesday Book but were bound into a second volume, referred to as Little Domesday. Incomplete as it was, Domesday represented a unique achievement.

William's administrators divided the country into groups of shires, called circuits—seven in all. To each circuit a body of commissioners was assigned, equipped with a standard set of questions to be answered. They held sessions of the shire courts within their circuits, at which both oral and written evidence was heard. The local administration was already complex by 1066. Each shire was subdivided into hundreds, units of fiscal and judicial administration, and each hundred had a court, whose members gave evidence before the commissioners. The records of the land tax (geld), which was collected through the shires and hundreds, were available and proved particularly useful, since they recorded the names of estates and their owners liable to geld. The vast estates of the king were administered by officials, called reeves, who made written returns about the royal lands, and each landholder within the shire had to submit a written description of his estates. In cases of disputed ownership, each of the contending parties gave evidence, and written evidence in the form of title deeds was recorded.

The commissioners organized this vast corpus of material shire by shire, under the names of the chief tenants, beginning with the land of the king. For each estate the information was compiled according to the set questions provided: who held the estate; what was it called; how much tax did it pay; how many peasants (of various types) were there; how much meadow, pasture, and woodland; what was the estate worth; and so forth. For each circuit a written return was compiled, and these were dispatched to Winchester. Little Domesday was one such return, and another exists for the southwestern shires, called Exon Domesday. Comparison of these circuit returns with Domesday itself reveals that the scribe did not simply copy the material but selected, abbreviated, and rearranged it into its final form.

The Purpose of Domesday. The reasons behind this mammoth investigation are not easily determined. By 1086 William had been reigning for 20 years, years that had seen a massive redistribution of wealth from English to Norman hands. Some of the original settlers had abandoned or forfeited their estates; others had died without heirs, and their land had been redistributed. It may be that the survey was intended to establish rights of tenure; certainly it was used for this purpose over the next 50 years. The main thrust of the inquiry, however, was to determine the rights of the king. In any case, the importance of Domesday to modern historians is that it provides a unique guide to 11th-century England.

Problems of Interpretation. It must be said, however, that as a data base Domesday has serious flaws. First, Domesday named only those landlords who held directly of the king (the tenants in chief) and their immediate subtenants. Of these groups, only the tenants in chief and their more important subtenants can be precisely identified.

Another problem occurs vis-à-vis the peasants and non-noble freemen, who were enumerated in groups for each estate. It seems likely that only heads of households were recorded, omitting wives, children, and dependents, and some multiplier (usually five) must be applied to obtain an estimate of total population for each estate. In the case of slaves, a further problem emerges: though it might be assumed that, in this case, the totals given were accurate, other evidence suggests that slaves too might be married and have children. The fact that slave women were recorded in some, but not all, areas would support this hypothesis. It is therefore possible that a multiplier (perhaps five again) should be applied to the slave totals also.

Finally, it should be noted that whole categories of people were omitted from the Domesday statistics: household retainers and servants of the great lords who did not hold land; the monks and clerks who staffed monasteries and collegiate churches; the families and dependents of the barons and their men. Most serious is the lack of any usable figures for urban communities. Nevertheless, the Domesday material, which allows for an estimated total of between 1½ million and 2 million inhabitants in 11th-century England, presents a better picture of a medieval population than is available from any other European kingdom.

THE BRITISH POST OFFICE

A 17-pence stamp featuring pictures of medieval husbandry was issued to celebrate the 900th anniversary of Domesday Book.

Ann Williams, lecturer at the Polytechnic of North London, was academic adviser to the "Domesday" exhibition, London, and academic consultant to the "Domesday 900" exhibition, Winchester. She was coeditor of the 1986 facsimile edition of Domesday Book.

(continued from page 317)
per woman. For white women the rate was 1.7 and for black women, 2.2. There were 770,355 births to unmarried women in 1984, 4% more than in 1983. The proportion of all births occurring to unmarried women, 21%, and the birthrate per 1,000 unmarried women aged 15–44, 31, were the highest ever recorded. All of the increase in nonmarital births between 1980 and 1984 was due to increases in births to unmarried women aged 20 and older. In 1984, 13% of births to white women and 59% of births to black women were to unmarried mothers.

The Alan Guttmacher Institute reported that annual legal abortions in the U.S. fell more than 4% between 1982 and 1984, from an estimated 1,574,000 to 1,508,000, after nearly a decade of increase.

According to recent estimates reported by the Population Reference Bureau, the birthrate per 1,000 population about 1986 averaged 27 for the world as a whole, 15 in more developed countries and 31 in less developed countries, all unchanged from a year earlier. Also unchanged were regional rates, which ranged from a high of 45 in Africa to a low of 13 in Europe. The total fertility rate in more developed countries was below the replacement level, averaging 1.9 births per woman and falling as low as 1.3 in West Germany. Although China's total fertility rate was at the replacement level of 2.1, the average for all less developed countries, though declining, was still 4.2. Because of current and past high fertility, the proportion of children under age 15 ranged between 40 and 50% of the total population in many less developed countries and was 39% for these countries as a whole, compared with 23% for more developed countries. As a result, these countries had a large built-in potential for future population growth.

Death Statistics. Provisional estimates put deaths in the U.S. at 2,084,000 in 1985, 37,000 more than in 1984 and a record annual high, although the death rate, 8.7 per 1,000 population, remained unchanged from 1984. The increase in numbers of deaths reflected the continuing rise in the proportion of persons aged 65 and over in the U.S. population and the influenza outbreak of early 1985. The leading causes of death in 1985 were:

Causes of death	Estimated rate per 100,000 population
1. Diseases of the heart	325.0
2. Malignant neoplasms	191.7
3. Cerebrovascular diseases	64.0
4. Accidents and adverse effects	38.6
5. Chronic obstructive pulmonary diseases	31.2
6. Pneumonia and influenza	27.9
7. Diabetes mellitus	16.2
8. Suicide	12.0
9. Chronic liver disease and cirrhosis	11.2
10. Atherosclerosis	9.9
11. Nephritis, nephrotic syndrome, and nephrosis	9.4
12. Homicide and legal intervention	8.1
13. Conditions of the perinatal period	7.6
14. Septicemia	7.1
15. Congenital anomalies	5.5

As in recent years, the first four of these causes continued to account for almost three out of four deaths, and death rates continued to rise slightly for cancer and to fall for stroke and accidents. The death rate for heart disease, which had been declining since the 1960s, rose slightly between 1984 and 1985, probably relative to the influenza outbreak of 1985.

The average death rate for the world as a whole remained unchanged from the previous three or four years at 11 per 1,000 population. The average rate of 11 in less developed countries was almost as low as the average of 10 in more developed countries but, combined with their birthrate of 31, it resulted in a high rate of natural increase of 2% a year. At that rate a population doubles in 34 years. Death rates were higher than birthrates in Denmark, Hungary, and West Germany.

Infant Mortality. The provisional infant mortality rate for the U.S. in 1985 was 10.6 deaths under one year of age per 1,000 live births. The insignificant difference from 10.7 in 1984 reflected the continued slowing in the rate of infant mortality decline observed since 1981. Detailed data for 1983 showed the rate for blacks at 19.2, compared with 9.7 for white infants, a relative gap that had remained unchanged for more than two decades. The latest estimates reported by the Population Reference Bureau put infant mortality rates at 82 for the world as a whole and 92 for less developed countries, both slightly higher than previous annual estimates, while the rate of 17 for more developed countries was down one point from the previous year. The rates were well over 100 in most African countries and lowest in Japan and Iceland (6.2 per 1,000 live births).

Life Expectancy. Life expectancy at birth for the total U.S. population in 1985 was estimated at 74.7 years, the same as in 1984. The figures were unchanged for white males (71.8 years) and black females (73.7) and had declined slightly for white females (78.8 to 78.7) and black males (65.5 to 65.3).

Worldwide, estimates of life expectancy remained unchanged at 62 years for the world as a whole, 73 in more developed countries, and 58 in less developed countries. Among regions, Africa, at 50 years, had the lowest life expectancy. The highest for men and women combined was 77 years, reported for Japan, Iceland, and Sweden.

Marriage and Divorce Statistics. Between 1984 and 1985, the number of marriages in the U.S. declined 2%, from 2,487,000 to 2,425,000, and the number of divorces rose 3%, from 1,155,000 to 1,187,000. These were both reversals of previous trends and were due in part to the aging of the large baby boom generation, born from 1946 to 1964. This generation was aging out of the early 20s, the usual ages for first marriage (in 1983 the median age at first marriage was 22.5 for women and 24.4 for men), and entering the early 30s, when most divorces occur. The increase in divorce also reflected the recovery from the 1981–83 recession. The marriage rate in 1985 was 10.2 per 1,000 population (10.5 in 1984), and the divorce rate was 5 (4.9 in 1984).

Surveys. In a summary of findings from the World Fertility Survey and Contraceptive Prevalence Survey programs conducted between the mid-1970s and 1985, the Population Information Program of Johns Hopkins University reported that in the 61 less developed countries surveyed, current use of contraception ranged from less than 1% among married women of childbearing age in Mauritania to 66% in Costa Rica. Among regions, rates were lowest in Africa and highest in Latin America. In a separate survey, China's "contraceptive prevalence" rate was found to be 69% in 1982, the highest current use of contraception among married women so far recorded in a less developed country. In 17 more developed countries participating in the World Fertility Survey, current contraceptive use among married women of reproductive age ranged from 51% in Spain (in 1977) to 75% or more in seven other European countries. In the U.S. the figure was 68% in both 1976 and 1982–83. (JEAN VAN DER TAK)

See also World Data.

INTERNATIONAL MIGRATION

Western European governments continued to tighten legislation curbing the flow of immigrants in 1986. The immigration issue became heavily politicized, particularly when visa controls were imposed that suggested discrimination on grounds of colour rather than age, skill, or some other, more general measure of status. A number of factors contributed to the attitudes of the European governments: the acceleration in the flow of would-be immigrants from the third world, the rise in crime and terrorism, and, perhaps the most important, rising unemployment and a general deterioration in social conditions. As opportunities diminished elsewhere in the world—most notably in the oil-producing countries of the Middle East—Western Europe, North America, and Australia grew in popularity. Within Europe, the poorer countries generated their own problems; in Ireland, for example, the lack of jobs produced a net emigration of 31,000.

Denmark, France, the U.K., Switzerland, and West Germany took action to reduce the flow of immigrants and refugees from the third world during 1986. In Britain deportation orders on children, alleged to be "adoptions of convenience," gave rise to considerable controversy, as did Home Office action to limit the right of members of Parliament to prevent the repatriation of a would-be immigrant until the case had been thoroughly investigated. The most dramatic and controversial action taken by the U.K. government was its imposition of a visa requirement for visitors from Bangladesh, Ghana, India, Nigeria, and Pakistan. The decision followed a threat of industrial action by immigration officers who claimed they could not cope with the increasing influx of foreign visitors-immigrants. The number of people refused entry rose from 277 a month in the period April–July 1985 to 672 a month in January–March 1986. The visa requirements also affected nationals of the specified countries who had been granted permanent resident status in the U.K. since Jan. 1, 1973, but did not hold U.K. passports.

In West Germany the Christian Democratic government mounted a campaign to amend the federal republic's constitutional requirement that "persons persecuted on political grounds shall enjoy the right of asylum." In the first nine months of 1986 some 72,600 third world refugees entered West Germany—half through East Germany into West Berlin—and requested asylum. On October 1 East Germany closed this route to refugees without visas for West Germany.

TOM ANSTEY—CANAPRESS

Sri Lankan Hindu Tamils gather on a fishing boat bound for Newfoundland after they and others were rescued from crowded lifeboats. The 155 refugees had paid for full passage to the safety of North America but apparently were abandoned short of their destination.

On October 17 the Danish Folketing (parliament) approved new immigration rules that required refugees to have a valid passport or visa. These rules were expected to reduce the flow of refugees by 50–80%; the number had risen from a total of 9,000 in 1985 to nearly 1,000 a week in 1986, mainly from North Africa. Under the previous law, once asylum seekers reached the frontiers they were given entry and could not be turned back without a tribunal ruling. In France the National Assembly passed a new law that restricted and tightened controls on foreign residents. In the future they could be expelled if the Ministry of the Interior decided they constituted a threat to public order, with no recourse to the courts. The expulsion of 101 Malians under this procedure in October provoked strong criticism from the Association of French Lawyers.

The Canadian government granted one-year residence and work permits to 155 Sri Lankan Tamils who were rescued from lifeboats at sea, the last stage of their journey, via West Germany, from their strife-torn homeland. They joined the 22,000 refugees already in Canada who were applying for permanent resident status; another 10,000–12,000 refugees had filed applications outside the country. Canada took 84,301 immigrants in 1985 and had a 1986 target of slightly under 100,000. Applicants with desired skills were given preference. Australia planned to take 95,-000 immigrants in 1986–87, compared with the 89,000 accepted in 1985–86. It increased the number of skilled migrants it would take from 14,000 to 16,000 and opened a new category—Independent and Concessional—which gave rights of entry to extended family members.

In the U.S. the flow of would-be immigrants increased as economic conditions elsewhere, particularly in Mexico, deteriorated. The six-month trial in Tucson, Ariz., of 11 members of the Sanctuary Movement, which aimed to assist those wishing to leave El Salvador and Guatemala, ended in May with the conviction of 8 defendants, including religious leaders. In October Congress passed a far-reaching immigration law giving amnesty to between one million and five million illegal aliens who had entered the U.S. before January 1982 and had lived there continuously ever since. At the same time, fines were to be imposed on employers who knowingly hired illegal immigrants. Because of the shortage of agricultural labour, foreign agricultural workers wanting to enter the U.S. were to be given preferential treatment. (LOUIS KUSHNICK)

REFUGEES

During 1986 there was a significant improvement in the critical refugee situation in Africa, which had dominated the work of the UN High Commissioner for Refugees (UNHCR) in the previous year, but a number of major refugee movements continued to occur on that continent. The relative stabilization of the exodus of refugees fleeing civil disturbance, drought, and famine was partially offset by new movements of refugees to Ethiopia from The Sudan, the result of civil war in that country. On a more positive note, there were repatriation movements from The Sudan to Ethiopia and Uganda and from the Central African Republic to Chad, while developments concerning the possible voluntary return home of Ethiopians from Somalia and Djibouti gave grounds for optimism.

The situation in southern Africa was cause for concern as attacks by the armed forces of the South African government on Botswana, Zambia, and Zimbabwe affected refugees in those countries and partially destroyed the UNHCR-supported transit centre at Makeni in Lusaka, Zambia. The security problems prevailing in Mozambique, where the Mozambique National Resistance continued to oppose the government, prompted tens of thousands of Mozambicans to seek safety in neighbouring countries, including Malawi, Swaziland, Zambia, and Zimbabwe. Although the setting up of assistance programs remained a major priority and involved the expenditure of some $198 million in 1986, UNHCR placed increasing emphasis on finding permanent solutions to the problems of refugees in the region. Priority was being given to voluntary repatriation and, failing this, to programs designed to promote self-reliance for refugees.

The largest single refugee problem in the world remained that of Afghans in Pakistan and Iran, where the numbers had reached three million and two million, respectively, according to the estimates of the governments concerned. During the year there was a shift in the emphasis of UNHCR programs in Pakistan from relief to the promotion of self-reliance. Many of the refugees in Iran had found local employment and were now self-sufficient, but large numbers continued to depend on assistance from the government. UNHCR was therefore planning a number of rural settlements, as well as providing vocational training and income-generating projects for this group.

Resettlement remained the main long-term solution for refugees in camps in Southeast Asia, though an increasing number of Indochinese "long-stayers" awaiting resettlement caused concern. The Orderly Departure Program from Vietnam suffered a setback in 1986, mainly as a result of procedural problems; nevertheless, as of September 1986 over 113,000 persons had left Vietnam under the program since its inception in 1979. On December 29 Thailand announced that it planned to phase out its refugee camps, starting with the closing of the huge Khao I Dang. Some 26,000 Kampucheans there would lose their refugee status and would be moved to settlements nearer the Kampuchean border. A Thai spokesman indicated that his country could no longer cope with the refugee presence.

In Latin America an increasing number of refugees from Nicaragua sought asylum in neighbouring countries, notably Honduras. The poor economic situation in the region impeded refugee integration. UNHCR sought to facilitate the voluntary repatriation of refugee groups, particularly Salvadorans and Nicaraguans from Honduras and Guatemalans from Mexico. The unrest in Chile provoked the departure of a number of refugees, mainly to Argentina. Former refugees from Argentina and Uruguay continued to return to their countries of origin.

Asylum-seekers continued to arrive in great numbers in Western Europe, particularly from other continents. The increase in applications for asylum under national procedures for the determination of refugee status resulted in additional delays in decision making in many countries. Asylum-seekers were thus compelled to endure extended waiting periods without the possibility of receiving assistance to integrate. Intergovernmental consultations with UNHCR participation were held to discuss the problem and to find common solutions. Some countries, however, took unilateral decisions in order to control and restrict the admission of asylum-seekers and other persons who arrived without visas.

The year began with the accession of Switzerland's Jean-Pierre Hocké, former director of operations at the International Committee of the Red Cross, to the position of UN High Commissioner for Refugees. Hocké was elected in December 1985 by the UN General Assembly to serve a three-year term starting Jan. 1, 1986. He succeeded Poul Hartling of Denmark, who retired after eight years in the post. (UNHCR)

This article updates the *Macropædia* article POPULATION.

Publishing

The publishing industry in 1986 was subjected to several major influences. Competition increased, but at the same time, new markets with rapidly growing readerships—particularly China and the Far East—were emerging to provide fresh challenges for the more adventurous. Traditional publishing activities continued to evolve as they gradually, or sometimes almost instantly, adopted the new technology that was giving newcomers the competitive edge on pricing.

The adoption of new technology generated its own problems, not least of which were those resulting from the change in skill requirements. Nowhere was this more apparent than in the U.K., where London's "Fleet Street"—for nearly 500 years the home of the nation's publishing and, since the 1700s, the newspaper industry—moved rapidly into obsolescence. Newspapers moved or were planning imminent moves out of central London in order to reduce their costs and take advantage of the new technology. New newspapers were being published that took immediate advantage of high technology and consequently were able to have lower cover prices and offer cheaper advertising rates. The main casualties of the changeover were the printers, and a number of serious labour disputes arose over the issue.

The impact of new technology not only revolutionized the way in which newspapers, magazines, and, to a lesser extent, books were printed but also affected the content. New systems allowed full-colour pictures to be transmitted in minutes around the world. In book and magazine publishing there were also significant electronic order-processing developments. The U.K. Teleordering Scheme added an international dimension, launched in Cairo and Vienna. Late in 1986 it was extended into France, Belgium, Scandinavia, and China, and there were plans to introduce it into Malaysia, Hong Kong, and Singapore.

Newspapers. For the U.K.'s national newspapers 1986 proved to be a revolutionary year, one that, regardless of subsequent events, would be remembered for the transformation in the economic structure of the industry. It was marked not just by a quickening shift to modern printing technologies, accompanied by a considerable loss of jobs, but by the launch of two new national daily titles to join the nine in an already strongly competitive marketplace. Some of the activity, such as the launch of a newspaper by Eddie Shah (*see* BIOGRAPHIES), had been foreseen. But no outsider expected the most radical and dramatic move, the virtually overnight shift of the four newspapers owned by Rupert Murdoch's News International Ltd. out of their existing plant and into a custom-built new technology centre at Wapping, east London.

News International had maintained that the plant was for a new evening paper, but in January, when printing unions threatened to strike over a "jobs for life" claim, Murdoch first had sections of *The Sunday Times* printed there and the following weekend dismissed 5,000 print union members and gave instruction for the four newspapers—*The Times, The Sunday Times,* the *Sun,* and *News of the World*—to be moved to Wapping. The well-protected Wapping premises had been prepared to produce all four newspapers with the help of U.S. advisers and non-London electricians. The move, an astonishingly well-kept industrial secret, not only caused deep bitterness within the British trade union movement (over the role of the electricians) but also instantly changed the economic base of the newspaper business; the production costs of the Murdoch papers, which spanned daily and Sunday, serious and popular, were slashed. Nearly one year later, however, union pickets were still outside "Fortress Wapping," and the staff still had to be bused through the barbed-wire barriers that protected the premises.

In the wake of the News International move, the launch in March of Shah's seven-day-a-week daily paper *Today* was inevitably an anticlimax. Shah, who was a publisher of small local papers in northwestern England, saw his creation as revolutionary both in production terms—it used a direct-input headquarters in London, several remote printing plants around England, and a franchise distribution system to avoid the existing strongly unionized one—and in its ability to use colour for news and feature presentation. The paper was directed at roughly the same readership that was attracted to the *Daily Mail* and *Daily Express* and aimed at a circulation of around one million. But at the launch the technology and distribution network both proved inadequate, and the full colour on editorial copy lacked the expected appeal. Sales quickly dropped to around the quarter-million mark, and by midyear *Today* had been taken over by Lonrho, a commercial conglomerate that already owned the upmarket liberal *Observer.* Shah remained as a minor shareholder and titular chairman. Efforts to relaunch the paper in September raised its weekday sales to 300,000 (fewer for the Sunday edition), and in December the editor, Brian McArthur, resigned to return to *The Sunday Times.*

The other U.K. newspaper launch was more auspicious. The *Independent* was conceived by Andreas Whittam Smith, once the city (financial) editor of the *Daily Telegraph,* who together with two colleagues raised £20 million to start an upmarket daily aimed at young professionals, whom he believed to be either nonreaders or sufficiently unhappy with *The Times,* the *Daily Telegraph,* or *The Guardian* to move to a well-written, politically independent newcomer. Because Whittam Smith was using direct-input technology and production costs were low, he was able to offer journalists high salaries and attract talent from *The Times* and *The Sunday Times* after the Wapping move. This enabled the *Independent* to build a strong editorial staff. The first edition of the *Independent,* on October 7, was greeted with admiration from both within and outside the industry. Its success in economic terms was less clear. Whittam Smith had estimated that if sales were 400,000 at the end of the first year, the newspaper would be a viable proposition. During its first two weeks the *Independent* sold about 650,000 copies daily, but by December it had slipped to 320,000 on its own estimate and 275,000 according to others. Losses suffered by the three main rivals were believed to be up to 50,000 copies daily, with *The Times* most affected.

In South Africa international protests from publishers and journalists greeted the stringent news censorship laws imposed by the government on all media in December. The move was the culmination of a year of political upheaval and violence. Black journalists were among those detained under emergency laws, and international as well as South African media were subjected to increased censorship.

A certain irony resulted when the situation in South Africa was juxtaposed with that in the U.S.S.R., where observers noted that Soviet leader Mikhail Gorbachev's efforts to reform the economic structure and morale of the country, involving a policy of *glasnost* (openness), were being extended to the media. Though they remained tools of the state, newspapers were printing articles and readers' letters that were more openly critical of shortcomings in society and the bureaucracy.

The face of a loading-dock worker and a plaintive headline summarize the lead story of Baltimore's *News-American* in its final issue after having been published since 1773.

© 1986 MARTY KATZ

In France a new law on press monopolies came into force in November. Less stringent than the previous one, it allowed 30% of combined national and provincial sales to have one owner, thus clearing the way for newspaper proprieter Robert Hersant to keep his empire—which included 38% of national sales—intact. (PETER FIDDICK)

The year started badly for proponents of diversity in the U.S. newspaper industry. In February the *St. Louis* (Mo.) *Globe-Democrat* ceased publication, leaving that city of 453,000 with only one daily, the *St. Louis Post-Dispatch.* In May the *Baltimore* (Md.) *News-American* closed after more than two centuries of publication, leaving that city of 787,000 with only one daily, the *Sun.*

And so it went throughout the year, as more and more U.S. cities became one-newspaper towns. Of the 1,676 general-purpose daily newspapers remaining in the U.S., fewer than three dozen had any local competition. Meanwhile, a number of major U.S. dailies came under chain ownership. The Gannett Co., the country's largest newspaper chain, with more than 90 papers, purchased the Evening News Association, publisher of the *Detroit News,* for $717 million. Two months later it was announced that Gannett and the Knight-Ridder Co., a large chain that owned Detroit's only other daily, the *Free Press,* planned to apply for an exemption from antitrust laws to enter a so-called joint operating agreement; that arrangement would allow the two Detroit newspapers to merge their business operations while maintaining separate editorial staffs. The day after the *Baltimore News-American* was closed, the Times Mirror Co., a major media conglomerate, announced that it intended to purchase the A. S. Abell Co. of Baltimore, the company that published the *Sun,* for $600 million.

In the minds of many critics, the decline of local competition and the supplanting of local ownership by distant newspaper chains threatened to limit the diversity of viewpoints in the U.S. newspaper industry and the accountability of newspapers to local readers. Monopoly- and chain-owned papers, according to this argument, are more likely to avoid controversy and less likely to invest money in provocative hometown reporting than are locally owned papers and those in competitive markets. The opposite view held that the economics of the newspaper industry made the decline of local competitiveness inevitable. One move, however, ran counter to the trend: Murdoch, forced to sell the *Chicago Sun-Times* after he acquired a TV station in Chicago, sold the paper to a local investor group headed by the publisher, Robert Page.

Whether the decline of competitive and locally owned newspapers was a cause for concern or not, the industry faced serious economic problems in 1986. Daily circulation, which had set records in the three previous years, declined by 315,508—or 0.5%—to 62,766,232, according to the 1986 *Editor & Publisher International Year Book.* Much of the loss was caused by higher newsstand prices charged by leading dailies. The *New York Post,* for instance, lost 126,000 customers after raising its price from 30 to 35 cents. Perhaps a larger part of the decline, however, simply reflected the uncertain economy and the dwindling number of newspapers. A total of 19 papers ceased daily publication; some were merged with other papers, others were converted to weeklies, and a few were shut down completely. At the same time, 7 new dailies were started, bringing the net loss of papers for the year to 12.

The trend toward morning papers continued as 26 dailies shifted from afternoon to morning distribution. That brought the total number of morning dailies to 482, up from the previous year's 458, and raised morning circulation by 2.6%, from 35,424,418 to 36,361,561. The number of evening newspapers dropped from 1,257 to 1,220, and evening circulation declined by 4.5%, from 27,657,322 to 26,404,671. The number of Sunday editions of daily newspapers rose from 783 to 798, and Sunday circulation increased by 2.2%, from 57,573,979 to 58,825,978.

There were not many major court cases involving newspapers during the year, but there were some noteworthy attempts by the executive branch of the government to intimidate and mislead the press. For the first time in memory, a director of the Central Intelligence Agency (CIA) threatened to prosecute a number of leading news organizations for allegedly publishing information harmful to the national security. Citing Section 798 of Title 18 of the U.S. Code, a seldom-used 1951 law banning the disclosure of classified information about U.S. ciphers, code breaking, and other communications intelligence, CIA Director William Casey persuaded the *Washington Post* not to publish details of U.S. eavesdropping on Soviet submarines. Casey also asked the Department of Justice to bring formal proceedings against news organizations that did publish the material. The information surfaced shortly before the trial of Ronald Pelton, a former employee of the National Security Agency, on charges of espionage.

The 1986 Pulitzer gold medal for public service, the most prestigious of the Pulitzer Prizes, was awarded to the *Denver* (Colo.) *Post* for a series of articles indicating that the nationwide concern over missing children was largely unwarranted. Among other findings, the paper reported that about 99% of "missing" children were in fact voluntary runaways, most of whom returned home within 72 hours, and that the number of children kidnapped by strangers is small, contrary to popular belief. Reporting prizes went to, among others, Edna Buchanan, a veteran police reporter for the *Miami* (Fla.) *Herald,* as well as to *Lexington* (Ky.) *Herald-Leader* reporters Jeffrey Marx and Michael York for a series of articles revealing payoffs to University of Kentucky basketball players. The *New York Times* won two Pulitzers for a series on the U.S. Strategic Defense Initiative (known popularly as "Star Wars") and for the music criticism of Donal Henahan. *New York Daily News* columnist Jimmy Breslin received the prize for commentary, and Jules Feiffer was cited for his cartoons in New York City's weekly *Village Voice.* (DONALD MORRISON)

Magazines. Three important court cases favoured U.S. magazine publishers in 1986. *Playboy* and the American Booksellers Association won a victory from the Attorney General's Commission on Pornography, which had linked hard-core pornography to sex crimes. On July 3 a U.S. federal district court judge ordered the commission to rescind a letter it had sent to 7,000 retail outlets of the 7-Eleven food stores chain. The letter requested that the retailers remove *Penthouse* and *Playboy* from their shelves.

The U.S. Supreme Court ruled in June that libel suits filed by public officials and figures must be dismissed by the judge before a trial unless the evidence suggests they can prove libel with "convincing clarity." In a third case the Supreme Court decided that even a private figure suing a news organization for libel must prove that damaging statements are false, at least "on matters of public concern."

According to the March 22 issue of *The Nation,* which celebrated its 120th year, the FBI had had a long interest in the magazine, from 1922 to 1982. In 2,000 pages of FBI documents, obtained under the Freedom of Information Act, it was revealed that the agency once conducted a nine-year analysis comparing the positions of the Communist Party and those expressed in articles published by *The Nation* and its rival, *The New Republic.*

If college bookstore sales were an indication, *Cosmopolitan* was favoured. According to a College Store Executive Magazine Survey, *Cosmopolitan* was the magazine most frequently read by U.S. college students. The runners-up, in order of sales, were *Glamour, Time, People, Playboy, Penthouse, Vogue, Mademoiselle, Newsweek,* and *TV Guide.*

The face-lift of the year was performed on *Newsweek.* It was totally overhauled from back to front in an effort to improve its circulation of three million, particularly the newsstand sales. *U.S. News & World Report,* purchased from its employees in 1984 for some $165 million, introduced a new design that by midyear had helped increase circulation by 250,000 to 2.3 million.

Several magazines celebrated new approaches and anniversaries during the year. *Boy's Life,* the nation's eighth oldest popular magazine, marked its 75th birthday. According to the editor, the readers never could get enough of hunting, fishing, music, and cars. With the death of its founders, *Reader's Digest* and its more than 2,000 employees turned to new management and a promise to "put profits No. 1 on the agenda." One thing would not change; the *Digest* would remain under private control. William Buckley's *National Review* marked its 30th year with a gala party at New York City's Plaza Hotel. Among the 730 guests to praise the conservative voice was U.S. Pres. Ronald Reagan. *Ebony,* founded to support blacks, noted its 40th anniversary.

One of the year's largest takeovers was the purchase for some $92 million of *Ladies' Home Journal* from Family Media by Meredith. The Des Moines, Iowa, publisher already issued *Better Homes and Gardens,* among seven other popular titles.

The venerable *Scientific American* was acquired by a West German publishing company for $52.6 million. Founded in 1845, it was one of the oldest continuously published magazines in the U.S. The reason for the sale was the drop in advertising and increased competition from such other scientific publications as *Discover, Science Digest,* and *Omni.*

Four science magazines took top honours in the 1986

National Magazine Awards. The four and the categories in which they won were *Science 85,* public interest; *The Sciences,* essays and criticism; *IEEE Spectrum,* single-topic issue; and *Discover,* general excellence.

Leading scholars in the humanities and the social sciences strongly criticized the content and editing of scholarly publications. An American Council of Learned Societies study found that scholars believed that their journals were biased in favour of established researchers. About one-third said that they rarely found articles of interest in their discipline's primary journal. (WILLIAM A. KATZ)

The British magazine market was relatively stable in 1986, though there appeared to be a slowdown in sales increases even in the more buoyant consumer sectors. This was partly because of increased competition and partly because more new free titles were being distributed, particularly to high-income urban areas.

The most notable new magazine, and one with possible future implications, was *Prima,* a women's monthly based on homecraft activities, the first title launched in Britain by the Gruner and Jahr group, already strong in West Germany and France; its first two editions sold well. It was seen as a rival mainly for the supermarket-distributed *Family Circle.* Equally notable was the closing of *Honey,* an International Publishing Corp. (IPC) fashion magazine launched in the 1960s; its circulation had fallen from over 250,000 to about 100,000. (PETER FIDDICK)

Books. During 1986 the word big took on new dimensions. The big books got bigger as publishers offered multimillion-dollar advances to authors, the biggest best-sellers sold more copies than ever before, and two large publishing companies grew even larger through mergers and acquisitions.

In January hardcover and paperback rights to *Whirlwind,* a new novel by James Clavell, author of *Shogun* and *Noble House,* were purchased by William Morrow and Avon for more than $5 million. The two publishers, both Hearst companies, were able to share the risk of the huge advance and by joining together in the deal could offer more money to the author than either could alone. Such "hard-soft" deals had become more common in recent years after paperback publishers such as Bantam and Warner found success with hardcover books. Simultaneously, hardcover publishers such as St. Martin's Press, Viking Penguin, and McGraw-Hill sought to establish a presence in mass market paperback publishing in order to compete as "full-line" publishers, though their move into paperbacks was notably less lucrative than the move by paperback publishers into hardcover.

Large advances continued to be in the news throughout the year, and Random House, long considered one of the most prestigious publishers in the U.S., made two of the biggest deals together with Ballantine Books, its paperback subsidiary. In July the house paid $4,333,000 for the hardcover and paperback rights to *California Gold,* an as-yet-unwritten novel by John Jakes, author of *North and South* and the best-selling Kent Family Chronicles, a series of paperback originals published in the late 1970s. In the next month Howard Kaminsky, president and chief executive officer of the Random House adult trade division, announced that a three-book contract had been signed with Barbara Taylor Bradford, author of *A Woman of Substance* and *Act of Will,* whose novels had more than 23 million copies in print worldwide. Bradford's next novel, still unwritten, was promised to her current publisher, Doubleday, and the contract with Random House would not take effect until the book following it. The price paid for the three books was not announced, but Morton Janklow, Bradford's agent, described the deal as having "very few analogies in publishing."

Random House also acquired several important political autobiographies during 1986, including books by recently released Soviet dissident Anatoly Shcharansky, due to be published in the fall of 1987; the autobiography of Philippine president Corazon Aquino, due in 1987; the memoirs of first lady Nancy Reagan, to be published in the fall of 1989, after Pres. Ronald Reagan had left office; and, most notably, an authorized biography of President Reagan by Edmund Morris, author of *The Rise of Theodore Roosevelt.* Random House paid $3 million for the president's biography, a record price for a nonfiction book. The price seemed especially high because it was not the president's autobiography, though he would be cooperating with biographer Morris.

Record high advances were matched in 1986 by record high sales figures and to some extent justified the hope of publishers that the upcoming books would be even more successful. During 1986 three nonfiction books in quick succession claimed the title "fastest selling hardcover book in history": *Iacocca,* the autobiography of Chrysler president Lee Iacocca, which sold nearly 2.7 million copies within 18 months of its October 1984 publication, according to Bantam, the book's publisher; *Fit for Life,* a diet book by Harvey and Marilyn Diamond that had sold more than two million copies since its June 1985 publication and was still high on best-seller lists at the end of 1986; and the biggest of them all, *Fatherhood,* by popular television performer Bill Cosby, published in May 1986 by Doubleday. Within 19 weeks of its publication, the book had sold more than two million copies, eclipsing both *Iacocca* and *Fit for Life,* and it was still the number one nonfiction best-seller at year's end. (Berkley paid $1.6 million for the paperback rights to this book, but with no end in sight to the sales success of the hardcover edition, paperback publication might be held off until as late as 1988.)

Alongside these successes stood at least one notable failure, David Stockman's *The Triumph of Politics: Why the Reagan Revolution Failed,* published by Harper & Row. The case of the Stockman book was an expensive lesson for Harper & Row, which in 1985 had paid a $2.4 million advance to the former director of the Office of Management and Budget under President Reagan. The book was only a moderate success when it was published in April 1986—it was on best-seller lists for less than three months, and though the publisher said the book had more than 350,-

AP/WIDE WORLD

Videocassettes featuring products normally advertised on commercial television were released by several companies in an attempt to reach videocassette-recorder owners who normally skip commercials when viewing programs they have recorded for later viewing.

Shoppers in Amsterdam crowd a display featuring the collected writings of Anne Frank, the young Jewish girl who was in hiding during World War II. The 744-page book contains all of Frank's existing writings and the findings of a government analysis that confirmed Frank's authorship of her famous diary.

AP/WIDE WORLD

000 copies in print by summer, most observers doubted that *The Triumph of Politics* would recoup its publisher's investment.

The embarrassment of the lesson was compounded when it was announced in October 1986 that Avon Books would publish its paperback edition of the Stockman book in January 1987, rather than wait the customary year after hardcover publication, and that the book's subtitle would be changed to "The Inside Story of the Reagan Revolution." Said the paperback house, "Avon is not convinced that the mass market is convinced that the Reagan Revolution has failed."

Sales of all books in the U.S. rose 8.3% to $9,880,-000,000 in 1985, and trade book (excluding textbooks) sales were up an even more gratifying figure—17.3% to $1,988,000,000. Record high book sales could be traced to the phenomenon of chain bookstores and discount bookselling. With the presence of a B. Dalton or Waldenbooks in every shopping mall, books were more widely available than ever before; and the rise of chain booksellers such as the Washington-based Crown organization, which sold new books at 35% off the cover price, made books available at low prices. Some found their profit margin shrinking on each title, and by the year's end Dayton-Hudson, the corporate parent of B. Dalton, had announced that the chain was for sale.

Hardcover and paperback prices rose to new highs in 1986, with the most popular hardcover fiction regularly priced at $19.95 to $22.95. Paperback prices of $4.95 and $5.95 were no longer unusual, but affluent readers were more willing to pay those prices than their parents had been to pay $5.95 to $10.95 for hardcovers a decade and more earlier.

In the fall of 1986 Bertelsmann AG, a West German publishing company, bought Doubleday, one of the last privately owned publishing companies in the U.S., for $475 million. The acquisition of Doubleday made Bertelsmann, which already owned Bantam, the second largest publisher in the U.S. after Simon & Schuster, which was owned by Gulf and Western. (WILLIAM W. GOLDSTEIN)

Although the British publishing industry continued to move out of recession in 1986, operating conditions were extremely competitive. In the home market institutional buying was constrained by government-imposed financial restrictions despite the availability of £20 million for books relevant to new school examinations, and the retail trade remained worryingly flat. In export markets the depreciation of the U.S. dollar reduced sales into the U.S. but improved U.K. publishers' competitive position in all other markets. The U.K.'s *Trade Year Book* for 1986 put U.K. book sales at £1,800 million for 1985, with home sales at £1,100 million and exports at £675 million. This reflected a 29% real growth rate by value since 1981.

Much of the recovery stemmed from improved marketing and good budget control. Book prices had been held back for two years, and average prices of university and general books actually fell between 1984 and 1985. The greater receptiveness to books was demonstrated by the steadily increased press coverage given to major book awards. In 1986 the Nobel Prize for Literature went for the first time to an African author, Wole Soyinka (*see* BIOGRAPHIES) from Nigeria, and this created much media attention. The Booker Prize went to Kingsley Amis of the U.K. for *The Old Devils*.

On the international front a number of legislative issues emerged. In June the U.S. manufacturing clause lapsed despite strenuous attempts by U.S. printers to achieve an extension. This clause had effectively withheld copyright protection from any U.S. author whose works were printed in significant quantities in other countries (except Canada) and imported into the U.S. For more than 90 years the clause had prevented U.S. accession to the Berne Copyright Convention and created the alternative Universal Copyright Convention. The lapse increased the chances of the U.S. upgrading its standard of protection to Berne. A dispute between the U.S. and Canada over wood products resulted in the imposition by Canada of a 10% tariff on English-language book imports. European Communities members protested vigorously, claiming that this was a breach of the General Agreement on Tariffs and Trade, and within Canada there were claims that the tariff breached the nation's constitution in that it discriminated between books published in the two official languages.

Elsewhere in the world both the Singapore and Malaysian parliaments received evidence on proposed new copyright laws that would bring them up to international standards. Strong U.S. pressure brought a pledge from South Korea to introduce international standard legislation by 1987; Indonesia also indicated a willingness to join the international literary community; and there were promises of significant amendments to existing laws in Pakistan. With vigorous antipiracy action taken throughout the world by the British Campaign Against Book Piracy and the U.S. Copyright Alliance, much progress was made on copyright issues during the year.

The big new fair in 1986 was the Beijing (Peking) International Book Fair, held in September. It was a successful event in terms of organization, participation, market response, and reported sales, but most participants found it expensive. It was to be repeated in 1988 and was likely to become a featured part of the international book fair circuit. The Frankfurt Book Fair theme for 1986 was India. The size of the fair and the number of participants grew again, but so did the costs of participation, and there were signs that the fair had reached its peak.

(ANTHONY A. READ)

See also Literature.

This article updates the *Macropædia* article PUBLISHING.

Race Relations

In 1986 religious and political leaders throughout the world publicly condemned racial prejudice. At the same time, there was an increase in the incidence of racial violence. Worldwide condemnation of apartheid in South Africa continued and led in a number of countries to the imposition of economic sanctions and to disinvestment by some investors.

Continental Western Europe. On June 11, 1986, the European Parliament, the Council of Ministers, and the Commission of European Communities (EC) issued a joint declaration against racism in a special ceremony at the European Parliament in Strasbourg, West Germany. Nonetheless, racial tension intensified throughout Western Europe during 1986.

In the French general elections in March, the extreme right-wing National Front won 35 seats in the National Assembly and gained 9.7% of the vote. This share was down from the 11% polled in the 1984 European elections, but it represented an increase of 500,000 votes. Some of the party's immigration views were reflected in the policies of the new government headed by Prime Minister Jacques Chirac. The police were given authority to carry out identity checks, and these were reported to be directed toward foreign workers; the Ministry of the Interior was given new powers of expulsion; and in October the Cabinet approved proposals to prevent automatic French citizenship from being given to anyone who was born in France of foreign parents or who married a French national. By early 1986 there were estimated to be 4.5 million immigrants in France, and most of the racial tension was focused on the North African community. In 1985 about 30,000 foreigners, mainly North Africans, obtained citizenship automatically under the above two categories.

There was evidence of growing tension and racial attacks in French cities that had a heavy concentration of immigrant communities. In the French dependency of New Caledonia in the Pacific, seven French settlers who had confessed to killing ten Kanaks (indigenous Melanesians) were released from prison without trial and declared innocent on the grounds that they had acted in self-defense.

In West Germany, Denmark, Sweden, and Switzerland, an increase in racial tension combined with high unemployment and declining government revenues led to the imposition of curbs on the entry of refugees and immigrants. (*See* POPULATIONS AND POPULATION MOVEMENTS: *International Migration.*) Chancellor Helmut Kohl declared that West Germany could not allow unrestricted entry to immigrants. Prejudice against Turkish guest workers and their families was reported to have increased, and the murder of a 26-year-old Turk in Hamburg led West German Pres. Richard von Weizsäcker to caution those who were expressing antiforeign feelings.

Great Britain. An advisory group appointed by Basil Cardinal Hume, Roman Catholic archbishop of Westminster, reported that "Racism permeates every part of British society. There is no area of society in Britain where it is not experienced by Black people." The report concluded that there was racism in the Roman Catholic Church and its institutions, and a 1986 Consultation on Anglicans and Racism found the same in the Church of England. Racism was found in the juvenile justice system, where young black people were treated more harshly than white people. Home Office figures published in June showed that the proportion of black men in prison was eight times that of the general population, and the ratio for black women was higher. These figures were believed by some to be a result of racial discrimination in society and in the criminal justice system.

Despite measures to combat racial discrimination in employment, it continued to be practiced. A study published in April by the Commission for Racial Equality found that the procedures established by the 1976 Race Relations Act allowing victims of racial discrimination in employment to go to an industrial tribunal had not helped victims to any great extent. A study of the 40 local councils in areas where

AP/WIDE WORLD

A march through downtown Atlanta, Georgia, honouring the 57th anniversary of the birth of Martin Luther King, Jr., is led by Atlanta's Mayor Andrew Young, Coretta Scott King, Bishop Desmond Tutu, and Martin Luther King III.

80% of Britain's black population lived found that these authorities were failing in the fight against racial bias even when they had made efforts to ensure equal opportunity.

The House of Commons Home Affairs Committee found that there was widespread violence against black people and described these attacks as "the most shameful and dispiriting aspect of race relations in Britain." The Joint Campaign Against Racism, an all-party pressure group backed by the British Council of Churches, estimated that racial attacks rose to 20,000 in 1985. The police received widespread criticism for their failure to take racial attacks seriously.

There were a number of independent reports on the causes of serious disturbances that occurred in several cities in September–October 1985. Racial discrimination and unemployment, a history of racist and oppressive policing, and a deterioration of police relations with the community were identified as the major causes of the disturbances.

South Africa. Conflict and repression continued to be the dominant themes of race relations in South Africa. It was estimated that some 2,000 South Africans, mainly blacks, had been killed by the security forces between September 1984 and July 1986. The Women for Peace organization estimated in a report published in May 1986 that there had been 9,400 serious injuries during that period, and that there were at least 350 deaths in the three months following the proclamation of the June 12 state of emergency. The Detainees' Parents Support Committee estimated that 23,000 people were detained after the emergency was declared. It was believed that nearly one-half of these were under 21 years of age and that more than 60% were under 25. A study at the University of Cape Town found that 93% of the black detainees interviewed claimed they had been tortured.

Under the state of emergency regulations, the minister of law and order was given virtually total powers in "unrest areas," including control of the press. On September 3 new press controls prohibited journalists from being "within sight" of any unrest, restricted gatherings, or "security action." On October 9 the government declared the United Democratic Front (UDF)—a federation of more than 600 affiliated black protest groups—an "affected organization," thus cutting off its foreign funding.

Efforts were made by the Commonwealth Eminent Persons Group mission and by U.K. Foreign Secretary Sir Geoffrey Howe to effect significant changes in the government's apartheid policies. The failure of these led to increased pressure for economic sanctions. On September 16 EC foreign ministers reached agreement on a truncated package of sanctions: an end to new investment and a ban on the imports of iron, steel, and gold coins. Coal imports were to continue because of insistence by West Germany. U.K. Prime Minister Margaret Thatcher and West German Chancellor Helmut Kohl were not in favour of the measures, though in an unexpected move the U.K.'s Barclays Bank decided to cease operating in South Africa. On October 2 the U.S. Senate overrode Pres. Ronald Reagan's veto of the Congressional Sanctions Bill by a vote of 78–21, following the House of Representatives's earlier 313–83 vote. The U.S. sanctions were much more severe than the EC measures and cut South Africa off from access to U.S. markets for its coal, steel, and textiles. They also banned new investments and withdrew the landing rights of South African Airlines in the U.S. These measures were expected to add to the pressures for disinvestment that had already led to the withdrawal of $18.5 billion by U.S. universities and state and local governments from companies involved in South Africa. In October General Motors and

In a march through the streets of Pulaski, Tennessee, home of the Ku Klux Klan, Klan members protest the first national observance of the anniversary of the birth of Martin Luther King, Jr.

AP/WIDE WORLD

IBM joined the 50 or so U.S. companies withdrawing from South Africa.

United States. The U.S. administration continued its efforts to dismantle the affirmative-action programs developed during the 1960s and early 1970s. Despite Justice Department intervention against such programs, the Supreme Court upheld two affirmative-action plans. In a case brought by the Cleveland chapter of the International Association of Firefighters challenging the agreement between the city and a group of minority firefighters to promote minorities, the Supreme Court upheld the plan by a vote of six to three. In a case involving a New York City local branch of the Sheet Metal Workers' Association that had been ordered by a federal court to increase its nonwhite membership to 29% and to hire an administrator to oversee the program, the court upheld the order by a vote of five to four.

A number of studies published during 1986 indicated a widening schism between blacks and whites in the U.S., and this was blamed on the policies of President Reagan's administration. The Children's Defense Fund in Washington, D.C., published a report in June that revealed that black children were twice as likely as whites to die in their first year, three times as likely to be poor, four times as likely not to live with either parent, and five times as likely to be receiving welfare benefits. The report also revealed a widening gap between the proportion of white and black high-school graduates who continued their education in college. Increasing poverty was blamed. Other studies found that the income gap between black and white families had increased and that black unemployment levels continued to be more than double the white rate—with black teenagers having an official unemployment rate of 41%. The Census Bureau reported in July that the average white income was almost double that of blacks.

The year ended with what was described as New York City's worst racial incident in some years. Although details were still unclear at year's end, it appeared that three black men were attacked by a group of white teenagers in the white community of Howard Beach, Queens, and one, fleeing across a busy highway, was struck and killed by a car. Tempers flared among both blacks and whites, and on December 27 an estimated 1,200 people marched through Howard Beach to protest the incident. (LOUIS KUSHNICK)

See also Human Rights.

Religion

Caught up in the enthusiasm of the moment after Corazon C. Aquino was inaugurated as president of the Philippines in March, Jaime Cardinal Sin, Roman Catholic archbishop of Manila, broke into a Mass to lead a throng of worshipers in a populist chant—"Cory, Cory, Cory"—hailing the new chief of state. In a nation where 85% of the population is Roman Catholic, the dominant church played a decisive role in the struggle to replace the regime of Ferdinand E. Marcos with a government headed by the widow of assassinated opposition leader Benigno S. Aquino, Jr. (*See* World Affairs [Southeast Asia]: *Philippines.*) Barred from other public platforms by Marcos, Aquino and her followers made their appeals from the church's pulpits. Denied access to the airwaves, Marcos's opponents used Radio Veritas, a Catholic station, to transmit their message.

After the transition, Sin went to the Vatican to explain to Pope John Paul II the role he and the church had played in the fight to drive Marcos from power. Sin said he told the pontiff that the church's involvement was not "political" but "moral." In response, Sin reported, John Paul "smiled because he understands. He came from Poland." Nonetheless, once the new government was in power, the cardinal withdrew somewhat from the centre of public political activity and instructed his clergy to do the same. In August he said: "The church—and here I speak of only the clergy—should have a low profile in its nation-building work, avoiding the limelight."

Other clashes between religious and secular authority took place in other parts of the world. The dividing line over legitimate authority was drawn most clearly and dramatically in South Africa, where the government of Pres. P. W. Botha was under increased international pressure to change its system of apartheid, or racial separation. (*See* Special Report.) Among the leaders involved in mobilizing world opinion against apartheid was Desmond Tutu, who had been awarded the Nobel Peace Prize in 1984. A day after the government imposed a strict state of emergency to quell riots, Tutu and Botha exchanged views in a 90-minute conversation. A month later the two met again to discuss what Tutu called "the serious and deteriorating situation." After U.S. Pres. Ronald Reagan stated in July that it would be a "historic act of folly" for the U.S. to impose more stringent economic sanctions on South Africa, the outspoken prelate said he found Reagan's speech "nauseating." In September, when he became the first black archbishop of Cape Town, the highest ranking official of the Anglican Church in southern Africa, Tutu seized the occasion to denounce "the violence of apartheid" before an international audience. After the formal rites, the archbishop invited many of his prominent guests to inspect conditions in a black "squatter camp," described later as "dramatically squalid" by the archbishop of Canterbury, Robert Runcie.

In Nicaragua the gap between church and state widened. Visiting the U.S. at a time when Congress was deciding whether to finance counterrevolutionary forces in Nicaragua, Miguel Cardinal Obando y Bravo, archbishop of Managua, accused his nation's government of persecuting the church. Tensions reached a new peak in July when the government expelled Bishop Pablo Antonio Vega Mantilla, vice-president of the Nicaraguan bishops' conference. Speaking during a visit to Colombia, Pope John Paul characterized the expulsion order as "an almost incredible act" that recalled "the dark ages" of anticlericalism in Latin America. Toward year's end the Vatican appointed a new papal nuncio, Msgr. Poalo Giglio, to negotiate an end to the rifts. Priests were among the targets of government wrath in Chile when a state of siege was declared following an unsuccessful attempt to assassinate Pres. Augusto Pinochet in September. Declaring that his nation was embroiled in "a war between Marxism and democracy," Pinochet ordered a crackdown on the press and house-to-house searches in centres of opposition. Among the first to be arrested were five Roman Catholic priests.

In the U.S. the courtroom was the primary place for resolving church-state conflicts. After a six-month trial in a U.S. District Court in Tucson, Ariz., a jury found six leaders of the Sanctuary Movement guilty of conspiracy to violate U.S. immigration laws. Two other defendants were found guilty on lesser charges. Officially founded in 1982, the movement had helped Salvadoran and Guatemalan refugees cross the U.S. border and enter an "underground railroad" system that guided them to 300 churches and synagogues offering sanctuary. All the defendants were placed on probation.

In its fall session the U.S. Supreme Court heard arguments over the place of "scientific creationism" in public school curricula. The case grew out of Louisiana's Creationism Act of 1981, which outlawed the teaching of evolution unless students also were exposed to the tenets of creationism, based on a literal interpretation of biblical accounts of the creation. Although that legislation was struck down by lower courts, fundamentalists took their case to the highest court, where they contended that "creationist science consists of scientific evidence and not religious concepts, and evolution is no more scientific and nonreligious than creation science." Fundamentalists also asserted themselves in Greeneville, Tenn., where a federal court heard complaints from parents in a small town who objected to books their children were required to read in school. Included on their list of offensive reading materials were a Hans Christian Andersen fairy tale, *The Diary of Anne Frank,* and a story in which a girl reads to a boy while he is cooking. The judge dismissed the case, but a U.S. Court of Appeals ruled that the children had the right not to attend classes containing "offensive" material and could read at home.

Questions about the authority of traditional religious teachings played a major role in the internal life of churches. In the Roman Catholic Church the Vatican intensified its campaign to enforce obedience to the magisterium, the church's teaching authority. In its first such action directed at an American Catholic priest, the Vatican withdrew the right of Charles E. Curran to teach theology at Catholic University in Washington, D.C., and in another unusual move it stripped Archbishop Raymond Hunthausen of Seattle, Wash., of much of his authority. (See *Roman Catholic Church,* below.) Meeting in Washington, D.C., in November, the National Conference of Catholic Bishops discussed the Hunthausen affair behind closed doors. The conference president, Bishop James Malone, had called for an audience with the pope to deal with "the growing and dangerous disaffection between the Vatican and key American Catholic leaders." In the end, however, the bishops extended sympathy to their colleague in Seattle but reaffirmed "unreservedly their loyalty to and unity with the Holy Father." Despite the controversy over doctrinal issues, however, the nation's bishops did reach agreement on a major pastoral letter on the U.S. economy calling for the alleviation of social and economic injustice and underscoring the church's commitment to all people, but "especially to the poor." Backing up their appeal for measures to correct economic inequalities, the bishops declared that current levels of poverty in the U.S. were a "social and political scandal."

The Vatican's worldwide crackdown on dissent continued to target religious orders. In midsummer, two letters from top Vatican officials to John Vaughn, international head of the Franciscan order, were leaked to the press. In one of them, Joseph Cardinal Ratzinger (*see* BIOGRAPHIES), prefect of the Sacred Congregation for the Doctrine of the Faith, called on Vaughn to "remedy, modify and help overcome a radical mentality of dissent" among Franciscans. In the U.S. another conflict broke out when a Jesuit, John J. McNeill, defied a directive to keep silent and sent a statement to two newspapers charging that a Vatican document reaffirming the church's position condemning homosexuality was "mean and cruel."

Conservative forces were in the ascendant in other sectors of the religious world. In the Southern Baptist Convention, conservatives consolidated their hold on the largest Protestant denomination in the U.S. by electing as its president the Rev. Adrian Rogers. (See *Baptist Churches,* below.) Capping a decade of intensified involvement in politics by Protestant evangelicals, Pat Robertson (*see* BIOGRAPHIES), president of the Christian Broadcasting Network and a prominent television preacher, announced that he would be a candidate for the Republican presidential nomination if he obtained three million signatures and $3 million by mid-1987. Months before Robertson's announcement, Vice-Pres. George Bush courted the votes of Protestant fundamentalists by telling a meeting of Jerry Falwell's Liberty Federation that "America is in crying need of the moral vision" brought into the political process by evangelists. To counter negative reactions to the political activism of fundamentalists, Falwell announced his intention to form a Christian Anti-Discrimination Committee.

In Israel ultra-Orthodox believers, insisting on a strict observance of traditional Jewish laws, campaigned for the closing of theatres and soccer stadiums on the Sabbath. Some of the religious engaged in acts of vandalism, spray-painting advertisements that offended them and burning down bus shelters where the ads were displayed. Some secular Jews were accused of retaliating by scrawling graffiti

(*continued on page 331*)

Pope John Paul II Visits Rome's Synagogue

The dome of the Roman Synagogue can be seen clearly from St. Peter's Basilica on the opposite side of the Tiber, but no pope in history had ever set foot there until April 13, 1986, when Pope John Paul II crossed its threshold. Chief Rabbi Elio Toaff welcomed the pope not with the expected handshake but with a warm embrace. "Toda rabba" ("many thanks") said the pope in Hebrew, taking his place before the seven-branched candelabrum that symbolizes Judaism.

Pope John Paul's words brought out the historic nature of the occasion. The Roman Catholic Church, he said, quoting a declaration of the Second Vatican Council, "deplores the hatred, persecutions, and displays of anti-Semitism directed against the Jews at any time and by anyone." At this point he added, "I repeat—by anyone," which was interpreted as Christian contrition on behalf of the papacy itself. The pope continued: "You are our dearly beloved brothers and, in a certain way, it could be said that you are our elder brothers." It followed that "no ancestral or collective blame can be imputed to the Jews as a people for what happened in Christ's passion." This removed the age-old pseudo-justification for "Christian anti-Semitism."

The pope's words evoked intense emotion among the congregation of 1,000. There were tears, and Pope John Paul closed his eyes while a choir sang the same slow anthem, "Ani Ma'amin," that had been chanted by victims on their way to Nazi gas chambers. Everyone knew that Auschwitz was very close to the pope's home city of Krakow, Poland, and he had friends who had experienced its concentration camp.

But this meeting was in Rome, where the Jewish presence was as ancient as that of the Christians. Because they were a minority, however, Roman Jews had often been victimized by the papacy. In 1553 the books of the Talmud were burned, and 1555 saw the establishment of the ghetto, which was dispersed only with the collapse of the Papal States in 1870. With such unhappy memories Rabbi Toaff contrasted the help given to Jews in the Nazi roundup of Oct. 16, 1943, when many thousands were hidden in convents and religious houses. That explained why Roman Jews had never shared in the negative judgment of Pope Pius XII's "silences."

Pope John Paul did not respond to Rabbi Toaff's invitation to recognize the State of Israel as "an irreversible good for the whole world." It was explained that this was a religious and not a political occasion. The Arab ambassadors to Italy, while applauding the pope's "noble sentiments," expressed the hope that nothing had changed in the Holy See's attitude to the Arab-Israeli conflict. For the Jewish community, this was the only disappointing aspect of the visit—and it was predictable. (PETER HEBBLETHWAITE)

DONATELLO BROGIONI—SYGMA

Special Report: Religion

Religion in a Troubled Land

BY MARTIN E. MARTY

Events in troubled South Africa made front-page or prime-time news daily during 1986. In many stories of the struggle over that country's policy of apartheid or racial separation, religion was the focus. The September 7 enthronement of Nobel Prize winner Desmond Tutu as archbishop of Cape Town and head of the Anglican Church in southern Africa drew religious leaders from around the world. Television images of the event attracted the attention of hundreds of millions.

The Religious Component. Tutu was only the best known of the religious leaders in South Africa. Receiving almost equal attention was the Rev. Allan Boesak, a political activist whose home base was the chaplaincy at the University of the Western Cape near Cape Town. Boesak was also president of the World Alliance of Reformed Churches and thus a traveled ecumenical veteran with influence in Europe and America as well as in southern Africa. Another figure to be reckoned with was Chief Gatsha Mangosuthu Buthelezi, chief minister of KwaZulu, a collection of northern Natal territories that had not chosen to be "independent" of South Africa, as the government wanted. A major leader among six million Zulus and head of a million-strong movement called Inkatha, he made a great point of his Christian faith as he asserted his place and position in helping determine South Africa's future.

While whites represented less than one-fifth of the population and while the majority of them sided with the government in support of apartheid, world religious leaders had also come to recognize some white clerics as credible dissenters. Best known of these was the Rev. Christiaan Beyers Naudé, who had been brought up in the militant far right wing of the Afrikaner church but who had made a 180-degree turn 30 years earlier. He directed the Christian Institute of South Africa, a now banned organization that set out to oppose the Dutch Reformed Church's pro-apartheid policies. Naudé himself was banned for seven years, meaning that he was removed from the public scene entirely for that time. Now a senior figure in the South African Council of Churches, he remained both an irritant and a conscience in the white churches and a signal of courage in world Christendom.

Religion shows up on both sides and all fronts of the South African tension lines. When the government imposed a state of emergency on June 12, it effectively banned black and other dissenting political gatherings. Soon it became clear that religious events, most notably ceremonies associated with burial of those killed by police in episodes of "unrest," were to be perceived as having political potency as, indeed, they often had. They also were banned. Ministers of white, Coloured (mixed-race), and black congregations alike were regularly detained by the police as part of a policy to intimidate or restrict clerical involvement in the racial struggle. International religious organizations like the World Council of Churches and their constituent churches kept exposing South African racial policies to view around the world.

The South African story had domestic American implications. When debate over imposing economic sanctions in order to induce change was raging in the U.S., the Roman Catholic bishops joined the leadership in many Protestant churches and some Jewish organizations in calling for sanctions. U.S. black religious leaders were vocal in criticizing legislatures and Pres. Ronald Reagan for resisting meaningful sanctions. In churches across the land, Americans examined their racial outlooks in the light of South African attitudes and policies.

South Africa thus was another illustration of a worldwide trend that developed late in the 20th century. Alongside ideological conflict such as that between the Soviet Union and the United States, and alongside traditional wars over territory, a religious dimension regularly appeared where tribes, parties, races, and nations battled. Both sides in such struggles tended to invoke the name of God for their cause, and both drew on long traditions. To understand the South African scene, some sort of religious map is vital.

Mapping the Churches. At base in a nation that is 73.8% black (24 million people, including the ten black national states or "homelands") is African traditional religion, a complex that survived the centuries of missionary work that began among the indigenous peoples in 1737. Traditional African ways are still celebrated in more remote areas, but they live on more significantly when fused with the Christianity that came to prevail in highly religious southern Africa. This traditional religion, however, is not prominent in the political mixture.

On that base is an enormous cluster of African Indigenous Churches, as they are now known. Nowhere else in the world are there so many self-starting prophetic and often pentecostal ("Spirit-filled") movements. In the 1980 census 3,270 AIC denominations turned up, with six million adherents. This amounts to 30% of the black population and 26% of the total Christian population of South Africa. These churches arose in opposition to more formal and less responsive churches and remain very close to the people, to whom they offer meaning and solace in times of sudden change. Attempts to account for them as mainly political phenomena, however, have fallen out of favour. They are also too disorganized and sometimes too "otherworldly" to be direct participants in the movements for political and social change.

At the opposite extreme from the traditional and indigenous black churches—and from the politically activist Roman Catholic and mainstream Protestant groups—is the Dutch Reformed Church (Nederduitse Gereformeerde Kerk), which dates back to 1652 when settlers from Holland first arrived. There have been schisms from this Reformed body, but it is by far the most important of the largely white churches. Its missionary endeavours resulted in a "Sendingkerk," which claims about half a million members, and there are a million more nonwhites in still another Reformed church. Boesak is active in the Reformed Church, which has been productive of dissent against apartheid.

The Dutch Reformed Church is best known as the church of most government leadership, and it is a kind of "pariah church" in much of the Christian world because on its soil the religious rationale for apartheid developed. While not an established church, it is certainly the privileged church of the establishment among the Afrikaners,

Martin E. Marty is Fairfax M. Cone distinguished service professor of history of modern Christianity at the University of Chicago and senior editor of The Christian Century.

who make up about 60% of the 4.8 million citizens who are white. During the 19th-century struggles by the Afrikaner "Boers" against black Africans and the British, people of this church developed a concept of themselves as a nation chosen by Divine Providence.

The Theology of Apartheid. Not until the middle of the 20th century—especially around 1948 when the National Party, which remains in power, came to ascendancy—did a theology and practice of apartheid fully develop. Its churchly proponents, all of whom cite the Bible and a version of Reformed theology to support their claims, insist that apartheid is not racist. They claim that just as God made all people one, and thus deserving of respect, God also intended that they engage in "separate development." There are to be separate cultures, separate polities, most of all separate places, for each group, and there should be no interracial marriage and only very restricted interaction between races. Thus the Indian population (900,000, or 2.7% of the total) is to be free to pursue Islam or Hinduism, but in separate cultural enclaves. Late in 1986 the Dutch Reformed Church declared that "forced separation of people cannot be seen as a prescription from the Bible," but this resolution, while bringing the church into line with the government's modest reforms, fell short of demands for one church for all races.

Just as God and church were called to promote apartheid, they came to serve the dissenting cause. The Anglican Church (which Bishop Tutu came to head) represents only about 7% of the total population, but it has been strategically placed in the English-speaking minority of the population. It has joined much of Roman Catholicism, with its similar percent of the population and its similar interracial character, to call for "liberation" from the apartheid pattern.

While black Lutherans have provided quite consistent protest leadership, the small white Lutheran population has an outlook similar to that of the white Dutch Reformed Church. Somewhat larger is the Methodist Church, with its important (11% of the African population) black component. Methodism, Presbyterianism, and Congregationalism, while not statistically huge, are to be reckoned with in any religious accounting on the antiapartheid front.

Over the past 15 years, the dissenting forces in the churches began to take risks in uttering prophetic denunciations of what they saw not as "separate development" but as dehumanizing racism. The South African Council of Churches has been a particular irritant. In the face of each repressive measure by the government, church leaders have come forth with a new protest document. Many of these documents breathe the spirit of the "confessing churches" of Germany during the Nazi period, and dissenters regularly draw analogies between the racist policies of that time and place and South Africa's own.

The statements of protest culminated in *The Kairos Document,* which was issued by 150 theologians at Soweto in 1985. "Kairos" is the Greek New Testament term for a time of special urgency. The authors reflect life in a time when black radicalism is moving beyond and outside the churches and when the language of nonviolent change is being muffled. The *Kairos* drafters radically protest apartheid and religious justification for the present government. They express some loss of confidence in nonviolent strategies in the face of governmental violence. To the government this "liberation" document looks like treason. The two forces dug in ever deeper during 1986 for what threatened to be a long and bloody confrontation involving all the forces of state and church along with the energies of private citizens.

(continued from page 329)

on Jewish centres of learning and attacking a vehicle from a religious burial society in Jerusalem. Israel's minister of the interior ruled that the word convert be stamped on the identity cards of those immigrating to Israel after being converted, reviving an old feud over the control of Israel's religious life by Orthodox rabbis who do not regard conversions overseen by non-Orthodox rabbis as authentic. However, he was overruled by the Israeli Supreme Court. (See *Judaism,* below.) Meanwhile, all Jews were united in shock and anger when Arab terrorists entered a synagogue in Istanbul and massacred 21 worshipers. One year after Indian Prime Minister Rajiv Gandhi and moderate Sikhs had reached an accord designed to reduce age-old disputes between Sikhs and Hindus in Punjab state, new acts of violence erupted. (See *Hinduism,* below.)

The year's events also included notable acts of reconciliation. In an effort to heal old wounds through a symbolic act, Pope John Paul in April made the first papal visit to a synagogue. (*See* Sidebar.) In February the pope and the archbishop of Canterbury crossed paths in India, where Christians constitute a tiny minority. While in India the pope also met with the Dalai Lama, the exiled leader of Tibetan Buddhists. In October John Paul, Runcie, and 700 leaders of 12 major world religious groups gathered in Assisi, Italy, the home village of St. Francis, to offer interfaith prayers for peace and appeal to world leaders to lay down their weapons for one day. Three major branches of Lutheranism in the United States—the Lutheran Church in America, the American Lutheran Church, and the Association of Evangelical Lutheran Churches—voted to merge into one denomination of 5.3 million members. (See *Lutheran Communion,* below.)

The bishops of the United Methodist Church, the second largest U.S. Protestant group, approved a pastoral letter to their 9.4 million members calling on all Methodists to say "a clear and unconditional 'no' to nuclear war and to any use of nuclear weapons." Two major religious newsmakers of 1986 were former hostages caught in the strife of the Middle East. In July Lawrence Martin Jenco, director of Catholic Relief Services in Lebanon, was freed by a radical Muslim Shi'ah group after being held hostage for more than 18 months. Benjamin Weir, a Presbyterian missionary who had been a hostage in Lebanon for 16 months before his release in 1985, was elected moderator of the Presbyterian Church (U.S.A.). A prominent role in negotiating the release of the hostages was played by Terry Waite, a special envoy of the archbishop of Canterbury.

In other developments Pope John Paul, in the fifth encyclical of his papacy, combined reflections on the doctrine of the Holy Spirit with a stinging critique of Marxist materialism. In the autumn the pilgrim pope undertook the longest trip of his pontificate when he took his evangelical message to Asia and the Pacific. Earlier in the year an Italian court, in a complex decision, acquitted three Bulgarians and three Turks of conspiring to assassinate the pope in 1981 but convicted Mehmet Ali Agca, already serving a life sentence as the would-be assassin, of complicity in smuggling the weapon used to shoot the pontiff into Italy. A former financial adviser to the Vatican, Michele Sindona, was sentenced to life imprisonment for murder and later committed suicide. William Wilson, the first U.S. envoy to the Vatican with the rank of ambassador, resigned his post after a controversy with the U.S. State Department that followed an unauthorized trip to Libya in 1985. In Gallup, N.M., Donald E. Pelotte became the first American Indian ordained as a bishop in the Roman Catholic Church.

(ROY LARSON)

PROTESTANT CHURCHES

Anglican Communion. Debate over such controversial issues as women's ministry, orthodox belief, and the troubles in South Africa continued in 1986. An event that was not controversial, however, was the visit by Robert Runcie to India in February. It was the first such visit by an archbishop of Canterbury and was made in response to an invitation from the (non-Anglican) churches of North and South India and the Mar Thoma church. Runcie had a brief meeting with Pope John Paul II when their itineraries crossed in Bombay.

At the same time, a dispute was developing in New Zealand over the election of Paul Oestreicher as bishop of Wellington. His appointment was not ratified by the other New Zealand dioceses, and eventually the post was filled by the newly chosen primate of New Zealand, Brian Davis. Oestreicher's rejection was thought to be because he had become a Quaker while being an Anglican and because he was regarded as too radical. In South Africa Desmond Tutu, whose political rhetoric attracted international attention, was elected archbishop of Cape Town and primate of the church for all southern Africa in April. (See *Introduction,* above.)

While much of the Anglican Communion was still preoccupied with resolving the question of women's ordination, Canada and the U.S. indicated their willingness to have women bishops. In each of those churches a woman just failed to win election as a bishop during the year. In Canterbury in April women priests and their supporters from all over the communion demonstrated their strength during a weekend of events to celebrate the ministry of women. Hopes that visiting women priests might soon be able to officiate legally in England were dashed in July, however, when the General Synod rejected the Women Ordained Abroad Measure. In October the Movement for the Ordination of Women defied the church law when it allowed a woman priest, ordained in Hong Kong, to celebrate the Eucharist during its annual meeting in Westminster, London. The act provoked the wrath of the archbishop of Canterbury, who ordered an immediate investigation.

The bishop of London, Graham Leonard, an Anglo-Catholic traditionalist and leading opponent of women's ordination, appeared to be aligning himself increasingly with the breakaway sections of the Anglican church. A particularly noteworthy action was his "adoption" of a parish and its priest in Tulsa, Okla., which had been dispossessed by the Episcopal Church, the U.S. branch of Anglicanism.

(SUSAN YOUNG)

Baptist Churches. The simmering eight-year controversy in the 14.4 million-member Southern Baptist Convention reached something of a peak with the June 1986 election of Adrian Rogers of Memphis, Tenn., an ardent fundamentalist conservative (as compared, according to the official SBC press, with the moderate conservatives), as president. The election of Rogers, though only by a 54–46% margin, gave a seeming victory to the fundamentalist faction and a sense that it had received a mandate to reform the four mission boards and six seminaries of the denomination. (Colleges and universities related to the Southern Baptists are usually controlled by state conventions and thus are not subject to the same pressures as the nationally controlled boards and seminaries.)

At the August meeting of the Home Mission Board, three months after the June annual meeting of some 40,000 "messengers" (delegates) in Atlanta, Ga., the search committee seeking a replacement for the recently retired chief executive was voted out by the fundamentalists. This powerful board, with an annual budget of $68 million, appointed and governed 3,600 missionaries in the U.S. and Canada. In spite of the chilling effect of the fundamentalist conservative victory on the seminaries—the essential posture of the fundamentalist is an inerrantist view of Scripture—and the fundamentalists' virtual control of the national boards, observers believed that the deep cultural commitment of the moderate conservatives would prevent any major schism or split in the SBC as a political entity.

The American Baptist Churches in the U.S.A. (Northern Baptists) announced a $30 million national campaign, Alive in Mission. Half the funds would be used to found 500 new churches, while the other half would go to churches in other lands affiliated with the denomination. The money for overseas would be disbursed by the ABC USA Board of International Ministries.

V. Carney Hargroves, president of the American Baptist Churches in the U.S.A. (1954–55) and of the Baptist World Alliance (1970–75), died June 25 at the age of 85. In England, Nell Alexander, playwright and the first woman president of the Baptist Union of Great Britain and Ireland, died May 29 at the age of 71. Alexander's play *Moment of Pointed Light* had been translated into eight languages.

(NORMAN R. DE PUY)

Christian Church (Disciples of Christ). The ecumenically minded Disciples of Christ became the first American denomination to have full-fledged voting members from other denominations on its governing board. The four, who took their seats on the 187-member General Board during the year, were from the Christian Methodist Episcopal Church, Presbyterian Church (U.S.A.), The United Church of Canada, and the United Church of Christ.

Leaders of American church bodies met at National City Christian Church in Washington, D.C., as a follow-up to the World Council of Churches emergency consultation on South Africa, held in Harare, Zimbabwe, in December 1985, and vowed to speak "with one voice" against apartheid. The Disciples' Division of Overseas Ministries board voted for the first time to make a social services grant from the church's general funds to South African liberation movements. The action was controversial since staff recommended continuing only gifts specifically designated to the special fund for southern Africa of the World Council of Churches' Program to Combat Racism.

In a growing relationship with the Christian Pentecostal Church of Cuba, the Disciples sent ten fraternal delegates to the Cuban church's convention. (See also *United Church of Christ,* below.)

(ROBERT LOUIS FRIEDLY)

Churches of Christ. Encouraging signs of renewal were apparent in many of the autonomous churches of Christ. The mission budgets of most larger congregations increased more rapidly than their general budgets. Gifts totaling $8.8 million were collected for foreign relief efforts.

Whites Ferry Road Church in Louisiana led in food programs for drought-stricken countries. Manna International concentrated on land development and water systems in Ethiopia and Kenya, while Bread for a Hungry World distributed $2 million to relief projects in Africa and Haiti.

Homes were constructed for more than 900 victims of the 1985 Mexico City earthquake, and 70 more units were planned. Ten tons of powdered milk were delivered to Poland, where high levels of radiation had resulted from the nuclear accident at the Chernobyl power plant in the U.S.S.R.

Outreach to visitors and newcomers to the U.S., pioneered by the International Mission at the Manhattan Church in New York City, was emphasized. The Central Church in Los Angeles, with services in English, Spanish, and Korean, was an example of a growing trend among urban churches. The Midtown Church in Fort Worth, Texas, began a school to train preachers among Thais and Laotians.

(M. NORVEL YOUNG)

Church of Christ, Scientist. At the church's annual meeting in Boston in June 1986, the board of directors stressed the denomination's founding purpose: to commemorate the teachings and life of Christ Jesus "which should reinstate primitive Christianity and its lost element of healing." Videotaped reports of spiritual healing from around the world were shown.

Inquiries from the media often reflected widespread confusion over the practice of spiritual healing in Christian Science. As a 1986 reader response in *U.S. News & World Report* pointed out, healing in Christian Science is not "'faith healing' that implores God to heal and says it was His will if nothing happens." Rather it is "responsible spiritual healing practiced now over a century by many perfectly normal citizens and caring parents."

The Christian Science Monitor expanded its monthly television news broadcasts to a weekly program. During 1986 the *Monitor*'s daily half-hour radio news program, "Monitoradio," was carried on some 100 stations, while the one-hour weekend edition aired on about 200 stations.

Jean K. Weida of Boston succeeded to the one-year post of church president.

(NATHAN A. TALBOT)

Church of Jesus Christ of Latter-day Saints. New temples were dedicated in late 1985 and 1986 in Lima, Peru; Johannesburg, South Africa; Seoul, South Korea; Buenos Aires, Arg.; Frankfurt, West Germany; Toronto, Ont.; and Denver, Colo. The church had 42 operating temples at the end of 1986. The drive toward internationalization was also reflected in the church's announcement, in June 1986, that the number of its missions had expanded to 193. In April the church's membership passed six million, approximately two-thirds of whom lived in the U.S. and Canada. By the end of 1986 the church had more than 1,600 stakes (dioceses).

During the year a small group of ultra-orthodox Jews demonstrated in Jerusalem and New York City against construction of the Brigham Young University Center for Near Eastern Studies on Mount Scopus in Jerusalem. After an eight-month investigation of the complaint, the Israeli Cabinet reaffirmed permission to the church-owned university to complete the structure, which was scheduled to open in 1987.

A hearing on the indictment of document dealer Mark Hoffman for murder, deception, and forgery produced testimony that some of the Mormon-related documents he had sold or traded to the Church Library and Archives might not have been authentic. His trial, at which this testimony would be explored more fully, was expected to take place in 1987.

(LEONARD J. ARRINGTON)

Jehovah's Witnesses. A primary concern of Jehovah's Witnesses is the prophetic injunction of Jesus to preach "this good news of the kingdom in all the world for a witness." Congregations of active house-to-house ministers rose from 47,869 in 1985 to 49,716 worldwide in 1986, and the number of kingdom proclaimers surpassed three million, representing a 7% increase over 1985. A total of 189,800 new Witnesses were baptized.

Witnesses working in 205 countries made extensive use of Bibles and Bible study aids, but the language barriers presented a problem. To overcome this obstacle, volunteer technical experts from among the Witnesses developed MEPS (Multilanguage Electronic Phototypesetting System), which processed nearly 200 languages and could add more. This made it possible for the journals *The Watchtower* and *Awake!* and other Watchtower Bible and Tract Society publications to be printed simultaneously in many languages. In 1986 MEPS text entry and graphics units, produced by Jehovah's Witnesses, were being used in 25 countries. Nonsalaried full-time volunteers also had been trained in laser scanner technology and other aspects of full-colour graphics, and by early 1987 nearly all publications produced by Jehovah's Witnesses would be in full colour. (FREDERICK W. FRANZ)

Lutheran Communion. In the U.S., simultaneous conventions of the Lutheran Church in America, American Lutheran Church, and Association of Evangelical Lutheran Churches approved plans to form one Evangelical Lutheran Church in America, effective Jan. 1, 1988. Its membership of 5.3 million would include approximately two-thirds of the country's 8.5 million Lutherans. To the north, the newly united Evangelical Lutheran Church in Canada, grouping about two-thirds of that country's 300,000 Lutherans, began operations at the beginning of the year. Most other Canadian Lutherans were part of the Lutheran Church-Canada, whose parent body, the U.S.-based Lutheran Church-Missouri Synod, voted to give the LCC autonomy, effective Jan. 1, 1989.

In Namibia, where the 500,000 Lutherans constituted about half the population, progress was reported on efforts to unite three Lutheran denominations. Efforts also continued to consolidate East Germany's eight regional Evangelical churches, three of them Lutheran, the rest products of earlier Reformed-Lutheran mergers. In August in Sweden, the nearly 40 Lutheran bishops of Iceland, Denmark, Norway, Finland, and Sweden met to increase cooperation and contact. El Salvador's Lutherans got their first bishop when Bishop Ake Kastlund of the Church of Sweden consecrated Medardo Ernesto Gómez.

In July, at its annual meeting, the executive committee of the Lutheran World Federation (LWF) urged "comprehensive economic sanctions" against South Africa. The LWF also announced it would withdraw funds from three banks because of their South African links. The committee condemned U.S. help for the *contras* in Nicaragua, though it said its criticism was not an "unqualified endorsement of the present direction of Nicaraguan political and social life."

The ongoing international Lutheran-Baptist, Lutheran-Reformed, and Lutheran-Roman Catholic dialogue groups met during the year. Gunnar Stålsett, the LWF general secretary, visited Pope John Paul II in June. Later in the year, eight U.S. Lutheran bishops met the pope as part of an "ecumenical pilgrimage" that included stops at the LWF and World Council of Churches headquarters in Geneva and at global centres of Orthodoxy (in Turkey) and Anglicanism (in England). As an expression of the four-year-old "interim eucharistic sharing" involving U.S. Anglicans and Lutherans, the archbishop of Canterbury gave a major address at the Lutheran Church in America convention in August.

(THOMAS HARTLEY DORRIS)

Methodist Churches. The 15th World Methodist Council (WMC) and Conference, held in the Kenyatta Conference Centre in Nairobi, Kenya, in July 1986, brought together 3,000 Methodists representing 90 countries. This was the first time the Council had met in Africa. The theme chosen was "Jesus Christ: God's 'Yes' for the World." The Social and International Affairs Committee produced a Social Affirmation for use in worship that drew attention to the responsibilities of Christians. A consultation on global survival recommended that Methodists concern themselves with the use of the Earth's resources and seek an improved quality of life for all humanity. The Evangelism Committee proposed a five-year program to include special events to celebrate the 250th anniversary of the meeting that confirmed John Wesley's faith in May 1738, as well as a third International Christian Youth Conference, to be held in Brisbane, Australia, in 1987.

Reports of the various ecumenical conversations with Roman Catholics, Lutherans, and the World Alliance of Reformed Churches were received. The Pastoral Exchange Committee reported that it had expanded operations to include 608 families from India, Korea, New Zealand, South Africa, Europe, and North America.

The South African situation dominated the conference. Bishop (later Archbishop) Desmond Tutu was a guest speaker and participated in many sessions. A resolution was adopted expressing deep concern about the policies of the South African government. It called on all member churches to divest themselves of funds in corporations and banks having links with South Africa and to advocate the imposition of economic sanctions to their governments. The resolution also called on the South African government to release Nelson Mandela and other political prisoners, lift the state of emergency, and begin negotiations with representatives of all South African people for a system in which all would participate with equal rights. The conference drew attention to Methodists imprisoned for political reasons. An open-air rally in the centre of Nairobi was attended by Pres. Daniel arap Moi of Kenya, who brought greetings as a "fellow Christian."

A document entitled "An Invitation to discover . . . re-affirm" was brought to the Council. It defined precisely those parts of the Christian faith essential to Methodist theology, and it was hoped that it would moderate the freethinking tendencies of some members. Kenyan Bishop Lawi Immathui was elected chairman of the WMC Executive Committee for a five-year term.

(PETER H. BOLT)

Pentecostal Churches. Pentecostal churches in the U.S. spoke out in 1986 on several social issues facing the nation. All of the churches had adopted positions strongly opposing pornography. In January the Assemblies of God published position papers on abortion and alcohol that reaffirmed the pro-life and total abstinence stands traditionally taken by the church. To deal with these and other problems, the first Pentecostal mental health centre was opened in Akron, Ohio. Known as Emerge Ministries, it was founded by Richard Dobbins and offered special counseling services to ministers.

Several new leaders were elected to head Pentecostal denominations in 1986. In August the General Assembly of the Church of God (Cleveland, Tennessee) elected Raymond E. Crowley as general overseer. With over 35,000 delegates meeting in Atlanta, this assembly also served as a centennial celebration for the church. Other leaders elected during the year included Cullen Hicks as head of the Congregational Holiness Church and Joe Edmonson to head the Church of God of the Apostolic Faith.

Meeting in Oklahoma City in October, the Pentecostal Fellowship of North America revised its format to that of a leadership forum. For the first time attendance was by invitation only. Pentecostals also were prominent in the New Orleans Leaders' Congress, which met in the Louisiana city in October. Some 10,000 Pentecostal and charismatic leaders from 30 denominations gathered under the theme "The Holy Spirit and World Evangelization."

(VINSON SYNAN)

Reformed, Presbyterian, and Congregational Churches. Several important anniversaries were celebrated in 1986. On Oct. 18, 1685, Louis XIV of France revoked the Edict of Nantes, which had granted some religious liberty to Protestants, and as a result the Huguenots emigrated to other countries. Many of the commemorative services, lectures, and exhibitions emphasized the continuing struggle for religious liberty. The year also marked the 450th anniversaries of Calvin's *Institutes* (March), of the adoption of the reform by the citizens of Geneva (May 21), and of Calvin's arrival in Geneva (July). The Geneva Church sponsored numerous events, among them a service at St. Pierre Cathedral on May 18 and a ceremony at the Reformation Wall on May 21. The World Alliance of Reformed Churches (WARC) cooperated in an international forum on "The Reformed Faith Today."

The situation in South Africa was a continuing cause for concern. The WARC general secretary, Edmond Perret, had visited WARC president Allan Boesak, then in detention, in September 1985. He paid a further visit in December 1985, following the World Council of Churches emergency consultation on South Africa in Harare, Zimbabwe. Other WARC churches facing difficulties included those in Lesotho and Guatemala. Under its new secretary, Jill Schaeffer of the U.S., the WARC Department of Cooperation and Witness was paying increasing attention to the local activities of member churches, and in this connection Schaeffer made a major tour of Latin America.

The WARC Executive Committee met in New Delhi, India. A consultation attached to its meeting challenged the membership on "Unity and Union in the Reformed Family of Churches." A new phase of international dialogue between WARC and the Lutheran World Federation was started, and dialogue between WARC and the Orthodox churches was planned to begin in 1988. The reformed responses to the World Council of Churches document on "Baptism, Eucharist and Ministry" were surveyed. WARC published *Mennonites and Reformed in Dialogue* (jointly with the Mennonite World Conference), *Reformed Theology and the Jewish People*, and *Saints: Visible, Orderly, and Catholic, the Congregational Idea of the Church*. The WARC European Committee published its study "Sola Scriptura."

A former WARC president, James I. McCord, became the 14th recipient of the Templeton Prize for his outstanding contribution to theological education.

(ALAN P. F. SELL)

Religious Society of Friends. Quakers were nowhere numerous, although British Friends in 1986 recorded an increase in membership for the first time in many years. Scattered groups in many parts of the world kept in touch through the Friends World Committee for Consultation, which in 1986 set up an Asia-West Pacific Section, based in Australia.

"Youthquake" was the title given to a gathering of young adults at Oaxtepec, Mexico. In North America many Quaker communities continued their wholehearted support of the Sanctuary Movement, receiving refugees from Central America in defiance of U.S. immigration laws.

At the London Yearly Meeting, which in 1986 was held at the University of Exeter, the Quaker Women's Group became the first collective presenter of the important Swarthmore Lecture, presenting its sufferings and hopes, as women, to the Society. Also dealt with at the meeting was the response of British Friends to the document on "Baptism, Eucharist and Ministry" of the World Council of Churches. An effort had been made, by a group not given to theological formulation, to translate these concepts into valid Quaker terms such as "Membership, Worship, and Service."

(DAVID FIRTH)

Salvation Army. On Jan. 9, 1986, two Salvation Army officers arrived on the island of Tonga to begin Army work. This brought the number of countries in which the Army operated to 90.

The High Council of the Salvation Army met in April at Sunbury-on-Thames, Middlesex, England, to elect a successor to Gen. Jarl Wahlström, who retired as the Army's international leader in July. Commissioner Eva Burrows (*see* BIOGRAPHIES) gained the majority vote of the 46 members on May 2 and became general of the Salvation Army on July 9. At 56, General Burrows was the youngest person to be elected international leader and only the second woman to hold the office in the movement's 121-year history. Gen. Frederick Coutts, the Army's international leader between 1963 and 1969, died in February at the age of 87.

Celebrations were held during 1986 to mark the centenary of the Salvation Army's Goodwill services through its inner-city community centres, known as "slum work" in the early days. Regional celebrations took place throughout Britain. The national celebration and service of thanksgiving was held in Southwark Cathedral, London, in November. (ROB GARRAD)

Seventh-day Adventist Church. Neal C. Wilson, the General Council president, headed an official delegation that visited Seventh-day Adventist churches in the Soviet Union and Hungary in June 1986. In Moscow Wilson met with representatives of both the government and the Russian Orthodox Church.

The Supreme Court of Canada on Dec. 18, 1985, ruled unanimously that an employer must take reasonable steps to accommodate the religious practice of a Seventh-day Adventist whose religious beliefs prevented her from working on her chosen day of worship.

Adventist World Radio in February began construction of KSDA, a $5 million, 100-kw shortwave radio station that would serve eastern and southern Asia from the island of Guam. Loma Linda (Calif.) University Medical Center continued its successful heart transplants for infants with hypoplastic left-heart syndrome. Major programs of the Adventist Development and Relief Agency International (ADRA) included drilling wells in drought-stricken Africa, developing child health-care programs in Africa and Haiti, building homes for victims of earthquake in Mexico City and volcanic eruption in Colombia, and providing emergency supplies for cyclone victims in the Solomon Islands.

World membership stood at 4,716,859 on Dec. 31, 1985, an increase of 6.6% over 1984. The Inter-American Division remained the largest division, with a membership of 889,893, but during 1985 the South American Division (697,486) took second place from the North American Division (689,507). (ROBERT W. NIXON)

Unitarian (Universalist) Churches. Nearly 2,000 registrants and friends attended the annual General Assembly of the Unitarian Universalist Association (UUA) on the campus of the University of Rochester, N.Y., June 23–28, 1986. The meeting marked the 25th anniversary of the merger of the Unitarian and Universalist denominations in North America. Five resolutions were selected for study in the year ahead; they dealt with abortion rights and open discussion, ending world hunger and distributing resources equitably, sex-biased wage discrimination, civil rights for victims of AIDS (acquired immune deficiency syndrome), and U.S. compliance with the 1979 SALT treaty and 1972 Anti-Ballistic Missile Treaty with the Soviet Union.

The growth in adult membership and religious education enrollment of recent years was sustained in 1985–86. Women now represented 18% of all settled ministers and 66% of theological school students. In protest against South Africa's policy of apartheid, the UUA had totally divested itself of all South Africa-related securities at a substantial loss. The continental headquarters buildings in Boston were declared a nuclear-free zone.

In Great Britain the 1986 Annual Meetings of the General Assembly of Unitarian and Free Christian Churches, held in Leicester during April, appointed Sheila Crosskey as the new president. The European Unitarian Universalists, the Provincial Assembly of Lancashire and Cheshire, and a Brussels group were granted recognition as affiliated societies of the General Assembly.

In East Melbourne, Victoria, Australia, the Melbourne Unitarian Peace Memorial Church was producing a "Unitarian Half-Hour" radio program.The Universalist Church of Tokyo, led by John Shidara, was operating a religious social service centre at Komagane. The Japan Free Religious Association, cofounded by John Nicholls Booth in 1948, was guided by Shinichiro Imaoka, who was approaching 100 years of age. (JOHN NICHOLLS BOOTH)

The United Church of Canada. The role of women in the church was celebrated by the election of the first laywoman as moderator of Canada's largest Protestant denomination at the meeting of its highest legislative body, the General Council, in Sudbury, Ont., in August 1986. Anne Squire of Ottawa, a former general secretary of the church's Division of Ministry, Personnel, and Education, was elected to succeed Robert F. Smith of Vancouver, B.C. One of Smith's last acts as moderator was to take part in an apology to native congregations for the church's failure "to recognize, learn from and share in, native spirituality. . . . In our zeal to tell you of the good news of Jesus Christ, we were blind to the value of your spirituality. . . . We ask you to forgive us." The apology was accepted by Indian commissioners (delegates), and the entire body then held a victory dance.

After lengthy debate, Council decided to divest itself of all investments "in corporations and companies having direct equity investment in South Africa until power is shared among all (its) peoples." The church had approximately $200 million invested in about 50 companies. The commissioners also voted to ask the federal government to implement its recently announced economic sanctions against South Africa as soon as possible.

On the controversial subject of (gender) inclusive language for God, Council moved to "celebrate the intention . . . to create a freer and more broadly inclusive community through the use of a variety of human metaphors, images and pronouns for God in church documents, worship and liturgy." Resolutions were approved calling for peace and disarmament in Central America and support of a nuclear freeze by the superpowers, as were requests to the Canadian government for greater financial support for peace work, a declaration of peace as an objective in its foreign policy, and the elimination of nuclear weapons by the year 2000. (NORMAN K. VALE)

United Church of Christ. The first two meetings of the 20-member committee to plan and provide oversight for the ecumenical partnership between the United Church of Christ (UCC) and the Christian Church (Disciples of Christ) were held during the year. Other ecumenical activities in the UCC included study of the theological consensus of the Consultation on Church Union, of which the UCC was a member, and the third round of theological dialogues between the Lutheran and Reformed churches.

Joining and expanding on the church's new priority of spiritual renewal were a number of new spiritual emphases, including the organization of a Spiritual Development Network, which had held a meeting at Elmhurst (Ill.) College, in September 1985. A new theological journal, *Prism,* published by seminaries of the UCC, provided a forum for articulating viewpoints in a period of unusual theological awareness throughout the church.

Following the participation of the UCC president in the World Council of Churches emergency consultation on South Africa, many members pressed for comprehensive economic sanctions against the South African government. In April 1986 the church's Executive Council endorsed the Harare Declaration framed at the Zimbabwe meeting.

In June more than 200 persons gathered in Cambridge, Mass., to celebrate 350 years of participation by the churches in higher education in the U.S. The Heritage and Horizon Convocation also celebrated the 140th anniversary of the American Missionary Association, founded in 1846 to defend freed slaves and to provide for their education.

James E. Wagner, former president of the Evangelical and Reformed Church and copresident of the UCC, died on Oct. 19, 1985. (AVERY D. POST)

ROMAN CATHOLIC CHURCH

The Extraordinary Synod held at the end of 1985 seemed to set the agenda for 1986: bishops united around Pope John Paul II, and the Roman Catholic Church recommitted itself firmly to the Second Vatican Council (1962–65). But an astonishing letter from the pope to the Brazilian bishops—with over 300 members, theirs was the world's largest episcopal conference—suggested that change was imminent. The letter, received on April 12, described liberation theology as "a new stage in theological reflection" and stated: "As pastors you are extraordinarily close to your people in their joys and in their sufferings." The Brazilian bishops were overwhelmed and, to add to their joy, the order of silence imposed in March 1985 on Leonardo Boff, their leading theologian, was lifted.

Commentators who concluded that the pope had changed his mind about liberation theology were proved wrong, however. The second "Instruction on Christian Freedom and Liberation," issued on April 5, repeated the condemnations of the first. During his visit to Colombia in July the pope reaffirmed that "the goods of creation are for everyone and should not be turned into the patrimony of a few," but at the same time he warned about "ideological temptations." Later in July, Joseph Cardinal Ratzinger (*see* BIOGRAPHIES), prefect of the Sacred Congregation for the Doctrine of the Faith, was in Lima, Peru, where he read another papal letter that made no concessions to liberation theology.

The pope's letter to the Brazilian bishops in April did confirm a change of approach. The Brazilians were in Rome for an informal meeting in March and had spoken frankly about the Roman Curia, which replied in kind. The pope was present throughout. It was clear that if the Brazilian church was to play any role in the return to democracy, it needed at least tacit Vatican approval.

Variations on the theme of "return to democracy" and liberation theology were heard throughout the year. In Chile democracy looked increasingly unlikely after the assassination attempt on President Pinochet; the role of the church as unofficial opposition grew, and the pope's planned spring 1987 visit was put in jeopardy. In the Philippines Jaime Cardinal Sin of Manila played a prominent role in the peaceful overthrow of Pres. Ferdinand Marcos's government. Another political cardinal, Obando y Bravo of Managua, Nicaragua, opposed the government as Marxist and was rebuked for being unpatriotic. (See *Introduction,* above.)

In the U.S. 1986 was marked by controversy. In August the Vatican decided that Charles E. Curran, theology professor at the Catholic University of America, Washington, D.C., could no longer teach Catholic theology. His views on sexual ethics were called into question. Curran's defense was that there could be legitimate dissent on "noninfallible" questions, as stipulated by the 1968 Norms of the U.S. Bishops, but Ratzinger refuted the usefulness of drawing a distinction between infallible and noninfallible. The incident provoked a statement of support for Curran by 29 eminent U.K. theologians in October.

The case of Archbishop Raymond Hunthausen of Seattle was even more notable. In December 1985 Hunthausen was given an auxiliary bishop, Donald Wuerl, a former member of the Roman Curia, who strenuously denied he had a watchdog function. On July 1, however, Hunthausen was informed by the Congregation of Bishops that he no longer had any authority over marriage tribunal operations, liturgical and parish programs, priests leaving the ministry, clergy formation and seminarians, and moral issues relating to health care and ministry to homosexuals. This left Hunthausen with no serious responsibilities, and although not forced to resign he was hamstrung. The action gave rise to fears that the Vatican had listened to denunciations from a group called Catholics United for the Faith (CUF) and that Hunthausen's opposition to nuclear weapons was a factor.

JOHN A. ZIERTEN

Donald E. Pelotte, first American Indian bishop of the Roman Catholic Church, wore a tribal headdress at his ordination celebration. He was to serve the New Mexico and Arizona diocese of Gallup.

This increase of discipline meant that the Roman Catholic Church lost appeal as an ecumenical partner, although this was not reflected in an ecumenical spectacular at Assisi, Italy, the birthplace of St. Francis, when international religious leaders gathered to pray for peace on October 27. Particularly remarkable was the attendance of the patriarch of Moscow and the archbishop of Canterbury. But relations with the Orthodox churches suffered a setback in June when members of the joint commission walked out of a meeting in southern Italy. (See *The Orthodox Church,* below.) This quarrel meant that a papal visit to the U.S.S.R. in 1988 to celebrate the millennium of Russian Christianity was in jeopardy. Superficially, relations with the Anglican Communion were much better. Ecumenical dialogue continued in the Anglican-Roman Catholic International Commission (ARCIC), and a September meeting in Wales "brought the reformation to an end" with the issuance of a joint statement on "Justification." But this success was offset by the dismissal of earlier agreements in *Theology* magazine (July) as "loftily grandiloquent statements" that idealized the papacy and romanticized the church.

In the autumn the pope spent four days in southeastern France attempting, in the words of a Vatican official, to "rekindle a sense of enthusiasm for the church in a country that . . . is now becoming Catholic in name only." The "Ostpolitik" of the Vatican continued to be dominated by Polish considerations and the prospect of a third papal visit in 1987. In September the prolonged effort of the Polish church to raise and administer its own agricultural fund collapsed, but most remaining political prisoners were given amnesty, which deprived Solidarity of a popular cause. Despite this a Czestochowa Workers' pilgrimage in September became a blatant pro-Solidarity demonstration. A Vatican delegation headed by France's Paul Cardinal Poupard went to Budapest in October to resume the "Christian-Marxist dialogue" abandoned in 1968 because of the Soviet invasion of Czechoslovakia.

(PETER HEBBLETHWAITE)

THE ORTHODOX CHURCH

Administratively independent from one another but united in faith, sacraments, and canonical discipline, the independent (autocephalous) churches of the Orthodox world seemed to have speeded the process—under way since the early 1960s—of preparing a "Holy and Great Council." A preconciliar commission met twice in Geneva in 1986 (February 15–23 and October 21–28) and adopted several consensus documents, which indicated broad agreement on such issues as the discipline of fasting and the attitude (positive but reserved) toward contemporary ecumenism. In the mind of the organizers, the absence of major theological tensions on these issues might help in the solution of the really difficult problems. Foremost among those was the issue of administrative unity in countries, like the U.S., where Orthodox witness was hampered by the existence of parallel jurisdictions, often dependent on centres abroad and following ethnic allegiances.

Following the death of Patriarch Justin of Romania (July 31), Metropolitan Teoktist of Moldavia was appointed to head the Romanian church temporarily. The largest in numbers—after the Russian church—among the Orthodox churches, the Romanian patriarchate controlled numerous schools and publications, an unusual phenomenon in Eastern Europe. However, its leadership had been sharply criticized recently by dissident priests seeking more freedom for preaching and youth work.

In the Soviet Union several factors contributed to an atmosphere of uncertainty. These included the illness of the aged patriarch Pimen and the recent changes in government leadership. The Communist Party program, adopted under General Secretary Mikhail Gorbachev, included appeals for the strengthening of antireligious activity. However, the church was allowed to make preparations for a celebration of the millennium of Christianity in Russia (1988). Several Orthodox activists were under arrest and some had their prison terms extended, but one, Vladimir Poresh, was freed. Some Russian-speaking persons from the U.S. were refused entry to attend ecclesiastical meetings, while others were allowed to take part in a symposium on the millennium, held in Kiev in July.

The fourth plenary session of the theological dialogue with the Roman Catholic Church (May 29–June 7) was indicative of the problems, both political and theological, connected with the situation in Eastern Europe and the policies of the Vatican. Representatives from the Soviet Union and Greece did not attend, while those from Yugoslavia, Poland, and Czechoslovakia left before the end of the meeting. (See *Roman Catholic Church,* above.) Another session was scheduled for May 1987. The visit paid by Metropolitan Dorotheos of Prague and Czechoslovakia to Metropolitan Theodosius of America (May 14–30), following the 1985 visit by Metropolitan Basil of Warsaw, was characteristic of the need of the smaller Orthodox churches in Eastern Europe to maintain their Western connections. A return visit by Metropolitan Theodosius to both Poland and Czechoslovakia took place on September 18–26. More significant still, in this respect, was the travel to the U.S. of the patriarch of Georgia (U.S.S.R.), also as a guest of Metropolitan Theodosius, in October 1986.

As the Greek Parliament was passing liberalized legislation on the issue, the Holy Synod of the Church of Greece issued a strong statement against abortion. A similar attitude was found in a text on family ethics adopted by the Council of the Orthodox Church in America, held in Washington, D.C., August 17–21.

(JOHN MEYENDORFF)

EASTERN NON-CHALCEDONIAN CHURCHES

The Coptic Church of Egypt—the largest single Christian group in the Middle East—felt relatively secure under the regime of Pres. Hosni Mubarak, but simmering Muslim extremism remained a threat to the Christian minority. Since his liberation from forced residence in a monastery, the Coptic patriarch, Shenuda III, had adopted a lower profile in order not to provoke hostile Muslim reaction. The future remained uncertain, however, and increasing numbers of Copts were immigrating to Western countries.

In India a visit by Pope John Paul II to Catholicos Mar Basileios Mar Thomas Matthew I was the occasion of public recrimination by the latter, in a speech addressed to the pope opposing what he called Roman Catholic "proselytism." Indian press comments on the same subject seemed to indicate a notable regression of the ecumenical spirit in India.

(JOHN MEYENDORFF)

JUDAISM

Orthodox, Reform, Reconstructionist, and Conservative Judaism had long worked together in uneasy partnership, but in 1986 the fringes of the partnership began to fray. Several indications pointed toward increasing factionalism and intolerance among the several Judaic groupings, in the U.S. as well as in the State of Israel. (See *Introduction,* above.) One was the decision by the Synagogue Council of America not to admit the Reconstructionist movement to the Council. Since the purpose of the SCA was to join all the Judaic movements, the Orthodox veto on inclusion of Reconstructionism marked a crisis.

Rabbi Reuven Bulka, a member of the Rabbinical Council of America (Orthodox), published in *The Coming Cataclysm* the observation that by the year 2000 fully 560,000 Jews would be deemed Jewish by Reform and Conservative Judaism but not by Orthodoxy. The question "Will there be one Jewish people by the year 2000?" was addressed by a meeting of the heads of the Reform, Orthodox, Reconstructionist, and Conservative rabbinical seminaries held at Princeton, N.J., on March 16–17. The divisive issues came down to one: the matter of personal status. Jewish law, observed by Orthodox and Conservative Judaism, requires a writ of divorce from a rabbinical court, as well as a civil divorce, before a wedding is dissolved and the partners may remarry. Without such a writ, the marriage remains in effect. If the woman remarries, she is regarded as an adulteress, and children from the second marriage are irremediably tainted. In the matter of conversion, Orthodoxy requires ritual immersion (baptism) as well as circumcision for males, and Reform Judaism does not. A third issue involves what is called patrilineal descent. In Jewish law the child automatically enjoys the status of the mother, not the father. Reform Judaism takes the position that either parent's status governs, so that the child of a Jewish father and a non-Jewish mother is Jewish. In these three areas Reform Judaism recognizes as Jewish persons whom Orthodoxy rejects.

At the Princeton meeting Rabbi Norman Lamm of Yeshiva University, New York City, made an important proposal; specifically, a Jewish court, or bet din, made up of three judges "chosen on the basis of scholarship and personal halahic [legal] observance, not institutional affiliation." This proposal left open the possibility that an authority would be accepted out of Conservative or Reform Judaism if that person were both qualified in learning and also appropriately pious and observant. The membership would be individual and not institutional. The reception of Lamm's proposal was positive, though whether the court would be set up in the near future was not clear.

Signs of renewed commitment to Jewish unity appeared as well. The president of the Rabbinical Assembly (Conservative), Alexander M. Shapiro, was invited to address the Orthodox Rabbinical Council of America. Five rabbis walked out, but 150 listened to him. Rabbi Henry I. Sobel of São Paulo, Brazil, a Reform rabbi, argued that the controversies had to be seen "as an argument between brothers, and not as a dispute between adversaries." His view, on the whole, still prevailed.

One point on which Orthodoxy differed from Reform and Conservative Judaism was the acceptance of women as rabbis. Since the ordination, a year earlier, of the first woman rabbi in Conservative Judaism, the women's revolution in that movement had proceeded apace. Fully a third of the students in the coming graduating classes of the Jewish Theological Seminary were women. In opposition, a Union for Traditional Conservative Judaism came into being within the Conservative movement, with the support of a large minority of the Conservative rabbinate. However, the Rabbinical Assembly affirmed the patrilineal principle, a position crucial to the traditional Conservative rabbis, and schism in 1986 was avoided.

REUTERS/BETTMANN NEWSPHOTOS

Orthodox Jewish seminary students in the Hedushei Harim yeshiva of Tel Aviv survey books ruined as part of the damage probably perpetrated by secular Jewish vandals.

The future of Judaism involved not just debates among rabbis but also the understanding of Judaism among lay people, Jewish and gentile. Discussing Hanukka, the December festival celebrating the miracle of the Jews' attainment of religious freedom in the struggle against the Syrians in the 2nd century BC, Rabbi Hillel Goldberg (*Intermountain Jewish News,* Dec. 20, 1985) commented, "Chanukah confronts very serious issues: religious freedom and Jewish self-hatred." He cited a report in the *Rocky Mountain News* by Terry Mattingly, who commented that the Jewish holiday "most carefully etched from the devastating lessons of assimilation" has become a kind of mimicking of the secular practices associated with the American Christmas.

(JACOB NEUSNER)

BUDDHISM

One of the most important developments in the Buddhist world during 1986 was the continuation of the apparent renewal of the Buddhist community in China. Temples in key regions such as Beijing (Peking), Shanghai, Chengdu (Chengtu; capital of Sichuan [Szechwan] Province), and Tibet continued to be restored and reopened, and monasteries and study institutes accepted more novices for training in Buddhist precepts and canonical languages. It remained unclear, however, whether these activities reflected an active piety or the government's desire to set up cultural museums.

Perhaps the most dramatic headlines of the year involving Buddhism centred around the continued violence in the predominantly Theravada Buddhist island country of Sri Lanka. Tamil separatist groups, mainly Hindu and ethnically linked to the major population group of southern India, carried out guerrilla attacks against military and civilian centres, while the military attacked Tamil sites. (*See* WORLD AFFAIRS [South Asia]: *Sri Lanka.*) In February Pres. J. R. Jayawardene asked Buddhist monks to prepare a strategy to end the conflict. Opposition parties as well as many Buddhist monks remained opposed to conceding Tamil demands for a separate state, although in 1985 the Buddhist leader Palipane Chandananda had called for broader national talks to include Tamils and consider their separatist demands. Throughout this crisis the Buddhist establishment in Sri Lanka appeared to move toward a larger role in national politics and security.

Two major projects to translate portions of the extensive Buddhist canon into English, announced in 1985, were under way in 1986. The Bukkyo Dendo Kyokai, based in Tokyo and founded by the Japanese industrialist and philanthropist Yehan Numata, launched a project to render the entire Chinese version of the canon into English. The project, which involved the worldwide participation of 70 scholars, was being directed from the Numata Center in Berkeley, Calif. Plans included the translation of 139 texts (in 100 volumes of translation) by the end of the century. Another major translation project was begun in 1985 in Burma, where the first volume of a new English translation of the Pali canon appeared. This project was supervised by the Burma Pitaka Association, whose president was former prime minister U Nu and whose general secretary was U Chan Htoon, former president of the World Fellowship of Buddhists.

In Japan there was controversy over the taxation of visitors to Buddhist temples. Art works from the Great Eastern Temple at Nara, never before shown outside Japan, were exhibited at the Art Institute of Chicago during the summer. (*See* ART EXHIBITIONS AND ART SALES.)

(FRANK E. REYNOLDS; ROBERT CAMPANY)

Some four million Hindu pilgrims flocked to bathe in the Ganges River in India during the Kumbha Mela, the greatest of Hindu pilgrimage festivals, held for the first time in 12 years. It is traditionally held every three years.

AP/WIDE WORLD

HINDUISM

Violent conflict continued to dominate the relationship between Hindu and Sikh communities in India during the year. (*See* WORLD AFFAIRS [South Asia]: *India.*) Although the ongoing violence was denounced by Sikh religious and political leaders, the chief minister of Sikh-dominated Punjab state agreed to perform public penance for having forcibly expelled, on April 30, terrorists and secessionists who had taken refuge in the Golden Temple of Amritsar, the holiest Sikh shrine.

Bloodshed marred the annual Rathayatra, or car festival, of Lord Jagannatha in Ahmedabad, Gujarat, when some Muslims hurled stones and flaming objects from rooftops on the thousands of Hindus escorting the sacred images through the streets. Over 70 people lost their lives in the ensuing riots. Muslim-Hindu violence also disrupted processions celebrating the 359th birth anniversary of the Hindu warrior saint Shivaji in parts of Maharashtra in May and the traditionally joyful spring festival of Holi in parts of Gujarat, Maharashtra, and Uttar Pradesh. The visit of Pope John Paul II in February was warmly received by the prime minister as contributing to an easing of tension between the Hindu and Christian communities in India, particularly over the issue of conversion to Christianity, which Hindu religious and political leaders had viewed as a threat to traditional Indian society.

The greatest of the Hindu pilgrimage festivals, the Kumbha Mela, celebrated every 3 years, was held for the first time in 12 years at Hardwar on the Ganges in April. Despite the presence of some 17,000 police, army, and volunteer personnel, some 50 persons were crushed to death in a stampede to bathe in the sacred river at the most auspicious time. The Rama Jamnabhumi temple at Ayodhya in Uttar Pradesh, regarded as the birthplace of the Lord Rama, was opened in February by court order after being locked for 37 years following a dispute between Hindus and Muslims over title to the present building. Muslims claimed that it was built by the emperor Babur as a mosque.

In the U.S. two Hindu-based sects experienced bad days. The International Society for Krishna Consciousness became the object of a federal grand jury investigation following the slaying in Los Angeles of a dissident member who had alleged that the sect's largest temple, in West Virginia, was built with the profits from criminal activities. In Oregon the former commune of Bhagwan Shree Rajneesh was placed on the market for an estimated $50 million, while the Bhagwan, expelled from the U.S. as an illegal alien, continued to seek a new location for his commune.

(H. PATRICK SULLIVAN)

ISLAM

The growing strength of Islamic fundamentalism over the past several years had become a primary concern for the governments of most Islamic nations. Organized fundamentalist movements had grown from small groups formed mainly around religious interests to much larger and in some cases well-structured organizations able to concentrate power on the established governing authorities. By 1986 most governments of Islamic nations were having to devote considerable time and attention to the powerful fundamentalist forces active among their own citizens and in other Islamic countries.

While some of these organizations had been in existence for many years, such as the Muslim Brotherhood in Egypt, others were fairly new and difficult to identify. Fundamentalism had deep roots in Islamic history, and in more recent periods Muslims concerned about Western influences had tended to take fundamentalist stances.

Fundamentalist movements often combined students, rural villagers, members of the urban lower classes, and lower and middle ranks in the military. These people viewed many aspects of modernity (in other words, westernization) as being principally responsible for the ills they saw about them. Their solution was to reform government and society in terms of Islamic principles. Thus these movements often became revolutionary opponents of the established governments.

Historically, most fundamentalist movements had not gained permanent or widespread power. Viewed in the perspective of years or decades, they were transient, though there was no guarantee that this would always be the case. What they had done from time to time was to upset established governments, cause periods of bloody violence and turmoil, and alter international relationships. In the 1980s the concurrent rise of non-Islamic fundamentalist movements suggested that the present world situation was causing many people to seek solutions in traditional religious values and to turn away from liberal Western idealism.

During 1986 Egypt, Jordan, Malaysia, The Sudan, Indonesia, and Pakistan were among the countries facing challenges from fundamentalist groups. In Indonesia the government's attempts to develop a state ideology were resisted by Islamic conservatives. Although Malaysia rejected legal moves toward islamization, Islamic influences there were clearly growing. In The Sudan the government's attempted islamization of the legal system was resisted strongly by southern Sudanese Christian groups. The Egyptian government in May refused to accept a court order calling for the release of jailed fundamentalists. Pres. Hosni Mubarak, who supported family planning because of Egypt's population crisis, found it politically difficult to implement population-limitation plans. Muslim separatist movements continued in northern Nigeria, while in Iran Ayatollah Ruhollah Khomeini, who was reported to be in ill health, exhorted his followers in November to continue his efforts on behalf of militant fundamentalism even after his death.

(REUBEN W. SMITH)

WORLD CHURCH MEMBERSHIP

The accompanying table serves to illustrate the articles on the various religions by placing each religion's continental statistics in the overall global context. Statistics, essential in the secular world, are also widely employed in the religious world. Over 100 countries, mainly in the third world, include a religion question in their official decennial population census and publish the results in great detail. India, for instance, analyzes its citizens' religions in several massive census volumes. Many other countries with no religious census enumerate religion through public opinion polls (in the West) and social scientific surveys (Communist countries).

Some 5,000 leading Christian denominations and 10,000 parachurch organizations collect and publish each year detailed statistics of Christian membership, practice, finances, and activities. So do a fair number of non-Christian religious bodies, especially for their renewal movements. For the churches especially, statistics have an important threefold value: understanding the past; operating in the present; and planning for the future.

(DAVID B. BARRETT)

This article updates the *Macropædia* articles The Buddha and BUDDHISM; CHRISTIANITY; EASTERN ORTHODOXY; HINDUISM; Muhammad and the Religion of ISLAM; JUDAISM; PROTESTANTISM; The Study and Classification of RELIGIONS; ROMAN CATHOLICISM; and *Micropædia* entries on the various denominations.

Adherents of All Religions by Eight Continental Areas, 1986

Religionists	Africa	East Asia	Europe	Latin America	Northern America	Oceania	South Asia	U.S.S.R.	**World**	%
Christians	259,544,680	74,614,270	415,529,010	388,863,450	231,539,720	21,143,000	125,954,640	102,083,790	**1,619,272,560**	32.9
Roman Catholics	98,557,180	8,904,140	253,852,110	365,973,680	88,144,650	7,310,180	72,863,900	4,940,000	**900,545,840**	18.3
Protestants	69,087,120	28,871,510	79,973,650	13,417,650	96,293,800	7,449,790	23,049,300	8,409,000	**326,551,820**	6.6
Orthodox	24,129,950	74,190	35,351,060	421,240	5,948,530	506,130	3,201,260	88,720,290	**158,352,650**	3.2
Anglicans	21,496,950	326,770	33,076,370	1,191,100	7,760,000	5,463,380	286,990	500	**69,602,060**	1.4
Other Christians	46,273,480	36,437,660	13,275,820	7,859,780	33,392,740	413,520	26,553,190	14,000	**164,220,190**	3.3
Muslims	237,067,660	24,143,740	9,042,340	625,180	2,675,720	93,520	535,079,210	31,494,020	**840,221,390**	17.1
Nonreligious	1,433,850	619,384,830	48,788,900	12,751,380	19,310,020	2,859,170	18,386,060	82,981,670	**805,895,880**	16.4
Hindus	1,395,390	9,740	585,540	636,340	764,200	284,080	644,218,360	1,300	**647,894,950**	13.2
Buddhists	13,850	155,159,650	209,600	496,980	193,440	16,880	150,975,920	349,710	**307,416,030**	6.2
Atheists	234,470	133,582,030	17,153,270	2,388,410	1,029,120	507,920	5,084,340	60,562,030	**220,541,590**	4.5
Chinese folk religionists	10,220	194,049,230	50,350	68,460	116,160	19,170	8,442,280	100	**202,755,970**	4.1
New Religionists	12,080	41,289,300	33,470	357,830	1,025,050	4,910	66,777,800	200	**109,500,640**	2.2
Tribal religionists	70,170,270	772,770	50	1,168,160	65,210	84,730	25,215,740	0	**97,476,930**	2.0
Jews	276,390	1,950	1,520,060	976,230	8,050,100	85,540	3,893,810	3,177,380	**17,981,460**	0.4
Sikhs	29,110	1,080	212,240	5,950	8,660	6,530	15,897,290	50	**16,160,910**	0.3
Shamanists	1,100	12,828,530	300	500	290	290	12,000	299,750	**13,142,760**	0.3
Confucians	550	5,635,590	990	500	1,020	290	1,500	200	**5,640,640**	0.1
Baha'is	1,319,350	44,200	67,090	543,460	300,110	56,540	2,228,260	4,900	**4,563,910**	0.1
Shintoists	50	3,423,960	390	990	710	590	200	100	**3,426,990**	0.1
Jains	49,980	430	9,870	1,980	2,040	980	3,304,650	20	**3,369,950**	0.1
Other religionists	63,400	58,500	296,140	6,725,010	685,050	23,270	215,750	5,000	**8,072,120**	0.2
World Population	**571,622,400**	**1,264,999,800**	**493,499,610**	**415,610,810**	**265,766,620**	**25,187,410**	**1,605,687,810**	**280,960,220**	**4,923,334,680**	**100.0**

NOTES:

Continents. UN demographic practice divides the world into eight continental areas as shown above (*see* United Nations, *World Population Prospects*, with populations of all countries covering the period 1950–2025).

Rows. The list of religions is arranged by descending order of magnitude of global adherents in 1986 (last two columns).

Adherents. As defined and enumerated for each of the world's countries in *World Christian Encyclopedia* (1982), projected to mid-1986.

Christians. Followers of Jesus Christ affiliated to churches (church members, including children), plus persons professing in censuses or polls though not so affiliated.

Other Christians. Catholics (non-Roman), marginal Protestants, crypto-Christians, and adherents of African, Asian, black, and Latin-American indigenous churches.

Muslims. 83% Sunnis, 16% Shi'ahs, 1% other schools.

Nonreligious. Persons professing no religion, nonbelievers, agnostics, freethinkers, dereligionized secularists indifferent to all religion.

Hindus. 70% Vaishnavites, 25% Shaivites, 2% neo-Hindus and reform Hindus.

Buddhists. 56% Mahayana, 38% Theravada, 6% Tantrayana.

Atheists. Persons professing atheism, skepticism, disbelief, or irreligion, including antireligious (opposed to all religion).

Chinese folk religionists. Followers of traditional Chinese religion (local deities, ancestor veneration, Confucian ethics, Taoism, universism, divination, some Buddhist elements).

New Religionists. Followers of Asian 20th-century New Religions, New Religious movements, radical new crisis religions, and non-Christian syncretistic mass religions, all founded since 1800 and mostly since 1945.

Jews. 84% Ashkenazis, 10% Orientals, 4% Sephardis.

Confucians. Non-Chinese followers of Confucius and Confucianism, mostly Koreans.

Other religionists. Including minor world religions, spiritist religions, New Age religions, quasi-religions, pseudo-religions, parareligions, religious systems, mystic systems, religious and semireligious brotherhoods of numerous varieties.

World Population. UN medium variant figures for mid-1986, computed from *World Population Prospects* (1985), pages 42–43.

(DAVID B. BARRETT)

Social Security and Welfare Services

During 1986 modest progress was recorded in social security on three fronts: unemployment benefits, equal treatment for men and women, and partial pensions designed to ease the transition from work to retirement. Otherwise, the year saw a certain number of improvements and one or two cutbacks in social security systems.

National Developments in Social Security. Two of the largest countries in the less developed world introduced unemployment benefits in 1986. In February a legislative decree was issued in Brazil that provided for the introduction of an unemployment insurance system. Benefits were equivalent to 50% of the worker's average earnings over the previous three months; minimum and maximum benefits were set at 0.7 and 1.5 times the minimum wage, respectively. Benefits were to be payable for up to four months in an 18-month period. To be eligible, workers must have: been either laid off or dismissed without good reason; paid social security contributions for 36 months in the previous four years; registered for work in the previous six months; and applied for benefit within 30 days of dismissal. The system was to be financed through contributions from employers, employees, and the government.

As part of a wider reform that replaced lifetime labour contracts in enterprises by a system of three-year fixed-term contracts, China passed legislation providing for the introduction of unemployment insurance with effect from October. The system, which was contributory and administered by local authorities, paid benefits of between 60 and 75% of previous earnings for up to 12 months. Workers who had been with their enterprise for more than five years qualified for extended benefit, set at 50% of earnings, for an additional 12-month period.

The equal treatment of men and women in social security schemes had been the subject of numerous reforms in recent years, and 1986 saw important new developments in this respect at both the international and national levels. In July the Council of the European Communities issued a directive "on the implementation of the principle of equal treatment for men and women in occupational social security schemes." Equal treatment in statutory schemes was the subject of an earlier directive issued in 1978 for implementation by the end of 1984, but since it did not require member states to eliminate all aspects of inequality, discrimination in statutory schemes still existed, notably concerning pension age and survivors' benefits.

The 1986 directive stated that there should be no sexual discrimination either directly or indirectly, especially as regards the scope of schemes and the conditions of access to them; the obligation to contribute and the calculation of contributions; the calculation of benefits, including supplementary benefits due in respect of a spouse or dependents; and the conditions governing the duration and retention of entitlements to benefits. Member states had to ensure that all occupational schemes conformed by Jan. 1, 1993.

In West Germany provisions governing survivors' pensions were revised with effect from Jan. 1, 1986, to eliminate inequality between men and women. Previously a widow was entitled to 60% of the pension earned by the husband's employment, irrespective of whether or not she was entitled to a pension of her own; widowers received no pension on the basis of their wives' employment unless the wife was the principal breadwinner. Under the new scheme, the surviving spouse (widow or widower) was to draw a survivor's pension of 60% of the pension to which the deceased spouse was or would have been entitled. The pension was payable in full, regardless of any other pension or income, provided the total did not exceed a specified level (for 1986 this was DM 900 monthly plus DM 190 for each dependent child). Where the total exceeded that level, the survivor's pension was reduced by 40% of the excess. There was a ten-year transitional period, and until the end of 1988 husbands and wives could opt by mutual agreement to continue under the old system if it was more favourable to them. The situation was unchanged for recipients of a survivor's pension granted before the revised system came into force. In addition, the plan introduced a bonus of one year's insurance per child for mothers or fathers who had remained at home to bring up a child and who reached age 65 in 1986 or later.

Under legislation that was being implemented in stages starting in April, Japan was reducing sexual discrimination in its social security system. The flat-rate basic pension became payable to all citizens, including economically inactive married and divorced women who were previously not protected by any plan. The pensionable age for women was to be raised gradually from 55 to 60 by the year 2000, age 60 being the present pensionable age for men. Pension contribution rates were increased more for women than for men, and rates for women would continue to rise more rapidly until parity was achieved.

Denmark and Finland followed the example of Sweden and from January 1987 were to give workers the right to draw a partial pension and reduce their working hours accordingly. The Danish scheme applied to all employees between the ages of 60 and 67, the statutory pension age, provided that they had worked in the country during the previous 12 months; had contributed to the complementary pension scheme for at least 10 of the previous 20 years; reduced their workweek by at least 9 hours; and worked 15 to 30 hours a week and at least 20 days per quarter. The basis for calculating the partial pension was the same as for cash sickness benefit, namely, 90% of average earnings over the previous four weeks; for each hour's reduction in the workweek, 1/39 of this amount was paid in benefit, up to a maximum of 65,500 kroner.

In Finland both employees and self-employed workers between the ages of 60 and 65 who were covered by the private-sector employment pension plan would be eligible for a partial pension if they had been working full-time for at least 12 out of the previous 18 months and if they had been covered by the employment pension plan for at least 5 out of the previous 15 years. The workweek had to be reduced to between 16 and 28 hours and earnings to between 35 and 70% of their former level. In the case of farmers and other self-employed persons, working time had to be reduced by at least half. Unlike the Danish or Swedish schemes, the amount of the partial pension varied according to age; at age 60 benefit was 44% of the reduction in earnings, but this figure rose by one-third of a percentage point for each month by which the beneficiary's age exceeded 60, reaching 64% by age 65. The partial pension could not exceed 75% of the worker's employment pension entitlement.

South Korea adopted legislation in May providing for a national pension scheme covering persons aged 18 to 60 working for companies with more than ten employees. The target pension was 40% of final pay after 20 years in insured employment. Contributions were 3% of insured earnings for employees and 4% for employers. The scheme was to start in 1989. In the Philippines the minimum monthly pension under social security was increased from

120 pesos to 200 pesos. Cash sickness benefits and the funeral grant were also raised. In Sweden unemployment benefits rose by 20% from July 1, and family allowances would increase by 21% from Jan. 1, 1987. In the U.S.S.R., where there was no mechanism for the regular adjustment of pensions, large increases in benefits were approved for persons disabled from childhood, ranging from 50 to 66.7%

A series of important changes in pensions, as well as social assistance and other benefits, were contained in the U.K.'s Social Security Act, which, according to Social Services Secretary Norman Fowler, represented "the culmination of the most fundamental review of social security" since World War II. Major long-term savings were made through cutbacks in the State Earnings-Related Pension Scheme (SERPS). Pensions were to be reduced from 25 to 20% of covered earnings and based not on the 20 best years but on average earnings over the individual's entire working life, and survivors' pensions were to be halved. Incentives were to be offered to encourage individual employees to contract out of SERPS by opting for a personal pension on a money-purchase basis. (ROGER A. BEATTIE)

Social programs engendered relatively little debate in the U.S. Congress in 1986, but comprehensive reform of the welfare system was expected to be a major domestic issue in 1987. Several important human service programs and antipoverty volunteer agencies were reauthorized, despite calls by Pres. Ronald Reagan for cutbacks or outright elimination.

In an omnibus bill, Congress authorized $15,470,000,000 over four years for social service programs targeted on low-income households. The largest of these ($8,710,000,000) was the Low Income Home Energy Assistance Program (LIHEAP), which helped needy families and individuals pay their heating and cooling bills and provided funds for weatherization assistance. An estimated seven million households received LIHEAP money in fiscal 1986. Other human service programs renewed for four years included Head Start, which provided educational, nutritional, social, and health services to almost 500,000 preschoolers from needy families; Follow Through, a demonstration program designed to meet the continuing needs of Head Start graduates; Community Service block grants, which provided seed money to community service agencies that fight poverty; community food and nutrition programs; and Dependent Care programs that helped states set up before- and after-school programs for children with no adult at home during the day. The omnibus bill also created a new program to increase the number of qualified day-care workers by giving states money to help fund scholarships for needy persons seeking child development associate credentials.

Reauthorized for three years in another measure were the major domestic antipoverty volunteer programs administered by ACTION. These included Volunteers in Service to America (VISTA) and the Older American Volunteer Programs, such as Foster Grandparents and the Retired Senior Volunteer Programs (RSVP). Congress also renewed vocational training programs for the handicapped and expanded Medicaid health care to, potentially, millions of additional infants, children, and pregnant women, and aged, blind, and disabled persons whose family incomes were below the poverty level.

The Social Security system got a new director during the year. Dorcas R. Hardy became the tenth head of the agency and the first woman in that post. The only major action in Congress involving Social Security was repeal of the "trigger" mechanism initiated in 1972, which required that inflation reach at least 3% in a given year before a cost-of-living allowance would be added to benefits. Future benefits would rise whenever the consumer price index had gone up in the preceding year. For 1987 the 37 million Social Security recipients would get a 1.3% cost-of-living increase in their monthly benefits. This meant that the average retired worker would receive $488 a month, a $6 increase, and the average retired couple would get $833, a boost of $11. The 1.3% increase also would go to about four million low-income aged, blind, and disabled persons receiving welfare benefits under federal Supplemental Security Income (SSI). Payroll taxes would increase for higher paid workers. The rate was to remain at 7.15%, but the maximum amount of wages on which a worker paid Social Security tax would rise from $42,000 in 1986 to $43,800. This meant that the maximum tax would increase from $3,003 to $3,131.70 for worker and employer. The maximum tax for a self-employed person would rise $221.41, to $5,387.40.

While there was less wrangling than usual over social programs in 1986, the groundwork was laid for a major debate in 1987 on overhaul of the U.S. welfare system. President Reagan called for welfare reform in his state of the union address in January and created a task force to evaluate current programs. Reporting in December, the task force recommended that President Reagan ask Congress to authorize states to use money from current welfare programs for innovative experiments and demonstrations aimed at getting people off welfare and into jobs. Meanwhile, Democrats in the House of Representatives had set up their own Social Policy Task Force, which urged greater emphasis on assisting the working poor and a renewed effort to help those on government assistance get education and training. The country's Roman Catholic bishops adopted a pastoral letter calling on the government

KEVIN HORAN—PICTURE GROUP

A Chicago welfare recipient pauses from a job he got through "workfare," a program that was growing along with public insistence that able people put in time and energy to earn their checks. Many U.S. states were requiring "workfare" measures.

to increase its efforts to create jobs and help poor people. (*See* RELIGION.) The American Public Welfare Association called for a "fundamental redesign" of the Aid to Families with Dependent Children (AFDC) program, with emphasis on providing young welfare parents with basic reading skills and job training.

Both Democrats and Republicans in Congress sponsored bills aimed at making it easier for welfare recipients to find and keep jobs, but no action was taken on them. The measures were mainly designed to stimulate discussion. Putting people to work had emerged as the key to welfare reform, but questions remained as to how much pressure should be used to accomplish this and what the respective roles of the states and federal government should be in education, training, and financing. Reformers would probably take a close look at two of the most successful state "workfare" programs, those in Massachusetts and California.

In all, more than 70 different welfare programs were operating in the U.S. In fiscal 1984 they provided cash or in-kind benefits amounting to $134 billion in federal and state assistance. Although Medicaid was the most expensive program ($37.6 billion), the heart of the welfare system was AFDC, which began in 1935 and cost $16.1 billion in 1984. Federal and state spending on AFDC had risen 21% since 1970, but the number of recipients had grown 45% in the same period. Benefit outlays declined slightly after 1981 because of tighter eligibility rules pushed by the White House, resulting in a widening gap between the government-set poverty level and the benefits received by AFDC recipients. In 1985 the poverty line for a family of four in the median state was $11,003, while the median-state AFDC level was $4,548.

The Census Bureau reported that 33.1 million Americans, or 14% of the population, lived in poverty in 1985; 33.1% of blacks were poor, 29% of Hispanics, 19.5% of children aged 6 to 17, and 12.6% of persons over 65. In another report, the bureau said that when values were assigned to noncash benefits (food, housing, medical care), estimates of the poverty population ranged from about 22 million to 30 million, depending on which benefits were included. (DAVID M. MAZIE)

See also Education; Health and Disease; Industrial Review: *Insurance.*

This article updates the *Macropædia* article SOCIAL WELFARE.

Space Exploration

Loss of the space shuttle *Challenger* in January followed by several other mishaps caused 1986 to be the worst year in space ever experienced by the United States. The disasters brought the U.S. space program to its slowest pace since the dawn of the space age and cast doubt upon the future of several ambitious space science programs that had been in development since the 1970s.

The National Aeronautics and Space Administration (NASA) had designated 1986 as the "Year for Space Science." It started with the successful flyby of Uranus by Voyager 2 almost five years after it flew past Saturn. This was to have been followed by several space shuttle launches, which were to have launched the Galileo orbiter-and-probe to Jupiter, the European Ulysses probe over the poles of the Sun (by way of a hairpin turn at Jupiter), and the Hubble Space Telescope into Earth orbit for observations of the cosmos. The shuttle was also scheduled to carry two Spacelab missions, ASTRO-1 and Earth Observation Mission-1, to study the stars in ultraviolet light and to study the middle atmosphere from low orbit.

Space Shuttle. The only successful U.S. manned mission of 1986, mission 61-C on January 12, was a leftover from the 1985 schedule. The crew of the orbiter *Columbia* included mission commander Robert Gibson, pilot Charles Bolden, mission specialists George Nelson, Steven Hawley, and Franklin Chang-Diaz, RCA engineer Robert Cenker, and Rep. William Nelson (Dem. Fla.). The payload included an RCA communications satellite, which was launched into space, and an automated materials science laboratory. Bad weather at Kennedy Space Center, the primary landing site for the mission, forced the crew to land shortly before dawn at Edwards Air Force Base in California, only the second time that a night landing had been made.

The ill-fated launch of the 51-L space shuttle *Challenger* mission brought to the fore the difficulties that NASA had been experiencing for many years in trying to accomplish too much with too little money. The mission experienced trouble at the outset as the launch was postponed for several days, partly because of delays in getting the previous shuttle orbiter back on the ground. On the night before the launch, central Florida was swept by a severe cold wave that deposited thick ice on the launch pad.

The primary goal of the mission was to launch the second Tracking and Data Relay Satellite (TDRS-B). It also carried the Spartan Halley spacecraft, a small satellite that was to be released by *Challenger* and picked up two days later after observing Halley's Comet during its closest approach to the Sun.

Greatest visibility among the crew went to teacher-in-space Sharon Christa McAuliffe of Concord, N.H., the winner of a national screening begun in 1984. McAuliffe was to conduct at least two lessons from orbit and then spend the following nine months lecturing students across the U.S. The goal was to highlight the importance of teachers and to interest students in high-tech careers. Other members of the crew were mission commander Francis "Dick" Scobee, pilot Michael Smith, mission specialists Ellison Onizuka, Judith Resnik, and Ronald McNair, and Hughes Aircraft engineer Gregory Jarvis.

Launch was delayed until 11:38 AM on January 28. All appeared to be normal from lift-off until after the vehicle emerged from "Max-Q," the period of greatest aerodynamic pressure. Mission Control told Scobee, "*Challenger,* go with throttle up." Scobee replied, "Roger, go with throttle up," and seconds later the vehicle disappeared in an explosion just 73 seconds after lift-off at an altitude of 14,240 m (47,000 ft). Tapes salvaged from the wreckage later showed that the instant before breakup Smith said, "Uh-oh," but nothing else was heard. Debris rained into the Atlantic Ocean for more than an hour after the explosion; searches revealed no sign of the crew.

The accident immediately grounded the shuttle program, until at least February 1988 and possibly later. An intensive investigation by NASA and by a commission appointed by U.S. Pres. Ronald Reagan and chaired by former secretary of state William Rogers followed. What emerged was an appalling pattern of assuming that because the vehicle had survived minor mishaps it could be pushed even further.

The immediate cause of the accident was suspected within days and was fully established within a few weeks. The severe cold reduced the resiliency of two rubber O-rings that sealed the joint between the lower two segments of the right-hand solid rocket booster (each booster had four almost identical segments). Under normal circumstances, when the shuttle's three main engines ignited they pressed the whole vehicle forward, like a giant leaf spring, and the boosters were ignited when the vehicle swung back to centre. On the morning of the accident an effect called joint rotation occurred, preventing the rings from resealing and opening a path for hot exhaust gas to escape from inside the booster. Puffs of black smoke appeared on the far side of the booster in a spot not visible to most cameras.

As the vehicle ascended, the leak expanded, and after 59 seconds a 2.4-m (8-ft) stream of flame emerged from the hole. This grew to 12 m (40 ft) and gradually eroded one of three struts that secured the booster's base to the large external tank carrying liquid hydrogen and liquid oxygen for the orbiter engines. At the same time, thrust in the booster lagged slightly, although within limits, and the nozzle steering systems tried to compensate. When the strut broke, the booster's base swiveled outward, forcing its nose through the top of the external fuel tank and causing the whole tank to collapse and explode. Through ground tracking cameras this was seen as a brief flame licking from a concealed spot on the right side of the vehicle a few seconds before everything disappeared in the fireball. Even if the plume had been seen at lift-off, there would have been no hope for crew escape because the shuttle orbiter could not survive high-speed separation from the tank until the last seconds of the boosters' two-minute burn.

Challenger broke up in the explosion but, miraculously, the forward section with the crew cabin was severed in one piece and continued to coast upward with other debris, including wings and still-flaming engines, then plummeted to the ocean. It was believed that the crew survived the initial breakup but that loss of cabin pressure rendered them unconscious within seconds since they did not wear pressure suits. Death probably resulted from oxygen deficiency minutes before impact.

The boosters also survived the fireball and righted themselves to continue flying, something totally unexpected. Range safety officers finally detonated their charges 30 seconds later to prevent them from overflying land.

An intensive salvage operation was organized to retrieve as much of the wreckage as possible and the bodies of the crew. The task was complicated by the force of the explosion and the altitude at which it occurred, as well as by the separate paths taken by the boosters. The Rogers Commission report, delivered June 6 to the president, faulted NASA as a whole, and its Marshall Space Flight Center in Huntsville, Ala., and contractor Morton Thiokol Inc. in Ogden, Utah, in particular, for poor engineering and management. Marshall was responsible for the shuttle boosters, engines, and tank, while Morton Thiokol manufactured the booster motors and assembled them at Kennedy. (*See* Special Report).

Other Flight Accidents. *Challenger* seemed to touch off a series of accidents. On April 18 a U.S. Air Force Titan 34D exploded 8.5 seconds after lift-off when one of its two solid-fuel boosters ruptured in a manner apparently unrelated to that of *Challenger.* The explosion damaged Space Launch Complex 4 at Vandenberg Air Force Base in California, putting it out of action until late 1986. More serious was the loss of the vehicle's payload, reportedly the last of the Big Bird reconnaissance satellites.

On May 3 a Delta carrying a badly needed GOES weather satellite lost power in its first-stage liquid-fuel engine 71 seconds after launch, and the vehicle went into a slide and had to be destroyed. Fault was laid to bad wiring insulation in a relay box. Finally, on May 30 a European Ariane carrying an Intelsat 5 communications satellite was lost when the third-stage engine failed to ignite properly.

Failures of sounding rockets made headlines with the loss on August 23 of an Aries rocket carrying an X-ray telescope. Such failures were common in the low-cost program but recently had attracted more interest.

Some successes were achieved. Europe on March 28 launched an Ariane 3, its first since an accident in September 1985, carrying the GTE Spacenet GStar 2 and Brasilsat S2 communications satellites. And on September 17 an Atlas E booster carried a NOAA-G weather satellite into polar orbit. Its launch had been delayed by the need to make sure that its engine package, similar to that of the Delta, would not suffer the same fate. France's advanced

(continued on page 344)

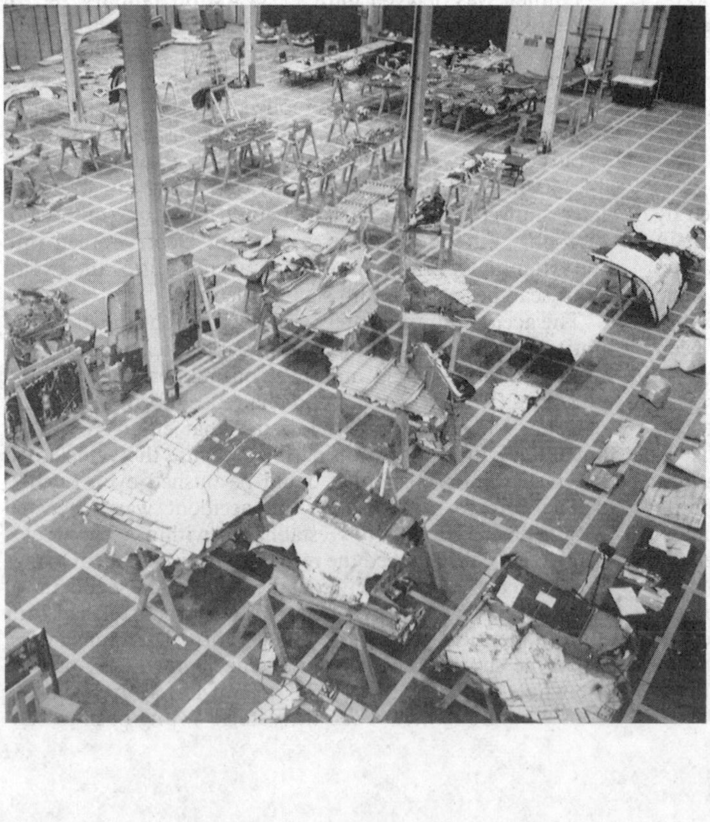

PHOTOGRAPHS, AP/WIDE WORLD

Battered debris from the space shuttle *Challenger*—probably a piece of a rocket it carried as cargo—is hoisted from the ocean by a navy salvage crew. Identified remains of the exploded shuttle were laid out on a huge floor grid at the Kennedy Space Center as part of NASA's detailed investigation of the January 28 accident, which claimed the lives of the seven crew members.

Special Report: Space Exploration

The Year the Space Program Stopped

BY TONY REICHHARDT

On New Year's Day 1986, not even the most expert observer of the U.S. space program could have predicted that six months later nearly every major space launch vehicle in the American fleet would be out of commission, sidelined by a catastrophic failure.

As 1986 began the National Aeronautics and Space Administration (NASA) was preparing eagerly for what it billed as a "Year for Space Science," which coincided with the 25th anniversary of manned space flight. No fewer than 15 space shuttle flights were planned for the year, including launches of the Galileo mission to Jupiter and the long-awaited Hubble Space Telescope. Following Voyager 2's flyby of Uranus in January, Halley's Comet (back in the sky after 76 years) was to be studied intensively by shuttle scientists in Earth orbit and by an international fleet of spacecraft that would fly past its shrouded nucleus.

Everything changed, however, on the morning of January 28, when a horrified world watched space shuttle *Challenger,* with a crew of seven aboard, explode in the chilly skies over Florida. The shock wave from that explosion was still being felt at the end of the year and would probably continue to affect national space policy at least for the rest of the decade.

Faulty Seals and Fundamental Problems. In the weeks immediately after the accident, NASA's own investigative teams and a special presidential commission focused on the nuts and bolts of what had gone wrong with shuttle mission 51-L. The physical cause of the accident—a faulty seal in one of the shuttle's two solid rocket boosters—was quickly pinpointed, and the space agency immediately began work on a redesigned solid booster for future launches.

But the presidential commission, headed by former secretary of state William P. Rogers, also heard disturbing testimony from a number of engineers who had been expressing concern about the reliability of the seals for at least two years and who had warned superiors about a possible failure the night before 51-L was launched. In June the Rogers commission released its report on the accident, and one of its strongest recommendations was to tighten the communications gap between shuttle managers and working engineers. In response to this implied criticism that its quality-control measures had become slack, NASA added several more checkpoints in the shuttle bureaucracy, including a new NASA safety office and a shuttle safety advisory panel, in order to prevent such a "flawed" decision to launch from being made again.

Aside from these internal fixes at NASA, however, the Rogers commission addressed a more fundamental problem. In NASA's effort to streamline shuttle operations in pursuit of its declared goal of flying 24 missions a year, the commission said, the agency had simply been pushing too hard. The shuttle program had neither the personnel nor the spare parts to maintain such an ambitious flight rate without straining its physical resources or overworking its technicians.

This judgment cut to the core of the way in which the national space program had been conducted in the shuttle era. Indeed, the *Challenger* accident merely focused attention on more deeply seated problems that had existed for as long as 15 years. When a succession of unmanned rocket explosions in April and May—a Titan 34D carrying a spy satellite, a Delta with a weather satellite aboard, and a European Ariane carrying a communications satellite—plunged Western space planning into further chaos, it merely seemed to strengthen a consensus that already was building; the unraveling space program required drastic rethinking.

From the time it was approved by Pres. Richard M. Nixon in 1972, the shuttle had been conceived as a "do-everything" vehicle for carrying every kind of space payload, from commercial and scientific satellites to military spacecraft to probes bound for the outer planets. NASA's fleet of conventional "expendable" rockets such as the Delta and Atlas had been phased out in the shuttle era as a result and were being used primarily to reach the polar orbits that the shuttle would be unable to achieve until its West Coast launch pad became available in mid-1986.

Although this reliance on the shuttle was the officially stated national space policy, the Defense Department had already begun to retreat from placing all its orbital eggs in one basket even before the *Challenger* accident. Concerned that shuttle launch delays would jeopardize the assured access to space of high-priority national security satellites, the Air Force in 1985 had begun a program of buying advanced Titan rockets as "complementary expendable launch vehicles" for its own use beginning in the late 1980s.

After the *Challenger* accident other, less powerful groups came forward to express their long-standing unhappiness with exclusive reliance on the shuttle for their access to space. Among those calling for a "mixed fleet" of shuttles and expendable launchers were scientists whose missions now faced long delays because the shuttle had become the only existing means of carrying their spacecraft. "The space shuttle can be used effectively to support some kinds of science," said Thomas Donahue, chairman of the Space Science Board of the National Academy of Sciences, "but much of space science involves . . . putting free flyer [spacecraft] into orbit or launching interplanetary probes. That's best done by the traditional method of expendable launch vehicles."

By July, when NASA announced that the shuttle would not be ready to fly again until early 1988, there still was no decision from Congress or the White House as to whether another orbiter would be built to replace *Challenger.* Proponents argued that another vehicle—perhaps two more—would be needed to meet the launch needs of the 1990s, which would include construction of NASA's international space station, a permanent facility in Earth orbit.

New Orbiter, Limited Business. In mid-August Pres. Ronald Reagan announced his decision—construction of a replacement shuttle orbiter would begin immediately. When the shuttle resumed service, however, it would no longer be in the business of launching satellites for paying

Tony Reichhardt is editor of the monthly feature magazine Space World *and a frequent writer on space issues.*

customers but would be devoted almost exclusively to defense and scientific payloads. The Reagan administration had long had the goal of stimulating a private space launch industry, and now, with the removal of a heavily subsidized competitor from the market, three different companies stepped forward within a week's time to announce plans for operating commercial versions of the Delta, Titan, and Atlas/Centaur launchers. Other private firms with new vehicles on the drawing board at last sensed a window of opportunity and put fresh effort into their designs.

Still, this inauguration of a new commercial era in U.S. space transportation came more with a whimper than with a bang. Proponents of the shuttle feared that it would lose its economic viability if it were forbidden to earn revenue from paying customers. As for the new, private launch businesses, they were sure to face significant competition from Europe's Ariane rocket, which recovered from its own 1986 launch failure to find itself on top of the world satellite market. And two new players, Japan and China, promised that even more low-cost, government-subsidized competitors would be on the scene sometime in the 1990s.

Whither NASA? With a string of launch accidents behind it and a two-year downtime for the shuttle ahead, the U.S. found itself in a sobering position toward the end of its first 25 years in space. Several conspicuous Soviet achievements—a spectacular dual mission to Venus and Halley's Comet, launch of the permanent Mir space station into Earth orbit, and announced plans for robot expeditions to Mars and Venus—led to much soul-searching about the United States' having surrendered the lead on the space frontier.

Perhaps the most important question currently facing the U.S. space program is also the most fundamental: What are its goals? Lost in the glare of publicity following the shuttle accident was the report of another presidential commission headed by Thomas Paine, a former NASA administrator, whose National Commission on Space had been asked in 1985 to recommend goals for the U.S. space program that would carry it boldly into the 21st century.

Based on a year of research and interviews with scientists and engineers, as well as with politicians and ordinary citizens, the Paine commission outlined a methodical plan for development of the solar system that would lead from a space station in Earth orbit in the 1990s to a lunar base in the first years of the next century and a permanently occupied outpost on Mars by 2035. Those ambitious goals are achievable, said the commission, if the nation commits itself to a sustained level of expenditure, fixed at approximately 1% of a continually rising gross domestic product.

Critics and proponents of the U.S. space program alike have argued that NASA functions best when it has a specific, ambitious goal, such as sending astronauts to the Moon. In the era of the space shuttle, which is a technology rather than a purpose, that goal has been largely missing.

The establishment of a permanent space station in Earth orbit is NASA's next major program, with construction scheduled to begin in 1993. Whether that project is challenging enough to reestablish U.S. predominance in space is a question that remained unanswered at the end of 1986. Meanwhile, the U.S. space program could look ahead to at least one more year of self-examination and restructuring before the beginning of a new, different shuttle era in 1988.

(continued from page 342)

Spot-1 Earth resources mapping satellite was launched on February 22 atop an Ariane 1 and became operational on May 6. It carried visible and infrared sensors capable of much finer resolution than the comparable U.S. Landsats.

Soviet Space Stations. On February 19 the Soviet Union launched its newest space station, Mir (Peace). It was not the long-awaited Cosmograd station, reportedly capable of supporting a crew of 12, but was a major improvement on the Salyut series. Tass described Mir as "a base unit for building in the future a permanently operated manned orbital complex with specialized modules to tackle scientific and national economic questions." Mir sported four additional docking ports in a ring around its nose port for laboratory modules supporting work in life sciences and astrophysics. The nose port was to be used for crews and the base port for supply craft. The only crew to board the station in 1986 comprised Vladimir Solovyov and Leonid Kizim, launched on March 13 aboard Soyuz T-15. On May 5 they flew their Soyuz T-15 from Mir to Salyut 7, and they boarded it on May 6 for almost two months of operations in the first station-to-station transfer ever accomplished. On May 28 and May 31 Solovyov and Kizim staged two spacewalks, during which they deployed a 15-m (50-ft) metal lattice tower in a demonstration of space construction techniques.

While the cosmonauts were away from Mir, the new Soyuz-TM spacecraft was launched, unmanned, on May 21 to dock with Mir two days later. It was later brought back to the Earth, unmanned. Solovyov and Kizim returned to Mir on June 25 for continued operations there and returned to Earth in their Soyuz T-15 on July 16 after 125 days in orbit.

The Soviets also began approach and landing tests with their own space shuttle, launched from the back of a modified Bison Myasishchev Mya-4 bomber. Unlike the U.S. shuttle the Soviet craft was equipped with jet engines for extended landing capabilities. It was designed to carry a 30,000-kg (66,000-lb) payload. A new unmanned cargo pod capable of orbiting 100,000 kg (220,000 lb), to be used

JET PROPULSION LABORATORY

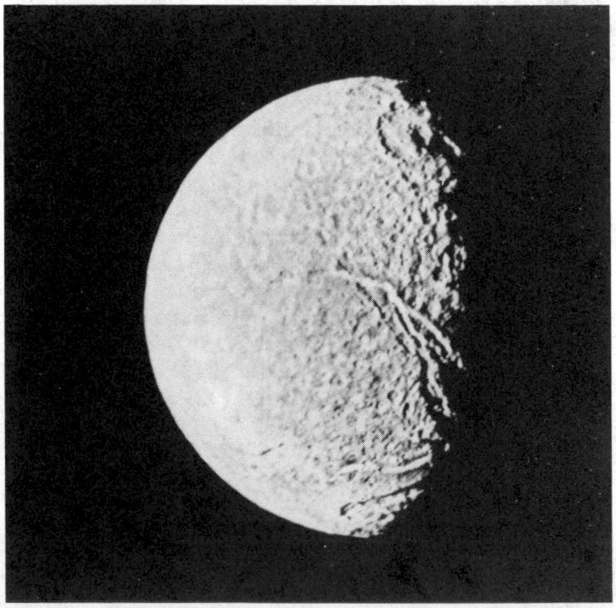

An image of Titania, one of ten newly discovered moons of Uranus, was captured in great detail by cameras aboard Voyager 2 and relayed to Earth as the spacecraft, launched in 1977, made its closest approach to the distant planet on January 24.

A mock-up of the latest manned Soviet space station, Mir, is assembled by technicians at a cosmonaut training complex. Reporters were allowed to view the completed structure in April.
SOVFOTO/EASTFOTO

in conjunction with the shuttle, also was reported to be under development. Both were expected to debut between 1987 and 1989.

Planetary Encounters. The only bright spot in space for the U.S. during the year was the flyby of Uranus by Voyager 2 just four days before the *Challenger* accident. Voyager 2 was launched Aug. 20, 1977, on a mission to fly past Jupiter and Saturn. The spacecraft's continued good health after the latter encounter in August 1981 led flight controllers to retarget it for Uranus. That planet, which rotates with its north pole inclined 7.9° below the plane of its orbit, was the first to be discovered by the telescope.

Several oddities emerged as the probe flew within 81,593 km (50,679 mi) of the planet's atmosphere. There was a puzzling absence of radio noise until shortly before closest approach, apparently because the magnetic pole is offset 55° from the geographic pole. The planet's period was refined to about 17.2 hours. It was also found to have a strong ultraviolet electroglow on the day side (stronger than those found on Jupiter and Saturn) and an ultraviolet aurora on the night side.

The planet itself remained largely featureless without intense image enhancement, which revealed methane clouds in the upper atmosphere and haze in the polar atmosphere. Its rings were found to be more sharply defined and delicate than expected. During the brief flyby Voyager 2 discovered ten satellites to add to the five already known. Voyager remained in good shape as it hurtled away from the planet and on to a flyby of Neptune in 1989.

Centre stage in 1986, of course, went to Halley's Comet. For the public it was a visual dud, as astronomers had warned, falling far short of the dazzling 1910 apparition. For the scientists, however, it yielded a bumper crop of data as they took their first close look at what were believed to be the icy leftovers from the birth of the solar system. Astronomer Fred Whipple had originated the theory that comets are "dirty snowballs." An international flotilla of probes showed the comet to be dirtier than he imagined.

Five probes were launched during 1984–85 to make ballistic intercepts of the comet. The U.S.S.R. launched two Vega spacecraft, which swung past Venus first to drop off atmospheric probes that drifted on balloons. The European Space Agency launched the Giotto, named for a 14th-century painter who depicted the comet as the Star of Bethlehem, and Japan launched the Suisei and Sakigake probes.

Vegas 1 and 2 flew past the comet on March 4 and 9, respectively, as close as 8,029 km (4,987 mi) to its nucleus, and provided final targeting data for Giotto. They also suffered severe dust erosion of solar arrays. Japan's Suisei followed at 151,000 km (94,000 mi) on March 8, while Sakigake provided images from 7.1 million km (4.4 million mi). The closest and most hazardous approach was made by Giotto, which was targeted to fly through the comet's tail and behind the nucleus in order to obtain images with the highest possible resolution. Those pictures, taken 595 km (370 mi) from the nucleus, showed the nucleus to be a velvet-black lump, approximately 15 x 10 km (9.4 x 6.2 mi) in size, spewing jets of water vapour and dust. As it flew through the tail, the spacecraft was showered by as many as 100 dust particles the size of sand grains each second, and it finally went silent after sending back more than 2,000 images. Surprisingly, Giotto resumed contact with the Earth 34 minutes later and reported that everything but the camera was working. If it could be revived, the probe might be retargeted for a 1992 flyby of Comet Grigg-Skjellerup. (*See* ASTRONOMY: *Special Report.*)

"Star Wars" Test. A major test of the U.S. Strategic Defense Initiative, nicknamed "Star Wars," was carried out on September 5 with the launch of a missile track-and-intercept experiment atop a Delta launcher. The vehicle's second stage carried a Maverick air-to-ground missile infrared imaging system, and the third stage carried a Phoenix missile air-to-air radar tracker. The two stages flew an orbital ballet as they observed each other's rocket plumes against the Earth, space, and Sun. The test ended after 2 hours and 45 minutes when the third stage intercepted an Aries sounding rocket launched from the White Sands Test Facility in New Mexico. (DAVE DOOLING)

See also Astronomy; Earth Sciences; Industrial Review: *Aerospace; Telecommunications;* Military Affairs; Television and Radio.

This article updates the *Macropædia* article EXPLORATION: *Space Exploration.*

Sports and Games

AERIAL SPORTS

In what pilot Dick Rutan called "the last 'first' in aviation," the twin-engined *Voyager* aircraft, made mostly of carbon-fibre cloth, paper, and epoxy, completed in 1986 an unprecedented nine-day, 40,269-km (25,012-mi), storm-tossed flight to become the first aircraft to fly around the Earth on a single load of fuel. It eclipsed unrefueled distance records of 18,253 km (11,337 mi) and 20,177 km (12,532 mi) set by U.S. Air Force B-52 pilots in 1962.

The *Voyager*'s journey, which began December 14 at Edwards Air Force Base in California, ended at the same place on December 23 after a global circumnavigation that took the aircraft over the Pacific Ocean, Southeast Asia, the Indian Ocean, central Africa, the mid-Atlantic, Central America, and back up the coast of California to Edwards. Throughout the epochal flight, monitored by chase planes, radar, radio, and meteorological equipment, pilot Rutan, 48, and copilot Jeana Yeager, 34, were confined in a cockpit measuring 1.6 m (5.6 ft) long and no more than 1 m (3.3 ft) wide. The elongated *Voyager* had a wingspan of 33.6 m (110.8 ft), longer than that of a Boeing 727, and its 17 fuel tanks carried 454 dekalitres (1,200 gal) of fuel, of which only about 3.8 dekalitres (10 gal) were left when it landed. It lost portions of its wingtips on takeoff.

Throughout much of the journey *Voyager* encountered extreme turbulence while running into storms over the Pacific, Africa, and the Atlantic, and Yeager suffered severe bruises. Rutan, a veteran of 325 combat missions in the Vietnam war, was unable to keep the aircraft from twice being knocked into steep, dangerous banks. Weighing just 844 kg (1,858 lb) without fuel, the *Voyager* reached a maximum altitude of approximately 5,450 m (18,000 ft) while climbing over a mountain range in East Africa. Its average speed was 186.4 km/h (115.8 mph), and it completed its last leg up the California coast at 108 km/h (67 mph).

Perhaps the flight of the *Voyager* was the "last first" for piston and powered aircraft, but the world of aerial sports still awaited the first around-the-world balloon flight, with at least one attempt scheduled for 1987. In September 1986 Dutch balloonists Evelien Brink, her husband, Henk Brink, and Willem Hageman set a new record for transatlantic balloon flight, flying from St. John's, Newfoundland, to Almere, Neth., in 51 hr 14 min.

In sport ballooning Coy Foster of the U.S. set four world's records in three flights over Texas. He achieved a world altitude mark for Class AX-3 hot-air balloons of 6,165 m (20,227 ft), flying from Plano to Jackass Flats in a Colt 21A on February 15, and a world altitude record for Class AX-4 balloons of 8,993.9 m (29,508.8 ft), flying from Plano to Brashear in a Colt 31A on February 23. Foster set distance and duration world records for Class AX-4 hot-air balloons with an 8 hr 1 min, 208.6-km (130.4-mi) flight from Plano to Bellfalls in a Colt AX4 on March 20. In another Texas flight on March 1 from Longview to Westlake, William E. Bussey of the U.S. set a world distance mark of 287 km (179.5 mi) for Class AX-5 hot-air balloons in a Firefly AX5. Joseph Starkbaum of Austria achieved a world record for altitude in a Class AX-6 balloon with a flight reaching 10,670 m (35,008 ft) over Tauplitz, Austria, June 10.

U.S. Army Sgt. Terry Vares was the star of the World Parachute Style and Accuracy Championships at Ankara, Turkey, September 1–14, taking two firsts and a third place. She won the women's combination contest with a score of 4, followed by Heike Glaw of East Germany with 12 and Cheryl Stearns of the U.S. with 13. The men's combination was won by Josef Pavlata of Czechoslovakia with 4, followed by Vyacheslav Zalyunas of the U.S.S.R. with 7 and Franck Bernachot of France with 8. Vares was first in women's individual style with 28.27, while Ronald Eilenstein of East Germany won men's individual style with 28.04. Stearns was first in women's individual accu-

LEO VOGELZANG—SYGMA

The *Dutch Viking* floats serenely in its flight from Newfoundland to The Netherlands. The three crew members were the first Europeans to make the Atlantic crossing via balloon, and the passage time of 51 hours 14 minutes set a new record for the feat.

racy with a mark of 0.05 cm from the target disk. In men's individual accuracy, Zalyunas won with 0.03 cm.

At the World Parachute Championships for Canopy Relative Work at Gatton, Australia, October 1–12, France finished first in the four-way sequential event with 77 points. The U.S. was second with 59 points, and Australia was third with 58. China was the winner in the four-way rotation with 148 points; the U.S. was second with 147 and The Netherlands third with 140. France also won the eight-way speed stacks with a time of 391.14 sec. Great Britain was second with 411.04 sec, and Australia placed third with 413.87 sec. The overall men's team performance event was won by the U.S.S.R. with a score of 5. France followed with 7, and Czechoslovakia was third with 14. In the women's overall competition the U.S.S.R. also finished first with a score of 5. East Germany came in second with 7, and Czechoslovakia was again third, with 11.

A new record for largest free-fall parachute formation was set July 5 by 100 U.S. jumpers over Muskogee, Okla. At the same location on June 26 four U.S. competitors set a record for four-canopy rotation by completing 20 formations in 180 sec. A women's world record for largest free-fall formation was set by 60 U.S. women over Deland, Fla., on March 24. On January 6 eight Australians set a record of 45.13 sec for eight-way speed formation.

In gliding a world's absolute record for altitude gained in a single-place glider was achieved February 17 by Robert Harris of the U.S., who attained 14,938 m (49,009 ft) in a Burkhart Grob G-102. Otto Wegscheider of West Germany flew an ASW 22M for 1,028.6 km (639.2 mi) at Kenilworth, South Africa, January 6 to set a world record for distance around a triangular course in a motor glider. Two other West Germans, Walter Binder and Martin Heide, attained 135.5 km/h (84.21 mph) at Fuentemilanos, Spain, on July 13 to set a multiplace motor glider record for speed over a 100-km (60-mi) course.

The Fédération Aéronautique Internationale (FAI) certified the Dec. 8, 1985, women's world record set by Inge Muller of West Germany, who flew her Ventus 138.7 km/h (86.2 mph) at Bitterwasser, South Africa, over a 300-km (180-mi) course. Also confirmed was the multiplace women's glider record of 123.3 km/h (76.6 mph) over a 300-km (180-mi) triangular course set Dec. 7, 1985, by Inge Muller and Christine Muller, flying a Janus at Bitterwasser.

In hang gliding the FAI confirmed the Dec. 29, 1985, world mark for distance over a triangular course set by Denis Cummings of Australia with a flight of 80.8 km (50.23 mi) in a Magic III launched from Parkes, New South Wales. In February Cummings launched from Parkes in a Magic III and set a world record of 15.6 km/h (9.7 mph) for speed around a 25-km (15-mi) triangular course. In the new field of man-powered aircraft, the FAI confirmed the Oct. 2, 1985, world speed record of 44.3 km/h (27.5 mph) over a closed circuit set by Holger Rochelt of West Germany in a Musculair II at Oberschleissheim Airport.

(MICHAEL D. KILIAN)

ARCHERY

International archery introduced in 1986 a new system of competition and a new scoring method designed to assure excitement until the final shots. Officials hoped that the changes would make the sport more attractive for the public and the media. The sport is governed by the Fédération Internationale de Tir à l'Arc (FITA), which in 1986 had 70 member nations. In the past major competition consisted of two so-called FITA rounds. In each round an archer took 36 shots at each of four distances, a total of 144 shots for each round.

The new format, known as the Grand FITA Round, is a four-day competition. The rules are the same for men and women except, as in the past, the men shoot from 30, 50, 70, and 90 m and the women from 30, 50, 60, and 70 m. In the Grand FITA Round each archer shoots 72 arrows the first day and 72 the second. Then eliminations begin, with the previous scores thrown out after every session. On the third morning the 24 leaders shoot 36 arrows each. That afternoon the 18 leaders shoot 36 arrows each. On the fourth morning the field is reduced to 12 for 36 more shots. On the fourth afternoon the six leaders shoot the final 36 arrows, and that performance decides the winner of the competition.

The Grand FITA Round, used only for target competition, was introduced in a two-day experiment on March 15–16 in Caserta, Italy. It was scheduled for use in the 1987 world championships and the 1988 Olympic Games.

A traditional scoring system was employed for the world field championships August 25–30 in Radstadt, Austria. This type of competition, more popular in Europe than in the U.S., was held over rugged terrain in fog, rain, mud, and treacherous footing. The champions were Goran Bjerendel of Sweden in men's freestyle (using bowsight or bowmark, but not both), Carita Jussila of Finland in women's freestyle, Mats Palmer of Sweden in men's barebow (no visual aids, bowsights, or bowmarks), and Annie Dardenne of France in women's barebow.

Richard McKinney of Gilbert, Ariz., placed fourth in men's freestyle in the world field championships. He won the U.S. field championship June 14–15 in Staunton, Va., and his eighth U.S. target championship August 5–8 in Oxford, Ohio. The U.S. women's champions were Debra Ochs of Howell, Mich., in target and Kitty Frazier of Cross Lanes, W.Va., in field. (FRANK LITSKY)

AUTOMOBILE RACING

Grand Prix Racing. In international Formula One automobile racing in 1986, the drivers' world championship was in doubt until the final contest in Australia, with Nigel Mansell (Great Britain) leading until then over Alain Prost (France) and Nelson Piquet (Brazil). In that race Mansell experienced a tire blowout while his Williams-Honda FW11 was traveling at some 320 km/h (1 km = 0.62 mi). He managed to avoid disaster, but his chance to win the championship was gone. Prost took the title for the second year in a row, driving for the McLaren team and using a Porsche TAG V6-cylinder engine. During the 1986 season Renault withdrew from competition, and the Italian Ferrari team had a poor year. The Williams-Honda team won the constructors' world championship.

The season opened well for Williams when Piquet won the Brazilian Grand Prix in the brand-new Honda V6-engined FW11 at 184.980 km/h, setting a record lap speed of 193.612 km/h for the Rio de Janeiro autodrome circuit. Second place went to Ayrton Senna of Brazil in a Lotus-Renault 98T and third to Jacques Laffite of France in a Ligier. The scene then moved to Jerez, Spain, where Senna won for Lotus-Renault at 167.486 km/h, followed by Mansell's Williams-Honda FW11, which had made the fastest lap at 174.186 km/h, a new record. Prost was third. Prost then won the San Marino Grand Prix in a McLaren-Porsche MP4/2C at 196.208 km/h after setting a new lap record of 204.631 km/h; Piquet was second and Gerhard Berger (Austria) third in a BMW-powered Benetton. Prost won again at Monaco at 134.634 km/h; he also established a new record of 86.607 sec for the altered circuit. Keke Rosberg of Finland, also driving a McLaren-Porsche MP4/2C, finished second, and Senna's Lotus-Renault was third.

Before the Belgian Grand Prix at Spa in May, the only Formula One fatality of the season befell Elio De Angelis (Italy) while he was testing tires at the Paul Ricard circuit. The race was won by Mansell at 203.548 km/h, with Senna's Lotus second and Stefan Johansson of Sweden third in a Ferrari F1/86. Prost lapped at a record speed of 209.453 km/h to finish sixth.

Racing then moved to North America. In the Canadian Grand Prix at Montreal, Mansell was victorious, winning at 178.225 km/h from Prost and Piquet. Because only a limited quantity of fuel is permitted at the start of a race, drivers must watch fuel gauges and drive accordingly, a misjudgment sometimes resulting in a well-placed car failing to complete the distance. Indeed, in this race Piquet had to conserve his fuel after making a record lap at 185.808 km/h. In the U.S. Grand Prix at Detroit, over an artificial downtown course, Senna finished first, followed by Laffite and Prost, the winning Lotus-Renault averaging 136.747 km/h. Piquet had the fastest lap at 143.076 km/h but crashed one lap later.

The French Grand Prix followed in July, with Mansell's Williams-Honda winning at 118.059 km/h from Prost and Piquet; Mansell also set a new short-course lap record of 196.117 km/h. Mansell then went on to win the British Grand Prix at Brands Hatch, beating Piquet and Prost, at 208.846 km/h. In the German Grand Prix at Hockenheim, Piquet won at 229.534 km/h, followed by Senna and Mansell, with Berger setting a surprise record lap in the Benetton-BMW at 218.46 km/h. The Hungarian Grand Prix at Budapest was won by Piquet at 151.805 km/h, with Senna second and Mansell third. Near the end of the race Piquet drove the fastest lap for the new Hungaroring circuit at 158.794 km/h.

Prost's McLaren returned to winning form in Austria, averaging 227.821 km/h at the Österreichring, followed by the two Ferraris. Berger again drove the quickest lap, at 232.157 km/h. The Williams-Honda cars placed first and second in the Italian Grand Prix at Monza, Piquet (228.373 km/h) leading Mansell home. Teo Fabi (Italy) set a record lap at 237.006 km/h in a Benetton-BMW. At the Portuguese Grand Prix Mansell won again, averaging 187.644 km/h at the Estoril Autodrome, with Prost's McLaren second and Piquet's Williams third.

In Mexico Berger won a well-deserved victory in his Benetton-BMW with an average speed of 162.79 km/h, followed by Prost, Senna, and Piquet. In the Australian Grand Prix at Adelaide, after Mansell's tire burst, Prost drove home to his second world driver's championship, averaging 162.60 km/h, with Piquet second and Johansson third. Piquet set a new lap record at 168.469 km/h. The Dutch Grand Prix did not take place in 1986.

AP/WIDE WORLD

Indianapolis 500 winner Bobby Rahal waves as he rides a victory lap after snatching first place in the closest three-car finish in Indy history. His car, a March-Cosworth 86C, was powered by an engine built in England.

Rallies and Other Races. The Rothmans team of Type 956 Porsches gained for Derek Bell of Great Britain his second successive world sports car drivers' championship; Jaguar just failed by one point to give Derek Warwick a place in the championship. Bell and Hans-Joachim Stuck (West Germany) won the Le Mans 24-hour race in France in a Rothmans 926C Porsche at 207.19 km/h. The Spa 24-hour race went to a Brun 2.8 Porsche, driven by Oscar Larrauri and Jesús Pareja, at 147.33 km/h; the Daytona (Fla.) 24-hour to a Porsche at 169.75 km/h; and the Tourist Trophy race at Silverstone in England to Jeff Allam and Denny Hulme in a Rover Vitesse saloon.

The Monte Carlo Rally was won by a Lancia Delta S4, while a Peugeot 205 T16 scored in the Swedish Rally, and a Renault 5 Turbo won the Portuguese event. Two Toyota Celica Turbos led a Peugeot home in the Safari Rally in Africa. In Corsica Henri Toivonen and Sergio Cresto were killed when their Lancia crashed and caught fire. Lancia withdrew, and the Tour de Corsica was won by Peugeot. In New Zealand two Lancias led a Peugeot home, and in Sweden Peugeot reversed the position in the Thousand Lakes Rally, clinching for Peugeot the world rally championship. Juho Kankkunen of Finland won the rally drivers' championship after he successfully appealed against disqualification from the San Remo rally.

(WILLIAM C. BODDY)

U.S. Racing. It was Bobby Rahal's year in U.S. racing with victories in the 70th Indianapolis 500 and a CART (Championship Auto Racing Teams) season title. He won $581,062 for his Indy heroics, driving his Budweiser/Truesports March-Cosworth to a 1.44-sec victory over Kevin Cogan and setting a record average speed of 170.722 mph (1 mi = 1.61 km). His final lap speed of 209.152 mph was another of 19 new speed marks in a race delayed almost a week by bad weather.

Drivers other than Rahal and Cogan provided the excitement during the race. Polesitter Rick Mears, a former winner, eventually finished third, but that was because he needed a late pit stop for fuel. And, at the beginning of the race, Michael Andretti moved to a commanding lead only to lose it on an unexpected pit stop. He eventually finished sixth.

The CART season was the richest and most successful ever held despite the fact that the United States Auto Club (USAC) continued to sponsor the Indianapolis 500. Throughout the season the main feature was a Rahal versus Michael Andretti duel.

The National Association for Stock Car Auto Racing (NASCAR) also enjoyed its greatest Winston Cup season as the cars gained equal billing with the drivers. If Ford's Talledega shape had been dominant in 1985, Chevrolet assumed primacy in 1986. Dale Earnhardt in a Chevrolet won the Winston Cup championship and one of stock car racing's classics, the Coca-Cola 600 at Charlotte, N.C. This was a prototypical Chevrolet versus Ford confrontation, with Bill Elliott, the 1985 Eljer Driver of the Year, in a Thunderbird finally running out of fuel 16 laps from the finish to drop to third place. Tim Richmond in a Chevrolet inherited second.

Geoff Bodine in a Chevrolet won the year's top stock car race, the Daytona 500, when Earnhardt exhausted his fuel three laps from the finish. Second was Terry Labonte in an Oldsmobile. As in other races to follow, it was the younger drivers pushing to the fore as the racing standbys,

Richard Petty, Cale Yarborough, and Bobby Allison, visited the victory circle less and less.

Road racing flourished in the U.S. The International Motor Sports Association (IMSA) began its best year ever with the 24 hours of Daytona; this again was a parade of Porsche 962s. Al Holbert, the eventual Camel GT (Grand Touring) prototype season champion and Porsche U.S. racing manager, won with the help of the Englishman Bell and Al Unser, Jr. The Holbert car set a record pace of 105.484 mph in traveling a record 2,534.72 mi. Winner of the Sebring 12-hour race was another Porsche 962, driven by Bob Akin, Sr., Hans Stuck, and Jo Gartner.

Mazda RX-7 won an unprecedented seventh straight GTUnder 2.8-litre manufacturers championship and with 81 victories became the most successful car in IMSA history. Tom Kendall, a student at UCLA, bested pro Roger Mandeville, also in an RX-7, for the drivers' championship. Kendall also won the Firestone Firehawk Grand Sport championship, driving a Nissan 300ZX with Max Jones. In the Kelly Challenge series Irv Hoerr and his Oldsmobile Toronado dominated the Buicks, Chevrolets, and Pontiacs. The Sports Car Club of America (SCCA) crowned a Chevrolet Camaro as its Trans-Am champion, and Wally Dallenbach, Jr., won the drivers' title. This series shared some cars with the IMSA Kelly series. In SCCA's pro rally division Audi Quattro's John Buffum easily defended his season crown. (ROBERT J. FENDELL)

BADMINTON

China rose to the top of the badminton world in 1986 by winning both the Thomas Cup for men and the Uber Cup for women. These two international team tournaments, held in Jakarta, Indon., from April 22 through May 4, were the main events of 1986.

In the semifinals of the Uber Cup, China defeated Korea 4–1, and Indonesia beat Japan 5–0. In the finals China won all three of the singles matches as Li Lingwei beat Ivana Lie 12–11, 11–3; Han Aiping defeated Elizabeth Latief 11–1, 11–3; and Wu Jianqiu beat Verawaty Fajrin (Indon.) 12–9, 11–7. Indonesia won both doubles matches with Imelda Kurtniawan and Rosiana Tendean beating Han Aiping and Li Lingwei 15–11, 15–12 and Verawaty Fajrin and Yanti Kusmiatie defeating Lin Ying and Wu Dixi 15–10, 15–13. China thus won the cup by 3–2.

In the semifinals of the Thomas Cup, China was pitted against Denmark, and Indonesia played Malaysia. Morten Frost of Denmark gave his country its only win in the semifinals by defeating Han Jian 15–8, 15–3. Malaysia also could garner only one victory in its semifinal match as Razif Sidek and Jalani Sidek triumphed over Liem Swie King and Bobby Ertanto in doubles 5–15, 15–6, 15–14.

The final five matches between China and Indonesia generated considerable excitement. At the end of the three singles matches, China led 2–1. Indonesia, however, was considered very strong in doubles play, the remaining two matches to be contested for the cup. Indonesia won the fourth match, tying the score at 2–2, and then called on a very tired Liem Swie King to partner Bobby Ertanto in the final match. However, the Indonesian could not rise to the occasion, and China won the final match and the cup. The scores of the matches between China and Indonesia were: Yang Yang (China) beat Icuk Sugiarto 15–7, 15–1; Lius Pongoh (Indon.) beat Ding Qiqing 15–12, 11–15, 15–1; Xiong Guobao (China) defeated Liem Swie King 15–13, 15–13; Christian Hadinata/Hadibowo (Indon.) beat Zhang Qiang/Zhou Jincan 15–13, 15–8; and Tian Bingyi/Li Yongbo (China) defeated Liem Swie King/Bobby Ertanto 15–12, 15–9. (C. R. ELI)

BASEBALL

Despite the lack of closely contested divisional races in the final weeks of the regular season, major league baseball witnessed a first in 1986—all 26 franchises attracted more than one million spectators. The 12 National League teams totaled 22,328,187 in paid attendance, for an average per game of 23,578. The American League's 14 teams averaged 22,697 on an aggregate of 25,171,447.

World Series. In the 25th year of their existence, the New York Mets achieved their second World Series title in rare fashion. After losing the opening two contests of the best-of-seven format at home, the Mets surged to defeat the Boston Red Sox four games to three. The Mets were only the second team in 83 World Series to rebound after going into an opponent's park down 0–2. Oddly enough, it had been in 1985 that a team accomplished this dramatic turnabout for the first time—the Kansas City Royals, who overcame the St. Louis Cardinals, winning also by four victories to three.

The Red Sox, decided underdogs, triumphed 1–0 in the World Series opener at Shea Stadium, New York City, on October 18. Bruce Hurst, a crafty left-hander, restricted the Mets to four hits through eight innings, striking out eight batters. Calvin Schiraldi, a former Met, pitched the ninth inning to secure the victory.

In the second game, at Shea Stadium on October 19, the Red Sox amassed 18 hits to wallop the Mets 9–3. Boston received three hits from each of three different batters in their lineup and knocked out New York's imposing young right-hander, Dwight Gooden, after five innings. Steve Crawford was credited with the Boston victory.

The World Series shifted to Fenway Park in Boston on October 21, and the Mets took an immediate liking to the new environs. Centre fielder Len Dykstra led off the game with a home run against Dennis ("Oil Can") Boyd, and before the first inning had ended, the Mets enjoyed a 4–0 advantage. Bob Ojeda, a left-hander whom the Red Sox had traded to New York during the off-season, conquered his former teammates 7–1 with a solid seven-inning effort. Roger McDowell contributed two innings of perfect relief. Gary Carter batted in three runs for the visiting Mets.

In game four, at Boston on October 22, Carter ripped two home runs and Dykstra another to power the Mets to a 6–2 victory behind Ron Darling, evening the series at two victories each. The losing pitcher for Boston was Al Nipper.

In the fifth game, however, the Red Sox finally won at home, 4–2. In the bottom of the second inning, when Spike Owen's sacrifice fly brought home Dave Henderson from third base for a 1–0 Boston margin, it marked the first time in the 1986 World Series that the home team had managed a lead in any game. Hurst worked the complete game for his second triumph; Gooden was the loser.

In the sixth game, at Shea Stadium on October 25, the Red Sox were on the verge of winning their first World Series title since 1918. But they failed, losing 6–5 in ten innings, and the series was deadlocked at three victories each. For the game the Red Sox entrusted the vital pitching assignment to their best regular-season starter, Roger Clemens (*see* BIOGRAPHIES), who was well-rested. The right-handed ace yielded no hits through four innings and had a 2–0 lead on runs batted in by Dwight Evans and Marty Barrett. The Mets tied the game 2–2 in the fifth, only to fall behind again 3–2 in the seventh when the Red Sox tallied off McDowell with the aid of a throwing error by New York third baseman Ray Knight. The Mets, however, again drew even at 3–3 in the eighth on Carter's

Boston Red Sox catcher Rich Gedman (left) walks away as victorious New York Mets Ray Knight, Howard Johnson, and Gary Carter share an outburst of joy following the sixth game of the World Series on October 25. Celebrating fans—an estimated 2.2 million—jammed New York City streets on October 28 as the world champion Mets paraded to City Hall after beating Boston in the final game.

(LEFT) AP/WIDE WORLD; (RIGHT) FOCUS ON SPORTS

bases-loaded sacrifice fly off Schiraldi. The 1986 World Series, deemed by some to be wanting in great theatre, then graduated to just that.

Henderson, leading off the tenth inning, clouted a home run for Boston off Rick Aguilera. Then Wade Boggs doubled and Barrett singled him in to give the Red Sox a 5–3 margin. In the Mets' tenth, Wally Backman flied out, as did Keith Hernández. The Red Sox were one out away from the world championship. Then Carter singled, followed by a single from pinch-hitter Kevin Mitchell. Knight, the next batter, went to an 0-2 count. Now the Red Sox were merely one strike away. But Knight looped a clutch single to centre, scoring Carter from second. Bob Stanley replaced Schiraldi as Boston's pitcher and promptly unleashed a wild pitch with Mookie Wilson at bat, thus allowing Mitchell to trot home with the tying run from third base. On a 3–2 delivery Wilson then slapped a ball to the right side of the infield, where first baseman Bill Buckner let the grounder slip through his legs for a crucial error. Knight scored from second, and New York won.

In the climactic seventh game Boston again called on Hurst, who had already beaten the Mets twice. He was strong for a time and through five innings was in command with a 3–0 lead. Homers by Evans and Rich Gedman and a run-batted-in (RBI) single by Boggs in the second inning produced that cushion. However, the resilient Mets would not be denied.

Keyed by Hernández's one-out bases-loaded single for two runs, the Mets staged a three-run rally in the sixth. Then the New Yorkers erupted for three more runs in the seventh, which Knight ignited by clubbing a tie-breaking homer. Mets reliefers Sid Fernández, McDowell, and Jesse Orosco held off the Red Sox, and the Mets won the clinching game, 8–5. Knight was voted most valuable player in the World Series.

Championship Series. The Mets and Red Sox qualified for the World Series only after enduring tense best-of-seven league play-off series. The Mets were defeated 1–0 in the opener of the National League Championship Series by the Houston Astros, whose brilliant right-hander Mike Scott struck out 14 New York batters. New York won the second game by 5–1 and the third by 6–5 on Dykstra's clutch two-run homer in the ninth inning. Scott beat the Mets again 3–1 in game four, but the Mets won the fifth contest in 12 innings, 2–1. Then, in the sixth game at Houston, the Mets scored three runs in the 9th to tie, one run in the 14th, and three more in the top of the 16th—just enough to outlast the Astros 7–6 for their third National League pennant, four games to two.

The Red Sox' route was no less hectic. Clemens was routed 8–1 by the California Angels in the opener of the American League play-offs. Boston won 9–2 to tie the series, but the Red Sox then lost two in a row, by scores of 5–3 and 4–3, the latter after the Angels collected three runs in the bottom of the 9th, all charged to Clemens, and the winning run in the 11th.

In the fifth game, another of the 1986 postseason contests that would not soon be forgotten, the Angels were leading 5–2 entering the ninth inning and were on the brink of their first pennant. But Don Baylor and Henderson each hit two-run homers to give the Red Sox a 6–5 lead. The Angels tied the game in their half of the 9th inning, but the Red Sox won in the 11th by 7–6 on a sacrifice fly from Henderson. The rejuvenated Red Sox then returned to Boston for 10–4 and 8–1 conquests, winning their first pennant since 1975.

Regular Season. The New York Mets, decided favourites in the National League East, did not disappoint their followers. With 108 victories, the best record in baseball, the Mets removed all vestiges of suspense early in the summer and finished 21½ games ahead of the second-place Philadelphia Phillies. The Houston Astros, meanwhile, responded to rookie manager Hal Lanier with splendid pitching and timely hitting to win a surprising victory in the National League West by ten games over the Cincinnati Reds.

In the American League East, deemed baseball's best, the Red Sox jumped into first place in May and never surrendered their position. They outdistanced the second-place New York Yankees by 5½ games. The California Angels also enjoyed a relatively trouble-free excursion in the American League West, which they won by five games over the Texas Rangers.

Boggs, Boston's third baseman, won his third American League batting crown with an average of .357. Meanwhile, teammate Clemens was clearly the league's domi-

Final Major League Standings, 1986

AMERICAN LEAGUE East Division					NATIONAL LEAGUE East Division				
Club	W.	L.	Pct.	G.B.	Club	W.	L.	Pct.	G.B.
Boston	95	66	.590	–	New York	106	54	.667	–
New York	90	72	.556	5½	Philadelphia	86	75	.534	21½
Detroit	87	75	.537	8½	St. Louis	79	82	.491	28½
Toronto	86	76	.531	9½	Montreal	78	83	.484	29½
Cleveland	84	78	.519	11½	Chicago	70	90	.438	37
Milwaukee	77	84	.478	18	Pittsburgh	64	98	.395	44
Baltimore	73	89	.451	22½					

West Division					West Division				
Club	W.	L.	Pct.	G.B.	Club	W.	L.	Pct.	G.B.
California	92	70	.568	–	Houston	96	66	.593	–
Texas	87	75	.537	5	Cincinnati	86	76	.531	10
Kansas City	76	86	.469	16	San Francisco	83	79	.512	13
Oakland	76	86	.469	16	San Diego	74	88	.457	22
Chicago	72	90	.444	20	Los Angeles	73	89	.451	23
Minnesota	71	91	.438	21	Atlanta	72	89	.447	23½
Seattle	67	95	.414	25					

nant pitcher; he won 24 games, lost only 4, and in a late-April contest struck out a record 20 Seattle Mariners, while walking none. Joe Carter of the Cleveland Indians led the league with 121 RBIs; Jesse Barfield of the Toronto Blue Jays paced the league in home runs with 40.

Scott, who hurled a no-hitter to clinch the Astros' division crown, was the preeminent pitcher in the National League. He won 18, lost 10, and struck out 306 batters. Tim Raines of the Montreal Expos captured the batting crown with a .334 average, while Philadelphia's veteran Mike Schmidt was the leading home-run hitter with 37. Schmidt also paced the league in RBIs with 119. Vince Coleman of the St. Louis Cardinals led the major leagues with 107 stolen bases.

Boston dominated the postseason awards in the American League as Clemens was named most valuable player and also won the Cy Young award as the league's best pitcher, while John McNamara was voted manager of the year. The American League's rookie of the year was outfielder Jose Canseco of Oakland. In the National League third baseman Schmidt of Philadelphia was most valuable player, and Scott of Houston won the Cy Young award. Lanier of Houston was voted manager of the year, and pitcher Todd Worrell of St. Louis was named the league's outstanding rookie. (ROBERT WILLIAM VERDI)

Latin America. A Mexican team, the Mexicali Eagles from the state of Baja California Norte, won the 1986 Caribbean Series played in Maracaibo, Venezuela, in February. The Mexicans had to come from behind in the tournament, as they were downed 11–0 by the La Guaira Sharks, their Venezuelan hosts, in their first game and later 6–0 by the Mayagüez Indians of Puerto Rico. The only game they won during the first round of the series, in fact, was an 11-inning cliff-hanger against the Cibao Eagles of the Dominican Republic, whom they defeated 6–5.

However, the second round was totally different for the Mexicans. They first avenged their loss against the Venezuelans by defeating them 14–0, and then they went on to edge the Dominicans 8–7 and the Puerto Ricans 5–4 (in ten innings). The Eagles' four wins and two losses were sufficient for the Caribbean crown, as both the La Guaira Sharks and the Cibao Eagles finished with an even 3–3 record. The Mayagüez Indians were last with two victories and four defeats.

The Mexicali Eagles had reached the Caribbean Series after defeating Hermosillo, Tijuana, and Culiacán in three consecutive play-off matchups to gain the Mexican Pacific League's pennant. In Venezuela the La Guaira Sharks qualified, even though the Caracas Sharks had actually won the national championship. The Cibao Eagles finished third in the Dominican tournament but later won the right to represent their country by prevailing over the Licey Tigers. The Mayagüez Indians won the Puerto Rican championship in a series against the San Juan Metropolitanos after Caguas—which finished the regular tournament in first place—failed during the play-offs.

Cuba continued its domination over amateur baseball as it overwhelmed its competition during the world amateur championship played in Haarlem, Neth., during the summer. The Cubans compiled a 10–1 record, against 8–3 for their nearest competitors, Taiwan and South Korea. The U.S. finished fourth with a 7–4 record.

(SERGIO SARMIENTO)

Japan. Tokorozawa's Seibu Lions of the Pacific League (PL) won the Japan Series championship in the best-of-seven postseason contest against the Hiroshima Carp of the Central League (CL). With the series opener tied, the Carp won the next three games, but the Lions came back to win four straight games and gain the championship. This was the second time that a team had bounced back to win the Series after three straight losses. The Nishitetsu Lions, the predecessors of the Seibu Lions, accomplished the feat in 1958. It was the Lions' third Japan Series title, their first in three years.

The Carp won the CL pennant for the fifth time. The triumph had to be attributed to the best pitching corps in the league; ace hurler Manabu Kitabeppu won 18 games (most victories in the league) and had an earned run average (ERA) of 2.43 (best in the league); Akihito Kaneishi had an ERA of 2.68 (second best); and rookie Hiroshi Nagatomi won ten games against two losses. Manager Junro Anan also had to be given credit. With no batter hitting .300 or over or 30 or more home runs, it was Anan's "magic" that helped win the CL championship.

Randy Bass of the Hanshin Tigers won the CL triple crown (.389 batting average, 47 home runs, 109 RBIs) for the second year in a row. His batting average set a record for Japanese professional baseball. Kitabeppu was voted most valuable player of the season.

In the PL the Lions won the pennant for the second straight year and the fourth time in six years. Contributing to their triumph were better-than-average pitching and the play of Koji Akiyama (41 homers, 115 RBIs) and rookie Kazuhiro Kiyohara (.304, 31 homers, 78 RBIs).

Hiromitsu Ochiai of the Lotte Orions won the batting triple crown for the second year in a row (.360, 50 home runs, 116 RBIs). It was the second straight year that Ochiai had belted 50 or more home runs, a feat nobody had accomplished before. Lions' shortstop Hiromichi Ishige was voted the league's most valuable player.

(RYUSAKU HASEGAWA)

BASKETBALL

United States. *College.* The world of college basketball was shaken to its foundations when tragedy marred the finish of the 1985–86 season. Len Bias, the University of Maryland's 2.03-m (6-ft 8-in) All-America forward, was seemingly at the pinnacle of success when his life ended with stunning swiftness in the early morning of June 19. Only 22 years old, Bias had just fulfilled a boyhood dream by signing a lucrative contract as the No. 1 draft choice of the Boston Celtics, the National Basketball Association (NBA) champions. Cocaine apparently turned the dream into a nightmare. Bias suffered a fatal heart attack, according to grand jury testimony, after ingesting the drug at a party with friends and Maryland teammates.

Shock waves of anger and frustration rippled across ev-

Louisville Cardinals' Herbert Crook begins to topple over Duke's Tommy Amaker as the latter lunges for a loose ball, in the first half of the NCAA championship game on March 31. The Cardinals defeated the No. 1-ranked Blue Devils of Duke 72-69.

AP/WIDE WORLD

ery campus. It became apparent that the pressure of big-time sports exposed players at many universities to the same conditions that had led to Bias's death. Evidence in the subsequent grand jury investigation confirmed that the "student-athlete" status of many athletes was a sham. Bias had been missing classes and failing courses, giving him little chance to earn a degree. Nor was he an exception. Some skilled players were recruited and exploited by college basketball programs that emphasized winning games, not education.

Before this unhappy chapter, college basketball had proved its appeal once again, both on the court and at the ticket windows. Record crowds were attracted by the trend toward parity in most conferences. With Patrick Ewing of Georgetown following Houston's Akeem Olajuwon into the NBA, the dynasties that had sent their teams into the National Collegiate Athletic Association (NCAA) tourney finals three times in four years were gone.

Duke emerged to fill the void. The Blue Devils pulled away from the rest of the Atlantic Coast Conference, putting together a 21-game victory streak en route to the NCAA championship game in Dallas, Texas. Louisiana State was the Cinderella team among the semifinalists, but Louisville overcame an early deficit to oust the Tigers 88–77 and move into the championship game. Duke became the other finalist by eliminating Kansas, 71–67.

The Duke–Louisville final was no David versus Goliath showdown to rival that of 1985, when Villanova toppled Georgetown, the overwhelming favourite. Duke had won 37 games in 1985–86, a one-season NCAA record, and was atop the polls conducted weekly by the Associated Press and United Press International. But Louisville, coming together at the right time, stretched its own victory string to 17 games in a row with a 72-69 triumph over the Blue Devils in the final. Coach Denny Crum thus became the first to claim two NCAA titles in the decade, adding an encore to the Cardinals' 1980 tournament triumph.

Dominant defense and a spectacular freshman, Pervis ("Never Nervous") Ellison, won the championship for Louisville. Ellison got 25 points and 11 rebounds, becoming the first freshman to be named most outstanding player of the Final Four since Utah's Arnie Ferrin in 1944. Crum's defensive game plan zeroed in on spectacular Duke guard Johnny Dawkins. A diamond-and-one alignment, with four Louisville players alternating as Dawkins's shadow, gradually turned the game around. The Cardinals' defense took its toll on Dawkins in the second half, holding him scoreless for 15 minutes and 25 seconds.

Duke's Dawkins made the coaches' All-America team, along with Bias of Maryland, Kenny Walker of Kentucky, Danny Manning of Kansas, and St. John's Walter Berry. Berry also was named player of the year.

More controversy was assured for the 1986–87 campaign when the NCAA Rules Committee approved a three-point field goal for men's competition. Successful shots from behind a line on the court, to be drawn at a distance of 19 ft 9 in (6 m) from the centre of the basket, would score three points. The unexpected move brought quick reaction from coaches. "A three-point shot from 19 ft is a little cheap," said Lou Carnesecca of St. John's. "The distance should be 22 ft." Added Kentucky's Eddie Sutton: "You'll see more teams using man-to-man defense. It should reduce congestion under the basket."

In women's basketball Texas swept all opposition aside with an unprecedented 34–0 record. The Lady Longhorns capped their perfect season by routing USC 97–81 in the NCAA championship game. Clarissa Davis of Texas was named most outstanding player of the women's Final Four, and her coach, Jody Conradt, took coach of the year laurels.

Professional. A new era in the National Basketball Association opened in 1985–86, even though it was sidetracked, at least temporarily, by the old order. The "Twin Towers" of the Houston Rockets began to loom large on the NBA

AP/WIDE WORLD

The Boston Celtics' Larry Bird holds onto the ball while seemingly trapped by towering Houston Rockets Akeem Olajuwon (left) and Ralph Sampson in the first quarter of game six of the NBA championship series.

NBA Final Standings, 1985–86

EASTERN CONFERENCE Atlantic Division			WESTERN CONFERENCE Midwest Division		
Team	Won	Lost	Team	Won	Lost
Boston	67	15	Houston	51	31
Philadelphia	54	28	Denver	47	35
New Jersey	39	43	Dallas	44	38
Washington	39	43	Utah	42	40
New York	23	59	Sacramento	37	45
			San Antonio	35	47
Central Division			Pacific Division		
Team	Won	Lost	Team	Won	Lost
Milwaukee	57	25	L.A. Lakers	62	20
Atlanta	50	32	Portland	40	42
Detroit	46	36	L.A. Clippers	32	50
Chicago	30	52	Phoenix	32	50
Cleveland	29	53	Seattle	31	51
Indiana	26	56	Golden State	30	52

skyline. In their second season together, 2.24-m (7-ft 4-in) Ralph Sampson and 2.12-m (7-ft) Akeem Olajuwon elevated the Rockets to the Western Division championship and a spot in the play-off finals.

In the end the league's power structure survived the assault when the Boston Celtics captured their 16th NBA crown. The Celtics vanquished Houston four games to two, in an acrimonious showdown, but there was a strong feeling that Sampson and Olajuwon were the most visible symbols of a budding dynasty.

The ease with which the Rockets dethroned the Los Angeles Lakers, defending NBA kings, in the Western Conference finals was a clear warning. Boston's poise, pride, and play-off experience ultimately prevailed over Houston's size and youth, though the losers were not intimidated.

Sampson was labeled a bully for fighting with the Celtics' Jerry Sichting, 38 cm (15 in) shorter and 23 kg (50 lb) lighter, in the fifth game of the final. His team was ousted three days later, with a Boston Garden crowd of 14,890 jeering Sampson's every move. Sampson accepted the blame for the 114–97 rout that put another world championship banner in the Garden rafters, issuing a prediction at the same time: "We'll be back."

Regardless of what the future might hold, 1985–86 belonged to the Celtics, both during the regular season and in the play-offs. They rolled up an NBA record of 82 victories in 100 games, won 41 straight home games after a setback on Dec. 6, 1985, by the Portland Trail Blazers, and finished with an astonishing 50–1 mark on their famed parquet floor. As usual, the spearhead for such excellence was 2.1-m (6-ft 9-in) forward Larry Bird, continuing his reign as the NBA's dominant force. Bird was voted the league's most valuable player, also adding a second play-off MVP trophy to the one he gained in 1984.

Surrounded by such stars as Dennis Johnson, Robert Parish, and Kevin McHale, Bird made Boston virtually unbeatable in pressure situations. Only once during the play-offs was Bird's status as the best player on the floor seriously challenged. That was on April 20, when Michael Jordan of the Chicago Bulls riddled the Celtic defense for a record 63 points in a play-off game. Jordan proved the broken foot that had limited him to 18 regular-season games had healed, but even his virtuoso performance could not prevent the Bulls from being swept 3–0 in their first-round series with Boston. (ROBERT G. LOGAN)

World Amateur. The United States achieved a double success in the world basketball championships in 1986, winning both the men's and women's titles. The men's tournament in Spain in July involved 24 nations. After two series of elimination matches the U.S. won its semifinal 96–80 against Brazil. The other semifinal produced a sensational finish. Yugoslavia led the Soviet Union 85–76 with less than a minute to play. Then the Soviets scored nine points to send the game into overtime, during which they grabbed a one-point lead and hung on to win 91–90. The final almost produced a similar sensation after the U.S. had led by 18 in the second half. The Soviet Union rallied but finally lost 87–85.

For the U.S., diminutive guard Tyrone Bogues, standing only 1.59 m (5 ft 3 in) tall, was a revelation, making no fewer than ten steals during the match. Kenny Smith, with 23 points, was top scorer in the final game for the victors, who were coached by Lute Olson from Arizona. Third place went to Yugoslavia with Brazil fourth, followed by Spain, Italy, Israel, Canada, China, Greece, Cuba, and Argentina.

The women's world championship took place in August in the Soviet Union, with the semifinals and finals played in Moscow. The U.S. defeated Canada in one semifinal, and the Soviet Union beat Czechoslovakia in the other. In the final the U.S. defeated the host country 108–88 to win the championship, while Canada took third place from Czechoslovakia. They were followed by China, Cuba, Bulgaria, Hungary, Australia, South Korea, Brazil, and Taiwan.

The 13th World Congress of the International Basketball Federation (FIBA) took place in Barcelona, Spain, in June and led to a modification of the rules aimed at reducing the number of fouls that are committed near the end of a game in order to stop the clock. This new rule was applied in the world championships and proved to be successful. At the congress the status of players was discussed with a view to recognizing that many players throughout the world were now effectively professional in all but name. Although the congress agreed to the deletion of all references to the word "amateur," the motion to allow open competition narrowly failed to be passed.

The major club competition during the 1985–86 European season, the European Champions' Cup, was won by KK Cibona of Zagreb, Yugos., which retained its title by defeating Zhalgiris of Kaunas, U.S.S.R., in the final at Budapest. In the other European Cup competitions FC Barcelona defeated Scavolini Pesaro, Italy, in the Cup Winners' Cup, and Banco di Roma beat Juventus Caserta in an all-Italian final of the Korac Cup. The women's European Champions' Cup was retained by AS Vicenza, Italy, which beat DJK Dusseldorf, West Germany, in the final. Dynamo Novosibirsk, U.S.S.R., defeated BSE Budapest, Hung., to win the Ronchetti Cup for women. The men's South American club championship, held in Buenos Aires in April, was won by Monte Libano of Brazil.

In competitions for national teams China won the Asian women's championships, held in Kuala Lumpur, Malaysia, in June, with South Korea in second place and Taiwan third. Brazil took the South American women's crown from Peru in a tournament at Guarantigueta, Brazil, in May. (MELVIN D. WELCH)

BILLIARD GAMES

Billiards. The Union Mondial de Billiard (UMB)-sanctioned 41st world three-cushion tournament was held in May in Las Vegas, Nev., with a field of 14 including 19-time (and defending) champion Raymond Ceulemans of Belgium. Ceulemans literally annihilated his six round-robin preliminary bracket foes. His torrid scoring pace set several new records, including best 50-point game (19 innings), best game average (2.6315), and best average for first six games (1.807). It was an epic start.

But a nontraditional UMB-dictated format sent the top

Englishman Joe Johnson, with his wife, Terry, proudly salutes fans with his newly won trophy at the world professional snooker championship finals at Sheffield, England, on May 5. Johnson, who was seeded 16th, defeated three-time winner Steve Davis.
AP/WIDE WORLD

two players from each preliminary bracket into a sudden-death play-off to determine the top positions, with all matches played to 50 points. There Ceulemans met the runner-up from the opposite bracket, Avelino Rico of Spain. At 55 Rico was the oldest contestant in the tournament and, though of world-class skill, had lost to Ceulemans all 20 times the two had played previously. As the match began, the Belgian master shot out to another huge lead (44–25 after 28 innings and then 48–35 after 35), and the usual die seemed cast once again.

Instead, one of the most electrifying finishes in the history of the game was fashioned by the imperturbable Rico: a brilliant, shot-making run of 15-and-out to capture the semifinal match 50–48. Due to the format and stunning upset, Ceulemans's best possible finish could be only third, which he later claimed with a 50–36 (28 innings) win over Marco Zanetti of Italy (who finished fourth). Ironically, Ceulemans's final tournament grand average was a new world record (1.746).

Rico's opponent in the finals was the fast-rising 23-year-old Torbjorn Blomdahl of Sweden. The game was a repeat of their meeting in the 44th European championship in 1986 in Luxembourg, when Blomdahl roared from far behind (25–41) to win 50–48. In the world tournament, though, the roles were reversed. Blomdahl started fast and built his own 41–25 lead. But then, as against Ceulemans, the veteran Spaniard caught fire, running an 8 followed closely by a 7. The young Swede began to wilt, missing some routine naturals. That was all the persistent Rico needed; soon he was the new champion, posting a second scintillating come-from-behind victory 50–46 and ending one of the most memorable world tournaments in UMB history.

Tokyo was the site for the 1986 42nd All-Japan three-cushion championship. Yoshio Yoshihara averaged 1.363, made a high run of 13, and edged out Nobuaki Kobayashi (1974 world champion), who also ran a 13.

The French Nationale three-cushion crown was won by Richard Bitalis in Chartres, with an average of 1.315 and high run of 7. In Vienna veteran Johann Scherz won his 27th Austrian three-cushion title; he averaged 1.351 and ran 10. The Danish national three-cushion championship in Copenhagen was won by Tony Carlsen.

The Billiard Federation of the USA (BFUSA) 19th annual national three-cushion tournament was held in San Jose, Calif. Carlos Hallon of Florida was undefeated in winning his second BFUSA title. Runner-up was Allen Gilbert, and third was Frank Torres.

The 67th annual national amateur three-cushion meet at the Cleveland (Ohio) Athletic Club (CAC), was won by Robert McManus of Creve Coeur Club, Peoria, Ill. He defeated CAC member Patrick Butler 50–35 in the final.

Pocket Billiards. Play on the U.S. professional winter tournament circuit's 4½-ft by 9-ft (1.3-m by 2.7-m) tables began in November 1985 at the tenth U.S. nine-ball open in Norfolk, Va., with $30,000 at stake. A strong field of 50 entered. Veteran Jimmy Reid won the men's division, and Belinda Beardon snared the women's title.

Beardon also triumphed at 14.1 Continuous (straight pool) in late November 1985 at Niagara Falls, N.Y., taking the women's crown at the $61,800 world 14.1 open. The men's division was won by Mike Sigel. In the year's other major 14.1 tournament, the $51,250 ninth Professional Pool Players Association world open in Philadelphia, Nick Varner was men's champ, Loree Jon Jones the women's titlist, and Paul Hultgren the top junior.

In other nineball competition Beardon won the seventh Women's Professional Billiard Association meet, her first WPBA crown. She also received the *Billiards Digest* woman Player of the Year award; the magazine's male honouree was Earl Strickland, a repeat winner from 1984.

The tour's richest tournament was the 128-player, $114,000 Resorts Last Call II event in Atlantic City, N.J., in April. There Jim Rempe gained pool's top prize of $35,000, aided by a run of six racks during his 11–7 finals victory over Efren Reyes. Reyes's Filipino countryman Jose Parica achieved a pair of notable wins at the fifth Childress Open in Richmond, Ky., and the Classic Cup V in Aurora, Ill. Sigel streaked to four of the year's biggest nine-ball wins on top of his 14.1 success, winning the Q-Master Spring Open in Norfolk, Va., the Glass City Open in Toledo, Ohio, the Busch Open in Moline, Ill., and the B.C. Open in Binghamton, N.Y. Danny Medina gained a major victory at one of the year's new events, the California Mixed Open in Anaheim.

Women's nine-ball divisions were played at the Classic Cup V, where Beardon won again; the Busch, with Kris Villalpando on top; the Charlotte Open, won by Peg Ledman; and the Cleveland Open and California Mixed, both taken by many-time U.S. and world champion Jean Balukas.

In bar table (3½-ft by 7-ft [1.1-m by 2.1-m]) eight-ball play, the Billiard Congress of America (BCA) All-American Team titles were won by MeMaws of Fort Worth, Texas, in the men's division and by Leisure Club of Phoenix, Ariz., in the women's. The BCA individual winners were Jesus Rivera (men's), Linda Hoffman (women's), and Stan Coscia (seniors).

The $51,000 Lite Beer World Series of Tavern Pool crowned Carson Wiley and Janet McKee in its fifth annual competition at Las Vegas, Nev. Las Vegas was also the site for the Valley International 8-Ball League championships; titles went to Scott Kitto over Mark Wilson (singles), Red Sails Resort over Caboto Club (men's teams), and defending champion Cannon Lanes over Shortshop Saloon (women's teams). Finalists at the eighth $34,500 Coors-

McDermott Team Cup in Milwaukee, Wis., were Iron City Pool League (Pittsburgh, Pa.) over Dedden's (Louisville, Ky.) in men's play, and Cannon Lanes (Cannon Falls, Minn.) over Sportsman's of New Glarus (Wis.) in women's action. (BRUCE H. VENZKE)

Snooker. Joe Johnson (England) won the world professional snooker title for the first time in 1986 when he defeated Steve Davis (England) by 18 frames to 12 in the final at Sheffield, England, in May. Davis, who had earlier won the Coral U.K. championship in Preston, England, and the Dulux British Open in Derby, retained his position as the world's top-ranked player. Jimmy White won the Mercantile Credit Classic by defeating Cliff Thorburn (Canada) 13–12 in the final at Warrington in January. Tony Meo won the English title by defeating Neal Foulds 9–7 in the final at Ipswich. Thorburn retained the Benson and Hedges Masters and the Scottish Masters.

(SYDNEY E. FRISKIN)

BOBSLEDDING

Veteran Swiss driver Erich Schaerer gained his fifth world title as captain of the winning four-man sled at Königsee, West Germany, in March 1986; it was his last championship tournament before retirement. The Austrians, led by Peter Kienast, were runners-up, and another Swiss sled, steered by Ralph Pichler, finished third. The two-man title was retained by Wolfgang Hoppe and Dietmar Schauerhammer of East Germany, with an aggregate time for the four runs that was 1.09 seconds better than that of Pichler and Celest Poltera, who earlier had set a new track record. Another East German bob, driven by Detlef Richter and braked by Steffen Grummt, placed third.

East Germany won all three medals in the two-man event at the European championships at Igls, Austria, in January. Hoppe and Schauerhammer finished ahead of Bernhard Lehmann and Bogdan Musiol, followed by Richter and Grummt. The four-man title went to the Swiss sled driven by Hans Hiltebrand, with Lehmann runner-up and Kienast third.

Titles in the second World Cup series, ending in February at Lake Placid, N.Y., were awarded for performances throughout the season at six locations. Maris Pojkans and Ivars Berzups of the U.S.S.R. won the two-man title, followed by their compatriots Vjacheslav Shavljev and Aleksandr Putschkov; Ekkehard Fasser and Kurt Meier of Switzerland finished third. Fasser drove the four-man title winner, ahead of Matt Roy of the U.S. and Walter Delle-Karth of Austria. The overall top driver was Fasser, with Roy runner-up and Nick Phipps of the U.K. third.

(HOWARD BASS)

BOWLING

World Tenpins. The ninth American Zone amateur championships of the Fédération Internationale des Quilleurs took place at Bogotá, Colombia, on Sept. 21–28, 1985. Bowlers from 17 countries participated in the 12 events, 6 each for men and women. The U.S. men captured the most medals—12, including 4 gold.

Enrique Sepúlveda of Mexico won the individual match game masters' title, defeating Larry Jones of the U.S. 383–331 in the final two-game roll-off. The women's title in that event was taken by Edda Piccini, also of Mexico, who defeated Debbie Bennett of the U.S. 363–354. In the men's division Juan Roguebert of Panama won the six-game singles with 1,200. The doubles title was won by Dan Nadeau and Scott Thomsen of the U.S. with 2,303. The trios and five-man events were also won by the U.S., with scores of 3,453 and 5,836. In the 24-game all-events, Nadeau was best with 4,646. The women's championships were won by Carmen Aguilar of Venezuela in the singles, 1,177; Ashie Gonzales and Algie Badovinac of Puerto Rico in the doubles, 2,214; Mexico in the trios, 3,204; and Mexico in the five-game event, 5,618. Aguilar also won the all-events, 4,410.

In Europe the national champions of 14 countries met in Oslo in April 1986 for the European individual championships. Remo Fornasari of Italy with a 212 average led the rest of the field in round-robin head-to-head matches, with Tony Rosenqvist (203) of Sweden runner-up. For the women Margot Simon of West Germany averaged 203, with Monica Johansson of Sweden (200) second. The European Team Cup took place in June in Frankfurt, West Germany. In the men's division Finland and Sweden recorded wins in 14 out of 17 matches, but the Finns knocked down 92 more pins than the Swedes to take first place. In the women's competition, the Swedes secured an 88-pin margin over the second-place Finnish team.

Fifteen nations attended the ninth Asian Zone amateur championships in June in Kuala Lumpur, Malaysia, where Ma Ying-chieh of Taiwan won the men's masters title, defeating former world champion Ollie Reformado of the Philippines 437 to 359. Bec Watanabe of the Philippines defeated Japan's Mitchio Hayashi in the final, 429 to 378, for the women's title. The other champions were: men—singles, Mike Wee, Singapore, 1,310; doubles, the Philippines 2,465; trios, Taiwan 3,624; fives, Taiwan 6,169; all-events, Ma Ying-chieh 4,921; women—singles, Atsuko Asai, Japan, 1,192; doubles, the Philippines 2,373; trios, Thailand 3,531; fives, Japan 5,629; all-events, Bong Coo, the Philippines, 4,830. Twenty new Asian records were bowled. (YRJÖ SARAHETE)

U.S. Tenpins. In a year that lacked a dominant figure in bowling, perhaps the most talked-about individual was one of the most unlikely heroes: Rose Walsh, of Pomona, Calif., a 60-year-old grandmother, who rolled a perfect game in the Women's International Bowling Congress (WIBC) tournament in Costa Mesa, Calif. This was just the second 300 in the tournament's 62-year history.

The champions of the WIBC tournament were: Open Division—team, Sillia's Pro Shop, Cleveland, Ohio, 2,891; singles, Dana Stewart, Morgan Hill, Calif., 698; doubles, Sally Gates and Marilyn Frazier, Palmdale/Lancaster, Calif., 1,260; all-events, Robin Romeo, Van Nuys, Calif., and Maria Lewis, Mantera, Calif. (tied), 1,877. Division I—team, Royal Buick, Tucson, Ariz., 2,676; singles, Diane Smith, Lake Cowichan, B.C., 688; doubles, Cindy Brennan and Joy Eckley, Missoula/Ronan, Mont., 1,188; all-events, Nancy Schubert-Balcer, Baltimore, Md., 1,780. The WIBC Queens tournament was won by Cora Fiebig of Madison Heights, Mich., who defeated Barbara Thorberg of St. Louis, Mo., 223–177, in the title game.

The No. 1 performer on the Professional Bowlers Association tour for more than a decade, Earl Anthony, was inducted into the American Bowling Congress Hall of Fame in a ceremony at the ABC tournament site in Las Vegas, Nev. Anthony won 41 PBA championships before his retirement in 1983. A record 10,019 five-man teams competed in the 83rd annual ABC tournament. The Regular Division winners: team, Faball Enterprises No. 2, Milwaukee, Wis., 3,253; singles, Jeff Mackey, Mexico, Mo., 774; doubles, Don Cook and Bob Larson, Milwaukee, 1,418; all-events, Ed Marzka, Detroit, 2,116.

In the Masters tournament, staged on the ABC meet lanes, Mark Fahy of Chicago won the $43,600 first prize by defeating Del Ballard, Jr., of Richardson, Texas, 222–193, in the championship game. (JOHN J. ARCHIBALD)

Michael Spinks (left) and Larry Holmes get tied up during their title bout for the International Boxing Federation heavyweight championship on April 19. Spinks retained his title.
FOCUS ON SPORTS

BOXING

Though Europe, the Commonwealth, and Great Britain declined affiliation to the International Boxing Federation (IBF) in 1986, the organization strengthened its bid for universal recognition when several of its championships were promoted in Europe and Britain; however, these were not recognized as title fights by the European Boxing Union (EBU) or British Boxing Board of Control. The greatest strength of the IBF was that its heavyweight champion, Michael Spinks (U.S.), who beat Larry Holmes (U.S.) for the second time before stopping European champion Steffen Tangstad (Norway) in four rounds, would continue to be accepted as the world's best heavyweight, undefeated in 29 fights.

Despite the big increase in the number of world champions, U.S. promoters Don King and Butch Lewis announced that they would be trying to unify the world heavyweight championship in 1987 with a series of elimination matches involving Tim Witherspoon (U.S.), the World Boxing Association (WBA) champion; Trevor Berbick (Canada), recognized by the World Boxing Council (WBC); and Spinks. This ambitious plan for unification was complicated by the arrival on the championship scene of Mike Tyson (U.S.), a 20-year-old who had won all his 27 contests and defeated Berbick by a technical knockout in the second round to win the WBC title in November.

Earlier Berbick had caused a surprise by winning the title at the age of 33 from Pinklon Thomas (U.S.). The WBA crown also changed when Witherspoon outpointed Tony Tubbs (U.S.). Witherspoon was found to have taken drugs before the contest and was ordered by the WBA to meet Tubbs again for the title, but Tubbs agreed to allow Witherspoon to defend the championship against Frank Bruno (England) before meeting him again. Witherspoon stopped Bruno in 11 rounds but was stopped in the first round by James ("Bonecrusher") Smith (U.S.), a late substitute for Tubbs, in December.

Two new champions emerged in the comparatively new cruiserweight division. The WBC version, for boxers up to 195 lb, was won by Carlos de León (P.R.), who outpointed Bernard Benton (U.S.). It was the third time de León had won the title, which he then retained by stopping Michael Greer (U.S.) in eight rounds. The WBA version, known as junior heavyweight, for competitors up to 190 lb, was won from Dwight Muhammad Qawi (U.S.) by Evander Holyfield (U.S.) in his 12th professional contest. The WBC light-heavyweight championship, vacated by Spinks after he gained the heavyweight crown, was won by J. B. Williamson (U.S.), who outpointed Prince Mama Mohammed (Ghana); Williamson, however, lost the title when he was outscored by Dennis Andries (England). Marvin Johnson (U.S.) became WBA champion again, winning the vacant title by stopping Leslie Stewart (Trinidad) in seven rounds and retaining it by defeating Jean-Marie Emebe (France) in 13 rounds.

Marvin Hagler (U.S.), who had dominated the middleweight division for more than six years and was accepted as undisputed champion by all ruling bodies, retained that title by knocking out John Mugabi (Uganda) in 11 rounds. It was Mugabi's first defeat in 27 contests. The 32-year-old Hagler, undefeated for ten years, did not box again during the year, but protests throughout the world followed the announcement that he had agreed to defend the championship against Sugar Ray Leonard (U.S.), former welterweight and junior middleweight champion, in 1987. Leonard had retired as undefeated welterweight champion in 1982 following an operation for a detached retina. He made a brief return in a nontitle fight, which he won but in which he suffered a knockdown, and he immediately retired again. Inactive for four years, he had not appeared in the ratings, but the WBC waived its rules and gave permission for the match to take place. After stopping Mark Medal (U.S.) in eight rounds, Thomas Hearns (U.S.) relinquished the WBC junior middleweight crown; Mike McCallum (Jamaica) retained the WBA version, halting Julian Jackson (Virgin Islands, U.S.) in two rounds and Said Skouma (France) in nine. Duane Thomas (U.S.) won the vacant WBC junior middleweight title by knocking out Mugabi in three rounds.

The biggest upset in some years was the decisive victory of Lloyd Honeyghan (England) against Don Curry (U.S.), the undisputed welterweight champion, in six rounds. Curry, who earlier had retained his title by knocking out Eduardo Rodríguez (Panama) in two rounds, had been regarded as a likely superchampion in the class of Leonard and Hagler. Curry not only had been undefeated in six years as a professional but had not lost a contest since he was a 16-year-old amateur. Honeyghan was later stripped of the WBA welterwieght title because he refused to fight against a South African. The WBC junior welterweight championship changed twice. René Arredondo (Mexico) took it from Lonnie Smith (U.S.) in five rounds. It was Smith's first defeat in 23 bouts. Arredondo's reign was short-lived—he was knocked out in the first round in his defense against Tsuyoshi Hamada (Japan). The WBA championship was won by Patrizio Oliva (Italy) when he outpointed defending champion Ubaldo Sacco (Arg.). Oliva later stopped Brian Brunette (U.S.) in three rounds.

Héctor Camacho (P.R.) kept the WBC lightweight title with victories on points against Edwin Rosario (P.R.) and Cornelius Boza-Edwards (Uganda). Livingstone Bramble (U.S.) retained the WBA crown by stopping Tyrone Crawley (U.S.) in 13 rounds but lost it when he was knocked out in two rounds by Rosario. Julio César Chávez (Mexico) retained the WBC junior lightweight championship by stopping Faustino Barrios (Arg.) in five rounds and Refugio Rojas (U.S.) in seven and by outpointing Rocky Lockridge (U.S.) over 12 rounds. The WBA title changed hands twice: Alfredo Layne (Panama) beat the champion Wilfredo Gómez (P.R.) in nine rounds but was stopped by Brian Mitchell (South Africa) in ten.

The WBC featherweight crown was retained by Azumah Nelson (Ghana) with a win on points over Marcos Villasana (Mexico) and a ten-round knockout against Danilo Cabrera (Dominican Republic). Barry McGuigan (Northern Ireland) retained the WBA championship by stopping Cabrera in 14 rounds but unexpectedly lost it to Steve Cruz (U.S.). Lupe Pintor (Mexico) was three pounds overweight for his defense of the WBC junior featherweight title against Samart Payakaroon (Thailand) and was knocked out in five rounds. Víctor Callejas (P.R.) continued as WBA champion.

Miguel Lora (Colombia) remained WBC bantamweight king by outpointing Wilfredo Vásquez (P.R.) and stopping Enrique Sánchez (Dominican Republic) in six rounds. Gaby Cañizales (U.S.) captured the WBA title from Richie Sandoval with a seventh-round knockout but lost the championship in his first defense when outpointed by Bernardo Pinango (Venezuela). Pinango retained the crown by stopping Ciro De Leva (Italy) in ten rounds.

Gilberto Román (Mexico) deposed WBC super flyweight champion Jiro Watanabe (Japan) with a win on points, while Kaosai Galaxy (Thailand) retained the WBA title by stopping Israel Contreras (Venezuela) in five rounds. Sot Chitalada (Thailand) retained the WBC flyweight title by outpointing Freddie Castillo (Mexico) at Kuwait in the first world championship bout ever held in the Middle

Flyweight boxer Anthony Arthur Johnson of the U.S. team accepts gifts after being presented with a gold medal for his performance against the Soviet Union's Rinvidas Biljus at the Moscow Goodwill Games in July. A jury decision declared the winner.

AP/WIDE WORLD

East. Hilario Zapata (Panama) retained the WBA version with points victories over Javier Lucas (Mexico), Shuichi Hozumi (Japan), Dodie Penalosa (Phil.), and Alberto Castro (Colombia). Chang Jung Koo (South Korea) retained the WBC junior flyweight title by outpointing Germán Torres (Mexico) and Francisco Montiel (Mexico). Yuh Myung Woo (South Korea) also held onto the WBA crown by outpointing José de Jesus (P.R.) and stopping Tomohiro Kiyuna (Japan) in 12 rounds.

In Europe the heavyweight championship changed hands. After Bruno gave it up to challenge Witherspoon for the WBA title, Tangstad, a former champion, regained it by outpointing John Westgarth (England). Later the EBU stripped Tangstad of the title for not defending it by a mandatory date. Alex Blanchard (Neth.) kept the light heavyweight crown by outpointing Ralf Rocchigiani (West Germany). Graham took the middleweight title from Ayub

European, Commonwealth, and British Boxing Champions
as of Dec. 31, 1986

Division	Europe	Commonwealth	Britain
Heavyweight	Vacant	Horace Notice, England	Horace Notice, England
Cruiserweight	Vacant	Chisanda Mutti, Zambia	Andy Straughn, England
Light heavyweight	Alex Blanchard, The Netherlands	Leslie Stewart, Trinidad	Vacant
Middleweight	Herol Graham, England	Tony Sibson, England	Brian Anderson, England
Junior middleweight	Chris Pyatt, England	Nick Wilshire, England	Vacant
Welterweight	José Varela, West Germany	Vacant	Vacant
Junior welterweight	Vacant	Vacant	Tony Laing, England
Lightweight	Gert Bo Jacobsen, Denmark	Langton Tinago, Zimbabwe	Tony Willis, England
Junior lightweight	Jean-Marc Renard, Belgium	John Sichula, Zambia	...
Super featherweight	...	...	Najib Daho, England
Featherweight	Jim McDonnell, England	Tyrone Downes, Trinidad	Robert Dickie, Wales
Junior featherweight	...	...	...
Bantamweight	Antoine Montero, France	Vacant	Ray Gilbody, England
Super flyweight	...	...	...
Flyweight	Duke McKenzie, England	Richard Clarke, Jamaica	Dave McAuley, Northern Ireland
Junior flyweight	...	...	...

For the table of world champions, see *Sporting Record*.

Kalule (Den.) in ten rounds and retained it by stopping Mark Kaylor (England) in eight rounds. After halting Angelo Liquori (Italy) in eight rounds and Alfonso Redondo (Spain) in four, Skouma gave up the junior middleweight crown. It was taken over by Chris Pyatt (England), who knocked out John van Elteren (Neth.) in 97 seconds.

The welterweight championship vacated by Honeyghan went to José Varela (West Germany), who stopped Brahim Messaoudi (France) in five rounds. Terry Marsh (England) held onto the junior welterweight crown by outpointing Tek Nkalankete (France) and Francesco Prezioso (Italy) but was subsequently stripped of his title by the EBU when his request for an extension because of injury was turned down.

Gert Bo Jacobsen (Den.) captured the lightweight title from René Weller (West Germany), who retired after eight rounds. Jacobsen then outpointed Alfredo Raininger (Italy). Jean-Marc Renard (Belgium) won the vacant junior lightweight championship by halting Marco Gallo (Italy) in eight rounds and retained the title by stopping Fernando Rodríguez (Spain), also in eight rounds, and Najib Daho (England) in five.

Jim McDonnell (England) kept the featherweight crown by outpointing Salvatore Bottiglieri (Italy). After retaining the bantamweight title with points wins over Ray Gilbody (England) and Vicente Fernández (Spain), De Leva relinquished it to bid for world honours. The vacant title went to Antoine Montero (France) with a first-round knockout of Gilbody. Duke McKenzie (England) won the flyweight championship from Charlie Magri (England) in five rounds.

In the Commonwealth Chisanda Mutti (Zambia), Leslie Stewart (Trinidad), Tony Sibson (England), Nick Wilshire (England), and John Sichula (Zambia) remained champions at cruiserweight, light heavyweight, middleweight, junior middleweight, and junior lightweight, respectively. New champions were Horace Notice (England), heavyweight; Langton Tinago (Zimbabwe), lightweight; Tyrone Downes (Trinidad), featherweight; and Richard Clarke (Jamaica), flyweight. (FRANK BUTLER)

CHESS

The year 1986 was an outstanding one for chess. For the first time since World War II part of a world championship match between two Soviets was held outside the Soviet Union, which created great publicity that stimulated increased interest in chess. In addition to playing host for the first half of this match, England again succeeded in winning the silver medal at the Dubai Olympiad and failed to take the gold by only the smallest margin.

The year started with the traditional Hastings (England) tournament, won by Margeir Petursson, a grand master from Iceland. Unfortunately, the Hastings tournament had fallen on hard times because of the lack of a commercial sponsor and was not nearly as strong as it had been previously.

Just after Hastings, British grand master Nigel Short, then only 20 years old, won a much stronger tournament at Wijk aan Zee, Neth., but the biggest surprise of the year was the performance of English international master Glenn Flear in winning the very strong Greater London Council (GLC) tournament in London in March. Flear was a last-minute replacement and the only player in the event who had not qualified for the grand master title; nevertheless, he defeated a host of strong competitors.

In March ex-world champion Anatoly Karpov took part in the SWIFT tournament in Brussels as preparation for his forthcoming title match with Garry Kasparov and won first place. Karpov then went on to the even stronger Bugojno double-round event, where he lost one game but still won the tournament.

In May the "Match of Champions," held in London between U.S. champion Lev Alburt and British titleholder Jonathan Speelman, resulted in a close win for Alburt. England's number one player, Tony Miles, fared less well in Basel, Switz., where he was trounced by Kasparov by the alarming margin of 5½ to ½. Kasparov's score in this match was the kind of performance formerly associated only with Bobby Fischer, and some observers began to predict that Kasparov might eventually reach and even surpass Fischer's rating of 2780.

The high point of the year was the World Championship Centenary Match between Kasparov and Karpov, the first half of which was held in London under the sponsorship of the GLC, Save and Prosper, and a number of other groups, while the second half was played in Leningrad. Kasparov said that the London half was the best organized event in which he had ever played. British television companies gave the event unprecedented coverage, with Thames Television showing programs three times each week, on the evening of every playing day, and the BBC offering a weekly summary of events. At the end of the London half Kasparov led by 1 point (2 wins to 1 with 9 games drawn), and he shared with Karpov the £10,000 brilliancy prize offered by Save and Prosper. This was the highest prize ever offered for a single game of chess and was paid in gold Victorian sovereigns.

11th game of the world championship match

White A. Karpov	Black G. Kasparov	White A. Karpov	Black G. Kasparov
1 d4 (000 min)	Nf6 (000)	22 Kh2 (079)	Qh5 (095)
2 c4 (000)	g6 (000)	23 Nexg6+(083)	hg (095)
3 Nc3 (002)	d5 (001)	24 Qxg6 (086)	Qe5 (098)
4 Bf4 (002)	Bg7 (001)	25 Rf7 (127)	Rxf7 (111)
5 e3 (003)	c5 (002)	26 Qxf7 (127)	Ng5 (111)
6 dc (003)	Qa5 (002)	27 Ng6+ (127)	Kh7 (111)
7 Rc1 (003)	dc (003)	28 Nxe5 (127)	Nxf7 (112)
8 Bxc4 (009)	0-0 (003)	29 Nxf7 (127)	Kg6 (112)
9 Nf3 (011)	Qxc5 (003)	30 Nd6 (127)	fe (113)
10 Bb3 (011)	Nc6 (004)	31 Nc4 (128)	ef (119)
11 0-0 (011)	Qa5 (004)	32 Rxf2 (128)	b5 (121)
12 h3 (013)	Bf5 (004)	33 Ne3 (128)	a5 (122)
13 Qe2 (013)	Ne4 (005)	34 Kg3 (136)	a4 (124)
14 Nd5 (014)	e5 (011)	35 Rc2 (139)	Rf8 (125)
15 Rxc6 (014)	ef (016)	36 Kg4 (144)	Bd4 (132)
16 Rc7 (015)	Be6 (053)	37 Re2 (146)	Bxe3 (141)
17 Qe1 (019)	Qb5 (058)	38 Rxe3 (146)	Rf2 (141)
18 Ne7+ (046)	Kh8 (059)	39 b3 (147)	Rxg2+(146)
19 Bxe6 (046)	fe (066)	40 Kf3 (147)	Rxa2 (146)
20 Qb1 (051)	Ng5 (078)	41 ba (147)	
21 Nh4 (079)	Nxh3+(090)	Draw agreed.	

In the second half of the match Kasparov quickly built up what appeared to be a decisive lead. By game 16 he led by 4 wins to 1, but overconfident play caused him to lose games 17, 18, and 19. In the final shoot-out Kasparov displayed the stronger nerves and again showed himself to be the better player, winning the match by 12½ to 11½. This was the first time that a reigning champion had successfully defended his title in a return match since 1896–97.

While this match was in progress, Andrey Sokolov of the U.S.S.R. defeated fellow countryman Artur Yusupov to earn the right to play a match with Karpov in the spring of 1987. The winner of that match would challenge Kasparov for the world title in October–November 1987.

Meanwhile, the women's world championship match was held half in Sofia, Bulg., and half in Borjomi, U.S.S.R. Maya Chiburdanidze of the U.S.S.R. retained her title by beating Elena Ahkmilovskaya, also of the U.S.S.R., 8½–5½.

The 1986 U.S.S.R. championship was won by Vitali Tseshkovsky, the British championship by Speelman (after a play-off), and the U.S. championship by Yasser Seirawan. After his defeat in the world championship Karpov was anxious to restore his fortunes as quickly as possible, and with very little time for rest he played in the Tilburg tournament in The Netherlands, which was won by Aleksandr Beljavsky (Karpov finished third).

The next important event of the year was the chess Olympiad in Dubai, from which Israel had been excluded by the chess federation. As a result, the event was boycotted by the teams of The Netherlands, Norway, Sweden, Denmark, and others.

The men's event was won by the U.S.S.R. with 40 points out of a possible 56. Second was England with 39 and third, the U.S. with 38½. Despite losing to Seirawan, Kasparov had the distinction of winning three gold medals in this Olympiad: a team gold because the U.S.S.R. won the event, the gold medal for the best performance on first board, and an individual gold for the best rating performance of the entire Olympiad. The U.S.S.R. also won the womens' Olympiad, with 33½ points from 42 games.

Immediately after the Olympiad, the OHRA tournament in Brussels provided a grand finale for the year. It was the strongest tournament since the Elo rating system was introduced in the early 1960s, with an average rating of 2636. Despite losing to Short during the first half of the event, Kasparov captured first prize with the incredible score of 7½ out of 10, two points ahead of Viktor Korchnoi of Switzerland. This result reinforced the view that Kasparov was a genuine rival for Fischer's position as the strongest player of all time. (RAYMOND KEENE)

CONTRACT BRIDGE

A novel one-day contract bridge tournament was played worldwide in June 1986. More than 100,000 players competed in their own clubs. The participation of sports and entertainment celebrities enhanced the event, and within 24 hours of its conclusion results and details were screened before an all-night audience at the Paris headquarters of the French Bridge Federation, with the bridge-playing film star Omar Sharif as host of the proceedings. Sponsored by the Japanese electronics firm Epson, the event was a success and would be repeated.

A further move to bring the average player into the rarefied atmosphere of world championship bridge took place during the 1986 world championship tournament, played in Miami Beach, Fla., in September. The three major championships—the knockout teams, the open, and the women's pairs—had previously been contested on a quota basis of participants according to the size of the country, augmented by pairs of world-ranking players. In 1986, however, these events were opened widely; additional pairs could enter and play the same deals as were being played in the championship proper, with a percentage of these new entrants qualifying for the main event.

Moves were made to limit the complexity and proliferation of new bidding conventions in pairs tournaments. A cleverly designed convention card was to be adopted as the World Bridge Federation (WBF) official card. Players would be required to complete this card, giving sufficient detail of their systems to permit opponents to understand them. Any methods that could not be properly explained in the space provided could not be played.

The United States took the honours in all the events in Miami Beach. In the mixed pairs Pam and John Wittes, Kerri Shuman and Bob Hamman, and Rozanna and Bill Pollack, all of the U.S., won the gold, silver, and bronze medals, respectively. In the open pairs Jeff Meckstroth and Eric Rodwell of the U.S. took the gold, followed by Wolfgang Meinl and Heinrich Berger of Austria; the bronze medal went to Stephen Burgess and Paul Marston of Australia. Amalya Kearse partnered world champion Jacqui Mitchell to win the gold in the women's pairs for the U.S., with Charlotte Palmond and Bettina Kalkerup of Denmark second ahead of Sally Horton and Sandra Landy of Great Britain.

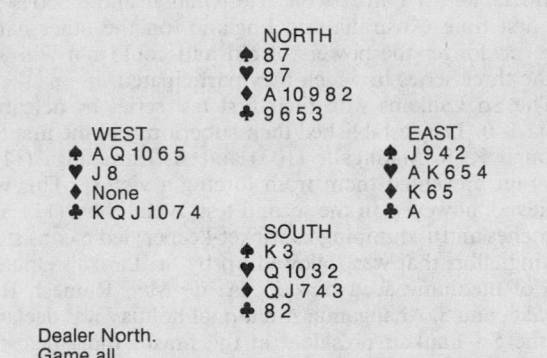

WEST	NORTH	EAST
	♠ 8 7 ♥ 9 7 ♦ A 10 9 8 2 ♣ 9 6 5 3	
♠ A Q 10 6 5 ♥ J 8 ♦ None ♣ K Q J 10 7 4		♠ J 9 4 2 ♥ A K 6 5 4 ♦ K 6 5 ♣ A
	SOUTH ♠ K 3 ♥ Q 10 3 2 ♦ Q J 7 4 3 ♣ 8 2	

Dealer North.
Game all.

In the closed room Woolsey and Manfield reached six spades after an uncontested auction. Their opponents, Mahmood and Fazli, had faint hopes of their partners reaching a grand slam. They were right in a sense. Nisar and Nishat held the East-West cards against Silverman and Robinson. Silverman threw a spanner in the works when he opened two diamonds, a bid that by that pair's methods showed a "weak two" in hearts, diamonds, or clubs. East doubled, South passed, and West and East had an uninterrupted auction up to seven clubs, as follows: 3♦ – 3♥ – 3♠ – 4♣ – 4♦ – 4♠ – 4 no trumps – 5♥ – 6♣ – 7♣. At this point North, Silverman, decided to double, and East, deciding that his partner's first bid showed a diamond suit, converted to seven diamonds. A thoroughly bemused West retreated to seven hearts. North took his life in his hands when he doubled, but all proved well since East-West decided to stay there. Declarer ruffed a diamond in dummy, cashed two top hearts, released the ace of clubs, and crossed to dummy with a spade finesse. He could now discard his losing diamonds on the clubs, and South made two trump tricks for a score of 500 and a swing of 1,970 points worth 18 match points. Doubled in seven spades (as they surely would have been), East-West would have scored 2,470 points and would have gained 14 match points to end the session with a lead of 32.

The U.S. completed its clean sweep when Steve Robinson, Neil Silverman, Bob Lipsitz, Ed Manfield, Kit Woolsey, and Peter Boyd beat Zia Mahmood, Nishat Abedi, Nisar Ahmed, and Jan-E-Alam Fazli of Pakistan in knockout team play. The first of four 32-board sessions ended in a tie, but one hand might have put the Pakistani team on the road to victory (*see* box). Pakistan failed to recover from the disaster and lost heavily. Sweden took the bronze medal with Bjorn Fallenius, Magnus Lindqvist, Nils Nilsland, and Anders Wirgren.

At the victory banquet Jaime Ortiz-Patino, retiring WBF president, handed over his gavel to the newly elected president, Denis Howard of Sydney, Australia. Howard, president of the Australian Federation and of Zone 7, had represented Australia both as player and as captain and had been a member of the WBF executive council since 1983. (HAROLD FRANKLIN)

CRICKET

In 1985–86 test cricket (competition between national teams) was notable for the continued preeminence of West Indies. The force of its fast bowling was unstoppable. New Zealand became recognized as the second best team, while India and Pakistan remained in the middle of the unofficial world table. Sri Lanka won a test match and a series for the first time. Australia and England, on the other hand, were no longer the powers of old and could not win any of the three series in which they participated.

The Sri Lankans won their first test series by defeating India 1–0. They established their superiority in the first test through R. S. Madugalle (103) and A. Ranatunga (111), but rain prevented them from forcing a victory. This was achieved, however, in the second test. Amal Silva (111 and 8 catches and 1 stumping as wicket-keeper) led a consistent batting effort that was followed up by Sri Lanka's efficient trio of medium-paced bowlers, A. de Mel, Rumesh Ratnayake, and S. Ahangama. A national holiday was declared by the Sri Lankan president at the finish. India held the upper hand in the third test, thanks largely to Mohinder Amarnath's unbeaten 116, but Sri Lanka held onto its lead by means of a partnership between Roy Dias and the captain, Duleep Mendis, who both made centuries.

Sri Lanka proceeded to Pakistan and lost a three-test series 2–0. The first game was a predictable draw on the high-scoring Faisalabad field, Aravinda de Silva's 122 for Sri Lanka being surpassed by Qasim Umar's 206 and Javed Miandad's 203 not out for Pakistan. The remaining matches were better balanced and were decided mainly by the fast bowling of Pakistan's Imran Khan, who returned to test cricket after a two-year absence and took 17 wickets in the series. The best bowling figures yet recorded for Sri Lanka, 8 wickets for 83 runs by Ravi Ratnayeke, could not prevent victory by 8 wickets for Pakistan in the second test; nor could another century by de Silva stop a 10-wicket win by Pakistan in the third.

Australia, meanwhile, had begun the home leg of two three-test series against New Zealand. It found the fast-medium bowling of R. J. Hadlee (*see* BIOGRAPHIES) to be overwhelmingly dominant. In Australia Hadlee took 33 wickets, including 15 in the first test at Brisbane (a record for New Zealand, as were his 9 wickets for 52 runs in the first innings). Although their captain, A. R. Border, maintained his world-class batting with 152 not out and G. R. J. Matthews made his first test hundred, the Australians went down by an innings in the first game. They recovered to beat New Zealand by 4 wickets in the second, thanks largely to the legspin of R. G. Holland, who took 10 wickets for 174 runs, but then went down by 6 wickets in the third test to lose the series 2–1. M. D. Crowe (188 in the first test) emerged as New Zealand's finest batsman.

Before the return series in New Zealand, Australia had first to play a three-test series against India. Their lack of success continued, but the Australians at least escaped from being defeated and drew the series 0–0. India's batsmen were all in fine form, led by Sunil Gavaskar, who scored two large centuries (166 not out and 172). K. Srikkanth and Amarnath hit one apiece. India's bowling, however, was not quite strong enough, and Australia twice narrowly avoided defeat. D. C. Boon made two centuries, while G. M. Ritchie, Border, and Matthews scored one each.

In New Zealand for the return leg, Australia lost again, this time 1–0. The first test was a rain-affected draw, Matthews's 130 being counteracted by J. V. Coney's 101 for New Zealand. The second test also ended in a draw but was a closer game. Border had to make a century in each innings (140 and 114 not out) to withstand New Zealand, for whom M. D. Crowe hit 137. The third test was decided by the off-spin of J. G. Bracewell, who took 10 wickets for 106. The batting of G. R. Marsh (118) and Boon, who carried his bat through the second innings for 58, could not prevent a comfortable New Zealand win.

Disputes over umpiring were an all too common feature of the season, especially when Pakistan paid a return visit to Sri Lanka. Pakistan won the first test by an innings (the off-spinner Tauseef Ahmed taking 9 wickets for 75) but then threatened to cancel the rest of the tour during the second test, which Sri Lanka won by 8 wickets. Sri Lanka's left-arm swing bowler K. Kuruppuarachchi took 5 wickets for 44 runs on his test debut, and seven leg-before-wicket decisions went against Pakistan, while none went against the home team. With the series at 1–1 the third test ended in a more amicable draw, Ranatunga (135 not out) and A. P. Gurusinghe (116 not out) batting well for the home side and Rameez Raja (122) for Pakistan.

Test Series Results, September 1985–September 1986

Test	Host country and its scores		Visiting country and its scores		Result
1st	Sri Lanka	347 and 61 for 4 wkt	India	218 and 251	Match drawn
2nd	Sri Lanka	385 and 206 for 3 wkt dec	India	244 and 198	Sri Lanka won by 149 runs
3rd	Sri Lanka	198 and 307 for 7 wkt	India	249 and 325 for 5 wkt dec	Match drawn
1st	Pakistan	555 for 3 wkt	Sri Lanka	479	Match drawn
2nd	Pakistan	259 and 100 for 2 wkt	Sri Lanka	157 and 200	Pakistan won by 8 wkt
3rd	Pakistan	295 and 98 for 0 wkt	Sri Lanka	162 and 230	Pakistan won by 10 wkt
1st	Australia	179 and 333	New Zealand	553 for 7 wkt dec	New Zealand won by an innings and 41 runs
2nd	Australia	227 and 260 for 6 wkt	New Zealand	293 and 193	Australia won by 4 wkt
3rd	Australia	203 and 259	New Zealand	299 and 164 for 4 wkt	New Zealand won by 6 wkt
1st	Australia	381 and 17 for 0 wkt	India	520	Match drawn
2nd	Australia	262 and 308	India	445 and 59 for 2 wkt	Match drawn
3rd	Australia	396 and 119 for 6 wkt	India	600 for 4 wkt dec	Match drawn
1st	New Zealand	379 for 6 wkt	Australia	435	Match drawn
2nd	New Zealand	339 and 16 for 1 wkt	Australia	364 and 219 for 7 wkt dec	Match drawn
3rd	New Zealand	258 and 160 for 2 wkt	Australia	314 and 103	New Zealand won by 8 wkt
1st	Sri Lanka	109 and 101	Pakistan	230	Pakistan won by an innings and 20 runs
2nd	Sri Lanka	273 and 32 for 2 wkt	Pakistan	132 and 172	Sri Lanka won by 8 wkt
3rd	Sri Lanka	281 and 323 for 3 wkt	Pakistan	318	Match drawn
1st	West Indies	307 and 5 for 0 wkt	England	159 and 152	West Indies won by 10 wkt
2nd	West Indies	399 and 95 for 3 wkt	England	176 and 315	West Indies won by 7 wkt
3rd	West Indies	418	England	189 and 199	West Indies won by an innings and 30 runs
4th	West Indies	312 and 39 for 0 wkt	England	200 and 150	West Indies won by 10 wkt
5th	West Indies	474 and 246 for 2 wkt dec	England	310 and 170	West Indies won by 240 runs
1st	England	294 and 180	India	341 and 136 for 5 wkt	India won by 5 wkt
2nd	England	102 and 128	India	272 and 237	India won by 279 runs
3rd	England	390 and 235	India	390 and 174 for 5 wkt	Match drawn
1st	England	307 and 295 for 6 wkt dec	New Zealand	342 and 41 for 2 wkt	Match drawn
2nd	England	256 and 230	New Zealand	413 and 74 for 2 wkt	New Zealand won by 8 wkt
3rd	England	388 for 5 wkt dec	New Zealand	287 and 7 for 0 wkt	Match drawn

In the only five-test series of the year, England was utterly outplayed by West Indies in the Caribbean and lost by the same margin (5–0) as in 1984. The fast bowling of Malcolm Marshall and Joel Garner (who each took 27 wickets) was reinforced by the Jamaican pair of M. A. Holding and B. P. Patterson, who were equally quick. No England batsman could score a century in the series, the captain D. I. Gower coming closest with an innings of 90. For West Indies R. B. Richardson made 102 in the second test and 160 in the third. In the fifth D. L. Haynes hit 131, while the West Indian captain, I. V. A. Richards, scored 110 not out off only 56 balls. This was the fastest century in test history in terms of balls received and completed England's ignominy.

England's performance did not improve when the team returned home to meet India and New Zealand. They lost 2–0 to India, for whom the batting of D. B. Vengsarkar was the decisive factor. In the first test Vengsarkar scored 126 not out; G. A. Gooch hit 114 for England but received insufficient support. In the second Vengsarkar hit 61 and 102 not out, while no England batsman could score more than 32. The third test was drawn, the new England captain M. W. Gatting scoring 183 not out and Chetan Sharma taking ten wickets for India. Sharma was well supported during the series by his fellow medium-pacers Kapil Dev and R. M. H. Binny and by the left-arm spin of R. J. Shastri and Maninder Singh.

England then lost a home series to New Zealand for the first time, 1–0. Having drawn the first test (Gooch hitting 183 against M. D. Crowe's 106 for New Zealand), England was undone in the second by the fast-medium bowling of Hadlee, who took 10 wickets for 140. Bracewell (110) helped New Zealand to build up a winning total. There was a little comfort for England in the third test, as it was on top after centuries by Gower and Gatting when the rain arrived.

In the English domestic season Essex won the Britannic Assurance county championship, Middlesex the Benson & Hedges Cup, Hampshire the John Player Special League, and Sussex the Nat West Trophy. In Australia, New South Wales won the Sheffield Shield and Western Australia the McDonald's Cup. In the Benson & Hedges World Series Cup finals, Australia beat India 2–0.

In the West Indies, Barbados took the Shell Shield, while Jamaica won the Geddes Grant-Harrison Line Trophy. In New Zealand, Otago won the Shell Trophy and Canterbury the one-day Shell Cup. Delhi won the Ranji Trophy, West Zone the Duleep Trophy, and Bombay the Irani Trophy in India. The Patron's Trophy in Pakistan was won by Karachi Whites, the Qaid-i-Azam Trophy by Karachi, and the PACO Cup by PACO. In South Africa the Currie Cup was won by Western Province. (SCYLD BERRY)

CURLING

With a cliff-hanging 4–3 triumph over Scotland in the final contest of the 28th men's world championships, watched by 5,724 fans at the Toronto Coliseum on April 6, 1986, Canada extended its record number of wins to 17 with a team from Alberta skipped by Ed Lukowich, supported by John Ferguson, Neil Houston, and Brent Simon. The Scottish four, from Perth, comprised David Smith (skip), Hammy McMillan, Michael Hay, and Peter Smith (the skip's brother). In 1967 Hay's father, Chuck, had led Scotland to its only world title.

Scotland led 1–0 after two ends, but Canada blanked the next four before scoring two in the seventh, when McMillan missed a key shot. David Smith failed to take advantage of a chance in the eighth, allowing Canada to steal one, but it was Lukowich's turn to miss in the ninth, enabling the Scots to tie the game at 3–3. In the tenth and final end, Lukowich knocked out a wide-open Scottish stone with a perfect final shot to gain the championship. On the Canadian team, Houston and Ferguson became the first curlers to win both world junior and world senior titles, having succeeded at the junior level in 1976 and 1978, respectively.

The Scots reached the final undefeated, having won all nine of their round-robin games before beating Steve Brown's U.S. team 3–1 in the semifinal. Canada ousted Stefan Hasselborg's Swedish team 6–3 in the other semifinal. Attendance for the tournament, which began on March 29, was 61,745.

Canada also won the eighth women's world championship, held at Kelowna, B.C., on March 23–30, by defeating Andrea Schopp's West German team 12–5 in the final. The victorious team, from St. Catherines, Ont., comprised Marilyn Darte (skip), Kathy McEdwards, Chris Jurgenson (the skip's sister), and Jan Augustyn. Canada advanced to the final by beating the Swedish team, led by Inga Arwidsson; Sweden then defeated Scotland 10–9 to finish third. It was Canada's third consecutive title.

The European championship, ending at Grindelwald, Switz., on Dec. 15, 1985, resulted in success in the men's competition for West Germany, which overcame Sweden 7–5 in the final. Norway finished third. The women's title went to the host nation with a 7–5 victory over Scotland in the final. The Norwegians again took the bronze medal. (HOWARD BASS)

CYCLING

Cycle racing in 1986 was dominated by a highly publicized struggle between France's Bernard Hinault and Greg LeMond of the U.S. in the three-week Tour de France (July 4–27). After 4,100 km (2,500 mi) of racing punctuated by accusations of betrayal between the two riders, who were competing for the same team, LeMond became the first non-European winner of the race since it was first held in 1903. LeMond crashed twice in the final four days but finished with an advantage of 3 min 10 sec over Hinault. Urs Zimmermann of Switzerland finished third, nearly 11 minutes behind the winner.

For the first time a full world championship road and track program was held in the United States at Colorado Springs, Colo., at high altitude. The benefits of the thin air at 1,800 m (6,000 ft) along with technological advances led to five world records on the 333.3-m cement track.

East Germany's Michael Hübner (amateur, 10.118 sec), Koichi Nakano of Japan (professional, 10.578 sec; *see* BIOGRAPHIES), and Connie Paraskevin of the U.S. (women, 11.245 sec) all set new records for a flying-start 200 m in time-trial qualifying rounds of the individual sprint competitions. Nakano went on to win the professional title for the tenth successive year before announcing his retirement from international competition. Hübner succeeded his compatriot Lutz Hesslich as amateur champion. Paraskevin was beaten in the semifinals, however, and Christa Rothenburger gave East Germany its first women's success.

In the 1,000-m time trial, Maik Malchow of East Germany improved his own world record, set as a junior six years earlier in Mexico, to 1 min 2.091 sec, and Czechoslovakia set a new outdoor mark of 4 min 17.710 sec for the 4,000-m team pursuit before its team went on to beat East Germany in the final by a mere 0.012 sec.

World best times were set under non-world-record conditions by Great Britain's Tony Doyle (professional 5,000-m

Greg LeMond of the U.S. passes close-contender Bernard Hinault of France on the outside in the Tour de France. The two rivals finished the 4,100-kilometre (2,500-mile) course only 3 min 10 sec apart, with LeMond taking first place.

DESPREZ—SIPA/SPECIAL FEATURES

pursuit, 5 min 40.338 sec), the U.S.S.R.'s Vyacheslav Ekimov (amateur 4,000-m pursuit, 4 min 28.953 sec), and France's Jeannie Longo (women's 3,000-m pursuit, 3 min 39.323 sec). Longo captured the pursuit title and went on to win the women's road race. The individual road program was staged over a 15.4-km circuit on the grounds of the U.S. Air Force Academy. (JOHN R. WILKINSON)

1986 Cycling Champions

Event	Winner	Country
WORLD AMATEUR CHAMPIONS—TRACK		
Men		
Sprint	M. Hübner	East Germany
Tandem sprint	R. Rehounek, V. Voboril	Czechoslovakia
Individual pursuit	V. Ekimov	U.S.S.R.
Team pursuit	S. Buchta, T. Cherny P. Soukup, A. Trcka	Czechoslovakia
1,000-m time trial	M. Malchow	East Germany
50-km points	D. Frost	Denmark
50-km motor paced	M. Gentili	Italy
Women		
Sprint	C. Rothenburger	East Germany
Individual pursuit	J. Longo	France
WORLD PROFESSIONAL CHAMPIONS—TRACK		
Sprint	K. Nakano	Japan
Individual pursuit	A. Doyle	Great Britain
50-km points	U. Freuler	Switzerland
One-hour motor paced	B. Vicino	Italy
Keirin	M. Vaarten	Belgium
WORLD AMATEUR CHAMPIONS—ROAD		
Men		
Individual road race	U. Ampler	East Germany
100-km team time trial	T. Cordes, R. Harmeling J. Talen, G. de Vries	The Netherlands
Women		
Individual road race	J. Longo	France
WORLD PROFESSIONAL CHAMPION—ROAD		
Individual road race	M. Argentin	Italy
WORLD CHAMPIONS—CYCLO-CROSS		
Amateur	V. Di Tano	Italy
Professional	A. Zweifel	Switzerland
MAJOR PROFESSIONAL ROAD-RACE WINNERS		
Tour de France	G. LeMond	U.S.
Tour of Italy	R. Visentini	Italy
Tour of Spain	A. Pino	Spain
Paris–Nice	S. Kelly	Ireland
Milan–San Remo	S. Kelly	Ireland
Tour of Flanders	A. van der Poel	The Netherlands
Paris–Roubaix	S. Kelly	Ireland
Flèche Wallonne	L. Fignon	France
Liège–Bastogne–Liège	M. Argentin	Italy
Dauphiné–Libéré	U. Zimmermann	Switzerland
Bordeaux–Paris	G. Glaus	Switzerland
G.P. de Midi Libre	C. Criquielion	Belgium
Tour of Switzerland	A. Hampsten	U.S.
Amstel Gold	S. Rooks	The Netherlands
G.P. Frankfurt	J.-M. Wampers	Belgium
Dunkirk 4-day	D. de Wolf	Belgium
Tirenno Adriatico	L. Rabottini	Italy
Ghent–Wevelgem	G. Bontempi	Italy
Tour of Romandie	C. Criquielion	Belgium
Tour de l'Avenir*	M. Indurain	Spain
Tour of Britain*	J. McLoughlin	Great Britain
Coors Classic*	B. Hinault	France
Berlin–Prague–Warsaw†	O. Ludwig	East Germany
Paris–Brussels	G. Bontempi	Italy
Tour of Lombardy	G. Baronchelli	Italy

*Mixed professional and amateur.
†Amateur.

FENCING

In one of the most keenly contested competitions in recent years, the Soviet Union won the Grand Prize of Champions award in the prestigious three-weapon world championship of fencing during the summer in Sofia, Bulg. The Soviets captured the coveted overall trophy by the slim margin of one point, outscoring Italy 87–86. West Germany was third with 83.

The Soviet Union emerged with three gold medals to lead in that department as well but, in contrast to recent years, it failed to monopolize the action. Italy and West Germany each carried off two golds in the eight-event meet, the French taking the remaining one.

Ten nations, an unusually high number, shared in first-, second-, and third-place medals. The big surprise was a silver medal won by Tulio Díaz of Cuba. It was the best showing by a competitor from that nation in six decades.

Competing in Sofia's suburban Winter Sports Stadium, Andrea Borella of Italy captured the individual foil crown by outscoring Díaz. In third place was Italy's Mauro Numa. The Italians then went on to win the team foil title.

France's only gold medal was gained by Philippe Riboud in épée. Romania's Miklos Bodoczi was the runner-up, while another Frenchman, Olivier Lenglet, carried off the bronze medal. In the team épée event France, despite its strong showing in the individual competition, failed to finish among the top three. West Germany won the gold medal, followed by the Soviet Union and Italy in that order.

Competition with the sabre was dominated by performers from Eastern Europe. The Soviet Union's Sergey Mindirgassov was the individual victor. Hungary's Imre Bujdoso and Bulgaria's Vasil Etropolski were second and third, respectively. In team sabre the order of finish was the Soviet Union, Poland, and Bulgaria.

In the only weapon with which women compete—the

foil—Anja Fichtel of West Germany outlasted Sabine Bau, her teammate, to win first place. Olga Vochtchakina of the Soviet Union finished third. Led by Vochtchakina the Soviets won the team foil gold medal. Italy placed second and West Germany third. (MICHAEL STRAUSS)

FIELD HOCKEY

At the sixth World Cup tournament in London in October 1986, Australia defeated England 2–1 in the final to win the trophy for the first time. England had finished first in group A and qualified with the Soviet Union for the semifinals, together with Australia and West Germany from group B. In the semifinals England beat West Germany 3–2 (in overtime), and Australia defeated the Soviet Union 5–0. West Germany finished third, followed by the Soviet Union, Spain, Argentina, The Netherlands, Poland, New Zealand, Canada, Pakistan, and India.

In World Cup preparatory matches England defeated Ireland 1–0 in London in January. In June a five-match series between The Netherlands and Pakistan was tied. In Moscow in July the Soviet Union defeated Pakistan 2–1, India 3–1, and France 2–1 to win a four-nation tournament. England defeated Belgium 4–0 in August at Marlowe, England. Australia, at home, beat Argentina in five successive matches. In September England beat West Germany 4–2 in Hamburg and Spain 3–2 in Barcelona; Spain defeated England 1–0 in Tarrasa, Spain. New Zealand won a three-nation tournament in Dundee, Scotland, defeating Scotland 4–1 and tying 1–1 with Poland.

In April West Germany won the eighth Champions Trophy tournament in Pakistan. Australia finished second, Pakistan third, Great Britain fourth, India fifth, and The Netherlands sixth. At the Asian Games in Seoul, South Korea, in September, South Korea won the gold medal by defeating Pakistan 2–1 in the final. India won the bronze medal. Indoors, Scotland retained the Home Countries championship by defeating England 4–3 at Crystal Palace, London.

In women's hockey The Netherlands won the sixth World Cup tournament in Amstelveen, Neth., in August 1986 by defeating West Germany 3–0 in the final. Other placings were (3) Canada, (4) New Zealand, (5) England, (6) Australia, (7) Argentina, (8) Soviet Union, (9) United States, (10) Scotland, (11) Spain, and (12) Ireland. Canada defeated England 3–1 at Wembley, London, in March, and later England won the Home Countries championship at Largs, Scotland, where Scotland finished second, Ireland third, and Wales fourth. In August the U.S. beat England 2–1 and 3–1 at Leicester, England. Indoors, England won the Home Countries championship in Cork, Ireland, where Ireland was second, Scotland third, and Wales fourth.

(SYDNEY E. FRISKIN)

FOOTBALL

Association Football (Soccer). Argentina's 3–2 victory over West Germany was the highlight of the 1986 World Cup competition, held in Mexico in May–June. The final round of the tournament, which takes place every four years, was enlarged in 1986 to include 24 countries. It was played first on a league basis, with the first two teams in each of the six groups of four proceeding to a single-game elimination round with a penalty shoot-out, after 30 minutes of extra time, to settle any tie games. Argentina had previously won the cup in 1978. The team's captain, Diego Maradona (*see* BIOGRAPHIES), was the outstanding player of the tournament.

Argentina opened with a 3–1 victory over South Korea in Mexico City's Olympic Stadium (June 2). Maradona, though closely marked and victim of some bruising challenges, created all three goals and popped in the tying goal in the next game against defending champion Italy in Puebla (June 5). Against Bulgaria, Argentina was in more commanding form than the 2–0 score indicated and as a result headed Group A, over Italy.

West Germany in Group E made hard work of qualifying and was beaten 2–0 by the smooth-flowing Danes in its final group game. Morocco headed Group F, over England, which after an unimpressive start (0–1) against Portugal in Monterrey finally triumphed over Poland when Gary Lineker of Everton (afterward transferred to Spanish club Barcelona for some £2 million) scored three goals. Brazil displayed its usual goal flair from the start, winning all three Group D matches; Spain finished second. The U.S.S.R. scored nine times in its Group C matches, with France second.

In the second round the U.S.S.R. was eliminated 4–3 by Belgium. In Argentina's 1–0 defeat of Uruguay the only goal was scored by Pedro Pasculli. Brazil pumped four goals past Poland to qualify for the quarterfinals, and Spain provided the biggest upset by downing Denmark 5–1. Other winners were West Germany, Mexico, England, and France.

In the quarterfinals West Germany had to struggle, scraping through on penalty shots in overtime against Mexico. France reached the semifinals in similar fashion although its victory over Brazil was closer. Socrates Oliveira, Brazil's captain, saw his penalty shot saved by Joel Bats, but the next six shots found their mark until the French captain, Michel Platini, missed and left the tally at 3–3. Brazil's Julio Cesar whacked his kick against a post, after which Luis Fernández rattled the back of the net to gain the victory for France. England lined up against Argentina in the quarterfinals and lost 2–1 as Maradona scored twice. The fourth quarterfinal contest went to a penalty shoot-out, with Belgium winning at the expense of Spain.

The semifinals ended in 2–0 victories for the West Ger-

ASSOCIATED PRESS LTD.

Diego Maradona, star player of the Argentine soccer team, is held high and raises the World Cup trophy in celebration of his team's victory over West Germany. The outcome at Mexico City's Aztec Stadium brought the cup back to South America.

mans and Argentines. France and West Germany battled it out at Guadalajara, where a critical error by goalkeeper Bats let a shot by defender Andreas Brehme slip under his body after the ball hit a post. Though the French had chances, their shooting was wayward, and West German goalkeeper Harald Schumacher was in top form. The final spot for Argentina was sealed by two goals from Maradona early in the second half of the game, played on the same day, June 25, in the Aztec Stadium in Mexico City. He completely unhinged the Belgian defense in a brilliant 12-minute spell.

The final game (June 29) sparkled from the opening minute when West Germany's Klaus Allofs forced a corner, and both sides went out for a win. Yet a strange error of judgment by Schumacher allowed José Luis Brown to storm through the defense and head home Jorge Burruchaga's free kick. Though Brown was injured later in the game, he stayed on to be the linchpin of Argentina's rear guard. Maradona inspired his team by example and exhortation and played a key part in all three goals, although he himself did not score. A foul on the Argentine skipper led to the free kick that resulted in Brown's goal after 21 minutes; then, ten minutes after the break, Maradona linked with Héctor Enrique and Jorge Valdano for the latter's inspired effort in which he slotted the ball tantalizingly wide of Schumacher's left hand and into the net. But if the South Americans thought they had the match sewn up, they reckoned without the skill and enthusiasm of "Kally" Rummenigge. He jabbed home the ball from close range following a corner on the left by Brehme; then nine minutes before the end of the game another similar corner allowed Rudolf Voeller to supply the finishing touch and tie the score. Scenting possible victory, West Germany surged forward only to have Maradona exploit gaps at the back by sending Burruchaga clear to put his country's name in the record books by clinching a second World Cup triumph with a fine goal.

Table I. Association Football National Champions

Nation	League winners	Cup winners
Albania	Dinamo	17 Nentori
Argentina	River Plate	
Austria	FK Austria	FK Austria
Belgium	Anderlecht	FC Brugge
Bolivia	Jorge Wilsteman	
Brazil	Curitiba	
Bulgaria	Beroe Stara Zagora	Vistosha
Chile	Cobresal	
Colombia	América de Cali	
Costa Rica	Alajuelense	
Cyprus	Apoel	Apollon
Czechoslovakia	Vitkovice	Spartak Trnava
Denmark	Brondby	B 1903 Copenhagen
Ecuador	Deportivo Quito	
El Salvador	FAS	
England	Liverpool	Liverpool
Finland	HJK Helsinki	Haka
France	Paris SG	Bordeaux
Germany, East	Dynamo Berlin	LOK Leipzig
Germany, West	Bayern Munich	Bayern Munich
Greece	Panathinaikos	Panathinaikos
Guatemala	Aurora	
Honduras	Olimpia	
Hungary	Honved	Vasas
Iceland	Valur	Fram
Ireland	Shamrock Rovers	Shamrock Rovers
Italy	Juventus	Roma
Luxembourg	Avenir Beggen	Union
Malta	Rabat Ajax	Rabat Ajax
Mexico	Monterrey	
Netherlands, The	PSV Eindhoven	Ajax Amsterdam
Northern Ireland	Linfield	Glentoran
Norway	Rosenborg	Lillestrøm
Paraguay	Olimpia	
Peru	Universidad Técnica de Cajamarca	
Poland	Gornik	GKS Katowice
Portugal	Porto	Benfica
Romania	Steaua Bucharest	Dinamo Bucharest
Scotland	Celtic	Aberdeen
Spain	Real Madrid	Real Zaragoza
Sweden	Malmö	AIK Stockholm
Switzerland	Young Boys	Sion
Turkey	Besiktas	Bursaspor
U.S.S.R.	Dynamo Kiev	Torpedo Moscow
U.S.	San Diego	
Uruguay	Peñarol	
Venezuela	Deportivo Táchira	
Wales	—	Wrexham
Yugoslavia	Red Star Belgrade	Velez Mostar

European Champions' Cup. Steaua Bucharest ended Romania's European trophy famine by edging out the expensively assembled Barcelona team on penalties in the final at Seville, Spain, on May 7. The shoot-out came when the score sheet was still blank. Barcelona started off like racehorses, whereas Steaua played a containing role. The pattern was repeated in the second half when Barcelona's Bernd Schuster controlled the midfield more, though Ladislav Boloni caused Javier Urruti to make two fine saves in the Barcelona goal and José Alesanco hooked clear from Victor Piturca during a Steaua attack. In the shoot-out the first four spot kicks were saved by the goalkeepers, but Marius Lacatus broke the deadlock for Steaua. Pichi Alonso's effort was then saved, Gavrilla Balint made it 2–0, and there it stayed.

European Cup-Winners' Cup. Dynamo Kiev, which in 1975 became the first Soviet team to win a European title, gained its second such championship by convincingly winning the Cup-Winners' Cup final in Lyon, France, on May 2 against Atletico Madrid. Dynamo set the seal on the game as early as the sixth minute when Aleksandr Zavarov scored. He controlled much of the play by using the flanks intelligently until he had to leave the game because of injury midway through the second half. Atletico's known ability to counter quickly was stifled by the efficient covering and tackling of the Ukrainian team. Two great saves by Viktor Chanov just after the break inspired Dynamo and its left-winger Oleg Blokhin to retain the initiative despite the exhortations of the largely partisan crowd of 39,000. Blokhin scored the second goal five minutes before the end of the game, and three minutes later Vadim Yevtushenko made the victory certain with a third goal.

North America. In the Major Indoor Soccer League, Cleveland and San Diego finished first in the Eastern and Western divisions, respectively. In the championship playoffs San Diego defeated Minnesota four games to three in the final round to gain the MISL title for the second year in a row. (TREVOR WILLIAMSON)

Latin America. Once again, Argentina was the dominant power in Latin-American soccer. The country's national team won the World Cup for the second time (*see* above), while River Plate gained the Libertadores de América Cup; it was the third year in a row that the coveted South American club championship was won by an Argentine team.

In contrast to its international success, though, the internal affairs of Argentine football were in disarray. The traditional national championship was played for the last time (Argentinos Juniors won it again), and a new first-division league was organized (won by River Plate). The new league was made up almost exclusively of teams from the city and province of Buenos Aires, with clubs from Córdoba and Rosario added for good measure. Although the quality of play improved after many of the weak provincial teams were discarded, any pretense to a national championship was also abandoned. Moreover, the stadia remained only half-filled as many Argentine stars—like Maradona, unquestionably the best player of the World Cup—were playing abroad.

The other traditional powerhouse of Latin-American soccer, Brazil, had a disappointing year. A hastily assembled national team played unevenly in the World Cup and was eliminated by France in the quarterfinals. Curitiba of

Paraná won the national Brazilian championship again but was knocked out early from the Libertadores de América Cup. Mexico, the World Cup host, also reached the quarterfinals, and like Brazil it was defeated in a penalty shoot-out. The Mexican league championship was won by Monterrey.

The other two Latin-American teams to reach the World Cup were Uruguay and Paraguay. Both advanced to the second round but were eliminated by Argentina and England, respectively. Uruguay's championship was won by Peñarol, and Paraguay's by Olimpia.

América de Cali won its fourth Colombian league championship in a row, and for the second time in as many years, it was the runner-up in the Libertadores de América Cup, an impressive performance by a team playing in a country with little soccer tradition. Other Latin-American club championships in 1986 included Jorge Wilsterman of Cochabamba in Bolivia, Cobresal in Chile, Deportivo Quito in Ecuador, Universidad Técnica de Cajamarca in Peru, and Deportivo Táchira in Venezuela.

(SERGIO SARMIENTO)

Rugby. *Rugby Union.* The 1985–86 rugby season was hectic as countries traveled on tours in preparation for the first World Cup, scheduled for 1987. Also taking place during the year were the centenary celebrations of the International Rugby Football Board (IB), held in England in April 1986. The IB staged a congress in Oxfordshire that was attended by representatives from more than 50 countries, and it also arranged two special matches involving the leading players from all of its eight member countries. In the first, held at Cardiff Arms Park, the Rest of the World defeated the British Lions 15–7; in the second, at Twickenham, a composite side representing Australia, New Zealand, and South Africa won 32–13 over a team selected from England, Scotland, Wales, Ireland, and France.

Immediately after those celebrations 31 of New Zealand's leading players undertook a tour of South Africa in defiance of the wishes of the New Zealand Rugby Union (NZRU). The "rebels," who called themselves the Cavaliers, did not claim to be representing their country, but the South Africans made the tour official from their own point of view by awarding caps for the tests. The South Africans won the test series 3–1. The NZRU subsequently banned the Cavaliers from selection for New Zealand's next two official tests.

France went on an ambitious tour, playing two test matches in Argentina and one each in New Zealand and Australia. The French were beaten 15–13 in the first test at Buenos Aires but won the second, also in Buenos Aires, 22–9. The French were then beaten 27–14 by Australia at Sydney and 18–9 by New Zealand (minus their Cavaliers) at Christchurch.

New Zealand was still without its Cavaliers for the first of the three tests against Australia in New Zealand in August and September, but some of them were recalled for the second and third tests. Australia won the first test 13–12 at Wellington, lost the second 12–13 at Dunedin, and won the third 22–9 at Auckland.

Wales toured Fiji, Tonga, and Western Samoa in May and June. They beat Fiji 22–15 at Suva, Tonga 15–7 at Nuku'alofa, and Western Samoa 32–14 at Apia. The Fijians had already made a tour of Wales and Ireland in October and November 1985. On that tour they lost to Wales 40–3 at Cardiff and to Ireland 16–15 in Dublin.

At the same time of the year, New Zealand toured Argentina, playing two tests in Buenos Aires. The New Zealanders won the first test 33–20, while the second was drawn 21–21. Japan had a disappointing tour of France in October 1985. In two international matches France defeated Japan 50–0 at Dax and 52–0 at Nantes.

The 1986 Five Nations' Championship resulted in France and Scotland becoming joint champions, with Wales and England tying for third and Ireland finishing last. Scotland won the Calcutta Cup, defeating England 33–6 at Murrayfield. The Scots then went to Bucharest and defeated Romania 33–18.

Rugby League. Honours were evenly divided when New Zealand toured Great Britain in October–November 1985, with each team winning a test and the third ending in a 6–6 draw. In the customary two tests between France and Great Britain, played in February–March 1986, the first resulted in a 10–10 draw and the second in a 24–10 win for Great Britain. The Challenge Cup was won by Castleford, which beat Hull Kingston Rovers 15–14 in the final on May 3. (DAVID FROST)

U.S. Football. *College.* Penn State won its second national championship in five years by defeating Miami of Florida 14–10 in the Fiesta Bowl at Tempe, Ariz., on Jan. 2, 1987. Coach Joe Paterno tied record holder Paul ("Bear") Bryant with his sixth undefeated regular season.

MCDONOUGH—FOCUS ON SPORTS

Penn State's D. J. Dozier, no. 42, breaks through the pack for the winning touchdown in the Fiesta Bowl, putting down the favoured University of Miami Hurricanes 14-10. Both teams had entered the competition unbeaten and untied.

Paterno also kept all his seniors on schedule to graduate in a year when academic and recruiting improprieties often upstaged the games.

Penn State and Miami went into the game with 11–0 records, the first time since 1973 that undefeated, untied teams had met in a bowl game. The match amplified support for a major-college tournament that would make such contests possible more often. Penn State and Miami were independents, and so the more prestigious Rose, Orange, Cotton, and Sugar Bowls could not pair them because of commitments to conference champions. The Fiesta Bowl attracted them by offering revenue from prime-time television.

Miami quarterback Vinny Testaverde won the Heisman Trophy as the most outstanding college player, before throwing five interceptions against Penn State. Testaverde, who swept most individual awards, was the national leader with 26 touchdown passes and 165.8 efficiency rating points. The Hurricanes' other national leader was Bennie Blades, with ten interceptions. In team categories Miami ranked second to Miami of Ohio's plus-24 turnover margin and Oklahoma's 42.4-point scoring average.

Oklahoma ranked third in the wire-service polls with an 11–1 record and set a major college record by leading in six of the eight basic offensive and defensive statistics. The Sooners ranked second in a seventh, total offense. Besides the scoring title their offense took the rushing championship with an average of 404.7 yd per game. Defensively, the Sooners won five shutouts and allowed top-ranked averages of 6.6 points, 169.6 total yards, 108.9 passing yards, and 60.7 rushing yards per game. Testaverde's passing accounted for four of the seven passing touchdowns and eight offensive touchdowns against Oklahoma.

Oklahoma linebacker Brian Bosworth, the team's leading tackler, was the most notable of at least 21 players disqualified from postseason games in the colleges' first year of drug testing. Because of his use of anabolic steroids, he was disqualified from the Orange Bowl, which the Sooners won 42–8 over Arkansas (9–3). Bosworth had already become a sensation with his hairstyles, jewelry, and war paint.

Arizona State (10–1–1), the Pacific Ten Conference champion, was ranked fourth in the Associated Press poll after winning the Rose Bowl 22–15 over eighth-ranked Michigan (11–2), the Big Ten champion. Fifth-rated Nebraska (10–2) won the Sugar Bowl 30–15 over tenth-ranked Louisiana State (9–3), the Southeast Conference champion. Auburn (10–2), rated sixth, beat Southern California (7–5) in the Florida Citrus Bowl. Seventh-ranked Ohio State (10–3) won the Cotton Bowl 28–12 over Texas A&M, the Southwest Conference champion. Alabama (10–3), rated ninth, was a 28–6 winner over Washington in the Sun Bowl.

Other conference champions included Clemson (8–2–2) in the Atlantic Coast, Pennsylvania (10–0) in the Ivy League, and San Diego State (8–4) in the Western Athletic. Pacific Coast Athletic Conference champion San Jose State (10–2) won the California Bowl 37–7 over Mid-American champion Miami of Ohio (8–4).

San Jose State won team statistical championships with 481.4 yd total offense and 312.5 yd passing offense per game, and it ranked second in rushing defense. San Jose State quarterback Mike Perez was the individual offensive leader with 329.9 yd per game.

Fresno State's Kevin Sweeney broke the major teams' Division I-A record with 10,623 passing yards for his career. The season passing leaders besides Testaverde were Michigan State's Dave Yarema with 2,581 yd and a 67.3% completion rate, Michigan's Jim Harbaugh with 10.1 yd per attempt, and Boston College's Shawn Halloran, whose six interceptions were only 2.3% of his passes.

Heisman runner-up Paul Palmer of Temple led all major-college players with 1,866 rushing yards and a record-setting 2,633 all-purpose yards, including catches and kick returns. Steve Bartalo of Colorado State led with 19 touchdowns and 114 points and set a career record with 1,215 carries. Auburn's Brent Fullwood had the top average running gain, 8.33 yd.

Long Beach State's Mark Templeton set records for running backs with 18 catches in a game and 99 for the season, which led all I-A players. He set a career record with 262 catches. Louisiana State's Wendell Davis led all receivers with 1,244 yd, as did Miami of Ohio's Andy Schillinger with 20.8 yd per catch and 12 touchdown catches. Cornelius Bennett of Alabama became the first linebacker to win the Vince Lombardi Trophy for best lineman.

In Division I-AA Georgia Southern at 13–2 won its second straight national championship with a 48–21 victory over Arkansas State (12–2–1). North Dakota State (13–

AP/WIDE WORLD

New York Giants quarterback Phil Simms steps back for a pass over Denver Broncos Rulon Jones (no. 75) in the Super Bowl first quarter. Simms, after an outstanding passing game that led to the Giants' 39–20 victory, was named most valuable player.

0) became the Division II champion for the third time in four years when it won 27–7 over South Dakota (11–3). Jeff Bentrim, who quarterbacked all four of those teams, won the Harlon Hill Trophy as the top Division II player, became the first player in any division to win three scoring championships, and broke Walter Payton's Division II record with 67 touchdowns. Augustana (Ill.) won an unprecedented fourth straight Division III championship 31–3 over Salisbury (Md.) State. Augustana's 12–0–1 record gave it a 50-game unbeaten streak.

Professional. The New York Giants won their first National Football League (NFL) championship since 1956 when they defeated the Denver Broncos 39–20 in the Super Bowl on Jan. 25, 1987, at Pasadena, Calif. Quarterback Phil Simms led the Giants to victory with an NFL play-off game record of 22 completions out of 25 pass attempts for 268 yd and three touchdowns; he was voted the game's most valuable player. Though they failed to capitalize on two scoring opportunities in the second quarter, the Broncos led 10–9 at halftime. But the Giants took control in the third quarter by shutting down Denver while scoring 17 points. In the conference championship games to qualify for the Super Bowl, the Giants defeated Washington 17–0 to win the National conference (NFC) title, and Denver beat Cleveland 23–20 in overtime to gain the American conference (AFC) honours.

Table II. NFL Final Standings and Play-offs, 1986

AMERICAN CONFERENCE	W	L	T	NATIONAL CONFERENCE	W	L	T
Eastern Division				Eastern Division			
*New England	11	5	0	*New York Giants	14	2	0
*New York Jets	10	6	0	*Washington	12	4	0
Miami	8	8	0	Dallas	7	9	0
Buffalo	4	12	0	Philadelphia	5	10	1
Indianapolis	3	13	0	St. Louis	4	11	1
Central Division				Central Division			
*Cleveland	12	4	0	*Chicago	14	2	0
Cincinnati	10	6	0	Minnesota	9	7	0
Pittsburgh	6	10	0	Detroit	5	11	0
Houston	5	11	0	Green Bay	4	12	0
				Tampa Bay	2	14	0
Western Division				Western Division			
*Denver	11	5	0	*San Francisco	10	5	1
*Kansas City	10	6	0	*Los Angeles Rams	10	6	0
Seattle	10	6	0	Atlanta	7	8	1
Los Angeles Raiders	8	8	0	New Orleans	7	9	0
San Diego	4	12	0				

*Qualified for play-offs.

Play-offs

Wild-card round	American finals
Washington 19, Los Angeles Rams 7 New York Jets 35, Kansas City 15	Denver 23, Cleveland 20 (two overtimes)
American semifinals	National finals
Clevoland 23, Now York Jets 20 Denver 22, New England 17	New York Giants 17, Washington 0
National semifinals	Super Bowl
Washington 27, Chicago 13 New York Giants 49, San Francisco 3	New York Giants 39, Denver 20

For the first time in one regular season, two teams, the New York Giants and the Chicago Bears, each won 14 games. The Giants were one of three teams to improve their won-lost record from the previous season by four games; the others were the Kansas City Chiefs and Cleveland Browns. The Giants won their first divisional championship since 1963 behind a defense that ranked second in yards and points allowed and first in rushing yards allowed. Linebacker Lawrence Taylor (*see* BIOGRAPHIES) sparked the Giants' defense with 20½ quarterback sacks, a league high, and was the second defensive player ever voted the NFL's most valuable player. Bill Parcells of the Giants was named coach of the year.

The Bears, despite starting four different quarterbacks because of injuries, set NFL records with 29 victories in two years and 39 in three years. They were the only team to win a third straight divisional championship. Their 168.8 rushing yards per game led the league for the fourth straight year, tying a 44-year-old record. They led in total defense for the third straight year, allowing 258.1 yd per game and ranking second against both the run and pass. They allowed the fewest points, 187, for the second straight year, setting an NFL record for a 16-game season. On the offense Walter Payton extended career records to 16,193 rushing yards, ten seasons of rushing, receiving passes, and returning kicks for more than 1,000 yd, and 77 games of more than 100 yd; Dennis Gentry's 28.8-yd kickoff return average led the NFL, and Kevin Butler led the NFC with 28 field goals and 120 points.

The San Francisco 49ers won their third divisional championship in four years with conference-leading averages of 256 passing yards and 380.1 total yards per game. Jerry Rice led the NFC and all wide receivers with 86 catches. He led all NFL pass catchers with 1,570 yd and 15 touchdowns. Roger Craig's 81 catches ranked second in the NFC and first among NFL backs. Safety Ronnie Lott made 10 of the 49er defense's 39 interceptions, both league highs. The 49ers also led in turnover differential, taking away 20 more than they lost.

The Washington Redskins defeated the Los Angeles Rams in the NFC's wild-card game for the two top teams that did not win divisional championships. Washington featured Dexter Manley, whose 18½ sacks ranked second in the league and led all defensive linemen, and George Rogers, who led the league with 18 rushing touchdowns. For the Rams, Eric Dickerson was offensive player of the year and led the NFL with 1,821 rushing yards, 404 rushing attempts, and 2,026 yd from scrimmage.

The Browns won their second straight divisional championship and their first play-off game since 1969. Quarterback Bernie Kosar, the NFL's youngest player, threw only ten interceptions for a league-low rate of 1.9%. The other AFC division winners were the Denver Broncos, with the conference's best rushing defense, and the New England Patriots, with its best pass defense. Denver's Sammy Winder led the AFC with 14 touchdowns. Stanley Morgan's 1,491 yd for New England led AFC receivers. The Patriots' Tony Franklin led the NFL with 32 field goals and 140 points.

The New York Jets' victory in the AFC's wild-card contest, which broke a five-game losing streak, ended Kansas City's first play-off appearance since 1971. Kansas City tied San Francisco for the NFL lead with 49 turnovers. Deron Cherry's 9 interceptions and the Chiefs' total of 31 led the AFC. Ten of the Chiefs' 41 touchdowns were scored by defenders or on kicking plays.

The Seattle Seahawks and the Cincinnati Bengals tied the Chiefs and the Jets with 10–6 records but lost play-off berths because their records were not as good against other AFC teams. Cincinnati's 405.6 yd per game led NFL offenses, with James Brooks averaging a league-high 5.3 yd per carry for the second-ranked rushing offense. For Seattle, Bobby Joe Edmonds's 12.3-yd punt-return average led the NFL; Curt Warner's 1,481 rushing yards led the AFC; and Steve Largent extended his streak of games with pass receptions to 139, an NFL record.

Other individual NFL leaders were the Minnesota Vikings' Tommy Kramer with a 92.6 passer rating, Los Angeles Raider tight end Todd Christensen with 95 catches, New Orleans Saints kicker Morten Andersen with an .867 field-goal rate (26 for 30), the Detroit Lions' Eric Hipple with a 63% pass-completion rate, and the Indianapolis Colts' Rohn Stark with a 45.2-yd punting average. The

St. Louis Cardinals led all teams in pass defense, allowing 164.8 yd per game. New Orleans running back Rueben Mayes was rookie of the year, and San Diego defensive end Leslie O'Neal was named the top defensive rookie.

The Miami Dolphins again were the league's top passing team. Their 298.7 yd per game and 17 sacks were league bests. Dan Marino's 44 touchdown passes led the NFL by 19, and his 92.5 rating led the AFC. But the Dolphins' defensive collapse made them one of four teams to finish four games worse than in 1985. The others were the Raiders, the San Diego Chargers, and the Green Bay Packers. The Raiders took slight consolation in their NFL-high 63 sacks, with Sean Jones's 15½ leading the AFC. When the Dallas Cowboys' record fell by three games, they experienced their first losing season since 1964. The Philadelphia Eagles allowed 104 sacks and broke the old record by 34.

The NFL gained its second highest average attendance, 60,365, in a season of mixed blessings. On the bright side, its first European exhibition was a success in London, and it suffered only a $1 judgment in losing an antitrust suit to the four-year-old United States Football League. The USFL then broke up, and its stars went to the NFL. They included former Heisman Trophy winners Herschel Walker, who caught 76 passes as a Dallas halfback, and Doug Flutie, the Bears' starting quarterback in the play-offs.

The year began ominously off the field with revelations after the Patriots' Super Bowl loss that at least six Patriots had used cocaine. Subsequent cocaine-induced deaths of basketball player Len Bias and Browns safety Don Rogers created public pressure for commissioner Pete Rozelle to institute an antidrug program, but an arbitrator disallowed the program because it had not been collectively negotiated with the players. Rozelle was more successful in reacting to heightened scrutiny of unnecessary violence on the field, for which he suspended three players.

Canadian Football. The Hamilton Tiger-Cats defeated the Edmonton Eskimos 39–15 in the Grey Cup on November 30 at Vancouver, B.C., to win the championship of the Canadian Football League (CFL). Hamilton led 29–0 at halftime in defeating the Western Division champions. The Tiger-Cats' 9–8–1 record was second best in the Eastern Division, but they defeated the first-place Toronto Argonauts (10–8) in the play-offs. The Grey Cup's most outstanding players, all Tiger-Cats, were quarterback Mike Kerrigan on offense, Grover Covington on defense, and Canadian Paul Osbaldiston, who kicked six field goals and three extra points.

For the season the Schenley Award for most outstanding player went to Winnipeg wide receiver James Murphy, who led league receivers with 116 catches, 1,746 yd, and 12 touchdowns. Winnipeg wide receiver Joe Paplawski was the most outstanding Canadian; Roger Aldag of Saskatchewan, the most outstanding offensive lineman; Calgary defensive lineman Harold Hallman, the most outstanding rookie; and British Columbia defensive end James ("Quick") Parker, the most outstanding defensive player and sack leader with 22. (KEVIN M. LAMB)

GOLF

Greg Norman of Australia was the dominant golfer of 1986. At Turnberry in Ayrshire, Scotland, he won the British Open convincingly, by five strokes from Gordon Brand of England. He was a player of immense talent, and only his nerve had seemed suspect as the major titles in the game consistently eluded him. But once he broke through to win the oldest championship of them all, Norman, at the age of 31, enjoyed an almost unprecedented run of success that established him as the head of the new Sony world rankings by winning six tournaments in a row. It began with the Panasonic European Open at Sunningdale, England, and continued through the Dunhill Cup at St. Andrews, Scotland (where Norman was captain of a three-man Australian team that also included David Graham and Rodger Davis); the Suntory world match-play championship at Wentworth, England; the Queensland Open; the New South Wales Open; and the South Australian Open.

Earlier in the year in the United States, Norman had won both the Panasonic Las Vegas International and the Kemper Open, and though he did not play during the last two months of the season in the U.S., he still finished as the leading money winner there with a record $653,296. He was only the second overseas player, after Gary Player of South Africa, to do so and also the first man whose worldwide prize money in a single season exceeded $1 million. He was the first man who had been, at different times in his career, leading money winner on the Australian tour, the European tour (1980), and the U.S. tour. Norman was also the first man to have held the lead going into the last round of the world's four major championships, the Masters, U.S. Open, British Open, and U.S. Professional Golfers' Association (PGA) championship; however, three of those titles eluded him.

In the Masters at Augusta, Ga., the first of the year's "majors," Norman had victory knocked from his grasp by Jack Nicklaus, who, at the age of 46 and apparently long since past his prime, won this title for the sixth time. It brought Nicklaus's tally of major championships to 20, for he could add to his six Masters, five PGAs, four U.S. Opens, three British Opens, and two U.S. amateur championships during a career that spanned more than a quarter of a century. With a round to go, Nicklaus was considered a serious contender by few people. Not only was he four strokes behind Norman but there were also eight players ahead of him, including Bernhard Langer, the defending champion from West Germany, Severiano Ballesteros of Spain, Tom Watson of the U.S., and Nick Price of South Africa, who in the third round had set a course record of 63. Nor did the picture change much over the first nine holes of the final round as Nicklaus completed them in 35. However, his 30 for the second nine with five birdies and an eagle three at the 15th hole, less a dropped stroke at the 12th, sent the challengers fleeing in all directions. Ballesteros had appeared to have the title in his grasp at the 15th, but on that hole a four-iron shot that he put into the water short of the green cost him not only the lead but ultimate victory. This left Norman, who had rallied late with four birdies in a row from the 14th, with the best chance of overtaking Nicklaus as he came to the last hole. Needing a fifth birdie to win, Norman instead missed the green with his approach shot, and then both he and Tom Kite (U.S.) failed to hole putts that would have earned each of them a tie with Nicklaus. Nicklaus's four rounds were 74, 71, 69, 65 (279).

In the U.S. Open at Shinnecock Hills, Long Island, which was being revisited for the first time in 90 years, Norman led Lee Trevino and Hal Sutton by a stroke with 18 holes to play. All three failed to sustain the challenge, Trevino and Sutton finishing in a tie for fourth place and Norman having to settle for a 75 and 12th place. Instead it was another apparently fading star, Raymond Floyd, who, at 43 years and 9 months, became the new and also the oldest U.S. Open champion. Floyd joined Gene Sarazen, Ben Hogan, Byron Nelson, Gary Player, and Jack Nicklaus as the only men to have won, in different years, the Masters, U.S. Open, and PGA. His rounds were 75, 68,

A joyful Jack Nicklaus (left) accepts the Augusta National Golf Club "Green Jacket" following his Masters tournament win there—his career's 20th major victory. Raymond Floyd (right) follows through on a stroke in his first successful bid for the coveted U.S. Open title. Both champions, Nicklaus at age 46 and Floyd at 43, were the oldest ever to win the respective competitions.

(LEFT) AP/WIDE WORLD; (RIGHT) BARTON SILVERMAN—THE NEW YORK TIMES

70, 66, and he won by two strokes from Lanny Wadkins and Chip Beck, both of the U.S.

Bad weather had marked the first round of the U.S. Open, and it was similarly rough at Turnberry for the first round of the British Open, only Ian Woosnam of Wales matching the par of 70. Because of these testing conditions, the Royal and Ancient Golf Club, which controlled the championship, was criticized for the manner in which it had "set up the course," fairways being considered too narrow and the rough too severe. But in the second round Norman made what proved to be his decisive move, with a 63 to equal the British Open record for a single round. There had been a distinct possibility that Norman would score even lower; if he had holed a 12-ft putt on the 17th green for an eagle three and then a birdie three on the 18th, he would have shot a 60. As it was, he could manage only a birdie at the 17th and then took three putts at the 18th. However, Norman was out in front, and this time he was there to stay. He led by a stroke from Tsuneyuki ("Tommy") Nakajima of Japan going into the last round, and when Nakajima took six at the round's first hole, it became a one-horse race, Norman's scores being 74, 63, 74, 69 (280, equal to par).

In the PGA at Toledo, Ohio, Norman was four strokes ahead of Bob Tway of the U.S. going into the last round, having led from the start with a 65 and then following that with rounds of 68 and 69. But his momentum was destroyed at the start of the final day when torrential rain flooded the course and play was suspended for 24 hours. Norman was not the same man the next day, and gradually his lead dwindled until he was even with Tway as they came to the 18th hole. Even then Norman after two shots was on the fringe of the green and Tway, at age 27 a leader of the next generation of U.S. golfers, in a bunker. But it was Tway who holed out from the sand for a birdie to snatch a spectacular victory. He had rounds of 72, 70, 64, and 70. With three other victories on the U.S. tour, Tway finished second to Norman on the U.S. money list.

It was only toward the end of the season that Norman replaced Ballesteros at the head of the Sony world rankings, based on the results of the three years 1984–86. Ballesteros long remained at the top because of a splendid season in Europe, where he won six tournaments: the Dunhill British Masters, the Carrolls Irish Open, the Johnny Walker Monte Carlo Open, the Peugeot French Open, the KLM Dutch Open, and the Lancôme Trophy, which he shared with Langer. This shared title was unprecedented. The two best players in Europe, having tied after 72 holes, still failed to reach a decision after four extra holes, and a draw was declared because of gathering darkness. Even so it was not the best of years for Ballesteros. In the major championships he made little impression other than in the Masters tournament, where he lost a fine opportunity and finished fourth. Ballesteros nevertheless set a new record in Europe with earnings of £242,208.

It was the arrival of another Spaniard, José-Maria Olazabal, that in many ways caused the biggest stir. It was Olazabal's first year as a professional, but he won two tournaments, the Ebel European Masters at Crans sur Sierre, Switz., and the Sanyo Open at El Prat, Barcelona, Spain. With some remarkably consistent golf throughout the season, Olazabal finished as the second leading money winner in Europe with £136,775. This automatically made him the Henry Cotton rookie of the year. Not even Ballesteros rose to the top so quickly in the professional ranks, although he was only 17 when he turned professional, whereas Olazabal was 20. Olazabal also received an unprecedentedly early invitation to play in the Suntory world match-play championship, losing in the second round to Nicklaus, who, in turn, was defeated by Norman, the ultimate winner against Sandy Lyle of Great Britain in the final. Unfortunately this win was marred, in Norman's opinion, by some unnecessarily biased crowd behaviour in favour of Lyle, and the Australian afterward threatened never to play in that tournament again.

An outstanding achievement of the year was the victory by Great Britain and Ireland in the women's Curtis Cup match at Prairie Dunes, Kan. They defeated the United States comfortably by 13–5, and it was only their third win in a series dating back to 1932. Moreover, it was the first time that any visiting British team, including Ryder and Walker Cup teams, had won in the U.S. For this, much of the credit went to the captain, Diane Bailey, and her inspirational leadership. Patricia Johnson, who won all her four games, Jill Thornhill, with three and a half points, and Belle Robertson, who at 50 was the oldest player ever

Golfer Jane Geddes shouts her delight in claiming the winner's trophy at the U.S. Women's Open in Kettering, Ohio. A finishing tie had put Geddes head to head with South African-born Sally Little in an 18-hole play-off—a measure needed for the first time since 1976.
AP/WIDE WORLD

to have appeared in the match, all made outstanding contributions as well.

The women's world amateur team championship for the Espirito Santo Trophy at Lagunita, Caracas, Venezuela, was won by the Spanish team of Macarena Campomanes, Mary Carmen Navarro, and Maria Orueta. France was second, the United States third, and Great Britain and Ireland fourth.

A week later at Lagunita, Canada won the men's amateur team championship to gain the Eisenhower Trophy, Mark Brewer, Brent Franklin, Jack Kay, and Warren Sye scoring 838 for the four rounds. The U.S. was second at three strokes behind, China third, and Sweden fourth.

At the Nissan Cup world championships contested between teams of six at Tokyo in November, Japan beat Europe 8–4, with a joint Australia-New Zealand team third, and the U.S. fourth. Nakajima made the best individual score.

For the second successive year Laura Davies was the leading money winner on the women's PGA circuit in Europe, clinching the honour by winning the last tournament of the year, the Spanish Open at La Manga, Spain. Altogether Davies had four wins, her most satisfying being that in the British Open at Royal Birkdale, when she had four rounds of 71, 73, 69, 70 for a 17-under-par aggregate of 283. Her total earnings for the season were a record £37,500.

Jane Geddes of the U.S. won the U.S. Women's Open at Kettering, Ohio, beating Sally Little of South Africa in an 18-hole play-off after they had tied at 287, Geddes with 74, 74, 70, 69 and Little with 73, 72, 72, 70. It was an eventful week at the Open; a derailed train released clouds of phosphorus smoke and forced the immediate area to be evacuated, heavy storms interrupted play on three of the five days, and then an earthquake measuring 4.2 on the Richter scale shook the course. Pat Bradley (*see* BIOGRAPHIES), with five victories on the U.S. Ladies' PGA tour, became leading money winner in the U.S. with official earnings of $492,021, a sum exceeded by only three players on the U.S. men's tour. (MICHAEL E. J. WILLIAMS)

GYMNASTICS

The 1986 World Cup tournament in gymnastics, held in Beijing (Peking), brought together the top gymnasts from the 1985 world championships, 17 men and 14 women. The Soviet Union dominated the tournament, as it had the world championships.

In the men's competition there was a tie for the all-around title, and there were three deadlocks in the individual events. Overall, the U.S.S.R. gained six gold medals to four for China and one for East Germany. For total medals, the U.S.S.R. won ten, China seven, East Germany three, and Italy one.

The U.S.S.R. won all five gold medals in the women's events and added two silvers and three bronzes. Romania accounted for the remaining five medals, three silvers and two bronzes.

Li Ning of China and Yury Korolev of the Soviet Union shared the gold medal for the men's all-around title, while world champion Elena Shushunova of the Soviet Union scored a narrow triumph by 0.125 points over Daniela Silivas of Romania in the women's all-around. The only perfect ten of the tournament was awarded to Shushunova in the vault.

In the individual World Cup events for men, Li Ning finished first in the free exercises and on the pommel horse. Korolev also earned a gold medal in the pommel horse and shared first place in the rings and vault. Valentin Mogilny of the Soviet Union shared the gold medal in the rings, and Silvio Kroll of East Germany shared first place with Korolev in the vault. Xu Zhiqiang of China and Mogilny shared first on the parallel bars.

In the women's individual events, Shushunova won gold medals in the free exercises, the uneven parallel bars, and the vault. The other gold medalist was Oksana Omeliantchik of the Soviet Union, who won the balance beam.

No U.S. men qualified for the tournament. In the all-around for women, Kelly Garrison and Sabrina Mar of the U.S. finished 13th and 14th, respectively.

(C. ROBERT PAUL, JR.)

HANDBALL

Naty Alvarado of Hesperia, Calif., won his eighth United States Handball Association (USHA) national open singles title in 1986 by defeating Vern Roberts, Jr., of Tucson, Ariz., 21–15, 21–4 at the Houston (Texas) Downtown YMCA. Alvarado's eighth title (his fifth in a row) set a new USHA record for number of championships won and left him only one short of the Amateur Athletic Union (AAU) record of nine singles titles set by Joe Platak in the 1930s and '40s.

Alvarado, teaming with Roberts, fell short in his attempt to win his fifth consecutive open doubles title. They were upset in the semifinals by the San Ramon, Calif., team of Rick Christian and Mike Connors, who were in turn upset in the finals by Chicago's Jon Kendler and Los Angeles's Poncho Monreal 12–21, 21–10, 11–1.

Peanut Motal of Martinez, Calif., won her second straight women's open singles title by defeating Rosemary Bellini of New York City 21–4, 21–15. Susan Oakleaf and LeaAnn Tyson of Austin, Texas, won the open doubles title, defeating Motal and Allison Roberts of Cincinnati, Ohio, 21–16, 21–14.

In other action Pat Kirby of Tucson convincingly regained the masters singles title (for players aged 40 and over), which he had lost in 1985 for the first time in five years, by defeating masters newcomer Larry Aguiar of Hayward, Calif., 21–7, 21–16. Stuffy Singer and Steve August of Los Angeles teamed to win the masters doubles title by defeating Kirby and Fred Munsch of New York City 21–7, 21–20. Other winners included Tom Natale of Tucson (golden singles for players 50 and over); Tom Ciasulli of Mountainside, N.J. (super singles for players 60 and over); and Monroe Seifer of New York City (diamond singles for players 70 and over).

Also in 1986 Kirby became the 21st player inducted into the Handball Hall of Fame. Kirby began his handball career in Ireland, the birthplace of modern handball, where he won 16 All-Ireland championships. After moving to the United States he won three national AAU championships and three Canadian national titles, the only player ever to win titles in all three countries. (TERRY CHARLES MUCK)

HORSE RACING

Thoroughbred Racing and Steeplechasing. *United States and Canada.* Lady's Secret won the Eclipse Award as champion older filly or mare of 1986 with a clean sweep of the 229 votes cast by representatives of the Thoroughbred Racing Associations, the National Turf Writers Association, and the *Daily Racing Form.* The four-year-old daughter of Secretariat was one of five Breeders' Cup winners to earn Eclipse Award honours. It marked the third time in as many years that the seven-race Cup series had produced five champions. Besides Lady's Secret the others were Manila, Brave Raj, Capote, and Smile.

Lady's Secret, favoured to succeed Spend a Buck as horse of the year, won 10 of 15 starts, all in graded stakes races. Eight of her victories came in Grade I stakes, making her the leading winner of such races since the Thoroughbred Owners and Breeders Foundation began grading stakes in 1973. She defeated male rivals in the Whitney Handicap and finished either second or third in three other stakes against males.

Lady's Secret also helped her owners, trainer, and jockey—Mr. and Mrs. Eugene Klein, D. Wayne Lukas, and Pat Day—win Eclipse Awards in their respective categories. Lukas, winning for a second consecutive year, had another Eclipse Award victor in the two-year-old champion colt Capote. It also was the second consecutive Eclipse Award for the Kleins, whose Thoroughbreds were trained by Lukas.

Flatterer, a seven-year-old gelding that had been voted champion steeplechaser the previous three years, was the only equine champion to repeat. Other Eclipse Award winners included: two-year-old filly, Brave Raj; three-year-old colt, Snow Chief; three-year-old filly, Tiffany Lass; older male horse, Turkoman; male turf horse, Manila; female turf horse, Estrapade; sprinter, Smile; breeder, Paul Mellon; and apprentice jockey, Allen Stacy. Mellon was previously honoured in 1971. Snow Chief and Brave Raj were trained by Mel Stute.

Lukas, who in 1978 changed from training quarter horses to training Thoroughbreds, for the third straight year set an international record for purse earnings with a total of $12,344,595. He led all trainers with 64 stakes victories, six fewer than his record total in 1985.

Day finished first in three categories: races won (429), stakes races won (55), and stakes earnings ($6,426,225). Winner of an Eclipse Award in 1984, he was champion jockey in number of races won for the fourth time in five years. Stacy, who competed primarily on the Maryland circuit, led the apprentice riders with 278 victories. Mr. and Mrs. Klein, who owned Lady's Secret in partnership with Mel Hatley and also were part owners of Capote, accumulated $3.6 million in stakes earnings with a comparatively small but talented stable.

Manila was successful in eight of ten starts, including six stakes, and defeated older horses the four times he faced them. He won his last six races of the year, capped by the Breeders' Cup Turf, and earned $1,814,729. Only Snow Chief, the year's top money earner with $1,875,200, and Lady's Secret ($1,871,053) earned more.

Snow Chief numbered the Florida Derby, Santa Anita Derby, and Preakness among his five victories. He was sidelined by injury in early summer. Besides Snow Chief in

JERRY COOKE/SPORTS ILLUSTRATED

An unexpected winner, Ferdinand thunders to lead the field in the 112th Kentucky Derby at Churchill Downs. The 17-1 underdog came from last place at the urging of famed jockey Bill Shoemaker, age 54, to pull away for a 2¼-length upset victory.

Far in front, Snow Chief crosses the line for a surprising finish in the 111th Preakness Stakes, just two weeks after losing the Kentucky Derby 19½ lengths behind the winner, Ferdinand. Snow Chief's win toppled hopes that Ferdinand would take the Triple Crown.

AP/WIDE WORLD

the Preakness, other winners of the triple crown for three-year-olds were Ferdinard (ridden by 54-year-old Bill Shoemaker) in the Kentucky Derby and Danzig Connection in the Belmont Stakes.

The stretch-running Turkoman amassed earnings of $1,531,664 from four firsts and three seconds in eight starts. He won two Grade I events, the Widener Handicap and the Marlboro Cup, and finished second to Skywalker in the Breeders' Cup Classic. Estrapade, another million-dollar earner, defeated males in the Budweiser-Arlington Million and in the Oak Tree Invitational.

Sam-Son Farm's Ruling Angel was voted Canada's horse of the year and also the two-year-old filly champion. It was the third consecutive year that Ernie Samuel's stable had raced a horse of the year. Dauphin Fabuleux won in 1984 and Imperial Choice in 1985. Sam-Son Farm had another 1986 champion, the two-year-old Blue Finn.

Carotene, owned by the Kinghaven Farms of D. G. ("Bud") Wilmot and his family, was voted champion three-year-old filly and champion turf runner in Canada. Among her triumphs was the Breeders' Stakes, one of Canada's triple crown races. Golden Choice won the other two, the Queen's Plate and the Prince of Wales, to clinch the three-year-old colt championship. Other winners of the Sovereign Awards denoting champions: sprinter, New Connection; older filly or mare, Bessarabian; and older male, Let's Go Blue. (JOSEPH C. AGRELLA)

Europe and Australia. A significant change of emphasis had entered European racing in recent years. The fashion had swung away from the exploitation of two-year-olds toward saving them for the classic races at three. So many of the best juveniles were failing to progress that the leading trainers altered their methods, particularly with colts. Shirley Heights, successful in 1978, was the last Epsom Derby winner that had won a group race at two. The fact that prize money for the two-year-old events had not kept pace with that for older horses helped the process, but the apparent frailty of the modern Thoroughbred seemed more significant. A succession of harsh winters and late springs in northern Europe also encouraged cautious handling of young talent.

Dancing Brave, the best three-year-old in Europe in 1986 (though he was to fail in California later when at less than his best), had won two minor contests at a mile in his only appearances during 1985, while Shahrastani, which beat him by ½ length in the Epsom Derby, had finished second in his only outing as a two-year-old. Dancing Brave won the Craven Stakes and Two Thousand Guineas and was the favourite to win the Derby. In that race he was beginning a move from the rear when he became hampered early in the straightaway and, although he finished fast, he could not catch Shahrastani. Shahrastani had prepared with victories at Sandown and York and later went on to claim the Irish Derby by eight lengths from Royal Ascot winner Bonhomie. The Irish Derby was sponsored by Budweiser beer for the first time and, with a much increased prize and already possessing a favourable date three and a half weeks after its rival, at the end rather than the beginning of June, it began to threaten the reputation of the Epsom Derby as the principal three-year-old classic race in Europe.

Dancing Brave, meanwhile, beat Triptych by four lengths in the Coral-Eclipse Stakes before gaining his revenge on Shahrastani in the King George VI and Queen Elizabeth Diamond Stakes at Ascot on July 26. He won by ¾ length and 4 lengths from Shardari and Triptych, respectively, with Shahrastani another 5 lengths behind. Shardari defeated Triptych in the Matchmaker International (the former Benson & Hedges Gold Cup).

Shahrastani was reported to have suffered from a breathing problem at Ascot and did not race again until the Prix de l'Arc de Triomphe on October 5. Dancing Brave was given a six-week break and then gained an easy success at Goodwood in preparation for his Arc clash with the French champion, Bering. This colt had won the second of his two races as a juvenile and began 1986 with a hat trick of triumphs, culminating in a comfortable victory in the Prix du Jockey-Club (French Derby) on June 8. Bering was rested until September, when he won the Prix Niel, over the Arc course and distance. The Arc drew its most competitive field in some years, thanks to greatly increased prize money. It was a thrilling affair, 10 of the 15 horses having a chance to win as they approached the final furlong. Bering then went to the front on the outside,

Major Thoroughbred Race Winners, 1986

Race	Won by	Jockey	Owner
United States			
Acorn	Lotka	J. Bailey	Henryk de Kwiatkowski
Arkansas Derby	Rampage	P. Day	Mr. and Mrs. John Reed
Arlington Classic	Sumptious	R. Romero	John A. Bell III
Arlington-Washington Futurity	Bet Twice	C. Perret	Blanche P. Levy
Arlington-Washington Lassie	Delicate Vine	G. Stevens	Greg Alsdorf, Robert Frankel, and Jerome Moss
Belmont	Danzig Connection	C. McCarron	Henryk de Kwiatkowski
Blue Grass	Bachelor Beau	L. Melancon	Richard A. Waterfield and Jack A. Tafel
Breeders' Cup Juvenile	Capote	L. Pincay, Jr.	Eugene Klein, Barry Beal, and L. R. French
Breeders' Cup Juvenile Fillies	Brave Raj	P. Valenzuela	Dolly Green
Breeders' Cup Sprint	Smile	J. Vásquez	Frances A. Genter Stable
Breeders' Cup Mile	Last Tycoon	Y. Saint-Martin	R. C. Strauss
Breeders' Cup Distaff	Lady's Secret	P. Day	Mr. and Mrs. Eugene Klein
Breeders' Cup Turf	Manila	J. Santos	B. M. Shannon
Breeders' Cup Classic	Skywalker	L. Pincay, Jr.	Oak Cliff Stable
Brooklyn	Little Missouri	J. Samyn	Loblolly Stable
Budweiser-Arlington Million	Estrapade	F. Toro	Allen E. Paulson
Champagne	Polish Navy	R. Romero	Ogden Phipps
Coaching Club American Oaks	Valley Victory	R. Romero	Richard N. Dick and others
Delaware Handicap	Shocker T.	G. St. Leon	Thomasina Caporella
Flamingo	Badger Land	J. Velásquez	Mel Hatley and Jeff Lukas
Florida Derby	Snow Chief	A. Solis	Carl E. Grinstead and Ben Rochelle
Futurity	Gulch	A. Cordero, Jr.	Peter M. Brant
Gulfstream Park Handicap	Skip Trial	R. Romero	Mrs. Ben Cohen
Hialeah Turf Cup	Sondrio	C. Perret	Craig B. Singer
Hollywood Derby (2 divisions)	Thrill Show	W. Shoemaker	Mary Jones Bradley, Richard Duchossois, and Charles Whittingham
	Spellbound	R. Sibille	Edward G. Brennan
Hollywood Futurity	Temperate Sil	W. Shoemaker	Frankfurt Stable and Charles Whittingham
Hollywood Gold Cup	Super Diamond	L. Pincay, Jr.	Roland Sahm
Jockey Club Gold Cup	Creme Fraiche	R. Romero	Brushwood Stable
Kentucky Derby	Ferdinand	W. Shoemaker	Mrs. Elizabeth A. Keck
Kentucky Oaks	Tiffany Lass	G. Stevens	Aaron U. Jones
Man o'War	Dance of Life	P. Day	Rokeby Stable
Marlboro Cup Invitational	Turkoman	G. Stevens	Saron Stable
Meadowlands Cup	Broad Brush	A. Cordero, Jr.	Robert E. Meyerhoff
Metropolitan	Garthorn	R. Meza	Mr. and Mrs. Jerome Moss
Preakness	Snow Chief	A. Solis	Carl Grinstead and Ben Rochelle
Santa Anita Derby	Snow Chief	A. Solis	Carl Grinstead and Ben Rochelle
Santa Anita Handicap	Greinton	L. Pincay, Jr.	Mary Jones Bradley
Suburban	Roo Art	P. Day	Barbara Holleran
Travers	Wise Times	J. Bailey	Russell L. Reineman
Turf Classic	Manila	J. Santos	B. M. Shannon
Washington (D.C.) International	Lieutenant's Lark	R. Davis	Lowell T. Stevens, Jr.
Widener	Turkoman	C. McCarron	Saron Stable
Wood Memorial Invitational	Broad Brush	V. Bracciale	Robert E. Meyerhoff
Woodward	Precisionist	C. McCarron	Fred W. Hooper
England			
One Thousand Guineas	Midway Lady	R. Cochrane	H. Ranier
Two Thousand Guineas	Dancing Brave	G. Starkey	K. Abdulla
Derby	Shahrastani	W. Swinburn	The Aga Khan
Oaks	Midway Lady	R. Cochrane	H. Ranier
St. Leger	Moon Madness	P. Eddery	Lavinia, duchess of Norfolk
Coronation Cup	Saint-Estèphe	P. Eddery	Y. Houyvet
Ascot Gold Cup	Longboat	W. Carson	R. Hollingsworth
Coral-Eclipse Stakes	Dancing Brave	G. Starkey	K. Abdulla
King George VI and Queen Elizabeth Diamond Stakes	Dancing Brave	P. Eddery	K. Abdulla
Sussex Stakes	Sonic Lady	W. Swinburn	Sheikh Mohammed
Matchmaker International	Shardari	W. Swinburn	The Aga Khan
Dubai Champion Stakes	Triptych	A. Cruz	A. Clore
France			
Poule d'Essai des Poulains	Fast Topaze	C. Asmussen	M. Fustok
Poule d'Essai des Pouliches	Baiser Volé	G. Guignard	R. Sangster
Prix du Jockey-Club	Bering	G. Moore	Mme A. Head
Prix de Diane Hermès	Lacovia	F. Head	G. Oldham
Prix Royal-Oak	El Cuite	S. Cauthen	Sheikh Mohammed
Prix Ganay	Baillamont	F. Head	S. Niarchos
Prix Lupin	Fast Topaze	C. Asmussen	M. Fustok
Grand Prix de Paris	Swink	W. Swinburn	N. B. Hunt
Grand Prix de Saint-Cloud	Acatenango	S. Cauthen	Gestüt Fährhof
Prix Vermeille	Darara	Y. Saint-Martin	The Aga Khan
Prix de l'Arc de Triomphe	Dancing Brave	P. Eddery	K. Abdulla
Grand Critérium	Danishkada	Y. Saint-Martin	The Aga Khan
Ireland			
Irish Two Thousand Guineas	Flash of Steel	M. Kinane	B. Firestone
Irish One Thousand Guineas	Sonic Lady	W. Swinburn	Sheikh Mohammed
Irish Derby	Shahrastani	W. Swinburn	The Aga Khan
Irish Oaks	Colorspin	P. Eddery	Helena Springfield, Ltd.
Irish St. Leger	Authaal	C. Roche	Sheikh Mohammed
Phoenix Champion Stakes	Park Express	J. Reid	P. Burns
Italy			
Derby Italiano	Tommy Way	W. Carson	Scuderia Eraseo
Grand Premio del Jockey-Club	Antheus	G. Moore	J. Wertheimer
West Germany			
Deutsches Derby	Philipo	D. Richardson	Stall Surinam
Grosser Preis von Baden	Acatenango	G. Bocskai	Gestüt Fährhof
Grosser Preis von Berlin	Acatenango	G. Bocskai	Gestüt Fährhof
Preis von Europa	Allez Milord	G. Starkey	J. Brody

but Dancing Brave swept past him some 100 m (330 ft) from the finish to win by 1½ lengths. Triptych, which ran well in top-class company all season, was ½ length back in third, closely followed by stable companions Shahrastani and Shardari. Acatenango, the best horse produced in West Germany in many years, finished seventh, while the 1985 Japanese Derby winner, Sirius Symboli, and the Chilean Oaks winner, Maria Fumata, filled the last two places.

Triptych gained a well-merited reward two weeks later by winning the Dubai Champion Stakes, at Newmarket, by ¾ length from Celestial Storm, previously runner-up to Moon Madness in the English St. Leger, and by four lengths from Park Express, which had won Ireland's richest all-ages event, the Phoenix Champion Stakes, in early September. Triptych was the fourth French-trained winner of a Group I race in England, the highest rate of success for cross-Channel raiders in many years. Her triumph followed the victories of Saint-Estèphe in the Coronation Cup and of Last Tycoon in both the King's Stand Stakes and William Hill Sprint Championship.

Midway Lady was the best filly early in the season in Britain, winning the One Thousand Guineas and Oaks. Because of injuries, however, those were her only races. Lacovia, victorious in the Prix de Diane (French Oaks), also broke down. Sonic Lady, a close third in the One Thousand Guineas, emerged as the leading European performer at a mile with six wins in eight attempts in 1986. In addition to winning the Irish One Thousand Guineas, she defeated all comers in the Sussex Stakes and Prix du Moulin de Longchamp. But she failed in the Breeders' Cup Mile in California, won by Last Tycoon, which thus displayed a remarkable versatility.

Pat Eddery was champion jockey in England after a brilliant season, and Michael Stoute was the leading trainer. Racing mourned the death of a former great jockey, Sir Gordon Richards (see OBITUARIES).

In Australia, At Talaq, fourth in the 1984 Epsom Derby and successful in the Grand Prix de Paris shortly thereafter, won the Melbourne Cup. However, the star of the year in Australasia was the New Zealand-bred gelding Bonecrusher, acclaimed locally as the best in the world.

Although not the best jumper anywhere, Dawn Run added to her already enormous popularity when she became the first horse to complete the Champion Hurdle (1984) and Cheltenham Gold Cup double. Sadly, the Irish mare was killed at Auteuil, Paris, in June, as the result of a fall in the Grande Course de Haies d'Auteuil, won by Le Rheusois from the three-time U.S. champion jumper Flatterer. West Tip was a well-backed winner of the Seagram Grand National. (ROBERT W. CARTER)

Harness Racing. In the U.S. in 1986 Forrest Skipper (best time, 1 min 51⅗ sec) posted his 13th consecutive victory in the $301,350 Breeders' Crown. Falcon Seelster (1 min 51⅗ sec) was the champion on the five-furlong and half-mile tracks. In a 1-min 52⅖-sec time trial at Lexington, Ky., Razzle Hanover became the fastest two-year-old pacer ever. The Hambletonian of $1,172,082 was won by Nuclear Kosmos in two heats of 1 min 54⅘ sec and 1 min 56⅕ sec. Amity Chief won the Messenger in 1 min 55⅘ sec, defeating Barberry Spur, winner of both the Little Brown Jug and the Cane Pace. Sugarcane Hanover took the 94th Kentucky Futurity in 1 min 55⅖ sec, while the Breeders' Crown for aged trotters was won by Grades Singing and the World Trotting Derby by Royal Prestige. Jate Lobell made it eight in a row by winning the Fox Stake in 1 min 54⅕ sec, while Laughs won the $1,025,500 Meadowlands Pace for three-year-olds in 1 min 52⅕ sec.

In New Zealand the $125,000 Benson & Hedges New Zealand two-year-old championship went to Race Ruler, and Bionic Chance took the Cigna $125,000 pace final. Free's Bret won the New Zealand Oaks and Alba's Reign the Pacers' Derby. Comedy Lad took the $250,000 Auckland Cup. The New Zealand Cup in late 1985 was won by Borana. In Australia Western Australia pacer Village Kid won the $125,000 Hunter Cup, the $155,000 JPS Miracle Mile, and also the Inter-Dominion Pacing championship. Wondai's Mate won the $100,000 JPS Championship in Brisbane, and True Delight took the Truer Memorial at Bankstown, also worth $100,000.

For the second consecutive year Utah Bulwark won the Swedish championship with a record time of 2 min 0.1 sec for the 2,640 m; at Göteborg Utah Bulwark beat a U.S. horse, Grades Singing, in a $55,000 team race. Norway's Rex Rodney won the Forus Open Trot, and at Stockholm he won the Elitlopp. Rebur won Sweden's five-year-old championship; the four-year-old championship went to Garrett Lobell.

In Norway Rex Rodney won the Oslo Grand Prix and at the New Biri track set a Norwegian record of 1 min 57.2 sec over 1,600 m against international competition. Norway's Jarlsberg Grand Prix final was won by Finland's Dynastic. Davidia Hanover beat Emile and Callit in a heat and in the final of the Finlandia. Black Laukko won the Finnish Derby with a time of 2 min 4.2 sec for 2,600 m. In Denmark Junior Lobell won the Copenhagen Cup with a time of 1 min 58.4 sec for 2,011 m, and he also won the Greyhound Rennen in West Germany. Every Way was victorious in the German Derby as well as the Prix Henri Crovoisier in France. The Netherlands Derby was won by All or Nothing in 2 min 0.3 sec over 2,600 m.

In France the Prix d'Amérique of $303,200 was won by Ourasi in a race record of 2 min 3.1 sec for 2,650 m. Ourasi went on to win 12 consecutive races, including the Prix d'Europe. At Cesena, Italy, Callit won the Campionato and Havios the Union Européenne du Trot (UET) five-year-old championship. Feystongal won the Italian Derby, and Mac The Knife won the Premio Duomo as well as the UET Grand Prix of approximately $125,000.

In the U.K. the Famous Musselburgh Pacing Handicap, with a purse of £3,000, was won by Airmail from Mayfields Classic and Trew Seas. The National Pacing Derby went to Donisthorpe King, the Two-Year-Old Futurity to Unique, and the Roosevelt Cup to Silver Glorie. The final of the colts' Sires Championship was won by Frisco Lobell in 2 min 6.6 sec, while Baby Bird won the Fillies Final.

(NOEL SIMPSON)

AP/WIDE WORLD

Nuclear Kosmos (no. 2, far right) noses across the line ahead of Royal Prestige (no. 3) at the Hambletonian in New Jersey on August 2. The winning driver (hidden) is Ulf Thoresen of Norway.

ICE HOCKEY

North America. After the unexpected early elimination of the previous year's finalists, it was a wide open race for the Stanley Cup in the 1986 National Hockey League (NHL) play-offs. In the end it was the enduring Montreal Canadiens who emerged from the pack, defeating the Calgary Flames, four games to one, to claim their 23rd championship. The Canadiens last won the cup in 1979, when they capped a four-year string of victories. The 1986 play-off team, a successful combination of rookies and veterans, included two members of the last championship team, Bob Gainey and Larry Robinson.

The defending champion Edmonton Oilers, who had finished the regular season with the league's best record, lost to the Calgary Flames in an arduous quarterfinal series that went to seven games. The Oilers, loaded with exceptionally talented players, had a brilliant year as Wayne Gretzky once again proved the top scorer in the league, breaking his own record with 215 points; teammate Paul Coffey, with 48 goals, broke Bobby Orr's record for goals by a defenseman. But in the play-offs, the Oilers' wide open, creative style was stymied by the muscular, disciplined Flames, who went on to beat St. Louis before meeting the Canadiens in the final series.

The Philadelphia Flyers, the runner-up team in 1985, met defeat in the play-offs' opening round, losing to the New York Rangers, three games to two. The Canadiens later handily defeated the Rangers in the best-of-seven semifinals, four games to one.

In the championship round the Canadiens performed with cool confidence, while Calgary, exhausted from a string of long series, could not produce the offense to complement its tight defense. The weariness was understandable—the Flames set a league record for most play-off games in a single season, 22. They did muster enough energy, however, for several bench-clearing brawls during the defensive battle of the series' fourth game, which Montreal won, 1–0. The Conn Smythe Trophy for the most valuable player in the play-offs went to rookie Patrick Roy, the Montreal goaltender.

The Oilers were more successful in the annual trophy races. Gretzky won his record seventh consecutive Hart Trophy as the league's most valuable player. Coffey won his second straight Norris Trophy as the top defenseman, and Edmonton coach Glen Sather won the Jack Adams Award as best coach. Mike Bossy of the New York Islanders won the Lady Byng Trophy as most gentlemanly player for the third time in the last four years. The Vezina Trophy for the league's best goaltender was awarded to John Vanbiesbrouck of the New York Rangers. Gary Suter of the Flames was voted the rookie of the year, and Troy Murray of the Chicago Blackhawks won the Selke Award as the top defensive forward. Bob Froese and Darren Jensen of Philadelphia won the William Jennings Trophy for the goaltending team with the fewest goals scored against it. Charlie Simmer of the Boston Bruins was the winner of the Bill Masterton Trophy for sportsmanship and dedication to hockey.

The top choice in the 1986 entry draft was Joe Murphy, who went to the Detroit Red Wings. Murphy, a Canadian, played for Michigan State University and was the first U.S. college student to be chosen number one in the NHL draft. Usually Canadian junior league players are the top choices. Of the 21 first-round selections in 1986, 6 were U.S. players—a record for the draft.

There were many coaching and managing changes after the season. Toronto's Dan Maloney left to coach Winnipeg, where general manager John Ferguson had been doing the coaching. John Brophy took over in Toronto. Scotty Bowman, Buffalo's general manager, assumed coaching duties as well, replacing Jim Schoenfeld. Coach Jacques Demers left St. Louis to succeed Brad Park at Detroit after the Red Wings finished the season with the league's worst record. It was the third coaching change in a year for Detroit. Halfway through the season Park had replaced first-year coach Harry Neale. In St. Louis Jacques Martin took over for Demers. The Rangers replaced manager Craig Patrick with the legendary Phil Esposito, a one-time Ranger captain.

Rookie goaltender Patrick Roy holds aloft the Stanley Cup that he helped the Montreal Canadiens win. In addition, the 20-year-old Roy became the youngest Stanley Cup most valuable player in the history of the league and won the Conn Smythe Trophy.

The exception to the revolving door of coaches and general managers had always been the New York Islanders, but after the 1985–86 season Al Arbour decided to retire as coach after 13 years. He had guided the team to four consecutive Stanley Cup championships. The Islanders named Terry Simpson as his successor. Another notable retirement was that of referee Ron Wicks, who had officiated more regular season games (1,073) than any referee in NHL history.

In the minor league play-offs the Adirondack Red Wings defeated the Hershey Bears, four games to two, for the American Hockey League title, and the Muskegon Lumberjacks defeated the Fort Wayne Komets, four games to none, for the International Hockey League championship.

(ROBIN CATHY HERMAN)

European and International. In the 51st world championships, the title hinged on the final match of the tournament contested by the eight Group A nations in Moscow on April 12–28, 1986. In that game the host nation gained a 3–2 victory over Sweden. Thus the U.S.S.R., which won all ten matches during the tournament, raised its total number of titles gained to 20, one more than Canada. The bronze medal was also decided on the closing day, when a goal by Vancouver's Tony Tanti $2\frac{1}{2}$ minutes before the end of the game gave Canada a 4–3 win over Finland, narrowly denying the Finns their first medal in the competition.

A major surprise was the poor showing made by the defending champion, Czechoslovakia, which was beaten 2–1 on the opening day of the tournament by Poland. The Poles subsequently finished last in the group. After the initial round-robin, only subsequent meetings between the four qualifiers for the championship section counted in the competition for medals, but points earned in the opening round were carried forward by teams competing in the relegation section.

Awards for the three best players in the group were presented to Peter Lindmark, the Swedish goaltender, and two Soviets, defenseman Vyacheslav Fetisov and forward Vladimir Krutov. Expanding public interest in the championships was reflected in much increased television coverage in 13 European countries.

Table I. NHL Final Standings, 1986

	Won	Lost	Tied	Goals	Goals against	Points
Clarence Campbell Conference						
NORRIS DIVISION						
*Chicago	39	33	8	351	349	86
*Minnesota	38	33	9	327	305	85
*St. Louis	37	34	9	302	291	83
*Toronto	25	48	7	311	386	57
Detroit	17	57	6	266	415	40
SMYTHE DIVISION						
*Edmonton	56	17	7	426	310	119
*Calgary	40	31	9	354	315	89
*Winnipeg	26	47	7	295	372	59
Vancouver	23	44	13	282	333	59
*Los Angeles	23	49	8	284	389	54
Prince of Wales Conference						
ADAMS DIVISION						
*Quebec	43	31	6	330	289	92
*Montreal	40	33	7	330	280	87
*Boston	37	31	12	311	288	86
*Hartford	40	36	4	332	302	84
Buffalo	37	37	6	296	291	80
PATRICK DIVISION						
*Philadelphia	53	23	4	335	241	110
*Washington	50	23	7	315	272	107
*New York Islanders	39	29	12	327	284	90
*New York Rangers	36	38	6	280	276	78
Pittsburgh	34	38	8	313	305	76
New Jersey	28	49	3	300	374	59

*Clinched play-off berth.

Table II. World Ice Hockey Championships, 1986

	Won	Lost	Tied	Goals	Goals against	Points
GROUP A Championship Section						
U.S.S.R.	3	0	0	18	6	6
Sweden	1	1	1	12	12	3
Canada	1	2	0	13	16	2
Finland	0	2	1	7	16	1
GROUP A Relegation Section						
Czechoslovakia	5	4	1	38	21	11
United States	4	6	0	41	43	8
West Germany	2	7	1	23	52	5
Poland	1	8	1	26	63	3
GROUP B						
Switzerland	6	1	0	38	20	12
Italy	4	3	0	21	18	8
East Germany	4	3	0	25	21	8
France	3	4	0	22	25	6
Netherlands, The	3	4	0	25	32	6
Austria	3	4	0	24	27	6
Yugoslavia	3	4	0	24	25	6
Japan	2	5	0	15	26	4
GROUP C Promotion Section						
Norway	2	0	1	19	7	5
China	2	0	1	16	7	5
Bulgaria	1	2	0	9	23	2
Romania	0	3	0	10	17	0
GROUP C Consolation Section						
Denmark	3	0	0	10	5	6
Hungary	1	2	0	16	17	2
North Korea	1	2	0	10	14	2
Spain	1	2	0	11	21	2
GROUP C Relegation Section						
South Korea	1	0	0	9	7	2
Australia	0	1	0	7	9	0

The 26 participating nations, two more than in preceding seasons, were divided, as usual, into three groups. The eight Group B countries competed at Eindhoven, Neth., on March 20–29. Switzerland, winning six of its seven games and losing only to East Germany, was promoted to Group A, changing places with the relegated Poland, for the 1987 competition in Vienna.

Yugoslavia and Japan, finishing at the bottom of Group B, were demoted to Group C for 1987. They were to be replaced by Norway and China, which placed first and second, respectively, in the Group C contest at Puigcerda, Spain, on March 23–April 1. Two nations, North Korea and Hong Kong, were asked to compete in the forthcoming season in a new Group D, where they would be joined possibly by Great Britain, the champion in 1936, which planned a return to the competition after an enforced spell in the wilderness brought about by a lack of rinks with adequate spectator accommodation.

At the 19th annual tournament for the Izvestia Trophy, held in Moscow during December 1985, Czechoslovakia caused an upset by defeating the second-place Soviet Union 3–1 in the final game, thus winning the contest for the first time in eight years. In finishing fourth behind Sweden and avoiding last place only through a 5–4 victory over Finland, Canada gave the most disappointing performance of the five competing nations.

Transatlantic competition was heightened by a series of eight matches played in Canada during March 1986 between teams from the host nation and the U.S.S.R. Six wins for the Moscow-based visitors whetted appetites for the next Canada Cup tournament, arranged for 1987. It was announced that the four best European nations, based on world championship results, would be eligible, along with Canada and the U.S.

The world junior (under 21) championship, played at Hamilton, Ont., on Dec. 26, 1985–Jan. 4, 1986, was regained by the U.S.S.R. Canada, the defending champion, was runner-up, and the U.S. finished third. The other Group A contestants included Sweden, Czechoslovakia, Finland, Switzerland, and West Germany. Fourteen other nations participated in tournaments of Groups B and C, held in Austria and France, respectively.

Ice hockey was given a boost in Sweden by the decision to build the ambitiously modernistic Prince Bertil Arena, with a capacity of more than 14,000 spectators, in Stockholm. That city had already been named by the International Ice Hockey Federation as the site for the senior world championships in 1989. Much interest centred on an enthusiastic renaissance of the sport in Great Britain after decades of comparative stagnation. The recovery was due largely to sponsorship worth £500,000 by the Heineken brewing concern. Progress was enhanced by the influence of imported players, restricted to three per club, and an outstanding signing was that of Garry Unger, a Canadian centre who had played 1,105 games in the NHL.

(HOWARD BASS)

ICE SKATING

Despite a continuing worldwide increase in the number of rinks built during 1986 and a consequent expansion of recreational participation, fewer spectators attended the major international competitions. One apparent reason for the decline was extensive television coverage, income from which was easily sufficient to pay for promotion of the events; the irony of the situation was by no means exclusive to ice skating. While a general rise in ice dance activity was experienced, there was little sign of a change in the decline of support for pairs skating, except in North America and

Debi Thomas, 18, of San Jose, California, edged out titleholder Katarina Witt of East Germany to capture the women's world figure skating championship in Geneva on March 21. Thomas was the first black to win the title.

STEVEN E. SUTTON—DUOMO

the U.S.S.R., a fact attributed to the increasing risk and excessive training time involved.

Decisions were made to build the world's first covered 400-m speed-skating circuits, at Heerenveen, Neth., and Calgary, Alta., to be used for the 1987 world championships and the 1988 Winter Olympics, respectively. Their construction reflected a marked increase of interest in this branch of the sport.

Figure Skating. Although all four titles were defended at the 76th world championships in Geneva on March 17–22, three changed hands and the fourth was retained narrowly, emphasizing that nobody stood head and shoulders above the competition. In the men's event, the triumph of Brian Boitano of the U.S., though well deserved, had to be termed a shock; his victory had appeared highly improbable before the final free skating, when each of the three competitors leading him made mistakes. Brian Orser of Canada, runner-up for the third time, twice failed to land his triple-axel specialty. Aleksandr Fadeev, the Soviet defending champion, finished third.

In the women's competition, Debi Thomas of the U.S. became the first black world champion, denying a third successive title to Katarina Witt, the East German Olympic gold medalist who, for once, narrowly failed to come from behind after winning the long free-skating segment. Tiffany Chin of the U.S. took the bronze medal for the second year in a row.

The pairs victory by Moscow's Sergey Grinkov and his diminutive partner, Ekatarina Gordeeva, only 14, signaled the emergence of a partnership with bright Olympic prospects. Deposing their Leningrad compatriots Oleg Vasiliev and Elena Valova, they denied the Olympic gold medalists a third world title in four years. Gordeeva, only 1.47 m and 35 kg (4 ft 10 in and 77 lb), captured the hearts of spectators as her powerfully built partner manipulated her like a puppet on a string, achieving overhead lifts and triple throws with consummate ease.

Only a 5–4 split by the judges enabled Andrey Bukin and Natalia Bestemianova to retain their ice dance crowns. Their win was in doubt to the end as their Soviet compatriots Sergey Ponomarenko and Marina Klimova almost snatched a triumph. In both the pairs and dance competitions, Canadian partnerships prevented the Soviets from completing a clean sweep of the medals, with Mark Rowsom and Cynthia Coull winning the bronze in the former event and Rob McCall and Tracy Wilson taking third place in the latter.

Speed Skating. For the second year in a row, Hein Vergeer of The Netherlands outpaced Oleg Bozhiev, the Soviet winner in 1984, to retain the men's world championship at Inzell, West Germany, on February 15–16. Another Soviet, Viktor Shasherin, gained the bronze medal. In the individual events, Bozhiev won the 500 m and the 1,500 m and Vergeer the 5,000 m; Geis Karlstad of Norway took the 10,000 m for a second time.

In the women's world championship, at The Hague, Neth., on February 8–9, Karin Kania led an East German sweep of the medals, with Andrea Ehrig (née Schöne), the former world champion, runner-up and Sabine Brehm third for the second successive year. Ehrig was first in the 5,000 m. The 500 m went to Edel-Therese Høiseth of Norway, and Yvonne van Gennip of The Netherlands took the 1,500 m.

In the separate world sprint championship, at Karuizawa, Japan, on February 22–23, Igor Zhelezovsky of the U.S.S.R. retained the men's title, with Dan Jansen of the U.S. runner-up and Akira Kuroiwa third for the host country. Kania captured the women's title, defeating the East German defender, Christa Rothenburger, with Bonnie Blair third for the U.S.

Two new men's world records were set, and all five women's records were broken during the year. Shasherin reduced the 3,000 m to 4 min 3.22 sec at Davos, Switz., and Karlstad achieved 10,000-m figures of 14 min 12.14 sec at Inzell. Kania shattered four of the women's times—39.52 sec for the 500 m, 1 min 59.30 sec for the 1,500 m, and 4 min 18.02 sec for the 3,000 m, all at Medeo, U.S.S.R., and 1 min 18.84 sec for the 1,000 m at Karuizawa. The fifth women's record was set by Ehrig with 7 min 20.99 sec for the 5,000 m at Medeo.

PAUL J. SUTTON—DUOMO

Brian Boitano of Sunnyvale, California, moved from fourth to first place to capture the men's world figure skating title. His graceful long program in the Geneva championship was capped by the only successful triple-axel jump in the competition.

At the sixth world indoor short-track championships, it was third time lucky for Tatsuyoshi Ishihara of Japan, the men's winner, who had been runner-up the two previous years. Guy Daigneault and Robert Dubreuil, both Canadians, finished second and third, respectively. Blair gained the women's crown, and she also was followed by two Canadians, runner-up Maryse Perreault and Nathalie Lambert.

As on the outdoor tracks, the women were in record-breaking form indoors. Two new world best times were set by Blair—48.12 sec in the 500 m and 2 min 35.21 sec in the 1,500 m—and Perreault lowered the 1,000-m record to 1 min 41.80 sec. All three times were accomplished at Chamonix, France, in April. (HOWARD BASS)

LACROSSE

Men. The world championships, contested every four years, took place in Toronto in July 1986. The United States won the series after beating Canada 18–9 in the final; Australia finished third. In the semifinals Canada beat Australia 17–14, and the U.S. defeated England 32–8; a feature of the latter match was the scoring of a goal by the England goalkeeper, the first time this had happened in an international contest. In earlier rounds the U.S. defeated Australia 18–12, Australia beat England 17–11, Canada beat England 15–12, and the U.S. beat Canada 21–11.

In U.S. lacrosse the North beat the South 21–15 in the Collegiate All Stars match, thus securing 22 wins to 21 over the previous 44 years. North Carolina was the champion university, defeating Virginia 10–9 in overtime. Individual awards were given to Peter Sheehan (Virginia, goalkeeper), Tom Haus (North Carolina, defense), Glen Miles (Naval Academy, midfield), and Roddy Marino (Virginia, attack). The champion team in U.S. club lacrosse was Long Island, which beat Maryland 11–9 to take the honours.

In Australia Victoria won the interstate championship. State champions were: in Victoria, Williamstown, with M. Lyons of Malvern "fairest and best" player; in South Australia, Sturt, with J. Hill of Sturt fairest and best; in Western Australia, Wembly, with J. Kennedy of East Fremantle fairest and best. In England, in the north, the Senior Flags were won by Heaton Mersey, which beat Stockport 10–8. Cheadle again won the league championship. In the south, Hampstead won the Senior League championship and also the Southern Flags, beating Hillcroft 9–8.

(CHARLES DENNIS COPPOCK)

Women. At the second World Cup, played in 1986 at Swarthmore (Pa.) College, the six participating countries engaged in round-robin matches and then positional playoffs. Australia defeated the U.S. 4–3, and 10–7 in the final, having previously beaten Canada 3–0, England 12–2, Scotland 6–0, and Wales 11–1. The U.S., runners-up, beat Canada 6–3, England 8–5, Scotland 10–4, and Wales 21–1. Scotland, bronze medal winners, drew 3–3 with Canada but then beat them 7–5 in the play-offs, having previously defeated England 7–6 and Wales 10–4. The Canadians played a baffling six-woman zone that proved almost impenetrable and kept scores against them low. They defeated England 3–2 and Wales 10–1 to finish fourth.

Snow and freezing temperatures wreaked havoc with the territorial championship in Britain. The first territorial weekend took place on snow-cleared fields at Harrogate, North Yorkshire, and after seven games only the West was unbeaten; snow forced the cancellation of the second weekend, and so for a second successive year the territorial championship remained unresolved. The Territorial Reserves Tournament was won by the Home Scots. Middlesex beat Surrey 3–2 in the All-England Counties Tournament, and West London won the Clubs and Colleges Tournament. Scotland won the home international championship for the first time, defeating England and Wales.

(MARGARET-LOUISE O'KEEFFE)

LAWN BOWLS

Australia's main international event, the Mazda Classic, was won in 1986 for the second successive year by its own Ken Williams, who withstood a strong overseas challenge. He was less successful on a visit to Britain, where he was defeated in the first round of the Embassy World indoor championship at Coatbridge, Scotland, by Roy Cutts, who later won the English indoor singles title. At Coatbridge Tony Allcock, a bowler for England, not only won the world indoor singles but also the first world indoor pairs championship, in company with David Bryant who, at the age of 55, was still rated the world's outstanding bowler. Bryant went on in June to win the Gateway International Masters outdoor singles title at Worthing for the sixth time, defeating Ian Dickison of New Zealand in the final. Later, also at Worthing, Wynne Richards beat David Taylor in the Gateway English Bowling Association singles final, and Cliff Simpson and David Kilner won the pairs championship.

Dickison, although used to a faster playing surface in his own country, revealed his aptitude on British grass by winning the Commonwealth Games singles gold medal at Edinburgh in midsummer. The other gold medals for bowls at the games went to U.K.-based players. Scotland's Grant Knox and George Adrain won the pairs, and the fours title was captured by a Welsh team—Robert Weale, William Thomas, Haford Thomas, and Jim Morgan. Wendy Line of England won the women's singles gold medal; Freda Elliott and Margaret Johnston of Northern Ireland took the pairs; and Wales scored a second fours success with a team of Rita Jones, Linda Evans, Joan Ricketts, and Linda Parker. (DONALD J. NEWBY)

MARTIAL ARTS

Judo. South Korea's spectacular defeat of Japan in the Asian Games highlighted judo activity in 1986, but the Japanese *judoka* bounced back during competition for the Jigoro Kano Cup. The fourth International University Tournament in Tokyo in mid-January was the year's first major event; Japan and the Soviet Union shared the honours with four gold medals apiece, while South Korea took one. The Soviets also won the team title. Irene de Kok of The Netherlands starred in the European women's championships by taking first place in both the open and light-heavyweight classes. In the all-Japan championships at the Budokan in Tokyo in April, Yoshimi Masaki pinned Takao Fujiwara to win the prestigious title. The Goodwill Games were held in Moscow in mid-July, with favoured Grigory Verichev of the Soviet Union winning the open title. During the Asian Games in Seoul, South Korea, in October, South Korea won six of the eight gold medals, while Japan was able to win only two. The women's world championships were staged in Maastricht, Neth., in October. Ingrid Berghmans of The Netherlands won the open title, and her compatriot Irene de Kok captured the middleweight class. In the year's final event, the Jigoro Kano Cup in November, Hitoshi Saito took the open title by defeating Verichev, thereby giving Japan five of the seven titles; Soviet and Brazilian athletes captured the other two. The Soviet Union also captured the team title.

Karate. The 1986 men's and women's individual *kumite* (free sparring) finals in the all-Japan all-styles karate-do championships in December at the Budokan were virtually repeat performances of the previous year's finals. Once again, second-degree *shotokan* specialist Yorihisa Uchida fought it out with Masamichi Yokomichi, a third-degree *karateka* also fighting in the *shotokan* style, in the final match. The 23-year-old Uchida narrowly edged his tenacious 27-year-old opponent 6–5. In the women's *kumite* competition, 22-year-old third-degree Tomoko Konishi outpointed 19-year-old second-degree Sayuri Watanabe 3–2 to capture the title. It was Uchida's third national title and Konishi's fourth. It was the first time the contestants had worn masks and gloves in this tournament.

In the all-Japan championships sponsored by the Japan Karate Association in September, Yasunori Ogura defeated Tomio Imamura with two upper straight punches (*jodan-zuki*) to capture the men's individual *kumite* title. Meanwhile, two-time world and national champion Masahiko Tanaka announced his retirement from active competition at age 47. Rika Saito took first place in the women's *kumite* competition, scoring a full point (*ippon*) with a front kick (*mae-geri*) after her opponent, Tomoko Taguchi, had tied near the end of their match. Minoru Kawawada won the men's *kata* (prescribed movements based on techniques) contest and Yoko Nakamura the women's title. At a national tournament in November at the Yoyogi National Gymnasium in Tokyo, third-degree *karateka* Akiyoshi Matsui won the men's championship in *kyokushin-kai* for the second year in a row by defeating his second-degree opponent Akira Masuda. *Kyokushin-kai* is the only style that features full contact karate without protective equipment. A world tournament was scheduled for Tokyo in November 1987.

Kendo. The spotlight in Japanese kendo in 1986 focused on an 18-year-old college coed named Miyuki Satake from Kumamoto Prefecture when she became the youngest winner of the all-Japan women's championships. Satake defeated Manami Ohori with a *men* (helmet) strike in the finals at the Osaka Central Gymnasium in May. Since kendo is part of the training for the Japanese police, it was no surprise that 34-year-old Osaka policeman Toru Iwahori won the all-Japan men's championships at the Budokan in November. During the overtime period in a close match, Iwahori penetrated the defenses of 32-year-old Toru Kamei in the final match between the two six-degree kendoists with a quick *men* strike to take the coveted title. In the men's national team competition, Tochigi Prefecture edged Chiba Prefecture 3–2. The all-Japan police championships at the Budokan in May was won by Toshiya Ishida, another Osaka policeman. Other key tournaments included the university championships in July, the all-Japan housewives tournament in August, and the all-Japan teachers' championships in August. The teachers' tournament was broken down into competition among high school, junior high, and elementary school teachers; women teachers also participated. (ANDREW M. ADAMS)

MOTORBOATING

With a late-season surge of luck and skill, Jim Kropfeld and his turbine-powered *Miss Budweiser* took the American Power Boat Association's (APBA's) unlimited hydroplanes competition by storm in 1986. Trailing defending world champion Chip Hanauer and his *Miller American* by 269 points, Kropfeld went into the final race of the season knowing that it was all or nothing. And all or nothing it was, as he and his boat came from behind to win both the national high point and world championship titles by only 31 points.

Despite failing to retain his title, Hanauer still managed to make a strong showing throughout the season. He won the coveted APBA Gold Cup for the fifth consecutive year, becoming the only unlimited driver to do so since the legendary Gar Wood in the 1920s. Hanauer also was awarded the Union of International Motorboating Gold Medal in honour of his racing achievements.

Tight competition marked the 1986 APBA Offshore season. Sitting at the top of the ladder at the season's end were Modified-class national champion John D'Elia and his *Special Edition.* He easily won the national high point title, scoring 3,228 points and winning six out of ten races. D'Elia's boat was the first in the Modified class to average over 100 mph (161 km/h) for an entire race, achieving 103.034 mph (165.884 km/h) over a 150-mi (240-km) course.

In the Open class there was a scant 230 points between first- and fourth-place boats, with Ben Kramer in *Team Apache* taking top honours. Other 1986 national high point winners in the Offshore category included Al Copeland driving *Popeye's/Diet Coke* in Superboat, Dominick Palombi driving *What-A-Package* in Pro-Stock, defending champion Bob Erickson driving *AME 4000 Express* in Stock A, and Bill Kaye driving *Captain Maintained* to continue his reign in Stock B.

The two-litre outboard tunnel boats once again competed for the International Harmsworth Trophy—known as the "America's Cup" of powerboat racing—and this time returned the historic prize to U.S. soil after a two-year absence. After winning first- and second-place positions in the first leg of the event, Bill and Mike Seebold went on to London to compete in the second. Turning in another first-place performance, Mike pushed the Seebolds' total points to 1,100, putting the Americans at the top of the standings.

A broken left sponson in the preliminaries was enough to keep veteran Gene Thibodaux out of the final in the last race of the APBA Formula One season but not enough to keep him from becoming the first U.S. driver ever to win a Formula One world championship. Even with the accident Thibodaux managed to maintain a seven-point lead over fellow countryman Art Kennedy in the final standings. (RENEE J. MAHN)

MOTORCYCLING

A hand injury kept 1985 champion Freddie Spencer of the U.S. out of serious contention in the 500-cc road-race world championship in 1986. In his absence Eddie Lawson, also of the U.S. and riding a Yamaha, established a commanding lead to win the 11-event championship; Wayne Gardner (Australia; Honda), despite wins in Spain, The Netherlands, and Britain, scored 117 points to Lawson's 139 and finished second.

In the 250-cc class Carlos Lavado (Venezuela; Yamaha) won five grands prix to gain the championship; Sito Pons (Spain; Honda) was second. The 125-cc class went to Luca Cadalora, with Fausto Gresini second (both Italy; Garelli). Jorge Martínez won the 80-cc contest from Martin Herreros (both Spain; Derbi). In the eight sidecar championship events the Dutch team of Egbert Streuer and Bernhard Schnieders (LCR-Yamaha) scored 75 points to finish in a tie with Alain Michel and Jean-Marc Fresc (France; LCR-Yamaha) but won the championship because of their greater tally of five outright victories.

In world endurance racing Honda supplied V-4 winning power in every round, with Patrick Igoa and Alix Vieira (both France) gaining the championship. In Formula One events Joey Dunlop (Northern Ireland; Honda) won his fifth successive title.

Defending champion Dave Thorpe (U.K.; Honda) won

the world 500-cc motocross title, and the trials championship went to Thierry Michaud (France, Fantic). The International Six Days Enduro was dominated by Italy, whose riders took the main World Trophy, with Sweden second. In the Motocross des Nations, held in northern Italy, the U.S. team of Johnny O'Mara, David Bailey, and Ricky Johnson was unapproachable; the U.K. team finished in second place. (CYRIL J. AYTON)

MOUNTAINEERING

During 1985–86 both large siege expeditions and small "alpine style" lightweight assaults suffered fatalities. Eastern European mountaineers dominated high-altitude climbing; lightweight alpine-style ascents included the west face of Gasherbrum IV (7,925 m; 25,990 ft) in the Karakorams by Voytek Kurtyka of Poland and Robert Schauer of Austria; the west face of Dhaulagiri (8,167 m; 26,790 ft) in the Himalayas by Czechoslovaks Stane Belak, Marjan Kregar, and Iztok Tomazin, in October 1985; and two new routes on K2 in the Karakorams (8,611 m; 28,250 ft)—the south face by Polish climbers Jerzy Kukuczka and Tadeusz Piotrowski (who was killed on the descent) and the south-southwest ridge by Poles Przemyslaw Piasecki and Wojciech Wroz (killed on descent) and Peter Bozik of Czechoslovakia during July–August 1986. During May Sharon Wood of Canada became the sixth woman to climb Everest, ascending by the west ridge from the Chinese side. Reinhold Messner of Italy became the first man to climb all 14 mountains higher than 8,000 m.

In July and August 14 people died in accidents on and around K2, including Italy's Renato Casarotto, who fell into a crevasse. The largest single tragedy occurred on the southeast (Abruzzi) ridge when an international team was trapped above 8,000 m (26,250 ft) in a week-long storm. Of the seven climbers involved, five perished—Alan Rouse (U.K.), Julie Tullis (U.K.), Alfred Imitzer (Austria), Hanns Wieser (Austria), and Dobroslawa Wolf (Poland). Two Austrians, Kurt Diemburger and Willi Bauer, reached safety during a lull in the storm. In May seven high-school students and two teachers died of exposure on Mt. Hood in Oregon when they lost their way during a storm.

Accident statistics for 1985 showed that 50 people died on expeditions and 7 while trekking; 60% occurred in autumn, 25% in summer, and 15% in spring. Of the 35 deaths in Nepal, 26 occurred in autumn. Causes included 20 avalanches and 13 falls. The weather in the Himalayas was consistently bad during 1985–86.

Alpine climbing featured speed solo climbing extravaganzas involving helicopters, parachutes, and hang gliders. A typical tour was made by Jean-Marc Boivin (France) on March 19 when he connected three north faces in 17 hours. He started on the Grassi Route on the Aiguille Verte (1½ hours), parachuted to the base of the Droites, and climbed the north face (3½ hours). He then glided to the foot of the Shroud on the Grandes Jorasses, which he climbed in 4½ hours, and finally glided back to Chamonix.

In South America a remarkable 13-hour solo ascent on Nov. 26, 1985, of Cerro Torre (3,128 m; 10,166 ft) via the Maestri Route was made by Marco Pedrini of Italy. He later repeated the feat for a film. Pedrini was killed in an abseiling accident on the Aiguille de Dru in the Alps in August 1986. The Sherpa mountaineer Tenzing Norgay died in May (*see* OBITUARIES). (BERNARD NEWMAN)

POLO

At the 1986 Cartier International Polo Day at the Guards Polo Club in England, Mexico (R. Gracida [7], C. Gracida [10], G. Gracida [10], A. Herrera [8]) defeated England (A. Kent [8], J. Hipwood [9], S. Mackenzie [8], and H. Hipwood [9]) by a score of 8–4 in the Coronation Cup. Chile (A. Fantini [6], R. Vial [5], S. Moreno [6], and F. Fantini [6]) defeated England II (P. Churchward [6], Lord Charles Beresford [6], O. Ellis [5], and the prince of Wales [4]) 5–3 in the supporting Silver Jubilee Cup. In the final of the Queen's Cup, Guy Wildenstein's Les Diables Bleus (G. Wildenstein [3], R. Vial [5], G. Gracida [10], and the prince of Wales [4]) beat Tramontana (A. Embericos [2], M. Brown [4], C. Gracida [10], and J. Baez [6]) 9–8. Tramontana won the British Open championship 11–4 against Cowdray Park (G. Waddington [2], S. Moreno [7], M. Glue [4], and P. Withers [7]).

The Argentine Open, at Buenos Aires, was won by La Españada (A. Pieres [10], G. Pieres [10], E. Trotz [9], and A. Herrera [8]), which defeated Chapaleufu II. The Piaget "World Cup," at Palm Beach, Fla., was won by White Birch (P. Peires [6], A. Pieres [9], G. Pieres [10], and P. Brant [3]) against Retama (R. Gracida [7], C. Gracida [10], G. Gracida [10], and S. Gose [3]). The American Cup, at Santa Barbara, Calif., went to Twyman Farms (J. Kahlbetzer [2], W. Naish [5], C. Merlos [8], and J. Henderson [5]) with a 9–8 victory over Tulsa. The U.S. women's handicap championship was won by Z92.5 (named after a local radio station), which defeated Piaget 8–3. (COLIN J. CROSS)

RACKETS

William Boone, world champion, and John Prenn, his predecessor, won the major singles events of the 1985–86 season, with one exception: James Male beat Boone by three games to two to take the amateur championship. Boone defeated Prenn four to two to regain the British Open title, three to one to win the U.S. amateur title, and by a similar score to win the U.S. Open. Prenn, however, beat his rival three to one to win the Tuxedo, N.Y., Centenary Gold Racquet tournament. Prenn also beat Male four times: in the semifinal rounds of the open and amateur singles championships and in the Tuxedo and Manchester Gold Racquet events. Prenn and Male joined forces to win the open doubles title, beating Boone and Randall Crawley, the amateur champions, four to one in the final.

In the Queen's Club Centenary (1886–1986) celebrations, Male and Christopher Pickwoad, an Englishman living in Canada, won the world invitation doubles tournament. The Clifton Boasters (David Mallinson and Edmund Popplewell) beat New York (Jimmy Knott and Nick Barham) in the world interclub doubles event. (ROY MCKELVIE)

RACQUETBALL

Mike Yellen of Southfield, Mich., won his fourth consecutive U.S. national championship, equaling the record for consecutive titles held previously by Marty Hogan of St. Louis, Mo. Playing the entire professional season with a radically new oversized racquet, Yellen won only 2 of the 14 season tournaments but reached the final round in all but three of the events he played.

Hogan, once the reigning monarch of the men's game, finished the season third. It was the first time he had finished outside the top two since 1978. Bret Harnett of Las Vegas, Nev., stormed into second place by winning four major tournaments, including the season-ending $100,000 DP national championships in Arlington, Texas.

Lynn Adams of Costa Mesa, Calif., achieved her long-sought goal of playing a perfect season. Adams won every ranking women's professional tournament, thus becoming the first player in the history of racquetball to complete a professional season undefeated. Her closest competitor was second-ranked Caryn McKinney of Atlanta, Ga., who

Lynn Adams of Costa Mesa, California, played a perfect racquetball season. In winning every ranking women's professional tournament, she became the first player in the history of racquetball to complete a professional season undefeated.
EKTELON

fell to Adams in the final match of every Women's Professional Racquetball Association event.

While the men's and women's professional tours continued to grow moderately, the American Amateur Racquetball Association (AARA) guided racquetball into the mainstream of U.S. sports. In January racquetball was granted Class A status, the highest level of recognition by the United States Olympic Committee. Shortly after this vote, the AARA was informed that racquetball would be a demonstration sport at the 1987 Pan American Games. Full participation in the Olympic Games was expected by 1992. (DREW W. STODDARD)

REAL TENNIS

Christopher Ronaldson of the U.K., the professional at Hampton Court, London, was unbeaten in major competition throughout the 1985–86 season. Ronaldson's successes included the British and U.S. Open titles, both of which he won from Wayne Davies of Australia in the finals, and the professional championships and the world invitation tournament, in both of which he defeated Lachlan Deuchar of Australia in the finals. In the world doubles Ronaldson and Deuchar lost to Graham Hyland of Australia and the British amateur Alan Lovell. Britain, led by Ronaldson, beat Australia, led by Hyland, by four games to three in a six-a-side match. Britain also won the Bathurst Cup, restricted to amateurs, beating France 5–0 and the U.S. 3–1. The British team included Lovell, Michael Dean, and Julian Snow.

In the final of the President's Cup, celebrating the Queen's Club Centenary (1886–1986), Lovell defeated Kevin McCollum, the U.S. amateur champion, 2–1. Lovell retained his British amateur title, though taken to five sets by the fast-improving Snow. Katrina Allen of the U.K. retained the women's title at the expense of Lesley Ronaldson, wife of the world champion, 2–0. (ROY MCKELVIE)

RIVER SPORTS

The white-water pre-world championships took place July 10–13 at Bourg St. Maurice, France. In the slalom Lubos Hilgert of Czechoslovakia won the men's kayaking, Elizabeth Sharman of the U.K. the women's, and Jon Lugbill of the U.S. the canoeing. Rolf Kilian of West Germany won the wild-water (downriver white-water) kayaking by less than a second over John Fishburn of the U.S.

Fishburn and Lugbill won their respective events at the U.S. national championships, contested May 31–June 2 on the Ocoee River in Tennessee. Chris Doughty triumphed in the men's slalom kayaking, and Cathy Hearn won the women's classes in both slalom and wild-water competition.

The marathon world cup was held September 6 in Hardenburg, Neth. Libor Dvorak of Czechoslovakia won the canoeing; John Jacobi of Australia took the men's kayaking; and Anne Plant of the U.K. won the women's kayaking. The U.S. championships took place August 15–17 in Bowling Green, Ky. Allan and Jennifer Rudquist dominated the men's and women's canoe classes; John Edwards won the solo kayaking; and Fletcher Anderson and Bill Schmitz won the tandem kayaking.

The world flat-water championships were held August 19–24 in Montreal. Competitors from Hungary, Romania, and the Soviet Union won the most medals, although Jeremy West of the U.K. won two solo kayak events. At the U.S. championships August 2–5 in Indianapolis, Ind., the most medals went to Greg Barton in the men's kayak events, Sheila Conover in the women's, and Bruce Merritt in canoeing. (ERIC LEAPER)

RODEO

In 1986 the Professional Rodeo Cowboys Association (PRCA), based in Colorado Springs, Colo., marked its 50th anniversary. Unfortunately, the year was filled with turmoil and change for the PRCA. Winston cigarettes announced that it was pulling out of its long, lucrative partnership with the association—a sponsorship that amounted to some $3 million for PRCA rodeo in 1986 alone. At the same time, all but two of the ten PRCA directors called for the resignation of Dan Taylor, the PRCA president, citing his recent criticism of the Winston Pro Tour rodeos as the cause of the sponsor's pullout. Taylor, elected in 1985, had opposed the Pro Tour rodeos because they were open to only a relatively small number of top cowboys and the money won at the contests was counted toward the qualifications for the national finals and world championships. Taylor refused to resign, and a recall election among the 8,000 members ousted him by 32 votes.

The PRCA also lost a measure of influence among the 600 sanctioned rodeos held throughout the U.S. A 1985 federal court ruling declared that the PRCA could no longer force its members to compete only in PRCA-sanctioned rodeos. A rival group, the United States Professional Rodeo Association, was formed, consisting of a handful of top PRCA rodeo committees. It forced the PRCA to revamp its board of directors and, in return, agreed to disband. The new PRCA board provided for equal representation of cowboys, livestock contractors, and rodeo committees.

The year ended on a positive note with the $1.9 million National Finals Rodeo in Las Vegas, Nev., in December. As always, the top 15 winners in each cowboy event, plus the top 15 in Women's Professional Rodeo Association barrel racing, competed at "the Super Bowl of rodeo."

The 1986 world champions, selected on the basis of the most money won over the entire season in each event, were named at the end of the National Finals. The title of world all-around champion cowboy was bestowed for the second straight year on Lewis Feild of Elk Ridge, Utah, who won a record $166,042 in bareback riding and saddle bronc riding. Feild also won the bareback championship for the second year in a row with $115,675 earned in that event. Other world champions for 1986 were Bud Munroe of Valley Mills, Texas, with $100,932 in saddle bronc riding; Tuff Hedeman of Gainesville, Texas, $137,061 in bull riding; Chris Lybbert of Argyle, Texas, $88,877 in calf roping; Steve Duhon of Opelousas, La., $114,535 in steer wrestling; Jake Barnes of Bloomfield, N.M., and Clay O'Brien Cooper of Gilbert, Ariz., $89,498 each in team roping; and 16-year-old Charmayne James of Clayton, N.M., $151,969 in barrel racing. Two weeks earlier Jim Davis of Bandera, Texas, won his second straight single steer roping championship with $33,372.

All-around championships in other, smaller rodeo associations were won by Tom Eirikson of Longview, Alta., in the Canadian Professional Rodeo Association and Dan Dailey of Tulsa, Okla., in the International Professional Rodeo Association (for 1985). The latter association's International Finals to determine its 1986 world champions were to be held in Tulsa in January 1987. Reigning champions in the National Intercollegiate Rodeo Association included Paul Latham of Oklahoma Panhandle State University in the men's all-around and Shelley Meter of Eastern Wyoming College in the women's all-around.

(RANDALL E. WITTE)

ROWING

The balance of power in world rowing continued to change in 1986 with the Eastern European countries' share of world titles continuing to fall. The East Germans still ranked first, but they only gained their ten wins through the dominance of their women, particularly in junior events. The Soviet Union won seven titles, and Italy moved into third place with four, just ahead of Romania and the U.S.

The world championships in Nottingham, England, attracted 271 entries from 37 nations, competing in 21 open and lightweight events. In men's events six titles changed hands, and the East German dominance of the 1970s and early 1980s vanished. Though the East Germans successfully defended their coxed fours title in beating New Zealand by 1.96 sec, they lost their double sculls title to Italy, finishing third.

The Soviet Union became the new quadruple sculls champion, with Canada, the defending champion, finishing third behind Poland. The Pimenov brothers retained the coxless pairs title with a 2.15 sec verdict over Italy to give the Soviet Union a second gold medal. However, the Soviet eight lost their title to Australia, the U.S. taking third place. In single sculls Peter Michael Kolbe of West Germany regained the title he first won at Nottingham in 1975.

The defeat of the Abbagnale brothers in coxed pairs was only the second for the Italian Olympic champions since 1982 and gave Great Britain its first men's heavyweight rowing title since the championships were founded in 1962. However, Italy did gain a world title by defeating Bulgaria in double sculls by 1.89 sec. The closest verdict was the defeat of West Germany, which lost the coxless fours title by 0.10 sec to the U.S.

In women's events East Germany surrendered the coxed fours to Romania, which also retained the coxless pairs; however, the East Germans retained their titles in the three sculling events and failed by 1.01 sec to depose the Soviet Union in eights. In the seven lightweight events Italy won both the men's rowing titles, while Australia and Great Britain shared the two sculling championships. The U.S. won twice in women's events, with Romania taking the single sculls.

The International Rowing Federation's under-23 championships were upgraded to the international level for the first time and were held in Hamburg, West Germany. Italy, Great Britain, France, and West Germany performed best in the ten men's events, while West Germany dominated the seven women's races.

In the world junior championships in Roudnice, Czech., the Soviet Union won four of the men's titles, and Czechoslovakia, East Germany, Italy, and Yugoslavia each gained one. Though the East Germans no longer dominated that competition, their women's team won five of the six titles; the sixth went to Bulgaria.

For the first time since 1962 rowing was restored to the Commonwealth Games, held in Scotland. England overshadowed Australia and Canada in the eight men's events, largely through the personal achievement of Steven Redgrave, who won gold medals in single sculls, coxless pairs, and coxed fours. In the women's seven events the honours were more evenly divided between Australia, Canada, England, and New Zealand.

In England the Henley Royal Regatta was extended to five days for the first time in its 147-year history. Charles River Rowing Association, U.S., was a double winner in the Wyfold Cup (coxless fours) and Double Sculls Cup, and Ridley College, Canada, also scored a double triumph in the Thames Cup (eights) and Stewards' Cup (coxless fours). Bjørn Eltang became the first Danish winner of the Diamond Sculls; Neptune RC, Ireland, captured the Ladies' Plate (eights); and AZS Szczecin & AZS Wroclaw took the Prince Philip Cup (coxed fours) to Poland. In the 132nd University Boat Race Cambridge broke Oxford's ten-year string of wins, triumphing decisively by seven lengths to increase its lead in the series to 69–62. (KEITH OSBORNE)

SAILING

The international yacht-racing circuit of 1985–86 began with the Southern Cross series, which culminated in the Sydney-to-Hobart classic. The British team of *Panda* (the 1985 Fastnet race winner), *Cifraline 3,* and *Highland Fling* won the series cup on Dec. 30, 1985; however, New Zealander Laurie Davidson's one-tonner *Mad Max* was top scorer in the five-race series. In the Sydney-to-Hobart race, the 22.8-m (75-ft) *Apollo,* owned by Jack Rooklyn of Australia, was first across the finish line; the Australian yacht *Sagacious,* skippered by Gary Appleby, was, after protest, declared the overall winner. The Southern Racing Circuit, run in February mostly off the coast of Florida, was won overall by *Abracadabra,* a 42-footer from the Joubert/Nivelt design team. The British one-ton world champion *Jade* won class 5 and beat Lowell North's *Sleeper* for second overall position.

Challengers for the 1987 America's Cup began work early in 1986, mostly in Australian waters. Thirteen 12-m yachts competed for the world championship, and *Australia III* in the hands of Colin Beashel was the winner; New Zealand's new fibreglass *KZ5* under Chris Dickson finished second ahead of *America II* under John Kolius. *French Kiss,* the French boat skippered by Marc Pajot and designed by Philippe Briand, won two races and was the most innovative 12-m yacht racing, on occasions showing startling speed.

The British team, led on the water by Harold Cudmore, had two yachts, both named *Crusader.* The newer boat, a radical design by David Hollom, appeared to be no faster than the more conventional earlier craft. In the first preliminary America's Cup qualifying series, the Royal Thames Yacht Club used the conventional yacht, renamed *White Crusader.*

Spinnakers full, *Australia III* (KA-9), *French Kiss* (F-7), *America II* (US-42), and *Australia II* (KA-6) lead the pack in race six of a seven-race pre-America's Cup shoot-out in the waters off Western Australia. *Australia III* took three of the first six races, a possible harbinger of the outcome of the cup race.
LEO MASON/TIME

In match racing the most sought-after series was the Congressional Cup. Cudmore won the competition, after tying with Dave Perry (U.S.) with seven wins and two losses, by beating Perry when they met on the water. The Lymington Cup series was won by Peter Isler (U.S.), Perry's tactician in the Congressional Cup. The Liberty Cup series was won by Gary Jobson (U.S.).

The 43,500-km (27,000-mi) Whitbread Round the World race, staged in four legs and starting (Sept. 28, 1985) and finishing (May 9, 1986) in Portsmouth, England, was won by the Swiss-owned and built *UBS Switzerland.* Designed by Bruce Farr and skippered by Pierre Fehlmann, it finished in 117 days 14 hours 31 minutes, beating the record set by *Flyer* in the 1981–82 race by 2 days 16 hours 2 minutes and winning the Long John Trophy. The handicap winner was the much smaller French entry *L'Esprit d'Equipe,* a 1981 Briand design that competed in the last Whitbread as *33 Export* but was now much altered. Under Lionel Pean, it raced with a crew of only eight.

In the two-handed Carlsberg Transatlantic Race in June, the French sailors Loic Caradec and Olivier Despaigne set a record of 13 days 6 hours 13 minutes for the crossing in their 25.7-m (85-ft) wing-masted catamaran *Royale.* The world speed sailing record, held since 1979 by Britain's *Crossbow II* at 36 knots, fell to Pascal Maka of France, who achieved 38.86 knots on his pencil-slim sailboard.

(ADRIAN JARDINE)

World Class Boat Champions

Class	Winner	Class	Winner
Cadet	Robert Drontmann (The Netherlands)	Optimist	Janvier Garcia (Spain)
Catapult	Mark Cooper (New Zealand)	Solo	Ken Falcon (United Kingdom)
Enterprise	Alan Gillard (United Kingdom)	Star	Vic Brun (United States)
Europe	Niklas Beckvid (Sweden)	Tasar	Rob Longbottom (Australia)
Flying Dutchman	Georg Diesch (West Germany)	Topper	Andrew Peters (United Kingdom)
Finn	José Doreste (Spain)	Tornado	Rob White (United Kingdom)
Fireball	Nigel Abbott (Australia)	12 Metre	Colin Beashel (Australia)
505	Peter Colclough (United Kingdom)	Wayfarer	Julian Redman (United Kingdom)
420	Bros. Goddard (France)	¼ Ton	David Birkill (Australia)
H-Boat	Herluf Jørgensen (Denmark)	½ Ton	Pierre Fountaine (France)
Hornet	Chris Bines (United Kingdom)	¾ Ton	Graham Walker (United Kingdom)
J24	Ken Read (United States)	1 Ton	Victor Greulich (Denmark)
OK	Mark Fisher (Australia)		

SHOOTING

Sixty nations participated in the 44th world shooting championships at Suhl, East Germany. The 300-m rifle world championships were held at Skovde, Sweden. Overall, the Soviet Union led the 1986 championships with 39 medals won. The U.S. was second with 16, and Czechoslovakia finished third with 7.

Trap and Skeet. The Czechoslovakian trap team broke 443 of a possible 450 targets to win first place and the gold medal. Italy took the silver medal with 440, and the Soviet Union the bronze with 439. The individual gold medal went to Miloslav Bednarik of Czechoslovakia for his final score of 224 of a possible 225. In the women's division the Soviet Union team placed first with a 427. China placed second with 423, and Italy third with 411. E. Gao of China took the women's individual gold medal with a score of 192 of a possible 200.

At skeet, the Italian men's team won the gold medal with 442 of a possible 450. The East German team, which shot the same score, was awarded the silver. The Soviet Union's 441 took the bronze. Matt Dryke of the U.S. won the individual gold medal with a world-record 224 of a possible 225. Andrea Benelli of Italy and Ioan Toman of Romania shot scores of 222, with Benelli awarded second place under the tie-breaking rules. In women's competition China placed first with a score of 430. The Soviet Union was second with 428, followed by Poland with 424. Svetlana Demina of the Soviet Union won the individual gold medal with a 196.

Rifles. The 300-m standard rifle event was won by Finland with a new world-record score of 1,729. The U.S. team placed second with 1,726. The Soviet Union finished third with 1,715. Malcolm Cooper of Great Britain fired a new world-record score of 586 to take the individual gold medal. Harald Stenvaag of Norway was second with 582, while Mauri Roppanen of Finland placed third with 578. The 300-m free rifle team competition was won by the Soviet Union with a score of 3,476. The U.S. placed second with 3,471, and Norway was third with 3,464.

Glenn Dubis of the U.S. won the individual gold medal with 1,174. Second place went to Malcolm Cooper firing the same score, while Roppanen took third with 1,166.

The 50-m free rifle, 3 x 40-shot competition was taken by Czechoslovakia with a world-record score of 3,522. The Soviet Union placed second with 3,512, and France was third with 3,509. Petr Kurra of Czechoslovakia shot a final score of 1,264.9 to win the individual gold medal. The 60-shot prone event was won by Australia with a score of 1,793 of a possible 1,800. East Germany placed second with 1,790, and Sweden third with 1,787. A final score of 704.2 won Sandor Bereczky of Hungary the individual gold medal. In the women's division Bulgaria took first place in the 3 x 20 event with a world-record 1,746. Yugoslavia won the women's 60-shot prone competition with 1,777. Individual gold medals went to Vesela Letcheva of Bulgaria for the 3 x 20 match and Eva Forian for the 60-shot prone. The 50-m running game contest was won by the Soviet Union team with a world-record score of 1,765. Sergey Luzov of the Soviet team fired a 691 to take the individual gold medal.

The 10-m standing air rifle event was won by West Germany with a score of 1,770. Johann Riederer of West Germany won the individual gold medal. Letcheva won the individual gold in the women's division. The team medal went to the Finnish women for their score of 1,165. High team score on the 10-m running game target was 1,121, shot by the Soviet Union. First place individual score was 382 by Luros Racansky of Czechoslovakia.

Handguns. The Soviet Union won all team events. In the 25-m standard pistol competition, Austria placed second and Finland third. The centrefire 25-m event ended with Switzerland second and Austria third. Hungary placed second and East Germany third in the 25-m rapid fire matches. In the 50-m free pistol competition, Sweden was second and East Germany third. France finished second and East Germany third in the air pistol matches. In the women's division East Germany placed second and Sweden third. Individual gold medals were won by Afanasij Kuzmin of the Soviet Union in 25-m standard pistol, Oleg Tkachev of the Soviet Union in centrefire, and Igor Basinskij of the Soviet Union in air pistol. Paavo Palokangas of Finland won the individual gold medal for 50-m free pistol, while that for 25-m rapid fire pistol went to Adam Kaczmarek of Poland. Anke Voelker of East Germany won the women's division in air pistol with a score of 387, which tied the world record. (ROBERT N. SEARS)

SHOW JUMPING AND EVENTING

The world show jumping championships were held at Aachen, West Germany, in July 1986. The team event was won by the United States, represented by Katie Monahan (Amadia), Conrad Homfeld (Abdullah), Katherine Burdsall (The Natural), and Michael Matz (Chef). The team's gold medal score was 23.63 penalty points. Great Britain finished second with 31.19, scored by Nick Skelton (Raffles Apollo), Michael Whitaker (Warren Point), Malcolm Pyrah (Towerlands Anglezarke), and John Whitaker (Hopscotch). France finished third with a score of 44.32. Canada, West Germany, Mexico, Italy, The Netherlands, and Switzerland followed. Gail Greenough of Canada won the individual title. Homfeld was second and Skelton third.

At Gawler, South Australia, in May, the defending champion British team won the team and individual titles in the world three-day event competition. Virginia Leng and Priceless did not put a foot wrong throughout the event, but, sadly, New Zealander Judith ("Tinks") Pottinger's Volunteer, the leader, went lame. Another dramatic defector was the dual world champion, Bruce Davidson of the U.S., whose horse, Doctor Peaches, was eliminated at the initial veterinary inspection. Britain scored 300.60 penalty points, France 443.60, and Australia 493.55. The winning team comprised Leng, Ian Stark (Oxford Blue), Lorna Clarke (Myross), and Clarissa Strachan (Delphy Dazzle).

(PAMELA MACGREGOR-MORRIS)

SKIING

With winter sports holidays proving increasingly popular, the still-growing demands of recreational skiers continued to be met during 1986 by the opening up of terrain at higher altitudes through the addition of mechanical lift facilities. More resorts also took the precaution of providing snow-manufacturing equipment in order to augment the natural substance in case of an unexpected shortage. Equipment continued to become more sophisticated as manufacturers competed more keenly.

Alpine Racing. In a season between world championships, the 20th Alpine World Cup series, contested at sites in ten European countries, the U.S., Canada, and Japan, gained added prestige. In a closely contested outcome, Marc Girardelli of Luxembourg won his second consecutive overall men's title despite failing to finish the final race at Bromont, Que., on March 23—a slalom in which his Swiss rival, Pirmin Zurbriggen, finished third but would have taken the overall title had he won. Zurbriggen finished as runner-up for the second straight year, with Markus Wasmaier of West Germany third.

Peter Wirnsberger of Austria proved the best downhiller, ahead of Peter Müller of Switzerland and Michael Mair of Italy. Rok Petrovic, in only his second World Cup season, won the slalom competition for Yugoslavia, and there was a triple tie for second place between the veteran Swede Ingemar Stenmark, Paul Frommelt of Liechtenstein, and another Yugoslav, Bojan Krizaj. After an unsuccessful season the previous year, Stenmark increased his record number of World Cup race wins to 83. The remarkable Swede also finished second in the giant slalom, behind Joel Gaspoz of Switzerland and ahead of Hubert Strolz of Austria.

The overall women's World Cup winner was Maria Walliser of Switzerland, who had finished third the year before. Runner-up Erika Hess and Vreni Schneider completed a Swiss grand slam. Walliser was top points scorer in the downhill, followed by Katrin Gutensohn of Austria and Laurie Graham of Canada. Roswitha Steiner of Austria won a tiebreaker to become top slalom skier, in front of Hess, with Perrine Pelen of France finishing third. Schneider maintained Swiss supremacy as giant slalom leader, with Traudl Haecher of West Germany second and Maleja Svet of Yugoslavia in third place.

The concurrently decided Nations Cup was retained by Switzerland, ahead of Austria and West Germany, in a repeat of the previous season's result.

Nordic Events. Gunde Svan of Sweden retained the men's title—his third straight win—in the seventh Nordic World Cup competition for cross-country racing, a series of nine meetings at locations in nine countries spanning four months. Svan's fellow countryman Torgny Mogren was runner-up, with Vladimir Smirnov of the U.S.S.R. third. Marjo Matikainen of Finland captured the women's crown, followed by two Norwegians, Marianne Dahlmo and Brit Pettersen.

The third World Cup in Nordic combination, linking cross-country racing and jumping, went to Hermann Weinbuch of West Germany. His compatriot Thomas Müller placed second, and Geir Andersen, the Norwegian title defender, finished third.

Peter Wirnsberger (left) of Austria flashes down the track on his way to winning the downhill title in the 20th Alpine World Cup series. Switzerland's Vreni Schneider (right) leans hard into a turn on her way to winning the women's World Cup giant slalom event in Oberstaufen, West Germany.
PHOTOGRAPHS, AP/WIDE WORLD

The World Cup for ski jumping, decided at locations in eight European countries, Japan, Canada, and the U.S., was won by Matti Nykänen of Finland, with Ernst Vettori and Andreas Felder of Austria second and third. It was the third success for Nykänen, who had also won in 1983 and 1985. The Nations Cup went to Austria, with Finland runner-up and Norway third. Felder equaled Nykänen's record for the longest jump when he cleared 191 m (626 ft) at Bad Mitterndorf, West Germany, on March 9.

In the world biathlon championships, combining cross-country ski racing with rifle shooting, in Oslo on February 20–23, newcomer Valery Medvedtsev of the U.S.S.R. won both the individual events. He was followed in the 10 km by Peter Angerer of West Germany and Franz Schuler of Austria. Runner-up in the 20 km was André Sehmisch of East Germany, and Alfred Eder of Austria was third. The 4 × 7.5-km relay title was retained by the Soviet team, including Medvedtsev, with the East Germans outpointing the West Germans for second place.

The World Cup biathlon contest was determined at meetings in Italy, Austria, East Germany, Finland, and Sweden. Sehmisch was the victor, with Angerer runner-up and Matthias Jacob of East Germany third. The team event was won by East Germany, followed by the U.S.S.R. and West Germany.

Other Events. The first world freestyle championships, held at Tignes, France, on February 1–6, resulted in victories for Alaine Laroche, representing the host nation, and Connie Kissling of Switzerland in the men's and women's competitions, respectively. With its emphasis on highly specialized acrobatics, freestyle skiing gained further prestige when it was decided to include it as a demonstration event in the 1988 Winter Olympics, prior to its inclusion as an official event four years later.

Between snow seasons there was greater demand than previously for grass skiing, which simulated the actions on snow through the use of roller skis on grass slopes and which had become a sport in its own right. Competitions on this medium became more numerous, and there was also greater skiing activity on indoor and outdoor plastic slopes, the purpose of which was to tone up the correct muscles and improve technical ability, particularly in lowland areas with mild winters. (HOWARD BASS)

SPELUNKING

During 1986 exploration in the Sieben Hengste Cave in Switzerland increased its length to 80.9 km (50.3 mi) and its depth to 912 m (2,992 ft). Also in Switzerland, accurate mapping of the Hölloch (133.1 km [82.7 mi] long and 867 m [2,844 ft] deep) required more than 21,000 survey stations. Links discovered between several large caves comprising the Réseau de l'Alpe in the French Alps increased its total length to about 55 km (34 mi).

One of the very deep caves of the world, the Sima del Trave in the Picos de Europa region of Spain, was extended to 1,256 m (4,121 ft) by a French expedition. The first cave in Africa to exceed a depth of 1,000 m (3,281 ft) was descended to 1,007 m (3,304 ft) by a group from Barcelona, Spain. The linking of Schnellzughöhle, Austria, with a nearby cave increased its total depth to 970 m (3,182 ft). Explorers from France, Poland, the U.K., and Yugoslavia descended the Vjetrena in southern Yugoslavia to 920 m (3,018 ft). A depth of 800 m (2,625 ft) was reached in Cabri Höhle, Austria, with an additional shaft at the end of the cave remaining unexplored. In New Zealand the discovery of a link between Bulmer Cave and Castlekeep gave a combined depth of 723 m (2,372 ft), thus exceeding the 695 m (2,280 ft) of Nettlebed, also in New Zealand, and becoming the deepest in the Southern Hemisphere.

The cave areas of Mexico continued to attract attention. A British expedition exploring the mountains of the Sierra Madre Oriental, some 320 km (200 mi) northeast of Mexico City, found many new caves, including the 3-km (1.86-mi)-long Mexicana and the 600-m (1,968-ft)-deep Arriba Suyo Sotano. At 16.7 km (10.4 mi) the river passage in the Rio Encantado Cave, Puerto Rico, became possibly the longest continuously traversed underground river in the world. An Australian team explored two river caves, 8.5 km (5.3 mi) and 9 km (5.6 mi) long, in Thailand.

An expedition of French cave divers camped 7.9 km (4.9 mi) inside the Rhou bou Maza Cave in Algeria; from there they were able to explore a further 3.75 km (2.3 mi) of passage. The sump in Gough's Cave, Cheddar, Somerset, England, was much shorter but of great historical importance. A 12th-century manuscript recorded an underground river at Cheddar, but it had never been rediscovered; penetration upstream by divers gave hopes that the ancient cave would be refound.

Because extensive caves in rocks that are neither soluble, like limestone or gypsum, nor lava are very uncommon, the exploration of one of the Greenhorn caves in southern California, formed entirely in granite, was of particular note. The cave was explored for a distance of 956 m (0.6 mi) and to a depth of 151 m (495 ft). (T. R. SHAW)

SQUASH RACKETS

The year 1986 concluded with Jahangir Khan's first competitive defeat since April 1981. It occurred in the final of the World Open championship, held in November in Toulouse, France. In the final he lost 9–5, 9–7, 7–9, 9–1 to Ross Norman (New Zealand), the world's number

Ross Norman of New Zealand proves his skill in the 1986 World Open squash championships final against Jahangir Khan of Pakistan, who had not been beaten in more than five years. Norman took the match, snapping Khan's string of five world titles.
STEPHEN LINE

two player, in 1 hour 50 minutes. This first triumph for Norman over Khan ended the Pakistani player's run of five consecutive world titles. Earlier, Khan had won his fifth British Open crown. Khan and Norman finished first and second in both the U.S. Open and the Canadian Open championships in softball (the version played internationally), while in hardball competition Khan won the Canadian Open and Mark Talbott took the North American Open title in Khan's absence.

In women's squash rackets Susan Devoy of New Zealand won both the French and British Open titles. In the British Open final she overcame Lisa Opie from Guernsey, ranked second in the world.

In January 1986 the British Under 19 Open was won by Del Harris from England. At the world junior championships in Brisbane, Australia, Jansher Khan of Pakistan defeated Rodney Eyles of Australia in the final. Australia won the team event, defeating England in the final. The British Under 23 Open was won by Rodney Martin of Australia, who beat Zarak Jahan of Pakistan in an exciting final. Martin was a product of the clearly successful Australian Institute for Sport, whose squash academy was coordinated by past world champion Geoff Hunt.

England led the development of team squash with its Premier League, featuring virtually every top world-ranked player competing on a weekly basis; its national teams dominated the men's and women's home internationals and the European championships. England's men's team beat Sweden 3–2 and the women's team overcame Ireland 5–0 in the finals. Pakistan remained best in the world after its December 1985 triumph over New Zealand in the world team championship finals. (ANDREW SHELLEY)

SURFING

Tom Curren of the U.S. placed first in the 14th annual Surfer Poll awards and also finished first during the Association of Surfing Professionals' 1985–86 season. Tom Carroll of Australia was second in the Poll but dropped from his first-place rank in 1984–85 to third place in the ASP final standings. Barton Lynch, also representing Australia, finished a close second to Curren in the world competition. Frieda Zamba of the U.S., the 1985 winner, again captured first place in the women's division in addition to winning the Surfer Poll. Both Curren and Carroll, along with five other top surfers, refused to participate in the ASP events held in South Africa during the 1986–87 world tour as a protest against that nation's racial policies.

Despite Curren, Australia continued to dominate professional surfing. Since 1976 Australians had won 82 of the 146 world tour contests, including 12 of 20 in the 1985–86 season, and had taken the world title eight of the last ten years. (JACK C. FLANAGAN)

SWIMMING

The last occasion when the United States and the nations of Eastern Europe had met in head-to-head national team confrontation in aquatics was in the IV World Aquatics Championships held at Guayaquil, Ecuador, in 1982. The V World Championships, held at Madrid from Aug. 17 to 23, 1986, was expected to produce the best swimming since the 1976 Olympic Games. Sixty-two nations entered the competition, which consisted of swimming, diving, synchronized swimming, men's water polo, and, for the first time, women's water polo. (For water polo results, see *Water Polo,* below.)

At the new multimillion-dollar Piscina Centro Natatorium complex, the U.S. team won 7 of 32 events, as compared with 8 of 29 at Guayaquil. East Germany won 14 gold medals, 12 silver, and 4 bronze; 13 of the gold medals were won by women, who finished first and second in five events and set five of the six world records. Along with the seven gold medals, the U.S. won seven silver and ten bronze. Five of the gold were won by men. West Germany finished third with four gold, two silver, and one bronze, followed by the Soviet Union with two gold, three silver, and four bronze and Hungary with three gold.

The seven-day tournament produced six women's world records. Five were set by East Germany and the sixth by Romania. The outstanding swimmer of the tournament was East Germany's 20-year-old Kristin Otto, who, leading off the 4 × 100-m freestyle relay, set a world record of 54.73 sec for her 100 m, 0.06 sec faster than teammate Barbara Krause's 1980 record. The quartet of Otto, Manuela Stellmach, Sabine Schulze, and Heike Friedrich lowered the 4 × 100-m freestyle relay record by 1.84 sec to 3 min 40.57 sec. The previous mark, 3 min 42.41 sec, had been set by East Germany in 1984. Otto won the 100-m freestyle and the 200-m individual medley, swam on two winning relays, and placed second in the 50-m freestyle.

Friedrich won four gold medals—the 200-m and 400-m freestyle titles and as a member of the 4 × 100- and 4 × 200-m freestyle relay teams. Silke Hoerner of East Germany shaved 0.80 sec off teammate Silvia Gerasch's seven-month-old 200-m breaststroke world mark with a time of 2 min 27.40 sec. Three days later Gerasch dropped 0.18 sec from her own two-year-old 100-m breaststroke record with a time of 1 min 8.11 sec. The women's 4 × 200-m freestyle relay, one of two new events added to the world championship program, produced a world record for East Germany of 7 min 59.33 sec; the old mark of 8 min 2.27 sec had been set by East Germany in 1983. The other new event, the 50-m freestyle, gave Romania's Tamara Costache an opportunity to lower to 25.28 sec her world mark of 25.31 sec set on August 2 at Sofia, Bulg.

The U.S. gold medalists were Betsy Mitchell in the

100-m backstroke and Mary T. Meagher in the 200-m butterfly. The U.S. women also won two silver medals in the relays.

In the men's events Michael Gross of West Germany successfully defended his 200-m butterfly title in the second fastest time ever, 1 min 56.53 sec; he also won the 200-m freestyle. Other double gold medalists were Tamas Darnyi of Hungary in the 200-m and 400-m individual medleys, Igor Poliansky of the Soviet Union in the 100-m and 200-m backstroke, and Rainer Henkel of West Germany in the 400-m and 1,500-m freestyle.

For the United States Matt Biondi, with seven medals, was the outstanding swimmer. He won the 100-m freestyle, placed second in the 100-m butterfly behind teammate Pablo Morales, finished third in the 50-m freestyle and the 200-m freestyle, and helped the U.S. win two gold medals and a bronze in relay events.

Earlier in the year four world records were set at the U.S. world championship trials in Orlando, Fla. Biondi set two world marks: 48.74 sec for the 100-m freestyle on June 24, lowering by 0.21 sec his previous world record set Aug. 6, 1985, and, two days later, a time of 22.33 sec for the 50-m freestyle, 0.07 sec faster than teammate Tom Jager's mark set on Dec. 6, 1985. On June 23 Morales erased 0.24 sec from the world record of 53.08 sec for the 100-m butterfly, set by Gross in the 1984 Olympics. On June 27 Mitchell lowered the 200-m backstroke record by 1.31 sec, from 2 min 9.91 sec to 2 min 8.60 sec. The previous record had been set by Cornelia Sirch in 1982.

At the West German Championships at Bonn on June 27, Gross lowered his one-year-old 200-m butterfly world record from 1 min 56.65 sec to 1 min 56.24 sec. In Moscow on July 4 Vladimir Salnikov of the Soviet Union set a new 800-m freestyle world mark of 7 min 50.64 sec. Alex Baumann of Canada on March 4 in Montreal equaled his world best of 2 min 1.42 sec in the 200-m individual medley. In women's competition, at East Berlin on June 18, Friedrich lowered the 200-m freestyle mark from 1 min 57.75 sec to 1 min 57.55 sec.

The second major international event in 1986 was the first Goodwill Games, held July 4–13 at Moscow. The U.S. swimmers won 49 medals, 15 of which were gold, as compared with the host team's 37, 12 of which were gold. The outstanding swimmer was Salnikov, who, in addition to setting the above-mentioned world record in the 800-m freestyle, also won the 1,500-m freestyle and placed second in the 400-m freestyle. Two U.S. women were double winners: Angel Myers in the 50-m and 100-m freestyle and Leslie Daland in the 800-m and 1,500-m freestyle. Also winning twice in women's events was Noemi Lung of Romania in the 200-m and 400-m individual medley. Winning two events for the men were Dmitry Volkov of the U.S.S.R., 100-m and 200-m breaststroke; Vadim Yaroshuk of the U.S.S.R., 200-m and 400-m individual medley; and Poliansky, 100-m and 200-m backstroke.

Sixteen-year-old Heike Friedrich won both the 200-metre and the 400-metre freestyle events at the fifth World Aquatics Championships, held in Madrid. The East German athlete was started as a swimmer by her grandfather, a shepherd.

HEINZ KLUETMEIER/SPORTS ILLUSTRATED

The third major international event in 1986 was the XIII Commonwealth Games at Edinburgh, Scotland, July 24–30. A boycott by 32 of the 58 nations entered in the Games took place in protest against U.K. Prime Minister Margaret Thatcher's refusal to impose economic sanctions against South Africa. Outstanding performances in the swimming were recorded by Britain's 17-year-old Sarah Hardcastle, who came within a fraction of a second of breaking the 800-m freestyle world record of 8 min 24.62 sec set in 1978; her time in the event was 8 min 24.77 sec. Hardcastle also won the 400-m freestyle event. Allison Higson of Canada

HEINZ KLUETMEIER/SPORTS ILLUSTRATED

American Matt Biondi, sometimes called "El Torpedo," won seven medals at the fifth World Aquatics Championships, held in Madrid. The 21-year-old University of California senior came away with three golds, one silver, and three bronzes.

became the youngest Commonwealth Games champion in any sport when the 13-year-old girl won both the 100-m and 200-m breaststroke events. Suzanne Landells of Australia won the 200-m and 400-m individual medleys.

Alex Baumann of Canada was the outstanding male swimmer of the Commonwealth Games, setting a Commonwealth record of 4 min 18.29 sec in the 400-m individual medley and retaining his 200-m individual medley title. Australia won five gold medals in men's races, followed by Canada with four and England with two. In women's competition Australia won six gold medals, Canada five, and England four.

Diving. At the world championships in Madrid, Greg Louganis of the U.S. made diving history, winning his fourth and fifth world titles. In the 3-m springboard he withstood the challenge of China's Tan Liangde and Li Hongping, achieving one of his five perfect marks of 10. His winning total of 750.06 points was 57.78 higher than that of silver medalist Tan. In the 10-m platform Louganis came from behind to score 668.58 points to Li Kongzheng's 624.33. In the women's springboard China's 15-year-old Gao Min, who had never before competed in an international meet, scored 582.90 points, the highest total in the history of women's springboard. Her teammate Li Yihua finished second with 549.42. In the platform China's Chen Lin with 449.67 and Lu Wei with 422.25 outpointed Wendy Wyland of the U.S., who scored 412.47 and was the sole U.S. woman to win a medal.

At the Goodwill Games Soviet divers Nikolay Droshin and Sergey Gurylev won the springboard and the platform, respectively. In the women's events Brita Baldus of East Germany won the springboard by less than a point over China's Lin Jianqing. Soviet diver Angela Stasulevich won the platform.

At the Commonwealth Games Shaun Panayi and Craig Rogerson, both of Australia, won the men's springboard and the platform, respectively. In women's competition Canada's Debbie Fuller won both events.

Synchronized Swimming. At the world championships Canada won all three events. Carolyn Waldo won the solo and paired with Michelle Cameron to win the duet. Waldo won her third gold medal when she and Cameron joined six teammates to gain the team championship. Sarah Josephson of the U.S. won the silver medal in the solo and with her sister Karen took the silver in the pairs. In the team competition the U.S. swimmers lost to the Canadians by 0.379 points. At the Commonwealth Games the Canadians won both the solo and duet titles. Sylvie Frechette won the solo, and Waldo and Cameron took the duet.

(ALBERT SCHOENFIELD)

TABLE TENNIS

The 1986 European top 12 male and female players tournaments got under way on January 31 in Södertälje, Sweden. Seven nations were represented in the men's division and eight in the women's. Only Czechoslovakia, Hungary, and the Soviet Union arrived with both male and female athletes. Sweden's four male players clearly dominated their opponents, winning four of the top six places in the final rankings. Jan-Ove Waldner was first, Erik Lindh third, Ulf Carlsson fourth, and Jorgen Persson sixth. Desmond Douglas, one of two entries from England, was runner-up, and Leszek Kucharski of Poland was sixth. The final women's standings showed Fliura Bulatova of the Soviet Union in first place and Olga Nemes of West Germany in second. Next in order were Dana Guergueltcheva of Bulgaria, Branka Batinic of Yugoslavia, Bettine Vriesekoop of The Netherlands, and Marie Alboiu of Romania.

1986 World Rankings

MEN	WOMEN
1. Jiang Jialiang (China)	1. Geng Lijuan (China)
2. Chen Longcan (China)	2. Dai Lili (China)
3. Wang Huiyuan (China)	3. Jiao Zhimin (China)
4. Chen Xinhua (China)	4. Tong Ling (China)
5. Andrzej Grubba (Poland)	5. Olga Nemes (West Germany)
6. Jan-Ove Waldner (Sweden)	6. He Zhili (China)
7. Lo Chuen Tsung (Hong Kong)	7. Csilla Batorfi (Hungary)
8. Teng Yi (China)	8. Yang Young Ja (South Korea)
9. Xie Saike (China)	9. Li Bun Hui (North Korea)
10. Jorgen Persson (Sweden)	10. Fliura Bulatova (U.S.S.R.)

During the European championships, which were played in Prague, Czech., in April, Sweden's men once again demonstrated their talents. Persson won the singles title with a four-set victory over Kucharski, and Waldner teamed with Lindh to capture the doubles crown by defeating fellow Swedes Mikael Appelgren and Carlsson. Sweden also won the men's team title; France was second, Poland third, Czechoslovakia fourth, and Hungary fifth. In the women's division, Hungary won the team title and the singles championship when Csilla Batorfi defeated Bulatova in four sets. Bulatova, however, teamed with her compatriot Elena Kovtun to win the doubles championship. They won two straight sets after dropping the first set to Vriesekoop and Marie Hrachova of Czechoslovakia. Jindrich Pansky and Hrachova won the doubles title for Czechoslovakia in straight sets. The Soviet Union finished second in the team competition ahead of West Germany, Czechoslovakia, and France.

Port-of-Spain, the capital of Trinidad and Tobago, was the site of World Cup competition in July. Chen Longcan and Jiang Jialiang, two of China's finest players, were ranked first and second, respectively, at the end of play. Next in order were Kim Wan of South Korea, Lo Chuen Tsung of Hong Kong, Mikael Appelgren of Sweden, Andrzej Grubba of Poland, and Kiyoshi Saito of Japan.

(ARTHUR KINGSLEY VINT)

TENNIS

The decline of U.S. dominance in men's tennis continued in 1986. Of 12 singles semifinal places in the three major championships, those of France, Wimbledon (England), and the U.S., only one, the French, was occupied by an American, Johan Kriek, a former South African. A contributing factor was the decline of Jimmy Connors, who won no important tournament and failed, for the first time in 15 years, to reach the last eight of the singles in any Grand Slam (French, Wimbledon, U.S., and Australian) championship. He celebrated his 34th birthday during the season. More striking was the absence for much of the season of John McEnroe, seven years younger. He lost in the first round of the Grand Prix Masters' tournament at Madison Square Garden, New York City, in January and did not play again until the late summer, having married and fathered a child. He lost in the opening round of the U.S. Open at Flushing Meadow, New York City, but in later tournaments he had more success.

The women's game provided a contrast. Martina Navratilova, Czechoslovak-born but American, was again the outstanding player of the year, though not immune to defeat. Chris Evert Lloyd, a U.S. native, was not far behind her, winning the French Open singles for the fifth time to complete a sequence of 13 years in which she never failed to win at least one Grand Slam title.

Ivan Lendl (*see* BIOGRAPHIES), a native of Czechoslovakia, was the best male player of the season. He won the Italian, French, and U.S. Open titles and failed only in

Martina Navratilova raises her hands in jubilation upon capturing her fifth Wimbledon crown in a row. It was her seventh Wimbledon singles championship, placing her second only to Helen Wills Moody, winner of eight Wimbledon women's crowns.

AP/WIDE WORLD

the final at Wimbledon, where Boris Becker of West Germany triumphed for the second straight year. The success of Czechoslovak players was marked. In the U.S. Open in September four of the singles finalists were Czechoslovak-born: Lendl and Miloslav Mecir in the men's competition, and Navratilova and Helena Sukova in the women's.

Increased attendances and increased prize money were the norm. In the U.S. Open a record 450,286 spectators attended its 23 sessions; total prize money was $3,450,800. The Australian authorities announced plans to build a new stadium in Melbourne with a movable roof over the main court. The date of the Australian national championship was changed, from December to January. Because of this change no Australian championship took place in the calendar year 1986. Nabisco maintained its sponsorship of the men's Grand Prix, and Virginia Slims of the women's circuit. The main international team competitions, the Davis Cup for men and the Federation Cup for women, continued to be sponsored by the Japanese corporation NEC. There was a trend toward professional court officials.

Men's Competition. Lendl was designated "world champion" by the International Tennis Federation (ITF). He headed the Grand Prix series for 1985 and won the bonus of $800,000. The Australian championship, played in Melbourne in December 1985, was won by Stefan Edberg of Sweden when he beat Lendl 6–7, 7–5, 6–1, 4–6, 9–7 in the semifinal and defending champion, Mats Wilander, another Swede, 6–4, 6–3, 6–3 in the final.

The Grand Prix Masters' tournament was staged in Madison Square Garden in early January with a field of 16 for the singles. Lendl did not lose a set in four matches and beat Becker 6–2, 7–6, 6–3 in the final. Lendl did not compete in the World Championship Tennis (WCT) finals in Dallas, Texas, in April. There, Anders Jarryd of Sweden beat Wilander 6–4, 7–5, 6–3 in the semifinal and Becker in the final 6–7, 6–1, 6–1, 6–4. The subsequent WCT event, the Tournament of Championships at Forest Hills, New York City, went to Yannick Noah of France. He beat Lendl 6–3, 7–5 in the semifinal and Guillermo Vilas of Argentina 7–6, 6–0 in the final.

Lendl defeated Emilio Sanchez of Spain in the Italian championships at Rome. In the subsequent Grand Slam event, the French Open in Paris, Lendl was never threatened. He won his quarterfinal against Andrés Gómez (Ecuador) 6–7, 7–6, 6–0, 6–0 and his semifinal against Kriek 6–2, 6–1, 6–0. Wilander, the titleholder, lost in the third round to Andrey Chesnokov (U.S.S.R.). Mikael Pernfors of Sweden was the surprise player of the meeting. A product of the U.S. college game and little known elsewhere, he played with flair and patience. In the second round he beat Edberg, the fifth seed. In the quarterfinal he defeated Becker, the third seed, 2–6, 6–4, 6–2, 6–0, and in the semifinal he beat Henri Leconte of France 2–6, 7–5, 7–6, 6–3. Lendl ended Pernfors's success with a final win 6–3, 6–2, 6–4.

Becker, as in 1985, flourished on the fast grass of Wimbledon with his heavy, aggressive volleying game and pace-making. He avenged himself against Pernfors with a fourth-round win 6–3, 7–6, 6–2. In the semifinal he beat Leconte 6–2, 6–4, 6–7, 6–3 to oppose Lendl for the title. Lendl, seeded first, won a quarterfinal against Tim Mayotte of the U.S. 6–4, 4–6, 6–4, 3–6, 9–7 and a semifinal against Slobodan Zivojinovic (Yugos.) 6–2, 6–7, 6–3, 6–7, 6–4. Becker, not taken to five sets in any match, defeated Lendl 6–4, 6–3, 7–5 to become champion for the second successive year.

Lendl reassumed his authority in the U.S. Open championships at Flushing Meadow in September. He won for the second successive year and conceded just one set in seven matches. That was in a quarterfinal against Leconte, 7–6, 6–1, 1–6, 6–1. In the semifinal he beat Edberg 7–6, 6–2, 6–3. The finalist against him was, surprisingly, Mecir, who had defeated Wilander 6–7, 6–3, 6–3, 6–4, Joakim

VIC DELUCIA/THE NEW YORK TIMES

Ivan Lendl grimaces as he rockets a backhand return in the first set of the men's singles final of the United States Open championship match. His win capped two weeks of almost flawless play in the prestigious Grand Slam event.

Nystrom (Sweden) 6–4, 6–2, 3–6, 6–2, and Becker 4–6, 6–3, 6–4, 3–6, 6–3, all seeded above him. In the final, however, Lendl routed him 6–4, 6–2, 6–0.

No pair dominated competition in the men's doubles. Paul Annacone (U.S.) and Christo Van Rensburg (South Africa) won the Australian championship, while Heinz Gunthardt (Switz.) and Balazs Taroczy (Hung.) took the "World Doubles Championship" at the Royal Albert Hall in London. French champions were John Fitzgerald (Australia) and Tomas Smid (Czech.). Wimbledon was won by Nystrom and Wilander, and the U.S. Open by Hans Gildemeister (Chile) and Zivojinovic.

The World Team Cup in Düsseldorf, West Germany, was won by France for the first time. In the final France (Leconte, Thierry Tulasne, Noah, Guy Forget) beat Sweden (Jarryd, Wilander) 2–1.

The Davis Cup had a record entry of 71 nations. A new zone was instituted, the African Zone, the two finalists in which qualified for sections "A" and "B" of the European Zone. From an entry of nine, Zimbabwe and Nigeria moved to the European Zone, and in "B" Nigeria survived the first round. European Zone "A" was won by France and "B" by Israel. Argentina won the American Zone and South Korea the Eastern. The four winners earned promotion to the World Group for 1987.

Among the 16 nations in the World Group, losses in both the first round and in the subsequent play-offs caused Ecuador, New Zealand, the U.S.S.R., and Denmark to be relegated to the zonal groups for 1987. In the quarterfinal round the U.S. beat Mexico 4–1, Australia defeated Great Britain 5–0, Czechoslovakia triumphed over Yugoslavia 5–0, and Sweden beat Italy 3–0. Australia (Paul McNamee, Pat Cash) beat the U.S. (Brad Gilbert, Mayotte, Annacone) 3–1 in the semifinal in Brisbane. It was the first win by Australia against the U.S. since 1973. Sweden (Kent Carlsson, Edberg, Pernfors, Jarryd) beat Czechoslovakia (Mecir, Milan Srejber, Smid) 4–1 in Prague in the other semifinal. Wilander was a notable omission from the Swedish team, as was Lendl from the Czechoslovakian. Sweden, champion in 1985 and 1984, met Australia in the final at Melbourne in December.

In the finals Australia dethroned Sweden 3–2 to regain the trophy it had last won in 1983. Cash led his team to victory by defeating Edberg 13–11, 13–11, 6–4 and Pernfors 2–6, 4–6, 6–3, 6–4, 6–3 and by teaming with John Fitzgerald to beat Edberg and Jarryd 6–3, 6–4, 4–6, 6–1.

Women's Competition. The ITF named Navratilova "world champion" for the fifth time for her 1985 record. She maintained almost as strong a superiority in 1986, her only singles defeat in a Grand Slam event coming in the French Open. In December 1985 she won the Australian title for the third time, and in 1986 she took Wimbledon for the seventh and the U.S. Open for the third time. Evert Lloyd, Hana Mandlikova (Czech.), Sukova, and Steffi Graf (West Germany) were her closest rivals.

Navratilova beat Evert Lloyd 6–2, 4–6, 6–2 in the Australian final. In the Virginia Slims championship at Madison Square Garden in March, she defeated Mandlikova 6–2, 6–0, 3–6, 6–1. In the German Open in Berlin, a leading event in the women's calendar, Graf beat Navratilova 6–2, 6–3 in the final, a striking feat for a player not then 17. The demands of slow, hard courts also taxed Navratilova's skill in Paris, where in the French Open in early June Evert Lloyd beat her 2–6, 6–3, 6–3 in the final.

At Wimbledon Mandlikova beat Evert Lloyd 7–6, 7–5 in the semifinal. At the same level Navratilova beat Gabriela Sabatini, a 16-year-old Argentine, 6–2, 6–2. Navratilova won the final against Mandlikova 7–6, 6–3 to win for the fifth successive year and for the seventh time since 1978. She did not lose a set in any round.

Navratilova's subsequent success in the U.S. Open was not as easily achieved. Her semifinal against Graf was arguably the best women's match of the year. In the third set Navratilova saved two match points at 4–5 and another in the tiebreaker before winning 6–1, 6–7, 7–6. In the other semifinal Sukova beat Evert Lloyd 6–2, 6–4. Navratilova defeated Sukova 6–3, 6–2 in the final.

In doubles Navratilova and Pam Shriver (U.S.) were again the most successful pair. They won the Australian, Wimbledon, and U.S. titles. With Andrea Temesvari (Hung.), Navratilova also took the French title.

The Federation Cup, with an entry of 42, was held in Prague, Czech., in July. The two dominant teams were the U.S. (Navratilova, Evert Lloyd, Shriver, Zina Garrison) and Czechoslovakia (Mandlikova, Sukova, Regina Marsikova, Andrea Holimova). The U.S. won for the 12th time when they beat Czechoslovakia, champions for the previous three years, by 3–0 in the final round. Navratilova, leader of the visiting U.S. team, had been the leader of the victorious Czechoslovak team of 1975. She was given an affectionate welcome in her native land.

The Wightman Cup was won by the U.S. for the 48th time in 58 contests. The U.S. (Bonnie Gadusek, Kathy Rinaldi, Elsie Burgin, Anne White) beat Great Britain (Jo Durie, Sara Gomer, Annabel Coft, Anne Hobbs) at the Royal Albert Hall, London, by 7–0. It was the eighth U.S. victory in a row. (LANCE TINGAY)

TOBOGGANING

While recreational tobogganing for all ages continued to be widely popular in 1986, luge racing, though still thriving in Austria, Italy, East and West Germany, and the U.S.S.R., failed elsewhere to capitalize on its Olympic status and did not maintain a public awareness comparable to that of bobsledding.

Sergey Danilin of the U.S.S.R. won the men's title in the European luge championships at Hamarstad, Norway, on February 1–2, followed by two East Germans, Jens Müller and the 1985 world champion, Michael Walter. Kerstin Schmidt led an East German clean sweep of the women's medals, with Steffi Martin runner-up and Ute Oberhoffner third. The pairs victors were Evgeny Belousov and Aleksandr Beliakov of the U.S.S.R., defeating Jörg Hoffman and Jochen Pietzsch, the East German 1985 world champions. Hansjötg Raffl and Norbert Huber finished third for Italy.

On the Cresta Run for skeleton tobogganing at St.-Moritz, Switz., Franco Gansser of the host nation lowered his own record for the full course by 1.37 sec to 51.31 sec, an average speed of 85.05 km/h (52.85 mph), on February 16. Seven days later another Swiss, Nico Baracchi, set a new record of 41.58 sec from the intermediate Junction station.

Gansser retained the title in the 77th Grand National classic, with James Sunley runner-up for the U.K. and Urs Nater of Switzerland third. Gansser also won the Curzon Cup from Junction, followed by his brother, Reto. Chris Bertschinger completed a Swiss grand slam by finishing third. (HOWARD BASS)

TRACK AND FIELD SPORTS

Most of the record-breaking action in track and field sports in 1986 was provided by women as athletes prepared for the second world championships in Rome, scheduled for the summer of 1987. Male athletes accounted for only 5 of the 26 world records established in 1986.

Men's International Competition. Three of the four men bettering global records in 1986 had done so at least twice before. The fourth, Jurgen Schult of East Germany, was the biggest surprise of the year. His discus throw of 74.08 m (243 ft) not only was far beyond his previous best (69.74 m, 228 ft 10 in) but created a shock in the world of field sports because of the amount by which he surpassed the existing best of 71.86 m (235 ft 9 in). Discus records seldom are improved that much.

Far better known and experienced in setting new marks was Soviet hammer thrower Yury Syedikh, who bettered the old mark twice, bringing his career total to six. He threw 86.66 m (284 ft 4 in) June 22 and reached 86.74 m (284 ft 7 in) on August 30. East Germany's 31-year-old Udo Beyer regained the shot-put record that he had first established in 1978 and then improved upon in 1983. His put of 22.64 m (74 ft 3½ in) took the record away from countryman Ulf Timmermann (22.62 m; 74 ft 2½ in). Far younger, as athletes go, was Sergey Bubka of the Soviet Union, but his experience with record breaking was difficult to surpass. After winning the pole vault in the world championships at the age of 19 in 1983, he set four world pole-vault records in 1984, another in 1985, and his sixth during 1986. He finished the year with a new world best of 6.01 m (19 ft 8½ in).

No records were broken by Morocco's Said Aouita, holder of the world standards in the 1,500 m and 5,000 m. Outspoken in his desire to accumulate all records from 1,500 m through 10,000 m, Aouita in 1986 had to settle for four very near misses. Over a period of 36 days he failed by a total of only 1.62 sec to break four world records. He began the chase on August 6, running 13 min 00.86 sec to miss the 5,000-m standard by 0.46 sec. A week later he came within 0.44 sec of the 3,000-m mark, running 7 min 32.54 sec. Just four days later Aouita again challenged the 3,000-m standard, running the distance in 7 min 32.23 sec and missing by a mere 0.13 sec. He fell short by 0.59 sec in a 2,000-m race on September 5. He also had the second fastest time in the world in the 10,000 m, 27 min 26.11 sec, in his first effort at the distance and was the fourth fastest miler of the year, with 3 min 50.33 sec.

Aouita never raced in 1986 against Sebastian Coe and Steve Cram, his two archrivals from the United Kingdom. Meanwhile, Coe surprised himself by running the year's fastest 1,500 m in 3 min 29.77 sec, just 0.31 sec off Aouita's world record. Coe, who had talked about running longer distances, also led the world at 1,000 m (2 min 14.90 sec). Cram led the world at 800 m (1 min 43.19 sec) and one mile (3 min 48.31 sec) and was second fastest at 1,000 and 1,500 m.

Slowed by a leg injury in 1985, after winning four gold medals in the 1984 Olympics, Carl Lewis of the U.S. again encountered physical problems in 1986. He lost his number one ranking in the 100 m, which he had held for five years, to Canada's Ben Johnson. But he remained unbeaten in the long jump, extending his consecutive victory record to 48. Also injured in 1985 after an Olympic Games triumph was veteran 400-m hurdler Edwin Moses (*see* BIOGRAPHIES). He returned to action in fine form in 1986, leading the world and extending his unbeaten string of victories to 104 races.

A javelin with changed specifications was put into use during the year in order to reduce the distance thrown and thus lessen the possibility of injury. The best throw of the year—and, therefore, the new unofficial world best—was 85.72 m (281 ft 3 in) by Klaus Tafelmeier of West Germany. The old record, held by Uwe Hohn, who did not compete in 1986, was 104.80 m (343 ft 10 in).

Jackie Joyner takes flight in one of her typical long jumps. Joyner smashed the heptathlon world record twice, in the Moscow Goodwill Games and at a meet in Houston, Texas. Both times she topped 7,100 points. No woman had even reached 7,000 before.
JOHN IACONO/SPORTS ILLUSTRATED

Indoor competition was highlighted by the pole vault. An amazing nine world records were achieved during a two-month period in competition that ranged from the Soviet Union to Los Angeles and from Osaka, Japan, to Saskatoon, Sask. The record was raised, with one exception, by one centimetre each time. Billy Olson of the U.S. started the chain with his 5.86 m (19 ft 2¾ in) on Dec. 28, 1985, and Bubka completed it with 5.95 m (19 ft 6¼ in) on February 28. Each vaulter set four new marks, with Joe Dial of the U.S. gaining the ninth.

Multiple records were also scored in the 60-m dash, where Johnson twice ran 6.50 sec, and in the triple jump, where Charles Simpkins of the U.S. reached 17.50 m (57 ft 5 in) only to be surpassed by Maris Bruziks of the U.S.S.R. with 17.54 m (57 ft 6½ in). Two other global bests were established, Thomas Schonlebe of East Germany running 400 m in 45.41 sec and Mark McKoy of Canada hurdling 60 m in 7.47 sec.

Although still regarded as amateurs by the international and national governing bodies, track and field athletes were given more opportunities to win cash prizes. During the second year of the Mobil Grand Prix competition, a total of $763,000 was distributed. Leading winners were Aouita and woman hurdler Yordanka Donkova of Bulgaria, each receiving $35,000 for scoring the most points in a series of international tournaments.

The most significant meet of the year was the 14th European championships, held at Stuttgart, West Germany, August 26–31. Four world records, the men's hammer

(continued on page 393)

The XIII Commonwealth Games

BY CHRIS BRASHER

The XIII Commonwealth Games took place in Edinburgh, Scotland, from July 24 to Aug. 2, 1986. They proved to be an occasion that contrasted sharply with the previous (1970) Edinburgh Games, which have been regarded as among the finest ever held.

The Political Games. In 1986 politics led to the withdrawal of 32 of the 58 countries that had originally accepted the invitation to compete. The problem was the racial policies of South Africa, a former member of the Commonwealth. The Asian, Caribbean, and black African countries of the Commonwealth wanted full economic sanctions imposed on South Africa; U.K. Prime Minister Margaret Thatcher refused to impose them, saying that sanctions would have a disastrous effect on black employment in South Africa. To express their displeasure more than 50% of the Commonwealth governments ordered their teams to stay away.

Some teams could not observe the boycott for the simple reason that they were already installed in the Games Village, just under the magnificent volcanic hill, known as Arthur's Seat, that dominates the city of Edinburgh. On the day before the Games were to be opened by Prince Philip, the Bermudan team was ordered by the Bermudan premier not to march in the opening ceremony. The team manager made long and impassioned calls to Bermuda overnight; at last, as the other teams were already assembling for the march, word came through that the Bermudans could join in. This they did, to great cheers from the packed stadium. But it was to be their first and last appearance. On the orders of their premier, they withdrew from the competition. So much for trying to keep politics out of sports.

Politics also entered into the financial side of the Games. When Edinburgh made its successful bid, the city council was controlled by the Conservative Party, but by 1986 the Labour Party was in power, and many councillors believed that the cost of the Games would fall too heavily on the people of Edinburgh. Indeed, the Organizing Committee was so starved for funds that, five weeks before the tournament was due to open, it was in grave danger of having to declare itself bankrupt. Passionate appeals to the British government produced no response, but the pleas were heard by Robert Maxwell of Mirror Group Newspapers Ltd. He flew to Edinburgh and announced himself to be the saviour of the Games. He managed to stave off the immediate threat of bankruptcy. At the end of the Games, however, a huge deficit of more than £4 million remained. Further pleas to the government fell on deaf ears, and several major creditors remained unpaid as discussions continued as to who was responsible for the debt.

Sporting Highlights. Despite the controversy some athletic competition took place but, not surprisingly, it was not as exciting or as significant as had been hoped. The centrepieces of the track and field program were to have been two clashes between English athletes Steve Cram, world champion and Olympic silver medalist over 1,500 m, and Sebastian Coe, twice the Olympic 1,500-m champion and the world record holder at 800 m. Both were scheduled to run in the 800 m and the 1,500 m. In early season competition both men had shown that they were fully fit; thus, the athletic world was eager to discover which of these fine athletes was the greatest.

But the dream matchup was not to be; in the second semifinal of the 800 m on July 28, Coe was in trouble from the start. Looking like a shadow of his normal self, he struggled to qualify for the final with a time of 1 min 48.07 sec—nearly seven seconds slower than his best—and declared afterward that he had never felt so bad in any race in his career. He took to his bed with influenza and did not run again in Edinburgh.

Three days later the 800-m final was controlled from the back of the field—such was his stature—by Cram. Peter Elliott, the ginger-haired Yorkshireman, set a world-class pace—51.03 sec for the first lap—and Cram cruised along comfortably at the back. In the back straightaway Cram unleashed his awesome power and within 150 m was in the lead. His winning time of 1 min 43.22 sec set a U.K. all-comers record (a record for an athlete of any nationality running in the U.K.). Later that same day Steve Ovett, the oldest of this great trio of English middle-distance runners, won the 5,000 m with equal ease in 13 min 24.11 sec—a respectable, but not world-class, time. On August 1 Robert de Castella (Australia) became the first person to win two consecutive Commonwealth marathon titles.

The 41 gold medals in the track and field events went to only six nations: England took 18, Canada 10, Australia 9, Wales 2, and Northern Ireland and Scotland 1 each. The absence of so many African and Caribbean countries was deeply damaging in those events, as it was in the boxing arena, where those countries traditionally dominate many of the weight classes. In their absence no nation was more impressive than Canada, which produced several polished and aggressive fighters and won 6 of the 12 finals.

Weight lifting and wrestling both suffered from the boycott, notably from the withdrawal of India, and the Malaysians were sorely missed in the badminton competition, but in other sports the level of competition was not greatly affected. There was keen rivalry between Canada (15 gold medals) and Australia (13) in the swimming and diving events.

Among the outstanding individual performances of the Games was that of Steven Redgrave (England), who made history by winning rowing gold medals in the single sculls, coxless pairs, and coxed fours. Most memorable of the double gold medalists was Olympic shooting champion Malcolm Cooper (England), who won the individual and (with his wife) the pairs contests in the three-position small-bore rifle event. On the controversial rebuilt cycling velodrome, which remained uncovered, the schedule was often disrupted by rain. Australia emerged wet but triumphant, winning five of a possible seven gold medals.

Indeed the weather added to the problems of these unlucky XIII Commonwealth Games. During the ten days of competition Edinburgh was the wettest place in Britain.

A gold medalist (3,000-m steeplechase) in the 1956 Olympic Games, Chris Brasher is sports correspondent of The Observer. *He has won the "Sports Writer of the Year" award on two occasions and is author of* Tokyo 1964, Mexico 1968, *and* Munich '72.

Champions of the XIII Commonwealth Games

Badminton

Men's singles	S. Baddeley (England)	Women's doubles	England
Women's singles	H. Troke (England)	Mixed doubles	Australia
Men's doubles	Scotland	Team event	England

Bowling

Men's singles	I. Dickison (New Zealand)	Women's pairs	Northern Ireland
Women's singles	W. Line (England)	Men's fours	Wales
Men's pairs	Scotland	Women's fours	Wales

Boxing

Light flyweight	S. Olson (Canada)	Welterweight	D. Dyer (England)
Flyweight	J. Lyon (England)	Lt. middleweight	D. Sherry (Canada)
Bantamweight	S. Murphy (England)	Middleweight	R. Douglas (England)
Featherweight	B. Downey (Canada)	Lt. heavyweight	J. Moran (England)
Lightweight	A. Dar (Canada)	Heavyweight	J. Peau (New Zealand)
Lt. welterweight	H. Grant (Canada)	Superheavyweight	L. Lewis (Canada)

Cycling

1,000-m sprint	G. Neiwand (Australia)	
1,000-m individual time trial	M. Vinnicombe (Australia)	1 min 06.23 sec
4,000-m individual pursuit	D. Woods (Australia)	4 min 43.92 sec
4,000-m team pursuit	Australia	4 min 26.94 sec
100-km team time trial	England	2 hr 13 min 16 sec
10-mi track race	W. McCarney (Australia)	19 min 40.61 sec
105-mi road race	P. Curran (England)	4 hr 8 min 50 sec

Rowing

Men (2,000-m course)

Lightweight single sculls	P. Antonie (Australia)	7 min 16.43 sec
Single sculls	S. Redgrave (England)	7 min 28.29 sec
Double sculls	Canada	6 min 19.43 sec
Pairs without coxswain	England	6 min 40.48 sec
Lightweight fours without coxswain	England	6 min 25.86 sec
Fours without coxswain	Canada	6 min 00.56 sec
Fours with coxswain	England	6 min 08.13 sec
Eights	Australia	5 min 44.42 sec

Women (2,000-m course)

Lightweight single sculls	A. Ferguson (Australia)	7 min 45.49 sec
Single sculls	S. Foster (New Zealand)	7 min 43.22 sec
Double sculls	New Zealand	7 min 21.52 sec
Pairs without coxswain	Canada	7 min 34.51 sec
Lightweight fours without coxswain	England	6 min 54.70 sec
Fours with coxswain	Canada	6 min 50.13 sec
Eights	Australia	6 min 43.69 sec

Shooting

Full-bore rifle (individual)	S. Golinski (Australia)	396 pt
Full-bore rifle (pairs)	Canada	583 pt
Small-bore rifle, prone (individual)	A. Smith (Australia)	599 pt
Small-bore rifle, prone (pairs)	Canada	1,175 pt
Small-bore rifle, three-position (individual)	M. Cooper (England)	1,170 pt
Small-bore rifle, three-position (pairs)	England	2,278 pt
Free pistol (individual)	G. Yelavich (New Zealand)	551 pt
Free pistol (pairs)	Canada	1,099 pt
Rapid-fire pistol (individual)	P. Murray (Australia)	591 pt
Rapid-fire pistol (pairs)	England	1,169 pt
Centre-fire pistol (individual)	R. Northover (England)	583 pt
Centre-fire pistol (pairs)	Australia	1,165 pt
Shotgun, skeet (individual)	N. Kelly (Isle of Man)	196 pt
Shotgun, skeet (pairs)	England	195 pt
Shotgun, Olympic trench (individual)	I. Peel (England)	195 pt
Shotgun, Olympic trench (pairs)	England	185 pt
Air rifle (individual)	G. Lorion (Canada)	588 pt
Air rifle (pairs)	Canada	1,167 pt
Air pistol (individual)	G. Yelavich (New Zealand)	575 pt
Air pistol (pairs)	England	1,143 pt

Swimming and Diving

Men

100-m freestyle	G. Fasala (Australia)	50.95 sec
200-m freestyle	R. Glaria (Australia)	1 min 50.57 sec
400-m freestyle	D. Armstrong (Australia)	3 min 52.25 sec
1,500-m freestyle	J. Plummer (Australia)	15 min 12.62 sec
100-m backstroke	M. Tewksbury (Canada)	56.45 sec
200-m backtstroke	S. Goss (Canada)	2 min 02.55 sec
100-m breaststroke	V. Davis (Canada)	1 min 03.01 sec
200-m breaststroke	A. Moorhouse (England)	2 min 16.35 sec
100-m butterfly	A. Jameson (England)	54.07 sec
200-m butterfly	R. Mosse (New Zealand)	1 min 57.27 sec
200-m individual medley	A. Baumann (Canada)	2 min 01.80 sec
400-m individual medley	A. Baumann (Canada)	4 min 18.29 sec
4 x 100-m medley relay	Canada	3 min 44.00 sec
4 x 100-m freestyle relay	Australia	3 min 21.58 sec
4 x 200-m freestyle relay	Australia	7 min 23.49 sec
springboard diving	S. Panayi (Australia)	648.33 points
highboard diving	C. Rogerson (Australia)	600.87 points

Women

100-m freestyle	J. Kerr (Canada)	57.62 sec
200-m freestyle	S. Baumer (Australia)	2 min 00.61 sec
400-m freestyle	S. Hardcastle (England)	4 min 07.68 sec
800-m freestyle	S. Hardcastle (England)	8 min 24.77 sec
100-m backstroke	S. Hume (New Zealand)	1 min 04.00 sec
200-m backstroke	G. Parkes (Australia)	2 min 14.88 sec
100-m breaststroke	A. Higson (Canada)	1 min 10.84 sec
200-m breaststroke	A. Higson (Canada)	2 min 31.20 sec
100-m butterfly	C. Cooper (England)	1 min 02.12 sec
200-m butterfly	D. McGinnis (Canada)	2 min 11.97 sec
200-m individual medley	S. Landells (Australia)	2 min 17.02 sec
400-m individual medley	S. Landells (Australia)	4 min 45.82 sec
4 x 100-m medley relay	England	4 min 13.48 sec
4 x 100-m freestyle relay	Canada	3 min 48.45 sec
4 x 200-m freestyle relay	Australia	8 min 12.09 sec
synchronized swimming (solo)	S. Frechette (Canada)	199.50 points
synchronized swimming (duet)	Canada	199.54 points
springboard diving	D. Fuller (Canada)	513.09 points
highboard diving	D. Fuller (Canada)	431.61 points

Track and Field

Men

100 m	B. Johnson (Canada)	10.07 sec
200 m	A. Mahorn (Canada)	20.31 sec
400 m	R. Black (England)	45.57 sec
800 m	S. Cram (England)	1 min 43.22 sec
1,500 m	S. Cram (England)	3 min 50.87 sec
5,000 m	S. Ovett (England)	13 min 24.11 sec
10,000 m	J. Solly (England)	27 min 57.42 sec
Marathon	R. de Castella (Australia)	2 hr 10 min 15 sec
110-m hurdles	M. McKoy (Canada)	13.31 sec
400-m hurdles	P. Beattie (N. Ireland)	49.60 sec
3,000-m steeplechase	G. Fell (Canada)	8 min 24.49 sec
4 × 100-m relay	Canada	39.15 sec
4 × 400-m relay	England	3 min 07.19 sec
30-km walk	S. Baker (Australia)	2 hr 7 min 47 sec
High jump	M. Ottey (Canada)	2.30 m
Long jump	G. Honey (Australia)	8.08 m
Pole vault	A. Ashurst (England)	5.30 m
Triple jump	J. Herbert (England)	17.27 m
Shot put	B. Cole (England)	18.16 m
Discus	R. Lazdins (Canada)	58.86 m
Hammer throw	D. Smith (England)	74.06 m
Javelin	D. Oltley (England)	80.62 m
Decathlon	D. Thompson (England)	8,663 points

Women

100 m	H. Oakes (England)	11.20 sec
200 m	A. Issajenko (Canada)	22.91 sec
400 m	D. Flintoff (Australia)	51.29 sec
800 m	K. Wade (Wales)	2 min 00.94 sec
1,500 m	K. Wade (Wales)	4 min 10.91 sec
3,000 m	L. Williams (Canada)	8 min 54.29 sec
10,000 m	E. Lynch (Scotland)	31 min 41.42 sec
Marathon	L. Martin (Australia)	2 hr 26 min 07 sec
100-m hurdles	S. Gunnell (England)	13.29 sec
400-m hurdles	D. Flintoff (Australia)	54.94 sec
4 × 100-m relay	England	43.39 sec
4 × 400-m relay	Canada	3 min 28.92 sec
High jump	C. Stanton (Australia)	1.92 m
Long jump	J. Oladapo (England)	6.43 m
Shot put	G. Martin (England)	19.00 m
Discus	G. Martin (Australia)	56.42 m
Javelin	T. Sanderson (England)	69.80 m
Heptathlon	J. Simpson (England)	6,282 points

Weight Lifting

52 kg	G. Hayman (Australia)	212.5 kg
56 kg	N. Voukelatos (Australia)	245.0 kg
60 kg	R. Williams (Wales)	252.5 kg
67.5 kg	D. Willey (England)	315.0 kg
75 kg	W. Stellios (Australia)	302.0 kg
82.5 kg	D. Morgan (Wales)	350.0 kg
90 kg	K. Boxell (England)	350.0 kg
100 kg	D. Garun (Canada)	360.0 kg
110 kg	K. Roy (Canada)	375.0 kg
110 kg+	D. Lukin (Australia)	392.5 kg

Wrestling

48 kg	R. Moncur (Canada)
52 kg	C. Woodcroft (Canada)
57 kg	M. Ostberg (Canada)
62 kg	P. Hughes (Canada)
68 kg	D. McKay (Canada)
74 kg	G. Holmes (Canada)
82 kg	C. Rinke (Canada)
90 kg	N. Loban (England)
100 kg	C. Davis (Canada)
130 kg	W. Brightwell (Canada)

(continued from page 391)

throw and women's 200 m, 400-m hurdles, and javelin throw, were achieved. At the opposite extreme was the Commonwealth Games in Edinburgh, Scotland, July 26–August 2. Of the 58 Commonwealth nations, 32 African and Caribbean countries boycotted the meet because Great Britain refused to impose strong sanctions on South Africa. Also encountering trouble was the Goodwill Games, sponsored by the Soviet Union and Ted Turner, a U.S. television magnate. Turner announced a loss of $26 million in a multisport meeting that primarily featured Soviet and U.S. athletes.

Continuing to expand, the International Amateur Athletic Federation, worldwide governing body of the sport, staged its first world junior championships, in Athens. The IAAF also decided to let professionals in other sports com-

Sergey Bubka is triumphant as he sets a new pole-vaulting record, clearing the bar at 6.01 metres (19 feet 8½ inches). Bubka made the vault at the Goodwill Games in Moscow's Lenin Stadium. He had set four world records in 1984 and another in 1985.

AP/WIDE WORLD

pete in track and to approve official world indoor records. The first world indoor championships were scheduled to be held in Indianapolis, Ind., in March 1987.

Women's International Competition. It was a productive year for multiple record breakers among the women. Twelve athletes broke a total of 22 world marks, with two outstanding performers gaining credit for four records each.

Heike Drechsler of East Germany led the way. Only 21, and a world champion since 1983, she added sprinting to her long-jumping capabilities and achieved a rare distinction. Only one other woman and two men had produced world records in both field events and running events, as Drechsler did. Until 1986 Drechsler was known only as a record-breaking long jumper, and she solidified that perception of herself. She raised her own long-jump record to 7.45 m (24 ft 5½ in) and then equaled that mark. On the track, she surprisingly matched the 21.71-sec record for 200 m set twice by countrywoman Marita Koch. And then she did it again. To top off her magnificent season, Drechsler in the 100 m narrowly missed beating Evelyn Ashford, world record holder and Olympic champion in that event. Both ran 10.91 sec, a time bettered only by Ashford's 10.88 sec.

Equally proficient in establishing new all-time bests was Donkova. In 28 days she equaled the 100-m hurdle mark of 12.36 sec and then broke the record three times, running 12.34 and 12.29 on the same day and culminating her great season with a best of 12.26 sec.

It took Ingrid Kristiansen (*see* BIOGRAPHIES) of Norway much longer to earn her two world records. Breaking the 5,000 mark took her 14 min 37.33 sec, and it took another 30 min 13.74 sec for her 10,000-m record. Her performances were the second best of the year in both the 3-km race and the 42.195-km marathon, in which she was the world record holder.

Marina Stepanova of the Soviet Union had an unusual season in two respects. Without much prior experience in the event, she twice bettered the 400-m hurdle standard. Her times of 53.32 sec and 52.94 sec were achieved at the unheard-of age of 36 years.

Records were broken in three of the five field events, including Drechsler's marks in the long jump. Keeping her company in the record book were Stefka Kostadinova of Bulgaria and Fatima Whitbread of the U.K. Kostadinova first equaled the high-jump standard by clearing 2.07 m (6 ft 9½ in) and then added a centimetre to the mark to achieve 2.08 m (6 ft 9¾ in). Whitbread had perhaps the most unexpected record of the year. A veteran javelin thrower but always short of the highest level, she hurled the javelin 77.44 m (254 ft 1 in) in the trials of the European championships. This added 2.04 m (6 ft 9 in) to the previous mark. She later won the championships with a throw of 76.32 m (250 ft 5 in) for the second best distance ever.

Among the most applauded achievements was the heptathlon season of U.S. athlete Jackie Joyner. She first defeated the best in Europe with a strong early-season total of 6,841 points and then scored 6,910 for a U.S. record, which was lost, however, when the automatic timer device did not function. But that unfortunate mishap was forgotten when she twice broke the world record. She first did it in the Goodwill Games by piling up 7,148 points, 202 points above the previous best. Then, in the heat and humidity of Houston, Texas, Joyner scored 7,161 points. She also was among the best in the world in the long jump and was coholder of the U.S. best of the year at 12.84 sec in the 100-m hurdles.

Four records were broken in walking races, only recently given official recognition by the IAAF. Wang Yan of China walked 5,000 m in 21 min 33.8 sec, and three women broke the 10,000-m mark. Xu Yongjiu of China walked the distance in 45 min 31.9 sec, followed by Kerry Saxby of Australia (45 min 8.13 sec) and Yelena Kuznetsova of the Soviet Union (44 min 32.50 sec).

A leader in two events, though not a threat to the all-time best, was Doina Melinte of Romania. She led the way in both the 800 m and 1,500 m, running those distances in 1 min 56.2 sec and 3 min 56.7 sec, respectively. Another Romanian, Maricica Puica, garnered a world record in the seldom-run 2,000 m with a time of 5 min 28.69 sec.

Records fell in four events indoors. Drechsler led the way with long jumps of 7.25 m (23 ft 9½ in) and 7.29 m (23 ft 11 in). The 3,000-m standard was bettered twice, first by Olga Bondarenko of the U.S.S.R. (8 min 42.30 sec) and then by Zola Budd of the U.K. (8 min 39.79 sec). On the straightaways Nellie Cooman of The Netherlands ran 60 m in 7.00 sec, and Cornelia Oschkenat of East Germany hurdled 50 m in 6.73 sec.

U.S. Competition. U.S. men threatened no world records and managed national records in only three events. The only track record was set in the 10,000 m when Mark Nenow ran the distance in 27 min 20.56 sec, a time bettered only by two men ever. More prolific were Joe Dial and Jud Logan. During two weeks Dial pole vaulted in record form three times, raising the national record to 5.86 m (19 ft 2¾ in), 5.88 m (19 ft 3½ in), and 5.90 m (19 ft 4¼ in). Logan's record count in the hammer throw was four, increasing the record first to 77.66 m (254 ft 9 in) and finally to 80.88 m (265 ft 4 in).

The National Collegiate Athletic Association's championship was won by Southern Methodist by the margin of one point over Washington State. Texas won the women's title.

Except for Joyner's two world records, U.S. women

gained only one national mark. The discus standard was raised to 66.10 m (216 ft 10 in) by Carol Cady. Indoors, Joyner raised the long-jump record three times, jumping 6.83 m (22 ft 5 in), 6.96 m (22 ft 10 in), and 6.97 m (22 ft 10½ in). The indoor record in the 400-m run went to Diane Dixon with a clocking of 52.13 sec.

Marathon Running and Cross Country. International marathon running competition continued to grow in 1986 and produced two double winners in the five top races of the year. On the men's side veteran Toshihiko Seko of Japan won the London marathon on April 20 and then triumphed at Chicago on October 26. For the women Grete Waitz of Norway won at London, where her time of 2 hr 24 min 54 sec was the fourth fastest ever by a woman. On November 2 she won at New York City for the eighth time, the fifth in a row.

Other winners of major marathons were Abebe Mekonnen of Ethiopia at Rotterdam, Neth., on April 19; Rob de Castella at Boston on April 21, with the third best performance of all time, 2 hr 7 min 51 sec; Kristiansen at Boston and Chicago; and Gianni Poli of Italy at New York City.

Victors in the world cross-country championships at Neuchatel, Switz., were John Ngugi of Kenya and Budd. The latter won for the second consecutive time and led the U.K. to a women's team victory, breaking the three-meet winning streak of the U.S. Kenya pushed Ethiopia, which had won five straight men's team titles, into second place.

Another streak was kept alive by Pat Porter, who won the U.S. men's championships for the fifth straight time. Victor in the women's competition was Lesley Welch. The college men's champion was Aaron Ramirez of Arizona, and Arkansas captured the men's team title. In the women's event Texas defeated defending champion Wisconsin by two points, the smallest margin since 1970. Angela Chalmers was the individual winner. (BERT NELSON)

VOLLEYBALL

The world championships for men and women were the focal points of volleyball for 1986. Each event qualified one team for the 1988 Olympic Games.

The United States won the 1986 men's title. Since the U.S. had already qualified for the 1988 Olympic Games by virtue of being the 1984 Olympic champion, and because the second-place Soviet Union had qualified for the 1988 Olympics by finishing second to the U.S. in the 1985 World Cup, third-place Bulgaria was awarded the position for the 1988 Games.

The men's world championship was played in late September throughout France with the finals in Paris. More than 16,000 spectators watched the United States defeat the Soviets to gain its first world title. The victory for the U.S. completed a rare triple crown—in succession, the Olympic Games (1984), the World Cup (1985), and the world championship (1986). Only the Soviets had accomplished this feat previously.

Finishing fourth through tenth, respectively, were Brazil, Cuba, France, Argentina, Czechoslovakia, Poland, and Japan. Rounding out the 16-team field were Italy, China, Greece, Egypt, Taiwan, and Venezuela.

China won the 1986 women's world championship, played in early September throughout Czechoslovakia with the finals in Prague. Because the Chinese had already qualified for the Olympic Games as the 1984 Olympic champions, second-place Cuba was awarded the 1988 Olympic position. The victory by the Chinese continued their dominance of world titles that began with the 1981 World Cup and included the 1982 world championship, the 1984 Olympic Games, and the 1985 World Cup. Peru finished third and East Germany fourth. Completing the top ten in order were Brazil, the Soviet Union, Japan, South Korea, Italy, and the U.S. The last six finishers were Czechoslovakia, Bulgaria, West Germany, North Korea, Canada, and Tunisia.

Pepperdine University in May captured its second straight National Collegiate Athletic Association (NCAA) men's championship over Southern California. Penn State finished third and Ohio State fourth. In NCAA women's play (completed in December 1985) the Division I title went to the University of the Pacific over Stanford, Division II to Portland State over California State (Northridge), and Division III to Elmhurst over Laverne.

(ALBERT M. MONACO, JR.)

WATER POLO

The premier event of 1986 was the fifth world championships, held in August in Madrid. For the first time in the history of this tournament, a championship game rather than a round-robin system was used to determine the gold medalist. In one of the most exciting matches ever held, Yugoslavia defeated Italy 12–11 with just one second to go in the eighth overtime period. The lead changed hands numerous times, each team thinking it had won, only to have its opponent tie the score and send the game into another overtime. In the competition for third place, the U.S.S.R. defeated the United States 8–6 in a thrilling four-overtime contest. Rounding out the top eight teams were Spain, West Germany, Cuba, and France.

Australia went undefeated in seven matches to capture the gold medal in the women's portion of the world championships. The Netherlands, losing only to Australia (8–7) in the third round, finished in second place, followed in order by the United States, Canada, Hungary, and West Germany.

Another major international water polo tournament was conducted as part of the first Goodwill Games, held in Moscow in July. The host Soviet Union went undefeated to win top honours, and the U.S. took home the silver medal. Hungary placed third, with West Germany fourth, The Netherlands fifth, and Greece sixth.

(WILLIAM ENSIGN FRADY)

WATER SKIING

For the fifth time in six years, Carl Roberge of Orlando, Fla., won the overall title in the men's open competition during the U.S. National Water Ski Championships, held in West Palm Beach, Fla. Deena Brush of West Sacramento, Calif., was the overall winner in the women's open competition.

Roberge also successfully defended his slalom crown with 60½ buoys. Other event winners in men's open competition were Tory Baggiano of Birmingham, Ala., in tricks with 8,730 points and Mike Morgan of Lake Wales, Fla., in jumping with a leap of 54 m (177 ft). Brush won women's tricks with 5,830 points and jumping at 43.6 m (143 ft). Kim Laskoff of Fort Walton Beach, Fla., took the slalom gold medal with 62 buoys.

In the U.S. Masters tournament at Callaway Gardens, Ga., Brush and Patrice Martin of France were the overall champions. Cory Pickos of Eagle Lake, Fla., set a new world record in men's tricks with a run of 10,510 points in the elimination finals. Andy Mapple and Mike Hazelwood, both of Great Britain, won slalom and jumping, respectively. Brush was the best jumper among the women, while Kristie Overton of Greenville, N.C., won tricks for the second year in a row, and Camille Duvall of Orlando took the slalom title.

On the eight-stop cash prize tour, another world record was set. Hazelwood leaped 61.9 m (203 ft) in the Birmingham, Ala., tournament, breaking the mark of 61.6 m (202 ft) held by Glen Thurlow of Australia since 1983. Hazelwood was the overall money winner on the tour as well as the top jumper.

The U.S. barefoot water ski team won the world title for the first time in five tries, defeating the defending champions from Australia at Kelheim, West Germany. Overall individual titles in the 14-nation competition went to Mike Seipel of the U.S. and Kim Lampart of Australia. Lampart also won wake slalom and tricks. Seipel was best in men's tricks, while his teammate Ron Scarpa won wake slalom. Gavin O'Mahoney of Australia and Michelle Doherty of Great Britain won the jumping championships.

(THOMAS C. HARDMAN)

WEIGHT LIFTING

Naum Shalamanov of Bulgaria continued in 1986 to be the number one weight lifter in the world. Only 19, he again won the world championship in the 60-kg (132-lb) division by breaking his own record with a total lift of 335 kg (738.5 lb). The world championships were held in Sofia, Bulg., on November 8–15. Shalamanov followed by winning his third straight World Cup title in Melbourne, Australia, and then defected there on December 10.

Bulgaria again was the dominant country in weight lifting, winning seven gold medals in the world championships and placing second in two other classes out of a total of ten. The Soviet Union won two gold and four silver medals. The other gold medal was earned by Romania. Hungary gained five bronze medals.

The other world record set in the championships was a total lift of 449 kg (990 lb) in the 110-kg (242-lb) class by Yury Zaharevich, U.S.S.R. Among the new champions was Assen Zlatev of Bulgaria, a 1980 Olympic Games champion. In the 82.5-kg (181.5-lb) class his total lift was 405 kg (892.75 lb), equaling the world record. Aleksandr Varbanov of Bulgaria equaled the world record in the 75-kg (165-lb) class with a total lift of 377.5 kg (832 lb).

In the world championships, individual medals are awarded for total lift, snatch, and clean and jerk, and points in all three determine the team rankings. Bulgaria finished first with 449 points, and the U.S.S.R. placed second with 388 points.

For the first time selected lifters were tested for drug use prior to the start of the competition. The tests resulted in two-year suspensions for ten lifters. During the year eight other lifters were suspended for testing positive.

(C. ROBERT PAUL, JR.)

WRESTLING

The 1986 world wrestling championships were held October 18–22 at Budapest, Hung. The Soviet Union continued to dominate freestyle wrestling, placing in all ten weights. With six individual champions, two finishing second, one third, and one sixth, the Soviets garnered a total of 91 points. The U.S. was second with 72 points, and Bulgaria placed third with 59. It was the best effort ever recorded by a U.S. team and included one individual champion, three second-place, and three third-place finishers.

The Greco-Roman championships followed from October 23 to 26, also in Budapest. Crowds of up to 8,000 people cheered as a strong Soviet Union team won five individual championships to score 82 points and win the tournament. Bulgaria placed second with 69 points, and Hungary was third with 47.5.

The U.S. National Collegiate Athletic Association tournament took place March 13–15 at the University of Iowa. Thousands of enthusiastic fans cheered as they watched the home team win its ninth straight NCAA championship with an impressive 158 points, breaking its own scoring record of 155 points established in 1983. The University of Oklahoma was second with 84¾ points, and Oklahoma State University finished third with 77¼ points.

(MARVIN G. HESS)

Sumo. Traditional Japanese sumo wrestling enjoyed an event-filled year with the promotion of one *yokozuna* (grand champion), the retirement of another, and the ouster from the sumo world of a third for running up massive debts. After finishing as runner-up in two successive tournaments, *ozeki* (champion) Kitao gained promotion to *yokozuna* in late July and promptly changed his name to Futahaguro. Rising young *sekiwake* (junior champion) Hoshi earned a boost to *ozeki* after the July tournament and also changed his name, to Hokutoumi. Earlier, grand champion Takanosato announced his retirement after his comeback attempt collapsed in the January tournament. Taka had fought in nine tournaments as a *yokozuna* and had won four *yusho* (tourney championships). Also hanging up his *mawashi* (wrestling belt) was 37-year-old Aobajo, who set an all-time record of 1,631 consecutive bouts in all six divisions of sumo. Former *yokozuna* Wajima, who won 14 *yusho* during his 11-year career, was forced to resign in December 1985 from the Sumo Association after pawning his certificate of stable mastership and incurring as much as $5 million in debts. Wajima then became a professional wrestler in Japan along with John Tenta of Canada, who abruptly quit sumo after winning three tournaments in a row in the lower divisions without a loss.

In other important events during the year, Kasugano Oyakata was elected to a seventh two-year term as chairman of the Sumo Association and named Futagoyama Oyakata as acting chief director and successor. A sumo troupe of more than 100 wrestlers and officials staged the first sumo tournament ever held in Europe when they performed in a three-day Paris tournament in mid-October, and former junior champion Takamiyama (Jesse Kuahaulua of Hawaii) and ex-*yokozuna* Kitanoumi opened their own sumo stables.

Chiyonofuji, the 31-year-old grand champion, continued to dominate sumo by winning five of the six 15-day tournaments, the other one going to his stablemate *sekiwake* Hoshi (later *ozeki* Hokutoumi). Chiyonofuji captured the year's first tournament, the Hatsu *basho,* in January in Tokyo with a fine 13–2 record. The Haru *basho,* or Spring tournament, in March in Osaka was won by Hoshi with a strong 13–2 mark. In the Natsu *basho,* or Summer tournament, in May in Tokyo, Chiyonofuji surged back to capture his second tourney title of the year with another 13–2 record. Then in the Nagoya *basho* in July, Chiyonofuji and *ozeki* Kitao fought down to the wire with identical 14–1 records, with the muscular *yokozuna* finally beating Kitao in a play-off. The two consecutive runner-up performances were enough to give Kitao promotion as the 60th *yokozuna.*

Chiyonofuji chalked up his 18th career *yusho* and third tourney title of the year when he earned a near-perfect 14–1 record in the Aki *basho,* or Autumn tournament, in September in Tokyo. Chiyonofuji extended his career *yusho* record to 19 when he won the year's final tournament, the Kyushu *basho,* in November at Fukuoka. His 13–2 record also won him his fifth tourney title in 1986 and his fourth in a row. (ANDREW M. ADAMS)

This article updates the *Macropædia* article Major Team and Individual SPORTS and *Micropædia* entries on the various sports.

SPORTING RECORD

Automobile Racing, 1986

Formula One Grand Prix race results:

Race	*Driver*	*Car*	*Average speed*
Brazilian	N. Piquet	Williams-Honda FW11	184.980 km/h
Spanish	A. Senna	Lotus-Renault 98T	167.486 km/h
San Marino	A. Prost	McLaren-Porsche MP4	196.208 km/h
Monaco	A. Prost	McLaren-Porsche MP4	134.634 km/h
Belgian	N. Mansell	Williams-Honda FW11	203.548 km/h
Canadian	N. Mansell	Williams-Honda FW11	178.225 km/h
U.S.	A. Senna	Lotus-Renault 98T	136.747 km/h
French	N. Mansell	Williams-Honda FW11	118.059 km/h
British	N. Mansell	Williams-Honda FW11	208.846 km/h
German	N. Piquet	Williams-Honda FW11	229.534 km/h
Hungarian	N. Piquet	Williams-Honda FW11	151.805 km/h
Austrian	A. Prost	McLaren-Porsche MP4	227.821 km/h
Italian	N. Piquet	Williams-Honda FW11	228.373 km/h
Portuguese	N. Mansell	Williams-Honda FW11	187.644 km/h
Mexican	G. Berger	Benetton-BMW B186	162.790 km/h
Australian	A. Prost	McLaren-Porsche MP4	162.600 km/h

World drivers' championship: A Prost, 72 pt; N. Mansell, 70 pt; N. Piquet, 69 pt
Constructors' world championship: Williams-Honda, 141 pt; McLaren-Porsche, 96 pt; Lotus-Renault, 58 pt
World endurance championship for teams: Rothmans-Porsche
World endurance championship for drivers: D. Bell
Le Mans 24-Hour endurance: Rothmans-Porsche 926C
World rally manufacturers' championship: Peugeot-Sport
CART (Championship Auto Racing Teams):
Individual champion: B. Rahal
NASCAR (National Association for Stock Car Auto Racing):
Driver champion: D. Earnhardt
SCCA (Sports Car Club of America):
Driver champion: W. Dallenbach, Jr.
Indianapolis 500: B. Rahal, March-Cosworth 86C; aver. speed: 170.722 mph (274.862 km/h)

Baseball, 1986

Hall of Fame inductees: Willie McCovey
World Series results: New York Mets (NL) 4 games, Boston Red Sox (AL) 3 games
Japan Series: Seibu Lions (PL) 4 games, Hiroshima Carp (CL) 3 games
Caribbean Series: Mexicali Eagles (round-robin tournament)
World amateur championship: Cuba 10 wins 1 loss

Basketball, 1986

World amateur champions: *men:* U.S. 87, U.S.S.R. 85; *women:* U.S. 108, U.S.S.R. 88
U.S. amateur champions
National Collegiate Athletic Association (NCAA): *men:* Louisville 72, Duke 69; *women:* Texas 97, USC 81
National Invitational Tournament (NIT): Ohio State 73, Wyoming 63
National Basketball Association (NBA) professional championship 1985–86: Boston Celtics 4 games, Houston Rockets 2 games

Bowling, 1986

Tenpins: World amateur zone championships:

	men	*women*
North America	E. Sepulveda (Mexico)	E. Piccini (Mexico)
Europe	R. Fornasari (Italy)	M. Simon (West Germany)
Asia	Ma Ying-chieh (Taiwan)	B. Watanabe (Phil.)

American Bowling Congress (ABC):
Regular Division:

Team:	Faball Enterprises No. 2, Milwaukee, Wis.
Singles:	Jeff Mackey
Doubles:	D. Cook and R. Larson
All-events:	E. Marzka

Women's International Bowling Congress (WIBC):
Open Division:

Team:	Sillias Pro Shop, Cleveland, Ohio
Singles:	D. Stewart
Doubles:	S. Gates and M. Frazier
All-events:	R. Romeo and M. Lewis (tie)

Boxing

Champions as of Dec. 31, 1986:

	World Boxing Council (WBC)	*World Boxing Assn. (WBA)*
Heavyweight	M. Tyson (U.S.)	J. Smith (U.S.)
Cruiserweight	C. de León (P.R.)	E. Holyfield (U.S.)
Lt. heavyweight	D. Andries (England)	M. Johnson (U.S.)
Middleweight	M. Hagler (U.S.)	vacant
Jr. middleweight	D. Thomas (U.S.)	M. McCallum (Jamaica)
Welterweight	L. Honeyghan (England)	vacant
Jr. welterweight	T. Hamada (Japan)	P. Oliva (Italy)
Lightweight	H. Camacho (P.R.)	E. Rosario (P.R.)
Jr. lightweight	J. C. Chávez (Mexico)	B. Mitchell (South Africa)
Featherweight	A. Nelson (Ghana)	S. Cruz (U.S.)
Jr. featherweight	S. Payakaroon (Thailand)	V. Callejas (P.R.)
Bantamweight	M. Lora (Colombia)	B. Pinango (Venezuela)
Super flyweight	G. Román (Mexico)	K. Galaxy (Thailand)
Flyweight	S. Chitalada (Thailand)	H. Zapata (Panama)
Jr. flyweight	Chang Jung Koo (South Korea)	Yuh Myung Woo (South Korea)

Cricket

All-time standings as of Aug. 30, 1986*:

	Eng.	Aust.	S.Af.	W.I.	N.Z.	Ind.	Pak.	Sri L.
England	—	86/74	46/38	21/34	30/29	29/34	13/23	1/1
Australia	96/74	—	29/13	27/16	9/7	20/14	11/9	1/0
South Africa	18/38	11/13	—	...	19/16	...	...	...
West Indies	35/34	19/16	...	—	7/11	22/27	7/8	...
New Zealand	4/29	5/7	2/6	3/11	—	4/11	3/14	4/1
India	11/34	8/14	...	5/27	10/11	—	4/25	1/2
Pakistan	3/23	8/9	...	4/8	10/14	6/25	—	5/3
Sri Lanka	0/1	0/0	...	...	0/1	1/2	1/3	—

*Reading across, the first figure is the all-time number of wins and the second is the number of drawn matches against a given opponent.

Cycling, 1986

World amateur champions—track:

men:	Sprint	M. Hübner (East Germany)
	Tandem sprint	R. Rehounek, V. Voboril (Czech.)
	Individual pursuit	V. Ekimov (U.S.S.R.)
	Team pursuit	S. Buchta, T. Cherny, P. Soukup, and A. Trcka (Czech.)
	1,000-m time trial	M. Malchow (East Germany)
	50-km points	D. Frost (Den.)
	50-km motor paced	M. Gentili (Italy)
women:	Sprint	C. Rothenburger (East Germany)
	Individual pursuit	J. Longo (France)

World professional champions—track:

men:	Sprint	K. Nakano (Japan)
	Individual pursuit	A. Doyle (U.K.)
	50-km points	U. Freuler (Switz.)
	One-hour motor paced	B. Vicino (Italy)
	Keirin	M. Vaarten (Belgium)

World amateur champions—road:

men:	Individual road race	U. Ampler (East Germany)
	100-km team time trial	T. Cordes, R. Harmeling, J. Talen, G. de Vries (Neth.)
women:	Individual road race	J. Longo (France)

World professional champion—road:

men:	Individual road race	M. Argentin (Italy)

World champions—cyclo-cross:

Amateur	V. Di Tano (Italy)
Professional	A. Zweifel (Switz.)

Tour de France: G. LeMond (U.S.)

Fencing, 1986

World champions:
Grand Prize of Champions: U.S.S.R.
Men's foil: *indiv.:* A. Borella (Italy), *team:* Italy
Men's épée: *indiv.:* P. Riboud (France), *team:* West Germany
Men's sabre: *indiv.:* S. Mindirgassov (U.S.S.R.), *team:* U.S.S.R.
Women's foil: *indiv.:* A. Fichtel (West Germany), *team:* U.S.S.R.

Football, 1986

Association football (soccer) major tournaments:
World Cup: Argentina 3, West Germany 2
European Champions' Cup won by Romania
European Cup-Winners' Cup won by Dynamo Kiev
UEFA Cup won by Real Madrid
Libertadores de América Cup won by River Plate, Argentina
U.S. Major Indoor Soccer League (MISL) won by San Diego
U.S. professional National Football League (NFL) results:
National Football Conference championship: New York Giants 17, Washington Redskins 0
American Football Conference championship: Denver Broncos 23, Cleveland Browns 20
Super Bowl XXI: New York Giants 39, Denver Broncos 20
U.S. college football:
Rose Bowl: Arizona State 22, Michigan 15
Cotton Bowl: Ohio State 28, Texas A&M 12
Orange Bowl: Oklahoma 42, Arkansas 8
Sugar Bowl: Nebraska 30, Louisiana State 15
Fiesta Bowl: Penn State 14, Miami of Florida 10
Heisman Trophy winner: Vinny Testaverde, Miami of Florida
Canadian Football League professional championship (Grey Cup): Hamilton Tiger-Cats 39, Edmonton Eskimos 15

Rugby Union international matches, 1871–Sept. 30, 1986:

	Eng.	Scot.	Ire.	Wales	Brit. Isles	S.Af.	N.Z.	Aust.	France
England	—	48/16	55/8	36/12	...	2/1	3/0	4/0	32/7
Scotland	38/16	—	48/4	37/2	...	3/0	0/2	6/0	27/2
Ireland	35/8	44/4	—	29/5	...	1/1	0/1	6/0	25/5
Wales	43/12	51/2	54/5	—	...	0/1	3/0	7/0	36/3
British Isles	...	...	...	...	—	14/6	5/3	12/0	...
South Africa	6/1	5/0	8/1	6/1	20/6	—	20/2	21/0	11/4
New Zealand	12/0	10/2	8/1	8/0	24/3	15/2	—	57/4	17/0
Australia	7/0	4/0	4/0	4/0	2/0	7/0	21/4	—	5/1
France	22/7	27/2	28/5	20/3	...	3/4	4/0	9/1	—

*Reading across, the first figure is the all-time number of wins and the second is the number of drawn matches against a given opponent.

Rugby League test matches, 1908–Sept. 30, 1986*:

	Great Britain	Australia	New Zealand	France
Great Britain	—	49/4	43/3	28/3
Australia	43/4	—	38/0	22/3
New Zealand	24/3	20/0	—	15/3
France	13/3	12/3	11/3	—

*Reading across, the first figure is the all-time number of wins and the second is the number of drawn matches against a given opponent.

Golf, 1986

Major tournament winners:

	men	women
U.S. Open	R. Floyd (U.S.)	J. Geddes (U.S.)
U.S. Amateur	B. Alexander (U.S.)	K. Cockerill (U.S.)
British Open	G. Norman (Australia)	L. Davies (U.K.)
U.S. PGA	B. Tway (U.S.)	P. Bradley (U.S.)
U.S. Masters	J. Nicklaus (U.S.)	
U.S. Tournament Players Championship	J. Mahaffey (U.S.)	
Curtis Cup (amat.)		Great Britain and Ireland
Eisenhower Trophy (amat.)	Canada	

PGA leading money winner: G. Norman (Australia) $653,296
LPGA leading money winner: P. Bradley (U.S.) $492,021

Gymnastics, 1986

World Cup:

	men	women
All-around	Li Ning (China) and Y. Korolev (U.S.S.R.) (tie)	E. Shushunova (U.S.S.R.)
Pommel horse	Li Ning (China) and Y. Korolev (U.S.S.R.) (tie)	
Floor exercise	Li Ning (China)	E. Shushunova (U.S.S.R.)
Rings	Y. Korolev (U.S.S.R.) and V. Mogilny (U.S.S.R.) (tie)	
Horse vault	Y. Korolev (U.S.S.R.) and S. Kroll (East Germany) (tie)	E. Shushunova (U.S.S.R.)
Parallel bars	V. Mogilny (U.S.S.R.) and Xu Zhiqiang (China) (tie)	
Uneven parallel bars		E. Shushunova (U.S.S.R.)
Balance beam		O. Omeliantchik (U.S.S.R.)

Ice Skating, 1986

World championships:
Figure skating:
Individual: *men:* B. Boitano (U.S.), *women:* D. Thomas (U.S.)
Pairs: E. Gordeeva and S. Grinkov (U.S.S.R.)
Ice dancing: N. Bestemianova and A. Bukin (U.S.S.R.)
Speed skating:
Overall: *men:* H. Vergeer (Neth.), *women:* K. Kania (East Germany)
Sprint: *men:* I. Zhelezovsky (U.S.S.R.), *women:* K. Kania (East Germany)
New world records:

men:	3,000 m	V. Shasherin (U.S.S.R.)	4:03.22
	10,000 m	G. Karlstad (Norway)	14:12.14
women:	500 m	K. Kania (East Germany)	39.52
	1,000 m	K. Kania (East Germany)	1:18.84
	1,500 m	K. Kania (East Germany)	1:59.30
	3,000 m	K. Kania (East Germany)	4:18.02
	5,000 m	A. Schöne Ehrig (East Germany)	7:20.99

Rowing, 1986

World champions:

	men	women
Single sculls	West Germany	East Germany
Double sculls	Italy	East Germany
Quadruple sculls	U.S.S.R.	East Germany
Coxless pairs	U.S.S.R.	Romania
Coxed pairs	U.K.	—
Coxless fours	U.S.	—
Coxed fours	East Germany	Romania
Eights	Australia	U.S.S.R.

Skiing, 1986

World Cup—Alpine:

	men	women
Overall	M. Girardelli (Luxembourg)	M. Walliser (Switz.)
Downhill	P. Wirnsberger (Austria)	M. Walliser (Switz.)
Slalom	R. Petrovic (Yugos.)	R. Steiner (Austria)
Giant slalom	J. Gaspoz (Switz.)	V. Schneider (Switz.)

Nations Cup—Alpine: Switzerland
World Cup—Nordic:
Individual: A. Sehmisch (East Germany), *Team:* East Germany
Cross-country: *men:* G. Svan (Sweden), *women:* M. Matikainen (Fin.)
Combined: *men:* H. Weinbuch (West Germany)
Jumping: *men:* M. Nykänen (Fin.)
Nations Cup—Nordic: Austria
Biathlon world champions:

10 km	V. Medvedtsev (U.S.S.R.)
20 km	V. Medvedtsev (U.S.S.R.)
4 × 7.5-km relay	U.S.S.R.

World freestyle champions: *men:* A. Laroche (France), *women:* C. Kissling (Switz.)

Swimming, 1986

World swimming records set—men:

50-m freestyle	M. Biondi (U.S.)	22.33 sec
100-m freestyle	M. Biondi (U.S.)	48.74 sec
800-m freestyle	V. Salnikov (U.S.S.R.)	7:50.64 sec
100-m butterfly	P. Morales (U.S.)	52.84 sec
200-m butterfly	M. Gross (West Germany)	1:56.24 sec
200-m individual medley	A. Baumann (Canada)	(tie) 2:01.42 sec

World swimming records set—women:

50-m freestyle	T. Costache (Rom.)	25.34 sec
	T. Costache (Rom.)	25.31 sec
	T. Costache (Rom.)	25.28 sec
100-m freestyle	K. Otto (East Germany)	54.73 sec
200-m freestyle	H. Friedrich (East Germany)	1:57.55 sec
200-m backstroke	B. Mitchell (U.S.)	2:08.60 sec
100-m breaststroke	S. Gerasch (East Germany)	1:08.11 sec
200-m breaststroke	S. Gerasch (East Germany)	2:28.20 sec
	S. Hoerner (East Germany)	2:27.40 sec
4 × 100-m freestyle relay	K. Otto, M. Stellmach, S. Schulze, H. Friedrich (East Germany)	3:40.57 sec
4 × 200-m freestyle relay	M. Stellmach, A. Strauss, N. Bergknecht, H. Friedrich (East Germany)	7:59.33 sec

Tennis, 1986

	men's singles	women's singles
French Open:	I. Lendl (Czech.)	C. Evert Lloyd (U.S.)
Wimbledon:	B. Becker (West Germany)	M. Navratilova (U.S.)
U.S. Open:	I. Lendl (Czech.)	M. Navratilova (U.S.)
Australian Open:	S. Edberg (Sweden)	M. Navratilova (U.S.)

Davis Cup: Australia 3, Sweden 2
World Team Cup: France
Wightman Cup: United States (B. Gadusek, K. Rinaldi, E. Burgin, A. White)
Federation Cup: United States (M. Navratilova, C. Evert Lloyd, P. Shriver, Z. Garrison)

Track and Field, 1986

World outdoor records set—men:

Pole vault	S. Bubka (U.S.S.R.)	6.01 m (19 ft 8½ in)
Shot put	U. Beyer (East Germany)	22.64 m (74 ft 3½ in)
Discus throw	J. Schult (East Germany)	74.08 m (243 ft)
Hammer throw	Y. Syedikh (U.S.S.R.)	86.66 m (284 ft 4 in)
	Y. Syedikh (U.S.S.R.)	86.74 m (284 ft 7 in)

World outdoor records set—women:

200 m	H. Drechsler (East Germany)	(tie) 21.71 sec
	H. Drechsler (East Germany)	(tie) 21.71 sec
2,000 m	M. Puica (Rom.)	5 min 28.69 sec
5,000 m	I. Kristiansen (Norway)	14 min 37.33 sec
10,000 m	I. Kristiansen (Norway)	30 min 13.74 sec
5,000-m walk	Wang Yan (China)	21 min 33.80 sec
10,000-m walk	Xu Yongjiu (China)	45 min 31.90 sec
	K. Saxby (Australia)	45 min 8.13 sec
	Y. Kuznetsova (U.S.S.R.)	44 min 32.50 sec
100-m hurdles	Y. Donkova (Bulg.)	12.36 sec
	Y. Donkova (Bulg.)	12.34 sec
	Y. Donkova (Bulg.)	12.29 sec
	Y. Donkova (Bulg.)	12.26 sec
400-m hurdles	M. Stepanova (U.S.S.R.)	53.32 sec
	M. Stepanova (U.S.S.R.)	52.94 sec
High jump	S. Kostadinova (Bulg.)	2.07 m (6 ft 9½ in)
	S. Kostadinova (Bulg.)	2.08 m (6 ft 9¾ in)
Long jump	H. Drechsler (East Germany)	7.45 m (24 ft 5½ in)
	H. Drechsler (East Germany)	7.45 m (24 ft 5½ in)
Javelin throw	F. Whitbread (U.K.)	77.44 m (254 ft 1 in)
Heptathlon	J. Joyner (U.S.)	7,148 points
	J. Joyner (U.S.)	7,161 points

Weight Lifting, 1986

weight class	
52.0 kg (114.4 lb)	S. Marinov (Bulg.)
56.0 kg (123.2 lb)	M. Grablev (Bulg.)
60.0 kg (132 lb)	N. Shalamanov (Bulg.)
67.5 kg (148.5 lb)	M. Petrov (Bulg.)
75.0 kg (165 lb)	A. Varbanov (Bulg.)
82.5 kg (181.5 lb)	A. Zlatev (Bulg.)
90.0 kg (198 lb)	A. Khrapaty (U.S.S.R.)
100.0 kg (220 lb)	N. Vlad (Rom.)
110.0 kg (242 lb)	Y. Zaharevich (U.S.S.R.)
+110.0 kg (+242 lb)	A. Krastev (Bulg.)

Wrestling, 1986

World champions:

weight class	*freestyle*	*Greco-Roman*
48 kg	Y. Li (North Korea)	M. Alahverdiev (U.S.S.R.)
52 kg	K. Sik (North Korea)	S. Dudiaev (U.S.S.R.)
57 kg	S. Beloglasov (U.S.S.R.)	E. Ivanov (Bulg.)
62 kg	K. Isaev (U.S.S.R.)	K. Madszidov (U.S.S.R.)
68 kg	A. Fadsaev (U.S.S.R.)	L. Dzulfalakian (U.S.S.R.)
74 kg	R. Cascaret (Cuba)	M. Mamiavvily (U.S.S.R.)
82 kg	V. Modozian (U.S.S.R.)	no first place awarded
90 kg	M. Khadartsev (U.S.S.R.)	A. Malina (Poland)
100 kg	A. Khadartsev (U.S.S.R.)	T. Gaspar (Hung.)
130 kg	B. Baumgartner (U.S.)	T. Johansson (Sweden)

Television and Radio

The dominance of radio and television as providers of entertainment and news throughout the world was evident in the numbers of receivers and broadcasting outlets in use during 1986. Some 1,300,000,000 radio receivers of all types were in service, according to estimates published by Unesco. About one-third of the world's sets—an estimated 479 million—were in the United States and 176 million in the Soviet Union. Other countries with large numbers of radio receivers included Japan (85 million), the U.K. (56 million), France (47 million), and West Germany (25 million).

The U.S. and U.S.S.R. also ranked first and second in the number of television sets in use. The U.S. had 185.3 million, more than 25% of the world total of some 650 million, and the U.S.S.R. total was about 103 million. Japan was third (66 million), followed by the U.K. (27 million), West Germany (22 million), and France (20 million).

Organization of Services. In the U.S. in 1986 the emphasis of the Federal Communications Commission (FCC) in its regulation of broadcasting and cable television remained on deregulation, as it had throughout the previous five years of the administration of Pres. Ronald Reagan. But the commission's major action during the year was to adopt a rule that would require cable television systems to carry the programming of local television stations. The rule was designed to replace a similar one that a U.S. Court of Appeals had declared unconstitutional because it violated the First Amendment guarantee of freedom of the press. Broadcasters protested against the court's decision, arguing that their financial well-being would be jeopardized it their programs were not carried on local cable systems. They appealed to the U.S. Supreme Court and lobbied members of Congress for relief. The Supreme Court declined to review the case, but congressional pressure helped persuade the FCC to adopt a new must-carry rule, one based largely on a compromise worked out between the broadcasting and cable industries.

The issue was not closed, however. Members of the cable industry were planning to ask the FCC to reconsider the matter, and Turner Broadcasting System, Inc., one of the parties that successfully appealed the original rule, indicated that it would appeal the new one as well. One aspect of the new rule was particularly troublesome to cable interests; it required cable systems to include so-called A/B switches as part of every new installation and provide such switches on request to existing subscribers. The equipment would enable subscribers to shift easily between cable and off-air service and was the commission's answer to broadcasters' complaints that, when the new must-carry rule expired in five years, they would have no assurance that subscribers would be able to receive signals over the air. The cable industry argued that the switches would be unduly burdensome for cable operators.

A three-judge panel of the same court that in 1985 outlawed the must-carry rule issued a ruling in 1986 that had far-reaching ramifications for the broadcasting industry. It held that the commission's fairness doctrine, which required a broadcasting station to carry all sides of a controversial issue of public importance if it carried one, is not a statutory obligation imposed by Congress. Many observers, including commission lawyers, had for years contended that Congress in 1959 had incorporated the doctrine into the law requiring broadcasters to afford equal time to all political candidates in a given contest. Congress, in easing the restrictions of the "equal-time" law, had specified that broadcasters would still be obligated to "afford reasonable opportunity for the discussion of conflicting views." But the appeals court panel, in a 2–1 decision, said that this language did not make the doctrine "a binding statutory obligation; rather, it ratified the commission's long-standing position that the public interest standard authorizes the fairness doctrine." Thus, the FCC would be free to repeal the doctrine.

The FCC had concluded an inquiry into the doctrine in August 1985 with the finding that it inhibited rather than enhanced free speech because it discouraged broadcasters from engaging in controversial programming, but it deferred to Congress the question of what should be done regarding it. However, as with the must-carry rule, the matter was not closed. Public interest groups that supported the doctrine petitioned the full appeals court to rehear the case. In addition, members of Congress, who were among the most vigorous supporters of the fairness doctrine, reminded the FCC of that fact. Congress approved a report calling on the FCC to consider alternative means of administering and enforcing the doctrine and to report on the matter by Sept. 30, 1987.

If the regulatory framework of the broadcasting industry appeared to be coming undone, so did its financial structure. The buy-outs and mergers of some of the largest companies in the business—made possible, if not encouraged, by the FCC's deregulatory policies—continued. The sale of American Broadcasting Cos., owner of the ABC-TV network, a variety of radio networks, television stations in five of the largest U.S. markets, and 12 important radio stations, to the much smaller but highly regarded Capital Cities Communications, Inc., was completed. Capcities, a major broadcaster, cable TV operator, and publisher, acquired ABC in a cash-and-stock transaction valued at $3.5 billion, but the merged company was required to dispose of broadcast and other interests to bring it into compliance with the FCC's ownership rules. An even larger sale—that of RCA and its broadcasting subsidiary, NBC, to General Electric Co.—was completed in June. The acquisition price was $6.3 billion. To comply with commission rules, GE was given 18 months to dispose of five radio stations. The

F. MEYLAN—SYGMA

Silvio Berlusconi, television magnate and part owner of La Cinq, France's first privately owned noncable television network, poses on a set. Berlusconi ran three networks in Italy that also competed with state-owned television channels.

CBS founder William S. Paley (left) and stockholder Laurence A. Tisch take on temporary roles as chairman and chief executive officer of CBS, Inc., respectively, after Thomas H. Wyman, who held both jobs, resigned in September after losing the backing of the board.
AP/WIDE WORLD

acquisition gave General Electric a total of six television stations, five that had been owned by NBC as well as KCNC-TV Denver, an NBC affiliate that had already been part of GE's holdings.

As for CBS, it managed to fend off a hostile takeover attempt by the relatively small Turner Broadcasting System, headed by Ted Turner. The cost was high, however; CBS incurred a debt of more than $1 billion to buy up 21% of its own stock. That led to major cost-cutting moves, including layoffs and an offer of early retirement that was taken by more than 700 executives and staffers. It also led to the sale of some properties, including one of CBS's television stations, KMOX-TV St. Louis, to Viacom for $122.5 million.

But those financial dealings were only symptomatic of how shaky CBS, long a major force in U.S. broadcasting, had become. During the summer Laurence Tisch (*see* BIOGRAPHIES), chairman of Loews Corp., emerged as the dominant force at the network. For much of the preceding year he had been viewed by CBS as a bulwark against future takeover attempts. Loews, which owned hotels and tobacco companies and also had a large investment portfolio, had been buying CBS stock, and Tisch had been invited to join the board. But by August Loews's ownership of CBS stock had climbed to 24.9%, and the board, concerned about a takeover, asked Tisch not to increase his holdings above 25%. He refused to make such a commitment, and at a heated meeting of the CBS board in September, Thomas Wyman, chairman and chief executive, resigned. His place was taken, at least on an interim basis, by Tisch as acting chief executive and by William Paley, the 84-year-old founder of CBS, as acting chairman.

Cable television continued to expand. The A. C. Nielsen Co., the leading TV audience measurement service, estimated that in July the number of cable-equipped homes in the U.S. totaled 41,248,380, over two million more than 12 months earlier and 47.8% of the 86,377,440 television households in the continental U.S.

The passion in the U.S. for videocassette recorders (VCRs), which record and play back television programs as well as playing prerecorded movies and other programming, showed no sign of cooling in 1986. The Electronic Industries Association reported that as of June the number of homes with VCRs totaled 35% of all U.S. television homes, compared with 28.1% a year earlier.

In the U.K. the British Broadcasting Corporation (BBC) came under the scrutiny of a government committee that had been expected to recommend that the BBC be partly financed by advertising. Instead, the committee, chaired by Alan Peacock, reported in July that it should continue to be financed by a license fee because advertising funds were limited and because standards might suffer and the range of programs be reduced. The Peacock Report proposed a three-stage development over the next 15 years, ending in a free market in which the BBC would largely be funded by subscription. The license fee would be indexed to the retail price index for ten years.

The report's recommendations met with a mixed response. They angered some broadcasters, who felt that the long-term scenario did not reflect the realities of public-service broadcasting, and they also conflicted with government thinking. Prime Minister Margaret Thatcher took the unprecedented step of chairing a special Cabinet committee to prepare the government's response. The top items on the agenda were the BBC license, Independent Television (ITV) contracts (with proposals for their extension), technical aspects of subscription TV, and the independent status of Channel Four. The BBC suffered a setback with the death in August of Stuart Young (*see* OBITUARIES), chairman of the board of governors. He was succeeded by Marmaduke ("Duke") Hussey (*see* BIOGRAPHIES), a former managing director of Times Newspapers Ltd. Reputed to be a tough negotiator, Hussey was expected to impose tighter controls on the corporation.

In December the Independent Broadcasting Authority awarded the contract for the U.K.'s first direct broadcasting by satellite service, and the first in the world to be wholly funded by the private sector, to the British Satellite Corporation. The consortium grouped Granada Television, Anglia Television, Amstrad Consumer Electronics, and the Pearson and Virgin groups. The service was expected to begin in 1990.

In France Pres. François Mitterrand's decision to deregulate television and radio broadcasting produced hasty attempts to initiate commercial television before the March elections. Two companies began transmissions on new fifth and sixth channels, but they were the subject of widespread protests that culminated in an appeal to the French Council of State by authors, filmmakers, and composers to abolish La Cinq, which was being run by and was 40% owned by Italian magnate Silvio Berlusconi. The concessions for the two channels were subsequently canceled. French Prime Minister Jacques Chirac later announced a comprehensive plan for the entire audiovisual sector. TF-1, the oldest of the three state channels, was to be privatized, and new licenses were to be issued for the fifth and sixth channels. By contrast, the government decided to tighten state control on Radio France International, its international broadcasting service.

Reforms being attempted in West Germany had far-reaching implications. The division between the Christian Democrats and the Social Democratic Party widened; the former wished to allow private television, while the latter preferred to bolster the existing public organizations. A key concern was the extent to which freedom of speech, as laid down by the federal constitution, might be limited by private television.

In Italy Berlusconi and his Fininvest group, based in Milan, emerged to establish a dominant hold on private television. Berlusconi ended the year with control not only of Canale 5 but also of two other major channels, Italia Uno and Retequartro. This enabled him to move into France, West Germany, and Spain. Berlusconi was widely seen as the precursor of a new kind of entrepreneur operating on a grand European scale.

Programming. News was making news in terms of television programming in the U.S. in 1986. There was, for instance, the decision of CBS to give up on "The CBS Morning News" after watching it year after year trail the ABC and NBC morning news shows in the ratings race. But CBS did not give up entirely on news in the morning. A news broadcast was being planned for the 6–7:30 AM time period, to be followed by a 90-minute program that would not be part of the CBS News Division's responsibility.

But while CBS retreated on the news front in the morning, the three major networks were seeking viewers with a total of four prime-time news programs (five, counting the 13 episodes of "West 57th Street" that CBS was scheduled to begin running in midseason). The others were NBC's "1986," CBS's "60 Minutes," and ABC's "20/20" and its new "Our World," a weekly piece of nostalgia that dealt more with specific years or periods in the past than with current events. According to NBC research, those four hours represented the most prime time ever set aside for news programming. In part, at least, the networks' interest in news programs reflected concern for cost cutting; news shows were far less expensive than most of the other programming on the network schedules.

Another trend of 1986 was the revival of network interest in half-hour comedies in prime time. All told, 11 new comedies were added to the 17 returning ones, the largest number of survivors since the 1981–82 season. The phenomenal success of NBC's "The Cosby Show" was seen as one reason for this renewed interest. Another was, again, cost. A half-hour situation comedy cost between $300,000 and $500,000 per episode, while the cost of a one-hour action show ranged between $750,000 and $1.2 million. Cost and a generally poor reception at the program bazaar of the National Association of Television Program Executives in January 1986 were said to be factors in the decision of producers to skip action programming for the year. The number of such shows at the start of the 1986–87 season was 28, two fewer than at the start of the 1985–86 season.

AP/WIDE WORLD

U.S. Sen. Robert Dole tunes in to Sen. Charles McC. Mathias, Jr., on a live broadcast of Senate sessions. The television coverage, begun in June, was part of a six-week network trial run. TV coverage of House activities had begun in 1979.

The 1985–86 season marked the 60th anniversary of NBC and the first time that the network had ever won the prime-time ratings race. NBC had been buried in third place for a number of years until 1984–85, when, under the direction of its chairman, Grant Tinker, its reliance on what critics generally regarded as quality programming produced a second-place finish, close behind CBS. In 1985–86 NBC toppled CBS as the ratings leader, with ABC finishing third.

The networks were not competing only with one another. Independents were also offering competition and in the form of fresh material, not reruns of network series. More than 40 new first-run syndicated programs began showing up on the nation's stations in September. They included a late-night offering, a talk show, and half-hour reenactments of court cases. Included also were six new first-run weekly situation comedies.

Probably the most exciting phenomenon in the development of cable television in 1986 was the emergence of home shopping service. An operation called Home Shopping Service had begun making its mark in 1985, and in the first nine months of the 1986 fiscal year it reported revenues of $107 million and operating income of $20.7 million. In most versions teleshopping was direct-response advertising; one or two hosts would demonstrate products on television, and viewers who were interested called a toll-free number and gave their credit-card number, to which the items of their choice could be billed. The services were transmitted to cable systems by satellite. One industry consultant predicted that the home shopping service network would be an $800 million business in 1987.

Some of the competition for viewers' time and attention was coming from public broadcasting. The Public Broadcasting Service said that, based on the Nielsen Television Index, 55.1% of all households tuned in to PBS at least once a week during the year that ended in September 1986. For prime time the comparable figures were 32.6% and 28 million. In 1986 the service offered a schedule that included 8 new series, 26 specials, and 10 continuing series. Many received critical acclaim; "The Story of English," for instance, was a nine-part series that examined the roots and development of the English language. PBS's readiness to depart from the mainstream of programming landed the service in a major controversy, however. At issue was "The Africans," a nine-part series produced by noncommercial WETA-TV that examined the history and politics of the African peoples in the context of their relationship with the industrialized world. Conservative groups denounced the series as "pro-Marxist and anti-Western." Ali A. Mazrui, the Kenyan-born political scientist who wrote and narrated the series, commented: "Exposure to an alien society is the first lesson in self-knowledge."

As for radio programming, a *Broadcasting* magazine survey found the adult contemporary sound to be the most widely employed format among the top 10 radio stations in the top 50 markets in 1986. The second most popular sound was found to be contemporary hit, followed by easy listening, country, and album-oriented rock. "Oldies"—classic rock and country—were also popular. However, radio programming was not limited to music. News and talk formats were popular as well.

NBC's success in programming was not limited to its victory in the ratings contest. In the 38th annual Emmy awards competition NBC won not only the most awards in the network's history but also, with 34, the most of any network in 1986. CBS finished with 22 awards; the Public Broadcasting Service, 11; and ABC, 6. The Academy of Television Arts and Sciences for the second year in a row

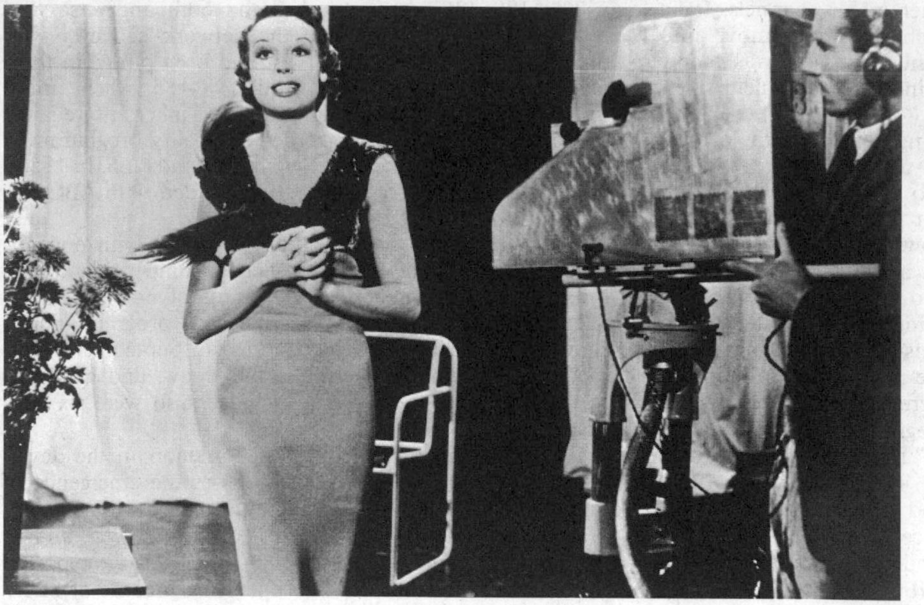

Adele Dixon sings on the first British Broadcasting Corporation television broadcast on Nov. 2, 1936. A half-century later BBC TV aired some 6,000 programs annually.
THE NEW YORK TIMES

named CBS's "Cagney and Lacey" the best dramatic show and NBC's "The Golden Girls" the best comedy series. NBC's "The Cosby Show," the most popular program on television, won three Emmys. NBC's "Peter the Great" was named the outstanding miniseries; NBC's "The Hallmark Hall of Fame: Love Is Never Silent," the outstanding drama or comedy special; and CBS's "The Kennedy Center Honors: A Celebration of the Arts," the outstanding variety, music, or comedy program.

In 1986 the BBC celebrated 50 years of television broadcasting, marking the first half-century of regular television broadcasting anywhere in the world. Sadly for the BBC, however, the year proved to be more memorable for the political controversy that some of its programs evoked than it was for their intrinsic qualities and appeal. In October the BBC reached an out-of-court settlement in the High Court libel action brought by two Conservative MPs alleged in a 1984 edition of the current affairs program "Panorama" to have links with extreme right-wing organizations; the BBC agreed to pay costs (amounting to almost £500,000) and to withdraw the allegations. Later the same month Norman Tebbit, chairman of the Conservative Party, accused the BBC of long-term left-wing bias, in particular in its news and current affairs programs; his criticisms centred on BBC coverage of the U.S. bombing raid on Libya, which in the view of the Conservative Party Central Office was overly sympathetic toward the Libyan regime. The BBC denied the charge.

Conservative MPs were also angered by the BBC's major drama serial "The Monocled Mutineer." Written by Alan Bleasdale, it depicted a British Army mutiny in the trenches of the Somme during World War I; the BBC's publicity material mistakenly gave the impression that the show was historically accurate. Both Bleasdale and the BBC were accused of rewriting history to promote left-wing ideologies. The peak viewing time Saturday drama series "Casualty" portrayed the doctors and nurses of a National Health Service hospital trying to run an emergency ward with inadequate staff, resources, and beds. It came under attack for its implied criticism of government health service policy. The allegations attracted little public interest, however, as did the serial itself.

The BBC drama that did appeal to wide audiences was the twice-weekly soap opera "EastEnders," which continued to hold the top two places in the popularity rankings. Dennis Potter's drama serial "The Singing Detective" (BBC) won critical and popular acclaim, while John Mortimer's "Paradise Postponed" (ITV's Thames Television) failed to make the expected impact. A major success for the BBC in terms of public appreciation and interest was a week of repeat programs scheduled to celebrate its 50th anniversary in November. Millions of viewers, many of them too young to remember the first showings of "That Was the Week That Was," "The Forsyte Saga," or "Dr. Finlay's Casebook" transmitted in the 1950s, 1960s, and 1970s, indulged themselves in an orgy of national nostalgia for five days.

In the U.S.S.R. television programs came under increasing criticism for their lack of imagination and poor news coverage that lacked objectivity. The disaster at the Chernobyl nuclear power plant highlighted the slowness of news coverage—the event was not reported until several days after it happened. Nevertheless, current affairs programs such as "International Panorama" continued to be extremely popular if only for the views of Western-style living that they provided. In Czechoslovakia music continued to dominate programming, with "Music from the Respirium"—regular live chamber music concerts—proving extremely popular. The 23rd Golden Prague International TV Festival in June attracted participants from 37 countries and, appropriately, 29 of the 62 entries were in the music category. Many of the entries dealt with social problems. Winners of the Grand Prix were Poland's "Greta" and the U.S.S.R.'s musical drama "Masquerade."

In the Middle East, where television was a relatively new media form, audiences were beginning to develop preferences. In particular, the increasingly sophisticated Dubai TV's daily program "Evening Theatre," which appeared on the Arabic Channel, proved popular. The hour of mystery and suspense had a large following among viewers, generating a demand for such material throughout the Middle East.

Many viewers throughout the world remained happy to rivet themselves to sports. It was estimated that the soccer World Cup in Mexico attracted 12,000,000,000 viewers in total and more than 500 million for the final match.

British television had less than its usual success in international competition. The Prix Italia Festival was traditionally an event in which British arts programs and documentaries prospered, but in 1987 the British collected only one prize—the host town of Luca's award for Channel 4's "Maids and Madames." The major arts award, the RAI Prize, went to "Seppau," made by SVT of Sweden, and the documentary prize was won by the Canadian Broadcasting Corporation for its "Final Offer." Belgian television won the Italian Prime Minister's Special Prize for a musical, "The Burgermeister of Veure."

(JOHN HOWKINS, PATRICK STODDART, LAWRENCE B. TAISHOFF, LEONARD ZEIDENBERG)

Amateur Radio. Ham radio operators over the years had put their hobby to use during times of earthquake, flood, or other natural disaster. And they continued in that tradition in 1986, providing vital communications links during the earthquake that rocked San Salvador. In the U.S. they offered communications support in connection with the Hands Across America fund-raising effort.

The FCC reported 421,082 licensed ham operators in the U.S. as of Sept. 30, 1986. In 1985 there were 413,127. The American Radio Relay League said that there were 1,625,000 hams throughout the world, up from 1,511,000 in 1985. Japan was said to have the largest number of licensed amateur operators, 675,000.

(LAWRENCE B. TAISHOFF; LEONARD ZEIDENBERG)

See also Industrial Review: *Advertising; Telecommunications;* Motion Pictures; Music.

This article updates the *Macropædia* article BROADCASTING.

Theatre

Great Britain and Ireland. The concern expressed in 1985 by the Arts Council of Great Britain (ACGB) and by arts organizations about the expected shortfall in revenues following the abolition of the Greater London Council (GLC) and six metropolitan councils in April 1986 proved to be only partly justified. Some local authorities previously reluctant to fund the arts had a change of heart, and private industry answered the call of Arts Minister Richard Luce to help out groups badly hit by the cuts, such as the historic Sadler's Wells Theatre. However, the fact that business sponsorship reached £10 million in 1986 failed to allay fears, since the ACGB could not honour all its existing commitments and the future of local authority funding was uncertain. The ACGB's grant for 1987–88 was set at £138.4 million, a reduction in real terms. There were fears that the freeze on ACGB grants to the National Theatre (NT), at £7.8 million, and to the Royal Shakespeare Company (RSC), at £5.2 million, could seriously jeopardize their artistic futures.

Most of the theatre awards of the Society of West End Theatre—the Laurence Olivier (LO) awards—and of the four publications, the *London Evening Standard (LS), Time Out (TO), Plays and Players (P&P),* and *Drama Magazine (DM),* went to the subsidized sector, with the RSC and the NT taking 13 between them. The *DM* and *P&P* best director award was won by Mike Alfreds for his stylized treatment of Chekhov's *The Cherry Orchard* at the NT's Cottesloe, while *TO,* entering the award lists for the first time but confining itself exclusively to the so-called Fringe, which included the Cottesloe and the RSC's Pit, chose the NT's Richard Eyre as the year's best director.

The designer awards were shared between William Dudley (LO award for Dusty Hughes's *Futurists* at the Cottesloe) and Ezio Frigerio of Italy (*DM* and *P&P* awards for Federico García Lorca's *The House of Bernarda Alba* at the Lyric, Hammersmith). Frigerio shared his *DM* award with Maria Bjørnson, who designed the costumes for *The Phantom of the Opera,* the Andrew Lloyd Webber musical at Her Majesty's. The LO award to Dudley was for three settings in all, including those for Alan Bennett's surreal comedy *Kafka's Dick* at the Royal Court and for the RSC production of *The Merry Wives of Windsor* at the Barbican. Bill Alexander won the LO director award for *The Merry Wives of Windsor* and Spanish guest director Nuria Espert, the "Sydney Edwards" (*LS*) award for her direction of *The House of Bernarda Alba,* in which Joan Plowright won the *DM* best actress prize. Two other awards for the NT were won by Steven Mackintosh in Neil Simon's *Brighton Beach Memoirs (P&P)* and Sally Dexter (LO most promising newcomer) in *Dalliance,* the Tom Stoppard adaptation of Arthur Schnitzler's *Liebelei.*

Other NT productions included Cicely Berry's touring production of *Hamlet,* Di Trevis's of Brecht's *The Mother,* and Sarah Daniels's feminist drama *Neaptide* at the Cottesloe; the final production of Jonathan Lynn's ensemble *Jacobowsky and the Colonel,* Robert David Macdonald's version of *The Threepenny Opera* with Tim Curry as Mack the Knife, and David Hare's Shakespearean directing debut with a vivid version of *King Lear,* dominated by Anthony Hopkins in the title role, at the Olivier; and Peter Hall's production of Brian Clark's bitter comedy *The Petition,* and two English comedies, *The Magistrate* and *Tons of Money,* staged by the Alan Ayckbourn Group, at the Lyttleton.

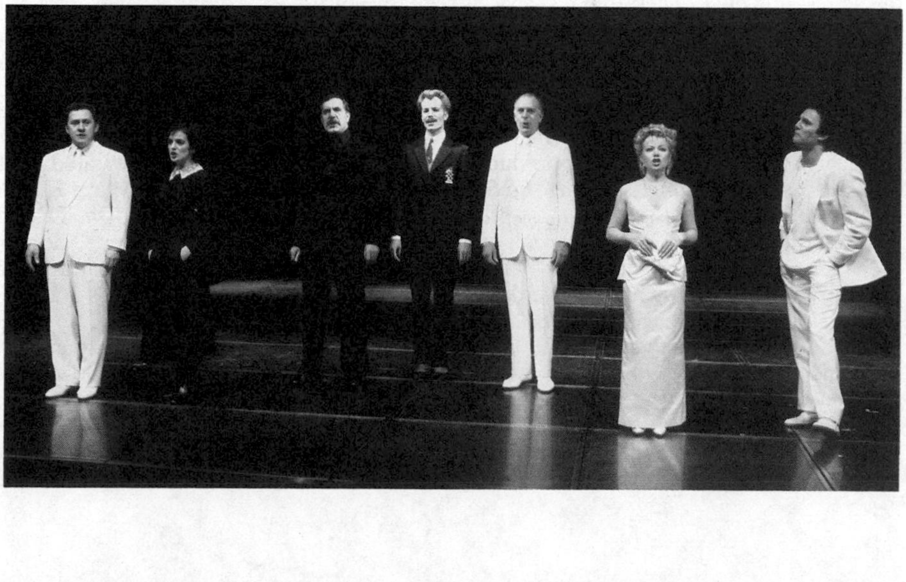

ALISTAIR MUIR

Cast members perform in the *Drama Magazine* musical award winner, *Chess*. The three-hour Anglo-Swedish pop-opera at London's Prince Edward Theatre featured lyrics by Tim Rice and music by members of the Swedish rock group Abba.

Moscow actors perform a scene from *Quotation,* a poetic comedy by Soviet dramatist Leonid Zorin, that criticizes materialistic values.
M. STROKOV—TASS/SOVFOTO

Christopher Hampton's *Les Liaisons Dangereuses,* the RSC production first seen at Stratford-upon-Avon and later in London, carried off two prizes as best play (LO and *LS*) and won for Lindsay Duncan the LO best actress award and for Howard Davies the *TO* best production award. Imogen Stubbs won the *P&P* award as the most promising actress in *The Two Noble Kinsmen* and *The Rover* at the new Swan Theatre at Stratford. (*See* Sidebar.) Other new RSC productions included Hughes's adaptation of Gorky's *Philistines;* Arthur Miller's *The Archbishop's Ceiling;* Deborah Levy's all-female view of the world, *Heresies;* U.S. author Richard Nelson's political drama of a writer's duties, *Principia Scriptoriae;* and two horror dramas by English writers Trevor Griffiths and Nick Darke.

In the subsidized sector the Lyric Theatre, Hammersmith, won a special LO award for *The House of Bernarda Alba.* The enterprising Bush Theatre won a similar award from *DM,* which also selected Jim Cartwright's peripatetic *Road* (at the Royal Court) as best new play. Cartwright was also listed as most promising writer by *P&P.* At the Royal Court Paul Jesson of the U.S. was LO best supporting actor in *The Normal Heart;* Ireland's Anne Devlin was cited as promising playwright by *TO* (alongside Robert Holman and Howard Barker) for *Ourselves Alone,* set in strife-torn Northern Ireland; Alison Steadman was *DM* best supporting actress in *Kafka's Dick;* and *TO* awards went to Howard Barker's reworking of Thomas Middleton's *Women Beware Women* and to Maggie Steed and Gary Oldman in the same drama. Two outstanding offerings at the Hampstead Theatre were Lyle Kessler's *Orphans,* which won Albert Finney three best actor awards (*P&P,* LO, and *LS*), and Michael Attenborough's moving production of *Observe the Sons of Ulster Marching Towards the Somme* by Ireland's Frank McGuinness, designated most promising playwright by *P&P* and *LS. TO* chose Deborah Warner, director of the Kick Theatre Company's *Coriolanus* at the Almeida, for a production award and Howard Sackler's *The Great White Hope* at the Tricycle for another, and *DM* divided its best actor award between Hugh Quarshie in the latter play and veteran Bill Fraser (also winner of the LO best comic actor award) in the West End production *When We Are Married.* This play also won the LO comedy award. *DM* considered Tom Wilkinson in *Ghosts* at the Young Vic the best supporting actor.

Other awards in the private sector went to Anthony Minghella's skit on British sexual mores *Made in Bangkok* (*P&P* best new play) and to *The Phantom of the Opera* (LO, *P&P,* and *LS* best new musical), which also won for Michael Crawford, in the title role, the LO award for best actor in a musical. The LO award for best actress in a musical went to Lesley Mackie in *Judy.* The *LS* best comedy production award went to Bob Larbey's *A Month of Sundays,* starring George Cole as a geriatric patient, and *P&P* and *LS* best actress honours were awarded to Julia McKenzie in Ayckbourn's fantasy drama *Woman in Mind.* Productions at the Theatre Royal, Haymarket, included *The Apple Cart* with Peter O'Toole, *The Taming of the Shrew* and *Antony and Cleopatra* with Vanessa Redgrave, and Derek Jacobi in Hugh Whitemore's *Breaking the Code.* At the Theatre of Comedy Ray Cooney produced *Rookery Nook* and *An Italian Straw Hat,* with minor success. As Ed Mirvish's Old Vic season faltered, the theatre went dark for three months; Mirvish decided to leave the direction to his son David and invited Jonathan Miller to take over as artistic director.

DM gave its musical award to the Anglo-Swedish spectacular *Chess,* staged by Trevor Nunn, on furlough from the RSC. Most of the other musicals—except for Dave Clark's electronic wonder *Time,* starring Cliff Richard and a talking effigy of Laurence Olivier—were revivals from the U.S.

The withdrawal of the Irish Arts Council's grant to the Dublin Festival prompted a rescue bid by the U.S.-based Ireland Foundation, supported by the Heinz Corp., which gave grants for 1986 and 1987. Samuel Beckett's 80th birthday was celebrated at the Abbey with a revival of *Happy Days* with Marie Kean and at the Gate by Barry McGovern's *I'll Go On.* The Peacock staged Tom McIntyre's *The Great Hunger.* Thomas Murphy's *A Thief at Christmas* at the Abbey and *Bailegangaire* with Siobhan McKenna (*see* OBITUARIES) at the Druid won him the Harvey's Irish Theatre Award for the writing category and gained the female acting award for McKenna. The production award went to Joe Dowling for *Juno and the Paycock* at the Gate and for three additional plays at the Gaiety. Donal McCann won the male acting award in *Juno.* For *Innocence* by McGuinness at the Gate, as well as for Dowling's *Heartbreak House* at the Gaiety, Joe Vaneck and Mick

Hughes shared the technical award for decor and lighting. The new work award was won by Paul Mercier's trilogy at the S.F.X. Centre.

France, Italy, Spain, Low Countries, Greece. Awards made by the French critics for 1985–86 included: first prize for best production to Peter Brook and his adapter Jean-Claude Carrière for *The Mahabharata;* Lerminier Prize for best regional production to Roger Planchon for *The Miser;* best play award to *The Toadstools* by Tilly; best actress to Nicole Garcia in *Two for the See-Saw;* best actor to Georges Bigot as Norodom Sihanouk in Ariane Mnouchkine's production of Hélène Sixous's epic drama at the Cartoucherie; best foreign-language production to Antoine Vitez's version of Marivaux's *The Triumph of Love* at the Milan Piccolo; and best artistic achievement to Sophie Loucachevsky's production of Yukio Mishima's *Madame de Sade* at the Chaillot. The Dominique direction prize went to Bernard Murat for Jean Anouilh's *The Rehearsal,* the Brigadier Prize to Laurent Terzieff, the Jean-Jacques Gautier Prize to Jean Mercure, and the Académie Française Prize to Raymond Devos.

Highlights at the Comédie Française, under its new director Jean Le Poulain, included Jorge Lavelli's Argentine-tango version of *A Midsummer Night's Dream* and a coproduction with Strasbourg of Brigitte Jacques's *Elvire Jouvet 40* at the Athénée, Jouvet's old theatre. At the Odéon, which Le Poulain and Giorgio Strehler agreed to occupy, each for half a year, two important novelties were Nella Bielski and John Berger's *Question of Geography* and Edvard Radzinsky's nostalgic drama about a retired actress hankering to appear in a Dostoyevsky play. Under Gérard Violette, Jean Mercure's successor as head of the Théâtre de la Ville, Marthe Keller appeared in Schiller's *Don Carlos,* and Benno Besson revived his famous version of Shvarts's *The Dragon.* Guy Rétoré staged *Purple Dust* at the Théâtre de l'Est Parisien. In the private sector there were new plays by Nathalie Sarraute, Georges Michel, Bernard Da Costa, Marguerite Duras, Pierre Rey, Arrabal, Jean-Claude Brisville, Victor Haim, Jean Poiret, Eduardo Manet, and Alain Page and many revivals, including four plays by Sacha Guitry.

At Milan's Piccolo Teatro there were two new plays by Alberto Moravia, and at the Sicilian Arts Centre at Gibellina, a revival of San Secondo's *The Rape of Proserpine.* Madrid paid homage to García Lorca with Nuria Espert's revival of *Yerma* and Luis Pasqual's coproduction with the Milan Piccolo of the previously unperformed *El Público.* In Amsterdam a new national company under Gerardjon Rijnden moved into the City Theatre. Salient features of the Greek season were Alexis Solomos's *Tartuffe* at the National and the unprecedented opening of the Epidaurus theatre to popular groups.

Switzerland, Austria, West and East Germany. In Zürich, Switz., Maria Becker scored two hits, as Mary Stuart at the Schauspielhaus and in Loleh Bellon's *Such Tender Bonds* with her own touring company. The Dance Group of the Grand Théâtre, Geneva, staged García Lorca's *El Público* at the Comédie. Friedrich Dürrenmatt was awarded both the Schiller and the Georg Büchner prizes.

Following objections, the British NT was forced to drop Peter Shaffer's *Yonadab* from its program at the Vienna Festival, substituting the Restoration comedy *Love for Love.* Claus Peymann, who succeeded Achim Benning as head of the Burgtheater, staged Thomas Bernhard's *Ritter, Dene, Voss,* written especially for three players in the company. Benno Besson made his Burg directing debut with *Don Juan,* while East Germany's Christoph Schroth directed the first performance at the Burg of the long-proscribed *Mother Courage,* starring Elisabeth Orth. No less memorable were Karl Maria Brandauer's *Hamlet,* the premiere of Havel's modern Faust drama *The Temptation,* and Peter Handke's *Prometheus Bound* in Salzburg, which earned him the City Prize.

Milestones in West German theatre were Robert Wilson's staging of Heiner Müller's *Hamletmachine* and Michael Bogdanov's of *Julius Caesar,* both in Hamburg; Augusto Boal's production of *El Público* at its world premiere in Wuppertal; and Peter Stein's of *The Hairy Ape* in Berlin. There were new plays by Harald Mueller, Tankred Dorst, Martin Walser, Friederike Roth, Thomas Bernhard, Stefan Schütz, and Heinrich Böll. Notable events in East Germany were the awarding of the National Prize to Müller; Alexander Lang's staging of his "Passion Trilogy" (Goethe's *Stella,* Strindberg's *The Dance of Death,* and Euripides' *Medea*) with Katja Paryla; and the Berliner Ensemble's Ekkehard Schall in *Krapp's Last Tape,* the first Beckett play to be performed in East Germany.

Eastern Europe, Scandinavia, Israel. The inauguration of a new permanent Jewish Dramatic Studio Theatre in Moscow, with simultaneous translation for non-Yiddish

AP/WIDE WORLD

A performance of *Richard III* opened a first-of-its-kind 12-day Shakespeare festival in Beijing (Peking) in April.

speakers, marked a cultural watershed in the U.S.S.R. A large number of new plays, by established and new playwrights, was another feature of the new regime. Anatoly Efros kept the nonconformist flag flying at the Taganka, where plays by Boris Mozhaev, Svetlana Alekseyevich, Viktor Sarsikov, and Viktor Slavkin were tried out, besides such popular hits as *The Lower Depths* and *The Misanthrope.* News that from Jan. 1, 1987, a larger measure of autonomy would be allowed in matters of finance, administration, and artistic policy confirmed that a wind of change was blowing.

In Warsaw Kazimierz Dejmek staged the premiere of Slawomir Mrozek's *Contract* at the Polski; Janusz Warminski revived *The Cherry Orchard* at the Ateneum; and an untried director, Edvard Myszky, showed his mettle with *Ghosts* at the National. Under its new head, Stanislaw Radwan, the Stary in Krakow had Andrzej Wajda direct the 150-year-old classic *The Revenge.* A satirical comedy, *Globe Lighting,* was Ivan Radoev's contribution at the Palace of Culture in Sofia, Bulg. Of special interest at Hungary's national theatre in Budapest were the rock musical *King Stephen,* Miklos Gabor as Shylock, and *Richard II,* the first of a cycle that was to include all of Shakespeare's historical dramas.

Two important events at the Royal Dramatic Theatre in Stockholm were Yury Lyubimov's debut, staging his own collage of Pushkin works entitled *The Banquet at the Time of the Plague,* and Ingmar Bergman's new *Hamlet* with Peter Stormare in the title role. The event of the year in Oslo was the return of Liv Ullmann to star in Peter Palitzsch's production of *Mother Courage* at the Norwegian Theatre, where she had made her debut 25 years earlier. The Norwegian tour of *Schweyk in the Second World War* was the big draw at the Tampere Festival in Finland, rivaled only by Adam Hanuszkiewicz's guest production of Turgenev's *A Month in the Country* at the Pyynikki Park Theatre. Decan Donnellan's production of *Macbeth* and Eugen Terttula's of Hella Wuolijoki's *The Farmer's Daughter* were staged at the Helsinki national theatre.

Significant developments in Israel included an increase in modern drama and the usual wave of foreign guest directors, including Robert Walker, who staged a Dario Fo farce at the Habimah. Jozef Szajna premiered the latest play in his concentration camp cycle, *Replika VII,* at the same theatre. Motti Lerner's drama *Kastner,* at the Cameri, won the Meskin Prize for the best new work. Other new plays of note were *The Optimist* by Emile Habibi and Joshua Sobol's controversial *The Palestinian Woman,* both at the Haifa City Theatre, and Yoram Gal's drama at the Jerusalem Khan about Zionist pioneer Y. H. Brenner, murdered in 1921. (OSSIA TRILLING)

United States. Broadway's downslide of the past few years went bone deep in 1986, when the fewest shows were produced of any year in the history of the New York stage. To make matters worse, the rate of success also declined. A mere 26 productions opened during the calendar year, compared with 31 in 1985, previously the worst year in Broadway history (the best was 1929, with more than 200 new shows).

Of the 26 productions, only 6 could be termed successful, and some of those were only borderline survivors. At Tony award time in June there was such a paucity of choice that older works such as Athol Fugard's *The Blood Knot* (1964) and John Guare's *The House of Blue Leaves* (1971) were pronounced eligible on the technicality that, having originally played off-Broadway, they were new as far as Broadway was concerned. This argument persuaded few voters and only underscored the despair of the situation.

The Tony for best play was won by Herb Gardner's *I'm Not Rappaport,* a popular favourite despite mixed reviews. It was Gardner's first success since his *A Thousand Clowns* of some 25 years earlier. The new play—a dramatic comedy about old age, grit, and survival—was not a profound

The Royal Shakespeare Company at 25

The year 1986 was one of major achievement for the Royal Shakespeare Company (RSC), despite a cut in state subsidy in real terms. In April the company, which had received its first subsidy from the Arts Council of Great Britain in 1963, became the first arts body to win the Queen's Award for Export for "boosting Great Britain's international prestige" and encouraging the tourist trade. The second major event of the year was the opening on April 26 of the new 430-seat Swan Theatre at Stratford-upon-Avon. This brought the number of RSC theatres to five in all; in addition, the company staged an annual season in Newcastle and toured productions at home and abroad. The RSC was also looking for a third theatre in London to which its Swan Theatre successes could be transferred, just as plays from the other two Stratford theatres might transfer to the Barbican or Pit theatres in London.

A festival of six plays in the Shakespeare tercentenary birthday year of 1864 had led the Stratford brewer Charles E. Flower to launch the yearly Stratford festival in 1875; from 1879 these had been staged in the Victorian-Gothic 800-seat Memorial Theatre until its destruction by fire in 1926, the year after it received its royal charter. On April 23, 1932, the prince of Wales unveiled the 1,150-seat Royal Shakespeare Theatre, alongside the shell of the old playhouse. The new Swan Theatre, designed as a three-tier house with a thrust stage by Stratford architect Michael Reardon, was built within the surviving brickwork of the gutted theatre. It was unveiled by Queen Elizabeth II in November 1986 in the presence of Frederick R. Koch, a businessman from Wichita, Kan., who had contributed £2 million toward its construction.

The RSC, until 1961 the Shakespeare Memorial Company, celebrated its 25th season with a record number of 36 productions, including 14 new plays or adaptations. The performances were attended by more than one million spectators in Britain alone and attracted over 200 national and international awards in Europe and the U.S. In October Trevor Nunn, who had succeeded Peter Hall in 1968, handed over the post of chief executive to Terry Hands, who had been his joint artistic director since 1978.

Despite some major criticisms of recent failures, Hands was set to carry on existing policies and to promote the Swan Theatre as the home of works by "Shakespeare's contemporaries and successors from 1570 to 1750." The first four works in this tradition at the Swan were *The Two Noble Kinsmen,* a romantic tragedy written by Shakespeare and John Fletcher; Ben Jonson's first comedy, *Every Man in His Humour; The Rover,* by Aphra Behn, Britain's first professional woman dramatist; and the romantic pirate saga *The Fair Maid of the West,* staged by Nunn and adapted from Thomas Heywood's two plays of that name.

(OSSIA TRILLING)

work of theatre, but it was a satisfying piece and was engagingly performed by Judd Hirsch and Cleavon Little (later replaced by the equally pleasing Hal Linden and Ossie Davis).

With this award the Tony voters seemed to be saying that audiences still appreciated the sentimentalism, social consciousness, and character drama that had been Broadway's style for decades. Yet the season's only other play of that type, George Furth's *Precious Sons,* failed to win an audience despite powerful performances by Ed Harris and Judith Ivey. When such efforts fail, it is not likely that producers will step up their output of serious plays.

Drama, however, had long been dormant on Broadway, which had become oriented toward musicals. That trend made the 1985–86 Tony awards even gloomier because there was no smash hit musical during the official season (June to June). The winner by default was *The Mystery of Edwin Drood,* a show that never played a sold-out week, reflecting a commercial theatre in serious trouble. Indeed, only two full-size Broadway productions opened from Labor Day through the year's end. These were the Marvin Hamlisch musical *Smile* and *Broadway Bound,* the final play in Neil Simon's autobiographical trilogy. Hamlisch's show was yet another multimillion-dollar failure.

A new musical hit did arrive during the summer, when Broadway traditionally shuts down. This was the British import *Me and My Girl,* and it inaugurated the Marquis Theater. The show was a revival, a very old-fashioned, good-time musical done as an affectionate send-up. With old songs, broad jokes, a music-hall style, and a captivating star in Robert Lindsay, it demonstrated anew that audiences will enjoy anything well done.

Oddly enough, *Me and My Girl* was one of three new musicals to open during the dog days of summer. It certainly outran the others. *Honky Tonk Nights* and *Rags* played a combined total of eight performances. *Rags* was a particularly shocking failure, created by composer Charles Strouse (*Annie*), lyricist Stephen Schwartz (*Pippin*), and librettist Joseph Stein (*Fiddler on the Roof*). It was only one of the year's $5 million flops, the other being Bob Fosse's *Big Deal,* based on the Italian movie *Big Deal on Madonna Street.* Fosse's notion was to reset the comedy about bungling burglars into a black, Depression-era milieu, using period songs. Like *Rags* it proved disorganized and without unifying character.

MARTHA SWOPE

Robert De Niro (right) plays a drug dealer in *Cuba and His Teddy Bear*. Ralph Macchio costars as his son. For the June sensation at Joseph Papp's Public Theater in New York, there was a live telecast to an adjacent space in the theatre to accommodate overflow crowds.

Fosse's failure with *Big Deal* was particularly distressing because so many of Broadway's directors were falling by the wayside. Michael Bennett, famous for staging *A Chorus Line* and *Dreamgirls,* fell ill and canceled all work indefinitely. Harold Prince was so rocked by four straight opening-night flops in as many years that he quit Broadway, only to make a spectacular splash in London staging Andrew Lloyd Webber's *The Phantom of the Opera.* But ever since *Jesus Christ Superstar* and *Evita,* Webber's shows had been consistently successful. In 1986 his *Song and Dance* ran the year, while his *Cats* became the most lucrative show in Broadway history.

The year's only other Broadway success did it without rave reviews or even advertising. All it needed was the presence of movie star Robert De Niro. This was the Rinaldo Povod play *Cuba and His Teddy Bear.* It was a merely promising work, but as recent history had proved for Dustin Hoffman and Al Pacino, audiences did not care whether the play was *Richard III* or *Death of a Salesman* when a movie star was in it. These appearances seemed the only way to attract audiences to current Broadway drama, and the actors who did it (at considerable financial sacrifice) were the true heroes of contemporary theatre.

Cuba and His Teddy Bear, like *The Mystery of Edwin Drood,* originated at Joseph Papp's New York Shakespeare Festival. This once-expansive institution was so crimped by shrinking sources of subsidy that its production choices seemed determined more by Broadway potential than by artistic value. New York's other major institution, the Circle in the Square, played a similar game. George C. Scott starred there in a shaky new play, *The Boys of Autumn,* and John Malkovich directed the Harold Pinter classic *The Caretaker,* in a production imported from Chicago's Steppenwolf Theatre Company.

So continued 1985's Chicago invasion of the New York stage. Gregory Mosher, having left that city's Goodman Theatre to reopen the long-dark theatre component in Lincoln Center, began the resurrection with *The House of Blue Leaves* in the studio theatre, the Newhouse. This was an all-star production featuring Christopher Walken, Swoosie Kurtz, Stockard Channing, and Julie Hagerty (it was also another Chicago import, having originated at the Goodman). It was so exuberantly staged by Jerry Zaks that audiences overstuffed the little theatre, forcing moves first upward into the Vivian Beaumont Theatre and then south to Broadway.

In Chicago itself the Goodman Theatre demonstrated how to succeed even when a successful artistic director has departed for New York. It imported Canada's Stratford Festival company for impeccable Shakespeare (*King Lear, Twelfth Night*) and borrowed Adrian Hall from Rhode Island's Trinity Rep to stage Brecht's *Galileo.* The aforementioned Steppenwolf Theatre Company presented contemporary works that ranged from Tennessee Williams's *Cat on a Hot Tin Roof* to new plays such as Laura Cunningham's *Bang.* (*See* Sidebar.)

Among the other regional theatres, in Los Angeles the established Mark Taper Forum began expanded operations at the James A. Doolittle Theatre in Hollywood with real rotating repertory and a diet of classics such as Lillian Hellman's *The Autumn Garden* and Shaw's *Heartbreak House.* Elsewhere most regional theatres presented professional productions of the established dramatic literature, which was precisely their reason for existence.

Theatre in Chicago

The regional theatre movement in the United States has had one of its most vigorous and visible profiles in the energetic, original work that is presented on the small stages of Chicago. Like many another large U.S. city that once depended on touring productions of Broadway shows to fill its theatres, Chicago in the last few decades has had to invent its own theatre as the formerly steady flow of "product" from New York was reduced to a trickle—or a brief seasonal spurt—in downtown playhouses. In Chicago, however, instead of a single, flagship edifice that drew most of the attention and customers, the resident theatre movement found expression in scores of small houses, almost all of them located away from the downtown area and converted from storefronts or second-floor spaces by young people just entering the profession.

This growth of "poor" theatre at first denied the city the glamour that attends the opening of a well-endowed instant institution, but, in its very poverty, it provided an opportunity for committed young theatre artists who were happy to survive and to develop their craft slowly, without living under the shadow of big budgets and high risks.

Studded with colleges and universities, Chicago always had been a central location for young actors, designers, and directors, and at least as long ago as 1959, with the opening of the Second City cabaret, it had been recognized as a springboard for talent. It was not until the mid-1970s, however, with the end of the Vietnam war, that the congregation of small theatres that had been slowly expanding since the 1960s exploded in activity.

It was a young playwright, David Mamet—26 when his first full-length play, *Sexual Perversity in Chicago,* was produced at the Organic Theater—who received the initial national recognition, through New York productions of his plays. As Mamet's reputation grew, climaxing with his 1984 Pulitzer Prize for *Glengarry Glen Ross,* so did the work of others of his theatrical generation.

Gregory Mosher, director of almost all of Mamet's plays in Chicago, became artistic director of the Goodman Theatre, the city's oldest and largest resident theatre, in 1978 and, partly because of his success in nurturing new work there, moved on in 1985 to become director of Lincoln Center Theater in New York City. A group of young actors who had banded together in 1976 as the Steppenwolf Theatre gained national recognition when their productions of Lanford Wilson's *Balm in Gilead* and Sam Shepard's *True West* hit New York in the early 1980s. Similarly, other actors from other theatres with oddball names such as Wisdom Bridge and Remains went on to gain choice stage, movie, and television assignments on the basis of their work in Chicago.

By 1986 many members of this '70s generation had left Chicago for the bigger opportunities and salaries their discovery had attracted. At the same time, Chicago's reputation as a "hot" theatre town had drawn dozens of small new groups eager to scramble for the acclaim their predecessors had achieved.

(RICHARD D. CHRISTIANSEN)

Canada. Northward in Canada, the Stratford Festival completed its first full season under its new artistic director, John Neville, presenting a risky program of three of Shakespeare's least popular plays, *Pericles, Cymbeline,* and *The Winter's Tale* (billed as "The Dark Romances"). As if to balance the risk, the 1938 Broadway musical *The Boys from Syracuse* was also presented in the main stage Festival Theatre. This Rodgers and Hart show, which is Shakespearean in that it is (casually) based on *A Comedy of Errors,* became the hit of the season, which in 1986 ran 26 weeks, from mid-May to late October.

Neville, as a new leader intent on blowing off the institutional dust that Stratford historically attracts, raided the nearby Shaw Festival for gifted but unknown Canadian actors, abandoning the star policy of recent years. He programmed the more informal Avon Theatre with a *Hamlet* that alternated with Tom Stoppard's *Rosencrantz and Guildenstern Are Dead* (which is a variation on *Hamlet*). Also, the "Young Company" was installed in Stratford's Third Stage theatre, and its *Macbeth* subsequently toured the province of Ontario. (MARTIN GOTTFRIED)

This article updates the *Macropædia* article The History of Western THEATRE.

See also Dance; Music.

Transportation

Achievements and new ideas in transportation and communications were exhibited by 54 countries in Vancouver, B.C., from May to October as part of Expo 86; the relationship between transportation and economic development was the recurrent theme. Elsewhere, liberalization of transport and increasing private-sector involvement continued. Deregulation of air transport and long-distance passenger buses and intercity truck (lorry) haulage in the U.S. and long-distance passenger buses in the U.K. led to a few companies becoming dominant, and sometimes overlapping, in the marketplace. (DAVID BAYLISS)

AVIATION

Far-reaching structural changes in the U.S. air transport industry took place in 1986, while for world airlines as a whole the dominant concerns were financial health and the effects of terrorism. The director general of the International Air Transport Association (IATA), representing almost 150 airlines, stated toward year's end that financial performance was "not encouraging." In the first seven months of 1986 capacity increased by 5.8%, compared with the same period of 1985, and outstripped the volume of traffic, which rose only 1.6%. As a result, load factors were badly affected. In addition, the important North Atlantic market was adversely affected by the U.S. perception of the terrorist threat in Europe, the aftereffects of the Chernobyl nuclear power station disaster in the U.S.S.R., and the progressive weakening of the U.S. dollar. IATA members' North Atlantic traffic was down by 8.9% in the first seven months of 1986, compared with the same period of 1985, and passenger load factor was down by 9.7 percentage points.

IATA estimated that its members would achieve a pretax profit of 1–2% of revenue on international scheduled services during 1986 and 1987. This compared with 3.9% in 1985 and 5.5% in 1984 and was about 7 percentage points below the minimum needed to finance investments and maintain profitability. IATA estimated that its members would need to acquire some 4,000 aircraft by the mid-1990s at a cost of about $150 billion–$200 billion.

The Hypersonic Future

In the ten years since the Concorde supersonic transport entered service, the airlines' interest in developing that class of aircraft had been at a low ebb, and it remained the only supersonic passenger plane. Yet Concorde, as exploited in particular by British Airways on transatlantic routes, retained a certain glamour and kept alive public interest in high-speed premium-class travel.

In the mid-1980s several new concepts came under discussion. They included a Concorde development that was economically superior to the original but offered only a modest increase in speed, put forward by Aerospatiale (the French partner in Concorde). More ambitious was the idea of a hypersonic aircraft or trans-atmospheric vehicle (TAV), which could fly in the atmosphere but also accelerate into space orbit. During acceleration in the atmosphere it would rely on the aerodynamic lift provided by its wings rather than on the pure thrust of a rocket. In 1986 this discussion gained impetus as a result of the U.S. government's emphasis on long-distance communications in developing transpacific trade.

One concept for such an application was McDonnell Douglas's Orient Express. It was envisioned to be a 300-seat airliner able to cruise at an altitude of 30,000 m (1 m = 3.3 ft) at a speed of Mach 5 (Mach number 1 corresponds to the speed of sound)—equivalent to about 4,800 km/h (1 km = 0.62 mi)—over a range of approximately 12,000 km. By comparison, Concorde carried 128 passengers at 2,150 km/h over approximately 4,900 km. The Orient Express could reduce the New York–Tokyo flight time from 14 hours by subsonic jet to a mere 2½ hours.

A British concept known as HOTOL (horizontal takeoff and landing) was being developed by British Aerospace with $4 million of government funding. The craft would be similar to Concorde in size, but its prime purpose would be to launch satellites in space. It would be able to take off from a 3,000-m runway and accelerate to Mach 5 by the time it reached an altitude of about 26,000 m. Continuing its flight by means of rocket propulsion, it would accelerate into a brief orbit to deliver its satellite or other payload and then return into the atmosphere.

Important unanswered questions concerned power plants and fuels. For operation in the atmosphere a TAV would need air-breathing engines that would also be capable of operating as a rocket to reach orbital velocity. Kerosene used in atmospheric flight would need to be supplemented by hydrogen in space. Methane also was proposed as a fuel.

With costs a major concern, the airline industry was bound to approach any new supersonic or hypersonic development with utmost caution. Before any development could become a commercial possibility, there might have to be an associated military requirement—probably from the U.S.—against which some of the costs could be offset. (DAVID WOOLLEY)

IATA members' 1985 results for total operations showed a net profit of $900 million on operating revenue of $77.1 billion; comparable figures for 1984 were $1.1 billion (the best figure in several years) on revenue of $73.9 billion. A few airlines were making good profits, while some, in the third world particularly, were doing very badly; the majority hovered around the break-even line.

AP/WIDE WORLD

A long-time employee of Frontier Airlines cleans out his work area after hearing that Frontier had filed for bankruptcy. Cost-cutting attempts by People Express, the new owner of the Denver-based line, proved unsuccessful, and a possible sale to United fell through.

The number of passengers carried on world scheduled services in 1985 totaled 890,893,000, an increase of 6%, according to preliminary estimates of the International Civil Aviation Organization. Passenger traffic amounted to 1,361,000,000,000 passenger-km (1 km = 0.62 mi), up by 7.1%. The growth in freight traffic slowed to only 0.4% following a marked acceleration in the period 1982–84; it amounted to 39,650,000,000 metric ton-km.

Security replaced safety as a major concern in 1986. Serious incidents included a bomb explosion on board a Trans World Airlines (TWA) 727 over the Mediterranean on April 2, resulting in the deaths of four passengers. The number of accidents declined sharply from 1985, when 1,710 passengers were killed, the highest number ever recorded. The passenger fatality rate for scheduled services was 0.09 per 100 million passenger-km, compared with 0.02 in 1984, but in five of the ten years 1976–85 the rate was 0.09 or higher.

Changes in the U.S. airline industry brought about by mergers and acquisitions made one relatively new airline, Texas Air Corp., the world's largest group outside the U.S.S.R. In developments that were unforeseen by the proponents of U.S. deregulation, the process of consolidation also put a handful of old-established major airlines in dominant positions and seriously weakened the challenge of the newer postderegulation carriers. The best-known and fastest growing postderegulation carrier, People Express, suffered financial problems in 1986 because of rapid expansion and its acquisition of the unprofitable Frontier Airlines. People Express failed to sell off Frontier, which was consequently forced to go into bankruptcy, and both People and the assets of Frontier were then acquired by

Aircraft designer Burt Rutan (left) and *Voyager* pilots Jeana Yeager and Dick Rutan (right) pause near the experimental plane at Mojave Airport in California. The crew had landed December 23 at Edwards Air Force Base after a nine-day, nonstop around-the-world flight.
AP/WIDE WORLD

Texas Air. Earlier, Texas Air had acquired Eastern Airlines, which had already absorbed Continental Airlines and New York Air. Under Texas Air control, Continental had become a low-cost operator with labour costs amounting to about 21% of its total outlays. The challenge for Texas Air was to reduce, against union opposition, the labour costs of the more traditionally structured Eastern, which stood at about 30%.

Other acquisitions concluded during 1986 were Republic by Northwest, Western Airlines by Delta, and Ozark by TWA. Major airlines with futures still clouded by poor financial performance were TWA and Pan American; the latter sold its profitable Pacific Division to United Airlines, with effect from January 1987. The net result of these changes was to establish Texas Air, United, American, Delta, and Northwest in commanding positions at the head of the U.S. industry.

In Western Europe moves toward a more liberal regulatory regime were made by the European Communities (EC), which wrote to flag carriers demanding an end to anticompetitive practices. Some EC countries were resistant to change, notably Italy and Greece, but the liberal policies of The Netherlands and the U.K. had already resulted in a significant increase in the number of airlines and capacity operating between the two countries. (DAVID WOOLLEY)

SHIPPING AND PORTS

Instead of the predicted slight improvement in world shipping markets in 1986, all major sectors—tanker, dry cargo, and gas—suffered near-disastrous conditions. The world merchant fleet again declined. The benefits of much lower operating costs for shipowners resulting from the sharp fall in oil prices were more than offset by the fact that 25% of the world merchant fleet was either idle or underused. An acceleration in the scrapping of older vessels still left too much cargo space. The car carriers, however, showed some improvement, and several new vessels entered service. The specialist reefer (refrigerator ship) industry did not escape the malaise, and although overall tonnage declined, there was still overcapacity. A relatively modest growth in container business, derived largely from the increasing trade with less developed countries, enabled two major containership operators to introduce round-the-world services using very large vessels that called at only a few ports.

The continuing oversupply in the bulk shipping sector kept freight rates low. In early 1986 the fleet (excluding tankers) comprised 4,968 vessels totaling 197.5 million metric tons deadweight (dw), and it was predicted that by the end of 1986 total tonnage would be 462 million metric tons dw. After a record decline in tonnage, in 1986 there were 2,515 tankers of 239.3 million metric tons dw. Despite an improvement in the supply-demand position, surplus tanker capacity was estimated at 102 million metric tons, or 23% of the world tanker fleet. The oil price collapse adversely affected liquefied natural gas (LNG) developments, and LNG exports from Algeria to the U.S. remained suspended.

The total tonnage of the world merchant fleet was reduced from 416 million gross registered tons (grt) in mid-1985 to 405 million grt in mid-1986. The Liberian registered fleet stood at 52.6 million grt and Panama's at 41.3 million grt; they were followed by Japan (38.5 million grt) and Greece (28.4 million grt). The U.K.'s fleet declined to 11.6 million grt, but the flag moved from ninth to eighth place. Because of the effect on U.K. and French ports, the decision to proceed with the Channel twin-bore rail tunnel between Dover (U.K.) and Calais (France) worried port operators and owners of the large cross-Channel fleet.

The first cargo of iron ore from Brazil's new Carajas export terminal reached Japan in 1986; initially 15 million metric tons a year were to be moved by vessels loading at 16,000 metric tons an hour. In the U.S. major container terminal projects went ahead at Los Angeles and Oakland in California and Houston, Texas. A $120 million container terminal for Pakistan's Karachi port was approved and expected to go on stream in 1992. The continuation of the Iran-Iraq war caused a slight fall in Suez Canal traffic. In October traffic through the Panama Canal was sharply reduced by a landslide at its eastern end. (W. D. EWART)

FREIGHT AND PIPELINES

While total freight was growing moderately, international, air, and road freight were buoyant in many parts of the world. In Western Europe rail freight was growing at 2–3% annually, reaching a total of 225,000,000,000 ton-km per year. This compared with 3,700,000,000,000 ton-km per year in the U.S.S.R., where rail freight traffic exceeded road freight by a ratio of 25:1. Double stacking on higher trains was the most rapidly growing mode of rail freight in North America.

Most pipeline construction activity was in non-Communist countries, where over 30,000 km of oil, natural gas, and petroleum products pipeline were laid. In the U.S.S.R. gas pipeline construction was still at a high level. Pipeline construction was also expanding in China.

The only coal slurry line being built was over the 259 km between Belovo and Novosibirsk in the U.S.S.R. In the U.S. 610 km of carbon dioxide lines had been commissioned, mainly to provide pressure to retrieve crude oil from exhausted fields. Work was finished on the gas pipeline from Yamburg in Western Siberia. Other major gas pipelines completed or well under way included the 1,450-km line from the Palm Valley field near Alice Springs, Australia, to Darwin, and the 1,600-km line between the western and northern regions of India.

Most crude oil pipelines opened were extensions, a notable exception being the California crude line running

(continued on page 412)

The Automobile's 100-Year Journey

BY HARRY SMALLENBURG

In 1887, a year after he obtained a patent for a gasoline-powered, internal-combustion-engine vehicle, Karl Benz sold his first automobile, and much of the world has not recovered since. Benz started simply enough by today's standards—with a three-wheeled "tricycle" car. It sped along at 15 km/h (9.3 mph) and developed 0.9 hp at 400 rpm. By 1888 he had a shop that employed 50 workmen. By 1890 he was ready to build a four-wheeler, the Benz Viktoria, which appeared in 1893. He followed that with the Benz Velo in 1894 and eventually became the latter half of Mercedes-Benz. Not bad for a man who, in 1885, got so excited demonstrating a test vehicle to neighbours that he ran it into his own brick wall.

Of course, Benz was not alone in Europe. Although historians date the automobile from Benz's patent and the unveiling of Gottlieb Daimler's first car a short time later, from the early 1880s on, inventors and engineers, carriage companies and bicycle makers were producing large, small, plain, fancy, gas-, steam-, or electricity-powered vehicles. In the U.S. the first successful gasoline car was built in 1893, the Duryea Motor Wagon Co. was founded in 1895, and both Henry Ford and Ransom Eli Olds were building experimental vehicles.

Back roads in two continents began to resound with popping, sputtering noises, and magnificent vehicles were built, including Hispano-Suizas and Bugattis. But the public at large held onto their horses and watched from a distance. And with good reason: in this first wave, cars were expensive and scarce, their availability limited by production methods. Labourers worked on one car at a time, traipsing down long rows of vehicles as though attending cows in a barn. To Karl Benz in 1895, "mass production" meant 135 cars per year.

MERCEDES BENZ OF NORTH AMERICA

The three-wheeler, the first car in the world to be powered by gasoline, was capable of a speed nearly 15 kilometres (just over nine miles) per hour. The model, patented by the German mechanical engineer Karl Benz on January 26, 1886, led to a series of four-wheelers.

The first model of the Italian Fiat automobile was ready for use in 1899. The firm, whose name is an acronym for the Fabbrica Italiana Automobili Torino company, turned to americanized mass production after World War I, giving its products the appeal of lowered cost.
AUTOMOTIVE INDUSTRIES

Then an American had the simple but astonishingly bright idea of making the cars move while the men stood still. Henry Ford combined interchangeability (proved effective by Henry Leland in 1908) and design simplicity (the secret of Olds's popular 1903 curved-dash car) and gave birth to that modern industrial miracle, the assembly line, first put into operation in 1913.

By 1915 Ford Motor Company had produced a record 300,000 cars in one year. By 1927 one U.S. citizen in seven owned an automobile. By 1935, 35 million vehicles were in operation worldwide.

In the wake of Ford's success with mass production, the '20s and '30s brought the rise of major European companies like Morris, Singer, Austin, Fiat, and Citroën, many of which had been founded earlier. This era produced "classic" cars, small (the Fiat Topolino and the Austin Seven) as well as large and luxurious (Rolls-Royce Phantom and the Packard Phaeton). Cars had also changed their appearance. No longer the high, squared-off carriage-like vehicles of earlier years, they became lower and longer, with more sweep and smoothness to the fenders (as with the Delahaye 135 of 1938) and more conscious dignity and elegance (like the Hispano-Suiza, the Mercedes-Benz, and the stunning 1940 Lincoln Continental).

During the '30s, also, the seeds of eventual change were being planted in Japan and Germany. In 1937 Toyota Motor Co. Ltd. began serious production. Perhaps most profound, however, was the appearance in 1936 of the first Volkswagen, designed by Ferdinand Porsche at the request of Adolf Hitler.

In the post-World War II period, industrial plants turned from wartime back to domestic production. Europeans and Japanese, inspired by design firms like Pininfarina, continued to emphasize modest coupés and sleek, attractive sports cars (Karmann Ghia, the Toyota Corolla and Corona series, the Porsche 356 series). American cars, on the other hand, stretched and expanded. The triumphs included the smooth, integrated 1949-model Ford, the Chevrolet Corvette (1953), and the classic Ford Thunderbird (1954). Now regarded as design failures, however, were cars that sported controversial fins and sprouted excessive excrescences of chrome (1956 Cadillac convertible). America went on to "muscle" cars.

Then came the Volkswagen Beetle, social reactions against all "establishments," including Detroit, and increasing gasoline prices. Volkswagen marketing hit the right note at the right time with the "think small" campaign, and conservation-conscious American consumers turned increasingly toward smaller, foreign cars. By 1960, 500,000 Beetles had reached the U.S. By 1986 imported vehicles accounted for some 30% of total sales. American compacts and sports cars (with some notable exceptions, like the Chevette and the Mustang) had not managed the same market appeal or the same quality.

The story of the mid-'80s was one of competition in styling, international jockeying for profitable markets, and recurrent concerns about protectionist trade legislation. During the '20s Ford and General Motors built plants in Japan and Europe. Now Japanese and European companies were building plants in America. They were also working out cooperative ventures and sharing technologies such as robotics as they prepared to meet the advance of yet another wave of inexpensive cars, this time from South Korea and Yugoslavia.

During its first hundred years the automobile was transformed from novelty to necessity. For rapid, convenient daily transportation, nothing surpasses it. No other machine has had its profound and extensive social impact. The horse, put finally out to pasture, reminds us of a more confined and leisurely past. Our cars—in the garage, the driveway, the parking structure, or the company fleet—keep us abreast of our present and propel us toward our future.

Harry Smallenburg is chairman of the Department of General Studies, Center for Creative Studies, Detroit, Michigan.

JIM BROWN/MOTOR TREND MAGAZINE

A 1934 Packard Dual Cowl Phaeton, one of fewer than 20 ever built, is still in use today—by choice of its Beverly Hills, California, owner. The classic vehicle, said to lend a look of honour, has had many grand uses such as lead car in the 1984 Olympics parade.

(continued from page 410)

for 2,850 km between Santa Barbara and Houston. Other major lines were completed in Alberta, Iraq, and Turkey. At the end of the year over 88,500 km of line worth more than $25 billion were at the planning stage.

ROADS AND TRAFFIC

The year 1986 marked the 30th anniversary of the inception of the U.S. Interstate Highway System—probably the largest engineering construction program in the world. It also brought completion of the world's longest metropolitan beltway (195 km) around London. Although the U.S. interstate system still had some gaps, the first transcontinental link was formed with the completion of the I-80 between San Francisco and the I-95 at Teaneck, N.J. In Japan the national expressway system was extended to 3,640 km, with an additional 2,250 km under construction. Completion of the Stuart Highway in Australia reduced by 150 km the drive from Port Augusta on the Spencer Gulf to Kulgera in the Northern Territory. The world's highest cross-border highway (4,575 m)—the Karrakoram Highway through the Kunjerab Pass—was opened to general traffic, as was the $436 million Riyadh Sudair Quasim expressway in Saudi Arabia, which was capable of withstanding very high temperatures. By contrast, the new 160-km road from Narvick, Norway, to Kiruna, Sweden, inside the Arctic Circle could withstand temperatures of −48°C (−55°F). In Hong Kong the opening of the highway between Sha Tin and Fanling marked another stage in the new orbital route around the New Territories.

Private financing of road projects continued with the second (toll) crossing of the River Thames in London and the Channel Tunnel, which was to provide a rolling highway and a rail link between France and the U.K. (*See* ENGINEERING PROJECTS: *Sidebar*.) The heavily used New Jersey Turnpike was to be widened to 12 lanes over its northern section at a cost of $1 billion.

Greater care was the focus of European Road Safety Year as fatalities in Europe reached 50,000 and another 1.5 million were injured. Little progress was made in developing non-oil fuels for road transport, and the ambitious C5 electric car project in the U.K. failed. In the U.S. sales of gasohol increased to over 25,000,000,000 litres (6,600,-000,000 gal; nearly 5% of the market).

INTERCITY RAIL

Continued development of high-speed rail projects in Western Europe led to plans for an integrated 14-system European intercity network reaching from Rome to Oslo and from Madrid to Stockholm and Vienna. While France still led high-speed services with its Train à Grand Vitesse (TGV), other European countries were developing faster trains. In France a TGV service between Rouen and Lyon began in September 1986, and construction was about half completed on the new line from Paris to Le Mans and Tours. In West Germany experimental train sets capable of 350 km/h were being built, although the service speed maximum was expected to be 255 km/h.

Passenger traffic growth was sluggish in Eastern Europe and the U.S.S.R., although heavy demand on some routes necessitated 24-coach trains, and there were plans for 32-coach trains. The first 355 km of the Baikal–Amur mainline was electrified. In Japan the imminent privatization of railways was designed to reduce the huge operating deficits ($8 billion in the year to March 1986). Six regional companies and a Shinkhansen (national high-speed rail network) company were to be formed. Development of intercity services continued, and work began on the 370-km line

West Germany's streamlined Intercity Experimental ICE, with 11,600 horsepower, is capable of running at speeds of 300 kilometres per hour (186 miles per hour).
HORST SCHAFER—PHOTO TRENDS

between Takasaki and Komatsu on the coast. The time between Tokyo and Osaka was reduced to less than three hours (average speed 190 km/h).

The future of the national passenger rail service in Canada was ensured by the government on condition that the subsidy be reduced from $450 million to $360 million by 1990. In Australia the railway between Gladstone and Rockhampton (Queensland) was electrified, as was the Pinwang to Beizhouzhong (P'in-wang to Pei-chou-chung) line in China. In The Netherlands the railway between Schipol Airport and Amsterdam Central opened. In the U.K. the link to London's third airport at Stansted was approved; this would give all three airports direct links with central London.

URBAN MASS TRANSIT

In industrialized countries there was a continuing trend toward greater involvement of the private sector in urban public transport. In the U.K. bus operations were deregulated to improve services and reduce costs; fears of resultant chaos proved ill-founded. Greater private-sector involvement was advocated in a 1986 World Bank Transport Sector Policy Study that cast doubt on costly infrastructure developments such as new and popular subways (metros).

Many new subway systems were opened in 1986, and 1,125 km of subway were under construction, including extensions to over 60 systems. The U.S.S.R. subway network was growing the fastest, with systems now operating in nine cities and under construction in five and a total length nearing 3,800 km. In the U.S. Los Angeles, famous for its dependence on the private automobile, began construction of a subway system.

Light rail (a rail system equipped only for light traffic) had become the equivalent of the subway for middle-sized, lower density cities. Many new systems were under construction, and existing ones were being extended. Conversion of lightly used suburban rail lines to light railways was becoming popular; two lines were converted in Melbourne, Australia, and proposals for a number of other industrial cities were at the planning stage.

In Japan doubts were cast over the future of many rural and secondary lines because the new semiprivate companies being formed to run these services were tending to use low-cost railbus technology. A Maglev "magnetically levitated" train system was opened in West Berlin, while a more conventional system was being planned in Paris. Most spending, however, was being directed toward the other end of the light rail technology spectrum—the profit-generating tramways and streetcars. In some European countries, small buses seating 15 to 20 were becoming increasingly popular. Since they ran more frequently than the large buses seating 50 or more, they attracted more passengers and revenue and, with their lower costs, were proving more viable. (DAVID BAYLISS)

See also Energy; Engineering Projects; Environment; Industrial Review: *Aerospace; Automobiles.*
This article updates the *Macropædia* article TRANSPORTATION.

World Affairs

The Geneva summit of Nov. 19–21, 1985, the first meeting between the heads of the two superpowers in many years, had produced no major tangible breakthroughs, even though the atmosphere, according to both sides, was "businesslike." There was general agreement to limit and reduce nuclear arms and enhance strategic stability. It was also agreed that a year later a second summit should take place in the United States. But the road to the meeting proved difficult; only modest progress was achieved at the arms talks in Geneva, a little more in Stockholm (concerning mutual inspection), and apparently none at all in Vienna (where conventional forces were discussed). Various regional disputes further complicated relations between the superpowers. The Daniloff affair—the arrest of an American reporter in Moscow on espionage charges—threatened for several weeks in September to end arms-control negotiations altogether. The Soviet leaders insisted on a "presummit," which took place in Reykjavík, Iceland, in early October 1986 and ended in failure. While both sides made greater concessions than ever before, Soviet leader Mikhail Gorbachev made an arms deal contingent on abandonment of the U.S. Strategic Defense Initiative, which was unacceptable to U.S. Pres. Ronald Reagan. The outcome of the conference reflected serious differences of opinion and interest; it was also the result of an over-

World Affairs: Contents

For your convenience this article groups the countries of the world by the geopolitical regions to which they belong. Certain related topics, such as United Nations, Dependent States, and various regional affairs articles (*e.g.*, Latin-American Affairs), are also included. An alphabetical list of these topics appears below, indicating the page where each may be found. Articles on the various countries update the *Macropædia* articles of the same name (except where otherwise noted), as do the more extensive statistical treatments in the *World Data* section.

ambitious agenda and insufficient preparation. However, enough common ground had emerged to induce both sides to continue negotiations.

Gorbachev consolidated his position in the Kremlin during the period under review. The stress in his approach was on *glasnost* (openness) and *perestroika* (reform of the economic system), but progress in both directions was modest. Given the urgency of Soviet domestic and economic problems, it came as no surprise that internal affairs figured more prominently on the Kremlin's agenda than foreign policies. There was no acute tension in Eastern Europe, and the Soviets made a determined attempt to normalize relations with China, a country engaged in a considerably more ambitious program of internal reforms.

Both superpowers suffered setbacks in the scientific-technological field. On January 28 the U.S. space shuttle *Challenger* exploded a few seconds after takeoff; on April 26 a major accident took place at the Soviet nuclear power plant at Chernobyl in the Ukraine, causing contamination well beyond the nation's borders. The *Challenger* explosion delayed the U.S. space program for a year or longer; Chernobyl caused rethinking of the future of nuclear power for civilian uses in many countries—paradoxically, much more in the West than in the Soviet bloc. (*See* ENERGY: *Sidebar;* SPACE EXPLORATION.)

No major political changes took place in Europe during the year under review, except the generally predicted victory of the French right-of-centre parties in March. Jacques Chirac became prime minister serving under François Mitterrand, the Socialist president. A plebiscite in Spain brought a qualified "yes" to NATO membership; after a prolonged government crisis in Italy, Prime Minister Bettino Craxi was reappointed.

Two of the most embattled third world regimes were overthrown. Pres. Ferdinand Marcos fled the Philippines in February after what amounted to a bloodless coup; that same month Jean-Claude ("Baby Doc") Duvalier escaped from Haiti, ending 28 years of family rule. But the problems of those two countries were far from over. Fighting continued in other global trouble spots, most notably the Iran–Iraq war and South Africa. The Pretoria government raided neighbouring countries to attack African National Congress strongholds, while at home riots in the black townships led to the imposition of a national state of emergency on June 12 and the arrest of thousands. These repressive measures, in turn, strengthened the movement to impose economic sanctions on South Africa.

Various insurgencies continued in Central America, as did the civil war in Lebanon. There were new surges of communal violence in India (especially in the Punjab) and Sri Lanka. Certain significant changes occurred in the pattern of global terrorism. While "internal" terrorism had been declining for almost a decade, there was an increase in both state-sponsored terrorism and "narco-terrorism"—cooperation between drug traffickers and terrorist groups. Israel, at one time one of the main targets of terrorism, was virtually free from attacks during the period under review, but major attacks occurred in France, Italy, Austria, Malta, Pakistan, and Turkey—not to mention individual acts of violence such as the murder of Olof Palme, the Swedish prime minister, on February 28 and the attempted murder of Indian Prime Minister Rajiv Gandhi.

While most of these attacks were carried out by very small groups of professionals, there was evidence that these groups were acting as proxies on behalf of certain Middle Eastern governments, primarily Libya and Syria. In a few cases diplomats were caught red-handed—as when evidence at the trial of a terrorist in London implicated the Syrian ambassador—although the accused countries vehemently denied all involvement. Claiming that Libya was behind many terrorist incidents, the United States retaliated on the night of April 14–15 with an air raid on Tripoli and Benghazi. The action provoked considerable criticism in Western Europe, but the U.S. stance against dealing with terrorists was somewhat compromised by the revelation that it had sold arms to Iran—at least partly, it appeared, to gain the release of U.S. hostages held by Shi'ah groups in Lebanon.

For all the publicity given to terrorism, its political and social effects were minute compared, for example, with major problems of the world economy. Global debt continued to rise—partly the result of the flight of capital from less developed countries, which reached about a trillion dollars in 1986. The continuing fall in the price of oil benefited the consumer countries but spelled disaster for producers such as Mexico. The summit of seven major industrialized nations in Tokyo (May 4–6) resolved to focus remedial efforts on underlying fundamentals such as budget deficits and surpluses, monetary policy, and interest rates, but the participants failed to agree on what the remedies should be. While the Europeans and Japan decried the fall of the dollar and the U.S. budget deficit, U.S. leaders stressed that the deficit had acted as a stimulus to world output and trade, whereas Japan and West Germany had done little to help in this respect. (WALTER LAQUEUR)

This article updates the *Macropædia* article 20th-Century International Relations.

UNITED NATIONS

Secretary-General Javier Pérez de Cuéllar reported to the General Assembly in the fall that in 1986 the UN faced the worst financial crisis in its history. The problem arose primarily because Congress cut the $210 million U.S. contribution by about 70%. As a result, in March the secretary-general stopped all recruiting and reduced staff and services, saving $60 million. During a resumed Assembly session (April 28–May 9) on the financial crisis, he urged the U.S. not to act unilaterally but to negotiate changes in UN budgetary procedures. Then, on November 3, he announced that he would not renew the contracts of six assistant and five undersecretaries-general.

The secretary-general underwent a quadruple coronary bypass operation on July 24, and on September 21 he warned that he might not be willing to succeed himself when his five-year term expired at the end of 1986 unless the U.S. and U.S.S.R. guaranteed the UN their financial support. Nonetheless, when, on October 10, the Assembly elected him on the unanimous recommendation of the Security Council, he accepted, saying that to decline "would have been tantamount to abandoning a moral duty."

Reports circulated that, before his election, the U.S. had "hinted" that it would ultimately pay most of its 1986 assessment, and on October 27 the U.S. said that it would contribute $100 million. A spokesman added that if the Assembly approved a package of wide-ranging budgetary changes recommended by an intergovernmental committee of experts (the "Group of 18"), the U.S. would try to reinstate at least $42 million more.

The Group of 18 completed its report in mid-August, recommending that, over three years, the UN reduce its staff by 15%; eliminate 25% of the assistant and undersecretary-general posts; lower UN salaries and fringe benefits; require host governments to finance UN meetings held away from headquarters; and consolidate activities relating to South West Africa/Namibia, now conducted by a council, an institute, a special committee, and a trust fund.

On December 19, the last day of the 1986 session, the Assembly approved, without a vote, a resolution containing

Senegal President Abdou Diouf (left), opening speaker at the UN General Assembly session on the African economic crisis, is greeted by chief U.S. delegate Vernon A. Walters. Herbert Okun, deputy U.S. delegate (right), and Aly Teymour, UN protocol officer, look on.
NEAL BOENZI—THE NEW YORK TIMES

most of the proposals of the Group of 18. New procedures would give major contributors to the UN a larger voice in formulating its budgets by guaranteeing them places on the 21-nation Committee for Program and Coordination that would now consider biennial budget proposals a year before they went into effect and set limits on appropriations. The committee was enjoined to act unanimously or by consensus—in effect, giving each member a veto—although the Assembly could, in theory, modify the committee decisions. On December 22 U.S. Pres. Ronald Reagan told the secretary-general that he regarded the new procedures as "historic" and that he would ask Congress in 1987 to allow the U.S. to pay its full UN contribution.

In the same resolution, the Assembly asked member states to pay their 1987 assessments as soon as possible. Affirmative responses came immediately from Denmark, Finland, Iceland, Norway, and Sweden; the U.S.S.R. announced that it would advance $25 million of its 1987 contribution of $71.4 million in December.

Stalemates. In September the secretary-general said that the UN's "credibility problem" arose in large measure from the superpowers' failure to agree on how best to deal with situations threatening international peace. Presumably he referred to UN agenda items on which, over the years, little progress had been made.

Nicaragua. On June 27 the International Court of Justice (ICJ) decided (12–3) that, by equipping and supporting *contra* forces fighting the Nicaraguan government and by mining Nicaraguan harbours in 1984, the U.S. had "breached its obligation under customary international law not to intervene in the affairs of another State" and should pay reparations. On July 31 and October 21 the U.S. defeated draft Security Council resolutions urging it to comply with the ICJ judgment. On December 18 eight Latin-American governments announced in Rio de Janeiro, Arg., that Pérez de Cuéllar would join with the secretary-general of the Organization of American States to assist them in attempting to persuade Costa Rica, El Salvador, Guatemala, Honduras, and Nicaragua to revive negotiations aimed at peace in Central America.

South Africa. Still seeking to implement its 1966 resolutions terminating South African control over Namibia, the UN convened two week-long conferences: a World Conference on Sanctions against Racist South Africa (Paris, June

16, the tenth anniversary of the Soweto uprising, to June 20) and the International Conference for the Immediate Independence of Namibia (Vienna, July 7–11). The first called for worldwide comprehensive mandatory economic sanctions against South Africa; the second acclaimed a 37-point Program of Action for Recovery and Development for Africa. Both criticized the U.S. and the U.K. for preventing the Security Council from acting effectively to support the Namibians against South Africa. (On February 13 those two powers abstained on a resolution strongly condemning South Africa for threatening acts of aggression against neighbouring states; on May 23 and June 18 they opposed draft resolutions calling for "selective economic and other sanctions" against South Africa.

In related efforts, the Assembly held a special session (September 17–19) on Namibia. The secretary-general reminded delegates that South Africa had agreed to implement a new electoral system in the territory on Aug. 1, 1986, but only on a condition, already rejected by the Security Council, that Cuba withdraw its forces from Angola. The Special Assembly again called (126–0–24) for South Africa to withdraw from Namibia and for the Security Council to implement its 1978 plan for Namibian independence. The regular Assembly endorsed these positions on November 10 by approving eight resolutions condemning South Africa and the policies of states, like the U.S., involved in "constructive engagement" and "similar policies of appeasement."

Afghanistan. On November 5 the Assembly adopted (122–20–11) its eighth annual resolution calling for foreign (*i.e.,* Soviet) troops to withdraw from Afghanistan and reaffirming the right of the Afghan people to self-determination. The secretary-general's personal representative, Diego Cordovez, spent two weeks in Afghanistan, Pakistan, and Iran in March. He reported that four agreements to end the fighting were "virtually complete," but that the timing and detailed arrangements for withdrawing Soviet troops remained unsettled. Further UN-sponsored talks seemed to break down in August. On December 9, however, Pakistan, Afghanistan, and the U.S.S.R. agreed on ways of monitoring a future Soviet withdrawal, though they still remained divided on the timetable.

Two UN reports (one to the UN Commission on Human Rights, meeting in Geneva at the end of February and in early March, and another issued on November 12) condemned the U.S.S.R. for pursuing a campaign of "systematic brutality" against Afghan civilians." However, it also cited reports that government opponents had "tortured, beaten and starved" Soviet soldiers.

Iran-Iraq. On March 21 the Security Council expressed profound concern over the unanimous conclusion of specialists who had visited Iran (February 26–March 3) that Iraqi forces had frequently violated the Geneva Protocol of 1925 by using chemical weapons against Iranian forces. On October 8 the Council unanimously called on Iran and Iraq to implement previous resolutions (including one adopted unanimously on February 24) urging them to observe an immediate cease-fire, stop all hostilities, and recall their forces to within their own borders. On December 22 the Security Council reiterated its call for the parties to settle their differences peacefully.

Cyprus. Pursuing negotiations in progress since 1984, the secretary-general met separately on March 29 with Greek and Turkish Cypriot "interlocutors" in an effort to solve the problem created when Turkey invaded Cyprus in 1974. He gave them a draft agreement for establishing a united Cypriot government with two autonomous states.

Kampuchea. On October 21 the Assembly called for all foreign troops to withdraw from Kampuchea, which Vietnam had invaded in 1978.

Lebanon. On January 17 a U.S. negative vote prevented the Security Council from adopting a draft resolution strongly deploring "Israeli acts of violence as well as abusive practices and measures against the civilian population in southern Lebanon." The U.S. said that the draft failed to deal fairly with southern Lebanon's security problems, including rocket attacks launched against Israel from Lebanese soil.

In September the secretary-general asked "whether it is still justifiable to keep in being [the UN Interim Force in Lebanon, or UNIFIL] which costs the international community some $140 million per annum and, after eight-and-a-half years, is still prevented from carrying out the task it was originally given" because Israel would not withdraw completely from Lebanon, perceiving conditions there as a threat to its security. On the other hand, Lebanese leaders, Syria, and Israel all wanted the force to stay, and he could not recommend withdrawing it.

On October 13 he reported that attacks on UNIFIL had decreased, although 16 casualties suffered during the year brought to 131 the number of its soldiers killed since 1978. On April 18 and 23 he expressed his outrage over the killing of hostages in Lebanon, including Alec Collett, a British journalist kidnapped in Beirut in 1985 while on assignment for the UN Relief and Works Agency for Palestine Refugees in the Near East (UNRWA).

Libya. A U.S. veto on February 6 prevented the Council from condemning Israel for forcibly intercepting and diverting a Libyan civilian aircraft in international airspace (April 4). On April 21 France and the U.K. joined the U.S. to defeat another draft resolution condemning the U.S. air attack on Tripoli and Benghazi (April 14). The U.S. said it had moved against Libya's "harsh policy of international terrorism." On November 20 the Assembly condemned (79–28–33) the U.S. raid as a violation of international law and affirmed Libya's "right to receive appropriate compensation."

Atomic Safety. The nuclear accident at Chernobyl in the U.S.S.R. in late April led 50 states to adopt two new conventions on nuclear safety at a special session of the General Conference of the International Atomic Energy Agency in Vienna on September 26. (*See* ENERGY: *Sidebar.*) The conventions oblige them to notify others of nuclear accidents as soon as possible and to provide assistance to one another in case of emergency.

Economic and Social Matters. From May 27 to June 1 the General Assembly met in its first special session devoted to the economic problems of a single region of the world and adopted a five-year program of action for Africa's economic recovery and development.

The U.S. informed the World Health Organization (WHO) in September that it would withhold $35 million of its assessed quota of about $137 million for the total biennial WHO budget of $550 million. On November 20 WHO announced that it would give its campaign against AIDS (acquired immune deficiency syndrome)—a "health disaster of pandemic proportions"—the kind of backing it gave to eradicating smallpox. It hoped to raise $1.5 billion a year by the 1990s for the campaign.

Amadou Mahtar M'Bow, the controversial director general of the UN Educational, Scientific and Cultural Organization (Unesco), announced on October 6 that he would not seek a third term in 1987.

Famine. The Food and Agriculture Organization (FAO) reported on April 20 that, despite a general improvement in harvests in Africa, six nations (Ethiopia, The Sudan, Angola, Botswana, Mozambique, and Cape Verde) continued to face food emergencies because of drought or civil strife. The effects of civil war were clearly seen in The Sudan when, on February 28, rebels controlling the south refused a UN request to allow a convoy to enter and take food to 900,000 people facing starvation. All international aid programs in The Sudan were suspended after opposition groups shot down a civilian aircraft in mid-August. On October 10, however, the World Food Program, the UN Children's Fund, and a consortium of agencies and donor states succeeded in airlifting 120 tons of food and medical supplies to the starving city of Juba.

Former Secretaries-General. During the campaign of former secretary-general Kurt Waldheim (*see* BIOGRAPHIES) to become president of Austria, evidence arose connecting him with atrocities committed by the Germans in Yugoslavia during World War II. On April 21 Pérez de Cuéllar indicated, through a spokesman, that he had passed no judgment on the charges and would not do so. In December the UN office in Vienna invited Waldheim to be guest of honour at a ceremony, in January 1987, when the UN would issue a stamp honouring the first secretary-general, Trygve Lie (d. 1968). Lie's daughter, Guri L. Zeckendorf, called the invitation "absolutely disgraceful" and said that neither she nor her sister would attend. On December 5 a UN spokesman said "scheduling difficulties" would prevent Pérez de Cuéllar from attending.

On September 18 the secretary-general honoured Dag Hammarskjöld on the 25th anniversary of his death. Pérez de Cuéllar quoted as still relevant Hammarskjöld's observations that the UN was "a body where ideologies are permitted to clash inside the wider framework of a fundamental unity of purpose for peace," an organization "not created in order to bring us to heaven, but in order to save us from hell."

Genocide. On February 19 the U.S. Senate consented (83–11) to U.S. ratification of the UN Convention on the Prevention and Punishment of the Crime of Genocide. The convention was adopted by the General Assembly in December 1948 and now had over 90 adherents.

(RICHARD N. SWIFT)

This article updates the *Macropædia* article UNITED NATIONS.

COMMONWEALTH OF NATIONS

The year 1986 proved to be a stressful one for the Commonwealth of Nations as it struggled with the legacies of the Commonwealth heads of government meeting held in Nassau, The Bahamas, in October 1985. The accord produced at Nassau was concerned with increasing pressure on South Africa (a member of the Commonwealth until 1961) to dismantle its apartheid system. To this end, the Commonwealth-appointed Eminent Persons' Group—cochaired by Malcolm Fraser, former prime minister of Australia, and Gen. Olusegun Obasanjo, former Nigerian head of state—made preliminary visits to South Africa in February and full visits in March and May. Its report, published in June, recorded the view that "at present there is no genuine intention on the part of the South African government to dismantle apartheid."

At Nassau it had been agreed that additional measures should be considered if the Nassau package did not produce results "within a reasonable period." A Commonwealth heads of government review meeting, attended by Australia, The Bahamas, Canada, India, the U.K., Zambia, and Zimbabwe, was held in London on August 3–5. All the governments at this "minisummit," with the exception of the U.K., agreed to introduce new economic sanctions, including a ban on new bank loans and on imports of

Commonwealth leaders meet in London for talks on sanctions against South Africa. Attendees (left to right) include Prime Ministers Brian Mulroney of Canada (foreground), Rajiv Gandhi of India, Margaret Thatcher of Great Britain, and Bob Hawke of Australia.

AP/WIDE WORLD

uranium, coal, iron, and steel from South Africa. Taking a different view of the likely impact of economic sanctions, the U.K. introduced voluntary bans on new investment and tourism promotion and agreed to observe any bans approved by the European Communities.

The strength of feeling among Commonwealth countries over the U.K.'s opposition to sanctions was demonstrated by the boycott of the Commonwealth Games held at Edinburgh, Scotland, in July–August. Of 58 countries originally expected to contest the Games, 32 withdrew. During the "minisummit" there had been widespread concern that the Commonwealth might break up over the failure to agree on a common policy toward South Africa, but at a meeting of Commonwealth parliamentarians held in London in October, a more conciliatory tone prevailed. Commonwealth Secretary-General Shridath ("Sonny") Ramphal declared that the organization had survived a test of its credibility.

The year saw the development of proposals to encourage collective support for small and vulnerable territories belonging to the Commonwealth, including a proposal to establish a regional defense force in the Eastern Caribbean. Among Commonwealth members, 26 were small island states with fewer than one million people; ten were classified as least developed by the UN. The role of nongovernmental organizations, commended at the Nassau meeting, was expanded through liaison groups set up to further social and economic contact.

A number of Commonwealth members suffered unease or outbreaks of violence. In the British colony of the Turks and Caicos Islands, direct British rule was imposed in July, following allegations of corruption and drug dealing made against government members. There were marked increases in sectarian violence in India and in Sri Lanka.

In 1985 the Commonwealth Development Corporation (CDC) made new commitments totaling £106.4 million in 16 countries; this brought total investment to £907.7 million, nearly half of which was directed to Africa. In the same year, some £300 million was contributed by other bodies for cofinancing CDC projects. In its new commitments, the CDC emphasized agricultural schemes to rehabilitate land and assist small-scale farmers. The Commonwealth Fund for Technical Cooperation, which approved expenditure of £28.6 million in 1986–87, received a gift of £1 million from Brunei.

(MOLLY MORTIMER)

POLITICAL PARTIES

The following table is a general world guide to the political parties of the world. All countries that were independent on Dec. 31, 1986, are included; there are a number for which no analysis of political activities can be given; for example, states where only one party is legal. Parties are included in most instances only if represented in parliaments (in the lower house in bicameral legislatures); the figures in the last column indicate the number of seats obtained in the last general election (figures in parentheses are those of the penultimate one). The date of the most recent election follows the name of the country.

The code letters in the affiliation column show the relative political positions of the parties within each country; there is, therefore, no entry in this column for single-party states. There are obvious difficulties involved in labeling parties within the political spectrum of a given country. The key chosen is as follows: F-fascist; ER-extreme right; R-right; CR-centre right; C-centre; L-non-Marxist left; SD-social democratic; S-socialist; EL-extreme left; and K-Communist.

The percentages in the column "Voting strength" indicate proportions of the valid votes cast for the respective parties, or the number of registered voters who went to the polls in single-party states.

Political Parties

Country Name of party	Affiliation	Voting strength (%)	Parliamentary representation	
Afghanistan				
Pro-Soviet government since April 27, 1978	—	—	—	
Albania (November 1982)				
Albanian Labour (Communist)	—	99.9	250	(250)
Algeria (March 1982)				
National Liberation Front	—	99.9	281	(261)
Angola (August 1980)				
Movimento Popular de Libertaçao de Angola (MPLA)	—	—	203	
Antigua and Barbuda (April 1984)				
Antigua Labour Party	C	...	16	(13)
Progressive Labour Movement	L	...	0	(3)
Independents	—	...	1	(1)
Argentina (November 1985)				
Movimiento Justicialista Nacional (Peronist)	CR	34.5	103	(111)
Unión Cívica Radical	C	43.0	130	(129)
Others	—	22.5	21	(14)
Australia (December 1984)				
National	R	...	21	(17)
Liberal	C	...	45	(33)
Labor	L	...	82	(75)
Austria (November 1986)				
Freiheitliche Partei Österreichs	R	9.7	18	(12)
Österreichische Volkspartei	C	41.3	77	(81)
Sozialistische Partei Österreichs	SD	43.3	80	(90)
Vereinigte Grüne Österreich (Greens)	—	4.8	8	(0)
Bahamas, The (June 1982)				
Progressive Liberal Party	CR	53	32	(30)
Free National Movement	L	43	8	(2)
Others	—	...	3	...
Bahrain				
Emirate, no parties	—	—	—	
Bangladesh (May 1986)				
Jatiya Party	—	...	183	
Awami League Party	—	...	76	
Other parties	—	...	39	
Independents	—	...	32	
Barbados (May 1986)				
Democratic Labour Party	C	59.5	24	(7)
Barbados Labour Party	L	40.4	3	(17)
Belgium (October 1985)				
Vlaams Blok	ER	1.4	1	(1)
Volksunie	R	7.8	16	(20)
Front Démocratique des Francophones	R	1.2	3	(8)
Liberals { Flemish	CR	10.7	22	(28)
Liberals { French	CR	10.2	24	(24)
Social Christians { Flemish	C	21.3	49	(43)
Social Christians { French	C	7.9	20	(18)
Socialists { Flemish	SD	14.5	32	(26)
Socialists { French	SD	13.7	35	(35)
Others	—	6.2	10	(11)
Belize (December 1984)				
United Democratic Party	R	...	21	(5)
People's United Party	C	...	7	(13)
Benin (November 1979)				
People's Revolutionary Party	—	—	336	
Bhutan				
A monarchy without parties	—	—	—	
Bolivia (July 1985)				
Acción Democrática Nacionalista	R	37.0	52	
Movimiento Nacionalista Revolucionario	C	42.0	60	
Christian Democratic Party	C	2.0	3	
Movimiento de la Izquierda Revolucionaria	L	11.0	16	
Small left-wing parties	L	15.0	22	
Botswana (September 1984)				
Botswana Democratic Party	C	...	29	(29)
Botswana People's Party	L	...	1	(1)
Botswana National Front	EL	...	4	(2)
Brazil (November 1986)				
Partido do Movimento Democrático Brasileiro (coalition)	R & L	...	479	(200)
Partido Democrático Social	SD	...	0	—
Partido Comunista Brasileiro	K	...	0	—
37 other parties	—	...	8	(277)
Brunei				
Legislative Council	—	...	33	
Bulgaria (June 1986)				
Fatherland Front				
Bulgarian Communist Party }			276	
Bulgarian Agrarian People's Union }	—	99.9	400	(400)
(Bulgarian Agrarian People's Union)			99	
Independents }			25	
Burkina Faso				
National Revolutionary Council since August 1983	—	—	—	
Burma (October 1985)				
Burma Socialist Program Party	—	...	489	(475)
Burundi (October 1974)				
Tutsi ethnic minority government	—	—	—	
Cameroon (May 1983)				
Cameroonian National Union	—	99.3	120	(120)
Canada (September 1984)				
Progressive Conservative	CR	50.0	211	(103)
Liberal	C	28.0	40	(147)
New Democratic	L	19.0	30	(32)
Others	—	—	1	(0)
Cape Verde (December 1985)				
African Party for the Independence of Cape Verde and independents	—	94	83	(56)
Central African Republic				
Military Committee of National Recovery took power on Sept. 1, 1981	—	...	—	
Chad				
Military government since 1975	—	—	—	
Chile				
Military junta since Sept. 11, 1973	—	—	—	
China, People's Republic of (February 1978)				
Communist (Kungchantang) National People's Congress	—	...	3,500	
Colombia (March 1986)				
Partido Conservador	R	...	82	(84)
Partido Liberal	C	49	100	(114)
Nuevo Liberalismo	C	...	7	—
Unión Patriótica	EL	...	10	—
Comoros (March 1982)				
Federal Assembly	—	...	38	
Congo (July 1979)				
Parti Congolais du Travail	—	—	115	
Costa Rica (February 1986)				
Partido de Liberación Nacional	L	...	29	(33)
Partido Unidad Social Cristiana	CR	...	25	(18)
Others	—	...	3	(6)
Cuba (December 1986)				
Partido Comunista Cubano	—	...	...	(499)
Cyprus				
Greek Zone (December 1985)				
Democratic Rally	CR	33.56	19	(12)
Democratic Party (DIKO)	C	27.65	16	(8)
Socialist Party (EDEK)	SD	11.07	6	(3)
Communist Party (AKEL)	K	27.43	15	(12)
Turkish Zone (June 1985)				
National Turkish Party	—	...	24	
Communal Liberation Party	—	...	10	
Turkish Republican Party	—	...	12	
New Dawn Party (Renaissance)	—	...	4	
Czechoslovakia (May 1986)				
National Front	—	99.4	200	(200)
Denmark (January 1984)				
Conservative	R	23.4	42	(26)
Liberal Democratic (Venstre)	CR	12.1	22	(21)
Christian People's	CR	2.7	5	(4)
Progress	C	3.6	6	(16)
Radical Liberal (Radikale Venstre)	C	5.5	10	(9)
Centre Democrats	C	4.6	8	(15)
Social Democrats	SD	31.6	56	(59)
Socialist People's	EL	11.5	21	(20)
Left Socialists	EL	2.7	5	(5)
Faeroe Islands and Greenland	—	—	4	(4)
Djibouti (May 1982)				
One-party state: National Assembly	—	...	65	
Dominica (July 1985)				
Freedom Party	C	59.0	15	(17)
Labour Party	L	...	5	(2)
Independents	—	...	1	(2)
Dominican Republic (May 1986)				
Partido Reformista Social Cristiano	R	...	56	
Partido Revolucionario Dominicano	L	...	48	
Partido de la Liberación Dominicana	EL	...	16	
Ecuador (June 1986)				
Frente de Reconstrucción Nacional				
Partido Social Cristiano }				15
Partido Conservador }				1
Partido Liberal Radical }				3
Concentración de Fuerzas Populares }	R & CR	35.3	27	4
Frente Radical Alfarista }				3
Others }				1
Frente Progresista Democrática				
Izquierda Democrática }				17
Democracia Popular }				8
Partido Socialista Ecuatoriano }				6
Movimiento Popular Democrático }	L & EL	55.5	43	4
Frente Amplio de Izquierda }				3
Partido Roldosista Ecuatoriano }				5
Others	—	—		1
Egypt (May 1984)				
New Wafd Party	R	15.12	57	
National Democratic Party	CR	72.99	391	
Socialist Labour Party	L	7.07	0	
National Progressive Unionist Party	L	4.17	0	
El Salvador (March 1985)				
Alianza Republicana Nacionalista	R	29	13	(19)
Partido Auténtico Institucional Salvadoreño	R	...	1	(0)
Partido de Conciliación Nacional	CR	8	12	(13)
Partido Acción Democrática	CR	...	1	(18)
Partido Cristiano Democrático	C	54	33	(40)
Equatorial Guinea (August 1983)				
National Assembly	—	...	41	
Ethiopia				
Military government since 1974	—	—	—	
Fiji (July 1982)				
Alliance Party (mainly Fijian)	—	...	28	(36)
National Federation (mainly Indian)	—	...	22	(15)
Others	—	...	2	(1)
Finland (March 1983)				
National Coalition Party (Conservative)	R	22.1	44	(47)
Swedish People's	R	4.6	11	(10)
Centre (including former Liberal) Party	C	17.6	38	(40)

Political Parties

Country / Name of party	Affiliation	Voting strength (%)	Parliamentary representation	
Christian League	C	3.0	3	(9)
Rural Party	C	9.7	17	(7)
Social Democratic	SD	26.7	57	(52)
People's Democratic League (Communist)	K	14.0	27	(35)
Green Party	—	1.5	2	—
Others	—	...	1	(0)
France (March 1986)				
Front National	F	9.7	35	(0)
Rassemblement pour la République	R	40.98	277: 147	(83)
Union pour la Démocratie Française	R		130	(64)
Diverse right	—	...	14	(11)
Parti Socialiste	SD	31.0	207	(269)
Diverse left	—	...	9	(20)
Parti Communiste	K	9.8	35	(44)
Gabon (February–March 1985)				
Parti Démocratique Gabonais	—	95.44	111	(84)
Gambia, The (April 1982)				
People's Progressive Party	C	61.7	27	(28)
Three other parties	—	...	8	(7)
German Democratic Republic (June 1986)				
National Front (Sozialistische Einheitspartei and others)	—	99.7	500	(500)
Germany, Federal Republic of (March 1983)				
Christlich-Demokratische Union	R	38.2	191	(174)
Christlich-Soziale Union		10.6	53	(52)
Freie Demokratische Partei	C	6.9	34	(53)
Sozialdemokratische Partei Deutschlands	SD	38.2	193	(218)
The Green (Ecology) Party	—	5.6	27	(0)
Ghana				
Military dictatorship since Dec. 31, 1981	—	—	—	
Greece (June 1985)				
New Democracy Party	CR	40.8	126	(115)
Panhellenic Socialist Movement (Pasok)	SD	45.8	161	(172)
Greek Communist Party (KKE)	K	9.4	12	(13)
Eurocommunists	K	1.4	1	(0)
Grenada (December 1984)				
New National Party	C	...	14	
Grenada United Labour Party	R	...	1	
Guatemala (November 1985)				
Movimiento de Liberación Nacional	ER	...	...	
Partido Democrático de Cooperación Nacional	CR	...	...	
Unión de Centro Nacional	C	...	...	
Democrácia Cristiana	C	...	...	
Partido Socialista Democrático	SD	...	...	
Guinea				
Military Committee for National Redress in power since April 1984	—	—	—	
Guinea-Bissau				
Governed by the Council of the Revolution since Nov. 14, 1980	—	—	—	
Guyana (December 1985)				
People's National Congress	R	77.0	42	(41)
People's Progressive Party	L	11.0	8	(10)
Others	...	0.5	3	(0)
Haiti				
Civilian-military council in power since February 1986	—	—	—	
Honduras (November 1985)				
Partido Nacional	R	...	63	(34)
Partido Liberal	CR	...	66	(44)
Others	C	...	3	(4)
Hungary (June 1985)				
Patriotic People's Front	—	...	361	
Independents	—	...	25	
Iceland				
Independence (Conservative)	R	38.7	23	(21)
Progressive (Farmers' Party)	C	19.0	14	(17)
Social Democratic	SD	11.7	6	(10)
Social Democratic Alliance	EL	7.3	4	—
People's Alliance	K	17.3	10	(11)
Feminists	—	5.5	3	—
India (December 1984; figures incomplete)				
Congress (I)	C	...	395	(351)
Communist Party of India (Marxist)	K	...	22	(35)
Communist Party (pro-Soviet)	K	...	6	(10)
Other opposition parties and independents	—	...	121	
Indonesia (May 1982)				
Golkar (Functional Groups)	—	64.3	342	
United Development Party	—	27.8	94	
Indonesian Democratic Party (merger of five nationalist and Christian parties)	—	7.9	24	
Iran (May 1984)				
Islamic Republican Party	R	...	251	
Iraq				
Military and Ba'th Party governments since 1958	—	...	...	
Ireland (November 1982)				
Fianna Fail (Sons of Destiny)	C	...	75	(81)
Fine Gael (United Ireland)	C	...	70	(63)
Irish Labour Party	L	...	16	(15)
Others	—	...	5	(7)
Israel (July 1984)				
Tehiya	ER	4.0	5	(3)
Kach	ER	1.2	1	—
Likud { Herut, Liberal }	R	31.9	41	(48)
National Religious	CR	3.5	4	(6)
Agudat Israel	C	1.7	2	(4)
Yahad	C	2.2	3	—
Ometz	C	1.2	1	—
Labour Alignment { Labour, Mapam }	SD	34.9	44	(47)
Civil Rights	SD	2.4	3	(1)
Shinui	SD	2.6	3	(2)
Progressive List for Peace	EL	1.8	2	—
Hadash	K	3.4	4	(4)
Others	—	—	7	(5)
Italy (June 1983)				
Movimento Sociale Italiano	F	6.8	42	(30)
Partito Liberale Italiano	CR	2.9	16	(9)
Democrazia Cristiana	C	32.9	225	(262)
Partito Repubblicano Italiano	C	5.1	29	(16)
Partito Social-Democratico Italiano	L	4.1	23	(20)
Partito Socialista Italiano	SD	11.4	73	(62)
Partito Radicale	EL	2.2	11	(18)
Partito Comunista Italiano	K	29.2	198	(201)
Südtiroler Volkspartei	—	0.5	3	(4)
Others	—	4.2	10	(8)
Ivory Coast (October 1980)				
Parti Démocratique de la Côte d'Ivoire	—	99.9	100	
Jamaica (December 1983)				
Jamaica Labour Party	L	...	60	(51)
People's National Party	SD	(Boycotted)		(9)
Japan (July 1986)				
Liberal-Democratic Party	R	49.6	300	(250)
Komeito (Clean Government)	C	...	57	(58)
Democratic Socialist Party	SD	...	28	(38)
Japan Socialist Party	S	...	87	(112)
Japanese Communist Party	K	...	27	(26)
Others	—	...	13	(27)
Jordan				
Royal government, no parties	—	—	60	
Kampuchea (May 1981)				
Kampuchean United Front for National Salvation (Vietnamese-backed)	—	99.0	117	
Kenya (September 1983)				
Kenya African National Union	—	48.0	158	
Kiribati (January 1983)				
House of Assembly, no formal parties	—	...	35	
Korea, North (November 1986)				
Korean Workers' (Communist) Party	—	...	...	
Korea, South (February 1985)				
Korea National Party	CR	9.2	20	(25)
Democratic Justice Party	C	35.3	148	(151)
New Korea Democratic Party	L	28.6	67	—
Democratic Korea Party	L	17.6	35	(81)
Independents and others	—	...	6	(19)
Kuwait (February 1985)				
Princely government with elected National Assembly, no parties	—	—	50	(30)
Laos, People's Democratic Republic of				
Lao People's Revolutionary Party	—	...	...	
Lebanon (April 1972)				
Maronites (Roman Catholics)	—	...	30	
Sunni Muslims	—	...	20	
Shi'ah Muslims	—	...	19	
Greek Orthodox	—	...	11	
Druzes (Muslim sect)	—	...	6	
Melchites (Greek Catholics)	—	...	6	
Armenian Orthodox	—	...	4	
Other Christian	—	...	2	
Armenian Catholics	—	...	1	
Lesotho				
Constitution suspended Jan. 30, 1970	—	—	—	
Liberia (October 1985)				
National Democratic Party of Liberia	R	...	45	
Opposition	L	...	19	
Libya				
Military government since Sept. 1, 1969	—	—	—	
Liechtenstein (February 1986)				
Vaterländische Union	CR	50.2	8	(8)
Fortschrittliche Bürgerpartei	C	42.7	7	(7)
Luxembourg (June 1984)				
Parti Chrétien Social	CR	...	25	(24)
Parti Libéral	C	...	14	(15)
Parti Ouvrier Socialiste	SD	...	21	(14)
Parti Communiste	K	...	2	(2)
Ecologists	—	...	2	(0)
Madagascar (August 1983)				
Advance Guard of the Malagasy Revolution (Arema)	C	64.8	117	(112)
Madagascar Independence Congress	L	8.8	9	(16)
Movement for Proletarian Power	L	11.1	3	—
People's Party for National Unity	L	10.6	6	(7)
Madagascar National Independence Movement (Monima)	L	3.7	2	—
Malawi (June 1983)				
Malawi Congress Party	—	...	101	(87)
Malaysia (August 1986)				
National Front (Barisan Nasional) Coalition				
United Malays National Organization		57.4	83	148 (133)
Malaysian Chinese Association			17	
Malaysian Indian Congress			6	
Malaysian People's Movement			5	
Sabah and Sarawak parties			37	
Opposition Parties				
Democratic Action Party		15.6	24	29 (21)
Pan-Malaysian Islamic Party		...	1	
Independents		...	4	
Maldives (February 1975)				
Presidential rule since 1975	—	—	—	
Mali (June 1985)				
Union Démocratique du Peuple Malien	—	...	82	
Malta (December 1981)				
Nationalist Party	R	...	31	(31)
Labour Party	SD	...	34	(34)
Mauritania				
Military government since April 25, 1981	—	—	—	
Mauritius (August 1983)				
Independence (Labour) Party	C	...	41	(2)
Parti Mauricien Social-Démocrate				(2)
Mouvement Socialiste Mauricien				—
Mouvement Militant Mauricien	L	...	19	(42)
Parti Socialiste Mauricien	—	—	—	(18)
Organisation du Peuple Rodriguais	—	...	2	(2)
Mexico (July 1985)				
Partido Revolucionario Institucional	CR	64.8	289	(299)
Partido Acción Nacional	CR	16.2	41	(101)
Partido Auténtico de la Revolución	CR	3.1	9	
Others	—	...	61	
Monaco (January 1978)				
Union Nationale et Démocratique	—	...	18	(17)
Mongolia (June 1986)				
Mongolian People's Revolutionary Party	—	99.9	370	(354)
Morocco (September 1984)				
Union Constitutionelle	CR	...	83	—
Rassemblement National des Indépendants	CR	...	61	(141)
Mouvement Populaire	CR	...	47	(44)
Istiqlal (Independence)	C	...	41	(49)
Union Socialiste des Forces Populaires	L	...	36	(16)
Others	—	...	38	(14)
Mozambique (November–December 1986)				
Frente da Libertação de Moçambique (Frelimo)	—	...	250	(210)
Nauru (December 1983)				
Independents	—	—	18	
Nepal (May 1986)				
140-member Parliament, 122 elected and 28 appointed by the king; no parties	—	—	—	
Netherlands, The (May 1986)				
Christen Democratisch Appèl	CR	34.6	54	(45)
Volkspartij voor Vrijheid en Democratie	C	17.4	27	(36)
Democraten 1966	C	6.1	9	(6)
Partij van de Arbeid	SD	33.3	52	(47)
Others	—	...	8	(16)
New Zealand (July 1984)				
New Zealand Party	CR	12.0	0	—
National (Conservative)	CR	36.0	37	(47)
Social Credit	C	8.0	2	(2)
Labour Party	L	43.0	56	(43)
Nicaragua (November 1984)				
Democratic Conservative Party	CR	14.0	14	
Independent Liberal Party	C	9.6	9	
Popular Social Christian Party	L	5.6	6	
Sandinista National Liberation Front	L	66.8	61	
Socialist Party of Nicaragua	EL	1.4	2	
Communist Party of Nicaragua	K	1.5	2	
Marxist-Leninist Popular Action Movement	K	1.0	2	

Political Parties

Country / Name of party	Affiliation	Voting strength (%)	Parliamentary representation	
Niger				
Military government since April 1974	—	—	—	
Nigeria				
Military government since December 1983	—	—	—	
Norway (September 1985)				
Høyre (Conservative)	R	30.1	50	(53)
Kristelig Folkeparti	CR	8.3	16	(15)
Senterpartiet (Agrarian)	C	6.7	12	(11)
Venstre (Liberal)	C	3.1	0	(2)
Progress Party	C	3.7	2	(4)
Arbeiderpartiet (Labour)	SD	41.2	71	(66)
Sosialistisk Venstreparti (Socialist Left)	S	5.4	6	(4)
Oman				
Independent sultanate, no parties	—	—	—	
Pakistan (February 1985)				
National Assembly (no parties)	—	...	237	
Panama				
Since July 1982 a civilian president under "indirect" military supervision	—	—	—	
Papua New Guinea (June 1982)				
Pangu Party	—	34.0	50	(39)
United Party	—	7.2	9	(38)
People's Progress Party	—	10.0	14	(18)
National Party	—	10.0	13	(3)
Independents	—	20.9	4	
Paraguay (February 1983)				
Partido Colorado (A. Stroessner)	R	90.0	40	
Opposition parties	—	10.0	20	
Peru (April 1985)				
Convergencia Democrática	R	...	12	
Acción Popular	CR	...	10	
Alianza Popular Revolucionaria Americana	SD	...	107	
Izquierda Unida	L	...	48	
Izquierda Nacionalista	L	...	1	
Independents	—	...	2	
Philippines				
Martial law lifted Jan. 17, 1981	—	—	—	
Poland (October 1985)				
Front of National Unity				
Polish United Workers' Party			245	(261)
United Peasants' party			106	(113)
Democratic Party	—	78.86	35	(37)
Non-party			74	(49)
Portugal (October 1985)				
Democratic and Social Centre	R	15.0	22	(30)
Democratic Renewal Party	CR	21.0	45	—
Social Democratic Party	C	29.0	88	(75)
Socialist Party	SD	20.0	57	(101)
United People's Alliance	K	15.0	38	(44)
Qatar				
Independent emirate, no parties	—	—	—	
Romania (March 1985)				
Social Democracy and Unity Front	—	99.99	389	(369)
Rwanda (December 1983)				
National Revolutionary Development Movement	—	...	70	
Saint Christopher and Nevis (June 1984)				
People's Action Movement	CR	...	6	(3)
Nevis Reformation Party	CR	...	3	(2)
Labour Party	L	...	2	(4)
Saint Lucia (May 1982)				
United Workers' Party	C	...	14	(5)
St. Lucia Labour Party	S	...	2	(12)
Progressive Labour Party	EL	...	1	(0)
Saint Vincent and the Grenadines (July 1984)				
St. Vincent Labour Party	CR	41.4	4	(11)
New Democratic Party	C	51.4	9	(2)
United People's Movement	L	3.2	0	(0)
San Marino (May 1983)				
Communist coalition				
Partito Comunista		...	15	(16)
Partito Social Democratico			9	(9)
Partito Socialista Unitario			8	(8)
Christian Democrats		...	26	(26)
São Tomé and Príncipe (1975)				
Movimento Libertaçao	—	—	—	
Saudi Arabia				
Royal government, no parties	—	—	—	
Senegal (February 1983)				
Parti Socialiste	CR	79.9	111	(83)
Parti Démocratique Sénégalais	L	14.0	8	(17)
Rassemblement National Démocratique	EL	2.6	1	—
Ligue Démocratique	K	1.1	0	—
Seychelles (August 1983)				
People's Progressive Front	—	59.3	23	
Sierra Leone (May–June 1986)				
All People's Congress and independents	—	...	105	(85)
Singapore (December 1984)				
People's Action Party	CR	64.38	77	(75)
Workers' Party	L	12.79	1	(0)
Democratic Party	—	3.70	1	(0)
Solomon Islands (October 1984)				
National Democratic Party	L	...	1	
United Party	—	...	13	
People's Alliance Party	—	...	12	
Solomone Ano Sagufenua	—	...	4	
Independents	—	...	7	
Somalia (December 1984)				
Somalian Revolutionary Socialist Party	—	99.86	171	(171)
South Africa (April 1981)				
Herstigte Nasionale Partij	ER	13.8	0	(0)
National Conservative Party	R	...	0	—
National Party	R	56.1	131	(134)
South Africa Party	CR	—	—	(3)
New Republic Party	C	7.7	8	(10)
Progressive Federal Party	L	19.1	26	(17)
Spain (June 1986)				
Alianza Popular	R	26	105	(105)
Centro Democrático y Social	C	9	19	(11)
Convergència (Catalan nationalists)	C	4	18	(12)
Partido Socialista Obrero Español	SD	44.1	184	(202)
Izquierda Unida (Communists)	K	4	7	—
Partido Nacionalista Vasco	—	1.5	6	(8)
Herri Batasuna (Basque radicals)	—	1.1	5	(2)
Others	—	...	6	(10)
Sri Lanka (July 1977)				
United National Party	R	...	140	(19)
Freedom Party	C	...	8	(91)
Tamil United Liberation Front	C	...	18	(12)
Communists and others	—	...	2	(44)
Sudan, The (April 1986)				
National Islamic Front	R	...	51	
National Umma Party	C	...	99	
Democratic Unionist Party	L	...	63	
South Sudan Political Alliance	—	...	9	
39 other parties	—	...	42	
Suriname				
National Military Council since 1980	—	—	—	
Swaziland				
Royal government, no parties	—	—	—	
Sweden (September 1985)				
Conservative	R	21.4	76	(86)
Centre	CR	12.5	44	(56)
Liberal	C	14.3	51	(21)
Social Democrats	SD	44.9	159	(166)
Communists	K	5.4	19	(20)
Switzerland (October 1983)				
Christian Democrats (Conservative)	R	...	42	(44)
Republican Movement	R	...	0	(1)
National Campaign	R	...	5	(2)
Evangelical People's	R	...	3	(3)
Swiss People's (ex-Middle Class)	CR	...	23	(23)
Radical Democrats	C	...	54	(51)
League of Independents	C	...	8	(8)
Liberal Democrats	L	...	8	(8)
Social Democrats	SD	...	47	(51)
Progressive Organization (Socialists)	EL	...	3	(3)
Communist Party	K	...	1	(3)
Environmentalist Party	—	...	3	—
Others	—	...	3	(3)
Syria (February 1986)				
Ba'th Party	—	...	129	
National Progressive Front	—	...	57	
Communist Party	—	...	9	
Taiwan (Republic of China)				
Nationalist (Kuomintang)	—	...	773	
Tanzania (October 1985)				
Chama Cha Mapinduzi	—	...	111	
Thailand (July 1986)				
Prachakorn Thai	ER	...	24	(36)
Chart Thai Nation	R	...	63	(73)
Democratic Party	C	...	100	(56)
Social Action Party	C	...	51	(92)
United Democratic Party	C	...	38	—
United Thai Party	—	...	19	(0)
Others	—	...	52	(67)
Togo (March 1985)				
Rassemblement du Peuple Togolais	—	96.0	77	(67)
Tonga (May 1981)				
Legislative Assembly (partially elected)	—	—	21	
Trinidad and Tobago (December 1986)				
People's National Movement	C	32	3	(26)
National Alliance for Reconstruction (four parties)	—	66	33	—
Tunisia (November 1986)				
National Front (led by the Parti Socialiste Destourien)	—	...	138	(136)
Turkey (November 1983)				
Nationalist Democracy Party	R	23.0	71	
Motherland Party	CR	45.0	212	
Populist Party	C	30.0	117	
Tuvalu (September 1985)				
House of Assembly, no political parties	—	—	12	
Uganda				
Military Council in power since July 1985	—	—	—	
Union of Soviet Socialist Republics (November 1984)				
Communist Party of the Soviet Union	—	99.99	1,500	(1,500)
United Arab Emirates				
Federal government of seven emirates	—	—	—	
United Kingdom (June 1983)				
Conservative	R	42.4	397	(339)
Alliance				
Liberal	C	25.4	17	(11)
Social Democratic	C		6	—
Labour	L	27.6	209	(268)
Communist	K	...	0	(0)
Scottish National Party	—	1.1	2	(2)
Plaid Cymru (Welsh Nationalists)	—	0.4	2	(2)
Ulster Unionists (three groups)	—	...	15	(10)
Social Democratic and Labour Party	—	...	1	(1)
Sinn Fein (Northern Ireland)	—	...	1	—
United States (November 1986)				
Republican	CR	...	177	(183)
Democratic	C	...	258	(252)
Uruguay (November 1984)				
Colorado Party (Conservative)	R	38.6	40	
Unión Civica	CR	2.3	2	
National (Blanco) Party	C	32.9	36	
Frento Amplio (Broad Front)	L	20.4		
Vanuatu (November 1983)				
Vanuaaku Pati	C	...	24	(26)
Others	—	...	15	(13)
Venezuela (December 1983)				
COPEI (Social Christians)	CR	28.31	...	(88)
Acción Democrática	L	44.25	118	(88)
Movimiento al Socialismo	SD	...	...	(11)
Partido Comunista Venezolano	K	...	...	(7)
Others	—	...	...	(7)
Vietnam, Socialist Republic of (April 1981)				
Communist Party	—	...	...	
Yemen, People's Democratic Republic of (October 1986)				
Yemen Socialist Party and independents	—	...	111	
Yemen Arab Republic				
Military government since 1974	—	—	—	
Yugoslavia (May 1986)				
Communist-controlled Federal Chamber	K	...	220	(220)
Zaire (October 1977)				
Legislative Council of the Mouvement Populaire de la Révolution	—	...	268	
Zambia (October 1983)				
United National Independence Party		67.0	125	
Zimbabwe (June–July 1985)				
Zimbabwe African National Union	—	77.0	63	(57)
Zimbabwe African People's Union	—	20.0	15	(20)
United African National Council	—	...	0	(3)
Zimbabwe African National Union (Sithole)	—	...	1	(0)
white roll				
Conservative Alliance of Zimbabwe	—	...	15	(20)
Independent Zimbabwe	—	...	4	—
Independent	—	...	1	(0)

(K. M. SMOGORZEWSKI)

Africa South of the Sahara

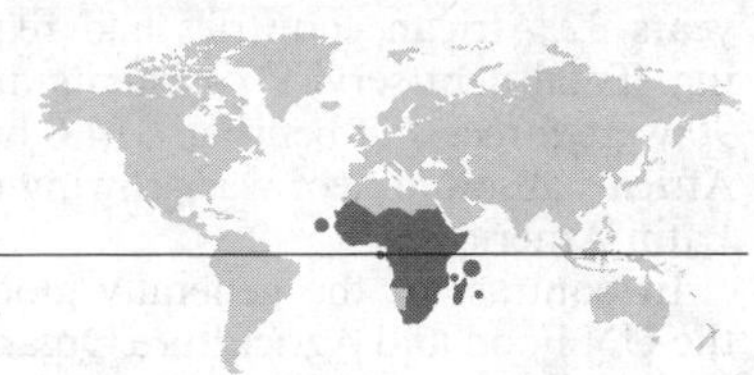

AFRICAN AFFAIRS

Having barely recovered from the most disastrous drought in its history, the African continent was afflicted by two new disasters in 1986—a plague of locusts, which did considerable damage to crops, and the spread of AIDS (acquired immune deficiency syndrome), now occurring in at least 20 countries. Health experts predicted that at least one million Africans would die from AIDS unless effective countermeasures were taken. The countries most affected were Zaire, Rwanda, and Uganda. (*See* HEALTH AND DISEASE.)

Organization of African Unity. The annual summit meeting of the Organization of African Unity (OAU), which met in Addis Ababa, Eth., in July, was devoted almost entirely to discussing the African Economic Recovery Plan prepared by a special committee of the OAU. The 200-page master plan gave top priority to developing and restructuring agriculture, and its main emphasis was on producing enough food to meet the continent's needs. The projected cost of the five-year plan was set at $128 billion, more than two-thirds of which was to be provided by African governments. OAU members affirmed their commitment to mobilizing all their resources for development purposes and undertaking, individually and collectively, all measures and policy reforms necessary for the recovery of African economies.

The summit meeting resolved to call for an extraordinary session of the UN General Assembly to discuss the recovery plan and to seek international support for it. While the General Assembly meeting in May unanimously endorsed the plan, major aid donors refused to commit themselves to specific financial contributions.

The other major topic at the summit meeting was the rapidly deteriorating security situation in southern Africa. Among the decisions made were support for the demand for comprehensive mandatory sanctions against South Africa and increased support for the guerrilla liberation movements of South Africa and South West Africa/Namibia.

Pres. Denis Sassou-Nguesso of Congo was elected as the 1986–87 chairman of the OAU, and Ide Oumarou, Niger's foreign minister, was appointed secretary-general. The OAU continued to suffer from a serious lack of funds because its members failed to pay their dues. Morocco, which in 1984 had become the first member to resign from the OAU, remained outside the organization, but Zaire, which had suspended its membership in sympathy with Morocco, returned.

Following its ratification by a majority of OAU members, the African Human Rights Charter came into force on October 21, more than five years after the decision to establish it was first made by the OAU. A special court of eminent jurists and others was to be set up to consider complaints of violations of human rights.

Southern Africa. The conflicts in southern Africa became so menacing in 1986 that they were near the top of the agenda of international concerns. The heightened concern was due to three main developments: increasingly violent conflicts within South Africa; transborder military attacks by the South African Army that threatened the security and economies of a number of neighbouring nations; and the escalation of arms supplies by the Soviet bloc to Angola. The Nkomati accord of 1984 between Mozambique and South Africa failed to live up to its promise and was rapidly eroded, while the Lusaka agreement between Angola and South Africa, also signed in 1984, failed to end the insurgency by South West Africa People's Organization (SWAPO) forces in Namibia and South Africa's attacks on Angola. No progress was made in implementing UN Resolution 435, which had established conditions for achieving Namibia's independence. The last remaining obstacle was the issue of linking the withdrawal of Cuban troops from Angola to the question of Namibian independence.

The death of Mozambican Pres. Samora Machel (*see* OBITUARIES) in an air crash on South African territory on October 19 dramatically heightened the sense of crisis. Even before Machel's death the Mozambican government was under such serious threat from the rebel Mozambique National Resistance (MNR) that the African frontline states (Angola, Botswana, Tanzania, Zambia, and Zimbabwe, in addition to Mozambique) considered plans to raise a pan-African army, with possible external support.

Frontline leaders accused Malawi of allowing the MNR to operate from its territory and Zaire of allowing U.S. arms destined for the rebel National Union for the Total Independence of Angola (UNITA) forces to pass through the country. Both governments denied the charges.

Coups and Inter-African Affairs. In January the government of Chief Leabua Jonathan in Lesotho was overthrown in a military coup. During the same month, Yoweri Museveni (*see* BIOGRAPHIES) proclaimed himself president of Uganda after his National Resistance Army captured the capital. These were the only two successful coups during the year, but in September there were two serious coup attempts, in Seychelles and Togo.

Following the military conflict between Burkina Faso and Mali over a disputed border area in late 1985, the International Court of Justice ordered the two countries to withdraw their troops in January 1986. In December the court ruled that the area should be divided equally between the two countries.

No significant new developments occurred in the conflict between Morocco and the Saharan Arab Democratic Republic (SADR) over the status of the former Spanish territory of Western Sahara. The Moroccan Army continued to maintain its military control over the territory despite OAU recognition of the SADR. Algeria remained closely involved in the conflict on the side of the SADR.

In the long-running civil war in Chad, the rebel forces led by Goukouni Oueddei began to disintegrate, and Goukouni's Libyan backers withdrew their support in favour of one of his rivals. Libya maintained its military presence in the north of Chad and pressed its claim to sovereignty over the Aozou Strip on the border.

Horn of Africa. The presidents of Ethiopia, Somalia, Djibouti, and The Sudan met together for the first time in April and agreed on a policy of détente. However, the spillover of the internal conflicts in Ethiopia and The Sudan prevented progress. The Eritreans, the Tigreans, and other resistance movements opposed to the Ethiopian regime all enjoyed limited facilities on Sudanese territory, while the rebel Sudan People's Liberation Army operated freely from bases inside Ethiopia. Several initiatives were taken by the new civilian government in Khartoum to reach a new understanding with the Ethiopians, whereby both sides would cease supporting each other's rebel movements. By the year's end there was no sign of either government's making progress toward suppressing its internal rebellions.

Political Systems. The Sudanese military regime kept its promise to hand back power to an elected civilian government in April, one year after the overthrow of Gen. Gaafar Nimeiry. No fewer than 20 political parties contested seats for a new constituent assembly, although security conditions prevented elections in a number of constituencies in the south.

In Zimbabwe progress was made toward establishing a single-party state through a tentative agreement on the merger of the ruling Zimbabwe African National Union-Patriotic Front and the opposition Zimbabwe African People's Union. Representatives of the white community had not yet agreed to support the idea.

External Relations. With the exception of South Africa, all African governments were represented at the eighth summit conference of the Nonaligned Movement held in Harare, Zimbabwe, in September, thereby affirming their commitment to the aspirations of the movement whether or not they always adhered strictly to its principles in practice. The 15 African members of the Commonwealth took the lead in committing that organization to support sanctions against South Africa, notwithstanding the adamant stand taken by U.K. Prime Minister Margaret Thatcher against such a policy. Her attitude strained relations within the Commonwealth and with many African governments. Relations with the U.S. were strained over a number of issues: the U.S. bombing of Libya was condemned by the OAU, and the administration's policy of "constructive engagement" toward South Africa and its opposition to sanctions were strongly criticized, as was its decision to provide direct military aid to UNITA. However, African hostility was diminished when the U.S. Congress overrode Pres. Ronald Reagan's veto of its proposed sanctions program.

A new initiative by the OAU to improve Afro-Arab cooperation made some progress but failed to establish the harmonious relationship envisaged by the decisions made at the first Afro-Arab summit in 1977. The OAU boycott of Israel, declared in 1973, was eroded further by the decisions of Côte d'Ivoire, Cameroon, and Liberia to follow the earlier example of Zaire in reestablishing diplomatic ties. Iran embarked on a diplomatic campaign to win African support for its war against Iraq and for its declared policy of exporting the Iranian revolution to the continent. The Soviet-bloc countries continued their policy of providing aid, mainly military, to African nations, in particular Libya, Angola, and Ethiopia. While many African countries welcomed offers of Soviet military aid, especially to liberation movements such as the African National Congress (ANC) in South Africa and SWAPO, the leaders of others, including Zambia, voiced dissatisfaction over the inadequacy of Soviet economic aid. Cuba increased the number of its combat troops in Angola to an estimated 40,000. China continued to maintain a low profile, focusing mainly on small-scale economic aid projects.

Social and Economic Conditions. Although the long years of drought finally broke over most of the continent in 1986, famine conditions persisted in the Sahel region and in such countries as Ethiopia, The Sudan, Mozambique, and Botswana. Overall, the economic outlook continued to be gloomy for reasons pinpointed by the UN Economic Commission for Africa; these included a vicious interaction between poverty and very low productivity levels in an environment marked by serious deficiencies in basic economic and social infrastructures, persistent poor performances of the agricultural sector, heavy dependence for domestic production on imports, and failure to diversify. Gross domestic product continued to grow at an average of 1%, slower than the 3% growth in population.

External debt reached $175 billion by 1986, having increased sevenfold since 1974. During the previous three years 32 African countries had requested debt rescheduling. Total debt service payments due in the period 1986–90 were forecast at between $14.6 billion and $24.5 billion. Africa's absolute debt was growing even faster than that of Latin America.

In contrast to the generally gloomy economic picture, the UN Food and Agriculture Organization (FAO) declared in a document on *African Agriculture—The Next 25 Years* that, given radical reforms in agricultural and economic policies, many countries could increase food production significantly. In 1986 Zimbabwe produced a bumper corn (maize) crop that enabled it to sell its surplus to other African countries and even to South Africa; The Sudan produced enough grain to feed its people and to keep a year's supply in reserve.

Population growth continued to be a major concern. The continent's average growth rate was 3%, compared with the world average of 1.8%. The World Bank predicted that unless the trend was reversed quickly the continent's population could soar from 460 million in 1985 to 1,800,000,000 by 2050.

The continent also held the unenviable record of having more refugees than any other part of the world. Latest estimates put the refugee population at over two million, with the largest numbers in The Sudan and Somalia (about 700,000 each), Zaire (300,000), Tanzania (160,000), Zambia and Angola (about 100,000 each), and Burundi and Zimbabwe (about 60,000 each). The majority of refugees came from Ethiopia, Uganda, Burundi, and Rwanda.

(COLIN LEGUM)

See also *Dependent States,* below.

ANGOLA

A people's republic, Angola is located on the Atlantic coast in southwestern Africa. The small exclave of Cabinda is separated from Angola by a strip of Zaire. Area: 1,246,700 sq km (481,350 sq mi). Pop. (1986 est.): 8,823,000. Cap.: Luanda. Monetary unit: kwanza, with (Oct. 1, 1986) a free rate of 29.92 kwanzas to U.S. $1 (43.23 kwanzas = £1 sterling). President in 1986, José Eduardo dos Santos.

During the congress of the Popular Movement for the Liberation of Angola-Party of Labour (MPLA/PT) held in December 1985, Pres. José Eduardo dos Santos had been unanimously reelected as party chairman for an additional five years. Under the terms of the constitution he would automatically retain the office of president for a similar period. At the same time, the party's Central Committee was enlarged from 59 members to 75 with 15 more alternates. A number of the older members who had served since the war of independence were dropped. Among these was Ludi Kissassunda, commissar for Malanje Province and chairman of the 9th military regional council, who was later charged with diamond smuggling. In February 1986 President dos Santos carried out an extensive reshuffle of his Cabinet, and in April he made a number of important changes among the provincial commissars.

These steps were taken primarily to help resolve Angola's economic difficulties, attributable in part to a lack of manual and technical skills. The main cause, however, was the continuing guerrilla war waged against the government by forces of the National Union for the Total Independence of Angola (UNITA), aided by South African troops and U.S.-supplied arms. During his visit to the U.S. in January, UNITA's leader, Jonas Savimbi (*see* BIOGRAPHIES), received a friendly reception from the State Department, which held the view that Soviet involvement on behalf of the Angolan government threatened U.S. interests in cen-

ANGOLA IN THE NEWS
RONALD REAGAN WANTS TO GIVE AID...
TO A CHINESE-TRAINED GUERRILLA...
WHO IS BANKROLLED BY SOUTH AFRICA...
Gulf
TO MAKE ATTACKS ON U.S.-OWNED OIL REFINERIES...
WHICH ARE GUARDED BY CUBAN TROOPS...
AT THE REQUEST OF THE MARXIST ANGOLAN GOVERNMENT.
THE WHITE HOUSE WANTS THE SUPPORT OF THE U.S. PEOPLE.
WASSERMAN

DAN WASSERMAN; © 1986 THE BOSTON GLOBE; REPRINTED WITH PERMISSION OF LOS ANGELES TIMES SYNDICATE

tral Africa. In late May the government, with the support of Cuban troops and arms from the U.S.S.R., launched a large-scale attack against the guerrillas. New weapons from the U.S. enabled UNITA to offer stiff resistance, but thousands of villagers from the battle area were forced to take refuge in Zambia. The central plateau, long the scene of guerrilla activity, had become so impoverished that in August the United Nations appealed for financial aid to launch an airlift of food to the deprived area.

This initiative was a clear indication of the continuing decline in the country's agricultural output. From being self-sufficient in food production, Angola had become increasingly dependent on food imports, and the production of export crops continued to fall. Industrial production, while still well below the levels of the early 1970s, was on the increase, though it continued to be hampered by a shortage of technical expertise. Income from the sale of petroleum, overwhelmingly the leading export earner, was seriously affected by the fall in world prices. Nevertheless, the sale of oil products was the most important factor in maintaining external debt at an acceptable level. Ironically, Angola's main customer for oil continued to be the U.S., despite the active sympathy shown by the leaders of that country toward the guerrilla movement.

In these circumstances the repeated incursions of South African troops, ostensibly to strike at guerrilla bases hostile to South Africa, were an additional embarrassment. Early in June the government charged South Africa with responsibility for a seaborne attack on the southern port of Namibe, but authorities in Pretoria refused to either admit or deny guilt. A fortnight earlier, however, South African troops had openly crossed the border and, according to the Angolan government, killed 56 Angolan soldiers. South Africa maintained that the casualties were South West Africa People's Organization guerrillas.

Relations with Angola's northern neighbour, Zaire, were strained because it was thought that the Zairians, acting in sympathy with the U.S., were providing sanctuary for UNITA guerrillas operating in the northeast. Although the Zairian prime minister denied the charge, some substance seemed to have been given to the accusation early in the year. In March 197 foreign hostages taken by UNITA forces during an attack on the northeastern diamond-mining town of Andrada were released to the International Committee of the Red Cross in Zaire's Shaba Province.

(KENNETH INGHAM)

This article updates the *Macropædia* article SOUTHERN AFRICA: *Angola.*

BENIN

The people's republic of Benin is on the southern coast of West Africa, on the Gulf of Guinea. Area: 112,600 sq km (43,450 sq mi). Pop. (1986 est.): 4,126,000. Cap.: Porto-Novo (official); Cotonou (de facto). Monetary unit: CFA franc, with (Oct. 1, 1986) a par value of CFAF 50 to the French franc and a free rate of CFAF 332.05 to U.S. $1 (CFAF 479.81 = £1 sterling). President in 1986, Brig. Gen. Mathieu Kerekou.

The closeness of Benin's relations with Libya was emphasized following the U.S. air raid on Tripoli in April 1986, when Cotonou was the only black African capital to witness demonstrations in support of Col. Mu'ammar al-Qadhdhafi and his regime. Also indicative of the two countries' cooperation was the establishment at Seme in southern Benin of a camp where refugees from Chad, recruited and paid by Libya, underwent training prior to returning to Chad to join Libyan-supported antigovernment forces there.

In April Benin chaired a conference of ministers of education of African and other French-speaking countries held in Cotonou. Attended by France's minister of national education, the conference had, as its main purpose, furtherance of the aims of the "Francophone summit" held in Paris in February. (*See* WORLD AFFAIRS [Western Europe]: *France:* Sidebar.) In May agreement was reached on a new bridge across the Niger River. The National Assembly approved administrative and development budgets for 1986 of CFAF 57,028,000,000 and CFAF 49,848,000,000, respectively. (PHILIPPE DECRAENE)

This article updates the *Macropædia* article WESTERN AFRICA: *Benin.*

BOTSWANA

A landlocked republic of southern Africa, Botswana is a member of the Commonwealth. Area: 581,730 sq km (224,607 sq mi). Pop. (1986 est.): 1,126,000. Cap.: Gaborone. Monetary unit: pula, with (Oct. 1, 1986) a free rate of 1.85 pula to U.S. $1 (2.67 pula = £1 sterling). President in 1986, Quett Masire.

During 1986 the government of Botswana came under increasing pressure from South Africa to curb the activities of African National Congress (ANC) guerrillas allegedly operating from the country. It was reported in February that Botswana had agreed to take action against the ANC. On May 19, however, South African forces attacked suspected ANC targets in Botswana, Zimbabwe, and Zambia; at least one person died in the raid on a village close to Gaborone.

Much of the government's economic planning had to take into account the fact that Botswana was in the front line of confrontation with South Africa. With Botswana experiencing its fifth successive year of drought conditions, Pres. Quett Masire appealed in April for international help. The U.K., West Germany, the U.S., and the European Communities responded.

The sixth national development plan, covering the period 1985–91, placed special emphasis on private enterprise. President Masire expressed his disappointment at the low level of foreign investment in Botswana. The U.S. agreed to provide 59 million pula for a work-force and skills training project, and a World Bank loan of 12.7 million pula was to be used for development in the Selebi-Pikwe area. With the first phase of the Morupule power project completed, the station began feeding power into the national grid. A Japanese loan to finance the second phase was arranged.

(GUY ARNOLD)

This article updates the *Macropædia* article SOUTHERN AFRICA: *Botswana.*

BURKINA FASO

Burkina Faso is a landlocked country of West Africa. Area: 274,200 sq km (105,869 sq mi). Pop. (1986 est.): 8,126,000. Cap.: Ouagadougou. Monetary unit: CFA franc, with (Oct. 1, 1986) a par value of CFAF 50 to the French franc and a free rate of CFAF 332.05 to U.S. $1 (CFAF 479.81 = £1 sterling). Chairman of the National Recovery Council (president) in 1986, Capt. Thomas Sankara.

During 1986 Burkina Faso and Mali sought to reconcile differences that had culminated in five days of cross-border conflict at the end of 1985. In February there was an exchange of prisoners taken during the hostilities, and in June diplomatic relations were resumed. In December the International Court of Justice ruled that the potentially mineral-rich Agacher Strip should be divided equally between the two countries. Plans for an eventual political union of Burkina with Ghana advanced further.

On August 18 Capt. Thomas Sankara dissolved his third government, formed in August 1985. Composition of the new government, appointed on August 29, was largely unchanged, but the number of women members was increased from three to five. During the year large numbers of political detainees were released, including former head of state Col. Saye Zerbo and labour union leader Soumane Touré. In February Sankara was received in Paris by French Pres. François Mitterrand, who paid a return visit to Burkina Faso in November. (PHILIPPE DECRAENE)

This article updates the *Macropædia* article WESTERN AFRICA: *Burkina Faso.*

BURUNDI

Burundi is a landlocked republic of central Africa. Area: 27,831 sq km (10,745 sq mi). Pop. (1986 est.): 4,830,000. Cap.: Bujumbura. Monetary unit: Burundi franc, with (Oct. 1, 1986) a free rate of FBu 101.29 to U.S. $1 (FBu 146.37 = £1 sterling). President in 1986, Col. Jean-Baptiste Bagaza.

During 1986 Burundi continued to recover from the effects of the 1984 drought. The government's principal economic effort was directed toward reducing the country's dependence on coffee exports by encouraging diversification. The economic recovery program, however, required a constant inflow of foreign aid. Burundi's principal donors were Belgium, France, West Germany, the European Communities' Economic Development Fund, and the Arab Bank for Economic Development in Africa.

Economic indicators were reasonable: debts at $344.4 million required only 7.5% of export earnings to service; the annual rate of inflation was just over 12%; domestic investment was running at 15% and growth of gross domestic product at 4.8%. Tea, the second most important export, was now earning $7 million a year. Nevertheless, three main problems affected Burundi's development prospects: its population density, one of the highest in the world; its reliance on coffee for 85% of foreign exchange; and the scarcity of natural resources.

In May Burundi was host to a two-day summit of 15 countries belonging to the east and southern African Preferential Trade Area. The meeting achieved a compromise on the definition of goods qualifying for preferential tariffs among member countries. (GUY ARNOLD)

This article updates the *Macropædia* article CENTRAL AFRICA: *Burundi.*

CAMEROON

A republic of western central Africa, Cameroon lies on the Gulf of Guinea. Area: 465,458 sq km (179,714 sq mi). Pop. (1986 est.): 9,873,000. Cap.: Yaoundé. Monetary unit: CFA franc, with (Oct. 1, 1986) a par value of CFAF 50 to the French franc and a free rate of CFAF 332.05 to U.S. $1 (CFAF 479.81 = £1 sterling). President in 1986, Paul Biya.

Cameroon suffered a massive natural disaster in 1986 when on August 21 clouds of toxic gas of volcanic origin emanating from Lake Nyos near Wum in the northwestern Bamenda region caused more than 1,700 deaths; initial estimates that some 20,000 people were affected in varying degrees were subsequently revised downward to about 3,000. International aid was flown in by the French Air Force via Gabon. (*See* DISASTERS; EARTH SCIENCES.)

The disaster occurred four days before the official visit to Cameroon of Israeli Prime Minister Shimon Peres, who took with him a medical team to help treat the casualties. During the visit, which marked a further step in Israel's moves toward reconciliation with black Africa, diplomatic relations between the two countries, severed in 1973, were restored.

Faced with criticism of continuing suppression of human rights in Cameroon, Pres. Paul Biya proceeded cautiously with liberalization measures. A number of political detainees were released, but the Paris-based Cameroonian Peoples' Union remained banned. (PHILIPPE DECRAENE)

This article updates the *Macropædia* article WESTERN AFRICA: *Cameroon.*

T. ORBAN—SYGMA

A surviving villager in Cameroon looks at empty homes and herds of dead cattle days after an eruption of lethal volcanic gas from Lake Nyos killed about 1,700 of his compatriots.

CAPE VERDE

The republic of Cape Verde occupies an island group in the Atlantic Ocean about 620 km (385 mi) off the west coast of Africa. Area: 4,033 sq km (1,557 sq mi). Pop. (1986 est.): 342,000. Cap.: Praia. Monetary unit: Cape Verde escudo, with (Oct. 1, 1986) a free rate of 89.27 escudos to U.S. $1 (128.99 escudos = £1 sterling). President in 1986, Aristides Pereira; prime minister, Pedro Pires.

On Jan. 13, 1986, Aristides Pereira, president of Cape Verde since independence in 1975, was unanimously reelected for an additional five-year term by the People's National Assembly. Following his reelection he formed a new government, expanding the Council of Ministers from 10 to 14. Pedro Pires remained as prime minister.

At the end of 1985 France signed three aid agreements worth F 10.5 million with Cape Verde and thus became one of the country's most important aid donors. The joint Cape Verde-Angola commission agreed on a number of projects for cooperation.

Cape Verde decided to establish diplomatic relations at the ambassadorial level with the Palestine Liberation Organization (PLO), following a visit to the islands by PLO leader Yasir Arafat, and with Zimbabwe, following a visit by President Pereira to Harare. (GUY ARNOLD)

This article updates the *Macropædia* article WESTERN AFRICA: *Cape Verde*.

CENTRAL AFRICAN REPUBLIC

The Central African Republic is a landlocked state in central Africa. Area: 622,436 sq km (240,324 sq mi). Pop. (1986 est.): 2,706,000. Cap.: Bangui. Monetary unit: CFA franc, with (Oct. 1, 1986) a par value of CFAF 50 to the French franc and a free rate of CFAF 332.05 to U.S. $1 (CFAF 479.81 = £1 sterling). Head of state in 1986, Gen. André Kolingba.

On Nov. 21, 1986, voters approved a new constitution and extended the mandate of Gen. André Kolingba as head of state for a further six years. The constitution allowed for parliamentary elections in which all candidates would be members of a single party, the Centrafrican Democratic Assembly.

The early months of the year saw a period of increasing discontent. On April 1 a bomb explosion destroyed part of the road leading to the airport at Bangui. The trial of 12 students on charges of "attacking state security" proved a major focus of unrest and provoked a student strike. On May 12 the authorities imposed a ban on unauthorized strikes in educational establishments. Intense anti-European sentiment followed the crash on March 27 of a Jaguar aircraft belonging to French forces stationed in the country. The plane crashed into an Islamic school in Bangui, killing some 35 people, many of them children.

Jean-Bédel Bokassa, whose rule as the self-styled Emperor Bokassa I had ended in a 1979 coup, returned to the Central African Republic from exile in France on October 23 and was immediately arrested. His trial on charges that included murder and cannibalism opened in late November but was adjourned to give the prosecution more time to prepare its case. The trial, which resumed on December 15, was expected to last at least three months.

(PHILIPPE DECRAENE)

This article updates the *Macropædia* article CENTRAL AFRICA: *Central African Republic*.

CHAD

Chad is a landlocked republic of central Africa. Area: 1,284,000 sq km (495,755 sq mi). Pop. (1986 est.): 5,139,000. Cap.: N'Djamena. Monetary unit: CFA franc, with (Oct. 1, 1986) a par value of CFAF 50 to the French franc and a free rate of CFAF 332.05 to U.S. $1 (CFAF 479.81= £1 sterling). President in 1986, Hissen Habré.

The year 1986 in Chad was characterized by the progressive consolidation of power by Pres. Hissen Habré, while the divisions among the groups opposed to his rule widened. In January Habré freed more than 100 political prisoners as part of his policy of "national reconciliation." He reshuffled his Cabinet in March to facilitate the entry into it of a number of people who had previously opposed his regime; Gen. Djibril Negue Djogo, former chief of staff in the opposition Transitional Government of National Unity (GUNT), was named justice minister.

Among a number of African initiatives to end the conflict was a proposal that Habré and former president Goukouni Oueddei, leader of GUNT and of its People's Armed Forces (FAP), should meet in Congo in March. Goukouni, however, refused to attend the reconciliation talks. Col. Wadal Abdelkader Kamougue, leader of a powerful opposition faction, resigned as GUNT vice-president in June in protest. In August another opposition faction, the Democratic Revolutionary Council (CDR), led by Acheikh ibn Oumar, broke away from GUNT. Later, fighting broke out around Fada in the north of Chad between FAP and CDR forces. Reports that Libyan troops had supported the CDR

ARNAUD BORREL—SIPA/SPECIAL FEATURES

French Jaguar bombers destroy the Libyan-built runway at Ouadi Doum in northern Chad in February. Libya supported the rebel cause, and France backed the pro-Western government forces in Chad's civil war.

were apparently confirmed by the news that Goukouni had been arrested and "gravely wounded" during a visit to Tripoli in October. In November Acheikh was chosen to replace Goukouni as head of GUNT. In late December there were serious clashes in northern Chad between Libyan troops and forces previously loyal to Goukouni, which had reportedly switched allegiance to Habré.

Following reports that government troops had been attacked by Libyan forces in central Chad, on February 16 French Jaguar bombers stationed in the Central African Republic destroyed the Libyan-built runway at Ouadi Doum in the north. The next day the airport at N'Djamena was slightly damaged during a rebel counterattack. When fighting flared in December, France stepped up its military support of the government, and the U.S. sent military and medical supplies. (PHILIPPE DECRAENE)

This article updates the *Macropædia* article WESTERN AFRICA: *Chad.*

COMOROS

The republic of Comoros is an island state in the Indian Ocean off the east coast of Africa. Area: 1,862 sq km (719 sq mi), excluding the island of Mayotte, which continued to be a de facto dependency of France. Pop. (1986 est., excluding Mayotte): 409,000. Cap.: Moroni. Monetary unit: Comorian franc, with (Oct. 1, 1986) a par value of CF 50 to the French franc and a free rate of CF 332.05 to U.S. $1 (CF 479.81 = £1 sterling). President in 1986, Ahmed Abdallah.

On Dec. 31, 1985, Pres. Ahmed Abdallah of Comoros granted an amnesty to 58 prisoners, including some imprisoned on political grounds. Reports differed as to whether they included any of those found guilty of involvement in the attempted coup of March 1985. In May 1986 15 prisoners convicted in connection with the coup attempt were released on condition that they not leave the country without permission.

President Abdallah attended the Bastille Day celebrations in France, and on October 19 French Prime Minister Jacques Chirac visited Comoros. Nevertheless, relations between the two countries remained strained by the question of the future status of the French dependency of Mayotte. Abdallah continued to press for the eventual reintegration of Mayotte into Comoros. The 1986 budget revealed that Comoros would have to spend 80% more on servicing its foreign debt than it had in 1985. (PHILIPPE DECRAENE)

This article updates the *Macropædia* article INDIAN OCEAN ISLANDS: *Comoros.*

CONGO

A people's republic, Congo is in central Africa on the Atlantic Ocean. Area: 342,000 sq km (132,047 sq mi). Pop. (1986 est.): 2,097,000. Cap.: Brazzaville. Monetary unit: CFA franc, with (Oct. 1, 1986) a par value of CFAF 50 to the French franc and a free rate of CFAF 332.05 to U.S. $1 (CFAF 479.81 = £1 sterling). President in 1986, Col. Denis Sassou-Nguesso; prime minister, Ange-Édouard Poungui.

In July 1986 Pres. Denis Sassou-Nguesso of Congo was elected to succeed Pres. Abdou Diouf of Senegal as chairman of the Organization of African Unity at the OAU summit in Addis Ababa, Eth. Sassou-Nguesso was outspoken in his condemnation of the apartheid system in South Africa. Earlier in the year Sassou-Nguesso visited Burkina Faso, Mali, and Senegal, and in July Congo appointed its first ambassador to Chad.

In August ten people were found guilty of involvement in a series of bomb attacks in Brazzaville in 1982. Claude-Ernest Ndalla, a founder of the ruling Congolese Labour Party, was sentenced to death.

In June Parliament approved a reduction of almost 50% in total spending in the 1986 budget. The measures cleared the way for an agreement with the International Monetary Fund on external-debt rescheduling, which came into effect in July. (PHILIPPE DECRAENE)

This article updates the *Macropædia* article CENTRAL AFRICA: *Congo.*

CÔTE D'IVOIRE

A republic of West Africa, Côte d'Ivoire lies on the Gulf of Guinea. Area: 320,763 sq km (123,847 sq mi). Pop. (1986 est.): 10,624,000. Cap., Abidjan; capital designate, Yamoussoukro. Monetary unit: CFA franc, with (Oct. 1, 1986) a par value of CFAF 50 to the French franc and a free rate of CFAF 332.05 to U.S. $1 (CFAF 479.81 = £1 sterling). President in 1986, Félix Houphouët-Boigny.

The question of who would eventually succeed Pres. Félix Houphouët-Boigny as leader of Côte d'Ivoire ceased to dominate the political arena in 1986. Following elections for the National Assembly in November 1985, Henri Konan Bédié was reelected president of the Assembly on Jan. 3, 1986, by a massive majority, and the following month a constitutional amendment strengthened the powers of the holder of that office in the event of the presidency falling vacant. When Philippe Yacé took over the presidency of the Economic and Social Council in February, he became the third most important person in the state hierarchy. On July 9 Houphouët-Boigny announced a new Cabinet, which at 40 members was his largest ever.

Despite its firm commitment to good relations with the West, Côte d'Ivoire experienced a temporary difficulty in relations with France. Following the publication in June of articles critical of the regime in two French Socialist journals, the government denounced "French interference." In his first official trip abroad after taking office, French Prime Minister Jacques Chirac visited Yamoussoukro, the capital designate of Côte d'Ivoire, in April.

Following the announcement in December 1985 that diplomatic links with Israel were to be reestablished, the government opened its embassy in Jerusalem in September. In retaliation the Arab Bank for Economic Development in Africa suspended loans to Côte d'Ivoire in January, and in late October, the Ivorian government announced that the embassy would be moved to Tel Aviv.

The October 1985 decision that Côte d'Ivoire should be the only approved version of the country's name was made in order to end confusion caused by the use of translations (such as the English-language Ivory Coast).

(PHILIPPE DECRAENE)

This article updates the *Macropædia* article WESTERN AFRICA: *Ivory Coast.*

DJIBOUTI

The republic of Djibouti is in the Horn of northeastern Africa on the Gulf of Aden. Area: 23,200 sq km (8,950 sq mi). Pop. (1986 est.): 456,000. Cap.: Djibouti. Monetary unit: Djibouti franc, with (Oct. 1, 1986) a free rate of DF 177 to U.S. $1 (DF 255.77 = £1 sterling). President in 1986, Hassan Gouled Aptidon; prime minister, Barkat Gourad Hamadou.

The trend toward an Issa-dominated ethnocracy in Djibouti, the former French territory of Afars and Issas, continued in 1986. Pres. Hassan Gouled Aptidon's personal power base was further consolidated in April when the Political Bureau of the People's Rally for Progress, the sole

A Soviet ship ferries foreigners to Djibouti from Aden, South Yemen, in January. More than 4,000 people were evacuated by British, French, and Soviet vessels following a coup and subsequent fighting among factions in South Yemen.

ERIC BOUVET—GAMMA/LIAISON

party, voted to expel Aden Robleh Awaleh, a party vice-president. In September 1986, after fleeing to Ethiopia, Robleh was sentenced in absentia to life imprisonment for attempting to destabilize the government.

Travel to South Yemen was suspended in August after South Yemeni fighter aircraft forced an Air Djibouti civil airliner en route from North Yemen to Djibouti to land at Aden. The plane was apparently searched for supporters of South Yemen's former president, Ali Nasir Muhammad, overthrown in January. On September 30 the government announced the reestablishment of diplomatic relations with Egypt, severed in 1979.

The first summit meeting of the Intergovernmental Authority on Drought and Development, grouping Ethiopia, Somalia, Kenya, The Sudan, Uganda, and Djibouti, took place in Djibouti in January. France maintained its military presence in the country. Nineteen French soldiers died in an accident involving a French surveillance aircraft on May 18. (PHILIPPE DECRAENE)

This article updates the *Macropædia* article EASTERN AFRICA: *Djibouti*.

EQUATORIAL GUINEA

The republic of Equatorial Guinea consists of Río Muni, on the Atlantic coast of West Africa, and the offshore islands of Bioko and Annobon. Area: 28,051 sq km (10,831 sq mi). Pop. (1986 est.): 324,000. Cap.: Malabo. Monetary unit: CFA franc, with (Oct. 1, 1986) a par value of CFAF 50 to the French franc and a free rate of CFAF 332.05 to U.S. $1 (CFAF 479.81 = £1 sterling). President of the Supreme Military Council in 1986, Lieut. Col. Teodoro Obiang Nguema Mbasogo; prime minister, Capt. Cristino Seriche Bioko.

On Jan. 17, 1986, Pres. Teodoro Obiang Nguema announced major changes in his Cabinet. The president took over the defense portfolio from Fructoso Mba Onana Nchama, his uncle, who remained deputy prime minister and became minister of public works. It was reported that on July 17 the government foiled an attempted coup in which several government ministers, including Mba Onana, were implicated. The following month Mba Onana received a prison sentence for his part in the coup attempt.

Throughout the year Equatorial Guinea maintained its delicate balancing act between Spain, the former colonial power, and France, whose economic influence was increasing, in part as a result of the country's adherence to the CFA franc zone. International donors showed guarded optimism at the way the economy was recovering. The International Monetary Fund approved a $9.2 million credit, and the Paris Club rescheduled $28 million of debts. There were signs that the external debt was being reduced.

Equatorial Guinea became the 31st African country to sign the Organization of African Unity's Human Rights Charter. The first meeting of the Morocco-Equatorial Guinea joint commission took place in Rabat in May. (GUY ARNOLD)

This article updates the *Macropædia* article WESTERN AFRICA: *Equatorial Guinea*.

ETHIOPIA

The socialist state of Ethiopia is in the Horn of northeastern Africa, on the Red Sea. Area: 1,223,500 sq km (472,400 sq mi). Pop. (1986 est.): 44,850,000. Cap.: Addis Ababa. Monetary unit: birr, with (Oct. 1, 1986) a par value of 2.07 birr to U.S. $1 (free rate of 2.98 birr = £1 sterling). Head of state and chairman of the Provisional Military Administrative Council in 1986, Lieut. Col. Mengistu Haile Mariam.

Twelve years after the transfer of power in Ethiopia from Emperor Haile Selassie to the Provisional Military Administrative Council (PMAC), final steps were taken during 1986 to present a new constitution. The establishment of a People's Democratic Republic of Ethiopia (PDRE) had become a widely publicized objective since the formation of the Workers' Party of Ethiopia (WPE) in September 1984. A constitutional drafting commission, which included a wide range of nationally known personalities but was clearly dominated in its executive and central drafting committees by the WPE and the Derg (the PMAC), was formed in February 1986. Four months later a first draft of the text was circulated. Following discussions of the draft at community-level associations throughout the nation, it was reviewed by the WPE Central Committee in September. On September 8 the Central Committee announced that the draft would be submitted for approval by a national referendum on a date to be announced. In his relatively short address on Revolution Day, September 12, PMAC chairman Mengistu Haile Mariam confirmed that the PMAC was "on the threshold of ending its mission."

Although in its basic proposals it reflected a standard Soviet-bloc model, the draft constitution contained interesting features that defined the issues and the processes on which "nation building"—a phrase often used by the PMAC—would depend. For example, it indicated that "the state shall transform the backward economy by strengthening socialist relations of production and by accelerating the development of the productive forces through the application of science and technology." There were references to the need for a "highly interdependent and integrated national economy" for strengthening the "economic relationship between rural and urban areas as well as between

Ethiopian refugees in Tug Wajale, Somalia, hoping to find a better life, wait in the overcrowded, disease-ridden conditions of a refugee camp. More than 40,000 people sought aid in a transit centre designed for only 2,000.

SHEILA RULE/THE NEW YORK TIMES

the periphery and the centre" and for establishing human settlement patterns that would "correspond to the distribution of natural resources." For the latter purpose "the state shall encourage the scattered rural population to aggregate"—a reference to the continuation of the "villagization" policy. A mixed economy was prescribed. "The ownership of the means of production is socialist, that is state and cooperative ownership, private ownership, and other forms of ownership as determined by law." Mengistu stated that Ethiopia was not yet socialist; any movement in that direction could be expected to take several generations.

Political power was to reside in a National Assembly to which an Amharic term, Shengo, was applied. Once elected from nominees of the WPE, the popular associations, and the military units, the Shengo would elect the head of state, who would occupy the post of president for five years.

During discussions at the community level there was concern, spoken and unspoken, about the degree to which the new constitutional framework would simply reproduce, in terms of personalities, the existing power structure. It was felt that the framework should facilitate the appearance at the top of new faces who might reflect more closely the complex of cultures within Ethiopia and the nation's growth in political experience. This growing consensus was also the outcome of 12 years of experience of the provisional and caretaker role assumed by the Derg. Although recognition could be given to the development of potentially useful political and social structures during those years, the material benefits to the average citizen stemming from the 1974 revolution were not so obvious. Instead there had been constant demands for struggle and sacrifice and frequent explanations that shortfalls were due to the iniquities of the previous regime and to natural disasters.

The growth of bureaucratic structures and the increasing gap between political priorities and technical reality had a serious impact on the economy. Following recalculation of its position after the 1984 population census, Ethiopia, with a per capita gross domestic product estimated at $110 per annum, was classified internationally as the least developed of the less developed countries. This caused some embarrassment and also some recognition that heavy investment in capital-intensive development in business and industry had diverted resources from peasant agriculture, which formed the backbone of the economy.

In 1985–86 agricultural production was targeted for a 21.5% increase over the previous year, which had been one of exceptionally low output. Overall, a 6.3% annual growth rate for the economy was set for the 1986–89 phase of the ten-year plan. Most development activity was still financed from Western and UN sources. The disruption of the agricultural economy resulted in the need for continuing emergency support for at least seven million of the rural population. In this context the defection to the U.S. of the commissioner for relief and rehabilitation, Maj. Ato Dawit Wolde Ghiorgis, at the end of 1985, claiming strong differences with the Derg over policies and practices, was a serious embarrassment to the government. The counteraccusation that he had embezzled funds remained unconvincing. An equally severe blow was the defection of Foreign Affairs Minister Goshu Wolde at the UN General Assembly in October 1986.

On the international scene, prospects of an accord with The Sudan faded as Ethiopia was accused of involvement in the rebellion in southern Sudan. However, serious attempts appeared to be under way to restore relations with Ethiopia's other neighbour, Somalia.

This article updates the *Macropædia* article EASTERN AFRICA: *Ethiopia.*

GABON

Gabon is a republic of central Africa, on the Atlantic Ocean. Area: 267,667 sq km (103,347 sq mi). Pop.: in 1986 estimates varied from 570,000 to 1.7 million. Cap.: Libreville. Monetary unit: CFA franc, with (Oct. 1, 1986) a par value of CFAF 50 to the French franc and a free rate of CFAF 332.05 to U.S. $1 (CFAF 479.81 = £1 sterling). President in 1986, Omar Bongo; prime minister, Léon Mébiame.

In presidential elections held in Gabon on Nov. 9, 1986, Omar Bongo, president since 1967 and the only candidate, was returned for a further term of office. On June 19 President Bongo granted an amnesty to all former members of the banned Movement for National Renewal (Morena). The third congress of the ruling Gabonese Democratic Party, the sole legal party, took place in Libreville in September. The party's Central Committee was enlarged to 297 members and the Political Bureau, which for the first time included a number of women, to 44.

The economy was badly affected by the low price of petroleum. To encourage cooperation among African producers and exporters of petroleum, Gabon called a meeting in Libreville in September. It was attended by Algeria, Gabon, Libya, and Nigeria (all members of the Organization of Petroleum Exporting Countries), as well as Angola, Benin, and Cameroon, which were not OPEC members.

Celebrations marking the 26th anniversary of independence in August were attended by Roland Dumas, formerly French foreign minister. In April the government adopted new measures to control the flow of illegal immigrants.

(PHILIPPE DECRAENE)

This article updates the *Macropædia* article CENTRAL AFRICA: *Gabon.*

GAMBIA, THE

A republic and member of the Commonwealth, The Gambia extends from the Atlantic Ocean along the lower Gambia River in West Africa; it is surrounded by Senegal, with which it has formed an administrative union called Senegambia. Area: 10,689 sq km (4,127 sq mi). Pop. (1986 est.): 764,500. Cap.: Banjul. Monetary unit: dalasi, with (Oct. 1, 1986) a free rate of 7.58 dalasis to U.S. $1 (10.95 dalasis = £1 sterling). President in 1986, Sir Dawda Jawara.

In January 1986 The Gambia floated the dalasi and lifted all restrictions on foreign exchange transactions. An International Monetary Fund (IMF) mission visited The Gambia in early July to report on its economic recovery program. The approval in August of a $30 million IMF-World Bank loan to cover an 18-month period indicated that The Gambia had achieved a certain economic respectability in the eyes of the world's bankers. Nevertheless, per capita income had declined by 1.6% a year.

On April 24, the 16th anniversary of The Gambia becoming a republic, Pres. Dawda Jawara remitted the sentences of 13 prisoners convicted for their involvement in the 1981 coup attempt. Two new political parties were formed during the year—the Gambia People's Party, led by former vice-president Assan Musa Camara, and the People's Democratic Organization for Independence and Socialism.

A quarrel with Senegal concerning passports was resolved when ministers of the Senegambian Confederation, including the presidents of both countries, met and called for movement between the two countries to be treated with greater understanding. (GUY ARNOLD)

This article updates the *Macropædia* article WESTERN AFRICA: *The Gambia.*

GHANA

A republic of West Africa and member of the Commonwealth, Ghana lies on the Gulf of Guinea. Area: 238,533 sq km (92,098 sq mi). Pop. (1986 est.): 13,144,000. Cap.: Accra. Monetary unit: cedi, with (Oct. 1, 1986) a free rate of 136 cedis to U.S. $1 (192.52 cedis = £1 sterling). Chairman of the Provisional National Defense Council in 1986, Jerry John Rawlings.

There were growing signs in 1986 that the International Monetary Fund (IMF) program adopted in 1983 by Jerry John Rawlings, chairman of the Provisional National Defense Council government, was working. The World Bank predicted a 5% growth in the economy for the third successive year. Export earnings had risen dramatically, while the decline in gold output had been reversed. The turnaround had been effected at the cost of devaluing the cedi to less than 3% of its value in December 1981, when Rawlings came to power. Ghana still depended for much of its revenue on loans from Western sources.

Seven people found guilty of plotting to overthrow the Rawlings government were executed in June. In late May security forces arrested another group of armed dissidents who apparently had crossed into the country from Togo. On April 25 the *Free Press,* the last independent newspaper, ceased publication.

A U.S. petroleum company began offshore exploration in conjunction with the Ghana National Petroleum Corporation. A new law was passed permitting the government to acquire at least a 30% interest in any mineral operation. (GUY ARNOLD)

This article updates the *Macropædia* article WESTERN AFRICA: *Ghana.*

GUINEA

The republic of Guinea is located in West Africa, on the Atlantic Ocean. Area: 245,857 sq km (94,926 sq mi). Pop. (1986 est.): 6,752,000. Cap.: Conakry. Monetary unit: Guinean franc, with (Oct. 1, 1986) a free rate of GF 340 to U.S. $1 (GF 491.30 = £1 sterling). President in 1986, Brig. Gen. Lansana Conté.

In April 1986 elections were held to fill district councils in Conakry as a first step toward establishing representative bodies at the local level throughout Guinea. The elections were the first since the Military Committee for National Recovery (CMRN) came to power in April 1984.

During the year the CMRN turned away from the isolationist policies of the previous régime by instituting a series of wide-ranging reforms on the advice of the International Monetary Fund (IMF). Following the replacement of Guinea's six state-owned banks with three private French banks in December 1985, the syli was devalued on January 3 and replaced three days later by the Guinean franc. Later the government revealed plans for a 30% reduction in the number of civil servants. Several state-owned industrial companies were privatized.

The IMF decision in February to grant a 13-month standby loan worth 33 million Special Drawing Rights was followed by a World Bank structural adjustment loan and, in April, by an agreement with 12 Western governments to reschedule some $200 million of public external debt. Four Franco-Guinean cooperation agreements were signed during a visit by French Minister of Cooperation Michel Aurillac in June. (PHILIPPE DECRAENE)

This article updates the *Macropædia* article WESTERN AFRICA: *Guinea.*

GUINEA-BISSAU

A republic of West Africa, Guinea-Bissau lies on the Atlantic Ocean. Area: 36,125 sq km (13,948 sq mi). Pop. (1986 est.): 891,000. Cap.: Bissau. Monetary unit: peso, with (Oct. 1, 1986) a free rate of 170.48 pesos to U.S. $1 (246.34 pesos = £1 sterling). President in 1986, João Bernardo Vieira.

The aftermath of the November 1985 coup plot dominated much of the political scene in Guinea-Bissau during 1986. In July six of the plotters, including former vice-president Paulo Correia, were executed. A subsequent Cabinet reshuffle was designed to restore government authority.

Changes in the law now allowed exploitation of minerals, including petroleum, by foreign companies. The changes were part of a general economic reform program that also included devaluation and the privatization of various trading enterprises. Strenuous efforts were being made to improve agricultural performance. Belgium and Brazil were supporting the economic recovery program. In August Pres. João Bernardo Vieira announced that liberalization measures were to be introduced into the import-export sector, which had been exclusively state controlled. As a consequence, much of the country's trade was likely to move into private hands.

In April the government revoked a decree under which the state had seized the assets of those people, almost all of them Portuguese, who had left the country when it achieved independence from Portugal in May 1974 and who had not returned by early 1975. Under conditions to be clarified at a later date, the government was to return the assets to the former owners. (GUY ARNOLD)

This article updates the *Macropædia* article WESTERN AFRICA: *Guinea-Bissau.*

KENYA

A republic and member of the Commonwealth, Kenya is in eastern Africa, on the Indian Ocean. Area: 582,646 sq km (224,961 sq mi), including 11,230 sq km of inland water. Pop. (1986 est.): 21,150,000. Cap.: Nairobi. Monetary unit: Kenya shilling, with (Oct. 1, 1986) a free rate of K Sh 15.85 to U.S. $1 (K Sh 22.91 = £1 sterling). President in 1986, Daniel arap Moi.

From an economic standpoint 1986 was a healthy year for Kenya. In December 1985 the International Monetary Fund approved a plan to provide financial assistance to Kenya so that it could pay for extra grain imports made necessary by the 1984 drought. In addition, improved weather conditions resulted in a surplus of corn (maize) for export from the 1985 crop. These benefits, coupled with a decline in world petroleum prices and an increase in the price paid for coffee, the nation's main export earner, allowed Kenya to look forward again to a favourable balance of trade. The price offered for tea had also stabilized after a fall. To ensure an improvement in the country's economic position, the government scaled down some ambitious spending projects and in January 1986 launched a program aimed at reducing the birthrate from 4 to 3% per annum. During the same month, Pres. Daniel arap Moi met the leaders of Uganda, The Sudan, Somalia, Ethiopia, and Djibouti with a view to establishing an intergovernmental authority that would deal with any future threat from drought and encourage agricultural development.

Two minor issues troubled the economic scene. In June Moi warned foreigners not to give their support to dissident groups and insisted that foreign businesses starting joint ventures in Kenya had to give their Kenyan partners a majority interest in the company. These announcements caused considerable dismay among foreign investors and, although the president responded by assuring them that their investments would be safe, a certain measure of unease persisted. In July and August there was a period of financial panic when a number of small banks, set up in response to the increasingly favourable economic climate in the country, were forced to close. Although Moi was quick to attribute these events to the machinations of saboteurs, informed opinion laid the blame upon the inexperience of managers. Moi ordered closer supervision by the central bank and promised stern action against corruption.

The agreement reached in 1983 concerning the disposal of assets of the defunct East African Community was finally approved at a meeting of the presidents of Kenya, Tanzania, and Uganda in July 1986. The previous month, during Tanzanian Pres. Ali Hassan Mwinyi's state visit to Nairobi, he and President Moi emphasized their commitment to East African economic cooperation.

At wide-ranging meetings between Moi and the leaders of Tanzania, Uganda, The Sudan, Zaire, Burundi, and Rwanda in January, March, July, and November, the participants announced their intention to forge closer political, economic, social, and cultural links between their countries.

Internal security was very much in the forefront of President Moi's thinking during the year. The appointment of Lieut. Gen. Haji Mahmoud Mohammed, leader of the forces loyal to the government during the attempted coup of August 1982, as chief of staff in July was part of a wider military reorganization aimed at ensuring the loyalty of the armed forces at all levels. Unrest among students at Kenyatta University, arising from the government's refusal to increase starting salaries for student teachers, led to the closing of the university from March 13 to May 6. During that period 17 people were given prison sentences for sedition. Many were recent graduates of Nairobi University. They were allegedly members of the Union of Nationalists to Liberate Kenya (Mwakenya), which was said to be plotting to overthrow the government and replace it with a socialist or Communist alternative. In December Parliament approved controversial constitutional amendments that increased the executive power of the president.

(KENNETH INGHAM)

This article updates the *Macropædia* article EASTERN AFRICA: *Kenya*.

LESOTHO

A constitutional monarchy of southern Africa and member of the Commonwealth, Lesotho forms a landlocked enclave within South Africa. Area: 30,355 sq km (11,720 sq mi). Pop. (1986 est.): 1,586,400. Cap.: Maseru. Monetary unit: loti (plural: maloti), at par with the South African rand, with (Oct. 1, 1986) a free rate of 2.22 maloti to U.S. $1 (3.21 maloti = £1 sterling). King, Moshoeshoe II; prime minister until Jan. 20, 1986, Chief Leabua Jonathan; chairman of the Military Council from January 24, Maj. Gen. Justin Metsino Lekhanya.

On Jan. 20, 1986, Maj. Gen. Justin Metsino Lekhanya (*see* BIOGRAPHIES) led a military coup that deposed Chief Leabua Jonathan, prime minister of Lesotho since 1965, and vested all executive and legislative power in King Moshoeshoe II. The new regime set up a six-member Military Council to advise the king and a Council of Ministers to assist in the administration of the country. General Lekhanya headed both bodies. Political activity was banned until the promulgation of a new constitution.

The coup followed a three-week blockade mounted by South Africa during which the republic's foreign minister, R. F. ("Pik") Botha, described Jonathan as the "greatest destabilizing factor in Lesotho." Although South Africa apparently precipitated, and probably even masterminded, the coup, Jonathan also had made many enemies at home. The new government did not hand over Lesotho's South African refugees to the republic, as Pretoria had demanded, but instead deported them to Zambia. Nonetheless, the blockade was subsequently lifted.

AP/WIDE WORLD

Members of the paramilitary forces in Lesotho celebrate their ousting of Prime Minister Chief Leabua Jonathan in January. Maj. Gen. Justin Metsino Lekhanya led the coup that gave power to King Moshoeshoe II with a six-member Military Council and a Council of Ministers.

The 1986–87 budget, announced in July, showed little change from that of the previous year, apart from a significant decline in revenue from the South African Customs Union. In September South Africa announced that agreement had been reached with Lesotho to go ahead with the long-planned water project in the Lesotho highlands. A treaty covering the first phase of the project was signed in October. (GUY ARNOLD)

This article updates the *Macropædia* article SOUTHERN AFRICA: *Lesotho.*

LIBERIA

The republic of Liberia is located in West Africa, on the Atlantic Ocean. Area: 99,067 sq km (38,250 sq mi). Pop. (1986 est.): 2,303,000. Cap.: Monrovia. Monetary unit: Liberian dollar, at par with the U.S. dollar, with a free rate (Oct. 1, 1986) of L$1.45 to £1 sterling. President in 1986, Gen. Samuel K. Doe.

A year of continuing criticism from both internal and international sources followed the general elections held in Liberia in October 1985. Many leading figures boycotted Gen. Samuel K. Doe's inauguration as president on Jan. 6, 1986. In June Doe granted an amnesty to thosc allcgedly involved in the coup attempt of November 1985. In March 1986 three opposition parties, the Liberia Unification Party (LUP), the Liberia Action Party (LAP), and the Unity Party (UP), formed a coalition. At the samc timc, the principal opposition party, the United People's Party (UPP), which had not been authorized to contest the elections, announced that it was "back in business." In April, however, more than 200 members of the UPP, including most of the leadership, were arrested. Gabriel Kpolleh of the LUP, Jackson Doe of the LAP, and Edward Kesselly of the UP were among those detained in a further crackdown on the opposition in August. They were released the following month. The ban on the UPP was lifted in September.

Much effort was made to improve Liberia's image in the U.S. Although a U.S. Senate resolution called for the suspension of $15 million worth of military aid to Liberia until democratic elections were held, in April the administration rescued the tottering Liberian economy by providing economic aid worth $42 million.

The International Monetary Fund declared Liberia ineligible for further loans because it was not meeting existing financial obligations. Foreign debt averaged $574 per capita, and by September the country was facing acute shortages of consumer goods. (GUY ARNOLD)

This article updates the *Macropædia* article WESTERN AFRICA: *Liberia.*

MADAGASCAR

The republic of Madagascar occupies the island of the same name and minor adjacent islands in the Indian Ocean off the southeast coast of Africa. Area: 587,041 sq km (226,658 sq mi). Pop. (1986 est.): 10,303,000. Cap.: Antananarivo. Monetary unit: Malagasy franc, with (Oct. 1, 1986) a free rate of FMG 748 to U.S. $1 (FMG 1,081 = £1 sterling). President in 1986, Didier Ratsiraka; prime minister, Lieut. Col. Désiré Rakotoarijaona.

On May 24, 1986, the defense minister, Rear Adm. Guy Sibon, and several other top-level defense personnel were killed in an air crash in central Madagascar. The appointment of a new defense minister, Gen. Christopher Raveloson Mahasampo, brother-in-law of Pres. Didier Ratsiraka, was announced on June 5. During the weekend of March 15–16 Cyclone Honorinnia struck central Madagascar. According to the Ministry of Information, the cyclone killed at least 30 people, left some 20,000 homeless, and caused an estimated $150 million worth of damage.

Following discussions between the government and the International Monetary Fund, a 20% devaluation of the Malagasy franc was announced on August 11. The following month the IMF approved a standby credit worth 30 million Special Drawing Rights. At a consultative meeting of the Paris Club of creditor nations in April, Madagascar secured commitments worth $600 million in external assistance.

The government continued its efforts to improve relations with France, building on the rapprochement achieved in 1985. President Ratsiraka's official visit to France in February was returned by French Minister for Cooperation Michel Aurillac, who visited Antananarivo in October. Two Sino-Malagasy economic cooperation agreements were signed during a visit by Chinese Pres. Li Xiannian (Li Hsien-nien) in March. (PHILIPPE DECRAENE)

This article updates the *Macropædia* article INDIAN OCEAN ISLANDS: *Madagascar.*

MALAWI

A republic and member of the Commonwealth, Malawi is a landlocked state in eastern Africa. Area: 118,484 sq km (45,747 sq mi). Pop. (1986 est.): 7,279,800. Cap.: Lilongwe. Monetary unit: Malawi kwacha, with (Oct. 1, 1986) a free rate of 1.98 kwacha to U.S. $1 (2.86 kwacha = £1 sterling). President in 1986, Hastings Kamuzu Banda.

On Jan. 2, 1986, Pres. Hastings Kamuzu Banda of Malawi dissolved his Cabinet. The new Cabinet, named two weeks later, contained the same personnel, though most of the ministers had been appointed to different portfolios.

Malawi's refusal to break its friendly links with South Africa continued to exacerbate its poor relations with other African neighbours. Those relations were further strained in August when Banda failed to attend a meeting of leaders of the Southern African Development Coordination Conference, intended to coordinate economic measures aimed at South Africa's apartheid policies.

Nor was the position improved when Banda welcomed the presidents of Mozambique, Zambia, and Zimbabwe to a meeting in Blantyre in September. Again the aim was to discuss sanctions against South Africa. Also on the agenda was regional cooperation, particularly the protection of railway communications through Mozambique, threatened by the Mozambique National Resistance (MNR) guerrillas; Mozambican Pres. Samora Machel (*see* OBITUARIES) believed that MNR fighters were taking refuge in Malawi. Following the discussions, Banda expelled several thousand people alleged to be deserters from the Mozambican Army, and they subsequently created havoc within the northern border of Mozambique. After the death of Machel in a plane crash in October, South Africa claimed that documents found in the wreckage showed that Mozambique and Zimbabwe were plotting to overthrow the Malawian government. (KENNETH INGHAM)

This article updates the *Macropædia* article SOUTHERN AFRICA: *Malawi.*

MALI

Mali is a landlocked republic of West Africa. Area: 1,240,192 sq km (478,841 sq mi). Pop. (1986 est.): 8,450,000. Cap.: Bamako. Monetary unit: CFA franc, with (Oct. 1, 1986) a par value of CFAF 50 to the French franc and a free rate of CFAF 332.05 to U.S. $1 (CFAF 479.81 = £1 sterling). President in 1986, Gen. Moussa Traoré; prime minister from June 6, Mamadou Dembelé.

Mali farmers wield simple but effective tools in digging a new irrigation canal, part of a cooperative project aimed at increasing rice production along the Niger River in spite of drought conditions that adversely affected much of the country's population.
AP/WIDE WORLD

During 1986 the government of Mali did everything in its power to improve relations with neighbouring Burkina Faso in the aftermath of the five-day war between the two countries over possession of the Agacher Strip in December 1985. (See *Burkina Faso,* above.) Diplomatic relations were resumed in June.

On June 6 Pres. Moussa Traoré announced a major Cabinet reshuffle in which a prime minister was appointed for the first time since 1971. The post was filled by Mamadou Dembelé. In October relations with France were strained by the French decision to expel 101 Malians under new legislation that granted the authorities increased power over foreign residents.

President Traoré's state visits to China in June and to the U.S.S.R. in July were expected to strengthen Mali's already cordial links with those countries. His three-day visit to Senegal in April was the first by a Malian head of state.

(PHILIPPE DECRAENE)

This article updates the *Macropædia* article WESTERN AFRICA: *Mali.*

MAURITANIA

The republic of Mauritania is on the Atlantic coast of West Africa. Area: 1,030,700 sq km (398,000 sq mi). Pop. (1986 est.): 1,689,000. Cap.: Nouakchott. Monetary unit: ouguiya, with (Oct. 1, 1986) a free rate of 74.80 ouguiya to U.S. $1 (108.89 ouguiya = £1 sterling). President of the Military Committee for National Salvation and prime minister in 1986, Col. Maaouya Ould Sidi Ahmed Taya.

Government reshuffles in August and October 1986 marked the continuing consolidation of power by Col. Maaouya Ould Sidi Ahmed Taya. In July the Military Committee for National Salvation announced that elections would be held to fill local councils.

The year was characterized by a serious resurgence of tension between Mauritania's black and Arab populations. Black Mauritanians apparently resented the fact that the minority Arab population held power and was implementing a policy of arabization. In September some 20 people were arrested and sentenced to prison for holding unauthorized meetings and publishing tracts "attacking national unity."

In April the International Monetary Fund, noting that Mauritania had achieved the objectives set out in the July 1985 economic recovery plan, approved a standby credit worth 12 million Special Drawing Rights. The following month a debt-rescheduling agreement was reached with the country's official Paris Club creditors.

In an effort to improve relations with neighbouring countries, Taya visited Tunisia, Mali, and Libya in late 1985–early 1986.

(PHILIPPE DECRAENE)

This article updates the *Macropædia* article WESTERN AFRICA: *Mauritania.*

MAURITIUS

The constitutional monarchy of Mauritius, a member of the Commonwealth, occupies an island in the Indian Ocean about 800 km (500 mi) east of Madagascar and includes the island dependencies of Rodrigues, Agalega, and Cargados Carajos Shoals. Area: 2,040 sq km (788 sq mi). Pop (1986 est.): 1,030,900. Cap.: Port Louis. Monetary unit: Mauritian rupee, with (Oct. 1, 1986) a free rate of Mau Rs 12.79 to U.S. $1 (Mau Rs 18.74 = £1 sterling). Queen, Elizabeth II; governor-general from Jan. 17, 1986, Sir Veerasamy Ringadoo; prime minister, Aneerood Jugnauth.

The popularity of the coalition government, comprising the Mauritius Socialist Movement (MSM), the Social Democratic Party (PMSD), and the Labour Party, was on the decline in 1986. In January four ministers resigned from the Cabinet immediately after four other members of Parliament belonging to the coalition parties had been arrested and charged with drug-smuggling offenses in The Netherlands. Some reports suggested that the two events were linked, but Anil Kumarsingh Gayan claimed that he had resigned as external affairs minister in order to fight for democracy. He argued that the democratic system could not function while leaders of the opposition Mauritian Militant Movement were suspended. Three more Cabinet ministers resigned in August. The subsequent appointment as external affairs minister of Sir Satcam Boolell, the Labour Party leader dismissed from the Cabinet in 1984, suggested that the rift between his party and Prime Minister Aneerood Jugnauth's MSM had healed.

The government decided to leave the Southern African Preferential Trade Area (PTA) on the grounds that it served the interests of only the larger member nations. Instead, Mauritius decided to concentrate on developing trade with its island neighbours—Madagascar, Réunion, Seychelles, and Comoros. Withdrawal from the PTA was to be effective from mid-1987.

In negotiations over raw sugar prices, the European Communities (EC) refused to accept the 1.33% increase demanded by the African, Caribbean, and Pacific (ACP) countries. Mauritius, in turn, was the only ACP country that refused to accept the EC ruling. The nation's foreign debts stood at approximately $332.4 million.

In January 1986 Sir Veerasamy Ringadoo was appointed governor-general in succession to Sir Seewoosagur Ramgoolam, who had died in office the previous month.

(GUY ARNOLD)

This article updates the *Macropædia* article INDIAN OCEAN ISLANDS: *Mauritius.*

MOZAMBIQUE

The people's republic of Mozambique is located in eastern Africa, on the Indian Ocean. Area: 799,380 sq km (308,642 sq mi). Pop. (1986 est.): 14,143,000. Cap.: Maputo. Monetary unit: metical, with (Oct. 1, 1986) a free rate of 40.05 meticais to U.S. $1 (57.87 meticais = £1 sterling). Presidents in 1986, Samora Machel to October 19 and, from November 6, Joaquim Chissanó; prime minister from July 17, Mário de Graça Machungo.

The death of Pres. Samora Machel (*see* OBITUARIES) in an air crash just inside the South African border on Oct. 19, 1986, was the climax of a bad year for Mozambique. Accusations that the South African government had been involved in the crash were firmly denied by spokesmen in Pretoria, but the fact that they had been made was a clear indication of the country's fear that its powerful neighbour would stop at nothing to undermine Mozambique's stability. Machel's successor was Joaquim Chissanó (*see* BIOGRAPHIES), who had been foreign minister for 11 years. He was a close friend of the former president and shared both Machel's Marxist views about internal policy and his pragmatic approach toward external relations. His position was not improved, however, when South Africa claimed to have discovered evidence at the scene of the crash demonstrating that Machel had been plotting with Zimbabwe to launch an attack on Malawi because of the aid given by that country to Mozambique National Resistance (Renamo, or MNR) rebel forces.

Mozambique's stability had already been rendered precarious by the activities of the Renamo rebels, who had played a major role in destroying the country's economy. Some 42% of government expenditure was devoted to the unsuccessful struggle against the rebels and to providing a defense against a possible attack from South Africa. Export earnings in 1985 had been particularly poor, and in 1986 two other sources of foreign exchange were threatened: Renamo attacks on the rail links to the Indian Ocean ports had caused the diversion of trade goods to other outlets, with a consequent loss of revenue to the Maputo government, and South Africa announced in October that there would be no further recruiting of workers from Mozambique and that those already working there would be repatriated when their work permits expired. When implemented, this would mean an annual loss for Mozambique of some $90 million in foreign currency earnings.

CAMERA PRESS

Citizens of Mozambique mourn their president, Samora Machel, killed in an airplane crash on October 19. Banners at the funeral encourage Mozambicans, under Machel's successor, Joaquim Chissanó, to continue the struggle against South African-backed rebels.

The reason given for South Africa's decision was that Mozambique, in contravention of the 1984 Nkomati accord between the two countries, was still giving sanctuary to guerrillas of the African National Congress operating against South Africa. Ironically, Machel had been firmly of the opinion that South Africa was assisting Renamo, thus breaking the accord in its turn. In order to weaken the influence of Renamo, Machel had been inclined to try to revive the accord at the time of his death. In December Chissanó announced that his government wished to maintain the accord.

With or without South African support, Renamo achieved an uncomfortable measure of success. In February rebel forces recaptured their former base of Casa Banana. They had lost the base in 1985 following an assault in which government forces were aided by Zimbabwean troops. (At least 6,000 Zimbabweans remained in Mozambique, where they had been sent originally to guard the oil pipeline.) The government troops left to guard Casa Banana were no match for the rebels, and although Zimbabwean soldiers recaptured the base in April, Renamo won control of the railway centre of Inhaminga.

In October the military situation became still more serious for the government. Machel, who suspected Malawi of harbouring Renamo rebels, had demanded that they should be handed over to his government. Malawian Pres. Hastings Kamuzu Banda responded by expelling several thousand Mozambicans, who at once began to ravage the border country in northern Mozambique, seizing control of a number of small towns. Emboldened by their success and by the death of Machel, Renamo then declared war on Zimbabwe. (KENNETH INGHAM)

This article updates the *Macropædia* article SOUTHERN AFRICA: *Mozambique.*

NIGER

Niger is a landlocked republic of West Africa. Area: 1,186,408 sq km (458,075 sq mi). Pop. (1986 est.): 6,423,000. Cap.: Niamey. Monetary unit: CFA franc, with (Oct. 1, 1986) a par value of CFAF 50 to the French franc and a free rate of CFAF 332.05 to U.S. $1 (CFAF 479.81 = £1 sterling). Chief of state and president of the Supreme Military Council in 1986, Brig. Gen. Seyni Kountché; prime minister, Ahmid Algabid.

During 1986 the regime of Pres. Seyni Kountché adopted an increasingly radical stance. The Supreme Military Council refused to release former president Hamani Diori, who—apart from a six-week period in April–June 1985—had been detained either in prison or under house arrest since he was deposed by Kountché in 1974. In January 1986 the National Charter Synthesis Commission adopted the preliminary draft of a charter, an important step toward reviving the constitution suspended at the start of Kountché's rule.

In February the International Monetary Fund indicated

its approval of Niger's economic and financial program for 1986, which aimed to reduce the budget deficit by keeping government spending at its 1985 level while boosting revenue. The Fund granted a standby credit worth 13.5 million Special Drawing Rights.

During Kountché's first state visit to France in June, he secured budgetary aid worth CFAF 2 billion. In September he visited Japan and North Korea. In April it was announced that Niger and Burkina Faso were to set up a commission to demarcate their common boundary.

(PHILIPPE DECRAENE)

This article updates the *Macropædia* article WESTERN AFRICA: *Niger.*

NIGERIA

A republic and member of the Commonwealth, Nigeria is located in West Africa, on the Gulf of Guinea. Area: 923,768 sq km (356,669 sq mi). Pop. (1986 est.): 98,916,000. Cap.: Lagos. Monetary unit: naira, with (Oct. 1, 1986) a free rate of 4.62 naira to U.S. $1 (6.68 naira = £1 sterling). President and chairman of the Armed Forces Ruling Council in 1986, Maj. Gen. Ibrahim Babangida.

During 1986 Maj. Gen. Ibrahim Babangida, the chairman of Nigeria's Armed Forces Ruling Council, insisted on an open style of government, in contrast to his predecessor, Maj. Gen. Mohammed Buhari, whom he had deposed in the August 1985 coup. General Babangida had set a deadline of Oct. 1, 1990, for a return to democratic rule. A 17-member Political Bureau was charged with searching for a suitable approach to civilian rule. The Political Bureau received a setback, however, when Chief Obafemi Awolowo, a respected elder statesman, refused to cooperate with it. Babangida reshuffled his Council of Ministers in January and again in September. Petroleum Resources Minister Tam David-West became minister of mines, power, and steel before being excluded from the government.

Widespread expressions of support for the government followed the December 1985 coup attempt. In March 1986 ten former military officers were executed for their part in the plot, while three others had their death sentences commuted to life imprisonment. On July 3 it was announced that former president Alhaji Shehu Shagari had been released, though his movements would continue to be restricted. Shagari had been detained since he was deposed in December 1983.

Nigeria joined the Organization of the Islamic Conference (OIC), a move apparently designed to appease the Muslim north of the country and possibly also Nigeria's Gulf state partners in the Organization of Petroleum Exporting Countries, with whom it had a delicate relationship. The Christian and non-Muslim south reacted with anger and suspicion, and fears were expressed that Nigeria might become an Islamic rather than a secular state.

An eruption of violence on a number of university campuses in May signaled the end of the government's honeymoon period. Riots broke out after disciplinary action was taken against two student leaders who had participated in a demonstration commemorating riots that had taken place in 1978; 15 people died during the violence. Although the public was appalled at the police reaction, there was little evidence of general support for the students. In an effort to quell the unrest, the government banned demonstrations, but the National Union of Nigerian Students said the ban was provocative and should be ignored. Student opposition to the government centred upon the decision to join OIC, the general economic climate, and the demand that the student body be allowed a greater say in national affairs.

The low price of oil dominated most economic decisions. Oil earnings for 1986 were estimated at 8.1 billion naira, representing over 80% of total foreign exchange earnings. The 1986 budget policy was designed to effect a gradual depreciation of the naira and to encourage non-oil sectors of the economy. There was a reduction in petroleum and other subsidies, and measures to promote exports were introduced. Following the earlier bans on imports of rice, corn (maize), and dried fish, imports of wheat were to be stopped as of 1987 in an effort to encourage local producers.

Although the government still refused to turn to the International Monetary Fund (IMF) for assistance, many of the economic measures it implemented during the year were in line with IMF policies. These included the establishment in October of a second-tier foreign exchange market. Government requirements, medical supplies, and debt servicing used the official first-tier rate, while other needs were met by central bank auctions of available foreign exchange. The government's privatization program gathered pace during the year. Minister of Finance Chu Okongwu called for a new debt strategy to enable less developed countries to stimulate economic growth while paying their debts. Nigeria's gross external liabilities stood at approximately $20 billion in 1986.

In February Nigeria reopened its borders with neighbouring Benin, Niger, and Cameroon. Its only other land border, with Chad, remained closed. The borders had been closed since April 1984, apart from a period in May 1985 when they had been opened to allow illegal immigrants to leave the country.

(GUY ARNOLD)

This article updates the *Macropædia* article WESTERN AFRICA: *Nigeria.*

RWANDA

The landlocked republic of Rwanda is situated in central Africa. Area: 26,338 sq km (10,169 sq mi). Pop. (1986 est.): 6,331,000. Cap.: Kigali. Monetary unit: Rwanda franc, with (Oct. 1, 1986) a free rate of RF 84.79 to U.S. $1 (RF 122.52 = £1 sterling). President in 1986, Maj. Gen. Juvénal Habyarimana.

In January 1986 Pres. Juvénal Habyarimana appointed a number of new members, including two women, to the Central Committee of the National Revolutionary Movement for Development, Rwanda's only political organization. He stressed that women should be encouraged to become more active in the country's development.

Despite considerable success in development plans, Rwanda still possessed one of the lowest per capita incomes ($280) in the world. Life expectancy, at 47 years, was also among the lowest. Nevertheless, confidence in the direction of the economy was reflected in the amount of aid Rwanda attracted. Aid from Belgium, the U.K., Canada, France, The Netherlands, Switzerland, and West Germany was supplemented by relatively massive loans from the World Bank's International Development Association.

Kenya and Rwanda agreed to speed up the development of transport and communications links between the two countries; Rwanda was to build transit warehouses in Mombasa, through which 90% of the country's trade passed. During a state visit in July by Pres. Ali Hassan Mwinyi of Tanzania, the two countries agreed to expand cooperation in all fields. In April Rwanda and Uganda established a joint commission to coordinate cooperation in several areas. The new international airport at Kigali was inaugurated on July 30.

(GUY ARNOLD)

This article updates the *Macropædia* article CENTRAL AFRICA: *Rwanda.*

SÃO TOMÉ AND PRÍNCIPE

The republic of São Tomé and Príncipe comprises two main islands and several smaller islets that straddle the Equator in the Gulf of Guinea, off the west coast of Africa. Area: 1,001 sq km (386 sq mi). Pop. (1986 est.): 109,600. Cap.: São Tomé. Monetary unit: dobra, with (Oct. 1, 1986) a free rate of 37.36 dobras to U.S. $1 (53.98 dobras = £1 sterling). President in 1986, Manuel Pinto da Costa.

In a reshuffle of his Cabinet announced in February 1986, Pres. Manuel Pinto da Costa of São Tomé and Príncipe reduced the number of ministers from 12 to 9 and divested himself of the foreign affairs and planning portfolios. In March two opposition groups based in Lisbon announced that they had formed the Democratic Opposition Coalition.

A violent outbreak of malaria during January and February caused the deaths of nearly 200 children. In response to a government appeal, the European Communities (EC) provided emergency aid to be used for treatment and a drainage program. The country was to benefit jointly with Equatorial Guinea from an EC aid program to develop trade in the Gulf of Guinca by improving port facilities at Bata, Equatorial Guinea, and São Tomé.

In late December 1985–January 1986, President da Costa visited Angola and Cape Verde, partly in his role as chairman for the year of thc Lusophone group of African countries. In both countries he reached agreements on closer cooperation. In October he visited Europe and the U.S., where he attended the 41st session of the United Nations. On his return to Africa he visited Libreville, Gabon, where he held talks with Pres. Omar Bongo.

(GUY ARNOLD)

This article updates the *Macropædia* article CENTRAL AFRICA: *São Tomé and Príncipe.*

SENEGAL

The republic of Senegal is located in West Africa, on the Atlantic Ocean; it surrounds the country of The Gambia, with which it has formed an administrative union called Senegambia. Area: 196,722 sq km (75,955 sq mi). Pop. (1986 est.): 6,699,000. Cap.: Dakar. Monetary unit: CFA franc, with (Oct. 1, 1986) a par value of CFAF 50 to the French franc and a free rate of CFAF 332.05 to U.S. $1 (CFAF 479.81 = £1 sterling). President in 1986, Abdou Diouf.

In January and February 1986 Pres. Abdou Diouf of Senegal announced changes to his Council of Ministers, reducing the membership slightly but leaving most of the major ministries unaltered. In June the Parti Démocratique Senegalais (PDS), the major opposition party, declared that it would boycott general elections due to be held in early 1988 unless the existing electoral code was amended to make it more "democratic." Among other things the PDS wanted the minimum voting age to be reduced from 21 to 18. Two prominent opposition politicians died during the year: Chiekh Anta Diop (62), leader of the Rassemblement National Démocratique, on February 7 and Seydou Cissokho (56), president of the Parti de l'Indépendance et du Travail (Communist Party), on March 10.

During celebrations marking the 26th anniversary of independence in April, President Diouf granted an amnesty to a number of detainees, among them eight who had been imprisoned for their part in the revolt by separatists in Casamance Province in 1983. The amnesty did not extend to some 60 others who had been similarly detained.

Once again relations with France dominated foreign policy. During the year a number of prominent French politicians visited Senegal, among them Minister of Cooperation Michel Aurillac in June and Michel Rocard of the Socialist Party in October. In January Senegal was host to the seventh summit of the Inter-African Committee to Combat Drought in the Sahel, during which Guinea-Bissau became the ninth member. Under an amendment to the terms of the Senegambian confederation, the decision to place troops on alert in response to a state of emergency was to be made jointly by the heads of state of Senegal and The Gambia, rather than by the former alone.

(PHILIPPE DECRAENE)

This article updates the *Macropædia* article WESTERN AFRICA: *Senegal.*

SEYCHELLES

A republic and member of the Commonwealth, the Seychelles consists of about 100 islands in the Indian Ocean, 1,450 km (900 mi) from the east coast of Africa. Area: 453 sq km (175 sq mi). Pop. (1986 est.): 66,100. Cap.: Victoria. Monetary unit: Seychelles rupee, with (Oct. 1, 1986) a free rate of SR 5.97 to U.S. $1 (SR 8.63 = £1 sterling). President in 1986, France-Albert René.

On Sept. 12, 1986, it was reported that a plot to depose Pres. France-Albert René of Seychelles on his return from the nonaligned movement summit in Harare, Zimbabwe, had been foiled. Apparently warned of the conspiracy, René left the summit early. The plot was reportedly masterminded by Defense and Youth Minister Col. Ogilvie Berlouis, who resigned and subsequently left the country. On September 19 René named a new Cabinet in which he took over the defense portfolio.

Presenting the 1986 budget in December 1985, René said that the government placed priority on developing tourism, oil exploration, fisheries, and manufacturing. Import duties and turnover tax were abolished in favour of a new tax levied on wholesalers, manufacturers, and retailers. In 1985 the current account was in surplus (by SR 12 million) for the first time since 1979, due largely to tourism. However, a reduction in grants and concessional aid meant that in 1986 a higher proportion of budget expenditure was allocated to debt servicing.

Seychelles was to resume oil exploration with assistance from the Indian Oil and Natural Gas Commission. The government sought to improve relations with Madagascar and Mauritius through the Indian Ocean Commission.

(GUY ARNOLD)

This article updates the *Macropædia* article INDIAN OCEAN ISLANDS: *Seychelles.*

SIERRA LEONE

A republic of West Africa and member of the Commonwealth, Sierra Leone lies on the Atlantic Ocean. Area: 71,740 sq km (27,699 sq mi). Pop. (1986 est.): 3,733,000. Cap.: Freetown. Monetary unit: leone, with (Oct. 1, 1986) a free rate of 28.50 leones to U.S. $1 (41.18 leones = £1 sterling). President in 1986, Maj. Gen. Joseph Saidu Momoh.

The general election held in Sierra Leone on May 30, 1986, more than a year early, strengthened the hand of Maj. Gen. Joseph Saidu Momoh, president since November 1985. More than half of the sitting members, many of them supporters of former president Siaka Stevens, lost their seats. Though the elections were free of violence, malpractices were uncovered in 17 constituencies, where the results were annulled and elections held again on June 6. Disappointment was expressed in some quarters that the new Cabinet, though reduced by two ministries, remained large (at 19 members) and contained a number of old faces from the Stevens years. President Momoh established a government Gold and Diamond Office and introduced measures to combat smuggling.

The 1986–87 budget presented in June revealed a major deficit of 833 million leones. In an effort to boost revenue, the government abolished subsidies on petroleum and rice, a necessary condition for a new standby credit from the International Monetary Fund, and floated the leone.

Momoh launched a three-year "green revolution" designed to return the country to self-sufficiency in food production. In an apparently contradictory move, immediately afterward he increased payments to farmers for coffee and cocoa to encourage exports. (GUY ARNOLD)

This article updates the *Macropædia* article WESTERN AFRICA: *Sierra Leone.*

SOMALIA

A republic in the Horn of northeastern Africa, the Somali Democratic Republic, or Somalia, lies on the Gulf of Aden and the Indian Ocean. Area: 637,000 sq km (246,000 sq mi). Pop. (1986 est.): 5,991,900. Cap.: Mogadishu. Monetary unit: Somali shilling, with (Oct. 1, 1986) a free rate of 36 Somali shillings to U.S. $1 (52.02 Somali shillings = £1 sterling). President in 1986, Maj. Gen. Muhammad Siyad Barrah.

On May 23, 1986, Pres. Muhammad Siyad Barrah of Somalia was severely injured in a motor accident. He was flown to the military hospital in Riyadh, Saudi Arabia, and placed in intensive care. Vice-Pres. Muhammad Ali Samater took over as interim president. Rumours that Barrah, in his late 70s, would not return to public life proved unfounded, and as sole candidate in the December 23 presidential election he was returned for a further seven-year term with 99.9% of the vote.

The antigovernment Somali National Movement continued its occasional guerrilla activities in the north of the country, where there was widespread disaffection against a regime perceived to favour the south. The other antigovernment movement, the Somali Democratic Salvation Front (SDSF), was apparently in disarray following a leadership crisis. The SDSF remained in control of the strip of land on the Somali-Ethiopian border that it had held, with backing from Ethiopian forces, since 1983.

A series of biweekly foreign currency auctions launched in September was intended to unify the former two-tier system of an official rate for government transactions and an adjustable market rate for private importers. The auctions were launched with the backing of a $67 million agricultural sector credit from the World Bank and $7.5 million from the U.K.'s Overseas Development Administration.

An order from Egypt for 100,000 head of cattle in July appeared to herald a revival of the livestock trade, which had been depressed since 1983 when Saudi Arabia, the principal market, banned beef imports from Somalia following a rinderpest scare. Livestock remained the mainstay of the economy. In November a five-member committee was set up to oversee a program to revitalize the economy through encouragement of local and foreign private investment. It was chaired by Muhammad Haji Ibrahim Egal, who had been prime minister of the civilian government before the 1969 coup that brought Barrah to power.

As of December 1985 an estimated 700,000 ethnic Somalis and Oromo were in 37 refugee camps, and an unknown number lived among the general population. Many had been refugees since the 1978–79 Ogaden war with Ethiopia, though a fresh influx had been entering the country from the northwest since 1984. In the early part of 1986, refugees were arriving at a rate of up to 1,000 a day.

In January President Barrah visited Djibouti to participate in the inaugural summit of the Intergovernmental Authority on Drought and Development. While there, he and Ethiopian leader Mengistu Haile Mariam set in motion a series of meetings intended to find a peaceful resolution to their long-standing territorial dispute. Meetings in Addis Ababa in May and Mogadishu in August produced statements of goodwill but no concrete proposals. In October it was announced that Somalia and the U.S.S.R. had agreed to improve links that had been strained (though never broken) since the U.S.S.R. supported Ethiopia in the Ogaden war. (VIRGINIA R. LULING)

This article updates the *Macropædia* article EASTERN AFRICA: *Somalia.*

SOUTH AFRICA

The Republic

South Africa occupies the southern tip of Africa, with the Atlantic Ocean to the west and the Indian Ocean to the east. It partially surrounds the four former black states of Bophuthatswana, Ciskei, Transkei, and Venda (whose independence is not recognized by the international community). Area: 1,123,226 sq km (433,680 sq mi). Pop. (1986 est.): 28,139,000. (Area and population figures exclude the four former black states.) Executive cap., Pretoria; judicial cap., Bloemfontein; legislative cap., Cape Town. Monetary unit: South African rand, with (Oct. 1, 1986) a free rate of R 2.22 to U.S. $1 (R 3.21 = £1 sterling). Executive state president in 1986, Pieter Willem Botha.

Domestic Affairs. South Africa began 1986 under a state of emergency in 30 districts. Lifted early in March, the state of emergency was reimposed nationwide in far harsher terms on June 12 and tightened further on December 11. Despite censorship of the media and incomplete official lists, reliable sources estimated that some 23,000 people had been held in detention after June, more than half of them under 25 years old and several thousand under 16. This was the government's response to the wave of unrest among the black majority that had begun in September 1984 and continued unabated—expanding in scope and depth and acquiring what many sober observers regarded as revolutionary proportions. School boycotts, rent strikes, consumer boycotts, and localized general strikes were combined with assaults on the structure and personnel of local government and on the security forces. A marked development was the emergence of street-level organizations, virtually parallel government of a localized kind. This was accompanied by an increasing rejection of "free enterprise" and a desire for "socialism" among blacks.

Violence, by the state and by those opposed to it, intensified. According to official figures (widely believed to underestimate the actual totals), during the two years to September 1986, 1,776 people had been killed, including 56 members of the security forces. At the same time, the government claimed that during the year there had been 170 actions by guerrillas of the banned African National Congress (ANC), compared with 136 in 1985. There was intensified violence in many areas, urban and rural, by black vigilante groups, accused by their victims of being supported by the police. In the Crossroads settlement, outside Cape Town, violence between vigilantes and their opponents in late May and early June resulted in 72 deaths and 80,000 people being rendered homeless. Among many other incidents of violence that attracted widespread attention were an upsurge in Alexandra Township, near Johannesburg, in February, during which 22 people were killed by police, and the shooting by police of 21 people in

Soweto in August in disorders arising from the eviction of rent strikers. Unofficial estimates put the death toll in the latter incident at 30–50.

Most of the black resistance to the government developed under the umbrella of the United Democratic Front (UDF), which claimed more than 600 affiliates with two million members. Some 13,000 of those detained were believed to have been UDF supporters. Three of 22 UDF leaders facing charges of treason in the Transvaal were acquitted in November, while similar charges against four UDF leaders on trial in Natal were dropped in June. In October the government prohibited the UDF from receiving funds from abroad. UDF patron Desmond Tutu was installed as Anglican archbishop of Cape Town in September.

The first of two major one-day national general strikes took place on May 1, with one of its demands the recognition of May Day as a paid public holiday; it was supported by about 1.5 million workers. The second, on June 16, held in part to commemorate the tenth anniversary of the Soweto massacre, was almost equally well supported, though it took place under the state of emergency. Other economic, educational, and political demands in these strikes included the removal of security forces from the townships and the release of detainees and political prisoners. Another widespread demand was the lifting of the ban on the ANC—generally seen as the most popular political organization among the black majority, with the imprisoned Nelson Mandela its most popular leader. His wife, Winnie Mandela (*see* BIOGRAPHIES), defied government restrictions and adopted an increasingly public profile during the first part of the year. At least 321 elected labour union leaders and officials were detained. Among them were Elijah Barayi, president of the Congress of South African Trade Unions (COSATU); he was subsequently released under severe restrictions.

During the first part of the year there were widespread expectations of accelerated reform by the National Party (NP) government. At the end of January Pres. Pieter W. Botha promised a series of measures, among them the establishment of a national statutory council, including leaders of African "communities and interest groups," to consider, among other matters, constitutional reform. In April it was announced that Parliament would be reconvened in August to finalize reform legislation and that, unusually, a federal congress of the National Party would be held shortly beforehand. Parliament repealed some 34 measures that formed the basis of urban influx control and the "pass laws." But the significance of this as a reform was qualified by the government's failure to carry through its January promise to restore South African citizenship to citizens of the "independent" homelands who resided in South Africa. Moreover, the government declared its intention of controlling urbanization in other ways.

Expectation of significant political change, heightened by the activities of the Commonwealth-appointed Eminent Persons Group (EPG), was to prove illusory. The renewal of the state of emergency was a signal of a hardening in the government's attitude. Botha's speeches in the latter part of the year reaffirmed that "group self-determination" and a refusal to "surrender" the position of the white minority remained essential pillars of government policy.

The government was partly influenced by a drift of white opinion further to the right, reflected most sharply in the growth of the Afrikaner Weerstandsbeweging, a neo-fascist organization claiming 50,000–100,000 members, which succeeded in disrupting several National Party meetings in April and May. Both the Conservative Party, the major party to the right of the NP, and the Herstigte Nasionale Partij (HNP) claimed increased support. In a by-election in Cape Province in September the NP held the seat, but the HNP doubled its vote from 1981. On December 31, in an apparent effort to renew the NP's mandate, President Botha announced a general election for the white electorate in 1987, two years earlier than expected.

The national statutory council was not introduced, largely because no significant African leader would agree to participate. KwaZulu leader Chief Gatsha Buthelezi, whose attitude was regarded as crucial, stated his unwillingness to participate unless Nelson Mandela was released and given the option of participating also. Instead, Buthelezi joined with other white and black politicians in Natal to present proposals for a multiracial parliament in the province in November. The scheme was rejected by Pretoria. Among blacks, the policies of Buthelezi and his Inkatha organization became increasingly controversial, especially with his formation of the United Workers Union of South Africa explicitly to rival COSATU and his vehement attacks on the exiled ANC leadership and the UDF.

Other political developments included the sudden resignation of Frederick van Zyl Slabbert, leader of the Progressive Federal Party (PFP) opposition, from Parliament, which he described as "a grotesque exercise in irrelevancy." He was followed by another leading PFP figure, Alex Boraine, and replaced by Colin Eglin. Legislation was passed to replace the elected provincial councils by executive organs, as part of the government's overall restructuring of second- and third-tier government (intermediate between central and local level).

After June the level of unrest slowly diminished. Attempts to challenge the emergency in the courts were largely unsuccessful. However, a rent strike already in progress in a number of townships had spread by September to 54. By that time the government had closed up to 250 black schools nationwide.

South Africa's worst gold-mining disaster, at Kinross mine, took place on September 16. Its death toll of 177 focused attention on mine safety and led to a one-day strike by more than 300,000 mine workers and 300,000 other members of COSATU.

Foreign Relations. South Africa's international isolation deepened further. Trying to forestall pressure for intensified Commonwealth sanctions, British Prime Minister Margaret Thatcher had secured the appointment of the EPG at the October 1985 Commonwealth conference in The Bahamas. Its aim was to assist in a "process of dialogue" between the government and the "true representatives of the majority black population of South Africa." Following discussions within and outside South Africa between December 1985 and May 1986, the EPG proposed a package of measures. Among them was a government declaration of "its commitment to dismantling the system of apartheid, to ending racial discrimination, and to broad-based negotiations leading to new constitutional arrangements for power-sharing by all the people of South Africa"; the EPG also urged removal of the military from the townships, the release of Nelson Mandela and other political prisoners and detainees, the lifting of the bans on the ANC and Pan Africanist Congress, and the suspension of violence by the ANC. On June 7 the EPG submitted a report concluding that the government had no genuine intention of dismantling apartheid.

The Commonwealth, with the exception of the U.K., agreed on further sanctions. The U.K., however, accepted the milder sanctions package agreed to by the European Communities (EC) in September. Both the EC and Japan decided to cease certain types of iron and steel imports, and the EC undertook to cease new investment and imports of gold coins. Overriding a veto by U.S. Pres. Ronald Reagan, the U.S. Congress in October imposed a wider range of measures, including a ban on loans, coal imports, and landing rights for South African Airways.

Intervention by South Africa in the southern African region increased. An economic blockade of Lesotho in January led to a coup that overthrew the government. South African commando raids on Botswana, Zambia, and (for the first time) Zimbabwe on May 19 against alleged ANC military targets coincided with the termination of the EPG mission. Following Zimbabwe's declaration in August that it would impose Commonwealth-agreed sanctions and possibly additional measures, South Africa imposed delays on traffic crossing to Zimbabwe and Zambia.

Tensions between South Africa and Mozambique sharpened dramatically in October. Following increased activity by Mozambique National Resistance (MNR) rebels on the Mozambique-Malawi border, the Mozambique government claimed it was threatened by an invasion from South Africa; at the same time, the South African government announced that recruitment of Mozambican workers to South Africa was to be terminated. In the midst of this, Mozambican Pres. Samora Machel (*see* OBITUARIES) was among those killed in a plane crash on South African territory. Despite vigorous denials by Pretoria, suspicion of its implication in the crash was evoked among blacks in southern Africa. The South African government claimed that documents found in the wreckage revealed that Zimbabwe and Mozambique were plotting to overthrow the government in Malawi.

No progress was made toward implementation of UN Resolution 435, calling for independence for South West Africa/Namibia and for democratic elections there. The government continued to insist that Cuban troops be withdrawn from Angola as a precondition. In June the Navy was reported by the Angolan government to have raided a southern Angolan port; in August and again later in the year the same sources reported that South African troops were active in southern Angola, supporting the National Union for the Total Independence of Angola rebels against an offensive by government and Cuban troops.

The Economy. At the start of 1986 the economy remained gripped by the recessionary conditions that had persisted almost unabated since 1982. In the period 1981–85 real gross domestic product (GDP) growth averaged 1.1% a year; in 1985 it fell by 1%, and in the first quarter of 1986 it continued downward. Neither domestic nor export demand, nor mild stimulatory policies introduced in September 1985 and continued in the March 1986 budget, were sufficient to turn the situation around substantially.

The slackness of the economy, by reducing demand for imports, produced a favourable current account balance of payments; there was a surplus of R 5.9 billion in 1985, which in the first six months of 1986 continued at an annual rate of R 5.2 billion. At the same time, the political situation accentuated a tendency toward net capital outflow, which reached R 9.2 billion in 1985 and R 2.6 billion in the first half of 1986. In part the outflow reflected disinvestment by foreign companies; the number of U.S. corporate investors, for example, was estimated to have fallen from 325 to 265 over the two years to October 1986. In part it reflected local money moving out. It also was affected by the debt-rescheduling agreement negotiated with foreign banks in March following the August 1985 freeze on debt-servicing payments.

By the latter part of the year there were mild signs of upturn, following a new "reflation package" of R 1.2 billion announced in June by the government and significant rises in the dollar price of gold from August. Nevertheless, original estimates of 3% growth in GDP were downgraded to 1–2%. Moreover, the mild upturn took place in conditions of a mounting backlog of social needs that had contributed substantially to the climate of unrest. Some estimates put unemployment as high as six million. Inflation was in the 18–20% range, the highest since 1920.

Strengthened sanctions intensified debate in government and business circles on possible strategies for economic growth. These varied from more highly controlled "siege economy" scenarios on the one hand to privatization and deregulation of industry on the other.

Bophuthatswana

The republic of Bophuthatswana consists of six discontinuous, landlocked geographic units, entirely surrounded by South Africa except for one unit that borders Botswana on the northwest. Area: 40,000 sq km (15,444 sq mi). Pop. (1986 est.): 1,564,000. Cap.: Mmabatho. Monetary unit: South African rand. President in 1986, Lucas Mangope.

AP/WIDE WORLD

Thousands of South African workers, among more than one million who stayed away from work, mass in Soweto's Orlando Stadium on May 1, International Labour Day. They demonstrated against the apartheid system and in favour of union demands that May Day be declared a paid public holiday.

Ciskei

Bordering the Indian Ocean in the south, Ciskei is surrounded on land by South Africa. Area: 5,386 sq km (2,080 sq mi). Pop. (1986 est.): 798,000. Cap.: Bisho. Monetary unit: South African rand. President in 1986, Lennox Sebe.

Transkei

Bordering the Indian Ocean and surrounded on land by South Africa, Transkei comprises three discontinuous geographic units, two of which are landlocked and one of which borders Lesotho. Area: 43,553 sq km (16,816 sq mi). Pop. (1986 est.): 2,755,000. Cap.: Umtata. Monetary unit: South African rand. Presidents in 1986, Kaiser Daliwonga Matanzima and, from February 20, Nyangelizwe Vulindlela Ndamase; prime minister, George Matanzima.

Venda

The landlocked republic of Venda is located in extreme northeastern South Africa. Area: 6,198 sq km (2,393 sq mi). Pop. (1986 est.): 448,000. Cap.: Thohoyandou. Monetary unit: South African rand. President in 1986, Patrick Mphephu.

The four former homelands, regarded as politically independent of South Africa only by the South African government, continued to depend overwhelmingly on revenue generated in the central South African economy, on the one hand in the form of wages paid to migrant workers and on the other in the form of direct and indirect payments from the South African government. In 1985–86 these amounted to R 740.7 million for Transkei, R 458.4 million for Bophuthatswana, R 194.4 million for Venda, and R 394.4 million for Ciskei.

Plans for the independence in December of a fifth homeland, KwaNdebele, were shelved after its legislative assembly itself withdrew the request in August. This was a consequence of near civil-war conditions that had raged intermittently since the start of the year, with mass resistance to independence combated by a quasi-official vigilante organization, Imbokotho. In January at least 24 were killed in resistance by the people of Moutse to incorporation in KwaNdebele. By August half the territory's business had been destroyed in the unrest. More than four-fifths of KwaNdebele's 200,000 inhabitants commuted to jobs in central South Africa.

The violent unrest within South Africa spilled over into other homelands, independent and nonindependent. A leaked Bophuthatswana government document claimed R 3 million damage to property between November 1985 and early February 1986. Documents on Transkei—published anonymously to protect identities—claimed 2,000 detained in the last six months of 1985 and a regime more repressive than ever before. Among major incidents were the death of 11 and wounding of 36 when Bophuthatswana police fired on a crowd of 10,000 demonstrating in the Winterveld squatter area. The police commander was subsequently assassinated.

In a bizarre incident in Ciskei, Charles Sebe, former government leader and brother of the president, who had been detained in 1983 and sentenced in June 1984 to 12 years in prison for terrorism, was freed from jail in September 1986 by a group including white mercenaries. He fled to Transkei, and from there he announced plans to "liberate" Ciskei from his brother's rule. Elections in Ciskei were canceled on the grounds that all government candidates were unopposed. (MARTIN LEGASSICK)

See also *Dependent States,* below.

SUDAN, THE

A republic of North Africa, The Sudan has a coastline on the Red Sea. Area: 2,503,890 sq km (966,757 sq mi). Pop. (1986 est.): 24,610,000. Cap.: Khartoum. Monetary unit: Sudanese pound, with (Oct. 1, 1986) an official rate of LSd 2.45 to U.S. $1 (LSd 3.54 = £1 sterling). Chairman of the Transitional Military Council to May 6, 1986, Gen. ʽAbd ar-Rahman Siwar ad-Dahab; chairman of the Supreme Council from May 6, Ahmad al-Mirghani; prime ministers, al-Jazuli Dafʽallah and, from May 6, Sadiq al-Mahdi.

In The Sudan's first democratic parliamentary elections in 18 years, held in April 1986, the Umma Party (UP) led by Sadiq al-Mahdi (*see* BIOGRAPHIES) won 99 of the 264 seats contested. (For tabulated results, see *Political Parties,* above.) Voting in 37 southern constituencies was postponed indefinitely because of rebel activities. The UP formed a coalition government with the Democratic Unionist Party and some southern Christian politicians; fundamentalist Muslim leaders were excluded.

The most pressing issue facing the new government was to make peace with the Sudan People's Liberation Army (SPLA), supported by Ethiopia, in the south. Prime Minister al-Mahdi's meeting with SPLA leader Col. John Garang (*see* BIOGRAPHIES) in Ethiopia on July 31 was unsuccessful. Garang asked for the lifting of the state of emergency in the south and repeal of Shariʽah (Islamic law) as preconditions for peace negotiations. Al-Mahdi offered to limit Shariʽah to the Muslim north but demanded a cease-fire before negotiations began. After a Sudan Airways civilian aircraft was shot down by the rebels on August 16, the government temporarily suspended all offers of negotiation.

An end to the civil war was vital on both economic and humanitarian grounds. Five million people in the south were threatened by famine. (See *United Nations,* above.) In February the government introduced austerity measures in response to an International Monetary Fund announcement that the country was ineligible for further loans because of its failure to meet debt repayments.

In March the government decided to dissolve the institutions set up jointly with Egypt by former president Gen. Gaafar Nimeiry in 1982. Egypt's refusal to hand over Nimeiry strained relations already weakened by the military assistance given to The Sudan by Egypt's enemy, Libya. (KENNETH INGHAM)

SWAZILAND

Swaziland is a landlocked monarchy of southern Africa and a member of the Commonwealth. Area: 17,364 sq km (6,704 sq mi). Pop. (1986 est.): 681,500. Administrative cap., Mbabane; royal and legislative cap., Lobomba. Monetary unit: lilangeni (plural: emalangeni), at par with the South African rand, with (Oct. 1, 1986) a free rate of 2.22 emalangeni to U.S. $1 (3.21 emalangeni = £1 sterling). King from April 25, 1986, Mswati III; regent until April 25, Queen Ntombi; prime ministers, Prince Bhekimpi Dlamini and, from October 6, Sotsha Dlamini.

On April 25, 1986, Prince Makhosetive was crowned King Mswati III (*see* BIOGRAPHIES) of Swaziland. The ceremonies, which lasted three days, were attended by representatives of 37 countries, including Pres. Pieter W. Botha of South Africa. The new king said that he would continue with the mixture of ancient and modern government that had characterized the reign of Sobhuza II, who died in 1982. One of Mswati's first acts, however, was to dissolve the Liqoqo, the Supreme Council of State established by the late king to advise the regent after his death. In October Mswati summarily dismissed Prince Bhekimpi Dlamini from his post as prime minister, appointing Sotsha Dlamini in his place.

The 1986–87 budget, presented in February, did nothing to relieve the effects of recession. South Africa, Lesotho, and Swaziland agreed to establish a Common Monetary Area to replace the Rand Monetary Area, and the rand ceased to be legal tender in Swaziland on July 1. The government accused the South African security forces of taking part in armed raids against alleged African National Congress bases in Mbabane in August and December. The incidents served as reminders of the pressures exerted on Swaziland by its neighbour. (GUY ARNOLD)

This article updates the *Macropædia* article SOUTHERN AFRICA: *Swaziland.*

TANZANIA

The republic of Tanzania, a member of the Commonwealth, consists of Tanganyika, on the east coast of Africa, and Zanzibar, just off the coast in the Indian Ocean, which includes Zanzibar Island, Pemba Island, and small islets. Area: 945,037 sq km (364,881 sq mi). Pop. (1986 est.): 22,463,000. Seat of government, Dar es Salaam; capital designate, Dodoma. Monetary unit: Tanzania shilling, with (Oct. 1, 1986) a free rate of 44.60 shillings to U.S. $1 (64.44 shillings = £1 sterling). President in 1986, Ali Hassan Mwinyi; prime minister, Joseph Warioba.

Ranked by the World Bank as one of the 25 least developed countries in the world, Tanzania found its economic problems continuing to loom large in 1986. Although coffee production improved after the higher rainfall of 1985, the benefits of increased output were offset by inadequate transport facilities and inefficient marketing. Sisal, once the country's largest export earner, continued to decline in importance as a result of low world prices and poor management. Even the supply of subsistence crops was adversely affected by the low prices offered to producers and by transport delays. In October the government called on farmers to use donkeys and oxcarts because the country lacked the means to pay for imported trucks and fuel.

In view of the impossibility of increasing export earnings, any prospect of an improvement in the economy depended on external finance. The new government of Pres. Ali Hassan Mwinyi, in power since November 1985, reversed the previous administration's attitude toward the International Monetary Fund. Former president Julius Nyerere had always refused to deal with the IMF because the heavy burden of servicing loans promptly would, in his view, have made development impossible. In early June the government of President Mwinyi agreed in principle to the terms imposed by the IMF in return for a standby credit. The 1986–87 budget, presented in June, introduced structural reforms, including an additional 33% devaluation of the Tanzania shilling. In August it was confirmed that the IMF had agreed to extend a standby facility of about 65 million Special Drawing Rights, and the following month the government secured a debt-rescheduling agreement with its Paris Club creditors.

Nyerere himself appeared to favour change in the political sphere. During a visit to Lusaka, Zambia, in June, he renounced his former opinion that a one-party state was essential to enable Africans to develop a sense of nationhood. The one-party system, he declared, had bred complacency among both voters and those elected to govern.The dismissal in February of 13 branch secretaries of Chama Cha Mapinduzi, the sole party, for corruption and embezzling party funds appeared to lend weight to his argument.

Relations with Kenya continued to improve. In June Mwinyi paid a three-day visit to Nairobi, where he and Pres. Daniel arap Moi agreed that the two countries should strengthen links and try to improve trade relations. From Tanzania's standpoint the latter proposal was difficult to implement because of the shortage of foreign exchange and the unavailability of produce to sell to its neighbour.

On another issue, however, the two countries found it easier to act together. On July 14 Tanzania followed the lead of Kenya and Uganda in withdrawing from the Commonwealth Games in Edinburgh, Scotland, as a protest against the U.K.'s refusal to support economic sanctions against South Africa. Addressing a meeting of the liberation committee of the Organization of African Unity in Arusha, Prime Minister Joseph Warioba called on Commonwealth countries to impose sanctions on South Africa even if the U.K. failed to cooperate. (KENNETH INGHAM)

This article updates the *Macropædia* article EASTERN AFRICA: *Tanzania.*

TOGO

A republic of West Africa, Togo is situated on the Bight of Benin. Area: 56,785 sq km (21,925 sq mi). Pop. (1986 est.): 3,072,000. Cap.: Lomé. Monetary unit: CFA franc, with (Oct. 1, 1986) a par value of CFAF 50 to the French franc and a free rate of CFAF 332.05 to U.S. $1 (CFAF 479.81 = £1 sterling). President in 1986, Gen. Gnassingbe Eyadema.

An attempt by a group of commandos to overthrow the regime of Pres. Gnassingbe Eyadema of Togo on the night of Sept. 23–24, 1986, was thwarted following fighting in the streets of Lomé during which a number of people died. The government claimed that the commandos had crossed into Togo from neighbouring Ghana and that they had been trained in both Ghana and Burkina Faso. The border with Ghana was subsequently closed. Following a request for assistance from President Eyadema, France sent a small force of paratroopers to Togo. In December 13 people were sentenced to death and 14 others to life imprisonment for involvement in the coup attempt.

In presidential elections held on December 21 Eyadema, the sole candidate, was returned for a further seven-year term of office. A government-appointed commission inquiring into prison conditions reported in January that in general prisoners were well treated. An Amnesty International report published in June was critical of the treatment of political detainees, claiming that torture was commonplace. (PHILIPPE DECRAENE)

This article updates the *Macropædia* article WESTERN AFRICA: *Togo.*

UGANDA

A landlocked republic and member of the Commonwealth, Uganda is located in eastern Africa. Area: 241,140 sq km (93,100 sq mi), including 44,081 sq km of inland water. Pop. (1986 est.): 15,638,100. Cap.: Kampala. Monetary unit: Uganda shilling, with (Oct. 1, 1986) a free rate of 1,380 shillings to U.S. $1 (1,995 shillings = £1 sterling). Chairman of the Military Council until Jan. 26, 1986, Gen. Tito Okello; president from January 29, Yoweri Museveni; prime ministers, Abraham Waligo and, from January 30, Samson Kisekka.

Following four months of negotiations, an agreement was signed in Nairobi, Kenya, on Dec. 17, 1985, between the government of Gen. Tito Okello and the main guerrilla force operating in Uganda, the National Resistance Army (NRA). Under its terms all troops would be withdrawn from Kampala, the armies would be disarmed, and the NRA would be given seats in a new Military Council. When no attempt was made to put the agreement into

(continued on page 442)

Special Report: Uganda

Ethnicity and the North-South Divide in Uganda Politics

BY ALI A. MAZRUI AND OMARI H. KOKOLE

An ethnically plural society, Uganda has also, for the first decades of its independence, been divided between a northern power base and a southern power base. The interplay of these factors has had a strong bearing on the struggle to evolve a democratic system in Uganda. On the attainment of independence (1962), there were two bases of state power—economic and military. British colonial policies had resulted in a situation in which economic power and prosperity were concentrated in the south of the country, while military power was in northern hands. The British had helped southerners construct wealthier, better educated, more urbanized, and more westernized societies than those existing in the north. The bulk of the crops for export and for home consumption were grown in southern districts of Uganda. The copper industry, when it was productive, was also part of the southern economy. On the other hand, the army that British colonial rule had created was recruited overwhelmingly from northern ethnic groups.

To some extent ethnicity reinforced the north-south divide. Northern groups primarily belong to the Nilotic and Sudanic families of "tribes." Southern groups tend to belong to the Bantu family of ethnic groups. Northern groups speak different languages, have different cultures, and to some extent even look different. Northerners tend to be not only taller but also more black in pigmentation than southerners.

North and South. Strictly in terms of indigenous values, the north has deeper democratic traditions than the south. Most southern societies before colonization were strong monarchies, whereas northern ones were decentralized republics. The southerners were further away from democracy. The Baganda in particular had a highly complex monarchical system operating on the basis of relatively centralized power. Other southern monarchies included Bunyoro, Ankole, and Toro. All four were not only monarchies but also imperial systems in dynastic terms. On the other hand, the Nilotic and Sudanic communities in the north were often virtually "tribes without rulers." If it is true, as classical American liberalism asserts, that "that government is best which governs least," the northern "tribes" of Uganda approximated that ideal the most closely. They had advisory elders rather than governors in their traditional systems.

The northern Ugandan communities produced Milton Obote, Idi Amin, and Tito Okello as rulers of Uganda. On the other hand, preeminent constitutional lawyers like Godfrey Binaisa (briefly president in 1979–80) and preeminent defenders of human rights like George Kanyeihamba (briefly attorney general in the same period) were descended from southern "tribes." The conclusion that emerges from this cultural and political complexity is that the greatest violators of human rights and of democratic principles in postcolonial Uganda have been descended from "tribes" whose ancestral origins were egalitarian and republican. On the other hand, the greatest defenders of postcolonial democracy have come from "tribes" whose traditional styles were monarchical and sometimes dictatorial. Particularly relevant are the former kingdoms of Buganda, Ankole, Bunyoro, and Toro.

While northern societies had traditionally been relatively egalitarian and basically nonhierarchical, partly because they were politically highly decentralized, colonization made them part of a country that included monarchical and highly hierarchical societies to the south. Economic and educational changes during the colonial period awakened northerners to their own deepening marginalization in the new country called "Uganda." The very name of the country was southern—derived from the name of the kingdom of Buganda. The capital of the new country—Kampala—was also in the Baganda heartland. Moreover, for a while the British had used the Baganda as their own colonial administrators in other parts of the country. Egalitarian northerners discovered the indignities of being at the lower end of the new hierarchy. The perceived "arrogance" of the Baganda was particularly resented. There was evidence that the Baganda and other southerners despised and looked down upon northerners as uncouth and more distant from Western civilization.

Idi Amin and the North-South Divide. The north acquired a kind of inferiority complex that it had never had in the days before the new political entity of "Uganda" was created. This was the breeding ground of the inflated "macho" of postcolonial northerners. Theirs was a level of cultural and gender assertiveness that was to attain excessive proportions under northerner Idi Amin (1971–79). What should be borne in mind is that although Amin himself was a northerner, allegiance under his administration was between pro-Amin and anti-Amin rather than between north and south. Amin killed more fellow northerners than southerners in his bid to retain power. This was partly because much of the power rivalry within his administration was within the contending factions of militarized northerners.

While on balance it must indeed be affirmed that Idi Amin's impact on Uganda weighed heavily on the side of national disintegration, there were factors in his administration that were *potentially* integrative. The first was the partial dilution of the north-south divide. That particular gulf could be bridged in theory only if southerners became militarily stronger or if the north became economically more prosperous. While Amin could not be expected to be interested in involving southerners more in military matters, he did attempt to make the north economically more prosperous. His expulsion from Uganda in 1972 of Asians who had opted not to give up British citizenship in favour of Ugandan citizenship was ostensibly designed to help black Ugandans become more successful in commerce and trade. On balance, black northerners benefited more from the expulsion and its aftermath than black southerners. The effect of Amin's arbitrary discrimination in favour of his ethnic compatriots and other supportive northerners was in the

Ali Al'Amin Mazrui is research professor at the University of Jos (Nigeria) and professor at the University of Michigan (U.S.). His numerous publications include Soldiers and Kinsmen in Uganda *and* The Africans: A Triple Heritage. *This article was written in collaboration with Omari H. Kokole, Ugandan lecturer at the University of Michigan.*

direction of restoring the economic balance between north and south. To that extent, his actions were—however unintentionally—nationally integrative.

Obote and the South. Another factor tending toward militarization and authoritarianization of the northern elite was their numerical insecurity. The population of northern Uganda was only a fraction of the population of the Bantu "tribes" of the south. In a liberal democracy based on number of votes, northern ethnic votes would be simply overwhelmed by southern ones. The only way in which northern leadership could win against southern politicians was either through popular ideology or through outright military intimidation. Obote's "Move to the Left" in the first republic of Uganda (1967–71) was a northern attempt to create a national base through a popular ideology, in spite of the north's numerical disadvantage as a region.

On the other hand, Obote's style during his second period in power (1980–85) resorted more to northern military intimidation of the south. The second Obote period was in many respects more militarized and more authoritarian than the first in its approach to southern Uganda.

Many southerners felt that their freedom ended not in 1971, when Amin overthrew Obote, but in 1966 and 1967 when Obote scrapped the jointly agreed independence constitution and unilaterally inaugurated a constitution of his own. Indeed, the Baganda were put under a state of emergency for five years, lived to see their monarchy destroyed and their king, hounded into exile, dying in a foreign and distant land. The great majority of the Baganda never forgave Obote for all of this.

For this and other reasons, the southerners found it easier to bear arms against Obote in the 1980s than they did against Amin in the 1970s. It seemed as if southern Uganda's democratization since the colonial days had found a new point of outrage. A number of southern groups went underground as guerrilla movements—some owed allegiance to Yusufu K. Lule (briefly president in 1979), others to former defense minister Yoweri Museveni (*see* BIOGRAPHIES), while still others rallied under separate southern banners. The best organized turned out to be Museveni's National Resistance Army (NRA).

By the middle of 1985 the pressures that southern resistance had placed on the national Army had become so great that tensions began to occur within the Obote government and between the Langi (Obote's "tribe") and the Acholi (the preponderant ethnic group in the national Army). The tensions culminated in the fall of Obote's government in July 1985 and his own second flight into exile. The new government under the leadership of northerner Gen. Tito Okello, an Acholi, was toppled by Museveni's NRA in January 1986. Museveni had restored the military balance between north and south—just as Amin had once attempted to restore the economic balance.

If democracy was to be reconstructed in Uganda on a more stable basis, however, it would require both economic and military forces to be in balance—the north sharing more equitably in the prosperity that the south had so far enjoyed, the south sharing more equitably in the power that the north had previously wielded. Long-term equilibrium would require much more than a peace conference or two, however. What was at stake was the prospect of a truly democratic and just society, defended by a genuinely *national* and *representative* army and based on more vigorous standards of distributive justice than the country had so far attempted.

Homeless children, the victims of war, pose with the staff of one of Uganda's government-run orphanages. The impoverished country, however, could provide little more than shelter. Food scarcity was a particularly difficult problem.

EDWARD A. GARGAN/THE NEW YORK TIMES

(continued from page 440)

effect, the NRA renewed its assault in mid-January 1986. By the end of the month, after heavy fighting in which civilian casualties were high, the NRA had taken Kampala. Okello's forces, which had sacked Kampala, withdrew eastward, pursued by the NRA.

NRA commander Yoweri Museveni (*see* BIOGRAPHIES) was sworn in as president on January 29 and soon afterward announced that he would also be minister of defense. True to his promise to form a broad-based government, he invited five members of the Democratic Party, including its leader, Paul Ssemogerere, three members of former president Milton Obote's Uganda People's Congress, and representatives of two small guerrilla groups to join his Cabinet, in which the NRA held a majority of the posts. In February a proclamation was issued stating that the NRA would rule by decree for a maximum of four years.

Okello's defeated forces, which had been reinforced in 1985 by troops previously belonging to former president Idi Amin's army, continued their retreat eastward almost to the Kenya border and then swung northwestward toward their home territory in the Acholi and West Nile districts. While offering little resistance to Museveni's pursuing troops, they devastated towns and villages through which they passed. Having failed to rally the civilian population against the NRA with stories of atrocities, they either discarded arms and uniforms and tried to blend in with villagers or took refuge in The Sudan or Zaire. The confidence of the northerners, in spite of their suspicion of an army drawn primarily from southern Uganda, was won by the restraint shown by the victorious troops.

National reconciliation was said to be the aim of the new government, which also said in March that it would seek to bring former presidents Amin and Obote to trial for crimes committed while they held office. In furtherance of its campaign to put an end to the widespread corruption, the government announced in April that a commission would be set up to investigate the activities of government ministers and heads of state-owned bodies. In November former vice-president Paul Muwanga was charged with kidnapping two Ugandans in 1981.

In May Museveni repeated Obote's promise to settle the claims of Asians who had forfeited property under Amin's government. This formed part of his plan to restore stability to an economy devastated by incompetence, corruption, and civil war. But a further promise to pay more to farmers for their produce was threatened by the low price offered for coffee, responsible for 90% of Uganda's foreign exchange earnings.

If the government provided evidence of its ability to restore order and set up a sound administration, its chances of attracting external financial aid were good. Its task was not helped by a demand from some of the more conservative Baganda that their monarchy be restored. Museveni replied that only after four years could the demand, along with other constitutional proposals, be considered. More serious was the endemic threat to peace in the northwest posed by former members of the Okello and Amin armies who continued to make incursions over the border from The Sudan. (KENNETH INGHAM)

This article updates the *Macropædia* article EASTERN AFRICA: *Uganda.*

ZAIRE

The republic of Zaire is located in central Africa with a short coastline on the Atlantic Ocean. Area: 2,344,885 sq km (905,365 sq mi). Pop. (1986 est.): 31,080,000. Cap.: Kinshasa. Monetary unit: zaire, with (Oct. 1, 1986) a free rate of 61.57 zaires to U.S. $1 (88.97 zaires = £1 sterling). President in 1986, Mobutu Sese Seko; first state commissioner (prime minister) until October 31, Kengo wa Dondo.

Early in 1986 a seminar held in Kinshasa under the auspices of the UN World Health Organization sought to assess Zaire's medical needs in the future. According to an estimate based upon an annual growth rate of 2.7%, the population would reach 43 million by the year 2000. A second seminar held in neighbouring Congo was intended to deal with the problems of migrant workers crossing the Congo-Zaire border. In May a government spokesman announced that the salaries of civil servants would be raised substantially, while the prices of water and electricity would be reduced in line with the cut in the price of oil products made in April. These measures were intended to help low-paid workers and to conform to the seven-year mandate for reform laid down by Pres. Mobutu Sese Seko.

This concern for the well-being of the people was offset by the stringent policy adopted toward dissidents. The main, though illegal, opposition party, the Union pour la Démocratie et le Progrès Social (UDPS), was a particular target of government attention. In January the minister of public affairs unsuccessfully called for a two-year prison sentence for two former members of the legislature, Tshisekedi wa Mulumba and Kanana Tshongo, for offenses against the head of state. Both were leading figures in the UDPS. In June, however, the two, together with five other prominent UDPS members, were restricted to "their places of origin" for allegedly writing and publishing seditious leaflets and urging university students to revolt. In March an Amnesty International report claimed that in late 1985 over 100 UDPS supporters had been arrested in Kinshasa and in Kasai-Oriental region and that some had been tortured and executed. Similar charges were made in regard to government counterinsurgency operations in Shaba region earlier in the year.

UDPS representatives in Paris appealed to the French government to intervene on their behalf to ensure that they had legal recognition. In reply President Mobutu, speaking at a mass rally on June 24 to celebrate the 19th anniversary of the founding of his ruling Mouvement Populaire de la Révolution, stated that his actions had been part of a new policy of firmness against those who were playing into the hands of evil forces outside the country that were trying to subvert peaceful political progress. He went on to deplore the proliferation of religious sects—in March he banned the Jehovah's Witnesses on the grounds that they constituted a threat to law and order—and the resurgence of tribalism. During a visit of inspection, Prime Minister Kengo wa Dondo said that Shaba had become an international centre of fraud.

In spite of his authoritarian rule, Mobutu continued to retain the support of external creditors. At the beginning of the year, a French private airline, UTA, undertook the reorganization of Air Zaire. In June the contract for the construction of the Mobayembongo hydroelectric power station on the Ubangi River in the Équateur region was awarded to a Yugoslav company, Energoinvest. In the same month, the U.K. announced that it planned to increase financial aid to $3 million in 1987–88, while British investment in Zaire would remain at a high level. A plan to expand electricity supplies in Kivu was backed by an International Development Association loan. The International Monetary Fund (IMF) also released further standby credits of $23.6 million as the first installment of a new 22-month standby aid program.

In late October Mobutu threw down the gauntlet to the IMF and World Bank, as well as to his other creditors, when he announced that he intended to reduce the servicing of foreign debts to 10% of export earnings and 20% of the government's operating income. This represented a reduction of 60% from the previous level of payment. He then abolished the office of prime minister, transferring Kengo wa Dondo to the Foreign Ministry, and appointed Mabi Mulumba, a critic of the high cost of servicing loans, as finance minister.

Mobutu made a deliberate effort to demonstrate his good intentions toward his African neighbours. He held several meetings with representatives of the new government in Uganda to discuss frontier security. On July 10 he visited Angola for talks aimed at improving cross-border relations after Zambia had accused Zaire of allowing U.S. arms to be transported to Angola's National Union for the Total Independence of Angola rebels through its territory. Jointly with Zambian Pres. Kenneth Kaunda, he even expressed the hope, though admitting that the task might not prove easy, that Zaire and Zambia might strive to improve relations. In July Zaire renewed its participation in the work of the Organization of African Unity, suspended in 1984 because of Zaire's disapproval of OAU recognition of the Saharan Arab Democratic Republic.

During a visit to Portugal Mobutu invited Portuguese Pres. Mário Soares to visit Zaire. Israel conveyed a message of goodwill and gratitude to Zaire for having been the first African country to renew diplomatic relations, and discussions took place on October 28 with a view to strengthening military cooperation between the two countries. Two months earlier there had been visits by senior politicians from both South and North Korea. As if to set the seal on his good intentions, in July Mobutu announced that the new ambassador to the U.S. would be the ever buoyant Nguza Karl-I-Bond, the former prime minister who in 1985 had renounced his opposition to the regime. (KENNETH INGHAM)

This article updates the *Macropædia* article CENTRAL AFRICA: *Zaire.*

ZAMBIA

A landlocked republic and member of the Commonwealth, Zambia is in eastern Africa. Area: 752,614 sq km (290,586 sq mi). Pop. (1986 est.): 6,896,000. Cap.: Lusaka. Monetary unit: kwacha, with (Oct. 1, 1986) a free rate of 6.99 kwacha to U.S. $1 (10.10 kwacha = £1 sterling). President in 1986, Kenneth Kaunda; prime minister, Kebby Musokotwane.

During 1986 external praise for the wholehearted manner in which Zambia had adopted the stringent conditions imposed by the International Monetary Fund (IMF) gave little satisfaction to Pres. Kenneth Kaunda. Zambia's desperate economic position was, he said in August, primarily the result of the unfavourable economic terms imposed by wealthy creditor nations. Earlier, however, he had insisted that the country had to retain freedom to condemn the policy of the Western powers toward South Africa, even if it lost external aid as a result. At the beginning of the year, Kaunda redistributed Cabinet posts with the intention of improving economic performance. In December a curfew was imposed for a week in the northern Copperbelt Province as protesters against food price increases rioted and looted in a number of towns. During the unrest, reported to be the worst Zambia had seen since independence, 15 people died.

On the recommendation of the IMF, a foreign exchange auction system had been introduced in 1985. The auction system proved highly controversial, but the government maintained that the auction was essential to Zambia's economic survival. In July the government introduced a number of administrative changes designed to minimize chances for abuse of the system. (KENNETH INGHAM)

This article updates the *Macropædia* article SOUTHERN AFRICA: *Zambia.*

ZIMBABWE

A republic and member of the Commonwealth, Zimbabwe is a landlocked state in eastern Africa. Area: 390,759 sq km (150,873 sq mi). Pop. (1986 est.): 8.4 million. Cap.: Harare. Monetary unit: Zimbabwe dollar, with (Oct. 1, 1986) a free rate of Z$1.65 to U.S. $1 (Z$2.39 = £1 sterling). President in 1986, the Rev. Canaan Banana; prime minister, Robert Mugabe.

Throughout 1986 attempts to achieve unity between the ruling Patriotic Front Party, the Zimbabwe African National Union (ZANU [PF]), and the Zimbabwe African People's Union (ZAPU) attracted a great deal of attention. Hopes were repeatedly raised, only to subside when one or another of the parties acted in a manner that discouraged optimism. Toward the end of January prospects looked dim when three senior officials of ZAPU were charged with treason. Yet a week later three other ZAPU officials, including Stephen Nkomo, brother of ZAPU leader Joshua Nkomo, were released after six months of detention. In March Joshua Nkomo indicated in a speech at a ZAPU rally in Bulawayo, Matabeleland Province, that the move toward unity was making no progress. Soon afterward, however, he and Enos Nkala, the Ndebele-speaking minister of home affairs regarded as strongly opposed to ZAPU, made a joint appeal for peace in Matabeleland.

On March 11 Vote Moyo, former secretary-general of ZAPU, was released after nearly four years' detention. He had consistently denied a charge of plotting to kill Prime Minister Robert Mugabe. Released at the same time, but for health reasons, was Lookout Masuku, former commander of the military wing of ZAPU. Although acquitted in 1983 of a charge of stockpiling arms with a view to overthrowing Mugabe's government, Masuku had been immediately detained under emergency regulations. He survived only a month after his release before dying of a rare brain disease. Speaking at his funeral, Nkomo again endangered the move toward unity by comparing the rule of Mugabe to Hitler's fascism.

In April Mugabe insisted that unity talks were still on course. He sharply criticized members of his own party who, he said, were fomenting tribalism. He was referring principally to Transport Minister Herbert Ushewokunze, who, in response to charges by the Public Accounts Committee of nepotism and general mismanagement of the national railways and Air Zimbabwe, claimed that his accusers—by implication, members of the Karanga subgroups of the Shona-speaking section of the population—had been motivated by tribal rivalry and were seeking to gain political control of the whole country. Justice Minister Eddison Zvobgo denied the charge, and Ushewokunze was removed from membership in the Politburo.

In June Michael Auret, national chairman of the Catholic Commission for Justice and Peace, and Nicholas Ndebele, acting director, were arrested. Attempts to obtain their release through the courts were frustrated by the severity of emergency regulations until Mugabe intervened personally on their behalf. In July more than 100 people were arrested under state of emergency regulations in the southern border town of Beitbridge, and once again senior officials of ZAPU were among those detained. On August 18 ten other leading ZAPU members were released.

In August Amnesty International was denounced as an enemy of the state by Nkala, who went on to issue a severe warning to anyone who might contemplate passing information to Amnesty. Yet in October Nkala announced that all remaining ZAPU detainees would be released. The release in December of Dumiso Dabengwa, regarded as one of the most influential ZAPU figures, removed a major stumbling block on the path to unity.

The uneasiness of ZANU (PF) regarding security was reflected in the fact that, although it was assumed that when the state of emergency was renewed in January it would be for the last time, it was subsequently renewed in July. This was done in spite of the fact that laws passed in April gave considerable emergency powers to the government. Continued guerrilla activity in Matabeleland by people claiming to be supporters of ZAPU provided some justification for the unease, but Nkomo himself denounced these actions as counterproductive.

Warnings of forthcoming constitutional changes were issued. In April, referring to the constitutional clause reserving 20 seats in the National Assembly for whites, the prime minister announced that racial representation in Parliament had to come to an end within 12 months. To achieve this end he needed support from at least some of Nkomo's followers so that he could obtain the 70 votes required to change the constitution. In October Justice Minister Zvobgo also confirmed that Zimbabwe would change its Westminster-style parliamentary system in 1987. There would be an executive president, and the Senate would be abolished.

While agriculture continued to prosper, the government announced its second five-year (1986–90) economic development plan. It emphasized both socialism and private enterprise. The previous plan had been ruined by three years of drought. The new scheme aimed at a moderate increase of 5% a year in gross domestic product. Other targets were to reduce foreign debts and budget deficits. For the first time since the government took office, guidelines were drawn up to encourage foreign investors.

Relations with South Africa, the main trading partner and transporter of a considerable proportion of Zimbabwe's produce, deteriorated. Trouble began in May when South African troops attacked alleged African National Congress targets in the centre and suburbs of Harare. Soon afterward Mugabe became one of the leaders of the Commonwealth campaign to impose economic sanctions to pressure South Africa to end apartheid. He was aware that the country was vulnerable to reprisals by South Africa but insisted that his people were prepared to suffer whatever ill effects might result. He strongly advised against withdrawing from the Commonwealth as a gesture of disapproval against the U.K.'s unwillingness to impose sanctions because he feared that to do so would benefit only South Africa.

Mugabe suffered embarrassment when it was revealed that Zimbabwe had just renewed a trade agreement with South Africa that gave Zimbabwe substantial benefits. He replied that he would tear up the treaty, and when he became chairman of the Nonaligned Movement at its meeting in Harare in September, he called for stricter economic measures against South Africa. He was also reassured by promises from four leading petroleum companies that they would find alternative routes for the importation of oil in the event of a South African boycott of Zimbabwe's trade. In spite of the criticism leveled by Mugabe, the U.K. made two further grants amounting to more than $16 million, bringing the total of British aid to Zimbabwe over the previous six years to nearly $240 million.

It was a severe blow to Mugabe when his friend and ally of many years, Pres. Samora Machel (*see* OBITUARIES) of Mozambique, was killed in an airplane crash in October. Zimbabwean troops, initially sent to Mozambique to protect the oil pipeline and railway from the coast to the interior, extended their range of activities considerably during 1986. They had successfully attacked strongholds held by the rebel Mozambique National Resistance (MNR), which was operating against the government of Mozambique. Fearing that the rebels, and possibly South Africa, might seize the opportunity provided by Machel's death to overthrow the Mozambican government, Mugabe announced that he would do all in his power to prevent such an occurrence. The MNR in its turn declared war on Zimbabwe in a statement issued in Lisbon on October 28.

(KENNETH INGHAM)

This article updates the *Macropædia* article SOUTHERN AFRICA: *Zimbabwe*.

Middle East and North Africa

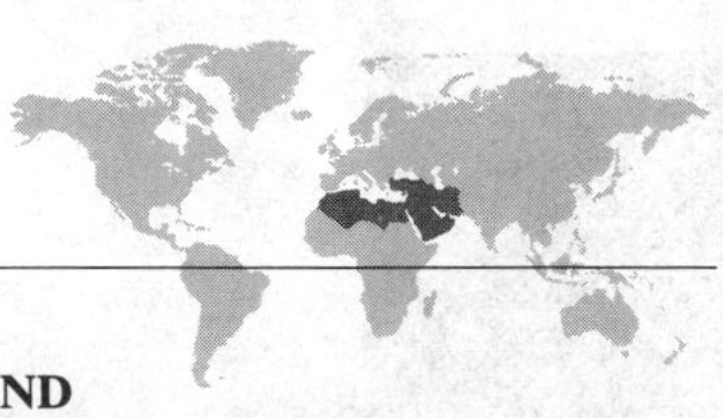

MIDDLE EASTERN AND NORTH AFRICAN AFFAIRS

The escalation of terrorism and the new level of danger posed by the Gulf war between Iran and Iraq characterized 1986, a year in which most new initiatives for peace were stillborn. The meeting of the year, between Morocco's King Hassan II (*see* BIOGRAPHIES) and Israeli Prime Minister Shimon Peres, brought bitter recriminations in the Arab world, while the first Egyptian-Israeli summit in five years similarly bore few tangible results. A slump in world energy prices in the first six months of 1986 brought fresh headaches for the rich Gulf states and further affected their ability to give aid to poorer countries. After several false starts, the Organization of Petroleum Exporting Countries finally agreed on a plan to raise oil prices, but at year's end it was too soon to assess the results.

Terrorism. The attacks by gunmen at check-in counters of the Israeli El Al airline at Rome and Vienna airports on Dec. 27, 1985, were blamed by the U.S. on Libya, which allegedly trained the Palestinian group responsible. Libya was also blamed for a mid-flight explosion on April 2, 1986, on board an Athens-bound U.S. Trans World Airlines plane, in which four Americans were killed, and the April 5 bombing of a West Berlin nightclub frequented by U.S. military personnel in which a U.S. serviceman and a Turkish woman were killed. The incidents provoked a crisis that resulted in the U.S. air strike on Tripoli and Benghazi in Libya. (*See* below.)

An even more serious spate of attacks was linked to extremists operating from Lebanon with covert support from Iran and Syria. Five bomb attacks that took place in France in early September were linked to demands for the release of a Lebanese, Georges Ibrahim Abdallah, who had been convicted of terrorist acts in France. Bomb explosions in Paris in September left 10 dead and more than 160 wounded. The attacks were also interpreted as a general offensive against French policy in the Middle East. On September 18 the French military attaché in Beirut, Christian Dutièrre, was assassinated.

In late autumn the spotlight was turned on Syria and Syrian Pres. Hafez al-Assad. On October 24 Nezar Hindawi, a Jordanian who held a Syrian passport, was convicted in th U.K. and sentenced to 45 years in prison for a plot—in which Syrian officials were implicated—to blow up an Israeli airliner. On November 25 a West Berlin court convicted two Arabs—one of them was Hindawi's brother—of carrying out a bombing in the city in March. The U.K. broke diplomatic links with Syria, and West Germany expelled five Syrian diplomats.

The attitude of Western countries was complicated by the fact that a number of their nationals were being held hostage by extremist groups in Lebanon. On November 2 U.S. hostage David Jacobsen, who had been held since May 1985 by the Islamic Jihad ("Islamic Holy War") group, was released in Beirut. Subsequently, two French hostages were freed via Damascus. The U.S. weapons deal with Iran that came to light shortly afterward provoked a major domestic crisis in the U.S. (*See* North America: *United States,* below.) The U.S. denied that the arms deliveries were directly related to the release of hostages held by pro-Iranian forces in Lebanon. The matter was still under investigation at year's end, but at best it was an embarrassing incident for an administration that had made the hard-line fight against terrorism the main plank of its Middle East policy.

The Gulf War. The Gulf war entered its seventh year in September with fighting, particularly in the air, at a new level of intensity. According to the shipping newspaper *Lloyd's List,* some 260 ships had been hit in the Gulf, with the deaths of 250 seamen, since May 1981. There were fears that the UN-brokered truce that ended the 1985 "war of the cities" would collapse completely. On November 25 Iraqi jets attacked Dezful and Andimeshk, killing more than 200 people. The following day Iran fired a missile at Baghdad, killing 53. Iraq also reported Iranian air and artillery strikes on Basra and the northern town of Arbil. In what appeared to be a widening of the war on November 25, Iranian fighter planes attacked an oil rig off the coast of Abu Dhabi, killing eight men. Iraqi jets struck the Iranian oil-loading terminal at Larak Island, hitting four tankers. The Iranians had been using a fleet of shuttle tankers to ferry petroleum down the 640-km (400-mi) "Exocet alley" (the Iraqi Air Force used Exocet missiles) from their main export terminal at Kharg Island to Larak in the Strait of Hormuz.

Iran had increased the pressure on Iraq in the land war in a number of ways. The Iranians joined forces with Iraqi Kurdish guerrillas to attack targets deep inside Iraqi territory, including the Dokan Dam. On May 14 Iraq claimed to have recaptured the strategic Kardamend peak, overlooking the Haj Omran Valley near the Iranian border. In February, however, Iran had demonstrated its ability to break through Iraqi defenses when it established a bridgehead at Fao in the south. On March 24 Iran's religious leaders announced that all able-bodied men should go to the front.

All diplomatic efforts to end the war appeared doomed to fail despite evidence of better contacts between Iran and Saudi Arabia, Iraq's principal guarantor. The deputy chairman of Iran's Majlis (parliament) visited the kingdom on March 23 for talks with Crown Prince Abdullah ibn Abdelaziz. Summing up the general view of the conservative Gulf states, Gulf Cooperation Council (GCC) Secretary-General Abdullah Bishara said on September 23 that it was "nightmarish" to compare the societies of the Gulf with what they might become if Iran won the Gulf war. Bishara issued a plea for "tolerance, moderation, and dialogue" to end the war and secure the future of the GCC.

Gulf Cooperation Council. Defense and security issues dominated the GCC summit, held in Abu Dhabi, United Arab Emirates, on November 2–5. The heads of state of the six member states—Saudi Arabia, Qatar, Kuwait, Oman, Bahrain, and the United Arab Emirates—called for an immediate cease-fire in the Gulf war and for an end to attacks on shipping in the Gulf. In a bid to improve collective security, the GCC had formed its own rapid deployment force, the Peninsula Shield, and there were suggestions that it would buy maritime patrol aircraft in 1987. After the summit Saudi Arabia issued a tender for the supply of submarines, which it was believed the kingdom might operate on behalf of GCC member states.

Procedures for imposing unified tariffs on foreign goods were expected to be completed by GCC states in March 1987. In the sphere of economic cooperation with the European Communities (EC), however, there were setbacks. In November the EC tightened its tariff system on petrochemical imports from Saudi Arabia and the other GCC nations. In other areas GCC states failed to take common action, although the interests of the small producers—Qatar, Oman, and Bahrain—were discussed at a GCC ministerial meeting in Abha, Saudi Arabia, on August 25–27.

A border dispute between two member states, Qatar and Bahrain, which resulted in a helicopter attack on a work site, was another setback to the cause of cooperation. To some extent, this was compensated for by the establishment of the first road link between Bahrain and Saudi Arabia, formally opened by King Fahd of Saudi Arabia and Sheikh Isa ibn Sulman al-Khalifah, emir of Bahrain, in a ceremony on November 26.

The Arab World and Arab-Israeli Relations. The quest for a lasting peace settlement was the subject of a surprise meeting between Israeli Prime Minister Shimon Peres and King Hassan of Morocco. The meeting in Rabat, Morocco, on July 21–23 was the first officially acknowledged meeting between an Israeli and an Arab leader since 1981 and invited comparison with the historic visit of Egyptian Pres. Anwar as-Sadat to Jerusalem in 1977. In 1986 the Moroccan monarch was, however, cast in the role of mediator rather than negotiator, since the key man on the Arab side in regard to the Palestinian issue remained King Hussein of Jordan. The Peres visit was prepared with the help of leaders of the Jewish community in Morocco. On the Arab side, reaction from Pres. Hosni Mubarak of Egypt was most cordial, but Syria responded by breaking off diplomatic relations with Morocco.

A much narrower agenda was prepared for a summit meeting in Alexandria, Egypt, between Mubarak and Peres on September 11–12, which took place after late-night agreement was reached to refer the territorial dispute over Taba, a strip of land in the Sinai Peninsula, to arbitration. The meeting, while it brought Peres some support at home, did not lead to the sort of breakthrough needed to end Egypt's isolation from the rest of the Arab world. In Alexandria the two leaders talked about an international conference to discuss a full Arab-Israeli peace. President Mubarak wanted to go on to Washington to pursue the idea, but he shelved the trip after the proposal met with a lukewarm response from the U.S.

Stumbling blocks existed on the road to an international conference: the Soviets wished to be included, and the Arabs were unable to agree on whether the Palestine Liberation Organization (PLO) should attend. In Helsinki, Fin., on August 18, the Israeli government held its first talks since 1967 with the Soviets, who reiterated their desire to be involved in any international conference on peace but were angered by Israel's determination to discuss the status of Soviet Jews.

The peace question was greatly complicated by the ac-

AP/WIDE WORLD

Moroccan King Hassan II (left) and Israeli Prime Minister Shimon Peres meet in Morocco in July for a rare summit with potentially broad implications for the Middle East.

tions of King Hussein of Jordan. Having worked for 12 months with PLO chairman Yasir Arafat on a joint peace initiative aimed at the U.S. and Israel, the Jordanian monarch on February 19 announced that he was "unable to coordinate politically with the PLO." The king said progress toward a peace deal had been blocked by the PLO's demand that any negotiations be preceded by U.S. recognition of the Palestinian people's right to self-determination. Hussein said the U.S. had offered to recognize the Palestinians' "legitimate rights"—a term used in the 1978 Camp David agreements—but not self-determination. Arafat's standing among Palestinians would have been compromised if he had accepted the U.S. conditions, since this would have gone against Palestine National Council resolutions.

On July 7 King Hussein closed the Jordanian offices of Arafat's al-Fatah group. Having also been nudged out of Tunisia, the PLO was forced to regroup in its old haunts in Lebanon. The Palestinian camps in the disputed south of Lebanon, especially those just outside Sidon, contained more guerrillas loyal to Arafat than at any other time since the Israeli invasion in 1982.

By moving against the PLO, King Hussein was in fact making a concession to Israel. It was thought that the most Peres could offer was a partial withdrawal from the West Bank, limited autonomy to the Palestinians in the occupied territory, and a freeze on new settlements. The major constraint on Peres was the fragile nature of the Israeli government; in accordance with the agreement made when the coalition government was formed, he handed over the prime ministership to the more hard-line Likud leader Yitzhak Shamir (*see* BIOGRAPHIES) in October. On taking office, Shamir called for increased settlement in the West Bank and Gaza Strip. His Cabinet colleague Ariel Sharon said Israel should assassinate Palestinian leaders and attack their command posts.

A wave of anti-Arab violence erupted in Jerusalem after the stabbing on November 15 of a Jewish religious student. After the attack, Israeli aircraft carried out two raids on Palestinian targets in Sidon. On the Arab side, the forces of restraint had also grown weaker. On November 22 a leading Palestinian moderate, Anwar Nusseibeh, died after a long illness, but his funeral at the al-Aqsa Mosque was marred by the activities of PLO members. The chairman of the Supreme Muslim Council for Jerusalem, Sheikh Saad ed-Din al-Alami, called on European and U.S. diplomats to ask for international protection of the city's Arab population.

Syria, regarded as central to any peace settlement, appeared to be moving its position closer to that of Jordan when President Assad visited Amman in May, but the promise was not fulfilled. Assad's internal difficulties over the terrorism issue made his own policies even more isolated: support for Iran in the Gulf war; backing for pro-Iranian bands of Muslim guerrillas in Lebanon; and opposition to any appeasement toward Israel on the Palestinian issue. Nevertheless, Assad was still considered to be a survivor, despite the fact that his regime was drawn from a minority group in Syria.

U.S. Policy. The U.S.-Iran weapons deal, first made public through a report in the Beirut weekly *al-Shiraa,* was damaging to U.S. interests in the Middle East, since it made a mockery of declared administration policy on terrorism. It was also revealed that Israel had been providing weapons to Iran almost continually since the start of the Gulf war. After talks with King Hussein in Cairo on November 23, President Mubarak expressed pained astonishment over the Iranian affair. U.S. dealings with fundamentalist Iran were of no help to the president in his own efforts to keep Egypt's religious extremists quiet.

It was clear that, despite the freeze in U.S.-Iranian relations since the Tehran U.S. embassy hostage crisis of 1979–81, the two sides had some things in common: hostility to Communism and opposition to any disruption of the flow of oil through the Strait of Hormuz. The need to block Soviet expansion toward the Gulf through Iran had been a constant theme in U.S. Middle East policy since World War II. The ground for a U.S.-Iran dialogue on the subject was laid in 1983, when Iran cracked down on the Communist Party. The covert arms deal with Iran was set up through U.S. Pres. Ronald Reagan's National Security Council.

More orthodox U.S. policy in regard to the Middle East was the subject of Vice-Pres. George Bush's visit to the region July 27–August 5. At the end of his four-day stay in Israel, Bush promised that the U.S. would continue to ensure Israel's qualitative military advantage over its potential enemies. Bush wanted to take advantage of the Peres-Hassan meeting, but King Hussein told the vice-president that he would not start direct negotiations with Israel about the future of the West Bank.

Despite the U.S.'s military commitment to Israel, President Reagan was able to secure passage through Congress of a truncated weapons deal for Saudi Arabia in June. Opponents of the deal pointed to Saudi Arabia's condemnation of the U.S. military attacks on Libya in April. The attacks, which had led to a call for an Arab summit, were made in response to alleged acts of Libyan-inspired terrorism against U.S. nationals. Israel was pleased by the raid, seeing it as a vindication of its own long-standing policy of massive retaliation against "terrorist bases." Canada and the U.K.—the raid was launched from bases in the U.K.—also supported the president's action, which came after a period of growing tension between Libya and U.S. forces in the Gulf of Sidra.

North Africa. The U.S. raid on Tripoli and Benghazi was a severe trial for Col. Muʿammar al-Qadhdhafi, whose own adopted daughter was killed when bombs damaged his barracks headquarters. (See *Libya,* Special Report, below.) The colonel was confident enough of his position to travel to the Nonaligned Movement's summit in Harare, Zimbabwe, in September. Libya expressed anger with Morocco following the July meeting between King Hassan and the Israeli prime minister, although it was in fact the Moroccan monarch who formally broke off the two-year political union between the two countries on August 29. The Libyan leader claimed it was still in force as "both peoples" had ratified it. Tripoli served notice of its new views of North African affairs by inviting the president of the self-proclaimed Saharan Arab Democratic Republic (SADR)—Morocco's rival for power in the Western Sahara—to attend a military parade marking the anniversary of Qadhdhafi's seizure of power. In the changing North African political scene, Algeria's Pres. Chadli Bendjedid was improving links with Libya, making a visit to Tripoli on December 3. Algeria had sponsored attempts to bring Libya and Tunisia into a regional alliance following the standoff between Morocco and Libya. Chadli also visited Tunisia on December 4.

The Tunisian authorities demonstrated their increasing reluctance to play host to the PLO in their capital by imposing travel restrictions on PLO officials. Their disaffection with the PLO dated from September 1985 when Israel struck at the PLO headquarters. Baghdad, Iraq, was viewed as the most likely site for the PLO's new home base.

(JOHN WHELAN)

ALGERIA

Algeria is a socialist republic of North Africa on the Mediterranean Sea. Area: 2,381,741 sq km (919,595 sq mi). Pop. (1986 est.): 22,566,000. Cap.: Algiers. Monetary unit: Algerian dinar, with (Oct. 1, 1986) a free rate of 4.63 dinars to U.S. $1 (6.69 dinars = £1 sterling). President in 1986, Col. Chadli Bendjedid; prime minister, Abdelhamid Brahimi.

During 1986 events in Algeria were dominated by the collapse in oil prices, which declined from their 1985 levels of around $27 a barrel to $11 a barrel by midyear before recovering to almost $15 a barrel. On April 21 the government revised its 1986 budget, originally drawn up at the end of 1985. The revision involved cuts of 11% in recurrent expenditure, 26% in investment expenditure, and a 300% growth in the budget deficit to 15 billion dinars. Hydrocarbon revenues were expected to fall by 40% and nonhydrocarbon revenues by 18%. Within the Organization of Petroleum Exporting Countries (OPEC), Algeria fought alongside the radicals to maintain high oil prices rather than increasing OPEC's market share. Concern over the size of the external debt added to the government's difficulties in raising loans on the international financial markets. A $500 million loan for the Banque Algerienne de Developpement was rejected by European banks in early 1986, although it was later taken up by Japanese banks at the lower level of $300 million. According to the Organization for Economic Cooperation and Development, the external debt stood at $18 billion at the start of the year.

At the same time, the government continued its policy of economic liberalization, approved in a referendum on the National Charter on January 16 by over 98% of the electorate. The National Popular Assembly approved austerity measures in mid-July. In November 186 people were sentenced to prison terms in the wake of violent demonstrations in Constantine that apparently began as a protest by students against poor living standards.

Limited development projects went ahead, with plans for a new steel plant at Bellara and an engine plant as a joint venture with Tunisia at Sakiet Sidi Youssef, Tunisia. The Assembly objected, however, to a new investment law that would have allowed foreign companies more than 50% ownership of joint companies. Pres. Chadli Bendjedid announced a Cabinet reshuffle in February in which Abdelaziz Khellef became finance minister in place of Boualem Benhamuda and Abdelmalek Nourani replaced Abderrahmane Belhayet as housing minister. Chadli also reinforced his position in the Army by promoting six supporters to the rank of general. Although he suffered from a slipped disk in July and was treated for the condition in Belgium, Chadli was able to visit Sweden and the U.S.S.R.

In foreign affairs Algeria maintained its support for the Polisario Front in the Western Sahara, although its straitened financial circumstances ensured that the struggle would take place on the diplomatic front. The major development in both regional and international terms was the surprise meeting between Chadli and Col. Mu'ammar al-Qadhdhafi of Libya on the Algerian-Saharan border on January 28. Subsequently, the two countries agreed to cooperate over electrical supply, oil exploration, industry, and mining, with Algeria also offering natural gas supplies and cooperation over aluminum production. At the end of the year Libya proposed a separate treaty of union, after Morocco broke off links with Libya. (See *Morocco,* below.)

(GEORGE JOFFÉ)

This article updates the *Macropædia* article NORTH AFRICA: *Algeria.*

BAHRAIN

The monarchy (emirate) of Bahrain consists of a group of islands in the Persian Gulf between the Qatar Peninsula and Saudi Arabia. Area: 685 sq km (264 sq mi). Pop. (1986): 435,000. Cap.: Manama. Monetary unit: Bahrain dinar, with (Oct. 1, 1986) a free rate of 0.38 dinar to U.S. $1 (0.54 dinar = £1 sterling). Emir in 1986, Isa ibn Sulman al-Khalifah; prime minister, Khalifah ibn Sulman al-Khalifah.

A territorial dispute between Bahrain and Qatar erupted in April 1986 when Qatari troops in helicopters landed on the island of Fasht al-Dibal, which lies roughly halfway between the two countries. They seized 30 men who were working on the construction of a coast guard station for a Dutch contractor employed by the Bahrain Ministry of Defense. The project was allegedly under the auspices of the Gulf Cooperation Council, to which both states belonged. Despite mediation by several Arab leaders, the matter was not resolved, and in early August the coast guard station structure was removed.

The incident brought to three the territorial disputes between Bahrain and Qatar, most notable of which was that over Hawar Island off the west coast of Qatar. A return to normal relations was indicated, however, by the visit of Bahrain's foreign affairs minister to Qatar in early August.

Plans to open a stock exchange were going forward despite the fact that recession in the region led several international banks to withdraw from Bahrain in 1986. The causeway to Saudi Arabia was officially opened at a ceremony by the heads of state of both countries on November 26. It was named the King Fahd Causeway in recognition of the fact that Saudi Arabia had borne the cost.

In December 1985 Bahrain announced that, unlike its Gulf neighbours, it would not afford diplomatic recognition to the U.S.S.R.

(JOHN WHELAN)

This article updates the *Macropædia* article ARABIA: *Bahrain.*

CYPRUS

An island republic and member of the Commonwealth, Cyprus is in the eastern Mediterranean Sea. Area: 9,251 sq km (3,572 sq mi). Pop. (1986 est.): 674,000. Area and population figures include the Turkish Cypriot state that has occupied the northern third of the island since 1974, though its existence is not internationally recognized. Official population estimates may not take into account the recent and reportedly extensive Turkish immigration and Greek emigration. Cap.: Nicosia. Monetary unit: Cyprus pound, with (Oct. 1, 1986) a free rate of £C 0.52 to U.S. $1 (£C 0.75 = £1 sterling). President in 1986, Spyros Kyprianou.

During 1986 efforts to bring the Greek and Turkish communities in Cyprus into a federation moved into complete deadlock. The UN continued its efforts to forge a federal republic, and a round of talks between the two communities early in the year resulted in a draft federal agreement prepared by UN Secretary-General Javier Pérez de Cuéllar in March. While Turkish Cypriots accepted the draft accord with reservations, Greek Cypriots promptly rejected it as pro-Turkish Cypriot for its failure to address some of their key concerns, such as the withdrawal of 23,000 Turkish troops in north Cyprus, international guarantees for a new state, and the rights of all citizens to move, live, and buy property anywhere on the island. Greek Cypriots counterproposed either an international conference or a meeting of Cypriot leaders. The conference proposal was aimed at accommodating a Soviet plan that included complete demilitarization of the island.

A visit to northern Cyprus by Turkish Prime Minister

Turgut Ozal in July sparked massive Greek Cypriot protests. Crossing points on the "green line" dividing Cyprus—used by diplomats, UN troops, and journalists—were closed by demonstrators. Ozal proposed an economic package to liberalize the ramshackle state-dominated economy in the north; this would lead to economic integration with Turkey and turn the Turkish Cypriot sector into a virtual free-trade zone. Left-wing opponents of the package withdrew from an uneasy coalition with Prime Minister Dervis Eroglu's right-wing nationalists in the northern Assembly, bringing down the government. Eroglu promptly formed a majority alliance with a small party of right-wing mainland Turkish settlers and headed a new administration.

Cyprus found itself at the centre of regional Arab feuds yet again. Two Cypriot students were kidnapped in Beirut and released in June in a trade-off with a jailed Lebanese, who, armed with grenades, had tried to board a Swissair plane. In August guerrillas attacked Britain's Akrotiri air base with rockets, mortars, grenades, and gunfire, injuring two women. In September gunmen hijacked an airliner in Karachi, Pak., and attempted to have it flown to Cyprus to free Arab prisoners held there for terrorist offenses.

An estimated 900,000 tourists helped generate an economic boom. Central bank figures showed real gross domestic product growth of 3.5% to £C 965 million in 1985. There was trouble on the export front, however, as exports dropped 17% in 1985, compared with a 33% rise in 1984. In the north per capita income was one-quarter of the $6,000-a-year average among Greek Cypriots, and tourism was virtually nonexistent. (THOMAS O'DWYER)

EGYPT

A republic of North Africa, Egypt has coastlines on the Mediterranean and Red seas. Area: 997,739 sq km (385,229 sq mi). Pop. (1986 est.): 49,851,000. Cap.: Cairo. Monetary unit: Egyptian pound (LE), with (Oct. 1, 1986) a par value of LE 1 = U.S. $1.43 and a main official rate (for most business transactions) of LE 0.70 = U.S. $1 (LE 1.01 = £1 sterling). President in 1986, Hosni Mubarak; prime ministers, Ali Lutfi and, from November 10, Atef Sedki.

A surge of unrest culminating in bloody riots on Feb. 25–26, 1986, presented a fresh challenge to Egypt's Pres. Hosni Mubarak, whose government also faced a determined drive by Islamic fundamentalists to unsettle the regime. The appointment of a new Cabinet in November was apparently motivated by concern about the economy. On the international front an agreement was reached with Israel to submit a dispute over a strip of land at Taba in the Sinai Peninsula to international arbitration.

AP/WIDE WORLD

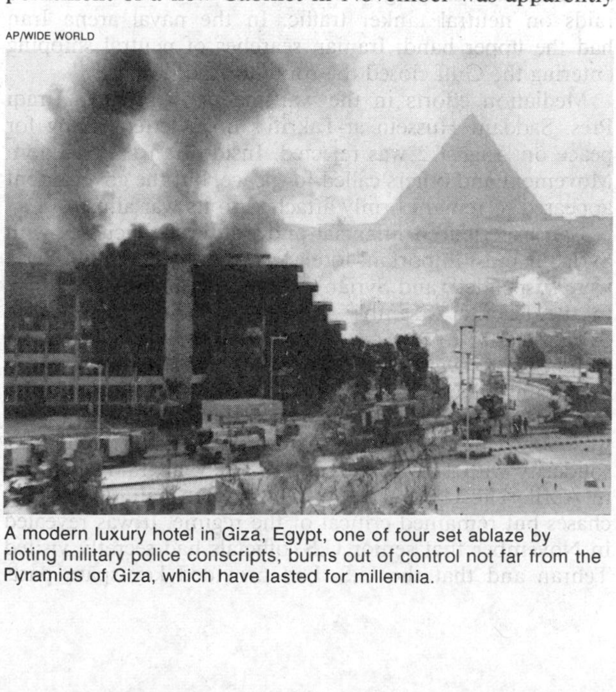

A modern luxury hotel in Giza, Egypt, one of four set ablaze by rioting military police conscripts, burns out of control not far from the Pyramids of Giza, which have lasted for millennia.

Domestic Affairs. The February riots apparently began because of dissatisfaction among security police conscripts. The disorders spread rapidly, inviting comparisons with the 1977 food riots that threatened the regime of the late president Anwar as-Sadat. The incidents started when conscripts at barracks near the Pyramids at Giza, outside Cairo, went on a rampage, ransacking the area's hotels and nightclubs, which pandered to the desires of visiting Arabs from the Gulf states. The Army intervened in strength, and the uprising was quelled at the cost of more than 100 deaths countrywide, according to official figures. About 2,000 conscripts were arrested, and the authorities subsequently announced that 1,240 people would be charged with various offenses.

Immediately after the riots, Interior Minister Ahmad Rushdi resigned and was replaced by Zaki Badr, who had put down an Islamic fundamentalist rebellion in Asyut in 1981–82. It was widely alleged that Islamic fundamentalists had incited the 1986 disturbances by circulating rumours that the conscripts were to have their period of national service extended. However, the Giza governorate subsequently decided to crack down on the red-light district in the area of the Pyramids as a concession to Muslim opinion. One immediate effect of the riots, following soon after the hijacking of the cruise liner *Achille Lauro* off the coast of Egypt in October 1985, was to blunt the drive for more tourists initiated by Tourism Minister Fouad Sultan.

In separate crackdowns on the fundamentalists on April 30, the authorities arrested the blind professor and theologian Omar Ahmad Rahman, along with 55 other people, under emergency powers. The state security court subsequently released them. The death on April 14 of a militant Islamic student shot by police caused mass protest. The government also faced labour trouble. In a dawn raid on February 9 police broke up an occupation by strikers at a textile factory in the Nile Delta town of Mehalla el-Kubra, arresting 111 workers. Troops had to intervene to break a strike by railway workers that began on July 7. Workers had initiated industrial action to support pay claims in the face of sharp increases in the cost of living.

Opposition parties boycotted elections to the 140 elective seats in the Majlis al-Shura (the consultative upper house of Parliament) on October 1. Interior Minister Bakr announced that 82% of those eligible had cast their votes.

In a surprise move reflecting concern about deteriorating economic conditions, on November 10 Mubarak dismissed the Cabinet and appointed Atef Sedki as prime minister. An economist with no previous experience of political office, Sedki retained several ministers from the previous Cabinet but appointed new ministers of finance and economy. On December 16 the authorities announced that they had uncovered a plan by an underground Communist group to overthrow the government. Two earlier plots against the regime reported since September were said to have involved Islamic fundamentalists.

The Economy. Egypt was in deep trouble with its international creditors because of its rising burden of debt, lower foreign exchange earnings from both oil and worker remittances, and failure to curb imports effectively. As a result of weak oil prices, Egypt was expected to lose $1.2 billion in oil revenue in 1986. On August 22 a package of economic reforms that had been under scrutiny for 18 months was announced. The measures sought to replace physical controls by price mechanisms as a way of limiting imports. The new tariff system was combined with a reform of the customs administration. A list of prohibited imports, including soap, was published.

In statements at the annual meeting of the International Monetary Fund (IMF) and World Bank, Egyptian officials stressed that no debt rescheduling would take place except on a bilateral basis, possibly with large creditor governments such as France and the U.S. External debt reached $38.6 billion, including military debts of some $7 billion owed to Western governments. By year's end the chances of securing a loan from the IMF appeared to have improved as the government was reported to be considering introducing changes to its interest rate system, domestic interest rates, and policy of subsidizing foodstuffs. It was expected that more than 200,000 workers would have returned to Egypt from the Gulf states by the end of the year, reducing a vital prop of the economy, worker remittances. The Suez Canal Authority said in late July that it was confident that in 1986–87 revenues would once again top $1 billion. On July 26 the authority celebrated the 30th anniversary of the canal's nationalization.

On September 3 the Egyptian General Petroleum Corporation acquired its first offshore concession from the government in fulfillment of a policy encouraging exploration work by local firms. In early September Egyptian oil exports were running at 250,000 bbl a day. President Mubarak was optimistic in his address on the state of the economy to the ruling National Democratic Party on July 20. He had just returned from a tour of Rome, Paris, London, and Bonn, during which it was revealed that the European Communities would increase aid to Egypt. In addition to converting some loans into grants, the EC would supply 40,000 metric tons of wheat, bringing the total value of its food aid in 1986 to $36 million. The government also took heart from the Egyptian Investment Authority's June decision in favour of General Motors Corp. of the U.S. establishing an integrated automobile industry. The venture would entail investment of $300 million and included a commitment from General Motors that some of the total would be invested in a local components industry with local partners.

Foreign Relations. President Mubarak and Israel's Prime Minister Shimon Peres discussed Middle Eastern issues in Alexandria on September 11–12. They agreed to explore the possibility of arranging an international conference on the Palestine question. The summit followed the signing of an agreement between the two countries to go to international arbitration over disputed land at the Taba enclave in Sinai. Both sides agreed to accept the arbitrator's decision as final. It was also announced that Egypt's chargé d'affaires in Israel would be promoted to ambassador.

While the summit deal was seen as helping Egypt in its attempt to get more aid from the U.S., it nevertheless represented a setback to President Mubarak's aim of fully reintegrating Egypt into the Arab fold. Following the summit about 20 political activists were arrested in Egypt for possessing tracts condemning the rapprochement. Although Mubarak remained on good terms with most moderate Arab countries, including Jordan, the banning of the semiofficial newspaper *al-Ahram* by Saudi Arabia in May gave a clear indication of Riyadh's displeasure over the Egyptian government's policy. It was the first time in 110 years that *al-Ahram,* the Arab world's foremost newspaper, had been banned in the kingdom, with the exception of a limited suspension in 1979 following the signing of the bilateral peace agreement between Egypt and Israel.

On August 31 Jordan's Prime Minister Zaid ar-Rifai briefed Mubarak about talks between King Hussein and officials of the U.S.S.R. Egypt's relations with Moscow had been improving gradually during the previous two years, ever since diplomatic relations were restored in 1984. Vladimir Polyakov of the Soviet Foreign Ministry had been the last Soviet ambassador before Sadat expelled the Soviets; on April 5 he visited Egypt for talks with his Egyptian counterparts about improving bilateral relations. Relations with Libya remained strained, despite Egypt's condemnation of the U.S. strike on Tripoli and Benghazi in April. In May it was alleged that the Libyan government had instigated a plot to persuade an Egyptian pilot to defect to Tripoli with his F-16 strike aircraft. Libya claimed it had broken up an Egyptian intelligence network that had provided guidance to U.S. jets. The existence of such a spy ring was denied by Egyptian officials. (JOHN WHELAN)

IRAN

The Islamic republic of Iran is in southwestern Asia on the Caspian and Arabian seas and the Persian Gulf. Area: 1,648,-380 sq km (636,443 sq mi). Pop. (1986 est.): 46 million. Cap.: Tehran. Monetary unit: rial, with (Oct. 1, 1986) an official rate of 76.20 rials to U.S. $1 (110.10 rials = £1 sterling). Supreme *faqih* (spiritual leader) in 1986, Ayatollah Ruhollah Khomeini; president, Sayyed Ali Khamenei; prime minister, Mir Hossein Moussavi.

The war with Iraq reached a critical stage in 1986 as Iranian leaders promised a final offensive to bring the conflict to a rapid and victorious end. It was claimed that between 750,000 and one million fighting men were mobilized, and new weapons supplies were acquired under a series of clandestine deals. Nevertheless, the front remained comparatively quiet. The main event in the land war was the drive by Iranian forces across the Shatt al-Arab on February 10, when the unused Iraqi port of Fao was captured. In late December Iran launched a new offensive in the area. The Iraqis used their supremacy in the air to carry the war to the Iranians, concentrating on destruction of the shuttle tanker fleet used to move oil from the export terminal at Kharg Island to safer ports farther south. In response to an air raid on August 12 on the Sirri terminal, formerly thought to be safe, a new temporary terminal was constructed at Larak Island, but on November 25 it too was bombed. Iranian retaliation to Iraqi air strikes on economic targets took the form of missile strikes on Kirkuk and Baghdad, shelling of Basra and border towns, and air raids on neutral tanker traffic. In the naval arena Iran had the upper hand. Iranian searches of neutral shipping entering the Gulf closed the route to Iraqi imports.

Mediation efforts in the war made no progress. Iraqi Pres. Saddam Hussein at-Takriti's open letter calling for peace on August 2 was rejected. Inside Iran the Freedom Movement and others called for peace, but the government appeared to remain firmly attached to its war aims.

Iran experienced financial and political difficulties with Syria, its most important foreign ally. Oil deliveries to Syria were suspended, and Syrian authorities came under attack in the Islamic Assembly for their policies in Lebanon. Syria's failure to pay an estimated $1 billion debt for oil supplies was eventually resolved, but there was renewed uncertainty about the relationship in June when a Jordanian-sponsored meeting between Syrian and Iraqi officials was only canceled at the last minute. Iran declared its solidarity with Libya following the U.S. air raid on Libya in April. The U.S.S.R. agreed to resume natural gas purchases but remained critical of the regime. It was revealed in November that senior U.S. officials had secretly visited Tehran and that the U.S. had provided key spare parts

Iranian soldiers ignite an American flag and brandish their own flags and photos of the Ayatollah Ruhollah Khomeini to celebrate their taking the Iraqi port of Fao. Despite superior firepower, Iraq's major counteroffensive failed to reclaim the ground.

KAZEMI—JB PICTURES

for aircraft and tanks. Though a number of U.S. hostages held in Lebanon were subsequently released, the U.S. administration denied that it had "negotiated with terrorists" for their freedom, claiming, instead, that it was trying to establish links with moderate elements inside Iran. (*See* North America: *United States,* below.)

Domestic politics were dominated by growing splits within the regime on the issue of the war and by reactions to a possible withdrawal of Ayatollah Ruhollah Khomeini from the centre of the political stage. Ayatollah Hussein Ali Montazeri, Khomeini's heir apparent, sought to withdraw from his position. In November it was confirmed that a number of his aides had been arrested and were to be put on trial. Ayatollah Shariat-Madari (*see* OBITUARIES), who died on April 3, had played a crucial role during the revolution but had opposed Khomeini's interpretations of the Islamic state. His ideas continued to play a part in separating many Shi'ah leaders from the Khomeini regime. A military campaign brought Kurdestan more firmly under central government control.

The economic situation deteriorated. Average oil production in the first half of the year was barely 2 million bbl a day, well under the 2.3 million-bbl-a-day quota set by the Organization of Petroleum Exporting Countries. Oil income fell dramatically to less than $10 billion, compared with some $13 billion in 1985. Despite efforts to reduce imports other than those vital to the war effort, the balance of payments deficit and trade-related debt increased. Agricultural performance was assisted by good weather conditions, but industrial output faltered.

(KEITH S. MCLACHLAN)

IRAQ

A republic of southwestern Asia, Iraq has a short coastline on the Persian Gulf. Area: 438,317 sq km (169,235 sq mi). Pop. (1986 est.): 15,946,000. Cap.: Baghdad. Monetary unit: Iraqi dinar, with (Oct. 1, 1986) a par value of 0.31 dinar to U.S. $1 (free rate of 0.45 dinar = £1 sterling). President in 1986, Saddam Hussein at-Takriti.

As the Gulf war entered its seventh year in September 1986, Iraq faced fresh Iranian attacks, pressure from its trade creditors, and little hope of a breakthrough in its relationship with Syria. Pres. Saddam Hussein at-Takriti could, however, count on friendship with Moscow, together with continued economic aid from Western countries, particularly France. On October 16 an explosion rocked Baghdad, hours after Iran had announced that it would attack Iraqi cities in retaliation for an Iraqi air raid on one of its airports. The prospect of a renewal of the 1985 "war of the cities" and continued attacks by both sides on shipping in the Gulf were constant features of the struggle in 1986. Iraq's success in regaining a series of mountain peaks in the north had to be weighed against disasters in the south. In February the Iraqi Army, caught by surprise, was unable to prevent the Iranians from establishing a bridgehead at the abandoned oil port of Fao in the south, but in December Iraq repulsed a renewed offensive by Iran in the area. Iranian troops also held Iraqi territory at Majnoun and Haj Omran in the north. The war was reported to be costing Iraq up to $1 billion a month.

At the regional conference of the ruling Ba'th Party on July 10, the first since 1982, President Hussein showed his political strength by securing the promotion of several longstanding party members loyal to him. Hussein also displayed his ruthlessness in dealing with alleged corruption. On October 2 it was announced on Baghdad television that seven men, including a former Oil Ministry undersecretary, had been hanged for accepting illegal commissions. At the same time, the government released 100,000 students from military camps to return to their studies.

Although domestic opposition to Hussein was muted, the opposition Al Amal al-Islami group claimed responsibility for the bombing of a Baghdad nightclub on April 6. The Kurdish Democratic Party, which was fighting for autonomy in the Kurdish region, claimed to control 10,000 sq km (3,860 sq mi) of land, but official sources said that the Army had regained control of Mangeish from the Kurds and that the leader of the rebellion, Jaafar Beselki, had been arrested.

An attempted hijack of an Iraq Airways airliner on December 25 ended when the plane crash-landed in Saudi Arabia. Reports suggested that either pro-Iranian groups in Lebanon or dissident Iraqis were responsible for the incident, in which at least 67 people died.

With the opening of the 500,000-bbl-a-day oil pipeline across Saudi Arabia, making it possible to export Iraqi oil without fear of Iranian attack, Iraq's economic prospects looked brighter at the start of 1986. The subsequent fall in the price of oil damaged the economy, however. Plans to cut the import bill by $2 billion in 1986 increased pressure on the government to reschedule the trade debt. In general, Iraq approached the debt problem by seeking bilateral talks with its trading partners. On May 22 Iraqi officials concluded an agreement with France to reschedule medium-term commercial debt, and in September Japanese banks and trading firms agreed to reschedule more than $600 million in commercial debt and contractors' payments. The second phase of the Saudi Arabian pipeline, scheduled for completion in late 1988, would give Iraq the capacity to pump 3.2 million bbl a day.

Although officially neutral in the war, the U.S. was reportedly moving toward advocating an end to the conflict based on Baghdad's terms. However, the situation was complicated late in the year by revelations of clandestine U.S. arms shipments to Iran. During a visit to Baghdad on August 26, Soviet Deputy Foreign Affairs Minister Vladimir Petrovsky told Hussein that his government backed Iraq's peace plan. On May 21 a contract was signed in Moscow for the Soviets to build the first stage of a trans-Iraq gas pipeline. A session of the Iraq-Soviet joint commission agreed to a five-year economic cooperation treaty. Prompted by King Hussein of Jordan, Pres. Hafez al-Assad of Syria was reported to be considering resolving his personal and ideological differences with his Iraqi counterpart.

In June President Hussein pronounced that Iraqi families should have at least five children. In his opinion childbearing was more important for Iraqi women than gaining postgraduate degrees. (JOHN WHELAN)

ISRAEL

A republic of southwestern Asia, Israel is situated on the Mediterranean Sea. Area: 20,700 sq km (7,992 sq mi), not including territory occupied in the June 1967 war. Pop. (1986 est.): 4,381,200. Cap.: Jerusalem (but see Israel table in Britannica World Data). Monetary unit: Israeli sheqel, with (Oct. 1, 1986) a free rate of 1.49 sheqalim to U.S. $1 (2.15 sheqalim = £1 sterling). President in 1986, Chaim Herzog; prime ministers, Shimon Peres and, from October 20, Yitzhak Shamir.

Domestic Affairs. To the surprise of the cynics and skeptics, on Oct. 20, 1986, Labour leader Shimon Peres stepped down as Israel's prime minister in accordance with the coalition agreement on which the government of national unity was based, and Likud leader Yitzhak Shamir (*see* BIOGRAPHIES) took his place. Peres took over as foreign minister and deputy prime minister. The changeover was accomplished without a hitch and with reasonably good grace.

Domestic crises, international complications, and dramatic encounters with Arab leaders marked the second and final year of Peres's premiership, but his most notable accomplishment was in an altogether different field. Before handing over office, Peres had been instrumental in achieving what many saw as the coalition's most significant and lasting success: the conquest of the runaway inflation that was threatening Israel's very existence when he became prime minister in September 1984. The soaring annual inflation rate of over 400% had been reduced to less than 20% by October 1986. The firm measures needed to control inflation were taken largely as a result of Peres's personal leadership and his unwavering insistence that Israel had to have a sound economy if his drive to further the peace process with the nation's Arab neighbours was to have any chance of success.

The candle of Israel's economic expansion had been burning at both ends for many years. Over three decades of Labour-controlled administrations, the economy had grown and flourished, but expansion in education, agriculture, and industry had been assisted by open-ended loans, credits, and subsidies. There had been no other way for a new, poor, arid country without natural resources and with a largely destitute immigrant population to become a flourishing multinational community with a defense force second to none in the region. Nevertheless, a day of reckoning was certain to come sooner or later. It was put off for a time by the Likud bloc, which, having achieved power for the first time in 1977, instituted a liberalized economic policy geared to a high rate of inflation and expansion in the private sector. With the formation of the government of national unity, however, it was evident that drastic measures were needed.

By the end of 1986 Israel's economy was clearly moving in the right direction. Inflation was under control. The sheqel had been revalued and stabilized and was holding its own. The banking system, which had been found to be seriously flawed, was being reformed and reorganized. Economic excesses were being checked and offenders prosecuted. Even so, there were still problems. For the first time Israel had to contend with an unusual degree of unemployment. The standard of living as measured on a per capita income basis had not yet recovered from the cutbacks necessitated by the war on inflation and remained below the 1983 level. While the national economy was back on course, recovery had not yet percolated down to the harder-hit communities. Among these were sectors that in previous years had been considered the showcases of the new Israel—the agricultural settlements and the developments in the Negev Desert. By the end of 1986 they were more like disaster areas than dreams. Having mastered inflation, the government now faced the task of overcoming the consequences. This provided a new and urgent range of priorities.

At the same time, the government was experiencing an unprecedented shortage of income, making it difficult to meet even the most pressing needs. Hitherto unimagined economies were forced on ministers and institutions. Funding shortfalls affected all levels of education, resulting in conflict with the teachers. Even defense, always the last sector to be trimmed, had to make heavy cuts that were considered unacceptable in terms of national security. Essential services suffered in both urban and rural areas. Funds urgently needed to ensure the civil and political well-being of Jerusalem were not forthcoming, despite the vigorous efforts of the city's mayor, Teddy Kollek.

The government was also forced to come to grips with a problem that traditionally had been ignored or sublimated by granting heavy subventions to the religious parties in the Knesset (parliament). Essentially, the religious parties owed their bargaining strength to the fact that they held the balance of power between the Likud "right" and the

UPI/BETTMANN NEWSPHOTOS

Shimon Peres (left) and Yitzhak Shamir officially exchange offices at midterm. The agreement to alternate prime minister and foreign minister posts gave Israel's two major parties equal influence in the coalition government of national unity.

Labour "left." With the establishment of the government of national unity, in which the parties of the right and left were finely balanced, there was an even greater proliferation of religious parties and associated institutions. The full extent of subventions extracted from the national exchequer by the religious groupings had never been fully disclosed, nor had the ultimate destination of these funds. All that was known was that they were very large and emanated primarily from the Ministry of the Interior and the Ministry of Religion, though these were not the only donors. Others included some municipalities and Jewish religious institutions in the U.S. and Europe.

No less disturbing was the influx of extremist ultra-religious students and others into Jerusalem and other towns. Some were well-organized and politically trained immigrants, principally from the U.S. They were seen by many Israelis as a disturbing element that did not reflect the interests or intentions of the majority. (*See* RELIGION.)

By comparison with these larger issues, the day-to-day crises tended to fade into relative insignificance, although they provided the media with short-term sensations. What concerned senior government officials was not the fact of a particular scandal but the evidence it provided of a lowering of standards in the public service. The cover-up of the killing of two Palestinians while in the custody of Israel's domestic intelligence agency, the General Security Services (Shin Bet), in April 1984 led to the resignation and dismissal of senior officials. Following revelations of serious infringement of government regulations by the head of Shin Bet, Avraham Shalom, he resigned in exchange for a promise of immunity from prosecution. In December it was reported that a Justice Ministry inquiry had cleared Shamir (prime minister at the time) of any involvement in the killings or the subsequent cover-up. The recommendations of the Beijski Commission on banking led to the resignations of the governor of the central bank and other leading bankers. These incidents raised questions about the accountability of such institutions as the secret services and the banking community. There was a growing suspicion that there were aspects of government outside the control or even the knowledge of elected officials and/or the responsible minister.

The government faced even greater difficulty in handling so-called rogue operations, such as the involvement of Jonathan Jay Pollard, a U.S. Navy analyst who pleaded guilty in the U.S. of spying for Israel. The entire affair as handled in Jerusalem revealed a degree of operational, organizational, and ministerial laxity that would not have been possible had the government laid down clear guidelines for the security service and retained strict political control over its activities. In November Mordechai Vanunu, a scientist who had worked at a nuclear research centre, was charged with treason for having revealed Israeli nuclear secrets to *The Sunday Times* of London.

A similar lack of governmental control over the activities of the religious parties and their institutions and settlements led to land-sale improprieties and, in November, to a serious outbreak of anti-Arab rioting by religious students in Jerusalem. In some ways both crises—the scandals in the security service and the violence of religious partisans—pointed to a malaise that remained evident despite the improvements in the economy and the positive achievements of the government. It was reflected, not least, in the fact that during 1986 more Jews emigrated from Israel than immigrated to it. While the government made substantial progress in political and economic matters, it seemed to have failed in its relations with the people and in winning credibility.

Following the changeover of the premiership, Peres's standing was suddenly deflated when he found it necessary to make political accommodations in the staffing of the Foreign Ministry. Senior officials of recognized stature found they had to make way for political appointees, and a ministry that had been marked by an exemplary professionalism was plunged into political wheeling and dealing. Following the achievements of his premiership, the start of his tenure as foreign minister was not Peres's finest hour.

Foreign Affairs. While still prime minister, Peres did succeed in infusing the conduct of foreign policy with a spirit of tolerance and demonstrating preparedness to seek accommodation with Israel's neighbours and with leading Arabs in the region. He sought a dialogue with King Hussein of Jordan, whom he saw as a central figure in the peacemaking process. In his efforts to achieve an understanding with Pres. Hosni Mubarak of Egypt, he made concessions, agreeing to refer the dispute over the Taba beach resort in the Sinai Peninsula to an international arbitration tribunal. Most dramatically, Peres traveled to Rabat, Morocco, to meet King Hassan II on July 22–23 and to Alexandria, Egypt, for a summit with President Mubarak on September 11–12. However, the benefits to Israel of these initiatives remained severely circumscribed. Perhaps the only significant element of these meetings—and of the indirect dialogue with King Hussein—lay in the circumstance that they represented, in effect, recognition of Israel as an integral part of the Middle East. Israeli troops remained in southern Lebanon throughout the year. (See *Lebanon,* below.)

Probably more important for Middle East peacemaking in the long run was the indirect, covert link that was established during confidential talks between Iran and Israel. It was no more than a first tentative step, but it suggested the ultimate achievement of a balance between Arab and non-Arab power in the Arabian Peninsula and the Gulf. However, the central themes of this important foreign policy operation, and the significance of the insight that it provided into the Iranian establishment's thinking about the future, were obscured by the controversy that erupted late in the year when details of arms dealings between the U.S and Iran emerged. Israel, which had played a crucial part in arranging the sale of U.S. arms to Iran, came under pressure to reveal the extent of its own arms shipments to that country. As the affair gained momentum in the U.S., Israel insisted that it had not known of any arrangement to trade arms for U.S. hostages in Lebanon or to transfer Iranian money to the Nicaraguan *contras.* (*See* North America: *United States,* below.)

The first diplomatic contact between Israel and the U.S.S.R. in 19 years took place in Helsinki, Fin., on August 18. The meeting apparently ended without agreement on an agenda for further meetings, although an Israeli spokesman said that contacts would continue.

(JON KIMCHE)

JORDAN

A constitutional monarchy, Jordan is located in southwestern Asia and has a short coastline on the Gulf of Aqaba. Area: 89,206 sq km (34,443 sq mi). Pop. (1986 est.): 2,750,000. Cap.: Amman. Monetary unit: Jordan dinar, with (Oct. 1, 1986) a free rate of 0.32 dinar to U.S. $1 (0.46 dinar = £1 sterling). King, Hussein I; prime minister in 1986, Zaid ar-Rifai.

A deterioration in relations with the Palestine Liberation Organization (PLO), abortive attempts to promote Arab unity, and an improvement in Jordan's relations with Syria were features of King Hussein's policies in 1986. He signaled the break with the PLO on February 19 when he said that Jordan was "unable to cooperate politically with the PLO leadership until such time as their word becomes their bond." Hussein accused PLO leader Yasir Arafat of unreliability and indecisiveness, but the real issue appeared to have been Arafat's conditions for starting Middle East peace negotiations. In July the Jordanian government ordered the closing of 25 offices of the PLO's al-Fatah group and expelled Arafat's second in command, Khalil al-Wazir (nom de guerre, Abu Jihad). Hussein accused al-Fatah of tampering with a by-election and promoting campus riots at Yarmuk University, Irbid, on May 15 that left 3 students dead and as many as 200 injured.

At the same time that he broke with Arafat, Hussein began a process of reconciliation with Pres. Hafez al-Assad of Syria. Assad and Hussein had cooperated in the past in taking action against the PLO, but the Jordanian leader was also eager to bring about a rapprochement between Syria and Iraq. Following Hussein's visit to Damascus in December 1985, on May 5 Assad made his first visit to Amman since 1977. However, the fact that no communiqué was issued indicated that the Jordanians had failed to persuade Syria to withdraw support for Iran in the Gulf war.

The meeting between Israel's Prime Minister Shimon Peres and Morocco's King Hassan II (*see* BIOGRAPHIES) on July 21–23 drew a muted reaction from Jordan. In subsequent meetings with U.S. Vice-Pres. George Bush, Hussein rejected suggestions that he enter into direct negotiations with Israel about the future of the West Bank. During talks with Soviet Deputy Foreign Affairs Minister Yury Vorontsov in Amman on August 28, Hussein discussed Moscow's call for an international conference on Middle East peace. In a gesture to refugees from the Israeli-occupied Gaza Strip, Jordan agreed to grant them temporary three-year passports on strictly humanitarian grounds.

In early September the Cabinet endorsed the five-year (1986–90) plan, which called for spending $9.7 billion and aimed at an annual growth rate of 5% in gross domestic product. Priority was given to the creation of new jobs, but the expected influx of workers returning from the Gulf states had yet to materialize. The fact that fewer than 450 families returned between January and August may have been the result of successful mediation with Kuwait over its plans to repatriate Arab workers. A government spokesman announced that all Jordanians in public-sector employment in the Gulf states had been assured of their jobs.

Features of the new plan included heavy investment in water supply, irrigation, roads, communications, and the social services. On September 27 Prime Minister Zaid ar-Rifai said huge oil reserves were awaiting discovery in the southern al-Jafr region, where seismic studies had been carried out by the Hunt Oil Co. of the U.S. In the first half of 1986 phosphate exports were 35% higher than in the corresponding period of 1985.

Opposition in the U.S. Congress resulted in the collapse in late January of a proposed deal under which the U.S. was to have sold weapons to Jordan, but the subject was largely bypassed when Hussein met with U.S. Pres. Ronald Reagan in Washington in June. Jordan concluded a missiles purchase with the U.S.S.R. and was exploring the possibility of buying Mirage interceptor jets from France and the Tornado fighter-bomber from Europe. Hussein's ten-day tour of Oman, Brunei, and Indonesia starting on March 28 included a visit to an Indonesian aircraft factory that was supplying the Jordanian Air Force with two transport aircraft. (JOHN WHELAN)

KUWAIT

A constitutional monarchy (emirate), Kuwait is in the northeastern Arabian Peninsula, on the Persian Gulf. Area: 17,818 sq km (6,880 sq mi). Pop. (1986 est.): 1,791,000. Cap.: Kuwait City. Monetary unit: Kuwaiti dinar, with (Oct. 1, 1986) a free rate of 0.29 dinar to U.S. $1 (0.42 dinar = £1 sterling). Emir, Sheikh Jabir al-Ahmad al-Jabir as-Sabah; prime minister in 1986, Crown Prince Sheikh Saad al-Abdullah as-Salim as-Sabah.

Kuwait's elected National Assembly was suspended on July 3, 1986, after a year of acrimony between its members and the government. Emir Sheikh Jabir implied that the Assembly had been working to "destabilize" Kuwait. On August 31 the last elected body in Kuwait, the Municipal Council, was dissolved, and its powers were handed over to a minister.

On July 1 the Cabinet had resigned to avoid impeachment of three members by the Assembly. The new Cabinet appointed on July 12 brought to the fore a number of technocrats but also redistributed top posts between the two competing branches of the ruling family. A key supporter of the emir, Sheikh Jabir Mubarak al-Hamad as-Sabah, was appointed to the portfolio of social affairs and labour. In a separate move, Sheikh Salim Abdul-Aziz as-Sabah was appointed governor of the central bank on September 28 in place of a leading technocrat who had resigned.

On June 17 explosions caused huge fires at oil export facilities at al-Ahmadi; sabotage was suspected and several arrests were made. On November 29 the death sentence was passed on one of five Iraqis accused of involvement in the assassination attempt on the emir in May 1985. A second accused was sentenced to life imprisonment, while the remaining three were acquitted.

Kuwait continued to emphasize the nonaligned nature of its foreign policy. In February Oil Minister Sheikh Ali al-Khalifah as-Sabah visited Moscow, where he discussed Soviet cooperation in hydrocarbons projects in Kuwait. In May Finance Minister Jassim al-Kharafi announced that plans were being drawn up for Kuwaiti investment in China, India, and the U.S.S.R. He maintained that the new strategy would not threaten Kuwait's investment in Western countries. (JOHN WHELAN)

This article updates the *Macropædia* article ARABIA: *Kuwait.*

LEBANON

A republic of southwestern Asia, Lebanon is situated on the Mediterranean Sea. Area: 10,230 sq km (3,950 sq mi). Pop. (1986 est.): 2,707,000. (The population of Lebanon, including about 500,000 Palestinian refugees, is thought to have declined since the outbreak of civil war in 1974, but reliable figures are not available.) Cap.: Beirut. Monetary unit: Lebanese pound, with (Oct. 1, 1986) a free rate of LL 43.85 to U.S. $1 (LL 63.36 = £1 sterling). President in 1986, Amin Gemayel; prime minister, Rashid Karami.

The civil war in Lebanon entered its 12th year in April 1986, with only fragile hopes of settlement. A comprehensive peace agreement signed in Damascus, Syria, on Dec. 28, 1985, by leaders of the three most powerful militia forces collapsed within a few weeks. In early July Syrian troops were deployed in Beirut for the first time in four years. Israel reinforced its troop deployments in the south in September, while the Palestine Liberation Organization (PLO) was building up its strength. To add to the confusion, rival wings of the (Christian) Lebanese Forces (LF) militia were fighting in Christian East Beirut in the same month.

Militiamen in Beirut, vying for control of a refugee camp, relax their vigilance during an unofficial truce to enjoy television coverage of the World Cup soccer play-offs half a world away in Mexico City.
AFP PHOTO

The Damascus accord had called for a total cease-fire followed by far-reaching political reforms designed to tackle the cause of the civil war. It was signed by Druze leader Walid Jumblatt, Shi'ah Muslim leader Nabih Berri, and Elie Hobeika, leader of the Maronite LF. The first blow to the settlement was the overthrow of Hobeika by Samir Geagea, the LF chief of staff. Infighting between supporters of the two leaders continued throughout the year. Pres. Amin Gemayel also spoke out against the cease-fire arrangement.

In April the PLO was reported to have established a strong presence in Sidon, prompting Israeli air raids on the city. The PLO was also consolidating its position in Beirut's refugee camps, where clashes with the (Shi'ah Muslim) Amal movement were reported. In a bid to seek help in ending the war, President Gemayel began a tour of Arab countries in May that took him to Tunisia and later to Kuwait, Qatar, Bahrain, Oman, and the United Arab Emirates; however, the initiative was vigorously condemned by his political opponents. The election on June 17 of George Saadeh as leader of the Christian Phalange Party, the country's largest Christian grouping, was also seen as a setback for Gemayel, who had given his support to a rival candidate.

In early July the Syrian government deployed members of its special forces in Muslim West Beirut. The aim was to reduce militia control of the city and violent crime, including the kidnapping of hostages. The Syrian move was described by Gemayel's aides as "illegitimate." On July 28–29 at least 60 people were killed in Beirut in two separate car bomb explosions, which appeared to be in reaction to the presence of Syrian troops in the capital.

On August 19 Prime Minister Rashid Karami met Christian members of the Cabinet for the first time in almost a year. The meeting related to political reforms. On September 2 the Cabinet agreed on a general truce and the establishment of a national charter based on "safeguarding Lebanon's unity, stressing its Arab identity, reforming its political system, setting up a national Army, and liberating the south." Syria's role in Lebanon was a source of dispute within the Cabinet. The Cabinet's subsequent call for the closing of illegal ports established by rival militia groups initially met with failure.

Sheikh Subhi al-Saleh, a prominent Sunni religious scholar who had been trying to promote dialogue between the warring factions, was assassinated in Beirut by unidentified gunmen on October 7. On October 20 Berri offered to exchange an Israeli airman, captured by members of his Amal movement, for Lebanese prisoners held by Israel. Amal fighters were in conflict with the PLO at year's end, laying siege to the Rashidiyeh Palestinian camp, south of Tyre. Palestinian forces tried to relieve pressure on the camp by overrunning villages controlled by Amal. The PLO accused Amal of trying to eliminate the Palestinian presence near the Israeli border.

The continued violence had severe effects on plans for economic recovery. The country faced imminent insolvency, despite desperate attempts by the Banque du Liban (central bank) to ensure monetary stability. Industry was operating at 40% of capacity. The appreciation of the U.S. dollar against the Lebanese pound—by more than 100% in 1985—led to a reduction in imports, but the government's failure to eliminate the illegal ports was also a drain on its ability to raise revenue through customs dues. Because of the fighting there was little benefit to show for the foreign aid money spent by the Council for Development and Reconstruction since 1983. One of Lebanon's best-run companies, Middle East Airlines, managed to contain losses for 1986 at around $1 million by cutting costs and improving security at Beirut airport.

In 1985 a $380 million overall payments surplus was recorded, compared with a $1.3 billion deficit the previous year. The surplus resulted from a fall in government weapons procurement and a rise in central bank assets. Lebanon's leaders, however, were increasingly aware that in the absence of a political solution economic prospects remained bleak. Per capita income was down to less than $250 a year, compared with $1,275 in 1975 (when Beirut, in particular, was a prosperous trading centre and had a large expatriate population).

In October it was reported that Saudi Arabia had agreed to hold talks in early 1987 about renewing a bilateral trade agreement. Trade talks were also to be held with Egypt and the U.S.S.R. Some Western countries, including the U.K., were reducing their diplomatic presence in Beirut because of the continuing strife. In May a representative of the European Communities held out little hope of agreement being reached on a new aid protocol.

Foreign diplomatic efforts centred on the plight of foreigners held hostage in Lebanon by extremist groups, some of which were demanding major changes in Western policy in the region. One U.S. hostage was released in July, and in November another American, one of three held by Islamic Jihad ("Islamic Holy War"), and two Frenchmen, held by the Revolutionary Justice Organization, were released. Following the November developments, both the U.S. and

French administrations faced criticism as details of their undercover negotiations with Iran and Syria, respectively, emerged. (See *Middle Eastern and North African Affairs*, above.) Among foreigners who remained in captivity were five (a sixth hostage was presumed dead) U.S., six French, and two British citizens. (JOHN WHELAN)

LIBYA

A socialist country of North Africa, Libya lies on the Mediterranean Sea. Area: 1,749,000 sq km (675,000 sq mi). Pop. (1986 est.): 3,955,000. Cap.: Tripoli. Monetary unit: Libyan dinar, with (Oct. 1, 1986) a free rate of 0.32 dinar to U.S. $1 (0.46 dinar = £1 sterling). Chief of state in 1986, Col. Mu'ammar al-Qadhdhafi; secretary-general of the General People's Committee (premier), Jadallah 'Azzuz al-Talhi.

On the night of April 14–15, 1986, flying from bases in the U.K. and from U.S. 6th Fleet aircraft carriers in the Mediterranean Sea, U.S. bombers carried out raids on the Libyan cities of Tripoli and Benghazi and their environs. The attack was in response to Libya's alleged involvement in terrorist activities in Europe and was precipitated by the death of a U.S. serviceman in the bombing of a discotheque in Berlin in early April. Following the raid, Libyan leader Col. Mu'ammar al-Qadhdhafi accused U.S. Pres. Ronald Reagan of being "the world's number one terrorist." Total military and civilian casualties were estimated at about 130, including, according to his own account, Qadhdhafi's adopted daughter.

World reaction was polarized between a minority of countries who supported the raid and a large majority, especially from the third world, who censured it loudly. Such was Qadhdhafi's reputation, however, that the favourable prominence forced on him by the raid, together with substantial international sympathy, was short-lived. The U.S.S.R. kept its distance, declined to ratify a treaty of friendship, and, ignoring Libya's weak economy, pressed for the settlement of arms bills said to total over $5 billion. The pressure on Libya to abandon any support of terrorism was sustained throughout the year. The U.S. fleet remained in the Mediterranean for some months, and other countries became involved in measures to discourage terrorism, although European governments did not cooperate comprehensively with the trade boycott proposed by the U.S. administration.

Rumours of the end of the Qadhdhafi leadership had circulated throughout his years in power, and his withdrawal from the public eye for some days after the bombing encouraged speculation that his control over the inner, family-dominated group that steered the country's affairs was slipping. The predictions of opposition groups outside the country were not fulfilled, however, and he survived a particularly difficult year. (*See* Special Report.) At the Nonaligned Movement summit in Harare, Zimbabwe, on September 3, when he harangued the participants and questioned the commitment of those present to the principle of nonalignment, he seriously embarrassed the chairman, Zimbabwean Prime Minister Robert Mugabe, and diminished his own international standing.

Libya's so-called union with Morocco was called off by Morocco's King Hassan II (*see* BIOGRAPHIES) in July. The unlikely union had been seriously impaired by the visit of Israeli Prime Minister Shimon Peres to Morocco earlier in the year; Libya remained the most implacable and unforgiving of all Arab countries in its attitude toward Israel. Relations with Tunisia remained strained. At a meeting in Algiers in August between Libyan and Tunisian representatives, the latter urged Libya to arrange compensation for the summary repatriation of Tunisian workers in Au-

(continued on page 458)

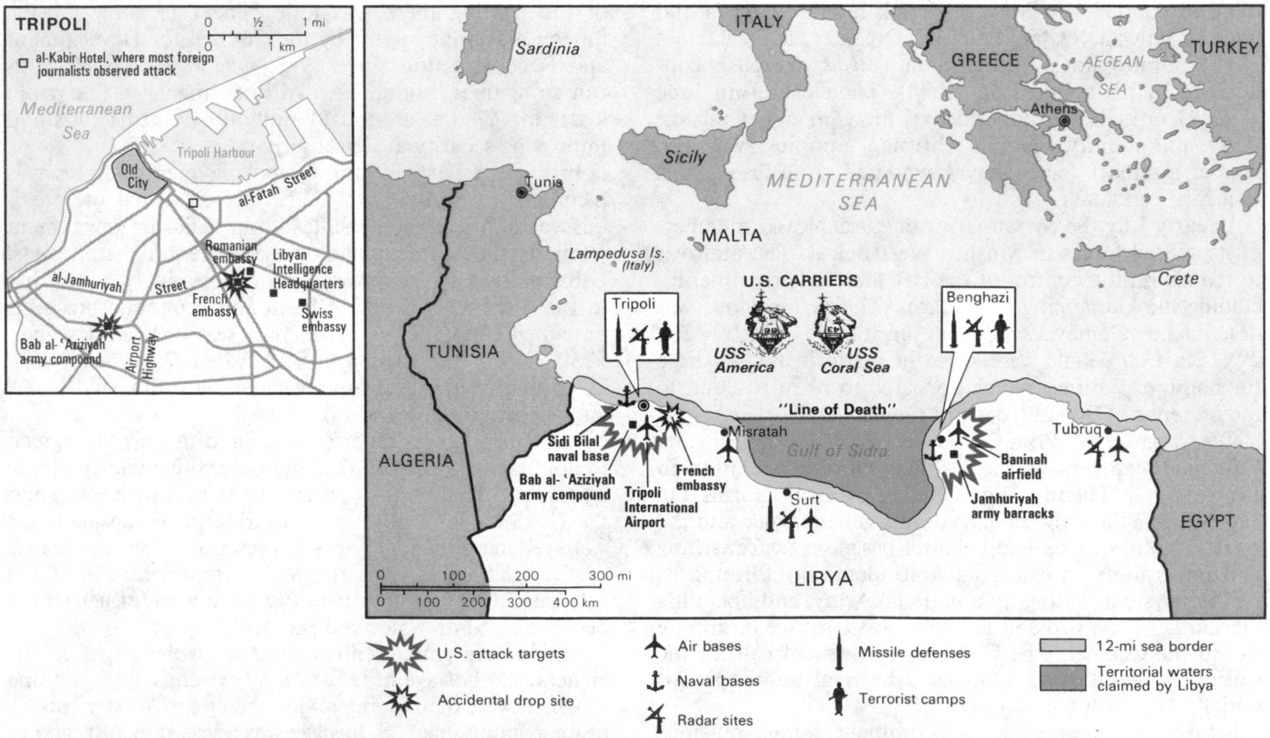

Libyan sites bombed by U.S. forces included five near Tripoli and Benghazi, crippling air defenses. A drop accidentally killed civilians near the French embassy. Territorial waters played a role in U.S.-Libyan grievances. The Law of the Sea convention (ratification pending) allowed a country to claim the area extending to 12 nautical miles from its coast. Libya defined a "line of death" that included the entire Gulf of Sidra and claimed 12 miles beyond it as its waters. The U.S. recognized only three nautical miles from a country's coast.

Special Report: Libya

Qadhdhafi Under Attack

BY ROBERT FISK

A dejected Col. Mu'ammar al-Qadhdhafi sits in the remains of his Tripoli barracks, bombed in a U.S. air raid in April.
BLACK STAR

There was a time, just after the U.S. air raid on Libya in April 1986, when Col. Mu'ammar al-Qadhdhafi needed Pres. Ronald Reagan almost as much as Reagan appeared to need Qadhdhafi. If the Libyan leader was the bogeyman of the Middle East, the soft but permissible target against which a nation pledged to confront "international terrorism" could demonstrate its sense of purpose, so the U.S. president conferred upon Libya the unique and historic distinction of being the one Arab state to "confront" the U.S. superpower in war. True, the Libyan antiaircraft barrage that was supposed to drive off the Americans began more than an hour after the last U.S. jets had disappeared over the dark horizon. True, the colonel retreated into introverted seclusion in the days that followed. True, most Arab rulers privately cursed the air raid more for its failure to eliminate Qadhdhafi than for the fact that it had taken place.

Most of the leaders of the region coveted invitations to the White House. Qadhdhafi preferred to be attacked by its incumbent. President Reagan obliged, and thus bestowed a peculiar and important status upon the Libyan leader. "I was the target," Qadhdhafi lamented afterward. "The Americans were trying to kill me in my own tent." Indeed, the colonel had been inside his patchwork Bedouin tent—pitched in the compound of his Tripoli residence—when the bombers arrived. The Americans thought this a trite, naive remark. They failed to see its significance within a tribal, Bedouin society, just as Qadhdhafi failed to understand why the Americans had come to regard him as a dangerous man.

The Suez Parallel. There was an obvious parallel in the military events that had engulfed Egypt 30 years earlier. Then another Arab potentate—identified by British and French prime ministers Anthony Eden and Guy Mollet as equally pernicious and disrespectful of international law—was assaulted by those two countries. They, too, had hoped to topple an Arab nation's ruler. Radio broadcasts to Egyptians had urged Gamal Abdel Nasser's overthrow; American radio broadcasts in 1986 suggested to Libyans the possibilities of a coup d'état. As it turned out, the Suez invasion cemented rather than fractured Nasser's power and made him a hero of the third world; the U.S. air raids on Tripoli and Benghazi certainly elevated Qadhdhafi in the eyes of many "nonaligned" nations, the speed of his ascent increasing with the distance separating these nations from Libya.

But there the parallel ended. Nasser was a truly titanic figure in the emerging world of Arab nationalism; Qadhdhafi, despite all his posturing in the great man's shoes, was a poor understudy. His credibility existed only with those states that needed the fruits of Libya's natural wealth—particularly the Europeans—and those that saw advantage in humouring his sense of self-importance in order to create a radical alliance—Syria and, to a lesser extent, Iran. Collapsing oil prices, growing evidence in Europe of Libyan involvement in bombings and assassinations, and the frank distrust of the U.S.S.R. deprived Qadhdhafi of the real victory he might have achieved had his regime maintained its early popular domestic support.

Within the Jamahiriyah. Instead, still trying to run his huge country and its tiny population according to the chauvinistic precepts of his own Third Universal Theory, Qadhdhafi moved around his nation like an internal exile, governing from a moving bus, fearful of the military coup with which the U.S. constantly taunted him. In one sense, the raids served to emphasize the sudden decline of Libya's economy as overseas nations chose this moment to assess the size of Qadhdhafi's external debts. Even before the raids, the "Green" shops—once stocked with plentiful supplies of imported goods—began to empty. Postraid consolation came only in changes of nomenclature. Libyans found that their nation—hitherto the Socialist People's Libyan Arab Jamahiriyah (the latter term meaning "government through the masses")—had been renamed the *Great* Socialist People's Libyan Arab Jamahiriyah, a reward for their courage during the air raids that now conveniently distinguished Libya from that other friendly Jamahiriyah, Burkino Faso. The months of the calendar were renamed, so that September became the First month—in honour, of course, of Qadhdhafi's Sept. 1, 1969, revolution.

The final break in trade ties between Libya and the U.S., which coincided with the departure of five oil companies ten weeks after the air raids, and the self-imposed import restrictions with which Libya tried to counter the drop in oil prices, completed the country's isolation. Almost every country trading with Libya was requested to accept deferred payments. One of the busiest men in Tripoli in midyear was the Indian-born commercial contract adviser whose premises were inundated with demands by foreign companies to renegotiate the terms of construction agreements with the Libyans.

The fall in oil prices halved earnings from Libyan exports, and there was no parallel production increase to offset the decline. A population accustomed to a plentiful supply of consumer goods thus found itself in a state of declining prosperity and enduring a spectacular fall in the standard of living. By mid-May one of the most prominent supermarkets in the old Tripoli souk contained dozens of yards of empty shelving. Its supplies consisted only of two varieties of powdered milk, shaving cream, razor blades, and tea. Libya's aspiration to be a leader

Robert Fisk is Middle East correspondent, The Times, *London.*

of the less developed world had taken a sorry turn. Only the "great man-made river" project, the monumental scheme to channel water from underground desert lakes to the agricultural lands along the Mediterranean coast, continued without interference, a sign that long-term planning had not been abandoned. No such claim could be made for Libya's body politic.

Return of the "World Leader." After an uncertain two-month period following the raid, during which he appeared to hand day-to-day control of the country to his four principal aides, Qadhdhafi, the "world leader" (as he was always described by Libyan television news broadcasters), returned to lecture the world and particularly his fellow Arabs on their iniquities and on his own innocence in fomenting what he himself referred to as terrorism. Soon he was once more calling on Egyptians to overthrow Pres. Hosni Mubarak and condemning King Hassan II of Morocco as a traitor because he met the Israeli prime minister. Qadhdhafi told Irish television viewers that he would again give his support to the Irish Republican Army in its efforts to "liberate" Northern Ireland and informed a stunned Nonaligned Movement summit conference in Harare, Zimbabwe, that it was irrelevant. For speaking his mind, Qadhdhafi could not be matched. By the end of the year, he was uttering sentiments every bit as provocative as those he vouchsafed before the U.S. raids.

This did not mean, however, that he had not changed. In the immediate aftermath of the air raids, the offices of the more radical Palestinian groups in Tripoli—curiously, they had been spared by the Americans—had their telephones disconnected. Visiting Palestinian extremists found themselves under close police guard in their hotels. The Americans and the British now traced responsibility for bomb attacks to Syria, rather than to Libya, and Qadhdhafi made no more public references to his relationship with Abu Nidal, whose assassination squads apparently took their inspiration from Damascus.

But there was no concomitant upsurge of popular discontent in Libya, no manifestation of unrest among a people whose long experience of Western occupation under Italy immunized them against U.S. exhortations to strike at Qadhdhafi. The professionals of the Libyan Army resented the political dominance of Qadhdhafi's followers. There were rumours in Tripoli of attempted mutinies following the air raids. But Qadhdhafi's own revolutionary cadres controlled the Army's infrastructure—they personally guarded the ammunition dumps—and if the U.S. attack had been intended to provoke a rebellion, then it failed. Even the "wandering dogs," as Qadhdhafi called his exiled opponents, took little advantage of the raids. And no Arab leader could outwardly support a Western assault on an Arab nation, however much he secretly supported it.

While the U.S. action might have softened Qadhdhafi's enthusiasm for giving armed or financial support to extremist groups, there was no proof of this. Few would deny that Libya was chosen as a target because it could not retaliate; Syria's air defenses and political power protected it from such punishment. For this reason the Arab world, despite its general contempt for Qadhdhafi, drew a rather different moral from the raids than the one the U.S. might have wished. Arab cynicism was substantially strengthened when, a few months later, the U.S. admitted that it had been supplying arms to Iran. A political ally of Libya, Iran furthermore had been accused by the U.S. of involvement in acts of "international terrorism" resulting in loss of life far greater than any action for which Libya could conceivably be blamed.

(continued from page 456)

gust 1985, sought improved border security arrangements, and demanded that Libya ease its interference in Tunisia's internal affairs. Maltese Prime Minister Carmelo Mifsud Bonnici announced support for Libya following the U.S. bombing, but this support faded; overall, Libya's relationship with Malta cooled significantly during the year.

Libya continued to occupy the Aozou Strip and to support the opposition Transitional Government of National Union (GUNT) forces in Chad. The regime's ambivalence toward Goukouni Oueddei, the GUNT leader, hardened into outright opposition in November, when he was reported to have been arrested in Tripoli. Goukouni's forces subsequently rebelled against the Libyans, and in late December fighting flared in northern Chad as the two groups fought for control of key towns. (*See* Africa South of the Sahara: *Chad,* above.)

The economy was dominated by the sharp decline in petroleum prices. Annual revenues of about $6 billion, much the same as in 1985, made it difficult to resume development spending except on priority projects. At home shortages of many consumer items were reported. There was some minor unrest, but nothing serious enough to lead to an overthrow of the government. (J. A. ALLAN)

This article updates the *Macropædia* article NORTH AFRICA: *Libya.*

MOROCCO

A constitutional monarchy of North Africa, Morocco has coastlines on the Atlantic Ocean and the Mediterranean Sea. Area: 458,730 sq km (177,117 sq mi). Pop (1986 est.): 22,455,000. (Area and population figures refer to Morocco as constituted prior to the purported division of Western Sahara between Morocco and Mauritania and the subsequent Moroccan occupation of the Mauritanian zone in 1979.) Cap.: Rabat. Monetary unit: dirham, with (Oct. 1, 1986) a free rate of 8.79 dirhams to U.S. $1 (12.70 dirhams = £1 sterling). King: Hassan II; prime ministers in 1986, Mohammad Karim Lamrani and, from September 30, Azzedine Laraki.

King Hassan II (*see* BIOGRAPHIES), who had long argued for realism over the issue of Israel and the Palestinians, shocked the Arab world on July 22, 1986, when he invited Israeli Prime Minister Shimon Peres to Morocco for discussions on the Arab-Israeli conflict. Although the discussions brought no concrete results—Hassan insisted on the rights of the Palestinians and the Palestine Liberation Organization (PLO) and Peres refused to consider negotiations with the PLO—Arab outrage was widespread. Hassan subsequently gave up his chairmanship of the standing committee for the Arab League summit. The decision to see Peres involved postponement of a visit to the U.S. that would have set the seal on the reconciliation between the two countries; Morocco's relations with the U.S. had been strained as a result of Morocco's 1984 treaty of union with Libya.

In any case, Hassan decided to cancel the treaty at the end of August, ostensibly because Libya associated itself with Syrian condemnation of the meeting with Peres. Moroccan enthusiasm for the treaty had been waning for some time. Morocco offered only formal support to Libya in the wake of the U.S. bombing of Libya in April, and Hassan had failed to make a long-anticipated visit to Tripoli. For Morocco the major purpose of the treaty had been to end Libyan support for the Polisario Front in the Western Sahara, but by now Morocco had established an apparently impregnable position over two-thirds of the territory. Although Polisario had obtained recognition from 65 states, mainly African and Latin American, Morocco still enjoyed support from Europe, the Middle East, and the U.S. Military and economic aid from the U.S. was expected to rise toward $150 million in fiscal 1987.

Celebrations marking the 25th anniversary of Hassan's accession to the throne on March 3 underlined Morocco's growing economic recovery. The 1986 harvest was a record 7.7 million metric tons, and no cereal imports were required. The trade deficit was declining as economic liberalization proceeded. Problems remained in relations with the European Communities, however, because of Spanish objections to concessions granted to Moroccan agricultural exports. There was also slight tension with Spain over the implications of a Spanish aliens law for the Moroccan populations of the Spanish enclaves of Ceuta and Melilla.

The International Monetary Fund suspended its standby credit arrangement in June following a dispute over the size of the Moroccan budget deficit, but a new standby on virtually identical terms was arranged in November. The foreign debt stood at about $14 billion. Foreign banks grudgingly agreed to reschedule $1.5 billion worth of commercial debt maturing in 1985–87. (GEORGE JOFFÉ)

This article updates the *Macropædia* article NORTH AFRICA: *Morocco.*

OMAN

The sultanate of Oman occupies the southeastern part of the Arabian Peninsula, facing the Persian Gulf, the Gulf of Oman, and the Arabian Sea. A small part of the country lies to the north and is separated from the rest of Oman by the United Arab Emirates. Area: 300,000 sq km (120,000 sq mi). Pop.: in 1986 estimates ranged from one million to an official two million; no census has ever been taken. Cap.: Muscat. Monetary unit: rial Omani, with (Oct. 1, 1986) a free rate of 0.39 rial to U.S. $1 (0.56 rial = £1 sterling). Sultan and prime minister in 1986, Qabus ibn Sa'id.

Following the announcement in September 1985 that diplomatic relations were to be established between the U.S.S.R. and Oman, each country named its envoy to Jordan as nonresident ambassador. Nevertheless, Oman maintained its pro-Western stance in 1986. In November the sultanate welcomed a visit by the prince and princess of Wales, and at the end of that month joint exercises with the U.K., code-named Saif Saria ("Swiftsword"), took place.

Weakness in petroleum prices caused a major adjustment to the third five-year (1986–90) development plan, which was cut by 5% to the equivalent of $22,935,000,000 in April. The plan placed emphasis on stimulating productive enterprises in agriculture, light industry, and fisheries. On January 25 the rial was devalued by 10.1% against the U.S. dollar in an attempt to cover the increasing balance of payments deficit resulting from weak energy prices. The move was expected to increase retail prices, but native Omanis enjoyed many subsidies on basic foodstuffs.

Changes in the petroleum market increased the pressure on the government to cooperate with the Organization of Petroleum Exporting Countries (OPEC), although Oman was not a member. Petroleum Minister Said Ahmad ash-Shanfari's announcement in early August that Oman was willing to cooperate with OPEC was followed by a cut of 50,000 bbl a day in the nation's output of crude petroleum from September 1. Government spokesmen maintained that, despite revenue constraints, the administration was paying its bills on time.

In the autumn semester the first 580 students were enrolled at Qabus University, near Muscat, the country's first university. It was built by the U.K. contractor Cementation International. (JOHN WHELAN)

This article updates the *Macropædia* article ARABIA: *Oman.*

QATAR

A monarchy (emirate) on the Arabian Peninsula, Qatar occupies a desert peninsula on the west coast of the Persian Gulf. Area: 11,400 sq km (4,400 sq mi). Pop. (1986 est.): 311,000. Cap.: Doha. Monetary unit: Qatar riyal, with (Oct. 1, 1986) a free rate of 3.64 riyals to U.S. $1 (5.26 riyals = £1 sterling). Emir and prime minister in 1986, Sheikh Khalifah ibn Hamad ath-Thani.

On April 26, 1986, Qatari armed forces attacked Fasht al-Dibal, an island lying halfway between Qatar and Bahrain, and arrested 30 employees of a Dutch contractor who were engaged in building a small coast guard station there for Bahrain. The incident involved a helicopter assault on the island, which had been reclaimed from a coral reef outcrop. Following mediation by fellow Gulf Cooperation Council (GCC) states, particularly Saudi Arabia, Qatar withdrew its forces from the site on June 15. On May 12 the workers seized by the Qatari forces were released, and in August it was reported that the works previously erected were being dismantled by the contractor. The Fasht al-Dibal dispute was one of a number of territorial disputes among member states of the GCC, though the military incident was the first to take place in several years.

Revised conceptual plans for development of Qatar's most important economic project—the $6 billion North Field gas scheme—were submitted at the end of September, but doubts now existed as to the scope of the overall development. The government was anxious to make progress in view of the declining supplies of gas feedstock for local industry being provided from existing sources. Because of weak world energy prices, petroleum income was expected to decline in 1986 by about 50%, compared with the 1985 total of $3.2 billion. Petroleum accounted for 90% of Qatar's exports. External reserves amounting to some $12.5 billion were, however, expected to be sufficient to allow Qatar to ride out the Gulf recession, at least in the short term. (JOHN WHELAN)

This article updates the *Macropædia* article ARABIA: *Qatar.*

SAUDI ARABIA

The kingdom of Saudi Arabia occupies four-fifths of the Arabian Peninsula, with coastlines on the Red Sea and the Persian Gulf. Area: 2,240,000 sq km (865,000 sq mi). Pop. (1986 est.): 11,670,000. Cap.: Riyadh. Monetary unit: Saudi riyal, with (Oct. 1, 1986) a free rate of 3.75 riyals to U.S. $1 (5.42 riyals = £1 sterling). King and prime minister in 1986, Fahd.

During 1986 oil policy moved to the forefront of Saudi Arabian affairs with the dismissal of veteran Petroleum and Mineral Resources Minister Sheikh Ahmed Zaki Yamani, who had held the post for almost 25 years, and a sustained campaign by King Fahd to force petroleum prices up to $18 a barrel in the wake of the dramatic slump early in the year. Speaking at a Cabinet meeting on November 10, Fahd implied that the kingdom would be seeking a higher production quota from the Organization of Petroleum Exporting Countries (OPEC) at the beginning of 1987. Saudi Arabia's share of OPEC's average 15 million-bbl-a-day quota for the last four months of 1986 was 4,350,000 bbl a day. In regional affairs the kingdom offered to cooperate with Iran on oil matters but continued support for Iraq in the Gulf war between Iran and Iraq by facilitating the passage of oil through an export pipeline to the Red Sea. Late in the year, however, it was revealed that large shipments of oil refined in Saudi Arabia had been transported by commercial U.S. traders to Iran. In addition, it was reported in November that a Saudi arms dealer, Adnan Khashoggi, had played an important role in financing the purchase by Iran of U.S. weapons.

The surprise dismissal of Yamani on Oct. 29, 1986, restored control of oil policy to King Fahd, in his capacity as chairman of the Supreme Petroleum Council. The appointment as petroleum minister of Hisham Nazer, previously planning minister, was seen as a temporary measure designed to pave the way for a leading member of the royal family to take over the portfolio. No official reason was given for the change, but Yamani, a choice of the late King Faisal (d. 1975), had never been close to Fahd.

During 1986 Fahd adopted the new title of "servant of the two shrines" instead of "your majesty," in clear reference to the Saud family's guardianship of Islam's holiest shrines, Medina and Mecca. He also urged his ministers to adopt an "open-door" policy in dealing with the public. Fahd's relations with Crown Prince Abdullah ibn Abdel-Aziz and Prince Sultan ibn Abdel-Aziz, the first and second deputy prime minister, respectively, remained good. However, the latter two men—the second and third most powerful members of the Saudi hierarchy—both underwent major surgery, Prince Abdullah for a heart bypass and Prince Sultan for removal of a tumour.

The kingdom's religious leaders legitimized kidney transplants, and early in the year television advertising appeared for the first time. The Hajj (annual pilgrimage) to Mecca was marked by incidents involving Iranian devotees, but the 103 people who were briefly detained in Jiddah represented only a small percentage of the 1.6 million who performed their religious duties.

The buildup of Saudi Arabia's military power provided major challenges to the government. A fourth branch of the military—the air defense force—was set up, in addition to the land, sea, and air forces already in existence. Prince Sultan, who was also defense minister, said on June 16 that the intention behind the move was purely defensive. Nevertheless, the motives of the Saudi government in seeking advanced weapons purchases were questioned in the U.S., where on June 5 the Senate approved by a single vote the sale of missiles to the kingdom worth $265 million—much reduced from its original proposed total. On June 18 U.S. Pres. Ronald Reagan said that Saudi Arabia had met the conditions for delivery of five airborne warning and control system (AWACS) surveillance aircraft.

Other countries were prepared to be more flexible in arms transactions. The U.K. contract to supply the Royal Saudi Air Forces with military aircraft went forward, with further protocols to augment the $7.5 billion agreement initialed in late 1985. The kingdom was, however, still seeking easy credit terms for the sale. France signed an agreement in early October to provide equipment and maintenance services to the Saudi Arabian Navy, which was seeking maritime aircraft and diesel-powered submarines.

Falling oil prices brought new pressures on government spending. The 1986–87 budget was postponed twice before being introduced on December 30. Spending was to be cut by 6% overall, but subsidies on basic foodstuffs remained largely unaffected. A new permanent starting date for the fiscal year—December 21—was established. Meanwhile, government spending was continuing at the monthly rate of one-twelfth of the total amount spent in fiscal 1985. Although foreign contractors complained about a worsening payments environment, the government maintained aid spending at the level that had made Saudi Arabia the world's leading aid donor in 1985 in terms of total spent in relation to gross national product. A senior Saudi spokesman, Prince Talal ibn Abdel-Aziz, formerly

Sheikh Ahmed Zaki Yamani, Saudi oil minister for nearly 25 years, put up with some of the headaches induced by an OPEC oil glut and price collapse. A royal decree by King Fahd in late October dismissed Yamani from his position.
AP/WIDE WORLD

prominent in UN relief organizations, was critical of the less developed African countries; he claimed that they had abused aid provided by Saudi Arabia and other Gulf states.

At the annual meeting of the World Bank board of governors in Washington, D.C., in September–October 1986, Saudi Arabia was elected to the board of executive directors. Jobarah E. Suraisry took up the kingdom's seat on the executive board on November 1.

On June 1 the riyal was devalued by 2.7% in an effort to reduce the balance of payments deficit, and the possibility of a further devaluation was not ruled out. Among the measures the government took to correct imbalances in the economy were the scaling down or rephasing of large projects and a propaganda drive to bring the private sector into productive investment in the kingdom. In January the Saudi Venture Capital Group, involving leading names from the merchant community, was formed. Its aim was to encourage investment in industrial projects by taking advantage of protectionist measures and cheap sources of finance from the government.

Efforts to promote investment were hampered, however, by the attitude of the Saudi Basic Industries Corporation (Sabic), which controlled many basic raw materials but was not prepared to make them available at reduced rates. Sabic was preoccupied with its own dispute with the European Communities over tariffs. During the first two weeks of January the EC imposed a duty of 13% on imports of methanol and 12.5% on imports of linear low-density polyethylene from Saudi Arabia.

As many Saudi infrastructure projects came to an end, the way was cleared for the services sector to play a greater role. The fourth five-year (1986–90) development plan placed a new emphasis on making the most of the kingdom's human resources by providing more training for Saudi Arabians. The question of whether the legal system would be reformed remained open. In the meantime, many joint-venture banks were coming under increasing pressure from the number of bad debts they were sustaining; Islamic prohibitions against the payment of interest and the issuing of mortgages as security for loans remained in effect.

In talks with U.S. Vice-Pres. George Bush on April 6, King Fahd reaffirmed the kingdom's policy on a comprehensive Middle East peace settlement. There were no major surprises in foreign policy, and the kingdom remained silent on the issue of restoring diplomatic links with the U.S.S.R., which had been broken off in 1938.

To improve European understanding of the recent development of Saudi Arabia, a major exhibition called "Riyadh Yesterday and Today" was staged in London; it featured exhibits staged by the Royal Commission for the two new industrial cities of Jubail and Yanbu. The exhibition proved extremely popular. In November the prince and princess of Wales visited Saudi Arabia. They were greeted by King Fahd in the absence of their expected host, Prince Abdullah; according to some reports Abdullah snubbed the royal visitors as a protest against the U.K.'s breaking of diplomatic links with Syria. (JOHN WHELAN)

This article updates the *Macropædia* article ARABIA: *Saudi Arabia.*

SYRIA

A republic of southwestern Asia, Syria is on the Mediterranean Sea. Area: 185,180 sq km (71,498 sq mi). Pop. (1986 est.): 10,612,000. Cap.: Damascus. Monetary unit: Syrian pound, with (Oct. 1, 1986) an official rate of 3.93 pounds to U.S. $1 (5.67 pounds = £1 sterling). President in 1986, Gen. Hafez al-Assad; prime minister, Abdul Rauf al-Kasm.

In elections held on Feb. 10–11, 1986, candidates of the Ba'th Party won 129 seats in the Syrian People's Council. The National Progressive Front gained 57 seats, and the Communist Party, which previously had no representation, took 9. The government faced two significant outbreaks of terrorism at home. A large car-bomb explosion in Damascus on March 13 represented the most serious threat to internal security since the 1982 rebellion by the Muslim Brotherhood in Hamah. Then on April 16 bombs exploded in as many as nine buses in various parts of the country, killing about 150 people. The terrorist attacks appeared to be related to the collapse of the Syrian-brokered peace agreement concluded in Lebanon in December 1985. The government blamed the Iraqi government for the car bomb and Israel for the later attacks.

The country's economic troubles were compounded by low oil prices, which led to a shortage of foreign exchange. Many factories were at a standstill because of a lack of raw materials and spare parts. The continuation of economic support from Saudi Arabia was considered vital to Syria, which would otherwise become much more dependent on the U.S.S.R. Syria in recent years had become the Soviet Union's biggest third world weapons buyer; some $19 billion worth of hardware had been supplied since 1980.

AFP PHOTO

The Rev. Lawrence Jenco (right), with British hostage negotiator Terry Waite (centre), speaks to reporters at Damascus Airport on his journey back to the U.S. after 19 months as a hostage in Beirut.

Syria's alleged role in promoting acts of international terrorism resulted in a decision by the U.K. to break diplomatic relations, a move that was praised by the U.S. administration but met with muted responses elsewhere. On November 10 the European Communities agreed to impose limited sanctions on Syria, including a ban on weapons sales and a review of the status of Syria's diplomatic missions. The action was complicated by Pres. Hafez al-Assad's role in securing the release of Western hostages in Lebanon and by his perceived status as a key factor in Middle East peace moves.

The conflict with the U.K. erupted after the conviction on October 24 of Nezar Hindawi, a Jordanian holding a Syrian passport, for an attempt to blow up an Israeli El Al aircraft in mid flight on April 17. Hindawi was sentenced to 45 years in prison. During the trial evidence was produced linking him to the Syrian embassy in London and suggesting that the Syrian government was involved in the bomb conspiracy. In an interview with *Time* magazine, President Assad denied any Syrian involvement in the plot and blamed it on Israeli secret service agents.

On May 6 U.S. Vice-Pres. George Bush said Syria's "fingerprints" were on international terrorist acts. He mentioned the presence of the Abu Nidal organization on Syrian soil. Syria maintained that Abu Nidal had only a press office in Damascus. In West Germany police claimed that the Syrian embassy in East Berlin had been involved in bombings on April 5 at a discotheque in West Berlin, which had prompted the U.S. raid on Libya. In November West Germany expelled five Syrian diplomats after testimony during the trial of two Jordanians that a Syrian agent had supplied explosives for an attack in West Berlin in March. Syria expelled three West German diplomats in protest.

In the context of the wider Middle East peace question, the major new initiative taken by Assad related to his dialogue with King Hussein of Jordan. Bilateral talks took place on July 26–27. Diplomatic ties with Morocco were cut as a protest against the visit of Israeli Prime Minister Shimon Peres to that nation in July. In contrast, relations with Iran were consolidated, though oil supplies were briefly interrupted in a dispute over payments.

The government's prestige in France was enhanced on June 20 with the release of two French hostages in Beirut, apparently due to mediation by the president. Government spokesmen in Paris denied that any weapons had been sold to Damascus but also agreed that the French administration had sold arms for strictly defensive purposes. France again thanked Syria following the release on November 11 of two more French hostages held in Lebanon.

(JOHN WHELAN)

TUNISIA

A republic of North Africa, Tunisia lies on the Mediterranean Sea. Area: 154,530 sq km (59,664 sq mi). Pop. (1986 est.): 7,326,000. Cap.: Tunis. Monetary unit: Tunisian dinar, with (Oct. 1, 1986) a free rate of 0.86 dinar to U.S. $1 (1.24 dinars = £1 sterling). President in 1986, Habib Bourguiba; prime ministers, Mohammed Mzali and, from July 8, Rashid Sfar.

The year 1986 was characterized by a series of changes within the government of Tunisia, with the question of who would eventually succeed the aging Pres. Habib Bourguiba the dominant issue. Under the constitution, the prime minister would take over if the office of president fell vacant. Mohammed Mzali, prime minister since 1980, was dismissed by President Bourguiba on July 8 and replaced by Finance Minister Rashid Sfar. No official reason for the change was given. In September Mzali was reported to have fled the country, and on October 1, after his parliamentary immunity was lifted, he was sentenced in absentia to a year in prison for having left the country illegally.

President Bourguiba dismissed his son from the post of special adviser to the government in January. A series of government reshuffles followed, and in September Hedi Mabrouk, the ambassador to France, was appointed foreign affairs minister. President Bourguiba's divorce from Wassila Bourguiba, his wife of 25 years, was announced on August 11. She was said to have had a powerful influence on her husband, especially in the late 1970s, and her fall from grace was connected by some to her desire to amend the existing succession process to allow for presidential elections.

In general elections held on November 2 candidates of the ruling Patriotic Union, led by the Parti Socialiste Destourien, ran virtually unopposed. A month before the elections the Mouvement des Démocrates Socialistes, the major opposition party, announced that it was boycotting the polls because it had secured no guarantee that they would be conducted on a free and fair basis. All the major opposition parties followed suit.

On July 31 death sentences were carried out on two of four Muslim fundamentalists sentenced earlier in the month. The other two had been sentenced in absentia.

In August the National Assembly approved an economic recovery program apparently drawn up in consultation with the International Monetary Fund (IMF). Its main features were a 10% devaluation of the dinar and cuts in public spending. Two World Bank loans totaling $275 million were to fund the restructuring of the industrial and agricultural sectors. In November the IMF approved a $250 million loan.

Government restrictions imposed in September on the entry of Palestinians holding Tunisian residence permits contributed to strains in relations with the Palestine Liberation Organization (PLO). The following month it was announced that the PLO would retain its political headquarters in Tunis but reduce its representation to essential staff. (PHILIPPE DECRAENE)

This article updates the *Macropædia* article NORTH AFRICA: *Tunisia.*

TURKEY

A republic of Asia Minor and southeastern Europe, Turkey has coastlines on the Aegean, Black, and Mediterranean seas. Area: 779,452 sq km (300,948 sq mi), including 23,764 sq km in Europe. Pop. (1986): 51.5 million. Cap.: Ankara. Monetary unit: Turkish lira, with (Oct. 1, 1986) a free rate of 706 liras to U.S. $1 (1,020 liras = £1 sterling). President in 1986, Gen. Kenan Evren; prime minister, Turgut Ozal.

The government of Prime Minister Turgut Ozal, leader of the right-of-centre Motherland Party, came under increasing pressure in 1986. In early May the Nationalist Democracy Party, favoured by the military in the November 1983 general elections, dissolved itself. Some of its members joined the Free Democratic Party, founded in the same month; others gravitated to either the Motherland Party or the Right Path Party, which grouped supporters of former prime minister Suleyman Demirel, overthrown by the military in September 1980. On April 2 the ban against making political statements (though not that against accepting party office) was officially lifted from Demirel and other leaders of the pre-1980 parties.

On September 28 by-elections were held to fill 11 vacant seats in the Assembly. The Motherland Party won six seats, though its share of the poll declined. The Right Path Party won four seats and emerged as the main contender for power. The remaining seat went to Erdal Inonu, elected leader of the Social Democratic Populist Party in May. Following the by-elections Ozal reshuffled his Cabinet. The economy grew strongly, at an estimated annual rate of almost 8%, but so did inflation, at approximately 35%. As a result, the value of the Turkish lira fell, and the balance of payments worsened.

Several major projects, notably the building of a second pipeline from Iraq to the Gulf of Iskenderun, had implications for Turkey's relations with its Muslim neighbours. Iran was warned that Turkey would not countenance any interruption in the supply of Iraqi oil. Relations with Iraq and Syria were dominated by Turkey's attempts to stop the infiltration of terrorists belonging to the PKK Kurdish separatist organization. Assurances on border security were received from Syria, but relations were strained when a Syrian diplomat was implicated in the July 1985 murder of a Jordanian diplomat in Ankara. On August 15, Turkish jets bombed Kurdish camps in northern Iraq, inflicting heavy casualties on terrorists who had killed 12 Turkish soldiers in an ambush on August 12. Nevertheless, the PKK campaign continued throughout the year. The most serious single terrorist incident of the year occurred in Istanbul on September 6, when two Arab terrorists, who died in the attack, killed 21 worshipers in a Jewish synagogue.

The return to normal parliamentary politics and the improvement in human rights—all the accused in the trials of members of the Turkish Peace Association and the Confederation of Revolutionary Trade Unions were released—led to closer relations with Europe. The Turkey-European Communities Association Council met in Brussels on September 16 for the first time in six years. In November Turkey took over the chair of the Council of Europe for a six-month period. The move was regarded as a vital step toward an eventual application to join the EC. The private meeting between Ozal and Greek Prime Minister Andreas Papandreou in Switzerland in February did not lessen tension between the two countries, which was increased by Ozal's visit to Cyprus in July and by Turkey's welcome of a new document on Cyprus prepared by the UN. (See *Cyprus,* above.)

Ozal visited the U.S.S.R. in July (where, however, he was not received by Soviet leader Mikhail Gorbachev), and in October work began on the Soviet gas line to Turkey. This working relationship between the two countries was, nevertheless, overshadowed by the question of alleged persecution of the Turkish minority in Bulgaria.

One of the Turkish Republic's founding fathers, Celal Bayar (*see* OBITUARIES), died on August 22. An earthquake in Malatya in southeastern Turkey on May 5 caused some 15 deaths. (ANDREW MANGO)

This article updates the *Macropædia* article TURKEY AND ANCIENT ANATOLIA.

UNITED ARAB EMIRATES

Consisting of Abu Dhabi, Ajman, Dubai, Fujairah, Ras al-Khaimah, Sharjah, and Umm al-Qaiwain, the United Arab Emirates is a federation of seven largely autonomous emirates located on the eastern Arabian Peninsula. Area: 77,700 sq km (30,000 sq mi). Pop. (1986 est.): 1.7 million. Cap.: Abu Dhabi. Monetary unit: United Arab Emirates dirham, with (Oct. 1, 1986) a free rate of 3.67 dirhams to U.S. $1 (5.31 dirhams = £1 sterling). President in 1986, Sheikh Zaid ibn Sultan an-Nahayan; prime minister, Sheikh Rashid ibn Said al-Maktum.

The Supreme Council of the United Arab Emirates (U.A.E.) met on Oct. 15, 1986, and renewed the provisional federal constitution, which had been introduced in December 1971, for another five years. The Supreme Council also reelected Sheikh Zaid as federal president.

The federal budget for fiscal 1986 was announced on October 20, just two months before the end of the fiscal year. The sharp fall in oil prices hit the government hard, although oil production was raised during the year. The new quota set by the Organization of Petroleum Exporting Countries was 950,000 bbl a day, but the U.A.E. was producing over one million bbl a day for most of the year.

Concern about security increased with the first attacks in July on shipping near Dubai, previously considered immune from attack by the combatants in the Iran-Iraq war. The U.A.E. permitted several Soviet shipping lines to call at its ports, and plans to open an embassy in Moscow were at an advanced stage. The government reestablished links with the Palestine Liberation Organization and called for a pan-Arab summit following the U.S. bombing raid on Libya in April. The Gulf Cooperation Council held its annual summit meeting in Abu Dhabi in November. The national carrier Emirates Airlines obtained clearance to fly to the U.K. and France. (JOHN WHELAN)

This article updates the *Macropædia* article ARABIA: *United Arab Emirates.*

YEMEN, PEOPLE'S DEMOCRATIC REPUBLIC OF

The People's Democratic Republic of Yemen (Yemen [Aden]; South Yemen) is located in the southern coastal region of the Arabian Peninsula, on the Gulf of Aden and the Arabian Sea. Area: 336,870 sq km (130,070 sq mi). Pop. (1986 est.): 2,365,000. Cap.: Aden. Monetary unit: Yemeni dinar, with (Oct. 1, 1986) a par value of 0.34 dinar to U.S. $1 (free rate of 0.50 dinar = £1 sterling). Chairman of the Presidium of the Supreme People's Council (president) in 1986, Ali Nasir Muhammad Husani until January 24; interim president from January 24 and president from November 6, Haidar Abu Bakr al-Attas; prime ministers, Haidar Abu Bakr al-Attas and, from February 8, Yasin Said Numan.

Pres. Ali Nasir Muhammad Husani of South Yemen was overthrown in a bloody coup that began on Jan. 13, 1986, and rapidly escalated into a full-scale civil war. Estimates of casualties in the fighting were as high as 10,000. Some 12,000 refugees fled, many to camps on the border with North Yemen. The cost of damage caused during the conflict was estimated at some $140 million.

Following a series of emergency meetings of the ruling Yemen Socialist Party, a new leadership emerged. Haidar Abu Bakr al-Attas, prime minister in the previous government, was sworn in as interim president on January 24. After elections to Parliament in October, he was elected president for a five-year term the following month. The new regime offered an amnesty to political opponents who returned by the end of 1986, but the offer was thought to exclude prominent members of the previous government, notably Muhammad himself, who was in exile in Ethiopia. On August 16 two South Yemeni fighter planes intercepted an Air Djibouti airliner and forced it to land at Aden, where a search was carried out for backers of the former president.

Following the coup the U.S.S.R. made a statement expressing its disavowal of Muhammad. While Saudi Arabia continued to fund projects in the country, the U.S. barred credits to Aden because it was considered to be economically dependent on the U.S.S.R. (JOHN WHELAN)

This article updates the *Macropædia* article ARABIA: *People's Democratic Republic of Yemen.*

YEMEN ARAB REPUBLIC

The Yemen Arab Republic (Yemen [San'a']; North Yemen) is situated in the southwestern coastal region of the Arabian Peninsula, on the Red Sea. Area: 200,000 sq km (77,200 sq mi). Pop. (1986 est.): 7,046,000. Cap.: San'a'. Monetary unit: Yemen rial, with (Oct. 1, 1986) a par value of 7.24 rials to U.S. $1 (free rate of 10.50 rials = U.S. $1; 15.17 rials = £1 sterling). President in 1986, Col. Ali Abdullah Saleh; prime minister, Abdel Aziz Abdel Ghani.

On Feb. 25, 1986, Prime Minister Abdel Aziz Abdel Ghani announced that the government of North Yemen remained committed to seeking a merger with South Yemen, despite the coup that had taken place in that country the previous month. In October reports of border clashes were denied by an official spokesman, who at the same time emphasized the government's desire to maintain good relations with both the East and West.

The economy suffered as a result of the decline in remittances from Yemenis working in the Persian Gulf states. Nevertheless, on October 22 the government signed its first commercially syndicated loan, for $50 million. The exploitation of oil discoveries made in 1984 began, and exports were scheduled to begin in early 1988 through a pipeline on which work started during 1986.

On October 7 Pres. Ali Abdullah Saleh ended a three-day visit to Saudi Arabia, his first in several years. Aid flows from Western countries, notably West Germany and the U.K., were vital to North Yemen, which had a fast-growing population and a crippling import bill of $1.2 billion a year. (JOHN WHELAN)

This article updates the *Macropædia* article ARABIA: *Yemen Arab Republic.*

East Asia

CHINA

The People's Republic of China is situated in eastern Asia, with coastlines on the Yellow Sea and the East and South China seas. Area: 9,572,900 sq km (3,696,100 sq mi), including Tibet and excluding Taiwan. (See *Taiwan*, below.) Pop. (1986 est., excluding Taiwan): 1,053,700,000. Cap.: Beijing (Peking). Monetary unit: renminbi yuan, with (Oct. 1, 1986) a free rate of 3.72 yuan to U.S. $1 (5.37 yuan = £1 sterling). General secretary of the Chinese Communist Party in 1986, Hu Yaobang (Hu Yao-pang); president, Li Xiannian (Li Hsien-nien); premier, Zhao Ziyang (Chao Tzu-yang).

China in 1986 broadened the scope of political and institutional reforms that had been designed to shift the nation toward market-oriented socialism and away from centralized control by the ruling Chinese Communist Party (CCP). But resistance to many of the proposed changes by conservative party officials and continuing problems in implementing various reforms clouded prospects for sustaining the policy breakthroughs of recent years. The question of China's future leadership added to the uncertainties because 82-year-old Deng Xiaoping (Teng Hsiao-p'ing), the principal architect of China's extraordinary political and economic transformation of the past decade, was fast approaching the end of his active career. Despite such tensions, China was still vigorously committed to economic development and increased commercial and technological ties with the industrialized world. China's pursuit of an independent foreign policy included the further expansion of relations with the United States as well as renewed efforts to improve ties with the Soviet Union.

Domestic Affairs. Political reform constituted the centrepiece of Deng's policy initiatives during the year. Although Deng did not offer a detailed program of action, he openly encouraged the nation's scientists and intellectuals to assume a more active political role, and he counseled the CCP to accept more fully the separation between party and government responsibilities. Deng hoped his appeals would evoke a vigorous response on the part of professionals and specialists, who had fewer vested interests in existing power relationships. At the same time, he sought to pressure reluctant middle-level officials into carrying out his reform programs. Deng also tried to reassure his more conservative colleagues that increased political openness would not undermine the authority of the party or pose a serious challenge to China's socialist system.

In December, however, Deng's reform strategy encountered an unexpected challenge from student activists dissatisfied with the pace and scope of political change. Student protests in nearly a dozen cities produced unprecedented calls for individual rights, freedom of expression, and increased democratization, including the right to elect officials of their choice. Although the demonstrations were largely peaceful, they constituted the boldest challenge to party authority since the upheavals of the Cultural Revolution during the mid-1960s. The government sought to avoid a major confrontation with the demonstrators, but the leadership feared that mushrooming protests in China's principal cities would be an enticement to other dissatisfied groups to join the students. Accordingly, after initial appeals to the students not to disrupt "stability and unity," the urban authorities banned demonstrations that had not been previously sanctioned. Despite the edict, some students continued to defy authorities, although they knew they were jeopardizing their chances for higher education and their future careers.

The boldness of the student protests provoked more conservative elements of the leadership troubled by the evident challenge to party authority. Some party officials called for harsher measures to halt the demonstrations, and several senior leaders described the events as evidence of what could happen when "bourgeois liberalism" and excessive westernization went unchecked. By year's end, pressures to curb recent dissent had mounted considerably, and a crackdown on intellectual freedom appeared to be in the offing.

The resurgence of debate among China's top leaders underscored not only the persistence of policy differences within the upper reaches of the party but also Deng's crucial role in furthering reforms. Although Deng had scored notable successes in securing the resignations of numerous aged officials and installing younger, more technically skilled personnel in their places, most senior leaders regarded his political involvement as essential if the accomplishments of recent years were to be solidified and further advanced. Deng remained crucial to resolving these policy differences.

Despite his oft-expressed wish to retire from the political scene, Deng acknowledged that others did not wish him to step aside. Although in apparent robust health at age 82, Deng repeatedly emphasized the urgency of transferring authority to younger officials. In recent years Deng had entrusted predominant responsibility to his principal lieutenants, 71-year-old Hu Yaobang (Hu Yao-pang), general secretary of the Communist Party, and 67-year-old Premier Zhao Ziyang (Chao Tzu-yang). An even younger generation of leaders, in particular 57-year-old Hu Qili (Hu Ch'i-li), 58-year-old Li Peng (Li P'eng), and 63-year-old Qiao Shi (Ch'iao Shih), were also increasingly prominent. But none had Deng's authority and prestige. Under such circumstances, the outlook for determining senior leadership posts at the upcoming 13th CCP National Congress, scheduled for the fall of 1987, remained clouded. The inability of the leadership to conclude a three-year party rectification campaign begun in 1983 suggested other unresolved differences that threatened to impede the implementation of Deng's reforms.

Notwithstanding these political uncertainties, economic development remained one of China's top priorities. All leaders appeared to recognize the compelling need to avoid the type of acute factionalism that plagued China during much of the 1960s and 1970s. The conflicts were rather symptomatic of the difficulty encountered in defining an authoritative ideology that both fostered dynamism of the marketplace and preserved China's socialist essence. In a major policy document issued in late September, the CCP Central Committee asserted that "advanced socialist culture and ideology" was fully compatible with the modernization program, including those parts that promoted economic reforms and an open-door policy toward the outside world. It appeared highly unlikely, however, that this document would end debate over the future shape of China's evolving political and economic structure.

The Economy. Chinese planners continued their efforts to curb overly rapid economic growth, which had approached a rate of 20% during 1985. Such excessive growth had overheated the economy and so taxed the capacities of an already overburdened transportation system that it impaired the efficient movement of fuel, raw materials, and finished products. Burgeoning investments in the industrial sector had greatly reduced China's foreign exchange reserves and contributed to inflation. With the onset of the seventh five-year plan in 1986, stress was placed on slower but steady growth. Runaway investments were curbed by limiting credit and by emphasizing the more efficient provision of goods and services. In these ways planners hoped to begin a period of sustained but more measured economic progress. As a result, the economic growth rate for 1986 remained robust at over 8%, and inflation slowed markedly.

The shifts in economic policy were linked to the goals enunciated in the new five-year plan, which projected an

AP/WIDE WORLD

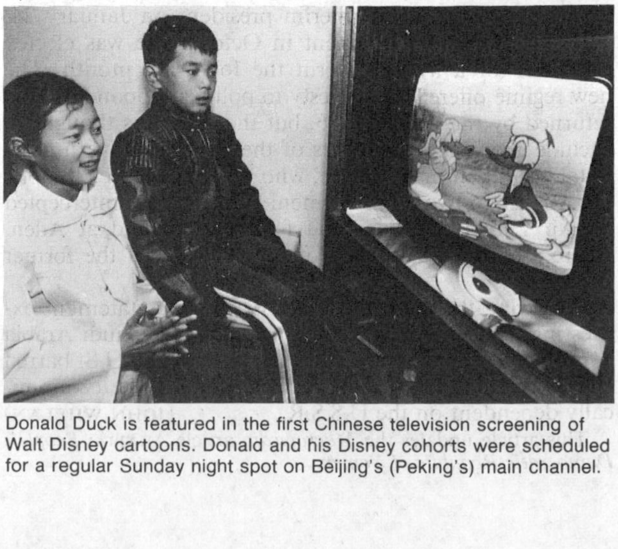

Donald Duck is featured in the first Chinese television screening of Walt Disney cartoons. Donald and his Disney cohorts were scheduled for a regular Sunday night spot on Beijing's (Peking's) main channel.

Zhang Ruipu (Chang Jui-p'u, second from right), the Chinese representative at talks with officials from Taiwan in May, announces China's decision to return a cargo plane and two crewmen to Taiwan. The pilot had defected to China.

AP/WIDE WORLD

annual growth of approximately 7.5%. For the first time since the introduction of five-year planning cycles in the 1950s, major details of the plan were published at the outset of the planning period. Priority was to be given to major infrastructural projects in transportation, communication, energy, and resource development. China also hoped to increase the export potential of various industries, thereby earning the foreign exchange needed to finance purchases of advanced technology from abroad. Planners envisioned the increased use of market forces, with macroeconomic control exercised more by indirect supervision of enterprises than by the more directive system of the past.

Despite such conspicuous economic successes as the doubling of agricultural output since the late 1970s, it was increasingly evident that future advances would prove to be more protracted and difficult. The agricultural sector was expected to grow at approximately 4% during the new five-year plan, but major improvements in productivity awaited a significant infusion of funds for technological and infrastructural development. More conservative leaders, notably veteran economic planner Chen Yun (Ch'en Yün), also voiced grave reservations about designating cultivable land for industrial development because such a policy could lead to future grain shortages. Agricultural output in 1986 was expected to surpass that of 1985, a year during which grain production declined.

The complications attending urban industrial reforms seemed even more daunting. Since the introduction of the responsibility system in industry in late 1984, numerous individual enterprises had become more accountable for their own economic performance and less responsive to priorities and quotas established by the state. But proponents of the urban reforms directly accused entrenched power holders of impeding or subverting the fuller introduction of market forces. Reform of the pricing system was especially slow to develop, although key reformers (including Premier Zhao) acknowledged the potential for instability in moving too rapidly on this highly sensitive issue.

Advocates of increased administrative supervision remained displeased by their loss of past prerogatives and used rampant overspending by individual enterprises as justification for reasserting some of their oversight responsibilities. All in all, however, growing numbers of enterprises in the industrial and service sectors were gaining more control over the allocation of their own resources, a development that made it increasingly difficult to plan and coordinate a mixed economy.

Additional uncertainties pervaded China's efforts to attract capital and technology from abroad. The country's hopes for upgrading the technological level of tens of thousands of inefficient industrial enterprises rested on the willingness of foreign firms to invest major resources in China's development program, especially that calling for the rapid development of coastal cities. Despite isolated successes, many foreign companies were noticeably reluctant to incur major risks by entering the China market. Chinese officials seemed especially vexed at Japanese firms, which seemed more intent on selling products to China than on making meaningful transfers of technology.

In an effort to attract increased foreign investment, the State Council in mid-October published new guidelines for such transactions. Although China offered certain concessions to foreign investors (notably increased access to China's domestic market, tax reduction, and various forms of preferential treatment for companies supplying advanced technology), it appeared doubtful that such steps would restore investors' confidence and reverse the 1986 figures, which showed the first decline in investments since China initiated its open-door policy at the end of the 1970s. The biggest constraint on investments remained China's acute shortage of hard currency and its unwillingness to permit foreign companies to convert large portions of their earnings from Chinese currency into foreign exchange.

Foreign Affairs. Three overlapping priorities dominated China's foreign policy during the year: enhanced national security, accelerated economic development, and the reduction of political and military tensions with neighbouring countries. The first two matters constituted the underpinning of China's relations with the U.S. After protracted discussions with U.S. defense officials, China agreed to a prospective $550 million purchase of modern equipment for 50 of its combat aircraft, by far the largest such transaction to date between the two countries. Following U.S. Defense Secretary Caspar Weinberger's visit to China in October, three ships from the U.S. Pacific fleet paid a port call to Qingdao (Tsingtao), the such visit since the Communist victory in 1949.

The importance of the U.S. in developing China's economic, technological, and scientific potential became increasingly evident during the year. U.S.-China trade, which surpassed $8 billion in 1985, seemed likely to go even higher in 1986, making the U.S. China's third largest trading partner. Owing to a more liberalized U.S. technology transfer policy, an increasingly large portion of this trade involved sophisticated U.S. technologies. In addition, more than 15,000 Chinese students were enrolled in U.S. universities, vastly exceeding the numbers in any other country. Although Chinese officials expressed intermittent dissatisfaction with continued U.S. weapons sales to Taiwan, the need for close relations with Washington constrained Beijing (Peking) from overemphasizing these grievances.

Sino-Japanese relations continued to encounter difficulties during the year, although both sides seemed determined to avoid a serious disruption in relations. China's principal grievance concerned the still yawning trade deficit with Japan, by far Beijing's largest trading partner. Trade between the two countries was curtailed significantly during the year as China sought to limit its purchase of Japanese goods. As a result, a trade gap that had approached $6 billion in 1985 seemed likely to narrow to about $4 billion in 1986. During Japanese Prime Minister Yasuhiro Nakasone's brief visit to China in November, Premier Zhao urged Japan to increase its purchases of Chinese goods, expand its investment in China, and provide more low-interest loans. The prime minister's attentiveness to Chinese sensibilities was also reflected by the September dismissal of his outspoken education minister, whose stridently nationalistic remarks had enraged officials in Beijing.

Sino-Soviet relations moved forward during the year, although China repeatedly emphasized that the deployment of Soviet military power opposite China still imposed a serious obstacle to better relations. Sino-Soviet trade was among the more notable developments in recent years, having increased ninefold during the first half of the 1980s. Trade between the two countries reached $2.6 billion in 1986, with the U.S.S.R. now ranking among China's half dozen leading trading partners. During a September visit to China by First Deputy Premier Nikolay Talyzin, the two sides discussed broadening scientific and technological cooperation, including Soviet help in refurbishing plants built by the Soviet Union during the 1950s.

The political dimension of the relationship stirred even greater interest. In a speech delivered in Vladivostok in late July, Soviet leader Mikhail Gorbachev offered China the most comprehensive overtures to come from a senior Soviet official in over 20 years. Gorbachev's speech called not only for a major expansion of Sino-Soviet economic cooperation but for negotiations leading to a mutual reduction of forces deployed along the Sino-Soviet border. He also indicated that Moscow would soon begin withdrawing some of the forces it had deployed in Mongolia. China responded to Gorbachev's speech with both skepticism and interest. Deng declared his willingness to meet with his Soviet counterpart if Moscow ceased to support Vietnam's occupation of Kampuchea, which Deng deemed the most serious of the security grievances between the two nations. During a meeting of the foreign ministers at the United Nations in October, Moscow and Beijing agreed to resume border negotiations in early 1987 after a nine-year hiatus. The two sides also engaged in limited discussions over the future of Kampuchea.

There was still very little indication, however, that Moscow was prepared to make major concessions on issues that Beijing continued to describe as the three major obstacles to improved relations: the deployment of Soviet military forces east of the Urals, the Soviet occupation of Afghanistan, and Soviet support for Vietnam in Kampuchea. But the Soviet Union did sanction visits to Beijing by the leaders of Poland and East Germany, thereby renewing party-to-party ties between the CCP and those of two of Moscow's closest allies.

Beijing's pursuit of a more visible foreign policy extended to the monarchical and athletic realms. Queen Elizabeth II of Britain visited China in October, reciprocating the visit of Hu earlier in the year. The good feeling that followed the signing of the Sino-British accord on returning Hong Kong to Chinese sovereignty in 1997 was evident in the extraordinary welcome extended to the queen by the Chinese. That same month a contingent of more than 500 Chinese athletes, officials, and journalists traveled to South Korea to participate in the Asian Games. Not surprisingly, the Chinese athletes garnered more medals than those of any other country. Despite the lack of formal relations between China and South Korea, Beijing indicated it would participate in the Summer Olympics of 1988, also to be held in Seoul. (JONATHAN D. POLLACK)

JAPAN

A constitutional monarchy in the northwestern Pacific Ocean, Japan comprises an archipelago with four main islands (Hokkaido, Honshu, Kyushu, and Shikoku), the Ryukyus (including Okinawa), and minor adjacent islands. Area: 377,801 sq km (145,870 sq mi). Pop. (1986 est.): 121,496,000. Cap.: Tokyo. Monetary unit: yen, with (Oct. 1, 1986) a free rate of 154.30 yen to U.S. $1 (222.96 yen = £1 sterling). Emperor, Hirohito; prime minister in 1986, Yasuhiro Nakasone.

Domestic Affairs. Japan's ruling Liberal-Democratic Party (LDP) made an impressive showing in July 1986 elections, and the term of Yasuhiro Nakasone (*see* BIOGRAPHIES) as party president (and hence as prime minister) was extended for a year. Late in 1985, as Nakasone had reached the halfway point in his second two-year term, he had reshuffled his Cabinet to sustain his foreign and domestic policies, to balance factional intraparty strength, and to keep LDP challengers for the leadership at bay. Thus he reappointed Foreign Minister Shintaro Abe, Finance Minister Noboru Takeshita, and Defense Agency Chief Koichi Kato. Kiichi Miyazawa (regarded, with Abe and Takeshita, as one of the "new leaders" of the party) was appointed chairman of the LDP executive council. Masaharu Gotoda, a member of the LDP's largest (Tanaka) faction, took the powerful position of chief Cabinet secretary. On January 27, in an address before the Diet, Nakasone promised to pursue policies of "economic harmony," to open the Japanese market further, to liberalize capital, and to internationalize the yen.

The 104th regular session of the Diet met from Dec. 22, 1985, to May 22, 1986, and approved 73 of 87 bills presented by the Cabinet. Legislation included the fiscal 1986 budget, improvement of the Japanese National Railways (JNR) management, and a bill to rectify disproportionate representation in the (lower) House of Representatives. In 1985 the Supreme Court had ruled that the 1983 general election was unconstitutional because of maldistribution of lower house seats among urban and rural districts. On May 22 the Diet adopted an "eight-for-seven" plan, which took one seat each from seven constituencies and added one seat to eight (total seats in the lower house increased to 512). Before redistribution, party strength in the lower house was LDP (including New Liberal Club allies) 262; Japan Socialist Party (JSP) 112; Clean Government Party (Komeito) 59; Democratic Socialist Party (DSP) 38; Japan Communist Party (JCP) 27; independents 8; vacancies 5 (total 511). In the upper house the LDP held 139 of the 252 seats.

On June 2, only hours after an extraordinary session was convened, Prime Minister Nakasone dissolved the House of Representatives. This step cleared the way for a dual election on July 6, the scheduled date for the regular election of half of the (upper) House of Councillors. Obviously, Nakasone hoped that the dual election would increase voter turnout and thus LDP chances and his own status. In a Tokyo Broadcasting System poll in April, 53% of those asked had stated that they supported the prime minister. By May, however, his image was somewhat damaged by what were seen to be concessions to the Western nations made at the summit of major industrial countries (*see* below). Moreover, party rules forbade a third term as LDP president. Nakasone carefully stated that he would, of course, "abide by party rules."

Prime Minister Nakasone called the results of the dual election "the voice of heaven." Participation was high (71.4% of eligible voters), and the LDP share of the popular

Brush in hand, Japan's Prime Minister Yasuhiro Nakasone shows how he painted an eye on a daruma doll. The act, symbolizing victory, marked the impressive gains made by Nakasone's Liberal-Democratic Party in the July elections.
AP/WIDE WORLD

vote (49.6%) was higher than in any election since 1963. The party won 300 seats outright and quickly absorbed 4 Diet members who had run as independents. In August, when the splinter New Liberal Club ended its ten-year history, five (of six) elected members returned to the LDP, giving the party control of all legislative committees. The lineup in the lower house was LDP 309; JSP 87; Komeito 57; DSP 28; JCP 27; independents 4 (total 512). In the upper house it was LDP 144; JSP 40; Komeito 25; DSP 12; JCP 16; independents 15 (total 252). On September 6 Masashi Ishibashi stepped down as chairman of the JSP, thus taking responsibility for the disastrous defeat of the largest opposition party. He was replaced by Takako Doi (*see* BIOGRAPHIES), who became the first female chief of a major political party in Japan's history.

Meanwhile, within the LDP there were maneuvers toward a "post-Nakasone era." Although a party task force approved an "extension" of Nakasone's term for one year beyond October 30, members denied him a third term as president. On July 1 Abe had announced his candidacy for the LDP presidency, and on July 14 he assumed the leadership of the fourth largest faction (Seiwakai, 82 Diet members), previously headed by former prime minister Takeo Fukuda. On September 4 Miyazawa replaced former prime minister Zenko Suzuki as chairman of the second largest faction (Kochikai, 88 Diet members). Takeshita continued to lead a splinter group (Soseikai, 40 members) within the Tanaka faction of 138 Diet members. Nakasone counted 83 members within his own faction, the third largest.

On July 22, after the Diet had reelected Nakasone prime minister, he again reorganized his Cabinet to reflect the strength of these factions. He chose Miyazawa as his finance minister, Takeshita as LDP secretary-general, and Abe as chairman of the party's executive council. Gotoda remained as chief Cabinet secretary; Tadashi Kuranari, a loyal Nakasone supporter, became foreign minister; and Shin Kanemaru took the rarely filled post of deputy prime minister. The press identified factional distribution as Tanaka 8, Nakasone 4, Abe 3, and Miyazawa 3. On September 8 the prime minister discharged Education Minister Masayuki Fujio, an ultranationalist, for extreme views aired in the opinion journal *Bungei Shunju.* He chose Masajuro Shiokawa (Abe faction) to replace Fujio.

On April 29 Emperor Hirohito turned 85, a special birthday because the government had chosen the day for a national celebration of his 60 years on the throne. In fact, he acceded as the Showa emperor on Dec. 25, 1926, the day his father, the Taisho emperor, died.

The Economy. In April the Diet approved the annual budget. General account expenditures totaled 54,088, 643,000,000 yen, an increase of just 3% over 1985. Only defense expenditures, increased by 6.6%, showed a greater rise. By June the 30% appreciation in the value of the yen was forcing painful adjustments in Japan's economy: a shift in employment from the industrial to the service sector, emphasis on new products catering to the domestic market, and a decline in corporate profits for the first time in three years. For example, the income of Toyota Motor Corp. fell over 17% in the year ended June 30. The almost free fall in the price of oil was a bright spot; official estimates put the 1986 savings on oil imports at more than $13 billion.

In calendar 1985 Japan's gross national product (GNP) rose 4.6% to a total of 290,683,000,000,000 yen ($1,219,000,000,000). In the last quarter (January–March) of fiscal 1985, however, GNP fell 0.5%, the first loss in a decade, and in the first quarter (April–June) of fiscal 1986 it rose only 0.9%. Forecasts for the year ranged from 2% growth (private estimate) to 4% (government estimate). In 1985 the rate of unemployment declined slightly to 2.6%, but by April 1986 it had reached a record 2.9%. Throughout 1985 inflation continued at a modest 2.1% pace.

In response to both sluggishness in the economy and foreign pressure, the government adopted policies to expand domestic demand. In April a 17-member advisory panel, headed by former Bank of Japan governor Haruo Maekawa, recommended that the nation reshape its economy to make it less dependent on exports and more amenable to domestic spending. The experts urged a variety of measures including income tax cuts, shortened working hours, and tax reform to discourage Japanese from saving so much. On January 30 the Bank of Japan cut the basic interest rate 0.5% (to 4.5%), the first reduction in three years. In coordination with Western central banks, the rate was lowered twice more, to 4% on March 10 and to 3.5% on April 21.

Meanwhile, the Nakasone administration was moving to aid small business hurt by the strengthened yen. On April 8 the government adopted a package of incentives, including lower interest on government loans. On September 19 the Cabinet approved a $19 billion supplementary budget for public works, housing, and help to small export-oriented businesses. More wide-ranging changes were proposed in early December, when LDP leaders outlined a revision of the tax code aimed at stimulating the economy; among the provisions were a reduction in income tax and introduction of a value-added tax. Later in the month government leaders agreed on a 1987 defense budget of $22 billion or 1.004% of GNP, breaking the ten-year-old 1% limit.

Foreign Affairs. As Japan prepared for the summit meeting of major industrial powers (the second to be held in Tokyo), the nation found itself in a strong, if uncomfortable, position. It accounted for 10% of global economic output, ranking second only to the U.S. In 1985 its trade surplus soared to $56 billion, and it replaced Britain as the world's largest creditor, with foreign assets exceeding liabilities by $129.8 billion. Holdings of foreign securities reached $145.8 billion, with 86% in the U.S. market.

In anticipation of the summit, Foreign Minister Abe visited the U.S., Britain, and West Germany early in the year. In January Prime Minister Nakasone consulted with his Canadian counterpart, Brian Mulroney (who remained in Tokyo after the summit for an official visit), and on April 13–14 Nakasone was in Washington, conferring with Pres. Ronald Reagan on U.S.-Japan trade relations. The president praised the prime minister's commitment to restructuring the Japanese economy. Both expressed the hope that such action would increase Japan's imports, decrease its exports, and reduce its massive trade surplus.

At the summit, held May 4–6, the leaders of the advanced industrial nations established a currency coordination system known as a "managed float." Five powers—Japan, the U.S., Britain, France, and West Germany—had been managing exchange rates; Canada and Italy were now added. These countries failed, however, to resolve the problem of trade, specifically in agricultural products. Some Japanese politicians and business leaders expressed disappointment over Nakasone's failure to persuade the allies to stem the steady rise in value of the yen as against the dollar.

Relations with the U.S. continued to revolve around trade issues. In 1985 the U.S. trade deficit with Japan rose to $49.7 billion, one-third of the total U.S. trade deficit of $148.5 billion. It was hoped that the shifting yen–dollar ratio would soon decrease Japan's exports and increase its imports. On February 10 the dollar hit a seven-year low against the yen, breaking the "magic 190" level, and on April 22 in New York the dollar traded at a postwar low of 170.90 yen, marking a 35% decline in the dollar over one year. Despite Bank of Japan intervention to stem the steep rise in value, on July 7 the yen traded at 158.90 against the dollar.

Meanwhile, talks between Tokyo and Washington were directed toward the removal of barriers to trade in pharmaceuticals, telecommunications, and electronic products. In April the U.S. Commerce Department determined that Japan had been dumping (selling below cost) semiconductors and computer memory chips. On July 31, after U.S. trade representative Clayton Yeutter set a deadline, the two nations signed a comprehensive pact on semiconductor trade. In return for its agreement to drop the antidumping cases, the U.S. was assured a "fair share" of the market.

On September 9 the Japanese Cabinet formally decided to cooperate in the U.S. Strategic Defense Initiative. Black and Hispanic leaders in the U.S. expressed outrage in September when two Japanese newspapers quoted Nakasone as saying that the presence of blacks and Hispanics in the U.S. population lowered the country's intellectual level. The Japanese government claimed the remarks were taken out of context, and Washington accepted the explanation.

Relations with the U.S.S.R. improved slightly in 1986. During the first visit to Tokyo by a Soviet foreign minister in a decade, Eduard Shevardnadze on January 19 agreed to resume negotiations on a peace treaty. Talks had been suspended because of the continued Soviet occupation of the "northern territories," islands northeast of Hokkaido regarded by Tokyo as Japanese territory. On May 29 Abe, in turn, became the first Japanese foreign minister to visit Moscow in eight years. He said he held "heated discussions" with Soviet leader Mikhail Gorbachev and Shevardnadze over the territorial issue but that the Soviet position remained "very rigid." On the other hand, in a humanitarian gesture, the Soviets did allow a 52-member group of elderly Japanese to visit ancestral graves on Etorofu, Kunashiri, Shikotan, and the Habomais.

China was represented in Tokyo by Foreign Minister Wu Xueqian (Wu Hsueh-ch'ien) on April 12. Nakasone promised to help China's seventh five-year development program and to reduce Japan's trade surplus with China ($6 billion in 1985). In May in Tokyo, Koichi Kato, chief of Japan's Defense Agency, and Yang Kezhi (Yang K'o-chih), chief of staff of the People's Liberation Army, agreed to promote defense ties between the two countries, including exchanges of uniformed personnel, technology transfers, and joint naval exercises.

Major newspapers in South Korea criticized an Education Ministry decision, made on May 27, to approve a controversial textbook for use by Japanese high school students. The text played down Japan's aggression on the Asian mainland 50 years earlier and referred to Japan's occupation of Korea (1910–45) in favourable terms. On July 19 the planned visit to Seoul by Crown Prince Akihito and the Princess Michiko was postponed, officially because of her surgery. Korean mass media and Christian groups had opposed the visit as an attempt to bolster the Chun Doo Hwan regime. A meeting in Tokyo September 10–11 between Foreign Minister Kuranari and his counterpart, Choi Kwang Soo, indicated that South Korea had accepted Japan's apology for remarks about the annexation of Korea made by Fujio before his dismissal as education minister. After Nakasone relieved the minister, he spoke directly to Choi: "I am sorry about the blunder made by Minister Fujio. I apologize."

On February 26 Tokyo moved quickly to recognize Corazon Aquino as the legitimate president of the Philippines. Less than 24 hours after Ferdinand Marcos fled Malacanang, Japan's Ambassador Kiyoshi Sumiya made a formal call at Aquino's headquarters to extend support for the new administration. Japan was the second largest provider of economic assistance to the Philippines, after the U.S. Early in September South African Foreign Minister R. F. ("Pik") Botha made an unofficial five-day visit to Tokyo. Foreign Minister Kuranari warned him that Japan would be forced to take further punitive measures against South Africa unless reforms of the apartheid system were enacted. Although LDP leaders were split over the issue, Japan had banned direct investment in South Africa by Japanese companies. (ARDATH W. BURKS)

KOREA

A country of northeastern Asia, bordered by the Sea of Japan, the Korea Strait, and the Yellow Sea, Korea is divided into two parts roughly at the 38th parallel.

The delicate relationship between the rival governments of North and South Korea weakened in January 1986 when North Korea unilaterally canceled scheduled two-way talks on economic, parliamentary, and humanitarian matters. The reason cited was the U.S.-South Korea military exercises to be held in March and April. South Korea protested that the maneuvers were routine and that the northerners had been invited to observe them, but to no avail.

In June, however, North Korea proposed an unprecedented meeting between top military leaders from each side, together with the commander of the 40,000-strong U.S. forces in the South. North Korean Defense Minister Oh Chin U sent letters directly to his southern counterpart, Lee Ki Baek, and to the U.S. commander, Gen. William Livesey. Observers saw the initiative as a minor breakthrough because the North had recognized the South's right to participate in military discussions on the Korean Peninsula. The South reacted skeptically, citing North Korea's continuing military buildup. The U.S. also responded coolly, insisting that the existing Military Affairs Commission under UN auspices provided an adequate channel for talks.

Some analysts, however, saw North Korea's gesture as indicative of a genuine desire to improve relations. They also cited Pyongyang's softer attitude at a June meeting in Lausanne, Switz., held to discuss its demand to stage half the events of the 1988 Olympic Games. Surprisingly, Communist representatives agreed in principle with the International Olympic Committee's suggestion that a few contests be held in the North. It was evident that new sporting facilities being built near Pyongyang were intended for that purpose. However, a bomb incident at Seoul airport in September, just before the Asian Games were due to begin, dimmed prospects for conciliation between the North and South. The bomb left 5 dead and about 30 injured, and North Korea was implicated.

AP/WIDE WORLD

The official flame marking the opening of the 10th Asian Games, held in Seoul's Olympic Stadium in September, has been lit by torchbearers as a large crowd looks on. The stadium was also to be the site of the 1988 Summer Olympics.

The most bizarre incident of the year occurred on November 17, when the South Korean Defense Ministry announced that Pres. Kim Il Sung of North Korea had been assassinated. The report was proved false the following day by the appearance of President Kim, alive and well, at Pyongyang airport. It was suggested that the original report was either the result of an attempt by North Korea to discredit the South Korean authorities or a mistaken interpretation of a broadcast concerning the death of the president's mother.

Republic of Korea (South Korea)

Area: 99,091 sq km (38,259 sq mi). Pop. (1986 est.): 41,569,000. Cap.: Seoul. Monetary unit: won, with (Oct. 1, 1986) a free rate of 877 won to U.S. $1 (1,267 won = £1 sterling). President in 1986, Chun Doo Hwan; prime minister, Lho Shin Yong.

In South Korea 1986 was dominated by the issue of constitutional reform. In February the New Korea Democratic Party (NKDP), the largest opposition grouping in the National Assembly, launched a campaign to collect ten million signatures from citizens. Its purpose was to force Pres. Chun Doo Hwan's agreement to an amendment of the constitution that would allow direct presidential elections by 1988, the year Chun had pledged to step down. At first the government declared the campaign illegal, but Chun moderated his attitude late in February, possibly because of events in the Philippines, where Pres. Ferdinand Marcos had just been deposed by popular consent. He invited NKDP's president, Lee Min Woo, to lunch at his Blue House residence and said the signature campaign could proceed and that police would not stop street demonstrations so long as they remained peaceful.

The security forces were less tolerant toward the country's politically minded university students. Police reported that between January and March some 70,000 of them took part in 299 antigovernment demonstrations; 455 were arrested, an 11-fold increase over the same period in 1985. As the year progressed, protests became increasingly violent and anti-American. The students' growing extremism led to a widening rift between them and the opposition politicians, who sensed that a compromise with the government on constitutional amendment might be possible.

Late in April Chun made a significant concession to his political foes: he dropped his long-standing insistence that the constitution must not be altered before 1988. The president's only condition was that any changes be debated in the National Assembly. On May 29 Roh Tae Woo, chairman of the ruling Democratic Justice Party (DJP), met the NKDP president and agreed to form a parliamentary committee "to revise the constitution in such a way as to guarantee the people a free choice of government." The opposition responded to Chun's concession by accepting some compromises. It no longer required, as preconditions for talks with the government, a promise of direct presidential polls, full amnesty for dissident leader Kim Dae Jung, and the release of all political prisoners.

Nevertheless, the form of future presidential elections remained a bone of contention. In August the DJP presented its plan for a draft constitution. It advocated that after 1988 the National Assembly elect a ceremonial president and a prime minister, with whom real power would rest. Another stipulation was that all presidential candidates must have resided in Korea for at least five years before the poll to be eligible. If accepted, such a requirement would effectively rule out the candidacy of Kim Dae Jung, who had returned to Korea in 1985 after two years of self-imposed exile in the U.S. The opposition continued to insist on direct balloting, arguing that indirect elections invariably favoured the ruling authorities. During the year Roh Tae Woo was increasingly mentioned as the government's choice to succeed Chun, but his success was likely to be determined by whether he could forge a workable agreement with the opposition on constitutional amendment. After a reshuffle in the DJP, in August Chun replaced 10 ministers out of 22 in the Cabinet.

South Korea's major international event of the year was the 10th Asian Games. For the Koreans, the Games were a rehearsal for the 1988 Olympics. The two-week event brought some 200,000 foreign visitors as well as 3,000 athletes to South Korea.

The economy gathered additional momentum in 1986, and gross national product was expected to grow by at least 8% following growth of 5% in 1985. Exports were buoyant, especially in the automotive and electronics sectors. For the first time since the Korean War, a trade surplus was forecast, amounting to $1.5 billion. Three factors provided the stimulus: low petroleum prices, falling global interest rates, and the strengthening Japanese yen. Less positively, low oil prices meant a falloff in Middle East demand for construction work, which severely affected Korea's already ailing construction industry. Some of the country's huge industrial *chaebol* (conglomerates), especially those in heavy machinery and shipping, had serious financial difficulties. The government responded with financial assistance and at the same time took measures to restructure the economy by encouraging smaller industrial concerns. The new five-year (1987–91) plan aimed to liberalize the economy by deregulating trade, investment, finance, and industry. Restrictions on imports and on foreign investment were gradually being relaxed.

Democratic People's Republic of Korea (North Korea)

Area: 122,370 sq km (47,250 sq mi). Pop. (1986 est.): 20,543,-000. Cap.: Pyongyang. Monetary unit: won, with (Oct. 1, 1986) a nominal exchange rate of 0.94 won to U.S. $1 (1.36 won = £1 sterling). General secretary of the Central Committee of the Workers' (Communist) Party of Korea and president in 1986, Marshal Kim Il Sung; chairmen of the Council of Ministers (premier), Kang Song San and, from December 29, Li Gunmo.

Speculation about whether Kim Chong Il would succeed his father, 74-year-old Kim Il Sung, as supreme leader of North Korea was brought firmly to an end in 1986. In May a visiting Japanese journalist was told by a Politburo member, Ho Dam, that "Kim Il Sung's heir is Kim Chong Il." Days later the elder Kim declared that the issue of his political successor had been "satisfactorily solved." The new leader, said Kim, would be "boundlessly faithful to the party and the revolution, and have personality and qualifications to realize fully political leadership over the whole people." In a partial reshuffle of the Cabinet in February, Hong Song Nam and Hong Si Hak were named as deputy premiers. Following elections to renew the Supreme People's Assembly in November, its members reelected Kim as president on December 29.

North Korea's relations with the U.S.S.R. continued to improve, to China's consternation. Besides helping build up Pyongyang's armed forces, Moscow supplied sophisticated weapons such as SA-3 antiaircraft missiles and MiG-23 fighter-interceptor jets. Exchanges of visits by senior officials led to Soviet promises of more economic and technical aid, including the building of North Korea's first nuclear power plant. For the first time, Soviet and North Korean warships visited each other's ports.

In April Finance Minister Yun Gi Jong presented the 1986 budget. Planned expenditure totaled about $15.8 billion, 4.2% more than in 1985, and defense spending took 14.1% of the total. Economic difficulties might have prompted statements by top government leaders early in the year that technological development would henceforth take high priority. (THOMAS HON WING POLIN)

MONGOLIA

A landlocked people's republic of eastern Asia, Mongolia occupies the geographic area known as Outer Mongolia. Area: 1,565,000 sq km (604,000 sq mi). Pop. (1986 est.): 1,938,000. Cap.: Ulan Bator. Monetary unit: tugrik, with (Oct. 1, 1986) a free rate of 3.36 tugriks to U.S. $1 (4.85 tugriks = £1 sterling). First secretary of the Mongolian People's Revolutionary (Communist) Party and chairman of the Presidium of the Great People's Hural (chief of state) in 1986, Zhambyn Batmunkh; chairman of the Council of Ministers (premier), Dumaagiyn Sodnom.

The 19th congress of the Mongolian People's Revolutionary Party (MPRP) met at Ulan Bator on May 28–31, 1986, with several hundred delegates in attendance. The general secretary, Zhambyn Batmunkh, presented the Central Committee's report, which reviewed the progress made during the seventh five-year plan period (1981–85) and outlined the plan for 1986–90. Between 1981 and 1985, national income rose 37%, social spending 40%, and average real incomes 12%. During 1986–90 real incomes were expected to rise by 20–25%. Industrialization was given priority and allocated a third of investment.

Batmunkh who, on his 60th birthday on March 10, 1986, had received the highest Soviet award, the Order of Lenin, was reelected general secretary of the MPRP. General elections took place to renew the Great People's Hural (parliament) in June.

In August diplomatic relations with China were established. In September, during an official visit by Polish leader Gen. Wojciech Jaruzelski, a treaty covering Polish-Mongolian economic collaboration for the period 1986–2000 was signed. In November Batmunkh paid an official visit to North Korea. (K. M. SMOGORZEWSKI)

TAIWAN

Taiwan, which consists of the island of Taiwan and surrounding islands off the coast of China, is the seat of the Republic of China (Nationalist China). Area: 36,000 sq km (13,900 sq mi), including the island of Taiwan and its 85 outlying islands, 21 in the Taiwan group and 64 in the Pescadores group. Pop. (1986 est.): 19,408,000. (Area and population figures exclude the Quemoy and Matsu groups, which are administered as an occupied part of Fujian [Fukien] Province.) Cap.: Taipei. Monetary unit: new Taiwan dollar, with (Oct. 1, 1986) an official rate of NT$36.71 to U.S. $1 (NT$53.05 = £1 sterling). President in 1986, Chiang Ching-kuo; president of the Executive Yuan (premier), Yu Kuo-hwa.

Taiwan achieved extraordinary economic progress in 1986, a year also memorable for significant political breakthroughs. Long noted for sustaining one of the most vibrant economies of the Pacific Rim, Taiwan experienced a growth rate that approached 11%, its best performance

Marching toward the American Institute, a semiofficial U.S. mission in Taiwan, Taiwanese demonstrators hold flags and signs that protest what they see as interference by U.S. congressmen in Taiwan's domestic affairs.
AP/WIDE WORLD

since 1979. Based on export-led growth, Taiwan steadily amassed currency reserves estimated at $46 billion, thereby taking its place among the world's largest holders of foreign exchange. Despite repeated efforts to narrow the U.S. trade deficit with Taiwan, the more than $14 billion imbalance was, in per capita terms, larger than that between the U.S. and Japan.

Taiwan's increased wealth brought with it growing demands for a less restrictive political structure. At the behest of Taiwan's aging but still powerful president, 76-year-old Chiang Ching-kuo, the political system underwent some of the most important reforms since the seat of the Nationalist government was moved to Taiwan in 1949. For the first time, the ruling Kuomintang (Nationalist Party) permitted opposition forces a degree of formal organization. This led to the formation of the Democratic Progressive Party (DPP) in late September. Despite its brief history, the DPP scored impressive victories in legislative elections in early December, garnering about 30% of the vote in Taiwan's major cities. Although the Kuomintang showed increased permissiveness toward a formal opposition party, it did not welcome expatriate politicians seeking to return to their native province prior to the elections. There were, however, other signs of major changes in the political arena. In mid-October the Kuomintang announced that in early 1987 it would lift martial law, which had been in effect since 1949. A new, less restrictive national security law would take its place.

Hints of change were also apparent in the Kuomintang's dealings with the mainland. Even though Taiwan officially forbade contact with the rival regime on the mainland, unofficial trade was estimated to have been in excess of $1 billion. Taiwan also decided to remain a member of the Asian Development Bank after China joined the organization. It meant that the Nationalist government would be known as "Taipei, China," but that designation had already been accepted to permit both Chinas to participate in the 1984 summer Olympic Games.

China and Taiwan were also involved in negotiating the return of a Boeing 747 cargo jet flown in mid-May to China by a pilot from Taiwan's flag carrier. At Taiwan's insistence, the talks were held in neutral Hong Kong and led to the speedy return of the aircraft. Although both governments publicly stated that only airline officials—not governments—were involved in the discussions, a new flexibility on Taiwan's part appeared to be emerging even as it continued to reject out of hand Beijing's (Peking's) overtures for closer contacts.

Taiwan was also concerned about the uncertain health of Chiang Ching-kuo. Although the constitution stipulated that power would pass to 63-year-old Vice-Pres. Lee Teng-hui, a native of Taiwan, there was talk of a possible power struggle should President Chiang become incapacitated or die.

Regardless of the island's current extraordinary prosperity, growing trade tensions with the U.S. and looming protectionist threats represented dark clouds on the economic horizon. Taiwan's heavy economic dependence on the U.S. and its anomalous international status (it maintained diplomatic relations with fewer than two dozen states) were causes of concern during a year that was otherwise one of significant accomplishments. (JONATHAN D. POLLACK)

South Asia

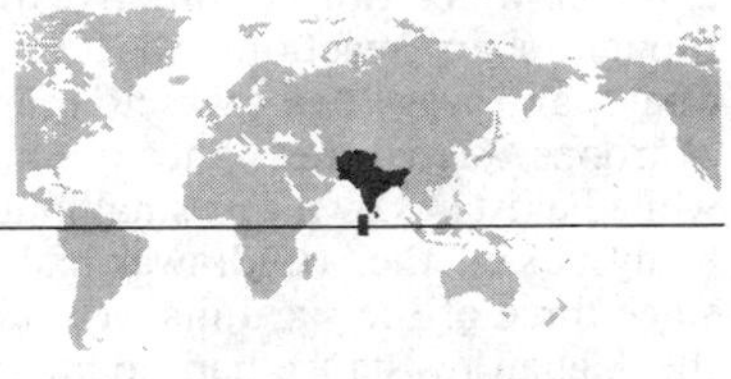

AFGHANISTAN

Afghanistan is a landlocked people's republic in central Asia. Area: 652,225 sq km (251,825 sq mi). Pop. (1986 est.): 16,892,000 (though estimates vary, by 1984 the exodus to Pakistan and Iran accounted for approximately 4.5 million). Cap.: Kabul. Monetary unit: afghani, with (Oct. 1, 1986) an official rate of 50.60 afghanis to U.S. $1 (73.12 afghanis = £1 sterling). General secretaries of the People's Democratic (Communist) Party in 1986, Babrak Karmal and, from May 4, Mohammad Najibullah; presidents of the Revolutionary Council, Karmal to November 20 and, from November 24, Haji Mohammad Chamkani; prime minister, Sultan Ali Keshtmand.

Two major events dominated Afghanistan in 1986. On May 4 Babrak Karmal, the country's president since 1979, resigned as general secretary of the People's Democratic (Communist) Party, retaining the less important position of president of the Revolutionary Council. The resignation of the 57-year-old Karmal was officially attributed to reasons of health—he had made no public appearance since March 30 and was reported to have been in the U.S.S.R. for medical treatment. It was widely thought, however, that the Soviet leadership was dissatisfied with his performance and wanted to create a broader power base. On November 20 Karmal resigned from the largely ceremonial post of president of the Revolutionary Council. His successor as party chief, Mohammad Najibullah (*see* BIOGRAPHIES), was formerly head of Khad, the country's secret police, and more recently had taken charge of security. In December Najibullah visited the U.S.S.R. to discuss prospects for ending the conflict in Afghanistan. A Cabinet reshuffle

Soviet troops prepare to leave Afghanistan, part of the pullout of 8,000 soldiers. The move fulfilled a promise made by Mikhail Gorbachev that was considered by some countries to be an inadequate gesture of military withdrawal.
FREDERIQUE HIBON—SYGMA

announced in the same month saw the elevation of Najibullah's supporters to the posts of foreign minister and defense minister.

The second major event was the announcement by the Soviet leader Mikhail Gorbachev that six regiments would be withdrawn from Afghanistan by the end of 1986. The withdrawal of troops began on October 15. Gorbachev's withdrawal offer was made from Siberia and was part of a much wider Soviet initiative in Asia. The withdrawal brought sharp reactions: the U.S. dismissed it as "inadequate" and suggested it was no more than a normal rotation of troops; Afghan resistance groups rejected it as a "bluff," while Pakistan saw it as a small but positive move. Strategic analysts said the withdrawal had no military significance since three of the six units were air-defense regiments and the Afghan resistance had no air capability. The regiments constituted only a little over 6% of an estimated 120,000 Soviet troops in Afghanistan.

In May, July, and August, for the fourth consecutive year, UN-sponsored talks were held in Geneva between Afghanistan and Pakistan with the object of ending the military presence in Kabul. None of the meetings produced any concrete results, though differences between the two countries had narrowed since the talks began in 1982. Discussions continued through diplomatic channels, and in December a UN spokesman announced that agreement had been reached on the monitoring of Soviet troop withdrawals. The remaining stumbling block was the timetable for a total withdrawal, with Pakistan insisting that this should take place as soon as technically feasible.

The war continued unabated, with many clashes between Soviet-backed Afghan troops and the resistance. Claims of success were made by both sides, but they were impossible to verify. A number of major offensives were launched during the year. In February the resistance shot down several military aircraft in Herat Province; the reported death toll was 200. In April, 700 resistance fighters were killed in Paktia Province. In July government troops clashed with resistance soldiers in Badakhshan Province, leaving 200 Soviet-Afghan soldiers and "dozens" of resistance soldiers dead. Also in July, 120 government troops died during an ambush on a military convoy in Zabol Province. In August a massive explosion destroyed an ammunition dump in the headquarters of the Afghan Army's 8th Division near Kabul, reportedly killing up to 100 people. The damage caused by the resistance fighters became increasingly costly; in April the government said it exceeded $712 million over an unspecified period.

A report by the U.S. State Department in February stated that the war had resulted in "one of the greatest mass migrations in history" and that Kabul's population had more than doubled to two million. "More than five million have been uprooted, nearly four million of them becoming refugees abroad. . . . In large areas of the countryside where resistance is active, wartime conditions and longstanding animosities among competing tribal groups have led to multiple taxation, arbitrary detention, and outright banditry," the report stated. (DILIP GANGULY)

BANGLADESH

A republic and member of the Commonwealth, Bangladesh is in the northeastern part of the Indian subcontinent, on the Bay of Bengal. Area: 143,998 sq km (55,598 sq mi). Pop. (1986 est.): 103.2 million. Cap.: Dhaka. Monetary unit: taka, with (Oct. 1, 1986) a free rate of 30.30 taka to U.S. $1 (43.78 taka = £1 sterling). President in 1986, Lieut. Gen. Hossain Mohammad Ershad; prime minister from July 9, Mizanur Rahman Chowdhury.

On Jan. 1, 1986, the ban on political activity in Bangladesh was lifted, and on May 7 the long-awaited parliamentary elections were held. They were the first since Lieut. Gen. Hossain Mohammad Ershad seized power in a bloodless coup in March 1982—the fourth military takeover in the country's 15-year history. The preelection period was marked by violence and alleged ballot rigging, and Ershad was accused of holding the election to strengthen his own power base. The result was a victory for the pro-government Jatiya Party, which took 183 of the 330 parliamentary seats, including the 30 reserved for women. The major opposition, an alliance of 15 parties led by Sheikh Hasina Wajad's Awami League Party, won 76 seats, but the other main opposition grouping, an alliance of 7 led by Begum Khalida Zia's Bangladesh Nationalist Party, boycotted the poll. The remaining seats were taken by smaller parties and independents.

On July 9 a new 26-member Cabinet was sworn in, including the first civilian prime minister since Ershad took power, Mizanur Rahman Chowdhury. The opposition boycotted the inaugural meeting of Parliament because martial law had not been lifted, and only 204 members attended. On August 28 Ershad resigned as army chief but retained the posts of chief martial law administrator and armed forces commander.

The election commission announced on September 1 that a presidential election would be held on October 15. At the same time, Ershad formally joined the Jatiya Party, and on the following day he was elected chairman, a post that had been vacant since the party's formation in January.

The major opposition parties boycotted the presidential election, in which Ershad received 83.6% of the vote. He was sworn in for a five-year term on October 23. The lifting of martial law and the revival of the constitution on November 10 coincided with the passing of a constitutional amendment ratifying all government actions during the period of martial law. The measure provided a new focus for opposition unrest.

On November 30 Ershad announced a major Cabinet reshuffle in which several key ministries changed hands. Four Awami League MPs were included in the new Cabinet. Law and Justice Minister A. K. M. Nurul Islam was named as vice-president and Ershad's successor.

During the year Ershad visited Pakistan, Nepal, India, and Bhutan. He made attempts to improve relations with the U.S.S.R., and in August the ambassador plenipotentiary of the Soviet Foreign Ministry visited Dhaka. Relations between the two countries had reached a low ebb in late 1983 and 1984 when at least 14 Soviet diplomats were expelled from Bangladesh on charges of meddling in the country's internal affairs. Links with China were strengthened by a three-day visit from China's Pres. Li Xiannian (Li Hsien-nien) in March, the first by a Chinese leader since 1971. China promised a generous interest-free loan to help finance economic development. Bangladesh boycotted the Commonwealth Games held in Edinburgh, Scotland, to protest British refusal to impose economic sanctions on South Africa.

AP/WIDE WORLD

Ballot boxes are stolen during Bangladesh's parliamentary elections in May, the first in seven years. The vote, accompanied by violence and accusations of fraud, followed the January 1 lifting of the ban on political activity.

Bangladesh remained one of the poorest countries in the world, with a per capita income of only $113. Gross domestic product during the 1986–87 fiscal year, which began July 1, was targeted to rise 5.2%. The country continued to be heavily dependent on foreign aid. Of the $1.4 billion in revenue projected by the 1986–87 budget, only $297 million was to be raised from domestic sources. Imports of 1.5 million metric tons of grain would be needed in 1986–87. Meanwhile, a government campaign was mounted to reduce the rat population, which consumes vast quantities of grain. (DILIP GANGULY)

BHUTAN

The monarchy of Bhutan is a landlocked state situated in the eastern Himalayas between China and India. Area: 47,000 sq km (18,100 sq mi). Pop. (1986 est.): 1,446,000. Cap.: Thimphu. Monetary unit: ngultrum, at par with the Indian rupee (which is also in use), with (Oct. 1, 1986) a free rate of 12.78 ngultrums to U.S. $1 (18.47 ngultrums = £1 sterling). Druk gyalpo (king) in 1986, Jigme Singye Wangchuk.

One of the most significant developments for Bhutan in 1986 was the progress made in its relations with China. This was of growing concern to India, which under the terms of a 1949 treaty guided Bhutan in its external relations and in all matters enjoyed considerable influence. A government delegation led by Ambassador Tashi Tobgyal visited Beijing (Peking) in June and met Premier Zhao Ziyang (Chao Tzu-yang), who promised that China would not interfere in Bhutan's internal affairs. Talks concentrated on the common border; there was no dispute concerning it, but China was seeking a formal demarcation. The outcome was inconclusive, and another meeting was planned for Thimphu in 1987. A Sino-Bhutan accord would make India the only non-Communist country having a border dispute with China.

The government launched a special training program designed to develop badly needed skills for trade and industry, with the aim of reducing its dependence on Indian personnel. The sixth five-year (1987–91) plan was to reflect this emphasis. The earlier plans gave high priority to developing the physical infrastructure and establishing a public administration and social services system, but progress was hampered by the lack of local skills. (DILIP GANGULY)

This article updates the *Micropædia* article BHUTAN.

INDIA

A federal republic of southern Asia and member of the Commonwealth, India is situated on a peninsula extending into the Indian Ocean with the Arabian Sea to the west and the Bay of Bengal to the east. Area: 3,166,414 sq km (1,222,559 sq mi), including the Indian-administered portion of Jammu and Kashmir. Pop. (1986 est.): 777 million, including Indian-administered Jammu and Kashmir. Cap.: New Delhi. Monetary unit: rupee, with (Oct. 1, 1986) a free rate of Rs 12.78 to U.S. $1 (Rs 18.47 = £1 sterling). President in 1986, Zail Singh; prime minister, Rajiv Gandhi.

Domestic Affairs. In 1986 Indian Prime Minister Rajiv Gandhi's attention was focused on attempts to consolidate his own position while grappling with the problems of the country and his party. There were also fears for Gandhi's safety. He escaped unhurt when a Sikh gunman attempted to assassinate him on October 2.

At home six-year-old problem of violent Sikh extremism in Punjab continuing to cause the most concern. There was no respite from terrorist activities in Punjab despite strong counterattacks by the police. In July, 15 bus passengers were shot dead in Muktsar. Gen. Arun Kumar Vaidya (*see* OBITUARIES), who had been chief of army staff when troops entered the Sikh Golden Temple at Amritsar in 1984 and had retired in January 1986, was assassinated in Pune on August 10. There was an attempt to kill the police chief, J. F. Ribeiro, in Jalandhar in October. Earlier, on April 29, a group of extremists at the Golden Temple announced plans to establish an independent Khalistan. The next day the police entered the temple to remove troublemakers. This led to resignations from S. S. Barnala's Cabinet, and 27 party legislators chose to sit as a separate group. There was also a split in the Shiromani Akali Dal, with the emergence of a dissident faction under P. S. Badal. The government told Parliament that during the 12-month period ended October 31, 418 persons had been killed in the Punjab, including 69 terrorists and 35 policemen, and that 1,322 terrorists had been arrested. The worst episode of the year occurred on November 29, when four Sikhs boarded a bus in a rural area of northern Punjab and massacred 24 passengers whom they identified as Hindus. The killings sparked riots and strikes in New Delhi and elsewhere.

The territorial dispute between Punjab and Haryana eluded settlement. In January the commission headed by K. K. Matthew reported that it was unable to identify the Punjab villages that could be transferred to Haryana. A new commission under E. S. Venkataramiah reported in June that 28,000 ha (70,000 ac) might be transferred, but specific areas were not indicated. The task was entrusted to yet another judge, D. A. Desai, but the Punjab government expressed inability to cooperate with his commission. A commission under Justice V. B. Eradi began examining the water dispute between the two states. In West Bengal violence flared in Darjeeling as the Gurkhas protested against discrimination and campaigned for a separate homeland. In Gujarat Muslim-Hindu violence in July led to heavy bloodshed, and in September an indefinite curfew was imposed in the town of Baroda as more violence brought the death toll to over 100 in two months.

On a more positive note, the 20-year-old insurgency problem in Mizoram, which borders Bangladesh and Burma, was brought to an end. The Mizo National Front, which represented the insurgents, signed an agreement in August with the Congress (I) by which Mizoram was to become a full-fledged state; in return, the insurgents agreed to lay down arms. In the meantime, Laldenga, who had been living in exile in London after having led the guerrilla movement for 20 years, took over as chief minister of the union territory. In the troubled Jammu and Kashmir state a power-sharing agreement between the National Conference and the Congress in November ended eight months of direct rule from Delhi. Farooq Abdullah, the Kashmiri Muslim leader, was appointed chief minister.

There were several Cabinet reshuffles during the year, and in May the Cabinet was expanded to 58 members—the largest in India's history—with the appointment of 2 new Cabinet ministers and 10 ministers of state. There was another major reshuffle in October, Gandhi's sixth since taking power. Two Cabinet ministers, S. B. Chavan and Bansi Lal, went back to their states—Maharashtra and Haryana—as chief ministers. Buta Singh, a Sikh, was made home minister in May. After B. R. Bhagat was dropped from the Cabinet, responsibility for external affairs passed to P. Shiv Shankar until October, when Narayan Dutt Tiwari took over the portfolio. Arjun Singh, who had left the Cabinet to become vice-president of the Congress in January, returned in October as communications minister. The exclusion of Arun Nehru, long regarded as close to the prime minister, caused widespread comment. Other new appointments in October were Bhajan Lal (environment and forest) and J. Vengala Rao (industry). G. S. Dhillon (agriculture and rural development) and Mufti Mohammed Sayeed (tourism) had been included earlier. The former finance minister, Pranab Mukherjee, and the former chief minister of Karnataka, R. Gundu Rao, were expelled from Congress (I) for antiparty activities. Mukherjee announced the formation of a separate Indian National Congress (Subhas-Indira) in October, and Gundu Rao floated a Congress (Indira Gandhi).

A Supreme Court judgment in a Muslim divorce case gave rise to Muslim protests that their religious practices were being curtailed. In response, the government brought forward a bill freeing husbands from paying alimony, and despite opposition by many parties and groups, it was passed by Parliament in May. A uniform civil code for voluntary adoption by followers of any religion was also introduced. Legislation was brought forward to establish a consumer protection commission and to regulate advertisements for breast-milk substitutes. By another enactment the strength of the Supreme Court was increased to 25. In January the death penalty was imposed on Balbir Singh, Satwant Singh, and Kehar Singh for the assassination of former prime minister Indira Gandhi; the High Court confirmed the sentences. A report on the circumstances of Indira Gandhi's death was not placed before Parliament because of a legal action by the government. India accepted the U.S. ruling that the petitions of victims of the poisonous gas leak from the Union Carbide plant in Bhopal in 1984 be heard in India. A court of inquiry confirmed

BALDEV—SYGMA

After attempting to assassinate Indian Prime Minister Rajiv Gandhi, gunman Karamjit Singh surrenders. The 26-year-old Sikh terrorist hid in bushes in a garden and shot at the prime minister with a homemade pistol, but the shot missed.

that the June 1985 crash of an Air-India jet in the Atlantic Ocean, which killed 329, had been caused by a bomb.

Two major developments were the announcement of a new education policy and the start of work on eliminating pollution from the Ganges River. A stampede at the Kumbha Mela festival at Hardwar on the Ganges in April resulted in some 50 deaths; 52 were killed when a train plunged into a river in Bihar in August. Notable personalities who died during the year included Tenzing Norgay, one of the first two people to climb Mt. Everest; the veteran politician Jagjivan Ram; and the nonconformist philosopher J. Krishnamurti (*see* OBITUARIES).

The Economy. The budget presented on February 28 set total expenditure at Rs 528,620,000,000, 3% more than in 1985. The deficit was envisaged at Rs 36.5 billion. Of total spending, some 42% was allocated to the development plan and 16.5% to defense. Agriculture and rural programs to reduce poverty were emphasized. Basic tax rates were unchanged, but taxes were increased on some luxury items. The national income was estimated at Rs 1,732,070,000,000 in 1984–85, an increase of 3.5% over 1983–84. Consumer prices were expected to rise by some 7% in 1986, reflecting a slight acceleration over 1985, as the lifting of some government subsidies took effect.

The Western Aid India Consortium approved aid of $4.5 billion in June. Loans were drawn from the Asian Development Bank for the first time. Significant developments included the award of a contract for the Hazir-Bijaipur-Jagdishpur gas pipeline to Spie-Capag-NKK, a French-Japanese consortium. The Helicopter Corporation signed an agreement with Aero Spatiale of France for 27 Dauphin helicopters. A protocol on computers was signed with the U.S.S.R. On a visit to New Delhi in October, U.S. Defense Secretary Caspar Weinberger announced U.S. readiness to supply advanced computers.

Foreign Policy. Rajiv Gandhi placed considerable emphasis on relations with Africa in 1986. He was active in getting economic sanctions imposed on South Africa, and to that end he toured four frontline African states (Zambia, Zimbabwe, Angola, and Tanzania) in May. India withdrew from the Commonwealth Games held in Scotland because of the U.K.'s attitude to South Africa. At the eighth conference of nonaligned countries, held in August–September in Harare, Zimbabwe, the chairmanship of the movement passed from India to Zimbabwe, and Gandhi was made chairman of a fund set up to help Africans. He traveled to Mexico in August for a meeting of the six-nation Five-Continent Peace Initiative (Argentina, Greece, India, Mexico, Sweden, Tanzania), where the group reiterated its call for an end to nuclear testing.

At a meeting of foreign ministers of nonaligned countries held in New Delhi in April, India joined in condemning the U.S. air raid on Libya. Among other countries visited by the prime minister were Maldives, Sweden, Mauritius, Indonesia, Australia, New Zealand, and Thailand. Pres. Zail Singh visited Nepal, Yugoslavia, Greece, and Poland. Notable visitors to India included Pope John Paul II, King Hussein of Jordan, the presidents of Nauru, Nicaragua, and Seychelles, the prime ministers of Greece, South Yemen, South Korea, Sweden, Turkey, and Yugoslavia, Oliver Tambo of the African National Congress, and Sam Nujoma of the South West Africa People's Organization, which was accorded diplomatic status. The second meeting of the South Asian Association for Regional Cooperation, held in Bangalore in November, was attended by the kings of Nepal and Bhutan and the presidents of Bangladesh, Maldives, Pakistan, and Sri Lanka.

During Soviet leader Mikhail S. Gorbachev's official visit to New Delhi on November 25–28, he and Gandhi issued a joint declaration on "principles for a nuclear-weapons-free and nonviolent world." An agreement on economic and technical cooperation envisaged Soviet assistance worth 1.5 billion rubles, mainly for four major projects in the industrial and energy sectors.

Relations with Pakistan continued to be marred by suspicions that Pakistan was pursuing an active nuclear program and that it was training Sikh separatists. A hijack incident in September at the Karachi airport, in which 14 Indians were killed, increased tension. On December 21 India and Pakistan agreed to increase cooperation in border security in an effort to prevent Sikh extremists from using Pakistan as a base for launching attacks against Indian territory. Relations with China were damaged by its reported incursion into Arunachal Pradesh. India continued to hope that Sri Lanka would produce a formula acceptable to the Tamils of the island. Pres. J. R. Jayawardene of Sri Lanka held talks with Gandhi on the issue in November.

(H. Y. SHARADA PRASAD)

MALDIVES

A republic and member of the Commonwealth in the Indian Ocean, the Maldives consists of about 2,000 small islands southwest of the southern tip of India. Area: 298 sq km (115 sq mi). Pop. (1986): 190,000 Cap.: Male. Monetary unit: rufiyaa, with (Oct. 1, 1986) a free rate of 7 rufiyaa to U.S. $1 (10.12 rufiyaa = £1 sterling). President in 1986, Maumoon Abdul Gayoom.

In December 1985, following years of negotiations, the first summit meeting of the newly formed South Asian Association for Regional Cooperation (SAARC) was held in Dhaka, Bangladesh. Maldives was by far the smallest nation in the group, whose other members were Bangladesh, Bhutan, India, Nepal, Pakistan, and Sri Lanka. Even Bhutan had a population almost eight times greater than that of Maldives. Having made its modest debut in two important organizations—the Commonwealth and SAARC—Maldives was learning both the problems and the advantages of being a small state.

The economy of Maldives, the most important sector of which was tourism, was so small that the pace of development was hampered at almost every turn. Lack of facilities, skills, and capital meant that only very limited advances were possible. One of the world's most diffuse island states, with a high proportion of its population under 15 years of age, Maldives sought from membership in the Commonwealth and SAARC to protect its economic development.

(GUY ARNOLD)

This article updates the *Macropædia* article INDIAN OCEAN ISLANDS: *Maldives.*

NEPAL

A constitutional monarchy, Nepal is a landlocked country in the Himalayas between India and the Tibetan Autonomous Region of China. Area: 147,181 sq km (56,827 sq mi). Pop. (1986 est.): 16,863,000. Cap.: Kathmandu. Monetary unit: Nepalese rupee, with (Oct. 1, 1986) a free rate of NRs 20.50 to U.S. $1 (NRs 29.62 = £1 sterling). King, Birendra Bir Bikram Shah Deva; prime ministers in 1986, Lokendra Bahadur Chand and, from June 15, Marich Man Singh Shrestha.

The elections for Nepal's national Panchayat (parliament) were held in May 1986. They were boycotted by the banned Nepali Congress Party and the Communists, but some 65% of the country's 8.7 million voters participated. Political parties had been banned by royal proclamation

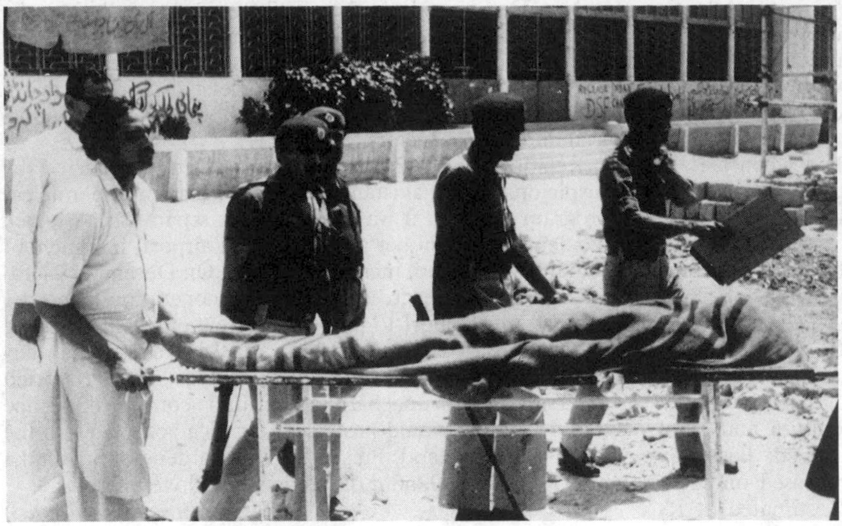

American passenger Rajesh Kumar, the first victim of terrorist shootings on hijacked Pan American flight 73 in Karachi, Pakistan, is wheeled, under police guard, to a hospital, where he died soon afterward.

AP/WIDE WORLD

since 1961. Some 69 new members were elected, many of whom were reported to be against the partyless system. The new prime minister was 44-year-old Marich Man Singh Shrestha. Perhaps the most momentous occasion for many Nepalese, however, was the visit by Queen Elizabeth II and Prince Philip from the U.K.

Nepal maintained cordial links with both China and India. The foreign minister visited China and renewed a ten-year-old bilateral trade treaty. U.S. companies agreed to carry out preliminary oil exploration in the south. The economy remained heavily dependent on foreign aid. The budget for the year starting in July set expenditure at $624.5 million, two-thirds of which was allocated for development. Only $227.5 million was to be internally generated. The Aid Nepal Consortium pledged $680 million in assistance over two years. (DILIP GANGULY)

PAKISTAN

A federal republic, Pakistan is in the northwestern part of the Indian subcontinent, on the Arabian Sea. Area: 796,095 sq km (307,374 sq mi), excluding the Pakistani-controlled section of Jammu and Kashmir. Pop. (1986 est., including some 3 million Afghan refugees and 1.6 million residents of Pakistani-controlled Jammu and Kashmir): 102,878,000. Cap.: Islamabad. Monetary unit: Pakistan rupee, with (Oct. 1, 1986) a free rate of PRs 17.01 to U.S. $1 (PRs 24.58 = £1 sterling). President in 1986, Gen. Mohammad Zia-ul-Haq; prime minister, Mohammad Khan Junejo.

Pakistan remained firmly under the control of Pres. Zia-ul-Haq during 1986 despite a high incidence of violence. Theoretically at least, martial law was lifted on Dec. 30, 1985, and on Jan. 18, 1986, Prime Minister Mohammad Khan Junejo formally adopted the Pakistan Muslim League as the country's ruling party. Soon afterward he reshuffled the Cabinet; the most significant change was the replacement of the controversial but competent finance minister, Mahbub ul-Haq, by Mian Mohammad Yasin Khan Wattoo.

The April return of Benazir Bhutto (*see* BIOGRAPHIES) from exile in London with a mandate from the government to relaunch her Pakistan People's Party (PPP), one of the ten parties in the Movement for the Restoration of Democracy (MRD), marked the start of another period of turbulence. Ironically, her pledge to lead "a peaceful revolution" became the cause of the worst violence the country had experienced in several years. The widespread welcome and support for Bhutto gave her the confidence to challenge President Zia to hold an election in late 1986, to which he responded that there was no justification before 1990 because the country had given him a vote of confidence in 1984. The euphoria that marked Bhutto's return was short-lived, and her call in early July for a nationwide "Black Day" to mark the ninth anniversary of the overthrow of her father (former prime minister Zulfikar Ali Bhutto) was supported by thousands of demonstrators but fell short of expectations. An outbreak of violence in Sind Province marked the occasion.

Events came to a head in the days before the Independence Day celebrations on August 14, which were to be the excuse for protest marches organized by the PPP. After a banned rally in Karachi, Bhutto and several other opposition leaders were arrested on August 14. There followed serious bloodshed and widespread antigovernment riots and demonstrations that persisted until September 6. In the meantime, while Bhutto served a 30-day detention order, her supporters lost faith in her, and the PPP leader, Ghulum Mustapha Jatoi, launched a new party that was blatantly anti-Bhutto.

Prime Minister Junejo formed a new Cabinet in late December in the wake of ethnic riots in Karachi that left more than 170 dead and hundreds injured. The riots were apparently triggered when ethnic Pathans, angered by an army sweep through their neighbourhood in search of illegal arms and narcotics, attacked Urdu-speaking areas.

Relations with the U.S. and China improved considerably in 1986. The U.S. pledged more than $4 billion in military and economic aid for 1987–93, a 35% increase over the previous package, which was to expire in 1987. The amount nevertheless fell short of Pakistan's request for $6.5 billion. U.S. aid had been increased since the U.S.S.R.'s invasion of Afghanistan in 1979 in order to curb Soviet advances in the region. Relations with China were boosted by the signing in September of an agreement to cooperate in the peaceful use of nuclear energy; it provided for safeguard inspections under the International Atomic Energy Agency. Further cooperation in industry, agriculture, and other areas.

The economy performed well, growing by 7.5% in fiscal 1985–86. This rate had been exceeded only twice during the previous 20 years, and it was in excess of the 6.5% increase targeted by the annual development plan. The rate of inflation declined to 4.9%, compared with 7.5% in 1984–85. The buoyant agricultural sector benefited from a World Bank loan of $220 million granted in May.

Pakistan continued to make progress in its effort to

check the production of and trafficking in drugs. During the year at least 140 kg (310 lb) of high-quality heroin and 1,125 kg (2,480 lb) of hashish were seized. In recognition of his efforts, President Zia was awarded Interpol's gold medal in January.

During the nine years that had elapsed since Pakistan decided to make its legal system conform with Islamic doctrine, only the most cosmetic changes had been made. The government was under increasing pressure to enforce Islamic laws—some 25,000 Muslim fundamentalists demonstrated in front of Parliament in July.

(DILIP GANGULY)

SRI LANKA

A republic and member of the Commonwealth, Sri Lanka occupies an island in the Indian Ocean off the southeast coast of peninsular India. Area: 65,610 sq km (25,332 sq mi). Pop. (1986 est.): 16,060,000. Cap., Colombo; capital designate, Sri Jayawardenapura. Monetary unit: Sri Lanka rupee, with (Oct. 1, 1986) a free rate of SL Rs 28.35 to U.S. $1 (SL Rs 40.96 = £1 sterling). President in 1986, Junius Richard Jayawardene; prime minister, Ranasingne Premadasa.

In 1986 Sri Lanka continued to suffer from endemic violence as extremists from the 2.5 million Tamil population fought for an autonomous state; the death toll over three years was estimated at 4,500. Relations with India had deteriorated as Sri Lanka alleged that Tamil guerrillas were being allowed to operate training camps and launch offensives from southern India.

The Tamil problem had proved costly for the economy, and the annual growth target for 1986–90 was revised from 5.8 to 4.4%. Defense spending had spiraled to $370 million in 1986, at a time when world prices for Sri Lanka's major exports had fallen. The country came near to self-sufficiency in rice, however, as a result of the aid-funded Mahaweli irrigation and power project. In June the consortium of principal donors approved $703 million in aid.

Sri Lanka's relations with China were given impetus by a visit from Pres. Li Xiannian (Li Hsien-nien), who pledged a $16.5 million interest-free loan. Other visitors included Pres. Hossain Mohammad Ershad of Bangladesh and, significantly, Israel's Pres. Chaim Herzog. Diplomatic relations with Israel had been severed in 1970, but there were reports that Israel's help might be sought in the effort to combat terrorism.

MICHEL PHILIPPOT—SYGMA

Tamil secessionist guerrillas get patrols underway in a city of the Sri Lankan Jaffna district. The power struggle between the country's Buddhist Sinhalese and Hindu Tamils had escalated since 1983, with some 300 reported killed within one week in April.

In November Pres. J. R. Jayawardene visited India for a summit meeting of the South Asian Association for Regional Cooperation. The Tamil issue was the subject of lengthy debate, and Tamil organizations based in India joined the negotiations. Concessions offered by the government included handing over part of the eastern province to Tamil control, along with the northern province, which they already held. The principal Tamil separatist group, the Liberation Tigers of Tamil Eelam, rejected the offer.

(DILIP GANGULY)

Southeast Asia

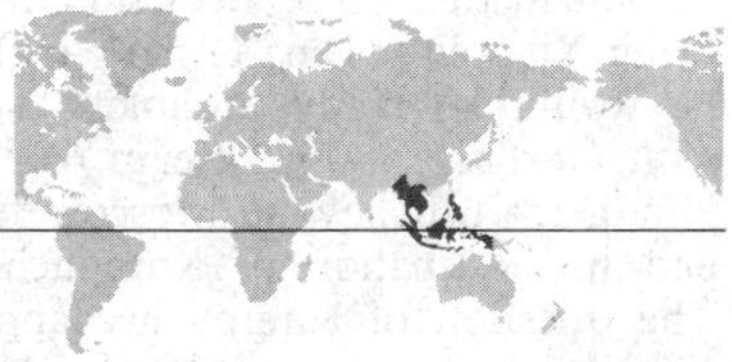

SOUTHEAST ASIAN AFFAIRS

Diplomatic efforts in Southeast Asia in 1986 continued to concentrate on finding a solution to the nine-year conflict over Kampuchea, where the regime was held in place by 160,000 Vietnamese troops, supported by the U.S.S.R. Major new developments gave a boost to prospects for peace. The chief impetus came from Soviet leader Mikhail Gorbachev, whose foreign policy speech in the Soviet Far East port of Vladivostok on July 28 was widely interpreted as marking a turning point. He called for better relations between his country and all of Asia and urged the amicable settlement of outstanding problems in the region. Gorbachev's initiative affected the attitudes of Vietnam, which annually received an estimated $1 billion in aid from Moscow. In support of the new Kremlin leadership's strong desire for improved ties with Vietnam's traditional enemy, China, Vietnamese leaders began a series of subtle diplomatic maneuvers that suggested a softening of their stance on the Kampuchean question.

Early in the year prospects for finding a solution had appeared gloomy. In January the foreign ministers of Vietnam, Laos, and Kampuchea met and again insisted that a withdrawal of Vietnamese troops would have to be preceded by the removal of the Khmer Rouge, which was leading the tripartite resistance in Kampuchea. Then the three-group resistance headed by Prince Norodom Sihanouk put forward an eight-point peace plan in March. It involved a phased withdrawal of Vietnamese troops under the auspices of the UN, to be followed by an election and formation of a new government presided over by Sihanouk but including members of the present Hanoi-backed regime. The plan received the support of members of the Association of Southeast Asian Nations (ASEAN) and some 40 other countries. However, Vietnam, strongly influenced by the U.S.S.R., rejected it. Later, in June, a meeting of ASEAN foreign ministers reiterated its criticism of Vietnam for not accepting the framework the plan provided, and this view was supported by Australia, Canada, and the European Communities (EC).

In July Gorbachev announced his Asian initiatives: "The Soviet state calls on all Asian and Pacific nations to cooperate for the sake of peace and security," he declared in the

Vladivostok speech. The U.S.S.R. desired "new, fair" relations with all nations in the region "without exception." Regarding Indochina, Gorbachev expressed "interest" in seeing an improvement in long-strained Sino-Vietnamese ties. He saw "no insurmountable obstacles" to friendlier relations between socialist Indochina and ASEAN.

Gorbachev's message was quickly reflected in Vietnamese policy. In August the Indochinese foreign ministers issued a joint communiqué that referred to "large public opinion calling for the withdrawal of Vietnamese forces" from Kampuchea. It also declared that Hanoi, Vientiane, and Phnom Penh were "prepared to discuss an early political solution" to the Kampuchean problem. Though there were fears that Moscow might sacrifice Vietnam's interests in Kampuchea for the sake of warmer Sino-Soviet ties, Vietnamese leaders publicly welcomed the budding rapprochement between the Communist giants.

Soon, however, China made its demands. In an interview with a U.S. television network, elder statesman Deng Xiaoping (Teng Hsiao-p'ing) said unequivocally that he would be ready to hold a summit in the U.S.S.R. with Gorbachev—the dream of every Soviet leader since Nikita Khrushchev—if Moscow "encouraged" Vietnam to end its occupation of Kampuchea by stopping its aid. The question of Kampuchea appeared for the first time on the Sino-Soviet agenda when the Soviet deputy foreign minister, Igor Rogachev, visited China in October. Previously, Moscow had refused to discuss the issue directly with Beijing (Peking) on the grounds that there could be no interference in the affairs of a third party (Vietnam). The Soviets, however, apparently rejected a Chinese request to pressure Vietnam on withdrawal. After Rogachev's departure, his Chinese counterpart, Qian Qichen (Ch'ien Ch'i-ch'en), reported that there had been "no substantial change" in Moscow's position on Kampuchea.

Nevertheless, momentum seemed to be gathering. India, the only major non-Communist country to recognize the Phnom Penh regime, promised ASEAN it would raise the issue of Kampuchea with its old friend, the U.S.S.R. Meeting in Jakarta, Indon., foreign ministers of ASEAN and the EC issued a communiqué calling on Vietnam "to begin serious negotiations" on the removal of its forces from Kampuchea. The ministers also reaffirmed that their governments would not provide Hanoi with aid that would "sustain and enhance" its occupation of Kampuchea. In a response to Gorbachev's Vladivostok policy statement, ASEAN representatives pointedly said that any improvement in their relations with the U.S.S.R. would depend on Moscow's helpfulness in resolving the Kampuchean conflict.

A major territorial dispute in Southeast Asia was moving closer to a final resolution. Since 1963 the former British territory of Sabah had been a part of the Malaysian federation. However, the Philippines had long argued its claim to the resource-rich region, and that claim was a source of constant irritation between the two neighbours and ASEAN partners. In April the Philippines foreign minister, Salvador Laurel, indicated that the new government of Pres. Corazon Aquino (*see* BIOGRAPHIES) wanted to settle the Sabah question with Malaysia, and the statement was immediately welcomed by Kuala Lumpur. After a May meeting with Malaysian Prime Minister Mahathir bin Mohamad in the Malaysian capital, Laurel announced that the issue would be settled "once and for all" in "a package

Facing the Economic Challenge

In 1986 it became clear to non-Communist Southeast Asian countries that their economic prospects had changed dramatically. The rapid growth of the 1970s and early 1980s was over. New strategies were needed to cope with low commodity prices, slower world trade, increasing protectionism, and growing competition from countries where costs were lower, such as China. Fundamental changes in direction could be detected. Privatization was being seen as a fund-raiser and a means to greater efficiency. The acquisition of high technology to improve competitiveness became a priority, and it was recognized that foreign assistance was needed.

The chances that the region could adapt successfully to the new world climate were good. It was operating from a strong base and, with the exception of the Philippines, had enjoyed strong and steady growth for more than a decade until 1984. Even in the less buoyant 1980–84 period, real growth rates were impressive, with annual averages exceeding 5% for Indonesia and Thailand, nearly 7% for Malaysia, and more than 8% for Singapore. Only the Philippines struggled along at 0.3%, not least because of the failure of an inept and corrupt government to control inflation. All five countries shared World Bank middle-income status. Economic expansion was accompanied by strong development, sound economic management, and, except in the Philippines, political stability.

In 1985 and in early 1986, however, the region felt the full impact of the collapse in oil and other commodity prices. Apart from Singapore, it continued to derive much of its wealth from the primary sector. Indonesia and Brunei and, to a lesser extent, Malaysia were heavily dependent on oil and gas. At the same time, growing protectionism and the slowdown in world trade affected newly developed manufacturing industries. Singapore's role in the region was diminished, and for the first time its gross domestic product declined, by 1.8%. Growth fell sharply in Malaysia (to +2.8%) and Indonesia (1.9%). Thailand fared better because of cheaper oil imports (4%), but in the Philippines there was a 3% contraction.

Restructuring was needed if economic stagnation and social unrest were to be avoided. Indonesia ignored possible political consequences and devalued its currency by 45% against the U.S. dollar to stimulate exports. In Malaysia Prime Minister Mahathir bin Mohamad (*see* BIOGRAPHIES), fresh from a resounding election victory in August, was strongly placed to announce that the cherished New Economic Policy had to take second place to economic growth and that foreign assistance would be welcomed. In Singapore severe wage constraints were imposed and conditions for foreign investment improved. The new Philippine government rescheduled its debt and subdued public expectations of greater affluence in the post-Marcos era. In Thailand the government tried to shift the emphasis to the private sector and sought more foreign help. By the year's end these strategies seemed to be working. (JANET H. CLARK) deal of some sort." He did not reveal details of the discussions. Officials of the two countries said they expected Manila to drop its claim to Sabah without preconditions, though it would want Kuala Lumpur's assurance that the state would not be used as a base for anti-Philippine activities. In July the Constitutional Commission responsible for drafting a new charter for the Philippines approved an article on national territory that virtually set aside the claim to Sabah.

The U.S. demonstrated its growing interest in Southeast Asia in two top-level visits to the region. In April U.S. Defense Secretary Caspar Weinberger visited the Philippines and Thailand. In Manila Weinberger told the fledgling Aquino administration that the U.S. was "ready to offer aid in terms [the Philippines] was willing to have." The assistance, he added, would be both economic and military. In Bangkok Weinberger and Thai Prime Minister Prem Tinsulanond agreed to start a "war reserve stockpile" of U.S. arms and munitions in Thailand. Its purpose, explained the Thai government, would be to "improve Thai forces' ability to resist external aggression."

Shortly afterward, U.S. Pres. Ronald Reagan stopped in Bali for a summit with President Suharto of Indonesia. The most substantive discussions of the four-day trip, however, were held at ministerial level, most notably between U.S. Secretary of State George Shultz and the ASEAN foreign ministers. Southeast Asian representatives drew U.S. attention to the dangers of trade protectionism. A confidential memorandum to Reagan said that "unless economic growth" in the region "can be nurtured and developed, ASEAN support for democratic ideals may be undermined." The U.S. promised to convey ASEAN's concerns about protectionism to other industrialized nations.

In a year that began with much of ASEAN in economic recession (*see* Sidebar), the association's member states sought help from Japan, their biggest trading partner. Japan's direct investment in Southeast Asia had declined dramatically, and ASEAN leaders called on the Japanese to reverse the trend. In July the eighth Japan-ASEAN Forum was attended by a hundred officials. The Southeast Asians asked Japan to expedite the opening of its markets to their exports as it had promised.

Economic cooperation within ASEAN itself was not without problems. When the group's economic ministers gathered in Manila for a meeting in August, they failed to produce any solutions or coordinated responses to such tough problems as slower growth, escalating protectionism, and plunging commodity prices. The Philippines' bold proposal for a common market met with a lukewarm response—as did another by Manila to make the currencies of the six member nations interchangeable for intraregional trade. The common market idea was expected to be discussed further during a summit of ASEAN heads of government scheduled for 1987. Agreement was easier to reach on external matters. The ministers endorsed united action to forge economic accords with the U.S. and appealed to Japan to help countries whose debt burdens had grown because of the increased strength of the yen.

(THOMAS HON WING POLIN)

BRUNEI

The sultanate of Brunei is located on the northern coast of the island of Borneo, on the South China Sea. Area: 5,765 sq km (2,226 sq mi). Pop. (1986 est.): 242,000. Cap.: Bandar Seri Begawan. Monetary unit: Brunei dollar, with (Oct. 1, 1986) a free rate of Br$2.17 to U.S. $1 (Br$3.14 = £1 sterling). Sultan and prime minister in 1986, Sir Muda Hassanal Bolkiah Mu'izzadin Waddaulah.

On Sept. 7, 1986, an era ended for Brunei when its redoubtable "Old Sultan," Sir Muda Omar Ali Saifuddin (*see* OBITUARIES), died at the age of 71. Though he had abdicated 19 years earlier in favour of his son, Sultan Sir Muda Hassanal Bolkiah, Omar had retained a major say in national affairs. In April the government released Ahmad bin Abdullah, who had been imprisoned in connection with the abortive uprising of 1962. Only one person was thought to remain in jail as a result of that event. Analysts believed the release—and a number of others in recent years—reflected the sultan's growing confidence.

Because of the decline in oil prices and falling production, the government announced an ambitious five-year plan designed to free the economy from its overwhelming dependence on the production of petroleum and natural gas. Priority areas for development were industry, agriculture, finance, and manpower training, especially in the technological sciences. Socially, there was growing concern about drug smuggling and usage. Since the opening of a direct air link with Australia in 1984, Brunei had become a transit point for drug traffic from the notorious Golden Triangle in mainland Southeast Asia.

Among revelations in the scandal over U.S. foreign policy emerging at year's end, the sultan was named as having contributed several million dollars to the U.S.-supported *contra* guerrillas in Nicaragua. (*See* North America: *United States,* below.) (THOMAS HON WING POLIN)

This article updates the *Macropædia* article EAST INDIES: *Brunei.*

BURMA

Burma is a people's republic of Southeast Asia with coastlines on the Bay of Bengal and the Andaman Sea. Area: 676,577 sq km (261,228 sq mi). Pop. (1986 est.): 38,438,000. Cap.: Rangoon. Monetary unit: kyat, with (Oct. 1, 1986) a free rate of 7.02 kyats to U.S. $1 (10.15 kyats = £1 sterling). Chairman of the State Council in 1986, U San Yu; prime minister, U Maung Maung Kha.

A turning point in the history of Burma was reached in 1986 when 75-year-old Gen. U Ne Win resigned as chairman of the governing Burma Socialist Program Party (BSPP) for reasons of old age and poor health. Ne Win had been the country's undisputed leader since he took power in a bloodless coup in 1962. The announcement was made at the BSPP's fourth congress, held in August, and the National Assembly elected U San Yu, chairman of the State Council since 1981 and a loyal follower of Ne Win, as his successor. Nevertheless, it was confidently expected that Ne Win would remain the real power in Burma until his health finally failed. San Yu was not expected to deviate from the "Burmese Road to Socialism."

Reports about the continuing insurgency problem conflicted. In April it was said that the banned Burmese Communist Party (BCP), with its 12,000 fighters, had united with the National Democratic Front (NDF)—a confederation of nine ethnic insurgent groups with 12,000 supporters—and made a joint declaration. But an August report disputed this, stating that there was no agreement within the NDF on whether to have links with the BCP and that the strongest NDF group, the Karens, wanted no association with the BCP.

Foreign loans were needed to finance the 1986–87 budget deficit, but the expected total of 2.6 billion kyats would be insufficient to prevent another balance of payments deficit. The trade deficit—the tenth since 1977–78—was expected to be around 1.4 billion kyats.

(DILIP GANGULY)

INDONESIA

A republic of Southeast Asia, Indonesia consists of the major islands of Sumatra, Java, Kalimantan (Indonesian Borneo), Celebes, and Irian Jaya (West New Guinea) and approximately 3,000 smaller islands and islets. Area: 1,919,443 sq km (741,101 sq mi). Pop. (1986 est.): 168,662,000. (Area and population figures include East [former Portuguese] Timor.) Cap.: Jakarta. Monetary unit: rupiah, with (Oct. 1, 1986) a free rate of 1,636 rupiah to U.S. $1 (2,364 rupiah = £1 sterling). President in 1986, Suharto.

Indonesian politics in 1986 were dominated by the general elections scheduled for 1987. One reason for heightened interest was that the membership of the House of People's Representatives was to be increased from 460 to 500, with 400 seats filled by election (previously 364) and 100 by presidential appointment (96). Above all, the balloting would reflect public opinion about President Suharto's 20-year rule and his suitability for another five-year term beginning in 1988. The government-backed Golkar held 246 parliamentary seats and seemed likely to maintain its dominant position. The largest opposition party was the Islam-oriented United Development Party (PPP), with 94 seats, but factional infighting had weakened its unity. The PPP based its policies on moral rectitude, clean government, and an equitable distribution of national wealth. The nationalist Indonesian Democratic Party, with 24 seats in Parliament, advocated less dependence on foreign assistance and greater government accountability.

In moves thought to be related to the election, the government put on trial several dissidents including H. R. Dharsono, a former top official who had served as secretary-general of the Association of Southeast Asian Nations. He was convicted of inciting young Muslims to riot in 1984 and of challenging the official version of the incident; he received a ten-year sentence in January. Dharsono's conviction followed soon after that of a fiery Muslim dissident preacher, Andi Mappetahang Fatwa, who, together with another Muslim preacher, was sentenced to 18 years in prison for subversion. Nine Communists who took part in the abortive coup of 1965 were executed in the fall. The tough actions were seen as a warning to would-be disturbers of the public peace in the preelection period.

Foreign relations were dominated by a period of friction with Australia. A diplomatic squabble erupted in April when an Australian newspaper published an article about alleged financial dealings of Suharto, his family and associates. Gen. Benny Murdani, the commander in chief of the armed forces, described the piece as representing an unacceptable "smear campaign." Australia's Prime Minister Robert Hawke responded that the press was not under his government's control, but Indonesia retaliated by suspending bilateral military cooperation and revoking visa-free entry for Australians for 24 hours. Relations between the two countries had just begun to ease when Canberra released a defense study that referred to potential military attack from or through the Indonesian archipelago. In September, in what was regarded as reprisal, the Indonesian military authority withdrew Australia's military landing rights for refueling in Indonesia, but within a week Australian protests had brought a reversal of the decision.

These events coincided with U.S. Pres. Ronald Reagan's four-day visit to Indonesia at the end of April, when two Australian journalists traveling in his entourage were refused entry. Talks between Suharto and Reagan focused on trade and investment problems. A four-day visit by Pres. François Mitterrand of France also concentrated on economic collaboration but was slightly clouded by Indonesia's earlier decision to purchase 12 fighter aircraft from the U.S. rather than from France. By contrast, Corazon Aquino of the Philippines, making her first foreign visit after becoming president, held talks with Suharto that were mainly of a political nature. Diplomatic relations with Zimbabwe were established in August.

For the economy 1986 was a testing time. Substantially reduced income from oil and natural gas exports necessitated a reduced budget for the first time in two decades. Expenditure for 1986–87 was down about 7% in rupiah terms from 1985–86. A long-expected but surprisingly large devaluation of the rupiah took place in September (45% against the U.S. dollar). A contraction in gross domestic product was expected following a rise of 1.9% in 1985. One positive factor was the low annual inflation rate of about 4%. (THOMAS HON WING POLIN)

This article updates the *Macropædia* article EAST INDIES: *Indonesia*.

KAMPUCHEA

A people's republic of Southeast Asia, Kampuchea occupies the southwestern part of the Indochinese Peninsula, on the Gulf of Thailand. Area: 181,035 sq km (69,898 sq mi). Pop. (1986 est.): 7,469,000. Cap.: Phnom Penh. Monetary unit: riel. Secretary-general of the People's Revolutionary (Communist) Party of Kampuchea and chairman of the Council of State (president) in 1986, Heng Samrin; chairman of the Council of Ministers (prime minister), Hun Sen.

The continuing struggle to wrest political and military control away from the Vietnam-backed Heng Samrin regime dominated developments in Kampuchea in 1986. After military successes in the 1984–85 dry season that decimated major bases of the Democratic Kampuchea (DK) resistance forces near the Thai-Kampuchean border, Vietnam pursued a two-pronged battlefield strategy. Its 140,000 troops conducted extensive search-and-destroy operations in Kampuchea's interior and tightened civilian security measures. At Hanoi's instigation, the administration in Phnom Penh erected a "defense line" along much of the border with Thailand to prevent infiltration into the interior by guerrillas of the UN-recognized coalition government made up of the nationalist Khmer People's National Liberation Front (KPNLF), the Armée Nationale Sihanoukist (ANS), and the Khmer Rouge (KR), the tripartite resistance alliance. Both measures, however, had limited effect.

Despite the loss of their large border bases, resistance forces performed well, and popular support for them was growing. Major efforts were made to reduce interfactional differences and cooperate more closely, with the KR actively adopting a non-Communist image. A joint military command was set up early in the year, followed by a two-tiered joint permanent committee on military coordination. In March all three combined for the first time to attack Batdambang, Kampuchea's second largest city. The attack was reportedly well planned and coordinated and raised hopes among the anti-Vietnamese coalition supporters that the forces could cooperate effectively. Despite instructions, however, some field commanders of the Khmer Rouge remained hostile to the two non-Communist groups. The ANS, which remained loyal to former head of state Prince Norodom Sihanouk, improved its military rating and achieved some success in recruitment.

Vietnam seemed to backtrack from its confident 1985 assertion that all its troops would be out of Kampuchea by 1990, by which time it had expected the resistance to be ineffectual. Vietnamese Deputy Foreign Minister Hoang

Bich Son stated in July: "We would like to withdraw [by 1990], but they [Phnom Penh] would like us to stay." A Vietnamese withdrawal would depend on the ability of the Phnom Penh regime to defend the country. Its 35,000-strong Army, despite having increased its strength some 20% in recent years, was still hampered by the extremely high rate of desertion.

Diplomatic efforts were made to break the imbroglio. The foreign ministers of Vietnam, Kampuchea, and Laos reaffirmed their position that Hanoi would pull its forces out if the KR and its leader Pol Pot were removed. A new initiative came from the DK alliance in March when it announced its first-ever eight-point peace plan after a conference in Beijing (Peking). It called for a two-phase withdrawal of Vietnamese troops, the formation of a four-party government that would include Heng Samrin, and nationwide elections to be supervised by the United Nations. The plan was favourably received by more than 40 countries, including the Association of Southeast Asian Nations (ASEAN)—the DK's strongest supporter—China, the U.S., Japan, and Australia. The U.S.S.R. and Vietnam rejected the proposal as "Beijing's usual farce." Phnom Penh, too, termed it "another theatrical scene masterminded by China." Late in the year reports were circulating in Bangkok to the effect that Pol Pot was in China suffering from a terminal illness.

Late in July the Soviet leader Mikhail Gorbachev in a speech at Vladivostok expressed his government's interest in seeing improved relations between Vietnam and China, adding that "it looks as though the moment is good." That fueled speculation on whether Moscow, as part of its effort to improve its relations with China and ASEAN, might pressure its ally Vietnam on the Kampuchean issue, which was China's precondition for friendlier Sino-Soviet relations. Such action would be compatible with the U.S.S.R.'s broader Asian objectives, but no positive moves had been made by the end of 1986.

In an extensive Cabinet reshuffle in early December, the positions of foreign minister and chairman of the party foreign relations commission, both formerly held by Prime Minister Hun Sen, went to Kong Korm and Yos San, respectively. Bou Thang was replaced as defense minister by his deputy, Koy Buntha. (THOMAS HON WING POLIN)

This article updates the *Macropædia* article Mainland SOUTHEAST ASIA: *Kampuchea.*

LAOS

A landlocked people's republic, Laos is in the northern part of the Indochinese Peninsula. Area: 236,800 sq km (91,400 sq mi). Pop. (1986 est.): 3,703,000. Cap.: Vientiane. Monetary unit: new kip, with (Oct. 1, 1986) a free rate of 35 new kip to U.S. $1 (50.57 new kip = £1 sterling). Presidents in 1986, Prince Souphanouvong and, from October 31 (interim), Phoumi Vongvichit; chairman of the Council of Ministers (prime minister), Kaysone Phomvihan.

In 1986 politics in Laos were dominated by preparations for the fourth congress of the ruling Lao People's Revolutionary Party (LPRP), its first since 1982. The country's official news agency (KPL) announced in August that there were to be nationwide lectures to teach citizens about the significance of the "conclave."

Foreign relations with Thailand continued to be strained because of disputes over three border villages. In June Bangkok accused Laotian soldiers of massacring 35 Lao refugees in a camp some 16 km (10 mi) inside Thai territory. Vientiane vigorously denied carrying out the massacre, claiming that Bangkok had "invented this extraordinary tale" to divert attention from domestic troubles. In August, however, tensions were eased by Laotian Prime Minister Kaysone Phomvihan's formal congratulations on the reappointment of the Thai prime minister.

Economic difficulties persisted; it was estimated that per capita income had fallen to $100 while the annual rate of inflation had risen to 30%. The lack of roads and other infrastructure hampered the distribution of rice and slowed the movement of exports and imports. The government introduced some capitalist measures in a desperate effort to boost production. Early in the year Vice-Pres. Khamphet Phengmuong announced reforms designed to expand economic links with non-Communist countries. The changes aimed to legitimize the profit motive for state enterprises, boost the private sector, and generally release the economy from rigid central planning. Government companies were to be allowed to trade directly and to reinvest part of their profits. Vientiane officially inaugurated its new economic strategy in August. It was stated that "under the new system managers will have greater autonomy from cadres." The government, however, continued to set quotas, pricing mechanisms, credit levels, salaries, and bonuses, and

AP/WIDE WORLD

American and Laotian soldiers sift through earth and debris where a U.S. C-130 gunship was downed in Laos during the Vietnam war. The search for clues as to the fate of 14 airmen reportedly aboard when the plane was hit uncovered some human remains.

the extent to which private interests would be allowed to develop was questionable.

On October 31 it was announced that 77-year-old Prince Souphanouvong, president of Laos since it became a republic in 1975, had resigned for reasons of health. A member of the Laotian royal family, he had led the revolutionary Pathet Lao movement during the two-decade-long civil war. (THOMAS HON WING POLIN)

This article updates the *Macropædia* article Mainland SOUTHEAST ASIA: *Laos.*

MALAYSIA

A federal constitutional monarchy of Southeast Asia and member of the Commonwealth, Malaysia consists of the former Federation of Malaya at the southern end of the Malay Peninsula (excluding Singapore) and Sabah and Sarawak on the northern part of the island of Borneo. Area: 330,434 sq km (127,581 sq mi). Pop. (1986 est.): 16,090,000. Cap.: Kuala Lumpur. Monetary unit: ringgit, with (Oct. 1, 1986) a free rate of 2.63 ringgits to U.S. $1 (3.80 ringgits = £1 sterling). Supreme head of state in 1986, with the title of *yang di-pertuan agong,* Tuanku Mahmood Iskandar ibni al-Marhum Sultan Ismail; prime minister, Datuk Seri Mahathir bin Mohamad.

The major political event in Malaysia in 1986 was the general election in August, in which the ruling National Front coalition retained power by an impressive margin. Given that the country's leadership also had to contend with several crises during the year, Prime Minister Mahathir bin Mohamad (*see* BIOGRAPHIES) had every right to be pleased by the electoral triumph. The National Front coalition, in which Mahathir's United Malays National Organization (UMNO) was the dominant party, took 148 of the 177 seats in an expanded Parliament. (For tabulated results, see *Political Parties,* above.) The results provided a new mandate for Mahathir's development-oriented policies and strengthened his position in the National Front as well as within UMNO.

AP/WIDE WORLD

Supporters carry a jubilant Prime Minister Mahathir bin Mohamad after his National Front coalition won a landslide victory in parliamentary and state assembly elections. The results provided a new mandate for Mahathir's policies.

One opposition party fared notably well. Led by political veteran Lim Kit Siang, the Chinese-based Democratic Action Party (DAP) secured 24 seats (compared with 7 in the last general election in 1982), making it the largest opposition grouping in Parliament. DAP won votes for its stance on education, culture, and job opportunities for Malaysia's Chinese. It was also helped by the government's extension of the controversial New Economic Policy (NEP), a 20-year (1970–90) economic and social restructuring program that sought to promote the interests of the Malay majority.

In addition, DAP benefited from the problems besetting the Malaysian Chinese Association (MCA), the National Front coalition's leading Chinese-based partner. MCA's new chief, business tycoon Tan Koon Swan, was indicted in January by a Singapore court for commercial crimes related to the 1985 collapse of Pan-Electric Industries, a Singapore-based conglomerate. After the election, Tan pleaded guilty to a charge of abetment of criminal breach of trust and was sentenced by a Singapore judge to two years' imprisonment and fined S$500,000. He was replaced as MCA president in September by his deputy, Ling Liong Sik. UMNO also suffered a rift at the top. Rumours that all was not well between Mahathir and his deputy party leader, Musa Hitam, were confirmed in late February when the latter resigned as deputy prime minister.

In resource-rich Sabah a simmering political crisis erupted in violence in March. Kota Kinabalu, the state capital, and several other cities were hit by a spate of bombings and arson, believed to have been inspired by opponents of Malaysia's only Christian state chief minister, Joseph Pairin Kitingan. In local elections in May, however, Pairin's Partai Bersatu Sabah won a two-thirds majority in the state assembly. Malaysia's stringent antidrug law came to world attention in July when two Australians (one British-born) were hanged. They were the first non-Asians executed under the law, which mandated capital punishment for trafficking in more than 15 g (½ oz) of heroin.

After two decades of high economic growth, Malaysia found itself in the trough of recession in 1986. Gross domestic product in 1985 contracted by 1%, and growth of 1% in 1986 was forecast. The biggest problem remained depressed global prices for commodities. Most of manufacturing industry also lacked buoyancy, though there were signs of recovery in the key electronics sector. In September the government approved a number of measures designed to attract more foreign and domestic investment. The NEP, rigid rules on foreign equity, and lengthy bureaucratic procedures had deterred some potential investors. The fifth Malaysia Plan (1986–90) envisaged annual average economic growth of 5%, with much of the stimulus coming from a 7% annual growth in private investment. The new incentives involved a weakening of the NEP, but Mahathir stated that NEP objectives and the redistribution of wealth would not be achieved without economic growth.

(THOMAS HON WING POLIN)

This article updates the *Macropædia* article Mainland SOUTHEAST ASIA: *Malaysia.*

PHILIPPINES

Situated in the western Pacific Ocean off the southeast coast of Asia, the republic of the Philippines consists of an archipelago of about 7,100 islands. Area: 300,000 sq km (115,800 sq mi). Pop (1986 est.): 55,768,000. Cap.: Manila. Monetary unit: Philippine peso, with (Oct. 1, 1986) a free rate of 20.46 pesos to U.S. $1 (29.56 pesos = £1 sterling). Presidents in 1986, Ferdinand E. Marcos and, from February 25, Corazon Aquino; prime ministers, Cesar Virata and, from February 25 to March 25, Salvador Laurel.

On the day of her inauguration, Pres. Corazon Aquino shakes hands with Fidel Ramos, whom she appointed to head the armed forces of the Philippines, as a smiling Salvador Laurel, her vice-president, looks on.
CHARLES STEINER—JB PICTURES

Corazon C. Aquino (*see* BIOGRAPHIES) became president of the Philippines on Feb. 25, 1986, when Ferdinand E. Marcos left the country amid a popular outcry against the official results of an election contest between the two. Salvador H. Laurel became vice-president, prime minister, and foreign minister.

Marcos, the president since 1966, had sought to renew his popular mandate by calling a snap election for February 7. "Cory" Aquino rallied the political opposition to Marcos. She blamed him for the murder in 1983 of her husband, Benigno S. Aquino, Jr., who had been Marcos's leading opponent. After an election campaign marked by violence, the Marcos-controlled National Assembly certified him as the winner, but many Filipino and foreign observers felt that fraud had robbed Aquino of victory.

On February 22 Defense Minister Juan Ponce Enrile (*see* BIOGRAPHIES) and Lieut. Gen. Fidel V. Ramos, the deputy chief of staff, occupied the Defense Ministry. They said they no longer accepted Marcos's authority because of election fraud and years of misconduct, and they called on Marcos to resign and turn over power to Aquino. Crowds of civilians rallied to their support, blocking moves by Gen. Fabian C. Ver, the chief of staff and a relative of Marcos, to launch an attack on them. The U.S. government warned against violence and called for "a peaceful transition," indicating that support had been withdrawn from Marcos.

Aquino staged a makeshift inauguration as president at 10:45 AM on February 25. At noon Marcos held his own inauguration for another term. But, under intensifying pressure from Washington, Marcos accepted a U.S. offer of asylum and left his palace at 9:05 PM with his family, Ver, and other close associates. Aquino was left in control.

She proclaimed a new provisional constitution on March 25, thus abolishing the National Assembly and the office of prime minister, and assumed broad powers to govern by decree. On May 25 she appointed a commission to write a new constitution. Its 48 members began work June 2. A final draft was approved on October 12, and the new document was to be submitted to the voters in January 1987.

In the spring supporters of Marcos began staging rallies, some of which turned violent, every Sunday in downtown Manila. At a rally on July 6 speakers urged Arturo M. Tolentino, who had run for vice-president with Marcos, to take an oath as acting president. He did, but the coup attempt quickly collapsed. A more serious threat emerged in late November, when antigovernment moves by troops loyal to Enrile, who had remained as defense minister, were blocked by Ramos, who had succeeded Ver as chief of staff. Aquino called for the resignation of her entire Cabinet and immediately replaced Enrile with his deputy, Rafaeo Ileto. The incidents emphasized the importance of military support for the Aquino regime.

Marcos denounced the Aquino government from his exile in Hawaii despite U.S. government rebukes. He also denied that he had looted the Philippines of billions of dollars. However, documents showed that his family had huge foreign holdings, and the Swiss government blocked his accounts in that country. Aquino sought to recover this money to relieve the Philippines' foreign debt of about $27 billion. The economy remained depressed.

On September 12 the Supreme Court ordered a retrial of 26 persons charged with Benigno Aquino's murder. The court said Marcos had arranged a sham trial that acquitted Ver and others on Dec. 2, 1985.

Preliminary negotiations for peace talks with the Communist New People's Army began on August 5, and a 60-day truce was agreed to on November 27. Some soldiers distrusted the Communists, and prior to the truce Ramos reported that more soldiers were being killed than before Aquino became president. On a well-received nine-day visit to the U.S. in September, Aquino asked for "understanding" of her handling of the Communist insurgency. Aquino made a truce agreement on September 5 with the leader of Muslim separatists in the southern Philippines. On September 13 Aquino arranged a truce with another rebel army in the north led by a renegade priest.

(HENRY S. BRADSHER)

See also Feature Article: *The Philippines: Is Democracy Restored?*

SINGAPORE

Singapore, a republic of Southeast Asia and member of the Commonwealth, occupies a group of islands, the largest of which is Singapore, at the southern extremity of the Malay Peninsula. Area: 618 sq km (239 sq mi). Pop. (1986 est.): 2,587,000. Monetary unit: Singapore dollar, with (Oct. 1, 1986) a free rate of S$2.17 to U.S. $1 (S$3.14 = £1 sterling). President in 1986, Wee Kim Wee; prime minister, Lee Kuan Yew.

In 1986 attention in Singapore focused on a series of new laws designed to give the government greater control over forces it deemed potentially detrimental to the republic's well-being. In August a bill was passed through Parliament—where the ruling People's Action Party (PAP) had a 77–2 majority— empowering the authorities to limit the sales of foreign publications judged to be "engaging in the domestic politics of Singapore." The move was condemned by the opposition and the local Law Society, while the usually pro-government *Straits Times* newspaper alleged it was an infringement of Singaporeans' right to information.

The penalties for MPs who abused parliamentary privileges were increased after an opposition member, J. B. Jeyaretnam, made allegations damaging to the attorney general and chief justice. Planned legislation would prevent any lawyer who had been debarred, suspended from practice, or convicted of a criminal offense from holding office in the Law Society's governing council. It was widely believed that the legislation was directed at the new president of the Law Society, Francis Seow, a former solicitor general who had been suspended for a year. Seow had favoured active public participation in public affairs. Meanwhile, Jeyaretnam was expelled from Parliament and sentenced to a month in prison for fraud and making false statements about his handling of party funds.

The long-ruling PAP attempted to enhance its image in April with the announcement of plans to form a youth wing. Young voters were believed to be responsible for the 13% swing against the PAP in the 1984 general elections.

The economy began to recover from the recession that had produced an unprecedented contraction of gross domestic product in 1985, and up to 2% growth over the year was predicted. (See *Southeast Asian Affairs:* Sidebar, above.) The improvement was led by the electronics industry and the transport and communications sector. The budget for fiscal 1986, presented in March, raised expenditure by 37% to S$22 billion. Reductions in taxation, including a 50% property-tax rebate, were aimed at improving the business climate. Estimates of investment were increased from S$1.1 billion to S$1.4 billion. Regulations governing the stock exchange were tightened following the 1985 collapse of the Pan-Electric Industries conglomerate.

(THOMAS HON WING POLIN)

This article updates the *Macropædia* article Mainland SOUTHEAST ASIA: *Singapore.*

THAILAND

Thailand is a constitutional monarchy in Southeast Asia, on the Andaman Sea and the Gulf of Thailand. Area: 513,115 sq km (198,115 sq mi). Pop. (1986 est.): 52,654,000. Cap.: Bangkok. Monetary unit: baht, with (Oct. 1, 1986) a free rate of 26.08 baht to U.S. $1 (37.69 baht = £1 sterling). King, Bhumibol Adulyadej; prime minister in 1986, Gen. Prem Tinsulanond.

Political activity in Thailand in 1986 focused on the snap general election held on July 27. After several members of Parliament crossed the floor to help defeat a government bill, Prime Minister Prem Tinsulanond dissolved Parliament and set the date of the election nine months before it was due. A record 61% of the electorate voted, but no one party was able to command a majority of seats, and yet another coalition had to be formed. Prem was chosen once again to head the government—his third successive term since he first came to power in 1980. His selection provoked opposition on the grounds that the position should go to an elected politician, but in general he was regarded as the leader most acceptable to the various political groupings, the military, and the monarchy.

A fire set by rioting protesters on June 23 destroys a $44 million tantalum-processing plant in Phuket. A state of emergency was declared to control some 50,000 angry residents of the resort town, who feared that factory pollution would discourage tourism.
AP/WIDE WORLD

The coalition was dominated by the Democratic Party (DP), which had won 100 seats, nearly double its total in the 1983 election. The DP was joined in the coalition by the Chart Thai (63), the Social Action Party (51), and the newly formed Rassadorn Party (18), each of which was proportionately represented in the 44-member Cabinet. The most notable change in the Cabinet was the handing over of the defense portfolio, previously held by Prem himself, to Panieng Kantarat. The appointment reflected increased sensitivity in the military arena. Just before the election Prem took the unprecedented step of dismissing the powerful army commander in chief, Gen. Arthit Kamlang-ek, and replaced him with Chaovalit Yongchaiyuth. Arthit had made it clear that he wanted to become prime minister and had indulged in considerable political and military maneuvering to that end. Prem had refused to grant Arthit a second extension in his top army job in March, and relations between the two had deteriorated thereafter.

The draft sixth five-year (1987–91) economic and social development plan was approved. It emphasized export development and job creation, and an economic growth target of 5% a year was set for the period. The budget for fiscal 1987 (begun Oct. 1, 1986) was intended to provide mild economic stimulus; it anticipated a deficit equal to 3.5% of gross domestic product (GDP), to be met by borrowing. The economy performed well in 1986, with GDP growth estimated at 4.5–5.5%. The trade position improved because of the reduced cost of oil imports, and in the first half of the year the trade deficit was 3.6 billion baht, compared with 36.9 billion baht in the previous six-month period. Exports in 1986 were running 15% above year-earlier levels. Tourism continued to be the major foreign exchange earner. The 2.4 million visitors in 1985 contributed 34 billion baht, and an increase of 6–

8% was expected in 1986. The annual inflation rate was not expected to exceed 2% in 1986. Investment slowed in both 1985 and 1986, inhibited by high interest rates, and business confidence was not particularly high. Thailand's foreign debt reached $14.9 billion at the end of 1985.

Two dramatic demonstrations during the year were rooted in economic issues. In January some 2,000 farmers from the central plains marched to Bangkok to protest that middlemen and rice mills were not paying them the prices mandated under the government's rice subsidy program. It took repeated government assurances that increased efforts would be made to enforce the prices before the farmers ended their sleep-in demonstration outside Government House. In June trouble erupted in the tourist-resort island of Phuket in the south. Worried about adverse environmental effects from a tantalum-processing plant, local inhabitants rioted, burned down the $44 million factory, and attacked a tourist hotel. Some 35 people were arrested, and a temporary state of emergency was imposed.

(THOMAS HON WING POLIN)

This article updates the *Macropædia* article Mainland SOUTHEAST ASIA: *Thailand.*

VIETNAM

The socialist republic of Vietnam occupies the eastern part of the Indochinese Peninsula in Southeast Asia and is bounded on the south and east by the South China Sea. Area: 331,653 sq km (128,052 sq mi). Pop. (1986 est.): 61,218,000. Cap.: Hanoi. Monetary unit: new dong, with (Oct. 1, 1986) a free rate of 11.76 new dong to U.S. $1 (17 new dong = £1 sterling). General secretaries of the Communist Party in 1986, Le Duan to July 10, Truong Chinh from July 14, and, from December 18, Nguyen Van Linh; chairman of the State Council (president), Truong Chinh; chairman of the Council of Ministers (premier), Pham Van Dong.

For Vietnam 1986 proved to be a watershed year. The death in July of Le Duan (*see* OBITUARIES), the veteran Communist Party general secretary, marked the end of an era. The country's top leader had long suffered from kidney problems, but it was rumoured that he was near death in February when he stayed on in the U.S.S.R. after a congress of the Communist Party of the Soviet Union. Eventually, Le Duan returned home and made some public appearances, but he was absent from important functions in May and June. On July 10 Radio Hanoi announced that "after a period of serious illness" the man who had been Vietnam's "first among equals" since the death of Ho Chi Minh in 1969 had died that morning. Since poor health had limited Le Duan's effectiveness for several years, his passing made little impact on national policy.

On July 14 the Politburo appointed its second-in-command, 79-year-old Truong Chinh, as the new general secretary. The choice surprised many observers, who had expected a younger and more vigorous successor. It was suggested that Chinh would be an interim party chief, who would provide continuity until the party could pick another candidate when it convened its sixth congress in December.

During the party congress, Truong Chinh, Prime Minister Pham Van Dong, and Le Duc Tho, who had negotiated the U.S. withdrawal from Vietnam, all resigned their party posts in a dramatic changing of the guard. On December 18 the congress chose Nguyen Van Linh, 73, former party secretary in Ho Chi Minh City, as the new general secretary. The session of the National Assembly that convened shortly afterward was expected to name replacements for Truong Chinh and Dong as president and prime minister, but it adjourned on December 29 without taking action.

During his short term as party secretary, Truong Chinh quickly involved himself in the burning issues of the day. In a major speech to cadres in October, Truong Chinh declared with unexpected candour: "We have tried to do too much too quickly. After making mistakes, we lacked the courage and determination to correct them." He listed the defects, from mismanagement and corruption to overcentralization and waste of resources.

The country's poor economic performance, in fact, had been the major focus of political attention during the year. In February the prominent economist Tran Phuong lost his job as vice-premier because of his key role in devaluing the currency the previous September. In June a major government reshuffle resulted in the dismissal of leading members of the economic team, including senior Vice-Premier To Huu, who was also a member of the Politburo. He was replaced as vice-premier by newly favoured Vo Chi Cong, also a Politburo member. Finance Minister Chu Tam Thuc lost his job to former minister of food industry Vu Tuan. The changes came in the wake of a party plenum, during which top party and government organizations had "scrupulously conducted criticism and self-criticism."

Given the growing consensus on the extent of the eco-

BARBARA CROSETTE/THE NEW YORK TIMES

A roadside market in the rural village of Di Su, featuring a variety of fresh produce and meat, gives residents an opportunity to earn private income. Greater freedom for farmers in the choice of their crops and in distribution of their goods was part of Vietnam's efforts toward economic reform.

nomic malaise, advocates of wide-ranging reform gained influence. Several radical reformist measures approved by the leadership and subsequently implemented were aimed at improving efficiency and productivity. Managers of enterprises were given greater independence from party control, and private industrial enterprises were permitted to operate with up to ten employees. State-employed workers were paid in cash instead of subsidized essential goods, and provincial governments were granted the authority to import and export. The establishment of export-processing zones was proposed, as was the promulgation of a new investment code that would permit 100% foreign ownership of enterprises and protect them from nationalization. Another measure sought to reduce the size of the burgeoning bureaucracy by up to one-quarter. Many of these measures had been first tried in the southern part of the country, where capitalist traditions remained embedded. There were fierce debates among Hanoi's leaders before the reforms were accepted. Departing from its earlier criticism of Ho Chi Minh City, the official press began to praise the former capital of South Vietnam for its "dynamism and innovativeness" in business activities.

A positive aspect of the economy was grain production, which in 1985 totaled a record 18.2 million metric tons, compared with an average of 17 million over the previous five years. Other indicators were less encouraging, however. According to the International Monetary Fund, as of 1984 Vietnam's external debt amounted to $6.7 billion, a quarter of which was owed to Western creditors; its trade deficit stood at $1 billion, and its foreign exchange reserves were estimated at below $10 billion in 1986. The value of the dong continued to depreciate. The black-market rate was only 400 to the U.S. dollar in September 1986, compared with the official rate of 11.8 dong. Inflation was running at an annual rate of 700%, and many basic goods remained in short supply. Even the gains in food production—estimated at 2% a year—were offset by a population increase of nearly 2.5%. Lack of confidence in the leadership was cited as an important factor in the economic decline. A Hanoi-based diplomat estimated that most people in the north were poorer than they were at the height of the Vietnam war (ended 1975).

Would-be refugees from Vietnam encountered a new obstacle. Since 1979 more than 100,000 Vietnamese had left the country for resettlement abroad through the Orderly Departure Program organized by the UN High Commissioner for Refugees and the Hanoi government. On Jan. 1, 1986, however, Vietnam refused to allow any new applicants to be interviewed. It complained that more than 60,000 people who had been approved for resettlement remained in the country because of tardiness on the part of receiving countries, especially the U.S. and Canada. U.S. officials responded that they were awaiting confirmation of the eligibility of some of the would-be migrants. In August the U.S. and Vietnam conducted talks to resolve the technical problems.

Vietnam moved in another area to improve its long-strained relations with Washington. In January U.S. officials led a seven-member team on the highest-level visit by Americans to Hanoi since the end of the war. The visitors accepted Vietnam's pledge, made in August 1985, that it would resolve within two years the question of the 1,797 U.S. servicemen still listed as missing in that conflict. In April Hanoi handed over the recovered remains of 21 such servicemen, bringing the total to more than 140 since 1982.

(THOMAS HON WING POLIN)

This article updates the *Macropædia* article Mainland SOUTHEAST ASIA: *Vietnam.*

Western Europe

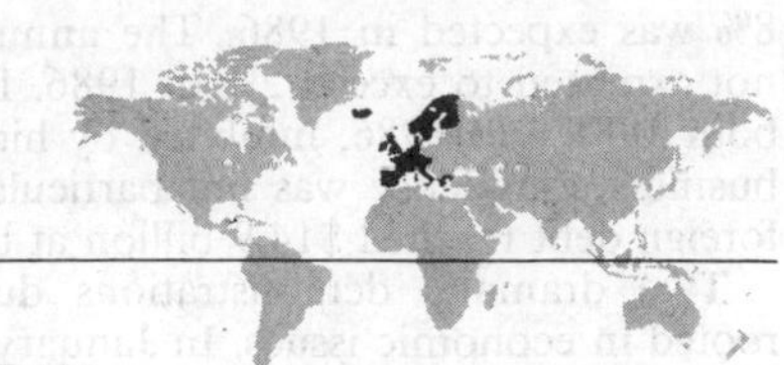

WESTERN EUROPEAN AFFAIRS

At the start of 1986 eight years of negotiations came to fruition with the enlargement of the European Communities (EC; the European Economic Community [EEC], the European Coal and Steel Community [ECSC], and Euratom) from 10 to 12 members. The accession of Portugal and Spain produced a common market of over 300 million people—by far the largest trading entity in the Western world as well as a major international political force. The new members would have a significant effect on the internal operations of the EC. The addition of the Iberian Peninsula states meant the appointment during January of three more members of the EC Commission, which had day-to-day responsibility for running the EC. Furthermore, late in 1985 there was an influx of Portuguese and Spanish officials and experts recruited to the EC's institutions and its international civil services. By March the political implications of the new members' accession were evident. Their effect on the composition of the elected European Parliament was to tilt the internal political balance to the left; the addition of 42 Socialist members from Portugal and Spain made the Socialists by far the largest single group, as well as giving the left parties a slight majority over the centre and right.

Celebrations to mark the enlargement of the EC were overshadowed by a general awareness of the serious internal and external problems that had to be faced. These had been the focus of attention in a two-day meeting of EC heads of state and government held in Luxembourg at the end of 1985. It was widely recognized that enlargement might exacerbate the already serious obstacles impeding effective decision making in the EC. The Commission had already warned the member governments that the frequency with which they invoked their right to veto majority decisions in the Council of Ministers had delayed enactment of much-needed legislation.

In spite of much public cynicism, some progress toward getting agreement on a reform of the decision-making procedures was made at the Luxembourg summit meeting in February 1986. The EC Council agreed to limit the use of the national veto on a range of issues affecting the development of the EC internal market. In addition, new areas, including monetary cooperation, technology, and environmental issues, were to be brought under the Treaty of Rome, which provided the legal framework of the EC. The summit also agreed on some modest steps to increase the role of the European Parliament in EC decision making and proposed a new treaty covering European political cooperation. This was highly significant, given the emphasis in recent years on efforts to coordinate a distinctive common European foreign policy—a development that had aroused some apprehension among U.S. policymakers.

These measures were to be formally adopted by the 12 member states in a so-called Single Act, but at least four countries—Denmark, Greece, Ireland, and Italy—had serious reservations. The Danish government, mindful of anti-EC sentiment among its electorate, was particularly worried about giving legal treaty status to EC foreign policy. Greece had similar reservations and was concerned that more emphasis on a European foreign policy might create conflicts, given its opposition to granting the EC defense responsibilities. Ireland took the view that the Single Act might compromise its neutral position as a nonmember of NATO. By contrast, Italy was disappointed over the lack of positive moves toward full political union. The Single Act was signed by all member governments on March 1, after a referendum among Danish voters had given strong endorsement to the Danish government's support for the measure. European parliamentarians in Strasbourg expressed dissatisfaction with the limited powers they had been given to shape Community laws, however, and it was clear that this would be a contentious issue in the future.

The accession of Portugal and Spain was seen as completing the enlargement of the Community for several years. The Turkish government, however, indicated to the Council of Ministers in February that it would pursue its right, enshrined in its present association agreement with the EC, to request full membership. This aroused bitter opposition from Greece on the grounds that Turkey did not have full parliamentary democracy, was violating human rights, and had troops in Cyprus. Also in February, the EC and the governments of the European Free Trade Association agreed to revise their comprehensive trade and commercial agreements to take into account the two new members.

Two other major internal issues that dominated developments during the year were reform of the EC common agricultural policy (CAP) and management of the crisis-ridden EC budget. These problems had beset the EC for more than a decade, and there were renewed fears in 1986 that, without fundamental changes, the CAP, with its system of farm production subsidies, could bankrupt the organization. After a marathon negotiating session in April, EC farm ministers agreed on a package of tough measures proposed by the Commission. This involved a continuing price freeze and price cuts on a wide range of farm products, including milk, meat, and certain cereals. Lower production quotas were agreed on in order to "drain" three million metric tons from the EC milk surplus. The measures evoked anger among the farming population, and this anger increased during the year as the cuts began to reduce farm incomes. Nevertheless, the CAP still accounted for more than 70% of the EC budget. From the middle of the year it became increasingly clear that the

European Communities
- Original member 1967
- Joined in 1973
- Joined in 1981
- Joined in 1986

European Free Trade Association
- Original member 1960
- Joined in 1970
- Joined in 1986

The European Coal and Steel Community (formed 1952), the European Economic Community, and the European Atomic Energy Community (both formed 1957) were merged to form a single organizational entity, the European Communities (EC), in 1967. Member nations of the EC became the Twelve in 1986, and the European Free Trade Association (EFTA) member total remained at six despite a shift. Spain joined the EC, as did Portugal, formerly an EFTA member. Finland's status with EFTA was formally changed from associate (effective 1961) to full member. Liechtenstein participates in special EFTA status via Switzerland although it is not a full member. The United Kingdom and Denmark left EFTA prior to joining the EC with Ireland in 1973. Greenland (not pictured) withdrew from the EC in 1985.

French Pres. François Mitterrand and British Prime Minister Margaret Thatcher exchange copies of the treaty for the Channel Tunnel project, signed on February 12 in Canterbury. The agreement was to be submitted to both parliaments for final approval.

GAYWOOD/SPOONER—GAMMA/LIAISON

budget was heading for another massive deficit and that there might have to be severe cuts in nonfarm spending. The main cause of the new crisis was the precipitate drop in the international value of the U.S. dollar, which, together with a slump in world agricultural prices, escalated the costs of EC food export subsidies. In December EC farm ministers meeting in Brussels agreed on a package of reforms, including a reduction in milk production and cuts in the guaranteed price paid for beef.

The CAP was also a cause of serious and continuing international trade conflict with the U.S. during 1986. The U.S. administration accused the EC of using illegal subsidies and protecting its farmers, and it complained of discrimination because it was not being given access to the Portuguese and Spanish markets after their entry into the EC. For its part, the EC had a long list of trade complaints against the U.S., including attempts to block imports of European special steels and synthetic textiles. Some of these disputes were temporarily defused as a result of the preparatory meeting in Uruguay for a new round of trade liberalization under the General Agreement on Tariffs and Trade. At the end of December the U.S. announced that it would increase tariffs on selected food and drink imports from the EC area by as much as 200% at the end of January 1987 if, in the meantime, the EC did not agree to compensate the U.S. for the loss of its markets for grain exports.

Disagreement on trade was only one of the contentious issues dividing the U.S. and its European allies during 1986. There was much European criticism of U.S. economic policies, particularly the size of the U.S. federal budget deficit and the use of high interest rates to finance it. The Western economic summit meeting held in Tokyo in May did little to reduce disagreement over what strategy the West should follow to tackle world currency instability and continuing high unemployment. There were also tensions over a variety of foreign and defense policy issues. Despite considerable U.S. pressure, when EC foreign ministers met in Brussels in January, they refused to adopt economic sanctions against Libya, which the U.S. held responsible for terrorist atrocities at European airports. After an allegedly Libyan-backed attack on a West Berlin nightclub in April, however, the EC did impose limited diplomatic sanctions. There was widespread criticism in Western Europe of U.S. Pres. Ronald Reagan's decision to approve a bombing raid by U.S. aircraft against Libya in April. In September, during the British presidency of the EC, the 12 EC members agreed to step up their common response to terrorism and to improve coordination among their police and security services. A further source of irritation was the revelation, late in the year, that the U.S. had secretly sent arms to Iran while publicly urging its allies not to deal with nations that supported terrorism, Iran among them.

Another cause of transatlantic tension during the year was the U.S. Strategic Defense Initiative (SDI; "Star Wars"). Virtually all Western European NATO governments were skeptical of it, and there was some dismay when the Reykjavík, Iceland, "presummit" meeting between President Reagan and Soviet leader Mikhail Gorbachev in October appeared to break down on the verge of a major agreement on nuclear weapons reductions because of U.S. refusal to limit testing of SDI. Although the European governments and the U.S. publicly closed ranks within NATO, it became clear that the Europeans, unlike the U.S., accepted the Soviet view that the Anti-Ballistic Missile Treaty ruled out the testing of SDI weapon systems in space. On the other hand, the British and West German governments were concerned that the abolition of U.S. medium-range missiles such as cruise and Pershing might make Western Europe more vulnerable to the superior conventional armed strength of the Warsaw Pact.

The accident at the Soviet nuclear power station at Chernobyl in April revived widespread opposition in some Western European countries to reliance on nuclear energy. The high levels of nuclear fallout and contamination of foodstuffs led the EC to impose a temporary ban on fruit and vegetable imports from all countries belonging to the Council for Mutual Economic Assistance (Comecon), with the exception of East Germany, which had a virtual customs union with West Germany. By the end of the summer, however, radioactivity readings had fallen to the point where EC restrictions on Eastern European food imports lapsed, although health checks continued in some countries. The Commission called for improved safety standards and more rigorous checks on EC power stations, and it was possible that both the U.K. and West Germany would decommission many of the nuclear power stations already built and rely increasingly on nonnuclear energy sources. On the other hand, the French government told its EC partners that it intended to go ahead with an accelerated program of nuclear power station construction.

Comecon responded positively to EC suggestions for closer trading links. Trade relations had improved in recent years, despite the debt-repayment problems experienced by Poland and some other Eastern European states.

The EC repeatedly condemned the policies of the South African government during 1986 and called for the release of Nelson Mandela, imprisoned leader of the African National Congress. An EC delegation, led by British Foreign Secretary Sir Geoffrey Howe, visited South Africa in July to try to persuade the government to moderate its apartheid policy, but it failed. In September EC members imposed modest trade sanctions and a ban on new investment. The insistence of the British and West German governments on restricting sanctions evoked fierce criticism inside and outside the Community.

The hopes of other EC governments that the U.K. would

join the exchange-rate mechanism at the heart of the European Monetary System (EMS) were frustrated, although in November there were indications that the decision might be reversed in the near future. In April a realignment of currency exchange rates within the EMS was necessary, but generally the system was thought to have demonstrated strong resilience in the face of international currency upheavals that followed the slump in the U.S. dollar.

Earlier in 1986 EC members welcomed the Anglo-French decision to construct a fixed-link Channel Tunnel to be financed through private investment. (*See* ENGINEERING PROJECTS: *Sidebar.*) In the regions close to the construction sites, however, there was considerable opposition on environmental and economic grounds. (JOHN PALMER)

See also Economic Affairs; Military Affairs.

ANDORRA

A landlocked independent coprincipality of Europe, Andorra is in the Pyrenees Mountains between Spain and France. Area: 464 sq km (179 sq mi). Pop. (1986 est.): 46,000. Cap.: Andorra la Vella. Monetary units: French franc and Spanish peseta. Coprinces: the president of the French Republic and the bishop of Urgel, Spain, represented by their *veguers* (provosts) and *batlles* (prosecutors). An elected Council General of 28 members elects the first syndic, in 1986 Francesc Cerqueda Pascuet; chief executive, Josep Pintat-Solans.

Following elections to renew Andorra's Council General in December 1985, Josep Pintat-Solans, Andorra's chief executive since May 1984, was reelected to that office in January 1986. Pintat-Solans received the votes of 27 of the 28 members of the Council General.

On September 26 French Pres. François Mitterrand paid an official visit to the coprincipality in his capacity as one of the two coprinces responsible for Andorra's foreign relations. At the banquet given in his honour, Mitterrand stated that Andorra was evidently prosperous; at the same time, he drew attention to the particular problems that the coprincipality faced. For example, only one-quarter of the people living in Andorra were citizens; the rest were foreign residents, mainly Spanish and French.

Now surrounded by European Communities (EC) territory, Andorra was seeking to negotiate some form of special status. Mitterrand suggested that, once Andorra had concluded separate negotiations with Spain and France, a tripartite delegation representing the two coprinces and the Andorran government should present the Andorran case to the EC Council of Ministers. (K. M. SMOGORZEWSKI)

This article updates the *Micropædia* article ANDORRA.

AUSTRIA

The republic of Austria is a landlocked state of central Europe. Area: 83,855 sq km (32,376 sq mi). Pop. (1986 est.): 7,551,600. Cap.: Vienna. Monetary unit: Austrian Schilling, with (Oct. 1, 1986) a free rate of 14.27 Schillings to U.S. $1 (20.62 Schillings = £1 sterling). Presidents in 1986, Rudolf Kirchschläger and, from July 8, Kurt Waldheim; chancellors, Fred Sinowatz and, from June 16, Franz Vranitzky.

The major event of 1986 in Austria was the election of Kurt Waldheim (*see* BIOGRAPHIES), former UN secretary-general, as the first non-Socialist federal president of the second republic; he stood as an independent with the support of the Austrian People's Party (ÖVP). His victory caused the resignation of federal Chancellor Fred Sinowatz of the Socialist Party of Austria (SPÖ) and several other ministers. The final ballot took place on June 8 between Waldheim and SPÖ candidate Kurt Steyrer. During the election campaign the World Jewish Congress attacked Waldheim because of his alleged membership in Nazi organizations and his activities in the Balkans as an officer in the German armed forces during World War II. Austria was criticized for alleged Fascist and anti-Semitic tendencies.

On June 16 the new federal chancellor, Franz Vranitzky, was sworn in, along with the new ministers for external affairs, Peter Jankowitsch; for finance, Ferdinand Lacina; for agriculture and forestry, Erich Schmidt; and for transport and nationalized industries, Rudolf Streicher. Sinowatz remained president of the SPÖ. The Socialist-led coalition government that emerged was fragile, however, and after the election of an extreme right-wing nationalist to the leadership of the Freedom Party (FPÖ), the junior party in the coalition, new general elections were called for November 23.

In the elections both major parties, the SPÖ and the ÖVP, lost support while the FPÖ and the Greens gained. The latter won representation in Parliament for the first time. (For tabulated results, see *Political Parties,* above.) With its total of 80 seats, the SPÖ remained the largest single party, and after resigning as chancellor on November 25 Vranitzky was immediately charged with the task of forming the new government.

Austria experienced severe contamination by radioactive fallout following the Chernobyl nuclear reactor disaster in the U.S.S.R., and thousands of metric tons of food had to be destroyed. The incident sensitized the population to the dangers of nuclear power, and fears about the West German reprocessing plant in Wackersdorf, Bavaria, led to demonstrations. Austria sought to negotiate treaties with all neighbouring countries having nuclear power stations to ensure the highest possible safety levels. The government ordered the dismantling of Zwentendorf, its only nuclear plant. Despite the government's conservation program, harmful emissions, principally from automobiles, continued to destroy the forests. Further measures being considered included an "environment tax," the compulsory introduction of catalytic converters on automobiles, and a lowering of the speed limit.

STEVENS—SIPA/SPECIAL FEATURES

A campaign billboard promoting Kurt Waldheim in the Austrian presidential elections is marked with a small but strategic swastika. During the campaign the former UN secretary-general was denounced for alleged past membership in Nazi organizations.

Despite specific concerns about the rise in unemployment, a high budget deficit, and structural defects in industry, the economy's performance in 1986 was good. The Organization for Economic Cooperation and Development forecast that real economic growth in 1986 would be 3%, unemployment 5%, and the rate of inflation 1.5%. The financial crisis that hit the Voest-Alpine group of state companies at the end of 1985 became an ongoing saga. Revelations about unsuccessful oil speculations and losses of billions of dollars led to the resignation of the entire board of directors. A rehabilitation plan drawn up in September involved huge job losses and heavy investment but was expected to bring Voest into profit in 1990.

The German-speaking majority in southern Tirol, part of Italy since the end of World War I, asked the Austrian government for help in April because Rome had still not issued any enforcement clauses for the autonomy statute of 1972. Austria subsequently lodged numerous diplomatic protests. In July the federal state of Niederösterreich (Lower Austria), previously governed from Vienna, was given its own capital, Sankt Pölten. (ELFRIEDE DIRNBACHER)

BELGIUM

A constitutional monarchy, the Benelux country of Belgium is situated on the North Sea coast of northwestern Europe. Area: 30,519 sq km (11,783 sq mi). Pop. (1986 est.): 9,880,000. Cap.: Brussels. Monetary unit: Belgian franc, with (Oct. 1, 1986) a commercial rate of BF 42.06 to U.S. $1 (BF 60.78 = £1 sterling) and a financial rate of BF 42.51 to U.S. $1 (BF 61.43 = £1 sterling). King, Baudouin I; prime minister in 1986, Wilfried Martens.

During 1986 the government of Prime Minister Wilfried Martens, reelected in October 1985, managed for the most part to avoid becoming embroiled in a new dispute between Belgium's Dutch- and French-language communities, concentrating instead on reducing the huge budget deficit and the public debt. Tension increased, however, when on September 30 the Council of State invalidated the appointment of José Happart as mayor of the small township of Voeren (Fourons), officially situated in Dutch-speaking Flanders, because of his refusal to speak Dutch. Minister of the Interior Charles-Ferdinand Nothomb immediately lodged an appeal against the decision, but Happart was nevertheless removed from office. Martens's offer to resign over the issue was rejected by King Baudouin. On October 18 Nothomb resigned over the issue and was replaced as interior minister by Joseph Michel.

Armed with special powers granted to it by Parliament, the government elaborated its austerity plan, aimed at reducing government expenditure in order to limit the budget deficit to 7% of gross national product by the end of 1987, as against 11.5% in 1986. Nearly BF 200 billion was pruned by imposing strict controls on all departments, but no new taxes were levied at the request of the Liberals, partners with the Social Christians in the coalition government. The education sector, which received BF 21.5 billion less than anticipated, bore the brunt of the cutbacks. Several thousand teachers were laid off, and plans for the construction of new school buildings were curtailed.

The government intervened to keep the Limburg coal mines, which in 1986 registered losses of nearly BF 13 billion, in operation. A new manager was appointed to implement a plan to restructure the mines. The steel industry also remained trouble-ridden. Despite drastic measures, the state-run Cockerill Sambre steel mills ran up losses of over BF 4.7 billion in 1985. Although several large firms reduced their staffs, and the French tire manufacturer, Michelin, closed its plant at Zuun, Brussels, with the loss of more than 1,000 jobs, a slight drop in unemployment was registered overall. Under pressure from the government, representatives of workers and employers finally reached agreement on a social pact for the first time in a decade. Its provisions dealt with employment, increased employee participation in decision making, the competitiveness of Belgian firms, and the purchasing power of wages.

The U.S. decision to manufacture new chemical weapons led to a lengthy debate both inside and outside Parliament. Several Social Christian politicians firmly opposed the storage of such weapons on Belgian territory, except in the case of serious international conflict or war. Even this proposal was unacceptable to the peace movements. Although long opposed to the installation of U.S. cruise missiles, which had arrived at the Florennes Air Force Base in 1985, Flemish Socialist chairman Karel van Miert no longer cited their withdrawal as a prerequisite for his party's participation in a future government.

With the arrest in late 1985 and early 1986 of several suspected members of the Cellules Communistes Combattantes, the urban guerrilla group that had claimed responsibility for more than two dozen bombings in the preceding year, terrorist activity ceased until September 30, when the headquarters of the Grand Lodge of Belgium was badly damaged. No group claimed responsibility for the new attack. Meanwhile, the government increased its powers to combat terrorism.

The projected extension to Belgium of the French Train à Grande Vitesse raised a storm of protest from environmentalists and the population in areas that would be most directly affected. (JAN R. ENGELS)

This article updates the *Macropædia* article The Low Countries: *Belgium*.

DENMARK

A constitutional monarchy of north central Europe, Denmark lies between the North and Baltic seas. Area: 43,080 sq km (16,633 sq mi), excluding the Faeroe Islands and Greenland. Pop. (1986 est.): 5,112,000. Cap.: Copenhagen. Monetary unit: krone, with (Oct. 1, 1986) a free rate of 7.66 kroner to U.S. $1 (11.06 kroner = £1 sterling). Queen, Margrethe II; prime minister in 1986, Poul Schlüter.

In 1986 Denmark took positive action to reduce its growing current account deficit, which had surged in 1984 and 1985. Three austerity packages were introduced by the government and passed in January, April, and October, respectively. The result was a record high level of taxation, both direct and indirect. However, the measures were slow in reducing the country's main economic problem, the huge balance of payments deficit. The latest official estimate was for a deficit in 1986 of more than 32 billion kroner, 4 billion kroner more than in the previous year, declining to 22 billion kroner in 1987.

In his opening statement to the Folketing (parliament) in October, Prime Minister Poul Schlüter played his last two cards before the upcoming general elections, which were expected to take place in the autumn of 1987. In an effort to cut back on consumer imports, the government introduced savings incentives and increased the cost of consumer credit. A whole range of measures were to be introduced to boost exports. The Schlüter government could point to four years of rapid economic growth. Unemployment was down from 280,000 to 214,000, and 210,000 new jobs, most of them in the private sector, had been created. Inflation had been halved, and the huge public deficit had been transformed into surplus for the first time since 1973.

A report by the Organization for Economic Cooperation and Development praised the achievements of the Danish government in fighting unemployment and inflation.

Government measures that limited wage increases to 2% a year for more than four years had created imbalances and problems, however, especially in the public sector. Teachers, nurses, and police, who fell toward the lower end of the income bracket, were demanding huge raises. It was anticipated that new wage agreements due early in 1987 could lead to strikes and unrest and to eventual abolition of an incomes policy that had provided higher increases for private-sector workers and key personnel than for public-sector workers.

The four parties in the coalition government—the Conservatives, the Liberal Democrats, the Centre Democrats, and the small Christian People's Party—had traditionally agreed with the main opposition party, the Social Democrats, on defense and security matters. However, the Social Democrats proposed a new "nonoffensive" approach to defense that caused an uproar. Inspired by ideas put forward within both the British Labour Party and, in particular, the West German Social Democratic Party, the proposal questioned the agreed NATO doctrine of flexible response. With the existing defense agreement due to run out by the end of the year, negotiations for a new one appeared likely to be extremely difficult and might well extend into 1988.

Following the opposition's rejection of a package of reforms agreed to by the European Communities (EC) in December 1985, the government won approval of the reforms, and of Denmark's continued membership in the EC, from 56.2% of voters in a referendum held on Feb. 27, 1986. In an extensive Cabinet reshuffle announced in March, six new government ministers were appointed in changes that affected a total of nine ministries.

After decades of discussions and plans, the Folketing agreed on legislation to build a combined tunnel and bridge across Great Belt, linking the two main islands of Sjælland and Fyn. Subsequently, talks were held with the Swedish government on another major project—the construction of a railway and road bridge linking the two countries. However, political and technical problems made it unlikely that an agreement would be reached before the end of the 1990s.

(JENS W. HOLSÖE)

FINLAND

The republic of Finland is in northern Europe, on the Gulf of Bothnia and the Gulf of Finland. Area: 338,145 sq km (130,559 sq mi). Pop. (1986 est.): 4,926,000. Cap.: Helsinki. Monetary unit: Finnish markka, with (Oct. 1, 1986) a free rate of 4.91 markkaa to U.S. $1 (7.09 markkaa = £1 sterling). President in 1986, Mauno Koivisto; prime minister, Kalevi Sorsa.

Finland was preoccupied in 1986 with the general elections due by March 1987 and the presidential election scheduled for January 1988. The fall in the oil price, which affected trade with the U.S.S.R., made an impact, as did the Chernobyl nuclear reactor disaster. (*See* ENERGY: *Sidebar.*)

The traditional consensus between the government and powerful business interests was damaged. In March a breakdown in negotiations over pay prompted several unions affiliated with the blue-collar SAK (Central Organization of Finnish Trade Unions) to hold the first major strike in 30 years. A two-year wage agreement ended the strike after 58 hours, but other groups subsequently withdrew their labour. A 45-day stoppage by government employees beginning April 2 seriously disrupted everyday services and traffic into and from the country.

The Israeli representatives stride briskly toward the Helsinki Council of State compound for talks with Soviet delegates in August. The first official contact between the two countries since 1967 broke up after only 90 minutes.

WITT—SIPA/SPECIAL FEATURES

Political calm ended in June when Paavo Väyrynen, the foreign minister and Centre Party leader, became the first official nominee for the presidential election. There was interparty friction within the government, in which the Social Democrats and Centre dominated, and the death on August 31 of former president Urho K. Kekkonen (*see* OBITUARIES) induced a widespread belief that politics had deteriorated into mediocrity. Pres. Mauno Koivisto retained a strong lead in the opinion polls, having elevated his "low profile" after Chernobyl. A Finnish observation station was the first outside the Soviet bloc to detect abnormal radioactivity, but officials were slow to break the news, giving rise to criticism both inside and outside Finland. Koivisto departed from the Kekkonen tradition of not criticizing other countries when he lambasted Sweden for "high-handedness" and singled out a Western journalist for rebuke. However, he did not criticize the U.S.S.R. for failing to inform its neighbours about the accident.

The long-expected split in Finland's Communist Party occurred, in effect. Following the expulsion of its district and branch organizations by the national-minded majority wing, the pro-Moscow minority faction set up its own "Democratic Alternative," a quasi-breakaway party.

Although the external balance gave no cause for concern and fiscal management remained sound, economic performance faltered. The Organization for Economic Cooperation and Development revised its predictions of steady 3% annual growth over the medium term to 2%. The Bank of Finland intervened to prevent a faster than usual depreciation of the markka. International speculation had been fueled by the belief that the markka would be devalued to improve Finland's export competitiveness. Economists estimated that a 10% increase in exports to the West would be required to compensate for loss of markets in the U.S.S.R. The halving of the price of oil, which constituted 80% of Soviet exports to Finland, meant that, to maintain balanced trade levels, Finland would have to cut back its exports to the Eastern bloc. Because of the country's heavy dependence on the U.S.S.R., which in the peak year of 1983 accounted for 26% of Finland's trade, extensive restructuring was necessary, and unemployment began to accelerate. On January 1 Finland became a full member of the European Free Trade Association.

Koivisto received assurances from senior Soviet officials concerning Moscow-Helsinki relations. He rebuked a retired Finnish general for publishing his experiences at a Soviet military academy. The censors banned a Finnish-produced film, *Born American,* because of its anti-Soviet undertones. A Helsinki correspondent for the Soviet news agency TASS who vanished with his family was thought to have gone to the U.S.

The most visible signs of neutral Finland's progress in developing its international relations were the visits by Chinese Foreign Minister Wu Xueqian (Wu Hsueh-ch'ien) to Finland in May and Finnish Prime Minister Kalevi Sorsa to China in September. (DONALD FIELDS)

FRANCE

A republic of western Europe, France includes the island of Corsica in the Mediterranean Sea and has coastlines on the English Channel, the Mediterranean, and the Atlantic Ocean. Area: 543,965 sq km (210,026 sq mi). Pop. (1986 est.): 55,406,000. Cap.: Paris. Monetary unit: franc, with (Oct. 1, 1986) a free rate of F 6.64 to U.S. $1 (F 9.60 = £1 sterling). President in 1986, François Mitterrand; prime ministers, Laurent Fabius and, from March 20, Jacques Chirac.

An important "first" for France occurred in 1986. Following legislative elections in March, in which the right overtook the left to win a majority of seats in the National Assembly, the country was faced with a situation unprecedented in the history of the Fifth Republic: "cohabitation" of a left-wing Socialist Party (PS) chief of state, Pres. François Mitterrand (who had reached only the fifth year of his seven-year term of office), and a right-wing head of government, Jacques Chirac (*see* BIOGRAPHIES), leader of the Rassemblement pour la République (RPR), the largest party in the new right-wing majority. A second factor that marked the year was the struggle against terrorism, which, beyond the implementation of its policy objectives, became an absolute priority for the government.

Domestic Affairs. From the start of the year, President Mitterrand threw himself into the electoral campaign, giving a positive picture of the successes of the left since he took office and calling on the electorate to preserve its "social gains." In the March 16 legislative elections nearly 7,000 candidates contested the seats in the National Assembly, newly enlarged to 577 deputies. The turnout in the single round of voting (a departure from the old system of two rounds, the second a runoff between the two leading candidates) was 78.3%. On the left the PS won 207 seats, the Left Radicals (MRG) 2 seats, and various other parties 7 seats, for a total of 216 seats and a 32.6% share of the vote. On the right the RPR took 147 seats and the Union pour la Démocratie Française (UDF) 130 seats; to this, 14 seats from various other right-wing parties could be added, giving a total of 291 seats (44.9%). The far-right National Front, led by Jean-Marie le Pen, entered the National Assembly for the first time with 35 seats (9.7%)—the same number as the Communist Party (PC), which, with only 9.8% of the poll, suffered a historic decline in support.

A majority of the French people had chosen a switch in direction and, after five years, rejected the Socialists. The tide had not turned against the left to such an extent since the presidential elections of 1969. On the other hand, far from experiencing a crushing defeat, the Socialists remained the largest single party in the National Assembly and passed the crucial threshold of 30% of the vote. In addition, few would have predicted that in Paris the PS vote would equal that of the right.

Firefighters carry the body of one of the victims of a terrorist bomb tossed from a car into a Paris clothing store on September 17. The blast was the fifth and last in a ten-day wave of bombings in the city that left 10 dead and more than 160 wounded.

AP/WIDE WORLD

The limited success of the National Front and the renewed failure of the Communist Party demonstrated that 80% of French voters rejected extremes. Although it had hoped for a better result, the UDF took twice the number of seats it had held in the previous National Assembly, while the RPR made considerable progress and won the right to form the new government. Raymond Barre (UDF), long the star of the opinion polls, did not have the kind of victory he had expected in the département of the Rhône, and he continued to oppose cohabitation. The narrow margin of seats held by the incoming majority, however, inspired Mitterrand to retain the presidency in an attempt to achieve cohabitation.

Elections to regional councils held on the same day were the first to take place under universal suffrage. The results were comparable to those in the legislative elections, although there was a more marked shift away from the left in general and the PS in particular, and the right finished with control of 20 of the 22 regions. The PS, which had controlled six regions before the election, retained only two (Nord-Pas-de-Calais and Limousin); it lost Auvergne, Languedoc-Roussillon, Midi-Pyrénées, and Provence-Alpes-Côte d'Azur. The RPR maintained its position, while the UDF took the lion's share, adding 3 regions to the 11 it already held and losing only Brittany, to the RPR. The National Front held the balance of power and in practice allowed the right to win in five regions, as it had done in Corsica in 1984.

The day after the RPR and the UDF had achieved a small absolute majority of seats in the legislative elections, President Mitterrand accepted the resignation of Laurent Fabius as prime minister. On the following day he received Jacques Chirac, who had previously been authorized by the RPR and the UDF to lead a new right-wing government, at the Élysée Palace. Mitterrand's first encounter with Chirac lasted more than two hours and apparently saw their new cohabitation off to a good start.

Some 48 hours later Chirac formed his Cabinet, which was composed of Chirac (RPR), prime minister; Edouard Balladur (RPR), minister of state for economy, finance, and privatization; Albin Chalandon (RPR), justice; André Giraud, defense; François Léotard (UDF-Republican Party [-PR]), culture and communications; Jean-Bernard Raimond, foreign affairs; Charles Pasqua (RPR), interior; Pierre Méhaignerie (UDF-Social Democratic Centre [-CDS], equipment, housing, and transport; Bernard Pons (RPR), overseas départements and territories; René Monory (UDF-CDS), education; Philippe Séguin (RPR), employment and social affairs; Alain Madelin (UDF-PR), industry, postal services, and tourism; François Guillaume, agriculture; Michel Aurillac (RPR), cooperation; and André Rossinot (UDF-Radical), parliamentary relations. The government team was completed with the addition of 13 delegate ministers and 15 secretaries of state. Three of the most influential ministers—defense, foreign affairs, and agriculture—were not members of any party.

After Chirac, the strong man in the government was undoubtedly Balladur, general secretary of the Élysée under Georges Pompidou and one of the former president's friends. He enjoyed an impressive amount of power since, as minister of state, he exercised influence on the budget, foreign trade, and denationalization measures. In addition, he was one of the leading experts on relationships between the presidency and the prime minister.

President Mitterrand's message to the new Parliament expressed the spirit of cohabitation and was followed by a vote of confidence in Chirac, which the traditional right carried by 292 votes to 285. In his speech the prime minister took the opportunity to outline his legislative policies, designed to lead to the economic revival of the country. Jacques Chaban-Delmas was elected president of the National Assembly on the second ballot.

Although the new parliamentary session was disrupted to some extent by incidents provoked by the National Front and the Communists, during his first months in office Chirac achieved a number of important successes. President Mitterrand, meanwhile, promulgated the enabling law allowing the government to act through *ordonnances* (that is, by decree without going through Parliament) in economic and social affairs. At the beginning of August the government's law on the privatization of 65 nationalized companies came into force. In addition, the passage of a bill on "freedom of communication," revised and corrected by Parliament, together with the annulment of concessions to the fifth and sixth public television channels, resulted in a delicate balance between the public and private sector in communications.

Elections to renew 120 seats (one-third of the total) in the Senate on September 28 resulted in a considerable advance by the RPR, which increased its representation from 59 to 77 seats and became the largest group in the upper house. The UDF underwent an adjustment, at the expense of the centrists and to the benefit of Léotard's Republican Party. The PC just managed to preserve its 15-seat group in the Senate, while the PS lost some ground. Following the elections, the right held 231 and the left 88 of the total of 319 Senate seats. The right apparently benefited in part from the temporary mood of national unity engendered by the struggle against terrorism. Opinion polls carried out at the end of October showed that both Chirac and Mitterrand had maintained their popularity and that cohabitation met with the approval of a majority of the French people.

For much of the year the government's main concern was with countering terrorism. Deaths and many injuries resulted from bomb attacks in February–March (including one on the Paris–Lyon express train) and in September, when during a ten-day period bombs hit targets in central Paris, among them a shopping arcade and a pub in the Champs-Élysées, the post office at the Hôtel de Ville, and police headquarters. Chirac announced a series of antiterrorist measures, including the introduction of visas for all foreign visitors except those from Switzerland and the European Communities (EC) countries and security checks of those entering public places and offices. Responsibility for most of the bombings was claimed by the Committee for Solidarity with Arab and Middle Eastern Political Prisoners, which was apparently seeking the release from a French prison of Georges Ibrahim Abdallah, leader of the Lebanese Armed Revolutionary Faction, and by the extreme left-wing Action Directe. Responsibility for the killing of Georges Besse, managing director of the state-owned Renault automobile-manufacturing company, who was shot in Paris on November 17, was claimed by Action Directe.

Parliament passed bills that increased the government's powers to combat terrorism and crime and tightened the conditions under which foreigners were allowed to reside in France. In the first exercise of its new powers, the government expelled 101 Malians from the country in October. The new powers were the source of some controversy because they allowed the authorities to expel illegal and undesirable aliens by means of administrative order and without the need to go through judicial processes.

The Chirac government suffered a defeat in November when student disorders—described as the worst since 1968 when students nearly brought down the government—forced it to withdraw a bill reorganizing the country's university system. During violent clashes between demonstrators and police, one student died and scores were injured. The measure, which among other things would have allowed universities to be more selective in their admissions and to issue their own diplomas, was attacked by the students as elitist.

In the economic field, retail prices fell in February by 0.2%, the first such decline in 20 years. Price rises remained under control, making an inflation rate of 2.3% for 1986 a credible forecast. After several favourable months, the balance of trade deteriorated again in midyear, and the government was hoping at best to bring it into balance for the whole year—a result that would prove insufficient to relaunch the economy. On the other hand, the first results of a program introduced by the new government to fund jobs for young people helped to produce a slight fall in unemployment to just under 2.5 million.

Paris was brought to a standstill in early 1986 by a transport strike called by six of the seven transport-sector unions. Further strikes in the public sector in October affected schools, the postal service, transport, electricity, and banks. The unions failed to combine their efforts, giving further proof of their disunity. Industrial action affecting the country's rail network, several major ports, and bus and subway transport in Paris began in mid-December and was in progress at year's end.

Following two days of negotiations, on April 6 the franc was devalued by 3% within the European Monetary System. Since the West German currency was revalued at the same time, the move represented a 5.8% devaluation of the franc against the Deutsche Mark. The fourth devaluation in less than five years, it was undertaken quite deliberately, in an effort to improve the competitiveness of exports, and ended the illusion of a firm franc in relation to the mark.

Foreign Affairs. In his book *Réflexions sur la politique extérieure de la France,* published at the start of the

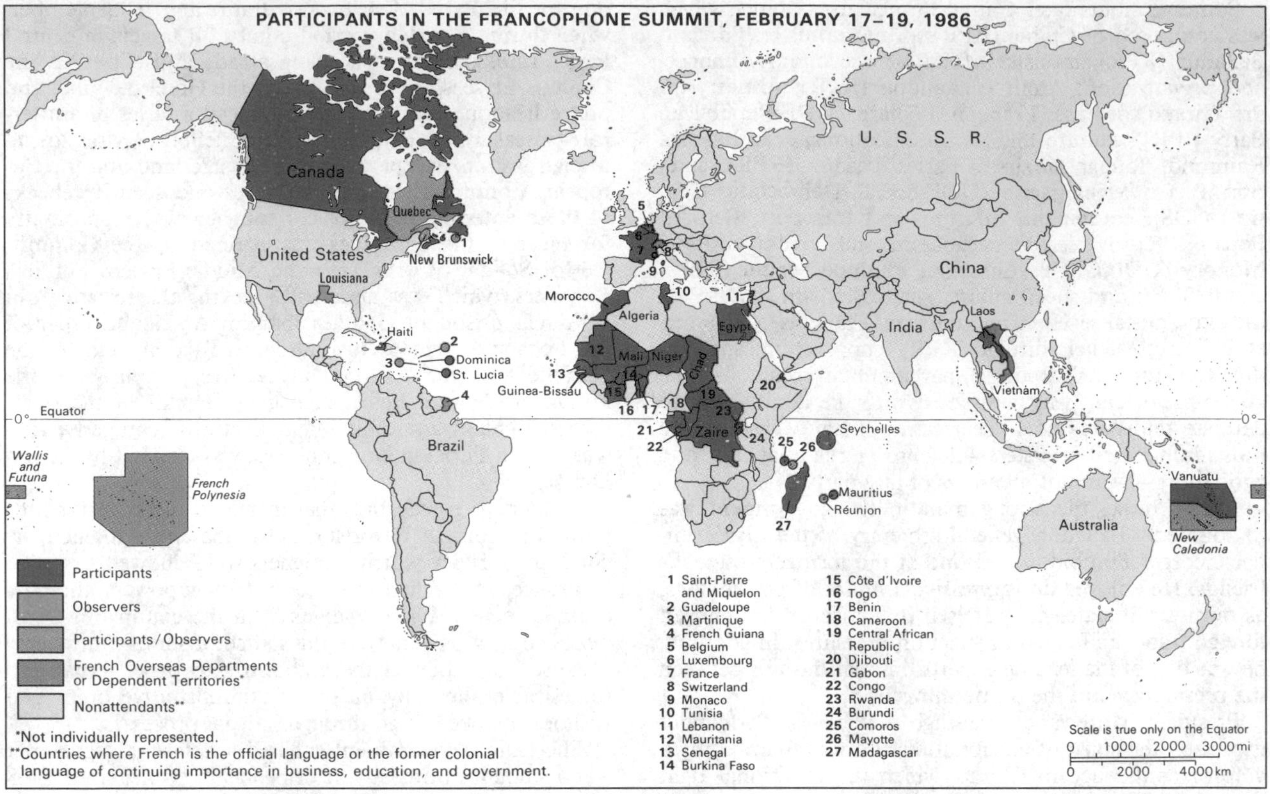

The Francophone Summit

Twenty-four years after Pres. Léopold Sédar Senghor of Senegal launched the idea of a French-speaking community, the French-speaking world finally united in 1986 to protect its heritage. During February 17–19, representatives of 120 million fluent French-speakers from five continents gathered in France at the first summit of countries where the language is spoken. The meeting was attended by 16 heads of state, 11 heads of government, and 15 other delegations.

Welcoming the visitors at Versailles before they moved to a conference centre in Paris, Pres. François Mitterrand of France underlined the threat. In accordance with the iron law of economic competition, countries that once played an active, creative part in the world economy were being pushed to the sidelines. Their best defense, he claimed, was a cultural identity based on a language that embodied one of the great civilizations known to history. Mitterrand also referred to an encouraging prediction that suggested the Romance languages would claim more speakers worldwide than English at the turn of the century. He failed to mention, however, that according to the same forecast, French would trail behind both Spanish and Portuguese within the Romance family of languages.

In a world of mass communications, high technology, computers, and data banks, defenders of the French language saw English as a careless giant ambling toward easy, undeserved victory. By 1984, for example, only 7% of papers in the main international scientific journals were being written in French. While English was widely recognized as being more streamlined and concise, Maurice Druon of the Académie Française had argued earlier that English was harder to master than French "which, being analytical, is more obedient to the laws of logic."

Mitterrand resisted any comparison with the Commonwealth—and, indeed, the summit backed away from political issues—but the meeting was an impressive example of unity in diversity. African presidents, European ministers, representatives from the Pacific, Haiti, Laos, Vietnam, Egypt, and even the U.S. state of Louisiana sat under one roof to discuss methods of cooperation. The problem of Canadian representation was solved when Brian Mulroney, the French-speaking prime minister of Canada, agreed that Robert Bourassa, premier of Quebec, and Richard Hatfield, premier of New Brunswick, should also attend in their own right. Mulroney was winningly enthusiastic in support of the cause, and in this harmonious climate the conference decided to hold the next summit in Quebec in 1988.

The summit approved 28 measures designed to strengthen the French-speaking world, including the establishment of a new agency to produce television programs in French, a school-leaving examination valid throughout the French-speaking world, and steps to encourage the publishing and distribution of books in French. The summit had met, cooperated, and decided. The French newspaper *Le Monde* welcomed the idea of a French-speaking community as an original way of resisting the "banalization" of the contemporary world. (CAMPBELL PAGE) year, Mitterrand wrote a long introduction in which he expressed a purely Gaullist attitude based on the ideas of national independence, a balance between the world's military blocs, and the creation of a strong Europe. Prime Minister Chirac, for his part, did not take issue with these main policy outlines.

While the official entry of Spain and Portugal into the EC was an important event, further progress in Europe would depend above all on the political will of member countries and their readiness to proceed with European integration. The Anglo-French decision to construct the Channel Tunnel was regarded as evidence of a more positive desire on the part of the U.K. for integration with the European continent. (*See* ENGINEERING PROJECTS: *Sidebar.*) Franco-West German cooperation was also strengthened in most fields, thanks to the 47th and 48th summit meetings between the French president and the West German chancellor in Paris and Frankfurt. Though some issues remained to be resolved, good relations between Paris and Bonn provided one of the chief reasons for optimism about the construction of a united Europe.

Two trips by Mitterrand in July, to the U.S. and the U.S.S.R., ensured that France was not absent from the East-West confrontation. In New York City Mitterrand and U.S. Pres. Ronald Reagan discussed disarmament and the perennial friendship between France and the U.S. on the occasion of the sumptuous festivities organized to commemorate the centenary of the Statue of Liberty, which celebrated that friendship. The following week in Moscow, after spending several hours in conversation with Soviet leader Mikhail Gorbachev, Mitterrand came away with the impression that the Soviet leader was "a modern man, a man of his time" but confirmed that "we remain allies of our allies." Speaking of the Chernobyl nuclear reactor catastrophe, Gorbachev recognized that it had created a disastrous situation for the whole region.

Both Mitterrand and Chirac attended the Franco-African summit held in Lomé, Togo, in November, and there appeared to be little dissent between the two leaders on the subject of French policy in Africa. During the year France sent military assistance to the government of Togo in the aftermath of the unsuccessful coup attempt in September, and French forces were active in supporting the government of Pres. Hissen Habré in Chad.

The release in November of two French citizens held hostage in Lebanon by a Shi'ah Muslim group linked with Syria brought questions in the National Assembly about how the government had obtained their freedom. Chirac thanked Syria, Algeria, and Saudi Arabia for their assistance but would not reveal details. Although another French hostage was released on December 24, at year's end a number of French citizens remained captive in Lebanon.

The third visit to France of Pope John Paul II, in October, inspired impressive demonstrations of the fidelity of many French people to the Roman Catholic Church and its head, who reminded them of the church's traditional views on the priesthood and on morals. (JEAN KNECHT)

See also *Dependent States,* below.

GERMANY, FEDERAL REPUBLIC OF

The Federal Republic of Germany (West Germany) is in central Europe, on the North and Baltic seas. Area: 248,717 sq km (96,030 sq mi). Pop. (1986 est., including West Berlin, which is an enclave within East Germany): 60,861,000. Provisional cap.: Bonn. Monetary unit: Deutsche Mark, with (Oct. 1, 1986) a free rate of DM 2.03 to U.S. $1 (DM 2.93 = £1 sterling). President in 1986, Richard von Weizsäcker; chancellor, Helmut Kohl.

A year of strong domestic economic growth in 1986 gave the centre-right coalition government confidence as it prepared for the federal elections scheduled to be held in January 1987. Under the leadership of federal Chancellor Helmut Kohl, the coalition of the Christian Democratic Union (CDU), its Bavarian wing, the Christian Social Union (CSU), and the Free Democratic Party (FDP) took credit for the virtual elimination of inflation and the creation of 600,000 new jobs in four years.

Domestic Affairs. Although the Christian Democrats suffered a severe setback in the elections for the state parliament of Lower Saxony on June 15, their position federally did not appear to be seriously challenged. Their state poll fell from 50.7% in 1982 to 44.5%, while the Social Democratic Party (SPD) managed to increase its share by nearly six percentage points to 42.1%. The FDP's performance remained unchanged at 5.9%, and the environmentalist Green Party marginally increased its strength to 7%. As a result, the Christian Democrats lost their absolute majority, but they stayed in power by forming a coalition with the FDP. The two parties commanded a majority of one. The CDU's loss of support was attributed to growing public opposition to nuclear energy in the wake of the nuclear power plant disaster at Chernobyl in the Ukraine, U.S.S.R.; dissatisfaction among farmers; and continuing doubts about Kohl's leadership despite his government's sound economic record. Certainly the outcome of the Lower Saxony elections did not denote a comeback for the Social Democrats on a federal scale.

The SPD sustained its worst defeat in the state elections in Bavaria on October 12, polling only 27.5% of the total vote, a drop of 4.4%. The CSU, led by the Bavarian minister president Franz-Josef Strauss, kept its absolute majority by winning 55.8%, though this was 2.5% below its poll in the 1982 elections. The Greens polled 7.5%, nearly 3% more than in 1982, and celebrated their entry into the state parliament for the first time. The Greens benefited from the opposition to construction of a nuclear fuel reprocessing plant at Wackersdorf, near the border with Czechoslovakia and Austria. The result augured badly for the SPD candidate for the federal chancellorship, Johannes Rau, minister president of North Rhine-Westphalia. He had said that in order to win an overall majority in the country, his party had to expand its vote in Bavaria. Instead, it seemed that the only chance for the SPD to regain power in the Bundestag (federal parliament) would be in collaboration with the Greens.

In state elections in Hamburg on November 8, the CDU and the SPD won 41.9 and 41.8% of the vote, respectively, compared with 43.2 and 42.8% in 1982. The Greens increased their share from 7.7 to 10.4%, while the FDP, with 4.8%, again failed to win representation. Although the CDU emerged as the biggest single party, it did not command a majority, and the state government was again formed by the SPD with the tacit support of the Greens.

At their Nürnberg conference in August, the Social Democrats called for an end to cooperation with the U.S. in space weapons research. An SPD government, they decided, would have the U.S. remove its nuclear missiles from West Germany and halt further deployment, and it would ask the U.S.S.R. to cut the number of its nuclear missiles directed toward Western Europe to 1979 levels. West Germany would remain a member of NATO. As for nuclear energy, all atomic power stations would be closed within ten years. The main emphasis of the party's federal election manifesto, adopted at a conference in Offenburg in October, was on combating mass unemployment, which still stood at more than two million, with public investments, funds to encourage the founding of many new small firms, and schemes to redistribute available work among more people. The SPD also promised lower taxes, especially for lower paid workers.

A federal parliamentary committee was appointed to investigate the affairs of Neue Heimat, the giant housing and construction group, which belonged to DGB, the trade-union confederation. Since World War II this concern had built more than half a million low-cost dwellings and had played a major role in helping to overcome the postwar housing shortage. In later years, however, it had become a source of scandal and had accumulated huge debts through the purchase of prospective building land on credit. The sale of the group to the head of a West Berlin baking concern for a nominal DM 1 in September was opposed by bank creditors, and in November DGB was forced to buy back the concern. It was expected that the parliamentary committee would recommend a reform of the laws on nonprofit housing. At the start of the federal election campaign, the Christian Democrats were quick to make political capital out of the affair, saying that once again Socialists had shown that they were bad at business. This caused the unions to abandon their pretense of political neutrality. They appealed to members to vote for candidates who clearly pursued policies beneficial to workers.

The country experienced a new wave of terrorism. In July a senior manager with the Siemens electrical concern, Karl-Heinz Beckurts, and his chauffeur died when their car was blown up by a booby-trap bomb in Munich. The killers, believed to be a new strain of the Red Army Faction or Baader-Meinhof gang of the 1970s, said they had struck against the Siemens "military industrial complex which is producing control and surveillance systems for military and police apparatuses all over the world." In October Gerold von Braunmühl, a senior civil servant, was shot and killed in Bonn as he got out of a taxi near his home. Braunmühl was political director of the Foreign Ministry and a close adviser of Foreign Minister Hans-Dietrich Genscher. The victim's crime, in the political jargon of a letter left at the scene, was to have been a "central figure in the formulation of West European policy in the global imperialist system." His murder confirmed a change in urban guerrilla strategy. While the original group fought the country's establishment, the new generation had turned its sights on wider targets—NATO, European unity, Western defense, and all forms of new technology.

The year's deaths brought to 30 the number of people killed by terrorists in West Germany since 1972. The security services believed that about 40 terrorists were currently active. Warrants were out for the arrest of most of them. During the year there were also attacks against U.S. troops and installations. The most serious was the bombing on April 5 of a West Berlin discotheque frequented by U.S. service personnel; 2 people were killed and 200 injured. The U.S. government, convinced that the Libyans had a hand in the attack, carried out a bombing raid on Libya soon afterward.

The number of third world refugees seeking political asylum in West Germany was expected to reach 100,000 by the end of the year. Many of them entered the country by flying to East Berlin and crossing, unhindered, to the Western sector. For many months the authorities appealed in vain to the East German government to stem the flow. Finally, in September, the East Germans ruled that the refugees would not be able to pass through to the West without visas. West Germany's constitutional guarantee of refuge to the politically persecuted had been abused for many years, and in 1986 the flood of refugees virtually exhausted temporary accommodation facilities, triggered racial incidents, and prompted demands that the asylum laws be tightened. Many of the refugees, notably large numbers of Tamils from Sri Lanka, paid extortionate fees to organized groups that arranged their journeys to the West.

The public prosecutor dropped investigations into allegations that Chancellor Kohl had given false testimony to parliamentary committees probing illegal donations to CDU funds. Kohl had consistently denied the accusation. West Berlin justice officials announced in October that they had decided against prosecuting members of the Nazis' infamous People's Court, which had sentenced more than 5,000 people to death during the Third Reich. The officials said the authorities had been negligent in failing to prosecute members earlier, when evidence against them was more readily available, but the West Berlin Justice Ministry said the main reason the six-year investigation was being closed was that old age and infirmity among the estimated 83 surviving prosecutors and justices of the People's Court made many of them unfit to stand trial. The People's Court, which opened in Berlin in 1934, had tried political dissidents for alleged treason, espionage, and "demoralization" of the Nazi war effort.

The government's privatization program was making steady progress. In July it reduced to 60% its holding in VIAG, a conglomeration of more than 100 firms in the chemicals, energy, and aluminum industries. Two months later 45% of IVG, a transport and warehousing concern, was sold to private investors. The biggest sell-off was planned for 1990, when the government was to dispose of its remaining stake in Volkswagen, the third largest company in the country. In 1986, 60% of Volkswagen belonged to private shareholders, 20% to the state government of Lower Saxony, and 20% to the federal government.

Foreign Affairs. Most commentators agreed that West German influence in international affairs, notably in the East-West dialogue, had diminished in recent years. This influence was probably at its height during the chancellorship of Social Democrat Helmut Schmidt, who liked to regard himself as an interpreter in the dealings between the superpowers. The U.S. air raid on Libya in April 1986 shed an illuminating light on relations between the U.S. and Europe. In West German eyes, it demonstrated that the U.S. was prepared to ride roughshod over the wishes of its allies when Washington felt it was in the national interest to do so.

The government could scarcely disguise its relief when it was not asked to allow U.S. bombers to take off from West German soil on their mission to Libya. Helmut Kohl did not envy U.K. Prime Minister Margaret Thatcher, who was asked and agreed to the request. West Germany emphasized the need for a political rather than a military solution to all international problems. As ever, the government feared that an increase in tension could have repercussions on its *Ostpolitik* and, in particular, on relations with East Germany. After discussions within the European Communities (EC) in April, however, the government told the Libyan people's bureau (embassy) to reduce its Libyan staff from 41 to 19. West German diplomatic representation in Libya was also reduced. During the trial of two Jordanians convicted on October 27 of carrying out a bomb attack in West Berlin on March 29, it was claimed that the Syrian embassy in East Berlin had supplied the explosives. The Bonn government subsequently expelled a number of Syrian diplomats.

In a speech to the West German-U.S. Chamber of Commerce in Munich in July, Foreign Minister Genscher said that Western Europe, while still firmly allied to the U.S., was developing its own profile. He said it had to be recognized that new generations had grown up on both sides of the Atlantic. Europe, he argued, had to strengthen its own identity in order to become an equal partner of the U.S.

The nuclear reactor disaster at Chernobyl caused great concern. In a statement to the Bundestag in May, Kohl noted that people were alarmed and were asking questions about the limitations of modern technology. He declared that the Chernobyl power plant would never have been licensed in West Germany and claimed that Soviet safety precautions were in no way comparable to those in West Germany, where safety standards were unsurpassed. Subsequently, the government put in a claim for damages from the U.S.S.R., but the Soviet government angrily rejected it.

In March the federal economics minister, Martin Bangemann, went to Washington to sign an agreement on participation in the U.S. administration's Strategic Defense Initiative (SDI). Members of the Bonn coalition parties were still quarreling, however, about whether the agreement safeguarded West German interests. Like the one the U.S. had concluded earlier with the U.K., the agreement was to remain confidential. It did not guarantee a minimum level of SDI orders for the country's firms, and the passage relating to West Germany's rights to make commercial use of technology developed in cooperation with the U.S. was said to be imprecise. Enthusiasm among industrialists for SDI business cooled somewhat as skepticism grew about the cash value of orders likely to be placed with European companies and about the amount of spin-off for civilian industries.

Soviet leader Mikhail Gorbachev commented that it was impossible to detect the logic in West German policies. He also noted, however, that despite the presence of U.S. missiles in the country and Bonn's support for the SDI program, Moscow was still prepared to develop "mutually advantageous relations."

REUTERS/BETTMANN NEWSPHOTOS

Israeli Prime Minister Shimon Peres pauses at the site of the Bergen-Belsen concentration camp in West Germany to read the inscription on a memorial decrying the Nazi extermination of 30,000 Jews there during World War II.

Although Kohl's government was no less opposed than Thatcher's to the imposition of serious sanctions against South Africa, there was no shortage of condemnation of the South African regime. In August Genscher called for the immediate abolition of apartheid and for equal civil rights for all, including the principle of one-man, one-vote. He said the situation in South Africa was ripe for revolution and that a necessary first step was to create a climate for negotiation. He demanded that the ban on black representative organizations, particularly the African National Congress, be lifted and that political prisoners, with Nelson Mandela at their head, be freed.

Pres. Richard von Weizsäcker visited the U.K. in July, and in a speech to both houses of Parliament—he was the first German head of state to be given this privilege—emphasized the importance of British membership in the EC. He said the Germans and the British had developed a close partnership. Opinion polls confirmed time and again the friendly attachment between the two peoples that was to be found in all sections of the population.

During Kohl's meeting with U.S. Pres. Ronald Reagan in Washington in October, he expressed support for the president's stance at his summit meeting with Gorbachev in Reykjavík, Iceland, earlier that month. The chancellor agreed with the U.S. refusal to conclude arms agreements in return for scrapping SDI. West Germany was again taken to task, however, for failing to give world trade a fillip by lowering interest rates. (NORMAN CROSSLAND)

This article updates the *Macropædia* article GERMANY: *Federal Republic of Germany*.

GREECE

The republic of Greece occupies the southern part of the Balkan Peninsula and several adjoining island groups in southeastern Europe, in and between the Ionian and Aegean seas. Area: 131,957 sq km (50,949 sq mi). Pop. (1986 est.): 9,987,000. Cap.: Athens. Monetary unit: drachma, with (Oct. 1, 1986) a free rate of 135.40 drachmas to U.S. $1 (195.65 drachmas = £1 sterling). President in 1986, Christos Sartzetakis; prime minister, Andreas Papandreou.

The ruling Panhellenic Socialist Movement (Pasok) suffered a significant setback in local elections held in Greece on Oct. 12, 1986, when it lost about one-quarter of its following, mainly to the Greek Communist Party (KKE). In the runoff one week later, it also lost the three biggest cities—Athens, Salonika, and Piraeus—to the conservative New Democracy Party. The defeat would have been even more substantial if, in the second round, the KKE had withheld its support from Socialist candidates in the provinces, as it did in Athens.

The sudden decline of Pasok's popularity, only 16 months after a major electoral victory (June 1985) that secured it a second four-year term, was attributed partly to growing discontent over economic austerity but also to left-wing reaction against government efforts to mend fences with the U.S. Prime Minister Andreas Papandreou chose to interpret the setback as a warning rather than as a sign of disaffection among voters. At the end of October he announced a reshuffle of his Cabinet in which the total number of ministers was reduced but key ministries remained unaffected. There was, however, little margin for a change in policy. After a year of rigid economies, a virtual wage freeze, and tightening of credit, the economy lost all its buoyancy. An improvement in the balance of payments reflected the decline in fuel prices and increased funding from the European Communities (EC) more than success of the government's stabilization measures.

Antinuclear protesters dressed as skeletons pour out possibly contaminated milk in Athens. Ten thousand people demonstrated to indicate disapproval of U.S.S.R. reluctance to disclose vital information following the nuclear accident at Chernobyl.

AP/WIDE WORLD

An overvalued currency, low productivity, and price controls continued to undermine competitiveness and discourage investments, resulting in higher unemployment. The EC, which had granted one-half of an emergency loan of 1,750,000,000 European Currency Units, would disburse the other half only if government spending was cut by one-fifth, inflation was lowered from 24 to 16%, and the government pledged to continue the austerity program throughout 1987. The earthquake on September 13, which killed 20 persons and seriously damaged two-thirds of the buildings in the southern port town of Kalamai, increased the government's economic burdens.

With the foreign debt hovering around $16 billion, Papandreou had no room to maneuver in his pursuit of better relations with the U.S. The goodwill of the administration appeared to be essential in order to keep open credit lines from U.S. banks, which enabled Greece to service debts and bridge deficits. Efforts were made to attract U.S. investments and encourage trade. Papandreou's overtures were not prompted exclusively by economic considerations. Repeated and massive Turkish air violations in the Aegean Sea, especially during NATO exercises (which Greece continued to boycott), reinforced Greek perceptions that Turkey posed a military threat. The government pressed the U.S. to continue allocating military assistance to Greece and Turkey at the established ratio of 7 to 10.

The continuation of military assistance to Greece, however, depended on U.S. military bases remaining in the country when the existing agreement expired in 1988. When U.S. Secretary of State George Shultz visited Athens in March to explore Papandreou's intentions, he left seemingly reassured that a compromise could be worked out after the October local elections. The U.S. administration agreed to be patient because, if Papandreou's approval of a new agreement could be secured, it could count on the consent of 85% of Greeks, since conservative approval was taken for granted. The results of the October elections, however, raised new questions about Papandreou's inclination to take a step that would further displease the left wing.

Washington decided to pay less attention to Papandreou's anti-Western rhetoric, designed to keep the left in tow, than to his actions. The U.S. administration checked its anger when terrorists blew the statue of former U.S. president Harry S. Truman off its pedestal in central Athens just before the Shultz visit, and the Socialist-Communist majority on the Athens city council decided not to put it back in place: the government first shrugged off the issue, then quashed the council's decision. Washington resented Papandreou's sharp condemnation of the U.S. air raid against Libya and his defiant refusal to join his EC partners in imposing sanctions on Libya for its role in international terrorism, but in July the staff of the Libyan mission in Athens was discreetly reduced by two-thirds.

Tourism continued to suffer from the reluctance of U.S. tourists to travel to Europe and particularly to Greece. Security at Athens airport was tightened enough for U.S. officials to award it high marks, but a midair bomb blast that killed four passengers on a Trans World Airlines airliner approaching Athens on April 2 set back the clock. So did the violent deaths in June and October of two Palestine Liberation Organization officials in central Athens, confirming that the city continued to serve as a transit base for terrorists. On September 23 Greece and Italy signed a secret agreement for cooperation on counterterrorism, and Greek policemen received special training in the U.S. and Britain.

Some aspects of Greece's foreign policy continued to puzzle its Western allies. The government pressed forward with a plan to establish a nuclear-free zone in the Balkans, but no headway was made during the year. On September 11 Greece and Bulgaria signed a protocol pledging not to allow the territory of one to be used for aggression against the other. The move appeared to be directly contrary to the two countries' obligations to their respective military alliances, NATO and the Warsaw Pact. The document seemed designed to intimidate Turkey, with which both Greece and Bulgaria had major differences. Finally, the motives behind Syrian Pres. Hafez al-Assad's surprise visit to Athens on May 27 remained obscure, although Western analysts believed it was prompted by fears of U.S. retaliation for Syria's suspected role in harbouring international terrorists. (MARIO MODIANO)

ICELAND

Iceland is an island republic in the North Atlantic Ocean, near the Arctic Circle. Area: 103,000 sq km (39,769 sq mi). Pop. (1986 est.): 243,100. Cap.: Reykjavík. Monetary unit: Icelandic króna, with (Oct. 1, 1986) a free rate of 40.40 krónur to U.S. $1 (58.38 krónur = £1 sterling). President in 1986, Vigdís Finnbogadóttir; prime minister, Steingrímur Hermannsson.

Iceland's position on the world map was highlighted when U.S. Pres. Ronald Reagan and Soviet leader Mikhail Gorbachev held their arms-reduction talks in Reykjavík on Oct. 11–12, 1986. (See *Introduction,* above.) The meeting brought some 3,000 public officials and journalists to Iceland's capital, which normally has a population of just under 90,000. The influx filled hotel rooms, restaurants, and telephone booths for ten days and stretched the resources of the town to the limit. The meeting as a whole passed off without incident, and security was kept to a minimum.

The economy performed well in 1986 as real gross national product rose by more than 5%, compared with 2.8% in each of the two previous years. The good growth record owed much to the rise in exports and improved domestic economic conditions resulting from lower oil prices and a sharp fall in inflation. The lower inflation rate was made possible by a nationwide wage agreement concluded in February whereby wage increases were kept low by the standards of previous years. Cost and price pressures could therefore be reduced, and inflation, as measured by the cost-of-living index, declined from 34% in 1985 to less than 10% in 1986. The decline represented a dramatic break in the spiral of wage and price increases that had plagued Iceland for years.

Relations with the U.S. had been soured in 1985 by the fact that the U.S. base in Iceland ceased to use Icelandic vessels for its transport needs, reverting instead to vessels of U.S. registry. This caused considerable income loss to Icelandic shippers, and the situation was compounded when the U.S. warned that it would apply trade sanctions against Iceland if it continued to export whale products on a substantial scale. Both issues angered Icelandic officials, and even those people who were normally well disposed toward the U.S. were showing a decidedly cooler attitude. Both disputes were resolved during the course of 1986. The freight dispute was settled by a compromise agreement whereby the U.S. administration undertook to seek U.S. Senate approval of a measure amending the Cargo Preference Act to allow Icelandic and U.S. shippers an equal right to bid on freight business. The whaling dispute was settled with the understanding that Iceland would use more than half of its whale products inside the country and export the remainder.

Iceland was one of the few remaining nations in the world that possessed a significant whale industry. Under international pressure it ceased commercial whaling in late 1985, but in 1986 it began a whaling program under which about 120 whales a year were to be caught for scientific research purposes. Previously, no such research program had existed. There was widespread criticism that this scientific whaling was no more than a front for continued commercial exploitation. The environmental action groups Greenpeace and Sea Shepherd were actively engaged in disrupting whaling and promoting a boycott of Icelandic products abroad. The issue took a more violent turn on November 7–9 when two saboteurs from the Sea Shepherd group scuttled two whaling boats in Reykjavík Harbour and wrecked control equipment in a whaling station. Both saboteurs escaped from the country before the crime was discovered.

GAMMA/LIAISON

Soviet leader Mikhail Gorbachev and U.S. Pres. Ronald Reagan meet in Reykjavík for "presummit" talks in October. Reports of possible breakthroughs on arms reduction faded when the two could not agree on U.S. Star War plans.

Early in 1986, following a period of heavy financial losses, the country's second largest shipping line, Hafskip Ltd., declared bankruptcy. The move left Iceland's second largest commercial bank, Útvegsbanki Íslands, with loan losses of $15 million–$20 million. During the subsequent inquiry it was alleged that the company's officers had acted illegally in their business dealings and that the bank had been lax in its attitude toward the company.

In August Reykjavík celebrated the 200th anniversary of the date when it was granted municipal status and designated the country's administrative centre. Emil Jónsson, former prime minister (1958–59) and foreign minister (1965–71) of Iceland, died in Reykjavík on November 30 at the age of 84. (BJÖRN MATTHIASSON)

IRELAND

The republic of Ireland, separated from Great Britain by the North Channel, the Irish Sea, and St. George's Channel, shares its island with Northern Ireland to the northeast. Area: 70,285 sq km (27,137 sq mi). Pop. (1986 est.): 3,547,000. Cap.: Dublin. Monetary unit: Irish pound (punt), with (Oct. 1, 1986) a free rate of Ir£0.74 to U.S. $1 (Ir£1.07 = £1 sterling). President in 1986, Patrick J. Hillery; prime minister, Garret FitzGerald.

Ireland's coalition government of Fine Gael and the Labour Party, led by Prime Minister Garret FitzGerald of Fine Gael, entered its fifth year in office in December 1986 beset by difficulties, both political and economic. It faced harsh and aggressive criticism from Fianna Fail, the opposition party, on its failure to reduce either unemployment, which was running at 18%, or the national debt, which, at 133% of national income, constituted the largest debt burden of any country in the industrialized world.

In an effort to restore the government's popularity, FitzGerald reshuffled his Cabinet in February. The personnel of the Cabinet remained unchanged, but nine portfolios changed hands. John Bruton became minister of finance in place of Alan Dukes, who took over the justice portfolio. Gemma Hussey, the only woman member of the Cabinet, moved from the Ministry of Education, where she was replaced by Patrick Cooney, to the Ministry of Social Welfare. The new defense minister was Patrick O'Toole, and the new industry and commerce minister was Michael Noonan.

With a certain amount of discontent evident among its backbenchers, the government was fortunate to survive a no-confidence vote introduced by the opposition in the Dail (lower house of Parliament) on October 23. The motion was defeated by 83 votes to 81. The tensions that preceded the parliamentary challenge confirmed the growing instability of the Fine Gael-Labour partnership. Although talk of an election was in the air, the survival of the administration led to the belief that the government would last long enough to introduce a tough budget early in 1987 before going to the country. General elections were due to be held by November 1987.

The government's position throughout 1986 was not made any easier by the formation in December 1985 of

Gasoline (petrol) bombs thrown in a crate explode as members of the police usher Ulster Loyalist protesters out of the town of Dundalk in the Irish Republic. The incident was part of the opposition by Loyalists to the Anglo-Irish agreement.
REUTERS/BETTMANN NEWSPHOTOS

the Progressive Democrats, a new political party led by Desmond O'Malley (*see* BIOGRAPHIES). He had been one of the chief dissidents involved in the attempt to oust Charles Haughey as the leader of Fianna Fail, and he was finally expelled from the party in 1985 on the issue of Northern Ireland policy. Deputies from both Fianna Fail and Fine Gael joined the Progressive Democrats, and support for the new party rapidly gathered momentum. Successive opinion polls estimated it at about 15%, making the new party a significant factor in the general elections.

At its annual conference in Dublin at the beginning of November, Provisional Sinn Fein, the political wing of the Provisional Irish Republican Army, voted to abandon its policy of refusing to allow its successful candidates to take up seats in the Dail. The motion secured the two-thirds majority required for a change in the party's constitution.

On June 26 a referendum was held on the issue of whether to remove the constitutional ban on divorce and allow the legislature to introduce a very limited form of divorce. Although the mood of the country, as reflected in opinion polls at the start of the campaign, indicated that the referendum would be carried by a small majority, the reverse proved to be the case. In the closing stages of the campaign it gradually became apparent that the opposition of the Roman Catholic Church, coupled with apparent confusion about the benefits to which the divorced wife would be entitled, had caused the public to change its mind. The reversal was particularly marked among women. Slightly more than half of the country's 2.3 million electorate went to the polls. The proposed amendment to the constitution was defeated overwhelmingly by two out of three voters; the result was 63.1% against, 36.3% in favour.

The pessimistic mood prevailing in the country was not helped by a second disastrous summer, which proved to be one of the worst on record. It culminated in one of the most violent rainstorms of the century. Flooding along the east coast in late August caused millions of pounds worth of damage. An interim payment of Ir£10 million was made by the government to farmers, householders, and industries in compensation. Two mainstays of the Irish economy, agriculture and tourism, suffered severe setbacks in 1986. Farm incomes dropped dramatically, and tourism was badly affected by the reluctance of U.S. tourists to travel abroad for fear of terrorism.

The Anglo-Irish agreement on Northern Ireland was sustained throughout its first year in the face of fierce opposition in Northern Ireland. (See *United Kingdom,* below.) It was reinforced by an international financial aid package, led by the U.S. with a donation authorized by Congress of $120 million over three years. The new U.S. ambassador to Ireland, Margaret Heckler, former U.S. secretary of health and human services, was one of the witnesses to the second Anglo-Irish agreement, signed in Dublin and London on September 18. Other participating countries included New Zealand, Canada, Australia, and member countries of the European Communities (EC).

Ireland was one of the last two countries in the EC to sign the Single European Act, a measure to harmonize the laws of member states. Domestic opposition was fueled by fears that the country's neutrality might be undermined and that laws might be passed damaging to Ireland's social and religious culture.

On May 21 thieves stole paintings from Sir Alfred Beit's collection at Russborough, County Wicklow, considered to be one of the finest private art collections in the world. The stolen haul, which included works by Vermeer, Murillo, and Rubens, had an estimated value of Ir$20 million. The pictures had been stolen previously in 1974, by a Republican gang led by Rose Dugdale. They were all later recovered. In the second robbery neither the thieves nor the paintings had been found by year's end. Irish pop star Bob Geldof was awarded an honorary knighthood by Queen Elizabeth II in recognition of his outstanding services in mobilizing public support for famine relief in Africa. As an Irish citizen he would be unable to use the title "Sir" but would be plain "Mr." Geldof KBE (Knight Commander Order of the British Empire). (MAVIS ARNOLD)

See also *United Kingdom,* below.

ITALY

A republic of southern Europe, Italy occupies the Apennine Peninsula, Sicily, Sardinia, and a number of smaller islands in the Mediterranean Sea. Area: 301,278 sq km (116,324 sq mi). Pop. (1986 est.): 57,298,000. Cap.: Rome. Monetary unit: Italian lira, with (Oct. 1, 1986) a free rate of 1,402 lire to U.S. $1 (2,025 lire = £1 sterling). President in 1986, Francesco Cossiga; prime minister, Bettino Craxi.

Domestic Affairs. The pattern of Italy's political experience in the post-World War II period—one of changing governments about twice a year on average—was altered early in 1986 when Prime Minister Bettino Craxi, in office since August 1983, overtook the late Aldo Moro's record for length of service. His premiership of the coalition government of Christian Democrats, Socialists, Republicans, Social Democrats, and Liberals remained an anomaly, in light of the fact that his Socialists controlled only 11% of the seats in Parliament, while the Christian Democrats controlled 33%. Nevertheless, Craxi expressed confidence that he would remain prime minister at least until 1987. The Christian Democrats, who had headed every postwar government without interruption until 1981, did not encourage such optimism.

Italy was said to be the only European country where parliamentary votes remained secret, though in fact this was true only in the Chamber of Deputies, where all balloting was secret except for votes on confidence motions. When Craxi foresaw any difficulty in passing a particular bill, therefore, he would declare that the vote would be a confidence vote. Toward the end of June 1986 the five coalition parties duly backed him in a routine vote of confidence. In two secret votes on a government bill just 20 minutes later, however, about 72 MPs belonging to the coalition parties voted against the government. Craxi, who was in Belgium at the time, flew back to Rome and submitted his resignation to Pres. Francesco Cossiga.

What followed was unprecedented, even in the chronicles of Italian politics. The Christian Democrats, still under the leadership of Ciriaco De Mita, said, in effect, that the Socialists had held the premiership too long and the "spirit of rotation" should be revived. They suggested that Craxi could, if he wished, withdraw his resignation if he promised to resubmit it in October. Craxi replied that he would accept no arrangement of this sort, but by the end of July he had made a pact with the Christian Democrats that he would resign sometime in March 1987, explaining that he wanted to take up the reins of his party again at that time. The Christian Democrats expected him to pass the prime minister's baton to them. While experts on constitutional law regarded such an arrangement as unethical at best, ordinary political observers expected Craxi's resignation to coincide with a call for elections, one year early. In December the Socialists were reported to be seeking support for proposed changes to the constitution that would reduce the membership of the Chamber of Deputies and allow for the election of the president by the people rather than by Parliament.

Craxi's second Cabinet, which was almost a carbon copy of his first, was sworn in at the beginning of August 1986. Alessandro Natta, who had stepped in as leader of the Italian Communist Party after Enrico Berlinguer's death in 1984, was reaffirmed as party chairman by acclamation in April. However, party membership had dropped in the previous two years, and Communist strength in by-elections appeared to be wavering.

What may have been the final chapter in the story of the attempted assassination of Pope John Paul II in May 1981 by the Turkish gunman Mehmet Ali Agca was written in March 1986 when a Rome court found three Bulgarians whom Agca had named as his accomplices not guilty "for lack of sufficient proof." One of the Bulgarians had been under arrest since November 1982, and the other two were already in Bulgaria when Agca began unfolding his barely credible story of a "Bulgarian connection." Three of four Turks named by Agca were also set free by the court. The would-be assassin continued to serve his life sentence in an Italian prison.

Thanks largely to confessions made in the U.S. by two former Mafia bosses in Sicily, Palermo saw the opening in February of what was called the *maxi-processo*—the trial of 474 alleged Mafia members (later reduced to 467). The hearings were expected to last until at least mid-1987. Sicily, Italy's largest island, was also in the government's thoughts in early 1986 when it commissioned a project to build a bridge across the Straits of Messina, linking Sicily with Calabria on the mainland. At 3,320 m (10,890 ft), the single-span suspension bridge would be the longest in the world. Work was to begin in 1989.

Michele Sindona, one of the great swindlers of the century, was found guilty by a Milan court of having hired an Italian-American in 1979 to kill Giorgio Ambrosoli, the court-appointed liquidator of Sindona's local bank. Sindona, who could boast of having been financial adviser to the Vatican in the late 1960s, among other things, had been extradited to Milan from the U.S., where he was serving a 25-year term for bank fraud. Two days after being sentenced in Milan, Sindona took his morning coffee in prison laced with cyanide. Inquiries ruled that his death was suicide, but with his last words—"They've poisoned me!"—the wily Sicilian managed to leave some doubts.

Tourism, Italy's leading industry, had earned £7,500 million in 1985. While tourists from the U.S. accounted for only 4% of arrivals in that year, their contribution to tourism earnings was as high as 17%. Tourist operators blamed the tragic shootout at Rome airport in December 1985, threats to Italy from Libya, and terrorism in general for what was expected to be a massive reduction—perhaps as high as 60%—in the number of U.S. tourists arriving in Italy in 1986.

Tourists may also have been discouraged by the fact that, following the explosions at the nuclear reactor at Chernobyl, U.S.S.R., in April, winds carried radioactive clouds over parts of northern Italy. (*See* ENERGY: *Sidebar.*) The two government agencies authorized to advise Italians of the risks from fallout to themselves and to their livestock and produce did not distinguish themselves by their often contradictory views. Yet another negative element was provided by the discovery in March that great quantities of Italian wine had been adulterated by the criminal addition of methyl alcohol. The deaths of ovcr 20 people were attributed to the wine, but the actual number might never be known. Italy was the world's largest wine producer and exporter, with France, West Germany, and the U.S. being major importers. None of the famous labels was involved, and all confiscated wine was cheap table wine in screw-top bottles. The government restored a small tax on the production of methyl alcohol as the only sure means of controlling its use and distribution.

One of the three Italian cities most favoured by tourists, Venice, suffered another exceptionally high tide which submerged St. Mark's Square under 1.5 m (5 ft 2 in) of lagoon water on February 1. It reminded Venetians that in November 1966 the same square had been awash under 1.8 m (6 ft) of water, and that the 300 billion lire allocated by the government in 1973, along with an additional 600 billion lire approved in 1984, had not been spent to contain the flooding. In October, after the local authorities finally took action, construction began on preventive measures.

A three-year project to restore the frescoes by Masaccio, along with Masolino and Filippino Lippi, in the Brancacci Chapel of the church of Sta. Maria del Carmine in Florence was completed. Dating from the 1420s, the frescoes were the most celebrated of Masaccio's works and had immense influence on Florentine painting of the Renaissance. The restoration work revealed not only the frescoes' original colours but also large sections that had been hidden from view.

Foreign Affairs. Italy began 1986 still suffering shock over the attack by Arab terrorists on Rome airport's check-in area at the end of December 1985. The official reaction was to require Italian visas for visitors from certain countries classified as high risk, to scrutinize the activities of foreigners residing in Italy, and to increase collaboration with other countries regarding security measures. In that context, in March U.K. Prime Minister Margaret Thatcher and Craxi signed a new extradition treaty, to replace the previous one dating from 1873, which would eventually allow the U.K. to hand over alleged terrorists living there to Italy.

In April, soon after the U.S. bombing of targets in Libya, the Libyans fired two Soviet-made missiles in the direction of the tiny Italian island of Lampedusa, which lies closer to Tunisia than to Sicily. The presumed target was a U.S. Coast Guard post on the island, but the two missiles landed some distance offshore. Libyan leader Col. Mu'ammar al-Qadhdhafi later claimed that he had reduced Lampedusa "to ruins," to which Craxi responded that if the missiles had hit the island, Qadhdhafi would no longer be head of Libya's government. In the aftermath of the attack, the U.S. military navigation post on the island was turned over to Italian personnel.

The Economy. After years in which Italy had experienced the highest inflation of any industrialized nation, ranging from 22 to 15% annually, in 1986 the inflation rate was expected to be between 6 and 8%. This was due largely to the steady depreciation of the U.S. dollar, bringing a fall in the price of oil and some raw materials. The 1986 trade deficit was down, but the dollar's loss in purchasing power also affected about one-third of Italy's exports. Italy was a country of serious savers, and recurring rumours that a tax was to be levied on government bonds caused savers to turn to the stock exchange, resulting in heavy speculative trading throughout the year. A plan to introduce the new lira—the old lira with the last three zeros chopped off—was promised for 1987, to the great relief of accountants, tourists, and others. With most major companies announcing that they expected dramatic increases in profits in 1986, there was general euphoria in financial circles.

(GEORGE ARMSTRONG)

LIECHTENSTEIN

A landlocked constitutional monarchy of central Europe, Liechtenstein is united with Switzerland by a customs and monetary union. Area: 160 sq km (62 sq mi). Pop. (1986 est.): 27,100. Cap.: Vaduz. Monetary unit: Swiss franc, with (Oct. 1, 1986) a free rate of Sw F 1.65 to U.S. $1 (Sw F 2.38 = £1 sterling). Sovereign prince, Francis Joseph II; deputy head of state in 1986, Prince Hans Adam; head of government, Hans Brunhart.

General elections held in Liechtenstein on Feb. 2, 1986, changed neither the principality's government nor the political composition of the 15-member Landtag (parliament). The Vaterländische Union (Patriotic Union) won 50.2% of the popular vote and retained its majority with eight deputies. The Fortschrittliche Bürgerpartei (Progressive Citizens' Party), with 42.7% of the vote, retained its seven seats. For the first time since 1974 a third party contested the elections. However, the Freie Wählerliste (Free Voters' List) failed to attract the 8% of valid votes required to gain representation in the Landtag. Hans Brunhart, appointed leader of the coalition government by Sovereign Prince Francis Joseph II in 1978, remained in office.

In the election, the first in which women could vote, the country's first woman deputy, Emma Eigenmann of the Progressive Citizens' Party, was returned. In April the last three communes where local elections were still confined to the male electorate voted to extend the franchise to women. (K. M. SMOGORZEWSKI)

This article updates the *Micropædia* article LIECHTENSTEIN.

LUXEMBOURG

The Benelux country of Luxembourg is a landlocked constitutional monarchy in western Europe. Area: 2,586 sq km (999 sq mi). Pop. (1986 est.): 365,900. Cap.: Luxembourg. Monetary unit: Luxembourg franc, at par with the Belgian franc, with (Oct. 1, 1986) a free rate of Lux F 42.06 to U.S. $1 (Lux F 60.78 = £1 sterling). Grand duke, Jean; prime minister in 1986, Jacques Santer.

The Social Christian-Socialist coalition government, which came to power in Luxembourg following general elections in June 1984, remained in office under the leadership of Social Christian Prime Minister Jacques Santer in 1986.

Luxembourg remained one of the most important banking centres in Europe. Early in the year it was alleged in the world press that Ferdinand Marcos, deposed president of the Philippines, held bank accounts in Luxembourg, as well as in several other countries. In response to the reports, Remy Kremer, president of the Grand Duchy Bankers' Association, declared, "There is no question of hiding criminality, but if the inquiry were motivated by tax reasons the bank secrecy would be 100% in this case." In April the government announced that it was considering introducing measures, including increased tax concessions for banks and their foreign clients, that would further enhance the attractiveness of Luxembourg as a financial centre. The proposals, likely to be brought into effect in early 1987, were prompted in part by a perceived threat to banking secrecy in Switzerland.

There was relatively little poverty in Luxembourg and, with the exception of the ruling dynasty, no aristocracy. The high standard of living continued to attract immigrants, who now represented around one-quarter of the total population. (K. M. SMOGORZEWSKI)

This article updates the *Macropædia* article THE LOW COUNTRIES: *Luxembourg*.

MALTA

The republic of Malta, a member of the Commonwealth, comprises the islands of Malta, Gozo, and Comino in the Mediterranean Sea between Sicily and Tunisia. Area: 316 sq km (122 sq mi). Pop. (1986 est.): 336,000. Cap.: Valletta. Monetary unit: Maltese lira (formerly Maltese pound), with (Oct. 1, 1986) a free rate of 0.38 lira to U.S. $1 (0.54 lira = £1 sterling). President in 1986, Agatha Barbara; prime minister, Carmelo Mifsud Bonnici.

During 1986 no accord was reached between Malta's two political parties on the organization of general elections due to be held in 1987; the opposition Nationalist Party pledged that it would not allow the ruling Labour Party to remain in office if it received only a minority of the popular vote. Late in the year there were several violent clashes between government and opposition supporters. On July 31 a provisional agreement was reached between the Roman Catholic Church and the state regarding the charging of fees in church schools over a two-year period, and the government later withdrew its stringent laws on the issuing of school licenses.

Malta continued to pursue a policy of neutrality and nonalignment, working to strengthen friendships with Libya and the Warsaw Pact states and to repair links with Western Europe. On November 10 Malta and Libya laid down guidelines for implementing the 1985 judgment of the International Court of Justice, which defined the median maritime line between the two countries. Prime Minister Carmelo Mifsud Bonnici visited Libyan leader Col. Mu'ammar al-Qadhdhafi on several occasions. Following the U.S. raid on Tripoli and Benghazi in April, Malta twice requested an urgent meeting of the UN Security Council.

On November 20 a four-year protocol for financial, economic, and technical aid was signed with Italy. The meeting between the Italian and Libyan foreign ministers in Malta on that occasion was the first ministerial-level meeting between the two countries since the Libyan missile attack on the Italian island of Lampedusa in April.

(ALBERT GANADO)

MONACO

A sovereign principality on the northern Mediterranean coast, Monaco is bounded on land by the French département of Alpes-Maritimes. Area: 1.90 sq km (0.73 sq mi). Pop. (1986 est.): 28,600. Monetary unit: French franc, with (Oct. 1, 1986) a free rate of F 6.64 to U.S. $1 (F 9.60 = £1 sterling). Chief of state, Prince Rainier III; minister of state in 1986, Jean Ausseil.

In September 1985 Jean Herly, who had been Monaco's minister of state since 1979, retired from the office. He was replaced by Jean Ausseil, who had previously served as France's ambassador to Ethiopia and Uruguay. In Monaco the minister of state, as head of the National Council, exercised the government's executive power under the authority of Prince Rainier III. The holder of the office was selected by Prince Rainier from among candidates nominated by the French government.

The sharp decline in tourist arrivals from the U.S. during 1986 did not affect Monaco as seriously as the surrounding French Riviera. According to Jacques Seydoux de Clausinne, chief executive of the Société des Bains de Mer, "Americans do not gamble much, but our Swiss, German, Italian, and Arab customers are still very much with us." With gambling continuing to thrive, deposits in the principality's banks rose appreciably. Jacques de Beer, chairman of an important Monegasque real-estate business, claimed that expensive properties were now much easier to sell than cheaper ones. (K. M. SMOGORZEWSKI)

This article updates the *Micropædia* article MONACO.

NETHERLANDS, THE

A constitutional monarchy of northwestern Europe, The Netherlands, a Benelux country, is on the North Sea. Area: 41,785 sq km (16,133 sq mi). Pop. (1986 est.): 14,582,000. Cap., Amsterdam; seat of government, The Hague. Monetary unit: guilder, with (Oct. 1, 1986) a free rate of 2.29 guilders to U.S. $1 (3.31 guilders = £1 sterling). Queen, Beatrix; prime minister in 1986, Ruud Lubbers.

On Feb. 27, 1986, the Dutch Parliament voted by a majority of ten (79 in favour, 69 against) to ratify the treaty with the U.S. under which 48 medium-range cruise missiles would be stationed in The Netherlands by the end of 1988. The opposition expressed doubts as to whether the treaty was constitutional.

The results of general elections held on May 21 went against opinion-poll predictions that left-wing parties would win a majority in Parliament for the first time. The Christian Democratic Appeal (CDA), led by Prime Minister Ruud Lubbers, and the right-wing Liberal Party (VVD) maintained their majority in the 150-seat lower house. Although the Labour Party (PvdA) increased its representation from 47 seats to 52, it lost its position as the biggest single party to the CDA (54 seats). The smaller parties on both left and right suffered severe losses; the Communist Party won no seats for the first time in many years. (For tabulated results, see *Political Parties,* above.)

Following the elections, both the PvdA and VVD chose new leaders. Wim Kok, former chairman of the country's largest trade union, succeeded former prime minister Joop den Uyl as PvdA leader. After some internal struggle, the VVD appointed Joris Voorhoeve as leader in place of Ed Nijpels. The performance of Nijpels in two important debates was perceived as having been damaging to the party, which lost support in the elections. While the VVD originally supported the opposition parties in calling for the liberalization of euthanasia laws, Nijpels withdrew his support from the proposal once Lubbers had vetoed it. The second issue concerned the follow-up to a 1985 parliamentary inquiry into the causes of the collapse of the RSV shipbuilding corporation, which had received massive injections of government money. Although the inquiry had held Gijs van Aardenne, at the time VVD minister of economic affairs, responsible for withholding information from Parliament and not exercising sufficient control over the situation, he was not forced to resign because he was protected by the Cabinet and Nijpels.

On July 14 Lubbers formed a new Cabinet that included nine CDA and five VVD members. Presenting his government's program to Parliament on July 30, he stated that the shortfall in revenue from natural gas resulting from the fall in oil prices would be made up by spending cuts and tax increases. In real terms, government spending was expected to stay below its 1985 level. Queen Beatrix's speech to Parliament on September 16 gave priority to stimulating trade and industry and reducing the budget deficit.

In October Parliament agreed to set up a parliamentary inquiry into an alleged corruption scandal in the construction trade. It was to investigate accusations that commissions had changed hands illicitly and that registered building costs had been manipulated in order to secure government subsidies. On October 4 the long-running project to protect Zeeland Province from flooding was completed with the opening of the flood barrier across the estuary of the Oosterschelde River. Built at a cost of 8 billion guilders, the barrier could be closed against North Sea storms by huge trapdoors. It was designed to prevent a recurrence of the disastrous flood of February 1953, in which over 1,800 people lost their lives.

The traditional "Elfstedentoch" skating race around 11 cities in Friesland Province took place on February 26 and was won for the second year in succession by Evert van Benthem, a farmer who thus achieved the status of a legend in his own lifetime. Among other competitors who finished the race was Crown Prince Willem Alexander. (KLAAS J. HOEKSEMA)

See also *Dependent States,* below.

This article updates the *Macropædia* article The Low COUNTRIES: *The Netherlands.*

NORWAY

A constitutional monarchy of northern Europe, Norway occupies the western part of the Scandinavian Peninsula, with coastlines on the Skagerrak, the North Sea, the Norwegian Sea, and the Arctic Ocean. Area: 323,878 sq km (125,050 sq mi), excluding the Svalbard Archipelago and Jan Mayen Island. Pop. (1986 est.): 4,166,000. Cap.: Oslo. Monetary unit: Norwegian krone, with (Oct. 1, 1986) a free rate of 7.38 kroner to U.S. $1 (10.66 kroner = £1 sterling). King, Olav V; prime ministers in 1986, Kåre Isaachsen Willoch and, from May 9, Gro Harlem Brundtland.

The serious economic problems created in Norway by plummeting oil and gas prices dominated developments during 1986. One result of the crisis was a change of government. In late April the three-party minority coalition headed by Conservative Prime Minister Kåre Willoch was defeated in a parliamentary vote on a proposed gasoline (petrol) tax increase, one of a number of emergency measures drawn up in the wake of the oil price collapse. The small, rightist Progress Party, which had held the balance of power in the Storting (parliament) since the September 1985 general election and usually supported the coalition of Conservative, Centre, and Christian Democratic parties, voted with the opposition Labour and Socialist Left parties against the increase.

Gro Harlem Brundtland (centre), Norway's new prime minister, poses with the female ministers in her Labour administration.
AP/WIDE WORLD

The Cabinet resigned and was replaced in early May by a minority Labour government headed by Gro Harlem Brundtland (*see* BIOGRAPHIES). The new administration promptly ordered a 12% devaluation of the krone, followed by a package of spending cuts and tax increases. The devaluation partly restored the competitive position of some key exports, hit by rising costs at home and the prolonged fall in the value of the U.S. dollar. Sales of forest products, in particular, benefited, but the important electrometallurgical industry continued to suffer from depressed world prices. At the same time, shipping companies with interests in offshore rigs and supply boats saw increasing numbers of their vessels lying idle as oil companies cut back exploration programs.

The spring wage adjustments contributed to the country's difficulties. In the course of unusually bitter bargaining, the Employers' Association locked out 100,000 employees in five trades and industries, creating Norway's worst labour dispute in 55 years. However, the lockout had inadequate support among individual employers and was called off after a week. The affected workers received generous, inflationary pay increases, and blue-collar workers won a cut in the workweek, to take effect from January 1987, bringing them into line with white-collar workers. Public-sector wage negotiations in progress as Brundtland took over also ended in substantial pay raises. The Labour government was forced to resort to compulsory arbitration to end a teachers' strike that disrupted final examinations at virtually all the country's secondary schools.

In June a group of continental European gas companies concluded a 27-year gas purchase agreement worth £60,000 million with Statoil, the national oil company. The deal paved the way for the development of the Sleipner and Troll gas fields and provided for a new pipeline from Norway's continental shelf to Zeebrugge, Belgium. With the addition of a short spur, the pipeline could eventually carry gas to the U.K. Sleipner was due to come on stream in 1993 and Troll three years later. Although the U.K. government in 1985 had vetoed a proposal that the British Gas Corporation (BGC) buy Sleipner gas, the Norwegians hoped that a new agreement might be reached with BGC after it became a private company in late 1986.

The Labour government proved more willing than its predecessor to cooperate with the Organization of Petroleum Exporting Countries (OPEC) in supporting world oil prices. After OPEC had agreed to observe output quotas in September and October, Norway cut its crude exports by 10% in November and December. The 1987 budget presented in October proposed significant tax increases to compensate for falling petroleum revenue, as well as a tax reform designed to close loopholes. Willoch stepped down as the Conservative leader in August and was replaced by Rolf Presthus, a former finance minister.

Certain parts of Norway suffered serious radioactive pollution from the Chernobyl nuclear plant disaster. (*See* ENERGY: *Sidebar.*) Large amounts of lamb and reindeer meat from contaminated areas had to be destroyed or used for animal fodder. Fears of fallout and terrorism hit the tourist trade. (FAY GJESTER)

See also *Dependent States,* below.

PORTUGAL

A republic of southwestern Europe, metropolitan Portugal is on the Atlantic coast of the Iberian Peninsula, which it shares with Spain. Area: 92,389 sq km (35,672 sq mi), including the Azores and Madeira island groups/archipelagoes in the Atlantic. Pop. (1986 est.): 10,250,000. Cap.: Lisbon. Monetary unit: Portuguese escudo, with (Oct. 1, 1986) a free rate of 146.88 escudos to U.S. $1 (212.24 escudos = £1 sterling). Presidents in 1986, Gen. Antônio dos Santos Ramalho Eanes and, from March 9, Mário Soares; prime minister, Aníbal Cavaco Silva.

Portugal's election for a new president, originally scheduled for December 1985, was postponed to allow municipal and legislative polls to proceed on schedule. On Jan. 26, 1986, the first round of the presidential election attracted a 75.6% turnout. Diogo Freitas do Amaral, former leader of the Democratic and Social Centre (CDS), led in the poll, gaining 46.3% of the vote. He was followed by Mário Soares (*see* BIOGRAPHIES), the Socialist Party (PSP) candidate, with 25.4%; Francisco Salgado Zenha, former minister of justice and of finance, for the new Democratic Renewal Party (PRD) of retiring president Antonió dos Santos Ramalho Eanes, with 20.9%; and finally by Maria de Lourdes Pintasilgo, who stood as an independent, with 7.4%.

Because no candidate gained 50%, a second round of voting was held on February 16 between the two leading candidates. Soares was elected with 51.3% of the votes cast in a 78.2% turnout. The Socialists appealed to the supporters of both Salgado Zenha and the Communists on the basis of blocking an extreme candidate of the right wing who was likely to return the country to a police state. Following his surprise election—few opinion polls had given him more than an even chance of success—Soares was sworn in on March 9. The ceremony was attended by leaders from other member countries of the European Communities (EC) and representatives of other NATO countries, as well as delegations from Portugal's former African colonies, the U.S.S.R., and the Socialist International.

Speaking after the inauguration, Prime Minister Aníbal Cavaço Silva, leader of the minority Social Democratic Party (PSD) government, which had come to power after the October 1985 general elections, stated that he would do everything possible to avoid conflict with the incoming president, while Soares for his part affirmed his support for any government commanding a majority in the Assembly. The minority government was to some extent dependent on the PRD, which appeared to have given its support in exchange for a program of rapid economic development and prompt payment of overdue wages to workers in both the private and state sectors. The PRD expressed its opposition, however, to plans for a thorough overhaul of the constitution. This prevented the government from relaxing Portugal's rigid labour laws or shrinking the overmanned state sector as radically or as quickly as it would have liked. Encouraged by his own party's popularity, as well as by favourable opinion polls and the PRD's success in the October 1985 election, Cavaço Silva threatened the Assembly with early elections if it proved too obstructive toward his efforts to modernize the country to take advantage of EC membership. Portugal's membership in the EC came into effect on Jan. 1, 1986.

The 1986 budget was approved in early April. However, the minority government was forced to accept amendments to its plans proposed by all three opposition parties. These involved reducing gasoline (petrol) prices and lowering the rate of income tax. As a result, the budget deficit rose to 11.8% of gross domestic product, compared with the official target of only 7% by 1991. The continuing rise in the deficit was explained by ballooning service payments on the country's public debt of 2,500,000,000,000 escudos. Interest payments alone would cost 18.8% of the total debt per year if payments were not to fall into arrears. The new government voiced particular concern over the financial state of those public-sector firms working in the steel, shipbuilding, chemicals, and fertilizer sectors; they accounted for a high proportion of the state sector's total operating losses of 54 billion escudos.

Lower income tax rates and other concessions designed to promote investment and saving were to be financed in part by higher indirect tax collections after the introduction of a value-added tax. The government also budgeted for a major expansion in public works to be supported by new funding from the EC, which became available on the country's accession to the Community. The control of inflation remained a priority. By mid-1986 the local rate was still running at over 11%, compared with an average of about 3% in EC countries. Imported inflation subsequently fell with the help of halved oil prices. The trend was assisted by two other factors: the suspension of the downward crawling peg devaluation of the escudo, in operation since November 1985, in April 1986; and weakening commodity prices resulting from the fall in U.S. dollar-denominated costs. Managed local interest rates had become strongly positive, and these were lowered 3 percentage points to about 18% by midyear.

At a PSP conference held on June 28–29, Vítor Constancio was elected to take over the leadership of the party from Soares, who resigned as secretary-general on February 20. The party refused to endorse the candidate (Jaime Gama) preferred by Soares himself. Constancio, a former governor of the central bank and chief negotiator with the EC on the accession treaty, told the party that it should follow more closely the successful model provided by the Socialist government of Prime Minister Felipe González in Spain. At the same meeting, Constancio indicated that he would like time to reorganize the party to his way of working rather than continuing in the footsteps of his predecessor. The PSP voted to delete all references to the ideas of Karl Marx from its statutes. The United People's Alliance, an electoral alliance between the Communist Party and the Democratic Movement, was dissolved on November 30 when the latter withdrew from the arrangement.

Mário Soares, three-time prime minister of Portugal and Socialist candidate for the presidency, casts his vote in the runoff election against Diogo Freitas do Amaral in February. Soares won the presidential post, the first civilian to do so in 60 years.

AP/WIDE WORLD

Conflict between the mainland government and the Azores, granted regional autonomy in 1976, flared up in midyear when leaders of the armed forces voiced their disapproval of parts of a proposed autonomy statute granting the flag and anthem of the Azores ceremonial status equal to those of Portugal. In September President Soares vetoed the measure. The statute was returned to the Assembly for further discussion. In October the Chinese Foreign Ministry announced that China and Portugal had come to an agreement on the return of Macau to China and that a working group would be established in the near future to settle the details. Portugal had previously recognized, in principle, Chinese sovereignty over the enclave on the southern China coast. (MICHAEL WOOLLER)

See also *Dependent States,* below.

SAN MARINO

The republic of San Marino is a landlocked enclave in northeastern Italy. Area: 61 sq km (24 sq mi). Pop. (1986 est.): 22,600. Cap.: San Marino. Monetary unit: Italian lira, with (Oct. 1, 1986) a free rate of 1,402 lire to U.S. $1 (2,026 lire = £1 sterling). The republic is governed by two *capitani reggenti,* or coregents, appointed every six months by a popularly elected Great and General Council. Executive power rests with the Congress of State, composed of the coregents, three secretaries of state, and seven ministers.

On July 26, 1986, a new coalition government of Christian Democrats and Communists won approval for its program from San Marino's Great and General Council (parliament). The previous left-wing coalition, comprising the Communists, Socialists, and United Socialists, had come to power following general elections in 1978; it fell apart in June 1986 as a result of foreign-policy disagreements. The secretaries of state in the new government were Gabriele Gatti (foreign affairs), Alvaro Selva (internal affairs), and Clara Boscaglia (finance and budget).

The Great and General Council elected Marino Venturini and Ariosto Maiani to serve as coregents for the six-month period beginning in April. They were succeeded by Giuseppe Arzilli and Maurizio Tomassoni, who would serve until March 1987.

An annual grant from the Italian government went some way toward meeting San Marino's budget expenditure, set at a total of approximately 160 billion lire in 1986. The remainder was to be covered by levying income tax and by issuing coins and postage stamps, an important source of income for the republic. The Autonomous Public Corporation was responsible for issuing gold, silver, and bronze coins which, while they were officially legal currency in both San Marino and Italy, were in practice reserved for collectors only. (K. M. SMOGORZEWSKI)

This article updates the *Micropædia* article SAN MARINO.

SPAIN

A constitutional monarchy of southwestern Europe with coastlines on the Bay of Biscay, the Atlantic Ocean, and the Mediterranean Sea, Spain shares the Iberian Peninsula with Portugal; it includes the Balearic and Canary island groups, in the Mediterranean and the Atlantic, respectively. Area: 504,750 sq km (194,885 sq mi). Pop. (1986 est.): 38,818,000. Cap.: Madrid. Monetary unit: peseta, with (Oct. 1, 1986) a free rate of 133.50 pesetas to U.S. $1 (192.91 pesetas = £1 sterling). King, Juan Carlos I; prime minister in 1986, Felipe González Márquez.

The most momentous event for Spain in 1986 was its long-awaited accession to the European Communities (EC) on January 1. It gave the country an immense psychological boost and at the same time presented it with a major economic challenge; suddenly the third poorest country in Europe was exposed to the harsh competition of its neighbours, with its protective barriers gradually being dismantled. A further boost to Spain's status was provided by the selection of Barcelona as host city for the 1992 summer Olympic Games—its rivals had included Amsterdam; Birmingham, England; Paris; and Belgrade, Yugos.

The first major political event of the year was the March 12 referendum on Spain's continued membership in the North Atlantic Treaty Organization (NATO). The outcome was crucial to the credibility of Prime Minister Felipe González Márquez (*see* BIOGRAPHIES), who had been a fervent opponent of Spain's joining NATO just four years earlier. His grounds for favouring membership now were European solidarity and the "modernization" of Spain. Although opinion polls suggested a strong negative vote, the outcome was 52.5% in favour and 39.8% against. It was a personal victory for González and his Partido Socialista Obrero Español (PSOE; Spanish Socialist Workers Party) government and a rejection for the conservative Alianza Popular (AP) opposition.

Quick to capitalize on the euphoria of the referendum success, González called an election for June 22—four months early. The PSOE won an absolute majority with 184 seats, although it lost 18 seats compared with its landslide victory in 1982. Manuel Fraga Iribarne's AP lost one seat, giving it 105 members. Beneficiaries were the Centro Democrático y Social (CDS) under former prime minister Adolfo Suárez, with 19 seats, and the Izquierda Unida, a new party formed as a result of fractures within the mainstream Partido Comunista Español (PCE), with 7 seats, compared with 4 for the PCE in 1982. Overall, the regional parties performed well, taking 35 seats in the lower house of the Cortes (parliament); the Catalan nationalists increased their representation to 18, the Partido Nacionalista Vasco (PNV; Basque Nationalist Party) representation fell to 6, while the Herri Batasuna (HB), with close links to the Euzkadi ta Azkatasuna (ETA; Basque Homeland and Liberty), won 5 seats, 3 more than in 1982. (For tabulated results, see *Political Parties,* above.)

AP/WIDE WORLD

A funeral gathering in Madrid honours eight of the ten paramilitary guard trainees killed in July by a car bombing attributed to members of a radical Basque separatist group.

Most senior Cabinet members were reappointed in July, including Foreign Minister Francisco Fernández Ordóñez and Carlos Solchaga, minister of economy, finance, and trade, who had both served for a year previously. Four new technical appointments were made: Joaquín Almunia, labour and social security minister in the previous Cabinet, was appointed to overhaul the civil service, while the labour portfolio went to Manuel Chaves, a lawyer and long-standing associate of González. Luis Carlos Croissier, an eminent industrialist, took over the industry portfolio. Julián García Vargas was given health and consumer affairs, while Virgilio Zapatero, minister for parliamentary relations, was elevated to Cabinet rank.

The worst terrorist act in over 12 years occurred on July 14 when an ETA bomb exploded in Madrid killing ten trainee Civil Guards and injuring many others. The following day, at the state opening of Parliament, King Juan Carlos called for a united effort to eradicate terrorism. Since 1975 the ETA had killed over 500 people, including 150 Civil Guards; some 34 people were murdered in the first ten months of 1986.

In early September 400 ex-members of the PNV launched a new nationalist but Conservative-based Basque party, the Eusko Abertzaleak (EA), led by Carlos Garaikoetxea, former president of the Basque government. The breakup of the ruling PNV followed the revelation that it had been negotiating with ETA against the wishes of González, who was strongly opposed to any communication with terrorists. The defection of 11 of the PNV's 32 members in the Basque parliament made it impossible for the state government to operate without the support of the Partido Socialista de Euzkadi (PSE) led by Txiki Benegas. To resolve the situation, regional premier José Ardanza called elections on November 30, some 15 months early. The PSE won 18 seats in the election, while the PNV obtained only 17, a drop of 15 seats. The HB retained its 18% share of the vote and increased its seats from 11 to 13. AP support in the region collapsed, and its representation plummeted from seven to two. The new EA party won 14 seats. More than two-thirds of the parliament was expected to be made up of nationalists, dedicated to home rule. Socialist efforts to create a sound coalition government for the region were intensified by fears of a complete breakdown of law and order should they fail.

In early October Fraga, the major opposition leader, saw his support crumble further when four members of his AP coalition defected to the mixed group benches in the Cortes. Among them was Jorge Verstrynge, a former protégé of Fraga, who was secretary-general of the AP until September. He had lost his position after proposing Fraga as a candidate for mayor of Madrid without permission, which Fraga interpreted as an attempt to remove him as party leader. On December 2 Fraga, who had played a leading role in democratizing Spain, resigned and was succeeded as interim leader of the party by Miguel Herrero de Miñón.

In November the Cabinet restructured the armed forces and appointed civilians to head the Civil Guard and paramilitary Policía Nacional—it was the first time in 150 years that civilians had held these posts. Lieut. Gen. Gonzalo Puigcerver, previously head of the King's Military Household, replaced Adm. Angel Liberal Lucini as chief of defense staff. The receptiveness of the armed services to the changes indicated how much the political climate had altered since Gen. Francisco Franco's death in 1975. The appointments marked the end of a generation of senior commanders who owed their ranks to their experience in the Spanish Civil War (1936–39). (MICHAEL WOOLLER)

SWEDEN

A constitutional monarchy of northern Europe, Sweden occupies the eastern side of the Scandinavian Peninsula, with coastlines on the North and Baltic seas and the Gulf of Bothnia. Area: 449,964 sq km (173,732 sq mi). Pop. (1986 est.): 8,361,-000. Cap.: Stockholm. Monetary unit: Swedish krona, with (Oct. 1, 1986) a free rate of 6.91 kronor to U.S. $1 (9.98 kronor = £1 sterling). King, Carl XVI Gustaf; prime ministers in 1986, Olof Palme to February 28 and, from March 12, Ingvar Carlsson.

The year 1986 proved to be one of trauma and grief, a year in which Sweden lost its innocence as it fell under the shadow of the gunman. On February 28, on a street in central Stockholm, Prime Minister Olof Palme (*see* OBITUARIES) was shot dead by an assassin whose identity remained unknown at year's end. Two weeks later 15 heads of state, 17 prime ministers, 19 foreign secretaries, representatives of various liberation movements, and celebrities from the world of arts and literature gathered in Stockholm for an intensely moving, essentially secular funeral service. Their presence was testimony to Palme's international stature. With his passing, Sweden seemed to shrink back into itself, to relinquish at least partially the role he had given it as "the conscience of the Western world."

His successor, Ingvar Carlsson (*see* BIOGRAPHIES), was a cautious, pragmatic man, lacking the personality and idealistic dynamism of Palme. However, since Swedes tend to distrust individuality, the indications were that they felt more comfortable with Carlsson. There seemed far more likelihood that he would prove capable of becoming a *landsfader*—the Swedish ideal of a benign national father figure, running the welfare state efficiently and keeping the nation on an even course. According to opinion polls, the popularity of the Social Democratic Party under his leadership increased. The trend was assisted, however, by disarray within the non-Socialist opposition.

Thorbjörn Fälldin resigned the chairmanship of the agrarian-based Centre Party and was replaced by Karin Söder; her main claims to fame were having closed state liquor stores on Saturdays and cracked down on Sweden's notorious sex clubs while she was minister for social affairs in Fälldin's second (1979–82) administration. Ulf Adelsohn resigned the leadership of the Conservative Party and was replaced by the party's defense spokesman, Carl Bildt.

The nuclear reactor disaster at Chernobyl in the Ukraine, U.S.S.R., deposited heavy fallout along the east coast and over Lappland and reawakened controversy over Sweden's own nuclear program. Following a national referendum in 1980, it had been agreed that the program's 12 reactors at four nuclear plants would be phased out by the year 2010. As a result of Chernobyl, the government was considering a proposal that would bring the deadline forward to 1996.

The welfare state was disrupted as public-sector unions staged industrial action in pursuit of pay parity with private industry. Hospitals, schools, and day-care centres were affected, and in many places public transport ground to a halt. The government maintained that pay parity would threaten anti-inflationary policies. In the end, the unions accepted a pay raise of 8.8%, which denied them parity with the private sector. The defeat of public-sector militancy, which in its mild way represented a watershed in Swedish political life, was achieved without the sort of dramatic personal intervention that had characterized Palme's era.

The difference between Carlsson and his predecessor was expected to be most apparent in the field of foreign relations. Carlsson risked incurring the wrath of the left wing by refusing to go too far too fast on the issue of

Ingvar Carlsson meets with the press at Swedish government headquarters on March 1 as bold headlines spread the word that Prime Minister Olof Palme is dead, assassinated by a gunman the previous day. Carlsson succeeded to the office of prime minister.

AP/WIDE WORLD

sanctions against South Africa, and of the right by maintaining a policy of improving relations with the U.S.S.R. despite renewed allegations of Soviet submarine violations of Swedish waters and proof that the Swedish embassy in Moscow had been bugged for 14 years. Pragmatism was the new order of the day.

The Stockholm Security Conference—the Conference on Confidence- and Security-Building Measures and Disarmament in Europe—concluded in September with the first East-West arms agreement since 1979. The principal provisions of the agreement were to limit the size of military maneuvers and to allow for the notification and inspection of military activity. (CHRIS MOSEY)

SWITZERLAND

A landlocked federal state in west central Europe, Switzerland consists of a confederation of 26 cantons (6 of which are demicantons). Area: 41,293 sq km (15,943 sq mi). Pop. (1986 est.): 6,556,000. Cap.: Bern. Monetary unit: Swiss franc, with (Oct. 1, 1986) a free rate of Sw F 1.65 to U.S. $1 (Sw F 2.38 = £1 sterling). President in 1986, Alphons Egli.

The Swiss themselves were surprised at the sheer size (75.7%) of their rejection, in a referendum on March 16, 1986, of the government's contention that the moment had arrived for the country to become a full member of the UN. It had confined itself to observer status, plus membership in UN specialized bodies. Even in cosmopolitan Geneva, host to half a dozen such institutions, no more than 30.2% voted in favour of UN membership. Countrywide, the conviction obviously prevailed that political neutrality should be preserved.

By the following month, however, fate seemed to be underlining the point that political detachment had diminished relevance in an age of increasing techno-scientific interrelationships. The accident at the Chernobyl nuclear reactor in the U.S.S.R. brought the fact home to the Swiss. Although its initial reaction, in the form of protective measures against radioactivity, was slow compared with that of neighbouring West Germany, the depth of public unease was reflected in a special two-day parliamentary debate. Almost 40% of the country's electricity was produced by five nuclear plants. A minor escape of radioactive dust from one plant was accorded more attention than would otherwise have been the case—even in the post-Chernobyl climate—because of inept delay in letting the facts become known. The long search continued, meanwhile, for a deep depository for nuclear waste storage; local consent was not forthcoming at some otherwise suitable sites.

Environmental fears again came to the fore when the population of Basel was awakened in the small hours of November 1 by police loudspeakers, instructing the people to close windows and remain indoors until further notice. A warehouse containing 1,246 metric tons of agrochemicals, including mercury compounds, was on fire at the Sandoz AG plant at Schweizerhalle. Toxic chemicals mixed with water from the fire hoses drained into the Rhine, exterminating fish for 160 km (100 mi) downstream and forcing West German cities with water-purification plants fed by the river to switch to standby artesian wells. In deploring that Switzerland's image as an ecologically caring country had been "destroyed in a single night," Interior Minister Alphons Egli, president in 1986, said controls in the chemical industry would have to be made stricter and Swiss environmental laws brought into line with the European Communities' "Seveso directive." International compensation claims would be dealt with expeditiously.

The government's other main preoccupation was the continuing influx of would-be refugees, mainly Turks, Tamils, Chileans, Africans, and Eastern Europeans, including numerous illicit border crossers. Some 20,000 were living on subsistence allowances from the authorities while they awaited the outcome of their applications for political asylum. Many had been waiting for years. They were being dealt with at the rate of almost 600 a month, with a 9.3% acceptance rate.

Banking secrecy came under scrutiny once again as the result of legal moves by successor governments in Haiti and the Philippines directed toward establishing entitlement to reputedly very large fortunes held in Switzerland by former presidents Jean-Claude Duvalier and Ferdinand Marcos. Procedures were expected to be protracted. In December the U.S. government asked Switzerland to lift banking secrecy regulations in connection with accounts through which, it was alleged, payments from Iran for arms deliveries had been directed to rebels fighting the Nicaraguan government.

A government proposal to increase the retirement age for women from 62 to 63, to bring it nearer that of men (65) and also to help replenish the state pension fund, was encountering steadily growing criticism from women as the year closed. Switzerland continued to have the highest proportion of AIDS (acquired immune deficiency syndrome) cases in Western Europe. Customs vigilance against drug smuggling was reinforced, with some success.

At the end of December two prominent personalities retired from the seven-member Federal Council (Cabinet): Kurt Furgler (economy minister) and Egli, both Christian Democrats, were replaced by Arnold Koller and Flavio Cotti, who became defense minister and interior minister respectively. The economy portfolio was taken over by Radical Democrat Jean-Pascal Delamuraz, who moved from defense. Foreign Minister Pierre Aubert, a Social Democrat, was chosen to serve as president in 1987. (ALAN MCGREGOR)

UNITED KINGDOM

A constitutional monarchy in northwestern Europe and member of the Commonwealth, the United Kingdom comprises the island of Great Britain (England, Scotland, and Wales) and Northern Ireland, together with many small islands. Area: 244,100 sq km (94,248 sq mi), including 3,218 sq km of inland water but excluding the crown dependencies of the Channel Islands and Isle of Man. Pop. (1986 est.): 56,678,000. Cap.: London. Monetary unit: pound sterling, with (Oct. 1, 1986) a free rate of £0.69 to U.S. $1 (U.S. $1.45 = £1 sterling). Queen, Elizabeth II; prime minister in 1986, Margaret Thatcher.

Domestic Affairs. For the government of U.K. Prime Minister Margaret Thatcher (*see* BIOGRAPHIES), which in 1986 entered its eighth year in office, the year could scarcely have opened more disastrously. Before the end of January Thatcher had lost two important ministers from her Cabinet, and the self-confidence of the government had been shaken to its foundations. The crisis grew out of a dispute about the future of the Westland Helicopter Co. Yet by the end of the year the affair had been largely forgotten, the government's fortunes had revived, and Thatcher was looking forward with growing confidence to general elections due to take place by mid-1988 and likely to be called some time in 1987.

In retrospect it seemed remarkable that a small helicopter company based in Yeovil, Somerset, could become the cause of a crisis that, at its height, seemed as if it might even bring the prime minister down. Westland was facing bankruptcy. The government had ruled out a public-sector rescue operation. The chairman of the Westland board, Sir John Cuckney, had become committed to a partnership led by the Sikorsky Aircraft Division of the U.S. United Technologies Corp. He regarded the alternative—European cooperation—as not feasible. The Cabinet decided to allow the Westland board and shareholders to make their own choice between an arrangement with Sikorsky or one with a European consortium. Secretary of State for Defence Michael Heseltine had meanwhile become an enthusiastic proponent of a European arrangement.

At a meeting of the Cabinet's economic subcommittee on Dec. 9, 1985, Heseltine had been given five days to put together a European deal. Ministers may have believed that he would be bound to fail, but he did not. The Cabinet, however, stuck to its decision to allow the company to decide its own fate, and at the end of the week its board decided to accept Sikorsky's reconstruction proposals. This was the background to the open row that ensued within the Cabinet. Heseltine continued to fight for the European alternative, which he believed to be in the best interests of the country. In the course of an unseemly battle the Department of Trade and Industry (DTI) and the Ministry of Defence engaged in a warfare of briefings that culminated on Jan. 6, 1986, with the leaking, by order of Trade and Industry Secretary Leon Brittan, of a letter to Heseltine commissioned from Solicitor General Sir Patrick Mayhew to correct the allegedly misleading impression that an earlier letter from Heseltine might have given to Westland shareholders. On January 9 Heseltine resigned from the Cabinet rather than accept a ruling that would have prevented him from further championing the European deal.

From that moment the Westland affair ceased to be about the future of the British helicopter industry and became a major political crisis, the most serious in the Thatcher government's history. The letter from the solicitor general, a confidential document, had been leaked without his authority and for the purpose of discrediting the secretary of state for defense. For some two weeks the crisis raged around the question of who had authorized the leak. Under pressure from the Law Officers' Department, Thatcher instituted an inquiry to be conducted by Sir Robert Armstrong, secretary to the Cabinet. But many questioned the point of such an inquiry if, as was widely suspected, the letter from the solicitor general had been commissioned at the instigation of the prime minister and leaked with her knowledge and approval.

Armstrong's report was presented to the prime minister on January 22. She subsequently insisted to the House of Commons that only then had she learned that Brittan had authorized the leak. DTI officials insisted that they had been authorized or, at the very least, "given cover" by the prime minister's office; the prime minister's officials denied that they had approved of the plan, although the prime minister's press secretary, Bernard Ingham, had discussed the logistics of the leak with the DTI press officer, Colette Bowe, on the assumption that the DTI was going to do, in any event, what Brittan had decided. Thatcher's statement to the Commons on January 23 did not satisfy her own backbenchers, and Brittan's position had become untenable. The following day he resigned, to be replaced by Paul Channon (*see* BIOGRAPHIES). Heseltine's replacement as defense secretary was George Younger.

In the aftermath of the affair the government had to abandon an attempt to sell off the various components of the publicly owned British Leyland (BL) motor-manufacturing company. General Motors of the U.S. had made a bid for BL's unprofitable truck division, but it was conditional on the inclusion of the successful Land Rover Co. as a sweetener. Secret talks with Ford Motor Co. about a takeover of BL's Austin Rover car division were at an earlier stage when the news leaked. Immediately there was patriotic uproar; if Ford took over Austin Rover, it would mean the end of British car assembly. Land Rover was a symbol, it soon became apparent, of British success. The "americanization" of BL, it was feared, would threaten the businesses of hundreds of small component suppliers, most of them in the West Midlands.

In vain the government argued that the European market was satiated with trucks and that to compete in the volume car business Austin Rover would need a huge injection of capital. But if these were the realities of Britain's industrial position in the world, the country was in no mood to recognize them. Conservative MPs were inundated with letters of protest. The Labour Party mounted a highly effective campaign in the House of Commons. First, the government was forced to break off talks with Ford. Then, as popular feeling mounted in defense of Land Rover, the prime minister—virtually isolated in her Cabinet—was advised that the deal with General Motors had become politically impossible. She was obliged to give way.

The patriotism aroused by the BL questions, and the latent anti-U.S. feeling that it revealed, exploded again a few weeks later when Thatcher, with a good deal of misgiving, acceded to a request from U.S. Pres. Ronald Reagan to use bases in Britain from which to launch the U.S. reprisal raids on Libya. Among Thatcher's reasons for agreeing were her loyalty to the U.S. and to the president, her gratitude for U.S. assistance during the Falkland Islands/Islas Malvinas conflict of 1982, and fear of the effects of congressional and public opinion in the U.S. if European allies refused to show solidarity against a common enemy. The instant reaction of the British public, however, and within much of Thatcher's own party, was hostile to the raids.

Although the government later regained a certain amount of public support on the Libyan issue, it remained generally unpopular, and Thatcher's own approval rating was re-

Soviet Foreign Minister Eduard Shevardnadze (left) and British Foreign Secretary Sir Geoffrey Howe shake hands and exchange documents of agreement related to economic cooperation, naval exercises, and finances after meeting in London in July.
AP/WIDE WORLD

ported by a Gallup Poll to be at its lowest since December 1981. Some MPs began to wonder whether, in the absence of another "Falklands factor," the "Thatcher factor" might not lose them the next elections. After the government had finished a humiliating third in the Fulham by-election (won by Labour) on April 10 and suffered reverses in local government elections on May 8, Thatcher's fortunes seemed at a nadir.

By the autumn, when the political conference season began, the government's popularity was reviving. The recovery was powerfully aided by the performance of the opposition parties. Most experts believed that for the Labour Party to stand a real chance of winning majority power at general elections, it should be scoring 40% or more in the opinion polls during the midterm period of unpopularity that was usual for governments. Labour's standing improved somewhat through the summer, and by the early autumn it was close to the 40% threshold. However, by and large, it had been the Liberal-Social Democratic Party Alliance that had benefited from the government's midterm "blues" and that subsequently suffered from its recovery. The Alliance was not helped by a fiasco at the Liberal Assembly held in September, when the leadership's defense policy was repudiated in favour of what was tantamount to a policy of unilateral nuclear disarmament. Nor was the Labour Party helped when during its conference attention was focused on its unilateral disarmament policies, which included the abandonment of Britain's nuclear deterrent and the expulsion of U.S. nuclear weapons from NATO bases in Britain. The Conservatives, for their part, staged a successful conference in which the emphasis was on unity and on plans for the future.

By November, with the conferences all over, opinion polls indicated that the government had recovered the ground lost since Westland; the Alliance had slipped substantially from its spring showings; and Labour appeared lodged once more around the 38% mark, where it had hovered since Neil Kinnock became leader in October 1983. Thus the anti-Socialist majority looked likely once again to have a more powerful effect on general election results than the anti-Thatcher majority.

Perhaps the happiest event of the year was the wedding on July 23 of Prince Andrew, second son of Queen Elizabeth II, to Sarah Ferguson. On the day of their marriage the couple were created duke and duchess of York (*see* BIOGRAPHIES). Perhaps the most ominous development of the year was the realization that AIDS (acquired immune deficiency syndrome) had the potential to become an epidemic plague on a scale that usually sober officials compared with the Black Death of the 14th century. (*See* HEALTH AND DISEASE.) By the end of the year a committee of senior Cabinet ministers was meeting twice a week, and £20 million had been budgeted for an advertising campaign to warn the public about the disease.

Economic Affairs. The Westland affair distracted public attention from what would otherwise have been seen as a new sterling crisis in January. The value of the U.S. dollar was falling, and with it the pound, no longer buoyed up on a tide of North Sea oil. By the end of January sterling had devalued 4% in the space of a month. The spot price of North Sea oil was down from $30 per barrel to $20 and was still falling. Although British interest rates were among the highest in the developed world, the authorities had to raise the base rate by another percentage point to 12.5%.

Yet none of these factors prevented Chancellor of the Exchequer Nigel Lawson from reducing the standard rate of income tax by one penny in the pound—from 30 pence to 29 pence in the pound—in his March budget. This marked a departure, since previously priority had been placed on raising tax thresholds in order to exempt low-income families from taxes altogether, and it was seen as an indication of Lawson's intention to fulfill his pledge to reduce the standard rate to 25 pence by the time of the elections.

It had become clear to most commentators that Lawson would be unable to satisfy both the desire of his Cabinet colleagues (to give priority to reducing unemployment and hospital waiting lists) and of Thatcher and himself (to cut taxes) without at least breaching public expenditure targets. When Lawson rose to make his autumn economic statement to the Commons on November 6, he announced an increase in real spending of £4,750 million for the 1987–88 financial year and a total of £10,250 million over two years. The education sector was to receive £5,000 million, chiefly to allow Education Secretary Kenneth Baker (*see* BIOGRAPHIES) to finance an end to the pay dispute with the teachers; social security would receive £3,400 million; and the health service would receive £1,300 million. Lawson insisted that the increases could be borne within a borrowing limit of £7,000 million and still leave £1,000 million–£2,000 million in hand for tax cuts.

The autumn "U-turn" was a historic moment of a kind, for it marked the final abandonment of "Thatcherism" except in the most general and rhetorical sense. Monetary targets had been regularly breached until, a few weeks earlier, the governor of the Bank of England, Robin Leigh-Pemberton, officially declared that monetarism had been abandoned. Now the commitment to hold down public spending in real terms was also gone, and the chancellor had no visible means of support for his continuing commitment to a borrowing target. As several commentators pointed out, he was taking a large gamble on the confidence of financial markets in sterling. High interest rates appeared to be the only means remaining for defending the currency. Unit labour costs continued to rise faster than in competitor countries as wages outstripped prices and productivity. Private forecasters were universally more pessimistic than the Treasury concerning the size of the balance of payments deficit in 1987, which would be the first in seven years. However, barring external crises—there had been an ominous minirun on the pound during the Conservative Party conference in early October—the medium-term economic forecasts could scarcely be better for a government seeking reelection. The economy was expanding, the consumer boom was continuing, incomes were rising considerably faster than prices, and there were signs that unemployment might be turning down.

Foreign Relations. The year was dominated by the problem of international terrorism and by the growing crisis in South Africa. The U.S. air strike on Libya in April put a severe—if temporary—strain on Anglo-U.S. relations, and there was continuing popular resentment that British collaboration in a mission that could have provoked terrorist reprisals had been rewarded by a general absence of U.S. tourists. In October, following a trial at the central criminal court (the "Old Bailey") in which the Syrian ambassador to the U.S. was implicated in a bomb plot against an Israeli airliner earlier in the year, the government broke off diplomatic relations with Syria and called upon its partners in the European Communities (EC) for general support. At the same time, however, France was dealing with the Syrians and Iranians in an effort to secure the release of French citizens kidnapped in Lebanon. It later transpired that the U.S. had for some time been supplying arms to Iran, its terrorist activities notwithstanding.

President Reagan's "presummit" meeting with Soviet leader Mikhail Gorbachev in Reykjavík, Iceland, in October was another cause of great unease in Europe and especially in London. The president had embraced the idea of a world without nuclear missiles. According to Thatcher and most other European leaders, the presence of nuclear weapons in Europe had deterred the U.S.S.R. from making use of its overwhelming superiority in conventional military might. Moreover, talk of a Europe without missiles undermined the U.K.'s status as a nuclear power, especially at a moment when Thatcher was preparing to fight an election in which the Trident submarine missile, to be purchased from the U.S., was likely to be an important issue. At a meeting with President Reagan in the U.S. in November, Thatcher succeeded in obtaining public assurances on these points. Nevertheless, the Libyan incident, Reykjavík, and U.S. duplicity and incompetence in handling the Iranian affair all added to the strain on transatlantic relations.

In the context of the South African situation the strain fell on the U.K.'s relations within the Commonwealth. From first to last Thatcher was adamantly opposed to sanctions. In light of Commonwealth opinion, the outspoken position she adopted was seen by some as unnecessarily provocative, a view that was said to be shared by Queen Elizabeth, head of the Commonwealth. When senior Commonwealth leaders met in London on August 3, Thatcher made only minimal concessions in her policy. (See *Commonwealth of Nations,* above.)

Northern Ireland. The year was one of smoldering violence during which there was no abatement in Protestant opposition to the Anglo-Irish agreement signed at Hillsborough Castle, County Down, on Nov. 15, 1985. By this historic accord the Republic of Ireland had, in effect, endorsed the union of Northern Ireland with Great Britain in return for a consultative role in the government of the province. Protestant Loyalists at once denounced the accord as the first stage of a conspiracy to bring about the unification of Ireland, and 1986 began with the 15 Northern Irish Protestant MPs in the British Parliament resigning their seats in order to provoke special elections that would serve as a protest against the Hillsborough agreement.

Thereafter a campaign of sullen resistance accompanied by spasmodic violence was maintained, and no progress was made toward the reconciliation of the Roman Catholic and Protestant communities at the expense of the Irish Republican Army (IRA), which had been the political aim of the agreement. Instead, its chief effect was to polarize still further the sectarian politics of the province as Loyalist extremists gained ground at the expense of the more moderate Official Unionists. Peter Robinson (*see* BIOGRAPHIES), deputy leader of the Rev. Ian Paisley's Democratic Unionist Party, held a dominant position in close association with the Ulster Defence Association and Ulster Volunteer Force paramilitary forces. Thus outflanked, the Official Unionists were unable to find any basis on which to resume political dialogue with the U.K. government without seeming to condone its pact with Dublin.

During the year the Hillsborough agreement, which provided for regular meetings of ministers from the two capitals, resulted in some improvement in security cooperation on the border (a British priority) and some largely symbolic steps toward reducing the alienation of the Roman Catholic minority (Ireland's chief concern). Policing and the judicial system were the main items under this latter heading, and steps were taken to establish a better police complaints procedure. The first anniversary of the agreement was accompanied by violence in which two were killed and some 70 injured. (PETER JENKINS)

See also *Commonwealth of Nations,* above; *Dependent States,* below.

VATICAN CITY STATE

The independent sovereignty of Vatican City State is surrounded by but is not part of Rome. As a state with territorial limits, it is properly distinguished from the Holy See, which constitutes the worldwide administrative and legislative body for the Roman Catholic Church. Area: 44 ha (109 ac). Pop. (1986 est.): 750. As sovereign pontiff, John Paul II is the chief of state. Vatican City is administered by a pontifical commission of five cardinals headed by the secretary of state, in 1986 Agostino Cardinal Casaroli.

Two important ecumenical developments took place during 1986. Pope John Paul II's visit to the Jewish synagogue in Rome in April was the first by a Roman Catholic pope. (*See* RELIGION: *Sidebar.*) In October the pope joined leaders and representatives of other major religions in a prayer for peace at Assisi, Italy.

During the year Pope John Paul visited India (January–February), Colombia (July), and France (October); in November he embarked on his longest-ever overseas tour, visiting Australia, New Zealand, the Seychelles, and Fiji and making stopovers in Singapore and Bangladesh. There was renewed speculation about a possible visit to the U.S.S.R. The Holy See expressed its concern for the people of the troubled Middle Eastern countries through two initiatives. Roger Cardinal Etchegaray, president of the Commission for Justice and Peace, went to Iran and Iraq in December 1985–January 1986 to visit prisoners taken in the war between those two countries. The following month Monsignor Achille Silvestrini, secretary of the Council for Public Affairs of the Church, journeyed to Beirut, Lebanon, and to Damascus, Syria.

Among those who were received by the pope in 1986 were Pres. Amin Gemayel of Lebanon; Jeanne Sauvé, governor-general of Canada; U.S. Secretary of State George Shultz; French Foreign Affairs Minister Jean-Bernard Raimond; Chilean Foreign Affairs Minister Jaime del Valle; Chancellor Helmut Kohl of West Germany; and Pres. José Sarney of Brazil. (MAX BERGERRE)

See also Religion: *Roman Catholic Church.*

This article updates the *Micropædia* article VATICAN CITY STATE.

Eastern Europe and the U.S.S.R

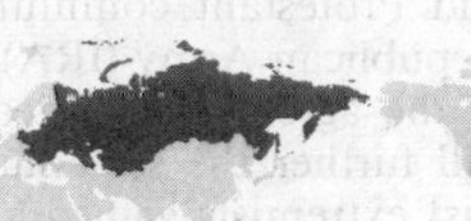

EASTERN EUROPEAN AFFAIRS

Broad trends in Eastern Europe in 1986 continued to be dominated by Soviet initiatives. As the Soviet leadership under Mikhail Gorbachev gradually revealed its international and, equally significantly, its domestic strategy, the Eastern European states were obliged to respond. At the centre of the relationship was the underlying tension between the interests of the Eastern Europeans (as defined by them) and those of the Soviet Union and the Eastern bloc (as defined by the Kremlin). Where state interests conflicted with bloc interests, the protagonists of the former had to struggle hard to validate them. The trend under Gorbachev was not wholly explicit, but there was evidence of Soviet distrust of closer links between individual Eastern European states and the West, together with dislike of any hard bargaining by Eastern Europeans with the Soviet Union over economic issues. A case in point was the price of Soviet oil. As world oil prices plummeted, the Soviet price was not adjusted or was adjusted only marginally, leaving the weaker Eastern Europeans with a serious debt problem. The Soviet Union professed to be uninterested.

A major development in this process was the December 1985 meeting of the CMEA (Council for Mutual Economic Assistance; Comecon) Council, which approved a new program for the next 15 years. For years there had been palpable drift in the CMEA; under Gorbachev there was movement in the direction of tighter constraints and tougher measures to modernize member states' economies. The broad objectives were to free the CMEA from its reliance on Western technology, to double productivity by 2000, to reduce energy consumption, and, in general, to shift toward a more modern production profile.

International economic integration dominated the hastily convened CMEA summit in November 1986. In essence, the Soviet Union seemed reluctant to continue its existing role of supplying raw materials to Eastern Europe in exchange for low-grade manufactured goods. At the same time, the Eastern Europeans were dissatisfied with adverse terms of trade (*i.e.,* the rising cost of Soviet deliveries) and exploitation of their economic vulnerability. Their underlying anxiety, that they would be cut off from access to Western technology by Soviet requirements, undoubtedly informed the discussions, which were described as "frank," the usual euphemism for discord in the Soviet world. The Eastern Europeans preferred to sell the small amount of goods of world market quality that they manufactured for hard currency, rather than to the Soviet Union. The outcome of the summit was a compromise of sorts. Closer international links were to be forged at the enterprise level, so that better consultation would bring about an improvement in the quality of Eastern European manufactures. But this was certain to mean growing Soviet preeminence, not least because CMEA exchanges were ultimately determined not by market criteria but by political power.

The need for modern technology was self-evident. Large tracts of Soviet and Eastern European industry were incapable of competing by world market standards. What was worse, they were being overtaken by later entrants to the club of industrialized nations, such as Taiwan, South Korea, and Singapore. Yet there was virtually no evidence that the Eastern European nations were ready to integrate the revolution in information technology into their economic, social, and, ultimately, political fabrics. Attitudes toward the challenge posed by information technology varied from complacency to noncomprehension, occasionally laced with fear that the far wider access to information required would undermine the existing distribution of power. The auguries were not favourable. Too many factors—a one-sided political power structure, conservatism, aversion to risk taking—inhibited the potential of information technology in Eastern Europe. The alternatives pointed toward growing irrelevance for the CMEA in world terms, since its products—apart from raw materials and food—would find no external markets.

Analogous themes were raised at the February congress of the Communist Party of the Soviet Union, where integration of the bloc economies and the diminishing of ideological differences received clear emphasis. Gorbachev's chosen instrument for achieving these aims was the holding of regular, all but continuous meetings of high-level representatives of all bloc countries. Notably, he argued that the ideas of socialism should be tested against the experience of not one but several states. At the congress of the Polish party in June, he added that there were traps for the unwary in trading with the West, above all that of dependence. The implication was that such contacts should be developed under a joint framework. Although it was still difficult to discern Gorbachev's vision of future patterns of development, there was evidence that he was looking for greater integration, greater discipline, tighter constraints, and fewer deviations from the line than had been the case in the previous few years.

The Eastern Europeans, who had become used to a fair degree of de facto autonomy in the late Brezhnev years, were not overwhelmingly enthusiastic about the Gorbachev strategy. The evidence of the past—not to mention the Soviet-Eastern European structural disparities—suggested that, all too often, so-called bloc interests would be little more than Soviet interests writ large. But any misgivings they may have had were kept private.

These misgivings may have multiplied in light of the Chernobyl disaster. Publicly all the Eastern European states held the line—that the explosion in the Chernobyl nuclear power plant was of no great significance, that everything was under control, that any countermeasures were a matter of caution, and that no changes would be made in nuclear programs—but in reality reactions varied from barely concealed anger in Poland to complacency in Bulgaria. At the very least, it was suggested unofficially in Poland, what kind of an alliance is the Warsaw Pact when one ally (the Soviet Union) fails to inform another (Poland) of a civilian nuclear accident; what would happen in the event of some similar military development?

Finally, there was an unprecedented initiative among the opposition movements of four Eastern European countries. Activists from Hungary, Czechoslovakia, East Gemany, and Poland (to which a few names from Romania were added later) signed a document proclaiming that the values of the 1956 revolution in Hungary—self-government, independence, and pluralism—were still valid. This initiative, which had been launched in Hungary, was unique in attracting support from so many Eastern European states. It marked the first time the human rights opposition in East Germany had joined with other like-minded groups in the area and showed its readiness to move from "peace-oriented" issues to a broader opposition.

(GEORGE SCHÖPFLIN)

See also Economic Affairs; Military Affairs.

ALBANIA

A socialist republic in the western Balkan Peninsula of southeastern Europe, Albania is situated on the Adriatic Sea. Area: 28,748 sq km (11,100 sq mi). Pop. (1986 est.): 3,020,000. Cap.: Tirane. Monetary unit: lek, with (Oct. 1, 1986) a free rate of 6.99 leks to U.S. $1 (10.10 leks = £1 sterling). First secretary of the Albanian (Communist) Party of Labour and chairman of the Presidium of the People's Assembly (president) in 1986, Ramiz Alia; chairman of the Council of Ministers (premier), Adil Carcani.

The ninth congress of the Albanian (Communist) Party of Labour was held Nov. 3–8, 1986, in Tirane, with some 700 delegates present. Ramiz Alia, the party's first secretary, opened the session by pledging unswerving commitment to the ideals of the late leader Enver Hoxha. The congress accepted the five-year (1986–90) plan setting out growth targets of 40% in industry and 30% in agriculture. Alia was reelected, and a new Central Committee was chosen which, in turn, elected a 13-member Politburo.

In terms of Albania's relations with the outside world, the most significant event of 1986 was the opening on August 6 of the railway linking Shkoder, in northwestern Albania, with Titograd, Yugos., providing Albania with access to the European rail network. The construction of the Albanian section of the line had been completed in December 1984. Work on the stretch between Titograd and the border, however, had been interrupted following the 1981 outburst of nationalism among ethnic Albanians in the Yugoslavian province of Kosovo, which had soured relations between Belgrade and Tirane.

Previously Albania had not been completely isolated. Airlines from Switzerland, Hungary, Romania, Greece, and Yugoslavia had been permitted to make once-weekly flights to Tirane, and a ferry service operated between Durres and Trieste, Italy. But the new link, at first used to carry freight only, was expected to provide a faster and cheaper route for the country's increasing trade with Europe.

(K. M. SMOGORZEWSKI)

BULGARIA

The socialist republic of Bulgaria is on the eastern Balkan Peninsula of southeastern Europe, along the Black Sea. Area: 110,912 sq km (42,823 sq mi). Pop. (1986 est.): 8,970,000. Cap.: Sofia. Monetary unit: lev, with (Oct. 1, 1986) a free rate of 0.93 lev to U.S. $1 (1.34 leva = £1 sterling). General secretary of the Bulgarian Communist Party and chairman of the State Council (president) in 1986, Todor Zhivkov; chairmen of the Council of Ministers (premiers), Grisha Filipov and, from March 21, Georgy Atanasov.

The 13th congress of the Bulgarian Communist Party (BCP), held April 2–5, 1986, in Sofia, was attended by over 2,600 party delegates as well as representatives of Communist parties and other organizations from over 100 countries. The Soviet delegation was led by Nikolay Ryzhkov, chairman of the Council of Ministers (premier) of the U.S.S.R. Todor Zhivkov, general secretary of the BCP since 1954, addressed the congress with a call for a new style of management and greater emphasis on technological innovation in the economy. Adopting a "gorbachevist" approach, he blamed managers for covering up weaknesses and failures and attacked a rising tide of absenteeism and lack of order and discipline. Since mid-1985 industrial and agricultural output had suffered badly as a result of unusually harsh weather conditions and a severe energy crisis.

The congress elected a new Central Committee, which in turn reelected the 75-year-old Zhivkov as general secretary and returned an unchanged Politburo and Secretariat. Two weeks before the congress, Grisha Filipov was replaced as premier by Georgy Atanasov, who was, at the same time, promoted from candidate (nonvoting) to full Politburo membership. In general elections to fill the 400-seat National Assembly on June 8, all candidates were approved by the Fatherland Front. (For tabulated results, see *Political Parties,* above.)

In March 1986 the trial in Rome of three Bulgarians and three Turks on charges of conspiracy to assassinate Pope John Paul II on May 13, 1981, ended with the acquittal of the defendants. The prosecution's principal witness was Mehmet Ali Agca, already serving a life sentence for his part in the attempt on the pontiff's life. His statements proved to be a mixture of apparent fact and complete fiction, with the result that the so-called Bulgarian connection was ruled "not proven." After the trial Sergey Antonov, a Bulgarian Airlines official arrested by the Italian authorities in November 1982, returned to Bulgaria to rejoin his two compatriots, who had been tried in absentia.

(K. M. SMOGORZEWSKI)

CZECHOSLOVAKIA

The federal socialist republic of Czechoslovakia is a landlocked state of central Europe. Area: 127,903 sq km (49,384 sq mi). Pop. (1986 est.): 15,550,000. Cap.: Prague. Monetary unit: koruna, with (Oct. 1, 1986) a commercial rate of 5.75 koruny to U.S. $1 (8.31 koruny = £1 sterling). General secretary of the Communist Party of Czechoslovakia and president in 1985, Gustav Husak; federal premier, Lubomir Strougal.

For the first time in several years, the atmosphere in Czechoslovakia in 1986 seemed subtly different, as if the long-standing political, economic, and social logjam might be on the verge of breaking up. There were no spectacular outward signs of such a change, but the expression of ideas in public appeared a shade less rigid and the regime commensurately more open to new ideas.

The main political event of the year was the 17th congress of the ruling Communist Party, held at the end of March. It produced no surprises. No major reform initiative was promised, but unease about the condition of the party did result in the launching of the idea of "activism." The party leader, the aging Gustav Husak, announced that it was time for party members to prepare themselves for new tasks, notably in the economy. In all probability, the pressure for greater effectiveness emanating from the Soviet Union under Mikhail Gorbachev had reached Prague. Presumably the Czechoslovak leadership was aware of the dilemma this presented. No change at all would be increasingly costly economically; too much change would have serious consequences for political stability. Husak's answer was on the conservative side. "Activism" was to be understood as not much more than another in the endless series of exhortatory mobilization campaigns.

Rather more interesting was the performance of the premier, Lubomir Strougal, who sketched Czechoslovakia's economic prospects up to the year 2000 and introduced a program of "intensification" in the economy. Although in many ways the country's economy and standard of living were superior to those of most other members of the Council for Mutual Economic Assistance, some slippage was becoming perceptible. Intensification was the preferred answer. This concept was close to Gorbachev-style streamlining, making the system function more effectively in its current parameters, with no radical adoption of market principles although some moves in that direction would not be excluded.

Strougal as much as admitted that the achievements of

the previous five years had been modest and that much activity had come to nothing as a result of incompetence and half-hearted compromises. He seemed to be arguing in favour of far-reaching systemic changes in the running of the economy, though in what direction was left vague. If these changes, and especially the necessary transformation in working and planning methods, were implemented, Strougal held out the promise of 18–19% growth of national income over the next five-year plan period. The main objective of the next three five-year plans (1986–2000) was to shift the main focus of Czechoslovak industry away from energy- and raw-materials-intensive industries (like heavy electrical machinery) and toward electronics and small-bulk chemicals. There could be no disguising the difficulties of such a move.

Other speakers at the congress revealed many of the negative aspects of the Czechoslovak system. There were extensive shortcomings in the work of party and state bodies, serious deficiencies in the performance of leading officials, and too many promotions of unsuitable people. Some observers pointed out that the hard-liners remained relatively silent at the congress, implying perhaps that their views would be less dominant in the coming years.

In common with other Central European countries, Czechoslovakia was one of the victims of the aftereffects of the nuclear power plant catastrophe at Chernobyl in the Ukraine. The official media minimized it, following the Soviet line closely, and, in contrast to the reporting in Poland, little or no technical and medical information was made available. Part of Czechoslovakia's problem was its own reliance on nuclear energy and the fact that its nuclear energy program had been built with Soviet help.

The popular mood in Czechoslovakia was surveyed by a group of social scientists, working without official permission, who published their results in France. Among the more striking results were findings that in a free election the Communist Party would receive 14% of the vote, that a Social Democratic identification attracted considerable support, and that religion continued to be a viable option for around a third of respondents (if Slovak results had been included, the figure would have been higher).

Environmental deterioration, which had been a source of mounting alarm both to unofficial domestic observers and to experts abroad, was beginning to receive attention in the official media. The party's position was largely to deny that Czechoslovak economic activity generated any pollution and to argue that other (*i.e.,* Western) countries were responsible. It was pointed out that at least 30% of the population of the Czech lands and 16% of Slovakia suffered from the harmful effects of air pollution (resulting mostly from combustion processes and traffic); that 54% of agricultural land was threatened by erosion and acid rain; and that solid wastes were accumulating far beyond the ability of recycling programs to deal with them.

The Charter 77 opposition continued its activities during the year. A number of documents were issued, notably on the peace process in Europe, control of employment by the state, how the secret police organized itself, and the philosophy of the Charter. Official repression of unorthodoxy fell with particular vehemence on the Jazz Section of the Union of Czech Musicians, a haven for a wide range of pop and rock music activities with some links to the Charter. In September the offices of the Section were closed down, and key figures were arrested. Several Czechoslovak activists signed a four-country declaration on the 30th anniversary of the Hungarian revolution in October 1956, and contacts were also maintained with Polish opposition groups.

(GEORGE SCHÖPFLIN)

GERMAN DEMOCRATIC REPUBLIC

A socialist republic, the German Democratic Republic (East Germany) is in central Europe on the Baltic Sea. Area: 108,333 sq km (41,827 sq mi). Pop. (1986 est.): 16,640,000. Cap.: Berlin (East). Monetary unit: Mark of Deutsche Demokratische Republik, with (Oct. 1, 1986) a free rate of M 2.03 to U.S. $1 (M 2.93 = £1 sterling). General secretary of the Socialist Unity (Communist) Party and chairman of the Council of State (president) in 1986, Erich Honecker; chairman of the Council of Ministers (premier), Willi Stoph.

In 1986 East Germany strengthened its position as the most successful economy in the Eastern bloc. The country's leader, Erich Honecker, told the congress of his Socialist Unity (Communist) Party in April that the economy had been growing steadily for 15 years, bringing a corresponding improvement in living standards. Few countries in the world, he claimed, could show more dynamic economic development. He attributed much of the growth to improvements in productivity, which had been brought about by the introduction of high technology. He highlighted better working conditions, which included a 40-hour week for shift workers and for mothers with at least two children. The minimum holiday entitlement had risen to three weeks and three days a year. Nearly five million women were in full-time employment, more than 90% of the female population of working age.

The new five-year (1986–90) plan was announced. It envisaged economic growth of 24–26% over the plan period, with industrial output rising by slightly less. Wages were planned to rise 21–22%. Emphasis was placed on improving social conditions. To stimulate an increase in the declining population, working mothers were to be given a year away from work with pay following the birth of a first child. The shortage of housing was to be solved by 1990, with over a million more apartments scheduled for construction or modernization by that time. At the closing session the party congress elected its Central Committee, which then elected the Politburo with its 22 full members and 5 candidate members. Honecker announced that he had been reelected as party general secretary.

The June 8 elections to the 500-seat Volkskammer (People's Chamber) were remarkable only for the lack of change they reflected. There were 703 candidates contesting the seats, and the 203 who were unsuccessful were made reserve deputies. The 25-member Council of State (Staatsrat), which had presidential powers, was approved unchanged on June 17.

Though Honecker could boast about economic achievements, his country's all-important relationship with the U.S.S.R. appeared to have weakened since Mikhail Gorbachev came to power in March 1985. The pace of improvement in East Germany's relations with West Germany, from which much of its economic success was derived, was thought to be a cause of concern to the U.S.S.R. For nearly two years Honecker had been planning to visit West Germany, but it was believed the Soviet leader did not approve and was suspicious about the special relationship between the two Germanys. Honecker nurtured ties with Bonn, but political pressure led him to declare that West Germany's pro-U.S. policy was likely to jeopardize its chances of improving relations with the Communist states.

The year saw a breakthrough in relations with China and, more important, the establishment of party links between the two countries when Honecker made a six-day visit to China in October. East Germany was the first Warsaw Pact country to restore relations with the Chinese

Communist Party. This occurred at a time when relations between the U.S.S.R. and China were visibly thawing, and it had the tacit approval of Gorbachev. However, the Chinese Communist Party continued to express its desire for diplomatic and party relations with Eastern European countries, "independent of the U.S.S.R."

Both German states commemorated, in greatly different ways, the 25th anniversary of the building of the Berlin Wall on August 13. In East Berlin Honecker attended a military parade. In West Berlin a ceremony took place in the old Reichstag building where Chancellor Helmut Kohl condemned the Wall as "this monument to inhumanity."

In May the East German Foreign Ministry informed all embassies in East Berlin that personnel would have to show passports before crossing into West Berlin instead of the usual identity cards. In the West the move was interpreted as another East German attempt to show that Berlin was its capital city. The West continued to contend that East Berlin was a city occupied by the four victorious powers in World War II, and that the eastern half was merely the Soviet sector of occupation. West German diplomats based in East Berlin refused to show passports and were not allowed entry to East Germany. Although the new "regulations" were supposed to apply to them, British, U.S., and French diplomats were permitted to cross the border without having to show passports. The U.S. protested to the U.S.S.R., and the requirement was retracted.

East Germany continued to demonstrate its individuality and detachment from the U.S.S.R. Honecker informed a Swedish newspaper that his country had changed its view of some historic events. In particular, it was now accepted that there had been widespread resistance to the Nazis and Hitler, by non-Communists as well as Communists.

The more liberal approach of the government was reflected in public behaviour. Following the accident at the Chernobyl nuclear power plant in the Ukraine, there were protests and petitions demanding a halt to nuclear programs. Workers who went on strike went unpunished; they wanted part of their wages in West German marks so they could buy goods made in the West. These were increasingly available but could be purchased only with "hard currency"—expensively bought on the black market.

(NORMAN CROSSLAND)

This article updates the *Macropædia* article GERMANY: *German Democratic Republic.*

ANNA CLOPET/USN&WR

A divided birthday cake and other graffiti adorning the Berlin Wall proclaim birthday wishes for the famed East-West divider, built 25 years earlier to deter the thousands of people per day who were attempting to leave East Berlin.

HUNGARY

A socialist republic, Hungary is a landlocked state in central Europe. Area: 93,036 sq km (35,921 sq mi). Pop. (1986 est.): 10,624,000. Cap.: Budapest. Monetary unit: forint, with (Oct. 1, 1986) a free rate of 46.69 forints to U.S. $1 (67.47 forints = £1 sterling). General secretary of the Hungarian Socialist Workers' (Communist) Party in 1986, Janos Kadar; chairman of the Presidential Council (chief of state), Pal Losonczi; chairman of the Council of Ministers (prime minister), Gyorgy Lazar.

On Oct. 23, 1956, a national uprising aimed at ending the Leninist-Stalinist political system erupted in Budapest. On October 30 Imre Nagy, a former premier, formed a government, and two days later he declared Hungary neutral by announcing its withdrawal from the Warsaw Pact. By November 4 the most important armed revolt against Communist rule had been crushed, with much loss of life, following the intervention of Soviet armoured divisions. Janos Kadar had been minister of home affairs in Nagy's government for the first two days of its existence before he formed a separate government and asked for support from the U.S.S.R. In the aftermath of the uprising he came to power as first secretary (later general secretary) of the Hungarian Socialist Workers' (Communist) Party.

Thirty years later Kadar's regime allowed no official ceremonies to mark the anniversary. Hungarian press reports emphasized that Hungarian and Soviet armed forces had cooperated in bringing the "counterrevolution" to an end. No mention was permitted of a proclamation issued in West Berlin by over 100 prominent dissidents from Hungary, Poland, East Germany, and Czechoslovakia to mark the anniversary. The anniversary was widely noted in the West. U.S. Pres. Ronald Reagan paid homage to the "shining example of idealism, patriotism, and sheer courage of the Hungarian revolution." At the same time, the British newspaper *The Guardian* commented that "there can be no doubt that Kadar has achieved a popular support which most European leaders can only dream of."

Figures released in February 1986 revealed that Hungary had failed to achieve a number of economic targets set in its sixth five-year (1981–85) plan. During that period national income (or gross national product) rose by 7%, compared with the plan target of 14 to 17%, and industrial output increased by 12%, compared with a 19–22% target. The seventh five-year (1986–90) plan, approved in December 1985, placed emphasis on technological improvements and modernization as well as encouraging economic growth.

The economy had performed particularly poorly in 1985, when industrial output rose by less than 1%. In an effort to reduce the country's hard-currency debt, the government had attempted to encourage an increase in exports and a reduction in imports. In 1985, however, while exports to other members of the Council for Mutual Economic Assistance showed a surplus, hard-currency exports fell. Hungary aimed to achieve a surplus of $350 million to $400 million in exports to Western countries in 1986. Hopes of meeting the target were diminished when agricultural output was badly hit by a severe drought. At the end of the year Laszlo Marothy, a former deputy prime minister, replaced Lajos Fulevegi as president of the National Planning Office, and Peter Medgyessy succeeded Istvan Hetenyi as finance minister. It was announced that as of Jan. 1, 1987, five profit-oriented banks would take over the management of state enterprise accounts.

Pres. Kenan Evren of Turkey and Soviet leader Mikhail Gorbachev visited Hungary in June 1986. In the course of an interview with *Time* magazine in August, Kadar commented on Hungary's relations with the U.S.S.R.: "Many things we do in this country Gorbachev cannot accept, which is quite understandable. The conditions and possibilities of the Soviet Union are quite different from ours. I can definitely say the Soviets understand and appreciate that we search for new solutions to present problems." The four-day visit by Pres. Richard von Weizsäcker to Hungary in October was the first by a West German head of state. Pal Losonczi, the chairman of the Presidential Council, paid a state visit to Finland in May.

Laszlo Cardinal Lekai (*see* OBITUARIES), the Roman Catholic primate of Hungary, died on June 30 at the age of 76. (K. M. SMOGORZEWSKI)

POLAND

A socialist republic of eastern Europe, Poland is on the Baltic Sea. Area: 312,683 sq km (120,727 sq mi). Pop. (1986 est.): 37,446,000. Cap.: Warsaw. Monetary unit: zloty, with (Oct. 1, 1986) an official rate of 199.60 zlotys to U.S. $1 (288.42 zlotys = £1 sterling). First secretary of the Polish United Workers' (Communist) Party and chairman of the Council of State (chief of state) in 1986, Gen Wojciech Jaruzelski; chairman of the Council of Ministers (premier), Zbigniew Messner.

The tenth congress of the Polish United Workers' (Communist) Party (PUWP) took place in Warsaw from June 30 to July 3, 1986. It was attended by 1,776 delegates representing just over 2,125,000 party members. The total membership of the party had declined by more than 600,000 since the ninth (extraordinary) PUWP congress, held in July 1981. Between August 1980 and December 1981, when Gen. Wojciech Jaruzelski, the PUWP first secretary, declared martial law, some 800,000 members had either resigned or been expelled.

The 1986 congress elected a new 230-member Central Committee (CC), which in turn selected the Politburo (of 15 full and 5 candidate members) and the Secretariat (of 10 secretaries, in addition to the first secretary). There was a high turnover of personnel. More than three-quarters of the CC members were new. Among the full Politburo members, five had previously been candidate members and four were new faces, while four candidate members and three secretaries were new appointments. Jaruzelski, Jozef Czyrek, Zbigniew Messner, Tadeusz Porebski, and Marian Wozniak (all elected in 1981) and Kazimierz Barcikowski (elected in 1980) retained their places as full Politburo members. In all, the posts in the three national policy-making bodies—the full and candidate Politburo and the Secretariat—were filled by 25 people, among them four generals: Jaruzelski himself, Florian Siwicki (also minister of national defense), Czeslaw Kiszczak (also minister of home affairs), and Jozef Baryla. In his address to the CC, Jaruzelski affirmed that Poland today was a different country from the Poland of five years earlier. He claimed: "Today, the strength of the authorities is no longer measured by the number of weakened opponents, but by the number of supporters won."

The congress was attended by delegations from other Communist parties, most notably a strong Soviet contingent headed by Mikhail Gorbachev, general secretary of the Communist Party of the Soviet Union. In his address to the congress, Gorbachev expressed "the sincere respect that the Soviet Communists have for their Polish associates and comrades." He also congratulated the PUWP for having "repulsed the enemies of socialism"—a reference to the banned trade-union movement Solidarnosc (Solidarity).

During the year there were a number of changes in the Council of Ministers. In July Bazyli Samojlik replaced Stanislaw Nieckarz as finance minister, and Jerzy Bajszczak succeeded Jozef Niewiadomski as minister of construction, regional planning, and municipal economy. In September Jan Szlachta (mining and energy) and Aleksander Krawczuk (culture and arts) entered the Council of Ministers in place of Czeslaw Piotrowski and Kazimierz Zygulski, respectively.

In an unexpected move, announced on September 10, the government freed all 225 political prisoners in the country, including Solidarity leader Zbigniew Bujak (*see* BIOGRAPHIES), who had been arrested in May after evading the authorities for almost five years. While Solidarity leaders expressed their jubilation, Home Affairs Minister Kiszczak's statement made it apparent that the government now regarded Solidarity as irrelevant. In February the government dropped court action against Solidarity leader Lech Walesa, who had been accused of slandering state officials after the October 1985 general election.

Among non-Communist Poles a debate was developing about what kind of freedom was both feasible and worth fighting for in Poland. On October 26 the Catholic *Tygodnik Powszechny* ("Universal Weekly") published a declaration signed by several well-known Catholics and a number of Solidarity leaders, including Walesa. The document stressed the view that the most urgent problem facing Poland was the revival of the national economy and that outside assistance from both Western and Eastern countries would be required.

On August 21, when asked why the U.S.S.R. occupied the dominant position among Poland's trading partners, Foreign Trade Minister Jerzy Urban replied that this was the result of the policy of Western powers, particularly the imposition of economic sanctions. Although some sanctions had been revoked following the lifting of martial law in July 1983, two remained: the suspension of Poland's most-favoured-nation trading status and the freeze on new credits. In the period 1980–85 Poland was granted credits amounting to 4.8 billion rubles by the U.S.S.R.

During a three-day visit to Poland in October, Soviet Premier Nikolay Ryzhkov and his Polish counterpart, Zbigniew Messner, signed three agreements on Polish-Soviet industrial collaboration. At the same time, the Polish and Soviet ministers of foreign trade signed three protocols on trading cooperation until the year 2000. The inauguration of a sea and rail link between Klaipeda in Lithuania, U.S.S.R., and Rugen Island, East Germany, which thus bypassed Poland, had serious repercussions for Poland's transport revenue. Previously all freight and passengers traveling by train between East Germany and the U.S.S.R. had passed through Poland.

During 1986 Jaruzelski accepted two invitations rarely proffered to Polish leaders. In February he traveled to Lithuania, and in September he became the first Polish leader in 27 years to visit China. During his three-day visit he discussed Sino-Polish political and economic relations with Chinese elder statesman Deng Xiaoping (Teng Hsiao-p'ing) and Premier Zhao Ziyang (Chao Tzu-yang). Late in the year Archbishop Francesco Cola-suonno of the Roman Curia arrived in Warsaw to arrange details of a visit by Pope John Paul II to Poland in the summer of 1987.

Premier Messner presented the government report on the economy to the PUWP congress on June 30. He reported that targets set in the three-year (1983–85) plan had been

Polish children drink doses of an iodine preparation, intended to prevent thyroid damage, part of a government-sponsored precautionary measure spurred by detection of radioactive fallout—and fear of its possible effects—from the Chernobyl reactor explosion.
UPI/BETTMANN NEWSPHOTOS

met. During that period national income had increased by 15%, compared with the plan target of 10%, while inflation had fallen from 23% in 1983 to 14.7% in 1985. While exports to socialist countries had risen, those to Western countries were below expectations. The zloty was devalued in February and September 1986 in an effort to boost exports. The socioeconomic five-year (1986–90) plan, which placed emphasis on improving productivity and speeding up modernization, was approved by the Council of Ministers in September. In June Poland joined both the International Monetary Fund and the World Bank. During the year Poland reached agreement with both government and commercial bank creditors on debt rescheduling.

(K. M. SMOGORZEWSKI)

ROMANIA

A socialist republic on the Balkan Peninsula in southeastern Europe, Romania has a coastline on the Black Sea. Area: 237,500 sq km (91,699 sq mi). Pop. (1986 est.): 22,808,000. Cap.: Bucharest. Monetary unit: leu, with (Oct. 1, 1986) a commercial rate of 10.71 lei to U.S. $1 (15.48 lei = £1 sterling). General secretary of the Romanian Communist Party, president of the republic, and president of the State Council in 1986, Nicolae Ceausescu; chairman of the Council of Ministers (prime minister), Constantin Dascalescu.

During 1986 Romania's relations with the U.S.S.R. improved. Pres. Nicolae Ceausescu made two visits to Moscow and on each occasion was warmly welcomed by Soviet leader Mikhail Gorbachev. The visits followed an important trade agreement signed in December 1985 whereby the U.S.S.R. was to increase oil supplies to Romania by 250% over the period 1986–90 as part of a general accord increasing bilateral trade by 70%. Domestic fuel shortages had become a problem for Romania, which until 1975 had been a net exporter of oil. By 1986, however, its reserves were seriously depleted, and output had fallen dramatically. A further agreement signed between the two countries in May provided for the development of economic, scientific, and technical cooperation until the end of the century. The U.S.S.R. also supported Romania's proposals for the Balkans to be designated a nuclear- and chemical weapons-free zone. Romania served as host to two important international Communist meetings in Bucharest during the year: in October a meeting of Warsaw Treaty foreign ministers and in November the 42nd meeting of the Council for Mutual Economic Assistance (Comecon).

In August there was a Cabinet reshuffle affecting key ministers. Although no reason was given for the changes, they were widely believed to be in response to the poor trade performance; in 1985 this had shown little change from 1984 and, in hard currency terms, had declined. As a result, foreign debt to the West totaled $6.6 billion in August. President Ceausescu pledged to pay the debt by 1990. The new foreign minister was Ioan Totu, the deputy prime minister who represented Romania at Comecon and who had negotiated the earlier economic agreements with the U.S.S.R. He replaced Ilie Vaduva, who was given the foreign trade and economic cooperation portfolio; Vaduva was a member of the Central Committee and formerly an academic specializing in economics. Cornel Pacoste replaced Totu as deputy prime minister. Finance Minister Petre Gigea was replaced by Alexandru Babe.

The mixed economic performance in 1986 reflected the fact that the country's reserves were run down; Western bankers agreed to reschedule $880 million of debt due in 1986 and 1987. Nevertheless, Ceausescu continued his ambitious plan of modernization. The prestigious Danube-Black Sea canal, opened in May 1984, had carried 6,000 vessels by August 1986. A new road and rail bridge opened in May 1986; crossing the Danube River near Fetesti, it brought to three the links with the (Romanian-Bulgarian) Dobruja region and provided the first direct road link between Bucharest and Constanta. A new branch of the canal was under construction linking Poarta Alba on the main Danube-Black Sea canal to Navodari on the Black Sea coast. Although the 1986 trade performance was poor, industrial output was estimated to have risen 7%, and there was a record grain harvest of 28 million metric tons.

In February King Michael I of Romania, who had been in forced exile since December 1947, was interviewed on Radio Free Europe. He stated that the rulers of Romania were not representing the people's wishes and that he would return to Romania when the regime collapsed.

In an unprecedented act of public participation, 99.99% of those eligible voted in a national referendum on November 23 to approve a 5% cut in defense expenditures that would reduce Romania's 190,000 armed forces by 10,000. Although the referendum had little significance—the defense cuts had already been approved—it demonstrated Ceausescu's determination "to consult the people." Within Western diplomatic circles the move was interpreted as an effort by Ceausescu to demonstrate that the whole nation supported his regime's stance of independence from Moscow.

(K. M. SMOGORZEWSKI)

UNION OF SOVIET SOCIALIST REPUBLICS

The Union of Soviet Socialist Republics is a federal state covering parts of eastern Europe and northern Asia. Area: 22,402,200 sq km (8,649,500 sq mi). Pop (1986 est.): 280 million. Cap.: Moscow. Monetary unit: ruble, with (Oct. 1, 1986) a free rate of 0.68 ruble to U.S. $1 (0.98 ruble = £1 sterling). General secretary of the Communist Party of the Soviet Union in 1986, Mikhail S. Gorbachev; chairman of the Presidium of the Supreme Soviet (president), Andrey A. Gromyko; chairman of the Council of Ministers (premier), Nikolay I. Ryzhkov.

Domestic Affairs. The year 1986 was dominated by three events: the 27th congress of the Communist Party of the Soviet Union (CPSU) in February–March, the explosion at the Chernobyl nuclear power plant in April, and the meeting of General Secretary Mikhail Gorbachev and U.S. Pres. Ronald Reagan in Reykjavík, Iceland, in October.

Gorbachev excelled at the party congress, which was attended by nearly 5,000 delegates. On the first day, February 25, he delivered the keynote speech. He spoke for almost six hours and portrayed himself as the national leader the country had lacked since the late 1970s. He was present during all nine days of the congress—held once every five years—but spoke only on the first and last days. In his speech Gorbachev expounded on the deficiencies of the Soviet system and claimed that when he came to power the economy and society were stagnant. He stated that the U.S.S.R. was a superpower but questioned whether it would still be one in the year 2000. It would, he said, but only if scientific-technical progress was accelerated and labour productivity improved. Gorbachev maintained that in foreign affairs the years before 1985 had been marked by diplomatic defeats. He asked why the optimism of the early 1970s, when the U.S.S.R. had achieved parity with the U.S. in armaments, had given way to pessimism a decade later. In answer he gave three main reasons. First, the bureaucracy was overburdened and quite incapable of administering the country; planning had to be streamlined and enterprises permitted to take more decisions. Second, scientific-technical progress was too slow. And finally, corruption had become so endemic that it was a national scandal, with many party officials using their offices for personal gain.

Premier Nikolay Ryzhkov delivered the main economic report. He continued the criticism begun by the general secretary, admonishing ministries and enterprises for wasting vast quantities of resources. Nevertheless, he outlined the country's prospects in the most ambitious terms, envisioning a doubling of national income and industrial output by the end of the century.

Great interest centred on the election of the new Central Committee (CC), which turned out to be smaller (307 full members) than the previous one elected at the 26th congress in 1981 (319 full members). If candidate (nonvoting) members were included, however, the new CC was larger than the old one. Despite the replacement of many government and party officials, 59.2% of the new CC had previously been full members. There was a slight decline in the proportion of members from government, compared with 1981, but overall the functional elites retained their relative positions, with party officials occupying about half the seats. The new CC was not markedly more youthful; 40% of the full members were over 60 (compared with 53% in 1981).

The first task of the new CC was to elect a new Politburo and Secretariat. There was at least one vacancy in the Politburo because Viktor Grishin, Gorbachev's challenger for supreme office in March 1985, had been dropped from the Politburo just before the congress. But the new 12-member Politburo that emerged included only one new full member, Lev Zaikov (62 years), CC secretary for defense industries. Two new candidate members were elected, and five new CC secretaries appeared in the Secretariat. The average age of Politburo full members was 64 years, of candidate members 62 years, and of the CC Secretariat 60 years. Of the 26 members of the party leadership only one, Georgy Razumovsky, was younger than Gorbachev. There was considerable racial imbalance in the leadership, which consisted of 19 Russians, 3 Belorussians, a Ukrainian, an Azerbaijani, a Kazakh, and a Georgian.

Before and during the congress the problem of corruption was discussed. So serious was it that Gorbachev, Egor Ligachev, the "second" secretary, and Boris Eltsin, the Moscow party leader, underlined that "social justice" had to be one of the party's primary goals. Social instability could result unless the abuse of privilege and position by officials was ended. More openness (*glasnost*) was needed, and the party had to criticize itself. This was necessary, as Gorbachev put it in a speech after the congress, because there was no opposition party in the U.S.S.R.

The process of the restructuring (*perestroika*) of the economy and society continued, especially in regard to top officials. By November 55% of the heads of CC departments in the Secretariat had been replaced since Gorbachev took over in March 1985. Corresponding figures for the Soviet government were 47%, for *oblast* (provincial) first secretaries 31%, and for first secretaries of the republics 28%. But turnover of personnel was more rapid at the centre than at the periphery. It was notable that during the first 20 months of the Brezhnev era (October 1964–June 1966), 45% of officials were replaced, compared with 58% during Gorbachev's first 20 months in office. The new appointees under Brezhnev had also been younger when they were appointed than were Gorbachev's new recruits.

Gorbachev was not completely at ease with the military. At the party congress he stressed that security was "becoming more and more a political task, which could be achieved only by political means." The time had come, he said, to "place interstate relations on a base other than armaments." Anatoly Dobrynin, the chief architect of the new political thinking in foreign affairs, went further and wrote in *Kommunist,* the party's theoretical journal, that modern weapons did not "afford any state the hope of defending itself by military-technical means only, by building the most powerful defense." National security and "international security had become inseparable concepts." Thus, the Brezhnev emphasis on equating the "progress of socialism" with the "correlation of forces" had been officially abandoned.

Gorbachev extended the moratorium banning the testing of nuclear weapons until Jan. 1, 1987. Gen. Nikolay Chervov of the General Staff and Marshal Sergey Akhromeyev, chief of the General Staff, both pointed out in articles that the Soviet Union was paying a price in doing so and that the decision on the test ban had been a difficult one, making it clear that there was disagreement between the military and political leaderships. In December a statement released by the new agency TASS said the U.S.S.R. would resume testing as soon as the U.S. conducted its first test of the new year.

Changes in the top military leadership continued as Gen. Pyotr Lushev, formerly commander in chief of the Group of Soviet Forces in Germany, became a first deputy minister of defense. It fell to him to deliver the main speech in Red Square on the 69th anniversary of the revolution when Marshal Sergey Sokolov (75), the minister of defense, could not attend because of illness. Lushev thereby became a serious contender for Sokolov's position.

The explosion in the fourth reactor at the Chernobyl nuclear power station near Kiev on April 26 became an important marker of the Gorbachev era. More long-term radiation was emitted into the Earth's atmosphere, water, and soil than from all previous nuclear explosions. The Politburo established a commission, headed by Boris Shcherbina, on the day of the explosion to cope with the tragedy, but it was not until May 11 that the danger of the possible penetration of the concrete base by the molten metal core and the consequent contamination of the subterranean water and subsoil was averted. At least 31 people died, over 200 suffered radiation burns, and another 135,-

000 were evacuated from the Chernobyl area and would have their health monitored for the rest of their lives.

If the human cost was high, the material loss was immense. An estimate of 2 billion rubles (about $2.7 billion) was almost certainly too low. A 30-km (18-mi) zone around Chernobyl was declared industrially and agriculturally dead. Shutting down the four reactors—and others of a similar type nationwide—resulted in the loss of 96 kw-hr of electricity daily. This led in September to electricity rationing in four republics. Also in September two *Pravda* articles focused on the electricity supply situation in the country. The energy sector was stated to be "guilty" of wasting resources and failing to prepare the country for what was expected to be an exceptionally harsh winter. So great was the need for electricity that on October 1 reactor No. 1 at Chernobyl was reported to be linked once again to the national grid and generating electricity. Reactor No. 2 was restarted in November, and it was announced that the third unit, which shared a control unit for ventilating equipment with the doomed reactor No. 4, would be operating again "in the second quarter of 1987." Plant workers were to perform 15-day shifts at the station without their families, confirmation that the area was still unsafe and that high risks were being taken in response to the urgent need to generate electricity.

The reason for the accident was officially stated to have been because workers were conducting an unauthorized test on the nuclear reactor. Of interest was the fact that a senior official dismissed as a result of the debacle was the deputy minister of the medium machine building industry and a member of the CC. This was the ministry primarily responsible for producing nuclear weapons for the armed forces. Military participation in the test was denied by the authorities. (For additional information on the accident, *see* ENERGY: *Sidebar*.)

The new policy of *glasnost* was not in evidence during the early phase of the disaster. On May 14 Gorbachev appeared on Soviet television for the first time—18 days after the accident—to explain the situation. Until then the CPSU had not made any official statement; that had been left to the government and press agencies. One result of Chernobyl was that public donations were accepted for the victims of a disaster for the first time in Soviet history. By July 20 some 400 million rubles had been collected. A special charity concert was staged by top Soviet rock musicians in Moscow.

During the year there were also two naval disasters. In August the *Admiral Nakhimov* sank after a collision with another vessel in the Black Sea, with the loss of 398 passengers and crew, and in October a Soviet nuclear-powered submarine sank in the Atlantic.

Infant mortality figures were published for the first time since 1974. Both the number of babies dying annually and the mortality rate for the whole population were about one-third higher in 1985 than in 1970. In April Boris Eltsin stated that life expectancy in the capital fell to 68 years in 1985 from 70 years in 1983. Infectious diseases were on the increase. For example, typhoid and paratyphoid cases rose to 18,900 in 1984 from 16,900 in 1980. (There were 300 cases in the U.S. in 1984.) Poor diet, vitamin deficiency, and alcohol abuse were some of the reasons for the deterioration.

There was evidence of a cultural thaw during the year as the Union of Writers and the Cinematographic Union acquired new leaders. Valentin Rasputin and Viktor Astafiev, leading writers on rural themes, published two novellas depicting the catastrophic moral collapse of contemporary Soviet society. Only those characters with some traces of Christian ethics in their behaviour were presented as morally healthy and socially responsible individuals. In September *Pravda* conceded that the church was not only surviving but had been "attempting to attract new members, especially youth."

Late in December it was reported that rioting had broken out in Alma-Ata in the Kazakh S.S.R., with more than 200 people injured and over a thousand arrested. The disorders were apparently triggered when Dinmukhamed Kunayev, a Kazakh and one of the last senior officials remaining from the Brezhnev era, was dismissed as head of the party in Kazakhstan and replaced by an ethnic Russian, Gennady Kolbin.

The Economy. Gorbachev saw a direct link between the performance of the economy and the authority of the CPSU. Success in modernizing the economy, he believed, would enhance his position and make it easier for him to launch new initiatives. The goals of the 12th five-year (1986–90) plan were reasonable: national income to increase annually by 3.5–4% and industrial output by 3.9–

TIME MAGAZINE

Two Soviet citizens take a moment to catch up on the news. A new government policy of openness in news reporting stimulated interest in readers long accustomed to reading nothing but the party line.

4.4%. Special importance was attached to machine tools, electrical equipment, and the electronic industries, which were to grow by 10% annually. Investment was envisioned at just over 4.5% more per annum, higher than during the period 1981–85 but still low, given the emphasis on industrial modernization. The increase in investment was intended to go into energy, agriculture, and industrial machinery. Between 1986 and 1990 some 80–95% of production was to meet "international quality standards" and 27–32% of equipment had to incorporate electronic components. (In 1985 the figure was only 5%.) The grain target for 1990 was 250 million metric tons. During the first nine months of 1986 the economy was on target: national income rose 4.3%, industrial output 5.2%, and labour productivity in industry 4.8%. Ligachev announced in November that the grain harvest was expected to reach 210 million metric tons, the best total since 1978.

New economic institutions continued to be established. Following U.S.S.R. Gosagroprom to run agriculture (set up in November 1985) and the Bureau for Machine Building (October 1985), the Bureau for the Fuel-Energy Complex was established in March 1986. The state monopoly of foreign trade was to be abolished on Jan. 1, 1987, after which more than 20 ministries and 70 enterprises would be permitted to enter foreign markets without reference to authority from the Ministry of Foreign Trade. This was to affect about 10% of foreign trade turnover. At the same time, wholesale trade was to be liberalized, but this would affect only some consumer goods.

A move that attracted international attention and surprised many observers was the passing of a new law in November that legalized individual private part-time business, to become effective May 1, 1987. In all, 29 categories of business were to be permitted, including taxi driving, tailoring, house and car repairs, and tutoring, and two million to three million people were affected. Those involved had to obtain a license and became liable to income tax; they were also required to have a full-time public-sector job. All the activities coming under control already existed, but previously they had been illegal. The legislation was restrictive and did not permit employment of a second person. It was undoubtedly in preparation for this that penalties were increased for those receiving "unearned incomes," with effect from July 1, 1986. This was intended to eliminate embezzlement and black market activity.

If enacted in 1987, as proposed, a law concerning cooperatives would have far-reaching implications. Leonid Abalkin, head of the Institute of Economics of the U.S.S.R. Academy of Sciences, in an interview looked forward to cooperatives being established by individuals. They would be involved in manufacturing and production of consumer goods and foodstuffs. Collective farms and the new cooperatives could contribute up to 25% of national income within ten years.

Foreign Policy. At the "presummit" at Reykjavík on October 11–12, Mikhail Gorbachev and President Reagan failed to reach agreement. On medium-range nuclear missiles, however, they agreed to aim for a global level of 100 warheads on each side and to reduce strategic missiles by 50% between 1986 and 1991. There was disagreement on the timetable for 1992–96. The U.S. wanted to discuss the elimination of all remaining ballistic missiles, while the U.S.S.R. wanted to eliminate all remaining strategic weapons; thus, the U.S. wanted to keep its bombers and its nonballistic missile force, which included cruise missiles. Whereas the U.S. wanted to observe the terms of the Anti-Ballistic Missile Treaty, the Soviets favoured strengthening it to restrict testing of the Strategic Defense Initiative (SDI) to the laboratory. SDI turned out to be the stumbling block. There appeared to be three main reasons why the Soviets feared SDI: militarily it could also lead to technological breakthroughs in conventional weapons unrelated to space research; economically it would result in the emergence of multinational high-technology corporations, thus strengthening the capitalist world economy; and politically those nations involved in research, such as the U.S., Japan, Western Europe, and Israel, would have even greater incentives for cooperation. The U.S.S.R. was clearly worried that the SDI might work.

Nicholas Daniloff, *U.S. News & World Report* correspondent held for 13 days in Moscow's Lefortovo Prison on charges of espionage, signals victory as he is driven away from the compound. A Soviet citizen arrested by the FBI was released about the same time.
AP/WIDE WORLD

On August 30 Nicholas Daniloff, a U.S. journalist, was arrested in Moscow and accused of spying. After lengthy negotiations he was allowed to leave the country, and Gennady Zakharov, a Soviet UN employee arrested for spying by the U.S. authorities, was permitted to return home. As part of the deal Yury Orlov, a noted physicist and founder of the now-defunct group set up to monitor Soviet compliance with the 1975 Helsinki Accords, was released from Siberian exile and flew with his wife to New York City. A few other Soviet citizens also moved to the West.

In February the human-rights campaigner Anatoly Shcharansky (*see* BIOGRAPHIES) was released with three others as part of an exchange deal; five Eastern-bloc spies who had been imprisoned in West Germany and the U.S. returned home. The dissident poet Irina Ratushinskaya was permitted to travel to the U.K. for medical treatment in December and announced that she planned to remain in the West. Also in December, the physicist and Nobel laureate Andrey Sakharov, whose banishment to internal exile in Gorky had become a cause célèbre in the West, was released and allowed to return to Moscow; his wife, Yelena Bonner, convicted of anti-Soviet activities in 1984, was pardoned. At about the same time, 50 émigrés who said they had become disillusioned with life in the United States returned to the Soviet Union.

Anatoly Dobrynin became the coordinator of Soviet foreign policy when he became head of the CC Secretariat's international department. His influence was soon felt in U.S.S.R.-U.S. relations as Gorbachev and Foreign Minister Eduard Shevardnadze launched initiative after initiative, especially on arms control. The Soviet goal was to capture the high moral ground and to seize and retain the initiative. For the first time in their history the Soviets displayed expertise in public relations and appeared as the victors after the Reykjavík summit. The Soviets argued that there was no deal on arms control because of Reagan's "obsession" with SDI. This line was adopted by the majority of the Western media despite the fact that it could have been plausibly argued that Gorbachev torpedoed the summit by his insistence that the U.S. abandon SDI.

New Soviet ambassadors were appointed to many countries; the new man in the U.S., Yury Dubinin, came as a surprise since a more senior diplomat had been expected. Shevardnadze continued to impress on the international stage and, for instance, concluded a successful visit to the U.K. in July by signing several agreements, including a final settlement of financial claims arising from the 1917 Revolution. In November Gorbachev paid a successful four-day visit to India.

Soviet diplomats and personnel continued to be expelled from Western countries: two from Italy and four from France in February. In September 25 Soviet UN personnel were asked to leave the U.S. In retaliation the U.S.S.R. expelled five U.S. diplomats. The U.S. countered by requiring 55 Soviets to leave, 5 of whom could be replaced. The Soviets then expelled another five U.S. diplomats and withdrew 260 local Soviet employees from the embassy in Moscow and the consulate in Leningrad. The U.S. objective was to reduce the number of Soviet diplomatic personnel in the U.S. to 251, the same as the number of Americans in the U.S.S.R.; this was achieved.

(MARTIN MCCAULEY)

YUGOSLAVIA

A federal socialist republic, Yugoslavia is in southern Europe on the Adriatic Sea. Area: 255,804 sq km (98,766 sq mi). Pop. (1986 est.): 23,289,000. Cap.: Belgrade. Monetary unit: Yugoslav dinar, with (Oct. 1, 1986) a free rate of 410.99 dinars to U.S. $1 (593.88 dinars = £1 sterling). Presidents of the Presidium of the League of Communists in 1986, Vidoje Zarkovic and, from June 28, Milanko Renovica; presidents of the Collective Presidency, Radovan Vlajkovic and, from May 15, Sinan Hasani; presidents of the Federal Executive Council (premiers), Milka Planinc and, from May 15, Branco Mikulic.

In 1986 Yugoslavia's political situation deteriorated. There was growing discord among the six republics and two autonomous provinces. The country's already weak financial and economic situation worsened and came under strong criticism from the International Monetary Fund. When Premier Milka Planinc's four-year term of office ended in May, she was replaced by another Croat, Branko Mikulic (see BIOGRAPHIES), a senior political leader from Bosnia with a reputation as a good organizer but also as a hardliner. Mikulic was replaced on the Collective Presidency by Hamdija Pozderac. Under "rotation" rules, Sinan Hasani, an ethnic Albanian from the autonomous province of Kosovo, became president of the Collective Presidency in May, with Lazar Mojsov, a Macedonian, as vice-president.

At its 13th congress in June, the Yugoslav League of Communists (Communist Party) elected a new, more youthful 165-seat Central Committee led by Milanko Renovica, a Serb from Bosnia, as president for one year and Radisa Gacic, from Serbia, as secretary; 127 new officials were appointed. The economic and political crisis and the reasons for it were vehemently debated, but proposals for party and state recentralization were rejected.

In October the Central Committee met to discuss the possibility of allowing the Socialist Alliance, which included the League of Communists, greater autonomy. It was suggested that it might be allowed to select its own (non-Communist Party) candidates from other permitted groups. Also in October, a memorandum to the Federal Assembly drafted by the prestigious Serbian Academy of Science and Art in Belgrade criticized the monopoly of the Communist Party and stated that without liberal reforms the federal system could collapse.

The Serbs, who were heavily outnumbered by Albanians in Kosovo Province, demonstrated in Belgrade in February, April, and November, alleging that local Albanians were pressuring them to move out of the province. Meanwhile, in Kosovo, the local authorities brought to trial Albanians accused of nationalism and "irredentism," and in July a law was passed prohibiting land sales to ethnic Albanians in "ethnically pure" Serbian villages.

There was a high degree of activity by opposition groups in Slovenia, notably the Greens, to which the authorities turned a blind eye. Slovenia's official youth organization, part of the Socialist Alliance, campaigned for nonmilitary forms of national service. In October the demand of the Slovene journalists' union that obligatory adherence to Marxism-Leninism be removed from the union's statutes was met. At the same time, a 26-year-old Croatian student, who had been imprisoned for four years for petitioning on human rights in 1980, sued the government for maltreatment while in prison. A similar lawsuit was started by a Serb from Bosnia who had been imprisoned for 22 months for preparing a private blueprint for a constitutional reorganization of Yugoslavia.

Yugoslavia's hard-currency debt was little changed in 1986 at around $20 billion. In January–October the annual rate of inflation was accelerating and had topped 90%, the highest in 40 years; in the same period, the dinar was devalued by 51% against a basket of major world currencies. A temporary freeze on prices imposed in July was lifted on November 1. The wheat harvest in 1986 totaled 4.8 million metric tons, 1% below 1985, but maize (corn) rose 23% to 12 million metric tons, reflecting recovery from the 1985 drought. Industrial production stagnated, and exports in the first nine months of 1986 were 3.4% below the same period of 1985, while imports fell 1.6%. In the same period, exports to the West fell 1.1% and imports rose 3.4%. The government's decree in July to withdraw "unjustified" wage raises led to a significant increase in the number of strikes.

(K. F. CVIIC)

North America

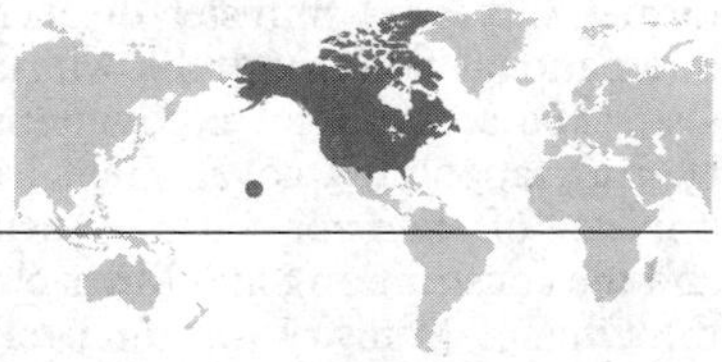

CANADA

Canada is a federal parliamentary state and member of the Commonwealth covering North America north of conterminous United States and east of Alaska. Area: 9,970,610 sq km (3,849,675 sq mi). Pop (1986 est.): 25,624,000. Cap.: Ottawa. Monetary unit: Canadian dollar, with (Oct. 1, 1986) a free rate of Can$1.39 to U.S. $1 (Can$2.01 = £1 sterling). Queen, Elizabeth II; governor-general in 1986, Jeanne Sauvé; prime minister, Brian Mulroney.

Domestic Affairs. The Conservative administration headed by Brian Mulroney reached the midpoint in its first term in the autumn of 1986. Elected to office in September 1984 with an overwhelming majority (211 of 282 members in the House of Commons), the Conservatives now appeared more assured as a government. Although their popularity in the country had fallen from 58% when they took office to the low 30s, their performance was better than their public image. They had been beset, since taking office, by minor scandals, adverse polls, and unfavourable press coverage. Yet on the larger questions their record was good. They had moved to rebuild confidence between the provinces and Ottawa by meeting the demands of the energy-producing provinces; they had introduced reforms into the parliamentary process by allowing more scope to private members; they had successfully held down federal expenditures; and they had skillfully managed the country's foreign relations. The economy had performed well under their guidance, with substantial real growth, an increase in employment, and lower inflation and interest rates. By mid-1986, however, this recovery had been checked, particularly for the Western provinces, by low world prices for petroleum and wheat.

The prime minister's personal style was still an uncertain aspect of the administration. Mulroney's credibility was often called into question by a tendency toward exaggeration and strong partisanship. He was sometimes irresolute, defending his government's policies vigorously, then hesitating and changing his position under pressure. A poll taken in September revealed that 60% of Canadians would prefer to have another prime minister. The same poll, however, showed elector dissatisfaction with all three national parties as well as a large element of uncommitted voters. As he moved toward a probable general election in 1988, Mulroney staked out three principal objectives: to achieve a free trade arrangement with the U.S.; to persuade Quebec to accept the national constitution it had rejected in 1982; and to undertake a thorough reform of Canada's taxation system. There was high risk involved in this program, since the first two goals depended on the cooperation of other parties, notably the U.S. and the ten Canadian provinces.

A reorganization of the Mulroney Cabinet on June 30 represented an attempt to form an effective team to secure the government's objectives. Eight new ministers were appointed, 4 were dropped, 2 were retired, and 19 others were given new posts in the 40-member Cabinet. Among those retired was the highly partisan and aggressive Erik Nielsen, deputy prime minister and minister of national defense. Three ministers emerged as key players in carrying out the government's strategy: Patricia Carney, the former successful minister of energy, who moved to the international trade portfolio with responsibility for supervising the commercial negotiations with the U.S.; Lowell Murray, appointed government leader in the Senate and minister of state for federal-provincial relations (Quebec and the constitution); and Michael Wilson, left in charge of the Finance Ministry (taxation reform). A senior Ontario minister, Sinclair Stevens, resigned as minister of regional industrial expansion on May 12 to face a judicial inquiry into alleged conflict of interest. His was the fifth resignation from the Mulroney Cabinet, although one of those who resigned, Marcel Masse, returned after being acquitted of election irregularities. Seeking to calm discontent in the Quebec wing of the party, Mulroney appointed Quebec Conservatives to four of the five major economic portfolios. One Quebec member left the party in May to sit in Parliament as an independent.

The 40 opposition Liberals were still in shock after their disastrous defeat in the 1984 election. One of their most popular members, Jean Chrétien, who had lost the leadership of the party to John Turner before the election, resigned his parliamentary seat on February 27. Chrétien had never been happy under Turner's leadership, and there was speculation that he might return to political life if Turner were to relinquish his post. At the Liberal Party convention on November 30, however, Turner's leadership was endorsed by a margin of 2,001 to 622.

The first two by-elections called by the new government took place on September 29. Chrétien's seat in the St. Maurice riding of Quebec was won by another Liberal, while a riding north of Edmonton in Alberta was narrowly retained by the Conservatives. The New Democratic Party, not previously prominent in Quebec or Alberta, made a surprisingly strong showing in both contests. The by-elections left party standings as follows: Progressive Conservatives 209; Liberals 40; New Democratic Party 29; independents 2; vacancies 2.

The first session of the 33rd Parliament ran from September 1984 to Sept. 30, 1986, when a second session began. During the 1985–86 sittings the Conservative government brought forward more of its own legislation than in the previous year. It introduced a no-fault divorce law and a new young offenders act and reduced the rate of growth in federal support payments to the provinces for health and higher education. In an effort to curb the growth of spending on social services, it limited cost-of-living increases in family allowances to rises in the consumer price index above 3% per year. An amendment to the National Parole Board Act, passed by the Commons on June 26, gave the parole board the right to keep violent offenders behind bars for the entire length of their sentences, rather than releasing them under supervision after they had served two-thirds of their terms. It was altered by the appointed upper house, the Senate, to permit appeal to the courts, but the change was overridden by an emergency sitting of Parliament on July 24.

The new Liberal government of Quebec, elected in December 1985, laid down five conditions on which it was prepared to sign the 1982 constitution. A statement on May 9 listed them as: an explicit recognition of Quebec as a distinct society; increased powers in immigration; the right of veto in constitutional amendments; participation in the naming of Supreme Court judges; and the limitation of federal spending powers. The first condition had always been opposed by former prime minister Pierre Trudeau, but Turner seemed prepared to accept it. Turner made it clear that the only conditions on which he had reservations were Quebec's desire to limit the federal spending power and the province's claim to a veto. The Quebec wing of the federal Liberal Party later passed a resolution affirming Quebec's "unique character as the home of Canadian francophones."

At the 27th annual premiers' meeting in Edmonton on August 11–12, Premier Robert Bourassa (*see* BIOGRAPHIES) spelled out a definition of a veto power for Quebec. Instead of the 1982 formula, which requires seven provinces with 50% of the country's population to approve constitutional amendments, Bourassa proposed seven provinces representing 75% of the population. This would mean that Quebec, with a little more than 26% of Canada's population, would have an effective veto on amendments. Alternatively, Bourassa claimed that Quebec should be entitled to compensation if the other provinces went ahead with amendments opposed by Quebec. The other premiers at Edmonton, while not directly agreeing with Bourassa's position, showed sympathy toward it, but the conference gave most of its attention to such issues as unemployment and regional economic development. All the provincial leaders except Howard Pawley of Manitoba (New Democratic Party) supported the federal government's free trade talks with the U.S.

The Economy. The Canadian economy grew slowly and erratically in 1986, showing elements of weakness. The gross national product, in current dollars and seasonally adjusted, stood at $485 billion at the end of six months. Over the entire year economic growth was projected to rise by 3.2%, slower than the 1985 rate. In July the country recorded its first merchandise trade deficit in ten years. The turnaround was blamed on the slowdown in U.S. growth and low world prices for primary products such as oil, gas, and wheat. In the Western oil-producing provinces fewer than 20% of drilling rigs were operating at midyear, resulting in a loss of 40,000 jobs.

The Canadian dollar was under severe attack from speculators in February, when it slipped to a low of 69.13 U.S. cents. It recovered following a vigorous defense by the Bank of Canada and hovered around 72 U.S. cents thereafter. The seasonally adjusted unemployment rate for September was 9.5%, little changed since the beginning of the year but an improvement over 1985. The consumer price index for September showed a year-to-year increase of 4.1%, about the same as for 1985. The Bank of Canada interest rate, influential in determining the chartered banks' loan rates, stood at 8.6% in early October.

Finance Minister Michael Wilson adopted a tough stance in his second budget, presented to Parliament on February 26. He introduced a 3% surtax on personal and corporate income taxes, a 1% increase in the sales tax (with a partial rebate to low-income earners), and higher excise taxes on tobacco and alcoholic beverages. About $1.5 billion would be raised by the new levies. On estimated expenditures of $116.8 billion, Wilson projected a deficit of $29.5 billion—well below the 1985–86 shortfall of $34.5 billion—based on an economic growth estimate of 3.7% for the year and oil prices of $22.50 a barrel. Both these forecasts proved incorrect as oil prices slumped to about U.S. $14 a barrel, wheat prices plummeted, and the economic growth rate had to be revised downward. On September 18 the minister stated that the deficit would inevitably increase to $32 billion. He ruled out more tax increases or reduced government spending, saying these measures would harm the areas of the country suffering economic distress.

Foreign Affairs. Trade issues dominated the Canada-U.S. relationship during 1986. The free trade negotiations started hesitantly when half the 20 members of the U.S. Senate Finance Committee announced they would vote against entering into the talks. Despite Pres. Ronald Reagan's efforts to change the senators' minds, the committee was deadlocked on April 23 when a resolution opposing the talks was brought to a vote. A tie vote defeated the resolution, however, and prepared the way for a "fast-track" approach to the question. This formula meant that the committee would have authority to approve or reject an eventual treaty proposal in its entirety but could not amend it. The close vote indicated that hard bargaining lay ahead for the trade negotiators. The two teams met for the first round of talks in Ottawa on May 21 and 22. The target date for the conclusion of a trade pact was the autumn of 1987.

As the talks got under way, the entire process was almost jeopardized by U.S. imposition of a 35% tariff on Canadian red cedar (redwood) shakes and shingles on May 22. The tariff was designed to decline over a five-year period. Imports of red cedar shingles from Canada, valued at $250 million annually, had captured some 73% of the U.S. market and had cost American producers about 2,000 jobs since 1978. The U.S. ambassador to Canada explained that the duty resulted from a quasi-judicial process begun by the U.S. International Trade Commission months before

A deserted oil rig in Canada's Alberta Province stands as a silent symbol of the industry's crisis. Canada's economy was severely affected, with some 40,000 oil-related jobs forfeited. Fewer than one-fifth of the Western provinces' drilling rigs were in use at midyear.
MIKE DOBEL—MASTERFILE

the trade negotiations with Canada began. The new tariff was intended as temporary relief for an industry badly hurt by imports.

The U.S. action created an uproar in Canada. Mulroney immediately sent a strong letter of protest to Reagan, and the House of Commons unanimously passed a resolution urging the president to reverse his stand. A Canadian request for compensation for the losses caused by the new duty was rejected by the Reagan administration. Canada banned the export of red cedar logs to the U.S., thus preventing American mills from making shingles and shakes at a time when British Columbia plants were shutting down. The Mulroney government also reimposed tariffs that had been suspended since 1979 on a range of U.S. books, periodicals, and computer components.

A further trade dispute came to the fore as the U.S. Commerce Department began an inquiry into Canadian softwood lumber exports. These exports, pines, spruces, and firs, were valued at over $3 billion in 1985. They had captured about one-third of the U.S. market, to some extent because of the decline of the Canadian dollar relative to that of the U.S. Arguing that stumpage fees on government-owned land in Canada were too low and constituted an indirect subsidy for Canadian exports, U.S. lumber interests demanded a 27% countervailing duty, which would cut Canadian imports by one-third. After defending Canadian stumpage arrangements for most of the summer, on September 30 Carney offered to increase stumpage fees and provincial taxes by 10% if the U.S. abandoned its consideration of the proposal to impose duties on lumber imports. The U.S. lumber industry rejected the minister's offer as inadequate. On October 16, in a preliminary ruling, the Commerce Department imposed a 15% duty on Canadian softwood lumber imports. On December 30 an agreement was reached under which the tariff was dropped in favour of a 15% Canadian export tax. While the pact avoided a formal finding of unfair subsidy by the Commerce Department and also kept the duties in Canada, it was strongly criticized by the Canadian lumber industry.

(continued on page 526)

Special Report: Canada

Expo 86

BY PETER WARD

For Canada, the brightest spot in 1986 was undoubtedly the rousing success of British Columbia's world's fair, Expo 86. In a year clouded by trade squabbles with the U.S., frequently violent labour clashes, unemployment, and pervasive national disillusionment with Prime Minister Brian Mulroney, the glittering $1.6 billion fair attracted millions of visitors and built bridges of understanding within Canada.

Traditionally, the rest of Canada has regarded British Columbia as laid back and a little flaky. People in British Columbia often complain about being isolated from the Canadian mainstream by psychology, as well as by the Rocky Mountains. So it was doubly sweet when, in 1986, the Pacific coast province became the national centre of attention. From the day Expo 86 opened on May 2 until it closed on the afternoon of October 13, more than 22 million people made their way through the turnstiles. The grand Vancouver summer party filled British Columbia—and all Canadians—with justifiable pride.

Expo 86 set records for attendance and came in under budget and on schedule, thanks chiefly to the combined talents of British Columbia businessman James Pattison (*see* BIOGRAPHIES) and then provincial premier William Bennett. At Bennett's request, Pattison took on the job of heading the corporation created to run Expo. Why did he agree to accept such a daunting task for a fee of only $1? "Because Bill Bennett asked me," said Pattison. "And because I've never done anything for my country, for my province, and I decided to do it."

The Birthday Party That Grew. The Expo idea had its genesis at a small dinner party at the Canadian High Commission in London. Canadian career diplomat Patrick Reid fell into conversation with Grace McCarthy, British Columbia's deputy premier, who was looking for a way to celebrate Vancouver's 100th birthday. Reid, then chairman of the Bureau of International Expositions, suggested an international fair for Vancouver in 1986. The provincial government liked the idea, and Reid was able to convince the Japanese to shift their scheduled fair from 1986 to 1985. Canada was designated as the 1986 fair site, and Vancouver won the right to be host city. Reid was appointed commissioner general of Expo 86 by the Canadian government, in charge of selling the fair to potential foreign exhibitors and ensuring its international character.

The idea of a fair was not without its detractors. Why spend millions on a circus when low-income housing and social services were needed, asked critics? Opposition politicians charged that the fair would be merely a promotion for Bennett's Social Credit Party. As the projected cost grew and money worries increased, two respected economists from the University of British Columbia produced figures to show that the fair would lose $558 million. There was further reason to be nervous: Montreal's Expo 67 lost so much money that the deficit was still being repaid a decade later. The New Orleans fair of 1984 left $200 million in unpaid bills.

In March 1982 the Expo corporation obtained agreement to use funds from a new Western Canada lottery to pay any Expo deficit. The federal government committed itself to building a huge pavilion on the Vancouver waterfront, which would become a cruise ship terminal and convention centre when the fair was over. A deal was hammered out giving the provincial government complete authority—as well as responsibility for any deficit—and the federal government agreed to commitments that would total nearly $300 million.

Getting Ready. With funding under control, Bennett and Pattison began planning the network of pavilions that would house Expo's exhibits on 69 ha (173 ac) along the inlet called False Creek, replacing the existing scrap metal dumps, sludge, and tidal mud flats. Labour problems posed the next threat. British Columbia is famous for its militant unions, and with recession deepening, the unions lobbied hard to ensure that all construction for the fair would be done by union crews in a closed shop environment. Bennett wanted the option of awarding either union or nonunion contracts, depending on who offered the best price. When a nonunion company was given one of the first construction contracts, it seemed that the unions might force cancellation of the fair entirely. Finally, Bennett's government declared Expo 86 an "economic development site," an act that made it illegal for union members to refuse to work alongside nonunion labourers. Union strife sputtered for a few days and then abated. Pattison later said those labour troubles were the worst situation he faced during his six years with Expo.

By this time, public opinion in the province was solidly behind Expo, forcing politicians who had condemned the fair as wasteful to change their tune. Opinion polls

AUTHENTICATED NEWS INTERNATIONAL

Highway 86, a walk-through, four-lane "road" with more than 200 present-day transportation items in a surreal setting, was one of the most popular exhibits at Expo 86. It provided visitors a hands-on means of experiencing the world of transportation.

Peter Ward operates Ward News Services Canada in the Parliamentary Press Gallery, Ottawa.

gave Expo an approval rating as high as 90%. Bennett and Pattison scored a public relations coup by making Expo apolitical. Together they covered 93 communities convincing the people that the fair would be for all British Columbians, not just Vancouver. Meanwhile, Reid, with his long-time connections on the international fair circuit, was able to obtain exhibition commitments from far more countries than expected.

Pattison, a one-time used car salesman and self-made billionaire, ran the Expo corporation with private-sector-style economy. As many as a dozen senior executives left the Expo organization suddenly during its operation, and there were frequent complaints about Pattison's tough attitude concerning expense accounts. Nobody complained about his 7 AM till after dark working schedule, however, and no one seemed to mind when he used his private Learjet without charge on Expo business. The Expo budget stayed on target, thanks largely to his management. He also shocked many of the provincial and city brass by decreeing that there would be no "freebee" passes; politicians and other local bigwigs who wanted to hand out Expo tickets would have to pay for them like anybody else.

Only people paying admission would make the fair a success, and to that end 1.6 million letters were sent out, inviting the recipients to come to Expo. British Columbia citizens suggested names of friends and relatives living outside the province, and each personalized invitation was signed by the premier. The goal was to attract 17 million visitors to keep the deficit between $300 million and $400 million. Prime ground for potential Expo visitors was judged to be the U.S. Pacific coast, particularly California. Expo conducted surveys that discovered that—even in 1984—what West Coast Americans wanted most in a vacation destination was safety, and advertising campaigns were mounted on that basis. The spate of hijackings and terrorist incidents that took place in Europe and the Mediterranean during 1985 and early 1986 undoubtedly helped the Expo cause.

In Vancouver optimism seemed to grow as the buildings took shape—the Canada Pavilion, with the Pan Pacific Hotel, the trade and convention centre on Burrard Inlet, and the dazzling array of exhibition buildings representing 54 countries, 9 of Canada's 12 provinces and 2 territories, several U.S. states, and dozens of private corporations. (*See* ARCHITECTURE.) By the time Expo opened, on May 2, 1986, most of Canada was interested and at least mildly envious. The prince and princess of Wales officially opened Expo in the 60,000-seat domed stadium of B.C. Place. The royal couple spent a few days enjoying Expo, for the benefit of international television.

Shortly after the opening, Premier Bill Bennett announced his resignation as leader of the ruling Social Credit Party. One of Bennett's Cabinet ministers, William Vander Zalm, won the leadership convention and took over from Bennett as premier on August 6.

A Grand Affair. Vancouver gets teased by the rest of Canada for being a rainy city, but not in 1986. About 130 of Expo's 165 days were without rainfall, providing great conditions for the visitors who munched 7.5 million hamburgers and downed 1.2 million imperial gallons of beer. In the Northwest Territories pavilion, customers went through 40 metric tons of musk-ox meat, 12 tons of reindeer meat, and 3.5 tons of ice from a 10,000-year-old glacier, flown in especially to cool the visitors' drinks. Only one accident marred Expo's safety record—a nine-year-old girl, watching a movie in the Canada Pavilion, was trapped and killed by the rotating auditorium. Crime was

A symbol of the Expo 86 world's fair, the Expo Center, a 17-story geodesic dome, rises high above visitors. The centre housed theatres and a restaurant. The highly successful fair was held in Vancouver, British Columbia, and had as its theme transportation and communication.

R. THOMPSON—PHOTO TRENDS

also remarkably light. Snatch-and-grab artists committed one major robbery, of a $15,000 night deposit, but a mere 79 pickpocket incidents were reported. Among the questions asked by visitors to Expo: "Does the Canadian flag come in any colours other than white and red?" and "Is this Canadian money any good off the Expo site?"

Eager to have attendance pass the 22 million mark, Pattison spent the last few weeks traveling the U.S. Pacific coast to promote Expo. The last-minute push worked. On Sunday, October 12, the final full day for Expo, 341,000 visitors crammed the site—113,000 more than on any other single day. Attendance topped 22 million the next day. Expo closed on October 13, Canadian Thanksgiving Day, with a gala party in the B.C. Place stadium. Young people from all the exhibiting nations joined hands with Commissioner General Reid to sing what had become the Expo 86 song, "Peace on Earth," and there wasn't a dry eye in sight. Pattison received a standing ovation.

The final cost of the fair—$1.6 billion—consisted of $804 million from the provincial government, $278 million from the federal government, and the rest from exhibitors, foreign and domestic. Pattison reported that the deficit would be lower than expected—less than $300 million—and that it would all be covered during the next three years by lottery proceeds. As a bonus, Vancouver got a domed stadium—the first in Canada—and $854 million worth of Advanced Light Rapid Transit system, 22 km (13.5 mi) linking the suburbs, the fair site, and downtown. Expo had created as many as 70,000 man-years of work, at a time when recession was threatening. The British Columbia government estimated that Expo brought $4 billion into the province. The federal and provincial governments picked up $742 million in revenue.

Expo made 1986 a memorable year for British Columbia and for all Canada. In the words of Prime Minister Mulroney: "The legacy of Expo 86 is one of optimism and opportunity. This exposition has demonstrated to the world that ours is a nation of 'doers.' " The day Expo closed, one of the chief "doers," Jimmy Pattison, resigned effective October 14 and flew to San Diego, Calif., for a holiday. "You know," he said, "I never did get that dollar Bill Bennett promised me for doing the job."

(continued from page 523)

To Canadians, the trade irritants pointed out the need for the free trade talks to continue. Even if a comprehensive pact could not be reached, it might be possible to create a permanent mechanism to deal with Canada-U.S. trade disputes. But the sentiment in Congress pointed toward making U.S. trade laws tougher, not easier. The achievement of free trade between the two countries would clearly be a supremely difficult accomplishment.

When Mulroney and Reagan met in Washington, March 18 and 19, they had before them a report on the controversial subject of acid rain. Issued in January, it called for the two countries to undertake a serious research and development program, to cost $5.5 billion over the next five years, into ways to burn coal more cleanly. The two leaders endorsed the report, indicating that the president had come to recognize the severity of transboundary pollution in North America. The leaders also signed an agreement extending the joint North American Aerospace Defense Command (NORAD) for a further five years.

Canada joined three other leading NATO members in an unsuccessful effort to persuade the U.S. to continue to comply with the terms of the 1979 Strategic Arms Limitation Treaty (SALT II), despite alleged Soviet violations. The request was made at a NATO foreign ministers' meeting in Halifax, Nova Scotia, May 29–30. Canada's external affairs minister, Joe Clark, placed blame on the Soviet Union for departing from the SALT II agreement through its deployment of SS-25 missiles. Previously, in the House of Commons on May 23, Clark had backed the U.S. in its plan to rebuild its stock of chemical weapons.

Canada continued to attempt to persuade Great Britain to adopt tough economic sanctions against South Africa. Following the Commonwealth meeting at Nassau in The Bahamas in October 1985, a Canadian, Archbishop Edward Scott of the Anglican Church, was appointed to the Group of Eminent Persons directed to open a dialogue on apartheid with the South African government. Although the group failed to do this, its report called firmly for economic sanctions against the regime. Canada imposed another group of sanctions, both economic and diplomatic, against South Africa on June 12. Mulroney went on to play a prominent part at a meeting of seven Commonwealth countries held in London, August 3–5. Six nations, Canada, Australia, India, Zambia, The Bahamas, and Zimbabwe, agreed to adopt and recommend to the entire Commonwealth a list of 11 punitive measures against South Africa. U.K. Prime Minister Margaret Thatcher accepted only two of the provisions recommended but agreed not to stand in the way of European Community sanctions, expected to be decided upon in September. Mulroney was credited with having played a major part in forging a consensus on the issue with Commonwealth states adjoining South Africa, such as Zimbabwe and Zambia. As a result, they dropped their threats to leave the Commonwealth.

Mulroney attended the economic summit meeting of the group of seven major industrialized nations in Tokyo, May 4–6. Although terrorism was the principal subject discussed, Canada gained a position in future meetings of finance ministers attempting to stabilize the exchange rates of major currencies. Mulroney went on to spend ten days visiting Japan, China, and South Korea. From February 14 to 22 he was in Paris attending a conference of French-speaking countries sponsored by France. He allowed the bilingual provinces of Quebec and New Brunswick to participate in the meeting as full members, a concession that Trudeau had always refused to make. (*See* FRANCE: *Sidebar.*)

(D. M. L. FARR)

UNITED STATES

The United States of America is a federal republic composed of 50 states, 49 of which are in North America and one of which consists of the Hawaiian Islands. Area: 9,372,571 sq km (3,618,770 sq mi), including 205,856 sq km of inland water but excluding the 156,492 sq km of the Great Lakes that lie within U.S. boundaries. Pop. (1986 est.): 241.5 million. Cap.: Washington, D.C. Monetary unit: U.S. dollar, with (Oct. 1, 1986) a free rate of U.S. $1.45 to £1 sterling. President in 1986, Ronald Reagan.

Foreign Affairs. After posting a record of achievement over nearly six years that even many of its severest critics acknowledged was impressive, the Reagan administration suffered a series of sharp setbacks toward the end of 1986. The first bad news came with the midterm election results of November 4. Despite extensive campaigning by Pres. Ronald Reagan (*see* BIOGRAPHIES), the Republican Party lost control of the U.S. Senate and additional seats in the House, which was already in Democratic hands.

Potentially more damaging, however, was a development that first came to public notice that same day. Newspapers carried the startling news that the U.S. had been secretly engaged for many months in shipping arms to Iran; this seemed tied to hopes of winning the release of American hostages held in Lebanon by radical Islamic groups with close ties to the Tehran regime, although the administration initially denied it. One of the hostages, David P. Jacobsen, was freed November 2 in Beirut after 17 months of captivity. The next day the pro-Syrian Lebanese magazine *al-Shiraa* reported that former U.S. national security adviser Robert C. McFarlane had traveled secretly to Iran. The magazine's account was confirmed November 4 by the speaker of the Iranian Majlis (parliament).

Complicating matters was the further disclosure that the contacts between Washington and Tehran involved a clandestine deal whereby the U.S. transferred military spare parts to Iran via Israel. The venture seemed to violate the Reagan administration's pledge never to negotiate with terrorists or with states that supported them, as well as the formal U.S. embargo on arms sales to Iran. By not issuing any specific denials of the news reports, high administration officials appeared to confirm the existence of the U.S.-Iran deal. Subsequent White House efforts to contain the damage were largely counterproductive. A nationally televised speech by Reagan on November 13 defending his administration's actions elicited media comment that was at best skeptical. At a news conference six days later, the president again sought to put the matter to rest by declaring that "the responsibility for the decision and the operation is mine and mine alone."

The developing crisis took still another turn on November 25, when U.S. Attorney General Edwin Meese III announced that $10 million of the $30 million paid by Iran for U.S. arms had been diverted to bank accounts in Switzerland controlled by *contra* guerrilla groups in Nicaragua; apparently this had taken place at a time when military aid to the *contras,* strongly supported by the administration, was forbidden by law. The same day, Reagan announced that his national security adviser, Vice-Adm. John M. Poindexter, had requested reassignment, and that Poindexter's deputy, Lieut. Col. Oliver L. North, had been "relieved" of his duties.

Reagan maintained his initially defiant public posture in an interview with *Time* magazine columnist Hugh Sidey—published in the December 8 issue—in which he defended North as a "national hero," but a partial change of heart apparently occurred over the next few days. Adopting a highly personal and apologetic tone, Reagan said in his weekly radio address of December 6 that the execution of his secret policy initiatives toward Iran was "flawed, and mistakes were made." At the same time, he refused to call the Iran venture a mistake, and he continued to insist that the secret diplomatic contacts were proper.

By then it was clear that what *The Economist* called the Iranagua affair was destined to remain in the public eye for some time. On November 26 the Justice Department expanded its probe of the weapons shipments to Iran into a full-scale investigation. A presidential commission was named, the courts appointed an independent counsel (special prosecutor), and both houses of Congress began probes of their own. While the president called for full disclosure of the facts, North and Poindexter, called before a congressional committee, claimed the protection of the Fifth Amendment, refusing to testify on grounds of possible self-incrimination. Another potential witness, William Casey, the head of the CIA, fell gravely ill. As the year ended it was still impossible to separate fact from rumour, and after the holiday lull it was expected that the various investigations would go into high gear.

The Iran-*contra* disclosures capped a turbulent year for the administration in its handling of foreign policy. As always, U.S. relations with the Soviet Union were of primary concern, and here also many media analysts concluded that the White House had stumbled. The year had begun on a positive note, however, with Reagan and Soviet leader Mikhail S. Gorbachev expressing their desire for peace in separate five-minute televised messages shown in each other's country on New Year's Day. The White House had proposed the messages in November 1985, before the Reagan-Gorbachev summit meeting in Geneva.

A second Reagan-Gorbachev meeting, at Reykjavík, Iceland, October 11–12, was to have set the agenda for a true summit in the U.S. at some future date. Instead, the talks turned into intense and detailed discussions over arms control. The parley fell apart October 12 after a vehement disagreement over the U.S. Strategic Defense Initiative (a space-based missile defense program that the media had nicknamed "Star Wars"). The stalemate was all the more disappointing because the superpowers had seemed to be on the verge of agreeing to a substantial reduction of offensive nuclear weapons.

Still, the failure at Reykjavík accorded with the up-and-down pattern that characterized U.S.-Soviet relations throughout 1986. An earlier episode centred on Nicholas S. Daniloff, the Moscow correspondent for *U.S. News & World Report* magazine, and Gennady F. Zakharov, a Soviet physicist attached to the UN in New York City. Zakharov was arrested by FBI agents August 23 on a New York subway platform as he exchanged money for three classified documents. Exactly one week later, Daniloff was detained in the Soviet capital on suspicion of espionage. At the time, he was preparing to leave the country with his family at the end of a five-year assignment for *U.S. News.* There followed a tense game of diplomatic parry and thrust that ended with the release of Daniloff on September 29 and of Zakharov on September 30 under an arrangement worked out by U.S. Secretary of State George P. Shultz and Soviet Foreign Minister Eduard A. Shevardnadze. In announcing the release of the two men on September 30, Reagan denied that a trade had taken place, although that assertion was challenged by many news commentators.

The incident did not end there. Over four days starting October 19, the U.S. and the Soviet Union traded diplomatic expulsions that cost the U.S. the services of 260 Soviet nationals employed at its Moscow embassy and Leningrad consulate. For the time, at least, the U.S. embassy staff was forced to perform routine housekeeping chores as well as conduct important diplomatic business.

U.S. Pres. Ronald Reagan, in the face of criticism regarding the authorization and purposes of secret weapons deals with Iran, addresses the nation via television on November 13. For the first time since he assumed office, the president's popularity rating fell dramatically.

AFP PHOTO

Official and unofficial U.S. reaction to the Soviet nuclear plant accident at Chernobyl in late April was generally marked by restraint and expressions of sympathy for the victims. (*See* ENERGY: *Sidebar.*) In his first public address on the subject, on May 14, Gorbachev thanked U.S. bone-marrow-transplant specialists Robert Gale (*see* BIOGRAPHIES) and Paul Terisaki for their help in treating victims of radiation poisoning. The White House response to the speech was mixed. A formal statement welcomed Gorbachev's proposal for an international early-warning system for nuclear accidents. However, the statement rebutted the Soviet leader's criticism of Western media coverage of Chernobyl, insisting that the nature of the coverage resulted from excessive secrecy on the part of the Kremlin.

For much of the first half of 1986, U.S. foreign-policy makers seemed preoccupied with Libya and its mercurial leader, Col. Muʿammar al-Qadhdhafi. The tone was set on January 7, when Reagan announced the imposition of U.S. economic sanctions against Libya and ordered the 1,000 to 1,500 Americans still living in that country to leave at once. The next day the president issued an order freezing all Libyan assets in the U.S. These drastic actions were prompted by alleged Libyan support of international terrorism, particularly the December 1985 attacks on the Israeli El Al airline's counters at Rome and Vienna airports that left 19 people dead. In March a U.S. Navy task force assembled in the Mediterranean Sea off Libya and began conducting "freedom of navigation" exercises in disputed waters of the Gulf of Sidra. Over a two-day period, Libya fired antiaircraft missiles at U.S. warplanes, while the U.S. responded by attacking a number of Libyan ships and a missile installation on the Libyan mainland.

The situation worsened on April 5, when a bomb exploded in a West Berlin discotheque, killing two people,

A billboard in Atlanta, Georgia, advertises a new U.S. federal holiday. The third Monday in January became Martin Luther King, Jr., Day in honour of the slain civil rights leader and Nobel Peace Prize winner.

ROB NELSON—PICTURE GROUP

one of whom was a U.S. serviceman. Once again Qadhdhafi was named by the U.S. as the likely instigator, and the Reagan administration mounted a campaign aimed at persuading its European allies to expel Libyan diplomats. The U.S. also indicated that it was prepared to retaliate militarily against Libya, and the threatened retaliation took place April 14, when U.S. warplanes bombed what were described as "terrorist-related targets" in the Libyan cities of Tripoli and Benghazi. With the exception of Great Britain, Western European governments expressed varying degrees of dismay over the raid. The Soviet Union condemned it in strong terms, as did Arab, Islamic, and other third world nations. The attack was generally approved in the U.S., however, although some members of Congress voiced reservations about the White House's lack of prior consultation, and Reagan was perceived as having finally used U.S. military power to back up years of tough rhetoric about terrorism. The president's standing in public opinion surveys soared to record levels.

Libya came back to haunt the administration later in the year. In an exclusive story in the *Washington Post* on October 2, it was disclosed that the White House had launched a secret campaign in August designed to convince Qadhdhafi that his country would be hit by another retaliatory strike and that he would be deposed in a coup. The revelation of planned deception, and of the U.S. news media's unwitting role in giving it credence, caused an uproar among publishers and broadcasters. Reagan acknowledged on October 2 that he had approved a plan in August to make Qadhdhafi "go to bed every night wondering what we might do" to deter him from backing terrorism. Referring specifically to the *Post*'s account, he added: "I challenge the veracity of that entire story I read this morning with great shock."

Even before the disclosure that money involved in the secret U.S.-Iran arms deal had made its way to *contra* rebel groups, Nicaragua was a major concern of the Reagan administration. After a battle of more than two years, the president persuaded Congress in 1986 to renew military assistance to the *contras,* who had been trying to overthrow the leftist Sandinista government. The omnibus spending bill for fiscal year 1987 contained $70 million in military aid and $30 million in nonmilitary aid for the *contras.* It also included $300 million in economic aid for other Central American nations. The deadlock on *contra* aid was broken June 25, when the House voted for the $100 million by 221 to 209. Perhaps more important than the money itself, however, the bill lifted most restrictions that Congress had imposed in 1984–85 on direct U.S. involvement with the *contras.* Among other things, the bill allowed the CIA to resume management of the *contra* aid program. However, the separate intelligence authorization bill for fiscal 1987 barred the CIA from tapping its multimillion-dollar contingency fund to give aid to the *contras* above the $100 million level set by Congress.

Nicaragua provided another embarrassing coda to the administration's foreign affairs record. The Nicaraguan government charged on October 7 that the CIA was responsible for a *contra* supply plane shot down over the southern part of the country two days earlier. Two Americans aboard the aircraft died when it crashed, but a third, a former U.S. marine named Eugene Hasenfus, parachuted from the plane and was captured. The White House and the CIA denied any link to the plane, despite a claim by

Texas Sesquicentennial

In 1986 Texas held the biggest birthday party of the year when it celebrated the 150th anniversary of its independence from Mexico. The Texas Sesquicentennial Commission, based in Austin, sanctioned some 10,000 events for the occasion, including the World's Largest Rattlesnake Roundup in Sweetwater, Buccaneer Days in Corpus Christi, a specially commissioned ballet in La Porte, tributes to the oil boomtowns in Odessa and Abilene, a reunion in Mexia of German prisoners of war held in Texas during World War II, and innumerable ethnic festivals, art fairs, and barbecues. A commemorative wagon train crisscrossed some 4,500 km (2,800 mi) of the state from January to July, while a steam train carrying special historic exhibits traveled 3,700 km (2,300 mi) from late February to April and July to September. Probably the most important observances were the ceremonies in San Antonio to honour the fall of the Alamo and the San Jacinto festival held near Houston to commemorate the decisive Battle of San Jacinto, where Gen. Sam Houston's forces defeated the Mexican Army and freed Texas from Mexican control.

The neighbouring state of Arkansas was also celebrating its 150th birthday in 1986, but even there Texas dominated the news. Organizers in Arkansas complained that many people did not even know about their own state's sesquicentennial.

Texas, however, was not celebrating its birth as a U.S. state (that came in 1845) but rather the founding of the independent Republic of Texas. Texans across the state used the occasion to rally together in a show of unity and optimism, and it came at a time when Texans needed something to celebrate. The oil boom of the 1970s had gone bust in the 1980s. Crude petroleum prices fell from a 1981 high of $35 per barrel to less than $10 in April 1986. They rose slightly to around $17 by the year's end, but prospects for recovery remained poor, and the damage to the oil industry had already spread throughout the economy. The real estate boom fueled by high oil prices collapsed, leaving housing developments half finished and new office high rises standing empty. The state government faced its first budget deficit in years when crucial oil revenues fell short. Gov. Mark White pushed through widespread budget cuts and a temporary sales tax increase. After his defeat for reelection in November there was a growing call for the state's first personal income tax. (MELINDA SHEPHERD)

A U.S. Navy F-14 Tomcat lights up the deck of the USS *America* on April 15, readying for catapult takeoff to begin its mission to Libya.
AP/WIDE WORLD

Hasenfus that the CIA had supervised not only that flight but also previous supply operations of a similar nature. As expected, Hasenfus was convicted by a government tribunal in Managua November 15 and sentenced to 30 years in prison for violating Nicaraguan security laws. While testifying in his defense, Hasenfus denied knowing who had funded or managed the operation that resulted in his capture. He maintained that he had taken the job only for the money, having had difficulty finding suitable employment at home. Shortly before Christmas he was pardoned and returned to the U.S.

South Africa continued to be a trouble spot for the U.S. in 1986. Handing Reagan the most important foreign policy defeat of his presidency, Congress enacted into law a bill imposing economic sanctions against South Africa. Reagan vetoed the bill September 26, saying it would hurt the South African blacks it was intended to help, but both houses voted overwhelmingly to override the veto, the House on September 29 by 313–83 and the Senate on October 2 by 78–21. The bill barred imports of South African iron, steel, textiles, agricultural goods, and other products and ordered the suspension of direct air travel between South Africa and the U.S. It also called for further sanctions in a year if the white minority government in Pretoria failed to move toward dismantling the system of apartheid (racial separation). Proponents acknowledged that the bill would not, by itself, force an end to apartheid, but they claimed the measure would demonstrate to South African blacks that the U.S. supported their aspirations for a freer life.

The administration's handling of U.S. relations with the Philippines may have constituted its main achievement of 1986 in foreign affairs. The Philippine presidential election of February 7, held amid allegations of widespread vote fraud, stirred indignation in the U.S.—especially after incumbent Pres. Ferdinand Marcos was declared the winner February 16 by the National Assembly. An independent tally the same day gave the victory to Marcos's opponent, Corazon Aquino. Events then moved swiftly. On February 19 the U.S. Senate voted 85–9 that the Philippine election had been marred by fraud. Five days later Reagan called on Marcos to resign, and on February 25, hours after holding an inaugural ceremony, Marcos fled to exile in Hawaii.

Aquino, inaugurated the same day as Marcos, scored a personal triumph on her first visit to the U.S. as Philippine president in September. After delivering a highly praised speech to a joint session of Congress, Aquino had the satisfaction of seeing that the U.S. lawmakers were willing to provide substantial aid to her financially pressed government. To encourage the Aquino government and bolster an economy that had suffered through years of Marcos's "crony capitalism," Congress twice voted aid increases for the Philippines. In a fiscal 1986 supplemental appropriations bill, Congress voted a bonus for the Philippines of $100 million in economic aid and $50 million in military assistance. That money was in addition to about $230 million already allocated in 1986. Then, in the omnibus spending bill for fiscal 1987, Congress set aside $200 million in "additional" economic aid. (*See* Feature Article: *The Philippines: Is Democracy Restored?*)

Domestic Affairs. Contrasting sharply with the fumbling performance of the White House in foreign affairs was the extraordinary record compiled by Congress on domestic legislation in 1986. It revised the tax code more extensively than at any other time since World War II, rewrote immigration law, and approved the most far-reaching environmental bills since the 1970s.

The tax reform bill, a product of more than two years'

AP/WIDE WORLD

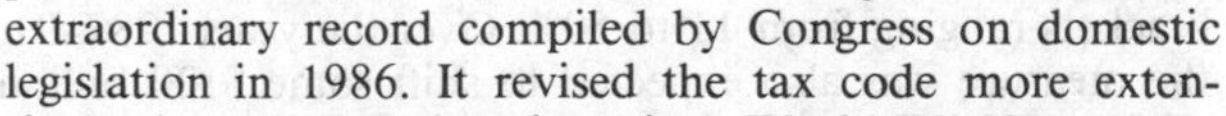

Rep. Dan Rostenkowski (left), chairman of the House Ways and Means Committee, chats with Speaker of the House Thomas P. ("Tip") O'Neill before the House vote on a major overhaul of the U.S. tax code.

Chinese sailors in Qingdao (Tsingtao) secure the USS *Reeves*, marking the first U.S. naval port call to China since 1949. The ship is a guided missile frigate.
AP/WIDE WORLD

work by Congress, the Treasury Department, and the White House, sharply reduced income-tax rates for corporations and individuals and curtailed or eliminated dozens of tax breaks. For individuals, the bill established just two basic rates of 15 and 28%, replacing the old structure of 14 brackets ranging from 11 to 50%. Over the years 1987–91, the measure was also expected to shift some $120 billion of the total income-tax burden from individuals to corporations. Even so, the corporate share of total income-tax collections was still projected to remain below the proportion that prevailed from 1940 through 1979.

Immigration law reform capped five years of effort. For the first time, employers were made subject to fines—and in repeat cases, jail terms—for knowingly hiring illegal aliens. At the same time, the bill included an amnesty program to give legal status to perhaps millions of illegals who could prove they had been in the U.S. since Jan. 1, 1982.

Environmental bills thought of as perennial losers also became winners. Three years of work on the Superfund toxic-waste cleanup program paid off when Congress cleared a bill in October mandating a fivefold increase in funding. The program, established in 1980, had expired in 1985 and was kept alive with such minimal funding that work had almost stopped. Congress reauthorized the 1972 Clean Water Act, including $18 billion for sewage- and pollution-treatment plants that set up what was described as the second-largest public works project in the nation's history, surpassed only by the Interstate Highway System. President Reagan killed the bill with a pocket veto, but supporters planned to reintroduce it in 1987. Still another environmental measure, the first major water projects bill in a decade, was cleared in the final hours of the 99th Congress. It authorized hundreds of dams, harbours, and recreational and flood-control projects but also required local users to pay more of the costs.

The Democratic Party staged what was seen as a surprisingly strong comeback in the November 4 midterm elections. Its margin of control in the Senate, 55 to 45, was slightly greater than the 53 to 47 Republican edge in the 99th Congress. In the House, Democrats increased their already sizable margin by 5 seats, to 258–177. The main effect of the election was to tilt the balance of political power for the Reagan administration's last two years, giving the president a Congress controlled by the opposition for the first time since he entered the White House.

The Democratic leaders of the 100th Congress consisted mainly of figures who had previously held positions of authority. Thomas P. ("Tip") O'Neill, Jr., of Massachusetts, who had served as speaker of the House for ten years before retiring from Congress, was succeeded—as had been expected—by Rep. James C. Wright of Texas. Wright's old post of House majority leader was taken over by Rep. Thomas S. Foley of Washington, while Rep. Tony Coelho of California was elected majority whip. In the Senate, Robert C. Byrd of West Virginia again assumed the office of majority leader, which he had held prior to the Republican election victory of 1980. Assisting him in the incoming Congress would be Alan Cranston of California as majority whip, Daniel K. Inouye of Hawaii as secretary of the Democratic Conference, and George J. Mitchell of Maine as deputy Senate president pro tempore.

AFP PHOTO

Former U.S. ambassador to Liberia Edward Perkins (right) poses with Pres. Ronald Reagan in the White House shortly after being named first black U.S. ambassador to South Africa.

Pres. Ronald Reagan announces changes in the Supreme Court as Warren E. Burger (not pictured), chief justice of the United States for 17 years, retires. Associate Justice William H. Rehnquist (right) takes the office. Reagan's choice for filling the vacant seat in the Supreme Court was federal appeals court Judge Antonin Scalia (left).
PAUL HOSEFROS—THE NEW YORK TIMES

Democratic efforts to portray the 1986 elections as a repudiation of the Republican Party were undermined by the strong GOP showing in gubernatorial contests. Republicans gained eight governorships on November 4. The Democrats, who entered the election campaign in control of 34 of 50 statehouses, saw their advantage drop to 26–24. Twenty-three blacks were elected to the 100th Congress, a record total. The number of women, by contrast, remained the same at 25. The election of four new women House members was offset by the retirement of four others, and the addition of a new female senator (Barbara Mikulski, Dem., Md.) was offset by the failure of Paula Hawkins (Rep., Fla.) to win a second term.

Though the news media naturally focused on elections for Congress and governor, voters in 43 states cast ballots on more than 200 state and local initiatives, bond issues, and referenda November 4. (See *Developments in the States in 1986,* below.) In a contest that claimed national attention, Rose Elizabeth Bird was rejected in her bid to remain chief justice of California. Her conservative oppo-

The Centennial of Lady Liberty

The 100th birthday of the Statue of Liberty was celebrated in 1986 with a four-day, $30 million extravaganza over the Fourth of July weekend. "Liberty Enlightening the World," conceived in 1871 as a gift from the French people for America's centennial in 1876, had her actual birthday on October 28, but the festivities were timed to coincide with the annual marking of the nation's independence. Millions of New Yorkers and tourists watched the dazzling kaleidoscope of events in and around New York Harbor, and many millions more viewed the spectacle on television.

With U.S. Pres. Ronald Reagan and French Pres. François Mitterrand presiding, the weekend's observances began on the evening of July 3 with a ceremony saluting the statue's restoration. Coordinated by television and film producer David Wolper (who had stage-managed the opening and closing ceremonies of the 1984 Olympic Games), it began with a flourish of 120 trumpets playing "The Liberty Fanfare" by Boston Pops conductor John Williams and ended with what was billed as the largest fireworks display ever staged in the United States.

TANNENBAUM—SYGMA

Another highlight was the July 4 harbour festival, with President Reagan, aboard the battleship *Iowa,* reviewing 33 warships—12 U.S. vessels and 21 representing 13 other nations. This was followed by Operation Sail, a parade of stately tall ships with an estimated 30,000 smaller craft in attendance. Recalling the millions of immigrants for whom the statue had been the first sight of a new home, several hundred new citizens were inducted by Chief Justice Warren Burger on Ellis Island (where the old facilities for processing immigrants were also being restored), and thousands of others across the country were sworn in via closed-circuit television.

The outsize celebration was not without its detractors. Some critics deplored what they considered to be overcommercialization and tasteless exploitation of a national symbol. Even before Liberty Weekend began, there had been disputes regarding the more than $66 million refurbishing of the statue. Lee Iacocca, the flamboyant chairman of Chrysler Corp., was fired by the secretary of the interior from a federal commission involved in the restoration, although he continued as the project's chief fund-raiser and emerged as something of a hero.

On the third day, the statue was reopened to the public for the first time in two years. Returned to the people, it would once again display its bronze-plaque inscription of the closing lines of Emma Lazarus's 1883 poem "The New Colossus":

Give me your tired, your poor,
Your huddled masses, yearning to breathe free,
The wretched refuse of your teeming shore.
Send these, the homeless, tempest-tost to me,
I lift my lamp beside the golden door!

(BONNIE OBERMAN)

Senate majority leader Robert Byrd flaunts a jacket bearing the Democrats' victory total following the November congressional elections. A surprising net gain of eight Senate seats gave Democrats 55 to the Republicans' 45.

ARTHUR GRACE—NEWSWEEK

nents drew attention to her votes to reverse all 61 death sentences that came before the court on appeal during her tenure. Three other liberal members of the seven-justice court also failed to win reconfirmation.

The nation was stunned on January 28 when the space shuttle *Challenger* exploded shortly after being launched from Cape Canaveral, Fla., killing all seven crew members. President Reagan, saying he and his wife, Nancy, were "pained to the core" by the tragedy, led the nation in mourning. The National Aeronautics and Space Administration (NASA) immediately grounded the remaining fleet of three shuttle orbiters. For weeks in advance, the *Challenger* flight had been the focus of intense interest because of the presence on the crew of Sharon Christa McAuliffe, a Concord, N.H., high school teacher chosen by NASA as the first "citizen observer" to ride the shuttle. Plans called for her to teach science lessons on television over the Public Broadcasting Service to schoolchildren across the country. McAuliffe's husband, two children, and parents were among the thousands who witnessed the disastrous flight in person.

On February 3 the president appointed an independent commission headed by former secretary of state William P. Rogers to investigate the *Challenger* explosion. Its mandate was "to take a hard look at the accident, to make a calm and deliberate assessment of the facts and ways to avoid repetition." The panel would attempt to determine "the probable cause or causes" of the disaster and present its findings to the White House within 120 days. In its final report, made public June 9, the Rogers commission severely criticized NASA, asserting that the *Challenger* tragedy could have been avoided. It identified the immediate cause of the accident as a leak of superhot gases from a faulty seal in the shuttle's right-side booster rocket: "The space shuttle's solid rocket booster problem began with the faulty design of its joint and increased as both NASA and contractor management [Morton Thiokol Inc.] first failed to recognize it as a problem, then failed to fix it and finally treated it as an acceptable flight risk." The commission also pointed to the shuttle's mission schedule as a contributing factor in the management malaise that had settled over NASA in recent years. Top agency officials apparently had deluded themselves into thinking that the shuttle had become "operational," although it was obviously highly risky and still well within the experimental phase. (*See* SPACE EXPLORATION: *Special Report.*)

The *Challenger* accident was not the only humiliation for the U.S. space program in 1986. On April 18 a Titan 34-D launch vehicle carrying a secret military payload exploded five seconds after lift-off from Vandenberg Air Force Base in California. Then, on May 3, an unmanned Delta rocket lost power shortly after being launched at Cape Canaveral. Veering out of control, it was destroyed by remote control signal from an air force range safety officer. On the brighter side, only four days before the *Challenger* explosion, the U.S. spacecraft Voyager 2 made its closest approach to the planet Uranus, passing within 82,000 km (50,000 mi) of the planet's surface. As had been the case in Voyager's earlier encounters with Jupiter and Saturn, some of the most intriguing photographic images transmitted to Earth were those of the planet's moons, which offered odd and unique examples of planetary physics. (*See* ASTRONOMY: *Special Report.*)

Warren E. Burger's decision to retire as chief justice of the United States, announced June 17, gave Reagan his second opportunity to fill a vacancy on the U.S. Supreme Court. He did so by nominating Associate Justice William H. Rehnquist (*see* BIOGRAPHIES) to be the new chief justice and naming federal appeals court Judge Antonin Scalia (*see* BIOGRAPHIES) to the vacant seat. The Senate voted on September 17 to confirm the nominations of both men, Scalia by 98–0 but Rehnquist by only 65–33. The negative vote on Rehnquist was the largest ever cast against any justice seated on the high court. During a bruising precon-

AP/WIDE WORLD

President and Mrs. Ronald Reagan (centre), at a memorial service for the space shuttle *Challenger* astronauts killed when the craft exploded after lift-off on January 28, mourn with crew family members (left to right) Rich Scobee, Kathi Scobee Krauss, June Scobee, Jane Smith, Scott Smith, and Alison Smith.

firmation battle, Rehnquist's opponents had questioned his judicial ethics, his candor and integrity, his record on civil rights, women's rights, and individual liberty in general, and whether he would serve to unite or divide the nation.

The Supreme Court was the focus of an unrelated controversy arising from a speech by Attorney General Edwin Meese at Tulane University in New Orleans, La., on October 21. Asserting that Supreme Court rulings were not "the 'supreme law of the land,' " Meese argued against what he said was a tendency to place judicial rulings "on a par with the Constitution." In his view, a Supreme Court decision "binds the parties in the case and also the executive branch for whatever enforcement is necessary. But such a decision does not establish 'a supreme law of the land' that is binding on all persons and parts of government, henceforth and forevermore." Meese's remarks provoked a storm of criticism from legal scholars, leading him to adopt a seemingly softer stance in later statements.

Wall Street was repeatedly shaken in 1986 by a series of insider-trading scandals exposed by the Securities and Exchange Commission (SEC). In what it described as the largest such case it had ever brought, on May 12 the agency charged Dennis B. Levine, a managing director in the mergers and acquisitions division of Drexel Burnham Lambert Inc. Levine was said to have cleared profits of at least $12.6 million through the use of nonpublic information in stock dealings. The SEC said his alleged scheme had lasted longer, netted higher profits, and involved more individual securities than any previous insider trading case it had taken to court. On June 5 Levine pleaded guilty to the insider-trading charges and also agreed to settle a suit brought against him by the SEC. He entered his plea as part of an arrangement under which he agreed to help investigators probing insider trading. Since Levine, 33, had built his banking career by exchanging information with contacts in the financial community, Wall Street expected that his cooperation with prosecutors would unleash a new round of indictments. Indeed, four other young Wall Street professionals pleaded guilty to federal charges of insider trading on the same day as Levine.

The biggest insider trading case of all came to light November 14. Shortly after the stock market closed that day, the SEC announced that securities speculator Ivan F. Boesky had agreed to pay $100 million in fines and illicit profits from trading based on inside information about corporate takeovers. Boesky also agreed to plead guilty to an unspecified criminal charge and would be barred from securities trading for life. The penalty, by far the most severe ever imposed for insider trading, grew out of the SEC's investigation of Levine. According to the agency's formal complaint, Levine had furnished Boesky with information obtained from his work at Shearson Lehman Brothers Inc. and Drexel Burnham Lambert. The most recent estimate in *Forbes* magazine's annual survey of the nation's wealthiest people had put Boesky's total fortune at $200 million. Although other estimates suggested he had even more money than that, Boesky's lawyer, Harvey Pitt, insisted that "very, very little" of his wealth would remain after he paid the penalty. (RICHARD L. WORSNOP)

See also *Dependent States,* below.

Church Membership in the United States

Religious body	Total clergy	Inclusive membership
Baptist bodies		
American Baptist Association	...	225,000
American Baptist Churches in the U.S.A.	7,822	1,559,683
Baptist Bible Fellowship, International	4,500	1,405,900
Baptist General Conference	1,560	132,546
Baptist Missionary Association of America	2,350	227,720
Conservative Baptist Association of America	...	225,000
Free Will Baptists	2,895	217,838
General Baptists (General Association of)	1,524	73,040
Liberty Baptist Fellowship	374	130,000
National Baptist Convention of America	28,574	2,668,799
National Baptist Convention, U.S.A., Inc.	27,500	5,500,000
National Primitive Baptist Convention	636	250,000
Primitive Baptists	...	72,000
Progressive National Baptist Convention	863	521,692
Regular Baptist Churches, General Association of	2,045	300,839
Southern Baptist Convention	62,900	14,477,364
Buddhist Churches of America	115	100,000
Christian and Missionary Alliance	2,181	227,846
Christian Congregation	1,449	103,990
Church of God (Anderson, Ind.)	3,227	185,593
Church of the Brethren	1,962	159,184
Church of the Nazarene	8,494	522,082
Churches of Christ—Christian Churches		
Christian Church (Disciples of Christ)	6,793	1,116,326
Christian Churches and Churches of Christ	6,238	1,051,469
Churches of Christ	...	1,604,000
Community Churches, International Council of	300	200,000
Congregational Christian Churches, Natl. Assn. of	826	108,115
Eastern Churches		
American Carpatho-Russian Orthodox Greek Catholic Ch.	68	100,000
Antiochian Orthodox Christian Archdiocese of N. Am.	180	280,000
Apostolic Catholic Assyrian Ch. of the East, N. Am. Dioc.	57	80,000
Armenian Apostolic Church of America	23	225,000
Armenian Church of America, Diocese of the	61	450,000
Bulgarian Eastern Orthodox Church	11	86,000
Coptic Orthodox Church	28	105,000
Greek Orthodox Archdiocese of N. and S. America	655	1,950,000
Orthodox Church in America	531	1,000,000
Romanian Orthodox Episcopate of America	67	60,000
Russian Orthodox Church Outside of Russia	168	55,000
Serbian Eastern Orth. Ch. in the U.S.A. and Canada	73	97,123
Ukrainian Orthodox Church in the U.S.A.	131	87,745
Episcopal Church	13,940	2,739,422
Evangelical Covenant Church of America	912	85,150
Evangelical Free Church of America	1,484	95,722
Friends United Meeting	621	57,433
Independent Fundamental Churches of America	1,366	120,446
Jehovah's Witnesses	None	730,441
Jews	6,500	5,834,635
Latter Day Saints (Mormons)		
Church of Jesus Christ of Latter-day Saints	28,598	3,860,000
Reorganized Church of Jesus Christ of L.D.S.	16,411	192,082
Lutherans		
American Lutheran Church	7,580	2,332,316
Evangelical Lutheran Churches, The Assn. of	665	110,934
Lutheran Church in America	8,484	2,898,202
Lutheran Church—Missouri Synod	7,954	2,638,164
Wisconsin Evangelical Lutheran Synod	1,462	415,380
Mennonite Church	3,399	91,167
Methodists		
African Methodist Episcopal Church	6,550	2,210,000
African Methodist Episcopal Zion Church	6,275	1,202,229
Christian Methodist Episcopal Church	2,650	718,922
Free Methodist Church of North America	1,773	72,223
United Methodist Church	37,483	9,266,853
Wesleyan Church	2,616	109,541
North American Old Roman Catholic Church	148	62,380
Pentecostals		
Apostolic Overcoming Holy Church of God	350	75,000
Assemblies of God	26,439	2,082,878
Church of God	2,737	75,890
Church of God (Cleveland, Tenn.)	9,638	505,775
Church of God in Christ	10,425	3,709,661
Church of God in Christ, International	1,600	200,000
Church of God of Prophecy	7,920	73,952
Full Gospel Fellowship of Churches and Ministers, Intl.	850	65,000
International Church of the Foursquare Gospel	3,482	177,787
Pentecostal Church of God	1,597	89,508
Pentecostal Holiness Church, International	3,422	113,000
United Pentecostal Church, International	6,796	500,000
Plymouth Brethren	500	98,000
Polish National Catholic Church of America	141	282,411
Presbyterians		
Cumberland Presbyterian Church	766	98,037
Presbyterian Church in America	1,641	179,696
Presbyterian Church (U.S.A.)	19,345	3,048,235
Reformed bodies		
Christian Reformed Church in North America	1,077	219,988
Reformed Church in America	1,641	342,275
Roman Catholic Church	57,183	52,654,908
Salvation Army	5,161	427,825
Seventh-day Adventist Church	4,308	651,954
Triumph the Church and Kingdom of God in Christ	1,375	54,307
Unitarian Universalist Association	1,041	171,838
United Church of Christ	10,085	1,683,777

Table includes churches reporting a membership of 50,000 or more and represents the latest information available.
Source: National Council of the Churches of Christ in the U.S.A.

(CONSTANT H. JACQUET)

Developments in the States in 1986

State governments experienced a particularly stormy year in their relations with the federal government in 1986, confronting Washington on a wide series of fronts. Federal plans for nuclear waste dumping, raising the drinking age, mandatory use of seat belts, and imposition of the 55-mph speed limit were challenged by various states, and debates over federal tax deductions, drug programs, education, and highway funding also raged.

Two women governors were elected in November 4 balloting, bringing the number of female state chief executives to a record high of three. Republicans made major advances in gubernatorial races, but Democrats offset those losses by picking up 200 seats in state legislatures nationwide.

A crisis over liability insurance was the most pressing problem facing state legislatures during the year, although responses around the country were anything but uniform. A national trend toward mandatory-seat-belt laws received what appeared to be a temporary setback in two state elections. The nation's state prison population continued to soar, but the long-awaited resumption of capital punishment on a large scale again failed to occur.

Forty-four states (all except Arkansas, Montana, Nevada, North Dakota, Oregon, and Texas) staged regular legislative sessions during the year, and eight (including Montana and Texas) called special sessions.

Party Strengths. Republicans made major gains in state gubernatorial elections in 1986, narrowing a 34–16 Democratic advantage to a 26–24 margin following the November balloting. GOP administrations in Oregon, Pennsylvania, and Tennessee were turned out in favour of Democrats, but Republican candidates replaced Democratic regimes in Alabama, Arizona, Florida, Kansas, Maine, Nebraska, New Mexico, Oklahoma, South Carolina, Texas, and Wisconsin.

Democrats made modest advances in state legislative races, however. After the November elections, Democrats had control of both chambers in 28 states, while Republicans held two chambers in only 10. For 1987, Democrats would enjoy total control in all states except Arizona, Colorado, Idaho, Indiana, Kansas, New Hampshire, North Dakota, South Dakota, Utah, and Wyoming (where Republicans controlled both chambers); Alaska, Michigan, Nevada, New York, Ohio, and Pennsylvania (where the House was dominated by Democrats and the Senate by Republicans); Delaware and New Jersey (where the House was Republican and the Senate Democratic); Montana (House Republican and Senate tied); New Mexico (House Democratic and Senate tied); Vermont (Senate Democratic and House tied); and Nebraska (which has a nonpartisan, unicameral legislature).

Women continued to gain influence in state government. A survey by the National Conference of State Legislatures found that 17.9% of state Cabinet officers were women in 1986, compared with 12.8% five years earlier, and some 15% of state legislators were also women, double the figure of ten years earlier. Nebraska laid claim to the first all-female governor's race, and the winner, Kay Orr, became the first Republican woman governor in the nation's history.

Followers of Lyndon LaRouche (*see* BIOGRAPHIES), a right-wing political extremist, scored a major upset by winning Democratic primary races for lieutenant governor and secretary of state in Illinois. The development alerted Democratic officials nationwide, however, and LaRouche candidates scored no additional victories. In Illinois the Democratic gubernatorial candidate, Adlai Stevenson III, refused to run on the same ticket with the LaRouchites and instead formed a third party, but Republicans swept all major state races in the general election.

Government Structures, Powers. The U.S. Supreme Court struck down Connecticut's "closed primary" law, which allowed only registered political party members to vote in primary elections. Similar laws in 35 states were presumably invalidated by the decision. Officials expressed interest in "motor voter" initiatives, which require officials to offer voter registration to driver's license renewal applicants. Arizona and Colorado, which had such regulations, were among only ten states that raised their voter turnout in 1986.

Rhode Island voters narrowly defeated an initiative rights amendment; the outcome left the number of states permitting citizen-initiated legislative elections at 23. Connecticut and Hawaii voters rejected a call for a state constitutional convention. Balloting in Alaska and Michigan resulted in defeat for legislative veto proposals, and voters in Arizona and Rhode Island turned down legislative pay increases. Idaho approved a reduction in the size of its legislature. Idaho, Mississippi, and Wisconsin approved prompt-pay legislation for the state, bringing to 44 the number of jurisdictions with similar laws. North Dakota voters rejected a proposal to end the state's Sunday closing law.

Government Relations. States stepped up lobbying activities in Washington to historic levels during 1986, attempting to influence the course of federal tax reform and to modify spending reductions dictated by the Gramm-Rudman-Hollings deficit-reduction measure. The efforts were only partially successful, and the year was a tumultuous one in federal-state relations.

Strenuous efforts to retain the major income tax provisions benefiting state governments—deductibility of state and local income and property taxes—bore fruit when Congress approved tax reform legislation at midyear. However, the new law eliminated deductibility of sales taxes, which furnish 48.5% of state revenue. State officials argued that any move to do away with state tax deductibility would increase citizen opposition to those taxes and impair the financial health of state governments.

Overall, however, the tax reform legislation was expected to provide a windfall for the 36 states that used the now-broadened federal tax base as the foundation for state income tax calculations. Four states that collected a percentage of federal tax liability projected reduced revenue. The federal tax changes suggested that many state legislators would face a happy decision—whether to spend or refund the generally increased revenues—in their 1987 sessions.

Money-saving tactics adopted by the U.S. Congress led to a struggle over motor fuel taxes during the year, with states accusing the federal government of returning only 68 cents of each dollar collected by the states for highway construction purposes. Virginia Gov. Gerald Baliles suggested the congressional foot-dragging meant that states should take back control of highway funding programs.

The federal government's budget problems led to what some commentators called "de facto new federalism," with states taking the lead in new initiatives as federal ability to fund innovations waned. Idaho Gov. John Evans declared that "More and more of the innovative ideas that are being considered as solutions to the problems of government have their roots in the states."

Finances. A regional recession in areas dependent on the oil and farming industries caused serious problems in the budgets of about half of the states. By year's end 18 states, most of them in the Midwest and Southwest, had been forced to cut their budgeted spending plans; only 3 had

UPI/BETTMANN NEWSPHOTOS

Democrat Helen Boosalis (left) and Republican Kay Orr, rivals in the race for Nebraska's governor's seat, meet after the state's primary. The state was the first to have two females as major-party contenders for governor. Orr was elected in the November general election.

made similar reductions in 1985. Programs to assist farmers were implemented in 18 states during 1986, with $1,250,000,000 expended on loans, loan guarantees, interest buy-downs, interest deferral, and loan forgiveness plans. Iowa and Minnesota required lenders to submit to mediation before foreclosing on farm properties.

Distressed farmers in the Southeast suffered another blow when the region was hit by what government meteorologists called the worst drought in the 115 years of official weather records. Threats to livestock prompted an outpouring of help, with state-assisted Operation Haylift shipments sent from 13 states in the Northeast and Midwest to hard-hit areas in 8 Southeastern states.

So-called tax amnesty programs continued to gain popularity, with Iowa, Michigan, Mississippi, New York, and West Virginia forgiving citizens who stepped forward to pay unreported or unpaid past obligations. The tax revolt of the 1970s seemed to lose momentum. Montana voters decided to freeze taxes at 1986 levels but rejected the abolition of property taxes. Oregon voters turned down four ballot measures aimed at cutting or shifting taxes, and Colorado citizens rejected an initiative to require voter approval of all state or local tax hikes. California voters approved Proposition 62, mandating a two-thirds council majority and voter approval for new or increased local taxes, but a court decision exempted charter cities, where a majority of Californians reside.

For the third consecutive year, only minor changes were made in state taxes. A survey by the Tax Foundation revealed that 16 states raised taxes by $2.4 billion during 1986, while 6 states trimmed levies by about $800 million. The most popular revenue raiser was the state sales tax, increased by Idaho, Kansas, Nebraska, New Mexico, Virginia, and Texas during the year. The motor fuels excise was boosted by Colorado, Delaware, Kentucky, Montana, North Carolina, Tennessee, Texas, and Virginia.

Cigarette taxes were increased in Colorado, Florida, New Mexico, Rhode Island, and Washington; by raising its rate from 23 to 31 cents per pack, Washington became the highest tobacco-taxing jurisdiction in the U.S. Four states—Colorado, Maine, New Mexico, and Washington—extended tobacco taxes to previously exempt products. New Mexico was the only state raising personal income taxes during the year. Colorado and Maine boosted corporate income taxes, and Maine doubled its excise on alcohol.

Connecticut, Delaware, Massachusetts, Michigan, Pennsylvania, and Vermont reduced personal income taxes. Pennsylvania also lowered corporate income tax rates, and California, Idaho, New Hampshire, and Utah adjusted their taxation of multinational corporate income from a worldwide to a water's edge basis, taxing corporations only on income produced in the U.S.

Figures compiled in 1986 revealed that state revenue from all sources totaled $438.6 billion during the 1985 fiscal year, an increase of 10.5% over the preceding 12 months. General revenue (excluding state liquor and state insurance trust revenue) amounted to $365.3 billion, also up 10.5%. Total state expenditures rose 11.2% to $390.8 billion, creating a technical surplus of $47.8 billion for the year. General expenditures, not including outlays of the liquor stores and insurance-trust systems, rose 11.4% to $345.1 billion. Of general revenue, 58.9% came from state taxes and licenses; 16.4% from charges and miscellaneous revenue, including educational tuition; and 24.7% from intergovernmental transfers (mostly from the federal government).

The largest state outlay was $128.6 billion for education, $44.3 billion of which went to state colleges and universities and $74.9 billion to local public schools. Other major outlays included $67.3 billion for public welfare, $33.2 billion for highways, and $27.5 billion for health and public hospitals.

Ethics. South Carolina state Rep. Phil Bradley was indicted for obstruction of justice after he refused to identify a fellow representative he allegedly saw using cocaine during a House session. Rhode Island's Superior Court ordered an investigation of the office of Attorney General Arlene Violet, who was defeated for reelection amid charges that her assistants withheld evidence from defense attorneys. West Virginia Attorney General Charlie Brown was acquitted by a jury on seven charges of illegally soliciting campaign funds from his staff. Brown admitted asking staffers to buy $100 tickets for a 1985 dinner but claimed the proceeds were used to repay debts, not influence the 1984 election.

Louisiana House speaker Joseph Delpit and state pardon board chairman Howard Marsellus, Jr., were indicted on three counts of public bribery; they were accused of taking $5,000 to $130,000 to assure successful pardon applications. Guam Gov. Ricardo J. Bordallo was indicted on charges that he solicited more than $100,000 in bribes and kickbacks; prosecutors said some of the money was delivered to Bordallo in a brown paper bag. William Huls, onetime head of the Louisiana Natural Resources Department, was indicted for helping to award a state oil lease to a company in which he had a secret interest. Georgia's public safety commissioner, Col. Hugh Hardison, was fired after being accused of allowing widespread fixing of traffic tickets and of using his position to gain personal financial advantages.

Arizona, Georgia, and Rhode Island toughened campaign finance and ethics laws during the year. In a case of great interest to the legal community, the state of Maryland filed a $450 million lawsuit against the prominent Baltimore law firm of Venable, Baetjer & Howard arising from the breakdown of the state-insured savings and loan industry in 1985. The state charged the law firm, which simultaneously represented the state thrift watchdog agency and numerous savings and loan executives, with "gross conflict of interest."

Education. A pilot program designed to reduce federal and state influence in local educational matters was approved during the year for 16 districts in Arkansas, Colorado, Missouri, New Hampshire, New Jersey, South Carolina, Tennessee, and Utah. The idea, designed to reverse the decades-old trend toward centralization of control over local education, was put forward by the National Governors' Association. It was labeled "the single most important event in American education in the last several years" by William Bennett, U.S. secretary of education.

California joined Texas in approving "pass-play," a controversial requirement that junior and senior high school students maintain a "C" average in order to be eligible for extracurricular activities. The South Dakota legislature, over a gubernatorial veto, abolished the two-year foreign language requirement for entrance to state colleges and universities.

Health, Welfare. Growing concern over the spread of AIDS (acquired immune deficiency syndrome) prompted heated debate but little legislative action during 1986. Some 200 bills on the subject were introduced in 30 state legislatures, but no state enacted the ideas most frequently advanced—a requirement for AIDS testing of marriage license applicants and restrictions on exposed children who want to attend public schools. California, Florida, and Wisconsin enacted measures restricting AIDS testing before the granting of insurance coverage or employment. California voters, by a solid 4 to 1 margin, rejected a LaRouche-inspired initiative that would have required quarantining of AIDS victims.

States continued to experiment with welfare reform ideas, and "workfare" spread during the year to a total of 30 states. Washington proposed replacing the Aid to Families with Dependent Children program with a private nonprofit corporation. Massachusetts offered money to welfare recipients seeking jobs or schooling. California required welfare mothers with children over six to receive training or work. Maryland provided economic assistance to firms that hired welfare recipients. Wisconsin, seeking to keep mothers off welfare, required a divorced parent to make payments to the spouse with child custody.

Enthusiasm for curbs on state funding of abortions continued to flounder. Antiabortion initiatives, usually including limits on state funding, were turned down by voters in Arkansas, Massachusetts, Oregon, and Rhode Island during the year.

North Dakota became the 36th state to inaugurate a statewide version of the Olympic Games in an attempt to promote health and fitness. Continuing a trend toward community-based mental health care, Rhode Island closed its major institution for the retarded; Gov. Edward D. DiPrete claimed the state was the first to adopt a formal policy of eliminating institutional care for retarded citizens.

Drugs. A nationwide crackdown on illegal drug use was reflected in numerous state actions during the year. State governments were granted a windfall of $602 million for education and law-enforcement purposes by a federal antidrug law signed by Pres. Ronald Reagan in October. Minnesota joined Arizona in imposing an excise tax on illegal drug sales, attempting to give lawmen another tool to prosecute dealers. However, South Dakota legislation requiring a tax stamp for drug dealing was ruled unconstitutional by the state supreme court as a violation of Fifth Amendment rights against self-incrimination.

Voters in Oregon, the first state to decriminalize possession of small amounts of marijuana, overwhelmingly rejected a proposal to legalize possession of the substance. Kansas voters approved sale of liquor by the drink. Florida became the first state to allow pharmacists to prescribe drugs for minor ailments.

Law and Justice. States struggled with responses to a national liability insurance crisis during 1986, generally endeavouring to temper huge jury verdicts and legal changes that had led to insurance premium increases and cancellations across a wide spectrum of U.S. society. A survey indicated that 1,400 bills on liability matters were introduced in state legislatures nationwide during the year, with 41 states taking action on tort reform, insurance regulation, or liability rules.

Florida and Washington overhauled the way tort claims are handled in the court system to make large recoveries in personal injury cases more difficult. Twelve other states put limits (from $200,000 to $875,000) on recoveries for pain and suffering. Nine states enacted laws preventing insurance companies from canceling coverage without adequate warning. Missouri and Wisconsin established limits on lawyers' fees. Michigan imposed a $225,000 ceiling on settlements in most medical malpractice cases. Eight states altered or abolished their laws allowing joint and several liability, which sometimes requires minor defendants to pay the entire cost of judgments.

The moves met with resistance in many cases. After West Virginia approved a new law limiting insurance company operations, most doctors and lawyers in the state received cancellation notices on their liability policies, and several insurers announced their intention to abandon business in the state. Acting on an antitrust complaint from the state attorney general, the West Virginia Supreme Court issued a restraining order against further cancellations. A special session of the state legislature ultimately relaxed the requirements on insurers but also set up a study that could lead to a state-run insurance company. (*See* INDUSTRIAL REVIEW: *Special Report.*)

California and Colorado approved new laws protecting persons who injure or kill intruders in their homes. Oregon voters approved a measure strengthening victims' rights and toughening criminal procedure methods. Maine voters rejected, by a 2 to 1 margin, a referendum making it a crime to sell or promote obscene material. Voters in Illinois, Oklahoma, and Rhode Island approved denial of bail to criminal suspects in certain circumstances.

Twelve additional jurisdictions, bowing to the threat of a cutoff of federal highway funds, raised the minimum drinking age for all alcoholic beverages to 21 during the year, leaving only four states—Idaho, Louisiana, Montana, and Wyoming—allowing under-21 drinking and in serious danger of federal sanctions. A Louisiana government spokesman noted that the federal fund cutoff would cost the state only $15 million in its first year, while an increase in the drinking age from 18 would cause a $30 million drop in revenue from the state excise taxes on alcohol.

The conflict over the federally imposed 55-mph speed limit continued to escalate during the year. The U.S. Department of Transportation announced plans to reduce highway funding for Arizona and Vermont because of lax state enforcement of speed limit laws. Nevada announced an increase to 70 mph for a short stretch of I-80 but backed down when the Federal Highway Administration ordered a cutoff of $66 million in highway funds. At year's end Nevada filed suit against the federal government, alleging infringement of states' rights.

Prisons. State prison populations continued to set new records during 1986, as laws mandating minimum sentences for certain crimes and trimming parole and probation procedures offset a leveling trend in the nation's crime rate. A midyear census by the U.S. Department of Justice found 484,615 prisoners in state institutions, up 7.2% from the 452,020 inmates on hand a year earlier. Much of the increase occurred in California's prison population, which rose 17.3% over the year and now comprised more than 10% of the national prisoner total.

A survey by the Legal Defense Fund of the National Association for the Advancement of Colored People revealed that 1,788 prisoners were occupying death row cells nationwide on October 1, compared with 1,590 a year earlier. More than 200 criminals received death sentences during 1986, but only 17 were actually executed.

Gambling. State-sponsored lotteries continued to gain public acceptance during the year, with voters in Montana, Kansas, South Dakota, Idaho, and Florida approving government-run games of chance in the November elections. A similar lottery proposal was defeated in North Dakota. That meant that 28 jurisdictions would have state lotteries by early 1987. Ten states in the Northeast and Midwest agreed to develop a regional lottery to promote maximum publicity and a multimillion-dollar payoff, with Illinois tentatively selected as the operating administrative centre.

Arizona, Iowa, and California began utilizing their lotteries to enforce child-support laws, often by confiscating the winnings of parents who were behind on support payments. Kansas approved pari-mutuel betting, and Missouri removed a local-refusal option that had prevented implementation of its 1984 horse-betting initiative. Florida voters decisively rejected a local-option proposal for legalizing casino gambling, and the Louisiana legislature killed a proposal by Gov. Edwin Edwards to set up three casinos near New Orleans.

Environment. Citizen concern over pollution and nuclear waste continued to preoccupy state governments during 1986, and tension between state and federal authorities was particularly evident. Voters in Massachusetts, New Jersey, and New York approved major toxic waste cleanup proposals, and California voters overwhelmingly passed a "safe drinking water and toxics enforcement" measure that was called the most far-reaching environmental initiative of the decade. Nevada voters appropriated $31 million for environmental land purchases.

Although the federal government increased funds for cleaning up toxic waste dumps from $1.6 billion to $9 billion over the next five years, Pres. Ronald Reagan pocket-vetoed a major water-quality bill that would have provided states with $18 billion in wastewater-treatment funds over eight years. Governors promised renewed lobbying for the legislation in 1987.

Concern over nuclear waste bubbled in several election campaigns. In an advisory vote, Washington voters overwhelmingly turned down a proposal for a high-level nuclear waste site in the states. Washington was a finalist, along with Nevada and Texas, for the first federal nuclear-waste depository. A presidential decision on the site was scheduled for 1991.

Energy. In a ruling universally applauded by the states, Exxon Corp. was ordered to repay $2.1 billion in oil overcharges made when oil price controls were in effect in the late 1970s. States divided the money according to petroleum consumption. The funds were to be used for consumer-related projects such as weatherizing hospitals and schools and helping the poor pay utility bills.

The Supreme Court ruled that states cannot require public utilities to include inserts from consumer groups with their customer bill mailings. The ruling, on a California case, affected similar programs in New York, West Virginia, and Wisconsin.

Equal Rights. Several states considered punitive measures against South Africa for its racial practices. California state agencies began selling off stock in corporations continuing to do business in South Africa, and Maryland became the first state to ban state agencies from purchasing goods produced in South Africa unless there was no alternative supplier.

Vermont voters narrowly rejected a state equal rights amendment backed by women's groups. By a 3 to 1 margin, California voters made English the state's official language, despite the concern of Hispanic groups that the measure would adversely affect the provision of bilingual ballots and other bilingual programs.

Consumer Protection. A federally backed trend toward mandatory-seat-belt laws continued during 1986, with new statutes approved or effective during the year in Indiana, Oklahoma, Utah, Minnesota, Iowa, Ohio, Louisiana, Washington, Idaho, Maryland, Nevada, Tennessee, Kansas, and Florida. However, voters in Nebraska and Massachusetts, reacting to what critics called excessive federal pressure, repealed their seat-belt laws in the November balloting, leaving the number of jurisdictions with mandatory-seat-belt strictures at 24 by year's end. Commentators proclaimed the two-state setback an exception to a general trend, and the Motor Vehicle Manufacturers Association predicted that 11 additional states would enact seat-belt legislation during 1987.

Idaho voters affirmed a new state right-to-work law over vigorous labour union opposition; it was the first such law to be passed since 1970 and brought to 21 the number of states with right-to-work legislation on the books. Nebraska became the first state to enact near-total deregulation of local telephone service, but voters in Maine and Oregon overwhelmingly banned inauguration of local measured phone rates. Texas voters approved intrastate branch banking. Maryland became the first jurisdiction to prohibit automobile dealers from placing their logo on new cars without compensating owners.

(DAVID C. BECKWITH)

Latin America and the Caribbean

LATIN-AMERICAN AFFAIRS

Latin America's economic difficulties eased slightly in 1986, but its external debt continued to be a cause for concern. Several elections took place, continuing the trend toward greater civilian rule that had begun in 1980. In Colombia the Liberal candidate, Virgilio Barco Vargas (*see* BIOGRAPHIES), easily defeated his Conservative rival, Alvaro Gómez Hurtado, in presidential elections in May, and the Liberals dominated the legislature following congressional elections in March. Following elections in May, Joaquín Balaguer began his fifth term as president of the Dominican Republic in August. In congressional elections held in Ecuador in June, Pres. León Febres Cordero's National Reconstruction Front lost control of Congress. In July the ruling Partido Revolucionario Institucional won state and municipal elections in Mexico.

There were elections in Brazil in November for two-thirds of the Senate, the Chamber of Deputies, and state governments and assemblies. Pres. José Sarney's supporters in the governing coalition, the Brazilian Democratic Movement Party and the Liberal Front Party, won a landslide victory, taking all the state governorships and over two-thirds of the seats in a constituent assembly, which was to replace Congress in February 1987 and decide on a new constitution and a date for direct presidential elections. Also in November, Peru's governing party, the Alianza Popular Revolucionaria Americana, won handily in municipal elections. In Central America civilian presidents took office in Guatemala and Honduras in January. In the Caribbean President-for-Life Jean-Claude Duvalier fled from Haiti in February and was replaced by an interim governing council; the opposition People's National Party won municipal elections in Jamaica in July; and in general elections held in Trinidad and Tobago in December the ruling People's National Movement was defeated by the National Alliance for Reconstruction.

Central America continued to be afflicted by economic and social disorders, and guerrilla activity persisted in El Salvador, Guatemala, and Honduras. Peace initiatives were made throughout the year. The Contadora Group, formed in January 1983 by Colombia, Mexico, Panama, and Venezuela, submitted a regional peace treaty at a presidential summit of the five member countries of the Central American Common Market (CACM)—Costa Rica, El Salvador, Honduras, Guatemala, and Nicaragua—at Esquipulas, Guatemala, in late May. The treaty was not signed, but it was agreed to set up a Central American Parliament similar to the European Parliament. A Contadora support group had been established by Argentina, Brazil, Uruguay, and Peru in late 1985, and in January 1986 they and the original Contadora Group members signed the Caraballeda Declaration, which pledged to continue the search for diplomatic means of solving conflicts in the region. All parties agreed to continue the Contadora peace process. In August the U.S. Congress approved $100 million in aid ($70 million military; $30 million nonmilitary) to the Nicaraguan *contras,* who were based largely in Honduras. In El Salvador peace talks between the administration of Pres. José Napoleón Duarte and the guerrillas broke down in September.

In April the vice-presidents of Costa Rica, El Salvador, Guatemala, and Honduras agreed to consider joining the General Agreement on Tariffs and Trade (GATT). A meeting of finance ministers and central bank presidents of the CACM countries was held in Guatemala City in July to study ways of increasing intraregional trade. One proposal was the creation of vouchers, denominated in U.S. dollars and backed by the central banks, for use in trade transactions between the CACM countries.

The San José Pact, originally signed in 1980, whereby Mexico and Venezuela supplied up to 130,000 bbl a day of oil on concessionary terms to Barbados, Costa Rica, the Dominican Republic, El Salvador, Guatemala, Honduras, Jamaica, and Panama, was renewed in August despite some misgivings on both sides. Buyers paid 80% of their bills in cash, and the remainder attracted preferential and extended terms, provided the resources so released were invested in development projects. Mexico and Venezuela were concerned about their own economic problems, which had resulted from the fall in international oil prices. At the same time, the beneficiaries under the pact were anxious about the price they had agreed to pay for the oil—about

AP/WIDE WORLD

Five Central American presidents are served a luncheon in Esquipulas, Guatemala, during a peace-seeking meeting in May. Seated (left to right) are Oscar Arias Sánchez of Costa Rica, José Napoleón Duarte of El Salvador, Vinicio Cerezo of Guatemala, José Azcona of Honduras, and Daniel Ortega of Nicaragua.

$19 a barrel, higher than the price then prevailing in world markets.

Neither the Latin American Integration Association (LAIA), which consisted of Argentina, Bolivia, Brazil, Chile, Colombia, Ecuador, Mexico, Paraguay, Peru, Uruguay, and Venezuela, nor the Andean Group of Bolivia, Colombia, Ecuador, Peru, and Venezuela made substantial progress during the year. LAIA foreign ministers held a meeting in Acapulco, Mexico, in July and reached a formal agreement to increase intraregional trade. Prior to that meeting, Mexico and Uruguay had signed an economic complementation agreement in May, the fifth under LAIA rules, which had as its objective an increase in bilateral trade in specific products. In the same month, Cuba was admitted to LAIA with observer status. In the Andean Group the only significant moves were directed toward attracting foreign capital. In Colombia legislation regulating export-processing assembly industries in free-trade zones permitted unrestricted foreign ownership, and companies were freed from foreign-exchange restrictions. A new liberal foreign-investment law in Venezuela eliminated the requirement that foreign firms become locally owned within 15 years, raised the amount of profits foreign companies could remit home, and made repatriation of such profits easier; certain industries such as tourism and agriculture were exempted from foreign-exchange restrictions.

A growing trend toward bilateral trade was evident in an increase in barter and countertrade agreements. Particularly important—and indicative of this trend—was a wide-ranging economic integration agreement reached in July between Argentina and Brazil, which both governments saw as the first move toward the eventual establishment of a Latin-American common market. The most important of the 12 protocols embodied an agreement providing for growth in capital goods trade. It was hoped that overall trade would rise from $1 billion to $3 billion within five years. Other protocols covered cooperation in food supplies, particularly wheat, oil prospecting, natural gas, nuclear energy, and iron ore. In another important trade-related move in June, Brazil reestablished diplomatic links with Cuba following a 22-year gap.

Initiatives were taken to increase direct investment in Latin America. In June the International Finance Corporation, an affiliate of the World Bank, set up an Emerging Countries Growth Fund to invest in stocks of locally owned companies in less developed countries and to open up capital markets in those countries to foreign portfolio investment. The U.S. and 30 other countries established the Inter-American Investment Corporation, with an initial capital of $200 million; its main objective was to encourage investment in small- and medium-sized companies.

Trade headed the agenda when the heads of government of the 23 Caribbean Community (Caricom) members met in Guyana in July. The members agreed to replace the Caricom Multilateral Clearing Facility, which had been suspended in April 1983, with an Export Credit Facility, a $75 million fund to provide preshipment and postshipment financing for maximum terms of two and five years, respectively. Traditional exports such as sugar and bananas were excluded. The U.S. Caribbean Basin Initiative (CBI) functioned fitfully during the year. As originally visualized, it was an integrated program of trade and tax measures, giving duty-free access to the U.S. market for 12 years (from 1984) for a wide range of Caribbean and Central American products, mostly manufactured goods. Declining imports from the Caribbean reduced the U.S. trade deficit with the area in 1985 to $854 million, while U.S. exports remained steady at about $6 billion.

An upturn in the world economy in 1985 helped Latin America to continue the modest recovery that had begun in 1984 after the 1981–83 recession. The region's gross domestic product (GDP) grew by 2.8% in 1985, compared with 3.2% in 1984, and output exceeded the 1981 peak. There was a small deterioration in trade; exports from Latin America reached $91.9 billion in 1985, against $97.5 billion in 1984, while imports totaled $57.6 billion, compared with $58.8 billion in the preceding year. The region's total external debt reached $360 billion at the end of 1985 and was estimated at $370 billion in November 1986. Interest payments amounted to $35 billion in 1985, and inflation remained a serious problem with a 1985 rate of 528%, against 185% in 1984. GDP estimates for 1986 envisaged a decline to 1.5–3% because of oil-related problems in Mexico and Venezuela and generally depressed international commodity prices. The region's average rate of inflation was expected to fall.

Latin-American governments expressed concern about the foreign debt but failed to develop a coordinated strategy to reduce it. A total of 13 countries in the region were involved in rescheduling negotiations in 1986. Brazil and Mexico were still the world's most indebted countries, with debts of $109 billion and $97 billion, respectively, in November 1986. In September an agreement with commercial bank creditors became effective, whereby $31.2 billion of the Brazilian debt was restructured, with 1985 and 1986 principal maturities being recycled into 1987 and trade and interbank lines maintained until March 1987. In October official and commercial bank creditors provided a financing package of $12 billion to Mexico, with further supplementary resources if oil prices fell and certain growth targets were not met. This was the largest financing package in Latin-American history and the first time such lending had been linked to economic growth objectives.

(ROBIN CHAPMAN)

ANTIGUA AND BARBUDA

A constitutional monarchy and member of the Commonwealth, Antigua and Barbuda comprises the islands of Antigua, Barbuda, and Redonda in the eastern Caribbean Sea. Area: 442 sq km (171 sq mi). Pop. (1986 est.): 81,400. Cap.: Saint John's. Monetary unit: Eastern Caribbean dollar, with (Oct. 1, 1986) a par value of EC$2.70 to U.S. $1 (free rate of EC$3.90 = £1 sterling). Queen, Elizabeth II; governor-general in 1986, Sir Wilfred E. Jacobs; prime minister, Vere Cornwall Bird.

During 1986 political life in Antigua and Barbuda was marked by persistent reports of factional disputes within the governing Antigua Labour Party. These focused on the leadership vacuum that was likely to occur in the event of the death or retirement of Prime Minister Vere Cornwall Bird, who was 76 years old. Deputy Prime Minister Lester Bird, Vere Bird's son, brought the issue into the open in June when he stated that he had no intention of succeeding his father. Frequent allegations of corruption continued in the weekly *Outlet,* edited by Tim Hector, leader of the left-wing Antigua Caribbean Liberation Movement. In May a high court judge ruled unconstitutional the section of the 1972 Public Order Act under which Hector had been imprisoned in 1985 for "undermining public confidence" in a government minister. The government appealed against the ruling.

In April the National Democratic Party and the United People's Movement merged to form the United National Democratic Party, with Ivor Heath as leader. Tourism remained the lifeblood of the economy, accounting for 60% of gross domestic product. Government borrowing for development projects increased to $63 million during the year. (ROD PRINCE)

This article updates the *Macropædia* article The West Indies: *Antigua and Barbuda.*

ARGENTINA

The federal republic of Argentina occupies the eastern section of the Southern Cone of South America, along the Atlantic Ocean. Area: 2,780,092 sq km (1,073,399 sq mi). Pop. (1986 est.): 31,030,000. Cap.: Buenos Aires. Monetary unit: austral, with (Oct. 1, 1986) a free rate of 1.05 australes to U.S. $1 (1.52 australes = £1 sterling). President in 1986, Raúl Alfonsín.

Domestic Affairs. Pres. Raúl Alfonsín surprised both supporters and opponents when he proposed in April 1986 that the capital of Argentina be moved from Buenos Aires to the neighbouring Patagonian towns of Viedma and Carmen de Patagones. The move was the most notable in a package of proposals for restructuring the political, administrative, and judicial systems in order to modernize the bureaucracy and decentralize decision making. A multiparty advisory committee had reviewed the package before it was submitted to Congress. Viedma and Carmen de Patagones were chosen because of their central location, 800 km (500 mi) south of Buenos Aires at the mouth of the Río Negro on the Atlantic coast. They were in an isolated and underdeveloped area, in contrast to the densely populated and heavily industrialized Buenos Aires location. The political reforms envisioned included a European-style parliamentary system with a prime minister, who could be reelected. It was speculated that Alfonsín would present himself as a candidate for the post if the reform was approved.

Labour unrest intensified. By September union leaders calculated that real wages had fallen 30% since June 1985. There had been seven general strikes and numerous industry-specific strikes since Alfonsín came into power in 1983. In October hospitals and train services were paralyzed, teachers and university lecturers stopped work, and legislation limiting the right to strike was threatened.

Investigations into military conduct during the 1982 Falkland Islands/Islas Malvinas conflict were completed in May. Three former leaders of the armed forces were found guilty of incompetence during the conflict and stripped of their rank and imprisoned. Former president Leopoldo Galtieri, who initiated the invasion of the islands, received a 12-year sentence; Adm. Jorge Isaac Anaya received 14 years for failing to give naval support to the Army and not taking an opportunity to negotiate an end to the hostilities; and Brig. Gen. Basilio Lami Dozo, the air force chief, was sentenced to 8 years.

President Alfonsín received international recognition for his fight against human rights violations. In July the Council of Europe announced that its Prize for Human Rights would be awarded to Alfonsín. It had never before been awarded to an individual. Alfonsín's reputation in the field later suffered, however; a law passed in late December granted exemption from prosecution on charges of human rights violations to all military and police officers not formally indicted within 60 days.

Jubilation gripped Argentina when its football team won the World Cup in Mexico, beating West Germany 3–2. During the celebrations in Buenos Aires, 2 people were killed and 376 were arrested when the crowd's enthusiasm got out of hand. The political parties took the opportunity to stress nationalistic issues.

Foreign Relations. Relations with the U.K. improved in the first half of the year but then deteriorated. In February a group of senior Argentine parliamentarians visited the

Argentine Pres. Raúl Alfonsín (left) chats with Australia's Prime Minister Bob Hawke before they shared a Saturday evening meal. The meeting took place during a visit by Alfonsín to Australia in July to improve trade relations.

AP/WIDE WORLD

U.K. at the invitation of the Interparliamentary Union and held informal talks with British MPs, academics, journalists, and businessmen. In October nine British MPs visited Buenos Aires for the 76th Interparliamentary Union Conference and held informal talks on normalization of relations.

In April Argentina relaxed its trade ban and adopted an open-door policy on visas for British subjects for the first time since the 1982 conflict. Exports of meat and the importation of British-made equipment were authorized. In September, however, the Senate passed a resolution urging Alfonsín not to authorize the resumption of trade with the U.K. unless Britain agreed to discuss sovereignty over the Falklands/Malvinas.

The sudden deterioration in relations with Britain in October occurred because of a disagreement over conservation of fish stocks. About 600 trawlers, mostly from the U.S.S.R. and other Eastern European countries, Japan, South Korea, and Taiwan, were fishing around the Falklands/Malvinas in 1986, compared with 485 in 1985 and 250 in 1984. An attempt to set up a multilateral agreement to conserve stocks under the auspices of the UN Food and Agriculture Organization failed when Argentina signed bilateral agreements with the U.S.S.R. and Bulgaria that implicitly recognized Argentina's jurisdiction over disputed territory. At the end of October the U.K. announced a 150-mi fishing zone where all fishing vessels would need a license from Feb. 1, 1987. Despite their claim to sovereign rights over a 200-mi area around the islands, British officials stressed that patrol vessels would not extend their policing beyond the 150-mi zone, apparently in an attempt to minimize disputes with Argentina. In turn, Argentina warned that foreign trawlers entering its own 200-mi exclusive economic zone could be fired on by coast guard boats.

Throughout 1986 emphasis was placed on improving foreign relations with a view to increasing trade. In July President Alfonsín visited New Zealand, Australia, Japan, the Philippines, Saudi Arabia, and Portugal to acquire high technology for industry and to improve trade. Argentina and Australia agreed on a common need to liberalize trade in agricultural produce—both countries' export markets had been damaged by the wheat export policies of the U.S. and the European Communities. A broad agreement with Japan to promote trade and economic cooperation resulted in a $100 million loan by the Japanese Export-Import Bank to finance Japanese imports.

An important trade agreement with the long-term aim of creating a common market in South America was signed with Brazil in July. The 12 protocols established a common barrier to imports from third countries; bilateral trade was to be balanced by the creation of two funds for investment and finance, to be used to expand production in either country if it was suffering a trade deficit in capital goods. Brazil agreed to purchase more grain from Argentina, and seasonal food shortages in both countries were to be eradicated through bilateral trade. Cooperation in energy development was also considered.

The Economy. The shortage of foreign exchange continued to dominate the economy. In February an agreement was finally reached with the International Monetary Fund (IMF) on new economic targets for the first quarter of the year that would release some $265 million in loans frozen since January. It was then decided, however, that because of the delay Argentina would forgo 235.5 million Special Drawing Rights (SDR) of its IMF standby program, cutting the total to SDR 1,180,000,000. Foreign banks agreed to a 180-day extension of $6.7 billion in debt falling due at the end of April, when the year-old debt-refinancing accord was to expire. In September Argentina obtained a further 180-day rollover of principal payments due in 1986 on its medium- and long-term foreign debt. Discussions began with the IMF for a new standby credit and compensatory finance because of a fall in its terms of trade.

In April the first changes were introduced to the nine-month-old austerity package, the Austral Plan. They included a 3.75% devaluation of the currency, the replacement of price controls by administered prices that would embrace input costs, and salary increases of 18 to 25% in the private sector and 18 to 21% for state company employees (but only 5% for central administration employees). The devaluation marked the start of a crawling peg exchange rate adjustment policy designed to encourage exports. Revisions to the Austral Plan also envisioned an acceleration of privatization, capitalization of the foreign debt to promote foreign investment, modifications to the tariff system to increase trade and competition, more incentives for exporters and investors, and a reduction of public-sector employment through attrition.

Disputes between the economy minister and the central bank over monetary policy resulted in inadequate controls on the money supply, while disputes within the ruling Unión Cívica Radical delayed privatization plans. The appointment in August of a technocrat from the Economy Ministry team, José Luis Machinea, as president of the central bank was expected to resolve monetary policy differences. Shortly after the new appointment, several cases of fraud were uncovered, involving central bank rediscounts authorized for suspected fraudulent export deals. This led to several small banks being taken over by the central bank and their directors being taken into police custody. The state prosecutor for administrative investigations also accused several former members of the central bank board of directors, including two members of the government, of fraud. In early October changes in banking regulations were announced designed to strengthen the commercial banking sector. (SARAH CAMERON)

BAHAMAS, THE

A constitutional monarchy and member of the Commonwealth, The Bahamas comprise an archipelago of about 700 islands in the North Atlantic Ocean just southeast of the United States. Area: 13,939 sq km (5,382 sq mi). Pop. (1986 est.): 236,000. Cap.: Nassau. Monetary unit: Bahamian dollar, with (Oct. 1, 1986) a par value of B$1 to U.S. $1 (free rate of B$1.45 = £1 sterling). Queen, Elizabeth II; governor-general in 1986, Sir Gerald Cash; prime minister, Sir Lynden O. Pindling.

Efforts to improve the image of The Bahamas continued in 1986, following the damage done by the royal commission report on drug-related corruption issued in December 1984. The former assistant commissioner of police, Howard Smith, was charged in November 1985 with receiving bribes. In July 1986 the government announced that it would introduce legislation to allow drug money handled by the banks to be traced, as well as the confiscation of property financed by drug trafficking. The U.S. agreed to supply the Bahamian police with helicopters and improved radio equipment. In May the government said it would start talks with the U.S. on an information-exchange agreement aimed at a tax treaty giving concessions to U.S. insurance companies and conventions.

While stopover tourist arrivals declined slightly in the first half of 1986 compared with the same period of 1985, cruise ship arrivals increased by one-third. Further development of tourist facilities was planned. In February deportation proceedings were started against a group of some 30,000 Haitians who, it was believed, had failed to register as illegal immigrants. (ROD PRINCE)

This article updates the *Macropædia* article The WEST INDIES: *The Bahamas.*

BARBADOS

The constitutional monarchy of Barbados, a member of the Commonwealth, occupies the most easterly island in the southern Caribbean Sea. Area: 430 sq km (166 sq mi). Pop. (1986 est.): 253,000. Cap.: Bridgetown. Monetary unit: Barbados dollar, with (Oct. 1, 1986) a free rate of BDS$2.01 to U.S. $1 (BDS$2.91 = £1 sterling). Queen, Elizabeth II; governor-general in 1986, Sir Hugh Springer; prime ministers, Bernard St. John and, from May 29, Errol Barrow.

In general elections held in Barbados on May 28, 1986, the Democratic Labour Party (DLP) won a sweeping victory over the incumbent Barbados Labour Party (BLP), gaining 24 out of 27 House of Assembly seats. The DLP leader, Errol Barrow (*see* BIOGRAPHIES), became prime minister, a post he had held from 1966 to 1976. His predecessor, Bernard St. John, indicated that he would retire from politics.

Soon after the election Barrow expressed reservations about U.S. influence in the region; he also criticized the twin-plant (contract-manufacturing) schemes promoted by Puerto Rico under the U.S.-sponsored Caribbean Basin Initiative. In August the U.S.-owned electronics company Intel, which had been planning a twin-plant operation, announced the phased closing of its Barbados factory.

Relations with Trinidad and Tobago improved after the Caribbean Community summit in July; talks among trade ministers in August produced agreement on trade in garments, processed meats, and vegetables. In July and August the new government announced tax cuts and mortgage interest rate reductions. (ROD PRINCE)

This article updates the *Macropædia* article The WEST INDIES: *Barbados.*

BELIZE

A constitutional monarchy and member of the Commonwealth, Belize is on the Caribbean coast of Central America. Area: 22,965 sq km (8,867 sq mi). Pop. (1986 est.): 171,000. Cap.: Belmopan. Monetary unit: Belize dollar, with (Oct. 1, 1986) a par value of BZ$2 to U.S. $1 (BZ$2.89 = £1 sterling). Queen, Elizabeth II; governor-general in 1986, Dame Minita Gordon; prime minister, Manuel Esquivel.

At the beginning of June 1986 Prime Minister Manuel Esquivel reshuffled his Cabinet. Several members who had been involved in public controversy lost their portfolios. The administration later published a five-year economic plan that envisaged a more diversified economy.

An International Monetary Fund staff report published at the end of June recognized Belize as the first country in the Western Hemisphere to implement an IMF austerity program with complete success. The 3.2% annual inflation rate augured well for the country's future development. In July Esquivel announced that his administration had adopted the Caricom trade rules agreed on in principle two years earlier. This automatically raised by 15% the tariffs on 83 categories of imports from all non-Caricom states. With production exceeding the forecast 80,000 tons by 13,000 tons, the sugar industry returned its first profit (BZ$3.5 million) since 1981.

On October 14 classes began at Belize's first university. The country already had the highest literacy rate in Central America. In February the U.S. State Department cited Belize as one of the few countries in the region that was making substantial headway in eradicating illicit drugs.

(INES T. BAPTIST)

This article updates the *Macropædia* article CENTRAL AMERICA: *Belize.*

BOLIVIA

Bolivia is a landlocked republic in central South America. Area: 1,098,581 sq km (424,164 sq mi). Pop. (1986 est.): 6,611,000. Judicial cap., Sucre; administrative cap., La Paz. Monetary unit: Bolivian peso, with (Oct. 1, 1986) a financial rate of 1,925 pesos to U.S. $1 (2,782 pesos = £1 sterling). President in 1986, Víctor Paz Estenssoro.

In 1986 the presidential party in Bolivia lacked the congressional majority required to enact new policies, and Pres. Víctor Paz Estenssoro was able to sustain political continuity only by means of a pact between his Movimiento Nacionalista Revolucionario (MNR) and the right-wing Acción Democrática Nacionalista (ADN). The alliance commanded 70% of votes in Congress, and the ADN was able to win certain concessions from the MNR. All but 7 of the 18 Cabinet members were replaced in January in a major reshuffle that increased the power of the private sector within government.

The most striking success of the conservative government during 1986 was its elimination of hyperinflation; in the six months ended in June, prices rose only 56.6%, compared with 8,274% for the previous 12 months. The reduction was achieved by strict fiscal and monetary restraint, a wage freeze, and a "controlled float" of the currency, which closely aligned the official and free exchange rates.

Plans to stimulate the economy were thwarted following the collapse of the London tin market in October 1985. Earnings from tin fell from 60% of total exports in 1978 to little over 25% in 1985. Faced with average production costs four to five times greater than tin prices for the forseeable future and mounting losses of the state mining company, Comibol, the government announced in August that it would close up to 16 mines with a probable loss of 8,000 jobs; 7,000 mining jobs were lost in 1985. The announcement provoked widespread strikes and protests by the powerful miners' union, supported by political and church leaders. On August 28 the government declared a 90-day state of siege, but it released detained labour leaders in mid-September with a pledge to modify plans for the mining industry in exchange for a return to work. A two-month teachers' strike in February–March was settled when the minimum wage was increased by 33%, the only wage increase permitted between the end of 1985 and July 1986.

Coca leaves for sale in a market in La Paz will yield cocaine if processed. U.S. and Bolivian troops raided processing labs in the jungle in an attempt to slow the export of hundreds of millions of dollars worth of coke from Bolivia.

SAMY SCHWARTZ—JB PICTURES

Agreement by Congress on tax reforms that would substantially increase government revenues led to approval by the International Monetary Fund of a one-year, $58 million standby loan in June, and a similar amount was pledged to compensate for the collapse of tin prices. Also in June, the government reached agreement to reschedule debt payments of $1,280,000,000. In December the IMF approved further loans to support structural economic adjustments. A new currency, the condor, equal to 1 million pesos, was to be introduced by early 1987.

Some 160 U.S. troops and six military helicopters arrived in Bolivia in July to assist in the struggle against cocaine trafficking. A series of joint U.S.-Bolivian raids reportedly resulted in the destruction of some drug laboratories, although the traffickers had apparently learned of the operation and fled. On July 30 the Bolivian ambassador to the U.S. told a U.S. Senate subcommittee that his country would need increased aid to compensate for lower cocaine exports.

(JANET KRENGEL)

BRAZIL

Brazil is a federal republic in eastern South America on the Atlantic Ocean. Area: 8,511,965 sq km (3,286,488 sq mi). Pop. (1986 est.): 138,403,000. Cap.: Brasília. Monetary unit: cruzado, with (Oct. 1, 1986) a free rate of 13.84 cruzados to U.S. $1 (20 cruzados = £1 sterling). President in 1986, José Sarney.

Domestic Affairs. During 1986 the political scene in Brazil was dominated by the elections on November 15 for the Chamber of Deputies, two-thirds of the Senate, and state governors and assemblies. Pres. José Sarney and his supporters won a landslide victory. The parties that made

Campaign literature litters the streets of São Paulo, Brazil, on the eve of national elections that were held November 15, the first since 21 years of military rule ended in 1985.
REUTERS/BETTMANN NEWSPHOTOS

up the governing coalition, the dominant Brazilian Democratic Movement Party (PMDB) and the Liberal Front Party (PFL), obtained all the state governorships and 77% of the seats in the Congress, which was to become the Constituent Assembly in February 1987. The PMDB and PFL ran separate candidates in many constituencies, and the PMDB, which represented centre-left elements in the coalition, obtained 22 governorships and 54% of the seats in the Assembly.

The most important PMDB victory was that of Wellington Moreira Franco in the state of Rio de Janeiro. The incumbent state governor, Leonel Brizola, had nominated Darcy Ribeiro, his deputy, on behalf of the Democratic Labour Party. The result was believed to be largely a consequence of Ribeiro's repeated attacks on the Cruzado Plan, the price stabilization package introduced on February 28, which was generally acclaimed as a success and as the main reason for the Sarney government's electoral victory. Brizola had been widely regarded as the most likely successor to Sarney as president.

The PFL, consisting mainly of conservative dissidents from the period of military rule between 1964 and 1985, had since February exerted a disproportionate influence on policy decisions, given its size. In a Cabinet reshuffle during that month, Sarney appointed PFL members to the main spending ministries. The PMDB began to exert greater influence on these decisions after the elections, and a sign of this was that Sarney called in the party leader, Ulysses Guimarães, for discussions on a package of supplementary measures to the Cruzado Plan. Sarney was reportedly planning Cabinet changes that would increase the PMDB representation.

The Constituent Assembly was to draft a new constitution and set a date for direct presidential elections. Sarney's mandate was legally for six years, to expire on March 15, 1991, but such had been his popularity that moves were expected aimed at allowing him to stay in office until 1990 and to run for a second term. His political future, however, appeared less certain following the imposition of austerity measures in November. On November 28 there were serious demonstrations in Brasília, and there were signs that Sarney could no longer depend on the support of key politicians within his own party. Proposals put forward for the new constitution included increased powers for the legislative branch of the government at the expense of the executive, a reduction in the workweek from 48 to 40 hours, enhanced labour rights, and a more restricted role for foreign investment.

The Economy. The introduction of the Cruzado Plan was precipitated by the spiraling inflation rate, which reached over 200% in the year to January 1986 and registered 14% in that month alone. The main purpose of the plan was to secure a permanent and sharp cut in the inflation rate so that the Sarney government could carry out its economic strategy. This was aimed at achieving an annual economic growth of approximately 6–7% in the period 1986–89, with the stimulus coming from expansion in the domestic market, social development programs, and increased investment.

The main components of the Cruzado Plan were the creation of a new currency, the cruzado; a temporary freeze on retail prices; elimination of most indexation (the tying of wages and interest rates to a cost-of-living index); and freezing of wages and other incomes to levels based on the average real values of the previous six months. The plan was quick to take effect. The rise in prices dropped to an average of 1–1.5% a month with no effect on Brazil's output, which continued to rise strongly. There were adverse consequences, however, as consumer spending rose dramatically, leading to shortages of some essential goods and eroding the trade surplus.

Amendments to the plan were made in July and November. In July measures such as "compulsory loans" (surcharges on automobiles, fuel oil, and gasoline) were introduced to restrain consumer demand and enforce savings, and a national development fund was set up to raise $20 billion (equivalent) for investments by 1989. The measures cut the spending power of the growing middle class. New taxes were introduced to stimulate investment. At the same time, more measures were announced to benefit the poor—better housing, free milk, and ambitious employment schemes. By November, however, the rate of inflation was accelerating, and there was a deterioration in the trade balance. To curb these trends, there were large price increases on beer, cigarettes, and automobiles; more restrictive conditions for wage increases; hefty tariff increases for telephones, electricity, and mail service; and the dismantling of the remaining indexation. These austerity moves led to widespread protests, and there were calls for a general strike in mid-December. The one-day strike, which took place on December 12, received only partial support from Brazilian workers.

Accumulated inflation fell sharply to 10% in March–October, making achievement of the official target of a March–December rate of 20% a real possibility. Gross domestic product was expected to increase by 7% in 1986, compared with 8.3% in 1985; consumer demand and exports remained buoyant. Overall industrial production grew by 12%, against 8.7% in 1985. Agriculture expanded by 5%, down from 13.9% in 1985 because of a drought from July through December 1985 in the southern regions. The external accounts remained sound, with a $9.3 billion trade surplus in January–October, and the current account for 1986 was expected to be in balance. Negotiations with creditor banks on a multiannual rescheduling of the external debt, estimated at $109 billion, were expected to begin in January 1987. (ROBIN CHAPMAN)

CHILE

The republic of Chile extends along the Pacific coast of the Southern Cone of South America. Area: 736,905 sq km (284,521 sq mi), not including Chile's Antarctic claim. Pop. (1986): 12,272,000. Cap.: Santiago. Monetary unit: Chilean peso, with (Oct. 1, 1986) an official rate of 195.04 pesos to U.S. $1 (281.83 pesos = £1 sterling). President in 1986, Maj. Gen. Augusto Pinochet Ugarte.

During 1986 political events in Chile were marked by a growing polarization between the military regime led by Gen. Augusto Pinochet Ugarte and the opposition, which developed a much stronger base and covered a wide spectrum of political interests. Spiraling violence climaxed in an assassination attempt on General Pinochet on September 7, the first to be reported during his 13-year rule. During the attack 5 bodyguards were killed and another 11 seriously injured, but Pinochet escaped with only a minor wound to his left hand. The Manuel Rodríguez Patriotic Front (FPMR) claimed responsibility for the attack. A state of siege was imposed for 90 days, and death squads, allegedly from a group calling itself the "September 11 Command," took their revenge with four political killings, including that of José Carrasco Tapia, foreign editor of the recently banned left-wing weekly *Análisis.* The campaign of terror continued with abductions and death threats to prominent opposition leaders, forcing some into hiding and others to leave the country.

The broad range of political parties (notably excluding the Communists) that had signed the National Accord for the Transition to Full Democracy under the auspices of Archbishop Juan Francisco Fresno in August 1985 tried to ease the situation. They attempted to counteract the extreme position taken by Pinochet of no dialogue and war on Communism and also that of the extreme left, which advocated violence to overthrow the regime. In response to a direct proposition by the National Party to achieve more consistent policies among members of the National Accord, the Christian Democratic Party abandoned its endeavours to change the Communist Party's stance of violent confrontation and on September 8 signed a coalition agreement with other political parties, ranging from conservative to democratic socialist. The document that emerged urged the armed forces to hold a plebiscite to amend the 1980 constitution and allow presidential, congressional, and local government elections ahead of schedule. It contained such guarantees as the right to work and to reasonable wages and security of private property.

The new agreement was also born out of the need to give a sense of direction to the opposition National Assembly of Civil Society (NACS), which had been established in May following the outright rejection of the National Accord by Pinochet. On Dec. 24, 1985, in a much-publicized meeting with Archbishop Fresno, Pinochet dismissed the subject and refused to return to it. The NACS, set up by social and human rights organizations, professional and student associations, and labour unions, claimed to have the support of three million Chileans. Apart from a return to democratic rule, it demanded public works programs to absorb the unemployed, increased public spending on welfare and education, an end to the privatization of state enterprises, satisfactory renegotiation of commercial debts and mortgages, and the lifting of restrictions on trade unions.

The NACS threatened Pinochet with various acts of civil disobedience if its demands had not been met by the end of May. Pinochet's intransigence evoked protests by university students in the middle of June, followed by a widespread 48-hour strike on July 2–3 during which the NACS was generally successful in mobilizing popular support. Its appeal lay in its request for people to register their grievances about fundamental social and economic issues

ALEXIS DUCLOS—GAMMA/LIAISON

The burned-out shell of an escort vehicle destroyed in a guerrilla ambush of Pres. Augusto Pinochet's motorcade gives evidence of deadly intent. Five guards were killed, but Pinochet escaped unharmed.

rather than purely political concerns. General dissatisfaction was also heightened at that time by extensive flooding in the country's central region that caused severe water shortages in Santiago. Measures taken by the government to deal with the crisis were seen as inadequate.

Demonstrations faced increased repression, and the troops were frequently called out. There were raids on Santiago's poor neighbourhoods in an effort to root out FPMR supporters. The NACS general strike in July brought the troops out again, but at that time there were eight deaths and more than 1,000 arrests. One of the victims was a young Chilean-born U.S. resident, Rodrigo Rojas de Negri, reportedly set on fire by soldiers. The leaders of the NACS, including its president, Juan Luis Gonzáles, were arrested and accused of contravening state security laws. This time, too, the crackdown extended to the media, and four radio stations had their broadcasting restricted to official news bulletins.

The brutality of the regime's reaction to the ground swell of opposition provoked international criticism, from the U.S. in particular. Early in 1986 the administration of Pres. Ronald Reagan called upon other governments to support a UN resolution that condemned Chile's human rights record. The draft resolution, based on a report prepared by a special UN envoy to Chile, Fernando Volio, was cosponsored by the U.S. and discussed at the UN in March. The Reagan administration later made clear its intention to veto the approval of multilateral loans to Chile if the human rights situation did not improve. In November the World Bank approved a $250 million loan covering balance of payments support. Failure to approve the loan would have jeopardized the last portion of private commercial funding for 1986 and made new loans for 1987 difficult to negotiate. Meanwhile, the new U.S. ambassador to Chile, Harry Barnes, continued to make contacts with members of the Chilean opposition.

Despite political instability the economic performance was good. Economic expansion slowed to 2.4% in 1985 as resources were switched away from consumption into investment and the foreign trade sector, but real gross domestic product rose by 5.8% in the first half of 1986. Official unemployment declined to 11%, but the statistics belied the true situation, given the large number of people engaged in emergency work programs and working in the informal sector. The rate of inflation declined and was not expected to exceed 20% for the year.

(ALEXANDER JOHNS CAMPBELL)

COLOMBIA

A republic in northwestern South America, Colombia has coastlines on the Caribbean Sea and the Pacific Ocean. Area: 1,141,748 sq km (440,831 sq mi). Pop. (1986 est.): 28,231,000. Cap.: Bogotá. Monetary unit: Colombian peso, with (Oct. 1, 1986) an official rate of 205.56 pesos to U.S. $1 (297.03 pesos = £1 sterling). Presidents in 1986, Belisario Betancur Cuartas and, from August 7, Virgilio Barco Vargas.

The political scene in Colombia was dominated in 1986 by elections: congressional in March and presidential in May. In the first the Liberal Party (PL) won a majority of 18 seats over the ruling Conservative Party (PC). In the presidential elections Virgilio Barco Vargas (*see* BIOGRAPHIES) of the LP won a landslide victory over his major opponent, Alvaro Gómez Hurtado (PC), and at the same time brought about a unification of the PL; the New Liberal faction withdrew from the presidential contest because of the poor results it had achieved in earlier elections.

Despite the peaceful transfer of government, President

Virgilio Barco Vargas, new president of Colombia, addresses Congress at his inauguration in Bogotá in August. His landslide victory helped unify the Liberal Party, which also won a majority of seats in congressional elections.

AP/WIDE WORLD

Barco took over a country engulfed by accelerating violence. The resurgence appeared to be a continuing response to the previous administration's decisive attempts to deal with the guerrilla movement and then with drug trafficking. When Pres. Belisario Betancur Cuartas assumed office in 1982, the guerrilla groups enjoyed both military and political strength; by August 1986 the members of the Colombian Revolutionary Armed Forces (FARC), the largest guerrilla group, were integrated into civilian life and had participated in the 1986 presidential, congressional, and local government elections as members of the Patriotic Union (UP). The other guerrilla groups, particularly the April 19 Movement (M-19), had put themselves in a precarious fringe position by refusing an offer of dialogue. Their violent actions following the elections discredited them, and they received little public support against the Army's antiguerrilla operations.

Betancur's drug-enforcement measures had sent many dealers into hiding, but killings and assassination attempts increased. Paradoxically, Interior Minister Jaime Castro had recommended the publication of a report by two jurists on the government's handling of the siege of the Palace of Justice, seized by M-19 guerrillas in November 1985, which commented on the Army's excessive use of force. He had also announced moves toward lifting the state of siege imposed in May 1984.

The consolidation of Betancur's limited progress in the peace effort was crucially dependent on the FARC's remaining in electoral politics. The prospects for this diminished, however, following the assassination of several UP leaders and the holding of army maneuvers in FARC areas. In September the new government held its first meeting with FARC leaders. Attorney General Carlos Jiménez Gómez voiced his concern about the armed forces' increasing use of torture and the alleged disappearances that had occurred during the fight against terrorism. Similar charges were leveled in an Amnesty International report published in July. During his seven-day visit to the country in early July, Pope John Paul II celebrated Mass in the wilderness that remained after the small town of Armero was devastated in the Nevado del Ruíz volcanic eruption of November 1985.

The introduction of an adjustment program in the second half of 1984 had helped reduce fiscal and external imbalances but caused economic growth to slow to 2.5% in 1985. Although a similar economic adjustment program was expected to continue under the auspices of the International Monetary Fund, the increase in gross domestic product in 1986 was forecast at 4.5%. This was the result of improved world coffee prices and new energy exports from the country's two largest projects, the El Cerrejón coal complex and the oil fields in the Llanos. Nevertheless, unemployment reached 15.2% in July, and public works lagged because of funding problems.

(ALEXANDER JOHNS CAMPBELL)

COSTA RICA

The Central American republic of Costa Rica has coastlines on the Caribbean Sea and the Pacific Ocean. Area: 51,100 sq km (19,730 sq mi). Pop. (1986 est.): 2,534,000. Cap.: San José. Monetary unit: Costa Rican colón, with (Oct. 1, 1986) a unified rate of 57.29 colones to U.S. $1 (82.78 colones = £1 sterling). Presidents in 1986, Luis Alberto Monge Álvarez and, from May 8, Oscar Arias Sánchez.

In presidential and legislative elections held on Feb. 2, 1986, voters gave a comfortable majority to Oscar Arias Sánchez (*see* BIOGRAPHIES) of the ruling centre-left Partido de Liberación Nacional (PLN). Arias polled 52%, compared with 45% for his only serious rival, the more stridently anti-Communist Rafael Angel Calderón Fournier of the centre-right Partido Unidad Social Cristiana (PUSC). The PLN took 29 of the 57 Assembly seats, while the PUSC increased its representation from 18 to 25 seats.

Although no supporter of Nicaragua's left-wing government, President Arias Sánchez promised to prevent anti-Sandinista (*contra*) forces from using Costa Rica as a base. Nonetheless, in July Nicaragua filed an action at the International Court of Justice to restrain Costa Rica from sheltering *contra* forces. The protest was prompted by cross-border fighting that resulted in Costa Rica's first official acknowledgement that *contra* forces were active near the country's northern border.

AP/WIDE WORLD

Contra leader Eden Pastora takes members of his army across the San Juan River to surrender to Costa Rican authorities and ask for asylum. Pastora had concluded that it would be impossible to win a military victory against the Sandinista government.

After persistent problems in servicing its $4.2 billion debt, Costa Rica embarrassed its commercial bank creditors at the end of October by requesting a 25-year rescheduling of $1.4 billion at below market interest rates. The banks refused. Improved prices for coffee exports and the reduced cost of oil imports were expected to help generate economic growth of 2–3% in 1986. (JANET KRENGEL)

This article updates the *Macropædia* article CENTRAL AMERICA: *Costa Rica.*

CUBA

The socialist republic of Cuba comprises the island of Cuba and several thousand smaller islands and cays in the Caribbean Sea. Area: 110,860 sq km (42,803 sq mi). Pop. (1986 est.): 10,191,000. Cap.: Havana. Monetary unit: Cuban peso, with (Oct. 1, 1986) a free rate of 0.80 peso to U.S. $1 (1.16 pesos = £1 sterling). President of the Councils of State and Ministers in 1986, Fidel Castro Ruz.

The Cuban Communist Party's third congress was held in February 1986 after several postponements (the second congress had been held in 1980). Pres. Fidel Castro Ruz was reelected first secretary, and his brother, Raúl Castro Ruz, was confirmed as the second most powerful figure in the Communist hierarchy. Four veteran leaders of the 1959 revolution, including former interior minister Ramiro Valdés Menéndez, were dropped from the Politburo. They were replaced by younger men and the first woman to be a full member of the Politburo, Vilma Espín Guillois, Raúl Castro's wife. Eight new members were appointed to the ten-member candidate Politburo. One-third of the 225-member Central Committee was also replaced. The moves were in line with a trend toward introducing younger technocrats into the administration. At the end of December the National Assembly reelected Fidel Castro president of the Council of State (head of state).

The government continued to enjoy success in its efforts to improve relations with other Latin-American countries. In June diplomatic links were restored with Brazil following a gap of 22 years. Uruguay had opened an embassy in Havana in October 1985. A more conciliatory approach toward dealing with Central American and Caribbean problems was adopted. In particular, full support was accorded to the Contadora process, whereby Colombia, Mexico, Panama, and Venezuela, along with Costa Rica, El Salvador, Guatemala, Honduras, and Nicaragua, were endeavouring to conclude a general peace treaty for Central America. An offer was made in April 1986 to withdraw military advisers from Nicaragua, while the number of teachers and technicians supplied to Managua was increased to 7,000 during the year.

Relations with the U.S. remained bad. In August the U.S. forbade the entry of Cuban immigrants through "third countries," such as Mexico, Spain, or Panama, and tightened controls on the export of goods into Cuba through Cuban front companies based in Panama and other countries. At the same time, however, it agreed that all Cuban political prisoners imprisoned for more than ten years could seek U.S. entry. As a result, in September 70 Cuban dissidents and their families arrived in Miami following two years of negotiations.

Cuba continued to be politically and economically dependent on the U.S.S.R., and aid (excluding military) was estimated at the equivalent of $4.5 billion in 1985. Four trade and economic cooperation agreements signed in April

Fidel Castro, beneath spectacular paintings of Marxist and nationalist heroes, reports to the third congress of the Cuban Communist Party in Havana.

AP/WIDE WORLD

1986 provided for a 50% increase in credits to Havana in the period 1986–90 as compared with the previous five years. Economic aid was to be increased for development of electricity generation, petroleum, machinery construction, transport, agriculture, sugar, and the electrical, chemical, metallurgical, and pharmaceutical industries. Under an accord concluded in May, Cuba's sugar shipments to the U.S.S.R. would remain fixed at four million metric tons a year in 1986–90, but the price paid was to be 7% lower than in 1981–85. Soviet oil supplies were to be maintained at the 1985 level of 13.4 million metric tons a year in 1986–90, at prices considerably below those in world markets. Much of the oil was reexported for hard currency.

The economy grew by 4.8% in 1985, compared with 7.4% in 1984. Four-fifths of 1985 growth was accounted for by manufacturing industry and construction, which recorded increases of 8.4 and 2.5%, respectively. The third five-year (1986–90) development plan, published in November 1985, provided for yearly growth of 3.5% and gave priority to exports, especially nonsugar exports, and to developing sugar output and energy self-sufficiency. The outlook for 1986 deteriorated because of a poor sugar crop, lower world oil prices, a decline in nickel production, and the appreciation of most Western currencies against the U.S. dollar.

The economy continued to be dominated by sugar, which provided 70% of exports in 1985, although its performance in both 1985 and 1986 was indifferent. The 1985–86 crop totaled 6.8 million metric tons, compared with 7.8 million in 1984–85. The decline was attributable to a prolonged drought followed by losses from Hurricane Kate, which swept across the country in November 1985, damaging 1 million ha (2.5 million ac) of cane. Harvesting was also adversely affected by absenteeism, labour shortages, and machinery failures. Cuba remained the world's largest cane producer after Brazil.

Cuba's convertible currency debt reached over $3.5 billion at the end of December 1985, and a persistent shortage of hard currency led to a rescheduling of debt repayments due to Paris Club and commercial bank creditors between 1983 and 1985. On July 1 Cuba suspended all payments on its medium-term and long-term debt, and later that month it also suspended payments on its short-term debt to Western countries because of its foreign exchange shortage. The 1986 rescheduling negotiations were still in progress at year's end, with Cuba refusing to pay interest unless new money was provided by commercial banks. Cuba's debt to the U.S.S.R. and other member countries of the Council for Mutual Economic Assistance was unknown but was estimated at between $6 billion and $22 billion. Cuba's first repayment to the U.S.S.R., equivalent to $125 million and falling due in 1986, had been rescheduled to 1990.

(ROBIN CHAPMAN)

This article updates the *Macropædia* article The WEST INDIES: *Cuba.*

DOMINICA

An island republic within the Commonwealth, Dominica is in the eastern Caribbean Sea. Area: 750 sq km (290 sq mi). Pop. (1986 est.): 86,200. Cap.: Roseau. Monetary unit: Eastern Caribbean dollar, with (Oct. 1, 1986) a par value of EC$2.70 to U.S. $1 (free rate of EC$3.90 = £1 sterling). President in 1986, Clarence Augustus Seignoret; prime minister, Eugenia Charles.

The governing Dominica Freedom Party (DFP) consolidated its control during 1986, winning a seat from the opposition Dominica Labour Party (DLP) in a by-election held on May 5. The seat had fallen vacant as a result of the imprisonment of former prime minister Patrick John, who had received a 12-year prison sentence in October 1985. The victory gave the DFP 16 of the 21 parliamentary seats. The DLP lost another member of Parliament in June when Eden Durand, community development minister in the shadow (opposition) cabinet, resigned to sit as an independent.

Former army commander Frederick Newton was hanged on August 8 for the murder of a policeman in 1981 during an attempt to free John from prison. It was the first execution since 1973. Five other former soldiers convicted at the same time as Newton had death sentences commuted to life imprisonment.

Prime Minister Eugenia Charles announced in June that the government was embarking on a structural adjustment program for the economy, backed by the World Bank and the International Monetary Fund. The aim was to achieve an annual growth rate of at least 4% in gross domestic product over the next three years; in 1985 the rate was 1.1%.

(ROD PRINCE)

This article updates the *Macropædia* article The WEST INDIES: *Dominica.*

DOMINICAN REPUBLIC

The Dominican Republic covers the eastern two-thirds of the Caribbean island of Hispaniola, which it shares with Haiti. Area: 48,442 sq km (18,704 sq mi). Pop. (1986 est.): 6,386,000. Cap.: Santo Domingo. Monetary unit: Dominican peso, with (Oct. 1, 1986) a free rate of 2.93 pesos to U.S. $1 (4.23 pesos to £1 sterling). Presidents in 1986, Salvador Jorge Blanco and, from August 16, Joaquín Balaguer.

The May 1986 presidential and parliamentary elections in the Dominican Republic brought victory to the Social Christian Reform Party (PRSC), which took 41.6% of the vote. Its leader, Joaquín Balaguer, was inaugurated in August for a fifth term as president. The outgoing Dominican

Revolutionary Party (PRD) led by Jacobo Majluta took 39.5% of the vote; the party had become increasingly divided, particularly when the popular José Francisco Peña Gómez, on the left of the PRD, failed to be nominated to the party's leadership. Many of his supporters deserted the PRD and helped to boost the vote of the (Marxist) Dominican Liberation Party (18.4%).

President Balaguer's pledge to form a government of national reconciliation was reflected in his Cabinet, which was made up of businessmen, technocrats, opposition members, and only four PRSC members—a choice that brought protests from the governing party. Economic policy was aimed at diversifying away from the country's heavy dependence on the ailing sugar industry. The economy deteriorated in 1985 when gross domestic product declined by 2.2%, and a similar decline was expected in 1986. The restructuring of the country's estimated $3.5 billion external debt brought an improvement to the balance of payments.

(PAUL MILLGATE)

This article updates the *Macropædia* article The West Indies: *Dominican Republic.*

ECUADOR

The republic of Ecuador is in western South America, on the Pacific Ocean. Area: 269,178 sq km (103,930 sq mi), including the Galápagos Islands. Pop. (1986 est.): 9,647,000. Cap.: Quito. Monetary unit: sucre, with (Oct. 17, 1986) an official intervention rate of 142 sucres to U.S. $1 (205.2 sucres = £1 sterling) and a free rate of 150.5 sucres to U.S. $1 (209.5 sucres = £1 sterling). President in 1986, León Febres Cordero Rivadeneira.

A state of emergency was declared in Ecuador in March 1986 when air force Gen. Frank Vargas Pazos led an antigovernment revolt at the Quito air base. It was ended quickly when government forces stormed the base, but widespread criticism of the handling of the affair contributed to the defeat of the ruling right-wing coalition in June midterm elections. The elections were combined with a national referendum in which Pres. León Febres Cordero was severely defeated when only 25% supported

AP/WIDE WORLD

Ecuadoran air force Gen. Frank Vargas Pazos joins his wife and son after ending his takeover of an air base in Manta. Vargas had been fired as chief of staff on March 7 after accusing the defense minister and the army commander of the misuse of public funds and demanding their dismissal. His renewed rebellion at the Quito air base on March 14 was put down by government forces.

his proposition that independents be permitted to stand in elections. The ruling seven-party National Reconstruction Front (FRN) lost its slim majority in the 71-seat Congress, and increased factionalism within the FRN meant the president could depend on only 17 votes, with a maximum of 31 on certain issues. The opposition centre-left Izquierda Democrática (17 seats) remained the largest single party in Congress.

Since Ecuador's constitution allowed impeachment of ministers by a simple majority vote and required congressional approval for certain changes in economic policy, President Febres Cordero faced a constitutional crisis until the next presidential election, due in mid-1988. Finance Minister Alberto Dahik was removed from office following impeachment proceedings by the opposition. His only economic package included interest rate liberalization and freeing the exchange rate, which hastened an International Monetary Fund (IMF) agreement for a standby facility of 75 million Special Drawing Rights (SDR).

Gross domestic product rose 3.8% in 1985, but the fall in oil prices was expected to lower the growth rate to 1.5% in 1986. A 32% drop in export earnings was forecast. The international financial community remained confident in the government's economic strategy: the U.S. Treasury provided a $150 million short-term loan, and the IMF provided a special facility of SDR 40 million.

(JANET KRENGEL)

EL SALVADOR

The republic of El Salvador is situated on the Pacific coast of Central America. Area: 21,041 sq km (8,124 sq mi). Pop. (1986 est.): 5,461,000. Cap.: San Salvador. Monetary unit: Salvadoran colón, with (Oct. 1, 1986) an official rate of 5.00 colones to U.S. $1 (7.23 colones = £1 sterling). President in 1986, José Napoleón Duarte.

The seven-year-old war persisted in 1986, and although El Salvador's government was partially successful in its fight against the guerrillas, support for Pres. José Napoleón Duarte declined. His position became increasingly difficult as the military, the right wing, and the U.S. pressed for continuation of the war against the Farabundo Martí National Liberation Front (FMLN), while much of the population was becoming disenchanted with the war effort.

To stimulate the economy, the government in January devalued the currency and set a single exchange rate of $1 to 5 colones to replace the dual rates of 2.50 and 4.85 colones. Other measures included public-sector wage increases, $200 million in industrial credits, and increased taxes (especially on coffee exports), but they were seen as insufficient to stimulate the economy.

El Salvador's weak economy became increasingly dependent on U.S. foreign assistance, which amounted to $435 million in fiscal 1986, bringing the total since 1979 to $2.3 billion. However, U.S. aid was contingent on a military victory against the FMLN. Military gains by government forces meant that the guerrillas increasingly resorted to economic sabotage (for instance, on power installations and processing plants) and mining of roads. Hopes that the war, in which an estimated 60,000 had died, would be ended by negotiation, faded when the guerrillas did not attend a September meeting with President Duarte in Sesori because the government would neither withdraw army units from the area nor agree to a temporary countrywide cease-fire.

The country suffered a further blow in October when an earthquake measuring 7.5 on the Richter scale struck San Salvador, leaving some 200,000 homeless and devastating

Survivors of an earthquake in El Salvador search through the rubble of their destroyed homes, looking for possessions and further victims of the disaster.

CLAUDE URRACA—SYGMA

the city centre. It was estimated that more than 1,000 people died. Rescuers employed techniques first used in the 1985 Mexico City earthquake to search for bodies.

(BEN BOX)

This article updates the *Macropædia* article CENTRAL AMERICA: *El Salvador.*

GRENADA

A constitutional monarchy within the Commonwealth, Grenada (with its dependency, the Southern Grenadines) is in the eastern Caribbean Sea. Area: 345 sq km (133 sq mi). Pop. (1986 est.): 97,500. Cap.: Saint George's. Monetary unit: Eastern Caribbean dollar, with (Oct. 1, 1986) a par value of EC$2.70 to U.S. $1 (free rate of EC$3.90 = £1 sterling). Queen, Elizabeth II; governor-general in 1986, Sir Paul Scoon; prime minister, Herbert A. Blaize.

During 1986 the governing New National Party (NNP) in Grenada continued to suffer internal strains. One of its 14 members of Parliament, Kenny Lalsingh, resigned in May to stand as an independent; he was followed in August by Phinsley St. Louis, the deputy speaker. Lalsingh had resigned as junior education minister in February following allegations of impropriety. In September he announced the formation of a new party, the Democratic Labour Congress. The ill health of Prime Minister Herbert Blaize led to speculation about a possible leadership struggle within the NNP.

AP/WIDE WORLD

U.S. Pres. Ronald Reagan speaks to thousands of Grenadians at a rally at Queen's Park in St. George's. Reagan promised continued aid and likened events in Nicaragua to those in Grenada in an attempt to gain support for increasing aid to anti-Sandinista forces.

The 1986 budget was presented in February. Blaize announced that income tax was to be abolished and replaced by a 20% value-added tax as part of a reform of the tax system, but complaints from the business community led to modifications later in the year. In July Blaize announced that public sector investments were being delayed and debt repayments postponed because of lack of revenue and cuts in U.S. budget support.

On December 4 death sentences were passed on 14 former members of the People's Revolutionary Government and army officers found guilty of murdering former prime minister Maurice Bishop in 1983. Those sentenced to death included former deputy prime minister Bernard Coard and former army chief Hudson Austin. Three defendants were convicted of manslaughter and sent to prison, and one was acquitted.

(ROD PRINCE)

This article updates the *Macropædia* article The WEST INDIES: *Grenada.*

GUATEMALA

A republic of Central America, Guatemala has coastlines on the Caribbean Sea and the Pacific Ocean. Area: 108,889 sq km (42,042 sq mi). Pop. (1986 est.): 8,640,000 (author's estimate). Cap.: Guatemala City. Monetary unit: quetzal, at par with the U.S. dollar, with (Oct. 1, 1986) an official market rate of 1 quetzal to U.S. $1 (1.45 quetzals = £1 sterling), a banking market rate of 2.79 quetzals to U.S. $1 (4.03 quetzals = £1 sterling), and an auction market rate established on an occasional basis by the Bank of Guatemala to govern certain import transactions. Chief of state to Jan. 14, 1986, Gen. Oscar Humberto Mejía Victores; president from January 14, Marco Vinicio Cerezo Arévalo.

On Jan. 14, 1986, the government of Guatemala was handed over to civilians—the first civilian government in 16 years and only the second since 1954. The new president was Marco Vinicio Cerezo Arévalo (*see* BIOGRAPHIES) of the Christian Democrats (DCG), who had won 68%

Vinicio Cerezo, his hand on a copy of a new constitution held by his wife, Raquel, takes the oath of office that makes him the first civilian president of Guatemala in 16 years. Alfonso Cabrera, president of the National Assembly, conducts the swearing in.

AP/WIDE WORLD

of the vote in December 1985 elections. The government abolished the secret police unit believed to be involved in political assassinations but left the army intelligence unit intact. Just before Cerezo's inauguration, the military regime decreed an amnesty to all security force members accused of human rights abuses in the period 1982–85.

Government policy was constrained by severe economic recession and strong military influence, and the failure to satisfy aspirations generated by the return to civilian rule brought widespread discontent. After a brief lull, there was a renewal of political violence from both left- and right-wing insurgents. In the fall, however, the leftist guerrillas indicated willingness to enter peace talks.

A package of economic measures introduced in May included simplification of the three-tier exchange rate. Given favourable coffee-export prices and low oil-import prices, the package was expected to generate marginal economic growth in 1986 following a contraction of 2.6% in 1985. The measure failed to reduce the inflation rate, which was expected to reach 40% by December.

Diplomatic relations with the U.K., severed in 1981 over Guatemala's claim to the former British colony of Belize, were restored on December 29. (JANET KRENGEL)

This article updates the *Macropædia* article CENTRAL AMERICA: *Guatemala.*

GUYANA

A republic and member of the Commonwealth, Guyana is situated in northeastern South America, on the Atlantic Ocean. Area: 215,000 sq km (83,000 sq mi). Pop. (1986 est.): 796,000. Cap.: Georgetown. Monetary unit: Guyana dollar, with (Oct. 1, 1986) a free rate of G$4.38 to U.S. $1 (G$6.33 = £1 sterling). President in 1986, Desmond Hoyte; prime minister, Hamilton Green.

Desmond Hoyte, who succeeded the late Forbes Burnham as president of Guyana in August 1985, announced early in 1986 that economic recovery was the overriding priority for his administration. During the year he took steps to encourage overseas private investment and to improve relations with Guyana's partners in the Caribbean Community (Caricom) and with Venezuela and the U.S. In August an aid agreement was signed with the U.S. government for the supply of 25,000 metric tons of wheat. The U.S. indicated that it had been influenced by domestic and foreign policy changes made by the Hoyte administration. Earlier in the year a fuel crisis caused by the acute foreign exchange shortage was resolved by a barter agreement under which Guyana undertook to supply bauxite to Venezuela in exchange for petroleum.

In January President Hoyte met several Caricom leaders on the island of Mustique, in St. Vincent and the Grenadines, to discuss allegations of fraud in Guyana's December 1985 general elections. Following the meeting, regional criticism of Guyana was moderated. The Cabinet resigned on December 30 to allow Hoyte to reorganize the government. (ROD PRINCE)

This article updates the *Macropædia* article The GUIANAS: *Guyana.*

HAITI

The republic of Haiti occupies the western one-third of the Caribbean island of Hispaniola, which it shares with the Dominican Republic. Area: 27,400 sq km (10,579 sq mi). Pop. (1986 est.): 5,427,000. Cap.: Port-au-Prince. Monetary unit: gourde, with (Oct. 1, 1986) a par value of 5 gourdes to U.S. $1 (free rate of 7.23 gourdes = £1 sterling). President until February 1986, Jean-Claude Duvalier; president of the interim governing council from February, Henri Namphy.

On Feb. 7, 1986, Haiti's Pres. Jean-Claude Duvalier and his family were flown by the U.S. to a temporary refuge in France following three months of demonstrations and violence that made his position untenable. An interim government council, made up of civilian and military members and headed by the army chief of staff, Lieut. Gen. Henri Namphy (*see* BIOGRAPHIES), took office and appointed a 19-member Cabinet. The council had difficulty in establishing its authority, and there were intermittent strikes and riots throughout the year. The Communist Party became increasingly active in organizing the opposition.

In March Namphy dismissed members of the council who had had close ties with the Duvalier regime and reduced it to three members: Namphy himself, Foreign Affairs Minister Jacques François, and Interior Minister Col. William Regala. In April, as part of an effort to promote confidence at home and abroad, a former World Bank official, Leslie Delatour, was named economy and

Haitians dance happily outside the presidential palace in Port-au-Prince in February after learning that Pres. Jean-Claude Duvalier, self-proclaimed president for life, had fled the country.
REUTERS/BETTMANN NEWSPHOTOS

finance minister. In June Namphy announced that presidential elections would be held in November 1987, with a new government taking office in February 1988. He also announced that he would not be standing as a candidate. Haiti's first nationwide democratic elections in nearly 30 years were held in October to choose 41 members of a constituent assembly, but the voter turnout was low.

The U.S. administration strongly backed the interim government by granting about $80 million in aid during the year. U.S. Secretary of State George Shultz visited Port-au-Prince in August and witnessed a treaty aimed at stopping the drug traffic through the island. Namphy visited Washington in November.

The economy deteriorated in 1986, and the new government was unable to pursue a consistent economic policy in the face of social and political conflicts. The unemployment rate rose to an estimated 50%. (ROBIN CHAPMAN)

This article updates the *Macropædia* article The WEST INDIES: *Haiti*.

HONDURAS

A republic of Central America, Honduras has coastlines on the Caribbean Sea and the Pacific Ocean. Area: 112,088 sq km (43,277 sq mi). Pop (1986 est.) 3,938,000. Cap.: Tegucigalpa. Monetary unit: lempira, with (Oct. 1, 1986) a par value of 2 lempiras to U.S. $1 (free rate of 2.89 lempiras = £1 sterling). Presidents in 1986, Roberto Suazo Córdova and, from January 27, José Azcona Hoyo.

Soon after being sworn in at the end of January 1986, Pres. José Azcona Hoyo (*see* BIOGRAPHIES) of Honduras helped formulate a National Patriotic Accord between the 46 Liberal Party deputies who supported him in Congress and the 63 National Party deputies who had backed his election opponent, Rafael Callejas. The Liberal supporters of former president Roberto Suazo Córdova were excluded. The accord sought to give the two parties a fair share in the leadership of the legislature and the Supreme Court.

Throughout 1986 controversy continued over the presence in Honduras of U.S. military personnel and of anti-Sandinista Nicaraguan Democratic Force guerrillas (*contras*). Unlike his predecessor, Azcona officially admitted that *contras* were operating from Honduran territory and lifted the ban on aid flows to the rebels. In a May visit to Washington, D.C., Azcona told U.S. Pres. Ronald Reagan that he would accept U.S. aid to support the estimated 15,000–20,000 *contras* because without it they would be uncontrollable. He stressed, however, that Honduras would "not be used as a launching platform for attacks against any neighbouring state" and that aid should be used to shift the war into Nicaragua. At the end of the visit a joint communiqué declared that U.S. aid of $61.2 million had been granted for Honduras's economic stabilization program. In March the U.S. had provided $20 million in emergency aid following an incursion into Honduras by Nicaraguan armed forces who were seeking to destroy *contra* bases. In December Honduran forces attacking Nicaraguan troops inside Honduras were ferried to the border area by U.S. military helicopters.

At a camp near the Honduran border, Nicaraguan *contra* rebels are taught how to operate 60-millimetre mortars like the one before them.
CLAUDIO URRACA—SYGMA

At the end of May Honduras and El Salvador agreed to take their long-standing border dispute, involving a mountain area and the Isla Meanguera, to the International Court of Justice at The Hague. (BEN BOX)

This article updates the *Macropædia* article CENTRAL AMERICA: *Honduras.*

JAMAICA

A constitutional monarchy within the Commonwealth, Jamaica occupies an island in the Caribbean Sea. Area: 10,991 sq km (4,244 sq mi). Pop. (1986 est.): 2,348,000. Cap.: Kingston. Monetary unit: Jamaica dollar, with (Oct. 1, 1986) a free rate of J$5.47 to U.S. $1 (J$7.90 = £1 sterling). Queen, Elizabeth II; governor-general in 1986, Sir Florizel Glasspole; prime minister, Edward Seaga.

Economic and political problems continued to preoccupy the government of Prime Minister Edward Seaga of Jamaica during 1986. On October 10 he tendered his resignation as leader of the Jamaica Labour Party, but withdrew it in early November. The year opened with an emergency package of tax measures to meet a shortfall in bauxite earnings of $50 million. Economic output fell by 3.7% in 1985, but there was some improvement in 1986. The International Monetary Fund (IMF) agreed to waive conditions on Jamaica's drawing rights in March, ending a six-month blockage of funds caused by failure to meet certain performance requirements, but on May 1 Seaga introduced an expansionary budget that ran counter to advice from IMF, World Bank, and U.S. Agency for International Development officials, who urged further austerity. In early October the government rejected an IMF requirement for devaluation of the Jamaica dollar to 6.06 to the U.S. dollar. Instead it offered a gradual devaluation.

Local government elections in July produced a decisive victory for the opposition People's National Party (PNP), led by former prime minister Michael Manley, which won 126 out of 187 seats and 57% of the vote. The polling was followed by a spate of violence and renewed calls from the PNP for an early general election. (ROD PRINCE)

This article updates the *Macropædia* article The WEST INDIES: *Jamaica.*

MEXICO

A federal republic of North America, Mexico has coastlines on the Pacific Ocean, the Gulf of Mexico, and the Caribbean Sea. Area: 1,958,201 sq km (756,066 sq mi). Pop. (1986 est.): 80,472,000. Cap.: Mexico City. Monetary unit: Mexican peso, with (Oct. 1, 1986) a free rate of 771 pesos to U.S. $1 (1,113 pesos = £1 sterling). President in 1986, Miguel de la Madrid Hurtado.

In 1986 the government of Mexico, led by Pres. Miguel de la Madrid Hurtado, was under unprecedented attack for its administration of elections, particularly in the northernmost state of Chihuahua in July. The ruling Partido Revolucionario Institucional (PRI), which had dominated politics in Mexico since 1929, saw its power base diminish as the country's economy moved into severe recession. Its image was also tarnished by the delay in rehabilitating the 100,000 people made homeless by the earthquake that devastated Mexico City in September 1986, many of whom were still living in the streets. In May the president suffered acute personal embarrassment when his opening address at the World Cup soccer finals was partially drowned out by disapproving shouts from some of the 100,000 spectators.

Of the state elections that took place, the one in Chihuahua, which borders Texas, attracted the most attention for alleged irregularities. The state was a stronghold of the opposition Partido Acción Nacional, which was expected to take a large—though not a majority—share of the vote. The outcome was an overwhelming victory for the PRI, a result that evoked widespread protests. Among the critics was the Roman Catholic Church, which was constitutionally banned from politics.

Recognition of the public's dissatisfaction with the country's economic performance was reflected in the removal of Finance Minister Jesús Silva Herzog from office in June, without explanation. He was, however, associated with the harsh austerity measures imposed by the International Monetary Fund (IMF), which were blamed for much of the economic malaise. At the same time, he was seen widely as a contender for the presidency in the 1988 election. Toward the end of the year President de la Madrid was making a concerted effort to improve the image of the PRI in preparation for the elections. Splits within the party led him to remove his personal friend Adolfo Lugo Verduzco as president of the party; Lugo was replaced by Jorge de la Vega Domínguez, also seen as a possible successor to de la Madrid.

Despite a series of austerity measures, Mexico's foreign debt continued to hover at near-crisis levels. By mid-1986 servicing the nearly $100 billion debt was the country's main cause for concern. Late in June the new finance minister, Gustavo Petricioli Iturbe, shocked creditors with his announcement that Mexico could no longer meet its debt obligations on "the terms agreed" and would be seeking new agreements, possibly on the basis of payments linked to oil revenue. At the end of September a new agreement was reached with the IMF, the World Bank, and the 500 or so commercial banks involved, which was linked to future economic growth (not oil revenue). Commercial banks agreed to provide $6 billion in new loans for repayment, delayed for seven years; $43.7 billion of restructured debt was to be repaid over 20 years with a seven-year grace period; and multilateral lenders were to contribute another $6 billion of new loans.

Many bankers were skeptical about the rescue package and about the country's ability to respond by achieving the planned 3–4% economic growth in 1987. Contingency finance built into the package was to be used if the oil price fell substantially.

In 1986 the already weak economy was stunned by the collapse of the international oil price. Oil revenue was vital to Mexico, and its budget was based on a price of $22.50 per barrel, but by the second quarter the price had dropped to $11.67 per barrel, with devastating effects. In the first half of 1986 the current account recorded a $1.2 billion deficit—the first since 1982—and the trade surplus more than halved to $1.6 billion, reflecting a 57% decline in oil earnings to $3.1 billion. Tourism earnings fell 11% to $961 million. It was expected that there would be continued deterioration for the remainder of the year, and a 3–5% decline in gross domestic product (GDP) was predicted. The weakness of the peso and the fall in reserves were additional depressing factors, and an acceleration in the rate of inflation produced fears of hyperinflation. The public deficit was forecast to rise to 15.8% of GDP by the end of 1986 instead of the targeted 4.9%, despite strong monetary controls that led to interest rates above 100% in September.

More positive was Mexico's entry to the General Agreement on Tariffs and Trade on August 24. This should have helped the country boost its non-oil exports, which were already growing strongly in the first half of the year, aided by their improved competitiveness following the depreciation in the value of the peso. The 1987 budget was

A sign outside a currency exchange centre in Juárez, Mexico, announces the late-July ratio in the plunge of the peso against the U.S. dollar.

ALLAN TANNENBAUM—SYGMA

announced in November, and more than half of spending was to go toward debt servicing.

Relations with the U.S., on which Mexico depended for some two-thirds of its trade, came under pressure early in the year. In the wake of the elections and the public criticism of the government that ensued, the U.S. strongly criticized Mexico for drug trafficking and corruption. However, the U.S. toned down its allegations as it perceived an intensifying threat of political instability in Mexico, and in June Pres. Ronald Reagan invited President de la Madrid to visit Washington in an effort to restore good relations. At the subsequent meeting in August, the two countries reached agreement on a $266 million program to reduce the massive flow of drugs across the 3,220-km (2,000-mi) border. Increased manning of the border and radar equipment were planned, which at the same time would assist in the effort to prevent illegal immigrants crossing into the U.S. Further evidence that good relations had been restored was an agreement reached in November whereby Mexico would supply 26 million bbl of oil to the U.S. strategic petroleum reserve. (PAUL MILLGATE)

NICARAGUA

A republic of Central America, Nicaragua has coastlines on the Caribbean Sea and the Pacific Ocean. Area: 127,849 sq km (49,363 sq mi). Pop. (1986 est.): 3,385,000. Cap.: Managua. Monetary unit: córdoba, with (Oct. 1, 1986) an official rate of 900 córdobas to U.S. $1 (1,300.50 córdobas = £1 sterling). President in 1986, Daniel Ortega Saavedra.

Throughout 1986 the five-year-old war against the right-wing opposition, or *contra* forces, continued to dominate events in Nicaragua. In August, after much debate, the U.S. Congress approved a $100 million package of military aid for the *contras,* which was expected to allow them to increase their military capacity and, for the first time, to establish permanent bases inside Nicaragua. Since the war intensified in 1983, *contra* forces had made only limited progress, and up to the first half of 1986 the Nicaraguan Army, helped by its Soviet-made helicopters, had won the upper hand in the conflict. Eugene Hasenfus, a U.S. citizen captured when a *contra* supply plane was shot down over

UPI/BETTMANN NEWSPHOTOS

Sandinista troops untie American Eugene Hasenfus's hands before he boards the helicopter in the background for a flight to Managua to stand trial for aiding the *contras.*

Nicaragua in October, claimed the CIA had been assisting the *contras,* despite a U.S. congressional prohibition. However, this was denied by the U.S. government. Hasenfus was tried by the People's Tribunal and sentenced to 30 years in prison, but Pres. Daniel Ortega pardoned him, and he returned to the U.S. in mid-December. There were indications that his testimony would be sought by investigators probing allegations that money received for secret U.S. arms shipments to Iran had been illegally diverted to the *contras.* Meanwhile, another U.S. citizen, Sam Hall, was arrested in Nicaragua for espionage.

The war was the main reason for the continued poor economic performance. Gross domestic product (GDP) fell 1.9% in 1985 and an estimated 2% in 1986. Food and other material goods supplies were disrupted, while 45% of government spending went to the war effort in 1986. Despite increased taxation and spending cutbacks, there was a fiscal deficit equivalent to over 20% of GDP, financed mainly by printing more money. One result was an inflation rate of approximately 300%. The U.S. economic embargo and low cotton prices caused export earnings to decline in 1986 to around $250 million.

Government emphasis on the distribution of basic goods and services to the war zones and other rural areas meant that shortages were particularly acute in Managua. Correspondingly, there was a much deeper erosion of political support for the Sandinista National Liberation Front government in the capital. Relations with the right-wing opposition parties, already poor, were further damaged by the expulsion of two Catholic clergymen and the closing in June 1986 of the newspaper *La Prensa.* In the countryside the government's standing was enhanced when a number of state farms and cooperatives, taken over in 1979, were subdivided and handed over to peasant farmers.

(RICHARD J. LAPPER)

This article updates the *Macropædia* article CENTRAL AMERICA: *Nicaragua.*

PANAMA

A republic of Central America, Panama lies between the Caribbean Sea and the Pacific Ocean on the Isthmus of Panama. Area: 77,082 sq km (29,762 sq mi). Pop. (1986 est.): 2,227,300. Cap.: Panama City. Monetary unit: balboa, at par with the U.S. dollar, with a free rate (Oct. 1, 1986) of 1.45 balboas to £1 sterling. President in 1986, Eric Arturo Delvalle.

For many Panamanians the year was not a pleasant one, for the general economy pointed to an economic recession. The national debt was approaching $4 billion, a per capita amount that was the highest in Latin America. Unemployment, also rising, reached about 20%. To improve the situation, Pres. Eric Arturo Delvalle proposed a number of measures, among which were the sale of some state-owned businesses, a tax increase on machinery and raw materials, and a reduction of subsidies to farmers and certain industries.

In response to the austerity package, the National Council of Organized Workers (Conato), an umbrella labour group of 200,000, led a crippling ten-day general strike in March. The strike was supported by 3,000 doctors, Texaco workers at the nation's only oil refinery at Colón, and 6,000 United Fruit Co. banana workers, who were demanding higher wages and better working conditions. The National Assembly approved the austerity measures but announced a reduction in fuel prices, a principal demand of the strike.

Many Panamanians believed that the spoon that stirred this brew of trouble was held by Gen. Manuel Antonio Noriega, commander of the National Guard. He was believed to have contrived the brutal murder of Hugo Spadafora, a severe critic of the regime, and to have forced the resignation of Pres. Nicolás Barletta in September 1985. President Delvalle and the National Assembly continued to support Noriega despite charges throughout the year of his connection to drug and arms smuggling, money laundering, and the selling of U.S. intelligence secrets to Cuba.

(ALMON R. WRIGHT)

This article updates the *Macropædia* article CENTRAL AMERICA: *Panama.*

PARAGUAY

Paraguay is a landlocked republic of central South America. Area: 406,752 sq km (157,048 sq mi). Pop. (1986 est.): 3,381,000. Cap.: Asunción. Monetary unit: guaraní, with (Oct. 1, 1986) an official rate of 320 guaraníes to U.S. $1 (462.40 guaraníes = £1 sterling). President in 1986, Gen. Alfredo Stroessner.

In response to growing pressures from within and outside the ruling Colorado Party, Pres. Alfredo Stroessner in July 1986 announced greater political freedom in Paraguay. Earlier in the year demonstrations against the government had become more frequent, and Stroessner promised that the state of siege in Asunción would be lifted, press freedom restored, and exiles might be allowed to return. Despite growing criticism within the Colorado Party, pro-Stroessner *militantes* won 17 of 25 districts in party elections in Asunción in July.

Domingo Laino of the Authentic Radical Liberal Party attempted to return to Paraguay in June, but he and former U.S. ambassador Robert White, who had accompanied him, were beaten by police at the airport. In July the U.S. suspended preferential tariff treatment for Paraguay until trade union freedom was established. Stroessner met with Radical Liberal Party leader Emilio Forestieri in September, the first meeting with an opposition leader in his 32-year presidency. Hopes that this marked the start of greater political freedom were dashed, however, when a prominent member of the Authentic Radical Liberal Party was arrested.

The economy continued to deteriorate. In August, after the World Bank had implemented its May threat to freeze development projects, the government succumbed to pressure and devalued the guaraní. (BEN BOX)

PERU

The republic of Peru is located in western South America, on the Pacific Ocean. Area: 1,285,216 sq km (496,225 sq mi). Pop. (1986 est.): 20,208,000. Cap.: Lima. Monetary unit: inti, with (Oct. 1, 1986) an official rate of 13.95 intis to U.S. $1 (20.16 intis = £1 sterling). President in 1986, Alan García Pérez; prime minister, Luis Alva Castro.

The most pressing domestic problem confronting Peru's new centre-left president, Alan García Peréz, in 1986 was how to suppress the activities of the Maoist guerrilla group Sendero Luminoso (Shining Path). García's attempts to negotiate failed, and attacks on key economic and political targets continued unabated. Of the country's 152 provinces, 19 were under state of emergency legislation, which suspended many civil rights. The restrictions were extended to Lima and Callao in February as the Sendero Luminoso campaign there intensified. In May the government announced that 7,307 people had been killed in the previous six years as a direct result of the guerrilla insurgency. While almost half these deaths were attributed to the armed forces, García's determination to ensure that

Relatives of prisoners of Peru's Lurigancho, El Fronton, and Santa Barbara prisons demonstrate in Lima. More than 250 prisoners had been killed when government security forces retook the three prisons following a coordinated mutiny.

N. BONNET—GAMMA/LIAISON

human rights were observed in the antiterrorist campaign appeared to be reducing military abuses. Unofficial estimates put total deaths much higher.

Responsibility for the most destabilizing incident was, however, placed on government forces. On June 18–19 Sendero Luminoso prisoners in three high-security prisons staged a coordinated mutiny, to coincide with the Socialist International's world congress in Lima. García ordered troops into the prisons to regain control, and in the struggle more than 250 prisoners were killed. The president was quick to condemn an outright massacre of more than 100 prisoners after their surrender, and a number of members of the paramilitary Republican Guard faced murder trials. The crisis led to the resignation of Justice Minister Luis González Posada and various minor officials. Gen. Jorge Rabanal, commander of the joint army, navy, and police action, was later arrested. Guerrilla attacks on civilian targets escalated and included the bombing of a tourist train to Machu Picchu. García escaped two bomb attacks.

Although the government's image was badly tainted by the prison killings, García retained the support of 70–80% of the population, according to opinion polls. One reason was his success in stimulating a modest economic boom. In 1986 gross domestic product (GDP) was officially projected to rise by 6%. The austerity package imposed in August 1985 held inflation to an annual average of 163% in 1985, but GDP growth was only 1.6%. In 1986 economic policy aimed to stimulate domestic demand by increasing wages, which in mid-1985 were only 69% of their 1980 value. Successive wage awards and the price freeze that continued until December (when it was replaced by a series of controls) permitted average real wages to rise by at least 50% in the 12 months to July. Increased consumer spending stimulated manufacturing and construction activity, reversing years of sluggish growth. Fish sales rose 51% in the first half of 1986, but the continued depression of world mineral prices meant that the trade surplus was not expected to exceed $350 million, compared with $1 billion in 1984 and 1985.

García's continued domestic popularity was helped by his stance on the country's $14 billion external debt and toward the International Monetary Fund (IMF). After one year in office, García announced that the restriction on service payments on the public sector debt to 10% of foreign exchange earnings would be extended by a year. Arrears on interest payments alone were expected to exceed $2 billion by the end of 1986. He also imposed a two-year ban on remittances abroad by all companies operating in Peru. International confidence fell, however, and in August the IMF declared Peru ineligible for further loans.

The results of the nationwide municipal elections on November 9 confirmed the popularity of García and the Alianza Popular Revolucionaria Americana. APRA took the lead in most of the country's 1,883 municipalities, holding its traditional northern base around Trujillo and unexpectedly wresting power in some of the opposition Izquierda Unida's southern strongholds.

(JANET KRENGEL)

SAINT CHRISTOPHER AND NEVIS

A constitutional monarchy and member of the Commonwealth, St. Christopher and Nevis is comprised of the islands of St. Christopher and Nevis in the eastern Caribbean Sea. Area: 267 sq km (103 sq mi). Pop (1986 est.): 46,000. Cap.: Basseterre. Monetary unit: Eastern Caribbean dollar, with (Oct. 1, 1986) a par value of EC$2.70 to U.S. $1 (free rate of EC$3.90 = £1 sterling). Queen, Elizabeth II; governor-general in 1986, Sir Clement Arrindell; prime minister, Kennedy A. Simmonds.

Despite an expected budget deficit of EC$3.4 million on current spending, incurred largely because of salary increases for government employees, the government of St. Christopher and Nevis (St. Kitts-Nevis) expected improved economic performance in 1986. The main stimulus again came from tourism, with a 24% increase in stopover visitors in January–May compared with the corresponding period a year earlier.

Loans were obtained from several international sources. These included $1.8 million from the U.S. Agency for International Development to construct a new road through the previously inaccessible region of southeastern St. Kitts, $3.5 million from Taiwan for residential construction, and an additional $3 million from the U.S., to be used for agricultural improvements and a basic needs program. A loan from the International Bank of Credit and Commerce was to go toward the EC$22 million being paid in compensation to former owners of land under sugarcane, which was compulsorily purchased in the 1970s. (ROD PRINCE)

This article updates the *Macropædia* article The WEST INDIES: *Saint Christopher and Nevis*.

Pope John Paul II greets islanders in July at the airport in Vieux Fort, St. Lucia, a stop on his way home following a visit to Colombia.
AP/WIDE WORLD

SAINT LUCIA

A constitutional monarchy and member of the Commonwealth, St. Lucia is the second largest of the Windward Islands in the eastern Caribbean Sea. Area: 617 sq km (238 sq mi). Pop. (1986 est.): 139,500. Cap.: Castries. Monetary unit: Eastern Caribbean dollar, with (Oct. 1, 1986) a par value of EC$2.70 to U.S. $1 (free rate of EC$3.90 = £1 sterling). Queen, Elizabeth II; governor-general in 1986, Sir Allen Lewis; prime minister, John Compton.

St. Lucia's political parties began preparations in late 1986 for general elections, constitutionally due by August 1987 but expected sooner. The St. Lucia Labour Party (SLP), which had lost the 1982 elections to the United Workers' Party headed by Prime Minister John Compton, promised to create 2,000 jobs in its first 30 months in office. It stated that agricultural diversification would be a priority, as would the strengthening of controls over banking and insurance. The SLP rejected proposals to unite with the left-wing Progressive Labour Party.

The 1986–87 budget, introduced in May, raised the income tax threshold from EC$2,000 to EC$3,000 and reduced the tax rate on higher income; direct taxes on luxuries were increased to pay for the concessions. Total spending rose, and a small surplus on current spending was envisaged. Projects under way included construction of a highway from Castries to Soufrière.

The economy expanded by an estimated 3–4% in 1985 but was expected to slow in 1986. Banana production rose 24% in 1985 to 80,664 metric tons. However, the new crop was damaged by storms, threatening the 100,000-ton target for 1986. (ROD PRINCE)

This article updates the *Macropædia* article The West Indies: *Saint Lucia.*

SAINT VINCENT AND THE GRENADINES

A constitutional monarchy within the Commonwealth, St. Vincent and the Grenadines comprises the islands of St. Vincent and the northern Grenadines in the eastern Caribbean Sea. Area: 389 sq km (150 sq mi). Pop. (1986 est.): 111,000. Cap.: Kingstown. Monetary unit: Eastern Caribbean dollar, with (Oct. 1, 1986) a par value of EC$2.70 to U.S. $1 (EC$3.90 = £1 sterling). Queen, Elizabeth II; governor-general in 1986, Joseph Lambert Eustace; prime minister, James Fitz-Allen Mitchell.

The improvement in the financial operations of the St. Vincent and the Grenadines government continued in 1986, and a surplus of EC$3 million was anticipated in the 1986–87 recurrent budget. Increased agricultural exports helped to reduce the trade deficit, but the banana industry was dealt a serious blow in September when a tropical storm destroyed about half the unharvested crop. Capital projects under way or planned included road building, water and sewerage improvements, and a comprehensive development scheme for the 1,200-ha (3,000-ac) Orange Hill estate, which was compulsorily acquired by the government in 1985 from a group of Danish investors.

In September Prime Minister James Mitchell and the new prime minister of Barbados, Errol Barrow, made public their opposition to a regional security treaty and to any increase in the military component of the Regional Security System. The leader of the opposition Labour Party and former foreign minister, Hudson Tannis, was killed in a plane crash on August 3. On the diplomatic front, Thailand agreed to establish links at an ambassadorial level with St. Vincent and the Grenadines, along with several other Caribbean countries. (ROD PRINCE)

This article updates the *Macropædia* article The West Indies: *Saint Vincent and the Grenadines.*

SURINAME

The republic of Suriname is in northeastern South America, on the Atlantic Ocean. Area: 163,820 sq km (63,251 sq mi), not including a 17,635-km area disputed with Guyana. Pop. (1986 est.): 403,000. Cap.: Paramaribo. Monetary unit: Suriname guilder, with (Oct. 1, 1986) a par value of 1.79 Suriname guilders to U.S. $1 (free rate of 2.58 Suriname guilders = £1 sterling). Chairman of the National Military Council in 1986, Dési Bouterse; acting president, L. F. Ramdat Misier; prime ministers, Wim Udenhout and, from July 17, Pretaapnarian Radhakishun.

On Feb. 25, 1986, the state of emergency in Suriname was lifted to mark the sixth anniversary of the military coup, and Dési Bouterse, chairman of the National Military Council (NMC), announced that the country would be returned to civilian rule by April 1987. An interim government led by acting president L. F. Ramdat Misier was formed, and a new Cabinet with 14 ministers made up of representatives of business, labour unions, and opposition parties was sworn in on July 17, 1986. Pretaapnarian

Radhakishun, formerly a businessman, succeeded Wim Udenhout as prime minister. Bouterse, however, retained overall control. Preparation of a new constitution was the priority.

The new government faced severe problems, with economic difficulties being compounded by an acceleration in rebel activity, led by a former bodyguard of Bouterse, Ronnie Brunswijk. Late in the year there were reports of atrocities committed during a government offensive against the rebels in eastern Suriname. A state of emergency in that area of the country was declared on December 2. Drug trafficking continued to be a problem, and one of Suriname's military leaders, a member of the NMC, was arrested in Miami, Fla., in late March by the U.S. Drug Enforcement Agency; the evidence suggested that Bouterse wanted to use cocaine money to stimulate the economy.

(KLAAS J. HOEKSEMA)

This article updates the *Macropædia* article The GUIANAS: *Suriname.*

TRINIDAD AND TOBAGO

A republic and member of the Commonwealth, Trinidad and Tobago consists of two islands in the Caribbean Sea off the coast of Venezuela. Area: 5,124 sq km (1,978 sq mi). Pop. (1986 est.): 1,202,000. Cap.: Port-of-Spain. Monetary unit: Trinidad and Tobago dollar, with (Oct. 1, 1986) a par value of TT$3.60 to U.S. $1 (free rate of TT$5.20 = £1 sterling). President in 1986, Sir Ellis Clarke; prime ministers, George Chambers and, from December 18, A. N. R. Robinson.

In 1986 Trinidad and Tobago suffered a serious economic decline for the fourth successive year. The 1986 budget, introduced on Dec. 17, 1985, was designed to stimulate the economy and improve competitiveness. In particular, the Trinidad and Tobago dollar was devalued by 33.3% against the U.S. dollar, to which it was linked. Oil continued to dominate the economy, contributing some three-quarters of all exports, although output declined 5.5% in the first half of 1986. The government's fiscal deficit was reduced, and the trade account remained in surplus; nevertheless, foreign reserves reached a record low of U.S. $676 million in July 1986.

Major investment projects included a $117 million natural gas production platform off southeastern Trinidad and a $250 million ammonia plant. In April 1986 a project was started to promote compressed natural gas as an alternative to motor fuel. The troubled state sugar company, Caroni, was placing increased emphasis on crop diversification. Difficulties in distribution and manufacturing led to several takeover bids and liquidation moves among business groups.

In the general elections held December 15, the National Alliance for Reconstruction (NAR) defeated the ruling People's National Movement in a landslide, winning all but 3 of the 36 seats in the House of Representatives. George Chambers, who lost his own seat, was replaced as prime minister by the NAR leader, Arthur Napoleon Raymond Robinson.

(ROD PRINCE)

This article updates the *Macropædia* article The WEST INDIES: *Trinidad and Tobago.*

URUGUAY

A republic of eastern South America, Uruguay lies on the Atlantic Ocean. Area: 176,215 sq km (68,037 sq mi). Pop. (1986 est.): 3,035,000. Cap.: Montevideo. Monetary unit: Uruguayan new peso, with (Oct. 1, 1986) a free rate of 161.50 new pesos to U.S. $1 (233.37 new pesos = £1 sterling). President in 1986, Julio María Sanguinetti Cairolo.

A salesman prepares a literature display with the theme "Uruguay Under Democracy" in Montevideo. A growing number of books, including leftist books once proscribed by the government, were being sold, marking the country's movement toward democracy.

ALAN RIDING/THE NEW YORK TIMES

Democracy in Uruguay strengthened in 1986, despite continued social and economic pressures arising from 12 years of military rule and 4 years of economic recession. However, the support that the opposition parties had pledged to the governing Colorado Party led by Julio María Sanguinetti was not always forthcoming. Trade unions were extremely militant, and there were many strikes. Attempts to reach political consensus through a national dialogue failed, and the government sought agreement with the main opposition parties on very specific areas of socioeconomic development. In April the principal political groups reached a national accord that should have ensured rapid congressional approval of necessary legislation over the next three years, but the executive had to make excessive use of the veto to get measures through the legislature. Opposition parties continued to refuse ministerial posts that were initially offered at the time of the first Cabinet reshuffle on April 3. After an emotional debate, a law granting amnesty to members of the armed forces accused of violating human rights during the period of military rule was passed on December 22.

The government succeeded in gaining support from the International Monetary Fund; a $126 million standby loan had been approved in September 1985. Agreement was also reached with commercial bank creditors in July 1986 to reschedule some $1,760,000,000 of external debt maturing in 1985–89.

(ALEXANDER JOHNS CAMPBELL)

VENEZUELA

A republic of northern South America, Venezuela lies on the Caribbean Sea. Area: 912,050 sq km (352,144 sq mi). Pop. (1986 est.): 17,791,000. Cap.: Caracas. Monetary unit: bolívar, with (Oct. 1, 1986) a main official rate of 7.50 bolivares to U.S. $1 (10.84 bolivares = £1 sterling). President in 1986, Jaime Lusinchi.

Unofficial campaigning was well under way in 1986 in both major parties for Venezuela's 1988 presidential election. Former president Carlos Andrés Pérez (1974–79) became eligible for reelection and was probably the most charismatic figure in Venezuelan politics. Although he was the most popular leader in the ruling Acción Democrática (AD) party, his support came from the electorate rather than the party organization. Pres. Jaime Lusinchi's favoured candidate, Octavio Lepage Barreto, resigned as interior minister to start his campaign. His contacts within the powerful ministry made him a favourite, though Reinaldo Leandro Mora, the president of the Senate, was favoured by AD's labour wing. Rafael Caldera, also a former president, was likely to find Eduardo Fernández his major rival to becoming the candidate of the Social Christian Party (COPEI).

Because of COPEI's lacklustre performance, the government maintained a substantial lead in the opinion polls, even though it showed errors of judgment during 1986. It managed to offend all sides when a plan to turn private foreign debt into 15-year bonds was dropped as quickly as it had been announced. Also during the year the government became increasingly sensitive to criticism, particularly in relation to the scandal of the so-called Wells of Death in Zulia State. Allegations of murder committed by a corrupt police force in Zulia prompted the government to order the editor of a leading Caracas newspaper to cease his exposés relating to the case.

The 1987 budget, introduced at the end of June, aimed to reduce Venezuela's heavy dependence on oil by stimulating alternative industries. On July 17 the president announced a 21-point economic recovery plan that included corporate tax reform, the maintenance of a price freeze on 30 basic goods, and revisions to the foreign investment law. In regard to the latter, prior approval by the foreign investment regulatory body was no longer essential; rules on conversion to joint ventures or locally owned companies were significantly relaxed; maximum payable dividends of 20% were raised; and more industries—including electronics, biotechnology, and informatics—joined agricultural and tourism in gaining exemptions from foreign investment rules. A further package of economic measures announced in December included a partial devaluation of the bolívar and a plan to assist eligible private-sector companies to repay foreign debts.

The collapse in oil prices intensified Venezuela's economic problems in 1986, especially in relation to the servicing of the $33 billion foreign debt. PDVSA, the state oil company, expected oil export income to plunge from $12.9 billion in 1985 (13.1% lower than in 1984) to $7.9 billion in 1986. In 1985 the total value of exports was $14.2 billion, and the current account surplus was $2.9 billion, down from $5.4 billion in 1984. Petroleum output fell by 3% in 1985. While non-oil gross domestic product (GDP) rose by a slight 0.6%, helped by healthy 10.7% and 5.7% rises in output in the negligible mining and agricultural sectors, total GDP rose by just 0.3%. In real terms GDP was expected to fall in 1986 and 1987.

The fall in oil prices had prompted the government to seek the renegotiation of its $21.2 billion public-sector foreign debt restructuring agreement, which was signed with commercial bank creditors on February 26. A $750 million down payment was to be made in 1986, but no principal was due in 1987. The Venezuelans sought both an extended period for amortization to the year 2000 and a debt-servicing formula that would take account of the price of oil, which determined Venezuela's ability to pay. In December Venezuela announced that it would seek to defer its first quarter 1987 payments. (PAUL MILLGATE)

Oceania

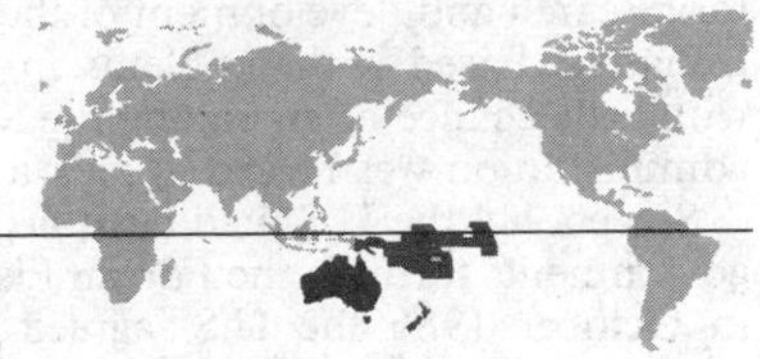

OCEANIAN AFFAIRS

A combination of commercial and strategic issues kept Oceania at the centre of great power attention in 1986.

Strategic Issues. A delegation from the South Pacific Forum took the South Pacific Nuclear Free Zone Treaty to the nuclear powers, seeking their agreement to protocols that would restrict their capacity to manufacture, test, or store nuclear weapons in the South Pacific but would not affect the transit of nuclear-powered vessels or the carriage of weapons. Although most Forum countries had signed the treaty, the number was insufficient for formal ratification. While Prime Minister Walter Lini of Vanuatu maintained that the treaty did not go far enough, Sir Tom Davis, premier of the Cook Islands, argued that it went too far and could threaten the security of the region.

The latter view emerged from Davis's concern over the effective termination of the ANZUS (Australia-New Zealand-U.S.) defense alliance and its replacement, through an exchange of letters, by a much weaker bilateral agreement between the U.S. and Australia. In light of its continuing differences with the U.S. over the nuclear issue, New Zealand was anxious to demonstrate its defense capability in the South Pacific and conducted a major army exercise in the Cook Islands. New Zealand was also taking an active role in the surveillance of the exclusive economic zones of some small countries. Meanwhile, after three years in office (and only, some observers argued, after Soviet intervention in the area), Australia's much-traveled foreign minister, William (Bill) Hayden, managed to fit a tour of island nations into his schedule.

Fisheries. Most great power interest in the region was in the fishing sector. The agreement signed between the U.S.S.R. and Kiribati in August 1985 was under renegotiation in 1986, with the Soviets reportedly seeking to reduce both ship numbers and fees payable because of poor catches but showing no inclination to quit the area. Talks on a similar agreement with Vanuatu were in progress at year's end. Unlike Kiribati, Vanuatu was prepared to consider port access to facilitate crew exchange and ship repairs. This, together with Vanuatu's establishment of diplomatic relations with Libya, Nicaragua, and the U.S.S.R., was creating some concern among Western countries. In a surprise move, in light of his earlier criticism of the Kiribati agreement, Prime Minister Ratu Sir Kamisese Mara of Fiji indicated that his country might also be prepared to negotiate with the U.S.S.R. on fisheries.

The most significant reaction to the Kiribati agreement came, however, from the U.S. Largely at the instigation of the American Tunaboat Association, the U.S. had emphatically denied any nation's ownership of highly migratory species of tuna, irrespective of exclusive economic zones. The Magnuson Act, invoked against the Solomon Islands when it seized the U.S. ship *Jeannette Diana* for illegal fishing in 1984, provided for mandatory trade sanctions against any country that restricted U.S. vessels fishing for highly migratory species. But it had become increasingly evident that this stand was working against U.S. foreign policy in the region. Moreover, U.S. officials argued that Soviet interest in the Central Pacific had less to do with fishing than with electronic surveillance of the Kwajalein missile base in the Marshall Islands, of growing significance for research and development of the U.S. Strategic Defense Initiative. Faced with problems in the South Pacific, and with little chance of amending the Magnuson Act, the U.S. administration was forced to seek a compromise.

Since 1984 the U.S. had been negotiating with 16 island governments through the Forum Fisheries Agency. Finally, in October 1986 the U.S. agreed to pay an annual fee of $12 million ($10 million from government sources; $2 million from the American Tunaboat Association), to be divided among the Forum countries in proportion to the catch from their respective waters.

The South Pacific Forum. At the 1986 meeting of the South Pacific Forum held in Suva, Fiji, in August, the New Caledonian issue was given prominence by a "Melanesian alliance" of the prime ministers of Vanuatu, the Solomon Islands, and Papua New Guinea. It was agreed to seek a listing of New Caledonia with the UN as a non-self-governing territory, thus bringing it under the jurisdiction of the Committee on Decolonization. The Forum, which had adopted a more conciliatory attitude toward France at meetings in previous years, was clearly perturbed over French Prime Minister Jacques Chirac's policy, which appeared designed to ensure that New Caledonia remained a French possession.

Following the appointment of a new director—Henry Faati Naisali, formerly Tuvalu's deputy prime minister and minister of finance—to the South Pacific Bureau of Economic Cooperation (SPEC), the South Pacific Forum was reviewing the rules and role of SPEC and also Forum membership. In the past, observer status had been conferred only on potential members on the brink of self-government; the Forum was considering extending it to nations in the wider Pacific region (from the Association of Southeast Asian Nations, for example) or to metropolitan countries with an interest in Oceania.

Television. Although private video facilities had proliferated, only the French and U.S. dependencies received a regular television service. In 1986 both Papua New Guinea and Fiji made a firm commitment to a comprehensive service, while several other countries had the matter under review. After Prime Minister Michael Somare's government in Papua New Guinea had signed an agreement with the Parry Corp.'s Newcastle Broadcasting Network (which established Niugini Television Network), the incoming government of Paias Wingti passed special legislation to prevent any broadcasting before 1988. In Fiji a 12-year monopoly agreement was signed with Australian Kerry Packer's Publishing and Broadcasting Ltd. The move caused disquiet in some quarters because of the company's heavy dependence on imported U.S. programs in its Australian operations. The most modest proposal was a U.S. cable network's offer to provide a service for Niue—a proposal that was attractive to Premier Sir Robert Rex, who hoped that it might help to stem the flow of migrants to New Zealand.

In response to all of these commercially based initiatives, Television New Zealand put forward a more limited proposal that would utilize the Intelsat facility to provide a regional service of Pacific-oriented material together with imported programs as a public broadcasting enterprise. The proposal was considered by the South Pacific Forum in August and referred to SPEC for evaluation. The Fiji experience, with broadcasting due to begin in March 1987, was expected to provide some lessons for Oceania. Norfolk Islanders rejected by referendum a proposal to introduce television, indicating that many people placed a higher priority on roads and other public works.

(BARRIE MACDONALD)

AUSTRALIA

A federal parliamentary state (formally a constitutional monarchy) and member of the Commonwealth, Australia occupies the smallest continent and includes the island state of Tasmania. Area: 7,682,300 sq km (2,966,200 sq mi). Pop. (1986 est.): 15,912,000. Cap.: Canberra. Monetary unit: Australian dollar, with (Oct. 1, 1986) a free rate of $A 1.59 to U.S. $1 ($A 2.29 = £1 sterling). Queen, Elizabeth II; governor-general in 1986, Sir Ninian Martin Stephen; prime minister, Robert J. Hawke.

Domestic Affairs. The Australian government of Prime Minister Robert (Bob) Hawke performed a difficult juggling act in 1986 as its popularity slumped to such an extent that, had elections been held after midyear, it might well have lost office. The prime minister's popularity, previously overwhelming, sank so low that he was pelted with flour bombs and greeted by protesters against his government during all public appearances.

Undeterred, Hawke continued to berate the opposition and said that he and his Australian Labor Party (ALP) government were prepared to make unpopular decisions when they were in the national interest. A turning point in the manifestation of electoral ill-feeling came in by-elections for two seats in the New South Wales state assembly in August. Barrie Unsworth, New South Wales premier, was only just reelected, and the swing against the ALP was so marked that the Liberal Party opposition began planning victory celebrations for the next federal elections. In defiance of opinion-poll predictions and allegations of corruption, the National Party was returned to power in Queensland's state elections on November 1. The result was seen as a personal triumph for state premier Sir Johannes Bjelke-Peterson.

Despite their best efforts, it seemed that almost nothing the ALP government did turned out well. An unprecedented fragmentation of traditional loyalties brought Australia's conservative farmers into alliance with the radical antinuclear lobby to demand the end of joint Australian-U.S. military facilities in Australia. The leader of the National Party, Ian Sinclair, called the 1986 ALP Cabinet "the Bollinger bolsheviks" and ridiculed their inability to use the North West Cape, Pine Gap, and Nurrungar military bases as bargaining chips in the dispute over the U.S. decision to subsidize sales of primary products to such areas as China and the U.S.S.R., where Australia had traditionally operated.

The Hawke ministry faced perennial problems with past and present ministers. In the most serious of these, attempts to conclude the long-running investigation into the conduct of Lionel Murphy (*see* OBITUARIES), former ALP attorney general and High Court judge, took a tragic turn when Murphy announced that he was unable to attend hearings of the parliamentary commission investigating allegations about him. Murphy explained that he was dying of inoperable cancer. Hawke moved swiftly to wind up the commission, only to find the ALP embarrassed by attacks from the opposition. Introducing the bill to abolish the Murphy commission, Attorney General Lionel Bowen said that Murphy and his family had already had to bear more stress in the last two and a half years than most people experienced in a lifetime; also, because of Murphy's grave illness, the commissioners would be unable to complete their inquiries. Bowen proposed that, under these circumstances, the allegations against Murphy be suppressed forever. However, the opposition spokesman on legal matters described this course of action as constituting an extraordinary and unprecedented restriction, giving a status and

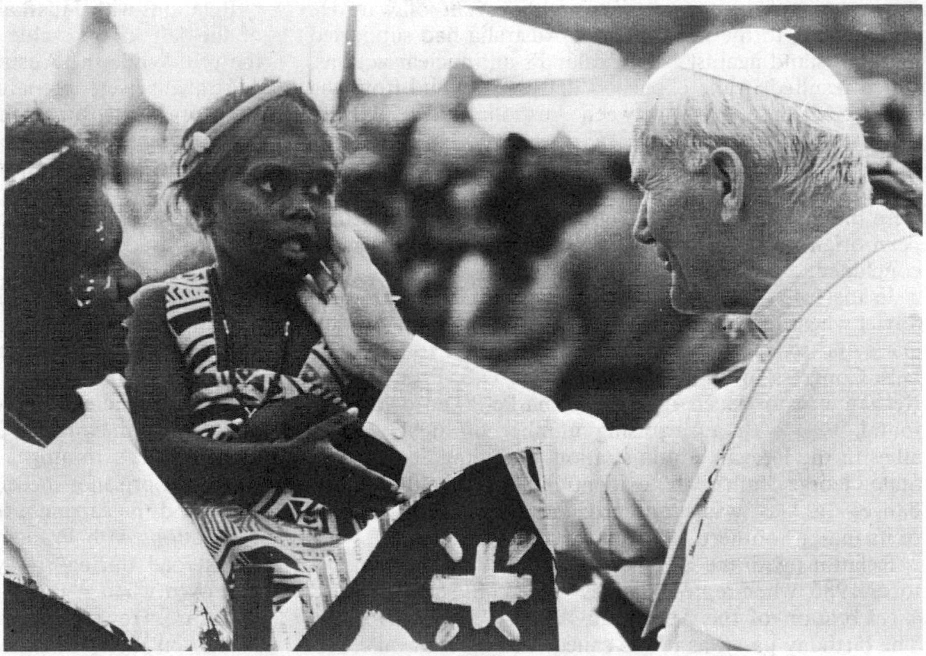

Pope John Paul II touches the cheek of an Aboriginal child in blessing during his week-long visit to Australia in November, during which he spoke strongly on behalf of the tribesmen's land rights.
AFP PHOTO

secrecy to the Murphy material that was unknown to Australia's democratic processes.

In another serious and disturbing case, Chris Hurford, minister for immigration and ethnic affairs, proposed in a letter to an Adelaide radio announcer that he would leak stories about the workings of government, and internal maneuvers within the ALP, in return for "a quid pro quo such as a regular time slot." Hurford called his letter "a little joke," but the *Australian* newspaper described it as a misuse of position that placed a moral obligation on the prime minister to demand Hurford's resignation. Hawke, however, accepted Hurford's explanation.

During the year a Sydney court heard the U.K. government's case for seeking an injunction against the publication in Australia of the memoirs of a former British intelligence agent, Peter Wright. The hearing ended on December 19 and a decision was not expected before February 1987.

The ALP was particularly worried by the emergence of a new spirit of conservatism that it termed the New Right. Special Minister of State Michael (Mick) Young identified the New Right as a major hurdle that the ALP would have to overcome, as it was gaining strength because of the legitimate disillusion over what was popularly taken to be the inordinate power of labour. The new hard-line right-wing reaction came from some industrialists who decided to mount an all-out assault on the ALP and on the arbitration system of powerful Industrial Courts. Peko-Wallsend Ltd. fired 1,100 workers at two of its operations in Western Australia, the Robe River iron-ore mine and the Cape Lambert port facilities in the Pilbara region. At the centre of the dispute was Charles Copeman, chief executive of Peko-Wallsend, who argued that the dispute was simply over the company's right and responsibility to manage. Hawke complained that employers who defied industrial commission rulings were hypocrites, but the leader of the Liberal Party opposition, John Howard, defended the company's action. On September 3 the court reinstated all the workers.

During her visit to Australia in March, Queen Elizabeth II signed a proclamation that, by immediately activating the Australia Act (1986), granted Australia full legal independence from the U.K. The act removed a number of controls, generally regarded as anachronistic, that the U.K. had maintained over Australian legislative and judicial processes.

A group calling itself the Australian Cultural Terrorists stole an uninsured Picasso painting worth $A 1.6 million from Victoria's National Gallery. When the painting, "Weeping Woman," was bought in December 1985, it had been Australia's most expensive art purchase. The group demanded that the state government of Victoria increase arts funding and establish a prize for young artists to be called "the Picasso ransom." The painting was returned within three weeks, after private companies announced new grants and prizes for young artists.

In late November Pope John Paul II undertook a six-day tour of Australia, visiting each state capital. The pope's visit to Canberra was marred by a number of threats to his life.

Foreign Affairs. Australia's international relations changed considerably during 1986. The alliance with the U.S. deteriorated rapidly as a result of the U.S. administration's decision to try to sell subsidized wheat to the U.S.S.R. Although little wheat was in fact sold to the Soviets, ill feeling and bitterness toward the U.S. reached a level not seen since the anti-U.S. protests during the Vietnam war. The difference in 1986, however, was that the protests came from conservative groups within Australia.

Minister for Foreign Affairs William (Bill) Hayden spoke without exaggeration of the "outrage" felt in Australia at the U.S. decision. In a series of not too thinly veiled threats, Hayden drew the attention of Americans to the presence of joint facilities and the access to ports and airfields afforded to U.S. ships and aircraft in Australia. While admitting that the joint defense facilities gave Australia access to defense technology of unmatched sophistication, Hayden pointed out that for this Australia paid more than $1 billion a year, largely as a result of which Australia was one of the few countries that had an adverse balance of trade with the U.S. Many Australians doubted the wisdom of such a close alliance. Referring to them, Hayden noted that although the joint facilities played a significant role in nuclear deterrence and arms control, they also made the country a prime target for enemy strikes in the event of war. He also referred to the way in which Australia had supported the U.S. stand against New Zealand's antinuclear actions, which resulted in the expulsion of New Zealand from the ANZUS defense treaty between Australia, New Zealand, and the U.S. (See *Oceanian Affairs,* above.) He added that as an ally of the U.S., Australia had lost many young men on the battlefields of Vietnam. Australia and New Zealand were the only nations with populations primarily of European origin who fought alongside the U.S. in Vietnam, he concluded.

In the face of the possible loss of Australia's traditional Soviet wheat market, all political parties buried their differences and sent representatives to Washington to lobby the U.S. Congress in an effort to persuade U.S. Pres. Ronald Reagan not to poach Australia's market. The delegation found itself with a surprising number of highly placed allies in the Reagan administration, including Secretary of State George Shultz, who evidently realized the diplomatic danger the U.S. was running in disregarding the interests of its major Southern Hemisphere ally.

Relations with the U.S. were also in the limelight in October 1986, when representatives of the U.S. Navy attended a celebration of the Australian Navy's 75th anniversary. The birthday party, as it was called, also drew naval representatives from the U.K., Canada, and France, but antinuclear protesters focused their hostility on the U.S. craft—one surfboard rider successfully hung onto the bow of a U.S. Navy warship as it sped through the waves of Sydney Harbour in a spectacular protest against the entry of nuclear-powered and nuclear-armed ships into Australian waters.

AP/WIDE WORLD

A protest banner and an effigy of a fisherman tip overboard from one of 40 crayfishing boats blockading Australia's Fremantle Harbour in reaction to new government regulations on fishing quotas.

Relations with Japan also deteriorated, mostly as a result of the fall in the value of the Australian dollar against the yen. While the Australian dollar was relatively strong, Australians were prepared to accept Japanese restrictive trade practices. But as the value of the dollar fell by 55% and Australia was unable to increase its volume of exports to Japan, the government tried to toughen its attitude. Minister for Trade John Dawkins blamed the fall in the value of exports to Japan for almost half of Australia's growing trade deficit. Dawkins described Japan as the country's most important trading partner and added that Australia, Japan's second most important trading partner in the developed world, provided a commercial link that had helped Japan to become a leading economic power. He maintained, however, that the relationship that had begun as a partnership of equals had in recent years become increasingly unequal, as Japan had dominated the market for Australia's mining and farming exports and had not paid a fair price for those goods. Dawkins called for fairness and urged the Japanese to rectify the emerging imbalance.

Relations with France followed a characteristically tortuous road during the year. For a time, relations were improved when Australia agreed to resume uranium sales to France. However, no sooner had the government ended its ban on uranium exports to France than French Prime Minister Jacques Chirac launched a strong personal attack on Hawke. Referring to comments by Hawke that France had an obligation to ensure that its policies did not result in violence and bloodshed in New Caledonia, the French territory in the Pacific Ocean, Chirac observed that he would welcome a change of government in Australia. Hawke described Chirac as "very stupid" and as completely misunderstanding the situation in New Caledonia.

Relations with Indonesia were strained following the publication in an Australian newspaper of an article about alleged financial dealings of Indonesia's President Suharto, his family and associates. There were a number of unpleasant exchanges culminating in Indonesia's withdrawal of Australia's military landing rights for refueling. Restoration of rights within one week put relations back on an even keel.

Relations with Malaysia continued on a cordial note despite the execution in Kuala Lumpur in July of two Australians (one British-born) convicted of drug smuggling. The sentences were carried out in the face of the Australian government's strong view that capital punishment was repugnant.

The Economy. In 1986 the economy suffered its worst year in a generation. The spectacular deterioration in economic fortune was brought to world notice when Treasurer Paul Keating observed that the country was in danger of becoming "a banana republic." Because he referred to the economic plight in such disparaging and colourful terms, Keating was blamed for triggering the mass exodus of capital that followed. It was argued that by drawing attention so dramatically to the economy's poor performance, Keating had actually accelerated the international downgrading of the country's currency. Whether he was to blame or not, the economy had its worst year in decades. A number of factors combined and interacted to cause a dramatic drop in the standard of living of most Australians.

One of the chief indicators of performance was the balance of payments figures. Each month brought bad news, and the July figures were described by most Australian economists as disastrous; in that month the balance of payments deficit was $A 1,557,000,000, second only to that of October 1985, when the account deficit reached $A 1,650,000,000. With such a severe decline in trade, the 1986–87

Kiwami Dai, in tribal ceremonial attire, is consecrated bishop of Australia's Anglican Church. He is the first Torres Strait islander to hold the office.
AP/WIDE WORLD

budget presented in August was of prime importance. In the weeks before budget day, Prime Minister Hawke and other members of the Cabinet prepared the country for the worst by pointing out that the collapse of world commodity prices had devastated the economy. Even the most radical forecasters, however, failed to predict the scope of the budget, which slashed government spending, deferred pension payments, increased the Medicare levy, and raised gasoline (petrol) and other taxes.

The federal government announced that it would press for wage discounting at the next national wage negotiations. The ALP placed high reliance on the budget as its major instrument of economic policy, and by cutting almost $A 3 billion from the government's existing programs, it hoped to safeguard the future. Welfare cuts accounted for $A 500 million, and the Medicare national health levy was increased from 1 to 1.25%. Australians were also expected to pay more through new and increased sales taxes. The tax on wine and cider was increased from 10 to 20%; the sales tax on luxury cars was increased from 20 to 30%; and new taxes were placed on swimming pools and flavoured milk.

The most controversial sections of the budget were the decisions to impose a charge of $A 250 a year on all students above the high-school level and to export uranium to France. Three government backbenchers walked out during the treasurer's budget speech when Keating announced the go-ahead for uranium sales to France, and university students immediately began a nationwide campaign to have the fee decision rescinded. The government's decision on uranium sales was a clear breach of one of the most sensitive sections of the ALP platform. The ALP conference in July endorsed the policy not to sell uranium to France until France ceased testing nuclear weapons in the Pacific region.

Although fewer days were lost through strikes in 1986 than in preceding years, there was industrial unrest in areas of vital importance to the export industries. Workers who had been fired by Woodside Petroleum Ltd. occupied a gas-drilling platform 140 km (87 mi) off the coast of Western Australia. They blockaded helicopter landings on the platform for a time but left quietly following negotiations between Woodside Petroleum and union representatives of the Amalgamated Metal Workers and the Electrical Trades.

When foreign exchange markets failed to support the Australian dollar after the budget was announced, the Reserve Bank tightened monetary policy. Within weeks domestic banks found that it was costing them about 18% to raise funds in the market, and accordingly they raised their prime lending rates. By September the ANZ Banking Group, for example, was charging its best corporate borrowers 19% for overdrafts. At that time, despite the continuing poor balance of payments figures, the dollar was gaining strength and the stock exchange was testing levels in the wake of an improvement in the world gold price.

At the local level state governments tried to devise ways to reduce their expenditures, and long-cherished work practices came under attack. In a watershed case workers were distressed by a Tasmanian Industrial Commission ruling that the Tasmanian state government did not have to pay its public servants their usual vacation bonus, which amounted to 17.5% of an employee's holiday pay. In the aftermath both employers and employees judged that for the first time the bonus was questionable under the relatively poor new economic conditions.

Within the federal Parliament, however, the opposition had some difficulty in capitalizing on the ALP's poor economic performance. While there was considerable bitterness caused in conservative circles by a new fringe benefits tax, there was indecision within the opposition on what constituted a taxable fringe benefit and what did not. In response to ALP backbench pressure, Prime Minister Hawke decided to amend fringe benefits legislation in order to eliminate unforeseen administrative injustices. Public opinion, however, saw the federal Parliament as being the home of some of the worst examples of unacceptable work practices in Australia. (A. R. G. GRIFFITHS)

FIJI

A constitutional monarchy and member of the Commonwealth, Fiji occupies an island group in the South Pacific Ocean. Area: 18,274 sq km (7,056 sq mi). Pop. (1986 est.): 710,000. Cap.: Suva. Monetary unit: Fiji dollar, with (Oct. 1, 1986) a free rate of F$1.17 to U.S. $1 (F$1.69 = £1 sterling). Queen, Elizabeth II; governor-general in 1986, Ratu Sir Penaia Ganilau; prime minister, Ratu Sir Kamisese Mara.

During 1986 Fiji's Indian-dominated opposition, the National Federation Party, remained torn by divisions that forced the resignation of its leader, Siddiq Koya. He was succeeded by Harish Sharma. The NFP also suffered defections to the newly formed Fiji Labour Party, which outpolled the governing Alliance Party in elections to the Suva city council.

Fiji was struck by Cyclone Martin in April, and later that month flooding in Suva caused eight deaths. This, together with a fall in the Australian dollar, caused continuing problems in the tourist industry, the country's largest foreign exchange earner in 1985. A shortfall in sugar production in 1985 forced Fiji to export its own crops while importing sugar to meet domestic requirements. The 1986 budget increased indirect taxes, established a fringe-benefits tax, and reduced direct taxation. In March–April there was a gradual 5% devaluation of the Fiji dollar. The wage freeze that had operated since November 1984 was lifted, but increases were still restricted.

In April Prime Minister Lee Kuan Yew of Singapore visited Fiji. In August Fiji was host to the South Pacific Forum. (See *Oceanian Affairs,* above.) The ban on Soviet cruise liners was lifted, and Prime Minister Ratu Sir Kamisese Mara indicated that Fiji might be interested in a fishing agreement with the U.S.S.R. In what was called

Fiji's worst air disaster, 11 people died when a light plane crashed at the international airport at Nadi on December 27. (BARRIE MACDONALD)

This article updates the *Macropædia* article PACIFIC ISLANDS: *Fiji.*

KIRIBATI

A republic in the western Pacific Ocean and member of the Commonwealth, Kiribati comprises the former Gilbert Islands, Banaba (Ocean Island), the Line Islands, and the Phoenix Islands. Area: 849 sq km (328 sq mi). Pop. (1986 est.): 65,000. Cap.: Bairiki. Monetary unit: Australian dollar, with (Oct. 1, 1986) a free rate of $A 1.59 to U.S. $1 ($A 2.29 = £1 sterling). President (*beritítenti*) in 1986, Ieremia Tabai.

International attention remained focused on Kiribati's fishing agreement with the U.S.S.R., signed in August 1985. Renewal talks were adjourned in September 1986; Soviet negotiators sought to reduce both the number of vessels and the fee payable by each because of low catches and other difficulties, but Kiribati would not agree to concessions on ship fees. Talks on the renewal of fishing agreements with Japanese interests also stalled, but in November an agreement was reached between the U.S. and 16 South Pacific Forum nations, including Kiribati, ending a long dispute over tuna fishing rights.

Fisheries license fees surpassed copra exports as the major source of overseas earnings. Kiribati also moved toward independence from U.K. budgetary assistance for recurrent expenditure—a development that would allow greater flexibility in the management of reserve funds. Even so, its large and continuing trade deficit caused Kiribati to seek least-developed-country status from the World Bank and International Monetary Fund. The causeway joining the administrative and commercial centres on Tarawa Atoll neared completion. (BARRIE MACDONALD)

This article updates the *Macropædia* article PACIFIC ISLANDS: *Kiribati.*

NAURU

An island republic within the Commonwealth, Nauru lies in the Pacific Ocean about 1,900 km (1,200 mi) east of New Guinea. Area: 21 sq km (8 sq mi). Pop. (1986 est.): 8,100. Cap.: Yaren. Monetary unit: Australian dollar, with (Oct. 1, 1986) a free rate of $A 1.59 to U.S. $1 ($A 2.29 = £1 sterling). Presidents in 1986, Hammer DeRoburt, Kennan Adeang from September 17, and DeRoburt from October 1.

Pres. Hammer DeRoburt continued to lead Nauru throughout 1986 with the exception of a two-week period beginning on September 17, when he lost office because of the defeat in Parliament of his proposed budget measures. Kennan Adeang was elected by the parliamentary deputies as the new president. DeRoburt's opponents subsequently changed sides, however, and he was returned to power on October 1 after a no-confidence motion against Adeang was carried by nine votes to eight.

Before the presidential upset occurred, DeRoburt made progress in consolidating the foreign relations of the phosphate-rich island. During the visit of Australian Minister for Foreign Affairs William (Bill) Hayden to Nauru in May, the president took the opportunity to discuss bilateral issues. Nauru was concerned in particular to continue the development of air and shipping services in the region and also to work against nuclear testing and the dumping of nuclear waste materials in the Pacific Ocean region by outside powers. (A. R. G. GRIFFITHS)

This article updates the *Micropædia* article NAURU.

NEW ZEALAND

New Zealand, a constitutional monarchy and member of the Commonwealth in the South Pacific Ocean, consists of North and South islands and Stewart, Chatham, and other minor islands. Area: 268,105 sq km (103,516 sq mi). Pop. (1986 est.): 3,288,522. Cap.: Wellington. Monetary unit: New Zealand dollar, with (Oct. 1, 1986) a free rate of $NZ 2.05 to U.S. $1 ($NZ 2.96 = £1 sterling). Queen, Elizabeth II; governor-general in 1986, Sir Paul Reeves; prime minister, David Russell Lange.

On Oct. 1, 1986, the New Zealand government introduced an all-embracing goods and services tax (GST) designed, along with accompanying income-tax changes, to shift the burden of taxation from earners to spenders. GST was set at 10%, while the top income-tax rate was lowered from 66 cents in the dollar on $NZ 38,000 or over to 48 cents on $NZ 30,000 or over. Thus the Labour Party government introduced a reform over which Conservative administrations had vacillated for years, and its reception did not appear to imperil Labour's chances of reelection.

The sudden removal of support programs, however, contributed to a catastrophic season for most kinds of farming, while provincial towns went hungry and unemployment deepened in the cities. Reduction of inflation, running at 13% for the year to the end of March, remained a priority. In mid-September, however, the Institute of Economic Research predicted that the effects of a wage round under negotiation, GST, and other factors would be to lift inflation

AP/WIDE WORLD

Queen Elizabeth II, at the opening of New Zealand's Parliament, formally reads a speech prepared by government officials for the occasion. Included was a statement against nuclear weapons. Prime Minister David Lange (left) and judges of the Supreme Court look on.

The Roots of Maori Nationalism

In the precolonial period of New Zealand's history, the indigenous people were divided into 42 tribes, but with the advent of European colonization in the 19th century, the tribes became conscious of a common ethnic identity. Thereafter they used the word Maori, meaning normal, to distinguish themselves from the white strangers, whom they called Pakeha.

After the Treaty of Waitangi between the British government and Maori chiefs was signed in 1840, massive land purchases and increased Pakeha settlement aroused fears among the Maori people that they might be outnumbered in their own land. In the hope of resolving the problem, the chiefs held intertribal meetings to discuss the concept of *kotahitanga* ("unification of the tribes"). These meetings culminated in the election of a Maori king in 1857.

The chiefs thought of the king as embodying a form of home rule. However, the British governor strongly opposed the concept.The king's capital was attacked and his land confiscated under the New Zealand Settlements Act (1863). Despite this setback the king established the Kauhanganui ("Great Council") of his own confederation of tribes in 1892. In the same year, tribes outside that confederation established Kotahitanga mo te Tiriti o Waitangi ("unity under the Treaty of Waitangi"), otherwise known as the Maori Parliament. Both the Kauhanganui and Kotahitanga attempted, unsuccessfully, to negotiate with the New Zealand House of Representatives for recognition of Maori rights.

At the turn of the century, when the Maori population had dropped to its lowest point of 45,000, a new educated elite formed the Young Maori Party and entered Parliament to negotiate a more equitable share of the nation's resources for the Maori people. The concept of *mana motuhake* ("Maori sovereignty") pursued by the chiefs in the previous century lapsed into the Maori subconscious. In the depression years of the 1920s and 1930s, however, the people became disillusioned with the elite leaders and turned to the prophet Ratana. The Ratana Church won the four Maori seats in Parliament and aligned them with the Labour Party. The alliance lasted 40 years but brought nothing substantive to the Maori people.

During the 1970s educated urban activists launched a Maori land-rights movement that challenged New Zealand's myth of racial harmony with marches and occupations of land. In 1980 Matiu Rata, former minister of Maori affairs, established the Mana Motuhake Party. Maori nationalism became concerned with self-determination over Maori land resources, language, and culture. According to Maori nationalists, sovereignty was never conceded under the Treaty of Waitangi; the movement in the 1980s sought recognition of that sovereignty within the nation-state of New Zealand. (RANGINUI J. WALKER)

over 16% by March 1987 and to create an internal deficit of around $NZ 2.7 billion, rather than the government's estimated $NZ 2.4 billion, in fiscal 1986. Independent agencies continued to predict that the recession would last for a limited period before the economy responded to the positive efforts being made to restructure it.

The National Party, still recovering from its losses in the 1984 general election, was so preoccupied with internal reorganization that it left practical opposition to Labour's own fragmented industrial wing. Jim McLay, the leader National had hurriedly elected to succeed former party leader and prime minister Sir Robert Muldoon, was deposed and replaced by James Bolger, a farmer and former minister of labour. The replacement of Bruce Beetham with Neil Morrison as leader of the Democratic (formerly Social Credit) Party failed to stem the party's decline in opinion polls. The New Zealand Party acknowledged that Labour was implementing its policies and disbanded.

The government maintained its nonnuclear policy in defiance of the U.S., which was determined to establish that, if U.S. nuclear-powered (or possibly nuclear-armed) warships were not welcome in New Zealand's ports, effective joint exercises were impractical and the ANZUS (Australia-New Zealand-U.S.) defense treaty had effectively lost a member. As the U.S. began to apply pressure, more New Zealanders joined the antinuclear cause. However, the government did not rush to enshrine New Zealand's nuclear-free status in legislation.

France threatened to impose trade sanctions to protest New Zealand's imprisonment of two French military agents who had pleaded guilty to charges of manslaughter following the bombing of the *Rainbow Warrior,* flagship of the environmental pressure group Greenpeace, in Auckland Harbour in July 1985. After New Zealand agreed to go to international arbitration, the UN secretary-general decided in July 1986 that the agents should serve out their sentences on French territory in the Pacific, while France should apologize to New Zealand for the incident and pay $NZ 13 million compensation.

During her visit in February, Queen Elizabeth II opened a session of Parliament with a speech that required her to pledge continued government opposition to nuclear weapons, an issue that caused the U.K. as well as the U.S. to curtail contact with New Zealand's Navy. Prime Minister David Lange made tours to Indonesia and to China. A less flippant tone in foreign affairs assisted Lange in maintaining strong support in opinion polls.

An exhibition of carvings and other indigenous art, "Te Maori," returned home after an enthusiastic reception in the U.S. As one indication of the growing influence of Maori nationalism, discord at national day commemorations at Waitangi, where the Treaty of Waitangi was signed, caused the government to transfer the ceremony to Parliament House. (*See* Sidebar.) (JOHN A. KELLEHER)

See also *Dependent States,* below.

PAPUA NEW GUINEA

A constitutional monarchy and member of the Commonwealth, Papua New Guinea is situated in the southwestern Pacific Ocean and comprises the eastern part of the island of New Guinea, the islands of the Bismarck, Trobriand, Woodlark, Louisiade, and D'Entrecasteaux groups, and parts of the Solomon Islands, including Bougainville. Area: 462,840 sq km (178,704 sq mi). Pop. (1986 est.): 3,399,000. Cap.: Port Moresby. Monetary unit: kina, with (Oct. 1, 1986) a free rate of 0.97 kina to U.S. $1 (1.40 kinas = £1 sterling). Queen, Elizabeth II; governor-general in 1986, Sir Kingsford Dibela; prime minister, Paias Wingti.

Prime Minister Paias Wingti, appointed in November 1985, proved an able successor to Michael Somare as Papua New Guinea's parliamentary leader. During 1986 he built up a coherent coalition government. The key position of finance minister was filled by Sir Julius Chan, who by mid-1986 had achieved a marked reduction in interest rates. Prime Minister Wingti himself took credit for lowering the level of lawlessness, and he placed strong emphasis on building up friendly relations with Indonesia. The government persuaded the Indonesians to approve the visit of a delegation from the UN High Commissioner for Refugees, which was then able to act on behalf of the estimated 10,000 refugees from Irian Jaya (West New Guinea), Indon., living in encampments in Papua New Guinea. The government also showed understanding of Australia's difficulties in maintaining its level of aid during its current balance of payments crisis.

The government planned to ban sex education in the country's schools and to remove all pictures of human reproductive organs from science textbooks. Explaining the reasons, Minister of Education Aruru Matiabe said that high school students, who were showing an increased incidence of venereal disease, had been practicing what they had learned in sex education classes.

(A. R. G. GRIFFITHS)

This article updates the *Macropædia* article EAST INDIES: *Papua New Guinea.*

SOLOMON ISLANDS

A parliamentary state and member of the Commonwealth, the Solomon Islands comprises a 1,450-km (900-mi) chain of islands and atolls in the western Pacific Ocean. Area: 27,556 sq km (10,640 sq mi). Pop. (1986 est.): 267,700. Cap.: Honiara. Monetary unit: Solomon Islands dollar, with (Oct. 1, 1986) a free rate of SI\$1.82 to U.S. \$1 (SI\$2.63 = £1 sterling). Queen, Elizabeth II; governor-general in 1986, Baddeley Devesi; prime ministers, Sir Peter Kenilorea and, from December 1, Ezekial Alebua.

Late in May 1986 Typhoon Namu struck the Solomon Islands out of season. The most serious damage was done by wind on Malaita and by torrential rain on Guadalcanal, where floodwaters stripped soil and trees from the hills and dumped them on the coastal plain where Honiara is located. More than a hundred people died, villages were washed away, and the emergent palm oil industry and a rice project were all but destroyed. Recovery aid was granted by Australia, New Zealand, the U.K., and the U.S. as well as international and regional organizations.

Allegations that relief from French Polynesia had been specified as being for the home village of Prime Minister Sir Peter Kenilorea on Malaita eventually led to his downfall. Following the withdrawal of one of the coalition partners in July, a vote of no confidence, which was tied 18-all, was judged by the speaker to have failed. After six more ministers left the Cabinet, however, Kenilorea resigned on November 17. His replacement as prime minister was Ezekial Alebua.

The Solomon Islands Council of Trade Unions was formed in September, largely in response to government public-service cuts. (BARRIE MACDONALD)

This article updates the *Macropædia* article PACIFIC ISLANDS: *Solomon Islands.*

TONGA

A monarchy and member of the Commonwealth, Tonga is an island group in the Pacific Ocean east of Fiji. Area: 747 sq km (288 sq mi). Pop. (1986 est.): 97,900. Cap.: Nuku'alofa. Monetary unit: pa'anga, with (Oct. 1, 1986) a free rate of 1.59 pa'anga to U.S. \$1 (2.29 pa'anga = £1 sterling). King, Taufa'ahau Tupou IV; prime minister in 1986, Prince Fatafehi Tu'ipelehake.

Tonga's chronic economic difficulties persisted in 1986. Of a budget of 57.3 million pa'anga, only 26.1 million pa'anga could be raised locally, leaving 31.2 million pa'anga to be covered by foreign aid and soft development loans. Inflation reached 35% in the first quarter but dropped to 28% and 25% in successive quarters. In an attempt to generate economic growth and investment, most income tax was cut from 40 to 10%, while company taxes were reduced to 30% for both resident and nonresident companies. To offset these reductions, a goods and services tax of 5% was imposed for a two-year period.

Although tourist numbers remained static, the average length of stay increased, bringing tourism receipts to a record 10 million pa'anga. Local processing of copra meant

AP/WIDE WORLD

An Australian helicopter that has been sent to help after the devastatingly destructive Typhoon Namu in May sweeps over bridge wreckage on the Ngalimbiu River near Honiara in the Solomon Islands.

that coconut oil earned half of Tonga's export receipts, while desiccated coconut exports increased following the completion of a new factory built with Australian aid. An Asian Development Bank grant of $3 million was to finance the development of other small industries. Japan allocated 4.5 million pa'anga to develop local fish markets. A seabed exploration project, conducted under UN auspices, discovered sulfite near Niuafo'ou in the northern part of the group. (BARRIE MACDONALD)

This article updates the *Macropædia* article PACIFIC ISLANDS: *Tonga.*

TUVALU

A constitutional monarchy within the Commonwealth, Tuvalu comprises nine main islands and their associated islets and reefs in the western Pacific Ocean. Area: 24 sq km (9 sq mi). Pop. (1986): 8,200. Cap.: Fongafale. Monetary unit: Tuvalu dollar, at par with the Australian dollar (also a legal currency), with (Oct. 1, 1986) a free rate of $T 1.59 to U.S. $1 ($T 2.29 = £1 sterling). Queen, Elizabeth II; governors-general in 1986, Fiatau Penitala Teo and, from March 1, Tupua Leupena; prime minister, Tomasi Puapua.

In 1986 Tuvalu continued to seek inclusion in the UN list of least developed countries. Against total budget expenditure of over $A 4 million, Tuvalu could raise a total of $A 1,760,000 from copra exports, philatelic sales, and fishing licenses. Most of the remaining income to cover recurrent expenditure was in the form of a $A 950,000 budgetary grant from the U.K. As an alternative to future dependence on uncertain budgetary assistance, Tuvalu attempted to establish an investment fund of $A 15 million. New Zealand allocated $A 400,000 (from the compensation it received from France for the 1985 *Rainbow Warrior* bombing) and promised $A 300,000 a year for ten years.

In March Tupua Leupena, former speaker of the legislature, became governor-general in succession to Sir Fiatau Penitala Teo, who had held the office since independence in 1978. In a constitutional review Tuvaluans voted decisively to retain Queen Elizabeth II as head of state but to bind the governor-general to accept the advice of the government.

In protest against continued nuclear testing at Mururoa Atoll, French Polynesia, the government rejected a French offer to send a warship to Tuvalu on a goodwill visit. (BARRIE MACDONALD)

This article updates the *Macropædia* article PACIFIC ISLANDS: *Tuvalu.*

VANUATU

The republic of Vanuatu, a member of the Commonwealth, comprises 12 main islands and some 60 smaller ones in the southwestern Pacific Ocean. Area: 12,189 sq km (4,706 sq mi). Pop. (1986 est.): 136,800. Cap.: Vila. Monetary unit: vatu, with (Oct. 1, 1986) a free rate of 90.81 vatu to U.S. $1 (131.22 vatu = £1 sterling). President in 1986, George Sokomanu; prime minister, the Rev. Walter Lini.

Vanuatu continued to pursue a foreign policy that was radical within the context of Oceania. In April 1986 Prime Minister Walter Lini sent a message of sympathy to Libya after the U.S. bombing raid. Over the next two months Vanuatu established diplomatic relations with Peru, Nicaragua, Libya, and the U.S.S.R. Talks with Soviet trade negotiators were under way at year's end, with Lini indicating that he was prepared to consider a fisheries agreement that included port access. (See *Oceanian Affairs,* above.) On September 30 it was announced that Vanuatu and the U.S. were to establish diplomatic relations.

Inflation, held at 2% in 1985 by government controls, was expected to rise in 1986 following a 10% devaluation of the vatu. Agricultural production declined in the wake of two cyclones in 1985, and commodity prices fell sharply in 1986. There were indications that U.K. budgetary aid worth about $A 1 million a year might be reduced and that $A 24 million in French aid was threatened by Vanuatu's strong opposition to French policies in the Pacific. A 30% reduction in fees for flag-of-convenience ship registration was designed to attract interest from Hong Kong. (BARRIE MACDONALD)

This article updates the *Macropædia* article PACIFIC ISLANDS: *Vanuatu.*

WESTERN SAMOA

A constitutional monarchy and member of the Commonwealth, Western Samoa occupies an island group in the South Pacific Ocean. Area: 2,831 sq km (1,093 sq mi). Pop. (1986 est.): 160,400. Cap.: Apia. Monetary unit: Western Samoa tala, with (Oct. 1, 1986) a free rate of 2.27 tala to U.S. $1 (3.28 tala = £1 sterling). Head of state (*O le Ao o le Malo*) in 1986, Malietoa Tanumafili II; prime minister, Va'ai Kolone.

Prime Minister Tofilau Eti Alesana of Western Samoa resigned at the end of 1985 after the legislature rejected his budget and the head of state refused to call a general election. He was succeeded in January 1986 by Va'ai Kolone, former prime minister and colleague of Tofilau Eti within the Human Rights Protection Party. Va'ai's government was a coalition of his own supporters and the Christian Democratic Party led by Tupuola Efi, another former prime minister.

Having been listed by the UN as one of the least developed countries, Western Samoa sought aid from the World Bank and the International Monetary Fund. Despite an adverse balance of trade in 1985, the country achieved a balance of payments surplus because of remittance income from Western Samoans living abroad. Remittances totaled more than 50 million tala, nearly twice total export earnings. At a national economic summit in October, delegates agreed that remittances were not a satisfactory foundation for the economy and that greater stress should be placed on tourism.

The Western Samoan Rugby Football Union accepted, then rejected, an invitation to tour South Africa. Officials denied that the tour had been called off because of a threat by Fiji to boycott regional rugby tournaments. (BARRIE MACDONALD)

This article updates the *Macropædia* article PACIFIC ISLANDS: *Samoa.*

Dependent States

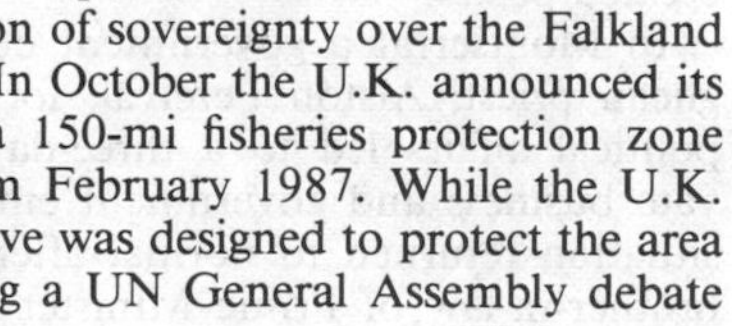

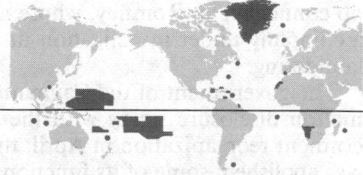

Europe and the Atlantic. Little progress was made in 1986 toward resolution of the dispute between the U.K. and Argentina over the question of sovereignty over the Falkland Islands/Islas Malvinas. In October the U.K. announced its intention to establish a 150-mi fisheries protection zone around the islands from February 1987. While the U.K. maintained that the move was designed to protect the area from overfishing, during a UN General Assembly debate in November Argentina claimed that the U.K.'s real motive was to "provoke armed incidents that will consolidate its colonial occupation" of the islands. At the end of the debate the General Assembly voted by 116 to 4, with 34 abstentions, in favour of a motion calling for negotiations to take place on "all aspects" of the islands' future. A number of European countries that had previously abstained in such UN votes backed the motion. Shortly before the debate the Argentine government offered to declare a formal end to hostilities in return for demilitarization of the zone around the islands.

Following the reopening of the Spanish frontier with Gibraltar in early 1985, economic links between Spain and the U.K. colony were rapidly reestablished. Air links had not resumed, however, and in September 1986 Spanish and British officials began talks in Madrid on the issue. The Spanish claimed that the isthmus on which the airport at Gibraltar was built was not included in the area originally ceded to the U.K.; they were seeking a separate terminal through which visitors to Spain could pass without going through Gibraltarian border controls. The idea was strongly resisted by the government of Gibraltar, which also protested the U.K.'s withdrawal of the ceremonial guard from the Gibraltar-Spain frontier in July.

General elections to the 24-seat House of Keys in the Isle of Man in November resulted in the return of 21 independent and 3 Labour members. The elections were the first to be held under a system of proportional representation. Miles Walker was elected to the post of chief minister, which replaced that of chairman of the board of governors.

Caribbean. In July the British government established an advisory council under the governor, Christopher Turner, to replace the government of Chief Minister Nathaniel Francis in the Turks and Caicos Islands. The new arrangement was expected to last for two years while a constitutional commission formulated a new government structure. The changes followed the report of a public inquiry ordered by the U.K. Foreign and Commonwealth Office, which found Francis and two ministers unfit to hold ministerial office and also severely criticized two opposition leaders. The four members of the advisory council were Ariel Misick and Emmanuel Missick, both former ministers; Clement Howell, an opposition leader; and Carlos Simons, a lawyer.

General elections in the British Virgin Islands held on September 30 produced a majority—five out of the nine elected legislative seats—for the Virgin Islands Party headed by Lavitty Stoutt, who was sworn in as chief minister. The outgoing United Party won two seats, and two were taken by independents, including the previous chief minister, Cyril Romney. The Legislative Council had been dissolved six days before it was due to debate a motion of no confidence in Romney, whose name had been linked to a company under investigation in connection with money laundering.

The government of the Cayman Islands signed an information disclosure treaty with the U.S. in July. In a government reorganization in April, the post of chief secretary was abolished; some of its functions were transferred to the financial secretary, Thomas Jefferson, while the remainder were taken over by the administrative secretary, a newly created post.

In Montserrat a government decision to expel an Anglican priest, Alston Percival, for alleged interference in political affairs led to a three-day protest strike by private business and government employees in August. The situation returned to normal after Percival, who was the brother-in-law of Prime Minister Kennedy Simmonds of St. Christopher and Nevis, announced that he would leave voluntarily by the end of the year. The government of Chief Minister John Osborne was also criticized for involvement in an abortive plan to lease part of the island for settlement and development by immigrants from Hong Kong and Taiwan. The government had a one-seat majority in the Legislative Council.

In the French overseas départements of Guadeloupe and Martinique, elections to the *conseils régionaux* in March produced narrow majorities for the left-wing parties. A Socialist-Communist coalition gained control in Guadeloupe with 22 out of 41 seats, and in Martinique a coalition of Socialists, Communists, and the Parti Populaire Martiniquais won 21 out of 41 seats. In French Guiana the left-wing parties, with the Socialists the dominant group, retained control.

The federation of the Netherlands Antilles was reduced from six members to five at midnight on January 1–2 when Aruba obtained separate status as a colony with internal self-government, aiming at independence in 1996. General elections held in November 1985 had brought changes of government in the federation and in Aruba. The ruling centre-right People's National Party failed to win a majority in the federal legislature, and Maria Liberia-Peters was replaced as prime minister on Jan. 1, 1986, by Domenico Martina of the New Antillean Movement, at the head of a seven-party coalition that gained 15 out of 22 seats. In Aruba Henny Eman of the Aruba People's Party defeated the veteran leader Betico Croes; his four-party coalition gained 13 out of 21 seats. In April the federal government introduced a package of emergency austerity measures that included drastic cuts in state spending.

AP/WIDE WORLD

Some 1,200 demonstrators march to the city limits of Papeete calling for Tahiti's independence and protesting French nuclear testing.

The administration of Puerto Rican Gov. Rafael Hernández Colón continued its campaign to promote twin-plant investment in Central America and the Caribbean using government revenues accumulated under Sec. 936 of the U.S. Internal Revenue Code and offering benefits under the Caribbean Basin Initiative. The scheme showed few concrete results in the first three-quarters of the year but was expected to pick up with the signing of a new U.S. tax bill guaranteeing the retention of Sec. 936.

Africa. Military conflict in the former Spanish territory of Western Sahara was at a low ebb as Morocco established a firm grip over some two-thirds of the area. The forces of the independence movement, the Popular Front for the Liberation of Saguia el Hamra and Río de Oro (Polisario Front), could mount only sporadic attacks, mainly against foreign fishing vessels off the coast. At its sixth congress, held in December 1985, Polisario once again expressed willingness to negotiate with Morocco over the future of Western Sahara, but it also declared its intention to escalate its military efforts in view of Morocco's rejection of the UN-proposed peace process.

On March 4, 1986, South African Pres. P. W. Botha announced in a speech to the South African Parliament that implementation of UN Resolution 435—which embodied a plan for achieving the independence of South West Africa/Namibia—should begin on August 1 on condition that Cuban troops withdraw from Angola by the same date. By the end of June, however, President Botha had renounced his pledge on the grounds that no agreement for a Cuban withdrawal had been reached, and the August 1 deadline passed without change.

Indian Ocean. Following elections to the *conseil régional* in the French overseas département of Réunion in March, Pierre Lagourgue was elected regional president with the backing of Socialist and Communist members. Réunion was visited by the French minister for overseas départements and territories, Bernard Pons, in September and by Prime Minister Jacques Chirac in October.

During his October trip to the Indian Ocean, Chirac also visited Mayotte and the republic of Comoros, where he discussed the continuing dispute between France and Comoros over the future status of Mayotte. In 1974 Mayotte had voted not to join Comoros in independence but to remain a dependency of France.

Pacific. Following nearly 20 years of negotiation, the U.S. trusteeship over Micronesia—the Trust Territory of the Pacific Islands—neared termination. Existing proposals were to give three of the four Micronesian governments—the Federated States of Micronesia, the Republic of the Marshall Islands, and the Republic of Palau (Belau)—self-government except on defense matters; these would remain the responsibility of the U.S., which would also maintain bases in the area, exercise the power of "strategic denial," and retain the right to secure land for military purposes. The same restrictions would apply to the fourth island group, the Northern Mariana Islands, which in 1975 had opted for commonwealth status (like that of Puerto Rico); this status meant that the Northern Marianas group retained closer ties with the U.S. and did not, for example, control its own exclusive economic zone. All four of the Micronesian governments would remain dependent on the U.S. for at least 90% of their funding.

A request to the Trusteeship Council of the UN for a formal end to trusteeship had stalled as a result of court action in Belau, where, on the petition of the high chief, Ibedul Yutaka Gibbons, the High Court ruled that the military clauses of the compact were in conflict with the constitutional requirement that a 75% majority by referendum was required to overturn the antinuclear clauses in Belau's constitution. In referenda in February and December, the latest in a series of such votes, 72 and 66%, respectively, voted in favour of the compact. Nevertheless, on October 21 a compact of free association with the U.S. came into force in the Marshall Islands, which thus became the first of the four island groups in which the trusteeship was terminated. The trusteeships for the Federated States of Micronesia and the Northern Marianas were terminated on November 3 and 4, respectively.

The three men arrested, then discharged, for the murder of Haruo Remeliik, president of Belau, in June 1985 were rearrested, tried, and convicted in 1986. They were subsequently released pending an appeal.

Guam's attempts to change from territorial to commonwealth status made little progress during the year. Ricardo Bordallo, the incumbent governor, won Democratic endorsement for reelection; along with his deputy, however, he faced charges of bribery, extortion, and conspiracy.

Following the discovery of abuses of the system, American Samoa canceled an agreement under which Western Samoans could enter the territory without a permit. Employment in American Samoa was threatened by a federal order that fixed new minimum wages and thus threatened the viability of the two fish canneries that provided 20% of the territory's employment. After an unsuccessful appeal, the order was amended, but not before the canneries had begun to explore the possibility of moving some of their operations to Western Samoa.

During a visit to New Caledonia in August, Prime Minister Chirac announced development plans worth CFPF 8 billion (120.75 CFP francs = U.S. $1 as of Oct. 1, 1986); most expenditure was to be in Kanak areas and was designed to generate 10,000 new jobs. Some saw the move as an attempt to woo Kanak support in anticipation of a 1987 referendum on the territory's future status. Tensions were evident, however, in the Kanak boycott of French legislative elections and when a local court ruled that the pro-French settlers responsible for the death of a pro-independence leader had acted in self-defense. In December the UN General Assembly approved by 89 votes to 24 a resolution affirming "the inalienable right of the people of New Caledonia to self-determination and independence" and demanding progress reports from France on moves toward those goals. The territory's problems were reflected in a sharp decline in tourism.

By contrast, French Polynesia was enjoying a tourism boom. There were attempts to reduce dependence on military spending, and High Commissioner Bernard Gérard foreshadowed the introduction of an income tax, the narrowing of the income gap between French expatriates and local residents, and the reduction of immigration from France—all moves designed to minimize socioeconomic inequalities and alleviate social tension. Gaston Flosse and his Tahoeraa Party won a clear majority in territorial elections that were called early because of the collapse of Flosse's coalition government.

In July France and New Zealand agreed to refer their dispute over the "Greenpeace affair"—the deliberate sinking of the Greenpeace environmentalist group's ship *Rainbow Warrior* in Auckland Harbour in July 1985—to the mediation of UN Secretary-General Javier Pérez de Cuéllar. Subsequently, the two French agents who had sabotaged the *Rainbow Warrior,* Alain Mafart and Dominique Prieur, were transferred from imprisonment in New Zealand to military postings on Hao Atoll in French Polynesia while France made a formal apology and paid compensation to New Zealand.

In October a special contingent of police was flown to Wallis and Futuna islands after public discontent and disorder arose over problems in the public service.

There was continuing tension between New Zealand and the Cook Islands, where Premier Sir Tom Davis remained a strong critic of New Zealand's antinuclear foreign policy and the South Pacific Nuclear Free Zone Treaty presented to the South Pacific Forum in 1985. Davis was reminded that the Cook Islands could, with independence, have an independent foreign policy, but that such a constitutional change could mean the reduction of aid from New Zealand and an end to open-entry immigration into New Zealand for Cook Islanders. During 1986 the Cook Islands assumed control of civil aviation—a contentious issue in the past—and established its own airline. Called Cook Islands International, it was to be managed by Ansett Airlines of Australia. The Cook Islands also planned to introduce its own currency.

With the population of Niue continuing to decline because of migration to New Zealand, the island's future, including its constitutional status, was being reviewed. Options included a continuation of self-government in free association with New Zealand; increased inward migration from non-Niueans, especially Tongans; and a reversion to dependent status.

East Asia. In the political evolution of Hong Kong, 1986 was a momentous year. One year after the U.K. and China ratified their joint declaration on the return of the territory to China in 1997, the forces that would shape that future were active. In March the committee (appointed by Beijing [Peking]) responsible for drawing up the post-1997 Basic Law for Hong Kong approved a draft outline. This indicated that the Basic Law would give more precise details than the Sino-British accord about the future relationship between China and its Hong Kong Special Administrative Region; a draft was likely in 1988. During her visit to Hong Kong in October, Queen Elizabeth II made a speech in which she sought to reassure the people that the joint declaration would preserve the "institutions, traditions, and way of life" of Hong Kong after 1997. Sir Edward Youde (*see* OBITUARIES), governor of Hong Kong since 1982, died in Beijing on December 4.

The Hong Kong government was due to review its political reform program in 1987, and this caused intense debate over the desired pace and extent of democratization. Beijing, however, made it clear that it preferred Hong Kong to concentrate on economic matters. The nuclear power plant that China proposed building at Daya (Ta-ya) Bay in Guangdong (Kwangtung) Province, bordering Hong Kong, was the cause of much controversy. Opposition to the $3.5 billion Sino-Hong Kong joint venture escalated after the nuclear accident at Chernobyl in the U.S.S.R., and more than one million people signed a petition against the project. Beijing proceeded, however, and in September signed key contracts with French and British equipment suppliers. The Hong Kong economy performed well and, following a surge in exports, forecasts of gross domestic product were revised upward to an increase of 5.6% in 1986 over 1985. The stock market reached new peaks.

In July Chinese and Portuguese diplomats met in Beijing to begin talks on the return of Macau to China. The Chinese wanted the transfer to take place no later than 1997, while the Portuguese wanted a few more years to complete major infrastructure developments. Another problem was the shortage of qualified ethnic Chinese to staff the local civil service. In May Joaquim Pinto Machado took over as governor of Macau in succession to Vasco Almeida e Costa, who had retired at the end of 1985.

(BARRIE MACDONALD; THOMAS HON WING POLIN; ROD PRINCE; LOUISE WATSON)

This article updates the *Macropædia* articles HONG KONG; INDIAN OCEAN ISLANDS; PACIFIC ISLANDS; SOUTHERN AFRICA: *South West Africa/Namibia;* THE WEST INDIES.

Dependent States*

Australia
- Christmas Island
- Cocos (Keeling) Islands
- Norfolk Island

Denmark
- Faeroe Islands
- Greenland

France
- French Guiana
- French Polynesia
- Guadeloupe
- Martinique
- Mayotte
- New Caledonia
- Réunion
- Saint Pierre and Miquelon
- Wallis and Futuna

Netherlands, The
- Aruba
- Netherlands Antilles

New Zealand
- Cook Islands
- Niue
- Tokelau

Norway
- Jan Mayen
- Svalbard

Portugal
- Macau

South Africa
- South West Africa/Namibia

United Kingdom
- Anguilla
- Bermuda
- British Virgin Islands
- Cayman Islands
- Falkland Islands
- Gibraltar
- Guernsey
- Hong Kong
- Isle of Man
- Jersey
- Montserrat
- Pitcairn Island
- Saint Helena
- Turks and Caicos Islands

United States
- American Samoa
- Guam
- Puerto Rico
- Trust Territory of the Pacific Islands
  - Marshall Islands
  - Federated States of Micronesia
  - Northern Marianas
  - Palau
- Virgin Islands (of the U.S.)

*Excludes territories (1) to which Antarctic Treaty is applicable in whole or in part, (2) without permanent civilian population, (3) without internationally-recognized civilian government (Western Sahara, Gaza Strip), or (4) representing unadjudicated unilateral or multilateral territorial claims.

Polar Regions

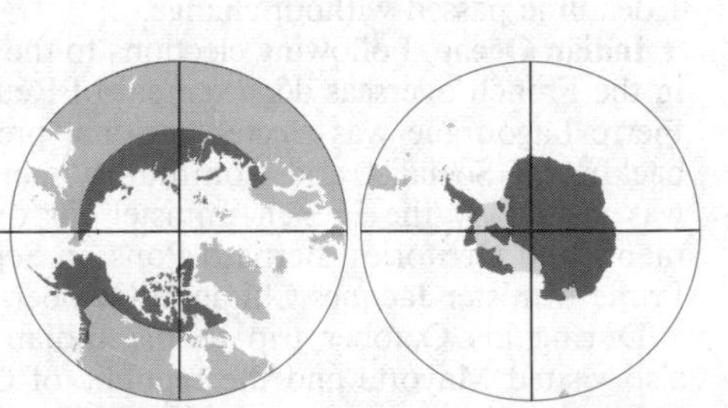

ANTARCTICA

The 1985–86 Antarctic summer field season was characterized by the most severe ice conditions since the mid-1960s. *Nella Dan,* under charter to Australia, and *John Biscoe* (U.K.) became trapped in two widely separate areas, and *Southern Quest,* the supply ship for the Footsteps of Scott Expedition, sank while attempting to reach Ross Island. *Greenpeace* and the Soviet ship *Kapitan Bondarenko* were also troubled by the severe ice conditions.

John Biscoe was caught near Adelaide Island in mid-November 1985, and conditions quickly became so severe that it was abandoned on November 18. *Polar Duke,* chartered by the United States, and *Polarstern* (West Germany) rescued the crew and scientific passengers. *Polarstern,* which was much more powerful than *Polar Duke,* broke *Biscoe* out two days later, and the ship was reclaimed by its crew.

Nella Dan was trapped off Enderby Land in late October 1985 by ice that was 4 m (13 ft) thick and was not released until the Japanese icebreaker *Shirase* freed it 52 days later. During the period that *Nella Dan* was trapped, the chartered *Icebird* attempted to assist but was almost trapped itself.

In the Ross Sea *Southern Quest,* a converted Icelandic trawler, failed in its efforts to approach Cape Hallett because of the ice and continued toward Cape Evans, the site of Jack Hayward Base, the expedition base camp. By early January the trawler was about 30 km (18.6 mi) from the

Expedition ship *MV Greenpeace,* in a summer attempt to penetrate the Ross Sea within the Antarctic Circle, is stymied by unexpectedly thick ice at about latitude 70° S.
AP/WIDE WORLD

base but was blocked by thick ice. An aircraft, which failed to recover three expedition members who had walked to the South Pole, was assembled on a nearby ice floe and sent to Ross Island. During the three days it took to assemble the aircraft, heavy ice closed in on the ship. On January 11 ice pressure split the hull, and the engine room was flooded. Shortly thereafter, *Southern Quest* went down stern first. The 21 men and women on board were rescued by U.S. Coast Guard helicopters and flown to McMurdo Station.

Greenpeace, an oceangoing tug and the flagship of the international environmental organization, attempted to reach Ross Island with materials for building a station and supplies for a four-man wintering party. Thick ice prevented it from approaching closer than 40 km (25 mi) from Cape Evans. After abandoning this attempt the ship steamed toward the Bay of Whales, the location of Adm. Richard Byrd's Little America bases, and expedition members were able to go ashore briefly.

Late in the season the Soviet Union's *Kapitan Bondarenko,* sister ship to *Mikhail Somov,* which had been trapped in ice for 133 days in 1985, suffered a broken rudder in the same area off Russkaya Station on the coast of Marie Byrd Land. Temporary repairs, accomplished by six days of round-the-clock work, enabled the ship to reach New Zealand for repairs in dry dock.

Worldwide attention was devoted to the discovery of a massive hole in the Earth's ozone shield centred over Antarctica. Scientists sent to McMurdo Station in August began to collect data that might lead to a discovery of the cause of this phenomenon. (*See* EARTH SCIENCES: *Meteorology.*)

National Programs. *Argentina.* The nation's scientific staff was tripled in size in an attempt to strengthen the research program. Geologists from the Argentine Antarctic Institute discovered 70 million-year-old dinosaur fossils on James Ross Island, northeast of the Antarctic Peninsula.

Australia. A new summer research station, Ellsworth David, was established at the Bunger Hills on the coast of Queen Maud Land. On January 6 scientists on board *Icebird* reached the South Magnetic Pole for only the fourth time in history. Located at latitude 65° 18′ S and longitude 140° 2′ E, about 150 km (93 mi) north of the French Dumont d'Urville Station, the South Magnetic Pole had first been reached in 1911, when it was on land.

Chile. A small-scale national program continued. It consisted primarily of uniformed forces maintaining the Antarctic bases.

France. Work on the year-round airstrip at Dumont d'Urville was temporarily suspended. However, some preliminary earthworks were continued as part of the plan to connect several small islands in order to establish an 1,100-m (3,608-ft) all-weather runway.

Japan. The Japanese continued to expand their Antarctic program. The two year-round stations, Syowa and Mizuho, were occupied, as was a new summer station, Asuka Camp.

New Zealand. Research by government and university scientists continued in the earth and biological sciences. Three sedimentary cores, containing evidence of as many as nine glacial advances, were recovered from Marshall Valley. A field party worked at Cape Hallett to reclaim the joint U.S.-New Zealand base last occupied in 1973.

Soviet Union. In February 1986 a wide-body IL-76 cargo plane was flown directly to Molodezhnaya in an attempt to speed the delivery of personnel and critical cargo. The plane landed on an improved snow and ice airstrip. The IL-76 could carry about 100 passengers and six tons of cargo. An alternative landing strip was also established at Novolazarevskaya. During the same month, an IL-14, a smaller cargo plane, crashed on the Philippi Glacier, killing six, while attempting an emergency landing in a whiteout.

A massive caving in of the Filchner-Ronne Ice Shelf apparently destroyed Druzhnaya I, a summer camp dedicated to geologic research. The event was discovered by researchers at Molodezhnaya while they were examining satellite photographs. A strip of ice 95 km (60 mi) wide and 195 km (120 mi) long was slowly drifting away from the new ice front.

United Kingdom. Field programs in glaciology and geology were successful despite damaged aircraft, severe weather, and the entrapment of *John Biscoe.* Glaciologic parties worked on Dolleman Island, the Ronne Ice Shelf, and the Rutford Ice Stream. Four automatic weather stations were deployed in a joint program with the U.S.

United States. Geologists working from the large Beardmore Glacier field camp discovered more than 350 vertebrate fossils in Gordon Valley near Mt. Falla. The bones, ranging in age from 190 million to 225 million years, included four new species of amphibians and reptiles. Other

Researchers in the cold waters of the Antarctic study the tiny crustaceans called krill. An abundant food source for marine animals, the creatures might some day become part of the human diet.
MICHAEL PARFIT

geologists discovered deposits of wood and twigs suggesting a partial deglaciation of parts of Antarctica as recently as two million years ago.

Glaciologists were successful in recovering ice cores from Siple Station for analysis in the laboratory, and others continued their studies of the large ice streams that drain Marie Byrd Land into the Ross Ice Shelf. Thirteen women and 150 men wintered at four U.S. bases during 1986.

Other Nations. South Korea sent an expedition to King George Island, after which part of the group continued on to climb Vinson Massif on the mainland. The South Korean government was considering the establishment of a base on King George Island, as were the governments of Peru and Spain. As of 1986 seven bases already existed on the small island. The Indian Antarctic Expedition base, Dakshin Gangotri, was occupied for the third consecutive winter. The first Italian Antarctic Expedition surveyed Terra Nova Bay, where a base was to be built during the 1986–87 field season.

International Activities. Meetings of the Antarctic Treaty System continued in an effort to develop a regime to regulate any future mineral activity in Antarctica. In December 1985 two Chilean pilots and eight U.S. tourists were killed when their light aircraft crashed while attempting a landing at the Chilean base on King George Island.

(PETER J. ANDERSON)

This article updates the *Macropædia* article ANTARCTICA.

ARCTIC REGIONS

Alaska. The precipitous drop in world oil prices was the most significant event affecting Alaska's North Slope in 1986. Many international oil analysts were predicting that crude oil prices would stay in the $15-a-barrel range for the next two years, compared with as much as $30 a barrel in the fall of 1985. Nevertheless, some major North Slope projects moved ahead with funds already committed. These included development of the $2 billion Endicott field, start-up of the new Lisburne field, and a new production facility in Kuparuk. Despite drilling cutbacks, no substantial decline in the North Slope work force was foreseen over the next two years.

In the spring the *Arctic News-Record* reported that Japanese and Alaskan interests had initiated the Alaska Asian Gas System prefeasibility study of North Slope gas reserves, estimated at 896,000,000,000 cu m (32 trillion cu ft). The study, expected to be completed by the end of 1986, was to determine the size of the liquefied natural gas market, establish production cost estimates, and test the significance of new technologies. In August ARCO Alaska announced it might wind down its two-year West Sak oil sands pilot project. If and when the project moved forward, it would involve 5,000 closely spaced wells to tap the huge resource base of heavy oil deposits—estimated at 40,000,000,000 bbl. In a major speech in June, the president of Standard Oil of Alaska indicated that, given current crude oil prices, projects such as West Sak and the movement of North Slope natural gas to market were "subeconomic for the foreseeable future."

ARCO Alaska's $717 million oil-recovery project at Prudhoe Bay was reported to be proceeding on schedule. Enriched natural gas would be injected into the Prudhoe Bay reserve with the aim of recovering 5.5% more oil from selected parts of the reservoir (115 million bbl over ten years). When the project started operations early in 1987, Prudhoe Bay would have the world's largest natural gas operation, handling some 84 million cu m (3,000,000,000 cu ft) daily. An additional benefit of the project was that, if a natural gas pipeline from Prudhoe Bay to southern or foreign markets was ever built, the gas-conditioning facilities—one of the largest components of gas-line capital costs—would be in place.

The Aleut Corporation recommended that the state consider using some of the native corporation's 400,000 ha (1 million ac) in the Aleutian Islands as disposal sites for Alaska's hazardous wastes. The corporation noted that abundant geothermal resources on the remote parcels of land could be used to power incinerators for destroying the wastes. The September issue of *Alaska Magazine* reported that Eskimo whalers were using satellite pictures to help locate migrating bowhead whales. As a result, the whalers reportedly landed more whales in 1986 than in any of the eight preceding seasons.

Canada. The mood in the Canadian oil and gas industry turned grim as oil prices fell. By autumn exploration activities from the Atlantic Ocean to the Beaufort Sea had ground to a halt. High-cost exploration in the Canadian Arctic required a crude oil price of at least $20 per barrel to be profitable. There were some heartening exceptions to the generally bad news, however. Early in the year Gulf Canada Ltd. announced the biggest oil discovery in

Canadian history at its Amauligak well in the Beaufort Sea. The announcement came after two decades of oil and gas exploration during which Canadian oil companies spent an estimated $6.5 billion plumbing the waters of the Beaufort Sea at the mouth of the Mackenzie River. Further test drilling was expected to confirm that the Amauligak reservoir contained an estimated 700 million–900 million bbl of reserves, with one well alone capable of producing almost 35,000 bbl per day.

Gulf Canada expressed optimism that successful results from the Amauligak field would eventually pave the way for commercial production in the Beaufort Sea, justifying the $1 billion to $2 billion pipeline extension needed to ship the oil to southern markets. The closest pipeline in Canada ended 800 km (500 mi) short of the sea at Norman Wells, N.W.T. Gulf and its competitors in the Beaufort had to be certain they could produce at least 50,000 bbl a day to justify a pipeline extension. Gulf spokesmen predicted that project evaluation would be completed by 1988, with commercial production possible by the mid-1990s.

Panarctic Oils Ltd. continued to ship oil from its modest Bent Horn facility on Cameron Island in the Northwest Territories. Although most of the once-a-year production of 108,000 bbl of oil (from a reserve estimated at 500 million bbl) was shipped south, the prime future market for Panarctic's oil was expected to be in the north as a replacement for expensive imported diesel fuel.

In April the Canadian government, stung by the unauthorized voyage of the U.S. icebreaker *Polar Sea* through the Northwest Passage in 1985, introduced legislation to extend Canadian criminal and civil law throughout the Arctic and to the offshore islands generally. The bill was part of a strategy to assert Canadian sovereignty over the Arctic Archipelago and to define the Northwest Passage as a Canadian waterway.

AP/WIDE WORLD

Susan Butcher, winner of the Anchorage-to-Nome Iditarod Trail Sled Dog Race, rewards one of her dogs with a hug. She and her team finished the course in just over 11½ days, paring some 16 hours off the record. The previous year's winner was also a woman.

In May the Steger International North Pole Expedition, which included two Canadians and four U.S. citizens, reached the North Pole after a 56-day trek across the unstable Arctic Ocean ice. Led by Will Steger of Ely, Minn., the five men and one woman re-created Robert Peary's 1909 conquest of the Pole, beginning at Ward Hunt Island off the northern tip of Ellesmere Island. This was the first expedition since Peary's to make the journey without aerial logistics support.

Debate continued over the division of the Northwest Territories into two new territories—Nunavut for the eastern Arctic and Denendeh for the west. One of the issues in dispute was which of the two new territories would include the oil-rich Beaufort Sea.

The Soviet North. The main aims of development in the Soviet northern regions for 1986–90 were reported in the *Arctic News-Record.* The chief goals were to relate the North more closely to the overall economy of the country and to improve the utilization of its vast resources. A more diversified economy was being planned, and social policies were to be implemented that would result in a better settlement pattern and higher living standards. The traditional livelihoods of the native peoples, especially reindeer husbandry, were to be promoted and mechanized where possible. The success of the plan would depend to a great extent on substantial increases in oil and gas production.

International. Falling metal prices and the depletion of high-grade ore reserves were reportedly forcing the closing of the Greenex lead and zinc mine in Maarmorilik, Greenland, after 13 years of operation. Greenex, the island's largest industrial employer, had a work force of about 340 people, including some 150 native Greenlanders.

At a meeting of the Inuit Circumpolar Conference (ICC) in July in Kotzebue, Alaska, 600 Inuit leaders, elders, and observers from Canada, Greenland, and the U.S. heard the ICC president, Hans-Pavia Rosing, urge them to continue to fight for their homelands and their culture, threatened by oil and mining interests and "so-called environmental groups." The conference approved a set of Arctic policy principles dealing with the increasing militarization and industrialization of the North, economic, social, and educational problems of the Inuit, and Arctic environmental issues.

Early in the year, the international environmental organization Greenpeace reportedly apologized to the Greenland and other Inuit for ruining the U.S. and European markets for seal pelts. The organization's campaign to stop the commercial killing of baby seals had put many traditional Inuit hunters out of business, although Greenpeace claimed this had not been its objective.

Fallout from the Chernobyl nuclear plant disaster in the U.S.S.R. was having a devastating effect on the reindeer-oriented economy of the Lapp people. (*See* ENERGY: *Sidebar.*) Radiation-laden rainfall had contaminated vegetation in the herding lands that stretch in a vast arc across northern Norway, Sweden, and Finland. The Swedish government was reportedly trying to assist the Lapps by buying and feeding contaminated deer meat to farmed mink and fox, which were grown for fur and thus were not part of the human food chain. (KENNETH DE LA BARRE)

This article updates the *Macropædia* article The ARCTIC.

CONTRIBUTORS

Adams, Andrew M. Free-lance Foreign Correspondent; Editor and Publisher, *Sumo World* magazine.
SPORTS AND GAMES: *Martial Arts; Wrestling (in part)*
Adler, Mortimer J. Philosopher, Author, and Chairman of the Board of Editors of Encyclopædia Britannica.
Feature Article: THE REAL AMERICAN BICENTENNIAL
Agrella, Joseph C. Correspondent, *Blood-Horse* magazine and Associated Press; former Turf Editor, *Chicago Sun-Times.*
SPORTS AND GAMES: *Horse Racing (in part)*
Allaby, Michael. Free-lance Writer and Lecturer. Author of *Who Will Eat?*
ENVIRONMENT *(in part)*
Allan, J. A. Reader in Geography, School of Oriental and African Studies, University of London.
WORLD AFFAIRS: *Libya*
Aloff, Mindy. Dance Critic, *The Nation;* Senior Critic, *Dance Magazine.* Editor, *Vassar Quarterly.*
DANCE *(in part)*
Amedeo, Michael. Writer, Encyclopædia Britannica Educational Corp.
BIOGRAPHIES *(in part)*
Anderson, Peter J. Assistant Director, Institute of Polar Studies, Ohio State University.
WORLD AFFAIRS: *Antarctica*
Andrews, John. Southeast Asia Bureau Chief, *The Economist,* London.
ECONOMIC AFFAIRS: Special Report
Archibald, John J. Feature Writer, *St. Louis Post-Dispatch;* Adjunct Professor, Washington University, St. Louis, Mo.
SPORTS AND GAMES: *Bowling (in part)*
Armstrong, George. Rome Correspondent, *The Guardian.*
WORLD AFFAIRS: *Italy*
Arnold, Guy. Free-lance Writer. Author of *Modern Nigeria; Aid in Africa.*
BIOGRAPHIES *(in part);* WORLD AFFAIRS: *Botswana; Burundi; Cape Verde; Equatorial Guinea; Gambia, The; Ghana; Guinea-Bissau; Lesotho; Liberia; Maldives; Mauritius; Nigeria; Rwanda; São Tomé and Príncipe; Seychelles; Sierra Leone; Swaziland*
Arnold, Mavis. Free-lance Journalist, Dublin.
BIOGRAPHIES *(in part);* WORLD AFFAIRS: *Ireland*
Arrington, Leonard J. Formerly Church Historian, Church of Jesus Christ of Latter-day Saints.
RELIGION: *Church of Jesus Christ of Latter-day Saints*
Ayton, Cyril J. Editor, *Motorcycle Sport,* London.
SPORTS AND GAMES: *Motorcycling*
Baptist, Ines T. Free-lance Writer.
WORLD AFFAIRS: *Belize*
Barford, Michael F. Editor and Director, *Tabacosmos,* London.
INDUSTRIAL REVIEW: *Tobacco*
Bargad, Warren. Associate Professor of Hebrew Literature and Director, Center for Jewish Studies, University of Florida.
LITERATURE: *Hebrew*
Barrett, David B. Missions Researcher, Foreign Mission Board, U.S. Southern Baptist Convention.
RELIGION: *World Church Membership*
Bass, Howard. Author, Journalist, and Broadcaster. Editor, *Winter Sports,* 1948–69.
SPORTS AND GAMES: *Bobsledding; Curling; Ice Hockey (in part); Ice Skating; Skiing; Tobogganing*
Bayliss, David. Director of Planning, London Regional Transport.
TRANSPORTATION *(in part)*
Beattie, Roger A. Secretariat Member, International Social Security Association, Geneva.
SOCIAL SECURITY AND WELFARE SERVICES *(in part)*
Beckwith, David C. National Correspondent, *Time* magazine, Washington, D.C.
INDUSTRIAL REVIEW: Special Report; WORLD AFFAIRS: *United States:* Developments in the States in 1986
Bergerre, Max. Vatican Affairs Correspondent, *La Vie Catholique,* Paris.
WORLD AFFAIRS: *Vatican City State*
Berkovitch, Israel. Writer and Consultant. Author of *Coal on the Switchback;* Editor of *World Energy: Looking Ahead to 2020.*
ENERGY: *Coal*
Berry, Scyld. Cricket Correspondent, *The Observer,* London.
BIOGRAPHIES *(in part);* SPORTS AND GAMES: *Cricket*
Beyer, Reginald Ian. Deputy Curator, Royal Botanic Gardens, Kew, England.
BOTANICAL GARDENS AND ZOOS *(in part)*
Bickelhaupt, David L. Professor of Insurance and Finance, College of Business, Ohio State University, Columbus.
INDUSTRIAL REVIEW: *Insurance*
Bilefield, Lionel. Technical Journalist.
INDUSTRIAL REVIEW: *Paints and Varnishes*
Bird, Thomas E. Director, Council for the Study of Ethics and Public Policy, Queens College, City University of New York.
LITERATURE: *Yiddish*
Bleibtreu, Hermann K. Professor of Anthropology, University of Arizona.
ANTHROPOLOGY
Boddy, William C. Editor, *Motor Sport.* Full Member, Guild of Motoring Writers.
SPORTS AND GAMES: *Automobile Racing (in part)*
Boden, Edward. Editor, *Veterinary Record.*
HEALTH AND DISEASE: *Veterinary Medicine*
Bolt, Peter H. Secretary, British Committee, World Methodist Council.
RELIGION: *Methodist Churches*
Booth, John Nicholls. Lecturer and Writer. Author of *The Quest for Preaching Power.*
RELIGION: *Unitarian (Universalist) Churches*
Boswall, Jeffery. Producer of Sound and Television Programs, BBC Natural History Unit, Bristol, England.
LIFE SCIENCES: *Ornithology*
Box, Ben. Free-lance Writer and Researcher.
BIOGRAPHIES *(in part);* WORLD AFFAIRS: *El Salvador; Honduras; Paraguay*
Boye, Roger. Coin columnist, *Chicago Tribune.*
PHILATELY AND NUMISMATICS: *Coins and Paper Money*
Bradsher, Henry S. Foreign Affairs Writer.
WORLD AFFAIRS: *Philippines*
Braidwood, Robert J. Professor Emeritus of Old World Prehistory, Oriental Institute and Department of Anthropology, University of Chicago. Author of *Prehistoric Men.*
ARCHAEOLOGY: *Eastern Hemisphere*
Brasher, Chris. Sports Correspondent, *The Observer,* London.
SPORTS AND GAMES: *Track and Field:* Special Report
Brazee, Rutlage J. Geophysical Consultant.
EARTH SCIENCES: *Geophysics*
Brecher, Kenneth. Professor of Astronomy and Physics, Boston University. Coauthor and coeditor of *Astronomy of the Ancients.*
ASTRONOMY; ASTRONOMY: Special Report
Brobyn, Allen F. Assistant Director (Marketing), Glass Manufacturers Federation, London.
INDUSTRIAL REVIEW: *Glass*
Burdin, Joel L. Professor of Educational Administration, City College of the City University of New York.
EDUCATION *(in part)*
Burke, Donald P. Executive Editor, *Chemical Week,* New York City.
INDUSTRIAL REVIEW: *Chemicals*
Burks, Ardath W. Emeritus Professor of Asian Studies, Rutgers University, New Brunswick, N.J.
WORLD AFFAIRS: *Japan*
Buss, Robin. Lecturer in French, Woolwich College of Further Education, London. Author of *Vigny's Chatterton.*
LITERATURE: *French (in part)*
Butler, Frank. Former Sports Editor, *News of the World,* London. Author of *The Good, the Bad and the Ugly: A Story of Boxing.*
SPORTS AND GAMES: *Boxing*
Cameron, Sarah. Regional Economist, Economics Department, Lloyds Bank PLC, London.
WORLD AFFAIRS: *Argentina*
Campany, Robert. Ph.D. Candidate, History of Religions, Divinity School, University of Chicago.
RELIGION: *Buddhism (in part)*
Campbell, Alexander Johns. Economist, Economics Department, Lloyds Bank PLC, London.
BIOGRAPHIES *(in part);* WORLD AFFAIRS: *Chile; Colombia; Uruguay*
Carter, Robert W. Journalist, London.
SPORTS AND GAMES: *Horse Racing (in part)*
Cassidy, Richard J. Senior Public Relations Officer, British Gas Corporation.
ENERGY: *Natural Gas*
Cegielski, Charles M. Senior Editor, Encyclopædia Britannica Yearbooks.
LIFE SCIENCES: *Introduction*
Chapman, Kenneth F. Former Editor, *Stamp Collecting* and *Philatelic Magazine.*
PHILATELY AND NUMISMATICS: *Stamps*
Chapman, Robin. Senior Economist, Economics Department, Lloyds Bank PLC, London.
BIOGRAPHIES *(in part);* WORLD AFFAIRS: *Brazil; Cuba; Haiti; Latin-American Affairs*
Chappell, Duncan. Professor, School of Criminology, Simon Fraser University, Vancouver, B.C.
CRIME, LAW ENFORCEMENT, AND PENOLOGY: *Crime; Law Enforcement*
Chapple, Abby. Writer, Consumer Communications, Annapolis, Md.
INDUSTRIAL REVIEW: *Furniture*
Christiansen, Richard D. Entertainment Editor, *Chicago Tribune.*
THEATRE: Sidebar
Chuprinin, Sergey. Journalist, Novosti Press Agency, Moscow.
LITERATURE: *Russian (in part)*
Clark, Janet H. Staff Editor, *Britannica Book of the Year,* London. Former Far East Editor, Economist Publications.
BIOGRAPHIES *(in part);* WORLD AFFAIRS: *Southeast Asian Affairs:* Sidebar
Clarke, R. O. Writer, Paris.
LABOUR–MANAGEMENT RELATIONS
Cleveland, William A. Editor, Britannica World Data and *Britannica Atlas.*
MINING
Cogle, T. C. J. Editor, *Electrical Review,* London.
INDUSTRIAL REVIEW: *Electrical*
Coppock, Charles Dennis. Honorary Member, English Lacrosse Union.
SPORTS AND GAMES: *Lacrosse (in part)*
Costin, Stanley H. British Correspondent,

Herrenjournal International, and others.
FASHION AND DRESS *(in part)*
Cross, Colin J. Editor, *The Polo Times;* U.K. Chairman, European Polo Academy.
SPORTS AND GAMES: *Polo*
Crossland, Norman. Former Bonn Correspondent, *The Economist,* London.
BIOGRAPHIES *(in part);* WORLD AFFAIRS: *German Democratic Republic; Germany, Federal Republic of*
Curley, Robert. Editorial Researcher, Encyclopædia Britannica, Inc.
BIOGRAPHIES *(in part)*
Cviic, K. F. East European Specialist, *The Economist,* London.
WORLD AFFAIRS: *Yugoslavia*
David, Tudor. Education Journalist; former Managing Editor, *Education,* London.
EDUCATION *(in part);* EDUCATION: Sidebar
Davies, C. R. M. Research Lecturer in Criminology and Penology, University of Liverpool, England.
CRIME, LAW ENFORCEMENT, AND PENOLOGY: *Prisons and Penology*
Davis, Donald A. Editor, *Drug & Cosmetic Industry* and *Cosmetic Insider's Report.*
INDUSTRIAL REVIEW: *Pharmaceuticals*
Deam, John B. Technical Director, National Machine Tool Builders Association, McLean, Va.
INDUSTRIAL REVIEW: *Machinery and Machine Tools*
Decraene, Philippe. Head, Center for Advanced Studies on Modern Africa and Asia, Paris.
WORLD AFFAIRS: *Benin; Burkina Faso; Cameroon; Central African Republic; Chad; Comoros; Congo; Côte d'Ivoire; Djibouti; Gabon; Guinea; Madagascar; Mali; Mauritania; Niger; Senegal; Togo; Tunisia*
de la Barre, Kenneth. Director, Katimavik, Montreal.
WORLD AFFAIRS: *Arctic Regions*
Denselow, Robin. Rock Music Critic, *The Guardian,* London; Current Affairs Reporter, BBC Television.
BIOGRAPHIES *(in part);* MUSIC: *Popular*
De Puy, Norman R. Minister, First Baptist Church, Newton Centre, Mass.; Columnist, *American Baptist* magazine.
RELIGION: *Baptist Churches*
Deshayes, Marie-Jose. Head of Documentation Service, International Vine and Wine Office, Paris.
INDUSTRIAL REVIEW: *Beverages (in part)*
Dirnbacher, Elfriede. Austrian Civil Servant.
WORLD AFFAIRS: *Austria*
Dixon, Bernard. Science Writer and Consultant. Editor (1969–79), *New Scientist* magazine. Author of *Magnificent Microbes.*
HEALTH AND DISEASE: *Mental Health; Overview (in part)*
Dooling, Dave. Manager, Program Development, Alabama Space and Rocket Center, Huntsville.
SPACE EXPLORATION
Dorris, Thomas Hartley. Editor, Ecumenical Press Service, Geneva.
RELIGION: *Lutheran Communion*
Eli, C. R. Former Executive Director, U.S. Badminton Association.
SPORTS AND GAMES: *Badminton*
Engels, Jan R. Director, Centre Paul Hymans; Editor, *Vooruitgang-Progrès* magazine.
WORLD AFFAIRS: *Belgium*
Ewart, W. D. Marine Consultant, London. Author of *Bunkers; Bulk Carriers.*
INDUSTRIAL REVIEW: *Shipbuilding;* TRANSPORTATION *(in part)*
Ewing, John. Professor and Chairman, Department of Mathematics, Indiana University. Author of *Puzzle It Out.*
MATHEMATICS
Farr, D. M. L. Professor of History, Carleton University, Ottawa.
WORLD AFFAIRS: *Canada*
Faust, Joan Lee. Garden Editor, *New York Times.*
GARDENING *(in part)*
Felknor, Bruce L. Editorial Consultant, Encyclopædia Britannica, Inc.
BRITANNICA AWARDS
Fendell, Robert J. Author of *The New Era Car Book and Auto Survival Guide; Encyclopedia of Auto Racing Greats.*
SPORTS AND GAMES: *Automobile Racing (in part)*
Ferrier, R. W. Group Historian, The British Petroleum Company PLC, London.
ENERGY: *Petroleum*
Fiddick, Peter. Media Editor, *The Guardian,* London.
BIOGRAPHIES *(in part);* PUBLISHING: *Newspapers (in part); Magazines (in part)*
Fields, Donald. Helsinki Correspondent, BBC, *Independent,* and *The Sunday Times,* London.
WORLD AFFAIRS: *Finland*
Firth, David. Editor, *The Friend,* London; formerly Editor, *Quaker Monthly,* London.
RELIGION: *Religious Society of Friends*
Fisher, David. Civil Engineer, Freeman Fox Ltd., Consulting Engineers, London.
ENGINEERING PROJECTS: *Bridges*
Fisk, Robert. Middle East Correspondent, *The Times,* London.
WORLD AFFAIRS: *Libya:* Special Report
Flanagan, Jack C. Travel Counselor.
SPORTS AND GAMES: *Surfing*
Frady, William Ensign, III. Editor, *Water Polo Scoreboard,* Newport Beach, Calif.
SPORTS AND GAMES: *Water Polo*
Franklin, Harold. Editor, *English Bridge Quarterly.* Bridge Correspondent, *Yorkshire Post.*
SPORTS AND GAMES: *Contract Bridge*
Franz, Frederick W. President, Watch Tower Bible and Tract Society of Pennsylvania.
RELIGION: *Jehovah's Witnesses*
Fridovich, Irwin. James B. Duke Professor of Biochemistry, Duke University Medical Center, Durham, N.C.
LIFE SCIENCES: *Molecular Biology (in part)*
Fridovich-Keil, Judith L. Graduate Student and Ph.D. Candidate, Biology Department, Massachusetts Institute of Technology.
LIFE SCIENCES: *Molecular Biology (in part)*
Friedly, Robert Louis. Vice President for Communication, Christian Church (Disciples of Christ), Indianapolis, Ind.
RELIGION: *Christian Church (Disciples of Christ)*
Friskin, Sydney E. Hockey Correspondent, *The Times,* London.
SPORTS AND GAMES: *Billiard Games (in part); Field Hockey*
Frost, David. Rugby Union Correspondent, *The Guardian,* London.
SPORTS AND GAMES: *Football (in part)*
Gaddum, Anthony H. Chairman, H. T. Gaddum and Company Ltd., Silk Merchants, Macclesfield, Cheshire, England.
INDUSTRIAL REVIEW: *Textiles (in part)*
Ganado, Albert. Lawyer, Malta.
WORLD AFFAIRS: *Malta*
Ganguly, Dilip. Special Correspondent, Agence France Presse, South Asia.
BIOGRAPHIES *(in part);* WORLD AFFAIRS: *Afghanistan; Bangladesh; Bhutan; Burma; Nepal; Pakistan; Sri Lanka*
Garrad, Rob. Director of Information Services, International Headquarters, Salvation Army.
BIOGRAPHIES *(in part);* RELIGION: *Salvation Army*
Gastil, Raymond Duncan. Director, Comparative Survey of Freedom, Freedom House, New York City.
HUMAN RIGHTS
Gibbons, J. Whitfield. Senior Research Ecologist, Savannah River Ecology Laboratory, Aiken, S.C.
LIFE SCIENCES: *Zoology*
Gillespie, Hugh M. Director of Communications, International Road Federation, Washington, D.C.
ENGINEERING PROJECTS: *Roads*
Gjester, Fay. Free-lance Journalist and Editor; formerly Oslo Correspondent, *Financial Times,* London.
BIOGRAPHIES *(in part);* WORLD AFFAIRS: *Norway*
Goldsmith, Arthur. Editor-at-Large, *Popular Photography,* New York City.
PHOTOGRAPHY
Goldstein, William W. Associate Editor, *Publishers Weekly.*
PUBLISHING: *Books (in part)*
Goodwin, Noël. Free-lance Writer and Broadcaster. Associate Editor (to 1983) and Contributor, *Dance & Dancers.*
DANCE *(in part)*
Gottfried, Martin. Drama Critic, New York City. Author of *A Theater Divided; Opening Nights; Broadway Musicals.*
THEATRE *(in part)*
Griffiths, A. R. G. Senior Lecturer in History, Flinders University of South Australia. Author of *Contemporary Australia.*
WORLD AFFAIRS: *Australia; Nauru; Papua New Guinea*
Grossman, Joel W. Archaeologist.
ARCHAEOLOGY: *Western Hemisphere*
Hallgren, Richard E. Assistant Administrator for Weather Services, National Oceanic and Atmospheric Administration.
EARTH SCIENCES: *Meteorology*
Hardman, Thomas C. Consulting Editor, *The Water Skier,* American Water Ski Assoc.
SPORTS AND GAMES: *Water Skiing*
Harper, Nicholas. Music Writer; Deputy Editor, *Classical CD,* England.
MUSIC: *Classical*
Hasegawa, Ryusaku. Editor, TBS-Britannica Co., Ltd., Tokyo.
SPORTS AND GAMES: *Baseball (in part)*
Havard-Williams, P. Professor, Department of Library and Information Studies, Loughborough University, Leicestershire, England.
LIBRARIES *(in part)*
Hawkland, William D. Chancellor and Professor of Law, Louisiana State University.
LAW: *Court Decisions*
Hebblethwaite, Peter. Vatican Affairs Writer, *National Catholic Reporter,* Kansas City, Mo.
BIOGRAPHIES *(in part);* RELIGION: *Roman Catholic Church; Roman Catholic Church:* Sidebar
Hébert, Pierre. Associate Professor, University of Toronto.
LITERATURE: *French (in part)*
Hendershott, Myrl C. Professor of Oceanography, Scripps Institution of Oceanography, La Jolla, Calif.
EARTH SCIENCES: *Oceanography*
Herman, Robin Cathy. Free-lance Journalist.
SPORTS AND GAMES: *Ice Hockey (in part)*
Hess, Marvin G. Executive Vice-President, National Wrestling Coaches Association.
SPORTS AND GAMES: *Wrestling (in part)*
Higgins, Fitzgerald. Editor and Reviewer.
LITERATURE: *United States*
Hoeksema, Klaas J. Assistant Professor, Department of Political Science, Free University, Amsterdam.
WORLD AFFAIRS: *Netherlands, The; Suriname*
Holsöe, Jens W. Diplomatic Correspondent, *Politiken,* Copenhagen.
WORLD AFFAIRS: *Denmark*
Hope, Thomas W. President, Hope Reports, Inc., Rochester, N.Y.
MOTION PICTURES *(in part)*
Howkins, John. Director, International Institute of Communications, London. Author of *Understanding Television.*
TELEVISION AND RADIO *(in part)*

Hunnings, Neville March. Editorial Director, European Law Centre, London. Editor, *Common Market Law Reports.*
LAW: *International Law*
IEIS. International Economic Information Services, London.
ECONOMIC AFFAIRS: *World Economy*
Ingham, Kenneth. Emeritus Professor of History, University of Bristol, England. Author of *Jan Smuts: The Conscience of a South African.*
WORLD AFFAIRS: *Angola; Kenya; Malawi; Mozambique; Sudan, The; Tanzania; Uganda; Zaire; Zambia; Zimbabwe*
Inglis, Kenneth. Professor of History, Australian National University.
Feature Article: AUSTRALIA'S BICENTENNIAL YEAR
Jacquet, Constant H. Staff Associate, National Council of Churches. Editor of *Yearbook of American and Canadian Churches.*
WORLD AFFAIRS: *United States (table)*
Jardine, Adrian. Company Director. Member, Guild of Yachting Writers.
SPORTS AND GAMES: *Sailing*
Jaspert, W. Pincus. Technical and Editorial Consultant. International Editor, *Amercian Printer* and *Worldwide Printer.*
INDUSTRIAL REVIEW: *Printing*
Jenkins, Peter. Political Columnist, *The Sunday Times,* London.
BIOGRAPHIES *(in part);* WORLD AFFAIRS: *United Kingdom*
Joffé, George. Journalist and Writer on North African Affairs.
BIOGRAPHIES *(in part);* WORLD AFFAIRS: *Algeria; Morocco*
Jones, D. A. N. Novelist and Critic. Author of *Parade in Pairs; Never Had It So Good.*
LITERATURE: *Introduction; United Kingdom*
Jones, W. Glyn. Professor of European Literature, University of East Anglia, Norwich, England.
LITERATURE: *Danish*
Joseph, Lou. Senior Science Writer, Hill and Knowlton, Chicago.
HEALTH AND DISEASE: *Dentistry*
Justin, Karen. Associate Editor, Encyclopædia Britannica Yearbooks.
BIOGRAPHIES *(in part)*
Katz, William A. Professor, School of Library Science, State University of New York, Albany.
PUBLISHING: *Magazines (in part)*
Keene, Raymond. Chess Correspondent, *The Times,* London; International Chess Grandmaster.
SPORTS AND GAMES: *Chess*
Kelleher, John A. Group Relations Editor, INL (newspapers), Wellington, N.Z.
WORLD AFFAIRS: *New Zealand*
Kennedy, Richard M. Agricultural Economist, International Economics Division of the Economic Research Service, U.S. Department of Agriculture.
AGRICULTURE AND FOOD SUPPLIES *(in part)*
Kilian, Michael D. Washington Columnist, *Chicago Tribune.* Author of *Flying Can Be Fun.*
SPORTS AND GAMES: *Aerial Sports*
Killheffer, John V. Associate Editor, *Encyclopædia Britannica.*
BIOGRAPHIES *(in part)*
Kimche, Jon. Formerly Editor, *New Middle East; Afro-Asian Affairs,* London. Author of *Second Arab Awakening; Palestine or Israel.*
BIOGRAPHIES *(in part);* WORLD AFFAIRS: *Israel*
Kind, Joshua B. Professor of Art History, Northern Illinois University, De Kalb. Author of *Rouault; Geometry as Abstract Art.*
MUSEUMS *(in part)*
Kloos, Jean Clark Cameron. Editor, *Timber Trades Journal.*
INDUSTRIAL REVIEW: *Wood Products*
Knecht, Jean. Formerly Assistant Foreign Editor, *Le Monde,* Paris.
BIOGRAPHIES *(in part);* WORLD AFFAIRS: *France*
Knox, Richard A. Technical Author; formerly Editor, *Nuclear Engineering International,* London.
INDUSTRIAL REVIEW: *Nuclear Industry*
Kokole, Omari H. Lecturer, Center for Afroamerican and African Studies, University of Michigan.
WORLD AFFAIRS: *Uganda:* Special Report *(in part)*
Kolata, Gina. Writer, *Science* magazine, Washington, D.C. Coauthor of *The High Blood Pressure Book.*
HEALTH AND DISEASE: *Overview (in part)*
Krengel, Janet. Economist, Economics Department, Lloyds Bank PLC, London.
BIOGRAPHIES *(in part);* WORLD AFFAIRS: *Bolivia; Costa Rica; Ecuador; Guatemala; Peru*
Kushnick, Louis. Lecturer, Department of American Studies, University of Manchester, England.
POPULATIONS AND POPULATION MOVEMENTS: *International Migration;* RACE RELATIONS
Lamb, Kevin M. Sportswriter, *Chicago Sun-Times.* Author of *Quarterbacks, Nickelbacks & Other Loose Change.*
BIOGRAPHIES *(in part);* SPORTS AND GAMES: *Football (in part)*
Lapper, Richard J. Free-lance Journalist.
WORLD AFFAIRS: *Nicaragua*
Laqueur, Walter. Codirector, Institute of Contemporary History and Wiener Library, London. Author of *Europe Since Hitler.*
WORLD AFFAIRS: *Introduction*
Larson, Roy. Editor and Publisher, *The Chicago Reporter.*
RELIGION: *Introduction*
Larsson, Gerd. Japan Correspondent, *Dagens Industri.*
BIOGRAPHIES *(in part)*
Leaper, Eric. Executive Director, National Organization for River Sports, Colorado Springs, Colo.
SPORTS AND GAMES: *River Sports*
Legassick, Martin. Coordinator (honorary), Southern Africa Labour Education Project; formerly Senior Lecturer in Sociology, University of Warwick, Coventry, England.
WORLD AFFAIRS: *South Africa*
Legum, Colin. Associate Editor (1947–81), *The Observer;* Editor, *Africa Contemporary Record,* London; and others.
BIOGRAPHIES *(in part);* WORLD AFFAIRS: *African Affairs*
Lennox-Kerr, Peter. Editor, *High Performance Textiles;* European Editor, *Textile World.* Author of *The World Fibres Book.*
INDUSTRIAL REVIEW: *Textiles (in part)*
Litsky, Frank. Sportswriter, *New York Times.*
SPORTS AND GAMES: *Archery*
Logan, Robert G. Sportswriter, *Chicago Tribune.* Author of *Cubs Win!; So You Think You're a Diehard Cub Fan.*
SPORTS AND GAMES: *Basketball (in part)*
Lucenet, Georges F. Secretary-General, International Union of Producers and Distributors of Electrical Energy (Unipede), Paris.
ENERGY: *Electricity*
Luling, Virginia R. Social Anthropologist.
WORLD AFFAIRS: *Somalia*
McCauley, Martin. Senior Lecturer in Soviet and East European Studies, School of Slavonic and East European Studies, University of London.
WORLD AFFAIRS: *Union of Soviet Socialist Republics*
Macdonald, Barrie. Reader in History, Massey University, Palmerston North, N.Z.
WORLD AFFAIRS: *Dependent States (in part); Fiji; Kiribati; Oceanian Affairs; Solomon Islands; Tonga; Tuvalu; Vanuatu; Western Samoa*
McGregor, Alan. General Correspondent, *The Times,* London; Swiss Radio International, Bern; ABC, Australia; and RNZ, New Zealand.
WORLD AFFAIRS: *Switzerland*
Macgregor-Morris, Pamela. Equestrian Correspondent, *Horse and Hound,* London.
SPORTS AND GAMES: *Show Jumping and Eventing*
McKelvie, Roy. Former Rackets and Real Tennis Correspondent, *The Times,* London.
SPORTS AND GAMES: *Rackets; Real Tennis*
McLachlan, Keith S. Senior Lecturer, School of Oriental and African Studies, University of London.
WORLD AFFAIRS: *Iran*
Magnus, Bernd. Professor of Philosophy, University of California, Riverside; Executive Secretary, North American Nietzsche Society.
Macropædia: NIETZSCHE
Mahn, Renee J. Publications Editor, American Power Boat Association.
SPORTS AND GAMES: *Motorboating*
Mallett, H. M. F. Editor, *Wool Record Weekly Market Report,* Bradford, England.
INDUSTRIAL REVIEW: *Textiles (in part)*
Mango, Andrew. Orientalist and Broadcaster.
WORLD AFFAIRS: *Turkey*
Marty, Martin E. Fairfax M. Cone Distinguished Service Professor of the History of Modern Christianity, University of Chicago.
RELIGION: Special Report
Mateja, James L. Auto Editor and Financial Reporter, *Chicago Tribune.* Author of *Used Cars: Finding the Best Buy.*
INDUSTRIAL REVIEW: *Automobiles (in part)*
Matthews, Ian D. Manager, International Affairs, British Steel Corp.
INDUSTRIAL REVIEW: *Iron and Steel*
Matthews, Peter. Athletics Commentator, ITV; Editor, *International Athletics Annual.*
BIOGRAPHIES *(in part)*
Matthíasson, Björn. Economist, Central Bank of Iceland.
WORLD AFFAIRS: *Iceland*
Mazie, David M. Associate of Carl T. Rowan, syndicated columnist. Free-lance Writer.
SOCIAL SECURITY AND WELFARE SERVICES *(in part)*
Mazrui, Ali Al'Amin. Research Professor, University of Jos, Nigeria; Professor, University of Michigan.
WORLD AFFAIRS: *Uganda:* Special Report *(in part)*
Mazze, Edward Mark. Professor of Marketing, School of Business Administration, Temple University, Philadelphia.
CONSUMER AFFAIRS *(in part);* INDUSTRIAL REVIEW: *Advertising*
Mermel, T. W. Consultant; formerly Chairman, Committee on World Register of Dams.
ENGINEERING PROJECTS: *Dams; Dams table*
Meyendorff, John. Professor, Dean of St. Vladimir's Orthodox Theological Seminary; Professor of History, Fordham University, New York City.
RELIGION: *The Orthodox Church; Eastern Non-Chalcedonian Churches*
Miles, Peter W. University of Adelaide, Australia.
LIFE SCIENCES: *Entomology*
Millgate, Paul. Economist, Group Economics Department, Lloyds Bank PLC, London.
WORLD AFFAIRS: *Dominican Republic; Mexico; Venezuela*
Millikin, Sandra. Architectural Historian.
ARCHITECTURE; ART EXHIBITIONS AND ART SALES: *Art Exhibitions;* MUSEUMS *(in part)*
Modiano, Mario. Athens Correspondent, *The Times,* London.
WORLD AFFAIRS: *Greece*
Monaco, Albert M., Jr. Executive Director, United States Volleyball Association.
SPORTS AND GAMES: *Volleyball*
Moore, John E. Hydrologist, Reston, Va.
EARTH SCIENCES: Hydrology
Morgenstern, Dan M. Director, Institute of Jazz Studies, Rutgers, The State University of

New Jersey. Author of *Jazz People.*
MUSIC: *Jazz*

Morris, Jacqui M. Editor, *Oryx* magazine.
ENVIRONMENT *(in part)*

Morrison, Donald. Senior Editor, *Time.*
PUBLISHING: *Newspapers (in part)*

Mortimer, Molly. Commonwealth Correspondent, *The Spectator,* London.
WORLD AFFAIRS: *Commonwealth of Nations*

Mosey, Chris. Associate Editor, *Sweden Now,* Stockholm; Nordic Correspondent, *The Observer;* Swedish Correspondent, *Daily Mail* and *The Times.*
BIOGRAPHIES *(in part);* WORLD AFFAIRS: *Sweden*

Muck, Terry Charles. Editor, *Leadership* magazine, Carol Stream, Ill.
SPORTS AND GAMES: *Handball*

Napier, Elspeth. Editor of publications of the Royal Horticultural Society.
GARDENING *(in part)*

Naylor, Ernest. Lloyd Roberts Professor of Zoology, University College of North Wales.
LIFE SCIENCES: *Marine Biology*

Nelson, Bert. Editor, *Track and Field News.* Author of *Olympic Track and Field.*
SPORTS AND GAMES: *Track and Field Sports*

Netschert, Bruce C. Vice-President, National Economic Research Associates, Inc., Washington, D.C.
ENERGY: *World Summary;* ENERGY: Sidebar

Neusner, Jacob. University Professor, Brown University, Providence, R.I. Author of *Judaism, The Evidence of the Mishnah.*
RELIGION: *Judaism*

Newby, Donald J. Bowls Correspondent, *Daily Telegraph,* London; former Editor, *World Bowls.*
SPORTS AND GAMES: *Lawn Bowls*

Newman, Bernard C. Editor, *Mountain.* Coauthor of *Extreme Rock.*
SPORTS AND GAMES: *Mountaineering*

Niwa, Takuzo. Deputy Editor, Commentary and Feature Department, *Japan Economic Journal.*
INFORMATION AND INFORMATION PROCESSING SYSTEMS *(in part)*

Nixon, Robert W. Director, Communication Department, General Conference of Seventh-day Adventists, Washington, D.C.
RELIGION: *Seventh-day Adventist Church*

Noblett, Geoffrey J. Senior Planning Engineer (Tunnels), Channel Tunnel Project Transmanche Link Joint Venture, London.
ENGINEERING PROJECTS: *Tunnels; Tunnels:* Sidebar

Noel, H. S. Editor, *World Fishing,* England.
AGRICULTURE AND FOOD SUPPLIES: *Fisheries*

Norman, Geraldine. Saleroom Correspondent, *The Times,* London. Author of *The Sale of Works of Art; Nineteenth Century Painters and Painting;* Coauthor of *The Fake's Progress.*
ART EXHIBITIONS AND ART SALES: *Art Sales*

Oberman, Bonnie. Writer and Editor.
BIOGRAPHIES *(in part)*; WORLD AFFAIRS: *United States:* Sidebar

Odell, Peter R. Director, Rotterdam Centre for International Energy Studies, Erasmus University, Rotterdam.
ENERGY: Special Report

O'Donoghue, Michael. Curator, Science Reference Library, London; Lecturer in Gemmology, City of London Polytechnic.
INDUSTRIAL REVIEW: *Gemstones*

O'Dwyer, Thomas. Director, Levant Bureau; Writer on East Mediterranean Affairs, Nicosia, Cyprus.
WORLD AFFAIRS: *Cyprus*

O'Keeffe, Margaret-Louise. Retired Press Officer, All England Women's Lacrosse Association.
SPORTS AND GAMES: *Lacrosse (in part)*

Olney, P. J. Curator of Birds and Reptiles, Zoological Society of London. Editor, *International Zoo Yearbook.*
BOTANICAL GARDENS AND ZOOS: *Zoos*

Osborne, Keith. Editor, *British Rowing Almanack.* Author of *Boat Racing in Britain, 1715–1975.*
SPORTS AND GAMES: *Rowing*

Osterbind, Carter C. Associate, Gerontology Center, and Professor Emeritus of Economics, University of Florida.
INDUSTRIAL REVIEW: *Building and Construction*

Page, Campbell. Paris Correspondent, *The Guardian,* London.
WORLD AFFAIRS: *France:* Sidebar

Palmer, John. Former European Editor, *The Guardian,* London.
WORLD AFFAIRS: *Western European Affairs*

Palmer, S. B. Reader, Department of Applied Physics, University of Hull, England.
PHYSICS

Parker, Sandy. Publisher of weekly international newsletter on fur industry; Copublisher, *Fur World.*
INDUSTRIAL REVIEW: *Furs*

Paul, Charles Robert, Jr. Special Assistant to the Secretary-General, U.S. Olympic Committee, Colorado Springs.
SPORTS AND GAMES: *Gymnastics; Weight Lifting*

Penfold, Robin C. Free-lance Writer in industrial topics. Editor, *Shell Petrochemicals.* Author of *A Journalist's Guide to Plastics.*
INDUSTRIAL REVIEW: *Plastics*

Pertile, Lino. Reader in Italian, University of Sussex, England.
LITERATURE: *Italian*

Petherick, Karin. Reader in Swedish, University of London.
LITERATURE: Swedish

Pfeffer, Irving. Attorney. Author of *The Financing of Small Business.*
ECONOMIC AFFAIRS: *Stock Exchanges (in part)*

Pinfold, Geoffrey M. Director, NCL Consulting Engineers, London. Author of *Reinforced Concrete Chimneys and Towers.*
ENGINEERING PROJECTS: *Buildings*

Plotnik, Arthur. Editor, *American Libraries* magazine, American Library Association.
LIBRARIES *(in part)*

Polin, Thomas Hon Wing. Assistant Managing Editor, *Asiaweek,* Hong Kong.
BIOGRAPHIES *(in part);* WORLD AFFAIRS: *Brunei; Dependent States (in part); Indonesia; Kampuchea; Korea; Laos; Malaysia; Singapore; Southeast Asian Affairs; Thailand; Vietnam*

Pollack, Jonathan D. Senior Staff Member, Political Science Department, Rand Corp., Santa Monica, Calif.
WORLD AFFAIRS: *China; Taiwan*

Poppeliers, John. International Liaison Officer for Cultural Affairs, National Parks Service, U.S. Department of the Interior.
HISTORIC PRESERVATION

Post, Avery D. President, United Church of Christ, New York City.
RELIGION: *United Church of Christ*

Prasad, H. Y. Sharada. Information Adviser to the Prime Minister, New Delhi, India.
WORLD AFFAIRS: *India*

Prince, Rod. Journalist specializing in Caribbean matters.
BIOGRAPHIES *(in part);* WORLD AFFAIRS: *Antigua and Barbuda; Bahamas, The; Barbados; Dependent States (in part); Dominica; Grenada; Guyana; Jamaica; Saint Christopher and Nevis; Saint Lucia; Saint Vincent and the Grenadines; Trinidad and Tobago*

Ranger, Robin. Associate Professor, Defense and Strategic Studies, School of International Relations, University of Southern California.
MILITARY AFFAIRS

Ravenholt, Albert. Foreign Correspondent, Manila; Associate, American Universities Field Staff International.
Feature Article: THE PHILIPPINES: IS DEMOCRACY RESTORED? *(in part)*

Ravenholt, Marjorie. Area Consultant on the Philippines and Southeast Asia, Manila.
Feature Article: THE PHILIPPINES: IS DEMOCRACY RESTORED? *(in part)*

Ray, G. F. Senior Research Fellow, National Institute of Economic and Social Research, London.
INDUSTRIAL REVIEW: *Introduction*

Read, Anthony A. Director, Book Development Council, London.
PUBLISHING: *Books (in part)*

Rebelo, L. S. Reader, Department of Portuguese Studies, King's College, University of London.
LITERATURE: *Portuguese (in part)*

Reichhardt, Tony. Editor, *Space World* magazine.
SPACE EXPLORATION: Special Report

Reid, J. H. Reader in German, University of Nottingham, England. Author of *Heinrich Böll: Withdrawal and Re-emergence.*
LITERATURE: *German*

Reid, Philip D. Professor of Biological Sciences, Smith College, Northampton, Mass.
LIFE SCIENCES: *Botany*

Reynolds, Frank E. Professor of the History of Religions and Buddhist Studies, Divinity School, University of Chicago.
RELIGION: *Buddhism (in part)*

Ripley, Michael D. Senior Public Relations Officer, Brewers' Society, U.K.
INDUSTRIAL REVIEW: *Beverages (in part)*

Robinson, David. Film Critic, *The Times,* London. Author of *A History of World Cinema; Chaplin: His Life and Art.*
BIOGRAPHIES *(in part);* MOTION PICTURES *(in part)*

Saeki, Shoichi. Professor of Literature, Chuo University, Tokyo. Author of *In Search of Japanese Ego.*
LITERATURE: *Japanese*

Sarahete, Yrjö. General Secretary, Fédération Internationale des Quilleurs, Helsinki.
SPORTS AND GAMES: *Bowling (in part)*

Sarmiento, Sergio. Editor in Chief, Spanish-language publications, Encyclopædia Britannica Publishers, Inc.
SPORTS AND GAMES: *Baseball (in part); Football (in part)*

Schoenfield, Albert. Formerly Publisher, *Swimming World;* Vice-Chairman, U.S. Olympic Swimming Committee; Honoree, International Swimming Hall of Fame.
SPORTS AND GAMES: *Swimming*

Schöpflin, George. Lecturer in East European Political Institutions, London School of Economics and School of Slavonic and East European Studies, University of London.
WORLD AFFAIRS: *Czechoslovakia; Eastern European Affairs*

Sears, Robert N. Firearms Consultant and Writer.
SPORTS AND GAMES: *Shooting*

Sell, Alan P. F. Theological Secretary, World Alliance of Reformed Churches, Geneva.
RELIGION: *Reformed, Presbyterian, and Congregational Churches*

Shackleford, Peter. Chief of Studies, World Tourism Organization, Madrid.
INDUSTRIAL REVIEW: *Tourism*

Shaw, T. R. Advisory Editor, *International Journal of Speleology.* Author of *History of Cave Science.*
SPORTS AND GAMES: *Spelunking*

Shelley, Andrew. Competitions Manager, Squash Rackets Association, England.
SPORTS AND GAMES: *Squash Rackets*

Shepherd, Melinda. Copy Editor, Encyclopædia Britannica, Inc.
BIOGRAPHIES *(in part);* WORLD AFFAIRS: *United States:* Sidebar

Sherwood, Martin A. Employed in the pharmaceutical industry. Author of *New Worlds in Chemistry.*

CHEMISTRY
Simpson, Noel. Managing Director, Sydney Bloodstock Proprietary Ltd., Sydney.
SPORTS AND GAMES: *Horse Racing (in part)*
Smallenburg, Harry Russell. Chairman, Department of General Studies, Center for Creative Studies, Detroit, Mich.
TRANSPORTATION: Special Report
Smith, Donald. Editor, *Rubber World* magazine, Akron, Ohio.
INDUSTRIAL REVIEW: *Rubber*
Smith, Reuben W. Dean, Graduate School, and Professor of History, University of the Pacific, Stockton, Calif.
RELIGION: *Islam*
Smogorzewski, K. M. Writer on contemporary history. Founder and Editor, *Free Europe,* London.
BIOGRAPHIES *(in part);* WORLD AFFAIRS: *Albania; Andorra; Bulgaria; Hungary; Liechtenstein; Luxembourg; Monaco; Mongolia; Poland; Political Parties; Romania; San Marino*
Stern, Irwin. Assistant Professor of Portuguese, Columbia University, New York City.
LITERATURE: *Portuguese (in part)*
Stoddard, Drew W. Commissioner, Men's Professional Racquetball; Editor, *National Racquetball Magazine.*
SPORTS AND GAMES: *Racquetball*
Stoddart, Patrick. Writer and Broadcaster; Film and Television Editor, *The Sunday Times,* London.
BIOGRAPHIES *(in part);* TELEVISION AND RADIO *(in part)*
Stoffels, Robert E. Editor, *Telephone Engineer & Management* magazine, Geneva, Ill.
INDUSTRIAL REVIEW: *Telecommunications*
Støverud, Torbjørn. Honorary Research Fellow, University College, London.
LITERATURE: *Norwegian*
Strauss, Michael. Ski, Sports, and Feature Writer, *New York Times* (retired); Sports Editor, *Palm Beach Daily News.*
SPORTS AND GAMES: *Fencing*
Sullivan, H. Patrick. Dean of the College and Professor of Religion, Vassar College, Poughkeepsie, N.Y.
RELIGION: *Hinduism*
Sully, Melanie. Senior Lecturer, North Staffs Polytechnic, Stafford, England.
BIOGRAPHIES *(in part)*
Sweetinburgh, Thelma. Fashion Writer, Paris.
FASHION AND DRESS *(in part);* MUSEUMS: Sidebar
Swift, Richard N. Professor Emeritus of Politics, New York University, New York City.
WORLD AFFAIRS: *United Nations*
Synan, Vinson. Former Assistant General Superintendent, Pentecostal Holiness Church. Author of *The Holiness-Pentecostal Movement.*
RELIGION: *Pentecostal Churches*
Taggart, Charles Johnson. Free-lance Writer.
BIOGRAPHIES *(in part)*
Taishoff, Lawrence B. President, Broadcasting Publications, Inc., and Publisher, *Broadcasting* magazine and others.
TELEVISION AND RADIO *(in part)*
Tak, Jean van der. Senior Editor, Population Reference Bureau, Inc.
POPULATIONS AND POPULATION MOVEMENTS: *Demography*
Talbot, Nathan A. Manager, Committees on Publication, The First Church of Christ, Scientist, Boston.
RELIGION: *Church of Christ, Scientist*
Tallan, Norman M. Chief, Metals and Ceramics Division, Materials Laboratory, Wright-Patterson Air Force Base, Dayton, Ohio.
INDUSTRIAL REVIEW: *Ceramics*
Tateishi, Kay K. Free-lance Writer and Translator.
BIOGRAPHIES *(in part)*
Teitelbaum, Michael S. Program Officer, Alfred P. Sloan Foundation, New York City.
Macropædia: POPULATION
Theiner, George. Editor, *Index on Censorship,* London. Coauthor of *The Kill Dog;* editor of *New Writing in Czechoslovakia.*
LITERATURE: *Eastern European; Russian (in part)*
Thomas, Theodore V. Free-lance Journalist and Press Consultant. Editor (1961–79), *British Toys and Hobbies.*
INDUSTRIAL REVIEW: *Games and Toys*
Tingay, Lance. Former Tennis Correspondent, *Daily Telegraph,* London. Author of *100 Years of Wimbledon; Tennis Facts and Feats.*
SPORTS AND GAMES: *Tennis*
Trigg, Robert H. Assistant Vice-President, Board Advisory Committees' Policies, New York Stock Exchange.
ECONOMIC AFFAIRS: *Stock Exchanges (in part)*
Trilling, Ossia. Coeditor and Contributor, *International Theatre.* Contributor, BBC, *The Times,* London, and other media.
THEATRE *(in part);* THEATRE: Sidebar
UNHCR. The Office of the United Nations High Commissioner for Refugees.
POPULATIONS AND POPULATION MOVEMENTS: *Refugees*
Utt, Roger L. Formerly Assistant Professor of Spanish, Department of Romance Languages and Literatures, University of Chicago.
LITERATURE: *Spanish (in part)*
Vale, Norman K. Retired Director of News Services, The United Church of Canada.
RELIGION: *The United Church of Canada*
Venzke, Bruce H. Associate Editor, *Pool & Billiard Magazine;* formerly Chief Correspondent, *National Billiard News;* Member, Statistics and Records Committee, Billiard Congress of America.
SPORTS AND GAMES: *Billiard Games (in part)*
Verdi, Robert William. Sports Columnist, *Chicago Tribune.*
SPORTS AND GAMES: *Baseball (in part)*
Vermeer, Ruth. Head, Development Programmes, International Organization of Consumer Unions, The Hague, Neth.
CONSUMER AFFAIRS *(in part)*
Vint, Arthur Kingsley. Counselor, International Table Tennis Federation.
SPORTS AND GAMES: *Table Tennis*
Waldman, Marilyn R. Associate Professor of History and Director, Center for Comparative Studies, Ohio State University, Columbus.
Macropædia: THE ISLAMIC WORLD
Walker, Ranginui J. Associate Professor of Maori Studies, Anthropology Department, University of Auckland, N.Z.
WORLD AFFAIRS: *New Zealand:* Sidebar
Ward, Peter. Owner and Operator, Ward News Services Canada, Parliamentary Press Gallery, Ottawa.
WORLD AFFAIRS: *Canada:* Special Report
Warner, Antony C. Editor, *Drinks Marketing,* London.
INDUSTRIAL REVIEW: *Beverages (in part)*
Warner, Edward S. Executive Editor, East Coast, *Infoworld* magazine, Palo Alto, Calif.
INFORMATION PROCESSING AND INFORMATION SYSTEMS *(in part);* INFORMATION PROCESSING AND INFORMATION SYSTEMS: Sidebar
Watson, Louise. London Editor, *Britannica Book of the Year.*
WORLD AFFAIRS: *Dependent States (in part)*
Way, Diane Lois. Historical Researcher.
BIOGRAPHIES *(in part)*
Webber, Frederick L. President, National Soft Drink Association, Washington, D.C.
INDUSTRIAL REVIEW: *Beverages (in part)*
Weinthal, John R. Writer on the automotive industry.
INDUSTRIAL REVIEW: *Automobiles (in part)*
Welch, Melvin D. Secretary, English Basket Ball Association; Editor (1971–78), *Basketball Magazine.*
SPORTS AND GAMES: *Basketball (in part)*
Whelan, John. Publisher, *Middle East Economic Digest* and *Africa Economic Digest.*
WORLD AFFAIRS: *Bahrain; Egypt; Iraq; Jordan; Kuwait; Lebanon; Middle Eastern and North African Affairs; Oman; Qatar; Saudi Arabia; Syria; United Arab Emirates; Yemen, People's Democratic Republic of; Yemen Arab Republic*
Whitney, Barbara. Senior Copy Editor, Encyclopædia Britannica, Inc.
BIOGRAPHIES *(in part)*
Wilkinson, John R. Sportswriter, East Midland Provincial Newspapers Ltd., U.K.
SPORTS AND GAMES: *Cycling*
Williams, Ann. Lecturer, Polytechnic of North London; Academic Advisor, Domesday Exhibition, London.
POPULATIONS AND POPULATION MOVEMENTS: Special Report
Williams, Brian. Free-lance Editor and Writer, London.
BIOGRAPHIES *(in part)*
Williams, Michael E. J. Golf Correspondent, *Daily Telegraph,* London.
SPORTS AND GAMES: *Golf*
Williams, Raymond Leslie. Associate Professor of Spanish, Washington University, St. Louis, Mo.
LITERATURE: *Spanish (in part)*
Williamson, Trevor. Chief Sports Subeditor, *Daily Telegraph,* London.
BIOGRAPHIES *(in part);* SPORTS AND GAMES: *Football (in part)*
Wilson, Michael. Free-lance Aviation Writer and Consultant.
INDUSTRIAL REVIEW: *Aerospace*
Witte, Randall E. Editor, *The Western Horseman* magazine, Colorado Springs, Colo.
SPORTS AND GAMES: *Rodeo*
Woods, Elizabeth. Writer. Author of *The Yellow Volkswagen; Gone; Men; The Amateur.*
LITERATURE: *English (in part)*
Woollen, Anthony. Editor (1959–79), *Food Manufacture,* London. Editor, *Food Industries Manual* (20th ed.).
AGRICULTURE AND FOOD SUPPLIES: *Food Processing*
Wooller, Michael. Economist, Economics Dept., Lloyds Bank PLC, London.
BIOGRAPHIES *(in part);* WORLD AFFAIRS: *Portugal; Spain*
Woolley, David. Air Transport Editor, *Interavia,* London.
TRANSPORTATION *(in part);* TRANSPORTATION: Sidebar
Worsnop, Richard L. Associate Editor, Editorial Research Reports, Washington, D.C.
WORLD AFFAIRS: *United States*
Wright, Almon R. Retired Senior Historian, U.S. Department of State.
WORLD AFFAIRS: *Panama*
Wyllie, Peter John. Chairman, Division of Geological and Planetary Sciences, California Institute of Technology.
EARTH SCIENCES: *Geology and Geochemistry*
Yang, Winston L. Y. Chairman, Department of Asian Studies, Seton Hall University, South Orange, N.J.
BIOGRAPHIES *(in part);* LITERATURE: *Chinese*
Yoshida, Nobuyoshi. Executive Editor, *Industrial Japan,* Tokyo.
INDUSTRIAL REVIEW: *Automobiles (in part)*
Young, M. Norvel. Chancellor Emeritus, Pepperdine University, Malibu, Calif. Author of *Preachers of Today.*
RELIGION: *Churches of Christ*
Young, Susan. News Editor, *Church Times,* London.
RELIGION: *Anglican Communion*
Zeidenberg, Leonard. Chief Correspondent, *Broadcasting* magazine, Washington, D.C.
TELEVISION AND RADIO *(in part)*
Zollo, Stephen M. New Products Editor, *Electronics* magazine, McGraw-Hill Inc.
INDUSTRIAL REVIEW: *Microelectronics*

Flags of the Nations

Afghanistan

Albania

Algeria

Andorra*

Angola

Antigua and Barbuda

Argentina*

Australia

Austria*

*State flag shown; national flag does not carry coat of arms.

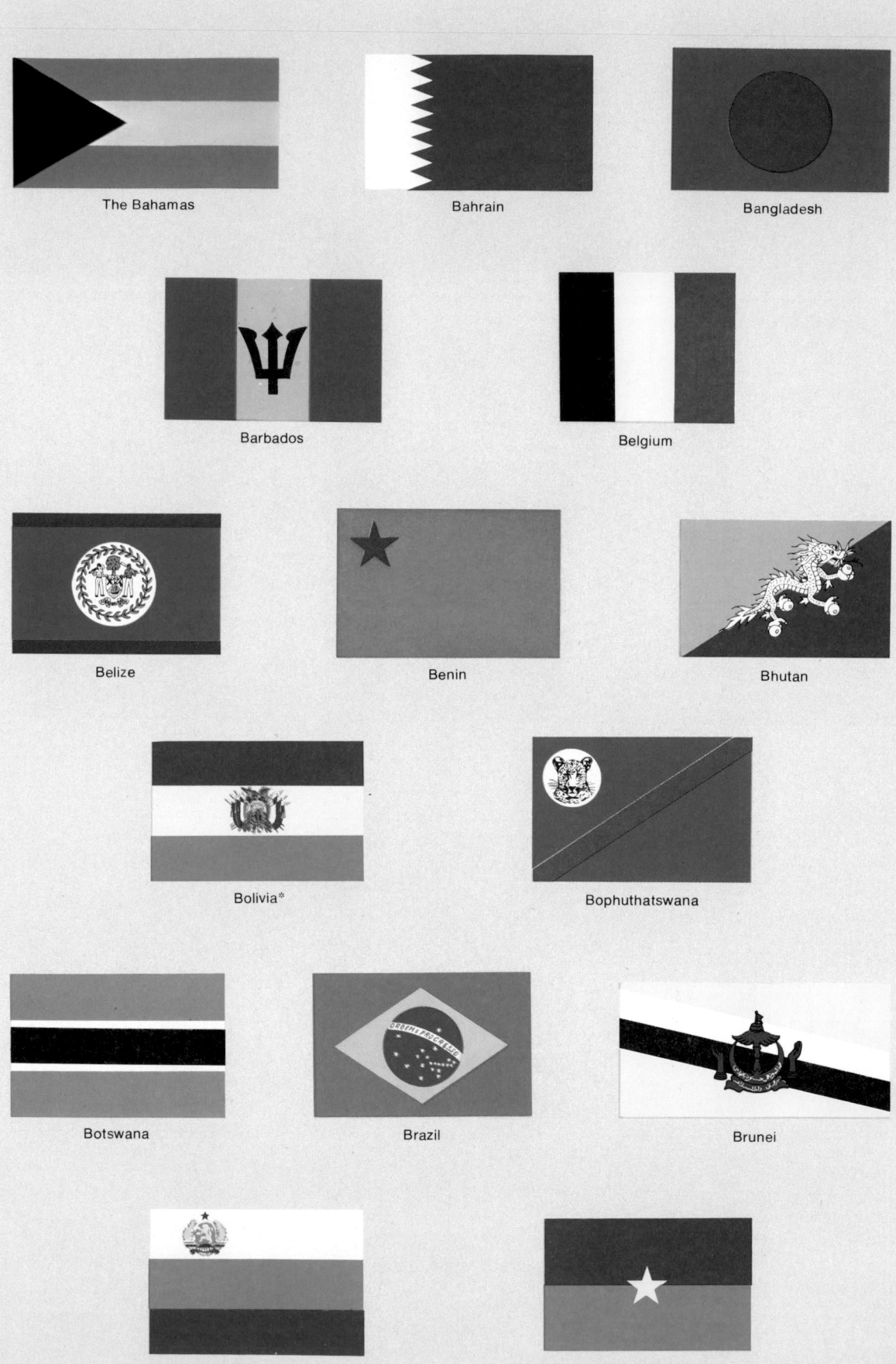

The Bahamas

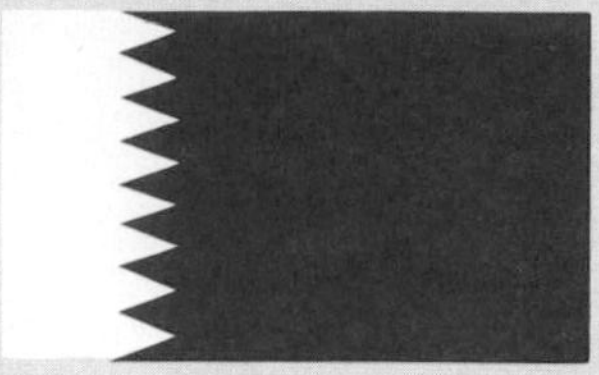
Bahrain

Bangladesh

Barbados

Belgium

Belize

Benin

Bhutan

Bolivia*

Bophuthatswana

Botswana

Brazil

Brunei

Bulgaria

Burkina Faso

*State flag shown; national flag does not carry coat of arms.

Burma

Burundi

Cameroon

Canada

Cape Verde

Central African Republic

Chad

Chile

China

Ciskei

Colombia

Comoros

Congo

Costa Rica*

Côte d'Ivoire

Cuba

*State flag shown; national flag does not carry coat of arms.

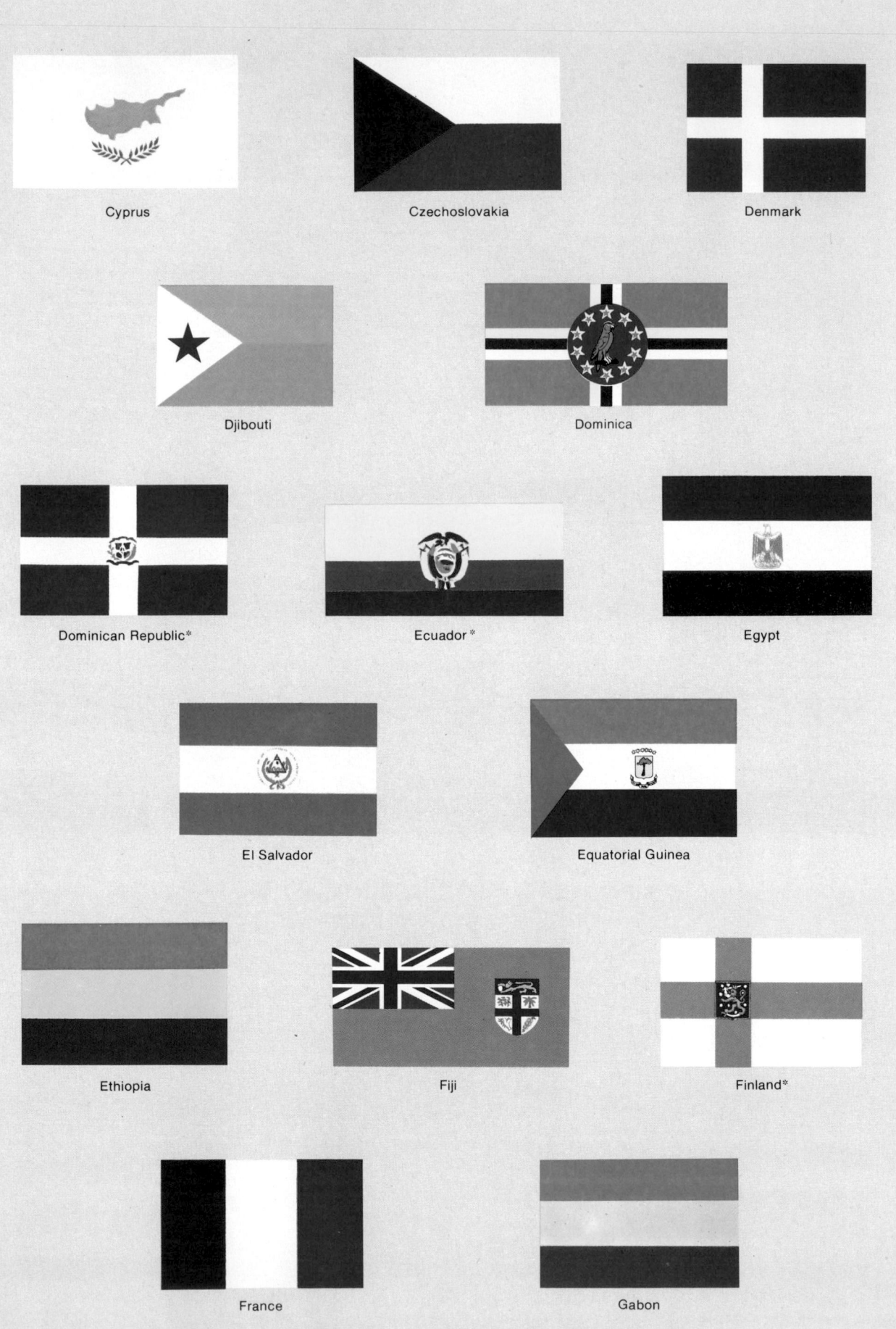

Cyprus

Czechoslovakia

Denmark

Djibouti

Dominica

Dominican Republic*

Ecuador*

Egypt

El Salvador

Equatorial Guinea

Ethiopia

Fiji

Finland*

France

Gabon

*State flag shown; national flag does not carry coat of arms.

The Gambia

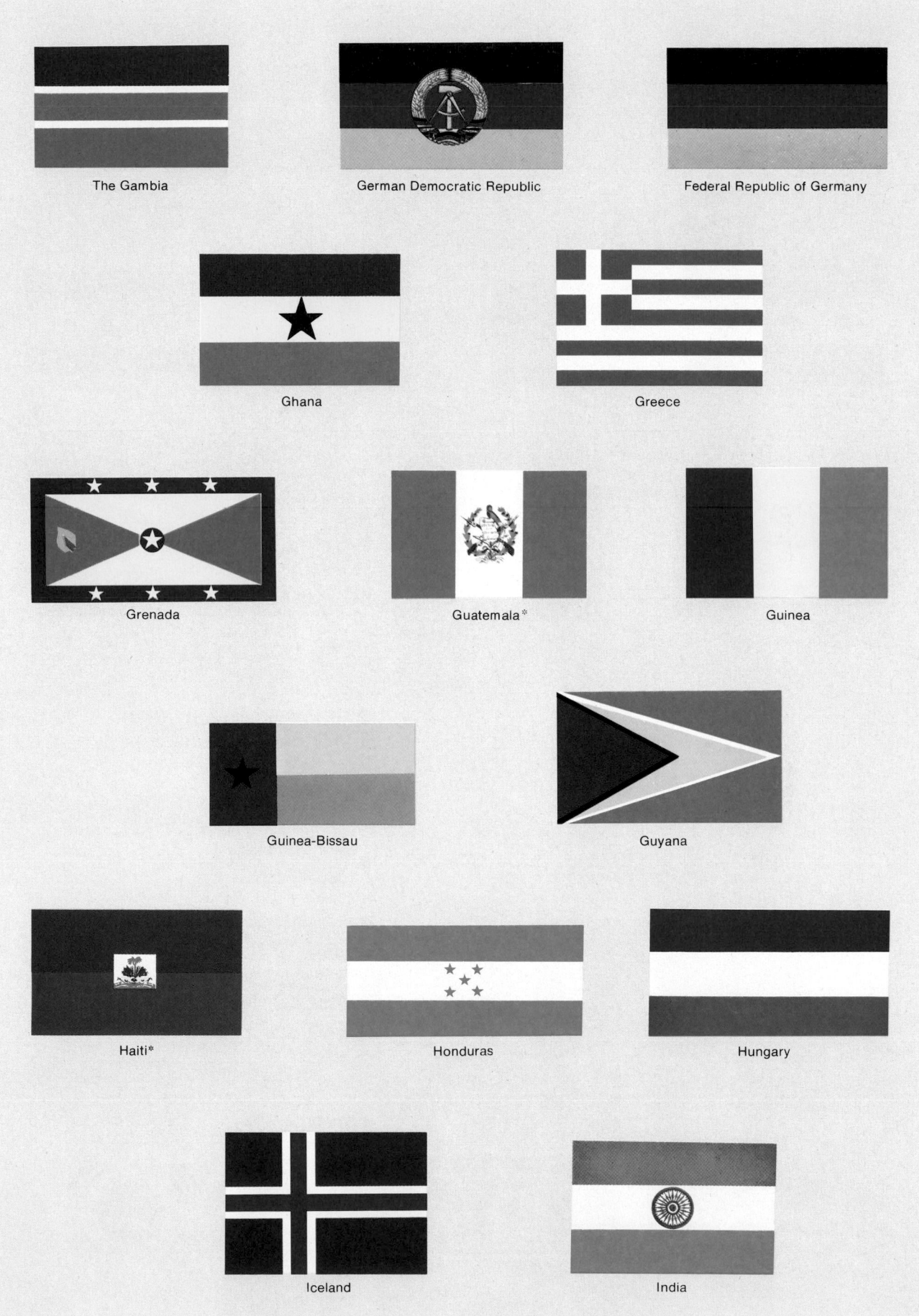

German Democratic Republic

Federal Republic of Germany

Ghana

Greece

Grenada

Guatemala*

Guinea

Guinea-Bissau

Guyana

Haiti*

Honduras

Hungary

Iceland

India

*State flag shown; national flag does not carry coat of arms.

Indonesia

Iran

Iraq

Ireland

Israel

Italy

Jamaica

Japan

Jordan

Kampuchea

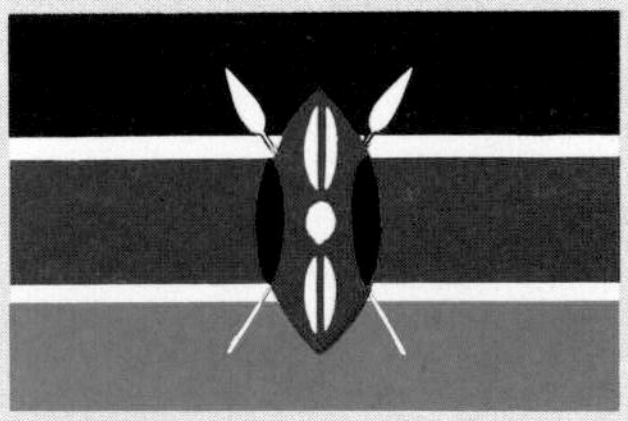
Kenya

Kiribati

North Korea

South Korea

Kuwait

Laos

Lebanon

Lesotho

Liberia

Libya

Liechtenstein

Luxembourg

Madagascar

Malaŵi

Malaysia

Maldives

Mali

Malta

Mauritania

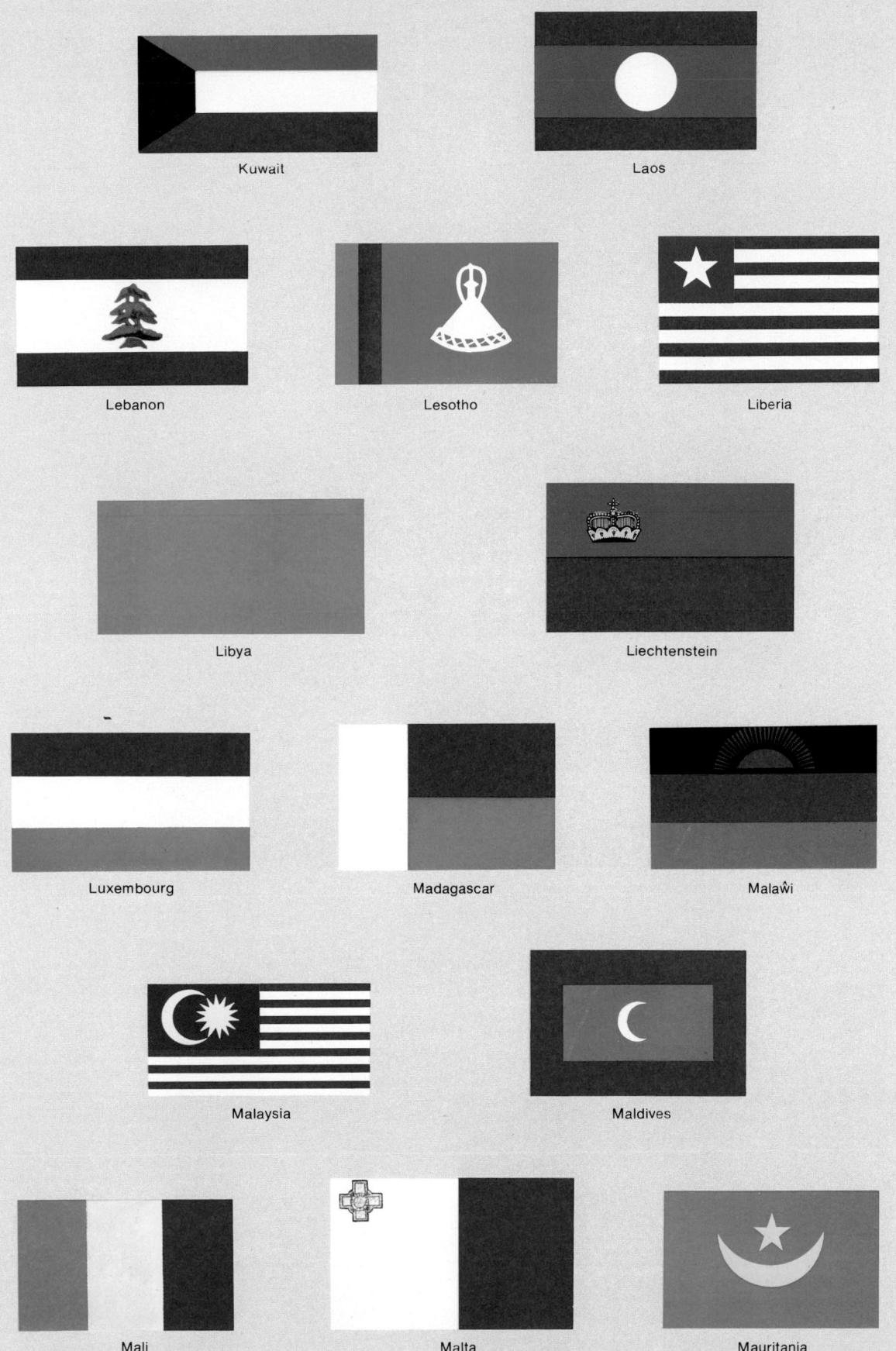

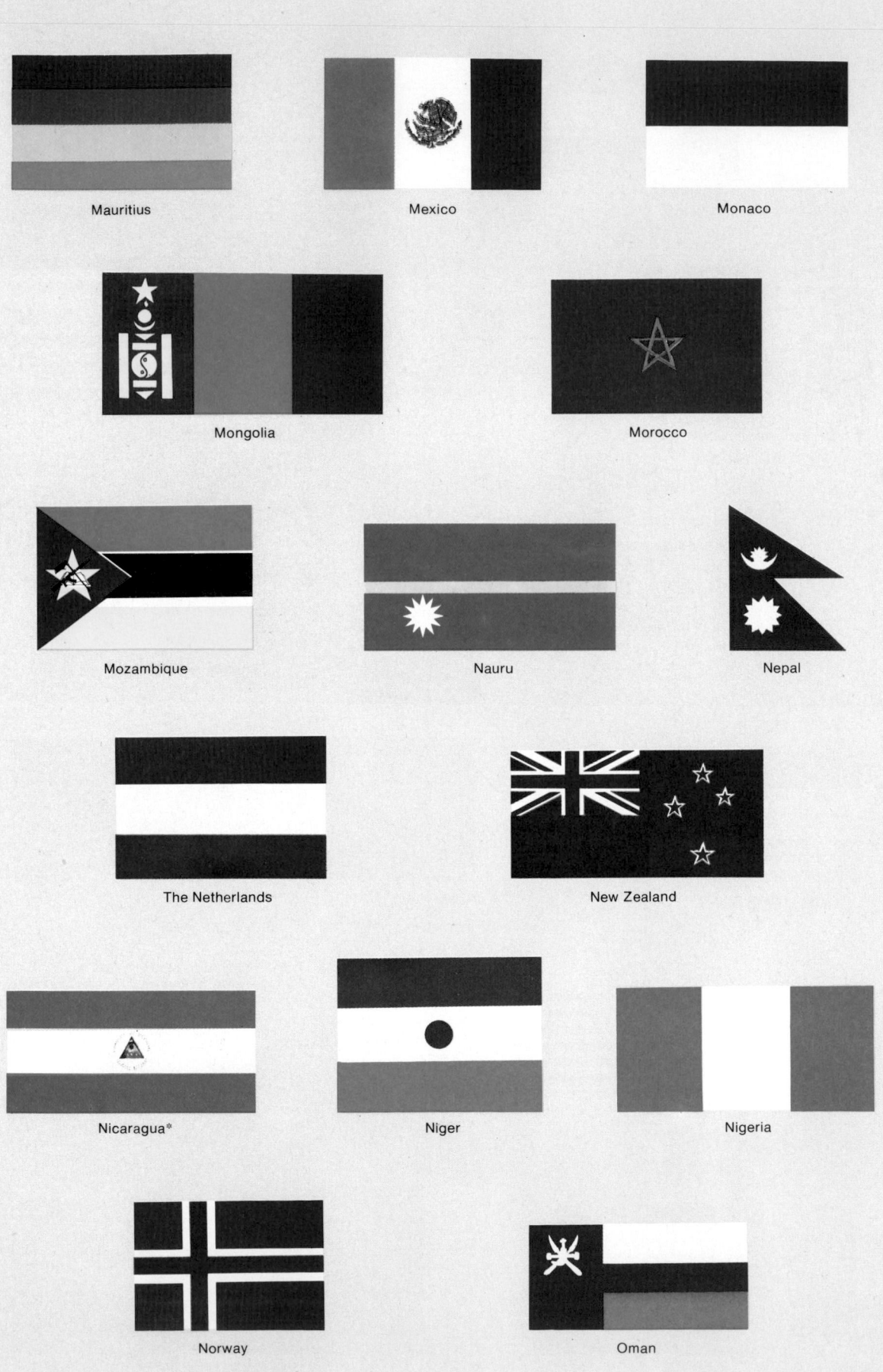

Mauritius

Mexico

Monaco

Mongolia

Morocco

Mozambique

Nauru

Nepal

The Netherlands

New Zealand

Nicaragua*

Niger

Nigeria

Norway

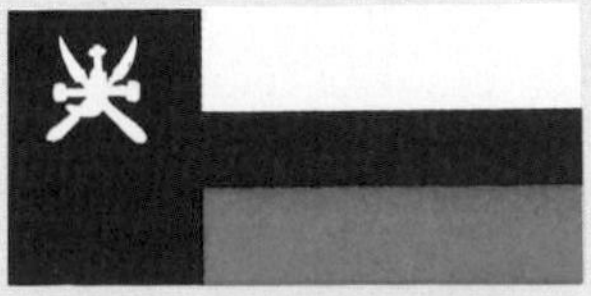
Oman

*State flag shown; national flag does not carry coat of arms.

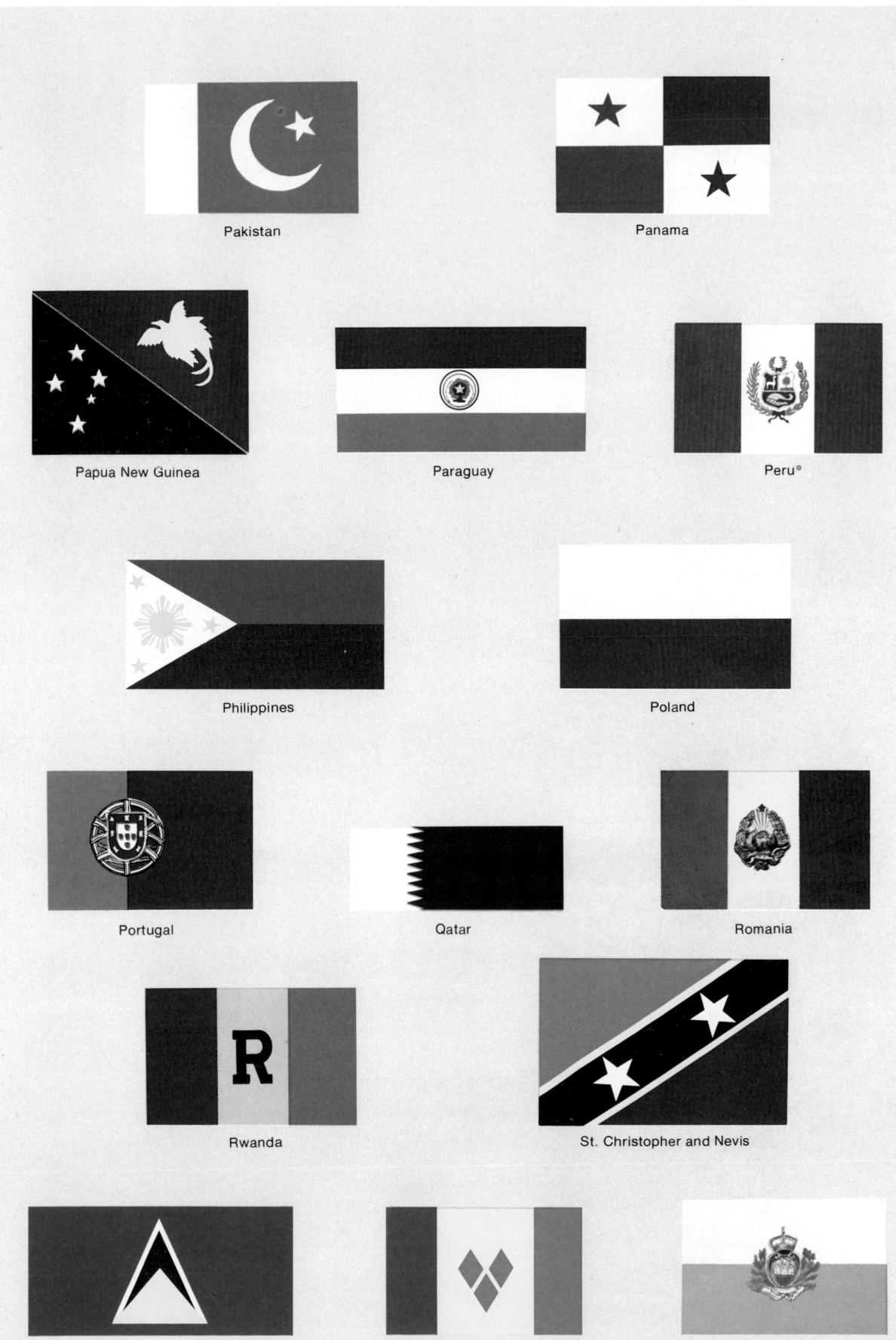

Pakistan

Panama

Papua New Guinea

Paraguay

Peru*

Philippines

Poland

Portugal

Qatar

Romania

Rwanda

St. Christopher and Nevis

St. Lucia

St. Vincent and the Grenadines

San Marino*

*State flag shown; national flag does not carry coat of arms.

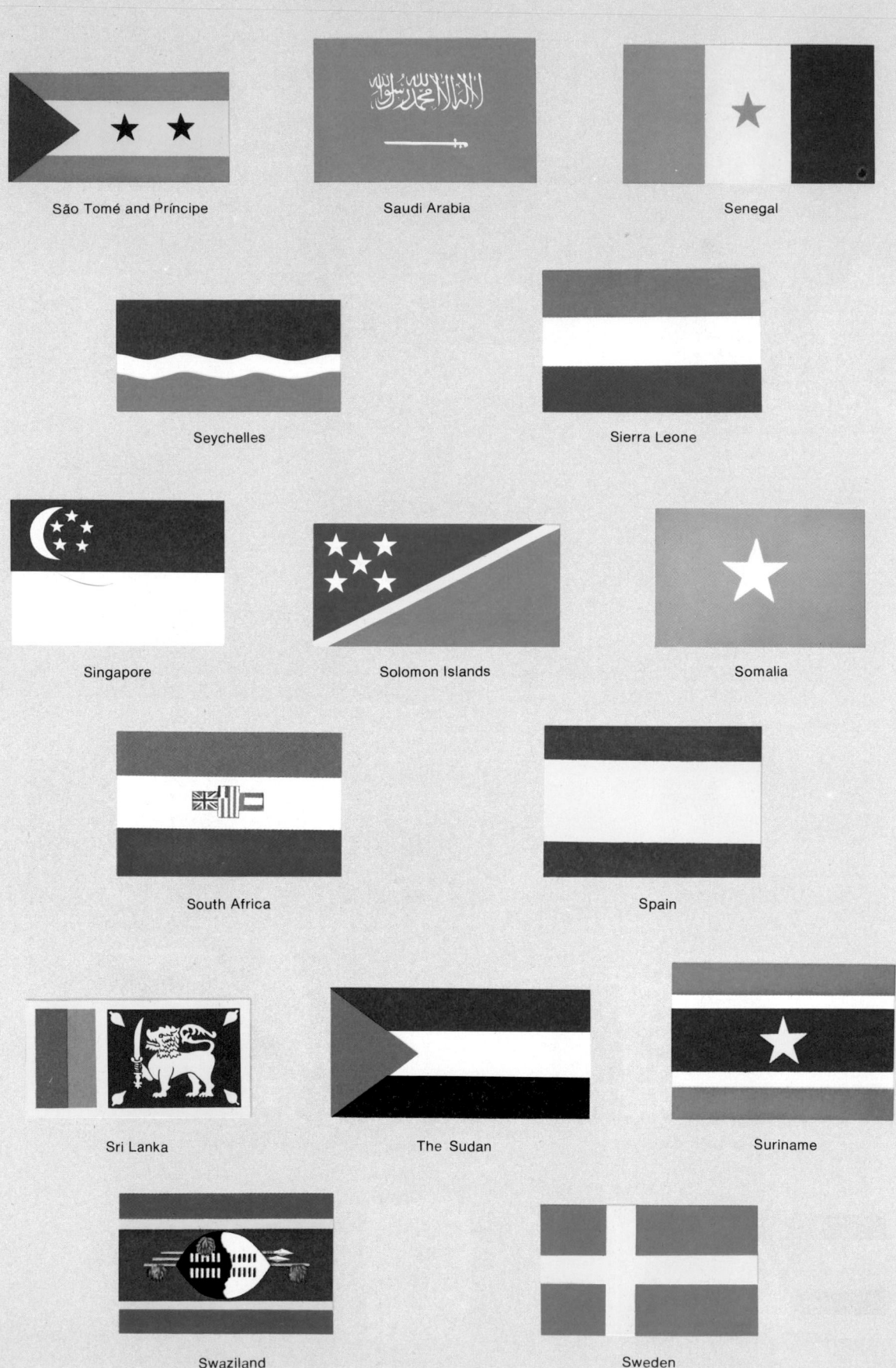

São Tomé and Príncipe

Saudi Arabia

Senegal

Seychelles

Sierra Leone

Singapore

Solomon Islands

Somalia

South Africa

Spain

Sri Lanka

The Sudan

Suriname

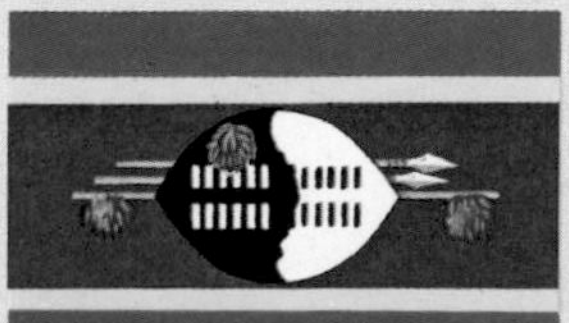
Swaziland

Sweden

Switzerland

Syria

Taiwan

Tanzania

Thailand

Togo

Tonga

Transkei

Trinidad and Tobago

Tunisia

Turkey

Tuvalu

Uganda

Union of Soviet Socialist Republics

United Arab Emirates

United Kingdom

United States

Uruguay

Vanuatu

Vatican City

Venda

Venezuela*

Vietnam

Western Samoa

People's Democratic Republic of Yemen

Yemen Arab Republic

Yugoslavia

Zaire

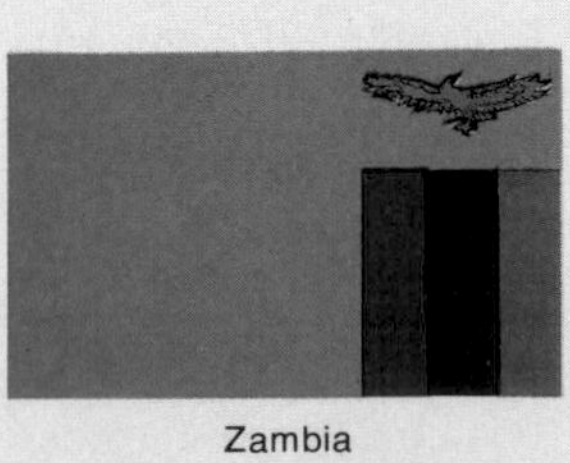
Zambia

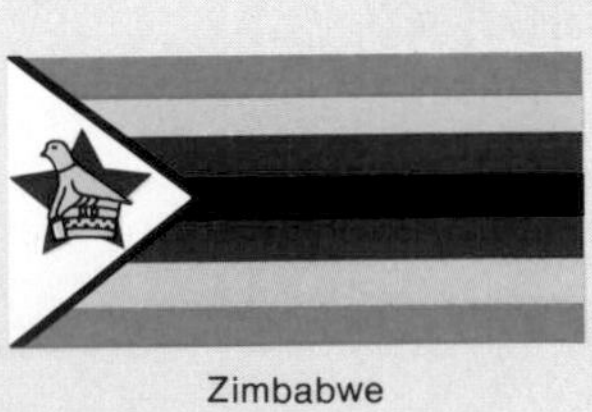
Zimbabwe

*State flag shown; national flag does not carry coat of arms.

1987
Britannica World Data

Encyclopædia Britannica, Inc.
Chicago
Auckland/Geneva/London/Manila/Paris/Rome
Seoul/Sydney/Tokyo/Toronto

CONTENTS

INTRODUCTION

Britannica World Data provides a statistical portrait of some 220 countries and dependencies of the world, at a level appropriate to the size and importance of each. It contains 186 country statements, ranging in length from one to four pages, for the largest and most significant of these, and permits, in the development of more than a score of major thematic subject areas (employment, agriculture, trade), simultaneous comparison among all of these larger countries and 34 additional smaller dependent states.

Updated annually, *Britannica World Data* can be consulted as a separate work of reference developing a particular body of subject matter, but it is particularly intended as direct, structured support for many of Britannica's other reference works—encyclopedias, yearbooks, atlases—at a level of detail that their editorial style or space requirements do not permit.

Like the textual, graphic, or cartographic modes of expression of these other products, statistics possess their own inherent editorial virtues and weaknesses. Two principal goals in the creation of *Britannica World Data* were up-to-dateness and comparability, each possible separately, but not always possible to combine. If, for example, research on some subject (say, registered motor vehicles) is completed during a particular year (x), figures may be available for 100 countries for the preceding year ($x-1$), for 140 countries for the year before that ($x-2$), and for 180 countries for the year before that ($x-3$).

Which year should be the basis of a thematic compilation for 220 countries so as to give the best combination of up-to-dateness and comparability? And, should $x-1$ be adopted for the thematic table, ought up-to-dateness in the country table (for which year x is already available) be sacrificed for agreement with the thematic table? In general, the editors have opted for maximum up-to-dateness in the country statistical boxes and maximum comparability in the thematic tables, so as to take the best advantage of late information, published and unpublished.

Comparability, however, also resides in the meaning of the numbers compiled, which may differ greatly from country to country. The headnotes to the thematic tables explain many of these definitional problems; the Glossary serves the same purpose for the country statistical pages. Since the researcher or editor does not always find a neat, unambiguous choice between a datum compiled on two different bases (say, railroad track length, or route length), one of which is wanted and the other not, a choice must be made between the latest official national data (which may be incomplete, published only after a delay of several years, politically suspect, compiled on the wrong basis [for international comparability], or may refer to some time period other than a standard Gregorian calendar year) and some external figure, often only an estimate, compiled by an international organization (such as the UN, FAO, or IMF), on the desired basis, but often at a considerable remove from the country's own most recent data, both in time and distance. Every effort has been made to obtain the best combination of comparability and up-to-dateness from available sources, and, when the completeness of a country's published data permitted, to analyze it further for better agreement in coverage, scope, and datedness, For certain subjects, especially population, the editors have prepared their own estimates.

The published basis of the information compiled is the statistical collections of Encyclopædia Britannica, Inc., some of the principal elements of which are enumerated in the Bibliography. All of these sources are held, and updated continuously for editorial use, in Britannica's editorial offices. The publications themselves are issued in some 75 languages in common use among the countries of the world; the information contained in them is supplemented by unpublished data received in correspondence from the countries concerned. Usual holdings for a country with a well-developed statistical and publishing program may include any of the following kinds of documents: the national statistical abstract; the most recent censuses of population; periodic or occasional reports on vital statistics, social indicators, agriculture, mining, labour, manufacturing, wholesale and retail trade, finance and banking, development planning, foreign trade, transportation, and communication. These primarily statistical sources are supplemented by other kinds of national reference works, such as gazetteers (of place names), national atlases, constitutions, and monographs by domestic or external analysts.

No reference work on the countries of the world can, or should, be used in isolation. To say that the population density of Hungary is about 300 persons per square mile will not be misleading, because the population is rather evenly distributed across the landscape outside the cities. To give a density for Greenland calculated on the same basis (total population ÷ total area) *would* be misleading (and would amount to only 0.06 persons per square mile) because much of Greenland is uninhabitable ice cap. Similarly, the great majority of the social, economic, and financial data contained in this work should not be interpreted in isolation. Interpretive text of long perspective, such as that of the *Encyclopædia Britannica* itself; political, geographic, and topical maps; and recent analysis of political events and economic trends, such as that contained in the articles of the *Book of the Year*, will all help to supply balance, physical framework, and analytical focus that numbers alone cannot provide. By the same token, study of those sources will be amplified and made more concrete by use of the *Britannica World Data* to supply up-to-date geographic, demographic, economic, and financial data to illuminate the generalized and more impressionistic methodology of those works.

GLOSSARY

A number of terms that are used to classify and report data in the "Nations of the World" section require some explanation.

Those italicized terms that are used regularly in the country compilations to introduce specific categories of information (*e.g., birth rate, budget*) appear in this glossary in italic boldface type, followed by a description of the precise kind of information being offered and how it has been edited and presented.

All other terms are printed here in roman boldface type. Many terms have quite specific meanings in statistical reporting, and they are so defined here. Other terms have less specific application as they are used by different countries or organizations. Data in the country compilations based on definitions markedly different from those below will usually be footnoted.

Terms that appear in small capitals in certain definitions are themselves defined at their respective alphabetical locations.

Terms whose definitions are marked by an asterisk (*) refer to data supplied only in the larger two- to four-page country compilations.

access to services, a group of measures indicating the general population's level of access to public services, including electrical power, treated public drinking water, sewage removal, and fire protection.*

age breakdown, the distribution of a given population by age, usually reported here as percentages (of total population) based on the number of persons in 15-year age brackets. When substantial numbers of persons censused do not know, or state, their exact age, reported distributions may not total 100.0%.

area and population, a tabulation usually including the first-order administrative subdivisions of the country (such as the states of the United States), with capital or administrative seat, area, and population. When these subdivisions are especially numerous, or, occasionally, nonexistent, a regional, political, electoral, census, or other nonadministrative scheme of subdivisions has been substituted.

associated state, *see* (free) association; *see* state.

autonomous, *see* self-governing.

balance of payments, a statistical statement for a given period showing the balance among: (1) transactions in goods, services, and income between a country and the rest of the world; (2) changes in ownership or valuation of that country's monetary gold, SPECIAL DRAWING RIGHTS, and claims on and liabilities to the rest of the world; and (3) unrequited transfers and counterpart entries needed (in an accounting sense) to balance transactions and changes among any of the foregoing types of exchange that are not mutually offsetting. The United Nations *System of National Accounts* (SNA) provides a framework for international comparability in classifying such transactions, but detail of local law as to what constitutes a transaction, basis of valuation, reporting periods, and the size of a transaction visible to fiscal authorities all result in differences in the meaning of a particular national statement.

balance of trade, the net value of all international goods trade of a country, usually excluding reexports (goods received only for transshipment), and the percentage that this net represents of total trade.

Balance of trade refers only to the "visible" international trade of goods as recorded by customs authorities and is thus a segment of a country's BALANCE OF PAYMENTS, which takes all visible and invisible trade with other countries into account. (Invisible trade refers to imports and exports of money, financial instruments, and services such as transport, tourism, and insurance.) A country has a favourable balance of trade when the value of exports exceeds that of imports.

barrel (bbl), a unit of liquid measure. The barrel conventionally used for reporting crude petroleum and petroleum products is equal to 42 U.S. gallons or 159 litres. The number of barrels of crude petroleum per metric ton ranging typically from 6.45 to 8.13, depends upon the specific gravity of the petroleum. The world average is roughly 7.33 barrels per ton.

birth rate, the number of live births annually per 1,000 of midyear population. Birth rates for individual countries may be compared with the world annual average of 29 births per 1,000 population between 1980 and 1985.

budget, the annual receipts and expenditures of the central government for its activities only; does not include state, provincial, or local governments unless otherwise specified. Figures for budgets are limited to ordinary (recurrent) receipts and expenditures and wherever possible exclude capital expenditures, *i.e.,* funds for development and other special projects originating as foreign-aid grants or loans.

When both a recurrent and a capital budget exist for a single country, the former is the budget funded entirely from national resources (taxes, duties, excises, etc.) that would recur (be generated by economic activity) every year. It funds the most basic governmental services, those least able to stand interruption. The capital budget is usually funded, particularly in less developed countries, by external aid and may change its size considerably from year to year. Sometimes a capital budget is funded by transfers from a recurrent budget.

capital, usually the actual seat of administration and government of a political entity. When more than one capital exists, each is identified by kind; when interim arrangements exist during the creation of a new national capital, the de facto situation is described.

Anomalous cases where the de jure designation under the country's laws differs from actual local practice, such as Benin's designation of one capital in constitutional law, but

Abbreviations

Measurements

cu m	cubic metre
kg	kilogram
km	kilometre
kW	kilowatt
kW-hr	kilowatt-hour
metric ton-km	metric ton-kilometre
mi	mile
passenger-km	passenger-kilometre
passenger-mi	passenger-mile
short ton-mi	short ton-mile
sq km	square kilometre
sq m	square metre
sq mi	square mile
troy oz	troy ounce
yr	year

Political Units and International Organizations

CARICOM	Caribbean Community and Common Market
CUSA	Customs Union of Southern Africa
EEC	European Economic Community
FAO	United Nations Food and Agriculture Organization
IMF	International Monetary Fund
OECS	Organization of Eastern Caribbean States
U.A.E.	United Arab Emirates
U.K.	United Kingdom
U.S.	United States
U.S.S.R.	Union of Soviet Socialist Republics

Months

Jan.	January	Oct.	October
Feb.	February	Nov.	November
Aug.	August	Dec.	December
Sept.	September		

Miscellaneous

avg.	average
c.i.f.	cost, insurance, and freight
est.	estimate
excl.	excluding
f.o.b.	free on board
GDP	gross domestic product
GNP	gross national product
govt.	government
incl.	including
mo.	month(s)
n.a.	not available (in text)
NMP	net material product
no.	number
pl.	plural
pos.	position
pub. admin.	public administration
SDR	Special Drawing Right
svcs.	services
teacher tr.	teacher training
transp.	transportation
voc.	vocational
$	dollar (of any currency area)
£	pound (of any currency area)
...	not available (in tables)
—	none, less than half the smallest unit shown, or not applicable (in tables)

another in actual practice; or where international recognition does not support a country's claim, as with the proclamation by Israel of a capital on territory not fully recognized as part of Israel; or the proclamation of both a state and a capital on territory recognized as part of another state, as with the Turkish Republic of Northern Cyprus, are footnoted.

capital budget, *see* budget.

causes of death, as defined by the World Health Organization, "the disease or injury which initiated the train of morbid events leading directly to death, or the circumstances of accident or violence which produced the fatal injury." This principle, the "underlying cause of death," is the basis of the medical judgment as to cause; the statistical classification system according to which these causes are grouped and named is the *International List of Causes of Death,* the latest revision of which is the Ninth, although a number of countries continue to report according to the Eighth, or even earlier, versions. Reporting is usually in terms of events per 100,000 population.

chief of state/head of government, as prescribed or practiced, although divergences between form and practice may be considerable.

In general usage, the chief of state is the formal head of a national state. The primary responsibilities of the chief of state are usually ceremonial—convening legislatures, greeting foreign officials, hosting state dinners, and bestowing honours. The head of government of a national state is the chief executive officer who effectively exercises the majority of actual executive powers. The head of government of a dependent political unit is the chief executive officer, either appointive or elective, who wields the most local executive powers, regardless of administrative prerogatives reserved elsewhere. In some countries the two positions may be merged.

In communist countries the official given as the chief of state is the chairman of the policy-making organ, and the official given as the head of government is the chairman of the nominal administrative/executive organ.

c.i.f. (trade valuation): *see* imports.

colony, an area annexed to, or controlled by, an independent state but not an integral part of it; a non-self-governing territory. A colony has a charter and may have a degree of self-government. A crown colony is a colony originally chartered by the British government.

commonwealth (U.S.), a self-governing political entity associated with the United States; examples are the Philippines from 1935 to 1946 and Puerto Rico since 1952.

communications, collectively, the means available for the public transmission of information within a country. Data are provided for daily newspapers, their number and total circulation, and the per capita rate of circulation implied by that total; for radio, television, and telephone receivers, total numbers and rates of availability are supplied.

constant prices, an adjustment to the members of a time series (of values) to eliminate the effect of inflation year by year. It consists of referring all data in the series to a single year so that "real" change may be seen.

constitutional monarchy, *see* monarchy.

consumer price index, also known as the retail price index or the cost-of-living index, a series of index numbers assigned to the price of a selected "basket," or assortment, of basic consumer goods and services in a country or region to measure changes over time in prices paid by a typical household for those goods and services. Items included in the consumer price index are ordinarily determined by governmental surveys of typical household expenditures, and are assigned weights relative to their proportion of those expenditures.

coprincipality, *see* monarchy.

current prices, the valuation of a financial aggregate as of the year reported, without adjustment for inflation.

daily per capita caloric intake (supply), the calories equivalent to the known average daily supply of foodstuffs for human consumption in a given country divided by the population of the country. This estimated measure may differ from actual daily per capita consumption of food as a result of waste, inefficient distribution, and exploitation of sources of food not included in the known supply of foodstuffs. The daily per capita caloric intake of a country may be compared with the corresponding daily per capita caloric requirement. The latter is calculated by the Food and Agriculture Organization (FAO) of the United Nations from the age and sex distributions, average body weights, and environmental temperatures in a given country to determine the calories needed to sustain a person there at normal levels of activity and health. The daily per capita caloric requirement ranges from 2,200 to 2,500.

See also food.

de facto population, for a given area, the population composed of those present at a particular time, including temporary visitors and excluding legal residents temporarily absent.

de jure population, for a given area, the population composed of those legally resident at a particular time, excluding temporary visitors and including legal residents temporarily absent.

deadweight tonnage, the maximum weight of cargo, fuel, fresh water, stores, and persons that may safely be carried by a ship. It is customarily measured in long tons of 2,240 pounds each, equivalent to 1.016 metric tons. Deadweight tonnage is the difference between the tonnage of a fully loaded ship and the fully unloaded tonnage of that ship.

death rate, the number of deaths annually per 1,000 of midyear population. Death rates for individual countries may be compared with the world annual average of 11 deaths per 1,000 population between 1980 and 1985.

density (of population), usually the total area of the country divided into its DE FACTO POPULATION. Special adjustment is made for inland water or other uninhabitable areas, *e.g.,* excluding the lake area of Finland or the ice area of Greenland.

department, a first-order civil administrative subdivision. *Overseas department* (France), an overseas subdivision of the French Republic, almost equivalent to a department of metropolitan France, with elected representation in the French Parliament.

dependency, any area outside of and under the jurisdiction of an independent state but not formally annexed to it.

direct taxes, taxes levied directly on firms and individuals, such as taxes on income, profits, and capital gains. The immediate incidence, or burden, of direct taxes is on the firms and individuals thus taxed; the incidence of direct taxes on firms may, however, be passed on to consumers and other economic units in the form of higher prices for goods and services, with the result that the distinction between direct and indirect taxes is not always clear.

distribution of income/wealth, the portion of personal income or wealth accruing to households or individuals comprising each respective decile (tenth) or quintile (fifth) of a country's households or individuals.*

See also household income and expenditures.

divorce rate, the number of legal, civilly recognized divorces annually per 1,000 population.

doubling time, the number of complete years required for a country to double its population at its current rate of natural increase; it does not take into account expected demographic change during the period, such as changes in birth rate, death rate, or population migration.

earnings index, a series of index numbers comparing average wages in a collective industrial sample for a country or region with the same industries at a previous period to measure changes over time in those wages. It is most commonly collected for wages paid on a daily, weekly, or monthly basis. The scope of the earnings index varies from country to country; the index is often limited to earnings in manufacturing industries. The index for each country applies to all wage earners in

Dependent states*

Australia
- Christmas Island
- Cocos (Keeling) Islands
- Norfolk Island

Denmark
- Faeroe Islands
- Greenland

France
- French Guiana
- French Polynesia
- Guadeloupe
- Martinique
- Mayotte
- New Caledonia
- Réunion
- Saint Pierre and Miquelon
- Wallis and Futuna

Netherlands, The
- Aruba
- Netherlands Antilles

New Zealand
- Cook Islands
- Niue
- Tokelau

Norway
- Jan Mayen
- Svalbard

Portugal
- Macau

South Africa
- South West Africa/Namibia

United Kingdom
- Anguilla
- Bermuda
- British Virgin Islands
- Cayman Islands
- Falkland Islands
- Gibraltar
- Guernsey
- Hong Kong
- Isle of Man
- Jersey
- Montserrat
- Pitcairn Island
- Saint Helena and Dependencies
- Turks and Caicos Islands

United States
- American Samoa
- Guam
- Puerto Rico
- Trust Territory of the Pacific Islands
  - Marshall Islands
  - Federated States of Micronesia
  - Northern Mariana Islands
  - Palau
- Virgin Islands (of the U.S.)

*Excludes territories (1) to which Antarctic Treaty is applicable in whole or in part, (2) without permanent civilian population, (3) without internationally recognized civilian government (Western Sahara, Gaza Strip), or (4) representing unadjudicated unilateral or multilateral territorial claims.

a designated group and ordinarily takes into account basic wages (overtime is normally distinguished), bonuses, cost-of-living allowances, and contributions toward social security. Some countries include payments in kind. Contributions toward social security by employers are usually excluded, as are social security benefits received by wage earners.

See also price and earnings indexes.

economically active population, *see* population economically active.

education, tabulation of the principal elements of the country's educational establishment, classified as far as possible according to the country's own system of primary, secondary, and higher levels (the usual age limits for these levels being identified in parentheses), with total number of schools (physical facilities) and of teachers and students (whether full- or part-time). The student–teacher ratio is calculated whenever available data permit.

educational attainment, the distribution of the population with completed educations (who may be as young as 6 years) by the highest level of formal education attained or completed.

emirate, *see* monarchy.

empire, *see* monarchy.

enclave, a portion of a state separated geographically from its main part and having boundaries only with some other state or states. The surrounded area is said to be an enclave with respect to the area that borders on it and an *exclave* with respect to the state of which it is a part.

enterprise, a legal entity formed to conduct a business, which it may do from more than one establishment (place of business or service point).

ethnic/linguistic composition, ethnic, racial, or linguistic composition of a national population, reported here according to the most reliable breakdown published in official sources (when available) or external analysis (when the subject is not addressed in national sources [usually because of social or political sensitivities]).

exchange rate, the value of one currency compared to another, or to a standardized value such as the SPECIAL DRAWING RIGHT, or as mandated by local statute when one currency is "tied" by a par value to another. Rates given usually refer to market values when the currency itself is traded, or to the value of trade transactions either averaged over the period of a year, or as of a single date during the year.

exclave, *see* enclave.

exports, material goods legally leaving a country (or customs area) and subject to customs regulations. The total value and distribution by percentage of the major items (in preference to groups of goods) exported are given, together with the distribution of trade among major trading partners (usually single countries or trading blocs). Figures given for goods exported are free on board (f.o.b.) unless otherwise specified. The value of goods exported and imported free on board (f.o.b.) is calculated from the cost of production and excludes the cost of transport.

external debt, public and publicly guaranteed debt with a maturity of more than one year that is owed to nonnationals of a country, and is repayable in foreign currency, goods, or services. The debt may be an obligation of a national or subnational governmental body (or an agency of either), of an autonomous public body, or of a private debtor that is guaranteed for repayment by a public entity. The debt is usually either outstanding (contracted) or disbursed (drawn).

external territory (Australia), *see* territory.

fabricated metal, refined metal that has been processed from ingots into finer or more finished forms, such as rolled shapes.

farm, economic unit comprising an operator and the land on which agricultural operations are conducted. The legal tenure of the farm may be under the control of a person, partnership, or corporation. In the United States, a farm is such a place with annual gross sales of farm products of $1,000 or more.

federal, consisting of first-order political subdivisions that are prior to and independent of the central government in certain functions.

federal republic, *see* republic.

federation, a union of coequal political entities that retain some degree of autonomy within the union.

fertility rate, *see* total fertility rate.

financial aggregates, tabulation of seven-year time series, providing principal measures of the financial condition of a country: the exchange rate of the national currency against the U.S. dollar, the pound sterling, and the International Monetary Fund's SPECIAL DRAWING RIGHT (SDR); the amount and kind of international reserves (holdings of SDRs, gold, and foreign currencies) and reserve position of the country in the IMF; principal economic rates and prices (central bank discount rate, government bond yields, and industrial stock [share] prices). For BALANCE OF PAYMENTS, the origin in terms of component balance of trade items and balance of invisibles (net) is given.*

fish catch, the live-weight equivalent of the aquatic animals (including fish, crustaceans, mollusks, etc., but excluding whales, seals, and other aquatic mammals) caught in freshwater or marine areas by national fleets and landed in domestic or foreign harbours for commercial, industrial, or subsistence purposes.

f.o.b. (trade valuation): *see* exports.

food, *see* daily per capita caloric intake.

form of government/political status, the structure of a country's administration provided for in normal constitutional operation, whether or not suspended by extralegal military or civil action, although such de facto administrations are identified; together with the number of members (elected, appointed, and ex officio) for each legislative house, named according to its English rendering. Dependent states (*see* Table) are classified according to the status of their political association with the administering country.

(free) association, late stage in the process by which U.K. and U.S. dependencies achieve independence; it usually implies a relation between a largely self-governing dependency and its administering power that is capable of termination in full independence at the instance of the dependent state, though always in consultation with the administering power.

global social product, *see* material product.

gross domestic product (GDP), the total value of the final goods and services produced by residents and nonresidents within a given country during a given year. The GDP excludes the value of net income earned abroad, which is included in the GROSS NATIONAL PRODUCT (GNP). Unless otherwise noted, the value is given in current prices of the year indicated.

gross national product (GNP), the total value of final goods and services produced both from within a given country *and* from external (foreign) transactions in a given year. Unless otherwise noted, the value is given in current prices of the year indicated. GNP is equal to GROSS DOMESTIC PRODUCT adjusted by net factor income from abroad. That income comprises the income residents receive from abroad for factor services (labour, investment, and interest) less similar payments made to nonresidents who contributed to the domestic economy.

gross output in factor values, the total market value of goods and services produced by a country, industry, or firm, less all INDIRECT TAXES on production but including all current subsidies received in support of production activity.

gross output value in producers' prices, the total market value of goods and services produced by a country, industry, or firm, including all INDIRECT TAXES on production but excluding subsidies.

gross (register) ton, unit of measure of the permanently enclosed volume of a ship, less certain exempted spaces such as those devoted to machinery, bunkers, crew accommodations, and so on; the gross register tonnage of a ship is thus a rough estimation of its volumetric cargo capacity. The gross register ton is equivalent to 100 cubic feet or 2.83 cubic metres.

head of government, *see* chief of state/head of government.

health, total number of accredited physicians (according to World Health Organization criteria) by specialization and their ratio to the total population; similarly for hospital beds.

household income and expenditure, data for average household size (by number of individuals) and average household income. Sources of income and expenditures for major items of consumption are reported as percentages.

In general, household income is the amount of funds, usually measured in monetary units, received by the members (generally those 14 years old and over) of a HOUSEHOLD in a given time period. The income can be derived from wages or salaries, nonfarm or farm SELF-EMPLOYMENT, pensions, investments, rental property, public assistance, unemployment benefits, etc. The income of a household is expressed as a gross amount before deductions for taxes. Data on expenditure refer to consumption of personal or household goods and services; they normally exclude savings, taxes, and insurance; practice with regard to inclusion of credit purchases differs markedly.

households, groups of related or unrelated individuals living in the same housing unit, distributed by size of household. A family household is one composed principally of individuals related by blood or marriage.*

immigration, usually the number and origin of those immigrants admitted to a nation in a legal status that would eventually permit the granting of the right to settle permanently or to acquire citizenship.*

imports, material goods legally entering a country (or customs area) and subject to customs regulations; excludes financial movements. The total value and distribution by percentage of the major items (in preference to groups of goods) imported are given, together with the direction of trade among major trading partners (usually single countries), trading blocs (such as the European Economic Community), or customs areas (such as Belgium–Luxembourg). The value of goods imported is given free on board (f.o.b.) unless otherwise specified; f.o.b. is defined above under EXPORTS.

The principal alternate basis for reporting valuation of goods in international trade is that of cost, insurance, and freight (c.i.f.); its use is restricted to imports, as it comprises the principal charges needed to bring the goods to the customs house in the country of destination. Because it inflates the value of imports relative to exports, more countries have, latterly, been providing estimates of imports on an f.o.b. basis as well.

incorporated territory (U.S.), *see* territory.

independent, of a state, autonomous and controlling both its internal and external affairs.

indirect taxes, taxes levied on sales or transfers of selected intermediate goods and services, including excises, value-added taxes, and tariffs, that are ordinarily passed on to the ultimate consumers of the goods and services. Figures given for individual countries are limited to indirect taxes levied by their respective central governments unless otherwise specified.

infant mortality rate, the number of children born live who die before their first birthday per 1,000 live births. Total infant mortality includes neonatal mortality, which is deaths of children within one month of birth.

kingdom, *see* monarchy.

land use, distribution by classes of vegetational cover or economic use of the land area only (excluding inland water, for example, but not marshland), reported as percentages.

leisure, the principal uses or reported preferences in the use of the individual's free time for recreation, rest, or self-improvement.*

life expectancy, the number of years a person born within a particular population group (age cohort) would be expected to live, based on actuarial calculations. Life expectancy at birth is usually lower than after the first year of life because of infant mortality and is often used to compare the general health of populations of different countries.

literacy, the ability to read and write a language with some degree of competence; the precise degree constituting the basis of a particular national statement is usually defined by the national census and is often tested by the census enumerator. Elsewhere, particularly where much adult literacy may be the result of literacy campaigns, rather than passage through a formal educational system, definition and testing of literacy may be better standardized, albeit of a lower overall standard.

major cities, usually the five largest cities proper whose population is at least one-tenth that of the primate (largest) city; fewer will be listed if the size disparity is very great or there are fewer urban localities in the country. For multipage tables, ten or more* will be listed without regard for the size of the primate city. All populations will refer to the most specific administrative or demographically defined city proper, unless a municipality or METROPOLITAN AREA is specified.

manufacturing, mining, and construction enterprises, a detailed tabulation of the principal industries in these three sectors, showing for each industry the number of enterprises and employees, wages in that industry as a percentage of the general average wage, and the value of that industry's output in terms of value added or turnover.*

marriage rate, the number of legal, civilly recognized marriages annually per 1,000 population.

material (or social) product, in the national accounting systems of the socialist countries, the aggregate (sometimes "global") value of all "productive" services, generally omitting personal (nonpublic) services, financial activities, and the like that in conventional Western national accounts would contribute to the GROSS DOMESTIC PRODUCT, a more comprehensive measure that not only includes material output but also every identifiable service element of a national economy. Socialist countries that are members of the International Monetary Fund have begun, however, to report gross domestic, and national, product according to the *System of National Accounts* that forms the basis of international reporting of national accounts.

material well-being, a group of measures indicating the percentage of households or dwellings possessing certain goods or appliances, including automobiles, telephones, television receivers, refrigerators, air conditioners, and washing machines.*

merchant marine, the privately or publicly owned ships of a nation (limited to those in Lloyd's of London statistical reporting of 100 or more GROSS REGISTER TONS) that are employed in commerce.

metropolitan area, comprises a city and the region of dense, predominantly urban, settlement around the city; the population of the whole is usually economically dependent upon the central city to some degree, for employment, shopping, transportation services, and the like. Such areas are usually compact and contiguous, containing no physically discontinuous elements.

military expenditure, the apparent value of all identifiable military expenditure by the central government on hardware, personnel, pensions, research and development, etc., reported here as a percentage of the GNP, with a comparison to the world average.

military personnel, *see* total active duty personnel.

mobility, a measure of the rate at which individuals or households change dwellings (or remain in them), usually measured between censuses and including international as well as domestic migration.*

monarchy, a government in which the CHIEF OF STATE holds office, usually hereditarily, but sometimes electively, and for life (sometimes electively for a term). The state may be a coprincipality, emirate, empire, kingdom, principality, shaykhdom, or sultanate. The powers of the monarch may range from absolute, *i.e.,* he or she both reigns and rules, through various degrees of limitation of authority, to merely nominal, as in a constitutional monarchy, in which the titular monarch reigns but others, as elected officials, participate in the ruling.

monetary unit, currency of issue, or that in official use in a given country; name, spelling, and abbreviation in English according to International Monetary Fund recommendations or local practice; valuation usually according to market or commercial rates.

See also exchange rate.

natural increase, also called natural growth or the balance of births and deaths, the excess of births over deaths in a population; the rate of natural increase is the difference between the BIRTH RATE and the DEATH RATE of a given population. Natural increase is added to the balance of migration to calculate the total growth of that population.

net material product, *see* material product.

nonferrous metal, metal that does not contain significant quantities of iron and its alloys; usually this term is reserved for base metals such as copper or lead.

official language(s), that (or those) prescribed for actual day-to-day conduct and publication of a country's official business. Other languages may have local protection, may be permitted in legal action (such as a trial), or may be "national languages," for the protection of which special provisions have been made, but these are not deemed official.

official name, the local official form(s) short or long, of a country's legal name(s) taken from the country's constitution or from other official documents. The English-language form is usually the protocol form in use by the country, the U.S. Department of State, and the United Nations.

official religion, generally, any religion prescribed or given special protection by the constitution or legal system of the country.

organized territory (U.S.), *see* territory.

overseas department (France), *see* department.

overseas territory (France), *see* territory.

parliamentary state, *see* state.

part of a realm, a dependent political entity with some degree of self-government and having a special status above that of a colony (*e.g.,* the prerogative of rejecting for local application any law enacted by the motherland).

participation rate, a measure of the extent to which any adult population is engaged in economically productive activities. It is usually calculated as the percentage of those employed or economically active as compared to the larger population from whom they are drawn—those over age 15, or between the ages of 15 and 64, or some other nationally or demographically standardized group.

passenger-miles or **passenger-kilometres,** carriage by public or commercial means of a single passenger a distance of one mile (or kilometre); in aggregate the total miles or kilometres traveled by all passengers in a given country via specified means of transportation. Figures given for countries are often calculated from ticket sales and ordinarily exclude passengers carried free of charge.

people's republic, *see* republic.

place of birth/national origin, if the former, numbers of native- and foreign-born population of a country by actual place of birth; if the latter, any of several classifications, including those based on origin of passport at original admission to country, on cultural heritage of family name, on self-designated (often multiple) origin of (some) ancestors, and on other systems for assigning national origin.*

political status, *see* form of government/political status.

population, the number of persons actually present within the borders of a country, state, or other civil entity at the date of a census of population, survey, cumulation of a civil register, or other estimate. Unless otherwise specified, populations given are DE FACTO, referring to those actually present, rather than DE JURE, those legally resident but not necessarily present on the referent date. If a time series, noncensus year, or per capita ratio referring to a country's total population is cited, it will usually refer to midyear of the calendar year indicated. Populations for cities will usually refer to the city proper, *i.e.,* the legally bounded corporate entity, or the most compact, contiguous, demographically urban portion of the entity defined by the local authorities. Occasionally it has been necessary to provide city figures for METROPOLITAN AREAS when the relevant civil entity at the core of a major agglomeration had an unrepresentatively small population.

population economically active, the total number of persons (above a set age for economic labour, usually 10–15 years) in all employment statuses—self-employed, wage- or salary-earning, part-time, seasonal, unemployed, etc. The United Nations' *Yearbook of Labour Statistics* defines the economically active population as "all persons of either sex who furnish the supply of labour for the production of economic goods and services." National practices vary between countries as regards the treatment of such groups as armed forces, inmates of institutions, persons living on reservations, persons seeking their first job, seasonal workers and persons engaged in part-time economic activities. In some countries, all or part of these groups may be included among the economically active while in other countries the same groups may be treated as inactive. However, in general, the data on economically active population do not include students, women occupied solely in domestic duties, retired persons, persons living entirely on their own means, and persons wholly dependent upon others.

population projection, the expected population in 1990 and 2000, embodying the country's own projections wherever possible. Estimates of the future size of a population are usually based on assumed future levels of fertility, mortality, and migration. Projections in the tables, whether based on external estimates by the United Nations, World Bank, U.S. Department of Commerce, or on those of the country itself, unless otherwise specified, are medium (*i.e.,* most likely) variants.

price and earnings indexes, tabulation comparing the change in the CONSUMER PRICE INDEX over a period of seven years with the change in the general labour force's EARNINGS INDEX for the same period.

principality, *see* monarchy.

production, the physical quantity or monetary value of the output of an industry, usually tabulated here as the most important items or groups of items (depending on the available detail) of primary (extractive) and secondary (manufactured) production. When a single consistent measure of value, such as "value added," can be obtained, this is given, ranked by value; otherwise, and usually, quantity of production is given.

public debt, the current outstanding debt of all periods of maturity for which the central government and its organs are obligated. Publicly guaranteed private debt is excluded. For many developing countries, only figures for long-term EXTERNAL DEBT are available.

quality of working life, a group of measures including weekly hours of work (including overtime); rates per 100,000 for job-connected injury, illness, and mortality; coverage of labour force by insurance for injury, permanent disability, and death; work days lost to labour strikes and stoppages; and commuting patterns (length of journey to work in minutes and usual method of transportation).*

railroads, mode of transportation by self-driven or locomotive-drawn cars over fixed rails. Length of track figures given for individual countries ordinarily include the total length of all mainline and spurline running track and exclude switching sidings and yard track. Route length, when given, does not compound multiple running tracks laid on the same trackbed.

recurrent budget, *see* budget.

religious affiliation, distribution of practicing or nominal religionists, as a percentage of total population. This usually assigns to children the religion of their parents, since few sources conform to any other practice.

republic, a state with elected leaders and a centralized presidential form of government, local subdivisions being subordinate to the national government. *Federal republic* (as distinguished from a unitary republic), a republic in which power is divided between the central government and local subdivisions (*e.g.,* states, provinces, or cantons) in whom it is held to originate, the division of power being defined in a written constitution and jurisdictional disputes usually being settled in a court; sovereignty usually rests with the authority that has the power to amend the constitution. *People's republic,* in the dialectics of Communism, the first stage of development toward a communist state, the second stage being a *socialist republic. Soviet republic,* a republic governed by an elected soviet (council). *Unitary republic* (as distinguished from a federal republic), a republic in which power is held by a central authority and not derived from constituent subdivisions.

retail price index, *see* consumer price index.

roundwood, wood obtained from removals from forests, felled or harvested (with or without bark), in all forms.

rural, *see* urban–rural.

self-employment, work in which income derives from direct employment in one's own business, trade, or profession, as opposed to work in which salary or wages are earned from an employer.

self-governing, of a state, in control of its internal affairs in degrees ranging from control of most internal affairs (though perhaps not of public order or of internal security) to complete control of all internal affairs (*i.e.,* the state is autonomous) but having no control of external affairs or defense. In this work the term self-governing refers to the final state in the successive stages of increasing self-government, generally followed by independence.

service/trade enterprises, a detailed tabulation for the largest sectors of the domestic service economy—personal and business (but not government) services and wholesale and retail trade—providing: number of enterprises and employees, wages as a percentage of the general average wage, and the value of that industry's output in terms of value added or turnover.*

sex distribution, ratios, calculated as percentages, of male and female population to total population.

shaykhdom, *see* monarchy.

social deviance, a group of measures, usually reported as rates per 100,000, for principal categories of socially deviant behaviour, including crime, alcoholism, drug abuse, and suicide.*

social participation, a group of measures indicative of the degree of social engagement possessed by a particular population, including rates of participation or membership in public activities such as elections, voluntary work (or non-job-connected organizational memberships), trade unions, and religion.*

social security, public programs designed to protect individuals and families from loss of income owing to unemployment, old age, sickness or disability, or death and to provide other assistance, such as medical care or other services. Such programs may include social insurance, health and welfare programs, income maintenance programs, or other modes of public aid.

socialist republic, *see* republic.

soviet republic, *see* republic.

Special Drawing Right (SDR), a unit of account utilized by the International Monetary Fund (IMF) to denominate monetary reserves available under a quota system to IMF members to maintain the value of their national currency unit in international transactions.

state, an autonomous political entity; also, a first-order civil administrative subdivision, especially of a federated union. *Associated state,* an autonomous state in free association with another that conducts its external affairs and defense. *Parliamentary state,* an independent state in the Commonwealth that is governed by a parliament and that may recognize the British monarch as its titular head.

structure of gross domestic product and labour force, tabulation of the principal elements of the national economy, according to standard industrial categories, together with the distribution of the labour force (when possible POPULATION ECONOMICALLY ACTIVE) that generates the GROSS DOMESTIC PRODUCT.

subsidy, financial aid or grant given by a government to a private or public enterprise deemed to be in the public interest. Subsidies may be employed for a wide range of purposes, such as to support a vital industry (*e.g.,* agriculture, steelmaking) or to keep prices of certain goods low or stable.

sultanate, *see* monarchy.

tenure, the legal or customary forms and methods by which real property is held, such as lease, fee, title, loan, communal grant, and the like. Tenure of housing is the legal form of occupancy (owned, rented, or subrented) by a HOUSEHOLD of its living quarters.

territory, a noncategorized political dependency; a first-order administrative subdivision; a dependent political entity with some degree of self-government, but with fewer rights and less autonomy than a colony since there is no charter. *External territory* (Australia), a territory situated outside the area of the country. *Incorporated territory* (U.S.), a part of the United States with nonvoting representation in the Congress, but with most constitutional provisions extended to its inhabitants (*e.g.,* Alaska until 1959). *Organized territory* (U.S.), a territory for which a system of laws and a settled government have been provided by an act of the United States Congress. *Overseas territory* (France), an overseas subdivision of the French Republic with elected representation in the French Parliament, having individual statutes, laws, and internal organization adapted to local conditions. *Trust territory,* a non-self-governing former mandate of the League of Nations, administered by an independent state under trust arrangements with the United Nations, with the goal of eventual self-government. *Unincorporated territory* (U.S.), a dependency of the United States with limited self-government, whose inhabitants can claim the fundamental but not all of the procedural rights (*e.g.,* trial by jury) guaranteed by the United States Constitution.

theocracy, a state governed by hierarchs, *i.e.,* by religious leaders.

ton-miles or **ton-kilometres,** aggregate measure of freight hauled in a specified period of time, equal to tons of freight multiplied by the miles (or kilometres) each ton is transported. Figures given for individual countries indicate the aggregate ton-miles (or ton-kilometres) traveled by freight via the means of transportation indicated. Figures are compiled from way-bills (nationally) and ordinarily exclude mail, specie, passengers' baggage, the fuel and stores of the conveyance in question, and goods carried free of charge.

total active duty personnel, full-time active duty military personnel (excluding militias and part-time, informal, or other paramilitary elements), with their distribution by percentages among the major services.
See also military expenditure.

total fertility rate, the sum of the current age-specific birth rates for each of the child-bearing years (usually 15–49). It is the probable number of births, given present fertility data, that would occur during the lifetime of each woman (should she live to the end of her child-bearing years).

tourism, service industry comprising activities connected with domestic and international travel for pleasure or recreation; confined here to international travel and reported as expenditures in U.S.$ by tourists of all nationalities visiting a particular country and, conversely, the estimated expenditures of that country's nationals in all countries of destination.

transport, all mechanical methods of moving persons or goods. Data reported for national establishments include: for railroads, length of track and volume of traffic for passengers and cargo (but excluding mail, etc.); for roads, length of network and numbers of passengers cars and of commercial vehicles, *i.e.,* trucks and buses (no data on traffic); for merchant marine, the number of vessels of more than 100 gross tons and their total deadweight tonnage (no data on traffic); for air transport, traffic data for passengers and cargo, and the number of airports with scheduled flights.

trust territory, *see* territory.

unincorporated territory (U.S.), *see* territory.

unitary republic, *see* republic.

urban–rural, social characteristic of local or national populations, defined by predominant economic activities, "urban" referring to a group of predominantly nonagricultural pursuits, "rural" to agricultural pursuits. The distinction is usually based on the country's own definition of urban, which may depend only upon the size (population) or a place, or upon factors like employment, administrative status, density of housing, public services, etc.

value added, also called value added by manufacture, the GROSS OUTPUT VALUE of a firm or industry minus the cost of inputs—raw materials, supplies, and other inputs for which other firms are paid—required to produce it. Value added is the portion of the sales value or gross output value that is actually created by the firm or industry. Value added generally includes labour costs, administrative costs, and operating profits.

The Nations of the World

Afghanistan

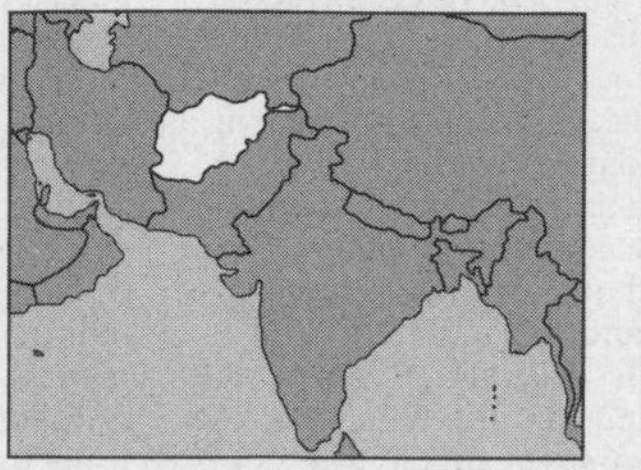

Official name: Da Afghānestān Dimukratik Jamhuriyat (Pashto); Jomhūrī-ye Demowkrātīk-e Afghānestān (Dari) (Democratic Republic of Afghanistan).
Form of government: unitary single-party people's republic with one transitional legislative body (Revolutionary Council [57])*.
Chief of state: President of the Revolutionary Council.
Head of government: Prime Minister.
Capital: Kābul.
Official languages: Pashto; Dari Persian.
Official religion: Islam.
Monetary unit: 1 afghani (AF) = 100 puls (puli); valuation (Oct. 1, 1986) 1 U.S.$ = AF 50.60; 1 £ = AF 73.12.

Area and population

	area		population
			1984
Regions	sq mi	sq km	estimate
Eastern	28,664	74,240	1,923,081
North-central	20,461	52,994	2,062,677
North-east	29,911	77,468	1,442,099
North-west	50,581	131,005	2,368,323
South-central	32,963	85,375	1,140,390
South-east	12,546	32,494	3,875,364
Western	76,699	198,649	1,554,500
TOTAL	251,825	652,225	14,366,434†

Demography

Density‡ (1986): persons per sq mi 67.1, persons per sq km 25.9.
Urban-rural§ (1985): urban 18.5%; rural 81.5%.
Sex distribution§ (1982): male 51.42%; female 48.58%.
Age breakdown§ (1982): under 15, 44.6%; 15–29, 26.8%; 30–44, 15.8%; 45–59, 8.5%; 60–74, 3.7%; 75 and over, 0.6%.
Population projection: (1990) 19,349,000; (2000) 24,180,000.
Doubling time§: 32 years.
Ethnic composition (1984): Pashtun 50%; Tadzhik 25%; Uzbek 9%; other 16%.
Religious affiliation (1983): Sunnī Muslim 87%; Shī'ī Muslim 12%; other 1%.
Major cities (1984): Kābul 1,373,572; Qandahār 277,508; Herāt 140,323.

Vital statistics

Birth rate per 1,000 population (1980–85): 48.9 (world avg. 29.0).
Death rate per 1,000 population (1980–85): 27.3 (world avg. 11.0).
Natural increase rate per 1,000 population (1980–85): 21.6 (world avg. 18.0).
Total fertility rate (avg. births per childbearing woman; 1980–85): 6.9.
Life expectancy at birth (1984): male 36.6 years; female 37.3 years.
Major reported illness (1981–82): tuberculosis 17,499 cases.

National economy

Budget (1981–82). Revenue: AF 40,464,100,000 (internal revenue sources 74.1%, of which natural gas revenues 43.9%; loans and grants-in-aid 25.9%). Expenditures: AF 40,464,100,000 (governmental ministries 50.0%; developmental budget 31.9%; foreign debt service 13.9%; surplus 1.6%).
Public debt (external, outstanding; 1982): U.S.$1,324,000,000.
Production (metric tons except as noted). Agriculture, forestry, fishing (1985): wheat 2,850,000, corn (maize) 800,000, grapes 510,000, rice 480,000, barley 340,000; livestock (number of live animals) 20,000,000 sheep, 3,750,000 cattle, 3,000,000 goats, 1,250,000 asses, 410,000 horses, 270,000 camels; roundwood 5,699,000 cu m; fish catch 1,500∥. Mining and quarrying (1983): salt 8,000; gypsum 5,000; barite 2,000. Manufacturing (by production value in afghanis; 1981–82): food products 3,762,000,000; textiles (all forms) 2,770,000,000; industrial chemicals (including fertilizers) 751,000,000; printing and publishing 539,000,000. Construction (1981–82): nonresidential 113,176 cu m, of which educational buildings 29,779, industrial buildings 21,171. Energy production (consumption): electricity (kW-hr; 1984) 1,045,000,000 (1,045,000,000); coal (metric tons; 1984) 170,000 (170,000); petroleum products (metric tons; 1984) 7,000 (322,000); natural gas (cu m; 1984) 2,715,000,000 (191,000,000).
Land use (1984): forested 2.9%; meadows and pastures 46.3%; agricultural and under permanent cultivation 12.4%; other 38.4%.
Gross national product (1984): U.S.$2,800,000,000 (U.S.$195 per capita).

Structure of net material product and labour force

	1982–83		1981–82	
	in value AF '000,000¶	% of total value	labour force	% of labour force
Agriculture	64,700	68.8	2,194,770	57.3
Manufacturing, mining, and public utilities	13,000	13.8	466,860	12.2
Construction	3,000	3.2	48,880	1.3
Transp. and commun.	3,300	3.5	65,650	1.7
Trade	8,600	9.1	126,100	3.3
Public administration	...	...	79,260	2.1
Public services	...	...	204,940	5.3
Other	1,500	1.6	642,360	16.8
TOTAL	94,000	100.0	3,828,820§	100.0

Population economically active§ (1981–82): total 3,828,820; activity rate of total population 27.8% (participation rates: ages 10–59, 43.8%; female 12.8%; unemployed 5.5%).

Price indexes (1980 = 100)

	1978	1979	1980	1981	1982	1983	1984
Consumer price index	78.8	99.1	100.0	104.9	111.0	107.7	116.0

Household size. Average household size§ (1979): 6.2.

Foreign trade

Balance of trade (current prices)♀

	1978	1979	1980	1981	1982	1983	1984
AF '000,000	−16,917	−8,586	5,432	3,555	629	−5,941	−4,569
% of total	35.9%	16.9%	9.7%	5.5%	0.9%	7.5%	5.4%

Imports (1981–82): AF 30,797,800,000 (vehicles 22.7%, petroleum products 18.0%, sugar 8.1%, woven fabrics of flax or ramie 7.9%, processed animal and vegetable oils 4.2%, tea 4.0%). *Major import sources:* U.S.S.R. 58.6%; Japan 12.6%; Hong Kong 4.4%; India 2.7%; West Germany 2.7%.
Exports (1981–82): AF 34,354,300,000 (natural gas 39.2%, dried fruit 25.2%, carpets and rugs 10.5%, fresh fruit 7.3%, wool and hides 3.4%). *Major export destinations:* U.S.S.R. 59.4%; Pakistan 8.8%; India 6.2%.

Transport and communications

Transport. Railroads (1984): length 6 mi, 10 km. Roads (1981–82): total length 11,789 mi, 18,974 km (paved 42%). Vehicles (1981–82): passenger cars 31,754; trucks and buses 30,997. Merchant marine: none. Air transport (1981–82): passenger-mi 117,750,000, passenger-km 189,500,000; short ton-mi cargo 14,500,000, metric ton-km cargo 21,169,000; airports (1986) 1.
Communications. Daily newspapers (1985): total number 12; total circulation 106,600; circulation per 1,000 population 5.9. Radio (1985): 135,000 receivers (1 per 118.5 persons). Television (1985): 12,800 receivers (1 per 1,250 persons). Telephones (1984): 31,200 (1 per 566 persons).

Education and health

Education (1984)	schools	teachers	students	student/ teacher ratio
Primary	754	14,865	545,959	36.7
Secondary	332	6,943	99,729	14.4
Voc., teacher tr.δ	16	666	7,360	11.1
Higher	5	1,283	13,450	10.5

Educational attainment (1980). Percent of population over age 25 having: no formal schooling 88.5%; some primary education 6.8%; complete primary 0.3%; some secondary 1.2%; postsecondary 3.2%. *Literacy* (1980): total population over age 15 literate 1,436,000 (20.0%); males 33.2%; females 5.8%.
Health (1981–82): physicians 1,215 (1 per 13,092 persons); hospital beds 6,875 (1 per 2,314 persons); infant mortality rate per 1,000 live births (1980–85) 194.0.
Food (1979–81): daily per capita caloric intake 2,055 (vegetable products 90%, animal products 10%); 84% of FAO recommended minimum.

Military

Total active duty personnel (1985): 47,000 (army 85.1%, air force 14.9%). *Military expenditure as percent of GNP* (1981): 3.0% (world 5.8%); per capita expenditure U.S.$6.

*The provisional Basic Principles of the Democratic Republic of Afghanistan, adopted in 1980, provides for the eventual election of a Grand National Assembly. †Total includes 2,615,000 nomads not distributed by region. Afghan refugees in Pakistan number almost 3,000,000 and in Iran 1,850,000. ‡Includes both settled and nomadic population. §Based on settled population only. ∥1983. ¶At 1978 prices. ♀Fiscal years beginning March 21. δIncludes technical institutes.

Albania

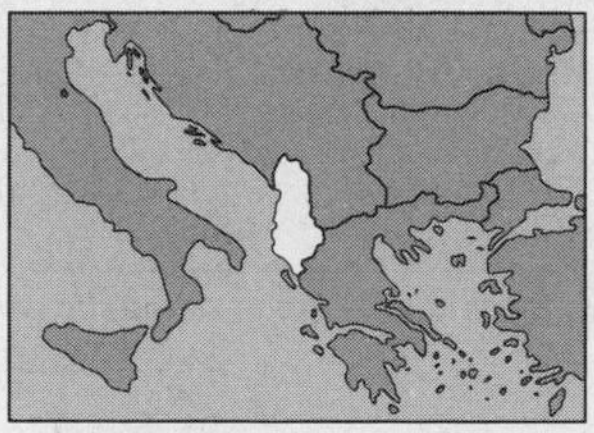

Official name: Republika Popullore Socialiste e Shqipërisë (People's Socialist Republic of Albania).
Form of government: unitary single-party socialist republic with one legislative house (People's Assembly [250]).
Chief of state: President (Chairman of the Presidium of the People's Assembly).
Head of government: Premier (Chairman of the Council of Ministers).
Capital: Tiranë.
Official language: Albanian.
Official religion: none.
Monetary unit: 1 lek = 100 qindars; valuation (Oct. 1, 1986) 1 U.S.$ = 6.99 leks; 1 £ = 10.10 leks.

Area and population

Provinces	Capitals	area sq mi	area sq km	population 1983 estimate
Berat	Berat	396	1,026	157,300
Dibër	Peshkopi	605	1,568	137,800
Durrës	Durrës	327	848	220,600
Elbasan	Elbasan	572	1,481	213,200
Fier	Fier	454	1,175	216,400
Gjirokastër	Gjirokastër	439	1,137	61,200
Gramsh	Gramsh	268	695	39,300
Kolonjë	Erseka	311	805	22,500
Korçë	Korçë	842	2,181	201,300
Krujë	Krujë	234	607	94,600
Kukës	Kukës	514	1,331	88,400
Lezhë	Lezhë	185	479	54,200
Librazhd	Librazhd	391	1,013	64,100
Lushnjë	Lushnjë	275	712	117,800
Mat	Burrel	397	1,028	68,700
Mirditë	Rrëshen	335	867	45,800
Përmet	Përmet	359	930	37,100
Pogradec	Pogradec	280	725	62,700
Pukë	Pukë	399	1,033	46,100
Sarandë	Sarandë	424	1,097	78,200
Shkodër	Shkodër	976	2,528	210,200
Skrapar	Çorovoda	299	775	42,500
Tepelenë	Tepelenë	315	817	46,100
Tiranë	Tiranë	478	1,238	316,100
Tropojë	Bajram	403	1,043	40,900
Vlorë	Vlorë	621	1,609	158,200
TOTAL		11,100*	28,748	2,841,300

Demography

Population (1986): 3,020,000.
Density (1986): persons per sq mi 272.0, persons per sq km 105.1.
Urban-rural (1984): urban 33.7%; rural 66.3%.
Sex distribution (1984): male 51.60%; female 48.40%.
Age breakdown (1980): under 15, 37.3%; 15–29, 28.9%; 30–44, 16.5%; 45–59, 10.2%; 60–74, 5.5%; 75 and over, 1.6%.
Population projection: (1990) 3,400,000; (2000) 4,000,000.
Doubling time: 28 years.
Ethnic composition (1980): Albanian 93.1%; Gypsy 2.5%; Greek 2.4%; other 2.0%.
Religious affiliation (1980): Muslim 20.5%; Christian 5.4%; atheist 18.7%; nonreligious 55.4%.
Major cities (1983): Tiranë 206,100; Durrës 72,400; Shkodër 71,200; Elbasan 69,900; Vlorë 61,100.

Vital statistics

Birth rate per 1,000 population (1985): 26.2 (world avg. 29.0).
Death rate per 1,000 population (1985): 5.8 (world avg. 11.0).
Natural increase rate per 1,000 population (1985): 20.4 (world avg. 18.0).
Total fertility rate (avg. births per childbearing woman; 1980): 3.6.
Marriage rate per 1,000 population (1984): 9.0.
Divorce rate per 1,000 population (1982): 0.8.
Life expectancy at birth (1983): male 67.9 years; female 72.9 years.
Major causes of death per 100,000 population: n.a.; however, major diseases include tuberculosis, hypertension, liver and stomach disorders; malaria and syphilis, formerly widespread, are now practically nonexistent.

National economy

Budget (1985). Revenue: 9,250,000,000 leks (surplus from state enterprises 93.0%, other 7.0%). Expenditures: 9,200,000,000 leks (national economy 52.5%, social and cultural services 26.7%, defense 18.5%, administration 1.5%).
Public debt (1984): U.S.$5,400,000,000†.
Tourism (1984): number of tourists 6,000; receipts from visitors, n.a.; expenditures by nationals abroad, n.a.
Production (metric tons except as noted). Agriculture, forestry, fishing (1984): wheat 600,000, corn (maize) 400,000, vegetables and fruit except grapes 353,000, sugar beets 320,000, potatoes 136,000, grapes 83,000, sunflower seeds 53,000, barley 34,000, oats 30,000, olives 25,000, tobacco 18,000; livestock (number of live animals) 1,200,000 sheep, 700,000 goats, 600,000 cattle, 200,000 pigs, 74,000 mules and asses, 43,000 horses; roundwood 2,330,000 cu m; fish catch (1983) 4,000. Mining and quarrying (1984): ferronickel ores 1,080,000; chromite ore 960,000; salt 70,000; copper (metal content) 12,600; nickel 6,000. Manufacturing (1983): bitumen (asphalt) 1,800,000; cement 1,100,000; distillate fuel oils 272,000; nitrogenous and phosphate fertilizers 102,000; raw sugar 40,000; paper and paperboard 17,000‡; olive oil 7,000; wine 220,000 hectolitres§; beer 160,000 hectolitres‡; cigarettes 6,200,000,000 units§; cotton and woolen fabrics 60,900,000 m§. Construction (1980): 1,821,000,000 leks. Energy production (consumption): electricity (kW-hr; 1984) 3,800,000,000 (3,800,000,000); coal (metric tons; 1984) 2,010,000 (1,985,000); crude petroleum (barrels; 1984) 25,020,000 (25,020,000); petroleum products (metric tons; 1984) 1,340,000 (1,340,000); natural gas (cu m; 1984) 427,077,000 (427,077,000).
Gross national product (at current market prices; 1982): U.S.$2,580,000,000 (U.S.$930 per capita).

Structure of net material product and labour force

	1983 value	% of total value	labour force	% of labour force
Agriculture	...	34.1	645,400 ‖	54.2
Manufacturing, mining, public utilities	...	43.3	252,700	21.2
Construction	...	7.8	80,700	6.8
Transportation and communication			33,400	2.8
Trade	...	14.8	53,900	4.6
Pub. admin., defense			87,200	7.3
Other			37,500	3.1
TOTAL	...	100.0	1,190,800	100.0

Population economically active (1983): total 1,090,800; activity rate of total population 38.4% (participation rates: ages 15–64, n.a.; female 46.0%; unemployed, n.a.).
Price and earnings indexes: n.a.
Household income and expenditure. Average household size (1984) 5.5; average annual income per household: n.a.; source of income: n.a.; expenditure: n.a.
Land use (1983): forested 45.3%; meadows and pastures 19.7%; agricultural and under permanent cultivation 25.9%; other 9.1%.

Foreign trade

Balance of trade (current prices)

	1978	1979	1980	1981	1982	1983
'000,000 leks	...	100	...	...	...	...
% of total	...	5.3	...	...	...	...

Imports (1982): U.S.$373,500,000 (mineral fuels and lubricants 33.3%, machinery and transport equipment 22.2%, chemicals and related products 16.6%, food and live animals 16.6%, consumer goods 5.9%). *Major import sources:* U.S.S.R. and Eastern European countries 35.6%; European Economic Community countries 28.7%; United States 4.6%; Japan 2.8%.
Exports (1982): U.S.$350,700,000 (mineral fuels 27.1%, crude minerals and metalliferous ores 26.2%, electricity 13.2%, food and food preparations 13.2%, consumer products 9.8%). *Major export destinations:* U.S.S.R. and Eastern European countries 35.7%; European Economic Community countries 31.2%; United States 3.8%; Japan 1.1%.

Transport and communications

Transport. Railroads (1984): length 253 mi, 408 km; passenger-mi 181,000,000§, passenger-km 291,000,000§; short ton-mi cargo 87,000,000§, metric ton-km cargo 127,000,000§. Roads (1981): total length 13,049 mi, 21,000 km (paved 14%). Vehicles (1970): passenger cars 3,500; trucks and buses 11,200. Merchant marine (1985): vessels (100 gross tons and over) 20; total deadweight tonnage 79,940. Air transport: passengers, n.a.; cargo, n.a.; airports (1986) with scheduled flights 1.
Communications. Daily newspapers (1982): total number 2; total circulation 145,000§; circulation per 1,000 population 52.0§. Radio (1985): total number of receivers 210,000 (1 per 13.3 persons). Television (1985): total number of receivers 185,740 (1 per 15 persons). Telephones, n.a.

Education and health

Education (1983)

	schools	teachers¶	students	student/teacher ratio
Primary (age 6–13)	1,621	26,440	557,300	...
Secondary (age 14–17)	20	1,250	32,500	...
Voc., teacher tr.	313	3,750	123,700	...
Higher	8	1,240	17,500	14.1

Educational attainment, n.a. *Literacy* (1970): total population over age 15 literate 1,234,376 (75.0%).
Health (1982): physicians 3,861 (1 per 720 persons); hospital beds (1978) 17,000 (1 per 151 persons); infant mortality rate per 1,000 live births 44.0.
Food (1980–82): daily per capita caloric intake 3,060 (vegetable products 87%, animal products 13%); 127% of FAO recommended minimum requirement.

Military

Total active duty personnel (1985): 40,400 (army 74.3%, navy 7.9%, air force 17.8%). *Military expenditure as percent of GNP* (1981): 8.1% (world 5.8%); per capita expenditure U.S.$69.

*Detail does not add to total given because of rounding. †Estimated total since 1949. ‡1980. §1981. ‖Partially estimated. ¶1982.

Algeria

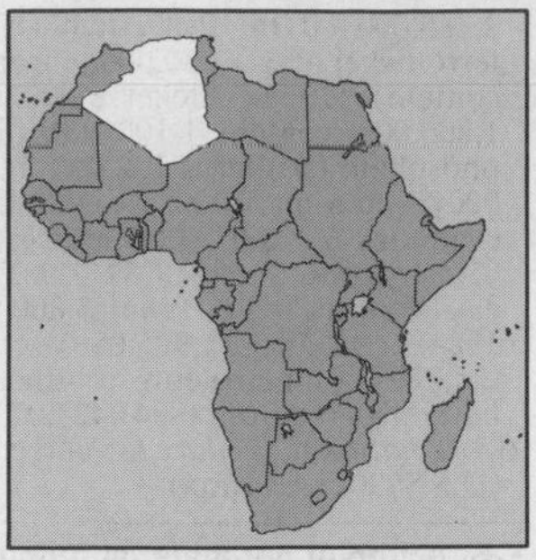

Official name: al-Jumhūrīyah al-Jazā'irīyah ad-Dīmuqrāṭīyah ash-Sha'bīyah (Arabic) (Democratic and Popular Republic of Algeria).
Form of government: socialist republic with one legislative house (The National People's Assembly [282]).
Head of state and government: President.
Capital: Algiers.
Official language: Arabic.
Official religion: Islam.
Monetary unit: 1 Algerian dinar (DA) = 100 centimes; valuation (Oct. 1, 1986) 1 U.S.$ = DA 4.63; 1 £ = DA 6.69.

Area and population

		area		population
Wilāyat*	**Capitals**	sq mi	sq km	1984 estimate
Adrar	Adrar	163,127	422,498	161,936
Alger	Algiers	304	786	2,442,303
Annaba	Annaba	1,347	3,489	650,096
Batna	Batna	5,746	14,882	691,079
Béchar	Béchar	118,147	306,000	184,069
Bejaïa	Bejaïa	1,329	3,442	659,040
Biskra	Biskra	42,366	109,728	662,778
Blida	Blida	1,430	3,704	1,126,303
Bouira	Bouira	1,744	4,517	454,805
ech-Cheliff	ech-Cheliff	3,350	8,677	1,040,563
Constantine	Constantine	1,375	3,562	809,245
Djelfa	Djelfa	8,844	22,905	403,500
Guelma	Guelma	3,330	8,624	633,733
Jijel	Jijel	1,431	3,705	604,319
Laghouat	Laghouat	43,264	112,052	391,817
Mascara	Mascara	2,257	5,846	526,644
Médéa	Médéa	3,361	8,704	575,305
Mostaganem	Mostaganem	2,712	7,024	896,767
M'Sila	M'Sila	7,654	19,825	540,013
Oran	Oran	703	1,820	889,800
Ouargla	Ouargla	215,921	559,234	261,760
Oum el-Bouaghi	Oum el-Bouaghi	3,136	8,123	464,806
Saïda	Saïda	41,227	106,777	450,594
Sétif	Sétif	3,996	10,350	1,176,673
Sidi bel Abbès	Sidi bel Abbès	4,497	11,648	604,773
Skikda	Skikda	1,833	4,748	597,530
Tamanrasset	Tamanrasset	214,673	556,000	62,680
Tébessa	Tébessa	6,400	16,575	439,638
Tíaret	Tíaret	9,056	23,456	731,542
Tizi Ouzou	Tizi Ouzou	1,450	3,756	1,028,864
Tlemcen	Tlemcen	3,585	9,284	678,025
TOTAL		919,595	2,381,741	20,841,000

Demography

Population (1986): 22,566,000.
Density (1986): persons per sq mi 24.5, persons per sq km 9.5.
Urban-rural (1984): urban 66.6%; rural 33.4%.
Sex distribution (1984): male 49.94%; female 50.06%.
Age breakdown (1984): under 15, 46.4%; 15–29, 26.6%; 30–44, 12.7%; 45–59, 8.3%; 60–74, 4.5%; 75 and over, 1.5%.
Population projection: (1990) 25,300,000; (2000) 36,000,000.
Doubling time: 22 years.
Ethnic composition (1980): Arab 83.5%; Berber 16.1%; French 0.4%.
Religious affiliation (1980): Sunnī Muslim 99.1%; Roman Catholic 0.5%; other 0.4%.
Major cities (1984): Algiers 2,442,303.

Vital statistics

Birth rate per 1,000 population (1983): 40.5† (world avg. 29.0); legitimate, n.a.; illegitimate, n.a.
Death rate per 1,000 population (1983): 8.8† (world avg. 11.0).
Natural increase rate per 1,000 population (1983): 31.7† (world avg. 18.0).
Total fertility rate (avg. births per childbearing woman; 1981): 6.4.
Marriage rate per 1,000 population (1982): 6.3†.
Divorce rate per 1,000 population: n.a.
Life expectancy at birth (1981): male 61.1 years; female 62.2 years.
Major infectious diseases per 100,000 population (1982): scarlet fever 696.5; chicken pox 151.4; dysentery 63.4.

National economy

Budget (1986). Revenue: DA 90,500,000,000 (hydrocarbons 32.0%). Expenditures: DA 104,500,000,000 (current expenditures 56.9%, investment 43.1%).
Public debt (external, outstanding; 1984): U.S.$12,052,000,000.
Tourism (1983): receipts from visitors, n.a.; expenditures by nationals abroad U.S.$476,000,000.
Production (metric tons except as noted). Agriculture, forestry, fishing (1985): wheat 1,650,000, barley 1,295,000, potatoes 800,000, grapes 469,000, tomatoes 305,000, oranges 260,000, dates 220,000; livestock (number of live animals) 13,111,000 sheep, 3,010,000 goats, 1,750,000 cattle, 180,000 camels; roundwood 1,688,000 cu m; fish catch 64,500‡. Mining and quarrying (1983): iron ore 4,200,000; barite 110,000; clay 57,000; zinc 52,700; sulfur 15,000; lead 6,000; copper 730; silver 120,000 troy oz. Manufacturing (1983): cement 4,776,000; pig iron and ferroalloys 1,113,400; crude steel 891,500; refined sugar 188,800. Construction (1981): residential 28,000 units. Energy production (consumption): electricity (kW-hr; 1984) 11,450,000,000 (11,440,000,000); coal (metric tons; 1984) 7,000 (1,197,000); crude petroleum (barrels; 1984) 233,175,000 (48,362,000); petroleum products (metric tons; 1984) 30,977,000 (19,577,000); natural gas (cu m; 1984) 24,269,000,000 (5,125,000,000).
Gross national product (at current market prices; 1984): U.S.$50,680,000,000 (U.S.$2,400 per capita).

Structure of gross domestic product and labour force

	1983			
	in value DA '000,000	% of total value	labour force§	% of labour force
Agriculture	16,607.6	8.2	960,000	27.0
Mining	62,356.6	31.0 }	475,000	13.3
Manufacturing	22,505.0	11.1 }		
Construction	30,577.1	15.1 }	609,000	17.1
Public utilities	2,073.9	1.0 }		
Transp. and commun.	11,162.1	5.5	158,000	4.4
Trade	31,322.8	15.5 }		
Finance	...	... }	568,000	15.9
Services	6,061.6	3.0 }		
Pub. admin., defense	...	...	797,000	22.3
Other	19,343.3	9.6	...	...
TOTAL	202,010.0	100.0	3,567,000	100.0

Population economically active (1982): total 4,163,643; activity rate of population 21.0% (participation rates: over age 10, 38.9%; female 6.8%; unemployed, n.a.).

Price and earnings indexes (1980 = 100)

	1979	1980	1981	1982	1983	1984	1985
Consumer price index	91.3	100.0	114.6	122.3	127.9	136.3	156.4
Earnings index	...	...	...	...	...	...	...

Household income and expenditure. Average household size (1980) 4.9; average annual income per household: n.a.; expenditure: n.a.
Land use (1984): forested 1.8%; meadows and pastures 13.5%; agricultural and under permanent cultivation 3.1%; built-up, wasteland, and other (mostly desert) 81.6%.

Foreign trade

Balance of trade (current prices)

	1979	1980	1981	1982	1983	1984
DA '000,000	+6,939	+19,493	+19,836	+11,151	+14,686	+18,672
% of total	10.4%	19.4%	19.0%	10.1%	13.9%	17.2%

Imports (1983): DA 49,782,000,000 (machines and transport equipment 36.0%, of which transport equipment 10.2%; food and food preparations 18.5%; consumer products 8.0%). *Major import sources:* France 23.5%; West Germany 11.2%; Italy 8.2%; Spain 7.0%; Japan 6.0%; United States 6.0%.
Exports (1983): DA 60,722,000,000 (mineral fuels and lubricants 98.5%, of which crude petroleum 23.4%). *Major export destinations:* European Economic Community 59.7%; United States 22.4%; Japan 1.9%.

Transport and communications

Transport. Railroads (1983): route length 2,576 mi, 4,146 km; passenger-mi 493,440,000, passenger-km 794,120,000; short ton-mi cargo 1,829,500,000, metric ton-km cargo 2,670,700,000. Roads (1981): total length 44,795 mi, 72,091 km (paved 54%). Vehicles (1983): passenger cars 574,506; trucks and buses 360,139. Merchant marine (1985): vessels (100 gross tons and over) 145; total deadweight tonnage 1,943,157. Air transport ‖ (1984): passenger-mi 1,560,772,000, passenger-km 2,511,824,000; short ton-mi cargo 9,073,000, metric ton-km cargo 13,246,000; airports (1986) with scheduled flights 22.
Communications. Daily newspapers (1985): total number 4; total circulation 480,000; circulation per 1,000 population 22.1. Radio (1985): 3,500,000 receivers (1 per 6 persons). Television (1985): 1,445,000 receivers (1 per 14 persons). Telephones (1983): 434,000 (1 per 47 persons).

Education and health

Education (1983–84)

	schools	teachers	students	student/teacher ratio
Primary (age 6–11)	10,266	109,173	3,336,536	30.6
Secondary (age 12–18)	1,178¶	61,098	1,452,389	23.8
Voc., teacher tr.♀	71	2,292	26,218	11.4
Higher	15¶	1,851¶	103,899	...

Educational attainment (1971). Percent of adult population over age 25 having: no formal schooling 84.4%; primary education 13.0%; secondary education 2.2%; higher 0.3%; unknown 0.4%. *Literacy* (1980): total population over age 15 literate 4,342,300 (41.8%); males literate 2,771,400 (55.6%); females literate 1,570,900 (29.1%).
Health (1983): physicians 7,464 (1 per 2,748 persons); hospital beds 41,188 (1 per 498 persons); infant mortality rate per 1,000 live births (1982) 92.2.
Food (1981–83): daily per capita caloric intake 2,663 (vegetable products 88%, animal products 12%); 108% of FAO recommended minimum requirement.

Military

Total active duty personnel (1986): 169,000 (army 88.8%, navy 4.1%, air force 7.1%). *Military expenditure as percent of GNP* (1984): 2.0% (world 6.1%); per capita expenditure U.S.$44.

*Separate area and population figures are not available for the 16 new wilāyāt created in February 1984. †For Algerian population only. ‡1983. §Employed persons only. ‖ Air Algérie international flights only. ¶1981–82. ♀1980–81.

Andorra

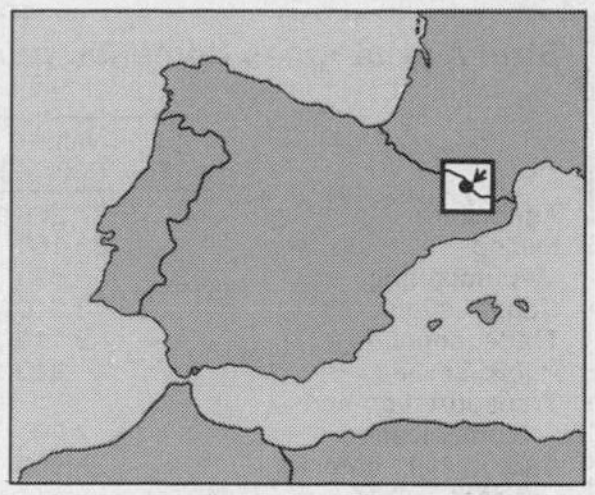

Official name: Principat (Co-Principat) or Senyoriu (Co-Senyoriu) d'Andorra; les Valls d'Andorra (Principality [or Co-Principality] of Andorra; the Valleys of Andorra).
Form of government: co-principality with one nonpartisan legislative house (General Council of the Valleys [28]).
Chiefs of state: President of France; Bishop of Urgel, Spain.
Head of government: Chief executive.
Capital: Andorra la Vella.
Official language: Catalan.
Official religion: Roman Catholicism.
Monetary unit: There is no local currency of issue; the French franc and Spanish peseta are both in circulation. 1 franc (F) = 100 centimes; 1 peseta (Pta) = 100 céntimos.
Valuation (Oct. 1, 1986)
1 U.S.$ = F 6.64, 1 £ = F 9.60;
1 U.S.$ = Ptas 133.50,
1 £ = Ptas 192.91.

Area and population

Parishes	Capitals	area sq mi	area sq km	population 1986 census
Andorra la Vella	Andorra la Vella	49*	127*	17,711
Canillo	Canillo	74	191	1,121
Encamp	Encamp			5,508
La Massana	La Massana	25	65	11,955
Les Escaldes-Engordany	—	*	*	3,140
Ordino	Ordino	33	85	1,015
Sant Julià de Lòria	Sant Julià de Lòria	*	*	5,427
TOTAL		181	468	45,877

Demography

Population (1986): 46,000.
Density (1986): persons per sq mi 255.9, persons per sq km 98.9.
Urban-rural (1986): urban 64.7%; rural 35.3%.
Sex distribution (1986): male 53.12%; female 46.88%.
Age breakdown (1986): under 15, 19.0%; 15–29, 27.3%; 30–44, 26.4%; 45–59, 14.8%; 60–74, 9.4%; 75 and over, 3.1%.
Population projection: (1990) 53,000; (2000) 80,000.
Doubling time: 93 years.
Ethnic composition (1986): Spanish 55.6%; Andorran 27.4%; French 7.2%; Portuguese 4.0%; British 1.5%; other 4.3%.
Religious affiliation (1980): Roman Catholic 94.2%; Jewish 0.4%; Jehovah's Witnesses 0.3%; Protestant 0.2%; other 4.9%.
Major cities (1986): Andorra la Vella 15,639; Les Escaldes 11,955; Encamp 3,535.

Vital statistics

Birth rate per 1,000 population (1984): 11.4 (world avg. 29.0).
Death rate per 1,000 population (1984): 4.0 (world avg. 11.0).
Natural increase rate per 1,000 population (1984): 7.4 (world avg. 18.0).
Total fertility rate (avg. births per childbearing woman): n.a.
Marriage rate per 1,000 population (1984): 3.1.
Divorce rate per 1,000 population: n.a.
Life expectancy at birth: (1980; both sexes) 70 years.
Major causes of death per 100,000 population: n.a.; however, health problems are those of a developed country—cardiovascular disease, hypertension, malignant neoplasms (cancers).

National economy

Budget (1983). Revenue: Ptas 3,719,700,000 (excise taxes on imported consumer goods and gasoline 93.9%; additional revenue is derived from a 3% tax on alcoholic beverages). Expenditures: Ptas 3,683,400,000 (primarily administrative services and education; Andorra has virtually no military or social welfare expenditures).
Production. Agriculture, forestry, fishing (1981): potatoes 472 metric tons, tobacco 264 metric tons, and unknown amounts of hay, rye, buckwheat, olives, and grapes; livestock (number of live animals; 1982) 9,000 sheep, 1,115 cattle, 217 horses. Mining and quarrying (1982): building stone and sometimes worked, small deposits of lead and iron ore. Manufacturing (1982): ceramics, cigars and cigarettes, alcoholic beverages (including anisette and brandy), clothing, jewelry, textiles, and wooden furniture. Construction (1984): 90 buildings totaling 83,834 sq m were authorized for construction. Energy production (consumption): electricity (kW-hr; 1984) 94,576,000 (166,675,000†); coal, none (n.a.); crude petroleum, none (n.a.); petroleum products, none (n.a.); natural gas, none (n.a.).
Population economically active (1986): total 21,484; activity rate of total population 46.8% (participation rates: ages 15–64, n.a.; female, n.a.; unemployed, n.a.).

Price and earnings indexes (1980 = 100)‡

	1979	1980	1981	1982	1983	1984	1985
Consumer price index	86.5	100.0	114.6	131.0	147.0	163.6	178.0
Earnings index	...	...	...	...	...	...	...

Public debt: n.a.
Gross national product (at current market prices; 1983): U.S.$360,000,000 (U.S.$9,000 per capita)§.

Structure of labour force

	1986 labour force	1986 % of labour force
Agriculture and forestry	132	0.6
Mining	571	2.7
Manufacturing	957	4.5
Construction	1,754	8.2
Public utilities	1,266	5.9
Transportation and communication	1,832	8.5
Trade	5,777	26.9
Finance	1,281	6.0
Pub. admin., defense	650	3.0
Services and hotel	5,209	24.3
Other	2,025	9.4
TOTAL	21,454	100.0

Household income and expenditure. Average household size: n.a.; income per household: n.a.; source of income: n.a.; expenditure: n.a.
Land use (1985): forested 23.7%; meadows and pastures 44.2%; agricultural and under permanent cultivation 4.0%; other 28.1%.
Tourism (1983): receipts from tourist arrivals, n.a.; expenditures by nationals abroad, n.a.; number of tourist arrivals, approximately 10,000,000 annually, most of whom do not stay overnight; number of hotels 235; number of hotel rooms 9,085.

Foreign trade

Balance of trade (current prices)

	1980	1981	1982	1983	1984
Ptas '000,000	−25,879	−28,090	−30,197	−32,011	−35,795
% of total	91.9%	94.8%	91.5%	91.6%	92.1%

Imports (1984): Ptas 37,335,000,000, of which from France Ptas 21,388,-000,000, from Spain Ptas 15,947,000,000 (includes fuels, food, perfumes, clothing, and radio and television sets) ‖ .
Exports (1984): Ptas 1,540,000,000, of which to France Ptas 773,000,000, to Spain Ptas 767,000,000 (includes wooden furniture, handicrafts, cigarettes, cigars, leather goods, and electricity).

Transport and communications

Transport. Railroads: none; however, both French and Spanish railways stop near the border. Roads (1981): total length 138 mi, 220 km (paved 55%). Vehicles (1985): passenger cars 25,000; trucks and buses, n.a. Merchant marine (1986): vessels (100 gross tons and over) none. Airports with scheduled flights (1986): none; the airport at nearby Seo de Urgel, Spain, has scheduled daily flights to Barcelona and Palma (on Majorca).
Communications. Daily newspapers (1983): total number 1; circulation (2 principal weeklies) 6,000; circulation per 1,000 population 144.5. Radio (1984): total number of receivers 8,000 (1 per 5.2 persons). Television (1984): total number of receivers 4,000 (1 per 10.4 persons). Telephones (1982): 17,719 (1 per 2.1 persons).

Education and health

Education (1985–86)

	schools	teachers	students	student/teacher ratio
Primary (age 6–12)	21	214	5,310	24.8
Secondary (age 12–18)	8	53	1,086	20.5
Voc., teacher tr.	5	37	692	18.7
Higher	...	...	...	...

Educational attainment, n.a.; education is compulsory to age 16, however. *Literacy* (1981): total population literate (virtually 100%).
Health: physicians (1984) 53 (1 per 784 persons); hospital beds (1981) 110 (1 per 325 persons); infant mortality rate per 1,000 live births (1980) 16.0.
Food (1980–82)¶: daily per capita caloric intake 3,420 (vegetable products 68%, animal products 32%); 137% of FAO recommended minimum requirement.

Military

Total active duty personnel (1982): none. France and Spain provide for Andorra's defense. The city of Barcelona police and French *gendarmerie* alternate year-by-year in assisting the 32-member Andorran police force. *Military expenditure as a percent of central government expenditure* (1981): 0.0001% (world 19.0%).

*Andorra la Vella includes Les Escaldes-Engordany and Sant Julià de Lòria. †Most of the consumption is produced within Andorra; the remainder is imported from Spain. ‡In Spanish pesetas. §Trade, tourism (including winter-season sports, fairs, and festivals), and the banking system (of some importance as a tax haven for foreign financial investment and transactions) are the primary sources of GNP. ‖ Imported manufactured items are less expensive in Andorra than in neighbouring countries because they are duty free. As a result, smuggling remains a profitable sideline for some. ¶Composite values derived from Spanish and French food data.

Angola

Official name: República Popular de Angola (People's Republic of Angola).
Form of government: people's republic with one legislative house (People's Assembly [208]).
Head of state and government: President.
Capital: Luanda.
Official language: Portuguese.
Official religion: none.
Monetary unit: 1 kwanza (Kw) = 100 lwei; valuation (Oct. 1, 1986) 1 U.S.$ = Kw 29.92; 1 £ = Kw 43.23.

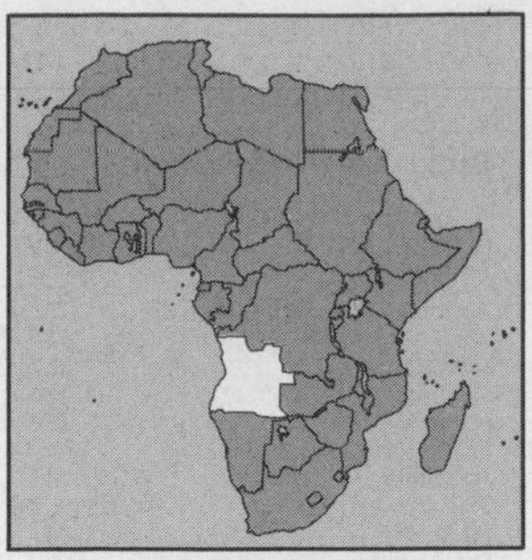

Area and population

		area*		population
Provinces	**Capitals**	sq mi	sq km	1986 estimate
Bengo	Caxito	14,173	36,708	140,000
Benguela	Benguela	15,116	39,151	681,000
Bié	Kuito	27,149	70,317	914,000
Cabinda	Cabinda	2,744	7,107	110,000
Huambo	Huambo	12,796	33,141	1,235,000
Huíla	Lubango	30,499	78,992	794,000
Kuando Kubango	Menongue	76,671	198,577	165,000
Kuanza Norte	N'Dalatando	7,717	19,988	451,000
Kuanza Sul	Sumbe	21,281	55,117	674,000
Kunene	N'Giva	29,327	75,956	239,000
Luanda	Luanda	570	1,477	1,082,000
Lunda Norte	Lucapa	39,685	102,784	296,000
Lunda Sul	Saurimo	29,860	77,336	142,000
Malanje	Malanje	33,686	87,247	809,000
Moxico	Lwena	77,870	201,683	270,000
Namibe	Namibe	22,043	57,090	75,000
Uíge	Uíge	23,728	61,455	574,000
Zaire	M'Banza Kongo	14,281	36,989	183,000
TOTAL		481,350†‡	1,246,700†‡	8,835,000‡§

Demography

Population (1986): 8,823,000.
Density (1986): persons per sq mi 18.3, persons per sq km 7.1.
Urban-rural (1986): urban 30%; rural 70%.
Sex distribution (1986): male 51.12%; female 48.88%.
Age breakdown (1986): under 15, 42.2%; 15–29, 27.5%; 30–44, 16.4%; 45–59, 9.5%; 60 and over, 4.4%.
Population projection: (1990) 9,700,000; (2000) 12,100,000.
Doubling time: 32 years.
Ethnic composition (1978): Ovimbundu 35.7%; Mbundu 22.3%; Kongo 12.6%; Luimbe 8.6%; Chokwe 8.2%; Nyaneka 4.2%; Humbe 2.5%; Ambo 2.4%; Lunda 0.9%; other 2.6%.
Religious affiliation (1980): affiliated Christian 65.7%, of which Roman Catholic 55.1%, Protestant 9.2%; nominal Christian 24.3%; tribal religionist 9.5%; other 0.5%.
Major cities (mid-1980s): Luanda 960,000; Lubango 105,000; Namibe 100,000 ‖.

Vital statistics

Birth rate per 1,000 population (1984): 47.0 (world avg. 29.0).
Death rate per 1,000 population (1983): 25.0 (world avg. 11.0).
Natural increase rate per 1,000 population (1983): 22.0 (world avg. 18.0).
Total fertility rate (avg. births per childbearing woman; 1984): 6.4.
Marriage rate per 1,000 population: n.a.
Divorce rate per 1,000 population: n.a.
Life expectancy at birth (1984): male 42.0 years; female 44.0 years.
Major causes of death per 100,000 population: n.a.; however, major diseases include malaria, tuberculosis, and tetanus.

National economy

Budget (1984). Revenue: Kw 74,556,000,000 (taxes 72.9%; state returns from mixed enterprises 14.0%; other 13.1%). Expenditures: Kw 82,302,000,000 (economic and social development 26.7%; education, health, and other social services 21.0%; administration 11.5%; defense 11.5¶; other 5.0%).
Public debt (external, outstanding; 1983): U.S.$799,000,000.
Tourism: receipts from visitors, n.a.; expenditures by nationals abroad, n.a.
Price and earnings indexes: n.a.
Production (metric tons except as noted). Agriculture, forestry, fishing (1984): cassava 1,950,000, sugarcane 360,000, bananas 280,000, corn (maize) 260,000, sweet potatoes 180,000, palm oil 40,000, coffee 27,000, peanuts (groundnuts) 20,000; livestock (number of live animals) 3,350,000 cattle, 955,000 goats, 460,000 pigs, 245,000 sheep; roundwood 9,003,000 cu m♀; fish catch 112,414♀. Mining and quarrying (1984): diamonds, of which gem quality 750,000 carats, industrial quality 250,000 carats; cement 350,000; salt 50,000. Manufacturing (1981): raw sugar 65,000; crude steel 10,000; soaps 6,000; paints 5,000; beer 1,250,000 hectolitres♂; matches 55,000 boxes; cigarettes 2,400,000,000 units; shirts 2,300,000 units; skirts 967,000 units; leather shoes 306,000 pairs. Construction: n.a. Energy production (consumption): electricity (kW-hr; 1984) 1,790,000,000 (1,790,000,000); coal (metric tons; 1984) none (negligible); crude petroleum (metric tons; 1984) 10,292,000 (3,250,000); petroleum products (metric tons; 1984) 971,000 (486,000); natural gas (cu m; 1984) 1,557,000,000 (n.a.).
Gross national product (at current market prices; 1982): U.S.$7,634,000,000 (U.S. $1,030 per capita).

Structure of gross domestic product and labour force

	1982		1981	
	in value Kw '000,000	% of total value	labour force	% of labour force
Agriculture	77,200	38.2	1,123,360	59.0
Mining	31,160	15.4		
Manufacturing	4,690	2.3		
Construction	3,310	1.6		
Trade, finance	9,110	4.5	304,640	16.0
Public utilities	810	0.4		
Transportation and communication	7,990	4.0		
Pub. admin., defense	23,580	11.7		
Services	...	...	476,000	25.0
Other	44,120	21.8		
TOTAL	201,970	100.0‡	1,904,000	100.0

Population economically active (1983): total 1,986,000; activity rate of total population 24.5% (participation rates: ages 15–64, n.a.; female 9.5%; unemployed, n.a.).
Household income and expenditure. Average household size (1980) 4.8; average annual income per household: n.a.; source of income: n.a.; expenditure: n.a.
Land use (1983): forested 42.9%; meadows and pastures 23.3%; agricultural and under permanent cultivation 2.8%; other 31.0%.

Foreign trade

Balance of trade (current prices)

	1979	1980	1981	1982	1983	1984
Kw '000,000	+11,400	+4,100	+3,200	+22,024	+32,959	+41,261
% of total	16.9%	3.8%	3.1%	26.6%	41.5%	52.3%

Imports (1984): U.S.$636,000,000 (mostly purchases of military hardware, food [particularly grains], and other machinery and transport equipment). *Major import sources* (1981): Portugal 15%; France 11%; U.S.S.R. 9%; South Africa 9%; Brazil 8%; United Kingdom 7%.
Exports (1984): U.S.$2,029,000,000 (1981; crude petroleum 74%, petroleum products 10%, diamonds 10%, coffee 5%). *Major export destinations* (1981): United States 49%; The Bahamas 15%; Spain 7%; Brazil 7%.

Transport and communications

Transport. Railroads (1986): route length 1,834 mi, 2,952 km; passenger journeys 7,622,000□; cargo transported 725,000 metric tons□. Roads (1984): total length 44,900 mi, 72,300 km (paved 12%). Vehicles (1984): passenger cars 56,625; trucks and buses 29,000. Merchant marine (1985): vessels (100 gross tons and over) 95; total deadweight tonnage 127,431. Air transport◇ (1984): passenger-mi 570,025,000, passenger-km 917,368,000; short ton-mi cargo 17,158,500, metric ton-km cargo 25,051,000; airports (1986) with scheduled flights 19.
Communications. Daily newspapers (1984): total number 4; total circulation 111,500; circulation per 1,000 population 13.5. Radio (1985): total number of receivers 230,000 (1 per 38 persons). Television (1985): total number of receivers 25,000 (1 per 343 persons). Telephones (1981): 65,900 (1 per 120 persons).

Education and health

Education (1982–83)

	schools	teachers	students	student/ teacher ratio
Primary (age 7–10)	6,308	32,004	1,178,430	36.8
Secondary (age 11–16)	...	3,870△	124,858	34.2
Voc., teacher tr.	...	410△	7,060	12.7
Higher	1	316	2,764	8.7

Educational attainment, n.a. *Literacy* (1980): total population over age 15 literate 1,196,000 (about 28%); males literate 771,000 (36.2%); females literate 425,000 (19.3%).
Health (1980): physicians 436 (1 per 17,000 persons); hospital beds 20,700 (1 per 359 persons); *infant mortality rate* per 1,000 live births (1984) 144.0.
Food (1979–81): daily per capita caloric intake 2,353 (vegetable products 92%, animal products 8%); 100% of FAO recommended minimum requirement.

Military

Total active duty personnel (1985): 43,000✝ (army 92.9%, navy 3.0%, air force 4.1%). *Military expenditure as percent of GNP* (1982): 18.6% (world 5.7%); per capita expenditure U.S.$99.

*Provincial detail and totals independently reported and converted. †Total contains adjustments of unspecified nature amounting to 2,156 sq mi (5,585 sq km). ‡Detail does not add to total given because of rounding. §Unified national estimates and projections based on sample surveys, partial censuses, and analysis of provincial vital statistics. ‖1981 estimate; population (1970 census) of other important towns was: Huambo 61,885; Lobito 59,258; and Benguela 40,996. ¶According to unofficial estimates, defense consumed more than 50% of the budget in 1981. ♀1983. ♂1979. □1981. ◇TAAG airline only. △1981–82. ✝In 1985, about 20,000 Cuban troops and several hundred other Soviet-bloc advisers and technicians were assisting government forces.

Antigua and Barbuda

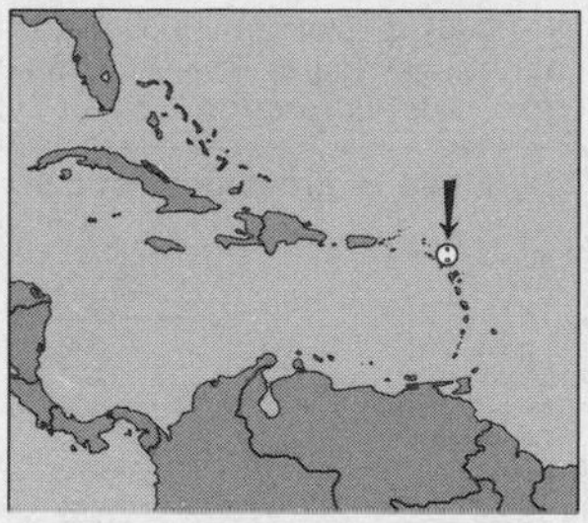

Official name: Antigua and Barbuda.
Form of government: constitutional monarchy with appointed Senate (17) and elected House of Representatives (17).
Chief of state: British Monarch represented by governor-general.
Head of government: Prime Minister.
Capital: Saint John's.
Official language: English.
Official religion: none.
Monetary unit: 1 East Caribbean dollar (EC$) = 100 cents; valuation (Oct. 1, 1986) 1 U.S.$ = EC$2.70; 1 £ = EC$3.90.

Area and population

	area		population
	sq mi	sq km	1984 estimate
Parishes*			
Saint George	10.2	26.4	
Saint John's	26.2	67.9	
Saint Mary	25.1	65.0	78,000
Saint Paul	17.7	45.8	
Saint Peter	12.8	33.2	
Saint Phillip	16.0	41.4	
Islands*			
Barbuda	62.0	160.6	1,500
Redonda	0.5	1.3	†
TOTAL	170.5	441.6	79,500

Demography

Population (1986): 81,400.
Density (1986): persons per sq mi 477.4, persons per sq km 184.3.
Urban-rural (1985): urban 30.8%; rural 69.2%.
Sex distribution (1983): male 48.00%; female 52.00%.
Age breakdown (1985): under 15, 37.2%; 15–29, 30.8%; 30–44, 12.8%; 45–59 11.5%; 60–74, 6.4%; 75 and over, 1.3%.
Population projection: (1990) 86,000; (2000) 99,000.
Doubling time: 72 years.
Ethnic composition (1980): black 94.4%; mulatto 3.5%; white 1.3%; other 0.8%.
Religious affiliation (1980): Anglican 44.5%; other Protestant (largely Moravian, Methodist, and Seventh-day Adventist) 41.6%; Roman Catholic 10.2%; Rastafarian 0.7%; other 3.0%.
Major cities (1982): Saint John's 30,000; Codrington 1,200.

Vital statistics

Birth rate per 1,000 population (1983): 15.0 (world avg. 29.0); legitimate 18.7%; illegitimate 81.3%.
Death rate per 1,000 population (1983): 5.2 (world avg. 11.0).
Natural increase rate per 1,000 population (1983): 9.8 (world avg. 18.0).
Total fertility rate (avg. births per childbearing woman; 1980–85): 2.1.
Marriage rate per 1,000 population (1983): 2.4.
Divorce rate per 1,000 population (1983): 0.4.
Life expectancy at birth (1982): 72.0 years.
Major causes of death per 100,000 population (1983): malignant neoplasms (cancers) 62.6; hypertensive heart disease 42.2; blood poisoning 30.7; cerebrovascular disease 28.1; pneumonia 25.6; diseases of pulmonary circulation 25.6.

National economy

Budget (1983). Revenue: EC$88,812,000 (indirect taxes 76.5%, of which consumer taxes 39.7%, import duties 27.9%; company income taxes 11.8%; transfer payments from abroad 4.6%). Expenditure: EC$94,595,000 (general public services 18.3%; education 13.8%; transportation and communication 10.3%; public order 9.3%; health 7.4%; interest on public debt 6.9%; defense 1.7%).
Tourism: receipts from visitors (1984) U.S.$65,000,000; expenditures by nationals abroad (1983) U.S.$6,000,000.
Production (metric tons except as noted). Agriculture, forestry, fishing (1983): sugarcane 4,600‡, sweet potatoes 353, tomatoes 285, yams 273, mangoes 249, pineapples 181, cabbage 166, carrots 148, cucumbers 140, pumpkins 116; livestock (number of live animals; 1984): 16,000 cattle, 12,000 sheep, 12,000 goats, 70,000 poultry§; fish catch (1983) marine fishes 1,013, lobsters 50. Mining and quarrying (1983): gravel 49,212. Manufacturing (value of production in EC$; 1983): clothing 24,000,000; mattresses 4,500,000; stoves 3,300,000; refrigerators 1,700,000; rum 1,200,000. Construction (1983): total building applications 557; gross value EC$60,400,000. Energy production (consumption): electricity (kW-hr; 1983) 65,500,000 (53,100,000); coal, none (none); crude petroleum (barrels; 1984) none (negligible); petroleum products (metric tons; 1984) negligible ‖ (47,000); natural gas, none (none).
Population economically active (1983): total 30,843; activity rate of total population 39.4% (participation rates: over age 15, 56.2%; female 39.6%; unemployed [1984] 21.0%).

Price and earnings indexes (1980 = 100)

	1978	1979	1980	1981	1982	1983	1984
Consumer price index	72.2	84.0	100.0	111.5	116.3	118.5	123.5
Weekly earnings index	76.5	85.8	100.0	...	...	...	...

Household income and expenditure. Average household size (1970) 4.2; average annual income per household: n.a.; source of income: n.a.; expenditure¶: food and nonalcoholic beverages 42.9%, housing 23.3%, transportation 10.0%, clothing and footwear 7.4%, energy 5.6%, alcoholic beverages and tobacco 3.6%, furniture, utensils, and other 7.2%.
Gross national product (at current market prices; 1984): U.S.$150,000,000 (U.S.$1,890 per capita).

Structure of gross domestic product and labour force

	1984		1982	
	in value EC$'000,000	% of total value	labour force♀	% of labour force
Agriculture, fishing	20.1	5.4	2,090	9.0
Quarrying	2.8	0.8	60	0.3
Manufacturing	18.2	4.9	1,718	7.4
Construction	22.8	6.2	2,577	11.1
Public utilities	10.0	2.7	340	1.5
Transp. and commun.	62.1	16.8	2,575	11.1
Trade, restaurants, and hotels	101.8	27.6	5,201	22.4
Finance, real estate	70.3	19.0	778	3.3
Pub. admin., defense	58.5	15.8	7,883	33.9
Services	20.2	5.5		
Other	−17.5ð	−4.7ð	...	...
TOTAL	369.30	100.0	23,222	100.0

Public debt (external, outstanding; 1983□): U.S.$20,000,000.
Land use (1983): forested 15.9%; meadows and pastures 6.8%; agricultural and under permanent cultivation 18.2%; other 59.1%.

Foreign trade◇

Balance of trade (current prices)

	1978	1979	1980	1981	1982	1983
EC$'000,000	−77	−169	−158	−207	−189	−178
% of total	53.2%	72.1%	51.2%	52.9%	63.6%	64.2%

Imports (1983): EC$227,859,000 (food and live animals 24.1%, of which meat 5.9%, cereals 4.0%, fruits and vegetables 3.8%; machinery and transport equipment 23.9%, of which motor vehicle parts 6.0%; chemicals 8.7%; clothing 6.4%; beverages 4.1%). *Major import sources:* United States 49.6%; United Kingdom 13.2%; Caricom states (The Bahamas, Barbados, Belize, Guyana, Jamaica, and Trinidad and Tobago) excluding the OECS 7.9%; Canada 5.5%.
Exports (1983): EC$49,688,000 (reexports 39.6%, of which miscellaneous manufactured articles 17.7%; machinery 15.6%; domestic exports 60.4%, of which miscellaneous manufactured articles 32.9%, machinery 7.9%, chemicals 4.7%, beverages and tobacco 4.5%). *Major export destinations:* Caricom states excluding the OECS 44.3%; United States 12.9%; other OECS 12.9%; United Kingdom 6.8%.

Transport and communications

Transport. Railroads△ (1982): 48 mi (78 km). Roads (1984): total length 341 mi, 548 km (paved 44%). Vehicles (1983): passenger cars 7,120; trucks and buses 1,271. Merchant marine (1985): vessels (100 gross tons and over) 3; total deadweight tonnage 443. Air transport (1981): passenger-mi 67,691,-000†; passenger-km 108,938,000†; short ton-mi cargo 14,812,000⊕, metric ton-km cargo 21,625,000⊕; airports (1986) with scheduled flights 1.
Communications. Daily newspapers: none. Radio (1985): total number of receivers 21,000 (1 per 3.8 persons). Television (1985): total number of receivers 17,000 (1 per 4.7 persons). Telephones (1983): 10,470 (1 per 7.5 persons).

Education and health

Education (1983)

	schools	teachers	students	student/ teacher ratio
Primary (age 5–10)	48	426	9,933	23.3
Secondary (age 11–16)	16	331	4,197	12.7
Voc., teacher tr.	1	...	...	...
Higher	...	...	...	...

Educational attainment (1970). Percent of total population having: no schooling 15.0%; primary education 79.2%; secondary 4.5%; higher 1.3%. *Literacy* (1980): total adult population literate 88%.
Health (1983): physicians 31 (1 per 2,523 persons); hospital beds 226** (1 per 346 persons); infant mortality rate per 1,000 live births (1982) 32.0.
Food (1980–82): daily per capita caloric intake 2,039 (vegetable products 72%, animal products 28%); 82% of FAO recommended minimum requirement.

Military

Total active duty personnel (1983): *c.* 700. *Military expenditure as percent of GNP:* n.a.

*Community councils are the actual organs of local governments. †Uninhabited. ‡No sugarcane harvested in 1984 or 1985 due to low prices and lack of rainfall. §1982. ‖ The country's oil refinery has been closed since 1974 except for a brief interval in 1982–83. ¶Weights of consumer price index components. ♀Wage earners and self-employed only. ðLess imputed bank service charges. □Includes external long-term private debt not guaranteed by the government. ◇Excludes crude petroleum and petroleum products. △Serving sugarcane plantations only. †Leeward Island Air Transport Company. ⊕1982 Seagreen airlines. **Excludes beds for mental patients.

Argentina

Official name: República Argentina (Argentine Republic).
Form of government: federal republic, with two legislative houses (Senate [46]; Chamber of Deputies [254]).
Head of state and government: President.
Capital: Buenos Aires.
Official language: Spanish.
Official religion: Roman Catholicism.
Monetary unit: 1 austral (pl. australes)* ($a) = 1,000 pesos; valuation (Oct. 1, 1986) 1 U.S.$ = $a 1.05; 1 £ = $a 1.52.

Area and population

Provinces	Capitals	area sq mi	area sq km	population 1985 estimate
Buenos Aires	La Plata	118,754	307,571	12,034,000
Catamarca	San Fernando del Valle de Catamarca	38,984	100,967	227,000
Chaco	Resistencia	38,469	99,633	777,000
Chubut	Rawson	86,752	224,686	307,000
Córdoba	Córdoba	65,161	168,766	2,598,000
Corrientes	Corrientes	34,054	88,199	715,000
Entre Ríos	Paraná	30,418	78,781	961,000
Formosa	Formosa	27,825	72,066	331,000
Jujuy	San Salvador de Jujuy	20,548	53,219	474,000
La Pampa	Santa Rosa	55,382	143,440	228,000
La Rioja	La Rioja	34,626	89,680	180,000
Mendoza	Mendoza	57,462	148,827	1,322,000
Misiones	Posadas	11,506	29,801	673,000
Neuquén	Neuquén	36,324	94,078	301,000
Río Negro	Viedma	78,384	203,013	460,000
Salta	Salta	59,759	154,775	751,000
San Juan	San Juan	34,614	89,651	512,000
San Luis	San Luis	29,633	76,748	231,000
Santa Cruz	Río Gallegos	94,187	243,943	134,000
Santa Fe	Santa Fe	51,354	133,007	2,647,000
Santiago del Estero	Santiago del Estero	52,222	135,254	651,000
Tucumán	San Miguel de Tucumán	8,697	22,524	1,090,000
Other federal entities				
Distrito Federal	Buenos Aires	77	200	2,924,000
Tierra del Fuego	Ushuaia	8,210	21,263	36,000
TOTAL		1,073,399†	2,780,092	30,564,000

Demography

Population (1986): 31,030,000.
Density (1986): persons per sq mi 28.9, persons per sq km 11.2.
Urban-rural (1985): urban 84.6%; rural 15.4%.
Sex distribution (1985): male 49.61%; female 50.39%.
Age breakdown (1980): under 15, 30.4%; 15–29, 23.9%; 30–44, 18.8%; 45–59, 15.1%; 60–74, 9.0%; 75 and over, 2.8%.
Population projection: (1990) 33,064,000; (2000) 38,752,000.
Doubling time: 44 years.
Ethnic composition (1983): European 98%; mestizo 2%.
Religious affiliation (1981): Roman Catholic 92.8%; other 7.2%.
Major cities (1980): Buenos Aires 2,924,000 (Greater Buenos Aires 9,766,000‡); Córdoba 969,000; Rosario 876,000; La Plata 455,000.

Vital statistics

Birth rate per 1,000 population (1985): 25.0 (world avg. 29.0); (1979) legitimate 70.2%; illegitimate 27.4%; unknown 2.4%.
Death rate per 1,000 population (1985): 9.0 (world avg. 11.0).
Natural increase rate per 1,000 population (1985): 16.0 (world avg. 18.0).
Total fertility rate (avg. births per childbearing woman; 1985): 3.4.
Marriage rate per 1,000 population (1983): 6.0.
Divorce rate per 1,000 population: §.
Life expectancy at birth (1981): male 68.6 years; female 73.3 years.
Major causes of death per 100,000 population (1981): circulatory diseases 371.9; malignant neoplasms (cancers) 148.8; respiratory diseases 51.8; accidents 42.8.

National economy

Budget (1983). Revenue: $a 106,321,000,000 ‖ (excise taxes 24.1%, social security taxes 19.9%, general sales tax 13.0%, export duties 8.9%, import duties 6.3%, income taxes 4.3%, property tax 3.2%). Expenditures: $a 148,792,000,000 ‖ (social security and welfare 33.3%, economic services 22.7%, defense 9.1%, general public services 8.8%, education 7.6%, health 1.4%).
Public debt (external, outstanding; 1984): U.S.$28,670,700,000.
Tourism (1984): receipts from visitors U.S.$602,000,000; expenditures by nationals abroad U.S.$681,000,000.
Production (metric tons except as noted). Agriculture, forestry, fishing (1985): sugarcane 14,140,000, wheat 13,600,000, corn (maize) 11,900,000, soybeans 6,500,000, sorghum 6,200,000, grapes 2,279,000, potatoes 2,097,000¶, alfalfa 1,522,000¶, flax 550,000, raw cotton 536,100; livestock (number of live animals; 1984) 53,500,000 cattle, 30,000,000 sheep; roundwood 13,375,000 cu m¶; fish catch 405,200. Mining and quarrying (1984): gold 24,000 troy oz; silver 2,500,000 troy oz; uranium 100. Manufacturing (by value in $a '000 ‖ ; 1985): motor vehicles 629,978; cast iron, steel, and ferroalloys 475,695; processed sugar 314,056; iron and steel pipes and tubes 291,232; paper and paper products 52,000; cigars and cigarettes 48,443. Construction (authorized; 1985) 1,255,700 sq m♀. Energy production (consumption): electricity (kW-hr; 1984) 44,914,000,000 (44,909,000,000); coal (metric tons; 1984) 509,000 (962,000); crude petroleum (barrels; 1984) 176,130,000 (174,822,000); petroleum products (metric tons; 1984) 21,700,000 (20,013,000); natural gas (cu m; 1984) 13,760,000,000 (15,971,000,000).
Gross national product (1984): U.S.$67,150,000,000 (U.S.$2,230 per capita).

Structure of gross domestic product and labour force

	1985♂ in value $a '000,000	1985♂ % of total value	1980 labour force	1980 % of labour force
Agriculture	1,400	15.8	1,200,992	12.0
Mining	245	2.8	47,171	0.5
Manufacturing	2,038	23.0	1,985,995	19.9
Construction	334	3.8	1,003,175	10.1
Public utilities	418	4.7	103,256	1.0
Transp. and commun.	1,034	11.7	460,476	4.6
Trade	1,129	12.7	1,702,080	17.0
Finance	687	7.7	395,704	4.0
Pub. admin., defense Services	1,579	17.8	2,399,039	24.0
Other	...	...	691,302	6.9
TOTAL	8,864	100.0	9,989,190	100.0

Population economically active (1983): total 10,815,000; activity rate of total population 36.5% (participation rates: over age 15, 50.2%; female 13.2%; unemployed 5.7%).

Price and earnings indexes (1980 = 100)

	1980	1981	1982	1983	1984	1985	1986□
Consumer price index	100.0	204.0	541.0	2,403	17,462	134,833	251,423
Monthly earnings index◇	100.0	183.3	434.3	2,496	22,056	138,698	...

Land use (1983): forested 21.9%; meadows and pastures 52.2%; agricultural and under permanent cultivation 13.0%; other 12.9%.

Foreign trade△

Balance of trade (current prices)

	1980	1981	1982	1983	1984	1985 ‖
$a '000,000	−270	+312	+4,834	+37,495	+184,460	+3,137
% of total	8.4%	4.2%	19.7%	30.0%	23.2%	42.9%

Imports (1985)✝: U.S.$3,814,229,000 (industrial chemicals 21.9%; nonelectrical machinery 14.4%; petroleum and petroleum products 10.0%; electrical machinery 8.4%; cast-iron and steel products 8.1%; road vehicles and transport equipment 7.7%; plastics, cellulose, and artificial resins 6.1%). *Major import sources:* United States 17.9%; Brazil 15.9%; West Germany 10.5%.
Exports (1985)✝: U.S.$8,396,114,000 (cereals 21.3%; vegetables, fruits, and nuts 15.4%; vegetable oils, fats, and waxes 12.7%; feeding stuff for animals 10.0%; meat and meat preparations 6.1%; hides and skins 4.3%; petroleum and petroleum products 4.0%, cast-iron and steel products 2.9%). *Major export destinations:* United States 12.5%; U.S.S.R. 11.8%; The Netherlands 10.9%; Brazil 6.0%; Japan 4.3%; Iran 4.0%; Italy 3.7%.

Transport and communications

Transport. Railroads (1985): length 21,335 mi, 34,336 km; passenger-km 10,740,000,000; metric ton-km cargo 9,504,000,000. Roads (1984): total length 131,920 mi, 212,305 km (paved 26%). Vehicles (1984): passenger cars 3,685,000; commercial vehicles and buses 1,388,000. Merchant marine (1985): vessels (100 gross tons and over) 549; total deadweight tonnage 3,568,739. Air transport (1985): passenger-km 4,803,850,000; metric ton-km cargo 538,339,000; airports (1986) 65.
Communications. Daily newspapers (1982): total number 159; total circulation 2,485,000⊕; circulation per 1,000 population 85. Radio (1984): 10,500,000 receivers (1 per 3.0 persons). Television (1984): 5,915,000 receivers (1 per 5.1 persons). Telephones (1983): 2,717,061 (1 per 11 persons).

Education and health

Education (1984)

	schools	teachers	students	student/teacher ratio
Primary (age 6–12)	20,619	218,520	4,430,513	20.3
Secondary (age 13–17)**	1,987	86,874	656,521	7.6
Vocational	3,117	119,309	905,755	7.6
Higher	1,251	64,230	677,535	10.5

Educational attainment (1980). Percent of adult population over age 25 having: no formal schooling 6.0%; less than primary education 32.0%; primary 34.6%; secondary 20.5%; higher 6.9%. *Literacy* (1980): total population over age 15 literate 94.9%; males literate 95.5%; females literate 94.4%.
Health: physicians (1979) 79,216 (1 per 351 persons); hospital beds (1980) 150,010 (1 per 182 persons); infant mortality rate per 1,000 live births (1984) 36.0.
Food (1980–82): daily per capita caloric intake 3,368 (vegetable products 67%; animal products 33%); 128% of FAO recommended minimum requirement.

Military

Total active duty personnel (1985): 108,000 (army 50.9%, navy 33.3%, air force 15.8%). *Military expenditure as percent of GNP* (1983): 2.7% (world 6.1%); per capita expenditure: U.S.$51.

*Introduced June 14, 1985, at the rate of 1 austral = 1,000 pesos. †Detail does not add to total given because of rounding. ‡1985. §Argentina has no legal provision for divorce. ‖ In new pesos, which prior to June 14, 1985, had a rate of 1 new peso = 10,000 old pesos. ¶1984. ♀Distrito Federal only. ♂At 1970 prices. □June. ◇Skilled workers in manufacturing only. △Import figures are f.o.b. (free on board) in balance of trade and c.i.f. (cost, insurance, and freight) for commodities and trading partners. ✝Commodities breakdown is for 1984. ⊕Partial circulation only. **Teacher training included with secondary.

Aruba

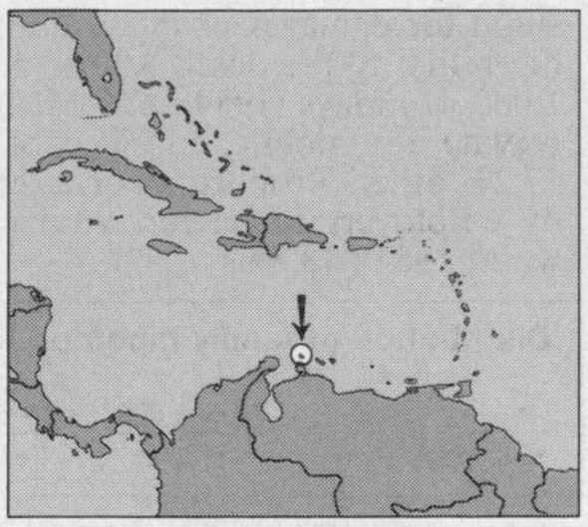

Official name: Aruba.
Political status: nonmetropolitan part of The Netherlands realm with one legislative house (Island Council [21])*.
Chief of state: Dutch Monarch represented by governor.
Head of government: Prime Minister.
Capital: Oranjestad.
Official language: Dutch.
Official religion: none.
Monetary unit: 1 Aruban guilder (A f.) at par with the Netherlands Antillean (NA f.) = 100 cents; valuation (Oct. 1, 1986) 1U.S.$ = A f. 1.80; 1 £ = A f. 2.60.

Area and population

Island	Capital	area sq mi	area sq km	population 1981 census
Aruba	Oranjestad	75	193	60,312
TOTAL		75	193	60,312

Demography

Population (1986): 62,000.
Density (1986): persons per sq mi 826.7, persons per sq km 321.2.
Urban–rural: n.a..
Sex distribution (1981): male 48.64%; female 51.36%.
Age breakdown (1981): under 15, 25.9%; 15–29, 30.6%; 30–44, 21.3%; 45–59, 12.7%; 60–74, 7.4%; 75 and over, 2.1%.
Population projection: (1990) 63,000; (2000) 66,000.
Doubling time: 63 years.
Ethnic composition (1980): mostly Netherlands Antillean (Dutch/Spanish/black/Amerindian) creole†.
Religious affiliation (1981): Roman Catholic 88.5%; Protestant 7.4%, of which Lutheran/Reformed tradition 2.5%, Methodist 2.4%; other Christian (Jehovah's Witness) 1.1%; Jewish 0.2%; nonreligious 1.6%; other 1.2%.
Major city (1980): Oranjestad 20,000.

Vital statistics

Birth rate per 1,000 population (1982): 15.7 (world avg. 29.0); legitimate 41.3%; illegitimate 58.7%.
Death rate per 1,000 population (1982): 4.7 (world avg. 11.0).
Natural increase rate per 1,000 population (1982): 11.0 (world avg. 18.0).
Total fertility rate (avg. births per childbearing woman): n.a.
Marriage rate per 1,000 population (1982): 7.1.
Divorce rate per 1,000 population (1982): 2.0.
Life expectancy at birth (1981): male 71.6 years; female 76.8 years.
Major causes of death per 100,000 population: n.a.

National economy

Budget (1979)‡. Revenue: NA f. 246,700,000 (tax revenue 76.9%, of which import duties 27.8%, corporate taxes 23.8%, excise taxes 15.2%; grants from abroad 13.5%; nontax revenue 9.5%). Expenditures: NA f. 255,800,000 (general public services 35.1%; economic services 11.5%; social security and welfare 11.4%; health 7.9%; education 5.4%; defense, negligible).
Public debt (external, outstanding; 1983)‡: U.S.$682,000,000§.
Tourism (1984): receipts from visitors U.S.$113,000,000; expenditures by nationals abroad, n.a.
Production (metric tons except as noted). Agriculture, forestry, fishing (1985): small amounts of tomatoes, beans, cucumbers, gherkins, watermelons, and lettuce are grown on hydroponic farms; aloe leaves, divi-divi pods, sour orange fruit, sorghum, and peanuts (groundnuts) are nonhydroponic crops of limited value; livestock (number of live animals; 1984‡) 23,000 goats, 9,000 cattle, 8,000 pigs, 8,000 sheep; roundwood, n.a.; fish catch, n.a. Mining and quarrying: excavation of sand for local use. Manufacturing: rum, cigarettes, and soft drinks‖. Construction: n.a. Energy production (consumption): electricity (kW-hr; 1984‡) 2,380,000,000 (2,380,000,000); coal, none (none); crude petroleum (barrels; 1984‡¶) none (149,900,000); petroleum products (metric tons; 1984‡¶) 18,970,000 (2,291,000); natural gas, none (none).
Gross national product (at current market prices; 1982‡): U.S.$1,370,000,000 (U.S.$5,870 per capita).

Structure of gross domestic product and labour force

	1981♀			
	in value A f. '000,000	% of total value	labour force	% of labour force
Agriculture	...	...	40	0.2
Mining	...	...	4	—
Manufacturing	...	...	2,020	8.6
Construction	...	...	1,882	8.0
Public utilities	...	...	484	2.1
Transportation and communication	...	...	1,277	5.4
Trade, restaurants, hotels	...	...	7,720	32.7
Finance	...	...	1,045	4.4
Pub. admin., defense	...	... }	9,082	38.5
Services	...	...		
Other	...	...	22	0.1
TOTAL	...	...	23,576	100.0

Population economically active (1981): total 26,031; activity rate of total population 43.2% (participation rates: ages 15–64, 62.3%; female 36.7%; unemployed [1985] 40.0%¶).

Price and earnings indexes (1980 = 100)‡

	1978	1979	1980	1981	1982	1983	1984
Consumer price index	78.3	87.2	100.0	112.2	119.0	122.4	125.0
Monthly earnings index♂	81.0	88.9	100.0	114.7	127.8	129.4	129.9

Household income and expenditure: average household size (1981) 4.0; average annual income per household: n.a.; source of income: n.a.; expenditure (1984)□: food 24.5%, housing 18.4%, transportation and communication 17.4%, household furnishings 9.1%, clothing and footwear 8.4%, recreation and education 5.0%, health 2.9%, beverages and tobacco 2.9%, other 11.4%.
Land use (1985): forested, negligible; meadows and pastures, negligible; agricultural and under permanent cultivation 5.0%; other (dry savanna and built-up) 95.0%.

Foreign trade◇

Balance of trade (current prices)

	1978	1979	1980	1981	1982	1983
NA f. '000,000	...	–317	–23	...	...	–33
% of total	...	3.9%	0.2%	...	...	0.4%

Imports (1983): NA f. 4,308,000,000 (crude petroleum 79.8%, petroleum products 8.5%, basic and miscellaneous manufactures 3.6%, machinery and transport equipment 2.9%, food 2.4%). *Major import sources:* Venezuela 83.0%; United States 9.4%; Saudi Arabia 2.2%; The Netherlands 1.5%.
Exports (1983): NA f. 4,275,000,000 (petroleum products 99.0%, sulfur pyrite 0.5%, crude petroleum 0.3%). *Major export destinations:* United States 55.5%; Puerto Rico 9.7%; United Kingdom 4.5%; Chile 2.7%; Colombia 2.6%.

Transport and communications

Transport. Railroads: none. Roads (1984): total length 236 mi, 380 km (paved, n.a.). Vehicles (1984): passenger cars 23,409; trucks and buses 582. Merchant marine: vessels (100 gross tons and over) n.a. Air transport: n.a.; airports (1986) with scheduled flights 1.
Communications. Daily newspapers (1985): total number 2; total circulation 11,519; circulation per 1,000 population 187. Radio: n.a. Television: n.a. Telephones (1983): 17,000 (1 per 3.6 persons).

Education and health

Education (1983)

	schools	teachers	students	student/teacher ratio
Primary (age 6–12)	33	373	6,763	18.1
Secondary (age 12–17)	10	189	3,082	16.3
Voc., teacher tr.	3	65	701	10.8
Higher	1	20	180	9.0

Educational attainment: n.a. *Literacy* (1985): total population over age 15 literate 95.0%.
Health (1985): physicians 59 (1 per 1,043 persons); hospital beds 279 (1 per 221 persons); infant mortality rate per 1,000 live births (1982) 8.0.
Food (1980–82)‡: daily per capita caloric intake 2,735 (vegetable products 69%; animal products 31%); 113% of FAO recommended minimum requirement.

Military

Total active duty personnel (1984): A small Dutch naval contingent is stationed permanently in the Netherlands Antilles and Aruba.

*Aruba withdrew from the Netherlands Antilles on Jan. 1, 1986, becoming an autonomous member of the Kingdom of the Netherlands, the same status as that of the whole of the Netherlands Antilles. †Nationality (1981): Dutch 93.8%, of which born in Aruba or the Netherlands Antilles 88.3%, born in The Netherlands 2.3%, born elsewhere 3.2%; citizen of the United Kingdom 1.3%; Colombian 0.8%; Venezuelan 0.7%; citizen of the Dominican Republic 0.7%; citizen of the United States 0.6%; other 2.1%. ‡Includes the Netherlands Antilles. §Includes external long-term private debt not guaranteed by the government. ‖ Servicing facilities, including a petroleum transshipment terminal and two ship repair and bunkering facilities, are underutilized. ¶Aruba's oil refinery was closed in early 1985. ♀Employed persons only. ♂Minimum wages in manufacturing as of January 1 of each year. □Weights of consumer price index components. ◇Imports c.i.f. (cost, insurance, and freight); exports f.o.b. (free on board).

Australia

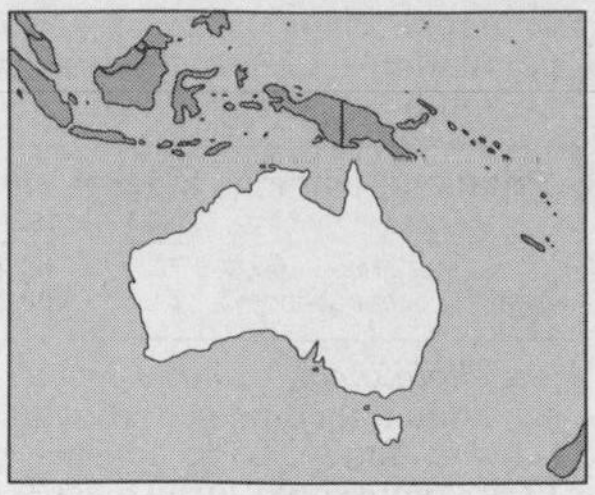

Official name: Commonwealth of Australia.
Form of government: constitutional monarchy with two legislative houses (Senate [76]; House of Representatives [148]).
Chief of state: British Monarch represented by governor-general.
Head of government: Prime Minister.
Capital: Canberra.
Official language: English.
Official religion: none.
Monetary unit: 1 Australian dollar ($A) = 100 cents; valuation (Oct. 1, 1986) 1 U.S.$ = $A 1.59; 1 £ = $A 2.29.

Area and population

		area		population
				1986
States	Capitals	sq mi	sq km	census*
New South Wales	Sydney	309,500	801,600	5,504,900
Queensland	Brisbane	666,900	1,727,200	2,567,200
South Australia	Adelaide	379,900	984,000	1,367,500
Tasmania	Hobart	26,200	67,800	444,200
Victoria	Melbourne	87,900	227,600	4,141,200
Western Australia	Perth	975,100	2,525,500	1,421,600
Territories				
Australian Capital Territory	Canberra	900	2,400	258,600
Northern Territory	Darwin	519,800	1,346,200	146,600
TOTAL		2,966,200	7,682,300	15,851,800

Demography

Population (1986): 15,912,000.
Density (1986): persons per sq mi 5.4, persons per sq km 2.1.
Urban-rural (1981): urban 85.7%; rural 14.3%.
Sex distribution (1986): male 49.87%; female 50.13%.
Age breakdown (1986): under 15, 23.2%; 15–29, 25.2%; 30–44, 22.1%; 45–59, 14.6%; 60–74, 11.0%; 75 and over, 3.9%.
Population projection: (1990) 16,678,000; (2000) 18,471,000.
Doubling time: 84 years.
Ethnic composition (1983): white 94.4%; Asian 2.1%; aboriginal 1.1%; other 2.4%.
Religious affiliation (1981): Christian 76.4%, of which Anglican Church of Australia 26.1%, Roman Catholic 26.0%, other Protestant 20.8% (Uniting Church 4.9%, Presbyterian 4.4%, Methodist 3.4%), Orthodox 2.9%; Muslim 0.5%; Jewish 0.4%; Buddhist 0.2%; no religion 10.8%; other 11.7%.
Major cities (1985): Sydney 3,391,600; Melbourne 2,916,600; Brisbane 1,157,200; Perth 1,001,000; Adelaide 987,100; Newcastle 423,300; Canberra 273,600; Wollongong 236,800; Gold Coast 208,100†; Hobart 178,100.
Place of birth (1984): 78.9% native-born; 21.1% foreign-born, of which United Kingdom 7.5%‡, Italy 1.8%, New Zealand 1.2%, Greece 1.0%, Yugoslavia 1.0%, East and West Germany 0.8%, The Netherlands 0.7%, Poland 0.4%, Malta 0.4%, Lebanon 0.3%, other 6.0%.
Mobility (1984). Population living in the same residence as in 1983: 83.2%; different residence, same state 15.5%; different states and territories 1.3%.
Households (1984). Total number of households 5,039,200. Average household size 2.8; (1981) 1 person 18.0%, 2 persons 29.2%, 3 persons 16.9%, 4 persons 19.1%, 5 persons 10.5%, 6 persons 4.1%, 7 or more persons 2.2%. Family households (1984): 3,868,900 (76.8%), nonfamily 1,170,300 (23.2%).
Immigration (1984): permanent immigrants admitted 73,110, from United Kingdom and Ireland 16.1%, Vietnam 13.5%, New Zealand 9.4%, South Asia (Bangladesh, India, Pakistan, Sri Lanka) 6.1%, Hong Kong 4.2%, China 3.6%, Malaysia and Singapore 3.5%, Lebanon 3.3%, United States 2.1%, South Africa 1.9%, Yugoslavia 1.8%, East and West Germany 1.6%. Refugee arrivals (1984) 15,761.

Vital statistics

Birth rate per 1,000 population (1986): 15.7 (world avg. 29.0); (1984) legitimate 85.2%; illegitimate 14.8%.
Death rate per 1,000 population (1986): 7.4 (world avg. 11.0).
Natural increase rate per 1,000 population (1986): 8.3 (world avg. 18.0).
Total fertility rate (avg. births per childbearing woman; 1985): 1.9.
Marriage rate per 1,000 population (1985): 7.2.
Divorce rate per 1,000 population (1985): 2.5.
Life expectancy at birth (1985): male 72.6 years; female 79.1 years.
Major causes of death per 100,000 population (1984): diseases of the circulatory system 349; malignant neoplasms (cancers) 168; diseases of the respiratory system 50; accidents, poisonings, and violence 47; diseases of the digestive system 24; endocrine, nutritional, and metabolic diseases and immunity disorders 15; diseases of the nervous system and sense organs 10.

Social indicators

Educational attainment (1982). Percent of adult population over age 20 having: primary and secondary education 57.6%; vocational 16.9%; certificate/diploma 17.1%; university 6.8%.
Quality of working life (1984). Average workweek: 35.7 hours (6.8% overtime). Annual rate per 100,000 workers for: injury or accident, n.a.; industrial illness, n.a.; death, n.a.. Proportion of employed persons insured for damages or income loss resulting from: injury 100%; permanent disability 100%; death 100%. Average days lost to labour stoppages per 1,000 workdays (1984): 0.7. Means of transportation to work (1981): 62.2% private automobile; 13.9% public transportation; 1.3% bicycle; 5.4% foot; 17.2% other. Proportion of unemployed workers discouraged (considered by employers to be too young or too old and no vacancies in line of work; 1984): 18.3%.

Distribution of family income (1982)

income group	$A 0–5,000	$A 6,000–13,000	$A 14,000–18,700	more than $A 18,700
% of population	11.2%	28.4%	32.4%	28.0%

Access to services (1976). Proportion of dwellings having access to: electricity 99.5%; bathroom 96.0%; flush toilet 92.2%; kitchen 97.9%; public sewer 73.4%.
Social participation. Eligible voters participating in last national election: 86.8%. Population over 16 years of age participating in voluntary work (1982): 4.2%. Trade union membership in total work force (1984): 55%. Practicing religious population in total affiliated population: n.a.
Social deviance (1984). Offense rate per 100,000 population for: murder 3.4; rape 13.8; serious assault 58.6; auto theft 584.7; burglary and housebreaking 1,754.3; fraud and forgery 473.8. Incidence per 100,000 in general population of (1984): alcoholism, n.a.; drug and substance abuse (charges) 360.8; suicide 12.3.
Leisure, n.a.
Material well-being (1983). Households possessing: automobile 86%; telephone 85%; refrigerator 99.6%; air conditioner 32.3%; washing machine 91.7%; hot water 98.7%; central heating 3.9%; swimming pool 10.1%.

National economy

Gross national product (at current market prices; 1984): U.S.$184,980,000,000 (U.S.$11,890 per capita).

Structure of gross domestic product and labour force

	1984–85		1985	
	in value $A '000,000	% of total value	labour force§	% of labour force
Agriculture	8,880	4.8	393,700	5.9
Mining	8,501	4.6	93,700	1.4
Manufacturing	32,615	17.8	1,137,000	17.1
Construction	11,921	6.5	485,100	7.3
Public utilities	6,940	3.8	132,900	2.0
Transportation and communication	15,045	8.2	512,700	7.7
Trade	24,574	13.4	1,318,500	19.9
Finance	42,094	23.0	652,200	9.8
Pub. admin., defense	7,895	4.3	323,900	4.9
Services	30,502	16.6	1,582,700	23.9
Other	−5,558‖	−3.0‖	...	...
TOTAL	183,409¶	100.0	6,632,400	100.0♀

Budget (1985–86). Revenue: $A 64,100,000,000 (income tax 61.9%, of which individual 51.0%, corporate 10.0%; excise duties 14.0%; sales tax 9.4%). Expenditures: $A 69,100,000,000 (social security and welfare 27.6%; transfers to state governments 19.6%; health 9.7%; interest on public debt 9.7%; defense 9.5%; education 7.2%; general public services 6.9%; economic services 6.3%; housing 2.0%; culture and recreation 1.2%).
External debt (1984–85): $A 33,100,000,000.
Tourism (1984): receipts from visitors U.S.$1,211,000,000; expenditures by nationals abroad U.S.$1,952,000,000.

Manufacturing, mining, and construction enterprises (1984–85)

	no. of establishments	no. of employees	weekly wages as a % of avg. of all wages	annual value added ($A '000,000)
Manufacturing				
Food, beverages, and tobacco	3,429	169,745	88.2	6,888
Paper, printing, and publishing	2,981	100,650	106.3	4,020
Basic metal products	536	76,908	124.0	4,106
Transport equipment	1,316	119,287	95.1	3,724
Chemical, petroleum, and coal products	887	55,039	112.7	3,376
Fabricated metal products	4,146	93,612	84.3	2,859
Wood, wood products, and furniture	4,069	72,300	76.5	2,174
Nonmetallic mineral products	1,707	38,708	101.5	1,913
Clothing and footwear	2,003	74,059	66.2	1,659
Textiles	649	33,315	86.3	986
Mining				
Coal, oil, and gas	158	38,646 }	150.5	6,924
Metaliic minerals	328	31,041 }		2,970
Construction♂	51,351	246,510	104.0	3,925

Production (gross value in $A '000 except as noted). Agriculture, forestry, fishing (1984–85): livestock slaughtered—cattle 2,147,500, sheep and lambs 549,500, pigs 437,800; wheat 3,256,300, wool 2,398,800; barley 757,000, sugarcane 512,200, cotton 309,900, grapes 254,800, sorghum 214,100, potatoes 178,400, apples 145,900, oranges 133,000, oats 128,500, rice 119,500, tomatoes 111,100, bananas 93,800, sunflower seeds 88,100, peanuts (groundnuts) 38,800, pears 38,200, pineapples 32,600, peaches 26,600; livestock (number of live animals; 1985) 149,248,000 sheep, 22,738,000 cattle, 2,463,000 pigs, 51,273,000 poultry; roundwood 18,286,000 cu m; fish catch 168,900 metric tons. Mining and quarrying (metric tons; 1984–85): iron ore 91,441,000; bauxite 22,790,000; refined metals—aluminum 822,315, zinc 299,386, lead 189,100, copper 165,491, tin 2,824, gold 40,501 kilograms. Manufacturing (metric tons; 1984–85): raw steel 6,311,000; cement 5,659,000; iron and steel slabs 3,992,000; super phosphate 2,582,000; sulfuric acid 1,774,000;

beef and veal 1,310,000; wheat flour 1,159,000; refined sugar 680,200; newsprint 371,857; lamb 300,800; pork 260,300; mutton 214,700; plaster sheets 69,584,000 sq m; textile floor coverings 41,503,000 sq m; woven cotton cloth 36,746,000 sq m; concrete roofing tiles 17,922,000 cu m; woven woolen cloth 9,903,000 sq m; automotive gasoline 155,290,000 hectolitres; furnace fuel 29,540,000 hectolitres; beer 18,500,000 hectolitres; finished and partly finished motor vehicles 375,812 units. Construction (building starts by value in $A '000; 1984–85): new dwellings 6,665,800; alterations and additions to dwellings 891,700; other buildings in private sector 4,756,400.

Retail sales and service enterprises (1979–80)

	no. of establishments	no. of employees	total wages and salaries ($A '000,000)	annual turnover ($A '000,000)
Motor vehicle dealers, gasoline and tire dealers	26,516	175,995	1,319	18,203
Food stores	39,416	260,266	1,131	12,747
Department and general stores	857	99,569	717	4,254
Clothing, fabrics, and furniture stores	17,908	81,797	519	4,143
Household appliances and hardware stores	8,196	43,542	320	2,966
Restaurants, hotels and accommodations	17,702	183,310	1,022	4,670
Licensed clubs	3,243	52,297	697	1,515
Laundries and dry cleaners	1,365	12,106	91	224
Motion picture theatres	577	6,777	45	178
Hairdressers and beauty salons	2,265	12,282	78	173

Energy production (consumption): electricity (kW-hr; 1984–85) 118,969,000,000 (112,947,000,000δ); coal (metric tons; 1984–85) 168,484,000 (71,968,000δ); crude petroleum (barrels; 1984) 169,700,000 (224,800,000δ); petroleum products (metric tons; 1984–85) 27,493,000 (25,600,000); natural gas (cu m; 1984–85) 12,958,000 (12,958,000).

Population economically active (July 1986): total 7,595,000; activity rate of total population 48.1% (participation rates: ages 15–64 [1985] 69.3%; female [1985] 54.2%; unemployed 7.6%).

Price and earnings indexes (1980 = 100)

	1980	1981	1982	1983	1984	1985	1986□
Consumer price index	100.0	109.7	121.9	134.2	139.6	149.0	157.3
Monthly earnings index	100.0	111.4	124.5	133.3	146.0	153.4	161.1

Household income and expenditure. Average household size (1984) 3.1; average annual income per household (1984–85) $A 11,543 (U.S.$10,153); sources of income (1984–85): wages and salaries 59.6%, government pensions and benefits 25.8%, income from property and entrepreneurship 14.6%; expenditure (1984–85): food and nonalcoholic beverages 19.7%, housing 12.8%, education and recreation 11.9%, household durable goods 7.7%, clothing and footwear 6.5%, health 3.9%, energy 2.9%.

Land use (1985): meadows and pastures 59.0%; agricultural and under permanent cultivation 4.3%; other 36.7%◇.

Financial aggregates

	1980	1981	1982	1983	1984	1985	1986 (8 mos.)
Exchange Rate, $A 1.00 per:							
U.S. Dollar	1.14	1.15	1.02	0.90	0.88	0.70	0.61
£	0.49	0.57	0.50	0.59	0.64	0.54	0.41
SDR	0.93	0.97	0.89	0.86	0.84	0.62	0.50
International reserves (U.S.$)							
Total (excl. gold; '000,000)	1,690	1,671	6,371	8,962	7,441	5,768	4,728
SDRs ('000,000)	---	52	86	81	209	310	330
Reserve pos. in IMF ('000,000)	325	294	---	114	183	207	228
Foreign exchange ('000,000)	1,365	1,325	6,285	8,768	7,049	5,250	4,170
Gold ('000,000 fine troy oz)	7.93	7.93	7.93	7.93	7.93	7.93	7.93
% world reserves	0.8	0.8	0.8	0.8	0.8	0.8	0.8
Interest and prices							
Central bank discount (%)	...	...	...	...	...	...	...
Gov't. Bond yield (%)	11.6	14.0	15.4	14.3	13.8	14.1	13.1△
Industrial share prices (1980 = 100)	100.0	104.2	79.5	100.4	117.0	143.5	194.0△
Balance of payments (U.S.$'000,000)							
Balance of visible trade	1,369	−2,333	−2,611	39	−815	...	
Imports, f.o.b.	20,190	23,549	23,407	19,470	23,653	...	
Exports, f.o.b.	21,559	21,216	20,796	19,510	22,838	...	
Balance of invisibles	−5,161	−5,517	−5,047	−5,335	−6,741	...	
Balance of payments, current account	−4,148	−8,359	−8,290	−5,787	−8,304	...	

Foreign trade

Balance of trade (current prices)

	1980–81	1981–82	1982–83	1983–84	1984–85	1985–86
$A '000,000	−1,755	−2,099	+1,331	+742	+613	−2,214.2
% of total	4.4%	4.6%	3.0%	1.5%	1.0%	3.3%

Imports (1984–85): $A 30,026,400,000 (machinery 25.4%, of which office machines and automatic data-processing equipment 5.3%; transport equipment 14.9%, of which road motor vehicles 7.9%; mineral fuels and lubricants 9.4%; chemicals and related products 8.7%; food and live animals 4.1%; crude materials (inedible) excluding fuels 3.4%; paper and paperboard 2.6%; beverages and tobacco 0.8%). *Major import sources:* Japan 22.1%; United States 21.9%; United Kingdom 7.0%; West Germany 6.0%; New Zealand 3.7%; Italy 2.8%; Saudi Arabia 2.4%; Hong Kong 2.3%; Singapore 2.3%; France 2.2%.

Exports (1984–85): $A 30,639,500,000 (metalliferous ores and metal scrap 16.2%; coal, coke, and briquettes 15.6%; cereals 9.6%; textile fibres and their waste 8.1%; petroleum, petroleum gases, and petroleum products 8.0%; nonferrous metals 7.8%; iron and steel 6.3%; meat 4.6%; sugar and honey 1.9%; dairy products 1.4%). *Major export destinations:* Japan 26.3%; United States 11.1%; New Zealand 5.9%; United Kingdom 3.7%; South Korea 3.6%; Singapore 3.4%; China 3.1%; West Germany 3.0%; Hong Kong 2.9%; Malaysia 2.0%; U.S.S.R. 2.5%; Papua New Guinea 1.9%.

Trade by commodity group (1984–85)

SITC Group	imports $A '000,000	imports %	exports $A '000,000	exports %
00 Food and live animals	1,284.1	4.3	7,284.0	23.8
01 Beverages and tobacco	225.4	0.7	72.3	0.3
02 Crude materials, excluding fuels	932.5	3.1	7,949.7	25.9
03 Mineral fuels, lubricants, and related materials	2,300.3	7.7	7,823.7	25.5
04 Animal and vegetable oils, fat and waxes	112.0	0.4	124.0	0.4
05 Chemicals and related products, n.e.s.	2,215.9	7.4	548.3	1.8
06 Basic manufactures	5,786.5	19.3	2,979.5	9.7
07 Machinery and transport equipment	11,333.3	37.7	1,482.9	4.8
08 Miscellaneous manufactured articles	3,865.8	12.9	592.8	1.9
09 Goods not classified by kind	1,000.1	3.3	952.1	3.1
Nonmerchandise trade	970.5	3.2	830.2	2.7
TOTAL	30,026.4	100.0	30,639.5	100.0♀

Direction of trade (1984–85)

	imports $A '000,000	imports %	exports $A '000,000	exports %
Africa	146.0	0.5	655.8	2.1
Asia	12,689.4	42.3	17,345.4	56.6
Japan	6,644.5	22.1	8,066.1	26.3
South America	273.5	0.9	172.6	0.6
North and Central America	7,484.0	24.9	3,977.4	13.0
United States	6,819.3	22.7	3,584.1	11.7
Europe	7,743.1	25.8	5,482.9	17.9
EEC	6,286.4	20.9	3,873.7	12.6
U.S.S.R.	28.9	0.1	873.4	2.9
Other Europe	1,427.8	4.8	735.8	2.4
Oceania	1,157.9	3.9	1,787.8	5.8
New Zealand	1,116.3	3.7	1,591.0	5.2
Other countries, including destinations unknown	532.5	1.8	1,217.6	4.0
TOTAL	30,026.4	100.0♀	30,639.5	100.0

Transport and communications

Transport. Railroads† (1984): route length 24,389 mi, 39,251 km; passenger-mi 1,359,051,000⊕, passenger-km 2,187,120,000⊕; short ton-mi cargo 27,018,000,000, metric ton-km cargo 39,447,800,000. Roads (1984): total length 500,049 mi, 804,753 km (paved 47%). Vehicles (1985): passenger cars 8,294,411; trucks and buses 1,095,633. Merchant marine (1985): vessels (100 gross tons and over) 652; total deadweight tonnage 3,094,094. Air transport (1985): passenger-mi 15,144,000,000, passenger-km 24,372,000,000; short ton-mi cargo 1,821,700,000, metric ton-km cargo 2,659,800,000; airports (1985) with scheduled flights 441.

Communications. Daily newspapers (1979): total number 63; total circulation 4,851,000; circulation per 1,000 population 337. Radio (1985): total number of receivers 20,000,000 (1 per 0.8 person). Television (1985): total number of receivers 6,500,000 (1 per 2.3 persons). Telephones (1985): 8,727,000 (1 per 1.8 persons).

Education and health

Education (1985)

	schools	teachers	students	student/teacher ratio
Primary (age 6–12)	8,460	96,087	1,727,897	18.0
Secondary (age 13–17)	1,603	101,043	1,278,272	12.7
Voc., teacher tr.	234	52,587	859,195	16.3
Higher	95	22,234	370,707	16.8

Literacy (1980): total population over age 15 literate 99.5%.

Health (1985): physicians (1982) 27,500 (1 per 552 persons); hospital beds 91,541 (1 per 172 persons); infant mortality rate per 1,000 live births 9.2.

Food (1980–82): daily per capita caloric intake 3,113 (vegetable products 66%, animal products 34%); 115% of FAO recommended minimum requirement.

Military

Total active duty personnel (1986): 69,555 (army 45.6%, navy 22.0%, air force 32.4%). *Military expenditure as percent of GNP* (1984): 2.9% (world 6.1%); per capita expenditure U.S.$323.

*Preliminary. †Includes Tweed Heads. ‡Includes both Northern Ireland and Republic of Ireland. §Employed persons only. ‖Less imputed bank service charges. ¶At factor cost. ♀Detail does not add to total given because of rounding. δ1983–84. □First quarter. ◇Urban areas, state forests and mining leases, unoccupied land (mainly desert). △June. †Government railways only. ⊕1978–79.

Austria

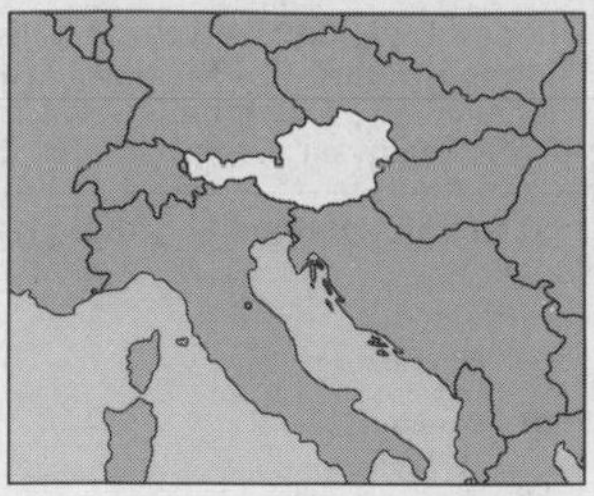

Official name: Republik Österreich (Republic of Austria).
Form of government: federal multiparty republic with two legislative houses (Federal Council [63]; National Council [183]).
Chief of state: President.
Head of government: Chancellor.
Capital: Vienna.
Official language: German.
Official religion: none.
Monetary unit: 1 schilling (S) = 100 groschen; valuation (Oct. 1, 1986) 1 U.S.$ = S 14.27; 1 £ = S 20.62.

Area and population

		area		population
				1985
States	Capitals	sq mi	sq km	estimate
Burgenland	Eisenstadt	1,531	3,965	267,700
Kärnten	Klagenfurt	3,681	9,534	540,300
Niederösterreich	Sankt Pölten	7,402	19,172	1,423,700
Oberösterreich	Linz	4,626	11,980	1,286,000
Salzburg	Salzburg	2,762	7,154	456,500
Steiermark	Graz	6,327	16,387	1,183,400
Tirol	Innsbruck	4,883	12,647	601,600
Vorarlberg	Bregenz	1,004	2,601	309,300
Wien	—	160	415	1,489,200
TOTAL		32,376	83,855	7,557,700

Demography

Population (1986): 7,552,000.
Density (1986): persons per sq mi 233.2, persons per sq km 90.1.
Urban-rural (1981): urban 55.1%; rural 44.9%.
Sex distribution (1984): male 47.37%; female 52.63%.
Age breakdown (1984): under 15, 18.6%; 15–29, 24.5%; 30–44, 20.5%; 45–59, 16.6%; 60–74, 13.3%; 75 and over, 6.5%.
Population projection: (1990) 7,579,000; (2000) 7,629,000.
Ethnic composition (national origin; 1981): Austrian 96.1%; Yugoslavian 1.7%; Turkish 0.8%; German 0.5%; other 0.9%.
Religious affiliation (1981): Roman Catholic 84.3%; Protestant 5.6%; nonreligious and atheist 6.0%; other 4.1%.
Major cities (1981): Vienna 1,505,800*; Graz 243,166; Linz 199,910; Salzburg 139,426; Innsbruck 117,287.

Vital statistics

Birth rate per 1,000 population (1985): 11.5 (world avg. 29.0); (1984) legitimate 78.5%; illegitimate 21.5%.
Death rate per 1,000 population (1985): 11.8 (world avg. 11.0).
Natural increase rate per 1,000 population (1984): −0.3 (world avg. 18.0).
Total fertility rate (avg. births per childbearing woman; 1984): 1.5.
Marriage rate per 1,000 population (1984): 6.1.
Divorce rate per 1,000 population (1984): 2.0.
Life expectancy at birth (1980–82): male 69.2 years; female 76.4 years.
Major causes of death per 100,000 population (1984): heart and circulatory disease 673.1, of which ischemic heart disease 181.8; malignant neoplasms (cancers) 248.6; accidents 63.7; diseases of the respiratory system 49.6.

National economy

Budget (1985). Revenue: S 325,700,000,000 (taxes 86.2%, of which direct income 31.5%, indirect 48.7%, corporate 6.0%). Expenditures: S 341,400,000,000 (goods and services 27.6%; interest on public debt 10.8%; subsidies 10.2%).
Tourism (1984): receipts from visitors U.S.$5,028,000,000; expenditures by nationals abroad U.S.$2,608,000,000.
Production (metric tons except as noted). Agriculture, forestry, fishing (1984): sugar beets 2,565,000, corn (maize) 1,542,000, barley 1,517,000, wheat 1,501,000, potatoes 1,138,000, grapes 360,000, rye 381,000, milk 3,650,000; livestock (number of live animals) 3,881,000 pigs, 2,633,325 cattle, 15,215,121 chickens; roundwood (1983) 13,647,000. Mining and quarrying (1985): iron ore 3,270,000; magnesite 1,183,409*; zinc 24,260†; lead 7,510†. Manufacturing (value in S '000,000; 1981) machinery 54,584, of which electrical 21,509, transport 11,382; metal products (including steel) 18,681; beverages and tobacco 17,469; textiles and apparel 16,068; chemical products 15,107; food products 12,587. Construction (dwellings completed; 1983): residential 3,800,000 sq m; nonresidential 100,000 sq m. Energy production (consumption): electricity (kW-hr; 1984) 42,358,000,000 (40,154,000,000); coal (metric tons; 1984) 2,900,000 (7,344,600); crude petroleum (barrels; 1984) 8,538,000 (50,148,800); petroleum products (metric tons; 1984) 7,076,000 (9,450,000); natural gas (cu m; 1984) 1,286,900,000 (4,928,000,000).
Population economically active (1984): total 3,411,500; activity rate of total population 45.1% (participation rates: ages 15–64, 65.2%; female 39.7%; unemployed 3.8%).

Price and earnings indexes (1980 = 100)

	1979	1980	1981	1982	1983	1984	1985
Consumer price index	94.0	100.0	106.8	112.6	116.3	122.9	126.9
Monthly earnings index	92.7	100.0	106.1	123.7	117.8	123.7	126.9

Gross national product (at current market prices; 1984): U.S.$68,800,000,000 (U.S.$9,110 per capita).

Structure of gross domestic product and labour force

	1984			
	in value S '000,000	% of total value	labour force	% of labour force
Agriculture	47,300	3.7	290,500	8.5
Mining	358,380	27.8	25,900	0.8
Manufacturing			1,038,700	30.4
Construction	91,110	7.1	293,000	8.6
Public utilities	38,780	3.0	41,000	1.2
Transportation and communication	73,400	5.7	218,100	6.4
Trade	206,920	16.0	454,100	13.3
Finance	183,140	14.2	190,700	5.6
Pub. admin., defense	183,100	14.2	685,100	20.1
Services	42,340	3.3	174,400	5.1
Other	65,200	5.0	...	...
TOTAL	1,289,670	100.0	3,411,500	100.0

Household income and expenditure. Average household size (1984) 2.7; income per household‡ (1983) S 171,000 (U.S.$9,520); sources of income (1980): wages and salaries 60.0%, social security benefits and social assistance grants 16.9%, self-employment 15.7%; expenditure (1983): food 26.7%, housing and utilities 23.8%, clothing and footwear 8.0%.
Land use (1983): forested 38.7%; meadows and pastures 24.4%; agricultural and under permanent cultivation 18.3%; other 18.6%.

Foreign trade

Balance of trade (current prices)

	1980	1981	1982	1983	1984	1985
S '000,000	−89,677	−82,741	−65,690	−71,200	−77,590	−77,010
% of total	16.5%	14.1%	11.0%	11.4%	11.0%	9.3%

Imports (1984): S 392,093,921,000 (machinery and transport equipment 28.0%, of which road vehicles 8.0%; manufactured goods 18.8%, of which textile yarn 4.6%, iron and steel 2.8%; petroleum and related materials 10.2%; chemicals and related products 10.0%). *Major import sources:* West Germany 39.9%; Italy 8.6%; U.S.S.R. 5.0%; Switzerland 4.4%; France 3.7%; Japan 3.3%.
Exports (1984): S 314,504,394,000 (manufactured goods 34.4%, of which iron and steel 9.4%; textile yarn 5.5%; machinery and transport equipment 29.9%, of which road vehicles 4.0%; chemicals 9.8%). *Major export destinations:* West Germany 29.6%; Italy 9.4%; Switzerland 6.9%; U.S.S.R. 4.5%; United Kingdom 4.4%; France 3.9%.

Transport and communications

Transport. Railroads (1984): length 4,146 mi, 6,672 km; passenger-mi 4,356,000,000, passenger-km 7,010,000,000; short ton-mi cargo 7,702,000,000, metric ton-km cargo 11,244,000,000. Roads (1984): total length 66,736 mi, 107,402 km (paved 100%). Vehicles (1984): passenger cars 2,468,452; trucks and buses 232,528. Merchant marine (1985): vessels (100 gross tons and over) 29; total deadweight tonnage 226,459. Air transport (1984): passenger-mi 872,400,000, passenger-km 1,404,000,000; short ton-mi cargo 16,093,000, metric ton-km cargo 23,496,000; airports (1986) with scheduled flights 6.
Communications. Daily newspapers (1984): total number 29; total circulation, 2,340,000§; circulation per 1,000 population, 310§. Radio (1984): total number of receivers 2,612,530 (1 per 2.9 persons). Television (1984): total number of receivers 2,418,584 (1 per 3.1 persons). Telephones (1983): 3,330,171 (1 per 2.3 persons).

Education and health

Education (1985–86)

	schools	teachers	students	student/ teacher ratio
Primary (age 6–9)	3,411	28,305	341,867	12.1
Secondary (age 10–18)	2,066	55,932	504,326	9.0
Voc., teacher tr.	1,241	22,910	374,424	16.3
Higher	44	10,252	168,060	16.4

Educational attainment (1981). Percent of adult population over age 25 having: secondary 47.5%; postsecondary 3.3%. *Literacy* (1983): virtually 100%.
Health (1985): physicians 21,513 (1 per 351 persons); hospital beds 84,125 (1 per 90 persons); infant mortality rate per 1,000 live births (1984) 11.4.
Food (1980–82): daily per capita caloric intake 3,595 (vegetable products 64%, animal products 36%); 130% of FAO recommended minimum requirement.

Military

Total active duty personnel (1985): 54,700 (army 91.4%; navy, none; air force 8.6%). *Military expenditure as percent of GNP* (1984): 1.2% (world 6.1%); per capita expenditure U.S.$105.

*1984. †Metal content only. ‡Represents net household or disposable income. §For 25 newspapers only.

Bahamas, The

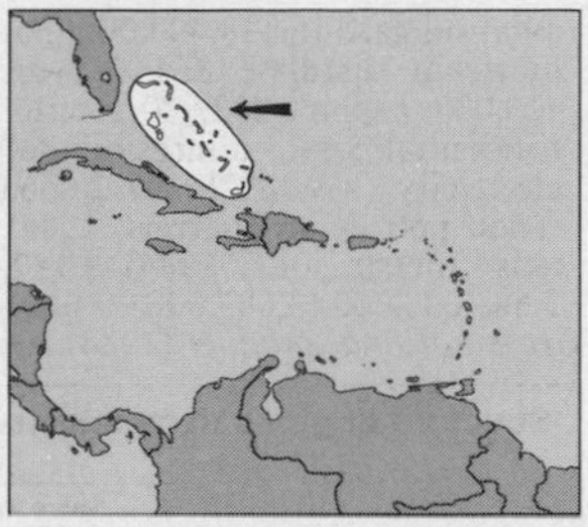

Official name: The Commonwealth of The Bahamas.
Form of government: constitutional monarchy with two legislative houses (Senate [16]; House of Assembly [43]).
Chief of state: British Monarch represented by governor-general.
Head of government: Prime Minister.
Capital: Nassau.
Official language: English.
Official religion: none.
Monetary unit: 1 Bahamian dollar (B$) = 100 cents; valuation (Oct. 1, 1986) 1 Bahamian dollar = U.S.$1.00 = £0.69.

Area and population

Islands and Island Groups†	Residence of Commissioner†	area* sq mi	area* sq km	population 1980 census
Abaco, Great and Little, and Mores Island and cays	Marsh Harbour	649	1,681	7,324
Acklins Island	Pompey Bay	192	497	616
Andros Island	Kemps Bay	2,300	5,957	8,397
Berry Islands	Nicolls Town	12	31	509
Biminis, North and South, Cay Lobos, and Cay Sal	Alice Town	11	28	1,432
Cat Island	Arthur's Town	150	388	2,143
Crooked Island	Colonel Hill	84	218	517
Eleuthera, Harbour Island, and Spanish Wells	Rock Sound	200	518	10,600
Exuma, Great and Little, and cays	George Town	112	290	3,672
Grand Bahama	Freeport	530	1,373	33,102
Inagua, Great and Little	Matthew Town	599	1,551	939
Long Cay	...	9	23	33
Long Island	Clarence Town	230	596	3,358
Mayaguana	Abraham's Bay	110	285	476
New Providence	Nassau	80	207	135,437
Ragged Island and cays	Duncan Town	14	36	146
San Salvador and Rum Cay	Cockburn Town	90	233	804
TOTAL		5,382‡	13,939‡	209,505§

Demography

Population (1986): 236,000.
Density (1986): persons per sq mi 43.8, persons per sq km 16.9.
Urban-rural (1985): urban 57.3%; rural 42.7%.
Sex distribution (1980): male 48.77%; female 51.23%.
Age breakdown (1985): under 15, 38.0%; 15–29, 27.9%; 30–44, 17.9%; 45–59, 10.5%; 60–74, 4.8%; 75 and over, 0.9%.
Population projection: (1990) 258,000; (2000) 310,000.
Doubling time: 41 years.
Ethnic composition (1980): black 72.3%; mixed 14.2%; white 12.9%; other 0.6%.
Religious affiliation (1980): non-Anglican Protestant (mostly Baptist and Church of God [Anderson Ind.]) 46.6%; Roman Catholic 25.5%; Anglican 20.7%; other 7.2%.
Major cities (1980): Nassau 110,000; Freeport 25,423.

Vital statistics

Birth rate per 1,000 population (1984): 22.2 (world avg. 29.0); legitimate 39.7%, illegitimate 60.3%.
Death rate per 1,000 population (1984): 5.0 (world avg. 11.0).
Natural increase rate per 1,000 population (1984): 17.2 (world avg. 18.0).
Total fertility rate (avg. births per childbearing woman; 1980–85): 3.2.
Marriage rate per 1,000 population (1983): 6.7.
Divorce rate per 1,000 population (1983): 0.8.
Life expectancy at birth (1980–85): male 66.9 years; female 70.9 years.
Major causes of death per 100,000 population (1982): malignant neoplasms (cancers) 107.8; heart diseases 80.7; accidents 39.0; chronic bronchitis, emphysema, and asthma 38.5; cerebrovascular disease 31.2.

National economy

Budget (1985). Revenue: B$365,845,000 (customs receipts 60.2%, nontax revenue 15.3%, stamp taxes 6.7%, service taxes 5.6%, business and professional licenses 3.8%, departure tax 3.8%). Expenditures: B$384,113,000 (education 21.8%, health 16.3%, interest on the public debt 12.4%, general administration 10.1%, police 9.3%, tourism 7.1%, defense 2.5%).
Public debt (external, outstanding; 1984): U.S.$208,600,000.
Tourism: receipts from visitors (1985) U.S.$865,000,000; expenditures by nationals abroad (1984) U.S.$106,000,000.
Production (metric tons except as noted). Agriculture, forestry, fishing, (1984): sugarcane 228,000, tomatoes 9,000, bananas 8,000, onions 2,000, corn (maize) 1,000, pulses 1,000; livestock (number of live animals) 38,000 sheep, 19,000 pigs, 18,000 goats, 4,000 cattle, 1,000,000 chickens; roundwood 115,000 cu m; fish catch (1983) 5,211, of which crayfish 2,808, groupers 660, conchs 510. Mining and quarrying (1983); aragonite 2,200,000; salt 870,000. Manufacturing (1983): residual fuel oils 4,050,000; gas-diesel oils 1,550,000; cement 26,000; rum 100,000 hectolitres ‖. Construction (value of new buildings¶ in B$'000,000; 1985): residential 78; nonresidential 23. Energy production (consumption): electricity (kW-hr; 1984) 870,000,000 (870,000,000); coal (metric tons; 1984) none (negligible); crude petroleum (barrels; 1984) none (41,964,000); petroleum products (metric tons; 1984) 4,740,000 (534,000); natural gas, none (none).
Gross national product (at current market prices; 1984): U.S.$960,000,000 (U.S.$4,250 per capita).

Structure of gross domestic product and labour force

	1984♀ in value B$'000,000	1984♀ % of total value	1979 labour force♁	1979 % of labour force
Agriculture	72.0	4.4	2,377	3.3
Mining	179.0	10.8	721	1.0
Manufacturing			3,934	5.5
Public utilities			1,190	1.7
Construction	48.0	2.9	4,034	5.6
Transp. and commun.	180.0	10.9	4,027	5.6
Trade	432.0	26.2	22,030	30.7
Finance	201.0	12.2	7,335	10.2
Pub. admin., defense	282.0	17.1	26,065	36.4
Services	257.0	15.5		
TOTAL	1,649.4□	100.0	71,713	100.0

Population economically active (1980): total 87,054; activity rate of total population 41.6% (participation rates: ages 15–64, 70.5%; female 44.5%; unemployed [1984] 20.0%).

Price and earnings indexes (1980 = 100)

	1979	1980	1981	1982	1983	1984	1985
Consumer price index	89.2	100.0	111.1	117.8	122.6	127.4	133.2
Annual earnings index◇	77.7	100.0	112.5	115.7	...	...	...

Household income and expenditure. Average household size (1980) 4.3; income per household (1979) B$13,537 (U.S.$13,537); source of income: n.a.; expenditure (1982): food and beverages 20.0%, expenditures in restaurants and hotels 16.1%, transport and communication 15.1%, housing 14.1%, recreation and entertainment 6.5%, household furnishings 6.0%.
Land use (1983): forested 32.2%; meadows and pastures 0.2%; agricultural and under permanent cultivation 0.9%; other△ 66.7%.

Foreign trade

Balance of trade (current prices)

	1979	1980	1981	1982	1983	1984	1985†
B$'000,000	+272	−2,536	−1,095	−1,814	−646	−535	−72
% of total	3.7%	20.2%	8.1%	16.7%	7.5%	6.8%	1.6%

Imports (1984): B$4,466,000,000 (petroleum [all forms] 83.9%, machinery and transport equipment 3.5%, food 3.3%). *Major import sources*⊕: United States 78.2%; United Kingdom 3.3%; Canada 2.9%.
Exports (1984): B$3,931,000,000 (petroleum [all forms] 92.8%, nonpetroleum reexports 1.1%, hormones 0.9%, rum 0.5%, crayfish 0.4%). *Major export destinations:* United States 72.5%; Canada 6.4%; United Kingdom 2.9%.

Transport and communications

Transport. Railroads: none. Roads (1984): total length 2,548 mi, 4,100 km (paved 40%). Vehicles (1984): passenger cars 88,000; trucks and buses 5,600. Merchant marine (1985): vessels (100 gross tons and over) 195; total deadweight tonnage 6,862,347. Air transport (1981)**: passenger-mi 72,313,000, passenger-km 116,377,000; short ton-mi cargo 162,000, metric ton-km cargo 236,000; airports (1986) with scheduled flights 21.
Communications. Daily newspapers (1984): total number 3; total circulation 34,600; circulation per 1,000 population 153. Radio (1985): total receivers 116,000 (1 per 2.0 persons). Television (1985): total receivers 51,000 (1 per 4.5 persons). Telephones (1983): 67,544 (1 per 3.3 persons).

Education and health

Education (1983)

	schools	teachers	students	student/ teacher ratio
Primary (age 5–11)	187	1,972	37,097	18.8
Secondary (age 11–16)	38	1,334	23,202	17.4
Higher††	1	135	2,000	14.8

Educational attainment (1970). Percent of adult population over age 25 having: no formal schooling 6.7%; primary education only 15.4%; secondary 63.0%; postsecondary or higher 14.9%. *Literacy* (1984): total population over age 15 literate 125,000 (89.0%).
Health (1983): physicians 218 (1 per 1,018 persons); hospital beds 948 (1 per 234 persons); infant mortality rate per 1,000 live births (1982) 25.3.
Food (1980–82): daily per capita caloric intake 2,490 (vegetable products 65%, animal products 35%); 90% of FAO recommended minimum requirement.

Military

Total active duty personnel (1985): 496‡‡. *Military expenditure as percent of central government budget* (1983): 2.6% (world 19.0%); per capita expenditure U.S.$37.

*Land area only of individual islands or island groups. †Out Islands (all islands and island groups other than New Providence) are governed by commissioners assigned by the central government. ‡10 sq mi (27 sq km) are unaccounted for in breakdown. §Census total includes Bahamian residents abroad, but excludes 14,010 nonresident visitors. ‖ 1982. ¶New Providence and Grand Bahama islands only. ♀Preliminary estimate at 1982 prices. ♁Insured employed persons as of January 1979. □Detail does not add to total given because of rounding. ◇Based on government salaries. △Mostly mangrove swamp and uncultivatable scrubland. †Through September. ⊕Excludes petroleum imports. **Bahamasair only. ††1985. ‡‡All paramilitary (coast guard) personnel.

Bahrain

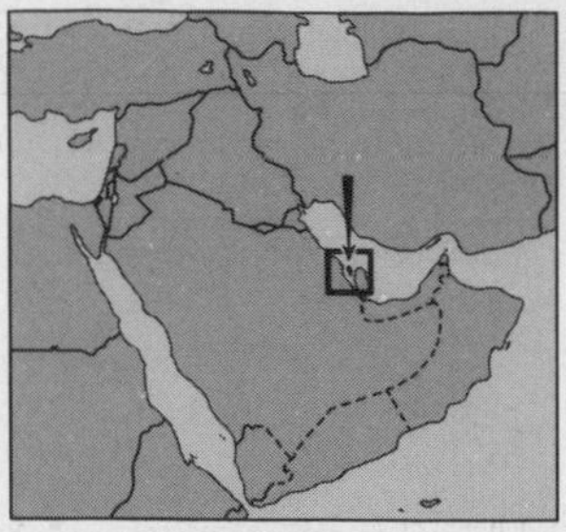

Official name: Dawlat al-Baḥrayn (State of Bahrain).
Form of government: monarchy (emirate) with a cabinet appointed by the Emir.
Chief of state: Emir.
Head of government: Prime Minister.
Capital: Manama.
Official language: Arabic.
Official religion: Islam.
Monetary unit: 1 Bahrain dinar (BD) = 1,000 fils; valuation (Oct. 1, 1986) 1 BD = U.S.$2.65 = £1.83.

Area and population

Regions	area sq mi	area sq km	population 1981 census
Towns/villages			
Central	13.6	35.2	16,776
Central villages	...	...	16,776
Judd Ḥafṣ	7.0	18.1	33,693
Judd Ḥafṣ	...	...	7,232
Judd Ḥafṣ villages	...	...	26,461
al-Manāmah	9.4	24.5	121,986
Manama	...	...	108,684
al-Manāmah villages	...	...	13,302
al-Muḥarraq	6.2	16.0	61,853
al-Muḥarraq	...	...	46,061
al-Muḥarraq villages	...	...	15,792
Northern	14.1	36.5	22,117
Northern villages	...	...	22,117
Rifā'	111.5	288.9	28,150
ar-Rifā'	...	...	22,408
Rifā' villages	...	...	5,742
Sitrah	11.0	28.5	22,993
Sitrah villages	...	...	22,993
Western	66.4	171.9	14,503
Western villages	...	...	14,503
Towns with special status			
al-Ḥadd	1.2	3.0	7,111
Madīnat 'Īsā	4.8	12.4	21,275
Islands			
Ḥawār and other	19.3	50.0	341
TOTAL	264.5*	685.0*	350,798

Demography

Population (1986): 435,000.
Density (1986): persons per sq mi 1,644.6, persons per sq km 635.0.
Urban-rural (1984): urban 78.9%; rural 21.1%.
Sex distribution (1986): male 59.75%; female 40.25%.
Age breakdown (1986): under 15, 32.0%; 15–29, 34.4%; 30–44, 21.3%; 45–59, 8.7%; 60–74, 2.9%; 75 and over, 0.7%.
Population projection: (1990) 479,000; (2000) 680,000.
Doubling time: 23 years.
Ethnic composition (1986): Bahraini 62.5%; non-Bahraini 37.5%.
Religious affiliation (1981): Muslim 85.0%; Christian 7.3%; other 7.7%.
Major cities (1981): Manama 121,986; al-Muḥarraq 61,853; ar-Rifā' 22,408.

Vital statistics

Birth rate per 1,000 population (1984): 36.8 (world avg. 29.0).
Death rate per 1,000 population (1984): 5.9 (world avg. 11.0).
Natural increase rate per 1,000 population (1984): 30.9 (world avg. 18.0).
Total fertility rate (avg. births per childbearing woman; 1984): 5.3.
Marriage rate per 1,000 population (1983): 6.2.
Divorce rate per 1,000 population (1983): 1.1.
Life expectancy at birth (1980–85): male 65.7 years; female 69.9 years.
Major causes of death per 100,000 population (1983): diseases of the circulatory system 97.3; accidents and acts of violence 30.2; ill-defined diseases 29.7%; malignant neoplasms (cancers) 23.9; respiratory diseases 17.2; diseases of the genito-urinary system 6.5; endocrine, nutritional, and metabolic diseases 6.2; certain causes of perinatal morbidity and mortality 5.2; infective and parasitic diseases 4.7.

National economy

Budget (1984). Revenue: BD 495,000,000 (petroleum company dividends and oil field receipts 64.4%; tax revenue 20.8%, of which taxes on international trade 9.9%; social security contributions 3.9%). Expenditures: BD 543,700,000 (public utilities 12.9%; defense 10.2%; education 10.2%; health 6.4%; roads 6.3%; social security and welfare 2.3%).
Population economically active (1984): total 176,853; activity rate of total population 44.2% (participation rates: over age 15, 64.6%; female 13.7%; unemployed 1.3%).

Price and earnings indexes (1980 = 100)

	1979	1980	1981	1982	1983	1984	1985
Consumer price index	96.3	100	111.3	121.2	124.8	125.2	122.0
Monthly earnings index	...	...	...	...	...	...	...

Production (metric tons except as noted). Agriculture, forestry, fishing (1984): dates 40,000, tomatoes 12,000, cow's milk 6,000; livestock (number of live animals) 15,000 goats, 7,000 sheep, 6,000 cattle. Manufacturing (barrels; 1982): fuel oil 19,889,000; gas oil 19,205,000; automotive and aviation gasoline 18,409,000; naphtha 7,886,000; kerosene 2,674,000; heavy lubricant distillate 364,000; diesel oil 310,000; liquefied petroleum gas 303,000; asphalt 232,000 metric tons. Construction (permits issued; 1983): residential 5,896; nonresidential 2,445. Energy production (consumption): electricity (kW-hr; 1984) 2,056,000,000 (2,056,000,000); coal, none (n.a.); crude petroleum (barrels; 1984) 14,801,000 (73,954,000); petroleum products (metric tons; 1984) 9,187,000 (384,000); natural gas (cu m; 1984) 3,685,000,000 (3,685,000,000).
Gross national product (1984): U.S.$4,260,000,000 (U.S.$10,640 per capita).

Structure of gross domestic product and labour force

	1982 value in BD '000,000	1982 % of total value	1984 labour force	1984 % of labour force
Agriculture	15.4	0.9	3,600	2.0
Mining	411.2	24.0	5,022	2.8
Manufacturing	340.0	19.9	14,654	8.3
Construction	110.2	6.4	37,565	21.2
Public utilities	15.0	0.9	3,391	2.0
Transp. and commun.	120.0	7.0	16,005	9.1
Trade	158.3	9.3	23,504	13.3
Finance	274.2	16.0	6,576	3.7
Pub. admin., defense	96.1	5.6	...	...
Services	72.9	4.3	64,093	36.2
Other	97.2	5.7	2,443†	1.4†
TOTAL	1,710.5	100.0	176,853	100.0

Households. Average household size (1984) 6.7.
Land use (1983): meadows and pastures 6.5%; agricultural and under permanent cultivation 3.2%; built-on and wasteland (mostly sand plains and salt marshes) 90.3%.
Public debt (external, outstanding; 1983): BD 91,200,000.
Tourism (1982): receipts from visitors U.S.$129,000,000; expenditures by nationals abroad U.S.$202,000,000.

Foreign trade‡

Balance of trade (current prices)

	1980	1981	1982	1983	1984	1985
BD '000,000	+173	+238	+201	+71	−16	−129.3
% of total	6.8%	7.9%	7.6%	3.0%	0.7%	5.8%

Imports (1984): BD 1,324,900,000 (crude petroleum 47.5%, machinery 21.8%, manufactured goods 17.1%, food 6.3%). *Major import sources*§: Japan 18.6%; United States 14.0%; United Kingdom 13.6%; Italy 11.8%.
Exports (1984): BD 1,179,000,000 (petroleum products 86.5%, aluminum 9.7%). *Major export destinations*§: Saudi Arabia 20.8%; Japan 19.4%; United Arab Emirates 11.0%; India 7.7%; United States 7.7%.

Transport and communications

Transport. Railroads: none. Roads (1984): total length 155 km (paved 100.0%). Vehicles (1983): passenger cars 65,588; trucks and buses 21,015. Merchant marine (1985): vessels (100 gross tons and over) 79; total deadweight tonnage 59,167. Air transport ‖ (1985): passenger-km 1,245,000,000; metric ton-km cargo 32,600,000; airports (1986) with scheduled flights 1.
Communications. Daily newspapers (1985): total number 3; total circulation 27,500; circulation per 1,000 population 65.9. Radio (1985): total number of receivers 142,000 (1 per 2.9 persons). Television (1985): total number of receivers 170,000 (1 per 2.5 persons). Telephones (1983): 87,607 (1 per 4.0 persons).

Education and health

Education (1980–81)

	schools	teachers	students	student/teacher ratio
Primary (age 6–11)	114	2,963	48,406	16.3
Secondary (age 12–17)	21	951	23,727	24.9
Voc., teacher tr.	5	233	2,846	12.2
Higher	2	159	3,650	22.9

Educational attainment (1981): Percent of population over age 10 having: no formal education 27.2%; knowledge of reading and writing 26.3%; primary education 24.9%; secondary 13.3%; higher 8.3%.
Literacy (1984): total population literate 202,429 (74.0%); males literate 139,715 (81.1%); females literate 62,714 (61.8%).
Health: physicians (1982) 397 (1 per 929 persons); hospital beds (1983) 1,177 (1 per 326 persons); infant mortality rate per 1,000 live births (1984) 44.1.

Military

Total active duty personnel (1985): 2,800 (army 82.1%, navy 10.7%, air force 7.2%). *Military expenditure as percent of GNP* (1983): 4.0% (world 6.1%); per capita expenditure U.S.$403.

*Total area includes numerous small uninhabited islands and dependencies of Bahrain. †Seeking work for the first time. ‡Import figures are f.o.b. (free on board) in balance of trade and c.i.f. (cost, insurance, and freight) for commodities and trading partners. §Percentage shares for trading partners derived from nonoil portion of foreign trade only. ‖ One-fourth apportionment of international flights of Gulf Air (jointly administered by the governments of Bahrain, Oman, Qatar, and the United Arab Emirates).

Bangladesh

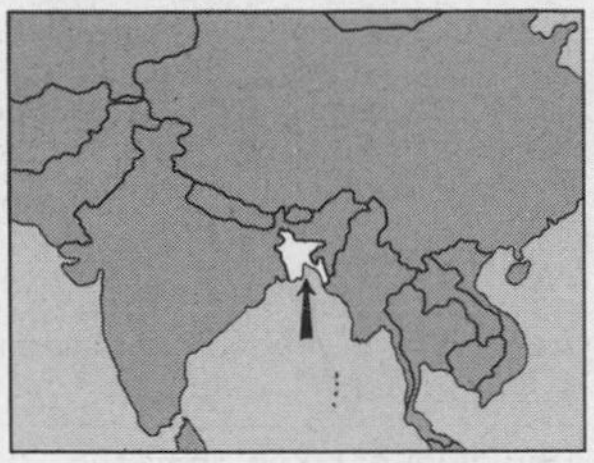

Official name: Gana Prajātantrī Bangladesh (People's Republic of Bangladesh).
Form of government: unitary multiparty republic with one legislative house (Parliament [330])*.
Head of state and government: President (Chief Martial Law Administrator).
Capital: Dhākā (formerly Dacca).
Official language: Bengali.
Official religion: Islam.
Monetary unit: 1 Bangladesh taka (Tk) = 100 paisa; valuation (Oct. 1, 1986) 1 U.S.$ = Tk 30.30; 1 £ = Tk 43.78.

Area and population

		area		population
Divisions†	**Administrative centres**	sq mi	sq km	1985 estimate
Chittagong	Chittagong	17,535	45,415	26,062,000
Dhākā	Dhākā	11,881	30,772	29,043,000
Khulna	Khulna	12,963	33,574	19,792,000
Rājshāhi	Rājshāhi	13,219	34,237	24,383,000
TOTAL		55,598	143,998	100,468,000‡

Demography

Population (1986): 103,204,000.
Density (1986): persons per sq mi 1,843, persons per sq km 717.
Urban-rural (1985): urban 20.3%; rural 79.7%.
Sex distribution (1985): male 51.51%; female 48.49%.
Age breakdown (1985): under 15, 44.3%; 15–29, 26.6%; 30–44, 15.2%; 45–59, 8.6%; 60 and over, 5.3%.
Population projection: (1990) 113,005,000; (2000) 139,693,000.
Doubling time: 26 years.
Ethnic composition (1980): Bengali 97.8%; Bihārī 1.5%; tribal (Chakmā, Gāro, Khāsi, Santāl, etc.) 0.7%.
Religious affiliation (1981): Muslim 86.6%; Hindu 12.1%; Buddhist 0.6%; Christian 0.3%; other 0.4%.
Major cities (1984): Dhākā 3,950,000; Chittagong 1,590,000; Khulna 740,000; Rājshāhi 300,000.

Vital statistics

Birth rate per 1,000 population (1985): 43.3 (world avg. 29.0).
Death rate per 1,000 population (1985): 16.6 (world avg. 11.0).
Natural increase rate per 1,000 population (1985): 26.7 (world avg. 18.0).
Total fertility rate (avg. births per childbearing woman; 1985): 5.8.
Marriage rate per 1,000 population (1982): 9.4.
Divorce rate per 1,000 population: n.a.
Life expectancy at birth (1985): male 49.2 years; female 48.2 years.
Major causes of death per 100 deaths (1976): diseases of the respiratory system 25.7, of which tuberculosis 4.8; malignant neoplasms (cancers) 19.8; infectious intestinal diseases 15.5; diseases of the liver and kidney 11.4; diseases of the circulatory system 5.9; virus fevers 4.5; childbirth related causes 4.4.; diabetes 3.6.

National economy

Budget (1985–86). Revenue: Tk 37,540,000,000 (tax receipts 79.8%, of which customs duties 30.9%, excise duties 22.0%, sales tax 12.3%, income taxes 11.5%, stamps [nonjudicial] 3.1%; dividends and profits from financial institutions 5.4%; interest receipts 4.5%). Expenditures: TK 33,130,000,000 (defense 15.1%; education 14.7%; debt service 11.8%; subsidy and grants-in-aid 11.6%; social and community services 5.1%; justice and police 4.1%; health and population control 3.9%; unexpected expenditures 11.8%).
Public debt (external, outstanding; 1985): U.S.$5,965,600,000.
Tourism: receipts from visitors (1984) U.S.$27,000,000; expenditures by nationals abroad (1983) U.S.$23,000,000.
Production (metric tons except as noted). Agriculture, forestry, fishing (1983–84): paddy rice 21,761,704, sugarcane 7,168,896, wheat 1,211,072, jute and jute-like fibres 953,008, sweet potatoes 713,232, bananas 674,624, mangoes 158,496, pineapples 136,144, tobacco leaves 47,752, tea 42,672, peanuts (groundnuts) 22,352, sesame seed 22,352; livestock (number of live animals) 22,490,000 cattle, 9,944,000 goats, 566,000 buffalo, 552,000 sheep, 55,621,000 chickens, 23,747,000 ducks; roundwood 26,359,000 cu m§; fish catch 728,500 ‖. Mining and quarrying (1983–84): sea salt 672,000; limestone 25,000. Manufacturing (1984–85)¶: chemical fertilizers 751,007; jute manufactures 452,900, of which jute sackings 219,400, burlap 209,600, carpet backing 22,200; iron and steel 253,631; paper and newsprint 89,702; sugar 87,849; petroleum products 9,473; chemicals 7,269; food products 1,964; cotton cloth 37,274,000 m; cotton yarn 160,000 bales; glass sheets 1,199,000 sq m; matches 431,000 gross. Construction: n.a. Energy production (consumption): electricity (kW-hr; 1984) 4,292,000,000 (4,292,000,000); coal (metric tons; 1984) none (175,000); crude petroleum (barrels; 1984) 147,000 (7,802,000); petroleum products (metric tons; 1984) 876,000 (1,314,000); natural gas (cu m; 1984) 10,053,200,000 (1,633,400,000).
Land use (1983): forested 16.0; meadows and pastures 4.5%; agricultural and under permanent cultivation 68.2%; other 11.3%.
Gross national product (at current market prices; 1984–85): U.S.$15,048,000,000 (U.S.$150 per capita).

Structure of gross domestic product and labour force

	1984–85		1983–84	
	in value Tk '000,000	% of total value	labour force	% of labour force
Agriculture	192,476	48.4	16,400,000	59.4
Mining	34,390	8.6	...	...
Manufacturing			2,400,000	8.7
Construction	20,939	5.3	500,000	1.8
Public utilities	2,424	0.6	25,000	0.1
Transp. and commun.	27,156	6.8	1,100.000	4.0
Trade	35,045	8.8	3,200,000	11.6
Finance	5,930	1.5	400,000	1.4
Public admin., defense	17,694	4.4	1,200,000	4.3
Services and other	61,692	15.5	2,400,000	8.7
TOTAL	397,746	100.0‡	27,625,000	100.0

Population economically active (1984): total 29,319,000; activity rate of total population 30.6% (participation rates: ages 15–64, 50.3%; female 8.8%; unemployed and underemployed [1983–84] 26.5%).

Price and earnings indexes (1980 = 100)

	1980	1981	1982	1983	1984	1985	1986♀
Consumer price index	100.0	116.2	130.7	143.0	158.1	175.0	195.1
Hourly earnings index♂	100.0	105.4	106.3	106.4	...	...	...

Household income. Average household size (1981) 5.8; median annual income per household (1977–78) Tk 8,332 (U.S.$549); sources of income: agriculture 44.7%, wages 26.9%, finance and trade 11.8%, real estate 6.0%, gifts and assistance 0.3%, pension 0.2%, other 10.1%; expenditure (1977–78): food and drink 70.5%, rent 9.3%, fuel and lighting 7.4%, clothing 6.5%, medical 1.6%, personal care 1.2%, education 0.8%, other 2.7%.

Foreign trade

Balance of trade (current prices)

	1980	1981	1982	1983	1984	1985
Tk '000,000	−24,380	−29,692	−28,508	−30,138	−40,882	−41,543
% of total	51.0%	51.2%	45.5%	45.8%	46.4%	42.6%

Imports (1984–85): Tk 68,738,000,000 (machinery and transport equipment 18.8%; food grains 17.7%, of which wheat 14.5%, rice 3.2%; petroleum and petroleum products 12.9%; edible oil and oil seeds 6.3%; chemicals 4.7%; fertilizers 3.8%; cotton 2.1%; cement 2.0%; textile yarn 1.6%). *Major import sources* (1983–84): Hong Kong 13.7%; Japan 12.5%; United States 11.2%; Singapore 10.8%; China 5.5%; United Kingdom 5.0%.
Export (1984–85): Tk 25,211,000,000 (jute manufactures 43.2%; raw jute and jute mesta 15.1%; ready-made garments 10.9%; fish, shrimp, and frog legs 10.2%; leather 8.7%; tea 5.8%; petroleum products 1.7%). *Major export destinations* (1983–84): United States 13.3%; Italy 8.6%; Japan 7.7%; United Kingdom 6.0%; Belgium 5.6%; Singapore 2.5%.

Transport and communications

Transport. Railroads (1983–84): route length 1,793 mi, 2,886 km; passenger-mi 3,890,000,000, passenger-km 6,260,000,000; short ton-mi cargo 496,000,000, metric ton-km cargo 724,000,000. Roads (1982): total length 98,522 mi, 158,551 km (paved 12%). Vehicles (1981–82): passenger cars 35,488; trucks and buses 21,401. Merchant marine (1985): vessels (100 gross tons and over) 260; total deadweight tonnage 480,422. Air transport (1985)□: passenger-mi 1,021,845,000, passenger-km 1,643,924,000; short ton-mi cargo 151,174,000, metric ton-km cargo 220,711,000; airports (1986) 8.
Communications. Daily newspapers (1984): total number 64; total circulation 546,000; circulation per 1,000 population 5.6. Radio (1985): 775,000 receivers (1 per 130 persons). Television (1985): 300,000 receivers (1 per 335 persons). Telephones (1984): 143,000 (1 per 685 persons).

Education and health

Education (1984–85)

	schools	teachers	students	student/ teacher ratio
Primary (age 5–9)	44,488	184,575	10,082,000	54.6
Secondary (age 10–14)	8,649	97,774	2,638,000	27.0
Voc., teacher tr.	158◇	2,851§	27,624§	9.9§
Higher ‖	...	14,685	386,542	26.3

Educational attainment (1974). Percent of adult population over age 25 having: no formal schooling 82.3%; primary education 10.0%; secondary 6.9%; postsecondary 0.9%. *Literacy* (1985): total population over age 15 literate 18,166,000 (33.1%); males literate 12,272,000 (43.3%); females literate 5,894,000 (22.2%).
Health: physicians (1982) 12,306 (1 per 7,560 persons); hospital beds (1984) 26,141 (1 per 3,748 persons); infant mortality rate per 1,000 live births (1980–85) 128.0.
Food (1980–82): daily per capita caloric intake 1,869 (vegetable products 96%, animal products 4%); 85% of FAO recommended minimum requirement.

Military

Total active duty personnel (1985): 91,300 (army 89.6%, navy 7.1%, air force 3.3%). *Military expenditure as percent of GNP* (1984): 1.4% (world 6.1%); per capita expenditure U.S.$2.

*Currently under martial law; constitution suspended and Parliament dissolved in 1982. †Geographic reorganization at the district level took place in 1984; each division is now divided into the following number of new districts: Chittagong 15, Dhākā 17, Khulna 16, and Rājshāhi 16. ‡Detail does not add to total given because of rounding. §1984. ‖ 1983. ¶Public sector except jute manufactures. ♀June. ♂Skilled wage earnings in manufacturing. □Bangladesh Biman only. ◇Public schools only.

Barbados

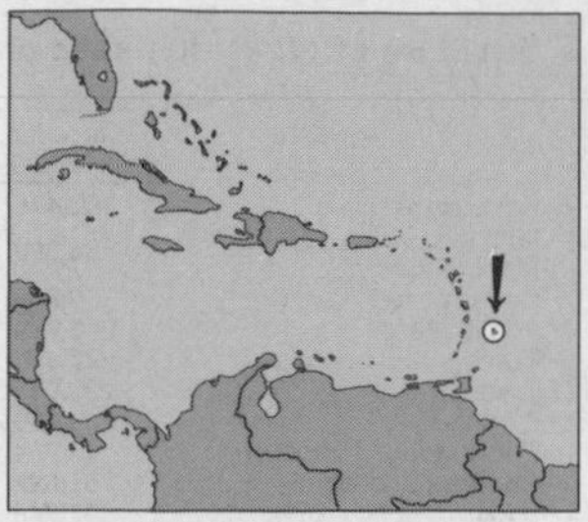

Official name: Barbados.
Form of government: constitutional monarchy with two legislative houses (Senate [21]; House of Assembly [27]).
Chief of state: British Monarch represented by governor-general.
Head of government: Prime Minister.
Capital: Bridgetown.
Official language: English.
Official religion: none.
Monetary unit: 1 Barbados dollar (BDS$) = 100 cents; valuation (Oct. 1, 1986) 1 U.S.$ = BDS$2.01; 1 £ = BDS$2.91.

Area and population

	area		population
			1980
Parishes*	sq mi	sq km	census
Christ Church	22	57	40,790
St. Andrew	14	36	6,731
St. George	17	44	17,361
St. James	12	31	17,255
St. John	13	34	10,330
St. Joseph	10	26	7,211
St. Lucy	14	36	9,264
St. Michael†	15	39	99,953
St. Peter	13	34	10,717
St. Philip	23	60	18,662
St. Thomas	13	34	10,709
TOTAL	166	430‡	248,983§

Demography

Population (1986): 253,000.
Density (1986): persons per sq mi 1,524, persons per sq km 588.
Urban-rural (1985): urban 42.3%; rural 57.7%.
Sex distribution (1985): male 47.40%; female 52.60%.
Age breakdown (1985): under 15, 27.3%; 15–29, 30.5%; 30–44, 17.2%; 45–59, 12.1%; 60–74, 9.4%; 75 and over, 3.5%.
Population projection: (1990) 257,000; (2000) 264,000.
Doubling time: 77 years.
Ethnic composition (1980): black 91.9%; white 3.3%; mulatto 2.6%; East Indian 0.5%; other 1.7%.
Religious affiliation (1980): Anglican 49.7%; other Protestant 38.3% (mainly Methodist, Pentecostal, and Seventh-day Adventist); Roman Catholic 5.9%; nonreligious 5.2%.
Major cities (1980): Bridgetown 7,552 (metropolitan area 99,953); other cities cannot be identified because no other bounded localities exist.

Vital statistics

Birth rate per 1,000 population (1984): 16.7 (world avg. 29.0); (1978) legitimate 27.9%; illegitimate 72.1%.
Death rate per 1,000 population (1984): 7.7 (world avg. 11.0).
Natural increase rate per 1,000 population (1984): 9.0 (world avg. 18.0).
Total fertility rate (avg. births per childbearing woman; 1980–85): 1.9.
Marriage rate per 1,000 population (1983): 5.0.
Divorce rate per 1,000 population (1983): 1.3.
Life expectancy at birth (1980–85): male 70.0 years; female 75.4 years.
Major causes of death per 100,000 population (1982): malignant neoplasms (cancers) 115.8; cerebrovascular disease 103.8; diseases of pulmonary circulation 85.1; acute myocardial infarction 45.5; diabetes mellitus 42.3.

National economy

Budget (1984–85). Revenue: BDS$571,974,000 (tax revenue 88.5%, of which individual income tax 21.9%, consumption tax 16.8%, import duties 14.7%, corporate tax 8.9%; nontax revenue 11.5%). Expenditures: BDS$559,810,000 (health 16.6%; general public services 15.7%; debt charges 11.6%; roads and other transportation 9.5%; social security and welfare 9.2%; defense 3.6%; agriculture 2.9%; education 2.4%).
Production (metric tons except as noted). Agriculture, forestry, fishing (1984): sugarcane 900,000, sweet potatoes 5,000, yams 5,000, carrots 3,000, cucumbers 2,000, corn (maize) 2,000; livestock (number of live animals) 54,000 sheep, 50,000 pigs, 32,000 goats, 18,000 cattle; roundwood, n.a.; fish catch (1983) 6,422, of which flying fishes 4,116. Manufacturing (1984): electronic assembly for reexport (including microprocessors and computer chips), n.a.; clothing, n.a.; cement 64,000; animal feed 43,000; cigarettes 238; barbed wire and chain link fencing 206; beer 58,000 hectolitres; rum 27,000 hectolitres. Construction, n.a. Energy production (consumption): electricity (kW-hr; 1984) 361,600,000 (382,000,000); coal, none (none); crude petroleum (barrels; 1985) 679,000 (1,457,000 ‖); petroleum products (metric tons; 1984) 192,000 (206,000); natural gas (cu m; 1985) 32,200,000 (10,300,000¶).
Population economically active (1986♀): total 116,700; activity rate of total population 46.1% (participation rates: ages 15–64, 73.7% ‖ ; female 47.1%; unemployed 15.6%).

Price and earnings indexes (1980 = 100)

	1980	1981	1982	1983	1984	1985	1986
Consumer price index	100.0	114.6	126.4	133.0	139.2	144.7	146.8δ
Monthly earnings index	100.0	109.8	121.6	128.3	140.5	...	...

Household income and expenditure. Average household size (1980) 3.7; income per household: n.a.; sources of income: n.a.; expenditure (1980): food 43.2%, housing 13.1%, household operations 9.6%, alcohol and tobacco 8.4%, fuel and light 6.2%, medical and personal care 6.0%, clothing and footwear 5.1%, transportation 4.6%, education and recreation 3.8%.
Public debt (external, outstanding; 1985): U.S.$220,800,000.
Tourism: receipts from visitors (1985) U.S.$298,000,000; expenditures by nationals abroad (1983) U.S.$26,000,000.
Gross national product (at current market prices; 1984): U.S.$1,100,000,000 (U.S.$4,370 per capita).

Structure of gross domestic product and labour force

	1984		1984	
	in value BDS$'000	% of total value	labour force	% of labour force
Agriculture, fishing	141,382	6.1	9,400	8.4
Mining	29,392	1.3 }	15,800	14.0
Manufacturing	264,056	11.5 }		
Construction	129,996	5.6	8,700	7.8
Public utilities	68,004	3.0	2,000	1.8
Transportation and communication	171,019	7.4	5,700	5.1
Trade	619,035	26.9	24,000	21.3
Finance	270,890	11.8	3,400	3.0
Pub. admin., defense, and services	381,223	16.5	39,400	35.1
Other	228,195□	9.9□	3,900◊	3.5◊
TOTAL	2,303,192	100.0	112,600	100.0

Land use (1983): forested, negligible; meadows and pastures 9.0%; agricultural and under permanent cultivation 77.0%; other 14.0%.

Foreign trade△

Balance of trade (current prices)

	1980	1981	1982	1983	1984	1985
BDS$'000,000	–507.1	–665.1	–498.6	–499.0	–427.7	–413.0
% of total	35.8%	46.0%	32.5%	27.9%	21.4%	22.6%

Imports (1985): BDS$1,221,500,000 (†electrical components 16.5%, machinery 16.0%, food and beverages 15.3%, fuels 5.3%; construction materials 4.9%, chemicals 4.7%). *Major import sources* (1984): United States 47.8%; Trinidad and Tobago 8.5%; United Kingdom 7.5%; Canada 5.7%; other EEC 4.5%.
Exports (1985): BDS$707,800,000 (⊕electrical components 61.3%, sugar 10.1%, clothing 9.1%, chemicals 4.3%, rum 1.6%). *Major export destinations* (1984): United States 27.6%; Trinidad and Tobago 9.5%; United Kingdom 6.9%; Guyana 6.7%; unspecified destinations 40.3% .

Transport and communications

Transport. Railroads: none. Roads (1984): total length 994 mi, 1,600 km (paved 95%). Vehicles (1984): passenger cars 30,984; trucks and buses 5,454. Merchant marine (1985): vessels (100 gross tons and over) 35; total deadweight tonnage 9,466. Air transport: passenger-mi 92,600,000**, passenger-km 149,000,000**; short ton-mi cargo 773,000††, metric ton-km cargo 1,128,000††; airports (1986) with scheduled flights 1.
Communications. Daily newspapers (1984): total number 2; total circulation 40,000; circulation per 1,000 population 159. Radio (1985): total number of receivers 180,000 (1 per 1.4 persons). Television (1985): total number of receivers 60,000 (1 per 4.2 persons). Telephones (1983): 72,850 (1 per 3.4 persons).

Education and health

Education (1984–85)

	schools	teachers	students	student/ teacher ratio
Primary (age 5–11)	130	1,464	30,792	21.0
Secondary (age 12–16)	36	1,449	28,815	19.9
Vocational	3	154	3,592	23.3
Higher	1	108	1,617	15.0

Educational attainment (1980). Percent of population over age 15 having: no formal schooling 0.6%; primary education 50.0%; secondary 41.0%; higher 3.8%. *Literacy* (1980): total population over age 15 literate‡‡ 169,894 (98.0%); males literate 78,022 (98.3%); females literate 91,872 (97.7%).
Health (1983): physicians 213 (1 per 1,179 persons); hospital beds 2,110 (1 per 119 persons); infant mortality rate per 1,000 live births (1984) 10.9.
Food (1980–82): daily per capita caloric intake 3,067 (vegetable products 74%, animal products 26%); 125% of FAO recommended minimum requirement.

Military

Total active duty personnel (1983): 154 (paramilitary marine and coast guard components only). *Military expenditure as percent of GNP* (1983): 0.7% (world 6.1%); per capita expenditure U.S.$26.

*Parishes have no local administrative function. †Includes Bridgetown. ‡Detail does not add to total given because of rounding. §Excludes nonresident visitors. ‖1983. ¶1984. ♀End of first quarter. δFebruary average. □Includes net indirect taxes. ◊Unemployed persons not previously employed. △Import figures are f.o.b. in balance of trade and c.i.f. in commodities and trading partners. †Breakdown based on retained imports only valued at BDS$1,010,000,000. ⊕Breakdown based on domestic exports only valued at BDS$496,500,000. **1983; Caribbean Airways only. ††1985; Caribbean Air Cargo only. ‡‡National literacy standard based solely on school attendance. Functional literacy may be appreciably lower.

Belgium

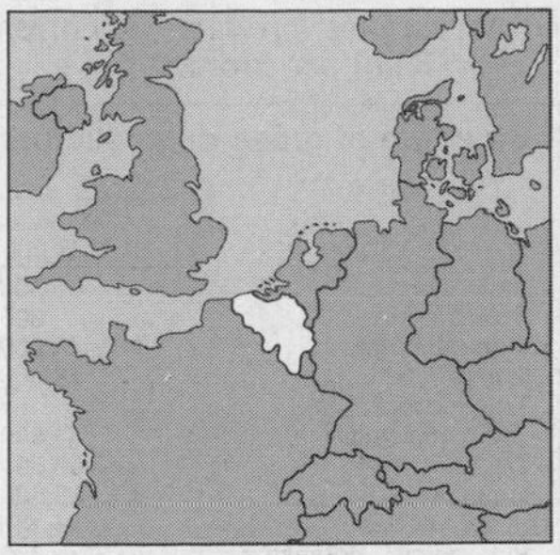

Official name: Koninkrijk België (Dutch); Royaume de Belgique (French) (Kingdom of Belgium).
Form of government: constitutional monarchy with two legislative houses (Senate [184]; House of Representatives [212]).
Chief of state: Monarch.
Head of government: Prime Minister.
Capital: Brussels.
Official languages: Dutch; French; German.
Official religion: none.
Monetary unit: 1 Belgian franc (BF) = 100 centimes; valuation (Oct. 1, 1986) 1 U.S.$ = BF 42.06; 1 £ = BF 60.78.

Area and population

		area		population
Provinces	**Capitals**	sq mi	sq km	1984 estimate
Antwerp	Antwerp	1,107	2,867	1,578,869
Brabant	Brussels	1,297	3,358	2,217,442
East Flanders	Ghent	1,151	2,982	1,331,193
Hainaut	Mons	1,462	3,787	1,285,936
Liège	Liège	1,491	3,862	992,061
Limburg	Hasselt	935	2,422	726,884
Luxembourg	Arlon	1,715	4,441	223,813
Namur	Namur	1,415	3,665	410,251
West Flanders	Brugge	1,210	3,134	1,086,574
TOTAL		11,783	30,518	9,853,023

Demography

Population (1986): 9,856,000.
Density (1986): persons per sq mi 836.5, persons per sq km 323.0.
Urban-rural (1980): urban 72.4%; rural 27.6%.
Sex distribution (1984): male 48.81%; female 51.19%.
Age breakdown (1983): under 15, 19.4%; 15–29, 23.6%; 30–44, 20.0%; 45–59, 18.1%; 60–74, 13.0%; 75 and over, 5.9%.
Population projection: (1990) 9,860,000; (2000) 9,890,000.
Doubling time: n.a.; doubling time exceeds 100 years.
Nationality (1981): Belgian 91.1%; Italian 2.8%; Moroccan 1.1%; French 1.1%; Dutch 0.7%; Turkish 0.6%; other 2.6%.
Religious affiliation (1980): Roman Catholic 91.8%; Protestant 3.5%; Muslim 1.1%.
Major cities (1984): Brussels 137,738 (982,434*); Antwerp 488,425; Ghent 235,401; Charleroi 213,041; Liège 203,065.

Vital statistics

Birth rate per 1,000 population (1985): 11.9 (world avg. 29.0); (1982) legitimate 94.8%; illegitimate 5.2%.
Death rate per 1,000 population (1985): 11.4 (world avg. 11.0).
Natural increase rate per 1,000 population (1985): 0.5 (world avg. 18.0).
Total fertility rate (avg. births per childbearing woman; 1985): 1.6.
Marriage rate per 1,000 population (1984): 5.8.
Divorce rate per 1,000 population (1982): 1.6.
Life expectancy at birth (1985): male 70.1 years; female 76.7 years.
Major causes of death per 100,000 population (1979): heart and circulatory diseases 359.9, of which cerebrovascular disease 127.0; malignant neoplasms (cancers) 264.8.

National economy

Budget (1985). Revenue: BF 1,417,671,000,000 (direct taxes 61.1%; value-added, stamp, and similar duties 26.0%; customs and excise duties 7.1%). Expenditures: BF 1,889,153,000,000 (government departments 43.0%; public debt 20.1%; educational and cultural services 15.1%; pension 8.9%; defense 5.6%).
Public debt (1984): U.S.$82,768,000,000.
Tourism (1984): receipts from visitors U.S.$1,700,000,000; expenditures by nationals abroad U.S.$1,953,000,000.
Production (metric tons except as noted). Agriculture, forestry, fishing (1984): sugar beets 5,723,000, potatoes 1,650,000, wheat 1,330,000, barley 935,000, apples 260,000, tomatoes 130,000, oats 118,000, corn (maize) 39,000, milk 4,150,000; livestock (number of live animals) 3,115,000 cattle, 5,300,000 pigs, 120,000 sheep, 35,000 horses; roundwood 3,086,000 cu m†; fish catch 48,580‡, of which European plaice (flounder) 10,591, Atlantic cod 7,715, Atlantic herring 5,970. Mining and quarrying (1984): quartz and quartzite 349,720; barite 39,000. Manufacturing (value added in BF '000,000; 1982): metal products and machinery 264,600; food and beverages 160,200; chemicals and chemical products 89,800, of which drugs and medicines 14,400; textiles 47,200; glass and glass products 38,200; furniture and fixtures 36,300; iron and steel 32,400; printing and publishing 28,500; paper and paper products 21,600; wearing apparel 20,800. Construction (1984): residential 14,976,000 cu m; nonresidential 18,168,000 cu m. Energy production (consumption): electricity (kW-hr; 1984) 53,699,000,000 (54,009,000,000); coal (metric tons; 1984) 6,301,000 (14,956,000); petroleum (barrels; 1984) none (170,027,000); natural gas (cu m; 1984) 46,480,000 (8,759,400,000).
Household income and expenditure. Average household size (1981) 2.7; sources of income (1984): wages and salaries 52.9%, self-employment 25.5%, transfer payments 20.9%; expenditure (1984): housing 30.9%, food 25.2%, personal care and health 11.0%, clothing and footwear 7.1%, other 25.8%.

Gross national product (at current market prices; 1984): U.S.$83,070,000,000 (U.S.$8,410 per capita).

Structure of gross domestic product and labour force

	1984		1983	
	in value BF '000,000	% of total value	labour force	% of labour force
Agriculture	112,300	2.5	106,100	2.5
Mining	26,900	0.6	26,700	0.6
Manufacturing	1,082,800	24.1	830,000	19.7
Construction	244,400	5.4	216,800	5.2
Public utilities	165,700	3.7	32,600	0.8
Transportation and communication	354,600	7.9	267,200	6.3
Trade	887,200	19.8	688,100	16.3
Finance	231,600	5.2	264,000	6.3
Pub. admin., defense	371,800	8.3 }	1,202,100	28.5
Services	896,800	20.0 }		
Other	111,900	2.5	579,800§	13.8
TOTAL	4,486,000	100.0	4,213,400	100.0

Population economically active (1983): total 4,213,400; activity rate of total population 42.7% (participation rates: ages 15–64, n.a.; female 38.8%; unemployed 12.9%).

Price and earnings indexes (1980 = 100)

	1980	1981	1982	1983	1984	1985	1986 ‖
Consumer price index	100.0	107.6	117.0	126.0	134.0	141.8	142.2
Hourly earnings index	100.0	110.1	116.9	122.0	128.0	136.4	...

Land use† (1983): forested 21.4%; meadows and pastures 20.7%; agricultural and under permanent cultivation 25.4%; other 32.5%.

Foreign trade†

Balance of trade (current prices)

	1980	1981	1982	1983	1984	1985
BF '000,000	−210,448	−236,884	−247,817	−166,257	−205,000	−151,800
% of total	5.3%	5.4%	4.9%	3.0%	3.3%	2.3%

Imports (1984): BF 3,192,525,000,000 (machinery and transport equipment 21.4%, of which road vehicles and parts 9.3%; mineral fuels and lubricants 18.6%, of which petroleum and petroleum products 14.1%, natural gas 2.8%; chemicals and chemical products 9.9%; food and live animals 9.4%; nonindustrial (gem) diamonds 5.9%). *Major import sources:* West Germany 19.9%; The Netherlands 18.8%; France 14.6%; United Kingdom 8.8%; United States 6.0%.
Exports (1984): BF 2,987,510,000,000 (machinery and transport equipment 21.0%, of which passenger cars 8.1%; chemicals and chemical products 12.6%, of which plastics 4.5%; food and live animals 9.3%; iron and steel 8.4%; petroleum and petroleum products 7.4%; nonindustrial (gem) diamonds 6.0%; textile yarns and fabrics 5.6%). *Major export destinations:* West Germany 19.7%; France 18.4%; The Netherlands 13.9%; United Kingdom 9.9%; United States 6.1%.

Transport and communications

Transport. Railroads (1984): route length 2,325 mi, 3,741 km; passenger-mi 4,007,000,000, passenger-km 6,444,000,000; short ton-mi cargo 5,391,000,000, metric ton-km cargo 7,871,000,000. Roads (1984): total length 79,341 mi, 127,688 km (paved 95%). Vehicles (1984): passenger cars 3,300,248; trucks and buses 310,685. Merchant marine (1985): vessels (100 gross tons and over) 344; total deadweight tonnage 3,853,651. Air transport (1985): passenger-mi 3,519,000,000, passenger-km 5,664,000,000; short ton-mi cargo 399,590,000; metric ton-km cargo 583,395,000; airports (1986) with scheduled flights 4.
Communications. Daily newspapers (1985): total number 38; total circulation 2,691,400¶; circulation per 1,000 population 272¶. Radio (1984): total number of receivers 4,610,000 (1 per 2.1 persons). Television (1984): total number of receivers 2,983,166 (1 per 3.3 persons). Telephones (1983): 3,984,295 (1 per 2.5 persons).

Education and health

Education (1982–83)

	schools	teachers	students	student/teacher ratio
Primary (age 6–12)	4,497	40,894	814,089	19.9
Secondary (age 12–18)	2,314	56,719	848,590	15.0
Voc., teacher tr.	209	6,864	218,717	31.9
Higher	19	...	108,689	...

Educational attainment (1977). Percent of population over age 14 having: less than secondary education 61.3%; lower secondary 17.8%; upper secondary 11.4%; vocational 3.6%; teacher's college 2.3%; university 3.6%.
Literacy (1984): virtually 100% literate.
Health (1983): physicians 28,365 (1 per 347 persons); hospital beds 92,138 (1 per 107 persons); infant mortality rate per 1,000 live births (1985) 9.4.
Food† (1980–82): daily per capita caloric intake 3,668 (vegetable products 59%, animal products 41%); 130% of FAO recommended minimum.

Military

Total active duty personnel (1985): 91,570 (army 73.4%, navy 5.0%, air force 21.6%). *Military expenditure as percent of GNP* (1984): 3.3% (world 6.1%); per capita expenditure U.S.$258.

*Région Bruxelloise. †Includes Luxembourg. ‡1983. §Includes 545,100 unemployed. ‖ June. ¶For 31 newspapers only.

Belize

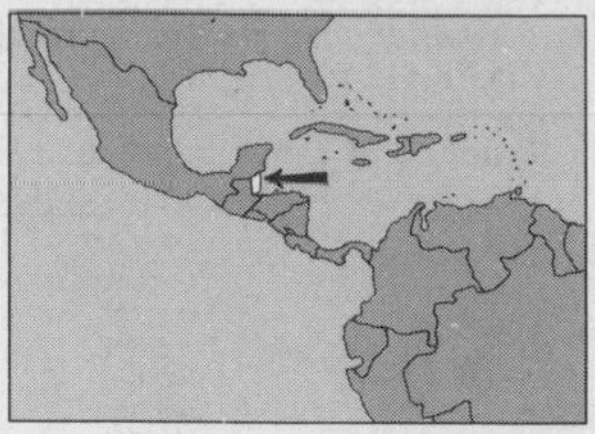

Official name: Belize.
Form of government: constitutional monarchy with two legislative houses (Senate [8]; House of Representatives [28]).
Chief of state: British Monarch represented by governor-general.
Head of government: Prime Minister.
Capital: Belmopan.
Official language: English.
Official religion: none.
Monetary unit: 1 Belize dollar (BZ$) = 100 cents; valuation (Oct. 1, 1986) 1 U.S.$ = BZ$2.00*; 1 £ = BZ$2.89.

Area and population

		area		population
Districts	Capitals	sq mi	sq km	1985 estimate
Belize	Belize City	1,624	4,206	54,500
Cayo	San Ignacio	2,061	5,338	27,400
Corozal	Corozal	718	1,860	28,000
Orange Walk	Orange Walk	1,829	4,737	26,600
Stann Creek	Dangriga	840	2,176	16,500
Toledo	Punta Gorda	1,795	4,649	13,400
TOTAL		8,867	22,965†	166,400

Demography

Population (1986): 171,100.
Density (1986): persons per sq mi 19.3, persons per sq km 7.5.
Urban-rural (1980): urban 51.7%; rural 48.3%.
Sex distribution (1984): male 50.63%; female 49.37%.
Age breakdown (1984): under 15, 45.3%; 15–29, 27.9%; 30–44, 11.8%; 45–59, 7.9%; 60–74, 5.0%; 75 and over, 2.1%.
Population projection: (1990) 190,300; (2000) 248,400.
Doubling time: 20 years.
Ethnic composition (1980): Creole 39.7%; mestizo 33.1%; Garifuna (black Carib) 7.6%; Maya 6.8%; white 4.2%; other 8.6%.
Religious affiliation (1980): Roman Catholic 61.7%; Anglican 11.8%; Methodist 6.0%; Mennonite 3.9%; Seventh-day Adventist 3.0%; Bahā'ī 2.5%; Pentecostal 2.2%; Nazarene 1.1%; Jehovah's Witnesses 1.0%; Baptist 0.9%; other 5.9%.
Major cities (1980): Belize City 39,770; Orange Walk 8,440; Corozal 6,900; Dangriga 6,660; Belmopan 2,940.

Vital statistics

Birth rate per 1,000 population (1985): 40.1 (world avg. 29.0); (1984) legitimate 46.1%; illegitimate 53.9%.
Death rate per 1,000 population (1985): 4.0 (world avg. 11.0).
Natural increase rate per 1,000 population (1985): 36.1 (world avg. 18.0).
Total fertility rate (avg. births per childbearing woman; 1980): 3.7.
Marriage rate per 1,000 population (1984): 5.3.
Divorce rate per 1,000 population (1984): 0.5.
Life expectancy at birth (1979–81): male and female 71.2 years.
Major causes of death per 100,000 population (1984): heart disease 43.8; bronchitis, emphysema, and asthma 42.6; malignant neoplasms (cancers) 34.5; pneumonia 32.0; perinatal mortality 24.7; cerebrovascular diseases 23.4.

National economy

Budget (1986–87). Revenue: BZ$213,800,000 (local revenue sources 65.8%, foreign sources 34.2%). Expenditures: BZ$213,800,000 (capital projects 45.8%, administration 11.9%, public debt payment 11.5%, education 9.0%, security 5.0%, health 4.9%).
Public debt (external, outstanding; 1984): U.S.$65,500,000.
Tourism (1984): receipts from visitors U.S.$11,000,000; expenditures by nationals abroad, n.a.
Production (metric tons except as noted). Agriculture, forestry, fishing (1984): sugarcane 1,038,000, oranges 46,000, grapefruits 28,000, bananas 19,000, corn (maize) 16,000, rice 4,000, coconuts 3,000, vegetables and melons 3,000, dry beans 3,000; livestock (number of live animals) 51,000 cattle, 20,000 pigs, 350,000 chickens; roundwood 164,000 cu m; fish catch 2,824‡. Mining and quarrying (1984): sand and gravel 554,370; limestone 608,860. Manufacturing (1983): sugar 103,100; molasses 33,500; fertilizer 4,641; wheat flour 1,264; beer 28,640 hectolitres; cigarettes 64,600,000 units; garments 1,966,000 units; batteries 5,555 units. Construction (1977): residential 7,150 sq m, nonresidential 2,018 sq m. Energy production (consumption): electricity (kW-hr; 1984) 58,000,000 (58,000,000); coal, none (n.a.); crude petroleum, none (n.a.); petroleum products (metric tons; 1984) none (58,000); natural gas, none (n.a.).
Population economically active (1984): total 47,325; activity rate of total population 29.2% (participation rates: over age 15, 63.0%; female 32.5%; unemployed 14.0%).

Price and earnings indexes (Feb. 1980 = 100)

	July 1980	July 1981	July 1982	July 1983	Feb. 1984	Feb. 1985
Consumer price index	109.1	119.9	128.1	133.9	135.5	142.6
Earnings index	...	...	...	...	...	...

Gross national product (at current market prices; 1984): U.S.$180,000,000 (U.S.$1,110 per capita).

Structure of gross domestic product and labour force

	1984			
	in value BZ$'000	% of total value	labour force	% of labour force
Agriculture	65,500	20.8	13,065	27.6
Mining	800	0.2	81	0.2
Manufacturing	46,000	14.6	4,192	8.9
Construction	18,000	5.7	1,994	4.2
Transportation and communication	34,800	11.0	2,035	4.3
Trade	55,000	17.5	4,558	9.6
Finance	33,400	10.6	570	1.2
Public utilities	6,100	1.9	611	1.3
Pub. admin., defense	32,800	10.4	6,268	13.2
Services	33,000	10.5	7,326	15.5
Other	11,000	3.5	6,625	14.0
TOTAL	314,800†	100.0†	47,325	100.0

Household income and expenditure. Average household size (1984) 5.2; income per household: n.a.; source of income: n.a.; expenditure (1980): food 51.5%, clothing 9.6%, energy and water 5.6%, housing 3.9%, health care 3.4%, education 1.5%.
Land use (1983): forested 44.4%; meadows and pastures 1.9%; agricultural and under permanent cultivation 2.3%; other 51.4%.

Foreign trade§

Balance of trade (current prices)

	1980	1981	1982	1983	1984	1985	March 1986
BZ$'000,000	11.7	+24.0	16.0	−24.9	−4.0	−6.4	−3.3
% of total	0.4%	5.3%	1.7%	7.4%	1.1%	1.8%	9.8%

Imports (1984): BZ$260,273,000 (manufactured goods 29.8%, food 21.5%, machinery and transport 19.9%, fuels 16.7%, chemicals 8.3%, beverages 2.4%). *Major import sources:* United States 43.6%; United Kingdom 8.3%; Canada 2.3%.
Exports (1984): BZ$145,719,000 (food 75.2%, manufactured goods 21.5%, crude materials except fuels 2.2%, chemicals 0.6%). *Major export destinations:* United States 57.8%; United Kingdom 20.5%; Canada 2.6%.

Transport and communications

Transport. Railroads: none. Roads (1984): total length 1,639 mi, 2,637 km (paved 16%). Vehicles (1984): passenger cars 3,707; trucks and buses 1,855. Merchant marine (1985): vessels (100 gross tons and over) 3; total deadweight tonnage 805. Scheduled international air transport (1984): passenger arrivals 40,064, passenger departures 43,157; cargo loaded 899 metric tons, cargo unloaded 1,301 metric tons; airports (1986) with scheduled flights 7.
Communications. Daily newspapers: none. Radio (1985): total number of receivers 88,000 (1 per 1.9 persons). Television: total number of receivers, n.a. Telephones (1984): 9,350 (1 per 17 persons).

Education and health

Education (1984)

	schools	teachers	students	student/ teacher ratio
Primary (age 5–14)	225	1,515	37,753	24.9
Secondary (age, n.a.)	24	491	6,532	13.3
Voc., teacher tr. / Higher	5	58	737	12.7

Educational attainment (1980). Percent of population over age 15 having: no formal schooling 7.3%; primary education 73.5%; secondary 14.2%; higher 1.6%; other 3.4%. *Literacy* (1982): total population over age 15 literate 95,400 (90%).
Health (1984): physicians 78 (1 per 2,078 persons); hospital beds 584 (1 per 278 persons); infant mortality rate per 1,000 live births (1985) 18.9.
Food (1980–82): daily per capita caloric intake 2,692 (vegetable products 74%, animal products 26%); 118% of FAO recommended minimum requirement.

Military

Total active duty personnel (1985): about 600; a British garrison of 1,800 troops remains in the country.

*The Belize dollar is officially pegged to the U.S. dollar. †Detail does not add to total given because of rounding. ‡1983. §Import value in balance of trade is f.o.b. (free on board) and in the major import categories section is c.i.f. (cost, insurance, and freight).

Benin

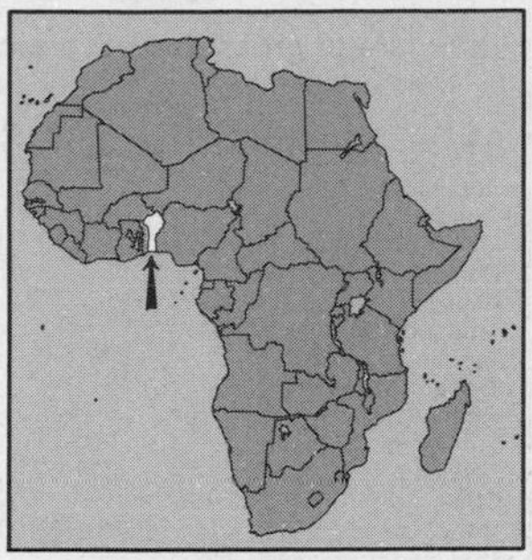

Official name: République Populaire du Bénin (People's Republic of Benin).
Form of government: unitary single-party people's republic with one legislative house (National Revolutionary Assembly [196]).
Head of state and government: President.
*Capitals**: Porto-Novo (official); Cotonou (de facto).
Official language: French.
Official religion: none.
Monetary unit: 1 CFA franc (CFAF) = 100 centimes; valuation (Oct. 1, 1986) 1 U.S.$ = CFAF 332.05; 1 £ = CFAF 479.81.

Area and population

		area		population
				1982
Provinces	Capitals	sq mi	sq km	estimate
Atacora	Natitingou	12,050	31,200	522,000
Atlantique	Cotonou	1,250	3,200	752,000
Borgou	Parakou	19,700	51,000	532,000
Mono	Lokossa	1,450	3,800	517,000
Ouémé	Porto-Novo	1,800	4,700	680,000
Zou	Abomey	7,200	18,700	618,000
TOTAL		43,450	112,600	3,621,000

Demography

Population (1986): 4,126,000.
Density (1986): persons per sq mi 94.9, persons per sq km 36.6.
Urban-rural (1984): urban 16.0%; rural 84.0%.
Sex distribution (1985): male 49.11%; female 50.89%.
Age breakdown (1985): under 15, 46.5%; 15–29, 25.7%; 30–44, 14.8%; 45–59, 8.5%; 60 and over, 4.5%.
Population projection: (1990) 4,661,000; (2000) 6,381,000.
Doubling time: 22 years.
Ethnic composition (1980): Fon 58.9%; Somba 10.4%; Yoruba 10.4%; Bariba 8.9%; Fulani 5.6%; other 5.8%.
Religious affiliation (1980): traditional beliefs 61.4%; Christian 21.6%, of which Roman Catholic 17.4%, Protestant 2.2%; Muslim 15.2%; other 1.8%.
Major cities (1982): Cotonou 487,000; Porto-Novo 208,000; Parakou 66,000; Abomey 54,000; Kandi 53,000.

Vital statistics

Birth rate per 1,000 population (1984): 49.0 (world avg. 29.0).
Death rate per 1,000 population (1984): 17.0 (world avg. 11.0).
Natural increase rate per 1,000 population (1984): 32.0 (world avg. 18.0).
Total fertility rate (avg. births per childbearing woman; 1984): 6.5.
Marriage rate per 1,000 population (1980–85): 12.8.
Divorce rate per 1,000 population (1980–85): 0.8.
Life expectancy at birth (1984): male 47.0 years; female 51.0 years.
Major causes of death per 100,000 population (1977): malaria 227.7; diseases of the respiratory system 206.5; diseases of the digestive system 200.7.

National economy

Budget (1985). Revenue: CFAF 50,800,000,000 (indirect taxes 59.1%, direct taxes 28.5%, other 12.4%). Expenditures: CFAF 50,800,000,000 (administration and services 70.4%, economic development 9.4%).
Production (metric tons except as noted). Agriculture, forestry, fishing (1984–85): yams 769,900, cassava 685,700, corn (maize) 373,500, seed cotton 87,800, millet and sorghum 85,300, palm kernels 75,000, peanuts (groundnuts) 58,000, sweet potatoes 48,000, dry beans 37,000, coconuts 20,000, taro 13,000, oranges 13,000, bananas 13,000, paddy rice 7,700, pineapples 3,000, coffee beans 3,000, cacao beans 1,300, tobacco 263; livestock (number of live animals; 1984) 1,050,000 sheep, 1,000,000 goats, 875,000 cattle, 520,000 pigs, 5,000,000 chickens; roundwood 4,234,000 cu m; fish catch (1983) 21,050. Mining and quarrying (1983): cement 315,000. Manufacturing (1984): sugar 49,000; palm oil and palm kernel oil 36,000; meat products 35,000; cotton fibre 16,000. Construction: n.a. Energy production (consumption): electricity (kW-hr; 1984) 160,062,000 (159,939,000); coal, none (n.a.); crude petroleum (barrels; 1984) 3,285,000 (n.a.); petroleum products (metric tons; 1984) none (101,000).
Gross national product (at current market prices; 1984): U.S.$1,060,000,000 (U.S.$270 per capita).

Structure of gross domestic product and labour force

	1981		1982	
	in value CFAF '000,000	% of total value	labour force	% of labour force
Agriculture	100,500	38.6	1,092,800	64.0
Mining, manufacturing, and public utilities	16,100	6.2	172,300	10.1
Construction	13,200	5.1		
Trade and finance	58,200	22.4		
Transportation and communication	15,700	6.0	441,900	25.9
Pub. admin., defense	26,000	10.0		
Other	—	—		
Net indirect taxes	30,400	11.7	—	—
TOTAL	260,100	100.0	1,707,000	100.0

Tourism (1984): receipts from visitors U.S.$12,000,000; expenditures by nationals abroad U.S.$4,000,000.
Population economically active (1984): total 1,749,000; activity rate of total population 45.9% (participation rates: ages 15–64 [1979] 58.9%; female [1979] 36.4%; unemployed, n.a.).

Price and earnings indexes (1977 = 100)

	1978	1979	1980	1981	1982	1983	1984
Consumer price index	106.9	117.8	130.7	147.8	...	...	...
Hourly earnings index	100.0	100.0	115.0	115.0	115.0	180.4	180.4†

Public debt (external, outstanding; 1985): U.S.$676,600,000.
Household income and expenditure. Average household size (1979) 5.4; income per household (1983): U.S.$240; source of income: n.a.; expenditure: n.a.
Land use (1983): forested 34.5%; meadows and pastures 4.0%; agricultural and under permanent cultivation 16.3%; other 45.2%.

Foreign trade‡

Balance of trade (current prices)

	1979	1980	1981	1982	1983	1984
CFAF '000,000	−49,450	−47,570	−119,120	−124,800	−109,470	−81,830
% of total	83.5%	64.2%	86.7%	94.1%	64.0%	46.2%

Imports (1982): CFAF 152,552,500,000 (manufactured goods 45.6%, of which cotton yarn and fabric 15.8%, chemical products 6.1%; machinery and transport equipment 22.8%, of which nonelectrical equipment 8.7%, electrical equipment 7.8%, transport equipment 6.3%; tobacco 13.7%; food products 11.8%, of which cereals 4.4%). *Major import sources* (1984): France 22.8%; Austria 8.8%; Brazil 7.7%; India 6.3%; The Netherlands 5.9%; Italy 5.2%; China 4.2%; Japan 4.1%; United States 3.8%; West Germany 2.2%.
Exports (1982): CFAF 7,837,000,000 (food products 32.1%, of which coffee 11.6%, cocoa beans 3.6%; palm kernel oil and palm oil 19.7%; cotton 18.7%; energy 7.0%; machinery and transport equipment 7.0%; cement 1.0%, chemical products 0.9%). *Major export destinations* (1984): Spain 31.9%; West Germany 20.6%; France 15.7%; Portugal 6.5%; The Netherlands 4.0%; Italy 2.2%; United Kingdom 2.2%.

Transport and communications

Transport. Railroads (1984): length 360 mi, 580 km; passenger-mi 116,600,000§, passenger-km 187,600,000§; short ton-mi cargo 120,900,000§, metric ton-km cargo 176,500,000§. Roads (1984): total length 5,219 mi, 8,400 km (paved 11%). Vehicles (1984): passenger cars 917; trucks and buses 506. Merchant marine (1985): vessels (100 gross tons and over) 15; total deadweight tonnage 4,880. Air transport ‖ (1985): passenger-mi 144,226,000, passenger-km 232,109,000; short ton-mi cargo 27,420,000, metric ton-km cargo 40,035,000; airports (1986) with scheduled flights 5.
Communications. Daily newspapers (1984): total number 3; total circulation 12,000¶; circulation per 1,000 population 3.5¶. Radio (1984): total number of receivers 290,000 (1 per 14 persons). Television (1984): total number of receivers 17,250 (1 per 203 persons). Telephones (1981): 18,000 (1 per 200 persons).

Education and health

Education (1982)

	schools	teachers	students	student/ teacher ratio
Primary	2,723	11,339	428,185	37.8
Secondary	133	1,816	117,724	64.8
Vocational	30	755	6,543	8.7
Higher	1	801	6,302	7.9

Educational attainment, n.a. *Literacy* (1980): total population over age 15 literate 530,000 (27.9%); males literate 368,000 (39.8%); females literate 162,000 (16.6%).
Health (1982): physicians 270 (1 per 13,570 persons); hospital beds 4,902 (1 per 749 persons); infant mortality rate per 1,000 live births (1984) 116.0.
Food (1980–82): daily per capita caloric intake 2,142 (vegetable products 96%, animal products 4%); 95%♀ of FAO recommended minimum requirement.

Military

Total active duty personnel (1985): 3,480 (army 92.0%, navy 3.4%, air force 4.6%). *Military expenditure as percent of GNP* (1983): 2.6% (world 6.1%); per capita expenditure U.S.$5.

*Porto-Novo is the official capital established under the constitution, but Cotonou, where the president and most government ministers reside, is de facto capital. †January. ‡Figures do not include unaccountable reexports of black market goods, which originate mainly in Nigeria and amounted to an estimated 90% of Benin's actual exports in 1981. Cross-border trade has been adversely affected by the recession in Nigeria and by the closure of the border in 1984; the border was reopened in March 1986. §1981. ‖ Cotonou airport only. ¶Circulation for government daily only. ♀1979–81.

Bermuda

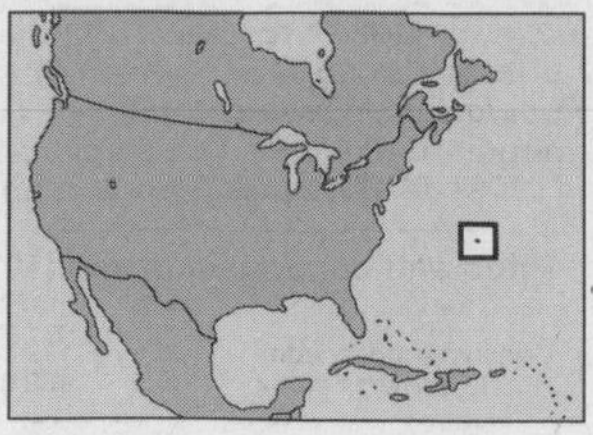

Official name: Bermuda.
Political status: colony (United Kingdom) with two legislative houses (Senate [11]; House of Assembly [40]).
Chief of state: British Monarch, represented by Governor.
Head of government: Premier.
Capital: Hamilton.
Official language: English.
Official religion: none.
Monetary unit: 1 Bermuda dollar (Ber$) = 100 cents; valuation (Oct. 1, 1986) 1 U.S.$ = Ber$1.00*; 1 £ = Ber$1.45.

Area and population

Municipalities	area sq mi	area sq km	population 1980 census
Hamilton	0.3	0.8	1,617
St. George	0.5	1.3	1,647
Parishes			
Devonshire	1.9	4.9	6,843
Hamilton	2.0	5.2	3,784
Paget	2.0	5.2	4,497
Pembroke†	1.8	4.7	10,443
St. George's‡	1.7	4.4	2,940
Sandys	1.9	4.9	6,255
Smith's	1.9	4.9	4,463
Southampton	2.2	5.7	4,613
Warwick	2.2	5.7	6,948
TOTAL	21.0§ ‖	54.0§ ‖	54,050¶

Demography

Population (1986): 57,400.
Density (1986): persons per sq mi 2,730, persons per sq km 1,060.
Urban-rural (1985): urban 100.0%; rural, none.
Sex distribution (1985): male 48.81%; female 51.19%.
Age breakdown (1985): under 15, 21.3%; 15–29, 24.6%; 30–44, 25.0%; 45–59, 16.1%; 60–74, 9.7%; 75 and over, 3.3%.
Population projection: (1990) 59,000; (2000) 63,000.
Doubling time: 86 years.
Ethnic composition (1980): black 61.3%; white 37.3%; other 1.4%.
Religious affiliation (1980): Anglican 37.0%; Methodist 16.0%; Roman Catholic 14.0%; Seventh-day Adventist 5.0%; other 28.0%.
Major cities (1985): St. George 1,707; Hamilton 1,676.

Vital statistics

Birth rate per 1,000 population (1984): 15.1 (world avg. 29.0); legitimate 67.5%; illegitimate 32.5%.
Death rate per 1,000 population (1984): 7.0 (world avg. 11.0).
Natural increase rate per 1,000 population (1984): 8.1 (world avg. 18.0).
Total fertility rate (avg. births per childbearing woman; 1980): 1.9.
Marriage rate per 1,000 population (1984): 11.8.
Divorce rate per 1,000 population (1984): 4.4.
Life expectancy at birth (1980): male 68.8 years; female 76.3 years.
Major causes of death per 100,000 population (1984): diseases of the circulatory system 354.0; malignant neoplasms (cancers) 163.0; accidents and violence 39.0; diseases of the respiratory system 37.0.

National economy

Budget (1985). Revenue: Ber$193,400,000 (customs duty 41.2%, hospital levy 11.0%, employment tax 9.5%, land tax 4.8%, international companies tax 4.4%, hotel occupancy tax 3.6%). Expenditures: Ber$203,800,000 (health and social services 20.8%, education 16.1%, public works and agriculture 15.6%, tourism 8.5%, police 8.1%).
Tourism (1985): receipts from visitors U.S.$356,700,000; expenditures by nationals abroad, n.a.
Production (value in Ber$ except as noted). Agriculture, forestry, fishing (1985): vegetables 3,770,000, milk 1,053,000, fruits 900,000, eggs 800,000, meat 400,000, honey 175,000, flowers 55,000♀; livestock (number of live animals) 3,000 pigs, 1,000 cattle, 1,000 horses, 1,000 goats; roundwood, n.a.; fish catch (1983) 481. Mining and quarrying: limestone quarried for construction material. Manufacturing: major industries are pharmaceuticals, electronics wares, fish processing, handicrafts, woodworking, small boat building, and textiles. Construction (value in Ber$; 1984): residential 59,000,000; nonresidential 36,700,000. Energy production (consumption): electricity (kW-hr; 1984) 382,000,000 (382,000,000); coal, none (none); crude petroleum, none (none); petroleum products (metric tons; 1984) none (142,000); natural gas, none (none).
Population economically active (1985)♂: total 25,442; activity rate of total population 44.7% (participation rates: ages 15–64, n.a.; female 49.3%; registered unemployed [1984] 0.1%).

Price and earnings indexes (1980 = 100)

	1979	1980	1981	1982	1983	1984	1985
Consumer price index	87.0	100.0	111.9	120.6	127.8	134.4	139.3
Weekly earnings index□	...	100.0	106.4	122.3	131.2	141.9	...

Gross national product (at current market prices; 1984–85): U.S.$1,087,000,000 (U.S.$19,190 per capita).

Structure of gross domestic product and labour force

	1984–85 in value Ber$'000	1984–85 % of total value	1984 labour force♂◇	1984 % of labour force
Agriculture, fishing	...	...	167	0.7
Quarrying	...	...	109	0.4
Manufacturing	...	...	962	3.8
Construction	...	...	1,957	7.7
Public utilities	...	...	382	1.5
Transportation and communication	...	...	1,989	7.8
Trade	...	...	9,140	36.1
Finance	...	...	3,285	13.0
Pub. admin., defense } Services	...	... }	7,115	28.1
Other	...	...	239△	0.9△
TOTAL	1,058,100	100.0	25,345	100.0

Public debt (external, outstanding; 1985): none.
Household income and expenditure. Average household size (1982) 2.7; income per household Ber$23,700 (U.S.$23,700); sources of income (1982): wages and salaries 72.2%, imputed income from owner occupancy 9.7%, investments including rents 8.0%, self-employment 6.7%; expenditure (1982): housing 22.6%, food, and nonalcoholic beverages 17.1%, household furnishings 15.2%, transportation 9.4%, foreign travel 6.9%, health 6.3%, entertainment and recreation 5.9%, clothing and footwear 5.8%.
Land use (1983): forested 14.7%; meadows and pastures, 0.6%; agricultural and under permanent cultivation, 4.7%; built-on, wasteland, and other 80.0%.

Foreign trade

Balance of trade (current prices)

	1980	1981	1982	1983	1984	1985
Ber$'000,000	–274.7	–293.4	–333.8	–355.0	–363.4	–364.0
% of total	78.9%	83.3%	90.6%	88.6%	81.7%	90.0%

Imports (1984): Ber$403,931,000 (food, beverages, and tobacco 20.3%, of which meat and meat preparations 5.6%, fruit and vegetables 3.9%; petroleum and petroleum products 12.5%; electrical machinery, including apparatus and appliances 10.2%; clothing 7.8%; chemicals 7.3%; transport equipment 7.1%; nonelectrical machinery 5.2%). *Major import sources:* United States 57.3%; United Kingdom 8.0%; Canada 6.5%; Japan 4.8%.
Exports (1984): Ber$40,544,500 (drugs and medicine 55.9%; electrical supplies 15.3%; electronic supplies 4.5%; scientific supplies 1.3%; books and papers 1.3%; aircraft supplies 0.7%; liquor 0.2%). *Major export destinations* (1983): Italy 30.7%; United States 24.9%; United Kingdom 7.5%; Canada 7.1%; The Netherlands 6.7%; Brazil 5.3%.

Transport and communications

Transport. Railroads: none. Roads (1985): total length 139 mi, 224 km (paved 100%). Vehicles (1985): passenger cars 17,240; trucks and buses 4,224. Merchant marine (1985): vessels (100 gross tons and over) 79; total deadweight tonnage 1,460,832. Air transport (passengers, 1984): arrivals 505,576, departures 505,212; short ton cargo handled 9,567†, metric ton cargo handled 8,679†; airports (1986) with scheduled flights 1.
Communications. Daily newspapers (1985): total number 1; total circulation 16,882; circulation per 1,000 population 297. Radio (1985): total number of receivers 100,000 (1 per 0.6 person). Television (1985): total number of receivers 66,600 (1 per 0.9 person). Telephones (1983): 51,374 (1 per 1.1 persons).

Education and health

Education (1984–85)

	schools	teachers	students	student/ teacher ratio
Primary (age 5–11)	22	312	5,413	17.3
Secondary (age 11–16)	13	350	4,134	11.8
Vocational	1	52	502	9.7
Higher	1	13	105	8.1

Educational attainment (1980). Percent of total population over age 16 having: no formal schooling 1.2%; primary education 25.1%; secondary 48.3%; some higher 19.6%; other 5.8%. *Literacy* (1980): total population over age 15 literate 39,577 (96.9%); males literate 19,026 (96.7%); females literate 20,551 (97.0%).
Health: physicians (1983) 108 (1 per 518 persons); hospital beds (1985) 408 (1 per 139 persons); infant mortality rate per 1,000 live births (1984) 5.9.
Food (1980–82): daily per capita caloric intake 2,521 (vegetable products 59%, animal products 41%); 106% of FAO recommended minimum requirement.

Military

Total active duty personnel (1985) British 700; U.S. 1,500.

*The Bermuda dollar is at par with the U.S. dollar. †Excludes the area and population of the city of Hamilton. ‡Excludes the area and population of the town of St. George. §Grand total includes 2.3 sq mi (5.4 sq km) leased to the United States for military bases. ‖ Detail does not add to total given (less area for the military bases) because of rounding. ¶Excludes 10,918 foreign workers and other visitors, 2,173 on-base military personnel, 620 institutionalized persons, and Bermudians residing abroad. ♀1982. ♂Excludes non-Bermudians totaling 6,748. □Hotel employees only. ◇Employed labour force. △Employment inadequately defined. †1983.

Bhutan

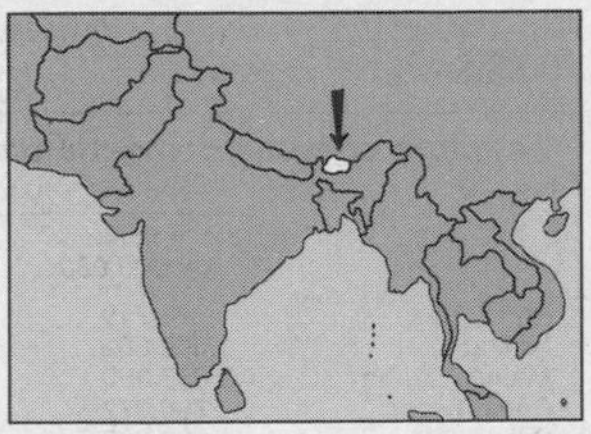

Official name: Druk-Yul (Kingdom of Bhutan).
Form of government: constitutional monarchy with one legislative house (National Assembly [150]).
Head of state and government: Monarch (*druk gyalpo*).
Capital: Thimphu.
Official language: Dzongkha (a Tibetan dialect).
Official religion: Mahāyāna Buddhism.
Monetary unit: 1 Ngultrum* (Nu) = 100 chetrum; valuation (Oct. 1, 1986) 1 U.S.$ = Nu 12.78; 1 £ = Nu 18.47.

Area and population

Districts	Capitals	area† sq mi	area† sq km	population 1982 estimate
Bumthang	Jakar	1,150	2,990	23,200
Chirang	Damphu	310	800	116,200
Dagana	Dagana	540	1,400	34,900
Gasa	Gasa	2,000	5,180	11,600
Gaylegphug	Gaylegphug	1,020	2,640	116,200
Ha	Paro	830	2,140	11,600
Lhuntsi	Lhuntshi	1,120	2,910	46,500
Mongar	Mongar	710	1,830	81,300
Paro	Paro	580	1,500	46,500
Pema Gatsel	Pema Gatsel	150	380	34,900
Samchi	Samchi	830	2,140	185,900
Samdrup Jongkhar	Samdrup Jongkhar	900	2,340	69,700
Shemgang	Shemgang	980	2,540	46,500
Tashigang	Tashigang	1,640	4,260	185,900
Thimphu	Thimphu	960	2,480	81,300
Tongsa	Tongsa	570	1,470	23,200
Wangdi Phodrang	Wangdi Phodrang	1,160	3,000	46,500
TOTAL		18,150	47,000	1,162,000‡

Demography

Population (1986): 1,446,000.
Density (1986): persons per sq mi 79.7, persons per sq km 30.8.
Urban-rural (1985): urban 4.5%; rural 95.5%.
Sex distribution (1985): male 51.59%; female 48.41%.
Age breakdown (1985): under 15, 40.0%; 15–29, 26.9%; 30–44, 17.4%; 45–59, 10.4%; 60–69, 3.7%; 70 and over, 1.8%.
Population projection: (1990) 1,569,000; (2000) 1,893,000.
Doubling time: 34 years.
Ethnic composition (1980): Bhutia 60.9%; Gurung 15.4%; Assamese 13.1%; other 10.6%.
Religious affiliation (1980): Buddhist 69.6%; Hindu 24.6%; Muslim 5.0%; other 0.8%.
Major cities (1985): Thimphu 20,000; Phuntsholing 10,000§.

Vital statistics

Birth rate per 1,000 population (1985): 37.7 (world avg. 29.0); legitimate, n.a.; illegitimate, n.a.
Death rate per 1,000 population (1985): 17.4 (world avg. 11.0).
Natural increase rate per 1,000 population (1985): 20.3 (world avg. 18.0).
Total fertility rate (avg. births per childbearing woman; 1985): 5.4.
Marital status of population 15 years and over (1985): married 71.3%; single 19.7%; widowed 7.5%; divorced 1.6%.
Divorce rate per 1,000 population: n.a.
Life expectancy at birth (1985): male 47.6 years; female 46.1 years.
Major causes of death per 100,000 population: n.a.; however, malaria, tuberculosis, gastrointestinal infectious diseases, goitre, and pneumonia are major health problems.

National economy

Budget (1985–86). Revenue: Nu 863,000,000 (grants from government of India 45.3%, internal sources 30.6%, loans 12.9%, grants from UN and other international agencies 11.2%). Expenditures: Nu 863,390,000 (public works 19.3%, agriculture 18.8% ∥, education 10.7%, health 6.2%, district administration 3.7%, foreign affairs 2.3%).
Public debt (external, outstanding): n.a.
Tourism (1984): receipts from visitors U.S.$2,000,000; expenditures by nationals abroad, n.a.
Production (metric tons except as noted). Agriculture, forestry, fishing (1984): corn (maize) 85,000, rice 61,000, fruit 48,000, potatoes 27,000, wheat 10,000, vegetables and melons 10,000, millet 7,000, barley 5,000, jute 4,000, tobacco 1,000; livestock (number of live animals) 315,000 cattle, 74,000 pigs, 45,000 goats, 43,000 sheep, 28,000 buffalo, 26,000 yaks§, 16,000 horses; roundwood 3,224,000 cu m; fish catch 1,000¶. Mining and quarrying: n.a.; however, some slate is quarried, and gypsum and graphite are mined. Manufacturing (value in Nu; 1980–81): distillery products 47,000,000; cement 36,000,000; chemical products 19,000,000; processed food 14,000,000; forest products 3,000,000. Construction (number of buildings completed; 1977–78): residential 10; nonresidential (guest house) 1. Energy production (consumption): electricity (kW-hr; 1984) 30,000,000 (36,000,000); coal (metric tons; 1984), none (1,000); crude petroleum, none (n.a.); petroleum products (metric tons; 1984) none (9,000); natural gas, none (n.a.).
Household income and expenditure. Average household size (1980): 5.4; income per household: n.a.; source of income: n.a.; expenditure: n.a.

Gross national product (at current market prices; 1983–84): U.S.$135,000,000 (U.S.$98 per capita).

Structure of gross domestic product and labour force

	1981–82			
	in value Nu '000,000	% of total value	labour force	% of labour force
Agriculture	478.9	40.1	613,000	94.3
Mining	9.6	0.8	6,000	0.9
Manufacturing	27.5	2.3		
Construction	21.5	1.8		
Trade	34.6	2.9	9,000	1.4
Public utilities	3.6	0.3	22,000	3.4
Transportation and communication	39.4	3.3		
Finance	16.7	1.4		
Pub. admin., defense	124.2	10.4		
Other	438.2♀	36.7		
TOTAL	1,194.2	100.0	650,000	100.0

Population economically active (1984): total 664,000; activity rate of total population 47.6% (participation rates: ages 15–64, n.a.; female, n.a.; unemployed, n.a.).

Price and earnings indexes (1980–81 = 100)

	1977–78	1978–79	1979–80	1980–81	1981–82
Consumer price index	71.8	80.4	91.3	100.0	110.3
Earnings index	...	...	...	...	...

Land use (1983): forested 69.8%; meadows and pastures 4.6%; agricultural and under permanent cultivation 2.1%; other 23.5%.

Foreign tradeð

Balance of trade (current prices)

	1978	1979	1980	1981	1982	1983
Nu '000,000	...	...	...	−298.6	−334.3	−260.9
% of total	...	...	...	46.5%	51.2%	48.2%

Imports (1981–82): Nu 404,521,000 (machinery and equipment 22.1%, petroleum products 14.2%, iron and steel products 8.1%, motor vehicles 7.3%, rice 3.9%, fabrics 3.0%, stationery and books 2.2%, wheat and wheat flour 1.6%). *Major import source:* India.
Exports (1981–82): Nu 177,981,000□ (cement 26.6%, oranges 9.6%, sawn timber 9.0%, potatoes 8.7%, talcum powder 6.1%, cardamom 6.1%, rosin 4.0%, menthol products 2.7%). *Major export destination:* India 96.5%.

Transport and communications

Transport. Railroads: none. Roads (1984): total length 1,270 mi, 2,050 km (paved about 50%). Vehicles (1984): passenger cars 1,939; trucks and buses 664. Merchant marine: none. Air transport: n.a.; airports (1986) with scheduled flights, none◇.
Communications. Daily newspapers: none△. Radio (1986): total number of receivers 12,500 (1 per 113 persons). Television (1983): total number of receivers 200 (1 per 6,800 persons). Telephones (1985): 1,990 (1 per 712 persons).

Education and health

Education (1984)

	schools†	teachers	students	student/ teacher ratio
Primary (age 7–11)	143	1,149	44,275	38.5
Secondary (age 12–16)	30	431	3,608	8.4
Voc., teacher tr.	8	150	2,264	15.1
Higher	2	16¶	204¶	12.8¶

Educational attainment, n.a. *Literacy* (1977): total population over age 15 literate 124,000 (18.0%); males literate 98,000 (31.0%); females literate 26,000 (9.0%).
Health (1983): physicians 65 (1 per 20,900 persons); hospital beds 831 (1 per 1,600 persons); infant mortality rate per 1,000 live births (1985) 134.0.
Food (1975–77): daily per capita caloric intake 2,058 (vegetable products 98%, animal products 2%); 89% of FAO recommended minimum requirement.

Military

Total active duty personnel (1985): about 4,000 (army 100%).

*Indian currency is also accepted legal tender; the Ngultrum is at par with the Indian rupee. †2,700 sq mi (7,000 sq km) are not included in the district area totals. ‡Detail does not add to total given because of rounding. §1982. ∥ Includes irrigation, animal husbandry, and forestry. ¶1983. ♀Includes tourism. ðImports and exports are based on trade with India only, which accounts for more than 90% of Bhutan's foreign trade. □An additional Nu 6,432,000 in commodities was exported to countries other than India. ◇An airport at Paro receives unscheduled air service from Calcutta. △A government weekly is published from Thimphu in Dzongkha, Nepalese, and English, circulation (1984) 5,000. †1985.

Bolivia

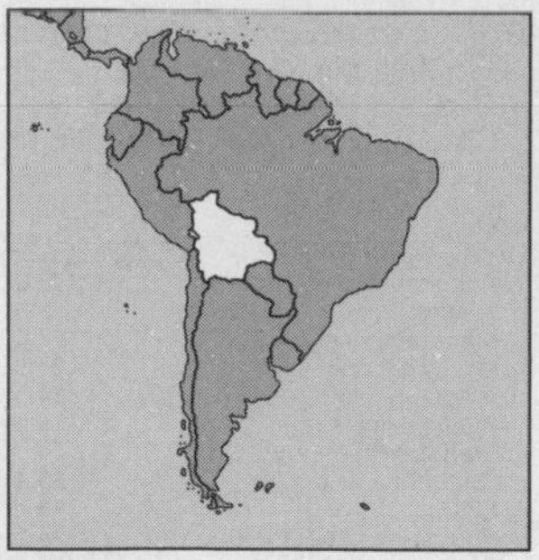

Official name: República de Bolivia (Republic of Bolivia).
Form of government: unitary, multiparty republic with two legislative houses (Chamber of Senators [27]; Chamber of Deputies [130]).
Head of state and government: President.
Capital: La Paz (administrative); Sucre (judicial).
Official languages: Spanish, Aymara, Quechua.
Official religion: Roman Catholicism.
Monetary unit: 1 Bolivian peso ($b) = 100 centavos; valuation (Oct. 1, 1986) 1 U.S.$ = $b 1,912,000; 1 £ = $b 2,763,000.

Area and population

		area		population
Departments	**Capitals**	sq mi	sq km	1985 estimate
Beni	Trinidad	82,458	213,564	240,000
Chuquisaca	Sucre	19,893	51,524	463,000
Cochabamba	Cochabamba	21,479	55,631	979,000
La Paz	La Paz	51,732	133,985	2,091,000
Oruro	Oruro	20,690	53,588	413,000
Pando	Cobija	24,644	63,827	47,000
Potosí	Potosí	45,644	118,218	878,000
Santa Cruz	Santa Cruz	143,098	370,621	1,048,000
Tarija	Tarija	14,526	37,623	270,000
TOTAL		424,164	1,098,581	6,429,000

Demography

Population (1986): 6,611,000.
Density (1986): persons per sq mi 15.6, persons per sq km 6.0.
Urban-rural (1986): urban 48.4%; rural 51.6%.
Sex distribution (1985): male 49.25%; female 50.75%.
Age breakdown (1984): under 15, 43.0%; 15–29, 26.6%; 30–44, 15.9%; 45–59, 9.3%; 60–74, 4.4%; 75 and over, 0.8%.
Population projection: (1990) 7,383,000; (2000) 9,731,000.
Doubling time: 25 years.
Ethnic composition (1982): mestizo 31.2%; Quechua 25.4%; Aymara 16.9%; white 14.5%; other 12.0%.
Religious affiliation (1981): Roman Catholic 94.0%; Bahā'ī 2.6%; other 3.4%.
Major cities (1985): La Paz 992,592; Santa Cruz 441,717; Cochabamba 317,251; Oruro 178,393; Sucre 86,609.

Vital statistics

Birth rate per 1,000 population (1980–85): 44.0 (world avg. 29.0).
Death rate per 1,000 population (1980–85): 16.0 (world avg. 11.0).
Natural increase rate per 1,000 population (1980–85): 28.0 (world avg. 18.0).
Total fertility rate (avg. births per childbearing woman; 1980–85): 6.3.
Marriage rate per 1,000 population (1980): 4.8.
Divorce rate per 1,000 population: n.a.
Life expectancy at birth (1980–85): male 48.6 years; female 53.0 years.
Major causes of death per 100,000 population: n.a.; however, major diseases are diseases of the respiratory system, gastrointestinal infections, measles, diphtheria, malaria, and tetanus.

National economy

Budget (1984). Revenue: $b 556,122,700,000 (internal taxes 39.9%, mining royalties 22.3%, customs duties 22.1%, royalties on petroleum 10.8%). Expenditures: $b 4,857,351,200,000 (public services 44.8%, transfers and contributions 8.6%, public debt service 5.4%, materials and equipment 2.5%).
Production (metric tons except as noted). Agriculture, forestry, fishing (1984): sugarcane 2,195,000, potatoes 650,000, corn (maize) 489,000, rice 194,000, bananas 160,000, oranges 95,000, wheat 69,000; livestock (number of live animals): 9,200,000 sheep, 4,300,000 cattle, 3,200,000 goats, 1,700,000 pigs, 800,000 asses, 420,000 horses; roundwood 1,282,000 cu m; fish catch 5,617*. Mining and quarrying (metric tons of pure metal; 1984): zinc 38,280; tin 17,875; antimony 9,675; lead 8,023; tungsten 2,590; copper 1,800; gold 1,100 kilograms. Manufacturing (gross value in $b; 1981): food and beverages 16,080,982,808, of which food 12,254,780,842; nonferrous metals 7,606,061,069; nonmetallic mineral products 1,328,121,249; metal products 1,194,120,108; wood and wood products 999,542,335; machinery and equipment 516,844,375. Construction† (1983): residential dwellings 323. Energy production (consumption): electricity (kW-hr; 1984) 1,695,000,000 (1,698,000,000); coal (metric tons; 1984) none (1,000); crude petroleum (barrels; 1984) 7,779,000 (7,884,000); petroleum products (metric tons; 1984) 1,078,000 (1,056,000); natural gas (cu m; 1984) 2,357,200,000 (295,300,000).
Population economically active (1982): total 1,871,600; activity rate of total population 31.6% (participation rates: over age 15, 31.6%; female 23.2%; unemployed 10.5%).

Price and earnings indexes (1980 = 100)

	1979	1980	1981	1982	1983	1984	1985
Consumer price index	50.0	100.0	204.0	541.0	2,403	17,462	134,833
Monthly earnings index	...	...	...	...	...	...	...

Gross national product (at current market prices; 1984): U.S.$2,560,000,000 (U.S.$410 per capita).

Structure of gross domestic product and labour force

	1984		1982	
	in value $b '000,000	% of total value	labour force‡	% of labour force
Agriculture	4,923,749	26.8	792,600	46.4
Mining	1,008,502	5.5	76,200	4.5
Manufacturing	3,853,350	21.0	155,500	9.1
Construction	780,372	4.3	56,500	3.3
Public utilities	100,669	0.5	7,200	0.4
Transportation and communication	1,001,792	5.5	94,700	5.5
Trade	2,534,178	13.8	128,800	7.5
Finance	1,889,497	10.3	13,300	0.8
Pub. admin., defense	1,483,825	8.1		
Services	648,543	3.5	382,600	22.4
Other§	122,853	0.7		
TOTAL	18,347,330 ‖	100.0	1,707,400	100.0¶

Public debt (external, outstanding; 1985): U.S.$3,277,000,000.
Tourism: receipts from visitors (1984) U.S.$37,000,000; expenditures by nationals abroad (1983) U.S.$42,000,000.
Land use (1983): forested 51.7%; meadows and pastures 24.9%; agricultural and under permanent cultivation 3.1%; other 20.3%.

Foreign trade♀

Balance of trade (current prices)

	1979	1980	1981	1982	1983	1984
U.S.$'000,000	−53.2	+261.8	+229.0	+399.0	+282.0	+311.9
% of total	3.4%	16.1%	14.4%	31.8%	23.0%	27.4%

Imports (1984): U.S.$473,651,000 (capital goods 48.5%, of which capital goods for industry 25.0%, transport equipment 12.5%; raw materials 41.0%, of which raw materials for industry 38.5%; consumer goods 9.5%, of which nondurable consumer goods 6.5%, durable consumer goods 3.0%). *Major import sources:* United States 22.0%; Argentina 17.0%; Brazil 12.0%; Japan 7.5%; West Germany 7.3%; Chile 3.6%; France 2.8%; Peru 2.7%; The Netherlands 2.6%; United Kingdom 2.3%.
Exports (1984): U.S.$782,115,600 (natural gas 48.0%; tin 31.7%; zinc 4.8%; silver 2.7%; tungsten 2.4%). *Major export destinations:* Argentina 48.8%; United States 18.4%; The Netherlands 9.7%; United Kingdom 5.2%; Belgium 3.5%; West Germany 3.2%; Switzerland 1.9%; Japan 1.1%; Brazil 1.0%.

Transport and communications

Transport. Railroads: route length (1985) 2,198 mi, 3,538 km; passenger-mi 479,000,000†, passenger-km 771,000,000†; short ton-mi cargo 404,000,000†, metric ton-km cargo 590,000,000†. Roads (1984): total length 25,468 mi, 40,987 km (paved 4%). Vehicles (1983): passenger cars 40,638; trucks and buses 36,951. Merchant marine (1985): vessels (100 gross tons and over) 2; total deadweight tonnage 18,934. Air transport (1985): passenger-mi 484,173,000, passenger-km 779,202,000; short ton-mi cargo 67,237,000, metric ton-km cargo 98,164,000; airports (1986) with scheduled flights 19.
Communications. Daily newspapers (1984): total number 14; total circulation 253,000; circulation per 1,000 population 40. Radio (1984): total number of receivers 482,000 (1 per 13 persons). Television (1984): total number of receivers 387,000 (1 per 16 persons). Telephones (1983): 204,747 (1 per 30 persons).

Education and health

Education (1983)

	schools	teachers	students	student/teacher ratio
Primary (age 6–13)	8,514	50,703	1,154,819	22.8
Secondary (age 14–17)	845	8,091	174,982	21.6
Higher	25	1,487	13,388	9.0

Educational attainment (1976). Percent of adult population over age 25 having: no formal schooling 48.6%; primary education 28.5%; secondary 17.9%; higher 5.0%. *Literacy* (1976): total population over age 15 literate 1,706,718 (63.2%); males literate 990,408 (75.8%); females literate 716,310 (51.4%).
Health (1978): physicians 3,410 (1 per 1,555 persons); hospital beds 9,353 (1 per 523 persons); infant mortality rate per 1,000 live births (1985) 110.0.
Food (1980–82): daily per capita caloric intake 2,116 (vegetable products 83%, animal products 17%); 89% of FAO recommended minimum requirement.

Military

Total active duty personnel (1985): 27,600 (army 72.5%, navy 13.0%, air force 14.5%). *Military expenditure as percent of GNP* (1982): 1.9% (world 6.1%); per capita expenditure U.S.$17.

*1983. †National government sponsored only. ‡Employed persons only. §Includes imputed bank service charges. ‖At current prices. ¶Detail does not add to total given because of rounding. ♀Import figures are f.o.b. (free on board) in balance of trade and c.i.f. (cost, insurance, and freight) for commodities and trading partners.

Botswana

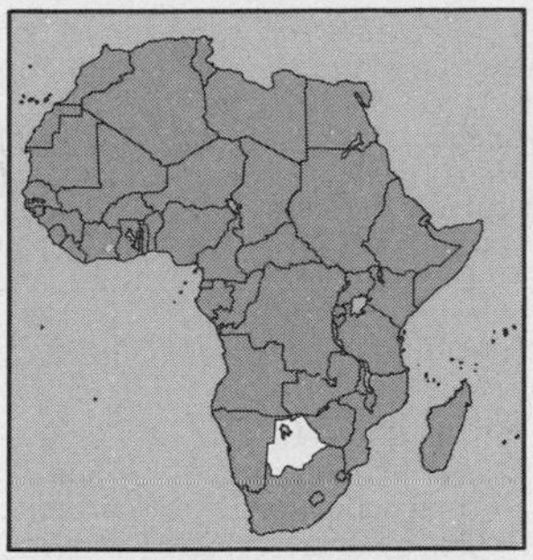

Official name: Republic of Botswana.
Form of government: multiparty republic with one legislative body (National Assembly [39]).
Head of state and government: President.
Capital: Gaborone.
Official language: English.
Official religion: none.
Monetary unit: 1 pula (P) = 100 thebe; valuation (Oct. 1, 1986) 1 U.S.$ = P 1.85; 1 £ = P 2.67.

Area and population

Districts	Capitals	area sq mi	area sq km	population 1984 estimate
Central	Serowe	57,039	147,730	355,000
Ghanzi	Ghanzi	45,525	117,910	21,000
Kgalagadi	Tsabong	41,290	106,940	26,000
Kgatleng	Mochudi	3,073	7,960	49,000
Kweneng	Molepolole	13,857	35,890	128,000
North East	Masunga	1,977	5,120	40,000
North West				
Chobe	Kasane	8,031	20,800	9,000
Ngamiland	Maun	42,135	109,130	75,000
Southern	Kanye	10,992	28,470	138,000
South East	Ramotswa	687	1,780	34,000
Towns*				
Francistown	—	31	79	36,000
Gaborone	—	37	97	79,000
Lobatse	—	12	30	22,000
Orapa	—	4	10	5,800
Selebi-Pikwe	—	19	50	33,000
TOTAL		224,607†	581,730	1,051,000†

Demography

Population (1986): 1,126,000.
Density (1986): persons per sq mi 5.0, persons per sq km 1.9.
Urban-rural (1985): urban 19.2%; rural 80.8%.
Sex distribution (1985): male 48.24%; female 51.76%.
Age breakdown (1981): under 15, 46.8%; 15–29, 24.7%; 30–44, 12.5%; 45–59, 8.0%; 60–74, 5.5%; 75 and over, 2.5%.
Population projection: (1990) 1,292,000; (2000) 1,865,000.
Doubling time: 19 years.
Ethnic composition (1980): Bantu 93.6%; Bushman 4.8%; European 0.7%; other 0.9%.
Religious affiliation (1980): folk religionist 49.2%; Protestant 26.6%; indigenous Christian 11.8%; Roman Catholic 9.4%; other 3.0%.
Major cities (1985): Gaborone 79,400; Francistown 38,000; Selebi-Pikwe 32,500; Lobatse 22,000; Kanye 22,000‡.

Vital statistics

Birth rate per 1,000 population (1980–85): 50.0 (world avg. 29.0); legitimate, n.a.; illegitimate, n.a.
Death rate per 1,000 population (1980–85): 13.0 (world avg. 11.0).
Natural increase rate per 1,000 population (1980–85): 37.3 (world avg. 18.0).
Total fertility rate (avg. births per childbearing woman; 1981): 6.2.
Marriage rate per 1,000 population: n.a.
Divorce rate per 1,000 population: n.a.
Life expectancy at birth (1981): male 52.7 years; female 59.3 years.
Major causes of death (as percent of total deaths; 1977): measles 16.3%; heart disease 8.4%; influenza and pneumonia 7.6%; diarrheal diseases 7.5%; malignant neoplasms (cancers) 6.0%.

National economy

Budget (1986–87)§. Revenue: P 1,195,000,000 (mineral royalties and dividends 57.4%; customs and excise taxes 16.2%; other income taxes 9.1%; nontax revenue 13.2%; foreign aid grants 3.4%). Expenditures: P 902,000,000 (recurrent expenditure 58.4%; development 38.7%, of which public works and communications 11.1%, mineral resources and water affairs 5.1%, drought relief 1.8%; education 12.0%; police and defense 1.6%).
Population economically active (1981): total 316,488; activity rate of total population 33.8% (participation rates: ages 15–64, 63.6%; female 40.3%; unemployed 10.2%).

Price and earnings indexes (1982 = 100)

	1980	1981	1982	1983	1984	1985	1986‖
Consumer price index	77.3	90.0	100.0	110.5	119.9	129.7	143.7
Earnings index¶	...	...	100.0	114.0	131.6	...	...

Production (metric tons except as noted). Agriculture, forestry, fishing (1984): cereals 10,000 (of which sorghum 6,000, corn [maize] 2,000, millet 1,000, wheat 1,000), vegetables and melons 16,000, pulses 15,000, fruit 11,000, roots and tubers 7,000, seed cotton 3,000, cotton seed 2,000, peanuts (groundnuts) 1,000; livestock (number of live animals) 2,900,000 cattle, 800,000 goats, 165,000 sheep, 144,000 mules and asses, 25,000 horses; roundwood 798,000 cu m; fish catch 1,250♀. Mining and quarrying (1984): diamonds 12,914,000 carats (P 616,000,000); nickel-copper matte 51,845, of which copper 21,471, nickel 18,604; cobalt 259. Manufacturing (1984): beer 155,000 hectolitres. Construction (1983): residential 81,900 sq m; nonresidential 82,600 sq m. Energy production (consumption): electricity (kW-hr; 1985) 438,000,000♂ (621,000,000♂); coal (metric tons; 1985) 437,000 (n.a.); crude petroleum, none (n.a.); petroleum products, n.a. (n.a.); natural gas, none (n.a.).
Public debt (external, outstanding; 1985): U.S.$334,100,000.
Tourism: receipts from visitors (1984) U.S.$53,000,000; expenditures by nationals abroad (1983) U.S.$16,000,000.
Gross national product (at current market prices; 1984): U.S.$940,000,000 (U.S.$900 per capita).

Structure of gross domestic product and labour force

	1983–84 in value P '000,000	1983–84 % of total value	1984 labour force□	1984 % of labour force
Agriculture	80.1	6.3	5,400	4.9
Mining	403.1	31.8	7,500◇	6.8
Manufacturing	85.4	6.7	9,500	8.6
Construction	51.6	4.1	11,100	10.0
Public utilities	34.5	2.7	2,000	1.8
Transportation and communication	30.9	2.4	5,500	5.0
Trade	289.4	22.8	18,100	16.5
Finance	48.6	3.8	6,200	5.6
Pub. admin., defense	198.4	15.6 }	44,700	40.6
Services	47.0	3.7 }		
TOTAL	1,269.0	100.0†	110,000	100.0†

Household income and expenditure. Average household size (1981) 5.7; average annual income per household, n.a.; sources of income (1980–81): wages and salaries 71.1%, self-employment 23.3%, transfers 5.5%; expenditure (1980): food, beverages, and tobacco 48.2%, rent and services 12.6%.
Land use (1983): forested 1.6%; meadows and pastures 75.2%; agricultural and under permanent cultivation 2.3%; other 20.9%.

Foreign trade△

Balance of trade (current prices)

	1980	1981	1982	1983	1984	1985
P '000,000	65.6	250.3	130.5	11.6	123.8	414.5
% of total	7.7%	28.4%	12.3%	0.8%	7.7%	17.8%

Imports (1985): P 1,142,000,000 (machinery and electrical goods 19.5%; food, beverages, and tobacco 18.1%; vehicles and transport equipment 14.3%; mineral fuels 11.0%; metal and metal products 8.0%; chemical and rubber products 7.5%; textiles and footwear 7.2%; wood and paper 3.2%). *Major import sources* (1984): CUSA (Customs Union of Southern Africa, which includes Botswana, Lesotho, South West Africa/Namibia, South Africa, and Swaziland) 78.1%; United Kingdom 3.1%; United States 2.4%.
Exports (1985): P 1,371,000,000 (diamonds 76.4%; copper-nickel matte 8.9%; meat and meat products 7.4%). *Major export destinations* (1984): United States 8.2%; CUSA 6.7%; United Kingdom 2.1%.

Transport and communications

Transport. Railroads (1983–84): length 444 mi, 714 km; number of passengers 487,298; short ton-mi cargo 733,789, metric ton-km cargo 1,071,314. Roads (1983): total length 4,987 mi, 8,026 km (paved 22%). Vehicles (1983): passenger cars 11,039; trucks and buses 20,739. Merchant marine: none. Air transport (1985)✝: passenger-mi 13,476,000, passenger-km 21,687,000; short ton-mi cargo 76,700, metric ton-km cargo 112,000; airports (1986) with scheduled flights 3.
Communications. Daily newspapers (1985): total number 1; total circulation 24,000; circulation per 1,000 population 22. Radio (1985): total number of receivers 77,000 (1 per 14 persons). Television (1984): none. Telephones (1984): 11,700 (1 per 90 persons).

Education and health

Education (1984–85)

	schools	teachers	students	student/ teacher ratio
Primary (age 7–13)	512	6,794	209,772	30.9
Secondary (age 14–19)	58	1,216	27,364	22.5
Voc., teacher tr.	26	69⊕	3,538	...
Higher	1	104	1,249	12.0

Educational attainment (1981). Percent of population over age 12 having: no formal schooling 42.9%; some primary education 34.9%; complete primary 14.5%; complete secondary 6.2%; higher 0.9%. *Literacy* (1985): total population over age 15 literate 385,000 (70.8%); males literate 179,000 (72.6%); females literate 206,000 (69.5%).
Health (1981): physicians (1984) 155 (1 per 6,748 persons); hospital beds 2,060 (1 per 455 persons); infant mortality rate per 1,000 live births 68.4.
Food (1980–82): daily per capita caloric intake 2,468 (vegetable products 84%, animal products 16%); 106% of FAO recommended minimum requirement.

Military

Total active duty personnel (1985): 3,000 (army 95.0%; navy, none; air force 5.0%). *Military expenditure as percent of GNP* (1983): 3.0% (world 6.1%); per capita expenditure U.S.$25.

*Areas included with respective district area totals. †Detail does not add to total given because of rounding. ‡1984. §Projected. ‖July. ¶Excludes government sector. ♀1983. ♂Botswana Power Corporation only. □Formal sector only. ◇18,894 Botswana were employed in South African mines in 1984. △Import figures are f.o.b. in balance of trade and c.i.f. in commodities and trading partners. ✝Air Botswana only. ⊕Teacher training only.

Brazil

Official name: República Federativa do Brasil (Federative Republic of Brazil).
Form of government: multiparty federal republic with 2 legislative houses (Federal Senate [72]; Chamber of Deputies [487]).
Chief of state and government: President.
Capital: Brasília.
Official language: Portuguese.
Official religion: none.
Monetary unit: 1 cruzado* (Cr$) = 1,000 cruzeiros; valuation (Oct. 1, 1986) 1 U.S.$ = 13.84 cruzados; 1 £ = 20.00 cruzados.

Area and population

States	Capitals	area† sq mi	area† sq km	population 1985 estimate
Acre	Rio Branco	58,915	152,589	366,837
Alagoas	Maceió	10,707	27,731	2,229,764
Amazonas	Manaus	604,035	1,564,445	1,722,250
Bahia	Salvador	216,613	561,026	10,681,907
Ceará	Fortaleza	58,159	150,630	5,867,861
Espírito Santo‡	Vitória	17,605	45,597	2,288,423
Goiás	Goiânia	247,913	642,092	4,441,482
Maranhão	São Luís	126,897	328,663	4,623,851
Mato Grosso	Cuiabá	340,156	881,001	1,483,095
Mato Grosso do Sul	Campo Grande	135,347	350,548	1,611,106
Minas Gerais	Belo Horizonte	226,708	587,172	14,564,489
Pará	Belém	482,906	1,250,722	4,345,763
Paraíba	João Pessoa	21,765	56,372	3,012,843
Paraná	Curitiba	77,048	199,554	8,067,161
Pernambuco	Recife	37,946	98,281	6,755,916
Piauí	Teresina	96,886	250,934	2,425,918
Rio Grande do Norte	Natal	20,469	53,015	2,116,782
Rio Grande do Sul	Pôrto Alegre	108,952	282,184	8,467,164
Rio de Janeiro	Rio de Janeiro	17,092	44,268	12,727,602
Rondônia	Pôrto Velho	93,840	243,044	904,298
Santa Catarina	Florianópolis	37,060	95,985	4,082,561
São Paulo	São Paulo	95,714	247,898	29,587,854
Sergipe	Aracaju	8,492	21,994	1,290,232
Other federal entities				
Distrito Federal	Brasília	2,245	5,814	1,576,657
Amapá	Macapá	54,161	140,276	217,881
Fernando de Noronha§	Fernando de Noronha	10	26	1,295
Roraima	Boa Vista	88,844	230,104	103,025
TOTAL		3,286,487‖	8,511,965	135,564,017

Demography

Population (1986): 138,403,000.
Density (1986): persons per sq mi 42.1, persons per sq km 16.3.
Urban-rural (1985): urban 72.7%; rural 27.3%.
Sex distribution (1985): male 49.92%; female 50.08%.
Age breakdown (1985): under 15, 36.4%; 15–29, 28.9%; 30–44, 17.8%; 45–59, 10.3%; 60–74, 5.2%; 75 and over, 1.4%.
Population projection: (1990) 150,368,000; (2000) 179,487,000.
Doubling time: 31 years.
Ethnic composition (1980): Brazilian white 53.0%, of which Portuguese 15.0%, Italian 11.0%, Spanish 10.0%, German 3.0%; mulatto 22.0%; mestizo 12.0%; black 11.0%; Japanese 0.8%; indigenous Indian 0.1%; other 1.1%.
Religious affiliation (1980): Roman Catholic 87.8%, of which Spiritist Catholic 15.7%¶, Evangelical Catholic 9.0%♀; Protestant (mostly Assemblies of God, other Pentecostal, and Baptist) 6.1%; Afro-American Spiritist 2.0%♂; Spiritist 1.7%□; nonreligious 1.0%; atheist 0.4%; Buddhist 0.3%; Jewish 0.2%; other 0.5%.
Major cities (1985)◇: São Paulo 10,099,086 (metropolitan area 15,280,375); Rio de Janeiro 5,615,149 (10,217,269); Belo Horizonte 2,122,073 (3,059,-727); Salvador 1,811,367 (2,125,792); Fortaleza 1,588,709; Brasília 1,576,-657; Nova Iguaçu△ 1,324,639; Recife 1,289,627; Curitiba 1,285,027; Porto Alegre 1,275,483.

Other principal *municipios* (1985)

	population		population		population
Belém	1,120,777	Santo André†	637,010	Teresina	476,102
Goiânia	928,046	Osasco†	594,249	Santos	461,096
Campinas	845,057	São Bernardo		São João de	
Manaus	834,541	do Campo	565,620	Meriti△	459,103
São Gonçalo	731,061	São Luís	564,434	Niterói△	442,706
Guarulhos†	717,723	Natal	512,241	Jaboatão	411,341
Duque de Caxias△	666,128	Maceió	484,094		

Total number of immigrants entering Brazil (1884–1973): 5,072,000; *place of national origin:* Portugal 31.1%; Italy 30.2%; Spain 13.8%; Japan 4.9%; Germany 4.0%; Russia (U.S.S.R.) 2.2%; other 13.8%.
Mobility (1980). Households living in same residence as in 1970: 25.0%.
Families (1983). Average family size 4.3; 1–2 persons 23.7%, 3 persons 19.7%, 4 persons 19.6%, 5–6 persons 23.1%, 7 or more persons 13.9%.
Immigration (1982–84): permanent immigrants admitted 7,673, from Portugal 28.4%, Uruguay 8.7%, Argentina 8.2%.

Vital statistics

Birth rate per 1,000 population (1980–85): 30.6 (world avg. 29.0).
Death rate per 1,000 population (1980–85): 8.4 (world avg. 11.0).
Natural increase rate per 1,000 population (1980–85): 22.2 (world avg. 18.0).
Total fertility rate (avg. births per childbearing woman; 1980–85): 3.8.
Marriage rate per 1,000 population (1984): 7.1.
Divorce rate per 1,000 population (1984): 0.2.
Life expectancy at birth (1980–85): male 60.9 years; female 66.0 years.
Major causes of death per 100,000 population (1980): diseases of the circulatory system 156.2, of which cerebrovascular disease 51.5, diseases of pulmonary circulation 40.5, acute myocardial infarction 30.7; ill-defined conditions 133.0; infectious and parasitic diseases 57.4; malignant neoplasms (cancers) 49.3; diseases of the respiratory system 36.9, of which pneumonia 29.3; accidents 32.0; homicide and other violence 22.6.

Social indicators

Educational attainment (1980). Percent of population over age 25 having: no formal schooling 32.9%; primary education 55.3%; secondary 6.9%; higher 5.0%.

Distribution of income (1984)⊕

percent of national income by decile

1	2	3	4	5	6	7	8	9	10 (highest)
1.0	2.0	2.6	3.6	4.4	5.2	7.6	10.5	16.5	46.6.

Quality of working life. Average workweek (1980): 80.6% of the labour force works 40 or more hours per week. Annual estimated rate per 100,000 insured urban workers (1982) for: injury or accident 5,500; industrial illness, n.a.; death 21. Proportion of labour force participating in national social insurance system: 51.8%. Average days lost to labour stoppages per 1,000 workdays: n.a. Average duration of journey and method of transport to work: n.a. Rate per 1,000 workers of discouraged (unemployed no longer seeking work): n.a.
Access to services (1980). Proportion of households having access to: electricity 67.4%, of which urban households having access 88.5%, rural households having access 20.5%; safe public (piped) water supply 53.2%, of which urban households having access 75.8%, rural households having access 3.2%; public sewage collection or septic tank 41.5%, of which urban households having access 57.4%, rural households having access 6.2%; public fire protection, n.a.
Social participation. Eligible voters participating in last national election: 82.7%**. Population participating in voluntary work: n.a. Trade union membership in total work force n.a.††. Practicing religious population in total affiliated population: Most men, and in particular Portuguese-Brazilian men, attend Mass only on special occasions. They believe religion is the domain and duty of women.
Social deviance: The incidence of crime is not accurately reported. Crimes resulting in imprisonment (1983): 243,958, of which murder 4.3%, rape 1.0%, other assault 19.5%, burglary and housebreaking 21.6%, armed robbery 0.3%, narcotics trafficking 3.8%, narcotics usage 4.5%. Suicides (1983): 5,368.
Leisure. Favourite leisure activities: n.a.
Material well-being (1980). Households possessing: automobile 22.4% (urban 28.3%, rural 9.5%); telephone 12.4% (urban 17.5%, rural 0.9%); television receiver 56.1% (urban 73.0%, rural 15.7%); refrigerator 50.4% (urban 65.7%, rural 13.6%); air conditioner, n.a.; washing machine, n.a.

National economy

Gross national product (at current market prices; 1984): U.S.$227,280,000,-000 (U.S.$1,710 per capita).

Structure of gross domestic product and labour force

	1985‡‡ in value U.S.$'000,000	1985‡‡ % of total value	1984 labour force§§	1984 % of labour force
Agriculture	25,147	10.1	14,974,441	29.8
Mining	2,680	1.1 }	7,997,553	15.9
Manufacturing	68,893	27.6 }		
Construction	13,645	5.5	2,926,441	5.8
Public utilities	9,667	3.9	...	...
Transportation and communication	19,124	7.7	1,818,407	3.6
Trade	40,757	16.4	5,354,165	10.7
Pub. admin., defense	17,323	6.9	2,133,540	4.3
Finance	24,797	9.9 }	13,445,733	26.8
Services	27,103	10.9 }		
Other	...	...	1,558,485	3.1
TOTAL	249,136	100.0	50,208,765	100.0

Budget (1986). Revenue: Cr$656,126,000,000 (current revenue 63.6%, of which property taxes 25.8%, taxes on goods and services 13.6%, social security contributions 5.9%, customs duties 3.7%; capital revenue 32.2%). Expenditures: Cr$656,126,000,000 (administration and planning 31.4%; transportation 14.3%; regional development 11.5%; education and culture 9.9%; social welfare 6.5%; agriculture and water supply 6.4%; national defense and public security 5.0%; health and sanitation 2.5%).
Public debt (external, outstanding; 1984): U.S.$66,502,100,000.
Population economically active (1984): total 52,443,100; activity rate of total population 39.6% (participation rates: ages 15–60, 63.5%; female 33.1%; unemployed [1986] 3.5%).

Price and earnings indexes (1980 = 100)

	1980	1981	1982	1983	1984	1985	1986‖ ‖
Consumer price index	100	206	407	984	2,924	9,556	23,556
Earnings index¶¶	100	203	403	865	2,374	8,018	...

Land use (1984): forested 66.9%; meadows and pastures 19.5%; agricultural and under permanent cultivation 8.9%; other 4.7%.
Tourism (1984): receipts from visitors U.S.$1,512,000,000; expenditures by nationals abroad U.S.$939,000,000.

Manufacturing enterprises (1981)

	no. of enter-prises	number of labourers	wages of labourers as a % of avg. of all wages	value added in producer's prices (in '000,000s of cruzeiros)
Chemicals	2,813	122,739	157.5	1,161,916
Metallurgy	9,032	391,670	113.9	799,797
Mechanical products	7,835	405,690	162.7	784,716
Food products	22,942	419,215	61.3	768,480
Textiles	5,295	380,828	73.8	458,510
Transportation equipment	2,634	196,632	153.6	531,123
Electric and communications equipment	2,752	186,490	120.2	500,213
Combustible fuels (not metals)	15,043	257,892	75.2	402,914
Clothing and footwear	8,966	354,625	55.3	314,594
Paper and paper products	1,377	80,498	102.4	183,214
Publishing and printing	5,004	103,074	117.5	207,294
Lumber	9,085	165,420	58.8	158,575
Plastics	2,145	104,301	89.6	158,452
Pharmaceutical products	443	22,688	113.7	145,835
Furniture	5,812	122,015	64.9	116,353

Production (value of production in '000,000,000s of cruzeiros except as noted). Agriculture, forestry, fishing (1984): soybeans 5,404, sugarcane 4,443, corn (maize) 3,515, coffee 3,217, rice 2,474, beans 1,894, cassava 1,873, cotton [all forms] 1,687, oranges 1,602, cocoa beans 1,020, wheat 916, bananas 645, potatoes 497, tomatoes 425, cashews 205, grapes 184, onions 166, pineapples 157, papayas 152, coconuts 144, black pepper 141, babassu oil 141, castor beans and oil 141, peanuts (groundnuts) 135; livestock (number of live animals; 1985) 134,500,000 cattle, 30,000,000 pigs, 17,500,000 sheep, 8,500,000 goats, 5,200,000 horses; roundwood (1984) 222,177,000 cu m; fish catch (metric tons; 1984) 946,000, of which sardines 266,000. Mining and quarrying (1984): iron ore 1,437; gold 1,073; tin 465; phosphate fertilizers 425; limestone 411; bauxite 371; granite 302; manganese 185; clay 147; magnesium 121. Manufacturing (1980): chemicals 1,850; food products 1,333; iron and steel and other worked metals 1,318; transport equipment 753; electric and nonelectric machinery 729; textiles 616; electrical goods (including computers, televisions, and radios) 498; cement and other worked nonmetals 403; clothing and footwear 370; paper and paper products 258; lumber 195; plastic products 194; tires and other rubber products 144. Construction (new buildings completed; 1983) residential 17,628,000 sq m; nonresidential 3,365,000 sq m.

Retail trade enterprises (1980)

	no. of enterprises	total no. of employees	annual wage as a % of all wages	annual value of sales (in '000,000s of cruzeiros)
General merchandise stores (including food products)	16,186	274,379	145.5	658,096
Gasoline stations	21,588	140,865	127.6	594,063
Food, beverages, and tobacco stores	538,638	963,106	16.5	586,249
Automobile dealers and auto parts stores	25,284	157,285	205.4	581,354
Stores selling clothing, fabrics, and textiles	117,595	452,641	102.3	434,793
Hardware stores	37,396	208,783	134.5	407,266
Stores selling radios, televisions, and related electronic goods	26,114	168,431	180.1	353,169
Drugstores	33,631	142,030	118.0	217,781
Agricultural machinery and heavy equipment dealers	6,565	59,244	329.5	204,332
General merchandise stores (excluding food products)	3,367	58,729	239.9	124,359
Book, magazine, and office supply stores	20,192	63,529	123.1	60,327

Energy production (consumption): electricity (kW-hr; 1984) 175,710,000,000 (175,634,000,000); coal (metric tons; 1984) 7,461,000 (13,708,000); crude petroleum (barrels; 1985) 205,787,000 [1984] (405,400,000); petroleum products (metric tons; 1984) 46,415,000 (36,461,000); natural gas (cu m; 1984) 2,069,700,000 (2,069,700,000); alcohol♀♀ (hectolitres; 1985) 120,000,000 (n.a.).

Household income and expenditure. Average household size (1980) 4.7; average annual income per household of families having income (1983)♁♁ 482,844 cruzeiros (U.S.$2,367); source of income: n.a.; expenditure (1974)□□: housing and household furnishings 33.5%, food 27.1%, clothing and footwear 7.0%, transportation 6.7%, health and hygiene 6.4%, education 2.7%, tobacco 2.0%, recreation 1.9%, other 12.7%.

Financial aggregates◇◇

	1981	1982	1983	1984	1985	1986
Exchange rate, cruzados per:						
U.S. dollar	0.128	0.253	0.984	3.184	10.490	13.840△△
£	0.244	0.408	1.427	3.682	15.153	20.068△△
SDR	0.149	0.279	1.030	3.121	11.522	16.794△△
International reserves (U.S.$)						
Total (excl. gold; '000,000)	6,604	3,928	4,355	11,508	10,605	9,240††
SDRs ('000,000)	452	—	—	1	1	2△△
Reserve pos. in IMF ('000,000)	264	287	—	—	—	—△△
Foreign exchange ('000,000)	5,888	3,641	4,355	11,507	10,604	9,225††
Gold ('000,000 fine troy oz)	2.20	0.15	0.54	1.47	3.10	3.37⊕⊕
% world reserves	0.23	0.02	0.06	0.16	0.33	0.35⊕⊕
Interest and prices						
Central bank discount (%)	49.0	49.0	156.6	215.3	...	...
Gov't. bond yield (%)	...	...	...	...	...	...
Industrial share prices	...	...	...	...	...	...
Balance of payments (U.S.$'000,000)						
Balance of visible trade	1,185	778	6,469	13,086	12,466	...
Imports, f.o.b.	22,091	19,395	15,429	13,916	13,168	...
Exports, f.o.b.	23,276	20,173	21,898	27,002	25,634	...
Balance of invisibles	−13,135	−17,082	−13,414	−13,215	−12,894	...
Balance of payments, current account	−11,751	−16,312	−6,837	+42	−273	...

Foreign trade

Balance of trade (current prices)***

	1980	1981	1982	1983	1984	1985
U.S.$'000,000	−2,823	+1,202	+780	+6,470	+13,089	+12,486
% of total	6.6%	2.6%	2.0%	17.3%	32.0%	32.2%

Imports (1984): U.S.$15,210,000,000 (mineral fuels 54.5%, of which crude petroleum 49.1%; chemicals 10.6%, of which organic chemicals 4.6%, fertilizers 2.0%; food products 8.5%, of which cereals 6.1%; electrical and nonelectrical machinery 6.6%; electrical and electronic goods 4.9%; transport equipment 3.5%, of which road vehicles 1.3%, boats [all kinds] 1.2%; metals [all forms] 2.9%, of which iron and steel 1.2%, copper 1.1%; photographic, surgical, and scientific instruments and apparatus 1.3%; plastics 1.2%; natural and synthetic rubber materials 1.1%). *Major import sources:* United States 16.6%; Iraq 14.5%; Saudi Arabia 9.7%; Nigeria 6.7%; West Germany 4.5%; Mexico 4.5%; Japan 4.0%; Venezuela 3.9%; Canada 3.8%; Argentina 3.5%; China 2.9%; France 2.6%; United Kingdom 2.0%.

Exports (1984): U.S.$27,005,000,000††† (metals [all forms] 10.9%, of which iron and steel 8.5%, bauxite 1.2%; coffee 9.5%; animal feedstuffs 5.9%; nonspecific vegetable and food products 5.5%; electrical and nonelectrical machinery 5.2%; textiles 4.5%, of which cotton products 1.8%; road vehicles 4.3%; footwear 4.0%; animal and vegetable fats and oils 3.2%; paper and paper products 2.8%; cocoa beans and cocoa 2.6%; sugar and confectionery 2.4%; organic chemicals 2.4%; electrical and electronic goods 2.2%; fresh and frozen meat 2.0%; tobacco products 1.7%; seeds of diverse fruits and products of industrial plants 1.7%; plastics 1.6%; lumber and wooden furniture 1.2%). *Major export destinations:* United States 28.6%; Japan 5.6%; The Netherlands 5.0%; West Germany 4.7%; Italy 4.1%; Argentina 3.2%; France 3.1%; United Kingdom 2.6%; Nigeria 2.4%; Belgium–Luxembourg 2.4%; Spain 1.8%; China 1.7%; Canada 1.5%.

Transport and communications

Transport. Railroads (1984): route length 17,984 mi, 28,942 km; passenger-mi 9,578,000,000, passenger-km 15,415,000,000; short ton-mi cargo 63,303,000,000, metric ton-km cargo 92,421,000,000. Roads (1984): total length 893,265 mi, 1,437,574 km (paved 8%). Vehicles (1984): passenger cars 10,008,000; trucks and buses 1,090,000. Merchant marine (1985): vessels (100 gross tons and over) 702; total deadweight tonnage 10,040,000. Air transport (1985)‡‡‡: passenger-mi 11,367,749,000, passenger-km 18,294,653,000; short ton-mi cargo 621,278,000, metric ton-km cargo 907,050,000; airports (1986) with scheduled flights 111.

Communications. Daily newspapers (1983): total number 265; total circulation 5,722,000; circulation per 1,000 population 44. Radio (1985): total number of receivers 53,000,000 (1 per 2.6 persons). Television (1985): total number of receivers 30,431,000 (1 per 4.5 persons). Telephones (1984): 10,803,000 (1 per 12 persons).

Education and health

Education (1984)

	schools	teachers	students	student/ teacher ratio
Primary (age 7–14)	190,904	1,022,014	24,821,301	24.3
Secondary (age 15–17)	9,104	214,969	2,946,657	13.7
Higher	847	120,632	1,399,539	11.6

Literacy (1985): total population over age 15 literate 66,255,000 (79.3%); males literate 32,757,000 (80.4%); females literate 33,498,000 (78.3%).

Health: physicians (1981) 103,000 (1 per 1,200 persons); hospital beds (1983) 534,055 (1 per 243 persons); infant mortality rate per 1,000 live births (1980–85) 71.0.

Food (1981–83): daily per capita caloric intake 2,564 (vegetable products 85%, animal products 15%); 108% of FAO recommended minimum requirement.

Military

Total active duty personnel (1986): 283,400 (army 64.5%, navy 17.6%, air force 17.9%). *Military expenditure as percent of GNP* (1983): 0.7% (world 6.1%); per capita expenditure U.S.$14.

*Introduced Feb. 28, 1986, at the rate of 1 cruzado = 1,000 old cruzeiros. †Total area, including 1,035 sq mi (2,680 sq km) in dispute between the states of Amazonas and Pará and 1,009 sq mi (2,614 sq km) in dispute between Ceará and Piauí. Land area excluding inland water is 3,265,075 sq mi (8,456,508 sq km). ‡Includes the islands of Trinidade and Martin Vaz. §Includes Rocas atoll and the rocks of São Pedro and São Paulo. ‖Detail does not add to total given because of rounding. ¶Spiritist Catholics are actively and regularly involved in the practice of medium religions; about 60,000,000 Roman Catholics defer to spiritist dogma and participate in organized spiritism occasionally. ♀Evangelical Catholics are persons who are officially regarded as Roman Catholic but who are affiliated to Protestant churches. ♁Non-Christian followers of Afro-Brazilian syncretistic religions ("low spiritism"). □Non-Christian followers of Kardecism ("high spiritism"). ◇First populations cited are for *municipios,* officially delimited areas including central city and adjacent urban and rural districts. Metropolitan areas are defined as urban and rural areas economically dependent on the central city. △*Municipio* within Rio de Janeiro metropolitan area. †*Municipio* within São Paulo metropolitan area. ⊕Excludes rural population of Acre, Amazonas, Pará, Rondônia, Amapá, and Roraima. **1982 election for state governors, federal senators, and federal deputies. Detail cited here is based on the electoral returns for federal deputies. ††Ban on trade union associations was repealed following the return to civilian government in March 1985. ‡‡1984 prices. §§Employed persons aged 10 years and over. ‖‖July average. ¶¶Minimum wages paid in the *municipio* of São Paulo. ♀♀Fuel produced from sugarcane used in the operation of locally produced automobiles as either hydrous alcohol or gasohol. ♁♁Prices of September 1984. □□State of Rio de Janeiro only. ◇◇Exchange rates, international reserves, and interest and prices are all based on end-of-year figures. △△September average. ††June average. ⊕⊕August average. ***Import figures are f.o.b. in balance of trade and c.i.f. in commodities and trading partners. †††Soybeans and products are 9.5% of total exports. ‡‡‡Cruzeiro do Sul, TransBrasil, Varig, and Vasp airlines only.

Brunei

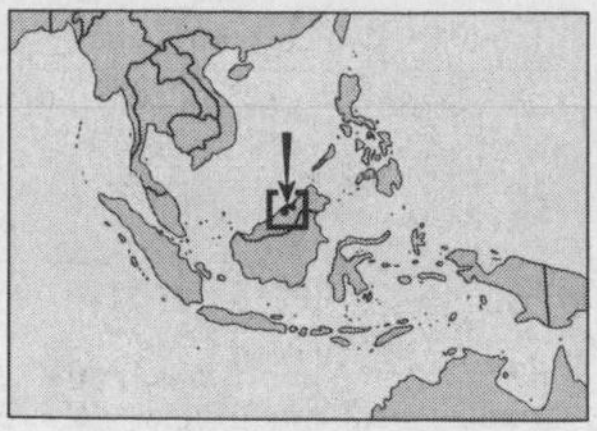

Official name: Negara Brunei Darussalam (State of Brunei, Abode of Peace).
Form of government: monarchy (sultanate).
Head of state and government: Sultan.
Capital: Bandar Seri Begawan.
Official language: Malay.
Official religion: Islam.
Monetary unit: 1 Brunei dollar (Br$) = 100 cents; valuation (Oct. 1, 1986) 1 U.S.$ = Br$2.17; 1 £ = Br$3.14.

Area and population

		area		population
Districts	Capitals	sq mi	sq km	1984 estimate
Belait	Kuala Belait	1,053	2,727	57,000
Brunei and Muara	Bandar Seri Begawan	220	570	129,400
Temburong	Bangar	503	1,303	6,800
Tutong	Tutong	450	1,165	22,700
TOTAL		2,226	5,765	215,900

Demography

Population (1986): 232,600.
Density (1986): persons per sq mi 104.5, persons per sq km 40.3.
Urban-rural (1981): urban 59.4%; rural 40.6%.
Sex distribution (1985): male 53.40%; female 46.60%.
Age breakdown (1985): under 15, 37.0%; 15–29, 30.3%; 30–44, 19.6%; 45–59, 8.5%; 60–69, 2.7%; 70 and over, 1.9%.
Population projection: (1990) 284,000; (2000) 354,000.
Doubling time: 26 years.
Ethnic composition (1985): Malay 64.6%; Chinese 20.0%; other indigenous 8.3%; other 7.1%.
Religious affiliation (1982): Muslim 63.4%; Buddhist 14.0%; Christian 9.7%; other 12.9%.
Major cities (1981): Bandar Seri Begawan 55,000*; Seria 23,511; Kuala Belait 19,281.

Vital statistics

Birth rate per 1,000 population (1985): 30.1 (world avg. 29.0); (1978) legitimate 99.3%; illegitimate 0.7%.
Death rate per 1,000 population (1985): 3.6 (world avg. 11.0).
Natural increase rate per 1,000 population (1985): 26.5 (world avg. 18.0).
Total fertility rate (avg. births per childbearing woman): n.a.
Marriage rate per 1,000 population (1985): 8.5.
Divorce rate per 1,000 population (1985): 0.7†.
Life expectancy at birth (1981): male 70.1 years; female 72.7 years.
Major causes of death per 100,000 population (1985): cardiovascular disease 69.0; malignant neoplasms (cancers) 64.0; cerebrovascular disease 40.0; pneumonia 29.0; bronchitis, emphysema, and asthma 25.0; hypertension 23.0; motor vehicle accidents 21.0; tuberculosis 19.0; signs, symptoms, and other ill-defined conditions 268.0.

National economy

Budget (1985). Revenue: Br$7,533,000,000 (government property 64.2%‡). Expenditures: Br$4,317,900,000 (defense 12.8%§, public works 8.7%§, education 8.2%§, development expenditure 7.7%).
Public debt (external, outstanding; 1985): none.
Tourism (1985): number of visitors 6,418.
Production (metric tons except as noted). Agriculture, forestry, fishing (1985): roots and tubers 5,000§, vegetables and melons 4,000§, cassava 4,000§, rice 1,065, sago 210, pepper 3, 108,810,000 fruits, 1,045,000 coconuts, eggs 2,320§; livestock (number of live animals) 15,000 pigs§, 15,000 buffalo§, 4,000 cattle§, 2,000 goats, 1,000,000 chickens§; roundwood 151,694 cu m; fish catch 1,850. Mining and quarrying (1984): other than petroleum and natural gas (see below), none except sand and gravel for construction. Manufacturing (1985): gasoline 104,600; distillate fuel oils 83,300; liquefied natural gas 29,400§, naphtha 6,800. Construction (number of buildings completed; 1983): residential 285, nonresidential, 9. Energy production (consumption): electricity (kW-hr; 1984) 831,000,000 (831,000,000); coal, none (none); crude petroleum (barrels; 1984) 55,762,000 (n.a.); petroleum products (metric tons; 1984) 746,000 (696,000); natural gas (cu m; 1984) 9,033,700,000 (1,467,800,000).
Population economically active (1981): total 70,690; activity rate of total population 36.4% (participation rates: ages 15–64, 61.1%; female 23.8%; unemployed [1984] 3.4%).

Price and earnings indexes (1980 = 100)

	1979	1980	1981	1982	1983	1984	1985
Consumer price index	...	100.0	129.0	137.2	138.8	143.1	146.4
Monthly earnings index ‖	86.4	100.0	107.5	...	...	...	...

Household income and expenditure. Average household size (1971) 5.8.; income per household: n.a.; source of income: n.a.; expenditure (1982): food 45.1%; transportation and communication 17.2%; recreation, education, and cultural services 8.9%; household furnishings 8.3%; clothing and footwear 6.1%; rent and utilities 5.0%.

Gross national product (at current market prices; 1983): U.S.$4,420,000,000 (U.S.$21,140 per capita).

Structure of gross domestic product and labour force

	1982		1981	
	in value Br$'000,000	% of total value	labour force	% of labour force
Agriculture	75.0	0.9	3,440	4.9
Mining	5,963.1	67.2	3,860	5.5
Manufacturing	879.8	9.9	2,780	3.9
Construction	268.5	3.0	12,650	17.9
Public utilities	13.1	0.2	1,960	2.8
Transportation and communication	63.9	0.7	4,530	6.4
Trade	868.3	9.8	7,360	10.4
Finance	282.2	3.2	2,010	2.8
Services	546.0	6.2	29,280	41.4
Other	−91.4¶	−1.0	2,820♀	4.0
TOTAL	8,868.5	100.0δ	70,690	100.0

Land use (1983): forested 78.7%; meadows and pastures 1.1%; agricultural and under permanent cultivation 1.3%; other 18.9%.

Foreign trade

Balance of trade (current prices)

	1980	1981	1982	1983	1984	1985
Br$'000,000	+8,622	+7,327	+6,582	+5,629	+5,482	+5,184.5
% of total	77.8%	74.3%	67.7%	64.6%	67.3%	65.8%

Imports (1985): Br$1,348,400,000 (machinery and transport equipment 33.8%, manufactured goods 21.5%, food and live animals 14.5%, miscellaneous manufactured articles 10.8%, chemicals 7.1%, beverages and tobacco 5.2%, mineral fuels 1.8%, animal and vegetables oils and fats 0.6%). *Major import sources:* Singapore 24.4%; Japan 19.8%; United States 15.6%; United Kingdom 9.2%; Malaysia 4.5%□; West Germany 3.8%; Thailand 3.1%; Australia 2.7%; Taiwan 2.7%.
Exports (1985): Br$6,532,900,000 (crude oil 54.4%, liquefied natural gas 42.6%, petroleum products 1.5%, other 1.5%). *Major export destinations:* Japan 61.2%; Thailand 10.6%; Singapore 8.7%; United States 7.3%; South Korea 7.0%; Taiwan 3.5%.

Transport and communications

Transport. Railroads◇ (1984): length 12 mi, 19 km. Roads (1985): total length 958 mi, 1,542 km (paved 35%). Vehicles (1985): passenger cars 79,428; trucks and buses 10,663. Merchant marine (1985): vessels (100 gross tons and over) 3; total deadweight tonnage 1,382. Marine transport (1985): cargo loaded 49,455,000 metric tons, cargo unloaded 680,400 metric tons. Air transport (1985): passenger arrivals 184,404, passenger departures 178,498; cargo loaded 432 metric tons, cargo unloaded 5,558 metric tons; airports (1986) with scheduled flights 1.
Communications. Daily newspapers (1985): none. Radio (1985): total number of receivers 70,000 (1 per 3.2 persons). Television (1985): total number of receivers 45,000 (1 per 5.0 persons). Telephones (1985): 32,865 (1 per 6.8 persons).

Education and health

Education (1984)

	schools	teachers	students	student/teacher ratio
Primary (age 5–11)	149	2,131	34,372	16.1
Secondary (age 12–20)	27	1,526	18,565	12.2
Voc., teacher tr.	6	275	1,339	4.9
Higher	1	△	187	...

Educational attainment (1981). Percent of adult population over age 25 having: no formal schooling 32.1%; primary education 28.3%; secondary 30.1%; postsecondary and higher 9.4%. *Literacy* (1984): total population over age 15 literate 108,900 (80.3%); males literate 64,300 (86.5%); females literate 44,600 (72.8%).
Health (1985): physicians 149 (1 per 1,505 persons); hospital beds 876 (1 per 256 persons); infant mortality rate per 1,000 live births 12.1.
Food (1980–82): daily per capita caloric intake 2,558 (vegetable products 82%, animal products 18%); 116% of FAO recommended minimum requirement.

Military

Total active duty personnel (1985): 4,050✝ (army 84.0%, navy 11.1%, air force 4.9%). *Military expenditure as percent of GNP* (1983): 5.8% (world 6.1%); per capita expenditure U.S.$1,200.

*1985 estimate. †For Muslim population only. ‡In 1983 more than 98% of state revenue was derived from exports of oil and gas. §1984. ‖ Nonagricultural sectors only. ¶Imputed bank service charge. ♀Includes unemployed. δDetail does not add to total given because of rounding. □Peninsular Malaysia only. ◇For industrial purposes only. △Teachers are included in vocational and teacher training. ✝All services form part of the army.

Bulgaria

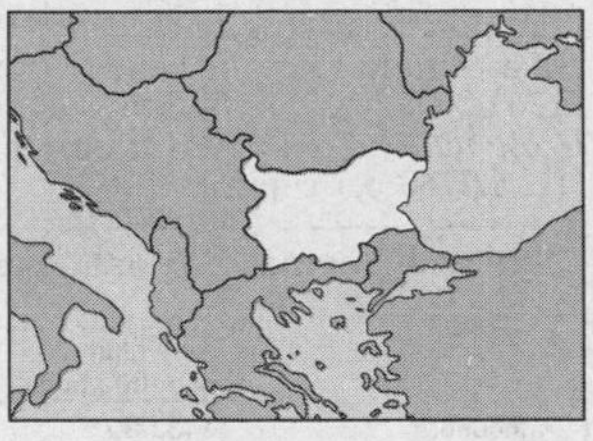

Official name: Narodna Republika Bŭlgaria (People's Republic of Bulgaria).
Form of government: unitary single-party socialist republic with one legislative house (National Assembly [400]).
Chief of state: Chairman of the State Council (president).
Head of government: Chairman of the Council of Ministers (premier).
Capital: Sofia.
Official language: Bulgarian.
Official religion: none.
Monetary unit: 1 lev (leva) = 100 stotinki; valuation (Oct. 1, 1986) 1 lev = U.S.$1.08; 1 £ = 1.56 leva.

Area and population

		area		population
				1984
Provinces	**Capitals**	sq mi	sq km	estimate
Blagoevgrad	Blagoevgrad	2,506	6,490	342,000
Burgas	Burgas	2,972	7,697	439,000
Gabrovo	Gabrovo	786	2,035	180,000
Khaskovo	Khaskovo	1,547	4,007	297,000
Kŭrdzhali	Kŭrdzhali	1,588	4,036	290,000
Kyustendil	Kyustendil	1,174	3,041	197,000
Lovech	Lovech	1,597	4,136	209,000
Mikhaylovgrad	Mikhaylovgrad	1,393	3,609	231,000
Pazardzhik	Pazardzhik	1,720	4,455	324,000
Pernik	Pernik	923	2,391	176,000
Pleven	Pleven	1,673	4,332	374,000
Plovdiv	Plovdiv	2,177	5,638	760,000
Razgrad	Razgrad	1,031	2,669	195,000
Ruse	Ruse	992	2,570	299,000
Shumen	Shumen	1,309	3,390	254,000
Silistra	Silistra	1,097	2,842	174,000
Sliven	Sliven	1,395	3,614	237,000
Smolyan	Smolyan	1,360	3,523	176,000
Sofiya	Sofia	2,767	7,166	306,000
Stara Zagora	Stara Zagora	1,956	5,066	414,000
Tolbukhin	Tolbukhin	1,816	4,704	253,000
Tŭrgovishte	Tŭrgovishte	1,055	2,732	173,000
Varna	Varna	1,477	3,825	467,000
Veliko Tŭrnovo	Veliko Tŭrnovo	1,807	4,680	342,000
Vidin	Vidin	1,161	3,006	169,000
Vratsa	Vratsa	1,527	3,955	290,000
Yambol	Yambol	1,587	4,111	205,000
City Commune				
Sofia		460	1,192	1,173,000
TOTAL		42,823*	110,912	8,946,000

Demography

Population (1986): 8,970,000.
Density (1986): persons per sq mi 209.4, persons per sq km 80.8.
Urban-rural (1985): urban 64.8%; rural 35.2%.
Sex distribution (1986): male 49.50%; female 50.50%.
Age breakdown (1985): under 15, 22.2%; 15–29, 20.4%; 30–44, 20.4%; 45–59, 19.4%; 60–74, 13.1%; 75 and over, 4.5%.
Population projection: (1990) 9,413,000; (2000) 9,698,000.
Doubling time: not applicable; population stable.
Ethnic composition (1980): Bulgarian 88.2%; Turkish 8.5%; other 3.3%.
Religious affiliation (1982): Eastern Orthodox 26.7%; Muslim 7.5%; Protestant 0.7%; Roman Catholic 0.5%; other 0.1%; atheist 64.5%.
Major cities (1984): Sofia 1,102,000†; Plovdiv 373,235; Varna 295,218; Burgas 183,477; Ruse 181,185.

Vital statistics

Birth rate per 1,000 population (1985): 13.2 (world avg. 29.0); (1980) legitimate 89.1%; illegitimate 10.9%.
Death rate per 1,000 population (1985): 12.0 (world avg. 11.0).
Natural increase rate per 1,000 population (1985): 1.2 (world avg. 18.0).
Total fertility rate (avg. births per childbearing woman; 1980): 2.2.
Marriage rate per 1,000 population (1984): 7.5.
Divorce rate per 1,000 population (1984): 1.6.
Life expectancy at birth (1984): male 68.0 years; female 74.0 years.
Major causes of death per 100,000 population (1983): diseases of the circulatory system 662.3; malignant neoplasms (cancers) 157.2.

National economy

Budget (1983). Revenue: 16,800,000,000 leva (turnover tax, taxes from state enterprises, and income tax 64.8%). Expenditures: 16,700,000,000 leva (economy 51.2%, education and health 18.1%, social security 17.4%).
Public debt (external, outstanding; 1984): U.S.$1,400,000,000.
Tourism (1984): number of tourists 6,138,000; receipts from visitors U.S.$288,000,000; expenditures by nationals abroad, n.a.
Production (metric tons except as noted). Agriculture, forestry, fishing (1984): wheat 3,600,000, corn (maize) 3,000,000, vegetables 1,963,000, barley 1,800,000, sugar beets 1,300,000; livestock (1985; number of live animals) 10,501,000 sheep, 3,734,000 pigs, 1,784,000 cattle; roundwood 4,841,000 cu m; fish catch 142,000. Mining and quarrying (1985): iron ore 2,063,000; lead 95,000; copper 75,000; zinc 68,000; manganese 45,000. Manufacturing (1984): cement 5,700,000; pig iron and crude steel 4,500,000; fertilizers 836,100; wood pulp and paper 556,500; cotton fabrics 363,200,000 m; motor vehicles 18,000 units; tractors 5,784 units; beer 91,800,000 hectolitres. Construction (1984): residential 4,483,000 sq m. Energy production (consumption): electricity (kW-hr; 1984) 44,601,000,000 (46,801,000,000); coal (metric tons; 1984) 32,482,000 (39,682,000); crude petroleum (barrels; 1984) 2,190,000 (93,400,000); petroleum products (metric tons; 1984) 11,390,000 (13,310,000); natural gas (cu m; 1984) 112,820,000 (2,164,000,000).
Gross national product (1984): U.S.$25,082,000,000 (U.S.$2,800 per capita).

Structure of net material product and labour force

	1984			
	in value '000,000 leva	% of total value	labour force	% of labour force
Agriculture	4,599.0	18.5	915,400	22.3
Mining } Manufacturing } Public utilities }	14,091.0	56.6 }	1,367,400	33.2
			51,700	1.3
Construction	2,367.0	9.5	354,400	8.6
Transp. and commun.	1,912.0	7.7	302,500	7.4
Trade	1,328.0	5.3	360,100	8.8
Finance	—	— }		
Pub. admin., defense	—	— }	709,900	17.3
Services	—	— }		
Other	611.0‡	2.4‡	46,500	1.1
TOTAL	24,908.0	100.0	4,107,900	100.0

Population economically active (1985): total 4,149,000; activity rate of total population 46.2% (participation rates [1983]: working age [male 16–60; female 16–55] 82.4%; female 49.2%; unemployed, n.a.).

Price and earnings indexes (1970 = 100)

	1978	1979	1980	1981	1982	1983	1984
Consumer price index	103.2	107.8	122.9	123.5	123.7	125.3	129.0
Monthly earnings index	126.6	133.1	155.6	163.7	167.7	170.1	174.8

Household income and expenditure. Average household size (1982) 3.3; income per household 5,092 leva (U.S.$5,249); sources of income: wages and salaries 62.9%, social welfare 20.0%, other 17.1%; expenditure (1981): food 36.5%, clothing and footwear 8.6%, housing 6.7%, transportation 5.4%.
Land use (1983): forested 34.9%; meadows and pastures 18.4%; agricultural and under permanent cultivation 37.5%; other 9.2%.

Foreign trade

Balance of trade (current prices)

	1979	1980	1981	1982	1983	1984
'000,000 leva	+303.4	+618.6	−97.6	−121.3	−148.5	+145.0
% of total	2.0%	3.5%	0.5%	0.6%	0.6%	0.6%

Imports (1984): 12,842,300,000 leva (fuels, mineral raw materials, and metals 46.9%; machinery and equipment 34.1%; of which transport equipment 14.0%; power and electrical machinery 4.4%, tractors and agricultural machinery 2.2%; chemical fertilizers and rubber 5.3%; crop and livestock crude material 5.0%). *Major import sources:* U.S.S.R. 59.0%; East Germany 5.5%; Poland 4.2%; Czechoslovakia 4.0%; West Germany 3.7%.
Exports (1984): 12,987,300,000 leva (machinery and equipment 47.7%, of which transport equipment 8.1%; fuels, mineral raw materials, and metals 10.8%; cigarettes 5.2%; fruit 3.9%). *Major export destinations:* U.S.S.R. 55.7%; East Germany 5.2%; Libya 4.5%; Czechoslovakia 4.0%.

Transport and communications

Transport. Railroads (1985): length 2,659 mi, 4,279 km; passenger-km 8,233,000,000§; metric ton-km cargo 18,060,000,000§. Roads (1984): total length 23,384 mi, 37,633 km (paved 91%). Vehicles (1983): passenger cars 937,579; trucks and buses 519,200. Merchant marine (1985): vessels (100 gross tons and over) 203; total deadweight tonnage 1,889,722. Air transport (1984): passenger-km 2,870,000,000; metric ton-km cargo 51,800,000; airports (1986) 13.
Communications. Daily newspapers (1984): total number 14; total circulation 2,315,000; circulation per 1,000 population 258. Radio (1985): 2,043,500 receivers (1 per 4.4 persons). Television (1985): 1,697,200 receivers (1 per 5.3 persons). Telephones (1985): 1,810,500 (1 per 5.0 persons).

Education and health

Education (1983–84)

	schools	teachers	students	student/ teacher ratio
Primary (age 7–15)	3,040	61,895	1,064,371	17.2
Secondary (age 16–18)	481	8,477	138,187	16.3
Voc., teacher tr.	528	17,884	217,552	12.2
Higher	33	14,738	102,525	7.0

Educational attainment‖ (1983): Percent of employed adult population having: postsecondary vocational certificate 15.6%; 4-year college 7.5%. *Literacy* (1980): total population over age 15 literate 95.5%.
Health (1985): physicians 24,700 (1 per 363 persons); hospital beds 82,300 (1 per 109 persons); infant mortality rate per 1,000 live births 15.8.
Food (1980–82): daily per capita caloric intake 3,663 (vegetable products 78%, animal products 22%); 146% of FAO recommended minimum.

Military

Total active duty personnel (1985): 148,500 (army 70.7%, navy 5.7%, air force 23.6%). *Military expenditure as percent of GNP* (1983): 8.1% (world 6.1%); per capita expenditure U.S.$461.

*Detail does not add to total given because of rounding. †1985. ‡Includes other material activities. §1984. ‖In labour force.

Burkina Faso*

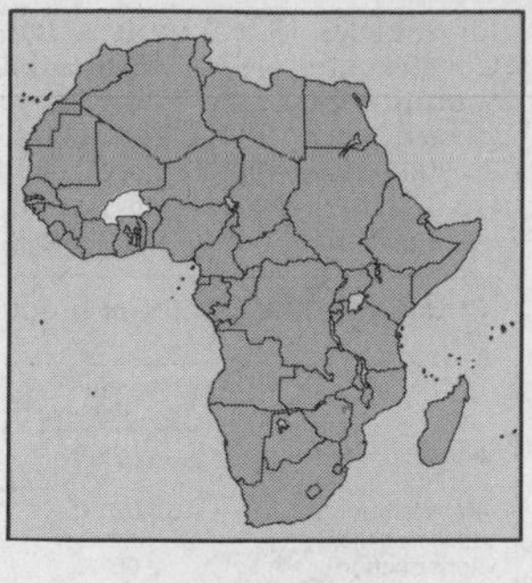

Official name: Burkina Faso (Burkina Faso).
Form of government: military regime†.
Head of state and government: President.
Capital: Ouagadougou.
Official language: French.
Official religion: none.
Monetary unit: 1 CFA franc (CFAF) = 100 centimes; valuation (Oct. 1, 1986) 1 U.S.$ = CFAF 332.05; 1 £ = CFAF 479.81.

Area and population

Provinces	Capitals	area sq mi	area sq km	population 1985 census
Bam	Kongoussi	1,551	4,017	164,263
Bazéga	Kombissiri	2,051	5,313	306,976
Bougouriba	Diébougou	2,736	7,087	221,522
Boulgou	Tenkodogo	3,488	9,033	403,358
Boulkiemde	Koudougou	1,598	4,138	363,594
Comoé	Banfora	7,102	18,393	250,510
Ganzourgou	Zorgho	1,578	4,087	196,006
Gnagna	Bogandé	3,320	8,600	229,249
Gourma	Fada N'Gourma	10,275	26,613	294,123
Houet	Bobo-Dioulasso	6,360	16,472	585,031
Kadiogo	Ouagadougou	451	1,169	459,138
Kénédougou	Orodara	3,207	8,307	139,722
Kossi	Nouna	5,088	13,177	330,413
Kouritenga	Koupéla	628	1,627	197,027
Mouhoun	Dédougou	4,032	10,442	289,213
Nahouri	Pô	1,484	3,843	105,273
Namentenga	Boulsa	2,994	7,755	198,798
Oubritenga	Ziniaré	1,812	4,693	303,229
Oudalan	Gorom Gorom	3,879	10,046	105,715
Passoré	Yako	1,575	4,078	225,115
Poni	Gaoua	4,000	10,361	234,501
Sanguie	Réo	1,994	5,165	218,289
Sanmatenga	Kaya	3,557	9,213	368,365
Sèno	Dori	5,202	13,473	230,043
Sissili	Léo	5,303	13,736	246,844
Soum	Djibo	5,154	13,350	190,464
Sourou	Tougan	3,663	9,487	267,770
Tapoa	Diapaga	5,707	14,780	159,121
Yatenga	Ouahigouya	4,746	12,292	537,205
Zoundwéogo	Manga	1,333	3,453	155,142
TOTAL		105,869‡	274,200	7,967,019

Demography

Population (1986): 8,126,000.
Density (1986): persons per sq mi 76.8, persons per sq km 29.6.
Urban-rural (1982): urban 7.6%; rural 94.2%.
Sex distribution (1985): male 48.23%; female 51.77%.
Age breakdown (1983): under 15, 45.7%; 15–29, 24.1%; 30–44, 15.4%; 45–59, 9.1%; 60 and over, 5.6%.
Population projection: (1990) 7,600,000; (2000) 9,300,000.
Doubling time: 27 years.
Ethnic composition (1980): Mossi 53.6%; Lobi 6.9%; Bobo 6.9%; Fulani 5.6%; Gurunsi 5.1%; Tuareg 4.1%; Gurma 4.0%; other 13.8%.
Religious affiliation (1980): tribal religionist 44.8%; Muslim 43.0%; Christian 12.2%, of which Roman Catholic 9.8%, Protestant 2.4%.
Major cities (1985): Ouagadougou 359,801; Bobo-Dioulasso 202,807; Koudougou 59,644; Ouahigouya 41,595.

Vital statistics

Birth rate per 1,000 population (1980–85): 47.8 (world avg. 29.0).
Death rate per 1,000 population (1980–85): 22.2 (world avg. 11.0).
Natural increase rate per 1,000 population (1980–85): 25.6 (world avg. 18.0).
Total fertility rate (avg. births per childbearing woman; 1980–85): 6.5.
Marriage rate per 1,000 population (1975): 9.4.
Divorce rate per 1,000 population (1975): 1.3.
Life expectancy at birth (1980–85): male 40.4 years; female 43.6 years.
Major causes of death per 100,000 population: n.a.; however, major diseases include bilharziasis, kwashiorkor, malaria, measles, and onchocerciasis ("river blindness").

National economy

Budget (1985). Revenue: CFAF 69,600,000,000 (taxes 77.7%, of which indirect 57.3%; direct 19.0%; other 23.7%). *Expenditures:* CFAF 76,700,000,000 (debt payment 23.6%; defense 20.7%§; education 19.6%§; public investment 12.3%; health 6.8%§).
Public debt (external, outstanding; 1984): U.S.$407,400,000.
Tourism: receipts from visitors (1984) U.S.$3,000,000; expenditures by nationals abroad (1983) U.S.$32,000,000.
Production (metric tons except as noted). Agriculture, forestry, fishing (1984): sorghum and millet 1,019,618, sugarcane 320,000, pulses 155,600, roots and tubers 119,000, seed cotton 79,287, peanuts (groundnuts) 78,000, corn (maize) 77,599, karite 66,675, sweet potatoes 43,000, rice 40,996, sesame 3,717; livestock (number of live animals; 1983) 2,950,000 cattle, 2,500,000 goats, 2,000,000 sheep, 14,000,000 chickens; roundwood 6,586,000 cu m; fish catch 7,000§. Mining and quarrying (1984): phosphates 3,000. Manufacturing (1983): flour 21,009; soap 10,006; cotton yarn 373; motorcycles and scooters 4,700 units; footwear 1,313,000 pairs; beer 701,447 hectolitres; soft drinks 139,558 hectolitres. Construction: n.a. Energy production (consumption): electricity (kW-hr; 1984) 121,217,000 (107,136,000); coal, none (n.a.); crude petroleum, none (n.a.); petroleum products (metric tons; 1984) 136,000 (135,000); natural gas, none (n.a.).
Gross national product (at current market prices; 1984): U.S.$1,040,000,000 (U.S.$160 per capita).

Structure of gross domestic product and labour force

	1982 in value CFAF '000,000	% of total value	labour force	% of labour force
Agriculture	143,030.2	41.2	2,763,000	82.0
Mining	27.5	‖	438,000	13.0
Manufacturing	43,010.7	12.4		
Construction	13,985.1	4.0		
Public utilities	4,876.4	1.4		
Transp. and commun.	24,460.6	7.0	168,000	5.0
Trade	40.599.8	11.7		
Pub. admin., defense; Services	56,516.9	16.3		
Other	20,481.5¶	5.9	...	...
TOTAL	346,988.7	100.0‡	3,369,000	100.0

Population economically active: total (1982) 3,369,000; activity rate of total population 47.6% (participation rates: over age 15 [1975] 44.6%; female 46.1%; unemployed, n.a.).

Price and earnings indexes (1980 = 100)

	1979	1980	1981	1982	1983	1984	1985
Consumer price index♀	89.1	100.0	107.6	120.5	130.6	133.4	146.3
Hourly earnings index	100.0	100.0	100.0	126.7	126.7	126.7	...

Household income and expenditure. Average household size (1984) 4.9; average annual income per household CFAF 303,000 (U.S.$640); source of income: n.a.; expenditure (1984): food 34.6%; transportation 18.6%; electricity and fuel 13.7%; beverages 9.0%; health 5.2%; housing 5.1%.
Land use (1983): forested 25.6%; meadows and pastures 36.5%; agricultural and under permanent cultivation 9.6%; other 28.3%.

Foreign trade♂

Balance of trade (current prices)

	1979	1980	1981	1982	1983	1984
CFAF '000,000	−36,150	−42,910	−55,030	−75,340	−68,100	−48,050
% of total	52.7%	52.9%	58.0%	67.5%	61.1%	46.7%

Imports (1984): CFAF 111,263,800,000 (manufactured goods 18.6%; machinery and transport equipment 18.3%, of which transport equipment 9.3%, electrical machinery 2.8%; cereals 15.6%; petroleum products 14.8%; chemicals 10.8%; preserved dairy products 4.2%; cement 3.0%; tobacco 2.6%). *Major import sources:* France 26.0%; Côte d'Ivoire 22.4%; United States 10.0%; The Netherlands 4.6%; Japan 3.8%; China 3.2%.
Exports (1984): CFAF 34,872,400,000 (raw cotton 55.0%; karite nuts 11.5%; live animals 11.0%; manufactured goods 6.2%; vegetables 2.6%). *Major export destinations:* Taiwan 25.2%; Côte d'Ivoire 14.8%; France 10.5%; United Kingdom 8.8%; West Germany 8.0%; Japan 7.2%; China 4.7%; Italy 3.6%.

Transport and communications

Transport. Railroads (1982)□: length 321 mi, 517 km; passenger-mi 532,000,000, passenger-km 856,000,000; metric ton-km cargo 668,000,000. Roads (1984): total length 5,395 mi, 8,684 km (paved 23%). Vehicles (1983): passenger cars 21,182; trucks and buses 5,729. Merchant marine: none. Air transport (1982): passenger-mi 134,000,000, passenger-km 215,000,000; metric ton-mi cargo 21,200,000; airports (1986) with scheduled flights 2.
Communications. Daily newspapers (1982): total number 1; total circulation 1,500; circulation per 1,000 population 0.2. Radio (1985): 116,000 receivers (1 per 68 persons). Television (1985): 18,000 receivers (1 per 436 persons). Telephones (1981): 10,625 (1 per 588 persons).

Education and health

Education (1984)

	schools	teachers	students	student/ teacher ratio
Primary	1,037	4,796	276,732	57.7
Secondary	79	1,553	43,001	27.7
Vocational	27	484	4,492	9.3
Higher	1	216	3,870	17.9

Educational attainment, n.a. *Literacy* (1985): total population over age 15 literate 509,700 (13.2%); males 392,100 (20.7%); females 119,900 (6.1%).
Health: physicians (1984) 118 (1 per 56,942 persons); hospital beds (1980) 4,587 (1 per 1,440 persons); infant mortality rate per 1,000 live births (1985) 137.0.
Food (1980–82): daily per capita caloric intake 1,922 (vegetable products 95%, animal products 5%); 82% of FAO recommended minimum requirement.

Military

Total active duty personnel (1985): 4,000 (army 97.5%; navy, none; air force 2.5%). *Military expenditure as percent of GNP* (1983): 2.8% (world 6.1%); per capita expenditure U.S.$4.

*Known as Upper Volta before Aug. 4, 1984. †The functions of the legislative house (National Assembly; [57]) and all political parties have been suspended since 1980. ‡Detail does not add to total given because of rounding. §1983. ‖ Less than 0.1%. ¶Import duties. ♀Ouagadougou only. ♂Import figures are f.o.b. in balance of trade and c.i.f. in commodities and trading partners. □Passenger-mi and short ton-mi cargo figures are based on traffic between Abidjan (Côte d'Ivoire) and Ouagadougou.

Burma

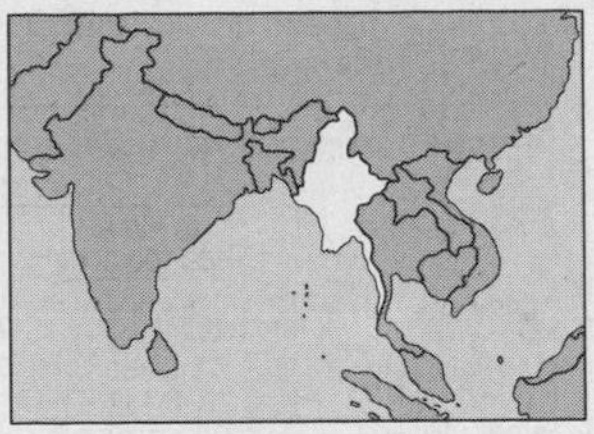

Official name: Pyeidaungzu Socialist Thammada Myanma Naingngandaw (Socialist Republic of the Union of Burma).
Form of government: single-party people's republic with one legislative house (People's Assembly [489*]).
Chief of state: President (Chairman).
Head of government: Prime Minister.
Capital: Rangoon.
Official language: Burmese.
Official religion: none.
Monetary unit: 1 Burmese kyat (K) = 100 pyas; valuation (Oct. 1, 1986) 1 U.S.$ = K 7.02; 1 £ = K 10.15.

Area and population

		area		population
				1983
Divisions	Capitals	sq mi	sq km	census
Irrawaddy	Bassein	13,567	35,138	4,991,057
Magwe	Magwe	17,305	44,820	3,241,103
Mandalay	Mandalay	14,295	37,024	4,580,923
Pegu	Pegu	15,214	39,404	3,800,240
Rangoon	Rangoon	3,927	10,171	3,973,782
Sagaing	Sagaing	36,535	94,625	3,855,991
Tenasserim	Tavoy	16,735	43,343	917,628
States				
Chin	Falam	13,907	36,019	368,985
Kachin	Myitkyinā	34,379	89,041	903,982
Karen	Pa-an	11,731	30,383	1,057,505
Kayah	Loi-kaw	4,530	11,733	168,355
Mon	Moulmein	4,748	12,297	1,682,041
Rakhine (Arakan)	Sittwe (Akyab)	14,200	36,778	2,045,891
Shan	Taunggyi	60,155	155,801	3,718,706
TOTAL		261,228	676,577	35,306,189

Demography

Population (1986): 38,438,000.
Density (1986): persons per sq mi 147.1, persons per sq km 56.8.
Urban–rural (1983): urban 24.0%; rural 76.0%.
Sex distribution (1983): male 49.59%; female 50.41%.
Age breakdown (1985): under 15, 41.2%; 15–29, 27.2%; 30–44, 15.3%; 45–59, 10.3%; 60–74, 5.0%; 75 and over, 1.0%.
Population projection: (1990) 41,351,000; (2000) 49,749,000.
Doubling time: 36 years.
Ethnic composition (1983): Burman 68.0%; Shan 8.9%; Karen 6.6%; Rakhine 4.4%; other 12.1%..
Religious affiliation (1980): Buddhist 87.2%; Christian 5.6%; Muslim 3.6%; tribal religions 1.9%; other 1.7%.
Major cities (1983): Rangoon 2,458,712; Mandalay 532,895; Moulmein 219,-991; Pegu 150,447; Bassein 144,092.

Vital statistics

Birth rate per 1,000 population (1985): 33.2 (world avg. 29.0).
Death rate per 1,000 population (1985): 13.7 (world avg. 11.0).
Natural increase rate per 1,000 population (1985): 19.5 (world avg. 18.0).
Total fertility rate (avg. births per childbearing woman; 1985): 4.5.
Marriage rate per 1,000 population, n.a.
Divorce rate per 1,000 population, n.a.
Life expectancy at birth (1985): male 51.2 years; female 54.3 years.
Major causes of death per 100,000 population (1978): pneumonia 16.1; heart diseases 10.5; enteritis and other diarrheal diseases 10.0; tuberculosis 9.4; malignant neoplasms (cancers) 6.5; cerebrovascular disease 4.1; malaria 3.5.

National economy

Budget (1982–83). Revenue: K 8,103,000,000 (taxes on goods and services 36.2%; property income 24.1%; import duties 17.6%; sales and excise taxes 10.9%; grants 8.1%; corporate and individual income taxes 2.9%). Expenditures: K 7,898,000,000 (agriculture, forestry, and fishing 25.7%; defense 19.0%; general public services 14.6%; education 11.2%; health 7.0%; social security and welfare 5.9%).
Public debt (external, outstanding; 1984): U.S.$2,219,300,000.
Tourism: receipts from visitors (1984) U.S.$10,000,000; expenditures by nationals abroad (1983) U.S.$4,000,000.
Production (metric tons except as noted). Agriculture, forestry, fishing (1984): rice 14,500,000, sugarcane 3,842,000, vegetables and melons 2,022,000, fruits 1,083,000, peanuts (groundnuts) 601,000, pulses 573,000 (of which dry beans 329,000, chick peas 183,000), plantains 438,000, corn (maize) 360,000, roots and tubers 242,000 (of which potatoes 155,000), sesame seed 216,000, wheat 191,000, seed cotton 108,000, millet 88,000, tobacco leaves 62,000, sunflower seed 60,000, jute 55,000, natural rubber 16,000; livestock (number of live animals) 9,550,000 cattle, 2,750,000 pigs, 2,100,000 water buffalo, 1,000,000 goats, 32,000,000 chickens; roundwood 19,497,000 cu m, of which teak 191,600; fish catch 585,800†, of which marine fishing areas 442,930†. Mining and quarrying (by metal content except as noted; 1984): lead 21,937; copper 12,000; zinc 5,320; tin 745; tungsten 216; jadeite 20,694 kg; silver 576,000 troy oz. Manufacturing (1984–85): cement 328,-000; fertilizer 150,000‡; sugar 62,000; soap 48,200; cotton yarn 14,100; cigarettes 2,760,000,000 units. Construction§ (units; 1976): residential 73; nonresidential 50. Energy production (consumption): electricity (kW-hr; 1984) 1,726,000,000 (1,726,000,000); coal (metric tons; 1984) 73,000 (248,-000); crude petroleum (barrels; 1984) 11,512,000 (10,272,000); petroleum products (metric tons; 1984) 1,070,000 (1,071,000); natural gas (cu m; 1984) 837,959,000 (837,959,000).
Gross national product (1984): U.S.$6,620,000,000 (U.S.$180 per capita).

Structure of gross domestic product and labour force

	1984–85			
	in value K'000,000	% of total value	labour force	% of labour force
Agriculture	25,927	48.0	9,772,000	66.1
Mining	607	1.1	85,000	0.6
Manufacturing	5,096	9.4	1,234,000	8.3
Construction	950	1.8	240,000	1.6
Public utilities	267 ‖	0.5	16,000	0.1
Transportation and communication	2,043	3.8	488,000	3.3
Trade	13,249	24.5	1,444,000	9.8
Finance, Public admin., Services	5,903 ‖	10.9	885,000	6.0
Other			628,000	4.2
TOTAL	54,042	100.0	14,792,000	100.0

Population economically active (1983–84): total 15,900,000; activity rate of total population 43.4% (participation rates: over age 15, n.a.; female [1981–82] 28.2%; unemployed 4.6%).

Price and earnings indexes (1980 = 100)

	1979	1980	1981	1982	1983	1984	1985
Consumer price index	89.1	100.0	107.6	120.5	130.6	136.9	146.3
Monthly earnings index¶	95.7	100.0	101.9	105.1	111.7	...	...

Household income and expenditure. Average household size (1980) 5.1; average annual income per household: n.a.; source of income: n.a.; expenditure (1976)♀: food and beverages 75.5%, fuel and power 7.5%, clothing 3.7%, household rent and utilities 3.4%, charities and ceremonials 1.9%, medical care 1.0%, education 1.0%, travel 0.8%.
Land use (1983): forested 48.9%; meadows and pastures 0.5%; agricultural and under permanent cultivation 15.3%; other 35.3%.

Foreign trade♁

Balance of trade (current prices)

	1978	1979	1980	1981	1982	1983	1984
K '000,000	−428.3	+625.2	+997.8	+1,006.2	+172.9	+1,084.1	+630.5
% of total	11.8%	14.0%	19.0%	17.0%	2.9%	21.7%	14.7%

Imports (1983–84): K 5,197,300,000 (nonelectrical machinery and transport equipment 21.1%; base metals and manufactures 8.8%; chemicals, fertilizers, and pharmaceuticals 5.4%; electrical machinery 3.9%). *Major import sources* (1983): Japan 30.8%; West Germany 24.4%; Singapore 9.3%; United Kingdom 5.7%; United States 2.6%.
Exports (1983–84): K 3,419,500,000 (rice and rice products 40.8%; teak 24.6%; base metals and ores 8.8%; rubber 1.8%). *Major export destinations* (1983): Singapore 20.3%; Indonesia 15.5%; Japan 14.8%; Hong Kong 5.4%.

Transport and communications

Transport. Railroads (1984): route length 1,949 mi, 3,137 km; passenger-mi 1,802,000,000, passenger-km 2,900,000,000; short ton-mi cargo 304,800,000, metric ton-km cargo 445,000,000. Roads (1984–85): total length 14,333 mi, 23,067 km (paved 17%). Vehicles (1980): passenger cars 43,300; trucks and buses 44,700. Merchant marine (1985): vessels (100 gross tons and over) 106; total deadweight tonnage 138,901. Air transport (1984–85): passenger-mi 118,402,000, passenger-km 190,544,000; short ton-mi cargo 1,604,000, metric ton-km cargo 2,342,000; airports (1986) with scheduled flights 20.
Communications. Daily newspapers (1985): total number 6; total circulation 509,000; circulation per 1,000 population 14. Radio (1985): total receivers 725,000 (1 per 52 persons). Television (1985): total receivers 35,000 (1 per 1,077 persons). Telephones (1984–85): 52,604 (1 per 710 persons).

Education and health

Education (1984–85)

	schools	teachers	students	student/ teacher ratio
Primary (age 5–9)	27,499	104,754	4,855,963	46.4
Secondary (age 10–15)	2,238	41,668	1,251,482	30.0
Voc., teacher tr.	74	1,036	14,570	14.1
Higher	35	5,524	174,279	31.5

Educational attainment, n.a. *Literacy* (1980): total population over age 15 literate 15,756,200 (65.9%); males literate 8,982,700 (75.9%); females literate 6,750,700 (56.3%).
Health (1984–85): physicians 9,481 (1 per 3,937 persons); hospital beds 25,599 (1 per 1,458 persons); infant mortality rate per 1,000 live births (1985) 106.
Food (1980–82): daily per capita caloric intake 2,360 (vegetable products 96%, animal products 4%); 109% of FAO recommended minimum.

Military

Total active duty personnel (1985): 186,000 (army 91.4%, navy 3.8%, air force 4.8%). *Military expenditure as percent of GNP* (1983–84): 3.4% (world 6.1%); per capita expenditure U.S.$6.

*Including 14 ex officio nonelected members of the People's Assembly who serve in the executive branch of government. †1983. ‡1983–84. §Government building activity only. ‖ Gas and water are included with finance, pub. admin., services, and other. ¶Males in manufacturing only. ♀Based on five rural townships. ♁Import figures are f.o.b. in balance of trade and c.i.f. in commodities and trading partners.

Burundi

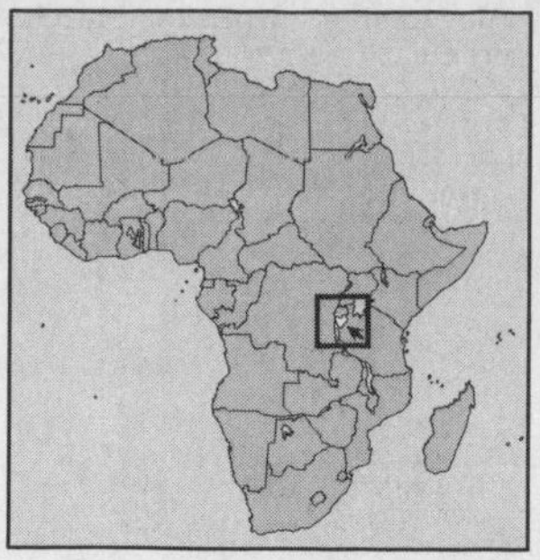

Official name: République du Burundi (French); Republika y'Uburundi (Rundi) (Republic of Burundi).
Form of government: unitary single-party republic with one legislative house (National Assembly [65]).
Head of state and government: President.
Capital: Bujumbura.
Official languages: French; Rundi.
Official religion: none.
Monetary unit: 1 Burundi franc (FBu) = 100 centimes; valuation (Oct. 1, 1986) 1 U.S.$ = FBu 101.29; 1 £ = FBu 146.37.

Area and population

		area		population
Provinces	Capitals	sq mi	sq km	1986 census*
Bubanza	Bubanza	422	1,093	193,109
Bujumbura	Bujumbura	515	1,334	565,782
Bururi	Bururi	971	2,515	364,798
Cankuzo	Cankuzo	749	1,940	125,724
Cibitoke	Cibitoke	633	1,639	226,574
Gitega	Gitega	768	1,989	548,016
Karuzi	Karuzi	563	1,459	251,376
Kayanza	Kayanza	475	1,229	436,297
Kirundo	Kirundo	661	1,711	348,515
Makamba	Makamba	761	1,972	149,984
Muramvya	Muramvya	591	1,530	428,558
Muyinga	Muyinga	705	1,825	306,106
Ngozi	Ngozi	567	1,468	463,500
Rutana	Rutana	733	1,898	173,278
Ruyigi	Ruyigi	913	2,365	200,789
TOTAL LAND AREA		10,026†	25,967	4,782,406
INLAND WATER		721	1,867	
TOTAL AREA		10,747	27,834	

Demography

Population (1986): 4,830,000.
Density‡ (1986): persons per sq mi 481.7, persons per sq km 186.0.
Urban–rural (1985): urban 2.5%; rural 97.5%.
Sex distribution (1985): male 48.79%; female 51.21%.
Age breakdown (1985): under 15, 44.3%; 15–29, 25.1%; 30–44, 15.7%; 45–59, 9.6%; 60–74, 4.5%; 75 and over, 0.8%.
Population projection: (1990) 5,305,000; (2000) 6,951,000.
Doubling time: 26 years.
Ethnic composition (1980): Hutu 83.3%; Tutsi 12.8%; Tutsi from Rwanda 1.6%; Zairian 1.2%; Twa Pygmy 1.0%; other 0.1%.
Religious affiliation (1980): affiliated Christian 79.5%, of which Roman Catholic 73.3%, Protestant 4.4%; tribal religionist 13.5%; nominal Christian 6.0%; Muslim 0.9%; other 0.1%.
Major cities (1986): Bujumbura 272,600; Gitega 95,300; Ngozi 20,000§.

Vital statistics

Birth rate per 1,000 population (1980–85): 47.6 (world avg. 29.0).
Death rate per 1,000 population (1980–85): 20.9 (world avg. 11.0).
Natural increase rate per 1,000 population (1980–85): 26.7 (world avg. 18.0).
Total fertility rate (avg. births per childbearing woman; 1980–85): 6.4.
Marriage rate per 1,000 population: n.a.
Divorce rate per 1,000 population: n.a.
Life expectancy at birth (1980–85): male 42.4 years; female 45.6 years.
Major causes of death per 100,000 population (1983) ‖ : measles 45.1; bacillary dysentery 26.2; other diarrheal diseases 7.9; malaria 7.4; pulmonary tuberculosis 2.6.

National economy

Budget (1984)¶. Revenue: FBu 15,064,400,000 (customs duties 31.7%, income tax 25.9%, other indirect taxes 22.6%, excise duties 14.9%, administrative receipts 4.3%, property tax 0.6%). Expenditures: FBu 15,828,000,000 (goods and services 57.4%, subsidies and transfers 17.6%, loans 0.5%, other 24.5%).
Public debt (external, outstanding; 1984): U.S.$334,400,000.
Tourism: receipts from visitors (1984) U.S.$27,000,000; expenditures by nationals abroad (1983) U.S.$18,000,000.
Production (metric tons except as noted). Agriculture, forestry, fishing (1984): bananas 980,000, sweet potatoes 450,000, cassava 430,000, pulses 292,000, sorghum 150,000, yams and taros 107,000, corn (maize) 103,000, millet 35,000, coffee 32,000, peanuts (groundnuts) 12,000, cotton seed 4,000, tea 2,000; livestock (number of live animals) 770,000 goats, 565,000 cattle, 315,000 sheep, 3,000,000 chickens; roundwood 3,466,000 cu m; fish catch 12,000♀. Mining and quarrying (1984): peat 14,000; kaolin clay 1,990; lime 42; gold 1,115 troy oz. Manufacturing (1983): beer 89,486,600 bottles; carbonated beverages 1,952,400 cases; cigarettes 293,950,000 units; blankets 358,800 units; footwear 300,900 pairs. Construction: n.a. Energy production (consumption): electricity (kW-hr; 1984) 2,000,000 (147,000,000); coal, none (n.a.); crude petroleum, none (n.a.); petroleum products (metric tons; 1984) none (36,000); natural gas, none (n.a.); peat♂ (metric tons; 1984) 8,000 (8,000).
Land use (1983): forested 2.4%; meadows and pastures 35.5%; agricultural and under permanent cultivation 50.9%; other 11.2%.

Gross national product (at current market prices; 1984): U.S.$1,010,000,000 (U.S.$220 per capita).

Structure of gross domestic product and labour force

	1984		1979	
	in value FBu '000,000	% of total value	labour force	% of labour force
Agriculture	55,084	52.2	2,246,200	93.1
Mining	□	□	1,400	0.1
Manufacturing	5,650	5.4	36,700	1.5
Construction	6,417	6.1	14,700	0.6
Public utilities	911□	0.9□	1,700	0.1
Transportation and communication	2,747	2.6	6,400	0.3
Trade	8,982	8.5	20,900	0.9
Finance	1,653	1.6	1,300	0.1
Pub. admin., defense	8,736	8.3	80,700	3.3
Services	5,262	5.0		
Other	10,061◇	9.5	3,100	0.1
TOTAL	105,503	100.0†	2,413,100	100.0†

Population economically active (1983): total 2,480,841; activity rate of total population 54.8% (participation rates: ages 15–64 [1979] 94.4%; female [1982] 52.5%; unemployed, n.a.).

Price and earnings indexes (1980 = 100)

	1980	1981	1982	1983	1984	1985	1986△
Consumer price index	100.0	112.0	118.4	128.3	146.7	152.1	152.7
Monthly earnings index✝	100.0	110.0	103.0	143.4	170.0	...	...

Household income and expenditure. Average household size (1980) 4.9; average annual income per household: n.a.; source of income: n.a.; expenditure⊕: food 59.6%, clothing and footwear 11.1%, furniture and household goods 6.0%, energy and water 5.8%, housing 4.4%, other 13.1%.

Foreign trade**

Balance of trade (current prices)

	1980	1981	1982	1983	1984	1985
FBu '000,000	−7,259	−5,873	−8,866	−7,352	−7,635	−6,506
% of total	38.2%	30.3%	35.9%	32.9%	24.4%	19.7%

Imports (1984): FBu 22,383,000,000 (intermediate goods 42.8%, consumer goods 31.8%, capital goods 25.4%). *Major import sources:* Belgium–Luxembourg 14.7%; France 14.0%; West Germany 8.8%; United States 5.5%; Japan 5.3%; Italy 4.0%.
Exports (1984): FBu 11,828,100,000 (coffee 83.6%; tea 7.3%; raw cotton 0.7%; animal hides and skins 0.7%). *Major export destinations:* West Germany 33.5%; Italy 2.9%; Belgium–Luxembourg 2.8%; United Kingdom 2.3%; United States 1.6%; The Netherlands 0.4%; France 0.3%.

Transport and communications

Transport. Railroads: none. Roads (1981): total length 3,196 mi, 5,144 km (paved 7%). Vehicles (1984): passenger cars 7,533; trucks and other vehicles 6,188. Merchant marine (1979): vessels (100 gross tons and over) 1; total gross tonnage 385. Air transport (1984)††: passenger arrivals 19,050, departures 19,091; cargo loaded 3,528 short tons (3,201 metric tons), unloaded 5,766 short tons (5,231 metric tons); airports (1986) with scheduled flights 1.
Communications. Daily newspapers (1984): total number 1; total circulation 20,000; circulation per 1,000 population 4.3. Radio (1985): total number of receivers 180,000 (1 per 26 persons). Television (1985): total number of receivers 250 (1 per 18,960 persons). Telephones (1983): 6,033 (1 per 750 persons).

Education and health

Education (1983–84)

	schools	teachers	students	student/ teacher ratio
Primary (age 6–11)	875	6,164	302,611	49.1
Secondary (age 12–18)	25	475	7,854	16.5
Voc., teacher tr.	36	594	6,033	10.2
Higher	6	372	2,479	6.7

Educational attainment, n.a. *Literacy* (1982): total population over age 10 literate 991,600 (33.8%); males literate 601,500 (42.8%); females literate 390,100 (25.7%).
Health (1983): physicians 216 (1 per 20,942 persons); hospital beds 5,709 (1 per 792 persons); infant mortality rate per 1,000 live births (1980–85) 124.
Food (1980–82): daily per capita caloric intake 2,244 (vegetable products 97%, animal products 3%); 96% of FAO recommended minimum requirement.

Military

Total active duty personnel (1985): 5,200 (army 96.2%, navy 0.9%, air force 2.9%). *Military expenditure as percent of GNP* (1983): 3.2% (world 6.1%); per capita expenditure U.S.$9.

*Beginning of year. †Detail does not add to total given because of rounding. ‡Based on land area. §1982. ‖ Data shown is for four provinces only. ¶1985: Revenue FBu 17,152,000,000; Expenditure FBu 18,757,000,000. ♀1983. ♂Peat is not yet popularly accepted as a fuel. It is mostly used by industries, schools, and the military. □Mining included with public utilities. ◇Indirect taxes, less subsidies. △May. ✝Nonagricultural activities in Bujumbura only; includes family allowances. ⊕Consumer price index components. **Import figures are f.o.b. in balance of trade and c.i.f. in commodities and trading partners. ††Bujumbura Airport only.

Cameroon

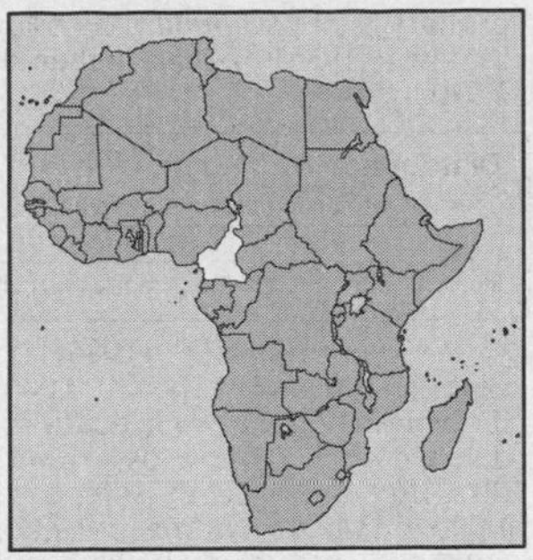

Official name: République du Cameroun (French); Republic of Cameroon (English).
Form of government: republic with one legislative house (National Assembly [120]).
Head of state and government: President.
Capital: Yaoundé.
Official languages: French; English.
Official religion: none.
Monetary unit: 1 CFA franc (CFAF) = 100 centimes; valuation (Oct. 1, 1986) 1 U.S.$ = CFAF 332.05; 1 £ = CFAF 479.81.

Area and population

		area		population
Provinces	Capitals	sq mi	sq km	1983 estimate
Adamoua	Ngaoundéré	24,680	63,910	350,000
Centre	Yaoundé	25,580	66,240	1,497,000
Est	Bertoua	42,080	109,000	433,000
Extrême-Nord	Maroua	13,250	34,320	1,549,000
Littoral	Douala	7,810	20,220	1,286,000
Nord	Garoua	25,410	65,820	549,000
Nord-Ouest	Bamenda	6,720	17,410	1,110,000
Ouest	Bafoussam	5,360	13,880	1,252,000
Sud	Ebolowa	19,190	49,700	372,000
Sud-Ouest	Buea	9,540	24,710	709,000
TOTAL		179,720*	465,460*	9,107,000

Demography

Population (1986): 9,873,000.
Density (1986)†: persons per sq mi 55.0, persons per sq km 21.2.
Urban-rural (1984): urban 36.1%; rural 63.9%.
Sex distribution (1984): male 49.99%; female 50.01%.
Age breakdown (1984): under 15, 44.6%; 15–29, 25.2%; 30–44, 15.6%; 45–59, 9.0%; 60 and over, 5.6%.
Population projection: (1990) 10,885,000; (2000) 13,893,000.
Doubling time: 29 years.
Ethnic composition (1982): Cameroon Highland Bantu 27%; Equatorial Bantu 25%; Kirdi 15%; Fulani 9.5%; Northwestern Bantu 8%; Hausa 8%; Baya and Bamum (Mbum) 6%; other 1.5%.
Religious affiliation (1980): Roman Catholic 35%; Protestant 18%; animist 25%; Muslim 22%.
Major cities (1985): Douala 852,700; Yaoundé 583,500; Nkongsamba 105,200; Maroua 100,200; Garoua 96,200.

Vital statistics

Birth rate per 1,000 population (1982–83): 45.0 (world avg. 29.0).
Death rate per 1,000 population (1982–83): 20.3 (world avg. 11.0).
Natural increase rate per 1,000 population (1982–83): 24.7 (world avg. 18.0).
Total fertility rate (avg. births per childbearing woman; 1982–83): 6.2.
Life expectancy at birth (1982–83): male 43.2 years; female 45.6 years.
Major causes of death per 100,000 population: n.a.; however, major health problems include measles, malaria, tuberculosis of respiratory system, anemias, meningitis, intestinal obstruction and hernia, avitaminoses and other nutritional deficiency diseases.

National economy

Budget (1985–86). Revenue: CFAF 740,000,000,000‡ (direct and assimilated taxes 49.5%; customs duties and taxes 26.9%; receipts for services 8.6%; indirect taxes 8.1%). Expenditures: CFAF 740,000,000,000 (investment 41.9%, of which development operations 31.1%; education 9.3%; armed forces 6.6%; health 3.6%; agriculture 2.3%).
Gross national product (1984): U.S.$8,000,000,000 (U.S.$850 per capita).

Structure of gross domestic product and labour force

	1983–84		1982	
	in value CFAF '000,000,000	% of total value	labour force	% of labour force
Agriculture	702.0	22.0	2,594,800	73.2
Mining	520.5	16.3	1,580	0.1
Manufacturing	358.5	11.2	159,560	4.5
Construction	192.6	6.0	62,860	1.8
Public utilities	35.2	1.1	3,230	0.1
Transp. and commun.	147.3	4.6	47,400	1.3
Trade	414.9	13.0	149,200 (Trade and Finance)	4.2
Finance	396.8	12.4		
Public admin., defense,	212.8	6.7	524,370 (Public admin., defense, Services, Other)	14.8
Services	79.4	2.5		
Other	135.0§	4.2		
TOTAL	3,195.0	100.0	3,543,000	100.0

Household income and expenditure. Average household size (1980) 5.2; average annual income per household ‖ (1983): U.S.$420; source of income: n.a.; expenditure ‖ (1983): food 33.6%, clothing and footwear 16.3%, housing 14.6%, transportation and communication 10.5%, recreation 5.1%, health 5.0%.
Population economically active (1982): total 3,543,000; activity rate of total population 45.5% (participation rates: ages 15–64, n.a.; female 37.5%; unemployed 4.6%).

Price index (1980 = 100)

	1979	1980	1981	1982	1983	1984	1985
Consumer price index	91.3	100.0	110.7	125.4	146.3	162.9	165.8
Earnings index	...	...	...	...	...	...	...

Production (metric tons except as noted). Agriculture, forestry, fishing (1984): sugarcane 1,100,000, plantains 970,000, cassava 620,000, vegetables 418,000, corn (maize) 400,000, millet and sorghum 400,000, yams 400,000, sweet potatoes 130,000, coffee 127,000, cocoa 115,000, dry beans 107,000, palm kernels 81,000, peanuts (groundnuts) 80,000, bananas 65,000, natural rubber 16,000; livestock (number of live animals) 3,730,000 cattle, 2,180,000 sheep, 2,000,000 goats, 1,000,000 pigs; roundwood 10,408,000 cu m; fish catch (1983) 84,277. Mining and quarrying (1984): marble 251,600; aluminum 74,100; limestone 50,700; tin ore and concentrate 14.0; gold 8 kilograms. Manufacturing (1983–84): cement 645,850; palm oil 64,500; sugar 58,655; rubber 16,233; fish products 8,331; cigarettes 2,795; sawnwood 463,497 cu m; beer 3,577,900 hectolitres. Construction (CFAF, gross value; 1983): 16,510,000,000. Energy production (consumption): electricity (kW-hr; 1984) 2,230,000,000 (2,230,000,000); coal, n.a. (none); petroleum (barrels; 1984) 47,462,000 (23,800,000); petroleum products (metric tons; 1984) 3,002,000 (2,845,000); natural gas, none (n.a.).
Land use (1983): forested 53.9%; meadows and pastures 17.7%; agricultural and under permanent cultivation 14.8%; other 13.6%.
Tourism: receipts from visitors (1984–85) U.S.$12,115,600; expenditures by nationals abroad (1983) U.S.$72,000,000.
Public debt (external, outstanding; 1984): U.S.$1,737,800,000.

Foreign trade

Balance of trade (current prices)

	1979	1980	1981	1982	1983	1984
CFAF '000,000,000	−30.6	−47.0	−89.3	−65.7	−94.8	−44.2
% of total	6.0%	7.5%	13.0%	9.2%	11.3%	4.8%

Imports (1984): CFAF 484,646,000,000 (machinery and transport equipment 34.3%, of which road transport equipment and parts 10.0%, drilling equipment 6.1%; chemical and pharmaceutical products 6.7%; textile yarn 6.6%; iron and steel 5.0%; cement 1.4%). *Major import sources:* France 42.8%; United States 10.2%; Japan 7.1%; West Germany 6.7%; Italy 4.6%; United Kingdom 3.5%; Belgium-Luxembourg 3.0%; The Netherlands 1.7%.
Exports (1984): CFAF 440,470,000,000 (cacao 22.8%; crude petroleum 21.6%; coffee 21.2%; aluminum and aluminum products 8.0%; sawnwood and logs 4.2%; cotton yarn and fabrics 3.2%; cocoa pulp and butter 3.2%; rubber 1.6%; bananas 1.5%). *Major export destinations:* France 33.3%; The Netherlands 24.9%; United States 12.4%; Belgium-Luxembourg 6.7%; Italy 6.3%; West Germany 6.1%; Japan 0.9%; United Kingdom 0.8%.

Transport and communications

Transport. Railroads (1985): length 729 mi, 1,173 km; passenger-mi 306,000,000, passenger-km 492,000,000; short ton-mi cargo 595,000,000, metric ton-km cargo 869,000,000. Roads (1985): total length 38,836 mi, 64,905 km (paved 5%). Vehicles (1985): passenger cars 72,449; trucks and buses 41,301. Merchant marine (1985): vessels (100 gross tons and over) 48; total deadweight tonnage 88,504. Air transport (1983): passenger-mi 345,511,000, passenger-km 547,999,000; short ton-mi cargo 34,291,000, metric ton-km cargo 50,064,000; airports (1986) with scheduled flights 10.
Communications. Daily newspapers (1984): 1; total circulation 35,000; circulation per 1,000 population 3.7. Radio (1985): total number of receivers 790,000 (1 per 12.0 persons). Television (1984) n.a.¶. Telephones (1981): 26,000 (1 per 333 persons).

Education and health

Education (1984–85)

	schools♀	teachers	students	student/ teacher ratio
Primary (age 6–14)	5,582	32,082	1,638,569	51.1
Secondary (age 15–24)	365	8,381	238,075	28.4
Voc., teacher tr.	199	3,239	77,555	23.9
Higher♂	1	572	13,753	24.0

Educational attainment (1976). Percent of population over age 15 having: no schooling 51,1%; primary education 41.7%; some postprimary 0.2%; secondary 5.7%; some postsecondary 0.3%; higher 0.2%; other 0.8%. *Literacy* (1980): total population literate (over age 15) 2,344,100 (55.2%); males literate 1,453,200 (70.2%); females literate 890,900 (41.0%).
Health: physicians (1982) 604 (1 per 14,800 persons); hospital beds (1984–85) 26,832 (1 per 377 persons); infant mortality rate per 1,000 births (1983) 116.
Food (1980–82): daily per capita caloric intake 2,148 (vegetable products 94%, animal products 6%); 93% of FAO recommended minimum requirement.

Military

Total active duty personnel (1985): 7,300 (army 90.4%, navy 4.8%, air force 4.8%). *Military expenditure as percent of GNP* (1983): 1.2% (world 6.0%); per capita expenditure U.S.$10.

*Total land area is 179,620 sq mi (465,214 sq km) and is shown for provinces; the total area (both land and water) is shown in the grand total. †Based on land areas. ‡Revenue breakdown is for 1982–83. §Includes import duties less imputed bank service charges. ‖ Capital city only. ¶A national television network was established in March 1985 and scheduled to become fully operational by July 1987. ♀1983–84. ♂Univerity of Yaoundé only.

Canada

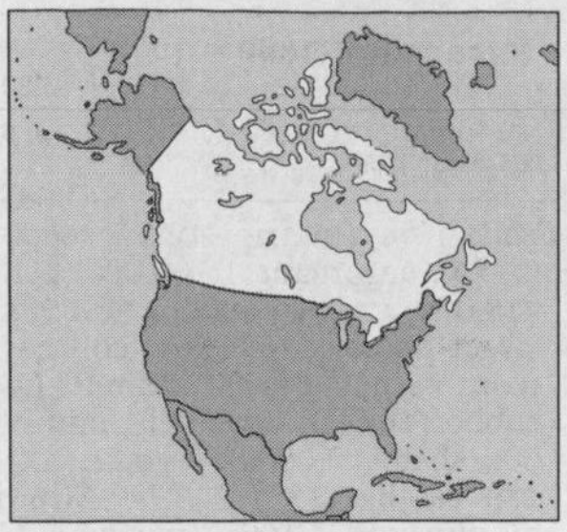

Official name: Canada.
Form of government: federal multiparty parliamentary state with two legislative houses (Senate [104]; House of Commons [282]).
Chief of state: British Monarch represented by governor-general.
Head of government: Prime Minister.
Capital: Ottawa.
Official languages: English; French.
Official religion: none.
Monetary unit: 1 Canadian dollar (Can$) = 100 cents; valuation (Oct. 1, 1986) 1 U.S.$ = Can$1.39; 1 £ = Can$2.01.

Area and population

		area		population
Provinces	**Capitals**	sq mi	sq km	1985* estimate
Alberta	Edmonton	248,800	644,390	2,348,800
British Columbia	Victoria	358,971	929,730	2,892,500
Manitoba	Winnipeg	211,723	548,360	1,069,600
New Brunswick	Fredericton	27,834	72,090	719,200
Newfoundland	Saint John's	143,510	371,690	580,400
Nova Scotia	Halifax	20,402	52,840	880,700
Ontario	Toronto	344,090	891,190	9,066,200
Prince Edward Island	Charlottetown	2,185	5,660	127,100
Quebec	Quebec	523,859	1,356,790	6,580,700
Saskatchewan	Regina	220,348	570,700	1,019,500
Territories				
Northwest Territories	Yellowknife	1,271,442	3,293,020	50,900
Yukon Territory	Whitehorse	184,931	478,970	22,800
TOTAL LAND AREA		3,558,096	9,215,430	25,358,400
INLAND WATER		291,579	755,180	
TOTAL AREA		3,849,675	9,970,610	

Demography

Population (1986): 25,638,000.
Density† (1986): persons per sq mi 7.2, persons per sq km 2.8.
Urban-rural (1985): urban 75.9%; rural 24.1%.
Sex distribution (1985): male 49.45%; female 50.55%.
Age breakdown (1985): under 15, 21.5%; 15–29, 26.5%; 30–44, 22.5%; 45–59, 14.7%; 60–74, 10.7%; 75 and over, 4.1%.
Population projection: (1990) 26,826,000; (2000) 29,028,000.
Doubling time: 88 years.
Ethnic origin (1981): British 40.2%; French 26.7%; German 4.1%; Italian 3.1%; Ukrainian 2.2%; Dutch 1.7%; other European 8.5%; Asiatic 2.1%; Amerindian and Inuktitut (Eskimo) 1.7%; multiple origin and other 9.7%.
Religious affiliation (1981): Roman Catholic 47.3%; Protestant 41.2%; Eastern Orthodox 1.5%; Jewish 1.2%; Muslim 0.4%; Hindu 0.3%; nonreligious 7.4%; other 0.7%.
Major metropolitan areas (1985): Toronto 3,202,400; Montreal 2,878,200; Vancouver 1,348,600; Ottawa–Hull 769,900; Edmonton 683,600; Calgary 625,600; Winnipeg 612,100; Quebec 593,500; Hamilton 559,700; Saint Catharines–Niagara 309,400.

Other metropolitan areas (1985)

	population		population		population
Chcoutimi-		Oshawa	172,800	Sudbury	147,600
Jonquière	139,400	Regina	174,800	Thunder Bay	123,500
Halifax	290,600	Saint John's	160,700	Trois Rivières	114,300
Kitchener	303,400	Saint John	116,800	Victoria	245,100
London	292,700	Saskatoon	170,100	Windsor	249,800

Place of birth (1981): 83.9% native-born; 16.1% foreign-born, of which United Kingdom 3.7%, other European 8.6%, Asian countries 1.7%, United States 1.3%, other 0.8%.
Mobility (1981). Population living in the same residence as in 1976: 52.4%; different residence, same province 24.9%; different province 22.7%.
Households (1985). Total number of households 9,079,000. Average household size 2.8; 1 person 20.5%, 2 persons 30.8%, 3 persons 18.0%, 4 persons 18.8%, 5 persons 8.1%, 6 or more persons 3.8%. Family households: 6,827,400 (75.2%), nonfamily 2,251,600 (24.8%, of which 1 person 20.5%).
Immigration (1984): permanent immigrants admitted 88,199, from Asia 47.5%, Europe 24.4%, United States 7.8%, West Indies 6.3%, other 14.0%.

Vital statistics

Birth rate per 1,000 population (1985): 14.9 (world avg. 29.0); (1983) legitimate 91.0%; illegitimate 9.0%.
Death rate per 1,000 population (1985): 7.0 (world avg. 11.0).
Natural increase rate per 1,000 population (1985): 7.9 (world avg. 18.0).
Total fertility rate (avg. births per childbearing woman; 1983): 1.7.
Marriage rate per 1,000 population (1985): 7.1.
Divorce rate per 1,000 population (1983): 2.8.
Life expectancy at birth (1983): male 73.0 years; female 79.0 years.
Major causes of death per 100,000 population (1983): diseases of the circulatory system 345.2; malignant neoplasms (cancers) 172.2; accidents 56.6; diseases of the respiratory system 53.5.

Social indicators

Educational attainment (1981). Percent of adult population over age 25 having: no formal schooling 2.0%; less than full primary education 14.2%; primary 9.5%; secondary 39.6%; postsecondary 34.7%, of which (graduates by level; 1986): 4-year higher degree 102,300, master's 15,480, doctorate 2,070.

Distribution of income (1984)

percent of national income by quintile

1	2	3	4	5 (highest)
2.5%	8.5%	15.1%	25.5%	48.4%

Quality of working life (1985). Average workweek: 38.8 hours (3.1% overtime). Annual rate per 100,000 workers for (1981): injury, accident, or industrial illness 4,956; death 4.0. Proportion of labour force insured for damages or income loss resulting from (1984): injury 99%; permanent disability 99%; death 99%. Average days lost to labour stoppages per 1,000 employee-workdays (1985): 1.6. Average duration of journey to work (1983): 23 minutes‡ (17.3% public transportation, 72.8% automobile, 9.9% other). Rate per 1,000 workers of discouraged (unemployed no longer seeking work; 1983): 10.5.
Access to services (1985). Proportion of households having access to: electricity 100.0%; public water supply 99.7%; public sewage collection 99.3%; public fire protection (1978) 90.4%.
Social participation. Eligible voters participating in last national election: 69.7%. Population over 18 years of age participating in voluntary work: n.a. Trade union membership in total work force: 29.2%. Practicing religious population in total affiliated population: 92.7%.
Social deviance (1982). Offense rate per 100,000 population for: murder 6.5; rape 10.2; auto theft 352.8; burglary and housebreaking 1,500.2. Incidence per 100,000 in general population of: alcoholism (1976) 27; drug and substance abuse 322.4; suicide (1983) 23.4.
Leisure (1981). Favourite leisure activities (hours weekly): television 13.3; social time 10.7; reading 3.5; recreation and culture 2.7.
Material well-being (1985). Households possessing: automobile 81.9%; telephone 98.2%; television receiver 98.4%; refrigerator 99.2%; central air conditioner 17.8%; automatic washing machine 77.4%; cable television and videocassette recorders 62.4%.

National economy

Gross national product (at current market prices; 1985): U.S.$335,800,000,000 (U.S.$13,240 per capita).

Structure of gross domestic product and labour force

	1984			
	in value Can$'000,000	% of total value	labour force	% of labour force
Agriculture	14,006	3.2	664,000	5.2
Mining	25,934	6.0	183,000	1.4
Manufacturing	71,875	16.6	2,031,000	16.0
Construction	18,040	4.2	627,000	4.9
Public utilities	15,412	3.6	130,000	1.0
Transportation and communication	32,188	7.4	757,000	6.0
Trade	40,035	9.3	1,942,000	15.3
Finance }			1,074,000	8.5
Pub. admin., defense }	215,210	49.7	} 3,928,000	31.0
Services }				
Other }			1,342,000§	10.6§
TOTAL	432,700	100.0	12,678,000	100.0‖

Budget (1984–85). Revenue: Can$67,326,000,000 (personal income tax 48.7%; corporation income tax 14.6%; sales tax 10.9%; excise taxes and import duties 9.8%). Expenditures: Can$98,200,000,000 (education, health, and welfare 40.4%; public debt interest 20.7%; economic development 11.5%; defense 8.9%).
National debt (1984): Can$163,419,000,000.
Tourism (1984): receipts from visitors U.S.$2,830,000,000; expenditures by nationals abroad U.S.$3,955,000,000.

Manufacturing, mining, and construction enterprises (1985)

	no. of enterprises¶	no. of employees	hourly wages as a % of avg. of all wages	annual shipments (Can$'000,000)
Manufacturing				
Transport equipment	1,202	181,431	112.1	42,363.8
Food and beverages	4,372	227,076	90.5	37,197.2
Paper and related products	773	118,119	122.4	18,191.8
Primary metals	446	103,495	124.0	16,477.7
Chemicals and related products	1,221	91,477	102.2	16,447.9
Metal fabricating	5,150	139,423	93.6	13,583.7
Electrical products	1,116	109,270	91.6	12,323.8
Wood	3,353	94,365	98.9	10,689.3
Printing, publishing, and related products	4,620	175,945	99.9	9,175.5
Machinery	1,679	80,732	97.7	7,407.7
Rubber and plastic	1,036	86,818	85.5	6,227.1
Clothing	2,107	85,364	57.8	5,394.3
Furniture and fixtures	2,489	49,272	72.4	3,233.8
Knitting mills	255	18,318¶	77.1	2,700.6
Textile	989	61,197	77.1	2,601.9
Tobacco products industries	24	8,711	90.5	1,645.1
Leather industries	419	22,714	59.3	1,284.0
Mining	125	178,852	131.2	25,740.1
Construction	...	384,315	116.7	19,523.0

Production (farm cash receipts in Can$'000 except as noted). Agriculture, forestry, fishing (1985): wheat 2,483,500, rapeseed 891,380, barley 638,310, corn (maize) 577,490, vegetables 544,270, floriculture 411,760, tobacco 360,070, potatoes 280,830, fruit 263,970, soybeans 229,770; livestock (number of live animals; 1984) 12,308,000 cattle, 10,655,000 pigs, 790,000 sheep, 96,300,000 poultry; roundwood 144,300,000 cu m; pelts 4,423,395 metric tons¶; fish catch 1,046,300 metric tons. Mining and quarrying (metric tons;

1985): iron ore 40,348,000; zinc 1,038,504; copper 730,347; lead 263,890; nickel 175,570; uranium 10,029; molybdenum 7,569; silver 1,209; gold 86. Manufacturing (metric tons; 1985): wood pulp 19,899,100; crude steel 14,637,500; pig iron 9,665,400; newsprint 8,998,000; cement 8,692,000; sulfuric acid 4,341,000; caustic soda 1,783,000; synthetic rubber 111,200; road motor vehicles 1,930,437 units, of which passenger cars 1,074,828 units, truck and buses 855,609 units; washing machines and dryers 741,190 units; refrigerators 509,990 units; footwear 44,394,000 pairs; beer 232,370,000 hectolitres. Construction (building permits; 1985): residential Can$10,883,100,000; nonresidential Can$8,640,800,000.

Service enterprises (1985)

	no. of enterprises	no. of employees♀	weekly wages as a % of all wages	annual sales (Can$'000,000)
Retail trade				
Food stores	...	213,400	...	32,189.6
Motor vehicle dealers	...	79,800	...	25,977.7
Department stores	...	δ	...	12,056.2
Service stations	...	63,700	...	12,096.7
Clothing stores	...	50,200	...	5,835.1
Pharmacies	...	52,400	...	5,328.9
Furniture and appliance stores	...	62,100	...	3,239.0
Automotive stores	...	31,500	...	2,801.4
General merchandise	...	231,700δ	...	2,575.4
General stores	...	δ	...	1,952.3
Sporting goods	...	...	...	1,748.6
Variety stores	...	45,100	...	1,262.6
Shoe stores	...	18,400	...	1,282.6
Hardware stores	...	17,300	...	1,137.0
Jewelry stores	...	14,000	...	927.8

Energy production (consumption): electricity (kW-hr; 1985) 446,412,000,000 (408,643,000); coal (metric tons; 1985) 60,681,000 (48,872,000); crude petroleum (barrels; 1985) 679,585,000 (594,533,000); petroleum products (metric tons; 1985) 86,634,000 (77,997,000); natural gas (cu m; 1985) 108,575,900,000 (50,122,100,000).

Population economically active (1985): total 12,639,000; activity rate of total population 49.8% (participation rates: over age 15, 65.2%; female 42.6%; unemployed 10.5%).

Price and earnings indexes (1981 = 100)

	1980	1981	1982	1983	1984	1985	1986□
Consumer price index	88.9	100.0	110.8	117.2	122.3	127.2	132.9
Monthly earnings index	89.3	100.0	111.8	118.1	123.3	127.6	...

Household income and expenditure. Average household size (1985) 2.8; average annual income per household (1984) Can$35,800 (U.S.$27,500); sources of income: wages and salaries 64.1%, social welfare 14.9%, interest, dividends, and other investment income 13.1%, other 7.9%; expenditure (1983): housing and energy 22.1%, food 17.8%, transportation and communication 15.4%, recreation 7.9%, household durable goods 7.4%, clothing 6.8%, health 3.5%, education 2.8%.

Land use (1983): forested 35.4%; meadows and pastures 2.6%; agricultural and under permanent cultivation 5.0%; built-on, wasteland, and other 57.0%.

Financial aggregates

	1980	1981	1982	1983	1984	1985	1986 (8 mos.)
Exchange rate, Can$ per:							
U.S. dollar	1.17	1.20	1.23	1.23	1.29	1.37	1.39
£	2.84	2.42	2.15	1.88	1.50	1.78	2.07
SDR	1.52	1.38	1.36	1.30	1.30	1.54	1.68
International reserves (U.S.$)							
Total (excl. gold; '000,000)	3,041	3,492	3,000	3,465	2,491	2,503	2,383
SDRs ('000,000)	453	174	71	21	72	218	125
Reserve pos. in IMF ('000,000)	579	402	365	703	678	711	748
Foreign exchange ('000,000)	2,009	2,916	2,564	2,741	1,741	1,574	1,510
Gold ('000,000 fine troy oz)	20.98	20.46	20.26	20.17	20.16	20.14	20.11
% world reserves	2.20	2.00	2.14	2.13	2.13	2.13	2.12
Interest and prices							
Central bank discount (%)	17.26	14.66	10.26	10.04	10.16	9.49	8.63□
Gov't. bond yield (%)	12.48	15.22	14.26	11.79	12.75	11.04	9.36□
Industrial share prices (1980 = 100)	100.0	97.4	76.8	111.4	110.2	130.5	147.1□
Balance of payments (U.S.$'000,000)							
Balance of visible trade,	8,002	6,609	14,959	14,877	16,585	...	...
of which:							
Imports, f.o.b.	59,475	65,940	55,470	60,829	72,369	77,444	...
Exports, f.o.b.	67,477	72,552	70,429	75,706	88,954	90,061	...
Balance of invisibles	−9,981	−12,925	−13,961	−14,147	−15,414	−15,321	...
Balance of payments, current account	−953	−5,055	2,110	1,365	1,893	−1,941	...

Foreign trade

Balance of trade (current prices)

	1979	1980	1981	1982	1983	1984	1985
Can$'000,000,000	2.8	6.9	4.5	15.8	19.4	16.6	14.3
% of total	2.2%	4.7%	2.8%	9.9%	11.8%	8.0%	6.4%

Imports (1985): Can$104,914,000,000 (machinery and transport equipment 58.4%, of which motor vehicle parts 13.8%, road motor vehicles 13.8%, electrical equipment 10.4%, nonelectrical machinery 9.2%; food, feed, beverages, and tobacco 5.6%; crude petroleum 3.5%; nonferrous metals 2.5%; chemicals 1.9%; plastics and synthetic rubber 1.7%; textiles 1.7%). *Major import sources:* United States 70.9%; Japan 5.8%; United Kingdom 3.1%; West Germany 2.6%; Mexico 1.3%; Taiwan 1.3%; France 1.3%; Hong Kong 0.8%.

Exports (1985): Can$119,241,000,000 (road motor vehicles and parts 26.2%; crude materials 16.1%, of which crude petroleum 5.0%, natural gas 3.3%; food 8.1%, of which wheat 3.2%; newsprint 4.5%; lumber 3.9%; machinery 3.0%; wood pulp 2.8%; chemicals 2.3%; iron and steel 2.0%; aluminum 1.7%). *Major export destinations:* United States 78.0%; Japan 4.8%; United Kingdom 2.0%; U.S.S.R. 1.4%; China 1.1%; West Germany 1.0%; The Netherlands 0.8%; Belgium–Luxembourg 0.7%; France 0.6%; Brazil 0.6%; South Korea 0.6%.

Trade by commodities (1985)

SITC Group	imports Can$'000,000	imports %	exports Can$'000,000	exports %
00 Food and live animals	5,183.8	4.9	9,282.8	8.0
01 Beverages and tobacco	725.7	0.7	352.0	0.3
02 Crude materials, excluding fuels	3,126.8	3.0	9,351.2	8.1
03 Mineral fuels, lubricants, and related materials	4,587.8	4.4	9,828.8	8.5
04 Animal and vegetable oils, fat, and waxes	143.5	0.1	843.2	0.7
05 Chemicals and related products, n.e.s.	3,792.8	3.6	5,128.0	4.4
06 Basic manufactures	31,847.0	30.3	31,652.5	27.3
07 Machinery and transport equipment	50,333.2	48.0	42,690.7	36.8
08 Miscellaneous manufactured articles	4,156.7	4.0	4,062.6	3.5
09 Goods not classified by kind	1,016.9	1.0	2,719.8	2.3
TOTAL	104,914.2	100.0	115,911.6◇	100.0‖

Direction of trade (1985)

	imports Can$'000,000	imports %	exports Can$'000,000	exports %
Africa	1,035.0	1.0	1,075.8	0.9
Asia	11,564.7	11.0	9,816.4	8.3
Americas	78,832.9	75.2	95,899.7	80.4
United States	74,377.0	70.9	92,986.7	78.0
South America	2,394.3	2.3	1,442.5	1.2
Central America	2,061.6	2.0	1,470.5	1.2
Europe	12,877.8	12.2	11,575.6	9.7
EEC	10,302.2	9.8	6,744.3	5.7
U.S.S.R. and Eastern Europe	323.4	0.3	3,515.9	2.9
Other Europe	2,252.2	2.1	1,315.4	1.1
Oceania	603.8	0.6	873.8	0.7
TOTAL	104,914.2	100.0	119,241.3	100.0

Transport and communications

Transport. Railroads (1984): length 74,564 mi, 120,000 km; passenger-mi 1,299,000,000, passenger-km 2,090,000,000; short ton-mi cargo 167,574,000,000, metric ton-km cargo 244,669,000,000. Roads (1984): total length 549,462 mi, 884,249 km (paved 81%). Vehicles (1983): passenger cars 10,731,000; trucks and buses 3,362,000. Merchant marine (1985): vessels (100 gross tons and over) 1,286; total deadweight tonnage 4,075,342. Air transport (1985): passenger-mi 45,528,555,000, passenger-km 73,271,248,000; short ton-mi cargo 3,233,289,000, metric ton-km cargo 4,720,522,000; airports (1986) with scheduled flights 61.

Communications. Daily newspapers (1984): total number 120; total circulation 5,570,000; circulation per 1,000 population 217. Radio (1985): total number of receivers 28,800,000 (1 per 0.9 person). Television (1985): total number of receivers 14,602,000 (1 per 1.7 persons). Telephones (1984): 16,480,000 (1 per 1.5 persons).

Education and health

Education (1986–87)

	schools	teachers	students	student/teacher ratio
Primary and secondary (age 6–18)	15,595	270,020	4,943,565	18.3
Higher	268	60,640	789,690	13.0

Literacy (1975): total population over age 14 literate 16,185,000 (95.6%); males literate 8,003,000 (95.6%); females literate 8,182,000 (95.7%).

Health (1982): physicians 45,542 (1 per 538 persons); hospital beds 180,935 (1 per 135 persons); infant mortality rate per 1,000 live births (1984) 9.3.

Food (1980–82): daily per capita caloric intake 3,438 (vegetable products 62%, animal products 38%); 129% of FAO recommended minimum requirement.

Military

Total active duty personnel (1985): 83,000 (army 25.3%, navy 6.6%, air force 18.4%, not identified by service 49.7%). *Military expenditure as percent of GNP* (1984): 2.1% (world 6.1%); per capita expenditure U.S.$265.

*June. †Based on land areas. ‡Urban areas. §Unemployed. ‖Detail does not add to total given because of rounding. ¶1982. ♀1984. δDepartment and general stores included with general merchandise. □July. ◇Domestic exports only. Reexports of Can$3,329,700,000 are excluded.

Cape Verde

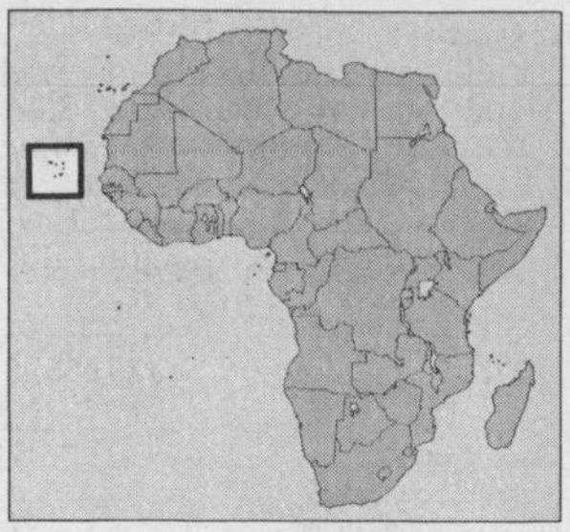

Official name: República de Cabo Verde (Republic of Cape Verde).
Form of government: unitary single-party republic with one legislative house (People's National Assembly [83]).
Chief of state: President.
Head of government: Prime Minister.
Capital: Praia.
Official language: Portuguese.
Official religion: none.
Monetary unit: 1 escudo (CV Esc) = 100 centavos; valuation (Oct. 1, 1986) 1 U.S.$ = CV Esc 89.27; 1 £ = CV Esc 128.99.

Area and population

Islands Counties	Capitals	area sq mi	area sq km	population 1980 census
Boa Vista		239	620	3,372
Boa Vista	Sal Rei			
Brava		26	67	6,985
Brava	Nova Sintra			
Fogo		184	476	30,978
Fogo	São Filipe			
Maio		104	269	4,098
Maio	Porto Inglês			
Sal		83	216	5,826
Sal	Santa Maria			
Santiago		383	991	145,957
Praia	Praia			57,748
Santa Catarina	Assomada			41,012
Santa Cruz	Pedra Badejo			22,995
Tarrafal	Tarrafal			24,202
Santo Antão		301	779	43,321
Paúl	Pombas			7,983
Porto Novo	Porto Novo			13,236
Ribeira Grande	Ponta Sol			22,102
São Nicolau		150	388	13,572
São Nicolau	Ribeira Brava			
São Vicente		88	227	41,594
São Vicente	Mindelo			
TOTAL		1,557*	4,033	295,703

Demography

Population (1986): 342,000.
Density (1986): persons per sq mi 219.7, persons per sq km 84.8.
Urban-rural (1980): urban 35.1%; rural 64.9%.
Sex distribution (1980): male 46.32%; female 53.68%.
Age breakdown (1980): under 15, 46.0%; 15–29, 27.6%; 30–44, 9.1%; 45–59, 9.0%; 60–74, 6.3%; 75 and over, 2.0%.
Population projection: (1990) 375,000; (2000) 420,000.
Doubling time: 29 years.
Ethnic composition (1986): mixed 71%; black 28%; white 1%.
Religious affiliation (1984): Roman Catholic 96.9%; Protestant and other 3.1%.
Major cities (1980): Praia 49,500†; Mindelo 36,746; São Filipe 4,370.

Vital statistics

Birth rate per 1,000 population (1985): 32.8 (world avg. 29.0); (1975) legitimate 55.2%; illegitimate 44.8%.
Death rate per 1,000 population (1985): 8.4 (world avg. 11.0).
Natural increase rate per 1,000 population (1985): 24.4 (world avg. 18.0).
Total fertility rate (avg. births per childbearing woman; 1980–85): 2.6.
Marriage rate per 1,000 population (1975): 5.4.
Divorce rate per 1,000 population: n.a.
Life expectancy at birth (1980–85): male 60.3 years; female 64.0 years.
Major causes of death per 100,000 population (1980): enteritis and other diarrheal diseases 85.5; heart disease 51.9; cerebrovascular disease 45.7; malignant neoplasms (cancers) 43.8; measles and other infectious and parasitic diseases 34.6; pneumonia 27.2; bronchitis, emphysema, and asthma 20.4; avitaminoses and other nutritional deficiencies 14.5.

National economy

Budget (1984). Revenue: CV Esc 1,630,000,000 (indirect taxes 46.8%, of which import duties 19.1%; direct taxes 25.5%, of which taxes from industry 7.3%; receipts from petroleum 5.0%). Expenditures: CV Esc 2,134,500,000 (no breakdown available).
Public debt (external, outstanding; 1984): U.S.$67,500,000.
Tourism: n.a.
Production (metric tons except as noted). Agriculture, forestry, fishing (1984): coconuts 10,000, sugarcane 9,000, fruit except bananas 9,000, pulses 5,000, vegetables 5,000, bananas 3,000, corn (maize) 3,000, potatoes 3,000, sweet potatoes 2,000, cassava 2,000, dates 2,000; livestock (number of live animals) 77,000 goats, 23,000 pigs, 13,000 cattle, 8,000 asses and mules, 2,000 horses, 1,000 sheep; roundwood, n.a.; fish catch (1983) 13,205, of which tuna 6,068 (46.0%), other marine fishes 5,838 (44.2%). Mining and quarrying (1985): salt CV Esc 12,236,000. Manufacturing (1985): meat 618,456; flour 10,824; bread 2,884; cacao powder 2,351; canned milk 2,000; cigars 74; goat skins 67; alcoholic beverages 151,100 litres; soft drinks 167,263 litres. Construction (1982): residential CV Esc 365,800,000; nonresidential CV Esc 1,700,000. Energy production (consumption): electricity (kW-hr; 1985) 12,132,572 (12,132,572); coal, none (none); crude petroleum, n.a. (n.a.); petroleum products (metric tons; 1984) n.a. (37,000); natural gas, n.a. (n.a.).
Gross national product (at current market prices; 1985): U.S.$123,000,000 (U.S.$400 per capita).

Structure of gross domestic product and labour force

	1981			
	in value CV Esc '000,000	% of total value	labour force	% of labour force
Agriculture, forestry, and fishing	560.0	17.6	58,000	55.8
Manufacturing and public utilities	125.0	3.9	1,700	1.6
Mining	9.0	0.3		
Construction	645.0	20.3		
Pub. admin., defense	550.0	17.3	44,300	42.6
Trade, finance, and other	1,290	40.6		
TOTAL	3,179	100.0	104,000	100.0

Population economically active (1980): total 102,000; activity rate of total population 34.5% (participation rates: ages 15–64, 57.7%; female 27.5%; unemployed 21.0%).

Price and earnings indexes (1975 = 100)

	1976	1977	1978	1979	1980	1981
Consumer price index	101.2	108.3	122.7	131.2	150.4	167.7
Monthly earnings index	...	...	...	...	...	...

Household income and expenditure. Average household size (1980) 4.3; average annual income per household: n.a.; source of income: n.a.; expenditure: n.a.
Land use (1983): forested 0.2%; meadows and pastures 6.2%; agricultural and under permanent cultivation 9.9%; other 83.7%.

Foreign trade

Balance of trade (current prices)

	1979	1980	1981	1982	1983	1984
CV Esc '000,000	−1,895	−2,743	−3,300	−3,978	−5,482	−5,766
% of total	91.1%	99.9%	91.5%	89.8%	92.0%	92.8%

Imports (1984): CV Esc 5,987,492,000 (machinery and transport equipment 22.2%, of which transport equipment 6.4%; mineral products 18.3%, foodstuffs and beverages 17.2%, of which vegetable products 13.5%; chemical products 5.6%; textiles and textile products 4.6%; plastics and resins 2.8%). *Major import sources:* Portugal 24.3%; The Netherlands 22.1%; France 10.1%; Spain 8.6%; Belgium–Luxembourg 5.8%; West Germany 5.1%; Brazil 4.2%; Argentina 2.7%.
Exports (1984): CV Esc 221,763,000 (fish 76.0%; bananas 13.0%; salt 8.0%). *Major export destinations:* Algeria 29.7%; Portugal 21.6%; Italy 18.9%; Nigeria 10.8%; Niger 5.4%; United Kingdom 5.4%.

Transport and communications

Transport. Railroads: none. Roads (1984): total length 1,398 mi, 2,250 km (paved 29%). Vehicles (1981): passenger cars 4,000; trucks and buses 1,343. Merchant marine (1985): vessels (100 gross tons and over) 25; total deadweight tonnage 22,092. Air transport (1985): passenger-mi 16,148,000, passenger-km 25,987,000; short ton-mi cargo 1,606,000, metric ton-km cargo 2,345,000; airports (1986) with scheduled flights 9.
Communications. Daily newspapers: none. Radio (1985): total number of receivers 47,000 (1 per 6.9 persons). Television: (1985): total number of receivers 500 (1 per 650 persons). Telephones (1981): 1,739 (1 per 168 persons).

Education and health

Education (1982–83)

	schools	teachers	students	student/ teacher ratio
Primary (age 7–10)	436	1,459	50,000	34.3
Secondary (age 10–17)	16	603	10,454	17.3
Voc., teacher tr.	4	76	923	12.1
Higher	...	...	...	...

Educational attainment, n.a. *Literacy* (1981): total population over age 15 literate 78,839 (49.3%); males literate 43,814 (55.3%); females literate 35,025 (43.4%).
Health (1980): physicians 51 (1 per 5,820 persons); hospital beds 632 (1 per 470 persons); infant mortality rate per 1,000 live births (1983) 30.0.
Food (1980–82): daily per capita caloric intake 2,716 (vegetable products 91%, animal products 9%); 116% of FAO recommended minimum requirement.

Military

Total active duty personnel (1985): 1,100 (army 90.9%, navy 6.8%, air force 2.3%). *Military expenditure as percent of GNP* (1982): 2.2% (world 6.0%); per capita expenditure U.S.$7.

*Detail does not add to total given because of rounding. †1985.

Central African Republic

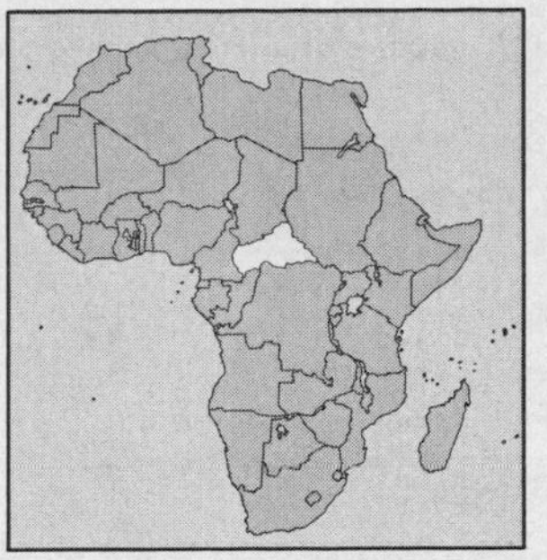

Official name: République Centrafricaine (Central African Republic).
Form of government: military dictatorship with one ruling body (Military Committee for National Recovery [23]).
Head of state and government: Chairman.
Capital: Bangui.
Official language: French.
Official religion: none.
Monetary unit: 1 CFA franc (CFAF) = 100 centimes; valuation (Oct. 1, 1986) 1 U.S.$ = CFAF 332.05; 1 £ = CFAF 479.81.

Area and population

Prefectures	Capitals	area sq mi	area sq km	population 1985* estimate
Bamingui-Bangoran	Ndélé	22,471	58,200	29,400
Bangui	Bangui	26	67	473,800
Basse-Kotto	Mobaye	6,797	17,604	187,200
Gribingui-Économique	Kaga-Bandoro	7,720	19,996	85,700
Haut-Mbomou	Obo	21,440	55,530	52,200
Haute-Kotto	Bria	33,456	86,650	233,100
Haute-Sangha	Berbérati	11,661	30,203	37,400
Kemo-Gribingui	Sibut	6,642	17,204	78,300
Lobaye	Mbaïki	7,427	19,235	160,700
Mbomou	Bangassou	23,610	61,150	132,900
Nana-Mambere	Bouar	10,270	26,600	197,600
Ombella-Mpoko	Bimbo	12,292	31,835	127,900
Ouaka	Bambari	19,266	49,900	216,200
Ouham	Bossangoa	19,402	50,250	269,300
Ouham-Pendé	Bozoum	12,394	32,100	242,100
Sangha-Économique	Nola	7,495	19,412	59,600
Vakaga	Birao	17,954	46,500	24,200
TOTAL		240,324†	622,436	2,607,600

Demography

Population (1986): 2,706,020.
Density (1986): persons per sq mi 11.3, persons per sq km 4.3.
Urban-rural (1983): urban 44.0%; rural 56.0%.
Sex distribution (1985): male 48.42%; female 51.58%.
Age breakdown (1985): under 15, 42.5%; 15–59, 25.5%; 30–44, 15.9%; 45–59, 10.1%; 60 and over, 6.0%.
Population projection: (1990) 2,965,000; (2000) 3,736,000.
Doubling time: 28 years.
Ethnic composition (1978): Banda 44.6%; Baya 14.3%; Ngbandi 10.7%; Azande 9.6%; Mbaka 4.3%; Sara 3.9%; Kare 2.5%; other 10.1%.
Religious affiliation (1980): Protestant 50.0%; Roman Catholic 33.1%; tribal 12.0%; Muslim 3.2%; Bahā'ī 0.3%; other 1.4%.
Major cities (1985): Bangui 473,800; Bambari 44,500; Bouar 42,000; Berberati 38,000; Bossangoa 35,800.

Vital statistics

Birth rate per 1,000 population (1983): 41.0 (world avg. 29.0); legitimate, n.a.; illegitimate, n.a.
Death rate per 1,000 population (1983): 17.0 (world avg. 11.0).
Natural increase rate per 1,000 population (1983): 24.0 (world avg. 18.0).
Total fertility rate (avg. births per childbearing woman; 1983): 5.5.
Marriage rate per 1,000 population: n.a.
Divorce rate per 1,000 population: n.a.
Life expectancy at birth (1983): male 46.0 years; female 49.0 years.
Major causes of death per 100,000 population (1978): infectious and parasitic diseases 59.0.

National economy

Budget (1984). Revenue: CFAF 38,500,000,000‡ (indirect taxes 52.4%, nonfiscal receipts 21.1%, direct taxes 20.3%). Expenditures: CFAF 48,000,000,000‡ (education and culture 13.9%, defense 8.3%, repayment of public debt 8.1%).
Public debt (external, outstanding; 1984): U.S.$224,400,000.
Tourism (1982): receipts from visitors U.S.$3,000,000; expenditures by nationals abroad, n.a.
Production (metric tons except as noted). Agriculture, forestry, fishing (1984): roots and tubers 1,154,000, cassava 235,500, peanuts (groundnuts) in shell 112,000, bananas 82,000, plantains 65,000, millet and sorghum 51,000, corn (maize) 40,000, seed cotton 20,000, coffee 15,000, rice 11,000, sesame seed 9,700; livestock (number of live animals) 2,000,060 cattle, 960,000 goats, 140,000 pigs, 82,000 sheep, 1,637,000 chickens; roundwood 3,158,000 cu m; fish catch (1983) 13,000. Mining and quarrying (1984): diamonds 337.1 carats; gold 235.5 kg. Manufacturing (1984): household aluminum articles 876; paints 556; hides and skins 368; footwear 381,136 pairs; motorcycles 4,030 units; bicycles 2,977 units; beer 234,241 hectolitres; soft drinks 50,472 hectolitres; cigarettes 20,654,000 units. Construction: n.a. Energy production (consumption): electricity (kW-hr; 1984) 73,201,000 (53,837,000); coal, none (n.a.); crude petroleum, none (n.a.); petroleum products (metric tons; 1984) none (60,000); natural gas, none (n.a.).

Land use (1983): forested 63.7%; meadows and pastures 4.8%; agricultural and under permanent cultivation 3.1%; other 28.4%.
Gross national product (at current market prices; 1984): U.S.$680,000,000 (U.S.$270 per capita).

Structure of gross domestic product and labour force

	1983 in value U.S.$'000,000	% of total value	labour force	% of labour force
Agriculture	177	35.5	1,114,000	85.8
Mining	16	3.2	55,000	4.2
Manufacturing	39	7.8		
Construction	22	4.4		
Public utilities	8	1.6		
Transportation and communication; Trade; Finance; Pub. admin., defense; Services	236	47.4	130,000	10.0
TOTAL	498§	100.0†	1,299,000	100.0

Population economically active (1984): total 1,322,000; activity rate of total population 51.3% (participation rates: over age 15 [1975] 50.2%; female [1981] 47.7%; unemployed, n.a.).

Price and earnings indexes (1980 = 100)

	1980	1981	1982	1983	1984	1985	1986 ‖
Consumer price index	100.0	112.6	127.5	144.5	151.1	161.3	169.4
Earnings index	...	...	...	...	...	...	...

Household income and expenditure. Average household size (1980) 4.3; average annual income per household CFAF 91,985 (U.S.$435); source of income: n.a.; expenditure¶ (1983): food 70.5%, clothing 9.5%, energy 6.5%, transportation and communication 4.1%, recreation 1.3%, health 1.0%, housing 0.6%.

Foreign trade

Balance of trade (current prices)

	1979	1980	1981	1982	1983	1984
U.S.$'000,000	+10.1	+34.7	−2.2	−16.1	−11.9	−9.4
% of total	6.8%	17.6%	1.1%	7.0%	6.2%	4.9%

Imports (1983): CFAF 52,100,000,000♀ (machinery and equipment 33.9%, food 20.9%, chemicals and plastics 12.2%, textiles 8.4%, fuels and lubricants 1.8%). *Major import sources:* France 45.9%; Zaire 12.4%; Japan 6.3%; West Germany 3.8%; Italy 1.7%.
Exports (1983): CFAF 43,700,000,000 (coffee 29.0%, diamonds 24.0%, wood 18.5%, cotton 12.8%). *Major export destinations:* France 30.3%; Belgium-Luxembourg 29.3%; Japan 11.4%; Italy 6.4%; West Germany 6.4%; Spain 4.0%; United States 3.2%.

Transport and communications

Transport. Railroads: none. Roads (1984): total length 12,600 mi, 20,278 km (paved 2%). Vehicles (1983): passenger cars 43,321; trucks and buses 3,861. Merchant marine: vessels (100 gross tons and over) none. Air transport (1982): passenger-mi 105,804,000, passenger-km 170,276,000; short ton-mi cargo 20,677,000, metric ton-km cargo 30,188,000; airports (1986) with scheduled flights 1.
Communications. Daily newspapers: none. Radio (1982): total number of receivers 135,000 (1 per 18 persons). Television (1982): total number of receivers 1,200 (1 per 2,000 persons). Telephones (1983): 2,737 (1 per 1,117 persons).

Education and health

Education (1983–84)

	schools♂	teachers	students	student/teacher ratio
Primary (age 6–11)	853	4,263	291,444	68.4
Secondary (age 12–18)	...	616	52,417	85.1
Voc., teacher tr.	...	90	1,712	19.0
Higher♂	7	297	4,571	15.4

Educational attainment, n.a. *Literacy* (1980): total population over age 15 literate 447,800 (38.5%); males literate 322,800 (58.8%); females literate 125,000 (20.4%).
Health (1980): physicians 108 (1 per 21,605 persons); hospital beds 3,605 (1 per 616 persons); infant mortality rate per 1,000 live births (1983) 142.0.
Food (1980–82): daily per capita caloric intake 2,151 (vegetable products 93%, animal products 7%); 94% of FAO recommended minimum requirement.

Military

Total active duty personnel (1985): 2,300 (army 87.0%; navy, none; air force 13.0%). *Military expenditure as percent of GNP* (1983): 2.0% (world 6.1%); per capita expenditure U.S.$5.

*Beginning of year. †Detail does not add to total given because of rounding. ‡Breakdown is for 1982. §At current factor cost. ‖January. ¶Capital city only. ♀Import breakdown is for 1980. ♂1981–82.

Chad

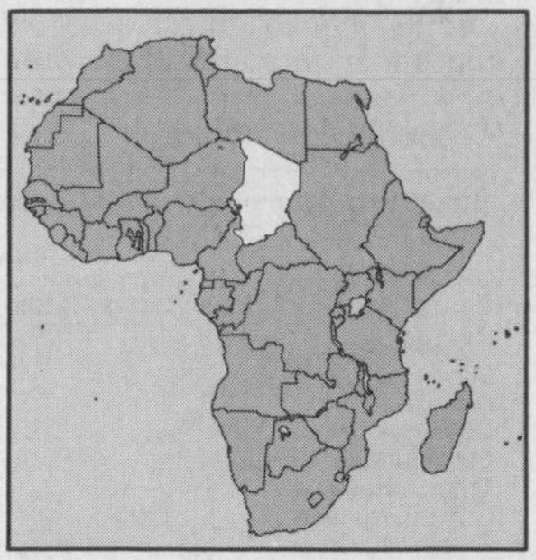

Official name: République du Tchad (Republic of Chad).
Form of government: military regime with no political parties or legislative bodies.
Head of state and government: President.
Capital: N'Djamena.
Official language: French.
Official religion: none.
Monetary unit: 1 CFA franc (CFAF) = 100 centimes; valuation (Oct. 1, 1986) 1 U.S.$ = CFAF 332.05; 1 £ = CFAF 479.81.

Area and population

Préfectures	Capitals	area sq mi	area sq km	population 1984 estimate
Batha	Ati	34,285	88,800	410,000
Biltine	Biltine	18,090	46,850	200,000
Borkou-Ennedi-Tibesti	Faya	231,795	600,350	103,000
Chari-Baguirmi	N'Djamena	32,010	82,910	719,000
Guéra	Mongo	22,760	58,950	234,000
Kanem	Mao	44,215	114,520	234,000
Lac	Bol	8,620	22,320	158,000
Logone Occidental	Moundou	3,355	8,695	324,000
Logone Oriental	Doba	10,825	28,035	350,000
Mayo-Kebbi	Bongor	11,625	30,105	757,000
Moyen-Chari	Sarh	17,445	45,180	582,000
Ouaddaï	Abéché	29,435	76,240	411,000
Salamat	Am Timan	24,325	63,000	121,000
Tandjilé	Laï	6,965	18,045	341,000
TOTAL		495,755*	1,284,000	4,944,000

Demography

Population (1986): 5,139,000.
Density (1986): persons per sq mi 10.4, persons per sq km 4.0.
Urban-rural (1986): urban 23.9%; rural 76.1%.
Sex distribution (1985): male 49.24%; female 50.76%.
Age breakdown (1985): under 15, 42.5%; 15–29, 26.0%; 30–44, 15.8%; 45–59, 9.9%; 60–74, 4.9%; 75 and over, 0.9%.
Population projection: (1990) 5,558,000; (2000) 7,063,000.
Doubling time: 33 years.
Ethnic composition (1980): Sudanic Arab 30.3%; Bagirmi, Sara, and Kreish 25.8%; Teda 7.7%; Mbum 6.7%; Masalit 6.5%; Tama 6.3%; Mubu 4.2%; Kanuri 2.3%; Hausa 2.2%; other 8.0%.
Religious affiliation (1980): Muslim 44.0%; Christian 33.0%, of which nominal only 15.5%, Protestant 8.8%, Roman Catholic 8.3%; traditional beliefs 22.8%; other 0.2%.
Major cities (1986): N'Djamena 511,700; Sarh 100,000; Moundou 90,000; Abéché 71,000; Kélo 27,000†.

Vital statistics

Birth rate per 1,000 population (1984): 43.0 (world avg. 29.0); legitimate, n.a.; illegitimate, n.a.
Death rate per 1,000 population (1984): 21.0 (world avg. 11.0).
Natural increase rate per 1,000 population (1984): 22.0 (world avg. 18.0).
Total fertility rate (avg. births per childbearing woman; 1984): 5.6.
Marriage rate per 1,000 population: n.a.
Divorce rate per 1,000 population: n.a.
Life expectancy at birth (1984): male 43.0 years; female 45.0 years.
Major causes of death per 100,000 population: n.a.

National economy

Budget (1986). Revenue: CFAF 18,694,000,000‡ (indirect taxes 73.2%, of which customs receipts 60.1%; direct taxes 21.7%). Expenditures: CFAF 22,700,000,000‡ (defense 46.5%; education 10.9%; community projects 9.1%; health 3.8%).
Public debt (external, outstanding; 1984): U.S.$109,000,000.
Tourism (1981): receipts from visitors U.S.$2,000,000; expenditures by nationals abroad, n.a.
Production (metric tons except as noted). Agriculture, forestry, fishing (1984): roots and tubers 436,000, millet 320,000, sugarcane 250,000, cassavas 210,000, seed cotton 115,000, peanuts (groundnuts) 80,000, cotton seed 72,000, rice 51,000, lint cotton 43,000, dry beans 35,000, sweet potatoes 35,000, mangoes 30,000, dates 30,000, raw sugar 22,000; livestock (number of live animals) 3,400,000 cattle, 2,200,000 sheep, 2,000,000 goats, 3,000,000 chickens; roundwood 3,482,000 cu m; fish catch 110,000. Mining and quarrying: clay and natron. Manufacturing (1984): beef and veal 24,000; mutton and lamb 8,000; goat meat 7,000; salted, dried, or smoked fish 20,000§; refined sugar 23,000; wheat flour 4,000§; woven cotton fabrics 15,600,000 metres§; beer 163,000 hectolitres§; cigarettes 349,000,000 units‡. Construction: n.a. Energy production (consumption): electricity (kW-hr; 1984) 65,000,000 (65,000,000); coal, none (n.a.); crude petroleum, none (n.a.); petroleum products (metric tons; 1984) none (69,000); natural gas, none (n.a.).
Household income and expenditure. Average household size (1980) 3.9; average annual income per household CFAF 96,806 (U.S.$458); source of income: n.a.; expenditure ∥ (1983): food 45.3%, health 11.9%, energy 5.8%, clothing 3.3%.
Gross national product (at current market prices; 1984): U.S.$360,000,000 (U.S.$70 per capita).

Structure of gross domestic product and labour force

	1983 in value U.S.$'000,000	% of total value	labour force	% of labour force
Agriculture	316.0	51.6	1,476,000	81.0
Mining	3.0	0.5		
Manufacturing	44.0	7.2	151,000	8.3
Construction	8.0	1.3		
Public utilities	3.0	0.5		
Transportation and communication				
Trade				
Finance	238.0	38.9	196,000	10.7
Pub. admin., defense				
Services				
TOTAL	612.0¶	100.0	1,823,000	100.0

Population economically active (1984): total 1,862,000; activity rate of total population 38.0% (participation rates: ages 15–64 [1980] 56.5%; female [1981] 23.6%; unemployed, n.a.).

Price and earnings indexes (1975 = 100)

	1972	1973	1974	1975	1976	1977	1978¶
Consumer price index	73.7	77.7	86.5	100.0	103.3	112.0	128.6
Earnings index	...	...	...	...	...	...	...

Land use (1983): forested 16.3%; meadows and pastures 35.7%; agricultural and under permanent cultivation 2.5%; other 45.5%.

Foreign trade♀

Balance of trade (current prices)

	1979	1980	1981	1982	1983	1984
CFAF '000,000	+644	−534	−6,684	−19,255	−31,793	−26,239
% of total	1.7%	1.7%	12.9%	36.1%	36.1%	21.3%

Imports (1983): CFAF 74,802,000,000 (petroleum products 16.8%; cereal products 16.8%; pharmaceutical products and chemicals 11.5%; machinery and transport equipment 8.5%, of which transport equipment 7.3%; electrical equipment 5.7%; textiles 2.9%; raw and refined sugar 2.3%). *Major import sources:* France 16.6%; Cameroon 9.2%; United States 8.9%; Italy 4.5%; West Germany 3.2%; United Kingdom 2.4%; The Netherlands 1.9%.
Exports (1983): CFAF 48,563,000,000 (raw cotton 91.1%; live cattle and frozen bovine meat 1.8%). *Major export destinations:* United States 36.6%; West Germany 8.0%; Portugal 8.0%; Cameroon 4.0%; France 3.1%; Italy 1.6%; Spain 1.3%; Japan 1.2%.

Transport and communications

Transport. Railroads: none. Roads (1983): total length 24,855 mi, 40,000 km (paved 1%). Vehicles (1982): passenger cars 7,000; trucks and buses 5,000. Merchant marine vessels (100 gross tons and over) none. Air transport♂ (1985): passenger-mi 144,226,000, passenger-km 232,109,000; short ton-mi cargo 27,420,000, metric ton-km cargo 40,035,000; airports (1986) with scheduled flights 2.
Communications. Daily newspapers (1983): total number 3; total circulation 1,500□; circulation per 1,000 population 3,300□. Radio (1984): total number of receivers 75,000 (1 per 65 persons). Television: none. Telephones (1981): 900 (1 per 5,085 persons).

Education and health

Education (1984)

	schools	teachers◇	students	student/teacher ratio
Primary (age 6–12)	783◇	2,610	288,478△	77.0
Secondary (age 13–19)	...	590	43,053	31.2
Voc., teacher tr.	...	...	2,559	...
Higher✝	1	85	550	6.5

Educational attainment, n.a. *Literacy* (1980): total population over age 15 literate 466,500 (17.8%); males literate 459,700 (35.6%); females literate 6,800 (0.5%).
Health: physicians (1980) 94 (1 per 47,640 persons); hospital beds (1978) 3,553 (1 per 1,190 persons); infant mortality rate per 1,000 live births (1984) 139.
Food (1980–82): daily per capita caloric intake 1,821 (vegetable products 92%, animal products 8%); 77% of FAO recommended minimum requirement.

Military

Total active duty personnel (1985): 12,200 (army 98.4%; navy, none; air force 1.6%). *Military expenditure as percent of GNP* (1983): 2.4% (world 6.1%); per capita expenditure U.S.$1.

*Detail does not add to total given because of rounding. †1979. ‡Breakdown is given for 1984. §1980. ∥ Capital city only. ¶At current factor cost. ♀Imports c.i.f. (cost, insurance, and freight); exports f.o.b. (free on board). ♂The airport at N'Djamena is underutilized because of the political and military unrest in Chad. □Partial circulation only. ◇1976–77. △Excluding Islamic private education (9,453 students in 1975). ✝1981–82.

Chile

Official name: República de Chile (Republic of Chile).
Form of government: military regime.
Head of state and government: President (general) assisted by a four-member junta.
Capital: Santiago.
Official language: Spanish.
Official religion: none.
Monetary unit: 1 peso (Ch$) = 100 centavos; valuation (Oct. 1, 1986) 1 U.S.$ = Ch$195.04; 1 £ = Ch$281.83.

Area and population

		area		population
Regions	Capitals	sq mi	sq km	1985 estimate*
Tarapacá	Iquique	22,422	58,073	266,400
Antofagasta	Antofagasta	48,381	125,306	336,200
Atacama	Copiapó	30,219	78,268	214,700
Coquimbo	La Serena	15,308	39,647	439,900
Valparaíso	Valparaíso	6,220	16,109	1,326,800
Libertador General Bernardo O'Higgins	Rancagua	7,024	18,193	589,300
Maule	Talca	11,783	30,518	739,300
Bío-Bío	Concepción	14,218	36,824	1,569,400
Araucanía	Temuco	12,263	31,760	678,000
Los Lagos	Puerto Montt	25,904	67,090	904,600
Aisén del General Carlos Ibáñez del Campo	Coihaique	42,085	108,999	71,400
Magallanes y de la Antártica Chilena	Punta Arenas	43,363†	112,310†	117,400
Región Metropolitana de Santiago	Santiago	5,331	13,808	4,722,500
TOTAL		284,520†‡	736,905†	11,976,000‡

Demography

Population (1986): 12,272,000.
Density (1986): persons per sq mi 43.1, persons per sq km 16.7.
Urban-rural (1985): urban 83.6%; rural 16.4%.
Sex distribution (1984): male 49.52%; female 50.48%.
Age breakdown (1984): under 15, 31.4%; 15–29, 29.0%; 30–44, 19.4%; 45–59, 11.9%; 60–74, 6.3%; 75 and over, 1.9%‡.
Population projection: (1990) 13,025,000; (2000) 15,116,000.
Doubling time: 47 years.
Ethnic composition (1980): mestizo 92%; Indian (mostly Mapuche) 6%; others (mainly European) 2%.
Religious affiliation (1982): Roman Catholic 79.2%; Protestant 6.0%; atheist and nonreligious 2.0%; other 12.8%.
Major cities (1985*): Greater Santiago 4,271,500; Viña del Mar 311,600; Valparaíso 266,900; Talcahuano 218,900; Concepción 215,800; Antofagasta 174,100; Temuco 170,200; Rancagua 149,700; Talca 143,000.

Vital statistics

Birth rate per 1,000 population (1984): 21.2 (world avg. 29.0); (1980) legitimate 72.4%; illegitimate 27.6%.
Death rate per 1,000 population (1984): 6.3 (world avg. 11.0).
Natural increase rate per 1,000 population (1984): 14.9 (world avg. 18.0).
Total fertility rate (avg. births per childbearing woman; 1981): 3.0.
Marriage rate per 1,000 population (1984): 6.8.
Divorce rate per 1,000 population (1982): 0.3.
Life expectancy at birth (1981): male 65.4 years; female 70.1 years.
Major causes of death per 100,000 population (1984): diseases of the circulatory system 177.6; malignant neoplasms (cancers) 100.9; accidents and poisonings 76.6; diseases of the respiratory system 65.8.

National economy

Budget (1984). Revenue: Ch$547,409,000,000 (excise taxes 40.0%, nontax revenue 20.4%, income taxes 11.3%, import and export duties 9.7%, social security contributions 8.3%, property taxes 4.0%). Expenditures: Ch$617,128,000,000 (social security and welfare 41.8%, education 13.1%, defense 11.6%, public services 11.1%, economic services 7.5%, health 6.2%).
Tourism: receipts from visitors (1984) U.S.$104,000,000; expenditures by nationals abroad (1983) U.S.$214,000,000.
Production (metric tons except as noted). Agriculture, forestry, fishing (1984): sugar beets 2,194,000, grapes 1,050,000, potatoes 988,000, wheat 988,000, corn (maize) 721,000, apples 235,000, tomatoes 162,000, oats 163,000; livestock (number of live animals) 6,300,000 sheep, 3,870,000 cattle, 1,150,000 pigs; roundwood 14,971,000 cu m; fish catch 3,978,078§. Mining (1984): iron ore 7,116,000,000; copper 1,308,000; nitrates 712,600; molybdenum 15,300; iodine 2,661; silver 465,159 kilograms; gold 17,716 kilograms. Manufacturing (1984): cement 1,296,000; crude steel ingots 684,000; pig iron 600,000; newsprint 172,800; beer 1,780,000 hectolitres; cigarettes 7,680,000,000 units§; tires 913,000 units; motor vehicles 6,744 units. Construction ‖ (value in '000,000 of Ch$; 1983) residential 16,174; nonresidential 4,643. Energy production (consumption): electricity (kW-hr; 1984) 13,490,000,000 (13,490,000,000); coal (metric tons; 1984) 1,224,000 (1,868,000); crude petroleum (barrels; 1984) 14,660,000 (30,022,000); petroleum products (metric tons; 1984) 3,975,000 (4,631,000); natural gas (cu m; 1984) 943,133,000 (943,133,000).
Gross national product (at current market prices; 1984): U.S.$20,340,000,000 (U.S.$1,710 per capita).

Structure of gross domestic product and labour force

	1983			
	in value Ch$'000,000	% of total value	labour force¶	% of labour force
Agriculture	138,400	9.4	509,400	15.8
Mining	131,800	8.9	59,400	1.8
Manufacturing	293,300	19.9	405,900	12.6
Construction	75,600	5.1	93,500	2.9
Public utilities	37,000	2.5	23,700	0.7
Transportation and communication	80,500	5.5	195,800	6.1
Trade	255,200	17.3	550,400	17.1
Finance	239,200	16.2	110,100	3.4
Pub. admin., defense	74,400	5.0	1,267,900	39.4
Services; Other	150,200	10.2		
TOTAL	1,475,600	100.0	3,216,100	100.0‡

Public debt (external, outstanding; 1984): U.S.$10,838,900,000.
Population economically active (1983): total 3,674,700; activity rate of total population 31.7% (participation rates: ages 15–64, 52.1%; female 16.2%; unemployed [1985] 13.1%).

Price and earnings indexes (1980 = 100)

	1980	1981	1982	1983	1984	1985	1986♀
Consumer price index	100.0	119.7	131.6	167.5	200.7	262.3	311.5
Monthly earnings index	100.0	130.3	142.9	162.5	195.0	...	...

Household income and expenditure. Average household size (1982) 4.5; income per household, n.a.; expenditure (1978): food 41.9%, housing 13.3%, transportation and communication 11.8%, recreation and education 8.2%, household goods 7.8%, clothing and footwear 7.6%.
Land use (1983): forested 20.7%; meadows and pastures 15.9%; agricultural and under permanent cultivation 7.4%; other 56.0%.

Foreign trade♂

Balance of trade (current prices)

	1979	1980	1981	1982	1983	1984	1985
U.S.$'000,000	+320	+329	−1,487	+720	+1,320	+953	+1,473
% of total	4.3%	3.6%	16.0%	10.7%	20.8%	15.0%	24.1%

Imports (1984): U.S.$3,481,000,000 (intermediate goods 62.0%; consumer goods 14.9%; capital goods 14.6%). *Major import sources* (1983): United States 25.5%; Venezuela 8.2%; Argentina 7.3%; Brazil 6.9%; West Germany 6.7%; Japan 5.9%.
Exports (1984): U.S.$3,657,600,000 (mining 54.2%, of which copper 43.4%; fruits and vegetables 8.0%; fish meal 7.5%; paper and paper products 7.1%; chemical and petroleum products 3.4%). *Major export destinations:* United States 26.0%; Japan 11.1%; West Germany 10.0%; Brazil 6.2%; United Kingdom 5.4%; France 4.5%; Italy 4.4%.

Transport and communications

Transport. Railroads (1985): length 5,300 mi, 8,500 km; passenger-mi 947,000,000, passenger-km 1,524,000,000; short ton-mi cargo 1,611,000,000, metric ton-km cargo 2,352,000,000. Roads (1984): total length 49,094 mi, 79,010 km (paved 11%). Vehicles (1984) passenger cars 622,000; trucks and buses 240,050. Merchant marine (1985): vessels (100 gross tons and over) 234; total deadweight tonnage 701,776. Air transport (1984): passenger-mi 969,337,000, passenger-km 1,560,000,000; short ton-mi cargo 77,393,000, metric ton-km cargo 112,992,000; airports (1986) with scheduled flights 13.
Communications. Daily newspapers (1983): total number 66; total circulation 1,407,300; circulation per 1,000 population 120. Radio (1984): 17,000,000 receivers (1 per 0.7 person). Television (1984): 2,645,000 receivers (1 per 4.5 persons). Telephones (1983): 608,200 (1 per 19 persons).

Education and health

Education (1984)

	schools	teachers□	students	student/teacher ratio
Primary (age 6–13)	8,862	62,746	2,092,069	...
Secondary (age 14–17)	1,401	...	581,243	...
Vocational	369	...	129,817	...
Higher	24	10,372	126,197	...

Educational attainment (1970). Percent of population over age 25 having: no formal schooling 12.4%; primary education 57.2%; secondary 26.6%; higher 3.8%. *Literacy* (1983): total population over age 12 literate 8,301,000 (95.6%); males 4,100,000 (95.0%)◇; females 4,201,000 (93.8%)◇.
Health: physicians (1981) 10,877 (1 per 1,038 persons); hospital beds (1982) 38,254 (1 per 300 persons); infant mortality rate per 1,000 live births (1984) 19.6.
Food (1980–82): daily per capita caloric intake 2,706 (vegetable products 84%, animal products 16%); 113% of FAO recommended minimum requirement.

Military

Total active duty personnel (1985): 101,000 (army 56.4%, navy 28.7%, air force 14.9%). *Military expenditure as percent of GNP* (1983): 4.5% (world 6.0%); per capita expenditure: U.S.$88.

*1984 year-end estimate. †Excludes 490,243 sq mi (1,269,723 sq km) of Antártica Chilena, portions of which are disputed with the United Kingdom and Argentina. ‡Detail does not add to total given because of rounding. §1983. ‖ Includes both private and public authorized construction. ¶Employed persons only. ♀June. ♂Import figures are f.o.b. (free on board) in balance of trade and c.i.f. (cost, insurance, and freight) for commodities and trading partners. □1982. ◇Calculated from the 1981 literacy rate of 94.4%.

China

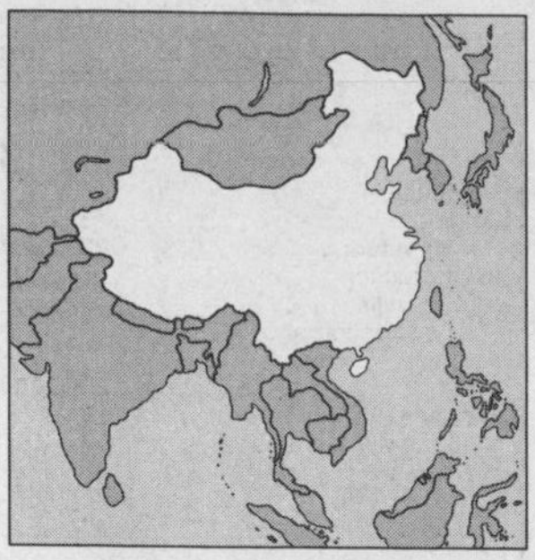

Official name: Chung-hua Jen-min Kung-ho-kuo (People's Republic of China).
Form of government: single-party people's republic with one legislative house (National People's Congress [2,978]).
Chief of state: President.
Head of government: Premier.
Capital: Peking (Beijing).
Official language: Mandarin Chinese.
Official religion: none.
Monetary unit: 1 Renminbi (yuan) (Y) = 10 jiao = 100 fen; valuation (Oct. 1, 1986) 1 U.S.$ = Y 3.72; 1 £ = Y 5.37.

Area and population*†

		area		population
Provinces	Capitals	sq mi	sq km	1985‡ estimate
Anhwei (Anhui)	Ho-fei (Hefei)	54,000	139,900	51,030,000
Chekiang (Zhejiang)	Hangchow (Hangzhou)	39,300	101,800	39,930,000
Fukien (Fujian)	Foochow (Fuzhou)	47,500	123,100	26,770,000
Heilungkiang (Heilongjiang)	Harbin (Harbin)	179,000	463,600	32,950,000
Honan (Henan)	Cheng-chou (Zhengzhou)	64,500	167,000	76,460,000
Hopeh (Hebei)	Shih-chia-chuang (Shijiazhuang)	78,200	202,700	54,870,000
Hunan (Hunan)	Ch'ang-sha (Changsha)	81,300	210,500	55,610,000
Hupeh (Hubei)	Wu-han (Wuhan)	72,400	187,500	48,760,000
Kansu (Gansu)	Lan-chou (Lanzhou)	141,500	366,500	20,160,000
Kiangsi (Jiangxi)	Nan-ch'ang (Nanchang)	63,600	164,800	34,210,000
Kiangsu (Jiangsu)	Nanking (Nanjing)	39,600	102,600	61,710,000
Kirin (Jilin)	Ch'ang-ch'un (Changchun)	72,200	187,000	22,840,000
Kwangtung (Guangdong)	Canton (Guangzhou)	89,300	231,400	61,660,000
Kweichow (Guizhou)	Kuei-yang (Guiyang)	67,200	174,000	29,320,000
Liaoning (Liaoning)	Shen-yang (Shenyang)	58,300	151,000	36,550,000
Shansi (Shanxi)	T'ai-yüan (Taiyuan)	60,700	157,100	26,000,000
Shantung (Shandong)	Tsinan (Jinan)	59,200	153,300	76,370,000
Shensi (Shaanxi)	Sian (Xi'an)	75,600	195,800	29,660,000
Szechwan (Sichuan)	Ch'eng-tu (Chengdu)	219,700	569,000	101,120,000
Tsinghai (Qinghai)	Hsi-ning (Xining)	278,400	721,000	4,020,000
Yunnan (Yunnan)	K'un-ming (Kunming)	168,400	436,200	33,620,000
Autonomous regions				
Inner Mongolia (Nei Monggol)	Hu-ho-hao-t'e (Hohhot)	454,600	1,177,500	19,850,000
Kwangsi Chuang (Guangxi Zhuang)	Nan-ning (Nanning)	85,100	220,400	38,060,000
Ningsia Hui (Ningxia Hui)	Yin-ch'uan (Yinchuan)	25,600	66,400	4,060,000
Sinkiang Uighur (Xinjiang Uygur)	Urumchi (Urumqi)	635,900	1,646,900	13,440,000
Tibet (Xizang)	Lhasa (Lhasa)	471,700	1,221,600	1,970,000
Municipalities				
Peking (Beijing)	—	6,500	16,800	9,470,000
Shanghai (Shanghai)	—	2,400	6,200	12,050,000
Tientsin (Tianjin)	—	4,400	11,300	7,990,000
TOTAL		3,696,100§	9,572,900§	1,034,750,000‖

Demography

Population (1986): 1,053,100,000.
Density (1985): persons per sq mi 284.9, persons per sq km 110.0.
Urban-rural (1984): urban 31.9%; rural 68.1%.
Sex distribution (1984): male 51.63%; female 48.37%.
Age breakdown (1982): under 15, 33.6%; 15–29, 29.1%; 30–44, 17.5%; 45–59, 12.2%; 60–74, 6.3%; 75 and over, 1.3%.
Population projection: (1990) 1,104,500,000; (2000) 1,244,400,000.
Doubling time: 60 years.
Ethnic composition (1982): Han (Chinese) 93.30%; Chuang 1.33%; Hui 0.72%; Uighur 0.59%; Yi 0.54%; Miao 0.50%; Manchu 0.43%; Tibetan 0.39%; Mongolian 0.34%; Tuchia 0.28%; Puyi 0.21%; Korean 0.18%; Tung 0.14%; Yao 0.14%; Pai 0.11%; Hani 0.11%; Kazakh 0.09%; Tai 0.08%; Li 0.08%; other 0.44%.
Religious affiliation (1980): nonreligious 59.2%; Chinese folk-religionist 20.1%; atheist 12.0%; Buddhist 6.0%; Muslim 2.4%; Christian 0.2%.
Major cities (1985)‡: Shanghai 6,880,000; Peking 5,760,000; Tientsin 5,300,000; Shen-yang 4,130,000; Wu-han 3,340,000; Canton 3,220,000; Chungking (Chongqing) 2,730,000; Harbin 2,590,000; Ch'eng-tu 2,540,000; Sian 2,280,000; Nanking 2,210,000; T'ai-yüan 1,840,000; Ch'ang-ch'un 1,810,000; Talien (Dalian) 1,590,000; K'un-ming 1,480,000; Lan-chou 1,460,000; Tsinan 1,390,000; An-shan (Anshan) 1,260,000; Ch'ing-tao (Qingdao) 1,230,000; Fu-shun (Fushun) 1,220,000.
Households (1984). Average rural household size 5.4; urban household size 4.0. Family households: 220,100,755 (99.5%); collective 1,073,010 (0.5%).

Vital statistics

Birth rate per 1,000 population (1984): 17.5 (world avg. 29.0); legitimate, n.a.; illegitimate, n.a.
Death rate per 1,000 population (1984): 6.7 (world avg. 11.0).
Natural increase rate per 1,000 population (1984): 10.8 (world avg. 18.0).
Total fertility rate (avg. births per childbearing woman; 1980–85): 2.3.
Marriage rate per 1,000 population (1982): 16.7.
Divorce rate per 1,000 population: n.a.
Life expectancy at birth (1980–85): male 65.5 years; female 69.4 years.
Major causes of death per 100,000 population (1981)¶: diseases of the heart 139.9; malignant neoplasms (cancers) 113.0; diseases of the circulatory system 111.2; diseases of the respiratory system 43.0; accidents (including suicide) 31.3; gastrointestinal diseases 25.9; infectious diseases 23.7.

Social indicators

Educational attainment (1982). Percent of population over age 5 having: no schooling or some primary 31.9%; completed primary 39.9%; completed junior secondary 20.0%; completed senior secondary 7.5%; some higher 0.2%; completed higher 0.5%.

Distribution of household income (1984)

percent of household income by quintile				
1	2	3	4	5 (highest)
1.7%	10.5%	38.9%	22.7%	26.2%

Quality of working life (1983). Average workweek: 48 hours. Annual rate per 100,000 workers for: injury or accident, n.a.; industrial illness, n.a.; death, n.a. Money spent on labour insurance and collective amenities (including pensions for the retired): Y 20,940,000,000. Average days lost to labour stoppages per 1,000 workdays: n.a. Average duration of journey to work: n.a. Method of transport: n.a. Rate per 1,000 workers of discouraged (unemployed no longer seeking work): n.a.
Access to services (1979). Proportion of communes having access to: electricity 87.1%; safe public water supply, n.a.; public sewage collection, n.a.; public fire protection, n.a.
Social participation. Eligible voters participating in last national election: n.a. Population participating in voluntary work: n.a. Trade union membership in total labour force (1984): 16.8%. Practicing religious population in total affiliated population: n.a..
Social deviance. Annual reported offense rate per 100,000 population (1979–81) for: theft 60.0; violent crime (including murder, rape, and robbery) 4.5; other 10.5♀.
Leisure. Favourite leisure activities: n.a.
Material well-being (1983). Urban families possessing (number per family): wristwatches 2.7; bicycles 1.6; sewing machines 0.8; radios 1.0; televisions 0.8. Rural families possessing (number per family): wristwatches 0.9; bicycles 0.6; sewing machines 0.4; radios 0.6; televisions 0.04.

National economy

Gross national product (at current market prices; 1984): U.S.$318,310,000,000 (U.S.$310 per capita).

Structure of national income and labour force

	1984		1985‡	
	in value Y '000,000,000	% of total value	labour force ('000)	% of labour force
Agriculture	249.9	44.3	325,380	68.4
Mining	...	...	63,380 (Mining and Manufacturing)	13.3 (Mining and Manufacturing)
Manufacturing	228.6	40.5		
Construction	29.3	5.2	18,580	3.9
Public utilities	...	...	...	...
Transp. and commun.	18.9	3.3	10,800	2.3
Trade	37.6	6.7	23,540	4.9
Finance	...	...	...	...
Pub. admin., defense	...	...	7,430	1.6
Services	..	...	17,790	3.7
Other	...	...	9,070	1.9
TOTAL	564.3	100.0	475,970	100.0

Budget (1984). Revenue: Y 146,500,000,000 (taxes 64.0%; receipts from state enterprises 17.7%). Expenditures: Y 151,500,000,000 (capital construction 31.6%; culture, education, public health 17.4%; defense 11.9%).
Tourism (1984): receipts from visitors U.S.$1,130,000,000; expenditures by nationals abroad, n.a.

Retail and service enterprises (1984)

	no. of enter-prises	no. of employees	annual wage as a % of all wages	annual gross output value (Y '000,000)
Retail trade	6,715,000	15,330,000	...	...
Grocery stores	158,000	1,142,000	...	...
Department stores	134,000	1,311,000	...	...
Other food shops	98,000	695,000	...	...
Agricultural supplies stores	64,000	303,000	...	...
Household supplies stores	57,000	286,000	...	...
Grain and oil shops	42,000	419,000	...	...
Textile stores	26,000	156,000	...	...
Electrical appliances stores	29,000	297,000	...	...
Drug stores	22,000	166,000	...	...
Book stores	20,000	89,000	...	...
Coal stores	13,000	148,000	...	...
Service trade	1,294,000	2,975,000	...	...
Repair shops	559,000	859,000	...	...
Barber shops	161,000	348,000	...	...
Hotels	79,000	567,000	...	...
Photo studios	68,000	171,000	...	...

Production (metric tons except as noted). Agriculture, forestry, fishing (1985): grains—rice 171,479,000, wheat 85,286,000, corn (maize) 62,250,000, sorghum 6,835,000, millet 6,302,000, barley 2,701,000; oilseeds—peanuts (groundnuts) 6,757,000, rapeseed 5,587,000, sunflower seed 1,901,000, sesame seed 692,000; fruits and nuts—apples 3,215,000, pears 2,331,000, oranges 1,700,000, bananas 560,000; others—roots and tubers 141,136,000, sugarcane 58,665,000, seed cotton 12,453,000, soybeans 10,519,000, sugar beets 8,091,000, pulses 5,840,000, jute fibre 3,200,000, tobacco leaves 2,036,000, tea 465,000; livestock (number of live animals) 313,010,000 pigs,

95,191,000 sheep, 63,427,000 goats, 51,375,000 cattle, 19,547,000 water buffalo, 10,978,000 horses, 9,962,000 asses, 531,000 camels; roundwood (1984) 231,650,000 cu m; fish catch (1983) 5,927,000, of which 2,250,000 freshwater fish, 1,509,000 marine fish, 413,000 clams, 321,000 marine crabs. Mining and quarrying (1984): metals (metal content of ores)—copper 180,000, zinc 160,000, lead 160,000, tin 15,000, tungsten 13,500, molybdenum 2,000; other metals—iron ore 75,000,000, bauxite 1,600,000, nickel 15,000, gold 1,900,000 troy oz; nonmetals—salt 16,000,000, gypsum 4,800,000, barite 1,000,000, talc 950,000, fluorspar 650,000, graphite 185,000, asbestos 160,000. Manufacturing (1984): cement 123,020,000; steel 43,470,000; chemical fertilizer 14,602,000; sugar 3,800,000; cloth 13,700,000,000 metres; wristwatches 37,982,000 units; bicycles 28,614,000 units; sewing machines 9,349,000 units; television sets 10,038,100 units. Construction (value in Y; 1983): residential 12,269,000,000; nonresidential 9,605,000,000. Distribution of industrial production (percent of total value of output by sector; 1978 [1984]): state-operated enterprises 80.6% (73.8%); collectives 19.2% (25.0%); privately operated enterprises 0.2% (1.2%). Retail sales (percent of total sales by sector; 1978 [1984]): state-operated enterprises 90.5% (45.8%); collectives 7.4% (39.6%); privately operated enterprises 2.1% (14.6%).

Manufacturing and mining enterprises (1984)◇

	no. of enterprises	no. of employees♂	annual wages as a % of avg. of all wages□	annual gross output value (Y '000,000)◇
Manufacturing				
Machinery, transport equipment, and basic manufactures,	107,600	10,382,000	96.7	175,710
of which,				
Industrial equipment	8,600	...	...	30,603
Transport equipment	3,300	...	...	22,298
Electronic goods	4,100	1,043,000	...	23,385
Metalware for daily use	12,100	...	...	14,801
Textiles,	19,700	4,114,000	95.5	108,294
of which,				
Cotton	5,700	...	...	57,688
Foodstuffs,	74,000	2,880,000	87.5	86,584
of which,				
Grains and edible oils	29,800	...	...	24,750
Processed meat	3,200	...	...	12,767
Tobacco manufactures	200	...	...	12,631
Chemicals,	28,700	3,267,000	92.1	83,032
of which,				
Organic chemicals	3,300	...	...	16,360
Fertilizers	3,700	1,110,000	...	13,117
Building materials,	59,100	2,055,000	93.0	28,727
of which,				
Brick, tile, other	37,000	...	...	11,931
Cement (all forms)	15,800	856,000	...	10,869
Secondary forest products (including paper and stationery)	23,100	1,132,000	96.1	24,414
Primary forest products	21,300	1,328,000	114.3	12,681
Mining				
Nonferrous and ferrous metals	5,700	3,336,000	107.6	57,936
Petroleum,	400	673,000	114.0	33,411
of which,				
Crude petroleum	24	...	...	14,250
Coal	10,500	4,268,000	119.8	19,472

Energy production (consumption): electricity (kW-hr; 1984) 376,990,000,000 (377,240,000,000); coal (metric tons; 1984) 789,230,000 (784,769,000); crude petroleum (barrels; 1984) 840,343,000 (678,694,000); petroleum products (metric tons; 1984) 65,424,000 (60,164,000); natural gas (cu m; 1984) 12,396,000,000 (12,396,000,000).

Population economically active (1982): total 474,384,000; activity rate of total population 47.1% (participation rates: over age 15, 70.9%; female 32.0%△; unemployed, n.a.). Urban work force by sector of employment, 1978 (1984): state-run enterprises 74,500,000 (86,700,000); collectives 20,000,000 (32,500,000); self-employment or privately run enterprises 150,000 (3,400,000).

Price and earnings indexes (1980 = 100)

	1978	1979	1980	1981	1982	1983	1984
Consumer price index	91.3	93.1	100.0	102.6	104.5	106.7	109.6
Earnings index✝	80.6	87.7	100.0	101.3	104.7	108.4	127.8

Land use (1984): forested 14.5%; meadows and pastures 30.6%; agricultural and under permanent cultivation 10.8%; other 44.1%.

Financial aggregates⊕

	1980	1981	1982	1983	1984	1985	1986**
Exchange rate, Y per:							
U.S. dollar	1.53	1.75	1.92	1.98	2.80	3.20	3.70
£	3.65	3.33	3.10	2.87	3.23	4.62	5.48
SDR	1.95	2.03	2.12	2.07	2.74	3.52	4.47
International reserves (U.S.$)							
Total (excl. gold; '000,000)	2,545	5,048	11,339	14,853	15,081	12,728	11,447
SDRs ('000,000)	92	275	214	335	406	483	553
Reserve pos. in IMF ('000,000)	191	—	—	176	223	332	365
Foreign exchange	2,262	4,773	11,125	14,342	14,420	11,913	10,529
Gold ('000,000 fine troy oz)	12.8	12.7	12.7	12.7	12.7	12.7	12.7
% world reserves	1.5	1.3	1.3	1.3	1.3	1.3	1.3
Interest and prices							
Central bank discount (%)	...	...	...	...	...	...	...
Gov't bond yield (%)	...	...	...	...	...	...	...
Industrial share prices	...	...	...	...	...	...	...
Balance of payments (Y '000,000)							
Balance of visible trade,	−290	3,030	8,610	5,130	1,590	−54,310	...
of which:							
Imports, f.o.b.	27,410	33,730	32,820	38,700	56,370	176,820	...
Exports, f.o.b.	27,120	36,760	41,430	43,830	57,960	122,510	...
Balance of invisibles	...	...	...	...	...	...	...
Balance of payments, current account	...	...	...	...	...	...	...

Household income and expenditure. Average household size (1984), n.a.; rural household 5.4, urban household 4.0. Average annual income per household, n.a.; rural household Y 1,908, urban household Y 2,667. Sources of income (1984): rural household—income from the collective and nonproductive sources 64.8%, sideline production 35.1%, of which selling privately tended livestock or poultry 11.1%, or crop or forest produce 10.1%; urban household♂—time wages 58.5%, subsidies 14.5%, bonuses 14.4%, piece-rate wages 9.5%. Expenditure (1984): rural household—food 59.0%, housing 11.7%, personal effects 11.0%, clothing 10.4%, fuel 5.5%, cultural activities 2.4%; urban household—food 58.0%, clothing 15.5%, personal effects 9.1%, cultural activities 5.8%, fuel 2.8%, transportation and communication 1.5%, housing 1.4%, other 5.9%.

Foreign trade††

Balance of trade (current prices)

	1980	1981	1982	1983	1984	1985
Y '000,000	−2,760	−10	+5,660	+1,650	−3,480	−70,220
% of total	4.8%	0.0%	7.3%	1.9%	2.9%	22.3%

Imports (1984): Y 62,047,000,000 (rolled steel 14.5%; wheat 6.1%; manufactured fertilizer 6.0%; aluminum, copper, and zinc (all forms) 3.6%; motor vehicles and chassis 3.4%; synthetic polymers 3.1%; synthetic fibres 2.9%; logs 2.5%; television sets 1.0%; ships 1.0%). *Major import sources:* Japan 31.3%; United States 14.8%; Hong Kong 10.9%; West Germany 4.8%; Canada 4.0%; Australia 3.4%; France 3.0%; U.S.S.R. 2.6%; United Kingdom 1.9%; Italy 1.7%.

Exports (1984): Y 58,056,000,000 (crude oil 16.1%; garments 5.8%; petroleum products 5.4%; cotton cloth 4.3%; cereals 2.8%; knitted fabrics 2.6%; polyester and cotton blend cloth 1.5%; canned foods 1.5%; cotton yarn 1.5%; tea 1.2%; aquatic products 1.2%). *Major export destinations:* Hong Kong 26.5%; Japan 20.6%; United States 9.3%; Jordan 5.0%; Singapore 5.0%; West Germany 3.1%; U.S.S.R. 2.4%; Brazil 1.5%; Syria 1.4%.

Transport and communications

Transport. Railroads (1985): length 35,200 mi, 56,600 km; passenger-mi 150,123,000,000, passenger-km 241,600,000,000; short ton-mi cargo 556,585,000,000, metric ton-km cargo 812,600,000,000. Roads (1986)‡: total length 584,000 mi, 940,000 km (paved 20%). Vehicles (1982): passenger cars 265,000; trucks 1,768,000. Merchant marine (1985): vessels (100 gross tons and over) 1,408; total deadweight tonnage 22,615,443‡‡. Air transport (1985): passenger-mi 7,270,000,000, passenger-km 11,700,000,000; short ton-mi cargo 288,000,000, metric ton-km cargo 420,000,000; airports (1986) with scheduled flights 76.

Communications. Daily newspapers (1986)‡: total number 222; total circulation, n.a.; circulation per 1,000 population, n.a. Radio (1985): total number of receivers 15,500,000 (1 per 67 persons). Television (1986): total number of receivers 69,650,000 (1 per 15 persons). Telephones (1984): 2,774,300 (1 per 371 persons).

Education and health

Education 1985

	schools	teachers	students	student/ teacher ratio
Primary (age 7–13)	832,309	5,377,000	133,702,000	24.9
Secondary (age 13–17)	93,221	2,652,000	47,060,000	17.7
Secondary specialized	12,655	361,000	4,424,000	12.3
Higher	1,016	344,000	1,703,000	5.0

Literacy (1982): total population over age 11 literate 511,000,000 (68.0%)§§; males literate, n.a.; females literate, n.a.

Health (1985): physicians 1,413,000 (1 per 737 persons); hospital beds 2,487,000 (1 per 419 persons); infant mortality rate per 1,000 live births (1980–85) 38.0.

Food (1983): daily per capita caloric intake 2,877 (vegetable products 92%, animal products 8%); 133% of FAO recommended minimum requirement.

Military

Total active duty personnel (1986): 2,950,000 (army 71.5%, navy 11.9%, air force 16.6%). *Military expenditure as percent of GNP* (1983): 8.6% (world 6.1%); per capita expenditure U.S.$34.

*Names of the provinces, autonomous regions, and municipalities are stated in conventional form followed by Pinyin transliteration; names of capitals are stated in conventional form or Wade–Giles transliteration followed by Pinyin transliteration. †Data for Taiwan, Quemoy, and Matsu are excluded. ‡Beginning of the year. §Includes 4,600 sq mi (11,900 sq km) not shown separately. ‖ Total includes servicemen not assigned to any political division. ¶Based on rural sample population of 3,800,000. ♀Excludes arrests for anti-Communist activities. ♂In state-owned industries only. □1979. ◇In 1980 constant prices. △Estimate. ✝Average annual wage of staff and workers. ⊕Exchange rates and international reserves are based on end of year figures. **August. ††Imports, c.i.f. (cost, insurance, and freight); exports, f.o.b. (free on board). ‡‡Deadweight tonnage includes 583 vessels of Taiwan (100 gross tons and over). §§Estimate of literacy excludes semiliterates.

Colombia

Official name: República de Colombia (Republic of Colombia).
Form of government: unitary, multiparty republic with two legislative houses (Senate [114]; House of Representatives [199]).
Head of state and government: President.
Capital: Bogotá.
Official language: Spanish.
Official religion: none.
Monetary unit: 1 peso (Col$) = 100 centavos; valuation (Oct. 1, 1986) 1 U.S.$ = Col$205.56; 1 £ = Col$297.03.

Area and population

		area		population
				1985
Commissariats	**Capitals**	sq mi	sq km	census*
Amazonas	Leticia	42,342	109,665	30,327
Guainía	San Felipe (Obando)	27,891	72,238	9,214
Guaviare	Guaviare	16,342	42,327	35,305
Vaupés	Mitú	25,200	65,268	18,935
Vichada	Puerto Carreño	38,703	100,242	13,770
Departments				
Antioquia	Medellín	24,561	63,612	3,888,067
Atlántico	Barranquilla	1,308	3,388	1,428,601
Bolívar	Cartagena	10,030	25,978	1,197,623
Boyacá	Tunja	8,953	23,189	1,097,618
Caldas	Manizales	3,046	7,888	838,094
Caquetá	Florencia	34,349	88,965	214,473
Cauca	Popayán	11,316	29,308	795,838
Cesar	Valledupar	8,844	22,905	584,631
Chocó	Quibdó	17,965	46,530	242,768
Córdoba	Montería	9,660	25,020	913,636
Cundinamarca	Bogotá	8,735	22,623	1,382,360
Huila	Neiva	7,680	19,890	647,756
La Guajira	Riohacha	8,049	20,848	255,310
Magdalena	Santa Marta	8,953	23,188	769,141
Meta	Villavicencio	33,064	85,635	412,312
Nariño	Pasto	12,845	33,268	1,019,098
Norte de Santander	Cúcuta	8,362	21,658	883,884
Quindío	Armenia	712	1,845	377,860
Risaralda	Pereira	1,598	4,140	625,451
Santander	Bucaramanga	11,790	30,537	1,438,226
Sucre	Sincelejo	4,215	10,917	529,059
Tolima	Ibagué	9,097	23,562	1,051,852
Valle	Cali	8,548	22,140	2,847,087
Intendancies				
Arauca	Arauca	9,196	23,818	70,085
Casanare	Yopal	17,236	44,640	110,253
Putumayo	Mocoa	9,608	24,885	119,815
San Andrés and Providencia	San Andrés	17	44	35,936
Special District				
Bogotá		613	1,587	3,982,941
TOTAL		440,831†	1,141,748	27,867,326

Demography

Population (1986): 28,231,000.
Density (1986): persons per sq mi 64.0, persons per sq km 24.7.
Urban–rural (1985): urban 69.9%; rural 30.1%.
Sex distribution (1985): male 49.49%; female 50.51%.
Age breakdown (1985): under 15, 35.5%; 15–29, 30.7%; 30–44, 17.0%; 45–59, 9.4%; 60 and over, 7.4%.
Population projection: (1990) 30,152,000; (2000) 35,544,000.
Doubling time: 28 years.
Ethnic composition (1980): mestizo 47.8%; mulatto 23.0%; white 20.0%; black 6.0%; Amerindian 1.6%; other 1.6%.
Religious affiliation (1983): Roman Catholic 97%; other 3%.
Major cities (1985): Bogotá 3,982,941; Medellín 1,418,554; Cali 1,323,944; Barranquilla 896,649; Cartagena 491,368.

Vital statistics

Birth rate per 1,000 population (1982): 30.6 (world avg. 29.0); legitimate 75.2%; illegitimate 24.8%.
Death rate per 1,000 population (1982): 5.8 (world avg. 11.0).
Natural increase rate per 1,000 population (1982): 24.8 (world avg. 18.0).
Total fertility rate (avg. births per childbearing woman; 1980–85): 3.9.
Marriage rate per 1,000 population (1977): 3.5.
Life expectancy at birth (1980–85): male 61.4 years; female 66.0 years.
Major causes of death per 100,000 population (1977): diseases of the circulatory system 129.2; infectious and parasitic diseases 86.6.

National economy

Budget (1984). Revenue: Col$486,073,000,000 (indirect taxes 38.1%, credit resources 38.1%, direct taxes 20.2%). Expenditures: Col$541,038,000,000 (education 22.0%, public debt 12.0%, defense 9.8%, public works 7.2%).
Public debt (external, outstanding; 1984): U.S.$7,980,400,000.
Tourism (1984): receipts from visitors U.S.$205,000,000; expenditures by nationals abroad U.S.$308,000,000.
Production (metric tons except as noted). Agriculture (1985): sugarcane 25,000,000, potatoes 2,017,000, rice 1,764,000, cassava 1,729,000, bananas 1,200,000, corn (maize) 882,000, coffee (green) 660,000, sorghum 537,000, tobacco 42,000; roundwood 16,916,000 cu m‡; fish catch 78,514‡; livestock (number of live animals) 21,935,000 cattle, 2,714,000 sheep, 2,378,000 pigs. Mining and quarrying (1985): iron ore 432,000; gold 840,000 troy oz; silver 100,000 troy oz. Manufacturing (value added in Col$'000,000; 1982): processed food 70,903; beverages 67,685; chemicals 62,112; textiles 41,854; nonmetal products 19,924; transport equipment 19,255. Construction (1983)§: residential 7,296,000 sq m; nonresidential 1,284,000 sq m. Energy production (consumption): electricity (kW-hr; 1984) 27,800,000,000 (27,793,000,000); coal (metric tons; 1984) 6,100,000 (5,650,000); crude petroleum (barrels; 1984) 60,965,000 (68,665,000); petroleum products (metric tons; 1984) 8,460,000 (6,614,000); natural gas (cu m; 1984) 4,796,135,000 (4,796,135,000).
Gross national product (at current market prices; 1984): U.S.$38,410,000,000 (U.S.$1,410 per capita).

Structure of gross domestic product and labour force

	1984		1980	
	in value Col$'000,000	% of total value	labour force	% of labour force
Agriculture	681,353	17.8	2,412,413	28.5
Mining	129,266	3.4	49,740	0.6
Manufacturing	843,181	22.0	1,136,735	13.4
Construction	206,618	5.4	242,191	2.9
Public utilities	81,722	2.1	44,233	0.5
Transp. and commun.	307,336	8.0	352,623	4.2
Trade	534,262	14.0 }	1,539,843	18.1
Finance }				
Pub. admin., defense }	1,044,844	27.3 }	1,998,460	23.6
Services }				
Other }			690,762	8.2
TOTAL	3,828,582	100.0	8,467,000	100.0

Population economically active (1980): total 8,467,000; activity rate of total population 33.1% (participation rates: over age 15, 52.3%; female 26.2%; unemployed 3.8%).

Price and earnings indexes (1980 = 100)

	1980	1981	1982	1983	1984	1985	1986‖
Consumer price index	100.0	127.5	158.8	190.2	220.8	273.9	325.4
Hourly earnings index¶	100.0	130.0	170.0	211.7	262.2	...	...

Average household size (1981) 5.4.
Land use (1984): forested 48.0%; meadows and pastures 28.9%; agricultural and under permanent cultivation 5.5%; other 17.6%.

Foreign trade

Balance of trade (current prices)

	1980	1981	1982	1983	1984	1985
U.S.$'000,000	−255.5	−1,729.0	−1,841.8	−1,390.7	−590.4	−179.9
% of total	3.1%	22.6%	22.9%	18.4%	7.9%	2.5%

Imports (1984): U.S.$4,051,948,000 (machinery 34.2%, chemicals 17.1%, crude petroleum and petroleum products 11.7%, base metals and metal manufactures 9.8%, paper 5.0%). *Major import sources* (1983): U.S. 34.7%; EEC countries 14.4%; Venezuela, Ecuador, and Peru 13.6%; Japan 7.9%.
Exports (1984): U.S.$3,461,583,000 (coffee 51.1%, crude petroleum and petroleum products 12.8%, bananas 5.8%, fresh-cut flowers 3.9%, chemicals 2.9%, cotton 2.8%). *Major export destinations* (1983): EEC countries 37.8%; U.S. 28.6%; Venezuela, Ecuador, and Peru 5.9%.

Transport and communications

Transport. Railroads (1985): route length 2,115 mi, 3,403 km; passenger-mi 142,000,000, passenger-km 228,000,000; short ton-mi cargo 534,000,000, metric ton-km cargo 780,000,000. Roads (1983): total length 65,369 mi, 105,201 km (paved 28%). Vehicles (1982): cars 476,417; trucks and buses 312,280. Merchant marine (1985): vessels (100 gross tons and over) 80; total deadweight tonnage 470,778. Air transport (1985): passenger-km 3,924,000,000; metric ton-km cargo 205,752,000; airports (1986) 78.
Communications. Daily newspapers (1984): 31; circulation 1,323,800; circulation per 1,000 population 47. Radio (1984): 3,025,000 receivers (1 per 9.3 persons). Television (1984): 1,801,000 receivers (1 per 16 persons). Telephones (1983): 2,547,222 (1 per 11 persons).

Education and health

Education (1986)

	schools	teachers	students	student/ teacher ratio
Primary	36,979	135,924	4,002,543	29.4
Secondary♀	6,336	107,084	2,136,239	19.9
Higher	231	43,447	402,438	9.3

Educational attainment (1973). Percent of population over age 20 having: no schooling 22.4%; primary education 55.9%; secondary 18.4%; higher 3.3%. *Literacy* (1981): population over age 15 literate 11,923,900 (74.2%).
Health: physicians (1983) 21,778 (1 per 1,969 persons); hospital beds (1982) 28,880 (1 per 586 persons); infant mortality rate (1981) 60.9.
Food (1981–83): daily per capita caloric intake 2,543 (vegetable products 86%, animal products 14%); 111% of FAO recommended minimum requirement.

Military

Total active duty personnel (1986): 66,200 (army 80.1%, navy 13.6%, air force 6.3%). *Military expenditure as percent of GNP* (1984): 1.1% (world 6.1%); per capita expenditure U.S.$15.

*Preliminary results. †Detail does not add to total given because of rounding. ‡1984. §Includes 56 urban centres. ‖August. ¶Manufacturing only. ♀Secondary includes vocational and teacher training.

Comoros*

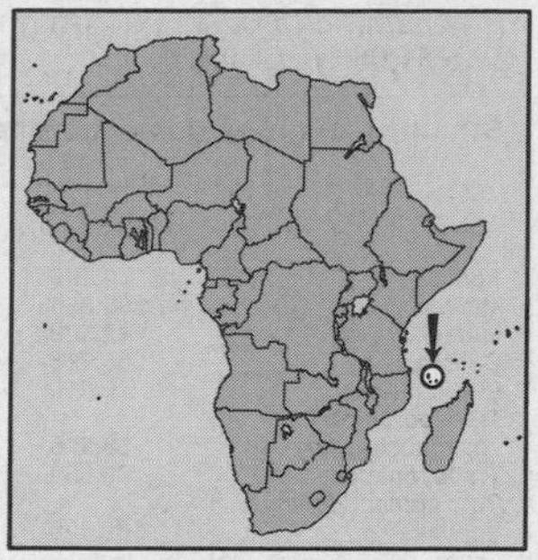

Official name: Jumhurīyat al-Qumur al-Ittihādīyah al-Islāmīyah (Arabic); République Fédéral Islamique des Comores (French) (Federal Islamic Republic of the Comoros).
Form of government: federal Islamic republic with one legislative house (Federal Assembly [38]).
Head of state and government: President.
Capital: Moroni.
Official languages: Arabic; French.
Official religion: Islam.
Monetary unit: 1 Comorian franc (CF) = 100 centimes; valuation (Oct. 1, 1986) 1 U.S.$ = CF 332.05; 1 £ = CF 479.81.

Area and population

		area		population
Governorates/Islands†	Capitals	sq mi	sq km	1986 estimate
Moili (Mohéli)	Fomboni	112	290	20,964
Ngazidja (Grande Comore)	Moroni	443	1,148	220,009
Ndzouani (Anjouan)	Mutsamudu	164	424	167,597
TOTAL		719	1,862	408,570

Demography

Population (1986): 409,000.
Density (1986): persons per sq mi 577.2; persons per sq km 222.9.
Urban-rural (1980): urban‡ 33.4%; rural 66.6%.
Sex distribution (1985): male 49.75%; female 50.25%.
Age breakdown (1985): under 15, 48.1%; 15–29, 24.8%; 30–44, 13.4%; 45–59, 8.6%; 60–74, 3.6%; 75 and over, 1.5%.
Population projection: (1990) 473,000; (2000) 661,000.
Doubling time: 21 years.
Ethnic composition (1980): Comorian (a mixture of Bantu, Arab, and Malagasy peoples) 96.9%; Makua (a Bantu people from East Africa) 1.6%; French 0.4%; other 1.1%.
Religious affiliation (1980): Sunnī Muslim 99.7%; Christian 0.2%; Bahā'ī 0.1%.
Major cities (1980): Moroni 17,267; Mutsamudu 16,883; Domoni 7,147; Ouani 6,936; Tsembehou 6,578.

Vital statistics

Birth rate per 1,000 population (1980–85): 49.3 (world avg. 29.0).
Death rate per 1,000 population (1980–85): 15.2 (world avg. 11.0).
Natural increase rate per 1,000 population (1980–85): 34.1 (world avg. 18.0).
Total fertility rate (avg. births per childbearing woman; 1980–85): 7.0.
Marriage rate per 1,000 population: n.a.
Divorce rate per 1,000 population: n.a.
Life expectancy at birth (1980–85): male 52.0 years; female 55.6 years.
Major causes of death per 100,000 population: n.a.; however, major diseases (1980) include malaria (afflicts 80% of the adult population), tuberculosis, leprosy, and kwashiorkor (a nutritional deficiency disease).

National economy

Budget (1984). Revenue: CF 6,659,000,000 (current revenues CF 6,066,000,000, of which indirect taxes on foreign trade 81.9%, turnover tax 7.2%, income from state enterprises 3.2%, registry and stamps 2.2%). Expenditures: CF 8,008,000,000 (current expenditure CF 7,008,000,000, of which defense 19.0%, education, youth, and recreation 18.7%, general administration 11.3%, foreign affairs 6.8%, community expenses 6.6%, public debt payments 6.5%, public works 4.1%, infrastructure and environment 3.9%, transport and tourism 3.4%, health 2.4%).
Public debt (external, outstanding; 1985): U.S.$129,100,000.
Tourism (1985): tourist arrivals 2,310.
Production (metric tons except as noted). Agriculture, forestry, fishing§ (1984): cassava 90,000, coconuts 43,000, bananas 34,000, sweet potatoes 17,000, rice 15,000, corn (maize) 6,000, copra 3,000, pulses 2,000, cloves 1,124 ‖ ¶, vanilla 181 ‖ ¶, ylang-ylang 60 ‖ ¶, coffee 8 ‖ ¶, basil 2 ‖ ¶; livestock (number of live animals) 92,000 goats, 83,000 cattle, 9,000 sheep, 4,000 asses, 300,000 chickens; roundwood, n.a.; fish catch (1983) 4,000. Mining and quarrying: sand and gravel for local construction. Manufacturing (1983): copra 684; ylang-ylang essence 49; other products are cement, handicrafts, soaps, and soft drinks. Construction: n.a. Energy production (consumption): electricity (kW-hr; 1985) 12,300,000 (10,450,000♀); coal, none (none); crude petroleum, none (none); petroleum products (metric tons; 1984) none (12,000); natural gas, none (none).
Population economically active (1980): total 99,463; activity rate of total population 29.7% (participation rates: ages 15–64, 41.1%; female 26.4%; unemployed 10.0%).

Price and earnings indexes (1979 = 100)

	1977	1978	1979	1980	1981	1982	1983
Consumer price index	75.5	87.9	100.0	111.2	131.9	177.2	188.5
Daily earnings index♁	...	...	100.0	...	...	...	133.3

Household income and expenditure. Average household size (1980) 5.3; average annual income per household: n.a.; source of income: n.a.; expenditure (1983)□: food and beverages 56.0%, energy 14.4%, clothing and footwear 10.0%, transportation and communication 6.6%, recreation 3.0%, tobacco 3.0%, other 7.0%.
Gross national product (at current market prices; 1983): U.S.$106,000,000 (U.S.$290 per capita).

Structure of gross domestic product and labour force

	1982		1980	
	in value CF '000,000	% of total value	labour force◇	% of labour force
Agriculture	12,972	44.8	1,349	10.6
Mining	—	—	—	—
Manufacturing	1,619	5.6	685	5.4
Construction	3,325	11.5	3,579	28.1
Public utilities	183	0.7	206	1.6
Transportation and communication	495	1.7	975	7.6
Trade, restaurants, hotels	4,288	14.8	1,210	9.5
Finance, insurance	789	2.7	146	1.1
Public admin., defense	5,010	17.3	4,597	36.1
Other services	259	0.9		
TOTAL	28,940	100.0	12,747	100.0

Land use§ (1983): forested 16.0%; meadows and pastures 7.0%; agricultural and under permanent cultivation 42.0%; other 35.0%.

Foreign trade△

Balance of trade (current prices)

	1980	1981	1982	1983	1984	1985
CF '000,000	−4,185	−4,330	−4,291	−5,680	−15,700	−8,961
% of total	51.6%	32.5%	25.0%	27.7%	71.7%	40.0%

Imports (1985): CF 15,675,000,000 (foodstuffs 19.1%, of which rice 7.6%; petroleum products 6.6%; automobiles 4.7%; cement 4.6%; unspecified commodities 65.0%). *Major import sources* (1981): France 51.1%; Pakistan 13.5%; Kenya and Tanzania 7.3%; Madagascar 6.2%; China 2.0%; United Kingdom 0.7%.
Exports (1985): CF 6,714,000,000 (vanilla 66.4%; cloves 20.3%; ylang-ylang 12.4%; copra 0.9%). *Major export destinations* (1984): France 43.0%; West Germany 10.0%; Singapore 9.0%; The Netherlands 7.0%; United States 6.0%; Mauritius 5.0%; United Kingdom 4.3%.

Transport and communications

Transport. Railroads: none. Roads (1983): total length 466 mi, 750 km (paved 35%). Vehicles (1983): passenger cars, 3,600; trucks and buses, 2,000. Merchant marine (1985): vessels (100 gross tons and over) 3; total deadweight tonnage 2,194. Air transport (1983)⸸: passenger arrivals and departures 30,537; cargo loaded and unloaded 172 metric tons; airports (1986) with scheduled flights 3.
Communications. Daily newspapers: none. Radio (1985): total number of receivers 40,000 (1 per 9.9 persons). Television: total number of receivers, n.a.⊕ Telephones (1981): 1,650 (1 per 208 persons).

Education and health

Education (1980–81)

	schools	teachers	students	student/teacher ratio
Primary (age 7–13)	236	1,292	59,709	46.2
Secondary	32	434	13,528	31.2
Voc., teacher tr.	4	27	327	12.1

Educational attainment (1980). Percent of total population over age 12 having: no formal schooling 47.4%; Qur'anic school education 7.2%; primary 9.3%; secondary 5.4%; higher 0.1%; not specified 30.6%. *Literacy* (1980): total population over age 12 literate 98,900 (47.4%); males literate 56,100 (56.3%); females literate 42,800 (41.5%).
Health (1982): physicians 20 (1 per 17,300 persons); hospital beds 813 (1 per 439 persons); infant mortality rate per 1,000 live births (1980) 121.7.
Food (1980–82)§: daily per capita caloric intake 2,291 (vegetable products 95%, animal products 5%); 98% of FAO recommended minimum requirement.

Military**

Total active duty personnel (1984): 700–800 (army 100%). *Military expenditure as percent of GNP* (1983): 1.9% (world 6.1%); per capita expenditure U.S.$6.

*Excludes Mayotte, a *collectivité territoriale* ("territorial collectivity") of France, unless otherwise indicated. †Island names in Comorian Swahili and French, respectively. ‡Settlements of more than 3,000 inhabitants. §Includes Mayotte. ‖ Excludes Mayotte. ¶1985; export only. ♀1984. ♁Construction sector only. □Weights of consumer price index components. ◇Wage earners only. △Import figures c.i.f. (cost, insurance, freight); export figures f.o.b. (free on board). ⸸Air Comores only. ⊕Television service began in 1986. **In 1983 France assumed sole responsibility for the defense of the Comoros.

Congo

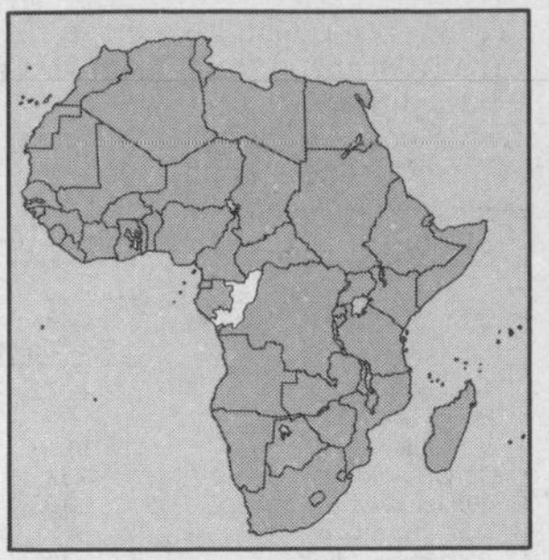

Official name: République Populaire du Congo (People's Republic of the Congo).
Form of government: people's republic with one legislative body (People's National Assembly [153]).
Head of state and government: President (Chairman of the Central Committee).
Capital: Brazzaville.
Official language: French.
Official religion: none.
Monetary unit: 1 CFA franc (CFAF) = 100 centimes; valuation (Oct. 1, 1986) 1 U.S.$ = CFAF 332.05; 1 £ = CFAF 479.81.

Area and population

		area		population
				1984
Regions	Capitals	sq mi	sq km	census
Bouenza	Nkayi	4,734	12,260	149,519
Cuvette	Owando	28,900	74,850	133,144
Kouilou	Pointe-Noire	5,274	13,660	76,216
Lékoumou	Sibiti	8,089	20,950	68,301
Likouala	Impfondo	25,500	66,044	48,993
Niari	Loubomo	10,011	25,930	123,456
Plateaux	Djambala	14,826	38,400	108,802
Pool	Kinkala	13,124	33,990	180,051
Sangha	Ouesso	21,544	55,800	46,367
Communes				
Brazzaville	—	25	65	595,102
Loubomo	—	5	12	49,458
Nkayi	—	2	5	35,628
Pointe-Noire	—	13	34	297,392
TOTAL		132,047	342,000	1,912,429

Demography

Population (1986): 2,097,000.
Density (1986): persons per sq mi 15.9, persons per sq km 6.1.
Urban-rural (1984): urban 51.1%; rural 48.9%.
Sex distribution (1985): male 49.31%; female 50.69%.
Age breakdown (1985): under 15, 43.6%; 15–29, 25.8%; 30–44, 15.6%; 45–59, 9.5%; 60–74, 4.6%; 75 and over, 0.9%.
Population projection: (1990) 2,450,000; (2000) 3,200,000.
Doubling time: 27 years.
Ethnic composition (1978): Kongo 52.3%; Teke 24.0%; Bubangui 5.2%; Kota 4.5%; Mboshi 3.4%; other 10.6%.
Religious affiliation (1980): Roman Catholic 53.9%; Protestant 24.4%; animist 19.0%; other 2.7%.
Major cities (1984): Brazzaville 595,102; Pointe-Noire 297,392; Nkayi 49,458; Loubomo 35,628.

Vital statistics

Birth rate per 1,000 population (1980–85): 44.5 (world avg. 29.0); legitimate, n.a.; illegitimate, n.a.
Death rate per 1,000 population (1980–85): 18.6 (world avg. 11.0).
Natural increase rate per 1,000 population (1980–85): 25.9 (world avg. 18.0).
Total fertility rate (avg. births per childbearing woman; 1980–85): 6.0.
Marriage rate per 1,000 population: n.a.
Divorce rate per 1,000 population: n.a.
Life expectancy at birth (1986): male 44.9 years; female 48.1 years.
Major causes of death per 100,000 population: n.a.; however, major diseases include malaria, diseases of the respiratory system, tuberculosis, and parasitic diseases.

National economy

Budget (1985). Revenue: CFAF 311,000,000,000 (petroleum revenue 58.0%, domestic taxes 19.3%, customs duties 15.0%). Expenditures: CFAF 311,000,000,000 (public works, construction, and housing 29.6%, hydraulic energy 18.1%, civil aviation and transport 9.5%, industries and crafts 6.5%, agriculture and livestock 6.1%, health 6.0%, defense 3.8%).
Public debt (external, outstanding; 1984): U.S.$1,395,000,000.
Tourism: receipts from visitors (1981) U.S.$13,000,000; expenditures by nationals abroad (1982) U.S.$54,000,000.
Production (metric tons except as noted). Agriculture, forestry, fishing (1984): cassava 600,000, sugarcane 250,000, bananas 32,000, palm oil 15,300, peanuts (groundnuts) 15,000, yams 14,000, sweet potatoes 13,000, corn (maize) 7,000, coffee 3,000, cacao beans 2,000, rice 2,000; livestock (number of live animals) 182,000 goats, 68,000 cattle, 60,000 sheep; roundwood (1983) 2,238,000 cu m; fish catch (1983) 31,926. Mining and quarrying (1983): cement 15,034; lead 4,000*; copper 35*; gold 8.3 kilograms*. Manufacturing (1983): cement 29,000; raw sugar 21,000; wheat flour 8,000; soap 5,100; peanut oil 1,000; cigarettes 895; beer 788,000 hectolitres; soft drinks 261,000 hectolitres; veneer sheets 61,000 cu m; footwear 928,000 pairs. Construction: n.a. Energy production (consumption): electricity (kW-hr; 1984) 237,000,000 (262,000,000); coal, none (n.a.); crude petroleum (barrels; 1984) 44,030,000 (n.a.); petroleum products (metric tons; 1984) none (84,000); natural gas (cu m; 1985) 34,000,000 (n.a.).
Land use (1983): forested 62.4%; meadows and pastures 29.3%; agricultural and under permanent cultivation 2.0%; other 6.3%.

Gross national product (at current market prices; 1984): U.S.$2,060,000,000 (U.S.$1,060 per capita).

Structure of gross domestic product and labour force

	1984		1981	
	in value CFAF '000,000	% of total value	labour force	% of labour force
Agriculture	70,299	7.7	180,200	34.0
Mining	395,854	43.0		
Manufacturing	42,509	4.6		
Construction	65.096	7.1		
Public utilities	9,510	1.0	137,800	26.0
Transportation and communication	68,576	7.5		
Trade, finance	98,659	10.7		
Pub. admin., defense / Services / Other	169,625	18.4	212,000	40.0
TOTAL	920,128	100.0	530,000	100.0

Population economically active (1983): total 563,000; activity rate of total population 34.1% (participation rates: ages 15–64, n.a.; female [1974] 44.6%; unemployed, n.a.).

Price and earnings indexes (1980 = 100)

	1979	1980	1981	1982	1983	1984	1985
Consumer price index	93.2	100.0	117.0	132.0	142.3	160.3	170.1
Earnings index	...	...	...	...	...	...	...

Household income and expenditure. Average household size (1980) 4.7; average annual income per household CFAF 1,016,000† (U.S.$ 4,500); source of income: n.a.; expenditure: n.a.

Foreign trade

Balance of trade (current prices)

	1979	1980	1981	1982	1983	1984
CFAF '000,000,000	55.1	92.1	121.5	120.4	194.9	297.2
% of total	34.0%	31.5%	38.0%	22.6%	31.8%	40.4%

Imports (1982): CFAF 225,200,000,000‡ (machinery 26.2%, of which electrical machinery 10.4%, transport equipment 9.7%; food and beverages 15.1%; iron and steel 12.3%; petroleum products 9.0%; chemicals and related products 5.9%; textiles 4.6%; plastic and rubber goods 2.5%; precision instruments 2.2%). *Major import sources:* France 61.1%; Brazil 7.0%; Belgium-Luxembourg 3.4%; Japan 3.3%; United States 3.0%; The Netherlands 2.2%; Italy 2.2%.
Exports (1982): CFAF 326,150,000,000 (crude petroleum 90.4%; wood and wood products 4.7%; pearls and precious stones 2.7%; petroleum products 0.8%; coffee, cocoa, and tobacco 0.4%). *Major export destinations:* United States 50.8%; Italy 21.0%; Spain 10.3%; France 10.0%; Belgium-Luxembourg 2.7%.

Transport and communications

Transport. Railroads (1983): length 498 mi, 802 km; passenger-mi 237,000,000, passenger-km 381,000,000; short ton-mi cargo 299,000,000, metric ton-km cargo 437,000,000. Roads (1985): total length 6,835 mi, 11,000 km (paved 5.1%). Vehicles (1982): passenger cars 30,500; trucks and buses 78,600. Merchant marine (1985): vessels (100 gross tons and over) 21; total deadweight tonnage 10,840. Air transport§ (1985): passenger-mi 144,226,000, passenger-km 232,109,000; short ton-mi cargo 27,422,000, metric ton-km cargo 40,035,000; airports (1986) with scheduled flights 17.
Communications. Daily newspapers (1985): total number 4; total circulation 23,850; circulation per 1,000 population 11.8. Radio (1985): total number of receivers 99,000 (1 per 20 persons). Television (1985): total number of receivers 5,000 (1 per 404 persons). Telephones (1982): 8,899 (1 per 202 persons).

Education and health

Education (1982–83)

	schools	teachers	students	student/ teacher ratio
Primary (age 6–13)	1,428	7,329	422,874	57.7
Secondary (age 14–18)	122 ‖	3,996	189,831	47.5
Voc., teacher tr.¶	36 ‖	1,448	20,744	14.3
Higher ‖	1	297	7,255	24.8

Educational attainment♀ (1974). Percent of population over age 15 having: secondary education 30%, of which males 37%, females 23%. *Literacy* (1985): total population over age 15 literate 620,000 (62.9%); males literate 332,000 (71.4%); females literate 288,000 (55.4%).
Health: physicians (1980) 278 (1 per 5,986 persons); hospital beds (1978) 6,876 (1 per 224 persons); infant mortality rate per 1,000 live births (1980–85) 81.0.
Food (1980–82): daily per capita caloric intake 2,466 (vegetable products 95%, animal products 5%); 111% of FAO recommended minimum requirement.

Military

Total active duty personnel (1984): 8,700 (army 92.0%, navy 2.3%, air force 5.7%). *Military expenditure as percent of GNP* (1983): 3.2% (world 6.0%); per capita expenditure U.S.$37.

*Metal content of ores. †Derived from GNP. ‡Import figures are c.i.f. (cost, insurance, and freight). §Air Afrique only. ‖ 1980–81. ¶1981–82. ♀For the Commune of Brazzaville only.

Costa Rica

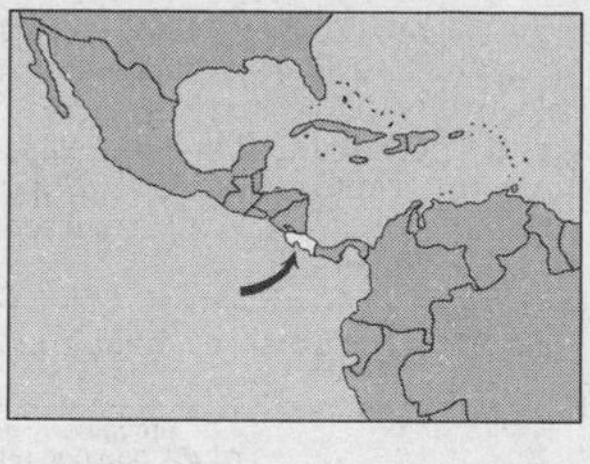

Official name: República de Costa Rica (Republic of Costa Rica).
Form of government: unitary multiparty republic with one legislative house (Legislative Assembly [57]).
Head of state and government: President.
Capital: San José.
Official language: Spanish.
Official religion: Roman Catholicism.
Monetary unit: 1 Costa Rican colón ₡ = 100 céntimos; valuation (Oct. 1, 1986) 1 U.S.$ = ₡57.29; 1 £ = ₡82.78.

Area and population

		area		population
Provinces	Capitals	sq mi	sq km	1984 census
Alajuela	Alajuela	3,766	9,753	427,962
Cartago	Cartago	1,206	3,125	271,671
Guanacaste	Liberia	3,915	10,141	195,208
Heredia	Heredia	1,026	2,656	197,575
Limón	Limón	3,548	9,188	168,076
Puntarenas	Puntarenas	4,354	11,277	265,883
San José	San José	1,915	4,960	890,434
TOTAL		19,730	51,100	2,416,809

Demography

Population (1986): 2,534,000.
Density (1986): persons per sq mi 128.4, persons per sq km 49.6.
Urban-rural (1985): urban 50.0%; rural 50.0%.
Sex distribution (1984): male 50.04%; female 49.96%.
Age breakdown (1984): under 15, 35.0%; 15–29, 31.3%; 30–49, 20.5%; 50–69, 9.9%; 70 and over and unknown, 3.3%.
Population projection: (1990) 2,779,000; (2000) 3,498,000.
Doubling time: 25 years.
Ethnic composition (1981): European 86.8%; mestizo 7.0%; other 6.2%.
Religious affiliation (1984): Roman Catholic 92.4%; other 7.6%.
Major cities (1984): San José 241,464; Limón 52,602; Alajuela 34,556; Puntarenas 29,224; Cartago 23,928.

Vital statistics

Birth rate per 1,000 population (1984): 32.7 (world avg. 29.0).
Death rate per 1,000 population (1984): 4.5 (world avg. 11.0).
Natural increase rate per 1,000 population (1984): 28.2 (world avg. 18.0).
Total fertility rate (avg. births per childbearing woman; 1980–85): 3.5.
Marriage rate per 1,000 population (1983): 7.9.
Divorce rate per 1,000 population (1983): 1.0.
Life expectancy at birth (1981): male 70.5 years; female 74.7 years.
Major causes of death per 100,000 population (1983): diseases of the circulatory system 115.5; malignant neoplasms (cancers) 78.4; accidents 27.2; birth trauma and other conditions originating from perinatal period 23.6; respiratory diseases 20.3; infections and parasitic diseases 17.5.

National economy

Budget (1983). Revenue: ₡28,115,100,000 (taxes on goods and services 31.0%, social security contributions 25.2%, taxes on foreign trade 22.4%, income taxes 19.9%). Expenditures: ₡30,490,000,000 (health 22.5%, economic services 20.2%, education 19.4%, social security and welfare 14.5%, general public services 8.8%, housing and community services 7.8%).
Public debt (external, outstanding; 1985): U.S.$3,523,700,000.
Gross national product (1984): U.S.$2,930,000,000 (U.S.$1,210 per capita).

Structure of gross domestic product and labour force

	1984			
	in value ₡'000,000	% of total value	labour force*	% of labour force
Agriculture	33,014	20.8	224,064	26.8
Mining / Manufacturing	35,808	22.6	131,954	15.8
Construction	6,546	4.1	46,479	5.5
Public utilities	5,533	3.5	48,267	5.8
Transp. and commun.	7,220	4.6		
Trade	31,108	19.6	155,875	18.7
Finance / Public admin., defense, services / Other	39,445	24.9	228,675	27.4
TOTAL	158,674	100.0†	835,314	100.0

Production (metric tons except as noted). Agriculture, forestry, fishing (1984): sugarcane 2,850,000, bananas 950,000, rice 127,000, coffee 124,000, corn (maize) 104,000, palm oil 24,000, dry beans 20,000, palm kernels 7,000, cocoa beans 3,000; livestock (number of live animals): 2,550,000 cattle, 223,000 pigs, 6,000,000 chickens; roundwood 3,395,000 cu m; fish catch 10,902‡. Mining and quarrying (1983): gold 30,000,000 troy oz, silver 2,000 troy oz. Manufacturing (production value in ₡; 1980): cigarettes and beer 3,449,000,000; chemical and rubber products 1,133,000,000; textiles and leather goods 731,000,000; machinery and fabricated metal products 716,000,000; lumber and wooden products 526,000,000. Construction (1983): residential 664,000 sq m; nonresidential 128,000 sq m. Energy production (consumption): electricity (kW-hr; 1984) 3,067,000,000 (2,417,000,000); coal, none (n.a.); crude petroleum (barrels; 1984) none (3,005,000); petroleum products (metric tons; 1984) 389,000 (590,000); natural gas, none (n.a.).
Population economically active (1984): total 835,314; activity rate of total population 34.6% (participation rates: over age 15, 52.2%; female 13.3%; unemployed 5.0%).

Price index (1980 = 100)

	1980	1981	1982	1983	1984	1985	May 1986
Consumer price index	100.0	137.1	260.6	345.6	386.9	445.1	479.6
Earnings index	...	...	...	...	...	...	...

Tourism (1984): receipts from visitors U.S.$117,339,000; expenditures by nationals abroad U.S.$36,000,000§.
Family income and expenditure: average family size (1977) 5.0; income per family ₡29,318 (U.S.$3,421); source of income: n.a.; expenditure (1975)‖: food 40.8%, housing 12.3%, clothing and footwear 10.0%, education 9.2%, household operations 8.2%, utilities 6.6%, transport 6.5%, health care 6.4%.
Land use (1983): forested 31.5%; meadows and pastures 42.8%; agricultural and under permanent cultivation 12.5%; other 13.2%.

Foreign trade¶

Balance of trade (current prices)

	1979	1980	1981	1982	1983	1984	1985
₡'000,000	−2,796	−3,308	−1,755	+2,600	−309	−556	−2,090
% of total	14.9%	16.2%	3.9%	4.2%	0.4%	0.6%	2.1%

Imports (1983): ₡42,870,520,000♀ (raw materials 48.8%, consumer nondurables 17.0%, oil and fuel 10.1%, consumer durables 4.8%, building materials 3.4%, machinery and equipment 3.1%). *Major import sources:* United States 37.8%; Guatemala 6.0%; Japan 5.3%; West Germany 4.7%; El Salvador 3.0%; United Kingdom 1.3%.
Exports (1983): ₡37,588,740,000♀ (bananas 27.8%, coffee beans 26.6%, cattle and meat 3.8%, raw sugar 2.0%). *Major export destinations:* United States 31.7%; West Germany 12.8%; Guatemala 10.2%; El Salvador 4.8%; United Kingdom 2.5%.

Transport and communications

Transport. Railroads (1986): route length 435 mi, 700 km; passenger-km, n.a.; metric ton-km cargo, n.a. Roads (1984): total length 18,078 mi, 29,094 km (paved 10%). Vehicles (1984): passenger cars 106,233; trucks and buses 69,875. Merchant marine (1985): vessels (100 gross tons and over) 28; total deadweight tonnage 20,286. Air transport (international; 1984): passenger-mi 336,000,000, passenger-km 540,000,000; short-ton mi cargo (1985) 15,156,000, metric ton-km cargo (1985) 22,128,000; airports (1986) with scheduled flights 8.
Communications. Daily newspapers (1985): total number 4; total circulation 180,000; circulation per 1,000 population 71. Radio (1984): total number of receivers 190,000 (1 per 12.5 persons). Television (1984): total number of receivers 450,000 (1 per 5.3 persons). Telephones (1983): 281,040 (1 per 8.5 persons).

Education and health

Education (1984)

	schools	teachers	students	student/ teacher ratio
Primary (age 5–11)	3,068	12,223	353,958	29.0
Secondary (age 12–17)	241	9,152	148,032	16.2
Vocational	...	...	...	...
Higher	14‡	...	54,466	...

Educational attainment (1973). Percent of adult population over age 25 having: no formal schooling 16.1%; less than primary education 49.1%; primary 17.8%; secondary 11.2%; postsecondary and higher 5.8%. *Literacy* (1984): total population over age 10 literate 93.1%; males literate 93.0%; females literate 93.1%.
Health: physicians (1979) 1,506 (1 per 1,432 persons); hospital beds (1980) 7,570 (1 per 295 persons); infant mortality per 1,000 live births (1984) 18.8.
Food (1980–82): daily per capita caloric intake 2,638 (vegetable products 82%, animal products 18%); 118% of FAO recommended minimum requirement.

Military

Military expenditure as percent of GNP (1983): 0.7% (world 6.1%); per capita expenditure U.S.$6. Army was officially abolished in 1948. About 8,000 long-term volunteers made up of 4,500 civil guards and 3,500 rural guards conduct both police and paramilitary activities.

*Employed only. †Detail does not add to total because of rounding. ‡1983. §1982. ‖ Based on the components of the consumer price index in San José only. ¶Import figures are f.o.b. (free on board) in balance of trade and c.i.f. (cost, insurance, and freight) for commodities and trading partners. ♀Based on conversion of U.S.$ (used in official government sources) into ₡ using the average exchange rate of 1983.

Côte d'Ivoire

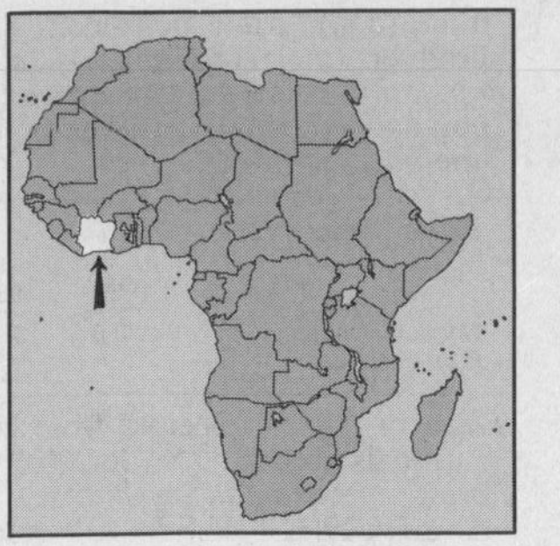

Official name: République de Côte d'Ivoire (Republic of Côte d'Ivoire [Ivory Coast]*).
Form of government: republic with one legislative house (National Assembly [175]).
Head of state and government: President.
Capital: Abidjan (Capital designate: Yamoussoukro).
Official language: French.
Official religion: none.
Monetary unit: 1 CFA franc (CFAF) = 100 centimes; valuation (Oct. 1, 1986) 1 U.S.$ = CFAF 332.05; 1 £ = CFAF 479.81.

Area and population

Departments	Capitals	area sq mi	area sq km	population 1975 census†
Abengourou	Abengourou	2,664	6,900	177,692
Abidjan	Abidjan	5,483	14,200	1,389,141
Aboisso	Aboisso	2,413	6,250	148,823
Adzopé	Adzopé	2,019	5,230	162,837
Agboville	Agboville	1,486	3,850	141,970
Biankouma	Biankouma	1,911	4,950	75,711
Bondoukou	Bondoukou	6,382	16,530	296,551
Bongouanou	Bongouanou	2,151	5,570	216,907
Bouaflé	Bouaflé	2,189	5,670	164,817
Bouaké	Bouaké	9,189	23,800	808,048
Bouna	Bouna	8,290	21,470	84,290
Boundiali	Boundiali	3,048	7,895	96,449
Dabakala	Dabakala	3,734	9,670	56,230
Daloa	Daloa	4,483	11,610	265,529
Danané	Danané	1,776	4,600	170,249
Dimbokro	Dimbokro	3,293	8,530	258,116
Divo	Divo	3,058	7,920	202,511
Ferkessedougou	Ferkessedougou	6,845	17,728	90,423
Gagnoa	Gagnoa	1,737	4,500	174,018
Guiglo	Guiglo	5,463	14,150	137,672
Issia	Issia	1,386	3,590	104,081
Katiola	Katiola	3,637	9,420	77,875
Korhogo	Korhogo	4,826	12,500	276,816
Lakota	Lakota	1,054	2,730	76,105
Man	Man	2,722	7,050	278,659
Mankono	Mankono	4,116	10,660	82,358
Odienné	Odienné	7,954	20,600	124,010
Oumé	Oumé	927	2,400	85,486
Sassandra	Sassandra	6,768	17,530	116,644
Séguéla	Séguéla	4,340	11,240	75,181
Soubré	Soubré	3,193	8,270	75,350
Tingréla	Tingréla	849	2,200	35,829
Touba	Touba	3,367	8,720	77,786
Zuénoula	Zuénoula	1,093	2,830	98,792
TOTAL		123,847‡	320,763	6,702,866

Demography

Population (1986): 10,624,000.
Density (1986): persons per sq mi 85.8, persons per sq km 33.1.
Urban-rural (1985): urban 42.0%; rural 58.0%.
Sex distribution (1985): male 51.09%; female 48.91%.
Age breakdown (1985): under 15, 45.1%; 15–29, 25.4%; 30–44, 15.6%; 45–59, 9.2%; 60–74, 4.0%; 75 and over 0.7%.
Population projection: (1990) 12,662,000; (2000) 19,088,000.
Doubling time: 23 years.
Ethnic composition (1980): Bete 19.7%; Senufo 14.7%; Baule 11.9%; Anui 10.7%; Malinke 6.5%; Dan 5.6%; Lobi 5.4%; other 25.5%.
Religious affiliation (1980): folk religionist 43.8%; Christian 32.0%; Muslim 24.0%; other 0.2%.
Major cities (1975): Abidjan 1,800,000§; Bouaké 175,264; Yamoussoukro 70,000§; Daloa 60,837; Man 50,288; Korhogo 45,250.

Vital statistics

Birth rate per 1,000 population (1984): 45.0 (world avg. 29.0); legitimate, n.a.; illegitimate, n.a.
Death rate per 1,000 population (1984): 14.0 (world avg. 11.0).
Natural increase rate per 1,000 population (1984): 31.0 (world avg. 18.0).
Total fertility rate (avg. births per childbearing woman; 1984): 6.5.
Life expectancy at birth (1984): male 51.0 years; female 54.0 years.
Major causes of death per 100,000 population: n.a.; however, the major infectious diseases include malaria, dysentery, yaws, pneumonia, leprosy, and syphilis and gonorrhea.

National economy

Budget (1986). Revenue: CFAF 549,300,000,000. Expenditures: CFAF 549,300,000,000.
Public debt (external, outstanding; 1984): U.S.$4,834,600,000.
Tourism: receipts from visitors (1984) U.S.$72,000,000; expenditures by nationals abroad (1983) U.S.$180,000,000.
Production (metric tons except as noted). Agriculture (1984): sugarcane 1,800,000, plantains 850,000, cassava 800,000, rice 490,000, corn (maize) 468,000, cacao beans 411,000, pineapples 220,000, cotton 212,000, coconuts 170,000, palm oil 145,000, coffee 85,000; livestock (number of live animals) 1,400,000 goats, 1,400,000 sheep, 760,000 cattle; roundwood 12,190,000 cu m; fish catch (1983) 93,960. Mining and quarrying (1982): diamonds 37,000 carats. Manufacturing (1983–84): cement 1,000,000; wheat flour 148,000; raw sugar 126,500; cocoa powder 74,000; cotton fibre 58,400. Construction (in CFAF; 1982): 229,000,000,000. Energy production (consumption): electricity (kW-hr; 1984) 1,918,000,000 (1,918,000,000); coal, none (n.a.); crude petroleum (barrels; 1984) 10,027,000 (12,095,000); petroleum products (metric tons; 1984) 1,627,000 (1,246,000).
Gross national product (at current market prices; 1984): U.S.$6,030,000,000 (U.S.$620 per capita).

Structure of gross domestic product and labour force

	1982 in value CFAF '000,000,000	% of total value	labour force	% of labour force
Agriculture	651.1	26.2	2,750,000	65.0
Mining, manufacturing, and public utilities	406.0	16.3	338,000	8.0
Construction	126.3	5.1		
Transp. and commun.	177.6	7.1		
Trade, finance	689.1	27.7		
Pub. admin., defense, and services	288.9	11.6	1,140,000	27.0
Other	147.5	6.0		
TOTAL	2,486.5 ‖	100.0	4,228,000	100.0

Population economically active (1985): total 5,497,800; activity rate of total population 54.0% (participation rates: ages 15–64, n.a.; female, n.a.; unemployed, n.a.).

Price and earnings indexes (1980 = 100)

	1979	1980	1981	1982	1983	1984	1985
Consumer price index	87.2	100.0	108.8	116.8	123.7	129.0	131.4
Annual wage index	...	100.0	107.0	117.4	...	...	...

Household income and expenditure. Average household size (1980) 4.5; average annual income per household CFAF 500,000; sources of income: self-employment 49.9%, wages 44.9%, transfers and other resources 5.2%; expenditure (1979): food 51.1%, housing 11.6%, clothing 8.4%.
Land use (1983): forested 26.3%; meadows and pastures 9.4%; agricultural and under permanent cultivation 12.5%; other 51.8%.

Foreign trade

Balance of trade (current prices)

	1978	1979	1980	1981	1982	1983	1984
CFAF '000,000,000	−1.8	+6.0	+49.5	+7.8	+36.8	+92.5	+525.8
% of total	0.1%	0.6%	3.9%	0.6%	2.0%	6.2%	28.5%

Imports (1984): CFAF 658,569,000,000 (machinery and transport equipment 23.4%, of which nonelectrical machinery 7.6%, electrical machinery 6.1%; crude petroleum 12.6%; chemicals 12.6%; cereals 7.5%; dairy products 3.1%). *Major import sources:* France 32.9%; Nigeria 8.9%; W.Ger. 5.1%; Japan 3.8%.
Exports (1984): CFAF 1,184,347,000,000 (cacao beans 33.5%; coffee 15.5%; wood 11.5%; energy products 11.5%; cacao butter 6.0%; cotton 2.9%; canned fish 1.7%; chemicals 1.5%). *Major export destinations:* France 16.4%; The Netherlands 16.4%; U.S. 15.0%; Italy 6.4%; W.Ger. 5.2%; U.K. 3.4%.

Transport and communications

Transport. Railroads (1984): length 761 mi, 1,225 km; passenger-mi 533,000,000, passenger-km 857,800,000; short ton-mi cargo 363,000,000, metric ton-km cargo 530,200,000. Roads (1984): total length 33,390 mi, 53,736 km (paved 7%). Vehicles (1984): passenger cars 182,956; trucks and buses 52,491. Merchant marine (1985): vessels (100 gross tons and over) 61; total deadweight tonnage 175,325. Air transport¶ (1985): passenger-mi 210,389,000, passenger-km 338,590,000; short ton-mi cargo 39,311,000, metric ton-km cargo 57,396,000; airports (1986) with scheduled flights 15.
Communications. Daily newspapers (1984): total number 1; total circulation 80,000; circulation per 1,000 population 8.2. Radio (1984): 900,000 receivers (1 per 10.8 persons). Television (1984): 340,000 receivers (1 per 28.7 persons). Telephones (1980): 88,000 (1 per 94 persons).

Education and health

Education (1984–85)

	schools♀	teachers	students	student/teacher ratio
Primary (age 6–11)	4,419	31,297♁	1,179,456	...
Secondary (age 12–18)	218	4,569♀	245,342	...
Voc., teacher tr.	38	1,947□	44,481♀	...
Higher	1	1,204□	12,755	...

Educational attainment (1975). Percent of population over age 6 having: no formal schooling 75.3%; primary education 17.3%; secondary 5.1%; higher 0.5%. *Literacy* (1980): total population literate 1,560,000 (35.0%).
Health (1982): physicians 502 (1 per 17,847 persons); hospital beds 10,062 (1 per 891 persons); infant mortality rate per 1,000 live births (1984) 106.
Food (1980–82): daily per capita caloric intake 2,658 (vegetable products 93%, animal products 7%); 115% of FAO recommended minimum.

Military

Total active duty personnel (1985): 7,720 (army 79.0%, navy 8.9%, air force 12.1%). *Military expenditure as percent of GNP* (1984): 1.2% (world 6.1%); per capita expenditure U.S.$7.

*From 1986 Côte d'Ivoire has requested that the French version of the country's name be utilized as the official protocol version in all languages. †Preliminary. ‡Detail does not add to total given because of rounding. §1983. ‖ At current factor cost. ¶Air Afrique only. ♀1979–80. ♁1982. □1981.

Cuba

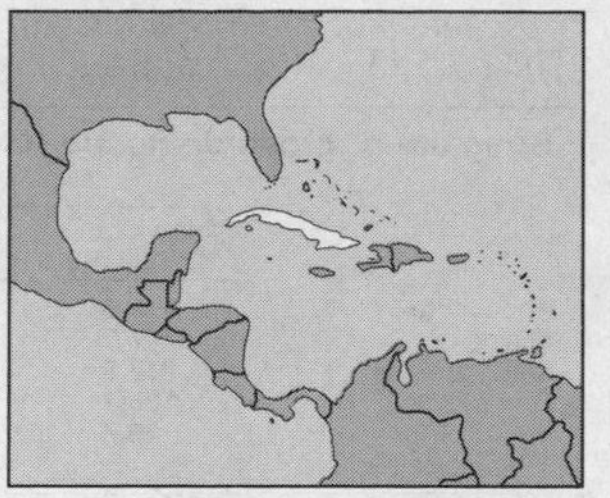

Official name: República de Cuba (Republic of Cuba).
Form of government: unitary socialist republic with one legislative house (National Assembly of the People's Power [499]).
Head of state and government: President.
Capital: Havana.
Official language: Spanish.
Official religion: none.
Monetary unit: 1 peso = 100 centavos; valuation (Oct. 1, 1986) 1 peso = U.S.$1.25 = £0.86.

Area and population

		area		population
Provinces	Capitals	sq mi	sq km	1985 estimate
Camagüey	Camagüey	5,466	14,158	697,200
Ciego de Avila	Ciego de Avila	2,441	6,321	337,900
Cienfuegos	Cienfuegos	1,613	4,177	339,500
Ciudad de la Habana*	—	281	727	1,992,600
Granma	Bayamo	3,229	8,362	758,400
Guantánamo	Guantánamo	2,388	6,184	473,100
Holguín	Holguín	3,589	9,295	941,000
La Habana†	Havana	2,197	5,691	606,600
Las Tunas	Las Tunas	2,542	6,584	457,300
Matanzas	Matanzas	4,532	11,739	577,600
Pinar del Río	Pinar del Río	4,194	10,861	660,700
Sancti Spíritus	Sancti Spíritus	2,599	6,732	411,000
Santiago de Cuba	Santiago de Cuba	2,382	6,170	942,700
Villa Clara	Santa Clara	3,067	7,944	782,100
Special municipality				
Isla de la Juventud	Nueva Gerona	849	2,200	65,500
TOTAL		42,803‡	110,860‡	10,043,200

Demography

Population (1986): 10,191,000.
Density (1986): persons per sq mi 238.1, persons per sq km 91.9.
Urban–rural (1986): urban 70.8%; rural 29.2%.
Sex distribution (1985): male 50.41%; female 49.59%.
Age breakdown (1985): under 15, 26.4%; 15–29, 29.5%; 30–44, 20.0%; 45–59, 12.8%; 60 and over, 11.3%.
Population projection: (1990) 10,653,000; (2000) 11,801,000.
Doubling time: 61 years.
Ethnic composition (1981): white 66.0%; mulatto 21.9%; black 12.0%; other 0.1%.
Religious affiliation (1980): nonreligious 48.7%; Roman Catholic 39.6%; atheist 6.4%; Afro-American Spiritist 1.6%; Protestant 1.4%; other 2.3%.
Major cities (1985): Havana 1,992,600; Santiago de Cuba 356,000; Camagüey 287,400; Holguín 194,100; Santa Clara 176,900.

Vital statistics

Birth rate per 1,000 population (1985): 18.0 (world avg. 29.0).
Death rate per 1,000 population (1985): 6.4 (world avg. 11.0).
Natural increase rate per 1,000 population (1985): 11.6 (world avg. 18.0).
Total fertility rate (avg. births per childbearing woman; 1980–85): 2.0.
Marriage rate per 1,000 population (1985): 7.9.
Divorce rate per 1,000 population (1985): 2.9.
Life expectancy at birth (1982–83): male 72.6 years; female 76.0 years.
Major causes of death per 100,000 population (1984): heart disease§ 175.3; malignant neoplasms (cancers) 117.1; cerebrovascular disease 61.3; accidents 39.5; pneumonia and influenza 37.1; suicide 21.0.

National economy

Budget (1983). Revenue: 12,128,200,000 pesos (government sector 98.6%; taxes 1.4%). Expenditures: 11,393,600,000 pesos (production capital 40.3%; education and public health 19.4%; social, cultural, and scientific activities 14.8%; defense, internal security 9.9%; housing, community services 5.5%).
Production (metric tons except as noted). Agriculture, forestry, fishing (1984): sugarcane 75,000,000, rice 555,000, oranges 410,000, sweet potatoes 335,000, potatoes 259,000, bananas 185,000, corn (maize) 97,000, tobacco 45,000, coffee 26,000; livestock (number of live animals): 6,400,000 cattle, 2,300,000 pigs, 759,000 horses; roundwood 3,132,000 cu m; fish catch (1985) 221,000, of which mackerel 72,000‖, spiny lobster 13,000. Mining and quarrying (1983): nickel 39,200; chromite 30,000. Manufacturing (1985): cement 3,182,300; fertilizers 1,159,700; crude steel 412,900; corrugated steel bars 300,500; cigarettes 17,961,200,000 units; cigars 366,300,000 units; tires 450,000 units; buses 2,393 units; sugarcane harvesters 606 units; beer 2,606,800 hectolitres¶; rum 489,700 hectolitres¶. Construction (1983): residential 2,035,900 sq m; nonresidential 1,389,500 sq m. Energy production (consumption): electricity (kW-hr; 1984) 12,300,000,000 (12,300,000,000); coal (metric tons; 1984) none (110,000); crude petroleum (barrels; 1984) 5,507,000 (50,797,000); petroleum products (metric tons; 1984) 6,226,000 (10,029,000); natural gas (cu m; 1984) 3,357,000 (3,357,000).
Household income and expenditure. Number of households (1981) 2,290,176; average household size (1981) 4.2; average annual income per household (1982) 3,680 pesos (U.S.$4,330); sources of income (1982): wages and salaries 57.3%, bonuses and other payments 42.7%; expenditure: n.a.
Population economically active (1981): total 3,617,620; activity rate of total population 37.2% (participation rates: ages 15–64, 58.5%; female 31.5%; unemployed *c.* 4.0%).

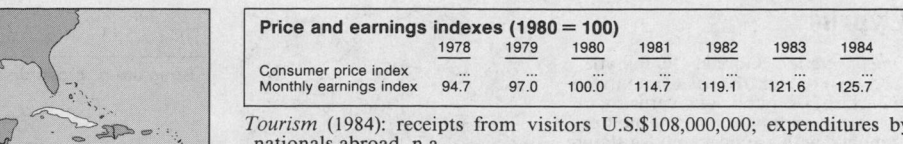

Price and earnings indexes (1980 = 100)

	1978	1979	1980	1981	1982	1983	1984
Consumer price index	...	...	...	...	...	...	...
Monthly earnings index	94.7	97.0	100.0	114.7	119.1	121.6	125.7

Tourism (1984): receipts from visitors U.S.$108,000,000; expenditures by nationals abroad, n.a.
Gross national product (1983): U.S.$15,760,000,000 (U.S.$1,590 per capita).

Structure of gross social product♀ and labour force

	1985		1984	
	in value '000,000 pesos	% of total value	labour force	% of labour force
Agriculture	3,815	13.9	608,600	19.5
Miningδ	295	1.1	665,700	21.4
Manufacturing	11,830	43.2		
Public utilities□	461	1.7		
Construction	2,393	8.7	308,500	9.9
Transportation and communication	2,030	7.4	212,700	6.8
Trade	6,435	23.5	367,200	11.8
Public administration	—	—	156,100	5.0
Services	—	—	781,600	25.1
Other	124	0.5	14,400	0.5
TOTAL	27,383	100.0	3,114,800	100.0

Public debt (external, outstanding; 1984◇): U.S.$5,403,000,000.
Land use (1983): forested 17.4%; meadows and pastures 22.5%; agricultural and under permanent cultivation 29.0%; other 31.1%.

Foreign trade

Balance of trade (current prices)

	1979	1980	1981	1982	1983	1984	1985△
'000,000 pesos	−187	−578	−1,290	−597	−693	−1,745	−250
% of total	2.6%	6.8%	13.2%	5.7%	5.9%	13.8%	2.3%

Imports (1984): 7,207,300,000 pesos (mineral fuels and lubricants 30.8%, machinery and transport equipment 30.5%, basic manufactures 13.3%, foodstuffs and beverages 11.2%). *Major import sources* (1985): U.S.S.R. 67.2%; East Germany 3.5%; China 2.9%; Japan 2.8%; Czechoslovakia 2.5%.
Exports (1984): 5,462,100,000 (sugar 74.9%, petroleum waste products 10.1%, nickel ore 5.3%, oranges 2.2%, shellfish 1.6%). *Major export destinations* (1985): U.S.S.R. 74.7%; East Germany 3.9%; Bulgaria 3.0%; China 2.7%.

Transport and communications

Transport. Railroads (1985)✝: route length 3,229 mi, 5,196 km; passenger-mi 1,466,000,000¶, passenger-km 2,360,000,000¶; short ton-mi cargo 1,927,000,000¶, metric ton-km cargo 2,814,000,000¶. Roads (1984): total length 21,000 mi, 34,000 km (paved 30%). Vehicles (1982): passenger cars 182,200; trucks and buses 152,400. Merchant marine (1985): vessels (100 gross tons and over) 423, total deadweight tonnage 1,236,163. Air transport (1985): passenger-mi 1,525,000,000, passenger-km 2,455,000,000; short ton-mi cargo 22,900,000‖, metric ton-km cargo 33,400,000‖; airports with scheduled flights, n.a.
Communications. Daily newspapers (1984): total number 16; total circulation 1,281,000; circulation per 1,000 population 128. Radio (1985): total number of receivers 2,140,000 (1 per 4.7 persons). Television (1985): total number of receivers 1,525,000 (1 per 6.6 persons). Telephones (1982): 406,355 (1 per 24 persons).

Education and health

Education (1984–85)

	schools	teachers	students	student/teacher ratio
Primary (age 6–11)	10,866	83,400	1,283,000	15.4
Secondary (age 12–17)	1,291	64,700	773,800	12.0
Voc., teacher tr.	605	23,600	312,900	13.3
Higher	33	15,900	192,900	12.1

Educational attainment (1981). Percent of adult population over age 25 having: no formal schooling and some primary education 39.6%; completed primary 26.6%; secondary 29.6%; higher 4.2%. *Literacy* (1980): total population over age 15 literate 6,087,000 (91.1%); males literate 3,101,000 (91.1%); females literate 2,986,000 (91.1%).
Health (1985): physicians (1984) 20,490 (1 per 493 persons); hospital beds 53,038 (1 per 190 persons); infant mortality rate per 1,000 live births 16.5.
Food (1980–82): daily per capita caloric intake 2,917 (vegetable products 77%, animal products 23%); 123% of FAO recommended minimum requirement.

Military

Total active duty personnel (1985)⊕: 161,500 (army 80.5%, navy 8.4%, air force 11.1%). *Military expenditure as percent of GNP* (1983): *c.* 8.0% (world 6.1%); per capita expenditure: *c.* U.S.$126.

*Province contiguous with the city of Havana. †Province bordering the city of Havana on the east, south, and west. ‡Includes 1,434 sq mi (3,715 sq km) of unpopulated cays not distributed by province. §Includes acute myocardial infarction, ischemic heart diseases, and diseases of pulmonary circulation. ‖1983. ¶1984. ♀Total domestic production excluding nonproductive services such as health, education, and defense. δIncludes metallurgy. □Electric energy production. ◇Includes external long-term private debt not guaranteed by the government. △First nine months only. ✝Figures exclude 5,989 mi (9,638 km) of railways serving sugar plantations or sugar factories. ⊕U.S. forces at Guantánamo total 2,400; Soviet forces total 4,600.

Cyprus

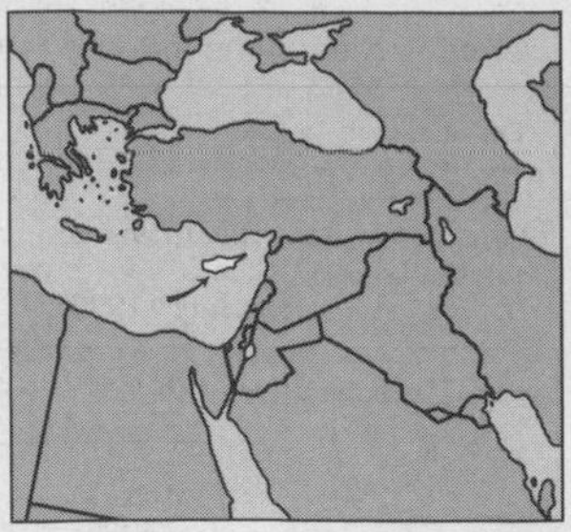

*Official name**: Kipriakí Demokratía (Kípros) (Greek)/Kıbrıs Cumhuriyeti (Turkish) (Republic of Cyprus).
Form of government: unitary multiparty republic with a unicameral legislature (House of Representatives [80]).
Head of state and government: President.
Capital: Nicosia.
Official languages: Greek; Turkish.
Official religion: none.
Monetary unit†: 1 Cyprus pound (£C) = 1,000 mils; valuation (Oct. 1, 1986) 1£C = U.S.$0.52 = £0.75.

Area and population

Districts	Capitals	area sq mi	area sq km	population‡ 1982 census
Famagusta	Famagusta	766	1,984	24,187
Kyrenia	Kyrenia	247	640	...
Larnaca	Larnaca	433	1,121	83,151
Limassol	Limassol	538	1,393	143,847
Nicosia	Nicosia	1,049	2,717	207,290
Paphos	Paphos	539	1,396	45,023
TOTAL		3,572	9,251	503,498

Demography

Population (1986): 674,000.
Density (1986): persons per sq mi 189.0, persons per sq km 73.0.
Urban-rural§ (1982): urban 63.6%; rural 36.4%.
Sex distribution§ (1983): male 49.76%; female 50.23%.
Age breakdown§ (1983): under 15, 25.0%; 15–29, 26.5%; 30–44, 20.3%; 45–59, 13.9%; 60–69, 7.2%; 70 and over, 7.1%.
Population projection: (1990) 708,000; (2000) 793,000.
Doubling time: 53 years.
Ethnic composition (1985): Greek 79.2%; Turk 18.7%; other 2.1%.
Religious affiliation (1980): Greek Orthodox 76.2%; Muslim 18.7%; other Christian 2.7%; other 2.4%.
Major cities (1982): Nicosia§ 123,298; Limassol 100,254; Larnaca 35,823.

Vital statistics§

Birth rate per 1,000 population (1984): 20.6 (world avg. 29.0); (1983) legitimate 99.7%; illegitimate 0.3%.
Death rate per 1,000 population (1984): 8.0 (world avg. 11.0).
Natural increase rate per 1,000 population (1984): 12.6 (world avg. 18.0).
Total fertility rate (avg. births per childbearing woman; 1983): 2.5.
Marriage rate per 1,000 population (1984): 7.8.
Divorce rate per 1,000 population (1984): 0.4.
Life expectancy at birth (1979–81): male 72.3 years; female 76.0 years.
Major causes of death per 100,000 population: n.a.; however major infectious diseases in 1983 included measles, leprosy, and tuberculosis.

National economy§

Budget ‖ (1987). £C 404,100,000 (1984; indirect taxes 45.9%; direct taxes 27.7%; interest, dividends, rents, and royalties 6.1%; sales of goods and services 5.8%). Expenditures: £C 540,300,000 (ordinary 81.3%; development 12.6%; special relief 6.1%).
Public debt (external, outstanding; 1985): U.S.$922,600,000.
Tourism¶ (1984): receipts from visitors U.S.$270,000,000; expenditures by nationals abroad U.S.$53,000,000.
Production (metric tons except as noted). Agriculture, forestry, fishing (1984): grapes 205,000, potatoes 180,000, oranges 147,000, barley 90,000, grapefruit 89,000, lemons 49,000, wheat 18,000; livestock (number of live animals) 500,000 sheep, 360,000 goats, 250,000 pigs, 43,000 cattle; roundwood 80,000 cu m; fish catch (1983) 2,058. Mining and quarrying (1984): iron pyrites 31,039; asbestos 8,215; terra umbra (brown earth) 7,362. Manufacturing (1984): cement 852,700; mosaic tiles 1,634,000 sq m; wine 442,100 hectolitres; beer 233,000 hectolitres; footwear 7,296,000 pairs; cigarettes 2,586,000,000 units. Construction (value added in £C; 1983) 130,500,000. Energy production (consumption): electricity (kW-hr; 1984) 1,250,000,000 (1,250,000,000); coal, none (none); crude petroleum (barrels; 1984) none (4,097,000); petroleum products (metric tons; 1984) 532,000 (830,000); natural gas, n.a. (n.a.).
Population economically active (1983): total 209,089; activity rate of total population 32.2% (participation rates: over age 15, 75.0%; female 39.2%; unemployed 3.7%).

Price and earnings indexes (1980 = 100)§

	1980	1981	1982	1983	1984	1985	1986♀
Consumer price index	100.0	110.6	117.7	123.6	131.1	137.6	139.5
Monthly earnings index	100.0	106.7	117.8	122.7	...	...	...

Household income and expenditure. Average household size§ (1982) 3.5; average annual income per household: n.a.; source of income: n.a.; expenditure (1981): food, beverages, and tobacco 28.1%, transport and communication 23.2%, household furnishings and operation 11.8%, clothing and footwear 10.8%, housing 8.4%, restaurants and hotels 8.4%, recreation 7.5%.
Land use (1983): forested 18.5%; meadows and pastures 10.1%; agricultural and under permanent cultivation 46.8%; other 24.6%.

Gross national product§♂ (at current market prices; 1984): U.S.$2,390,000,000 (U.S.$3,640 per capita).

Structure of gross domestic product and labour force§

	1984 in value £C '000,000	1984 % of total value	1984 labour force	1984 % of labour force
Agriculture	119.6	9.1	43,219	18.1
Mining	7.6	0.6	1,127	0.5
Manufacturing	212.5	16.2	44,237	18.6
Construction	135.1	10.3	21,901	9.2
Public utilities	25.7	1.9	1,528	0.6
Transportation and communication	117.8	8.9	11,515	4.8
Trade	233.8	17.8	40,695	17.1
Finance	} 462.1	} 35.2	8,569	3.6
Pub. admin., defense / Services			45,432	19.1
Other			20,059	8.4
TOTAL	1,314.2	100.0	238,282	100.0

Foreign trade§□

Balance of trade (current prices)

	1980	1981	1982	1983	1984	1985
£C '000,000	−236.6	−251.9	−322.8	−376.6	−381.4	−471.0
% of total	38.7%	34.7%	38.4%	41.5%	36.1%	44.8%

Imports (1985): £C 762,311,000 (machinery and transport equipment 26.2%, petroleum and petroleum products 16.9%, food and live animals 10.8%, cereals and cereal preparations 4.6%, iron and steel 3.9%, beverages and tobacco 2.1%). *Major import sources:* United Kingdom 13.6%; Italy 12.5%; France 9.4%; Japan 8.9%; Iraq 5.9%; United States 4.5%; U.S.S.R. 2.5%.
Exports (1985): £C 290,610,000 (clothing and accessories 17.1%, vegetables and fruit 15.9%, beverages and tobacco 8.5%, footwear 5.7%, machinery and transport equipment 4.5%, chemicals 3.7%). *Major export destinations:* United Kingdom 15.7%; Libya 7.2%; Saudi Arabia 7.0%; Iraq 3.8%; U.S.S.R. 3.1%; Egypt 2.6%; United Arab Emirates 2.5%; Yemen (Ṣan'ā') 1.7%.

Transport and communications

Transport. Railroads: none. Roads (1984): total length 7,156 mi, 11,517 km (paved 48%). Vehicles (1984): passenger cars 118,078; trucks and buses 43,095. Merchant marine (1985): vessels (100 gross tons and over) 844; total deadweight tonnage 14,299,321. Air transport (1984): passenger-mi 700,905,000, passenger-km 1,128,000,000; short ton-mi cargo 18,222,000, metric ton-km cargo 26,604,000; airports (1986) with scheduled flights 3.
Communications. Daily newspapers (1985): total number 11; total circulation 122,974; circulation per 1,000 population 91.7. Radio (1985): total number of receivers 300,000 (1 per 2.3 persons). Television (1985): total number of receivers 158,300 (1 per 4.1 persons). Telephones (1983): 164,000 (1 per 4.0 persons).

Education and health§

Education (1984–85)

	schools	teachers	students	student/teacher ratio
Primary (age 5–12)	396	2,193	47,381	21.6
Secondary (age 12–18)	93	2,644	43,511	16.5
Vocational	16	492	5,375	10.9
Higher	15	250	2,580	5.2

Educational attainment (1976). Percent of population over age 20 having: primary education 54.9%; secondary 36.7%; higher 7.7%. *Literacy* (1980): total population over age 10 literate 416,000 (89.0%); males literate 216,000 (93.5%); females literate 200,000 (84.5%).
Health (1983): physicians 741 (1 per 875 persons); hospital beds 3,576 (1 per 181 persons); infant mortality rate per 1,000 live births (1984) 14.9.
Food (1979–81): daily per capita caloric intake 3,378 (vegetable products 74%, animal products 26%); 136% of FAO recommended minimum requirement.

Military

Total active duty Greek Cypriot personnel (1986): 13,000 (army 100.0%). *Military expenditure* (1985): U.S.$62,183,000; per capita expenditure U.S.$31. *Total active duty Turkish Cypriot personnel* (1986): 4,500. *Military expenditure* (1985): U.S.$5,297,000; per capita expenditure U.S.$32.4.

*In July 1974 Turkey invaded Cyprus, and an autonomous Turkish-Cypriot administration was established in the northern part of the island. On Feb. 13, 1975, the occupied territory was declared the "Turkish Federated State of Cyprus." Following a unilateral declaration of independence in November 1983, the autonomous sector was renamed the "Turkish Republic of Northern Cyprus." The state is not recognized internationally. †Monetary unit of the Turkish sector is the Turkish lira (LT); valuation (Oct. 1, 1986) 1 U.S.$ = LT 706.37; 1 £ = LT 1,020.70. ‡Population for government-controlled areas (the Greek south) was officially 503,498. The 1986 estimated population for the Turkish sector was given as 163,000; the total population of the island therefore amounted to about 674,000 in that year. Its size, distribution, and makeup have been extensively altered since the Turkish invasion, now embodying internal refugees no longer resident in their home districts, recent Turkish immigrants, and international immigrants. §Data refer to government-controlled area only. ‖ *Budget* for the Turkish sector (1985). Revenue: LT 33,026,700,000 (foreign aid 40.9%, local taxes 33.2%, local loans 25.9%). Expenditures: LT 33,026,700,000 (investment 30.6%, personnel 28.6%, defense 8.1%). ¶The Turkish sector contains the two most popular resorts, Famagusta and Kyrenia. ♀July. ♂GDP for Turkish sector (1982) U.S.$206,000,000 (U.S.$1,346 per capita). □*Foreign trade* for the Turkish sector (1985). *Imports:* LT 74,747,536,000. *Major import sources* (1983): Turkey 38.4%; United Kingdom 17.1%. *Exports:* LT 23,697,892,000 (citrus fruit, potatoes, carob, tobacco). *Major export destinations* (1983): United Kingdom 45.4%; Turkey 12.8%.

Czechoslovakia

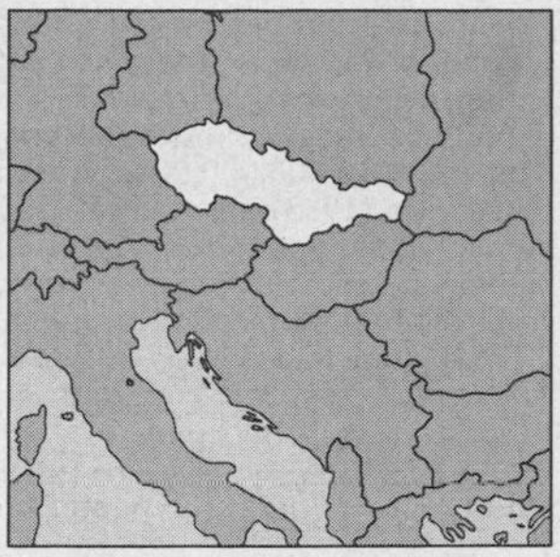

Official name: Československá Socialistická Republika (Czechoslovak Socialist Republic).
Form of government: federal socialist republic with two legislative houses (House of the People [200]; House of Nations [150]).
Chief of state: President.
Head of government: Premier.
Capital: Prague.
Official languages: Czech; Slovak.
Official religion: none.
Monetary unit: 1 koruna (Kčs) = 100 halura; valuation (Oct. 1, 1986) 1 U.S.$ = Kčs 5.75; 1 £ = Kčs 8.31.

Area and population

Republics / Regions	Capitals	area sq mi	area sq km	population 1985 estimate
Czech Socialist Republic	Prague			
Jihočeský	České Budějovice	4,380	11,345	694,900
Jihomoravský	Brno	5,802	15,028	2,057,200
Severočeský	Ústí nad Labem	3,015	7,810	1,181,800
Severomoravský	Ostrava	4,273	11,067	1,956,700
Středočeský	Prague	4,248	11,003	1,139,100
Východočeský	Hradec Králové	4,340	11,240	1,245,500
Západočeský	Plzeň	4,199	10,876	874,100
Slovak Socialist Republic	Bratislava			
Středoslovenský	Banská Bystrica	6,944	17,986	1,575,900
Východoslovenský	Košice	6,253	16,195	1,457,500
Západoslovenský	Bratislava	5,595	14,491	1,713,800
Capital Cities				
Prague	—	191	495	1,190,600
Bratislava	—	142	367	413,000
TOTAL		49,384*	127,903	15,500,100

Demography

Population (1986): 15,550,000.
Density (1986): persons per sq mi 314.9, persons per sq km 121.6.
Urban-rural (1985): urban 74.1%; rural 25.9%.
Sex distribution (1985): male 48.71%; female 51.29%.
Age breakdown (1985): under 15, 24.2%; 15–29, 21.4%; 30–44, 22.0%; 45–59, 15.9%; 60–74, 11.7%; 75 and over, 4.6%.
Population projection: (1990) 15,758,000; (2000) 16,278,000.
Doubling time: n.a.; population growth is negligible.
Ethnic composition (1984): Czech 63.8%; Slovak 31.0%; Hungarian 3.8%; Polish 0.4%; German 0.4%; Ukrainian 0.3%; other 0.3%.
Religious affiliation (1980): Roman Catholic 65.6%; atheist 20.1%; Czechoslovak Church 4.4%; Evangelist Church of Czech Brethren 1.4%; other 8.5%.
Major cities (1985): Prague 1,193,500; Bratislava 417,100; Brno 385,900; Ostrava 327,800; Košice 222,200.

Vital statistics

Birth rate per 1,000 population (1985): 14.5 (world avg. 29.0); (1983) legitimate 93.5%; illegitimate 6.5%.
Death rate per 1,000 population (1985): 11.8 (world avg. 11.0).
Natural increase rate per 1,000 population (1985): 2.7 (world avg. 18.0).
Total fertility rate (avg. births per childbearing woman; 1982): 2.3.
Marriage rate per 1,000 population (1985): 7.7.
Divorce rate per 1,000 population (1985): 2.5.
Life expectancy at birth (1985): male 67.2 years; female 74.4 years.
Major causes of death per 100,000 population (1985): cerebrovascular disease 340.4; ischemic heart disease 325.1; malignant neoplasms (cancers) 232.0; bronchitis, emphysema, and asthma 85.5; accidents, poisoning, and violence 76.3; diseases of the digestive system 47.1.

National economy

Budget (1984). Revenue: Kčs 343,805,000,000 (receipts from enterprises 71.7%; taxes 13.3%). Expenditures: Kčs 342,192,000,000 (education, health, social welfare, and culture 40.8%; national economy 39.2%; defense 11.8%).
Tourism: receipts from visitors (1984) U.S.$328,000,000; expenditures by nationals abroad (1983) U.S.$229,000,000.
Production (metric tons except as noted). Agriculture, forestry, fishing (1984): sugar beets 7,600,000, wheat 5,317,000, potatoes 3,700,000, barley 3,276,000, corn (maize) 722,000; livestock (number of live animals, 1985) 6,743,000 pigs, 5,150,000 cattle, 48,519,000 chickens; roundwood 18,800,000 cu m; fish catch 19,900. Mining and quarrying (1984): iron ore 1,869,000; copper 25,500; zinc 9,100. Manufacturing (1985): crude steel 15,036,000; rolled steel 11,037,000; cement 10,265,000; wood pulp and paper 1,700,000; sulfuric acid 1,298,000; plastic and resins 1,100,109; chemical fertilizers 935,376; cotton fabrics 606,365,000 m; beer 22,365,000 hectolitres; wine 1,205,000 hectolitres; road motor vehicles 231,657 units. Construction (1984): 7,052,000 sq m. Energy production (consumption): electricity (kW-hr; 1985) 80,628,000,000 (82,960,000,000); coal (metric tons; 1985) 128,532,000 (133,108,000); crude petroleum (barrels; 1984) 669,000 (126,570,000); petroleum products (metric tons; 1984) 13,373,000 (13,373,000); natural gas (cu m; 1984) 758,000,000 (11,274,000,000).
Public debt (external, outstanding, to the West; 1984): U.S.$3,600,000,000.
Land use (1985): agricultural 40.4%; forested 35.8%; meadows and pastures 13.0%; other 10.8%.
Gross national product (at current market prices; 1984): U.S.$83,947,000,000 (U.S.$5,400 per capita).

Structure of net material product and labour force

	1984 in value Kčs '000,000	% of total value	labour force	% of labour force
Agriculture	45,332	8.4	1,034,000	13.7
Mining and manufacturing	318,004	58.7	2,848,000	37.8
Construction	59,486	11.0	723,000	9.6
Public utilities	—	—	138,000	1.8
Transportation and communication	29,133	5.4	497,000	6.6
Trade	86,349	15.9	807,000	10.7
Finance	—	—	†	†
Pub. admin., defense	—	—	215,000	2.9
Services	—	—	1,272,000†	16.9†
Other	3,157‡	0.6‡	...	...
TOTAL	541,461	100.0	7,534,000	100.0

Population economically active§ (1985): total 7,580,450; activity rate of total population 49.0% (participation rates: working age, 86.9%; female 46.0%; unemployed, n.a.).

Price and earnings indexes (1977 = 100)

	1978	1979	1980	1981	1982	1983	1984
Consumer price index	103.3	106.4	109.5	110.4	116.0	117.1	118.2
Monthly earnings index	103.0	105.5	107.9	109.5	112.0	114.1	116.1

Household income and expenditure. Average household size (1984) 3.1; income per household Kčs 80,860 (U.S.$12,120); sources of income: wages and salaries 75.3%, welfare 10.4%, other 14.3%; expenditure (1984): clothing and footwear 26.9%, food 26.3%, services 12.6%.

Foreign trade

Balance of trade (current prices)

	1979	1980	1981	1982	1983	1984
Kčs '000,000	−5,604	−1,377	+1,413	+1,345	+826	+493
% of total	3.8%	0.9%	0.8%	0.7%	0.4%	0.2%

Imports (1984): Kčs 113,737,000,000 (machinery and transport equipment 31.6%, of which industrial machinery 9.6%, agricultural and construction machinery 8.4%, transport equipment 7.2%; crude petroleum and petroleum products 21.4%; food 7.2%; chemicals 6.7%; nonferrous metals 3.5%; iron and steel 3.2%). *Major import sources:* U.S.S.R. 46.8%; East Germany 10.4%; Poland 7.2%; Hungary 5.6%; West Germany 4.2%.
Exports (1984): Kčs 114,230,000,000 (machinery and transport equipment 56.3%, of which industrial machinery 13.4%, road vehicles and parts 9.3%, textile and leather machinery 4.6%; iron and steel 6.8%; mineral fuels and lubricants 6.5%; footwear 3.5%). *Major export destinations:* U.S.S.R. 43.4%; East Germany 8.8%; Poland 7.1%; Hungary 5.0%; West Germany 4.7%; Yugoslavia 4.1%; Bulgaria 2.8%; Austria 2.6%; Romania 1.7%.

Transport and communications

Transport. Railroads (1984): length 8,149 mi, 13,114 km; passenger-mi 11,734,000,000, passenger-km 18,884,000,000; short ton-mi cargo 46,785,000,000, metric ton-km cargo 68,309,000,000. Roads (1984): total length 46,535 mi, 74,891 km (paved 100%). Vehicles (1984): passenger cars 2,639,564; trucks and buses 412,860. Merchant marine (1985): vessels (100 gross tons and over) 19; total deadweight tonnage 276,647. Air transport (1984): passenger-mi 1,233,000,000, passenger-km 1,985,000,000; short ton-mi cargo 35,864,000, metric ton-km cargo 52,360,000; airports (1986) 14.
Communications. Daily newspapers (1984): total number 30; total circulation 4,353,000 ‖; circulation per 1,000 population 284. Radio (1985): total number of receivers 4,208,538 (1 per 3.7 persons). Television (1985): total number of receivers 4,346,022 (1 per 3.6 persons). Telephones (1985): 3,489,022 (1 per 4.4 persons).

Education and health

Education (1985–86)

	schools	teachers	students	student/ teacher ratio
Primary (age 6–14)	6,332	96,414	2,074,403	21.5
Secondary (age 15–18)	343	9,465	134,392	14.2
Voc., teacher tr.	562	16,740	261,422	15.6
Higher	36	19,131	168,699	8.8

Educational attainment (1980). Percent of adult population having: less than full primary education 1.2%; primary and less than full secondary 52.6%; full secondary 41.2%; higher 5.0%. *Literacy* (1980): total population over age 15 literate 11,524,716 (99.6%); males literate 5,525,860 (99.6%); females literate 5,998,856 (99.5%).
Health (1985): physicians 46,492 (1 per 333 persons); hospital beds 121,603 (1 per 127 persons); infant mortality rate per 1,000 live births 14.0.
Food (1980–82): daily per capita caloric intake 3,508 (vegetable products 67%, animal products 33%); 140% of FAO recommended minimum requirement.

Military

Total active duty personnel (1985): 203,300 (army 71.3%; navy, none; air force 28.7%). *Military expenditure as percent of GNP* (1983): 5.9% (world 6.1%); per capita expenditure U.S.$445.

*Detail does not add to total given because of rounding. †Finance is included with services. ‡Includes other activities of the material sphere. §Excludes women on maternity leave and includes workers of working age, which is 15–59 for men and 15–54 for women. ‖ 27 newspapers only.

Denmark

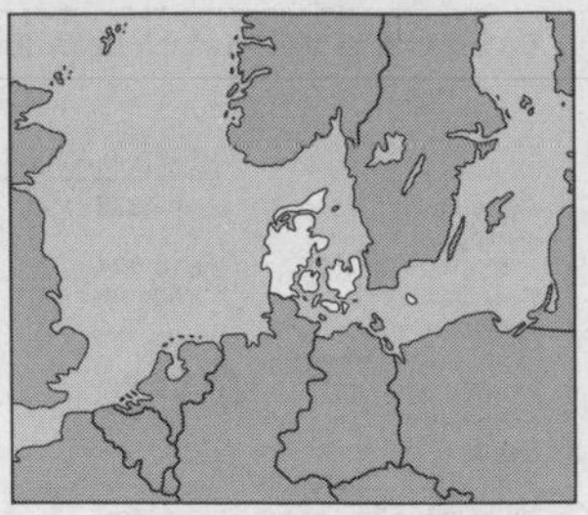

Official name: Kongeriget Danmark (Kingdom of Denmark).
Form of government: parliamentary state and constitutional monarchy with one legislative house (Folketing [179]).
Chief of state: Danish Monarch.
Head of government: Prime Minister.
Capital: Copenhagen.
Official language: Danish.
Official religion: Evangelical Lutheran.
Monetary unit: 1 krone (Dkr; plural kroner) = 100 øre; valuation (Oct. 1, 1986) 1 U.S.$ = Dkr 7.66; 1 £ = Dkr 11.06.

Area and population*

		area		population
Counties	**Capitals**	sq mi	sq km	1985 estimate†
Århus	Århus	1,761	4,561	582,200
Bornholm	Rønne	227	588	47,200
Frederiksborg	Hillerød	520	1,347	335,000
Fyn	Odense	1,346	3,486	454,300
København	—	202	522	612,200
Nordjylland	Ålborg	2,383	6,173	482,000
Ribe	Ribe	1,209	3,132	215,400
Ringkøbing	Ringkøbing	1,874	4,853	264,500
Roskilde	Roskilde	344	891	209,000
Sønderjylland	Åbenrå	1,517	3,930	249,700
Storstrøm	Nykøbing	1,312	3,398	257,100
Vejle	Vejle	1,157	2,997	326,800
Vestjælland	Sorø	1,152	2,984	278,800
Viborg	Viborg	1,592	4,122	230,400
Cities				
Copenhagen (København)	—	34	88	478,600
Frederiksberg	—	3	9	88,000
TOTAL		16,633	43,080‡	5,111,100‡

Demography

Population (1986): 5,112,000.
Density (1986): persons per sq mi 307.3, persons per sq km 118.7.
Urban-rural (1984): urban 84.2%; rural 15.8%.
Sex distribution (1986): male 49.27%; female 50.73%.
Age breakdown (1986): under 15, 18.3%; 15–29, 22.7%; 30–44, 22.6%; 45–59, 16.1%; 60–74, 13.9%; 75 and over, 6.4%..
Population projection: (1990) 5,098,800; (2000) 5,114,000.
Doubling time: n.a.; population has been declining since 1980.
Ethnic composition (1986): Danish 97.7%; other Scandinavian 0.5%; Turkish 0.4%; Yugoslavian 0.2%; other 1.2%.
Religious affiliation (1985): Evangelical Lutheran 91.5%; Roman Catholic 0.5%; Methodist 0.1%; Jewish 0.1%; other 7.8%.
Major cities (1985): Greater Copenhagen 1,358,540; Århus 252,071; Odense 171,468; Ålborg 154,750.

Vital statistics

Birth rate per 1,000 population (1985): 10.6 (world avg. 29.0); (1984) legitimate 58.1%; illegitimate 41.9%.
Death rate per 1,000 population (1985): 11.4 (world avg. 11.0).
Natural increase rate per 1,000 population (1985): −0.8 (world avg. 18.0).
Total fertility rate (avg. births per childbearing woman; 1984): 1.4.
Marriage rate per 1,000 population (1984): 5.6.
Divorce rate per 1,000 population (1984): 2.8.
Life expectancy at birth (1983–84): male 71.5 years; female 77.5 years.
Major causes of death per 100,000 population (1984): ischemic heart disease 325.3; malignant neoplasms (cancers) 284.2; cerebrovascular disease 101.2.

National economy

Budget (1985). Revenue: Dkr 201,162,000,000 (customs and excise taxes 45.5%, income and property taxes 41.1%, other 13.4%). Expenditures: Dkr 237,537,000,000 (social services 24.3%, education 6.8%, defense 5.0%, other 63.9%).
Public debt (1984): U.S.$40,612,000,000.
Tourism (1984): receipts from visitors U.S.$1,292,000,000; expenditures by nationals abroad U.S.$1,227,000,000.
Population economically active (1984): total 2,764,000; activity rate of total population 54.1% (participation rates: ages 15–64, 78.9%; female 47.6%; unemployed 10.0%).

Price and earnings indexes (1980 = 100)

	1979	1980	1981	1982	1983	1984	1985
Consumer price index	89.0	100.0	111.7	123.0	131.5	139.8	147.8
Hourly earnings index	89.8	100.0	109.0	120.6	128.5	134.6	140.5§

Household income and expenditure. Average household size (1986) 2.3; income per household (1981) Dkr 105,218 (U.S.$14,772); principal sources of income (1981): wages and salaries 59.1%, self-employment 14.3%, pensions and other 26.6%; expenditure (1983): housing 33.7%, food and beverages 22.0%, transportation and communication 15.8%, education, recreation, and culture 9.4%, clothing and footwear 5.7%.
Production (metric tons except as noted). Agriculture, forestry, fishing (1985): barley 5,252,000, sugar beets 3,516,000, wheat 1,996,000, milk 5,099,000; livestock (number of live animals) 2,617,700 cattle, 9,089,000 pigs; roundwood 2,194,000 cu m ‖; fish catch 1,657,500. Manufacturing (value added in kroner; 1984): fabricated metal products and machinery 41,516,000,000; food, beverages, and tobacco 22,561,000,000; chemicals and petroleum products 12,606,000,000; paper and printed products 10,606,000,000. Construction (1983): residential 2,264,000 sq m; nonresidential 3,184,800 sq m. Energy production (consumption): electricity (kW-hr; 1984) 22,361,000,000 (29,245,000,000); coal (metric tons; 1983) none (9,317,000); crude petroleum (barrels; 1984) 17,702,000 (49,888,000); petroleum products (metric tons; 1984) 7,052,000 (9,203,000); natural gas (1984) 242,175,000 (113,374,000).
Gross national product (at current market prices; 1984): U.S.$57,700,000,000 (U.S.$11,290 per capita).

Structure of gross domestic product and labour force

	1985		1984	
	in value Dkr '000,000	% of total value	labour force	% of labour force
Agriculture	29,932	5.8	165,000	6.0
Mining	6,826	1.3	3,000	0.1
Manufacturing	108,552	21.0	482,000	17.4
Construction	30,864	6.0	157,000	5.7
Public utilities	6,042	1.2	17,000	0.6
Transportation and communication	41,313	8.0	178,000	6.4
Trade	71,004	13.7	369,000	13.4
Finance	16,184	3.1	185,000	6.7
Pub. admin., defense	114,128	22.1	764,000	27.6
Services	109,556	21.2	147,000	5.3
Other	−17,025¶	−3.3	297,000♀	10.8
TOTAL	517,376	100.0‡	2,764,000	100.0

Land use (1983): forested 11.6%; meadows and pastures 5.7%; agricultural and under permanent cultivation 62.3%; other 20.4%.

Foreign trade

Balance of trade (current prices)

	1980	1981	1982	1983	1984	1985
Dkr '000,000	−13,717	−10,373	−10,692	−3,325	−6,972	−12,111
% of total	6.7%	4.3%	4.0%	1.1%	2.1%	3.3%

Imports (1985): Dkr 191,371,000,000 (machinery and transportation equipment 26.4%, of which road vehicles 7.4%; mineral fuels 17.0%, of which crude petroleum and petroleum products 13.7%; manufactured goods 15.7%, of which iron and steel 4.5%; chemicals and related products 8.7%; food and live animals 8.7%). *Major import sources:* West Germany 21.1%; Sweden 13.0%; United Kingdom 9.4%; United States 5.9%; The Netherlands 5.2%.
Exports (1985): Dkr 179,338,900,000 (food and live animals 26.8%, of which meat and meat preparations 11.5%, fish and shellfish 5.0%; dairy products 4.1%, machinery and transport equipment 21.8%; chemicals and related products 7.9%). *Major export destinations:* West Germany 15.8%; United Kingdom 12.2%; Sweden 12.1%; United States 10.1%; Norway 6.7%.

Transport and communications

Transport. Railroads (1984): length 1,521 mi, 2,448 km; passenger-mi 2,710,000,000, passenger-km 4,362,000,000; short ton-mi cargo 1,120,000,000, metric ton-km cargo 1,635,000,000. Roads (1984): total length 43,602 mi, 70,170 km (paved 100%). Vehicles (1984): passenger cars 1,439,993; trucks and buses 251,697. Merchant marine (1985): vessels (100 gross tons and over) 1,070; total deadweight tonnage 7,419,442. Air transport (1985): passenger-mi 1,937,000,000, passenger-km 3,118,000,000; short ton-mi cargo 87,447,000, metric ton-km cargo 127,671,000; airports (1986) with scheduled flights 12.
Communications. Daily newspapers (1984): total number 47; total circulation 1,837,000; circulation per 1,000 population 359. Radio (1985): total number of receivers 2,101,078 (1 per 2.4 persons). Television (1985): total number of receivers 1,945,551 (1 per 2.6 persons). Telephones (1984): 3,828,000 (1 per 1.3 persons).

Education and health

Education (1984–85)

	schools	teachers	students	student/teacher ratio
Primary (age 7–12)	2,557	34,541	415,148	12.0
Secondary (age 13–18)	3,247	36,105	339,835	9.4
Vocational	282	...	144,024	...
Higher	96δ	10,411δ	124,144	...

Educational attainment (1983). Percent of population over age 14 having: primary and secondary education 84.5%; some postsecondary 6.7%; graduated from university 8.8%. *Literacy* (1983): 99.5%.
Health (1984): physicians 12,806 (1 per 399 persons); hospital beds 36,405 (1 per 140 persons); infant mortality rate per 1,000 live births 7.7.
Food (1979–81): daily per capita caloric intake 3,548 (vegetable products 55%, animal products 45%); 127% of FAO recommended minimum requirement.

Military

Total active duty personnel (1985): 29,600 (army 57.4%, navy 19.3%, air force 23.3%). *Military expenditure as percent of GNP* (1983): 2.4% (world 6.1%); per capita expenditure U.S.$256.

*Excluding Greenland (*q.v.*) and the Faeroe Islands. †January 1. ‡Detail does not add to total given because of rounding. §June 1985. ‖ 1984. ¶Includes imputed bank service charges. ♀Includes 276,000 unemployed. δ1982–83.

Djibouti

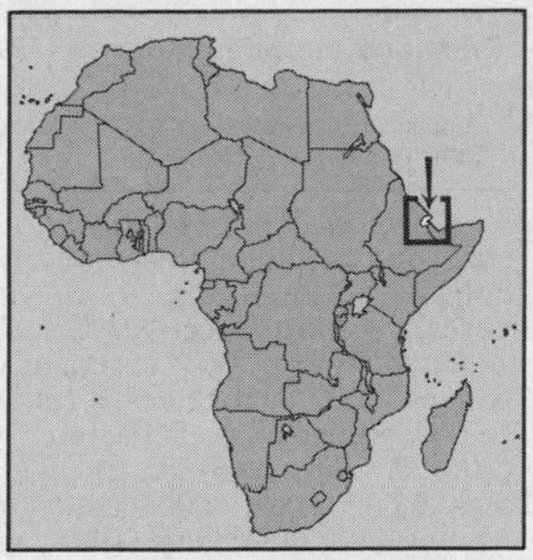

Official name: Jumhūrīyah Jībūtī (Arabic); République de Djibouti (French) (Republic of Djibouti).
Form of government: unitary single-party republic with one legislative house (National Assembly [65]).
Chief of state: President.
Head of government: Prime Minister.
Capital: Djibouti.
Official languages: Arabic; French.
Official religion: none.
Monetary unit: 1 Djibouti franc (DF) = 100 centimes; valuation (Oct. 1, 1986) 1 U.S.$ = DF 177.00; 1 £ = DF 255.77.

Area and population

Districts	Capitals	area* sq mi	area* sq km	population 1982 estimate
‘Ali Sabīḥ (Ali-Sabieh)	‘Ali Sabīḥ	925	2,400	15,000
Dikhil	Dikhil	2,775	7,200	30,000
Djibouti	Djibouti	225	600	200,000
Obock	Obock	2,200	5,700	15,000
Tadjoura (Tadjourah)	Tadjoura	2,825	7,300	30,000
TOTAL		8,950	23,200	335,000†

Demography

Population (1986): 456,000‡.
Density (1986): persons per sq mi 49.5, persons per sq km 19.1.
Urban-rural (1985): urban 75.0%; rural 25.0%.
Sex distribution (1982): male 49.28%; female 50.72%.
Age breakdown (1983): under 15, 38.0%; 15–29, 34.0%; 30–44, 17.0%; 45–50, 3.0%; 51 and over, 8.0%.
Population projection: (1990) 498,000; (2000) 670,000.
Doubling time: 23 years.
Ethnic composition (1984): Issa 47%; Afar 37%; European (mostly French) 8%; Arabic (mostly Yemeni) 6%; other 2%.
Religious affiliation (1983): Sunnī Muslim 94%; Christian 6%, of which Roman Catholic 4%, Protestant 1%, Orthodox 1%.
Major city and towns (1982): Djibouti 200,000§; ‘Ali Sabīḥ 4,000; Tadjoura 3,500; Dikhil 3,000.

Vital statistics

Birth rate per 1,000 population (1980–85): 49.2 (world avg. 29.0).
Death rate per 1,000 population (1980–85): 18.3 (world avg. 11.0).
Natural increase rate per 1,000 population (1980–85): 30.9 (world avg. 18.0).
Total fertility rate (avg. births per childbearing woman; 1980–85): 6.8.
Marriage rate per 1,000 population (1982): 6.7.
Divorce rate per 1,000 population (1982): 1.9.
Life expectancy at birth (1985): 45 years.
Major causes of death‖ (1984): percentage of total deaths from diarrhea and acute dehydration 16.0%; malnutrition 16.0%; intoxication 11.0%; tuberculosis 6.0%; acute respiratory disease 6.0%; malaria 6.0%; anemia 6.0%; heart disease 2.0%; kidney disease 1.0%; other ailments 19.0%; no diagnosis 11.0%.
Major reported diseases per 100,000 population (1984): diarrhea 2,219.0; gonorrhea 542.2, of which men 437.5, women 104.7; tuberculosis 380.0; malaria 296.8; syphilis 181.2, of which men 84.2, women 97.0; measles 64.0; viral hepatitis 59.3; whooping cough 21.5; leprosy 8.1; acute poliomyelitis 7.4; tetanus 2.5.

National economy

Budget (1985). Revenue: DF 22,585,800,000 (customs duties 47.4%; direct taxes 29.2%, of which licences and patent fees 7.1%, income tax 6.6%; foreign aid grants 6.6%; excises and stamps 4.1%). Expenditures: DF 22,-585,800,000 (general administration 41.7%; defense 21.0%; health 7.5%; education 6.8%; economic development 6.1%; debt payment 3.4%).
Public debt (external, outstanding; 1984): U.S.$62,600,000.
Tourism: n.a.
Production (metric tons except as noted). Agriculture¶, forestry, fishing (1984): vegetables and melons 12,000; livestock (number of live animals) 543,000 goats, 400,000 sheep, 54,000 camels, 44,000 cattle, 7,000 asses; fish catch 426♀. Mining and quarrying (1984): mineral production limited to locally used construction material and evaporated salt. Manufacturing (1984): n.a.; main items produced are furniture, nonalcoholic beverages, light electromechanical goods, and mineral water. Construction (1985): residential 32,214 sq m; nonresidential 21,722 sq m. Energy production (consumption): electricity (kW-hr; 1985) 164,245,000 (164,245,000); coal, none (n.a.); crude petroleum, none (n.a.); petroleum products (metric tons; 1984) none (64,000); natural gas, none (n.a.).
Population economically active: n.a.; unemployed (1985) *c.* 60%.

Price and earnings indexes (1975 = 100)

	1977	1978	1979	1980	1981	1982	1983
Consumer price index	136.6	163.4	187.6	210.5	222.2	217.0	...
Monthly earnings index	...	...	...	...	...	...	...

Gross national product (at current market prices; 1984): U.S.$301,540,000 (U.S.$740 per capita).

Structure of gross domestic product and labour force

	1984 in value DF '000,000	1984 % of total value	1982 labour force♂	1982 % of labour force
Agriculture	2,690	4.5	63	0.4
Mining	—	—	—	—
Manufacturing	4,920	8.2	726	4.5
Construction	4,490	7.5	2,309	14.3
Public utilities	1,942	3.2	456	2.8
Transportation and communication	6,010	10.0	2,711	17.0
Trade	9,400	15.6	3,148	19.5
Finance	6,530	10.8	1,296	8.0
Pub. admin., defense	16,170	26.8	3,347	20.7
Services	950	1.6	915	5.6
Other	7,132□	11.8□	1,168	7.2
TOTAL	60,234	100.0	16,139	100.0

Household income and expenditure. Average household size◇ (1982) 5.6; income per household: n.a.; source of income: n.a.; expenditure: n.a.
Land use (1983): forested 0.3%; meadows and pastures 9.1%; agricultural and under permanent cultivation¶; other 90.6%.

Foreign trade△

Balance of trade (current prices)

	1977	1978	1979	1980	1981	1982	1983
DF '000,000	−15,585	−25,963	−31,431	−35,699	−28,311	−37,965	−12,599
% of total	69.8%	80.4%	88.7%	88.9%	90.1%	89.5%	24.7%

Imports (1983): DF 39,307,000,000 (machinery and transport equipment 23.0%, of which electrical machinery and appliances 10.9%; food and live animals 19.1%; textiles and clothing 12.0%; petroleum products 9.4%; kat [a narcotic leaf] 9.0%; special transactions, including importation of gold coins, personal effects, and military goods, 4.8%; tobacco and tobacco products 4.3%). *Major import sources* (1983): France 35.4%; Ethiopia 9.7%; Japan 7.6%; The Netherlands 5.3%; Italy 4.3%; United Kingdom 3.8%.
Exports (1983): DF 1,919,000,000 (unspecified special transactions 89.6%, of which live animals [including camels] 30.8%, food and food products 18.6%). *Major export destinations* (1981): France 31.0%; Yemen (Ṣan‘ā’) 29.8%; Somalia 9.1%; Ethiopia 7.7%; The Netherlands 6.6%; United States 5.9%.

Transport and communications

Transport. Railroads (1984): length 66 mi, 106 km; short ton-mile cargo 90,-140,000, metric ton-km cargo 131,600,000✝. Roads (1983): total length 1,806 mi, 2,906 km (paved 11%). Vehicles (1985): passenger cars 12,049; trucks and buses 951. Merchant marine (1985): vessels (100 gross tons and over) 6; total deadweight tonnage 2,650. Air transport⊕ (1985): passenger arrivals 55,023, passenger departures 48,256; cargo loaded 1,655 metric tons, cargo unloaded 6,627 metric tons; airports (1986) with scheduled flights 3.
Communications. Daily newspapers: none. Radio (1985): total number of receivers 30,000 (1 per 14 persons). Television (1985): total number of receivers 11,300 (1 per 38 persons). Telephone subscribers (1985): 3,986 (1 per 108 persons).

Education and health

Education (1985–86)

	schools	teachers	students	student/ teacher ratio
Primary (age 6–14)	58	511**	25,212	...
Secondary (age 12–20)	8	231**	4,978	...
Voc., teacher tr.	12	110	1,984	12.5
Higher††	—	—	161	—

Educational attainment, n.a. *Literacy* (*c.* 1980): population over age 14 literate 11.9%; 8.8% if discounting the expatriate population.
Health (1985): physicians 68 (1 per 6,323 persons); hospital beds 1,283 (1 per 335 persons); infant mortality rate per 1,000 live births 200.
Food: n.a.

Military

Total active duty personnel (1985): 3,000 (army 95.7%, navy 1.0%, air force 3.3%)‡‡. *Military expenditure as percent of GNP* (1984): 9.0% (world, n.a.); per capita expenditure U.S.$67.

*Approximate figures given in sq km; sq mi equivalent rounded to appropriate level of generality. †Including 45,000 unaccounted, not shown separately. ‡About 17,000 Ethiopian refugees were still residing in Djibouti in late 1985. §District population. ‖ Infants and children to age 10, district of Djibouti only. ¶In 1985 only 900 ac (400 ha) of land were cultivated. ♀1983. ♂Salaried employees only. □Import duties, less imputed bank service charge. ◇City of Djibouti only. △The value of imports includes merchandise destined for Ethiopia and northern Somalia; that of exports excludes reexports coming from those areas. In 1980 the value of reexports from Ethiopia and northern Somalia was approximately five times greater than the value of domestic exports. ✝Based on total weight of Ethiopian exports and imports transported to and from the port of Djibouti. ⊕Djibouti International Airport only. **1984–85. ††1983–84. ‡‡In 1985, 3,800 French military personnel were also stationed in Djibouti.

Dominica

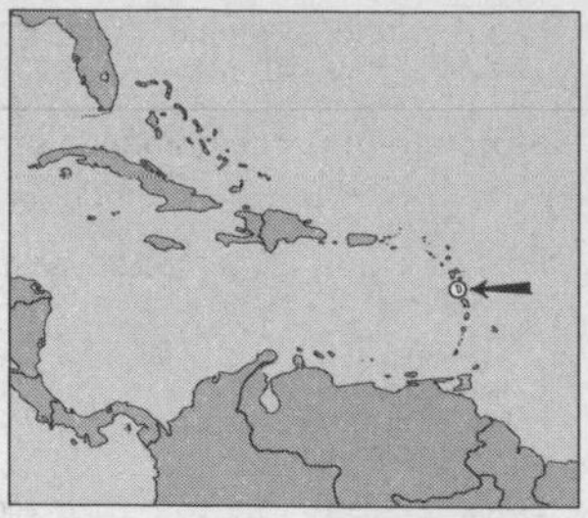

Official name: Commonwealth of Dominica.
Form of government: multiparty republic with one legislative house (House of Assembly [31]).
Chief of state: President.
Head of government: Prime Minister.
Capital: Roseau.
Official language: English.
Official religion: none.
Monetary unit: 1 East Caribbean dollar (EC$) = 100 cents; valuation (Oct. 1, 1986) 1 U.S.$ = EC$2.70*; 1 £ = EC$3.90.

Area and population

	area		population
Parishes	sq mi	sq km	1981 census
St. Andrew	69	179	12,748
St. David	49	127	7,337
St. George	21	54	20,501
St. John	23	60	5,412
St. Joseph	46	119	6,606
St. Luke	4	10	1,503
St. Mark	4	10	1,921
St. Patrick	32	83	9,780
St. Paul	26	67	6,386
St. Peter	11	29	1,601
TOTAL	290†‡	750†	73,795§ ‖

Demography

Population (1986): 86,200.
Density (1986): persons per sq mi 297.2, persons per sq km 114.9.
Urban-rural: n.a.
Sex distribution (1981)§: male 49.81%; female 50.19%.
Age breakdown (1981)§: under 15, 39.8%; 15–29, 28.6%; 30–44, 11.9%; 45–59, 9.2%; 60–74, 7.4%; 75 and over, 3.1%.
Population projection: (1990) 94,000; (2000) 119,000.
Doubling time: 45 years.
Ethnic composition (1981): black 91.2%; mixed race 6.0%; Amerindian 1.5%; white 0.5%; not stated 0.6%; other 0.2%.
Religious affiliation (1981): Roman Catholic 76.9%; Protestant 15.5%, of which Methodist 5.0%, Seventh-day Adventist 3.2%, Pentecostal 2.9%; other 7.6%.
Major towns (1981): Roseau 8,346; Marigot 3,554; St. Joseph 2,665; Portsmouth 2,220.

Vital statistics

Birth rate per 1,000 population (1984): 20.8 (world avg. 29.0); (1980) legitimate 35.0%; illegitimate 65.0%.
Death rate per 1,000 population (1984): 5.2 (world avg. 11.0).
Natural increase rate per 1,000 population (1984): 15.6 (world avg. 18.0).
Total fertility rate (avg. births per childbearing woman; 1980–85): 3.5.
Marriage rate per 1,000 population: n.a.
Divorce rate per 1,000 population: n.a.
Life expectancy at birth (1980–85): male 72.8 years; female 76.5 years.
Major causes of death per 100,000 population (1984): diseases of the circulatory system 197.8; malignant neoplasms (cancers) 88.6; diseases of the respiratory system 27.9; endocrine and metabolic disorders 26.7.

National economy

Budget (1983–84). Revenue: EC$106,300,000 (grants from abroad 34.4%, consumption tax 21.2%, income tax 17.6%, import duties 9.6%). Expenditures: EC$71,000,000 (education 18.0%, general administration 16.8%, health 14.3%, public debt 12.7%, police 9.3%, pensions 6.0%, transportation and communication 5.3%).
Tourism: receipts from visitors (1984) U.S.$4,500,000; expenditures by nationals abroad (1983) U.S.$700,000.
Gross national product (1984): U.S.$80,000,000 (U.S.$940 per capita).

Structure of gross domestic product and labour force

	1984		1981	
	in value EC$'000,000	% of total value	labour force	% of labour force
Agriculture	56.3	29.6	7,843	31.0
Mining	1.5	0.8	8	—
Manufacturing	13.8	7.3	1,417	5.6
Construction	14.7	7.7	2,306	9.1
Public utilities	5.5	2.9	245	1.0
Transportation and communication	21.7	11.4	914	3.6
Trade, hotels, restaurants	16.9	8.9	1,613	6.3
Finance, real estate, insurance	19.7	10.4	257	1.0
Pub. admin., defense	45.5	24.0	4,980	19.7
Services	2.4	1.3		
Other	−8.1¶	−4.3¶	5,700♀	22.7
TOTAL	189.9	100.0	25,333	100.0

Population economically active (1981); total 25,333; activity rate of total population 34.3% (participation rates: ages 15–64, 61.7%; female 34.1%; unemployed 18.7%♁).

Price and earnings indexes (1975 = 100)

	1979	1980	1981	1982	1983	1984	1985
Consumer price index	76.6	100.0	113.3	118.4	123.2	125.9	128.5
Earnings index	...	...	...	...	...	...	...

Household income and expenditure. Average household size (1981) 4.3; average annual income per household: n.a.; expenditure□: food and nonalcoholic beverages 56.9%, clothing and footwear 9.5%, housing 8.9%, alcoholic beverages and tobacco 8.3%, fuel and light 5.4%, other 11.0%.
Production (metric tons except as noted). Agriculture, forestry, fishing (1984): bananas 37,000, root crops (mostly dasheens and tanias) 25,000, coconuts 15,000, grapefruits 8,000, limes 6,000, oranges 2,000, cucumbers 1,800, cocoa 429, coffee 366, ginger 177; livestock (number of live animals) 9,000 pigs, 6,000 goats, 4,000 cattle; roundwood, n.a.; fish catch (1983) 1,500. Mining and quarrying (1983): pumice and volcanic ash 110,000. Manufacturing (1984): galvanized sheets 2,739; laundry soap 2,424; toilet soap, 1,644; coconut meal 789; edible coconut oil 6,600 hectolitres. Construction: n.a. Energy production (consumption): electricity (kW-hr; 1984) 20,200,000 (16,300,000); coal, none (none); crude petroleum, none (none); petroleum products (metric tons; 1984) none (12,000); natural gas, none (none).
Public debt (external, outstanding; 1983)◇: U.S.$42,000,000.
Land use (1983): forested 41.0%; meadows and pastures 3.0%; agricultural and under permanent cultivation 23.0%; other 33.0%.

Foreign trade

Balance of trade (current prices)△

	1980	1981	1982	1983	1984	1985†
EC$'000,000	−102.4	−82.3	−62.2	−47.5	−86.9	−57.5
% of total	66.1%	44.3%	32.0%	24.3%	38.6%	35.4%

Imports (1984): EC$156,104,000 (food 16.1%, of which meat 5.0%, flour 3.3%, dairy products 2.8%; electric and nonelectric machinery 13.9%; transport equipment 11.1%; metals and their manufactures 9.4%; petroleum products 6.1%; cardboard boxes 4.2%). *Major import sources:* United States 26.7%; United Kingdom 12.8%; Trinidad and Tobago 7.7%; Canada 7.7%; St. Lucia 5.5%; The Netherlands 3.2%.
Exports (1984): EC$69,226,000 (⊕bananas 44.6%; toilet soap 13.5%; galvanized sheets 9.8%; household soap 8.6%; refined coconut oil 4.3%; crude coconut oil 2.4%; grapefruit 2.3%). *Major export destinations:* United Kingdom 45.7%; Jamaica 15.6%; Trinidad and Tobago 14.1%; Antigua and Barbuda 4.3%; Barbados 3.0%; Grenada 2.7%.

Transport and communications

Transport. Railroads: none. Roads (1984): total length 489 mi, 787 km (paved 60%). Vehicles (1983): passenger cars 2,713; trucks and buses 1,250. Merchant marine (1985): vessels (100 gross tons and over) 4; total deadweight tonnage 2,144. Air transport (1984): passenger arrivals 33,954, passenger departures 34,381; cargo unloaded 196 metric tons, cargo loaded 271 metric tons; airports (1986) with scheduled flights 2.
Communications. Daily newspapers: none. Radio (1985): total number of receivers 35,000 (1 per 2.4 persons). Television: total number of receivers, n.a**. Telephones (1983): 4,505 (1 per 18.0 persons).

Education and health

Education (1982–83)

	schools	teachers	students	student/ teacher ratio
Primary††	66	584	17,456	29.9
Secondary	8	145	3,234	22.3
Voc., teacher tr.	1	13	121	9.3
Higher‡‡	...	59	284	4.8

Educational attainment (1981). Percent of population over age 15 having: no formal schooling 5.1%; primary education 78.5%; secondary 13.5%; higher 1.3%; other 0.5%. *Literacy* (1981): total population over age 15 literate 42,100 (94.9%).
Health (1984): physicians (1983) 26 (1 per 3,100 persons); hospital beds 237 (1 per 350 persons); infant mortality rate per 1,000 live births 23.9.
Food (1980–82): daily per capita caloric intake 2,155 (vegetable products 82%, animal products 18%); 89% of FAO recommended minimum requirement.

Military

Total active duty personnel (1985): none§§.

*Since July 1976 the par value has been U.S.$1.00 = EC$2.70. †Includes inland water area. ‡Detail does not add to total given because of rounding. §Excludes institutionalized population. ‖ Total population including institutionalized residents equalled 74,785. ¶Less imputed service charges. ♀Includes unemployed totaling 4,746. ♁1984 estimate of unemployment equalled 13.0%. □Weights of consumer price index components. ◇Includes external long-term private debt not guaranteed by the government. △Imports c.i.f. (cost, insurance, and freight); exports f.o.b. (free on board). Exports include reexports. †First nine months only. ⊕Breakdown based on domestic exports only totaling EC$67,307,000. **Dominica has no national television service. Cable television service is available in Roseau. ††1983–84. ‡‡1980–81. §§Defense force officially disbanded in 1981. 250-member police force has residual responsibilities for defense.

Dominican Republic

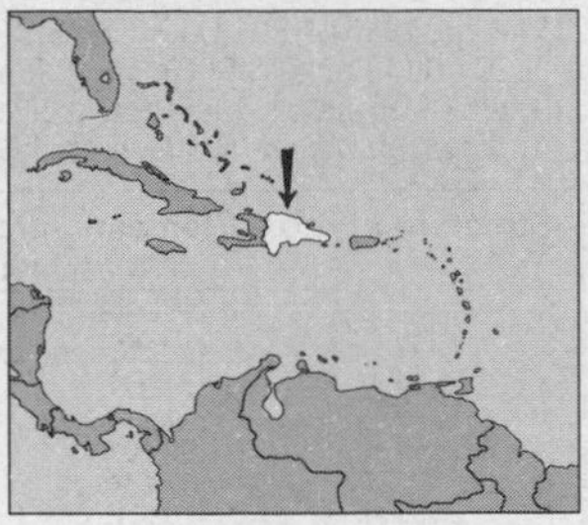

Official name: República Dominicana (Dominican Republic).
Form of government: multiparty republic with two legislative houses (Senate [27]; Chamber of Deputies [120]).
Head of state and government: President.
Capital: Santo Domingo.
Official language: Spanish.
Official religion: none.
Monetary unit: 1 Dominican peso (RD$) = 100 centavos; valuation (Oct. 1, 1986) 1 U.S.$ = RD$2.94; 1 £ = RD$4.25.

Area and population

Provinces	Capitals	area sq mi	area sq km	population 1981 census
Azua	Azua	938	2,430	142,770
Bahoruco (Baoruco)	Neiba	531	1,376	78,636
Barahona	Barahona	976	2,528	137,160
Dajabón	Dajabón	344	890	57,709
Duarte	San Francisco de Macorís	499	1,292	235,544
El Seibo	El Seibo	1,154	2,989	157,866
Espaillat	Moca	386	1,000	164,017
Independencia	Jimaní	719	1,861	38,768
La Altagracia	Higüey	1,191	3,084	100,112
La Estrelleta	Elías Piña	690	1,788	65,384
La Romana	La Romana	209	541	109,769
La Vega	La Vega	1,304	3,377	385,043
María Trinidad Sánchez	Nagua	506	1,310	112,629
Montecristi	Montecristi	768	1,989	83,407
Pedernales	Pedernales	373	967	17,006
Peravia	Baní	626	1,622	168,123
Puerto Plata	Puerto Plata	726	1,881	206,757
Salcedo	Salcedo	206	533	99,191
Samaná	Samaná	382	989	65,699
Sánchez Ramírez	Cotuí	453	1,174	126,567
San Cristóbal	San Cristóbal	1,445	3,743	446,132
San Juan	San Juan	1,375	3,561	239,957
San Pedro de Macorís	San Pedro de Macorís	450	1,166	152,890
Santiago	Santiago de los Caballeros	1,205	3,122	550,372
Santiago Rodríguez	Sabaneta	394	1,020	55,411
Valverde	Mao	220	570	100,319
National district				
Santo Domingo	—	570	1,477	1,550,739
TOTAL		18,704*	48,442*	5,647,977

Demography

Population (1986): 6,386,000.
Density (1986): persons per sq mi 341.4, persons per sq km 131.8.
Urban-rural (1985): urban 55.7%; rural 44.3%.
Sex distribution (1985): male 50.31%; female 49.69%.
Age breakdown (1985): under 15, 40.7%; 15–29, 30.7%; 30–44, 15.4%; 45–59, 8.5%; 60–74, 3.7%; 75 and over, 1.0%.
Population projection: (1990) 6,971,000; (2000) 8,407,000.
Doubling time: 28 years.
Ethnic composition (1982): mulatto 75%; white 15%; black 10%.
Religious affiliation (1984): Roman Catholic 93.7%; other 6.3%.
Major cities (1983): Santo Domingo 1,410,000; Santiago de los Caballeros 285,000; La Romana 101,000; San Pedro de Macorís 81,000.

Vital statistics

Birth rate per 1,000 population (1980–85): 33.1 (world avg. 29.0); (1976) legitimate 32.8%; illegitimate 67.2%.
Death rate per 1,000 population (1980–85): 8.0 (world avg. 11.0).
Natural increase rate per 1,000 population (1980–85): 25.1 (world avg. 18.0).
Total fertility rate (avg. births per childbearing woman; 1980–85): 4.2.
Marriage rate per 1,000 population (1981): 4.9.
Divorce rate per 1,000 population: (1981): 1.7.
Life expectancy at birth (1980–85): male 60.7 years; female 64.6 years.
Major causes of death per 100,000 population (1982): diseases of the circulatory system 87.1; infectious and parasitic diseases 47.8; diseases of the respiratory system 29.9; malignant neoplasms (cancers) 27.3.

National economy

Budget (1983). Revenue: RD$1,000,700,000 (tax revenue 82.3%, of which excise taxes 26.0%, import duties 23.6%, taxes on corporate profits 11.5%; nontax revenue 16.2%). Expenditures: RD$1,205,300,000 (general services 15.3%; education 15.3%; agriculture 12.9%; health 10.5%; defense 8.7%).
Public debt (external, outstanding; 1984): U.S.$2,388,300,000.
Tourism: receipts from visitors (1984) U.S.$277,000,000; expenditures by nationals abroad (1983) U.S.$87,000,000.
Production (metric tons except as noted). Agriculture (1984): sugarcane 11,750,000, plantains 605,000, rice 344,000, bananas 320,000, tomatoes 181,000, cassava 118,000, corn (maize) 76,000, coffee 49,000, cacao 44,000, tobacco 35,000; livestock (number of live animals) 1,994,000 cattle, 832,000 pigs, 465,000 goats, 204,000 horses; roundwood (1984) 969,000 cu m; fish catch (1983) 13,169. Mining (1984): ferronickel 64,000; silver 1,208,000 troy oz.; gold 338,000 troy oz. Manufacturing (1982): cement 958,600; fertilizers 175,200; cigarettes 3,612,000,000 units; molasses 295,100,000 litres; beer 86,300,000 litres. Construction (1983†): residential 777,000 sq m; nonresidential 398,000 sq m. Energy production (consumption): electricity (kW-hr; 1984) 4,009,000,000 (4,009,000,000); coal, none (none); crude petroleum (barrels; 1984) none (11,691,000); petroleum products (metric tons; 1984) 1,395,000 (2,021,000); natural gas, none (none).
Gross national product (at current market prices; 1984): U.S.$6,040,000,000 (U.S.$990 per capita).

Structure of gross domestic product and labour force

	1984 in value U.S.$'000,000‡	1984 % of total value	1981 labour force	1981 % of labour force
Agriculture	1,246	17.1	420,463	22.0
Mining	306	4.2	4,743	0.2
Manufacturing	1,281	17.6	224,437	11.7
Construction	505	6.9	80,850	4.3
Public utilities	128	1.8	13,891	0.7
Transp. and commun.	584	8.0	40,470	2.1
Trade	1,173	16.1	192,181	10.0
Finance, real estate	662	9.1	22,369	1.2
Pub. admin., defense	741	10.2	363,125	18.9
Other services	654	9.0		
Other	—	—	552,859§	28.9§
TOTAL	7,280	100.0	1,915,388	100.0

Population economically active (1981): total 1,915,388; activity rate of total population 33.9% (participation rates: ages 15–64, 53.6%; female 28.9%; unemployed [1986] 28.0%).

Price and earnings indexes (1980 = 100)

	1979	1980	1981	1982	1983	1984	1985
Consumer price index	85.7	100.0	107.5	115.8	121.3	154.0	207.5 ‖
Earnings index¶	95.4	100.0	107.2	118.5	...	...	...

Household income and expenditure. Average household size (1981) 5.1; average annual income per family (1975) urban family RD$2,299, rural family RD$654; source of income: n.a.; expenditure♀: food, beverages, and tobacco 51.7%, housing 23.9%, clothing and footwear 6.0%, other 18.4%.
Land use (1983): forested 13.0%; meadows and pastures 43.2%; agricultural and under permanent cultivation 30.2%; other 13.6%.

Foreign trade♁

Balance of trade (current prices)

	1980	1981	1982	1983	1984	1985
RD$'000,000	−463.8	−262.8	−491.3	−493.8	−389.0	−540.7
% of total	19.4%	9.9%	24.1%	23.9%	18.3%	26.9%

Imports (1983): RD$1,279,000,000 (crude petroleum 25.6%; food 9.5%, of which cereals 5.2%; petroleum products 9.3%; nonelectrical machinery 8.3%; iron and steel 3.6%; medicinal products 3.5%). *Major import sources* (1984): United States 32.4%; Venezuela 26.5%; Mexico 11.7%; Japan 4.7%.
Exports (1983): RD$785,200,000 (raw sugar 33.6%; gold alloy 19.2%; ferronickel 10.6%; coffee 9.7%; cacao 7.1%; furfural 2.9%). *Major export destinations* (1984): U.S. 72.1%; The Netherlands 7.0%; Puerto Rico 5.0%.

Transport and communications

Transport. Railroads (1985): length 994 mi, 1,600 km□. Roads (1982): total length 10,788 mi, 17,362 km (paved 29%). Vehicles (1983): passenger cars 94,601; trucks and buses 55,346. Merchant marine (1985): vessels (100 gross tons and over) 39; total deadweight tonnage 73,243. Air transport (1983)◇: passenger departures 684,000, arrivals 668,000; cargo loaded 22,400 metric tons, cargo unloaded 16,700 metric tons; airports (1986) 3.
Communications. Daily newspapers (1985): total number 9; total circulation 208,000; circulation per 1,000 population 33. Radio (1985): 227,000 receivers (1 per 28 persons). Television (1985): 392,000 receivers (1 per 16 persons). Telephones (1983): 175,054 (1 per 35 persons).

Education and health

Education (1983–84)

	schools	teachers	students	student/ teacher ratio
Primary (age 7–12)△	6,009	23,578	1,092,838	46.3
Secondary (age 13–18)			352,328	...
Voc., teacher tr.	...	...	27,670	...
Higher	5	...	91,115	...

Educational attainment (1970). Percent of adult population over age 25 having: no formal schooling 40.1%; primary education 45.9%; secondary 12.1%; higher 1.9%. *Literacy* (1985): total population over age 15 literate 2,860,000 (77.3%); males literate 1,447,000 (77.7%); females literate 1,413,000 (76.8%).
Health (1980)☨: physicians 2,142 (1 per 2,600 persons); hospital beds 8,953 (1 per 620 persons); infant mortality rate per 1,000 live births (1980–85) 75.0.
Food (1980–82): daily per capita caloric intake 2,147 (vegetable products 87%, animal products 13%); 95% of FAO recommended minimum.

Military

Total active duty personnel (1985): 22,200 (army 58.5%, navy 22.1%, air force 19.4%). *Military expenditure as percent of GNP* (1983): 1.5% (world 6.1%); per capita expenditure U.S.$20.

*Total includes 63 sq mi (163 sq km) of offshore islands not shown separately. †New building construction authorized. ‡At 1982 prices. §Includes not adequately defined work categories and unemployed persons not previously employed. ‖ Average of first nine months. ¶Monthly earnings index in manufacturing. ♀Weights of consumer price index components. ♁Imports and exports f.o.b. (free on board). □All track serves the sugar industry only except for 65 mi (104 km) for public transport. ◇Santo Domingo and Puerto Plata airports only. △1982–83. ☨Physicians and hospital beds under the auspices of the Institute of Social Security only.

Ecuador

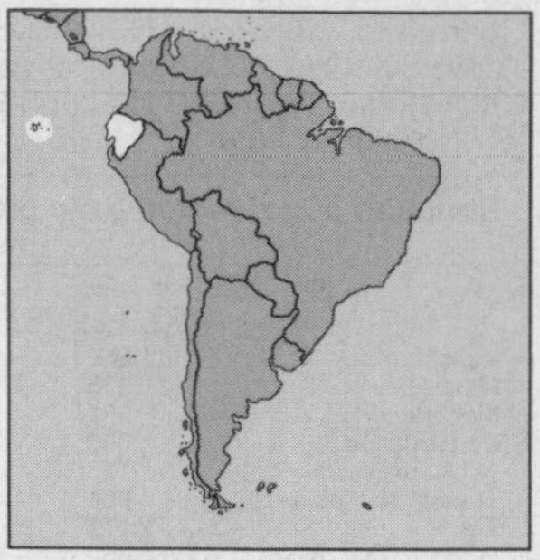

Official name: República del Ecuador (Republic of Ecuador).
Form of government: unitary multiparty republic with one legislative house (National Congress [71]).
Head of state and government: President.
Capital: Quito.
Official language: Spanish.
Official religion: none.
Monetary unit: 1 Sucre (S/.) = 100 centavos; valuation (Oct. 1, 1986) 1 U.S.$ = S/. 141.75; 1 £ = S/. 204.83.

Area and population

Regions / Provinces	Capitals	area sq mi	area sq km	population 1984 estimate
Coastal				
El Oro	Machala	2,281	5,908	337,800
Esmeraldas	Esmeraldas	5,854	15,162	279,700
Guayas	Guayaquil	8,256	21,382	2,317,400
Los Ríos	Babahoyo	2,459	6,370	506,800
Manabí	Portoviejo	6,990	18,105	998,800
Eastern				
Morona-Santiago	Macas	10,200	26,418	79,400
Napo	Tena	20,200	52,318	134,700
Pastaza	Puyo	11,687	30,269	35,900
Zamora-Chinchipe	Zamora	7,102	18,394	53,700
Sierra				
Azuay	Cuenca	3,124	8,092	490,000
Bolívar	Guaranda	1,599	4,142	163,100
Cañar	Azogues	1,344	3,481	191,200
Carchi	Tulcán	1,446	3,744	139,500
Chimborazo	Riobamba	2,338	6,056	362,000
Cotopaxi	Latacunga	2,007	5,198	302,900
Imbabura	Ibarra	1,921	4,976	271,500
Loja	Loja	4,429	11,472	393,200
Pichincha	Quito	6,404	16,587	1,581,900
Tungurahua	Ambato	1,201	3,110	360,100
Island territory				
Galápagos Islands	Puerto Baquerizo Moreno	3,086	7,994	7,200
TOTAL		103,930*	269,178	9,114,900†

Demography

Population (1986): 9,647,000.
Density (1986): persons per sq mi 92.8, persons per sq km 35.8.
Urban-rural (1986): urban 52.8%; rural 47.2%.
Sex distribution (1986): male 50.30%; female 49.70%.
Age breakdown (1982): under 15, 41.9%; 15–29, 28.1%; 30–44, 15.4%; 45–59, 8.6%; 60–74, 4.5%; 75 and over, 1.5%.
Population projection: (1990) 10,816,000; (2000) 14,395,000.
Doubling time: 24 years.
Ethnic composition (1980): Quechua 49.9%; mestizo 40.0%; white 8.5%; Amerindian 1.6%.
Religious affiliation (1984): Roman Catholic 92.1%; other 7.9%.
Major cities (1986): Guayaquil 1,509,100; Quito 1,093,300; Cuenca 193,000; Portoviejo 134,400; Machala 122,100.

Vital statistics

Birth rate per 1,000 population: (1984) 36.8 (world avg. 29.0); (1982) legitimate 67.9%; illegitimate 32.1%.
Death rate per 1,000 population (1984): 8.1 (world avg. 11.0).
Natural increase rate per 1,000 population (1984): 28.7 (world avg. 18.0).
Total fertility rate (avg. births per childbearing woman; 1985): 4.8.
Marriage rate per 1,000 population (1984): 5.9.
Divorce rate per 1,000 population (1984): 0.4.
Life expectancy at birth (1981): male 59.8 years; female 63.6 years.
Major causes of death per 100,000 population (1979)‡: respiratory diseases 127.1; intestinal diseases 105.3; circulatory diseases 97.0; accidents 61.9.

National economy

Budget (1985). Revenue: S/. 182,902,900,000 (income from petroleum 59.7%, production and sales tax 13.8%, import duties 12.7%, income taxes 7.8%). Expenditures: S/. 183,014,000,000 (education 24.3%, public debt service 24.0%, general public services 23.6%, transport and communication 12.7%, health 6.9%).
Public debt (external, outstanding; 1985): U.S.$7,084,000,000.
Tourism (1983): receipts from visitors U.S.$120,000,000; expenditures by nationals abroad U.S.$152,000,000.
Production (metric tons except as noted). Agriculture, forestry, fishing (1984): bananas 1,924,000, rice 470,000, potatoes 363,000, oranges 350,000, raw sugar 328,000, corn (maize) 300,000, cassava 243,000, pineapples 92,000, coffee (green) 90,000, cacao 60,000, palm oil 43,000; livestock (number of live animals) 4,278,000 pigs, 2,311,000 sheep, 3,300,000 cattle, 42,000,000 chickens; roundwood 8,228,000 cu m; fish catch 307,288§. Mining and quarrying (1984): limestone 1,600,000; silver 400 troy oz, gold 1,000 troy oz. Manufacturing (value in S/. '000,000; 1983): food products 19,432; petroleum products 16,446; textiles and clothing 6,495; beverages (including liquors) 2,706. Construction (in S/. ‖; 1983): residential 12,235,300,000; nonresidential 1,920,000,000. Energy production (consumption): electricity (kW-hr; 1985) 4,806,000,000 (3,817,000,000); crude petroleum (barrels; 1984) 99,207,000 (52,545,000); petroleum products (metric tons; 1984) 4,324,000 (3,978,000); natural gas (cu m; 1984) 410,300,900 (410,300,900).
Gross national product (1984): U.S.$10,340,000,000 (U.S.$1,130 per capita).

Structure of gross domestic product and labour force

	1984 in value S/. '000,000	1984 % of total value	1982 labour force	1982 % of labour force
Agriculture	106,041	13.5	786,530	33.0
Mining	127,135	16.2	7,050	0.3
Manufacturing	152,207	19.4	284,780	11.9
Construction	37,744	4.8	158,530	6.6
Public utilities	3,973	0.5	14,560	0.6
Transp. and commun.	54,232	6.9	103,850	4.4
Trade	131,678	16.8	266,640	11.2
Finance	43,734	5.6	38,420	1.6
Pub. admin., defense	55,245	7.0	614,240	25.7
Services	66,652	8.5		
Other	6,250	0.8	112,650	4.7
TOTAL	784,891	100.0	2,387,250	100.0

Population economically active (1982): total 2,387,250; activity rate of total population 29.7% (participation rates: ages 15–64, 50.1%; female 21.0%; unemployed [1981] 1.9%).

Price and earnings indexes (1980 = 100)

	1979	1980	1981	1982	1983	1984	1985
Consumer price index	88.5	100.0	116.4	135.3	200.8	263.6	337.3
Annual earnings index¶	75.0	100.0	116.3	126.9	...	...	...

Household income and expenditure. Average household size (1982) 5.1; average annual income per household (1982) S/. 28,747 (U.S.$956); sources of income (1982): self-employment 53.6%, wages and salaries 38.0%, interest, dividends, and rent 2.9%, social security 2.9%; expenditure (1982): food, beverages, and tobacco 33.8%, transportation and communication 13.0%, clothing 10.7%, housing and utilities 10.7%.
Land use (1983): forested 51.5%; meadows and pastures 16.6%; agricultural and under permanent cultivation 9.0%; other 22.9%.

Foreign trade♀

Balance of trade (current prices)

	1980	1981	1982	1983	1984	1985
U.S.$'000,000	+532.1	+646.4	+425.8	+971.6	+1,124.3	+1,285.9
% of total	12.0%	14.6%	11.0%	28.0%	27.8%	30.4%

Imports (1985): U.S.$1,690,020,900 (chemical products 18.1%, mineral products 12.9%, industrial machinery 10.9%, food products 6.2%, transport equipment parts 6.0%). *Major import sources:* United States 35.1%; Japan 9.4%; West Germany 7.8%; Brazil 6.6%; Italy 2.9%.
Exports (1985): U.S.$2,760,535,100 (crude petroleum 62.5%, bananas 6.9%, coffee 6.6%, cacao 4.9%, petroleum products 4.2%). *Major export destinations:* United States 54.6%; Panama 4.8%; Taiwan 3.7%; Colombia 2.5%.

Transport and communications

Transport. Railroads: (1985) route length 600 mi, 965 km; (1981) passenger-mi 40,600,000, passenger-km 65,300,000; (1981) short ton-mi cargo 21,900,000, metric ton-km cargo 32,100,000. Roads (1984): total length 22,194 mi, 35,718 km (paved 16%). Vehicles (1984): passenger cars 248,575; trucks and buses 32,624. Merchant marine (1985): vessels (100 gross tons and over) 152; total deadweight tonnage 624,779. Air transport (1982): passenger-mi 455,000,000, passenger-km 732,000,000; short ton-mi cargo 20,800,000, metric ton-km cargo 30,400,000; airports (1986) 14.
Communications. Daily newspapers (1985): total number 7; total circulation 538,000; circulation per 1,000 population 57. Radio (1985): 1,900,000 receivers (1 per 4.9 persons). Television (1985): 600,000 receivers (1 per 16 persons). Telephones (1982): 290,200 (1 per 28 persons).

Education and health

Education (1983–84)

	schools	teachers	students	student/teacher ratio
Primary (age 4–12)	13,011	50,347	1,677,364	33.3
Secondary (age 12–18)♂	1,315	29,319	459,647	15.7
Vocational	466	10,590	190,631	18.0
Higher	17	11,186	267,900	23.9

Educational attainment (1982). Percent of adult population over age 25 having: no formal schooling 25.4%; primary education 34.1%; secondary 7.9%; higher 7.6%. *Literacy* (1982): total population over age 10 literate 4,875,974 (85.2%); males literate 2,492,827 (87.9%); females literate 2,383,147 (82.6%).
Health (1984): physicians 11,000 (1 per 829 persons); hospital beds 15,455 (1 per 590 persons); infant mortality rate per 1,000 live births 68.4.
Food (1980–82): daily per capita caloric intake 2,081 (vegetable products 82%, animal products 18%); 92% of FAO recommended minimum requirement.

Military

Total active duty personnel (1985): 42,500 (army 82.3%, navy 10.6%, air force 7.1%). *Military expenditure as percent of GNP* (1983): 1.6% (world 6.1%); per capita expenditure U.S.$21.

*Detail does not add to total given because of rounding. †Total includes 66,100 persons not shown separately. ‡Excludes nomadic Indian tribes. §1983. ‖ Authorized construction. ¶For salaried industrial workers. ♀Import figures are f.o.b. in balance of trade and c.i.f. for commodities and trading partners. ♂Includes teacher training.

Egypt

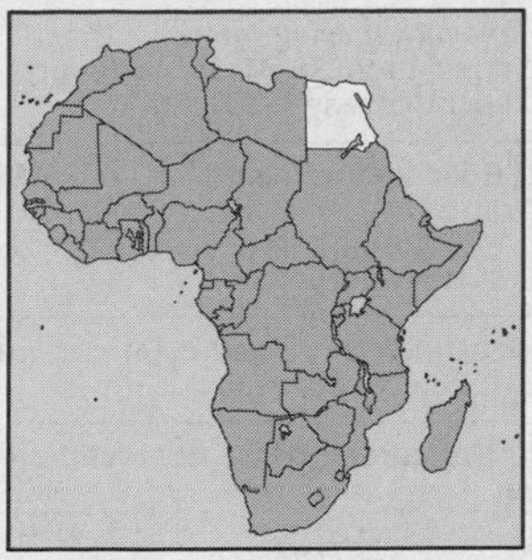

Official name: Jumhūrīyah Miṣr al-ʿArabīyah (Arab Republic of Egypt).
Form of government: republic with one legislative house (People's Assembly [458]).
Chief of state: President.
Head of government: Prime Minister.
Capital: Cairo.
Official language: Arabic.
Official religion: Islam.
Monetary unit: 1 Egyptian pound (LE) = 100 piastres = 1,000 millièmes; valuation (Oct. 1, 1986) 1 LE = U.S.$1.43 = £1.01.

Area and population

Regions / Governorates	Capitals	area sq mi	area sq km	population 1985 estimate
Desert				
al-Baḥr al-Aḥmar	al-Ghurdaqah	78,643	203,685	70,000
Maṭrūḥ	Marsā Maṭrūḥ	81,897	212,112	173,000
Sīnāʾ al-Janūbīyah	aṭ-Ṭūr	12,796	33,140	24,000
Sīnāʾ ash-Shamālīyah	al-ʿArīsh	10,646	27,574	152,000
al-Wādī al-Jadīd	al-Khārijah	145,369	376,505	113,000
Lower Egypt				
al-Buḥayrah	Damanhūr	3,911	10,130	3,199,000
ad-Daqahlīyah	al-Manṣūrah	1,340	3,471	3,469,000
Dumyāṭ (Damietta)	Dumyāṭ	227	589	728,000
al-Gharbīyah	Ṭanṭā	750	1,942	2,847,000
Kafr ash-Shaykh	Kafr ash-Shaykh	1,327	3,437	1,795,000
al-Minūfīyah	Shibīn al-Kawm	592	1,532	2,157,000
al-Qalyūbīyah	Banhā	387	1,001	2,186,000
ash-Sharqīyah	az-Zaqāzīq	1,614	4,180	3,318,000
Upper Egypt				
Aswān	Aswān	262	679	781,000
Asyūṭ	Asyūṭ	600	1,553	2,179,000
Banī Suwayf	Banī Suwayf	510	1,322	1,424,000
al-Fayyūm	al-Fayyūm	705	1,827	1,495,000
al-Jīzah	al-Jīzah	32,878	85,153	3,159,000
al-Minyā	al-Minyā	873	2,262	2,692,000
Qinā	Qinā	715	1,851	2,159,000
Sawhāj	Sawhāj	597	1,547	2,455,000
Urban				
Būr Saʿīd (Port Said)	—	28	72	374,000
al-Iskandarīyah (Alexandria)	—	1,034	2,679	2,821,000
al-Ismāʿīlīyah (Ismailia)	—	557	1,442	465,000
al-Qāhirah (Cairo)	—	83	214	6,205,000
as-Suways (Suez)	—	6,888	17,840	254,000
TOTAL		385,229	997,739	46,694,000

Demography

Population (1986): 48,009,000.
Density (1986): persons per sq mi 124.6, persons per sq km 48.1.
Urban–rural (1985): urban 48.8%; rural 51.2%.
Sex distribution (1985): male 50.90%; female 49.10%.
Age breakdown (1984): under 15, 39.0%; 15–29, 27.8%; 30–44, 16.1%; 45–59, 10.8%; 60–74, 5.3%; 75 and over, 1.0%.
Population projection: (1990) 52,536,000; (2000) 63,941,000.
Doubling time: 26 years.
Ethnic composition (1980): Egyptian 99.7%; other 0.3%.
Religious affiliation (1980): Sunnī Muslim 81.8%; Christian 17.8%; other 0.4%.
Major cities (1985): Cairo 6,205,000; Alexandria 2,821,000; al-Jīzah 1,608,400; Shubrā al-Khaymah 515,500; al-Maḥallah al-Kubrā 362,700.

Vital statistics

Birth rate per 1,000 population (1984): 37.4 (world avg. 29.0).
Death rate per 1,000 population (1984): 10.9 (world avg. 11.0).
Natural increase rate per 1,000 population (1984): 26.5 (world avg. 18.0).
Total fertility rate (avg. births per childbearing woman; 1984): 5.4.
Marriage rate per 1,000 population (1979): 9.4.
Divorce rate per 1,000 population (1979): 1.8.
Life expectancy at birth (1984): male 58.0 years; female 61.1 years.
Major causes of death per 100,000 population (1979): symptoms and ill-defined conditions 221.4; bronchitis, emphysema and asthma 53.4; pneumonia 47.3; ischemic heart disease 15.8.

National economy

Budget (1986–87). Revenue: LE 14,451,000,000 (sovereign tax 66.3%, oil revenue 5.3%, Suez Canal revenue 1.6%). Expenditures: LE 20,000,000,000 (debt servicing 13.5%, subsidies 8.7%, increase in the wages in the civil service and the state sector 5.9%).
Public debt (external, outstanding; 1984): U.S.$15,807,600,000.
Tourism (1983): receipts from visitors U.S.$285,000,000; expenditures by nationals abroad U.S.$151,000,000.
Production (metric tons except as noted). Agriculture, forestry, fishing (1984): corn (maize) 3,600,000, tomatoes 2,600,000, rice 2,230,000, wheat 1,815,000, watermelons 1,250,000, potatoes 1,200,000, millet 625,000, dates 450,000, dry onions 400,000, cotton (lint) 390,000; livestock (number of live animals) 2,410,000 buffalo, 1,825,000 cattle, 1,780,000 asses, 1,500,000 goats, 1,450,000 sheep, 82,000 camels, 28,000,000 chickens; roundwood 1,958,000 cu m; fish catch (1983) 140,000. Mining and quarrying (1983): iron ore 2,223,000; crude gypsum and anhydrite 721,340; fire clay 205,000. Manufacturing (1983): cement 3,794,000; cotton yarn 229,200; jute textiles 29,640; cotton textiles 7,716. Construction (1981): residential units 151,169.
Energy production (consumption): electricity (kW-hr; 1984) 22,870,000,000 (22,870,000,000); coal (metric tons; 1984) 1,100,000 (1,100,000); crude petroleum (barrels; 1984) 299,071,000 (141,790,000); petroleum products (metric tons; 1984) 18,206,000 (16,116,000); natural gas (cu m; 1984) 2,773,507,000 (2,773,507,000).
Gross national product (at current market prices; 1984): U.S.$33,340,000,000 (U.S.$700 per capita).

Structure of gross domestic product and labour force

	1986–87 in value LE '000,000	1986–87 % of total value	1984 labour force	1984 % of labour force
Agriculture	4,660.0	16.1	4,347,879	39.1
Mining }	9,598.3	33.2	39,730	0.3
Manufacturing }			1,703,955	15.3
Construction	1,384.0	4.8	588,267	5.3
Public utilities	266.9	0.9	76,750	0.7
Transp. and commun.	2,262.3	7.8	616,013	5.5
Trade	3,811.3	13.2	954,128	8.6
Finance	1,524.0	5.3	123,289	1.1
Pub. admin., defense	4,286.4	14.8 }	2,098,601	18.8
Services	1,126.8	3.9 }		
Other	...	...	584,589*	5.3*
TOTAL	28,920.0	100.0	11,133,201	100.0

Population economically active (1984): total 11,133,201; activity rate of total population 24.5% (participation rates: over age 15, 40.2%; female 5.7%; unemployed, n.a.).

Price and earnings indexes (1980 = 100)

	1979	1980	1981	1982	1983	1984	1985
Consumer price index	82.9	100.0	110.4	126.8	147.2	172.3	195.2
Earnings index	...	...	...	...	...	...	...

Household income and expenditure. Average household size (1984) 5.4; average annual income per household: n.a.; source of income: n.a.; expenditure† (1974–75): food 49.7%, clothing and footwear 14.2%, housing 12.4%, transportation 5.2%, tobacco 4.9%, recreation 1.3%.
Land use (1983): meadows and pastures 0.1%; agricultural and under permanent cultivation 2.5%; built-on, wasteland, and other 97.4%.

Foreign trade

Balance of trade (current prices)

	1980	1981	1982	1983	1984	1985
LE '000,000	−1,269.8	−3,924.5	−4,170.4	−4,982.0	−5,338.1	−4,373.1
% of total	22.9%	46.4%	48.8%	52.3%	54.8%	45.7%

Imports (1983): LE 7,192,700,000 (foodstuffs 25.2%, machinery and electrical apparatus 18.6%, transport equipment 12.1%, chemical products 6.1%). *Major import sources:* United States 16.1%; West Germany 10.6%.
Exports (1983): LE 2,250,300,000 (petroleum and petroleum products 56.8%, textile fibre and products 22.7%). *Major export destinations:* Italy 18.1%; France 9.5%; U.S.S.R. 7.3%; United States 6.6%; The Netherlands 3.9%.

Transport and communications

Transport. Railroads (1983–84): route length 2,700 mi, 4,346 km; passenger-mi 14,977,200,000, passenger-km 24,103,500,000; short ton-mi cargo 1,779,000,000, metric ton-km cargo 2,597,000,000. Roads (1983): total length 18,684 mi, 30,069 km (paved 47%). Vehicles (1983): passenger cars 597,869; trucks and buses 227,224. Merchant marine (1985): vessels (100 gross tons and over) 399; total deadweight tonnage 1,307,108. Inland water (1985): Suez Canal, number of transits 19,791; metric ton-km cargo 59,233,272,000. Air transport (1984): passenger-km 4,385,501,000; metric ton-km cargo 88,243,000; airports (1986) 11.
Communications. Daily newspapers (1985): total number 17; total circulation 4,822,350; circulation per 1,000 population 99.4. Radio (1985): 12,000,000 receivers (1 per 4.0 persons). Television (1985): 3,860,000 receivers (1 per 12.6 persons). Telephones (1982): 521,625 (1 per 82.4 persons).

Education and health

Education (1981–82)

	schools	teachers‡	students	student/teacher ratio
Primary (age 6–11)	11,761	140,146	4,748,414	...
Secondary (age 12–17)‡	2,715	78,086	2,060,100	26.4
Voc., teacher tr.‡	519	38,635	672,362	17.4
Higher	12	11,910	594,597	...

Educational attainment (1976). Percent of population over age 10 having: no formal education 82.9%; primary 9.9%; secondary 5.0%; higher 2.1%; postgraduate 0.1%. *Literacy* (1984): total population over age 15 literate 11,914,209 (43.0%); males literate 8,230,021 (58.9%); females literate 3,684,188 (26.8%).
Health (1984): physicians 73,300 (1 per 635 persons); hospital beds 85,350 (1 per 545 persons); infant mortality rate per 1,000 live births 104.5.
Food (1980–82): daily per capita caloric intake 3,157 (vegetable products 93%, animal products 7%); 127% of FAO recommended minimum requirement.

Military

Total active duty personnel (1985): 445,000 (army 71.9%, navy 4.5%, air force 23.6%). *Military expenditure as percent of GNP* (1983): 8.3% (world 6.1%); per capita expenditure U.S.$56.

*Unemployed seeking work for the first time. †Urban only. ‡1980–81.

El Salvador

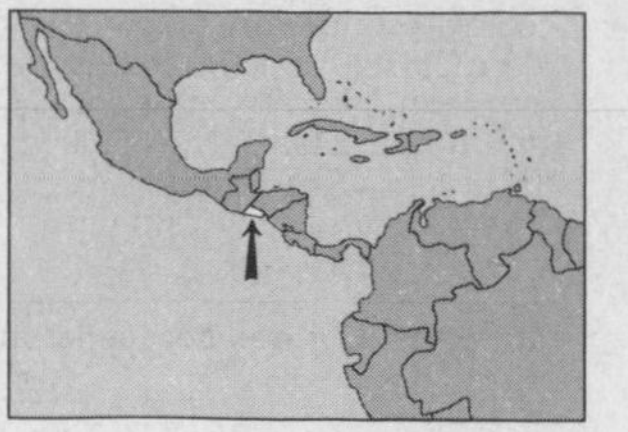

Official name: República de El Salvador (Republic of El Salvador).
Form of government: republic with one legislative house (Legislative Assembly [60]).
Chief of state and government: President.
Capital: San Salvador.
Official language: Spanish.
Official religion: none.
Monetary unit: 1 colón (₡) = 100 centavos; valuation (Oct. 1, 1986) 1 U.S.$ = ₡5.00*; 1 £ = ₡7.23.

Area and population

		area		population
Departments	Capitals	sq mi	sq km	1983 estimate
Ahuachapán	Ahuachapán	479	1,240	258,500
Cabañas	Sensuntepeque	426	1,104	191,000
Chalatenango	Chalatenango	779	2,017	248,100
Cuscatlán	Cojutepeque	292	756	215,000
La Libertad	Nueva San Salvador	638	1,653	417,200
La Paz	Zacatecoluca	473	1,224	266,100
La Unión	La Unión	801	2,074	331,900
Morazán	San Francisco (Gotera)	559	1,447	227,200
San Miguel	San Miguel	802	2,077	462,000
San Salvador	San Salvador	342	886	1,043,800
Santa Ana	Santa Ana	781	2,023	471,700
San Vicente	San Vicente	457	1,184	215,000
Sonsonate	Sonsonate	473	1,226	346,000
Usulután	Usulután	822	2,130	422,200
TOTAL		8,124	21,041	5,115,800†

Demography

Population (1986): 5,461,000.
Density (1986): persons per sq mi 672.2, persons per sq km 259.5.
Urban-rural (1985): urban 41.8%; rural 58.2%.
Sex distribution (1985): male 50.01%; female 49.99%.
Age breakdown (1985): under 15, 45.3%; 15–29, 27.8%; 30–44, 14.4%; 45–59, 7.8%; 60–74, 3.7%; 75 and over, 1.0%.
Population projection: (1990) 5,958,000; (2000) 7,406,000.
Doubling time: 30 years.
Ethnic composition (1980): mestizo (white and Indian) 93.7%; Indian 5.3%; white 1.0%.
Religious affiliation (1980): Roman Catholic 96.2%; Protestant 2.4%; other 1.4%.
Major cities (1984): San Salvador 455,300; Santa Ana 135,200; Mejicanos 89,000; San Miguel 86,700; Delgado 66,200.

Vital statistics

Birth rate per 1,000 population (1984): 29.8 (world avg. 29.0); (1980) legitimate 31.1%; illegitimate 68.9%.
Death rate per 1,000 population (1984): 6.0 (world avg. 11.0).
Natural increase rate per 1,000 population (1984): 23.8 (world avg. 18.0).
Total fertility rate (avg. births per childbearing woman; 1980–85): 5.6.
Marriage rate per 1,000 population (1982): 4.1.
Divorce rate per 1,000 population (1982): 0.4.
Life expectancy at birth (1981): male 61.7 years; female 65.3 years.
Major causes of death per 100,000 population (1983): signs, symptoms, and ill-defined conditions 141.6; homicide and injury and other violence 87.3; direct obstetric causes 71.4; intestinal and infectious diseases 46.5; accidents 42.0; bronchitis, emphysema, and asthma 18.5.

National economy

Budget (1984). Revenue: ₡1,701,000,000 (taxes on goods and services 37.0%, taxes on foreign trade 21.9%, income taxes 16.0%, foreign grants 9.4%, fees and charges 4.9%, property taxes 4.7%). Expenditures: ₡2,087,900,000 (defense 24.6%, economic services 18.4%, education 15.5%, general public services 14.6%, health 8.1%, social security and welfare 3.7%).
Public debt (1985): U.S.$1,400,400,000.
Tourism (1984): receipts from visitors U.S.$5,000,000; expenditures by nationals abroad (1983) U.S.$74,000,000.
Production (metric tons except as noted). Agriculture, forestry, fishing (1984): sugarcane 3,140,000, corn (maize) 509,000, coffee 166,000, sorghum 141,000, seed cotton 77,000, rice 60,000, bananas 55,000, dry beans 49,000, cassava 23,000, tobacco 5,000; livestock (number of live animals) 937,000 cattle, 379,000 pigs, 14,000 goats, 4,000,000 chickens; roundwood 4,620,000 cu m; fish catch (1983) 7,603. Manufacturing (value in ₡'000; 1984): processed food 1,827,983; refined petroleum products 617,361; beverages 357,224; chemical products 310,922; textiles 273,573; clothing and footwear 218,287; nonmetallic products 155,102; tobacco products 115,747. Construction (value in ₡'000; 1983): private residential 129,500, public and private nonresidential 213,900. Energy production (consumption): electricity (kW-hr; 1984) 1,671,463,000 (1,415,346,000); coal, none (n.a.); petroleum (barrels; 1984), none (4,501,000); petroleum products (metric tons; 1984) 575,000 (508,000); natural gas, none (n.a.).
Household income and expenditure. Average household size (1978) 5.1; income per household ₡8,650 (U.S.$3,460); source of income: n.a.; expenditure (1978): food 39.3%, housing 20.4%, transportation and communication 10.8%, clothing and footwear 9.4%, recreation 4.4%.

Population economically active (1980): total 1,593,353; activity rate of total population 35.5% (participation rates: over age 15, 60.3%; female 21.2%; unemployed [1982] 30%).

Price and earnings indexes (1980 = 100)

	1980	1981	1982	1983	1984	1985	1986‡
Consumer price index	100.0	114.8	128.3	145.3	162.1	198.1	265.8
Monthly earnings index	...	...	...	...	...	...	...

Gross national product (at current market prices; 1984): U.S.$3,820,000,000 (U.S.$730 per capita).

Structure of gross domestic product and labour force

	1984		1980	
	in value ₡'000,000	% of total value	labour force	% of labour force
Agriculture	2,354.9	20.6	636,617	40.0
Mining	17.7	0.2	4,394	0.3
Manufacturing	1,767.5	15.5	247,621	15.5
Construction	365.8	3.2	80,089	5.0
Public utilities	281.9	2.5	9,681	0.6
Transportation and communication	482.0	4.2	65,593	4.1
Trade	2,924.4	25.6	256,086	16.1
Finance	1,006.0	8.8	15,863	1.0
Public admin., defense	1,261.9	11.1	250,158	15.7
Services	947.7	8.3		
Other	—	—	27,251§	1.7§
TOTAL	11,409.8	100.0	1,593,353	100.0

Land use (1983): forested 5.9%; meadows and pastures 29.4%; agricultural and under permanent cultivation 35.0%; other 29.7%.

Foreign trade ‖

Balance of trade (current prices)

	1980	1981	1982	1983	1984	1985
₡'000,000	+457.8	−287.3	−234.6	−225.3	−449.1	−474.9
% of total	9.3%	6.7%	6.3%	5.8%	11.0%	12.3%

Imports (1984): ₡2,443,575,000 (chemical products 23.0%, of which medicinal and pharmaceutical products 6.2%, basic chemicals 4.4%; food products 13.8%, of which wheat 2.5%, corn 1.7%; crude petroleum 13.3%; electrical machinery and appliances 5.4%). *Major import sources:* United States 33.2%; Guatemala 19.2%; Mexico 10.0%; Venezuela 6.7%; Costa Rica 4.8%; West Germany 4.4%; Japan 4.3%.
Exports (1984): ₡1,793,432,000 (food products 71.4%, of which coffee 61.7%, unrefined sugar 3.6%, shrimp 3.3%; chemical products 5.6%; cotton and cotton products 3.4%). *Major export destinations:* United States 37.4%; West Germany 22.5%; Guatemala 16.4%; Japan 5.5%; Costa Rica 3.8%; Spain 2.1%; Netherlands Antilles 1.7%.

Transport and communications

Transport. Railroads (1984): route length 374 mi, 602 km; passenger-mi 2,903,000, passenger-km 4,672,000; short ton-mi cargo 17,417,000, metric ton-km cargo 25,429,000. Roads (1984): total length 7,549 mi, 12,149 km (paved 14%). Vehicles (1984): passenger cars 128,976; trucks and buses 19,284. Merchant marine (1985): vessels (100 gross tons and over) 11; total deadweight tonnage 3,318. Air transport (1985): passenger-mi 274,393,000, passenger-km 441,594,000; short ton-mi cargo 25,434,000, metric ton-km cargo 37,133,000; airports (1986) with scheduled flights 1.
Communications. Daily newspapers (1985): total number 6; total circulation 300,000; circulation per 1,000 population 57. Radio (1985): total number of receivers 1,000,000 (1 per 5.2 persons). Television (1985): total number of receivers 350,000 (1 per 15 persons). Telephones (1982): 86,316 (1 per 56 persons).

Education and health

Education (1983)

	schools	teachers	students	student/ teacher ratio
Primary	2,454	17,633	851,895	48.3
Secondary	279	5,642	82,573	14.6
Vocational	17	667	10,392	15.6
Higher	19	3,300	42,421	12.9

Educational attainment (1980). Percent of population over age 10 having: no formal schooling 30.2%; primary education 60.7%; secondary 6.9%; higher 2.3%. *Literacy* (1980): total population over age 15 literate 1,771,431 (69.0%); males literate 880,908 (73.2%); females literate 890,523 (65.3%).
Health: physicians (1981) 1,793 (1 per 2,701 persons); hospital beds (1979) 7,848 (1 per 584 persons); infant mortality rate per 1,000 live births (1984) 35.1.
Food (1979–81): daily per capita caloric intake 2,155 (vegetable products 88%, animal products 12%); 94% of FAO recommended minimum requirement.

Military

Total active duty personnel (1984): 41,650 (army 93.7%, navy 0.7%, air force 5.6%). *Military expenditure as percent of GNP* (1983): 4.3% (world 6.1%); per capita expenditure U.S.$32.

*Official rate. †Detail does not add to total given because of rounding. ‡July. §Includes unemployed. ‖ Import figures are f.o.b. (free on board) in balance of trade and c.i.f. (cost, insurance, and freight) for commodities and trading partners.

Equatorial Guinea

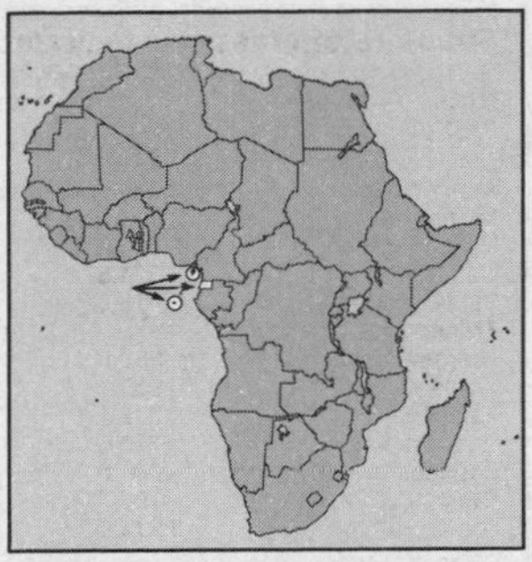

Official name: República de Guinea Ecuatorial (Republic of Equatorial Guinea).
Form of government: unitary single-party republic with one legislative house (National Assembly [41]).
Head of state and government: President.
Capital: Malabo.
Official language: Spanish.
Official religion: none.
Monetary unit: 1 ekwele (EK, plural bikwele) = 100 céntimos; valuation (Oct. 1, 1986) 1 U.S.$ = EK 332.05; 1 £ = EK 479.81.

Area and population

	area		population
			1983
Districts	sq mi	sq km	census
Annobón	7	17	2,000
Bioko Norte	779	2,017	46,000
Bioko Sur			10,969
Centro-Sur			52,393
Kie-Ntem			70,202
Litoral	10,038	26,000	66,370
Wele-Nzas			51,839
TOTAL	10,831*	28,051*	300,000†

Demography

Population (1986): 324,000.
Density (1986): persons per sq mi 29.9, persons per sq km 11.6.
Urban-rural (1985): urban 40.3%; rural 59.7%.
Sex distribution (1985): male 48.98%; female 51.02%.
Age breakdown (1980): under 15, 41.5%; 15–29, 25.8%; 30–44, 15.6%; 45–59, 10.6%; 60–74, 5.4%; 75 and over, 1.1%.
Population projection: (1990) 359,000; (2000) 438,000.
Doubling time: 27 years.
Ethnic composition (1978): Fang 71.5%; Bubi 14.3%; Duala 2.9%; Ibibio 1.4%; other 9.9%.
Religious affiliation (1980): Christian (mostly Roman Catholic) 88.8%; tribal 4.6%; atheist 1.4%; Muslim 0.5%; other 0.2%; none 4.5%.
Major city (1983): Malabo 37,500.

Vital statistics

Birth rate per 1,000 population (1980–85): 42.2 (world avg. 29.0); legitimate, n.a.; illegitimate, n.a.
Death rate per 1,000 population (1980–85): 17.6 (world avg. 11.0).
Natural increase rate per 1,000 population (1980–85): 24.6 (world avg. 18.0).
Total fertility rate (avg. births per childbearing woman; 1980–85): 5.7.
Marriage rate per 1,000 population: n.a.
Divorce rate per 1,000 population: n.a.
Life expectancy at birth (1980–85): male 46.9 years; female 50.1 years.
Major causes of death per 100,000 population: n.a.; however, major diseases include cholera, leprosy, trypanosomiasis (sleeping sickness), malaria, and waterborne (especially gastrointestinal) diseases.

National economy

Budget (1982). Revenue: EK 2,980,000,000 (direct and indirect taxes 75.9%, sales of goods and services 13.7%). Expenditures: EK 4,038,000,000 (1981; wages and salaries 65.9%, goods and services 20.4%, capital expenditure 10.6%).
Public debt (external, outstanding; 1984): U.S.$102,600,000.
Tourism (1986):‡.
Gross national product (at current market prices; 1983): U.S.$60,000,000 (U.S.$197 per capita).

Structure of gross domestic product and labour force

	1983		1985	
	in value EK '000,000	% of total value	labour force	% of labour force
Agriculture	2,490	41.3	103,000	60.9
Manufacturing			...	...
Construction			...	...
Public utilities	710	11.8	...	...
Transportation and communication			...	...
Trade			...	...
Finance			...	...
Pub. admin., defense	2,830	46.9	...	...
Services			...	...
Other			66,000	39.1
TOTAL	6,030	100.0	169,000	100.0

Production (metric tons except as noted). Agriculture, forestry, fishing (1985): roots and tubers 90,000, cassava 55,000, sweet potatoes 35,000, bananas 18,000, fruit excluding melons 18,000, coconuts 8,000, coffee 7,000, cacao beans 7,000, palm oil 5,000, palm kernels 2,800; livestock (number of live animals) 35,000 sheep, 7,000 goats, 5,000 pigs, 4,000 cattle, 160,000 chickens; roundwood (1984) 587,000 cu m; fish catch (1984) 4,000. Mining and quarrying: n.a.; however, iron ore, lead, zinc, manganese, and molybdenum are present in the sedimentary rocks; traces of gold, diamonds, and radioactive ores have also been located. Manufacturing (1979): sawn wood 16,000 cu m. Construction: n.a. Energy production (consumption): electricity (kW-hr; 1983) 15,000,000 (15,000,000); coal, none (n.a.); crude petroleum (1984)§, none (n.a.); petroleum products (metric tons; 1983) none (26,000); natural gas, none (n.a.).
Population economically active (1984): total 111,000; activity rate of total population 36.5% (participation rates: over age 15, 61.0%; female, n.a.; unemployed, n.a.).
Price and earnings indexes: n.a.
Household income and expenditure. Average household size (1980) 4.5; average annual income per household: n.a.; source of income: n.a.; expenditure: n.a.
Land use (1984): forested 46.2%; meadows and pastures 3.7%; agricultural and under permanent cultivation 8.2%; built-on, wasteland, and other 41.9%.

Foreign trade

Balance of trade (current prices)

	1978	1979	1980	1981	1982‖	1983‖
EK '000,000	+547.6	+351.9	−4,704.0	−5,400.0	−6,657.0	−9,326.0
% of total	18.6%	9.8%	54.8%	51.1%	27.5%	29.3%

Imports (1981): EK 7,982,000,000 (food, beverages, and tobacco 24.9%; petroleum and petroleum products 22.4%; motor vehicles and machinery 17.4%; iron and steel products 12.4%; clothing 6.0%). *Major import sources* (1985): Spain 30.2%; France 23.6%; Italy 14.6%; The Netherlands 4.8%; West Germany 4.1%; Belgium–Luxembourg 3.0%; China 2.4%; United States 1.9%; Japan 1.7%; Norway 1.5%; United Kingdom 1.1%; Switzerland 0.9%.
Exports (1981): EK 2,582,000,000 (cacao 71.5%; timber 24.4%; coffee 2.8%). *Major export destinations* (1985): The Netherlands 37.6%; Spain 31.5%; West Germany 16.4%; Italy 5.0%; France 2.2%; Switzerland 1.4%; Portugal 1.3%; Belgium–Luxembourg 0.7%; Greece 0.3%.

Transport and communications

Transport. Railroads: none. Roads (1982): total length 1,715 mi, 2,760 km (paved 12%). Vehicles (1979): passenger cars 4,000; trucks and buses 3,000. Merchant marine (1985): vessels (100 gross tons and over) 2; total deadweight tonnage 6,700. Air transport (1980): passenger-mi 4,000,000, passenger-km 7,000,000; short ton-mi cargo 700,000, metric ton-km cargo 1,000,000; airports (1986) with scheduled flights 2.
Communications. Daily newspapers (1985): total number 2; total circulation 1,000; circulation per 1,000 population 3. Radio (1984): total number of receivers 90,000 (1 per 3.5 persons). Television (1984): total number of receivers 2,100 (1 per 148 persons). Telephones (1982): 1,366 (1 per 220 persons).

Education and health

Education (1980–81)

	schools	teachers	students	student/ teacher ratio
Primary (age 6–11)	511	647	40,110	62.0
Secondary (age 12–17), voc., teacher tr.¶	14	288	3,013	10.5

Educational attainment, n.a. *Literacy* (1980): total population literate, about 55%.
Health: physicians (1977) 5 (1 per 64,000 persons); hospital beds (1982) 3,200 (1 per 95 persons); infant mortality rate per 1,000 live births (1983) 137.
Food (1981–83): daily per capita caloric intake, n.a.; FAO recommended minimum daily requirement for the region is 2,300 calories.

Military

Total active duty personnel (1986): 2,300 (army 87.0%, navy 6.5%, air force 6.5%). *Military expenditure as percent of GNP* (1981): 1.8% (world 5.8%); per capita expenditure U.S.$9.

*Total area includes the coastal islands of Corisco (6 sq mi [15 sq km]), Great Elobey (1 sq mi [2 sq km], and Little Elobey. †Detail does not add to total given because of rounding; total population includes the coastal islands of Corisco, Great Elobey, and Little Elobey. ‡Tourism remains undeveloped. §A group of petroleum companies signed an exploration and production-sharing agreement with the government in 1984. The agreement covered a 2,200-sq-km area off Rio Muni and called for sonar exploration and two exploratory wells during the initial 3-year period. ‖ Estimate. ¶Efforts are being undertaken to provide the level of training necessary to nondegree teachers in service. Also, teacher training schools will be expanded in order to increase the number of primary school teachers.

Ethiopia

Official name: Hebretasebawit Etiyop'iya (Socialist Ethiopia).
Form of government: socialist state ruled by a Provisional Military Administrative Council (PMAC).
Head of state and government: Chairman of the PMAC and of the Council of Ministers.
Capital: Addis Ababa.
Official language: Amharic.
Official religion: none.
Monetary unit: 1 Ethiopian Birr (Br) = 100 cents; valuation (Oct. 1, 1986) 1 U.S.$ = Br 2.07; 1 £ = Br 2.98.

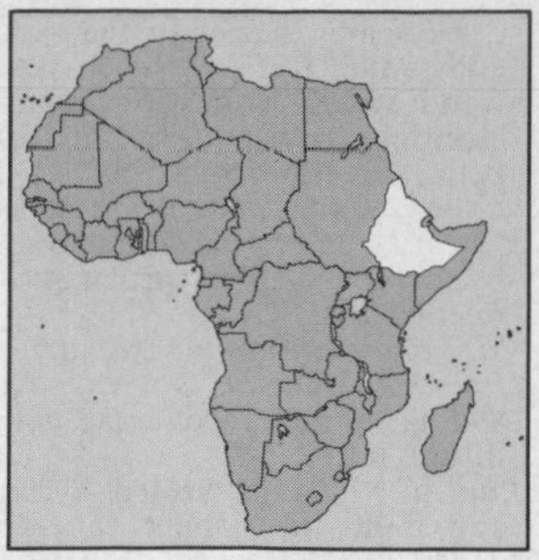

Area and population

		area		population
				1984
Regions	Capitals	sq mi	sq km	census
Arsi	Asela	9,500	24,600	1,662,233
Bale	Goba	49,500	128,300	1,006,491
Eritrea*	Asmera	45,300	117,400	2,704,000
Gemu Gofa	Arba Minch	15,400	40,100	1,248,034
Gojam	Debre Markos	24,900	64,400	3,244,882
Gonder	Gonder	28,300	73,400	2,905,362
Hararge	Harer	98,400	254,800	4,151,706
Ilubabor	Metu	19,600	50,800	963,327
Kefa	Jima	20,500	53,000	2,450,369
Shewa*	Addis Ababa	33,000	85,500	9,503,140
Sidamo	Awasa	45,100	116,700	3,790,579
Tigray	Mekele	25,400	65,700	2,409,700
Welega	Nekemte	27,000	69,800	2,369,677
Welo	Dese	30,500	79,000	3,609,918
TOTAL		472,400	1,223,500	42,019,418

Demography

Population (1986): 44,675,700.
Density (1986): persons per sq mi 94.6, persons per sq km 36.5.
Urban-rural (1984): urban 11.3%; rural 88.7%.
Sex distribution (1984): male 49.85%; female 50.15%.
Age breakdown (1984): under 15, 46.6%; 15–29, 22.7%; 30–44, 15.6%; 45–59, 8.9%; 60–74, 4.5%; 75 and over, 1.7%.
Population projection: (1990) 50,290,000; (2000) 66,920,000.
Doubling time: 26 years.
Ethnolinguistic composition (1983): Amhara 30.0%; Galla 26.0%; Tigrinya 9.0%; Tigre 5.0%; Kafa 4.0%; Somali 3.0%; Gurage 3.0%; Nilotes 3.0%, of which Nuer 1.3%; Arabic 1.3%; Afar 1.0%; other 14.7%.
Religious affiliation (1980): Ethiopian Orthodox 48.9%; Muslim 31.4%; traditional religion 11.4%; other Christian 7.3%; other 1.0%.
Major cities (1984): Addis Ababa 1,423,111; Asmera 275,385; Dire Dawa 98,104; Gonder 68,958; Dese 68,848.

Vital statistics

Birth rate per 1,000 population (1985): 49.7 (world avg. 29.0).
Death rate per 1,000 population (1985): 23.1 (world avg. 11.0).
Natural increase rate per 1,000 population (1985): 26.6 (world avg. 18.0).
Total fertility rate (avg. births per childbearing woman; 1985): 6.7.
Life expectancy at birth (1985): male 39.5 years; female 42.6 years.
Major causes of death (1977–78)†: infectious and parasitic diseases 24.0%; digestive system diseases 17.6%; allergy, endocrine, metabolic, nutritional, and circulatory diseases 14.9%; respiratory diseases 9.9%.

National economy

Budget (1984). Revenue: Br 1,866,100,000 (taxes 74.6%, of which income and profit tax 24.7%, excise tax 15.5%, import duties 16.8%, export duties 10.2%; nontax revenue 25.4%). Expenditures: Br 2,431,200,000 (general government 47.3%; economic development 23.1%, of which agriculture and settlement 7.3%, road construction 3.0%; social services 10.7%, of which education 5.2%, public health 2.5%; debt service 8.4%).
Tourism (1984): receipts from visitors U.S.$6,000,000; expenditures by nationals abroad U.S.$4,000,000.
Production (metric tons except as noted). Agriculture, forestry, fishing (1984): sugarcane 1,650,000, corn (maize) 1,275,000, barley 848,000, wheat 675,000, vegetables and melons 513,000, coffee 240,000, fruits 210,000, millet 145,000, seed cotton 73,000, treenuts 59,000, cotton seed 48,000, sesame seed 36,000, lentils 32,000, linseed 30,000, peanuts (groundnuts) 28,000; livestock (number of live animals) 26,000,000 cattle, 23,450,000 sheep, 17,250,000 goats, 6,945,000 horses, mules, and asses, 1,020,000 camels; roundwood 31,154,000 cu m; fish catch 3,900‡. Mining and quarrying (1983): cement 150,000; salt 125,000; kaolin 9,000; limestone 5,000; gold 435 kilograms; platinum 3 kilograms. Manufacturing (gross value in Br '000§; 1984): food products 394,600; textiles 346,353; beverages 262,997; leather and shoes 155,481; metal products 124,574; chemicals 109,371; paper and printing 86,921; wood 21,174. Construction (authorized; 1981): residential 162,000 sq m; nonresidential 32,300 sq m, of which commercial 24,800 sq m. Energy production (consumption): electricity (kW-hr; 1984) 740,400,000 (751,100,000); coal, none (n.a.); crude petroleum (barrels; 1984) n.a. (5,294,000); petroleum products (metric tons; 1984) 680,000 (444,000); natural gas, n.a. (n.a.).
Gross national product (at current market prices; 1985): U.S.$4,744,000,000 (U.S.$110 per capita ‖).

Structure of gross domestic product and labour force

	1984–85		1984	
	in value Br '000,000	% of total value	labour force	% of labour force
Agriculture	3,928.3	44.1	10,956,000	76.8
Mining	15.8	0.2		
Manufacturing	1,017.3	11.4		
Construction	374.5	4.2		
Public utilities	73.6	0.8		
Transportation and communication	583.8	6.5	3,308,000	23.2
Trade	962.1	10.8		
Finance	347.1	3.9		
Pub. admin., defense	770.0	8.6		
Services	644.8	7.2		
Other	196.7	2.2		
TOTAL	8,914.0	100.0¶	14,264,000	100.0

Public debt (external, outstanding; 1984): U.S.$1,384,200,000.
Population economically active (1984): total 18,492,300; activity rate of total population 43.9% (participation rates: ages 15–64, 74.3%; female 39.2%; unemployed, n.a.).

Price and earnings indexes (1980 = 100)

	1980	1981	1982	1983	1984	1985	1986♀
Consumer price index	100.0	106.1	112.4	111.6	121.0	144.1	132.6
Monthly earnings index	...	...	...	...	...	...	...

Household income and expenditure. Average household size (1984) 4.5; income per household *c.* U.S.$600; source of income: n.a.; expenditureδ: food 49.0%, housing 14.6%, household utilities 14.6%, clothing and footwear 6.7%, miscellaneous goods and services 5.4%, transportation 4.5%, recreation and reading 2.6%, medical care 1.8%, personal care 0.8%.
Land use (1983): forested 24.0%; meadows and pastures 41.1%; agricultural and under permanent cultivation 12.7%; other 22.2%.

Foreign trade

Balance of trade (current prices)

	1979	1980	1981	1982	1983	1984
Br '000,000	−300.6	−614.2	−723.8	−775.6	−980.4	−1,086.7
% of total	14.7%	25.9%	31.0%	31.7%	37.0%	38.6%

Imports (1984): Br 1,949,098,000 (machinery 24.3%, petroleum and petroleum products 18.5%, motor vehicles 10.1%, food 8.8%, chemicals 5.4%, electrical materials 4.2%). *Major import sources:* U.S.S.R. 22.1%; United States 15.7%; West Germany 10.5%; Italy 9.9%; Japan 6.6%.
Exports (1984): Br 846,550,000 (coffee 64.5%, hides 11.4%, kat [a narcotic leaf] 3.8%, oilseeds 2.2%, pulses 2.0%). *Major export destinations:* United States 19.5%; West Germany 18.0%; Japan 7.5%; Italy 7.4%; Djibouti 6.9%.

Transport and communications

Transport. Railroads□ (1985): length 485 mi, 781 km; passenger-mi 191,000,000◇, passenger-km 307,000,000◇; short ton-mi cargo 74,000,000◇, metric ton-km cargo 108,000,000◇. Roads (1983): total length 23,305 mi, 37,506 km (paved 33%). Vehicles (1984): passenger cars 43,558; trucks and buses 13,069. Merchant marine (1985): vessels (100 gross tons and over) 23; total deadweight tonnage 71,989. Air transport (1983): passenger-mi 473,697,000, passenger-km 762,343,000; short ton-mi cargo 18,587,000, metric ton-km cargo 27,136,000; airports (1986) with scheduled flights 37.
Communications. Daily newspapers (1984): total number 3; total circulation 47,000; circulation per 1,000 population 1.1. Radio (1985): 2,000,000 receivers (1 per 22 persons). Television (1985): 40,000 receivers (1 per 1,085 persons). Telephones (1983): 100,783 (1 per 408 persons).

Education and health

Education (1983–84)

	schools	teachers	students	student/ teacher ratio
Primary (age 7–12)	7,096	46,674	2,497,114	53.5
Secondary (age 13–18)	1,066	13,192	579,834	44.0
Voc., teacher tr.	...	...	...	...
Higher	11	1,446	15,776	10.9

Educational attainment, n.a. *Literacy* (1980)△: total population over age 15 literate 1,000,000 (4.8%); males (9.3%); females (0.5%).
Health (1982): physicians 504 (1 per 79,365 persons); hospital beds 10,993 (1 per 3,639 persons); infant mortality rate per 1,000 live births (1980–85) 155.0.
Food (1979–81): daily per capita caloric intake 2,149 (vegetable products 93%, animal products 7%); 92% of FAO recommended minimum requirement.

Military

Total active duty personnel (1985): 217,000† (army 96.8%, navy 1.4%, air force 1.8%). *Military expenditure as percent of GNP* (1982): 8.6% (world 6.1%); per capita expenditure (1982) U.S.$12.

*Eritrea includes Aseb Administration, and Shewa includes Addis Ababa region. †Percentage of deaths in a sample population of hospital inpatients. ‡1983. §At constant prices of 1978–79. ‖ Per capita figures are based on population calculated from 1984 census; the census population was about 16% higher than previous estimates. ¶Detail does not add to total given because of rounding. ♀April. δWeights of consumer price index components, Addis Ababa only. □Includes 62 mi (100 km) of the Chemin de Fer Djibouti–Ethiopien (CDE) in Djibouti; excludes 190 mi (306 km) of Northern Ethiopia Railway, not in use since 1978. ◇1982. △Adult illiteracy is reported to have been reduced to about 46% in 1983. †In 1985 about 6,600 Cuban and other Soviet-bloc advisers were assisting government forces.

Fiji

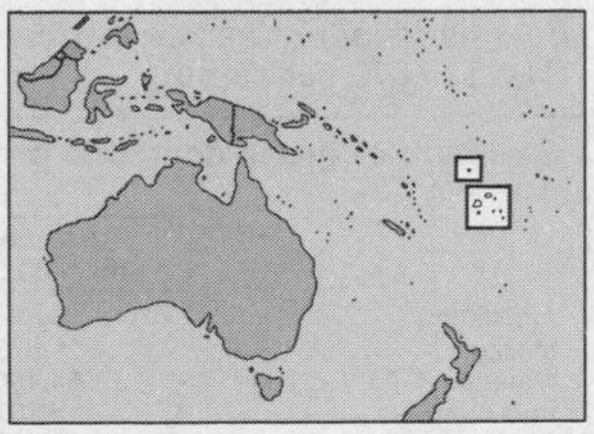

Official name: Fiji.
Form of government: constitutional monarchy with two legislative houses (Senate [22]; House of Representatives [52]).
Chief of state: British Monarch represented by governor-general.
Head of government: Prime Minister.
Capital: Suva.
Official language: English.
Official religion: none.
Monetary unit: 1 Fiji dollar (F$) = 100 cents; valuation (Oct. 1, 1986) 1 U.S.$ = F$1.17; 1£ = F$1.69.

Area and population

Divisions Provinces*	Capitals	area sq mi	area sq km	population 1984 estimate
Central	Suva			
Naitasiri		643	1,666	86,000
Rewa		105	272	103,600
Serua-Namosi		540	1,400	18,100
Tailevu		369	955	44,800
Eastern	Levuka			
Kandavu		185	478	8,800
Lau		188	487	13,800
Lomaiviti		159	411	13,700
Rotuma		18	46	2,600
Northern	Labasa			
Mathuata		774	2,004	69,300
Mbua		532	1,379	12,800
Thakaundrove		1,087	2,816	39,100
Western	Lautoka			
Mba		1,017	2,634	192,200
Nandronga-Navosa		921	2,385	53,200
Ra		518	1,341	28,100
TOTAL		7,056	18,274	686,000†

Demography

Population (1986): 714,000.
Density (1986): persons per sq mi 101.2, persons per sq km 39.1.
Urban-rural (1983): urban 38.4%; rural 61.6%.
Sex distribution (1985): male 50.46%; female 49.54%.
Age breakdown (1985): under 15, 36.6%; 15–29, 29.8%; 30–44, 18.3%; 45–59, 9.7%; 60–74, 4.3%; 75 and over, 1.3%.
Population projection: (1990) 768,000; (2000) 927,000.
Doubling time: 28 years.
Ethnic composition (1985): Indian 49.9%; Fijian 45.2%; part-European 1.7%; Rotuman 1.2%; Chinese 0.7%; European 0.5%; other 0.8%.
Religious affiliation (1980): Christian 49.7%; Hindu 40.9%; Muslim 7.8%; other 1.6%.
Major cities (1985): Suva 75,000; Lautoka 27,000; Nadi 8,000; Ba 7,000; Labasa 5,000.

Vital statistics

Birth rate per 1,000 population (1984): 29.8 (world avg. 29.0); (1978) legitimate 82.7%; illegitimate 17.3%.
Death rate per 1,000 population (1984): 5.3 (world avg. 11.0).
Natural increase rate per 1,000 population (1984): 24.5 (world avg. 18.0).
Total fertility rate (avg. births per childbearing woman; 1983): 3.3.
Marriage rate per 1,000 population (1983): 10.1.
Divorce rate per 1,000 population (1979): 0.7.
Life expectancy at birth (1980–85): male 70.5 years; female 74.6 years.
Major causes of death per 100,000 population (1983): heart disease 133.1; ill-defined conditions 59.5; hypertensive and cerebrovascular diseases 48.1; malignant neoplasms (cancers) 44.1; pneumonia 32.6; accidents 15.0.

National economy

Budget (1985). Revenue: F$359,700,000 (direct taxes 42.3%, indirect taxes 33.6%, current transfers 16.0%, capital transfers 4.1%). Expenditures: F$442,000,000 (education 17.3%, economic services 12.9%, general public services 10.6%, health 7.1%, defense 3.4%).
Public debt (external, outstanding; 1984): U.S.$289,600,000.
Tourism: receipts from visitors (1984) U.S.$149,900,000; expenditures by nationals abroad (1981) U.S.$19,000,000.
Production (metric tons except as noted). Agriculture, forestry, fishing (1985): sugarcane 3,042,000, paddy rice 27,400, copra 21,100, ginger 3,100; livestock (number of live animals) 158,000 cattle, 56,000 goats, 29,000 pigs; roundwood 205,855 cu m; fish catch 10,741. Mining and quarrying (1985): gold 1,865 kilograms; silver 459 kilograms. Manufacturing (1985): refined sugar 340,000; cement 93,200; coconut oil 11,600; soap 6,100; beer 178,400 hectolitres; paint 23,000 hectolitres. Construction (1985): residential 72,000 sq m; nonresidential 36,000 sq m. Energy production (consumption): electricity (kW-hr; 1985) 372,000,000 (372,000,000); coal (metric tons; 1984) none (22,000); crude petroleum, none (n.a.); petroleum products (metric tons; 1984) none (155,000); natural gas, none (n.a.).
Household income and expenditure. Average household size (1980) 4.6; income per household F$2,837 (U.S.$3,546); sources of income (1973): wages and salaries 81.5%, self-employment 9.1%, other 9.4%; expenditure (1985): food 33.9%, housing 18.6%, transportation 11.3%, household furnishings 7.6%, clothing and footwear 6.3%, energy 4.9%.

Gross national product (at current market prices; 1984): U.S.$1,250,000,000 (U.S.$1,820 per capita).

Structure of gross domestic product and labour force

	1984 in value F$'000,000	1984 % of total value	1983 labour force	1983 % of labour force
Agriculture	216.2	18.7	85,059	40.6
Mining	6.1	0.5	1,171	0.6
Manufacturing	114.4	9.9	14,348	6.8
Construction	69.6	6.0	7,450	3.6
Public utilities	26.2	2.3	2,449	1.2
Transportation and communication	110.7	9.6	7,450	3.6
Trade	204.1	17.6	15,792	7.5
Finance	161.8	14.0	5,148	2.4
Pub. admin., defense, services	272.9	23.6	25,600	12.2
Other	−24.1‡	−2.1‡	45,703§	21.8
TOTAL	1,157.9	100.0†	209,703	100.0

Population economically active (1985): total 230,000; activity rate of total population 33.0% (participation rates: ages 15–64 [1982], 55.2%; female 19.0%; unemployed 8.1%).

Price and earnings indexes (1979 = 100)

	1980	1981	1982	1983	1984	1985	1986 ‖
Consumer price index	114.5	127.3	136.2	145.4	153.1	159.8	161.7
Annual earnings index	107.8	118.2	131.3	139.5	149.6	...	...

Land use (1983): forested 64.9%; agricultural and under permanent cultivation 12.9%; meadows and pastures 3.3%; other 18.9%.

Foreign trade

Balance of trade (current prices)

	1980	1981	1982	1983	1984	1985
F$'000,000	−153.2	−270.9	−208.0	−248.2	−206.8	−244.3
% of total	20.0%	33.5%	28.0%	33.6%	27.0%	31.6%

Imports (1985): F$508,191,000 (mineral fuels and related materials 22.7%; manufactured goods 19.8%; machinery and transport equipment 18.0%; food, beverages, and tobacco 16.6%; chemicals 7.6%). *Major import sources:* Australia 33.8%; New Zealand 17.0%; Japan 15.0%; United Kingdom 6.6%; Singapore 4.9%; United States 4.1%; Taiwan 2.5%; China 2.2%; Hong Kong 1.8%.
Exports (1985)¶: F$183,217,000 (sugar 56.7%; gold 11.9%; fish 6.4%; coconut oil 4.2%; manufactured goods 4.0%; molasses 3.8%; wood and by-products 3.2%). *Major export destinations*♀: United Kingdom 42.4%; Australia 18.1%; Malaysia 10.9%; New Zealand 4.6%; Japan 4.1%; United States 4.0%.

Transport and communications

Transport. Railroads (1983): length 660 mi, 1,062 km. Roads (1985): total length 2,564 mi, 4,127 km (paved 13%). Vehicles (1986): passenger cars 32,453; trucks and buses 22,799. Merchant marine (1985): vessels (100 gross tons and over) 60; total deadweight tonnage 26,764. Air transport* (1985)♂: passenger-mi 327,600,000, passenger-km 527,300,000; short ton-mi cargo 92,500,000, metric ton-km cargo 135,000,000; airports (1986) with scheduled flights 20.
Communications. Daily newspapers (1985): total number 2; total circulation 53,000; circulation per 1,000 population 76. Radio (1985): total number of receivers 400,000 (1 per 1.8 persons). Television: none. Telephones (1985): 53.228 (1 per 13.1 persons).

Education and health

Education (1984)

	schools	teachers	students	student/teacher ratio
Primary (age 5–15)	672	4,374	123,340	28.2
Secondary (age 16–19)	139	2,656	43,277	16.3
Voc., teacher tr.	39	272	3,820	14.0
Higher□	5	...	3,947	...

Educational attainment (1976). Percent of adult population 25 years old and over having: no schooling 19.7%, some primary education 45.8%, primary 20.5%, some secondary 6.7%, secondary 3.9%, postsecondary 3.3%. *Literacy* (1985): total population over age 15 literate 374,300 (85.5%); males literate 197,300 (90.2%); females literate 177,000 (80.9%).
Health (1984): physicians 339 (1 per 2,024 persons); hospital beds 1,736 (1 per 395 persons); infant mortality rate per 1,000 live births 22.5.
Food (1980–82): daily per capita caloric intake 3,046 (vegetable products 86%, animal products 14%); 115% of FAO recommended minimum requirement.

Military

Total active duty personnel (1985): 2,670 (army 93.6%; navy 6.4%; air force, none). *Military expenditure as percent of GNP* (1982): 1.2% (world 6.1%); per capita expenditure: U.S.$22.

*The provinces are autonomous only with respect to local affairs. †Detail does not add to total given because of rounding. ‡Other activities less imputed bank service charges. §Self-employed and unemployed. ‖May. ¶Excludes reexports, valued at F$80,670,000. ♀Based on exports of local products only. ♂Domestic airlines only including South Pacific service. □1983.

Finland

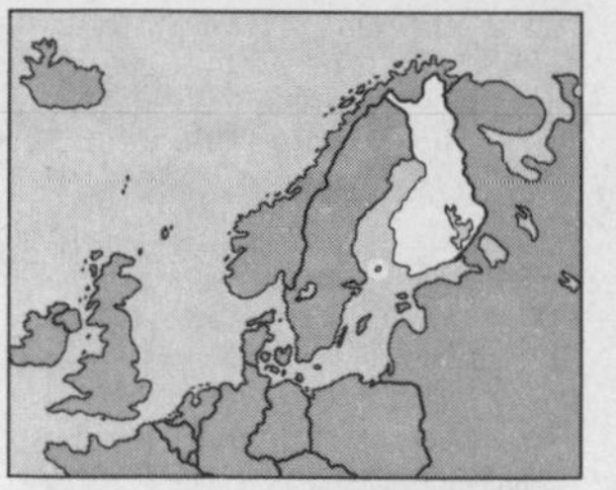

Official name: Suomen Tasavalta (Finnish); Republiken Finland (Swedish) (Republic of Finland).
Form of government: multiparty parliamentary republic with one legislative house (Eduskunta [200]).
Chief of state: President.
Head of government: Prime Minister.
Capital: Helsinki.
Official languages: Finnish; Swedish.
Official religion: none.
Monetary unit: 1 markka (Fmk) = 100 penni; valuation (Oct. 1, 1986) 1 U.S.$ = Fmk 4.91; 1 £ = Fmk 7.09.

Area and population

		land area		population
Provinces	Capitals	sq mi	sq km	1986 estimate*
Åland (Ahvenanmaa)	Mariehamn (Maarianhamina)	590	1,527	23,600
Häme	Hämeenlinna	6,568	17,010	677,700
Keski-Suomi	Jyväskylä	6,266	16,230	247,800
Kuopio	Kuopio	6,375	16,511	256,200
Kymi	Kouvola	4,163	10,783	340,700
Lappi	Rovaniemi	35,930	93,057	201,100
Mikkeli	Mikkeli	6,310	16,342	209,000
Oulu	Oulu	21,956	56,866	432,000
Pohjois-Karjala	Joensuu	6,866	17,782	177,600
Turku ja Pori	Turku	8,559	22,170	712,800
Uusimaa	Helsinki	3,822	9,898	1,187,500
Vaasa	Vaasa	10,211	26,447	444,700
TOTAL LAND AREA		117,616	304,623	4,910,700
INLAND WATER		12,943	33,522	
TOTAL AREA		130,559	338,145	

Demography

Population (1986): 4,926,000.
Density† (1986): persons per sq mi 41.9, persons per sq km 16.2.
Urban-rural (1985): urban 59.8%; rural 40.2%.
Sex distribution (1985): male 48.41%; female 51.59%.
Age breakdown (1985): under 15, 19.5%; 15–29, 22.9%; 30–44, 23.6%; 45–59, 16.7%; 60–74, 12.4%; 75 and over, 4.9%.
Population projection: (1990) 5,006,000; (2000) 5,073,000.
Doubling time: n.a.; doubling time exceeds 100 years.
Ethnolinguistic composition (1983): Finnish 93.6%; Swedish 6.2%; other 0.2%‡.
Religious affiliation (1985): Lutheran 89.4%; Greek Orthodox 1.1%; nonaffiliated 8.6%; other 0.9%.
Major cities (1985): Helsinki 484,410; Tampere 168,271; Turku 161,540; Espoo 154,243; Vantaa 143,188.

Vital statistics

Birth rate per 1,000 population (1985): 12.8 (world avg. 29.0); (1984) legitimate 84.9%; illegitimate 15.1%.
Death rate per 1,000 population (1985): 9.8 (world avg. 11.0).
Natural increase rate per 1,000 population (1985): 3.0 (world avg. 18.0).
Total fertility rate (avg. births per childbearing woman; 1983): 1.7.
Marriage rate per 1,000 population (1985): 5.3.
Divorce rate per 1,000 population (1984): 2.0.
Life expectancy at birth (1984): male 70.4 years; female 78.8 years.
Major causes of death per 100,000 population (1983): ischemic heart disease 276.4; malignant neoplasms (cancers) 194.4; cerebrovascular diseases 112.7; accidents 44.4; pneumonia 38.4; suicide and self-inflicted injuries 24.4.

National economy

Budget (1986). Revenue: Fmk 100,781,000,000 (tax revenue 76.8%, of which income and property taxes 27.1%, sales tax 26.2%, excise duties 13.1%, vehicle taxes 3.1%, stamp duties 2.9%). Expenditures: Fmk 100,781,000,000 (social security 17.2%; education 15.9%; health 8.4%; agriculture and forestry 8.5%; transportation 8.3%; administration 5.8%; defense 5.2%).
Public debt (1986): U.S.$8,562,000,000.
Tourism (1984): receipts from visitors U.S.$489,000,000; expenditures by nationals abroad U.S.$681,000,000.
Production (metric tons except as noted). Agriculture, forestry, fishing (1984): barley 1,715,300, oats 1,320,900, sugar beets 823,400, potatoes 745,100, milk 3,173,000§, pork 166,000, beef 121,000; livestock (number of live animals) 1,591,600 cattle, 1,255,800 pigs, 201,600 reindeer; roundwood (1985) 43,600,000 cu m; fish catch (1983) 119,496. Mining and quarrying (1984): iron ore 812,600‖; chromite 369,000; copper 31,000‖. Manufacturing (value added in Fmk; 1983): machinery 15,999,000,000, of which transport equipment 4,732,000,000, electrical equipment 3,789,000,000; paper and paper products 8,991,000,000; processed food 8,891,000,000; chemical products 8,299,000,000. Construction (1984): residential 18,430,000,000 cu m; nonresidential 28,940,000,000 cu m. Energy production (consumption): electricity (kW-hr; 1984) 43,311,000,000 (48,519,000,000); coal (metric tons; 1984) none (3,733,000); crude petroleum (barrels; 1984) none (70,544,000); petroleum products (metric tons; 1984) 9,184,000 (8,848,000); natural gas (cu m; 1984) none (762,000,000).
Household income and expenditure. Average household size (1983) 2.5; income per household Fmk 87,668 (U.S.$15,740); sources of income (1985): wages and salaries 67.8%, self-employment 15.2%, income from property 3.0%; expenditure (1984): food 27.2%, housing 18.4%, transportation and communications 17.1%, recreation and education 9.0%, clothing 5.2%.

Gross national product (at current market prices; 1984): U.S.$53,090,000,000 (U.S.$10,870 per capita).

Structure of gross domestic product and labour force

	1984		1985	
	in value Fmk '000,000	% of total value	labour force	% of labour force
Agriculture	16,534	7.7	280,000	10.8
Mining	972	0.4	537,000	20.6
Manufacturing	54,406	4		
Public utilities	5,737	2.7	60,000	2.3
Construction	14,260	6.7	179,000	6.9
Transportation and communication	15,005	7.0	186,000	7.2
Trade	21,986	10.3	354,000	13.6
Finance	29,932	14.0	155,000	6.0
Pub. admin., defense	29,002	13.6	680,000	26.2
Services	10,716	5.0		
Other	15,494	7.2	168,000	6.5
TOTAL	214,044¶	100.0	2,600,000♀	100.0♀

Population economically active (1985): total 2,600,000; activity rate of total population 53.0% (participation rates: ages 15–64, 77.1%; female 47.7%; unemployed 6.5%).

Price and earnings indexes (1980 = 100)

	1979	1980	1981	1982	1983	1984	1985
Consumer price index	89.6	100.0	112.0	122.4	132.7	142.0	150.4
Hourly earnings index	89.0	100.0	113.0	124.8	137.8	150.8	163.4

Land use (1983): forested 76.3%; meadows and pastures 0.5%; agricultural and under permanent cultivation 7.8%; other 15.4%.

Foreign trade

Balance of trade (current prices)

	1980	1981	1982	1983	1984	1985
Fmk '000,000	−1,410.0	+3,107.0	+1,725.0	+1,242.1	+6,222.0	+2,618
% of total	1.3%	2.6%	1.4%	0.9%	4.0%	1.6%

Imports (1985): Fmk 81,408,000,000 (raw materials and producer goods 62.5%, of which crude petroleum 15.3%; machinery and transport equipment 14.3%, of which transport vehicles 5.6%; fuels and lubricants 6.8%). *Major import sources:* U.S.S.R. 21.0%; West Germany 14.9%; Sweden 11.8%; United Kingdom 7.2%; United States 5.4%.
Exports (1985): Fmk 84,026,000,000 (forestry products 37.8%, of which paper and paper products 29.8%, wood products 8.0%; metal and engineering products 36.5%, of which metal products and machines 29.0%, basic metals 7.5%; chemical products 11.7%; textiles and clothing 6.3%; food and beverages 2.6%). *Major export destinations:* U.S.S.R. 21.5%; Sweden 13.2%; United Kingdom 10.8%; West Germany 9.3%; United States 6.3%; Norway 4.2%.

Transport and communications

Transport. Railroads (1985): length 5,644 mi, 9,116 km; passenger-mi 2,003,000,000, passenger-km 3,224,000,000; short ton-mi cargo 5,525,000,000, metric ton-km cargo 8,067,000,000. Roads (1984): total length 47,130 mi, 75,848 km (paved 54%). Vehicles (1984): passenger cars 1,473,975; trucks and buses 182,853. Merchant marine (1985): vessels (100 gross tons and over) 307; total deadweight tonnage 2,853,850. Air transport (1985): passenger-mi 1,817,000,000, passenger-km 2,924,000,000; short ton-mi cargo 57,784,000, metric ton-km cargo 84,364,000; airports (1986) 21.
Communications. Daily newspapers (1984): total number 67; total circulation 2,600,000; circulation per 1,000 population 533. Radio (1984): total number of receivers 2,515,000 (1 per 1.9 persons). Television (1984): total number of receivers 1,738,432 (1 per 2.8 persons). Telephones (1984): 2,899,000 (1 per 1.7 persons).

Education and health

Education (1983–84)

	schools	teachers	students	student/ teacher ratio
Primary (age 7–12)	4,238	25,139	369,047	14.7
Secondary (age 13–19)	1,082	22,356	316,740	14.2
Voc., teacher tr.	550	15,000	116,906	7.8
Higherδ	21	5,191	119,902	23.1

Educational attainment (1983). Percent of population over age 14 having: lower secondary education 51.5%; higher secondary 28.4%; some postsecondary 8.8%; undergraduate 4.3%; graduate 6.1%; postgraduate 0.6%; other 0.3%. *Literacy* (1985): virtually 100% literate.
Health (1984): physicians 9,979 (1 per 489 persons); hospital beds 61,103 (1 per 80 persons); infant mortality rate per 1,000 live births 6.2.
Food (1980–82): daily per capita caloric intake 3,080 (vegetable products 57%, animal products 43%); 114% of FAO recommended minimum.

Military

Total active duty personnel (1985): 36,500 (army 84.6%, navy 7.4%, air force 8.0%). *Military expenditure as percent of GNP* (1984): 1.4% (world 6.1%); per capita expenditure U.S.$154.

*January 1. †Based on land area only. ‡Includes English 0.04%; German 0.04%; Russian 0.04%; Lappish 0.03%; and other 0.1%. §1983. ‖Metal content of ores. ¶At 1980 prices. ♀Detail does not add to total given because of rounding. δUniversities only.

France

Official name: République Française (French Republic).
Form of government: republic with two legislative houses (Parliament; National Assembly [577], Senate [317]).
Chief of state: President.
Head of government: Prime Minister.
Capital: Paris.
Official language: French.
Official religion: none.
Monetary unit: 1 Franc (F) = 100 centimes; valuation (Oct. 1, 1986) 1 U.S.$ = F 6.64; 1 £ = F 9.60.

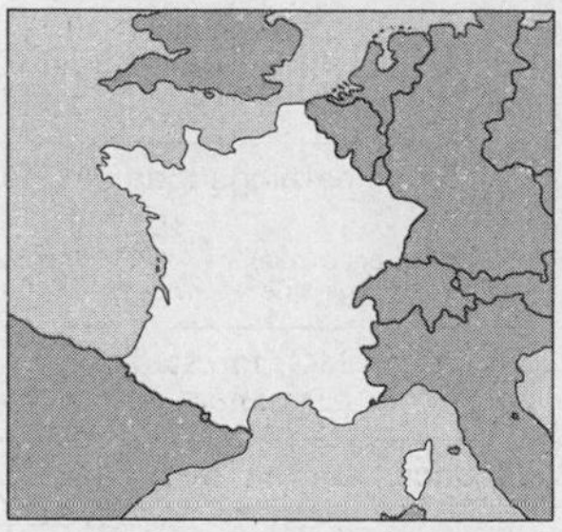

Area and population

Regions / Departments	Capitals	area sq mi	area sq km	population 1985 estimate
Alsace				
Bas-Rhin	Strasbourg	1,836	4,755	933,000
Haut-Rhin	Colmar	1,361	3,525	659,000
Aquitaine				
Dordogne	Périgueux	3,498	9,060	380,000
Gironde	Bordeaux	3,861	10,000	1,157,000
Landes	Mont-de-Marsan	3,569	9,243	302,000
Lot-et-Garonne	Agen	2,070	5,361	302,000
Pyrénées-Atlantiques	Pau	2,952	7,645	564,000
Auvergne				
Allier	Moulins	2,834	7,340	366,000
Cantal	Aurillac	2,211	5,726	161,000
Haute-Loire	Le Puy	1,922	4,977	207,000
Puy-de-Dôme	Clermont-Ferrand	3,077	7,970	600,000
Basse Normandie				
Calvados	Caen	2,142	5,548	601,000
Manche	Saint Lô	2,293	5,938	472,000
Orne	Alen	2,356	6,103	296,000
Bretagne				
Côtes-du-Nord	Saint-Brieuc	2,656	6,878	543,000
Finistère	Quimper	2,600	6,733	838,000
Ille-et-Vilaine	Rennes	2,616	6,775	768,000
Morbihan	Vannes	2,634	6,823	601,000
Bourgogne				
Côte-d'Or	Dijon	3,383	8,763	480,000
Nièvre	Nevers	2,632	6,817	237,000
Saône-et-Loire	Mâcon	3,311	8,775	572,000
Yonne	Auxerre	2,866	7,424	316,000
Centre				
Cher	Bourges	2,793	7,235	322,000
Eure-et-Loire	Chartres	2,270	5,880	375,000
Indre	Châteauroux	2,622	6,791	240,000
Indre-et-Loire	Tours	2,366	6,127	517,000
Loiret	Orléans	2,616	6,775	555,000
Loir-et-Cher	Blois	2,449	6,343	301,000
Champagne-Ardenne				
Ardennes	Charleville-Mézières	2,019	5,229	300,000
Aube	Troyes	2,370	6,139	292,000
Haute-Marne	Chaumont	2,398	6,211	211,000
Marne	Châlons-sur-Marne	3,151	8,162	549,000
Corse				
Corse-du-Sud	Ajaccio	1,550	4,014	112,000
Haute-Corse	Bastia	1,802	4,666	135,000
Franche-Comté				
Doubs	Besançon	2,021	5,234	477,000
Haute-Saône	Vesoul	2,070	5,360	236,000
Jura	Lons-le-Saunier	1,930	4,999	245,000
Territoire de Belfort	Belfort	235	609	134,000
Haute-Normandie				
Eure	Évreux	2,332	6,040	480,000
Seine-Maritime	Rouen	2,424	6,278	1,203,000
Île-de-France				
Essonne	Évry	696	1,804	1,017,000
Hauts-de-Seine	Nanterre	68	176	1,370,000
Paris	Paris	41	105	2,140,000
Seine-et-Marne	Melun	2,284	5,915	953,000
Seine-Saint-Denis	Bobigny	91	236	1,330,000
Val-de-Marne	Créteil	95	245	1,186,600
Val-d'Oise	Pontoise	481	1,246	960,000
Yvelines	Versailles	882	2,284	1,250,000
Languedoc-Roussillon				
Aude	Carcassonne	2,318	6,004	283,000
Gard	Nîmes	2,260	5,853	548,000
Hérault	Montpellier	2,356	6,101	732,000
Lozère	Mende	1,995	5,167	74,000
Pyrénées-Orientales	Perpignan	1,589	4,116	348,000
Limousin				
Corrèze	Tulle	2,261	5,857	242,000
Creuse	Guéret	2,149	5,565	138,000
Haute-Vienne	Limoges	2,131	5,520	357,000
Lorraine				
Meurthe-et-Moselle	Nancy	2,024	5,241	713,000
Meuse	Bar-le-Duc	2,400	6,216	199,000
Moselle	Metz	2,400	6,216	1,009,000
Vosges	Épinal	2,268	5,874	394,000
Midi-Pyrénées				
Ariège	Foix	1,888	4,890	135,000
Aveyron	Rodez	3,373	8,736	278,000
Gers	Auch	2,416	6,257	173,000
Haute-Garonne	Toulouse	2,436	6,309	845,000
Haute-Pyrénées	Tarbes	1,724	4,464	228,000
Lot	Cahors	2,014	5,712	156,000
Tarn	Albi	2,223	5,758	340,000
Tarn-et-Garonne	Montauban	1,435	3,718	193,000
Nord-Pas-de-Calais				
Nord	Lille	2,217	5,743	2,513,000
Pas-de-Calais	Arras	2,576	6,671	1,421,000

Area and population (continued)

Regions / Departments	Capitals	area sq mi	area sq km	population 1985 estimate
Pays de la Loire				
Loire-Atlantique	Nantes	2,631	6,815	1,021,000
Maine-et Loire	Angers	2,767	7,166	694,000
Mayenne	Laval	1,998	5,175	276,000
Sarthe	Le Mans	2,396	6,206	510,000
Vendée	La Roche-sur-Yon	2,595	6,721	496,000
Picardie				
Aisne	Laon	2,845	7,369	535,000
Oise	Beauvais	2,263	5,860	682,000
Somme	Amiens	2,382	6,170	549,000
Poitou-Charentes				
Charente	Angoulême	2,300	5,956	342,000
Charente-Maritime	La Rochelle	2,650	6,684	518,000
Deux-Sèvres	Niort	2,316	5,999	344,000
Vienne	Poitiers	2,699	6,990	376,000
Provence-Côte d'Azur				
Alpes-Maritimes	Nice	1,660	4,299	890,000
Alpes-de-Haute-Provence	Digne	2,674	6,925	122,000
Bouches-du-Rhône	Marseille	1,964	5,087	1,737,000
Hautes-Alpes	Gap	2,142	5,549	107,000
Var	Toulon	2,307	5,974	742,000
Vaucluse	Avignon	1,377	3,567	436,000
Rhône-Alpes				
Ain	Bourg-en-Bresse	2,225	5,762	438,000
Ardèche	Privas	2,135	5,529	272,000
Drôme	Valence	2,521	6,530	402,000
Haute-Savoie	Annecy	1,694	4,388	516,000
Isère	Grenoble	2,869	7,431	970,000
Loire	Saint-Étienne	1,846	4,781	739,000
Rhône	Lyon	1,254	3,249	1,456,000
Savoie	Chambéry	2,327	6,028	332,000
TOTAL		210,026	543,965	55,063,000*

Demography

Population (1986): 55,406,000.
Density (1986): persons per sq mi 263.8, persons per sq km 101.9.
Urban–rural (1985): urban 77.2%; rural 22.8%.
Sex distribution (1985): male 49.16%; female 50.84%.
Age breakdown (1985): under 15, 20.0%; 15–29, 23.2%; 30–44, 21.0%; 45–59, 17.1%; 60–74, 11.9%; 75 and over, 5.8%.
Population projection: (1990) 55,900,000; (2000) 58,600,000.
Doubling time: n.a.; doubling time exceeds 100 years.
Ethnic composition (1980): French 82.9%; German (Alsatian) 2.6%; Italian 2.2%; Breton 2.0%; Algerian 1.7%; Portuguese 1.4%; Spanish 1.0%; Jewish 1.0%.
Religious affiliation (1980): Roman Catholic 76.4%; other Christian 3.7%; atheist 3.4%; Muslim 3.0%; other 13.5%.
Major cities (1982): Paris 2,165,892 (metropolitan area 10,210,059); Marseille 868,435 (1,227,901); Lyon 410,455 (1,533,305); Toulouse 344,917 (648,267); Nice 331,165 (865,492); Strasbourg 247,068 (613,380); Nantes 237,789 (558,-814); Bordeaux 201,965 (843,411); Saint-Étienne 193,938 (547,729).
Place of national origin (1982): French 90.6%; Algerians 1.5%, Portuguese 1.4%, Moroccans 0.8%, Spanish 0.6%, Italian 0.6%, other 4.5%.
Mobility (1982). Population living in same residence as in 1975: n.a.; same region 91.7%; different region 5.8%; different country 2.5%.
Households (1982). Average household size 2.7; 1 person 24.6%, 2 persons 28.5%, 3 persons 18.8%, 4 persons 16.1%, 5 persons 7.4%, 6 persons or more 4.6%. Family households: 14,118,940 (72.1%), nonfamily 5,471,460 (27.9%, of which 1-person 24.6%).
Immigration (1984): permanent immigrants admitted 40,185, from Portugal 39.9%, Morocco 17.0%, Spain 10.3%, Tunisia 6.5%, Turkey 5.6%.

Vital statistics

Birth rate per 1,000 population (1985): 13.9 (world avg. 29.0); (1983) legitimate 84.1%; illegitimate 15.9%.
Death rate per 1,000 population (1985): 10.0 (world avg. 11.0).
Natural increase rate per 1,000 population (1985): 3.9 (world avg. 18.0).
Total fertility rate (avg. births per childbearing woman; 1983): 1.5.
Marriage rate per 1,000 population (1985): 4.9.
Divorce rate per 1,000 population (1984): 2.0.
Life expectancy at birth (1980–82): male 70.4 years; female 78.6 years.
Major causes of death per 100,000 population (1984): malignant neoplasms (cancers) 237.8; heart disease 218.3; cerebrovascular disease 121.2.

Social indicators

Educational attainment (1974). Percent of adult employed population having: less than full primary education 36.2%, primary 30.4%, secondary 21.0%, some postsecondary 7.0%, 4-year degree 2.4%, postgraduate 2.8%.

Distribution of income (1975)

percent of household income by quintile

1	2	3	4	5 (highest)
5.3%	11.1%	16.0%	21.8%	45.8%.

Quality of working life. Average workweek (1985): 38.9 hours (overtime, n.a.). Annual rate per 100,000 workers (1982) for: injury or accident 27.7; industrial illness 0.5; death 0.003. Proportion of labour force insured for damages or income loss resulting from: injury, n.a.; permanent disability, n.a.; death, n.a. Average days lost to labour stoppages per 1,000 workers (1984): 57.6. Average duration of journey to work (1974): 53 minutes.
Access to services (1982). Proportion of dwellings having: central heating 67.5%; piped water 99.2%; indoor plumbing 85.0%; natural gas 48.9%.
Social participation. Eligible voters participating in last national election: 65.9%. Population over 15 years of age participating in voluntary associations: 28%. Trade union membership in total workforce: n.a.

Social deviance. Offense rate per 100,000 population (1984) for: murder 4.2; rape 5.2; other assault 69.4; theft, including burglary and housebreaking, 3,005.7. Incidence per 100,000 in general population of: alcoholism† (late 1970s) 3,500–4,000; drug and substance abuse, n.a.; suicide (1984) 19.9.
Leisure (1974–75). Favourite leisure activities: television 34%; reading 14%; knitting 10%; conversations 10%; games 8%; walking 4%; radio 4%.
Material well-being (1984). Households possessing: automobile 72.9%; television receiver 92.1%, of which colour 64.7%; refrigerator 96.9%; washing machine 83.6%.

National economy

Gross national product (at current market prices; 1984): U.S.$542,960,000,000 (U.S.$9,880 per capita).

Structure of gross domestic product and labour force

	1984			
	in value F '000,000	% of total value	labour force	% of labour force
Agriculture	167,592	4.1	1,659,300	7.0
Mining	66,870	1.6	121,800	0.5
Manufacturing	1,054,191	25.8	4,991,900	21.2
Construction	240,918	5.9	1,578,900	6.7
Public utilities	109,480	2.7	217,200	0.9
Transp. and commun.	216,621	5.3	1,369,900	5.8
Trade	385,111	9.9	3,454,400	14.7
Finance	497,431	12.2	1,655,700	7.0
Other (incl. pub. admin., defense, and services)	1,341,125	32.9	8,524,200‡	36.2
TOTAL	4,079,339	100.0*	23,573,300	100.0

Budget (1985). Revenue: F 954,300,000,000 (value-added taxes 46.6%, income tax 23.4%, corporate taxes 9.8%). Expenditure: F 994,909,000,000 (education 23.4%, health and social services 19.7%, defense 15.7%, administration 11.4%).
Public debt (internal; 1985): F 897,100,000,000.
Tourism (1984): receipts from visitors U.S.$7,598,000,000; expenditures by nationals abroad U.S.$4,270,000,000.

Manufacturing and mining enterprises (1983)

	no. of enterprises	no. of employees	hourly wages as a % of avg. of all wages§	annual value added (F '000,000)
Food products	...	545,000	100	133,600
Transport equipment	709	624,000	115	125,200
Electrical machinery	674	494,000	101	74,700
Petroleum refineries	49	28,000	...	57,300
Industrial chemicals	304	128,000	117	53,700
Metal products	3,417	254,000	109	47,100
Iron and steel	144	232,000	...	44,400
Textiles	1,910	258,000	83	33,100
Printing, publishing	1,745	213,000	117	27,200
Beverages	...	53,000	100	26,400
Paper and products	642	110,000	109	24,100
Wearing apparel	2,601	238,000	79	22,200
Rubber products	176	99,000	97	15,300
Tobacco	...	9,000	100	12,700
Glass products	146	65,000	112	11,800

Production (metric tons except as noted). Agriculture, forestry, fishing (1984): wheat 32,884,000, sugar beets 27,790,000, barley 11,543,000, corn (maize) 10,321,000, grapes 9,400,000, potatoes 6,200,000, apples 2,935,000, oats 1,875,000, rapeseed 1,345,000, sunflower seeds 1,000,000, tomatoes 790,000, carrots 551,000, pears 485,000, peas 480,000, peaches 454,000, rye 349,000, sorghum 256,000; livestock (number of live animals) 23,570,000 cattle, 12,260,000 sheep, 11,400,000 pigs, 1,200,000 goats; roundwood 38,681,000 cu m; fish catch 784,000 ‖. Mining and quarrying (1985): iron ore 4,400,000¶, potash salts 1,750,000, bauxite 1,454,000, zinc 40,200¶, lead 1,800¶, gold 88,200 troy oz. Manufacturing (1985): cement 22,224,000; crude steel 19,008,000; pig iron 15,420,000; sulfuric acid 4,251,000; rubber products 544,080, of which tires 46,224,000 units; aluminum 463,200; automobiles 2,784,000 units. Construction (dwelling units; 1983) 314,143.

Retail trade enterprises (1982)

	no. of enterprises	no. of employees	weekly wages as a % of all wages	annual purchases (F '000,000)
Large food stores	1,864	289,765	...	203,245
Small food stores	128,664	377,241	...	117,833
butcher shops	49,833	153,241	...	39,501
Clothing stores	70,821	200,995	...	40,502
Pharmacies	20,508	106,934	...	30,359
Department stores	1,732	76,853	...	27,101
Gas, coal, and other energy products	4,780	20,673	...	26,377
Furniture stores	7,698	58,299	...	20,842
Electrical and electronics stores	11,550	51,546	...	16,034
Publishing and paper	20,047	61,245	...	11,284

Energy production (consumption): electricity (kW-hr; 1984) 306,800,000,000 (282,000,000,000); coal (metric tons; 1984) 20,698,000 (40,516,000); crude petroleum (barrels; 1984) 15,040,000 (529,022,000); petroleum products (metric tons; 1984♀) 68,298,000 (75,284,000); natural gas (cu m; 1984) 6,579,800,000 (29,071,000,000).
Household income and expenditure. Average household size (1985) 2.7; average annual income per household (1984) F 156,830 (U.S.$17,945). Sources of income (1984): wages and salaries 52.8%, social security 25.4%, self-employment 21.5%; expenditure (1984): housing 28.5%, food and beverages 20.3%, health 10.6%, transportation 10.1%, clothing and footwear 7.4%, recreation 6.8%.

Population economically active (1984): total 23,573,300; activity rate of total population 42.9% (participation rates: ages 15–64, 65.6%; female 40.9%; unemployed 9.8%).

Price and earnings indexes (1980 = 100)

	1979	1980	1981	1982	1983	1984	1985
Consumer price index	87.9	100.0	113.4	126.8	139.0	149.3	157.9
Hourly earnings index	86.2	100.0	114.4	137.5	155.1	168.2	178.4

Land use (1984): forested 26.7%; meadows and pastures 23.0%; agricultural and under permanent cultivation 34.4%; other 15.9%.

Financial aggregates

	1980	1981	1982	1983	1984	1985
Exchange rate, F per:						
U.S. dollar	4.52	5.75	6.73	8.35	9.59	8.98
£	10.78	10.97	10.87	12.11	11.09	11.65
SDR	5.76	6.69	7.42	8.74	9.40	8.30
International reserves (U.S.$)						
Total (excl. gold; '000,000)	27,340	22,262	16,531	19,851	20,940	26,589
SDRs ('000,000)	935	1,257	979	442	572	900
Reserve pos. in IMF ('000,000)	1,067	1,029	958	1,352	1,265	1,370
Foreign exchange	25,338	19,976	14,594	18,057	19,102	24,319
Gold ('000,000 fine troy oz)	81.85	81.85	81.85	81.85	81.85	81.85
% world reserves	8.6	8.6	8.6	8.7	8.6	8.6
Interest and prices						
Central bank discount (%)	9.50	9.50	9.50	9.50	9.50	9.50
Gov't. bond yield (%)	12.99	15.66	15.56	13.61	12.41	10.94
Industrial share prices (1980 = 100)	100.0	88.1	74.8	101.0	136.4	159.3
Balance of payments (U.S.$'000,000)						
Balance of visible trade	−13,419	−9,970	−15,785	−8,754	−4,089	−4,532
Imports, f.o.b.	120,934	110,843	107,289	98,460	96,392	100,565
Exports, f.o.b.	107,515	100,873	91,504	89,706	92,303	96,033
Balance of invisibles	13,360	9,393	8,326	7,664	6,965	8,039
Balance of payments, current account	−4,208	−4,809	−12,082	−4,904	−14	907

Foreign trade

Balance of trade (current prices)

	1980	1981	1982	1983	1984	1985
F '000,000,000	−55.4	−54.6	−100.5	−48.3	−53.2	−24.2
% of total	4.6%	3.8%	6.1%	2.7%	3.0%	1.3%

Imports (1985): F 967,920,000,000 (fuels 22.0%, of which crude petroleum 13.1%; machinery 20.3%; chemicals and chemical products 14.0%; agricultural products 12.4%; transport equipment 7.0%, of which automobiles 3.7%). *Major import sources:* West Germany 16.4%; Italy 10.0%; Belgium–Luxembourg 8.5%; U.K. 8.2%; U.S. 7.6%; The Netherlands 6.0%.
Exports (1985): F 906,912,000,000 (machinery 27.5%; agricultural products 16.7%; chemicals and chemical products 15.2%; transportation equipment 11.0%, of which automobiles 5.4%). *Major export destinations:* West Germany 14.4%; Italy 10.5%; U.S. 8.3%; Belgium–Luxembourg 8.2%; U.K. 7.1%; The Netherlands 4.7%.

Transport and communications

Transport. Railroads: (1985) route length 21,547 mi, 34,676 km; (1985) passenger-mi 37,766,000,000, passenger-km 60,780,000,000; short ton-mi cargo 40,061,000,000, metric ton-km cargo 58,488,000,000. Roads (1984): total length 499,945 mi, 804,585 km (paved 92%). Vehicles (1985): passenger cars 20,800,000; trucks and buses 3,310,000. Merchant marine (1985): vessels (100 gross tons and over) 1,136; total deadweight tonnage 13,712,614. Air transport (1985): passenger-mi 24,390,000,000, passenger-km 39,252,000,000; short ton-mi cargo 2,041,489,000, metric ton-km cargo 2,980,524,000; airports (1986) with scheduled flights 60.
Communications. Daily newspapers (1985): total number 102; total circulation 13,490,000; circulation per 1,000 population 244. Radio (1983): total number of receivers 20,000,000 (1 per 2.7 persons). Television (1985): total number of receivers 17,655,000 (1 per 3.1 persons). Telephones (1983): 29,373,663 (1 per 1.9 persons).

Education and health

Education (1983–84)

	schools	teachers	students	student/teacher ratio
Primary (age 2–10)	66,497	299,823	6,720,960	22.4
Secondary (age 11–18) / Voc., teacher tr.	11,181	319,292	5,225,994	16.4
Higher	1,094δ	44,156	1,135,941	25.7

Literacy (1980): total population literate 41,112,000 (98.8%); males literate 19,933,000 (98.9%); females literate 21,179,000 (98.7%).
Health (1983): physicians 114,951 (1 per 475.0 persons); hospital beds 496,896 (1 per 109.9 persons); infant mortality rate per 1,000 live births (1985) 8.0.
Food (1980–82): daily per capita caloric intake 3,525 (vegetable products 62%, animal products 38%); 140% of FAO recommended minimum requirement.

Military

Total active duty personnel (1985): 476,560 (army 63.0%, navy 14.2%, air force 20.3%, other 2.5%). *Military expenditure as percent of GNP* (1984): 3.2% (world 6.1%); per capita expenditure U.S.$289.

*Detail does not add to total given because of rounding. †Estimated as per a narrowly defined meaning of alcoholism. ‡Includes 2,318,700 unemployed persons. §1982. ‖ 1983. ¶Metal content only. ♀Includes Monaco. δ1980–81.

French Guiana

Official name: Département de la Guyane française (Department of French Guiana).
Political status: overseas department of France with two legislative houses (General Council [19]; Regional Council [31]).
Chief of state: President of France.
Heads of government: Commissioner of the Republic (for France); President of the General Council (for French Guiana); President of the Regional Council (for French Guiana).
Capital: Cayenne.
Official language: French.
Official religion: none.
Monetary unit: 1 franc (F) = 100 centimes; valuation (Oct. 1, 1986) 1 U.S.$ = F 6.64; 1 £ = F 9.60.

Area and population

		area		population
Arrondissements	Capitals	sq mi	sq km	1982 census
Cayenne	Cayenne	17,600*	45,600*	61,587
Saint-Laurent-du-Maroni	Saint-Laurent-du-Maroni	15,800*	40,900*	11,435
TOTAL		34,700†	90,000†	73,022

Demography

Population (1986): 85,700.
Density (1986): persons per sq mi 2.5, persons per sq km 1.0.
Urban-rural (1982): urban 73.4%; rural 26.6%.
Sex distribution (1982): male 52.66%; female 47.34%.
Age breakdown (1982): under 15, 34.2%; 15–29, 29.2%; 30–44, 19.9%; 45–59, 9.8%; 60–74, 5.1%; 75 and over, 1.8%.
Population projection: (1990) 99,000; (2000) 142,000.
Doubling time: 30 years.
Ethnic composition (1982): Guianese (mixed) Creole 42.6%; Guiana Chinese 14.0%; French (metropolitan) 10.7%; Haitian 7.5%; French West Indian 6.6%; Bush Negro 4.7%; Brazilian 4.6%; Amerindian 4.1%; other (other West Indian, Surinamese, Hmong, and other Southeast Asian) 5.2%.
Religious affiliation (1980): Roman Catholic 87.1%; Protestant 3.9%; nonreligious 2.5%; Afro-American spiritist 2.0%; animist 1.5%; Chinese folk-religionist 1.3%; Muslim 1.0%; Bahā'ī 0.7%.
Major cities (1982): Cayenne 37,097; Kourou 6,465; Rémire-Montjoly 5,921; Saint-Laurent-du-Maroni 5,042.

Vital statistics

Birth rate per 1,000 population (1984): 29.0 (world avg. 29.0); legitimate 23.0%; illegitimate 77.0%.
Death rate per 1,000 population (1984): 6.2 (world avg. 11.0).
Natural increase rate per 1,000 population (1984): 22.8 (world avg. 18.0).
Total fertility rate (avg. births per childbearing woman; 1975–79): 3.1.
Marriage rate per 1,000 population (1984): 3.9.
Divorce rate per 1,000 population (1984): 0.4.
Life expectancy at birth (1975–79): male 63.4 years; female 69.7 years.
Major causes of death per 100,000 population (1981): diseases of the circulatory system 119.3; accidents and violence 89.8; malignant neoplasms (cancers) 49.1; diseases of the digestive system 47.7; infectious and parasitic diseases 43.5.

National economy

Budget (1984). Revenue: F 675,000,000 (receipts from French central government 30.2%, taxes on fuels 12.0%, customs duties 7.6%, new loans 4.9%, unspecified sources 36.0%). Expenditures: F 675,000,000 (health and social services 21.5%, public works 19.0%, departmental administration 6.8%, construction of departmental buildings 3.6%, debt payments 1.3%; unspecified services 35.6%).
Public debt (external, outstanding; 1983‡): $25,000,000.
Tourism: n.a.
Production (metric tons except as noted). Agriculture, forestry, fishing (1984): cassava 8,000, rice 7,790§, sugarcane 5,009§, plantains 1,000, corn (maize) 1,000, limes 650, bananas 500, hearts of palm 659,000 buds; livestock (number of live animals) 14,000 cattle, 10,000 pigs, 100,000 chickens; roundwood 254,000 cu m; fish catch—shrimps and prawns caught by foreign vessels and landed in French Guiana for processing 1,582, local catch of shrimps and prawns 280, other 403. Mining and quarrying (1985): gold 407 kg; stone, sand, and gravel 407,000‖. Manufacturing (1984): canned hearts of palm 438; yogurt 1,762,000 cups; sawnwood and veneer sheets 34,679 cu m; finished wood products 729 cu m; rum 2,128 hectolitres§; passion fruit juice 207 hectolitres; lime juice 96 hectolitres; other products include leather goods, clothing, handicrafts, and beer. Construction (1984): residential 49,398 sq m; nonresidential authorized 17,361 sq m. Energy production (consumption): electricity (kW-hr; 1984) 181,100,000 (153,000,000); coal, none (none); crude petroleum, none (none); petroleum products (metric tons; 1984) none (105,000); natural gas, none (none).
Household income and expenditure. Average household size (1982) 3.3; income per household (1980) F 75,762 (U.S.$16,776); sources of income (1980): salaries 76.4%, industrial and commercial profits 12.3%, pensions and rents 3.8%, noncommercial profits 2.5%, income from stocks and bonds 1.6%, other 3.4%; expenditure (1980)¶: food and nonalcoholic beverages 44.9%, clothing and footwear 8.4%, housing 7.3%, household furnishings 7.0%, alcoholic beverages 5.1%, transportation and communication 5.0%, energy 4.1%, recreation 3.6%, health 2.2%, other 12.4%.
Land use (1983): forested 81.9%; meadows and pastures 0.1%; agricultural and under permanent cultivation♀; other 18.0%.
Gross national product (at current market prices; 1983): U.S.$180,000,000 (U.S.$2,340 per capita).

Structure of gross domestic product and labour force

	1982			
	in value	% of total value	labour force	% of labour force
Agriculture, forestry fishing	...	...	3,706	11.9
Mining	...	...	...	...
Manufacturing	...	...	1,522	4.9
Construction	...	...	2,837	9.1
Public utilities	...	...	380	1.2
Transp. and commun.	...	...	1,347	4.3
Trade	...	...	2,025	6.5
Finance, real estate	...	...	444	1.4
Pub. admin., services, other	...	...	18,922♁	60.7
TOTAL	...	...	31,183	100.0

Population economically active (1982): total 31,183; activity rate of total population 42.7% (participation rates: ages 15–64, 67.2%; female 37.2%; unemployed 15.3%).

Price and earnings indexes (December 1980 = 100)□

	1979	1980	1981	1982	1983	1984	1985
Consumer price index	88.9	100.0	116.5	130.3	151.5	163.0	172.8
Earnings index◇	87.4	100.0	120.1	139.9	154.0	168.0	179.6

Foreign trade

Balance of trade (current prices)

	1980	1981	1982	1983	1984	1985
F '000,000	−973	−1,163	−1,431	−1,843	−1,831	−1,956
% of total	82.2%	75.2%	77.1%	75.8%	73.7%	74.7%

Imports (1984): F 2,158,000,000 (food products 25.2%; electrical and nonelectrical machinery 16.4%; mineral fuels 16.1%; transport vehicles 10.4%; metals and metal products 6.5%; chemicals and chemical products 5.1%). *Major import sources:* France 54.7%; Trinidad and Tobago 13.0%; EEC (excluding France) 11.7%; Japan 4.7%; United States 2.9%.
Exports (1984): F 326,700,000 (shrimps and prawns 59.3%; basic metal products 10.9%; tires 9.9%; veneers, plywood, and finished wooden products 6.7%). *Major export destinations:* United States 38.2%; EEC (excluding France) 23.4%; Japan 16.7%; France 8.4%; Martinique 6.4%; Guadeloupe 5.6%.

Transport and communications

Transport. Railroads (1985): none. Roads (1984): total length 691 mi, 1,112 km (paved 65%). Vehicles (1984): passenger cars 14,440; trucks and buses 625. Merchant marine: n.a. Air transport (1985)△: passenger arrivals 75,056, passenger departures 76,934; cargo unloaded 2,608 metric tons, cargo loaded 1,237 metric tons; airports (1985): with scheduled flights 5.
Communications. Daily newspapers (1985): total number 2; total circulation 16,000△; circulation per 1,000 population 194†. Radio (1985): 43,000 receivers (1 per 1.9 persons). Television (1985): 6,400 receivers (1 per 13 persons). Telephones (1983): 22,143 (1 per 3.7 persons).

Education and health

Education (1984–85)

	schools	teachers	students	student/teacher ratio
Primary (age 6–11)	76	748	15,620⊙	...
Secondary (age 12–18)	8	470	5,529⊙	...
Voc., teacher tr.	...	177	...	...
Higher	1	...	239	...

Educational attainment (1982). Percent of population over age 25 having: no formal schooling 20.8%; primary education 40.4%; secondary 32.4%; higher 6.4%. *Literacy* (1982): total population over age 16 literate 38,964 (82.0%); males literate 21,021 (82.5%); females literate 17,943 (81.3%).
Health: physicians (1982) 62 (1 per 1,194 persons); hospital beds (1981) 907 (1 per 79 persons); infant mortality rate per 1,000 live births (1984) 22.6.
Food (1980–82): daily per capita caloric intake 2,818 (vegetable products 71%, animal products 29%); 105% of FAO recommended minimum requirement.

Military

Total active duty personnel (1984): 2,700**.

*Areas designated by arrondissement, including area south of the confluence of the Maroni and Litany rivers disputed between French Guiana and Suriname. †Approximate total area. ‡Includes external long-term private debt not guaranteed by the government. §1985. ‖1984. ¶Weights of consumer price index components. ♀Less than 0.01%. ♁Includes 8,927 in nonsaleable services, 3,218 in saleable services, 2,017 in categories not clearly defined, and 4,760 unemployed. □Indexes based on end-of-year figures. ◇Based on minimum hourly wages paid. △Rochambeau international airport (Cayenne) only. †Circulation for one daily. ⊙1985–86. **Includes metropole troops, local conscripts serving in French Guiana, and French Foreign Legion troops assigned to guard the Kourou Space Centre.

French Polynesia

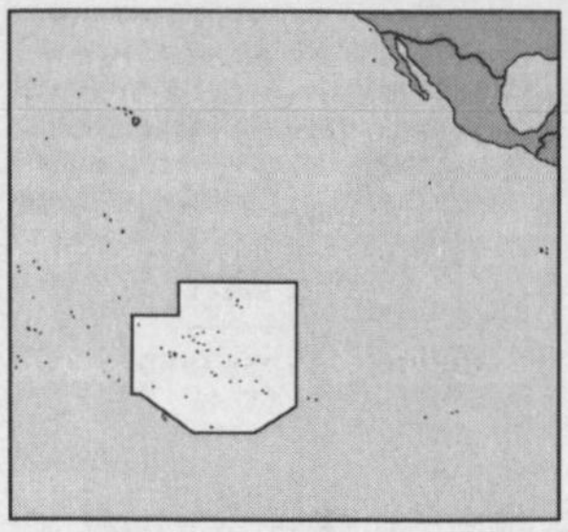

Official name: Territoire de la Polynésie française (French); Polynesia Farani (Tahitian) (Territory of French Polynesia).
Political status: overseas territory (France) with one legislative house (Territorial Assembly [30]), two representatives in the French National Assembly, and one senator in the French Senate.
Chief of state: President of France.
Head of government: High Commissioner (for France); President of the Territorial Assembly (for French Polynesia).
Capital: Papeete.
Official languages: French; Tahitian.
Official religion: none.
Monetary unit: 1 Franc de la Comptoirs française du pacifique (CFPF) = 100 centimes; valuation (Oct. 1, 1986) 1 U.S.$ = CFPF 120.75; 1 £ = CFPF 174.48.

Area and population

		area		population
Circumscriptions	Capitals	sq mi	sq km	1983 census
Îles Australes	Mataura	57	148	6,283
Îles Marquises	Taiohae	405	1,049	6,548
Îles sous le Vent	Uturoa	156	404	19,060
Îles Tuamotu et Gambier	Papeete	280	726	11,793
Îles du Vent	Papeete	461	1,194	123,069
TOTAL		1,550*	4,000*	166,753

Demography

Population (1986): 180,000.
Density (1985)†: persons per sq mi 132.5, persons per sq km 51.1.
Urban-rural (1985): urban 73.4%‡; rural 26.6%.
Sex distribution (1983): male 52.12%; female 47.88%.
Age breakdown (1985): under 15, 37.9%; 15–29, 30.0%; 30–44, 16.5%; 45–59, 10.5%; 60–74, 4.3%; 75 and over, 0.8%.
Population projection: (1990) 202,000; (2000) 269,000.
Doubling time: 28 years.
Ethnic composition (1983): Polynesian 68.5%; mixed 14.5%, of which Polynesian-European 9.5%, Polynesian-Chinese 3.8%, European-Chinese 0.3%; European (mostly French) 11.6%; Chinese 4.5%; other 0.9%.
Religious affiliation (1980): Protestant 46.6%, of which Evangelical Church of French Polynesia 32.8%; Roman Catholic 39.4%; other Christian 8.2%, of which Mormon 3.5%; nonreligious 5.0%; other 0.8%.
Major cities (1983): Papeete 23,496; Faaa 21,927; Punaauia 12,414; Pirae 12,023; Mahina 8,954.

Vital statistics

Birth rate per 1,000 population (1985): 30.5 (world avg. 29.0); (1980) legitimate 45.1%; illegitimate 54.9%.
Death rate per 1,000 population (1985): 5.3 (world avg. 11.0).
Natural increase rate per 1,000 population (1985): 25.2 (world avg. 18.0).
Total fertility rate (avg. births per childbearing woman; 1985): 3.5.
Marriage rate per 1,000 population (1985): 6.6.
Divorce rate per 1,000 population (1980): 1.2.
Life expectancy at birth (1980–85): male 61.3 years; female 65.1 years.
Major causes of death per 100,000 population (1984): diseases of the circulatory system 120.1; ill-defined conditions 94.2; malignant neoplasms (cancers) 67.7; accidents, suicide, and violence 58.9.

National economy

Budget (1984) Revenue: CFPF 37,591,000,000 (custom duties and taxes 73.4%, of which indirect taxes 56.9%; loans 7.5%; visa and postal registrations 3.7%; property taxes 3.1%). Expenditures: CFPF 29,205,000,000 (grants and subsidies 39.2%; operating and service expenses 34.5%; public debt service 10.3%; infrastructure expenses and maintenance 7.4%).
Public debt (external, outstanding; 1982): U.S.$114,000,000.
Tourism (1984): receipts from visitors U.S.$66,000,000; expenditures by nationals abroad, n.a.
Production (metric tons except as noted). Agriculture, forestry, fishing§ (1985): coconuts 65,000 ‖, cassava 5,000 ‖, potatoes 3,000 ‖, watermelon 1,470, pineapples 1,240, tomatoes 1,150, cucumbers 960, bananas 333, carrots 272, plantains 206, coffee 55, vanilla 14, flowers CFPF 655,000,000 ‖; livestock (number of live animals; 1984) 32,000 pigs, 10,000 cattle, 3,000 goats; roundwood, n.a.; fish catch 2,028, of which skipjack tuna 457, black cultured pearls 206 kilograms. Mining and quarrying: none. Manufacturing (1985): copra 12,520; crude coconut oil 7,449; *monoï* oil (a base used in cosmetics and suntan lotions) 81¶; beer 100,000 hectolitres♀; printed cloth 200,000 metres♂; sandals 600,000 pairs♂. Construction (value added in CFPF '000,000; 1984): residential 2,848; nonresidential 3,639. Energy production (consumption): electricity (kW-hr; 1984) 193,700,000 (176,700,000); coal, none (none); crude petroleum, none (none); petroleum products (metric tons; 1984) none (145,000); natural gas, none (none).

Gross national product (at current market prices; 1983): U.S.$1,374,000,000 (U.S.$8,330 per capita).

Structure of gross domestic product and labour force

	1982		1983	
	in value CFPF '000,000	% of total value	labour force	% of labour force
Agriculture	6,514	4.8	8,032	13.1
Manufacturing	11,091	8.1	4,155	6.8
Construction	12,843	9.4	6,231	10.2
Public utilities	1,330	1.0	392	0.7
Transportation and communication	8,790	6.4	3,439	5.6
Trade }	33,029	24.1	13,698	22.4
Finance }			1,253	2.1
Pub. admin., defense	32,520	23.7 }	20,663	33.8
Services	30,836	22.5 }		
Other□	—	—	3,258	5.3
TOTAL	136,953	100.0	61,121	100.0

Population economically active (1983): total 61,121; activity rate of total population 36.7% (participation rates: ages 15–64, *c.* 58.0%; female 31.6%◇; unemployed 5.3%).

Price and earnings indexes (1980 = 100)

	1979	1980	1981	1982	1983	1984	1985
Consumer price index	89.8	100.0	116.7	133.6	151.9	168.1	181.1
Monthly earnings index	86.8	100.0	119.8	149.4	177.2	199.2	217.1

Household income and expenditure. Average household size (1983) 5.0; average annual income per household (1977) CFPF 2,118,161 (U.S.$23,624); sources of income (1980): salaries 50.7%, self-employment 38.5%, transfer payments 9.1%, other 1.7%; expenditure△: food and beverages 36.5%, clothing 9.0%, other manufactures 42.0%, services 12.5%.
Land use (1983): forested 31.4%; meadows and pastures 5.5%; agricultural and under permanent cultivation 20.5%; other 42.6%.

Foreign trade

Balance of trade (current prices)

	1980	1981	1982	1983	1984	1985
CFPF '000,000	−39,690	−51,982	−58,957	−69,421	−80,358	−82,376
% of total	89.5%	90.0%	90.0%	87.8%	88.8%	86.3%

Imports (1985): CFPF 88,940,000,000 (food products 19.0%, electrical machinery and appliances 17.7%, petroleum products 13.3%, transport equipment 13.0%, metal manufactures 7.8%, chemical products 5.0%, textiles 4.5%. *Major import sources* (1983): France 45.8%; United States 15.8%; New Zealand 6.0%; Singapore 4.6%; Japan 4.3%.
Exports (1985): CFPF 6,564,000,000 (reexports [primarily ammunition, aeronautical parts, and machinery] 63.5%, black cultured pearls 21.2%, coconut oil 11.5%, vanilla 0.6%, *monoï* oil 0.2%). *Major export destinations* (1983): France 68.0%; Italy 14.5%; United States 7.0%; Japan 6.5%.

Transport and communications

Transport. Railroads: none. Roads (1984): total length 495 mi, 797 km (paved 33%¶). Vehicles (1975): passenger cars 16,500; trucks and buses 8,500. Merchant marine: vessels (100 gross tons and over), n.a. Air transport (1985): passenger arrivals 340,900, passenger departures 324,400; cargo unloaded 5,091 metric tons†, cargo loaded 663 metric tons†; airports (1985) with scheduled flights 32.
Communications. Daily newspapers (1984): total number 2; total circulation 21,700; circulation per 1,000 population 128. Radio (1985): total number of receivers 80,000 (1 per 2.2 persons). Television (1984): total number of receivers 25,600 (1 per 6.6 persons). Telephones (1983): 27,612 (1 per 6.0 persons).

Education and health

Education (1984–85)

	schools	teachers⊙	students	student/ teacher ratio
Primary (age 6–10)	253	1,361	40,803	...
Secondary (age 11–17)	24	789	12,970	...
Voc., teacher tr.	17	197	3,822	...
Higher⊙	...	12	68	5.7

Educational attainment (1983): Percent of population over age 20 having: no formal schooling 7.7%; primary education 58.0%; secondary 28.7%; higher 5.6%. *Literacy* (1983): total population over age 14 literate 98,314 (95.0%); males literate 51,910 (94.9%); females literate 46,404 (95.0%).
Health (1983): physicians 88** (1 per 1,895 persons); hospital beds 900** (1 per 185 persons); infant mortality rate per 1,000 live births (1985) 20.8.
Food (1980–82): daily per capita caloric intake 2,874 (vegetable products 79%, animal products 21%); 108% of FAO recommended minimum requirement.

Military

Total active duty personnel (1985): 5,300 French military personnel. *Military expenditure as percent of GNP:* n.a.

*Approximate total area including inland water; total land area is 1,359 sq mi (3,521 sq km). †Based on land area. ‡Urban agglomeration of Papeete. §Includes marine-produced commodities, *e.g.*, pearls. ‖ 1984. ¶1982. ♀1980. ♂1979. □Unemployed. ◇Based on employed total of 57,863. △Weights of consumer price index components. †Excludes 540 metric tons of nondifferentiated domestic cargo. ⊙1982–83. **Public health facilities only.

Gabon

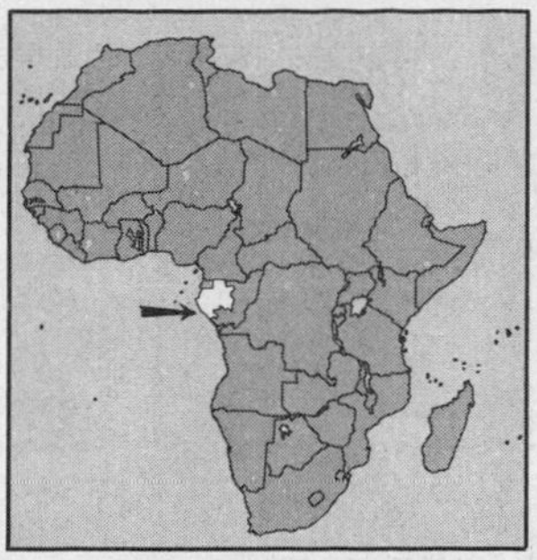

Official name: République Gabonaise (Gabonese Republic).
Form of government: unitary single-party republic with one legislative house (National Assembly [120]).
Chief of state: President.
Head of government: Prime Minister.
Capital: Libreville.
Official language: French.
Official religion: none.
Monetary unit: 1 CFA franc (CFAF) = 100 centimes; valuation (Oct. 1, 1986) 1 U.S.$ = CFAF 332.05; 1 £ = CFAF 479.81.

Area and population

		area		population
				1978
Provinces	Capitals	sq mi	sq km	estimate
Estuaire	Libreville	8,008	20,740	359,000
Haut-Ogooué	Franceville	14,111	36,547	213,000
Moyen-Ogooué	Lambaréné	7,156	18,535	49,000
Ngounié	Mouila	14,575	37,750	118,000
Nyanga	Tchibanga	8,218	21,285	98,000
Ogooué-Ivindo	Makokou	17,790	46,075	53,000
Ogooué-Lolo	Koulamoutou	9,799	25,380	49,000
Ogooué-Maritime	Port-Gentil	8,838	22,890	194,000
Woleu-Ntem	Oyem	14,851	38,465	166,000
TOTAL		103,347*	267,667	1,300,000*

Demography

Population (1986): 1,187,000.
Density (1986): persons per sq mi 11.5, persons per sq km 4.4.
Urban-rural (1985): urban 40.9%; rural 59.1%.
Sex distribution (1985): male 49.14%; female 50.86%.
Age breakdown (1985): under 15, 35.4%; 15–29, 24.1%; 30–44, 18.1%; 45–59, 13.1%; 60–74, 7.5%; 75 and over, 1.8%.
Population projection: (1990) 1,282,000; (2000) 1,611,000.
Doubling time: 50 years.
Ethnic composition (1980): Fang 34.5%; Mpongwe 14.5%; Mbete 13.6%; Punu 10.9%; French 6.0%; other 20.5%.
Religious affiliation (1980): Christian 94.5%, of which Roman Catholic 63.8%, Protestant 18.4%, African indigenous 12.1%; traditional religion 2.9%; Muslim 0.8%; other 1.8%.
Major cities (1983): Libreville 257,000; Port-Gentil 123,000; Franceville 38,030.

Vital statistics

Birth rate per 1,000 population (1980–85): 33.7 (world avg. 29.0).
Death rate per 1,000 population (1980–85): 19.9 (world avg. 11.0).
Natural increase rate per 1,000 population (1980–85): 13.8 (world avg. 18.0).
Total fertility rate (avg. births per childbearing woman; 1980–85): 4.7.
Marriage rate per 1,000 population: n.a.
Divorce rate per 1,000 population: n.a.
Life expectancy at birth (1980–85): male 48.0 years; female 51.4 years.
Major causes of death per 100,000 population: n.a.; however, major diseases include malaria, measles, shigellosis (infection with dysentery), trypanosomiasis, and tuberculosis.

National economy

Budget (1986). Revenue: CFAF 720,000,000,000 (taxes on petroleum organizations and petroleum fees 50.3%; loans 16.7%; customs duties 14.9%). Expenditures: CFAF 720,000,000,000 (current expenditure 44.4%; development expenditure 33.1%, of which infrastructure 17.8%; public debt 22.5%).
Public debt (external, outstanding; 1984): U.S.$724,500,000.
Tourism: receipts from visitors (1984) U.S.$4,000,000; expenditures by nationals abroad (1983) U.S.$92,000,000.
Production (metric tons except as noted). Agriculture, forestry, fishing (1984): roots and tubers 416,000, cassava 265,000, plantains 170,000, sugarcane 155,600, corn (maize) 10,000, peanuts (groundnuts) 10,000, bananas 8,000, palm oil 3,200, cacao beans 2,500, coffee 1,400; livestock (number of live animals) 150,000 pigs, 80,000 sheep, 2,000,000 chickens; roundwood (1985) 1,382,000 cu m; fish catch (1983) 52,638. Mining and quarrying (1985): manganese 2,300,000; uranium 918. Manufacturing (1984): cement 207,900; flour 21,600; raw sugar 15,000; beer 500,000 hectolitres; soft drinks 198,172 hectolitres; cigarettes 17,800,000 packs; textiles CFAF 2,420,000,000. Construction: n.a. Energy production (consumption): electricity (kW-hr; 1984) 535,000,000 (535,000,000); crude petroleum (barrels; 1985) 63,038,000 (9,000,000); petroleum products (metric tons; 1984) 1,121,000 (660,000); natural gas (cu m; 1984) 205,016,000 (205,016,000); fuelwood and bagasse (cu m; 1984) 1,315,000 (1,315,000).
Population economically active (1984): total 533,000; activity rate (1977) of total population 39.4% (participation rates: ages 15–64 [1977], 9.6%; female [1977] 47.2%; unemployed, n.a.).

Price and earnings indexes (1980 = 100)

	1980	1981	1982	1983	1984	1985	1986†
Consumer price index	100.0	108.7	126.8	137.0	148.2	159.1	163.7
Earnings index	100.0	101.1	126.6	156.3	...	...	...

Gross national product (at current market prices; 1984): U.S.$2,830,000,000 (U.S.$2,470 per capita).

Structure of gross domestic product and labour force

	1983			
	in value CFAF '000,000	% of total value	labour force	% of labour force
Agriculture	75,800	5.9	14,118‡	10.2‡
Mining	605,700	47.2	3,919	2.9
Manufacturing	57,200	4.5	4,123	3.0
Construction	93,000	7.3	13,154	9.5
Public utilities	19,500	1.5	§	§
Transportation and communication	50,600	4.0	§	§
Trade	105,000	8.2	3,732	2.7
Finance	10,000	0.8	§	§
Pub. admin., defense	102,600	8.0	42,678	31.0
Services	85,100	6.6	§	§
Other, including taxes on imports	77,500	6.0	56,143§	40.7§
TOTAL	1,282,000	100.0	137,867‡	100.0

Household income and expenditure. Average household size (1980) 4.0; average annual income per household: n.a.; sources of income‡ (1983): private sector 73.4%, public sector 26.6%; expenditure ‖ (1983): food and tobacco 54.7%, clothing and footwear 17.5%, housing 13.0%, transportation and communication 6.3%.
Land use (1983): forested 77.6%; meadows and pastures 18.2%; agricultural and under permanent cultivation 1.8%; other 2.4%.

Foreign trade

Balance of trade (current prices)

	1980	1981	1982	1983	1984	1985
CFAF '000,000	+351,000	+371,100	+252,100	+421,700	+492,600	+500,500
% of total	48.8%	45.0%	32.4%	39.4%	40.8%	40.9%

Imports (1983): CFAF 324,900,000,000 (machinery and mechanical equipment 23.8%; transport equipment and parts 15.1%; food, beverages, and tobacco products 12.3%; metal and metal products 10.7%; household and consumer products 5.3%; clothing and textiles 4.6%). *Major import sources:* France 54.2%; United States 11.0%; Japan 7.4%; West Germany 5.1%; The Netherlands 3.8%; United Kingdom 3.6%; Italy 3.1%; Spain 2.5%; Belgium-Luxembourg 1.8%.
Exports (1983): CFAF 746,600,000,000 (crude petroleum and petroleum products 83.5%; wood 7.4%, of which okoumé and ozigo 5.5%; manganese ore and concentrate 4.2%; uranium ore and concentrate 3.3%). *Major export destinations:* France 30.4%; United States 25.6%; Spain 6.7%; Italy 5.5%; The Netherlands 4.8%; Brazil 4.4%; Canada 4.4%; United Kingdom 4.1%.

Transport and communications

Transport. Railroads (1984): length 210 mi, 338 km; passengers carried 135,913; short ton cargo carried 731,065, metric ton cargo carried 664,605. Roads (1984): total length 4,668 mi, 7,513 km (paved 8%). Vehicles (1983): passenger cars 16,043; trucks and buses 10,695. Merchant marine (1985): vessels (100 gross tons and over) 21; total deadweight tonnage 169,612. Air transport (1983): passengers carried 850,000; cargo carried 36,376 short tons (33,000 metric tons); airports (1986) with scheduled flights 25¶.
Communications. Daily newspapers (1984): total number 2; total circulation 33,000; circulation per 1,000 population 35. Radio (1985): total number of receivers 100,000 (1 per 12 persons). Television (1985): total number of receivers 21,000 (1 per 55 persons). Telephones (1984): 11,600 (1 per 99 persons).

Education and health

Education (1982–83)

	schools	teachers	students	student/ teacher ratio
Primary	901	3,781	165,559	43.8
Secondary	47	1,161	22,350	19.3
Voc., teacher tr.	29	582	10,545	18.1
Higher	1	297	2,651	8.9

Educational attainment, n.a. *Literacy* (1978): total population over age 15 literate 800,000 (77%); males literate, n.a.; females literate, n.a.
Health (1980): physicians 265 (1 per 4,053 persons); hospital beds 4,617 (1 per 253 persons); infant mortality rate per 1,000 live births (1980–85) 121.6.
Food (1980–82): daily per capita caloric intake 2,808 (vegetable products 88%, animal products 12%); 120% of FAO recommended minimum requirement.

Military

Total active duty personnel (1985): 2,400 (army 70.8%, navy 8.3%, air force 20.9%), not including 600 French troops. *Military expenditure as percent of GNP* (1983): 2.7% (world 6.1%); per capita expenditure U.S.$84.

*Detail does not add to total given because of rounding. †January. ‡Official government figures for salaried workers only, not including traditional agricultural workers; agricultural workers (FAO estimate, 1984) totaled 395,000 (74.0% of the labour force). §Public utilities, transportation and communication, finance, and service employees included with other. ‖ Libreville only. ¶Includes airfields.

Gambia, The

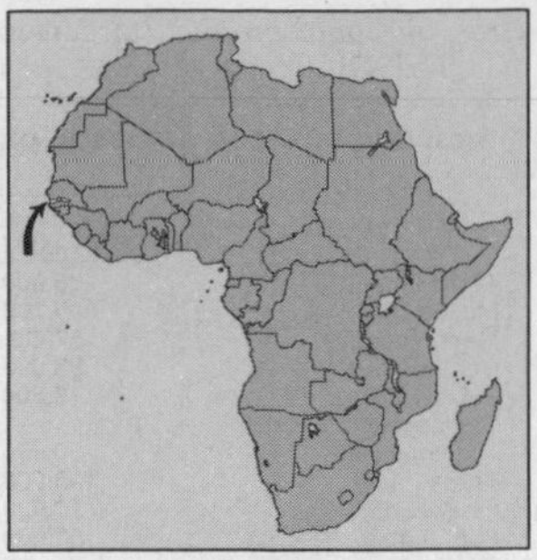

Official name: Republic of The Gambia.
Form of government: multiparty republic with one legislative house (House of Representatives [49]).
Head of state and government: President.
Capital: Banjul.
Official language: English.
Official religion: none.
Monetary unit: 1 dalasi (D) = 100 butut; valuation (Oct. 1, 1986) 1 U.S.$ = D 7.58; 1 £ = D 10.95.

Area and population

		area		population
				1983*
Divisions	**Capitals**	sq mi	sq km	census
Kombo Saint Mary	Kanifing	29	76	101,504
Lower River	Mansakonko	625	1,618	55,263
MacCarthy Island	Kuntaur/Georgetown	1,117	2,894	126,004
North Bank	Kerewan	871	2,256	112,225
Upper River	Basse	799	2,069	111,388
Western	Brikama	681	1,764	137,245
City				
Banjul	—	5	12	44,188
TOTAL		4,127	10,689	687,817

Demography

Population (1986): 764,500.
Density† (1986): persons per sq mi 229.9, persons per sq km 88.7.
Urban-rural (1983): urban 21.2%; rural 78.8%.
Sex distribution (1983): male 49.74%; female 50.26%.
Age breakdown (1983): under 15, 43.8%; 15–29, 26.5%; 30–44, 15.7%; 45–59, 9.4%; 60–74, 4.0%; 75 and over, 0.6%.
Population projection: (1990) 887,000; (2000) 1,244,000.
Doubling time: 20 years.
Ethnic composition (1983): Malinke 40.4%; Fulani 18.7%; Wolof 14.6%; Dyola 10.3%; Soninke 8.2%; other 7.8%.
Religious affiliation (1983): Muslim 95.4%; Christians 3.7%; traditional beliefs and other 0.9%.
Major cities (1983): Serekunda 102,600‡; Banjul 44,188; Brikama 24,300‡; Basse 5,612; Kau-Ur 5,338; Bansang 4,137.

Vital statistics

Birth rate per 1,000 population (1980–85): 47.5 (world avg. 29.0); legitimate, n.a.; illegitimate, n.a.
Death rate per 1,000 population (1980–85): 21.7 (world avg. 11.0).
Natural increase rate per 1,000 population (1980–85): 25.8 (world avg. 18.0).
Total fertility rate (avg. births per childbearing woman; 1980–85): 6.4.
Marriage rate per 1,000 population: n.a.
Divorce rate per 1,000 population: n.a.
Life expectancy at birth (1980–85): male 40.9 years; female 44.1 years.
Major causes of death per 100,000 population: n.a.; however, major infectious diseases include malaria, gonococcal infections and syphilis, leprosy (Hansen's disease), chicken pox, schistosomiasis, tetanus, tuberculosis, and trypanosomiasis (sleeping sickness).

National economy

Budget (1984–85§). Revenue: D 172,642,000 (import and excise duties 52.3%; income tax 14.8%; export duties 5.5%). Expenditures: D 335,801,000 (current expenditure D 180,912,000, of which education, sports, and culture 13.0%; health, labour, and social welfare 8.0%; public works, transport, and communications 7.2%; agriculture, forestry, fisheries, and mineral resources 7.0%).
Production (metric tons except as noted). Agriculture, forestry, fishing (1984): peanuts (groundnuts) in shell 114,000, millet and sorghum 33,000, paddy rice 22,000, corn (maize) 11,000, cassava 6,000, palm oil 2,500, palm kernels 2,000; livestock (number of live animals) 280,000 cattle, 185,000 goats, 175,000 sheep, 12,000 pigs, 4,000 asses, 310,000 chickens; roundwood 777,000 cu m, of which fuel wood 756,000 cu m, saw logs, veneer logs and logs for sleepers 14,000 cu m, industrial wood 7,000 cu m; fish catch (1983) 9,598, of which inland water 598, Atlantic Ocean 9,000. Mining and quarrying: n.a.; however, deposits of kaolin, tin, ilmenite, zircon, and rutile are significant locally. Manufacturing: n.a.; however, major agriculture-based industries include peanut and palm kernel processing for oil and cake, fish preservation (salting, drying, and smoking), and brewing of alcoholic beverages; other industries include plastics, confectionery, furniture, and toiletries. Construction: n.a. Energy production (consumption): electricity (kW-hr; 1984) 42,000,000 (42,000,000); coal, none (n.a.); crude petroleum, none (n.a.); petroleum products (metric tons; 1984) none (55,000); natural gas, none (n.a.).
Population economically active (1983): total 325,600; activity rate of total population 47.3% (participation rates: ages 15–64 [1980] 79.0%; female [1980] 42.2%; unemployed, n.a.).

Price and earnings indexes (1980 = 100)

	1980	1981	1982	1983	1984	1985	1986 ‖
Consumer price index	100.0	106.1	117.6	130.1	158.9	188.0	269.3
Earnings index	...	...	...	...	...	...	...

Household income and expenditure. Average household size (1980) 4.9; average annual income per household: n.a., source of income: n.a., expenditure¶ (1985): food, beverages, and tobacco 58.0%, clothing and footwear 17.5%, energy and water 5.4%, housing 5.1%, education, health, transportation and communication, recreation and other 14.0%.
Gross national product (1984): U.S.$180,000,000 (U.S.$250 per capita).

Structure of gross domestic product and labour force

	1982–83		1983	
	in value D'000,000	% of total value	labour force	% of labour force
Agriculture	154.1	27.2	239,940	73.7
Mining	0.5	0.1	66	0.0
Manufacturing	41.1	7.2	8,144	2.5
Construction	45.7	8.1	4,373	1.3
Public utilities	2.6	0.5	1,233	0.4
Transportation and communication	47.8	8.4	8,014	2.5
Trade	134.4	23.7	♀	♀
Finance	60.8	10.7	14,570	4.5
Public administration	79.6	14.0	8,295	2.5
Services	14.2	2.5	9,381	2.9
Other	−13.6♂	♂	31,607♀	9.7♀
TOTAL	567.2	100.0	325,623	100.0

Tourism: receipts from visitors (1984) U.S.$22,000,000; expenditures by nationals abroad (1983) U.S.$2,000,000.
Public debt (external, outstanding; 1984): U.S.$161,000,000.
Land use (1983): forested 19.8%; meadows and pastures 9.0%; agricultural and under permanent cultivation 16.0%; built-on area, wasteland, and other 55.2%.

Foreign trade□

Balance of trade (current prices)

	1980	1981	1982	1983	1984	1985
D '000,000	−189.1	−156.8	−90.6	−133.4	−140.1	−189.2
% of total	63.3%	60.4%	31.5%	34.5%	30.1%	35.3

Imports (1984): D 354,160,000 (food and live animals 37.3%, machinery and transport equipment 17.1%, basic manufactured goods 16.1%, mineral fuels and lubricants 12.3%, beverages and tobacco 5.0%, chemicals and related products 4.4%, animal and vegetable oils and fats 1.1%). *Major import sources:* United States 15.9%; United Kingdom 14.9%; France 10.0%; China 8.8%; U.S.S.R. and Eastern European countries 7.9%; Thailand 7.2%; West Germany 6.7%; Italy 5.3%; Senegal 4.9%; Japan 4.7%; Algeria 4.2%; The Netherlands 3.7%.
Exports (1984): D 162,568,000 (peanut oil 27.4%, shelled peanuts 24.2%, peanut meal and cake 2.4%, fish and fish preparations 2.2%). *Major export destinations:* Ghana 26.5%; France 20.3%; Switzerland 19.2%; Belgium-Luxembourg 12.8%; United Kingdom 8.6%; Guinea 6.5%; Italy 5.9%.

Transport and communications

Transport. Railroads: none. Roads (1983): total length 1,916 mi, 3,083 km (paved 15%). Vehicles (1983): passenger cars 6,100; trucks and buses 1,030. Merchant marine (1985): vessels (100 gross tons and over) 6; total deadweight tonnage 4,046. Air transport: passengers, n.a.; cargo, n.a.; airports (1986) with scheduled flights 1.
Communications. Daily newspapers: none. Radio (1985): total number of receivers 105,000 (1 per 7.0 persons). Television: none. Telephones (1980): 3,476 (1 per 182 persons).

Education and health

Education (1984–85)

	schools	teachers	students	student/ teacher ratio
Primary (age 8–14)	189	2,640	66,257	25.1
Secondary (age 15–21)	8	587	10,309	17.6
Voc., teacher tr.	8	150	1,141	7.6

Educational attainment (1973). Percent of adult population over age 20 having: no formal schooling 90.8%; primary education 6.2%; secondary 2.6%; higher 0.4%. *Literacy* (1980): total population over age 15 literate 67,700 (20.1%); males literate 47,700 (29.1%); females literate 20,000 (11.6%).
Health (1980): physicians 66 (1 per 9,571 persons); hospital beds 756 (1 per 835 persons); infant mortality rate per 1,000 live births (1980–85) 174.0.
Food (1980–82): daily per capita caloric intake 2,223 (vegetable products 93%, animal products 7%); 95% of FAO recommended minimum requirement.

Military

Total active duty personnel (1985): 475 (army 84.2%, navy 10.5%, air force 5.3%). *Military expenditure as percent of GNP* (1982): 0.0% (world 6.0%).

*Preliminary. †Based on land area, which is 8,613 sq km (3,325 sq mi). ‡1986. §Estimate. ‖ April. ¶Low-income population in Banjul and Kombo St. Mary only. ♀Trade is included with other. ♂Less imputed bank charges. □Import figures are f.o.b. (free on board) in balance of trade and c.i.f. (cost, insurance, and freight) for commodities and trading partners.

German Democratic Republic

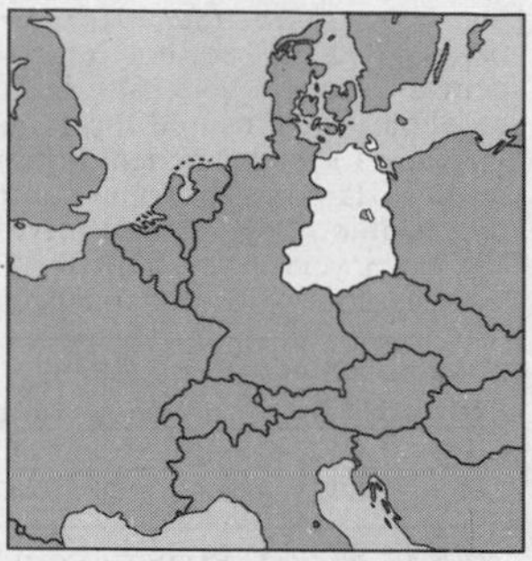

Official name: Deutsche Demokratische Republik (German Democratic Republic).
Form of government: unitary single-party republic with one legislative house (People's Chamber [500]).
Chief of state: Chairman, Council of State.
Head of government: Premier.
Capital: Berlin.
Official language: German.
Official religion: none.
Monetary unit: 1 Mark of Deutsche Demokratische Republik (M) = 100 Pfennige; valuation (Oct. 1, 1986) 1 U.S.$ = M 2.03; 1 £ = M 2.93.

Area and population

Districts	Capitals	area sq mi	area sq km	population 1985 estimate
Berlin, capital city	—	156	403	1,196,900
Cottbus	Cottbus	3,190	8,262	883,500
Dresden	Dresden	2,602	6,738	1,783,200
Erfurt	Erfurt	2,837	7,349	1,237,100
Frankfurt	Frankfurt	2,775	7,186	706,800
Gera	Gera	1,546	4,004	742,200
Halle	Halle	3,386	8,771	1,800,800
Karl-Marx-Stadt	Karl-Marx-Stadt	2,320	6,009	1,889,100
Leipzig	Leipzig	1,917	4,966	1,384,000
Magdeburg	Magdeburg	4,450	11,526	1,254,800
Neubrandenburg	Neubrandenburg	4,227	10,948	620,100
Potsdam	Potsdam	4,853	12,568	1,121,500
Rostock	Rostock	2,731	7,074	897,500
Schwerin	Schwerin	3,348	8,672	592,200
Suhl	Suhl	1,489	3,856	550,300
TOTAL		41,827	108,333*	16,660,000

Demography

Population (1986): 16,640,000.
Density (1986): persons per sq mi 397.8; persons per sq km 153.6.
Urban–rural (1985): urban 76.6%; rural 23.4%.
Sex distribution (1985): male 47.23%; female 52.77%.
Age breakdown (1985): under 15, 19.3%; 15–29, 22.2%; 30–44, 19.7%; 45–59, 19.4%; 60–74, 12.1%; 75 and over, 7.3%.
Population projection: (1990) 16,604,000; (2000) 16,483,000.
Doubling time: not applicable; population is declining.
Ethnic composition (1986): German 99.7%; other 0.3%.
Religious affiliation (1986): Protestant 47.0%; Roman Catholic 7.0% unaffiliated and other 46.0%.
Major cities (1985): Berlin (East) 1,196,900; Leipzig 555,800; Dresden 520,100; Karl-Marx-Stadt 317,200; Magdeburg 288,900; Rostock 241,900.

Vital statistics

Birth rate per 1,000 population (1985): 13.2 (world avg. 29.0); (1983) legitimate 74%; illegitimate 26%.
Death rate per 1,000 population (1985): 13.4 (world avg. 11.0).
Natural increase rate per 1,000 population (1985): −0.2 (world avg. 18.0).
Total fertility rate (avg. births per childbearing woman; 1985): 1.6.
Marriage rate per 1,000 population (1985): 7.8.
Divorce rate per 1,000 population: (1985): 2.9.
Life expectancy at birth (1983): male 69.1 years; female 75.1 years.
Major causes of death per 100,000 population (1983): circulatory diseases 825.0; malignant neoplasms (cancers) 212.0; pneumonia 23.0; stomach and intestinal diseases 9.0; tuberculosis 4.0.

National economy

Budget (1985). Revenue: M 231,084,000,000 (revenue from state-owned enterprises 79.7%, social security contributions 7.5%, taxes and dues 7.4%, health care contributions 3.5%). Expenditures: M 230,944,000,000 (economic development 31.4%, social welfare and health 19.3%, economic subsidies and price supports 17.3%, education 5.7%, defense 5.6%, general administration 4.5%, cultural activities 2.4%).
Public debt (external, outstanding; 1984): U.S.$11,300,000,000.
Tourism (1984): total tourist arrivals 1,039,811.
Production (metric tons except as noted). Agriculture, forestry, fishing (1984): potatoes 7,753,000, sugar beets 6,500,000, barley 4,400,000, wheat 4,100,000, rye 2,300,000, oats 700,000; livestock (number of live animals; 1985) 13,191,000 pigs, 5,848,000 cattle, 2,528,000 sheep, 51,300,000 chickens; commercial timber 10,984,000 cu m, firewood 860,000 cu m; fish catch 300,000. Mining and quarrying (metal content except as noted; 1984): bauxite (gross amount) 58,000; iron ore 20,000; copper ore 12,000; nickel 2,000; tin 1,800; silver 1,360,000 troy oz. Manufacturing (1984): cement 11,555,000; steel 7,573,000; fertilizer 4,733,000; pig iron 2,357,000; plastics and synthetic resins 1,056,500; sulfuric acid 885,000; paper 871,000; sugar 870,000; lumber 2,275,000 cu m; 1,248,000 vacuum cleaners; 1,110,000 radios; 895,000 refrigerators; 639,000 television receivers; 525,000 washing machines. Construction (sq m; 1984): residential 7,316,000; nonresidential, n.a. Energy production (consumption): electricity (kW-hr; 1984) 110,093,000,000 (114,301,000,000); coal (metric tons; 1984) 296,341,000 (300,041,000); crude petroleum (barrels; 1984) 3,333,000 (3,501,000); petroleum products (metric tons; 1984) 10,272,600 (10,560,000); natural gas (cu m; 1984) 7,722,000,000 (13,877,000,000).
Gross national product (at current market prices; 1984): U.S.$93,631,000,000 (U.S.$5,600 per capita).

Structure of net material product and labour force

	1984 in value M '000,000	1984 % of total value	1984 labour force†	1984 % of labour force
Agriculture	19,190	8.1	914,200	10.7
Mining, manufacturing	165,280‡	70.0‡	3,482,500	41.0
Construction	13,770	5.8	583,100	6.9
Transportation and communication	9,620	4.1	626,800	7.4
Trade	21,250	9.0	861,400	10.1
Services	—	—	2,030,500§	23.9§
Other	6,900 ‖	3.0 ‖	—	—
TOTAL	236,100¶	100.0	8,498,500	100.0

Population economically active (1984): total 8,498,500†; activity rate of total population 51.0% (participation rates: ages 15–64, n.a.; female 49.4; unemployed, n.a.).

Price and earnings indexes (1970 = 100)

	1978	1979	1980	1981	1982	1983	1984
Consumer price index	97.8	98.4	98.6	98.9	98.9	98.9	98.9
Monthly earnings index	128.8	132.8	135.2	138.5	142.2	144.1	145.2

Household income and expenditure. Average household size (1984) 3.1; average annual income per household M 29,040 (U.S.$10,900); sources of income: wages and salaries 68.6%, social welfare 31.4%; expenditure (1984): food 20.5%, education and recreation 15.2%, clothing 10.2%, housing 9.7%, health 6.1%, energy 1.3%.
Land use (1984): forested 27.3%; meadows and pastures 11.8%; agricultural and under permanent cultivation 47.3%; other 13.6%.

Foreign trade

Balance of trade (current prices)

	1979	1980	1981	1982	1983	1984
M '000,000	−4,005	−5,840	+1,073	+5,353	+8,031	+6,901
% of total	3.7%	4.9%	0.8%	3.7%	5.0%	4.0%

Imports (1984): M 83,500,600,000 (combustibles, minerals, and unfabricated metals 41.6%; machinery, equipment, and transportation equipment 26.0%; fabricated and partially fabricated industrial materials 17.7%; chemicals and related products 9.0%; consumer goods 5.7%).
Exports (1984): M 90,401,900,000 (machinery, equipment, and transportation equipment 46.9%; combustibles, minerals, and unfabricated metals 17.5%; consumer goods 15.1%; chemical products 12.2%; fabricated industrial materials 8.3%). *Direction of total trade*♀: U.S.S.R. 38.6%; Czechoslovakia 7.4%; West Germany 6.0%; Poland 5.0%; Hungary 4.9%; Bulgaria 2.8%.

Transport and communications

Transport. Railroads (1984): length 8,840 mi, 14,226 km; passenger-mi 14,200,000,000, passenger-km 22,900,000,000; short ton-mi cargo 38,800,000,000, metric ton-km cargo 56,700,000,000. Roads (1984): total length 29,440 mi, 47,380 km (paved 100%). Vehicles (1984): passenger cars 3,157,077; trucks and buses 272,914. Merchant marine (1985): vessels (100 gross tons and over) 402; total deadweight tonnage 1,815,995. Air transport (1984): passenger-mi 1,535,000,000, passenger-km 2,470,000,000; short ton-mi cargo 51,700,000, metric ton-km cargo 75,500,000; airports (1986) with scheduled flights 4.
Communications. Daily newspapers (1984): total number 39; total circulation 8,950,000; circulation per 1,000 population 537. Radio (1985): 6,509,932 receivers (1 per 2.6 persons). Television (1985): 6,015,400 receivers (1 per 2.8 persons). Telephones (1985): 3,527,000 (1 per 4.7 persons).

Education and health

Education (1983–84)

	schools	teachers	students	student/teacher ratio
Primary (age 6–10)	5,666	54,971	766,745	13.9
Secondary (age 10–18)	5,711	112,172	1,265,349	11.3
Vocational	4,500	56,577	414,044	7.3
Higher	54	29,700	434,326	14.6

Educational attainment (1984). Percent of employed population over age 20 having: primary education, virtually 100%; academic secondary 15.6%; vocational 75.7%; higher 8.7%. *Literacy* (1985): total population over age 15 literate, virtually 100%.
Health (1985): physicians 37,000 (1 per 450 persons); hospital beds 170,000 (1 per 98 persons); infant mortality rate per 1,000 live births (1984) 10.0.
Food (1980–82): daily per capita caloric intake 3,720 (vegetable products 65%, animal products 35%); 142% of FAO recommended minimum requirement.

Military

Total active duty personnel (1985): 174,000 (army 69.0%, navy 8.6%, air force 22.4%). *Military expenditure as percent of GNP* (1983): 6.4% (world 6.1%); per capita expenditure U.S.$563.

*Detail does not add to total given because of rounding. †Employed. ‡Includes public utilities. §Includes finance, public administration, and defense. ‖ Other material activities. ¶At 1980 prices. ♀Separate figures are not available for import sources and export destinations.

Germany, Federal Republic of

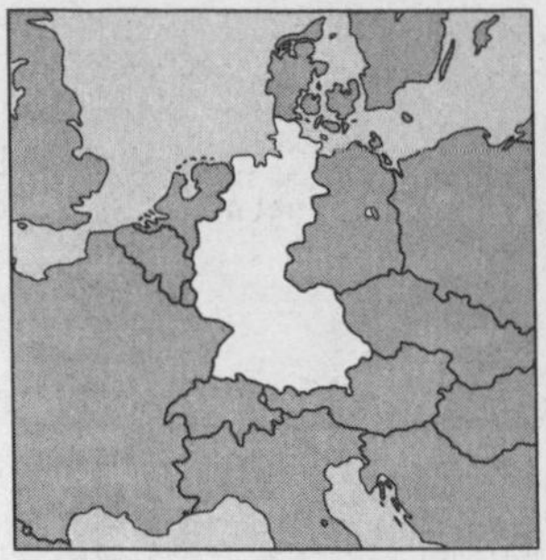

Official name: Bundesrepublik Deutschland (Federal Republic of Germany).
Form of government: federal multiparty republic with two legislative houses (Federal Council [45]; Federal Diet [520]).
Chief of state: President.
Head of government: Chancellor.
Capital: Bonn (provisional).
Official language: German.
Official religion: none.
Monetary unit: 1 Deutsche Mark (DM) = 100 Pfennige; valuation (Oct. 1, 1986) 1 U.S.$ = DM 2.03; 1 £ = DM 2.93.

Area and population

		area		population
States	**Capitals**	sq mi	sq km	1986 estimate*
Baden-Württemberg	Stuttgart	13,804	35,751	9,271,000
Bayern	Munich	27,241	70,553	10,974,000
Bremen	Bremen	156	404	660,000
Hamburg	Hamburg	292	755	1,580,000
Hessen	Wiesbaden	8,152	21,114	5,529,000
Niedersachsen	Hannover	18,320	47,450	7,197,000
Nordrhein-Westfalen	Düsseldorf	13,153	34,068	16,674,000
Rheinland-Pfalz	Mainz	7,663	19,847	3,615,000
Saarland	Saarbrücken	992	2,568	1,046,000
Schleswig-Holstein	Kiel	6,072	15,727	2,614,000
Berlin (West)†	Berlin (West)	185	480	1,860,000
TOTAL		96,030	248,717	61,020,000

Demography

Population (1986): 60,852,000.
Density (1986): persons per sq mi 635.4, persons per sq km 245.3.
Urban-rural (1980): urban 84.7%; rural 15.3%.
Sex distribution (1986): male 47.84%; female 52.16%.
Age breakdown (1985): under 15, 15.3%; 15–29, 24.4%; 30–44, 20.4%; 45–59, 19.6%; 60–74, 13.5%; 75 and over 6.8%.
Population projection: (1990) 59,600,000; (2000) 58,800,000.
Doubling time: not applicable; population has been declining since about 1980.
Ethnic composition (1985): German 92.8%; Turk 2.3%; Yugoslav 1.0%; Italian 0.9%; Greek 0.5%; Austrian 0.3%; Spanish 0.3%; Dutch 0.2%; other 1.7%.
Religious affiliation (1980): Christian 92.8%, of which Protestant 46.7% (including Lutheran-Reformed tradition 23.5%, Lutheran tradition 21.7%, Reformed tradition 0.7%, other 0.8%), Roman Catholic 43.8%, New Apostolic (non-Roman) Catholic 0.8%, Greek Orthodox 0.6%, other 0.9%; nonreligious 3.7%; Muslim 2.4%; atheist 0.9%; Jewish 0.1%; other 0.1%.
Major cities (1985): Berlin (West) 1,852,700; Hamburg 1,585,900; Munich 1,266,100; Cologne 919,300; Essen 622,000; Frankfurt am Main 598,000; Dortmund 575,200; Düsseldorf 563,000; Stuttgart 561,200; Bonn 292,600.
Place of birth: n.a.
Mobility: n.a.
Households (1982). Number of households 25,336,000; average household size 2.4; 1 person 31.3%, 2 persons 28.7%, 3 persons 17.6%, 4 persons 14.4%, 5 or more persons 8.0%. Family households: 17,410,000 (68.7%); nonfamily 7,926,000.
Immigration (1984): immigrants admitted 457,093, from Poland 18.0%, German Democratic Republic 9.3%, Italy 8.8%, Turkey 7.6%, United States 5.3%, Yugoslavia 4.4%, Romania 4.2%, Austria 3.4%, United Kingdom 2.9%.

Vital statistics

Birth rate per 1,000 population (1985): 9.6 (world avg. 29.0); legitimate, 90.6%; illegitimate, 9.4%.
Death rate per 1,000 population (1985): 11.5 (world avg. 11.0).
Natural increase rate per 1,000 population (1985): −1.9 (world avg. 18.0).
Total fertility rate (avg. births per childbearing woman; 1984): 1.3.
Marriage rate per 1,000 population (1985): 6.0.
Divorce rate per 1,000 population (1984): 2.1.
Life expectancy at birth (1982–84): male 70.8 years; female 77.5 years.
Major causes of death per 100,000 population (1984): diseases of the circulatory system 576.4, of which cerebrovascular disease 152.3, acute myocardial infarction 132.0; malignant neoplasms (cancers) 259.6, of which stomach, colon, and rectum 63.0, bronchial, lung, and tracheal 41.9, breast 21.4; pulmonary diseases 70.8, of which chronic bronchitis 36.0, pneumonia 26.5; chronic liver disease and cirrhosis 23.7; suicide 20.5.

Social indicators

Educational attainment (1982). Percent of adult population over age 14 having: less than full primary education, virtually zero; primary and secondary 34.9%, of which primary with general secondary 15.9%; some postsecondary in preparation for higher education 10.0%; completion of more advanced education 55.1%, of which trade school graduates with apprenticeship 44.7%, skilled technicians or craftsmen 4.6%, engineers 1.9%, university graduates (all levels) 3.9%.
Quality of working life (1984). Average workweek: 40.8 hours‡. Annual rate per 100,000 workers for: injury or accident at work 5,258; injury or accident on way to work 548; industrial illness 121; death 13.4§. Proportion of labour force insured for damages or income loss resulting from: injury, virtually 100%; permanent disability, virtually 100%; death, virtually 100%. Average days lost to labour stoppages per 1,000 workers (1983): 2. Principal means of journey to work: private automobile 32.4%; public transportation 19.2%; bicycle 6.2%; foot 37.5%; other 4.7%. Percentage of unemployed workers not eligible for unemployment benefits (1984): 28.9%.

Distribution of income (1978)

percent of household income by quintile				
1	2	3	4	5 (highest)
6.9	11.0	15.9	21.9	44.8

Access to services. Proportion of dwellings having: electricity 99.7%; piped water supply 99.2%; flush sewage disposal 94.2%; public fire protection, n.a.
Social participation. Eligible voters participating in last national election 89.1%. Population participating in voluntary work: n.a. Trade union membership in total work force (1984): 26.6%. Practicing religious population in total affiliated population: n.a.
Social deviance (1983). Offense rate per 100,000 population for: murder 4.4; sexual abuse 69.4, of which child molestation 17.8, rape 17.6; assault and battery 107.5; larceny 4,302.5, of which burglary 367.2, auto theft 130.6. Incidence per 100,000 in general population (late 1970s) of: alcoholism 2,500 to 3,000; drug and substance abuse 650; suicide 21‡.
Leisure (late 1970s). Favourite leisure activities: watching television 56%; reading 30%.
Material well-being (1983). Households possessing: automobile 65%; telephone 88%; colour television receiver 73%; refrigerator 79%; air conditioner 56% ∥; electric washing machine 83%.

National economy

Gross national product (at current market prices; 1984): U.S.$678,880,000,000 (U.S.$11,100 per capita).

Structure of gross domestic product and labour force

	1985		1984	
	in value DM '000,000	% of total value	labour force	% of labour force
Agriculture	30,870	1.7	1,396,000	4.8
Mining	71,100¶	3.9¶	332,000	1.1
Manufacturing	595,770	32.6	8,448,000	29.3
Construction	93,290	5.1	1,960,000	6.8
Public utilities	¶	¶	243,000	0.8
Transportation and communication } Trade	274,630	15.0	1,553,000	5.4
Trade			4,071,000	14.1
Finance } Services	473,000	25.8 }	1,659,000	5.8
Services			7,090,000	24.6
Pub. admin., defense	207,570	11.3		
Other	84,290	4.6	2,063,000♀	7.2
TOTAL	1,830,430	100.0	28,815,000	100.0♂

Budget (1983). Revenue: DM 493,990,000,000 (tax revenue 93.5%, of which social security contributions from employers 26.1%, from employees 21.8%, taxes on individual wages 13.9%, value added tax on goods and services 12.7%, taxes paid by self-employed or nonemployed 8.2%, mineral oil tax 4.9%, tobacco tax 2.9%; nontax revenue 6.0%, of which income from property 4.7%). Expenditures: DM 520,050,000,000 (social security and welfare 50.0%; health 18.6%; defense 9.3%; economic services 7.0%, of which transportation and communication 3.1%; education 0.8%).
Total national debt (1985) DM 392,360,000,000.
Tourism (1984): receipts from visitors U.S.$4,096,000,000; expenditures by nationals abroad U.S.$13,914,000,000.

Manufacturing, mining, and construction enterprises (1984)

	no. of enterprises	no. of tradesmen and professionals	wages as a % of avg. of all wages	annual gross production value‡ (DM '000,000)
Road motor vehicle	1,798	793,000	109.5	159,022
Chemical	1,943	568,000	122.8	156,168
Food and beverage	3,862	453,000	87.8	148,023
Machinery (nonelectric)	4,545	927,000	105.5	135,381
Machinery and appliances (electric)	2,299	932,000	102.2	131,767
Petroleum and natural gas	50	36,000	158.9	107,741
Iron and steel	101	234,000	104.5	44,198
Calculator, computer	2,012	274,000	91.1	35,887
Mining	83	222,000	109.4	33,814
Textile	1,419	236,000	76.8	32,530
Cement, sand, and gravel	2,130	161,000	101.7	30,539
Plastics	1,659	191,000	89.5	28,592
Wood and wood products	2,197	197,000	88.4	26,591
Metalware	1,279	147,000	103.8	22,461
Construction	16,384	1,032,000	89.1	...

Production (metric tons except as noted). Agriculture, forestry, fishing (1984): sugar beets 20,018,000, barley 10,284,000, wheat 10,223,000, potatoes 7,753,000, oats 2,083,000, rye 1,930,000; livestock (number of live animals) 23,449,000 pigs, 15,552,000 cattle; 1,218,000 sheep; roundwood 26,778,000 cu m; fish catch (1983) 305,620, of which Atlantic cod 68,832, Atlantic redfish 45,942, blue mussel 31,634. Mining and quarrying (1985): iron ore 330,900□, zinc 117,800□, lead 20,500□, copper 900□. Manufacturing (value added at factor cost in DM; 1983): machinery and transport equipment 152,129,000,000, of which electrical equipment 52,045,000,000, transport equipment 48,913,000,000; chemicals (including medicinal products) 41,900,000,000; food and beverages 24,426,000,000; calculators and computers 13,364,000,000; semiprocessed iron and steel 10,440,000,000; textiles 9,931,-

000,000; furniture and other wood products 9,434,000,000; plastics and other synthetic products 8,998,000,000; metalware 8,651,000,000; printed matter 7,798,000,000; clocks and other precision products 6,656,000,000; clothing 6,410,000,000; office machines 6,195,000,000; cast metals 4,806,-000,000. Construction (1983): residential 173,681,000 cu m; nonresidential 147,639,000 cu m; restoration and conversion 2,275,000 cu m.

Service enterprises (1984)

	no. of enter-prises	no. of employees	weekly wage as a % of all wages	annual turnover (DM '000,000)
Gas	108	23,000	...	32,175
Water	158	18,000	...	3,811
Electrical power	459	232,000	...	110,583
Transport				
air	174	36,000	...	11,224
buses, trains	5,769	142,000	...	10,869
shipping	1,904	11,000	...	...
Communication				
press	2,100	204,000	...	25,155
film	615	3,000	...	836
Mail	17,960	503,000	...	45,954
Hotels and restaurants	117,035	649,000	...	41,066
Wholesale trade◇	132,000	1,239,000	...	...
Retail trade◇	507,000	2,282,000	...	...
Health services◇	88,000	318,000	...	...
Financial services◇	36,000	427,000	...	...

Energy production (consumption): electricity (kW-hr; 1984) 376,600,000,000 (380,646,000,000); hard coal (metric tons; 1984) 84,866,000 (87,469,000); lignite-brown coal (metric tons; 1984) 126,740,000 (129,380,000); crude petroleum (barrels; 1984) 24,400,000 (527,100,000); petroleum products (metric tons; 1984) 75,457,000 (100,962,000); natural gas (cu m; 1984) 17,-525,000,000 (47,718,000,000).

Population economically active (1984): total 28,542,000; activity rate of total population 47.1% (participation rates: ages 15–64, 66.5%; female 39.1%; unemployed 7.9%).

Price and earnings indexes (1980 = 100)

	1980	1981	1982	1983	1984	1985	1986△
Consumer price index	100.0	106.3	111.9	115.6	118.4	121.0	121.1
Hourly earnings index	100.0	105.5	110.5	114.1	116.8	121.3	...

Household income and expenditure. Average household size (1985) 2.4; average annual net income per household (1985) DM 43,192 (U.S.$14,670); sources of take home income (1985): wages 83.9%, self-employment 7.7%, investments 8.5%; expenditure (1985): food 25.7%, rent 19.6%, transportation 14.8%, entertainment and education 9.0%, clothing and footwear 8.2%, household expenses 8.0%, electricity and gas 7.3%, other 7.4%.

Land use (1983): forested 30.0%; meadows and pastures 19.0%; agricultural and under permanent cultivation 30.5%; other 20.5%.

Financial aggregates

	1979	1980	1981	1982	1983	1984	1985
Exchange rate, DM per:							
U.S. dollar	1.7315	1.9590	2.2548	2.3765	2.7238	3.1480	2.9440
£	3.8509	4.6722	4.3022	3.8369	3.9511	3.6407	3.8163
SDR	2.2810	2.4985	2.6245	2.6215	2.8517	3.0857	2.7035
International reserves (U.S.$)							
Total (excl. gold; '000,000)	52,549	48,592	43,719	44,762	42,674	40,141	44,380
SDRs ('000,000)	2,076	1,840	1,609	2,054	1,613	1,362	1,547
Reserve pos. in IMF ('000,000)	3,125	2,291	2,465	3,088	3,748	3,750	3,808
Foreign exchange	47,348	44,461	39,645	39,620	37,313	35,028	39,025
Gold ('000,000 fine troy oz)	95.25	95.18	95.18	95.18	95.18	95.18	95.18
% world reserves	10.09	9.99	10.00	10.05	10.06	10.06	10.03
Interest and prices							
Central bank discount (%)	6.0	7.5	7.5	5.0	4.0	4.5	4.0
Gov't. bond yield (%)	7.7	8.7	10.6	9.1	8.0	7.8	6.9
Industrial share prices (1980 = 100)	106.8	100.0	100.4	99.0	133.5	150.4	199.9
Balance of payments (U.S.$ '000,000)							
Balance of visible trade	16.85	8.99	16.58	25.26	22.25	22.24	28.82
Imports, f.o.b.	148.89	176.50	154.49	143.67	140.40	141.18	145.32
Exports, f.o.b.	165.75	185.48	171.07	168.93	162.65	163.42	174.14
Balance of invisibles	12.19	12.14	10.73	10.58	7.55	4.92	4.42
Balance of payments, current account	−6.17	−15.91	−5.03	3.93	4.22	6.77	13.77

Foreign trade

Balance of trade (current prices)

	1980	1981	1982	1983	1984	1985
DM '000,000	+8,947	+27,720	+51,277	+42,089	+53,967	+73,353
% of total	1.5%	3.6%	6.4%	5.1%	5.8%	7.3%

Imports (1985): DM 463,811,000,000 (machinery and transport equipment 22.8%, of which transport equipment 4.7%, electrical machinery 4.2%, office equipment 3.5%; mineral fuels 19.9%, of which crude petroleum and petroleum products 15.3%, natural gas 3.9%; food and beverages 9.6%, of which fruits and vegetables 3.0%, coffee, tea, and spices 1.8%, meat and meat products 1.3%; chemicals and chemical products 8.9%, of which plastics and synthetics 2.3%, medicinal products 0.9%; clothing and wearing apparel 4.4%; iron and steel 3.5%; textiles and yarn 3.2%; metallic ores and scrap metal 2.0%; paper and paper products 1.9%). *Major import sources:* The Netherlands 12.6%; France 10.6%; Italy 8.0%; United Kingdom 8.0%; United States 7.0%; Belgium–Luxembourg 6.3%; Japan 4.5%.

Exports (1985): DM 537,164,000,000 (machinery and transport equipment 45.9%, of which transport equipment 16.1%, specialized equipment for specific industries 6.2%, electrical machinery 5.7%; chemicals and chemical products 13.2%, of which plastics and synthetics 3.3%, medicinal products 1.3%, dyes and dye products 1.2%; iron and steel 5.1%; food and beverages 4.0%, of which dairy products 1.0%, meat and meat products 0.6%; textiles and yarn 3.3%; paper and paper products 1.9%). *Major export destinations:* France 11.9%; United States 10.3%; The Netherlands 8.6%; United Kingdom 8.6%; Italy 7.8%; Belgium–Luxembourg 6.9%; Switzerland 5.4%; Austria 5.1%.

Trade by commodity group (1985)

	imports		exports	
SITC Group	U.S.$'000,000	%	U.S.$'000,000	%
00 Food and live animals	15,066	9.6	7,317	4.0
01 Beverages and tobacco	1,562	1.0	1,193	0.6
02 Crude materials, excluding fuels	10,829	6.9	3,641	2.0
03 Mineral fuels, lubricants, and related materials	31,308	19.9	5,188	2.8
04 Animal and vegetable oils, fat, and waxes	936	0.6	949	0.5
05 Chemicals and related products, n.e.s.	14,017	8.9	24,170	13.2
06 Basic manufactures	25,450	16.2	34,081	18.7
07 Machinery and transport equipment	35,986	22.8	83,773	45.9
08 Miscellaneous manufactured articles	17,967	11.4	18,216	10.0
09 Goods not classified by kind	4,426	2.8	3,910	2.1
TOTAL	157,547	100.0δ	182,438	100.0δ

Direction of trade (1985)

	imports		exports	
	U.S.$'000,000	%	U.S.$'000,000	%
Africa	7,094	4.5	5,261	2.9
Asia	18,761	11.9	19,283	10.5
Middle East	5,291	3.4	8,720	4.7
Japan	7,120	4.5	2,707	1.5
other Asia	6,350	4.0	7,856	4.3
South America	5,333	3.4	2,532	1.4
North and Central America	13,262	8.4	23,246	12.6δ
United States	10,982	7.0	19,047	10.4
other North and Central Am.	2,280	1.4	4,199	2.3
Europe	111,678	71.0δ	131,754	71.6δ
EEC	76,560	48.6	86,575	47.1
U.S.S.R.	4,690	3.0	3,603	2.0
other Europe	30,428	19.3	41,576	22.6
Oceania	1,253	0.8	1,868	1.0
TOTAL	157,381	100.0	183,944	100.0

Transport and communications

Transport. Railroads (1985): length 42,571 mi✝, 68,512 km✝; passenger-mi 26,258,000,000, passenger-km 42,258,000,000; short ton-mi cargo 43,086,-000,000, metric ton-km cargo 62,905,000,000. Roads (1983): total length 302,764 mi, 487,251 km (paved 99%). Vehicles (1985): passenger cars 25,844,500; trucks and buses 1,350,200. Merchant marine (1985): vessels (100 gross tons and over) 1,816; total deadweight tonnage 9,240,871. Air transport (1985): passenger-mi 15,180,000,000, passenger-km 24,430,000,-000; short ton-mi cargo 1,711,314,000, metric ton-km cargo 2,498,477,000; airports (1986) with scheduled flights 28.

Communications. Daily newspapers (1985): total number 633; total circulation⊕ 27,300,000; circulation per 1,000 population 447.4. Radio (1985): total number of receivers 25,265,633 (1 per 2.4 persons). Television (1985): total number of receivers 22,130,000 (1 per 2.8 persons). Telephones (1983): 31,370,022 (1 per 2.0 persons).

Education and health

Education (1984–85)

	schools	teachers	students	student/teacher ratio
Primary (age 6–10)	22,445	304,357	4,511,122	14.8
Secondary (age 10–19)	5,412	191,624	3,026,721	15.8
Voc., teacher tr.**	7,816	87,975	2,718,404	30.9
Higher**	...	311,460	1,267,263	4.1

Literacy (1985): virtually 100%.

Health (1985): physicians 153,895 (1 per 396 persons); hospital beds (1984) 678,708 (1 per 90 persons); infant mortality rate per 1,000 live births 9.0.

Food (1980–82): daily per capita caloric intake 3,448 (vegetable products 62%, animal products 38%); 129% of FAO recommended minimum requirement.

Military

Total active duty personnel (1985): 478,000 (army 70.2%, navy 7.6%, air force 22.2%). *Military expenditure as percent of GNP* (1984): 3.3% (world 6.1%); per capita expenditure U.S.$334.

*January 1. †Berlin (West) is under tripartite (France, United Kingdom, United States) jurisdiction and is only administratively a part of West Germany. ‡1983. §1982. ‖1979. ¶Public utilities included with mining. ♀Includes some unemployed. δDetail does not add to total given because of rounding. □Metal content only. ◇1970. △June. ✝1984. ⊕For 612 newspapers only. **1983–84.

Ghana

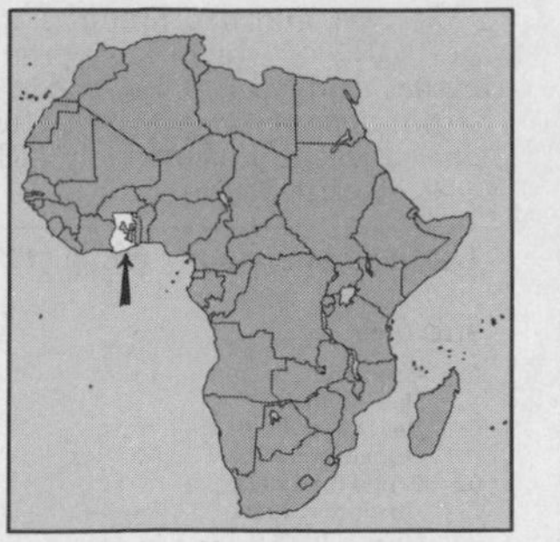

Official name: Republic of Ghana.
Form of government: republic with one ruling body (Provisional National Defense Council [10]).
Head of state and government: Chairman of the Provisional National Defense Council.
Capital: Accra.
Official language: English.
Official religion: none.
Monetary unit: 1 cedi (₵) = 100 pesewas; valuation (Oct. 1, 1986) 1 U.S.$ = ₵136.00; 1 £ = ₵196.52.

Area and population

		area		population
				1984
Regions	Capitals	sq mi	sq km	census
Ashanti	Kumasi	9,417	24,389	2,089,683
Brong-Ahafo	Sunyani	15,273	39,557	1,179,407
Central	Cape Coast	3,794	9,826	1,145,520
Eastern	Koforidua	7,461	19,323	1,679,483
Greater Accra	Accra	1,253	3,245	1,420,066
Northern	Tamale	27,175	70,384	1,162,645
Upper East	Bolgatanga	3,414	8,842	771,584
Upper West	Wa	7,134	18,476	439,161
Volta	Ho	7,942	20,570	1,201,095
Western	Sekondi-Takoradi	9,236	23,921	1,116,930
TOTAL		92,098*	238,533	12,205,574

Demography

Population (1986): 13,144,000.
Density (1986): persons per sq mi 142.7, persons per sq km 55.1.
Urban-rural (1984): urban 31.3%; rural 68.7%.
Sex distribution (1984): male 49.11%; female 50.89%.
Age breakdown (1985): under 15, 46.6%; 15–29, 26.1%; 30–44, 14.5%; 45–59, 8.3%; 60–74, 3.8%; 75 and over, 0.7%.
Population projection: (1990) 14,500,000; (2000) 18,700,000.
Doubling time: 22 years.
Ethno-linguistic composition (1983): Akan 44.1%; Mossi-Dagomba 15.9%; Ewe 13.0%; Ga-Adangme 8.3%; Gurma 3.5%; Yoruba 1.6%; other 13.6%.
Religious affiliation (1980): Christian 62.6%, of which Protestant 27.9%, Roman Catholic 18.7%, African indigenous 16.0%; traditional beliefs 21.4%; Muslim 15.7%, of which Aḥmadīyah 7.9%; other 0.3%.
Major cities (1984): Accra 859,600; Kumasi 348,900; Tamale 136,800; Tema 99,600; Sekondi-Takoradi 93,900.

Vital statistics

Birth rate per 1,000 population (1980–85): 46.9 (world avg. 29.0); legitimate, n.a.; illegitimate, n.a.
Death rate per 1,000 population (1980–85): 14.6 (world avg. 11.0).
Natural increase rate per 1,000 population (1980–85): 32.3 (world avg. 18.0).
Total fertility rate (avg. births per childbearing woman; 1980–85): 6.5.
Life expectancy at birth (1980–85): male 50.3 years; female 53.7 years.
Major causes of death per 100,000 population: n.a.; however, major infectious diseases include malaria, tuberculosis, leprosy, trypanosomiasis (sleeping sickness), and onchocerciasis (river blindness).

National economy

Budget (1986). Revenue: ₵85,200,000,000 (taxes on international trade 40%; domestic taxes 60%). Expenditures: ₵90,000,000,000 (recurrent expenditures 70.0%; development 29.0%, of which roads and highways 3.2%; health 0.7%; education 0.6%).
Public debt (external, outstanding; 1984): U.S.$1,122,400,000.
Tourism: receipts from visitors (1984) U.S.$2,000,000; expenditures by nationals abroad (1983) U.S.$25,000,000.
Production (metric tons except as noted). Agriculture, forestry, fishing (1984): roots and tubers 3,510,000 (of which cassava 1,900,000, yams 880,000, cocoyams 750,000, taro 730,000), cereals 872,000 (of which corn [maize] 534,000, sorghum 140,000, millet 132,000, rice 66,000), plantains 650,000, cocoa 188,000, coconuts 160,000, sugarcane 110,000, peanuts (groundnuts) 90,000, oranges 35,000, lemons 30,000, palm kernels 30,000, pulses 11,000; livestock (number of live animals) 2,000,000 goats, 2,000,000 sheep, 800,000 cattle, 375,000 pigs, 13,000,000 chickens; roundwood 8,075,000 cu m; fish catch (1983) 228,000 (of which anchovies 30,700). Mining and quarrying (1984): manganese ore 286,700; bauxite 48,500; gold 8,923 kg; diamonds 348,800 carats. Manufacturing (1984): kerosine, gasoline, and diesel 476,000; cement 235,000; wheat flour 39,590; cocoa cake, cocoa butter, and cocoa liquor 9,662; soap 5,465; iron rods 1,914; toothpaste 12; cloth 10,300,000 metres; beer 452,000 hectolitres; evaporated milk 110,000 hectolitres; ice cream 7,460 hectolitres; cigarettes 2,008,000,000 units. Construction (value added in ₵'000; 1982): 2,421,900. Energy production (consumption): electricity (kW-hr; 1984) 1,830,000,000 (1,480,000,000); coal (metric tons; 1984) none (2,000); crude petroleum (barrels; 1984) 678,000 (7,721,000); petroleum products (metric tons; 1984) 781,000 (560,000); natural gas, none (n.a.).
Household income and expenditure. Average household size (1980) 5.1; average annual income per household (1978) ₵9,600 (U.S.$ †); source of income: n.a.; expenditure (1978): food and beverages 57.4%, housing 15.3%, clothing and footwear 14.3%, transport and communication 3.3%, health care 1.3%.

Gross national product (at current market prices; 1984): U.S.$4,730,000,000 (U.S.$380 per capita).

Structure of gross domestic product and labour force

	1982		1983	
	in value ₵'000,000	% of total value	labour force	% of labour force
Agriculture	52,798.0	58.2	2,501,000	53.0
Mining	360.4	0.4		
Manufacturing	3,116.8	3.4	944,000	20.0
Construction	2,421.9	2.7		
Public utilities	513.4	0.6		
Transportation and communication	2,567.8	2.8		
Trade	22,950.5	25.3		
Finance	1,843.7	2.0	1,274,000	27.0
Pub. admin., defense	4,052.4	4.5		
Services	548.7	0.6		
Other	−435.3‡	−0.5		
TOTAL	90,738.3§	100.0	4,719,000	100.0

Population economically active (1984): total 4,763,000; activity rate of total population 38.1% (participation rates: ages 15–64, n.a.; female [1981] 41.1%; unemployed 10.8%).

Price and earnings indexes (1980 = 100)

	1980	1981	1982	1983	1984	1985	1986‖
Consumer price index	100.0	216.5	264.8	590.1	824.1	909.1	1,095.2
Earnings index	100.0	...	139.9	240.8	...	...	...

Land use (1983): forested 37.2%; meadows and pastures 15.0%; agricultural and under permanent cultivation 12.0%; other 35.8%.

Foreign trade¶

Balance of trade (current prices)

	1979	1980	1981	1982	1983	1984
₵'000,000	+605.8	+816.2	+159.5	+639.3	−946.5	+637.1
% of total	12.4%	13.4%	2.8%	15.4%	6.3%	1.6%

Imports (1981): ₵3,484,310,000 (petroleum products 30.3%; machinery and transport equipment 27.3%; chemicals 11.9%; basic manufactures 11.3%; food and live animals 7.1%, of which wheat and flour 1.5%, rice 1.4%). *Major import sources:* Nigeria 26.3%; United Kingdom 17.2%; United States 11.9%; West Germany 11.4%; Japan 3.8%.
Exports (1981): ₵2,685,633,000 (cocoa beans 40.8%; gold 16.2%; logs and timber 3.8%; cocoa products 1.8%; industrial diamonds 0.8%). *Major export destinations:* United States 22.3%; Switzerland 18.1%; Japan 12.8%; The Netherlands 12.7%; United Kingdom 10.7%; West Germany 9.0%; U.S.S.R. 7.0%.

Transport and communications

Transport. Railroads (1984): length 592 mi, 953 km; passenger-mi 97,800,000, passenger-km 157,400,000; short ton-mi cargo 29,800,000, metric ton-km cargo 43,500,000. Roads (1985): total length 17,600 mi, 28,300 km (paved 20%). Vehicles (1983): passenger cars 52,864; trucks and buses 24,312. Merchant marine (1985): vessels (100 gross tons and over) 123; total deadweight tonnage 177,158. Air transport (1982): passenger-mi 181,000,000, passenger-km 291,000,000; short ton-mi cargo 21,200,000, metric ton-km cargo 31,000,000; airports (1986) with scheduled flights 4.
Communications. Daily newspapers (1985): total number 4; total circulation 490,000; circulation per 1,000 population 38. Radio (1985): total number of receivers 2,500,000 (1 per 5.1 persons). Television (1985): total number of receivers 140,000 receivers (1 per 92 persons). Telephones (1982): 70,653 (1 per 168 persons).

Education and health

Education (1984–85)

	schools	teachers♀	students	student/teacher ratio
Primary (6–11)	8,965	51,631♂	1,464,624	...
Secondary (12–18)	5,589	32,795♂	723,385	...
Voc., teacher tr.	61	1,727	24,827	...
Higher	3	1,041□	7,878	...

Educational attainment (1970). Percent of adult population over age 25 having: no formal schooling 77.7%; primary education 5.8%; some secondary 12.8%; complete secondary 3.3%; higher 0.4%. *Literacy* (1985): total population over age 15 literate 3,835,000 (53.2%); males literate 2,261,000 (64.1%); females literate 1,574,000 (42.8%).
Health: physicians (1982) 1,435 (1 per 8,278 persons); hospital beds (1981) 20,582 (1 per 563 persons); infant mortality rate per 1,000 live births (1980–85) 98.
Food (1980–82): daily per capita caloric intake 1,657 (vegetable products 94%, animal products 6%); 82% of FAO minimum recommended requirement.

Military

Total active duty personnel (1985): 15,100 (army 82.8%, navy 7.9%, air force 9.3%). *Military expenditure as percent of GNP* (1982): 0.7% (world 6.0%); per capita expenditure U.S.$16.

*Detail does not add to total given because of rounding. †Unofficial exchange rate (7.5 to 9.9 times the official rate) does not allow direct conversion into other currencies. ‡Import duties, less imputed bank service charge. §At current prices. ‖April. ¶Import figures are f.o.b. in balance of trade and c.i.f. in commodities and trading partners. ♀1983–84. ♂Includes untrained teachers. □1980–81.

Greece

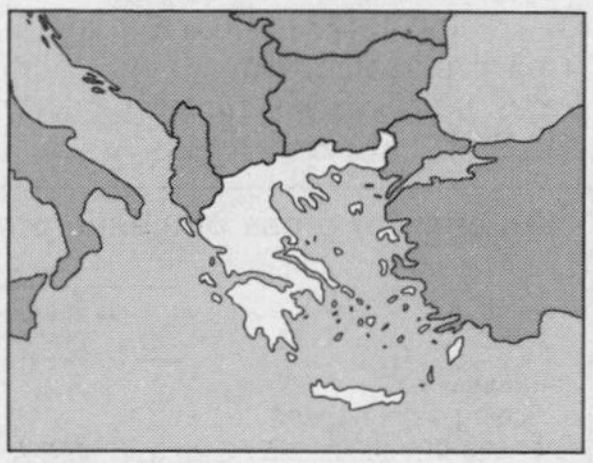

Official name: Ellinikí Dimokratía (Hellenic Republic).
Form of government: unitary multiparty republic with one legislative house (Greek Chamber of Deputies [300]).
Chief of state: President.
Head of government: Prime Minister.
Capital: Athens.
Official language: Greek.
Official religion: Eastern Orthodox.
Monetary unit: 1 drachma (Dr) = 100 leptae; valuation (Oct. 1, 1986) 1 U.S.$ = Dr 135.40; 1 £ = Dr 195.65.

Area and population*

Regions	area sq mi	area sq km	population 1981 census
Aegean Islands	3,522	9,122	428,533
Central Greece and Évvoia	9,417	24,391	1,099,841
Crete	3,219	8,336	502,165
Greater Athens	165	427	3,027,331
Ionian Islands	891	2,307	182,651
Ípiros	3,553	9,203	324,541
Macedonia	13,066	33,841	2,120,481
Pelopónnisos	8,254	21,379	1,012,528
Thessalía	5,420	14,037	695,654
Thráki	3,312	8,578	345,220
Autonomous administration			
Ayion Oros (Mt. Athos)	130	336	1,472
TOTAL	50,949	131,957	9,740,417

Demography

Population (1986): 10,008,000.
Density (1986): persons per sq mi 196.4, persons per sq km 75.8.
Urban-rural (1981): urban 58.1%; rural 41.9%.
Sex distribution (1984): male 49.18%; female 50.82%.
Age breakdown (1984): under 15, 21.3%; 15–29, 22.0%; 30–44, 19.1%; 45–59, 19.8%; 60–74, 12.4%; 75 and over, 5.4%.
Population projection: (1990) 10,200,000; (2000) 10,700,000.
Doubling time: n.a.; doubling time exceeds 100 years.
Ethnic composition (1982): Greek 94.9%; Macedonian 1.8%; Turkish 0.6%; Albanian 0.6%; other 2.1%.
Religious affiliation (1982): Christian 98.1%, of which Greek Orthodox 97.6%, Roman Catholic 0.4%, Protestant 0.1%; Muslim 1.5%; other 0.4%.
Major cities (1981): Athens 885,737; Thessaloníki 406,413; Piraiévs 196,389; Pátrai 142,163; Iráklion 102,398.

Vital statistics

Birth rate per 1,000 population (1985): 11.8 (world avg. 29.0); legitimate 96.6%; illegitimate 3.4%.
Death rate per 1,000 population (1985): 9.3 (world avg. 11.0).
Natural increase rate per 1,000 population (1985): 2.5 (world avg. 18.0).
Total fertility rate (avg. births per childbearing woman; 1984): 2.3.
Marriage rate per 1,000 population (1985): 6.3.
Divorce rate per 1,000 population (1982): 0.7.
Life expectancy at birth (1980): male 72.2 years; female 76.4 years.
Major causes of death per 100,000 population (1985): malignant neoplasms (cancers) 182.6; cerebrovascular disease 184.3; diseases of pulmonary circulation and other forms of heart disease 138.8; ischemic heart disease 102.4.

National economy

Budget (1984). Revenue: Dr 929,263,000,000 (indirect taxes 64.0%; direct taxes 27.2%; government entrepreneurship 4.5%). Expenditures: Dr 1,116,215,000,000 (personnel outlays 37.3%, of which salaries 28.9%, pensions 8.4%; servicing of public debt 16.2%; grants 12.5%; subsidies 9.2%).
Tourism (1984): receipts from visitors U.S.$1,313,000,000; expenditures by nationals abroad U.S.$339,000,000.
Production (metric tons except as noted). Agriculture, forestry, fishing (1984): tomatoes 2,345,000, wheat 2,309,000, corn (maize) 2,091,000, sugar beets 1,789,000, grapes 1,565,000, olives 1,400,000, potatoes 1,053,000, barley 890,000, oranges 757,000, cotton 431,000, tobacco 142,000, rice 92,000, oats 67,000; livestock (number of live animals) 8,252,000 sheep, 4,753,000 goats, 1,065,000 pigs, 754,000 cattle, 199,000 asses, 37,000,000 chickens; roundwood 2,824,000 cu m†; fish catch 100,000. Mining and quarrying (1985): bauxite 2,461,200; iron ore 1,452,000‡; zinc ore 40,605; lead ore 30,835. Manufacturing (value added in Dr; 1983): food, beverages, and tobacco 95,100,000,000; textiles 74,270,000,000; chemicals 62,660,000,000; clothing 44,380,000,000; transport equipment 33,919,000,000. Construction (cu m; 1984): residential 28,004,000; nonresidential 12,364,000. Energy production (consumption): electricity (kW-hr; 1985) 26,292,000,000 (24,075,000,000); coal (metric tons; 1984) 32,502,000 (32,823,000); crude petroleum (barrels; 1984) 9,057,000 (92,607,000); petroleum products (metric tons; 1984) 11,599,000 (9,484,000); natural gas (cu m; 1984) 72,820,000 (72,820,000).
Household income and expenditure. Average household size (1982) 3.3; income per household (1982) Dr 252,300 (U.S.$3,777); sources of income (1984): wages and salaries 43.0%, property and entrepreneurship 40.8%, transfer payments 13.3%, other 2.9%; expenditure (1984): food, beverages, and tobacco 42.5%, housing 14.9%, clothing and footwear 8.2%, other 34.4%.
Gross national product (at current market prices; 1984): U.S.$36,940,000,000 (U.S.$3,730 per capita).

Structure of gross domestic product and labour force

	1984 in value Dr '000,000	1984 % of total value	1983 labour force	1983 % of labour force
Agriculture	615,150	18.5	1,054,600	27.7
Mining	69,700	2.1	30,500	0.8
Manufacturing	602,200	18.1	717,200	18.8
Construction	211,700	6.4	302,000	7.9
Public utilities	66,950	2.0	29,700	0.8
Transportation and communication	261,800	7.9	267,000	7.0
Trade	432,930	13.0	551,100	14.5
Finance	84,820	2.5	125,900	3.3
Pub. admin., defense	557,800	16.7	564,600	14.8
Services	246,850	7.4		
Other	180,750	5.4	165,600§	4.4
TOTAL	3,330,650	100.0	3,808,200	100.0

Public debt (1982): U.S.$4,955,000,000.
Population economically active (1983): total 3,808,200; activity rate of total population 38.7% (participation rates: ages 16–64, 54.5%; female 34.1%; unemployed 4.6%).

Price and earnings indexes (1980 = 100)

	1980	1981	1982	1983	1984	1985	1986‖
Consumer price index	100.0	124.5	150.6	181.1	214.5	255.9	314.3
Hourly earnings index	100.0	127.2	169.8	202.7	256.0	306.8	...

Land use (1983): forested 20.0%; meadows and pastures 40.2%; agricultural and under permanent cultivation 30.1%; other 9.7%.

Foreign trade

Balance of trade (current prices)

	1980	1981	1982	1983	1984	1985
Dr '000,000	−231.8	−255.8	−379.6	−456.6	−541.3	−783.6
% of total	34.4%	35.0%	40.6%	36.8%	33.3%	38.4%

Imports (1985): Dr 1,412,797,300,000 (machinery and transport equipment 23.6%, of which passenger cars 3.2%; crude petroleum 25.8%; food, beverages, and tobacco 12.2%, of which meat products 4.1%, milk and cream 1.4%, coffee 0.8%; chemical products 8.6%, of which plastics and resins 2.1%, medicinal and pharmaceutical products 1.2%). *Major import sources:* West Germany 17.0%; Italy 9.3%; Saudi Arabia 8.0%; France 6.4%; Japan 6.4%; The Netherlands 5.8%; U.S.S.R. 5.2%.
Exports (1985): Dr 629,188,300,000 (food, beverages, and tobacco 25.9%, of which tobacco 3.3%, concentrated tomato puree 1.9%, olive oil 1.5%; clothing 13.8%; petroleum products 9.9%; textile yarn 5.9%). *Major export destinations:* West Germany 20.1%; Italy 11.3%; United States 8.1%; France 8.0%; United Kingdom 6.9%.

Transport and communications

Transport. Railroads (1985): route length 1,540 mi, 2,479 km; passenger-mi 932,100,000, passenger-km 1,500,000,000; short ton-mi cargo 501,400,000, metric ton-km cargo 732,000,000. Roads (1984): total length 66,055 mi, 106,306 km (paved 83%). Vehicles (1985): passenger cars 1,151,037; trucks and buses 589,256. Merchant marine (1985): vessels (100 gross tons and over) 2,599; total deadweight tonnage 55,356,085. Air transport (1984): passenger-mi 3,915,000,000, passenger-km 6,300,000,000; short ton-mi cargo 54,182,000, metric ton-km cargo 79,104,000; airports (1986) with scheduled flights 29.
Communications. Daily newspapers (1983): total number 124; total circulation 981,200¶; circulation per 1,000 population, n.a. Radio (1984): total number of receivers 4,000,000 (1 per 2.5 persons). Television (1984): total number of receivers 1,715,000 (1 per 5.8 persons). Telephones (1983): 3,113,000 (1 per 3.2 persons).

Education and health

Education (1983–84)

	schools	teachers	students	student/teacher ratio
Primary (age 6–12)	9,194	34,955	896,399	25.6
Secondary (age 13–17)	2,399	37,826	690,382	18.3
Voc., teacher tr.	575	8,035	101,748	12.7
Higher	161	12,067	148,515	12.3

Educational attainment (1981). Percent of population over age 14 having: primary education 42.3%; lower secondary 10.3%; higher secondary 15.0%; some postsecondary 4.2%; a degree from higher education school 4.4%. *Literacy* (1985): total population over age 15 literate 7,600,000 (92.3%); males literate 3,705,000 (97.1%); females literate 3,895,000 (87.8%).
Health (1984): physicians (1983) 27,607 (1 per 357 persons); hospital beds 57,081 (1 per 173 persons); infant mortality rate per 1,000 live births 14.1.
Food (1980–82): daily per capita caloric intake 3,564 (vegetable products 78%, animal products 22%); 143% of FAO recommended minimum requirement.

Military

Total active duty personnel (1985): 201,500 (army 78.4%, navy 9.7%, air force 11.9%). *Military expenditure as percent of GNP* (1984): 6.7% (world 6.1%); per capita expenditure U.S.$223.

*For reasons of space, the principal political subdivisions, or departments (*nomoi*), are not included in the table. Regions given are purely geographic entities except for Ayion Oros (Mt. Athos), which is a self-governing monastic community. †1983. ‡1984. §Mostly unemployed. ‖July. ¶For 22 dailies only.

Greenland

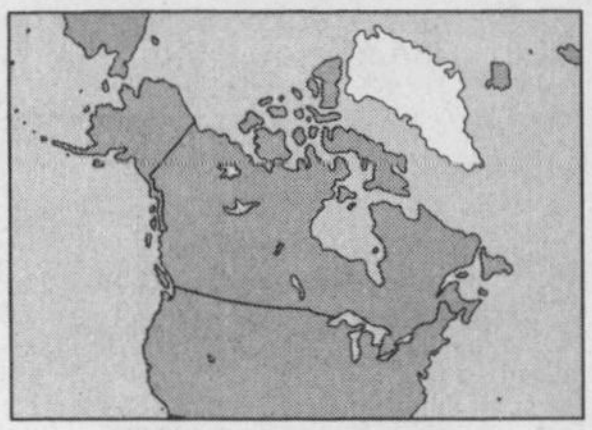

Official name: Kalaallit Nunaat (Greenlandic); Grønland (Danish) (Greenland).
Political status: integral part of the Danish realm with a local legislative house (Landsting [26]).
Chief of state: Danish Monarch.
Heads of government: High Commissioner (for Denmark); Prime Minister (for Greenland).
Capital: Nuuk (Godthåb).
Official languages: Greenlandic; Danish.
Official religion: Lutheran Church of Greenland (Evangelical Lutheran).
Monetary unit: 1 Danish krone (DKr) = 100 øre; valuation (Oct. 1, 1986) 1 U.S.$ = DKr 7.66; 1 £ = DKr 11.06.

Area and population

	area		population
Counties	sq mi	sq km	1986 estimate*
Communes			
Avanersuaq (Nordgrønland)	41,200	106,700	
Qaanaaq (Thule)	...	...	811
Kitaa (Vestgrønland)	46,000	119,100	
Aasiaat (Egedesminde)	...	...	3,499
Ilulissat (Jakobshavn)	...	...	4,425
Ivittuut (Ivigtut)	...	...	36
Kangaatsiaq (Kangåtsiaq)	...	...	1,259
Maniitsoq (Sukkertoppen)	...	...	4,006
Nanortalik	...	...	2,752
Narsaq (Narssaq)	...	...	2,120
Nuuk (Godthåb)	...	...	11,438
Paamiut (Frederikshåb)	...	...	2,739
Qaqortoq (Julianehåb)	...	...	3,291
Qasigiannguit (Christianshåb)	...	...	1,811
Qeqertarsuaq (Godhavn)	...	...	1,062
Sisimiut (Holsteinsborg)	...	...	4,817
Upernavik	...	...	2,198
Uummannaq (Umanaq)	...	...	2,582
Tunu (Østgrønland)	44,800	115,900	
Illoqqortoormiut (Scoresbysund)	...	...	535
Tasiilaq (Angmagssalik)	...	...	2,794
TOTAL (ICE-FREE)	131,900	341,700	53,406†
Permanent ice‡	708,100	1,833,300	
TOTAL	840,000	2,175,000	

Demography

Population (1986): 54,000.
Density‡ (1986): persons per sq mi 0.41, persons per sq km 0.16.
Urban-rural (1986): urban (town) 78.8%; rural (settlement) 21.2%.
Sex distribution (1986): male 54.31%; female 45.69%.
Age breakdown (1986): under 15, 24.7%; 15–29, 33.7%; 30–44, 23.2%; 45–59, 12.6%; 60–74, 4.6%; 75 and over, 1.2%.
Population projection: (1990) 56,000; (2000) 61,000.
Doubling time: 62 years.
Ethnic composition (by place of birth; 1986): born in Greenland 82.5%; born elsewhere 17.5%.
Religious affiliation (1980): Protestant 97.8%; other 2.2%.
Major towns (1985): Nuuk (Godthåb) 11,026; Sisimiut (Holsteinsborg) 4,754; Ilulissat (Jakobshavn) 4,348; Maniitsoq (Sukkertoppen) 4,092; Aasiaat (Egedesminde) 3,534.

Vital statistics

Birth rate per 1,000 population (1984): 20.0 (world avg. 29.0); legitimate 32.3%; illegitimate 67.7%.
Death rate per 1,000 population (1984): 8.3 (world avg. 11.0).
Natural increase rate per 1,000 population (1984): 11.7 (world avg. 18.0).
Total fertility rate (avg. births per childbearing woman; 1984): 2.1.
Marriage rate per 1,000 population (1984): 6.0.
Divorce rate per 1,000 population (1984): 2.6.
Life expectancy at birth (1976–80): male 59.7 years; female 67.3 years.
Major causes of death per 100,000 population (1984): malignant neoplasms (cancers) 138.7; accidents 119.7; heart disease 89.3; suicide 62.7.

National economy

Budget (1984). Revenue: DKr 1,156,700,000 (contributions from Danish government 54.4%, duties 17.3%, income tax 14.7%, other taxes and duties 5.1%). Expenditures: DKr 1,156,700,000 (education 41.6%, social welfare 29.0%, construction 13.8%, administration 10.1%).
Public debt (external, outstanding): n.a.
Tourism: receipts from visitors, n.a.; expenditures by nationals abroad, n.a.
Production (metric tons except as noted). Agriculture, forestry, hunting, fishing (1983): fish catch 107,360; livestock (number of live animals) 21,129 sheep, 3,000 reindeer; hunting (number of animals killed) 92,794 seals, 2,308 whales, of which 601 white whales, 492 narwhals; hunting products (number; 1984) 52,517 seal skins, 1,384 fox skins, 45 polar bear skins. Mining and quarrying (1984): zinc concentrates 71,800, cryolite 67,200, lead concentrates 17,800. Manufacturing (1983): principally handicrafts and food processing. Housing (1983): residential 39,900 sq m; nonresidential 18,800 sq m. Energy production (consumption): electricity (kW-hr; 1984) 181,700,000 (181,700,000); coal (1983) none (1,000); crude petroleum, none (n.a.); petroleum products (1985) none (150,400); natural gas, none (n.a.).
Gross national product (at current market prices; 1983): U.S.$380,000,000 (U.S.$7,290 per capita).

Structure of gross domestic product and labour force

	1979		1976	
	in value DKr '000,000	% of total value	labour force	% of labour force
Agriculture, fishing, hunting, and sheep breeding	335.3	16.0	3,222	15.1
Mining, manufacturing	661.2	31.6	3,205	15.0
Construction	574.9	27.4	3,112	14.5
Transportation and communication	100.4	4.8	1,842	8.6
Trade	167.8	8.0	2,153	10.1
Public utilities	}	}	293	1.4
Public administration, education	255.0	12.2	3,233	15.1
Social and health services	}	}	2,141	10.0
Other	}	}	2,177	10.2
TOTAL	2,094.6	100.0	21,378	100.0

Population economically active (1976): total 21,378; activity rate of total population 43.0% (participation rates: ages 15–64, n.a.; female 33.1%; unemployed, n.a.).

Price and earnings indexes (January 1980 = 100)

	1980	1981	1982	1983	1984	1985	1986
Consumer price index§	100.0	113.3	129.9	145.7	157.4	172.2	181.5
Monthly earnings index§	100.0	110.9	128.4	141.2	155.8	169.7	177.6

Household income and expenditure. Average household size (1976) 3.9; taxable income per taxpayer (1980) DKr 84,160 (U.S.$9,200); source of income: n.a.; expenditure (1985): food 33.6%, housing 13.8%, clothing 9.2%, fuel and light 7.8%, transportation and communications 7.8%.
Land use (1983): forested 0.1%; meadows and pastures 0.7%; agricultural and under permanent cultivation, none; other (principally ice cap) 99.3%.

Foreign trade

Balance of trade (current prices)

	1980	1981	1982	1983	1984	1985
DKr '000,000	−802	−772	−875	−779	−1,085	−1,303
% of total	27.7%	22.4%	23.4%	19.2%	23.6%	26.3%

Imports (1985): DKr 3,131,000,000 (machinery and transport equipment 27.2%, of which ships and aircraft 6.9%, automobiles 1.1%; food 18.1%; mineral fuels 16.8%; metal products and semimanufactures 16.4%). *Major import sources:* Denmark 59.2%; Norway 8.4%; Japan 3.7%; United States 3.6%.
Exports (1985): DKr 1,828,000,000 (shrimp, prawns, and mollusks 62.8%; zinc 15.9%; fish and fish products 14.5%; lead 2.3%). *Major export destinations:* Denmark 75.4%; West Germany 6.9%; Belgium-Luxembourg 4.2%; United States 1.7%.

Transport and communications

Transport. Railroads: none. Roads: n.a. Vehicles (1985): passenger cars 1,494; trucks and buses 958. Merchant marine (1985): vessels (100 gross tons and over) 45; total deadweight tonnage, n.a. Air transport (1983): passenger-mi 8,664,000, passenger-km 13,944,000; short ton-mi cargo 162,000, metric ton-km cargo 236,000. Passenger conveyance within Greenland (1982): by ship 57,322; by aircraft 90,443.
Communications. Daily newspapers (1985): none. Radio (1984): total number of receivers 13,500 (1 per 3.9 persons). Television (1984): total number of receivers 10,000 (1 per 5.2 persons). Telephone subscribers (1984): 11,554 (1 per 4.6 persons).

Education and health

Education (1985–86)

	schools ‖	teachers	students	student/ teacher ratio
Primary (age 6–15)	97	}	7,040	...
Secondary (age 15–19)	37	1,069	2,273¶	...
Voc., teacher tr.	5	}	1,258♀	...

Educational attainment (1970). Percent of adult population ages 14 through 39 having: primary education 61.7%; secondary 25.9%. *Literacy* (1979); virtually 100%.
Health (1984): physicians 59 (1 per 892 persons); hospital beds 585 (1 per 90 persons); infant mortality rate per 1,000 live births 28.5.
Food: daily per capita caloric intake, n.a.

Military

*Total active duty personnel*δ (1980): 320.

*January 1. †Includes 1,231 people not distributed by county. ‡Area of permanent ice not distributable by county; population density calculated with reference to ice-free area only. §Based on January only. ‖ 1979–80. ¶Does not include 67 students studying in Denmark. ♀1984–85. δForeign troops only. Mostly air force personnel from the United States.

Grenada

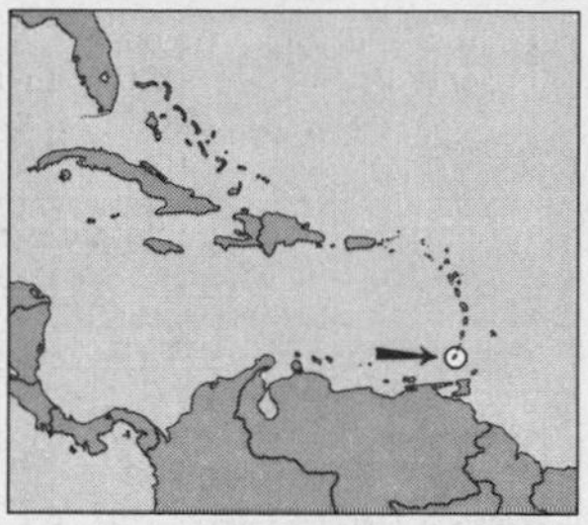

Official name: Grenada.
Form of government: constitutional monarchy with two legislative houses (Senate [13]; House of Representatives [15]).
Chief of state: British Monarch, represented by a governor-general.
Head of government: Prime Minister.
Capital: St. George's.
Official language: English.
Official religion: none.
Monetary unit: 1 East Caribbean dollar (EC$) = 100 cents; valuation (Oct. 1, 1986) 1 U.S.$ = EC$2.70; 1 £ = EC$3.90.

Area and population*

Parishes	Capitals	area sq mi	area sq km	population 1981 census
Carriacou	—	13	34	4,671
St. Andrew	—	35	91	22,425
St. David	—	18	47	10,195
St. George's	—	26	67	29,369
St. John	—	15	39	8,328
St. Mark	—	9	23	3,968
St. Patrick	—	17	44	10,132
TOTAL		133	345	89,088

Demography

Population (1986): 97,500.
Density (1986): persons per sq mi 733.1, persons per sq km 282.6.
Urban-rural (1980)†: urban 5.4%; rural 94.6%.
Sex distribution (1981): male 48.58%; female 51.42%.
Age breakdown (1985): under 15, 35.1%; 15–29, 35.1%; 30–44, 12.4%; 45–59, 9.3%; 60–74, 6.2%; 75 and over, 2.1%.
Population projection: (1990) 106,000; (2000) 130,000.
Doubling time: 31 years.
Ethnic composition (1983): black 84%; mixed 12%; East Indian 3%; white 1%.
Religious affiliation (1980): Roman Catholic 64.4%; Protestant 34.5%, of which Anglican 20.7%, Seventh-day Adventist 3.1%, Methodist 2.1%; other 1.1%.
Major locality (1981): St. George's 4,788.

Vital statistics

Birth rate per 1,000 population (1983): 31.2 (world avg. 29.0); (1979) legitimate 22.5%; illegitimate 77.5%.
Death rate per 1,000 population (1983): 8.6 (world avg. 11.0).
Natural increase rate per 1,000 population (1983): 22.6 (world avg. 18.0).
Total fertility rate (avg. births per childbearing woman; 1980–85): 3.6.
Marriage rate per 1,000 population (1979): 3.9.
Divorce rate per 1,000 population (1979): 0.2.
Life expectancy at birth (1980–85): male 65.4 years; female 69.4 years.
Major causes of death per 100,000 population (1981): diseases of the circulatory system 186.3; ill-defined conditions 158.3; malignant neoplasms (cancers) 90.9; endocrine, nutritional, and metabolic diseases 48.3; diseases of the respiratory system 41.5; diseases of the digestive system 31.4.

National economy

Budget (1984)‡. Revenue: EC$87,400,000 (import duties 46.9%; income taxes 25.4%; property taxes 5.4%; export duties 3.7%; post office 3.7%). Expenditures: EC$158,600,000 (current expenditure 54.7%, of which wages and salaries 27.8%, purchases of goods and services 10.1%, transfer payments 8.2%, charges on public debt 6.8%; development expenditure 45.3%).
Public debt (external, outstanding; 1984): U.S.$39,900,000.
Tourism: receipts from visitors (1985) U.S.$23,500,000; expenditures by nationals abroad (1983) U.S.$3,000,000.
Gross national product (1984): U.S.$80,000,000 (U.S.$860 per capita).

Structure of gross domestic product and labour force

	1984		1981	
	in value EC$'000,000	% of total value	labour force§	% of labour force
Agriculture	37.9	21.7	7,987	28.7
Quarrying	1.8	1.0	75	0.3
Manufacturing	4.7	2.7	1,566	5.6
Construction	13.6	7.8	2,863	10.3
Public utilities	3.7	2.1	371	1.3
Transportation and communication	13.1	7.5	1,689	6.1
Trade	39.4	22.6	3,902	14.0
Finance	11.9	6.8	367	1.3
Pub. admin., defense	37.7	21.6	1,682	6.0
Services	10.5	6.0	2,566	9.2
Other	—	—	4,779	17.2
TOTAL	174.3	100.0 ‖	27,847	100.0

Production (metric tons except as noted). Agriculture, forestry, fishing (1984): bananas 14,000, coconuts 8,000, sugarcane 6,000, citrus fruits 4,000, roots and tubers 4,000, nutmeg 2,418¶, cacao 2,000, mangoes 2,000, avocados 1,500, breadfruit 935¶, peas and beans 645¶, soursop 555¶, mace 150¶; livestock (number of live animals) 16,000 sheep, 13,000 goats, 11,000 pigs, 6,000 cattle, 260,000 chickens♀; roundwood, n.a.; fish catch (1983) 1,801. Mining and quarrying: excavation of gravel for local use. Manufacturing (1983): clothing EC$6,500,000 in export sales♀; beer 11,200 hectolitres; malt 4,700 hectolitres; edible coconut oil 2,600 hectolitres; rum 2,100 hectolitres; coconut meal 105; laundry soap 26. Construction: n.a. Energy production (consumption): electricity (kW-hr; 1984) 25,000,000 (25,000,000); coal, none (none); crude petroleum, none (none); petroleum products (metric tons; 1984) none (20,000); natural gas, none (none).
Household income and expenditure. Average household size (1970) 4.7; average annual income per household: n.a.; source of income: n.a.; expenditure♂: food 59.0%, clothing and footwear 8.0%, housing 6.5%, household furnishings 6.5%, fuel and light 6.0%, transportation 4.0%, alcohol and tobacco 2.5%, other 7.5%.
Population economically active (1984): total 46,000; activity rate of total population c. 48.0% (participation rates: ages 15–64, n.a.; female, n.a.; unemployed [1985] 25.0%).

Price and earnings indexes (1980 = 100)

	1979	1980	1981	1982	1983	1984
Consumer price index	84.0	100.0	121.6	131.0	...	...
Monthly earnings index□	...	...	...	...	...	...

Land use (1982): forested 9.0%; meadows and pastures 6.0%; agricultural and under permanent cultivation 41.0%; other 44.0%.

Foreign trade◇△

Balance of trade (current prices)

	1980	1981	1982	1983	1984	1985
U.S.$'000,000	−36.7	−41.7	−46.5	−45.7	−38.3	−46.7
% of total	51.3%	52.3%	55.6%	54.7%	51.5%	51.4%

Imports (1983): U.S.$64,600,000 (food 21.1%; machinery and transportation equipment 19.5%; estimated unrecorded imports for international airport project 13.2%; miscellaneous manufactured goods 13.2%; mineral fuels 9.6%). *Major import sources*†: United Kingdom 19.5%; United States 17.4%; Trinidad and Tobago 17.0%; East Germany 10.2%; Canada 4.6%.
Exports (1983): U.S.$18,920,000 (domestic exports 97.4%, of which fresh fruit 21.9%, cocoa beans 21.4%, nutmeg 17.2%, bananas 17.1%, clothing 9.4%, mace 4.0%; reexports 2.6%). *Major export destinations*⊕: Trinidad and Tobago 34.3%; United Kingdom 25.7%; West Germany 11.1%; The Netherlands 11.1%; U.S.S.R. 5.1%.

Transport and communications

Transport. Railroads: none. Roads (1984): total length 609 mi, 980 km (paved 66%). Vehicles (1981): passenger cars 4,784; trucks and buses 981. Merchant marine (1985): vessels (100 gross tons and over) 3; total deadweight tonnage 577. Air transport (1982): passenger arrivals and departures, n.a.; cargo loaded 59 metric tons, cargo unloaded 116 metric tons; airports (1986) with scheduled flights 3.
Communications. Daily newspapers: none. Radio (1985): total number of receivers 50,000 (1 per 1.9 persons). Television: total number of receivers, n.a. Telephones (1985): 5,650 (1 per 17 persons).

Education and health

Education (1982–83)

	schools	teachers	students	student/ teacher ratio
Primary (age 5–11)	64	764	17,704	23.2
Secondary (age 12–18)	20**	264	8,578	32.5
Vocational**	1	21	213	10.1
Higher	...	40	519	13.0

Educational attainment (1970). Percent of adult population over age 25 having: no schooling 2.9%; primary education 90.4%; secondary 5.8%; higher 0.9%. *Literacy* (1981): total population over age 15 literate 46,000 (85.0%).
Health (1985): physicians 38 (1 per 2,513 persons); hospital beds 304 (1 per 314 persons); infant mortality rate per 1,000 live births (1983) 21.2.
Food (1980–82): daily per capita caloric intake 2,162 (vegetable products 78%, animal products 22%); 90% of FAO recommended minimum requirement.

Military

Total active duty personnel (1986):††. *Military expenditure as percent of GNP:* n.a.; per capita expenditure, n.a.

*Grenada is divided into seven parishes for administrative purposes only. Local governmental bodies, the first since 1968, were to be established in mid-1986. The new system was to include six district boards for the island of Grenada itself, a single combined council for the islands of Carriacou and Petite Martinique, and a municipal borough council for the locality of St. George's. †Urban defined as locality of St. George's only. ‡*Budget* (1985). Revenue: EC$95,000,000. Expenditures: EC$249,900,000 (current expenditure 49.3%; development expenditure 50.7%, most of which is for road, agricultural, health, and international airport projects). §Employed labour force only, including 5,932 self-employed. ‖ Detail does not add to total given because of rounding. ¶1983. ♀1982. ♂Weights of consumer price index components in 1979. □Grenada does not have a systematically computed index of wage rates. ◇Imports c.i.f. (cost, insurance, and freight); exports f.o.b. (free on board). △The 1979–83 period includes estimated unrecorded imports for the airport project at Point Salines. †Recorded imports only. ⊕Domestic exports only. **1981–82. ††The 550-member police force includes a paramilitary unit.

Guadeloupe

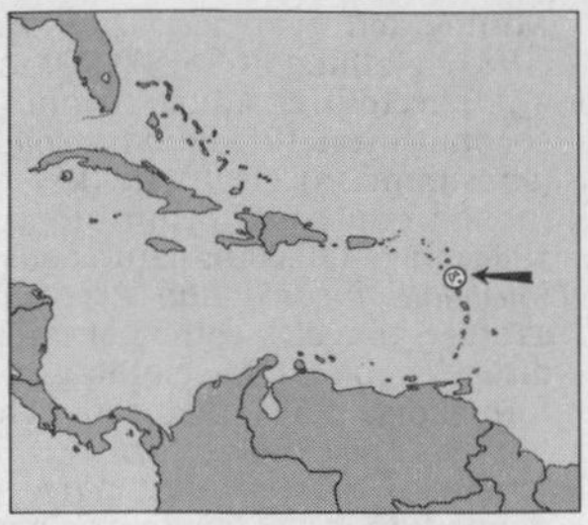

Official name: Département de la Guadeloupe (Department of Guadeloupe).
Political status: overseas department (France), with two legislative houses (General Council [43]; Regional Council [41]).
Chief of state: President of France.
Heads of government: Commissioner of the Republic (for France); President of the General Council (for Guadeloupe); President of the Regional Council (for Guadeloupe).
Capital: Basse-Terre.
Official language: French.
Official religion: none.
Monetary unit: 1 Franc (F) = 100 centimes; valuation (Oct. 1, 1986) 1 U.S.$ = F 6.64; 1 £ = F 9.60.

Area and population

		area		population
Arrondissements	**Capitals**	sq mi	sq km	1982 census
Basse-Terre*	Basse-Terre	332	861	138,242
Pointe-à-Pitre†	Pointe-à-Pitre	297	769	179,027
Saint-Martin–Saint-Barthélemy‡	Marigot	29	75	11,131
TOTAL		687§	1,780§	328,400

Demography

Population (1986): 334,000.
Density (1986) ‖ : persons per sq mi 486.2, persons per sq km 187.6.
Urban–rural (1985): urban 45.6%; rural 54.4%.
Sex distribution (1982): male 49.10%; female 50.90%.
Age breakdown (1982): under 15, 31.1%; 15–29, 29.2%; 30–44, 16.6%; 45–59, 12.0%; 60–74, 7.8%; 75 and over, 2.8%; not specified 0.5%.
Population projection: (1990) 338,000; (2000) 350,000.
Doubling time: 52 years.
Ethnic composition (1980): Creole (mulatto) 77.0%; black 10.0%; Guadeloupe mestizo (French–Amerindian) 10.0%; white 2.0%; other 1.0%.
Religious affiliation (1980): Roman Catholic 90.2%; Protestant (mostly Seventh-day Adventist and Reformed Church of France) 3.9%; Jehovah's Witness 1.9%; Hindu–Catholic spiritist 0.9%; Muslim 0.9%; other 2.2%.
Major cities (1982): Les Abymes 51,837; Pointe-à-Pitre 25,151; Le Gosier 13,741; Basse-Terre 13,397.

Vital statistics

Birth rate per 1,000 population (1984): 20.2 (world avg. 29.0); (1980) legitimate 47.9%; illegitimate 52.1%.
Death rate per 1,000 population (1984): 6.8 (world avg. 11.0).
Natural increase rate per 1,000 population (1984): 13.4 (world avg. 18.0).
Total fertility rate (avg. births per childbearing woman; 1980–85): 2.5.
Marriage rate per 1,000 population (1984): 5.0.
Divorce rate per 1,000 population (1984): 1.5.
Life expectancy at birth (1980–85): male 67.8 years; female 73.2 years.
Major causes of death per 100,000 population (1979): chronic rheumatic heart disease 103.8; malignant neoplasms (cancers) 81.4; cerebrovascular disease 66.4; homicide and other violence 54.2; accidents 31.2; hypertensive disease 31.2; diabetes mellitus 25.4.

National economy

Budget (1984). Revenue: F 1,799,000,000 (receipts from French central government 31.0%; carried over receipts 30.1%; taxes on motor fuels 21.3%). Expenditures: F 1,801,000,000 (health and social services 32.1%; carried over expenses 30.1%; capital investments and works 18.2%; agriculture, trade, and industry 5.8%).
Public debt (external, outstanding; 1984¶): U.S.$47,000,000.
Tourism (1984): receipts from visitors U.S.$98,000,000; expenditures by nationals abroad, n.a.
Production (metric tons except as noted). Agriculture, forestry, fishing (1984): sugarcane 590,200♀, bananas 150,000, roots and tubers 27,000, eggplant 5,000, coconuts 3,000, cucumbers 3,000, pineapples 2,000, commercially grown flowers (mostly anthuriums) 127,000 stems; livestock (number of live animals) 93,000 cattle, 40,000 pigs, 40,000 goats, 310,000 chickens♂; roundwood 17,000 cu m; fish catch 8,940. Mining and quarrying (1984): pozzolan, sand, and gravel for local use. Manufacturing (1985): cement 160,000□; raw sugar 53,100; molasses 18,100□; rum 74,900 hectolitres; other products include clothing, wooden furniture and posts, and metalware. Construction (1981): residential 261,400 sq m; nonresidential 124,000 sq m. Energy production (consumption): electricity (kW-hr; 1985) 474,000,000 (428,200,000); coal, none (none); crude petroleum, none (none); petroleum products (metric tons; 1984) none (213,000); natural gas, none (none).
Land use (1983): forested 40.0%; meadows and pastures 12.0%; agricultural and under permanent cultivation 22.0%; other 26.0%.
Household income and expenditure. Average household size (1982) 3.7; income per household (1980) F 72,898 (U.S.$16,142); sources of income: salaries 76.8%, industrial and commercial benefits 9.3%, pensions and rents 4.0%, noncommercial benefits 3.9%, income from stocks and bonds 2.6%, other 3.4%; expenditure (1979)◊: food 34.4%, transportation 16.3%, housing 12.2%, clothing and footwear 9.2%, education and recreation 6.6%, household furnishings 6.0%, energy 5.7%, other 9.6%.
Gross national product (at current market prices; 1983): U.S.$1,180,000,000 (U.S.$3,580 per capita).

Structure of gross domestic product and labour force

	1980		1982	
	in value F '000,000	% of total value	labour force	% of labour force
Agriculture	449	7.7	12,997	10.5
Manufacturing	372	6.3	6,643	5.3
Construction	259	4.4	9,997	8.1
Public utilities	12	0.2	703	0.6
Transportation and communication	267	4.6	4,819	3.9
Trade, restaurants, hotels	1,071	18.3	10,062	8.1
Finance, insurance, real estate△	1,560	26.6	15,109	12.2
Pub. admin., defense, services†, other	1,870	31.9	63,558⊕	51.3⊕
TOTAL	5,860	100.0	123,888	100.0

Population economically active (1982): total 123,888; activity rate of total population 37.9% (participation rates: ages 15–64, 63.7%; female 42.5%; unemployed 19.7%).

Price and earnings indexes (1978 = 100)††**

	1979	1980	1981	1982	1983	1984	1985
Consumer price index	112.5	129.3	147.4	162.5	178.6	192.5	202.6
Monthly earnings index	114.3	130.9	157.1	183.1	201.5	219.9	235.1

Foreign trade

Balance of trade (current prices)

	1980	1981	1982	1983	1984	1985
F '000,000	−2,628	−3,025	−3,569	−4,412	−4,480	−5,076
% of total	85.9%	74.8%	76.5%	77.9%	74.9%	79.1%

Imports (1984): F 5,231,000,000 (food 22.8%, petroleum products 18.3%, electrical machinery 12.8%, transport vehicles 9.0%, chemical products 7.7%, metal manufactures 5.8%). *Major import sources:* France 59.0%; Martinique 11.0%; Netherlands Antilles 4.0%; Italy 4.0%.
Exports (1984): F 751,000,000 (bananas 57.0%, sugar 12.9%, rum 4.5%, and eggplant, fruits, fresh-cut flowers, and plants of unknown value). *Major export destinations:* France 72.0%; Martinique 15.0%.

Transport and communications

Transport. Railroads (1984): only private, narrow-gauge railways serving sugar plantations. Roads (1984): total length 1,279 mi, 2,059 km (paved 60%). Vehicles (1984): passenger cars 89,369; trucks and buses 26,806. Merchant marine: n.a. Air transport (1985)‡‡: passenger arrivals 496,239, passenger departures 499,468; cargo loaded 4,226 metric tons, cargo unloaded 7,419 metric tons; airports (1986) with scheduled flights 6.
Communications. Daily newspapers (1985): total number 1; total circulation 25,000; circulation per 1,000 population 75. Radio (1985): total number of receivers 60,000 (1 per 5.5 persons). Television (1985): total number of receivers 47,000 (1 per 7.1 persons). Telephones (1983): 68,518 (1 per 4.8 persons).

Education and health

Education (1982–83)

	schools	teachers	students	student/teacher ratio
Primary (age 6–10)	232	2,408	50,576	21.0
Secondary (age 11–17)	...	2,394	33,218	13.9
Vocational	...	570	15,844	27.8
Higher§§	1	92	4,809	52.3

Educational attainment (1982). Percent of population over age 25 having: no schooling 10.7%; primary education 54.6%; secondary 29.5%; higher 5.2%.
Literacy (1980): total population literate 217,900 (91.5%); males literate 106,500 (92.7%); females literate 111,400 (90.3%).
Health (1983): physicians 418 (1 per 789 persons); hospital beds 4,235 (1 per 78 persons); infant mortality rate per 1,000 live births (1984) 17.7.
Food (1980–82): daily per capita caloric intake 2,512 (vegetable products 76%, animal products 24%); 104% of FAO recommended minimum requirement.

Military

Total active duty personnel (1984): 1,800 ‖ ‖ .

*Comprises Basse-Terre 327 sq mi (848 sq km) and Îles des Saintes 5 sq mi (13 sq km), pop. 2,901. †Comprises Grand-Terre 228 sq mi (590 sq km); Marie-Galante 61 sq mi (158 sq km), pop. 13,757; La Désirade 8 sq mi (20 sq km), pop. 1,602; and the small, uninhabited Îles de la Petite-Terre. ‡Comprises the French part of Saint-Martin 20 sq mi (52 sq km), pop. 8,072; Saint-Barthélemy 8 sq mi (21 sq km), pop. 3,059; and the small, uninhabited island of Tintamarre. §Total area includes 29 sq mi (75 sq km) not allocated by arrondissement. ‖ Based on total area. ¶Includes external long-term private debt not guaranteed by the government. ♀1985. ♂1981. □1984. ◊Weights of consumer price index components. △Includes business services. †Includes nonsaleable services. ⊕Includes 29,427 unemployed, 4,984 of whom were not previously employed. **Actual base year is average of April 1, 1978, through March 31, 1979. ††All figures are end of year unless otherwise indicated. ‡‡Raizet international airport only. §§1984–85. ‖ ‖ Includes metropole troops, local conscripts in military service, and police.

Guam

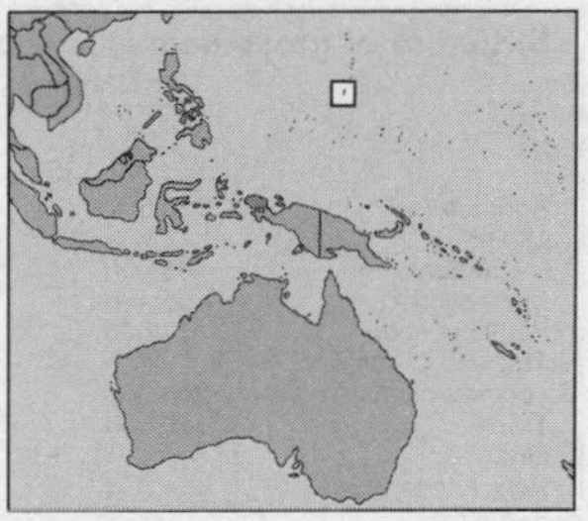

Official name: Guam.
Political Status: self-governing organized unincorporated territory of the United States with one legislative house (21).
Chief of state: President of the United States.
Head of government: Governor.
Capital: Agana.
Official language: English.
Official religion: none.
Monetary unit: 1 United States dollar (U.S.$) = 100 cents; valuation (Oct. 1, 1986) 1 U.S.$ = £ 0.69.

Area and population

	area		population*
Election Districts	sq mi	sq km	1986 estimate
Agana	1	3	1,000
Agana Heights	1	3	3,700
Agat	10	26	4,600
Asan	6	16	2,300
Barrigada	9	23	8,900
Chalan Pago-Ordot	6	16	3,600
Dededo	30	78	27,000
Inarajan	19	49	2,400
Mangilao	10	26	7,800
Merizo	6	16	1,900
Mongmong-Toto-Maite	2	5	6,000
Piti	7	18	3,300
Santa Rita	17	44	10,500
Sinajana	1	3	2,800
Talofofo	17	44	2,300
Tamuning	6	16	15,500
Umatac	6	16	800
Yigo	35	91	11,800
Yona	20	52	4,800
TOTAL	209	541†	121,000

Demography

Population (1986): 121,000.
Density (1986): persons per sq mi 578.9, persons per sq km 223.7.
Urban–rural (1980): urban‡ 39.5%; rural 60.5%.
Sex distribution (1980): male 52.20%; female 47.80%.
Age breakdown (1980): under 15, 34.9%; 15–29, 30.6%; 30–44, 19.4%; 45–59, 10.5%; 60–74, 3.9%; 75 and over, 0.7%.
Population projection: (1990) 129,900; (2000) 137,000.
Doubling time: 49 years.
Ethnic composition (1980): Chamorro 41.8%; Filipino 21.2%; German 2.1%; Korean 1.8%; Japanese 1.8%; other§ 31.3%.
Religious affiliation (1980): Roman Catholic 79.5%; Protestant 15.7%; other 4.8%.
Major populated places (1980): Tamuning 8,862; Apra Harbor 5,633; Andersen Air Force Base 4,892; Mangilao 4,029.

Vital statistics

Birth rate per 1,000 population (1985): 17.8 (world avg. 29.0); legitimate 64.5%; illegitimate 35.5%.
Death rate per 1,000 population (1985): 3.4 (world avg. 11.0).
Natural increase rate per 1,000 population (1985): 14.4 (world avg. 18.0).
Total fertility rate (avg. births per childbearing woman; 1980): 3.2.
Marriage rate per 1,000 population (1985): 11.3.
Divorce rate per 1,000 population (1985): 5.3.
Life expectancy at birth (1980–82): male 69.6 years; female 74.5 years.
Major causes of death per 100,000 population (1983): heart disease 117.7; malignant neoplasms (cancers) 51.5; motor vehicle accidents 24.9; cerebrovascular diseases 18.9; pneumonia 14.6; homicide 13.7; other diseases of the central nervous system 12.9; diabetes mellitus 12.9.

National economy

Budget (1984). Revenue: U.S.$212,920,869 (local income taxes 37.9%, gross business receipts taxes 19.6%, revenues from United States agencies ‖ 10.4%, federal grants-in-aid 2.3%). Expenditures: U.S.$179,102,238 (general government operations 39.8%, public education 32.1%, law and public safety 12.6%, public health and community services 11.2%, economic development 2.1%).
Public debt (external, outstanding): n.a.
Tourism (1984): receipts from visitors U.S.$200,000,000; expenditures by nationals abroad, n.a.
Production. Agriculture, forestry, fishing (value of production in U.S.$ except as noted; 1984): watermelons 1,197,378, head cabbages 264,567, cucumbers 236,160, bananas 169,715, tomatoes 161,611, long beans 155,100, pepino melons 152,685, sweet potatoes 124,576, pineapples 115,920, eggs 902,462; livestock (number of live animals) 4,120 pigs, 1,300 goats, 650 cattle, 90 carabaos; fish catch (metric tons) 388¶. Mining and quarrying (1983): sand and gravel. Manufacturing (value of gross business receipts in U.S.$; 1980): petroleum refining and related products 322,083,000; food processing 11,742,000; printing and publishing 6,039,000; industrial and medical goods and materials 412,000. Construction (gross value of building and construction permits in U.S.$; 1985): residential 33,099,000; nonresidential 30,675,000. Energy production (consumption): electricity (kW-hr; 1984) 1,000,000,000 (1,000,000,000); coal, none (n.a.); crude petroleum (barrels; 1984) none (10,662,000); petroleum products (metric tons; 1984) 1,375,000,000 (795,000); natural gas, none (n.a.).
Gross national product (at current market prices; 1984): U.S.$760,000,000 (U.S.$6,340 per capita).

Structure of gross business income and labour force

	1982		1986	
	in value U.S.$'000,000	% of total value	labour force♀	% of labour force
Agriculture	1.4	0.2	110	0.3
Manufacturing	107.3	13.1	1,320	3.2
Construction	64.6	7.9	3,960	9.7
Trade	422.3	51.5	7,690	18.8
Transp. and commun.	45.3	5.5	1,850δ	4.5
Finance	80.8	9.9	1,690	4.1
Pub. admin., defense	...	...	17,640	43.1
Services	99.6	12.2	6,630	16.2
TOTAL	819.2†	100.0†	40,890	100.0†

Population economically active (1986): total 35,590□; activity rate of total population 29.0% (participation rates: over age 16, 60.4%; female 40.3%; unemployed 6.0%).

Price and earnings indexes (1978 = 100)

	1979	1980	1981	1982	1983	1984	1985
Consumer price index	112.1	134.0	161.4	169.6	179.3	195.6	198.3
Hourly earnings index	116.5	123.0	...	...	...	134.4	141.6

Household income and expenditure. Average household size (1980) 3.7; median annual income per household (1979) U.S.$16,203; source of income: n.a.; expenditure (1978): housing 28.6%, food 24.1%, transportation 18.0%, clothing 10.6%, entertainment 5.1%, medical care 4.7%.
Land use (1983): forested 18.2%; meadows and pastures 14.5%; agricultural and under permanent cultivation 21.8%; other 45.5%.

Foreign trade

Balance of trade (current prices)

	1978	1979	1980	1981	1982	1983
U.S.$'000	−236,227	−403,144	−483,141	...	...	−571,519
% of total	76.7%	82.5%	79.8%	...	...	87.9%

Imports (1983): U.S.$610,743,985 (mineral fuels 46.9%, of which crude petroleum 28.8%; machinery and transport equipment 19.1%, of which passenger cars 12.4%; food and live animals 12.0%, of which beef and veal 1.5%; beverages and tobacco 4.5%, of which cigarettes 1.3%; manufactured goods 4.4%; chemicals 2.3%). *Major import sources:* United States 23.4%; Japan 19.2%; Taiwan 4.6%; Hong Kong 3.1%; Philippines 1.3%.
Exports (1983): U.S.$39,224,728 (clothing 16.9%; beverages and tobacco 12.0%, of which alcoholic beverages 4.4%, cigarettes 3.5%, nonalcoholic beverages 1.9%; machinery and transport equipment 11.4%; travel goods 3.0%; lubricating oils and greases 2.7%; fish and fish products 2.6%; cosmetics 2.6%; watches and watch cases 1.5%; cement 1.5%). *Major export destinations:* United States 24.9%; Japan 4.8%; Hong Kong 2.0%.

Transport and communications

Transport. Railroads: none. Roads (1984): total length 419 mi, 674 km (paved 100%). Vehicles◇ (1984): passenger cars 57,856; trucks and buses 16,521. Merchant marine (1984): vessels (100 gross tons and over), n.a.; surface cargo loaded, unloaded, or transshipped (1984) 977,000 metric tons. Air transport (1984): passenger arrivals 361,423; passenger departures, n.a.; cargo loaded 3,565 metric tons; cargo unloaded 5,797 metric tons; airports (1986) with scheduled flights 1.
Communications. Daily newspapers (1985): total number 1; total circulation 18,050; circulation per 1,000 population 153. Radio (1985): total receivers 100,000 (1 per 1.2 persons). Television (1985): total receivers 79,000 (1 per 1.5 persons). Telephones (1984): 23,354 (1 per 5.0 persons).

Education and Health

Education (1984–85)

	schools	teachers	students	student/ teacher ratio
Primary (age 5–12)	39△	522**†**	17,609	25.4**†**
Secondary (age 13–18)	19⊕	533**†**	14,223	21.6**†**
Voc., teacher tr.△	1⊕	66	868	13.2
Higher⊕	2**	162	3,499	21.6

Educational attainment (1980). Percent of population 25 years old and over having: primary education 21.3%; some secondary 13.1%; secondary 31.2%; college 34.4%. *Literacy* (1985): *c.* 90%.
Health: physicians (1982): 83 (1 per 1,334 persons); hospital beds (1979) 223 (1 per 470 persons); infant mortality rate per 1,000 live births (1983) 7.5.
Food: daily per capita caloric intake, n.a.

Military

Total active duty U.S. personnel (1984): 10,900 (navy 45.0%, air force 35.8%, other 19.2%).

*Includes about 23,000 active duty personnel, Department of Defense employees, and dependents. †Detail does not add to total given because of rounding. ‡Places of 2,500 or more. §Includes various Pacific Island groups (mostly Micronesian) and persons of multiple ethnic origin. ‖ Consists largely of federal income tax. ¶An additional 48 metric tons were produced through aquaculture. ♀Employed persons only. δIncludes public utilities. □Excludes nonimmigrant aliens and civilians living on military reservations. ◇Excludes military vehicles. △1983. **†**Public schools only. ⊕1981–82. **1982–83.

Guatemala

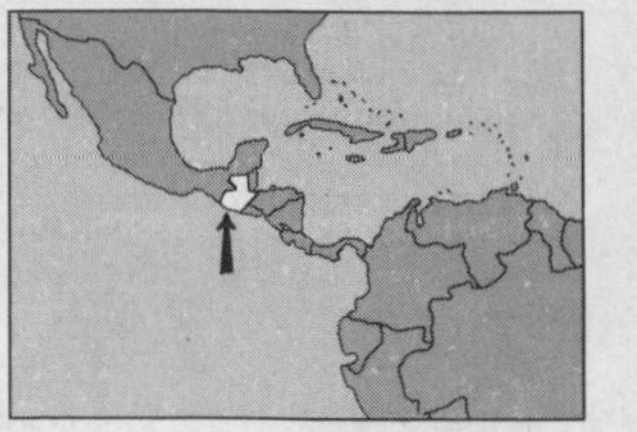

Official name: República de Guatemala (Republic of Guatemala).
Form of government: republic with one legislative house (Legislative Assembly [100]).
Head of state and government: President.
Capital: Guatemala City.
Official language: Spanish.
Official religion: none.
Monetary unit: 1 Guatemalan quetzal (Q) = 100 centavos; valuation (Oct. 1, 1986) 1 U.S.$ = Q 1.00*; 1 £ = Q 1.45.

Area and population

Departments	Capitals	area sq mi	area sq km	population 1985 estimate
Alta Verapaz	Cobán	3,354	8,686	393,400
Baja Verapaz	Salamá	1,206	3,124	160,600
Chimaltenango	Chimaltenango	764	1,979	283,900
Chiquimula	Chiquimula	917	2,376	220,100
El Progreso	Progreso	742	1,922	106,100
Escuintla	Escuintla	1,693	4,384	565,200
Guatemala	Guatemala City	821	2,126	2,050,700
Huehuetenango	Huehuetenango	2,857	7,400	571,300
Izabal	Puerto Barrios	3,490	9,038	330,500
Jalapa	Jalapa	797	2,063	171,500
Jutiapa	Jutiapa	1,243	3,219	348,000
Petén	Ciudad Flores	13,843	35,854	118,100
Quezaltenango	Quezaltenango	753	1,951	478,100
Quiché	Santa Cruz	3,235	8,378	461,000
Retalhuleu	Retalhuleu	717	1,856	228,600
Sacatepéquez	Antigua Guatemala	180	465	148,600
San Marcos	San Marcos	1,464	3,791	590,200
Santa Rosa	Cuilapa	1,141	2,955	263,100
Sololá	Sololá	410	1,061	181,800
Suchitepéquez	Mazatenango	969	2,510	327,800
Totonicapán	Totonicapán	410	1,061	249,100
Zacapa	Zacapa	1,039	2,690	155,500
TOTAL		42,042†	108,889	8,403,000† ‡

Demography

Population (1986)§: 8,195,000.
Density (1986): persons per sq mi 194.9, persons per sq km 75.3.
Urban-rural (1985)§: urban 32.7%; rural 67.3%.
Sex distribution (1985): male 50.56%; female 49.44%.
Age breakdown (1985): under 15, 45.9%; 15–29, 26.5%; 30–44, 14.3%; 45–59, 8.6%; 60–74, 3.8%; 75 and over, 0.9%.
Population projection: (1990) 9,197,000; (2000) 12,222,000.
Doubling time: 21 years.
Ethnic composition (1983): Maya 55%; mestizo 42%; white or black 3%.
Religious affiliation (1983): Roman Catholic *c.* 80%; Protestant *c.* 20%.
Major cities (1981)§: Guatemala City 754,200; Quezaltenango 62,700; Escuintla 36,900; Izabal 24,200.

Vital statistics

Birth rate per 1,000 population (1985): 41.7 (world avg. 29.0).
Death rate per 1,000 population (1985): 7.5 (world avg. 11.0).
Natural increase rate per 1,000 population (1985): 34.2 (world avg. 18.0).
Total fertility rate (avg. births per childbearing woman; 1980–85): 6.1.
Marriage rate per 1,000 population (1984): 3.8.
Divorce rate per 1,000 population (1983): 0.2.
Life expectancy at birth (1981): male 57.3 years; female 60.5 years.
Major causes of death per 100,000 population (1981): typhoid and other intestinal infectious diseases 260.0; respiratory diseases 143.2; homicide 113.6; birth trauma and other conditions originating in the perinatal period 67.9; diseases of the circulatory system 57.2.

National economy

Budget (1984). Revenue: Q 961,800,000 (tax revenue 51.5%, treasury bills and foreign loans 30.5%). Expenditures: Q 1,131,600,000 (defense 16.0%, education 12.2%, transportation 8.1%, health 7.6%, public works and communication 7.2%, agriculture 3.8%).
Public debt (external, outstanding; 1985): U.S.$1,926,000,000.
Tourism (1984): receipts from visitors U.S.$57,000,000; expenditures by nationals abroad U.S.$100,000,000 ∥.
Production (metric tons except as noted). Agriculture, forestry, fishing (1984): sugarcane 6,410,000, corn (maize) 1,038,000, bananas 680,000, coffee 140,000, tomatoes 93,000, dry beans 90,000, sorghum 82,000, cottonseed 78,000; livestock (number of live animals) 2,605,000 cattle, 810,000 pigs, 660,000 sheep, 15,000,000 chickens; roundwood 7,000,000 cu m; fish catch 4,284 ∥. Mining and quarrying (1984): feldspar 5,000; zinc 1,000¶; iron ore 365; copper concentrate 700 ∥; silver 8,000 ∥ troy oz. Manufacturing (1984): raw sugar 508,000; cheese 15,000♀; butter 5,000♀; beer 700,000 hectolitres♁; cigarettes 2,008,000,000 units; cement 401,000. Construction (1982)□: residential 147,200 sq m; nonresidential 73,600 sq m. Energy production (consumption): electricity (kW-hr; 1984) 1,625,000,000 (1,625,000,000); coal, none (n.a.); crude petroleum (barrels; 1984) 1,709,000 (5,472,000); petroleum products (metric tons; 1984) 672,000 (963,000); natural gas, none (n.a.).
Gross national product (at current market prices; 1984): U.S.$9,110,000,000 (U.S.$1,180 per capita).

Structure of gross domestic product and labour force

	1984 in value Q '000	1984 % of total value	1983 labour force	1983 % of labour force
Agriculture	758,800	25.7	1,347,381	58.1
Mining	7,800	0.3	2,319	0.1
Manufacturing	468,400	15.8	315,394	13.6
Construction	53,400	1.8	95,082	4.1
Public utilities	54,000	1.8	6,957	0.3
Transportation and communication	204,800	6.9	57,977	2.5
Trade	770,500	26.0 }	169,292	7.3
Finance }				
Pub. admin., defense }	639,500	21.6 }	278,289	12.0
Services }				
Other }			46,381	2.0
TOTAL	2,958,200◇	100.0†	2,319,072	100.0

Population economically active (1984): total 1,678,000; activity rate of total population 22.1% (participation rates: over age 15 [1981] 48.1%; female [1981] 7.1%; unemployed 16.1%).

Price and earnings indexes (1980 = 100)

	1979	1980	1981	1982	1983	1984	1984
Consumer price index	90.3	100.0	111.4	111.6	115.0	120.8	143.4
Annual earnings index△	90.2	100.0	131.2	139.3	135.3	...	...

Household income and expenditure. Average household size (1980) 4.5; income per household: n.a.; source of income: n.a.; expenditure✝ (1975): food 43.9%, housing 12.8%, clothing and footwear 12.6%, transport 5.2%, household furnishings 4.7%.
Land use (1983): forested 39.7%; meadows and pastures 12.3%; agricultural and under permanent cultivation 16.7%; other 31.3%.

Foreign trade⊕

Balance of trade (current prices)

	1979	1980	1981	1982	1983	1984
Q '000,000	−125.1	+84.5	−286.3	−116.7	+125.0	−53.3
% of total	4.7%	2.8%	10.2%	4.8%	5.6%	2.3%

Imports (1984): Q 1,278,496,000 (mineral fuels and lubricants 23.7%; chemical products 23.3%; basic manufactures 18.5%; machinery and transport equipment 16.4%). *Major import sources:* United States 30.9%; Mexico 9.1%; Venezuela 8.1%; El Salvador 7.6%; Netherlands Antilles 7.2%.
Exports (1984): Q 1,132,190,000 (coffee 31.9%; cardamon 8.9%; cotton 6.4%; sugar 6.3%; bananas 4.9%; beans and legumes 2.1%). *Major export destinations:* United States 34.9%; El Salvador 15.6%; West Germany 5.2%; Costa Rica 4.8%; Japan 4.4%; Italy 3.2%.

Transport and communications

Transport. Railroads (1986): route length 375 mi, 603 km. Roads (1985): total length 11,200 mi, 18,000 km (paved 15.8%). Vehicles (1983): passenger cars 188,100; trucks and buses 58,500. Merchant marine (1985): vessels (100 gross tons and over) 8; total deadweight tonnage 24,138. Air transport (1985): passenger-mi 89,370,000, passenger-km 143,827,000; short ton-mi cargo 14,543,000, metric ton-km cargo 21,232,000; airports (1986) 2.
Communications. Daily newspapers (1983): total number 8; total circulation 224,500; circulation per 1,000 population 30. Radio (1985): 325,000 receivers (1 per 24 persons). Television (1985): 207,000 receivers (1 per 37 persons). Telephones (1983 est.): 161,520 (1 per 47 persons).

Education and health

Education (1984)

	schools	teachers	students	student/ teacher ratio
Primary (age 7–12)	7,820	26,963	979,888	36.3
Secondary (age 13–18)**	...	12,023	174,653	14.5
Voc., teacher tr.**	...	...	...	...
Higher ∥	5	4,490	51,556	11.5

Educational attainment (1981). Percent of adult population over age 25 having: no formal schooling 52.9%; some primary education 26.2%; complete primary 8.3%; some secondary 5.4%; complete secondary 3.4%. *Literacy* (1980): total population over age 15 literate 2,076,500 (51.1%); males literate 1,203,000 (58.6%); females literate 873,500 (43.5%); Maya literate 450,000 (20.0%).
Health: physicians (early 1980s) 1,250 (1 per 5,700 persons); hospital beds (1982) 9,881 (1 per 720 persons); infant mortality rate per 1,000 live births (1985) 56.0.
Food (1980–82): daily per capita caloric intake 2,111 (vegetable products 91%, animal products 9%); 96% of FAO recommended minimum requirement.

Military

Total active duty personnel (1985): 31,700 (army 94.6%, navy 3.2%, air force 2.2%). *Military expenditure as percent of GNP* (1983): 2.4% (world 6.1%); per capita expenditure U.S.$25.

*The value of the quetzal is fixed at par with that of the U.S.$; the nonofficial rate is 179% higher. †Detail does not add to total given because of rounding. ‡Based on estimated de facto population. §Based on de jure population. ∥ 1983. ¶1982. ♀1981. ♁1979. □Authorized private construction in Guatemala City. ◇At 1958 prices. △Includes real annual wages and salaries paid to workers affiliated with the Guatemalan Institute of Social Security. ✝Urban families. ⊕Import figures are f.o.b. (free on board) in balance of trade and c.i.f. (cost, insurance, and freight) for commodities and trading partners. **Secondary includes vocational and teacher training.

Guinea

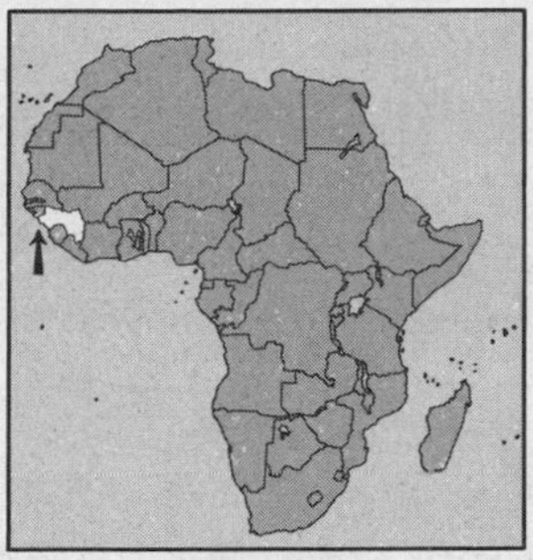

Official name: République de Guinée (Republic of Guinea).
Form of government: interim military regime ruling through the Military Committee for National Recovery (CMRN [20]) with an appointed government (41).
Head of state and government: President.
Capital: Conakry.
Official language: French.
Official religion: none.
Monetary unit: 1 Guinean franc* (GF) = 100 cauris; valuation (Oct. 1, 1986) 1 U.S.$ = GF 340.00; 1 £ = GF 491.30.

Area and population

		area		population
Regions	Capitals	sq mi	sq km	1983 census
Beyla	Beyla	6,738	17,452	161,347
Boffa	Boffa	1,932	5,003	141,719
Boké	Boké	3,881	10,053	225,207
Conakry	Conakry	119	308	705,280
Coyah (Dubréka)	Coyah	2,153	5,576	134,190
Dabola	Dabola	2,317	6,000	97,986
Dalaba	Dalaba	1,313	3,400	132,802
Dinguiraye	Dinguiraye	4,247	11,000	133,502
Faranah	Faranah	4,788	12,400	142,923
Forécariah	Forécariah	1,647	4,265	116,464
Fria	Fria	840	2,175	70,413
Gaoual	Gaoual	4,440	11,500	135,657
Guéckédou	Guéckédou	1,605	4,157	204,757
Kankan	Kankan	7,104	18,400	229,861
Kérouané	Kérouané	3,070	7,950	106,872
Kindia	Kindia	3,409	8,828	216,052
Kissidougou	Kissidougou	3,425	8,872	183,236
Koubia	Koubia	571	1,480	98,053
Koundara	Koundara	2,124	5,500	94,216
Kouroussa	Kouroussa	4,647	12,035	136,926
Labé	Labé	973	2,520	253,214
Lélouma	Lélouma	830	2,150	138,467
Lola	Lola	1,629	4,219	106,654
Macenta	Macenta	3,363	8,710	193,109
Mali	Mali	3,398	8,800	210,889
Mamou	Mamou	2,378	6,160	190,525
Mandiana	Mandiana	5,000	12,950	136,317
Nzérékoré	Nzérékoré	1,460	3,781	216,355
Pita	Pita	1,544	4,000	227,912
Siguiri	Siguiri	7,626	19,750	209,164
Télimélé	Télimélé	3,119	8,080	243,256
Tougué	Tougué	2,394	6,200	113,272
Yomou	Yomou	843	2,183	74,417
TOTAL		94,926†	245,857	5,781,014

Demography

Population (1986): 5,563,000.
Density (1986): persons per sq mi 58.6, persons per sq km 22.6.
Urban-rural (1985): urban 26.0%; rural 74.0%.
Sex distribution (1985): male 48.63%; female 51.37%.
Age breakdown (1985): under 15, 43.1%; 15–29, 26.2%; 30–44, 16.2%; 45–59, 9.6%; 60–74, 4.2%; 75 and over, 0.7%.
Population projection: (1990) 6,145,000; (2000) 7,935,000.
Doubling time: 30 years.
Ethnic composition (1980): Fulani 40.9%; Malinke 25.9%; Susu 11.4%; Kissi 8.4%; Kpelle 4.8%; other 8.6%.
Religious affiliation (1980): Muslim 69.0%; tribal religionist 29.5%; Roman Catholic 1.1%; other 0.4%.
Major cities (1983): Conakry 705,280‡; Kankan 88,760; Labé 65,439; Kindia 55,904.

Vital statistics

Birth rate per 1,000 population (1980–85): 46.8 (world avg. 29.0).
Death rate per 1,000 population (1980–85): 23.5 (world avg. 11.0).
Natural increase rate per 1,000 population (1980–85): 23.3 (world avg. 18.0).
Total fertility rate (avg. births per childbearing woman; 1980–85): 6.2.
Life expectancy at birth (1980–85): male 38.7 years; female 41.8 years.
Major causes of death per 100,000 population: n.a.; however, major diseases include malaria, venereal disease, tuberculosis, intestinal infections, measles, and schistosomiasis.

National economy

Budget (1986). Revenue: GF 109,602,000,000 (customs duties 42.2%, income tax 14.1%, excise tax 3.1%). Expenditures: GF 136,999,000,000 (material expenses 24.1%, wages 22.1%, debt service 17.1%, infrastructure 14.3%, rural development 7.6%, industry and mining development 7.5%).
Public debt (external, outstanding; 1984): U.S.$1,168,200,000.
Tourism: n.a.
Production (metric tons except as noted). Agriculture, forestry, fishing (1984): roots and tubers 848,000 (of which cassava 650,000, sweet potatoes 83,000, yams 79,000), fruits 566,000 (of which plantains 235,000, bananas 115,000, pineapples 20,000), cereals 530,000 (of which rice 400,000, corn [maize] 56,000), vegetables and melons 389,000, sugarcane 225,000, peanuts (groundnuts) 75,000, milk 43,000, palm kernels 35,000, pulses 28,000, coffee 15,000, eggs 10,710; livestock (number of live animals) 1,850,000 cattle, 455,000 sheep, 450,000 goats, 45,000 pigs, 10,000,000 chickens; roundwood 3,635,000 cu m; fish catch 18,453§. Mining and quarrying (1984): bauxite ‖ 12,000,000; alumina 508,000; gem diamonds 34,000 carats; industrial diamonds 14,000 carats. Manufacturing (value of production in GS '000; 1985): corrugated and sheet iron 571,081; plastics 462,242; tobacco products 375,154; cement 326,138; printed matter 216,511; fruit juice 75,763; beer 69,934; matches 22,449. Construction: n.a. Energy production (consumption): electricity (kW-hr; 1984) 499,000,000 (499,000,000); coal, none (n.a.); crude petroleum, none (n.a.); petroleum products (metric tons; 1984) none (289,000); natural gas, none (n.a.).
Gross national product (at current market prices; 1984): U.S.$1,810,000,000 (U.S.$290 per capita).

Structure of gross domestic product and labour force

	1985		1983	
	in value GS '000,000	% of total value	labour force	% of labour force
Agriculture	16,195	40.0	1,968,000	82.0
Mining	5,420	13.4		
Manufacturing	724	1.8		
Construction	2,593	6.4		
Public utilities	133	0.3	264,000	11.0
Transp. and commun.	531	1.3		
Trade	8,697	21.5		
Finance	1,295	3.2		
Pub. admin., defense	4,765	11.8	38,400	1.6
Services			129,600	5.4
Other	127	0.3	...	...
TOTAL	40,481¶†	100.0	2,400,000	100.0

Population economically active (1984): total 2,306,000; activity rate of total population 43.5% (participation rates: ages 15–64, n.a.; female [1981] 40.7%; unemployed, n.a.).
Household income and expenditure. Average household size (1980) 4.7; average annual income per capita (1984) GS 7,660 (U.S.$305); source of income: n.a.; expenditure (1985): food 61.5%, health care 11.2%, clothing and footwear 7.9%, housing and energy 7.3%, transportation 5.1%, recreation 4.2%, durable goods 2.9%.
Land use (1983): forested 42.1%; meadows and pastures 12.2%; agricultural and under permanent cultivation 6.4%; other 39.3%.

Foreign trade♀

Balance of trade (current prices)

	1979	1980	1981	1982	1983	1984
GS '000,000	−400	+1,000	+1,611	+2,511	+2,617	+3,467
% of total	2.7%	4.8%	9.9%	16.3%	16.6%	18.7%

Imports (1984): GS 7,542,000,000 (food, machinery and transport equipment, petroleum products, building materials, textiles). *Major import sources:* France 31.9%; Brazil 12.3%; U.S. 11.6%; W.Ger. 6.9%; Belgium 6.4%; Spain 5.3%.
Exports (1984): GS 11,009,000,000 (bauxite and alumina 90% to 95%; coffee, pineapples, bananas, palm kernels). *Major export destinations:* U.S. 27.5%; W.Ger. 18.9%; Spain 16.3%; Ireland 10.1%; Italy 5.8%.

Transport and communications

Transport. Railroads (1985): route length 584 mi, 940 km. Roads (1984): total length 17,600 mi, 28,400 km (paved 4%). Vehicles (1982): passenger cars 9,948; trucks and buses 9,992. Merchant marine (1985): vessels (100 gross tons and over) 19; total deadweight tonnage 2,927. Air transport (1982): passenger-mi 89,500,000, passenger-km 144,000,000; metric ton-km cargo 700,000; airports (1986) with scheduled flights 1.
Communications. Daily newspapers (1979): total number 1; total circulation 20,000; circulation per 1,000 population 4. Radio (1985): 100,000 receivers (1 per 54 persons). Television (1985): 7,700 receivers (1 per 705 persons). Telephones (1981): 15,800 (1 per 310 persons).

Education and health

Education (1983)

	schools	teachers	students	student/teacher ratio
Primary (age 7–12)	2,635δ	7,867	246,129	31.3
Secondary (age 13–18)	...	5,091	89,756	17.6
Voc., teacher tr.	...	744δ	7,963	...
Higherδ	...	1,373	13,182	9.6

Educational attainment, n.a. *Literacy* (1985): total population over age 15 literate 874,000 (28.3%); males 603,000 (39.7%); females 271,000 (17.2%).
Health: physicians (1980) 301 (1 per 17,000 persons); hospital beds□ (1976) 7,650 (1 per 579 persons); infant mortality rate per 1,000 live births (1980–85) 159.
Food (1979–81): daily per capita caloric intake 1,880 (vegetable products 96%, animal products 4%); 82% of FAO recommended minimum requirement.

Military

Total active duty personnel (1985): 9,900 (army 85.8%, navy 6.1%, air force 8.1%). *Military expenditure as percent of GNP* (1981): 4.9% (world 5.8%); per capita expenditure U.S.$10.

*In January 1986 the Guinean syli (GS) was replaced at par by the Guinean franc (GF), and its value was depreciated by 92.5% in terms of foreign currency. The exchange rate given for the Guinean franc is the official rate only; the public transaction rate is 11.8% lower. †Detail does not add to total given because of rounding. ‡Metropolitan area. §1983. ‖ Dry basis. ¶In constant prices of 1981. ♀Trade with the Socialist bloc is not included in major import sources and major export destinations; the U.S.S.R., however, is a major trading partner. δ1982. □Government hospitals only.

Guinea-Bissau

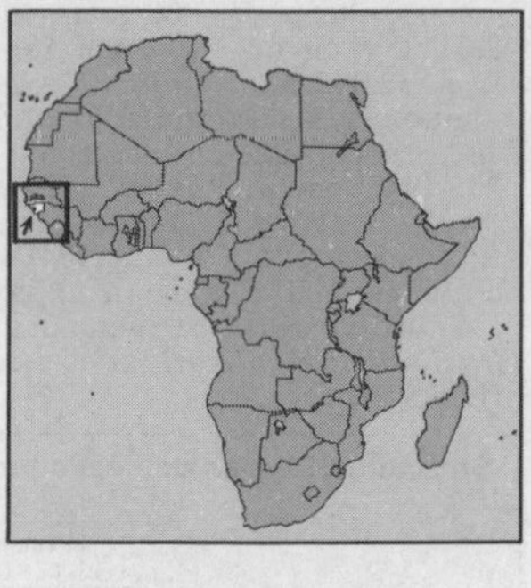

Official name: Républica da Guiné-Bissau (Republic of Guinea-Bissau).
Form of government: single-party republic with one legislative house (National People's Assembly [150]).
Head of state and government: President.
Capital: Bissau.
Official language: Portuguese.
Official religion: none.
Monetary unit: 1 peso (PG) = 100 centavos; valuation (Oct. 1, 1986) 1 U.S.$ = PG 170.48; 1 £ = PG 246.34.

Area and population

Regions	Capitals	area sq mi	area sq km	population 1979 census*
Bafatá	Bafatá	2,309	5,981	115,656
Bissau†	Bissau	324	840	51,796
Bolama	Bolama	1,013	2,624	25,449
Cacheu	Cacheu	1,998	5,175	127,514
Gabú	Gabú	3,533	9,150	103,683
Oio	Farim	2,086	5,403	131,271
Quinara	Fulacunda	1,212	3,138	35,567
Tombali	Catió	1,443	3,736	55,088
Autonomous Sector				
Bissau	—	30	78	107,281
TOTAL		13,948	36,125	753,305

Demography

Population (1986): 891,000.
Density (1986): persons per sq mi 63.9, persons per sq km 24.7.
Urban-rural (1985): urban 27.0%; rural 73.0%.
Sex distribution (1985): male 48.42%; female 51.58%.
Age breakdown (1985): under 15, 42.9%; 15–29, 25.6%; 30–44, 15.7%; 45–59, 10.2%; 60–74, 4.7%; 75 and over, 0.9%.
Population projection: (1990) 987,000; (2000) 1,229,000.
Doubling time: 37 years.
Ethnic composition (1979): Balante 24.9%; Fulani 20.2%; Malinke 12.2%; Mandyako 10.6%; Pepel 10.0%; Bafata 3.3%; other 18.8%.
Religious affiliation (1985): traditional beliefs 65%; Muslim 30%; Christian 5%.
Major cities (1979): Bissau 107,281; Bafatá 13,429; Gabú 7,803; Mansôa 5,390; Catió 5,179.

Vital statistics

Birth rate per 1,000 population (1980–85): 41.0 (world avg. 27.0); legitimate, n.a.; illegitimate, n.a.
Death rate per 1,000 population (1980–85): 22.0 (world avg. 11.0).
Natural increase rate per 1,000 population (1980–85): 19.0 (world avg. 18.0).
Total fertility rate (avg. births per childbearing woman; 1980–85): 5.4.
Marriage rate per 1,000 population: n.a.
Divorce rate per 1,000 population: n.a.
Life expectancy at birth (1975–80): male 39.4 years; female 42.6 years.
Major causes of death per 100,000 population: n.a.; however, major diseases include tuberculosis of the respiratory system, whooping cough, typhoid fever, bacillary dysentery and amoebiasis, malaria, pneumonia, and meningococcal infections.

National economy

Budget (1981). Revenue: PG 1,137,000,000 (indirect taxes 49.6%; direct taxes 25.8%; duties, fines, and other penalties 3.0%). Expenditures: PG 1,944,000,000.
Tourism: n.a.; however, the island of Bubaque is being developed as a tourist resort, with 110 rooms in 1979; work began in 1985 on a 180-room hotel in Bissau.
Production (metric tons except as noted). Agriculture, forestry, fishing (1984): rice 105,000, roots and tubers (sweet potatoes and cassava) 40,000, fruit 40,000, peanuts (groundnuts) 30,000, coconuts 25,000, plantains 25,000, vegetables 20,000, millet 16,000, sorghum 13,000, corn (maize) 10,000, palm kernels 10,000, cashews 10,000, copra 5,000, sugarcane 5,000, papayas 2,000, pulses 2,000; livestock (number of live animals) 225,000 cattle, 150,000 goats, 133,000 pigs, 420,000 chickens‡; roundwood 558,000 cu m; fish catch (1983) 2,617. Mining and quarrying: n.a.; however, prospecting for bauxite, petroleum, and phosphates was being carried out in the mid-1980s. Manufacturing (in PG '000,000; 1982): beverages 143.7, of which beer 122.3, orangeade and lemonade 16.5; clothing 14.0§; peanut oil 7.0; palm oil 2.4. Construction (in PG '000,000; 1982): total buildings 2.5. Energy production (consumption): electricity (kW-hr; 1984) 14,000,000 (14,000,000); coal, none (n.a.); crude petroleum (barrels; 1981) none (210,000); petroleum products (metric tons; 1984) none (25,000); natural gas, none (n.a.).
Population economically active (1979): total 213,000; activity rate of total population 38.7% (participation rates: ages 15–64, 42.0%; female 3.6%; unemployed 0.5%).

Price and earnings indexes (1975 = 100)

	1975	1976	1977	1978	1979	1980	1981
Consumer price index	100.0	101.5	104.5	114.1	136.6	147.4	147.4
Monthly earnings index	...	...	...	...	...	...	...

Land use (1983): forested 38.2%; meadows and pastures 45.7%; agricultural and under permanent cultivation 10.3%; other 5.8%.
Gross national product (1984): U.S.$160,000,000 (U.S.$190 per capita).

Structure of gross domestic product and labour force

	1983 in value U.S.$'000,000	1983 % of total value	1979 labour force	1979 % of labour force
Agriculture	37	48.7	157,320	79.2
Mining	1	1.3	...	...
Manufacturing	1	1.3	3,006	1.5
Construction	2	2.6	1,727	0.9
Public utilities			270	0.1
Transportation and communication			2,438	1.2
Trade	35	46.1	5,250	2.6
Finance			207	0.1
Pub. admin., defense; Services			27,417	13.8
Other	...	...	940	0.5
TOTAL	76‖	100.0	198,575	100.0¶

Public debt (external, outstanding; 1984): U.S.$149,400,000.
Household income and expenditure. Average household size (1981) 4.1; average annual income per household: n.a.; source of income: n.a.; expenditure: n.a.

Foreign trade

Balance of trade (current prices)

	1978	1979	1980	1981	1982	1983
PG '000,000	−1,308.8	−1,588.0	−1,477.6	−1,334.1	−1,500.8	−1,227.5
% of total	60.0%	62.3%	65.9%	56.0%	61.1%	63.2%

Imports (1983): PG 1,585,600,000 (food and beverages 33.7%, of which cereals 22.7%; textiles and clothing 15.8%; transport equipment 12.8%; machinery and apparatus, including electrical 8.2%). *Major import sources* (1984): Portugal 29.7%; Italy 14.7%; Spain 9.1%; West Germany 5.6%; The Netherlands 5.3%; France 4.7%; Burma 4.0%; Senegal 3.4%; U.S.S.R. 3.0%; China 2.4%; Eastern European countries 1.8%.
Exports (1983): PG 358,100,000 (vegetables and fruits, including peanuts and cashew nuts 66.1%; fish, including shrimp 23.7%; cork and wood 4.5%). *Major export destinations* (1984): Romania 35.4%; Portugal 35.3%; China 9.2%; France 6.1%; Spain 4.4%; Senegal 3.0%; The Netherlands 2.2%.

Transport and communications

Transport. Railroads: none. Roads (1983): total length 3,143 mi, 5,058 km (paved, 8.0%). Vehicles (1982): private motor vehicles 4,100. Merchant marine (1985): vessels (100 gross tons and over) 15; total deadweight tonnage 2,523. Air transport (1980): passenger-mi 5,000,000, passenger-km 8,000,000; short ton-mi cargo 700,000, metric ton-km cargo 1,000,000; airports (1986) with scheduled flights 1.
Communications. Daily newspapers (1984): total number 1; total circulation 6,000; circulation per 1,000 population 7.0. Radio (1985): total number of receivers 26,000 (1 per 34 persons). Television: none. Telephones (1981): 5,000 (1 per 161 persons).

Education and health

Education (1983–84)

	schools	teachers	students	student/ teacher ratio
Primary (age 7–13)	658	2,455	65,405	26.6
Secondary (age 13–18)	10	660	8,561	13.0
Voc., teacher tr.	4	58	578	10.0

Educational attainment (1979). Percent of population over age 7 having: no formal schooling or knowledge of reading and writing 90.4%; primary education 7.9%; secondary 1.0%; technical 0.5%; higher 0.2%. *Literacy* (1979): total population over age 7 literate 46,513 (26.8%).
Health: physicians (1980) 108 (1 per 7,287 persons); hospital beds (1983) 1,593 (1 per 526 persons); infant mortality rate per 1,000 live births (1980–85) 143.0.
Food (1980–82): daily per capita caloric intake 2,230 (vegetable products 93%, animal products 7%); 96% of FAO recommended minimum requirement.

Military

Total active duty personnel (1986): 8,550♀ (army 95.9%, navy 3.2%, air force 0.9%). *Military expenditure as percent of GNP* (1983): 8.4% (world 6.1%); per capita expenditure U.S.$11.

*Preliminary. †Bissau region excludes Bissau city. ‡1982. §Production figure for first three quarters only. ‖At current factor cost. ¶Detail does not add to total given because of rounding. ♀Includes Gendarmerie.

Guyana

Official name: Co-operative Republic of Guyana.
Form of government: unitary single-party republic with one legislative house (National Assembly [65]).
Chief of state: President.
Head of government: Prime Minister.
Capital: Georgetown.
Official language: English.
Official religion: none.
Monetary unit: 1 Guyana dollar (G$) = 100 cents; valuation (Oct. 1, 1986) 1 U.S.$ = G$4.38; 1 £ = G$6.33.

Area and population

Administrative Regions		area sq mi	area sq km	population 1980 census
Region 1	(Barima/Waini)	...	...	18,297
Region 2	(Pomeroon/Supenaam)	...	...	42,268
Region 3	(Essequibo Islands/West Demerara)	...	...	104,747
Region 4	(Demerara/Mahaica)*	...	...	318,952
Region 5	(Mahaica/Berbice)	...	...	53,862
Region 6	(East Berbice/Corentune)	...	...	152,517
Region 7	(Cuyuni/Mazaruni)	...	...	14,142
Region 8	(Potaro/Siparuni)	...	...	4,265
Region 9	(Upper Takutu/Upper Essequibo)	...	...	13,051
Region 10	(Upper Demerara/Berbice)	...	...	36,518
TOTAL		83,000†	215,000†	758,619

Demography

Population (1986): 796,000.
Density (1986): persons per sq mi 9.6, persons per sq km 3.7.
Urban-rural (1985): urban 31.2%; rural 68.8%.
Sex distribution (1985): male 50.16%; female 49.84%.
Age breakdown (1982): under 15, 40.2%; 15–29, 31.3%; 30–44, 13.8%; 45–59, 8.8%; 60–74, 4.8%; 75 and over, 1.1%.
Population projection: (1990) 867,000; (2000) 1,075,000.
Doubling time: 32 years.
Ethnic composition (1980): East Indian 50.8%; Black African 30.4%; other 18.8%.
Religious affiliation (1980): Hindu 34.4%; Protestant 18.0%; Roman Catholic 18.0%; Anglican 16.0%; Muslim 9.0%; other 4.6%.
Major cities (1980): Georgetown 167,839 (200,000‡); Linden 30,043; New Amsterdam 19,287; Corriverton 13,718; Rosehill 5,311.

Vital statistics

Birth rate per 1,000 population (1984): 29.3 (world avg. 29.0); legitimate, n.a.; illegitimate, n.a.
Death rate per 1,000 population (1984): 7.6 (world avg. 11.0).
Natural increase rate per 1,000 population (1984): 21.7 (world avg. 18.0).
Total fertility rate (avg. births per childbearing woman; 1980–85): 3.2.
Marriage rate per 1,000 population: n.a.
Divorce rate per 1,000 population: n.a.
Life expectancy at birth (1980–85): male 67.7 years; female 73.3 years.
Major causes of death per 100,000 population (1977): circulatory diseases 223.6; symptoms and ill-defined conditions 90.8; infectious and parasitic diseases 83.4; respiratory diseases 65.6.

National economy

Budget (1984). Revenue: G$762,700,000 (excise duties 29.3%, income tax 28.8%, import and export duties 10.1%). Expenditures: G$1,375,900,000 (economic services 15.6%, education 7.4%, defense 5.4%, health 2.9%, social security and welfare 2.7%).
Public debt (external, outstanding; 1985): U.S.$721,100,000.
Tourism (1983): receipts from visitors U.S.$4,200,000; expenditures by nationals abroad, n.a.
Production (metric tons except as noted). Agriculture, forestry, fishing (1985): sugarcane 3,520,000, rice 300,000, coconuts 40,000, bananas and plantains 20,000, oranges 11,000, hen eggs 4,200; livestock (number of live animals) 148,000 pigs, 140,000 cattle, 118,000 sheep, 15,000,000 chickens; roundwood 201,000 cu m; fish catch 27,630§. Mining and quarrying (1984): bauxite 1,556,000, alumina 73,157‖, gold 10,000 troy oz, diamonds 6,000 metric carats. Manufacturing (1982): rum 151,300 hectolitres¶, cigarettes 590,000,000 units, refined sugar 241,900§, stock feeds 55,000¶, flour 32,000, margarine 3,000¶. Construction: n.a. Energy production (consumption): electricity (kW-hr; 1984) 390,000,000 (390,000,000); coal, none (n.a); crude petroleum, n.a. (n.a.); petroleum products (metric tons; 1984) none (400,000); natural gas, n.a. (n.a.).
Population economically active (1984): total 320,000; activity rate of total population 40.8% (participation rates: over age 15, 68%; female [1980] 24.8%; unemployed [1980] 18.7%).

Price and earnings indexes (1980 = 100)

	1977	1978	1979	1980	1981	1982	1983
Consumer price index	64.6	74.4	87.7	100.0	124.7	147.8	169.9
Weekly earnings index	60.8	90.0	95.2	100.0	110.0	...	...

Household income and expenditure. Average household size (1980) 5.0; average annual income per household: n.a.; sources of income (1974): wages and salaries 73.0%, transfer payments 6.3%, other 20.7%; expenditure: n.a.

Gross national product (at current market prices; 1984): U.S.$470,000,000 (U.S.$600 per capita).

Structure of gross domestic product and labour force

	1984 in value G$'000,000	1984 % of total value	1980 labour force	1980 % of labour force
Agriculture	347	20.4	48,603	25.0
Mining	65	3.8	9,389	4.8
Manufacturing	183	10.8	27,939	14.4
Construction	100	5.9	6,574	3.4
Public utilities	...	...	2,772	1.4
Transportation and communication	100	5.9	9,160	4.7
Trade	125	7.4	14,690	7.7
Finance			2,878	1.5
Pub. admin., defense	780	45.9	57,416	29.5
Services				
Other			15,260	7.8
TOTAL	1,700	100.0♀	194,681	100.0♀

Land use (1983): forested 83.2%; meadows and pastures 6.2%; agricultural and under permanent cultivation 2.5%; other 8.1%.

Foreign trade

Balance of trade (current prices)

	1978	1979	1980	1981	1982	1983
G$'000,000	+107.0	+9.4	+74.1	−155.6	−20.7	−34.7
% of total	7.6%	0.6%	3.9%	7.4%	1.4%	3.0%

Imports (1983): G$745,000,000 (fuels and lubricants 39.3%; machinery and transport equipment 8.2%; chemicals 6.7%; building materials 4.5%; food, beverages, and tobacco 3.9%). *Major import sources* (1984): Trinidad and Tobago 34.1%; United States 24.2%; United Kingdom 9.5%; Barbados 7.5%.
Exports (1983): G$580,000,000 (sugar 37.0%; calcined bauxite 24.6%; dried bauxite 11.9%; rice 11.2%; timber 2.3%; rum 1.9%). *Major export destinations* (1984): United States 23.5%; United Kingdom 22.3%; Venezuela 16.7%; Canada 6.4%; Trinidad and Tobago 6.3%; West Germany 4.6%; France 3.3%; Jamaica 1.9%.

Transport and communications

Transport. Railroads♂: length (1980) 80 mi, 130 km. Roads (1984): total length 3,426 mi, 5,513 km (paved 9%). Vehicles (1984): passenger cars 20,000; trucks and buses 4,610. Merchant marine (1985): vessels (100 gross tons and over) 103; total deadweight tonnage 22,662. Air transport (1982): total passengers 155,000; total cargo 3,100 metric tons; airports (1986) with scheduled flights 19.
Communications. Daily newspapers (1985): total number 2; total circulation 78,000; circulation per 1,000 population 99. Radio (1985): total number of receivers 350,000 (1 per 2.3 persons). Television: none. Telephones (1982): 28,500 (1 per 32 persons).

Education and health

Education (1979–80)

	schools	teachers	students	student/teacher ratio
Primary (age 6–11)	424	6,021	164,830	27.4
Secondary (age 12–17)	87	2,513	46,595	18.5
Voc., teacher tr.	15	348	4,647	13.4
Higher	1	...	1,889	...

Educational attainment (1970). Percent of adult population over age 25 having: no formal schooling 12.2%; primary education 77.6%; secondary 9.2%; higher 1.0%. *Literacy* (1980): total population over age 15 literate 505,300 (95.5%); males literate 255,200 (97.1%); females literate 250,100 (94.0%).
Health: physicians (1982) 270 (1 per 2,857 persons); hospital beds (1979) 4,002 (1 per 188 persons); infant mortality rate per 1,000 live births (1983) 45.0.
Food (1980–82): daily per capita caloric intake 2,329 (vegetable products 88%, animal products 12%); 102% of FAO recommended minimum requirement.

Military

Total active duty personnel (1985): 6,600□ (army 90.9%, navy 4.5%, air force 4.6%). *Military expenditure as percent of GNP* (1982): 4.5% (world 6.1%); per capita expenditure U.S.$26.

*Includes Greater Georgetown. †Estimated; no dated survey available. ‡1985 estimate. §1983. ‖1982. ¶1980. ♀Detail does not add to total given because of rounding. ♂The two railways are used solely for mining and not for passenger transport. □All services are part of the army.

Haiti

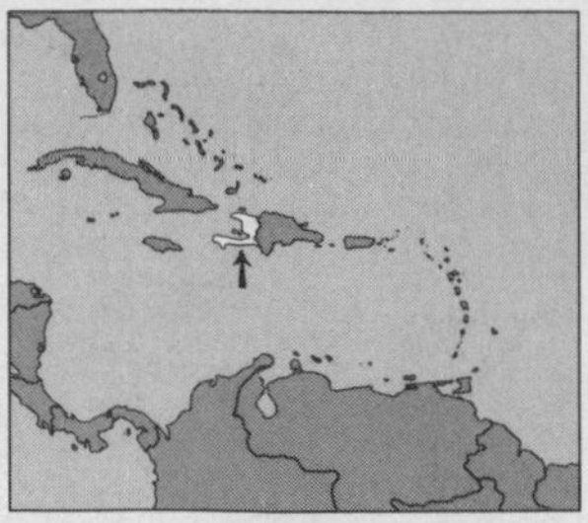

Official name: République d'Haïti (Republic of Haiti).
Form of government: interim military–civilian regime*.
Head of state and government: President assisted by National Council of Government.
Capital: Port-au-Prince.
Official language: French.
Official religion: Roman Catholicism.
Monetary unit: 1 gourde (G) = 100 centimes; valuation (Oct. 1, 1986) 1 U.S.$ = G 5.00; 1 £ = G 7.23.

Area and population

		area		population
Departements	**Capitals**	sq mi	sq km	1986 estimate
Centre	Hinche	1,429	3,700	380,000
Grande Anse	Jérémie	1,268	3,284	510,000
L'Artibonite	Gonaïves	1,750	4,532	777,000
Nord	Cap-Haïtien	790	2,045	594,000
Nord-Est	Fort-Liberté	676	1,752	196,000
Nord-Ouest	Port-de-Paix	899	2,330	315,000
Ouest	Port-au-Prince	1,795	4,649	1,756,000
Sud	Les Cayes	1,117	2,894	522,000
Sud-Est	Jacmel	855	2,215	377,000
TOTAL		10,579	27,400†	5,427,000

Demography

Population (1986): 5,427,000.
Density (1986): persons per sq mi 513.0, persons per sq km 198.1.
Urban–rural (1982): urban 20.6%; rural 79.4%.
Sex distribution (1982): male 48.48%; female 51.52%.
Age breakdown (1982): under 15, 39.2%; 15–29, 26.9%; 30–44, 15.6%; 45–59, 10.0%; 60–74, 5.4%; 75 and over, 2.9%.
Population projection: (1990) 5,829,000; (2000) 6,967,000.
Doubling time: 31 years.
Ethnic composition (1980): black 95.0%; mulatto 5.0%.
Religious affiliation (1982): Roman Catholic 80.3%; Baptist 9.7%; Pentecostal 3.6%; other (mostly Protestant) 6.4%.
Major cities (1986): Port-au-Prince 457,600; Cap-Haïtien 70,500; Gonaïves 36,500; Les Cayes 35,500; Pétionville 35,333‡.

Vital statistics

Birth rate per 1,000 population (1980–85): 35.6 (world avg. 29.0).
Death rate per 1,000 population (1980–85): 13.0 (world avg. 11.0).
Natural increase rate per 1,000 population (1980–85): 22.6 (world avg. 18.0).
Total fertility rate (avg. births per childbearing woman; 1980–85): 5.7.
Marriage rate per 1,000 population (1980): 0.7§.
Divorce rate per 1,000 population (1980): 0.1§.
Life expectancy at birth (1980–85): male 51.2 years; female 54.4 years.
Major causes of death per 100,000 population (1982) ‖: ill-defined conditions 115.2; infectious intestinal diseases 21.9; tuberculosis 13.1; diseases associated with malnutrition 8.5; endocrine and metabolic disorders 8.0; pneumonia 6.4; diseases of the circulatory system 5.9.

National economy

Budget (1981–82). Revenue (excluding foreign grants and loans): G 732,000,000 (customs duties 35.0%, other 65.0%). Expenditures: G 961,000,000 (debt 26.1%, development budget 15.0%, health 9.7%, education 8.9%, defense 7.9%, public relations and information 3.9%).
Production (metric tons except as noted). Agriculture, forestry, fishing (1984): sugarcane 3,000,000, sweet potatoes 350,000, mangoes 340,000, plantains 315,000, cassava 265,000, bananas 235,000, corn (maize) 186,000, rice 124,000, sorghum 123,000, dry beans 52,000, coffee 38,000, oranges 32,000, sisal 11,000; livestock (number of live animals) 1,350,000 cattle, 1,100,000 goats, 500,000 pigs, 425,000 horses; roundwood 5,761,000 cu m; fish catch 4,000¶. Mining and quarrying (1984): construction materials for local use. Manufacturing (value of production in G '000,000; 1981): refined flour 218; cement 128; baseballs and softballs 92; electronic equipment 73; livestock feed 12; edible oils 23,883 metric tons; cigarettes 932,000,000 units♀; beer and malt 1,539,000 bottles; cotton clothing 2,575,000 pieces. Construction (new buildings completed; 1982♁): 358. Energy production (consumption): electricity (kW-hr; 1984) 375,000,000 (375,000,000); coal, none (none); crude petroleum, none (none); petroleum products (metric tons; 1984) none (210,000); natural gas, none (none).
Tourism: receipts from visitors (1984) U.S.$91,000,000; expenditures by nationals abroad (1983) U.S.$39,000,000.
Household income and expenditure. Average household size (1982) 4.5; source of income: n.a.; expenditure (1976)□: food and beverages 77.9%, housing 8.3%, household furnishings 4.0%, clothing and footwear 3.2%, other 6.6%◇.
Population economically active (1982)△: total 2,129,658; activity rate of total population 42.1% (participation rates: ages 15–64, 66.2%; female 41.0% (unemployed [1986] unofficially 60.0%).

Price and earnings indexes (1980 = 100)

	1979	1980	1981	1982	1983	1984	1985
Consumer price index	84.9	100.0	110.9	119.0	131.2	139.6	151.9†
Monthly earnings index⊕	72.7	100.0	120.0	120.0	...	...	...

Public debt (external, outstanding; 1985): U.S.$534,200,000.
Gross national product (1984): U.S.$1,710,000,000 (U.S.$330 per capita).

Structure of gross domestic product and labour force

	1984**		1982	
	in value U.S.$'000,000	% of total value	labour force△	% of labour force
Agriculture	512	32.0	1,222,859	57.4
Mining	2	0.1	19,260	0.9
Manufacturing	280	17.5	121,208	5.7
Construction	90	5.6	22,192	1.0
Public utilities	13	0.8	2,057	0.1
Transp. and commun.	34	2.1	16,386	0.8
Trade	289	18.0	285,728	13.4
Finance	86	5.4	4,030	0.2
Pub. admin., defense	170	10.6	...	...
Services	126	7.9	124,475	5.8
Other	...	...	311,463	14.6
TOTAL	1,602	100.0	2,129,658	100.0†

Land use (1983): forested 3.6%; meadows and pastures 18.2%; agricultural and under permanent cultivation 32.6%; other 45.6%.

Foreign trade††

Balance of trade (current prices)

	1978	1979	1980	1981	1982	1983
G '000,000	−287.5	−410.0	−516.0	−1,045.0	−624.0	−638.5
% of total	16.1%	22.9%	19.3%	40.9%	26.1%	25.5%

Imports (1982–83): G 1,890,000,000 (basic manufactures 19.5%, machinery and transport equipment 19.4%, food and live animals 18.7%, petroleum products 12.8%, chemicals 9.0%). *Major import sources* (1984): United States 66.9%; Netherlands Antilles 5.0%; Japan 4.7%; Argentina 3.0%; France 2.7%; Canada 2.3%.
Exports (1982–83): G 951,800,000 (light industrial products [including baseballs, clothing, electronic equipment] 50.4%, coffee 26.9%, perfume resinoids 3.7%, cordage 2.6%, cocoa 2.1%). *Major export destinations* (1984): United States 79.6%; West Germany 3.4%; France 3.3%; Canada 2.9%; Italy 2.8%; Dominican Republic 2.4%.

Transport and communications

Transport. Railroads (1985): ‡‡. Roads (1983): total length 2,292 mi, 3,688 km (paved 18%). Vehicles (1983): passenger cars 34,025; trucks and buses 4,257. Merchant marine (1985): vessels (100 gross tons and over) 8; total deadweight tonnage 1,705. Air transport (1983)§§: passenger arrivals 226,000, passenger departures 242,000; cargo unloaded 12,100 metric tons, cargo loaded 14,700 metric tons; airports (1986) with scheduled flights 2.
Communications. Daily newspapers (1985): total number 6; total circulation 21,500; circulation per 1,000 population 4.0. Radio (1985): total number of receivers 120,000 (1 per 44 persons). Television (1985): total number of receivers 75,000 (1 per 71 persons). Telephones (1983): 38,400 (1 per 134 persons).

Education and health

Education (1982–83)

	schools	teachers	students	student/ teacher ratio
Primary (age 6–12)	3,241	16,986	723,041	42.6
Secondary (age 13–18)	290	5,367	117,081	21.8
Higher	1	582	3,464	6.0

Educational attainment (1982)◇. Percent of adult population over age 25 having: no formal schooling 76.9%; primary education 15.2%; secondary 7.2%; higher 0.7%. *Literacy* (1982): total population over age 15 literate 1,066,966 (34.7%); males literate 547,318 (37.1%); females literate 519,648 (32.5%).
Health (1982): physicians 482 (1 per 10,500 persons); hospital beds 5,250 (1 per 963 persons); infant mortality rate per 1,000 live births (1980–85) 117.7.
Food (1980–82): daily per capita caloric intake 1,906 (vegetable products 95%, animal products 5%); 84% of FAO recommended minimum requirement.

Military

Total active duty personnel (1985): 6,900 (army 92.8%, navy 4.3%, air force 2.9%) ‖ ‖. *Military expenditure as percent of GNP* (1983): 1.4% (world 6.1%); per capita expenditure U.S.$4.

*Constitution suspended and National Assembly dissolved on Feb. 9, 1986. †Detail does not add to total given because of rounding. ‡1982 preliminary census figure. §Registered only. ‖ Public health facilities only. ¶1983. ♀1982–83. ♁Port-au-Prince and Pétionville only. □Excludes alcoholic beverages and tobacco. ◇Port-au-Prince metropolitan area only (1976): food and beverages 64.5%, housing 11.4%, household furnishings 5.8%, education 4.8%, recreation and leisure 4.0%, clothing and footwear 3.2%, transportation and communication 1.1%, health 0.7%, other 4.5%. △Based on a 2.5% sample tabulation of census returns. †Average through September. ⊕Minimum wages paid in industrial enterprises. **In 1982 prices. ††Import figures are f.o.b. in balance of trade and c.i.f. in commodities and trading partners. ‡‡The only railway is privately owned and used to transport sugarcane. §§Port-au-Prince airport only. ‖ ‖ By 1987 the military is to be increased to 10,000 troops.

Honduras

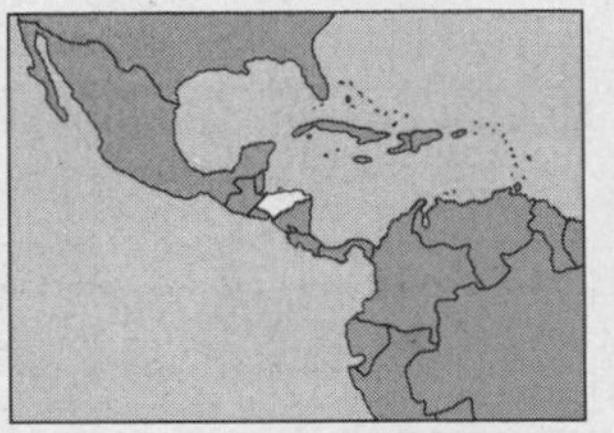

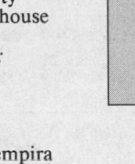

Official name: República de Honduras (Republic of Honduras).
Form of government: multiparty republic with one legislative house (National Congress [132]).
Head of state and government: President.
Capital: Tegucigalpa.
Official language: Spanish.
Official religion: none.
Monetary unit: 1 Honduran lempira (L) = 100 centavos; valuation* (Oct. 1, 1986) 1 U.S.$ = L 2.00; 1 £ = L 2.89.

Area and population

Departments	Administrative centres	area sq mi	area sq km	population 1983 estimate†
Atlántida	La Ceiba	1,641	4,251	242,200
Choluteca	Choluteca	1,626	4,211	289,600
Colón	Trujillo	3,427	8,875	128,400
Comayagua	Comayagua	2,006	5,196	211,500
Copán	Santa Rosa de Copán	1,237	3,203	217,300
Cortés	San Pedro Sula	1,527	3,954	624,100
El Paraíso	Yuscarán	2,787	7,218	206,600
Francisco Morazán	Tegucigalpa	3,068	7,946	736,300
Gracias a Dios	Puerto Lempira	6,421	16,630	35,500
Intibucá	La Esperanza	1,186	3,072	111,400
Islas de la Bahía	Roatán	100	261	18,700
La Paz	La Paz	900	2,331	86,600
Lempira	Gracias	1,656	4,290	174,900
Ocotepeque	Nueva Ocotepeque	649	1,680	64,100
Olancho	Juticalpa	9,402	24,351	228,100
Santa Bárbara	Santa Bárbara	1,975	5,115	286,800
Valle	Nacaome	604	1,565	125,600
Yoro	Yoro	3,065	7,939	304,300
TOTAL		43,277	112,088	4,092,200‡

Demography

Population (1986): 3,938,000.
Density (1986): persons per sq mi 91.0, persons per sq km 35.1.
Urban–rural (1985): urban 38.2%; rural 61.8%.
Sex distribution (1985): male 50.14%; female 49.86%.
Age breakdown (1982): under 15, 47.6%; 15–29, 26.3%; 30–44, 13.6%; 45–59, 8.0%; 60–74, 3.7%; 75 and over 0.8%.
Population projection: (1990) 4,502,000; (2000) 6,289,000.
Doubling time: 21 years.
Ethnic composition (1982): mestizo 90.0%; black (including Black Caribs) 5.0%; Indian 4.0%; white 1.0%.
Religious affiliation (1980): Roman Catholic 93.6%; Protestant 3.0%; Afro-American spiritist 0.5%; Muslim 0.3%; other 2.6%.
Major cities (1985): Tegucigalpa 571,400; San Pedro Sula 372,800; La Ceiba 61,900; Choluteca 57,200; El Progreso 55,500.

Vital statistics

Birth rate per 1,000 population (1983): 38.7 (world avg. 29.0); legitimate, n.a.; illegitimate, n.a.
Death rate per 1,000 population (1983): 4.7 (world avg. 11.0).
Natural increase rate per 1,000 population (1983): 34.0 (world avg. 18.0).
Total fertility rate (avg. births per childbearing woman; 1981): 6.6.
Marriage rate per 1,000 population (1981): 4.0.
Divorce rate per 1,000 population (1981): 0.2.
Life expectancy at birth (1980–85): male 58.2 years; female 61.7 years.
Major causes of death: n.a.; however, principal causes include diseases of early infancy, gastritis and other enteric diseases (particularly typhoid fever), pneumonia and influenza, accidents, and cardiovascular diseases.

National economy

Budget (1985). Revenue: L 3,054,000,000 (current revenue 60.2%, of which nontax revenue 20.1%; import and export duties 13.4%; tax on production and internal trade 11.4%; individual income tax 7.9%). Expenditures: L 3,054,000,000 (current expenditure 58.2%, of which wages and salaries 27.9%; capital expenditure 21.8%; payment on public debt 17.3%; net allowance on loans 2.7%).
Tourism (1983): receipts from visitors U.S.$23,000,000; expenditures by nationals abroad U.S.$41,000,000.
Production (metric tons except as noted). Agriculture, forestry, fishing (1985): sugarcane 3,226,000, bananas and plantains 1,213,000, corn (maize) 434,000, palm nut 296,000, coffee 79,000, dry beans 52,000, millet 39,000, rice 35,000, seed cotton 15,000; livestock (number of live animals; 1984) 2,434,000 cattle, 400,000 pigs; roundwood 4,937,000 cu m; fish catch 8,432§. Mining and quarrying (1984): limestone 500,000; zinc ore and concentrate 41,483; marble 40,000; salt 30,000; lead 20,544; gold 2,550 troy oz. Manufacturing (1985): cement 348,000; iron and steel semimanufactures 20,000‖; raw sugar 215,600; beef and veal 69,000§; palm oil 7,500§; soft drinks 1,412,300 hectolitres; beer 391,000 hectolitres; cigarettes 115,594,000 units; matches 65,166,000 units. Construction (value added in lempiras; 1985)¶: residential 67,300,000; commercial 21,400,000; industrial 4,600,000. Energy production (consumption): electricity (kW-hr; 1985) 1,382,500,000 (1,199,700,000); coal, none (n.a.); crude petroleum (barrels; 1984), none (1,942,000); petroleum products (metric tons; 1984) 259,000 (564,000); natural gas, none (n.a.).
Gross national product (at current market prices; 1984): U.S.$2,980,000,000 (U.S.$700 per capita).

Structure of gross domestic product and labour force

	1984 in value L '000,000	1984 % of total value	1985 labour force	1985 % of labour force
Agriculture	1,544	24.2	584,800	52.9
Mining	137	2.1	5,300	0.5
Manufacturing	831	13.0	146,600	13.3
Construction	348	5.5	47,900	4.3
Public utilities	140	2.2	4,000	0.4
Transportation and communication	433	6.8	44,100	4.0
Trade	750	11.8	106,900	9.7
Finance	677	10.6	12,900	1.2
Public admin., defense	300	4.7		
Services	512	8.0	152,700	13.8
Other	703♀	11.0		
TOTAL	6,375	100.0‡	1,105,200	100.0‡

Public debt (external, outstanding; 1985): U.S.$2,030,900,000.
Population economically active (1984): total 1,133,263; activity rate of total population 30.5% (participation rates: ages 15–64, 53.6%; female 9.4%; unemployed [1983] 21.0%).

Price and earnings indexes (1980 = 100)

	1979	1980	1981	1982	1983	1984	1985
Consumer price index	86.5	100.0	110.2	121.2	132.7	138.8	141.0
Monthly earnings index	...	...	...	...	...	...	...

Household income and expenditure: Average household size (1979) 5.7; average annual income per household: n.a.; source of income: n.a.; expenditure (1982): food, beverage, tobacco 45.0%, utilities and rent 22.3%, clothing and footwear 9.1%, household furnishings and operation 8.3%, medical and health care 7.0%, transportation 3.0%, recreation 2.9%, other 2.4%.
Land use (1983): forested 34.1%; meadows and pastures 30.4%; agricultural and under permanent cultivation 15.8%; other 19.7%.

Foreign trade♂

Balance of trade (current prices)

	1979	1980	1981	1982	1983	1984
L '000,000	−26.9	−103.8	−114.8	−101.7	−133.0	−242.6
% of total	1.7%	5.7%	6.8%	3.7%	4.6%	7.5%

Imports (1984): L 1,791,000,000 (basic manufactures 22.4%, mineral fuels and lubricants 21.1%, machinery and transport equipment 20.6%, chemical products 19.0%; food products 9.6%). *Major import sources:* United States 35.7%; Venezuela 10.3%; Mexico 6.5%; Costa Rica 5.0%; Japan 4.9%; West Germany 3.9%.
Exports (1984): L 1,471,600,000 (bananas 30.0%, coffee 23.0%, lead and zinc 5.8%, shrimp and lobsters 5.3%, wood 4.6%, refrigerated meat 3.3%, silver 2.8%). *Major export destinations:* United States 51.1%; Japan 8.7%; West Germany 5.6%; Belgium 5.1%; Italy 4.6%.

Transport and communications

Transport. Railroads (1985): route length 370 mi, 595 km; passengers, n.a.; cargo, n.a. Roads (1985): total length 10,577 mi, 17,022 km (paved 12%). Vehicles (1985): passenger cars 66,666; trucks and buses 18,759. Merchant marine (1985): vessels (100 gross tons and over) 291; total deadweight tonnage 516,210. Air transport (1983): passenger-mi 216,200,000, passenger-km 348,000,000; short ton-mi cargo 1,619,000, metric ton-km cargo 2,364,000; airports (1986) with scheduled flights 3.
Communications. Daily newspapers (1984): total number 6; total circulation 236,300□; circulation per 1,000 population 58. Radio (1983): total number of receivers 1,534,620 (1 per 2.7 persons). Television (1984): total number of receivers 136,000 (1 per 31 persons). Telephones (1985): 62,786 (1 per 61 persons).

Education and health

Education (1985)

	schools	teachers	students	student/ teacher ratio
Primary (age 7–13)	6,492	20,724	858,061	41.4
Secondary (age 14–19)	452	6,799	582,287	85.6
Voc., teacher tr.	11§	...	103,941	...
Higher	7	2,692	34,478	14.0

Educational attainment (1974). Percentage of adult population over age 25 having: no formal schooling 52.8%; less than primary education 34.4%; primary 6.0%; some secondary 3.5%; secondary 1.8%; postsecondary 1.0%. *Literacy* (1980): total population over age 15 literate 1,309,500 (68.6%); males literate 676,700 (71.1%); females literate 632,800 (66.2%).
Health (1985): physicians 1,900 (1 per 2,000 persons); hospital beds 5,220 (1 per 733 persons); infant mortality rate per 1,000 live births (1983) 78.6.
Food (1980–82): daily per capita caloric intake 2,170 (vegetable products 88%, animal products 12%); 96% of FAO recommended minimum requirement.

Military

Total active duty personnel (1985): 16,600 (army 88.0%, navy 3.0%, air force 9.0%). *Military expenditure as percent of GNP* (1982): 2.3% (world 6.0%); per capita expenditure U.S.$15.

*The Honduran lempira is officially pegged to the U.S. dollar at L 2.00 per U.S.$1. †Based on a different population series. ‡Detail does not add to total given because of rounding. §1983. ‖ 1982. ¶Tegucigalpa, San Pedro Sula, and La Ceiba only. ♀Includes net indirect taxes. ♂Import figures are f.o.b. (free on board) in balance of trade and c.i.f. (cost, insurance, and freight) for commodities and trading partners. □Circulation for 5 dailies only.

Hong Kong

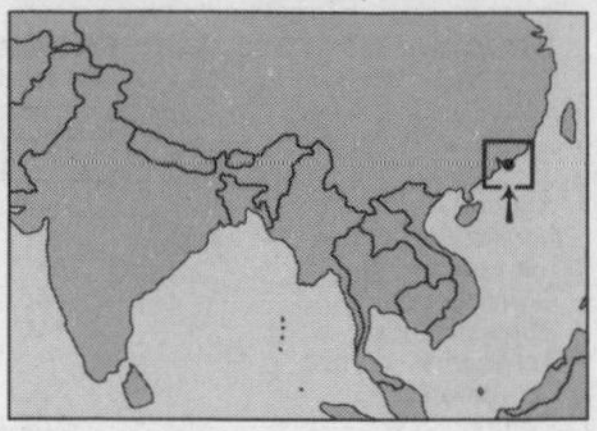

Official name: Hsiang Kang (Chinese); Hong Kong (English).
Political status: colony (United Kingdom) with three nominated advisory councils (Executive Council [15], Legislative Council [57], Urban Council [30]).
Chief of state: British Monarch.
Head of government: Governor.
Capital: Victoria.
Official languages: Chinese; English.
Official religion: none.
Monetary unit: 1 HK dollar (HK$) = 100 cents; valuation (Oct. 1, 1986) 1 U.S.$ = HK$7.80; 1 £ = HK$11.28.

Area and population

	area*		population†
			1981
Districts	sq mi	sq km	census
Hong Kong Island	29.9	77.4	1,203,342
Kowloon	17.0	44.1	2,458,279
New Territories	353.6	915.7	1,324,939
TOTAL	400.5	1,037.2	4,986,560

Demography

Population (1986): 5,533,000.
Density‡ (1986): persons per sq mi 13,815, persons per sq km 5,335.
Urban-rural (1985): urban 90.8%; rural 9.2%.
Sex distribution (1985): male 51.68%; female 48.32%.
Age breakdown (1985): under 15, 23.1%; 15–29, 30.4%; 30–44, 20.6%; 45–59, 14.4%; 60–74, 8.9%; 75 and over, 2.6%.
Population projection: (1990) 5,802,000; (2000) 6,534,000.
Doubling time: 77 years.
Ethnic composition (1984): Chinese 98.6%; British 0.9%; other 0.5%.
Religious affiliation (1983): predominantly Buddhist; some Confucianist and Taoist; approximately 500,000 Christian.
Major cities (1981): New Kowloon 1,649,950; Kowloon 799,123; Victoria 590,771.

Vital statistics

Birth rate per 1,000 population (1985): 14.1 (world avg. 29.0).
Death rate per 1,000 population (1985): 4.7 (world avg. 11.0).
Natural increase rate per 1,000 population (1985): 9.4 (world avg. 18.0).
Total fertility rate (avg. births per childbearing woman; 1983): 1.7.
Marriage rate per 1,000 population (1985): 8.3.
Divorce rate per 1,000 population (1985): 0.9.
Life expectancy at birth (1985): male 72.5 years; female 78.4 years.
Major causes of death per 100,000 population (1985): malignant neoplasms (cancers) 137.5; diseases of circulatory system 136.2; diseases of respiratory system 76.6; diseases of the genitourinary system 20.5.

National economy

Budget (1985–86 est.). Revenue: HK$37,401,200,000 (earnings and profit taxes 39.2%, income from properties and investments 10.6%, fees and charges 8.5%, excise duties 8.4%). Expenditures: HK$38,361,600,000 (education 18.7%, medical 9.1%, law and order 8.5%, social welfare 6.0%, defense 4.2%, housing 4.1%).
Public debt (external, outstanding; 1984): U.S.$270,400,000.
Gross national product (at current market prices; 1984): U.S.$33,970,000,000 (U.S.$6,330 per capita).

Structure of gross domestic product and labour force

	1984			
	in value HK$'000,000	% of total value	labour force	% of labour force
Agriculture	1,257	0.5	30,000	1.1
Mining	323	0.1	500	0.1
Manufacturing	57,238	24.6	988,300	37.3
Construction	11,816	5.1	212,800	8.1
Public utilities	5,635	2.4	12,400	0.5
Transportation and communication	19,340	8.3	210,300	7.9
Trade	49,946	21.5	571,600	21.6
Finance	62,525	26.9	132,800	5.1
Pub. admin., defense, and services	36,718	15.8	464,200	17.5
Other	−12,138§	−5.2	20,800	0.8
TOTAL	232,660	100.0	2,643,700	100.0

Production (metric tons except as noted). Agriculture, forestry, fishing (1985): vegetables 151,000, fruits and nuts 1,150, rice 20, milk 2,900; livestock (number of live animals) 590,000 pigs ‖, 810 cattle; roundwood 180,000 cu m¶; fish catch 196,000, of which marine 178,000. Mining and quarrying (1985): feldspar sand 82,446; feldspar 26,777; kaolin 9,602; quartz 116. Manufacturing (value added in HK$; 1983): wearing apparel 11,131,856,000; electrical machinery 7,246,432,000; textiles 6,409,130,000; plastic products 3,251,844,000; publishing and printed material 2,029,141,000; food, beverages, and tobacco 1,815,334,000. Construction (1985): residential 1,461,000 sq m; nonresidential 1,443,000 sq m. Energy production (consumption): electricity (kW-hr; 1984) 17,923,000,000 (17,183,000,000); coal (metric tons; 1984) none (4,262,000); petroleum products (metric tons; 1984) none (3,823,000); natural gas (cu m; 1985) none (204,500,000).
Population economically active (1985): total 2,621,000; activity rate of total population 48.3% (participation rates: over age 15, 64.6%; female 47.9%; unemployed 3.4%).

Price and earnings indexes (1979–80 = 100)

	1979	1980	1981	1982	1983	1984	1985
Consumer price index	89.5	103.3	117.9	130.3	143.2	154.9	159.8
Daily earnings index	92.5	107.5	125.0	140.4	150.7	163.8	173.9

Household income and expenditure. Average household size (1981) 3.9; income per household HK$47,000 (U.S.$7,800); source of income: n.a.; expenditure (1979–80): food 38.3%, housing 20.1%, personal services and entertainment 11.1%, clothing and footwear 7.8%, transportation and vehicles 6.4%, durable goods 4.6%, fuel and light 2.8%.
Tourism (1984): receipts from visitors U.S.$1,734,100,000; expenditures by nationals abroad, n.a.
Land use (1984): forested 13.0%; meadows and pastures 1.0%; agricultural and under permanent cultivation 8.0%; built-on, scrub lands, and other 78.0%.

Foreign trade

Balance of trade (current prices)

	1980	1981	1982	1983	1984	1985
HK$'000,000	−13,408	−16,212	−15,508	−14,743	−1,929	+3,733
% of total	6.4%	6.2%	5.7%	4.4%	0.4%	0.8%

Imports (1985): HK$231,419,710,000 (machinery and transport equipment 25.6%, of which electrical machinery 8.3%; textile yarn and fabrics 14.5%; food and live animals 8.6%, of which vegetables and fruits 2.2%; chemicals and related products 7.0%; photographic apparatus, watches, and clocks 5.9%; petroleum and petroleum products 3.8%). *Major import sources:* China 25.5%; Japan 23.1%; United States 9.5%; Taiwan 9.0%; Singapore 4.9%.
Exports (1985): HK$235,152,270,000♀ (machinery and transport equipment 25.4%, of which electrical machinery 8.1%; clothing accessories and wearing apparel 22.4%; textile yarn and fabrics 10.1%; travel goods 1.6%). *Major export destinations:* United States 30.8%; China 26.0%; Japan 4.2%; West Germany 4.1%; United Kingdom 3.6%.

Transport and communications

Transport. Railroads (1984): length 21 mi, 34 km; passenger-mi 919,640,000, passenger-km 1,480,020,000; short ton-mi cargo 63,668,000, metric ton-km cargo 92,954,000. Roads (1985): total length 823 mi, 1,325 km (paved 100%). Vehicles (1985): passenger cars 184,681; trucks and buses 90,420. Merchant marine (1985): vessels (100 gross tons and over) 396; total deadweight tonnage 11,332,555. Air transport (1985): passenger arrivals 4,256,000, passenger departures 4,356,000; airports (1986) with scheduled flights 1.
Communications. Daily newspapers (1985): total number 69; total circulation 3,189,000♂; circulation per 1,000 population 602♂. Radio (1985): total number of receivers 2,720,000 (1 per 2.0 persons). Television (1985): total number of receivers 1,310,000 (1 per 4.1 persons). Telephones (1985): 2,312,000 (1 per 2.3 persons).

Education and health

Education (1984–85)

	schools	teachers	students	student/ teacher ratio
Primary (age 6–11)	757	19,824	537,345	27.1
Secondary (age 12–18)	412	...	426,553	...
Vocational	24		17,827	
Higher	21	3,169	36,316	11.5

Educational attainment (1981). Percent of population over age 5 having: no schooling 15.5%; primary education 39.8%; secondary 39.2%; higher 5.5%. *Literacy* (1985): total population over age 15 literate 3,668,000 (88.1%); males literate 2,040,000 (94.7%); females literate 1,628,000 (80.9%).
Health (1985): physicians 4,887 (1 per 1,110 persons); hospital beds 24,638 (1 per 220 persons); infant mortality rate per 1,000 live births 7.6.
Food (1979–81): daily per capita caloric intake 2,771 (vegetable products 70%, animal products 30%); 121% of FAO recommended minimum requirement.

Military

Total active duty personnel (1985)□: 8,741 (army 87.7%, navy 9.3%, air force, n.a.). *Military expenditure as percent of GNP* (1983): 0.6% (world 6.1%); per capita expenditure U.S.$39.

*Excludes the surface areas of reservoirs. †Excludes 13,906 transients and 20,600 Vietnamese refugees but includes 49,747 marine population. ‡Density based on land area. §Less imputed bank service charges. ‖ Excludes local pigs not slaughtered in abattoirs. ¶1984. ♀Includes reexports. ♂Thirty-five newspapers only, 1984. □British forces with a few locally enlisted personnel in the navy.

Hungary

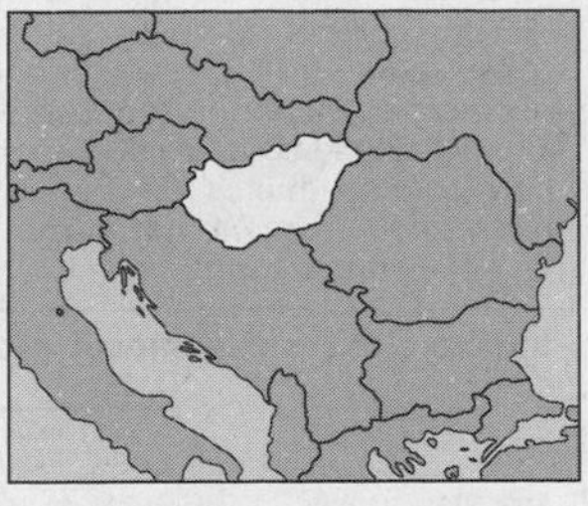

Official name: Magyar Népköztársaság (Hungarian People's Republic).
Form of government: unitary single-party republic with one legislative house (National Assembly [387]).
Chief of State: President.
Head of government: Premier.
Capital: Budapest.
Official language: Hungarian.
Official religion: none.
Monetary unit: 1 forint (Ft) = 100 filler; valuation (Oct. 1, 1986) 1 U.S.$ = Ft 46.69; 1 £ = Ft 67.47.

Area and population

		area		population
Counties	**Capitals**	sq mi	sq km	1986* estimate
Baranya	Pécs	1,732	4,487	432,000
Bács-Kiskun	Kecskemét	3,229	8,362	558,000
Békés	Bekéscsaba	2,175	5,632	422,000
Borsod-Abaúj-Zemplén	Miskolc	2,798	7,248	791,000
Csongrád	Szeged	1,646	4,263	457,000
Fejér	Székesfehérvár	1,689	4,374	426,000
Győr-Sopron	Győr	1,549	4,012	428,000
Hajdú-Bihar	Debrecen	2,398	6,212	551,000
Heves	Eger	1,404	3,637	342,000
Komárom	Tatabánya	869	2,250	321,000
Nógrád	Salgótarján	982	2,544	233,000
Pest	Budapest†	2,469	6,394	985,000
Somogy	Kaposvár	2,331	6,036	353,000
Szabolcs-Szatmár	Nyiregyháza	2,293	5,938	578,000
Szolnok	Szolnok	2,165	5,608	436,000
Tolna	Szekszárd	1,430	3,704	266,000
Vas	Szombathely	1,288	3,337	280,000
Veszprém	Veszprém	1,810	4,689	388,000
Zala	Zalaegerszeg	1,461	3,784	313,000
Capital City				
Budapest†		203	525	2,080,000
TOTAL		35,921	93,036	10,640,000

Demography

Population (1986): 10,622,000.
Density (1986): persons per sq mi 295.7, persons per sq km 114.2.
Urban-rural (1986): urban 56.8%; rural 43.2%.
Sex distribution (1986): male 48.28%; female 51.72%.
Age breakdown (1986): under 15, 21.4%; 15–29, 19.8%; 30–49, 28.5%; 50–59, 12.1%; 60 and over, 18.2%.
Population projection: (1990) 10,920,000; (2000) 10,964,000.
During the intercensal period 1970–80, the average growth rate was 0.2%; since 1980, however, the population has been decreasing.
Ethnic composition (1980): Magyar 98.8%; German 0.3%; other 0.9%.
Religious affiliation (1980): Christian 83.2%, of which Roman Catholic 53.9%, Protestant 21.6%; Jewish 0.9%; nonreligious 8.7%; atheist 7.2%.
Major cities (1986): Budapest 2,080,000; Miskolc 212,000; Debrecen 212,000; Szeged 183,000; Pécs 177,000; Győr 129,000.

Vital statistics

Birth rate per 1,000 population (1985): 12.2 (world avg. 29.0); (1984) legitimate 91.2%; illegitimate 8.8%.
Death rate per 1,000 population (1985): 13.8 (world avg. 11.0).
Natural increase rate per 1,000 population (1985): −1.6 (world avg. 18.0).
Total fertility rate (avg. births per childbearing woman; 1980–85): 2.1.
Marriage rate per 1,000 population (1985): 6.9.
Divorce rate per 1,000 population (1985): 2.7.
Life expectancy at birth (1984): male 65.6 years; female 73.7 years.
Major causes of death per 100,000 population (1985): diseases of the circulatory system 747.3; malignant neoplasms (cancers) 267.4.

National economy

Budget (1984). Revenue: Ft 563,200,000,000 (payments by enterprises 82.6%, personal income tax 7.2%). Expenditures: Ft 566,700,000,000 (social welfare and health 26.1%, economic tasks 23.9%, interest on public debt 9.5%, education 9.2%, defense 6.0%).
Public debt (external, outstanding; 1984): U.S.$7,379,800,000.
Tourism (1985): receipts from visitors U.S.$506,000,000; expenditures by nationals abroad U.S.$206,000,000.
Production (metric tons except as noted). Agriculture, forestry, fishing (1985): corn (maize) 6,613,000, wheat 6,548,000, sugar beets 4,024,000, barley 1,040,000; potatoes 971,000; sunflower seeds 669,000; rye 163,000; livestock (number of live animals) 8,280,000 pigs, 2,465,000 sheep, 1,766,000 cattle, 62,000,000 poultry; roundwood 6,600,000 cu m; fish catch 38,976,000. Mining and quarrying (1985): bauxite 2,815,000‡; dolomite 1,480,000; iron ore 385,000. Manufacturing (1985): cement 3,678,000; crude steel 3,647,000; rolled steel 2,860,000; pig iron 2,382,000; chemical fertilizers 1,069,100; aluminum 73,800; cotton fabrics 310,314,000 sq m; leather footwear 42,-800,000 pairs; buses and trucks 15,181 units. Construction (1985): residential 5,723,500 sq m. Energy production (consumption): electricity (kW-hr; 1985) 26,770,000,000 (31,705,000,000); coal (metric tons; 1985) 24,042,000 (26,030,000‡); crude petroleum (barrels; 1985) 15,352,000 (67,508,000‡); petroleum products (metric tons; 1985) 8,813,000 (10,210,000‡); natural gas (cu m; 1985) 7,441,000,000 (10,918,000,000‡).

Land use (1985): forested 17.7%; meadows and pastures 13.4%; agricultural and under permanent cultivation 56.9%; other 12.0%.
Gross national product (1985): U.S.$18,253,000,000 (U.S.$1,710 per capita).

Structure of net material product and labour force

	1984			
	in value Ft '000,000,000	% of total value	labour force	% of labour force
Agriculture	105.6	13.1	916,000	18.6
Mining and manufacturing	301.9	37.5	1,607,000	32.7
Construction	84.5	10.5	366,000	7.4
Public utilities	6.1	0.8	76,000	1.5
Transportation and communication	58.8	7.3	397,000	8.1
Trade	93.0	11.6	506,000	10.3
Services	...	...	1,010,000	20.6
Other	154.2§	19.2§	41,000‖	0.8‖
TOTAL	804.1	100.0	4,919,000	100.0

Population economically active (1985): total 4,912,900; activity rate of total population 46.1% (participation rates: ages 15–64, 80.7%; female 45.7%; unemployed, n.a.).

Price and earnings indexes (1980 = 100)

	1980	1981	1982	1983	1984	1985	1986¶
Consumer price index	100.0	104.6	111.8	120.0	129.9	138.9	140.9
Monthly earnings index	100.0	107.2	114.0	119.7	127.5	141.0	145.4

Household income and expenditure. Average household size (1984) 2.7; income per household Ft 178,000 (U.S.$3,700); sources of income: wages 65.0%, social income 34.1%, other 0.9%; expenditure (1984): food 28.2%, services 25.9%, consumer goods 19.0%, beverages and tobacco 15.1%, clothing and footwear 8.1%.

Foreign trade

Balance of trade (current prices)

	1979	1980	1981	1982	1983	1984	1985
Ft '000,000,000	−21.9	+13.6	−8.4	+5.5	+15.0	+30.0	+22.6
% of total	3.7%	2.4%	1.2%	0.8%	2.0%	3.8%	2.7%

Imports (1984): Ft 383,990,000,000 (machinery and transport equipment 26.0%; crude petroleum and petroleum products 15.0%; chemicals and related products 13.7%; food 6.3%; textile yarn and fabrics 3.3%; iron and steel 3.0%; nonferrous metals 2.9%; paper and paperboard 1.8%). *Major import sources:* U.S.S.R. 29.1%; West Germany 10.7%; East Germany 6.4%; Austria 5.1%; Czechoslovakia 5.0%; Poland 4.4%; Yugoslavia 3.9%.
Exports (1984): Ft 413,956,900,000 (machinery and transport equipment 30.1%, of which road vehicles and parts 9.0%; food 17.8%, of which meat 6.6%; chemicals 10.9%; petroleum products 8.4%; iron and steel 3.6%). *Major export destinations:* U.S.S.R. 30.1%; West Germany 7.4%; East Germany 5.9%; Austria 5.3%; Czechoslovakia 5.2%; Poland 4.2%; Yugoslavia 3.4%; Italy 3.3%.

Transport and communications

Transport. Railroads (1985): length 8,140 mi, 13,100 km; passenger-mi 6,965,-000,000, passenger-km 11,209,000,000; short ton-mi cargo 15,278,000,000, metric ton-km cargo 22,307,000,000. Roads (1985): total length 18,413 mi, 29,633 km (paved 98.3%). Vehicles (1986): passenger cars 1,435,900; trucks and buses 157,797. Merchant marine (1985): vessels (100 gross tons and over) 19; total deadweight tonnage 109,739. Air transport (1985): passenger-mi 828,300,000, passenger-km 1,333,000,000; short ton-mi cargo 14,930,000, metric ton-km cargo 21,800,000; airports (1986) 4.
Communications. Daily newspapers (1984): total number 29; total circulation 2,994,700; circulation per 1,000 population 281.0. Radio (1985): 5,500,-000 (1 per 2.0 persons). Television (1985): 2,911,000 (1 per 2.7 persons). Telephones (1985): 1,433,336 (1 per 7.4 persons).

Education and health

Education (1985–86)

	schools	teachers	students	student/ teacher ratio
Primary (age 6–13)	3,546	88,066	1,297,800	14.7
Secondary (age 14–18)	175♀	7,709♀	126,190	...
Vocational	729♀	21,801♀	370,918	...
Higher	58	14,850	99,344	6.7

Educational attainment (1984). Percent of population over age 7 having: no formal schooling 1.3%; primary education 65.5%; secondary 27.1%; higher 6.1%. *Literacy* (1984): total population over age 10 literate 9,033,597 (98.9%); males literate 4,331,597 (99.2%); females literate 4,702,000 (98.7%).
Health (1985): physicians 34,758 (1 per 306 persons); hospital beds 102,346 (1 per 104 persons); infant mortality rate per 1,000 live births 20.4.
Food (1982): daily per capita caloric intake 3,226 (vegetable products 67%; animal products 33%); 134% of FAO recommended minimum.

Military

Total active duty personnel (1985): 106,000 (army 79.2%, air force 20.8%). *Military expenditure as percent of GNP* (1983): 4.3% (world 6.1%); per capita expenditure U.S.$281.

*Beginning of the year. †Budapest has separate county status. The area and population of the city are excluded from the larger county (Pest), which it administers. ‡1984. §Includes other material activities, balance of taxes on products and value differences, and cost of nonmaterial services. ‖ Other material activities. ¶April. ♀1984–85.

Iceland

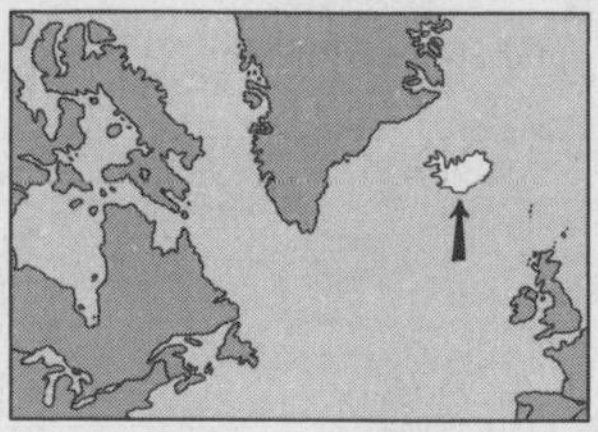

Official name: Lýdhveldidh Ísland (Republic of Iceland).
Form of government: unitary multiparty republic with two legislative houses (Upper House [20]; Lower House [40]).
Head of state and government: President.
Capital: Reykjavík.
Official language: Icelandic.
Official religion: Evangelical Lutheran.
Monetary unit: 1 króna (ISK) = 100 aurar; valuation (Oct. 1, 1986) 1 U.S.$ = ISK 40.40; 1 £ = ISK 58.38.

Area and population

Regions / Counties*	Administrative centres	area sq mi	area sq km	population 1984 estimate
Austurland		8,683	22,490	13,100
Austur-Skaftafellssýsla	Höfn	2,347	6,080	2,300
Nordhur-Múlasýsla	Seydhisfjördhur	4,799	12,430	3,300
Sudhur-Múlasýsla	Eskifjördhur	1,537	3,980	7,500
Nordhurland eystra		8,370	21,680	26,200†
Eyjafjardharsýsla	Akureyri	1,602	4,150	19,000
Nordhur-Thingeyjarsýsla	Húsavík	2,077	5,380	1,700
Sudhur-Thingeyjarsýsla	Húsavík	4,691	12,150	5,400
Nordhurland vestra		4,973	12,880	10,700†
Austur-Húnavatnssýsla	Blönduós	1,900	4,920	2,600
Skagafjardharsýsla	Saudhárkrókur	2,077	5,380	6,500
Vestur-Húnavatnssýsla	Blönduós	996	2,580	1,500
Rekjavíkursvaedhi og Reykjanessvaedhi		741	1,920	142,600
Gullbringusýsla	Keflavík	405	1,050	32,600
Kjósarsýsla	Hafnarfjördhur	336	870	110,000
Sudhurland		9,649	24,990	20,100†
Árnessýsla	Selfoss	3,401	8,810	10,400
Rangárvallasýsla	Hvolsvöllur	3,197	8,280	8,300
Vestur-Skaftafellssýsla	Vík	3,050	7,900	1,300
Vestfirdhir		3,676	9,520	10,400
Austur-Bardhastrandarsýsla	Patreksfjördhur	444	1,150	400
Nordhur-Ísafjardharsýsla	Ísafjördhur	1,181	3,060	5,200
Strandasýsla	Hólmavík	1,015	2,630	1,100
Vestur-Bardhastrandarsýsla	Patreksfjördhur	598	1,550	2,000
Vestur-Ísafjardharsýsla	Ísafjördhur	436	1,130	1,700
Vesturland		3,676	9,520	15,100
Borgarfjardharsýsla	Borgarnes	753	1,950	6,800
Dalasýsla	Budhardalur	815	2,110	1,100
Mýrasýsla	Borgarnes	1,262	3,270	2,600
Snaefellsnessýsla	Stykkishólmur	846	2,190	4,600
TOTAL		39,768	103,000	238,200†

Demography

Population (1986): 243,000.
Density (1986): persons per sq mi 6.1, persons per sq km 2.4.
Urban–rural (1983): urban 88.8%; rural 11.2%.
Sex distribution (1984): male 50.21%; female 49.79%.
Age breakdown (1983): under 15, 26.7%; 15–29, 27.4%; 30–44, 18.6%; 45–59, 13.6%; 60–74, 9.5%; 75 and over, 4.3%.
Population projection: (1990) 250,000; (2000) 270,000.
Doubling time: 79 years.
Ethnic composition (1983): native Icelander 97.2%; other European 2.2%; other 0.6%.
Religious affiliation (1983): Lutheran 96.9%; Roman Catholic 0.7%; other 2.4%.
Major cities (1984): Reykjavík 88,745; Kópavogur 13,711; Akureyri 12,979; Hafnarfjördhur 12,683‡; Keflavík 6,886‡.

Vital statistics

Birth rate per 1,000 population (1985): 15.9 (world avg. 29.0); legitimate 52.9%; illegitimate 47.1%.
Death rate per 1,000 population (1985): 7.1 (world avg. 11.0).
Natural increase rate per 1,000 population (1985): 8.8 (world avg. 18.0).
Total fertility rate (avg. births per childbearing woman; 1983): 2.1.
Marriage rate per 1,000 population (1984): 5.9.
Divorce rate per 1,000 population (1984): 1.9.
Life expectancy at birth (1985): male 73.5 years; female 79.5 years.
Major causes of death per 100,000 population (1983): heart and circulatory diseases 312.6; malignant neoplasms 166.2; accidents, suicide, etc. 59.9.

National economy

Budget (1985). Revenue: ISK 26,889,000,000 (indirect taxes 84.0%, of which sales tax 52.9%, import duties 15.8%; income taxes 9.4%). Expenditures: ISK 29,260,000,000 (social services 59.4%, of which social security and welfare 26.4, education 17.1%, health 10.2%; industrial services 23.5%; other 7.5%).
Public debt (1984): U.S.$852,218,000.
Tourism (1984): receipts from visitors U.S.$74,710,000; expenditures by nationals abroad U.S.$76,900,000.
Production (metric tons except as noted). Agriculture, forestry, fishing (1985): fodder crops 3,943,000§, potatoes 2,000§, milk 108,000§; livestock (number of live animals) 709,000 sheep, 72,700 cattle, 52,200 horses; fish catch, capelin 993,000, cod 322,800, herring 49,400, lobster, shrimp, and shellfish 27,300. Mining and quarrying (1984): diatomite 25,000. Manufacturing (1984): marine products 377,883‡, of which frozen fish 146,891‡, salted fish 75,048‡; cement 118,000; aluminum, refined 82,391; ferrosilicon 55,000. Construction (1983): residential 849,400 cu m, nonresidential 1,094,400 cu m. Energy production (consumption): electricity (kW-hr; 1984) 3,853,000,000 (3,853,000,000); coal (1984) none (40,000); petroleum, none (none); petroleum products (1984) none (468,000); natural gas, none (none).
Gross national product (at current market prices; 1984): U.S.$2,250,000,000 (U.S.$9,390 per capita).

Structure of gross domestic product and labour force

	1984 in value ISK '000,000	1984 % of total value	1984 labour force	1984 % of labour force
Agriculture	...	7.3	7,630	6.7
Fishing and processing	...	16.4	16,280	14.3
Manufacturing	...	15.5	18,445	16.2
Construction	...	9.8	11,615	10.2
Transportation and communication	...	8.9	7,980	7.0
Trade	...	17.4 ‖	17,630 ‖	15.5 ‖
Pub. admin., defense, services, and other	...	24.7	34,270	30.1
TOTAL	81,532	100.0	113,850	100.0

Population economically active (1984): total 113,850; activity rate of total population 47.5% (participation rates: 15–64, n.a.; female [1983] 31.5%; unemployed 1.3%).

Price and earnings indexes (1980 = 100)

	1980	1981	1982	1983	1984	1985	1986¶
Consumer price index	100.0	150.6	224.7	418.2	547.0	721.8	882.1
Hourly wages index	100.0	152.7	228.5	339.0	403.2	531.6	...

Household income and expenditure. Average household size: n.a.; disposable income per person (1982) ISK 82,240 (U.S.$6,660); sources of income (1982): wages, salaries, and self-employment 80.0%, transfer payments and other 20.0%; expenditure (1984): food 25.3%, housing 25.3%, transportation and communication 18.8%, education and recreation 10.1%, clothing and footwear 8.8%, health 1.7%, other 9.4%.
Land use (1983): forested 1.2%; meadows and pastures 22.7%; agricultural and under permanent cultivation 0.1%; other 76.0%♀.

Foreign trade

Balance of trade (current prices)

	1980	1981	1982	1983	1984	1985
ISK '000,000	+153	−196	−1,885	−1,973	−2,620	−3,850
% of total	1.8%	1.5%	10.0%	5.0%	5.2%	5.4%

Imports (1985): ISK 37,600,000,000 (machinery and transport equipment 17.8%, of which ships and aircraft 2.9%; fuels and lubricants 14.4%, of which petroleum 2.6%; construction materials 5.7%). *Major import sources:* West Germany 13.2%; U.K. 9.6%; Denmark 9.1%; The Netherlands 8.9%; U.S.S.R. 8.0%; Sweden 8.0%.
Exports (1985): ISK 33,750,000,000 (fish and fish products 64.7%, of which frozen fish fillets 32.6%, dried, salted, and smoked fish 16.5%; aluminum, refined 9.9%; agricultural products 1.4%). *Major export destinations:* U.S. 27.0%; U.K 18.7%; West Germany 8.3%; U.S.S.R. 6.7%; Portugal 5.6%.

Transport and communications

Transport. Railroads (1986): none. Roads (1984): total length 7,220 mi, 11,619 km (paved 11.5%). Vehicles (1984): passenger cars 100,260; trucks and buses 12,950. Merchant marine (1985): vessels (100 gross tons and over) 395; total deadweight tonnage 168,627. Air transport (1985): passenger-mi 1,489,000, passenger-km 2,397,000; short ton-mi cargo 15,398,000, metric ton-km cargo 22,480,000; airports (1986) with scheduled flights 23.
Communications. Daily newspapers (1984): total number 5; total circulation 114,000; circulation per 1,000 population 507. Radio (1984): 73,088 receivers (1 per 3.2 persons). Television (1984): 64,747 receivers (1 per 3.7 persons). Telephones (1983): 116,856 (1 per 2.0 persons).

Education and health

Education (1982–83)

	schools	teachers	students	student/teacher ratio
Primary (age 7–12)	187	2,600	25,000	9.6
Secondary (age 12–19)	157	...	21,800	...
Voc., teacher tr.	44	...	4,280	...
Higher	4	280	4,780	17.1

Educational attainment, n.a. *Literacy* (1984): total population over age 14 literate 175,029 (100.0%).
Health (1983): physicians 545 (1 per 435 persons); hospital beds 2,678 (1 per 88 persons); infant mortality rate per 1,000 live births (1984) 6.1.
Food (1980–82): daily per capita caloric intake 3,129 (vegetable products 54%, animal products 46%); 123%♂ of FAO recommended minimum.

Military

Iceland maintains no domestic military forces; external security is guaranteed by the NATO-sponsored U.S.-manned Iceland Defense Force, numbering about 2,700 (mostly air force). A domestic coast guard of about 120 is maintained.

*Counties include county cities and towns, which are within, but administratively independent of, the counties. †Detail does not add to total given because of rounding. ‡1983. §1984. ‖ Trade includes finance and public utilities. ¶July. ♀Glaciated, covered with peat bogs, or lava desert. ♂1979–81.

India

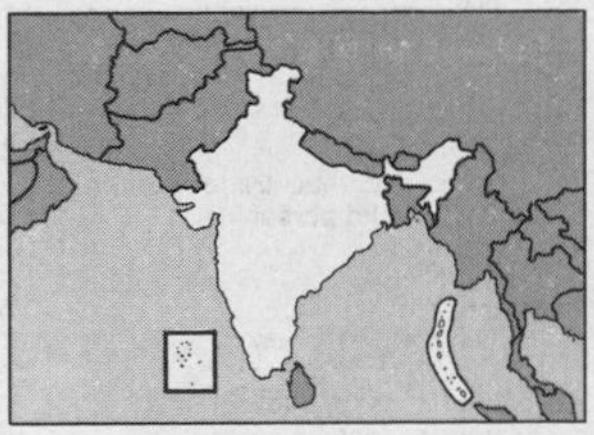

Official name: Bhārat (Hindī); Republic of India (English).
Form of government: multiparty federal republic with two legislative houses (Council of States [244], House of the People [544]).
Chief of state: President.
Head of government: Prime Minister.
Capital: New Delhi.
Official languages: Hindī; English.
Official religion: none.
Monetary unit: 1 Indian rupee (Rs) = 100 paisa; valuation (Oct. 1, 1986) 1 U.S.$ = Rs 12.78; 1 £ = Rs 18.47.

Area and population

		area		population
States	Capitals	sq mi	sq km	1981 census
Andhra Pradesh	Hyderābād	106,204	275,068	53,549,673
Assam	Prāgjyotiṣapura	30,285	78,438	19,896,843*
Bihār	Patna	67,134	173,877	69,914,734
Gujarāt	Gāndhīnagar	75,685	196,024	34,085,799
Haryāna	Chandīgarh	17,070	44,212	12,922,618
Himāchal Pradesh	Simla	21,495	55,673	4,280,818
Jammu and Kashmir	Srinagar	39,145†	101,387†	5,987,389
Karnātaka	Bangalore	74,051	191,791	37,135,714
Kerala	Trivandrum	15,005	38,863	25,453,680
Madhya Pradesh	Bhopāl	171,215	443,446	52,178,844
Mahārāshtra	Bombay	118,800	307,690	62,784,171
Manipur	Imphāl	8,621	22,327	1,420,953
Meghālaya	Shillong	8,660	22,429	1,335,819
Nāgāland	Kohīma	6,401	16,579	774,930
Orissa	Bhubaneswar	60,119	155,707	26,370,271
Punjab	Chandīgarh	19,445	50,362	16,788,915
Rājasthān	Jaipur	132,140	342,239	34,261,862
Sikkim	Gangtok	2,740	7,096	316,385
Tamil Nādu	Madras	50,216	130,058	48,408,077
Tripura	Agartala	4,049	10,486	2,053,058
Uttar Pradesh	Lucknow	113,673	294,411	110,862,013
West Bengal	Calcutta	34,267	88,752	54,580,647
Union Territories				
Andaman and Nicobar Islands	Port Blair	3,185	8,249	188,741
Arunāchal Pradesh	Itanagar	32,333	83,743	631,839
Chandīgarh	Chandīgarh	44	114	451,610
Dādra and Nagar Haveli	Silvassa	190	491	103,676
Delhi	Delhi	572	1,483	6,220,406
Goa, Daman, and Diu	Panaji	1,473	3,814	1,086,730
Lakshadweep	Kavaratti	12	32	40,249
Mizorām	Aizawl	8,140	21,081	493,757
Pondicherry	Pondicherry	190	492	604,471
TOTAL		1,222,559†	3,166,414†	685,184,692

Demography

Population (1986): 777,230,000.
Density (1986): persons per sq mi 612.3, persons per sq km 236.4.
Urban–rural (1985): urban 25.5%; rural 74.5%.
Sex distribution (1985): male 51.74%; female 48.26%.
Age breakdown‡ (1981): under 15, 39.5%; 15–29, 25.9%; 30–44, 17.4%; 45–59, 10.7%; 60 and over, 6.5%.
Population projection: (1990) 827,152,000; (2000) 964,072,000.
Doubling time: 31 years.
Linguistic composition (1971): Hindī 28.0%; Telugu 8.2%; Bengali 8.1%; Marāṭhī 7.6%; Tamil 6.9%; Urdū 5.2%; Gujarāti 4.7%; Malayālam 4.0%; Kannaḍa 3.9%; Oṛiyā 3.6%; Bhojpurī 2.6%; Punjābī 2.5%; Assamese 1.6%; Chhattisgarhī 1.2%; Magadhī 1.2%; Maithilī 1.1%; other 9.6%.
Religious affiliation (1981)‡: Hindu 82.6%; Muslim 11.4%; Christian 2.4%; Sikh 2.0%; Buddhist 0.7%; Jain 0.5%; other 0.4%.
Major cities (1981): Greater Bombay 8,243,405; Delhi 5,729,283§; Calcutta 3,305,006; Madras 3,276,622; Bangalore 2,476,355; Hyderābād 2,150,580; Ahmadābād 2,059,725; Kānpur 1,481,789; Nāgpur 1,219,461; Pune 1,203,351; Jaipur 977,165; Lucknow 895,721; Indore 829,327; Madurai 820,891; Coimbatore 704,514.

Other principal cities (1981)

	population		population		population
Āgra	694,191	Jamshedpur	438,385	Sholāpur (Solapur)	511,103
Ajmer	375,593	Jodhpur	506,345	South Suburban	378,765
Alīgarh	320,861	Jullundur	408,196	Srīnagar	586,038
Allahābād	616,051	Kolhāpur	340,625	Surat	776,583
Amritsar	594,844	Kota	358,241	Thāna (Thane)	309,897
Bareilly	386,734	Kozhidkode (Calicut)	394,447	Tiruchchirāppalli	362,045
Bhavnagar	307,121	Lucknow	895,721	Trivandrum	483,086
Bhopāl	671,018	Ludhiāna	607,052	Vadodara (Baroda)	734,473
Chandīgarh	373,789	Meerut	417,395	Vārānasi (Benares)	708,647
Cochin	513,249	Morādābād	330,051	Vijayawāda	454,577
Dhārwār-Hubli	527,108	Mysore	441,754	Vishākhapatnam	565,321
Durgāpur	311,798	Patna	776,371	Warangal	335,150
Faridābād	330,864	Raipur	338,245		
Guntūr	367,699	Rājkot	445,076		
Gwalior	539,015	Rānchi	489,626		
Howrah (Haora)	744,429	Salem	361,394		
Jalapur	614,162				

Place of birth (foreign born; 1981): other Asia 7,875,399, of which Bangladesh 4,170,524, Pakistan 2,736,038, Nepal 501,292, Sri Lanka 211,514, Burma 134,783; Africa 42,726; Europe 13,046; United States and Canada 5,923.
Mobility (1981). Population living in same district but at different residence as in 1971: 47,604,000; different district, same state 22,557,000; different state 10,860,000; moved outside the country 1,179,000.
Households. Average household size (1981) 5.7; number of rooms per household (1971): 1 room 47.8%, 2 rooms 28.2%, 3 rooms 12.0%, 4 rooms 6.0%, 5 or more rooms 5.9%, unspecified number of rooms 0.1%. Average number of persons per room (1971) 2.8. Population in households (1981) 665,287,849 (97.1%), houseless population 2,330,000 (0.34%), institutional population (1971) 2,693,000 (0.5%).
Emigration (1984): persons living abroad 11,644,000 (accepting foreign citizenship, 7,394,000), of which in Nepal 3,800,000 (2,388,000); Malaysia 1,170,000 (1,030,000); Sri Lanka 1,028,000 (426,000); United Kingdom 719,000 (359,000); Mauritius 697,000 (696,000); Guyana 500,000 (500,000); United States 440,000 (320,000); Trinidad and Tobago 421,000 (420,000); Burma 350,000 (50,000); Fiji 326,000 (326,000).

Vital statistics

Birth rate per 1,000 population (1983): 33.7 (world avg. 29.0); legitimate, n.a.; illegitimate, n.a.
Death rate per 1,000 population (1983): 11.9 (world avg. 11.0).
Natural increase rate per 1,000 population (1983): 21.8 (world avg. 18.0).
Total fertility rate (avg. births per childbearing woman; 1981): 4.7.
Marriage rate per 1,000 population: n.a.
Divorce rate per 1,000 population: n.a.
Life expectancy at birth (1981): male 53.9 years; female 52.9 years.
Major causes of death (rural areas only; 1982): asthma and bronchitis 8.7%; tuberculosis of the lungs 5.5%; pneumonia 5.2%; heart attack 4.7%; typhoid fever 3.1%; anemias 2.9%; gastroenteritis 2.5%; malignant neoplasms (cancers) 2.5%; influenza 2.1%; tetanus 1.6% (excludes diseases of the newborn).

Social indicators

Educational attainment (1981). Percent of adult population over age 25 having: no formal schooling (illiterate) 64.8%; literate population with no formal schooling 0.9%; some primary education only 11.2%; some secondary only 6.2%; completed secondary 7.1%; higher 2.5%; other 7.3%.

Distribution of income (1975–76)

percent of household income by quintile:				
1	2	3	4	5 (highest)
7.0%	9.2%	13.9%	20.5%	49.4%

Quality of working life (1981). Average workweek: 45 hours. Rate of fatal (nonfatal) injuries per 100,000 workers (1981–82): industrial workers 16 (7,657); miners 34 (371); railway workers 20 (1,531). Employees covered under Employee's State Insurance Scheme (1983) 7,187,000, number of beneficiaries 27,886,000. Average days lost to labour stoppages per 1,000 workdays (1982): 1.4. Average duration of journey to work: n.a. Rate per 1,000 workers of discouraged (unemployed no longer seeking work): n.a.
Access to services. Proportion of villages having: access to electricity (1982–83) 55.7%; adequate water supply (1977) 68.7%. Urban population with adequate water supply (1977) 98.0%.
Social participation. Eligible voters participating in last national election: 61.5%. Trade union membership in total workforce (1980): 6,126,816 ‖. Practicing religious population in total affiliated population: n.a.
Social deviance (1984). Offense rate per 100,000 population for: murder 3.4; dacoity (gang robbery) 1.4; theft and housebreaking 43.7; rape 0.8. Incidence in general population of: alcoholism, n.a.; drug and substance abuse, n.a.¶. Rate per 100,000 population of suicide (1980): 6.1.
Leisure (1985). Favourite leisure activities in urban areas: listening to the radio and attending the cinema.
Material well-being (1983). Households possessing: automobile 0.8%; telephone 2.3%; television receiver 1.6%; radio receiver 17.2%; air conditioner, n.a.; washing machine, n.a.

National economy

Gross national product (at current market prices; 1984): U.S.$197,210,000,000 (U.S.$264 per capita).

Structure of gross domestic product and labour force

	1984–85		1981	
	in value Rs '000,000,000	% of total value	labour force	% of labour force
Agriculture	570.7	32.8	153,015,000	62.5
Mining	80.4	4.6	1,264,000	0.5
Manufacturing }			25,143,000	10.3
Construction }	399.9	22.9	3,565,000	1.5
Public utilities }			974,000	0.4
Transportation and communication	102.7	5.9	6,069,000	2.5
Trade	270.2	15.5	12,165,000	5.0
Finance	108.9	6.3	1,764,000	0.7
Pub. admin., defense	102.1	5.9	...	...
Services	106.9	6.1	18,557,000	7.6
Other	...	...	22,089,000	9.0
TOTAL	1,741.8	100.0	244,605,000	100.0

Budget (1985–86). Revenue: Rs 476,354,100,000 (tax revenue 53.6%, of which excise taxes 25.2%, customs duties 16.5%, taxes on corporations 5.9%; nontax revenue 16.5%, of which interest receipts 9.8%). Expenditures: Rs 512,952,900,000 (interest payments 13.8%; defense 13.2%; social and community services 4.7%; industry and minerals 4.2%; agriculture 3.5%).
Public debt (external, outstanding; 1984): U.S.$22,403,100,000.
Production (metric tons except as noted). Agriculture, forestry, fishing (1985): sugarcane 173,569,000, cereals 164,573,000, rice 91,500,000, vegetables and melons 45,420,000, wheat 44,229,000, fruit excluding melons

23,955,000, roots and tubers 19,733,000, potatoes 12,642,000, pulses 12,085,-000, sorghum 10,000,000, mangoes 9,200,000, cotton (all forms) 7,600,000, corn (maize) 7,000,000, peanuts (groundnuts) 5,600,000, cassava 5,569,000, coconuts 4,550,000, rapeseed 3,030,000, dry beans 2,900,000, cottonseed 2,800,000, jute 1,780,000, spices♀—chilies 525,000, turmeric 173,000, black pepper 26,000, cardamom 5,400; livestock (number of live animals) 182,-410,000 cattle, 81,500,000 goats, 64,500,000 water buffalo, 41,300,000 sheep, 1,100,000 camels; roundwood (1984) 238,861,000 cu m; fish catch (1984) 2,858,914, of which freshwater fishes 1,083,891. Mining and quarrying (1985): limestone 48,492,000; iron ore 42,036,000; copper ore 4,152,000; dolomite 2,208,000; bauxite 2,016,000; gypsum 1,260,000; manganese ore 1,236,000; phosphorite 900,000; kaolin 720,000; barite 564,000; chromite 552,000; magnesite 420,000; zinc concentrates 88,692; lead concentrates 35,400; kyanite 30,000; tungsten concentrates 4,452 kg; gold 152 kg; diamond 1,357 carats. Manufacturing (1985): cement 31,080,000; steel ignots 10,962,000; salt 9,876,000; refined sugar 7,980,000; fertilizer 5,580,000; wheat flour 3,429,600; printing and writing paper 866,400; steel pipes and tubes 847,200; soda ash 813,600; caustic soda 704,400; tea 652,800; man-made fibre 300,108; aluminum 260,016; paperboard 249,600; plastic resins 101,520; steel castings 92,400; zinc 70,812; refined copper cathode 28,020; lead 15,756; bicycles 5,646,000 units. Construction (value in Rs; 1983) residential 76,085,000,000; nonresidential 56,706,000,000.

Manufacturing enterprises (1981)

	no. of factories	no. of employees	annual wages as a % of avg. of all wages	annual value added (Rs '000,000)
Chemicals and chemical products	237	730,754	...	14,299
Cotton textiles	7,189	1,070,941	...	13,271
Basic metals and alloys	5,779	578,007	...	12,343
Machinery except electrical	7,011	401,028	...	8,885
Transport equipment and parts	2,815	484,484	...	8,556
Electrical machinery	3,406	317,349	...	8,339
Food products	17,067	1,289,509	...	7,072
Rubber, plastic, petroleum and coal products	3,498	172,877	...	5,360
Paper, paper products, printing, publishing, etc.	4,798	272,965	...	4,343
Nonmetallic mineral products	6,440	339,713	...	4,033
Wool, silk, and synthetic textiles	3,743	216,282	...	3,787
Metal products	6,457	191,498	...	3,312
Jute, hemp, mesta textiles	265	272,439	...	3,003
Beverages and tobacco products	8,901	403,104	...	2,314
Textile production (wearing apparel except footwear)	2,889	98,678	...	1,193

Energy production (consumption): electricity (kW-hr; 1984) 165,440,000,000 (165,378,000,000); coal (metric tons; 1984) 152,519,000 (147,616,000); crude petroleum (barrels; 1984) 212,291,000 (267,786,000); petroleum products (metric tons; 1984) 27,692,000 (32,339,000); natural gas (cu m; 1984) 3,213,-800,000 (3,213,800,000).

Financial aggregates♁

	1980	1981	1982	1983	1984	1985	1986□
Exchange rate, Rs per:							
U.S. dollar	7.93	9.10	9.63	10.49	12.45	12.17	12.61
£	18.91	17.36	15.55	15.22	14.40	17.59	18.79
SDR	10.11	10.59	10.63	10.99	12.20	13.36	15.48
International reserves (U.S.$)							
Total (excl. gold; '000,000)	6,944	4,693	4,315	4,937	5,842	6,420	5,977
SDRs ('000,000)	480	545	374	110	331	336	253
Reserve pos. in IMF ('000,000)	420	384	402	510	477	535	586
Foreign exchange ('000,000)	6,043	3,764	3,539	4,318	5,034	5,549	5,138
Gold ('000,000 fine troy oz)	8.594	8.594	8.594	8.594	8.737	9.397	10.449
% world reserves	0.9	0.9	0.9	0.9	0.9	0.9	0.9
Interest and prices							
Central bank discount (%)	9.0	10.0	10.0	10.0	10.0	10.0	10.0
Gov't. bond yield (%)	6.7	7.2	7.6	8.0	8.7	8.9	...
Industrial share prices (1980 = 100)	100.0	122.7	120.1	126.2	134.8	200.0	243.0
Balance of payments (U.S.$'000,000)							
Balance of visible trade	−5,644	−5,712	−4,820	4,098	...	...	...
Imports, f.o.b.	13,947	14,149	14,046	13,868	...	...	...
Exports, f.o.b.	8,303	8,437	9,226	9,770	...	...	...
Balance of invisibles	+525	+7	−621	−917	...	...	...
Balance of payments, current account	−1,785	−2,698	−2,524	1,953	...	...	...

Population economically active (1981): total 244,605,000; activity rate of total population 35.7% (participation rates: over age 15, 59.0%; female 26.0%; unemployed 7.3%).

Price and earnings indexes (1980 = 100)

	1980	1981	1982	1983	1984	1985	1986□
Consumer price index	100.0	113.0	121.9	136.3	147.7	155.9	171.3
Earnings index◇	100.0	102.4	113.5	...	...	...	...

Household income and expenditure. Number of households (1981) 119,772,-545. Average household size (1981) 5.7; average annual income per household: n.a.; sources of income (1980–81): self-employment 44.9%, salaries and wages 38.7%, interest 7.6%, profits and dividends 4.8%, rent 4.0%; expenditure (1982–83): food 53.2%, transportation and communication 10.3%, clothing and footwear 9.2%, housing 5.5%, fuel and energy 5.0%, tobacco and alcoholic beverages 3.4%, education 2.8%, medical care and health expenses 2.1%.

Service enterprises (1980)‡

	no. of enter-prises	no. of em-ployees	annual wage as a % of all wages	annual value added (Rs '000,000)△
Wholesale and retail trade	6,046,200	10,228,700	...	157,094
Community and personal services	3,177,700	13,128,800	...	57,455
Construction	152,000	451,200	...	53,540
Transportation	307,400	1,194,300	...	43,705
Finance and insurance	273,500	1,570,800	...	33,868
Electricity, gas, and water	33,700	363,500	...	15,993
Restaurants and hotels	807,000	2,080,500	...	11,939
Communications	98,900	530,900	...	7,203
Storage and warehousing	122,400	356,900	...	1,353

Tourism: receipts from visitors (1983) U.S.$1,203,000,000; expenditures by nationals abroad (1981) U.S.$220,000,000.
Land use (1984): forested 22.7%; meadows and pastures 4.0%; agricultural and under permanent cultivation 56.6%; other 16.7%.

Foreign trade

Balance of trade (current prices)

	1980	1981	1982	1983	1984	1985
Rs '000,000	−49,254	−61,599	−51,275	−50,214	−63,003	−82,368
% of total	26.7%	30.0%	22.5%	22.3%	22.7%	29.5%

Imports (1984–85): Rs 198,000,000,000 (petroleum and petroleum products 31.5%; pearls, precious and semiprecious stones 6.0%; iron and steel 4.5%; nonelectrical machinery, components, and parts 2.7%; nonferrous metals 2.0%; transport equipment and parts 1.7%; cereals and cereal preparations 1.0%). *Major import sources:* U.S.S.R. 10.6%; United States 9.8%; West Germany 7.6%; Japan 7.3%; Saudi Arabia 7.3%; United Kingdom 6.0%; Belgium 4.6%; The Netherlands 2.1%.
Exports (1984–85): Rs 113,000,000,000 (crude petroleum 13.5%; handicrafts 13.2%; pearls, precious and semiprecious stones 9.5%; ready-made garments 7.4%; machinery and transport equipment 6.4%; tea and maté 6.1%; leather and leather manufactures including footwear 4.0%; iron ore 3.9%; fish and fish preparations 2.9%; spices 1.5%). *Major export destinations:* United States 15.3%; U.S.S.R. 14.3%; Japan 9.2%; United Kingdom 5.8%; West Germany 4.1%; Saudi Arabia 2.1%; Belgium 1.6%; The Netherlands 1.6%.

Transport and communications

Transport. Railroads (1985): route length 38,200 mi, 61,478 km; passenger-mi 149,000,000,000, passenger-km 240,000,000,000; short ton-mi cargo 134,-583,000,000, metric ton-km cargo 196,488,000,000. Roads (1984–85): total length 1,101,000 mi, 1,772,000 km (paved 47%). Vehicles (1984–85): passenger cars 1,517,000; trucks and buses 952,000. Merchant marine (1985): vessels (100 gross tons and over) 741; total deadweight tonnage 10,760,881. Air transport (1985): passenger-mi 9,246,000,000, passenger-km 14,880,-000,000; short ton-mi cargo 358,033,000, metric ton-km cargo 522,720,000; airports (1986) with scheduled flights 75.
Communications. Daily newspapers (1985): total number 1,423; total circulation 12,895,680✝; circulation per 1,000 population 16.9✝. Radio (1985): total number of receivers 25,000,000 (1 per 30 persons). Television (1985): total number of receivers 2,200,000 (1 per 346 persons). Telephones (1984–85): 3,714,000 (1 per 205 persons).

Education and health

Education (1984–85)

	schools	teachers	students	student/ teacher ratio
Primary (age 5–10)	550,000	1,391,912⊕	85,400,000	...
Secondary (age 10–17)	200,000	1,910,781⊕	43,500,000	...
Voc., Teacher tr.	5,000	...	468,993**	...
Higher	135	259,745**	3,442,000	...

Literacy (1981): total population over age 14 literate 168,900,000 (40.8%); males literate 117,600,000 (54.8%); females literate 51,300,000 (25.7%).
Health (1983–84): physicians 284,000 (1 per 2,629 persons); hospital beds 599,000 (1 per 1,246 persons); infant mortality rate per 1,000 live births (1985) 105.
Food (1981–83): daily per capita caloric intake 2,088 (vegetable products 95%, animal products 5%); 92% of FAO recommended minimum requirement.

Military

Total active duty personnel (1986): 1,260,000 (army 87.3%, navy 3.7%, air force 9.0%). *Military expenditure as percent of GNP* (1984): 3.9% (world 6.1%); per capita expenditure U.S.$9.

*Estimate; state not censused. †Excludes 46,660 sq mi (120,849 sq km) of territory claimed by India as part of Jammu and Kashmir but occupied by Pakistan or China. Final status of these claims is not determined. ‡Excluding Assam. §Including New Delhi (population 273,036). ‖ Total of reporting unions only (about 50%). ¶India's codeine consumption in 1983 was fourth highest in the world. ♀All data for spices, 1981–82. ♁Excepting 1986, exchange rates and international reserves are end-of-year figures, and other categories are yearly averages. □July. ◇Average daily wage rate of male agricultural workers. △1980–81. ✝Circulation of 114 main dailies only. ⊕1983–84. **1982–83.

Indonesia

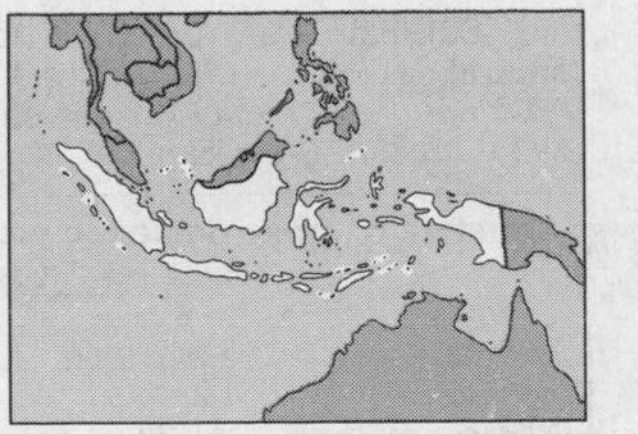

Official name: Republik Indonesia (Republic of Indonesia).
Form of government: unitary multiparty republic with two legislative houses (People's Consultative Assembly [920]; House of People's Representatives [460]).
Head of state and government: President.
Capital: Jakarta.
Official language: Bahasa Indonesia.
Official religion: monotheism.
Monetary unit: 1 Indonesian rupiah (Rp) = 100 sen; valuation (Oct. 1, 1986) 1 U.S.$ = Rp 1,636.00; 1 £ = Rp 2,364.02.

Area and population

		area		population
		sq mi	sq km	1986 estimate
Metropolitan district	**Capitals**			
Jakarta Raya	Jakarta	228	590	8,164,400
Provinces				
Bali	Denpasar	2,147	5,561	2,709,200
Bengkulu	Bengkulu	8,173	21,168	985,600
Irian Jaya	Jayapura	162,928	421,981	1,363,500
Jambi	Jambi	17,345	44,924	1,822,200
Jawa Barat	Bandung	17,877	46,300	31,876,400
Jawa Tengah	Semarang	13,207	34,206	27,755,900
Jawa Timur	Surabaya	18,503	47,922	31,639,300
Kalimantan Barat	Pontianak	56,664	146,760	2,827,000
Kalimantan Selatan	Banjarmasin	14,541	37,660	2,328,000
Kalimantan Tengah	Palangkaraya	58,919	152,600	1,159,000
Kalimantan Timur	Samarinda	78,162	202,440	1,690,500
Lampung	Tanjung Karang	12,860	33,307	6,422,100
Maluku	Ambon	28,767	74,505	1,659,100
Nusa Tenggara Barat	Mataram	7,790	20,177	3,107,700
Nusa Tenggara Timur	Kupang	18,485	47,876	3,048,900
Riau	Pakanbaru	36,511	94,562	2,583,900
Sulawesi Selatan	Ujung Pandang	28,101	72,781	6,669,500
Sulawesi Tengah	Palu	26,921	69,726	1,604,800
Sulawesi Tenggara	Kendari	10,690	27,686	1,122,400
Sulawesi Utara	Menado	7,345	19,023	2,406,400
Sumatera Barat	Padang	19,219	49,778	3,851,500
Sumatera Selatan	Palembang	40,034	103,688	5,586,900
Sumatera Utara	Medan	27,331	70,787	9,667,500
Timor Timur*	Dili	5,743	14,874	618,500
Special autonomous districts				
Aceh	Banda Aceh	21,387	55,392	3,078,400
Yogyakarta	Yogyakarta	1,224	3,169	2,913,400
TOTAL		741,101†	1,919,443	168,662,000

Demography

Population (1986): 168,662,000.
Density (1986): persons per sq mi 227.6, persons per sq km 87.9.
Urban-rural (1980): urban 22.4%; rural 77.6%.
Sex distribution (1985): male 49.75%; female 50.25%.
Age breakdown (1985): under 15, 39.2%; 15–29, 28.0%; 30–44, 16.8%; 45–59, 10.7%; 60–74, 4.4%; 75 and over, 0.9%.
Population projection: (1990) 183,456,800; (2000) 222,753,000.
Doubling time: 38 years.
Ethnolinguistic composition (1980): Javanese 40.1%; Sundanese 15.3%; Bahasa Indonesian 12.0%; Madurese 4.8%; other 27.8%.
Religious affiliation (1980): Muslim 87.1%; Christian 8.8%, of which Roman Catholic 3.0%; Hindu 2.0%; Buddhist 0.9%; other 1.2%.
Major cities (1984): Jakarta 7,585,000; Surabaya 2,271,000; Bandung 1,613,-000; Medan 1,506,000; Semarang 1,077,000.

Vital statistics

Birth rate per 1,000 population (1985): 30.4 (world avg. 29.0).
Death rate per 1,000 population (1985): 12.0 (world avg. 11.0).
Natural increase rate per 1,000 population (1985): 18.4 (world avg. 18.0).
Total fertility rate (avg. births per childbearing woman; 1985): 3.8.
Marriage rate per 1,000 population (1982): 7.5.
Divorce rate per 1,000 population (1982): 1.2.
Life expectancy at birth (1985): male 53.4 years; female 56.2 years.
Major causes of death: n.a.; however, major diseases include tuberculosis, malaria, dysentery, cholera, and plague.

National economy

Budget (1986–87 est.). Revenue: Rp 21,421,600,000,000 (taxes from energy production 45.5%, foreign aid receipts 16.8%, income tax 13.4%, excise tax 10.0%, customs duties 7.6%). Expenditures: Rp 21,421,600,000,000 (development 38.7%, of which education 5.3%, defense 2.6%, health 1.5%; debt service 19.7%; salaries and pensions 15.0%).
Public debt (external, outstanding; 1984): U.S.$22,882,800,000.
Tourism: receipts from visitors (1984): U.S.$519,000,000; expenditures by nationals abroad (1983) U.S.$523,000,000.
Production (metric tons except as noted). Agriculture, forestry, fishing (1984): paddy rice 37,500,000, sugarcane 23,726,000, cassava 14,000,000, rubber 1,150,000, nutmeg 7,751‡; livestock (number of live animals) 7,910,000 goats, 6,800,000 cattle, 4,790,000 sheep, 2,391,000 water buffalo; roundwood 148,194,000 cu m; fish catch 2,217,170. Mining and quarrying (1985): nickel ore 995,604; bauxite 830,471; copper ore§ 233,446; iron ore§ 130,930; tin ore§ 22,414; silver 2,151,821 kg. Manufacturing (1984): cement 6,607,400; paper 84,578; cotton yarn 129,903 bales; beer 474,040 hectolitres; transportation vehicles 155,400 units‖. Energy production (consumption): electricity (kW-hr; 1984) 21,345,000,000 (21,345,000,000); coal (metric tons; 1984) 1,084,652 (303,000); crude petroleum (barrels; 1984) 517,859,000 (193,749,000); petroleum products (metric tons; 1984) 23,433,000 (22,954,-000); natural gas (cu m; 1984) 24,102,000,000 (6,492,000,000).
Gross national product (1984): U.S.$78,881,000,000 (U.S.$486 per capita).

Structure of gross domestic product and labour force

	1984		1982	
	in value Rp'000,000	% of total value	labour force	% of labour force
Agriculture	18,746.6	24.0	31,593,314	54.7
Mining	14,608.3	18.7	390,661	0.7
Manufacturing	9,621.9	12.3	6,021,929	10.4
Construction	4,527.8	5.8	2,146,210	3.7
Public utilities	588.2	0.8	61,666	0.1
Transp. and commun.	4,317.0	5.5	1,796,112	3.1
Trade	12,104.5	15.5	8,553,919	14.8
Finance, real estate	4,273.9	5.5	112,859	0.2
Pub. admin., defense	6,086.2	7.8	7,126,131	12.3
Services and other	3,122.4	4.0		
TOTAL	77,996.8¶	100.0†	57,802,801	100.0

Population economically active: total (1982) 59,598,626; activity rate of total population 38.5% (participation rates [1980]: ages 15–64, 59.2%; female 32.8%; unemployed 1.8%).

Price and earnings indexes (1980 = 100)

	1979	1980	1981	1982	1983	1984	1985
Consumer price index	84.4	100.0	112.2	122.9	137.4	151.7	180.5
Monthly earnings index♀	87.2	100.0	108.5	122.6	155.5	175.0	...

Household income and expenditure. Average household size (1983) 4.7; income per household: n.a.; source of income: n.a.; expenditure (1984): food 63.3%, housing and utilities 17.4%, clothing 4.6%, durable goods 3.1%.
Land use (1983): forested 67.2%; meadows and pastures 6.6%; agricultural and under permanent cultivation 11.2%; other 15.0%.

Foreign trade

Balance of trade (current prices)

	1980	1981	1982	1983	1984	1985
U.S.$'000,000	+12,235	+10,410	+7,240	+6,545	+9,508	+9,430
% of total	38.7%	30.5%	19.4%	18.3%	27.7%	34.0%

Imports (1985): U.S.$10,259,090,000 (machinery 35.0%, chemicals 14.8%, mineral fuels 14.1%, base metals 13.0%, food and live animals 6.7%). *Major import sources:* Japan 25.8%; U.S. 16.8%; Singapore 8.2%.
Exports (1985): U.S.$18,586,712,000 (petroleum and petroleum products 48.9%, natural gas 19.6%, rubber 15.2%, wood products 6.1%, coffee 3.0%). *Major export destinations:* Japan 46.2%; U.S. 21.7%; Singapore 8.7%.

Transport and communications

Transport. Railroads: (1985) length 4,004 mi, 6,444 km; (1984) passenger-km 6,376,000,000; (1984) metric ton-km cargo 1,175,000,000. Roads (1984): total length 110,539 mi, 177,896 km (paved 64%). Vehicles (1985): passenger cars 958,919; trucks and buses 1,030,809. Merchant marine (1985): vessels (100 gross tons and over) 1,653; total deadweight tonnage 2,673,698. Air transport (1984): passenger-km 9,402,000,000; metric ton-km cargo 169,-800,000; airports (1985) 94.
Communications. Daily newspapers (1982): total number 89; total circulation 2,603,190; circulation per 1,000 population 16.8. Radio (1985): 32,-800,000 receivers (1 per 5.1 persons). Television (1985): 4,900,000 receivers (1 per 34 persons). Telephones (1984): 795,647 (1 per 209 persons).

Education and health

Education (1983–84)

	schools	teachers	students	student/ teacher ratio
Primary (age 7–12)	129,388	925,834	25,804,380	27.9
Secondary (age 13–18)	18,630	384,219	6,447,030	16.8
Voc., teacher tr.	2,752ð	65,528ð	934,527□	...
Higher	50ð	56,322ð	692,700◇	...

Educational attainment (1982). Percent of population over age 10 having: no formal education 23.6%; less than primary 37.9%; primary 25.6%; less than secondary 7.3%; secondary 5.0%; postsecondary 0.3%; higher 0.2%. *Literacy* (1985): total population over age 15 literate 79,197,000 (74.1%); males literate 41,450,000 (83.0%); females literate 33,708,000 (65.4%).
Health: physicians (1983) 10,262 (1 per 15,542 persons); hospital beds (1984) 103,500 (1 per 1,586 persons); infant mortality rate per 1,000 live births (1985) 79.0.
Food (1980–82): daily per capita caloric intake 2,363 (vegetable products 98%, animal products 2%); 109% of FAO recommended minimum.

Military

Total active duty personnel (1985): 278,050 (army 77.7%, navy 13.3%, air force 9.0%). *Military expenditure as percent of GNP* (1983): 2.8%; (world 6.1%); per capita expenditure U.S.$15.

*Indonesian sovereignty over former Portuguese East Timor is not recognized by the United Nations. †Detail does not add to total given because of rounding. ‡1983 export figure only. §Concentrates. ‖1983. ¶In constant 1983 prices. ♀Based on prices received by farmers for sale of produce. ð1981–82. □Excludes students enrolled in religious schools. ◇1982–83.

Iran

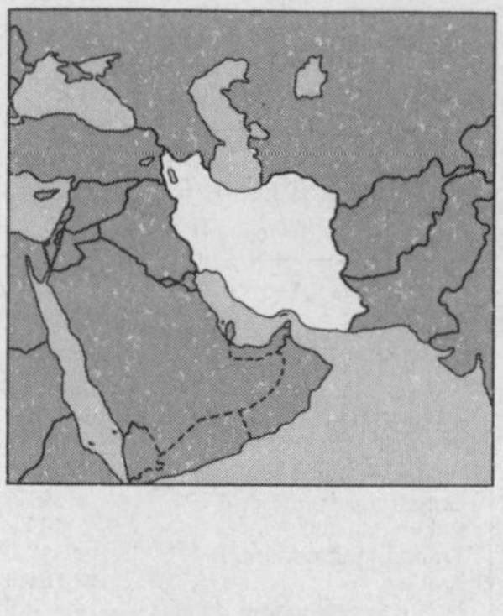

Official name: Jomhūrī-ye Eslamī-ye Īrān (Islamic Republic of Iran).
Form of government: unitary Islamic republic with a single legislative house (Islamic Consultative Assembly [270]).
Chief of state: Velayat Faghih (religious leader).
Head of state: President.
Head of government: Prime Minister.
Capital: Tehrān.
Official language: Farsī (Persian).
Official religion: Islam.
Monetary unit: 1 rial (Rls) = 100 dinars; valuation (Oct. 1, 1986) 1 U.S.$ = Rls 76.20; 1£ = Rls 110.10.

Area and population

Provinces	Capitals	area sq mi	area sq km	population 1984 estimate
Azārbāijān-e Gharbī	Orūmīyeh	15,000	38,850	1,915,000
Azārbāijān-e Sharqī	Tabrīz	25,908	67,102	4,097,000
Bakhtarān	Bakhtarān	9,137	23,667	1,177,000
Boyer Aḥmad-e Kohkilūyeh	Yāsūj	5,506	14,261	390,000
Būshehr	Būshehr	10,676	27,653	519,000
Chahār Mahāl-e Bakhtīārī	Shahr Kord	5,741	14,870	601,000
Eşfahān	Eşfahān	40,405	104,650	3,012,000
Fārs	Shīrāz	51,466	133,298	2,806,000
Gīlān	Rasht	5,679	14,709	2,069,000
Hamadān	Hamadān	7,638	19,784	1,407,000
Hormozgān	Bandar 'Abbās	25,818	66,870	694,000
Īlām	Īlām	7,352	19,044	308,000
Kermān	Kermān	71,997	186,472	1,535,000
Khorāsān	Mashhad	120,980	313,337	4,441,000
Khūzestān	Ahvāz	24,981	64,702	2,284,000
Kordestān	Sanandaj	9,651	24,998	906,000
Lorestān	Khorramābād	12,117	31,383	1,306,000
Markazī	Arāk	15,403	39,895	1,430,000
Māzandarān	Sarī	18,291	47,375	2,880,000
Semnān	Semnān	34,764	90,039	370,000
Sīstān-e Balūchestān	Zāhedān	70,107	181,578	997,000
Tehrān	Tehrān	7,381	19,118	7,243,000
Yazd	Yazd	24,673	63,905	569,000
Zanjān	Zanjān	14,053	36,398	1,488,000
TOTAL		634,724	1,643,958	44,444,000

Demography

Population (1986): 45,895,000.
Density (1986): persons per sq mi 72.3, persons per sq km 27.9.
Urban-rural (1984–85): urban 51.4%; rural 48.6%.
Sex distribution (1984–85): male 51.65%; female 48.6%.
Age breakdown (1984–85): under 15, 43.4%; 15–29, 25.9%; 30–44, 15.9%; 45–59, 9.3%; 60–74, 4.4%; 75 and over, 1.1%.
Population projection: (1990) 51,315,000; (2000) 65,161,000.
Doubling time: 25 years.
Ethnic composition (1980): Persian 45.0%; Azerbaijani 16.0%; Kurdish 8.2%; Luri 2.2%; Bakhtiari 1.9%; Baluchi 1.9%; Arab 1.6%; other 23.2%.
Religious affiliation (1985): Muslim 98% (Shīʿī 93.0%, Sunnī 5%); other 2%.
Major cities (1985): Tehrān 5,751,500; Eşfahān 1,121,200; Mashhad 1,103,300; Shīrāz 834,800; Ahvaz 508,500.

Vital statistics

Birth rate per 1,000 population (1985): 39.7 (world avg. 29.0).
Death rate per 1,000 population (1985): 11.4 (world avg. 11.0).
Natural increase rate per 1,000 population (1985): 28.3 (world avg. 18.0).
Total fertility rate (avg. births per childbearing woman; 1985): 5.4.
Marriage rate per 1,000 population (1984–85): 8.9.
Divorce rate per 1,000 population (1984–85): 0.8.
Life expectancy at birth (1985): male 58.0 years; female 58.3 years.
Major causes of death per 100,000 population (1984–85)*: diseases of the circulatory system 52.7; accidents, poisonings, and suicides 29.7; ill-defined conditions and symptoms 19.4; diseases of early infancy 15.2; malignant neoplasms (cancers) 14.0; diseases of the respiratory system 13.1; diseases of the nervous system 5.9.

National economy

Budget (1983–84). Revenue: Rls 3,727,943,000,000 (oil and gas 53.5%, taxes 19.3%, trade and services 5.1%). Expenditures: Rls 3,727,943,000,000 (social affairs 34.1%, economic affairs 25.7%, national defense 9.5%).
Tourism (1984): receipts from visitors U.S.$42,000,000; expenditures by nationals abroad, n.a.
Production (metric tons except as noted). Agriculture, forestry, fishing (1984): wheat 5,500,000, potatoes 1,550,000, barley 1,550,000, grapes 1,300,000, rice (paddy) 1,230,000, watermelons 950,000; livestock (number of live animals) 34,000,000 sheep, 13,600,000 goats, 8,200,000 cattle, 1,800,000 asses, 350,000 horses, 74,000,000 chickens; roundwood 6,739,000 cu m; fish catch (1983) 34,500. Mining and quarrying (1984): iron ore 850,000; copper ore 150,000; kaolin 100,000; barite 90,000; chromium ore (oxide content) 50,000; zinc ore 50,000; lead 28,000. Manufacturing (value in Rls; 1983–84): machinery 513,148,000,000; textiles 388,755,000,000; chemicals 226,085,000,000; iron and steel 135,688,000,000. Construction (1983–84): residential 21,065,000 sq m; nonresidential 1,448,000 sq m. Energy production (consumption): electricity (kW-hr; 1983) 37,168,000,000 (37,168,000,000); coal (metric tons; 1984) 850,000 (900,000); crude petroleum (barrels; 1984) 808,741,000 (255,542,000); petroleum products (metric tons; 1984) 31,690,000 (31,400,000); natural gas (cu m; 1984) 8,314,000,000 (8,314,000,000).
Gross national product (at current market prices; 1984): U.S.$162,710,725,893 (U.S.$3,770 per capita).

Structure of gross domestic product and labour force

	1983 in value Rls '000,000	1983 % of total value	1976 labour force	1976 % of labour force
Agriculture	2,138.5	15.6	2,755,680	36.3
Mining	1,951.8	14.2	89,875	1.2
Manufacturing	1,072.9	7.8	1,027,506	13.5
Construction	1,088.6	7.9	1,169,056	15.4
Public utilities	90.9	0.7	59,718	0.8
Transp. and commun.	947.6	6.9	424,919	5.6
Trade	2,842.8	20.7	651,940	8.6
Finance	1,627.5	11.8	90,837	1.2
Services	782.0	5.7	520,508	6.9
Pub. admin., defense } Other }	1,200.2	8.7	733,066	9.7
			61,188	0.8
TOTAL	13,742.8	100.0	7,584,293	100.0

Population economically active (1983–84): total 11,969,000; activity rate of total population 28.4% (participation rates: over age 10, 86.1%; female [1981] 15.4%; unemployed 13.9%).

Price and earnings indexes (1980 = 100)

	1980	1981	1982	1983	1984	1985	1986†
Consumer price index*	100.0	124.2	147.4	176.5	198.6	207.4	227.2
Monthly earnings index‡	100.0	108.9	19.7	138.1	158.8	180.3	...

Household income and expenditure. Average household size (1984–85) 4.2; income per household (1975) Rls 298,761 (U.S.$4,235); sources of income: wages 40.8%, self-employment 28.2%, assistance 4.5%; expenditure* (1982–83): food and tobacco 40.9%, housing and energy 25.7%, clothing and footwear 7.5%, transportation 6.9%, furniture and household equipment 6.5%.
Land use (1983): forested 11.0%; meadows and pastures 26.9%; agricultural and under permanent cultivation 8.4%; other 53.7%.

Foreign trade

Balance of trade (current prices)§

	1980	1981	1982	1983	1984	1985
Rls '000,000	+228,200	+119,200	+587,500	+275,800	−65.1	+303.5
% of total	12.9%	6.5%	27.0%	8.9%	2.8%	14.2%

Imports (1983–84): Rls 1,582,719,000,000 (machinery and transport equipment 35.1%, food and live animals 12.5%, chemicals 11.8%). *Major import sources* (1985): West Germany 16.3%; Japan 13.4%; United Kingdom 6.7%; Italy 6.0%; Singapore 3.9%; Australia 2.1%.
Exports (1985): Rls 1,218,600,000,000 (petroleum and petroleum products 98.0%). *Major export destinations* (1985): Japan 16.5%; Italy 9.8%; Spain 5.8%; France 5.2%; United States 5.0%; West Germany 4.2%.

Transport and communications

Transport. Railroads (1984–85): route length 2,837 mi, 4,567 km; passenger journeys 7,200,000; freight carried 10,600,000 tons. Roads (1983): total length 67,710 mi, 108,970 km (paved 31%). Vehicles (1981): passenger cars 1,532,269; trucks and buses 313,006. Merchant marine (1985): vessels (100 gross tons and over) 347; total deadweight tonnage 3,864,513. Air transport (1985): passenger-mi 2,468,000,000, passenger-km 3,972,000,000; short ton-mi cargo 78,462,000, metric ton-km cargo 114,552,000; airports (1986) 13.
Communications. Daily newspapers (1984): 14; circulation 962,000 ‖ ; circulation per 1,000 population 22.2 ‖ . Radio (1985): total receivers 10,000,000 (1 per 4.5 persons). Television (1985): total receivers 2,085,000 (1 per 19.4 persons). Telephones (1983): 2,118,080 (1 per 19.1 persons).

Education and health

Education (1985–86)

	schools	teachers	students	student/ teacher ratio
Primary (age 7–11)	48,982	268,606	6,343,300	23.6
Secondary (age 12–18)	13,818	167,769	2,922,576	17.4
Voc., teacher tr.	1,325	20,683	277,609	13.4
Higher	114¶	13,698	145,809	10.6

Educational attainment (1976). Percent of population over age 10 having: no formal schooling 16.1%; Qur'anic education 10.7%; primary education 43.0%; secondary 23.7%; higher 6.4%; certificate not reported 0.1%. *Literacy* (1980): total population over age 15 literate 10,980,000 (42.8%); males literate 7,163,000 (55.4%); females literate 3,817,000 (30.1%).
Health: physicians (1982–83) 15,945 (1 per 2,582 persons); hospital beds (1984–85) 70,152 (1 per 616 persons); infant mortality rate per 1,000 live births (1985) 111.
Food (1978–80): daily per capita caloric intake 2,912 (vegetable products 90%, animal products 10%); 121% of FAO recommended minimum requirement.

Military

Total active duty personnel (1985): 555,000 (revolutionary guard corps 45.1%, army 45.0%, navy 3.6%, air force 6.3%). *Military expenditure as percent of GNP* (1983): 5.0% (world 6.1%); per capita expenditure U.S.$124.

*For urban areas only. †April. ‡Compensation paid to employees in large manufacturing establishments. §Imports derived from the Direction of Trade Statistics (DOTS). ‖ Circulation based on 10 dailies only. ¶1982–83.

Iraq

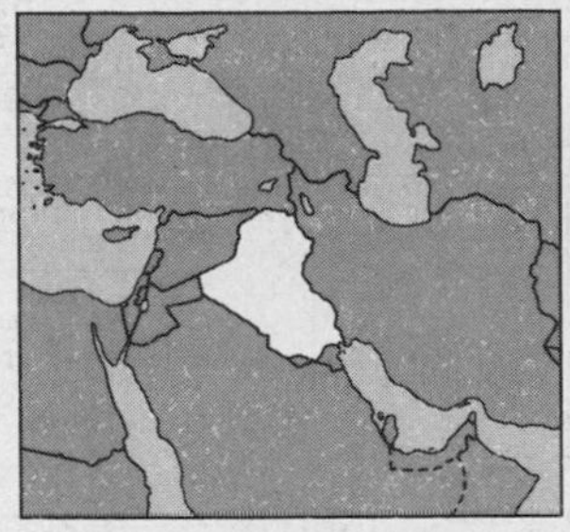

Official name: al-Jumhūrīyah al-ʿIrāqīyah (Republic of Iraq).
Form of government: unitary single-party republic with one legislative house (National Assembly [250]).
Head of state and government: President.
Capital: Baghdād.
Official language: Arabic.
Official religion: Islam.
Monetary unit: 1 Iraqi dinar (ID) = 20 dirhams = 1,000 fils; valuation (Oct. 1, 1986) 1 ID = U.S.$3.22; 1 ID = £2.23.

Area and population

		area*		population
		sq mi	sq km	1985 estimate
Governorates	**Capitals**			
al-Anbār	ar-Ramādī	53,175	137,723	582,058
Bābil	al-Ḥillah	2,030	5,258	739,031
Baghdād	Baghdād	1,992	5,159	4,648,609
al-Başrah	Basra	7,363	19,070	1,304,153
Dhī Qār	an-Nāṣirīyah	5,261	13,626	725,913
Diyālā	Baʿqūbah	7,449	19,292	691,350
Karbalā'	Karbalā'	1,944	5,034	329,234
Maysān	al-ʿAmārah	5,445	14,103	411,843
al-Muthannā	as-Samāwah	19,702	51,029	253,816
an-Najaf	an-Najaf	10,751	27,844	472,103
Nīnawā	Mosul	14,555	37,698	1,358,082
al-Qādisiyah	ad-Dīwānīyah	3,285	8,507	511,799
Şalāḥ ad-Dīn	Sāmarrā'	11,198	29,004	442,782
at-Ta'mīm	Kirkūk	4,012	10,391	650,965
Wasiṭ	al-Kūt	6,683	17,308	483,716
Kurdish Autonomous Region				
Dahūk	Dahūk	2,363	6,120	330,356
Irbīl	Irbīl	5,587	14,471	742.682
as-Sulaymānīyah	as-Sulaymānīyah	6,083	15,756	906,495
LAND AREA		168,878	437,393	15,584,987
INLAND WATER		357	924	
TOTAL AREA		169,235	438,317	

Demography

Population (1986): 15,946,000.
Density (1986): persons per sq mi 94.4, persons per sq km 36.5.
Urban-rural (1984): urban 66.0%; rural 34.0%.
Sex distribution (1984): male 51.44%; female 48.56%.
Age breakdown (1984): under 15, 45.7%; 15–29, 27.6%; 30–44, 13.8%; 45–59, 7.6%; 60–74, 3.9%; 75 and over, 1.4%.
Population projection: (1990) 18,136,000; (2000) 24,198,000.
Doubling time: 21 years.
Ethnic composition (1978): Arab 76.9%; Kurd 18.6%; Turkmen 1.5%; Persian 1.3%; Assyrian 0.8%; other 0.9%.
Religious affiliation (1980): Muslim 95.8% (of which Shīʿī 53.5%, Sunnī 42.3%); Christian 3.5%; other 0.7%.
Major cities (1985): Baghdād 3,400,000†; Dahūk 570,926; Basra 616,700; Mosul 570,926.

Vital statistics

Birth rate per 1,000 population (1980–85): 45.1 (world avg. 29.0).
Death rate per 1,000 population (1980–85): 11.5 (world avg. 11.0).
Natural increase rate per 1,000 population (1980–85): 33.6 (world avg. 18.0).
Total fertility rate (avg. births per childbearing woman; 1980–85): 6.7.
Marriage rate per 1,000 population (1982): 4.0.
Divorce rate per 1,000 population (1981): 0.1.
Life expectancy at birth (1980–85): male 55.9 years; female 59.1 years.
Major causes of death per 100,000 population (1975): heart disease (except ischemic) 69.9; accidents (all types) 27.6; pneumonia 27.2; malignant neoplasms (cancers) 19.6; during the early 1980s, however, there were high war casualities and high incidence of trachoma, influenza, measles, whooping cough, and tuberculosis.

National economy

Budget (1981). Revenue: ID 5,025,000,000 (revenue from oil and public enterprises 88.5%, sales tax 7.7%, income tax 1.3%). Expenditures: ID 5,025,000,000 (economic services 44.9%, defense 24.0%, local government 8.3%, internal security 5.2%, health 4.6%, education 2.9%).
Public debt (external, outstanding; 1980): U.S.$481,000,000.
Tourism (1981): receipts from visitors U.S.$170,000,000; expenditures by nationals abroad, n.a.
Production (metric tons except as noted). Agriculture, forestry, fishing (1984): wheat 300,000, barley 300,000, sugarcane 200,000†, potatoes 110,000†, rice 95,000, corn (maize) 90,000, eggs 22,000,000, milk 1,125,000; livestock (number of live animals) 8,300,000 sheep, 3,000,000 cattle, 2,300,000 goats, 250,000 camels, 250,000† buffalo, 45,000,000 poultry; roundwood 137,000 cu m; fish catch 26,219†. Mining and quarrying (1983): elemental sulfur 340,000; gypsum 170,000; salt 80,000. Manufacturing (1983): cement 5,600,000; paper and paperboard 12,186‡; beer 669,390 hectolitres‡. Construction (1983): authorized residential 9,338,000 sq m; authorized nonresidential 823,000 sq m. Energy production (consumption): electricity (kW-hr; 1984) 18,460,000,000 (18,460,000,000); coal, n.a. (n.a.); crude petroleum (barrels; 1984) 442,824,000 (71,944,000); petroleum products (metric tons; 1984) 8,110,000 (5,260,000); natural gas (cu m; 1984) 276,774,000 (276,774,000).
Gross national product (at current market prices; 1981): U.S.$31,300,000,000 (U.S.$2,300 per capita).

Structure of gross domestic product and labour force

	1982		1984	
	in value ID '000,000	% of total value	labour force	% of labour force
Agriculture	1,277.8	10.0	1,121,523	29.7
Mining	2,962.6	23.3	47,356	1.2
Manufacturing	875.1	6.9	351,391	9.3
Construction	2,080.6	16.3	387,876	10.2
Public utilities	65.0	0.5	30,327	0.8
Transportation and communication	1,102.1	8.7	229,289	6.1
Trade	1,478.7	11.6	285,953	7.6
Finance	826.2	6.5	40,272	1.1
Pub. admin., defense	...	... }	1,252,184	33.1
Services	2,230.3	17.5 }		
Other	−169.9§	−1.3§	33,800 ‖	0.9 ‖
TOTAL	12,728.5	100.0	3,779,971	100.0

Population economically active (1984): total 3,779,971; activity rate of total population 25.1% (participation rates: over age 15, 46.1%; female 15.1%; unemployed 0.9%).

Price and earnings indexes (1973 = 100)

	1981	1982	1983
Consumer price index	129.4	157.9	177.1
Earnings index	...	...	...

Household income and expenditure. Average household size (1984) 6.9; average annual income per household: n.a.; source of income: n.a.; expenditure (1971–72): food and beverages 55.4%, housing 18.2%, clothing and footwear 10.3%, transport and communications 5.3%, medical care and health 2.4%, recreation 1.2%.
Land use (1982): forested 3.4%; meadows and pastures 9.2%; agricultural and under permanent cultivation 12.6%; built-on, wasteland, and other 74.8%.

Foreign trade¶

Balance of trade (current prices)

	1977	1978	1979	1980	1981
ID '000,000	+1,668	+2,155	+4,776	+5,789	+1,026
% of total	41.4%	49.2%	60.6%	59.5%	19.8%

Imports (1981): ID 2,333,845,000 (machines electrical and nonelectrical, airplanes, and other 63.2%; consumer goods 20.7%; chemical and pharmaceutical products 3.4%). *Major import sources* (1984): West Germany 9.7%; Japan 9.0%; France 7.7%; United States 7.5%.
Exports (1981): ID 16,859,000 (foodstuffs 55.9%; rubber, paper, and fertilizers 23.0%). *Major export destinations* (1984): Brazil 20.7%; Yugoslavia 11.3%; Italy 9.5%; France 7.3%.

Transport and communications

Transport. Railroads (1983): route length 1,516 mi, 2,439 km; passenger-mi 34,087,000, passenger-km 54,858,000; short ton-mi cargo 777,285,000, metric ton-km cargo 1,134,817,000. Roads (1981): total length 15,699 mi, 25,265 km (paved 65%). Vehicles (1981): passenger cars 229,530; trucks and buses 152,768. Merchant marine (1985): vessels (100 gross tons and over) 148; total deadweight tonnage 1,685,917. Air transport (1982): passenger-mi 917,000,000, passenger-km 1,476,000,000; short ton-mi cargo 37,463,000, metric ton-km cargo 54,696,000; airports (1986) with scheduled flights 3.
Communications. Daily newspapers (1985): total number 6; total circulation 324,000; circulation per 1,000 population 21. Radio (1985): total number of receivers 2,200,000 (1 per 7 persons). Television (1985): total number of receivers 600,000 (1 per 26 persons). Telephones (1983): 624,685 (1 per 23 persons).

Education and health

Education (1984–85)

	schools	teachers	students	student/ teacher ratio
Primary (age 6–11)	10,463	119,734	2,827,109	23.6
Secondary (age 12–17)	2,109	33,466	996,622	29.8
Voc., teacher tr.	228	6,266	106,312	17.0
Higher	25♀	6,952	116,179	16.7

Educational attainment, n.a. *Literacy* (1984): total population over age 15 literate 2,815,895 (45.9%); males literate 2,034,011 (65.9%); females literate 781,884 (26.0%).
Health (1982): physicians 7,634 (1 per 1,773 persons); hospital beds 24,772 (1 per 570 persons); infant mortality rate per 1,000 live births (1984) 81.8.
Food (1979–81): daily per capita caloric intake 2,789 (vegetable products 88%, animal products 12%); 116% of FAO recommended minimum requirement.

Military

Total active duty personnel (1985): 520,000 (army 91.3%, navy 1.0%, air force 7.7%). *Military expenditure as percent of GNP* (1983): 47.2% (world 6.1%); per capita expenditure U.S.$787.

*Excluding Iraq–Saudi Arabia Neutral Zone. †1983. ‡1981. §Less indirect taxes. ‖Unemployed. ¶Balance of trade is based on f.o.b. (free on board) valuation of imports and exports; however, commodities traded and trade partners information are based on c.i.f. (cost, insurance, and freight). ♀1982–83.

Ireland

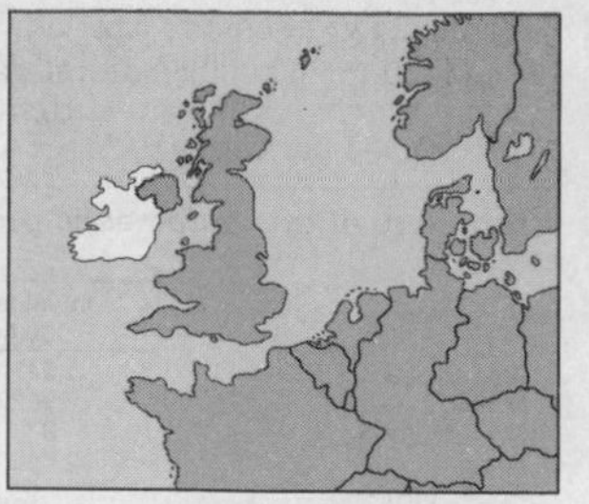

Official name: Éire (Irish); Ireland* (English).
Form of government: unitary multiparty republic with two legislative houses (Senate [60]; House of Representatives [166]).
Chief of state: President.
Head of government: Prime Minister.
Capital: Dublin.
Official languages: Irish; English.
Official religion: Roman Catholic.
Monetary unit: 1 Irish pound (I£) = 100 new pence; valuation (Oct. 1, 1986) 1 I£ = U.S.$1.35 = £0.94.

Area and population	area		population
Provinces / Counties	sq mi	sq km	1986 census
Connacht	6,611	17,122	430,726
Galway†	2,293	5,940	178,180
Leitrim	581	1,525	27,000
Mayo	2,084	5,398	115,016
Roscommon	951	2,463	54,551
Sligo	693	1,796	55,979
Leinster	7,580	19,633	1,851,134
Carlow	346	896	40,958
Dublin†	356	922	1,020,796
Kildare	654	1,694	116,015
Kilkenny	796	2,062	73,094
Laoighis	664	1,719	53,270
Longford	403	1,044	31,491
Louth	318	823	91,698
Meath	902	2,336	103,762
Offaly	771	1,998	59,806
Westmeath	681	1,763	63,306
Wexford	908	2,351	102,456
Wicklow	782	2,025	94,482
Munster	9,315	24,127	1,019,694
Clare	1,231	3,188	91,343
Cork†	2,880	7,460	412,623
Kerry	1,815	4,701	123,922
Limerick†	1,037	2,686	164,204
Tipperary North Riding	771	1,996	59,453
Tipperary South Riding	872	2,258	77,051
Waterford†	710	1,838	91,098
Ulster	3,093	8,012	235,641
Cavan	730	1,891	53,881
Donegal	1,865	4,830	129,428
Monaghan	498	1,291	52,332
TOTAL LAND AREA	26,600	68,895‡	3,537,195
INLAND WATER	537	1,390	
TOTAL AREA	27,137	70,285	

Demography

Population (1986): 3,547,000.
Density (1986): persons per sq mi 133.3, persons per sq km 51.5.
Urban-rural (1985): urban 57.0%; rural 43.0%.
Sex distribution (1985): male 50.06%; female 49.94%.
Age breakdown (1985): under 15, 30.5%; 15–29, 24.4%; 30–44, 17.4%; 45–59, 12.7%; 60–74, 10.8%; 75 and over, 4.2%.
Population projection: (1990) 3,676,000; (2000) 4,021,000.
Doubling time: 77 years.
Ethnic composition (1981): more than 94% Irish nationality.
Religious affiliation (1983): Catholic 94.0%; Anglican 4.0%; other 2.0%.
Major cities§ (1986): Dublin 502,337; Cork 133,196; Limerick 56,241; Galway 47,008; Waterford 39,516.

Vital statistics

Birth rate per 1,000 population (1985): 17.6 (world avg. 29.0); (1980) legitimate 95.0%; illegitimate 5.0%.
Death rate per 1,000 population (1985): 9.4 (world avg. 11.0).
Natural increase rate per 1,000 population (1985): 8.2 (world avg. 18.0).
Total fertility rate (avg. births per childbearing woman; 1980–85): 3.2.
Marriage rate per 1,000 population (1985): 5.2.
Life expectancy at birth (1980–85): male 70.4 years; female 75.7 years.
Major causes of death per 100,000 population (1984): heart and circulatory diseases 454.3; malignant neoplasms (cancers) 189.2; pneumonia 57.8.

National economy

Budget (1985). Revenue: I£6,400,000,000 (income taxes 33.3%, value-added tax 23.2%, excise taxes 20.6%). Expenditures: I£7,634,000,000 (debt service 26.1%, social welfare 18.2%, health 12.5%, education 11.1%, defense 3.6%).
Public debt (1986): U.S.$21,133,710,000.
Tourism: receipts from visitors (1984) U.S.$461,000,000; expenditures by nationals abroad (1981) U.S.$511,000,000.
Production (metric tons except as noted). Agriculture, forestry, fishing (1984): sugar beets 1,650,000, barley 1,600,000, potatoes 1,000,000, wheat 660,000, oats 140,000, milk 5,880,000; livestock (number of live animals) 6,759,000 cattle, 3,754,000 sheep, 1,117,000 pigs; roundwood (1983) 1,026,000 cu m; fish catch (1984) 207,615. Mining and quarrying (1985): gypsum 304,000; barite 213,000; zinc ore 191,700 ‖; lead ore 34,600 ‖. Manufacturing (value added in I£; 1981): food and beverages 950,200,000; machinery and transport equipment 619,900,000; chemical products 511,300,000; nonmetallic mineral products 181,700,000; textiles 160,100,000; printing and publishing 144,200,000. Construction (1984): residential 2,461,000 sq m. Energy production (consumption): electricity (kW-hr; 1984) 11,568,000 (11,568,000); coal (metric tons; 1984) n.a. (1,386,000); crude petroleum (barrels; 1984) none (8,670,000); petroleum products (metric tons; 1984) 1,235,000 (3,777,000); natural gas (cu m; 1984) 2,207,200,000 (2,207,300,000).
Gross national product (1984): U.S.$17,500,000,000 (U.S.$4,950 per capita).

Structure of gross domestic product and labour force

	1985		1984	
	in value I£'000,000	% of total value	labour force	% of labour force
Agriculture	1,660	10.7	182,000	13.9
Mining	5,475	35.4	10,000	0.8
Manufacturing			212,000	16.1
Construction			83,000	6.3
Public utilities			15,000	1.1
Transp. and commun.	2,957	19.1	69,000	5.2
Trade			212,000¶	16.1
Pub. admin., defense	1,063	6.9	73,000	5.6
Services	4,303	27.8	...♀	...
Finance			...¶	...
Other			458,000♂	34.9
TOTAL	15,458	100.0‡	1,314,000	100.0

Population economically active (1983): total 1,473,000; activity rate of total population 42.2% (participation rates: ages 15–64, 56.1%; female 29.7%; unemployed 14.1%).

Price and earnings indexes (1980 = 100)

	1980	1981	1982	1983	1984	1985	1986□
Consumer price index	100.0	120.4	141.0	155.8	169.2	178.4	185.5
Weekly earnings index	100.0	116.7	131.7	147.1	165.1	177.5	...

Household income and expenditure. Average household size (1983) 3.9; income per household: n.a.; sources of income (1983): wages and salaries 60.4%, self-employment 15.8%, interest and dividends 4.5%; expenditure (1983): food 39.0%, rent and household goods 19.4%, transportation 11.9%.
Land use (1983): forest 4.9%; pasture 70.5%; agricultural 14.1%; other 10.5%.

Foreign trade

Balance of trade (current prices)

	1980	1981	1982	1983	1984	1985
I£'000,000	−1,342	−1,698	−1,120	−420	−15.3	+862
% of total	14.3%	15.1%	9.1%	2.9%	0.1%	4.6%

Imports (1984): I£8,912,900,000 (machinery and transport equipment 31.2%, chemical products 11.6%, petroleum and petroleum products 11.0%, food products 3.9%, textiles 3.6%, paper and paper products 2.8%, iron and steel 1.9%). *Major import sources:* United Kingdom 42.9%; United States 16.5%; West Germany 7.6%; France 4.8%; The Netherlands 3.8%; Japan 3.4%.
Exports (1984): I£8,897,600,000 (machinery and transport equipment 28.7%, of which office machinery and data-processing equipment 17.3%, electrical machinery 6.1%; food and beverages 23.2%, of which meat and meat products 6.0%, dairy products 5.3%). *Major export destinations:* United Kingdom 34.4%; West Germany 10.2%; United States 9.7%; France 8.4%.

Transport and communications

Transport. Railroads (1984): route length (1986) 1,205 mi, 1,940 km; passenger-km 816,000,000; metric ton-km cargo 552,000,000. Roads (1984): total length 57,354 mi, 92,303 km (paved 94%). Vehicles (1984): passenger cars 711,098; trucks and buses 88,040. Merchant marine (1985): vessels (100 gross tons and over) 152; total deadweight tonnage 226,548. Air transport (1985): passenger-km 2,460,000,000; metric ton-km cargo 85,692,000; airports (1986) 5.
Communications. Daily newspapers (1983): 10; circulation 939,000; circulation per 1,000 population 269. Radio (1985): total number of receivers 2,050,000 (1 per 1.7 persons). Television (1985): total number of receivers 851,000 (1 per 4.1 persons). Telephones (1983): 779,600 (1 per 4.5 persons).

Education and health

Education (1983–84)

	schools	teachers	students	student/teacher ratio
Primary (age 6–14)	3,385	20,732	563,509	27.2
Secondary (age 12–18)	568	14,012	243,778	17.4
Voc., teacher tr.	256	5,100	79,131	15.5
Higher	26	3,690	45,910	12.4

Educational attainment (1981). Percent of population over age 14 having: primary education 45.6%; secondary 27.3%; some postsecondary 19.4%; university or like institution 7.6%. *Literacy* (1985): virtually 100% literate.
Health (1984): physicians 4,250 (1 per 830 persons); hospital beds (1980) 33,028 (1 per 103 persons); infant mortality rate per 1,000 live births 10.1.
Food (1980–82): daily per capita caloric intake 3,970 (vegetable products 62%, animal products 38%); 143% of FAO recommended minimum requirement.

Military

Total active duty personnel (1986): 13,984 (army 87.8%, navy 6.8%, air force 5.4%). *Military expenditure as percent of GNP* (1984): 1.6% (world 6.1%); per capita expenditure U.S.$80.

*As provided by the constitution; the 1948 Republic of Ireland Act provides precedent for this longer formulation of the official name but, per official sources, "has not changed the usage *Ireland* as the name of the state in the English language." †Includes county borough(-s). ‡Detail does not add to total given because of rounding. §County boroughs. ‖ Metal content only. ¶Trade includes Finance. ♀Other includes Services. ♂Includes unemployed. □May.

Israel

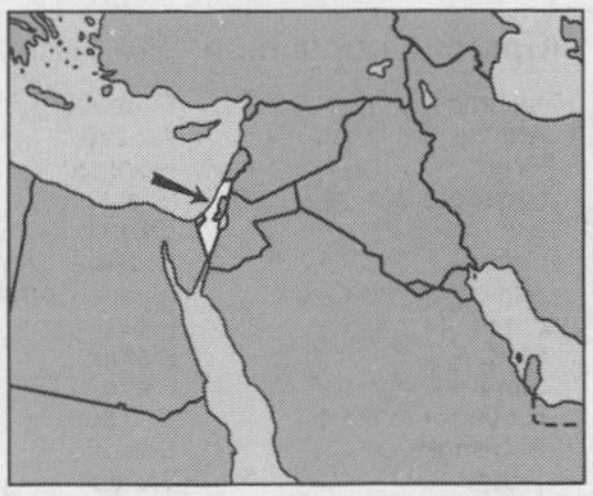

Official name: Medinat Yisra'el (Hebrew); Isrā'īl (Arabic) (State of Israel).
Form of government: multiparty republic with one legislative house (Knesset [120]).
Chief of state: President.
Head of government: Prime Minister.
Capital: Jerusalem is the proclaimed capital of Israel (from Jan. 23, 1950) and the actual seat of government, but recognition of its status as capital by the international community has largely been withheld pending final settlement of territorial and other issues through peace talks between Israel and the Arab parties concerned.
Official languages: Hebrew; Arabic.
Official religion: none.
Monetary unit: 1 Israeli sheqel (IS) = 100 agorot; valuation (Oct. 1, 1986) 1 U.S.$ = IS 1.49; 1 £ = IS 2.15.

Area and population

Districts	Capitals	area* sq mi	area* sq km	population 1983 census†
Central (Ha Merkaz)	Ramla	479	1,242	830,700
Haifa (Ḥefa)	Haifa	330	854	575,300
Jerusalem (Yerushalayim)	Jerusalem	215	557	472,900
Northern (Ha Ẕafon)	Tiberias	1,347	3,490	656,000
Southern (Ha Darom)	Beersheba	5,555	14,387	478,800
Tel Aviv	Tel Aviv–Yafo	66	170	1,000,200
TOTAL		7,992	20,700	4,037,600

Demography†

Population (1986): 4,381,000.
*Density** (1986): persons per sq mi 548.2, persons per sq km 211.6.
Urban-rural (1983): urban 86.9%; rural 13.1%.
Sex distribution (1984): male 49.91%; female 50.09%.
Age breakdown (1984): under 15, 32.6%; 15–29, 24.6%; 30–44, 18.4%; 45–59, 12.0%; 60–74, 9.2%; 75 and over, 3.2%.
Population projection‡: (1990) 4,638,800; (2000) 5,339,600.
Doubling time: 41 years.
Ethnic composition (1980): Jewish 83.1%; Arab 16.7%; other 0.2%.
Religious affiliation (1984): Jewish 82.7%; Muslim (mostly Sunnī) 13.3%; Christian 2.3%; Druze and other 1.7%.
Major cities (1983): Jerusalem 431,800; Tel Aviv–Yafo 330,400; Haifa 227,900; Ḥolon 133,900; Bat Yam 129,700.

Vital statistics†

Birth rate per 1,000 population (1985): 23.5 (world avg. 29.0); (1980) legitimate 97.5%; illegitimate 2.5%.
Death rate per 1,000 population (1985): 6.6 (world avg. 11.0).
Natural increase rate per 1,000 population (1985): 16.9 (world avg. 18.0).
Total fertility rate (avg. births per childbearing woman; 1984): 2.8.
Marriage rate per 1,000 population (1985): 6.9.
Divorce rate per 1,000 population (1985): 1.2.
Life expectancy at birth (1983): male 72.8 years; female 76.2 years.
Major causes of death per 100,000 population (1983): heart disease 195.6; malignant neoplasms (cancers) 124.6; cerebrovascular disease 74.8.

National economy

Budget (1985–86). Revenue: IS 11,156,500,000,000 (direct taxes 42.4%; indirect taxes 22.7%). Expenditures: IS 12,806,500,000,000 (consumption expenditure 45.6%; interest on loans 35.2%; subsidies 10.8%, of which on credit 3.7%, on exports 3.6%, on price stabilization 3.5%).
Tourism (1985): receipts from visitors U.S.$1,109,000,000; expenditures by nationals abroad U.S.$531,000,000.
Production (metric tons except as noted). Agriculture, forestry, fishing (1984): oranges 921,000, tomatoes 359,000, potatoes 207,000, wheat 130,000, apples 118,000, watermelons 82,000, lemons and limes 62,000, cucumbers 59,000, onions 57,000, grapes 43,000; livestock (number of live animals) 330,000 cattle, 240,000 sheep, 115,000 goats, 26,000,000 chickens; roundwood 118,000 cu m; fish catch 22,402§. Mining and quarrying (1984–85): phosphate rock 2,250,000; potash 1,825,000; phosphoric acid 150,000; bromine and bromine compounds 136,000; periclase 47,000. Manufacturing (1985): wheat flour 508,000; polyethylene 73,879; ammonium sulfate 60,389; writing and printing paper 53,899; cardboard 45,746; tires 31,316; cotton yarn 15,235. Construction (1985): residential 2,816,000 sq m; nonresidential 1,380,000 sq m. Energy production (consumption): electricity (kW-hr; 1985) 15,697,800,000 (15,400,400,000); coal (metric tons; 1984) none (2,678,300); crude petroleum (barrels; 1985) 65,237 (51,700,000); petroleum products (metric tons; 1984) 6,084,000 (4,928,000); natural gas (cu m; 1984) 53,300,000 (53,300,000).
Land use (1983): forested 5.7%; meadows and pastures 40.2%; agricultural and under permanent cultivation 21.5%, other 32.6%.
Population economically active (1985) ‖: total 1,444,000; activity rate of total population 33.7% (participation rates: over age 14, 73.9%; female 34.7%; unemployed 5.9%).

Price and earnings indexes (1980 = 100)

	1980	1981	1982	1983	1984	1985	1986¶
Consumer price index	100.0	216.8	477.8	1,173.5	5,560.4	22,498	32,265
Monthly earnings index	100.0	245.4	553.8	1,414.8	7,028.0	24,789	37,879

Public debt (external, outstanding; 1984): U.S.$15,415,200,000.
Gross national product (1984): U.S.$21,290,000,000 (U.S.$5,070 per capita).

Structure of gross domestic product and labour force

	1984 in value IS '000,000	1984 % of total value	1985 labour force	1985 % of labour force
Agriculture	227,025	3.8	76,700	5.6
Manufacturing, mining	1,306,831	21.8	309,800	22.6
Construction	427,236 }	7.1	72,300	5.3
Public utilities			13,000	0.9
Transp. and commun.	388,128	6.5	83,800	6.1
Trade	735,259	12.3	164,100	12.0
Finance	1,411,936	23.6	133,400	9.7
Public and community services	1,330,747	22.2	411,200	30.0
Services, other	163,350	2.7	105,400	7.8
TOTAL	5,990,512	100.0	1,369,700	100.0

Household income and expenditure. Average urban household size (1984) 3.7; monthly income per household IS 470,900 (U.S.$938); sources of income (1984): salaries and wages 90.8%, property, interest and dividends, pensions, allowances and assistance 8.4%, self-employment 0.8%; expenditure (1984): food, beverages, and tobacco 26.2%, housing and furnishings 26.0%, clothing, footwear, and personal effects 4.5%, fuel and light 4.0%, transportation 2.9%, other goods and services 36.4%.

Foreign trade

Balance of trade (current prices)

	1980	1981	1982	1983	1984	1985
IS '000,000	−16,310	−40,089	−68,787	−212,187	−1,198	−3,716
% of total	21.5%	22.9%	21.2%	26.2%	26.0%	20.1%

Imports (1985): US$8,319,600,000 (fuel and lubricants 18.2%; investment goods 17.0%; diamonds 15.5%; foodstuffs 2.8%). *Major import sources:* United States 20.2%; West Germany 10.8%; United Kingdom 9.1%; Switzerland 6.6%; Francc 3.6%.
Exports (1985): US$6,256,400,000 (metals, machinery, and electronics 30.8%; diamonds 22.9%; agricultural products 7.5%; food, beverages, and tobacco 6.1%; textiles, clothing, and leather 6.1%). *Major export destinations:* United States 34.2%; United Kingdom 7.6%; West Germany 5.3%; The Netherlands 4.4%; France 4.2%; Italy 4.0%.

Transport and communications

Transport. Railroads (1986): route length 323 mi, 520 km; passenger-mi 127,000,000, passenger-km 205,000,000; short ton-mi cargo 645,400,000, metric ton-km cargo 942,200,000. Roads (1984): total length 7,848 mi, 12,630 km (paved 100%). Vehicles (1984): passenger cars 599,294; trucks and buses 125,050. Merchant marine (1985): vessels (100 gross tons and over) 64; total deadweight tonnage 657,458. Air transport (1985): passenger-mi 337,000,000, passenger-km 542,000,000; short ton-mi cargo 33,936,000, metric ton-km cargo 49,546,000; airports (1986) with scheduled flights 4.
Communications. Daily newspapers (1985): total number 25; total circulation 843,000; circulation per 1,000 population 196. Radio (1985): 400,000 receivers (1 per 10.7 persons). Television (1985): 606,000 receivers (1 per 7.1 persons). Telephones (1983): 1,410,000 (1 per 2.9 persons).

Education and health

Education (1984–85)♀

	schools	teachers	students	student/teacher ratio
Primary (age 6–13)	1,853	46,266	621,858	13.4
Secondary (age 14–17)♂	542 }	38,193	235,062 }	8.6
Voc., teacher tr.	368 }		95,145 }	
Higher	7□	8,112◇	96,810	...

Educational attainment (1984). Percent of population over age 14 having: no formal schooling 6.5%; primary education 24.5%; secondary 47.8%; higher 21.2%. *Literacy* (1979): total population over age 15 literate 2,412,200 (91.6%); males literate 1,241,900 (95.6%); females literate 1,170,300 (87.7%).
Health: physicians (1981) 10,200 (1 per 387 persons); hospital beds (1983) 26,402 (1 per 155 persons); infant mortality rate per 1,000 live births (1985) 12.3.
Food (1983–84): daily per capita caloric intake 3,036 (vegetable products 77%, animal products 23%); 119%△ of FAO recommended minimum.

Military

Total active duty personnel (1986): 149,000 (army 75.2%, navy 6.0%, air force 18.8%). *Military expenditure as percent of GNP* (1984): 24.4% (world [1983] 6.1%); per capita expenditure U.S.$1,380.

*Excluding West Bank, Gaza Strip, Golan Heights, and East Jerusalem. †De jure; includes population of East Jerusalem and about 23,700 Israeli residents living in occupied territories. ‡Based on migration balance of +5,000 per year in the 1980s and nil in the 1990s. §1983. ‖ Excludes armed forces; includes Israelis in occupied territories. ¶April. ♀Includes schools run by UNRWA in East Jerusalem. ♂Includes intermediate education age 12–14. □Universities only. ◇University full-time equivalents only. △1979–81.

Italy

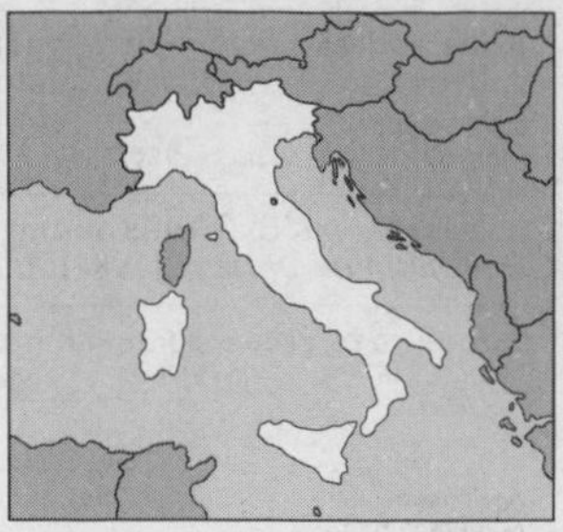

Official name: Repubblica Italiana (Italian Republic).
Form of government: republic with two legislative houses (Senate [323]; Chamber of Deputies [630]).
Chief of state: President.
Head of government: Prime Minister.
Capital: Rome.
Official language: Italian.
Official religion: none; Roman Catholicism disestablished 1985.
Monetary unit: 1 lira (Lit, plural lire) = 100 centesimi; valuation (Oct. 1, 1986) 1 U.S.$ = Lit 1,402; 1 £ = Lit 2,026.

Area and population

Regions / Provinces	Capitals	area sq mi	area sq km	population 1985 estimate
Abruzzi	L'Aquila	4,168	10,794	1,244,403
Chieti	Chieti	999	2,587	379,426
L'Aquila	L'Aquila	1,944	5,034	296,866
Pescara	Pescara	473	1,225	291,883
Teramo	Teramo	752	1,948	276,228
Basilicata	Potenza	3,858	9,992	617,265
Matera	Matera	1,331	3,447	206,464
Potenza	Potenza	2,527	6,545	410,801
Calabria	Catanzaro	5,823	15,080	2,116,749
Catanzaro	Catanzaro	2,026	5,247	764,527
Cosenza	Cosenza	2,568	6,650	766,219
Reggio di Calabria	Reggio di Calabria	1,229	3,183	586,003
Campania	Naples	5,249	13,595	5,607,718
Avellino	Avellino	1,078	2,792	443,426
Benevento	Benevento	800	2,071	294,250
Caserta	Caserta	1,019	2,639	788,100
Napoli	Naples	452	1,171	3,041,808
Salerno	Salerno	1,900	4,922	1,040,134
Emilia-Romagna	Bologna	8,542	22,123	3,947,140
Bologna	Bologna	1,429	3,702	922,423
Ferrara	Ferrara	1,016	2,632	376,561
Forlì	Forlì	1,123	2,910	606,444
Modena	Modena	1,039	2,690	596,505
Parma	Parma	1,332	3,449	398,938
Piacenza	Piacenza	1,000	2,589	276,063
Ravenna	Ravenna	718	1,859	355,530
Reggio nell'Emilia	Reggio nell'Emilia	885	2,292	414,676
Friuli-Venezia Giulia	Trieste	3,030	7,847	1,224,221
Gorizia	Gorizia	180	467	143,006
Pordenone	Pordenone	878	2,273	276,691
Trieste	Trieste	82	212	274,673
Udine	Udine	1,890	4,895	529,851
Lazio	Rome	6,642	17,203	5,080,060
Frosinone	Frosinone	1,251	3,239	473,834
Latina	Latina	869	2,251	453,028
Rieti	Rieti	1,061	2,749	144,607
Roma	Rome	2,066	5,352	3,735,020
Viterbo	Viterbo	1,395	3,612	273,571
Liguria	Genoa	708	5,416	1,778,024
Genova	Genoa	2,091	1,834	1,019,140
Imperia	Imperia	446	1,155	223,854
La Spezia	La Spezia	341	882	238,896
Savona	Savona	596	1,545	296,134
Lombardia	Milan	9,211	23,857	8,885,224
Bergamo	Bergamo	1,066	2,760	906,399
Brescia	Brescia	1,846	4,782	1,026,918
Como	Como	798	2,067	781,629
Cremona	Cremona	684	1,771	330,646
Mantova	Mantova	903	2,339	375,054
Milano	Milan	1,066	2,762	3,991,521
Pavia	Pavia	1,145	2,965	506,599
Sondrio	Sondrio	1,240	3,212	175,708
Varese	Varese	463	1,199	790,750
Marche	Ancona	3,743	9,694	1,424,378
Ancona	Ancona	749	1,940	437,604
Ascoli Piceno	Ascoli Piceno	806	2,087	357,094
Macerata	Macerata	1,071	2,774	294,176
Pesaro e Urbino	Pesaro	1,117	2,893	335,504
Molise	Campobasso	1,713	4,438	332,667
Campobasso	Campobasso	1,123	2,909	239,642
Isernia	Isernia	590	1,529	93,025
Piemonte	Turin	9,807	25,399	4,411,921
Alessandria	Alessandria	1,375	3,560	457,815
Asti	Asti	583	1,511	212,613
Cuneo	Cuneo	2,665	6,903	548,363
Novara	Novara	1,388	3,594	504,769
Torino	Turin	2,637	6,830	2,298,841
Vercelli	Vercelli	1,159	3,001	389,520
Puglia	Bari	7,470	19,348	3,978,058
Bari	Bari	1,980	5,129	1,498,529
Brindisi	Brindisi	710	1,838	402,508
Foggia	Foggia	2,774	7,185	695,047
Lecce	Lecce	1,065	2,759	793,749
Taranto	Taranto	941	2,437	588,225
Sardegna	Cagliari	9,301	24,090	1,628,690
Cagliari	Cagliari	2,662	6,895	749,942
Nuoro	Nuoro	2,720	7,044	276,758
Oristano	Oristano	1,016	2,631	158,339
Sassari	Sassari	2,903	7,520	443,651
Sicilia (Sicily)	Palermo	9,926	25,708	5,051,413
Agrigento	Agrigento	1,175	3,042	483,989
Caltanissetta	Caltanissetta	822	2,128	292,849
Catania	Catania	1,371	3,552	1,042,832
Enna	Enna	989	2,562	195,875
Messina	Messina	1,254	3,247	681,719
Palermo	Palermo	1,927	4,992	1,234,091
Ragusa	Ragusa	623	1,614	284,238
Siracusa	Siracusa	814	2,109	403,559
Trapani	Trapani	951	2,462	432,261

Area and population (continued)

Regions / Provinces	Capitals	area sq mi	area sq km	population 1985 estimate
Toscana	Florence	8,877	22,992	3,580,589
Arezzo	Arezzo	1,248	3,232	313,537
Firenze	Florence	1,498	3,879	1,199,988
Grosseto	Grosseto	1,739	4,504	220,672
Livorno	Livorno	468	1,213	347,108
Lucca	Lucca	684	1,773	384,428
Massa-Carrara	Massa-Carrara	447	1,157	205,503
Pisa	Pisa	945	2,448	389,422
Pistoia	Pistoia	373	965	265,493
Siena	Siena	1,475	3,821	254,438
Trentino-Alto Adige	Bolzano	5,259	13,620	877,205
Bolzano-Bozen	Bolzano	2,857	7,400	433,229
Trento	Trento	2,402	6,220	443,976
Umbria	Perugia	3,265	8,456	814,942
Perugia	Perugia	2,446	6,334	588,353
Terni	Terni	819	2,122	226,589
Valle d'Aosta	Aosta	1,259	3,262	113,587
Veneto	Venice	7,090	18,363	4,366,244
Belluno	Belluno	1,420	3,678	218,504
Padova	Padova	827	2,142	814,820
Rovigo	Rovigo	691	1,789	252,145
Treviso	Treviso	956	2,477	728,262
Venezia	Venice	950	2,460	839,088
Verona	Verona	1,195	3,096	780,195
Vicenza	Vicenza	1,051	2,721	733,230
TOTAL		116,324	301,277	57,080,498

Demography

Population (1986): 57,291,000.
Density (1986): persons per sq mi 492.5, persons per sq km 190.2.
Urban–rural (1985): urban 71.7%; rural 28.3%.
Sex distribution (1985): male 48.96%; female 51.04%.
Age breakdown (1985): under 15, 19.9%; 15–29, 22.8%; 30–44, 19.8%; 45–59, 18.7%; 60–74, 13.2%; 75 and over 5.6%.
Population projection: (1990) 57,400,000; (2000) 58,100,000.
Doubling time: n.a.; doubling time exceeds 100 years.
Ethnic composition (1980): Italian 98.1%; other 1.9%.
Religious affiliation (1980): Roman Catholic 83.2%; nonreligious 13.6%; atheist 2.6%; other 0.2%.
Major cities (1985): Rome 2,826,733; Milan 1,535,722; Naples 1,206,955; Turin 1,049,997; Genoa 746,785; Palermo 716,149; Bologna 442,307.
National origin (1980): Italian 98.1%; foreign 1.9%, of which Austrian 0.2%, French 0.2%, Slovene 0.2%, Albanian 0.1%, other 1.2%.
Mobility (1977). Population living in the same residence as in 1967: 52.0%.
Households. Average household size (1984) 3.0; composition of households (1981) 1 person 17.9%, 2 persons 23.6%, 3 persons 22.1%, 4 persons 21.5%, 5 persons 9.5%, 6 or more persons 5.4%. Family households (1981): 13,-088,040 (74.3%); nonfamily 4,527,088 (25.7%), of which 1-person 13.9%.
Immigration (1982): immigrants admitted 92,423, from Europe 76.9%, of which West Germany 34.3%, Switzerland 25.7%, France 6.0%; Africa 6.0%; Latin America 5.7%; United States 5.2%; Asia 2.6%.

Vital statistics

Birth rate per 1,000 population (1985): 10.1 (world avg. 29.0); (1984) legitimate 95.0%; illegitimate 5.0%.
Death rate per 1,000 population (1985): 9.5 (world avg. 11.0).
Natural increase rate per 1,000 population (1985): 0.6 (world avg. 18.0).
Total fertility rate (avg. births per childbearing woman; 1983): 1.5.
Marriage rate per 1,000 population (1984): 5.2.
Divorce rate per 1,000 population: (1984): 0.3.
Life expectancy at birth (1983): male 73.0 years; female 79.0 years.
Major causes of death per 100,000 population (1983): diseases of the circulatory system 459.0, of which myocardial infarction 72.4, ischemic heart disease 66.5; malignant neoplasms (cancers) 225.4; diseases of the respiratory system 69.0; diseases of the digestive system 55.3.

Social indicators

Educational attainment (1981). Percent of adult population having: less than full primary education 21.3%; primary 40.6%; junior secondary 23.8%; upper secondary 11.5%; 4-year higher degree 2.8%.

Distribution of income (1980)

percent of household income by quintile

1	2	3	4	5 (highest)
7.0	11.0	16.0	22.0	45.0

Quality of working life. Average workweek (1983): 38.5 hours. Annual rate per 100,000 workers (1978) for: injury or accident 5,928; industrial illness 405; death 66. Proportion of labour force insured for damages or income loss (1982) resulting from: injury 100%; permanent disability 100%; death 100%. Average days lost to labour stoppages per 1,000 workdays (1984): 0.8. Average duration of journey to work: n.a. Rate per 1,000 workers of discouraged (unemployed no longer seeking work; 1982): 0.9.
Access to services (1981). Proportion of dwellings having access to: electricity 99.5%; safe water supply 98.7%; toilet facilities 98.5%; bath facilities 86.4%.
Social participation. Eligible voters participating in last national election (1983): 89.0%. Population participating in voluntary work: n.a. Trade union membership in total workforce (1984): *c.* 70%. Practicing religious population in total affiliated population (1980): 65.7%, of which weekly 28.0%.
Social deviance (1984). Offense rate per 100,000 population for: murder 11.4; rape 60.2; other assault 48.9; theft, including burglary and housebreaking 2,313. Incidence per 100,000 in general population of: alcoholism (1978) 2.0; drug and substance abuse (1978) 25.1; suicide (1984) 5.6.
Leisure (1982). Favourite leisure activities (as percent of public spending on culture): cinema 35.6%; sporting events 16.3%; theatre 10.6%.

Material well-being. Rate per 1,000 of population possessing (1983): automobile 345; telephone 380. Households possessing (1979): television 72%; refrigerator 91%; air conditioner 9%; washing machine 88%.

National economy

Gross national product (at current market prices; 1984): U.S.$367,040,000,000 (U.S.$6,440 per capita).

Structure of gross domestic product and labour force

	1984			
	in value 000,000,000 lire	% of total value	labour force	% of labour force
Agriculture	32,294	5.3	2,426,000	10.4
Mining	20,060	3.3	206,000	0.9
Manufacturing	146,406	23.9	4,881,000	20.8
Construction	46,686	7.6	1,956,000	8.4
Public utilities	30,285	4.9	206,000	0.9
Transportation and communication	40,300	6.6	1,069,000	4.6
Trade	95,284	15.6	4,293,000	18.3
Finance	76,821	12.5	658,000	2.8
Pub. admin., defense	86,631	14.2	5,320,000	22.7
Services	48,999	8.0		
Other	−11,544*	−1.9*	2,390,000†	10.2†
TOTAL	612,112	100.0	23,405,000	100.0

Budget (1984). Revenue: Lit 203,529,000,000,000 (property and income taxes 44.9%, business taxes 23.5%, transfer payments 14.2%, sales taxes 9.6%). Expenditures: Lit 296,350,000,000,000 (social services 21.5%, regional and local subsidies 13.8%, education and culture 9.7%, transportation and communication 7.8%, national defense 4.5%).

Tourism (1984): receipts from visitors U.S.$8,595,000,000; expenditures by nationals abroad U.S.$2,098,000,000.

Manufacturing, mining, and construction enterprises (1981)

	no. of enterprises	no. of employees	hourly wages as a % of avg. of all wages	annual value added (Lit '000,000,000)
Transport equipment	730	402,000	117.7	10,388
Industrial chemicals	1,037	244,000	119.7	10,128
Machinery, nonelectrical	2,484	299,000	98.0	9,777
Electrical machinery	1,145	310,000	112.1	8,249
Pottery, ceramics, and glass	2,427	207,000	83.4	6,767
Iron and steel	872	236,000	122.6	6,702
Food products	1,607	172,000	92.2	6,429
Textiles	2,935	275,000	84.4	6,348
Metal products	2,379	197,000	86.7	5,734
Wearing apparel	1,729	165,000	75.8	3,157
Printing, publishing	776	85,000	103.2	3,075
Petroleum and gas	7	7,000	138.6	2,460
Plastic products	916	71,000	84.4	2,090
Paper and paper products	607	64,000	102.1	2,030
Nonmetal mining and quarrying	301	18,000	82.9	536
Construction	326,000	1,199,000	...	31,920

Production (metric tons except as noted). Agriculture, forestry, fishing (1984): sugar beets 11,591,400, grapes 11,300,000, wheat 10,136,700, corn (maize) 6,816,000, tomatoes 6,719,400, potatoes 2,519,300, olives 2,130,000, apples 2,036,600, oranges 1,945,800, barley 1,634,000, peaches 1,360,000, pears 1,069,000, rice 998,000; livestock (number of live animals) 9,113,000 cattle, 9,228,000 sheep, 9,187,000 pigs, 110,000,000 chickens; roundwood 80,444,000 cu m; fish catch 428,674. Mining and quarrying (1985): rock salt 3,175,700; potash 1,701,500; feldspar 1,116,400; asbestos 136,000; barite 127,200; magnesium 89,400; zinc 82,200; lead 25,000. Manufacturing (1985): cement 37,152,000; crude steel 23,784,000; pig iron 12,036,000; olive oil 3,900,000‡; plastics and resins 2,640,000; sulfuric acid 2,520,000; pasta 2,485,000‡; chemical fertilizers 1,830,000§; caustic soda 1,031,000; soaps and detergents 1,058,600‡; textiles and cloth 253,400§; wine 71,200,000 hectolitres ‖; beer 9,333,000 hectolitres ‖; 2,437,300 motorized road vehicles, of which 1,395,500 automobiles, 853,900 motorcycles, scooters, and mopeds‡, 187,800 trucks and buses; 331,500,000 pairs of shoes‡; 50,000,000 women's dresses‡. Construction (buildings completed 1984): residential 199,701; commercial, industrial, and other 7,359.

Service enterprises (1981)

	no. of enterprises	no. of employees	hourly wage as a % of all wages	annual value added (Lit '000,000,000)
Public utilities	61	11,000	...	5,082
Electrical power	49	125,000	...	4,017
Transportation	195,828	1,135,950	...	24,760
Communication			...	5,842
Finance	234,334	938,904	...	46,343
Wholesale and retail trade	1,589,785	3,694,238	...	61,884
Pub. admin., services	494,153	3,553,304	...	57,333

Energy production (consumption): electricity (kW-hr; 1984) 188,000,000 (193,962,000,000); coal (metric tons; 1984) 1,805,845 (22,550,000); crude petroleum (barrels; 1984) 15,300,000 (570,000,000); petroleum products (metric tons; 1984) 68,741,000 (72,538,000); natural gas (cu m; 1984) 13,853,910,000 (31,378,500,000).

Population economically active (1985): total 23,213,000; activity rate of total population 40.6% (participation rates: ages 15–64 [1984] 63.0%; female [1984] 34.7%; unemployed 10.6%).

Price and earnings indexes (1980 = 100)

	1979	1980	1981	1982	1983	1984	1985
Consumer price index	82.5	100.0	117.8	137.2	157.3	174.3	190.3
Monthly earnings index	68.8	100.0	123.9	145.7	167.9	186.7	207.5

Land use (1983): forested 21.6%; meadows and pastures 17.4%; agricultural and under permanent cultivation 42.2%; other 18.8%.

Financial aggregates

	1980	1981	1982	1983	1984	1985
Exchange rate, Lit per:						
U.S. dollar	856.4	1,136.8	1,352.5	1,518.8	1,757.0	1,909.4
£	1,992.2	2,305.3	2,367.6	2,304.0	2,347.9	2,759.1
SDR	1,186.8	1,396.8	1,511.3	1,737.4	1,897.6	1,843.7
International reserves (U.S.$)						
Total (excl. gold; '000,000)	23,140	20,134	14,090	19,840	20,796	15,515
SDRs ('000,000)	665	783	785	591	633	326
Reserve pos. in IMF ('000,000)	823	734	696	990	1,074	1,160
Foreign exchange ('000,000)	21,652	18,617	12,610	18,259	19,089	14,029
Gold ('000,000 fine troy oz)	66.67	66.67	66.67	66.67	66.67	66.67
% world reserves	7.0	7.0	7.0	7.1	7.1	7.0
Interest and prices						
Central bank discount (%)	16.50	19.00	18.00	17.00	16.50	15.00
Gov't. bond yield (%)	16.11	20.58	20.90	18.02	14.95	13.00
Industrial share prices (1980 = 100)	100.0	151.7	123.1	153.1	171.9	286.7
Balance of payments (U.S.$'000,000)						
Balance of visible trade	−16,417	−10,901	−8,130	−4,390	−5,994	7,041
Imports, f.o.b.	−93,236	−85,803	−80,678	−75,215	−78,976	−84,722
Exports, f.o.b.	76,819	74,902	72,548	70,827	72,982	77,681
Balance of invisibles	5,402	1,537	1,701	2,555	2,026	1,739
Balance of payments, current account	−9,801	−8,604	−5,684	555	−2,871	−4.206

Public debt (1985): U.S.$390,000,000,000.

Household income and expenditure. Average household size (1984) 3.0; average annual income per household Lit 19,692,000 (U.S.$11,208); sources of income: salaries and wages 49.2%, self-employment 31.1%, social security 11.8%; expenditure (1983): food and beverages 29.1%, housing 26.0%, transport and communications 13.7%, recreation and education 5.9%.

Foreign trade

Balance of trade (current prices)

	1980	1981	1982	1983	1984	1985
Lit '000,000,000	−15,716	−14,056	−16,966	−11,465	−19,163	−23,262
% of total	9.2%	6.7%	7.9%	4.9%	6.9%	7.8%

Imports (1984): Lit 148,177,782,000,000 (machinery and transport equipment 20.6%, of which transport equipment 8.0%, precision machinery 4.3%; crude petroleum 15.7%; chemicals and chemical products 9.9%; food and live animals 8.3%; metal and semiprocessed metal 8.3%; refined petroleum products 7.1%). *Major import sources:* West Germany 15.9%; France 12.4%; United States 6.1%; The Netherlands 4.9%; U.S.S.R. 4.8%; Switzerland 4.1%.

Exports (1984): Lit 129,014,607,000,000 (nontransport machinery 25.5%; transport equipment 10.0%, of which automobiles 3.3%, tractors and construction equipment 0.7%; textiles 8.9%; metal and processed metal 8.9%; clothing and wearing apparel 8.7%, of which shoes 4.2%; chemicals and chemical products 7.9%; refined petroleum products 4.8%). *Major export destinations:* West Germany 16.1%; France 14.0%; United States 10.9%; United Kingdom 6.7%; Switzerland 4.1%; Saudi Arabia 3.2%.

Transport and communications

Transport. Railroads (1985): route length 12,272 mi, 19,750 km; passenger-mi 24,397,000,000, passenger-km 39,264,000,000; short ton-mi cargo 12,465,000,000, metric ton-km cargo 18,198,000,000. Roads (1983): total length 184,981 mi, 297,698 km (paved 100%). Vehicles (1983): passenger cars 20,450,000; trucks and buses 1,720,000. Merchant marine (1985): vessels (100 gross tons and over) 1,573; total deadweight tonnage 14,373,122. Air transport (1985): passenger-mi 9,056,000,000, passenger-km 14,575,000,000; short ton-mi cargo 534,282,000, metric ton-km cargo 780,038,000; airports (1986) 36.

Communications. Daily newspapers (1985): total number 66; total circulation 6,238,000¶; circulation per 1,000 population 109. Radio (1985): 14,015,000 receivers (1 per 4.1 persons). Television (1985): 13,900,000 receivers (1 per 4.1 persons). Telephones (1983): 21,670,001 (1 per 2.6 persons).

Education and health

Education (1983–84)

	schools	teachers♀	students♂	student/ teacher ratio
Primary (age 6–10)	28,786	276,716	3,909,365	...
Secondary (age 11–13)	13,135	333,062	3,301,625	...
Voc., teacher tr.	4,430	199,268	2,042,913	...
Higher	74	47,844	1,096,454	...

Literacy (1985): total population over age 15 literate 38,421,342 (97.0%); males literate 18,767,897 (97.9%); females literate 19,653,445 (96.3%).

Health: physicians (1981) 97,003 (1 per 583.9 persons); hospital beds (1983) 500,828 (1 per 113.5 persons); infant mortality rate per 1,000 live births (1985) 10.9.

Food (1980–82): daily per capita caloric intake 3,589 (vegetable products 76%, animal products 24%); 143% of FAO recommended minimum requirement.

Military

Total active duty personnel (1985): 385,100 (army 70.1%, navy 11.6%, air force 18.3%). *Military expenditure as percent of GNP* (1984): 2.8% (world 6.1%); per capita expenditure U.S.$174.

*Imputed bank charges less indirect duties on import. †Unemployed. ‡1984. §1983. ‖ 1982. ¶For 51 newspapers only. ♀1982–83. ♂1984–85.

Jamaica

Official name: Jamaica.
Form of government: constitutional monarchy with two legislative houses (Senate [21]; House of Representatives [60]).
Chief of state: British Monarch represented by governor-general.
Head of government: Prime Minister.
Capital: Kingston.
Official language: English.
Official religion: none.
Monetary unit: 1 dollar (J$) = 100 cents; valuation (Oct. 1, 1986) 1 U.S.$ = J$5.47; 1 £ = J$7.90.

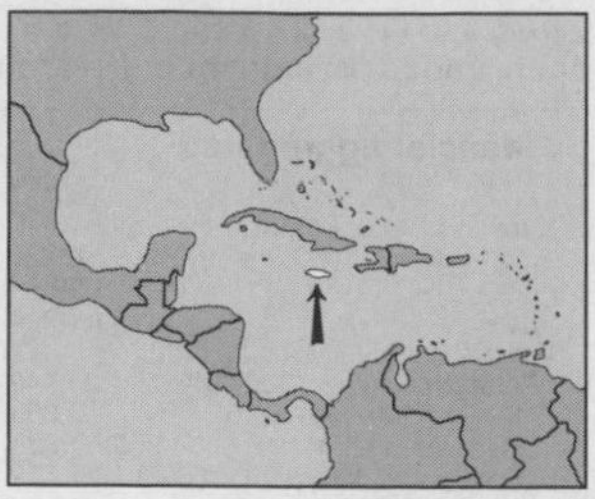

Area and population

Parishes	Capitals	area sq mi	area sq km	population 1985 estimate
Clarendon	May Pen	462	1,196	212,100
Hanover	Lucea	174	450	64,000
Kingston	*	8	22	†
Manchester	Mandeville	321	830	153,800
Portland	Port Antonio	314	814	76,200
Saint Andrew	*	166	431	625,800†
Saint Ann	Saint Ann's Bay	468	1,213	144,600
Saint Catherine	Spanish Town	460	1,192	388,000
Saint Elizabeth	Black River	468	1,212	142,400
Saint James	Montego Bay	230	595	145,300
Saint Mary	Port Maria	236	611	109,900
Saint Thomas	Morant Bay	287	743	83,800
Trelawny	Falmouth	338	875	72,200
Westmorland	Savanna-la-Mar	312	807	125,600
TOTAL		4,244	10,991	2,343,700‡

Demography

Population (1986): 2,348,000.
Density (1985): persons per sq mi 553.3, persons per sq km 213.6.
Urban-rural (1982): urban 47.8%; rural 50.94%.
Sex distribution (1982): male 49.06%; female 50.94%.
Age breakdown (1982): under 15, 38.4%; 15–29, 28.8%; 30–44, 13.9%; 45–59, 9.4%; 60–64, 2.6%; 65 and over, 6.9%.
Population projection: (1990) 2,535,000; (2000) 2,872,000.
Doubling time: 37 years.
Ethnic composition (1983): black 76.3%; Afro-European 15.1%; East Indian and Afro-East Indian 3.4%; white 3.2%; other 2.0%.
Religious affiliation (1980): Protestant (mostly Anglican, Baptist, Seventh-day Adventist) 70.7%; Roman Catholic 9.6%; indigenous Christian 8.6%; spiritist (mostly Rastafarian) 7.1%; other 4.0%.
Major cities (1982): Kingston 104,000§ (metropolitan area 524,600); Spanish Town 89,100; Portmore 73,400; Montego Bay 70,300.

Vital statistics

Birth rate per 1,000 population (1984): 25.2 (world avg. 29.0).
Death rate per 1,000 population (1984): 5.9 (world avg. 11.0).
Natural increase rate per 1,000 population (1984): 19.3 (world avg. 18.0).
Total fertility rate (avg. births per childbearing woman; 1982): 3.3.
Marriage rate per 1,000 population (1984): 4.6.
Divorce rate per 1,000 population (1984): 0.3.
Life expectancy at birth (1980–85): male 67.9 years; female 71.9 years.
Major causes of death per 100,000 population (1978): cerebrovascular disease 81.7; malignant neoplasms (cancers) 74.8; heart disease 72.4; diseases of the respiratory system 41.7%; infectious and parasitic diseases 39.3.

National economy

Budget (1984). Revenue: J$2,335,800,000 (tax revenue 77.5%, of which income taxes 34.5%, consumption taxes 21.2%, stamps 7.0%; transfers from capital development funds 17.9%). Expenditures: J$3,592,600,000 (public debt 26.1%; general administration 21.7%; health 14.4%; education 9.5%; public order and defense 7.0%).
Public debt (external, outstanding; 1984): U.S.$2,174,700,000.
Tourism: receipts from visitors (1985) U.S.$394,000,000; expenditures by nationals abroad (1983) U.S.$11,000,000.
Production (metric tons except as noted). Agriculture, forestry, fishing (1984): sugarcane 2,655,000, roots and tubers 186,000, coconuts 120,000, vegetables (including pumpkins, tomatoes, and carrots) 91,000, citrus fruits 87,000, bananas 40,000, plantains 29,000, cocoa 7,000, tobacco 2,000, coffee 1,800; livestock (number of live animals) 420,000 goats, 318,000 cattle, 270,000 pigs; roundwood (1984) 117,000 cu m; fish catch (1983) 8,653. Mining and quarrying (1985): bauxite 6,140,000; gypsum 180,000 ‖. Manufacturing (1984): cement 259,000; sugar 188,000; fertilizer 46,000; stout and beer 431,000 hectolitres; rum 142,000 hectolitres; cigarettes 1,255,000,000 units; tires 209,000 units; cloth 1,754,000 metres. Construction (private sector only; 1983): residential completions 54,500 sq m; nonresidential starts 21,500 sq m. Energy production (consumption): electricity (kW-hr; 1984) 2,400,000,000 (2,400,000,000); coal, none (none); crude petroleum (barrels; 1984) none (7,110,000); petroleum products (metric tons; 1984) 896,000 (1,886,000); natural gas, none (none).
Land use (1983): forested 27.9%; meadows and pastures 18.5%; agricultural and under permanent cultivation 24.8%; other 28.8%.
Gross national product (at current market prices; 1984): U.S.$2,480,000,000 (U.S.$1,090 per capita).

Structure of gross domestic product and labour force

	1984 in value J$'000,000	% of total value	labour force	% of labour force
Agriculture	525.5	5.6	245,000	25.2
Mining	825.7	8.8	7,500	0.8
Manufacturing	1,667.7	17.8	116,200	12.0
Construction	840.9	9.0	44,700	4.6
Public utilities	305.0	3.2	39,600	4.1
Transportation and communication	619.9	6.6		
Trade	1,917.3	20.5	119,700	12.3
Pub. admin., defense	1,126.0	12.0	111,600	11.5
Finance, real estate	1,403.1	15.0	287,100¶	29.5
Other	136.6	1.5		
TOTAL	9,367.7	100.0	971,400	100.0

Population economically active (1984): total 971,400; activity rate of total population 42.6% (participation rates: ages 14–64, 72.2%; female 46.6%; unemployed [1985] 25.6%).

Price and earnings indexes (1980 = 100)

	1980	1981	1982	1983	1984	1985	1986♀
Consumer price index	100.0	112.7	120.1	134.0	171.3	215.3	248.6
Monthly earnings index	...	...	...	...	...	...	...

Household income and expenditure. Average household size (1982) 4.2; income per household, n.a.; sources of income (1982): wages and salaries 70.9%, self-employment 27.3%, transfers 1.8%; expenditure (1982): food and beverages 36.8%, transportation 13.2%, housing 8.5%, cafe and hotel expenditures 7.4%, household furnishings 5.3%, tobacco 4.9%, energy 4.6%, recreation 3.3%, health care 2.5%, clothing 2.3%, other 11.2%.

Foreign trade

Balance of trade (current prices)

	1980	1981	1982	1983	1984	1985
J$'000,000	−107.4	−556.1	−841.2	−1,071.2	−1,103.8	−2,388.8
% of total	3.0%	13.8%	24.5%	27.8%	16.5%	28.2%

Imports (1984): J$4,510,000,000 (crude petroleum and petroleum products 30.2%, chemical products 9.7%, cereals and cereal preparations 8.1%, industrial machinery and parts 7.3%, textile yarn and fabrics 3.5%). *Major import sources:* United States 45.2%; Netherlands Antilles 13.4%; Venezuela 7.9%; Canada 5.5%; United Kingdom 5.4%.
Exports (1984): J$2,896,000,000 (alumina 44.0%, bauxite 20.4%, raw sugar 5.9%, clothing 4.6%, petroleum products 2.5%, cigars and cigarillos 1.5%, coffee 1.2%, rum 1.0%). *Major export destinations:* United States 47.5%; Canada 14.1%; United Kingdom 12.7%; U.S.S.R. 5.0%.

Transport and communications

Transport. Railroads: length♁ 215 mi, 346 km; passenger-mi□ 49,280,000, passenger-km 79,309,000; short ton-mi cargo◇ 88,514,000, metric ton-km cargo 129,228,000. Roads (1985): total length 7,680 mi, 12,360 km (paved 39%). Vehicles (1983): passenger cars 40,271; trucks and buses 20,167. Merchant marine (1985): vessels (100 gross tons and over) 13; total deadweight tonnage 12,878. Air transport (1985): passenger-mi 918,000,000, passenger-km 1,477,000,000; short ton-mi cargo 13,336,000, metric ton-km cargo 19,470,000; airports (1986) with scheduled flights 6.
Communications. Daily newspapers (1985): total number 2; total circulation 84,100; circulation per 1,000 population 36. Radio (1985): total number of receivers 860,000 (1 per 2.7 persons). Television (1985): total number of receivers 215,000 (1 per 11 persons). Telephones (1984): 136,778 (1 per 17 persons).

Education and health

Education (1983–84)

	schools	teachers△	students	student/teacher ratio
Primary (age 6–11)	881	10,374	341,748	...
Secondary (age 12–16)	...	8,139	224,846	...
Voc., teacher tr.△	...	508	8,508	16.7
Higher	...	...	5,176✝	...

Educational attainment (1981). Percent of population over age 14 having: no formal schooling 2.0%; primary education 69.7%; secondary and higher 28.3%. *Literacy* (1980): total population over age 14 literate 1,100,600 (88.6%); males literate 542,600 (88.2%); females literate 558,000 (89.1%).
Health: physicians (1985) 317⊕ (1 per 7,290 persons); hospital beds (1984) 6,066 (1 per 376 persons); infant mortality rate per 1,000 live births (1984) 13.2.
Food (1980–82): daily per capita caloric intake 2,531 (vegetable products 85%, animal products 15%); 113% of FAO recommended minimum requirement.

Military

Total active duty personnel (1985): 2,100** (army 84.8%; navy 7.1%; air force 8.1%). *Military expenditure as percent of GNP* (1983): 1.3% (world 6.1%); per capita expenditure U.S.$16.

*The parishes of Kingston and Saint Andrew are jointly administered from the Half Way Tree section of Saint Andrew. †Kingston included with Saint Andrew. ‡Later estimate equals 2,311,000. §City of Kingston is contiguous with Kingston parish. ‖1984. ¶Includes 104,000 unemployed not previously employed. ♀July average. ♁1985. □1978. ◇1981. △Public education only. ✝University of the West Indies, Mona campus. ⊕Government-employed only. **Excludes paramilitary forces.

Japan

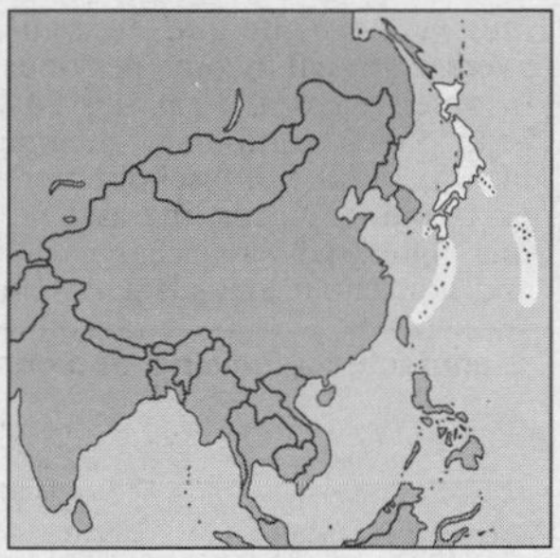

Official name: Nihon (Japan).
Form of government: constitutional monarchy with a National Diet consisting of two legislative houses (House of Councillors [252]; House of Representatives [512]).
Chief of state: Emperor.
Head of government: Prime Minister.
Capital: Tōkyō.
Official language: Japanese.
Official religion: none.
Monetary unit: 1 yen (¥) = 100 sen; valuation (Oct. 1, 1986) 1 U.S.$ = ¥154.30; 1 £ = ¥222.96.

Area and population

Regions / Prefectures	Capitals	area sq mi	area sq km	population 1985 census*
Chūbu				
Aichi	Nagoya	1,984	5,138	6,477,200
Fukui	Fukui	1,618	4,191	822,000
Gifu	Gifu	4,091	10,596	2,038,300
Ishikawa	Kanazawa	1,620	4,197	1,157,700
Nagano	Nagano	5,245	13,585	2,170,400
Niigata	Niigata	4,857	12,579	2,448,900
Shizuoka	Shizuoka	3,001	7,773	3,582,000
Toyama	Toyama	1,642	4,252	1,125,400
Yamanashi	Kōfu	1,723	4,463	823,100
Chūgoku				
Hiroshima	Hiroshima	3,269	8,466	2,820,200
Okayama	Okayama	2,737	7,090	1,914,100
Shimane	Matsue	2,559†	6,628†	797,500
Tottori	Tottori	1,349†	3,493†	620,200
Yamaguchi	Yamaguchi	2,358	6,106	1,588,500
Hokkaidō				
Hokkaidō (Territory)	Sapporo	32,247	83,519	5,688,500
Kantō				
Chiba	Chiba	1,988	5,150	5,168,100
Gumma	Maebashi	2,454	6,356	1,913,200
Ibaraki	Mito	2,353	6,094	2,717,500
Kanagawa	Yokohoma	927	2,402	7,380,200
Saitama	Urawa	1,467	3,799	5,854,900
Tochigi	Utsunomiya	2,476	6,414	1,883,800
Kinki				
Hyōgo	Kōbe	3,235	8,378	5,275,600
Mie	Tsu	2,231	5,778	1,738,300
Nara	Nara	1,425	3,692	1,303,900
Shiga	Ōtsu	1,551	4,016	1,165,900
Wakayama	Wakayama	1,824	4,725	1,086,600
Kyūshū				
Fukuoka	Fukuoka	1,915	4,960	4,753,200
Kagoshima	Kagoshima	3,539	9,165	1,833,600
Kumamoto	Kumamoto	2,860	7,408	1,836,200
Miyazaki	Miyazaki	2,986	7,735	1,183,500
Nagasaki	Nagasaki	1,588	4,112	1,599,500
Ōita	Ōita	2,447	6,337	1,246,300
Saga	Saga	939	2,433	890,700
Ryukyu				
Okinawa	Naha	870	2,254	1,177,000
Shikoku				
Ehime	Matsuyama	2,190	5,672	1,533,600
Kagawa	Takamatsu	727	1,882	1,034,000
Kōchi	Kōchi	2,744	7,107	843,400
Tokushima	Tokushima	1,600	4,145	831,400
Tohoku				
Akita	Akita	4,483‡	11,612‡	1,252,900
Aomori	Aomori	3,713‡	9,617‡	1,521,200
Fukushima	Fukushima	5,322	13,784	2,054,200
Iwate	Morioka	5,899	15,279	1,454,600
Miyagi	Sendai	2,815	7,292	2,167,900
Yamagata	Yamagata	3,601	9,327	1,251,200
Metropolis				
Tōkyō§	Tōkyō	835	2,162	11,780,500
Urban prefectures				
Kyōto ‖	Kyōto	1,781	4,613	2,565,400
Ōsaka ‖	Ōsaka	721	1,868	8,653,300
TOTAL		145,870¶♀	377,801¶♀	121,025,700♀

Demography

Population (1986): 121,510,000.
Density (1986): persons per sq mi 833.0, persons per sq km 321.6.
Urban-rural (1980): urban 76.2%; rural 23.8%.
Sex distribution (1986): male 49.15%; female 50.85%.
Age breakdown (1986): under 15, 21.1%; 15–29, 20.8%; 30–44, 23.6%; 45–59, 19.4%; 60–69, 8.2%; 70 and over, 6.9%.
Population projection: (1990) 122,834,000; (2000) 128,119,000.
Doubling time: n.a.; doubling time exceeds 100 years.
Composition by nationality (1986): Japanese 99.4%; other (mainly Korean) 0.6%.
Religious affiliation (1984): most Japanese consider themselves to be adherents of both Shintō (93.4%), a body of indigenous beliefs and practices, and Buddhism (74.1%). A small proportion of the population is Christian (1.4%). Most of the others are members of the "new religions," which incorporate to varying degrees Shintō, Buddhist, Taoist, and Christian beliefs.
Major cities (1986): Tōkyō 8,386,000; Yokohama 3,037,000; Ōsaka 2,642,000; Nagoya 2,128,000; Sapporo 1,562,000; Kyōto 1,481,000; Kōbe 1,420,000; Fukuoka 1,172,000; Kawasaki 1,104,000; Kitakyūshū 1,053,000; Hiroshima 1,044,129♁.

Other principal cities (1985)

	population		population		population
Akashi	263,365	Kasugai	256,991	Sagamihara	482,778
Akita	296,381	Kawagoe	285,435	Sakai	818,368
Amagasaki	509,115	Kawaguchi	403,012	Sasebo	250,635
Aomori	294,050	Kōchi	312,253	Sendai	700,248
Asahigawa	363,630	Koriyama	301,672	Shimonoseki	269,167
Chiba	788,920	Koshigaya	253,483	Shizuoka	468,362
Fujisawa	328,387	Kumamoto	555,722	Suita	348,946
Fukushima	270,752	Kurashiki	413,644	Takamatsu	327,001
Fukuyama	360,264	Machida	321,182	Takatsuki	348,783
Funabashi	506,967	Maebashi	277,319	Tokorozawa	275,165
Gifu	411,740	Matsudo	427,479	Tokushima	257,886
Hachiōji	426,650	Matsuyama	426,646	Toyama	314,111
Hakodate	319,190	Miyazaki	279,118	Toyohashi	322,142
Hamamatsu	514,118	Nagano	336,967	Toyonaka	413,219
Higashiosaka	522,798	Nagasaki	449,382	Toyota	308,106
Himeji	452,916	Naha	303,680	Urawa	377,233
Hirakata	382,257	Nara	327,702	Utsunomiya	405,384
Ibaraki	250,468	Neyagawa	258,230	Wakayama	401,357
Ichikawa	397,806	Niigata	475,633	Yahatanishi	251,984
Ichinomiya	257,392	Nishinomiya	421,267	Yao	276,397
Iwaki	350,566	Ōita	390,105	Yokkaichi	263,003
Kagoshima	530,496	Okayama	572,423	Yokosuka	427,087
Kanazawa	430,480	Okazaki	284,996		
Kashiwa	273,130	Ōmiya	373,015		

Place of birth (1984): 99.4% native-born; 0.6% foreign-born (mainly Korean).
Mobility (1980). Population living in same residence as in October 1975: 68.0%; different residence, same prefecture 24.2%; different prefecture 7.7%.
Households (1986). Total households 38,987,773; average household size 3.1; composition of households (1985) 1 person 20.8%, 2 persons 18.4%, 3 persons 17.9%, 4 persons 23.6%, 5 persons 11.0%, 6 persons 5.2%, 7 or more persons 2.9%. Family households (1985) 30,021,000 (79.0%); nonfamily 7,967,000 (21.0%), of which 1-person 7,900,000 (20.8%).

Type of households (1983)

Total number of dwelling units: 34,705,000

	number of dwellings	percent of total
by kind of dwelling		
exclusive entry (do not share bathroom or kitchen)	31,935,000	94.0
combined with nondwelling	2,770,000	8.0
detached house	22,306,000	64.3
apartment building	9,329,000	26.9
tenement (substandard or overcrowded building)	2,882,000	8.3
by legal tenure of householder		
owned	21,650,000	62.4
rented	12,951,000	37.3
by government	2,645,000	7.6
by private owner	8,487,000	24.5
other	1,819,000	5.2
by kind of amenities		
running water	32,637,000	94.0
flush toilet	20,198,000	58.2
bathroom	30,633,000	88.3
by year of construction		
prior to 1945	3,670,000	10.6
1945–60	4,738,000	13.7
1961–70	8,870,000	25.6
1971–80	14,473,000	41.7
1981–83	2,705,000	7.8

Immigration (1985): permanent immigrants/registered aliens 850,612, from South Korea 80.3%, Taiwan 8.8%, United States 3.4%, Philippines 1.4%, United Kingdom 0.8%, Vietnam 0.5%, West Germany 0.4%.

Vital statistics

Birth rate per 1,000 population (1985): 11.9 (world avg. 29.0); (1980) legitimate 99.2%; illegitimate 0.8%.
Death rate per 1,000 population (1985): 6.1 (world avg. 11.0).
Natural increase rate per 1,000 population (1985): 5.8 (world avg. 18.0).
Total fertility rate (avg. births per childbearing woman; 1984): 1.8.
Marriage rate per 1,000 population□ (1985): 6.1.
Divorce rate per 1,000 population□ (1985): 1.4.
Life expectancy at birth (1984): male 74.5 years; female 80.2 years.
Major causes of death per 100,000 population (1985): malignant neoplasms 155.4; heart diseases 116.8; cerebrovascular diseases 111.8; pneumonia and bronchitis 42.5; accidents and adverse effects 24.3; senility without mention of psychosis 23.0; suicide 19.4; cirrhosis of the liver 14.2; nephritis, nephrotic syndrome, and nephrosis 11.2; hypertensive diseases 10.5.

Social indicators

Educational attainment (1980). Percent of population 15 years old and over having: no schooling 0.3%; primary and lower secondary education 38.5%; higher secondary 38.0%; junior college and technical college 5.7%; university and postgraduate 8.0%; still in school 9.5%.

Distribution of income (1980)

percent of average household income by decile

1	2	3	4	5	6	7	8	9	10 (highest)
35.8	53.6	64.6	73.5	82.9	93.2	105.2	120.4	145.4	224.8.

Quality of working life. Average workweek (1985): 46.7 hours ([1984] 10.7% overtime). Annual rate of industrial deaths per 100,000 workers (1984): 3.7. Proportion of labour force insured for damages or income loss resulting from injury, permanent disability, and death (1986): 46.8%. Average man-

days lost to labour stoppages per 1,000 workdays (1985): 0.18. Average duration of journey to work (1983): 32 minutes (26.7%◇ private automobile, 67.4%◇ public transportation, 5.5%◇ taxi, 0.4%◇ other). Rate per 1,000 workers of discouraged (unemployed no longer seeking work; 1982): 64.7.
Access to services (1980). Proportion of households having access to: gas supply 63.0%; safe public water supply 91.4%; public sewage collection 89.4%.
Social participation. Eligible voters participating in last national election (December 1983): 67.9%. Population over 15 years of age participating in social service activities on a voluntary basis (1981): 26.0%. Trade union membership in total work force (1985): 20.8%.
Social deviance (1984). Offense rate per 100,000 population for: murder 1.5; rape 1.6; larceny and theft 1,137.9; robbery 1.8. Incidence in general population of: alcoholism, n.a.; drug and substance abuse, n.a. Rate of suicide per 100,000 population (1985) 19.4.

Leisure/use of personal time
Daily activities (1981)
(both sexes)

Social activities	daily average hrs./min.	% of day
Work	4.35	19.1
Meals	1.50	7.6
Housekeeping and childcare	1.49	7.6
Commuting to work/school	.36	2.5
Schoolwork	.32	2.2
Shopping	.22	1.5
Personal activities		
Sleep	7.57	33.1
Rest and relaxation	1.19	5.5
Personal care and grooming	.57	4.0
Transportation (excluding commuting)	.12	.8

Recreational activities (1981)

	weekday hrs./min.	% of total leisure time	weekend hrs./min.	% of total leisure time
Males				
Personal associations and friendships	2.30	18.7	3.20	18.2
Television, radio, newspapers, and magazines	2.27	18.4	2.59	16.3
Study and research (excluding schoolwork)	2.23	17.9	2.45	15.0
Hobbies and amusements	2.12	16.5	3.18	18.1
Voluntary social activities	2.11	16.3	3.04	16.8
Sports	1.38	12.2	2.51	15.6
Females				
Television, radio, newspapers, and magazines	2.29	19.1	2.37	16.3
Study and research (excluding schoolwork)	2.24	18.4	2.34	16.0
Voluntary social activities	2.21	18.1	2.32	15.7
Hobbies and amusements	2.07	16.3	2.48	17.4
Personal associations and friendships	2.06	16.1	2.51	17.7
Sports	1.34	12.0	2.43	16.9

Material well-being (1985). Households possessing: automobile 67.4%; telephone, virtually 100%; colour television receiver 99.1%; refrigerator, virtually 100%; air conditioner 52.3%; washing machine, virtually 100%; videocassette recorder 27.8%.

National economy

Gross national product (at current market prices; 1984): U.S.$1,255,400,000,000 (U.S.$10,460 per capita).

Structure of gross domestic product and labour force

	1984		1986△	
	in value ¥'000,000,000	% of total value	labour force	% of labour force
Agriculture	9,655.0	3.2	5,580,000	9.2
Mining	1,194.5	0.4	70,000	0.1
Manufacturing	88,700.3	29.8	14,290,000	23.5
Construction	22,219.4	7.5	5,340,000	8.8
Public utilities	10,430.5	3.5	340,000	0.6
Transportation and communication	18,755.9	6.3	3,420,000	5.6
Trade	42,685.1	14.3	13,760,000	22.6
Finance	45,341.5	15.2	2,280,000	3.7
Pub. admin., defense	13,774.6	4.6	1,940,000	3.2
Services	55,842.5	18.7	12,040,000	19.8
Other	−10,515.2†	−3.5	1,870,000⊕	3.1
TOTAL	298,084.2♀	100.0	60,930,000	100.0♀

Budget (1986)**. Revenue: ¥54,089,000,000,000 (income tax 31.1%; corporation tax 23.5%; public bonds 20.2%; liquor tax 3.7%; stamp duties 2.7%; custom duties 1.0%). Expenditures: ¥54,089,000,000,000 (national debt 20.9%; transfers to local governments 18.8%; social security 18.2%; public works 11.5%; culture, education, and science promotion 9.0%; national defense 6.2%; pensions 3.4%; measures for energy 1.2%; economic cooperation 1.2%; foodstuff control 1.1%; small enterprises 0.4%).
Public debt (1984): U.S.$496,439,471,000.
Population economically active (1986)△: total 60,930,000; activity rate of total population 50.1% (participation rates: ages 15–64 [1985] 68.6%; female [1985] 39.7%; unemployed 2.7%).

Price and earnings indexes (1980 = 100)

	1980	1981	1982	1983	1984	1985	1986††
Consumer price index	100.0	104.9	107.8	109.9	112.3	114.6	115.1
Monthly earnings index	100.0	105.1	110.6	115.0	119.8	124.6	129.7

Household income and expenditure‡‡ (1985). Average household size 3.8; average annual income per household ¥5,338,150 (U.S.$22,380); sources of income: wages and salaries 94.3%, of which regular income of household head 63.9%, temporary income and bonuses of household head 18.6%, income of other household members 11.8%; expenditure: food 20.6%, transportation 7.8%, reading and recreation 7.0%, clothing and footwear 5.6%, fuel, light, and water charges 4.7%, housing 3.8%, education 3.4%, furniture and household utensils 3.4%, medical care 1.9%, net savings 10.8%.

Manufacturing, mining, and construction enterprises (1983)

	no. of establishments	avg. no. of persons engaged§§	monthly as a % of avg. of all contract wages	annual value added (¥'000,000,000)
Electrical machinery	32,344	1,626,000	102.0	12,100
Nonelectrical machinery	42,313	1,084,000	102.0	8,295
Transport equipment	15,549	901,000	104.3	8,152
Food products	53,692	1,138,000	92.5	7,749
Chemical products	5,411	402,000	111.8	7,188
Iron and steel	7,050	407,000	111.0	4,054
Fabricated metal products	51,277	764,000	93.7	4,689
Printing and publishing	30,431	508,000	110.6	4,280
Ceramic, stone, and clay	22,074	483,000	92.9	3,766
Ordnance and miscellaneous	19	1,600	94.1	9.4
Textiles	37,899	647,000	91.3	2,935
Paper and paper products	12,364	278,000	97.2	2,074
Nonferrous metal products	4,351	182,000	106.7	1,594
Apparel products	31,031	525,000	83.5	1,525
Precision instruments	8,074	265,000	97.2	1,591
Petroleum and coal products	1,007	42,000	120.9	1,197
Lumber and wood products	24,485	301,000	79.1	1,400
Furniture and fixtures	18,697	243,000	84.3	1,200
Rubber products	5,643	159,000	100.0	1,064
Leather products	5,790	77,000	87.8	354
Mining	869	50,229	100.4	406‖‖
Construction	550,798¶¶	5,410,000	94.9	21,674

Tourism (1984): receipts from visitors U.S.$416,000,000; expenditures by nationals abroad U.S.$334,000,000.

Financial aggregates

	1980	1981	1982	1983	1984	1985	1986 (6 mo.)
Exchange rate♀♀ ¥ per:							
U.S. dollar	203.00	219.90	235.00	232.20	251.10	200.50	165.00
£	484.16	419.57	379.41	336.83	290.40	289.62	252.50
SDR	258.91	255.95	259.23	243.10	246.13	220.23	194.30
International reserves (U.S.$)♀♀							
Total (excl. gold; '000,000)	24,636	28,208	23,334	24,602	26,429	26,719	34,034
SDRs ('000,000)	1,738	1,934	2,091	1,935	1,927	2,116	2,231
Reserve pos. in IMF ('000,000)	1,331	1,558	2,071	2,303	2,219	2,275	2,354
Foreign exchange ('000,000)	21,567	24,716	19,172	20,364	22,283	22,328	29,450
Gold ('000,000 fine troy oz)	24.23	24.23	24.23	24.23	24.23	24.23	24.23
% world reserves	2.5	2.5	2.6	2.6	2.6	2.6	2.6
Interest and prices							
Central bank discount (%)	7.25	5.50	5.50	5.00	5.00	5.00	3.50
Gov't. bond yield (%)	9.22	8.66	8.06	7.42	6.81	6.34	4.98
Industrial share prices (1980 = 100)	100.0	116.3	115.8	136.5	172.1	210.2	280.5
Balance of payments (U.S.$'000,000,000)							
Balance of visible trade	2.1	20.0	18.1	31.5	44.4	56.0	...
Imports, f.o.b.	124.6	129.6	119.6	114.0	123.9	118.0	...
Exports, f.o.b.	126.7	149.5	137.7	145.5	168.3	174.0	...
Balance of invisibles	−11.4	−13.6	−9.9	−9.1	−7.8	−5.2	...
Balance of payments, current account	−10.8	4.8	6.9	20.8	35.0	49.2	...

Production (metric tons except as noted). Agriculture, forestry, fishing (1985): rice 11,662,000, potatoes 3,727,000, radishes 2,544,000, mandarin oranges 2,491,000, cabbages 1,589,000, sweet potatoes 1,527,000, Chinese cabbages 1,478,000, onions 1,326,000, cucumbers 1,033,000, apples 909,800, wheat 874,000, watermelons 820,400, tomatoes 802,300, carrots 662,600, eggplants 598,500, Welsh onions 552,800, Japanese pears 461,700, lettuce 458,600, spinach 382,500, taro 375,000, grapes 311,200, persimmons 290,000, pumpkins 273,400, summer oranges 268,700, burdocks 263,400, turnips 208,600, peaches 205,400, strawberries 195,700, Spanish paprika 171,600, cauliflowers 128,800, soybeans 115,500, string peas 93,900, string beans 66,500, cow's milk 7,380,000 (of which marketed as fluid milk 4,307,000), hen's eggs 2,140,000; livestock (number of live animals) 10,718,000 pigs, 4,698,000 cattle (of which 2,111,000 dairy cows), 51,000 goats, 23,000 horses, 177,477,000 hens, 150,215,000 broiler chickens; roundwood (1984) 65,079,000 cu m (of which coniferous species 20,418,000 cu m, broadleaved species 12,093,000 cu m); fish catch 12,197,000 (of which sardines 3,914,000, mackerel 931,000 [jack mackerel 16.3%], tuna 391,000, bonito 316,000, sauries 243,000, salmon and trout 201,000, squid 125,000, yellowtails 33,000). Mining and quarrying (1984): limestone 169,825,000; quicklime 7,753,000; gypsum 6,050,000; dolomite 4,268,000; fire clay 1,287,484; pyrophyllite 1,073,000; iron ore 324,419; zinc 252,700; talc 84,522; barite 66,018; lead 48,735; copper 43,309; chromium 7,420; silver 323,575 kg; gold 3,220 kg. Manufacturing (1985): crude steel 105,279,000; semifinished steel 96,512,000; hot-rolled steel products 82,731,000; pig iron 80,569,000; cement 72,847,000; cold-rolled steel strips 20,527,000; plastic products 4,390,800, of which film 1,203,800; compound fertilizers 3,679,100; spun yarn 1,224,900; raw silk 959,100; finished products (in number of units) 324,778,000 fluorescent lamps, 182,752,000 watches, 149,513,000 motor vehicle tires, 86,032,000 electronic desk calculators, 39,355,000 motor vehicle tubes, 28,283,000 videocassette recorders, 16,880,000 colour television receivers, 16,520,000 35-mm cameras, 7,909,000 microwave ovens, 7,646,800 passenger cars, 5,466,991 trucks and buses, 5,354,000 electric refrigerators, 5,092,000 automatic washing machines, 4,536,300 motorcycles, 4,448,800 typewriters, 2,700,800 copying machines. Construction (floor area started; 1985): residential 103,132,000 sq m; nonresidential 199,560,000 sq m, of which government and public owned 20,463,000 sq m, private owned 179,098,000 sq m.

Service enterprises (1984)

	no. of establish-ments¶¶	avg. no. of em-ployees	monthly contract wages as a % of all contract wages	gross output at producers' value (¥'000,000,000)
Eating and drinking services	794,758	139,000	80.8	...
Real estate	238,358	90,000	103.4	33,674
Transport and communication	160,643	2,276,000	99.6	31,954
Road passenger transport	45,499	537,000	95.5	...
Road freight transport	48,267	658,000	102.3	...
Finance and insurance	84,136	676,000	126.8	22,016
Public utilities	10,914	232,000	117.0	17,694
Retail trade	1,781,075	952,000	88.3	63,192 (retail and wholesale)
Wholesale trade	445,447	1,768,000	100.0	
Medical services	157,879	173,000	130.2	...
Educational services	82,059	222,000	116.6	...

Energy production (consumption): electricity (kW-hr; 1985) 603,930,000,000 (541,390,000,000); coal (metric tons; 1985) 16,383,000 (110,620,000); crude petroleum (barrels; 1985) 3,931,000 (3,985,000,000); petroleum products (metric tons; 1985) 150,994,000, of which (by volume) heavy fuel oil 39.2%, gasoline 22.0%, kerosine and jet fuel 17.2%, diesel 15.3%, naphtha 6.2% (165,063,000 of which [by volume] heavy fuel oil 37.2%, gasoline 20.1%, kerosine and jet fuel 15.2%, diesel 14.0%, naphtha 13.4%); natural gas (cu m; 1985) 2,225,000,000 (27,847,000,000♁♁).

Land use (1984): forested 67.7%; meadows and pastures 1.7%; agricultural and under permanent cultivation 12.8%; other 17.8%.

Foreign trade□□

Balance of trade (current prices)

	1980	1981	1982	1983	1984	1985
¥'000,000,000	+55	+4,603	+4,473	+7,373	+10,674	+13,238
% of total	0.1%	7.4%	6.9%	11.8%	20.9%	18.7%

Imports (1985): ¥31,084,900,000,000 (crude petroleum 26.7%; machinery and equipment 9.6%, of which office machinery 1.2%, aircraft 1.2%; chemicals 6.2%; metal ores and scrap 4.8%, of which iron ore 2.4%, nonferrous metal ores 1.7%; petroleum products 4.6%; coal 4.0%; fish and shellfish 3.5%; nonferrous metals 3.2%; textiles 3.0%; wood 2.9%). *Major import sources:* United States 20.0%; Saudi Arabia 8.0%; Indonesia 7.8%; United Arab Emirates 6.8%; Australia 5.7%; China 5.0%; Canada 3.7%; Malaysia 3.3%; South Korea 3.1%; Oman 2.4%.

Exports (1985): ¥41,955,700,000,000 (motor vehicles 19.5%; iron and steel 7.8%; tape recorders 4.8%; chemicals 4.4%, of which plastic materials 1.3%; office machinery 4.4%; scientific and optical equipment 3.9%; textiles and allied products 3.6%, of which synthetic fabrics 1.2%; vessels 3.4%; electron tubes, etc. 2.7%; power-generating machinery 2.2%; television receivers 1.5%; radio receivers 1.5%). *Major export destinations:* United States 37.1%; China 7.1%; South Korea 4.0%; West Germany 3.9%; Hong Kong 3.7%; Australia 3.1%; Taiwan 2.9%; United Kingdom 2.7%; Canada 2.6%; Saudi Arabia 2.2%.

Trade by commodity group (1984)

SITC group	imports U.S.$'000,000	imports %	exports U.S.$'000,000	exports %
00 Food and live animals	15,191	11.1	1,290	0.8
01 Beverages and tobacco	836	0.6	150	0.1
02 Crude materials, excluding fuels	19,153	14.0	1,250	0.7
03 Mineral fuels, lubricants, and related materials	60,337	44.2	505	0.3
04 Animal and vegetable oils, fats, and waxes	372	0.3	148	0.1
05 Chemicals and related products, n.e.s.	8,346	6.1	7,626	4.5
06 Basic manufactures	11,932	8.7	30,137	17.7
07 Machinery and transport equipment	10,809	7.9	102,680	60.4
08 Miscellaneous manufactured articles	6,088	4.5	24,654	14.5
09 Goods not classified by kind	3,439	2.5	1,674	1.0
TOTAL	136,503	100.0♀	170,114	100.0♀

Direction of trade (1984)

	imports U.S.$'000,000	imports %	exports U.S.$'000,000	exports %
Africa	3,112	2.3	6,358	3.7
Asia	70,778	51.9	56,912	33.5
South America	4,247	3.1	2,466	1.4
North America and Central America	34,804	25.5	70,319	41.3
United States	26,862	19.7	59,937	35.2
other North and Central Am.	7,942	5.8	10,382	6.1
Europe	14,909	10.9	27,170	16.0
EEC	9,336	6.8	19,404	11.4
U.S.S.R.	1,394	1.0	2,518	1.5
other Europe	4,179	3.1	5,248	3.1
Oceania	8,650	6.3	6,890	4.1
TOTAL	136,500	100.0	170,114	100.0

Transport and communications

Transport. Railroads: length (1984) 16,714 mi, 26,899 km; rolling stock (1983) locomotives 4,000, passenger cars 47,022, freight cars 65,142; passengers carried (1985) 18,987,000,000; passenger-mi (1985) 205,101,000,000, passenger-km 330,097,000,000; short ton-mi cargo (1985) 15,161,000,000, metric ton-km cargo 22,134,000,000. Roads (1984): total length 699,200 mi, 1,125,200 km (paved 56%). Vehicles (1986): passenger cars 27,844,580; trucks 17,139,806; buses 231,228. Merchant marine (1985): vessels (100 gross tons and over) 10,288; total deadweight tonnage 63,451,188. Air transport (1985): passengers carried 50,337,000; passenger-mi 40,716,000,000, passenger-km 65,527,000,000; short ton-mi cargo 2,116,320,000, metric ton-km cargo 3,089,770,000; airports (1986) with scheduled flights 65. Shares of domestic passenger traffic by mode of transportation (1984): automobiles 43.9%; railway 39.0%; buses 12.4%; ships and airplanes 4.7%.

Distribution of traffic (1984)

	cargo carried ('000,000 tons)	% of nat'l total	passengers carried ('000,000)	% of nat'l total
Road	5,115.0	90.2	34,030	47.8
Rail (intercity)	107.0	1.9	18,753	26.3
Urban transport	—	—	18,262	25.6
road	—	—	7,551	10.6
rail	—	—	10,711	15.0
Inland water	450.0	7.9	155	0.2
Air	0.5	0.0	45	0.1
Pipeline	...	...	—	—
TOTAL	5,673.0♀	100.0	71,245	100.0

Communications. Daily newspapers (1985): total number 124; total circulation 68,710,000; circulation per 1,000 population 569. Radio (1985): total number of receivers 94,500,000 (1 per 1.3 persons). Television (1985): total number of receivers 30,225,000 (1 per 4.0 persons). Telephones (1984): 66,636,000 (1 per 1.8 persons).

Other communication media (1985)

	titles		traffic ('000)
Print		**Electronic**	
Books (new titles)	31,221	Telegrams♁♁	43,526
of which		Domestic	41,684
Social sciences	7,178	International	1,842
Fiction	6,290	Telex (in minutes)	165,822‖ ‖
Business	1,266	Domestic	111,103‖ ‖
Children's	2,310	International	133,386
Natural sciences	2,605		
History	1,983	**Post♁♁**	
Arts	3,107	Mail	16,579,443
Magazines/journals	3,683	Domestic	16,344,000
Weekly	98	International	235,443
Monthly	2,435	Parcels	144,528
		Domestic	140,636
Cinema		International	3,892
Feature films (greater than 1,600 m)	319		

Radio and television broadcasting (1984): commercial radio stations 270, commercial television stations 6,068. Commercial broadcasters' broadcasting hours (by percentage of programs; 1984): reports—radio 13.3%, television 15.5%; education—radio 5.1%, television 12.0%; culture—radio 18.6%, television 24.0%; entertainment—radio 21.4%, television 42.7%; music—radio 34.7%, television 0%; sports—radio 5.9%, television 4.4%; other—radio 1.0%, television 1.4%. Advertisements (daily avg.; 1984): radio 166, television 235.

Education and health

Education (1985)

	schools	teachers	students	student/teacher ratio
Primary (age 6–11)	25,040	461,249	11,095,711	24.1
Secondary (age 12–17)	16,584	551,962	11,168,212	20.2
Higher	1,066	133,867	2,445,206	18.3

Literacy (1985): total population over age 15 literate 94,385,000 (100%); males literate 45,883,000 (100%); females literate 48,502,000 (100%).

Health (1984): physicians 181,101 (1 per 663 persons); dentists 63,145 (1 per 1,901 persons); nurses 303,734◇◇ (1 per 395 persons); pharmacists 129,700 (1 per 925 persons); midwives 24,649 (1 per 4,869 persons); hospital beds (1984) 1,467,050 (1 per 81.8 persons), of which general 71.6%, mental 22.6%, tuberculosis 4.1%, other 1.7%; infant mortality per rate 1,000 live births (1985) 5.5.

Food (1983): daily per capita caloric intake 2,858 (vegetable products 79%, animal products 21%); 122% of FAO recommended minimum requirement.

Military

Total active duty personnel (1985): 243,000 (army 63.8%, navy 18.1%, air force 18.1%). *Military expenditure as percent of GNP* (1984): 1.0% (world, n.a.); per capita expenditure U.S.$99.

*Oct. 1, 1985. †Excludes Lake Naka (38 sq mi [98 sq km]), which is part of both Tottori and Simane prefectures. ‡Excludes Lake Towada (23 sq mi [60 sq km]), which is part of both Akita and Aomori prefectures. §Part of Kanto geographical region. ‖Part of Kinki geographical region. ¶1985 survey; includes Lake Naka and Lake Towada. ♀Detail does not add to total given because of rounding. ♁1985. □Figures relate only to Japanese nationals in Japan. ◇Applies to passengers carried within the metropolitan areas of Tōkyō, Ōsaka, and Nagoya only. △June. †Import duties and statistical discrepancy less imputed bank service charge. ⊕Includes unemployed. **Initial budget. ††July. ‡‡Worker's household. §§Consists of employees, proprietors, unpaid family workers, and salaried managers and directors. ‖ ‖1982. ¶¶1981. ♀♀End of period. ♁♁1984. □□Import figures are f.o.b. in balance of trade and c.i.f. in commodities and trading partners. ◇◇Clinical nurses only.

Jordan

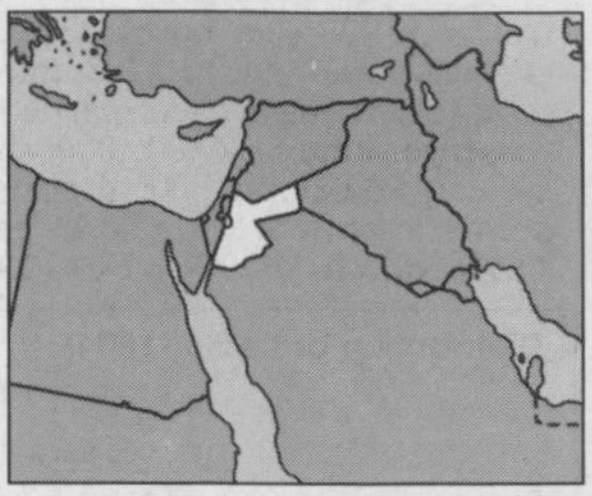

Official name: al-Mamlakah al-Urdunnīyah al-Hāshimīyah (al-Urdun) (Hashemite Kingdom of Jordan).
Form of government: constitutional monarchy with two legislative houses (Senate [30 appointed by king]; House of Deputies [130 elected]).
Chief of state: Monarch.
Head of government: Prime Minister.
Capital: Amman.
Official language: Arabic.
Official religion: Islam.
Monetary unit: 1 Jordan Dinar (JD) = 1,000 fils; valuation (Oct. 1, 1986) JD 1.00 = U.S.$3.13 = £2.17.

Area and population

		area		population
Governorates	Capitals	sq mi	sq km	1985 estimate*
al-ʿĀṣimah	Amman	6,904	17,882	1,427,300
al-Balqāʾ	as-Salt	413	1,069	179,100
al-Karak	al-Karak	1,777	4,601	153,100
Irbid	Irbid	8,747	22,654	744,800
Maʿān	Maʿān	16,602	43,000	90,800
TOTAL		34,443	89,206	2,595,000

Demography

Population (1986): 2,750,000.
Density (1986): persons per sq mi 79.8, persons per sq km 30.8.
Urban–rural (1984): urban 71.5%; rural 28.5%.
Sex distribution (1985): male 52.31%; female 47.69%.
Age breakdown (1984): under 15, 48.1%; 15–29, 27.4%; 30–44, 12.5%; 45–59, 8.0%; 60–74, 3.1%; 75 and over, 0.9%.
Population projection: (1990) 3,213,000; (2000) 4,743,000.
Doubling time: 20 years.
Ethnic composition (1982): Arab 98.0%; Circassian 1.0%; Armenian 1.0%.
Religious affiliation (1980): Sunnī Muslim 93.0%; Christian 4.9%; other 2.1%.
Major cities (1985): Amman 800,000; az-Zarqā 274,300; Irbid 144,650; ar-Raṣayfah 63,100.

Vital statistics

Birth rate per 1,000 population (1980–85): 45.3 (world avg. 29.0).
Death rate per 1,000 population (1980–85): 9.1 (world avg. 11.0).
Natural increase rate per 1,000 population (1980–85): 36.2 (world avg. 18.0).
Total fertility rate (avg. births per childbearing woman; 1980–85): 7.1.
Marriage rate per 1,000 population (1984): 7.1.
Divorce rate per 1,000 population (1984): 1.0.
Life expectancy at birth (1980–85): male 60.3 years; female 64.2 years.
Major causes of death per 100,000 population: n.a.; however, major diseases include tuberculosis, typhoid, and paratyphoid fevers, salmonella, hepatitis, and dysentery; nonvenereal syphilis is widespread in the southern desert region.

National economy

Budget† (1983). Revenue: JD 762,000,000 (foreign grants and loans 44.4%, indirect taxes 21.6%, fees 8.0%, direct taxes 10.4%). Expenditures: JD 775,370,000 (development expenditure 39.2%, defense 21.7%, education 7.6%, police 3.3%, health and social welfare 2.8%).
Public debt (external, outstanding; 1984): U.S.$2,336,300,000.
Tourism (1984): receipts from visitors U.S.$416,000,000; expenditures by nationals abroad U.S.$334,000,000.
Production (metric tons except as noted). Agriculture, forestry, fishing (1984): tomatoes 208,700, eggplant 51,100, olives 50,000, wheat 49,700, citrus fruit (mostly oranges and lemons) 48,300, squash 42,700, hot and sweet peppers 16,200, bananas 14,300, watermelons 14,000, cauliflower 12,400, barley 11,900, grapes 8,600, tobacco 2,400; livestock (number of live animals; 1983) 980,000 sheep, 442,000 goats, 34,000 cattle, 17,000 camels; roundwood 9,000 cu m; fish catch (1983) 17. Mining and quarrying (1984): phosphate ore 6,120,000; potash 486,000; gypsum 41,000. Manufacturing (1984): cement 1,994,000; phosphate fertilizer 365,000‡; steel 112,000; cigarettes 460; beer 50,200 hectolitres; arrack 8,500 hectolitres; wine 4,200 hectolitres. Construction (1983): residential 2,378,100 sq m; nonresidential 632,300 sq m. Energy production (consumption): electricity (kW-hr; 1984) 2,304,000,000 (2,304,000,000); coal, none (n.a.); crude petroleum (barrels; 1984) none (18,977,000); petroleum products (metric tons; 1984) 2,387,000 (2,327,000); natural gas none (n.a.).
Population economically active (1984): total 552,357; activity rate of total population 21.3% (participation rates: over age 15, 40.9%; female 11.1%; unemployed 6.0%).

Price and earnings indexes (1975 = 100)

	1978	1979	1980	1981	1982	1983	1984
Consumer price index	136.6	156.0	173.3	194.2	200.5	210.6	218.7
Daily earnings index	152.7	164.7	200.0	213.3	...	...	...

Household income and expenditure. Average household size (1984) 6.9; income per household (1979) JD 1,820§ (U.S.$6,055); source of income: n.a.; expenditure (1980): food and nonalcoholic beverages 42.3%, household supplies 20.4%, rent 14.6%, education 7.2%, clothing and footwear 6.6%, health care 2.4%, transportation 1.5%, tobacco 0.9%, recreation 0.3%, other 3.8%.
Gross national product (at current market prices; 1984): U.S.$4,908,000,000 (U.S.$1,960 per capita).

Structure of gross domestic product and labour force

	1984			
	in value JD '000,000	% of total value	labour force	% of labour force
Agriculture	157.0	5.6	22,455	4.1
Mining	94.0	3.4	6,658	1.2
Manufacturing	675.0	24.1	35,945	6.5
Construction	327.0	11.7	56,836	10.3
Public utilities	68.0	2.4	2,370	0.4
Transportation and communication	387.0	13.8	46,971	8.5
Trade	324.0	11.6	58,369	10.6
Finance	170.0	6.1	15,835	2.9
Pub. admin., defense	371.0	13.3	} 273,956	49.6
Services	70.0	2.5		
Other	155.0	5.5	32,962 ‖	5.9 ‖
TOTAL	2,798.0	100.0	552,357	100.0

Land use (1983): forested 0.4%; meadows and pastures 1.0%; agricultural and under permanent cultivation 4.3%; wasteland (mostly desert), built-on, and other 94.3%.

Foreign trade

Balance of trade (current prices)¶

	1980	1981	1982	1983	1984	1985
JD '000,000	−545	−805	−878	−893	−781	−763
% of total	51.3%	52.9%	52.9%	61.0%	45.7%	55.1%

Imports (1984): JD 1,071,300,000 (mineral fuels [mostly crude petroleum] 19.9%; nonelectrical machinery and equipment 6.1%; cereals [including wheat, wheat flour, rice, and corn] 6.1%; iron and steel 5.7%; motor vehicles 5.4%; electrical machinery and equipment 4.8%; metal manufactures [mostly structures and parts] 4.4%). *Major import sources:* Saudi Arabia 19.5%; United States 11.1%; Japan 7.4%; United Kingdom 6.8%; West Germany 6.3%; Italy 5.8%.
Exports (1984)♀: JD 261,100,000 (worked building stone and asbestos cement 28.1%; natural phosphate fertilizer 22.6%; food and live animals [mostly assorted vegetables, tomatoes, olives, citrus fruit, and spices] 14.0%; wearing apparel, textiles, and yarn 4.9%; pharmaceuticals 4.3%; wood and wooden products 3.2%). *Major export destinations:* Iraq 26.0%; Saudi Arabia 14.8%; India 13.1%; Romania 4.9%; Pakistan 4.3%; Kuwait 4.0%.

Transport and communications

Transport. Railroads (1985): route length 385 mi, 619 km; passenger traffic, n.a.; short ton-mi cargo 864,000,000, metric ton-km cargo 1,262,000,000. Roads (1984): total length 3,934 mi, 6,332 km (paved 74.4%). Vehicles (1982): passenger cars 118,852; trucks and buses 48,884. Merchant marine (1985): vessels (100 gross tons and over) 8; total deadweight tonnage 76,155. Air transport (1984): passenger-mi 2,243,264,000, passenger-km 3,610,191,000; short ton-mi cargo 95,815,000, metric ton-km cargo 139,888,000; airports (1986) with scheduled flights 2.
Communications. Daily newspapers (1985): total number 5; total circulation 188,000; circulation per 1,000 population 69.7. Radio (1985): total number of receivers 551,000 (1 per 4.9 persons). Television (1985): total number of receivers 181,000 (1 per 14.9 persons). Telephones (1982): 86,074 (1 per 27.3 persons).

Education and health

Education (1983–84)

	schools	teachers	students	student/ teacher ratio
Primary (age 5–11)	1,148	15,179	487,890	32.1
Secondary (age 12–17)	1,515	13,153	286,092	21.8
Vocational	19	1,290	25,310	19.6
Higher	47	2,465δ	55,575	...

Educational attainment (1979). Percent of population over age 14 having: no formal schooling 47.9%; primary education 19.8%; secondary 26.4%; higher 5.9%. *Literacy* (1984): total population over age 15 literate 1,006,785 (74.6%); males literate 593,556 (83.9%); females literate 413,229 (64.4%).
Health (1984): physicians 2,310 (1 per 1,102 persons); hospital beds 3,578 (1 per 711 persons); infant mortality rate per 1,000 live births 63.0.
Food (1979–81): daily per capita caloric intake 2,498 (vegetable products 89%, animal products 11%); 102% of FAO recommended minimum requirement.

Military

Total active duty personnel (1985): 70,300 (army 89.3%, navy 0.5%, air force 10.2%). *Military expenditure as percent of GNP* (1982): 21.3% (world 6.0%); per capita expenditure U.S.$298.

*January 1. †*Budget* (1986). Revenue: JD 580,000,000. Expenditures: JD 635,000,000. ‡1983. §Households involved in nonagricultural activities only. ‖ Unemployed persons. ¶Includes reexports. ♀Domestic exports only. δ1982–83.

Kampuchea

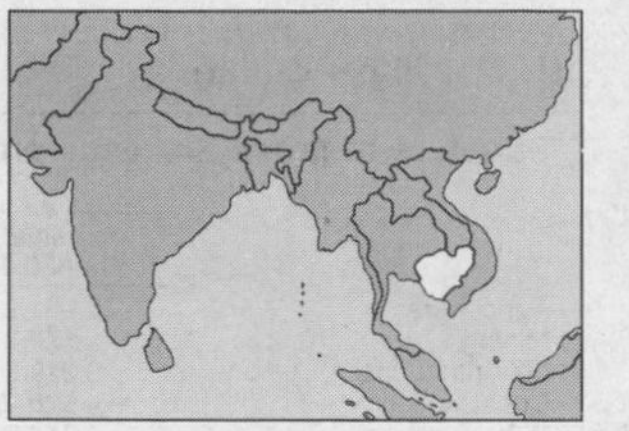

Official name: Sathearanakrath Pracheachon Kampuchea (People's Republic of Kampuchea)*.
Form of government: single-party people's republic with one legislative house (National Assembly [117]).
Chief of state: President, Council of State.
Head of government: Prime Minister.
Capital: Phnom Penh.
Official language: Khmer.
Official religion: none.
Monetary unit: 1 riel = 100 sen; valuation (Dec. 31, 1983) 1 U.S.$ = 4.00 riels; 1 £ = 5.81 riels.

Area and population

		area		population
Provinces	Capitals	sq mi	sq km	1981 census
Bătdâmbâng	Bătdâmbâng	7,407	19,184	719,000
Kâmpóng Cham	Kâmpóng Cham	3,783	9,799	1,070,000
Kâmpóng Chhnăng	Kâmpóng Chhnăng	2,132	5,521	221,000
Kâmpóng Saôm	Kâmpóng Saôm	26	68	53,000
Kâmpóng Spoe	Kâmpóng Spoe	2,709	7,017	340,000
Kâmpóng Thum	Kâmpóng Thum	10,657†	27,602†	379,000
Kâmpôt	Kâmpôt	2,320	6,008	354,000
Kândal	...	1,472	3,812	720,000
Kaôh Kŏng	Krŏng Kaôh Kŏng	4,309	11,161	25,000
Krâchéh	Krâchéh	4,283	11,094	157,000
Môndól Kiri	Senmonorom	5,517	14,288	16,000
Phnom Penh	Phnom Penh	18	46	329,000
Poŭthisăt	Poŭthisăt	4,900	12,692	175,000
Preăh Vihéar	Phnum Tbéng Meanchey	†	†	70,000
Prey Vêng	Prey Vêng	1,885	4,883	672,000
Rôtânôkiri	Lumphăt	4,163	10,782	45,000
Siĕmréab	Siĕmréab	6,354	16,457	477,000
Stŏeng Trêng	Stŏeng Trêng	4,283	11,092	39,000
Svay Riĕng	Svay Riĕng	1,145	2,966	292,000
Takêv	Takêv	1,376	3,563	531,000
TOTAL LAND AREA		68,721	177,987	6,684,000
INLAND WATER		1,177	3,048	
TOTAL AREA		69,898	181,035	

Demography

Population (1986): 7,469,000.
Density‡ (1986): persons per sq mi 108.7, persons per sq km 42.0.
Urban-rural (1985): urban 15.6%; rural 86.4%.
Sex distribution (1985): male 49.74%; female 50.26%.
Age breakdown (1985): under 15, 32.8%; 15–29, 34.2%; 30–44, 19.7%; 45–59, 9.2%; 60–74, 3.6%; 75 and over 0.5%.
Population projection: (1990) 8,572,000; (2000) 9,772,000.
Doubling time: 27 years.
Ethnic composition (1982): Khmer 93%; Chinese 3%; Vietnamese 4% (although recent Vietnamese immigration may have raised their proportion to as much as 8%).
Religious affiliation (1980): Buddhist 88.4%; Muslim 2.4%; other 9.2%.
Major cities (1971): Phnom Penh 600,000§; Kâmpóng Cham 34,706; Kâmpóng Chhnăng 15,813; Kratié 14,765; Pursat 14,736; Svay Riĕng 13,766.

Vital statistics

Birth rate per 1,000 population (1985): 43.5 (world avg. 29.0); legitimate, n.a.; illegitimate, n.a.
Death rate per 1,000 population (1985): 18.2 (world avg. 11.0).
Natural increase rate per 1,000 population (1985): 25.3 (world avg. 18.0).
Total fertility rate (avg. births per childbearing woman; 1985): 4.9.
Marriage rate per 1,000 population: n.a.
Divorce rate per 1,000 population: n.a.
Life expectancy at birth (1985): male 44.5 years; female 47.4 years.
Major causes of death per 100,000 population (registered deaths only; 1966): tuberculosis of the respiratory system 154; all accidents other than vehicle accidents 111; malaria 55; pneumonia 51.

National economy

Budget. The lack, since the mid-1970s, of a taxable domestic economic base or of any income-earning export markets has left Kampuchea without a central governmental budget other than the dispersal of foreign aid and the management of development investments.
Public debt: n.a.
Tourism: none.
Production (metric tons except as noted). Agriculture, forestry, fishing (1984): rice 1,300,000, roots and tubers 130,000, cassava 95,000, corn (maize) 75,000, beans 30,000, sweet potatoes 26,000, tobacco 5,000, rubber 13,000; livestock (number of live animals) 1,466,000 cattle, 1,008,000 pigs, 600,000 buffalo, 6,000,000 chickens; roundwood 5,215,000 cu m; fish catch 62,700. Mining and quarrying (1984): salt 40,000. Manufacturing (1983): cement 50,000§; pork 20,000; beef and veal 14,000; sawn wood 27,200 cu m; plywood 2,000 cu m; cigarettes 4,100,000,000 units§. Construction: n.a. Energy production (consumption): electricity (kW-hr; 1984) 70,000,000 (70,000,000); coal, n.a. (n.a.); crude petroleum, n.a. (n.a.); petroleum products (metric tons; 1984), none (10,000); natural gas, n.a. (n.a.).
Household income and expenditure. Average household size (1980) 5.6; average annual income per household: n.a.; source of income: n.a.; expenditure: n.a.

Gross national product (at current market prices; 1975): U.S.$1,132,000,000 (U.S.$159 per capita).

Structure of gross domestic product and labour force

	1966		1980	
	in value '000,000 riels	% of total value	labour force	% of labour force
Agriculture	13,100	40.9	2,454,000	74.4
Mining and manufacturing	3,300	10.3		
Construction	1,700	5.3		
Public utilities	400	1.3	220,000	6.7
Transportation and communication	700	2.2		
Trade	7,300	22.8		
Public admin., defense	3,900	12.2	625,000	18.9
Services	1,600	5.0		
TOTAL	32,000	100.0	3,299,000	100.0

Population economically active (1985): total 3,602,000; activity rate of total population 49.5% (participation rates: ages 15–64, 64.5%; female 39.9%; unemployed, n.a.).

Price and earnings indexes (1970 = 100)

	1967	1968	1969	1970	1971	1972	1973
Consumer price index ‖	79.5	84.1	89.4	100.0	172.0	215.2	556.1
Earnings index	...	...	...	...	...	...	...

Land use (1983): forested 75.8%; meadows and pastures 3.3%; agricultural and under permanent cultivation 17.2%; other 3.7%.

Foreign trade¶

Balance of trade (current prices)

	1978	1979	1980	1981	1982	1983
U.S.$'000,000	...	...	...	−60	...	−20
% of total	...	...	...	41.1%	...	67.0%

Imports (1973): 14,200,100,000 old riels (agricultural and food products 54.4%, textiles 12.4%, mineral products 11.7%, pharmaceuticals 9.8%, metals and metal products 9.0%, chemicals 2.3%). *Major import sources* (1972): Japan 17.8%; Thailand 16.5%; Hong Kong 14.9%; France 14.4%; United States 10.1%; Singapore 5.3%.
Exports (1973): 2,732,500,000 old riels (rubber 93.1%, haricot beans 4.4%, sesame seeds 2.0%, rice 0.5%). *Major export destinations* (1972): South Vietnam 54.8%; Hong Kong 18.3%; Singapore 10.2%; Japan 4.1%; France 4.1%; United States 3.0%.

Transport and communications

Transport. Railroads (1981): length 403 mi, 649 km; passenger-mi 33,554,000, passenger-km 54,000,000; short ton-mi cargo 6,850,000, metric ton-km cargo 10,000,000. Roads (1981): total length 8,296 mi, 13,351 km (paved 20%). Vehicles (1981): passenger cars 700; trucks 1,800. Merchant marine (1985): vessels (100 gross tons and over) 3; total deadweight tonnage 3,839. Air transport (1977): passenger-mi 26,098,800, passenger-km 42,000,000; short ton-mi cargo 274,000, metric ton-km cargo 400,000; airports (1986) with scheduled flights 1.
Communications. Daily newspapers (1984): total number 16; total circulation, n.a. Radio (1985): total number of receivers 200,000 (1 per 36 persons). Television (1985): total number of receivers 52,000 (1 per 140 persons). Telephones (1981): 7,315 (1 per 790 persons).

Education and health

Education (1983–84)

	schools	teachers	students	student/ teacher ratio
Primary (age 6–11)	3,629♀	36,520	1,504,840	41.2
Secondary	207	4,494	145,730	32.4
Voc., teacher tr.	13	278	7,334	26.4
Higher	2♂	...	586♂	...

Educational attainment, n.a. *Literacy* (1980): total population over age 15 literate 48.0%.
Health (1984): physicians 200 (1 per 36,000 persons); hospital beds 16,200 (1 per 441 persons); infant mortality rate per 1,000 live births (1985) 145.0.
Food (1980–82): daily per capita caloric intake 1,930 (vegetable products 95%, animal products 5%); 87% of FAO recommended minimum requirement.

Military

Total active duty personnel (1984): 30,000□. *Military expenditure as percent of GNP:* n.a.; per capita expenditure, n.a.

*The UN continues to seat Democratic Kampuchea (DK), whose present leadership calls itself the Coalition Government of Democratic Kampuchea and is composed of Khmer People's National Liberation Front, the DK (Khmer Rouge), and the organization of Norodom Sihanouk. †Area of Preăh Vihéar included with Kâmpóng Thum. ‡Based on land area. §1982. ‖ Phnom Penh only. ¶In 1981 imports were estimated to be U.S.$103,000,000; exports were estimated to be U.S.$43,000,000. Major trading partners are the U.S.S.R., Vietnam, Czechoslovakia, Bulgaria, East Germany, Hungary, Cuba, Poland, Mongolia, and Laos. ♀1981–82. ♂1982–83. □Excludes about 160,000 Vietnamese troops and about 45,000 opposition forces of Democratic Kampuchea.

Kenya

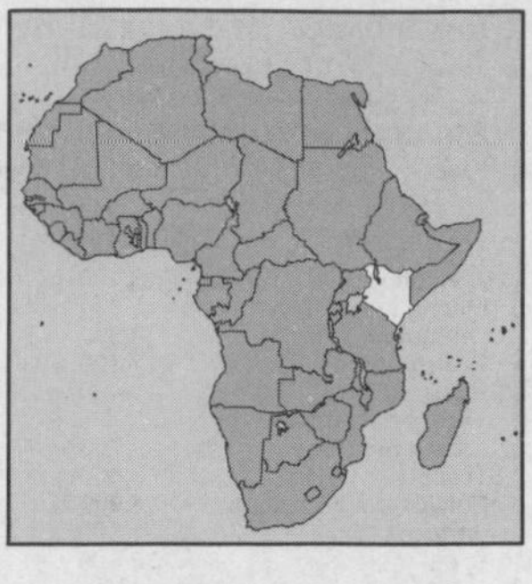

Official name: Jamhuri ya Kenya (Swahili); Republic of Kenya (English).
Form of government: unitary single-party republic with one legislative house (National Assembly [172]).
Head of state and government: President.
Capital: Nairobi.
Official languages: Swahili; English.
Official religion: none.
Monetary unit: 1 Kenyan shilling (K Sh) = 100 cents; valuation (Oct. 1, 1986) 1 U.S.$ = K Sh 15.85; 1 £ = K Sh 22.91.

Area and population

Provinces	Provincial headquarters	area sq mi	area sq km	population 1984 estimate
Central	Nyeri	5,087	13,176	2,926,200
Coast	Mombasa	32,279	83,603	1,688,000
Eastern	Embu	61,734	159,891	3,423,500
Nairobi	Nairobi	264	684	1,103,600
North Eastern	Garissa	48,997	126,902	484,700
Nyanza	Kisumu	6,240	16,162	3,508,500
Rift Valley	Nakuru	67,131	173,868	4,132,400
Western	Kakamega	3,228	8,360	2,269,400
TOTAL LAND AREA		220,625	571,416	19,536,300
INLAND WATER		4,336	11,230	
TOTAL AREA		224,961	582,646	

Demography

Population (1986): 21,150,000.
*Density** (1986): persons per sq mi 95.9, persons per sq km 37.0.
Urban-rural (1985): urban 16.7%; rural 83.3%.
Sex distribution (1985): male 49.77%; female 50.23%.
Age breakdown (1984): under 15, 52.0%; 15–29, 22.7%; 30–44, 12.6%; 45–59, 7.9%; 60–74, 3.6%; 75 and over, 0.9%.
Population projection: (1990) 24,872,000; (2000) 37,505,000.
Doubling time: 17 years.
Ethnic composition (1979): African 98.5% (Kikuyu 20.9%, Luhya 13.8%, Luo 12.8%, Kamba 11.3%, Kalenjin 10.8%); Asian 0.5%; Arab 0.3%; European 0.3%; other 0.4%.
Religious affiliation (1980): Roman Catholic 26.4%; Protestant 19.3%; other Christian 27.3%; tribal religionist 18.9%; Muslim 6.0%; other 2.1%.
Major cities (1984): Nairobi 1,103,600; Mombasa 425,600; Kisumu 167,100; Nakuru 101,700; Machakos 92,300†.

Vital statistics

Birth rate per 1,000 population (1980–85): 55.1 (world avg. 29.0).
Death rate per 1,000 population (1980–85): 14.0 (world avg. 11.0).
Natural increase rate per 1,000 population (1980–85): 41.1 (world avg. 18.0).
Total fertility rate (avg. births per childbearing woman; 1984): 7.7.
Life expectancy at birth (1980–85): male 51.2 years; female 54.7 years.
Major causes of death per 100,000 population: n.a.; however, major health problems include malaria, gastroenteritis, venereal diseases, diarrhea and dysentery, trachoma, and schistosomiasis.

National economy

Budget‡ (1984–85). Revenue: K Sh 22,017,000,000 (sales tax 27.5%, income tax 24.5%, import duties 15.9%, excise duties 7.7%). Expenditures: K Sh 25,783,000,000 (economic services 35.2%, education 20.8%, public administration 15.5%, defense 8.9%, health 6.7%).
Production (metric tons except as noted). Agriculture, forestry, fishing (1984): sugarcane 3,910,000, corn (maize) 1,275,000, cassava 680,000, potatoes 416,000, sweet potatoes 350,000, plantains 255,000, pulses 250,000, pineapples 165,000, sorghum 150,000, bananas 142,000, tea 115,000, coconuts 110,000, wheat 100,000, coffee 95,000, barley 85,000, millet 75,000, tomatoes 57,000, sisal 50,000, seed cotton 27,000, sunflower seeds 17,000, cottonseed 17,000, cashew nuts 15,000, copra 10,000; livestock (number of live animals) 12,000,000 cattle, 8,000,000 goats, 6,700,000 sheep; roundwood 31,115,000 cu m; total fish catch 78,442, of which freshwater fish 93.6%. Mining and quarrying (metric tons; 1984): soda ash 226,000, fluorspar 50,883; salt 49,449; lime and limestone 20,855§; corundum (ruby) 98 kilograms†. Manufacturing (metric tons except as noted; 1983): wheat flour 221,600 ‖; corn meal 302,200 ‖; animal feeds 154,006; refined salt 54,470; cotton woven fabrics 61,733,000 sq m; bedsheets 513,000 sq m; shirts 3,074,000 units; blankets 2,303,000 units. Construction (1982): residential 252,000 sq m; nonresidential 91,000 sq m. Energy production (consumption): electricity (kW-hr; 1984) 1,949,000,000 (1,845,000,000); coal (metric tons; 1984) none (118,000); crude petroleum (barrels; 1984) none (14,250,000); petroleum products (metric tons; 1984) 1,766,000 (1,043,000).
Population economically active (1984): total 7,283,000; activity rate of total population 37.3% (participation rates: ages 15–64, n.a.; female [1981] 33.5; unemployed, n.a.).

Price and earnings indexes (1980 = 100)

	1980	1981	1982	1983	1984	1985	1986¶
Consumer price index	100.0	111.8	134.7	150.2	165.4	187.0	193.5
Annual earnings index	100.0	116.6	124.5	132.7	145.3	...	...

Gross national product (at current market prices; 1984): U.S.$5,748,000,000 (U.S.$290 per capita).

Structure of gross domestic product and labour force

	1984 in value K Sh '000,000	% of total value	labour force♀	% of labour force
Agriculture	22,961.2	26.7	235,600	21.1
Mining	170.2	0.2	4,100	0.4
Manufacturing	9,219.2	10.7	153,100	13.7
Construction	4,626.2	5.4	49,200	4.4
Public utilities	1,314.0	1.5	17,500	1.6
Transp. and commun.	4,378.8	5.1	54,100	4.9
Trade	9,684.8	11.3	84,800	7.6
Finance	5,703.2	6.6	50,200	4.5
Pub. admin., defense	10,558.4	12.3	142,000	12.7
Services	7,979.4	9.3	324.100	29.1
Other	9,285.8δ	10.8	—	—
TOTAL	85,881.2	100.0□	1,114,700	100.0

Public debt (external, outstanding; 1984): U.S.$2,633,400,000.
Tourism (1984): receipts from visitors U.S.$673,000,000; expenditures by nationals abroad U.S.$576,000,000.
Household income and expenditure. Average household size (1980) 6.2; average annual income per household: n.a.; source of income: n.a.; expenditure (1980): food 46.5%, housing 10.0%, furniture and utensils 9.4%, transportation 8.4%, clothing and footwear 7.7%, health 2.2%, education 1.0%.
Land use (1983): forested 4.2%; meadows and pastures 6.6%; agricultural and under permanent cultivation 4.2%; other 85.0%.

Foreign trade◊

Balance of trade (current prices)

	1980	1981	1982	1983	1984	1985
K Sh '000,000	−6,365	−5,446	−4,383	−2,706	−3,636	−6,049
% of total	23.6%	20.4%	16.2%	9.3%	10.5%	16.1%

Imports (1984): K Sh 22,297,060,000 (crude petroleum 27.4%; machinery and transport equipment 26.4%, of which transport equipment 10.4%; chemicals 11.9%, of which pharmaceuticals 1.8%, fertilizers 1.3%; iron and steel 5.8%). *Major import sources:* U.K. 13.7%; United Arab Emirates 11.8%; Japan 10.0%; W.Ger. 8.8%; Saudi Arabia 7.2%; Iran 6.3%; France 5.0%; U.S. 4.6%.
Exports (1984): K Sh 15,096,270,000 (coffee, not roasted, 27.0%; tea 25.1%; petroleum products 18.9%; vegetables and fruit 7.2%, of which canned pineapples 3.4%; cement 2.3%; sisal fibre 1.7%; soda ash 1.6%; pyrethrum extract 1.4%; meat and meat products 1.0%). *Major export destinations:* U.K. 18.3%; W.Ger. 12.6%; Uganda 8.7%; The Netherlands 6.8%; U.S. 5.0%.

Transport and communications

Transport. Railroads (1984): route length (1986) 1,649 mi, 2,654 km; passenger-mi 323,100,000, passenger-km 520,000,000; short ton-mi cargo 1,546,000,000, metric ton-km cargo 2,246,000,000. Roads (1984): total length 33,900 mi, 54,500 km (paved 12%). Vehicles (1983): passenger cars 116,852; trucks and buses 88,912. Merchant marine (1985): vessels (100 gross tons and over) 28; total deadweight tonnage 4,859. Air transport△ (1984): passenger-mi 635,400,000, passenger-km 1,022,500,000; short ton-mi cargo 84,800,000, metric ton-km cargo 123,800,000; airports (1986) with scheduled flights 9.
Communications. Daily newspapers: total number (1985) 5; total circulation (1982) 220,000; circulation per 1,000 population (1982) 12. Radio (1985): 1,600,000 receivers (1 per 13 persons). Television (1985): 100,000 receivers (1 per 203 persons). Telephones (1983): 216,674 (1 per 87 persons).

Education and health

Education (1983)

	schools	teachers	students	student/ teacher ratio
Primary (age 5–11)	11,966	117,475	4,323,822	36.8
Secondary (age 12–17)	2,230	18,960	493,710	26.0
Voc., teacher tr.	40	1,212	20,554	17.0
Higher	4	...	22,157	...

Educational attainment (1979). Percent of population over age 25 having: no formal schooling 58.6%; primary education 32.2%; some secondary 7.9%; complete secondary and higher 1.3%. *Literacy* (1985): total population over age 15 literate 5,758,000 (59.2%); males literate 3,311,000 (69.6%); females literate 2,447,000 (49.2%).
Health (1984): physicians 2,591 (1 per 7,540 persons); hospital beds 30,886 (1 per 633 persons); infant mortality rate per 1,000 live births (1983) 81.
Food (1980–82): daily per capita caloric intake 2,036 (vegetable products 89%, animal products 11%); 87% of FAO recommended minimum requirement.

Military

Total active duty personnel (1985): 13,650 (army 95.2%; navy 4.8%; air force reorganized as part of army since 1982, air force personnel about 2,300 in 1983). *Military expenditure as percent of GNP* (1983): 2.1% (world 6.1%); per capita expenditure U.S.$7.

*Land area only. †1983. ‡Budget for 1986–87: Revenue K Sh 38,962,000,000; Expenditure K Sh 38,962,000,000. §Excludes limestone used in making cement. ‖ 1984. ¶June. ♀Employed persons only. δIndirect taxes less subsidies and imputed bank service charges. □Detail does not add to total given because of rounding. ◊Import figures are f.o.b. in balance of trade and c.i.f. in commodities and trading partners; exports excludes reexports valued at K Sh 441,880,000. △Kenya Airways only.

Kiribati

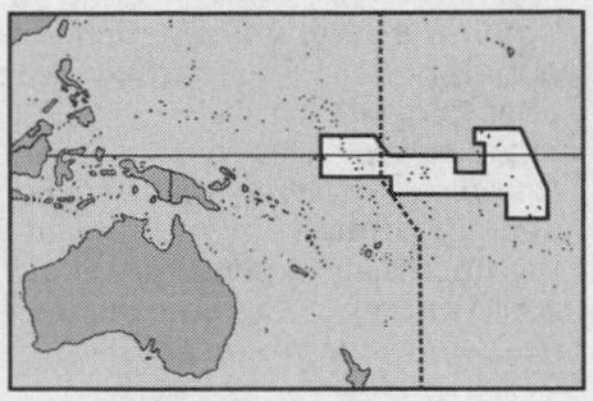

Official name: Republic of Kiribati.
Form of government: unitary republic with one legislature (House of Assembly [37]).
Head of state and government: President.
Capital: Bairiki, on Tarawa Atoll.
Official language: English.
Official religion: none.
Monetary unit: 1 Australian Dollar ($A) = 100 cents; valuation (Oct. 1, 1986) 1 U.S.$ = $A 1.59; 1 £ = $A 2.29.

Area and population

Island Groups / Islands	Capitals	area* sq mi	area* sq km	population 1985 census
Gilberts Group	Bairiki Islet	110	285	61,369
Abaiang	Tuarabu	7	17	4,386
Abemama	Kariatebike	11	27	2,966
Aranuka	Takaeang	4	12	984
Arorae	Roreti	4	9	1,470
Banaba	Anteeren	2	6	189
Beru	Taubukinberu	7	18	2,702
Butaritari	Butaritari	5	13	3,622
Kuria	Tabontebike	6	15	1,052
Maiana	Tebangetua	6	17	2,141
Makin	Makin	3	8	1,777
Marakei	Rawannawi	5	14	2,693
Nikunau	Rungata	7	19	2,061
Nonouti	Teuabu	8	20	2,930
Onotoa	Buariki	6	16	1,927
Tabiteuea North	Utiroa	10	26	3,171
Tabiteuea South	Buariki	5	12	1,322
Tamana	Bakaka	2	5	1,378
Tarawa North	Abaokoro	6	15	3,205
Tarawa South	Bairiki	6	16	21,393
Line Group	Kiritimati	207	535	2,598
Northern		167	432	2,598
Kiritimati (Christmas)	London	150	388	1,737
Tabuaeran (Fanning)	Paelau	13	34	445
Teraina (Washington)	Washington	4	10	416
Southern (Caroline, Flint, Malden, Starbuck, Vostok)		40	103	—
Phoenix Group (Birnie, Enderbury, Kanton [Canton], McKean, Manra [Sydney], Nikumaroro [Gardner], Orona [Hull], Rawaki [Phoenix])	Kanton	11	29	24
TOTAL		328	849	63,991

Demography

Population (1986): 65,000.
Density (1986)†: persons per sq mi 234.7, persons per sq km 90.7.
Urban–rural (1985): urban 33.4%; rural 66.6%.
Sex distribution (1985): male 49.56%; female 50.44%.
Age breakdown (1985)‡: under 15, 38.9%; 15–29, 29.9%; 30–44, 16.1%; 45–59, 9.3%; 60–74, 4.9%; 75 and over, 0.9%.
Population projection: (1990) 69,800; (2000) 77,000.
Doubling time: 40 years.
Ethnic composition (1985): I-Kiribati 96.2%; mixed (part I-Kiribati and other) 2.5%; Tuvaluan 0.7%; European 0.4%; other 0.2%.
Religious affiliation (1985)‡: Roman Catholic 52.7%; Kiribati Protestant (Congregational) 40.9%; Bahā'ī 2.4%; Seventh-day Adventist 1.4%; other 2.6%.
Major cities (1985): Urban Tarawa 21,393.

Vital statistics

Birth rate per 1,000 population (1980–85): 34.9 (world avg. 29.0); legitimate, n.a.; illegitimate, n.a.
Death rate per 1,000 population (1980–85): 13.9 (world avg. 11.0).
Natural increase rate per 1,000 population (1980–85): 21.0 (world avg. 18.0).
Total fertility rate (avg. births per childbearing woman; 1980–85): 4.5.
Marriage rate per 1,000 population (1973): 4.5.
Divorce rate per 1,000 population: n.a.
Life expectancy at birth (1978): male 50.3 years; female 53.8 years.
Major causes of death per 100,000 population (1979)§: n.a.; however, the major causes include tuberculosis, diarrheal and respiratory diseases, and nutritional disorders.

National economy

Budget (1984). Revenue: $A 18,791,000 (current revenue 81.8%, of which taxes 34.0%, nontax revenue 47.8%; external aid and income 18.2%). Expenditures: $A 18,737,000 (current expenditure 83.2%, of which education 14.4%, health 10.0% ‖, police 6.6% ‖; capital expenditure 16.8%).
Public debt: n.a.
Tourism (1977): visitors 796.
Production (metric tons except as noted). Agriculture, forestry, fishing (1984): coconuts 85,000, roots and tubers 13,000 (of which taro 3,000), copra 12,000, fruit 5,000, vegetables and melons 4,000, bananas 4,000, eggs 113; livestock (number of live animals) 10,000 pigs, 191,000 chickens ‖; fish catch 24,212¶, of which snapper 3,000, emperor 2,500, yellowfin tuna 2,100, skipjack tuna 2,000. Mining and quarrying: none♀. Manufacturing (1981): copra $A 2,930,000; other important products are processed fish, baked goods, clothing, boats, and handicrafts. Energy production (consumption): electricity (kW-hr; 1984) 6,000,000 (6,000,000) coal: none (n.a.); crude petroleum: none (n.a.); petroleum products (metric tons; 1984) none (9,000); natural gas: none (n.a.).
Gross national product (at current market prices; 1984): U.S.$30,000,000 (U.S.$480 per capita).

Structure of gross domestic product and labour force

	1982 in value $A '000	1982 % of total value	1985 labour forceδ	1985 % of labour force
Agriculture	7,094	24.9	327	4.7
Mining	—	—	13	0.2
Manufacturing	760	2.7	87	1.3
Construction	1,149	4.0	411	5.9
Public utilities	540	1.9	231	3.3
Transportation and communication	6,100	21.5	1,011	14.6
Trade	4,492	15.8	902	13.0
Finance	684	2.4	80	1.1
Pub. admin., defense } Services	3,903	13.7	3,258	46.9
Other, including unemployed	3,716	13.1	625	9.0
TOTAL	28,438	100.0	6,945	100.0

Population economically active (1985): total 26,337; activity rate of total population 41.2% (participation rates: over age 15, 67.8%; female 36.1%, unemployed 2.4%).

Price and earnings indexes (1980 = 100)

	1978	1979	1980	1981	1982	1983	1984
Consumer price index	80.3	86.1	100.0	107.7	113.7	120.8	128.1
Monthly earnings index	...	...	...	...	...	...	...

Household income and expenditure. Average household size (1985) 6.1; income per household: n.a.; sources of income (1978): agriculture 35.9%, wages only 27.5%, wages and other 19.3%, agriculture and other 12.6%, other 4.7%; expenditure (1982): food 50.0%, tobacco and alcohol 14.0%, clothing 8.0%, transportation 8.0%, housing and household operation 7.5%.
Land use (1983): forested 2.8%; agricultural and under permanent cultivation 50.7%; other 46.5%.

Foreign trade

Balance of trade (current prices)

	1978	1979	1980	1981	1982	1983	1984
$A '000	+7,281	+5,664	−14,422	−16,312	−15,681	−15,900	−10,381
% of total	20.5%	15.4%	74.8%	−71.2%	77.2%	65.4%	28.5%

Imports (1984): $A 23,387,000 (machines and transport equipment 36.6%, food and live animals 23.2%, basic manufactured goods 13.4%, petroleum products 9.5%, miscellaneous manufactured articles 5.7%, beverages and tobacco 5.0%, chemicals 4.8%). *Major import sources:* Australia 35.9%; Japan 15.5%; New Zealand 7.8%; Italy 2.5%; United Kingdom 2.5%.
Exports (1984): $A 13,006,000 (copra 53.7%, fish and fish preparations 17.6%). *Major export destinations:* Western Europe 97%; Asia 3%.

Transport and communications

Transport. Roads (1984): total length 398 mi, 640 km (paved, n.a.). Vehicles (1978): passenger cars and trucks 163; motorcycles 2,822. Merchant marine (1985): vessels (100 gross tons and over) 4; total deadweight tonnage 1,297. Air transport (1978): passengers carried 14,593; airports (1986) with scheduled flights 17.
Communications. Daily newspapers: none. Radio (1985): total number of receivers 10,000 (1 per 6.4 persons). Television (1985): none. Telephones (1984): 1,400 (1 per 45.7 persons).

Education and health

Education (1985)

	schools	teachers	students	student/ teacher ratio
Primary (age 6–13)	112	460	13,440	29.2
Secondary (age 14–18)	8	117	2,024	17.3
Voc., teacher tr.	2	31	75	2.4
Higher□	1	12	97	8.1

Educational attainment (1985)‡: Percent of population over age 15 having: no schooling 3.5%, less than full primary education 38.4%, primary 37.1%, some secondary 15.5%, secondary 4.4%, higher 0.4%. *Literacy* (1985): total population over age 15 literate 7,900 (20.0%).
Health (1981): physicians 16 (1 per 3,690 persons); hospital beds 283 (1 per 208 persons); infant mortality rate per 1,000 live births (1978) 87.
Food (1980–82): daily per capita caloric intake 3,120 (vegetable products 76%, animal products 24%); 117% of FAO recommended minimum requirement.

*Includes uninhabited islands. †Density based on inhabited island areas (277 sq mi, 717 sq km). ‡Indigenous population only, who constitute 98.5% of the total population. §Leading causes of death at Tungary Central Hospital. ‖ 1982. ¶1983. ♀Mining of phosphates on Banaba (Ocean Island) ceased in 1979. δIndigenous population active in cash economy only. □Teachers college.

Korea, North

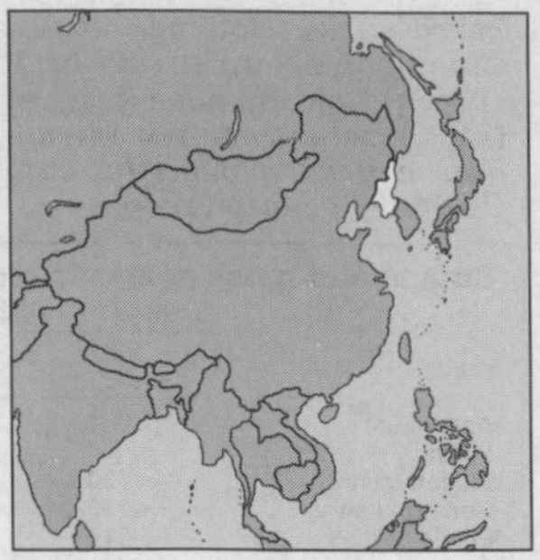

Official name: Chosŏn Minjujuŭi In'min Konghwaguk (Democratic People's Republic of Korea).
Form of government: unitary single-party republic with one legislative house (Supreme People's Assembly [615]).
Chief of state: President.
Head of government: Premier.
Capital: P'yŏngyang.
Official language: Korean.
Official religion: none.
Monetary unit: 1 won = 100 chon; valuation (Oct. 1, 1986) 1 U.S.$ = 0.94 won; 1 £ = 1.36 won.

Area and population

		area*		population
				1968
Provinces	**Capitals**	sq mi	sq km	estimate
Chagang-do	Kanggye	6,300	16,200	780,000
Hamgyŏng-namdo	Hamhŭng	7,400	19,200	1,315,000
Hamgyŏng-pukto	Ch'ŏngjin	6,100	15,900	1,110,000
Hwanghae-namdo	Haeju	2,900	7,600	1,340,000
Hwanghae-pukto	Sariwŏn	3,300	8,600	1,060,000
Kangwŏn-do	Wŏnsan	4,100	10,700	1,030,000
P'yŏngan-namdo	P'yŏngsan	4,700	12,300	2,250,000
P'yŏngan-pukto	Sinŭiju	4,600	12,000	1,760,000
Yanggang-do	Hyesan	5,400	14,100	435,000
Special cities				
Ch'ŏngjin-si	—	700	1,900	385,000
Hamhŭng-si	—	300	800	530,000
P'yŏngyang-si	P'yŏngyang	700	1,800	1,275,000
Special district				
Kaesŏng-chigu	Kaesŏng	500	1,200	289,000
TOTAL		47,300†	122,400†	13,559,000

Demography

Population (1986): 20,543,000.
Density (1986): persons per sq mi 434.3, persons per sq km 167.8.
Urban–rural (1985): urban 62.0%; rural 38.0%.
Sex distribution (1985): male 49.58%; female 50.42%.
Age breakdown (1985): under 15, 38.1%; 15–29, 29.4%; 30–44, 16.6%; 45–59, 9.9%; 60–74, 4.9%; 75 and over, 1.1%.
Population projection: (1990) 22,443,000; (2000) 27,256,000.
Doubling time: 29 years.
Ethnic composition (1980): Korean 99.3%; other 0.7%.
Religious affiliation (1980): atheist or nonreligious 67.9%; traditional beliefs 15.6%; Ch'ŏndogyo 13.9%; Buddhist 1.7%; Christian 0.9%.
Major cities (1981): P'yŏngyang 1,283,000; Hamhŭng-Hŭngnam 775,000; Ch'ŏngjin 490,000; Kaesŏng 240,000; Wŏnsan 240,000.

Vital statistics

Birth rate per 1,000 population (1984): 30.0 (world avg. 29.0).
Death rate per 1,000 population (1984): 6.0 (world avg. 11.0).
Natural increase rate per 1,000 population (1984): 24.0 (world avg. 18.0).
Total fertility rate (avg. births per childbearing woman; 1984): 3.8.
Marriage rate per 1,000 population: n.a.
Divorce rate per 1,000 population: n.a.
Life expectancy at birth (1984): male 65 years; female 72 years.
Major causes of death: n.a.; however, major diseases include endemic diseases (typhoid fever, dysentery, clonorchiasis [liver fluke], paragonimiasis [lung fluke], encephalitis, poliomielitis, diphtheria, measles, tuberculosis of respiratory system, bronchitis, malignant neoplasms (cancers), hypertensive and ischemic heart diseases, and intestinal obstruction and hernia.

National economy

Budget (1985). Revenue: 27,384,000,000 won (detail, n.a.). Expenditures: 27,384,000,000‡ (national economy 59.0%, social and cultural affairs 23.0%, defense 15.1%, other 2.9%).
Public debt (external, outstanding; 1983): U.S.$3,000,000,000.
Production (metric tons except as noted). Agriculture, forestry, fishing (1984): rice 5,400,000, corn (maize) 2,580,000, potatoes 1,700,000, vegetables 1,545,000, apples 560,000, millet 500,000, barley 500,000, soybeans 400,000, sweet potatoes 400,000, sugarcane 181,000, millet and sorghum 127,000, pears 87,000, peaches 85,000, tobacco 50,000, dry onions 35,000, pulses 29,000, seed cotton 11,000, sesame seed 8,000, avocado 7,000; livestock (number of live animals) 2,700,000 pigs, 1,025,000 cattle, 340,000 sheep, 260,000 goats, 18,100,000 chickens; roundwood 4,462,000 cu m; fish catch (1983) 1,600,000. Mining and quarrying (1984): iron ore 8,000,000; crude magnesite 1,900,000; calcined magnesite 800,000; pyrites 620,000; salt 570,000; zinc 140,000; barite 110,000; lead (metal content) 75,000; copper 15,000; silver 1,600,000 troy oz; gold 160,000 troy oz. Manufacturing (1984): cement 8,910,000; pig iron 5,750,000; chemical fertilizers 3,900,000§; crude steel 3,500,000; steel semimanufactures 3,400,000; television sets 200,000 units; machine tools 29,000 units; cars 18,000 units; textile fabrics 600,000,000 m. Construction: n.a. Energy production (consumption): electricity (kW-hr; 1984) 45,000,000,000 (45,000,000,000); coal (metric tons; 1984) 49,000,000 (49,400,000); crude petroleum (barrels; 1984) none (17,600,000); petroleum products (metric tons; 1984) 2,330,000 (2,820,000); natural gas, none (n.a.).
Population economically active (1980): total 7,838,000; activity rate of total population 45.3% (participation rates: ages 15–64, 75.1%; female 45.9%; unemployed, n.a.).
Price and earnings indexes: n.a.
Household income and expenditure. Average household size (1980) 5.7; average annual income per household 3,677 won (U.S.$4,275); source of income: n.a.; expenditure ‖ (1984): food 46.5%; clothing 29.9%; furniture 3.8%; energy 3.3%; housing 0.6%.
Gross national product (1984): U.S.$14,700,000,000 (U.S.$760 per capita).

Structure of gross domestic product and labour force

	1982			
	in value '000,000 won	% of total value	labour force	% of labour force
Agriculture	...	...	3,276,000	44.1
Mining and manufacturing	...	...	} 2,790,000	33.0
Construction	...	...		
Public utilities	...	...		
Transp. and commun.	...	...	418,000	4.9
Trade	...	...	} 1,521,000	18.0
Finance	...	...		
Pub. admin., defense	...	...		
Services	...	...		
Other	...	...		
TOTAL	11,800	100.0	8,455,000	100.0

Land use (1983): forested 74.4%; meadows and pastures 0.4%; agricultural and under permanent cultivation 18.7%; other 6.5%.
Tourism: n.a.

Foreign trade

Balance of trade (current prices)

	1974	1976	1978	1979	1980	1981
'000,000 won	−601	−176	−53	+165	−256	−285
% of total	31.6%	11.5%	3.3%	6.3%	9.4%	10.3%

Imports (1984): U.S.$1,390,000,000 (crude petroleum, coal and coke, industrial machinery and transport equipment [including trucks], industrial chemicals, textile yarn and fabrics, and grain are among the major imports). *Major import sources* (1981): U.S.S.R. 22.0%; Japan 18.0%; China 17.0%; East European countries 7.6%.
Exports (1984): U.S.$1,340,000,000 (minerals [including lead, magnesite, and zinc], metallurgical products [iron and steel, nonferrous metals], cement, agricultural products [including fish, grain, fruit and vegetables, tobacco], and manufactured goods [textile fabrics, clothing], are among the major exports). *Major export destinations* (1981): U.S.S.R. 26.0%; China 17.0%; Japan 9.0%; Saudi Arabia 9.0%; India 5.0%.

Transport and communications

Transport. Railroads (1985): length 2,779 mi, 4,473 km; passengers, n.a.; cargo, n.a. Roads (1985): total length 13,670 mi, 22,000 km (paved 2%). Vehicles (1982): passenger cars 180,000. Merchant marine (1985): vessels (100 gross tons and over) 89; total deadweight tonnage 829,392. Air transport (1979): passenger-mi 52,200,000, passenger-km 84,000,000; short ton-mi cargo 1,370,000, metric ton-km cargo 2,000,000; airports (1986) with scheduled flights 1.
Communications. Daily newspapers (1984): total number 10; total circulation, n.a. Radio (1984): total number of receivers 4,100,000 (1 per 5 persons). Television (1984): total number of receivers 1,050,000 (1 per 19 persons). Telephones (1983): 10,000 (1 per 2,000 persons).

Education and health

Education (1982)

	schools	teachers	students	student/ teacher ratio
Primary (age 5–9)	4,700¶ }		*c.* 2,500,000	...
Secondary (age 10–15)	...	} *c.* 100,000	*c.* 2,500,000♀	...
Voc., teacher tr.	...		...	...
Higher	175	9,244	200,000	21.6

Educational attainment, n.a. *Literacy* (1979): 90%.
Health (1982): physicians 45,000 (1 per 417 persons); hospital beds 244,000 (1 per 77 persons); infant mortality rate per 1,000 live births (1984) 28.
Food (1980–82): daily per capita caloric intake 3,065 (vegetable products 94%, animal products 6%); 130% of FAO recommended minimum requirement.

Military

Total active duty personnel (1985): 838,000 (army 89.5%, navy 4.2%, air force 6.3%). *Military expenditure as percent of GNP* (1984): 23.3% (world 6.1%); per capita expenditure U.S.$177.

*Areas approximate. †Detail does not add to total given because of rounding. ‡Revenue and expenditure breakdown given is for 1979. §1983. ‖ Workers and clerical workers only. ¶1976. ♀Includes vocational students.

Korea, South

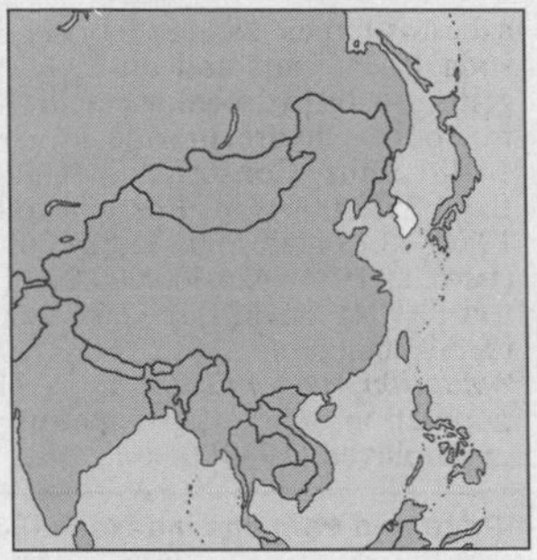

Official name: Taehan Min'guk (Republic of Korea).
Form of government: unitary republic with a National Assembly (276 members).
Chief of state: President.
Head of government: Prime Minister.
Capital: Seoul.
Official language: Korean.
Official religion: none.
Monetary unit: 1 won (W) = 100 chon; valuation (Oct. 1, 1986) 1 U.S.$ = W 877; 1 £ = W 1,267.

Area and population

		area		population
Provinces	**Capitals**	sq mi	sq km	1985 census
Cheju-do	Cheju	705	1,825	489,458
Chŏlla-namdo	Kwangju	4,720	12,225	3,748,442
Chŏlla-pukto	Chŏnju	3,108	8,050	2,202,218
Ch'ungch'ŏng-namdo	Taejŏn	3,410	8,833	3,001,538
Ch'ungch'ŏng-pukto	Ch'ŏngju	2,869	7,431	1,391,084
Kangwŏn-do	Ch'unch'ŏn'	6,523	16,894	1,726,029
Kyŏnggi-do	Inch'ŏn*	4,191	10,856	4,794,240
Kyŏngsang-namdo	Masan	4,576	11,851	3,013,276
Kyŏngsang-pukto	Taegu*	7,501	19,428	3,519,121
Special cities				
Inch'ŏn-si	Inch'ŏn	78	202	1,387,475
Pusan-si	Pusan	168	434	3,516,768
Sŏul-t'ŭkpyŏlsi	Seoul	234	605	9,645,824
Taegu-si	Taegu	176	455	2,030,649
TOTAL		38,259	99,091	40,466,577†

Demography

Population (1986): 41,568,600.
Density (1986): persons per sq mi 1,094, persons per sq km 422.2.
Urban–rural (1985): urban 65.4%; rural 34.6%.
Sex distribution (1985): male 50.12%; female 49.88%.
Age breakdown (1985): under 15, 30.6%; 15–29, 31.0%; 30–44, 19.4%; 45–59, 12.3%; 60–74, 5.4%; 75 and over, 1.3%.
Population projection: (1990) 44,108,000; (2000) 50,582,000.
Doubling time: 46 years.
Ethnic composition (1982): Korean 99.9%; other 0.1%.
Religious affiliation (1981): Buddhist 37.4%; Protestant 25.7%; Confucian 17.5%; Roman Catholic 4.8%; Ch'ondogyo 3.6%; Wonbulgyo 3.2%; other 7.8%.
Major cities (1985): Seoul 9,645,824; Pusan 3,516,768; Taegu 2,030,649; Inch'ŏn 1,387,475; Kwangju 843,500‡.

Vital statistics

Birth rate per 1,000 population (1984): 23.0 (world avg. 29.0).
Death rate per 1,000 population (1984): 6.2 (world avg. 11.0).
Natural increase rate per 1,000 population (1984): 16.8 (world avg. 18.0).
Total fertility rate (avg. births per childbearing woman; 1985): 2.4.
Marriage rate per 1,000 population (1981): 3.1.
Divorce rate per 1,000 population (1981): 0.4.
Life expectancy at birth (1985): male 64.5 years; female 70.9 years.
Major causes of death per 100,000 population: n.a.

National economy

Budget (1986). Revenue: W 13,197,500,000,000 (income and excise taxes 61.5%, customs duties 14.4%, defense surtax 14.1%, monopoly profits 7.4%). Expenditures: W 14,461,900,000,000 (defense 31.2%, education 20.1%, economic development and social programs 26.7%).
Tourism (1984): receipts from visitors U.S.$673,000,000; expenditures by nationals abroad U.S.$576,000,000.
Production (metric tons except as noted). Agriculture, forestry, fishing (1984): fruits and vegetables 10,351,000 (of which cabbages 3,457,000, apples 528,000, oranges 261,000, garlic 200,000), rice 7,970,000, barley 804,000, potatoes 436,000, soybeans 226,000, corn (maize) 133,000; livestock (number of live animals) 2,215,000 cattle, 3,649,000 pigs, 350,000 goats; roundwood 6,675,000 cu m; fish catch 2,990,000. Mining and quarrying (1985): iron ore 670,000; zinc ore 92,509; lead ore 18,947; tungsten ore 4,643; refined silver 126,123 kilograms. Manufacturing (1985): cement 20,420,000; pig iron 8,833,000; crude steel 4,851,000; urea fertilizer 839,000; man-made fibres 1,046,000,000 sq m; cotton fabrics 470,000,000 sq m; passenger cars 261,600 units. Construction (1985): residential 20,600,000 sq m; nonresidential 17,700,000 sq m. Energy production (consumption): electricity (kW-hr; 1985) 58,000,000 (62,338,000,000§); coal (metric tons; 1985) 23,630,000 (36,820,000§); crude petroleum (barrels; 1984) none (203,972,000); petroleum products (metric tons; 1984) 23,437,000 (23,516,000).
Household income and expenditure. Average household size (1985) 4.2; income per household W 4,538,700 (U.S.$5,150); sources of income: wages and salaries 60.3%, other 39.7%; expenditure (1984): food 37.6%, housing including utilities 11.8%, education 9.9%, clothing and footwear 9.8%, health 7.5%, transportation 6.2%.
Public debt (external, outstanding; 1984): U.S.$24,642,100,000.
Gross national product (at current market prices; 1986): U.S.$90,600,000,000 (U.S.$2,180 per capita).

Structure of gross domestic product and labour force

	1985			
	in value W '000,000,000	% of total value	labour force	% of labour force
Agriculture	7,893.4	14.5	3,909,000	26.1
Mining	794.0	1.5	142,000	0.9
Manufacturing	16,757.8	30.7	3,351,000	22.4
Construction	4,632.7	8.5	903,000	6.1
Public utilities	1,740.1	3.2	36,000	0.2
Transportation and communication	4,164.9	7.6	663,000	4.4
Trade	7,073.7	13.0	3,148,000	21.0
Finance	6,197.8	11.4	500,000	3.3
Pub. admin., defense	3,186.0	5.8	1,765,000	11.8
Services	2,677.6	4.9		
Other	−5,732 ‖	−1.1 ‖	567,000¶	3.8¶
TOTAL	54,544.8	100.0	14,984,000	100.0

Population economically active (1985): total 15,554,000; activity rate of total population 38.4% (participation rates [1984]: ages 15–64, 54.6%; female 38.4%; unemployed 3.5%).

Price and earnings indexes (1980 = 100)

	1980	1981	1982	1983	1984	1985	1986♀
Consumer price index	100.0	121.3	130.1	134.5	137.6	141.0	140.6
Monthly earnings index	100.0	120.0	137.7	154.6	167.1	184.1	164.6

Land use (1983): forested 66.5%; meadows and pastureland 0.7%; agricultural and under permanent cultivation 22.0%; other 10.8%.

Foreign trade

Balance of trade (current prices)

	1980	1981	1982	1983	1984	1985
US$'000,000	−4,384	−3,628	−2,400	−1,970	−1,386	−853
% of total	11.3%	8.1%	5.4%	3.9%	2.3%	1.4%

Imports (1985): U.S.$31,135,700,000 (machinery and transport equipment 34.2%, mineral fuels and related products 23.6%, crude materials except fuels 12.4%, chemicals and chemical products 9.0%). *Major import sources:* Japan 24.5%; United States 20.8%; Australia 3.5%; Malaysia 3.5%; West Germany 2.8%; Saudi Arabia 2.4%; Oman 2.0%; United Kingdom 1.6%.
Exports (1985): U.S.$30,283,100,000 (manufactured goods 51.0%, machinery and transport equipment 37.6%, food and live animals 3.8%, chemicals and chemical products 3.1%). *Major export destinations:* United States 35.4%; Japan 15.1%; Hong Kong 5.2%; Canada 4.1%; Saudi Arabia 3.2%; West Germany 2.9%; Kuwait 0.7%.

Transport and communications

Transport. Railroads (1986): length 3,905 mi, 6,285 km; passenger-mi (1984) 13,477,000,000, passenger-km 21,689,000,000; short ton-mi cargo 7,965,000,000, metric ton-km cargo 11,630,000,000. Roads (1986): total length 31,692 mi, 51,003 km (paved 46%). Vehicles (1985): passenger cars 465,149; trucks and buses 556,659. Merchant marine (1985): vessels (100 gross tons and over) 1,847; total deadweight tonnage 11,712,926. Air transport (1985): passenger-mi 6,386,594,000, passenger-km 10,278,246,000; short ton-mi cargo 1,413,851,000, metric ton-km cargo 2,064,318,000; airports (1986) with scheduled flights 3.
Communications. Daily newspapers (1985): total number 25; total circulation 6,748,100‡; circulation per 1,000 population 171§. Radio (1984): total number of receivers 10,250,000 (1 per 4.0 persons). Television (1984): total number of receivers 8,113,483 (1 per 5.0 persons). Telephones (1985): 6,517,395 (1 per 6.2 persons).

Education and health

Education (1986)

	schools	teachers	students	student/teacher ratio
Primary (age 6–13)	6,519	126,785	4,856,752	36.9
Secondary (age 14–19)	3,338	109,593	4,049,013	35.5
Vocational	746	56,176	1,836,020	32.7
Higher	287	1,977	82,452	41.7

Educational attainment (1980). Percent of adult population over age 25 having: no formal schooling 21.1%; primary education 36.1%; secondary 16.7%; postsecondary 7.2%. *Literacy* (1981): total population literate 13,191,432 (92.7%); males literate 6,937,242 (97.5%); females literate 6,254,190 (87.9%).
Health (1984): physicians 28,015 (1 per 1,448 persons); hospital beds 68,700 (1 per 588 persons); infant mortality rate per 1,000 live births (1985): 27.0.
Food (1980–82): daily per capita caloric intake 2,938 (vegetable products 91%, animal products 9%); 125% of FAO recommended minimum requirement.

Military

Total active duty personnel (1985): 598,000 (army 87.0%, navy 7.5%, air force 5.5%). *Military expenditure as percent of GNP* (1986): 5.5% (world *c.* 6.0%); per capita expenditure: U.S.$107.

*During 1981–82 Inch'ŏn and Taegu also became special cities. †Includes 455 people not distributed by provinces. ‡1983. §1984. ‖ Includes import duties less imputed bank service charges. ¶Unemployed. ♀May.

Kuwait

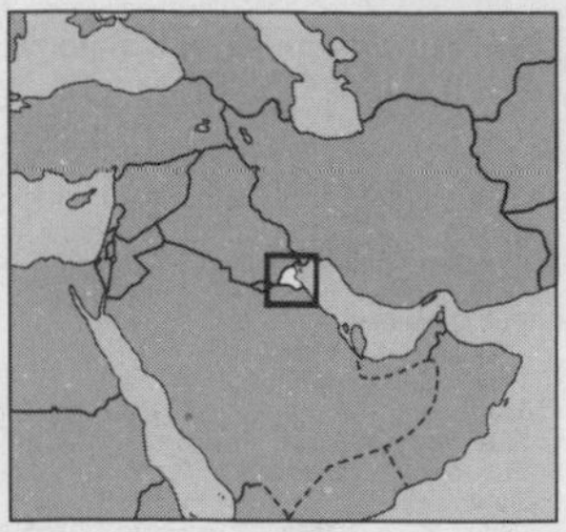

Official name: Dawlat al-Kuwayt (State of Kuwait).
Form of government: Constitutional monarchy with a single parliamentary house (National Assembly [64])*.
Chief of state: Emir.
Head of government: Prime Minister.
Capital: Kuwait City.
Official language: Arabic.
Official religion: Islam.
Monetary unit: 1 Kuwaiti dinar (KD) = 1,000 fils; valuation (Oct. 1, 1986) 1 KD = U.S.$3.42 = £2.37.

Area and population

		area		population
Governorates	Capitals	sq mi	sq km	1986 estimate
al-Aḥmadī	al-Aḥmadī	1,984	5,138	321,350
al-Jahrāʾ	al-Jahrāʾ	4,372	11,324	293,780
Capital	Kuwait City	38	98	177,008
Ḥawallī	Ḥawallī	138	358	998,375
Islands†	—	348	900	...
TOTAL		6,880	17,818	1,790,513

Demography

Population (1986): 1,791,000.
Density (1986): persons per sq mi 260.3, persons per sq km 100.5.
Urban-rural (1985): urban 93.7%; rural 6.3%.
Sex distribution (1985): male 58.10%; female 41.90%.
Age breakdown (1984): under 15, 39.9%; 15–29, 28.4%; 30–44, 21.8%; 45–59, 7.7%; 60–74, 1.8%; 75 and over, 0.4%.
Population projection: (1990) 2,143,000; (2000) 2,936,000.
Doubling time: 24 years.
Ethnic composition (1980): Kuwaiti 41.7%; other Arab 42.3%; Asian 15.0%; other 1.0%.
Religious affiliation (1980): Muslim 91.5% (Sunnī about 80%, Shīʿah about 20%); Christian 6.4%; other 2.1%.
Major cities (1980): Ḥawallī 152,402; as-Sālimīyah 145,991; al-Jahrāʾ 67,311; Kuwait City 60,525; al-Farwānīyah 57,841.

Vital statistics

Birth rate per 1,000 population (1985): 31.7 (world avg. 29.0); legitimate, n.a.; illegitimate, n.a.
Death rate per 1,000 population (1985): 2.7 (world avg. 11.0).
Natural increase rate per 1,000 population (1985): 29.0 (world avg. 18.0).
Total fertility rate (avg. births per childbearing woman; 1980–85): 6.2.
Marriage rate per 1,000 population (1985): 5.4.
Divorce rate per 1,000 population (1985): 1.6.
Life expectancy at birth (1980–85): male 68.0 years; female 72.9 years.
Major causes of death per 100,000 population (1982): circulatory diseases 81.4; accidents, poisonings, and violence 53.5; malignant neoplasms (cancers) 35.6; certain causes of perinatal morbidity and mortality 31.9; respiratory diseases 26.5; symptoms and ill-defined conditions 20.3; infectious and parasitic diseases 18.5; congenital anomalies 16.3; endocrine, nutritional, and metabolic diseases 13.7; diseases of the digestive system 7.2

National economy

Budget (1986–87). Revenue: KD 1,912,700,000 (oil revenue 86.6%). Expenditures: KD 3,244,100,000 (wages and salaries 23.4%, construction and expropriations 22.3%, goods and services 8.4%, reserve fund for future generations 5.9%, transport equipment 0.8%).
Public debt: none.
Tourism (1983): receipts from visitors U.S.$31,000,000; expenditures by nationals abroad U.S.$1,492,000,000.
Gross national product (at current market prices; 1984): U.S.$27,570,000,000 (U.S.$16,850 per capita).

Structure of gross domestic product and labour force

	1985			
	in value KD '000,000	% of total value	labour force	% of labour force
Agriculture	28.2	0.5	12,632	2.0
Mining (oil sector)	2,808.3	45.9	7,033	1.1
Manufacturing	363.9	5.9	51,089	7.6
Construction	203.0	3.3	124,156	18.5
Public utilities	178.7	2.9	7,466	1.1
Transportation and communication	234.8	3.8	37,205	5.5
Trade	582.0	9.5	75,931	11.3
Finance	542.0	8.9	20,347	3.0
Pub. admin., defense, services	1,180.6	19.3	326,729	48.7
Other	...	...	7,797	1.2
TOTAL	6,121.5	100.0	670,385	100.0

Production (metric tons except as noted). Agriculture, forestry, fishing (1984): milk 31,000, poultry meat 20,000, tomatoes 14,000, melons 3,000, onions 2,000; livestock (number of live animals) 600,000 sheep, 8,000,000 chickens; fish catch 4,566. Mining and quarrying (1985): sulfur 202,377; asphalt 945,000 barrels. Manufacturing (1985): flour 144,221; bran 36,833; asbestos pipes 29,688; salt 21,326; cattle feed 13,771; liquefied caustic soda 10,845; fats and oil 10,162; chlorine gas 8,611; biscuits 2,223; detergents 1,440; hydrochloric acid 464,200 gallons; hydrogen gas 3,045,000 cu m; sodium hydrochloride 17,457 cu m; standard accumulators (batteries) 14,481 units. Construction (1985): residential 1,375,000 sq m; nonresidential 1,358,000 sq m. Energy production (consumption): electricity (kW-hr; 1984) 13,894,000,000 (11,827,000,000); coal, none (none); crude petroleum (barrels: 1984) 424,400,000,000 (176,343,000); petroleum products (metric tons; 1984) 24,362,000 (2,799,000); natural gas (cu m; 1984) 5,816,000,000 (5,199,000,000).
Population economically active (1984): total 598,098; activity rate of total population 36.6% (participation rates: over age 15, 60.9%; female 14.0%; unemployed [1980] 0.3%).

Price and earnings indexes (1980 = 100)

	1979	1980	1981	1982	1983	1984	1985
Consumer price index	93.5	100.0	107.4	115.7	121.2	122.6	124.4
Monthly earnings index	...	...	...	...	...	...	...

Household income and expenditure. Average household size (1984) 7.4; annual income per household (1973)‡ KD 4,246 (U.S.$12,907); sources of income: wages and salaries 53.8%, self-employment 20.8%, other 25.4%; expenditure (1983): food 35.7%, housing and maintenance 18.7%, transportation 15.3%, household appliances 11.0%, clothing and footwear 10.0%, other 9.3%.
Land use (1983): forested 0.1%; meadows and pastures 7.5%; agricultural and under permanent cultivation 0.1%; other, built-up, and wasteland 92.3%.

Foreign trade

Balance of trade (current prices)

	1979	1980	1981	1982	1983	1984
KD '000,000	+3,652	+3,604	+2,585	+885	+1,204	+1,239
% of total	56.6%	50.5%	39.9%	16.8%	23.1%	21.4%

Imports (1984): KD 1,039,000,000 (machinery and transport equipment 43.6%, manufactured goods 22.1%, miscellaneous manufactured articles 15.3%, food and live animals 12.3%, chemicals 3.6%). *Major import sources:* Japan 20.6%; France 10.3%; United States 9.1%; United Kingdom 5.8%.
Exports (1984): KD 2,277,800,000 (crude petroleum 49.7%, refined petroleum 37.1%). *Major export destinations:* Japan 13.6%; Italy 9.9%; Singapore 7.6%; The Netherlands 7.5%; Iraq 6.8%.

Transport and communications

Transport. Railroads: none. Roads (1984): total length 1,208 mi, 1,944 km (paved 100%). Vehicles (1985): passenger cars 411,629; trucks and buses 200,461. Merchant marine (1985): vessels (100 gross tons and over) 245; total deadweight tonnage 3,505,829. Air transport (1984): passenger-mi 2,334,000,000, passenger-km 3,756,000,000; short ton-mi cargo 121,662,000, metric ton-km cargo 177,624,000; airports (1986) with scheduled flights 1.
Communications. Daily newspapers (1985): total number 7; total circulation 453,000; circulation per 1,000 population 265. Radio (1985): total number of receivers 950,000 (1 per 1.8 persons). Television (1985): total number of receivers 600,000 (1 per 2.8 persons). Telephones (1983): 258,325 (1 per 6.5 persons).

Education and health

Education (1985–86)

	schools	teachers	students	student/ teacher ratio
Primary (age 6–10)	270	9,620	172,659	17.9
Secondary (age 11–18)	384	18,685	239,595	12.8
Voc., teacher tr.	6	788	12,272	15.6
Higher	1	858	16,359	19.1

Educational attainment (1980). Percent of adult population over age 25 having: no formal schooling 60.1%; primary education 7.9%; secondary education 21.0%; higher education 11.0%. *Literacy* (1985): total population over age 10 literate 964,324 (77.5%); males literate 519,683 (70.7%); females literate 372,641 (73.1%).
Health (1984): physicians 2,983 (1 per 548 persons); hospital beds 5,523§ (1 per 296 persons); infant mortality rate per 1,000 live births 19.5.
Food (1980–82): daily per capita caloric intake 3,404 (vegetable products 74%, animal products 26%); 147% of FAO recommended minimum requirement.

Military

Total active duty personnel (1985): 13,100 (army 76.3%, navy 8.4%, air force 15.3%). *Military expenditure as percent of GNP* (1983): 4.0% (world 6.1%); per capita expenditure U.S.$662.

*Parliament dissolved on July 3, 1986, and several articles of the constitution were suspended, under pressure from the Persian Gulf war and falling oil prices. †Bubian Island and Warba Island. ‡Kuwaiti households only. §Government hospitals only.

Laos

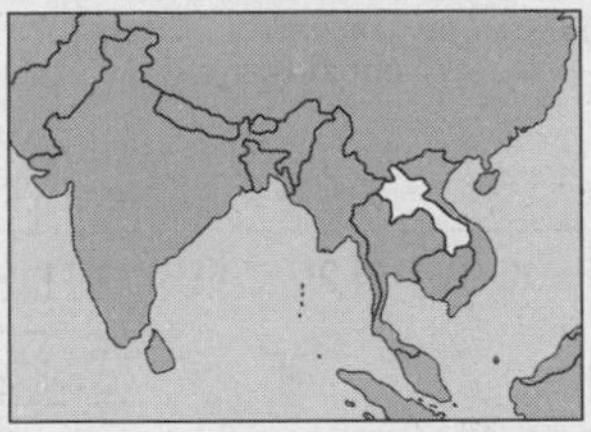

Official name: Sathalanalat Paxathipatai Paxaxôn Lao (Lao People's Democratic Republic).
Form of government: unitary single-party people's republic with one legislative house (National Congress of People's Representatives [264]).
Chief of state: President.
Head of government: Prime Minister.
Capital: Vientiane.
Official language: Lao.
Official religion: none.
Monetary unit: 1 kip (KN) = 100 at; valuation (preferential rate; Oct. 1, 1986) 1 U.S.$ = KN 35.00; 1 £ = KN 50.57.

Area and population

Provinces	Capitals	area sq mi	area sq km	population 1985 census
Attapu	Attapu	...	...	69,631
Bokeo	Houayxay	...	...	54,925
Bolikhamxay	Pakxan	...	...	122,300
Champasak	Pakxé	...	...	403,041
Houaphan	Xam Nua	...	...	209,921
Khammouan	Thakhek	...	...	213,462
Louang Namtha	Louang Namtha	...	...	97,028
Louangphrabang	Louangphrabang	...	...	295,475
Oudomxay	Xay	...	...	187,115
Phôngsali	Phôngsali	...	...	122,984
Saravan	Saravan	...	...	187,515
Savannakhét	Savannakhét	...	...	543,611
Vientiane	Vientiane	...	...	264,277
Xaignabouri	Xaignabouri	...	...	223,611
Xékong	Thong	...	...	50,909
Xiangkhoang	Phônsavan	...	...	161,589
Municipalities				
Vientiane	—	...	...	377,409
TOTAL		91,400	236,800	3,584,803

Demography

Population (1986): 3,703,000.
Density (1986): persons per sq mi 40.5, persons per sq km 15.6.
Urban-rural (1985): urban 15.9%; rural 84.1%.
Sex distribution (1985): male 49.02%; female 50.98%.
Age breakdown (1985): under 15, 42.8%; 15–29, 26.5%; 30–44, 16.1%; 45–59, 9.6%; 60–74, 4.3%; 75 and over, 0.7%.
Population projection: (1990) 4,028,000; (2000) 5,082,000.
Doubling time: 28 years.
Ethnic composition (1983): Lao 48%; Mon-Khmer peoples 25%; Thai peoples 14%; Sino-Tibetan peoples, including the Hmong (Meo) and Yao 13%.
Religious affiliation (1980): Buddhist 57.8%; tribal religionist 33.6%; Christian 1.8%, of which Roman Catholic 0.8%, Protestant 0.2%; Muslim 1.0%; atheist 1.0%; Chinese folk-religionist 0.9%; none 3.8%; other 0.1%.
Major cities (1975): Vientiane 200,000*; Savannakhét 53,000; Pakxé 47,000; Louangphrabang 46,000.

Vital statistics

Birth rate per 1,000 population (1985): 39.5 (world avg. 29.0).
Death rate per 1,000 population (1985): 14.8 (world avg. 11.0).
Natural increase rate per 1,000 population (1985): 24.7 (world avg. 18.0).
Total fertility rate (avg. births per childbearing woman; 1985): 5.6.
Marriage rate per 1,000 population: n.a.
Divorce rate per 1,000 population: n.a.
Life expectancy at birth (1985): male 49.4 years; female 52.4 years.
Major causes of death per 100,000 population: n.a; however, during the 1970s malaria, influenza, dysentery, and pneumonia were among the country's major health problems.

National economy

Budget (1981). Revenue: KN 930,000,000 (state enterprises 75.3%, private sector taxes 15.1%). Expenditures: KN 2,160,000,000 (current expenditure 56.0%, capital expenditure 44.0%).
Public debt (external, outstanding; 1982): U.S.$60,000,000.
Tourism (1982): total number of tourists 29,000.
Population economically active (1984): total 2,002,000; activity rate of total population 55.8% (participation rates: ages 15–64, 52.0%; female 44.9%; unemployed, n.a.).

Price and earnings indexes (1976 = 100)

	1980
Consumer price index	793
Monthly earnings index	...

Production (metric tons except as noted). Agriculture, forestry, fishing (1984): rice 1,322,000, cassava 76,000, potatoes 46,000, corn (maize) 40,000, pineapples 38,000, sweet potatoes 38,000, onions 35,000, melons 30,000, sugarcane 30,000, oranges 26,000; livestock (number of live animals) 1,350,000 pigs, 915,000 water buffalo, 500,000 cattle, 60,000 goats, 6,000,000 chickens; roundwood 4,236,000 cu m; fish catch 20,000. Mining and quarrying (1984): gypsum 82,000; rock salt 10,000; tin (metal content) 315. Manufacturing (1983): domestic animal feed 3,000; washing powder 970; plastic products 185; textiles 1,451,400 metres; clothing 474,900 pieces; cigarettes 12,000,000 packets; bricks 10,900,000 units; rubber tires and tubes 1,000,000 units; beer 13,000 hectolitres; soft drinks 12,370 hectolitres. Construction: n.a. Energy production (consumption): electricity (kW-hr; 1984) 990,000,000 (330,000,000); coal (metric tons; 1981) 1,000 (1,000); crude petroleum, n.a. (n.a.); petroleum products (metric tons; 1984) none (49,000); natural gas, n.a. (n.a.).
Gross national product (at current market prices; 1984): U.S.$765,220,000 (U.S.$220 per capita).

Structure of gross domestic product and labour force

	1983 in value KN '000,000	1983 % of total value	1983 labour force	1983 % of labour force
Agriculture	12,994	72.0	1,342,000	72.0
Manufacturing	1,263	7.0		
Mining				
Construction				
Public utilities				
Transportation and communication	3,790	21.0	521,000	28.0
Trade				
Finance				
Pub. admin., defense				
Services				
TOTAL	18,047	100.0	1,863,000	100.0

Household income and expenditure. Average household size (1980) 5.3; average annual income per household KN 3,710 (U.S.$371); source of income: n.a.; expenditure: n.a.
Land use (1984): forested 55.0%; meadows and pastures 3.5%; agricultural and under permanent cultivation 3.9%; other 37.6%.

Foreign trade

Balance of trade (current prices)

	1979	1980	1981	1982	1983	1984
U.S.$'000,000	−67.0	−100.0	−68.1	−61.9	−66.8	−36.7
% of total	65.9%	68.2%	66.8%	54.7%	56.7%	61.9%

Imports (1984): U.S.$47,994,000 (important imports include cereals, other food products, petroleum products, and agricultural and general machinery). *Major import sources:* Thailand 39.6%; Singapore 14.3%; Japan 11.8%; United Kingdom 2.2%; Vietnam 1.6%; unspecified countries 20.7%.
Exports (1984): U.S.$34,300,000 (electricity 67.0%; other important exports include wood [76.5% of all exports in 1980], coffee, and tin). *Major export destinations:* Thailand 69.6%; China 14.3%; United States 5.8%; Belgium–Luxembourg 1.7%; Iran 1.7%; unspecified countries 6.9%.

Transport and communications

Transport. Railroads: none. Roads (1985): total length 8,067 mi, 12,983 km (paved 31%). Vehicles (1982): passenger cars 15,000; trucks and buses 3,000. Merchant marine: none. Air transport (1982): passenger-mi 5,000,000, passenger-km 8,000,000; short ton-mi cargo 70,000, metric ton-km cargo 100,000; airports (1986) with scheduled flights 7.
Communications. Daily newspapers (1983): total number 2; total circulation 12,500; circulation per 1,000 population 3.0. Radio (1984): total number of receivers 225,000 (1 per 18 persons). Television (1984): total number of receivers 30,000 (1 per 134 persons). Telephones (1983): 4,300 (1 per 921 persons).

Education and health

Education (1982–83)

	schools	teachers	students	student/teacher ratio
Primary (age 6–10)	6,525	16,454	480,871	29.2
Secondary (age 11–16)	419	3,709	64,500	17.4
Voc., teacher tr.	115†	2,413‡	30,624‡	12.7‡
Higher	1	‡	‡	...

Educational attainment, n.a. *Literacy* (1980): total population over age 15 literate 997,600 (45.2%); males literate 586,600 (52.8%); females literate 412,500 (37.6%).
Health (1985): physicians 430 (1 per 8,336 persons); hospital beds 11,650 (1 per 307.7 persons); infant mortality rate per 1,000 live births 116.
Food (1980–82): daily per capita caloric intake 1,927 (vegetable products 90%, animal products 10%); 87% of FAO recommended minimum requirement.

Military

Total active duty personnel (1986): 53,000 (army 94.3%, navy 1.9%, air force 3.8%). *Military expenditure as percent of GNP* (1981): 9.0% (world 5.8%); per capita expenditure U.S.$7.

*1984. †Includes third-level vocational. ‡Vocational, teacher training includes higher.

Lebanon

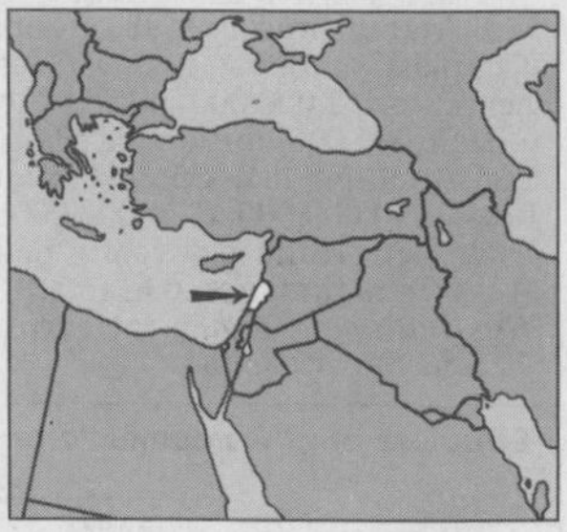

Official name: al-Jumhūrīyah al-Lubnānīyah (Republic of Lebanon).
Form of government: multiparty republic with one legislative house (National Assembly [99]).
Chief of state: President.
Head of government: Prime Minister.
Capital: Beirut.
Official language: Arabic.
Official religion: none.
Monetary unit: 1 Lebanese pound (LL) = 100 piastres; valuation (Oct. 1, 1986) 1 U.S.$ = LL 43.85; 1 £ = LL 63.36.

Area and population

		area		population
Governorates	**Capitals**	sq mi	sq km	1970 estimate
Bayrūt	Beirut (Bayrūt)	7	18	474,870
al-Biqāʿ	Zaḥlah	1,653	4,280	203,520
Jabal Lubnān	Bʿabdā	753	1,950	833,055
al-Janūb	Ṣaydā	364	943	249,945
an-Nabaṭīyah*	an-Nabaṭīyah	408	1,058	...
ash-Shamāl	Tripoli (Ṭarābulus)	765	1,981	364,935
TOTAL		3,950	10,230	2,126,325

Demography

Population (1986): 2,707,000.
Density (1986): persons per sq mi 685.3, persons per sq km 264.6.
Urban-rural (1985): urban 83.7%; rural 16.3%.
Sex distribution (1985): male 48.53%; female 51.47%.
Age breakdown (1984): under 15, 35.6%; 15–29, 30.4%; 30–44, 15.0%; 45–59, 11.0%; 60–74, 6.0%; 75 and over, 2.0%.
Population projection: (1990) 3,301,000; (2000) 3,992,000.
Doubling time: in the period 1970–75 the average growth rate was 2.6%; however, since 1976 the population is decreasing from the massive emigration resulting from the civil war.
Ethnic composition (1983): Lebanese 82.6%; Palestinian 9.6%; Armenian 4.9%; Syrian, Kurd, and other 2.9%.
Religious affiliation: no official data exist subsequent to the 1932 census, when Christians (predominantly Maronite Roman Catholic) were a slight majority; it is thought that Muslims today constitute the majority but by what margin is highly uncertain. An unofficial estimate (1984) indicated that the main religious groups were distributed as follows: Shīʿi Muslim 32%; Maronite Christian 24.5%; Sunnī Muslim 21%; Druze 7%; Greek Orthodox 6.5%; Greek Catholic 4%; Armenian Christian 4%; other 1.0%.
Major cities (1985): Beirut 1,500,000; Tripoli 500,000; Zaḥlah 200,000; Ṣaydā 100,000.

Vital statistics

Birth rate per 1,000 population (1984): 29.8 (world avg. 29.0); legitimate, n.a.; illegitimate, n.a.
Death rate per 1,000 population (1984): 8.8 (world avg. 11.0).
Natural increase rate per 1,000 population (1984): 21.0 (world avg. 18.0).
Total fertility rate (avg. births per childbearing woman; 1984): 3.8.
Marriage rate per 1,000 population (1973): 7.0.
Divorce rate per 1,000 population (1973): 0.6.
Life expectancy at birth (1980–85): male 65.0 years; female 68.9 years.
Major causes of death (mid-1970s): heart ailments and gastrointestinal diseases, including typhoid and dysentery; violence and acts of war have been principal causes of mortality for the last decade.

National economy

Budget (1985). Revenue: LL 8,217,000,000 (customs duties *c.* 35%). Expenditure: LL 10,892,000,000 (defense 21.6%, education 15.0%, public works 6.7%, housing 0.1%).
Production (metric tons except as noted). Agriculture, forestry, fishing (1984): oranges 200,000, grapes 160,000, apples 128,000, tomatoes 125,000, potatoes 120,000, lemons and limes 50,000, olives 50,000, sugar beets 50,000, apricots 25,000, peaches and nectarines 22,000, wheat 18,000, bananas 13,000, olive oil 10,000, centrifugal sugar (raw value) 6,000, almonds 5,500, tobacco 4,000; livestock (number of live animals) 440,000 goats, 130,000 sheep, 45,000 cattle, 9,000,000 chickens; roundwood 470,000 cu m; fish catch (1983) 1,400. Mining and quarrying (1982): gypsum 5,000. Manufacturing (1982): cement 1,980,000. Construction (1981): 5,863,000 sq m. Energy production (consumption): electricity (kW-hr; 1984) 1,355,000,000 (1,385,000,000); coal, n.a. (none); crude petroleum (barrels; 1984) n.a. (5,570,000); petroleum products (metric tons; 1984) 735,000 (1,511,000); natural gas, none (n.a.).
Population economically active (1984): total 701,783; activity rate of total population 26.5% (participation rates: over age 15, 42.4%; female 20.5%; unemployed, n.a.).

Price and earnings indexes (1980 = 100)

	1976	1977	1978	1979	1980	1981	1982
Consumer price index	...	...	...	...	...	...	...
Monthly earnings index†	...	61.5	...	77.8	100.0	118.5	137.0

Public debt (external, outstanding; 1984): U.S.$178,700,000.
Tourism (1980): number of visitors 135,548.
Household income and expenditure. Average household size (1980) 5.3; average annual income per household: n.a.; source of income: n.a.; expenditure: n.a.
Gross national product (at current market prices; 1983): U.S.$4,600,000,000–$5,500,000,000 (U.S.$1,636–$1,956 per capita).

Structure of gross domestic product and labour force

	1977		1982	
	in value LL '000,000	% of total value	labour force	% of labour force
Agriculture	700	8.5	238,188	20.7
Mining	...	...		
Manufacturing	1,070	13.1	223,136	19.4
Construction	280	3.4	71,698	6.2
Public utilities	445	5.4	8,503	0.7
Transportation and communication	630	7.7	62,161	5.4
Finance	...	...		
Trade	2,320	28.3	203,258	17.7
Pub. admin., defense	835	10.2		
Services	1,920	23.4	342,057	29.8
Other	...	...	...	...
TOTAL	8,200	100.0	1,149,001	100.0‡

Land use (1983): forested 6.8%; meadows and pastures 0.9%; agricultural and under permanent cultivation 29.1%, wasteland, built-up, and other areas 63.2%.

Foreign trade

Balance of trade (current prices)

	1980	1981	1982	1983	1984	1985
LL '000,000	−8,631	−8,906	−9,890	−12,461	−13,987	−25,581
% of total	59.1%	45.0%	48.5%	69.0%	64.9%	61.8%

Imports (1982): LL 15,146,000,000 (consumer goods 40.0%; machinery and transport equipment 35.0%; petroleum products 20.0%). *Major import sources:* Italy 15.2%; France 10.3%; United States 9.1%; West Germany 7.6%; Saudi Arabia 5.7%.
Exports (1982): LL 5,256,000,000 (agricultural products 21.3%, of which vegetables 15.9%; textile products 11.3%; metal products 8.5%; precious metals, jewelry, and coins 5.0%). *Major export destinations:* Saudi Arabia 29.7%; Iraq 22.1%; Jordan 10.8%; Syria 7.4%; Kuwait 5.5%.

Transport and communications

Transport. Railroads (1982): length 258 mi, 415 km; passenger-mi 5,325,000, passenger-km 8,570,000; short ton-mi cargo 28,770,000, metric ton-km cargo 42,010,000. Roads (1982): total length 4,300 mi, 7,000 km (paved 80%). Vehicles (1982): passenger cars 460,400; trucks and buses 35,000. Merchant marine (1985): vessels (100 gross tons and over) 247; total deadweight tonnage 790,014. Air transport§ (1984): passenger-mi 516,117,000, passenger-km 830,612,000; short ton-mi cargo 13,544,000, metric ton-km cargo 19,774,000; airports (1986) with scheduled flights 1.
Communications. Daily newspapers (1985): total number 38; total circulation 601,954; circulation per 1,000 population 225.6. Radio (1984): total number of receivers 1,500,000 (1 per 1.8 persons). Television (1985): total number of receivers 451,000 (1 per 5.8 persons). Telephones (1973): 227,000 (1 per 12 persons).

Education and health

Education (1981–82)

	schools	teachers	students	student/ teacher ratio
Primary (age 5–9)	1,116	53,450	398,977	...
Secondary (age 10–16)	1,405		250,028	...
Voc., teacher tr.	181	3,563	39,045	11.0
Higher	18	...	70,314	...

Educational attainment (1970). Percent of population over age 25 having: no formal schooling 45.6%; ability to read and write 35.6%; primary education 10.8%; secondary 4.9%; higher 3.1%. *Literacy* (1980): total population over age 10 literate 1,183,000 (73.4%); males literate 643,000 (82.6%); females literate 540,000 (64.2%).
Health (1982): physicians 3,000 (1 per 1,000 persons); hospital beds 11,400 (1 per 263 persons); infant mortality rate per 1,000 live births (1984) 44.4.
Food (1979–81): daily per capita caloric intake 2,995 (vegetable products 84%, animal products 16%); 121% of FAO recommended minimum requirement.

Military

Total active duty personnel (1985): 17,400 (army 91.5%, navy 1.7%, air force 6.3%); factional armies (1985) Lebanese forces (Maronite) 5,000; Progressive Socialist Party/Druze forces 2,500; Amal (Shīʿī) 5,500; Murābiṭūn (Sunnī) 2,500. *Military expenditure as percent of GNP* (1983): 8.2% (world 6.1%); per capita expenditure: U.S.$161.

*Created in 1975; includes the districts of Nabaṭīyah, Bint Jubayl, Marj ʿUyūn, and Ḥāṣbayya, which were formerly part of al-Janūb. †Excludes banking sector. ‡Detail does not add to total given because of rounding. §International flights only.

Lesotho

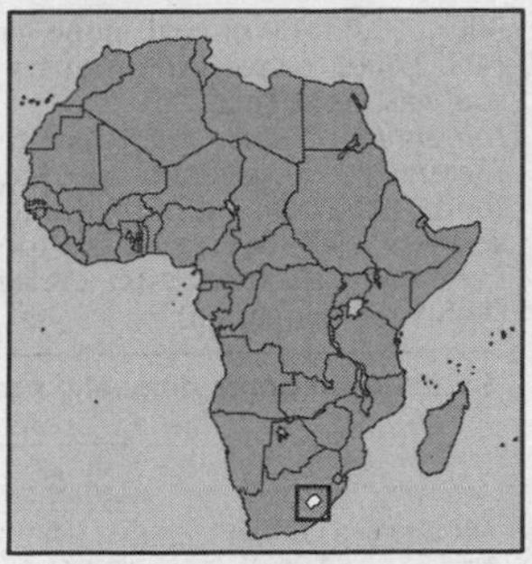

Official name: Lesotho (Sotho); Kingdom of Lesotho (English).
Form of government: constitutional monarchy with two legislative houses (National Assembly [80]; Senate [30])*.
Chief of state: King.
Head of government: Chairman of the Military Council.
Capital: Maseru.
Official languages: Sotho; English.
Official religion: Christianity.
Monetary unit: 1 loti (plural maloti [M]) = 100 lisente; valuation (Oct. 1, 1986) 1 U.S.$ = M 2.22; 1 £ = M 3.21.

Area and population

		area		population
Districts	Capitals	sq mi	sq km	1986 census
Berea	Teyateyaneng	858	2,222	194,631
Butha-Buthe	Butha-Buthe	682	1,767	100,644
Leribe	Leribe	1,092	2,828	257,988
Mafeteng	Mafeteng	818	2,119	195,591
Maseru	Maseru	1,652	4,279	311,159
Mohale's Hoek	Mohale's Hoek	1,363	3,530	164,392
Mokhotlong	Mokhotlong	1,573	4,075	74,676
Qacha's Nek	Qacha's Nek	907	2,349	63,984
Quthing	Quthing	1,126	2,916	110,376
Thaba-Tseka	Thaba-Tseka	1,649	4,270	104,095
TOTAL		11,720	30,355	1,577,536

Demography

Population (1986): 1,586,400.
Density (1986): persons per sq mi 135.4, persons per sq km 52.3.
Urban-rural (1985): urban 5.8%; rural 94.2%.
Sex distribution (1986): male 48.21%; female 51.79%.
Age breakdown (1985): under 15, 42.3%; 15–29, 25.9%; 30–44, 16.2%; 45–59, 9.9%; 60–74, 4.7%; 75 and over, 1.0%.
Population projection: (1990) 1,731,000; (2000) 2,251,000.
Doubling time: 27 years.
Ethnic composition (1984): Sotho 99.7%; other 0.3%.
Religious affiliation (1980): Roman Catholic 43.5%; Protestant (mostly Lesotho Evangelical) 29.8%; Anglican 11.5%; other Christian 8.0%; tribal 6.2%; other 1.0%.
Major urban centres (1976): Maseru 55,031 (Maseru-Roma-Morija metropolitan area [1986] 109,382); Maputsoe 15,823; Teyateyaneng 8,589.

Vital statistics

Birth rate per 1,000 population (1980–85): 41.7 (world avg. 29.0); legitimate, n.a.; illegitimate, n.a.
Death rate per 1,000 population (1980–85): 16.4 (world avg. 11.0).
Natural increase rate per 1,000 population (1980–85): 25.3 (world avg. 18.0).
Total fertility rate (avg. births per childbearing woman; 1980–85): 5.8.
Life expectancy at birth (1980–85): male 47.7 years; female 51.0 years.
Major causes of death: n.a.

National economy

Budget (1985–86). Revenue: M 250,000,000 (tax revenue 84.4%, of which customs receipts 64.4%, sales tax 7.6%, income tax 6.4%, company tax 3.4%; grants 6.8%). Expenditures: M 311,300,000 (recurrent expenditure 74.8%, of which personal emoluments 35.3%, education 9.5%, interest payments 8.6%, subsidies and transfers 5.5%, other goods and services 15.8%; capital expenditure 25.2%).
Production (metric tons except as noted). Agriculture, forestry, fishing (1984): corn (maize) 90,000, sorghum 26,000, vegetables and melons 25,000, fruit 15,000, pulses 15,000, roots and tubers 6,000, wheat 5,000; livestock (number of live animals) 1,350,000 sheep, 1,020,000 goats, 560,000 cattle, 105,000 horses, 105,000 asses, 72,000 pigs, 1,000,000 chickens: roundwood 293,000 cu m; fish catch 20†. Mining and quarrying (1982)‡: diamonds 42,000 carats. Manufacturing (1983): n.a.; however, food processing, cottage industry weaving, and handicrafts were the main manufacturing activities. Construction: n.a. Energy production (consumption): electricity (kW-hr; 1985) 1,000,000 (n.a.); coal, none (n.a.); petroleum, none (n.a.); natural gas, none (n.a.).
Gross national product (at current market prices; 1984): U.S.$790,000,000 (U.S.$520 per capita).

Structure of gross domestic product and labour force

	1981–82		1981	
	in value M '000,000	% of total value	labour force	% of labour force
Agriculture	142.4	24.5	430,000	60.0
Mining	0.7	0.1		
Manufacturing	43.7§	7.5	107,000	15.0
Construction	62.4	10.7		
Public utilities	‖	‖		
Transp. and commun.	‖	‖		
Trade	‖	‖		
Finance	‖	‖	179,000	25.0
Pub. admin., defense	110.8	19.1		
Services	140.3‖	24.1‖		
Other	81.0¶	13.9		
TOTAL	581.3	100.0♀	716,000δ	100.0

Public debt (external, outstanding; 1984): U.S.$134,300,000.
Tourism (1981): number of tourists entered 153,528.
Population economically active (1984): total 757,000□; activity rate of total population 50.3% (participation rates: ages 15–64, n.a.; female [1978–79] 46.1%; unemployed [1978–79] 2.2%).

Price and earnings indexes (1980 = 100)

	1980	1981	1982	1983	1984	1985	1986◇
Consumer price index	100.0	114.9	125.9	147.1	164.0	188.2	214.5
Annual earnings index△	100.0	145.6	311.2	441.8	518.8	577.6	...

Household income and expenditure. Average household size (1980) 4.4; average annual income per household (1979–80) M 1,550 (U.S.$1,150); sources of income (1978–79): agriculture 49.2%, wages and salaries 42.0% (of which migrant workers' remittances 32.4%), home industry 2.4%, other 6.4%; expenditure (1975): food 34.0%, clothing 19.3%, housing 9.7%, transportation 9.5%, education 4.1%, health 1.8%.
Land use (1983): meadows and pastures 65.9%; agricultural and under permanent cultivation 9.8%; other 24.3%.

Foreign trade†

Balance of trade (current prices)

	1979	1980	1981	1982	1983	1984	1985
M '000,000	−251.2	−298.3	−384.6	−501.1	−571.7	−650.7	−780.0
% of total	76.8%	76.7%	81.7%	86.5%	89.6%	89.0%	89.7%

Imports (1981): M 439,375,000 (manufactured goods [excluding chemicals, machinery, and transport equipment] 37.4%, of which clothing 8.4%, blankets and traveling rugs 3.6%, footwear 3.3%; food and live animals 18.9%, of which cereals [all forms] 5.9%, sugar [all forms] 2.6%; machinery and transport equipment 17.0%, of which trucks and vans 3.5%; petroleum products 8.6%). *Major import sources:* Customs Union of Southern Africa 97.1%; European Economic Community 1.5%.
Exports (1981): M 43,124,000 (diamonds 42.1%; food and live animals 10.3%; umbrellas, brooms, brushes, and basketwork 8.1%; mohair 8.0%; road vehicles 3.1%; footwear 3.0%). *Major export destinations:* Customs Union of Southern Africa 46.7%; Switzerland 41.8%; West Germany 7.0%.

Transport and communications

Transport. Railroads (1985): length 1 mi, 2 km. Roads (1985): total length 2,623 mi, 4,221 km (paved 12%). Vehicles (1982): passenger cars 5,129; trucks and buses 11,962. Merchant marine (1985): vessels (100 gross tons and over) none. Air transport (1981): passenger-mi 8,000,000, passenger-km 13,000,000; short ton-mi cargo 70,000, metric ton-km cargo 100,000; airports (1986) with scheduled flights 15.
Communications. Daily newspapers (1985): total number 3; total circulation 44,000; circulation per 1,000 population 28. Radio (1985): total number of receivers 43,000 (1 per 36 persons). Television (1985): total number of receivers 500 (1 per 3,092). Telephones (1981): 7,910 (1 per 173 persons).

Education and health

Education (1984–85)⊕

	schools	teachers	students	student/teacher ratio
Primary (age 6–12)	1,141	5,663	314,003	55.4
Secondary (age 13–17)	143	1,676	35,423	21.1
Voc., teacher tr.	9	221	2,221	10.0
Higher◇	1	146	1,119	7.7

Educational attainment (1976). Percent of population over age 10 having: no formal education 28.8%; primary 64.6%; secondary 2.3%; higher 0.6%. *Literacy* (1985): total population over age 15 literate 655,400 (73.6%); males literate 273,800 (62.4%); females literate 381,600 (84.5%).
Health (1982): physicians 114 (1 per 12,265 persons); hospital beds 2,300 (1 per 608 persons); infant mortality rate per 1,000 live births (1983) 109.
Food (1980–82): daily per capita caloric intake 2,355 (vegetable products 93%, animal products 7%); 103% of FAO recommended minimum requirement.

Military

Total active duty personnel (1980): 1,500**. *Military expenditure as percent of GNP* (1981): 1.8% (world 5.7%); per capita expenditure U.S.$9.

*Following a military coup in January 1986, it was announced that executive and legislative powers were to be vested in the King, assisted by a six-member Military Council and a Council of Ministers. †1983. ‡Mining activities ended in late 1982 with the closure of Lesotho's one commercial mine. Plans to reopen the mine were being considered in 1984. §Includes handicrafts. ‖Public utilities, transportation and communication, trade, and finance included with services. ¶Indirect taxes less subsidies. ♀Detail does not add to total given because of rounding. δIn 1981 about 23% of the total labour force were employed in South Africa, and in 1985 15.6%, or 116,603 workers, were employed there mostly as gold miners. □The total labour force, defined as the population between 18 and 64 years, was estimated at 749,000 in 1985. ◇January. △Based on Basotho miners working in South Africa. †Import figures are f.o.b. in balance of trade and c.i.f. in commodities and trading partners. ⊕Excludes private schools. **Lesotho Paramilitary Force.

Liberia

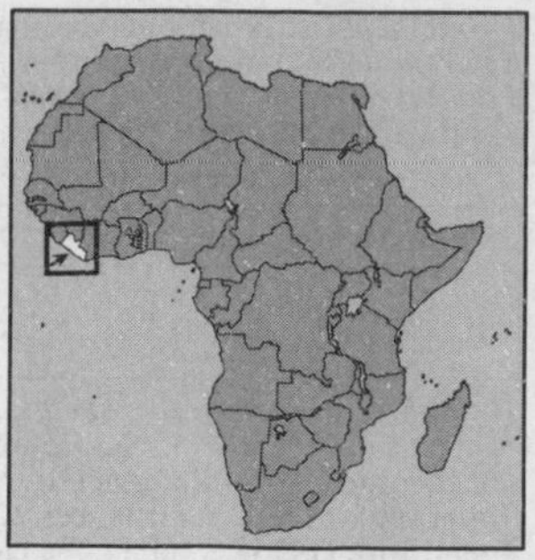

Official name: Republic of Liberia.
Form of government: multiparty republic with two legislative houses (Senate [26]; House of Representatives [64]).
Head of state and government: President.
Capital: Monrovia.
Official language: English.
Official religion: none.
Monetary unit: 1 Liberian dollar (L$) = 100 cents; valuation (Oct. 1, 1986) 1 U.S.$ = L$1.00; 1 £ = L$1.45.

Area and population

Counties	Capitals	area sq mi	area sq km	population 1982 estimate
Bong	Gbarnga	3,127	8,099	231,000
Grand Bassa	Buchanan	3,382	8,759	169,600
Grand Cape Mount	Robertsport	2,250	5,827	71,400
Grand Gedeh	Zwedru	6,575	17,029	111,800
Lofa	Voinjama	7,475	19,360	235,600
Maryland	Harper	1,202	3,113	81,200
Montserrado*	Bensonville	1,058	2,740	459,600
Nimba	Sanniquellie	4,650	12,044	379,500
Sinoe	Greenville	3,959	10,254	71,500
Territories				
Bomi	Tubmanburg	755	1,955	84,100
Gibi	...	846	2,191	72,700
Kru Coast	Barclayville	473	1,225	26,500
Marshall	...	414	1,072	25,100
Rivercess	...	1,693	4,385	29,800
Sasstown	...	391	1,013	12,000
TOTAL		38,250	99,067†	2,061,500

Demography

Population (1986): 2,303,000.
Density (1986): persons per sq mi 60.2, persons per sq km 23.2.
Urban-rural (1985): urban 39.5%; rural 60.5%.
Sex distribution (1985): male 49.57%; female 50.43%.
Age breakdown (1985): under 15, 46.8%; 15–29, 24.9%; 30–44, 14.7%; 45–59, 8.7%; 60–74, 4.1%; 75 and over, 0.8%.
Population projection: (1990) 2,571,000; (2000) 3,564,000.
Doubling time: 22 years.
Ethnic composition (1980): Bakwe 26.7%; Kpelle 20.8%; Gere and Basse 14.4%; Loma 8.0%; Mano 6.9%; Gola 6.9%; Liberians 1.3%; other 15.0%.
Religious affiliation (1983): traditional beliefs 75%; Muslim 15%; Christian 10%.
Major cities (1984): Monrovia 425,000; Yekepa 14,189‡; Tubmanburg 14,089‡; Gbarnga 10,860§.

Vital statistics

Birth rate per 1,000 population (1980–85): 48.7 (world avg. 29.0).
Death rate per 1,000 population (1980–85): 17.2 (world avg. 11.0).
Natural increase rate per 1,000 population (1980–85): 31.5 (world avg. 18.0).
Total fertility rate (avg. births per childbearing woman; 1980–85): 6.9.
Marriage rate per 1,000 population: n.a.
Divorce rate per 1,000 population: n.a.
Life expectancy at birth (1980–85): male 47.4 years; female 50.7 years.
Major causes of death per 100,000 population ‖ (1983): complications during pregnancy 866.0; malaria 225.3; pneumonia 123.2; anemia 77.9; malnutrition 48.4.

National economy

Budget (1985). Revenue: L$189,100,000¶ (income and profits taxes 38.1%; import duties 25.3%; tax on foreign vessels 9.5%; excise tax 7.9%). Expenditures: L$371,800,000 (current expenditure 82.4%, of which wages and salaries 36.8%, interest on public debt 12.2%, goods and services 5.5%, subsidies and grants 2.2%; development expenditure 17.6%).
Public debt (external, outstanding; 1984): U.S.$756,700,000.
Tourism: n.a.
Population economically active (1981): total 742,500; activity rate of total population 37.9% (participation rates: ages 10–64, 60.2%; female 31.4%; unemployed 12.5%).

Price and earnings indexes (1980 = 100)

	1980	1981	1982	1983	1984	1985	1986♀
Consumer price index	100.0	107.6	114.0	117.2	118.6	117.9	118.6
Monthly earnings index	...	...	...	...	...	...	...

Production (metric tons except as noted). Agriculture, forestry, fishing (1984): cassava 300,000, rice 230,000, sugarcane 155,000, bananas 79,000, natural rubber 78,000, plantains 33,000, sweet potatoes 17,000, green coffee 12,000, oranges 7,000, pineapples 7,000, cocoa beans 6,000; livestock (number of live animals) 235,000 sheep, 234,000 goats, 120,000 pigs, 42,000 cattle, 3,000,000 chickens; roundwood 4,174,000 cu m; fish catch (1983) 13,553. Mining and quarrying (1984): iron ore 15,100,000; diamonds 240,000 carats; gold 10,500 troy oz. Manufacturing (1982): cement 79,000; palm oil 20,000; cigarettes 20,000,000 units; beer 161,000 hectolitres♂. Construction: n.a. Energy production (consumption): electricity (kW-hr; 1984) 897,000,000 (897,000,000); coal, none (n.a.); crude petroleum (barrels; 1984) none (4,853,000); petroleum products (metric tons; 1984) 627,000 (502,000); natural gas, none (n.a.).
Household income and expenditure. Average household size (1980) 5.8; income per household: n.a.; source of income: n.a.; expenditure (1985)□: food 34.4%, rent 14.9%, clothing and footwear 13.8%, household goods and services 6.1%, beverages and tobacco 5.7%, fuel and light 5.0%.
Gross national product (at current market prices; 1984): U.S.$990,000,000 (U.S.$460 per capita).

Structure of gross domestic product and labour force

	1983		1981	
	in value L$'000,000	% of total value	labour force◊	% of labour force
Agriculture	135.1	18.5	515,000	79.3
Mining	127.2	17.4	20,000	3.1
Manufacturing	62.5	8.6	11,000	1.7
Construction	30.2	4.1	7,500	1.2
Public utilities	21.3	2.9	1,500	0.2
Transportation and communication	48.0	6.6	12,000	1.8
Trade	69.0	9.4	32,000	4.9
Finance	93.6	12.8		
Pub. admin., defense; Services	128.5	17.6	32,000	4.9
Other	15.3	2.1	18,500	2.9
TOTAL	730.7	100.0	649,500	100.0

Land use (1983): forested 39.0%; meadows and pastures 2.5%; agricultural and under permanent cultivation 3.9%; other 54.6%△.

Foreign trade

Balance of trade (current prices)

	1980	1981	1982	1983	1984	1985
L$'000,000	+114.4	+120.8	+105.5	+52.9	+116.9	+189.4
% of total	10.5%	12.9%	12.4%	6.6%	14.9%	27.8%

Imports (1983): L$411,622,000 (machinery and transportation equipment 26.5%, food and live animals 22.6%, petroleum and petroleum products 21.6%, basic manufactures 17.0%, miscellaneous manufactured articles 5.9%, chemicals 4.9%, beverages and tobacco 2.2%, animal and vegetable oils 1.3%). *Major import sources:* United States 24.9%; West Germany 12.3%; The Netherlands 9.9%; Japan 8.1%; United Kingdom 5.2%; France 3.6%; China 3.3%; Denmark 2.3%; Belgium–Luxembourg 1.4%.
Exports (1983): L$427,600,000 (iron ore 62.6%, rubber 17.1%, logs and timber 5.5%, coffee 4.3%, diamonds 4.0%, cocoa 2.7%). *Major export destinations:* West Germany 30.6%; United States 17.9%; Italy 17.6%; France 7.0%; The Netherlands 5.3%; Spain 4.9%; Belgium–Luxembourg 4.7%; United Kingdom 2.8%; Japan 1.5%.

Transport and communications

Transport. Railroads† (1985): route length 304 mi, 490 km; short ton-mi cargo 1,682,500,000⊕, metric ton-km cargo 2,456,400,000⊕. Roads (1983): total length 6,404 mi, 10,306 km (paved 7%). Vehicles (1983): passenger cars 12,064; trucks and buses 7,319. Merchant marine (1985): vessels (100 gross tons and over) 1,808; total deadweight tonnage 113,552,239. Air transport (1980): passenger-mi 10,600,000, passenger-km 17,000,000; short ton-mi cargo 68,000, metric ton-km cargo 100,000; airports (1986) with scheduled flights 8.
Communications. Daily newspapers (1985): total number 2; total circulation 27,000; circulation per 1,000 population 12. Radio (1985): total number of receivers 325,000 (1 per 6.9 persons). Television (1985): total number of receivers 35,000 (1 per 64 persons). Telephones (1983): 8,510 (1 per 246 persons).

Education and health

Education (1980)

	schools	teachers	students	student/teacher ratio
Primary (age 6–12)	1,232	9,099	227,431	25.0
Secondary (age 13–18)	419	1,129	51,666	45.8
Voc., teacher tr.	6	63	2,322	36.9
Higher	3	190	3,789	19.9

Educational attainment, n.a. *Literacy* (1985): total population over age 15 literate 425,100 (35.0%); males literate 285,400 (47.3%); females literate 139,700 (22.8%).
Health (1981): physicians 236 (1 per 8,305 persons); hospital beds 3,000 (1 per 653 persons); infant mortality rate per 1,000 live births (1980–85) 112.0.
Food (1980–82): daily per capita caloric intake 2,261 (vegetable products 95%, animal products 5%); 99% of FAO recommended minimum requirement.

Military

Total active duty personnel (1984): 6,750 (army 93.3%**, navy 6.7%). *Military expenditure as percent of GNP* (1983): 2.8% (world 6.1%); per capita expenditure U.S.$12.

*Area and population of the commonwealth district of Monrovia are included with Montserrado county. †Detail does not add to total given because of rounding. ‡1974 census. §1980 estimate. ‖ Hospital inpatient morbidity rates. ¶Domestic revenue only. ♀1980. ♂April. □Weights of consumer price index components. ◊Employed persons only. △Primarily swampy lowland. †For iron-ore transport only. ⊕Refers to Liberian American-Swedish Minerals Company railroad only. **Army includes 250 air force personnel.

Libya

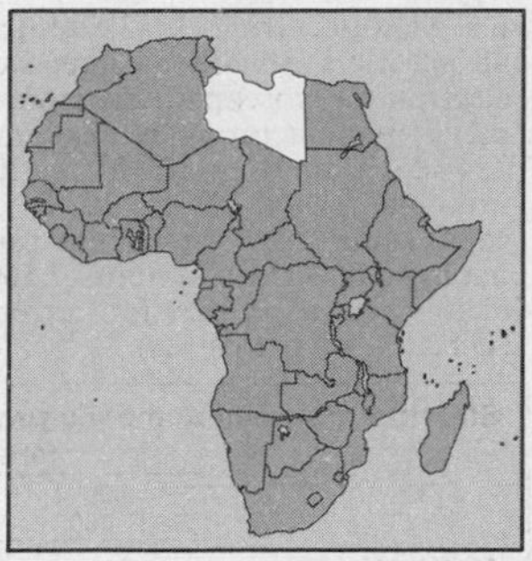

Official name: al-Jamāhīrīyah al-ʿArabīyah al-Lībīyah ash-Shaʿbīyah al-Ishtirākīyah (Socialist People's Libyan Arab Jamahiriya).
Form of government: socialist state with one policy-making body (General People's Congress [approx. 1,000]).
Chief of state:* Muʿammar al-Qadhdhafi.
Head of government: Secretary-general of the General People's Committee (premier).
Capital: Tripoli.
Official language: Arabic.
Official religion: Islam.
Monetary unit: 1 Libyan dinar (LD) = 1,000 dirhams; valuation (Oct. 1, 1986) 1 Libyan dinar = U.S.$3.13 = £2.17.

Area and population

Baladīyāt	Capitals	area sq mi	area sq km	population 1984 census
Ajdābiyā	Ajdābiyā	...	...	100,547
Awbārī	Awbārī	...	...	48,701
al-ʿAzīzīyah	al-ʿAzīzīyah	...	...	85,068
Banghāzī	Banghāzī	...	...	485,386
Darnah	Darnah	...	...	105,031
al-Fataḥ	al-Marj	...	...	102,763
Ghadamis	Ghadamis	...	...	52,247
Gharyān	Gharyān	...	...	117,073
al-Jabal al-Akhḍar	al-Bayḍāʾ	...	...	120,662
al-Khums	al-Khums	...	...	149,642
al-Kufrah	al-Kufrah	...	...	25,139
Marzuq	Marzuq	...	...	42,294
Miṣrātah	Miṣrātah	...	...	178,295
Nigāt al-Khums	Zuwārah	...	...	181,584
Sabhā	Sabhā	...	...	76,171
Sawfajjīn	Banī Walīd	...	...	45,195
ash-Shāṭi	Birāk	...	...	46,749
Surt	Surt	...	...	110,996
Ṭarābulus	Tripoli (Ṭarābulus)	...	...	990,697
Tarhunah	Tarhunah	...	...	84,640
Ṭubruq	Ṭubruq	...	...	94,006
Yafran	Yafran	...	...	73,420
az-Zāwiyah	az-Zāwiyah	...	...	220,075
Zlīṭan	Zlīṭan	...	...	101,107
TOTAL		685,524	1,775,500	3,637,488

Demography

Population (1986): 3,955,000.
Density (1986): persons per sq mi 5.8, persons per sq km 2.2.
Urban–rural (1985): urban 64.5%; rural 35.5%.
Sex distribution (1985): male 52.72%; female 47.28%.
Age breakdown (1980): under 15, 46.6%; 15–29, 25.1%; 30–44, 16.2%; 45–59, 8.3%; 60–74, 3.2%; 75 and over, 0.6%.
Population projection: (1990) 4,416,700; (2000) 6,538,800.
Doubling time: 20 years.
Ethnic composition (1982): Libyan (Berber and Arab with some Negro stock) 82.4%; foreign nationals 17.6%.
Religious affiliation (1982): Sunnī Muslim 97.0%; other 3.0%.
Major cities (1979): Tripoli 587,400; Banghāzī 267,700; Miṣrātah 52,200.

Vital statistics

Birth rate per 1,000 population (1980–85): 46.0 (world avg. 29.0).
Death rate per 1,000 population (1980–85): 11.2 (world avg. 11.0).
Natural increase rate per 1,000 population (1980–85): 34.8 (world avg. 18.0).
Total fertility rate (avg. births per childbearing woman; 1980–85): 7.2.
Marriage rate per 1,000 population (1979): 6.0.
Divorce rate per 1,000 population (1979): 1.5.
Life expectancy at birth (1980–85): male 56.1 years; female 59.4 years.
Major causes of death per 100,000 population: n.a.; however, major diseases include trachoma, tuberculosis, malaria, and dysentery.

National economy

Budget (1986). Revenue and expenditure: LD 4,475,000,000 (development expenditures: investment 38.0%, trade 31.5%, development 30.5%).
Public debt (external, outstanding; 1982): U.S.$844,000,000.
Tourism: receipts from visitors (1984) U.S.$12,000,000; expenditures by nationals abroad (1981) U.S.$645,000,000.
Production (metric tons except as noted). Agriculture, forestry, fishing (1984): tomatoes 245,000, wheat 150,000, potatoes 120,000, olives 110,000, dates 98,000, barley 70,000, oranges 45,000, grapes 23,000, peanuts (groundnuts) in shells 14,000; livestock (number of live animals) 4,800,000 sheep, 1,500,000 goats, 200,000 cattle, 135,000 camels, 60,000 asses; roundwood 633,000 cu m; fish catch (1983) 7,500. Mining and quarrying (1983): gypsum 180,000; salt 12,000. Manufacturing (1985): lime 270,000,000; cement 4,600,000; urea 668,300; ammonia 495,000; methanol 495,000; ethylene 247,500; asphalt 150,000; crude steel 10,000. Construction (gross value in LD; 1981): residential 61,671,000; nonresidential 256,904,000. Energy production (consumption): electricity (kW-hr; 1983) 7,270,000,000 (7,270,000,000); coal (metric tons; 1984) none (1,000); crude petroleum (barrels; 1984) 396,792,000 (46,668,000); petroleum products (metric tons; 1984) 5,470,000 (5,972,000); natural gas (cu m; 1984) 4,612,900,000 (3,331,510,000).

Gross national product (at current market prices; 1983): U.S.$29,790,000,000 (U.S.$8,220 per capita).

Structure of gross domestic product and labour force

	1982		1985	
	in value LD '000,000	% of total value	labour force	% of labour force
Agriculture	217	2.5	178,000	16.8
Mining	4,265	48.2	24,500	2.3
Manufacturing	305	3.4	112,000	10.5
Construction	1,054	11.9	256,500	24.2
Public utilities	69	0.8	25,500	2.4
Transportation and communication	387	4.4	93,000	8.7
Trade	523	5.9	41,000	3.9
Finance			13,000	1.2
Pub. admin., defense	2,026	22.9	69,000	6.5
Services			183,500	17.3
Other			66,000	6.2
TOTAL	8,846	100.0	1,062,000	100.0

Population economically active (1985): total 1,062,000; activity rate of total population 29.3% (participation rates: working age, n.a.; female 9.4%; unemployed, n.a.).

Price and earnings indexes (1975 = 100)

	1973	1974	1975	1976	1977	1978	1979
Consumer price index	85.3	91.6	100.0	105.4	112.1	145.0	137.1
Monthly earnings index	...	...	...	...	...	...	...

Household income and expenditure. Average household size (1980) 5.1; average annual income per household: n.a.; source of income: n.a.; expenditure (1977): food 37.2%, housing 32.2%, transportation 9.4%, education and recreation 8.5%, clothing 6.9%, medical care 3.3%.
Land use (1983): forested 0.4%; meadows and pastures 7.6%; agricultural and under permanent cultivation 1.2%; desert and built-up areas 90.8%.

Foreign trade

Balance of trade (current prices)

	1980	1981	1982	1983	1984	1985
LD '000,000	+4,674	+2,238	+1,894	+1,348	+1,486.2	+1,790.5
% of total	56.3%	32.0%	29.8%	25.9%	69.4%	38.3%

Imports (1981): LD 2,481,422,000 (food and live animals 16.3%, transport equipment and parts 14.9%, nonelectrical machinery 13.1%, electrical machinery 10.2%, metal manufactured products 9.7%, textiles and clothing 6.2%, iron and steel 5.1%, chemicals 4.5%). *Major import sources* (1984): Italy 26.6%; West Germany 12.9%; Japan 6.6%; United Kingdom 5.3%; Austria 1.6%.
Exports (1981): LD 4,609,851,000 (crude petroleum 99.6%, chemicals 0.4%). *Major export destinations* (1984): Italy 24.0%; West Germany 19.0%; Spain 9.2%; Switzerland 3.8%; The Netherlands 3.5%; United Kingdom 1.8%.

Transport and communications

Transport. Railroads: none. Roads (1982): total length 12,000 mi, 19,300 km (paved 56%). Vehicles (1982): passenger cars 415.509; trucks and buses 334,405. Merchant marine (1985): vessels (100 gross tons and over) 100; total deadweight tonnage 1,513,747. Air transport† (1981): passenger-mi 831,027,000, passenger-km 1,337,411,000; short ton-mi cargo 9,004,000, metric ton-km cargo 13,146,000; airports (1986) with scheduled flights 11.
Communications. Daily newspapers (1985): total number 1; circulation 40,000; circulation per 1,000 population 10.7. Radio (1985): total number of receivers 167,000 (1 per 22.7 persons). Television (1985): total number of receivers 175,000 (1 per 21.6 persons). Telephones (1976): 59,000 (1 per 42.0 persons).

Education and health

Education (1982–83)

	schools	teachers	students	student/teacher ratio
Primary (age 6–12)	2,744	42,202	741,502	17.6
Secondary (age 13–18)	1,555	25,044	301,415	12.0
Voc., teacher tr.	195	3,883	50,363	12.9
Higher‡	8	1,340§	25,700	...

Educational attainment (1973). Percent of population over age 10 having: no formal schooling (illiterate) 43.1%; ability to read only 8.7%; ability to read and write 32.1%; primary education 9.8%; secondary 5.8%; higher 0.5%. *Literacy* (1985): total population over age 10 literate 2,701,446 (74.4%); males literate 1,666,170 (85.0%); females literate 1,035,276 (62.0%).
Health (1982): physicians 5,210 ‖ (1 per 637 persons); hospital beds 16,051 (1 per 207 persons); infant mortality rate per 1,000 live births (1981) 97.5.
Food (1980–82): daily per capita caloric intake 3,667 (vegetable products 84%, animal products 16%); 156%¶ of FAO recommended minimum requirement.

Military

Total active duty personnel (1985): 73,000 (army 79.5%, navy 8.9%, air force 11.6%). *Military expenditure as percent of GNP* (1983): 17.5% (world 6.1%); per capita expenditure U.S.$6,608.

*No formal titled office exists. †International scheduled flights only. ‡1981–82. §1979–80. ‖ Personnel in government services only. ¶1979–81.

Liechtenstein

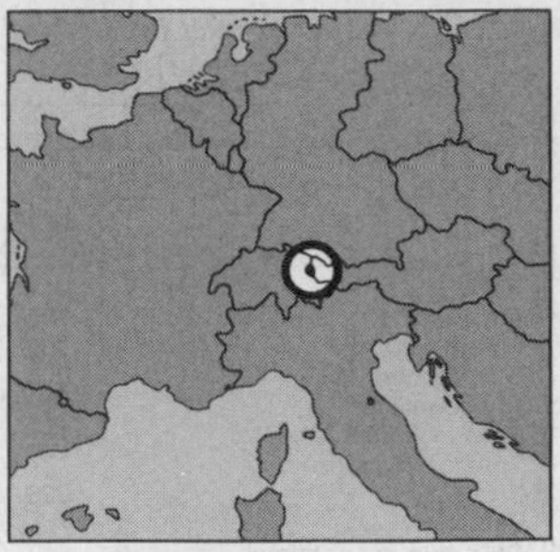

Official name: Fürstentum Liechtenstein (Principality of Liechtenstein).
Form of government: constitutional monarchy with one legislative house (Diet [15]).
Chief of state: Prince.
Head of government: Head of the Government..
Capital: Vaduz.
Official language: German.
Official religion: none.
Monetary unit: 1 Swiss franc (Sw F) = 100 centimes; valuation (Oct. 1, 1986) 1 U.S.$ = Sw F 1.65; 1 £ = Sw F 2.38.

Area and population

Communes	area sq mi	area sq km	population 1986 estimate*
Balzers	7.6	19.6	3,500
Eschen	4.0	10.3	2,800
Gamprin	2.4	6.1	900
Mauren	2.9	7.5	2,700
Planken	2.0	5.3	300
Ruggell	2.9	7.4	1,300
Schaan	10.4	26.8	4,700
Schellenberg	1.4	3.5	700
Triesen	10.2	26.4	3,000
Triesenberg	11.5	29.8	2,200
Vaduz	6.7	17.3	4,900
TOTAL	61.8†	160.0	27,100†

Demography

Population (1986): 27,100.
Density (1986): persons per sq mi 438.5, persons per sq km 169.4.
Urban–rural: n.a.
Sex distribution (1986): male 48.91%; female 51.09%.
Age breakdown (1986): under 15, 20.4%; 15–29, 27.1%; 30–44, 25.0%; 45–59, 14.0%; 60–74, 9.8%; 75 and over, 3.7%.
Population projection: (1990) 27,700; (2000) 29,600.
Doubling time: not applicable; population growth is negligible.
Ethnic composition (1986): Liechtensteiner 63.8%; Swiss 16.0%; Austrian 8.2%; German 4.0%; other 8.0%.
Religious affiliation (1986): Roman Catholic 86.9%; Protestant 8.5%; other 4.6%.
Major cities (1985): Vaduz 4,872; Schaan 4,653.

Vital statistics

Birth rate per 1,000 population (1985): 13.9 (world avg. 29.0); legitimate 94.6%; illegitimate 5.4%.
Death rate per 1,000 population (1985): 6.4 (world avg. 11.0).
Natural increase rate per 1,000 population (1985): 7.5 (world avg. 18.0).
Total fertility rate: n.a.
Marriage rate per 1,000 population (1985): 12.6.
Divorce rate per 1,000 population (1984): 7.3.
Life expectancy at birth (1980–84): male 71.1 years; female 77.8 years.
Major causes of death per 100,000 population (1984): diseases of the circulatory system 213.6, of which heart disease 161.2 (including ischemic heart disease 71.2); malignant neoplasms (cancers) 157.4; diseases of the digestive system 52.5; accidents, poisonings, and acts of violence 52.5; diseases of the respiratory system 26.2.

National economy

Budget (1984). Revenue: Sw F 275,872,000 (taxes and interest 67.8%; post, telephone, and telegraph 19.2%; other revenue sources include real estate capital-gains taxes and death and estate taxes). Expenditures: Sw F 267,988,000 (financial affairs 46.0%; education 13.4%; post, telephone, and telegraph 12.2%; social affairs 10.4%).
Public debt: none.
Tourism (1984): 83,589 tourist arrivals; receipts from visitors, n.a.; expenditures by nationals abroad, n.a.
Population economically active (1986): total 12,851; activity rate of total population 47.4% (participation rates: ages 15–64, n.a.; female [1984] 34.4%; unemployed 0.4%).

Price and earnings indexes (1980 = 100)

	1979	1980	1981	1982	1983	1984	1985‡
Consumer price index§	96.1	100.0	106.6	112.4	115.8	118.1	120.4
Monthly earnings index	...	...	...	...	...	...	...

Household income and expenditure. Average household size (1980) 3.0; average annual income per household: n.a.; sources of earned income (1984): wages and salaries 92.1%, self-employment 7.9%; expenditure (1983): insurance 14.9%, rent 12.7%, education and self-improvement 12.7%, food 12.5%, taxes 10.3%, transportation 10.1%, health 5.5%, clothing 4.7%.
Production (metric tons except as noted). Agriculture, forestry, fishing (1984): silo corn (maize) 25,000, milk 11,916, potatoes 400, barley 210, wheat 160; livestock (number of live animals; 1985) 6,373 cattle, 2,701 pigs, 2,545 sheep; commercial timber (1984) 8,918 cu m. Mining and quarrying: n.a. Manufacturing (1983): whipped cream 1,578; yogurt 54; cheese 8; wine 48,540 litres; small-scale precision manufacturing includes optical lenses, electron microscopes, electronic equipment, and high-vacuum pumps; metal manufacturing is also important. Construction (1984): residential 184,486 cu m; nonresidential 226,622 cu m. Energy production (consumption): electricity (kW-hr; 1984) 55,506,000 (163,813,000); coal (metric tons; 1984) none (132); petroleum products (metric tons; 1984) none (38,507); natural gas (kg; 1984) none (2,560,179).
Gross national product (at current market prices; 1980): U.S.$523,960,000 (U.S.$20,960 per capita).

Structure of gross domestic product and labour force

	1980 in value Sw F '000	1980 % of total value	1986 labour force	1986 % of labour force
Agriculture	...	...	364	2.8
Mining	...	...	60	0.5
Manufacturing	...	...	4,402	34.2
Construction	...	...	1,064	8.3
Public utilities	...	...	127	1.0
Transportation and communication	...	...	388	3.0
Trade	...	...	1,614	12.6
Finance	...	...	784	6.1
Pub. admin., defense	...	...	602	4.7
Services	...	...	3,165	24.6
Other	...	...	281	2.2
TOTAL	876,000	100.0	12,851	100.0

Land use (1983): forested 18.7%; meadows and pastures 37.5%; agricultural and under permanent cultivation 25.0%; other 18.8%.

Foreign trade

Balance of trade (current prices)

	1979	1980	1981	1982	1983	1984
Sw F '000,000	+398.0	+454.6	+531.9	+523.5	+560.7	+625.4
% of total	35.3%	34.1%	38.6%	39.3%	41.6%	41.8%

Imports (1984): Sw F 434,916,000 (machinery and transport equipment 33.6%; hardware 14.0%; chemical products 5.0%; unrefined and semifabricated metal 4.9%; limestone, cement, and other building materials 3.5%; food, beverages, and tobacco 2.3%, of which fruits and vegetables 0.6%; wood and cork 1.2%). *Major import sources:* n.a.
Exports (1984): Sw F 1,060,326,000 (machinery and transport equipment 47.2%; hardware 22.9%; other finished goods 19.1%; chemical products 7.8%; limestone, cement, and other building materials 1.6%). *Major export destinations:* European Economic Community countries 35.3%; Switzerland 21.0%; other European Free Trade Association countries 7.5%.

Transport and communications

Transport. Railroads (1984): length 11.5 mi, 18.5 km; passenger and cargo traffic, n.a. Roads (1979): total length 205 mi, 330 km. Vehicles (1985): passenger cars 14,804; trucks and buses 1,631. Merchant marine: none. Air transport: none.
Communications. Daily newspapers (1984): total number 2; total circulation 14,500; circulation per 1,000 population 545. Radio (1984): total number of receivers 8,736 (1 per 3.0 persons). Television (1984): total number of receivers 8,210 (1 per 3.2 persons). Telephones (1984): 24,265 (1 per 1.1 persons).

Education and health

Education (1986–87)

	schools	teachers	students	student/teacher ratio
Primary (age 7–12)	14	101	1,690	16.7
Secondary (age 13–19)	9	113	1,673	14.8
Vocational ‖	1	30	117	...

Educational attainment, n.a.; 9 years of formal education are compulsory, however. *Literacy:* virtually 100%.
Health (1984): physicians 20 (1 per 1,330 persons); hospital beds, n.a; infant mortality rate per 1,000 live births 7.4.
Food: daily per capita caloric intake 3,530 (vegetable products 62%, animal products 38%); 130% of FAO recommended minimum requirement¶.

Military

Total active duty personnel: none. *Military expenditure as percent of GNP:* none.

*January 1, 1986. †Detail does not add to total given because of rounding. ‡August. §The index is for Switzerland, which is united with Liechtenstein in a customs and monetary union. ‖ One evening school with part-time teachers. ¶Figures are derived from statistics for Switzerland and Austria.

Luxembourg

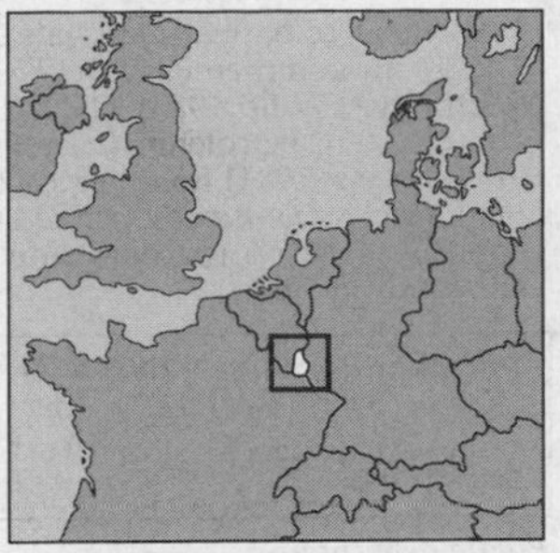

Official name: Grand-Duché de Luxembourg (French); Grossherzogtum Luxemburg (German) (Grand Duchy of Luxembourg).
Form of government: constitutional monarchy with one legislative house (Chamber of Deputies [64]).
Chief of state: Grand Duke.
Head of government: Prime Minister.
Capital: Luxembourg.
Official languages: French; German.
Official religion: none.
Monetary unit: 1 Luxembourg franc (LFr., plural LFr.) = 100 centimes; valuation (Oct. 1, 1986) 1 U.S.$ = LFr. 42.06; 1 £ = LFr. 60.78.

Area and population

Districts / Cantons	area sq mi	area sq km	population 1981 census
Diekirch	447	1,157	53,353
Clervaux	128	332	9,574
Diekirch	92	239	21,872
Redange	103	267	10,268
Vianden	21	54	2,642
Wiltz	102	265	8,997
Grevenmacher	203	525	38,846
Echternach	72	186	10,649
Grevenmacher	82	211	16,403
Remich	49	128	11,794
Luxembourg	349	904	272,403
Capellen	77	199	27,153
Esch	94	243	114,483
Luxembourg (Ville et Campagne)	92	238	114,225
Mersch	86	224	16,542
TOTAL	999	2,586	364,602

Demography

Population (1986): 365,900.
Density (1986): persons per sq mi 366.3, persons per sq km 141.5.
Urban–rural (1985): urban 81.8%; rural 18.2%.
Sex distribution (1985): male 48.67%; female 51.33%.
Age breakdown (1981): under 15, 18.5%; 15–29, 23.7%; 30–44, 21.2%; 45–59, 18.8%; 60–74, 12.8%; 75 and over, 5.0%.
Population projection: (1990) 366,000; (2000) 367,000.
Doubling time: n.a.; doubling time exceeds 100 years.
Ethnic composition (1981): Luxemburger 73.7%; Portuguese 8.0%; Italian 6.1%; French 3.3%; German 2.4%, other 6.5%.
Religious affiliation (1980): Roman Catholic 93.0%; Protestant 1.2%; other 5.8%.
Major cities (1981): Luxembourg 78,924; Esch-sur-Alzette 25,142; Dudelange 14,074; Differdange 8,588.

Vital statistics

Birth rate per 1,000 population (1985): 11.2 (world avg. 29.0); (1984) legitimate 91.8%; illegitimate 8.2%.
Death rate per 1,000 population (1985): 11.0 (world avg. 11.0).
Natural increase rate per 1,000 population (1985): 0.2 (world avg. 18.0).
Total fertility rate (avg. births per childbearing woman; 1984): 1.4.
Marriage rate per 1,000 population (1985): 5.3.
Divorce rate per 1,000 population (1985): 1.8.
Life expectancy at birth (1984): male 66.9 years; female 73.5 years.
Major causes of death per 100,000 population (1984): circulatory diseases 554.9, of which cerebrovascular disease 188.1, ischemic heart disease 179.6; malignant neoplasms (cancers) 261.9; accidents and suicides 67.5, of which suicide 18.9.

National economy

Budget (1985). Revenue: LFr. 74,010,585,000 (income and excise taxes 50.5%, customs taxes 11.8%). Expenditures*: LFr. 73,172,200,000 (social security 25.7%, transport and power 21.8%, education and arts 14.0%, debt service 12.6%, administration 7.8%, defense 3.0%).
Public debt (1985): U.S.$760,400,000.
Tourism: receipts from visitors, n.a.; expenditures by nationals abroad, n.a.
Production (metric tons except as noted). Agriculture, forestry, fishing (1984): barley 65,300, wheat 39,400, potatoes 34,400, oats 30,300; livestock (number of live animals) 226,761 cattle, 70,542 pigs; roundwood 336,000 cu m. Mining and quarrying (1984): metal ores, none; nonmetals 10,465,-000, of which stone 4,460,000, sand and gravel 3,900,000, gypsum 450,000. Manufacturing (1984): steel ingots and castings 3,987,000; finished rolled products 3,550,800; pig iron 2,768,000; meat products 20,465, of which beef and veal 13, 756, pork 6,709; wine 152,250 hectolitres. Construction (1983): residential and semiresidential 304,804 sq m; nonresidential 213,683 sq m. Energy production (consumption): electricity (kW-hr; 1984) 905,251,000 (3,818,693,000); coal (metric tons; 1984) none (189,000); crude petroleum, none (n.a.); petroleum products (metric tons; 1984) none (995,335); natural gas (cu m; 1984) none (317,326,000).
Gross national product (at current market prices; 1984): U.S.$4,980,000,000 (U.S.$13,610 per capita).

Structure of gross domestic product and labour force

	1983 in value LFr.'000,000,000	1983 % of total value	1984 labour force	1984 % of labour force
Agriculture	5.6	2.7	7,000	4.4
Mining	0.2	0.1 }	37,800	23.5
Manufacturing	52.9	25.7 }		
Construction	12.1	5.9	13,900	8.6
Public utilities	5.4	2.6	1,300	0.8
Transportation and communication	11.1	5.4	10,400	6.5
Trade	30.5	14.8	56,900	35.3
Finance	32.9	16.0	10,100	6.2
Pub. admin., defense	23.9	11.6	17,800	11.1
Services	31.3	15.2	3,100	1.9
Other	...	...	2,700†	1.7†
TOTAL	205.9‡	100.0	161,000	100.0

Population economically active (1984): total 161,000; activity rate of total population 44.0% (participation rates: ages 15–64 [1981] 61.3%; female [1981] 33.3%; unemployed 1.7%).

Price and earnings indexes (1980 = 100)

	1979	1980	1981	1982	1983	1984	1985
Consumer price index	93.8	100.0	109.3	118.2	128.4	135.7	141.2
Hourly earnings index§	92.4	100.0	104.6	116.9	127.6	137.6	...

Household income and expenditure. Average household size (1982) 2.8; income per household LFr. 751,800 (U.S.$16,455); sources of income (1984): wages and salaries 87.7%, self-employment 9.7%, transfer payments 2.6%; expenditure (1984): food and beverages 18.1%, transportation and communication 17.8%, housing 17.3%, household goods and furniture 7.8%, health 7.1%, clothing and footwear 6.6%.
Land use (1984): forested 31.7%; meadows and pastures 27.3%; agricultural and under permanent cultivation 21.6%; other 19.4%.

Foreign trade ‖

Balance of trade (current prices)

	1979	1980	1981	1982	1983	1984
LFr. '000,000	−6,062	−12,704	−17,192	−15,868	−16,492	−14,503
% of total	3.4%	6.7%	8.8%	7.2%	6.9%	4.7%

Imports (1984): LFr. 160,064,000,000 (metal products, machinery, and transport equipment 35.0%, of which electrical machinery 12.2%, transport equipment 8.4%; mineral products 17.4%; chemical products 8.6%; food, beverages, and tobacco 8.6%). *Major import sources:* Belgium 37.1%; West Germany 30.7%; France 13.1%; The Netherlands 3.9%; United States 2.9%; Italy 2.6%.
Exports (1984): LFr. 145,560,000,000 (metal products, machinery, and transport equipment 61.4%, of which electrical machinery 9.2%; plastic materials and rubber manufactures 12.7%; textile yarn, fabrics, and related products 5.2%; chemical products 4.2%; food, beverages, and tobacco 2.1%). *Major export destinations:* West Germany 27.2%; Belgium 15.5%; France 15.1%; The Netherlands 6.2%; United States 5.7%; United Kingdom 5.0%; Italy 3.6%.

Transport and communications

Transport. Railroads (1985): route length 168 mi, 270 km; passenger-mi 179,000,000, passenger-km 288,000,000; short ton-mi cargo 443,000,000, metric ton-km cargo 648,000,000. Roads (1984): total length 3,204 mi, 5,157 km (paved 99%). Vehicles (1985): passenger cars 151,640; trucks and buses 13,691. Merchant marine: vessels (100 gross tons and over) n.a.; total deadweight tonnage, n.a. Air transport (1984): passenger arrivals 377,000, departures 405,000; cargo loaded and unloaded 74,648 metric tons; airports (1985) with scheduled flights 1.
Communications. Daily newspapers (1984): total number 6; total circulation 130,000; circulation per 1,000 population 365. Radio (1985): 227,000 receivers (1 per 1.6 persons). Television (1984): 91,300 receivers (1 per 4.0 persons). Telephones (1984): 147,074 (1 per 2.5 persons).

Education and health

Education (1984–85)

	schools	teachers¶	students	student/ teacher ratio
Primary (age 6–15)	...	1,685	21,979	...
Secondary (age 12–18)	...	}	8,705	...
Voc., teacher tr.	...	} 3,482♀	16,571	...
Higher	...	}	785	...

Educational attainment, n.a. *Literacy* (1983): virtually 100% literate.
Health (1984): physicians 637 (1 per 574 persons); hospital beds 4,688 (1 per 78 persons); infant mortality rate per 1,000 live births (1985) 9.0.
Food (1980–82): daily per capita caloric intake ‖ 3,668; (vegetable products 59%, animal products 41%); 142% of FAO recommended minimum requirement.

Military

Total active duty personnel (1985): 720 (army 100.0%). *Military expenditure as percent of GNP* (1984): 0.7% (world 6.1%); per capita expenditure U.S.$109.

*Percentage breakdown is for 1984, LFr. 67,656,400,000. †Unemployed only. ‡At factor cost and current prices. §Manufacturing only. ‖ Figures for Belgium–Luxembourg. ¶1982–83. ♀Includes part-time teachers.

Macau

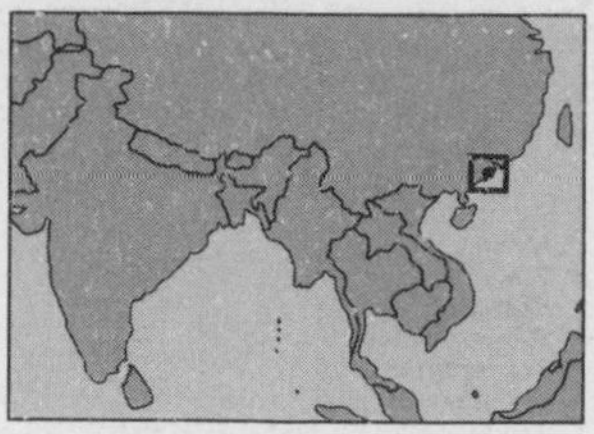

Official name: Macau.
Political status: overseas territory (Portugal).
Head of state and government: Governor (appointed).
Capital: Macau.
Official language: Portuguese.
Official religion: Roman Catholicism.
Monetary unit: 1 pataca* = 100 avos; valuation (Oct. 1, 1986) 1 U.S.$ = 8.11 patacas; 1 £ = 11.72 patacas.

Area and population

		area		population
Districts	**Capital**	sq mi	sq km	1981 census
Parishes				
Marine Area	—	—	—	13,011
Islands		3.9	10.1	9,478
São Francisco Xavier (Coloane)	—	1.4	3.5	4,082
Nossa Senhora Carmo (Taipa)	—	2.5	6.6	5,396
Macau	Macau	2.1	5.4†	225,337
Santo António	—	0.3	0.9	78,325
São Lázaro	—	0.3	0.8	20,787
São Lourenço	—	0.3	0.8	38,941
Sé	—	0.4	1.0	28,495
Nossa Senhora Fátima	—	0.8	2.0	58,789
TOTAL		6.0	15.5	247,826

Demography

Population (1986 est.): 433,000.
Density (1986): persons per sq mi 72,167, persons per sq km 27,935.
Urban-rural (1981): urban 94.9%‡.
Sex distribution (1981): male 51.88%; female 48.12%.
Age breakdown (1981): under 15, 22.9%; 15–29, 36.2%; 30–44, 16.7%; 45–59, 12.7%; 60 and over, 11.5%.
Population projection: (1990) 455,000; (2000) 727,000.
Doubling time: 47 years.
Nationality (1981): Chinese 73.5%; Portuguese 20.3%; English 0.9%; other 5.3%.
Religious affiliation (1984): Buddhist and Taoist 69.9%; Roman Catholic 6.2%; nonreligious 14.1%; other 9.8%.
Major city (1981): Macau 223,581.

Vital statistics

Birth rate per 1,000 population (1984): 19.4 (world avg. 29.0); legitimate, n.a.; illegitimate, n.a.
Death rate per 1,000 population (1984): 4.6 (world avg. 11.0).
Natural increase rate per 1,000 population (1984): 14.8 (world avg. 18.0).
Total fertility rate (avg. births per childbearing woman; 1980–85): 3.4.
Marriage rate per 1,000 population (1984): 8.6.
Divorce rate per 1,000 population (1982): 0.1.
Life expectancy at birth (1979): male 68.0 years; female 73.0 years.
Major causes of death per 100,000 population (1983): diseases of the circulatory system 138.7; malignant neoplasms (cancers) 80.8; signs, symptoms, and ill-defined conditions 69.8; diseases of the respiratory system 40.2; accidents and violence 36.9; infectious and parasitic diseases 31.4; diseases of the digestive system 21.0; endocrinal and metabolic diseases 12.2.

National economy

Budget (1984). Revenue: 1,442,800,000 patacas (1983; direct taxes 25.3%, indirect taxes 14.0%, transitory accounts 9.6%). Expenditures: 1,153,900,000 patacas (1983; security forces 14.1%, health and social welfare 4.6%, education 4.0%).
Gross national product (at current market prices; 1983): U.S.$780,000,000 (U.S.$2,270 per capita).

Structure of labour force

	1981	
	labour force	% of labour force
Agriculture	7,551	6.0
Mining	71	0.1
Manufacturing	56,304	45.0
Construction	9,937	7.9
Public utilities	876	0.7
Transportation and communication	5,776	4.6
Trade	14,134	11.3
Finance	2,191	1.8
Public administration	4,056	3.2
Services	8,714	7.0
Other	15,450	12.4
TOTAL	125,060	100.0

Production (metric tons except as noted). Agriculture, forestry, and fishing (1985): grapes 5,000, eggs 625; livestock (number of live animals) 8,000 cattle, 6,000 pigs; fish catch 7,000§. Mining and quarrying (1982): granite 656,920. Manufacturing (1983): clothing 27,184; knitwear 13,230; meat 9,021; furniture 2,335; wine 796; explosive and pyrotechnic products 586; footwear 376; optical materials 312. Construction (1984): residential 207,472 sq m; commercial 217,177 sq m. Energy production (consumption): electricity (kW-hr; 1984) 425,000,000 (425,000,000); coal (metric tons; 1984) none (1,000); petroleum (barrels; 1981) none (2,559); petroleum products (metric tons; 1984) none (180,000); natural gas, none (n.a.).
Population economically active (1981): total 127,359; activity rate of total population 42.7% (participation rates: over age 10, 61.5%; female 37.1%; unemployed 2.4%).

Price and earnings indexes (Oct. 1982–Sept. 1983 = 100)

	1983 ‖	1984 ‖	1985 ‖
Consumer price index	100	112.2	115.9
Earnings index	...	...	...

Public debt: none.
Tourism (1984): number of tourist arrivals 4,155,343.
Household income and expenditure. Average household size: n.a.; income per household: n.a.; source of income: n.a.; expenditure (1982–83): food 42.0%, rent 21.2%, education, health, and other services 8.1%, clothing and footwear 7.3%, transportation 4.9%.
Land use (1979): forested 50.0%; agricultural and under permanent cultivation 4.0%; built-on area, wasteland, and other 46.0%.

Foreign trade

Balance of trade (current prices)

	1979	1980	1981	1982	1983	1984
'000,000 patacas	+196.4	−38.0	−112.2	+38.5	+250.3	+919.4
% of total	5.1%	−0.7%	−1.4%	0.4%	2.3%	6.7%

Imports (1984): 6,385,600,000 patacas (industrial raw materials 51.6%, food and beverages 10.3%, machinery and electrical equipment 7.9%, building materials 6.8%, mineral fuels 6.0%, transport equipment 1.9%). *Major import sources:* Hong Kong 39.5%; China 28.0%; Japan 10.0%; United States 7.0%; United Kingdom 1.6%; Australia 1.3%; West Germany 1.3%; France 0.6%.
Exports (1984): 7,305,000,000 patacas (textiles and garments 70.0%, toys 10.0%, artificial flowers 3.8%, electronics 3.2%, leather articles 2.1%, ceramics 0.7%, fish and seafood 0.8%, furniture 0.8%, optical products 0.7%). *Major export destinations:* United States 30.4%; Hong Kong 20.1%; West Germany 10.6%; France 10.5%; United Kingdom 6.7%; China 5.2%; Italy 3.6%; Australia 1.9%; Japan 1.5%.

Transport and communications

Transport. Railroads: none. Roads (1982): total length 56 mi, 90 km (paved 100%). Vehicles (1984): passenger cars 17,543; trucks and buses 4,647. Merchant marine (1982): vessels 311¶; total gross tonnage 15,288. Air transport: none.
Communications. Daily newspapers (1985): total number 10; total circulation 242,000♀; circulation per 1,000 population 629. Radio (1984): total number of receivers 80,000 (1 per 3.9 persons). Television (1979): total number of receivers 59,000 (1 per 4.8 persons). Telephones (1985): 27,716 (1 per 11 persons).

Education and health

Education (1984–85)

	schools	teachers	students	student/teacher ratio
Primary (age 6–11)	73	1,057	31,468	29.8
Secondary (age 12–18)	30	744	12,612	17.0
Voc., teacher tr.	1	12	29	2.4
Higher	1	86	4,172	48.5

Educational attainment (1981). Percent of economically active population over age 10 having: no formal schooling 13.8%; primary education 22.6%; some secondary 27.2%; complete secondary 20.5%; some postsecondary 13.0%; higher 2.9%. *Literacy* (1981): total population over age 10 literate 127,359 (61.3%); males literate 80,102 (76.4%); females literate 47,257 (46.2%).
Health (1984): physicians (1982) 386 (1 per 772 persons); hospital beds 1,360 (1 per 227 persons); infant mortality rate per 1,000 live births 12.0.
Food (1981–83): daily per capita caloric intake 2,008 (vegetable products 74%, animal products 26%); 107% of FAO recommended minimum requirement.

Military

Total active duty personnel (1982): 1,800 (army 100%).

*The pataca free floats with the Hong Kong dollar and has a parity of 1 pataca = HK$0.96. †Detail does not add to total given because of rounding. ‡5.1% of Macau's population lives on sampans and other vessels. §1984. ‖ March. ¶All registered vessels including barges, tugboats, floating casinos, sampans, dredgers, but excluding barges used for restaurants and recreation. ♀Partial circulation only.

Madagascar

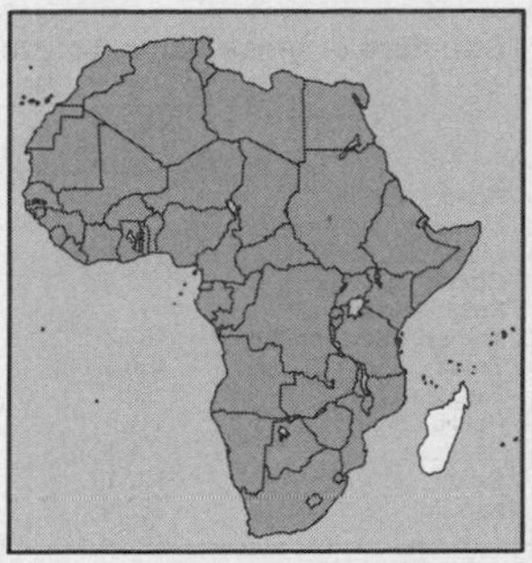

Official name: Repoblika Demokratika Malagasy (Malagasy); République Démocratique de Madagascar (French) (Democratic Republic of Madagascar).
Form of government: multiparty republic with one legislative house (National People's Assembly [137]).
Chief of state: President.
Head of government: Prime Minister.
Capital: Antananarivo.
Official languages: Malagasy; French.
Official religion: none.
Monetary unit: 1 franc (FMG) = 100 centimes; valuation (Oct. 1, 1986) 1 U.S.$ = FMG 748.37; 1 £ = FMG 1,081.40.

Area and population

		area		population
Provinces	Capitals	sq mi	sq km	1985 estimate
Antananarivo	Antananarivo	22,503	58,283	3,195,800
Antsiranana	Antsiranana	16,620	43,046	689,800
Fianarantsoa	Fianarantsoa	39,526	102,373	2,209,700
Mahajanga	Mahajanga	57,924	150,023	1,075,300
Toamasina	Toamasina	27,765	71,911	1,444,700
Toliara	Toliara	62,319	161,405	1,396,700
TOTAL		226,658	587,041	10,012,000

Demography

Population (1986): 10,303,000.
Density (1986): persons per sq mi 45.5, persons per sq km 17.6.
Urban-rural (1985): urban 21.8%; rural 78.2%.
Sex distribution (1985): male 49.61%; female 50.39%.
Age breakdown (1985): under 15, 44.0%; 15–29, 25.4%; 30–44, 15.5%; 45–59, 9.6%; 60–74, 4.6%; 75 and over, 0.9%.
Population projection: (1990) 11,575,000; (2000) 15,552,000.
Doubling time: 25 years.
Ethnic composition (1978): Malagasy 98.8%, of which Merina 25.9%, Betsimisaraka 14.6%, Betsileo 12.0%, Tsimihety 7.3%, Sakalava 6.1%; Antandroy 54.4%; Comorian 0.3%; Indian and Pakistani 0.2%; French 0.2%; other 0.5%.
Religious affiliation (1980): Christian 51.0%, of which Roman Catholic 26.0%, Protestant 22.8%; traditional beliefs 47.0%; Muslim 1.7%; other 0.3%.
Major cities (1980): Antananarivo 662,600*; Toamasina 95,505; Fianarantsoa 83,250; Mahajanga 80,881.

Vital statistics

Birth rate per 1,000 population (1984): 47.0 (world avg. 29.0); legitimate, n.a.; illegitimate, n.a.
Death rate per 1,000 population (1984): 15.0 (world avg. 11.0).
Natural increase rate per 1,000 population (1984): 32.0 (world avg. 18.0).
Total fertility rate (avg. births per childbearing woman; 1984): 6.5.
Marriage rate per 1,000 population: n.a.
Divorce rate per 1,000 population: n.a.
Life expectancy at birth (1980–85): male 48.9 years; female 50.4 years.
Major causes of death per 100,000 population: n.a.; however, major diseases include malaria, leprosy, and tuberculosis.

National economy

Budget (1985). Revenue: FMG 241,000,000,000 (no breakdown available). Expenditures: FMG 436,200,000,000 (current expenditure 71.8%, of which education 15.5%, defense 10.7%, health 5.9%, agriculture 1.9%, public works 0.9%).
Public debt (external, outstanding; 1984): U.S.$1,636,400,000.
Tourism: receipts from visitors (1984) U.S.$5,000,000; expenditures by nationals abroad (1983) U.S.$38,000,000.
Production (metric tons except as noted). Agriculture, forestry, fishing (1984): roots and tubers 2,866,000 (of which cassava 2,047,000, sweet potatoes 463,000, potatoes 264,000, taro 93,000), rice 2,132,000, sugarcane 1,660,000, fruit 741,000, vegetables and melons 302,000, bananas 224,000, corn (maize) 141,000, coffee 81,000, pulses 57,000, peanuts (groundnuts) 32,000, sisal 20,000, cloves 2,800†, black pepper 2,600†, cacao 2,000, vanilla 500†; livestock (number of live animals) 10,400,000 cattle, 1,800,000 goats, 1,350,000 pigs, 700,000 sheep; roundwood 6,262,000 cu m; fish catch 54,500‡. Mining and quarrying (1984): chromite concentrate 59,765; graphite 13,973; industrial calcite 2,000; mica 720; beryl 45,723 kg; celestite 30,000 kg; tourmaline 26,560 kg; jasper 17,000 kg; agate 9,300 kg. Manufacturing (1984): raw sugar 73,377; cement 36,580; gasoline 13,755; soap 13,424; cigarettes 2,537; chewing tobacco 1,328; beer 228,577 hectolitres. Construction (1983): residential 25,800 sq m; nonresidential 14,800 sq m. Energy production (consumption): electricity (kW-hr; 1984) 452,000,000 (452,000,000); coal (metric tons; 1984) 11,000 (11,000); crude petroleum (barrels; 1984) none (1,838,300); petroleum products (metric tons; 1984) 214,000 (306,000); natural gas, none (n.a.).
Population economically active: total (1984) 4,629,000; activity rate of total population 47.5% (participation rates: ages 15–64 [1975] 82.5%; female [1981] 44.5%; unemployed [1982] 0.6%).

Price and earnings indexes (1980 = 100)

	1980	1981	1982	1983	1984	1985	1986§
Consumer price index	100.0	130.5	172.0	205.3	225.5	249.3	283.4
Earnings index	...	...	...	...	...	...	...

Gross national product (at current market prices; 1984): U.S.$2,600,000,000 (U.S.$270 per capita).

Structure of gross domestic product and labour force

	1983		1982	
	in value U.S.$'000,000	% of total value	labour force	% of labour force
Agriculture	1,011	44.3	3,335,000	75.0
Mining	6	0.3	89,000	2.0
Manufacturing	251	11.0	445,000	10.0
Construction	103	4.5		
Public utilities	26	1.1		
Transportation and communication, Trade, Finance, Services, Pub. admin., defense	883	38.7	578,000	13.0
TOTAL	2,280	100.0 ‖	4,447,000¶	100.0

Household income and expenditure. Average household size (1980) 4.7; average annual income per household (1981) FMG 4,485 (U.S.$1,650); source of income: n.a.; expenditure♀: food 60.4%, fuel and light 9.1%, clothing and footwear 8.6%, household goods and utensils 2.4%.
Land use (1983): forested 22.3%; meadows and pastures 58.5%; agricultural and under permanent cultivation 5.2%; other 14.0%.

Foreign trade♁

Balance of trade

	1977	1978	1979	1980	1981	1982	1983
FMG '000,000,000	+14.6	+6.5	−25.7	−17.9	−34.1	−12.7	−21.6
% of total	9.6%	3.8%	13.3%	9.5%	16.6%	5.6%	8.7%

Imports (1984): FMG 198,294,000,000□ (mineral products 27.0%, of which crude petroleum 6.5%; chemical products 14.6%; machinery 9.7%; metal products 8.5%; vehicles and parts 7.8%; electrical equipment 4.6%; textiles 3.8%). *Major import sources:* France 36.2%; United States 6.8%; West Germany 4.3%; Japan 3.5%; United Kingdom 2.8%; Italy 2.6%.
Exports (1984): FMG 192,267,000,000 (coffee 40.6%; vanilla 15.8%; cloves and clove oil 12.5%; sugar 2.9%; petroleum products 0.4%). *Major export destinations:* France 41.8%; United States 14.7%; Japan 8.5%; West Germany 7.1%; Italy 6.5%; The Netherlands 5.8%.

Transport and communications

Transport. Railroads (1984): route length 644 mi, 1,036 km; passenger-mi 127,000,000, passenger-km 205,000,000; short ton-mi cargo 153,000,000, metric ton-km cargo 224,000,000. Roads (1985): total length 10,700 mi, 17,300 km (paved 30%). Vehicles (1983): passenger cars 23,412; trucks and buses 6,067. Merchant marine (1985): vessels (100 gross tons and over) 69; total deadweight tonnage 97,712. Air transport (1984): passenger-mi 253,500,000, passenger-km 408,000,000; short ton-mi cargo 14,600,000, metric ton-km cargo 21,300,000; airports (1986) with scheduled flights 35.
Communications. Daily newspapers (1985): total number 7; total circulation, n.a. Radio (1985): total number of receivers 900,000 (1 per 11 persons). Television (1985): total number of receivers 70,000 (1 per 143 persons). Telephones (1983): 37,100 (1 per 255 persons).

Education and health

Education (1978)

	schools	teachers	students	student/ teacher ratio
Primary (age 6–11)	8,002	23,937	1,311,000	54.8
Secondary (12–18)	104◇	5,088△	131,836△	25.9△
Voc., teacher tr.◇	126	759	9,213	12.1
Higher	3✝	706⊕	32,599⊕	46.2⊕

Educational attainment, n.a. *Literacy* (1985): total population over age 15 literate 3,778,000 (67.5%); males literate 2,004,000 (73.7%); females literate 1,774,000 (61.6%).
Health (1982): physicians 940 (1 per 9,851 persons); hospital beds 20,800 (1 per 442 persons); infant mortality rate per 1,000 live births (1984) 110.
Food (1980–82): daily per capita caloric intake 2,522 (vegetable products 93%, animal products 7%); 110% of FAO recommended minimum requirement.

Military

Total active duty personnel (1985): 21,100 (army 94.8%, navy 2.8%, air force 2.4%). *Military expenditure as percent of GNP* (1983): 2.1% (world 6.1%); per capita expenditure U.S.$6.

*1985. †Quantity exported; 1983–84. ‡1983. §March. ‖ Detail does not add to total given because of rounding. ¶Includes unemployed. ♀Consumer price index components in Antananarivo only; housing not included. ♁Import figures are f.o.b. in balance of trade and c.i.f. in commodities and trading partners. □Excludes gold and military equipment. ◇1971–72. △1975. ✝1984; two colleges and one university with six regional centres. ⊕1982.

Malaŵi

Official name: Malaŵi (Chewa); Republic of Malaŵi (English).
Form of government: single-party republic with one legislative house (National Assembly [101]).
Head of state and government: President.
Capital: Lilongwe.
Official languages: Chewa; English.
Official religion: none.
Monetary unit: 1 Malaŵi kwacha (MK) = 100 Tambala; valuation (Oct. 1, 1986) 1 U.S.$ = MK 1.98; 1 £ = MK 2.86.

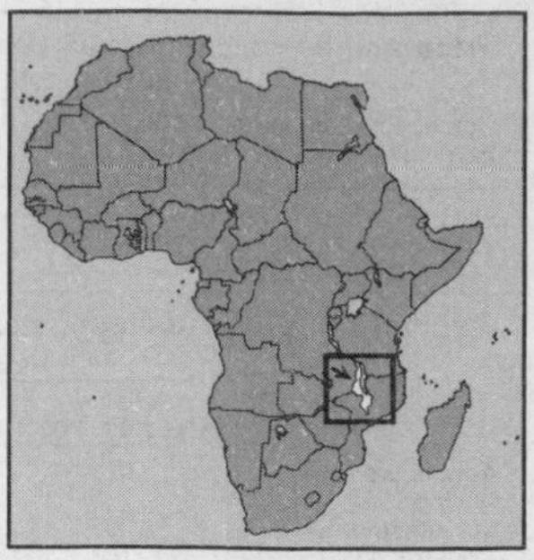

Area and population

Regions / Districts	Capitals	area* sq mi	area* sq km	population 1985 estimate
Central	Lilongwe	13,742	35,592	2,835,900
Dedza	Dedza	1,399	3,624	395,000
Dowa	Dowa	1,174	3,041	327,300
Kasungu	Kasungu	3,042	7,878	257,500
Lilongwe	Lilongwe	2,378	6,159	931,300
Mchinji	Mchinji	1,296	3,356	209,800
Nkhotakota	Nkhotakota	1,644	4,259	124,800
Ntcheu	Ntcheu	1,322	3,424	299,500
Ntchisi	Ntchisi	639	1,655	116,000
Salima	Salima	848	2,196	174,700
Northern	Mzuzu	10,398	26,931	794,300
Chitipa	Chitipa	1,353	3,504	88,300
Karonga	Karonga	1,141	2,955	131,100
Mzimba	Mzimba	4,027	10,430	368,600
Nkhata Bay	Nkhata Bay	1,579	4,090	129,600
Rumphi	Rumphi	2,298	5,952	76,700
Southern	Blantyre	12,260	31,753	3,428,600
Blantyre	Blantyre	777	2,012	508,100
Chikwawa	Chikwawa	1,836	4,755	241,700
Chiradzulu	Chiradzulu	296	767	219,400
Machinga	Machinga	2,303	5,965	425,200
Mangochi	Mangochi	2,422	6,272	376,100
Mulanje	Mulanje	1,332	3,450	594,500
Mwanza	Mwanza	886	2,295	89,200
Nsanje	Nsanje	750	1,942	135,400
Thyolo	Thyolo	662	1,715	400,500
Zomba	Zomba	996	2,580	438,500
TOTAL		45,747	118,484	7,058,800

Demography

Population (1986): 7,279,000.
Density (1986): persons per sq mi 200.0, persons per sq km 77.2.
Urban-rural (1985): urban 12.3%; rural 87.7%.
Sex distribution (1985): male 48.54%; female 51.46%.
Age breakdown (1985): under 15, 47.6%; 15–29, 25.5%; 30–44, 14.5%; 45–59, 8.1%; 60–74, 3.6%; 75 and over, 0.6%.†
Population projection: (1990) 8,224,000; (2000) 11,161,000.
Doubling time: 23 years.
Ethnic composition (1980): Maravi (including Nyanja, Chewa, Tonga, and Tumbuka) 58.6%; Lomwe 18.4%; Yao 13.4%; Ngoni 6.7%; other 2.9%.
Religious affiliation (1980): Christian 57.2%, of which Protestant 25.7%, Roman Catholic 25.0%; traditional beliefs 19.0%; Muslim 16.2%; other 7.6%.
Major cities (1984): Blantyre 333,800; Lilongwe 172,100; Mzuzu 70,200.

Vital statistics

Birth rate per 1,000 population (1983): 54.0 (world avg. 29.0).
Death rate per 1,000 population (1983): 23.0 (world avg. 11.0).
Natural increase rate per 1,000 population (1983): 31.0 (world avg. 18.0).
Total fertility rate (avg. births per childbearing woman; 1985): 7.6.
Marriage rate per 1,000 population (1977): 7.8.
Divorce rate per 1,000 population (1977): 1.4.
Life expectancy at birth (1981): male 42.7 years; female 45.4 years.
Major causes of death per 100,000 population‡ (1981): pneumonia 14.7; measles 11.1; malnutrition 10.4; anemia 8.9; diarrheal diseases 7.9.

National economy

Budget (1984–85). Revenue: MK 329,500,000 (surtax 25.8%, import duties 20.4%, corporate taxes 17.3%, income tax 12.4%). Expenditures: MK 363,000,000 (debt charges 36.2%, goods and services 27.3%, wages 24.7%).
Public debt (external, outstanding; 1984): U.S.$730,600,000.
Tourism (1984): receipts from visitors U.S.$6,000,000; expenditures by nationals abroad, n.a.
Production (metric tons except as noted). Agriculture (1984): sugarcane 1,670,000, corn (maize) 1,400,000, peanuts (groundnuts) 180,000, sorghum 140,000, potatoes 122,000, tobacco 70,000, tea 34,000; livestock (number of live animals) 910,000 cattle, 770,000 goats, 220,000 pigs, 89,000 sheep; roundwood 6,444,000 cu m; fish catch 58,416§. Mining and quarrying (1984): limestone 100,000; cement 70,000. Manufacturing (1982): beer 657,000,000 hectolitres; cigarettes 743,000,000 units. Construction (value in MK; 1983) ‖ : residential 2,923,000; nonresidential 1,661,000. Energy production (consumption): electricity (kW-hr; 1985) 473,160,000 (400,090,000); coal (metric tons; 1984) none (39,000); crude petroleum, none (none); petroleum products (metric tons; 1984) none (130,000); natural gas, none (n.a.).
Gross national product (at current market prices; 1984): U.S.$1,430,000,000 (U.S.$210 per capita).

Structure of gross domestic product and labour force

	1985 in value MK '000,000	1985 % of total value	1982 labour force¶	1982 % of labour force
Agriculture♀	313.9	36.4	179,215	52.1
Mining	...	...	609	0.2
Manufacturing	106.6	12.4	31,397	9.1
Construction	33.4	3.9	24,725	7.2
Public utilities	17.1	2.0	4,272	1.2
Transp. and commun.	53.4	6.2	16,729	4.9
Trade	156.5	18.1	21,812	6.3
Finance	56.6	6.6	10,036	2.9
Public administration	112.1	13.0	} 55,257	} 16.1
Services	35.5	4.1		
Other	−22.7δ	−2.6δ		
TOTAL	862.4□	100.0†	344,052	100.0

Population economically active (1977): total 2,967,000◇; activity rate of total population 41.3% (participation rates: over age 15, 80.2%, female 46.2%; unemployed 1.9%).

Price and earnings indexes (1980 = 100)

	1978	1979	1980	1981	1982	1983	1984
Consumer price index	75.7	84.0	100.0	111.8	122.8	139.4	167.3
Monthly earnings index	81.5	85.7	100.0	112.9	131.9	124.3	...

Household income and expenditure (1979–80). Average household size△ 4.5; income per household MK 1,934 (U.S.$2,419†); sources of income: wages 83.3%, household enterprise 6.0%; expenditure: food 23.7%, transportation and communication 13.7%, household equipment 9.9%, clothing and footwear 8.0%, housing 7.6%.
Land use (1983): forested 44.0%; meadows and pastures 19.6%; agricultural and under permanent cultivation 24.9%; other 11.5%.

Foreign trade⊕

Balance of trade (current prices)

	1979	1980	1981	1982	1983	1984
MK '000,000	−103.7	−82.9	−31.7	−26.5	−54.0	+72.0
% of total	22.2%	15.2%	6.1%	4.9%	9.2%	9.4%

Imports (1984): MK 381,573,000 (fertilizer 12.4%, diesel fuel 6.9%, motor spirit 4.5%, motor vehicles 4.3%, clothing and garments 2.6%). *Major import sources:* South Africa 40.4%; United Kingdom 13.0%; Japan 8.2%; Zimbabwe 6.1%; Zambia 4.5%.
Exports (1984): MK 436,541,000 (tobacco 52.7%, tea 25.9%, corn 6.7%, sugar 6.6.%, beans and peas 1.5%, unbleached cotton fabric 1.2%). *Major export destinations:* United Kingdom 31.5%; West Germany 9.2%; United States 8.8%; South Africa 7.4%; The Netherlands 6.6%.

Transport and communications

Transport. Railroads (1984): route length 490 mi, 789 km; passenger-mi 67,100,000, passenger-km 108,000,000; short ton-mi cargo 82,200,000, metric ton-km cargo 120,000,000. Roads (1983): total length 7,172 mi, 11,542 km (paved 19%). Vehicles (1981): passenger cars 14,102; trucks and buses 17,247. Merchant marine (1985): vessels (100 gross tons and over) 1; total deadweight tonnage 300. Air transport (1985): passenger-mi 52,200,000, passenger-km 84,000,000; short ton-mi cargo 616,000, metric ton-km cargo 948,000; airports (1986) with scheduled flights 4.
Communications. Daily newspapers (1985): total number 2; total circulation 32,000; circulation per 1,000 population 4.5. Radio (1985): total number of receivers 1,060,000 (1 per 6.7 persons). Television (1983): total number of receivers, n.a. Telephones (1981): 15,130 (1 per 412 persons).

Education and health

Education (1982–83)

	schools	teachers	students	student/teacher ratio
Primary (age 6–13)	2,411	13,714	868,849	63.4
Secondary (age 14–18)	60	825	17,232	20.9
Teacher tr., voc.**	10	155	2,322	15.0
Higher	4	305	1,849	6.1

Educational attainment (1977). Percent of adult population over age 25 having: primary education 4.7%; secondary 2.5%; higher 0.2%. *Literacy* (1983): total population over age 15 literate 1,121,934 (31.3%).
Health (1982): physicians 121 (1 per 51,461 persons); hospital beds 6,596 (1 per 840 persons); infant mortality rate per 1,000 live births (1985) 152.0.
Food (1980–82): daily per capita caloric intake 2,220 (vegetable products 96%, animal products 4%); 95% of FAO recommended minimum requirement.

Military

Total active duty personnel (1985): 5,250 (army 95.2%, navy 1.9%, air force 2.9%). *Military expenditure as percent of GNP* (1983): 1.7% (world 6.1%); per capita expenditure U.S.$3.

*Total land area is 36,400 sq mi (94,276 sq km) and is shown for regions and districts; the total area (both land and water) is shown in the grand total. †Detail does not add to total given because of rounding. ‡Reported inpatient deaths in hospitals. §1983. ‖ New construction in the cities of Blantyre and Lilongwe only. ¶Employed persons only. ♀Both estate and smallholder agriculture. δLess imputed bank service charges. □At 1978 prices. ◇1984; includes 2,402,000 people working in agriculture. △Based on a sample survey of the city of Blantyre. †Based on end of 1979 conversion factor. ⊕Import figures are f.o.b. (free on board) in balance of trade and c.i.f. (cost, insurance, and freight) for commodities and trading partners. **Public only.

Malaysia

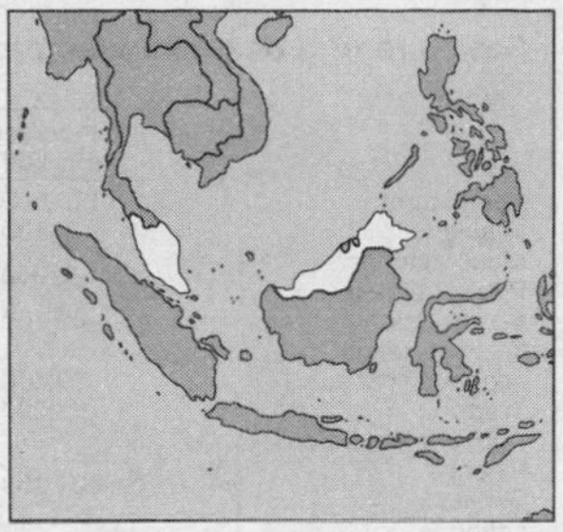

Official name: Malaysia.
Form of government: federal constitutional monarchy with two legislative houses (Senate [69]; House of Representatives [154]).
Chief of state: Yang di-Pertuan Agong.
Head of government: Prime Minister.
Capital: Kuala Lumpur.
Official language: Malay.
Official religion: Islam.
Monetary unit: 1 ringgit, or Malaysian dollar (M$) = 100 cents; valuation (Oct. 1, 1986) 1 U.S.$ = M$2.63; 1 £ = M$3.80.

Area and population

Regions / States	Capitals	area sq mi	area sq km	population 1984 estimate
East Malaysia				
Sabah*	Kota Kinabalu	28,460	73,711	1,176,400
Sarawak	Kuching	48,050	124,449	1,442,100
West Malaysia				
Johor	Johor Baharu	7,330	18,985	1,818,900
Kedah	Alor Setar	3,639	9,425	1,233,000
Kelantan	Kota Baharu	5,765	14,931	1,016,200
Melaka	Melaka	640	1,658	511,500
Negeri Sembilan	Seremban	2,565	6,646	631,500
Pahang	Kuantan	13,884	35,960	895,000
Pinang	Pinang	398	1,031	1,029,300
Perak	Ipoh	8,110	21,005	1,976,900
Perlis	Kangar	307	795	162,900
Selangor	Shah Alam	3,072	7,956	1,682,800
Terengganu	Kuala Terengganu	5,002	12,955	617,000
Federal Territory				
Kuala Lumpur	—	94	243	1,076,100
TOTAL LAND AREA		127,317	329,750	15,269,600
INLAND WATER		264	684	
TOTAL AREA		127,581	330,434	

Demography

Population (1986): 16,090,000.
Density (1986): persons per sq mi 126.4, persons per sq km 48.8.
Urban-rural (1985): urban 38.2%; rural 61.8%.
Sex distribution (1985): male 50.36%; female 49.64%.
Age breakdown (1980): under 15, 39.5%; 15–29, 29.1%; 30–44, 16.5%; 45–59, 9.2%; 60–74, 4.6%; 75 and over, 1.1%.
Population projection: (1990) 17,830,000; (2000) 23,050,000.
Doubling time: 30 years.
Ethnic composition (1985): Malay 59.0%; Chinese 32.0%; Indian 9.0%.
Religious affiliation (1980): Muslim 52.9%; Buddhist 17.3%; Chinese folk-religionist 11.6%; Hindu 7.0%; Christian 6.4%; other 4.8%.
Major cities (1980): Kuala Lumpur 1,103,200†; Ipoh 293,849; Pinang 248,241; Johor Baharu 246,395; Petaling Jaya 207,805.

Vital statistics

Birth rate per 1,000 population (1985): 29.0 (world avg. 29.0).
Death rate per 1,000 population (1985): 6.2 (world avg. 11.0).
Natural increase rate per 1,000 population (1985): 22.8 (world avg. 18.0).
Total fertility rate (avg. births per childbearing woman; 1985): 3.6.
Marriage rate per 1,000 population (1979): 1.7.
Divorce rate per 1,000 population (1979): 0.02.
Life expectancy at birth (1985): male 65.8 years; female 69.8 years.
Major causes of death per 100,000 population (1981)‡: heart disease 29.1; infectious and parasitic diseases 19.2; malignant neoplasms (cancers) 18.6; cerebrovascular diseases 14.4; pneumonia 10.6.

National economy

Budget (1986). Revenue: M$22,121,000,000 (income tax 39.8%, import and export duties 21.9%, sales and excise taxes 14.1%). Expenditures: M$29,564,000,000 (economic development 25.7%, debt service 20.0%, education 13.7%, administration 8.3%, defense 8.1%, internal security 5.0%, health 4.0%).
Tourism: receipts from visitors (1984) U.S.$546,000,000; expenditures by nationals abroad (1983) U.S.$579,000,000.
Production (metric tons except as noted). Agriculture (1984): palm oil 3,717,000, rice 1,755,000, rubber 1,530,000, palm kernels 1,046,000, pineapples 181,000, cacao 93,000, peppers 23,800; livestock (number of live animals) 2,100,000 pigs, 575,000 cattle, 335,000 goats, 255,000 buffalo, 69,000 sheep, 78,000,000 chickens; roundwood 40,212,000 cu m; fish catch 741,089§. Mining and quarrying (1984): bauxite 680,000; copper 141,000; iron ore 194,000; tin concentrates 41,300; gold 89,527 troy oz. Manufacturing (1983) ‖ : cement 3,231,000; iron and steel products 287,900; bars and rods for reinforced concrete 241,000; condensed milk 113,800; tin 53,300; soap 46,400; biscuits 45,500; canned pineapple 39,300; cigars, cigarettes, and other tobacco products 14,500; rubber compounds 12,000; footwear 26,105,000 pairs; rubber tires and tubes 10,280,000 units. Construction: n.a. Energy production (consumption): electricity (kW-hr; 1984) 13,700,000,000 (13,750,000,000); coal (metric tons; 1984) none (300,000); petroleum (barrels; 1984) 165,588,000 (53,296,000); petroleum products (metric tons; 1984) 5,818,000 (8,474,000); natural gas (cu m; 1984) 5,080,000,000 (359,000,000).
Gross national product (at current market prices; 1984): U.S.$30,280,000,000 (U.S.$1,980 per capita).

Structure of gross domestic product and labour force

	1984 in value M$'000,000	1984 % of total value	1985 labour force	1985 % of labour force
Agriculture	7,157	21.3	1,980,900	35.5
Mining	1,638	4.9	63,400	1.1
Manufacturing	6,185	18.4	876,300	15.7
Construction	1,825	5.4	386.800	6.9
Public utilities	876	2.6	¶	¶
Transp. and commun.	2,758	8.2	272,300	4.9
Trade	4,597	13.7	773,500	13.9
Finance	2,704	8.0		
Pub. admin., defense	4,410	13.1	895,500	16.1
Services	852	2.5		
Other	625♀	1.9♀	327,000¶♁	5.9¶♁
TOTAL	33,627□	100.0	5,575,900	100.0

Public debt (external, outstanding; 1984): U.S.$11,846,000,000.
Population economically active (1985): total 5,575,900; activity rate of total population 35.6% (participation rates: over age 15, 58.8%; female [1980] 33.6%; unemployed [1984] 6.2%).

Price and earnings indexes (1980 = 100)

	1980	1981	1982	1983	1984	1985	1986◇
Consumer price index	100.0	109.7	116.1	120.4	125.1	125.5	126.2

Household income and expenditure. Average household size (1980) 5.2; average annual income per household: n.a.; source of income: n.a.; expenditure (1980): food 36.2%, housing 24.1%, transportation 16.6%, recreation and education 6.7%, clothing and footwear 4.7%, health 1.3%.
Land use (1983): forested 66.0%; meadows and pastures 0.1%; agricultural and under permanent cultivation 13.2%; other 20.7%.

Foreign trade△

Balance of trade (current prices)

	1980	1981	1982	1983	1984	1985
M$'000,000	+7,045	+3,141	+1,961	+5,028	+8,954	+10,664
% of total	14.3%	6.1%	3.6%	8.3%	13.1%	16.2%

Imports (1984): M$32,968,000,000 (machinery and transport equipment 45.3%, basic manufactures 15.5%, mineral fuels 10.4%, food and live animals 9.8%, chemicals 8.1%, crude materials excluding fuels 3.5%). *Major import sources:* Japan 26.3%; United States 16.3%; Singapore 13.1%; West Germany 4.2%; Australia 4.0%.
Exports (1984): M$38,654,000,000 (crude and partly refined petroleum 22.6%, palm oil 11.8%, saw logs and sawn lumber 10.2%, rubber 9.5%, tin 3.0%). *Major export destinations:* Japan 22.8%; Singapore 20.4%; United States 13.5%; Netherlands 4.0%; United Kingdom 2.5%.

Transport and communications

Transport. Railroads (1984): route length 1,666 mi, 2,681 km; passenger-mi 940,000,000 ‖ , passenger-km 1,512,000,000 ‖ ; short ton-mi cargo 740,000,000 ‖ , metric ton-km cargo 1,080,000,000 ‖ . Roads (1984): total length 17,975 mi, 28,928 km (paved 80%). Vehicles (1984): passenger cars 1,075,328; trucks and buses 313,528. Merchant marine (1985): vessels (100 gross tons and over) 467; total deadweight tonnage 2,582,744. Air transport (1984): passenger-mi 3,705,800,000, passenger-km 5,964,000,000; short ton-mi cargo 137,000,000, metric ton-km cargo 200,000,000; airports (1986) with scheduled flights 39.
Communications. Daily newspapers (1985): total number 42; circulation, n.a. Radio (1983): total number of receivers 282,893✝ (1 per 52.5 persons). Television (1983): total number of receivers 1,672,845✝ (1 per 8.9 persons). Telephones (1983): 976,500 (1 per 15 persons).

Education and health

Education (1985)

	schools	teachers	students	student/teacher ratio
Primary (age 7–12)	6,629	91,099	2,191,676	24.1
Secondary (age 13–19)	1,132	56,290	1,273,666	22.6
Voc., teacher tr.	45	1,699	20,720	12.2
Higher	41	8,415	96,212	11.4

Educational attainment (1980). Percent of population over age 5 having: no formal education 25%; primary 44%; some secondary 18%; secondary and higher 13%. *Literacy* (1980): total population over age 10 literate 7,133,775 (75.0%); males literate 3,913,865 (83.0%); females literate 3,219,910 (67.1%).
Health: physicians (1983) 4,234 (1 per 3,510 persons); hospital beds (1981) 34,538 (1 per 411 persons); infant mortality rate per 1,000 live births (1985) 28.0.
Food (1980–82): daily per capita caloric intake 2,636 (vegetable products 87%, animal products 13%); 113% of FAO recommended minimum requirement.

Military

Total active duty personnel (1985): 110,000 (army 81.8%, navy 8.2%, air force 10.0%). *Military expenditure as percent of GNP* (1983): 8.1% (world 6.1%); per capita expenditure U.S.$160.

*Includes Labuan federal territory. †1985. ‡Medically certified deaths only. §1983. ‖ Peninsular Malaysia only. ¶Public utilities included with other. ♀Includes import duties and bank service charges. ♁Includes unemployed. □At constant 1970 prices. ◇May. △Import figures are f.o.b. (free on board) in balance of trade and c.i.f. (cost, insurance, and freight) for commodities and trading partners. ✝Licenses issued and renewed.

Maldives

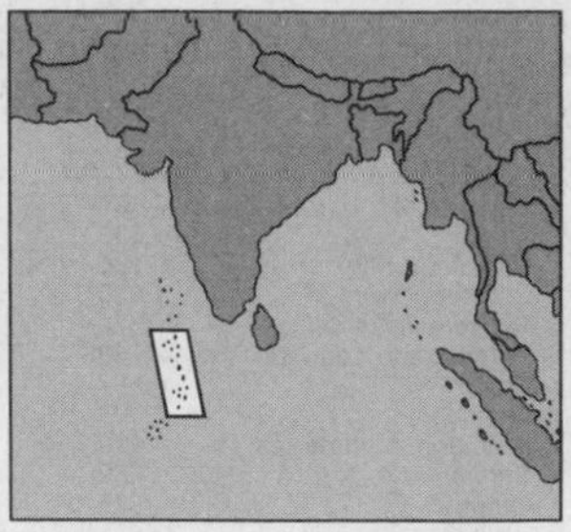

Official name: Divehi Jumhuriyya (Republic of Maldives).
Form of government: republic with one legislative house (People's Council [48]).
Head of state and government: President.
Capital: Male.
Official language: Divehi.
Official religion: Islam.
Monetary unit: 1 Maldivian Rufiyaa (Rf) = 100 laaris; valuation (Oct. 1, 1986) 1 U.S.$ = Rf 7.00; 1 £ = Rf 10.12.

Area and population*

Administrative atolls	Capitals	area sq mi	area sq km	population 1985 census
Haa-Alifu	Dhidhdhoo	...	...	9,891
Haa-Dhaalu	Nolhivaranfaru	...	...	10,848
Shaviyani	Farukolhu Funadhoo	...	...	7,529
Noonu	Manadhoo	...	...	6,874
Raa	Ugoofaaru	...	...	9,516
Baa	Eydhafushi	...	...	6,945
Lhaviyani	Naifaru	...	...	6,402
Kaafu	Male	...	...	54,908
Alifu	Mahibadhoo	...	...	7,695
Vaavu	Felidhoo	...	...	1,423
Meemu	Muli	...	...	3,493
Faafu	Magoodhoo	...	...	2,148
Dhaalu	Kudahuvadhoo	...	...	3,576
Thaa	Veymandhoo	...	...	6,942
Laamu	Hithadhoo	...	...	7,158
Gaafu-Alifu	Viligili	...	...	6,081
Gaafu-Dhaalu	Thinadhoo	...	...	8,870
Gnyaviyani	Foah Mulah	...	...	6,189
Seenu	Hithadhoo	...	...	14,965
TOTAL		115	298	181,453

Demography

Population (1986): 190,000.
Density (1986): persons per sq mi 1,652.2, persons per sq km 637.6.
Urban–rural (1985): urban 25.5%; rural 74.5%.
Sex distribution (1985): male 51.84%; female 48.16%.
Age breakdown (1977): under 15, 44.6%; 15–29, 24.8%; 30–44, 16.4%; 45–59, 9.6%; 60 and over, 4.6%.
Population projection: (1990) 217,000; (2000) 303,000.
Doubling time: 19 years.
Ethnic composition: the majority is principally of Sinhalese and Dravidian extraction; Arab, African, and Negrito influences are also present.
Religious affiliation: virtually 100% Sunnī Muslim.
Major cities (1985): Male 46,334.

Vital statistics

Birth rate per 1,000 population (1984): 46.3 (world avg. 29); legitimate, n.a.; illegitimate, n.a.
Death rate per 1,000 population (1984): 9.3 (world avg. 11.0).
Natural increase rate per 1,000 population (1984): 37.0 (world avg. 18.0).
Total fertility rate (avg. births per childbearing woman; 1984): 6.6.
Marriage rate per 1,000 population (1981): 34.6.
Divorce rate per 1,000 population (1981): 25.5.
Life expectancy at birth (1984): male 57.0 years; female 58.0 years.
Major causes of death per 100,000 population: n.a.; however, waterborne diseases (including gastroenteritis, cholera, and typhoid fever), are principal health problems, as are malaria, shigellosis, filariasis, leprosy, and tuberculosis.

National economy

Budget (1984). Revenue: Rf 171,200,000 (import duties 28.6%; foreign aid 23.4%, of which cash receipts 17.1%, food aid 3.5%, nonbudgetary fund receipts 2.8%; revenue from tourism 16.2%; charges associated with all aspects of fishing 11.2%; charges associated with the airline industry 6.7%). Expenditures: Rf 182,800,000 (defense 11.9%; Islamic centre 11.5%; education 10.8%; main airport 10.4%; president's office and residence 8.2%; finance 6.9%; administration 5.7%; social services 5.7%; health 5.5%; reclamation 3.4%).
Public debt (external, outstanding; 1985) U.S.$52,100,000.
Production (metric tons except as noted). Agriculture, forestry, fishing (1985): vegetables and melons 18,000, coconuts 10,000, roots and tubers 8,000 (including cassava, sweet potatoes, and yams), fruits excluding melons 8,000, copra 2,000; fish catch 47,500, of which skipjack tuna 24,400, yellowfin tuna 7,100. Mining and quarrying: n.a. Manufacturing: n.a.; however, major industries are boat building and repairing, coir yarn and mat weaving, coconut and fish processing, lacquer work, garment manufacturing, and handicrafts. Construction: n.a. Energy production (consumption): electricity (kW-hr; 1984) 11,000,000 (11,000,000); coal, none (n.a.); petroleum products (metric tons; 1984) none (8,000); natural gas, none (n.a.).
Tourism: receipts from visitors (1984) U.S.$30,000,000; expenditures by nationals abroad (1983) U.S.$3,000,000.
Household income and expenditure. Average household size (1985) 6.1; income per household: n.a.; source of income: n.a.; expenditure: n.a.
Gross national product (at current market prices; 1983): U.S.$56,028,000 (U.S.$320 per capita).

Structure of gross domestic product and labour force

	1984 in value Rf '000	1984 % of total value	1980 labour force†	1980 % of labour force
Agriculture‡	156,500	29.2	35,900	54.9
Mining	6,500	1.2	...	...
Manufacturing }	25,000	4.7	13,600	20.8
Public utilities }			200	0.3
Construction	40,700	7.6	3,100	4.7
Transportation and communication	30,600	5.7	3,300	5.0
Trade	53,200	9.9	2,000	3.1
Pub. admin., defense }	224,000	41.8	...	...
Finance }			...	...
Services }			5,300	8.1
Other }			2,000	3.1
TOTAL	536,500	100.0§	65,400	100.0

Population economically active (1980): total 65,410; activity rate of total population 42.2% (participation rates: ages 15–59, 79.8%; female 38.8%; unemployed, n.a.).
Land use (1984): forested 3.3%; meadows and pastures 3.3%; agricultural and under permanent cultivation 10.0%; built-on, wasteland, and other 83.4%.

Foreign trade‖

Balance of trade (current prices)

	1980	1981	1982	1983	1984	1985
Rf '000,000	−119.9	−35.6	−91.2	−269.9	−217.5	−177.5
% of total	50.5%	21.4%	39.4%	58.7%	46.7%	35.3%

Imports (1984): U.S.$51,565,000 (food, beverages, and tobacco 27.1%, of which rice 4.1%, sugar and sugar products 3.4%, tobacco 2.5%, alcoholic and nonalcoholic beverages 2.2%; machinery and transport equipment 26.2%; petroleum products 12.9%; chemicals 6.3%; wood and wood products 3.5%; steel 3.3%; cement products 2.3%). *Major import sources* (1983): Singapore 62.1%; Japan 11.4%; Sri Lanka 7.9%; India 4.5%; Hong Kong 3.1%; United Kingdom 1.9%.
Exports (1984): U.S.$17,625,000 (clothing and wearing apparel 40.1%; fresh skipjack tuna 37.8%; canned fish 8.0%; dried skipjack 7.6%; salted reef fish [including grouper, perch, and snapper] 2.2%; shark liver oil 1.9%). *Major export destinations:* United States 39.0%; Thailand 32.5%; Sri Lanka 10.0%; Switzerland 6.5%; Japan 6.1%; Singapore 1.9%.

Transport and communications

Transport. Railroads: none. Roads: total length, n.a. Vehicles (1984): passenger cars 310; trucks 107. Merchant marine (1985): vessels (100 gross tons and over) 35; total deadweight tonnage 205,327. Air transport (1984): passenger arrivals 88,877, passenger departures 88,742; cargo loaded 78 metric tons, cargo unloaded 2,161 metric tons; airports (1986) with scheduled flights 1.
Communications. Daily newspapers (1985): total number 2; circulation, n.a. Radio (1984): total number of receivers 17,444 (1 per 10 persons). Television (1985): total number of receivers 3,686 (1 per 50 persons). Telephones (1982): 1,540 (1 per 103 persons).

Education and health

Education (1983–84)

	schools	teachers	students	student/teacher ratio
Primary (age 6–11)	65	590	42,598	72.2
Secondary (age 11–18)	4	93	841	9.0
Voc., teacher tr.	3	27	206	7.6
Higher	—	—	—	—

Educational attainment (1977). Percent of adult population over age 25 having: no formal schooling 80.2%; primary education 15.1%; secondary 3.9%; postsecondary 0.1%; higher 0.1%; not stated 0.6%. *Literacy* (1982): total population over age 15 literate 62,365 (81.1%); males literate 31,896 (80.2%); females literate 30,469 (82.0%).
Health (1984): physicians 20 (1 per 8,850 persons); hospital beds¶ (1977) 40 (1 per 3,863 persons); infant mortality rate per 1,000 live births 68.0.
Food (1979–81): daily per capita caloric intake 1,983 (vegetable products 91%, animal products 9%); 90% of FAO recommended minimum requirement.

Military

Total active duty personnel: Maldives maintains one security force numbering about 700–1,000; it performs both army and police functions.

*Maldives is divided into 19 administrative districts corresponding to atoll groups; arrangement shown here is from north to south; total area excludes 34,634 sq mi (89,702 sq km) of water. †Employed persons only. ‡Primarily fishing. §Detail does not add to total given because of rounding. ‖Import figures are f.o.b. (free on board) in balance of trade and c.i.f. (cost, insurance, and freight) for commodities and trading partners. ¶In government establishments only.

Mali

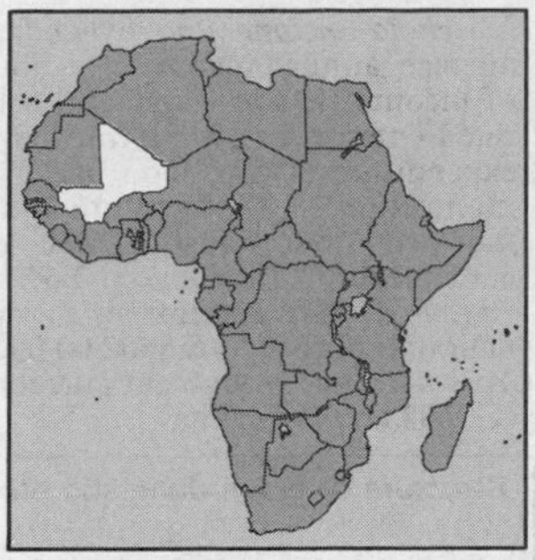

Official name: République du Mali (Republic of Mali).
Form of government: unitary single-party republic with one legislative house (National Assembly [82]).
Head of state and government: President.
Capital: Bamako.
Official language: French.
Official religion: none.
Monetary unit: 1 CFA franc (CFAF)* = 100 centimes; valuation (Oct. 1, 1986) 1 U.S.$ = CFAF 332.05; 1 £ = CFAF 479.81.

Area and population

		area		population
Regions	Capitals	sq mi	sq km	1985 estimate
Gao	Gao	124,323	321,996	451,800
Kayes	Kayes	76,356	197,760	1,071,300
Koulikoro	Koulikoro	34,685	89,833	1,144,200
Mopti	Mopti	34,257	88,752	1,384,600
Ségou	Ségou	21,671	56,127	1,297,200
Sikasso	Sikasso	29,529	76,480	1,348,200
Tombouctou†	Tombouctou	157,907	408,977	590,300
District				
Bamako	Bamako	103	267	801,500
TOTAL		478,841	1,240,192	8,089,500

Demography

Population (1986): 8,450,000.
Density (1986): persons per sq mi 17.6, persons per sq km 6.8.
Urban-rural (1985): urban 20.8%; rural 79.2%.
Sex distribution (1985): male 48.39%; female 51.61%.
Age breakdown (1985): under 15, 46.0%; 15–29, 25.8%; 30–44, 14.9%; 45–59, 8.7%; 60–74, 3.9%; 75 and over, 0.7%.
Population projection: (1990) 9,430,000; (2000) 12,404,000.
Doubling time: 25 years.
Ethnic composition (1980): Bambara 32.9%; Fulani 12.2%; Senufo 11.5%; Malinke 9.0%; Soninke 8.6%; Dogon 7.4%; Songai 6.0%; Tuareg 5.4%; Dyula 3.2%; Bobo 2.5%; other 1.3%.
Religious affiliation (1983): Muslim 90%; traditional beliefs 9%; Christian 1%.
Major cities (1976): Bamako 801,500‡; Ségou 64,890; Mopti 53,885; Sikasso 47,030; Kayes 44,736.

Vital statistics

Birth rate per 1,000 population (1980–85): 50.2 (world avg. 29.0); legitimate, n.a.; illegitimate, n.a.
Death rate per 1,000 population (1980–85): 22.4 (world avg. 11.0).
Natural increase rate per 1,000 population (1980–85): 27.8 (world avg. 18.0).
Total fertility rate (avg. births per childbearing woman; 1980–85): 6.7.
Marriage rate per 1,000 population: n.a.
Divorce rate per 1,000 population: n.a.
Life expectancy at birth (1980–85): male 40.4 years; female 43.6 years.
Major causes of death per 100,000 population: n.a.; however, major infectious diseases include malaria, syphilis and gonococcal infections, influenza, measles, amebiasis, and strep throat.

National economy

Budget (1986). Revenue: CFAF 69,180,000,000 (indirect taxes 35.8%, direct taxes 16.3%, customs duties 15.4%, carryover revenue from previous fiscal years 9.7%). Expenditures: CFAF 69,080,000,000 (defense 18.7%, education 12.6%, foreign affairs 3.3%, commerce and finance 2.9%).
Tourism: receipts from visitors (1984) U.S.$13,000,000; expenditures by nationals abroad (1983) U.S.$18,000,000.
Population economically active (1982): total 3,906,000; activity rate of total population 52.0% (participation rates: ages 15–64, 52.3%; female [1976] 17.0%; unemployed 1.3%§).

Price and earnings indexes (1970 = 100)

	1979	1980	1981	1982	1983	1984	1985
Consumer price index‖	313.0	382.7	429.5	439.4	482.6	...	...
Hourly earnings index¶	84.3	100.0	100.0	113.1	113.1	113.1	113.1

Production (metric tons except as noted). Agriculture, forestry, fishing (1984): millet 800,000, seed cotton 152,000, rice 125,000, sugarcane 107,000, peanuts (groundnuts) in shell 100,000, cottonseed 96,000, cassava 75,000, sweet potatoes 54,000, cotton lint 54,000, corn (maize) 50,000, wheat 2,000, tobacco 1,100; livestock (number of live animals) 6,300,000 sheep, 6,000,000 goats, 6,000,000 cattle, 800,000 asses, 400,000 camels, 75,000 horses, 14,000,000 chickens; roundwood 4,751,000 cu m; fish catch 54,000. Mining and quarrying (1984): gold 16,100 troy oz, salt 4,500. Manufacturing (1985): cotton fibre 67,900; goat, mutton, and lamb 47,000♀; soft drinks 43,700; beef and veal 34,000♂; cement 25,400♂; sugar 24,000; molasses 8,400; butter 4,355♀; beer 9,500 hectolitres□. Construction: n.a. Energy production (consumption): electricity (kW-hr; 1985) 158,177,000 (117,060,000); coal, none (n.a.); crude petroleum, none (n.a.); petroleum products (metric tons; 1984) none (150,000); natural gas, none (n.a.).

Gross national product (at current market prices; 1984): U.S.$1,060,000,000 (U.S.$130 per capita).

Structure of gross domestic product and labour force

	1982			
	in value MF '000,000,000	% of total value	labour force	% of labour force
Agriculture	388.7	53.1	3,355,300	85.9
Mining Manufacturing	53.8	7.3	195,300	5.0
Construction	42.1	5.7		
Public utilities	4.7	0.6		
Transportation and communication	25.2	3.4		
Trade	120.9	16.5	355,400	9.1
Finance Pub. admin., defense Services Other	97.5	13.3		
TOTAL	732.9	100.0◇	3,906,000	100.0

Public debt (external, outstanding; 1985): U.S.$1,327,400,000.
Household income and expenditure. Average household size (1980) 5; average annual income per household: n.a.; source of income: n.a.; expenditure: n.a.
Land use (1983): forested 7.1%; meadows and pastures 24.6%; agricultural and under permanent cultivation 1.7%; other 66.6%.

Foreign trade

Balance of trade (current prices)

	1980	1981	1982	1983	1984	1985
CFAF '000,000,000	−25.6	−35.7	−33.0	−36.9	−35.3	−43.8
% of total	22.8%	29.8%	25.6%	22.7%	17.4%	22.1%

Imports (1983): U.S.$254,900,000 (machinery, appliances, and transportation equipment 35.5%; petroleum products 19.1%; construction materials 11.8%; food products 10.5%; chemicals and pharmaceutical products 10.5%). *Major import sources:* Côte d'Ivoire 25.6%; France 22.6%; West Germany 10.0%; United Kingdom 7.0%; Senegal 4.2%; Japan 2.9%; United States 2.9%; Italy 2.6%; Spain 2.6%; The Netherlands 2.2%; Belgium–Luxembourg 1.9%; Hong Kong 1.2%; China 1.2%; Switzerland 1.0%.
Exports (1983): U.S.$166,800,000 (raw cotton and cotton products 40.9%; live animals 30.4%; salted, dried, or smoked fish 1.2%; peanuts 1.0%). *Major export destinations:* Belgium–Luxembourg 24.6%; France 15.6%; West Germany 10.1%; Japan 7.0%, United Kingdom 5.4%; China 4.4%; The Netherlands 4.0%; Niger 3.7%; Italy 3.6%; Côte d'Ivoire 2.6%.

Transport and communications

Transport. Railroads (1985): route length (1986) 398 mi, 641 km; passenger-mi 107,349,000, passenger-km 172,761,000; short ton-mi cargo 165,301,000, metric ton-km cargo 241,335,000. Roads (1986): total length 9,756 mi, 15,700 km (paved 11%). Vehicles (1982): passenger cars 20,000; trucks and buses 5,000. Merchant marine: vessels (100 gross tons and over) none. Air transport (1982): passenger-mi 59,000,000, passenger-km 95,000,000; short ton-mi cargo 411,000, metric ton-km cargo 600,000; airports (1986) with scheduled flights 7.
Communications. Daily newspapers (1985): total number 1; total circulation 40,000; circulation per 1,000 population 4.9. Radio (1985): total number of receivers 110,000 (1 per 75 persons). Television (1985): total number of receivers 500 (1 per 16,420 persons). Telephones (1983): 9,537 (1 per 789 persons).

Education and health

Education (1982–83)

	schools	teachers	students	student/ teacher ratio
Primary (age 6–14)	1,558	10,912	364,382	33.4
Secondary (age 15–17)	20	3,870	64,148	16.6
Voc., teacher tr.	11	890	12,612	14.2
Higher	7	499	5,792	11.6

Educational attainment (1976). Percent of adult population over age 25 having: no formal schooling 95.4%; primary education 3.8%; secondary 0.6%; postsecondary and higher 0.2%. *Literacy* (1980): total population over age 15 literate 361,800 (10.1%); males literate 329,200 (18.6%); females literate 32,600 (1.8%).
Health (1980): physicians 337 (1 per 21,068 persons); hospital beds 4,056 (1 per 1,722 persons); infant mortality rate per 1,000 live births (1980–85) 149.0.
Food (1980–82): daily per capita caloric intake 1,749 (vegetable products 91%, animal products 9%); 81% of FAO recommended minimum requirement.

Military

Total active duty personnel (1986): 5,050 (army 91.1%, navy 1.0%, air force 7.9%). *Military expenditure as percent of GNP* (1984): 5.0% (world [1983] 6.1%); per capita expenditure U.S.$7.

*In June 1984, the Mali franc (MF) was replaced by the CFA franc at the rate of 1 CFA franc = 2 Mali francs; older data may be reported in Mali francs. †Area for Tombouctou region is estimated as a residue between total reported area and the remainder of the regions. ‡1985 estimate. §Urban areas, estimated. ‖Includes food index for Bamako only. ¶Minimum hourly wages of industrial workers. ♀1982. ♂1984. □1983. ◇Detail does not add to total given because of rounding.

Malta

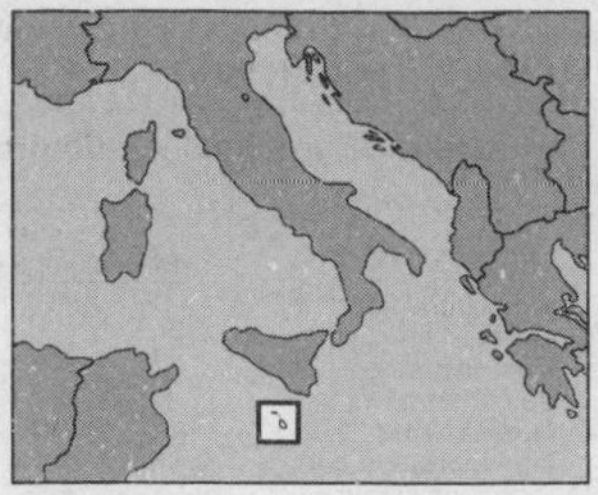

Official name: Repubblika ta' Malta (Maltese); Republic of Malta (English).
Form of government: unitary multiparty republic with one legislative house (House of Representatives [65]).
Chief of state: President.
Head of government: Prime Minister.
Capital: Valletta.
Official languages: Maltese; English.
Official religion: Roman Catholicism.
Monetary unit: 1 Maltese lira (Lm) = 100 cents = 1,000 mils; valuation* (Oct. 1, 1986) 1 Lm = U.S.$2.65 = £3.83.

Area and population

	area		population
Census regions†	sq mi	sq km	1985 estimate
Gozo and Comino	27	70	23,800
Inner Harbour	6	15	119,700
Northern	30	78	25,900
Outer Harbour	12	32	86,200
South Eastern	20	53	38,100
Western	27	69	38,300
TOTAL	122	316‡	332,000

Demography

Population (1986): 336,000.
Density (1986): persons per sq mi 2,755.8, persons per sq km 1,064.0.
Urban-rural (1985): urban 85.4%; rural 14.6%.
Sex distribution (1986): male 48.72%; female 51.28%.
Age breakdown (1986): under 15, 24.2%; 15–29, 22.5%; 30–44, 25.0%; 45–59, 15.0%; 60–74, 9.7%; 75 and over, 3.6%.
Population projection: (1990) 345,000; (2000) 360,000.
Doubling time: 87 years.
Ethnic composition (1980): Maltese 95.7%; British 2.1%; other 2.2%.
Religious affiliation (1980): Roman Catholic 97.3%; Anglican 1.2%; other 1.5%.
Major cities (1984): Sliema 20,071; Birkirkara 18,041; Qormi 17,130; Hamrun 14,087; Valletta 14,013.

Vital statistics

Birth rate per 1,000 population (1984): 16.8 (world avg. 29.0); legitimate 99.3%; illegitimate 0.7%.
Death rate per 1,000 population (1984): 8.8 (world avg. 11.0).
Natural increase rate per 1,000 population (1983): 8.0 (world avg. 18.0).
Total fertility rate (avg. births per childbearing woman; 1980–85): 2.0.
Marriage rate per 1,000 population (1984): 8.0.
Divorce rate per 1,000 population: n.a.
Life expectancy at birth (1984): male 70.7 years; female 75.2 years.
Major causes of death per 100,000 population (1984): diseases of the circulatory system 481.6; malignant neoplasms (cancers) 158.5; endocrine, nutritional, and metabolic diseases of the blood and blood-forming organs 93.1; diseases of the respiratory system 27.3; diseases of the digestive system 27.3; accidents, poisoning, and violence 24.9.

National economy

Budget (1984). Revenue: Lm 212,840,000 (national insurance 23.6%, income tax 20.3%, customs and excise taxes 20.3%, property income 9.7%). Expenditures: Lm 183,074,000 (national insurance benefits 28.8%, health 10.9%, education 8.5%).
Public debt (1985): U.S.$147,965,000.
Production (value added in Lm except where noted). Agriculture, forestry, fishing (1983): vegetables 7,912,000 (of which tomatoes 2,751,000, melons 387,000, onions 223,000), cereals 2,417,000 (of which wheat 929,000, barley 333,000), fruits 1,900,000 (of which citrus fruits 731,000, strawberries 553,000), potatoes 1,617,000; livestock (number of live animals) 53,366 pigs, 12,794 cattle, 3,395 sheep, 1,062,900 chickens; fish catch 1,032,000. Mining and quarrying (1983): quarrying 971,100, of which building stone 968,300. Manufacturing (1983): textiles and wearing apparel 35,193,100, of which clothing 26,684,000, textiles 4,144,000, footwear 4,020,000; food and beverages 18,426,000, of which wine, beer, and malt products 4,678,800, nonalcoholic beverages 4,291,500, bakery products 3,076,300; machinery and transport equipment 17,286,900, of which electrical equipment 11,566,200, transport equipment 2,140,800; chemicals 7,406,700, of which rubber tires and rubber products 2,826,100, plastics 1,585,000; wood, cork, and furniture 5,738,800; tobacco and tobacco products 3,005,000. Construction (1983): 20,584,800. Energy production (consumption): electricity (kW-hr; 1984) 722,600,000 (722,600,000); coal (metric tons; 1984) none (94,000); crude petroleum, none (n.a.); petroleum products (metric tons; 1984) none (871,000); natural gas, none (342,700,000).
Population economically active (1983): total 120,922; activity rate of total population 36.7% (participation rates: ages 15–64, n.a.; female 24.5%; unemployed 8.5%).

Price and earnings indexes (1980 = 100)

	1980	1981	1982	1983	1984	1985	1986§
Consumer price index	100.0	111.5	118.0	117.0	116.5	116.2	117.9
Annual earnings index	100.0	108.7	120.2	...	...	...	...

Household income and expenditure. Average household size (1982) 3.6; average annual income per household Lm 4,736 (U.S.$11,399); sources of income (1984): wages and salaries 48.9%, professional and unincorporated enterprises 17.0%, transfer payments 14.6%, property income 12.1%; expenditure (1984): food and beverages 33.2%, transportation and communication 14.2%, furniture and household operations 9.9%, clothing and footwear 7.6%, housing 7.1%, recreation, entertainment, and education 6.3%, health 3.7%, tobacco 3.6%.
Tourism (1984): receipts from visitors U.S.$130,000,000; expenditures by nationals abroad U.S.$50,000,000.
Gross national product (at current market prices; 1984): U.S.$1,210,000,000 (U.S.$3,660 per capita).

Structure of gross domestic product and labour force

	1984			
	in value Lm '000	% of total value	labour force	% of labour force
Agriculture	19,346	4.6	5,486	4.5
Manufacturing	124,706	29.6	34,118	28.0
Mining, Construction	19,660	4.7	5,807	4.8
Public utilities	24,985	5.9	1,288	1.1
Transportation and communication	23,391	5.5	6,148	5.0
Trade	66,077	15.7	11,472	9.4
Finance	18,631	4.4	3,286	2.7
Pub. admin., defense	56,090	13.3	27,042	22.2
Services	33,605	8.0	15,523	12.8
Other	34,886	8.3	11,592‖	9.5‖
TOTAL	421,377	100.0	121,762	100.0

Land use (1983): agricultural and under permanent cultivation 43.8%; other (infertile clay soil with underlying limestone) 56.2%.

Foreign trade

Balance of trade (current prices)

	1980	1981	1982	1983	1984	1985
Lm '000,000	−124.9	−125.6	−123.8	−128.1	−149.1	−114.1
% of total	27.3%	26.6%	26.8%	28.9%	29.1%	21.8%

Imports (1985): Lm 354,139,000 (semimanufactures 28.0%, of which textile fabrics and yarn 12.6%, metal and metal manufactures 6.3%; machinery and transport equipment 24.1%, of which electrical equipment 8.3%, transport equipment 3.9%; food and beverages 13.8%, of which cereals 2.9%, meats 2.6%, fruits and vegetables 1.6%; fuels 12.0%; chemicals 7.2%; tobacco 1.6%). *Major import sources:* Italy 23.1%; United Kingdom 18.6%; West Germany 17.8%; United States 5.7%; Spain 4.2%; France 4.1%; The Netherlands 3.0%.
Exports (1985): Lm 187,099,000 (clothing and footwear 35.1%; machinery and transport equipment 22.1%, of which electrical equipment 14.7%; semimanufactures 10.1%, of which rubber 2.9%; printed material 5.2%; food and beverages 3.6%; chemicals 1.3%). *Major export destinations:* West Germany 30.6%; United Kingdom 16.0%; Italy 9.4%; United States 6.3%; U.S.S.R. 5.4%; The Netherlands 4.7%.

Transport and communications

Transport. Railroads: none. Roads (1984): total length 823 mi, 1,324 km (paved 92%). Vehicles (1984): passenger cars 77,419; trucks and buses 17,368. Merchant marine (1985): vessels (100 gross tons and over) 235; total deadweight tonnage 2,988,755. Air transport (1985): passenger-mi 750,092,000, passenger-km 1,207,159,000; short ton-mi cargo 3,307,500, metric ton-km cargo 4,828,000; airports (1986) with scheduled flights 1.
Communications. Daily newspapers (1981): total number 4; total circulation 81,000; circulation per 1,000 population 245. Radio (1985): total number of receivers 151,000 (1 per 2.2 persons). Television (1985): total number of receivers 90,500 (1 per 3.7 persons). Telephones (1983): 98,125 (1 per 3.3 persons).

Education and health

Education (1984–85)

	schools	teachers	students	student/ teacher ratio
Primary (age 5–13)	124	1,777	35,411	19.9
Secondary (age 11–20)	65	1,624	21,759	13.4
Voc., teacher tr.	23	555	6,140	11.1
Higher	1	156	1,408	9.0

Educational attainment, n.a. *Literacy* (1980): total population over age 14 literate 261,900 (81.4%); males literate 129,500 (83.4%); females literate 132,400 (79.7%).
Health: physicians (1982) 413 (1 per 786 persons); hospital beds (1980) 3,431 (1 per 93 persons); infant mortality rate per 1,000 live births (1984) 11.7.
Food (1980–82): daily per capita caloric intake 2,918 (vegetable products 72%, animal products 28%); 118% of FAO recommended minimum requirement.

Military

Total active duty personnel (1986): 775 (army 100%). *Military expenditure as percent of GNP* (1984): 1.5% (world [1983] 6.1%); per capita expenditure U.S.$43.

*The Maltese lira is tied to the currencies of several principal trading partners. †Malta has no first-order administrative subdivisions; data are reported according to census regions. ‡Detail does not add to total given because of rounding. §August. ‖ Mostly unemployed.

Martinique

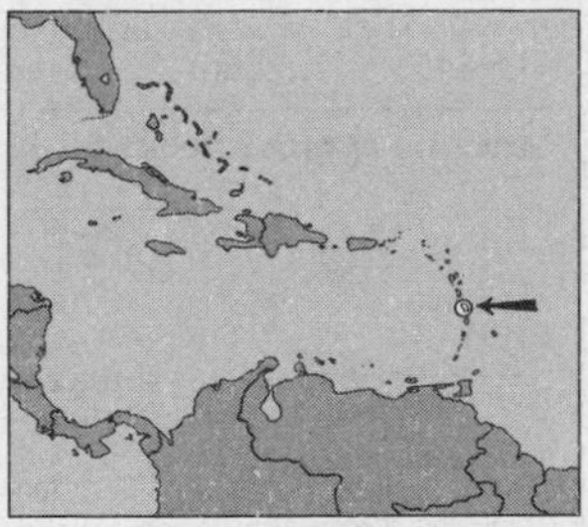

Official name: Département de la Martinique (Department of Martinique).
Political status: overseas department (France) with two legislative houses (General Council [44]; Regional Council [41]).
Chief of state: President of France.
Heads of government: Commissioner of the Republic (for France); President of the General Council (for Martinique); President of the Regional Council (for Martinique).
Capital: Fort-de-France.
Official language: French.
Official religion: none.
Monetary unit: 1 Franc (F) = 100 centimes; valuation (Oct. 1, 1986) 1 U.S.$ = F 6.64; 1 £ = F 9.60.

Area and population

		area		population
				1982
Arrondissements	Capitals	sq mi	sq km	census
Fort-de-France	Fort-de-France	141	365	176,749
Le Marin	Le Marin	154	399	78,329
La Trinité	La Trinité	126	327	73,488
TOTAL		421	1,091	328,566

Demography

Population (1986): 328,000.
Density (1986): persons per sq mi 779.1, persons per sq km 300.6.
Urban–rural (1982): urban 57.1%; rural 42.9%.
Sex distribution (1982): male 48.49%; female 51.51%.
Age breakdown (1982): under 15, 28.3%; 15–29, 30.3%; 30–44, 16.2%; 45–59, 13.2%; 60–74, 8.5%; 75 and over, 3.3%; not specified, 0.2%.
Population projection: (1990) 330,000; (2000) 352,000.
Doubling time: 64 years.
Ethnic composition (1980): mulatto 94.7%; French (metropolitan) 2.3%; East Indian 1.9%; Creole (Martinique white) 0.7%; other 0.4%.
Religious affiliation (1980): Roman Catholic 91.4%; Protestant (mostly Seventh-day Adventist) 4.7%; syncretist 1.6%; nonreligious 1.2%; other 1.1%.
Major cities (1982): Fort-de-France 96,649; Schoelcher 16,412; Le Lamentin 6,872; Saint-Pierre 4,923.

Vital statistics

Birth rate per 1,000 population (1985): 17.5 (world avg. 29.0); legitimate 36.1%; illegitimate 63.9%.
Death rate per 1,000 population (1985): 6.6 (world avg. 11.0).
Natural increase rate per 1,000 population (1985): 10.9 (world avg. 18.0).
Total fertility rate (avg. births per childbearing woman; 1980–85): 2.4.
Marriage rate per 1,000 population (1985): 4.1.
Divorce rate per 1,000 population (1985): 1.1.
Life expectancy at birth (1980–85): male 68.4 years; female 73.5 years.
Major causes of death per 100,000 population (1982): diseases of the circulatory system 192.3; malignant neoplasms (cancers) 100.2; mental disorders (including deaths associated with chronic alcoholism) 30.6; accidents 25.4; diseases of the respiratory system 24.5; diabetes mellitus 23.9.

National economy

Budget (1984). Revenue: F 1,645,000,000 (receipts from French central government 30.8%; carried over and supplementary receipts 24.0%; taxes on motor fuels 17.1%; new loans 4.6%; receipts from public health and social welfare clinics 2.6%). Expenditures: F 1,643,000,000 (health and social assistance 28.2%, of which health 12.0%; infrastructure and public works 26.0%; deferred and supplementary expenses 23.9%; debt 1.2%).
Production (metric tons except as noted). Agriculture, forestry, fishing (1984): bananas 157,777*†, sugarcane 117,522*, pineapples 23,000, yams 9,000, sweet potatoes 7,000, avocados 6,500, carrots 5,000, tomatoes 4,000, cucumbers 3,000, limes 2,300, flowering and nonflowering plants 67*†, anthuriums 47*†; livestock (number of live animals) 72,000 sheep, 55,000 cattle, 40,000 pigs, 26,000 goats; roundwood 17,000 cu m; fish catch 5,174. Mining and quarrying (1984): pumice 165,000; sand and gravel for local construction. Manufacturing (1985): petroleum products 700,000‡; cement 189,000‡; sugar 8,610*; pineapple compote 1,394*; pineapple juice 1,330*; rum 93,327* hectolitres; other products include leather goods, clothing, fabricated metals, and yawls and sails. Construction: n.a. Energy production (consumption): electricity (kW-hr; 1985) 442,000,000 (390,000,000); coal, none (none); crude petroleum (barrels; 1985) none (3,523,000); petroleum products (metric tons; 1984) 700,000 (361,000); natural gas, none (none).
Population economically active (1982): total 130,500; activity rate of total population 39.9% (participation rates: ages 15–64, 62.2%; female 44.7%; unemployed [1984] 25.0%).

Price and earnings indexes (1979 = 100)§

	1979	1980	1981	1982	1983	1984	1985
Consumer price index	100.0	118.5	136.8	150.4	166.6	179.7	190.8
Monthly earnings index	100.0	114.5	137.4	160.1	176.3	192.3	205.6

Tourism (1984): receipts from visitors U.S.$87,000,000; expenditures by nationals abroad, n.a.
Public debt (external, outstanding; 1984 ‖): U.S.$32,000,000.
Gross national product (at current market prices; 1983): U.S.$1,330,000,000 (U.S.$4,070 per capita).

Structure of gross domestic product and labour force

	1980		1982	
	in value F '000	% of total value	labour force	% of labour force
Agriculture	396,200	6.5	9,844	7.5
Manufacturing	316,200	5.2	5,854	4.5
Construction	236,100	3.9	7,832	6.0
Public utilities	104,100	1.7	1,006	0.8
Transportation and communication	232,100	3.8	5,197	4.0
Trade, restaurants, hotels	1,092,700	17.9	9,864	7.6
Finance, real estate¶	588,300	9.6	2,063	1.6
Services♀	948,600	15.5	15,815	12.1
Pub. admin., defense, other	2,189,100ð	35.9	73,025□	55.9
TOTAL	6,103,400	100.0	130,500	100.0

Household income and expenditure. Average household size (1982) 3.8; income per household (1979) F 70,009 (U.S.$17,415); sources of income (1979): salaries 74.2%, industrial and commercial profits 10.0%, pensions and rents 4.8%, income from stocks and bonds 3.9%, noncommercial profits 3.4%, other 3.7%; expenditure (1980)◇: food and beverages 31.7%, transportation 13.3%, housing 11.2%, clothing and footwear 8.2%, recreation 7.5%, household furnishings 7.4%, health 3.5%, energy 2.7%, other 14.5%.
Land use (1983): forested 26.0%; meadows and pastures 30.0%; agricultural and under permanent cultivation 18.0%; other 26.0%.

Foreign trade

Balance of trade (current prices)

	1980	1981	1982	1983	1984	1985
F '000,000	−3,011	−3,211	−3,819	−4,359	−4,632	−4,750
% of total	73.1%	62.2%	65.3%	62.4%	63.2%	64.6%

Imports (1984): F 5,983,000,000 (crude petroleum and petroleum products 24.6%, food products 20.2%, electrical machinery and equipment 11.7%, chemical products 8.2%, metal manufactures [including iron and steel] 5.6%, textiles and clothing 4.5%). *Major import sources:* France 54.0%; Venezuela 11.0%; Saudi Arabia 5.0%; United Arab Emirates 5.0%; Italy 3.0%; United States 3.0%.
Exports (1984): F 1,351,000,000 (bananas 37.6%, petroleum products 29.4%, rum 6.6%, canned pineapples 5.8%, fertilizer 3.8%). *Major export destinations:* France 54.2%; Guadeloupe 35.8%; West Germany 5.6%; French Guiana 1.9%.

Transport and communications

Transport. Railroads: none. Roads (1984): total length 1,130 mi, 1,819 km (paved 83%). Vehicles (1984): passenger cars 140,000; trucks and buses 3,700. Fishing fleet (1984): vessels (100 gross tons and over) 2. Air transport (1985): passenger arrivals 407,151, passenger departures 408,110; cargo unloaded 5,282 metric tons, cargo loaded 4,887 metric tons; airports (1986) with scheduled flights 1.
Communications. Daily newspapers (1985): total number 1; total circulation 30,000; circulation per 1,000 population 92. Radio (1985): total number of receivers 48,000 (1 per 6.8 persons). Television (1985): total number of receivers 43,000 (1 per 7.6 persons). Telephones (1983): 83,600 (1 per 3.9 persons).

Education and health

Education (1982–83)

	schools	teachers	students	student/teacher ratio
Primary (age 6–11)	226	1,927△	41,928	...
Secondary (age 12–18)	...	2,489△	31,677	...
Vocational	...	653△	15,410	...
Higher	1	40	1,220	30

Educational attainment (1982). Percent of population over age 15 having: no formal schooling 7.2%; primary education 46.2%; secondary 41.8%; higher 4.8%. *Literacy* (1982): total population over age 15 literate 206,807 (92.5%); males literate 97,538 (91.8%); females literate 109,269 (93.2%).
Health: physicians (1982) 393 (1 per 830 persons); hospital beds (1984) 4,200 (1 per 78 persons); infant mortality rate per 1,000 live births (1985) 14.0.
Food (1980–82): daily per capita caloric intake 2,671 (vegetable products 81%, animal products 19%); 110% of FAO recommended minimum requirement.

Military

Total active duty personnel (1984): 2,800†.

*1985. †Quantity of production for export only. ‡1984. §All figures are end of year unless otherwise indicated. ‖ Includes external long-term private debt not guaranteed by the government. ¶Includes rent. ♀Business services only. ðIncludes nonsaleable (community, social, and personal) services. □Includes 7,707 not adequately defined and 35,936 unemployed (including previously and not previously employed). ◇Weights of consumer price index components. △Public schools only. †Includes metropole troops, local conscripts in military service, and police.

Mauritania

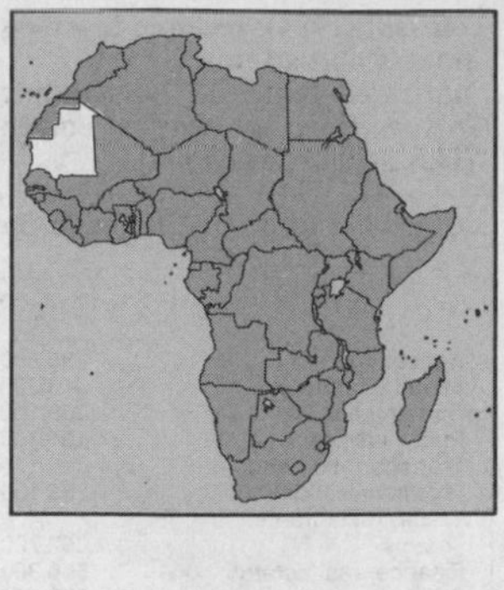

Official name: al-Jumhūrīyah al-Islāmīyah al-Mūrītānīyah (Arabic), République Islamique de Mauritanie (French) (Islamic Republic of Mauritania).
Form of government: military regime.
Head of state and government: President assisted by Military Committee for National Salvation (24).
Capital: Nouakchott.
Official languages: Arabic; French.
Official religion: Islam.
Monetary unit: 1 Mauritanian Ouguiya (UM) = 5 khoums; valuation (Oct. 1, 1986) 1 U.S.$ = UM 74.80; 1 £ = UM 108.09.

Area and population

		area		population
				1982
Regions	**Capitals**	sq mi	sq km	estimate
el-'Açâba	Kiffa	14,100	36,600	149,000
Adrar	Atar	83,100	215,300	59,000
Brakna	Aleg	12,700	33,000	165,000
Dakhlet Nouadhibou	Nouadhibou	8,600	22,300	30,000
Gorgol	Kaédi	5,200	13,600	163,000
Guidimaka	Sélibaby	4,000	10,300	100,000
Hodh ech-Chargui	Néma	70,500	182,700	230,000
Hodh el-Gharbi	'Ayoûn el-'Atroûs	20,600	53,400	150,000
Inchiri	Akjoujt	18,100	46,800	20,000
Tagant	Tidjikdja	36,800	95,200	80,000
Tiris Zemmour	Fdérik	97,600	252,900	25,000
Trarza	Rosso	26,200	67,800	240,000
District				
Nouakchott	Nouakchott	46	120	150,000
TOTAL		397,700*	1,030,020	1,561,000

Demography

Population (1986): 1,689,000.
Density (1986): persons per sq mi 4.2, persons per sq km 1.6.
Urban-rural (1983): urban 25.0%; rural 75.0%†.
Sex distribution (1985): male 49.48%; female 50.52%.
Age breakdown (1985): under 15, 46.4%; 15–29, 26.0%; 30–44, 14.6%; 45–59, 8.4%; 60–74, 3.9%; 75 and over, 0.7%.
Population projection: (1990) 1,828,000; (2000) 2,229,000.
Doubling time: 37 years.
Ethnic composition (1980): Moor 79.6%; Tukulor 12.2%; Fulani 5.0%; Soninke 3.0%; other 0.2%.
Religious affiliation (1980): Muslim 99.4%; Christian 0.4%; other 0.2%.
Major cities (1981): Nouakchott 350,000‡; Nouadhibou 22,000; Kaédi 21,000; Zouérate (Zouîrât) 17,500§.

Vital statistics

Birth rate per 1,000 population (1984): 45.0 (world avg. 29.0); legitimate, n.a.; illegitimate, n.a.
Death rate per 1,000 population (1984): 26.0 (world avg. 11.0).
Natural increase rate per 1,000 population (1984): 19.0 (world avg. 18.0).
Total fertility rate (avg. births per childbearing woman; 1984): 6.2.
Marriage rate per 1,000 population: n.a.
Divorce rate per 1,000 population: n.a.
Life expectancy at birth (1984): male 45.0 years; female 48.0 years.
Major causes of death per 100,000 population: n.a.; however, major diseases include malaria, typhoid fever, and cholera.

National economy

Budget (1986)‖. Revenue: UM 18,600,000,000 (tax revenue 69.5%, of which taxes on international trade 42.8%, taxes on income and profits 16.6%; capital receipts 10.1%; loans 8.7%; subsidies and grants 7.4%). Expenditures: UM 18,600,000,000 (administration 56.6%, of which defense 18.1%, education 12.4%, health and social affairs 3.6%; public debt service 12.6%; investments 4.9%).
Public debt (external, outstanding; 1984): U.S.$1,170,600,000.
Tourism (1981): receipts from visitors U.S.$6,000,000; expenditures by nationals abroad U.S.$15,000,000.
Land use (1984): forested 14.7%; meadows and pastures 38.1%; agricultural and under permanent cultivation 0.2%; desert 47.0%.
Production (metric tons except as noted). Agriculture, forestry, fishing (1985): millet 32,000, pulses 24,000, rice 15,000, dates 12,000, vegetables 9,000, roots and tubers 6,000, sweet potatoes 2,000, peanuts (groundnuts) 2,000, corn (maize) 1,000; livestock (number of live animals) 5,200,000 sheep, 3,250,000 goats, 1,350,000 cattle, 785,000 camels, 161,000 horses and asses, 4,000,000 chickens; roundwood 12,000 cu m; fish catch 60,000. Mining and quarrying (1984): iron ore (gross weight) 9,500,000; hydraulic cement 60,000; gypsum 4,000. Manufacturing (1985): milk 93,000; meat 43,000, of which fresh beef and veal 17,000, fresh mutton and lamb 7,000, goat meat 5,300; hides and skins 5,200; cheese 1,700; butter 700. Construction (value added in U.S.$; 1982): 60,000,000. Energy production (consumption): electricity (kW-hr; 1984) 102,000,000 (102,000,000); coal (metric tons; 1984) none (7,000); crude petroleum, none (n.a.); petroleum products (metric tons; 1984) none (195,000); natural gas, none (n.a.).

Gross national product (at current market prices; 1984): U.S.$750,000,000 (U.S.$450 per capita).

Structure of gross domestic product and labour force

	1981			
	in value UM '000,000	% of total value	labour force	% of labour force
Agriculture	8,545	25.2	353,000	69.0
Mining	2,898	8.5		
Manufacturing } Public utilities }	2,249	6.6	40,000	8.0
Construction	2,141	6.3		
Transportation and communication	2,700	8.0		
Trade and finance	6,024	17.7		
Pub. admin., defense	5,910	17.4	118,000	23.0
Services	...	...		
Other	3,477	10.2		
TOTAL	33,944	100.0*	511,000	100.0

Population economically active (1980): total 516,000; activity rate of total population 31.6% (participation rates: ages 15–64, 55.2%; female 20.0%; unemployed, n.a.).

Price and earnings indexes (1980 = 100)

	1978	1979	1980	1981	1982	1983	1984
Consumer price index	82.8	90.3	100.0	119.1	134.1	135.3	144.9
Earnings index	...	...	...	...	...	...	...

Household income and expenditure. Average household size (1980) 5.0; average annual income per household: n.a.; source of income: n.a.; expenditure¶ (1983): food and beverages 61.0%; housing 24.0%; clothing and footwear 5.2%.

Foreign trade

Balance of trade (current prices)

	1980	1981	1982	1983	1984	1985
UM '000,000	−2,694	+1,178	−530	+4,969	+7,877	+13,129
% of total	13.1%	4.9%	2.1%	18.4%	27.0%	29.4%

Imports (1984): UM 10,620,000,000♀ (machinery and transport equipment 40.0%, food 25.0%, crude petroleum and petroleum products 18.6%). *Major import sources:* France 21.9%; Spain 19.8%; West Germany 9.6%; United States 7.6%; Senegal 6.9%; Algeria 6.0%; Thailand 5.7%; China 3.0%; Egypt 3.0%; Italy 2.7%; Belgium–Luxembourg 2.6%; The Netherlands 2.5%; Japan 1.4%; Denmark 1.3%; United Kingdom 1.1%; Canada 0.9%; Côte d'Ivoire 0.8%; India 0.8%; South Korea 0.4%.
Exports (1984): UM 15,982,000,000 (fish 50.3%, iron ore 49.7%). *Major export destinations:* Italy 23.9%; Japan 22.1%; Belgium 17.9%; France 15.1%; Spain 7.3%; United Kingdom 5.0%; West Germany 3.2%; Algeria 1.5%; Portugal 1.0%; Senegal 0.9%; Greece 0.9%; Turkey 0.6%; United States 0.4%.

Transport and communications

Transport. Railroads (1984): route length 428 mi, 689 km; passenger-mi 4,350,000, passenger-km 7,000,000; short ton-mi cargo 4,207,000,000, metric ton-km cargo 6,142,000,000. Roads (1981): total length 4,685 mi, 7,540 km (paved 18%). Vehicles (1981): passenger cars 11,262; trucks and buses 8,437. Merchant marine (1985): vessels (100 gross tons and over) 48; total deadweight tonnage 8,337. Air transport♂ (1982): passenger-mi 137,000,000, passenger-km 221,000,000; short ton-mi cargo 14,600,000, metric ton-km cargo 21,300,000; airports (1986) with scheduled flights 8.
Communications. Daily newspapers (1985): total number 1; total circulation, n.a. Radio (1985): total number of receivers 95,000 (1 per 17 persons). Television (1985): total number of receivers 750 (1 per 2,208). Telephones (1982): 3,161 (1 per 493 persons).

Education and health

Education (1982)

	schools	teachers	students	student/ teacher ratio
Primary (age 6–11)	637	2,401	107,390	44.7
Secondary (age 12–17)	...	864	25,700	29.7
Voc., teacher tr.□	...	57	1,027	18.0
Higher	3◇	25△	1,374◇	...

Educational attainment, n.a. *Literacy* (1978): total adult population literate 17.0%.
Health: physicians (1980) 103 (1 per 14,500 persons); hospital beds (1979) 561 (1 per 2,653 persons); infant mortality rate per 1,000 live births (1984) 133.0.
Food (1981–83): daily per capita caloric intake 2,162 (vegetable products 76%, animal products 24%); (1982) 97% of FAO recommended minimum requirement.

Military

Total active duty personnel (1986): 8,470 (army 94.4%, navy 3.8%, air force 1.8%). *Military expenditure as percent of GNP* (1983): 5.8% (world 6.1%); per capita expenditure U.S.$25.

*Detail does not add to total given because of rounding. †The percentage of nomads in Mauritania declined from about 80% of the total population in 1970 to about 25% of the total population in 1983. ‡1984. §1977. ‖Breakdown for revenue and expenditure is for 1982. ¶Capital city only. ♀Import commodities breakdown is for 1983. ♂Includes part of Air Afrique traffic. □Teacher training only. ◇1983. △1980–81.

Mauritius

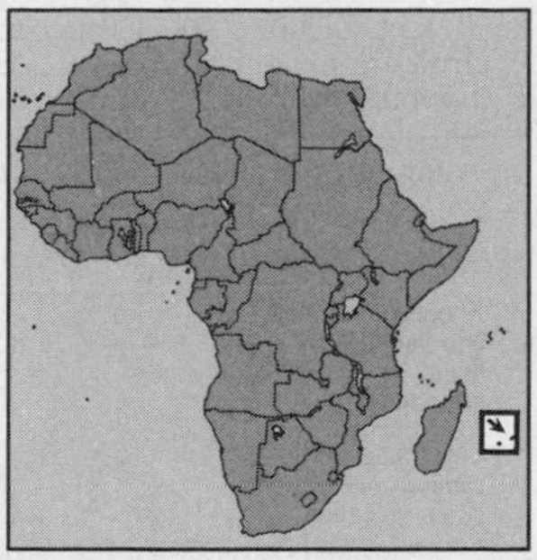

Official name: Mauritius.
Form of government: constitutional monarchy with one legislative house (Legislative Assembly [70]).
Chief of state: British Monarch represented by governor-general.
Head of government: Prime Minister.
Capital: Port Louis.
Official language: English.
Official religion: none.
Monetary unit: 1 Mauritian Rupee (Mau Re; plural Mau Rs) = 100 cents; valuation (Oct. 1, 1986) 1 U.S.$ = Mau Rs 12.97; 1 £ = Mau Rs 18.74.

Area and population

Islands / Districts	area sq mi	area sq km	population 1983 census*
Mauritius	720	1,865	960,200
Black River	100	259	36,700
Flacq	115	298	107,400
Grand Port	101	262	92,300
Moka	89	230	61,300
Pamplemousses	69	179	90,200
Plaines Wilhems	78	202	301,300
Port Louis	17	44	132,200
Rivière du Rampart	57	148	80,500
Savanne	94	243	58,300
Rodrigues	40	104	33,000
Agelega	27	70	350
Saint Brandon	1	3	150
TOTAL	788	2,041†	993,700

Demography

Population (1986): 1,031,000.
Density (1986): persons per sq mi 1,308.4, persons per sq km 505.1.
Urban-rural‡ (1985): urban 41.6%; rural 58.4%.
Sex distribution (1985): male 50.32%; female 49.68%.
Age breakdown‡ (1983): under 15, 32.4%; 15–29, 32.0%; 30–44, 17.7%; 45–59, 11.0%; 60–74, 5.7%; 75 and over, 1.2%.
Population projection: (1990) 1,073,000; (2000) 1,185,000.
Doubling time: 58 years.
Ethnolinguistic composition (1983): Creole 55.5%; Indian 39.6%; European 3.8%; Chinese 0.6%; other 0.5%.
Religious affiliation‡ (1983): Hindu 52.5%; Roman Catholic 25.7%; Muslim 12.9%; Protestant 4.4%; Buddhist 0.4%; other 4.1%.
Major cities (1983): Port Louis 148,040; Beau Bassin–Rose Hill 87,520; Quatre Bornes 56,676; Vacoas–Phoenix 56,011; Curepipe 57,613.

Vital statistics

Birth rate per 1,000 population (1985)‡: 19.0 (world avg. 29.0).
Death rate per 1,000 population (1985)‡: 6.8 (world avg. 11.0).
Natural increase rate per 1,000 population (1985)‡: 12.2 (world avg. 18.0).
Total fertility rate (avg. births per childbearing woman; 1984)‡: 2.1.
Marriage rate per 1,000 population (1985)‡: 11.3.
Divorce rate per 1,000 population (1983)‡: 0.4.
Life expectancy at birth (1982–84): male 64.4 years; female 71.2 years.
Major causes of death per 100,000 population (1983): heart diseases 293.0; respiratory diseases, including pneumonia, bronchitis, emphysema, and asthma 80.2; injury and poisoning 48.2; malignant neoplasms (cancers) 46.9.

National economy

Budget (1985–86 est.). Revenue: Mau Rs 3,888,000,000 (import duties 26.2%, stamp duties 16.3%, export duties 10.2%, income tax 8.5%, excise duties 6.9%). Expenditures: Mau Rs 4,686,000,000 (debt servicing 44.2%, education and cultural affairs 11.6%, general administration 11.5%, social security 7.8%, health 6.5%, transfers to local government 5.6%).
Public debt (external, outstanding; 1984): U.S.$354,200,000.
Tourism: receipts from visitors (1984) U.S.$44,000,000; expenditures by nationals abroad (1983) U.S.$13,000,000.
Gross national product (at current market prices; 1984): U.S.$1,100,000,000 (U.S.$1,090 per capita).

Structure of gross domestic product and labour force

	1985 in value Mau Rs '000,000	% of total value	labour force§	% of labour force
Agriculture	1,965	14.3	52,651	24.4
Mining	20	0.1	165	0.1
Manufacturing	2,730	19.9	62,949	29.2
Construction	750	5.5	5,012	2.3
Public utilities	465	3.4	3,772	1.8
Transportation and communication	1,490	10.9	8,714	4.0
Trade	1,840	13.4	9,198	4.3
Finance	2,225	16.2	5,164	2.4
Pub. admin., defense	1,460	10.7 }	63,183	29.3
Services	755	5.5 }		
Other	...	...	4,546	2.1
TOTAL	13,700 ‖	100.0†	215,354	100.0†

Production (metric tons except as noted). Agriculture, forestry, fishing (1984): sugarcane 5,009,000, tea (green) 40,726, potatoes 20,680, tomatoes 10,500, bananas 4,750, peanuts (groundnuts) 2,420, tobacco 925, corn (maize) 3,265; livestock (number of live animals) 70,000 goats, 59,000 cattle, 10,000 pigs, 4,000 sheep; roundwood 30,000 cu m; fish catch (1983) 9,536. Manufacturing (1985): sugar, refined 645,800; molasses 160,000; fertilizers 51,010¶; processed tea 8,100; soft drinks 272,000 hectolitres; beer and stout 171,900 hectolitres; rum 42,900 hectolitres; matches 196,000 boxes. Construction (1985): residential 315,000 sq m; nonresidential 102,000 sq m. Energy production (consumption): electricity (kW-hr; 1984) 455,000,000 (455,000,000); coal (metric tons; 1984) none (1,000); crude petroleum, none (n.a.); petroleum products (metric tons; 1984) none (183,000); natural gas, none (n.a.).
Population economically active (1984): total 367,000; activity rate of total population 38.0% (participation rates: over age 15, 58.5%; female 15.1%; unemployed 19.1%).

Price and earnings indexes (1980 = 100)

	1979	1980	1981	1982	1983	1984	1985	June 1986
Consumer price index	70.4	100.0	114.5	127.5	134.7	144.6	154.3	157.4
Monthly earnings index	79.8	100.0	117.9	129.9	138.7	144.5	148.1	...

Household income and expenditure. Average household size‡ (1983) 4.8; income per household (1979) Mau Rs 15,540 (U.S.$2,430); sources of income (1984): salaries and wages 53.1%, entrepreneurial income 32.4%, transfer payments 7.3%, interest and dividends 4.3%, other 2.9%; expenditure (1982): food and nonalcoholic beverages 43.9%, clothing, footwear, and furnishings 10.5%, housing 10.4%, transportation 10.0%, alcohol and tobacco 6.5%.
Land use (1983): forested 31.4%; meadows and pastures 3.8%; agricultural and under permanent cultivation 57.8%; other 7.0%.

Foreign trade♀

Balance of trade (current prices)

	1980	1981	1982	1983	1984	1985
Mau Rs '000,000	−560.7	−1,260.9	−330.0	−161.6	−482.8	−352.0
% of total	7.7%	17.4%	4.0%	1.8%	4.5%	2.6%

Imports (1985): Mau Rs 8,041,200,000 (manufactured goods classified chiefly by material 32.3%, food 16.8%, mineral fuels and lubricants 14.3%, machinery and transport equipment 13.3%, chemicals 6.9%, inedible crude materials excluding fuels 4.9%, animal and vegetable oils and fats 3.3%). *Major import sources:* France 12.7%; South Africa 8.6%; United Kingdom 8.0%; Kuwait 7.4%; Japan 6.0%; China 5.4%; Bahrain 4.7%.
Exports (1985): Mau Rs 6,636,500,000 (sugar 43.2%, clothing 38.5%, tea 2.7%, watches and clocks 2.2%, fish and fish preparations 2.1%, pearls and precious and semiprecious stones 1.9%, textile yarn and fabric 1.4%). *Major export destinations:* United Kingdom 43.5%; France 20.8%; United States 15.1%; West Germany 6.3%; Italy 3.2%; Belgium 1.7%; Réunion 1.7%.

Transport and communications

Transport. Railroads: none. Roads (1983): total length 1,110 mi, 1,787 km (paved 92%). Vehicles (1984): passenger cars 26,143; trucks and buses 17,531. Merchant marine (1985): vessels (100 gross tons and over) 20; total deadweight tonnage 53,829. Air transport (1984): passenger-mi 276,000,000, passenger-km 444,000,000; short ton-mi cargo 5,712,400, metric ton-km cargo 8,340,000; airports (1986) with scheduled flights 2.
Communications. Daily newspapers (1985): total number 8; total circulation 76,000; circulation per 1,000 population 74. Radio (1984): total number of receivers 129,414 (1 per 7.8 persons). Television (1984): total number of receivers 98,130 (1 per 10 persons). Telephones (1985): 64,597 (1 per 15 persons).

Education and health

Education (1985)

	schools	teachers	students	student/ teacher ratio
Primary (age 5–12)	280	6,450	140,714	21.8
Secondary (age 12–20)	127	3,603	71,686	19.9
Voc., teacher tr.¶	7	69δ	444	...
Higher¶	2	184δ	610	...

Educational attainment (1983). Percent of adult population over age 25 having: no formal education 24.4%, less than primary 0.1%, primary 51.5%, secondary 20.4%, higher 3.6%. *Literacy* (1980): total population over age 15 literate 557,100 (84.6%); males literate 297,700 (90.5%); females literate 259,400 (78.8%).
Health (1985)‡: physicians 711 (1 per 1,404 persons); hospital beds 2,850 (1 per 350 persons); infant mortality rate per 1,000 live births 23.8.
Food (1980–82): daily per capita caloric intake 2,811 (vegetable products 90%, animal products 10%); 119% of FAO recommended minimum requirement.

Military

Total active duty personnel: none; however, a special police mobile unit ensures internal security. *Military expenditure as percent of GNP* (1983): 0.2% (world 6.1%); per capita expenditure U.S.$2.

*Preliminary. †Detail does not add to total given because of rounding. ‡Island of Mauritius only. §Employed persons as of September 1985. ‖ At current prices. ¶1984. ♀Import figures are f.o.b. (free on board) in balance of trade and c.i.f. (cost, insurance, and freight) for commodities and trading partners. δ1982.

Mayotte

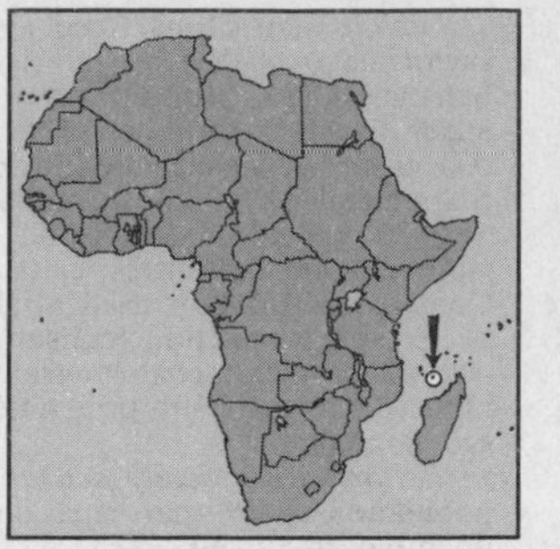

Official name: Collectivité Territoriale de Mayotte (Territorial Collectivity of Mayotte).
Political status: overseas dependency of France with one legislative house (General Council [17])*.
Chief of state: President of France.
Head of government: Commissioner of the Republic (for France); President of the General Council (for Mayotte).
Capital: Dzaoudzi (Capital designate, Mamoudzou).
Official language: French.
Official religion: none.
Monetary unit: 1 French (metropolitan) franc (F) = 100 centimes; valuation (Oct. 1, 1986) 1 U.S.$ = F 6.64; 1 £ = F 9.60.

Area and population

Islands / Communes	Capitals	area sq mi	area sq km	population 1985 census†
Grande Terre				
Acoua	—	4.9	12.6	2,714
Bandraboua	—	12.5	32.4	3,510
Bandrele	—	14.1	36.5	2,989
Boueni	—	5.4	14.1	3,000
Chiconi	—	3.2	8.3	4,035
Chirongui	—	10.9	28.3	3,380
Dembeni	—	15.0	38.8	2,369
Kani-Keli	—	7.9	20.5	2,785
Koungou	—	11.0	28.4	3,458
Mamoudzou	—	16.2	41.9	12,119
Mtsamboro	—	5.3	13.7	3,978
M'tsangamouji	—	8.4	21.8	3,248
Ouangani	—	7.3	19.0	2,586
Sada	—	4.3	11.2	4,163
Tsingoni	—	13.4	34.8	3,029
Petite Terre				
Dzaoudzi	—	2.6	6.7	5,675
Pamandzi	—	1.7	4.3	4,100
TOTAL		144.1	373.2‡	67,138

Demography

Population (1986): 70,300.
Density (1986): persons per sq mi 487.9, persons per sq km 188.4.
Urban-rural: n.a.§.
Sex distribution (1978): male 49.94%; female 50.06%.
Age breakdown (1978): under 15, 50.2%; 15–29, 23.4%; 30–44, 13.9%; 45–59, 7.0%; 60–74, 3.8%; 75 and over, 1.7%.
Population projection: (1990) 86,000; (2000) 141,000.
Doubling time: 14 years.
Ethnic composition (1985): Comorian (a mixture of Bantu, Arab, and Malagasy peoples) 96.9%; Europeans 2.5%; other 0.5%.
Religious affiliation (1985): Sunnī Muslim 96.9%; Christian, principally Roman Catholic, 3.0%; other 0.1%.
Major towns (1985) ‖ : Mamoudzou 12,119; Dzaoudzi 5,675.

Vital statistics

Birth rate per 1,000 population (1978): 49.8 (world avg. 30.0); legitimate (monogamous marriage) 70.8%; legitimate (polygamous marriage) 18.4%; illegitimate 10.8%.
Death rate per 1,000 population: n.a.
Natural increase rate per 1,000 population: n.a.
Total fertility rate (avg. births per childbearing woman): n.a.
Marriage rate per 1,000 population: n.a.; *marital status of adult population* (1978): monogamous marriage 51.8%; unmarried 27.3%; polygamous marriage 11.0%; divorced 6.6%; widowed 3.3%.
Divorce rate per 1,000 population: n.a.
Life expectancy at birth: n.a.
Major causes of death per 100,000 population: n.a.; however, malaria is a significant contagion; filariasis, formerly widespread, and leprosy are now practically nonexistent.

National economy

Budget (1984). Revenue: F 137,089,000 (subsidies 44.0%, indirect taxes 22.9%, receipts from public property 17.7%, loans 8.5%, direct taxes 6.8%). Expenditures: F 148,393,000 (roads 14.1%, health 11.5%, debt service 10.9%, education 9.9%, construction 6.9%, water supply 3.9%).
Public debt: n.a.
Tourism: n.a.
Production (metric tons except as noted). Agriculture, forestry, fishing (1985): rice 2,000–2,500, mangoes 1,500¶, bananas 1,300¶, breadfruit 700¶, citrus fruit 600¶, cassava 500¶, pineapples 200¶, corn (maize) 150¶, ylang-ylang 18,000 kilograms♀, coffee 9,200 kilograms♀, copra 4,000 kilograms♀, vanilla 3,800 kilograms♀, cloves 600 kilograms♀, cinnamon 193 kilograms♀; coconut palm trees (number of producing trees) 350,000; livestock (number of live animals; 1984) 10,000–15,000 goats, 3,000–4,000 cattle, 1,500–2,000 sheep; fish catch (1982) *c.* 500. Mining and quarrying: negligible. Manufacturing (1983): mostly involves processing of agricultural products for export. Construction (gross value in F '000; 1985): residential, none; nonresidential 50,200. Energy production (consumption): electricity (kW-hr; 1982) 5,000,000 (5,000,000); coal, none (n.a.); crude petroleum, none (n.a.); petroleum products, none (n.a.); natural gas, none (n.a.).
Gross national product (at current market prices): n.a.

Structure of gross domestic product and labour force

	1978 in value	% of total value	labour force	% of labour force
Agriculture, forestry, and fishing	...	...	9,298	61.6
Mining	...	...	19	0.1
Manufacturing	...	...	833	5.5
Construction	...	...	1,361	9.0
Public utilities	...	...	133	0.9
Transportation and communication	...	...	287	1.9
Trade	...	...	672	4.5
Finance	...	...	220	1.5
Pub. admin., defense	...	...	218	1.4
Education, health	...	...	348	2.3
Other	...	...	1,697♂	11.2
TOTAL	...	...	15,086	100.0‡

Population economically active (1978): total 14,214; activity rate of total population 32.1% (participation rates: ages 15–64, 65.0%; female 35.9%; unemployed 5.8%).

Price and earnings indexes (1982 = 100)□

	1980	1981	1982	1983	1984	1985	1986
Consumer price index	...	...	100.0	113.3	137.2	143.8	153.4
Hourly earnings index	72.8	81.7	100.0	106.3	117.2	152.6	...

Household income and expenditure. Average household size (1978) 4.7; average annual income per household: n.a.; source of income: n.a.; expenditure: n.a.
Land use (1984): agricultural 64.3%, of which 21.4% is under permanent cultivation; other 35.7%.

Foreign trade◇

Balance of trade (current prices)

	1980	1981	1982	1983	1984	1985
F '000,000	−69	−96	−110	−140	−173	−185
% of total	83.8%	83.9%	91.1%	90.1%	89.6%	89.1%

Imports (1985): F 196,047,000 (food products 26.5%; mineral fuels 15.5%; metals and metal products 14.9%; machinery 11.9%; chemical products 7.0%; transport equipment 6.5%; wood and wood products 3.8%; textiles and clothing 3.7%). *Major import sources* (1984): France 52.9%; Bahrain 11.3%; Kenya 7.7%; Thailand 7.0%; South Africa 5.9%; Réunion 2.8%.
Exports (1985): F 10,693,000 (reexports 64.2%; domestic exports 35.8%, of which ylang-ylang 22.5%, vanilla 11.2%, coffee 2.0%). *Major export destinations* (1984): France 81%; Réunion 6%; United States 6%.

Transport and communications

Transport. Railroads: none. Roads (1984): total length 143 mi, 230 km (paved 49%). Vehicles (1984): 1,528. Merchant marine: n.a. Air transport (1985)△: passenger arrivals and departures 17,426; cargo loaded and unloaded (metric tons) 172; airports (1986) with scheduled flights 1.
Communications. Daily newspapers (1985): total number 1; total circulation, n.a. Radio (1985): total number of receivers 6,000 (1 per 11 persons). Television: total number of receivers, n.a. Telephone subscribers (1981): 400 (1 per 137 persons).

Education and health

Education (1984–85)

	schools△	teachers	students	student/ teacher ratio
Primary (age 6–11)	72	407	14,992	36.8
Secondary (age 12–18)♰	3	66	1,374	20.0
Voc., teacher tr.♰	...	...	...	...
Higher	—	—	—	—

Educational attainment (1978). Percent of population 15 years and over having: no formal education 82.0%; some primary 10.6%; early secondary 5.4%; late secondary 1.5%; postsecondary and higher 0.5%. *Literacy* (1978): total population over age 15 literate 4,279 (18.0%); males literate 3,230 (27.5%); females literate 1,049 (8.7%).
Health: physicians (1980) 9 (1 per 5,857 persons); hospital beds (1981) 86 (1 per 638 persons); infant mortality rate per 1,000 live births, n.a.
Food: daily per capita caloric intake, n.a.

Military

Total active duty personnel (1985): 300 French troops.

*Final status of Mayotte is not yet determined; it is claimed by the Comoros as an integral part of that country. †Preliminary figure. ‡Detail does not add to total given because of rounding. §In the late 1970s, 87% of all residents of Mayotte lived in villages of less than 1,000 inhabitants. ‖ Populations cited are for villages with adjoining communes. ¶1983. ♀Export production only. ♂Includes 872 unemployed. □Base period is January 1982. Indexes are based on prices and minimum hourly wages paid in January of each year. ◇Export figures include reexports in balance of trade and commodities but exclude reexports for data on trading partners. △Excludes 8,487 military personnel and 789 metric tons of military cargo. ♰General secondary includes vocational and teacher training.

Mexico

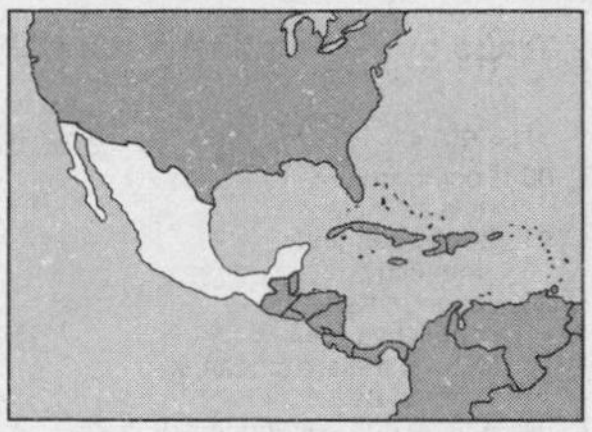

Official name: Estados Unidos Mexicanos (United Mexican States).
Form of government: federal republic with two legislative houses (Senate [64] and Chamber of Deputies [400]).
Chief of state and head of government: President.
Capital: Mexico City.
Official language: Spanish.
Official religion: none.
Monetary unit: 1 peso (Mex$) = 100 centavos; valuation (Oct. 1, 1986) 1 U.S.$ = Mex$770.50; 1 £ = Mex$1,113.37.

Area and population

States	Capitals	area* sq mi	area* sq km	population 1985 estimate
Aguascalientes	Aguascalientes	2,112	5,471	629,600
Baja California Norte	Mexicali	26,997	69,921	1,328,700
Baja California Sur	La Paz	28,369	73,475	279,300
Campeche	Campeche	19,619	50,812	533,300
Chiapas	Tuxtla Gutiérrez	28,653	74,211	2,392,800
Chihuahua	Chihuahua	94,571	244,938	2,188,800
Coahuila	Saltillo	57,908	149,982	1,806,700
Colima	Colima	2,004	5,191	398,300
Durango	Durango	47,560	123,181	1,328,100
Guanajuato	Guanajuato	11,773	30,491	3,369,600
Guerrero	Chilpancingo	24,819	64,281	2,423,700
Hidalgo	Pachuca	8,036	20,813	1,745,400
Jalisco	Guadalajara	31,211	80,836	4,972,400
México	Toluca	8,245	21,355	10,176,500
Michoacán	Morelia	23,138	59,928	3,233,000
Morelos	Cuernavaca	1,911	4,950	1,160,600
Nayarit	Tepic	10,417	26,979	813,100
Nuevo León	Monterrey	25,067	64,924	2,969,200
Oaxaca	Oaxaca	36,275	93,952	2,587,800
Puebla	Puebla	13,090	33,902	3,850,500
Querétaro	Querétaro	4,420	11,449	882,700
Quintana Roo	Chetumal	19,387	50,212	330,800
San Luis Potosí	San Luis Potosí	24,351	63,068	1,916,200
Sinaloa	Culiacán	22,521	58,328	2,198,800
Sonora	Hermosillo	70,291	182,052	1,716,300
Tabasco	Villahermosa	9,756	25,267	1,228,800
Tamaulipas	Ciudad Victoria	30,650	79,384	2,176,900
Tlaxcala	Tlaxcala	1,551	4,016	633,100
Veracruz	Jalapa	27,683	71,699	6,258,900
Yucatán	Mérida	14,827	38,402	1,230,100
Zacatecas	Zacatecas	28,283	73,252	1,226,900
Federal District				
Distrito Federal	—	571	1,479	9,931,400
TOTAL		756,066	1,958,201	77,938,300

Demography

Population (1986): 80,472,000.
Density† (1986): persons per sq mi 106.4, persons per sq km 41.1.
Urban-rural (1985): urban 69.7%; rural 30.3%.
Sex distribution (1984): male 50.07%; female 49.93%.
Age breakdown (1980): under 15, 43.0%; 15–29, 27.8%; 30–44, 14.9%; 45–59, 8.5%; 60–74, 4.0%; 75 and over, 1.8%.
Population projection: (1990) 88,690,000; (2000) 113,000,000.
Doubling time: 28 years.
Ethnic composition (1981): mestizo 55.0%; Amerindian 29.0%; Caucasian 15.0%; black 0.5%; other 0.5%.
Religious affiliation (1980): Roman Catholic 92.6%; Protestant (including Evangelical) 3.3%; Jewish 0.1%; other 0.9%; none 3.1%.
Major cities (1980): Mexico City 8,831,079; Guadalajara 1,626,152; Ciudad Netzahualcóyotl 1,341,230; Monterrey 1,090,009; Puebla 835,759; León 593,002; Juárez 544,496; Tijuana 429,500; Mérida 400,142; Chihuahua 385,603.
Place of birth (1980): 98.4% native-born; 1.6% foreign-born and unknown.
Mobility (1970). Population living in the same state as in 1960: 87.2%; different state 12.8%.
Households (1980). Total households 12,074,609; average household size 5.5; 1 person 5.4%, 2 persons 10.2%, 3 persons 12.4%, 4 persons 14.3%, 5 persons 13.5%, 6 persons 11.7%, 7 or more persons 32.5%. Family households: 11,421,286 (94.6%); nonfamily 653,323 (5.4%).
Immigration (1980): permanent immigrants admitted 73,260.
Emigration (1984): legal immigrants to the United States 57,600.

Vital statistics

Birth rate per 1,000 population (1983): 32.7 (world avg. 29.0); (1978) legitimate 91.0%, illegitimate 7.9%, unspecified 1.1%.
Death rate per 1,000 population (1983): 7.0 (world avg. 11.0).
Natural increase rate per 1,000 population (1983): 25.7 (world avg. 18.0).
Total fertility rate (avg. births per childbearing woman; 1980–85): 4.9.
Marriage rate per 1,000 population (1982): 7.2.
Divorce rate per 1,000 population (1981): 0.3.
Life expectancy at birth (1980–85): male 63.9 years; female 68.2 years.
Major causes of death per 100,000 population (1981): diseases of the circulatory system 100.2; accidents, including alcohol-related deaths 97.6; diseases of the respiratory system 77.2; infectious and parasitic diseases 73.0; diseases of the digestive system 43.8; malignant neoplasms (cancers) and nonmalignant tumours 41.7; signs, symptoms, and ill-defined conditions 37.9; conditions originating in the perinatal period 36.9.

Social indicators

Educational attainment (1980). Percent of population 15 years and over having: no primary education 13.7%; up to 3 years of primary 19.0%; 4 to 6 years of primary 28.0%; some postprimary 26.7%; unspecified 12.6%.

Distribution of income (1977)

percent of household income by quintile

1	2	3	4	5 (highest)
2.9	7.0	12.0	20.4	57.7

Quality of working life. Average workweek (1980): 46.0 hours. Annual rate (1979) per 100,000 workers for: temporary disability 2,789; indemnification 41; death 7. Labour conflicts (1982): 51,420, involving 146,419 workers. Labour stoppages (1982): 1,925, involving 25,173 workers. Average duration of journey to work: n.a. Method of transport: n.a. Rate per 1,000 workers of discouraged (unemployed no longer seeking work): n.a.
Access to services (1980). Proportion of dwellings having access to: electricity 74.6%; safe public water supply 71.2%; public sewage collection 49.2%.
Social participation. Eligible voters participating in last national election: 74.9%. Population participating in voluntary work: n.a. Trade union membership in total work force: n.a. Practicing religious population in total affiliated population (1970): weekly 10% of urban dwellers, 25% of rural dwellers; yearly 55% of urban dwellers, 73% of rural dwellers.
Social deviance (1975). Criminal cases tried by local authorities per 100,000 population for: murder 10.4; rape 3.0; other assault 31.4; theft 21.0. Incidence per 100,000 in general population of: alcoholism, n.a.; drug and substance abuse, n.a.‡; suicide 0.86§.
Leisure (1982). Favourite leisure activities (average daily attendance): cinema 430,486; museums and archaeological sites 29,220; live theatre 7,676; sporting events 5,056; bullfights 330.
Material well-being (1970). Households possessing: radio 46.3%; television 1.8%; radio and television 29.4% .

National economy

Gross national product (at current market prices; 1984): U.S.$158,310,000,000 (U.S.$2,062 per capita).

Structure of gross domestic product and labour force

	1985 in value U.S.$'000,000	1985 % of total value	1980 labour force	1980 % of labour force
Agriculture	16,825	9.4	5,699,971	23.8
Mining	6,747	3.8	477,017	2.0
Manufacturing	43,810	24.6	2,575,124	10.7
Construction	8,373	4.7	1,296,337	5.4
Public utilities	3,292	1.8	115,932	0.5
Transportation and communication	13,645	7.7	672,011	2.8
Trade	42,473	23.8	1,729,296	7.2
Finance	15,973	9.0	405,754	1.7
Pub. admin., defense	6,633	3.7	‖	‖
Services	20,518	11.5	2,418,114	10.1
Other	—	—	8,598,128 ‖	35.8 ‖
TOTAL	178,289¶	100.0	23,987,684	100.0

Budget (1985). Revenue: Mex$7,896,100,000,000 (revenue from state petroleum company 45.5%, income taxes 23.9%, value added taxes 16.2%, import duties 5.1%, excise taxes 4.8%). Expenditures: Mex$11,478,200,000,000 (interest on public debt 36.9%, transfer payments and subsidies 29.6%, goods and services 18.2%).
Public debt (external, outstanding; 1985): U.S.$97,700,000,000.
Tourism (1985): receipts from visitors U.S.$1,727,000,000; expenditures by nationals abroad U.S.$694,300,000.

Manufacturing, mining, and construction enterprises (1983)

	no. of large enterprises	no. of employees (000)	yearly wages as a % of avg. of all wages	annual value added (Mex$'000,000)
Manufacturing	1,209	526.5♀	100.0	2,167,421♀
Food, beverages, and tobacco	476	150.5	78.1	586,032
Metal products	149	92.5	109.8	472,463
Chemicals	141	59.4	120.2	333,228
Nonelectrical machinery and transport equipment	47	53.8	132.2	224,053
Paper and printing	96	29.0	107.0	145,781
Nonmetallic mineral products	54	25.7	103.9	130,516
Textiles and apparel	153	58.8	78.6	107,828
Electrical machinery	66	31.4	87.8	84,239
Wood and wood products	6	5.0	100.7	19,129
Other manufactures	21	20.3	110.6	64,154
Mining (petroleum and coal products)	14	5.1	97.5	35,358
Construction	...	...	...	...

Production (metric tons except as noted). Agriculture, forestry, fishing (1985): sugarcane 37,800,000, corn (maize) 15,103,000, sorghum 6,648,000, wheat 5,228,000, oranges 2,000,000, tomatoes 1,665,000, bananas 1,500,000, dry beans 1,085,000, rice 988,000, soybeans 911,000, potatoes 840,000, barley 629,000, lemons and limes 603,000, grapes 600,000, cottonseed 560,000, coffee 269,000, cotton lint 196,000, tobacco 56,000; livestock (number of live animals) 37,450,000 cattle, 19,000,000 pigs, 10,500,000 goats, 6,500,000 sheep, 6,135,000 horses, 3,183,000 asses, 3,130,000 mules, 200,000,000 chickens; roundwood (1984) 17,739,000 cu m; fish catch (1984) 1,103,658, of which sardines 278,331, anchovies 132,738. Mining and quarrying (metals by metal content; 1985): iron ore 4,982,000; zinc 273,840; lead 206,640; copper 181,560; manganese 168,000; silver 69,453,000 troy oz; gold 233,438 troy oz; (nonmetals; 1985) sulfur 1,997,000; fluorite 695,000; phosphate rock 518,300♁; barite 484,000; graphite 41,500♁. Manufacturing (value added

Mex$'000,000,000; 1983): iron and steel products 358.2; transport vehicles 202.4; printing and paper products 145.8; animal and vegetable oil and margarine 105.4; beer 98.5; plastic and other artificial fibres 88.6; beverages 83.8; cereals and cereal preparations 82.4; cement 81.3; soaps, detergents, and other products 80.7; rubber tires and tubes 77.3; electrical machinery and appliances 71.1; meat and dairy products 58.0; cotton, linen, and other finished products 47.1. Construction (gross value of new construction in Mex$'000,000,000; 1982): residential 453.9; nonresidential 107.0.

Service enterprises (1970)

	no. of establish-ments	no. of employees	weekly wage as a % of all wages	annual value added (Mex$'000,000)
Food and beverage preparation	71,524	177,399	...	3,236
Recreation and resorts	20,850	78,149	...	3,189
Food and beverage service	51,884	141,105	...	2,539
Lodging	6,708	54,509	...	2,515
Exhibitions and shows	3,550	33,323	...	2,143
Repair, excluding industries requiring parts	41,572	95,553	...	1,908
Professional services	9,522	32,058	...	1,772
Medical and social assistance	16,244	43,731	...	1,449
Educational services	5,016	43,781	...	1,355
Personal grooming and cleaning	29,708	65,060	...	1,212
Automobile repair	18,848	51,588	...	1,105
Alcoholic beverages	19,640	36,294	...	697
Mechanical repair	8,195	17,562	...	404
Shoe repair	4,532	6,737	...	73

Energy production (consumption): electricity (kW-hr; 1984) 87,083,000,000 (86,988,000,000); coal (metric tons; 1984) 7,800,000 (7,975,000); crude petroleum (barrels; 1985) 1,050,800,000 (444,000,000δ); petroleum products (metric tons; 1984) 66,174,000 (62,506,000); natural gas (cu m; 1985) 28,081,000,000 (24,695,000,000δ).

Population economically active (1980): total 23,987,684; activity rate of total population 35.9% (participation rates: ages 15–64, 57.1%; female 27.8%; unemployed 4.5%.)

Price and earnings indexes (1980 = 100)

	1980	1981	1982	1983	1984	1985	1986□
Consumer price index	100.0	127.9	203.3	410.2	679.0	1,071.2	2,131.2
Monthly earnings index	100.0	129.5	207.2	311.3	494.2	...	...

Household income and expenditure. Average household size (1980) 5.5; average annual income per household: n.a. Source of income: n.a.; expenditure (1983): food, beverages, and tobacco 35.0%, housing 20.7%, transportation and communication 11.8%, clothing and footwear 11.0%, recreation and entertainment 5.0%, health and medical services 5.0%.

Land use (1984): forested 23.8%; meadows and pastures 38.7%; agricultural and under permanent cultivation 12.8%; other 24.7%.

Financial aggregates◇

	1981	1982	1983	1984	1985	1986△
Exchange Rate, Mex$ per:						
U.S. Dollar	24.51	56.40	120.09	167.83	256.87	555.54
£	49.70	98.73	182.18	224.89	332.98	837.9
SDR	28.90	62.27	128.38	171.80	408.28	677.57
International reserves (U.S.$)						
Total (excl. gold; '000,000)	4,074	834	3,913	7,272	4,906	3,461
SDRs ('000,000)	178	6	23	3	—	8
Reserve pos. in IMF ('000,000)	187	—	95	—	—	—
Foreign exchange	3,709	828	3,795	7,269	4,906	3,453
Gold ('000,000 fine troy oz)	2.26	2.07	2.31	2.42	2.36	2.54
% world reserves	0.24	0.22	0.24	0.26	0.25	0.26
Interest and prices						
Treasury bill rate	30.77	45.75	59.19	49.47	63.36	84.00
Balance of payments (U.S.$'000,000)						
Balance of visible trade, of which:	−4,099	+7,646	+14,507	+12,941	+8,407	...
Imports, f.o.b.	24,037	14,435	7,721	11,255	13,460	...
Exports, f.o.b.	19,938	22,081	22,228	24,196	21,867	...
Balance of invisibles	−10,089	−13,660	−9,654	−9,112	−8,317	...
Balance of payments, current account	−13,899	−5,753	+5,208	+540	...	...

Foreign trade†

Balance of trade (current prices)

	1980	1981	1982	1983	1984	1985
U.S.$'000,000	−4,667	−5,642	+6,173	+13,340	+12,943	+8,396
% of total	13.4%	12.7%	17.0%	45.3%	36.2%	23.8%

Imports (1985): U.S.$13,992,800,000 (machinery and transport equipment 40.4%, of which transport equipment 10.9%, electrical machinery 8.6%; chemical products 14.7%; unprocessed agricultural products 9.3%, of which soybeans 2.0%, sorghum 1.9%, corn 1.8%; livestock and fish 3.4%). *Major import sources* (1984): United States 62.2%; Japan 4.3%; West Germany 4.1%; France 2.2%; Canada 1.9%; Brazil 1.9%; Italy 1.9%.

Exports (1985): U.S.$21,835,100,000 (crude petroleum 61.0%; machinery and transport equipment 10.5%; petroleum products 6.2%; unprocessed agricultural products [including livestock] 5.9%, of which coffee 2.2%, tomatoes 0.9%, live cattle 0.7%; chemical products 3.1%). *Major export destinations* (1984): United States 58.0%; Japan 7.8%; Spain 7.1%; United Kingdom 4.2%; France 3.8%; Brazil 2.3%; Israel 2.0%; Canada 2.0%.

Trade by commodity group (1983)

	imports		exports	
SITC group	U.S.$'000,000	%	U.S.$'000,000	%
00 Food and live animals	1,622	20.1	1,543	7.2
01 Beverages and tobacco	—	—	90	0.4
02 Crude materials, excluding fuels	580	7.2	587	2.7
03 Mineral fuels, lubricants, and related materials	599	7.4	15,979	74.7
04 Animal and vegetable oils, fats, and waxes	101	1.2	—	—
05 Chemicals and related products, n.e.s.	644	8.0	895	4.2
06 Basic manufactures	1,039	12.9	1,189	5.6
07 Machinery and transport equipment	3,351	41.6	1,044	4.9
08 Miscellaneous manufactured articles	119	1.5	67	0.3
09 Goods not classified by kind	4	0.1	5	—
TOTAL	8,059	100.0	21,399	100.0

Direction of trade (1984)

	imports		exports	
SITC group	U.S.$'000,000	%	U.S.$'000,000	%
Africa	42	0.4	53	0.2
Asia	568	5.3	2,723	11.2
South America	404	3.7	829	3.4
North and Central America	6,956	64.6	15,912	65.2
United States	6,695	62.2	14,612	59.9
other North and Central Am.	261	2.4	1,300	5.3
Europe	1,731	16.1	4,656	19.0
EEC	1,411	13.1	4,442	18.2
U.S.S.R.	4	—	14	—
other Europe	316	2.9	200	0.8
Oceania	73	0.7	15	0.1
unknown }	987	9.2	219	0.9
freight and insurance charges }			—	—
TOTAL	10,761	100.0	24,407	100.0

Transport and communications

Transport. Railroads (1985): route length§ 16,031 mi, 25,799 km; passenger-mi 3,691,000,000, passenger-km 5,940,000,000; short ton-mi cargo 31,126,000,000, metric ton-km cargo 45,444,000,000. Roads (1983): total length 133,265 mi, 214,470 km (paved 50%). Vehicles (1982): passenger cars 5,221,159; trucks and buses 1,978,327. Merchant marine (1985): vessels (100 gross tons and over) 638; total deadweight tonnage 2,077,451. Air transport⊕ (1985): passenger-mi 10,991,000,000, passenger-km 17,688,000,000; short ton-mi cargo 118,825,000, metric ton-km cargo 173,481,000; airports (1986) 72.

Communications. Daily newspapers (1983): total number, more than 350; total circulation, n.a.; circulation per 1,000 population, n.a. Radio (1985): total number of receivers 22,250,000 (1 per 3.5 persons). Television (1985): total number of receivers 7,750,000 (1 per 10.1 persons). Telephones (1983): 5,845,400 (1 per 12.8 persons).

Education and health

Education (1984–85)

	schools	teachers	students	student/teacher ratio
Primary (age 6–12)	76,183	437,408	15,219,245	34.8
Secondary (age 12–18)	17,620	230,656	4,396,087	19.1
Voc., teacher tr.	4,815	126,705	1,845,512	14.6
Higher	1,305	92,338	1,121,252	12.1

Literacy (1980): total population literate 31,475,670 (82.6%); males literate 15,955,272 (85.8%); females literate 15,520,398 (79.5%).

Health: physicians (1980) 53,053 (1 per 1,308 persons); hospital beds (1984) 72,000 (1 per 1,070 persons); infant mortality rate per 1,000 live births (1983) 53.0.

Food (1981–83): daily per capita caloric intake 2,966 (vegetable products 86%, animal products 14%); 124% of FAO recommended minimum requirement.

Military

Total active duty personnel (1986): 139,500 (army 75.3%, navy 20.1%, air force 4.6%). *Military expenditure as percent of GNP* (1984): 0.3% (world 6.1%); per capita expenditure U.S.$7.

*Total land area is 754,107 sq mi (1,953,128 sq km); the area shown for the states, federal district, and the grand total includes both land and water area. †Based on land area. ‡Through 1982, cannabis remained the most abused drug. §1983. ‖Public administration, defense, and unemployed persons are included with other. ¶In 1984 dollars. ♀Detail does not add to total given because of rounding. δ1984. □July. ◇Exchange rates and treasury bill rates are expressed in period averages; international reserves are expressed in end of period rates. △June. †All exports f.o.b. (free on board), imports c.i.f. (cost, insurance, and freight). ⊕All scheduled traffic of Mexicana and AeroMexico airlines.

Micronesia, Federated States of

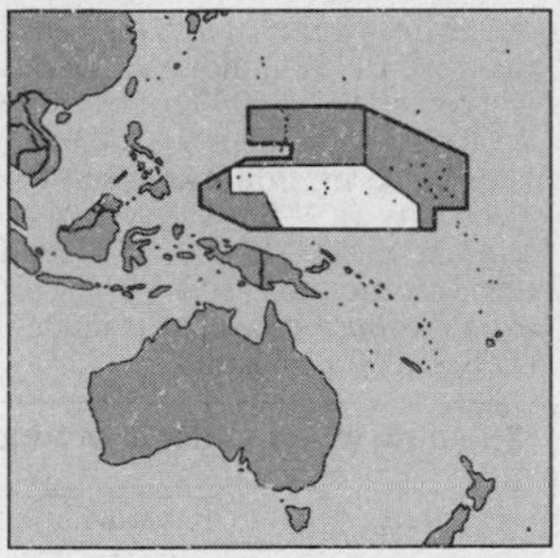

Official name: Federated States of Micronesia.
Political status: federal republic in free association with the United States with one legislative house (National Congress [14])*.
Head of state and government: President.
Capital: Kolonia.
Official language: none.
Official religion: none.
Monetary unit: 1 U.S. dollar (U.S.$) = 100 cents; valuation (Oct. 1, 1986) 1£ = U.S.$1.44.

Area and population

States / Major Islands	area sq mi	area sq km	population 1985 estimate
Kosrae	42.3	109.6	6,462
Kosrae Island	42.3	109.6	6,462
Pohnpei	133.3	345.2	27,871
Pohnpei Island	129.0	334.1	24,788
Truk	49.1	127.2	46,159
Moen Islands	7.0	18.1	14,218
Yap	45.9	118.9	10,948
Yap Island	38.7	100.2	6,951
TOTAL	270.8†	701.4†	91,440

Demography

Population (1986): 94,700.
Density (1986): persons per sq mi 349.7, persons per sq km 135.0.
Urban–rural (1980): urban 19.4%; rural 80.6%.
Sex distribution (1980): male 51.12%; female 48.88%.
Age breakdown (1980): under 15, 46.4%; 15–29, 26.8%; 30–44, 12.6%; 45–59, 8.5%; 60–74, 4.5%; 75 and over, 1.2%.
Population projection: (1990) 109,000; (2000) 154,000.
Doubling time: 20 years.
Ethnic composition (1980): Trukese 41.1%; Pohnpeian 25.9%; Mortlockese 8.3%; Kosraean 7.4%; Yapese 6.0%; Ulithian, or Woleaian, 4.0%; Pingelapese, or Mokilese, 1.2%; Western Trukese 1.0%; Palauan 0.4%; Filipino 0.2%; other 4.5%.
Religious affiliation (1984): Christianity is the predominant religious tradition, with the Kosraeans, Pohnpeians, and Trukese being mostly Protestant and the Yapese mostly Roman Catholic.
Major cities (1980): Moen 10,351; Tol 6,705; Kolonia 5,549; Sokehs 3,632; Kitti 3,401; Madolenihmw 3,376; Dublon 3,223; Fefan 3,076.

Vital statistics

Birth rate per 1,000 population (1984): 29.4 (world avg. 29.0); legitimate, n.a.; illegitimate, n.a.
Death rate per 1,000 population (1984): 2.7‡ (world avg. 11.0).
Natural increase rate per 1,000 population (1984): 26.7 (world avg. 18.0).
Total fertility rate (avg. births per childbearing woman; 1985): 5.3§.
Marriage rate per 1,000 population: n.a.
Divorce rate per 1,000 population: n.a.
Life expectancy at birth (1985)‡: male 64.0 years; female 68.1 years.
Major causes of death per 100,000 population (1984): diseases of the cerebrovascular system 53.2; pulmonary diseases 47.5; suicide and accidents 23.8.

National economy

Budget (1985). Revenue: U.S.$80,965,900 (U.S. Department of the Interior 49.8%, other U.S. government grants and federal program funds 40.2%, local revenue sources 10.0%). Expenditures: n.a.
Public debt (external, outstanding): n.a.
Tourism (1985): number of visitors 11,805.
Production (metric tons except as noted). Agriculture, forestry, fishing (1985): n.a.; however, Micronesia's major crops include coconuts (from which more than 4,000 tons of copra is produced), cassava, sweet potatoes, and a variety of tropical fruits (including bananas); livestock comprises mostly pigs and poultry; fish catch, n.a., however, tuna is one of the major natural resources of Micronesia. Mining and quarrying: quarrying of sand and aggregate for local construction only. Manufacturing: n.a.; however, copra is the most important product, and the manufacture of handicrafts and personal items (clothing, mats, boats, etc.) by individuals is also important. Construction: n.a. Energy production (consumption): electricity ‖ (kW-hr; 1984) 150,000,000 (150,000,000); coal, none (n.a.); crude petroleum, none (n.a.); petroleum products (metric tons; 1984) none (50,000 ‖); natural gas, none (n.a.).
Price and earnings indexes: n.a.
Household income and expenditure: average household size (1980) 7.0; average annual income per household, n.a.; sources of income (as percent of workers over age 16): wage and salary workers (private) 22.8%, wage and salary workers (government) 51.5%, self-employed persons 2.7%, primarily subsistence workers 5.7%; expenditure: n.a.
Land use (1984) ‖ : forested 22.5%; meadows and pastures 13.5%; agricultural and under permanent cultivation 33.5%; other 30.5%.

Gross national product (at current market prices; 1983): U.S.$106,500,000 (U.S.$1,250 per capita).

Structure of gross domestic product and labour force

	1983 in value U.S.$'000,000	1983 % of total value	1980 labour force	1980 % of labour force
Agriculture	...	...	196	2.0
Mining	...	...	¶	¶
Manufacturing	...	...	115	9.7
Construction	...	...	946¶	1.2¶
Trade	...	...	864	4.8
Public utilities	...	... }	472	8.8
Transportation and communication	...	... }		
Finance	...	...	121	1.2
Pub. admin., defense	...	...	1,765	18.0
Services	...	...	3,086	31.5
Other	...	...	2,233♀	22.8♀
TOTAL	106.5	100.0	9,798♁	100.0

Population economically active (1982): total 37,602; activity rate of total population 51.4% (participation rates: ages 15–64, n.a.; female 48.9%; unemployed 4.4%).

Foreign trade

Balance of trade (current prices)

	1978	1979	1980	1981	1982	1983
U.S.$'000,000	...	...	...	...	...	−54.94
% of total	...	...	...	...	...	88.4%

Imports (1983): U.S.$58,530,000 (much of Micronesia's food must be imported, including fruits, vegetables, meat, and fish; nearly all manufactured goods must be imported, including such necessities as medicine and fuel oil. *Major import sources:* United States; Japan; Guam; Australia.
Exports (1983): U.S.$3,590,000 (primarily from copra, but black pepper, handicrafts, and a few marine products are also exported). *Major export destinations:* United States; Japan.

Transport and communications

Transport. Railroads: none. Roads (1985): total length 19 mi□, 31 km□. Vehicles: passenger cars, trucks, and buses, n.a. Merchant marine: n.a. Air transport: n.a.; airports (1986) with scheduled flights 2.
Communications. Daily newspapers (1985): there are no private newspapers. Radios (1984): total number of receivers 15,800 (1 per 5.4 persons). Television (1984): total number of receivers 500 (1 per 170.8 persons). Telephones: n.a.

Education and health

Education (1980–81)

	schools	teachers	students	student/teacher ratio
Elementary (age 3–5)	...	...	1,690	...
Elementary (age 6–13)	...	...	13,866	...
Elementary (over age 14)	...	...	1,557	...
High school (age 12–18)	...	...	3,104	...
High school (over age 18)	...	...	777	...
College◇	...	...	720	...

Educational attainment (1980). Percent of population over age 15 having: no formal schooling 18.1%; primary education 48.8%; secondary education 26.2%; higher 6.9%. *Literacy* (1980): total population over age 15 literate 30,074 (76.7%); males literate 13,710 (67.0%); females literate 16,364 (87.2%).
Health (1985): physicians 36△ (1 per 2,540 persons); hospital beds, n.a.; infant mortality rate per 1,000 live births (1984) 36.5.
Food: daily per capita caloric intake, n.a.

Military

External security is provided by the United States.

*On Nov. 3, 1986, the United States unilaterally terminated the UN trusteeship it held over the Federated States of Micronesia, the Republic of the Marshall Islands, the Republic of Palau, and the Commonwealth of the Northern Mariana Islands, thus formally initiating their free-association political status. The United Nations has thus far not recognized the termination of the trusteeship. †Detail does not add to total given because of rounding. ‡For registered deaths only. §Includes other islands in geographic Micronesia. ‖ Includes the area formerly comprising the U.S. Trust Territory of the Pacific Islands. ¶Construction includes mining. ♀Includes unemployed. ♁Excludes more than 4,500 persons employed in nonmarket subsistence activities. □Paved road only. ◇In 1985, 1,200 students were enrolled in colleges and universities in the United States. △Excludes medical officers.

Mongolia

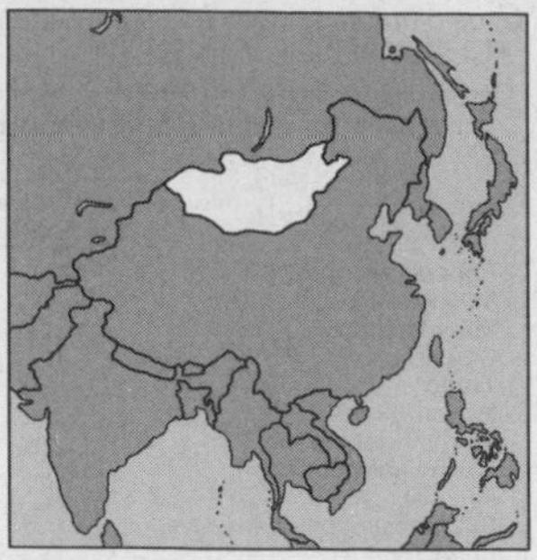

Official name: Bŭged Nayramdah Mongol Arad Ulas (Mongolian People's Republic).
Form of government: unitary single-party republic with one legislative house (People's Great Hural [370]).
Chief of state: Chairman of the Presidium of the People's Great Hural.
Head of government: Premier.
Capital: Ulaanbaatar (Ulan Bator).
Official language: Khalkha Mongolian.
Official religion: none.
Monetary unit: 1 tugrik = 100 möngös; valuation (Oct 1, 1986) 1 U.S.$ = 3.36 tugriks; 1 £ = 4.85 tugriks.

Area and population

Provinces	Capitals	area sq mi	area sq km	population 1984 estimate
Arhangay	Tsetserleg	21,000	55,000	83,800
Bayanhongor	Bayanhongor	45,000	116,000	69,500
Bayan-Ölgiy	Ölgiy	18,000	46,000	84,000
Bulgan	Bulgan	19,000	49,000	46,000
Dornod	Choybalsan	47,000	122,000	67,800
Dornogovĭ	Saynshand	43,000	111,000	47,400
Dundgovĭ	Mandalgov	30,000	78,000	44,100
Dzavhan	Uliastay	32,000	82,000	88,100
Govĭ-Altay	Altay	55,000	142,000	62,500
Hentiy	Öndörhaan	32,000	82,000	60,500
Hovd	Hovd	29,000	76,000	71,600
Hövsgöl	Mörön	39,000	101,000	96,600
Ömnögovĭ	Dalandzadgad	64,000	165,000	35,500
Övörhangay	Arvayheer	24,000	63,000	93,200
Selenge	Sühbaatar	16,000	42,000	76,400
Sühbaatar	Baruun-urt	32,000	82,000	47,200
Töv	Dzuunmod	31,000	81,000	90,200
Uvs	Ulaangom	27,000	69,000	81,400
Autonomous municipalities				
Darhan	—	100	200	63,600
Erdenet	—	300	800	40,500
Ulaanbaatar	—	800	2,000	470,500
TOTAL		604,000*	1,565,000	1,820,400

Demography

Population (1986): 1,938,000.
Density (1986): persons per sq mi 3.2, persons per sq km 1.2.
Urban-rural (1985): urban 51.7%; rural 48.3%.
Sex distribution (1985): male 50.00%; female 50.00%.
Age breakdown (1985): under 15, 42.7%; 15–29, 26.2%; 30–44, 16.1%; 45–59, 9.7%; 60–74, 4.4%; 75 and over, 0.9%.
Population projection: (1990) 2,170,000; (2000) 2,837,000.
Doubling time: 26 years.
Ethnic composition (1979): Khalkha Mongol 77.5%; Kazakh 5.3%; Dörbed Mongol 2.8%; Bayad 2.0%; Buryat Mongol 1.9%; Dariganga Mongol 1.5%; other 9.0%.
Religious affiliation: Although formal freedom of worship, or of propagandization against religion, exists, all traditional religious practice (lamaistic Buddhism, shamanism, Islam, and others) has become vastly attenuated during the 20th century; reliable data on the current situation do not exist.
Major cities (1985): Ulaanbaatar (Ulan Bator) 488,200; Darhan 69,800; Erdenet 42,900.

Vital statistics

Birth rate per 1,000 population (1984): 37.0 (world avg. 29.0); legitimate, n.a.; illegitimate, n.a.
Death rate per 1,000 population (1984): 11.1 (world avg. 11.0).
Natural increase rate per 1,000 population (1984): 25.9 (world avg. 18.0).
Total fertility rate (avg. births per childbearing woman; 1985): 5.0.
Marriage rate per 1,000 population (1984): 6.1.
Divorce rate per 1,000 population (1984): 0.3.
Life expectancy at birth (1985): male 61.3 years; female 65.4 years.
Major causes of death per 100,000 population: n.a.; however, major diseases include brucellosis, helminthiasis (an infection with worms), bacillary dysentery and amoebiasis, enteritis and other diarrheal diseases, cerebrospinal meningitis, trachoma, and tuberculosis of the respiratory system. Typhus, diphtheria, and acute poliomyelitis, formerly widespread, have reportedly been eliminated.

National economy

Budget (1985). Revenue: 5,735,000,000 tugriks (turnover tax 63.6%, deductions from profits 20.9%, social insurance contributions 3.5%). Expenditures: 5,720,000,000 tugriks (economy 42.0%, social and cultural services 39.1%, defense 13.4%, administration and other 5.5%).
Public debt: heavily dependent on U.S.S.R.
Tourism (1983): number of tourists 170,000; receipts from visitors, n.a.; expenditures by nationals abroad, n.a.
Production (metric tons except as noted). Agriculture, forestry, fishing (1985): wheat 482,000, potatoes 114,000, barley 94,000, oats 53,000; livestock (number of live animals) 13,391,000 sheep, 4,298,000 goats, 2,374,000 cattle, 1,961,000 horses, 47,600 pigs; roundwood 1,500,000 cu m; fish catch 400. Mining and quarrying (1984): fluorspar 700,000; copper 118,000. Manufacturing (1984): flour 185,200; cement 140,700; lime 108,900; meat 68,600; woolen cloth 980,000 m; leather shoes 2,696,000 pairs; sheep and goat skins 2,940,000 sq m; beer 97,300,000 hectolitres. Construction (1984): residential 190,000 sq m; nonresidential 838 units. Energy production (consumption): electricity (kW-hr; 1984) 2,264,000,000 (2,526,000,000); coal (metric tons; 1984) 5,431,000 (5,442,500); crude petroleum, none (n.a.); petroleum products (metric tons; 1984) none (696,000); natural gas, none (n.a.).
Gross national product (at current market prices; 1984): U.S.$1,820,400,000 (U.S.$1,000 per capita).

Structure of net material product and labour force

	1984 value	% of total value	labour force	% of labour force
Agriculture	...	17.7	382,900	55.4
Mining and manufacturing	...	32.3	86,900	12.6
Construction	...	6.0	27,800	4.0
Public utilities	...		16,600	2.4
Transportation and communication	...	11.0	35,400	5.1
Trade	...	33.0	40,900	5.9
Services†	...	...	100,500	14.5
TOTAL	...	100.0	691,000	100.0*

Population economically active (1984): total 691,000; activity rate of total population 37.1% (participation rates: ages 15–64, 67.2%; female 51.3%; unemployed, n.a.)
Price and earnings indexes: n.a.
Household income and expenditure. Average household size (1980) 5.0; average annual income per household: n.a.; source of income: n.a.; expenditure: n.a.
Land use (1984): forested 9.7%; meadows and pastures 78.8%; agricultural and under permanent cultivation 0.8%; other 10.7%.

Foreign trade

Balance of trade (current prices)

	1979	1980	1981	1982	1983	1984
U.S.$'000,000	−207.5	−138.7	−225.7	−220.0	−305.0	−230.0
% of total	18.5%	15.2%	20.1%	17.0%	20.7%	18.1%

Imports (1984): U.S.$750,000,000 (machinery and equipment 34.2%; fuels, minerals, and metals 29.9%; consumer goods 18.8%; food products 9.9%; chemical products, fertilizers, and rubber 7.2%). *Major import sources:* U.S.S.R. and socialist countries 97.4%; capitalist countries 1.0%.
Exports (1984): U.S.$520,000,000 (raw materials and food products 43.7%; minerals and metals 41.3%; consumer goods 13.8%; chemicals and related products 1.0%). *Major export destinations:* U.S.S.R. and socialist countries 94.0%; capitalist countries 4.4%.

Transport and communications

Transport. Railroads (1984): length 1,086 mi, 1,748 km; passenger-mi 248,500,000, passenger-km 400,000,000; short ton-mi cargo 3,524,000,000, metric ton-km cargo 5,100,000,000. Roads (1985): total length 29,000 mi, 47,600 km (paved 2%). Vehicles: n.a. Merchant marine: vessels (100 gross tons and over) none. Air transport (1984): passenger-mi 173,000,000, passenger-km 278,000,000; short ton-mi cargo 4,040,000, metric ton-km cargo 5,900,000; airports (1986) with scheduled flights 1.
Communications. Daily newspapers (1985): total number 2; total circulation 170,000; circulation per 1,000 population 91.0. Radio (1985): total number of receivers 194,000 (1 per 9.6 persons). Television (1985): total number of receivers 78,100 (1 per 24 persons). Telephones (1985): 46,700 (1 per 40 persons).

Education and health

Education (1984–85)

	schools	teachers	students	student/teacher ratio
Primary and secondary (age 8–18)	673	16,500	418,000	25.3
Voc., teacher tr.	40	1,200	25,700	21.4
Higher	8	1,500	25,100	16.7

Educational attainment (1979). Percent of population over age 10 having: primary education 48.0%; some secondary 29.7%; complete secondary 9.5%; vocational secondary 7.0%; some higher and complete higher 5.8%.
Literacy (1980): total population over age 15 literate 849,000 (89.5%); males literate 443,000 (93.4%); females literate 406,000 (85.5%).
Health (1985): physicians 4,234 (1 per 444 persons); hospital beds 20,400 (1 per 92 persons); infant mortality rate per 1,000 live births 49.0.
Food (1981–83): daily per capita caloric intake 2,744 (vegetable products 67%, animal products 33%); 114% of FAO recommended minimum requirement.

Military

Total active duty personnel (1986): 25,500 (army 86.3%; navy, none; air force 13.7%). *Military expenditure* as percent of GNP (1984): 11.5% (world 6.1%); estimated foreign military assistance $600,000; per capita expenditure U.S.$200.

*Detail does not add to total given because of rounding. †Includes finance, public administration, and defense.

Morocco

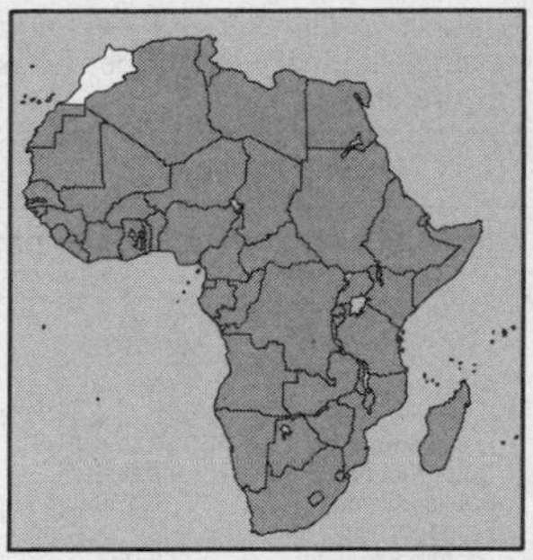

Official name: al-Mamlakah al-Maghribīyah (Kingdom of Morocco).
Form of government: constitutional monarchy with one legislative house (House of Representatives [306]).
Chief of state: King.
Head of government: Prime Minister.
Capital: Rabat.
Official language: Arabic.
Official religion: Islam.
Monetary unit: 1 Moroccan dirham (DH) = 100 Moroccan francs; valuation (Oct. 1, 1986) 1 U.S.$ = DH 8.79; 1 £ = DH 12.70.

Area and population

		area		population
Provinces	**Capitals**	sq mi	sq km	1984 estimate
Agadir	Agadir	2,282	5,910	623,000
Azilal	Azilal	3,880	10,050	396,000
Béni Mellal	Béni Mellal	2,732	7,075	720,000
Ben Slimane	Ben Slimane	1,066	2,760	181,000
Boulemane	Boulemane	5,558	14,395	136,000
Chaouen (Chefchaouen)	Chaouen (Chefchaouen)	1,680	4,350	320,000
Essaouira	Essaouira	2,446	6,335	403,000
Fès	Fès	2,085	5,400	852,000
Figuig	Figuig	21,618	55,990	104,000
Guelmim*	Guelmim	11,100	28,750	136,000
al-Hoceima	al-Hoceima	1,371	3,550	324,000
Ifrane	Ifrane	1,278	3,310	104,000
el-Jadida	el-Jadida	2,317	6,000	800,000
el-Kelaa des Srarhna	el-Kelaa Srarhna	3,888	10,070	601,000
Kénitra	Kénitra	1,832	4,745	758,000
Khémisset	Khémisset	3,207	8,305	421,000
Khénifra	Khénifra	4,757	12,320	381,000
Khouribga	Khouribga	1,641	4,250	460,000
Laayoune†	el-Aaiún	...	...	119,000
Marrakech	Marrakech	5,697	14,755	1,325,000
Meknès	Meknès	1,542	3,995	654,000
Nador	Nador	2,367	6,130	633,000
Ouarzazate	Ouarzazate	16,043	41,550	558,000
Oujda	Oujda	7,992	20,700	821,000
er-Rachidia	er-Rachidia	23,006	59,585	439,000
Safi	Safi	2,813	7,285	737,000
Settat	Settat	3,764	9,750	714,000
Sidi Kacem	Sidi Kacem	1,568	4,060	533,000
Tangier	Tangier	461	1,195	462,000
Tan-Tan	Tan-Tan	6,678	17,295	49,000
Taounate	Taounate	2,156	5,585	549,000
Taroudannt	Taroudannt	6,355	16,460	581,000
Tata	Tata	10,010	25,925	102,000
Taza	Taza	5,799	15,020	636,000
Tétouan	Tétouan	2,326	6,025	739,000
Tiznit	Tiznit	2,687	6,960	328,000
Prefectures				
Ain Chok-Hay Hassani	—			324,000
Ain Sebaa-Hay Mohammadi	—			453,000
Ben Msik-Sidi Othmane	—	623	1,615	701,000
Casablanca-Anfa	—			957,000
Mohammadia-Znata	—			165,000
Rabat-Salé	—	492	1,275	1,115,000
TOTAL		177,117	458,730	21,414,000

Demography

Population (1986): 22,455,000.
Density (1986): persons per sq mi 126.8, persons per sq km 48.9.
Urban-rural (1985): urban 43.9%; rural 56.1%.
Sex distribution (1984): male 50.08%; female 49.92%.
Age breakdown (1982): under 15, 42.1%; 15–29, 28.3%; 30–44, 14.1%; 45–59, 9.2%; 60 and over 6.3%.
Population projection: (1990) 27,840,000; (2000) 36,509,000.
Doubling time: 21 years.
Ethnic composition (1982): Arab-Berber 99.1%; other 0.9%.
Religious affiliation (1982): Muslim (mostly Sunnī) 98.7%; Christian 1.1%.
Major cities (1984): Casablanca 2,600,000; Fès 852,000; Rabat 556,000.

Vital statistics

Birth rate per 1,000 population (1980–85): 44.1 (world avg. 29.0).
Death rate per 1,000 population (1980–85): 11.7 (world avg. 11.0).
Natural increase rate per 1,000 population (1980–85): 32.4 (world avg. 18.0).
Total fertility rate (avg. births per childbearing woman; 1980–85): 6.4.
Life expectancy at birth (1980–85): male 56.1 years; female 59.4 years.
Major causes of death per 100,000 population (1978)‡: ill-defined conditions and symptoms, and senility 137.2; parasitic and infectious diseases 80.5.

National economy

Budget (1986). Revenue: DH 55,420,000,000 (loans 38.7%). Expenditures: DH 68,310,000,000 (current 32.5%, investment 30.0%).
Public debt (external, outstanding; 1984): U.S.$10,169,200,000.
Tourism: receipts from visitors (1984) U.S.$440,000,000; expenditures by nationals abroad (1982) 83,000,000.
Production (metric tons except as noted). Agriculture, forestry, fishing (1984): wheat 1,989,000, barley 1,405,000, oranges 746,000, potatoes 550,000; livestock (number of live animals) 12,000,000 sheep, 4,500,000 goats, 3,300,000 cattle; roundwood 1,717,000 cu m; fish catch 461,182. Mining and quarrying (1984): phosphate rock 21,517,000; lead 143,655; zinc 20,247. Manufacturing (value in DH; 1985): foodstuffs 16,662,000,000; chemicals 9,450,000,000; textiles and leather 6,146,000,000. Construction (value added in DH; 1984): 4,714,808,000. Energy production (consumption): electricity (kW-hr; 1984) 6,617,000,000 (6,617,000,000); coal (metric tons; 1984) 820,000 (1,010,000); crude petroleum (barrels; 1984) 136,800 (33,516,000); petroleum products (metric tons; 1984) 3,996,000 (3,856,000); natural gas (cu m; 1984) 83,544,000 (83,544,000).
Gross national product (at current market prices; 1984): U.S.$14,340,000,000 (U.S.$630 per capita).

Structure of gross domestic product and labour force

	1984		1982	
	in value DH '000,000	% of total value	labour force	% of labour force
Agriculture	17,547	16.6	2,351,629	39.2
Mining	7,709	7.3	63,360	1.1
Manufacturing	17,360	16.4	930,615	15.5
Construction	6,903	6.5	437,464	7.3
Public utilities	1,486	1.4	22,465	0.4
Transp. and commun.	5,685	5.4	140,981	2.3
Trade	14,685	13.9	498.130	8.3
Finance	458	0.4	...	...
Pub. admin., defense	13,182	12.5	532,803	8.9
Services	13,504	13.0	474,109	7.9
Other	7,016	6.6	547,704	9.1
TOTAL	105,535	100.0	5,999,260	100.0

Population economically active (1982): total 5,999,260; activity rate of total population 29.6% (participation rates: over age 15, 47.9%; female 18.1%; unemployed 4.7%).

Price and earnings indexes (1980 = 100)

	1979	1980	1981	1982	1983	1984	1985
Consumer price index	91.4	100.0	112.5	124.4	132.1	148.5	160.0

Household income and expenditure. Average household size (1982) 5.9; income per household: n.a.; source of income: n.a.; expenditure (1981): food 54.0%, transportation 18.5%, housing 13.5%, clothing 8.5%.
Land use (1983): forested 11.6%; meadows and pastures 28.0%; agricultural and under permanent cultivation 18.8%; other 41.6%.

Foreign trade

Balance of trade (current prices)

	1980	1981	1982	1983	1984	1985
DH '000,000	−5,136	−7,406	−10,405	−8,173	−15,287	−16,424
% of total	21.0%	23.1%	29.5%	22.2%	28.6%	27.2%

Imports (1984): DH 34,396,000,000 (petroleum 24.4%; food, beverages, and tobacco 16.9%; vegetable oil 3.1%; chemical products 2.7%). *Major import sources:* France 18.3%; United States 12.5%; Saudi Arabia 12.1%.
Exports (1984): DH 19,110,000,000 (phosphates 24.2%; food, beverages, and tobacco 22.4%; phosphoric acid 18.4%; clothing 5.4%). *Major export destinations:* France 21.7%; Spain 7.5%; India 7.4%; West Germany 7.0%.

Transport and communications

Transport. Railroads (1984): route length 1,105 mi, 1,779 km; passenger-km 1,608,000,000; metric ton-km cargo 4,572,000,000. Roads (1984): total length 35,778 mi, 57,577 km (paved 45%). Vehicles (1983): passenger cars 470,239; trucks and buses 232,857. Merchant marine (1985): vessels (100 gross tons and over) 293; total deadweight tonnage 679,513. Air transport (1985): passenger-km 2,124,000,000; metric ton-km cargo 38,796,000; airports (1986) 13.
Communications. Daily newspapers (1985): total number 8; total circulation 282,000; circulation per 1,000 population 12.3. Radio (1985): 2,550,000 receivers (1 per 9.3 persons). Television (1985): 1,032,956 receivers (1 per 22.8 persons). Telephones (1983): 265,672 (1 per 86.9 persons).

Education and health

Education (1984–85)

	schools	teachers	students	student/teacher ratio
Primary (age 7–12)	3,443	73,038§	2,278,734	...
Secondary (age 14–21)	1,145	52,920§	1,419,595	...
Voc., teacher tr.	17 ‖	952	16,257	17.1
Higher	19¶	4,566	119,920	26.3

Educational attainment, (1982). Percent of population over age 5 having: no formal education 78.0%; Qur'anic education 5.0%; primary education 9.0%; secondary 5.0%; higher 0.7%; not specified 2.3%. *Literacy* (1980): total population over age 15 literate 7,655,000 (70.7%); males literate 4,459,000 (82.4%); females literate 3,196,000 (58.7%).
Health (1984): physicians 2,957 (1 per 7,727 persons); hospital beds 26,538 (1 per 805 persons); infant mortality rate per 1,000 live births (1975–80) 114.4.
Food (1980–82): daily per capita caloric intake 2,635 (vegetable products 93%, animal products 7%); 109% of FAO recommended minimum requirement.

Military

Total active duty personnel (1985): 149,000 (army 87.3%, navy 4.0%, air force 8.7%). *Military expenditure as percent of GNP* (1983): 8.2% (world 6.1%); per capita expenditure U.S.$55.

*Excludes area and population of the portion of the provincial territory in Moroccan-occupied Western Sahara. †Area is not available. Excludes population of the portion of the provincial territory in Moroccan-occupied Western Sahara. ‡Urban centres only. §Public schools only. ‖ Teacher's training establishments. ¶1982.

Mozambique

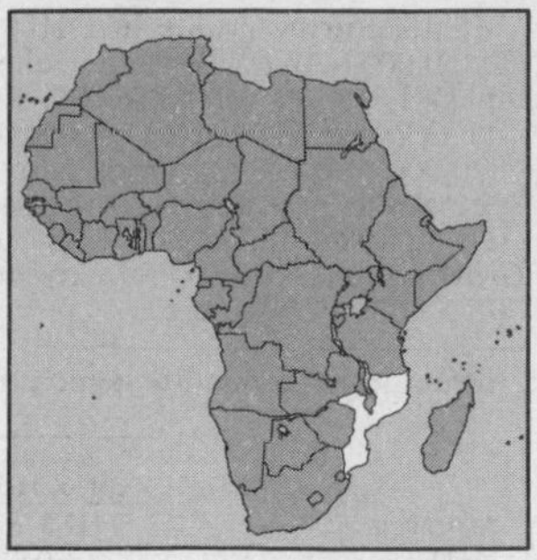

Official name: República Popular de Moçambique (People's Republic of Mozambique).
Form of government: people's republic with a single legislative house (People's Assembly [226]).
Chief of state and head of government: President.
Capital: Maputo.
Official language: Portuguese.
Official religion: none.
Monetary unit: 1 metical (Mt., plural meticais) = 100 centavos; valuation (Oct. 1, 1986) 1 U.S.$ = Mt. 40.05; 1 £ = Mt. 57.87.

Area and population

Provinces	Capitals	area* sq mi	area* sq km	population 1986 estimate
Cabo Delgado	Pemba	31,902	82,625	1,098,700
Gaza	Xai-Xai	29,231	75,709	1,158,200
Inhambane	Inhambane	26,492	68,615	1,166,000
Manica	Chimoio	23,807	61,661	749,500
Maputo	Maputo	9,944	25,756	574,800
Nampula	Nampula	31,508	81,606	2,808,300
Niassa	Lichinga	49,829	129,056	600,900
Sofala	Beira	26,262	68,018	1,245,000
Tete	Tete	38,890	100,724	971,300
Zambézia	Quelimane	40,544	105,008	2,922,300
City				
Maputo	—	232	602	882,800
TOTAL LAND AREA		303,623	786,380	14,177,900†
INLAND WATER		5,019	13,000	
TOTAL AREA		308,642†	799,380	

Demography

Population (1986 est.): 14,177,900.
Density‡ (1986): persons per sq mi 46.7, persons per sq km 18.0.
Urban-rural (1980): urban 13.2%; rural 86.8%.
Sex distribution (1985): male 48.77%; female 51.23%.
Age breakdown (1980): under 15, 43.7%; 15–29, 25.2%; 30–44, 16.0%; 45–59, 9.7%; 60–74, 4.6%; 75 and over, 0.8%.
Population projection: (1990) 15,696,000; (2000) 20,463,000.
Doubling time: 26 years.
Ethnic composition (1980): Makua 52.3%; Tsonga 23.6%; Malawi 12.0%; Shona 5.8%; Yao 3.2%; Swahili 0.7%; Makonde 0.5%; Portuguese 0.2%; other 1.7%.
Religious affiliation (1980): tribal religionist 47.8%; Muslim 16.5%; Christian 16.5%, of which Roman Catholic 14.3%; other 19.2%.
Major cities (1986): Maputo 882,800; Beira 269,700; Nampula 182,600.

Vital statistics

Birth rate per 1,000 population (1975–80): 47.1 (world avg. 30.0); (1974) legitimate 73.1%; illegitimate 26.9%.
Death rate per 1,000 population (1975–80): 20.6 (world avg. 12.0).
Natural increase rate per 1,000 population (1975–80): 26.5 (world avg. 18.0).
Total fertility rate (avg. births per childbearing woman; 1975–80): 6.4.
Marriage rate per 1,000 population (1974): 0.7.
Divorce rate per 1,000 population (1973): 0.01.
Life expectancy at birth (1975–80): male 42.1 years; female 45.0 years.
Major infectious diseases per 100,000 population (1980): measles 227.4; pulmonary tuberculosis 55.9; viral hepatitis 19.2; leprosy 13.8; cholera 4.6; tetanus 4.5.

National economy

Budget (1985). Revenue: Mt. 18,911,900,000 (indirect taxes 38.5%, direct taxes 34.5%, profits from state enterprises 9.0%). Expenditures: Mt. 25,490,300,000 (education 16.3%, health 7.1%).
Production (metric tons except as noted). Agriculture, forestry, fishing (1984): cassava 3,150,000, sugarcane 1,000,000, corn (maize) 330,000, sorghum 180,000, bananas 70,000, copra 65,000, peanuts (groundnuts) 70,000; livestock (number of live animals) 1,320,000 cattle, 19,000,000 chickens; roundwood 15,029,000 cu m; fish catch 42,440§. Mining and quarrying (1984): marine salt 28,000; hydraulic lime 10,000; copper 1,000; bentonite 500; garnet 12,000 kg. Manufacturing (1985): cement 75,800; sugar 23,600; feed 21,300; edible oils 3,800; soap 7,900; hoes 113,200 units; tires 125,000 units; inner tubes 69,800; beer 228,000 hectolitres. Construction (1974): residential 247,000 sq m; nonresidential 121,000. Energy production (consumption): electricity (kW-hr; 1984) 1,945,000,000 (1,540,000,000); coal (metric tons; 1984) 390,000 (440,000); crude petroleum (barrels; 1984) none (4,031,500); petroleum products (metric tons; 1984) 501,000 (485,000); natural gas, none (none).
Population economically active (1980): total 5,671,290; activity rate of total population 45.0% (participation rates: over age 15, 79.9%; female 52.4%; unemployed 1.7%).

Price and earnings indexes (1970 = 100)

	1971	1973	1975	1977
Consumer price index	115.7	130.6	164.2	195.5
Monthly earnings index	...	...	...	...

Household income and expenditure. Average household size (1980) 4.2; average annual income per household: n.a.; source of income: n.a.; expenditure: n.a.
Gross national product (at current market prices; 1981): U.S.$4,466,000,000 (U.S.$360 per capita).

Structure of gross domestic product and labour force

	1981 in value Mt. '000,000	1981 % of total value	1980 labour force	1980 % of labour force
Agriculture	64,374	40.0	4,754,831	83.8
Mining	684	0.4 }	346,794	6.1
Manufacturing	13,276	8.3 }		
Construction	8,925	5.6	42,121	0.7
Public utilities	2,168	1.3	‖	‖
Transportation and communication	6,032	3.8	77,025	1.4
Trade and finance	38,482	23.9	112,244	2.0
Pub. admin., defense	12,816	8.0 }	243,449 ‖	4.3 ‖
Services	...	... }		
Other	14,002	8.7	94,826	1.7
TOTAL	160,759¶	100.0	5,671,290	100.0

Public debt (external, outstanding; 1982): U.S.$583,000,000.
Tourism: n.a.
Land use (1983): forested 19.3%; meadows and pastures 56.1%; agricultural and under permanent cultivation 3.9%; other 20.7%.

Foreign trade

Balance of trade (current prices)

	1979	1980	1981	1982	1983	1984♀
Mt. '000,000	−10,264	−16,897	−18,392	−22,918	−20,286	−22,000
% of total	38.2%	48.2%	48.1%	57.0%	65.7%	64.7%

Imports (1985): Mt. 18,298,146,000 (foodstuffs 28.5%, crude petroleum and derivatives 16.3%, capital equipment 11.5%, machinery and spare parts 11.0%, chemicals 5.9%, metals 4.4%). *Major import sources:* U.S.S.R. 19.5%; South Africa 11.7%; United States 11.5%; France 5.7%; Italy 5.3%; The Netherlands 4.6%.
Exports (1985): Mt. 309,244,000 (shrimps 43.6%, cashew nuts 15.1%, sugar 8.9%, cotton fibre 7.0%, copra 6.6%, petroleum products 5.1%). *Major export destinations:* Spain 23.2%; United States 18.6%; Japan 16.3%; East Germany 12.4%; Portugal 5.6%.

Transport and communications

Transport. Railroads: track length (1984) 2,388 mi, 3,843 km; passenger-mi (1985) 140,057,000, passenger-km 225,400,000; short ton-mi cargo (1985) 198,359,000, metric ton-km cargo 289,600,000. Roads (1982): total length 16,200 mi, 26,000 km (paved, n.a.). Vehicles (1981): passenger cars 49,500; trucks and buses, n.a. Merchant marine (1985): vessels (100 gross tons and over) 101; total deadweight tonnage 36,240. Air transport (1984): passenger-mi 365,000,000, passenger-km 588,000,000; short ton-mi cargo 9,115,000, metric ton-km cargo 13,308,000; airports (1986) with scheduled flights 7.
Communications. Daily newspapers (1985): total number 2; total circulation 54,000; circulation per 1,000 population 3.8. Radio (1985): total number of receivers 450,000 (1 per 31 persons). Television (1985): total number of receivers 6,500 (1 per 2,165 persons). Telephones (1982): 56,000 (1 per 231 persons).

Education and health

Education (1984–85)

	schools	teachers	students	student/ teacher ratio
Primary (age 5–9)δ	4,649	20,286	1,311,014	64.6
Secondary (age 10–16)	202	3,377	135,068	40.0
Voc., teacher tr.	38	961	12,887	13.4
Higher	1	323	1,351	4.2

Educational attainment (1980). Percent of population over age 5 having: no schooling 83.0%; primary education 14.9%; secondary 1.9%; higher 0.2%. *Literacy* (1985): total population over age 15 literate 1,270,389 (16.6%); males literate 743,101 (20.0%); females literate 527,288 (13.3%).
Health (1985): physicians 317 (1 per 43,468 persons); hospital beds 12,472 (1 per 1,105 persons); infant mortality rate per 1,000 live births 101.0.
Food (1980–82): daily per capita caloric intake 1,864 (vegetable products 97%, animal products 3%); 80% of FAO recommended minimum requirement.

Military

Total active duty personnel (1985): 15,800 (army 88.6%, navy 5.1%, air force 6.3%). *Military expenditure as percent of GNP* (1982): 3.4% (world 6.0%); per capita expenditure U.S.$13.

*Total area is shown for the provinces. †Detail does not add to total given because of rounding. ‡Density is based on land area. §1983. ‖ Public utilities are included with services. ¶At current prices. ♀At 1983 prices. δIncludes initiation classes in which pupils learn Portuguese.

Nauru

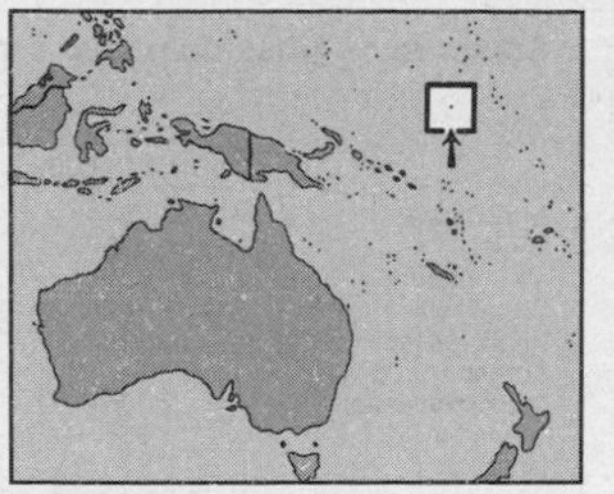

Official name: Naoero (Republic of Nauru).
Form of government: republic with one legislative house (Parliament [18]).
Head of state and government: President.
Capital: Yaren*.
Official language: Nauruan.
Official religion: none.
Monetary unit: 1 Australian dollar ($A) = 100 cents; valuation (Oct. 1, 1986) 1 U.S.$ = $A 1.59; 1 £ = $A 2.29.

Area and population

	area		population
Districts	sq mi	sq km	1983† census
Aiwo	0.4	1.1	812‡
Anabar	0.6	1.5	226
Anetan	0.4	1.0	265
Anibare	1.2	3.1	87
Baitsi	0.5	1.2	363
Boe	0.2	0.5	578
Buada	1.0	2.6	467
Denigomodu	0.3	0.9	2,600‡
Ewa	0.5	1.2	269
Ijuw	0.4	1.1	132
Meneng	1.2	3.1	1,024
Nibok	0.6	1.6	338
Uaboe	0.3	0.8	272
Yaren	0.6	1.5	559
TOTAL	8.2	21.2	8,043§

Demography

Population (1986): 8,400.
Density (1986): persons per sq mi 1,024.4, persons per sq km 396.2.
Urban-rural (1985): urban 100%; rural 0%.
Sex distribution‖ (1981): male 51.30%; female 48.70%.
Age breakdown‖ (1981): under 15, 43.8%; 15–24, 23.0%; 25–34, 13.7%; 35–44, 8.2%; 45–55, 6.1%; 55–64, 3.1%; 65 and over, 2.1%.
Population projection: (1990) 8,800; (2000) 10,100.
Doubling time: 52 years.
Ethnic composition¶ (1977): Nauruan 57.5%, of whom Eamwit 30.2%, Irvwa 25.2%, Eamwidamwit 17.7%; other Pacific islander 26.1%, of whom Gilbertese 67.9%, Tuvaluan 32.1%; Chinese 8.6%; European and other 7.8%.
Religious affiliation (1980): Nauruan Protestant Church (Congregational) 57.6%; Roman Catholic 24.0%; Confucian and Taoist 8.4%; Buddhist 1.7%; Bahā'ī 1.7%; nonreligious 6.6%.
Major cities: none.

Vital statistics

Birth rate per 1,000 population (1981): 24.0 (world avg. 29.0); legitimate, n.a.; illegitimate, n.a.
Death rate per 1,000 population (1981): 10.5 (world avg. 11.0).
Natural increase rate per 1,000 population (1981): 13.5 (world avg. 18.0).
Total fertility rate (avg. births per childbearing woman): n.a.
Marriage rate per 1,000 population‖ (1977): 6.3.
Divorce rate per 1,000 population‖ (1977): 0.3.
Life expectancy at birth‖ (1976–81): male 48.9 years; female 62.1 years.
Major causes of death per 100,000 population (1976–81)‖♀: accidents, suicide, and violence 116.0; diseases of the circulatory system 89.0; diseases of the digestive system 53.0; malignant neoplasms (cancers) 38.0; infectious and parasitic diseases 33.0.

National economy

Budget (1984–85). Revenue: $A 88,273,000♁ (no breakdown available). Expenditures: $A 88,130,600 (no breakdown available).
Public debt (external, outstanding): none.
Tourism: receipts from visitors, n.a; expenditures by nationals abroad, n.a.
Gross national product (at current market prices; 1981): U.S.$155,400,000 (U.S.$19,200 per capita).

Distribution of gross domestic product and labour force

	1982		1981	
	value in $A '000,000	% of total value	labour force	% of labour force
Agriculture	...	...	...	...
Mining	...	...	...	...
Manufacturing	...	...	...	...
Construction	...	...	...	...
Public utilities	...	...	...	...
Transportation and communications	...	...	...	...
Trade	...	...	...	...
Finance	...	...	...	...
Services	...	...	...	...
Pub. admin., defense	...	...	...	...
Other	...	...	...	...
TOTAL	100	100.0	4,769□	100.0

Production (metric tons except as noted). Agriculture, forestry, fishing (1985): coconuts 2,000, and noncommercial quantities of bananas, pineapples, and vegetables are produced, but most foodstuffs and beverages are imported; livestock (number of live animals) 2,000 pigs; roundwood, none; fish catch, n.a. (fish caught are for local consumption only). Mining and quarrying (1984): phosphate rock 1,636,000. Manufacturing: none. Construction (1977): 65 units. Energy production (consumption): electricity (kW-hr; 1984) 28,000,000 (28,000,000); coal, none (n.a.); crude petroleum, none (n.a.); petroleum products (metric tons; 1984) none (41,000); natural gas, none (n.a.).
Population economically active‖ (1981): total 1,758; activity rate of total population 35.2% (participation rates: over age 15, 61.5%; female, n.a.; unemployed, n.a.).
Price and earnings indexes: n.a.
Household income and expenditure. Average household size (1977) 8.0; average annual income per household: ◇; source of income: n.a.; expenditure: n.a.
Land use (1983): forested 40%; meadows and pastures, nil; agricultural and under permanent cultivation, nil; built-on, wasteland, and other *c.* 60%△.

Foreign trade

Balance of trade (current prices)

	1978	1979	1980	1981	1982	1983
$A '000,000	+42.9	+66.8	+81.6	+61.9	...	+98.6
% of total	65.4%	75.9%	59.2%	67.5%	...	57.4%

Imports (1979): $A 10,600,000 (food, fuel, water, machinery for phosphate industry, and building materials). *Major import sources:* Australia 58.0%; United Kingdom, New Zealand, and Japan.
Exports (1979): $A 77,400,000 (phosphate 100%). *Major export destinations* (1984): Australia 68.3%; New Zealand 27.4%; Philippines 2.3%; South Korea 1.5%; Japan 0.5%.

Transport and communications

Transport. Railroads (1985): length 3 mi, 5 km; (1983–84) passenger traffic, n.a.; short ton-mi cargo 4,670,000, metric ton-km cargo 6,820,000. Roads (1985): total length 12 mi, 19 km (paved 100%). Vehicles (1984): passenger cars, trucks, and buses 1,788. Merchant marine (1985): vessels 8; total deadweight tonnage, 93,391. Air transport (1982): passenger-mi 147,886,000, passenger-km 238,000,000; short ton-mi cargo 1,096,000, metric ton-km cargo 1,600,000; airports (1986) with scheduled flights 1.
Communications. Daily newspapers: none; 1 bimonthly, total circulation 750; circulation per 1,000 population, about 95. Radio (1985): total number of receivers 4,000 (1 per 2.1 persons). Television: no broadcast TV; videotaped television is commonplace, however. Telephones (1979): 1,500 (1 per 5.3 persons).

Education and health

Education (1985)

	schools	teachers	students	student/ teacher ratio
Primary (age 6–13)	7	102	1,451	14.2
Secondary (age 14–17)	2	36	465	12.9
Vocational	1	4	60	15.0
Teacher training (at second level)†	1	1	10	10.0
Higher	—	—	88⊕	—

Educational attainment. n.a. *Literacy* (1979): total population over age 15 literate 99.0%.
Health (1980): physicians, 11 (1 per 700 persons); hospital beds 200 (1 per 40.0 persons); infant mortality rate per 1,000 live births (1981) 31.2.
Food (1978–80): daily per capita caloric intake 3,202 (vegetable products 64%, animal products 36%); 120% of FAO recommended minimum requirement.

Military

Total active duty personnel (1985): Nauru does not have any military establishment. The defense is assured by Australia, but no formal agreement exists. There is a police force of about 57 Nauruans.

*Seat of government. †Preliminary. ‡Includes expatriates and their dependents. §Total includes 51 Nauruans unable to complete census forms; not distributable by district. ‖Nauruan population only. ¶According to 1983 preliminary census results, Nauruans constitute 63.8% of total population. ♀Average for the period. Of the 191 deaths during the six years, the leading specific causes by actual number were: motor vehicle accidents 31; viral hepatitis 17; acute cerebrovascular disease 16; diabetes mellitus 11; drownings 9; cirrhosis 8; diabetes 6. ♁Largely from phosphate exports. □The Nauruan economy is heavily dependent on contract immigrant labour, largely engaged in phosphate production. In 1981 Nauruans constituted only 36.9% of the employment structure (most of whom worked in the administrative-governmental sector); foreign contract labour as a percent of labour force included I-Kiribati 26.7%, Tuvaluans 17.0%, Chinese 8.0%, Filipinos 3.6%, and others 7.8%. Government employed 1,700 people, Nauru Phosphate Corporation employed 2,832 in 1981. ◇Individual landownership, distribution of phosphate royalties according to landownership, and sequential working of phosphate deposits have combined to produce considerable inequities in income distribution among Nauruans. Similar inequities exist between the Nauruans and the alien work force, especially the phosphate workers from Kiribati and Tuvalu. Minimum Nauruan annual salary was $A 4,503 in 1981. △About 80% of Nauru's land area is classified as phosphate-bearing, of which about 60% had been mined out by the early 1980s. †1980. ⊕Nauruans studying overseas at secondary and tertiary levels.

Nepal

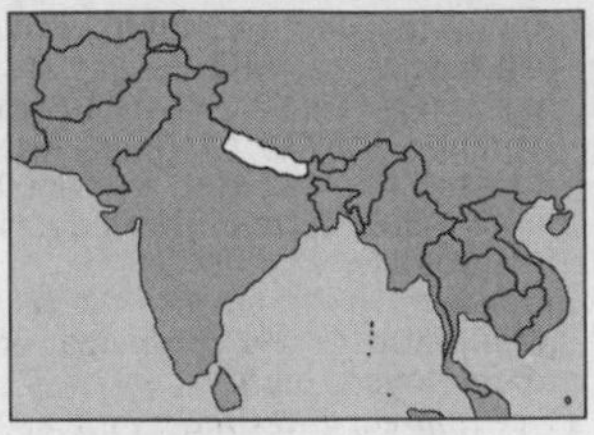

Official name: Nepāl Adhirājya (Kingdom of Nepal).
Form of government: constitutional monarchy with one legislative house (National Panchayat [140]).
Chief of state: King.
Head of government: Prime Minister.
Capital: Kāthmāndu.
Official language: Nepālī.
Official religion: none.
Monetary unit: 1 Nepalese rupee (NRs) = 100 paisa (pice); valuation (Oct. 1, 1986) 1 U.S.$ = NRs 20.50; 1 £ = NRs 29.62.

Area and population

Development regions / Geographic regions	Capitals	area sq mi	area sq km	population 1981 census
Eastern	Dhankūtā	10,987	28,456	3,708,923
Mountain				338,439
Hill				1,257,042
Tarai				2,113,442
Central	Kāthmāndu	10,583	27,410	4,909,357
Mountain				413,143
Hill				2,108,433
Tarai				2,387,781
Western	Pokharā	11,351	29,398	3,128,859
Mountain				19,951
Hill				2,150,939
Tarai				957,969
Mid-western	Surkhet	16,362	42,378	1,955,611
Mountain				242,486
Hill				1,042,365
Tarai				670,760
Far-western	Dipāyal	7,544	19,539	1,320,089
Mountain				288,877
Hill				604,336
Tarai				426,876
TOTAL		56,827	147,181	15,022,839

Demography

Population (1986): 16,863,000.
Density (1986): persons per sq mi 296.7, persons per sq km 114.6.
Urban–rural (1985): urban 8.0%; rural 92.0%.
Sex distribution (1981): male 51.22%; female 48.78%.
Age breakdown (1981): under 15, 41.4%; 15–29, 25.5%; 30–44, 17.4%; 45–59, 10.0%; 60–74, 4.7%; 75 and over, 1.0%.
Population projection: (1990) 18,469,000; (2000) 23,184,000.
Doubling time: 30 years.
Ethnic composition (1981): Nepalese 58.4%; Bihārī (including Maithilī and Bhojpurī) 18.7%; Tharu 3.6%; Tamang 3.5%; Newār 3.0%; other 12.8%.
Religious affiliation (1981): Hindu 89.5%; Buddhist 5.3%; Muslim 2.7%; Jain 0.1%; other 2.4%.
Major cities (1981): Kāthmāndu 235,160; Birātnagar 93,544; Lalitpūr 79,875; Bhaktapūr 48,472; Pokharā 46,642.

Vital statistics

Birth rate per 1,000 population (1985): 40.6 (world avg. 29.0).
Death rate per 1,000 population (1985): 17.6 (world avg. 11.0).
Natural increase rate per 1,000 population (1985): 23.0 (world avg. 18.0).
Total fertility rate (avg. births per childbearing woman; 1985): 6.0.
Marriage rate per 1,000 population: n.a.
Divorce rate per 1,000 population: n.a.
Life expectancy at birth (1984): male 47.2 years; female 45.7 years.
Major causes of death per 100,000 population: n.a.; however, major diseases include cholera, malaria, tuberculosis, and typhoid.

National economy

Budget (1984–85). Revenue: NRs 4,190,100,000 (taxes on goods and services 39.4%, customs duties 20.7%, income tax 10.7%, interest on loans 9.5%, registration taxes 6.9%, land revenue 6.3%, government services 5.5%). Expenditures: NRs 3,079,200,000 (loan repayment 22.5%, defense 17.2%, general administration 13.6%, social services 8.5%, economic services 6.9%, education 5.4%, revenue and economic administration 3.2%).
Tourism: receipts from visitors (1984) U.S.$32,000,000; expenditures by nationals abroad (1983) U.S.$20,000,000.
Production (metric tons except as noted). Agriculture, forestry, fishing (1985): rice 2,800,000, corn (maize) 710,000, wheat 534,000, potatoes 420,000, sugarcane 408,000, millet 125,000, jute 33,000, tobacco 6,000, milk (cow, buffalo, goat) 812,000, eggs 17,500; livestock (number of live animals) 7,500,000 cattle, 4,500,000 buffalo, 2,650,000 goats, 2,480,000 sheep, 400,000 pigs; roundwood 15,435,000 cu m; fish catch 2,112*. Mining and quarrying (1984): limestone 45,000; magnesite 14,603; talc 7,595; garnet 20,000 kilograms. Manufacturing (1983–84): jute 20,528; sugar 18,464; cement 10,355; cotton textiles 11,973,000 metres; synthetic textiles 3,639,000 metres; beer 27,840 hectolitres; cigarettes 3,709,000,000 units; shoes 68,000 pairs. Construction: n.a. Energy production (consumption): electricity (kW-hr; 1984) 350,000,000 (424,000,000); coal (metric tons; 1984) none (63,000); petroleum products (metric tons; 1984) none (107,000); natural gas, none (none).
Gross national product (at current market prices; 1984): U.S.$2,630,000,000 (U.S.$160 per capita).

Structure of gross domestic product and labour force

	1983–84 in value NRs '000,000	1983–84 % of total value	1981 labour force	1981 % of labour force
Agriculture	22,087	57.8	6,244,289	91.1
Mining	96	0.3	971	†
Manufacturing	1,650	4.3	33,029	0.5
Construction	2,502	6.6	2,022	†
Public utilities	140	0.4	3,013	†
Transportation and communication	2,306	6.0	7,424	0.1
Trade	1,355	3.5	109,446	1.6
Finance	8,048‡ (Finance, Services, Other)	21.1‡ (Finance, Services, Other)	9,850	0.1
Services			313,570	4.6
Other			127,272§	1.9§
TOTAL	38,184	100.0	6,850,886	100.0 ‖

Public debt (external, outstanding; 1985): U.S.$527,200,000.
Population economically active (1981): total 6,850,886; activity rate of total population 37.4% (participation rates: ages 15–64, 67.5%; female 22.6%; unemployed, n.a).

Price and earnings indexes (1980 = 100)

	1979	1980	1981	1982	1983	1984	1985
Consumer price index	87.2	100.0	111.1	124.1	139.5	143.4	155.0
Monthly earnings index	...	...	...	...	...	...	...

Household income and expenditure. Average household size (1981) 5.8; income per household (1973–74) NRs 791 (U.S.$75); sources of income (1973–74)¶: wages and salaries 39.2%, self-employment 33.6%, owner-occupied dwellings 17.5%; expenditure (1973–75)¶: food and beverages 48.0%, housing 20.0%, clothing and footwear 8.8%, fuel and power 4.2%, recreation 3.4%, education 3.2%.
Land use (1984): forested 32.5%; meadows and pastures 13.1%; agricultural and under permanent cultivation 17.0%; other 37.4%.

Foreign trade♀

Balance of trade (current prices)

	1980	1981	1982	1983	1984	1985
NRs '000,000	−2,947.5	−2,601.2	−3,827.2	−5,064.2	−4,411.4	−5,048.0
% of total	60.4%	42.9%	62.2%	65.0%	51.1%	46.3%

Imports (1983–84): NRs 6,514,300,000 (basic manufactured goods 27.7%; machinery and transport equipment 25.3%; mineral fuels 11.5%; food and live animals, chiefly for food 11.2%; chemicals 10.7%; miscellaneous manufactured articles 7.2%; crude materials except fuels 4.1%). *Major import sources:* India 46.9%; Japan 24.8%; South Korea 7.5%; Singapore 4.7%; United States 4.2%; Hong Kong 2.3%.
Exports (1983–84): NRs 1,703,900,000 (food and live animals, chiefly for food 34.3%; basic manufactures 32.6%; crude materials except fuels 21.8%; machinery, transport equipment, and other manufactured articles 4.9%; animal and vegetable oils 4.0%). *Major export destinations:* India 68.1%; United Kingdom 12.9%; United States 8.5%; Singapore 3.8%; Japan 3.0%.

Transport and communications

Transport. Railroads (1982–83): route length 32 mi, 52 km; passengers carried 114,500; freight handled 19,800 tons. Roads (1983–84): total length 3,485 mi, 5,608 km (paved 46%). Vehicles (1978): passenger cars 14,201; trucks and buses 9,988. Merchant marine: none. Air transport (1984): passenger-mi 186,000,000, passenger-km 300,000,000; short ton-mi cargo 3,041,000, metric ton-km cargo 4,440,000; airports (1986) with scheduled flights 6.
Communications. Daily newspapers (1983): total number 51; total circulation, n.a.; circulation per 1,000 population, n.a. Radio (1984): total number of receivers 310,000 (1 per 50 persons). Television: total number of receivers, n.a. Telephones (1984): 23,500.

Education and health

Education (1984–85)

	schools	teachers	students	student/teacher ratio
Primary (age 6–11)	11,660	46,484	1,747,857	37.6
Secondary (age 12–17)	4,631	17,069	454,511	26.6
Higher	69	3,654	48,229	13.2

Educational attainment (1981). Percent of adult population over age 25 having: no formal schooling 41.2%; primary education 29.4%; secondary 22.7%; higher 6.8%. ‖ *Literacy* (1981): total population over age 6 literate 2,833,440 (23.3%); males literate 2,117,030 (34.0%); females literate 716,410 (12.0%).
Health (1983–84): physicians 571 (1 per 28,270 persons); hospital beds 3,048 (1 per 5,296 persons); infant mortality rate per 1,000 live births (1985) 132.0.
Food (1981–83): daily per capita caloric intake 2,008 (vegetable products 93%, animal products 7%); 91% of FAO recommended minimum requirement.

Military

Total active duty personnel (1986): 30,000 (army 100.0%). *Military expenditure as percent of GNP* (1984): 1.3% (world 6.1%); per capita expenditure U.S.$2.

*1984. †Less than 0.1%. ‡Includes indirect taxes less subsidies. §Includes activities not adequately defined. ‖ Detail does not add to total given because of rounding. ¶For Kāthmāndu only. ♀Import figures are f.o.b. (free on board) in balance of trade and c.i.f. (cost, insurance, and freight) for commodities and trading partners.

Netherlands, The

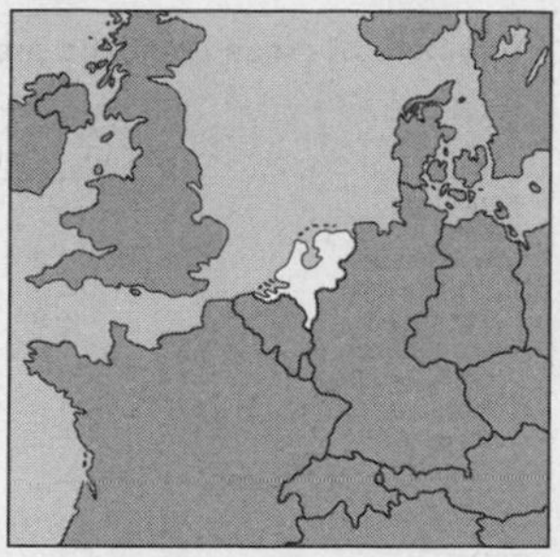

Official name: Koninkrijk der Nederlanden (Kingdom of The Netherlands).
Form of government: constitutional monarchy with two legislative houses (First Chamber [75]; Second Chamber [150]).
Chief of state: Monarch.
Head of government: Prime Minister.
Seat of government: The Hague.
Capital: Amsterdam.
Official language: Dutch.
Official religion: none.
Monetary unit: 1 Netherlands guilder (f.) = 100 cents; valuation (Oct. 1, 1986) 1 U.S.$ = f. 2.29; 1 £ = f. 3.31.

Area and population

		area		population
Provinces	Capitals	sq mi	sq km	1986 estimate*
Drenthe	Assen	1,025	2,654	432,000
Flevoland	Lelystad	548	1,420	177,300
Friesland	Leeuwarden	1,295	3,357	598,100
Gelderland	Arnhem	1,935	5,011	1,761,500
Groningen	Groningen	905	2,344	560,000
Limburg	Maastricht	838	2,170	1,088,300
Noord-Brabant	's-Hertogenbosch	1,910	4,946	2,124,600
Noord-Holland	Haarlem	1,031	2,672	2,322,700
Overijssel	Zwolle	1,289	3,339	998,800
Utrecht	Utrecht	514	1,331	944,400
Zeeland	Middelburg	691	1,790	355,800
Zuid-Holland	's-Gravenhage	1,123	2,908	3,164,600
TOTAL LAND AREA		13,105†	33,943†	14,529,400
INLAND WATER		3,028	7,842	
TOTAL AREA		16,133†	41,785†	

Demography

Population (1986): 14,582,000.
Density (1986): persons per sq mi 1,112.0, persons per sq km 429.4.
Urban–rural (1985): urban 88.5%; rural 11.5%.
Sex distribution (1985): male 49.46%; female 50.54%.
Age breakdown (1985): under 15, 19.7%; 15–29, 25.6%; 30–44, 22.4%; 45–59, 15.6%; 60–74, 11.7%; 75 and over, 5.0%.
Population projection: (1990) 14,783,000; (2000) 15,380,000.
Doubling time: n.a.; vital rates and net migration in near balance.
Ethnic composition (by nationality; 1984): Netherlander 96.1%; Turkish 1.1%; Moroccan 0.8%; German 0.3%; other 1.7%.
Religious affiliation (1984): Roman Catholic 36.2%; Dutch Reformed Church 18.1%; Reformed Churches 8.3%; other 2.7%; no religion 34.7%.
Major cities (1986): Amsterdam 679,100; Rotterdam 571,400; 's-Gravenhage 444,000; Utrecht 229,900; Eindhoven 190,800.

Vital statistics

Birth rate per 1,000 population (1985): 12.1 (world avg. 29.0); legitimate 92.3%; illegitimate 7.7%.
Death rate per 1,000 population (1985): 8.5 (world avg. 11.0).
Natural increase rate per 1,000 population (1985): 3.6 (world avg. 18.0).
Total fertility rate (avg. births per childbearing woman; 1984): 1.5.
Marriage rate per 1,000 population (1984): 5.7.
Divorce rate per 1,000 population (1984): 2.4.
Life expectancy at birth (1984): male 73.0 years; female 79.5 years.
Major causes of death per 100,000 population (1985): malignant neoplasms (cancers) 226.3, of which lung cancer 56.0; ischemic heart diseases 176.1; cerebrovascular diseases 80.9; accidents, poisoning, and violence 37.3.

National economy

Budget (1985). Revenue: f. 140,368,000,000 (income and corporate taxes 35.2%, natural gas royalties 10.9%, excise and import taxes 7.4%). Expenditures: f. 170,037,000,000 (social security and public health 18.7%, education and culture 17.1%, defense 7.9%).
Public debt (1985): U.S.$68,731,000,000.
Tourism (1984): receipts from visitors U.S.$1,531,000,000; expenditures by nationals abroad U.S.$3,014,000,000.
Production (metric tons except as noted). Agriculture (1985): sugar beets 6,955,000, potatoes 6,673,000, vegetables and melons 2,855,000, wheat 1,131,000; livestock (number of live animals) 5,248,000 cattle, 12,383,000 pigs, 814,000 sheep; roundwood 906,000 cu m; fish catch 503,275. Manufacturing (value of sales in f. '000,000; 1984): foodstuffs 73,300; synthetic fibres 41,400; petroleum products 31,200; electrical machinery 12,800; transport equipment 11,800. Construction (1982): residential 58,947,000 cu m; nonresidential 51,620,000 cu m. Energy production (consumption): electricity (kW-hr: 1984) 62,778,000,000 (62,421,000,000); coal (metric tons; 1984) none (9,900,000); crude petroleum (barrels; 1984) 21,140,000 (333,984,000); petroleum products (metric tons; 1984) 62,059,000 (34,943,500,000); natural gas (cu m; 1984) 77,251,000,000 (28,198,000,000).
Household income and expenditure. Average household size (1985) 2.6; income per household (1984) f. 74,500 (U.S.$23,200); sources of income: wages 40.0%, transfer payments 28.2%, self-employment 19.6%, other 12.2%; expenditure (1983): housing 31.8%, food 11.2%, clothing 4.7%.
Gross national product (at current market prices; 1984): U.S.$135,830,000,000 (U.S.$9,420 per capita).

Structure of gross domestic product and labour force

	1984			
	in value f. '000,000	% of total value	labour force	% of labour force
Agriculture	14,610	4.5	62,500	1.0
Mining	29,770	9.4	8,300	0.1
Manufacturing	56,720	17.8	932,500	15.4
Construction	20,610	6.5	338,600	5.6
Public utilities	5,520	1.7	46,400	0.8
Transportation and communication	20,870	6.6	304,900	5.0
Trade	47,650	15.0	730,800	12.1
Pub. admin., defense	46,260	14.5	293,400	4.8
Finance }	92,390	29.1	451,000	7.4
Services }			1,127,900	18.6
Other	−16,410‡	−5.1‡	1,758,700§	29.0§
TOTAL	317,990	100.0	6,055,000	100.0†

Population economically active (1984): total 6,055,000; activity rate of total population 42.0% (participation rates: ages 15–64, 59.9%; female 35.5%; unemployed 12.6%).

Price and earnings indexes (1980 = 100)

	1979	1980	1981	1982	1983	1984	1985
Consumer price index	93.9	100.0	106.7	113.0	116.2	120.0	122.7
Hourly earnings index	96.0	100.0	103.0	110.0	113.0	115.0	120.0

Land use (1983): forested 8.7%; meadows and pastures 33.7%; agricultural and under permanent cultivation 25.5%; other 32.1%.

Foreign trade

Balance of trade (current prices)

	1980	1981	1982	1983	1984	1985
f. '000,000	−2,813	9,704	12,453	12,410	17,792	18,284
% of total	1.0%	3.2%	4.0%	3.8%	4.8%	4.6%

Imports (1985): f. 215,467,000,000 (manufactured goods 26.3%; mineral fuels 22.3%, of which crude petroleum 14.1%; machinery and transport equipment 20.5%; foodstuffs, beverages, and tobacco 12.2%; chemicals 10.1%). *Major import sources:* West Germany 22.4%; Belgium–Luxembourg 12.3%; United Kingdom 10.0%; United States 8.3%; France 6.7%.
Exports (1985): f. 225,568,000,000 (mineral fuels 23.1%; manufactured goods 20.2%, of which metal products 6.0%; food and beverages 18.0%; chemical products 16.6%; machinery and transport equipment 14.6%). *Major export destinations:* West Germany 30.0%; Belgium–Luxembourg 14.1%; France 10.4%; United Kingdom 9.5%; Italy 5.8%.

Transport and communications

Transport. Railroads (1984): length 2,852 km; passenger-km 8,938,000,000; metric ton-km cargo 3,120,000,000 ‖. Roads (1984): total length 110,140 km (paved 86.5%). Vehicles (1984): passenger cars 4,772,000; trucks and buses 352,700. Merchant marine (1985): vessels (100 gross tons and over) 1,344; total deadweight tonnage 5,949,419. Air transport ‖ (1985): passenger-km 18,240,000,000; metric ton-km cargo 1,485,000,000; airports (1986) 6.
Communications. Daily newspapers (1984): total number 79; total circulation 4,500,000; circulation per 1,000 population 312. Radio (1985): total number of receivers 4,750,000 (1 per 3.1 persons). Television (1985): total number of receivers 4,454,000 (1 per 3.2 persons). Telephones (1983): 8,023,000 (1 per 1.8 persons).

Education and health

Education (1984–85)

	schools	teachers	students	student/teacher ratio
Primary (age 6–12)	9,467	75,998	1,193,338	15.8
Secondary (age 12–18)	1,409	53,375	822,615	15.4
Voc., teacher tr.	2,031	54,560	640,737	11.7
Higher	456	30,396	305,126	10.0

Educational attainment (1983). Percent of population ages 15–64 having: primary education 17.7%; secondary 65.2%; higher 17.1%. *Literacy* (1986): virtually 100% literate.
Health (1985): physicians 31,185 (1 per 465 persons); hospital beds 68,343 (1 per 212 persons); infant mortality rate per 1,000 live births 7.9.
Food (1980–82): daily per capita caloric intake 3,553 (vegetable products 57%, animal products 43%); 132% of FAO recommended minimum requirement.

Military

Total active duty personnel (1985): 105,975 (army 68.3%, navy 15.8%; air force 15.9%). *Military expenditure as percent of GNP* (1984): 3.2% (world 6.1%); per capita expenditure U.S.$274.

*January 1st estimate; includes about 1,300 persons having no fixed municipality of residence. †Detail does not add to total given because of rounding. ‡Imputed bank service charge. §Includes 758,000 unemployed persons. ‖ KLM (Royal Dutch Airlines) only.

Netherlands Antilles

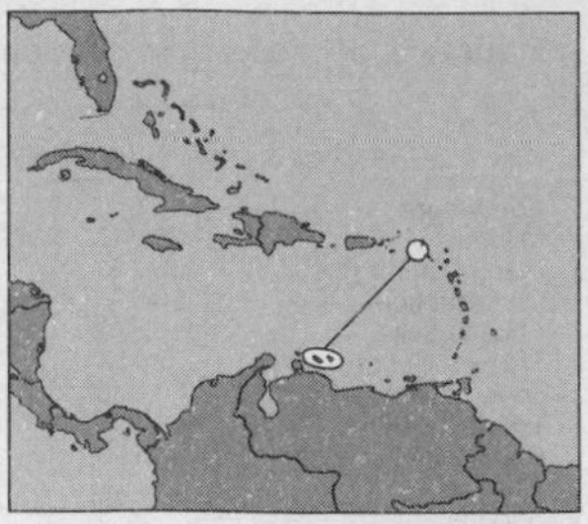

Official name: Nederlandse Antillen (Netherlands Antilles).
Political status: nonmetropolitan territory of The Netherlands with one legislative house (States of the Netherlands Antilles [22])*.
Chief of state: Dutch Monarch represented by the governor.
Head of government: Prime Minister.
Capital: Willemstad.
Official language: Dutch.
Official religion: none.
Monetary unit: 1 Netherlands Antillean guilder (NA f.) = 100 cents; valuation (Oct. 1, 1986) 1 U.S.$ = NA f. 1.80; 1 £ = NA f. 2.60.

Area and population

		area		population
Island councils	Capitals	sq mi	sq km	1981 census
Leeward Islands				
Bonaire	Kralendijk	111	288	8,753
Curaçao	Willemstad	171	444	147,388
Windward Islands				
Saba	The Bottom	5	13	965
Sint Eustatius or Statia	Oranjestad	8	21	1,358
Sint Maarten (Dutch part only)	Philipsburg	13	34	13,156
TOTAL		308	800	171,620

Demography

Population (1986): 176,000.
Density (1986): persons per sq mi 571.4, persons per sq km 220.0.
Urban-rural (1985)†: urban 92.4%; rural 7.6%.
Sex distribution (1981): male 48.25%; female 51.75%.
Age breakdown (1981): under 15, 30.0%; 15–29, 29.9%; 30–44, 19.5%; 45–59, 11.3%; 60–74, 6.7%; 75 and over, 2.6%.
Population projection: (1990) 178,000; (2000) 185,000.
Doubling time: 47 years.
Ethnic composition (1980)†: Netherlands Antillean (Dutch/Spanish/black/Amerindian) creole 84.0%; white 6.1%; other West Indian 4.9%; Suriname creole 2.9%; other 2.1%.
Religious affiliation (1981): Roman Catholic 83.8%; Protestant 10.2%, of which Lutheran/Reformed tradition 3.3%, Methodist 3.2%, Seventh-day Adventist 1.5%; Jewish 0.3%; nonreligious 2.6%; other 3.1%.
Major cities (1980): Willemstad (urban area) 100,000; Philipsburg 10,000.

Vital statistics

Birth rate per 1,000 population (1982): 20.7 (world avg. 29.0); legitimate 52.3%; illegitimate 47.7%‡.
Death rate per 1,000 population (1982): 5.5 (world avg. 11.0).
Natural increase rate per 1,000 population (1982): 15.2 (world avg. 18.0).
Total fertility rate (avg. births per childbearing woman; 1980–85): 3.5.
Marriage rate per 1,000 population (1982): 5.6.
Divorce rate per 1,000 population (1982): 2.8.
Life expectancy at birth (1981)§: male 71.1 years; female 75.7 years.
Major causes of death per 100,000 population (1983): diseases of the circulatory system 206.0; malignant neoplasms (cancers) 128.6; accidents 40.4; diseases of the digestive system 31.2; diseases of the respiratory system 27.1; nephritis and nephrosis 23.7.

National economy

Budget (1984). Revenue: NA f. 342,300,000 ‖ (tax revenue 50.7%, of which import duties 24.0%, foreign exchange commission 6.8%, gasoline tax 6.5%; revenue sharing transfers from island governments 28.7%; other 20.6%). Expenditures: NA f. 394,500,000¶ (current expenditures 97.9%; capital expenditures 2.1%).
Public debt (external, outstanding; 1983)†: U.S.$682,000,000♀.
Tourism: receipts from visitors (1984)ŏ U.S.$218,000,000, of which Sint Maarten U.S.$131,000,000, Curaçao U.S.$83,000,000, Bonaire U.S.$4,000,000; expenditures by nationals abroad (1981)† U.S.$63,000,000.
Production (metric tons except as noted). Agriculture, forestry, fishing (value of production in NA f. '000; 1982): eggs 3,863, fruits and vegetables 2,850□, pork 1,250, goat meat 555; livestock (number of live animals; 1984†) 23,000 goats, 9,000 cattle, 8,000 pigs, 8,000 sheep; roundwood, n.a.; fish 11,000. Mining and quarrying (1984): unrefined salt 230,000. Manufacturing (1982)†◇: heavy fuel oils 19,400,000; beer 134,000 hectolitres△; other manufactures include electronic parts, cigarettes, textiles, rum and curaçao liqueur. Construction: n.a. Energy production (consumption): electricity (kW-hr; 1984†) 2,380,000,000 (2,380,000,000); coal, none (none); crude petroleum (barrels; 1984†) none (149,900,000); petroleum products (metric tons; 1984†) 18,970,000 (2,291,000); natural gas, none (none).
Household income and expenditure. Average household size (1981) 4.2; average annual income per household: n.a.; source of income: n.a.; expenditure (1984)†⊕: food 22.1%, transportation and communication 19.4%, housing 18.8%, household supplies 10.0%, clothing and footwear 8.7%, recreation and education 5.9%, beverages and tobacco 2.3%, health 2.2%, other 10.6%.
Gross national product (at current market prices; 1982†): U.S.$1,370,000,000 (U.S.$5,870 per capita).

Structure of gross domestic product and labour force

	1980†		1981**	
	in value NA f. '000,000	% of total value	labour force	% of labour force
Agriculture	22.7 (with Mining)	0.9 (with Mining)	280	0.5
Mining			173	0.3
Manufacturing	543.3	22.3	6,408	11.2
Construction	188.2	7.7	5,147	9.0
Public utilities	40.9	1.7	1,213	2.1
Transportation and communication	361.1	14.8	4,599	8.0
Trade	511.8	21.0	14,145	24.8
Finance	289.0	11.9	3,896	6.8
Pub. admin., defense	402.4	16.5	21,150 (with Services)	37.0 (with Services)
Services	145.7	6.0		
Other	−69.2††	−2.8††	143	0.3
TOTAL	2,435.9	100.0	57,154	100.0

Population economically active (1981): total 70,162; activity rate of total population 40.9% (participation rates: ages 15–64, 63.6%; female 40.6%; unemployed [1985] 35.0%§).

Price and earnings indexes† (1980 = 100)

	1978	1979	1980	1981	1982	1983	1984
Consumer price index	78.3	87.2	100.0	112.2	119.0	122.4	125.0
Monthly earnings index‡‡	81.0	88.9	100.0	114.7	127.8	129.4	129.9

Land use (1983): forested, negligible; meadows and pastures, negligible; agricultural and under permanent cultivation 8.0%; other (dry savanna) 92.0%.

Foreign trade

Balance of trade (current prices)† §§

	1978	1979	1980	1981	1982	1983	1984
NA f. '000,000	−254	+74	+169	+328	...	+661	+239
% of total	2.3%	0.5%	0.9%	1.7%	...	4.3%	1.8%

Imports (1983)§ ‖ ‖ : NA f. 3,824,000,000 (crude petroleum 78.0%, basic and miscellaneous manufactures 7.0%, machinery and transport equipment 5.5%, food 4.6%, petroleum products 2.7%). *Major import sources* (1984): Venezuela 50.0%; Mexico 15.4%; United States 10.3%; Libya 3.9%; The Netherlands 3.4%.
Exports (1983)§: NA f. 2,951,000,000 (petroleum products 90.0%, crude petroleum 6.7%, organic chemicals 1.2%). *Major export destinations* (1984): United States 17.4%; Jamaica 9.3%; Puerto Rico 8.7%; Cuba 8.4%; The Netherlands 6.0%; Colombia 5.3%.

Transport and communications

Transport. Railroads: none. Roads (1984): total length 474 mi, 763 km (surfaced 100.0%). Vehicles (1982†): passenger cars 55,000; trucks and buses 8,000. Merchant marine vessels (100 gross tons and over) n.a. Air transport (1982)¶¶: passenger-mi 234,000,000, passenger-km 377,000,000; short ton-mi cargo 1,243,000, metric ton-km cargo 1,815,000; airports (1986) with scheduled flights 5.
Communications. Daily newspapers (1985): total number 4; total circulation 44,500; circulation per 1,000 population 255. Radio (1985)†: 160,000 receivers (1 per 1.5 persons). Television (1985)†: 58,000 receivers (1 per 4.1 persons). Telephones (1983): 48,000 (1 per 3.6 persons).

Education and health

Education (1983)

	schools	teachers	students	student/teacher ratio
Primary (age 6–12)	91	1,248	24,578	19.7
Secondary (age 12–17)	22	633	8,623	13.6
Voc., teacher tr.	3	79	732	9.3
Higher	1	53	677	12.8

Educational attainment (1981). Percent of population over age 15 having: no formal schooling or incomplete primary education 27.8%; completed primary 24.9%; completed vocational and secondary 36.1%; completed higher 0.8%; other 10.4%♀♀. *Literacy* (1985): total population over age 15 literate 95.0%.
Health (1985): physicians 184 (1 per 950 persons); hospital beds 1,500 (1 per 117 persons); infant mortality rate per 1,000 live births (1982) 8.4.
Food (1980–82)†: daily per capita caloric intake 2,735 (vegetable products 69%, animal products 31%); 113% of FAO recommended minimum requirement.

Military

Total active duty personnel (1984): A small Dutch naval contingent is stationed permanently in the Netherlands Antilles.

*Aruba withdrew from The Netherlands Antilles on Jan. 1, 1986, becoming an autonomous member of the Kingdom of The Netherlands, the same status as the whole of the Netherlands Antilles. †Includes Aruba. ‡Excludes Sint Eustatius. §Curaçao only. ‖ Excludes development aid from The Netherlands. ¶Excludes development projects. ♀Includes external long-term private debt not guaranteed by the government. ŏExcludes Saba and Sint Eustatius. □Mostly tomatoes, beans, cucumbers, gherkins, melons, and lettuce grown on hydroponic farms; aloe leaves, divi-divi pods, and sour orange fruit are non-hydroponic crops. ◇Curaçao's oil refinery was operational in mid-1986, but the oil refinery on Aruba was closed in early 1985. △1981. †Weights of consumer price index components. ⊕Curaçao and Bonaire only. **Employed persons only. ††Less imputed bank service charges. ‡‡Minimum wages in manufacturing as of January 1 of each year. §§Import and export figures are f.o.b. (free on board). ‖ ‖ Imports c.i.f. (cost, insurance, and freight). ¶¶ALM airlines only. ♀♀All population over age 15 attending school; educational attainment is unavailable for this group.

New Caledonia

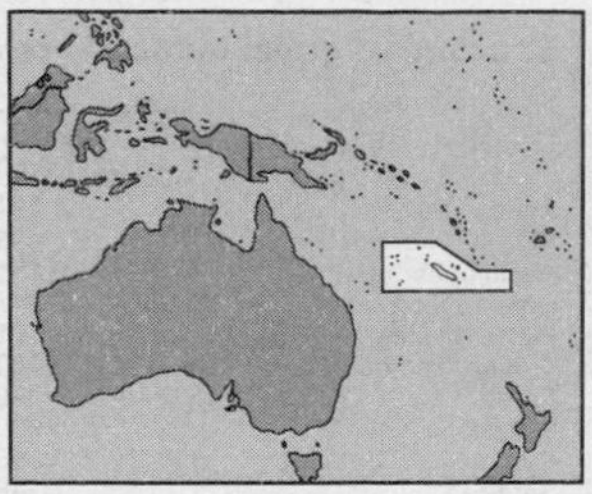

Official name: Territoire de la Nouvelle-Calédonie et Dépendances (Territory of New Caledonia and Dependencies).
Political status: overseas territory (France) with four autonomous regional councils forming one advisory legislative house (Territorial Congress [46])*.
Chief of state: President of France.
Head of government: High Commissioner (for France); President of Territorial Congress assisted by the presidents of the four autonomous regional councils (for New Caledonia)*.
Capital: Nouméa.
Official language: French.
Official religion: none.
Monetary unit: 1 franc of the Comptoirs français du Pacifique (CFPF) = 100 centimes; valuation (Oct. 1, 1986) 1 U.S.$ = CFPF 120.75; 1 £ = CFPF 174.48.

Area and population

		area		population
Regions	Capitals	sq mi	sq km	1983 census
Loyauté	...	765	1,981	15,510
Nord	...	2,837	7,348	21,512
Nouméa	Nouméa	637	1,650	85,098
Sud	...	2,995	7,757	23,248
TOTAL		7,233† ‡	18,734† ‡	145,368

Demography

Population (1986): 151,000.
Density (1986): persons per sq mi 20.9, persons per sq km 8.1.
Urban-rural (1983): urban 58.5%; rural 41.5%.
Sex distribution (1983): male 51.10%; female 48.90%.
Age breakdown (1983): under 15, 36.2%; 15–29, 26.9%; 30–44, 19.5%; 45–59, 11.2%; 60–74, 5.1%; 75 and over, 1.1%.
Population projection: (1990) 159,000; (2000) 180,000.
Doubling time: 40 years.
Ethnic composition (1983): Melanesian 42.6%; European 37.1%; Polynesian 12.2%, of which Wallisian 8.4%, Tahitian 3.8%; Indonesian 3.7%; Vietnamese 1.6%; other 2.8%.
Religious affiliation (1980): Roman Catholic 71.6%; Protestant 19.0%; nonreligious 4.5%; Sunnī Muslim 4.0%, other 0.9%
Major cities (1983)§: Nouméa 60,112; Mont-Doré 14,614; Dumbéa 5,538.

Vital statistics

Birth rate per 1,000 population (1984): 22.8 (world avg. 29.0); (1980) legitimate 57.5%; illegitimate 42.5%.
Death rate per 1,000 population (1984): 5.3 (world avg. 11.0).
Natural increase rate per 1,000 population (1984): 17.5 (world avg. 18.0).
Total fertility rate (avg. births per childbearing woman; 1980–85): 3.6.
Marriage rate per 1,000 population (1983): 5.7.
Divorce rate per 1,000 population (1983): 1.1.
Life expectancy at birth (1980–85): male 64.6 years; female 68.5.
Major causes of death per 100,000 population (1978): malignant neoplasms (cancers) 35.1; perinatal mortality 24.9; cerebrovascular diseases 24.1; heart diseases 13.9; cranial fractures 13.9.

National economy

Budget (1985). Revenue: CFPF 33,890,000,000 (indirect taxes 29.5%; French government grants 25.5%; direct taxes 16.3%; loans 8.6%). Expenditures: CFPF 33,890,000,000 (current expenditure 87.8%, of which repayment of loans and advances 28.9%, social and cultural services 28.3%, public debt 9.7%, public works 6.6%; capital expenditure 12.2%).
Public debt (external, outstanding; 1984 ‖): U.S.$201,000,000.
Production (metric tons except as noted). Agriculture, forestry, fishing (1985): coconuts 11,000¶, vegetables 3,800¶, bananas 2,000¶, potatoes 1,689, corn (maize) 1,638, yams 1,600♀, plantains 1,000¶, taro 900♀, coffee 520, sorghum 443, wheat 367; livestock (number of live animals; 1984) 100,000 cattle, 20,000 pigs, 10,000 horses; roundwood (1984) 12,000 cu m; fish catch (1983) 2,400, of which trochus shells 501. Mining and quarrying (1985): nickel ore 3,630,000 (ferronickel [metal content] 36,103, nickel matte [metal content] 8,905); chromite ore 149,496 (concentrate 78,820); cobalt (metal content) 280¶. Manufacturing (1984): corrugated iron sheets 3,147♂, beef 2,410♀, soap 362, coconut oil 263, beer 42,406 hectolitres♂. Construction (dwellings authorized; 1983): residential 40,900 sq m; nonresidential, n.a. Energy production (consumption): electricity (kW-hr; 1985) 1,120,000,000 (1,113,000,000); coal (metric tons; 1984) none (103,000); crude petroleum, none (none); petroleum products (metric tons; 1984) none (291,000); natural gas, none (none).
Population economically active (1983): total 58,154; activity rate of total population 40.0% (participation rates: ages 15–64, n.a.; female, n.a.; unemployed 6.0%).

Price and earnings indexes (1980 = 100)□

	1979	1980	1981	1982	1983	1984	1985
Consumer price index	89.3	100.0	115.9	131.3	145.8	156.2	164.3
Hourly earnings index	89.6	100.0	115.9	138.3	153.2	164.2	172.3

Land use (1983): forested 51.2%; meadows and pastures 13.3%; agricultural and under permanent cultivation 0.5%; other 35.0%.
Gross national product (at current market prices; 1983): U.S.$1,212,000,000 (U.S.$8,320 per capita).

Structure of gross domestic product and labour force

	1982		1983	
	in value CFPF '000,000	% of total value	labour force	% of labour force
Agriculture	1,820	1.7	19,700	33.9
Mining	13,476	12.5	7,244	12.5
Manufacturing	4,985	4.6		
Construction	6,782	6.3		
Public utilities	2,091	1.9	593	1.1
Transportation and communication	4,761	4.4	2,659	4.6
Trade	28,395◇	26.3	4,370△	7.5
Finance	16,900◇	15.6	1,025	1.7
Services			18,922△	32.5
Pub. admin., defense	27,791	25.7		
Other	1,092	1.0	3,641†	6.3
TOTAL	108,093	100.0	58,154	100.0†

Household income and expenditure. Average household size (1983) 4.1; average annual income per household (1980) CFPF 1,670,000 (U.S.$20,600); sources of income (1980): salaries 71.6%, welfare 5.1%, pensions 4.5%, other 18.8%; expenditure (1980): food 28.4%, transportation and communication 15.1%, housing 13.3%, energy 8.3%, recreation 6.4%, clothing and footwear 5.6%, household supplies 3.7%, health 2.6%, other 16.6%.
Tourism (1983): receipts from visitors U.S.$46,000,000⊕; expenditures by nationals abroad, n.a.

Foreign trade

Balance of trade (current prices)

	1980	1981	1982	1983	1984	1985
CFPF '000,000	−4,236	−7,734	−16,323	−18,971	−12,902	−11,993
% of total	6.4%	10.6%	22.9%	28.4%	14.9%	12.0%

Imports (1985): CFPF 55,931,000,000 (mineral products 25.6%, food 21.7%, transportation equipment 14.0%, machinery and electrical goods 9.9%). *Major import sources* (1984): France 39.9%; other EEC countries 12.0%; Australia 9.7%; United States 6.4%; Japan 5.0%.
Exports (1985) CFPF 43,938,000,000 (ferronickel and nickel matte 72.0%, nickel ore 11.4%, chromite 3.5%). *Major export destinations* (1984): France 58.6%; Japan 22.7%; United States 6.0%; Singapore 1.7%.

Transport and communications

Transport. Railroads: none. Roads (1983): total length 3,716 mi, 5,980 km (paved 13%). Vehicles (1984): passenger cars 35,000; trucks and buses 1,650. Merchant marine: vessels (100 gross tons and over) n.a. Air transport (1984)**: passengers arriving 118,774, passengers departing 119,307; cargo unloaded 3,811 metric tons, cargo loaded 1,670 metric tons; airports (1986) with scheduled flights 6.
Communications. Daily newspapers (1984): total number 1; total circulation 13,000; circulation per 1,000 population 88. Radio (1985): total number of receivers 80,000 (1 per 1.9 persons). Television (1984): total number of receivers 31,000 (1 per 4.7 persons). Telephones (1983): 32,578 (1 per 4.5 persons).

Education and health

Education (1985)

	schools	teachers	students	student/ teacher ratio
Primary (age 6–10)	263	1,529	31,589	20.7
Secondary (age 11–17)	45	976§	11,445	...
Vocational	28	309§	6,906	...
Higher	6	63	761	12.1

Educational attainment (1983). Percent of adult population over age 20 having: no formal schooling 17.4%; primary education 51.8%; secondary 25.9%; higher 4.8%. *Literacy* (1976): total population over age 13 literate 75,819 (89.4%); males literate 40,296 (90.1%); females literate 35,523 (88.7%).
Health (1983): physicians 194 (1 per 751 persons); hospital beds 1,224 (1 per 121 persons); infant mortality rate per 1,000 live births 11.2.
Food (1980–82): daily per capita caloric intake 2,821 (vegetable products 80%, animal products 20%); 106% of FAO recommended minimum requirement.

Military

Total active duty personnel (1985): 2,400 French troops. *Military expenditure as percent of GNP:* n.a.

*Interim governmental structure effective as of November 18, 1985. †Detail does not add to total given because of rounding. ‡Total area per new survey equals 7,172 sq mi (18,576 sq km); regional areas are not available. §Populations cited are for communes. ‖ Includes external long-term private debt not guaranteed by the government. ¶1984. ♀1983. ♂1981. □All figures are end of year. ◇Finance/Services includes restaurants and hotels. △Services/Pub. admin., defense includes restaurants and hotels. †Includes 3,500 unemployed. ⊕Number of visitors: (1983) 90,335; (1984) 91,512; (1985) 51,190. **Tontouta international airport only.

New Zealand

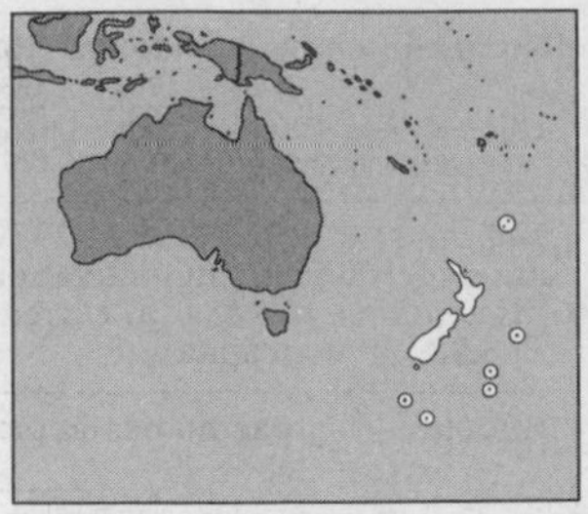

Official name: New Zealand.
Form of government: constitutional monarchy with one legislative house (House of Representatives [95]).
Chief of state: British Monarch, represented by governor-general.
Head of government: Prime Minister.
Capital: Wellington.
Official language: English.
Official religion: none.
Monetary unit: 1 New Zealand dollar ($NZ) = 100 cents; valuation (Oct. 1, 1986) 1 U.S.$ = $NZ 2.05; 1£ = $NZ 2.96.

Area and population

	area		population
Statistical areas*	sq mi	sq km	1985 estimate
North Island			
Central Auckland	2,155	5,581	894,000
East Coast	4,214	10,914	49,500
Hawke's Bay	4,359	11,289	152,800
Northland	4,885	12,653	124,400
South Auckland-Bay of Plenty	14,248	36,902	522,500
Taranaki	3,756	9,729	108,200
Wellington	10,721	27,766	587,700
South Island			
Canterbury†	16,826	43,579	422,200
Marlborough	4,278	11,080	37,200
Nelson	6,824	17,675	79,400
Otago	14,326	37,105	182,100
Southland‡	11,245	29,124	108,200
Westland	5,952	15,415	23,100
TOTAL	103,789	268,812	3,291,300

Demography

Population (1986): 3,280,400.
Density (1986): persons per sq mi 31.6, persons per sq km 12.2.
Urban-rural (1985): urban 83.7%; rural 16.3%.
Sex distribution (1986): male 49.66%; female 50.34%.
Age breakdown (1986): under 15, 23.3%; 15–29, 25.6%; 30–44, 21.2%; 45–59, 14.3%; 60–74, 11.3%; 75 and over, 4.3%.
Population projection: (1991) 3,485,000; (2001) 3,695,000.
Doubling time: 83 years.
Ethnic composition (1981): European 85.8%; Maori 8.9%; Pacific Island Polynesian 2.8%; other and not specified 2.5%.
Religious affiliation (1981): Anglican 25.7%; Presbyterian 16.5%; Roman Catholic 14.4%; Methodist 4.7%; other 38.7%.
Major cities (1985): Manukau 182,800; Christchurch 161,700; Auckland 143,600; Wellington 133,200; Waitemata 99,000.

Vital statistics§

Birth rate per 1,000 population (1985): 15.5 (world avg. 29.0); legitimate 76.2%; illegitimate 23.8%.
Death rate per 1,000 population (1985): 7.8 (world avg. 11.0).
Natural increase rate per 1,000 population (1985): 7.7 (world avg. 18.0).
Total fertility rate (avg. births per childbearing woman; 1986): 1.9.
Marriage rate per 1,000 population (1985): 7.5.
Divorce rate per 1,000 population (1984): 0.3.
Life expectancy at birth (1985): male 71.0 years; female 76.8 years.
Major causes of death per 100,000 population (1983): heart disease 270.1; malignant neoplasms (cancers) 184.1; cerebrovascular disease 91.1; accidents 39.6; pneumonia 39.5.

National economy

Budget (1984–85). Revenue: $NZ 12,539,100,000 (income tax 66.6%; customs, sales tax, and beer duty 20.5%; interest and profits 5.0%; highways tax 2.7%). Expenditures: $NZ 15,322,600,000 (social services 29.1%; debt services and investment 17.7%; health 12.5%; education 11.3%; development of industry 11.2%).
Public debt (external, outstanding; 1985): U.S.$12,409,500,000.
Tourism (1984): receipts from visitors U.S.$309,000,000; expenditures by nationals abroad U.S.$477,000,000.
Production (metric tons except as noted). Agriculture, forestry, fishing (1985): barley 644,400, fruits 397,000, wheat 309,600, potatoes 272,000, corn (maize) 174,600, oats 51,000; livestock (number of live animals) 67,854,000 sheep, 7,921,000 cattle, 454,000 pigs, 136,000 goats; roundwood (1984) 8,934,000 cu m; fish catch (1984) 143,058. Mining and quarrying (1984): limestone 3,718,700; aluminum 243,100; serpentine 76,900; lead 6,000; gold 21,605 troy oz. Manufacturing (value added, $NZ '000; 1981–82): food, beverages, and tobacco 1,540,430, of which meat 743,343, dairy products 242,801, wine 28,535; fabricated metal products, machinery, and equipment 1,444,158; paper and paper products 684,629; textiles, wearing apparel, and leather 612,657; chemicals and chemical, petroleum, coal, rubber, and plastic products 605,934; wood and wood products 395,378. Construction ($NZ '000; 1986): residential 1,715,988; nonresidential 1,648,095. Energy production (consumption): electricity (kW-hr; 1985) 26,765,000,000 (23,994,000); coal (metric tons; 1985) 2,408,500 (2,345,800); petroleum (barrels; 1984) 16,500,000 (25,039,300); petroleum products (metric tons; 1985) 3,345,000 (3,345,000); natural gas ‖ (cu m; 1985) 3,700,900,000 (2,880,920,000¶).
Gross national product (1984): U.S.$23,530,000,000 (U.S.$7,280 per capita).

Structure of gross domestic product and labour force

	1985		1984	
	in value $NZ '000,000	% of total value	labour force	% of labour force
Agriculture	4,291	11.0	143,000	10.4
Mining	435	1.1	5,000	0.4
Manufacturing	9,191	23.7	302,000	22.0
Construction	2,047	5.3	88,000	6.4
Public utilities	1,081	2.8	16,000	1.2
Transp. and commun.	3,280	8.5	103,000	7.5
Trade	7,098	18.3	221,000	16.1
Finance	5,880	15.2	99,000	7.2
Pub. admin., defense	4,380	11.3	302,000	22.0
Services	1,745	4.5		
Other	−699♀	−1.8♀	92,000♂	6.7♂
TOTAL	38,729□	100.0□	1,371,000	100.0□

Population economically active (1984): total 1,371,000; activity rate of total population 41.9% (participation rates: ages 15–64 [1981] 65.4%; female 35.2%; unemployed 5.7%).

Price and earnings indexes (1980 = 100)

	1980	1981	1982	1983	1984	1985	1986◇
Consumer price index	100.0	115.3	134.0	143.8	152.7	176.2	193.1
Weekly earnings index	100.0	119.0	133.0	134.0	137.0	149.0	155.0

Household income and expenditure. Average household size (1981) 3.2; income per household $NZ 15,810 (U.S.$13,755); source of income: n.a.; expenditure (1984): food 22.5%, transportation 19.3%, housing 18.5%, household durable goods 13.7%; clothing 6.8%, energy 2.8%, education 2.2%, health 1.4%.
Land use (1983): forested 38.3%; meadows and pastures 52.5%; agricultural and under permanent cultivation 1.7%; other 7.5%.

Foreign trade

Balance of trade (current prices)

	1980	1981	1982	1983	1984	1985
$NZ '000,000	+392.6	+383.6	+351.1	+811.5	+425.9	−868.5
% of total	3.7%	3.1%	2.4%	5.3%	2.5%	3.6%

Imports (1985): $NZ 12,472,600,000 (machinery and electrical equipment 20.3%; mineral fuels 12.4%, of which petroleum 7.7%; chemicals 10.7%; transport equipment 10.1%; iron, steel, and nonferrous metals 6.0%; textiles, clothing, and footwear 6.0%). *Major import sources:* Japan 20.2%; Australia 18.8%; United States 16.6%; United Kingdom 8.7%; West Germany 4.8%.
Exports (1985): $NZ 11,604,100,000 (food and live animals 45.2%, of which meat and meat preparations 19.7%, dairy products and eggs 12.6%; wool 12.7%; forest products 6.6%; chemicals 5.2%). *Major export destinations:* Australia 15.7%; Japan 14.3%; United States 14.3%; United Kingdom 8.9%; Iran 3.8%; U.S.S.R. 1.3%.

Transport and communications

Transport. Railroads (1984): length 2,692 mi, 4,332 km; passenger-mi 284,687,000, passenger-km 458,160,000; short ton-mi cargo 2,168,000,000, metric ton-km cargo 3,165,000,000. Roads (1984): total length 57,731 mi, 92,909 km (paved 53%). Vehicles (1985): passenger cars 1,534,064; trucks and buses 314,682. Merchant marine (1985): vessels (100 gross tons and over) 117; total deadweight tonnage 334,243. Air transport (1985): passenger-mi 4,857,143,000, passenger-km 7,816,828,000; short ton-mi cargo 725,679,000, metric ton-km cargo 1,059,540,000; airports (1986) with scheduled flights 36.
Communications. Daily newspapers (1984): total number 33; total circulation 1,055,000; circulation per 1,000 population 323. Radio (1985): total number of receivers 2,800,000 (1 per 1.2 persons). Television (1985): total number of receivers 938,228 (1 per 3.4 persons). Telephones (1983): 1,939,488 (1 per 1.7 persons).

Education and health

Education (1984)

	schools	teachers	students	student/teacher ratio
Primary (age 5–12)	2,503	18,583	459,009	24.7
Secondary (age 13–17)	330	12,949	228,621	17.7
Voc., teacher tr.	28	2,867	141,527	49.4
Higher△	7	2,958	33,875	11.5

Educational attainment (1981). Percent of population over age 15 having: no formal schooling 1.0%; primary education 14.9%; secondary 57.7%; vocational, postsecondary, and higher 26.4%. *Literacy* (1983): total population over age 15 literate 825,470 (100.0%).
Health (1984): physicians 7,750 (1 per 421 persons); hospital beds 31,621 (1 per 103 persons); infant mortality rate per 1,000 live births (1985) 10.8.
Food (1980–82): daily per capita caloric intake 3,492 (vegetable products 54%, animal products 46%); 136% of FAO recommended minimum requirement.

Military

Total active duty personnel (1985): 12,443 (army 43.6%, navy 21.6%, air force 34.8%). *Military expenditure as percent of GNP* (1983): 2.2% (world 6.1%); per capita expenditure U.S.$162.

*The statistical areas listed have no administrative significance; adjacent islands and land reclamations are included where appropriate. †Includes Chatham Island county. ‡Includes Stewart Island county. §Vital statistics figures are for December 1985. ‖Since 1979, data include manufactured gas. ¶1984. ♀Includes import duties less imputed bank service charges. ♂Includes unemployed. □Detail does not add to total given because of rounding. ◇Second quarter. △Universities only.

Nicaragua

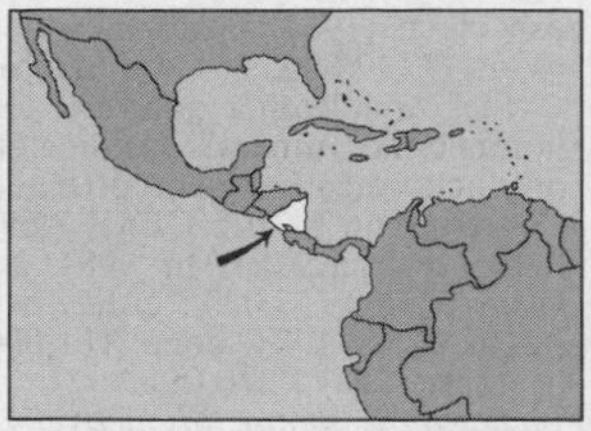

Official name: República de Nicaragua (Republic of Nicaragua).
Form of government: unitary multiparty republic with one legislative house (National Assembly [96]).
Head of state and government: President (coordinator of the junta).
Capital: Managua.
Official language: Spanish.
Official religion: none.
Monetary unit: 1 Nicaraguan córdoba (C$) = 100 centavos; valuation (Oct. 1, 1986) 1 U.S.$ = C$900.00;* 1 £ = C$1,301.

Area and population

Zones / Departments	Capitals	area† sq mi	area† sq km	population 1985 estimate
Atlantic				
Río San Juan	San Carlos	2,876	7,448	34,330
Zelaya	Bluefields	22,816	59,094	325,454
North Central				
Boaco	Boaco	1,924	4,982	97,432
Chontales	Juigalpa	1,910	4,947	111,786
Estelí	Estelí	849	2,199	115,333
Jinotega	Jinotega	3,697	9,576	143,264
Madriz	Somoto	756	1,958	80,268
Matagalpa	Matagalpa	2,623	6,794	263,649
Nueva Segovia	Ocotal	1,290	3,341	139,116
Pacific				
Carazo	Jinotepe	398	1,032	97,106
Chinandega	Chinandega	1,800	4,662	285,506
Granada	Granada	372	964	136,068
León	León	2,021	5,234	257,815
Managua	Managua	1,389‡	3,597‡	903,998‡
Masaya	Masaya	224	581	179,114
Rivas	Rivas	830	2,149	101,825
National District				
Distrito Nacional		‡	‡	‡
TOTAL LAND AREA		45,775	118,558	
INLAND WATER		3,588	9,291	
TOTAL AREA		49,363	127,849	3,272,064

Demography

Population (1986): 3,385,000.
Density (1986)§: persons per sq mi 73.9, persons per sq km 28.6.
Urban-rural (1985): urban 57.2%; rural 42.8%.
Sex distribution (1985): male 49.97%; female 50.03%.
Age breakdown (1985): under 15, 46.7%; 15–29, 27.5%; 30–44, 14.2%; 45–59, 7.5%; 60–74, 3.4%; 75 and over, 0.7%.
Population projection: (1990) 3,874,000; (2000) 5,428,000.
Doubling time: 21 years.
Ethnic composition (1980): mestizo (Spanish/Indian) 68.8%; white 14.0%; black 8.0%; Zambo (black/Indian) 5.0%; Amerindian 4.0%; other 0.2%.
Religious affiliation (1983): Roman Catholic 90.9%; Protestant 5.3%; other 3.8%.
Major cities (1985): Managua 682,111; León 100,982; Granada 88,636.

Vital statistics

Birth rate per 1,000 population (1984): 44.2 (world avg. 29.0).
Death rate per 1,000 population (1984): 9.7 (world avg. 11.0).
Natural increase rate per 1,000 population (1984): 34.5 (world avg. 18.0).
Total fertility rate (avg. births per childbearing woman; 1980–85): 5.9.
Marriage rate per 1,000 population (1984): 4.3.
Divorce rate per 1,000 population (1984): 0.4.
Life expectancy at birth (1982): male 56 years; female 60 years.
Major causes of death per 100,000 population (1978): heart disease 56.7; diarrheal diseases 37.3; accidents, poisoning, and violence 29.8; malignant neoplasms (cancers) 12.8.

National economy

Budget (1984). Revenue: C$11,459,800,000 (sales tax 41.2%, import duties 16.2%, social security 10.2%, property tax 7.8%). Expenditures: C$14,311,000,000 (goods and services 47.4% ‖, current transfers and subsidies 12.0% ‖, interest payments 4.6% ‖).
Tourism (1984): receipts from visitors U.S.$5,000,000; expenditures by nationals abroad U.S.$7,000,000 ‖.
Production (metric tons except as noted). Agriculture, forestry, fishing (1984): sugarcane 3,144,000, corn (maize) 216,000, bananas and plantains 213,000, rice 191,000, seed cotton 188,000, milk 125,000, sorghum 116,000, coffee 107,000, lint cotton 85,000, dry beans 60,000, cassava 28,000; livestock (number of live animals) 2,000,000 cattle, 540,000 pigs, 5,000,000 chickens; roundwood 3,491,000 cu m; fish catch 4,548 ‖. Mining and quarrying (1984): gold 32,666 troy oz; salt 20,000 ‖. Manufacturing (gross value in C$'000,000; 1983): processed foods 90,787; beverages 198,340; chemical products 314; petroleum products 413; textiles 442¶; footwear and clothing 256; metal products 115. Construction (1983): residential 20,300 sq m; nonresidential 26,800 sq m. Energy production (consumption): electricity (kW-hr; 1984) 973,000,000 (1,238,000,000); coal, none (n.a.); crude petroleum (barrels; 1984) none (3,151,900); petroleum products (metric tons; 1984) 437,000 (541,000); natural gas, none (n.a.).
Gross national product (at current market prices; 1984): U.S.$2,700,000,000 (U.S.$850 per capita).

Structure of gross domestic product and labour force

	1984 in value C$'000,000	1984 % of total value	1980 labour force	1980 % of labour force
Agriculture	10,785.3	23.5	391,963	45.4
Mining	349.6	0.8	6,568	0.7
Manufacturing	11,404.7	24.9	91,403	10.6
Construction	1,370.0	3.0	37,322	4.3
Public utilities	905.8	2.0	6,652	0.8
Transportation and communication	2,673.6	5.8	30,064	3.4
Trade	8,794.0	19.2	105,053	12.2
Finance	3,036.3	6.6	16,761	2.0
Pub. admin., defense	4,208.5	9.2	158,789	18.4
Services	2,296.3	5.0		
Other	...	...	19,352	2.2
TOTAL	45,824.1	100.0	863,925	100.0

Public debt (external, outstanding; 1985): U.S.$4,702,400,000.
Population economically active (1982): total 868,000; activity rate of total population 29.4% (participation rates: over age 15, 56.5%; female [1981] 22.6%; unemployed [1981] 13.4%).

Price and earnings indexes (1980 = 100)

	1979	1980	1981	1982	1983	1984	1985
Consumer price index	73.9	100.0	123.9	154.6	202.6	274.4	876.7
Hourly earnings index♀	77.7	100.0	125.1	...	...	...	...

Household income and expenditure. Average household size (1980) 6.9; average annual income per household: n.a.; sources of income (1978): wages and salaries 70.8%, property and entrepreneurial income 27.6%, other 1.6%; expenditure (1981): food 34.0%, housing 24.2%, clothing and footwear 24.0%.
Land use (1984): forested 20.3%; meadows and pastures 42.3%; agricultural and under permanent cultivation 12.2%; other 25.2%.

Foreign trade♂

Balance of trade (current prices)

	1979	1980	1981	1982	1983	1984
C$'000,000	+2,198.9	−3,735.4	−4,263.7	−3,196.6	−3,158.4	−3,626.5
% of total	26.5%	29.2%	29.4%	28.2%	27.9%	34.1%

Imports (1984): U.S.$790,975,000 (chemical and pharmaceutical products 12.6%; crude petroleum 12.3%; industrial machinery 10.3%; inedible agricultural products 7.6%; food products 6.7%; road motor vehicles 5.1%). *Major import sources:* United States 17.0%; Japan 7.5%; Guatemala 3.5%; Costa Rica 2.4%; Honduras 1.8%.
Exports (1984): U.S.$398,478,000 (cotton 33.7%; coffee 32.8%; traditional food products 12.5%; chemical products 4.4%; bananas 4.1%). *Major export destinations:* Japan 24.2%; United States 13.3%; Guatemala 3.9%; Costa Rica 3.7%.

Transport and communications

Transport. Railroads (1984): route length (1986) 153 mi, 247 km; passenger-mi 37,566,000, passenger-km 60,465,000; short ton-mi cargo 3,253,000, metric ton-km cargo 4,750,000. Roads (1984): total length 9,057 mi, 14,576 km (paved 11%). Vehicles (1982): passenger cars 24,887; trucks and buses 9,789. Merchant marine (1985): vessels (100 gross tons and over) 19; total deadweight tonnage 25,409. Air transport (1980): passenger-mi 47,000,000, passenger-km 76,000,000; short ton-mi cargo 3,800,000, metric ton-km cargo 5,500,000; airports (1986) with scheduled flights 1.
Communications. Daily newspapers (1985): total number 3; total circulation 149,000; circulation per 1,000 population 46. Radio (1985): 200,000 receivers (1 per 16 persons). Television (1985): 160,000 receivers (1 per 20 persons). Telephones (1984): 51,237 (1 per 57 persons).

Education and health

Education (1984)

	schools	teachers	students	student/ teacher ratio
Primary (age 7–12)	4,783	16,997	553,939	32.6
Secondary (age 13–18)	467	4,104	91,374	22.3
Voc., teacher tr.		1,954	70,471	36.1
Higher	16	2,666	33,062	12.4

Educational attainment (1971). Percent of adult population over age 25 having: no formal schooling 53.9%; primary or secondary education 37.4%; some postsecondary 4.4%. *Literacy* (1983): total population over age 15 literate 88.0%.
Health (1984): physicians 2,172 (1 per 1,456 persons); hospital beds 5,045 (1 per 627 persons); infant mortality rate per 1,000 live births 76.4.
Food (1979–81): daily per capita caloric intake 2,188 (vegetable products 84%, animal products 16%); 97% of FAO recommended minimum requirement.

Military

Total active duty personnel (1985): 62,850 (army 95.5%, navy 1.3%, air force 3.2%). *Military expenditure as percent of GNP* (1983): 10.2% (world 6.1%); per capita expenditure U.S.$97.

*Official rate only; the nonofficial rate is 66.7% higher. †Total land area only is shown for the departments and the national district; the total area (both land and water) is shown only in the grand total. ‡Distrito Nacional is included with Managua. §Based on land area. ‖1983. ¶1982. ♀Nonagricultural activities. ♂Import figures are f.o.b. (free on board) in balance of trade and c.i.f. (cost, insurance, and freight) for commodities and trading partners.

Niger

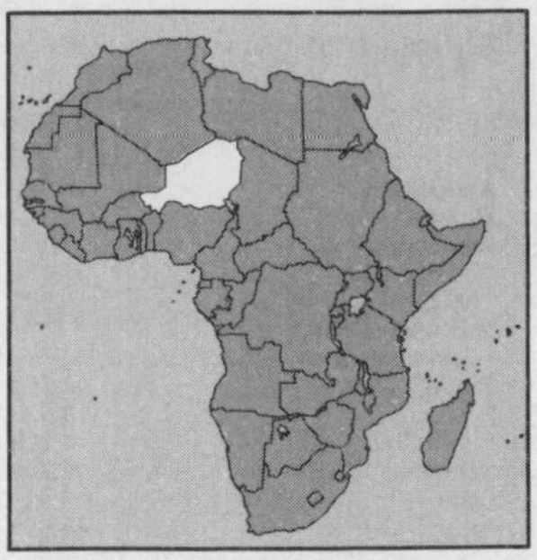

Official name: République du Niger (Republic of Niger).
Form of government: military government with one advisory body (National Development Council* [150]).
Head of state and government: President in conjunction with the Supreme Military Council.
Capital: Niamey.
Official language: French.
Official religion: none.
Monetary unit: 1 CFA franc (CFAF) = 100 centimes; valuation (Oct. 1, 1986) 1 U.S.$ = CFAF 332.05; 1 £ = CFAF 479.81.

Area and population

		area		population
Departments	Capitals	sq mi	sq km	1984 estimate
Agadez	Agadez	244,869	634,209	176,900
Diffa	Diffa	54,138	140,216	186,000
Dosso	Dosso	11,970	31,002	798,700
Maradi	Maradi	14,896	38,581	1,117,700
Niamey	Niamey	34,862	90,293	1,423,000
Tahoua	Tahoua	41,188	106,677	1,126,600
Zinder	Zinder	56,151	145,430	1,177,700
TOTAL		458,075†	1,186,408	6,006,600

Demography

Population (1986): 6,423,000.
Density (1986): persons per sq mi 14.0, persons per sq km 5.4.
Urban-rural (1985): urban 16.2%; rural 83.8%.
Sex distribution (1985): male 49.53%; female 50.47%.
Age breakdown (1985): under 15, 46.7%; 15–29, 25.6%; 30–44, 14.9%; 45–59, 8.0%; 60–74, 3.9%; 75 and over, 0.9%.
Population projection: (1990) 7,148,000; (2000) 9,339,000.
Doubling time: 26 years.
Ethnic composition (1980): Hausa 52.4%; Zerma 15.0%; Fulani 10.2%; Kanuri 9.0%; Songhai 8.0%; Tuareg 3.0%; Moors 1.9%; other 0.5%.
Religious affiliation (1983): Sunnī Muslim 97.5%; other 2.5%.
Major cities (1983): Niamey 399,100; Zinder 82,800; Maradi 65,100; Tahoua 41,900.

Vital statistics

Birth rate per 1,000 population (1980–85): 51.0 (world avg. 29.0).
Death rate per 1,000 population (1980–85): 22.9 (world avg. 11.0).
Natural increase rate per 1,000 population (1980–85): 28.1 (world avg. 18.0).
Total fertility rate (avg. births per childbearing woman; 1980–85): 7.1.
Marriage rate per 1,000 population: n.a.
Divorce rate per 1,000 population: n.a.
Life expectancy at birth (1980–85): male 40.9 years; female 44.1 years.
Major causes of death per 100,000 population (1976): malaria 317; measles 229; meningitis 145; other major diseases include bacillary dysentery and amoebiasis, typhoid fever, enteritis and other diarrheal diseases, avitaminoses and other nutritional deficiency diseases, tuberculosis of the respiratory system, and bronchitis.

National economy

Budget (1986). Revenue: CFAF 162,400,000,000 (external aid 51.1%, indirect taxes 29.5%, direct taxes 9.1%). Expenditures: CFAF 162,400,000,000 (capital expenses 49.3%, administration 16.6%, national debt 15.3%).
Public debt (external, outstanding; 1984): U.S.$677,900,000.
Tourism (1984): receipts from visitors U.S.$3,000,000; expenditures by nationals abroad, n.a.
Gross national product (at current market prices; 1984): U.S.$1,190,000,000 (U.S.$200 per capita).

Structure of gross domestic product and labour force

	1984		1981	
	in value CFAF '000,000	% of total value	labour force	% of labour force
Agriculture	268,200	43.6	1,481,000	87.2
Mining	53,600	8.7		
Manufacturing	25,400	4.1		
Construction	19,200	3.1		
Public utilities	10,300	1.7		
Transportation and communication	26,900	4.4	217,000	12.8
Trade and finance	83,000	13.5		
Pub. admin., defense	52,800	8.6		
Services	52,000	8.4		
Other	24,000	3.9		
TOTAL	615,400	100.0	1,698,000	100.0

Production (value of production in CFAF except as noted). Agriculture, forestry, fishing (1983–84): millet 2,712,000,000, beans 1,177,000,000, rice 426,000,000, cotton 390,000,000, sorghum 288,000,000, peanuts (groundnuts) 200,000,000, gum arabic 20,000,000; livestock (number of live animals; 1985) 7,530,000 goats, 3,530,000 cattle, 3,530,000 sheep, 505,000 asses, 414,000 camels, 290,000 horses; roundwood (1984) 3,807,000 cu m; fish catch (1984) 6,840 metric tons. Mining and quarrying (1984): uranium 97,712,000,000. Manufacturing (1980): food products 29,035,000,000; textiles and leather goods 15,298,000,000; metal products 6,420,000,000; nonmetallic mineral products (mostly cement) 4,280,000,000; chemical products (mostly plastic products) 4,280,000,000; beverages 2,791,000,000. Construction (1980): CFAF 75,937,000,000. Energy production (consumption): electricity (kW-hr; 1984) 245,000,000 (375,000,000); coal (metric tons; 1984) 55,000 (55,000); crude petroleum, none (n.a.); petroleum products (metric tons; 1984) none (181,000); natural gas, none (n.a.); uranium (metric tons; 1984) 3,276 (n.a.).
Population economically active (1982): total 1,745,000; activity rate of total population 30.2% (participation rates: ages 15–64, 51.0%; female, n.a.; unemployed, n.a.).

Price index (1980 = 100)

	1980	1981	1982	1983	1984	1985	1986‡
Consumer price index	100.0	122.9	137.2	133.8	145.0	143.7	150.0
Hourly earnings index§	100.0	107.3	107.2	107.3	107.3	...	...

Household income and expenditure. Average household size (1980) 5.2; average annual income per household: n.a.; sources of income (1977): self-employment 59.5%, family 30.1%, salary or wages 4.8%, employer 0.7%; (1983): food and beverages 50.5%, household expenses 19.1%, clothing 7.3%.
Land use (1984): forested 2.1%; meadows and pastures 7.3%; agricultural and under permanent cultivation 3.0%; other 87.6%.

Foreign trade

Balance of trade (current prices)

	1977	1978	1979	1980	1981	1982
CFAF '000,000	−8,900	−5,200	−2,800	−5,900	−14,900	−55,500
% of total	10.1%	3.9%	1.5%	2.4%	5.7%	19.8%

Imports (1982): CFAF 168,041,000,000 (food products 27.8%, of which cereals 13.9%, sugar and sugar products 5.5%; nonelectrical machinery 9.5%; petroleum products 9.3%; road vehicles 9.3%; chemical products 9.0%; cotton thread and fabrics 6.6%). *Major import sources:* France 31.1%; Nigeria 15.0%; Côte d'Ivoire 6.3%; United States 6.1%; West Germany 3.9%.
Exports (1982): CFAF 112,497,000,000 (uranium 80.6%; live animals 9.8%; cotton thread and fabrics 1.7%). *Major export destinations:* France 58.0%; Japan 14.5%; Nigeria 11.7%; Spain 4.4%.

Transport and communications

Transport. Railroads (1984): none‖. Roads (1984): total length 11,891 mi, 19,137 km (paved 17%). Vehicles (1984): passenger cars 23,102; trucks and buses 9,052. Air transport (1984)¶: passenger arrivals 49,828, passenger departures 47,448; cargo unloaded 4,318 metric tons, cargo loaded 1,261 metric tons; airports (1986) with scheduled flights 6.
Communications. Daily newspapers (1985): total number 1; total circulation 5,000; circulation per 1,000 population 0.8. Radio (1985): total number of receivers 160,000 (1 per 39 persons). Television (1985): total number of receivers 12,000 (1 per 521 persons). Telephones (1981): 9,320 (1 per 603 persons).

Education and health

Education (1980–81)

	schools	teachers	students	student/ teacher ratio
Primary (age 7–12)	1,664	5,518	228,855	41.5
Secondary (age 13–19)	64	1,371	32,892	24.0
Voc., teacher tr.	8	120	2,351	19.6
Higher♀	1	189	1,825	9.7

Educational attainment (1977). Percent of population over age 9 having: no formal schooling 88.6%; primary education 10.3%; secondary 0.9%; higher 0.2%. *Literacy* (1980): total population over age 15 literate 278,000 (9.8%); males literate 195,000 (14.0%); females literate 83,000 (5.8%).
Health: physicians (1980) 136 (1 per 40,209 persons); hospital beds (1979) 3,261 (1 per 1,633 persons); infant mortality rate per 1,000 live births (1980–85) 140.0.
Food (1981–83): daily per capita caloric intake 2,380 (vegetable products 93%, animal products 7%); 101% of FAO recommended minimum requirement.

Military

Total active duty personnel (1986): 2,270 (army 94.7%, air force 5.3%). *Military expenditure as percent of GNP* (1984): 0.7% (world 6.1%); per capita expenditure U.S.$2.

*The legislature (National Assembly) was suspended in 1974. In 1983 the National Development Council assumed the role of a constituent assembly. †Detail does not add to total given because of rounding. ‡July. §Guaranteed minimum wage for professionals. ‖Niger is a cofounder of the Common Benin-Niger Organization for Railroads and Transport, currently maintaining rail operations only in Benin, but having the purpose of extending rail services from the sea at Cotonou, Benin, to Dosso and, ultimately, Niamey, Niger. ¶Niamey airport only. ♀Université de Niamey.

Nigeria

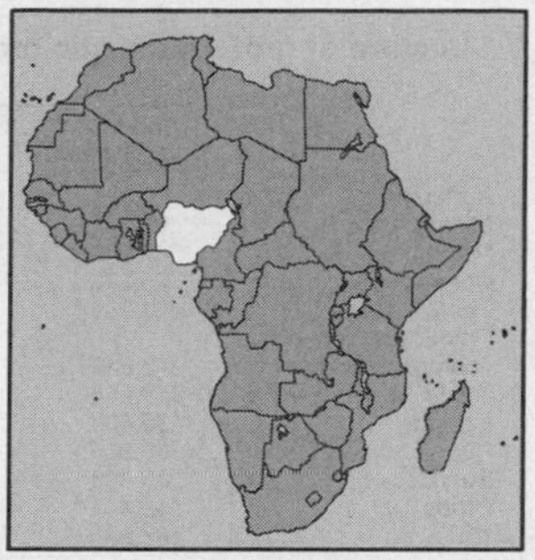

Official name: Federal Republic of Nigeria.
Form of government: federal republic (constitution suspended in part Dec. 31, 1983); temporarily governed under emergency powers by Armed Forces Ruling Council (AFRC).
Head of state and government: President.
Capital: Lagos (Capital designate: Abuja).
Official language: English.
Official religion: none.
Monetary unit: 1 Nigerian naira (₦) = 100 kobo; valuation (Oct. 1, 1986) 1 U.S.$ = ₦4.62; 1 £ = ₦6.68.

Area and population

		area		population
				1983
States	Capitals	sq mi	sq km	estimate
Anambra	Enugu	6,824	17,675	5,880,600
Bauchi	Bauchi	24,944	64,605	3,975,200
Bendel	Benin City	13,707	35,500	4,023,700
Benue	Makurdi	17,442	45,174	3,968,200
Borno	Maiduguri	44,942	116,400	4,901,000
Cross River	Calabar	10,516	27,237	5,686,800
Gongola	Yola	35,286	91,390	4,259,700
Imo	Owerri	4,575	11,850	6,004,900
Kaduna	Kaduna	27,122	70,245	6,700,800
Kano	Kano	16,712	43,285	9,442,000
Kwara	Ilorin	25,818	66,869	2,803,200
Lagos	Ikeja	1,292	3,345	2,733,500
Niger	Minna	25,111	65,037	1,953,100
Ogun	Abeokuta	6,472	16,762	2,535,900
Ondo	Akure	8,092	20,959	4,463,100
Oyo	Ibadan	14,558	37,705	8,516,700
Plateau	Jos	22,405	58,030	3,313,600
Rivers	Port-Harcourt	8,436	21,850	2,812,100
Sokoto	Sokoto	39,589	102,535	7,421,000
Federal Capital Territory		2,824	7,315	...
TOTAL		356,669*	923,768	91,395,100

Demography

Population (1986): 98,112,000.
Density (1986): persons per sq mi 275.1, persons per sq km 106.2.
Urban-rural (1985): urban 16.1%; rural 83.9%.
Sex distribution (1985): male 49.50%; female 50.50%.
Age breakdown (1985): under 15, 48.3%; 15–29, 25.8%; 30–44, 14.1%; 45–59, 7.8%; 60–74, 3.4%; 75 and over, 0.6%.
Population projection: (1990) 108,430,000; (2000) 139,200,000.
Doubling time: 28 years.
Ethnic composition (1980): Hausa 21.5%; Yoruba 21.2%; Igbo 18.4%; Fulani 11.2%; Ebe 5.6%; Kanuri 4.2%; Edo 3.4%; Nupe 2.5%; Tiv 2.2%; Ijaw 1.8%; Bura 1.7%; other 6.3%.
Religious affiliation (1980): Muslim 45.0%; Protestant 26.3%; Roman Catholic 12.1%; African indigenous 10.6%; tribal religionist 5.6%; other 0.4%.
Major cities (1983): Lagos 1,097,000; Ibadan 1,060,000; Ogbomosho 527,400; Kano 487,100; Oshogbo 344,500.

Vital statistics

Birth rate per 1,000 population (1980–85): 50.4 (world avg. 29.0).
Death rate per 1,000 population (1980–85): 17.1 (world avg. 11.0).
Natural increase rate per 1,000 population (1980–85): 33.3 (world avg. 18.0).
Total fertility rate (avg. births per childbearing woman; 1980–85): 7.1.
Marriage rate per 1,000 population: n.a.
Life expectancy at birth (1980–85): male 46.9 years; female 50.2 years.
Major causes of death per 100,000 population: n.a.; major diseases include malaria, tuberculosis, trypanosomiasis, onchocerciasis, and leprosy.

National economy

Budget (1986). Revenue ₦15,600,000,000 (traditional sources, including petroleum revenues 84.0%; import duties 6.4%; special funds 5.8%). Expenditures: ₦10,900,000,000 (recurrent expenditure 51.4%, of which debt service 10.7%, rural development 4.5%, education 4.1%, transportation 3.8%, police 1.9%, health 0.7%; capital expenditure 48.6%).
Public debt (1985): U.S.$13,015,600,000.
Tourism: receipts from visitors (1984) U.S.$102,000,000; expenditures by nationals abroad (1983) U.S.$454,000,000.
Production (metric tons except as noted). Agriculture, forestry, fishing (1984): cassava 11,800,000, millet 3,000,000, sorghum 3,000,000, corn (maize) 1,600,000, sugarcane 1,200,000, pulses 890,000, rice 800,000, palm oil 750,000, peanuts (groundnuts) 550,000, cacao 160,000, cotton lint 55,000; livestock (number of live animals) 11,800,000 cattle, 26,000,000 goats, 12,800,000 sheep; roundwood 92,042,000 cu m; fish catch 515,250†. Mining and quarrying (1984): limestone 867,133; cassiterite 1,768; tin metal 1,422. Manufacturing (value added in producers' prices ₦'000,000; 1980): beverages and tobacco 737.9; transport equipment 717.5, of which motor vehicles 688.7; chemical products 417.1, of which drugs and medicines 116.2; textiles 334.9; food products 315.7; rubber products 43.3. Construction (1978): residential ₦884,830,000; nonresidential ₦1,769,640,000. Energy production (consumption): electricity (kW-hr; 1984) 8,835,000,000 (8,700,000,000); coal (metric tons; 1984) 83,460 (50,000); crude petroleum (barrels; 1984) 500,404,000 (54,400,000); petroleum products (metric tons; 1984) 7,310,000 (9,125,000); natural gas (cu m; 1984) 5,638,000,000 (5,638,000,000).
Gross national product (at current market prices; 1984): U.S.$74,120,000,000 (U.S.$790 per capita).

Structure of gross domestic product and labour force

	1983–84		1985	
	in value ₦'000,000	% of total value	labour force	% of labour force
Agriculture	12,165.7	25.0	20,865,000	57.8
Mining	9,923.0	20.4	144,000	0.4
Manufacturing	2,372.5	4.9	6,570,000	18.2
Construction	3,268.3	6.7	433,000	1.2
Public utilities	460.3	0.9		0.2
Transp. and commun.	2,187.7	4.5	216,600	0.6
Trade	10,490.3	21.6	5,776,000	16.0
Other (including finance, pub. admin., defense, and services)	7,783.8	16.0	2,095,400	5.6
TOTAL	48,651.7*	100.0	36,100,000	100.0

Population economically active (1984): total 33,708,000; activity rate of total population 35.9% (participation rates: ages 15–64, 73.3%; female [1983] 39.8%; unemployed [registered] 0.5%).

Price and earnings indexes (1980 = 100)

	1979	1980	1981	1982	1983	1984	1985
Consumer price index	90.9	100.0	120.8	130.1	160.3	223.8	236.1
Earnings index‡	98.1	100.0	...	...	...	...	...

Household income and expenditure. Average household size (1982) 5.0; average annual income per household ₦2,600 (U.S.$3,875); sources of income (1979): self-employment 49.4%, wages and salaries 36.2%, interest 5.4%, rent 4.7%, transfer payments 4.3%; expenditures (1979): food 53.0%, of which beverages and tobacco 4.9%; fuel and light 11.4%, clothing 6.0%, transportation 4.7%, household goods 3.8%, other 21.1%.
Land use (1983): forested 15.4%; meadows and pastures 23.0%; agricultural and under permanent cultivation 33.4%; other 28.2%.

Foreign trade

Balance of trade (current prices)

	1980	1981	1982	1983	1984	1985
₦'000,000	+6,066	−511	−1,411	−447	+2,679	+4,132
% of total	27.2%	2.3%	7.9%	2.9%	17.3%	22.6%

Imports (1983): ₦9,723,000,000 (machinery and transport equipment 41.3%; manufactured goods 21.8% [important sectors include iron and steel products, textiles, paper products, and rubber products]; food and live animals 15.2%; chemicals 10.3%; mineral fuels 1.5%). *Major import sources:* United Kingdom 21.0%; United States 14.2%; West Germany 13.3%; France 12.5%; Japan 9.3%; The Netherlands 4.7%; Italy 4.4%.
Exports (1983): ₦7,612,300,000 (crude petroleum 96.4%; other important exports include cocoa, rubber, and palm kernels). *Major export destinations* (1982): United States 46.2%; The Netherlands 12.1%; France 10.1%; West Germany 6.6%; United Kingdom 2.3%; Ghana 1.2%.

Transport and communications

Transport. Railroads (1985): length 2,178 mi, 3,505 km; passenger-mi 1,275,000,000§, passenger-km 2,053,000,000§; short ton cargo handled 1,819,000, metric ton cargo handled 1,650,000. Roads (1984): total length 77,000 mi, 124,000 km (paved 48%). Vehicles (1981): passenger cars 262,550; trucks 90,731. Merchant marine (1985): vessels (100 gross tons and over) 191; total deadweight tonnage 607,095. Air transport (1983): passenger-mi 1,506,000,000, passenger-km 2,424,000,000; short ton-mi cargo 23,458,000, metric ton-km cargo 34,248,000; airports (1986) with scheduled flights 15.
Communications. Daily newspapers (1984): total number 15; total circulation 510,000§; circulation per 1,000 population 5.7§. Radio (1985): 6,000,000 receivers (1 per 16 persons). Television (1985): 500,000 receivers (1 per 193 persons). Telephones (1983): 708,365 (1 per 129 persons).

Education and health

Education (1982–83)

	schools	teachers	students	student/ teacher ratio
Primary (age 6–12)	37,692	424,717	15,021,100	35.4
Secondary (age 12–17)	5,498	78,117	2,421,625	31.0
Voc., teacher tr.	475	...	395,732	...
Higher	80	...	...	...

Educational attainment, n.a. *Literacy* (1985): total population over age 15 literate 20,208,000 (42.4%); males literate 12,551,000 (53.8%); females literate 7,657,000 (31.5%).
Health (1983): physicians 11,294 (1 per 8,059 persons); hospital beds 60,840 (1 per 1,496 persons); infant mortality rate per 1,000 live births 113.
Food (1980–82): daily per capita caloric intake 2,444 (vegetable products 95%, animal products 5%); 104% of FAO recommended minimum requirement.

Military

Total active duty personnel (1985): 94,000 (army 85.1%, navy 5.3%, air force 9.6%). *Military expenditure as percent of GNP* (1983): 2.5% (world 6.1%); per capita expenditure U.S.$19.

*Detail does not add to total given because of rounding. †1983. ‡For wages earned in nonagricultural activities only. §1982.

Norway

Official name: Kongeriket Norge (Kingdom of Norway).
Form of government: constitutional monarchy with one legislative house (Parliament [157]).
Chief of state: King.
Head of government: Prime Minister.
Capital: Oslo.
Official language: Norwegian.
Official religion: Evangelical Lutheran.
Monetary unit: 1 Norwegian krone (NKr) = 100 øre; valuation (Oct. 1, 1986) 1 U.S.$ = NKr 7.38; 1 £ = NKr 10.66.

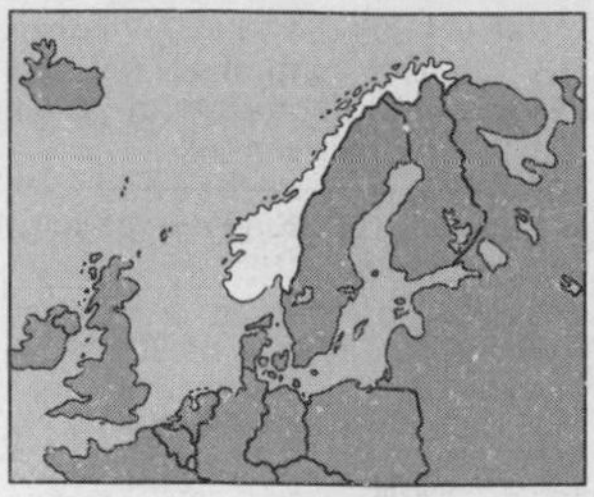

Area and population

Counties	Capitals	area* sq mi	area* sq km	population 1986† estimate
Akershus	—	1,898	4,917	393,217
Aust-Agder	Arendal	3,557	9,212	94,688
Buskerud	Drammen	5,763	14,927	219,967
Finnmark	Vardø	18,779	48,637	75,667
Hedmark	Hamar	10,575	27,388	186,355
Hordaland	Bergen	6,036	15,634	399,702
Møre og Romsdal	Molde	5,832	15,104	237,290
Nordland	Bodø	14,798	38,327	242,268
Nord-Trøndelag	Steinkjer	8,673	22,463	126,692
Oppland	Lillehammer	9,753	25,260	181,791
Oslo	Oslo	175	454	449,337
Østfold	Moss	1,615	4,183	234,941
Rogaland	Stavanger	3,529	9,141	323,365
Sogn og Fjordane	Leikanger	7,195	18,634	106,116
Sør-Trøndelag	Trondheim	7,271	18,831	246,824
Telemark	Skien	5,913	15,315	162,547
Troms	Tromsø	10,021	25,954	146,736
Vest-Agder	Kristiansand	2,811	7,281	140,232
Vestfold	Tønsberg	856	2,216	191,600
TOTAL		125,050	323,878	4,159,335‡

Demography

Population (1986): 4,166,000.
Density (1986): persons per sq mi 33.3, persons per sq km 12.9.
Urban-rural (1985): urban 80.3%; rural 19.7%.
Sex distribution (1985): male 49.45%; female 50.55%.
Age breakdown (1985): under 15, 20.2%; 15–29, 23.2%; 30–44, 20.9%; 45–59, 14.5%; 60–74, 14.7%; 75 and over, 6.5%.
Population projection: (1990) 4,214,000; (2000) 4,319,000.
Doubling time: n.a.; doubling time exceeds 100 years.
Ethnic composition (by country of citizenship; 1985): Norway 97.6%; Denmark 0.4%; United Kingdom 0.3%; United States 0.2%; Pakistan 0.2%; Sweden 0.2%; other 1.1%.
Religious affiliation (1980): Lutheran 87.9%; other 3.8%; nonreligious 3.2%.
Major cities (1986): Oslo 449,300; Bergen 207,900; Trondheim 134,400; Stavanger 95,100; Baerum 84,700; Kristiansand 62,600; Drammen 50,900.

Vital statistics

Birth rate per 1,000 population (1985): 12.4 (world avg. 29.0); (1984) legitimate 78.7%; illegitimate 21.3%.
Death rate per 1,000 population (1985): 10.6 (world avg. 11.0).
Natural increase rate per 1,000 population (1985): 1.8 (world avg. 18.0).
Total fertility rate (avg. births per childbearing woman; 1984): 1.7.
Marriage rate per 1,000 population (1984): 5.0.
Divorce rate per 1,000 population (1984): 1.9.
Life expectancy at birth (1984): male 72.9 years; female 79.6 years.
Major causes of death per 100,000 population (1984): ischemic heart disease 267.3; malignant neoplasms (cancers) 223.1; cerebrovascular disease 132.4.

National economy

Budget (1985). Revenue: NKr 160,767,000,000 (value added taxes 30.2%, taxes on petroleum income 21.7%, taxes on interest and dividends 12.8%, tax on petroleum extraction 8.1%, ordinary income tax 6.8%). Expenditures: NKr 123,071,000,000 (social security 22.3%, general subsidies 17.8%, public services 17.8%, defense 11.5%).
Tourism (1985): receipts from visitors U.S.$583,000,000; expenditures by nationals abroad U.S.$1,324,000,000.
Public debt (1983): U.S.$13,150,000,000.
Production (metric tons except as noted). Agriculture, forestry, fishing (1984): barley 700,000, oats 527,000, potatoes 470,000; livestock (number of live animals) 2,351,000 sheep, 976,100 cattle, 719,500 pigs; roundwood 9,553,000 cu m; fish catch (1984) 2,419,500, of which capelin 944,000, Atlantic cod 174,900, prawn and shrimp 85,600. Mining and quarrying (1985): iron ore 2,267,000§, titanium 661,000§, zinc 28,600§, copper 22,900§. Manufacturing (value added in NKr '000,000; 1984): machinery and equipment 20,404, of which transport equipment 5,255, electrical equipment 4,068; paper and paper products 9,021; food products 8,547; chemical products 7,256; wood and wood products 4,249. Construction (1983): residential 3,664,000 ‖ sq m; nonresidential 2,242,000 sq m. Energy production (consumption): electricity (kW-hr; 1985) 103,189,000,000 (87,750,000,000¶); coal (metric tons; 1985) 569,000 (777,000¶); crude petroleum (barrels; 1985) 286,610,000 (51,136,000¶); petroleum products (metric tons; 1985) 7,692,000 (6,042,000); natural gas (cu m; 1985) 26,667,000,000 (1,112,000,000¶).
Gross national product (at current market prices; 1984): U.S.$57,080,000,000 (U.S.$13,790 per capita).

Structure of gross domestic product and labour force

	1985 in value NKr '000,000	% of total value	labour force	% of labour force
Agriculture	17,874	3.6	144,000	7.0
Mining	97,281	19.5	23,000	1.1
Manufacturing	67,272	13.5	365,000	17.7
Construction	25,878	5.2	151,000	7.3
Public utilities	21,962	4.4	21,000	1.0
Transportation and communication	42,647	8.6	171,000	8.3
Trade	58,956	11.8	343,000	16.6
Finance	35,603	7.2	132,000	6.4
Pub. admin., defense	88,990	17.9		
Services	30,898	6.2	714,000♀	34.6
Other	10,474	2.1		
TOTAL	497,835	100.0	2,064,000	100.0

Population economically active (1985): total 2,064,000; activity rate of total population 49.7% (participation rates: ages 15–64 [1984] 74.6%; female [1984] 42.9%; unemployed 2.5%).

Price and earnings indexes (1980 = 100)

	1979	1980	1981	1982	1983	1984	1985
Consumer price index	89.1	100.0	113.6	126.2	141.1	149.9	154.2
Hourly earnings index	91.0	100.0	110.0	121.0	132.0	143.0	154.0

Household income and expenditure. Average household size (1982) 2.7; consumption expenditure per household NKr 88,000 (U.S.$13,600); sources of income: wages and salaries 63.0%, social security 18.8%, self-employment and property income 17.0%, other 1.2%; expenditure (1982): food 20.6%, transportation 17.5%, housing 13.1%, household furniture and equipment 8.7%, clothing 8.7%, recreation 8.2%.
Land use (1984): forested 27.1%; meadows and pastures 0.3%; agricultural and under permanent cultivation 2.8%; built-up and other 69.8%.

Foreign trade

Balance of trade (current prices)

	1980	1981	1982	1983	1984	1985
NKr '000,000	8,070	14,578	13,489	32,989	40,933	37,795
% of total	4.6%	7.5%	6.3%	14.4%	15.3%	11.1%

Imports (1985): NKr 132,549,000,000 (machinery and transport equipment 23.9%, of which road vehicles 9.2%; raw materials 16.7%, of which fuels 8.8%; metals and metal products 9.4%, of which iron and steel 3.8%; food products 5.3%, of which fruits and vegetables 1.4%). *Major import sources:* Sweden 17.9%; West Germany 16.1%; U.K. 10.0%; U.S. 7.2%.
Exports (1985): NKr 170,344,000,000 (fuels and fuel products 53.7%, of which crude petroleum 32.7%, natural gas 17.2%; metals and metal products 12.8%, of which aluminum 4.8%, iron and steel 3.1%; machinery and transport equipment 12.2%; food products 5.2%, of which fish and fish products 4.6%). *Major export destinations:* U.K. 35.8%; West Germany 15.6%; Sweden 8.8%; The Netherlands 6.1%.

Transport and communications

Transport. Railroads (1985): length 2,652 mi, 4,258 km; passenger-mi 1,387,000,000, passenger-km 2,232,000,000; short ton-mi cargo 2,006,000,000, metric ton-km cargo 2,928,000,000. Roads (1984): total length 52,216 mi, 84,033 km (paved 62%). Vehicles (1984): passenger cars 1,429,710; trucks and buses 214,051. Merchant marine (1985): vessels (100 gross tons and over) 2,219; total deadweight tonnage 25,721,469. Air transport (1984): passenger-mi 2,331,000,000, passenger-km 3,752,000,000; short ton-mi cargo 91,149,000, metric ton-km cargo 133,075,000; airports (1985) 41.
Communications. Daily newspapers (1984): total number 64; total circulation 1,882,000; circulation per 1,000 population 454. Radio (1985): total number of receivers 1,505,000 (1 per 2.8 persons). Television (1985): total number of receivers 1,339,369 (1 per 3.1 persons). Telephones (1985): 2,578,812 (1 per 1.6 persons).

Education and health

Education (1984–85)

	schools	teachers	students	student/ teacher ratio
Primary (age 7–15)	3,539	30,795	550,136	17.9
Secondary (age 14–18) and vocational	930	16,377	196,317	12.0
Higher	229	6,883	90,381	13.1

Educational attainment (1980). Percent of population over age 15 having: lower secondary education 56.8%; higher secondary 32.1%; graduated university or technical school 11.1%. *Literacy* (1985): virtually 100% literate.
Health: physicians (1983) 9,722 (1 per 425 persons); hospital beds (1985) 18,418 (1 per 161 persons); infant mortality rate per 1,000 live births (1984) 8.3.
Food (1980–82): daily per capita caloric intake 3,319 (vegetable products 62%, animal products 38%); 124% of FAO recommended minimum.

Military

Total active duty personnel (1985): 37,000. *Military expenditure as percent of GNP* (1984): 2.8% (world avg. 6.1%); per capita expenditure U.S.$376.

*Excludes Svalbard and Jan Mayen (24,360 sq mi [63,080 sq km]). †January 1. ‡Includes the Norwegian population of Svalbard and Jan Mayen registered as residents in municipalities on the mainland. §Metal content only. ‖1982. ¶1984. ♀Includes 52,000 unemployed.

Oman

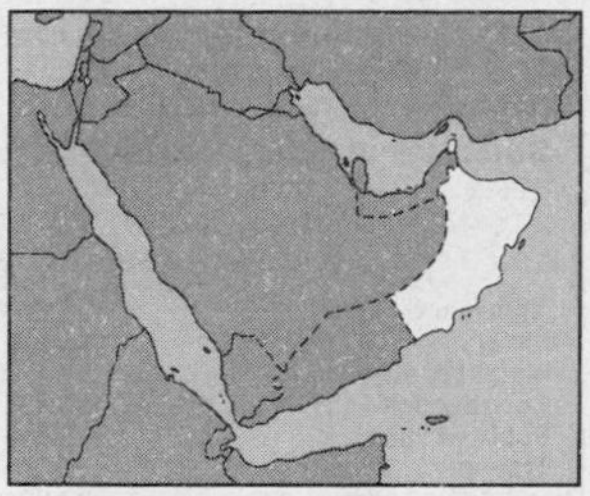

Official name: Salṭanat ʿUmān (Sultanate of Oman).
Form of government: monarchy with a consultative council (55) appointed by the Sultan.
Chief of state: Sultan.
Head of government: Prime Minister.
Capital: Muscat.
Official language: Arabic.
Official religion: Islam.
Monetary unit: 1 rial Omani (RO) = 1,000 baizas; valuation (Oct. 1, 1986) 1 RO = U.S.$2.60 = £1.80.

Area and population

	area*		population†
Region	sq mi	sq km	1986 estimate
Area			
Dhofar	40,000	100,000	...
Southern	...	...	...
Musandam (R'ūs al-Jibāl)	800	2,000	13,000
Musandam	...	...	...
Other	79,200	198,000	...
al-Baṭinah	...	...	...
al-Jaww and al-Buraymī	...	...	...
Dhahirah (aẓ-Ẓāhirah)	...	...	...
Capital	...	...	...
Eastern al-Ḥajar	...	...	...
Jaʿlān and Sur (Jaʿlān)	...	...	...
Sharqiyah	...	...	...
ʿUman Interior	...	...	...
Western al-Ḥajar	...	...	...
TOTAL	120,000	300,000	1,271,000

Demography

Population (1986): 1,271,000.
Density (1986): persons per sq mi 10.6, persons per sq km 4.2.
Urban-rural (1985): urban 8.8%; rural 91.2%.
Sex distribution (1985): male 52.85%; female 47.15%.
Age breakdown (1984): under 15, 44.1%; 15–29, 24.9%; 30–44, 18.1%; 45–59, 8.8%; 60–74, 3.5%; 75 and over, 0.6%.
Population projection: (1990) 1,430,000; (2000) 1,909,000.
Doubling time: 33 years.
Ethnic composition (1984): Omani Arab 77%; Indian 15%; Pakistani (mostly Baluchi) 3½%; Bengali 2½%; other 2%.
Religious affiliation (1984): Muslim 86%; Hindu 13%; other 1%.
Major city (1981): Muscat 50,000.

Vital statistics

Birth rate per 1,000 population (1980–85): 47.7 (world avg. 29.0).
Death rate per 1,000 population (1980–85): 16.7 (world avg. 11.0).
Natural increase rate per 1,000 population (1980–85): 31.0 (world avg. 18.0).
Total fertility rate (avg. births per childbearing woman; 1980–85): 7.1.
Marriage rate per 1,000 population: n.a.
Divorce rate per 1,000 population: n.a.
Life expectancy at birth (1980–85): male 48.7 years; female 50.9 years.
Major causes of death per 100,000 population: n.a; however, principal health problems and major infectious diseases include shigellosis, tuberculosis, influenza, malaria, and trachoma.

National economy

Budget (1985). Revenue: RO 1,873,000,000 (oil revenue 80.6%, customs duties 2.2%, gas revenue 2.0%, corporate income tax 1.4%, interest from investments 1.0%). Expenditures: RO 1,928,300,000 (defense 38.6%, financing of civil ministries 31.1%, development 27.7%).
Gross national product (1984): U.S.$7,380,000,000 (U.S.$6,250 per capita).

Structure of gross domestic product and labour force

	1985		1984	
	in value RO '000,000	% of total value	labour force‡	% of labour force‡
Agriculture	98.5	2.8	9,360	3.4
Mining	1,654.1	47.7	3,460	1.3
Manufacturing	111.1	3.2	5,558	2.1
Construction	242.3	7.0	226,172	84.0
Public utilities	36.8	1.1	185	0.1
Transp. and commun.	95.1	2.7	2,716	1.0
Trade	445.8	12.9	...	...
Finance	289.6	8.4	4,499	1.7
Pub. admin., defense	477.9	13.8 }	10,219	3.8
Services	35.3	1.0 }		
Other	−22.3§	−0.6§	7,241	2.6
TOTAL	3,464.2	100.0	269,410	100.0

Public debt (external, outstanding; 1984): U.S.$1,231,600,000.
Tourism (1983): receipts from visitors U.S.$4,248,000,000; expenditures by nationals abroad, n.a.
Household income and expenditure. Average household size (1980) 5.5; average annual income per household: n.a.; source of income: n.a.; food expenditure (1978): meat and eggs 20.6%, cereals 15.2%, fruits and nuts 12.4%, vegetables 11.9%, dairy products 10.3%, other foods 29.6%.
Production (metric tons except as noted). Agriculture, forestry, fishing (1984): vegetables and melons 182,000, fruit excluding melons 124,000, dates 75,000, bananas 35,000, tomatoes 14,000, limes 10,000, watermelons 10,000, onions 9,000, mangoes 4,000, tobacco leaf 2,000, wheat 1,000, roots and tubers 1,000, potatoes 1,000. livestock (number of live animals) 700,000 goats, 135,000 sheep, 125,000 cattle, 1,000,000 chickens; fish catch (1983) 108,766. Mining and quarrying (1982): stone 6,220,000; sand and gravel 1,343,000; marble 50,000; copper 12,000 ‖. Manufacturing (1985): major products include cement blocks and floors, furniture, aluminum products, household utensils, fertilizers, and fibreglass products. Construction (1983): number of residential buildings completed 418. Energy production (consumption): electricity (kW-hr; 1984) 1,675,000,000 (1,675,000,000); coal, none (none); crude petroleum (barrels; 1984) 152,110,000 (8,432,000); petroleum products (metric tons; 1984) 5,700,000 (5,333,000); natural gas (cu m; 1984) 5,781,450,000 (5,781,450,000).
Population economically active (1984): total 269,410; activity rate of total population 22.6% (participation rates: over age 15, 40.8%; female, n.a.; unemployed, n.a.).

Price and earnings indexes (1978 = 100)

	1978	1979	1980	1981	1982	1983	1984
Consumer price index¶	100.0	108.5	119.3	122.7	124.0	118.6	108.8
Monthly earnings index	...	...	...	...	...	...	...

Land use (1983): meadows and pastures 4.7%; agricultural and under permanent cultivation 0.2%; other (mostly desert and developed area) 95.1%.

Foreign trade

Balance of trade (current prices)

	1978	1979	1980	1981	1982	1983
RO '000,000	+224.8	+356.9	+696.3	+831.6	+600.4	+634.9
% of total	25.6%	29.3%	36.8%	34.5%	24.5%	29.2%

Imports (1984): RO 949,200,000 (transport equipment 18.6%, manufactured goods 15.5%, food 12.9%, petroleum products 1.3%). *Major import sources:* Japan 21.3%; United Arab Emirates 17.8%; United Kingdom 16.6%; West Germany 9.5%; United States 7.6%; The Netherlands 3.1%; France 2.9%; India 2.3%..
Exports (1984): RO 1,527,000,000 (crude petroleum 98.9%, fish 0.4%, copper 0.4%, fruits and vegetables 0.2%). *Major export destinations:* Japan 58.8%; Singapore 7.6%; United States 4.1%; United Kingdom 2.7%; Philippines 1.4%; France 0.7%.

Transport and communications

Transport. Railroads: none. Roads (1984): total length 14,071 mi, 22,646 km (paved 15%). Vehicles (1984): private vehicles 93,359; commercial vehicles 85,889. Merchant marine (1985): vessels (100 gross tons and over) 28; total deadweight tonnage 12,434. Air transport (1983)♀: passenger-mi 553,268,000, passenger-km 890,400,000; short ton-mi cargo 16,313,000, metric ton-km cargo 23,817,000; airports (1986) with scheduled flights 7.
Communications. Daily newspapers (1985): total number 2; total circulation 16,000; circulation per 1,000 population 17. Radio (1984): total number of receivers 800,000 (1 per 1.9 persons). Television (1984): total number of receivers 46,000 (1 per 32.6 persons). Telephones (1984): 23,391 (1 per 50.5 persons).

Education and health

Education (1985–86)

	schools	teachers	students	student/ teacher ratio
Primary (age 6–11)	351	7,109	177,685	25.0
Secondary (age 12–17)	290	4,840	48,828	10.1
Voc., teacher tr.	14	707	3,141	4.4
Higher	none	none	2,316ð	---

Educational attainment, n.a. *Literacy* (1979): total population over age 6 literate 38%; males literate 55%; females literate 20%.
Health (1985): physicians 581 (1 per 1,792 persons); hospital beds 2,565 (1 per 406 persons); infant mortality rate per 1,000 live births (1984) 113.4.
Food: daily capita caloric intake, n.a.

Military

Total active duty personnel (1985): 21,500 (army 76.7%, navy 9.3%, air force 14.0%); foreign troops 3,700. *Military expenditure as percent of GNP* (1983): 27.9% (world 6.1%); per capita expenditure U.S.$1,695.

*Cadastral areas have not been calculated. †No census has ever been taken in Oman; the total given is an unofficial estimate. For planning purposes the Omani government uses a 1985 estimate of 2,000,000. ‡Civilian employees and non-Omani workers only. §Less imputed bank service charges. ‖ 1984. ¶Applies to food and beverages in the capital area only. ♀International flights only. ðOmani students studying abroad.

Pakistan

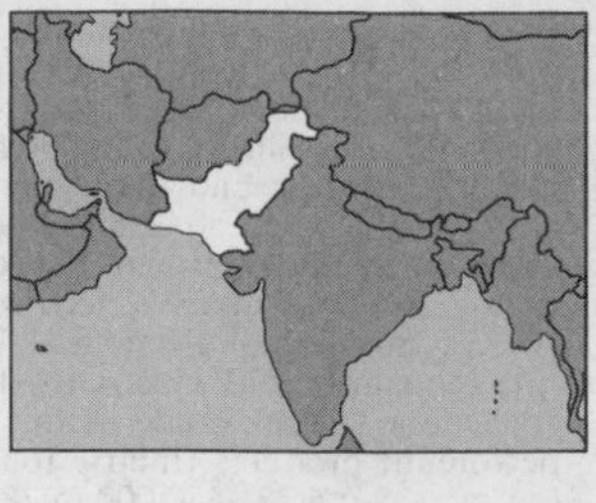

Official name: Islām-ī Jamhūrīya-e Pākistān (Islamic Republic of Pakistan).
Form of government: federal republic with two legislative houses (Senate [87]; National Assembly [237]).
Head of state and government: President (Chief Martial Law Administrator).
Capital: Islāmābād.
Official language: Urdū.
Official religion: Islam.
Monetary unit: 1 Pakistan Rupee (PRs) = 100 paisa; valuation (Oct. 1, 1986) 1 U.S.$ = PRs 17.01; 1 £ = PRs 24.58.

Area and population

		area		population
Provinces	Capitals	sq mi	sq km	1983 estimate*
Baluchistān	Quetta	134,050	347,188	4,611,000
North-West Frontier	Peshāwar	28,773	74,522	11,658,000
Punjab	Lahore	79,284	205,345	50,460,000
Sind	Karāchi	54,407	140,913	20,312,000
Federally Administered Tribal Areas	...	10,510	27,221	2,329,000
Federal Capital Area				
Islāmābād	...	350	906	359,000
TOTAL		307,374	796,095	89,729,000

Demography

Population (1986): 102,878,000*.
Density (1986): persons per sq mi 334.7, persons per sq km 129.2.
Urban-rural (1985): urban 29.8%; rural 70.2%.
Sex distribution (1981): male 52.47%; female 47.53%.
Age breakdown (1981): under 15, 45.2%; 15–29, 23.9%; 30–44, 15.0%; 45–59, 9.2%; 60–74, 5.1%; 75 and over, 1.6%.
Population projection: (1990) 113,558,000; (2000) 145,364,000.
Doubling time: 26 years.
Linguistic composition (1981): Punjābī 48.2%; Pashto 13.1%; Sindhī 11.8%; Saraiki 9.8%; Urdū 7.6%; other 9.5%.
Religious affiliation (1981): Muslim 96.7%; Christian 1.6%; Hindu 1.5%; other 0.2% .
Major cities (1981): Karāchi 5,208,100; Lahore 2,952,700; Faisalābād 1,104,200; Rāwalpindi 806,000; Hyderābād 795,000.

Vital statistics

Birth rate per 1,000 population (1985): 41.7 (world avg. 29.0).
Death rate per 1,000 population (1985): 14.6 (world avg. 11.0).
Natural increase rate per 1,000 population (1985): 27.1 (world avg. 18.0).
Total fertility rate (avg. births per childbearing woman; 1985): 5.6.
Marriage rate per 1,000 population (1975–80): 10.7.
Divorce rate per 1,000 population (1975–80): 0.3.
Life expectancy at birth (1985): male 52.0 years; female 50.2 years.
Major causes of death per 100,000 population: n.a.; however, major diseases include tuberculosis, cancer, poliomyelitis, typhoid, and dysentery.

National economy

Budget (1985–86). Revenue: PRs 88,897,000,000 (customs duties 29.1%, excise taxes 19.9%, income taxes 12.0%, general sales tax 6.1%). Expenditures: PRs 82,650,200,000 (national defense 40.0%, interest on public debt 27.1%, grants to provinces 8.7%, subsidies 8.7%, general administration 4.5%, education and health 3.8%).
Public debt (external, outstanding; 1985): U.S.$9,732,100,000†.
Tourism (1984): receipts from visitors U.S.$178,000,000; expenditures by nationals abroad U.S.$207,000,000.
Production (metric tons except as noted). Agriculture, forestry, fishing (1984–85): sugarcane 32,950,000, wheat 11,000,000, rice 3,457,000, cottonseed 1,800,000, corn (maize) 1,027,000, cotton 1,017,000, tobacco 79,600; livestock (number of live animals) 29,700,000 goats, 25,200,000 sheep, 16,500,000 cattle, 13,100,000 buffalo, 910,000 camels, 113,700,000 poultry; roundwood 19,952,000 cu m; fish catch 390,600. Mining and quarrying (1984–85): limestone 4,634,000; dolomite 120,867; fire clay 76,551; barite 20,827; feldspar 5,661; chromite 3,090; bauxite 2,035; magnesite 3,137. Manufacturing (1984–85): cement 4,698,000; chemical fertilizers 2,714,139, of which urea 1,814,666; steel products 718,485; chemicals 248,657; jute textiles 78,209; paper and paperboard 50,083; tea 46,916; cotton textiles 271,831,000 sq m; beverages 914,134,000 bottles; cigarettes 38,921,000,000 units; bicycles 462,604 units; road motor vehicles 83,646 units. Construction (value in PRs; 1983): residential 7,767,000,000; nonresidential 11,285,000,000. Energy production (consumption): electricity (kW-hr; 1984) 21,873,000,000 (21,873,000,000); coal (metric tons; 1984) 1,869,000 (1,868,000); crude petroleum (barrels; 1984) 4,771,800 (60,802,000); petroleum products (metric tons; 1984) 4,321,000 (5,291,000); natural gas (cu m; 1984) 8,897,000,000 (8,897,000,000).
Household income and expenditure. Average household size (1981) 6.7; income per household PRs 20,530 (U.S.$2,075); sources of income (1979): self-employment 53.1%, wages and salaries 30.7%, property 11.2%, other 5.0%; expenditure (1979): food 50.8%, housing 17.5%, clothing and footwear 9.6%, recreation 0.4%, other 21.7%.

Gross national product (at current market prices; 1984): U.S.$35,420,000,000 (U.S.$360 per capita).

Structure of gross domestic product and labour force

	1984–85			
	in value PRs '000,000	% of total value	labour force	% of labour force
Agriculture	105,663	24.7	14,490,000	50.7
Mining	5,912	1.4	27,000	0.1
Manufacturing	84,452	19.7	3,693,000	12.9
Construction	20,436	4.8	1,319,000	4.6
Public utilities	8,845	2.1	311,000	1.1
Transportation and communication	33,334	7.8	1,261,000	4.4
Trade	71,529	16.7	3,281,000	11.5
Finance	13,476	3.1	225,000	0.8
Pub. admin., defense	36,165	8.4	} 2,800,000	9.7
Services	35,575	8.3		
Other	12,792	3.0	1,189,000‡	4.2
TOTAL	428,179§	100.0	28,596,000	100.0

Population economically active (1983–84): total 27,740,000; activity rate of total population 28.4% (participation rates: over age 10, 46.1%; female 11.6%; unemployed 3.9%).

Price and earnings indexes (1980 = 100)

	1980	1981	1982	1983	1984	1985	1986‖
Consumer price index	100.0	111.9	118.5	125.8	134.1	141.9	147.4
Monthly earnings index	100.0	...	...	...	...	...	...

Land use (1983): forested 3.8%; meadows and pastures 6.4%; agricultural and under permanent cultivation 26.3%; built-on, wasteland, and other 63.5%.

Foreign trade¶

Balance of trade (current prices)

	1980	1981	1982	1983	1984	1985
PRs '000,000	–22,450	–22,374	–30,823	–23,475	–38,927	–42,029
% of total	30.2%	28.2%	35.3%	22.5%	35.1%	32.5%

Imports (1984–85): PRs 89,799,700,000 (mineral fuels and lubricants 24.2%, nonelectrical machinery 13.8%, transport equipment 8.7%, tea 3.9%, electrical goods 3.9%, iron and steel 3.7%, grains, pulses, and flour 3.1%, drugs and medicines 2.2%). *Major import sources:* Japan 13.4%; United States 12.3%; Saudi Arabia 10.7%; Kuwait 7.8%; United Kingdom 5.9%; West Germany 5.8%; Malaysia 5.5%.
Exports (1984–85): PRs 38,414,700,000 (cotton fabrics 12.1%, raw cotton 11.7%, cotton yarn 10.5%, ready-made garments and hosiery 8.9%, rice 8.7%, leather 6.2%, carpets and rugs 5.3%). *Major export destinations:* Japan 12.0%; United States 10.4%; Saudi Arabia 6.8%; United Kingdom 6.6%; West Germany 5.8%; Italy 4.1%; China 2.7%; Hong Kong 2.7%.

Transport and communications

Transport. Railroads (1985): route length 5,452 mi, 8,775 km; passenger-mi 11,065,000,000, passenger-km 17,808,000,000; short ton-mi cargo 4,932,000,000, metric ton-km cargo 7,200,000,000. Roads (1985): total length 62,954 mi, 101,315 km (paved 40%). Vehicles (1984): passenger cars 211,752; trucks and buses 66,722. Merchant marine (1985): vessels (100 gross tons and over) 77; total deadweight tonnage 654,682. Air transport (1985): passenger-km 6,891,631,000; metric ton-km cargo 291,262,000; airports (1986) with scheduled flights 30.
Communications. Daily newspapers (1984): total number 118; total circulation 1,991,000♀; circulation per 1,000 population 22♀. Radio (1984): total number of receivers 5,200,000 (1 per 18 persons). Television (1985): total number of receivers 1,055,089 (1 per 95 persons). Telephones (1985): 533,000 (1 per 200 persons).

Education and health

Education (1984–85)

	schools	teachers	students	student/ teacher ratio
Primary (age 5–9)	75,532	214,500	5,645,000	26.3
Secondary (age 10–14)	10,503	143,600	2,306,000	16.1
Voc., teacher tr.	270	4,070	55,000	13.5
Higher	647	25,214	148,797	5.9

Educational attainment (1981). Percent of population over age 10 having: no formal schooling 73.8%; primary education 10.2%; secondary 9.6%; some postsecondary 1.5%; higher degree 1.3%. *Literacy* (1981): total population over age 15 literate 11,938,790 (25.6%); males literate 8,709,162 (36.0%); females literate 3,229,628 (15.2%).
Health (1985): physicians (1986) 42,501 (1 per 2,426 persons); hospital beds 55,886 (1 per 1,796 persons); infant mortality rate per 1,000 live births 115.0.
Food (1980–82): daily per capita caloric intake 2,232 (vegetable products 89%, animal products 11%); 103% of FAO recommended minimum requirement.

Military

Total active duty personnel (1985): 482,800 (army 93.2%, navy 3.2%, air force 3.6%). *Military expenditure as percent of GNP* (1983): 5.4% (world 6.1%); per capita expenditure U.S.$20.

*Provincial estimates exclude and 1986 estimate includes Afghan refugees and residents of Pakistani-occupied Jammu and Kashmir. †As of June 30. ‡Includes unemployed. §At factor cost. ‖July. ¶Import figures are f.o.b. (free on board) in balance of trade and c.i.f. (cost, insurance, and freight) for commodities and trading partners. ♀1983.

Panama

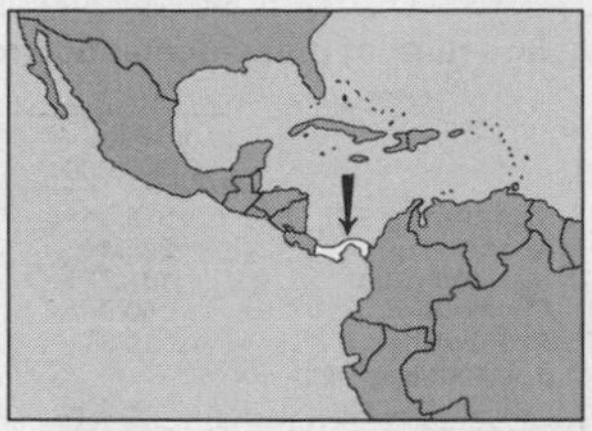

Official name: República de Panamá (Republic of Panama).
Form of government: multiparty republic with two legislative houses (Legislative Assembly [67]; National Assembly [505]).
Head of state and government: President.
Capital: Panama City.
Official language: Spanish.
Official religion: none.
Monetary unit: 1 balboa (B) = 100 cents; valuation (Oct. 1, 1986) 1 U.S.$ = B 1.00; 1 £ = B 1.45.

Area and population

		area*		population
Provinces	Capitals	sq mi	sq km	1986 estimate
Bocas del Toro	Bocas del Toro	3,443	8,917	75,400
Chiriquí	David	3,381	8,758	353,000
Coclé	Penonomé	1,944	5,035	161,700
Colón	Colón	1,915	4,961	160,200
Darién	La Palma	6,488	16,803	37,200
Herrera	Chitré	937	2,427	99,800
Los Santos	Las Tablas	1,493	3,867	81,000
Panamá	Panama City	4,642	12,022	1,012,200
Veraguas	Santiago	4,280	11,086	206,900
Special territory				
Comarca de San Blas	El Porvenir	1,238	3,206	39,800
TOTAL LAND AREA		29,341	75,992	2,227,300†
INLAND WATER		421	1,090	
TOTAL AREA		29,762†	77,082	

Demography

Population (1985): 2,227,300.
Density (1986): persons per sq mi 75.9, persons per sq km 29.3.
Urban-rural (1985): urban 52.0%; rural 48.0%.
Sex distribution (1983): male 51.02%; female 48.98%.
Age breakdown (1983): under 15, 38.7%; 15–29, 28.9%; 30–44, 16.5%; 45–59, 9.4%; 60–74, 5.1%; 75 and over, 1.4%.
Population projection: (1990) 2,420,000; (2000) 2,979,000.
Doubling time: 31 years.
Ethnic composition (1982): mestizo (and mulatto) 70%; white 12%; black 12%; Indian and other 6%.
Religious affiliation (1980): Roman Catholic 89.0%; Protestant 5.0%; Muslim 4.5%; Bahā'ī 1.0%; Hindu 0.3%; other 0.2%.
Major cities (1986): Panama City 434,668; San Miguelito 221,512; Colón 67,885; David 49,472‡.

Vital statistics

Birth rate per 1,000 population (1984): 26.3 (world avg. 29.0); (1980) legitimate 28.6%; illegitimate 71.4%.
Death rate per 1,000 population (1984): 3.9 (world avg. 11.0).
Natural increase rate per 1,000 population (1984): 22.4 (world avg. 18.0).
Total fertility rate (avg. births per childbearing woman; 1980–85): 3.6.
Marriage rate per 1,000 population (1984): 4.7.
Divorce rate per 1,000 population (1984): 0.4.
Life expectancy at birth (1980–85): male 69.2 years; female 72.9 years.
Major causes of death per 100,000 population (1983): heart disease 68.3, of which acute myocardial infarction 26.5; malignant neoplasms (cancers) 48.8; accident, suicide, homicide, and other violence 44.9, of which motor vehicle traffic accidents 14.1; cerebrovascular disease and atherosclerosis 38.9; signs, symptoms, and ill-defined conditions 34.3; congenital anomalies including birth injury, difficult labour, and other complications of pregnancy 32.2; pneumonia, influenza, and bronchitis 21.4; diabetes mellitus 9.0.

National economy

Budget (1985). Revenue: B 1,562,494,000 (loans 31.3%, direct taxes 23.1%, indirect taxes 22.8%, income from state enterprises 8.8%, income from state assets 1.9%). Expenditures: B 1,562,494,000 (payments on public debt 49.6%, education 10.4%, capital expenditure 9.9%, home affairs and justice 7.1%, health 4.9%, public works 2.1%).
Public debt (external, outstanding; 1985): U.S.$3,107,300,000.
Tourism (1984): receipts from visitors U.S.$186,000,000; expenditures by nationals abroad U.S.$67,000,000.
Production (metric tons except as noted). Agriculture, forestry, fishing (1984): sugarcane 2,134,000, bananas and plantains 1,183,000, rice 175,000, corn (maize) 80,000, coffee 9,000, cacao 1,000; livestock (number of live animals) 1,470,000 cattle, 200,000 pigs; roundwood 2,047,000 cu m; fish catch 166,075§. Manufacturing (value added in B; 1983): processed food 697,981,000, of which prepared meat 135,456,000, chemical products 97,305,000; refined sugar 82,292,000; wood pulp and paper products 57,877,000; textile products 56,422,000. Construction (value added in B; 1983 ‖): residential 51,972,400; nonresidential 32,941,000. Energy production (consumption): electricity (kW-hr; 1984) 2,360,000,000 (2,360,000,000); coal (metric tons; 1984) none (3,000); crude petroleum (barrels; 1984) none (13,375,000); petroleum products (metric tons; 1984) 1,715,000 (957,000).
Land use (1983): forested 53.7%; meadows and pastures 15.3%; agricultural and under permanent cultivation 7.7%; other 23.3%.

Gross national product (at current market prices; 1984): U.S.$4,210,000,000 (U.S.$1,970 per capita).

Structure of gross domestic product and labour force

	1984		1983	
	in value B '000,000	% of total value	labour force¶	% of labour force
Agriculture	409.9	9.0	169,900	28.3
Mining	6.0	0.1	800	0.1
Manufacturing	408.2	9.0	61,900	10.3
Construction	242.6	5.3	35,700	6.0
Public utilities	194.9	4.3	9,100	1.5
Transportation and communication	910.7	20.1	37,300	6.2
Trade	650.5	14.3	86,700	14.5
Finance	790.3	17.4	27,700	4.6
Pub. admin., defense	659.9	14.5	158,600	26.5
Services	433.8	9.6		
Other	−166.3	−3.7	11,600♀	1.9
TOTAL	4,540.5	100.0†	599,300	100.0†

Population economically active (1984): total 681,000; activity rate of total population 31.9% (participation rates: over age 15 [1983] 51.8%; female, n.a.; unemployed 9.9%).

Price and earnings indexes (1980 = 100)

	1980	1981	1982	1983	1984	1985	1986♂
Consumer price index	100.0	107.3	111.9	114.2	116.0	117.2	116.5
Monthly earnings index	100.0	104.2	110.7	...	...	...	...

Household income and expenditure. Average household size (1980) 4.6; median income per household (1980) B 2,950 (U.S.$2,950); sources of income (1979): wages and salaries 85.3%, transfers 9.2%, other 5.5%; expenditure (1978): food 47.3%, housing 12.7%, transportation 6.8%, health care 4.9%, clothing 4.8%.

Foreign trade□

Balance of trade (current prices)

	1979	1980	1981	1982	1983	1984
B '000,000	−760.03	−928.41	−1,064.86	−1,032.59	−943.67	−993.77
% of total	55.6%	56.3%	61.9%	57.9%	59.4%	64.3%

Imports (1984): B 1,269,820,000 (crude petroleum 26.8%, machinery and transport equipment 20.8%, manufactured products 17.7%, chemical products 12.6%, food products 8.2%). *Major import sources:* United States 30.3%; Mexico 9.8%; Venezuela 8.0%; Japan 7.7%; Ecuador 6.3%; Costa Rica 2.6%; West Germany 2.0%.
Exports (1984): B 256,316,000 (bananas 29.1%, shrimp 19.2%, sugar 13.0%, coffee 5.1%, petroleum products 2.1%). *Major export destinations:* United States 59.2%; Costa Rica 8.0%; West Germany 6.6%; Italy 4.1%; Puerto Rico 3.7%; Guatemala 1.2%; El Salvador 0.9%.

Transport and communications

Transport. Railroads: route length (1986) 281 mi, 452 km; passengers carried (1984) 53,731. Roads (1984): total length 5,925 mi, 9,535 km (paved 32%). Vehicles (1984): passenger cars 120,995; trucks and buses 41,753. Merchant marine (1985): vessels (100 gross tons and over) 5,512; total deadweight tonnage 67,266,670. Panama Canal traffic (1985): oceangoing transits 11,654; cargo 141,132,244 metric tons. Air transport (1985): passenger-mi 342,433,000, passenger-km 551,094,000; short ton-mi cargo 38,221,000, metric ton-km cargo 55,802,000; airports (1986) with scheduled flights 6.
Communications. Daily newspapers (1984): total number 7; total circulation 132,300; circulation per 1,000 population 62. Radio (1985): 295,000 receivers (1 per 7.4 persons). Television (1985): 400,000 receivers (1 per 5.5 persons). Telephones (1984): 213,400 (1 per 10 persons).

Education and health

Education (1984)◇

	schools	teachers	students	student/ teacher ratio
Primary (age 6–11)	2,438	12,969	338,363	26.1
Secondary (age 12–17)	321	9,568	181,774	19.0
Voc., teacher tr.	76	665	11,580	17.4
Higher	11	2,489	36,965	14.9

Educational attainment (1980). Percent of adult population over age 25 having: no formal schooling 17.5%; primary education 50.0%; secondary 23.1%; higher 8.2%; other 1.2%. *Literacy* (1980): total population over age 10 literate 1,193,800 (88.9%); males literate 604,800 (88.7%); females literate 589,000 (89.1%).
Health (1984): physicians 2,438 (1 per 875 persons); hospital beds 7,669 (1 per 278 persons); infant mortality rate per 1,000 live births (1985) 23.0.
Food (1980–82): daily per capita caloric intake 2,388 (vegetable products 81%, animal products 19%); 103% of FAO recommended minimum requirement.

Military

Total active duty personnel (1985): 12,000 (army 95.8%, navy 2.5%, air force 1.7%). *Military expenditure as percent of GNP* (1982): 0.8% (world 6.0%); per capita expenditure U.S.$16.

*Area figures shown for provinces and special territory include both land and water area. †Detail does not add to total given because of rounding. ‡1980. §1983. ‖ Private only. ¶Employed persons only. ♀Includes persons employed in the Canal Zone. ♂May. □Import figures are f.o.b. (free on board) in balance of trade and c.i.f. (cost, insurance, and freight) for commodities and trading partners. ◇Preliminary.

Papua New Guinea

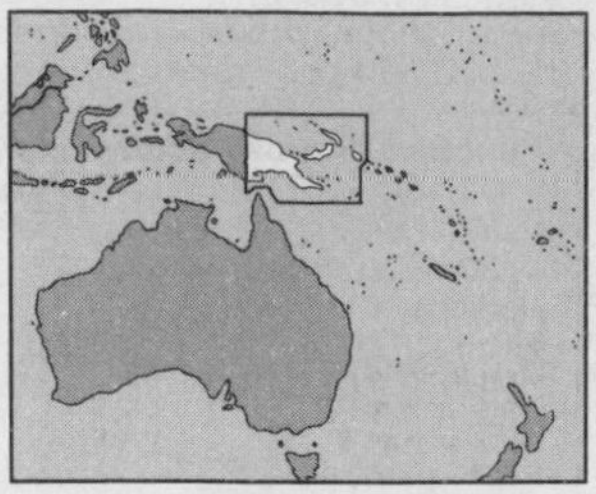

Official name: Papua New Guinea.
Form of government: constitutional monarchy with one legislative house (National Parliament [109]).
Chief of state: British Monarch represented by governor-general.
Head of government: Prime Minister.
Capital: Port Moresby.
Official language: English.
Official religion: none.
Monetary unit: 1 Papua New Guinea kina (K) = 100 toea; valuation (Oct. 1, 1986) 1 U.S.$ = K 0.97; 1 £ = K 1.40.

Area and population

		area		population
				1985
Provinces	Administrative centres	sq mi	sq km	estimate*
Central	Port Moresby	11,400	29,500	129,400
Chimbu	Kundiawa	2,350	6,100	184,400
Eastern Highlands	Goroka	4,300	11,200	299,600
East New Britain	Rabaul	6,000	15,500	149,400
East Sepik	Wewak	16,550	42,800	247,900
Enga	Wabag	4,950	12,800	175,300
Gulf	Kerema	13,300	34,500	70,000
Madang	Madang	11,200	29,000	238,400
Manus	Lorengau	800	2,100	29,000
Milne Bay	Alotau	5,400	14,000	145,900
Morobe	Lae	13,300	34,500	346,800
National Capital District	Port Moresby	100	240	136,200
New Ireland	Kavieng	3,700	9,600	74,800
Northern	Popondetta	8,800	22,800	87,600
North Solomons	Kieta	3,600	9,300	148,800
Southern Highlands	Mendi	9,200	23,800	254,100
Western	Daru	38,350	99,300	89,000
Western Highlands	Mount Hagen	3,300	8,500	293,000
West New Britain	Kimbe	8,100	21,000	103,800
West Sepik	Vanimo	14,000	36,300	125,300
TOTAL		178,703†	462,840	3,353,700‡

Demography

Population (1986): 3,397,000.
Density (1986): persons per sq mi 19.0, persons per sq km 7.3.
Urban-rural (1980): urban 13.1%; rural 86.9%.
Sex distribution (1980): male 52.35%; female 47.65%.
Age breakdown (1980): under 15, 43.0%; 15–29, 25.9%; 30–44, 17.0%; 45–59, 10.4%; 60–74, 3.5%; 75 and over, 0.2%.
Population projection: (1990) 3,691,000; (2000) 4,544,000.
Doubling time: 31 years.
Ethnic composition (1980): New Guinea Papuan 83.1%; New Guinea Melanesian 15.5%; other 1.4%.
Religious affiliation (1980): Protestant 58.4%; Roman Catholic 32.8%; Anglican 5.4%; traditional beliefs 2.5%; Bahā'ī 0.6%; other 0.3%.
Major cities (1984): Port Moresby 144,300; Lae 73,400; Madang 23,700; Wewak 22,100; Goroka 20,900.

Vital statistics

Birth rate per 1,000 population (1985): 35.0 (world avg. 29.0); legitimate, n.a.; illegitimate, n.a.
Death rate per 1,000 population (1985): 12.5 (world avg. 11.0).
Natural increase rate per 1,000 population (1985): 22.5 (world avg. 18.0).
Total fertility rate (avg. births per childbearing woman; 1985): 5.3.
Marriage rate per 1,000 population: n.a.
Divorce rate per 1,000 population: n.a.
Life expectancy at birth (1980–85): male 53.5 years; female 53.0 years.
Major causes of death per 100,000 population: n.a.; however, major infectious diseases include malaria, intestinal infections, and tuberculosis.

National economy

Budget (1984). Revenue: K 770,056,000 (foreign government grants 30.1%, customs and excise taxes 22.2%, personal income tax 16.8%, loans 8.3%). Expenditures: K 747,113,000 (no breakdown available).
Public debt (external, outstanding; 1984): U.S.$925,200,000.
Tourism (1984): receipts from visitors U.S.$12,000,000; expenditures by nationals abroad U.S.$31,000,000.
Production (metric tons except as noted). Agriculture, forestry, fishing (1984): bananas 920,000, coconuts 782,000, sweet potatoes 464,000, sugarcane 382,000, copra 140,000, palm oil 108,000, cassava 101,000, coffee 57,000, palm kernels 44,700, cocoa 28,000, pineapples 10,000, tea 9,000, pulses 2,000, peanuts (groundnuts) 1,000; livestock (number of live animals) 1,460,000 pigs, 123,000 cattle, 16,000 goats, 1,000,000 chickens; roundwood 6,910,000 cu m; fish catch 1,395§. Mining and quarrying (1984): copper 164,447; silver 44,400 kg; gold 25,971 kg. Manufacturing (value added in K; 1983): food, beverages, and tobacco 126,670,000; wood and wood products 36,695,000; metals, metal products, machinery, and equipment 35,428,000. Construction (value ‖; 1985): residential K 28,279,000; nonresidential K 11,018,000. Energy production (consumption): electricity (kW-hr; 1984) 1,495,000,000 (1,495,000,000); coal, none (n.a.); crude petroleum (barrels; 1981) none (4,266,060); petroleum products (metric tons; 1984) none (674,000); natural gas, none (n.a.).
Gross national product (at current market prices; 1984): U.S.$2,480,000,000 (U.S.$760 per capita).

Structure of gross domestic product and labour force

	1980			
	in value K '000,000	% of total value	labour force	% of labour force
Agriculture	575.0	33.7	564,500	77.0
Mining	225.4	13.2	4,300	0.6
Manufacturing	161.7	9.5	14,000	1.9
Construction	60.9	3.6	21,600	2.9
Public utilities	10.8	0.6	2,800	0.4
Transportation and communication	84.8	5.0	17,400	2.4
Trade	143.1	8.4	25,100	3.4
Finance	99.3	5.8	4,500	0.6
Pub. admin., defense	122.1	7.1	77,100	10.5
Services	202.1	11.8		
Other	22.9	1.3	1,500	0.2
TOTAL	1,708.1	100.0	732,800	100.0†

Population economically active (1980): total 1,148,000; activity rate of total population 38.2% (participation rates: ages 15–64, 67.1%; female 37.5%; unemployed 12.8%¶).

Price and earnings indexes (1980 = 100)

	1979	1980	1981	1982	1983	1984	1985♀
Consumer price index	89.2	100.0	108.1	114.0	123.0	132.2	137.2
Monthly earnings index	...	...	...	...	...	...	...

Household income and expenditure. Average household size (1980) 4.6; income per household (1975–76) K 2,771 (U.S.$3,483); source of income: n.a.; expenditure (1977): food, beverages, and tobacco 60.9%, transportation and communication 13.0%, housing and public utilities 7.2%, clothing and footwear 6.2%, household equipment and operation 5.3%.
Land use (1983): forested 71.2%; agricultural and under permanent cultivation 0.8%; meadows and pastures 0.2%; other 27.8%.

Foreign trade♂

Balance of trade (current prices)

	1978	1979	1980	1981	1982	1983	1984
K '000,000	+72.1	+125.3	+7.5	−173.7	−180.8	−138.0	−64.7
% of total	7.0%	10.0%	0.5%	13.3%	13.7%	9.2%	3.9%

Imports (1984): K 866,831,000 (machinery and transport equipment 28.1%; mineral fuels, lubricants, and related materials 18.0%; food and live animals 17.8%; manufactured goods 16.2%). *Major import sources:* Australia 39.8%; Japan 15.7%; Singapore 11.8%; United States 10.3%; United Kingdom 3.5%; Hong Kong 2.3%.
Exports (1984): K 802,155,000 (copper ore and concentrates 37.2%; coffee 14.1%; cocoa beans 8.4%; timber 8.0%; palm oil 7.9%; copra 6.2%; copra oil 5.0%). *Major export destinations:* Japan 28.3%; West Germany 20.5%; United Kingdom 11.2%; Australia 9.8%; Spain 3.4%; United States 3.4%.

Transport and communications

Transport. Railroads: none. Roads (1982): total length 11,523 mi, 18,545 km (paved 6%). Vehicles (1984): passenger cars 22,757; trucks and buses 39,481. Merchant marine (1985): vessels (100 gross tons and over) 84; total deadweight tonnage 35,059. Air transport (1984): passenger-mi 358,000,000, passenger-km 576,000,000; short ton-mi cargo 8,500,000, metric ton-km cargo 12,500,000; airports (1986) with scheduled flights 62.
Communications. Daily newspapers (1985): total number 1; total circulation 27,000; circulation per 1,000 population 8.1. Radio (1985): total number of receivers 222,000 (1 per 15 persons). Television (1985): total number of receivers 230,000 (1 per 14 persons). Telephones (1984): 51,483 (1 per 63 persons).

Education and health

Education (1984)

	schools	teachers	students	student/teacher ratio
Primary (age 7–12)	2,332	11,184	351,064	31.4
Secondary (age 13–16)	118	1,873	47,124	25.2
Voc., teacher tr.	99	601	8,583	14.3
Higher	2	387	3,510	9.1

Educational attainment (1980). Percent of population over age 5 having: no formal schooling 78.0%; some primary education 7.8%; completed primary 9.6%; some secondary, secondary, and higher 4.6%. *Literacy* (1980): total population over age 15 literate 757,500 (42.3%); males literate 490,100 (52.4%); females literate 267,400 (31.3%).
Health (1984): physicians 280 (1 per 11,635 persons); hospital beds 14,661 (1 per 222 persons); infant mortality rate per 1,000 live births (1985) 68.0.
Food (1980–82): daily per capita caloric intake 2,074 (vegetable products 90%, animal products 10%); 78% of FAO recommended minimum requirement.

Military

Total active duty personnel (1985): 3,232 (army 88.0%, navy 9.3%, air force 2.7%). *Military expenditure as percent of GNP* (1983): 1.2% (world 6.1%); per capita expenditure U.S.$9.

*De jure. †Detail does not add to total given because of rounding. ‡Includes 25,000 noncitizens. §1983. ‖ Private only. ¶1977; in six urban centres. ♀Third quarter. ♂Import figures are f.o.b. (free on board) in balance of trade and c.i.f. (cost, insurance, and freight) for commodities and trading partners.

Paraguay

Official name: República del Paraguay (Republic of Paraguay).
Form of government: republic with two legislative houses (Senate [30]; Chamber of Deputies [60]).
Head of state and government: President.
Capital: Asunción.
Official language: Spanish.
Official religion: Roman Catholicism.
Monetary unit: 1 Paraguayan Guaraní (₲) = 100 céntimos; valuation* (Oct. 1, 1986) 1 U.S.$ = ₲320.00; 1£ = ₲462.40.

Area and population

Regions / Departments	Capitals	area sq mi	area sq km	population 1985 estimate
Occidental		95,338	246,925	50,400
Alto Paraguay	Fuerte Olimpio	17,754	45,982	10,100
Boquerón	Dr. Pedro P. Peña	18,034	46,708	12,000
Chaco	Mayor Pablo Lagerenza	14,041	36,367	300
Nueva Asunción	General Eugenio A. Garay	17,359	44,961	200
Presidente Hayes	Pozo Colorado	28,150	72,907	27,800
Oriental		61,710	159,827	3,228,600
Alto Paraná	Puerto Presidente Stroessner	5,751	14,895	255,000
Amambay	Pedro Juan Caballero	4,994	12,933	69,400
Asunción	Asunción	45	117	477,100
Caaguazú	Coronel Oviedo	4,430	11,474	333,000
Caazapá	Caazapá	3,666	9,496	111,400
Canendiyú	Salto del Guairá	5,663	14,667	77,100
Central	Asunción	952	2,465	572,500
Concepción	Concepción	6,970	18,051	143,000
Cordillera	Caacupé	1,910	4,948	194,000
Guairá	Villarrica	1,485	3,846	149,600
Itapúa	Encarnación	6,380	16,525	284,500
Misiones	San Juan Bautista	3,690	9,556	80,100
Ñeembucú	Pilar	4,690	12,147	69,500
Paraguarí	Paraguarí	3,361	8,705	201,900
San Pedro	San Pedro	7,723	20,002	210,500
TOTAL		157,048	406,752	3,279,000

Demography

Population (1986): 3,381,000.
Density (1986): persons per sq mi 21.5, persons per sq km 8.3.
Urban–rural (1985): urban 43.9%; rural 56.1%.
Sex distribution (1984): male 50.20%; female 49.80%.
Age breakdown (1982): under 15, 41.1%; 15–29, 28.1%; 30–44, 15.4%; 45–59, 9.1%; 60–74, 4.8%; 75 and over, 1.5%.
Population projection: (1990) 3,823,000; (2000) 5,198,000.
Doubling time: 23 years.
Ethnic composition (1980): mestizo (Spanish–Guaraní) 90.8%; Amerindian 3.0%; German 1.7%; other 4.5%.
Religious affiliation (1980): Roman Catholic 96.0%; Protestant 1.8%; other 2.2%.
Major cities (1985): Asunción 477,000; Lambaré 84,000; Fernando de la Mora 80,000; Puerto Presidente Stroessner 64,000.

Vital statistics

Birth rate per 1,000 population (1984): 38.9 (world avg. 29.0); (1981) legitimate 67.4%; illegitimate 32.6%.
Death rate per 1,000 population (1984): 7.7 (world avg. 11.0).
Natural increase rate per 1,000 population (1984): 31.2 (world avg. 18.0).
Total fertility rate (avg. births per childbearing woman; 1980–85): 5.2.
Marriage rate per 1,000 population (1982): 4.3.
Divorce rate per 1,000 population: n.a.
Life expectancy at birth (1980–85): male 62.8 years; female 67.5 years.
Major causes of death per 100,000 population (1984): diseases of the circulatory system 113.2; ill-defined conditions 70.6; malignant neoplasms (cancers) 39.2; perinatal causes 19.2.

National economy

Budget (1984). Revenue: ₲79,191,500,000 (domestic taxes on goods and services 36.8%, income tax 12.6%, customs duties 10.0%, sales tax 7.5%, pension funds 5.8%, real estate taxes 4.5%, alcohol tax 3.8%). Expenditures: ₲118,283,100,000 (public works 14.9%, defense 13.3%, education 12.2%, ministry of interior 8.1%, public health 8.0%, public debt 6.7%).
Public debt (external, outstanding; 1985): U.S.$1,460,400,000.
Tourism: receipts from visitors (1984) U.S.$96,000,000; expenditures by nationals abroad (1983) U.S.$46,000,000.
Production (metric tons except as noted). Agriculture, forestry, fishing (1984): cassava 2,553,688, sugarcane 2,465,350, soybeans 975,404, corn (maize) 730,159, bananas 325,000, seed cotton 282,000, oranges 230,000, palm kernels 150,000, wheat 139,071, sweet potatoes 120,000, lint cotton 105,000; livestock (number of live animals) 6,794,868 cattle, 1,109,138 pigs; roundwood 6,852,000 cu m; fish catch 3,500†. Mining and quarrying (1984): limestone 175,000; kaolin 50,000; gypsum 6,000. Manufacturing (1983): cement 109,000‡; sugar 85,200‡; beef and veal 85,000‡; tung oil 17,000; hides 11,000; edible coconut oil 4,500; coconut pulp 3,400; woven cotton fabrics 6,134,000 metres‡; beer 455,930 hectolitres; alcohol 42,200 hectolitres; matches 2,979,000 boxes. Construction (1982): residential 116,800 sq m; nonresidential 210,600 sq m. Energy production (consumption): electricity (kW-hr; 1984) 1,095,000,000 (1,291,000,000); coal, none (none); crude petroleum (barrels; 1984) none (1,100,000); petroleum products (metric tons; 1984) 147,000 (474,000); natural gas, none (none).
Gross national product (at current market prices; 1984): U.S.$4,120,000,000 (U.S.$1,260 per capita).

Structure of gross domestic product and labour force

	1984 in value ₲'000,000	1984 % of total value	1982 labour force	1982 % of labour force
Agriculture	307,113	28.7	445,720	43.3
Mining	4,359	0.4	1,130	0.1
Manufacturing	172,003	16.1	124,840	12.1
Construction	66,873	6.2	67,170	6.5
Public utilities	26,064	2.4	2,540	0.3
Transportation and communication	44,059	4.1	26,230	2.6
Trade	272,599	25.5	78,650	7.6
Finance	177,374§ (Finance, Pub. admin., defense, Services, Other)	16.6§ (Finance, Pub. admin., defense, Services, Other)	29,140	2.8
Pub. admin., defense / Services			168,980	16.4
Other			85,110	8.3
TOTAL	1,070,444	100.0	1,029,510	100.0

Population economically active (1982): total 1,029,510; activity rate of total population 33.9% (participation rates: ages 15–64, 57.1%; female 11.8%; unemployed 29.0%).

Price and earnings indexes (1980 = 100)

	1980	1981	1982	1983	1984	1985	1986‖
Consumer price index	100.0	114.0	121.7	138.0	166.1	207.9	260.4
Monthly earnings index	...	...	...	...	...	...	...

Household income and expenditure: average household size (1982) 5.2; sources of income (1982): self-employment and business profits 56.0%, wages and salaries 40.8%, transfer payments from government 3.2%.
Land use (1983): forested 51.5%; meadows and pastures 39.1%; agricultural and under permanent cultivation 4.9%; other 4.5%.

Foreign trade

Balance of trade (current prices)

	1980	1981	1982	1983	1984	1985
₲'000,000	−26,071	−26,532	−32,301	−26,519	−42,316	−75,892
% of total	25.0%	26.3%	25.5%	23.5%	21.7%	28.2%

Imports (1984): U.S.$513,054,500 (fuels and lubricants 26.8%, of which crude petroleum 9.4%, gasoline 3.4%; transport equipment 20.0%; machines, apparatus, and engines 17.9%; food, beverages, and tobacco 7.7%; iron and iron manufactures 4.5%.). *Major import sources:* Brazil 32.7%; Argentina 15.7%; Japan 11.8%; Algeria 9.4%; United States 8.7%.
Exports (1984): U.S.$334,502,000 (cotton fibres 39.2%; soybeans 29.7%; timber 6.8%; tobacco 4.6%; tung oil 2.8%; cowhide 2.1%; processed meat 1.3%; sugar 1.2%). *Major export destinations:* Brazil 16.0%; The Netherlands 12.5%; Argentina 12.2%; West Germany 11.2%; United States 5.4%.

Transport and communications

Transport. Railroads (1980): route length (1986) 274 mi, 441 km; passenger-mi 13,900,000, passenger-km 22,400,000; short ton-mi cargo 23,600,000, metric ton-km cargo 34,400,000. Roads (1983): total length 7,034 mi, 11,320 km (paved 19%). Vehicles (1984): passenger cars 90,655; trucks and buses 35,150. Merchant marine (1985): vessels (100 gross tons and over) 40; total deadweight tonnage 50,957. Air transport (1982): passenger-mi 290,000,000, passenger-km 466,000,000; short ton-mi cargo 1,400,000, metric ton-km cargo 2,000,000; airports (1986) with scheduled flights 1.
Communications. Daily newspapers (1985): total number 5; total circulation 198,000; circulation per 1,000 population 60. Radio (1984): total number of receivers 598,000 (1 per 5.4 persons). Television (1984): total number of receivers 266,200 (1 per 12 persons). Telephones (1984): 83,490 (1 per 39 persons).

Education and health

Education (1984)

	schools	teachers	students	student/teacher ratio
Primary (age 7–12)	3,796	22,091	559,080	25.3
Secondary (age 13–18)¶	713	9,044	149,019	16.5
Higher	2	649	30,222	11.2

Educational attainment (1982). Percent of population over age 12 having: no formal schooling 9.6%; less than full primary education 47.4%; primary 17.9%; less than full secondary 15.4%; secondary 4.2%; higher 2.9%. *Literacy* (1982): total population over age 15 literate 1,534,810 (85.7%); males literate 782,560 (88.7%); females literate 752,250 (82.9%).
Health (1982): physicians 2,201 (1 per 1,379 persons); hospital beds 3,345 (1 per 907 persons); infant mortality rate per 1,000 live births (1984) 52.9.
Food (1980–82): daily per capita caloric intake 2,824 (vegetable products 80%, animal products 20%); 123% of FAO recommended minimum requirement.

Military

Total active duty personnel (1985): 14,370 (army 77.9%, navy 15.3%, air force 6.8%). *Military expenditure as percent of GNP* (1983): 1.9% (world 6.1%); per capita expenditure U.S.$25.

*Official rate only; nonofficial rate is 99.8% higher. †1983. ‡1984. §Includes hotels and restaurants. ‖February. ¶Includes vocational education and teacher training.

Peru

Official name: República del Perú (Spanish) (Republic of Peru).
Form of government: unitary multiparty republic with two legislative houses (Senate [60]; Chamber of Deputies [180]).
Head of state and government: President.
Capital: Lima.
Official languages: Spanish; Quechua.
Official religion: Roman Catholicism.
*Monetary unit**: 1 Inti (I/.) = 100 céntimos = 1,000 soles; valuation (Oct. 1, 1986) 1 U.S.$ = I/. 13.95; 1 £ = I/. 20.16.

Area and population

Departments	Capitals	area sq mi	area sq km	population 1986 estimate
Amazonas	Chachapoyas	15,945	41,297	304,200
Ancash	Huaraz	14,158	36,669	921,800
Apurímac	Abancay	7,934	20,550	358,100
Arequipa	Arequipa	24,528	63,528	858,400
Ayacucho	Ayacucho	17,058	44,181	548,300
Cajamarca	Cajamarca	13,486	34,930	1,178,400
Cuzco	Cuzco	29,471	76,329	961,300
Huancavelica	Huancavelica	8,139	21,079	369,800
Huánuco	Huánuco	13,088	33,897	559,900
Ica	Ica	8,205	21,251	497,200
Junín	Huancayo	15,944	41,296	1,012,900
La Libertad	Trujillo	8,973	23,241	1,120,900
Lambayeque	Chiclayo	5,304	13,737	828,700
Lima	Lima	13,058	33,821	5,922,700
Loreto	Iquitos	146,342	379,025	590,300
Madre de Dios	Puerto Maldonado	30,271	78,403	43,000
Moquegua	Moquegua	6,065	15,709	119,900
Pasco	Cerro de Pasco	9,356	24,233	260,500
Piura	Piura	14,055	36,403	1,335,400
Puno	Puno	27,947	72,382	971,700
San Martín	Moyobamba	20,197	52,309	399,000
Tacna	Tacna	5,881	15,232	181,200
Tumbes	Tumbes	1,827	4,732	127,500
Ucayali	Pucallpa	38,931	100,831	205,800
Constitutional Province				
Callao	Callao	57	148	530,200
TOTAL		496,225†	1,285,216†	20,207,100

Demography

Population (1986): 20,207,000.
Density (1986): persons per sq mi 40.7, persons per sq km 15.7.
Urban–rural (1985): urban 70.2%; rural 29.8%.
Sex distribution (1985): male 50.38%; female 49.62%.
Age breakdown (1985): under 15, 40.5%; 15–29, 28.2%; 30–44, 16.3%; 45–59, 9.5%; 60–74, 4.5%; 75 and over, 1.0%.
Population projection: (1990) 22,392,000; (2000) 28,944,000.
Doubling time: 27 years.
Ethnic composition (1981): Quechua 47.1%; mestizo 32.0%; white 12.0%; Aymara 5.4%; jungle Amerindian 1.7%; other 1.8%.
Religious affiliation (1983): Roman Catholic 92.4%; other 7.6%.
Major cities (1985): Lima 5,169,000; Arequipa 531,800; Callao 515,200; Trujillo 438,700; Chiclayo 347,700.

Vital statistics

Birth rate per 1,000 population (1985): 35.5‡ (world avg. 29.0); (1977) legitimate 57.8%; illegitimate 42.2%.
Death rate per 1,000 population (1985): 10.0‡ (world avg. 11.0).
Natural increase rate per 1,000 population (1985): 25.5‡ (world avg. 18.0).
Total fertility rate (avg. births per childbearing woman; 1985): 4.7.
Marriage rate per 1,000 population (1982): 6.0‡.
Life expectancy at birth (1985): male 58.3 years; female 62.2 years.
Major causes of death per 100,000 population (1981): respiratory diseases 104.4, of which pneumonia 71.7; infectious and parasitic diseases 95.9; diseases of the circulatory system 59.3; symptoms and ill-defined conditions 35.3; malignant neoplasms (cancers) 33.8.

National economy

Budget (1984). Revenue: S/. 9,215,000,000,000 (tax on fuel 25.2%; tax on external trade 23.1%; tax on goods and services 19.7%; property tax 15.4%). Expenditures: S/. 17,013,000,000,000 (current expenditure 59.6%, of which defense and interior 19.8%, interest payments 17.3%, wages 13.0%).
Public debt (external, outstanding; 1985): U.S.$10,510,000,000.
Tourism (1984): receipts from visitors U.S.$258,000,000; expenditures by nationals abroad U.S.$160,000,000.
Production (metric tons except as noted). Agriculture, forestry, fishing (1985): sugarcane 7,425,000, potatoes 1,590,000, rice 964,000, corn (maize) 708,000, seed cotton 291,000, coffee 93,000, wheat 92,000; livestock (number of live animals [1984]) 14,500,000 sheep, 2,825,000 cattle, 2,400,000 alpacas§, 1,775,000 pigs; roundwood 7,775,000 cu m; fish catch (1985) 3,117,000. Mining and quarrying (1985): iron ore 4,807,000; zinc 589,000; copper 397,000; lead 210,000; silver 1,879. Manufacturing (value added in S/. '000,000; 1980): food, beverages, and tobacco 370.7; nonferrous metals 183.7; chemicals and plastics 159.0; textiles 151.6. Construction (value in S/. '000,000; 1982): buildings 1,147,369‖. Energy production (consumption): electricity (kW-hr; 1984) 11,769,000,000 (11,769,000,000); coal (metric tons; 1984) 85,000 (140,000); crude petroleum (barrels; 1984) 67,541,000 (59,344,000); petroleum products (metric tons; 1984) 7,591,000 (6,590,000); natural gas (cu m; 1984) 1,114,144,000 (1,114,144,000).
Gross national product (1984): U.S.$17,960,000,000 (U.S.$940 per capita).

Structure of gross domestic product and labour force

1984	in value S/. '000,000	% of total value	labour force	% of labour force
Agriculture	43,321	14.0	2,381,700	37.5
Mining	29,910	9.7	133,400	2.1
Manufacturing	66,611	21.5	666,900	10.5
Construction	15,368	5.0	241,300	3.8
Public utilities			19,100	0.3
Transp. and commun.	127,060	41.1	273,100	4.3
Trade			889,200	14.0
Finance			152,400	2.4
Services¶	27,066	8.7	1,594,200	25.1
Other	...	...	...	...
TOTAL	309,336	100.0	6,351,300	100.0

Population economically active (1982): total 6,394,700; activity rate of total population 35.1% (participation rates: over age 15, 57.1%; female 29.3%; unemployed [1984] 10.9%).

Price and earnings indexes (1980 = 100)

	1980	1981	1982	1983	1984	1985	1986♀
Consumer price index	100.0	175.4	288.4	609.0	1,280.2	3,372.0	6,323.3
Monthly earnings index	100.0	190.5	313.2	542.4	1,041.8	2,395.6	...

Household income and expenditure. Average household size (1981) 4.8; income per household (1971–72) S/. 51,170 (U.S.$1,322); source of income: n.a.; expenditure (1983)♂: food, drink, and tobacco 38.1%, rent and utilities 15.6%, transportation 9.8%, recreation and education 7.4%.
Land use (1983): forest 54.8%; pasture 21.2%; agricultural 2.7%; other 21.3%.

Foreign trade

Balance of trade (current prices)

	1980	1981	1982	1983	1984	1985
I/. '000,000	+510.9	+134.2	+457.8	+1,845.0	+5,206.6	+17,914.2
% of total	29.5%	5.2%	11.0%	22.7%	31.2%	37.5%

Imports (1984): S/. 6,118,800,000,000 (capital goods 36.0%, of which public sector 18.7%, private sector 17.3%; food items 13.5%, of which wheat 6.6%). *Major import sources:* United States 33.1%; Japan 8.8%; Argentina 8.1%; West Germany 7.4%; Brazil 5.8%.
Exports (1984): S/. 10,951,500,000,000 (petroleum [all forms] 19.6%; copper 14.0%; zinc 10.8%; lead 7.4%; silver 7.2%). *Major destinations:* United States 34.5%; Japan 9.8%; Belgium–Luxembourg 5.9%; United Kingdom 5.0%; West Germany 3.8%; Taiwan 3.3%; Italy 3.1%.

Transport and communications

Transport. Railroads (1983): route length (1985) 2,179 mi, 3,506 km; passenger-km 563,024,000; metric ton-km cargo 839,718,000. Roads (1984): total length 40,400 mi, 65,000 km (paved 11%). Vehicles (1982): passenger cars 359,700; trucks and buses 196,013. Merchant marine (1985): vessels (100 gross tons and over) 650; total deadweight tonnage 1,096,603. Air transport (1985): passenger-km 1,601,210,000; metric ton-km cargo 192,301,000; airports (1986) 22.
Communications. Daily newspapers (1985): total number 66; total circulation 1,121,900□; circulation per 1,000 population 57□. Radio (1985): 2,225,000 receivers (1 per 8.9 persons). Television (1985): 1,370,000 receivers (1 per 14 persons). Telephones (1983): 519,703 (1 per 36 persons).

Education and health

Education (1985)

	schools	teachers	students	student/teacher ratio
Primary (age 6–11)	24,939	109,039	3,787,569	34.7
Secondary (age 12–16)	4,178	74,135	1,597,839	21.6
Voc., teacher tr.	1,032	10,620	226,321	21.3
Higher	44	21,083	358,337	17.0

Educational attainment (1981). Percent of population over age 25 having: no formal schooling 20.1%; less than primary education 33.2%; primary 21.1%; secondary 20.8%; higher 4.8%. *Literacy* (1981): total population literate 11,458,810 (78.7%); males 6,092,490 (84.3%); females 5,366,320 (73.1%).
Health (1982): physicians 14,751 (1 per 1,236 persons); hospital beds 29,991 (1 per 608 persons); infant mortality rate per 1,000 live births (1985) 92.7.
Food (1980–82): daily per capita caloric intake 2,141 (vegetable products 87%, animal products 13%); 93% of FAO recommended minimum requirement.

Military

Total active duty personnel (1986): 127,000 (army 66.9%, navy 21.3%, air force 11.8%). *Military expenditure as percent of GNP* (1984): 7.8% (world [1983] 6.1%); per capita expenditure U.S.$67.

*The inti was introduced on Feb. 1, 1985, to replace the Peruvian sol (S/.), and effective Jan. 1, 1986, all operations in the financial system were expressed in intis. †Detail does not add to total given because of rounding. ‡Excludes Indian jungle population; based on incomplete information. §1983. ‖Includes new construction and capital repairs. ¶Services includes public administration and defense. ♀August. ♂Estimate for Lima metropolitan area only. □Partial circulation.

Philippines

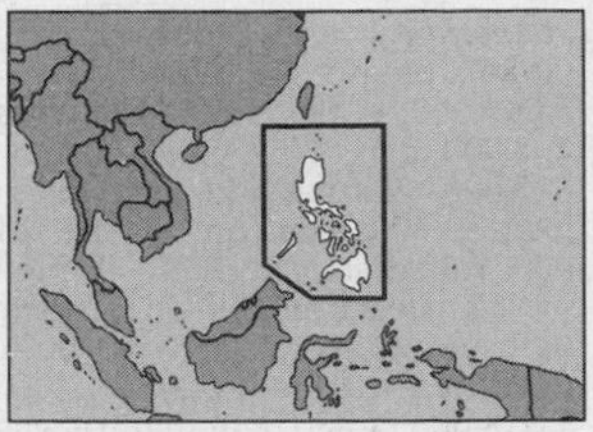

Official name: Republika ñg Pilipinas (Pilipino); Republic of the Philippines (English).
Form of government: parliamentary state operating under interim constitution pending approval of new constitution.
Chief of state and head of government: President.
Capital: Manila.
Official languages: Pilipino; English.
Official religion: none.
Monetary unit: 1 Philippine peso (₱) = 100 centavos; valuation (Oct. 1, 1986) 1 U.S.$ = ₱ 20.46; 1 £ = ₱ 29.56.

Area and population

	area		population
Regions	sq mi	sq km	1985 estimate
Bicol	6,808	17,633	3,830,000
Cagayan Valley	14,055	36,403	2,508,000
Central Luzon	7,039	18,231	5,429,000
Central Mindanao	8,994	23,293	2,493,000
Central Visayas	5,773	14,951	4,201,000
Eastern Visayas	8,275	21,432	3,086,000
Ilocos	8,328	21,568	3,838,000
National Capital Region	246	636	6,915,000
Northern Mindanao	10,937	28,328	3,206,000
Southern Mindanao	12,237	31,693	3,931,000
Southern Tagalog	18,117	46,924	7,084,000
Western Mindanao	7,214	18,685	2,828,000
Western Visayas	7,808	20,223	5,031,000
TOTAL	115,800*	300,000	54,378,000*

Demography

Population (1986): 56,004,000.
Density (1986): persons per sq mi 483.6, persons per sq km 186.7.
Urban-rural (1986): urban 40.5%; rural 59.5%.
Sex distribution (1986): male 50.20%; female 49.80%.
Age breakdown (1983): under 15, 41.0%; 15–29, 28.7%; 30–44, 16.2%; 45–59, 8.8%; 60–74, 4.3%; 75 and over, 1.0%.
Population projection: (1990) 61,480,000; (2000) 74,057,000.
Doubling time: 29 years.
Ethnic composition (by mother tongue; 1980): Tagalog 29.7%; Cebuano 24.2%; Ilocano 10.3%; Hiligaynon Ilongo 9.2%; Bicol 5.6%; Samar-Leyte 4.0%; Pampango 2.8%; Pangasinan 1.8%; other 12.5%*.
Religious affiliation (1980): Roman Catholic 84.1%; Aglipayan (Philippine Independent Church) 6.2%; Muslim 4.3%; Protestant 3.5%; other 1.9%.
Major cities (1980): Manila 1,630,485; Quezon City 1,165,865; Davao 610,-375; Cebu 490,281; Caloocan 467,816.

Vital statistics

Birth rate per 1,000 population (1985): 32.1 (world avg. 29.0); (1980) legitimate 96.3%; illegitimate 3.7%.
Death rate per 1,000 population (1985): 8.0 (world avg. 11.0).
Natural increase rate per 1,000 population (1985): 24.1 (world avg. 18.0).
Total fertility rate (avg. births per childbearing woman; 1985): 4.2.
Marriage rate per 1,000 population (1982): 6.9.
Life expectancy at birth (1986): male 61.6 years; female 65.2 years.
Major causes of death per 100,000 population (1983): pneumonia 86.0; tuberculosis 37.6; heart diseases 33.7; vascular diseases 28.7; diarrhea 19.0; malignant neoplasms (cancers) 17.9; accidents 15.1.

National economy

Budget (1986). Revenue: ₱ 87,500,000,000 (tax revenue 82.9%, of which tax on foreign trade 30.1%, tax on domestic goods and services 28.8%, income tax 19.1%; nontax revenue 9.4%). Expenditures: ₱ 92,888,000,000 (interest on debt 25.3%; education 12.5%; transport and communications 9.4%; defense 8.7%; health 4.4%; agriculture 4.1%; public services 4.1%).
Public debt (external, outstanding; 1984): U.S.$11,175,700,000.
Tourism: receipts from visitors (1984) U.S.$350,000,000; expenditures by nationals abroad (1983) U.S.$221,000,000.
Production (metric tons except as noted). Agriculture, forestry, fishing (1984): rice 7,840,900, bananas 3,887,600, corn (maize) 3,346,200, sugarcane 3,260,200, cotton (lint) 73,000, peanuts (groundnuts) 42,300, copra 34,000; livestock (number of live animals) 3,022,000 buffalo, 1,849,000 cattle, 2,362,000 goats, 7,613,000 pigs; roundwood 35,559,000 cu m; fish catch 2,207,000. Mining and quarrying (1984): limestone 7,000,000; copper 303,000; chromite 250,000; silver 50,000 kilograms; gold 24,000 kilograms. Manufacturing (gross value added in constant prices of 1972 in ₱ '000,000; 1983): food items 9,246; chemicals and chemical products 2,315; electrical machinery 1,717; coal and petroleum products 1,351; footwear and wearing apparel 1,247; tobacco manufactures 1,117. Construction† (authorized; 1983): residential 3,576,000 sq m; nonresidential 3,276,000 sq m. Energy production (consumption): electricity (kW-hr; 1984) 18,925,000,000 (15,519,000,000); coal (metric tons; 1984) 1,143,000 (1,193,000); petroleum (barrels; 1984) 4,405,000 (60,802,000); petroleum products (metric tons; 1984) 7,521,000 (9,623,000); natural gas, n.a. (n.a.).
Gross national product (at current market prices; 1984): U.S.$35,040,000,000 (U.S.$660 per capita).

Structure of gross domestic product and labour force

	1984			
	in value ₱ '000,000	% of total value	labour force	% of labour force
Agriculture	138,505	25.3	9,733,000	46.4
Mining	9,714	1.8	141,000	0.7
Manufacturing	137,251	25.0	1,940,000	9.3
Construction	31,209	5.7	743,000	3.5
Public utilities	7,113	1.3	75,000	0.4
Transp. and commun.	33,820	6.2	891,000	4.2
Trade	99,711	18.2	2,464,000	11.8
Finance	42,140	7.7	385,000	1.8
Services } Other }	48,864	8.9	4,597,000‡	21.9
TOTAL	548,327	100.0*	20,969,000	100.0

Population economically active (1984): total 20,969,000; activity rate of total population 40.3% (participation rates: over age 15, 64.2%; female [1983] 39.4%; unemployed 6.2%).

Price and earnings indexes (1980 = 100)

	1980	1981	1982	1983	1984	1985	1986§
Consumer price index	100.0	113.1	124.6	137.1	206.2	253.8	252.8

Household income and expenditure. Average household size (1980) 5.6; income per family (1975) ₱ 5,840 (U.S.$777.5); sources of income (1971): wages and salaries 44.8%, self-employment 40.3%, owner-occupied dwellings 7.1%, pensions, social security, and related benefits 2.1%, other 5.7%; expenditure (1982): food, beverages, and tobacco 54.6%, housing 12.0%, household furnishings and operations 7.0%, clothing 6.2%, transport and communication 3.4%, education 2.7%.
Land use (1983): forested 40.4%; meadows and pastures 3.8%; agricultural and under permanent cultivation 37.7%; other 18.1%.

Foreign trade ‖

Balance of trade (current prices)

	1980	1981	1982	1983	1984	1985
₱ '000,000	−14,898	−18,153	−22,674	−28,566	−10,907	−8,113
% of total	14.7%	16.9%	20.9%	20.7%	5.8%	4.5%

Imports (1984): ₱ 107,670,000,000 (mineral fuels and lubricants 27.2%; electrical machinery 7.0%; nonelectrical machinery 6.9%; base metals 4.1%; cereals 4.0%; chemicals 3.9%; transport equipment 3.6%). *Major import sources:* United States 26.9%; Japan 13.4%; Saudi Arabia 6.9%; Kuwait 6.3%; Malaysia 6.0%; Hong Kong 3.9%; China 3.6%.
Exports (1984): ₱ 88,339,000,000 (electrical and electronic equipment and components 23.6%; coconut products 13.5%, of which coconut oil 10.8%; clothing 11.1%; fruits and vegetables 7.3%; sugar and sugar products 6.1%; forest products 6.0%; mineral products 4.9%). *Major export destinations:* United States 38.0%; Japan 19.3%; Singapore 5.9%; Hong Kong 4.3%; United Kingdom 4.2%; West Germany 3.4%; Malaysia 3.3%.

Transport and communications

Transport. Railroads (1985): route length 658 mi, 1,059 km; passenger-mi 99,000,000, passenger-km 144,000,000; short ton-mi cargo 8,000,000, metric ton-km cargo 12,000,000. Roads (1984): total length 97,641 mi, 157,139 km (paved 14%). Vehicles (1984): passenger cars 894,927; trucks and buses 128,083. Merchant marine (1985): vessels (100 gross tons and over) 1,000; total deadweight tonnage 7,571,141. Air transport¶ (1985): passenger-mi 4,853,801,000, passenger-km 7,811,451,000; short ton-mi cargo 662,243,000, metric ton-km cargo 966,859,000; airports (1986) with scheduled flights 42.
Communications. Daily newspapers (1984): total number 25; circulation 2,379,145; circulation per 1,000 population 44. Radio (1985): 3,550,000 receivers (1 per 15 persons). Television (1985): 2,700,000 receivers (1 per 20 persons). Telephones (1983): 658,415 (1 per 79 persons).

Education and health

Education (1983–84)

	schools	teachers	students	student/ teacher ratio
Primary (age 7–12)	32,809	272,479♀	8,717,469	...
Secondary (age 13–16)	5,430	89,019♀	3,204,551	...
Voc., teacher tr. } Higher }	1,157	51,337	165,012 / 1,411,486	... / ...

Educational attainment (1975). Percent of adult population over age 15 having: less than elementary education 10.0%; elementary 52.9%; secondary 22.9%; college 12.3%; not stated 1.9%. *Literacy* (1980): total population over age 15 literate 25,139,700 (88.7%); males literate 12,772,200 (89.9%); females literate 12,367,500 (87.5%).
Health: physicians (1982) 46,579 (1 per 1,090 persons); hospital beds (1984) 70,608 (1 per 756 persons); infant mortality rate per 1,000 live births (1985) 56.0.
Food (1980–82): daily per capita caloric intake 2,405 (vegetable products 90%, animal products 10%); 106% of FAO recommended minimum requirement.

Military

Total active duty personnel (1985): 114,800 (army 61.0%, navy 24.4%, air force 14.6%). *Military expenditure as percent of GNP* (1983): 1.9% (world 6.1%); per capita expenditure U.S.$14.

*Detail does not add to total given because of rounding. †Private only. ‡Includes unemployed. §July. ‖ Import figures are f.o.b. (free on board) in balance of trade and c.i.f. (cost, insurance, and freight) for commodities and trading partners. ¶Philippines Airlines only. ♀1981–82.

Poland

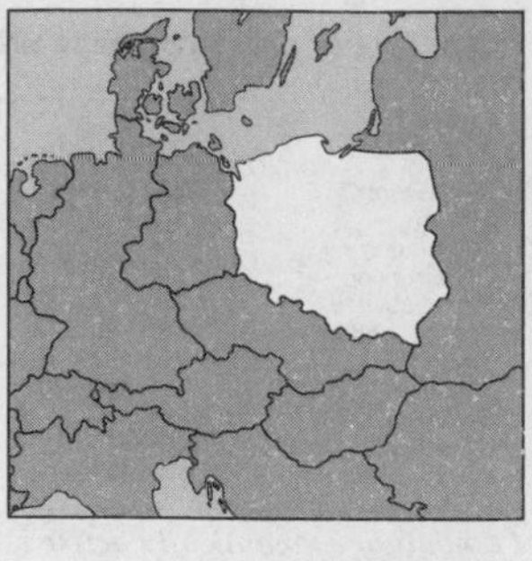

Official name: Polska Rzeczpospolita Ludowa (Polish People's Republic).
Form of government: unitary single-party socialist republic with one legislative house (Sejm [460]).
Chief of state: President (Chairman).
Head of government: Prime Minister.
Capital: Warsaw.
Official language: Polish.
Official religion: none.
Monetary unit: 1 złoty = 100 groszy; valuation (Oct. 1, 1986) 1 U.S.$ = 199.60 złotys; 1 £ = 288.42 złotys.

Area and population

Provinces	Capitals	area sq mi	area sq km	population 1985 estimate
Biała Podlaska	Biała Podlaska	2,065	5,348	295,600
Białystok	Białystok	3,882	10,055	666,100
Bielsko	Bielsko Biala	1,430	3,704	865,300
Bydgoszcz	Bydgoszcz	3,996	10,349	1,074,100
Chełm	Chełm	1,493	3,866	239,100
Ciechanów	Ciechanów	2,456	6,362	415,800
Częstochowa	Częstochowa	2,387	6,182	762,800
Elbląg	Elbląg	2,356	6,103	462,500
Gdańsk	Gdańsk	2,855	7,394	1,387,400
Gorzów	Gorzów Wielkopolski	3,276	8,484	479,200
Jelenia Góra	Jelenia Góra	1,690	4,378	507,000
Kalisz	Kalisz	2,514	6,512	691,300
Katowice	Katowice	2,568	6,650	3,895,500
Kielce	Kielce	3,556	9,211	1,101,300
Konin	Konin	1,984	5,139	455,400
Koszalin	Koszalin	3,270	8,470	483,700
Kraków	Kraków	1,256	3,254	1,205,400
Krosno	Krosno	2,202	5,702	470,100
Legnica	Legnica	1,559	4,037	484,700
Leszno	Leszno	1,604	4,154	372,500
Łódź	Łódź	588	1,523	1,149,100
Łomża	Łomża	2,581	6,684	336,600
Lublin	Lublin	2,622	6,792	976,900
Nowy Sącz	Nowy Sącz	2,153	5,576	659,300
Olsztyn	Olsztyn	4,759	12,327	717,000
Opole	Opole	3,295	8,535	1,006,000
Ostrołęka	Ostrołęka	2,509	6,498	381,800
Piła	Piła	3,168	8,205	460,500
Piotrków	Piotrków Trybunalski	2,419	6,266	628,400
Płock	Płock	1,976	5,117	507,300
Poznań	Poznań	3,147	8,151	1,289,100
Przemyśl	Przemyśl	1,713	4,437	392,500
Radom	Radom	2,816	7,294	724,600
Rzeszów	Rzeszów	1,698	4,397	682,600
Siedlce	Siedlce	3,281	8,499	633,000
Sieradz	Sieradz	1,880	4,869	399,100
Skierniewice	Skierniewice	1,529	3,960	407,500
Słupsk	Słupsk	2,878	7,453	390,800
Suwałki	Suwałki	4,050	10,490	443,300
Szczecin	Szczecin	3,854	9,981	933,100
Tarnobrzeg	Tarnobrzeg	2,426	6,283	577,000
Tarnów	Tarnów	1,603	4,151	634,000
Toruń	Toruń	2,065	5,348	633,600
Wałbrzych	Wałbrzych	1,609	4,168	731,900
Warszawa	Warszawa	1,463	3,788	2,395,600
Włocławek	Włocławek	1,700	4,402	424,100
Wrocław	Wrocław	2,427	6,287	1,109,200
Zamość	Zamość	2,695	6,980	485,700
Zielona Góra	Zielona Góra	3,424	8,868	638,900
TOTAL		120,727	312,683	37,063,300

Demography

Population (1986): 37,455,700.
Density (1986): persons per sq mi 310.8, persons per sq km 120.0.
Urban-rural (1985): urban 60.3%; rural 39.7%.
Sex distribution (1985): male 48.76%; female 51.24%.
Age breakdown (1985): under 15, 25.4%; 15–29, 23.3%; 30–44, 20.9%; 45–59, 16.6%; 60–74, 9.9%; 75 and over, 3.9%.
Population projection: (1990) 38,967,000; (2000) 41,217,000.
Doubling time: 87 years.
Ethnic composition (1981): Polish 98.7%; Ukrainian 0.6%; other 0.7%.
Religious affiliation (1980): Roman Catholic 81%; other 19%.
Major cities (1986): Warsaw 1,659,400; Łódź 847,900; Kraków 740,100.

Vital statistics

Birth rate per 1,000 population (1985): 18.2 (world avg. 29.0).
Death rate per 1,000 population (1985): 10.3 (world avg. 11.0).
Natural increase rate per 1,000 population (1985): 7.9 (world avg. 18.0).
Total fertility rate (avg. births per childbearing woman; 1982): 2.3.
Marriage rate per 1,000 population (1984): 7.7.
Divorce rate per 1,000 population (1984): 1.3.
Life expectancy at birth (1982): male 67.2 years; female 75.2 years.
Major causes of death per 100,000 population (1984): diseases of the circulatory system 492.9; malignant neoplasms (cancers) 179.0.

National economy

Budget (1984). Revenue: 3,297,300,000,000 złotys (tax on state enterprises 74.7%). Expenditures: 3,362,800,000,000 złotys (economy 46.6%, health and welfare 11.2%, education 11.2%, defense 8.3%).
Public debt (external, outstanding; 1984): U.S.$26,530,000,000.
Tourism (1983): receipts U.S.$85,000,000; expenditures U.S.$195,000,000.

Production (metric tons except as noted). Agriculture, forestry, fishing (1984): potatoes 37,400,000, sugar beets 16,000,000, rye 9,500,000, wheat 6,000,000, barley 3,600,000; livestock (1985; number of live animals) 17,207,000 pigs, 10,906,000 cattle; roundwood 23,963,000 cu m; fish catch 725,000. Mining and quarrying (1984): copper ore 431,000; zinc 148,000; lead 52,800; iron ore 48,000. Manufacturing (1984): crude steel 16,500,000; rolled steel 13,121,000; pig iron 9,369,000; cotton fabrics 808,900,000 m. Construction (1984): residential 13,305,000 sq m. Energy production (consumption): electricity ('000,000 kW-hr; 1985) 137,712 (128,183); coal ('000 metric tons; 1985) 241,800 (197,000); crude petroleum (barrels; 1984) 1,398,600 (1,480,000); natural gas ('000,000 cu m; 1985) 6,373 (12,400).
Gross national product (1984): U.S.$143,000,000,000 (U.S.$3,890 per capita).

Structure of net material product and labour force

	1984 in value '000,000 złotys	% of total value	labour force	% of labour force
Agriculture	1,256.4	17.5	5,295,000	30.9
Mining and manufacturing }	3,561.8	49.6	4,999,400	29.1
Public utilities }			206,700	1.2
Construction	832.9	11.6	1,242,600	7.2
Transp. and commun.	420.3	5.9	1,057,000	6.2
Trade	982.3	13.7	1,325,000	7.7
Finance	—	—	156,300	0.9
Public admin., defense	—	—	253,000	1.5
Services	—	—	2,627,000	15.3
Other	128.1	1.7	1,800	0.0
TOTAL	7,181.8	100.0	17,163,800	100.0

Population economically active (1985): total 18,007,000; activity rate of total population 48.6% (participation rates: over age 15, 65.1%; female 45.9%; unemployed, n.a.).

Price and earnings indexes (1980 = 100)

	1978	1979	1980	1981	1982	1983	1984
Consumer price index	85.4	91.4	100.0	121.2	243.4	294.5	345.2
Monthly earnings index	81.8	86.2	100.0	139.3	215.9	237.8	272.7

Household income and expenditure. Average household size (1983) 3.4; average annual income 1,453,000 złotys (U.S.$11,900); sources of income: wages 82.9%, social welfare 17.1%; expenditure (1983): food 46.8%, clothing 12.5%, housing 12.3%.
Land use (1984): forested 27.9%; meadows 13.0%; agricultural and under permanent cultivation 47.3%; other 11.8%.

Foreign trade

Balance of trade (current prices)

	1978	1979	1980	1981	1982	1983	1984
'000,000,000 złotys	−6.2	−4.1	−6.4	−7.5	+82.2	+90.0	+126.2
% of total	6.5%	3.9%	5.8%	7.7%	4.5%	4.4%	5.0%

Imports (1984): 1,209,965,000,000 złotys (machinery and transport equipment 30.4%, fuel and power 23.1%, chemicals 13.3%, iron and steel products 9.5%, food 4.5%). *Major import sources:* U.S.S.R. 36.4%; W.Ger. 7.4%; E.Ger. 6.3%; Czechoslovakia 6.1%; Yugoslavia 3.5%.
Exports (1984): 1,336,125,000,000 złotys (machinery and transport equipment 39.3%, fuel and power 17.5%, chemicals 9.8%, food 6.3%, building materials 5.3%). *Major export destinations:* U.S.S.R. 29.6%; W.Ger. 8.5%; Czechoslovakia 5.6%; E.Ger. 4.6%; U.K. 4.1%; Hungary 3.2%.

Transport and communications

Transport. Railroads (1984): length 27,070 km; passenger-km 59,100,000,000; metric ton-km cargo 124,000,000,000. Roads (1985): total length 254,000 km (paved 62%). Vehicles (1985): passenger cars 3,179,000; trucks and buses 732,000. Merchant marine (1985): vessels (100 gross tons and over) 761; total deadweight tonnage 4,439,947. Air transport (1985): passenger-km 2,859,486,000; metric ton-km cargo 256,793,000; airports (1986) 12.
Communications (1983). Daily newspapers (1985): total number 45; circulation 7,960,000; circulation per 1,000 population 215. Radio (1985): 9,286,663 receivers (1 per 4.0 persons). Television (1985): 8,864,768 receivers (1 per 4.2 persons). Telephones (1985): 4,028,000 (1 per 9.5 persons).

Education and health

Education (1985–86)

	schools	teachers	students	student/ teacher ratio
Primary (age 7–15)	16,791	267,600	4,879,100	18.2
Secondary (age 15–19)	896	21,300	338,000	15.9
Voc., teacher tr.	7,328	82,900	1,359,800	16.4
Higher	92	57,300	265,800	4.6

Educational attainment (1983). Percent of population over age 15 having: less than full primary education 8.0%; primary and secondary 85.9%, of which secondary 22.2%; higher 5.3%. *Literacy* (1983): total population over age 15 literate 27,352,000 (99.2%).
Health (1985): physicians 71,097 (1 per 521 persons); hospital beds 242,334 (1 per 153 persons); infant mortality rate per 1,000 live births (1984) 19.1.
Food (1980–82): daily per capita caloric intake 3,356 (vegetable products 68%, animal products 32%); 133% of FAO recommended minimum.

Military

Total active duty personnel (1985): 319,000 (army 65.8%, navy 6.0%, air force 28.2%). *Military expenditure as percent of GNP* (1983): 5.8% (world 6.1%); per capita expenditure U.S.$321.

Portugal

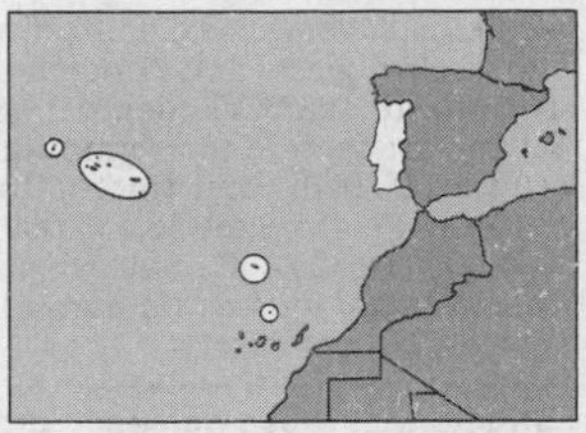

Official name: República Portuguesa (Republic of Portugal).
Form of government: parliamentary state with one legislative house (Assembly of the Republic [250]).
Chief of state: President.
Head of government: Prime Minister.
Capital: Lisbon.
Official language: Portuguese.
Official religion: none.
Monetary unit: 1 Escudo (Esc) = 100 centavos; valuation (Oct. 1, 1986) 1 U.S.$ = Esc 146.88; 1 £ = Esc 212.24.

Area and population

Continental Portugal Districts	Capitals	area sq mi	area sq km	population 1985 estimate*
Aveiro	Aveiro	1,084	2,808	648,796
Beja	Beja	3,948	10,225	183,994
Braga	Braga	1,032	2,673	747,701
Bragança	Bragança	2,551	6,608	186,905
Castelo Branco	Castelo Branco	2,577	6,675	230,306
Coimbra	Coimbra	1,524	3,947	444,699
Évora	Évora	2,854	7,393	178,248
Faro	Faro	1,915	4,960	334,598
Guarda	Guarda	2,131	5,518	202,393
Leiria	Leiria	1,357	3,515	432,509
Lisboa	Lisbon (Lisboa)	1,066	2,761	2,113,400
Portalegre	Portalegre	2,342	6,065	140,493
Porto	Porto	925	2,395	1,629,399
Santarém	Santarém	2,605	6,747	459,999
Setúbal	Setúbal	1,955	5,064	723,000
Viana do Castelo	Viana do Castelo	871	2,255	263,506
Vila Real	Vila Real	1,671	4,328	266,010
Viseu	Viseu	1,933	5,007	427,397
Azores (Açores) Autonomous Region	Ponta Delgada	868	2,247	250,699
Madeira Autonomous Region	Funchal	306	794	264,787
TOTAL		35,672†	92,389†	10,128,839

Demography

Population (1986): 10,250,000.
Density (1986): persons per sq mi 287.3, persons per sq km 110.9.
Urban-rural (1981): urban 29.6%; rural 70.4%.
Sex distribution (1985): male 48.25%; female 51.75%.
Age breakdown (1985): under 15, 23.8%; 15–29, 24.2%; 30–44, 18.3%; 45–59, 16.9%; 60–74, 12.3%; 75 and over, 4.5%.
Population projection: (1990) 10,450,500; (2000) 10,748,400.
Nationality (1981): Portuguese 98.9%; Angolan 0.2%; Cape Verdean 0.2%; French 0.1%; Brazilian 0.1%; Spanish 0.1%; other 0.4%.
Religious affiliation (1981): Christian 96.0%, of which Roman Catholic 94.5%, Protestant 0.6%, other Christian (mostly Apostolic Catholic and Jehovah's Witness) 0.9%; nonreligious 3.8%; Jewish 0.1%; Muslim 0.1%.
Major cities (1981): Lisbon 807,167; Porto 327,368; Amadora 95,518.

Vital statistics

Birth rate per 1,000 population (1985): 12.8 (world avg. 29.0); (1984) legitimate 88.5%; illegitimate 11.5%.
Death rate per 1,000 population (1985): 9.6 (world avg. 11.0).
Natural increase rate per 1,000 population (1985): 3.2 (world avg. 18.0).
Total fertility rate (avg. births per childbearing woman; 1980–85): 2.3.
Marriage rate per 1,000 population (1985): 6.7.
Divorce rate per 1,000 population (1984): 0.7.
Life expectancy at birth (1985): male 68.6 years; female 75.3 years.
Major causes of death per 100,000 population (1984): circulatory diseases 426.0, of which cerebrovascular diseases 241.3; ischemic heart disease 84.6; malignant neoplasms 155.4; liver disease 60.3; pneumonia 24.6.

National economy

Budget (1984). Revenue: Esc 603,167,000,000 (indirect taxes 52.7%; direct taxes 35.2%; property income 9.6%). Expenditures: Esc 976,213,000,000 (public debt 32.8%; education 9.8%; health 8.2%; defense 7.0%; public works 3.7%).
Public debt (external, outstanding; 1984): U.S.$10,582,800,000.
Tourism (1984): receipts from visitors U.S.$949,000,000; expenditures by nationals abroad U.S.$222,000,000.
Production (metric tons except as noted). Agriculture, forestry, fishing (1984): potatoes 1,080,000, grapes 1,020,000, tomatoes 881,000, corn (maize) 530,000, wheat 344,000, olives 300,000, oats 195,000, cork 99,200‡; livestock (number of live animals) 5,000,000 sheep, 3,450,000 pigs, 1,020,000 cattle; roundwood (1983) 8,278,000 cu m; fish catch (1983) 246,470. Mining and quarrying (1985): copper pyrites 355,000; anthracite 237,000; kaolin 53,900; tungsten 2,975. Manufacturing (value of production in Esc '000,000; 1985): refined petroleum 286,111; cotton and synthetic fibres 172,298; animal feedstuffs 84,533; clothing 73,778; radios, televisions, and telecommunications equipment 54,579; iron and steel 59,547; netting 45,947; motor vehicles 39,895; cement 35,610; alcoholic beverages 20,085. Construction (1983): residential 5,447,000 sq m; nonresidential 2,007,000 sq m. Energy production (consumption): electricity (kW-hr; 1984) 19,033,000,000 (20,333,000,000); coal (metric tons; 1984) 194,900 (673,000); crude petroleum (barrels; 1984) none (55,430,000); petroleum products (metric tons; 1984) 6,760,000 (7,837,000); natural gas, none (n.a.).
Gross national product (at current market prices; 1984): U.S.$20,050,000,000 (U.S.$1,990 per capita).

Structure of gross domestic product and labour force

	1984 in value Esc '000,000	% of total value	labour force	% of labour force
Agriculture	256,600	9.2	998,000	22.3
Mining }	889,100	31.8	13,000	0.3
Manufacturing }			1,017,000	22.7
Construction	172,300	6.2	350,000	7.8
Public utilities	61,700	2.2	31,000	0.7
Transp. and commun. }	550,900	19.7	158,000	3.5
Trade }			523,000	11.7
Finance	172,800	6.2	116,000	2.6
Pub. admin., defense	329,400	11.8 }	857,000	19.2
Services }	359,900	12.9 }		
Other }			413,000§	9.2
TOTAL	2,792,700	100.0	4,476,000	100.0

Population economically active (1984): total 4,476,000; activity rate of total population 44.4% (participation rates: ages 15–64, 68.6%; female 41.5%; unemployed 8.4%).

Price and earnings indexes (1980 = 100)

	1979	1980	1981	1982	1983	1984	1985
Consumer price index	85.7	100.0	120.0	147.3	184.3	237.6	284.2
Daily earnings index	82.6	100.0	121.6	148.0	172.7	203.6	244.1

Household income and expenditure. Average household size (1981) 2.9; income per household: n.a.; sources of income (1985): property and entrepreneurial income 42.3%; wages and salaries 36.4%, transfer payments 12.1%; expenditure (1981): food 34.8%, transportation and communication 14.6%, housing 13.2%, clothing and footwear 11.2%, cafes and hotels 8.8%, health 4.3%, recreation 3.9%, other 9.2%.
Land use (1983): forested 39.7%; meadows and pastures 5.8%; agricultural and under permanent cultivation 38.7%; other 15.8%.

Foreign trade

Balance of trade (current prices)

	1980	1981	1982	1983	1984	1985
Esc '000,000	−243,870	−352,100	−422,240	−390,740	−377,210	−248,260
% of total	34.5%	40.7%	38.9%	27.8%	19.9%	11.4%

Imports (1985): Esc 1,302,737,000,000 (crude petroleum 24.1%, machinery and transport equipment 13.8%, of which road vehicles 7.3%; chemicals 8.6%, cereals 4.3%). *Major import sources:* West Germany 11.4%; United States 9.7%; France 8.0%; United Kingdom 7.5%; Italy 5.2%.
Exports (1985): Esc 967,404,000,000 (clothing 9.3%; paper products 6.9%; chemicals 6.0%; crude petroleum 4.4%; iron and steel products 3.6%; cork products 3.5%; alcoholic beverages 3.3%). *Major export destinations:* United Kingdom 14.6%; West Germany 13.8%; France 12.7%; United States 9.2%; The Netherlands 6.9%.

Transport and communications

Transport. Railroads (1985): route length 2,245 mi, 3,613 km; passenger-km 5,722,000,000; metric ton-km cargo 1,307,000,000. Roads (1981): total length 32,282 mi, 51,953 km (paved 86%). Vehicles (1984): passenger cars 1,600,738; trucks and buses 103,285. Merchant marine (1985): vessels (100 gross tons and over) 367; total deadweight tonnage 2,405,741. Air transport (1984)‖: passenger-km 4,273,953,000; metric ton-km cargo 125,556,000; airports (1986) 20.
Communications. Daily newspapers (1985): total number 28; total circulation 593,900¶; circulation per 1,000 population 58. Radio (1984): total number of receivers 2,155,000 (1 per 4.7 persons). Television (1984): total number of receivers 1,523,000 (1 per 6.6 persons). Telephones (1983): 1,567,000 (1 per 6.4 persons).

Education and health

Education (1982–83)

	schools	teachers	students	student/teacher ratio
Primary (age 5–11)	13,069	76,141	1,305,724	17.1
Secondary (age 12–19)	629	38,809	582,495	15.0
Voc., teacher tr.	368	...	26,003	...
Higher	21	10,578	89,964	8.5

Educational attainment (1981). Percent of population over age 14 having: no formal schooling 21.8%; primary education 58.5%; secondary 15.9%; higher 3.8%. *Literacy* (1981): total population over age 14 literate 5,729,000 (78.2%); males literate 2,967,000 (84.0%); females literate 2,762,000 (72.7%).
Health (1985): physicians 24,095 (1 per 420 persons); hospital beds 53,566 (1 per 190 persons); infant mortality rate per 1,000 live births 11.6.
Food (1980–82): daily per capita caloric intake 3,106 (vegetable products 80%, animal products 20%); 127% of FAO recommended minimum requirement.

Military

Total active duty personnel (1985): 73,040 (army 62.6%, navy 19.1%, air force 18.3%). *Military expenditure as percent of GNP* (1984): 3.2% (world 6.1%); per capita expenditure U.S.$81.

*January 1. †Includes 156 sq mi (404 sq km) of inland water. ‡1983. §Mostly unemployed. ‖ TAP (Air Portugal) only. ¶For 16 newspapers only.

Puerto Rico

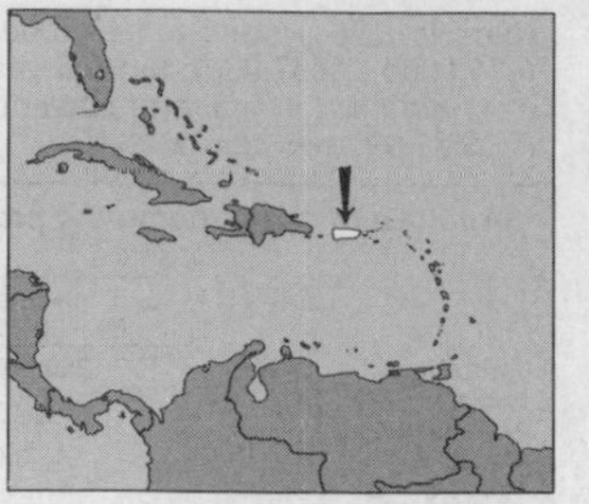

Official name: Estado Libre Asociado de Puerto Rico (Spanish); Commonwealth of Puerto Rico (English).
Political status: self-governing commonwealth associated with the United States, having two legislative houses (Senate [27]; House of Representatives [51]).
Chief of state: President of the United States.
Head of government: Governor.
Capital: San Juan.
Official languages: Spanish; English.
Official religion: none.
Monetary unit: 1 U.S. dollar (U.S.$) = 100 cents; valuation (Oct. 1, 1986) 1 U.S.$ = £0.69.

Population 1984 estimate

Municipio	population	Municipio	population	Municipio	population
Adjuntas	18,900	Fajardo	33,200	Naguabo	21,300
Aguada	32,400	Florida	7,600	Naranjito	25,100
Aguadilla	55,000	Guánica	18,800	Orocovis	20,900
Agunas Buenas	23,000	Guayama	40,300	Patillas	17,900
Aibonito	22,500	Guayanilla	21,000	Peñuelas	20,200
Añasco	24,400	Guaynabo	85,100	Ponce	190,900
Arecibo	87,000	Gurabo	25,000	Quebradillas	19,700
Arroyo	18,200	Hatillo	30,400	Rincón	12,400
Barceloneta	19,600	Hormigueros	15,200	Río Grande	37,700
Barranquitas	22,800	Humacao	52,400	Sabana Grande	21,100
Bayamón	202,500	Isabela	38,200	Salinas	26,600
Cabo Rojo	35,000	Jayuya	15,000	San Germán	34,200
Caguas	121,100	Juana Díaz	43,600	San Juan	428,900
Camuy	26,200	Juncos	27,000	San Lorenzo	33,300
Canóvanas	32,400	Lajas	21,300	San Sebastián	36,100
Carolina	165,700	Lares	28,000	Santa Isabel	19,500
Cataño	25,900	Las Marías	8,600	Toa Alta	33,400
Cayey	43,300	Las Piedras	23,100	Toa Baja	77,700
Ceiba	15,100	Loíza	24,600	Trujillo Alto	50,800
Ciales	17,200	Luquillo	15,400	Utuado	34,600
Cidra	29,600	Manatí	38,000	Vega Alta	30,000
Coamo	32,200	Maricao	6,700	Vega Baja	48,800
Comerío	18,400	Maunabo	11,800	Vieques	7,800
Corozal	29,600	Mayagüez	101,000	Villalba	22,500
Culebra	1,300	Moca	29,900	Yabucoa	31,400
Dorado	26,700	Morovis	21,900	Yauco	39,200
				TOTAL	3,270,000

Demography

Area: 3,515 sq mi, 9,104 sq km.
Population (1986): 3,287,000.
Density (1986): persons per sq mi 935.1, persons per sq km 361.1.
Urban-rural (1985): urban 70.7%; rural 29.3%.
Sex distribution (1980): male 48.70%; female 51.30%.
Age breakdown (1980): under 15, 31.6%; 15–29, 26.5%; 30–44, 18.4%; 45–59, 12.3%; 60–74, 8.3%; 75 and over, 2.9%.
Population projection: (1990) 3,320,000; (2000) 3,424,000.
Doubling time: 54 years.
Ethnic composition (1980): white 80.0%; black 20.0%.
Religious affiliation (1984): Roman Catholic 85.3%; Protestant 4.7%; other 10.0%.
Major cities (1984): San Juan 428,900; Bayamón 202,500; Ponce 190,900; Carolina 165,700; Caguas 121,100.

Vital statistics

Birth rate per 1,000 population (1984): 19.5 (world avg. 29.0); (1980) legitimate 79.0%; illegitimate 21.0%.
Death rate per 1,000 population (1984): 6.6 (world avg. 11.0).
Natural increase rate per 1,000 population (1984): 12.9 (world avg. 18.0).
Total fertility rate (avg. births per childbearing woman; 1980–85): 2.4.
Marriage rate per 1,000 population (1983): 9.1.
Divorce rate per 1,000 population (1983): 4.0.
Life expectancy at birth (1980–85): male 70.8 years; female 76.9 years.
Major causes of death per 100,000 population (1982): diseases of the circulatory system 267.9; malignant neoplasms (cancers) 101.1; diseases of the respiratory system 64.8; diseases of the digestive system 44.4; diabetes mellitus 27.8; accidents 26.8; homicide and other violence 15.8.

National economy

Budget (1983–84). Revenue: U.S.$3,771,000,000* (income taxes 33.1%, federal grants 18.2%, local excise taxes 15.9%, federal excise taxes 9.7%). Expenditures: U.S.$3,688,000,000 (health and welfare 32.2%, education 28.1%, public safety 9.2%, debt payment 7.4%, general government 6.9%).
Public debt (outstanding; 1984): U.S.$8,690,900,000.
Tourism: receipts from visitors (1984) U.S.$659,000,000; expenditures by nationals abroad (1983) U.S.$551,000,000.
Production (value of production in U.S.$'000,000 except as noted). Agriculture, forestry, fishing (1984): milk 164, starchy vegetables 57, coffee 48, fruit 33, sugarcane 29, eggs 24; livestock (number of live animals) 591,000 cattle, 203,000 pigs; roundwood, n.a.; fish catch 1,256 metric tons. Mining (1984): stone 28. Manufacturing (net income in U.S.$'000,000; 1984): chemicals 2,513, of which pharmaceuticals 2,245, petrochemicals 89; metal products and machinery 2,146; foods 584, of which meat products 150, alcoholic beverages 83, confectionery 80; apparel and related products 452; stone, clay, glass, and concrete products 85. Construction (new buildings authorized; 1983): residential 1,655,000 sq m; nonresidential 23,400 sq m. Energy production (consumption): electricity (kW-hr; 1984) 12,281,000,300 (10,154,600,000); coal (metric tons; 1984) none (50,000); crude petroleum (barrels; 1984) none (36,555,000); petroleum products (metric tons; 1984) 5,519,000 (6,320,000); natural gas, none (none).
Gross national product (at current market prices; 1984): U.S.$14,031,000,000 (U.S.$4,290 per capita).

Structure of gross domestic product and labour force

	1984			
	in value US$'000,000	% of total value	labour force	% of labour force
Agriculture	396.7	2.1	39,000	4.1
Manufacturing	7,274.6	38.0	143,000	15.0
Mining	361.6	1.9	2,000	0.2
Construction			34,000	3.6
Public utilities	1,675.6	9.0	11,000	1.2
Transp. and commun.			30,000	3.2
Trade	2,645.5	14.2	145,000	15.2
Finance	2,409.2	12.9	22,000	2.3
Pub. admin., defense	2,153.1	11.5	177,000	18.6
Services	1,742.8	9.3	140,000	14.7
Other	11.9	0.1	209,000†	21.9
TOTAL	18,671.0	100.0	952,000	100.0

Population economically active (1985): total 967,400; activity rate of total population 29.5% (participation rates: ages 16–64, 48.2%; female 35.3%; unemployed [1986] 20.3%).

Price and earnings indexes (1980 = 100)

	1979	1980	1981	1982	1983	1984	1985
Consumer price index	90.7	100.0	109.8	113.9	114.6	116.8	117.3
Earnings index‡	92.1	100.0	109.2	115.4	120.1	121.4	...

Household income and expenditure. Average family size (1984) 4.1; income per family U.S.$16,794; sources of income (1984): wages and salaries 54.4%, transfers 30.4%, self-employment 6.7%, other 8.5%; expenditure (1984): food and beverages 21.2%, household furnishings 13.8%, housing 12.7%, transportation 12.4%, clothing 11.6%, recreation 9.0%, health care 5.3%, foreign travel 3.9%, education 2.0%, other 8.1%.
Land use (1981): forested 20.3%; meadows and pastures 38.1%; agricultural and under permanent cultivation 15.7%; other 25.9%.

Foreign trade

Balance of trade (current prices)

	1978	1979	1980	1981	1982	1983	1984
U.S.$'000,000	−1,795	−1,295	−2,442	−2,282	+721	−466	−690
% of total	14.9%	9.0%	15.7%	13.9%	4.2%	2.7%	3.3%

Imports (1983–84): U.S.$9,528,300,000 (petroleum products 13.1%, chemicals [all forms] 11.9%, food 11.9%, crude petroleum 9.2%, automobiles 5.9%, textiles [all forms] 5.6%). *Major import sources:* U.S. 57.3%; Japan 5.4%; Venezuela 4.7%; Netherlands Antilles 4.0%; Ecuador 4.0%.
Exports (1983–84): U.S.$9,145,900,000 (chemicals, crude petroleum, and petroleum products 33.5%, metal products and machinery 23.1%, food and alcoholic beverages 17.4%, textiles [all forms] 8.3%). *Major export destinations:* U.S. 82.7%; U.S. Virgin Islands 2.1%; Dominican Republic 1.8%.

Transport and communications

Transport. Railroads (1985)§: length 59 mi, 96 km. Roads (1984): total length 8,810 mi, 14,178 km (paved 86%). Vehicles (1984): passenger cars 1,020,700; trucks and buses 157,100. Merchant marine: n.a. Air transport (1983–84): passenger arrivals 2,533,352, passenger departures 2,571,012; cargo loaded and unloaded 165,258 metric tons; airports (1986) with scheduled flights 9.
Communications. Daily newspapers (1985): total number 5; total circulation 577,000; circulation per 1,000 population 176. Radio (1985): 2,000,000 receivers (1 per 1.6 persons). Television (1985): 818,000 receivers (1 per 4.0 persons). Telephones (1984): 808,736 (1 per 4.0 persons).

Education and health

Education (1980–81)

	schools	teachers	students	student/teacher ratio
Primary (age 5–12)	1,618	23,154	470,089	20.3
Secondary (age 13–18)	619	13,297	337,153	25.4
Voc., teacher tr.	68	2,600	60,045	23.1
Higher	34	3,300	159,972 ‖	...

Educational attainment (1980). Percent of adult population over age 25 having: no formal schooling 8.0%; primary education 39.8%; secondary 33.8%; higher 18.4%. *Literacy* (1980): total population over age 15 literate 1,924,100 (90.8%); males literate 934,400 (91.8%); females literate 989,700 (89.8%).
Health (1983): physicians 7,133 (1 per 458 persons); hospital beds (1984) 12,493 (1 per 262 persons); infant mortality rate per 1,000 live births 17.4.

Military

Total active duty personnel (1985): 3,900¶.

*Excludes federal government grants to specific local government agencies equaling U.S.$1,200,000,000. †Unemployed. ‡Hourly earnings in manufacturing. §Privately owned railway for sugarcane transport only. ‖ 1984. ¶Excludes paramilitary personnel. The United States is responsible for defense.

Qatar

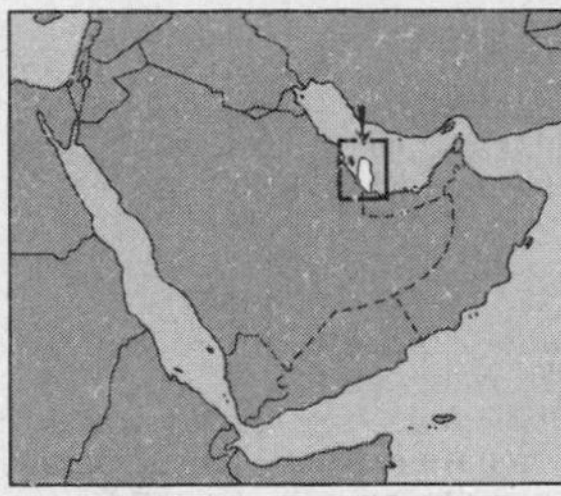

Official name: Dawlat Qaṭar (State of Qatar).
Form of government: constitutional monarchy; Islamic law is the basis of legislation in the state.
Head of state and government: Emir.
Capital: Doha.
Official language: Arabic.
Official religion: Islam.
Monetary unit: 1 riyal (QR) = 100 dirhams; valuation (Oct. 1, 1986) 1 U.S.$ = QR 3.64; 1 £ = QR 5.26.

Area and population

	area		population
			1970
Municipalities*	sq mi	sq km	estimate
Doha	...	...	68,400
al-Khawr	...	...	1,900
ar-Rayyān	...	...	5,800
ash-Shamāl†	...	...	2,300
Umm aṣ-Ṣilāl	...	...	2,000
al-Wakrah	...	...	1,800
nonmunicipal area			
Dukhān	...	...	700
other‡	...	...	28,200
TOTAL	4,400	11,400	111,100

Demography

Population (1986): 311,000.
Density (1986): persons per sq mi 70.7, persons per sq km 27.3.
Urban–rural (1985): urban 88.0%; rural 12.0%.
Sex distribution (1985)§: male 66.11%; female 33.89%.
Age breakdown (1984): under 15, 36.2%; 15–29, 30.4%; 30–44, 23.2%; 45–59, 7.6%; 60 and over, 2.6%.
Population projection: (1990) 354,000; (2000) 469,000.
Doubling time: 29 years.
Ethnic composition (1983): South Asian 34%; Qatari 20%; other Arab 25%; Iranian 16%; other 5%.
Religious affiliation (1980): Muslim 92.4% ‖ ; Christian 5.9%; Hindu 1.1%; Bahā'ī 0.2%; other 0.4%.
Major cities (1983): Doha 190,000; Musay'īd 40,000.

Vital statistics

Birth rate per 1,000 population (1985): 30.6 (world avg. 29.0); legitimate, n.a.; illegitimate, n.a.
Death rate per 1,000 population (1985): 2.6 (world avg. 11.0).
Natural increase rate per 1,000 population (1985): 28.0 (world avg. 18.0).
Total fertility rate (avg. births per childbearing woman; 1984): 4.6.
Marriage rate per 1,000 population (1985): 3.6.
Divorce rate per 1,000 population (1985): 1.0.
Life expectancy at birth (1980–85): male 68.2 years; female 73.2 years.
Major causes of death per 100,000 population (1985): injury and poisoning 61.5; diseases of the circulatory system 45.8; symptoms, signs, and ill-defined conditions 43.2; malignant neoplasms (cancers) 27.5; endocrine, nutritional, and metabolic disease and immunity disorders 11.3; diseases of the digestive system 7.9.

National economy

Budget (1985–86). Revenue: QR 9,737,000,000 (crude oil 85.0%). Expenditures: QR 17,048,000,000 (state capital development projects 22.3%, of which industry and agriculture 4.9%, housing and public buildings 4.1%, electricity and water 1.0%, education 0.1%; foreign commitments 8.5%; other capital development projects 7.9%).
Public debt: none.
Production (metric tons except as noted). Agriculture, forestry, fishing (1985): tomatoes 5,574, dates 4,921, squash 1,673, melons 1,586, barley 1,399, eggplant 808, wheat 140; livestock (number of live animals) 72,540 goats, 67,661 sheep, 10,759 camels, 6,108 cattle, 2,300 deer, 700 horses; roundwood, n.a.; fish catch 3,362. Mining and quarrying (1983): limestone 1,600,000; clay, sand, and gypsum are also mined for local use. Manufacturing (1985): ammonia 743,800; urea 639,600; concrete reinforcing steel bars 503,700; propane 329,161; cement 227,700; butane 219,557; ethylene 184,900; sulphur 27,600; organic fertilizer 22,400; flour 17,900; bran 5,700. Construction (1984): residential 421,400 sq m; nonresidential 68,000 sq m. Energy production (consumption): electricity (kW-hr; 1984) 3,425,000,000 (3,425,000,000); coal, none (n.a.); crude petroleum (barrels; 1984) 139,389,000 (20,152,000); petroleum products (metric tons; 1984) 3,996,000 (485,000); natural gas (cu m; 1984) 4,167,000,000 (4,167,000,000).
Population economically active¶ (1984): total 113,149; activity rate of total population 40.3% (participation rates: over age 15, 63.2%; female 9.8%; unemployed, n.a.).

Price and earnings indexes (1980 = 100)

	1979	1980	1981	1982	1983	1984
Consumer price index	93.6	100.0	...	113.9	119.5	117.3
Earnings index	...	...	...	...	...	...

Household income and expenditure. Average family size (1984) 6.4; income per family: n.a.; source of income: n.a.; expenditure: n.a.

Gross national product (at current market prices; 1984): U.S.$6,020,000,000 (U.S.$20,690 per capita).

Structure of gross domestic product and labour force

	1985		1984	
	in value QR '000,000	% of total value	labour force	% of labour force
Agriculture	230	1.7	267	0.2
Mining	...	...	6,658	5.9
Manufacturing	1,660	12.5	12,763	11.3
Construction	1,428	10.7	28,347	25.1
Public utilities	173	1.3	6,998	6.2
Transportation	478	3.6	4,737	4.2
Trade	1,484	11.2	16,151	14.3
Finance	1,830	13.7	3,713	3.3
Pub. admin., defense	6,065	45.6	...	...
Services	325	2.4	33,515	29.5
Other	−364♀	−2.7♀	...	...
TOTAL	13,309	100.0	113,149	100.0

Tourism (1985): receipts and expenditures, n.a.; total number of tourists staying in hotels 96,307.
Land use (1983): meadows and pastures 4.5%; agricultural and under permanent cultivation 0.3%; built-up, desert, and other 95.2%.

Foreign trade♂

Balance of trade (current prices)

	1979	1980	1981	1982	1983	1984
QR '000,000	+9,282	+16,040	+15,757	+9,138	+7,419	+12,698
% of total	44.1%	63.0%	61.4%	41.9%	43.9%	63.0%

Imports (1985): QR 4,195,000,000 (machinery and transport equipment 38.7%, food and live animals 15.0%, chemicals and chemical products 5.1%, beverages and tobacco 2.2%, cork and wood 0.6%). *Major import sources:* Japan 18.2%; United Kingdom 16.3%; West Germany 8.7%; France 7.6%; United States 6.5%; Italy 4.9%; The Netherlands 2.8%; United Arab Emirates 2.6%.
Exports (1985): QR 12,895,000,000 (crude petroleum 91.1%, liquefied gas and other nonpetroleum exports 8.9%). *Major export destinations:* Japan 56.6%; France 8.9%; Singapore 3.8%; Italy 2.2%; Australia 2.0%; The Netherlands 2.0%; United Kingdom 1.1%; China 0.9%.

Transport and communications

Transport. Railroads: none. Roads (1983): total length 671 mi, 1,080 km (paved, n.a.). Vehicles (1985) new passengers cars 10,001; truck and buses 3,558. Merchant marine (1985): vessels (100 gross tons and over) 60; total deadweight tonnage 525,099. Air transport (1983): passenger arrivals 402,400, passenger departures 399,100; cargo unloaded 17,062 metric tons, cargo loaded 4,193 metric tons; airports (1986) with scheduled flights 1.
Communications. Daily newspapers (1985): total number 5; total circulation 55,500; circulation per 1,000 population 184.4. Radio (1985): total number of receivers 120,000 (1 per 2.5 persons). Television (1985): total number of receivers 150,000 (1 per 2.0 persons). Telephones (1984): 105,666 (1 per 2.8 persons).

Education and health

Education (1984–85)□

	schools	teachers	students	student/ teacher ratio
Primary (age 6–11)	92	2,505	30,515	12.2
Secondary (age 12–17)	70	2,090	18,261	8.7
Vocational	3	88	581	6.6
Higher	1	401	4,621	11.5

Educational attainment (1981). Percent of population over age 10 having: no formal education (including illiterates) 48.9%; primary 15.0%; preparatory (lower secondary) 11.7%; secondary 12.8%; postsecondary 11.6%. *Literacy* (1981): total population over age 10 literate 96,565 (51.1%); males literate 65,151 (51.2%); females literate 31,414 (50.1%).
Health: physicians (1985) 505 (1 per 596 persons); hospital beds (1983) 891 (1 per 315 persons); infant mortality rate per 1,000 live births (1980–85) 45.0.
Food: daily per capita caloric intake, n.a.

Military

Total active duty personnel (1985): 6,000 (army 83.3%, navy 11.7%, air force 5.0%). *Military expenditure as percent of GNP* (1981): 13.1% (world 5.7%); per capita expenditure U.S.$3,896.

*Towns under the supervision of the Ministry of Municipal Affairs. All such locales are subject to urban plan and construction projects. †Includes ar-Ruways. ‡Includes other towns, islands, and nomads. Qatar's main industrial centre, Musay 'īd (Umm Sa'īd), grew substantially after the construction of an oil refinery in 1974. It is not yet a municipality. §Sex distribution (1970): Qatari (male 50.33%, female 49.67%); non-Qatari (male 74.21%, female 25.79%); total (male 64.53%, female 35.47%). ‖ Qatari nationals are almost all Sunnī Muslims of the Wahhābīyah sect. ¶Includes foreign workers. ♀Includes QR 120,000,000 import duties less QR 484,000,000 imputed bank service charge. ♂Import figures are f.o.b. (free on board) in balance of trade and c.i.f. (cost, insurance, and freight) for commodities and trading partners. □There were 13,050 students and 926 teachers in private schools. There were also 1,138 Qatari university students studying abroad.

Réunion

Official name: Département de la Réunion (Department of Reunion).
Political status: overseas department (France) with two legislative houses (General Council [36]; Regional Council [45]).
Chief of state: President of France.
Heads of government: Commissioner of the Republic (for France); President of General Council (for Réunion); President of Regional Council (for Réunion).
Capital: Saint-Denis.
Official language: French.
Official religion: none.
Monetary unit: 1 Franc (F) = 100 centimes; valuation (Oct. 1, 1986) 1 U.S.$ = F 6.64; 1 £ = F 9.60.

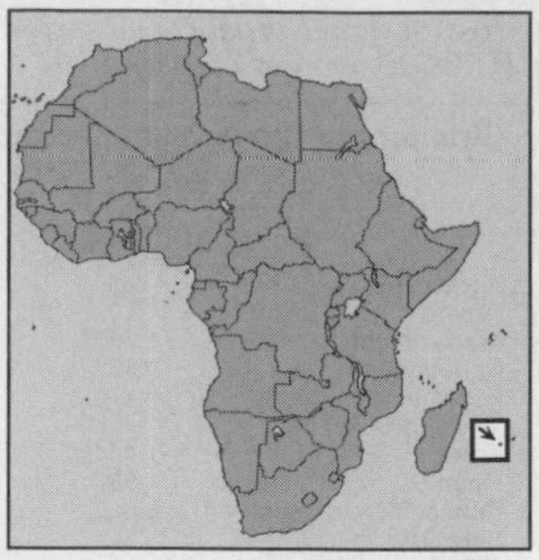

Area and population

		area		population
Arrondissements	Capitals	sq mi	sq km	1982 census
Saint-Benoit	Saint-Benoit	284	736	74,312
Saint-Denis	Saint-Denis	164	423	180,647
Saint-Paul	Saint-Paul	180	467	94,378
Saint-Pierre	Saint-Pierre	339	878	166,461
TOTAL		969* †	2,510* †	515,798†

Demography

Population (1986): 555,000.
Density (1986): persons per sq mi 573.8, persons per sq km 221.5.
Urban-rural (1982): urban 52.8%; rural 47.2%.
Sex distribution (1982): male 49.05%; female 50.95%.
Age breakdown (1982): under 15, 35.6%; 15–29, 29.8%; 30–44, 17.2%; 45–59, 11.1%; 60 and over, 6.3%.
Population projection: (1990) 595,000; (2000) 706,000.
Doubling time: 38 years.
Ethnic composition (1980): mixed race 63.1%; East Indian 27.5%; French 3.1%; other (including Chinese, Comoran, East African, Malagasy, and Arab) 6.3%.
Religious affiliation (1980): Roman Catholic 96.3%; Muslim 2.2%; Protestant 0.6%; Bahā'ī 0.3%; Hindu 0.2%; other 0.4%.
Major cities (1982)‡: Saint-Denis 126,323; Saint-Pierre 90,627; Saint-Joseph 31,141; Le Port 25,377.

Vital statistics

Birth rate per 1,000 population (1985): 24.1 (world avg. 29.0); legitimate 52.9%; illegitimate 47.1%.
Death rate per 1,000 population (1985): 5.6 (world avg. 11.0).
Natural increase rate per 1,000 population (1985): 18.5 (world avg. 18.0).
Total fertility rate (avg. births per childbearing woman; 1980–85): 2.5.
Marriage rate per 1,000 population (1985): 5.8.
Divorce rate per 1,000 population (1985): 1.2.
Life expectancy at birth (1980–85): male 64.6 years; female 68.2 years.
Major causes of death per 100,000 population (1984): diseases of the circulatory system 174.0; accidents, poisoning, violence 71.1; malignant neoplasms (cancers) 46.4; diseases of the respiratory system 38.7; diseases of the circulatory system 36.5; endocrine and metabolic disorders 22.4.

National economy

Budget (1984). Revenue: F 3,123,000,000 (grants from the French central government 39.8%; indirect taxes 24.8%, of which taxes on fuels 19.7%; new loans 7.4%; supplementary receipts from unreported sources 27.5%). Expenditures: F 3,123,000,000 (health and social services 33.6%; general administration 15.3%; public works 12.5%; debt charges 1.0%; nondesignated supplementary expenditures 27.5).
Public debt (external, outstanding; 1984§): U.S.$54,000,000.
Tourism (1984): tourist arrivals 78,952.
Gross national product (1983): U.S.$1,917,000,000 (U.S.$3,640 per capita).

Structure of gross domestic product and labour force

	1980		1982	
	in value F '000,000	% of total value	labour force ‖	% of labour force
Agriculture	500	5.9	17,390	14.7
Mining	...	...	...	...
Manufacturing	800	9.5	7,369	6.2
Construction	401	4.7	11,176	9.4
Public utilities	132	1.6	697	0.6
Transportation and communication	348	4.1	5,871	5.0
Trade	1,240	14.7	14,328	12.1
Finance, real estate, insurance	2,076¶	24.6	15,915♀	13.4
Pub. admin., defense, and services	2,661	31.5	44,576	37.6
Other	290	3.4	1,168	1.0
TOTAL	8,448	100.0	118,490	100.0

Production (metric tons except as noted). Agriculture, forestry, fishing (1985): sugarcane 2,077,000, corn (maize) 14,000, bananas 4,520, potatoes 3,940, mangoes 3,858, tomatoes 3,620, onions 1,420, carrots 1,354, avocados 800, tobacco 232, vanilla 132, geranium extract 23, khuskhus (vetiver) extract 13; livestock (number of live animals; 1984) 72,000 pigs, 43,000 goats, 20,000 cattle; roundwood (1984) 33,000 cu m; fish catch 2,180. Mining and quarrying (1984): gravel and sand for local use. Manufacturing (1985): sugar 227,900; cement 172,800δ; molasses 67,400; rum 102,400 hectolitres. Construction: n.a. Energy production (consumption): electricity (kW-hr; 1984) 521,000,000 (513,300,000); coal, none (none); crude petroleum, none (none); petroleum products (metric tons; 1984) none (301,000); natural gas, none (none).
Population economically active (1982): total 172,828; activity rate of total population 33.5% (participation rates: ages 15–65, 54.3%; female 35.9%; unemployed [1985] 40.0%).

Price and earnings indexes (December 1980 = 100)□

	1979	1980	1981	1982	1983	1984	1985
Consumer price index	...	100.0	113.9	124.3	134.4	144.0	152.9
Earnings index◇	85.6	100.0	122.2	142.4	156.8	171.0	182.9

Household income and expenditure. Average household size (1982) 4.2; income per household (1981) F 82,240 (U.S.$15,133); sources of income (1981): wages and salaries 66.4%, self-employment 17.4%, transfer payments 12.4%, other 3.8%; expenditure△: food and beverages 38.8%, clothing and footwear 11.5%, housing 8.2%, energy 7.4%†, transportation 7.2%, household furnishings 6.2%, food away from home 2.7%, other 18.0%.
Land use (1983): forested 35.2%; meadows and pastures 4.0%; agricultural and under permanent cultivation 21.6%; other 39.2%.

Foreign trade

Balance of trade (current prices)

	1980	1981	1982	1983	1984	1985
F '000,000	–3,368	–3,522	–4,548	–5,536	–6,077	–6,654.8
% of total	75.3%	69.9%	75.0%	76.0%	78.8%	80.6%

Imports (1984): F 6,894,600,000 (food and agricultural products 24.1%, electrical and nonelectrical machinery 13.5%, mineral fuels 12.3%, transport equipment 10.4%, chemical products 8.6%). *Major import sources* (1985): France 65.0%; Bahrain 5.1%; United Arab Emirates 3.4%; Italy 3.1%; South Africa 3.0%.
Exports (1984): F 816,600,000 (sugar 75.0%, rum 4.2%, spiny lobster 2.9%, geranium extract 2.6%, khuskhus (vetiver) extract 1.6%). *Major export destinations* (1985): France 52.8%; Portugal 26.8%; West Germany 3.2%; Madagascar 3.1%.

Transport and communications

Transport. Railroads, none. Roads (1984): total length 1,684 mi, 2,710 km (paved, n.a.). Vehicles (1984): passenger cars 128,228; trucks and buses 41,841. Merchant marine: n.a. Air transport (1985): passenger arrivals 205,772, passenger departures 209,685; cargo unloaded 6,757 metric tons, cargo loaded 3,673 metric tons; airports (1986) with scheduled flights 1.
Communications. Daily newspapers (1985): total number 3; total circulation 61,500; circulation per 1,000 population 113. Radio (1985): total number of receivers 122,000 (1 per 4.5 persons). Television (1985): total number of receivers 88,000 (1 per 6.2 persons). Telephones (1986): 90,015 (1 per 6.1 persons).

Education and health

Education (1984–85)

	schools	teachers	students	student/ teacher ratio
Primary (age 6–11)	508	5,087	113,330	22.3
Secondary (age 12–18) / Voc., teacher tr.	85	3,947	69,417	17.6
Higher	1	74	2,420	32.7

Educational attainment (1974). Percent of population over age 15 having: no formal schooling 26.2%; primary education 31.9%; secondary 39.3%; higher 2.0%; not specified 0.6%. *Literacy* (1982): total population over age 15 literate 270,200 (78.7%).
Health (1985): physicians (1986) 750 (1 per 734 persons); hospital beds 3,498 (1 per 156 persons); infant mortality rate per 1,000 live births 10.3.
Food (1980–82): daily per capita caloric intake 2,694 (vegetable products 83%, animal products 17%); 119% of FAO recommended minimum requirement.

Military

Total active duty personnel (1985): 2,200 French troops⊕.

*Includes 2 sq mi (6 sq km) not assigned by arrondissement. †Distant Indian Ocean islets administered by France from Réunion are excluded from total. Areas of these islets with no permanent population are: Îles Glorieuses 1.7 sq mi (4.3 sq km), Île Juan de Nova 1.9 sq mi (4.8 sq km), Île Tromelin 0.3 sq mi (0.8 sq km), Bassas da India 0.1 sq mi (0.2 sq km), Île Europa 7.8 sq mi (20.2 sq km). ‡Populations cited are for urban agglomerations. §Includes long-term private debt not guaranteed by the government. ‖ Employed labour force. ¶Includes business services and rent. ♀Includes business services. δ1984. □Indexes cited are for December. ◇Based on minimum hourly wage. △Weights of consumer price index components. †Includes motor fuels. ⊕Includes troops stationed on Mayotte.

Romania

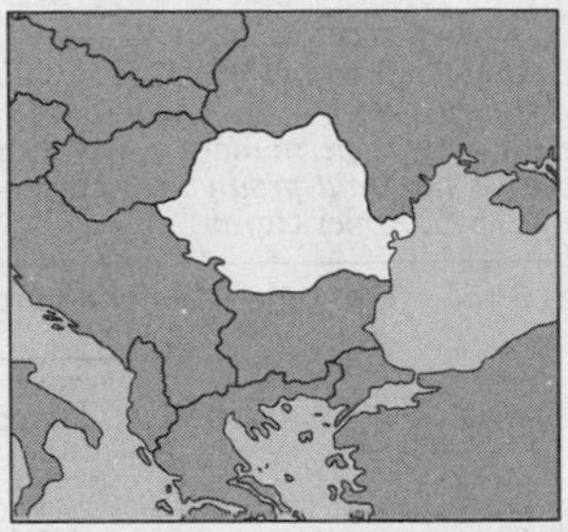

Official name: Republika Socialistă România (Socialist Republic of Romania).
Form of government: unitary single-party socialist republic with one legislative house (Grand National Assembly [369]).
Chief of state: President.
Head of government: Prime Minister.
Capital: Bucharest.
Official language: Romanian.
Official religion: none.
Monetary unit: 1 Romanian leu (plural lei) = 100 bani; valuation (Oct. 1, 1986) 1 U.S.$ = 4.35* lei; 1 £ = 6.29* lei.

Area and population

		area		population
		sq mi	sq km	1984 estimate
Districts	**Capitals**			
Alba	Alba Iulia	2,406	6,231	423,400
Arad	Arad	2,954	7,652	501,200
Arges	Piteşti	2,626	6,801	662,900
Bacău	Bacău	2,551	6,606	707,500
Bihor	Oradea	2,909	7,535	652,300
Bistriţa-Năsăud	Bistriţa	2,048	5,305	314,400
Botoşani	Botoşani	1,917	4,965	463,500
Brăila	Brăila	1,824	4,724	395,300
Braşov	Braşov	2,066	5,351	669,500
Buzău	Buzău	2,344	6,072	521,000
Caraş-Severin	Resita	3,283	8,503	402,200
Calaraşi	Calaraşi	1,915	4,959	342,300
Cluj	Cluj-Napoka	2,568	6,650	738,500
Constanţa	Constanţa	2,724	7,055	689,800
Covasna	Sfîntu Gheorghe	1,431	3,705	226,800
Dîmboviţa	Tîrgovişte	1,558	4,035	554,900
Dolj	Craiova	2,862	7,413	770,600
Galaţi	Galaţi	1,708	4,425	625,700
Giurgiu	Giurgiu	1,471	3,810	374,200
Gorj	Tîrgu Tiu	2,178	5,641	369,700
Harghita	Miercurea-Ciuc	2,552	6,610	354,000
Hunedoara	Deva	2,709	7,016	549,200
Ialomiţa	Slobozia	1,763	4,565	301,900
Iaşi	Iaşi	2,112	5,469	779,100
Maramureş	Baia Mare	2,400	6,215	535,700
Mehedinţi	Drobeta-Turnu-Severin	1,892	4,900	328,800
Mureş	Tîrgu Mureş	2,585	6,696	614,100
Neamţ	Piatra Neamţ	2,274	5,890	565,900
Olt	Slatina	2,126	5,507	531,800
Prahova	Ploieşti	1,812	4,694	858,600
Sălaj	Zalău	1,486	3,850	267,700
Satu Mare	Satu Mare	1,701	4,405	409,000
Sibiu	Sibiu	2,093	5,422	504,300
Suceava	Suceava	3,303	8,555	672,500
Teleorman	Alexandria	2,224	5,760	509,400
Timiş	Timişoara	3,356	8,692	709,600
Tulcea	Tulcea	3,255	8,430	265,300
Vaslui	Vaslui	2,045	5,297	454,900
Vîlcea	Rîmnicu Vîlcea	2,203	5,705	423,700
Vrancea	Focşani	1,878	4,863	385,600
Muncipality				
Bucharest	Bucharest	587	1,521	2,197,700
TOTAL		91,699	237,500	22,624,500

Demography

Population (1986): 22,807,600.
Density (1986): persons per sq mi 248.7, persons per sq km 96.0.
Urban-rural (1984): urban 50.8%; rural 49.2%.
Sex distribution (1984): male 49.35%; female 50.65%.
Age breakdown (1984): under 15, 25.1%; 15–29, 22.6%; 30–44, 19.4%; 45–59, 18.8%; 60–74, 10.5%; 75 and over, 3.6%.
Population projection: (1990) 23,994,000; (2000) 25,728,000.
Doubling time: not applicable; population growth is negligible.
Ethnic composition (1980): Romanian 88.5%; Hungarian 7.8%; other 3.7%.
Religious affiliation (1980): Romanian Orthodox 70.0%; Greek Orthodox 10.0%; Muslim 1.0%; atheists 7.0%; other 3.0%; none 9.0%.
Major cities (1984): Bucharest 1,961,000†; Braşov 335,000; Constanţa 318,800; Iaşi 310,200; Timişoara 309,300; Cluj-Napoca 299,800.

Vital statistics

Birth rate per 1,000 population (1984): 15.5 (world avg. 29.0).
Death rate per 1,000 population (1984): 10.3 (world avg. 11.0).
Natural increase rate per 1,000 population (1984): 5.2 (world avg. 18.0).
Total fertility rate (avg. births per childbearing woman; 1982): 2.4.
Marriage rate per 1,000 population (1984): 7.3.
Divorce rate per 1,000 population (1984): 1.5.
Life expectancy at birth (1984): male 67.0 years; female 72.6 years.
Major causes of death per 100,000 population (1982): diseases of the circulatory system 603.4; diseases of the respiratory system 144.7.

National economy

Budget (1984). Revenue: 310,937,600,000 lei (corporate tax 45.6%, turnover tax 24.5%, income tax 15.9%). Expenditures: 260,207,200,000 lei (national economy 59.5%, social services 33.4%, defense 4.6%).
Public debt (external, outstanding; 1984): U.S.$6,967,900,000.
Tourism: receipts from visitors (1984) U.S.$230,000,000; expenditures by nationals abroad (1983) U.S.$92,000,000.
Production (metric tons except as noted). Agriculture (1984): corn (maize) 13,274,300, wheat 7,900,000, sugar beets 7,018,500, potatoes 6,391,000; livestock (1985; number of live animals) 18,636,800 sheep, 14,776,700 pigs, 6,752,000 cattle; roundwood 24,126,000 cu m; fish catch 253,000. Mining and quarrying (1984): iron ore 2,160,000; bauxite 620,000; lead and zinc 74,000. Manufacturing (1984): crude steel 14,436,700; cement 14,016,000; rolled steel 10,329,400; fertilizers 3,072,700; plastics and synthetic rubber 633,000. Construction (1982): 12,689,000 sq m. Energy production (consumption): electricity (kW-hr; 1984) 72,530,000,000 (75,530,000,000); coal (metric tons; 1984) 44,279,600 (44,279,600); crude petroleum (barrels, 1984) 83,943,000 (183,155,000); petroleum products (metric tons; 1984) 23,029,000 (13,510,000); natural gas (cu m; 1984) 40,769,000,000 (42,603,000,000).
Gross national product (at current market prices; 1984): U.S.$45,536,300,000 (U.S.$2,020 per capita).

Structure of net material product and labour force

	1984			
	in value '000,000 lei	% of total value	labour force	% of labour force
Agriculture	108,500	15.3	3,067,900	29.2
Mining, manufacturing, and public utilities	432,500	61.0	3,865,500	36.8
Construction	54,600	7.7	779,900	7.4
Transp. and commun.	42,500	6.0	716,900	6.8
Trade	‡	‡	617,000	5.9
Pub. admin., defense	...	...	57,100	0.5
Services	...	...	1,242,500	11.9
Other	70,900‡	10.0‡	153,100	1.5
TOTAL	709,000	100.0	10,499,900	100.0

Population economically active (1984): total 10,499,900; activity rate of total population 46.7% (participation rates: over age 15, 62.4%; female 45.9%; unemployed, n.a.).

Price and earnings indexes (1980 = 100)

	1978	1979	1980	1981	1982	1983	1984
Consumer price index	96.1	98.5	100.0	102.2	119.5	125.7	127.1
Monthly earnings index	92.3	93.5	100.0	103.7	110.8	113.9	122.6

Household income and expenditure. Average household size (1984) 3.1; income per household 62,310 lei (U.S.$3,500); sources of income (1982): wages 62.6%, other 37.4%; expenditure (1980): food 62.7%, clothing 13.8%.
Land use (1984): forested 26.7%; meadows and pastures 20.2%; agricultural and under permanent cultivation 45.3%; other 7.8%.

Foreign trade

Balance of trade (current prices)

	1979	1980	1981	1982	1983	1984
'000,000 lei	−5,325	−8,043	+3,031	+26,987	+34,379	+67,300
% of total	5.8%	7.3%	0.9%	9.8%	12.4%	17.3%

Imports (1984): 160,816,300,000 lei (mineral fuels 57.7%, machinery 19.8%). *Major import sources:* U.S.S.R. 19.8%; Iran 9.3%; Egypt 8.3%; Syria 6.5%; Poland 5.7%; East Germany 5.4%; West Germany 4.0%.
Exports (1984): 228,122,900,000 lei (fuels 30.7%, machinery and transport equipment 28.4%, chemicals 11.8%). *Major export destinations:* U.S.S.R. 15.5%; Italy 8.7%; West Germany 7.0%; China 4.1%; East Germany 4.1%.

Transport and communications

Transport. Railroads (1984): length 6,940 mi, 11,169 km; passenger-km 28,785,000,000; metric ton-km cargo 75,159,000,000. Roads (1985): length 45,235 mi, 72,800 km (paved 64%). Vehicles (1980): cars 250,000; trucks and buses 130,000. Merchant marine (1985): vessels (100 gross tons and over) 410; total deadweight tonnage 4,502,639. Air transport (1984): passenger-km 2,652,000,000; metric ton-km cargo 80,000,000; airports (1986) 15.
Communications. Daily newspapers (1985): total number 36; total circulation 4,228,000§; circulation per 1,000 population 187§. Radio (1984): 3,350,000 (1 per 6.7 persons). Television (1985): 3,935,000 (1 per 5.7 persons). Telephones (1984): 1,859,768 (1 per 11 persons).

Education and health

Education (1984–85)

	schools	teachers	students	student/ teacher ratio
Primary (age 6–13)	14,134	148,407	3,035,209	20.4
Secondary (age 14–17)	1,973	49,547	1,500,193	30.3
Higher	44	13,252	166,238	12.5

Educational attainment (1977). Percent of population over age 25 having: primary education 55.6%; secondary 39.8%; postsecondary 4.6%. *Literacy* (1983) 95.8%.
Health (1985): physicians 47,400 (1 per 480 persons); hospital beds 212,670 (1 per 106 persons); infant mortality rate per 1,000 live births (1984) 23.4.
Food (1980–82): daily per capita caloric intake 3,343 (vegetable products 76%, animal products 24%); 126% of FAO recommended minimum.

Military

Total active duty personnel (1985): 189,500 (army 79.2%, navy 3.9%, air force 16.9%). *Military expenditure as percent of GNP* (1983): 4.7% (world 6.1%); per capita expenditure U.S.$219.

*Official rate only; the commercial rate is 1U.S.$ = 10.71 lei; 1£ = 15.48 lei. †1985. ‡Other includes trade and other material activities. §1984.

Rwanda

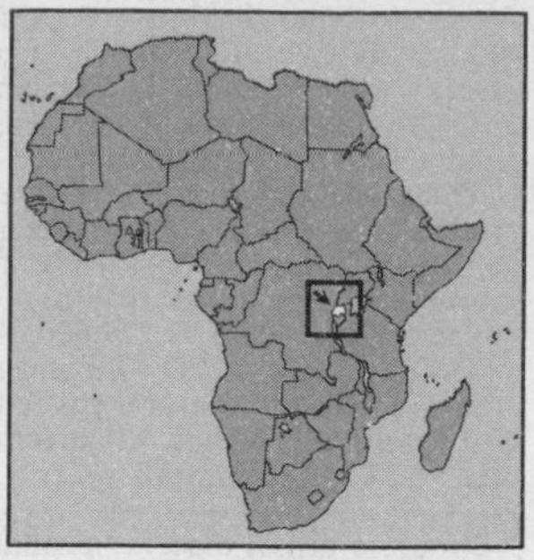

Official name: Repubulika y'u Rwanda (Rwanda); République Rwandaise (French) (Republic of Rwanda).
Form of government: republic with one legislative house (National Development Council [70]).
Head of state and government: President.
Capital: Kigali.
Official languages: Rwanda; French.
Official religion: none.
Monetary unit: 1 Rwanda franc (RF); valuation (Oct. 1, 1986) 1 U.S.$ = RF 84.79; 1 £ = RF 122.52.

Area and population

		area		population
Prefectures	Capitals	sq mi	sq km	1983 estimate
Butare	Butare	707	1,830	682,500
Byumba	Byumba	1,925	4,987	623,600
Cyangugu	Cyangugu	859	2,226	343,500
Gikongoro	Gikongoro	846	2,192	401,900
Gisenyi	Gisenyi	925	2,395	566,400
Gitarama	Gitarama	865	2,241	706,200
Kibungo	Kibungo	1,596	4,134	420,200
Kibuye	Kibuye	510	1,320	500,600
Kigali	Kigali	1,255	3,251	835,400
Ruhengeri	Ruhengeri	680	1,762	581,200
TOTAL		10,169*	26,338	5,661,400*

Demography

Population (1986): 6,331,000.
Density (1986): persons per sq mi 622.6, persons per sq km 240.4.
Urban-rural (1985): urban 5.1%; rural 94.9%.
Sex distribution (1985): male 49.37%; female 50.63%.
Age breakdown (1985): under 15, 48.7%; 15–29, 25.8%; 30–44, 13.4%; 45–59, 7.9%; 60–74, 3.5%; 75 and over, 0.7%.
Population projection: (1990) 7,105,000; (2000) 9,845,000.
Doubling time: 22 years.
Ethnic composition (1985): Hutu 90%; Tutsi 9%; Twa 1%.
Religious affiliation (1985): Roman Catholic 56%; Protestant 12%; Muslim 9%; traditional belief systems 23%.
Major cities (1978): Kigali 156,700†; Butare 21,691; Ruhengeri 16,025; Gisenyi 12,436.

Vital statistics

Birth rate per 1,000 population (1984): 52.0 (world avg. 29.0); legitimate, n.a.; illegitimate, n.a.
Death rate per 1,000 population (1984): 19.0 (world avg. 11.0).
Natural increase rate per 1,000 population (1984): 33.0 (world avg. 18.0).
Total fertility rate (avg. births per childbearing woman; 1984): 8.0.
Marriage rate per 1,000 population (1983): 2.2‡.
Divorce rate per 1,000 population: n.a.
Life expectancy at birth (1984): male 46.0 years; female 49.0 years.
Major causes of death per 100,000 population: n.a.; however, major diseases include malaria, typhoid fever, trypanosomiasis (sleeping sickness), pneumonia, tuberculosis of respiratory system, bacillary dysentery and amoebiasis, diphtheria, meningococcal infection, and acute poliomyelitis.

National economy

Budget§ (1986). Revenue: RF 22,354,000,000 (import and export duties 39.6%, taxes on goods and services 25.3%, income tax 18.1%, property taxes 1.9%). Expenditures: RF 22,354,000,000 (education 28.0%, defense 14.7%, general administration 14.8%, economy and finance 13.3%, health 5.3%).
Public debt (external, outstanding; 1984): U.S.$307,706,000.
Production (metric tons except as noted). Agriculture, forestry, fishing (1984): plantains 2,200,000, roots and tubers 1,878,000 (of which sweet potatoes 950,000, cassava 950,000, potatoes 330,000), cereals 291,000 (of which sorghum 200,000, corn [maize] 80,000), coffee 26,000, tea 8,000, tobacco 3,000; livestock (number of live animals) 2,213,000 goats, 826,000 cattle, 693,000 sheep, 284,000 pigs; roundwood 5,461,000 cu m; fish catch (1983) 1,210. Mining and quarrying (1984): cassiterite (tin ore) 1,561; wolframite (tungsten ore) 482; gold 240 troy oz. Manufacturing (value added at producers' prices in RF '000,000; 1983): food, beverages, and tobacco products 20,800; textile industry 1,534; building materials 1,168; nonmetal minerals 1,099; wood products 667; industrial chemicals 510; printing and published materials 211. Construction (1981): residential 59,600 sq m; nonresidential 34,400 sq m. Energy production (consumption): electricity (kW-hr; 1984) 135,000,000 (150,000,000); coal, none (n.a.); petroleum products (metric tons; 1984) none (123,000); natural gas (cu m; 1984) 1,025,600 (1,025,600).
Population economically active (1983): total 2,718,000; activity rate of total population 47.7% (participation rates: ages 15–64 [1978] 94.3%; female [1978] 55.1%; unemployed, n.a.).

Price and earnings indexes (1980 = 100)

	1980	1981	1982	1983	1984	1985	1986‖
Consumer price index	100.0	106.6	119.9	127.7	134.6	137.0	137.0
Earnings index	...	...	...	...	...	...	...

Tourism: receipts from visitors (1984) U.S.$4,100,000; expenditures by nationals abroad (1981) U.S.$12,000,000.
Land use (1983): forested 10.4%; meadows and pastures 17.6%; agricultural and under permanent cultivation 40.5%; other 31.5%.
Gross national product (at current market prices; 1984): U.S.$1,610,000,000 (U.S.$270 per capita).

Structure of gross domestic product and labour force

	1984		1983	
	in value RF '000,000	% of total value	labour force	% of labour force
Agriculture	68,692	43.2	2,394,000	88.1
Mining	572	0.3		
Manufacturing	26,053	16.4		
Construction	7,885	5.0		
Public utilities	910	0.6		
Transportation and communication	4,425	2.8	324,000	11.9
Trade	21,725	13.7		
Finance	7,119	4.5		
Pub. admin., defense; Services	16,908	10.6		
Other	4,641	2.9		
TOTAL	158,930	100.0	2,718,000	100.0

Household income and expenditure: Average household size (1983) 5.2; average annual income per household RF 122,870 (U.S.$1,300); sources of income (1977): self-employment (profits, interest, etc.) 71.0%, salaries and wages 16.5%, transfers 9.5%; expenditure: n.a.

Foreign trade

Balance of trade (current prices)

	1979	1980	1981	1982	1983	1984
RF '000,000	−3,324	−11,093	−13,390	−12,861	−17,840	−13,858
% of total	13.2%	44.3%	46.8%	43.4%	54.6%	45.2%

Imports (1984): RF 27,121,815,200¶ (machinery and transport equipment 24.0%, of which transport equipment 12.3%, electrical equipment 6.3%; mineral fuels and lubricants 16.5%; textiles, clothing, and footwear 10.9%; construction materials 8.5%; food 7.6%). *Major import sources:* Belgium-Luxembourg 14.4%; Kenya 12.7%; Japan 10.1%; France 9.3%; China 8.2%; Iran 6.4%; West Germany 5.6%; United States 2.5%; The Netherlands 2.3%; Italy 2.0%.
Exports (1984): RF 15,701,300,000 (coffee 82.0%; tin ores and concentrates 6.2%; tea 3.7%). *Major export destinations:* Mombasa consignment 82.0%; Belgium-Luxembourg 7.6%; Kenya 3.2%; Italy 2.2%; West Germany 1.1%.

Transport and communications

Transport. Railroads: none. Roads (1984): total length 7,500 mi, 12,070 km (paved 5.0%). Vehicles (1984): passenger cars 9,838; trucks and buses 5,523. Merchant marine: none. Air transport (1983): passenger arrivals 51,000, passenger departures 56,000; metric ton cargo loaded 16,742; metric ton cargo unloaded 12,176; airports (1986) with scheduled flights 2.
Communications. Daily newspapers (1984): total number 1; total circulation per 1,000 population, n.a. Radio (1978): total number of receivers 202,695 (1 per 24 persons). Television: none. Telephones (1984): 6,598 (1 per 894 persons).

Education and health

Education (1984–85)

	schools	teachers♀	students	student/ teacher ratio
Primary (age 7–12)	1,572♀	14,005	790,198	...
Secondary (age 13–19)	...	1,082	45,158δ	...
Voc., teacher tr.	...	...	δ	...
Higher	3	184	1,527	...

Educational attainment (1978). Percent of economically active population having: no formal schooling 63.3%; some primary education 26.3%; complete primary education 8.2%; some secondary and complete secondary education 0.9%; some postsecondary vocational education 1.2%; higher education, less than 0.1%. *Literacy* (1980): total population literate 1,295,900 (49.4%); males literate 798,800 (62.2%); females literate 497,100 (37.2%).
Health (1983): physicians 258 (1 per 22,093 persons); hospital beds 9,015 (1 per 632 persons); infant mortality rate per 1,000 live births (1984) 128.0.
Food (1980–82): daily per capita caloric intake 2,115 (vegetable products 97%, animal products 3%); 91% of FAO recommended minimum requirement.

Military

Total active duty personnel (1985): 5,150 (army 97.1%; navy, none; air force 2.9%). *Military expenditure as percent of GNP* (1983): 1.4% (world 6.1%); per capita expenditure U.S.$3.

*Detail does not add to total given because of rounding. †1981. ‡Excludes marriages not registered in court. §Revenue and expenditure breakdowns are for 1984. ‖February. ¶Import commodity breakdown is given for 1983. ♀1983–84. δIncludes agricultural and technical vocational students.

Saint Christopher and Nevis

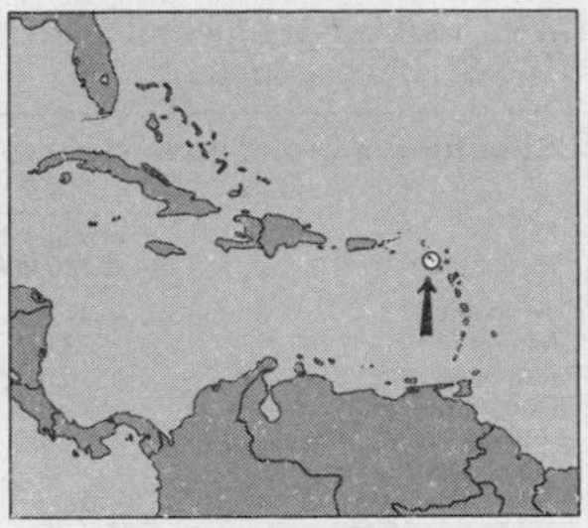

Official name: Federation of Saint Christopher and Nevis*.
Form of government: constitutional monarchy with one legislative house (National Assembly [15]).
Chief of state: British Monarch represented by governor-general.
Head of government: Prime Minister.
Capital: Basseterre.
Official language: English.
Official religion: none.
Monetary unit: 1 Eastern Caribbean dollar (EC$) = 100 cents; valuation (Oct. 21, 1985) 1 U.S.$ = EC$2.70; 1 £ = EC$3.90.

Area and population

Islands / Parishes	Capitals	area sq mi	area sq km	population 1980 census
Saint Christopher	Basseterre	67.2	174.1	33,881
Christ Church Nichola Town		7.2	18.6	1,989
Saint Anne Sandy Point		4.9	12.8	3,145
Saint George Basseterre		11.1	28.7	14,283
Saint John Capisterre		9.6	24.8	3,163
Saint Mary Cayon		5.8	15.1	3,308
Saint Paul Capisterre		5.3	13.8	2,080
Saint Peter Basseterre		8.0	20.7	2,497
Saint Thomas Middle Island		9.4	24.3	2,255
Trinity Paimetto Point		6.0	15.4	1,161
Nevis	Charlestown	35.7	92.5	9,428
Saint George Gingerland		7.1	18.5	2,295
Saint James Windward		12.0	31.1	1,691
Saint John Figtree		8.2	21.3	2,224
Saint Paul Charlestown		1.4	3.5	1,243
Saint Thomas Lowland		7.0	18.1	1,975
TOTAL		102.9	266.6	43,309

Demography

Population (1986): 46,000.
Density (1986): persons per sq mi 447.0, persons per sq km 172.5.
Urban-rural (1980): urban 35.8%; rural 64.2%.
Sex distribution (1980): male 48.12%; female 51.88%.
Age breakdown (1980): under 15, 37.2%; 15–29, 30.4%; 30–44, 9.5%; 45–59, 9.4%; 60–74, 10.0%; 75 and over, 3.5%.
Population projection: (1990) 50,000; (2000) 53,000.
Doubling time: 55 years.
Ethnic composition (1980): black 94.3%; mixed 3.3%; white 0.9%, other 1.3%.
Religious affiliation (1980): Anglican 32.6%; Methodist 28.8%; Moravian 8.7%; Roman Catholic 7.2%; Church of God 3.5%; other 19.2%.
Major towns (1980): Basseterre 14,283; Charlestown 1,243.

Vital statistics

Birth rate per 1,000 population (1985): 22.3 (world avg. 29.0); (1980) legitimate 18.6%; illegitimate 81.4%.
Death rate per 1,000 population (1985): 9.6 (world avg. 11.0).
Natural increase rate per 1,000 population (1985): 12.7 (world avg. 18.0).
Total fertility rate (avg. births per childbearing woman; 1982): 3.3.
Marriage rate per 1,000 population (1977): 3.5.
Divorce rate per 1,000 population (1977): 0.2.
Life expectancy at birth (1983): male 62.0 years; female 67.0 years.
Major causes of death per 100,000 population (1983): cerebrovascular diseases 176.3; malignant neoplasms (cancers) 145.1; diseases of pulmonary circulation 93.7; diseases of the respiratory system 84.2; infectious and parasitic diseases 69.2.

National economy

Budget (1982). Revenue: EC$51,098,000 (import duties and excise taxes 22.3%, consumer taxes 16.3%, stamps 7.3%, interest and currency exchange premiums 7.2%, charges on electricity, ice, and cold storage 6.9%). Expenditures: EC$62,606,000 (general administration 27.6%, economic services 18.6%, education 18.6%, health 9.7%, debt payment 3.1%).
Public debt (external, outstanding; 1983†): U.S.$11,000,000.
Production (metric tons except as noted). Agriculture, forestry, fishing (1984): sugarcane 310,000, coconuts 2,000, fruits 2,000, vegetables 1,000, sweet potatoes 600, peanuts (groundnuts) 300, tanias 122‡, cotton lint 7§; livestock (number of live animals) 14,000 sheep, 10,000 pigs, 10,000 goats, 6,000 cattle; roundwood, n.a.; fish catch (1983) 1,100. Mining and quarrying: excavation of sand for local use. Manufacturing (value of production in EC$'000; 1982): sugar 29,291 ‖; clothing 4,597‡ ‖; assembly of electrical appliances 3,781 ‖; footwear 1,851‡ ‖; molasses 1,429 ‖; aerated water 26,500 hectolitres; beer 10,460 hectolitres. Construction: n.a. Energy production (consumption): electricity (kW-hr; 1984) 34,000,000 (26,300,000); coal, none (none); crude petroleum, none (none); petroleum products (metric tons; 1984) none (17,000); natural gas, none (none).
Household income and expenditure. Average household size (1980) 3.7; average annual income per household: n.a.; source of income: n.a.; expenditure (1982)¶: food and beverages 55.6%, household supplies 9.4%, housing 7.6%, clothing and footwear 7.5%, fuel and light 6.6%, transportation 4.3%, other 9.0%.

Gross national product (at current market prices; 1984): U.S.$60,000,000 (U.S.$1,360 per capita).

Structure of gross domestic product and labour force

	1983 in value EC$'000,000	1983 % of total value	1984 labour force♀	1984 % of labour force
Agriculture	23.7	17.1	4,380	29.6
Mining	0.3	0.2	—	—
Manufacturing	17.8	12.8	2,170	14.7
Construction	11.0	7.9	400	2.7
Public utilities	1.6	1.2	1,030	7.0
Transportation and communication	18.3	13.2	450	3.0
Trade	20.4	14.7	940	6.3
Finance, real estate	16.3	11.7	280	1.9
Pub. admin., defense	28.7	20.7	4,700	31.7
Services	7.8	5.6		
Other	−7.1ð	−5.1ð	460	3.1
TOTAL	138.8	100.0	14,810	100.0

Population economically active (1980): total 17,125; activity rate of total population 39.5% (participation rates: ages 15–64, 69.5%; female 40.9%; unemployed□).

Price and earnings indexes (1980 = 100)

	1978	1979	1980	1981	1982	1983	1984
Consumer price index	77.2	85.4	100.0	111.2	117.8	121.2	...
Earnings index◊	72.7	80.0	100.0	110.0	113.3	115.0	117.3

Tourism: receipts from visitors (1984) U.S.$11,300,000; expenditures by nationals abroad, n.a.
Land use (1983): forested 17.0%; meadows and pastures 3.0%; agricultural and under permanent cultivation 39.0%; other 41.0%.

Foreign trade△

Balance of trade (current prices)

	1978	1979	1980	1981	1982	1983
EC$'000,000	−20.2	−41.2	−55.9	−63.3	−67.2	−86.3
% of total	18.3%	31.2%	30.0%	32.6%	39.8%	45.2%

Imports (1983): EC$138,700,000 (manufactured goods 22.7%; food 19.6%; machinery 19.0%; mineral fuels 9.8%; chemicals 8.0%). *Major import sources:* United States 35.0%; United Kingdom 15.4%; Trinidad and Tobago 10.0%; Canada 6.1%; Puerto Rico 5.9%.
Exports (1983): EC$52,400,000 (domestic exports 95.0%, of which sugar 55.2%, clothing 9.4%, footwear 8.8%, electronic goods 8.3%, beer and ale 5.5%; reexports 5.0%). *Major export destinations:* United States 47.9%; United Kingdom 18.5%; Trinidad and Tobago 13.4%.

Transport and communications

Transport. Railroads (1985): length 36 mi, 58 km†. Roads (1984): total length 198 mi, 318 km (paved 44%). Vehicles (1984): passenger cars 2,392; trucks and buses 465. Merchant marine (1985): vessels (100 gross tons and over) 2; total deadweight tonnage 459. Air transport (1982): passenger arrivals 51,940, passenger departures 52,410; cargo handled, n.a.; airports (1986) with scheduled flights 2.
Communications. Daily newspapers (1985): none. Radio (1985): total number of receivers 21,000 (1 per 2.2 persons). Television (1985): total number of receivers 5,000 (1 per 9.2 persons). Telephones (1983): 3,259 (1 per 14 persons).

Education and health

Education (1984–85)

	schools	teachers	students	student/teacher ratio
Primary (age 5–12)	32	339	7,655	22.6
Secondary (age 13–17)	7	286	4,436	15.5
Voc., teacher tr.	2	29	240	8.3
Higher	—	—		

Educational attainment (1980). Percent of population over age 15 having: no formal schooling 1.0%; primary education 22.0%; secondary 74.5%; higher 1.5%; other 1.0%. *Literacy* (1980): total population over age 15 literate 24,887 (91.5%); males literate 11,533 (90.8%); females literate 13,354 (92.2%).
Health (1985): physicians 20 (1 per 2,300 persons); hospital beds 248 (1 per 185 persons); infant mortality rate per 1,000 live births 30.2.
Food (1980–82): daily per capita caloric intake 2,231 (vegetable products 74%, animal products 26%); 92% of FAO recommended minimum requirement.

Military

Total active duty personnel (1985): the country maintains a police force and a small defense force of volunteers.

*Saint Kitts and Nevis and Federation of Saint Kitts and Nevis are both officially acceptable, variant, short- and long-form names of the country. †Includes external long-term private debt not guaranteed by the government. ‡1981. §1982. ‖ Export figure. ¶Weights of consumer price index components. ♀Employed persons only. ðLess imputed bank service charges. □1985: unemployment during tourist and sugarcane-harvesting seasons (overlapping periods, December through July) *c.* 10.0%; off-season *c.* 20.0%. ◊Average wages paid sugar industry employees. △Imports c.i.f. (cost, insurance, freight); exports f.o.b. (free on board), including reexports. †Light railway serving the sugar industry on Saint Christopher.

Saint Lucia

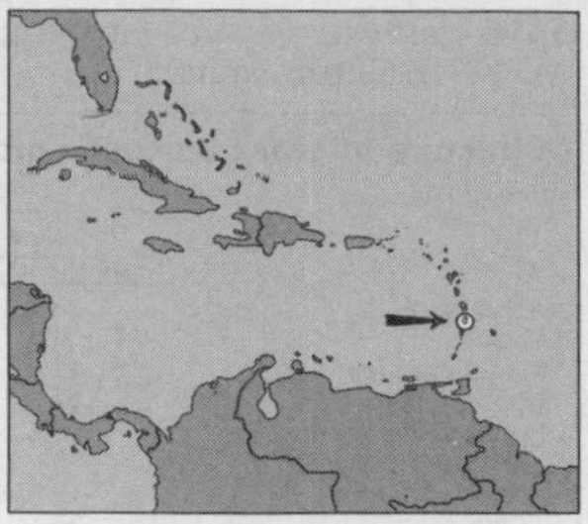

Official name: Saint Lucia.
Form of government: constitutional monarchy with two legislative houses (Senate [11]; House of Assembly [17]).
Chief of state: British Monarch represented by governor-general.
Head of government: Prime Minister.
Capital: Castries.
Official language: English.
Official religion: none.
Monetary unit: 1 Eastern Caribbean Dollar (EC$) = 100 cents; valuation (Oct. 1, 1986) 1 U.S.$ = EC$2.70; 1 £ = EC$3.90.

Area and population

		area		population
				1984
Quarters*	Capitals	sq mi	sq km	estimate
Anse-la-Raye	Anse-la-Raye	11.1	28.8	5,872
Canaries	Canaries	7.4	19.2	2,467
Castries	Castries	30.7	79.5	50,798
Choiseul	Choiseul	12.1	31.3	7,682
Dennery	Dennery	27.2	70.4	11,409
Gros Islet	Gros Islet	40.0	103.6	12,012
Laborie	Laborie	14.7	38.1	8,151
Micoud	Micoud	32.3	83.7	14,104
Soufrière	Soufrière	19.5	50.5	8,620
Vieux Fort	Vieux Fort	17.3	44.8	12,951
TOTAL		238.3†	617.2†	134,066

Demography

Population (1986): 140,000.
Density (1986): persons per sq mi 585.5, persons per sq km 226.1.
Urban-rural (1982): urban 52.1%; rural 47.9%.
Sex distribution (1984): male 48.54%; female 51.46%.
Age breakdown (1984): under 15, 44.5%; 15–29, 27.7%; 30–44, 11.3%; 45–59, 8.5%; 60–74, 5.8%; 75 and over, 2.2%.
Population projection: (1990) 151,000; (2000) 184,000.
Doubling time: 28 years.
Ethnic composition (1982): black 90.3%; mixed 5.5%; East Indian 3.2%; white 0.8%; other 0.2%.
Religious affiliation (1980): Roman Catholic 86.3%; Protestant 11.3%, of which Anglican 3.0%, Seventh-day Adventist 2.5%; Rastafarian 2.2%; other 0.2%.
Major cities (1984): Castries 50,798; Vieux Fort 12,951.

Vital statistics

Birth rate per 1,000 population (1985): 29.1 (world avg. 29.0); legitimate 15.9%; illegitimate 84.1%.
Death rate per 1,000 population (1985): 5.8 (world avg. 11.0).
Natural increase rate per 1,000 population (1985): 23.3 (world avg. 18.0).
Total fertility rate (avg. births per childbearing woman; 1980–85): 4.4.
Marriage rate per 1,000 population (1985): 3.1.
Divorce rate per 1,000 population (1985): 0.3.
Life expectancy at birth (1985): male 68.6 years; female 75.5 years.
Major causes of death per 100,000 population (1984): heart diseases 117.9; malignant neoplasms (cancers) 73.9; cerebrovascular diseases 68.6; accidents 32.8; diseases of the respiratory system 26.1; diabetes mellitus 20.9.

National economy

Budget (1983–84). Revenue: EC$120,700,000 (tax revenue 81.6%, of which import duties 28.3%, income taxes 27.2%, consumption taxes 12.8%; nontax revenue 10.6%; grants 7.8%). Expenditures: EC$139,800,000 (current expenditure 81.2%, of which interest payments 5.8%; capital expenditure 18.8%).
Public debt (external, outstanding; 1983‡): U.S.$34,000,000.
Tourism: receipts from visitors (1984) U.S.$42,400,000; expenditures by nationals abroad (1983) U.S.$10,000,000.
Production (metric tons except as noted). Agriculture, forestry, fishing (1984): bananas 61,000, mangoes 45,000, coconuts 30,000, yams 4,000, sweet potatoes 2,000, plantains 1,542§, citrus fruits 784§, vegetables (mostly tomatoes and cabbages) 710§, ginger 115§, cocoa beans 44; livestock (number of live animals) 15,000 sheep, 12,000 cattle, 12,000 pigs, 11,000 goats; roundwood, n.a.; fish catch (1983) 2,635. Mining and quarrying: excavation of sand for local construction and pumice. Manufacturing (value of production in EC$'000; 1984): cardboard boxes 22,000§; clothing 17,427; raw coconut oil 6,729; nonalcoholic beverages 6,561; copra 5,392; rum 2,743; other manufactures include soap, beer, electrical components, scuba-diving suits, and wooden toys. Construction: n.a. Energy production (consumption): electricity (kW-hr; 1984) 65,800,000 (54,300,000); coal, none (none); crude petroleum, none (none); petroleum products (metric tons; 1984) none (36,000); natural gas, none (none).
Population economically active (1980): total 49,451; activity rate of total population 41.1% (participation rates: ages 15–64, n.a.; female 55.2%; unemployed, n.a.).

Price and earnings indexes (1980 = 100)

	1980	1981	1982	1983	1984	1985	1986‖
Consumer price index	100.0	115.1	120.4	122.2	123.7	125.3	127.8
Weekly earnings index¶	100.0	...	115.0	...	...	...	...

Gross national product (at current market prices; 1984): U.S.$150,000,000 (U.S.$1,120 per capita).

Structure of gross domestic product and labour force

	1984		1983♀	
	in value EC$'000,000	% of total value	labour force	% of labour force
Agriculture	47.9	13.8	13,000	29.7
Mining	3.6	1.0		
Manufacturing	35.5	10.2	2,600	5.9
Construction	22.9	6.6	1,500	3.4
Public utilities	13.5	3.9	15,800	36.1
Transportation and communication	37.4	10.7		
Trade	77.5	22.3		
Finance	25.9	7.4		
Pub. admin., defense	72.9	20.9		
Services	34.3	9.9		
Other	−23.2δ	−6.7	10,900□	24.9
TOTAL	348.2	100.0	43,800	100.0

Household income and expenditure. Average household size (1980) 4.6; average annual income per household: n.a.; source of income: n.a.; expenditure (1984)◇: food 46.8%, housing 13.5%, clothing and footwear 6.5%, transportation and communication 6.3%, household furnishings 5.8%, fuel and light 4.5%, recreation and entertainment 3.2%, beverages and tobacco 2.8%, health care 2.3%, other 8.3%.
Land use (1983): forested 13.0%; meadows and pastures 5.0%; agricultural and under permanent cultivation 28.0%; other 54.0%.

Foreign trade△

Balance of trade (current prices)

	1980	1981	1982	1983	1984	1985
EC$'000,000	−210.0	−237.6	−206.0	−160.1	−190.9	−197.0
% of total	45.8%	51.6%	47.8%	38.4%	42.5%	41.2%

Imports (1984): EC$320,000,000 (machinery and transport equipment 17.5%, chemicals and chemical products 11.4%, crude petroleum and petroleum products 10.4%, paper and paperboard 6.6%, meat and meat preparations 5.7%, cereals and cereal preparations 5.0%, clothing 4.2%, textile yarn and fabrics 4.0%, metal manufactures 3.5%). *Major import sources:* United States 36.5%; United Kingdom 13.6%; Trinidad and Tobago 8.7%; Japan 6.1%; Canada 4.2%.
Exports (1984): EC$129,100,000✝ (bananas 49.8%, clothing 15.3%, cardboard boxes 10.3%, refined coconut oil 5.0%, electrical components and parts 3.7%, beer and ale 2.4%). *Major export destinations:* United Kingdom 50.8%; United States 16.7%; Trinidad and Tobago 6.6%; Barbados 4.7%.

Transport and communications

Transport. Railroads: none. Roads (1984): total length 426 mi, 686 km (paved 65%). Vehicles (1984): passenger cars 7,049; trucks and buses 2,084. Merchant marine (1985): vessels (100 gross tons and over) 6; total deadweight tonnage 2,142. Air transport (1984): passenger arrivals 116,495, passenger departures 115,381; cargo unloaded 736 metric tons⊕, cargo loaded 624 metric tons⊕; airports (1986) with scheduled flights 2.
Communications. Daily newspapers: none. Radio (1985): total number of receivers 92,000 (1 per 1.5 person). Television (1985): total number of receivers 5,000 (1 per 27 persons). Telephones (1983): 9,587 (1 per 14 persons).

Education and health

Education (1984–85)

	schools	teachers	students	student/teacher ratio
Primary (age 5–11)	85	1,139	33,534	29.4
Secondary (age 12–16)	11	280	5,321	19.0
Voc., teacher tr.	4	48	358	7.5
Higher	—	—	—	—

Educational attainment (1970). Percent of adult population over age 25 having: no formal schooling 28.7%; primary education 65.6%; secondary 4.7%; higher 1.0%. *Literacy* (1984): total population over age 15 literate 44,484 (59.7%).
Health (1984): physicians 58 (1 per 2,311 persons); hospital beds 522 (1 per 257 persons); infant mortality rate per 1,000 live births (1985) 22.7.
Food (1980–82): daily per capita caloric intake 2,381 (vegetable products 79%, animal products 21%); 98% of FAO recommended minimum requirement.

Military

Total active duty personnel (1985):**.

*During 1986 St. Lucia was to be reorganized into 8 administrative regions. †Includes the uninhabited 26.0 sq mi (67.3 sq km) Central Forest Preserve. ‡Includes external long-term private debt not guaranteed by the government. §1982. ‖August average. ¶Wages in nonagricultural activities excluding mining. ♀Wage earners and self-employed. δLess imputed bank charges. □Unemployed. ◇Weights of consumer price index components. △Imports c.i.f. (cost, insurance, freight); exports f.o.b. (free on board). Reexports included in balance of trade and commodities, excluded in trading partners. ✝Reexports comprise 4.1% of all exports. ⊕1983. **The 500-member police force includes a specially trained paramilitary unit.

Saint Vincent and the Grenadines

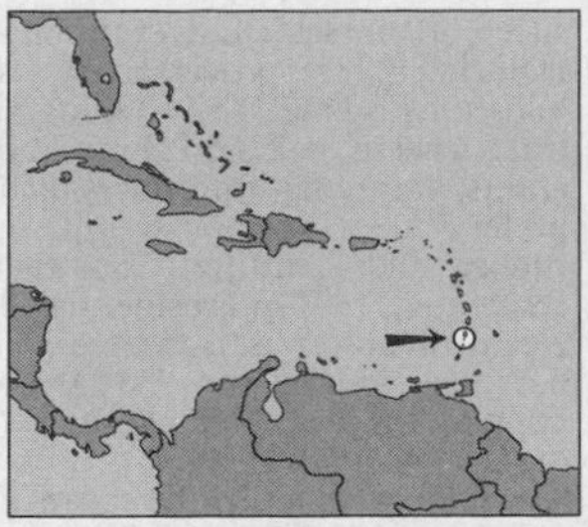

Official name: Saint Vincent and the Grenadines.
Form of government: constitutional monarchy with one legislative house (House of Assembly [6 senators, 13 representatives]).
Chief of state: British Monarch represented by governor-general.
Head of government: Prime Minister.
Capital: Kingstown.
Official language: English.
Official religion: none.
Monetary unit: 1 Eastern Caribbean Dollar (EC$) = 100 cents; valuation (Oct. 1, 1986) 1 U.S.$ = EC$2.70; 1 £ = EC$3.90.

Area and population

	area		population
Census divisions	sq mi	sq km	1985 estimate*
Island of Saint Vincent			
Barrouallie	14.2	36.8	5,187
Bridgetown	7.2	18.6	7,515
Calliaqua	11.8	30.6	19,379
Chateaubelair	30.0	77.7	6,786
Colonarie	13.4	34.7	8,015
Georgetown	22.2	57.5	7,221
Kingstown (city)	1.9	4.9	18,378
Kingstown (suburbs)	6.4	16.6	9,570
Layou	11.1	28.7	6,123
Marriaqua	9.4	24.3	9,341
Sandy Bay	5.3	13.7	3,186
Saint Vincent Grenadines			
Northern Grenadines	9.0	23.3	5,263
Southern Grenadines	7.5	19.4	2,784
TOTAL	150.3†	389.3†	108,748

Demography

Population (1986): 111,000.
Density (1986): persons per sq mi 738.5, persons per sq km 285.1.
Urban-rural‡ (1985): urban 25.7%; rural 74.3%.
Sex distribution (1984): male 48.45%; female 51.55%.
Age breakdown (1985): under 15, 37.4%; 15–29, 32.7%; 30–44, 14.9%; 45–59, 7.5%; 60–74, 5.6%; 75 and over, 1.9%.
Population projection: (1990) 117,000; (2000) 133,000.
Doubling time: 36 years.
Ethnic composition (1980): black 65.5%; mulatto 19.9%; East Indian 5.5%; white 3.5%; other (including Amerindian, mestizo, and Arab) 5.6%.
Religious affiliation (1980): Protestant 77.3%, of which Anglican 36.0%, Methodist 20.4%, Seventh-day Adventist 4.1%, Plymouth Brethren 3.9%; Roman Catholic 19.3%; other 3.4%.
Major cities (1984)§: Kingstown 18,378.

Vital statistics

Birth rate per 1,000 population (1984): 26.2 (world avg. 29.0); legitimate, n.a.; illegitimate, n.a.
Death rate per 1,000 population (1984): 6.5 (world avg. 11.0).
Natural increase rate per 1,000 population (1984): 19.7 (world avg. 18.0).
Total fertility rate (avg. births per childbearing woman; 1980–85): 3.0.
Marriage rate per 1,000 population (1984): 3.6.
Divorce rate per 1,000 population (1980): 0.2.
Life expectancy at birth (1980–85): male 67.5 years; female 71.4 years.
Major causes of death per 100,000 population (1984): diseases of the circulatory system 192.3; malignant neoplasms (cancers) 78.6; endocrine and metabolic disorders 37.0; homicide and other violence 36.0; infectious and parasitic diseases 28.7; diseases of the respiratory system 26.8.

National economy

Budget (1983). Revenue: EC$79,660,000 (tax revenue 77.1%, of which import duties 35.3% [including customs duties 18.8%] and taxes on income, profits, and capital gains 28.0%; nontax revenue 17.0%). Expenditures: EC$80,000,000 (general public services 19.7%; education 16.7%; health 11.3%; public order 6.5%; unspecified 45.8%).
Public debt (external, outstanding; 1985): U.S.$23,200,000.
Tourism (1984): receipts from visitors U.S.$29,000,000; expenditures by nationals abroad, n.a.
Production (metric tons except as noted). Agriculture, forestry, fishing (1984): bananas 41,000‖, coconuts 20,000, eddoes and dasheens 16,068, other roots and tubers 12,607, plantains 3,099, mangoes 2,000, arrowroot 783, ginger 122, tobacco 41; livestock (number of live animals) 13,000 sheep, 8,000 cattle, 7,000 pigs, 4,000 goats; roundwood, n.a.; fish catch (1983) 547. Mining and quarrying (1984): sand and gravel for local use. Manufacturing (1984): copra 2,000; cigarettes 20,000,000 units; rum 3,068 hectolitres; other products include flour, carbonated drinks, condensed milk, packing boxes for bananas, boats, concrete, and furniture. Construction (1984): 42,765 sq m. Energy production (consumption): electricity (kW-hr; 1984) 33,703,051 (25,867,011); coal, none (none); crude petroleum, none (none); petroleum products (metric tons; 1984) none (13,000); natural gas, none (none).

Gross national product (at current market prices; 1984): U.S.$100,000,000 (U.S.$920 per capita).

Structure of gross domestic product and labour force

	1984		1970	
	in value EC$'000,000	% of total value	labour force	% of labour force
Agriculture	38.2	17.4	6,882	29.0
Mining	0.7	0.3	48	0.2
Manufacturing	22.0	10.0	1,851	7.8
Construction	24.5	11.2	2,871	12.1
Public utilities	6.9	3.1	214	0.9
Transportation and communication	35.9	16.3	1,068	4.5
Trade	30.7	14.0	2,871	12.1
Finance	23.0	10.5		
Pub. admin., defense	43.2	19.7	7,190	30.3
Services	6.4	2.9		
Other	−11.9¶	−5.4	736	3.1
TOTAL	219.6	100.0	23,731	100.0

Population economically active (1980)♀: total 32,617; activity rate of total population 31.7% (participation rates: ages 14–64, 57.2%; female 34.5%; unemployed [1986] 30.0%).

Price and earnings indexes (1980 = 100)

	1979	1980	1981	1982	1983	1984	1985
Consumer price index	85.3	100.0	112.7	120.9	127.5	130.9	133.6
Earnings index♂	87.0	100.0	117.5	143.0	150.1	...	...

Household income and expenditure. Average household size (1978) 5.0; average annual income per household: n.a.; source of income: n.a.; expenditure (1981)□: food and nonalcoholic beverages 59.8%, clothing and footwear 7.7%, household furnishings 6.5%, housing 6.3%, energy 6.2%, transportation and communication 3.7%, tobacco and alcohol 2.8%, other 7.0%.
Land use (1983): forested 41.0%; meadows and pastures 6.0%; agricultural and under permanent cultivation 50.0%; other 3.0%.

Foreign trade◇

Balance of trade (current prices)

	1980	1981	1982	1983	1984	1985△
EC$'000,000	−111.3	−91.2	−77.1	−79.1	−62.2	−39.4
% of total	56.4%	40.9%	30.6%	26.3%	17.7%	14.1%

Imports (1984): EC$206,800,000 (food 24.6%, machinery and transport equipment 18.2%, chemicals and chemical products 10.8%, mineral fuels 8.6%, miscellaneous manufactured goods 31.0%). *Major import sources:* United States 37.0%; United Kingdom 14.8%; Trinidad and Tobago 11.4%; Japan 5.4%; Canada 3.1%.
Exports (1984): EC$144,600,000 (bananas 22.1%, basic and miscellaneous manufactures [including garments, linens, and furniture] 18.2%, eddoes and dasheens 16.7%, flour 11.9%, tanias 6.7%). *Major export destinations:* Trinidad and Tobago 45.4%; United Kingdom 24.1%; United States 10.6%; Saint Lucia 5.3%; Antigua and Barbuda 3.3%.

Transport and communications

Transport. Railroads: none. Roads (1984): total length 450 mi, 724 km (paved 48%). Vehicles (1984): passenger cars 4,460; trucks and buses 2,040. Merchant marine (1985): vessels (100 gross tons and over) 71; total deadweight tonnage 359,486. Air transport (1984): passenger arrivals 72,970, passenger departures 72,769; airports (1986) with scheduled flights 4.
Communications. Daily newspapers: none. Radio (1985): total number of receivers 55,000 (1 per 2.0 persons). Television (1985): total number of receivers 6,000 (1 per 18 persons). Telephones (1983): 6,074 (1 per 17 persons).

Education and health

Education (1982–83)

	schools	teachers	students	student/ teacher ratio
Primary (age 5–15)	62	1,251	24,551	19.6
Secondary (age 11–19)	19	292	5,170	17.7
Voc., teacher tr.	5	39	275	7.1
Higher	1	19	105	5.5

Educational attainment (1970). Percent of adult population over age 25 having: no formal schooling 5.8%; primary education 88.2%; secondary 5.2%; higher 0.8%. *Literacy* (1983): total population over age 14 literate 54,000 (85.0%).
Health (1984): physicians 24 (1 per 4,300 persons); hospital beds 350 (1 per 309 persons); infant mortality rate per 1,000 live births 26.5.
Food (1980–82): daily per capita caloric intake 2,353 (vegetable products 87%, animal products 13%); 97% of FAO recommended minimum requirement.

Military

Total active duty personnel (1983): 489 (police 100%). *Military expenditure as percent of GNP* (1982): 6.0% (world 6.0%); per capita expenditure U.S.$18.

*End of year figure. †Includes 0.9 sq mi (2.5 sq km) not distributed by census division. ‡Urban being defined as Kingstown and suburbs. §Populations of other locales are not available. ‖1985. ¶Less imputed service charges. ♀Based on projection of 1970 census except for unemployment rate. ♂Wages in manufacturing. □Weights of retail price components. ◇Imports c.i.f. (cost, insurance, and freight); exports f.o.b. (free on board), including reexports. △First nine months only.

San Marino

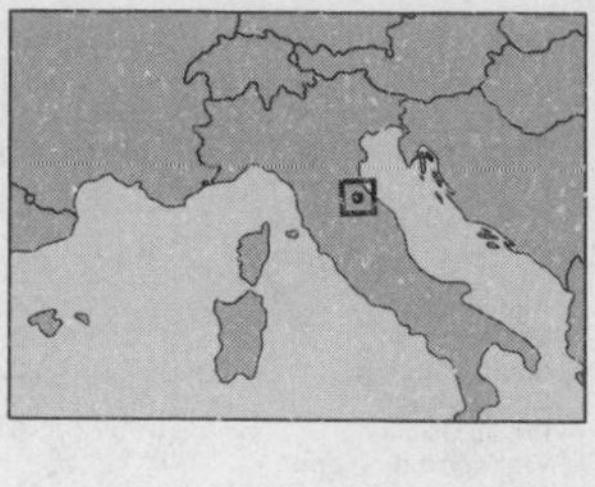

Official name: Serenissima Repubblica di San Marino (Most Serene Republic of San Marino).
Form of government: unitary multiparty republic with one legislative house (Great and General Council [60]).
Head of state and government: Captains-Regent (2).
Capital: San Marino.
Official language: Italian.
Official religion: none.
Monetary unit: 1 Italian lira (Lit; plural lire) = 100 centesimi; valuation (Oct. 1, 1986) 1 U.S.$ = Lit 1,402; 1 £ = Lit 2,026.

Area and population

		area		population
Castles	Capitals	sq mi	sq km	1986 estimate
Acquaviva	Acquaviva	1.88	4.86	1,148
Borgo Maggiore	Borgo	3.48	9.01	4,341
Città	San Marino	2.74	7.09	4,201
Chiesanuova	Chiesanuova	2.11	5.46	712
Domagnano	Domagnano	2.56	6.62	1,840
Faetano	Faetano	2.99	7.75	750
Fiorentino	Fiorentino	2.53	6.56	1,477
Montegiardino	Montegiardino	1.28	3.31	561
Serravalle/Dogano	Serravalle	4.07	10.53	6,941
TOTAL		23.63*	61.19	21,971

Demography

Population (1986): 22,600.
Density (1986): persons per sq mi 956.4, persons per sq km 369.4.
Urban-rural (1986): urban 90.4%; rural 9.6%.
Sex distribution (1986): male 50.12%; female 49.88%.
Age breakdown (1986): under 15, 19.0%; 15–29, 25.0%; 30–44, 21.3%; 45–59, 17.4%; 60–74, 12.8%; 75 and over, 4.5%.
Population projection: (1990) 23,000; (2000) 25,000.
Doubling time: not applicable; natural population growth is negligible, averaging only 0.3% during 1980–84.
Ethnic composition (1985): Sammarinesi 88.0%; Italian 11.7%; other 0.3%.
Religious affiliation (1980): Roman Catholic 95.2%; no religion 3.0%; other 1.8%.
Major cities (1986): Serravalle/Dogano 4,644; San Marino 2,447; Borgo Maggiore 2,086; Murata 1,316; Domagnano 884.

Vital statistics

Birth rate per 1,000 population (1985): 9.3 (world avg. 29.0); (1981) legitimate 96.5%; illegitimate 3.5%.
Death rate per 1,000 population (1985): 8.4 (world avg. 11.0).
Natural increase rate per 1,000 population (1985): 0.9 (world avg. 18.0).
Total fertility rate (avg. births per childbearing woman): n.a.
Marriage rate per 1,000 population (1984): 8.5.
Divorce rate per 1,000 population: negligible.
Life expectancy at birth (1980–85): male 70.7 years; female 76.2 years.
Major causes of death per 100,000 population (1985): diseases of the circulatory system 282.1; malignant neoplasms (cancers) 245.8; accidents, violence, and suicide 48.1.

National economy

Budget (1985). Revenue: Lit 207,193,000,000 (mainly receipts from postage stamp sales, tourism, and customs duties [collected by Italy and paid as a subsidy]). Expenditures: Lit 207,193,000,000 (†finance and economic planning 31.0%, internal affairs 11.3%, health and social security 9.0%, education and culture 7.1%, public works 6.3%).
Public debt: n.a.
Tourism: tourist arrivals (1985) 2,812,134; receipts from visitors (1983) U.S.$56,454,000; expenditures by nationals abroad, n.a.
Gross national product (at current market prices; 1980): U.S.$176,760,000 (U.S.$8,250 per capita).

Structure of labour force (1986)

	labour force	% of labour force
Agriculture	363	3.1
Manufacturing	4,130	35.4
Construction and public utilities	912	7.8
Transportation and communication	127	1.1
Trade	1,918	16.4
Finance and insurance	233	2.0
Services	602	5.2
Public administration and defense	1,770	15.2
Other	1,620‡	13.9‡
TOTAL	11,675	100.0*

Production (metric tons except as noted). Agriculture, forestry, fishing (1976): wheat *c.* 4,400†; grapes *c.* 700†; barley 456; livestock (number of live animals; 1985) 1,046 cattle (of which 539 dairy cattle), 1,598 pigs, 1,447 sheep, 81 horses§, 12,045 rabbits§, 50,040 quails§, 19,479 chickens§ Manufacturing (1985): processed meats 485,091 kilograms, of which beef 248,320 kilograms, swine 185,090 kilograms, veal 31,870 kilograms; milk 1,389,134 litres; cheese 86,276 kilograms; butter 11,644 kilograms; yogurt 9,112 kilograms; other major products include textiles, cement, paper, leather, bricks, pottery, tiles, postage stamps, gold and silver jewelry, paints, synthetic rubber, and furniture. Construction (new units completed; 1985): urban residential 160; nonresidential 38. Energy production (consumption): all electrical power is imported via electrical grid from Italy, consumption n.a.; coal (metric tons; 1984) none (n.a); crude petroleum (barrels; 1984) none (n.a.); petroleum products (metric tons; 1984) none (n.a.); natural gas (cu m; 1984) none (n.a.).
Population economically active (1986): total 11,479; activity rate of total population 50.9% (participation rates: ages 15–64, n.a.; female 40.6%; unemployed 6.1%).

Price and earnings indexes (1980 = 100)

	1981	1982	1983	1984	1985	1986 ‖ ¶
Consumer price index	139.2	150.1	165.1	174.9	196.1	200.8
Monthly earnings index	...	...	...	...	...	...

Household income and expenditure. Total number of households (1985): 7,653; average household size (1985) 3.0; average annual income per household: n.a.; source of income: n.a.; expenditure♀ (1980): food, beverages, and tobacco 33.5%, transportation and communication 12.6%, clothing and footwear 10.2%, furniture, appliances, and goods and services for the home 8.0%, recreation, entertainment, education, and culture 7.9%, housing, fuel, and electrical energy 7.6%, health and sanitary services 4.0%, other goods and services 15.7%.
Land use (1983): agricultural and under permanent cultivation 74%; meadows and pastures 17%; forested, built-on, wasteland, and other 9%.

Foreign trade

Balance of trade: n.a. San Marino and Italy form a single customs area; separate figures for San Marino are not available.
Imports (1985): manufactured goods of all kinds, oil, and gold. *Major import source:* Italy.
Exports (1985): wine, wheat, woolen goods, furniture, wood, ceramics, building stone, dairy products, meat, and postage stamps. *Major export destination:* Italy.

Transport and communications

Transport. Railroads: none (nearest rail terminal is at Rimini, Italy, 17 mi [27 km] northeast). Roads (1980): total length 137 mi, 220 km. Vehicles (1986): passenger cars 16,021; trucks and buses 1,742. Merchant marine: vessels (100 gross tons and over) none. Air transport: airports with scheduled flights, none; however, there is a heliport that provides passenger and cargo service between San Marino and Rimini, Italy, during the summer months.
Communications. Daily newspapers (1985): none; however, there are several journals of lesser frequency; total circulation of the oldest of these, *Il Nuovo Titano,* 1,300; circulation per 1,000 population 58.1. Radio (1982): total number of receivers 8,994 (1 per 2.4 persons). Television (1982): total number of receivers 6,000 (1 per 3.6 persons). Telephones (1983): 9,576 (1 per 2.9 persons).

Education and health

Education (1985–86)

	schools	teachers	students	student/ teacher ratio
Primary (age 6–10)	13	158	1,411	8.9
Secondary (age 11–18)	4	183	1,248	6.8
Vocational	...	...	701♂	...
Teacher tr.	...	...	48♂	...
Higher	...	...	343♂	...

Educational attainment (1985). Percent of the adult labour force having: basic literacy or primary education 41.0%; secondary 28.3%; some post-secondary 15.2%; higher degree 5.6%. *Literacy* (1985): total population over age 14 literate 17,852 (98.0%); males literate 8,842 (98.6%); females literate 9,010 (97.5%).
Health: physicians (1979) 10□ (1 per 2,115 persons); hospital beds (1980) 61 (1 per 351 persons); infant mortality rate per 1,000 live births (1985) 14.5.
Food (1978–80): daily per capita caloric intake 3,643 (vegetable products 75%, animal products 25%); 145% FAO recommended minimum requirement.

Military

Total active duty personnel (1984): none△. *Military expenditure as a percent of national budget* (1984): 2.0% (world 6.1%); per capita expenditure (1984) *c.* U.S.$2.

*Detail does not add to total given because of rounding. †Early 1980s. ‡Includes 548 unemployed persons. §1975. ‖ Weighting coefficients for component expenditures are those of the 1976 official Italian consumer price index. ¶March. ♀Italian household expenditure survey. ♂In Italy. □Panel physicians only. △Defense is provided by a public security force of about 50; all fit males 16–55 constitute a militia.

São Tomé and Príncipe

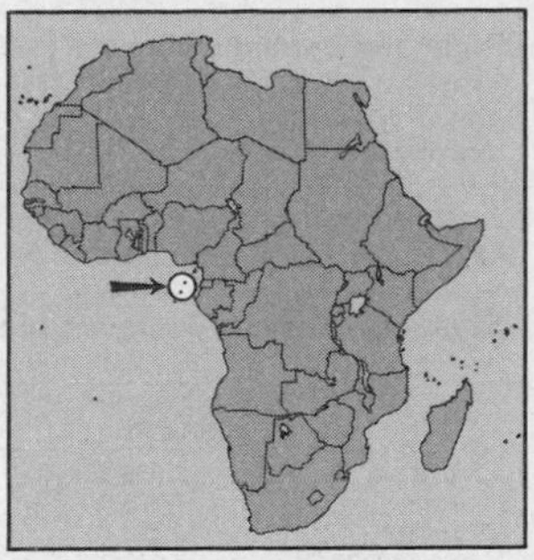

Official name: República democrática de São Tomé e Príncipe (Democratic Republic of São Tomé and Príncipe).
Form of government: republic with one legislative house (National People's Assembly [40]).
Head of state and government: President.
Capital: São Tomé.
Official language: Portuguese.
Official religion: Roman Catholicism.
Monetary unit: 1 dobra (Db) = 100 centavos; valuation (Oct. 1, 1986) 1 U.S.$ = Db 37.36; 1 £ = Db 53.98.

Area and population

Islands / Districts	Capitals	area sq mi	area sq km	population 1984 estimate
Príncipe	São António	55	142	5,671
Paguê	Príncipe	55	142	5,671
São Tomé		332	859	98,693
Aqua Grande	São Tomé	7	17	34,997
Cantagalo	Santana	46	119	11,270
Caué	São João Angolares	103	267	4,972
Lemba	Neves	88	229	8,537
Lobata	Guadalupe	41	105	12,717
Mé-zóchi	Trinidade	47	122	26,200
TOTAL		386	1,001	104,304

Demography

Population (1986): 109,600.
Density (1986): persons per sq mi 283.2, persons per sq km 109.5.
Urban-rural (1981): urban 33.5%; rural 66.5%.
Sex distribution (1981): male 49.72%; female 50.28%.
Age breakdown (1981): under 15, 46.3%; 15–29, 25.0%; 30–44, 11.6%; 45–59, 10.0%; 60–74, 5.3%; 75 and over, 1.8%.
Population projection: (1990) 114,000; (2000) 144,000.
Doubling time: 50 years.
Ethnic composition: mestiços, angolares (descendants of Angolan slaves), forros (descendants of freed slaves), serviçais (alien contract labourers), tongas (children of serviçais), and Europeans.
Religious affiliation (1985): Roman Catholic, about 80%; remainder mostly Protestant, predominantly Seventh-day Adventist and an indigenous Evangelical Church.
Major city (1984): São Tomé 34,997.

Vital statistics

Birth rate per 1,000 population (1985): 36.3 (world avg. 29.0); legitimate, n.a.; illegitimate, n.a.
Death rate per 1,000 population (1985): 8.8 (world avg. 11.0).
Natural increase rate per 1,000 population (1985): 27.5 (world avg. 18.0).
Total fertility rate (avg. births per childbearing woman; 1980–85): 5.2.
Marriage rate per 1,000 population: n.a.
Divorce rate per 1,000 population: n.a.
Life expectancy at birth (1980–85): male 47.1 years; female 50.0 years.
Major causes of death per 100,000 population (1972): senility without mention of psychosis, and ill-defined and unknown causes 367.5; gastritis, duodenitis, enteritis, and colitis, except diarrhea of the newborn, 95.5; pneumonia 62.4; heart disease 51.7; malaria 49.1.

National economy

Budget (1984). Revenue: Db 654,900,000* (indirect taxes 26.1%, import duties 13.5%, direct taxes 7.5%, export duties 6.3%, other sources 66.4%). Expenditures: Db 921,000,000* (services 64.4%, wages and salaries 46.0%, interest on the public debt 0.5%).
Tourism: virtually nonexistent in the mid-1980s, although development planners expected to establish a centre at Praia das Concas (on São Tomé), with an initial capacity of 400 tourists per week.
Public debt (external, outstanding; 1984): U.S.$82,000,000.
Production (metric tons except as noted). Agriculture, forestry, fishing (1985): coconuts 35,000, cacao 5,000, copra 4,000, melons 4,000, bananas 3,000, cassava 3,000, palmetto 3,000, vegetables 3,000, cereals 1,000, palm kernels 500; livestock (number of live animals) 4,000 goats, 3,000 cattle, 3,000 pigs, 2,000 sheep, 123,000 poultry; roundwood 6,000 cu m; fish catch (1984) 4,289, principally marine fish and shellfish. Mining and quarrying: some quarrying to support local construction industry. Manufacturing (1975): sawn wood 3,000 cu m†; bread and biscuits 1,831; palm oil 1,100‡; soap 470; ice 191; limes 22; corn (maize) flour 18; other products include soft drinks, beer, clothing, and bricks and clay products. Construction: (1972) buildings authorized 44 (5,561 sq m, of which residential 3,698, mixed residential–commercial 1,361, commercial 502). Energy production (consumption): electricity (kW-hr; 1984) 15,000,000 (15,000,000); coal, none (n.a.); crude petroleum, none (n.a.); petroleum products (metric tons; 1984) none (11,000); natural gas, none (n.a.).
Household income and expenditure: average household size: n.a.; income per household: n.a.; sources of income: n.a.; expenditure: n.a.
Gross national product (at current market prices; 1984): U.S.$34,243,000 (U.S.$330 per capita).

Structure of gross domestic product and labour force

	1981 in value Db '000,000	% of total value	labour force	% of labour force
Agriculture	207.3	31.3	16,486	54.4
Mining	...	...	—	—
Manufacturing	28.7	4.3	1,629	5.4
Construction	13.3	2.0	1,805	6.0
Public utilities	3.0	0.5	287	1.0
Transportation and communication	24.7	3.7	1,036	3.4
Trade	108.0	16.3	2,040	6.7
Pub. admin., defense	112.7	17.0	5,902	19.5
Finance }	165.4	24.9	187	0.6
Services }			1,235	4.1
Other }				
TOTAL	663.1	100.0	30,289	100.0

Population economically active (1981): total 30,607; activity rate of total population 31.7% (participation rates: ages 15–64, 61.1%; female 32.4%; unemployed, n.a.).

Price and earnings indexes (1974 = 100)

	1974	1975	1976	1977	1978	1979
Consumer price index	100.0	...	...	126.0	139.0	146.7
Earnings index	...	...	...	...	...	...

Land use (1984): meadows and pastures 1.0%; agricultural and under permanent cultivation 37.5%; forest, built-on, wasteland, and other 61.5%.

Foreign trade

Balance of trade (current prices)

	1980	1981	1982	1983	1984	1985
U.S.$'000,000	−11.7	−12.6	−15.9	−3.6	−4.9	−7.6
% of total	22.5%	31.5%	47.7%	23.1%	25.4%	42.7%

Imports (1984): Db 485,900,000 (food and other agricultural products 27.4%, mineral fuels and lubricants 16.3%, consumer goods 14.7%, machinery and transport equipment 12.9%, construction materials 8.6%). *Major import sources:* Portugal 29.8%; Angola 14.0%; France 12.3%; United Kingdom 10.7%; Belgium–Luxembourg 7.4%; Sweden 6.6%; East Germany 5.0%; Italy 4.1%; Japan 3.3%; Spain 1.7%; The Netherlands 0.8%; Norway 0.8%.
Exports (1984): Db 539,600,000 (cacao 80.0%, copra 15.0%, coffee 1.0%, palm kernels 0.4%). *Major export destinations:* East Germany 34.7%; The Netherlands, 18.1%; Portugal 15.3%; France 9.7%; United Kingdom 4.2%; Austria 2.8%; Italy 1.4%; Switzerland 1.4%.

Transport and communications

Transport. Railroads: none. Roads (1975): total length 179 mi, 288 km (paved 69%). Vehicles (1975): passenger cars 1,774; trucks and buses 265. Merchant marine (1985): vessels (100 gross tons and over) 3; total deadweight tonnage 1,172. Air transport (1975): passenger arrivals 10,050, passenger departures 9,240; short ton cargo loaded 19, unloaded 112; metric ton cargo loaded 28, unloaded 164; airports (1986) with scheduled flights 1.
Communications. Daily newspapers: none; 2 government weeklies (circulation, n.a.). Radio (1985): total number of receivers 26,000 (1 per 4.1 persons). Television: none. Telephones (1983): 2,187 (1 per 46.3 persons).

Education and health

Education (1984–85)

	schools	teachers	students	student/ teacher ratio
Primary (age 6–13)	63	517	19,086	36.9
Secondary (age 14–18)	11	300	6,186	20.6
Voc., teacher tr.	2	35	370	10.6
Higher	...	...	700§	...

Educational attainment, n.a. *Literacy* (1981): total population over age 15 literate 28,114 (54.2%); males literate 17,689 (70.2%); females literate 10,425 (39.1%).
Health: physicians (1981) 38 (1 per 2,500 persons); hospital beds (1978) 665 (1 per 129 persons); infant mortality rate per 1,000 live births (1985) 61.7.
Food (1981–83): daily per capita caloric intake 2,511 (vegetable products 87%, animal products 13%); 107% of FAO recommended minimum requirement.

Military

Total active duty personnel (1985): 700 Angolan and 200 Cuban troops (distribution by branch of service, n.a.). *Military expenditure as percent of GNP* (1980): 1.8% (world 5.6%).

*Breakdown given is for 1977. †1983. ‡1982. §Students abroad, 1982–83.

Saudi Arabia

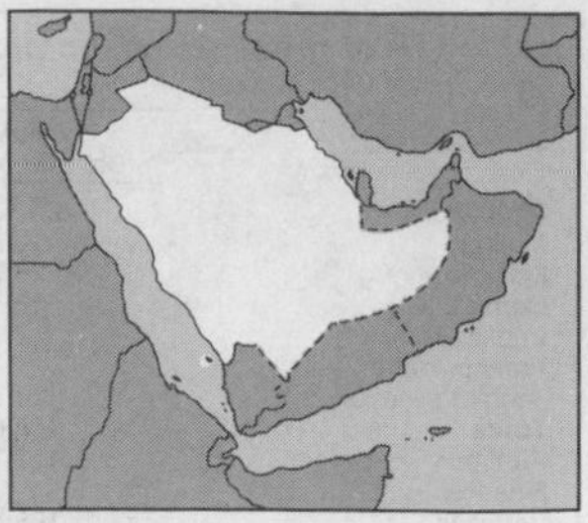

Official name: al-Mamlakah al-ʿArabīyah as-Saʿūdīyah (Kingdom of Saudi Arabia).
Form of government: monarchy.
Chief of state: King.
Head of government: Prime Minister.
Capital: Riyadh.
Official language: Arabic.
Official religion: Islam.
Monetary unit: 1 Saudi riyal (SRls) = 100 halalah; valuation (Oct. 1, 1986) 1 U.S.$ = SRls 3.75; 1 £ = SRls 5.42.

Area and population

Administrative Districts	Capitals	area sq mi	area sq km	population 1974 census*
ʿAsīr	Abha	...	...	682,000
al-Bāḥah	al-Bāḥah	...	...	186,000
Ḥā'il	Ḥā'il	...	...	260,000
al-Ḥudūd ash-Shamālīyah	ʿArʿar	...	...	129,000
al-Jawf	Sakākah	...	...	65,000
Jīzān	Jīzān	...	...	403,000
al-Madīnah	Medina (al-Madīnah)	...	...	519,000
Makkah	Mecca (Makkah)	...	...	1,754,000
Najrān	Najrān	...	...	148,000
al-Qaṣīm	Buraydah	...	...	316,000
al-Qurayyāt	an-Nabk	...	...	31,000
ar-Riyāḍ	Riyadh (ar-Riyāḍ)	...	...	1,272,000
ash-Sharqīyah	ad-Dammām	...	...	770,000
Tabūk	Tabūk	...	...	194,000
TOTAL		865,000	2,240,000	6,939,000†

Demography

Population (1986): 11,670,000.
Density (1986): persons per sq mi 13.5, persons per sq km 5.2.
Urban-rural (1985): urban 73.0%; rural 27.0%.
Sex distribution (1985): male 54.59%; female 45.41%.
Age breakdown (1984): under 15, 44.7%; 15–29, 28.7%; 30–44, 15.1%; 45–59, 7.8%; 60 and over, 3.7%.
Population projection: (1990) 13,724,000; (2000) 20,327,000.
Doubling time: 23 years.
Ethnic composition (1974): Saudi 88.2%; North Yemeni 5.6%; South Yemeni 1.0%; other 5.2%.
Religious affiliation (1980): Muslim (mostly Sunnī) 98.8%; Christian 0.8%; other 0.4%.
Major cities (1980): Riyadh 1,308,000‡; Jidda (Jiddah) 1,500,000§; Mecca 550,000; aṭ-Ṭa'if 300,000.

Vital statistics

Birth rate per 1,000 population (1980–85): 43.7 (world avg. 29.0).
Death rate per 1,000 population (1980–85): 12.6 (world avg. 11.0).
Natural increase rate per 1,000 population (1980–85): 31.1 (world avg. 18.0).
Total fertility rate (avg. births per childbearing woman; 1980–85): 3.5.
Marriage rate per 1,000 population: n.a.
Divorce rate per 1,000 population: n.a.
Life expectancy at birth (1980–85): male 54.5 years; female 57.6 years.
Major causes of death per 100,000 population: n.a.; however, major diseases include cholera, cerebrospinal meningitis, yellow fever, typhoid, tuberculosis, lung infections, and asphyxia.

National economy

Budget (1985–86). Revenue ‖: SRls 200,000,000,000 (oil 77.1%). Expenditures: SRls 200,000,000,000 (defense and security 32.0%, public administration and other government spending 15.0%, human resources development 11.9%, transport and communications 8.3%).
Public debt: none.
Tourism (1981): receipts from visitors U.S.$1,573,000,000; expenditures by nationals abroad U.S.$2,761,000,000.
Production (metric tons except as noted). Agriculture, forestry, fishing (1984): wheat 1,300,000, watermelons 480,000, dates 450,000, tomatoes 350,000, sorghum 87,000, grapes 75,000, onions 75,000, pumpkins, squash, and gourds 38,000, eggplants 25,000, cucumbers and gherkins 23,000, barley 12,000, millet 8,000, pulses 7,000, corn (maize) 4,000, potatoes 3,000, cabbages 1,000; livestock (number of live animals) 3,600,000 sheep, 2,350,000 goats, 550,000 cattle, 165,000 camels, 110,000 asses, 32,000,000 poultry; fish catch (1983) 26,425. Mining and quarrying (1984): gypsum 300,000; lime 12,000. Manufacturing (1985): cement 10,167,000; methanol 1,287,000; steel rods and bars 948,000; ethylene 927,900; urea 825,000; ehtylene glycol 310,000; industrial ethanol 200,000; ethylene dychloride 190,000; styrene 125,000; caustic soda 125,000; nitrogen 82,000; citric acid 75,000; oxygen 55,000; melamine 14,000. Construction (value added in SRls; 1981): 51,689,000,000. Energy production (consumption): electricity (kW-hr; 1984) 36,985,000,000 (36,985,000,000); coal, n.a. (n.a.); crude petroleum (barrels; 1984) 1,674,900,000 (302,015,000); petroleum products (metric tons; 1983) 43,619,000 (26,020,000); natural gas (cu m; 1984) 1,281,350,000 (1,281,350,000).
Land use (1983): forested 0.7%; meadows and pastures 39.5%; agricultural and under permanent cultivation 0.5%; other, built-on, and waste 59.3%.
Population economically active (1984): total 2,673,316; activity rate of total population 24.5% (participation rates: over age 15, 44.3%; female 2.3%; unemployed, n.a.).

Price and earnings indexes (1980 = 100)

	1979	1980	1981	1982	1983	1984	1985
Consumer price index	96.4	100.0	102.7	103.8	104.8	103.7	100.2
Monthly earnings index	...	...	...	...	...	...	...

Gross national product (at current market prices; 1984): U.S.$116,380,000,000 (U.S.$10,750 per capita).

Structure of gross domestic product and labour force

	1984–85 in value SRls '000,000	1984–85 % of total value	1984 labour force	1984 % of labour force
Agriculture	7,056.3	2.5	223,383	8.3
Mining	1,795.0	0.6	163,979	6.1
Oil sector	113,289.9	39.9		
Manufacturing	12,511.4	4.4	408,058	15.3
Construction	40,170.6	14.1	515,175	19.3
Public utilities	794.7	0.3	61,591	2.3
Transportation and communication	22,177.6	7.8	116,629	4.4
Trade	27,069.1	9.5	730,124	27.3
Finance	20,631.3	7.3	104.330	3.9
Pub. admin., defense	30,944.2	10.9	350,047	13.1
Services and other	7,674.8	2.7		
TOTAL	284,114.9	100.0	2,673,316	100.0

Household income and expenditure. Average household size (1984) 6.6; income per household: n.a.; source of income: n.a.; expenditure (1980): food 52.2%, housing 17.2%, clothing 6.6%, furniture and utensils 5.9%, transport and communication 4.5%, health care 2.1%.

Foreign trade

Balance of trade (current prices)

	1978	1979	1980	1981	1982	1983	1984
SRls '000,000	+59.2	+110.6	+238.9	+262.9	+120.5	+49.4	+37
% of total	29.9%	40.4%	54.4%	52.2%	30.2%	17.6%	12.7%

Imports (1984): SRls 127,698,000,000 (machinery and appliances 18.5%, foodstuffs 16.2%, transport equipment 13.7%, textiles and clothing 9.3%). *Major import sources:* Japan 18.5%; United States 18.3%; Italy 7.9%; France 7.6%; West Germany 7.4%; United Kingdom 6.1%; The Netherlands 2.4%; Switzerland 2.2%; Singapore 2.1%; Sweden 1.2%; Australia 1.2%; Canada 0.9%.
Exports (1984): SRls 165,060,000,000 (crude petroleum 89.7%, refined petroleum 10.3%). *Major export destinations:* Japan 31.3%; United States 8.5%; Singapore 5.7%; France 4.6%; Italy 4.2%; Brazil 3.2%; Indonesia 2.9%; West Germany 2.1%; Spain 2.1%; Thailand 1.9%; United Kingdom 1.5%; Pakistan 1.2%.

Transport and communications

Transport. Railroads (1986–87): route length 544 mi, 875 km; (1984–85) passenger-mi 51,041,000, passenger-km 82,413,000; short ton-mi cargo 667,080,000, metric ton-km cargo 973,920,000. Roads (1984–85): total length 50,878 mi, 81,881 km (paved 36%). Vehicles (1983): passenger cars 1,856,398; trucks and buses 1,704,300. Merchant marine (1985): vessels (100 gross tons and over) 398; total deadweight tonnage 5,247,299. Air transport (1985): passenger-mi 9,604,000,000, passenger-km 15,456,000,000; short ton-mi cargo 330,186,000, metric ton-km cargo 482,064,000; airports (1986) with scheduled flights 23.
Communications. Daily newspapers (1985): total number 10; total circulation 498,000; circulation per 1,000 population 44.3. Radio (1985): total number of receivers 2,800,000 (1 per 4.0 persons). Television (1985): total number of receivers 3,700,000 (1 per 3.0 persons). Telephones (1985): 927,803 (1 per 12.1 persons).

Education and health

Education (1984–85)

	schools	teachers	students	student/teacher ratio
Primary (age 6–12)	7,433	75,047	1,184,593	15.8
Secondary (age 13–18)	2,880	36,009	471,997	13.1
Voc., teacher tr.	26¶	881¶	9,235	...
Higher	77♀	8,561	91,978	10.7

Educational attainment, n.a. *Literacy* (1984): total population over age 15 literate 2,946,026 (48.8%); males literate 2,124,781 (58.0%); females literate 821,245 (34.6%).
Health (1985): physicians 14,267 (1 per 788 persons); hospital beds 26,410 (1 per 425 persons); infant mortality rate per 1,000 live births (1984) 109.8.
Food (1980–82): daily per capita caloric intake 2,969 (vegetable products 82%, animal products 18%); 122% of FAO recommended minimum requirement.

Military

Total active duty personnel (1985): 52,500 (army 66.7%, navy 6.7%, air force 26.6%). *Military expenditure as percent of GNP* (1983): 24.3% (world 6.1%); per capita expenditure U.S.$2,508.

*Official census data are of uncertain reliability; external estimates poorly founded. Total population may number as few as 4,000,000. †Total includes 210,000 nomads not distributable by district. ‡1981 estimate. §1983 estimate. ‖ A decision was taken to defer implementation of the 1986–87 budget in view of low oil prices. ¶1983–84. ♀Includes colleges, institutions of advanced study, and universities.

Senegal

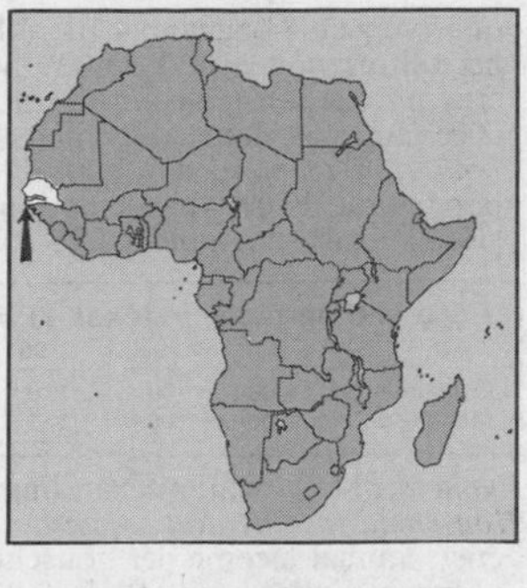

Official name: République du Sénégal (Republic of Senegal).
Form of government: republic with one legislative house (National Assembly [120]).
Head of state and government: President.
Capital: Dakar.
Official language: French.
Official religion: none.
Monetary unit: 1 CFA franc (CFAF) = 100 centimes; valuation (Oct. 1, 1986) 1 U.S.$ = CFAF 332.05; 1 £ = CFAF 479.81.

Area and population

Regions	Capitals	area sq mi	area sq km	population 1984 estimate
Dakar	Dakar	212	550	1,380,700
Diourbel	Diourbel	1,683	4,359	501,000
Fatick	Fatick	3,064	7,935	506,500
Kaolack	Kaolack	6,181	16,010	741,600
Kolda	Kolda	8,112	21,011	517,600
Louga	Louga	11,270	29,188	493,900
Saint-Louis	Saint-Louis	17,038	44,127	612,100
Tambacounda	Tambacounda	23,012	59,602	355,000
Thiès	Thiès	2,549	6,601	837,900
Ziguinchor	Ziguinchor	2,834	7,339	361,000
TOTAL		75,955	196,722	6,307,300

Demography

Population (1986): 6,699,000.
Density (1986): persons per sq mi 88.2, persons per sq km 34.1.
Urban-rural (1980): urban 25.4%; rural 74.6%.
Sex distribution (1985): male 49.49%; female 50.51%.
Age breakdown (1985): under 15, 45.0%; 15–29, 25.8%; 30–44, 15.4%; 45–59, 9.0%; 60–74, 4.1%; 75 and over, 0.7%.
Population projection: (1990) 7,430,000; (2000) 9,747,000.
Doubling time: 26 years.
Ethnic composition (1980): Wolof 35%; Serer 16%; Fulani (Peul) 14%; Tukulor 9%; Diola (Jola) 9%; Mandingo 7%; other 10%.
Religious affiliation (1980): Sunnī Muslim 91.0%; Roman Catholic 5.6%; tribal religionist 3.2%; other 0.2%.
Major cities (1984): Dakar 671,000; Thiès 126,886*; Kaolack 126,900; Ziguinchor 105,200; Saint-Louis 96,594*.

Vital statistics

Birth rate per 1,000 population (1980–85): 47.9 (world avg. 29.0).
Death rate per 1,000 population (1980–85): 21.1 (world avg. 11.0).
Natural increase rate per 1,000 population (1980–85): 26.8 (world avg. 18.0).
Total fertility rate (avg. births per childbearing woman; 1984): 6.6.
Marriage rate per 1,000 population: n.a.
Divorce rate per 1,000 population: n.a.
Life expectancy at birth (1984): male 45.0 years; female 48.0 years.
Major causes of death per 100,000 population (officially confirmed transmissible diseases only; 1978): malaria 12.7; measles 11.4, tetanus 5.5, leprosy 4.8.

National economy

Budget (1985–86). Revenue: CFAF 163,856,500,000 (no breakdown available). Expenditures: CFAF 153,012,100,000 (education 28.3%, defense 18.5%, public health 6.7%, economy and finance 6.6%).
Production (metric tons except as noted). Agriculture, forestry, fishing (1984): millet and sorghum 949,570†, sugarcane 800,000, peanuts (groundnuts) 682,000, paddy rice 147,000†, corn (maize) 98,000, beans 79,700†, cotton 56,000, tomatoes 40,000, cotton seed 34,000, onions 30,000, cotton lint 21,000, oranges 19,000, bananas 6,000, coconuts 5,000; livestock (number of live animals) 2,200,000 cattle, 2,100,000 sheep, 1,000,000 goats; roundwood 4,049,000 cu m; fish catch (1983) 212,895. Mining and quarrying (1985): calcium phosphate 1,809,800; cement 395,300; aluminum phosphate 365,640. Manufacturing (1982): peanut oil 219,000; wheat flour 70,000; refined sugar 44,000; soap 35,900; canned fish 23,900; cigarettes 2,176; nitrogenous fertilizers 5,000; woven cotton fabrics 6,900,000 sq m; carbonated beverages 287,000 hectolitres; beer 176,000 hectolitres; footwear 4,769,000 pairs. Construction (authorized; 1982): residential 203,600 sq m; nonresidential 44,500 sq m. Energy production (consumption): electricity (kW-hr; 1984) 684,000,000 (684,000,000); coal, none (n.a.); crude petroleum (barrels; 1984) none (2,570,000); petroleum products (metric tons; 1984) 334,000 (742,000); natural gas, none (n.a.).
Public debt (external, outstanding; 1984): U.S.$1,555,100,000.
Population economically active (1984): total 2,938,000; activity rate of total population 46.0% (participation rates: ages 15–64, 76.0%; female 40.5%; unemployed, n.a.).

Price and earnings indexes (1980 = 100)

	1980	1981	1982	1983	1984	1985	1986‡
Consumer price index	100.0	105.9	124.2	138.7	155.1	175.2	187.1
Hourly earnings index	100.0	105.0	105.0	113.6	113.6	...	...

Household income and expenditure§. Average household size (1975) 8.6; average annual income per household CFAF 1,105,800 (U.S.$5,160); sources of income: wages and salaries 51.6%, remittances and gifts 17.5%, pensions, social security, and related benefits 12.5%, other 18.4%; expenditure (1979): food and tobacco 57.5%, housing, maintenance, and utilities 18.4%, clothing 11.9%, transport 5.4%, other 6.8%.
Gross national product (at current market prices; 1984): U.S.$2,440,000,000 (U.S.$380 per capita).

Structure of gross domestic product and labour force

	1984 in value CFAF '000,000,000	1984 % of total value	1982 labour force ‖	1982 % of labour force
Agriculture	174.1	17.1	10,654	9.1
Mining			1,918	1.6
Manufacturing	281.4	27.7	30,736	26.4
Public utilities			3,221	2.8
Construction			8,402	7.2
Transportation and communication			24,789	21.2
Trade			14,648	12.6
Finance	561.0	55.2	7,921	6.8
Services; Pub. admin., defense, and other			14,339	12.3
TOTAL	1,016.5	100.0	116,628	100.0

Tourism: receipts from visitors (1984) U.S.$56,000,000; expenditures by nationals abroad (1983) U.S.$42,000,000.
Land use (1983): forested 30.9%; meadows and pastures 29.7%; agricultural and under permanent cultivation 27.2%; other 12.2%.

Foreign trade

Balance of trade (current prices)

	1979	1980	1981	1982	1983	1984
CFAF '000,000,000	−84.1	−121.5	−156.5	−145.9	−174.4	−203.1
% of total	27.0%	37.6%	36.5%	28.8%	27.5%	30.3%

Imports (1984): CFAF 437,099,000,000 (crude petroleum 23.9%, basic manufactures 15.0%, cereals 11.5%, mechanical equipment 8.4%, chemical products 8.4%, motor vehicle parts 5.3%, electrical equipment 2.6%). *Major import sources:* France 26.2%; Nigeria 11.2%; Algeria 8.2%; Thailand 6.2%; United States 5.1%; West Germany 3.5%; Côte d'Ivoire 3.3%; Italy 2.6%; The Netherlands 2.4%.
Exports (1984): CFAF 233,974,000,000 (petroleum products 18.5%, peanut oil 15.3%, calcium phosphate 10.9%, canned fish 9.1%, chemicals 9.0%, fresh or frozen fish 7.2%, fresh or frozen crustaceans 4.9%, cotton fabrics 3.1%, peanut oilcake 2.9%, footwear 0.6%). *Major export destinations:* France 30.7%; United Kingdom 5.7%; Côte d'Ivoire 5.2%; Italy 4.1%; Mali 2.8%; Mauritania 2.7%; India 2.3%; Japan 1.6%.

Transport and communications

Transport. Railroads (1984): route length 642 mi, 1,033 km; passenger-mi 82,600,000¶, passenger-km 133,000,000¶; short ton-mi cargo 212,000,000♀, metric ton-km cargo 309,000,000♀. Roads (1982): total length 8,679 mi, 13,968 km (paved 26%). Vehicles (1980): passenger cars 50,875; trucks and buses 27,767. Merchant marine (1985): vessels (100 gross tons and over) 144; total deadweight tonnage 44,261. Air transport♂ (1983): passenger-mi 129,310,000, passenger-km 208,106,000; short ton-mi cargo 26,217,000, metric ton-km cargo 38,278,000; airports (1986) with scheduled flights 12.
Communications. Daily newspapers (1984): total number 1; total circulation 31,000; circulation per 1,000 population 4.9. Radio (1985): total number of receivers 350,000 (1 per 19 persons). Television (1985): total number of receivers 52,000 (1 per 125 persons). Telephones (1979): 40,218 (1 per 137 persons).

Education and health

Education (1983–84)

	schools	teachers	students	student/teacher ratio
Primary (age 6–11)	2,150	12,934	533,394	41.2
Secondary (age 12–18)	192	2,346□	88,815	...
Voc., teacher tr.	5	1,475□	4,791	...
Higher	6	497	11,293	22.7

Educational attainment (1970). Percent of population over age 6 having: no formal schooling 95.3%; primary education 3.9%; secondary 0.7%; higher 0.1%. *Literacy* (1980): total population over age 15 literate 1,274,000 (22.5%); males literate 1,755,000 (31.0%); females literate 804,000 (14.2%).
Health (1982): physicians 470 (1 per 12,987 persons); hospital beds 6,200 (1 per 973 persons); infant mortality rate per 1,000 live births (1980–85) 141.0.
Food (1980–82): daily per capita caloric intake 2,364 (vegetable products 92%, animal products 8%); 99% of FAO recommended minimum requirement.

Military

Total active duty personnel (1985): 9,700 (army 87.6%, navy 7.2%, air force 5.2%). *Military expenditure as percent of GNP* (1983): 2.3% (world 6.1%); per capita expenditure U.S.$9.

*1979. †1985. ‡March. §Among traditional African households in Dakar. ‖ Private sector only. ¶1983. ♀1980. ♂International flights only. □1979–80.

Seychelles

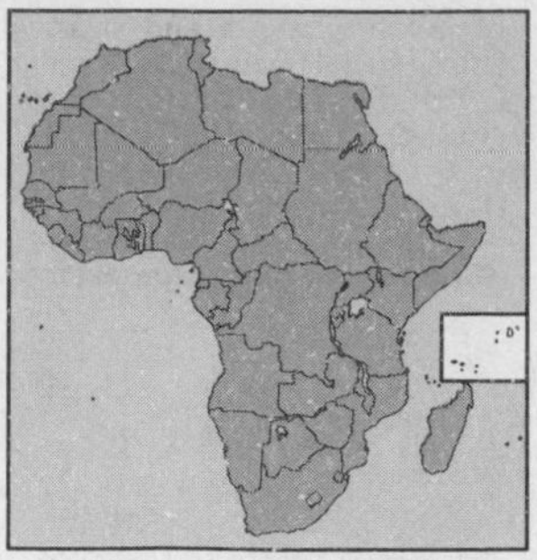

Official name: Republic of Seychelles (English); République des Seychelles (French); Repiblik Sesel (Creole).
Form of government: unitary single-party republic with one legislative house (People's Assembly [25]).
Head of state and government: President.
Capital: Victoria.
Official languages: English; French; Creole.
Official religion: none.
Monetary unit: 1 Seychelles rupee (SR) = 100 cents; valuation (Oct. 1, 1986) 1 U.S.$ = SR 5.97; 1 £ = SR 8.63.

Area and population

		area		population
Central (granitic) group	**Capital**	sq mi	sq km	1984 estimate
La Digue and satellites		6	15	2,000
Mahé and satellites	Victoria	61	158	57,400
Praslin and satellites		16	42	4,650
Silhouette		8	20	200
Other islands		2	4	50
Outer (coralline) islands		83	214	400
TOTAL		175*	453	64,700

Demography

Population (1986): 66,112.
Density (1986): persons per sq mi 377.8, persons per sq km 145.9.
Urban-rural (1977): urban 37.2%; rural 62.8%.
Sex distribution (1985): male 50.26%; female 49.74%.
Age breakdown (1985): under 15, 36.3%; 15–29, 31.5%; 30–44, 12.9%; 45–64, 12.9%; 65 and over, 6.4%.
Population projection: (1990) 69,600; (2000) 82,400.
Doubling time: 36 years.
Ethnic composition (1980): Seychellois 98.0%; non-Seychellois 2.0%.
Religious affiliation (1986): Roman Catholic 90.0%; Anglican 2.0%; other 8.0%.
Major city (1977): Victoria 23,012.

Vital statistics

Birth rate per 1,000 population (1985): 26.5 (world avg. 29.0); (1984) legitimate 33.2%; illegitimate 66.8%.
Death rate per 1,000 population (1985): 7.2 (world avg. 11.0).
Natural increase rate per 1,000 population (1985): 19.3 (world avg. 18.0).
Total fertility rate (avg. births per childbearing woman; 1984): 3.5.
Marriage rate per 1,000 population (1984): 6.0.
Divorce rate per 1,000 population (1984): 0.8.
Life expectancy at birth (1980–85): male 66.2 years; female 73.5 years.
Major causes of death per 100,000 population (1984): diseases of the circulatory system 146.8; ill-defined conditions 127.3; malignant neoplasms (cancers) 92.7; cerebrovascular diseases 64.9; pneumonia 40.2; diseases of the digestive system 38.6; accidents and adverse effects 37.1.

National economy

Budget (1985). Revenue: SR 447,700,000 (import duties 30.3%; income tax 20.8%; turnover tax and excise duties 17.8%; nontax revenue 17.7%; public entities 8.5%). Expenditures: SR 632,900,000 (debt payment 25.1%; general administration 20.9%, of which defense, police, and prisons 10.9%; education and information 13.9%; health 6.6%; economic services 6.5%; public enterprises 3.7%).
Gross national product (at current market prices; 1984): U.S.$145,000,000 (U.S.$2,240 per capita).

Structure of gross domestic product and labour force

	1984			
	in value SR '000,000	% of total value	labour force†	% of labour force
Agriculture	74.1	6.9	2,074	11.6
Mining and manufacturing	100.3	9.4	1,767	9.9
Construction	52.8	4.9	1,635	9.1
Public utilities	19.2	1.8	‡	‡
Transportation and communication	453.8§	42.4§	2,143	12.0
Trade	84.7	7.9	3,185	17.8
Finance	84.8	7.9	800	4.5
Public admin., defense	173.6	16.2	2,211	12.3
Services	28.0	2.6	4,077‡	22.8‡
Other	...	...	...	...
TOTAL	1,071.3	100.0	17,892	100.0

Tourism: receipts from visitors (1985) U.S.$47,000,000; expenditures by nationals abroad (1984) U.S.$6,400,000.
Production (metric tons except as noted). Agriculture, forestry, fishing (1984): coconuts 26,000, copra 3,722, mangoes 4,000, bananas 2,000, cinnamon bark 1,378, tea 87; livestock (number of live animals) 14,000 pigs, 4,000 goats, 1,600 cattle, 185,200 chickens; fish catch (1985) 4,351. Mining and quarrying (1984): guano 4,700. Manufacturing (1985): beer and stout 41,400 hectolitres; soft drinks 35,000 hectolitres; cigarettes 59,800,000 units. Energy production (consumption): electricity (kW-hr; 1985) 62,000,000 (62,000,000); coal, none (n.a.); petroleum, none (n.a.); natural gas, none (n.a.).
Population economically active (1984): total 25,221; activity rate of total population 39.0% (participation rates: ages 15–64 [1981] 62.3%; female [1981] 39.5%; unemployed 23.2%).

Price and earnings indexes (1980 = 100)

	1980	1981	1982	1983	1984	1985	1986 ‖
Consumer price index	100.0	110.6	109.7	116.3	120.9	122.0	121.4
Monthly earnings index	100.0	111.0	120.2	129.5	132.3	134.2	...

Public debt (external, outstanding; 1984): U.S.$43,100,000.
Household income and expenditure. Average household size (1978) 4.6; average annual income per household (1978) SR 18,480 (U.S.$2,658); sources of income: wages and salaries 88.8%, agricultural sales 3.8%, pensions 1.9%; expenditure (1984): food 37.3%, beverages and tobacco 18.7%, housing 15.8%, clothing and footwear 9.0%, household and personal goods 7.5%, services and recreation 5.6%, transportation 4.1%.
Land use (1983): forested 18.5%; agricultural and under permanent cultivation 18.5%; built-on, wasteland, and other 63.0%.

Foreign trade¶

Balance of trade (current prices)

	1980	1981	1982	1983	1984	1985
SR '000,000	−496.2	−480.7	−541.2	−456.8	−354.8	−524.7
% of total	64.7%	68.9%	73.0%	62.5%	49.4%	57.5%

Imports (1985): SR 718,700,000 (petroleum, petroleum products, and related materials 25.8%; machinery and transport equipment 25.8%; manufactured goods 23.6%; food, beverages, and tobacco 16.5%; chemicals and related products 5.8%; nonmetallic mineral manufactures 5.7%; textile yarn, fabrics, and finished articles 3.8%). *Major import sources:* United Kingdom 14.7%; Italy 9.5%; France 8.9%; South Africa 8.9%; United States 5.4%; United Arab Emirates 5.1%; Singapore 5.0%; Japan 4.7%; Kenya 4.7%; Bahrain 3.2%.
Exports (1985): SR 201,180,000♀ (petroleum products 83.3%δ; fish 4.0%; copra 3.9%; cinnamon bark 1.2%). *Major export destinations*□ (1984): Pakistan 38.6%; Japan 26.1%; Réunion 14.9%; United Kingdom 4.9%; France 2.7%.

Transport and communications

Transport. Railroads: none. Roads (1986): total length 161 mi, 259 km (paved 61%). Vehicles (1984): passenger cars 3,420; trucks and buses 1,161. Merchant marine (1985): vessels (100 gross tons and over) 4; total deadweight tonnage 821. Air transport (1985): passenger arrivals 76,000, passenger departures 76,000; metric ton cargo unloaded 1,326, metric ton cargo loaded 171; airports (1986) with scheduled flights 5.
Communications. Daily newspapers (1984): total number 2; total circulation 3,400; circulation per 1,000 population 52.5. Radio (1985): total number of receivers 16,000 (1 per 4.1 persons). Television (1985): total number of receivers 4,000 (1 per 16 persons). Telephones (1981): 7,105 (1 per 9 persons).

Education and health

Education (1986)

	schools	teachers	students	student/ teacher ratio
Primary (age 6–15)	26	681	14,663	21.5
Secondary (age 16–18)	4	112	2,433	21.7
Voc., teacher tr.	1	160	1,541	9.6

Educational attainment (1977). Percent of population over age 15 having: no formal schooling 13.7%; primary education 50.1%; some secondary 32.4%; complete secondary 1.4%; postsecondary 1.8%. *Literacy* (1971): total population literate 17,066 (57.3%); males literate 8,103 (54.9%); females literate 8,963 (59.6%).
Health (1984): physicians 34 (1 per 1,900 persons); hospital beds 359 (1 per 180 persons); infant mortality rate per 1,000 live births (1985) 17.9.
Food: daily per capita caloric intake, n.a.

Military

Total active duty personnel (1985): 1,200 (army 83%, navy 8.5%, air force 8.5%). *Military expenditure as percent of GNP* (1982): 5.8% (world 6.0%); per capita expenditure U.S.$129.

*Detail does not add to total given because of rounding. †Employed persons only. ‡Services include public utilities. §Includes import duties. ‖ March. ¶Imports c.i.f. (cost, insurance, freight), exports f.o.b. (free on board). ♀Includes SR 176 million of reexports. δItems reexported. □Domestic export only.

Sierra Leone

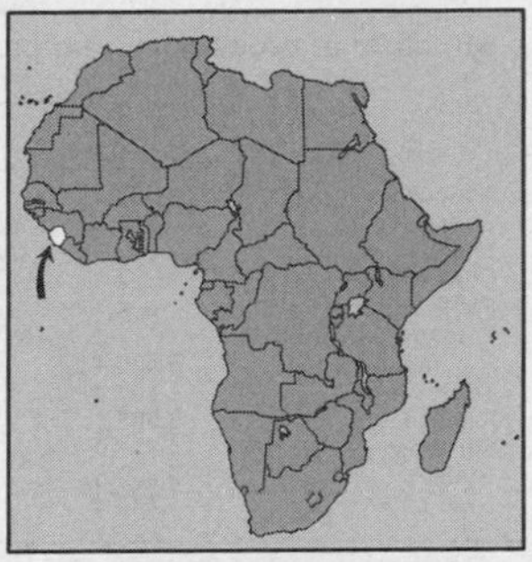

Official name: Republic of Sierra Leone.
Form of government: a unitary single-party republic with one legislative house (House of Representatives [124]).
Head of state and government: President.
Capital: Freetown.
Official language: English.
Official religion: none.
Monetary unit: 1 leone (Le) = 100 cents; valuation* (Oct. 1, 1986) 1 U.S.$ = Le 28.50; 1 £ = Le 41.18.

Area and population

Provinces Districts	Capitals	area sq mi	area sq km	population 1985 census†
Eastern Province	Kenema	6,005	15,553	960,551
Kailahun	Kailahun	1,490	3,859	233,839
Kenema	Kenema	2,337	6,053	337,055
Kono	Sefadu	2,178	5,641	389,657
Northern Province	Makeni	13,875	35,936	1,262,226
Bombali	Makeni	3,083	7,985	315,914
Kambia	Kambia	1,200	3,108	186,231
Koinaduga	Kabala	4,680	12,121	183,286
Port Loko	Port Loko	2,208	5,719	329,344
Tonkolili	Magburaka	2,704	7,003	247,451
Southern Province	Bo	7,604	19,694	740,510
Bo	Bo	2,015	5,219	268,671
Bonthe (incl. Sherbro)	Bonthe	1,339	3,468	105,007
Moyamba	Moyamba	2,665	6,902	250,514
Pujehun	Pujehun	1,585	4,105	116,318
Western Area	Freetown	215	557	554,243
TOTAL		27,699	71,740	3,517,530

Demography

Population (1986): 3,732,000.
Density (1986): persons per sq mi 134.7, persons per sq km 52.0.
Urban-rural (1985): urban 24.5%; rural 75.5%.
Sex distribution (1985): male 49.60%; female 50.40%.
Age breakdown (1985): under 15, 40.9%; 15–29, 25.9%; 30–44, 17.0%; 45–59, 10.7%; 60–74, 4.8%; 75 and over, 0.7%.
Population projection: (1990) 3,950,000; (2000) 4,771,000.
Doubling time: 25 years.
Ethnic composition (1978): Mende 34.4%; Temne 31.3%; Kono 5.6%; Bullom 3.7%; Fulani 3.7%; Koranko 3.7%; Limba 3.7%; Kissi 2.5%; other 11.4%.
Religious affiliation (1980): traditional beliefs 51.5%; Sunnī Muslim 39.4%; Protestant 4.7%; Roman Catholic 2.2%; Anglican 1.2%; other 1.0%.
Major cities (1985): Freetown 496,776; Koidu-New Sembehun 80,000; Bo 26,000; Kenema 13,000; Makeni 12,000.

Vital statistics

Birth rate per 1,000 population (1980–85): 45.3 (world avg. 29.0); legitimate, n.a.; illegitimate, n.a.
Death rate per 1,000 population (1980–85): 17.4 (world avg. 11.0).
Natural increase rate per 1,000 population (1980–85): 27.9 (world avg. 18.0).
Total fertility rate (avg. births per childbearing woman; 1980–85): 6.1.
Marriage rate per 1,000 population: n.a.
Divorce rate per 1,000 population: n.a.
Life expectancy at birth (1980–85): male 46.7 years; female 50.0 years.
Major causes of death per 100,000 population: n.a.; however, the major diseases are malaria, tuberculosis, leprosy, whooping cough, measles, tetanus, and diarrhea.

National economy

Budget (1984–85). Revenue: Le 262,100,000 (direct taxes 25.2%, excise duties 23.5%, import duties 19.5%, export duties 11.0%, other including grants 20.8%). Expenditures: Le 431,700,000 (public debt charges 33.9%, education and social welfare 19.0%, general administration 8.4%, defense 6.2%, construction and development 5.6%, police and justice 4.5%, agriculture development 4.0%).
Public debt (external, outstanding; 1984): U.S.$390,600,000.
Tourism (1983): receipts from visitors U.S.$8,000,000; expenditures by nationals abroad U.S.$4,000,000.
Production (metric tons except as noted). Agriculture, forestry, fishing (1985): rice 500,000, cassava 110,000, palm oil 44,000, pulses 33,000, palm kernels 30,000, millet 20,000, sorghum 20,000, corn (maize) 20,000, peanuts (groundnuts) 14,000, sweet potatoes 13,000, cocoa beans 10,000, coffee 9,000; livestock (number of live animals) 330,000 cattle, 320,000 sheep, 170,000 goats, 44,000 pigs, 5,000,000 chickens; roundwood (1984) 7,632,000 cu m; fish catch (1984) 52,500. Mining and quarrying (1984): bauxite 1,041,200; rutile (a titanium ore) 91,289; iron ore 325,000; diamonds 263,000 carats. Manufacturing (1984): salt 19,200; nails 2,300; paint 1,140 hectolitres; beer and stout 35,670 hectolitres; plastic footwear 477,000 pairs‡; cigarettes 1,346,000 units. Construction (value added in Le; 1981): 53,900,000. Energy production (consumption): electricity (kW-hr; 1984) 112,000,000 (112,000,000); coal, none (n.a.); crude petroleum (barrels; 1984) none (1,800,000); petroleum products (metric tons; 1984) 216,000 (163,000); natural gas, none (n.a.).
Household income and expenditure. Average household size (1980) 4.9; average annual income per household (1984): U.S.$320; sources of income (1984): self-employment 61.6%, wages and salaries 27.9%, other 10.5%; expenditure (1984): food, beverages, and tobacco 55.1%, clothing and footwear 12.9%, transport and communication 9.2%, furniture, furnishings, and household durable goods 8.0%, housing 7.4%, recreation, entertainment, and education 3.8%, health 1.3%.
Gross national product (at current market prices; 1984): U.S.$1,120,000,000 (U.S.$320 per capita).

Structure of gross domestic product and labour force

	1981–82 in value Le '000,000	1981–82 % of total value	1983–84 labour force§	1983–84 % of labour force
Agriculture	460.4	33.1	5,835	7.9
Mining	71.2	5.1	6,075	8.2
Manufacturing	66.4	4.8	8,046	10.9
Construction	78.1	5.6	8,986	12.2
Public utilities	7.4	0.5	2,134	2.9
Transportation and communication	184.8	13.3	7,211	9.8
Trade	180.4	13.0	6,161	8.3
Finance	141.0	10.1		
Pub. admin., defense	147.7	10.6	23,821	32.2
Services	61.6	4.4		
Other	−7.2‖	−0.5‖	5,639¶	7.6¶
TOTAL	1,391.8♀	100.0	73,908	100.0

Population economically active (1985): total 1,352,000; activity rate of total population 36.5% (participation rates: ages 15–64 [1980] 64.0%; female [1980] 34.7%; unemployed [registered; 1984] 0.4%).

Price and earnings indexes (1980 = 100)

	1980	1981	1982	1983	1984	1985	1986♂
Consumer price index	100.0	123.3	161.8	274.2	456.3	806.6	1,001

Land use (1984): forested 29.2%; meadows and pastures 30.8%; agricultural and under permanent cultivation 24.7%; other 15.3%.

Foreign trade

Balance of trade (current prices)

	1979	1980	1981	1982	1983	1984
Le '000,000	−129.9	−230.1	−205.9	−231.5	−85.0	−46.7
% of total	24.1%	34.6%	40.0%	45.8%	17.4%	5.9%

Imports (1984): Le 417,647,000 (minerals, fuels, and lubricants 39.0%; machinery and transport equipment 19.3%; basic manufactured goods 15.9%; food and live animals 13.0%; chemicals 5.1%). *Major import sources:* United Kingdom 11.4%; West Germany 11.0%; Japan 6.1%; The Netherlands 5.0%; France 4.9%; United States 4.6%; China 2.3%.
Exports (1984): Le 370,946,000 (diamonds 34.5%; rutile 16.1%; cacao 15.6%; bauxite 13.8%; coffee 9.2%; palm kernels 3.5%). *Major export destinations:* The Netherlands 16.5%; United Kingdom 11.9%; United States 8.8%; West Germany 1.7%.

Transport and communications

Transport. Railroads (1981): length 52 mi, 84 km. Roads (1980): total length 4,635 mi, 7,459 km (paved 16%). Vehicles (1984): passenger cars 19,040; trucks and buses 6,763. Merchant marine (1985): vessels (100 gross tons and over) 25; total deadweight tonnage 1,324. Air transport□ (1984): passenger-mi 75,698,000, passenger-km 121,825,000; short ton-mi cargo 1,337,000, metric ton-km cargo 1,952,000; airports (1986) with scheduled flights 6.
Communications. Daily newspapers (1985): total number 1; total circulation 12,000; circulation per 1,000 population 3.4. Radio (1984): total number of receivers 100,000 (1 per 38 persons). Television (1984): total number of receivers 21,700 (1 per 175 persons). Telephones (1981): 220,000 (1 per 15.4 persons).

Education and health

Education (1984–85)

	schools	teachers	students	student/teacher ratio
Primary (age 5–11)	1,219	10,451	350,160	33.5
Secondary (age 12–18)	171	3,829	81,879	21.4
Voc., teacher tr.	12	406	4,774	11.8
Higher	2	296	2,445	8.3

Educational attainment (1974). Percent of population over age 5 having: no formal schooling 81.3%; primary education 12.1%; secondary 5.9%; higher 0.7%. *Literacy* (1980): total population over age 15 literate 460,300 (23.6%); males literate 294,500 (31.2%); females literate 165,800 (16.5%).
Health (1983): physicians 197 (1 per 17,906 persons); hospital beds 4,754 (1 per 742 persons); infant mortality rate per 1,000 live births (1984) 134.0
Food (1981–83): daily per capita caloric intake 2,010 (vegetable products 96%, animal products 4%); 84% of FAO recommended minimum requirement.

Military

Total active duty personnel (1986): 3,100 (army 96.8%, navy 3.2%, air force, none). *Military expenditure as percent of GNP* (1984): 1.0% (world 6.1%); per capita expenditure U.S.$2.

*Free rate. †Preliminary. ‡1982. §Registered employment only. ‖Import duties less imputed bank service charge. ¶Registered unemployed. ♀At factor cost. ♂First quarter. □International flights only.

Singapore

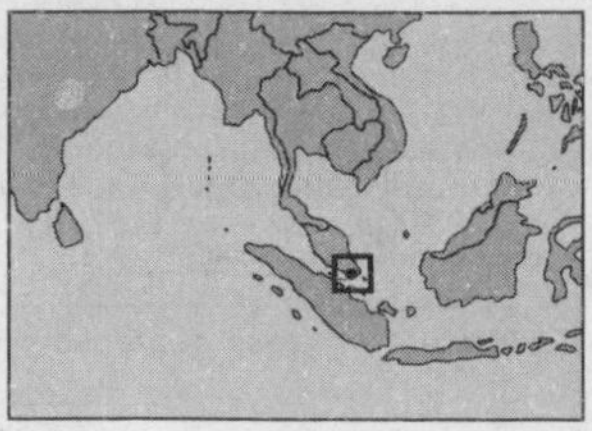

Official name: Hsin-chia-p'o Kung-ho-kuo (Mandarin Chinese); Republik Singapura (Malay); Singapore Kudiyarasu (Tamil); Republic of Singapore (English).
Form of government: unitary multiparty republic with one legislative house (Parliament [79]).
Chief of state: President.
Head of government: Prime Minister.
Capital: Singapore.
Official languages: Chinese; Malay; Tamil; English.
Official religion: none.
Monetary unit: 1 Singapore dollar (S$) = 100 cents; valuation (Oct. 1, 1986) 1 U.S.$ = S$2.17; 1 £ = S$3.14.

Area and population

	area		population
Census areas*	sq mi	sq km	1984 estimate
Central city area	3	8	157,000
City periphery	18	46	942,800
North	7	19	228,100
Northeast	4	9	301,500
West	7	18	413,200
Suburbs	49	127	754,700
East	7	19	195,000
North	13	34	309,900
West	29	74	249,800
Outlying areas	169	437	674,600
East	46	118	301,100
North	53	137	177,500
West	70	182	196,000
TOTAL	239	618	2,529,100

Demography

Population (1986): 2,587,000.
Density (1986): persons per sq mi 10,824, persons per sq km 4,186.
Urban–rural (1986): urban 100.0%.
Sex distribution (1985): male 50.93%; female 49.07%.
Age breakdown (1985): under 15, 24.4%; 15–29, 31.9%; 30–44, 23.3%; 45–59, 12.6%; 60 and over, 7.8%.
Population projection: (1990) 2,708,000; (2000) 3,036,000.
Doubling time: 61 years.
Ethnic composition (1985): Chinese 76.4%; Malay 14.9%; Indian† 6.4%; other 2.3%.
Religious affiliation (1980): Taoist 29.3%; Buddhist 26.7%; Muslim 16.3%; Christian 10.3%; Hindu 3.6%; nonreligious 13.2%; other 0.6%.

Vital statistics

Birth rate per 1,000 population (1985): 16.6 (world avg. 29.0).
Death rate per 1,000 population (1985): 5.2 (world avg. 11.0).
Natural increase rate per 1,000 population (1985): 11.4 (world avg. 18.0).
Total fertility rate (avg. births per childbearing woman; 1985): 1.6.
Marriage rate per 1,000 population (1985): 9.2.
Divorce rate per 1,000 population (1985): 0.9.
Life expectancy at birth (1985): male 69.7 years; female 75.2 years.
Major causes of death per 100,000 population (1985): diseases of the circulatory system 177.5, of which heart and hypertensive diseases 118.8; malignant neoplasms (cancers) 112.5; diseases of the respiratory system 84.8, of which pneumonia 48.6; accidents, poisoning, and violence 48.9.

National economy

Budget (1986–87). Revenue: S$14,552,911,000 (premiums on land sales 44.8%; income tax 17.5%; interest and dividends 12.5%; import and excise duties 6.0%; property tax 5.8%; sales of goods and services 4.3%; motor vehicle taxes 4.0%). Expenditures: S$22,193,618,000 (social welfare and housing 42.4%; defense, justice, and police 12.0%; transport and communication 9.2%; education 8.1%; agricultural, industrial, and commercial development 4.6%; general services 4.0%; health 2.4%).
Public debt (external, outstanding; 1984): U.S.$1,910,900,000.
Tourism: receipts from visitors (1984) U.S.$2,076,000,000; expenditures by nationals abroad (1983) U.S.$531,000,000.
Production (metric tons except as noted). Agriculture, forestry, fishing (1985): vegetables 28,648, fruits 5,610, sugarcane 370, tobacco 16; livestock (number of live animals; 1984) 1,310,000 pigs, 4,000 cattle, 2,000 goats, 2,000 buffalo; fish catch 25,042. Mining and quarrying (value added in S$; 1985): granite 132,900,000. Manufacturing (value added in S$; 1985): electronic products and components 2,729,100,000; transport equipment 939,300,000; petroleum refining and petroleum products 845,800,000; nonelectrical machinery 774,900,000; paints, pharmaceuticals, and chemical products 704,500,000; fabricated metal products except machinery and equipment 689,100,000; printing and publishing 550,400,000. Construction (1985): residential 9,222,000 sq m; nonresidential 2,202,000 sq m. Energy production (consumption): electricity (kW-hr; 1985) 9,876,300,000 (8,871,200,000); coal (metric tons; 1984) none (1,000); crude petroleum (barrels; 1984) none (285,687,000); petroleum products (metric tons; 1984) 31,598,000 (11,671,000); natural gas, none (none).
Gross national product (at current market prices; 1984): U.S.$18,390,000,000 (U.S.$7,270 per capita).

Structure of gross domestic product and labour force

	1984			
	in value S$'000,000	% of total value	labour force	% of labour force
Agriculture	308.6	0.8	8,100	0.7
Quarrying	112.8	0.3	2,400	0.2
Manufacturing	9,233.8	24.0	293,800	24.4
Construction	4,237.3	11.0	102,800	8.5
Public utilities	804.7	2.1	7,700	0.6
Transportation and communication	5,489.4	14.3	117,000	9.7
Trade	7,106.2	18.5	271,100	22.5
Finance	8,803.1	22.9	100,700	8.4
Services	4,825.0	12.5	248,300	20.6
Othar	−2,472.5‡	−6.4‡	52,200§	4.3
TOTAL	38,448.4	100.0	1,204,100	100.0 ‖

Population economically active (1985): total 1,204,000; activity rate of total population 47.1% (participation rates: ages 15–64, 62.2%; female 36.4%; unemployed 4.2%).

Price and earnings indexes (1980 = 100)

	1979	1980	1981	1982	1983	1984	1985
Consumer price index	92.2	100.0	108.3	112.4	113.8	116.8	117.3
Weekly earnings index	88.5	100.0	113.8	128.3	137.2	149.0	156.9

Household income and expenditure. Average household size (1984) 3.9; income per household S$20,800 (U.S.$9,700); source of income: n.a.; expenditure (1984): food and beverages 25.0%, transportation and communication 13.9%, recreation and education 11.7%, housing 9.3%, furniture and household equipment 8.8%, clothing and footwear 8.1%, health 3.0%.
Land use (1984): forested 4.6%; agricultural and under permanent cultivation 9.5%; built-up area 47.6%; other 38.3%.

Foreign trade¶

Balance of trade (current prices)

	1980	1981	1982	1983	1984	1985
S$'000,000	−7,170	−10,973	−12,361	−10,140	−6,497	−4,521
% of total	8.0%	11.0%	12.2%	9.9%	6.0%	4.3%

Imports (1985): S$57,817,500,000 (crude petroleum 22.2%, petroleum products 7.2%, office machines 3.2%, telecommunications apparatus 3.0%, woven textile fabrics 2.3%, electric power machinery 2.3%, scientific and optical instruments 2.0%). *Major import sources:* Japan 17.1%; United States 15.2%; Malaysia 14.4%; China 8.6%; Saudi Arabia 3.5%; Taiwan 3.3%; United Kingdom 2.9%.
Exports (1985): S$50,178,800,000 (petroleum products 26.7%, office machines 6.0%, telecommunications apparatus 5.5%, electrical circuit apparatus 3.1%, crude rubber 3.0%, clothing 2.3%, vegetable oils 2.2%). *Major export destinations:* United States 21.1%; Malaysia 15.5%; Japan 9.4%; Hong Kong 6.4%; Thailand 4.2%; Australia 3.3%; United Kingdom 2.7%.

Transport and communications

Transport. Railroads (1985): length 16 mi, 26 km. Roads (1984): total length 1,612 mi, 2,594 km (paved 89%). Vehicles (1985): passenger cars 236,553; trucks and buses 120,051. Merchant marine (1985): vessels (100 gross tons and over) 824; total deadweight tonnage 11,038,251. Air transport (1985): passenger-mi 13,511,000,000, passenger-km 21,744,000,000; short ton-mi cargo 701,798,000, metric ton-km cargo 1,024,608,000; airports (1986) with scheduled flights 1.
Communications. Daily newspapers (1985): total number 11; total circulation 713,866; circulation per 1,000 population 279. Radio (1985): total number of receivers 108,735 (1 per 24 persons). Television (1985): total number of receivers 373,172 (1 per 6.9 persons). Telephones (1986): 1,074,000 (1 per 2.4 persons).

Education and health

Education (1985)

	schools	teachers	students	student/ teacher ratio
Primary (age 6–13)	252	10,625	278,060	26.2
Secondary (age 12–18)	149	8,562	190,328	22.2
Voc., teacher tr.	15	1,686	18,894	11.2
Higher	5	3,708	39,693	10.7

Educational attainment (1980). Percent of population over age 10 having: no schooling 34.9%; primary education 44.3%; secondary 12.4%; upper secondary 5.7%; higher (degree or diploma holders from universities) 2.7%. *Literacy* (1984): total population over age 10 literate 1,822,800 (85.6%); males literate 998,300 (92.3%); females literate 824,500 (78.6%).
Health (1985): physicians 2,631 (1 per 972 persons); hospital beds 9,866 (1 per 259 persons); infant mortality rate per 1,000 live births 9.3.
Food (1980–82): daily per capita caloric intake 2,937 (vegetable products 79%, animal products 23%); 128% of FAO recommended minimum requirement.

Military

Total active duty personnel (1985): 55,500 (army 81.1%, navy 8.1%, air force 10.8%). *Military expenditure as percent of GNP* (1983): 5.8% (world 6.1%); per capita expenditure U.S.$432.

*The census areas have no administrative function. †Includes Sri Lankan. ‡Less imputed bank service charges. §Includes unemployed persons. ‖ Detail does not add to total given because of rounding. ¶Import figures are f.o.b. (free on board) in balance trade and c.i.f. (cost, insurance, and freight) for commodities and trading partners.

Solomon Islands

Official name: Solomon Islands.
Form of government: parliamentary state with one legislative house (National Parliament [38]).
Chief of state: British Monarch represented by governor-general.
Head of government: Prime Minister.
Capital: Honiara.
Official language: English.
Official religion: none.
Monetary unit: 1 Solomon Islands dollar (SI$) = 100 cents; valuation (Oct. 1, 1986) 1 U.S.$ = SI$1.82; 1 £ = SI$2.63.

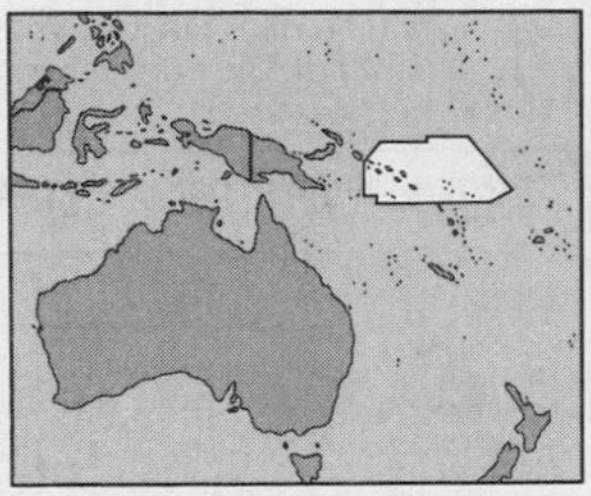

Area and population

Provinces	Capitals	area sq mi	area sq km	population 1986 estimate
Central Islands	Tulagi	493	1,276	19,900
Guadalcanal	Honiara	2,047	5,302	42,300
Isabel	Buala	1,550	4,014	15,000
Makira	Kira Kira	1,231	3,188	20,100
Malaita	Auki	1,638	4,243	77,900
Temotu	Santa Cruz	358	926	14,800
Western	Gizo	3,310	8,573	60,100
Capital Territory				
Honiara	Honiara	13	34	26,500
TOTAL		10,640*	27,556	276,770*

Demography

Population (1986): 276,700.
Density (1986): persons per sq mi 26.0, persons per sq km 10.1.
Urban–rural (1984): urban 24.0%; rural 76.0%.
Sex distribution (1976): male 52.23%; female 47.77%.
Age breakdown (1985): under 15, 49.1%; 15–29, 24.2%; 30–49, 16.4%; 50–59, 4.8%; 60 and over, 5.5%.
Population projection: (1990) 318,700; (2000) 459,100.
Doubling time: 21 years.
Ethnic composition (1976): Melanesian 93.3%; Polynesian 4.0%; Micronesian 1.4%; European 0.7%; Chinese 0.2%; other 0.4%.
Religious affiliation (1980): Christian 95.3%, of which Protestant 71.4%, Roman Catholic 19.1%; Melanesian indigenous 4.7%.
Major cities (1981): Honiara 24,975†; Gizo 1,925; Tulagi 916; Auki 853.

Vital statistics

Birth rate per 1,000 population (1982): 44.6 (world avg. 29.0).
Death rate per 1,000 population (1982): 11.7 (world avg. 11.0).
Natural increase rate per 1,000 population (1982): 32.9 (world avg. 18.0).
Total fertility rate (avg. births per childbearing woman; 1982): 7.3.
Marriage rate per 1,000 population: n.a.
Divorce rate per 1,000 population: n.a.
Life expectancy at birth (1982): male 54 years; female 54 years.
Major causes of death per 100,000 population: n.a.; however, major diseases are malaria, tuberculosis, and leprosy‡.

National economy

Budget (1984). Revenue: SI$65,500,000 (recurrent revenue SI$53,300,000, of which import duties 32.1%, government earnings 22.8%, export duties 18.9%; foreign aid grants 5.2%). Expenditures: SI$66,400,000 (recurrent expenditure SI$50,500,000, of which administrative infrastructure 51.1%; development expenditure 35.2%, of which commerce and industry 6.9%, natural resources 6.1%; education 8.5%; health 6.7%).
Gross national product (at current market prices; 1983): U.S.$160,000,000 (U.S.$640 per capita).

Structure of gross domestic product and labour force

	1984 in value SI$'000,000	1984 % of total value	1985 labour force§	1985 % of labour force
Agriculture	...	...	8,039	33.5
Mining	...	...	77	0.3
Manufacturing	...	...	1,738	7.2
Construction	...	...	1,466	6.1
Public utilities	...	...	315	1.3
Transportation and communication	...	...	2,149	9.0
Trade	...	...	2,566	10.7
Finance	...	...	525	2.2
Pub. admin., defense; Services	...	... }	7,121	29.7
Other	...	...	...	...
TOTAL	227.5 ‖	100.0	23,996	100.0

Household income and expenditure. Average household size (1983) 5.4; average annual income per household (1983): SI$1,010¶ (U.S.$1,160); sources of income (1983): wages and salaries 74.1%, self-employment, remittances, gifts, and other assistance 25.9%; expenditure (1984)♀: food 47.0%, housing 15.5%, drink and tobacco 9.5%, clothing 5.0%, transportation 1.1%.
Population economically active (1985): total 23,996§; activity rate of total population, n.a. (participation rates: ages 15–64, n.a.; female 16.8%§; unemployed, n.a.).

Price and earnings indexes (1980 = 100)

	1981	1982	1983	1984	1985	1986ô
Consumer price index	116.4	131.5	140.5	155.9	170.9	193.2
Annual earnings index¶	108.0	118.8	131.4	145.9	...	...

Production (metric tons except as noted). Agriculture, forestry, fishing (1985): coconuts 255,000□, sweet potatoes 49,000□, copra 41,904, palm oil 20,000, yams 19,000□, paddy rice 5,945, cocoa 1,715; livestock (number of live animals; 1983) 48,000 pigs, 23,000 cattle; roundwood 378,000 cu m; fish catch 31,106. Mining and quarrying (1983): gold 34 kilograms; silver 8 kilograms. Manufacturing: n.a.; however, major industries are palm oil, rice and saw milling, fish canning and freezing, soap and tobacco manufacturing, weaving, wood carving, fibreglass products, boatbuilding, and leather working. Construction (gross value in SI$; 1980): residential 1,858,000; nonresidential 693,000. Energy production (consumption): electricity (kW-hr; 1984) 28,000,000 (28,000,000); coal, none (n.a.); petroleum products (metric tons; 1984) none (44,000); natural gas, none (n.a.).
Public debt (external, outstanding; 1984): U.S.$25,800,000.
Tourism (1985): tourist arrivals 6,929.
Land use (1983): forested 93.0%; meadows and pastures 1.4%; agricultural and under permanent cultivation 1.9%; other 3.7%.

Foreign trade

Balance of trade (current prices)

	1980	1981	1982	1983	1984	1985
SI$'000	−664	−8,419	−929	+592	+34,725	+1,142
% of total	0.5%	6.8%	0.8%	0.4%	17.2%	0.6%

Imports (1985): SI$102,664,000 (machinery and transport equipment 26.3%, mineral fuels and lubricants 20.3%, manufactured goods 15.8%, food 15.3%, chemicals 6.0%). *Major import sources:* Australia 37.2%; Japan 19.6%; Singapore 10.2%; New Zealand 9.0%; United Kingdom 4.0%; China 3.7%; Hong Kong 3.0%; United States 2.1%.
Exports (1985): SI$103,806,000 (fish 30.8%, of which fresh and frozen 26.6%, canned 3.4%, smoked 0.7%; wood 23.8%, of which logs 22.8%, sawn 1.0%; copra 22.6%; palm oil 11.9%; cocoa 4.8%; gold 0.8%). *Major export destinations:* Japan 51.9%; United Kingdom 14.1%; The Netherlands 10.4%; Thailand 8.4%; United States 2.5%; South Korea 2.4%; Australia 2.3%; Sweden 2.3%.

Transport and communications

Transport. Railroads (1985): none. Roads◇ (1984): total length 1,300 mi, 2,100 km (paved, n.a.). Vehicles (1982): passenger cars 1,122; trucks and buses 1,323. Merchant marine (1985): vessels (100 gross tons and over) 26; total deadweight tonnage 4,552. Air transport (1984)△: passenger-mi 6,852,000, passenger-km 11,027,000; short ton-mi cargo 25,000, metric ton-km cargo 37,000; airports (1986) with scheduled flights 24.
Communications. Daily newspapers (1985): none. Radio (1985): total number of receivers 35,000 (1 per 7.6 persons). Television (1985): none. Telephones (1985): 3,827 (1 per 70 persons).

Education and health

Education (1984)

	schools	teachers	students	student/teacher ratio
Primary (age 7–12)	423	1,536	37,522	24.4
Secondary (age 13–18)	20	267	5,118	19.2
Voc., teacher tr.	2	63	1,142	18.1

Educational attainment (1976)ŧ. Percent of adult population over age 25 having: no schooling 55.5%; primary education 39.5%; secondary 3.3%; higher 1.6%. *Literacy* (1976): total population over age 15 literate 55,500 (54.1%); males 33,600 (62.4%); females 21,900 (44.9%).
Health: physicians (1985) 32 (1 per 8,352 persons); hospital beds (1983) 1,398 (1 per 178 persons); infant mortality rate per 1,000 live births (1982) 46.
Food (1980–82): daily per capita caloric intake 2,048 (vegetable products 89%, animal products 11%); 77% of FAO recommended minimum requirement.

Military

Total active duty personnel: no military forces are maintained, but a police force of about 500 provides internal security.

*Detail does not add to total given because of rounding. †1985. ‡Reported cases of these diseases in 1983 were: malaria 84,343, tuberculosis 302, and leprosy 33. §Wage earners only. ‖ Provisional. ¶Public service earnings. ♀Consumer price index components. ôSecond quarter. □1984. ◇Includes 500 mi (800 km) of privately maintained roads mainly for plantation use. △Solair only. ŧIndigenous population only.

Somalia

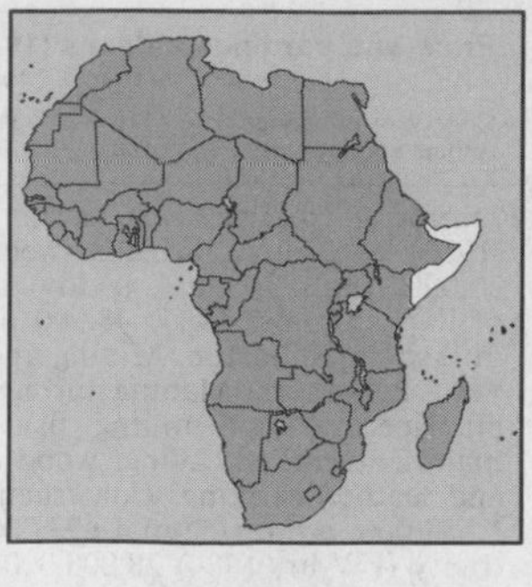

Official name: Jamhuuriyadda Dimuqraadiga Soomaaliya (Somali); Jumhūrīyah aṣ-Ṣūmāl ad-Dīmuqrāṭīyah (Arabic) (Somali Democratic Republic).
Form of government: military-dominated, single-party republic with one legislative house (People's Assembly [177]).
Head of state and government: President.
Capital: Mogadishu.
Official languages: Somali; Arabic.
Official religion: Islam.
Monetary unit: 1 Somali shilling (So.Sh.) = 100 cents; valuation (Oct. 1, 1986) 1 U.S.$ = So.Sh. 36.00; 1 £ = So.Sh. 52.02.

Area and population

		area		population
Regions	Capitals	sq mi	sq km	1980 estimate
Bakool	Xuddur	10,000	27,000	148,700
Bari	Boosaaso	27,000	70,000	222,300
Banaadir	Mogadishu	400	1,000	520,100
Bay	Baydhabo	15,000	39,000	451,000
Galguduud	Dhuusa Mareeb	17,000	43,000	255,900
Gedo	Garbahaarrey	12,000	32,000	235,000
Hiiraan	Beled Weyne	13,000	34,000	219,300
Jubbada Dhexe	Bu'aale	9,000	23,000	147,800
Jubbada Hoose	Kismaayo	24,000	61,000	272,400
Mudug	Gaalkacyo	27,000	70,000	311,200
Nugaal	Garoowe	19,000	50,000	112,200
Sanaag	Ceerigaabo	21,000	54,000	216,500
Shabeellaha Dhexe	Towhar	8,000	22,000	352,000
Shabeellaha Hoose	Marca	10,000	25,000	570,700
Togdheer	Burko	16,000	41,000	383,900
Woqooyi Galbeed	Hargeysa	17,000	45,000	655,000
TOTAL		246,000*	637,000	5,074,000

Demography

Population (1986): 5,991,900.
Density (1986): persons per sq mi 24.4, persons per sq km 9.4.
Urban-rural (1984): urban 33.0%; rural 67.0%.
Sex distribution (1985): male 45.78%; female 54.22%.
Age breakdown (1985): under 15, 43.7%; 15–29, 25.0%; 30–44, 14.7%; 45–59, 10.1%; 60–74, 5.9%; 75 and over, 0.6%.
Population projection: (1990) 6,476,000; (2000) 7,134,000.
Doubling time: 23 years.
Ethnic composition (1980): Somali 95.0%; Bantu 2.9%; Arab 1.5%; other 0.6%.
Religious affiliation (1980): Sunnī Muslim 99.8%; Christian 0.1%; other 0.1%.
Major city (1981): Mogadishu 500,000; Hargeysa 70,000; Kismaayo 70,000; Berbera 65,000; Marca 60,000.

Vital statistics

Birth rate per 1,000 population (1984): 49.0 (world avg. 29.0); legitimate, n.a.; illegitimate, n.a.
Death rate per 1,000 population (1984): 20.0 (world avg. 11.0).
Natural increase rate per 1,000 population (1984): 29.0 (world avg. 18.0).
Total fertility rate (avg. births per childbearing woman; 1984): 6.8.
Marriage rate per 1,000 population: n.a.
Divorce rate per 1,000 population: n.a.
Life expectancy at birth (1984): male 44.0 years; female 47.0 years.
Major causes of death per 100,000 population: n.a.; however, major diseases include leprosy, malaria, tetanus, and tuberculosis.

National economy

Budget (1985)†. Revenue: So.Sh. 7,753,500,000 (taxes on international transactions 36.1%, import duties 29.4%, income from government property 7.6%, income tax 1.3%). Expenditures: So.Sh. 7,753,500,000 (finance and central services 38.9%, defense 23.3%, economic services 12.8%, education 6.9%, foreign affairs 5.5%, health 2.3%, general administration 1.8%).
Tourism (1982): receipts from visitors U.S.$13,000,000; expenditures by nationals abroad U.S.$13,000,000.
Production (metric tons except as noted). Agriculture, forestry, fishing (1984): sugarcane 500,000, sorghum 235,000, corn (maize) 120,000, bananas 98,900, vegetables 82,000, sesame seed 59,500, roots and tubers 40,000, beans 20,800, cotton 4,000, rice 3,000, wheat 1,000; livestock (number of live animals) 15,700,000 goats, 9,700,000 sheep, 5,700,000 camels, 3,600,000 cattle; roundwood 5,168,000 cu m; fish catch (1983) 15,500. Mining and quarrying (1984): salt 30,000. Manufacturing (1983): sugar 30,800; pasta and flour 10,600; boxes and bags 6,800; canned meat and fish 1,100. Construction (value added in So.Sh.; 1982): 1,687,200,000. Energy production (consumption): electricity (kW-hr; 1984) 75,000,000 (75,000,000); coal, none (n.a.); crude petroleum (barrels; 1984) n.a. (2,675,000); petroleum products (metric tons; 1984) 350,000 (364,000); natural gas, none (n.a.).
Household income and expenditure. Average household size (1980) 4.9; average annual income per household: n.a.; source of income: n.a.; expenditure‡ (1983): food and tobacco 62.3%, housing 15.3%, clothing 5.6%, energy 4.3%, other 12.1%.
Public debt (external, outstanding; 1984): U.S.$1,233,000,000.
Gross national product (at current market prices; 1984): U.S.$1,360,000,000 (U.S.$240 per capita).

Structure of gross domestic product and labour force

	1982			
	in value So.Sh. '000,000	% of total value	labour force	% of labour force
Agriculture	4,774	34.7	1,588,000	82.0
Mining	744	5.4		
Manufacturing	1,207	8.8		
Construction	700	5.1	155,000	8.0
Public utilities	222	1.6		
Transportation and communication	1,074	7.8		
Trade	973	7.1		
Finance	1,008	7.3	194,000	10.0
Pub. admin., defense	1,519	11.0		
Services	1,542	11.2		
TOTAL	13,763	100.0	1,937,000	100.0

Population economically active (1984): total 2,025,000; activity rate of total population 35.7% (participation rates: ages 15–64, n.a.; female [1980] 22.1%; unemployed, n.a.).

Price and earnings indexes (1980 = 100)

	1979	1980	1981	1982	1983	1984	1985
Consumer price index	83.0	100.0	144.4	178.5	241.4	464.1	639.5
Earnings index	...	...	...	...	...	...	...

Land use (1983): forested 13.9%; meadows and pastures 46.0%; agricultural and under permanent cultivation 1.8%; other 38.3%.

Foreign trade

Balance of trade (current prices)

	1980	1981	1982	1983	1984	1985
So.Sh. '000,000	−1,069.9	−1,841.4	−73.5	−1,421.4	−995.3	−275.0
% of total	39.0%	48.9%	1.8%	33.3%	35.8%	3.7%

Imports (1983): So.Sh. 2,844,400,000 (petroleum 31.0%; food 16.0%; machinery and transport equipment 15.0%, of which transport equipment 7.4%; construction materials 11.8%; manufacturing raw materials 4.5%; medicinal and chemical products 4.5%; beverages and tobacco 3.9%; textiles and household goods 1.3%). *Major import sources* (1984): United States 20.3%; Italy 20.2%; Saudi Arabia 12.6%; West Germany 5.2%; United Kingdom 4.9%; France 4.8%; Bahrain 3.8%; Djibouti 3.3%; Thailand 2.9%; China 2.7%; Belgium 2.2%; The Netherlands 1.7%; Japan 1.5%; India 1.4%; Canada 1.1%; Kenya 1.0%; Denmark 1.0%; Australia 0.8%; Austria 0.7%.
Exports (1983): So.Sh. 1,423,000,000 (live animals 78.8%; bananas 7.3%; myrrh 6.3%; petroleum products 3.0%; fish 2.3%; undressed hides, skins, and furs 1.5%). *Major export destinations* (1984): Saudi Arabia 59.1%; Yemen (Ṣan'ā') 11.5%; Italy 5.8%; China 5.4%; United Arab Emirates 4.7%; Iran 3.7%; Yemen (Aden) 2.6%; Hong Kong 1.5%; France 0.9%.

Transport and communications

Transport. Railroads: none. Roads (1983): total length 13,233 mi, 21,297 km (paved 13%). Vehicles (1981): passenger cars 17,754; trucks and buses 9,533. Merchant marine (1985): vessels (100 gross tons and over) 27; total deadweight tonnage 31,051. Air transport (1984): passenger-mi 176,513,000, passenger-km 284,070,000; short ton-mi cargo 3,369,000, metric ton-km cargo 4,919,000; airports (1986) with scheduled flights 3.
Communications. Daily newspapers (1984): total number 1; total circulation, n.a. Radio (1985): total number of receivers 100,000 (1 per 45 persons). Television§: total number of receivers, n.a. Telephones (1981): 4,800 (1 per 782 persons).

Education and health

Education (1983)

	schools	teachers	students	student/teacher ratio
Primary (age 6–14)	1,308	9,460	220,680	23.3
Secondary (age 15–18)	51 ‖	2,201	53,591	24.3
Voc., teacher tr.	26 ‖	817	9,664	11.8
Higher ‖	1	262	2,332	8.9

Educational attainment, n.a. *Literacy* (1984): total adult population literate 60%.
Health: physicians (1981) 292 (1 per 17,865 persons); hospital beds (1978) 5,232 (1 per 917 persons); infant mortality rate per 1,000 live births (1984) 153.0.
Food (1980–82): daily per capita caloric intake 2,077 (vegetable products 72%, animal products 28%); 90% of FAO recommended minimum requirement.

Military

Total active duty personnel (1985): 62,700 (army 95.7%, navy 1.1%, air force 3.2%). *Military expenditure as percent of GNP* (1984): 8.1% (world 6.1%); per capita expenditure U.S.$23.

*Detail does not add to total given because of rounding. †Estimated. ‡Capital city only. §Since the end of 1983 television service covers Mogadishu area and Hargeysa. ‖ 1980–81.

South Africa

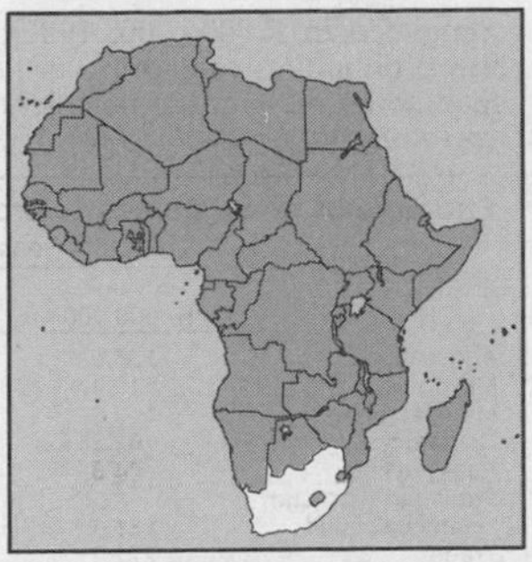

Official name: Republiek van Suid-Afrika (Afrikaans); Republic of South Africa (English).
Form of government: multiparty republic with three legislative houses (House of Assembly [178]; House of Representatives [85]; House of Delegates [45])*.
Head of state and government: State President.
Capitals: Pretoria (executive); Bloemfontein (judicial); Cape Town (legislative).
Official languages: Afrikaans; English.
Official religion: none.
Monetary unit: 1 rand (R) = 100 cents; valuation (Oct. 1, 1986) 1 U.S.$ = R 2.22; 1 £ = R 3.21.

Area and population†

		area		population‡	
				1983	1985
Provinces	**Capitals**	sq mi	sq km	estimate	census
Cape	Cape Town	247,638	641,379	5,374,000	5,044,419
Natal	Pietermaritsburg	35,272	91,355	2,842,000	2,147,902
Orange Free State	Bloemfontein	49,418	127,993	2,080,000	1,775,722
Transvaal	Pretoria	101,352	262,499	8,950,000	7,579,888
National states					
Gazankulu	Giyani	2,606	6,750	585,000	495,993
KaNgwane	Louieville	1,436	3,720	184,000	390,103
KwaNdebele	Siyabuswa	355	920	226,000	232,726
KwaZulu	Ulundi	12,664	32,800	3,792,000	3,744,380
Lebowa	Lebowakgomo	8,757	22,680	1,869,000	1,844,315
Qwaqwa	Phuthaditjhaba	185	480	306,000	183,142
TOTAL		433,680	1,123,226	26,945,000	23,438,590

Demography

Population (1986): 28,139,000‡.
Density (1986): persons per sq mi 64.9, persons per sq km 25.1.
Urban–rural (1985)§: urban 55.9%; rural 44.1%.
Sex distribution (1985)§: male 49.58%; female 50.42%.
Age breakdown (1985)§: under 15, 41.0%; 15–29, 26.9%; 30–44, 16.1%; 45–59, 9.8%; 60–74, 5.0%; 75 and over, 1.2%.
Population projection§: (1990) 36,754,000; (2000) 46,918,000.
Doubling time: 28 years.
Ethnic composition (1984): black 68.2%, of which Zulu 23.7%, North Sotho 9.8%, Xhosa 9.7%, South Sotho 7.3%, Tswana 5.7%, other 12.0%; white 18.0%; Coloured 10.5%; Asian 3.3%.
Religious affiliation (1980): tribal religionist 20.4%; Afrikaans Reformed 15.5%; Roman Catholic 9.5%; Methodist 8.5%; Anglican 6.5%; other 39.6%.
Major cities (mun.; 1983): Johannesburg 1,713,000‖; Cape Town 1,567,000; Durban 714,000; Pretoria 712,000; Port Elizabeth 560,000.

Vital statistics

Birth rate per 1,000 population (1983): 33.6 (world avg. 29.0); (1978) legitimate 75.9%¶; illegitimate 24.1%¶.
Death rate per 1,000 population (1983): 11.0 (world avg. 11.0).
Natural increase rate per 1,000 population (1983): 22.6 (world avg. 18.0).
Total fertility rate (avg. births per childbearing woman; 1980–85)§: 5.1.
Life expectancy at birth (1980–85)§: male 51.8 years; female 55.2 years.
Major causes of death per 100,000 population (1977)¶: heart disease 215.3; malignant neoplasms (cancers) 107.3; cerebrovascular disease 90.2; pneumonia 75.2; enteritis and other diarrheal diseases 49.1.

National economy

Budget (1986–87). Revenue: R 34,430,000,000 (income tax 58.8%, sales tax 27.4%, customs duty and excise tax 7.4%). Expenditures: R 37,751,000,000 (development 17.5%, education 16.2%, defense 14.0%, interest on public debt 13.9%, welfare services 8.4%, health 7.4%).
Tourism (1981–82): receipts from visitors U.S.$630,000,000; expenditures by nationals abroad, n.a.
Production (metric tons except as noted). Agriculture, forestry, fishing (1985): sugarcane 20,736,000, corn (maize) 7,550,000, wheat 1,600,000; livestock (number of live animals) 30,256,000 sheep, 12,733,000 cattle; forestry (1984) 18,944,000 cu m; fish catch (1984) 598,785. Mining and quarrying (1984): iron ore 24,496,000; manganese ore 3,049,000; chrome 3,006,000; phosphate concentrate 2,496,000; gold 681,300 kg; silver 217,600 kg; diamonds 10,118,910 carats. Manufacturing (value of sales in R; 1982): chemicals 10,386,000,000; food 8,329,000,000; metal products 4,998,000,000; motor vehicles 4,357,000,000; iron and steel 3,807,000,000; nonelectrical machinery 3,756,000,000; beverages and tobacco 3,755,000,000; electrical machinery 2,446,000,000. Construction (units; 1985): 34,300. Energy production (consumption): electricity♀ (kW-hr; 1985) 140,718,000,000 (140,718,000,000); coal♀ (metric tons; 1984) 140,554,000 (103,554,000); petroleum♀ (barrels; 1984) none (117,300); petroleum products♀ (metric tons; 1984)13,715,000 (10,418,000); natural gas, none (none).
Household income and expenditure. Average household size (1980) 5.1; average annual income per household R 8,829 (U.S.$11,349); sources of income (1983): wages and salaries 81.8%, transfer payments 4.8%; expenditure (1983): food and beverages 31.8%, housing 17.8%, transportation and communication 12.4%, clothing and footwear 8.1%, energy 6.8%.
Gross national product (1985): U.S.$112,671,000,000 (U.S.$4,000 per capita).

Structure of gross domestic product and labour force

	1984		1980	
	in value R '000,000	% of total value	labour force	% of labour force
Agriculture	4,905	5.0	1,299,840	15.0
Mining	13,082	13.5	820,300	9.5
Manufacturing	22,810	23.5	1,456,760	16.8
Construction	3,651	3.8	452,440	5.2
Public utilities	3,897	4.0	79,240	0.9
Transp. and commun.	9,360	9.6	424,040	4.9
Trade	11,601	11.9	1,008,340	11.6
Finance	13,627	14.0	285,840	3.3
Pub. admin., defense	12,489	12.9 }	1,986,240	22.9
Services	3,769	3.9 }		
Other	−2,020	2.1	852,660	9.9
TOTAL	97,171δ	100.0	8,665,700	100.0

Population economically active‡ (1982): total 8,983,000; activity rate of total population 35.1% (participation rates: ages 15–64 [1970] 68.3%; female [1981] 34.4%; unemployed [1985] 8.4%).

Price and earnings indexes (1980 = 100)

	1980	1981	1982	1983	1984	1985	1986□
Consumer price index	100.0	115.2	132.1	148.4	165.7	192.6	232.3
Monthly earnings index	100.0	121.5	149.0	158.1	...	...	...
white (black)	(100.0)	(120.6)	(156.6)	(158.7)	...	...	...

Total debt (external; 1985): U.S.$4,852,000,000.
Land use (1984): forested 3.4%; meadows and pastures 65.2%; agricultural and under permanent cultivation 11.2%; other 20.2%.

Foreign trade

Balance of trade (current prices)

	1980	1981	1982	1983	1984	1985
R '000,000	+5,780	−231	+914	+4,479	+3,705	13,748
% of total	16.9%	0.6%	2.4%	12.1%	7.9%	23.0%

Imports (1984): R 21,635,800,000 (machinery 29.4%; transport equipment 12.3%; chemicals 8.2%; metal products 5.0%; textiles 4.8%). *Major import sources:* U.S. 19.1%; W.Ger. 15.8%; Japan 12.9%; U.K. 11.2%.
Exports (1984): R 25,340,900,000 (gold 46.1%, of which gold coins 5.4%; minerals 12.1%; base metals 9.5%; diamonds 5.4%; food and tobacco 4.1%; textiles 3.0%). *Major export destinations:* U.S. 9.7%; Japan 7.7%; Switzerland 6.6%; U.K. 4.2%; W.Ger. 3.9%; Italy 2.6%.

Transport and communications

Transport. Railroads (1985): length 14,392 mi, 23,162 km; passenger mi 11,722,000,000, passenger-km 18,864,600,000; short ton-mi cargo 62,915,900, metric ton-km cargo 91,861,404. Roads (1984): total length 114,540 mi, 184,330 km (paved 27%). Vehicles (1984): passenger cars 2,800,000; trucks and buses 1,226,000. Merchant marine (1985): vessels 273; total deadweight tonnage 673,223. Air transport (1985): passenger-mi 5,429,800,000, passenger-km 8,738,430,000; short ton-mi cargo 272,231,000, metric ton-km cargo 397,476,000; airports (1986) with scheduled flights 32.
Communications. Daily newspapers (1985): total number 20; total circulation 1,277,000; circulation per 1,000 population 46.6. Radio (1985): 10,000,000 receivers (1 per 2.7 persons). Television (1985): 2,100,000 receivers (1 per 13.0 persons). Telephones (1984): 3,471,519 (1 per 7.4 persons).

Education and health

Education (1985)

	schools	teachers	students	student/ teacher ratio
Primary (age 6–12)	17,180◇	199,949◇	4,583,905	...
Secondary (age 13–17)	◇	◇	1,428,637	...
Vocational	132	3,733	130,428	...
Higher△	84	12,858	222,950	17.3

Educational attainment (1970). Percent of population over age 25 having: no formal schooling 42.1%; some primary 21.4%; complete primary 5.3%; some secondary 20.7%; postsecondary 3.7%. *Literacy* § (1984): percent of adult population literate 50%; white 93%; Asians 69%; Coloured 62%; black 32%.
Health: physicians (1983) 21,143 (1 per 1,219 persons); hospital beds (1980) 98,308 (1 per 246 persons); infant mortality rate (1980–85) 83.0.
Food (1981–83): daily per capita caloric intake 2,929 (vegetable products 85%, animal products 15%); 117% of FAO recommended minimum requirement.

Military

Total active duty personnel (1986): 106,400 (army 79.3%, navy 8.5%, air force 12.2%). *Military expenditure as percent of GNP* (1984): 4.1% (world 6.1%); per capita expenditure U.S.$98.

*For representation of whites, Coloureds, and Asians (mainly Indians), respectively. †Data exclude Bophuthatswana, Ciskei, Transkei, and Venda, which are treated as sovereign nations by the South African government. Together these entities have an area of 36,733 sq mi (95,137 sq km) and a population (1983) of 5,096,000. ‡Preliminary 1985 census figure released but incompletely processed, including adjustment for underenumeration. 1983 and 1986 estimates are continuations of a demographic series incorporating the 1980 census but predating the 1985 census. §Includes Bophuthatswana, Ciskei, Transkei, and Venda. ‖1984. ¶Whites, Asians, and Coloureds only. ♀Data apply to the Customs Union of Southern Africa comprising South Africa, Botswana, Lesotho, South West Africa/Namibia, and Swaziland. δAt factor cost. □September. ◇Primary includes secondary. △Includes universities, teacher-training colleges, and technikons (advanced technical colleges), but not ordinary technical colleges and institutes.

South West Africa/ Namibia

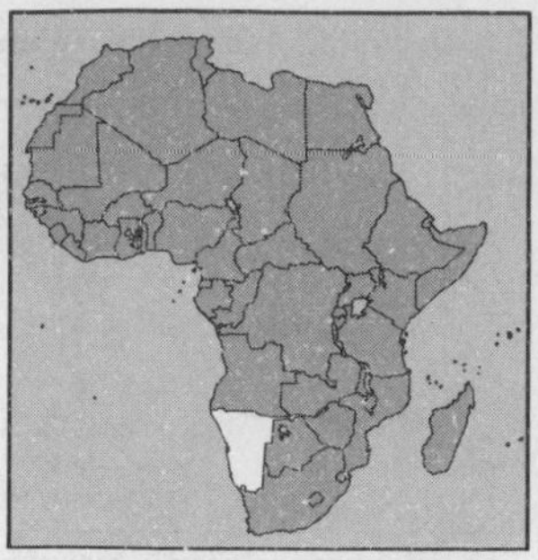

Official name: Suidwes-Afrika/Namibië (Afrikaans); South West Africa/ Namibia (English).
Political status: dependency of South Africa with one legislative house (National Assembly [62]).
Head of state and government: Administrator-General*.
Capital: Windhoek.
Official languages: Afrikaans; English.
Official religion: none.
Monetary unit: 1 South African rand (R) = 100 cents; valuation (Oct. 1, 1986) 1 U.S.$ = R 2.22; 1 £ = R 3.21.

Area and population†

Magisterial Districts	Capitals	area sq mi	area sq km	population 1981 census‡§
Bethanien	Bethanien	6,951	18,004	2,808
Boesmanland	Tsumkwe	7,131	18,468	2,453
Caprivi Oos	Katima Mulilo	4,453	11,533	37,923
Damaraland	Khorixas	17,977	46,560	24,214
Gobabis	Gobabis	16,003	41,447	22,079
Grootfontein	Grootfontein	10,239	26,520	20,720
Hereroland-Oos	Otjinene	20,058	51,949	18,918
Hereroland-Wes	Okakarara	6,371	16,500	15,411
Kaokoland	Opuwo	22,467	58,190	16,637
Karasburg	Karasburg	14,717	38,116	9,502
Karibib	Karibib	5,108	13,230	8,953
Kavango	Rundu	19,674	50,955	105,690
Keetmanshoop	Keetmanshoop	14,788	38,302	17,608
Lüderitz	Lüderitz	20,488	53,063	14,314
Maltahöhe	Maltahöhe	9,874	25,573	4,751
Mariental	Mariental	18,413	47,689	20,578
Namaland	Gibeon	8,154	21,120	12,766
Okahandja	Okahandja	6,811	17,640	13,336
Omaruru	Omaruru	3,253	8,425	5,498
Otjiwarongo	Otjiwarongo	7,934	20,550	16,126
Outjo	Outjo	14,951	38,722	8,866
Owambo	Ondangwa	20,000	51,800	452,036
Rehoboth	Rehoboth	5,476	14,182	27,664
Swakopmund	Swakopmund	17,258	44,697	15,473
Tsumeb	Tsumeb	6,340	16,420	19,447
Windhoek	Windhoek	12,930	33,489	110,644
TOTAL		317,818	823,144	1,031,927

Demography

Population (1986): 1,203,900§.
Density (1986): persons per sq mi 3.8, persons per sq km 1.5.
Urban-rural (1985): urban 51.3%; rural 48.7%.
Sex distribution (1985): male 49.48%; female 50.52%.
Age breakdown (1985): under 15, 44.3%; 15–29, 26.1%; 30–44, 15.3%; 45–59, 9.2%; 60–74, 4.3%; 75 and over, 0.8%.
Population projection: (1990) 1,360,000; (2000) 1,822,000.
Doubling time: 25 years.
Ethnic composition (1983): Ovambo 49.3%; Kavango 9.6%; Herero 7.3%; Damara 7.1%; white 6.8%; Nama 4.7%; other 15.2%.
Religious affiliation (1981): Lutheran 51.2%; Roman Catholic 19.8%; Dutch Reformed 6.1%; Anglican 5.0%; other 17.9%.
Major cities (1983): Windhoek 105,100; Rundu 15,000; Rehoboth 14,000; Swakopmund 13,500; Keetmanshoop 12,000.

Vital statistics

Birth rate per 1,000 population (1980–85): 45.1 (world avg. 29.0).
Death rate per 1,000 population (1980–85): 17.3 (world avg. 11.0).
Natural increase rate per 1,000 population (1980–85): 27.8 (world avg. 18.0).
Total fertility rate (avg. births per childbearing woman; 1980–85): 6.1.
Marriage rate per 1,000 population: n.a.
Life expectancy at birth (1980–85): male 47.0 years; female 49.5 years.
Major causes of death per 100,000 population: n.a.; however, major diseases include malaria, tuberculosis, and trypanosomiasis (sleeping sickness).

National economy

Budget (1985–86). Revenue: R 1,163,800,000 (taxes 31.4%, grants from South Africa 28.8%, customs and duties 21.5%). Expenditures: R 1,392,500,000 (finance 24.2%, defense and police 15.0%, transportation 6.1%, water affairs 4.7%, education 4.6%, health 1.8%).
Public debt (external, outstanding; 1984): U.S.$352,000,000.
Tourism (1981): receipts from visitors U.S.$45,960,000; expenditures by nationals abroad, n.a.
Production (metric tons except as noted). Agriculture, forestry, fishing (1984): roots and tubers 140,000, corn [maize] 40,000, fruit 25,000, vegetables and melons 20,000, millet 20,000, pulses 4,000, sorghum 3,000; wool 4,470‖, karakul pelts 1,500,000 units¶; livestock (number of live animals) 6,000,000 sheep, 2,300,000 goats, 2,000,000 cattle; fish catch¶ 340,981, of which anchovies 183,391, mackerel 105,273, South African pilchard 44,014. Mining and quarrying (1984): diamonds 930,200 carats, of which gem quality 884,000 carats; salt 84,900; copper 47,406; lead 33,255; zinc 32,195; uranium 4,400; limestone and marble 200; gold 6,302 troy oz; silver 3,255 troy oz. Manufacturing (gross output in R '000,000; 1976): food and beverages 140.8; metal products 34.2; wood products 6.6; chemical products 3.6; printing and publishing 2.4; other 12.4. Construction (value of buildings completed in R '000,000; 1983): residential 17.0; nonresidential 10.8. Energy production (consumption): electricity (kW-hr; 1985) 700,000,000 (n.a.); coal, none (n.a.); crude petroleum, none (n.a.); natural gas, none (n.a).
Gross national product (1984): U.S.$1,660,000,000 (U.S.$1,470 per capita).

Structure of gross domestic product and labour force

	1984		1981	
	in value R '000,000	% of total value	labour force	% of labour force
Agriculture	136.8	7.0	71,402	35.0
Mining	510.4	26.1	15,515	7.6
Manufacturing	102.6	5.3	8,017	3.9
Construction	62.2	3.2	17,654	8.7
Public utilities	74.3	3.8	1,922	0.9
Transportation and communication	131.3	6.7	9,615	4.7
Trade	272.2	13.9	22,253	10.9
Finance	150.4	7.7	3,764	1.8
Services	39.9	2.0	22,417	11.0
Public admin., defense	411.5	21.1	31,079	15.2
Other	60.9	3.1	360	0.2
TOTAL	1,952.5	100.0	203,998	100.0♀

Population economically active: total (1984) 471,000; activity rate of total population 41.6% (participation rates: ages 15–64, n.a.; female [1977] 38.8%; unemployed 21.0%).

Price and earnings indexes (1980 = 100)♁

	1979	1980	1981	1982	1983	1984	1985□
Consumer price index	88.9	100.0	114.8	132.7	148.5	162.1	173.9
Earnings index	...	...	...	...	...	...	...

Household income and expenditure. Average household size (1981) 4.8; average annual income per household (1980) R 3,223 (U.S.$4,143); sources of income (1980): wages 80.8%, self-employment 19.2%; expenditure: n.a.
Land use (1983): forested 12.7%; meadows and pastures 64.3%; agricultural and under permanent cultivation 0.8%; other 22.2%.

Foreign trade

Balance of trade (current prices)

	1979	1980	1981	1982	1983	1984
R '000,000	374.7	243.0	−130.1	−94.3	−70.7	−11.9
% of total	23.2%	12.2%	6.7%	4.5%	3.7%	0.5%

Imports (1984): R 1,094,400,000 (no breakdown available). *Major import sources:* South Africa (nearly 100%).
Exports (1984): R 1,082,500,000 (minerals 80%, including diamonds, uranium, copper, zinc, lead, tin; karakul pelts; fish and fish products). *Major export destinations:* South Africa; United States; West Germany.

Transport and communications

Transport. Railroads: length (1985) 1,454 mi, 2,340 km; (1981) metric ton-km cargo 1,900,000,000. Roads (1985): total length 28,748 mi, 46,266 km (paved 8.9%). Number of registered vehicles (1981): passenger cars 27,100; trucks and buses 19,400. Merchant marine: vessels (100 gross tons and over), none. Air transport (1984)◇: passengers handled 200,000; cargo handled 2,200 metric tons; airports (1986) with scheduled flights 8.
Communications. Daily newspapers (1982): total number 3; total circulation 20,000; circulation per 1,000 population 19.0. Radio (1985): 200,000 receivers (1 per 5.8 persons). Television (1985): 16,000 receivers (1 per 73 persons). Telephones (1984): 62,812 (1 per 18 persons).

Education and health

Education (1982–83)

	schools	teachers	students	student/ teacher ratio
Primary (age 6–12)	1,069	7,120	232,306	32.6
Secondary (age 13–19)	78	1,864	40,359	21.6
Voc., teacher tr.	6	81	1,200	14.8
Higher	4	137	537	3.9

Educational attainment, n.a. *Literacy* (1985): total population over age 15 literate 474,000 (72.5%); males literate 239,000 (74.2%); females literate 235,000 (70.8%).
Health (1984): physicians 276 (1 per 4,104 persons); hospital beds 7,900 (1 per 143 persons); infant mortality rate per 1,000 live births (1980–85) 116.
Food (1979–81): daily per capita caloric intake 2,197 (vegetable products 77%, animal products 23%); 96% of FAO recommended minimum requirement.

Military

Total active duty personnel△ (1985): 21,000 (army 100%). *Military expenditure as percent of GNP* (1984): 7.7% (world 6.1%); per capita expenditure U.S.$113.

*In June 1985 most executive authority was transferred to the cabinet, and the role of the South African-appointed administrator-general was downgraded to that of a constitutional figurehead. †Excludes area and population of Walvis Bay (part of South Africa), administered as part of South West Africa/Namibia until 1977. ‡Preliminary; total includes 7,512 transients not distributed by subdivision. §Unofficial external sources have estimated South West Africa/Namibia's population to be as much as a third higher than the government's estimates, implying that per capita values indicated herein might be reduced proportionately. ‖1980. ¶1983. ♀Detail does not add to total given because of rounding. ♁Windhoek only. □First quarter. ◇South West Africa/Namibia's four largest airports only. △The South West Africa Territory Force (SWATF), largely controlled by the Republic of South Africa.

Spain

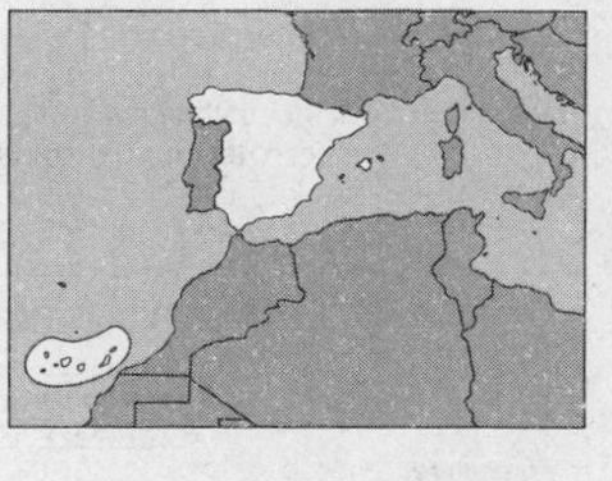

Official name: Reino de España (Kingdom of Spain).
Form of government: constitutional monarchy with two legislative houses (Senate [253]; Congress of Deputies [350]).
Chief of state: King.
Head of government: Prime Minister.
Capital: Madrid.
Official language: Spanish.
Official religion: none.
Monetary unit: 1 peseta (Pta) = 100 céntimos; valuation (Oct. 1, 1986) 1 U.S.$ = Ptas 133.50; 1 £ = Ptas 192.91.

Area and population

		area		population
Autonomous communities	**Capitals**	sq mi	sq km	1986 estimate
Andalucía	Seville (Sevilla)	33,694	87,268	6,735,600
Aragón	Zaragoza	18,398	47,650	1,215,600
Asturias	Oviedo	4,079	10,565	1,140,100
Baleares	Palma de Mallorca	1,936	5,014	675,400
Canarias	Santa Cruz de Tenerife	2,796	7,242	1,442,500
Cantabria	Santander	2,042	5,289	527,400
Castilla-La Mancha	Toledo	30,591	79,230	1,670,100
Castilla-León	Valladolid	36,368	94,193	2,602,300
Cataluña	Barcelona	12,328	31,930	6,057,200
Extremadura	Mérida	16,063	41,602	1,084,400
Galicia	Santiago de Compostela	11,365	29,434	2,870,900
La Rioja	Logroño	1,944	5,034	263,100
Madrid	Madrid	3,087	7,995	4,907,100
Murcia	Murcia	4,370	11,317	1,007,500
Navarra	Pamplona	4,023	10,421	522,500
País Vasco	Vitoria	2,803	7,261	2,176,800
Valencia	Valencia	8,998	23,305	3,790,200
TOTAL SPAIN		194,885	504,750	38,688,400*
Enclaves in Northern Morocco				
Ceuta	—	7.1	18.5	71,400
Melilla	—	5.4	14	58,600
Chafarinas	—	.24	.61	...
Vélez de la Gomera	—	.02	.04	...
Alhucemas	—	.004	.01	...
TOTAL		194,897.79*	504,783.16	38,818,400*

Demography

Population (1986): 38,818,000.
Density (1986): persons per sq mi 199.2, persons per sq km 76.9.
Urban-rural (1985): urban 77.4%; rural 22.6%.
Sex distribution (1985): male 48.98%; female 51.02%.
Age breakdown (1985): under 15, 24.6%; 15–29, 24.2%; 30–44, 18,5%; 45–59, 16.8%; 60–74, 11.6%; 75 and over, 4.3%.
Population projection: (1990) 39,517,000; (2000) 41,027,000.
Doubling time: n.a.; doubling time exceeds 100 years.
Ethnic composition (1984): Spanish 72.8%; Catalan 16.4%; Galician 8.2%; Basque 2.3%; other 0.3%.
Religious affiliation (1980): Roman Catholic 97.0%; Protestant 0.4%.
Major cities (1986): Madrid 3,217,461; Barcelona 1,756,905; Valencia 763,-949; Sevilla 673,574.

Vital statistics

Birth rate per 1,000 population (1983): 12.5 (world avg. 29.0).
Death rate per 1,000 population (1983): 7.8 (world avg. 11.0).
Natural increase rate per 1,000 population (1983): 4.7 (world avg. 18.0).
Total fertility rate (avg. births per childbearing woman; 1980–85): 2.4.
Marriage rate per 1,000 population (1983): 4.8.
Life expectancy at birth (1980–85): male 71.3 years; female 77.5 years.
Major causes of death per 100,000 population (1979): malignant neoplasms (cancers) 154.3; ischemic heart disease 79.5; respiratory diseases 7.8.

National economy

Budget (1985). Revenue: Ptas 4,422,000,000,000 (indirect taxes 41.0%, personal income taxes 34.4%, direct taxes on enterprises 15.6%). Expenditures: Ptas 4,867,000,000,000† (current transfers 57.0%, wages and salaries 31.0%).
Public debt (1981): U.S.$44,149,000,000.
Production (metric tons except as noted). Agriculture, forestry, fishing (1984): barley 10,695,000, sugar beets 9,064,000, wheat 6,044,000, potatoes 5,949,000, grapes 5,569,000, tomatoes 2,553,000, corn 2,505,000, oranges 1,310,000, onions 1,114,000, apples 1,019,000, oats 790,000; livestock (number of live animals) 5,050,000 cattle, 12,400,000 pigs, 2,400,000 goats, 1,660,000 sheep; roundwood 14,823,000 cu m‡; fish catch 1,250,000‡. Mining and quarrying (metal content in metric tons; 1984): iron ore 3,732,000, zinc 222,400, lead 95,800, copper 63,600. Manufacturing (1985): crude steel 14,152,000; pig iron 5,700,000; wine 3,554,000§; sulfuric acid 3,406,000§; wheat flour 2,366,000 ‖ ; sugar 1,328,000§; fertilizers 1,301,000‡, of which nitrogenous 852,000‡; plastic resin 1,250,000‡. Construction (1984): residential dwellings 207,168. Energy production (consumption): electricity (kW-hr; 1984) 115,450,000,000 (114,500,000,000); coal (metric tons; 1984) 39,950,000 (46,914,000); crude petroleum (barrels; 1984) 17,376,000 (318,-080,000); petroleum products (metric tons; 1984) 37,754,000 (34,711,000); natural gas (cu m; 1983) n.a. (2,668,536,000).
Gross national product (1984): U.S.$172,360,000,000 (U.S.$4,490 per capita).

Structure of gross domestic product and labour force

	1984			
	in value Ptas '000,000	% of total value	labour force	% of labour force
Agriculture	1,640,000	6.3	2,076,200	15.7
Mining	} 6,978,000	} 27.0	89,900	0.7
Manufacturing			2,945,800	22.3
Public utilities			82,000	0.6
Construction	1,658,000	6.4	1,202,300	9.1
Transp. and commun.	} 15,594,000	} 60.3	659,000	5.0
Trade			2,371,300	17.9
Finance			445,600	3.4
Pub. admin., defense			} 2,237,500	} 16.9
Services				
Other			1,118,600¶	8.5
TOTAL	25,870,000	100.0	13,228,200	100.0*

Tourism (1984): receipts from visitors U.S.$7,717,000,000; expenditures by nationals abroad U.S.$835,000,000.
Population economically active (1984): total 13,228,200; activity rate of total population 34.5% (participation rates: ages 15–64, 56.9%; female 24.7%; unemployed 20.6%).

Price and earnings indexes (1980 = 100)

	1979	1980	1981	1982	1983	1984	1985
Consumer price index	86.5	100.0	114.6	131.1	147.0	163.6	178.0
Monthly earnings index	84.4	100.0	119.9	138.1	158.8	178.7	197.7

Household income and expenditure. Average household size (1983) 2.8; income per household Ptas 1,250,000 (U.S.$8,700); sources of income (1984): wages and salaries 52.3%, profits and self-employment 28.6%, social security 16.8%; expenditure (1981): food 35.9%, housing 21.8%, transportation 11.8%, clothing and footwear 8.1%, health 6.0%, education 4.3%.
Land use (1983): forested 31.3%; meadows and pastures 21.4%; agricultural and under permanent cultivation 41.1%; other 6.2%.

Foreign trade

Balance of trade (current prices)

	1980	1981	1982	1983	1984	1985
Ptas '000,000	−957,466	−1,086,250	−1,207,600	−1,337,900	−850,900	−974,000
% of total	24.3%	22.3%	21.1%	19.1%	10.1%	10.6%

Imports (1985): Ptas 5,073,200,000,000 (petroleum and petroleum products 35.6%; machinery and transport equipment 20.7%, of which cars and trucks 4.6%; food 11.1%; chemicals, plastics, and rubber 10.0%; metals and metal products 6.8%). *Major import sources:* U.S. 10.9%; West Germany 10.6%; France 9.3%; Middle East 9.3%; U.K. 6.5%.
Exports (1985): Ptas 4,099,200,000,000 (machinery and transport equipment 27.1%, of which cars and trucks 13.0%; metals and metal products 15.4%; food 15.3%; petroleum products 10.7%). *Major export destinations:* France 15.5%; U.S. 10.0%; West Germany 9.6%; U.K. 8.6%; Italy 7.1%.

Transport and communications

Transport. Railroads (1985): route length 8,435 mi, 13,575 km; passenger-km 15,972,000,000; metric ton-km cargo 11,636,000,000. Roads (1984): total length 197,936 mi, 318,548 km (paved 56%). Vehicles (1984): passenger cars 8,874,442; trucks and buses 1,523,250. Merchant marine (1985): vessels (100 gross tons and over) 2,477; total deadweight tonnage 10,820,000. Air transport (1984): passenger-km 17,460,000,000; metric ton-km cargo 517,152,000; airports (1986) with scheduled flights 29.
Communications. Daily newspapers (1983): total number 113; total circulation 3,400,000; circulation per 1,000 population 89. Radio (1985): 10,800,-000 receivers (1 per 3.7 persons). Television (1985): 9,915,000 receivers (1 per 3.9 persons). Telephones (1983): 12,820,190 (1 per 3.0 persons).

Education and health

Education (1983–84)

	schools	teachers	students	student/ teacher ratio
Primary (age 2–13)	23,105♀	257,107	6,804,701	26.5
Secondary (age 14–17)	2,547	71,256	1,142,308	16.0
Vocational	2,397	45,339	695,180	15.3
Higher, teacher tr.♀	33	43,037	692,152	16.1

Educational attainment (1970). Percent of population over age 13 having: less than primary education 27.1%, of which no formal schooling 11.2%; primary 65.0%; lower secondary 2.6%; upper secondary 2.2%; some post-secondary 1.8%; university degree 1.3%. *Literacy* (1983): total population over age 15 literate 26,004,225 (92.8%); males literate 12,950,282 (95.9%); females literate 13,053,943 (89.9%).
Health: physicians (1984) 121,362 (1 per 316 persons); hospital beds (1981) 193,895 (1 per 195 persons); infant mortality rate per 1,000 live births (1983) 10.5.
Food (1980–82): daily per capita caloric intake 3,307 (vegetable products 74%, animal products 26%); 134% of FAO recommended minimum requirement.

Military

Total active duty personnel (1985): 320,000 (army 71.9%, navy 17.8%, air force 10.3%). *Military expenditure as percent of GNP* (1984): 2.4% (world 6.1%); per capita expenditure U.S.$101.

*Detail does not add to total given because of rounding. †Percentage breakdown is for 1984. ‡1983. §1984. ‖ 1982. ¶Unemployed persons not previously employed. ♀1982–83.

Sri Lanka (Ceylon)

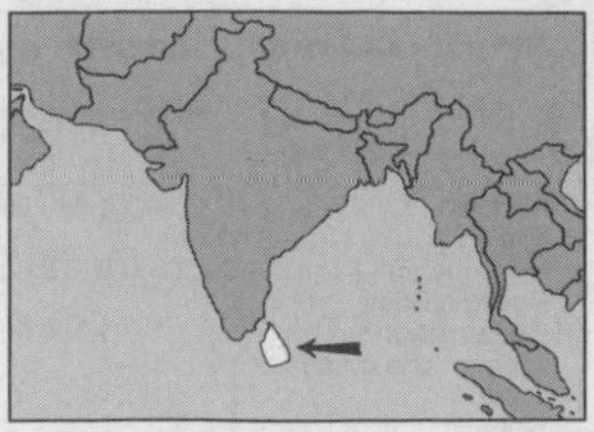

Official name: Sri Lankā Prajathanthrika Samajavadi Janarajaya (Democratic Socialist Republic of Sri Lanka).
Form of government: unitary multiparty republic with one legislative house (Parliament [168]).
Head of state and government: President.
Capital: Colombo (Capital designate, Sri Jayawardenapura).
Official language: Sinhala.
Official religion: none.
Monetary unit: 1 Sri Lanka rupee (SL Rs) = 100 cents; valuation (Oct. 1, 1986) 1 U.S.$ = SL Rs 28.35; 1 £ = SL Rs 40.96.

Area and population

		area		population
Districts	Capitals	sq mi	sq km	1983 estimate*
Amparai	Amparai	1,778	4,604	411,000
Anuradhapura	Anuradhapura	2,809	7,275	622,000
Badulla	Badulla	1,090	2,822	649,000
Batticaloa	Batticaloa	1,017	2,633	352,000
Colombo	Colombo	268	695	1,761,000
Galle	Galle	652	1,689	844,000
Gampaha	Gampaha	540	1,399	1,427,000
Hambantota	Hambantota	1,013	2,623	449,000
Jaffna	Jaffna	833	2,158	868,000
Kalutara	Kalutara	624	1,615	858,000
Kandy	Kandy	833	2,158	1,154,000
Kegalle	Kegalle	642	1,663	700,000
Kurunegala	Kurunegala	1,844	4,776	1,269,000
Mannar	Mannar	778	2,014	113,000
Matale	Matale	768	1,989	373,000
Matara	Matara	481	1,247	677,000
Moneragala	Moneragala	2,188	5,666	298,000
Mullaitivu	Mullaitivu	798	2,066	81,000
Nuwara Eliya	Nuwara Eliya	555	1,437	508,000
Polonnaruwa	Polonnaruwa	1,332	3,449	278,000
Puttalam	Puttalam	1,172	3,036	520,000
Ratnapura	Ratnapura	1,251	3,239	826,000
Trincomalee	Trincomalee	1,048	2,714	274,000
Vavuniya	Vavuniya	1,021	2,645	102,000
TOTAL		25,332†	65,610†	15,414,000

Demography

Population (1986): 16,060,000.
Density (1986): persons per sq mi 634.0, persons per sq km 244.8.
Urban-rural (1985): urban 21.1%; rural 78.9%.
Sex distribution (1985): male 50.55%; female 49.45%.
Age breakdown (1983): under 15, 35.3%; 15–29, 29.6%; 30–44, 17.9%; 45–59, 10.6%; 60–74, 5.2%; 75 and over, 1.4%.
Population projection: (1991) 17,719,000; (2001) 20,767,000.
Doubling time: 39 years.
Ethnic composition (1981): Sinhalese 74.0%; Tamil 18.2%; Sri Lankan Moor 7.1%; other 0.7%.
Religious affiliation (1981): Buddhist 69.3%; Hindu 15.5%; Muslim 7.6%; Christian 7.5%; other 0.1%.
Major cities (1983): Colombo 623,000; Dehiwala–Mount Lavinia 181,000; Moratuwa 137,000; Jaffna 128,000; Kandy 114,000.

Vital statistics

Birth rate per 1,000 population (1984): 24.8 (world avg. 29.0).
Death rate per 1,000 population (1984): 6.5 (world avg. 11.0).
Natural increase rate per 1,000 population (1984): 18.3 (world avg. 18.0).
Total fertility rate (avg. births per childbearing woman; 1985): 3.1.
Marriage rate per 1,000 population (1983): 7.9.
Divorce rate per 1,000 population (1983): 0.1.
Life expectancy at birth (1985): male 67.6 years; female 70.9 years.
Major causes of death per 100,000 population (1980): senility without mention of psychosis 116.9; diseases of the circulatory system 99.0; infectious and parasitic diseases 74.5; signs, symptoms, and ill-defined conditions 58.7; respiratory diseases 47.2.

National economy

*Budget** (1984). Revenue: SL Rs 37,371,000,000 (general sales and turnover tax 21.6%; import duties 21.1%; selective sales taxes 15.3%; income taxes 14.5%; export duties 8.4%). Expenditures: SL Rs 48,447,300,000 (finance and planning 29.5%; Mahaveli [river basin] development 14.6%; education 7.0%; transport and communication 6.1%; defense 5.1%).
Public debt (external, outstanding; 1985): U.S.$2,815,100,000.
Tourism: receipts from visitors (1984) U.S.$105,000,000; expenditures by nationals abroad (1983) U.S.$93,000,000.
Production (metric tons except as noted). Agriculture, forestry, fishing (1984): rice 2,270,000, coconuts 1,460,000, cassava 650,000, tea 230,000, natural rubber 145,000, sweet potatoes 130,000, copra 100,000, mangoes 75,000; livestock (number of live animals) 1,738,000 cattle, 951,000 buffalo, 535,000 goats; roundwood 8,497,000 cu m; fish catch 170,000. Mining and quarrying (1984): clays 131,890‡; salt 110,000; ilmenite 102,000; rutile 6,000; graphite 6,000; gemstones SL Rs 936,783,600‡. Manufacturing (1984): cement 401,000; raw sugar 18,000; cigarettes 5,750; beer 72,000 hectolitres‡. Construction (1983): residential 914,200 sq m. Energy production (consumption): electricity (kW-hr; 1984) 2,261,000,000 (2,261,000,000); coal (metric tons; 1984) none (1,000); crude petroleum (barrels; 1984) none (12,615,000); petroleum products (metric tons; 1984) 1,513,000 (1,154,000); natural gas (cu m; 1982) 3,063,000 (n.a.).
Gross national product (1984): U.S.$5,660,000,000 (U.S.$360 per capita).

Structure of gross domestic product and labour force

	1984		1980–81	
	in value SL Rs '000,000	% of total value	labour force	% of labour force
Agriculture	35,874	24.3	2,374,870	48.2
Mining	1,290	0.9	66,170	1.3
Manufacturing	24,378	16.5	531,065	10.8
Construction	11,621	7.9	223,750	4.5
Public utilities	2,345	1.6	18,999	0.4
Transp. and commun.	15,526	10.5	208,470	4.2
Trade	28,830	19.5	497,855	10.1
Finance	6,121	4.1	48,093	1.0
Pub. admin., defense, and services	8,574	5.8	650,981	13.2
Other§	12,957	8.9	310,092	6.3
TOTAL	147,516	100.0	4,930,345	100.0

Population economically active: total (1983) 5,594,000; activity rate of total population 36.3% (participation rates: over age 15, 56.1%; female [1981] 27.4%; unemployed [1981] 13.5%).

Price and earnings indexes (1980 = 100)

	1980	1981	1982	1983	1984	1985	1986‖
Consumer price index	100.0	117.9	130.7	149.0	173.8	176.3	190.9
Average wage index¶	100.0	100.2	118.0	129.3	162.9	178.0	187.2

Household income and expenditure. Average household size (1981) 5.2; income per household (1973) SL Rs 3,936 (U.S.$611); sources of income (1982): wages 49.0%, property income 38.8%, government transfers 9.1%; expenditure (1983): food 50.8%, transportation 14.6%, beverages and tobacco 9.3%, housing 9.2%, clothing 5.9%, recreation 3.9%, health 1.6%.
Land use (1983): forested 36.8%; meadows and pastures 6.8%; agricultural and under permanent cultivation 33.8%; other 22.6%.

Foreign trade

Balance of trade (current prices)

	1980	1981	1982	1983	1984	1985
SL Rs '000,000	−12,442	−10,768	−15,021	−14,519	−3,993	−9,890
% of total	26.1%	20.4%	25.9%	22.4%	5.1%	12.0%

Imports (1984): SL Rs 46,913,000,000 (petroleum products 22.8%, machinery and equipment 11.4%, wheat 5.3%, sugar 2.9%). *Major import sources:* Japan 16.7%; Saudi Arabia 16.6%; U.S. 8.9%; India 6.0%.
Exports (1984): SL Rs 36,541,000,000 (tea 43.2%, rubber 9.0%, desiccated coconut 3.2%, precious and semiprecious stones 1.9%). *Major export destinations:* U.S. 19.5%; Iraq 7.2%; U.K. 5.9%; W.Ger. 4.9%; U.S.S.R. 4.5%.

Transport and communications

Transport. Railroads (1985): route length 903 mi, 1,453 km; passenger-mi 1,312,000,000, passenger-km 2,111,000,000; short ton-mi cargo 169,229,000, metric ton-km cargo 247,070,000. Roads (1984): total length 53,573 mi, 86,218 km (paved 35%). Vehicles (1984): passenger cars 141,730; trucks and buses 125,654. Merchant marine (1985): vessels (100 gross tons and over) 91; total deadweight tonnage 974,235. Air transport (1985): passenger mi 1,558,000,000, passenger-km 2,508,000,000; short ton-mi cargo 47,779,000, metric ton-km cargo 69,756,000; airports (1986) with scheduled flights 1.
Communications. Daily newspapers (1985): total number 15; total circulation 850,000; circulation per 1,000 population 53. Radio (1985): 3,010,000 receivers (1 per 5 persons). Television (1985): 350,000 receivers (1 per 46 persons). Telephones (1982): 109,900 (1 per 135 persons).

Education and health

Education (1983)

	schools	teachers	students	student/teacher ratio
Primary (age 5–10)	3,983	18,693	593,009	31.7
Secondary (age 11–17)	5,629	113,148	2,930,070	25.9
Voc., teacher tr.	25	466	8,382	18.0
Higher♀	8	2,168	18,073	8.3

Educational attainment (1981). Percent of adult population over age 30 having: less than primary education 30.3%; primary 37.2%; postprimary 14.7%; secondary 13.7%; higher 2.7%. *Literacy* (1981): population over age 15 literate 86.1%; males literate 90.8%; females literate 81.2%.
Health (1984): physicians♂ 1,951 (1 per 7,999 persons); hospital beds 44,919 (1 per 347 persons); infant mortality rate per 1,000 live births 34.0.
Food (1980–82): daily per capita caloric intake 2,331 (vegetable products 96%, animal products 4%); 105% of FAO recommended minimum requirement.

Military

Total active duty personnel (1985): 37,660 (army 79.7%, navy 10.5%, air force 9.8%). *Military expenditure as percent of GNP* (1983): 1.5% (world 6.1%); per capita expenditure U.S.$5.

*Provisional. †Detail does not add to total given because of rounding. ‡1983. §Includes import duties. ‖June. ¶Agricultural minimum rates. ♀Universities only. ♂Includes only those in Department of Health Services.

Sudan, The

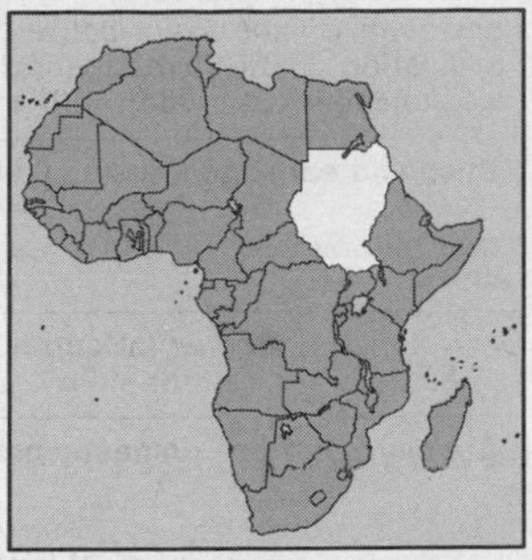

Official name: Jumhūrīyat as-Sūdān (Republic of the Sudan).
Form of government: multiparty republic with one legislative house (People's Assembly [301])*.
Chief of state: Chairman†.
Head of government: Prime Minister.
Capital: Khartoum.
Official language: Arabic.
Official religion: Islam.
Monetary unit: 1 Sudanese pound (LSd) = 100 piastres; valuation (Oct. 1, 1986) 1 U.S.$ = LSd 2.45; 1 £ = LSd 3.54.

Area and population

Regions / Provinces	Capitals	area sq mi	area sq km	population 1983 census
A'ālī an-Nīl (Upper Nile)	Malakāl	92,198	238,792	1,599,605
A'ālī an-Nīl (Upper Nile)	Nāṣir	45,231	117,148	802,354
Junqulī (Jongley)	Bor	46,781	121,164	797,251
Baḥr al-Ghazāl (Bahr el-Ghazal)	Wāu	77,566	200,894	2,265,510
Baḥr al-Ghazāl al-Gharbīyah (Western Bahr el-Ghazal) } Baḥr al-Ghazāl ash-Sharqīyah (Eastern Bahr el-Ghazal)	Raga } Uwayl	51,960	134,576	1,492,597
al-Buḥayrāh (El Buheyrah)	Rumbek	25,606	66,318	772,913
Dārfūr (Darfur)	al-Fāshir	196,404	508,684	3,093,699
Dārfūr al-Janūbīyah (Southern Darfur)	Nyala	62,753	162,529	1,765,752
Dārfūr ash-Shamālīyah (Northern Darfur)	al-Fāshir	133,651	346,155	1,327,947
al-Istiwā'īyah (Equatoria)	Jūbā	76,436	197,969	1,406,181
al-Istiwā'īyah al Gharbīyah (Western Equatoria)	Yambio	30,398	78,732	359,056
al-Istiwā'īyah ash-Sharqīyah (Eastern Equatoria)	Jūbā	46,038	119,237	1,047,125
Kurdufān (Kordofan)	al-Ubayyiḍ	146,817	380,255	3,093,294
Kurdufān al-Janūbīyah (Southern Kordofan)	Kāduqlī	61,141	158,355	1,287,525
Kurdufān ash-Shamālīyah (Northern Kordofan)	al-Ubayyiḍ	85,676	221,900	1,805,769
ash-Shamālīyah (Northern)	ad-Dāmir	183,800	476,040	1,083,024
an-Nīl (Nile)	ad-Dāmir	49,167	127,343	649,633
ash-Shamālīyah (Northern)	Dunqulah	134,633	348,697	433,391
ash-Sharqīyah (Eastern)	Kassalā	128,987	334,074	2,208,209
al-Baḥr al-Aḥmar (Red Sea)	Port Sudan	84,912	219,920	695,874
Kassalā (Kassala)	Kassalā	44,075	114,154	1,512,335
al-Wastā (Central)	Wad Madanī	53,675	139,017	4,012,543
an-Nīl al-Abyaḍ (White Nile)	ad-Duwaym	16,149	41,825	933,136
al-Jazīrah (El-Gezira)	Wad Madanī	13,536	35,057	2,023,094
an-Nīl al-Azraq (Blue Nile)	ad-Damazin	23,990	62,135	1,056,313
National Capital				
Kharṭūm (Khartoum)	Khartoum	10,875	28,165	1,802,299
TOTAL		966,757‡	2,503,890	20,564,364

Demography

Population (1986): 24,610,000.
Density (1986): persons per sq mi 25.5, persons per sq km 9.8.
Urban-rural (1983): urban 30.6%; rural 69.4%.
Sex distribution (1983): male 50.98%; female 49.02%.
Age breakdown (1985): under 15, 44.6%; 15–29, 26.0%; 30–44, 15.7%; 45–59, 8.9%; 60–74, 4.0%; 75 and over, 0.8%.
Population projection: (1990) 24,949,800; (2000) 32,885,000.
Doubling time: 25 years.
Ethnic composition (1980): Sudanese Arab 46.0%; Nilotic 25.5%; Azande 5.6%; Nuba 5.6%; Beja 5.0%; other 12.3%.
Religious affiliation (1980): Sunnī Muslim 73.0%; traditional beliefs 16.7%; Roman Catholic 5.6%; Anglican 2.3%; other 2.4%.
Major cities (1983): Omdurman 526,287; Khartoum 476,218; Khartoum North 341,146; Port Sudan 206,727.

Vital statistics

Birth rate per 1,000 population (1980–85): 45.3 (world avg. 29.0).
Death rate per 1,000 population (1980–85): 16.6 (world avg. 11.0).
Natural increase rate per 1,000 population (1980–85): 28.7 (world avg. 18.0).
Total fertility rate (avg. births per childbearing woman; 1980–85): 6.5.
Life expectancy at birth (1980–85): male 48.0 years; female 50.0 years.
Major causes of death per 100,000 population (1979)§: pneumonia 26.4; tuberculosis 1.8; meningitis 1.3; infectious hepatitis 1.1.

National economy

Budget (1986–87). Revenue: LSd 2,682,800,000 (tax revenue 62.2%; nontax revenue 37.8%). Expenditures: LSd 5,542,000,000 (current expenditures 65.3%; development budget 24.9%, of which agriculture 6.2%, transport and communications 3.5%, energy and mining 0.5%).
Public debt (external, outstanding; 1984): U.S.$5,658,800,000.
Tourism (1983): receipts from visitors U.S.$6,000,000; expenditures by nationals abroad U.S.$72,000,000.
Production (metric tons except as noted). Agriculture, forestry, fishing (1984): sugarcane 4,700,000, sorghum 1,450,000, seed cotton 640,000, peanuts (groundnuts) 420,000, millet 270,000, lint cotton 219,000, sesame seeds 150,000; livestock (number of live animals) 19,600,000 cattle, 20,000,000 sheep, 13,000,000 goats, 2,500,000 camels; roundwood 18,973,000 cu m; fish catch (1983) 29,500. Mining and quarrying (1984): hydraulic cement 176,000; salt 75,000; chromite concentrate 20,000; gypsum and anhydrite 8,000. Manufacturing (1982): raw sugar 270,000; wheat flour 265,000; cement 211,000; cigarettes 740,000,000 units. Construction: n.a. Energy production (consumption): electricity (kW-hr; 1984) 1,032,000,000 (1,032,000,000); crude petroleum (barrels; 1984) none (8,063,000); petroleum products (metric tons; 1984) 1,010,000 (1,073,000).
Gross national product (1984): U.S.$7,360,000,000 (U.S.$320 per capita).

Structure of gross domestic product and labour force

	1982–83 in value LSd '000,000	1982–83 % of total value	1979–80 labour force	1979–80 % of labour force
Agriculture	2,095.0	30.0	3,432,600	65.8
Mining } Manufacturing	482.0	6.9	183,300	3.5
Construction	300.0	4.3	107,600	2.1
Public utilities	123.0	1.8	59,200	1.1
Transp. and commun.	580.0	8.3	198,800	3.8
Trade	1,350.0	19.3 }	220,800	4.2
Finance	395.0	5.7 }		
Pub. admin., defense	620.0	8.9	...	...
Services	150.0	2.1	679,800	13.0
Other	886.0	12.7	340,500	6.5
TOTAL	6,981.0	100.0	5,222,600	100.0

Population economically active (1981): total 5,973,000; activity rate of total population 31.6% (participation rates: over age 15, 53.1%; female 10.9%; unemployed, n.a.).

Price indexes (1980 = 100)

	1979	1980	1981	1982	1983	1984	1985
Consumer price index	79.8	100.0	124.6	156.6	204.5	274.3	398.8

Household income and expenditure. Average household size (1980) 5.3; average annual income per household: n.a.; source of income: n.a.; expenditure (1980)‖: food, beverages, and tobacco 66.5%, education, health, transportation, and recreation 15.2%, housing 12.4%, clothing 5.9%.
Land use (1983): forested 20.2%; meadows and pastures 23.6%; agricultural and under permanent cultivation 5.2%; desert and other 51.0%.

Foreign trade

Balance of trade (current prices)

	1980	1981	1982	1983	1984	1985
LSd '000,000	−516.9	−509.7	−707.1	−761.5	−673.8	−894.4
% of total	48.8%	41.7%	44.0%	32.0%	29.2%	34.6%

Imports (1982): LSd 1,156,404,000 (machinery 28.3%; petroleum and petroleum products 27.1%; chemicals 8.2%; sugar 5.4%). *Major import sources* (1985): Japan 8.8%; Thailand 8.0%; Italy 7.6%.
Exports (1982): LSd 449,338,000 (cotton 25.1%; unmilled cereals 23.3%; sheep, lambs, and goats 12.3%). *Major export destinations* (1985): United States 17.2%; United Kingdom 9.5%; West Germany 8.0%.

Transport and communications

Transport. Railroads (1981–82): route length, 4,786 km; passenger-km 1,149,000; metric ton-km cargo 1,600,000,000. Roads (1982): total length 9,018 km (paved 33%). Vehicles (1982): passenger cars 150,000; trucks and buses 22,000. Merchant marine (1985): vessels (100 gross tons and over) 23; total deadweight tonnage 126,381. Air transport (1982): passenger-km 657,000,000; metric ton-km cargo 6,000,000; airports (1986) with scheduled flights 13.
Communications. Daily newspapers (1985): total number 2; total circulation 120,000; circulation per 1,000 population 5.1. Radio (1985): total number of receivers 1,340,000 (1 per 17.7 persons). Television (1985): total number of receivers 125,000 (1 per 189.5 persons). Telephones (1983): 68,838 (1 per 318.6 persons).

Education and health

Education (1985)

	schools	teachers	students	student/ teacher ratio
Primary (age 7–12)	6,707	47,750	1,653,491	34.6
Secondary (age 13–18)	2,167	17,591	490,583	27.9
Voc., teacher tr.	98	968¶	29,650	...
Higher	16	1,934♀	35,596	...

Educational attainment, n.a. *Literacy* (1980): total population over age 15 literate 2,507,200 (21.6%); males 36.5%; females 6.5%.
Health (1981): physiciansδ 2,169 (1 per 9,369 persons); hospital beds 17,328 (1 per 1,110 persons); infant mortality rate per 1,000 live births (1982) 119.
Food (1980–82): daily per capita caloric intake 2,332 (vegetable products 87%, animal products 13%); 101% of FAO recommended minimum.

Military

Total active duty personnel (1986): 56,750 (army 93.4%, navy 1.3%, air force 5.3%). *Military expenditure as percent of GNP* (1983): 1.7% (world 6.1%); per capita expenditure U.S.$8.

*Elections in 37 of the 301 constituencies, all in the south, have been postponed indefinitely. †A civilian and a coalitionist government representing several political parties was appointed in May 1986 to replace the joint military–civilian transitional government that existed since April 1985. The country is headed by a Supreme Council, which is composed of a chairman and four members. ‡Detail does not add to total given because of rounding. §Reported by hospitals and dispensaries. ‖ Low-income households. ¶Vocational only. ♀1980. δIncludes dentists.

Suriname

Official name: Republiek Suriname (Dutch); Republic of Suriname (English).
Form of government: military dictatorship with one ruling body (National Assembly [31]).
Head of state and government: Commander in Chief of the National Army.
Capital: Paramaribo.
Official languages: Dutch; English.
Official religion: none.
Monetary unit: 1 Suriname guilder (Sf) = 100 cents; valuation (Oct. 1, 1986) 1 U.S.$ = Sf 1.79; 1 £ = Sf 2.58.

Area and population

		area*		population
				1980
Districts	**Capitals**	sq mi	sq km	census†
Brokopondo	Brokopondo	8,278	21,440	20,249
Commewijne	Nieuw Amsterdam	1,587	4,110	14,351
Coronie	Tottness	626	1,620	2,777
Marowijne	Albina	17,753	45,980	23,402
Nickerie	Nieuw Nickerie	24,946	64,610	34,480
Para	Onverwacht	378	980	14,867
Saramacca	Groningen	9,042	23,420	10,335
Suriname	...	629	1,628	166,494
Town district				
Paramaribo	Paramaribo	12	32	67,905
TOTAL		63,251	163,820	354,860

Demography

Population (1986): 393,000.
Density (1986): persons per sq mi 6.2, persons per sq km 2.4.
Urban-rural (1985): urban 45.2%; rural 54.8%.
Sex distribution (1985): male 49.60%; female 50.40%.
Age breakdown (1980): under 15, 39.3%; 15–29, 29.5%; 30–44, 13.8%; 45–59, 10.0%; 60–74, 4.5%; 75 and over, 2.8%‡.
Population projection: (1990) 422,000; (2000) 505,000.
Doubling time: 32 years.
Ethnic composition (1980): Hindustani 35%; Creole 32%; Indonesian 15%; Bush Negro 10%; Amerindian 3%; Chinese 3%; other 2%.
Religious affiliation (1980): Hindu 27.4%; Roman Catholic 22.8%; Muslim 19.6%; Protestant 18.8%; other 11.4%.
Major cities (1980): Paramaribo 67,905; Nieuw Nickerie 6,078; Meerzorg 5,355; Marienburg 3,633.

Vital statistics

Birth rate per 1,000 population (1984): 29.7 (world avg. 29.0); legitimate, n.a.; illegitimate, n.a.
Death rate per 1,000 population (1984): 7.4 (world avg. 11.0).
Natural increase rate per 1,000 population (1984): 22.3 (world avg. 18.0).
Total fertility rate (avg. births per childbearing woman; 1980): 5.7.
Marriage rate per 1,000 population (1980): 6.7.
Divorce rate per 1,000 population (1980): 1.1.
Life expectancy at birth (1980–85): male 67.0 years; female 71.9 years.
Major causes of death per 100,000 population (1981): diseases of the circulatory system 164.0, of which cerebrovascular disease 49.0, ischemic heart disease 38.2; malignant neoplasms (cancers) 47.6; infectious and parasitic diseases 42.5; accidents 41.1, of which motor vehicle 15.6; diseases of the respiratory system 39.7; suicide 14.7.

National economy

Budget (1984). Revenue: Sf 518,980,000 (import duties 21.0%, individual income tax 18.2%, corporate tax 11.0%, export duties 9.3%, property income tax 8.3%). Expenditures: Sf 768,120,000 (general public services 24.5%, general administration 16.6%, education 11.9%, social security 5.8%, defense 5.4%, agriculture 2.8%).
Public debt (external, outstanding; 1985): U.S.$24,000,000.
Tourism (1983): receipts from visitors U.S.$4,000,000; expenditures by nationals abroad U.S.$35,000,000.
Production (metric tons except as noted). Agriculture, forestry, fishing (1984): rice 270,000, sugarcane 150,000, fruits and vegetables 102,000 (of which bananas 41,000, oranges 7,000, other citrus fruits 2,000, cabbage 1,000, tomatoes 1,000, cucumbers 1,000), coconuts 6,000; livestock (number of live animals) 53,000 cattle, 18,000 pigs, 10,000 goats, 4,000 sheep, 1,100,000 chickens; roundwood 260,000 cu m; fish catch (1983) 3,592. Mining and quarrying (1984): bauxite 3,454,000; gravel and crushed stone 66,000; clay 100,000; gold 322 troy oz. Manufacturing (1984): alumina 1,240,000; cement 50,000; aluminum 23,000; sugar 6,500; plywood 13,900 cu m; shoes 335,246 pairs; soft drinks 266,600 hectolitres; beer 145,600 hectolitres; cigarettes 521,000,000 units. Construction (1983): residential Sf 34,800,000; nonresidential Sf 10,100,000. Energy production (consumption): electricity (kW-hr; 1984) 1,250,000,000 (1,250,000,000); hard coal (metric tons; 1984) none (1,000); crude petroleum (barrels; 1984) 220,000 (220,000); petroleum products (metric tons; 1984) none (349,000); fuelwood (cubic metres; 1982) 19,000 (19,000); bagasse (metric tons; 1982) 36,000 (36,000).
Land use (1983): forested 96.1%; meadows and pastures 0.1%; agricultural and under permanent cultivation 0.4%; other 3.4%.

Population economically active (1982): total 83,461; activity rate of total population 23.8% (participation rates: over age 10 [1980] 36.9%; female, n.a.; unemployed [1986] 25.0%).

Price and earnings indexes (1980 = 100)

	1980	1981	1982	1983	1984	1985	1986§
Consumer price index ‖	100.0	108.7	116.6	121.8	126.2	140.0	150.0
Earnings index	...	...	...	...	...	...	...

Gross national product (at current market prices; 1984): U.S.$1,350,000,000 (U.S.$3,550 per capita).

Structure of gross domestic product and labour force

	1982		1980	
	in value Sf '000,000	% of total value	labour force	% of labour force
Agriculture	201	9.1	7,600	7.8
Mining	261	11.8	5,580	5.7
Manufacturing	198	9.0	7,260	7.4
Construction	63	2.9	3,940	4.1
Public utilities	39	1.8	1,260	1.3
Transportation and communication	113	5.1	2,930	3.0
Trade	268	12.2	11,420	11.6
Finance			1,970	2.1
Pub. admin., defense				
Services	1,062	48.2	38,040	38.9
Other			17,690	18.1
TOTAL	2,205	100.0‡	97,690	100.0

Household income and expenditure. Average household size (1980) 3.9; average annual income per household: n.a.; source of income: n.a.; expenditure ‖ (1968–69): food and drink 40.0%, household furniture and furnishings 12.3%, clothing and footwear 10.6%, transport and communications 9.5%, recreation 6.1%, fuel and power 5.5%.

Foreign trade

Balance of trade (current prices)

	1979	1980	1981	1982	1983	1984
Sf '000,000	+137.8	+114.4	−59.3	−49.9	−67.2	+84.1
% of total	9.5%	6.6%	3.4%	3.2%	4.9%	7.1%

Imports (1982): Sf 921,200,000 (raw materials and semimanufactured goods 38.7%, fuel and lubricants 22.8%, machinery and equipment 12.8%). *Major import sources* (1981): Caribbean countries 29%; United States 28%; The Netherlands 9%.
Exports (1982): Sf 765,100,000 (alumina 53.8%, aluminum 16.2%, rice 9.4%, shrimp 7.0%, bauxite 6.8%, plywood 2.7%, bananas 1.7%). *Major export destinations* (1981): United States 35%; The Netherlands 14%; Norway 13%; United Kingdom 7%.

Transport and communications

Transport. Railroads (1983): length 104 mi, 167 km; passengers, n.a.; cargo, n.a. Roads (1983): total length 5,523 mi, 8,889 km (paved 29%). Vehicles (1983): passenger cars 31,170; trucks and buses 12,850. Merchant marine (1985): vessels (100 gross tons and over) 25; total deadweight tonnage 19,187. Air transport (1980): passenger-mi 152,240,000, passenger-km 245,000,000; short ton-mi cargo 2,466,000, metric ton-km cargo 3,600,000; airports (1986) with scheduled flights 5.
Communications. Daily newspapers (1984): total number 8; total circulation 30,000¶; circulation per 1,000 population 80¶. Radio (1985): total number of receivers 188,000 (1 per 2.1 persons). Television (1985): total number of receivers 44,000 (1 per 8.8 persons). Telephones (1982): 27,495 (1 per 13 persons).

Education and health

Education (1983–84)

	schools	teachers	students	student/ teacher ratio
Primary (age 6–12)	319	3,796	91,595	24.1
Secondary (age 13–17)	51	789	15,501	19.6
Voc., teacher tr.	64	1,253	15,428	12.3
Higher	6	485	3,489	7.2

Educational attainment, n.a. *Literacy* (1980): total population over age 15 literate 170,700 (80.7%); males literate 88,286 (85.4%); females literate 82,414 (76.3%).
Health: physicians (1979) 224 (1 per 1,612 persons); hospital beds (1980) 3,169 (1 per 160.0 persons); infant mortality rate per 1,000 live births (1984) 32.5.
Food (1980–82): daily per capita caloric intake 2,470 (vegetable products 87%, animal products 13%); 110% of FAO recommended minimum requirement.

Military

Total active duty personnel (1985): 2,020♀ (army 89.1%, navy 7.9%, air force 3.0%). *Military expenditure as percent of GNP* (1983): 2.2% (world 6.1%); per capita expenditure U.S.$68.

*Area excludes 6,809 sq mi (17,635 sq km) of territory disputed with Guyana. †Preliminary. ‡Detail does not add to total given because of rounding. §February. ‖ For Paramaribo and environs. ¶Partial circulation only. ♀All services are part of the army.

Swaziland

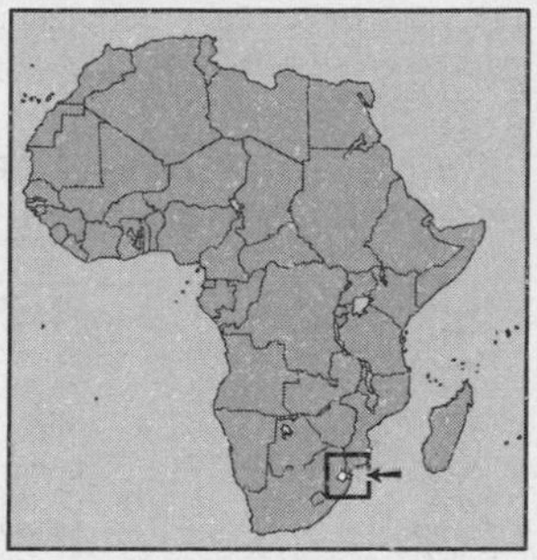

Official name: Umbuso weSwatini (Swazi); Kingdom of Swaziland (English).
Form of government: monarchy with two legislative houses (Senate [20]; House of Assembly [50]).
Chief of state: King.
Head of government: Prime Minister.
Capitals: Mbabane (administrative); Lobamba (royal and legislative).
Official languages: Swazi; English.
Official religion: none.
Monetary unit: 1 lilangeni (plural emalangeni [E]) = 100 cents; valuation (Oct. 1, 1986) 1 U.S.$ = E 2.22*; 1 £ = E 3.21.

Area and population

		area		population
Districts	Capitals	sq mi	sq km	1986 estimate†
Hhohho	Mbabane	1,378	3,569	186,000
Lubombo	Siteki	2,296	5,947	137,700
Manzini	Manzini	1,571	4,068	197,200
Shiselweni	Nhlangano	1,459	3,780	148,800
TOTAL		6,704	17,364	669,700

Demography

Population (1986): 681,500.
Density (1986): persons per sq mi 101.7, persons per sq km 39.2.
Urban-rural (1985): urban 26.3%; rural 73.7%.
Sex distribution (1985): male 48.84%; female 51.16%.
Age breakdown (1985): under 15, 46.1%; 15–29, 25.7%; 30–44, 14.6%; 45–59, 8.6%; 60–74, 4.2%; 75 and over, 0.8%.
Population projection: (1990) 828,000; (2000) 1,098,000.
Doubling time: 23 years.
Ethnic composition (1980): Swazi 87.8%; Zulu 9.2%; European 2.0%; other 1.0%.
Religious affiliation (1980): Christian 77.0%, of which Protestant 37.3%, Roman Catholic 10.8%, African indigenous 28.9%; traditional beliefs 20.9%; other 2.1%.
Major cities (1985): Mbabane 45,000; Manzini 17,000; Havelock Mine 6,500; Mhlume 5,000; Piggs Peak 2,900.

Vital statistics

Birth rate per 1,000 population (1980–85): 47.5 (world avg. 29.0); legitimate, n.a.; illegitimate, n.a.
Death rate per 1,000 population (1980–85): 17.2 (world avg. 11.0).
Natural increase rate per 1,000 population (1980–85): 30.2 (world avg. 18.0).
Total fertility rate (avg. births per childbearing woman; 1980–85): 6.5.
Marriage rate per 1,000 population: n.a.
Divorce rate per 1,000 population: n.a.
Life expectancy at birth (1980–85): male 45.3 years; female 51.9 years.
Major causes of death (1982)‡: intestinal infectious diseases 15.6%; tuberculosis 13.2%; diseases of the circulatory system 8.7%; diseases of the respiratory system 7.4%; diseases of the digestive system 5.5%; nutritional deficiencies 4.8%; malignant neoplasms (cancers) 4.4%.

National economy

Budget (1985–86)§. Revenue: E 218,300,000 (receipts from Customs Union of Southern Africa 62.0%). Expenditures: E 217,300,000 (current expenditure 79.1%, of which education and training 23.8%; economic development 20.9%, of which transport and communications 9.3%, agriculture 2.8%; debt payment 16.1%).
Tourism: receipts from visitors (1984) U.S.$7,000,000; expenditures by nationals abroad (1983) U.S.$22,000,000.
Land use (1983): forested 5.9%; meadows and pastures 66.8%; agricultural and under permanent cultivation 8.0%; other 19.4%.
Public debt (external, outstanding; 1984): U.S.$178,000,000.
Gross national product (1984): U.S.$590,000,000 (U.S.$930 per capita).

Structure of gross domestic product and labour force

	1983		1984	
	in value E '000,000	% of total value	labour force	% of labour force
Agriculture	101.5	25.3	20,134	26.8
Mining	10.7	2.7	2,238	3.0
Manufacturing	94.0	23.5	11,577	15.4
Construction	17.4	4.3	6,817	9.1
Public utilities	5.0	1.3	1,137	1.5
Transportation and communication	22.1	5.5	4,709	6.2
Trade	35.8	8.9	7,900	10.5
Finance	26.3	6.6	2,612	3.5
Pub. admin., defense	69.8	17.4		
Services	14.3	3.6	18,009	24.0
Other	3.7	0.9		
TOTAL	400.5 ‖	100.0	75,133	100.0

Population economically active (1984): total 281,000; activity rate of total population 44.1% (participation rates: ages 15–64, n.a.; female [1982] 51.7%; unemployed [1983] 4.0%).

Price and earnings indexes (1980 = 100)

	1979	1980	1981	1982	1983	1984	1985
Consumer price index	84.3	100.0	120.0	133.0	148.5	167.1	201.3
Monthly earnings index¶	141.3	100.0	136.4	172.1	181.3	...	...

Production (metric tons except as noted). Agriculture, forestry, fishing (1984): sugarcane 3,500,000, fruit excluding melons 143,000, cereals 115,000 (of which corn [maize] 110,000, rice 3,000, sorghum 2,000), pineapples 35,000, seed cotton 32,000, roots and tubers 17,000 (of which sweet potatoes 11,000, potatoes 6,000), lint cotton 12,000, pulses 3,000; livestock (number of live animals) 614,000 cattle, 298,000 goats, 40,000 sheep, 19,000 pigs, 1,000,000 chickens; roundwood 2,223,000 cu m; fish catch (1983) 44. Mining and quarrying (1984): asbestos 25,832; diamonds 16,837 carats. Manufacturing (producers' prices in E; 1981): food products and beverages 174,057,000; paper products 63,671,000; industrial chemicals 55,628,000; textiles 21,679,000; wood products, furniture, and fixtures 21,161,000. Construction (value in E; 1982): residential♀ 3,798,000; nonresidential 2,822,000. Energy production (consumption): electricity (kW-hr; 1981) 310,200,000 (n.a.); coal (metric tons; 1984) 124,569 (26,350); crude petroleum, n.a. (n.a.); petroleum products, n.a. (n.a.); natural gas, n.a. (n.a.).
Household income and expenditure. Average household size (1980) 5.0; average annual income per household: n.a.; source of income: n.a.; expenditures♂: food, drinks, and tobacco 39.3%, transportation and communication 15.3%, clothing and footwear 10.0%, furniture and utensils 9.0%, health and education 8.0%, energy and water 6.5%.

Foreign trade□

Balance of trade (current prices)

	1979	1980	1981	1982	1983	1984
E '000,000	−152.0	−159.4	−153.9	−167.9	−285.3	−252.3
% of total	27.9%	21.7%	18.4%	18.5%	30.6%	26.3%

Imports (1983–84): E 626,961,000 (machinery and transport equipment 27.7%, of which motor vehicles and parts 5.8%; manufactured goods 17.8%; mineral fuels and lubricants 15.5%, of which refined petroleum products 12.9%; chemicals 13.1%, of which artificial fertilizers 6.9%; food and live animals 9.4%; beverages and tobacco 2.4%). *Major import sources:* South Africa 84.7%; United States 7.0%; United Kingdom 2.3%; Japan 1.3%; West Germany 0.9%.
Exports (1983): E 323,688,700 (sugar 37.9%; wood and wood products 17.4%, of which woodpulp 13.8%; chemicals 13.2%; canned fruit and juices 6.9%; manufactured goods 6.7%; chrysotile asbestos 6.0%; citrus fruit 4.6%). *Major export destinations:* South Africa 32.4%; United Kingdom 22.1%.

Transport and communications

Transport. Railroads (1983): route length 194 mi, 312 km; passengers, n.a.; short ton-mi cargo 82,800,000, metric ton-km cargo 120,900,000. Roads (1983): total length 1,692 mi, 2,723 km (paved 23%). Vehicles (1983): passenger cars 17,238; trucks and buses 8,558. Merchant marine: n.a. Air transport (1984): passenger-mi 13,977,000, passenger-km 22,494,000; short ton-mi cargo 1,508,000, metric ton-km cargo 2,201,000; airports (1986) with scheduled flights 1.
Communications. Daily newspapers (1984): total number 3; total circulation 22,000; circulation per 1,000 population 34.5. Radio (1985): total number of receivers 87,000 (1 per 7.6 persons). Television (1985): total number of receivers 7,500 (1 per 88 persons). Telephones (1983): 7,456 (1 per 83 persons).

Education and health

Education (1984)

	schools	teachers	students	student/ teacher ratio
Primary (age 6–13)	467	4,039	134,528	33.3
Secondary (age 14–18)	89	1,569	28,833	18.4
Voc., teacher tr.	4	121	1,473	12.2
Higher	1	131	1,063	8.1

Educational attainment (1976). Percent of adult population over age 25 having: no formal schooling 53.6%; some primary education 25.4%; complete primary 9.2%; some secondary 7.9%; secondary and higher 3.9%. *Literacy* (1985): total population over age 15 literate 238,400 (67.9%); males literate 119,500 (70.3%); females literate 118,900 (65.7%).
Health (1984): physicians 80 (1 per 7,971 persons); hospital beds 1,608 (1 per 396 persons); infant mortality rate per 1,000 live births (1980–85) 129.
Food (1980–82): daily per capita caloric intake 2,526 (vegetable products 87%, animal products 13%); 109% of FAO recommended minimum requirement.

Military

Total active duty personnel (1983): 2,657. *Military expenditure as percent of GNP* (1983): 3.1% (world 6.1%); per capita expenditure U.S.$29.

*The lilangeni is at par with the South African rand. †De facto African population projection only. ‡Percentage of deaths of known cause at government, mission, and private hospitals. §Proposed budget (1986–87). Revenue: E 252,400,000 (receipts from Customs Union of Southern Africa 47.5%, tax receipts 14.6%); expenditure: (current expenditure 68.7%, of which education and training 18.9%). ‖ At factor cost, prices of 1980; detail does not add to total given because of rounding. ¶Based on earnings of skilled male workers in manufacturing. ♀Includes hotels, hostels, etc. ♂Weights of consumer price index components. □Import figures are f.o.b. in balance of trade and c.i.f. in commodities and trading partners.

Sweden

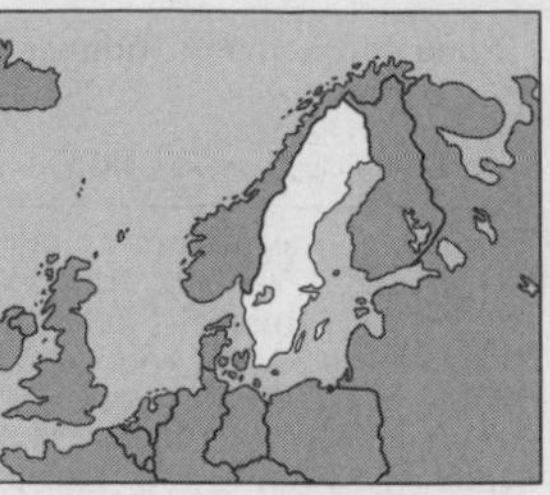

Official name: Konungariket Sverige (Kingdom of Sweden).
Form of government: constitutional monarchy and parliamentary state with one legislative house (Parliament [349]).
Chief of state: King.
Head of government: Prime Minister.
Capital: Stockholm.
Official language: Swedish.
Official religion: Church of Sweden (Lutheran).
Monetary unit: 1 Swedish krona (SKr) = 100 ore; valuation (Oct. 1, 1986) 1 U.S.$ = SKr 6.91; 1 £ = SKr 9.98.

Area and population

Counties	Capitals	area sq mi	area sq km	population 1986 estimate*
Älvsborg	Vänersborg	4,400	11,395	426,698
Blekinge	Karlskrona	1,136	2,941	150,959
Gävleborg	Gävle	7,024	18,191	289,153
Göteborg och Bohus	Göteborg	1,985	5,141	715,728
Gotland	Visby	1,212	3,140	56,144
Halland	Halmstad	2,106	5,454	240,063
Jämtland	Östersund	19,090	49,443	134,190
Jönköping	Jönköping	3,839	9,944	300,753
Kalmar	Kalmar	4,313	11,170	238,176
Kopparberg	Falun	10,886	28,194	283,880
Kristianstad	Kristianstad	2,350	6,087	280,354
Kronoberg	Växjö	3,266	8,458	173,972
Malmöhus	Malmö	1,907	4,938	750,140
Norrbotten	Luleå	38,191	98,913	262,300
Örebro	Örebro	3,289	8,519	270,211
Östergötland	Linköping	4,078	10,562	393,585
Skaraborg	Mariestad	3,065	7,937	270,468
Södermanland	Nyköping	2,340	6,060	249,701
Stockholm	Stockholm	2,505	6,488	1,578,299
Uppsala	Uppsala	2,698	6,989	251,852
Värmland	Karlstad	6,789	17,584	279,183
Västerbotten	Umeå	21,390	55,401	245,255
Västernorrland	Härnösand	8,370	21,678	262,314
Västmanland	Västerås	2,433	6,302	254,761
TOTAL LAND AREA		158,661†	410,929	8,358,139
INLAND WATER		15,071	39,035	
TOTAL		173,732†	449,964	

Demography

Population (1986): 8,361,000.
Density (1986)‡: persons per sq mi 52.5, persons per sq km 20.3.
Urban–rural (1985): urban 85.5%; rural 14.5%.
Sex distribution (1986): male 49.38%; female 50.62%.
Age breakdown (1985): under 15, 18.2%; 15–29, 20.7%; 30–44, 22.0%; 45–59, 16.1%; 60–74, 15.7%; 75 and over, 7.3%.
Population projection: (1990) 8,344,500; (2000) 8,328,600.
Ethnic composition (1985): Swedish 91.2%; Finnish 3.2%; other 5.6%.
Religious affiliation (1984): Church of Sweden 90.4% (nominally; about 30% nonpracticing); Roman Catholic 1.4%; other 8.2%.
Major cities (1986): Stockholm 659,030; Göteborg 425,495; Malmö 229,936; Uppsala 154,859; Norrköping 118,567.

Vital statistics

Birth rate per 1,000 population (1986): 11.8 (world avg. 29.0); (1984) legitimate 56.4%; illegitimate 43.6%.
Death rate per 1,000 population (1986): 11.3 (world avg. 11.0).
Natural increase rate per 1,000 population (1986): 0.5 (world avg. 18.0).
Total fertility rate (avg. births per childbearing woman; 1984): 1.6.
Marriage rate per 1,000 population (1986): 4.6.
Divorce rate per 1,000 population (1986): 2.4.
Life expectancy at birth (1983): male 73.1 years; female 79.1 years.
Major causes of death per 100,000 population (1983): heart disease 432.8; malignant neoplasms (cancers) 227.3; cerebrovascular disease 111.0.

National economy

Budget (1985–86). Revenue: SKr 261,952,800,000 (value-added tax 22.3%, income and capital gains taxes 21.0%, social security contributions 20.9%, nontax revenue 11.3%). Expenditures: SKr 323,389,000,000 (health and social affairs 24.5%, interest on national debt 23.9%, education and culture 11.8%, defense 7.8%, manpower 5.5%).
Public debt (1984): U.S.$64,629,000,000.
Tourism (1984): receipts from visitors U.S.$1,128,000,000; expenditures by nationals abroad U.S.$1,709,000,000.
Production (metric tons except as noted). Agriculture, forestry, fishing (1984): barley 2,733,000, sugar beets 2,508,000, oats 1,904,000, wheat 1,776,000, potatoes 1,307,000; livestock (number of live animals) 1,875,000 cattle, 2,670,000 pigs, 440,000 sheep; roundwood 24,800,000 cu m; fish catch 259,300, of which Baltic herring 120,900. Mining and quarrying (1985): iron ore 21,738,000, zinc 388,000§, copper 378,000§, lead 113,000§. Manufacturing (1984): crude and manufactured steel 9,176,000; paper and paperboard 6,869,000; cement 2,319,000; wood pulp 2,264,000; automobiles 314,600 vehicles. Construction (1985): 32,925 dwellings completed. Energy production (consumption): electricity (kW-hr; 1984) 119,589,000,000 (120,005,000,000); coal (metric tons; 1984) 13,000 (3,592,000); crude petroleum (barrels; 1984) 95,000 (104,800,000); petroleum products (metric tons; 1984) 13,950,000 (14,937,000); natural gas, n.a. (n.a.).
Gross national product (1984): U.S.$99,060,000,000 (U.S.$11,880 per capita).

Structure of gross domestic product and labour force

	1983		1984	
	in value SKr '000,000	% of total value	labour force	% of labour force
Agriculture	21,374	3.0	218,000	5.0
Mining	3,287	0.5	15,000	0.3
Manufacturing	146,891	20.8	953,000	21.7
Construction	46,708	6.6	260,000	5.9
Public utilities	18,520	2.6	40,000	0.9
Transportation and communication	40,764	5.8	294,000	6.7
Trade	75,189	10.7	586,000	13.3
Finance	81,550	11.6	316,000	7.2
Pub. admin., defense	153,438	21.8 }	1,574,000	35.8
Services	27,237	3.9 }		
Other	89,516	12.7	136,000 ‖	3.1
TOTAL	704,474	100.0	4,392,000	100.0†

Population economically active (1984): total 4,392,000; activity rate of total population 52.6% (participation rates: ages 15–64, 82.0%; female 46.9%; unemployed 3.1%).

Price and earnings indexes (1980 = 100)

	1980	1981	1982	1983	1984	1985	1986¶
Consumer price index	100.0	112.1	121.7	132.6	143.2	153.8	159.9
Hourly earnings index	100.0	110.2	118.2	127.4	141.2	154.1	...

Household income and expenditure. Average household size (1980) 2.4; income per household (1983) SKr 98,400 (U.S.$15,165); sources of income (1982): wages and salaries 62.1%; transfer payments 21.1%, of which social security 14.8%, self-employed 17.1%, other 31.1%; expenditure (1984): housing 33.3%, food 26.1%, transportation 15.8%, recreation 9.7%.
Land use (1983): forested 64.2%; meadows and pastures 1.7%; agricultural and under permanent cultivation 7.2%; other 26.9%.

Foreign trade

Balance of trade (current prices)

	1980	1981	1982	1983	1984	1985
SKr '000,000	−10,700	−1,160	−5,800	10,150	24,710	16,080
% of total	3.9%	0.4%	1.7%	2.5%	5.4%	3.2%

Imports (1985): SKr 244,380,000,000 (machinery and transport equipment 32.7%, of which transport equipment 8.7%, electrical machinery 8.4%; chemicals 9.5%; food and tobacco products 6.1%; clothing and footwear 4.8%). *Major import sources:* West Germany 17.8%; United Kingdom 14.1%; United States 8.4%; Denmark 6.8%; Finland 6.5%; Norway 6.0%.
Exports (1985): SKr 260,460,000,000 (machinery and transport equipment 41.7%, of which transport equipment 15.8%, electrical machinery 8.0%; paper products 9.7%; wood and wood pulp 7.4%; iron and steel products 6.6%; chemicals 6.2%). *Major export destinations:* United States 11.6%; West Germany 11.5%; Norway 10.4%; United Kingdom 9.9%; Denmark 8.2%.

Transport and communications

Transport. Railroads (1984): length 7,496 mi, 12,063 km; passenger-mi 4,040,000, passenger-km 6,501,000; short ton-mi cargo 11,988,000, metric ton-km cargo 17,503,000. Roads (1985): total length 108,300 mi, 174,291 km (paved 68%). Vehicles (1984): passenger cars 3,081,000; trucks and buses 223,590. Merchant marine (1985): vessels (100 gross tons and over) 694; total deadweight tonnage 4,230,771. Air transport (1985): passenger-mi 3,155,000,000, passenger-km 5,078,000,000; short ton-mi cargo 130,257,000, metric ton-km cargo 190,172,000; airports (1986) 36.
Communications. Daily newspapers (1984): total number 169; total circulation 4,782,100; circulation per 1,000 population 574. Radio (1984): 3,327,000 receivers (1 per 2.5 persons). Television (1984): 3,251,000 receivers (1 per 2.6 persons). Telephones (1984): 7,410,000 (1 per 1.1 persons).

Education and health

Education (1983–84)

	schools	teachers	students	student/ teacher ratio
Primary (age 7–12)	5,346♀	123,206♀	647,557	...
Secondary (age 13–18)	♀	♀	604,067	...
Higher	...	17,608	223,255	...

Educational attainment (1979). Percent of adult population over age 24 having: lower secondary education 7.3%; higher secondary 35.7%; some post-secondary 15.4%. *Literacy* (1985): virtually 100%.
Health (1983): physicians 19,300 (1 per 432 persons); hospital beds 116,688 (1 per 71 persons); infant mortality rate per 1,000 live births (1984) 6.4.
Food (1984): daily per capita caloric intake 3,000 (vegetable products 65%, animal products 35%); 112% of FAO recommended minimum requirement.

Military

Total active duty personnel (1985): 65,650 (army 71.6%, navy 14.7%, air force 13.7%). *Military expenditure as percent of GNP* (1984): 2.2% (world 6.1%); per capita expenditure U.S.$235.

*January 1. †Detail does not add to total given because of rounding ‡Density based on land area only. §Ore concentrates. ‖ Unemployed only. ¶August. ♀Primary includes secondary.

Switzerland

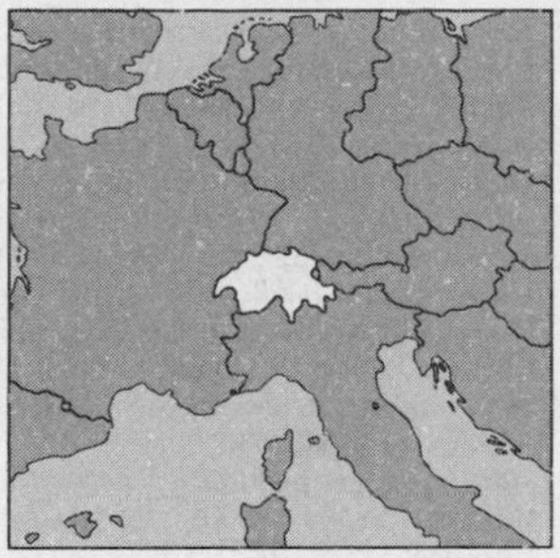

Official name: Confédération Suisse (French); Schweizerische Eidgenossenschaft (German); Confederazione Svizzera (Italian) (Swiss Confederation).
Form of government: federal state with two legislative houses (Council of States [46]; National Council [200]).
Head of state and government: President.
Capital: Bern.
Official languages: French; German; Italian.
Official religion: none.
Monetary unit: 1 Swiss Franc (Sw F) = 100 centimes; valuation (Oct. 1, 1986) 1 U.S.$ = Sw F 1.65; 1 £ = Sw F 2.38.

Area and population

		area		population
Cantons	Capitals	sq mi	sq km	1986 estimate*
Aargau	Aarau	542	1,405	468,200
Appenzell Ausser-Rhoden†	Herisau	94	243	49,100
Appenzell Inner-Rhoden†	Appenzell	66	172	13,100
Basel-Landschaft†	Liestal	165	428	225,000
Basel-Stadt†	Basel	14	37	195,900
Bern	Bern	2,335	6,049	922,900
Fribourg	Fribourg	645	1,670	192,400
Genève	Geneva	109	282	362,100
Glarus	Glarus	264	684	36,400
Graubünden	Chur	2,744	7,106	165,600
Jura	Delémont	323	837	64,600
Luzern	Luzern	576	1,492	303,900
Neuchâtel	Neuchâtel	308	797	154,900
Nidwalden†	Stans	107	276	30,600
Obwalden†	Sarnen	189	491	27,300
Sankt Gallen	Sankt Gallen	778	2,014	401,200
Schaffhausen	Schaffhausen	115	298	69,600
Schwyz	Schwyz	351	908	102,100
Solothurn	Solothurn	305	791	218,700
Thurgau	Frauenfeld	391	1,013	190,700
Ticino	Bellinzona	1,085	2,811	275,300
Uri	Altdorf	416	1,076	33,500
Valais	Sion	2,018	5,226	229,500
Vaud	Lausanne	1,243	3,219	543,700
Zug	Zug	92	239	80,300
Zürich	Zürich	668	1,729	1,128,200
TOTAL		15,943	41,293	6,484,800‡

Demography

Population (1986): 6,556,000.
Density (1986): persons per sq mi 411.2, persons per sq km 158.8.
Urban–rural (1985): urban 60.4%; rural 39.6%.
Sex distribution (1985): male 48.72%; female 51.28%.
Age breakdown (1985): under 15, 17.8%; 15–29, 23.2%; 30–44, 22.5%; 45–59, 17.5%; 60–74, 12.8%; 75 and over, 6.2%.
Population projection: (1990) 6,660,000; (2000) 6,870,000.
Ethnolinguistic composition (1980)‡: German 65.0%; French 18.4%; Italian 9.8%; Spanish 1.6%; Romansch 0.8%; Turkish 0.6%; other 3.8%.
Religious affiliation (1980): Rom. Cath. 47.6%; Protestant 44.3%; other 8.1%.
Major cities (1986): Zürich 351,500; Basel 174,600; Geneva 159,900.

Vital statistics

Birth rate per 1,000 population (1985): 13.2 (world avg. 29.0); (1983) legitimate 94.3%; illegitimate 5.7%.
Death rate per 1,000 population (1985): 9.7 (world avg. 11.0).
Natural increase rate per 1,000 population (1985): 3.5 (world avg. 18.0).
Total fertility rate (avg. births per childbearing woman; 1984): 1.8.
Marriage rate per 1,000 population (1984): 5.9.
Divorce rate per 1,000 population (1984): 1.7.
Life expectancy at birth (1981–82): male 72.7 years; female 79.6 years.
Major causes of death per 100,000 population (1983): circulatory system diseases 371.0; malignant neoplasms (cancers) 225.3.

National economy

Budget (1984). Revenue: Sw F 21,196,300,000 (taxes on consumption 53.1%, of which turnover tax 30.3%, customs duties 16.0%; taxes on income and wealth 39.8%). Expenditures: Sw F 21,643,800,000 (social security 21.9%; defense 21.2%; communications and energy 14.9%; education 8.2%).
Public debt (1983): U.S.$12,028,500,000.
Tourism (1984): receipts from visitors U.S.$3,163,000,000; expenditures by nationals abroad U.S.$2,282,000,000.
Production (metric tons except as noted). Agriculture, forestry, fishing (1984): potatoes 944,000, sugar beets 860,000, wheat 577,000, apples 360,000, barley 311,000, grapes 153,000; livestock (number of live animals; 1985) 1,998,000 pigs, 1,926,000 cattle, 357,000 sheep; roundwood (1985) 4,561,000 cu m; fish catch 3,917§. Mining and quarrying (1984): salt 300,000; gypsum 75,000. Manufacturing (1983): cement 4,116,000; wine 3,554,000; soaps and detergents 149,000; aluminum 76,000; chocolate 61,000; woolen carpets 15,000,000 sq m; 16,500,000 watches; 1,600,000 clocks. Construction (buildings completed; 1982): residential 17,678; nonresidential 9,058. Energy production (consumption) ‖: electricity (kW-hr; 1984) 48,141,000,000 (43,446,000,000); coal (metric tons; 1984) none (712,000); crude petroleum (barrels; 1984) none (29,173,000); petroleum products (metric tons; 1984) 4,075,000 (10,697,000); natural gas (cu m; 1984) none (1,443,390,000).
Gross national product (at current market prices; 1984): U.S.$105,060,000,000 (U.S.$16,150 per capita).

Gross domestic product and structure of labour force

	1984			
	in value Sw F '000	% of total value	labour force	% of labour force
Agriculture	...	...	210,700	6.7
Mining	...	...	937,900	29.8
Manufacturing	...	...		
Construction	...	...	223,700	7.1
Public utilities	...	...	29,300	0.9
Transp. and commun.	...	...	194,700	6.2
Trade	...	...	589,300	18.8
Finance	...	...	161,700	5.2
Pub. admin., defense	...	...	266,100	8.5
Services	...	...	528,700	16.8
TOTAL	214,085,000	100.0	3,142,100	100.0

Population economically active (1984): total 3,142,100; activity rate of total population 48.1% (participation rates: over age 14, 58.9%; female 36.9%; unemployed 1.1%).

Price and earnings indexes (1980 = 100)

	1979	1980	1981	1982	1983	1984	1985
Consumer price index	96.1	100.0	106.5	112.5	115.9	119.3	123.4
Hourly earnings index	94.6	100.0	102.4	109.0	113.1	...	...

Household income and expenditure (1982). Average household size 2.5¶; average income per household Sw F 61,000 (U.S.$30,045); sources of income: wages and salaries 64.7%, self-employment 15.9%, social security 11.3%; expenditure: food and beverages 27.7%, housing 24.9%, transportation and communication 11.6%, recreation and education 9.2%, health 8.2%.
Land use (1983): forested 26.4%; meadows and pastures 40.5%; agricultural and under permanent cultivation 10.4%; other 22.7%.

Foreign trade

Balance of trade (current prices)

	1980	1981	1982	1983	1984	1985
Sw F '000,000	−11,251	−7,272	−5,401	−7,341	−8,370	−8,099
% of total	10.2%	6.4%	4.9%	6.4%	6.4%	5.7%

Imports (1984): Sw F 69,024,400,000 (machinery and transport equipment 24.2%, chemical products 11.4%, mineral fuels 9.5%, precious metals and jewelry 9.5%. clothing and textiles 8.3%). *Major import sources:* West Germany 29.2%; France 11.0%; Italy 9.9%; United Kingdom 7.2%; United States 6.6%; The Netherlands 4.4%.
Exports (1984): Sw F 60,654,100,000 (nonelectrical machinery 18.2%, electrical machinery 10.6%, precious-metal articles and jewelry 10.2%, pharmaceuticals 7.6%, watches 6.3%). *Major export destinations:* West Germany 19.5%; United States 9.8%; France 8.3%; United Kingdom 8.0%; Italy 7.4%.

Transport and communications

Transport. Railroads (1984): length§ 3,105 mi, 4,997 km; passenger-mi 5,845,000,000, passenger-km 9,408,000,000; short ton-mi cargo 4,825,000,000, metric ton-km cargo 7,044,000,000♀. Roads (1983): total length 42,740 mi, 68,784 km. Vehicles (1984): passenger cars 2,552,132; trucks and buses 203,561. Merchant marine (1985): vessels (100 gross tons and over) 33; total deadweight tonnage 535,810. Air transport (1984): passenger-mi 7,494,000,000, passenger-km 12,060,000,000; short ton-mi cargo 465,920,000, metric ton-km cargo 680,232,000; airports (1986) with scheduled flights 5.
Communications. Daily newspapers (1985): total number 101; total circulation 3,207,584; circulation per 1,000 population 491. Radio (1985): 2,467,733 receivers (1 per 2.7 persons). Television (1985): 2,179,792 receivers (1 per 3.0 persons). Telephones (1983): 4,954,828 (1 per 1.3 persons).

Education and health

Education (1985–86)

	schools	teachers	students	student/ teacher ratio
Primary (age 6–11)	...	...	408,800	...
Secondary (age 11–18)	...	...	382,500	...
Voc., teacher tr.	...	...	252,100	...
Higher	...	...	110,100	...

Educational attainment (1970). Percent of population over age 12 having: no formal schooling 0.4%; primary education 73.5%; secondary 7.2%; some postsecondary 10.3%; university degree 2.6%. *Literacy:* virtually 100.0%.
Health (1984): physicians 14,712 (1 per 442 persons); hospital beds 66,192 (1 per 98 persons); infant mortality rate per 1,000 live births 7.6.
Food (1980–82): daily per capita caloric intake 3,465 (vegetable products 61%, animal products 39%); 129% of FAO recommended minimum.

Military

Total active duty personnel♂ (1985): 625,000 (army 92.8%, air force 7.2%).
Military expenditure as percent of GNP (1984): 2.2% (world 6.1%); per capita expenditure U.S.$301.

*January 1. †Demicanton; functions as a full canton and has the same legal prerogatives as a full canton. ‡Includes 960,674 resident aliens, but excludes seasonal workers. §1983. ‖ Figures include Liechtenstein. ¶1981. ♀Federal railway only. ♂Mobilized personnel.

Syria

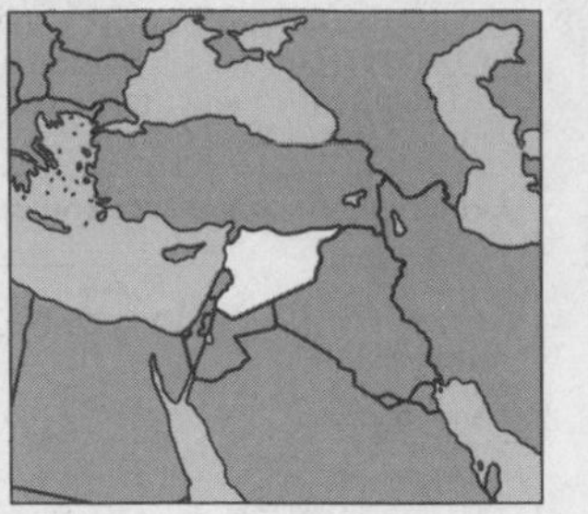

Official name: al-Jumhūrīyah al-'Arabīyah as-Sūrīyah (Syrian Arab Republic).
Form of government: unitary multiparty* republic with one legislative house (People's Council [195]).
Chief of state: President.
Head of government: Prime Minister.
Capital: Damascus.
Official language: Arabic.
Official religion: none.†
Monetary unit: 1 Syrian Pound (LS) = 100 piastres; valuation (Oct. 1, 1986) 1 U.S.$ = LS 3.93; 1£ = LS 5.67.

Area and population

		area		population
Governorates	Capitals	sq mi	sq km	1986 estimate
Dar'ā	Dar'ā	1,440	3,730	442,000
Dayr az-Zawr	Dayr az-Zawr	12,765	33,060	472,000
Dimashq	al-Iarmouk	6,962	18,032	1,088,000
Ḥalab	Aleppo	7,143	18,500	2,196,000
Ḥamāh	Ḥamāh	3,430	8,883	862,000
al-Ḥasakah	al-Ḥasakah	9,009	23,334	784,000
Ḥimṣ	Homs	16,302	42,223	971,000
Idlib	Idlib	2,354	6,097	695,000
al-Lādhiqīyah	Latakia	887	2,297	647,000
al-Qunayṭirah	al-Qunayṭirah	719‡	1,861‡	32,000
ar-Raqqah	ar-Raqqah	7,574	19,616	408,000
as-Suwaydā'	as-Suwaydā'	2,143	5,550	232,000
Ṭarṭūs	Tartous	730	1,892	524,000
Municipality				
Dimashq	Damascus	41	105	1,259,000
TOTAL		71,498‡	185,180‡	10,612,000

Demography

Population (1986): 10,612,000.
Density (1986): persons per sq mi 148.4, persons per sq km 57.3.
Urban-rural (1986): urban 49.1%; rural 50.9%.
Sex distribution (1986): male 51.07%; female 48.93%.
Age breakdown (1986): under 15, 49.3%; 15–29, 22.4%; 30–44, 14.3%; 45–59, 7.5%; 60–74, 4.8%; 75 and over, 1.7%.
Population projection: (1990) 12,774,000; (2000) 17,085,000.
Doubling time: 20 years.
Ethnic composition (1981): Arab 88.8%; Kurdish 6.3%; other 4.9%.
Religious affiliation (1980): Muslim (mostly Sunnī) 89.6%; Christian 8.9%; other 1.5%.
Major cities (1984): Damascus 1,178,000; Aleppo 1,109,100; Homs 406,300; Latakia 222,500; Ḥamāh 190,000.

Vital statistics

Birth rate per 1,000 population (1984): 43.0 (world avg. 29.0).
Death rate per 1,000 population (1984): 8.3 (world avg. 11.0).
Natural increase rate per 1,000 population (1984): 34.7 (world avg. 18.0).
Total fertility rate (avg. births per childbearing woman; 1980–85): 7.2.
Marriage rate per 1,000 population (1984): 8.2§.
Divorce rate per 1,000 population (1984): 0.6§.
Life expectancy at birth (1984): male 63.3 years; female 67.0 years.
Major causes of death per 100,000 population (1981): signs, symptoms, and ill-defined conditions 207.3; diseases of the circulatory system 60.7; infectious and parasitic diseases 15.1.

National economy

Budget (1985). Revenue: LS 42,984,000,000 (investment proceeds 61.1%, taxes and duties 27.4%). Expenditures: LS 42,984,000,000 (defense 30.2%, education 7.9%, national security 1.2%).
Public debt (external, outstanding; 1984): U.S.$2,453,300,000.
Tourism (1984): receipts from visitors U.S.$130,000,000; expenditures by nationals abroad U.S.$282,000,000.
Gross national product (at current market prices; 1984): U.S.$18,540,000,000 (U.S.$1,870 per capita).

Structure of gross domestic product and labour force

	1984			
	in value LS '000,000	% of total value	labour force	% of labour force
Agriculture	14,920	19.9	1,064,331	44.7
Mining	6,062	8.1	18,216	0.8
Manufacturing	6,511	8.7	280,103	11.8
Construction	4,949	6.6	219,680	9.2
Public utilities	213	0.3	6,829	0.3
Transportation and communication	6,209	8.2	110,645	4.6
Trade	17,529	23.3	248,281	10.4
Finance			21,373	0.9
Pub. admin., services	18,733	24.9	345,058	14.5
Other			67,270 ‖	2.8 ‖
TOTAL	75,126	100.0	2,381,786	100.0

Production (metric tons except as noted). Agriculture, forestry, fishing (1984): wheat 1,051,000, sugar beets 900,000, watermelons 850,000, tomatoes 740,000, grapes 440,000, olives 370,000, barley 302,000, potatoes 280,000, cucumbers 280,000, melons 280,000, cotton 160,000; livestock (number of live animals) 14,000,000 sheep, 1,000,000 goats, 770,000 cattle; roundwood 44,000 cu m; fish catch (1983) 3,777. Mining and quarrying (1984): phosphate rock 1,515,000; asphalt 52,000; salt 38,000; sand and gravel 14,283,000 cu m; stone 496,000 cu m; gypsum 191,000 cu m. Manufacturing (market value in LS; 1984): textiles 2,011,233; cement 1,376,202; chemical products 1,208,685; sugar 1,024,485. Construction (1984): residential 3,901,000 sq m; nonresidential 686,000 sq m. Energy production (consumption): electricity (kW-hr; 1984) 6,757,000,000 (6,622,000,000); coal (metric tons; 1984) none (2,000); crude petroleum (barrels; 1984) 66,145,000 (66,111,000); petroleum products (metric tons; 1984) 8,199,000 (6,058,000); natural gas (cu m; 1984) 64,068,000 (64,068,000).
Population economically active (1984): total 2,381,786; activity rate of total population 23.6% (participation rates: over age 15, 46.5%; female 9.8%; unemployed [1983] 5.1%).

Price and earnings indexes (1980 = 100)

	1978	1979	1980	1981	1982	1983	1984
Consumer price index	80.2	84.1	100.0	118.4	135.3	143.4	157.2
Annual earnings index¶	...	...	100.0	123.4	153.3	173.2	180.6

Average household size (1984): 6.4.
Land use (1983): steppe and pasture 45.6%; cultivable 30.5%; forested 2.7%; other 21.2%.

Foreign trade

Balance of trade (current prices)

	1979	1980	1981	1982	1983	1984
LS '000,000	−5,590	−6,647	−9,977	−6,569	−10,281	−8,879
% of total	30.2%	28.7%	37.7%	29.2%	40.5%	37.9%

Imports (1984): LS 16,153,708 (mineral fuels and related materials 34.3%; machinery and transport equipment 19.1%; foods, beverages, and tobacco 18.1%; chemical and pharmaceutical products 7.4%; metals and metal manufactures 1.8%). *Major import sources:* Iran 22.7%; Libya 7.7%; West Germany 5.9%; France 5.1%; Italy 4.8%; Japan 4.6%.
Exports (1984): LS 7,274,793 (petroleum and petroleum products 63.1%; textiles, wearing apparel, and leather 16.1%; food and live animals 5.4%). *Major export destinations:* Romania 28.2%; Italy 19.8%; France 12.1%; U.S.S.R. 11.5%; Iran 2.3%.

Transport and communications

Transport. Railroads (1984): route length 1,250 mi, 2,013 km; passenger-mi 464,000,000, passenger-km 746,000,000; short ton-mi cargo 661,888,000, metric ton-km cargo 966,340,000. Roads (1983): total length 14,062 mi, 22,632 km (paved 93%). Vehicles (1984): passenger cars 114,303; trucks and buses 85,544. Merchant marine (1985): vessels (100 gross tons and over) 53; total deadweight tonnage 83,770. Air transport (1985): passenger-mi 585,000,000, passenger-km 942,000,000; short ton-mi cargo 10,744,000, metric ton-km cargo 15,687,000; airports (1986) with scheduled flights 5.
Communications. Daily newspapers (1985): total number 9; total circulation 186,400; circulation per 1,000 population 18.2. Radio (1985): total number of receivers 1,802,000 (1 per 5.7 persons). Television (1985): total number of receivers 400,000 (1 per 25.7 persons). Telephones (1984): 474,298 (1 per 20.9 persons).

Education and health

Education (1983–84)

	schools	teachers	students	student/ teacher ratio
Primary (age 6–11)	8,489	67,086	1,823,684	27.2
Secondary (age 12–18)	1,598	26,366	701,330	26.6
Voc., teacher tr.	138	5,447	64,596	11.9
Higher	41	...	123,735	...

Educational attainment (1976). Percent of population having: no schooling 40.0%; knowledge of reading and writing 27.4%; primary education 18.1%; secondary 13.1%; higher 1.4%. *Literacy* (1984): total population over age 15 literate 2,284,264 (44.6%); males literate 1,661,453 (64.8%); females literate 622,811 (24.3%).
Health (1984): physicians 5,543 (1 per 1,792 persons); hospital beds 11,595 (1 per 857 persons); infant mortality rate per 1,000 live births (1980–85) 57.0.
Food (1980–82): daily per capita caloric intake 3,032 (vegetable products 86%, animal products 14%); 122% of FAO recommended minimum requirement.

Military

Total active duty personnel (1985): 402,500 (army 67.1%, navy 0.6%, air force 17.4%; forces abroad 7.7%, frontier force 0.5%, Palestine Liberation army 1.1%, paramilitary 5.6%). *Military expenditure as percent of GNP* (1983): 13.0% (world 6.1%); per capita expenditure U.S.$209.

*Parties other than the Communist Party form a coalition (National Progressive Front). †Islam is required to be the religion of the head of state and is the basis of the legal system. ‡Includes territory in the Golan Heights recognized internationally as part of Syria (located between the 1949 Israel–Syria Armistice line [west] and the 1974 UN Disengagement of Forces zone [east]) that has been occupied by Israel since 1967. Israel's unilateral annexation of this territory in December 1981 has received no international recognition. §Syrian Arabs only. ‖Seeking work for the first time. ¶Public sector only.

Taiwan

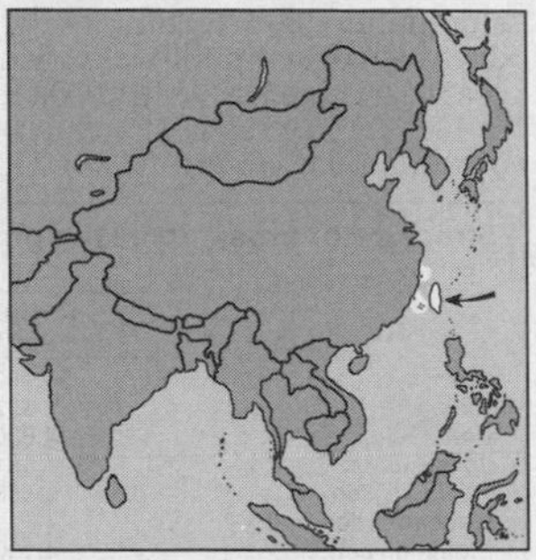

Official name: Chung-hua Min-kuo (Republic of China).
Form of government: unitary republic with a National Assembly (1,173).
Chief of state: President.
Head of government: Premier.
Capital: Taipei.
Official language: Mandarin Chinese.
Official religion: none.
Monetary unit: 1 New Taiwan dollar (NT$) = 100 cents; valuation (Oct. 1, 1986) 1 U.S.$ = NT$36.71; 1£ = NT$53.05.

Area and population

		area		population
				1986
Counties	Capitals	sq mi	sq km	estimate*
Chang-hua	Chang-hua	415	1,074	1,224,388
Chia-i	Chia-i	734	1,902	567,920
Hsin-chu	Hsin-chu	551	1,428	366,882
Hua-lien	Hua-lien	1,787	4,629	361,200
I-lan	I-lan	825	2,137	450,050
Kao-hsiung	Feng-shan	1,078	2,793	1,077,086
Miao-li	Miao-li	703	1,820	549,965
Nan-t'ou	Nan-t'ou	1,585	4,106	535,591
P'eng-hu	Ma-kung	49	127	101,981
P'ing-tung	P'ing-tung	1,072	2,776	901,035
T'ai-chung	Feng-yuan	792	2,051	1,149,785
T'ai-nan	Hsin-ying	778	2,016	1,003,744
T'ai-pei	Pan-ch'iao	792	2,052	2,687,949
T'ai-tung	T'ai-tung	1,357	3,515	274,915
T'ao-yüan	T'ao-yüan	471	1,221	1,219,979
Yün-lin	Tou-liu	498	1,291	788,647
Municipalities				
Chia-i	—	23	60	253,893
Chi-lung	—	51	133	351,089
Hsin-chu	—	40	104	304,660
Kao-hsiung	—	59	154	1,309,348
T'ai-chung	—	63	163	682,990
T'ai-nan	—	68	176	642,295
Taipei	—	105	272	2,534,423
TOTAL		13,900†	36,000	19,339,815

Demography

Population (1986): 19,408,000.
Density (1986): persons per sq mi 1,396.3, persons per sq km 539.1.
Urban–rural (1984): urban 71.6%; rural 28.4%.
Sex distribution (1986): male 51.88%; female 48.12%.
Age breakdown (1985): under 15, 29.6%; 15–29, 30.1%; 30–44, 19.5%; 45–59, 12.6%; 60–74, 6.8%; 75 and over, 1.4%.
Population projection: (1990) 20,518,000; (2000) 23,578,000.
Doubling time: 54 years.
Ethnic composition (1986): Taiwanese 84.0%; mainland Chinese 14.0%; aborigine 2.0%.
Religious affiliation (1980): Chinese folk-religionist 48.5%; Buddhist 43.0%; Christian 7.4%; Muslim 0.5%; other 0.6%.
Major cities (1986): Taipei 2,534,423; Kao-hsiung 1,309,348; T'ai-chung 682,990; T'ai-nan 642,295; Chi-lung 351,089; Hsin-Chu 304,660.

Vital statistics

Birth rate per 1,000 population (1985): 18.0 (world avg. 29.0).
Death rate per 1,000 population (1985): 4.8 (world avg. 11.0).
Natural increase rate per 1,000 population (1985): 13.2 (world avg. 18.0).
Total fertility rate (avg. births per childbearing woman; 1984): 2.3.
Marriage rate per 1,000 population (1985): 8.0.
Divorce rate per 1,000 population (1985): 1.1.
Life expectancy at birth (1984): male 70.5 years; female 75.5 years.
Major causes of death per 100,000 population (1984): cardiovascular diseases 141.9; malignant neoplasms (cancers) 82.0; respiratory diseases 35.6.

National economy

Budget (1984). Revenue: NT$552,649,000,000 (taxes 67.3%, of which income taxes 20.0%; customs duties 18.3%). Expenditures: NT$539,053,000,000 (defense 47.9%; general administration 16.2%; economy 14.3%; social welfare and health 14.0%; education 5.7%).
Tourism (1984): receipts from visitors U.S.$1,066,000,000; expenditures by nationals abroad, n.a.
Production (metric tons except as noted). Agriculture, forestry, fishing (1985): sugarcane 6,823,094, vegetables 3,243,364, rice 2,173,536, citrus fruits 418,864, sweet potatoes 369,461, corn (maize) 226,010, bananas 198,596, pineapple 149,745, peanuts 89,105; livestock (number of live animals; 1984) 5,888,198 pigs, 196,987 goats and sheep, 129,852 cattle; timber 474,584 cu m; fish catch 1,037,721. Mining and quarrying (1984): silver 10,739 kilograms; gold 1,629 kilograms. Manufacturing (1985): cement 14,417,700; crude steel 1,642,000; paperboard 1,487,400; man-made fibre 1,028,700; fertilizers 888,500; sulfuric acid 733,000; plastics and resins 674,000; cotton yarn 544,000; electronic calculators 48,194,071 units; audio recorders 16,127,903 units. Construction (1985): total residential and nonresidential 28,113,000 sq m. Energy production (consumption): electricity (kW-hr; 1985) 52,553,000,000 (33,802,275,000‡); coal (metric tons; 1985) 1,857,858 (2,013,458§); petroleum (barrels; 1985) 743,187 (n.a.); natural gas (cu m; 1985) 1,125,050,000 (n.a.).
Public debt (domestic and foreign; 1984): U.S.$1,139,000,000 ‖.
Gross national product (1985): U.S.$60,078,000,000 (U.S.$3,180 per capita).

Structure of gross domestic product and labour force

	1985			
	in value NT$'000,000	% of total value	labour force	% of labour force
Agriculture	140,837	6.0	1,297,000	16.9
Mining	14,353	0.6	35,000	0.5
Manufacturing	960,229	40.7	2,488,000	32.5
Construction	99,133	4.2	521,000	6.8
Public utilities	97,727	4.1	34,000	0.4
Transp. and commun.	144,569	6.1	388,000	5.1
Trade	328,011	13.9	1,336,000	17.5
Finance	223,285	9.5	190,000	2.5
Pub. admin., defense	242,942	10.3	1,141,000	14.9
Services	163,091	6.9		
Other	−57,443¶	−2.4¶	222,000	2.9
TOTAL	2,356,734	100.0†	7,652,000	100.0

Population economically active (1985): total 7,652,000; activity rate of total population 40.0% (participation rates: over age 15, 59.5%; female 43.5%; unemployed 2.9%).

Price and earnings indexes (1981 = 100)

	1979	1980	1981	1982	1983	1984	1985
Consumer price index	72.2	86.0	100.0	103.0	104.4	104.3	104.2
Monthly earnings index	68.7	84.2	100.0	109.7	116.6	134.6	132.1

Household income and expenditure. Average household size (1985) 4.5; income per household NT$38,459 (U.S.$966); sources of income (1984): mixed entrepreneurial and property income 26.2%, transfer payments 25.3%, mixed wages and entrepreneurial income 24.2%, wages and salaries 17.7%, entrepreneurial income 6.5%; expenditure (1985): food 32.7%, housing 28.5%, recreation and education 7.9%, transportation 6.7%, clothing and footwear 6.6%, household equipment and operation 6.2%, health 3.4%.
Land use (1980): forested 55.0%; agricultural and under permanent cultivation 25.2%; other 19.8%.

Foreign trade

Balance of trade (current prices)

	1979	1980	1981	1982	1983	1984	1985
NT$'000,000	46,371	762	51,123	128,164	191,518	333,836	421,057
% of total	4.2%	0.1%	3.2%	8.0%	10.5%	16.1%	20.8%

Imports (1985): NT$801,847,000,000 (petroleum and petroleum products 17.1%; electronic components 5.3%; unmilled grains 3.0%; iron and steel 2.8%; nonelectrical machinery 2.3%; telecommunication equipment 2.0%). *Major import sources:* Japan 27.6%; United States 23.6%; Saudi Arabia 6.8%; West Germany 4.2%; Australia 4.0%; Kuwait 3.3%.
Exports (1985): NT$1,222,904,000,000 (electronic products and appliances 10.9%; articles of apparel and clothing 9.8%; textile yarns and fabrics 5.8%; articles of plastic 5.6%; processed food 1.9%; dolls and toys 1.9%). *Major export destinations:* United States 48.1%; Japan 11.3%; Hong Kong 8.3%.

Transport and communications

Transport. Railroads (1985): length 4,900 km; passenger-km 8,309,300,000; metric ton-km cargo 2,299,800,000. Roads (1984): total length 19,306 km (paved 83%). Vehicles (1985): passenger cars 915,598; trucks and buses 429,371. Merchant marine (1985): vessels (100 gross tons and over) 583; total gross tonnage 4,327,487. Air transport (1985): passenger-km 11,246,414,000; metric ton-km cargo 1,838,986,000; airports (1986) 9.
Communications. Daily newspapers (1984): total number 31; total circulation 4,917,000; circulation per 1,000 population 259. Radio (1985): 13,500,000 receivers (1 per 1.4 persons). Television (1985): 6,080,000 receivers (1 per 3.1 persons). Telephones (1985): 4,227,992 (1 per 4.5 persons).

Education and health

Education (1985–86)

	schools	teachers	students	student/ teacher ratio
Primary (age 6–12)	2,459	71,853	2,313,240	32.2
Secondary (age 13–18)	839	60,346	1,250,840	20.7
Vocational	200	15,783	420,212	26.6
Higher	105	20,848	428,576	20.6

Educational attainment (1984). Percent of total population over age 6 having: no formal schooling 8.8%; less than primary education 18.1%; primary education 47.9%; secondary 19.9%; higher 3.1%; other 2.2%. *Literacy* (1984): total population aged 6 and over literate 15,205,733 (91.2%); males literate 8,282,417 (95.5%); females literate 6,923,316 (86.5%).
Health (1984): physicians 15,182 (1 per 1,243 persons); hospital beds 62,467 (1 per 302 persons); infant mortality rate per 1,000 live births 7.5.
Food (1983): daily per capita caloric intake 2,721 (vegetable products 77%, animal products 23%); 118% of FAO recommended minimum requirement.

Military

Total active duty personnel (1985): 471,000 (army 70.1%, navy 13.6%, air force 16.3%). *Military expenditure as percent of GNP* (1983): 7.5% (world 6.1%); per capita expenditure U.S.$209.

*As of May 1986. †Detail does not add to total given because of rounding. ‡By industry only. §1984. ‖ Based on the 1984 average exchange rate of NT$39.54 = U.S.$1.00. ¶Imputed bank service charge.

Tanzania

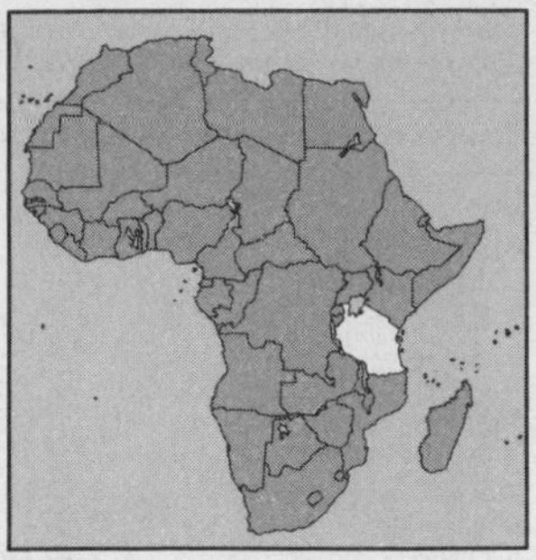

Official name: Jamhuri ya Mwungano wa Tanzania (Swahili); United Republic of Tanzania (English).
Form of government: unitary single-party republic with one legislative house (National Assembly [244]).
Chief of state: President.
Head of government: Prime Minister.
Seat of government: Dar es Salaam (Capital designate, Dodoma).
Official languages: Swahili; English.
Official religion: none.
Monetary unit: 1 Tanzanian shilling (T Sh) = 100 cents; valuation (Oct. 1, 1986) 1 U.S.$ = T Sh 44.60; 1 £ = T Sh 64.44.

Area and population

		area		population
				1985
Regions	Capitals	sq mi	sq km	estimate
Arusha	Arusha	31,698	82,098	1,183,000
Coast	Dar es Salaam	12,566	32,547	578,000
Dar es Salaam	Dar es Salaam	538	1,393	1,394,000
Dodoma	Dodoma	15,950	41,311	1,171,000
Iringa	Iringa	21,950	56,850	1,100,000
Kigoma	Kigoma	14,301	37,040	782,000
Kilimanjaro	Moshi	5,116	13,250	1,093,000
Lindi	Lindi	25,498	66,040	604,000
Mara	Musoma	8,402	21,760	862,000
Mbeya	Mbeya	23,301	60,350	1,335,000
Morogoro	Morogoro	27,268	70,624	1,134,000
Mtwara	Mtwara	6,452	16,710	878,000
Mwanza	Mwanza	7,600	19,683	1,736,000
Pemba North	Wete			
Pemba South	Chake Chake	380	984	*
Rukwa	Sumbawanga	26,500	68,635	603,000
Ruvuma	Songea	24,583	63,669	691,000
Shinyanga	Shinyanga	19,598	50,760	1,662,000
Singida	Singida	19,050	49,340	730,000
Tabora	Tabora	29,402	76,150	1,089,000
Tanga	Tanga	10,300	26,677	1,236,000
West Lake	Bukoba	10,987	28,456	1,298,000
Zanzibar North	Mkokotoni			
Zanzibar South and Central	Koani	641	1,660	571,000*
Zanzibar West	Zanzibar			
TOTAL LAND AREA		342,081	885,987	21,730,000
INLAND WATER		22,800	59,050	
TOTAL		364,881	945,037	

Demography

Population (1986): 22,463,000.
Density† (1986): persons per sq mi 63.5, persons per sq km 24.5.
Urban-rural (1983): urban 14.0%; rural 86.0%.
Sex distribution (1980): male 49.49%; female 50.51%.
Age breakdown (1980): under 15, 45.9%; 15–29, 25.3%; 30–44, 14.9%; 45–59, 8.9%; 60–74, 4.2%; 75 and over, 0.8%.
Population projection: (1990) 25,635,000; (2000) 36,008,000.
Doubling time: 21 years.
Ethnic composition (1980): Nyamwezi and Sukuma 21.2%; Swahili 8.9%; Hehet and Bena 6.7%; Makonde 6.1%; Haya 5.6%; other 51.5%.
Religious affiliation (1984): Christian 40%, of which Roman Catholic 26%; Muslim 30%; traditional beliefs and other 30%.
Major cities (1978): Dar es Salaam 900,000‡; Mwanza 110,553.

Vital statistics

Birth rate per 1,000 population (1984): 50.0 (world avg. 29.0).
Death rate per 1,000 population (1984): 16.0 (world avg. 11.0).
Natural increase rate per 1,000 population (1984): 34.0 (world avg. 18.0).
Total fertility rate (avg. births per childbearing woman; 1984): 7.0.
Marriage rate per 1,000 population (1967): 9.8.
Life expectancy at birth (1984): male 50.0 years; female 53.0 years.
Major causes of death per 100,000 population: n.a.; however, the major diseases include malaria, bilharziasis, tuberculosis, and sleeping sickness.

National economy

Budget (1985–86). Revenue: T Sh 18,031,000,000 (sales tax 54.5%, income tax 23.5%, customs and excise tax 8.3%). Expenditures: T Sh 19,908,000,000 (economic development 37.8%, public administration 23.5%, defense 18.5%, education 10.1%, health 4.9%).
Public debt (external, outstanding; 1984): U.S.$2,593,700,000.
Tourism (1984): receipts from visitors U.S.$13,000,000; expenditures by nationals abroad U.S.$12,000,000.
Production (metric tons except as noted). Agriculture (1984): cassava 5,600,000, corn (maize) 1,131,000, sweet potatoes 500,000, rice 400,000, coconuts 320,000, millet 285,000, seed cotton 140,000, unshelled peanuts (groundnuts) 59,000, chick peas 8,000, palm kernels 5,400; livestock (number of live animals) 14,500,000 cattle, 6,100,000 goats, 4,100,000 sheep, 26,000,000 chickens; roundwood 38,700,000 cu m; fish catch (1983) 272,498. Mining and quarrying (1984): diamonds 265,976 carats; phosphate minerals 14,536. Manufacturing (1984): cement 369,000; fertilizer 51,565; wheat flour 30,000; iron sheets 23,012; rolled steel 12,104§; sisal twine and ropes 11,273§; aluminum 6,000; textiles 69,194,000 sq m. Construction: n.a. Energy production (consumption): electricity (kW-hr; 1984) 870,000,000 (870,000,000); coal (metric tons; 1984) 1,000 (1,000); crude petroleum (barrels; 1984) none (4,141,000); petroleum products (metric tons; 1984) 522,000 (576,000).
Gross national product (1984): U.S.$4,460,000,000 (U.S.$210 per capita).

Structure of gross domestic product and labour force

	1984		1982	
	in value T SH '000,000	% of total value	labour force ‖	% of labour force
Agriculture	36,982	48.9	137,419	20.3
Mining	337	0.4	7,231	1.1
Manufacturing	4,630	6.1	118,234	17.5
Construction	1,551	2.1	51,377	7.6
Public utilities	553	0.7	21,460	3.2
Transportation and communication	4,100	5.4	60,166	8.9
Trade	9,127	12.1	38,030	5.6
Finance			16,900	2.5
Pub. admin., defense, Services	18,378¶	24.3¶	225,170	33.3
Other			...	...
TOTAL	75,658	100.0	676,017	100.0

Population economically active (1984): total 8,648,000; activity rate of total population 41.1% (participation rates: ages 15–64, 83.3%; female 51.4%; unemployed, n.a.).

Price and earnings indexes (1980 = 100)

	1979	1980	1981	1982	1983	1984
Consumer price index	76.8	100.0	125.6	162.0	205.8	279.5
Monthly earnings index	94.0	100.0	...	...	...	...

Household income and expenditure. Average household size (1980) 5.1; average annual income per household: n.a.; source of income: n.a.; expenditures (1981): food, beverages, and tobacco 54.1%, housing 8.6%, clothing 10.8%, energy 6.6%, transportation 6.4%.
Land use (1983): forested 47.2%; meadows and pastures 39.5%; agricultural and under permanent cultivation 5.9%; other 7.4%.

Foreign trade

Balance of trade (current prices)

	1980	1981	1982	1983	1984	1985
T Sh '000,000	−4,730.0	−4,853.0	−4,917.0	−3,384.0	−5,506.0	−10,659
% of total	36.1%	34.1%	36.8%	29.5%	32.3%	51.8%

Imports (1984): T Sh 11,267,000,000 (machinery and other industrial goods 36.4%, fuel 22.6%, consumer goods 14.3%, transport equipment 11.7%, construction materials 11.0%). *Major import sources:* United Kingdom 9.7%; Japan 9.4%; West Germany 8.2%; Italy 7.9%; United States 5.2%; Thailand 4.2%; India 3.4%; Bahrain 2.6%; China 2.1%.
Exports (1984): T Sh 5,761,000,000 (coffee beans 38.6%, cotton 12.4%, cashew nuts 7.6%, tea 5.7%, diamonds 5.7%, sisal 2.5%, cloves 2.4%, tobacco 1.9%). *Major export destinations:* West Germany 19.9%; United Kingdom 11.4%; India 7.3%; Algeria 4.7%; Japan 3.4%; Hong Kong 2.8%; United States 2.5%; France 2.4%.

Transport and communications

Transport. Railroads (1982): length 2,222 mi, 3,576 km; passenger-mi 577,000,000♀, passenger-km 929,000,000♀; short ton-mi cargo 475,000,000♀, metric ton-km cargo 694,000,000♀. Roads (1984): length 50,887 mi, 81,895 km. Vehicles (1984): cars, trucks, and buses 84,190. Merchant marine (1985): vessels (100 gross tons and over) 40; deadweight tonnage 59,048. Air transport (1985): passenger-mi 162,253,000, passenger-km 261,123,000; short ton-mi cargo 18,576,000, metric ton-km 27,122,000; airports (1986) 19.
Communications. Daily newspapers (1984): total number 3; total circulation 101,000; circulation per 1,000 population 5.0. Radio (1985): 2,000,000 receivers (1 per 11 persons). Television (1985): 10,000 receivers (1 per 2,170 persons). Telephones (1983): 99,885 (1 per 204 persons).

Education and health

Education (1981–82)

	schools	teachers	students	student/teacher ratio
Primary (age 7–13)	9,980	88,370	3,512,799	39.8
Secondary (age 14–19)	175	3,262	69,145	21.2
Voc., teacher tr.	40	744	17,914	24.1
Higher	1	893	3,780	4.2

Educational attainment (1978). Percent of population over age 10 having: no schooling 48.6%; some primary education 32.0%; completed primary 8.7%; secondary and higher 1.9%. *Literacy* (1983): 79.0%.
Health (1984): physicians 1,065 (1 per 19,775 persons); hospital beds 22,800 (1 per 924 persons); infant mortality rate per 1,000 live births 111.
Food (1980–82): daily per capita caloric intake 2,409 (vegetable products 94%, animal products 6%); 101% of FAO recommended minimum requirement.

Military

Total active duty personnel (1985): 40,350 (army 95.4%, navy 2.1%, air force 2.5%). *Military expenditure as percent of GNP* (1983): 2.5% (world 6.1%); per capita expenditure U.S.$6.

*Pemba North and Pemba South are included with Zanzibar. †Based on land areas. ‡1983. §1982. ‖ Employed persons only. ¶Includes indirect taxes, net of subsidies less imputed bank service charges. ♀For Tanzania Railways Corporation only.

Thailand

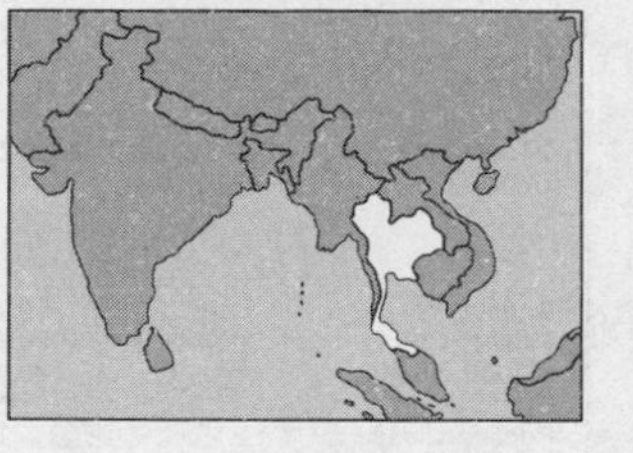

Official name: Muang Thai, or Prathet Thai (Kingdom of Thailand).
Form of government: constitutional monarchy with a multiparty National Assembly (Senate [261]; House of Representatives [347]).
Chief of state: King.
Head of government: Prime Minister.
Capital: Bangkok.
Official language: Thai.
Official religion: Buddhism.
Monetary unit: 1 Thai Baht (B) = 100 stangs; valuation (Oct. 1, 1986) 1 U.S.$ = B 26.08; 1 £ = B 37.69.

Area and population

Regions	area sq mi	area sq km	population 1984 estimate
Bangkok Metropolis	604	1,565	5,018,300
Central*	7,236	18,742	3,393,100
Eastern	14,481	37,507	3,746,000
Northeastern	65,195	168,854	17,219,300
Northern	65,500	169,644	10,106,000
Southern	27,303	70,715	6,166,100
Western	17,795	46,088	3,866,300
TOTAL	198,115†	513,115	49,515,100

Demography

Population (1986): 52,654,000.
Density (1986): persons per sq mi 265.8, persons per sq km 102.6.
Urban-rural (1985): urban 19.8%; rural 80.2%.
Sex distribution (1986): male 50.27%; female 49.73%.
Age breakdown (1984): under 15, 37.1%; 15–29, 30.5%; 30–44, 17.7%; 45–59, 9.3%; 60–69, 3.4%; 70 and over, 1.9%.†
Population projection: (1990) 56,796,000; (2000) 68,558,000.
Doubling time: 37 years.
Ethnic composition (1980): Thai 53.6%; Lao 27.6%; Chinese 10.6%; Malay 3.7%; Khmer 2.7%; other 1.8%.
Religious affiliation (1980): Buddhist 95.0%; Muslim 3.8%; Christian 0.5%; other 0.7%.
Major cities (1980): Bangkok 4,697,071; Chiang Mai 101,595; Hat Yai 93,519; Khon Kaen 85,863; Nakhon Ratchasima 78,246.

Vital statistics

Birth rate per 1,000 population (1985): 26.4 (world avg. 29.0).
Death rate per 1,000 population (1985): 7.6 (world avg. 11.0).
Natural increase rate per 1,000 population (1985): 18.8 (world avg. 18.0).
Total fertility rate (avg. births per childbearing woman; 1985): 3.2.
Marriage rate per 1,000 population (1983): 7.7.
Divorce rate per 1,000 population (1979): 0.5.
Life expectancy at birth (1985): male 61.0 years; female 66.9 years.
Major causes of death per 100,000 population (1983): accidents, poisonings, and violence 35.6; heart disease 33.8; malignant neoplasms (cancers) 27.0; tuberculosis 11.0; pneumonia 10.1; malaria 5.9.

National economy

Budget (1986–87). Revenue: B 227,500,000,000 (taxes 72.6%, of which indirect taxes 55.3%, direct taxes 17.4%; borrowing, state enterprises, and sale of assets and services 27.4%). Expenditures: B 227,500,000,000 (debt services 24.7%; education 18.1%; defense 18.0%; economic services 15.6%; public utilities and health 10.8%; internal security 4.8%; general administration 2.7%).
Public debt (external, outstanding; 1985): U.S.$9,799,900,000.
Tourism: receipts from visitors (1984) U.S.$ 1,156,000,000; expenditures by nationals abroad (1983) U.S.$344,000,000.
Production (metric tons except as noted). Agriculture, forestry, fishing (1984): sugarcane 24,894,000, rice 19,200,000, tapioca root 18,000,000, corn (maize) 4,150,000, coconuts 1,000,000, rubber 593,000, cotton 123,000, tobacco 90,000, coffee 19,000; livestock (number of live animals) 6,150,000 buffalo, 4,620,000 cattle, 4,150,000 pigs, 30,000 goats, 65,000,000 chickens; roundwood 40,857,000 cu m; fish catch (1983) 2,259,000. Mining and quarrying (1984): limestone 9,223,000; gypsum 1,110,700; fluorite 295,200; barite 174,900; iron ore 60,700; tin 22,000. Manufacturing (1984): cement 8,271,000; tin plate 92,000; detergent 91,548; cigarettes 29,200; commercial vehicles 74,910 units. Construction (value in B; 1982): residential 22,717,000,000; nonresidential 41,334,000,000. Energy production (consumption): electricity (kW-hr; 1984) 22,029,000,000 (22,717,000,000); coal (metric tons; 1984) 2,362,000 (2,522,000); crude petroleum (barrels; 1984) 5,776,000 (58,200,000); petroleum products (metric tons; 1984) 7,726,000 (11,073,000); natural gas (cu m; 1984) 2,421,279,000 (2,421,279,000).
Population economically active (1984): total 26,580,000; activity rate of total population 53.7% (participation rates: over age 15 [1982] 83.1%; female [1982] 47.1%; unemployed 5.1%).

Price and earnings indexes (1980 = 100)

	1980	1981	1982	1983	1984	1985	1986‡
Consumer price index	100.0	112.7	118.6	123.0	124.1	127.1	129.4
Monthly earnings index	...	...	...	...	...	...	...

Household income and expenditure. Average household size (1983) 5.3; median income per household (1983) B 43,476 (U.S.$1,890); sources of income (1982): interest and profits 33.8%, wages and salaries 32.6%, agriculture 20.1%, transfer payments 8.4%, property 3.2%; expenditure (1982): food 39.1%, transportation and communication 11.7%, clothing and footwear 10.2%, miscellaneous goods and services 8.6%, alcoholic beverages and tobacco 7.1%, housing 6.3%, household utilities including furniture 5.9%, medical care and health 4.7%, recreation 4.3%, education 0.5%.
Gross national product (at current market prices, 1984): U.S.$42,760,000,000 (U.S.$850 per capita).

Structure of gross domestic product and labour force

	1984		1983	
	in value B '000,000	% of total value	labour force§	% of labour force
Agriculture	193,438	19.5	17,401,300	69.1
Mining	21,291	2.2	50,700	0.2
Manufacturing	196,793	19.9	1,842,500	7.3
Construction	52,772	5.3	511,600	2.0
Public utilities	18,884	1.9	106,400	0.4
Transportation and communication	83,588	8.4	534,800	2.1
Trade	219,336	22.1	2,193,900	8.7
Finance, Pub. admin., defense, Services	205,457	20.7	2,536,600	10.1
Other			4,800	0.0
TOTAL	991,559	100.0	25,183,500†	100.0†

Land use (1983): forested 30.3%; meadows and pastures 0.6%; agricultural and under permanent cultivation 37.8%; other 31.3%.

Foreign trade‖

Balance of trade (current prices)

	1980	1981	1982	1983	1984	1985
B '000,000	−36,637	−42,090	−17,244	−66,497	−45,425	−33,285
% of total	12.1%	12.1%	5.1%	18.5%	11.5%	7.9%

Imports (1984): B 245,155,025,000 (mineral fuels and oils 23.5%, boiler machinery 13.5%, electrical machinery 8.8%, iron and steel 7.8%, motor vehicles 6.0%, organic chemicals 3.6%). *Major import sources:* Japan 26.9%; United States 13.3%; Saudi Arabia 8.5%; Singapore 7.9%; Malaysia 4.9%; West Germany 4.2%; China 3.0%; South Korea 2.8%; Taiwan 2.8%; United Kingdom 2.3%.
Exports (1984): B 175,237,200,000 (rice 14.8%, tapioca products 8.3%, rubber 7.4%, corn 5.7%, sugar and sugar products 3.5%, unwrought tin 3.1%, shrimps 1.6%). *Major export destinations:* United States 17.2%; Japan 13.0%; The Netherlands 10.0%; Singapore 8.4%; Malaysia 4.7%; Hong Kong 3.8%; West Germany 3.3%; Saudi Arabia 2.6%; China 2.5%; United Kingdom 2.2%.

Transport and communications

Transport. Railroads (1984): route length 2,321 mi, 3,735 km; passenger-mi 5,992,000,000, passenger-km 9,643,000,000; short ton-mi cargo 1,793,071,000, metric ton-km cargo 2,617,840,000. Roads (1984): total length 47,420 mi, 76,315 km (paved 39%). Vehicles (1983): passenger cars 411,982; trucks and buses 789,837. Merchant marine (1985): vessels (100 gross tons and over) 244; total deadweight tonnage 863,424. Air transport (1984): passenger-mi 5,920,000,000, passenger-km 9,528,000,000; short ton-mi cargo 285,728,000, metric ton-km cargo 417,156,000; airports (1986) with scheduled flights 9.
Communications. Daily newspapers (1985): total number 31; total circulation 2,564,500¶; circulation per 1,000 population 50. Radio (1985): total number of receivers 7,759,709 (1 per 6.7 persons). Television (1984): total number of receivers 3,000,000 (1 per 17 persons). Telephones (1983): 623,368 (1 per 79 persons).

Education and health

Education (1981)

	schools	teachers	students	student/teacher ratio
Primary (age 7–12)	33,712	333,351	7,449,219	22.3
Secondary (age 13–18)	1,437	76,339	1,572,587	20.6
Voc., teacher tr.	1,528	27,484♀	418,279	...
Higher	62	35,731	911,166	25.5

Educational attainment (1980). Percent of population over age 6 having: no formal schooling 15.8%; primary education 71.4%; secondary 9.3%; university 2.2%; other education 1.3%. *Literacy* (1980): total population over age 10 literate 29,793,848 (88.8%); males literate 15,316,986 (92.4%); females literate 14,476,862 (85.3%).
Health (1983): physicians 7,902 (1 per 6,266 persons); hospital beds 88,504 (1 per 559 persons); infant mortality rate per 1,000 live births (1985) 53.0.
Food (1980–82): daily per capita caloric intake 2,312 (vegetable products 94%, animal products 6%); 103% of FAO recommended minimum requirement.

Military

Total active duty personnel (1985): 235,300 (army 68.0%, navy 13.7%, air force 18.3%). *Military expenditure as percent of GNP* (1983): 4.1% (world 6.1%); per capita expenditure U.S.$33.

*Excluding Bangkok Metropolis. †Detail does not add to total given because of rounding. ‡June. §Employed persons 11 years and over. ‖Import figures are f.o.b. (free on board) in balance of trade and c.i.f. (cost, insurance, and freight) for commodities and trading partners. ¶Excludes circulation for two dailies. ♀1980.

Togo

Official name: République Togolaise (Republic of Togo).
Form of government: republic with one legislative body (National Assembly [77]).
Head of state and government: President.
Capital: Lomé.
Official language: French.
Official religion: none.
Monetary unit: 1 CFA franc (CFAF) = 100 centimes; valuation (Oct. 1, 1986) 1 U.S.$ = CFAF 332.05; 1 £ = CFAF 479.81.

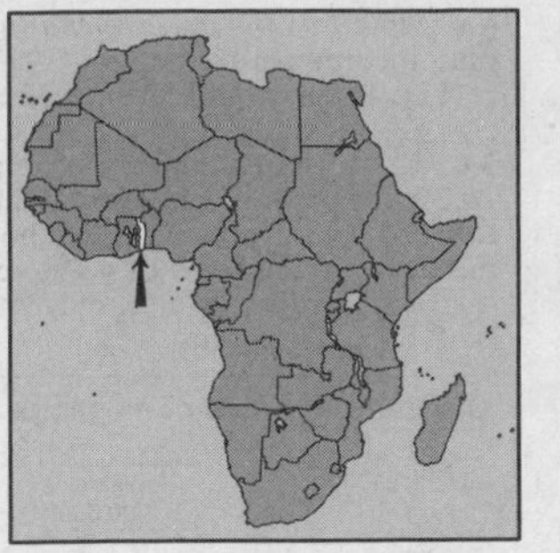

Area and population

Regions / Prefectures	Capitals	area sq mi	area sq km	population 1981 census
Centrale	Sokodé			269,174
Sotouboua	Sotouboua	2,892	7,490	128,617
Tchamba	Tchamba	*	*	44,912
Tchaoudjo	Sokodé	2,198*	5,692*	95,645
De la Kara	Kara			432,626
Assoli	Bafilo	362	938	32,444
Bassar	Bassar	2,444	6,330	118,345
Binah	Pagouda	180	465	50,077
Doufelgou	Niamtougou	432	1,120	66,120
Kéran	Kandé	653	1,692	44,762
Kozah	Kara	419	1,085	120,878
Des Plateaux	Atakpamé			561,656
Amou	Amlamé	1,692†	4,382†	72,951
Haho	Notsé	1,412	3,658	109,995
Kloto	Kpalimé	1,077	2,790	106,429
Ogou	Atakpamé	2,373	6,145	163,906
Wawa	Badou	†	†	108,375
Des Savanes	Dapaong			326,826
Oti	Sansanné-Mango	1,453	3,762	77,747
Tône	Dapaong	1,869	4,840	249,079
Maritime	Lomé			1,039,700
Golfe	Lomé	133	345	438,110
Lacs	Aného	275	712	140,006
Vo	Vogan	290	750	150,313
Yoto	Tabligbo	483	1,250	100,387
Zio	Tsévié	1,289	3,339	210,884
TOTAL		21,925‡	56,785	2,700,982§

Demography

Population (1986): 3,072,000.
Density (1986): persons per sq mi 140.1, persons per sq km 54.1.
Urban–rural (1981): urban 15.2%; rural 84.8%.
Sex distribution (1981): male 48.20%; female 51.80%.
Age breakdown (1980): under 15, 46.2%; 15–29, 25.8%; 30–44, 14.8%; 45–59, 8.6%; 60–74, 3.9%; 75 and over, 0.7%.
Population projection: (1990) 3,431,000; (2000) 4,522,000.
Doubling time: 24 years.
Ethnic composition (1978): Ewe 46.5%; Kabre 22.4%; Gurma 14.2%; Tem 4.2%; other African 11.7%; European 1.0%.
Religious affiliation (1980): animist 45.8%; Christian 37.0%; Sunnī Muslim 17.0%; other 0.2%.
Major cities (1983): Lomé 366,476; Sokodé 48,098‖; Kpalimé 27,669‖.

Vital statistics

Birth rate per 1,000 population (1980–85): 47.8 (world avg. 29.0); legitimate, n.a.; illegitimate, n.a.
Death rate per 1,000 population (1980–85): 17.1 (world avg. 11.0).
Natural increase rate per 1,000 population (1980–85): 30.7 (world avg. 18.0).
Total fertility rate (avg. births per childbearing woman; 1980–85): 6.5.
Marriage rate per 1,000 population (1979): 2.3.
Life expectancy at birth (1980–85): male 46.9 years; female 50.2 years.
Major illnesses per 100,000 population (1978): infectious and parasitic diseases 26,926; diseases of the respiratory system 9,296; diseases of the digestive system 8,007; accidents, poisoning, and traumas 7,172.

National economy

Budget (1986). Revenue: CFAF 87,300,000,000 (indirect tax revenue 45.1%, direct tax revenue 39.7%, stamps 2.3%). Expenditures: CFAF 87,300,000,000 (administrative expenditures 30.6%, public debt 27.6%).
Public debt (external, outstanding; 1984): U.S.$659,200,000.
Tourism: receipts from visitors (1983) U.S.$12,000,000; expenditures by nationals abroad (1979) U.S.$19,000,000.
Production (metric tons except as noted). Agriculture, forestry, fishing (1985): roots and tubers 805,000, cassava 439,000, tomatoes 420,000, yams 336,000, corn (maize) 208,000, sorghum 110,000, millet 71,000, pulses 41,000, cottonseed 30,000, peanuts (groundnuts) 22,000, cacao beans 16,000, rice 16,000, bananas 16,000, palm kernels 15,000, coconuts 14,000, palm oil 13,800, coffee 10,000; livestock (number of live animals) 850,000 sheep, 850,000 goats, 240,000 pigs, 240,000 cattle, 4,000,000 chickens; roundwood (1984) 735,000 cu m; fish catch (1984) 14,547. Mining and quarrying (1984): phosphate rock 2,700,000; salt 600,000¶; marble 15,087¶. Manufacturing (1980): cement 279,000¶; beer 385,000 hectolitres; woven cotton fabrics 20,000,000 m; footwear 1,155,000 pairs. Construction (value added in CFAF; 1981): 11,000,000,000. Energy production (consumption): electricity (kW-hr; 1985) 33,960,000 (249,318,000); crude petroleum (barrels; 1983) none (2,336,000); petroleum products (metric tons; 1984) none (122,000).

Gross national product (at current market prices; 1984): U.S.$730,000,000 (U.S.$250 per capita).

Structure of gross domestic product and labour force

	1983 in value CFAF '000,000	1983 % of total value	1984 labour force	1984 % of labour force
Agriculture	90.1	32.0	745,000	65.5
Mining	28.7	10.2		
Manufacturing	20.1	7.1		
Construction	8.1	2.9		
Public utilities	5.7	2.0		
Transp. and commun.	18.1	6.4	392,000	34.5
Trade	61.9	22.0		
Finance	...	...		
Pub. admin., defense	27.8	10.0		
Services	...	...		
Other	20.8	7.4		
TOTAL	281.3	100.0	1,137,000	100.0

Population economically active: total (1981) 1,104,000; activity rate of total population 40.8% (participation rates: over age 15, 76.7%; female [1980] 34.9%; unemployed [1980] 2.3%).

Price and earnings indexes (1980 = 100)

	1980	1981	1982	1983	1984	1985	1986
Consumer price index	100.0	119.7	133.0	145.5	140.3	137.8	...
Hourly earning index	100.0	100.0	110.0	110.0	110.0	110.0	110.0

Household income and expenditure. Average household size (1980) 5.6; average annual income per household CFAF 102,000 (U.S.$452); source of income: n.a; expenditure (1985): food 47.9%, housing 14.9%, clothing 7.7%, services 6.6%; other 22.9%.
Land use (1984): forested 27.6%; meadows and pastures 3.7%; agricultural and under permanent cultivation 26.2%; other 42.5%.

Foreign trade

Balance of trade (current prices)

	1979	1980	1981	1982	1983	1984
CFAF '000,000,000	−63.8	−45.1	−60.3	−70.2	−46.2	−18.2
% of total	40.7%	24.0%	34.4%	37.6%	27.2%	9.8%

Imports (1984): CFAF 118,460,000,000 (food and food products 19.6%, cotton textiles 9.4%, transport equipment and parts 8.3%, machinery and mechanical equipment 7.9%). *Major import sources:* France 32.3%; The Netherlands 10.3%; Côte d'Ivoire 7.1%; West Germany 6.9%; United Kingdom 5.6%; Japan 5.2%.
Exports (1984): CFAF 83,588,000,000 (phosphates 49.0%, cacao beans 25.1%, raw cotton 8.9%, clinker and cement 4.7%, coffee 3.6%). *Major export destinations:* The Netherlands 23.2%; France 21.1%; Yugoslavia 8.3%; U.S.S.R. 5.9%; Poland 4.7%; Tunisia 2.8%.

Transport and communications

Transport. Railroads (1982): length 321 mi, 516 km; passenger-mi 65,000,000, passenger-km 105,000,000; short ton-mi cargo 11,000,000, metric ton-km cargo 16,000,000. Roads (1982): total length 4,638 mi, 7,464 km (paved 20%). Vehicles (1984): passenger cars 36,372; trucks and buses 17,963. Merchant marine (1985): vessels (100 gross tons and over) 11; total deadweight tonnage 77,989. Air transport (1983): passenger-mi 129,311,000, passenger-km 208,106,000; short ton-mi cargo 26,218,000, metric ton-km cargo 38,278,000; airports (1986) with scheduled flights 1.
Communications. Daily newspapers (1985): total number 2; total circulation 10,000♀; circulation per 1,000 population 3.3♀. Radio (1985): total number of receivers 250,000 (1 per 12 persons). Television (1985): total number of receivers 14,000 (1 per 213 persons). Telephones (1983): 11,105 (1 per 255 persons).

Education and health

Education (1983)

	schools	teachers	students	student/ teacher ratio
Primary (age 6–11)	2,317	10,145	457,376	45.0
Secondary (age 12–18)	248δ	4,200	95,941	22.8
Voc., teacher tr.	22δ	348□	6,048	...
Higher	1	308	3,734	12.2

Educational attainment (1970). Percent of population over age 15 having: no formal schooling 80.8%; knowledge of reading and writing 11.1%; primary education 6.4%; secondary 1.6%; higher 0.1%. *Literacy* (1985): total population over age 15 literate 631,700 (39.1%); males literate 401,800 (51.7%); females literate 229,900 (27.5%).
Health: physicians (1980) 132 (1 per 19,900 persons); hospital beds (1982) 3,655 (1 per 752 persons); infant mortality rate per 1,000 live births (1975–80) 124.0.
Food (1981–83): daily per capita caloric intake 2,213 (vegetable products 96%, animal products 4%); 92% of FAO recommended minimum requirement.

Military

Total active duty personnel (1986): 5,110◇ (army◇ 93.0%, navy 1.9%, air force 5.1%). *Military expenditure as percent of GNP* (1984): 2.6% (world 6.1%); per capita expenditure U.S.$6.

*Tchaoudjo includes Tchamba. †Amou includes Wawa. ‡Detail does not add to total given because of rounding. §Total includes 71,000 persons not counted separately. ‖1981. ¶1982. ♀For one daily only. δ1981–82. □1979–80. ◇Includes gendarmerie.

Tonga

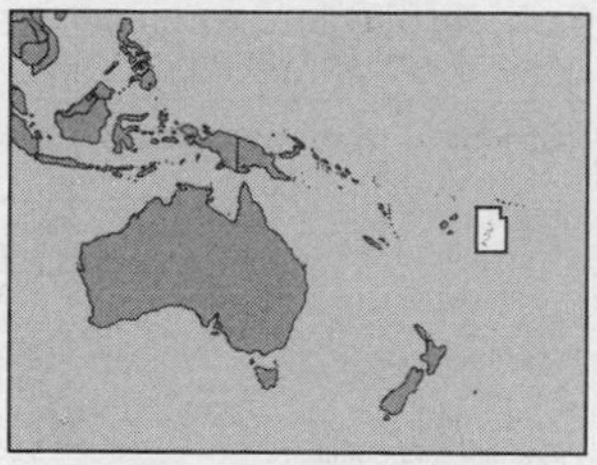

Official name: Pule'anga Fakatu'i 'o Tonga (Tongan); Kingdom of Tonga (English).
Form of government: constitutional monarchy with one legislative house (Legislative Assembly [28]).
Head of state and government: King.
Capital: Nukualofa.
Official languages: Tongan; English.
Official religion: none.
Monetary unit: 1 pa'anga (T$)* = 100 seniti; valuation (Oct. 1, 1986) 1 U.S.$ = T$1.59; 1 £ = T$2.29.

Area and population

Divisions / Districts	Capitals	area sq mi	area sq km	population 1984 census
Eua	Ohonua	33.7	87.4	4,017
Eua Foou		...	...	1,812
Eua Proper		...	...	2,205
Haapai	Pangai	42.2	109.3	8,561
Foa		...	...	1,299
Haano		...	...	881
Lulunga		...	...	1,461
Muomua		...	...	895
Pangai		...	...	2,665
Uiha		...	...	1,360
Niuas	Hihifo	27.7	71.7	2,517
Niuafoou		...	...	830
Niuatoputapu		...	...	1,687
Tongatapu	Nukualofa	99.8	258.6	66,420
Kolofoou		...	...	15,846
Kolomotua		...	...	13,371
Kolovai		...	...	4,356
Lapaha		...	...	7,668
Nukunuku		...	...	6,159
Tatakamotonga		...	...	7,280
Vaini		...	...	11,740
Vavau	Neiafu	46.0	119.2	15,077
Hahake		...	...	2,314
Hihifo		...	...	2,035
Leimatua		...	...	2,760
Motu		...	...	1,359
Neiafu		...	...	5,501
Pangaimotu		...	...	1,108
TOTAL LAND AREA		277.1	717.7	96,592
INLAND WATER		11.4	29.6	
TOTAL		288.5†	747.3†	

Demography

Population (1986): 97,900.
Density‡ (1986): persons per sq mi 353.3, persons per sq km 136.4.
Urban-rural (1980): urban 31.8%; rural 68.2%.
Sex distribution (1984): male 50.44%; female 49.56%.
Age breakdown (1976): under 15, 44.2%; 15–29, 26.0%; 30–44, 14.7%; 45–59, 9.5%; 60–74, 4.0%; 75 and over, 1.6%.
Population projection: (1990) 122,000; (2000) 139,000.
Doubling time: 25 years.
Ethnic composition (1976): Tongan 98.3%; other 1.7%.
Religious affiliation (1976): Free Wesleyan 47.4%; Roman Catholic 16.1%; Free Church of Tonga 13.7%; Latter-day Saints 9.3%; Church of Tonga 8.9%; Seventh-day Adventist 2.1%; other 2.5%.
Major city (1984): Nukualofa 27,740.

Vital statistics

Birth rate per 1,000 population (1984): 30.5 (world avg. 29.0); legitimate, n.a.; illegitimate, n.a.
Death rate per 1,000 population (1984): 2.8 (world avg. 11.0).
Natural increase rate per 1,000 population (1984) 27.7 (world avg. 18.0).
Total fertility rate (avg. births per childbearing woman; 1980–85): 4.3.
Marriage rate per 1,000 population (1983): 4.3.
Divorce rate per 1,000 population (1983): 0.6.
Life expectancy at birth (1980–85): male 61.0 years; female 64.8 years.
Major causes of death per 100,000 population: n.a.; however, major diseases include gastroenteritis, infantile diarrhea, and acute respiratory infections.

National economy

Budget (1981)§. Revenue: T$12,230,000 (import duties 31.4%; income and wealth tax 13.6%; licenses, stamp duties, registration fees 1.3%). Expenditures: T$16,275,000 (investments 37.2%; social services 22.2%; economic services 13.9%; defense 2.7%).
Tourism: receipts from visitors (1984) U.S.$6,000,000; expenditures by nationals abroad (1981) U.S.$1,000,000.
Production (metric tons except as noted). Agriculture, forestry, fishing (1984): roots and tubers 92,000, coconuts 56,000, sweet potatoes 17,000, cassava 11,000, fruits excluding melons 11,000, copra 7,000, bananas 3,000; livestock (number of live animals) 101,000 pigs, 17,000 goats, 12,000 horses, 11,000 cattle; roundwood 3,000 cu m; fish catch 1,055. Mining and quarrying (1982): coral 150,000; sand 25,000. Manufacturing (value added in T$; 1982): food products and beverages 2,623,000; furniture fixtures and wood products 328,000; metal products 252,000; glass and china products 203,000; paper and products 26,000. Construction (value in T$; 1981): residential 2,041,400; nonresidential 5,898,600. Energy production (consumption): electricity (kW-hr; 1984) 12,000,000 (12,000,000); coal, none (n.a.); petroleum, none (n.a.); petroleum products (metric tons; 1984) n.a. (15,000); natural gas, none (n.a.).
Gross national product (1983): U.S.$80,000,000 (U.S.$780 per capita).

Structure of gross domestic product and labour force

	1983 in value T$'000	1983 % of total value	1976 labour force	1976 % of labour force
Agriculture	35,790	41.5	9,529	44.5
Mining	394	0.5	16	0.1
Manufacturing	4,271	4.9	386	1.8
Construction	3,354	3.9	1,153	5.4
Public utilities	404	0.5	114	0.5
Transportation and communication	4,950	5.7	829	3.9
Trade	12,774	14.8	825 ‖	3.8 ‖
Finance	5,189	6.0	61	0.3
Pub. admin., defense	...	... }	4,082	19.0
Services	...	...		
Other	19,149¶	22.2	4,440♀	20.7
TOTAL	86,275	100.0	21,435	100.0

Public debt (external, outstanding; 1982): U.S.$16,000,000.
Population economically active (1984): total 30,900; activity rate of total population 32.1% (participation rates: ages 15–64, n.a.; female [1976] 14.7%; unemployed 4.5%).

Price and earnings indexes (1980 = 100)

	1979	1980	1981	1982	1983	1984	1985ð
Consumer price index	81.7	100.0	114.9	127.4	139.8	140.0	154.2
Earnings index	94.4	100.0	120.3	...	...	...	...

Household income and expenditure. Average household size (1980) 6.0; average annual income per household: n.a.; source of income: n.a.; expenditure (1983): food 55.1%, household goods 12.4%, tobacco and beverages 8.5%, clothing and footwear 6.2%, transportation 6.1%, housing 3.8%.
Land use (1982): forested 11.9%; meadows and pastures 6.0%; agricultural and under permanent cultivation 80.6%; other 1.5%.

Foreign trade

Balance of trade (current prices)

	1979	1980	1981	1982	1983	1984
T$'000,000	−19.4	−23.0	−27.3	−37.0	−35.2	−36.6
% of total	58.7%	61.7%	63.9%	81.5%	73.2%	64.7%

Imports (1984): T$46,614,129 (food and live animals 23.5%, mineral fuels 14.0%, machinery and transport equipment 13.6%, chemicals 6.0%, beverages and tobacco 5.6%). *Major import sources:* New Zealand 37.6%; Australia 24.0%; Japan 11.4%; Singapore 5.7%; United States 5.4%; Fiji 5.0%.
Exports (1984): T$9,995,621 (coconut oil products 50.1%, bananas 8.8%, desiccated coconut 7.7%). *Major export destinations:* New Zealand 59.4%; Australia 20.8%.

Transport and communications

Transport. Railroads: none. Roads (1984): total length 269 mi, 433 km (paved 60%). Vehicles (1983): passenger cars 443, commercial vehicles 1,343. Merchant marine (1985): vessels (100 gross tons and over) 20; total deadweight tonnage 22,447. Air transport (1980): passengers embarked and disembarked, international 44,000, domestic 14,000; cargo, n.a.; airports (1986) with scheduled flights 5.
Communications. Daily newspapers: none. Radio (1985): total number of receivers 66,000 (1 per 1.5 persons). Television: total number of receivers, n.a.□. Telephones (1983): 3,485 (1 per 30.0 persons).

Education and health

Education (1984)

	schools	teachers	students	student/teacher ratio
Primary (age 6–10)	111	810	16,921	20.9
Secondary (age 13–18)	50	789	14,549	18.4
Voc., teacher tr.	12	14◇	635	...
Higher△	1	...	125	...

Educational attainment (1976). Percent of adult population over age 25 having: no schooling 0.4%; less than primary education 37.3%; primary 12.4%; postprimary 45.6%; secondary 0.1%; postsecondary 0.1%; higher 0.6%; special education 2.4%; other 1.1%. *Literacy* (1976): total population over age 15 literate 46,456 (92.8%); males 92.9%; females 92.8%.
Health (1982): physicians 35 (1 per 2,881 persons); hospital beds 307 (1 per 328 persons); infant mortality rate per 1,000 live births (1983) 26.0.
Food (1980–82): daily per capita caloric intake 3,202 (vegetable products 84%, animal products 16%); 120% of FAO recommended minimum requirement.

Military

Total active duty personnel: Tonga had a national defense force of about 250 in the early 1980s.

*The pa'anga is at par with the Australian dollar. †Also includes 39.0 sq mi (101.1 sq km) of uninhabited islands. ‡Density is based on land area. §Estimated budget for 1984–85 was: revenue T$22,788,160; expenditures T$22,760,034. ‖ Trade includes hotels and restaurants. ¶Includes indirect taxes less subsidies. ♀Includes 2,809 persons seeking work for the first time. ðSecond quarter. □Tonga has no authorized television service, but a "pirate" station began transmitting in mid-1984. ◇1983. △1982.

Trinidad and Tobago

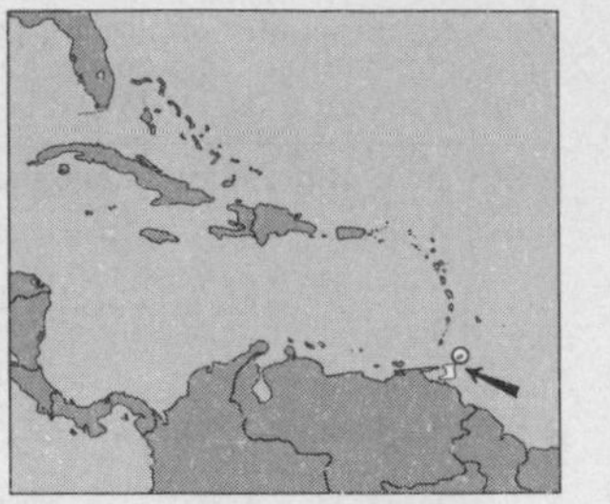

Official name: Republic of Trinidad and Tobago.
Form of government: multiparty republic with two legislative houses (Senate [31]; House of Representatives [36]).
Chief of state: President.
Head of government: Prime Minister.
Capital: Port-of-Spain.
Official language: English.
Official religion: none.
Monetary unit: 1 Trinidad and Tobago dollar (TT$) = 100 cents; valuation (Oct. 1, 1986) 1 U.S.$ = TT$2.41; 1 £ = TT$3.48.

Area and population

		area		population
Counties	Capitals	sq mi	sq km	1984 estimate
Caroni	Chaguanas	213	552	156,500
Nariva/Mayaro	Rio Claro	350	906	35,000
St. Andrew/St. David	Sangre Grande	364	943	54,900
St. George	...	350	907	406,700
St. Patrick	Siparia	255	660	137,800*
Tobago	Scarborough	117	303	42,100
Victoria	Princes Town	314	814	210,300
City				
Port-of-Spain	—	4	10	60,700
Boroughs				
Arima	—	3	7	26,700
Point Fortin	—	6	16	...*
San Fernando	—	2	6	37,400
TOTAL		1,978	5,124	1,168,100

Demography

Population (1986): 1,202,000.
Density (1986): persons per sq mi 607.7, persons per sq km 234.6.
Urban-rural (1985): urban 49.3%; rural 50.7%.
Sex distribution (1985): male 49.74%; female 50.26%.
Age breakdown (1985): under 15, 32.9%; 15–29, 30.6%; 30–44, 16.9%; 45–59, 11.2%; 60–74, 6.8%; 75 and over, 1.6%.
Population projection: (1990) 1,262,000; (2000) 1,410,000.
Doubling time: 32 years.
Ethnic composition (1980): black 40.8%; East Indian 40.7%; mixed 16.3%; white 0.9%; Chinese 0.5%; Arab 0.1%; other 0.7%.
Religious affiliation (1980): Christian 61.9%, of which Roman Catholic 33.0%, Protestant 28.1% (including Anglican 14.7%, Presbyterian 3.8%, Pentecostal 3.5%, Seventh-day Adventist 2.5%); Hindu 25.0%; Muslim 6.0%; other (including Rastafarian and Yoruba syncretist) 7.1%.
Major cities (1984): Port-of-Spain 60,700; San Fernando 37,400; Arima 26,700; Point Fortin 16,710†.

Vital statistics

Birth rate per 1,000 population (1982): 29.0 (world avg. 29.0); (1979) legitimate 56.9%; illegitimate 43.1%.
Death rate per 1,000 population (1982): 7.0 (world avg. 11.0).
Natural increase rate per 1,000 population (1982): 22.0 (world avg. 18.0).
Total fertility rate (avg. births per childbearing woman; 1980–85): 2.9.
Marriage rate per 1,000 population (1984): 7.2.
Divorce rate per 1,000 population (1984): 0.8.
Life expectancy at birth (1980–85): male 67.8 years; female 72.6 years.
Major causes of death per 100,000 population (1978): diseases of the circulatory system 244.1; malignant neoplasms 65.3; diabetes mellitus 48.2; accidents, poisoning, and violence 47.5; diseases of the respiratory system 41.5.

National economy

Budget (1985): Revenue: TT$6,300,400,000 (non-oil sector 60.8%, of which tax revenue 53.2% [including individual income taxes 22.3%, taxes on goods and services 11.9%, import duties 9.7%]; oil sector 39.2%, of which corporation taxes 29.7%, royalties 7.2%). Expenditure: TT$7,543,600,000 (current expenditure 78.5%, of which education 13.2%, welfare 8.3%, health 7.4%, justice and police 5.3%, public debt 4.7%, defense 0.9%; development expenditure 21.5%).
Tourism (1984): receipts from visitors U.S.$197,900,000; expenditures by nationals abroad U.S.$130,000,000.
Production (metric tons except as noted). Agriculture, forestry, fishing (1984): sugarcane 1,030,000‡, coconuts 57,000, rice 18,000, taro 18,000, tomatoes 8,000, oranges 7,000, coffee 2,135‡, cocoa 1,307‡; livestock (number of live animals) 76,000 cattle, 62,000 pigs, 49,000 goats; roundwood 57,000 cu m; fish catch (1983) 4,461. Mining and quarrying (1985): natural asphalt 21,300. Manufacturing (1985): nitrogenous fertilizers 1,660,000; methanol 358,200; cement 328,500; iron and steel billets 166,900; urea 155,000; iron and steel rods 102,900; sugar 91,700§; 22,900 motor vehicles ‖; 21,800 refrigerators ‖; 19,200 television receivers ‖; rum 757,000 hectolitres ‖; beer 223,000 hectolitres. Construction (new building authorized; 1984): residential 474,000 sq m; nonresidential 168,300 sq m. Energy production (consumption): electricity (kW-hr; 1984) 2,725,000,000 (2,725,000,000); coal, none (none); crude petroleum (barrels; 1985) 64,100,000 (35,704,000 ‖); petroleum products (metric tons; 1984) 4,300,000 (1,335,000); natural gas (cu m; 1984) 2,956,000,000 (2,956,000,000).

Gross national product (at current market prices; 1984): U.S.$8,350,000,000 (U.S.$7,150 per capita).

Structure of gross domestic product and labour force

	1985¶		1980	
	in value TT$'000,000	% of total value	labour force♀	% of labour force
Agriculture	653	3.4	37,530	9.8
Mining	4,461	23.5	21,060	5.5
Manufacturing	1,282	6.8	41,900	11.0
Construction	2,099	11.1	70,440	18.5
Public utilities	419	2.2	9,070	2.3
Transp. and commun.	1,917	10.1	33,670	8.8
Trade	1,769	9.3	50,510	13.2
Finance	1,912	10.1	16,590	4.3
Pub. admin., defense	2,910	15.3	88,890	23.2
Services	1,550	8.2		
Other	...	...	12,830	3.4
TOTAL	18,972	100.0	382,490	100.0

Public debt (external, outstanding; 1985): U.S.$1,087,400,000.
Population economically active (1983): total 449,400; activity rate of total population 39.2% (participation rates: ages 15–64, 64.4%; female 32.4%; unemployed [1985] 15.4%).

Price and earnings indexes (1980 = 100)

	1980	1981	1982	1983	1984	1985	1986δ
Consumer price index	100.0	114.3	127.4	148.7	168.6	181.4	190.5
Weekly earnings index	100.0	118.4	139.8	167.9	193.3	...	...

Household income and expenditure. Average household size (1980) 4.2; average annual income per household: n.a.; source of income: n.a.; expenditure (1981–82): food and beverages 27.7%, housing 22.7%, clothing and footwear 15.5%, transportation 13.2%, household furnishings 8.8%, health 2.2%, education 1.5%, recreation 1.4%, energy 1.1%, other 5.9%.
Land use (1983): forested 44.2%; meadows and pastures 2.2%; agricultural and under permanent cultivation 30.8%; other 22.8%.

Foreign trade

Balance of trade (current prices)□

	1980	1981	1982	1983	1984	1985
TT$'000,000	+2,729	+2,103	−694	+77	+1,079	+2,045
% of total	16.2%	13.2%	4.5%	0.7%	11.5%	23.3%

Imports (1985): TT$3,738,975,000 (machinery and transport equipment 30.1%; food 15.2%; base metals and products 9.0%; chemical products 8.0%). *Major import sources:* United States 37.7%; Japan 9.6%; United Kingdom 9.2%; Canada 7.2%; Argentina 4.4%
Exports (1985): TT$5,247,127,000 (domestic exports 96.6%, of which crude petroleum 46.7%, petroleum products 32.6%, anhydrous ammonia 7.6%, urea 2.4%, methanol 1.6%; reexports [mostly aircraft parts and oil-mining machinery] 3.4%). *Major export destinations:* United States 62.6%; Italy 3.9%; United Kingdom 3.9%; Guyana 3.0%; Barbados 2.8%.

Transport and communications

Transport. Railroads: none. Roads (1984): total length 4,909 mi, 7,900 km (paved 46%). Vehicles (1984): passenger cars 210,425; trucks and buses 60,401. Merchant marine (1985): vessels (100 gross tons and over) 49; total deadweight tonnage 12,376. Air transport (1985)◇: passenger-mi 1,278,500,000, passenger-km 2,057,500,000; short ton-mi cargo 6,843,000, metric ton-km cargo 9,991,000; airports (1986) with scheduled flights 2.
Communications. Daily newspapers (1985): total number 4; total circulation 177,000; circulation per 1,000 population 150. Radio (1985): 350,000 receivers (1 per 3.4 persons). Television (1985): 300,000 receivers (1 per 3.9 persons). Telephones (1983): 86,859 (1 per 13 persons).

Education and health

Education (1983–84)

	schools	teachers	students	student/ teacher ratio
Primary (age 5–11)	464	7,346	169,853	23.1
Secondary (age 12–19)	93	4,723	92,036	19.5
Voc., teacher tr.	...	...	...	...
Higher△	1	280	3,389	12.1

Educational attainment (1980). Percent of adult population over age 25 having: no formal schooling 7.1%; primary education 66.5%; secondary 21.7%; higher 2.7%; other 2.0%. *Literacy* (1980): total population over age 15 literate 653,100 (95.1%).
Health (1980): physicians 786 (1 per 1,376 persons); hospital beds 4,321 (1 per 250 persons); infant mortality rate per 1,000 live births (1982) 26.0.
Food (1980–82): daily per capita caloric intake 3,051 (vegetable products 81%, animal products 19%); 126% of FAO recommended minimum requirement.

Military

Total active duty personnel (1985): 2,130↑. *Military expenditure as percent of GNP* (1983): 3.1% (world 6.1%); per capita expenditure U.S.$202.

*St. Patrick includes the population of the borough of Point Fortin. †1980. ‡1985. §1986. ‖1984. ¶At factor cost. ♀Employed economically active population. δApril average. □Import figures are f.o.b. (free on board) in balance of trade and c.i.f. (cost, insurance, and freight) in commodities and trading partners. ◇BWIA International airways only. △1984–85; University of the West Indies, St. Augustine campus. ↑Includes 580 coast guard and 50 air force personnel forming part of the army.

Tunisia

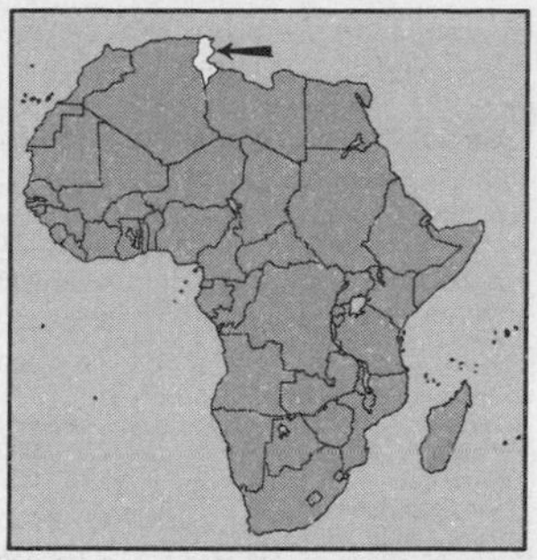

Official name: al-Jumhūrīyah at-Tūnisīyah (Republic of Tunisia).
Form of government: multiparty republic with one legislative house (Chamber of Deputies [125]).
Head of state and government: President.
Capital: Tunis.
Official language: Arabic.
Official religion: Islam.
Monetary unit: 1 dinar (D) = 1,000 millimes; valuation (Oct. 1, 1986) D 1.00 = U.S.$1.17 = £0.81.

Area and population

Governorates	Capitals	area sq mi	area sq km	population 1985 estimate
Aryānah	Aryānah	602	1,558	389,200
Bājah	Bājah	1,374	3,558	285,900
Banzart	Banzart	1,423	3,685	411,000
Bin ʿArūs	Bin ʿArūs	294	761	256,100
Jundūbah	Jundūbah	1,198	3,102	374,700
al-Kāf	al-Kāf	1,917	4,965	258,300
Madaniyīn	Madaniyīn	3,316	8,588	309,100
al-Mahdīyah	al-Mahdīyah	1,145	2,966	281,500
al-Munastīr	al-Munastīr	393	1,019	290,100
Nābul	Nābul	1,076	2,788	480,600
Qābis	Qābis	2,770	7,175	250,600
Qafṣah	Qafṣah	3,471	8,990	246,300
al-Qaṣrayn	al-Qaṣrayn	3,114	8,066	311,300
al-Qayrawān	al-Qayrawān	2,591	6,712	439,300
Qibilī	Qibilī	8,527	22,084	99,700
Ṣafāqis	Ṣafāqis	2,913	7,545	602,200
Sīdī Bū Zayd	Sīdī Bū Zayd	2,700	6,994	301,300
Silyānah	Silyānah	1,788	4,631	231,500
Sūsah	Sūsah	1,012	2,621	336,100
Taṭāwīn	Taṭāwīn	15,015	38,889	105,400
Tawzar	Tawzar	1,822	4,719	71,700
Tūnis	Tunis (Tūnis)	134	346	805,300
Zaghwān	Zaghwān	1,069	2,768	123,900
TOTAL		59,664	154,530	7,261,100

Demography

Population (1986): 7,326,000.
Density (1986): persons per sq mi 122.8, persons per sq km 47.4.
Urban-rural (1984): urban 52.8%; rural 47.2%.
Sex distribution (1985): male 50.84%; female 49.16%.
Age breakdown (1985): under 15, 39.6%; 15–29, 28.8%; 30–44, 14.2%; 45–59, 10.7%; 60–74, 5.4%; 75 and over, 1.3%.
Population projection: (1990) 7,989,000; (2000) 9,856,000.
Doubling time: 29 years.
Ethnic composition (1980): Arab 97.9%; Berber 1.5%; French 0.2%; Italian 0.1%; other 0.3%.
Religious affiliation (1980): Sunnī Muslim 99.4%; Christian 0.3%; Jewish 0.1%; other 0.2%.
Major cities (commune; 1984): Tunis 596,654; Ṣafāqis 231,911; Aryānah 98,655.

Vital statistics

Birth rate per 1,000 population (1985): 31.3 (world avg. 29.0); (1974) legitimate 99.8%; illegitimate 0.2%.
Death rate per 1,000 population (1985): 6.7 (world avg. 11.0).
Natural increase rate per 1,000 population (1985): 24.6 (world avg. 18.0).
Total fertility rate (avg. births per childbearing woman; 1984): 4.3.
Marriage rate per 1,000 population (1985): 7.0.
Divorce rate per 1,000 population (1983–84): 1.1.
Life expectancy at birth (1980–85): male 60.1 years; female 61.1 years.
Major causes of death per 100,000 population: n.a.; however, major illnesses include intestinal infections, trachoma, hepatitis, tuberculosis, and syphilis.

National economy

Budget (1984): Revenue: D 2,613,000,000 (indirect taxes 34.1%, investment 16.7%, direct taxes 11.0%). Expenditures: D 2,574,800,000 (education 11.2%, agriculture 7.9%, defense 7.5%, health 6.4%, interior affairs 4.2%, social welfare 1.1%).
Public debt (external, outstanding; 1984): U.S.$3,707,400,000.
Tourism: receipts from visitors (1984) U.S.$463,000,000; expenditures by nationals abroad (1982) U.S.$102,000,000.
Land use (1983): forested 3.6%; meadows and pastures 19.3%; agricultural and under permanent cultivation 30.2%; other 46.9%.
Production (metric tons except as noted). Agriculture, forestry, fishing (1985): wheat 1,380,000, barley 686,000, olives 525,000, tomatoes 420,000, watermelons 320,000, sugar beets 155,800, potatoes 150,000, oranges 122,000, grapes 120,000, dates 71,000, almonds 51,000, alfalfa 35,000, tobacco 4,000; livestock (number of live animals; 1984) 5,230,000 sheep, 1,030,000 goats, 600,000 cattle, 177,000 camels, 16,000,000 chickens; roundwood (1984) 2,751,000 cu m; fish catch 89,000. Mining and quarrying (1985): phosphate rock 4,505,000; iron ore 472,000; zinc 10,100; lead 6,500. Manufacturing (1984): cement 2,772,000; sulfuric acid 2,715,000; crude steel 168,000; pig iron and ferroalloys 144,000; tires 252,000 units. Construction (1982): residential building authorized 2,679,000 sq m. Energy production (consumption): electricity (kW-hr; 1984) 3,590,000,000 (3,590,000,000); coal (metric tons; 1984) none (20,000); crude petroleum (barrels; 1984) 41,220,000 (11,960,000); petroleum products (metric tons; 1984) 1,375,000 (2,786,000); natural gas (cu m; 1984) 393,008,000 (393,008,000).
Gross national product (at current market prices; 1984): U.S.$8,840,000,000 (U.S.$1,260 per capita).

Structure of gross domestic product and labour force

	1984		1984	
	in value* D '000,000	% of total value	labour force	% of labour force
Agriculture	550.0	13.3	475,000	26.6
Mining	416.4	10.1	38,000	2.2
Manufacturing	571.1	13.8	345,100	19.3
Construction	247.4	6.0	237,500	13.3
Public utilities	72.7	1.8	...	...
Transportation and communication	220.2	5.3	86,700	4.9
Trade	875.2	21.2	153,900	8.6
Finance	...	...	13,100	0.7
Pub. admin., defense	462.0	11.2	305,600	17.1
Services	...	...		
Other	715.0	17.3	131,100	7.3
TOTAL	4,130.0	100.0	1,786,000	100.0

Population economically active (1984): total 1,786,400; activity rate of total population 25.5% (participation rates: over age 15, 63.7%; female 23.3%; unemployed 13.7%).

Price and earnings indexes (1980 = 100)

	1979	1980	1981	1982	1983	1984	1985
Consumer price index	90.9	100.0	108.9	123.8	134.9	146.2	158.0
Monthly earnings index†	...	100.0	123.6	147.2	...	...	...

Household income and expenditure. Average household size (1984) 5.5; income per household: n.a.; source of income: n.a.; expenditure (1980): food 41.7%, housing 29.0%, clothing and footwear 8.5%, recreation 7.6%, transportation 4.9%.

Foreign trade

Balance of trade (current prices)

	1980	1981	1982	1983	1984	1985
D '000,000	−522.5	−632.9	−840.0	−845.0	−1,075.7	−844.0
% of total	22.4%	20.4%	26.4%	25.0%	27.8%	22.6%

Imports (1985): D 2,286,987,000 (petroleum and petroleum products 14.2%, plastic material 2.6%, chemical products 2.4%, pharmaceutical products 2.4%). *Major import sources:* France 27.6%; Italy 12.7%; Algeria 5.7%; The Netherlands 2.3%; United Kingdom 1.8%.
Exports (1985): D 1,443,032,000 (petroleum and petroleum products 42.2%, clothing 13.8%, fodder 9.9%, electrical machinery 2.1%, shoes 1.2%, rugs and tapestries 0.5%). *Major export destinations:* France 26.6%; Italy 16.8%; West Germany 11.0%, United States 10.4%; Spain 6.9%; China 0.8%.

Transport and communications

Transport. Railroads (1985): route length 1,316 mi, 2,118 km; passenger-mi 462,000,000, passenger-km 744,000,000; short ton-mi cargo 1,167,000,000, metric ton-km cargo 1,704,000,000. Roads (1982): total length 15,752 mi, 25,352 km (paved 52%). Vehicles (1982): passenger cars 141,185; trucks and buses 147,571. Merchant marine (1985): vessels (100 gross tons and over) 67; total deadweight tonnage 449,259. Air transport (1984): passenger-mi 987,376,000, passenger-km 1,589,032,000; short ton-mi cargo 13,100,000, metric ton-km cargo 19,100,000; airports (1986) with scheduled flights 6.
Communications. Daily newspapers (1985): total number 5; total circulation 250,000; circulation per 1,000 population 35.7. Radio (1985): total number of receivers 1,150,000 (1 per 6.0 persons). Television (1985): total number of receivers 275,000 (1 per 25.3 persons). Telephones (1983): 218,808 (1 per 31.4 persons).

Education and health

Education (1985–86)

	schools	teachers	students	student/teacher ratio
Primary (age 6–11)	3,358	40,703	1,291,490	31.7
Secondary (age 12–18)	380	21,269	457,630	21.5
Voc., teacher tr.	...	...	...	...
Higher	...	5,194	41,594	8.0

Educational attainment (1984). Percent of population over age 10 having: no formal schooling 46.2%; Qur'anic education 0.7%; primary 33.5%; secondary 17.0%; higher 2.1%; no certificate 0.5%. *Literacy* (1984): total population over age 10 literate 2,699,700 (46.2%); males literate 1,662,100 (65.4%); females literate 1,037,600 (41.9%).
Health: physicians (1982) 1,732 (1 per 3,883 persons); hospital beds (1983) 14,727 (1 per 464 persons); infant mortality rate per 1,000 live births (1984) 12.4.
Food (1980–82): daily per capita caloric intake 2,745 (vegetable products 91%, animal products 9%); 115% of FAO recommended minimum requirement.

Military

Total active duty personnel (1985): 35,100 (army 85.5%, navy 7.4%, air force 7.1%). *Military expenditure as percent of GNP* (1983): 2.9% (world 6.1%); per capita expenditure U.S.$35.

*At constant prices of 1980. †Government workers only.

Turkey

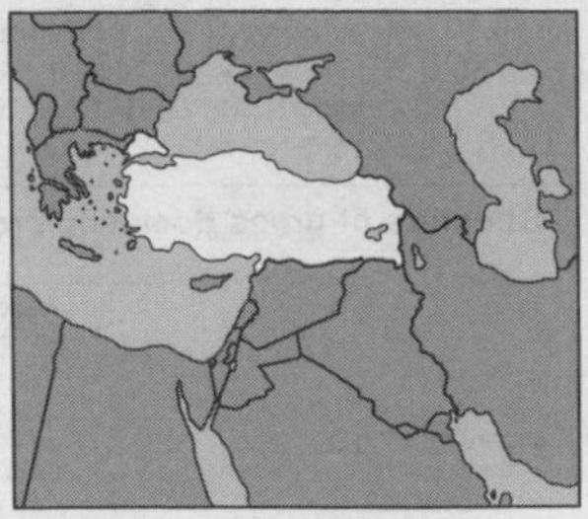

Official name: Türkiye Cumhuriyeti (Republic of Turkey).
Form of government: multiparty republic with one legislative house (Turkish Grand National Assembly [400]).
Chief of state: President.
Head of government: Prime Minister.
Capital: Ankara.
Official language: Turkish.
Official religion: none.
Monetary unit: 1 Turkish lira (LT) = 100 kurush; valuation (Oct. 1, 1986) 1 U.S.$ = LT 706.37; 1 £ = LT 1,020.70.

Area and population

Geographical regions	area sq mi	area sq km	population 1985 census*
Akdeniz kıyısı (Mediterranean Coast)	22,933	59,395	4,731,243
Batı Anadolu (West Anatolia)	29,742	77,031	3,574,865
Doğu Anadolu (East Anatolia)	68,074	176,311	6,411,702
Güneydoğu Anadolu (Southeast Anatolia)	15,347	39,749	2,532,816
İç Anadolu (Central Anatolia)	91,254	236,347	12,463,807
Karadeniz kıyısı (Black Sea Coast)	31,388	81,295	6,752,262
Marmara ve Ege kıyıları (Marmara and Aegean coasts)	33,035	85,560	9,852,161
Trakya (Thrace)	9,175	23,764	5,101,901
TOTAL	300,948	779,452	51,420,757

Demography

Population (1986): 51,542,000.
Density (1986): persons per sq mi 171.3, persons per sq km 66.1.
Urban-rural (1980): urban 43.9%; rural 56.1%.
Sex distribution (1980): male 50.65%; female 49.35%.
Age breakdown (1980): under 15, 38.5%; 15–29, 27.7%; 30–44, 16.0%; 45–59, 11.2%; 60–64, 1.8%; 65 and over, 4.8%†.
Population projection: (1990) 54,633,000; (2000) 67,166,000.
Doubling time: 28.5 years.
Ethnic composition (1978): Turkish 87.1%; Kurdish 9.5%; Arab 1.7%; other 1.7%.
Religious affiliation (1980): Sunnī Muslim 99.2%; Eastern Orthodox 0.3%; other 0.5%.
Major cities (1985): Istanbul 5,494,916; Ankara 2,251,533; İzmir 1,489,817; Adana 776,000; Bursa 614,133.

Vital statistics

Birth rate per 1,000 population (1980–85): 33.6 (world avg. 29.0).
Death rate per 1,000 population (1980–85): 9.3 (world avg. 11.0).
Natural increase rate per 1,000 population (1980–85): 24.3 (world avg. 18.0).
Total fertility rate (avg. births per childbearing woman; 1980–85): 4.5.
Marriage rate per 1,000 population (1983): 6.4.
Divorce rate per 1,000 population (1983): 0.4.
Life expectancy at birth (1980–85): male 60.3 years; female 64.9 years.
Major causes of death per 100,000 population (1983): heart disease 87.0; malignant neoplasms (cancers) 25.0; birth injury and difficult labour 19.7; cerebrovascular disease 17.8.

National economy

Budget (1985). Revenue: LT 5,313,639,000,000 (tax revenue 71.2%, special revenue and funds 6.4%). Expenditures: LT 5,724,050,000,000 (breakdown: n.a.).
Public debt (external, outstanding; 1984): U.S.$15,774,000,000.
Tourism (1984): receipts from visitors U.S.$548,000,000; expenditures by nationals abroad U.S.$277,000,000.
Production (metric tons except as noted). Agriculture, forestry, fishing (1985): wheat 17,000,000, sugar beets 9,830,000, barley 6,200,000, potatoes 4,110,000, grapes 3,308,000, corn (maize) 1,890,000, apples 1,772,000, cotton 1,399,000, dry onions 1,290,000, sunflower seed 752,000, olives 600,000, oranges 503,000, rye 323,000, figs 322,000, oats 288,000, rice 272,000; livestock (number of live animals; 1984) 40,930,000 sheep, 13,100,000 goats, 12,410,000 cattle; roundwood (1984) 18,927,000 cu m, fuelwood 12,488,000 cu m; fish catch 567,304‡. Mining and quarrying (1984): iron 3,887,097; copper 2,468,654; boron minerals 1,400,355. Manufacturing (1985): cement 17,581,000; petroleum products 13,587,000; crude iron 3,094,356; sulfuric acid 592,000; pig iron 276,672; motor vehicles 60,353 units. Construction (1985): residential 27,049,000 sq m; nonresidential 6,700,000 sq m. Energy production (consumption): electricity (kW-hr; 1984) 30,630,000,000 (33,268,000,000); coal (metric tons; 1984) 26,492,000 (28,226,000); crude petroleum (barrels; 1984) 14,841,000 (126,185,000); petroleum products (metric tons; 1984) 15,744,000 (17,635,000); natural gas (cu m; 1984) 1,128,000 (1,128,000).
Land use (1983): forested 26.2%; meadows and pastures 11.9%; agricultural and under permanent cultivation 34.2%; other 27.7%.
Household income and expenditure§. Average household size (1975) 5.0; income per household (1979) LT 11,880 (U.S.$385); sources of income: self-employment 46.8%, wages and salaries 38.9%, transfer grants 9.4%, other 4.9%; expenditure (1979): food 41.2%, housing 25.2%, clothing 14.8%, recreation and entertainment 6.1%, transportation 5.5%, health 3.3%, other 3.9%.

Gross national product (at current market prices; 1984): U.S.$57,810,000,000 (U.S.$1,160 per capita).

Structure of gross domestic product and labour force

	1985			
	in value LT '000,000	% of total value	labour force	% of labour force
Agriculture	4,486,000	16.3	9,390,000	51.4
Mining	} 8,195,000	29.7	133,000	0.7
Manufacturing			1,775,000	9.7
Construction	979,000	3.5	626,000	3.4
Transportation and communication	2,587,000	9.4	529,000	2.9
Trade	4,718,000	17.1	742,000	4.1
Finance	1,788,000	6.5	229,000	1.3
Public utilities	} 1,568,000	5.7	135,000	0.7
Pub. admin., defense			...	
Services	1,433,000	5.2	2,339,000	12.8
Other	1,836,000	6.6	2,371,000 ‖	13.0 ‖
TOTAL	27,590,000	100.0	18,269,000	100.0

Population economically active (1982): total 19,027,000; activity rate of total population 41.1% (participation rates: over age 15, 66.3%; female 32.9%; unemployed 17.7%).

Price and earnings indexes (1980 = 100)

	1979	1980	1981	1982	1983	1984	1985
Consumer price index	47.6	100.0	136.6	178.7	230.8	352.4	510.9
Daily earnings index ‖	68.9	100.0	127.4	161.8	221.2	306.1	...

Foreign trade

Balance of trade (current prices)

	1980	1981	1982	1983	1984	1985
U.S.$'000,000	−4,999	−4,230	−3,097	−3,507	−3,624	−3,386
% of total	46.2%	31.0%	21.2%	23.4%	20.3%	17.5

Imports (1985): U.S.$11,343,600,000 (crude oil 29.3%, iron and steel 9.3%, machinery 5.8%, organic chemicals 4.3%). *Major import sources:* West Germany 12.9%; United States 11.5%; Italy 6.3%; United Kingdom 5.3%; France 4.9%; Japan 3.9%.
Exports (1985): U.S.$7,958,100,000 (clothes 10.1%, agricultural products 9.3%, tobacco 4.2%, livestock and animal products 3.3%). *Major export destinations:* West Germany 14.0%; United Kingdom 9.4%; United States 9.1%; Italy 6.5%; France 4.4%; The Netherlands 2.2%.

Transport and communications

Transport. Railroads (1985): route length (1986) 5,076 mi, 8,169 km; passenger-mi 4,032,000,000, passenger-km 6,489,000,000; short ton-mi cargo 5,307,000,000, metric ton-km cargo 7,748,000,000. Roads (1983): total length 188,136 mi, 302,776 km (paved, n.a.). Vehicles (1985): passenger cars 983,743; trucks and buses 553,119. Merchant marine (1985): vessels (100 gross tons and over) 817; total deadweight tonnage 6,291,799. Air transport (1984): passenger-mi 1,467,544,000, passenger-km 2,361,789,000; short ton-mi cargo 17,991,000, metric ton-km cargo 26,266,000; airports (1986) with scheduled flights 16.
Communications. Daily newspapers (1979): total number 364; total circulation 3,878,000; circulation per 1,000 population 89.1. Radio (1985): total number of receivers 4,320,000 (1 per 11.8 persons). Television (1985): total number of receivers 5,000,000 (1 per 10.2 persons). Telephones (1983): 2,664,753 (1 per 18.6 persons).

Education and health

Education (1984–85)

	schools	teachers	students	student/ teacher ratio
Primary (age 5–12)	47,192	209,911	6,527,036	31.1
Secondary (age 13–18)	4,358	42,653	1,576,875	36.9
Voc., teacher tr.	1,995	90,261	1,169,500	12.9
Higher¶	153	16,454	225,622	13.7

Educational attainment (1980). Percent of population over age 6 having: primary education 37.9%; secondary 5.1%; higher 2.2%. *Literacy* (1980): total population over age 6 literate 25,307,000 (67.4%); males literate 15,185,000 (79.9%); females literate 10,122,000 (54.6%).
Health (1983): physicians 32,265 (1 per 1,495 persons); hospital beds 99,396 (1 per 475 persons); infant mortality rate per 1,000 live births (1982) 83.0.
Food (1980–82): daily per capita caloric intake 3,053 (vegetable products 90%, animal products 10%); 119% of FAO recommended minimum requirement.

Military

Total active duty personnel (1985): 630,000 (army 82.6%, navy 8.7%, air force 8.7%). *Military expenditure as percent of GNP* (1983): 4.9% (world 6.1%); per capita expenditure U.S.$55.

*Preliminary results. †Including those of unknown age. ‡1983. §Urban areas only. ‖ Insured workers only. ¶1983–84.

Tuvalu

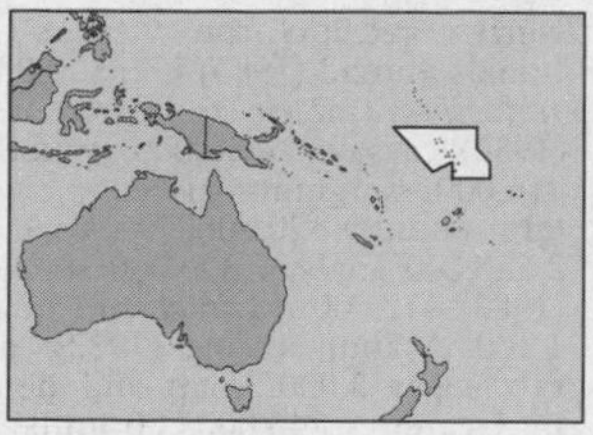

Official name: Tuvalu.
Form of government: constitutional monarchy with one legislative house (House of Assembly [13]).
Chief of state: British Monarch, represented by governor-general.
Head of government: Prime Minister.
Capital: Fongafale, on Funafuti Atoll.
Official language: English; Tuvaluan is widely spoken.
Official religion: none.
*Monetary unit**: 1 Tuvalu Dollar = 1 Australian Dollar ($T = $A) = 100 Tuvalu and Australian cents; valuation (Oct. 1, 1986) 1 U.S.$ = $A 1.59; 1 £ = $A 2.29.

Area and population

		area		population
Islands	Capital	sq mi	sq km	1985 census
Funafuti	Funafuti	0.91	2.36	2,810
Nanumaga		1.00	2.59	672
Nanumea		1.38	3.57	879
Niulakita		0.16	0.41	74
Niutao		0.82	2.12	904
Nui		1.27	3.29	604
Nukufetau		1.18	3.06	694
Nukulaelae		0.64	1.66	315
Vaitupu		1.89	4.90	1,231
TOTAL		9.25	23.96	8,229†

Demography

Population (1986): 8,200.
Density (1986): persons per sq mi 886.5, persons per sq km 342.2.
Urban-rural (1985): urban 34.2%; rural 65.8%.
Sex distribution (1985): male 47.42%; female 52.58%.
Age breakdown (1979): under 15, 33.8%; 15–29, 31.0%; 30–44, 14.3%; 45–59, 13.2%; 60–74, 6.1%; 75 and over, 1.6%.
Population projection: (1990) 9,000; (2000) 10,000.
Doubling time: n.a.; during 1979–85, no consistent trend was apparent.
Ethnic composition (1979): Tuvaluan (Polynesian) 91.2%; mixed (part I-Kiribati or other) 6.0%; I-Kiribati 1.3%; European and other Pacific 1.5%.
Religious affiliation (1979): Church of Tuvalu (Congregational) 96.9%; Seventh-day Adventist 1.4%; Bahā'ī 1.0%; Roman Catholic 0.2%; other 0.5%.
Major city (1985): Funafuti (urban) 2,810.

Vital statistics

Birth rate per 1,000 population (1985): 24.5 (world avg. 29.0); legitimate 82.2%; illegitimate 17.8%.
Death rate per 1,000 population (1985): 11.2 (world avg. 11.0).
Natural increase rate per 1,000 population (1985): 13.3 (world avg. 18.0).
Total fertility rate (avg. births per childbearing woman; 1985): 2.7.
Marriage rate per 1,000 population: n.a.
Divorce rate per 1,000 population: n.a.
Life expectancy at birth (1979): male 56.9 years; female 60.1 years.
Major causes of death per 100,000 population (1985): diseases of the digestive system 170.1; diseases of the circulatory system 145.8; diseases of the respiratory system 121.5; diseases of the nervous system 121.5; malignant neoplasms (cancers) 72.9; infectious and parasitic diseases 36.5; endocrine and metabolic disorders 24.3.

National economy

Budget (1983)‡. Revenue: $A 3,492,902 (British grant-in-aid 27.1%; philately tax 23.3%; customs duties 19.8%; personal tax 6.3%). Expenditures: $A 3,542,902 (works and communications 32.8%; social services 27.5%; office of Prime Minister 12.2%; financial services 10.8%; commerce and natural resources 5.3%; police, prisons, and immigration 4.1%; pensions and gratuities 4.0%; parliament 1.5%).
Gross national product (at current market prices; 1981): U.S.$5,000,000 (U.S.$680 per capita).

Structure of gross domestic product and labour force

	1979			
	in value $A	% of total value	labour force§	% of labour force
Agriculture	597,100	16.0	42	4.5
Mining	—	—	1	0.1
Manufacturing	37,300	1.0	62	6.6
Construction	485,200	13.0	229	24.5
Public utilities	...	...	14	1.5
Transportation and communication	149,300	4.0	111	11.9
Trade	1,268,900	34.0	100	10.7
Finance }			13	1.4
Pub. admin., defense }	1,194,200	32.0	182	19.4
Services }			181	19.3
Other	...	...	1	0.1
TOTAL	3,732,000	100.0	936	100.0

Production (metric tons except as noted). Agriculture ‖, forestry, fishing (1984): coconuts 2,000, hens' eggs 13, honey 2, other agricultural products include breadfruit, pulaka (taro), bananas, pandanus fruit, and pawpaws; livestock (number of live animals) n.a.¶; forestry, n.a.; fish catch 793♀♂. Mining and quarrying: n.a. Manufacturing (1983): copra 200 metric tons; handicrafts; beche-de-mer; baked goods. Construction: n.a. Energy production (consumption): electricity (kW-hr; 1981) 3,000,000 (3,000,000); coal, none (n.a.); crude petroleum, none (n.a.); petroleum products, none (n.a.); natural gas, none (n.a.).
Public debt: n.a.
Tourism (1979): number of visitors 474.
Population economically active (1979): total 4,010; activity rate of total population 54.6% (participation rates: over age 15, 81.1%; female 51.3%; employed 4.0%).

Price and earnings indexes (1978 = 100)

	1978	1979	1980	1981	1982	1983	1984
Consumer price index	100.0	104.1	117.9	129.2	141.2	150.7	156.0
Monthly earnings index	...	...	...	...	...	...	...

Household income and expenditure. Average household size (1979) 6.8; average annual income per household: $A 2,575; sources of income: agriculture and other 61.2%, cash economy only 17.9%, agriculture only 14.9%, other 6.0%; expenditure (1983): food 45.5%, housing and household operations 11.5%, transportation 10.5%, alcohol and tobacco 10.5%, clothing 7.5%, other 14.5%.
Land use (1983): agricultural and under permanent cultivation 75%□; other 25%.

Foreign trade

Balance of trade (current prices)

	1978	1979	1980	1981	1982	1983
$A '000	−1,527	−1,594	−3,061	−2,556	−2,853	−2,877
% of total	94.3%	75.6%	94.7%	98.6%	97.5%	95.0%

Imports (1983): $A 2,953,000 (food and live animals 27.0%, manufactured goods 16.9%, petroleum and petroleum products 14.0%, machinery and transport equipment 12.4%, chemicals 7.0%, beverages and tobacco 5.3%, animal and vegetable oils and fats 0.3%). *Major import sources:* Australia 39.5%; New Zealand 15.4%; United Kingdom 2.1%; Japan 2.1%; United States 0.5%.
Exports (1983): $A 76,000◇ (copra 100%). *Major export destinations* (1982): Fiji 47.5%; Australia 39.7%; New Zealand 5.3%.

Transport and communications

Transport. Railroads: none. Roads (1983): total length 5 mi, 8 km (paved, none). Vehicles: passenger cars, n.a.; trucks and buses, n.a.△ Merchant marine (1985): vessels (100 gross tons and over) 2; total deadweight tonnage 458. Air transport (1977): passenger arrivals (Funafuti) 1,443; cargo, n.a.; airports (1986) with scheduled flights 1†.
Communications. Newspapers (1984): total number 1 (fortnightly); total circulation 300; circulation per 1,000 population 36.1. Radio (1984): total number of receivers 1,100 (1 per 7.5 persons). Television: none. Telephones (1984): 120 (1 per 69 persons).

Education and health

Education (1984)

	schools	teachers	students	student/ teacher ratio
Primary (age 6–14)	11	61	1,349	22.1
Secondary (age 12–18)	1	15⊕	243	...
Vocational⊕	8	16	354	22.1
Higher	—	—	—	—

Educational attainment (1979). Percent of adult population over age 20 having: no formal schooling 0.4%; primary education 90.5%; secondary 7.7%; higher 0.5%. *Literacy* (1983): total population literate 5,509 (95.5%); males literate 2,443 (95.5%); females literate 3,066 (95.5%).
Health: physicians (1985) 4 (1 per 2,050 persons); hospital beds (1984) 36 (1 per 231 persons); infant mortality rate per 1,000 live births (1979) 42.
Food: daily per capita caloric intake, n.a.

Military

Total active duty personnel (1985): There is a police force of 31 men.

*The value of the Tuvalu Dollar is pegged to the value of the Australian Dollar, which is also legal currency in Tuvalu. †Total includes 46 persons unaccounted for in island populations. ‡Provisional budget for 1984 was balanced at $A 3,647,836, of which 24.7% was to be financed by foreign aid grants. §Employment in the cash economy only (excludes primarily fishermen and subsistence agriculturalists). ‖ Because of poor soil quality, only limited subsistence agriculture is possible on the islands. ¶Livestock largely consists of pigs, goats, and poultry; efforts are being made to increase their number to reduce dependence on imported meat, dairy products, and eggs. ♀1983. ♂Fish catch refers to marine fishes only and is largely used for local consumption, except for the export of some beche-de-mer to Fiji and Hong Kong. □Capable of supporting coconut palms, pandanus, and breadfruit. ◇Sales of postage stamps to overseas philatelists was becoming an important source of foreign exchange in the mid-1980s. △There are several cars, tractors, trailers, and light lorries on Funafuti; a few motorcycles are in use on most islands. †Six atoll lagoons have unscheduled seaplane service. ⊕1982–83.

Uganda

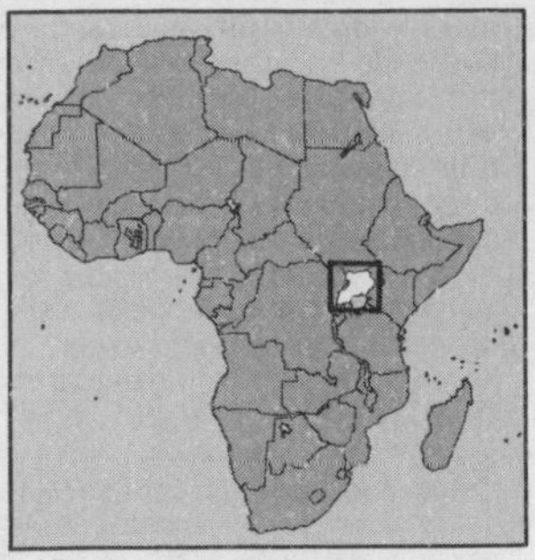

Official name: Republic of Uganda.
Form of government: multiparty republic with one legislative house (National Assembly [156]).
Chief of state: President.
Head of government: Prime Minister.
Capital: Kampala.
Official language: English.
Official religion: none.
Monetary unit: 1 Uganda shilling (U Sh) = 100 cents; valuation (Oct. 1, 1986) 1 U.S.$ = U Sh 1,381; 1 £ = U Sh 1,995.

Area and population

Provinces Districts	Capitals	area sq mi	area sq km	population 1980 census
Busoga	Jinja	5,150	13,340	1,221,872
Iganga	Bulamogi	3,190	8,250	643,801
Jinja	Jinja	280	730	228,520
Kamuli	Namwendwa	1,680	4,360	349,551
Central	Kampala	2,420	6,270	1,117,648
Kampala	Kampala	70	190	478,895
Mpigi	Mpigi	2,350	6,080	638,753
Eastern	Mbale	8,600	22,260	2,015,530
Kapchorwa	Kaptanya	670	1,740	74,517
Kumi	Kumi	1,100	2,860	238,809
Mbale	Bunkoko	990	2,550	557,241
Soroti	Soroti	4,080	10,560	476,629
Tororo	Sukulu	1,760	4,550	668,334
Karamoja	Moroto	10,410	26,960	350,908
Kotido	Kotido	5,120	13,270	161,445
Moroto	Katikekile	5,290	13,690	189,463
Nile	Arua	6,070	15,730	811,755
Arua	Olaki	3,020	7,830	472,283
Moyo	Moyo	1,930	5,010	106,492
Nebbi	Nebbi	1,120	2,890	232,980
North Buganda	Bombo	10,430	27,010	1,554,371
Luwero	Luwero	3,550	9,200	412,474
Mubende	Bageza	3,980	10,310	510,260
Mukono	Kawuga Mukono	2,900	7,500	631,637
Northern	Gulu	16,030	41,520	1,261,364
Apac	Apac	2,510	6,500	313,333
Gulu	Bungatira	4,500	11,660	270,185
Kitgum	Labongo	6,210	16,090	307,594
Lira	Lira	2,810	7,270	370,252
South Buganda	Masaka	6,170	15,970	905,754
Masaka	Kaswa Bukoto	4,520	11,700	631,156
Rakai	Byakabanda	1,650	4,270	274,598
Southern	Mbarara	8,210	21,280	1,963,428
Bushenyi	Bumbaire	1,960	5,080	522,495
Kabale	Rubale	940	2,430	455,471
Mbarara	Kakika	4,320	11,200	687,803
Rukungiri	Kagunga	990	2,570	297,659
Western	Butebe	11,960	30,980	1,427,446
Bundibugyo	Busaru	720	1,880	112,126
Hoima	Hoima	3,120	8,080	294,221
Kabarole	Karambe	3,410	8,820	520,141
Kasese	Rukoki	1,200	3,120	277,708
Masindi	Nyangeya	3,510	9,080	223,250
TOTAL LAND AREA		85,450	221,320	12,630,076
INLAND WATER		7,650	19,820	
TOTAL		93,100	241,140	

Demography

Population (1986): 15,638,000.
*Density** (1986): persons per sq mi 183.0, persons per sq km 70.7.
Urban-rural (1985): urban 14.4%; rural 85.6%.
Sex distribution (1985): male 49.57%; female 50.43%.
Age breakdown (1985): under 15, 48.5%; 15–29, 25.8%; 30–44, 14.1%; 45–59, 7.4%; 60–74, 3.6%; 75 and over, 0.6%.
Population projection: (1990) 17,851,500; (2000) 24,856,400.
Doubling time: 21 years.
Ethnic composition (1980): Ganda 18.0%; Nyoro 14.4%; Turkana 11.0%; Gisu 10.3%; Nkole 8.2%; Soga 8.2%; Chiga 7.0%; Lango 6.5%; other 16.4%.
Religious affiliation (1980): Roman Catholic 47.5%; Protestant 31.7%; Muslim 15.8%; other 5.0%.
Major cities (1980): Kampala 458,000; Jinja 45,100; Masaka 29,120; Mbale 28,039; Mbarara 23,160.

Vital statistics

Birth rate per 1,000 population (1984): 50.0 (world avg. 29.0).
Death rate per 1,000 population (1984): 16.0 (world avg. 11.0).
Natural increase rate per 1,000 population (1984): 34.0 (world avg. 18.0).
Total fertility rate (avg. births per childbearing woman; 1984): 6.9.
Life expectancy at birth (1984): male 49.0 years; female 53.0 years.
Major causes of death per 100,000 population: n.a.; however, major diseases include malaria, measles, venereal diseases, whooping cough, shigellosis (infection with dysentery), chicken pox, and leprosy.

National economy

Budget (1983–84). Revenue: U Sh 90,258,000,000 (export duties 45.7%, sales tax on imported goods 23.5%, customs duties 16.6%, taxes on income and profits 13.5%, excise tax 3.9%). Expenditures: U Sh 112,812,000,000 (general public services 23.8%, defense 17.0%, education 11.9%, economic services 8.8%, health 4.2%).
Public debt (external, outstanding; 1984): U.S.$695,200,000.
Tourism: receipts from visitors (1984) U.S.$8,000,000; expenditures by nationals abroad (1983) U.S.$10,000,000.
Production (metric tons except as noted). Agriculture, forestry, fishing (1984): cassava 1,650,000, millet 549,000, seed cotton 528,000, corn (maize) 416,000, sorghum 410,000, sugarcane 400,000, coffee 204,000, peanuts (groundnuts) 120,000; livestock (number of live animals) 5,200,000 cattle, 2,500,000 goats, 1,300,000 sheep; roundwood 12,230,000 cu m; fish catch (1983) 172,000. Mining and quarrying (1984): copper ore (metal content) 1,100. Manufacturing (1982): meat 141,000; cement 17,000; tea 14,000; raw sugar 3,000; soap and detergents 200; cotton fabrics 20,000,000 sq m; cigarettes 746,000,000 units; beer 10,000 hectolitres. Construction: n.a. Energy production (consumption): electricity (kW-hr; 1984) 655,000,000 (440,000,000); petroleum products (metric tons; 1984) none (210,000).
Gross national product (at current market prices; 1984): U.S.$3,290,000,000 (U.S.$230 per capita).

Structure of gross domestic product and labour force

	1981 in value U Sh '000,000	1981 % of total value	1978 labour force†	1978 % of labour force
Agriculture	353,347	68.1	81,100	21.8
Mining	145	0.0	3,600	1.0
Manufacturing	16,839	3.2	51,700	13.9
Construction	2,143	0.4	48,900	13.2
Transp. and commun.	5,842	1.1	10,000	2.7
Trade	33,999	6.6	18,300	4.9
Pub. admin., defense, and services	25,007	4.8	158,200	42.5
Other	81,489	15.7	...	...
TOTAL	518,811	100.0‡	371,800	100.0

Population economically active (1980): total 6,163,000; activity rate of total population 47.0% (participation rates: ages 15–64, 80.4%; female 42.8%; unemployed, n.a.).

Price and earnings indexes (1981 = 100)

	1980	1981	1982	1983	1984	1985	1986§
Consumer price index	83.2	100.0	200.3	248.3	343.3	799.8	1,346.5
Earnings index	...	...	...	...	...	...	...

Household size. Average household size (1980) 5.2; average annual income per household: n.a.; expenditure‖ (1984): food 63.8%, housing 9.2%, clothing 7.8%, transportation 2.2%, education 2.1%, health 1.0%.
Land use (1983): forested 29.6%; meadows and pastures 25.0%; agricultural and under permanent cultivation 31.5%; other 13.9%.

Foreign trade

Balance of trade (current prices)

	1979	1980	1981	1982	1983	1984
U Sh '000,000	+2,068	+818	+3,347	+858	+6,997	+27,245
% of total	46.7%	19.0%	12.1%	1.3%	6.3%	10.9%

Imports (1983): U Sh 52,313,000,000 (machinery and transport equipment 42.0%, other manufactured goods 29.0%, fuels 23.0%, food 5.0%). *Major import sources:* Kenya and Tanzania 29.0%; West Germany 8.6%; United Kingdom 8.2%; India 4.7%.
Exports (1983): U Sh 59,310,000,000 (unroasted coffee 88.0%). *Major export destinations:* United States 27.0%; United Kingdom 10.9%; France 9.6%; West Germany 9.3%; Spain 8.8%; Japan 4.4%.

Transport and communications

Transport. Railroads (1986): route length 788 mi, 1,268 km; passengers, n.a.; cargo, n.a. Roads (1985): total length 17,289 mi, 27,824 km (paved 15%). Vehicles (1982): passenger cars 10,633; trucks and buses 11,245. Merchant marine (1985): vessels (100 gross tons and over) 2; total deadweight tonnage 5,900. Air transport♀ (1985): passenger-mi 47,117,000, passenger-km 75,828,000; short ton-mi cargo 12,278,000, metric ton-km cargo 17,927,000; airports (1986) with scheduled flights 7.
Communications. Daily newspapers (1984): total number 5; total circulation 23,800♂; circulation per 1,000 population 1.7♂. Radio (1985): 285,000 receivers (1 per 53 persons). Television (1985): 77,000 receivers (1 per 196 persons). Telephones (1982): 55,000 (1 per 249 persons).

Education and health

Education (1982)

	schools	teachers	students	student/teacher ratio
Primary (age 6–12)	5,300	44,426	1,616,791	36.4
Secondary (age 13–18)	257	6,287	132,051	21.0
Voc., teacher tr.	23	735	13,338	18.1
Higher	4	640	7,312	11.4

Educational attainment, n.a. *Literacy* (1980): total population literate 47.9%.
Health (1982): physicians 665 (1 per 20,562 persons); hospital beds 19,650 (1 per 696 persons); infant mortality rate per 1,000 live births (1984) 110.0.
Food (1980–82): daily per capita caloric intake 1,781 (vegetable products 93%, animal products 7%); 77% of FAO recommended minimum requirement.

Military

Total active duty personnel (1985): 18,000 (army 100%). *Military expenditure as percent of GNP* (1983): 1.0% (world 6.1%); per capita expenditure U.S.$4.

*Based on land areas. †Employed only. ‡Detail does not add to total given because of rounding. §February. ‖Middle- to high-income families only. ♀Uganda Airlines only. ♂Partial circulation.

Union of Soviet Socialist Republics

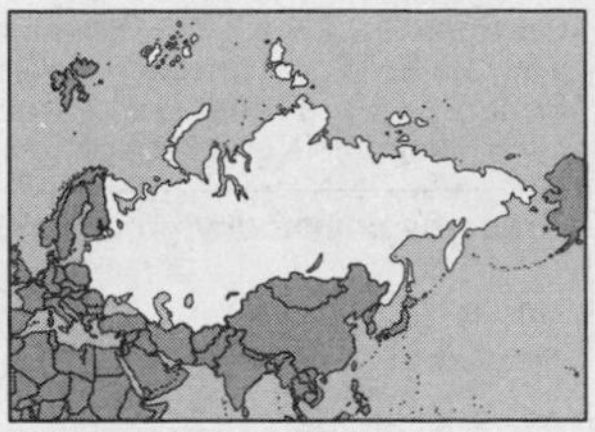

Official name: Soyuz Sovetskykh Sotsialisticheskikh Respublik (Sovetsky Soyuz) (Union of Soviet Socialist Republics [Soviet Union]).
Form of government: federal socialist republic with one legislative house (Supreme Soviet) comprising two chambers: Soviet of the Union [750] and Soviet of the Nationalities [750].
Chief of state: President (Chairman of the Supreme Soviet).
Head of government: Premier (Chairman of the Council of Ministers).
Capital: Moscow.
Official language: Russian.
Official religion: none.
Monetary unit: 1 ruble = 100 kopecks; valuation (Oct. 1, 1986) 1 ruble = U.S.$1.48 = £1.02.

Area and population

		area		population
Soviet Federated Socialist Republic	Capitals	sq mi	sq km	1985 estimate
Russian S.F.S.R.	Moscow	6,592,800	17,075,400	143,090,000
Soviet Socialist Republics				
Armenian	Yerevan	11,500	29,800	3,317,000
Azerbaijan	Baku	33,400	86,600	6,614,000
Belorussian	Minsk	80,200	207,600	9,942,000
Estonian	Tallinn	17,400	45,100	1,530,000
Georgian	Tbilisi	26,900	69,700	5,201,000
Kazakh	Alma-Ata	1,049,200	2,717,300	15,842,000
Kirgiz	Frunze	76,600	198,500	3,967,000
Latvian	Riga	24,600	63,700	2,604,000
Lithuanian	Vilnius	25,200	65,200	3,570,000
Moldavian	Kishinyov	13,000	33,700	4,111,000
Tadzhik	Dushanbe	55,300	143,100	4,499,000
Turkmen	Ashkhabad	188,500	488,100	3,189,000
Ukrainian	Kiev	233,100	603,700	50,840,000
Uzbek	Tashkent	172,700	447,400	17,974,000
TOTAL LAND AREA		8,600,400	22,274,900	276,290,000
INLAND WATER		49,100	127,300	
TOTAL		8,649,500	22,402,200	

Demography

Population (1986): 280,036,000.
Density (1986): persons per sq mi 32.6, persons per sq km 12.6.
Urban-rural (1985): urban 65.3%; rural 34.7%.
Sex distribution (1985): male 46.90%; female 53.10%.
Age breakdown (1985): under 15, 24.8%; 15–29, 24.8%; 30–44, 18.4%; 45–59, 18.9%; 60–74, 9.4%; 75 and over, 3.7%.
Population projection: (1990) 290,155,000; (2000) 310,236,000.
Doubling time: 82 years.
Ethnic composition (1979): Russian 52.4%; Ukrainian 16.2%; Uzbek 4.8%; Belorussian 3.6%; Kazakh 2.5%; Tatar 2.4%; Azerbaijani 2.1%; Armenian 1.6%; Georgian 1.4%; Moldavian 1.1%; Tadzhik 1.1%; other 10.8%.
Religious affiliation (1980): Christian 25.5%, of which Orthodox 22.5%, Protestant 1.6%, Roman Catholic 1.4%; Muslim 11.3%; Jewish 1.2%; nonreligious 29.1%; atheist 22.1%; other 10.8%.
Major cities (1985): Moscow 8,642,000; Leningrad 4,867,000; Kiev 2,448,000; Tashkent 2,030,000; Baku 1,693,000; Kharkov 1,554,000; Minsk 1,472,000; Gorky 1,399,000; Novosibirsk 1,393,000; Sverdlovsk 1,300,000; Kuybyshev 1,257,000; Tbilisi 1,158,000; Dnepropetrovsk 1,153,000.

Other principal cities (1985)

	population		population		population
Alma-Ata	1,068,000	Krasnoyarsk	872,000	Tolyatti	594,000
Barnaul	578,000	Krivoy Rog	684,000	Tula	532,000
Chelyabinsk	1,096,000	Lvov	742,000	Ufa	1,064,000
Donetsk	1,073,000	Novokuznetsk	577,000	Ulyanovsk	544,000
Dushanbe	552,000	Odessa	1,126,000	Ustinov	611,000
Frunze	604,000	Omsk	1,108,000	Vilnius	544,000
Irkutsk	597,000	Orenburg	519,000	Vladivostok	600,000
Karaganda	617,000	Penza	527,000	Volgograd	974,000
Kazan	1,047,000	Perm	1,056,000	Voronezh	850,000
Kemerovo	507,000	Riga	883,000	Yaroslavl	626,000
Khabarovsk	576,000	Rostov-na-Donu	986,000	Yerevan	1,133,000
Kishinyov	624,000	Samarkand	517,000	Zaporozhye	852,000
Krasnodar	609,000	Saratov	899,000	Zhdanov	522,000

Place of birth (1983): 99.9% native-born; 0.1% foreign-born.
Mobility (1985). Population living in the same residence from birth: 57.0%; 15 years and more 20.1%; 14–10 years 5.7%; 9–6 years 5.1%; 5–2 years 7.2%; less than 2 years 4.9%.
*Households** (1979). Average household size 3.5; 2 persons 29.7%, 3 persons 28.8%, 4 persons 23.0%, 5 persons 9.5%, 6 persons 4.1%, 7 or more persons 4.9%. Family households population: 232,075,245 (86.9%), nonfamily population 30,360,755 (13.1%).
Emigration: (1985) 1,140; (1979) 51,230.

Vital statistics

Birth rate per 1,000 population (1985): 19.4 (world avg. 29.0); legitimate, n.a.; illegitimate, n.a.
Death rate per 1,000 population (1985): 10.9 (world avg. 11.0).
Natural increase rate per 1,000 population (1985): 8.5 (world avg. 18.0).
Total fertility rate (avg. births per childbearing woman; 1982): 3.1.
Marriage rate per 1,000 population (1984): 9.6.
Divorce rate per 1,000 population (1984): 3.4.
Life expectancy at birth (1980): male 61.9 years; female 72.0 years.
Major causes of death per 100,000 population (1983): diseases of the circulatory system 554.3, of which cardiovascular atherosclerosis 228.2, cerebrovascular disease 121.6, hypertensive heart disease 82.7, ischemic heart disease 73.0, other diseases of the circulatory system 48.8; malignant neoplasms (cancers) 148.1.

Social indicators

Educational attainment (1984). Percent of population over age 10 having: less than full primary education 0.2%; primary or secondary 91.0%, of which secondary 60.4%; some postsecondary and higher 8.2%; postgraduate 0.6%.
Distribution of wealth: n.a.
Quality of working life (1985). Average workweek: 39.4 hours (3.0% overtime). Annual rate per 100,000 workers for: injury or accident, n.a.; industrial illness, n.a.; death, n.a. Proportion of labour force insured for damages or income loss resulting from: injury 100.0%; permanent disability 100.0%; death 100.0%. Average days lost to labour stoppages per 1,000 workdays: n.a. Average duration of journey to work: 58–68 minutes (mostly by public transportation and foot). Rate per 1,000 workers of discouraged (unemployed no longer seeking work): n.a.
Access to services† (1984). Proportion of dwellings having access to: electricity, virtually 100%; safe public water supply 91.0%; public sewage collection 89.0%; central heating 88.4%; gas 78.5%; hot water 71.0%; bathroom 82.0%.
Social participation. Eligible voters participating in last national election (1984): 99.9%. Population participating in voluntary work (1984): 76.5%. Trade union membership in total work force: 100.0%. Practicing religious population in total affiliated population: n.a; estimated at 10%.
Social deviance. Offense rate per 100,000 population for: murder, n.a.; rape, n.a.; other assault, n.a.; grand and auto theft, n.a.; burglary and housebreaking, n.a. Incidence per 100,000 in general population of: alcoholism, n.a.; drug and substance abuse, n.a.; suicide, n.a.
Leisure (1984). Favourite leisure activities (annual attendance): movies 3,968,000,000; lectures 301,500,000; museums 180,900,000; library 146,200,-000; concerts 138,300,000; theatre 123,500,000.
Material well-being (1985). Households possessing: automobile, n.a.; telephone 28.5%; television receiver 96.0%; refrigerator 91.0%; air conditioner, none; washing machine 70.0%; motorcyle 14.0%; bicycle 54.0%.

National economy

Global social product (at current market prices; 1984): U.S.$1,925,000,000,-000 (U.S.$7,000 per capita).

Structure of net material product and labour force

	1984			
	in value '000,000,000 rubles	% of total value	labour force	% of labour force
Agriculture	112.7	19.8	25,363,000	19.6
Mining and manufacturing }	262.2	46.0	37,957,000	29.3
Public utilities }			4,785,000	3.7
Construction	60.7	10.7	11,349,000	8.8
Transportation and communication	34.0	6.0	12,487,000	9.6
Trade	100.0	17.5	9,954,000	7.7
Finance	...	...	684,000	0.5
Pub. admin., defense	...	...	2,658,000	2.1
Services	...	...	22,703,000	17.5
Other	...	...	1,589,000	1.2
TOTAL	569.6	100.0	129,529,000	100.0

Budget (1984). Revenue: 376,700,000,000 rubles (share in profits of the state enterprises 30.7%, turnover tax 27.3%, income tax 7.6%). Expenditures: 371,200,000,000 rubles (national economy 57.0%, education and science 12.7%, social welfare 8.0%, defense 4.6%, health 4.6%).

Manufacturing, mining, and construction enterprises (1982)

	no. of enterprises	no. of employees	monthly wages as a % of avg. of all wages	annual gross output ('000,000 rubles)
Manufacturing				
Machinery and metal products	8,180	15,011,000	111.2	182,400
Food products	7,538	2,717,000	99.2	104,100
Chemicals and chemical products	1,493	1,148,000	112.8	75,500
Textiles	1,996	2,210,000	88.4	72,700
Clothing	5,118	2,250,000	88.4	30,900
Nonmetallic products	3,200	2,088,000	103.8	24,800
Wood, furniture, and paper	2,275	1,619,000	112.8	22,300
Beverages	1,726	374,000	95.5	7,700
Iron and steel	408	1,044,000	131.1	6,200
Footwear	406	494,000	95.8	5,500
Leather and leather products	266	199,000	95.9	4,200
Tobacco	88	40,000	95.5	3,800
Glass and pottery	333	376,000	99.3	3,300
Building materials	3,938	...	107.1	2,300
Rubber and plastic	...	433,000	103.5	...
Mining				
Petroleum and gas }	853	1,105,000	161.1 }	34,400
Coal }			153.9 }	
Metal ores	1,070	194,000	153.9	15,900
Construction	...	11,299,000	103.3	...

Public debt (1984): U.S.$26,000,000,000.
Tourism: tourist arrivals (1984) 7,249,000; tourists abroad (1982) 4,500,000.
Production (metric tons except as noted). Agriculture, forestry, fishing (1985): sugar beets 82,100,000, wheat 76,000,000‡, potatoes 73,000,000, barley 44,000,000, oats 18,000,000, corn (maize) 14,000,000‡, rye 13,500,000‡, flax fibre 9,200,000, raw cotton 8,750,000, grapes 7,500,000, sunflower seeds 5,230,000, dry pears 5,200,000‡, millet and sorghum 2,400,000‡, tobacco 360,000; livestock (number of live animals) 142,876,000 sheep, 121,055,000 cattle, 77,914,000 pigs, 6,325,000 goats, 5,783,000 horses, 1,143,000,000 poultry; roundwood 296,000,000 cu m‡; fish catch 10,400,000. Mining and quarrying (1984): iron ore 247,000,000; phosphate rock 76,400,000; salt 16,500,000; potash salts 9,800,000; bauxite 4,600,000; chromium ore 3,450,000; manganese (metal content) 3,000,000; magnesite 2,500,000; asbestos 2,300,000; copper 850,000; zinc 805,000‡; lead 435,000; nickel 176,000; molybdenum 11,200; tungsten 9,100‡; mercury 64,000 flasks‡; diamonds 10,900,000 carats. Manufacturing (1985): crude steel 155,000,000; cement 131,000,000; pig iron 110,500,000; rolled steel 108,300,000; mineral fertilizers 33,200,000; sulfuric acid 26,000,000; steel pipes 19,300,000; meat 17,100,000; sugar 11,800,000; paper and paperboard 6,000,000; resins and plastics 5,020,000; soda ash 4,800,000; caustic soda 3,100,000; cotton fibre 2,750,000; vegetable oil 2,500,000; cotton yarn 1,710,000; butter 1,515,000; man-made fibres 1,500,000; margarine 1,400,000; synthetic detergents 1,200,000; soap 1,098,000‡; insecticides 595,000; woolen yarn 447,000‡; woolen fibre 369,000‡; flax fibre 365,000‡; leather 126,000‡; cotton fabrics 7,523,000,000 sq m; rayon fabrics 1,914,000,000 sq m; linen fabrics 782,000,000 sq m; woolen fabrics 684,000,000 sq m; fish products 7,300,000,000 rubles; machine tools 2,674,000,000 rubles; food-processing equipment 963,000,000 rubles; forge press machines 662,000,000 rubles; leather footwear 787,000,000 pairs; tires 65,200,000 units; television receivers 9,400,000 units; radio receivers 8,800,000 units; refrigerators 5,900,000 units; bicycles 5,060,000 units; washing machines 5,100,000 units; passenger cars 1,332,000 units; motorcycles 1,100,000 units; buses 85,093 units; railroad freight cars 58,433 units‡; railroad passenger cars 1,916 units‡; beer 66,081,000 hectolitres‡; wine 35,101,000 hectolitres‡. Construction (1985): residential 114,000,000 sq m, of which urban 112,100,000 sq m, rural 1,900,000 sq m.

Service enterprises (1984)

	no. of enter-prises§	no. of employees	monthly wage as a % of all wages
Public utilities	...	3,875,000	77.6
Electrical power	1,433	910,000	116.8
Transport: rail	...	2,665,000	116.5
Transport: road	...	7,699,000	116.8
Transport: water	...	451,000	139.8
Communication	90,883	1,672,000	84.3
Finance	...	684,000	95.1
Wholesale trade	...	...	79.0
Retail trade	699,900	...	79.0
Tourism	...	...	...
Education	275,255	9,960,000	76.8
Public services and administration	...	2,658,000	87.4
Other services	276,000	22,703,000	...

Energy production (consumption): electricity (kW-hr; 1985) 1,545,000,000,000 (1,468,000,000,000‡); coal (metric tons; 1985) 726,000,000 (654,000,000‡); crude petroleum (barrels; 1985) 4,337,000,000 (3,642,000,000‡); petroleum products (metric tons; 1984) 409,260,000 (348,010,000); natural gas (cu m; 1985) 643,000,000,000 (524,000,000,000‡).
Population economically active (1984): total 129,529,000; activity rate of total population 46.9% (participation rates: ages [male] 15–60, [female] 15–55, 51.8%; female 46.0%; unemployed, n.a.).

Price and earnings indexes (1980 = 100)

	1979	1980	1981	1982	1983	1984
Consumer price index	96.9	100.0	101.2	104.5	105.2	104.0
Monthly earnings index	97.3	100.0	102.3	105.4	107.3	108.8

Household income and expenditure. Average household size (1984) 3.0; average annual income per household 5,600 rubles (U.S.$8,000); sources of income: wages and salaries 69.8%, social welfare 24.3%, other 5.9%; expenditure (1984): food 30.2%, alcohol 17.0%, clothing 15.6%, education and culture 15.6%, taxes 8.8%, housing 2.7%.
Land use (1983): forested 35.6%; meadows and pastures 16.7%; agricultural and under permanent cultivation 10.5%; other 37.2%.

Foreign trade

Balance of trade (current prices)

	1979	1980	1981	1982	1983	1984
'000,000,000 rubles	4.6	5.2	4.5	6.7	8.3	9.1
% of total	5.7%	5.5%	4.1%	5.6%	6.5%	6.5%

Imports (1984): 65,327,000,000 rubles (machinery and transport equipment 36.6%; cereals and food products 22.5%; consumer goods 11.7%; raw materials 8.3%; mineral fuels and lubricants 5.1%; chemicals and related products 4.5%; textiles and clothing 1.2%). *Major import sources:* East Germany 11.3%; Czechoslovakia 9.2%; Bulgaria 8.6%; Poland 8.1%; Hungary 6.8%; Cuba 5.3%; West Germany 5.0%; United States 4.3%; Yugoslavia 4.2%; Finland 3.5%; Japan 3.0%; Romania 2.7%; France 2.7%; Italy 2.0%; India 1.9%; Libya 1.7%; Argentina 1.7%; Austria 1.4%; United Kingdom 1.3%; Iraq 1.0%; China 0.8%; Belgium 0.8%.
Exports (1984): 74,384,000,000 rubles (crude petroleum and petroleum products 41.5%; mineral fuels and natural gas 12.9%; machinery and transport equipment 12.5%; raw materials 7.2%; chemicals, fertilizers, and resins 3.5%; wood and paper products 2.8%). *Major export destinations:* East Germany 10.1%; Czechoslovakia 8.9%; Bulgaria 8.2%; Poland 8.2%; Hungary 5.8%; West Germany 5.8%; Cuba 5.0%; Italy 4.2%; Yugoslavia 4.1%; Finland 3.3%; France 3.3%; Romania 2.4%; India 2.1%; United Kingdom 1.9%; Belgium 1.6%; Mongolia 1.4%; Vietnam 1.3%; Afghanistan 0.8%.

Trade by commodity group (1984)

	imports		exports	
SITC Group	'000 rubles	%	'000 rubles	%
00 Food and live animals	14,699,000	22.5	1,116,000	1.5
02 Raw materials, excluding fuels	5,422,000	8.3	5,356,000	7.2
03 Mineral fuels, lubricants, and related materials	3,332,000	5.1	40,465,000	54.4
05 Chemicals and related products	2,940,000	4.5	2,603,000	3.5
65 Textile yarn, fabrics and related materials	1,045,000	1.6	893,000	1.2
07 Machinery and transport equipment	23,909,000	36.6	9,298,000	12.5
08 Miscellaneous manufactured articles	7,643,000	11.7	1,338,000	1.8
09 Goods not classified by kind	6,337,000	9.7	13,315,000	17.9
TOTAL	65,327,000	100.0	74,384,000	100.0

Direction of trade (1984)

	imports		exports	
	'000 rubles	%	'000 rubles	%
Communist				
Comecon	34,587,000	52.9	38,165,000	51.3
Other	3,633,000	5.6	3,941,000	5.3
Market Economy				
Industrial countries	19,574,000	30.0	21,350,000	28.7
Developing countries	7,533,000	11.5	10,928,000	14.7
TOTAL	65,327,000	100.0	74,384,000	100.0

Transport and communications

Transport. Railroads (1985): length 89,562 mi, 144,136 km; passenger-mi 226,000,000,000, passenger-km 364,000,000,000; short ton-mi cargo 2,492,000,000,000, metric ton-km cargo 3,639,000,000,000. Roads (1985): total length 605,000 mi, 974,000 km (paved 81%). Vehicles (1980): passenger cars 8,255,000; trucks and buses 7,254,000. Inland waterways (1985): length 84,940 mi, 136,700 km; passenger-mi 3,670,000,000, passenger-km 5,900,000,000; short ton-mi cargo 181,019,000,000, metric ton-km cargo 264,300,000,000. Merchant marine (1985): vessels (100 gross tons and over) 7,154; total deadweight tonnage 28,153,312. Air transport (1985): passenger-mi 117,100,000,000, passenger-km 188,400,000,000; short ton-mi cargo 2,294,000,000, metric ton-km cargo 3,350,000,000; airports (1986) with scheduled flights 52. Shares of domestic passenger traffic by mode of transportation (1984): buses 43.7%; railway 36.8%; ships and airplanes 19.5%. Oil and gas pipelines (1985): length 151,180 mi, 243,300 km; short ton-mi cargo 1,621,400,000,000§, metric ton-km cargo 2,367,300,000,000§.

Distribution of traffic (1984)

	cargo carried ('000,000 tons)	% of nat'l total	passengers carried ('000,000)	% of nat'l total
Road	6,357.0	49.9	45,800.0	45.6
Rail	3,909.5	30.7	4,155.0	4.1
Urban transport	—	—	50,080.0	49.9
road	—	—	31,900.0	31.8
rail	—	—	18,180.0	18.1
Inland water	854.5	6.7	186.6	0.2
Air	3.1	0.0	112.3	0.1
Pipeline	1,621.4	12.7	—	—
TOTAL	12,745.5	100.0	100,333.9	100.0‖

Communications. Daily newspapers (1985): total number 724; total circulation 34,126,000,000; circulation per person 123. Radio (1985): 178,000,000 (1 per 1.5 persons). Television (1985): number of receivers 80,300,000 (1 per 3.4 persons). Telephones (1985): 29,462,000 (1 per 9.3 persons).

Education and health

Education (1984–85)

	schools	teachers	students	student/teacher ratio
Primary (age 6–13)	67,500	2,430,000	35,800,000	...
Secondary (age 14–17)	59,900		4,512,000	...
Vocational	4,471	246,000	4,500,000	18.2
Higher	892	377,000	5,280,100	14.0

Literacy (1984): total population over age 15 literate 99.0%.
Health (1986): physicians 1,170,000¶ (1 per 239 persons); hospital beds 3,613,000 (1 per 78 persons); infant mortality rate per 1,000 live births (1985) 26.0.
Food (1980–82): daily per capita caloric intake 3,358 (vegetable products 74%, animal products 26%); 130% of FAO recommended minimum requirement.

Military

Total active duty personnel (1986): 5,130,000 (army 38.8%, command and general support troops 28.4%, paramilitary forces 11.1%, navy 8.8%, air force 8.8%, forces abroad 4.1%). *Military expenditure as percent of GDP* (1985): 12–17%♀ (world 6.1%); per capita expenditure U.S.$1,000.

*Family households only. †Only urban dwellings. ‡1984. §1982. ‖Detail does not add to total given because of rounding. ¶Includes dentists. ♀Estimated by Western sources.

United Arab Emirates

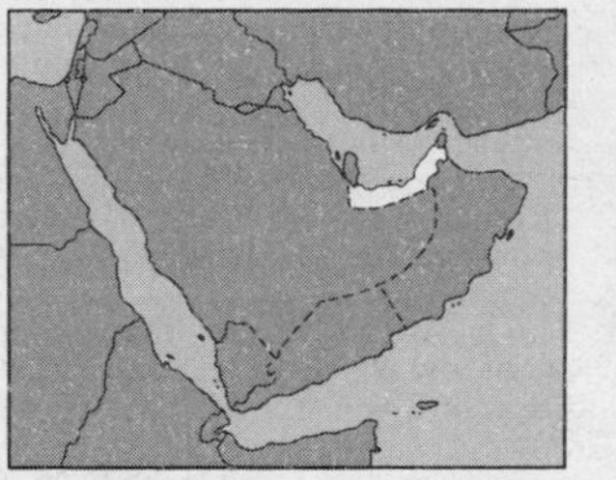

Official name: Ittiḥād al-Imārāt al-ʿArabīyah (United Arab Emirates).
Form of government: monarchy; federal union of seven emirates with one legislative house (Federal National Council [40]).
Chief of state: President.
Head of government: Prime Minister.
Capital: Abu Dhabi.
Official language: Arabic.
Official religion: Islam.
Monetary unit: 1 U.A.E. Dirham (Dh) = 100 fils; valuation (Oct. 1, 1986) 1 U.S.$ = Dh 3.67; 1 £ = Dh 5.31.

Area and population

		area		population
Emirates	**Capitals**	sq mi	sq km	1983 estimate
Abu Dhabi (Abū Ẓaby)	Abu Dhabi	26,000	67,340	521,000
Ajman (ʿAjmān)	Ajman	100	260	44,000
Dubai (Dubayy)	Dubai	1,500	3,890	307,000
Fujairah (Al-Fujayrah)	Fujairah	450	1,170	38,000
Ras al-Khaimah (Ra's al-Khaymah)	Ras al-Khaimah	650	1,680	86,000
Sharjah (Ash-Shāriqah)	Sharjah	1,000	2,590	185,000
Umm al-Qaiwain (Umm al-Qaywayn)	Umm al-Qaiwain	300	770	14,000
TOTAL		30,000	77,700	1,195,000

Demography

Population (1986): 1,342,000.
Density (1986): persons per sq mi 44.7, persons per sq km 17.3.
Urban–rural (1984): urban 78.1%; rural 21.9%.
Sex distribution (1984): male 68.85%; female 31.15%.
Age breakdown (1984): under 15, 28.4%; 15–29, 34.4%; 30–44, 29.3%; 45–59, 6.3%; 60–74, 1.3%; 75 and over, 0.3%.
Population projection: (1990) 1,570,000; (2000) 1,916,000.
Doubling time: 30 years.
Ethnic composition (1982): South Asian (mainly Indian and Pakistani) 50%; Arab 42%; other (mainly European, East Asian, and Iranian) 8%.
Religious affiliation (1980): Muslim 94.9% (Sunnī 80%, Shīʿī 20%); Christian 3.8%; other 1.3%.
Major cities (1980): Dubai 266,000; Abu Dhabi 243,000; Sharjah 125,000; al-ʿAyn 102,000; Ras al-Khaimah 42,000.

Vital statistics

Birth rate per 1,000 population (1980–85): 27.0 (world avg. 29.0); legitimate, n.a.; illegitimate, n.a.
Death rate per 1,000 population (1980–85): 4.0 (world avg. 11.0).
Natural increase rate per 1,000 population (1980–85): 23.0 (world avg. 18.0).
Total fertility rate (avg. births per childbearing woman; 1980–85): 6.7.
Marriage rate per 1,000 population (1984): 3.3*.
Divorce rate per 1,000 population (1984): 1.4*.
Life expectancy at birth (1980–85): male 61.6 years; female 65.6 years.
Major infectious diseases per 100,000 population (1984)*: chicken pox 358.7; malaria 224.8; measles 85.6; mumps 79.2; hepatitis 44.6; tuberculosis 40.4.

National economy

Budget (1986). Revenue: Dh 12,837,000,000 (breakdown, n.a.; consists largely of oil concession receipts). Expenditures: Dh 14,023,000,000 (defense 41.5%, investments 8.1%, capital spending 3.9%).
Gross national product (at current market prices; 1984): U.S.$28,480,000,000 (U.S.$23,250 per capita).

Structure of gross domestic product and labour force

	1983		1984	
	in value Dh '000,000	% of total value	labour force	% of labour force
Agriculture	1,130	1.1	35,895	4.9
Mining	45,304	44.8	14,866	2.0
Manufacturing	9,045	9.0	47,178	6.4
Construction	11,000	10.9	187,720	25.4
Public utilities	1,976	1.9	14,082	1.9
Transportation and communication	5,110	5.1	54,530	7.4
Trade	9,936	9.8	99,722	13.5
Finance }	17,607	17.4	21,920	3.0
Pub. admin., defense }			...	...
Services }			260,520	35.3
Other }			1,545†	0.2†
TOTAL	101,108	100.0	737,978	100.0

Public debt (external, outstanding; 1982): U.S.$1,117,000,000.
Production (metric tons except as noted). Agriculture, forestry, fishing (1984): dates 58,000, tomatoes 37,000, watermelons 26,000, cantaloupes and other melons 18,000, pumpkins and squash 9,000, eggplants 8,000, cabbages 5,000, cucumbers and gherkins 5,000, lemons and limes 5,000, milk 5,000, cauliflower 4,000, leaf tobacco 2,000, mangoes 2,000, green peppers 2,000, wheat 1,000, barley 1,000, carrots 1,000, corn (maize) 1,000, roots and tubers 1,000, potatoes 1,000, almonds 320; livestock (number of live animals) 450,000 goats, 150,000 sheep, 70,000 camels, 30,000 cattle, 3,000,000 chickens, eggs 3,800; fish catch (1983) 73,115. Mining and quarrying (1984): lime 45,000; also marble, shale for ceramic applications, and aggregate for cement. Manufacturing (1984): cement 9,000,000; aluminum 155,355; steel 65,000; sulfur 15,000; mutton and lamb meat 5,000; cow milk 5,000; goat meat 4,000; beef and veal meat 3,000; butter and ghee 150. Construction (value added in Dh; 1982): 11,015,000,000. Energy production (consumption): electricity (kW-hr; 1984) 6,636,000,000 (6,636,000,000); coal, none (n.a.); crude petroleum (barrels; 1984) 419,100,000 (36,682,000); petroleum products (metric tons; 1984) 10,060,000 (5,675,000); natural gas (cu m; 1984) 3,815,348,000 (987,408,000).
Tourism (1982): 9,836 rooms for tourists.
Population economically active (1984): total 737,978; activity rate of total population 54.5% (participation rates: over age 15, 76.1%; female 18.3%; unemployed, n.a.).
Price and earnings indexes: n.a.
Household income and expenditure: Average household size (1980) 3.8; average annual income per household: n.a.; source of income: n.a.; expenditure: n.a.
Land use (1983): forested, none; meadows and pastures 2.4%; agricultural and under permanent cultivation 0.2%; built-up, wasteland, and other 97.4%.

Foreign trade

Balance of trade (current prices)

	1978	1979	1980	1981	1982	1983
Dh '000,000	+38,885	+29,382	+25,673	+14,668	+18,187	+24,430
% of total	35.4%	31.2%	32.6%	26.1%	31.6%	28.5%

Imports (1983): Dh 30,675,000,000 (1981; nonelectrical machinery 16.7%, electrical machinery 9.5%, transport equipment 9.5%, food and live animals 9.1%, iron and steel 6.9%, textile yarn and fabric 5.8%, chemicals 5.1%). *Major import sources* (1984): Japan 17.8%; United States 12.1%; United Kingdom 9.9%; Italy 7.1%; West Germany 6.7%; Bahrain 5.4%; France 4.6%; The Netherlands 2.8%; Australia 2.3%; Singapore 1.7%; China 1.6%; Belgium–Luxembourg 1.5%; Switzerland 1.4%; Saudi Arabia 0.9%; Thailand 0.9%; Turkey 0.6%.
Exports (1983): Dh 55,105,000,000 (crude petroleum 86.2%, nonpetroleum exports 9.8%). *Major export destinations* (1984): Japan 49.4%; United States 8.2%; France 6.0%; Singapore 4.2%; Oman 3.1%; Italy 2.5%; Pakistan 2.1%; West Germany 1.8%; Australia 1.5%; Saudi Arabia 1.1%; Portugal 1.1%; Bangladesh 0.8%; United Kingdom 0.8%; The Netherlands 0.4%; Belgium–Luxembourg 0.3%; Bahrain 0.2%.

Transport and communications

Transport. Railroads: none. Roads (1981): total length 800 mi, 1,300 km (paved, n.a.). Vehicles (1981): passenger cars 130,700; trucks and buses 77,600. Merchant marine (1985): vessels (100 gross tons and over) 232; total deadweight tonnage 1,523,669. Air transport (1983): passenger-mi 2,213,000,000, passenger-km 3,562,000,000; short ton-mi cargo 65,300,000, metric ton-km cargo 95,300,000; airports (1986) with scheduled flights 2.
Communications. Daily newspapers (1985): total number 11; total circulation 272,500; circulation per 1,000 population 212.4. Radio (1985): total number of receivers 240,000 (1 per 5 persons). Television (1985): total number of receivers 112,000 (1 per 11 persons). Telephones (1983): 319,246 (1 per 4 persons).

Education and health

Education (1983–84)

	schools	teachers	students	student/ teacher ratio
Primary (age 6–11) }	327	5,278‡	125,923	...
Secondary (age 12–18) }		3,462‡	50,244	...
Vocational	9	273	2,442	8.9
Higher	...	443	4,502	10.2

Educational attainment (1975). Percent of adult population over age 25 having: no formal schooling 72.2%; primary education 5.2%; secondary education 16.6%; higher education 6.0%. *Literacy* (1984): total population over age 15 literate 689,845 (71.2%); males literate 534,182 (72.7%); females literate 155,663 (66.3%).
Health (1984): physicians 1,840 (1 per 666 persons); hospital beds 4,853 (1 per 252 persons); infant mortality rate per 1,000 live births (1980–84) 49.6.
Food (1980–82): daily per capita caloric intake 3,524 (vegetable products 73%, animal products 27%); 146% of FAO recommended minimum requirement.

Military

Total active duty personnel (1985): 43,000 (army 93.0%, navy 3.5%, air force 3.5%). *Military expenditure as percent of GNP* (1983): 7.9% (world 6.1%); per capita expenditure U.S.$1,492.

*Abu Dhabi Emirate only. †Unemployed seeking work for the first time. ‡Public schools only.

United Kingdom

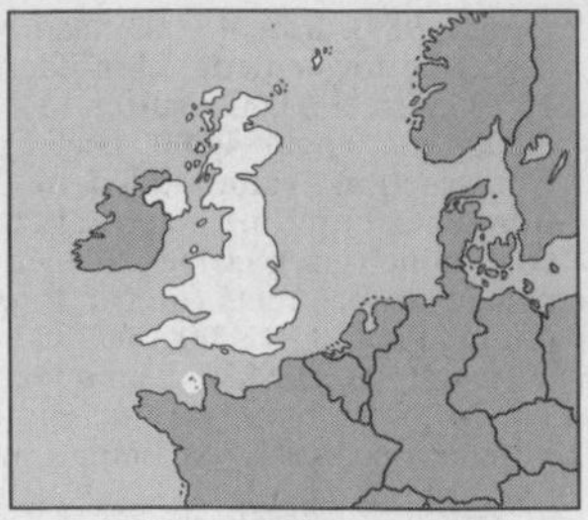

Official name: United Kingdom of Great Britain and Northern Ireland.
Form of government: constitutional monarchy with two legislative houses (House of Lords [1,178]; House of Commons [650]).
Chief of state: Sovereign.
Head of government: Prime Minister.
Capital: London.
Official language: English.
Official religion: Churches of England and Scotland "established" (protected and maintained by the state, but not "official") in their respective countries; no established church in Northern Ireland or Wales.
Monetary unit: 1 pound sterling (£) = 100 new pence; valuation (Oct. 1, 1986) 1 £ = U.S.$1.44.

Area and population

		area		population
Countries	**Capitals**	sq mi	sq km	1985 estimate
England	London	50,363	130,439	47,111,700
Counties				
Avon		520	1,346	942,000
Bedfordshire		477	1,235	516,700
Berkshire		486	1,259	724,000
Buckinghamshire		727	1,883	601,600
Cambridgeshire		1,316	3,409	621,400
Cheshire		899	2,329	942,400
Cleveland		225	583	559,900
Cornwall		1,376	3,564	443,800
Cumbria		2,629	6,810	484,400
Derbyshire		1,016	2,631	912,400
Devon		2,591	6,711	988,000
Dorset		1,025	2,654	627,700
Durham		941	2,436	600,900
East Sussex		693	1,795	682,400
Essex		1,418	3,672	1,504,700
Gloucestershire		1,020	2,643	511,400
Greater London*		610	1,579	6,767,500
Greater Manchester*		497	1,287	2,582,600
Hampshire		1,458	3,777	1,523,900
Hereford & Worcester		1,516	3,927	650,800
Hertfordshire		631	1,634	986,100
Humberside		1,356	3,512	850,000
Isle of Wight		147	381	122,900
Kent		1,441	3,731	1,495,200
Lancashire		1,183	3,064	1,380,300
Leicestershire		986	2,553	872,200
Lincolnshire		2,284	5,915	560,300
Merseyside*		252	652	1,481,000
Norfolk		2,073	5,368	719,100
Northamptonshire		914	2,367	546,100
Northumberland		1,943	5,032	300,600
North Yorkshire		3,208	8,309	696,600
Nottinghamshire		836	2,164	1,005,900
Oxfordshire		1,007	2,608	565,400
Shropshire		1,347	3,490	390,300
Somerset		1,332	3,451	447,000
South Yorkshire*		602	1,560	1,303,200
Staffordshire		1,049	2,716	1,020,400
Suffolk		1,466	3,797	624,200
Surrey		648	1,679	1,013,700
Tyne and Wear*		208	540	1,139,900
Warwickshire		765	1,981	479,700
West Midlands*		347	899	2,641,800
West Sussex		768	1,989	687,700
West Yorkshire*		787	2,039	2,052,800
Wiltshire		1,344	3,480	540,800
Northern Ireland†	Belfast	5,462	14,147	1,568,000
Scotland	Edinburgh	29,794‡	77,167	5,136,500
Regions				
Borders		1,804	4,672	101,700
Central		1,016	2,631	272,400
Dumfries and Galloway		2,459	6,370	146,600
Fife		505	1,307	344,100
Grampian		3,361	8,704	500,600
Highland		9,803	25,391	198,600
Lothian		678	1,755	745,200
Strathclyde		5,227	13,537	2,358,700
Tayside		2,893	7,493	394,300
Island areas (TOTAL)		2,049	5,307	74,300
Wales	Cardiff	8,019	20,768	2,811,800
Counties				
Clwyd		937	2,427	397,900
Dyfed		2,227	5,768	335,900
Gwent		531	1,376	440,200
Gwynedd		1,494	3,869	233,600
Mid Glamorgan		393	1,018	533,900
Powys		1,960	5,077	111,400
South Glamorgan		161	416	394,800
West Glamorgan		316	817	364,100
TOTAL		94,248	244,100	56,628,000

Demography

Population (1986): 56,678,000.
Density (1986): persons per sq mi 601.4, persons per sq km 232.2.
Urban-rural (1985): urban 92.5%; rural 7.5%.
Sex distribution (1986): male 48.68%; female 51.32%.
Age breakdown (1986): under 15, 19.0%; 15–29, 23.7%; 30–44, 20.3%; 45–59, 16.3%; 60–74, 14.3%; 75 and over, 6.4%.
Population projection: (1990) 57,900,000; (2000) 59,600,000.
Doubling time: more than 100 years.
Ethnic composition (1984): white 94.1%; Indian 1.5%; West Indian 1.0%; Pakistani 0.7%; African 0.2%; Chinese 0.2%; Bangladeshi 0.2%; Arab 0.1%; other and not stated 2.0%.
Religious affiliation (1980): Christian 87.8%, of which Anglican 57.0%, Roman Catholic 13.0%, Presbyterian 7.0%, Methodist 4.3%, Baptist 1.4%; nonreligious 8.2%; Muslim 1.3%; Jewish 0.8%; Hindu 0.5%; Sikh 0.4%; other 1.0%.
Major cities (1984): Greater London 6,767,500‡; Birmingham 1,009,400; Glasgow 733,800‡; Leeds 712,200; Sheffield 540,500; Liverpool 497,200; Bradford 464,400; Manchester 451,100; Edinburgh 439.700; Bristol 396,600.
Place of birth (1984): 93.2% (50,400,000) native-born; 5.6% foreign-born, of which Ireland 1.0%, India 0.7%, Caribbean 0.4%, Pakistan 0.3.%; not stated 1.2%
Mobility (1981). Population living in the same residence as 1980: 90.9%; different residence, same country (of the U.K.) 8.2%; different residence, different country within the U.K. 0.4%; from outside the U.K. 0.5%.
Households§ (1984). Average household size 2.6 (3.1); 1 person 25% (20%), 2 persons 32% (26%), 3 persons 16% (16%), 4 persons 18% (17%), 5 persons 6% (10%), 6 or more persons 3% (11%). Family households: 16,079,300 (74.3%), nonfamily 5,593,100 (25.7%, of which 1-person 22.5%).
Immigration (1985): permanent residents 270,000, from EEC 19.6%, Australia, New Zealand, and Canada 14.1%, United States 11.1%, South Africa 7.8%, Middle East 7.4%, Bangladesh and India 5.2%, Pakistan 4.4%.

Vital statistics

Birth rate per 1,000 population (1985): 13.3 (world avg. 29.0); legitimate 81.1%; illegitimate 18.9%.
Death rate per 1,000 population (1985): 11.7 (world avg. 11.0).
Natural increase rate per 1,000 population (1985): 1.6 (world avg. 18.0).
Total fertility rate (avg. births per childbearing woman; 1985): 1.8.
Marriage rate per 1,000 population (1985): 6.9.
Divorce rate per 1,000 population (1985): 2.8.
Life expectancy at birth (1982–84): male 71.6 years; female 77.6 years.
Major causes of death per 100,000 population (1985): diseases of the circulatory system 564.0, of which ischemic heart disease 319.4, cerebrovascular disease 145.0; malignant neoplasms (cancers) 279.2; diseases of the respiratory system 117.1, of which pneumonia 53.2; diseases of the digestive system 34.4; accidents 27.0; diseases of the endocrine system 16.5, of which diabetes mellitus 12.3; diseases of the genitourinary system 15.5.

Social indicators

Educational attainment (1981): Percent of adult population over age 18 having: primary or secondary education only, *c.* 90%; some postsecondary 4.5%; bachelor's or equivalent degree 4.7%; higher university degree 0.5%.

Distribution of disposable income (1983)

percent of household income by quintile

1	2	3	4	5 (highest)
6.9	11.9	17.6	24.0	39.6

Quality of working life (1984). Average workweek (hours): male 41.4, female 37.2 (overtime male 7.7%, female 1.3%). Annual rate per 100,000 workers for: injury or accident 61.0; industrial diseases 0.5; death 2.1. Proportion of labour force (employed persons) insured for damages or income loss resulting from: injury 100%; permanent disability 100%; death 100%. Average days lost to labour stoppages per 1,000 employee workdays: 1.3. Principal means of transport to work: 55% private automobile, 20.5% public transportation, 15% foot, 2.5% bicycle, 7% other.
Access to services (1982). Proportion of households having access to: bath or shower 96%; toilet 95%; central heating 63%.
Social participation. Eligible voters participating in last national election: 75.9%. Population over 16 years of age participating in voluntary work (1983): 23%. Trade union membership in total work force (1983) 41.1%.
Social deviance (1984). Offense rate per 100,000 population for: theft and handling stolen goods 3,837.4; burglary 1,589.0; fraud and forgery 268.4; violence against the person 212.9; robbery 56.5; sexual offense 38.7. Incidence per 100,000 population of: notified drug addicts 7.9; suicide 8.8.
Leisure (1984). Favourite leisure activities (hours weekly): watching television 9.6; listening to radio 8.7; reading 2.6; cultural activities 1.5.
Material well-being§ (1983). Households possessing: automobile 62.1% (58%), telephone 77.3% (66%), television receiver 96.9% (95%), refrigerator 97.0% (89%), heating (full or partial) 63.9% (64%), washing machine 81.3% (73%).

National economy

Gross national product (at current market prices; 1985): U.S.$507,603,000,000 (U.S.$8,960 per capita).

Structure of gross domestic product and labour force

	1985			
	in value £'000,000	% of total value	labour force	% of labour force
Agriculture	5,485	1.8	338,000	1.2
Mining }	76,800	25.1	276,000	1.0
Manufacturing }			5,533,000	20.1
Construction	18,651	6.1	970,000	3.6
Public utilities	34,335	11.2	338,000	1.2
Transp. and commun.	20,957	6.9	1,304,000	4.7
Trade	40,384	13.2	4,470,000	16.2
Finance	60,248	19.7	1,971,000	7.1
Pub. admin., defense	21,599	7.1	1,583,000	5.7
Services	44,165	14.4	4,684,000	17.0
Other	−16,883 ‖	−5.5 ‖	6,126,000¶	22.2¶
TOTAL	305,741	100.0	27,593,000	100.0

Budget (1985). Revenue: £147,363,000,000 (taxes on expenditures 38.6%, income tax 35.3%, national insurance contributions 16.3%). Expenditures: £147,363,000,000 (social security benefits 25.2%, debt interest 12.1%, military defense 12.3%, national health service 9.6%, education and science 9.2%).
Total national debt (1984): £143,000,000,000.

Financial aggregates

	1980	1981	1982	1983	1984	1985	1986
Exchange rate:							
U.S. Dollar per £	2.33	2.03	1.75	1.52	1.34	1.30	1.47♀
SDRs per £	1.87	1.64	1.46	1.39	1.18	1.32	1.20♀
International reserves (U.S.$)							
Total (excl. gold; '000,000,000)	20.65	15.24	12.40	11.34	9.44	12.86	18.59♀
SDRs ('000,000,000)	0.57	0.99	1.17	0.52	0.50	1.13	1.35♀
Reserve pos. in IMF ('000,000,000)	1.33	1.44	1.55	2.10	1.97	1.99	2.00♀
Foreign exchange ('000,000,000)	18.75	12.81	9.67	8.72	6.97	9.74	15.24♀
Gold ('000,000 fine troy oz)	18.84	19.03	19.01	19.01	19.03	19.03	19.03♀
% world reserves	27.7	27.7	27.8	27.8	27.8	27.7	27.6ð
Interest and prices◇							
Central bank discount (%)	14.00	...	...	...	...	...	
Gov't. Bond yield (%) long term	13.79	14.74	12.88	10.81	10.69	10.62	9.41ð
Industrial share prices (1980 = 100)	100.0	112.8	130.7	164.9	196.2	242.2	301.5ð
Balance of payments (U.S.$'000,000)							
Balance of visible trade,	+3,362	+7,171	+3,906	−1,312	−5,859	−2,283	−2,578□
Imports, f.o.b.	106,891	95,594	93,175	93,391	99,480	103,240	27,967
Exports, f.o.b.	110,253	102,765	97,081	92,078	93,621	100,957	25,389
Balance of invisibles	9,790	11,190	8,578	10,043	9,693	12,116	...
Balance of payments, current account	7,460	13,059	6,872	4,730	1,928	5,341	229□

Tourism (1984): receipts from visitors U.S.$5,546,000,000; expenditures by nationals abroad U.S.$6,142,000,000.

Manufacturing, mining, and construction enterprises (1984)

	no. of enterprises	no. of employees	annual wages as a % of avg. of all wages	annual gross output (£'000,000)◇
Manufacturing				
Food, drink, and tobacco	3,282	556,700	103.0	40,085.0
Chemical engineering	1,354	291,700	118.1	20,960.0
Mechanical engineering	3,023	623,500	108.4	19,859.0
Electrical and electronic engineering	2,412	527,500	96.8	18,362.0
Paper and paper products; printing and publishing	3,237	379,900	133.8	14,096.0
Motor vehicles	1,000	302,000	116.1	12,050.0
Metal manufacturing	901	303,400	102.8	10,281.0
Other transport equipment	671	335,300	105.2	8,565.0
Timber and wood products	2,091	139,800	98.1	6,330.0
Rubber and plastic	1,529	179,000	118.1	6,183.0
Footwear and clothing	2,727	245,500	85.6	5,501.0
Textiles	1,883	217,500	79.2	5,439.0
Mining				
Extraction of minerals other than fuels			103.1	40,455.0
Extraction of coal, mineral oil, and natural gas	1,649	292,000	118.1	18,664.0
Mineral oil processing			118.1	14,318.0
Construction	147,330△	989,000	...	29,263.5△

Production (metric tons except as noted). Agriculture, forestry, fishing (1985): wheat 12,050,000, barley 9,740,000, sugar beets 7,715,000, potatoes 6,895,000, turnips and rutabagas 3,300,000, corn (maize) 770,000, oats 615,000; livestock (number of live animals) 24,540,000 sheep, 12,865,000 cattle, 7,930,000 pigs; roundwood (1984) 3,780,000 cu m; fish catch (1984) 715,100. Mining (metric tons; 1984): iron ore 382,000; lead 331,300; aluminum 278,900; zinc 85,600; copper 69,400; tin 4,100. Manufacturing (total sales in £'000,000; 1985): motor vehicles and parts 8,275; aerospace equipment 4,371; electronic data processing and telecommunication equipment 3,267; radios and televisions 2,674; telephone and telegraph equipment 1,668; boilers 1,575; packaging containers of metal 1,569; mechanical lifting and handling equipment 1,559; constructional steelwork 1,476; precision instruments 1,433. Construction (value in £; 1985): residential 5,289,000,000; nonresidential 10,054,000,000, of which public 3,877,000,000, industrial 2,149,000,000, commercial 4,028,000,000.

Retail trade enterprises (1982)

	no. of enterprises	no. of employees	weekly wage as a % of all wages	annual turnover (£'000,000)✝
Food and grocery, of which	82,625	818,000	...	27,211
large grocery	113	379,000	...	16,703
other grocery	38,277	164,000	...	4,368
meats	14,954	84,000	...	2,405
Household goods, of which	39,112	269,000	...	9,358
electrical and musical goods	8,044	74,000	...	2,959
furniture	9,533	64,000	...	2,505
Drink, confectionery, and tobacco, of which	40,862	264,000	...	7,641
tobacco and confectionery	37,525	230,000	...	5,888
Clothing and footwear, of which	28,923	269,000	...	5,911
womens', girls', and infants' wear	15,105	99,000	...	2,020
footwear	3,422	77,000	...	1,467
men's and boys' wear	3,965	44,000	...	1,231
Mail order	21	44,000	...	2,421
Pharmaceuticals	7,921	66,000	...	2,074

Energy production (consumption): electricity (kW-hr; 1984) 280,491,000,000 (280,491,000,000); coal (metric tons; 1984) 51,182,000 (77,901,000); crude petroleum (barrels; 1984) 892,000,000 (597,000,000); natural gas (cu m; 1984) 43,102,000,000 (51,139,000,000).

Population economically active (1985): total 27,594,000; activity rate of total population 48.7% (participation rates: ages 15–64, 74.3%; female 32.9%; unemployed 11.5%).

Price and earnings indexes (1980 = 100)

	1980	1981	1982	1983	1984	1985	1986
Consumer price index	100.0	111.9	121.5	127.1	133.4	141.5	146.3ð
Monthly earnings index	100.0	113.4	126.3	137.1	144.9	161.1	173.8⊕

Household income and expenditure. Average household size (1983) 2.6; average annual income per household £9,550 (U.S.$14,520); sources of income: wages and salaries 64.9%, social security benefits 15.2%, rent, dividends, and interest 9.8%, income from self-employment 8.9%; expenditure (1986): food 18.5%, transport and communication 17.8%, housing 15.3%, recreation, entertainment, and education 8.8%, clothing and footwear 7.5%, household goods and services 6.3%, energy 6.2%.
Land use (1984): forested 8.9%; meadows and pastures 50.2%; agricultural and under permanent cultivation 27.5%; other 13.4%.

Foreign trade**

Balance of trade (current prices)

	1980	1981	1982	1983	1984	1985
£'000,000	−2,409	−471	−1,420	−5,459	−8,194	−6,459
% of total	2.5%	0.5%	1.3%	4.3%	5.5%	4.0%

Imports (1985): £84,789,600,000 (machinery and transport equipment 31.7%, of which road vehicles 8.0%, data-processing equipment 5.3%; petroleum and petroleum products 9.6%; food and live animals 9.5%, of which vegetables and fruits 2.4%, meat and meat preparations 1.7%; chemicals and chemical products 8.1%, of which organic chemicals 2.2%; textile yarn and fabrics 3.6%; paper and paperboard 3.0%; nonferrous metals 2.6%; apparel and clothing accessories 2.5%). *Major import sources:* West Germany 14.9%; United States 11.7%; The Netherlands 7.7%; France 7.7%; Norway 5.2%; Italy 5.1%; Japan 4.9%; Belgium 4.7%; Ireland 3.3%; Sweden 2.9%.
Exports (1985): £78,331,400,000 (machinery and transport equipment 31.5%, of which road vehicles 5.0%, data-processing equipment 4.8%, power generating machinery and equipment 3.9%, machinery specialized for particular industries 3.9%; petroleum and petroleum products 20.5%; chemicals and chemical products 12.0%, of which organic chemicals 3.5%; nonmetallic mineral manufactures 2.8%; professional, scientific, and controlling instruments 2.7%; nonferrous metals 1.8%). *Major export destinations:* United States 14.7%; West Germany 11.4%; France 9.9%; The Netherlands 9.4%; Ireland 4.7%; Italy 4.4%; Belgium 4.3%; Sweden 3.8%; Australia 1.8%.

Transport and communications

Transport. Railroads†† (1985): length 25,885 mi, 41,659 km; passenger-mi 18,796,000,000, passenger-km 30,249,000,000; short ton-mi cargo 8,752,000,000, metric ton-km cargo 12,700,000,000. Roads (1984): total length 230,253 mi, 370,557 km (paved 97%). Vehicles (1984): passenger cars 18,152,900; trucks and buses 2,312,400. Merchant marine (1985): vessels (100 gross tons and over) 2,378; total deadweight tonnage 21,794,712. Air transport (1985): passenger-mi 32,064,200,000, passenger-km 51,602,400,000; short ton-mi cargo 1,080,172,000, metric ton-km cargo 1,577,124,000; airports (1986) with scheduled flights 40.
Communications. Daily newspapers (1984): total number 112; total circulation 30,412,400; circulation per 1,000 population 538. Radio (1985): total number of licenses 18,460,000 (1 per 3 persons). Television (1985): total number of licenses 18,716,000 (1 per 3 persons). Telephones (1984): 29,336,000 (1 per 1.9 persons).

Education and health

Education (1983–84)‡‡

	schools	teachers	students	student/teacher ratio
Primary (age 5–10)	25,326	207,100	4,549,700	22.0
Secondary (age 11–19)	5,328	274,500	4,384,200	16.0
Voc., teacher tr.§§	755	‖ ‖	605,724	...
Higher	46¶¶	53,000 ‖ ‖	204,276	...

Literacy (1984): total population literate, virtually 100%.
Health (1984): physicians 83,690 (1 per 675 persons); hospital beds 430,915 (1 per 131 persons); infant mortality rate per 1,000 live births (1985) 9.4.
Food (1980–82): daily per capita caloric intake 3,210 (vegetable products 63%, animal products 37%); 127% of FAO recommended minimum requirement.

Military

Total active duty personnel (1986): 323,800 (army 50.1%, navy 21.1%, air force 28.8%). *Military expenditure as percent of GNP* (1984): 5.5% (world 6.1%); per capita expenditure U.S.$416.

*Metropolitan county. †Comprises 26 local government districts not shown separately. ‡1985. §Percent given in parentheses is for Northern Ireland. ‖ Less imputed bank charges. ¶Includes self-employed and unemployed. ♀October. ðAugust. □First quarter. ◇1983. △1982. ✝Includes value-added taxes. ⊕April. **Import figures are c.i.f. (cost, insurance, and freight); export figures are f.o.b. (free on board). ††British railways only. ‡‡Public sector only. §§Third level. ‖ ‖ Included with higher. ¶¶Universities only.

United States

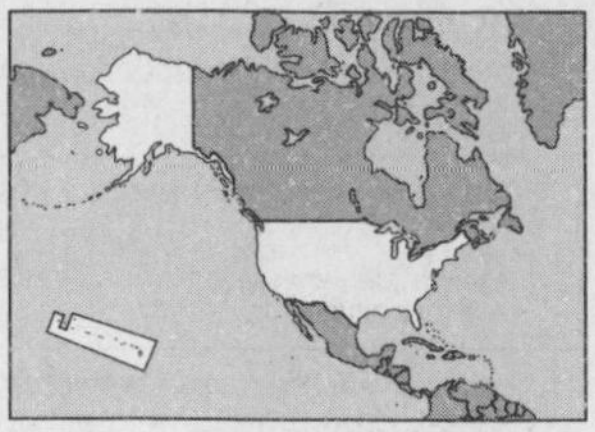

Official name: United States of America.
Form of government: federal republic with two legislative houses (Senate [100] and House of Representatives [435]).
Head of state and government: President.
Capital: Washington, D.C.
Official language: English.
Official religion: none.
Monetary unit: 1 dollar (U.S.$) = 100 cents; valuation (Oct. 1, 1986) 1 U.S.$ = £0.69; 1 £ = U.S.$1.45.

Area and population

		area*		population
States	Capitals	sq mi	sq km	1986 estimate
Alabama	Montgomery	51,705	133,915	4,053,000
Alaska	Juneau	591,004	1,530,693	534,000
Arizona	Phoenix	114,000	295,259	3,317,000
Arkansas	Little Rock	53,187	137,754	2,372,000
California	Sacramento	158,706	411,047	26,981,000
Colorado	Denver	104,091	269,594	3,267,000
Connecticut	Hartford	5,018	12,997	3,189,000
Delaware	Dover	2,044	5,294	633,000
Florida	Tallahassee	58,664	151,939	11,675,000
Georgia	Atlanta	58,910	152,576	6,104,000
Hawaii	Honolulu	6,471	16,760	1,062,000
Idaho	Boise	83,564	216,430	1,003,000
Illinois	Springfield	57,871	149,885	11,553,000
Indiana	Indianapolis	36,413	94,309	5,504,000
Iowa	Des Moines	56,275	145,752	2,851,000
Kansas	Topeka	82,277	213,096	2,461,000
Kentucky	Frankfort	40,409	104,659	3,728,000
Louisiana	Baton Rouge	47,752	123,677	4,501,000
Maine	Augusta	33,265	86,156	1,174,000
Maryland	Annapolis	10,460	27,091	4,463,000
Massachusetts	Boston	8,284	21,455	5,832,000
Michigan	Lansing	97,102	251,493	9,145,000
Minnesota	St. Paul	86,614	224,329	4,214,000
Mississippi	Jackson	47,689	123,514	2,625,000
Missouri	Jefferson City	69,697	180,514	5,066,000
Montana	Helena	147,046	380,847	819,000
Nebraska	Lincoln	77,355	200,349	1,598,000
Nevada	Carson City	110,561	286,352	963,000
New Hampshire	Concord	9,279	24,032	1,027,000
New Jersey	Trenton	7,787	20,168	7,620,000
New Mexico	Santa Fe	121,593	314,924	1,479,000
New York	Albany	52,735	136,583	17,772,000
North Carolina	Raleigh	52,669	136,412	6,331,000
North Dakota	Bismarck	70,702	183,117	679,000
Ohio	Columbus	44,787	115,998	10,752,000
Oklahoma	Oklahoma City	69,956	181,185	3,305,000
Oregon	Salem	97,073	251,418	2,698,000
Pennsylvania	Harrisburg	46,043	119,251	11,889,000
Rhode Island	Providence	1,212	3,139	975,000
South Carolina	Columbia	31,113	80,582	3,378,000
South Dakota	Pierre	77,116	199,730	708,000
Tennessee	Nashville	42,144	109,152	4,803,000
Texas	Austin	266,807	691,027	16,682,000
Utah	Salt Lake City	84,899	219,887	1,665,000
Vermont	Montpelier	9,614	24,900	541,000
Virginia	Richmond	40,767	105,586	5,787,000
Washington	Olympia	68,139	176,479	4,463,000
West Virginia	Charleston	24,231	62,758	1,919,000
Wisconsin	Madison	66,215	171,496	4,785,000
Wyoming	Cheyenne	97,809	253,324	507,000
District				
Dist. of Columbia	—	69	179	626,000
TOTAL		3,679,192†	9,529,063	241,077,000†

Demography

Population (1986): 241,077,000.
Density (1986): persons per sq mi 65.5, persons per sq km 25.3.
Urban-rural (1980): urban 73.7%; rural 26.3%.
Sex distribution (1985): male 48.75%; female 51.25%.
Age breakdown (1985): under 15, 21.7%; 15–29, 25.8%; 30–44, 21.8%; 45–59, 14.2%; 60–74, 11.7%; 75 and over, 4.8%.
Population projection: (1990) 249,657,000; (2000) 267,955,000.
Doubling time: 78 years.
Composition by race (1985): white 84.9%; black 12.1%; other races 3.0%.
Religious affiliation (1980): Protestant 40.0%; Roman Catholic 30.0%; Jewish 3.2%; Eastern Orthodox 2.1%; Muslim 0.8%; Hindu 0.2%; nonreligious and atheist 6.9%; other 16.8%.
Place of birth (foreign-born; 1980): Mexico 2,199,221; Germany (East and West) 849,384; Canada 842,859; Italy 831,922; United Kingdom 669,149; Cuba 607,814; Philippines 501,440; Poland 418,128; U.S.S.R. 406,022; South Korea 289,885; China 286,120; Vietnam (South) 231,120; Japan 221,794; Portugal 211,614; Greece 210,998; India 206,087.
Mobility (1984). Population living in the same residence as in 1983: 82.7%; different residence, same county 10.4%; different county, same state 3.6%; different state 2.8%; moved from abroad 0.5%.
Immigration (1981): permanent immigrants admitted 596,600, from Mexico 17.0%, Caribbean countries 12.3%, Vietnam 9.3%, Philippines 7.3%, South America 6.0%, Korea 5.5%, Taiwan 4.3%, Central America 4.1%, India 3.6%, Laos 2.6%, African countries 2.5%, United Kingdom 2.5%, Kampuchea 2.1%, Canada 1.9%, Iran 1.9%, U.S.S.R. 1.5%, Portugal 1.2%, West Germany 1.1%, Pakistan 0.9%, Poland 0.8%.

Major cities (1985): New York 7,183,984; Los Angeles 3,186,459; Chicago 2,998,841; Houston 1,746,375; Philadelphia 1,640,102; Detroit 1,090,581; Dallas 997,467; San Diego 988,284; Phoenix 890,746; San Antonio 862,878.

Other principal cities (1985)

	population		population		population
Akron	226,704	Fresno	275,125	Omaha	362,883
Albuquerque	357,051	Honolulu	817,083	Pittsburgh	400,969
Anaheim	240,283	Indianapolis	471,656	Portland	367,571
Anchorage	229,579	Jackson	210,024	Richmond	221,857
Arlington	156,140	Jacksonville	601,007	Rochester	243,212
Atlanta	436,214	Jersey City	224,401	Sacramento	312,944
Austin	406,469	Kansas City	444,942	St. Louis	431,109
Baltimore	771,097	Lexington	210,364	St. Paul	267,896
Baton Rouge	245,830	Long Beach	389,728	St. Petersburg	249,879
Birmingham	281,973	Louisville	290,069	San Francisco	733,456
Boston	573,131	Memphis	654,626	San Jose	706,062
Buffalo	339,890	Miami	385,892	Santa Ana	231,937
Charlotte	335,690	Milwaukee	621,931	Seattle	495,190
Cincinnati	317,198	Minneapolis	361,021	Shreveport	220,888
Cleveland	546,126	Mobile	206,505	Tampa	285,280
Colorado Springs	251,886	Nashville	481,286	Toledo	343,677
Columbus	565,682	Newark	316,356	Tucson	381,473
Corpus Christi	264,221	New Orleans	561,364	Tulsa	374,875
Denver	513,048	Norfolk	283,219	Virginia Beach	312,584
El Paso	474,870	Oakland	362,095	Washington, D.C.	626,000
Fort Worth	424,449	Oklahoma City	443,575	Wichita	284,915

Households (1985). Total households 86,789,000 (percent married-couple families 58.0%). Average household size 2.7; 1 person 23.7%, 2 persons 31.6%, 3 persons 17.8%, 4 persons 15.8%, 5 persons 7.0%, 6 persons 2.6%, 7 or more persons 1.5%. Family households: 62,700,000 (72.2%), nonfamily 24,100,000 (27.8%, of which 1-person 23.7%).

Vital statistics

Birth rate per 1,000 population (1986): 15.5 (world avg. 29.0); (1984) legitimate 80.6%; illegitimate 19.4%.
Death rate per 1,000 population (1986): 8.7 (world avg. 11.0).
Natural increase rate per 1,000 population (1986): 6.8 (world avg. 18.0).
Total fertility rate (avg. births per childbearing woman; 1985): 1.8.
Marriage rate per 1,000 population (1986): 10.0; median age at first marriage, men 25.5 years, women 23.3 years.
Divorce rate per 1,000 population (1986): 4.9.
Life expectancy at birth (1985): white male 71.8 years, black male 65.3 years; white female 78.8 years, black female 73.7 years.
Major causes of death per 100,000 population (1986): cardiovascular diseases 403.4, of which ischemic heart diseases 220.1, other forms of heart disease 83.5, cerebrovascular diseases 62.1, atherosclerosis 10.2, other cardiovascular diseases 9.1; malignant neoplasms (cancers) 193.1; diseases of the respiratory system 55.2, of which pneumonia 26.7; accidents and adverse effects 38.6, of which motor-vehicle accidents 18.8; diabetes mellitus 15.4; suicide 12.4; chronic liver disease and cirrhosis 11.0; nephritis and nephrosis 9.2; homicide 8.5.
Morbidity rates of infectious diseases per 100,000 population (1983): gonorrhea 383.3; chicken pox 75.6; syphilis 31.9; hepatitis B (serum) 10.4; hepatitis A (infectious) 9.2; salmonellosis 18.9; shigellosis 8.4; aseptic meningitis 5.4; mumps 1.4; measles (rubeola) 0.6.
Incidence of chronic health conditions per 1,000 population (per 1,000 population over age 65) (1982): arthritis 133.0 (495.8); hypertension 116.9 (390.4); hearing impairment 87.1 (299.7); heart conditions 74.5 (256.8).

Social indicators

Educational attainment (1984). Percent of population over age 25 having: less than full primary education 7.8%; primary 6.6%; less than full secondary 12.4%; secondary 38.4%; some postsecondary 15.8%; 4-year higher degree and more 19.1%, of which postgraduate 6.8%. Number of earned degrees (1986–87): bachelor's degree 950,000; master's degree 276,000; doctor's degree 33,700; first-professional degrees (in fields such as medicine, theology, and law) 78,000.

Distribution of income (1983)

percent of national household income by quintile

1	2	3	4	5 (highest)
4.7	11.2	17.1	24.3	42.7

Quality of working life (1985). Average workweek: 40.5 hours (8.1% overtime). Annual rate per 100,000 workers for (1984): injury or accident 1,900; death 11.0. Proportion of labour force insured for damages or income loss resulting from: injury, permanent disability, and death (1984) 61.0%. Average days lost to labour stoppages per 1,000 workdays (1985): 0.7. Average duration of journey to work (1979): 22.5 minutes (85.7% private automobile, 5.9% public transportation, 1.3% bicycle or motorcycle, 3.9% foot, 2.3% work at home, 0.9% other). Rate per 1,000 workers of discouraged (unemployed no longer seeking work; 1983): 53.5.
Access to services (1984). Proportion of dwellings having access to: electricity 100.0%; safe public water supply 98.2%; public sewage collection 98.1%‡; public fire protection, n.a.
Social participation. Eligible voters participating in last national election (1984): 59.9%. Population over age 13 participating in voluntary work (1974): 22.9%. Trade union membership in total work force (1984): 18.8%. Practicing religious population in total affiliated population (weekly church attendence; 1984): Roman Catholic 52%; Protestant 39%, of which Baptist 41%, Methodist 37%, Lutheran 35%, Episcopal 30%, Presbyterian 28%.
Social deviance (1985). Offense rate per 100,000 population for: murder 7.9; rape 36.6; robbery 208.5; aggravated assault 302.9; motor vehicle theft 462.0; burglary and housebreaking 1,287.3; larceny-theft 2,901.2. Adult drug

and substance users (1982): alcohol 56.7%; cigarettes 34.6%; marijuana 6.6%; hallucinogens 1.2%; tranquilizers 1.2%; heroin 0.6%. Rate per 100,000 population of suicide (1986) 12.4.

Crime rates per 100,000 population in metropolitan areas (1985)

	violent crime				
	total	murder	rape	robbery	assault
Atlanta	742.6	10.9	53.3	288.6	389.9
Baltimore	1,132.0	11.5	44.9	420.3	655.3
Boston	663.6	4.7	31.5	293.0	334.5
Chicago	1,073.2	12.1	35.8	482.5	542.9
Dallas	842.6	17.2	70.5	321.2	433.8
Detroit	970.2	18.3	68.0	502.4	381.5
Houston	675.3	18.3	67.0	352.0	238.0
Los Angeles	1,179.5	16.3	54.7	582.1	526.4
Miami	1,692.0	21.8	55.4	744.2	870.6
Minneapolis	400.9	2.5	40.3	152.2	205.8
New York	1,658.0	17.0	48.3	969.7	623.0
Philadelphia	572.0	8.0	36.7	271.9	255.3
Pittsburgh	339.0	3.5	22.4	179.8	133.2
St. Louis	659.7	11.4	33.4	214.7	400.1
San Francisco	792.3	7.8	43.8	378.7	362.1
Washington, D.C.	640.9	7.0	32.4	292.4	309.0

	property crime				
	total	burglary	larceny	auto theft	arson§
Atlanta	6,042.0	1,668.3	3,785.9	587.9	66.7
Baltimore	5,039.7	1,357.0	3,193.7	489.0	85.6
Boston	4,841.4	1,222.0	2,485.8	1,233.7	27.6
Chicago	5,623.5	1,313.5	3,334.0	975.9	67.6
Dallas	8,506.4	2,291.6	5,523.5	691.3	76.2
Detroit	6,810.7	1,836.7	3,494.5	1,479.5	114.9
Houston	6,431.1	1,904.4	3,272.0	1,254.7	113.3
Los Angeles	6,008.8	1,765.3	3,135.9	1,107.6	167.5
Miami	9,578.0	2,598.1	5,620.8	1,359.1	64.5
Minneapolis	4,934.1	1,356.8	3,211.5	365.9	74.8
New York	6,061.2	1,610.0	3,455.7	995.5	106.9
Philadelphia	3,631.6	950.3	2,167.5	513.7	20.1
Pittsburgh	2,685.2	769.9	1,351.3	564.0	70.1
St. Louis	4,663.2	1,352.5	2,801.5	509.2	99.0
San Francisco	5,253.5	1,225.1	3,481.7	546.7	53.6
Washington, D.C.	4,504.1	1,035.3	2,980.5	488.4	47.0

Leisure (1976). Favourite leisure activities (weekly hours): watching television 9.6; social time 7.6; reading 3.7; cultural activities 1.5; recreation 1.2.
Material well-being (1982). Occupied dwellings with householder possessing: automobile 86.1%; telephone 97.0%; television receiver 84.8%; refrigerator 63.5%; air conditioner 58.0%; washing machine 71.4%.
Recreational expenditures (1985): U.S.$176,300,000,000 (television and radio receivers 19.9%; toys and sport supplies 11.6%; golfing, bowling, and other participatory activities 8.3%; magazines and newspapers 7.5%; spectator amusements 5.5%, of which movies 2.1%, theatre and opera 1.7%, spectator sports 1.7%; parimutuel receipts 1.5%).

National economy

Gross national product (at current market prices; 1985): U.S.$3,998,100,000,000 (U.S.$16,750 per capita).

Gross national product and national income
in U.S.$000,000,000

	1981	1982	1983	1984	1985
Gross national product	2,957.8	3,069.3	3,304.8	3,774.7	3,988.5
By type of expenditure					
Personal consumption expenditures	1,849.1	1,984.9	2,155.9	2,423.0	2,582.3
Durable goods	235.4	245.1	279.8	331.1	361.5
Nondurable goods	730.7	757.5	801.7	872.4	912.2
Services	883.0	982.2	1,074.4	1,219.6	1,308.6
Gross private domestic investment	484.2	414.9	471.6	674.0	669.3
Fixed investment	458.1	441.0	485.1	607.0	661.8
Changes in business inventories	26.0	−26.1	−13.5	67.1	7.5
Net exports of goods and services	30.0	19.0	−8.3	−59.2	−78.5
Exports	369.9	348.4	336.2	384.6	369.9
Imports	341.9	329.4	344.4	443.8	448.4
Government purchases of goods and services	596.5	650.5	685.5	736.8	815.4
Federal	228.9	258.9	269.7	312.9	335.4
State and local	367.6	391.5	415.8	423.9	460.0
By major type of product					
Goods output	1,294.8	1,276.8	1,355.7	1,506.4	1,532.4
Durable goods	530.5	499.9	555.3	665.4	676.5
Nondurable goods	764.4	776.9	800.4	851.0	855.9
Services	1,373.0	1,510.8	1,639.3	1,615.4	1,644.2
Structures	289.9	281.7	309.8	370.2	393.4
National income	2,363.8	2,446.8	2,646.7	3,039.3	3,211.3
By type of income					
Compensation of employees	1,765.4	1,864.2	1,984.9	2,221.3	2,372.5
Proprietors' income	125.1	111.1	121.7	183.6	193.0
Rental income of persons	42.3	51.5	58.3	54.0	57.3
Corporate profits	189.9	159.1	225.2	273.3	295.5
Net interest	241.0	260.9	256.6	300.2	287.4
By industry division					
Agriculture, forestry, fishing	74.8	69.6	60.9	81.3	70.3
Mining and construction	154.2	154.3	152.3	195.2	206.0
Manufacturing	581.3	549.6	579.9	667.0	677.8
Durable	340.5	311.4	329.5	393.4	405.1
Nondurable	240.8	238.3	250.4	273.5	272.7
Transportation	84.3	83.3	87.7	103.2	107.1
Communications, public utilities	106.2	117.0	124.4	135.1	139.5
Wholesale and retail trade	349.4	359.0	386.4	460.8	485.3
Finance, insurance, real estate	326.0	355.1	394.0	391.2	406.4
Services	350.6	387.0	426.6	512.9	561.5
Government and government enterprise	337.0	364.1	391.7	437.7	469.9

Structure of gross domestic product and labour force

	1985			
	in value U.S.$'000,000,000	% of total value	labour force	% of labour force
Agriculture	91.5	2.3	3,179,000	2.7
Mining	122.8	3.1	969,000	0.8
Manufacturing	795.8	20.1	19,424,000	16.6
Construction	182.2	4.6	4,661,000	4.0
Public utilities	121.4	3.0	5,301,000 (with transportation and communication)	4.5 (with transportation and communication)
Transportation and communication	253.0	6.4		
Trade	652.5	16.5	23,188,000	19.8
Finance	626.6	15.8	5,924,000	5.1
Public administration, defense	477.4	12.1	16,294,000	13.9
Services	639.4	16.2	21,931,000	18.7
Other	−5.6‖	−0.1	16,296,000¶	13.9
TOTAL	3,957.0	100.0	117,167,000	100.0

Budget (1986). Revenue: U.S.$793,700,000,000 (individual income tax 45.2%, social insurance taxes and contributions 36.5%, corporation income tax 9.3%, excise taxes 4.4%, customs duties 1.5%). Expenditures: U.S.$973,700,000,000 (defense 29.3%, social security and medicare 27.7%, interest on debt 14.6%; income security 11.9%, health 3.6%, education 3.0%, veteran benefits and services 2.7%).
Total national debt (1985): U.S.$1,415,100,000,000.

Manufacturing, mining, and construction enterprises (1984)

	no. of enterprises	no. of employees	weekly wage as a % of all wages	annual value of shipments (U.S.$'000,000)
Manufacturing				
Food and kindred products	20,208	1,619,000	100.6	295,050
Transportation equipment	8,466	1,906,000	146.7	288,306
Chemical and allied products	11,363	1,048,000	133.0	211,833
Machinery, except electrical	48,947	2,197,000	119.6	210,168
Petroleum and coal products	2,165	189,000	161.2	200,588
Electrical and electronic machinery	15,116	2,208,000	108.5	182,534
Fabricated metal products	32,793	1,464,000	112.6	139,213
Primary metals	7,048	858,000	137.7	131,152
Paper and allied products	6,160	681,000	125.0	95,944
Textile mill products	6,192	746,000	77.6	55,078
Stone, clay, and glass products	15,591	595,000	114.9	54,993
Apparel and other related products	21,367	1,197,000	85.7	...
Instruments and related products	7,661	714,000	106.2	53,511
Rubber and plastic products	12,348	782,000	99.5	52,147
Tobacco products	117	65,000	135.3	16,918
Leather and leather products	2,558	192,000	68.4	4,850
Lumber and wood	28,293	707,000	96.4	...
Furniture and fixtures	9,160	487,000	82.2	...
Miscellaneous manufacturing industries	14,532	1,372,000	84.5	...
Mining				
Oil and gas extraction	23,577	613,000	139.6 (all mining)	121,100 (all mining)
Coal mining	4,133	361,000 (coal, metal, nonmetallic)		
Metal mining	985			
Nonmetallic, except fuels	5,126			
Construction				
General contractors and operative builders	112,963	1,158,000	145.5 (all construction)	148,100 (all construction)
Heavy construction contractors	29,055	1,072,000		
Special trade contractors	243,729	2,115,000		

Business activity (1982): number of businesses 9,103,688 (sole proprietorships 76.3%, active corporations 18.2%, active partnerships 5.5%), of which services 5,772,241, wholesaling and retailing 3,331,447; business receipts $2,776,933,000,000 (active corporations 83.8%, sole proprietorships 11.3%, active partnerships 4.9%), of which wholesaling and retailing $2,222,319,000,000, services $554,614,000,000; net profit $89,105,000,000 (sole proprietorships 44.3%, active corporations 40.0%, active partnerships 15.7%), of which services $51,587,000,000, wholesaling and retailing $37,518,000,000. New business concerns and business failures (1985): total number of new incorporations 668,904; total failures 57,067; failure rate per 10,000 concerns 85; current liabilities of failed concerns $33,375,900,000, average liability $584,000. Business expenditures for new plant and equipment (1985): total $384,400,000,000, of which manufacturing businessess $153,600,000,000 (nondurable goods 51.2%, durable 48.8%), trade, services, and communication $148,300,000,000, public utilities $48,400,000,000, transportation $17,500,000,000, mining $16,500,000,000, other $100,000,000.
Production (metric tons except as noted). Agriculture, forestry, fishing (1985): corn (maize) 225,181,520,000, wheat 66,000,540,000, soybeans 57,112,650,000, sorghum 28,260,160, sugarcane 25,594,400, sugar beets 20,535,030, potatoes 18,466,060, barley 12,875,840, tomatoes 8,180,000, oats 7,559,390, oranges 6,814,770, rice 6,170,760, grapes 5,084,500, cottonseed 4,789,030, apples 3,605,590, cotton 2,924,500, grapefruit 2,180,000, peanuts (groundnuts) 1,870,050, onions 1,860,000, peaches and pears 1,652,030, sunflower seeds 1,430,180, cabbages 1,380,000, green peas 1,115,000, carrots 1,030,000, dry beans 1,010,050, tobacco 685,470, rye 524,200, strawberries 462,117, almonds 335,480, milk 64,954,000, cheese 2,543,456, butter 571,576, eggs 4,041,400; livestock (number of live animals) 109,749,000 cattle, 54,073,000 pigs, 10,580,000 horses, 10,443,000 sheep, 1,550,000 goats, 1,155,000,000 poultry; roundwood (1984) 247,241,000 cu m; fish catch 2,897,100,000. Mining and quarrying (1985): iron ore 48,386,000; phosphate rock 50,800,000; copper 1,110,700; bauxite 565,000; lead 409,400; zinc 217,500; molybdenum 49,000; uranium 4,500; silver 1,294; nickel 400; tin 100; gold 72. Manufacturing (1985): crude steel 79,355,000; cement 70,284,000; paper and paper products 61,128,000; wood pulp 49,245,000; pig iron 45,465,000; sulfuric acid 35,872,000; plastic and resins 15,700,000; nitrogenous and phosphate fertilizers 15,475,000; gypsum and gypsum products 13,440,000; caustic soda 9,942,000; newsprint 4,923,000; aluminum 3,499,000; man-made fibre 3,775,700; synthetic rubber 1,907,000; machine

tools U.S.$5,073,300,000; industrial material handling equipment U.S.$4,272,400,000; cotton fabric 3,278,000 m; footwear 266,042,000 pairs; motor vehicle tires 195,972,000 units; radio receivers 58,684,000 units; television receivers 40,606,000 units; household appliances 41,797,000 units, of which 10,883,000 microwave ovens, 6,080,000 refrigerators, 5,278,000 washing machines, 3,914,000 clothes dryers, 3,575,000 dishwashers, 3,529,000 water heaters. Construction (1985): private U.S.$292,800,000,000, of which residential U.S.$158,800,000,000, commercial and industrial U.S.$82,700,000,000, other U.S.$51,300,000,000; federal, state, and local U.S.$62,800,000,000.

Retail and wholesale trade and services (1982)

	no. of enterprises	no. of employees	weekly wage as a % of all wages	annual sales (U.S.$'000,000♀)
Retail trade	1,923,228	14,467,813	...	1,373,941
Durable goods	...	...	...	514,207
Automotive dealers	91,068	1,051,174	...	312,793
Building materials, hardware, garden supply, and mobile home dealers	34,002	306,657	...	74,062
Furniture, home furnishings, equipment stores	93,734	542,635	...	68,112
Nondurable goods	...	...	...	859,734
Food stores	176,219	2,347,603	...	282,198
General merchandise group stores	34,145	1,839,158	...	159,456
Eating and drinking places	319,873	4,665,830	...	131,035
Gasoline service stations	116,188	603,886	...	100,767
Apparel and accessory stores	133,920	986,155	...	69,673
Drugstores and proprietary stores	49,527	496,217	...	46,014
Liquor stores	34,861	167,286	...	17,802
Wholesale trade	415,829	4,984,480	...	1,374,752
Durable goods	256,103	2,912,848	...	630,312
Machinery, equipment, and supplies	99,250	1,192,023	...	165,820
Motor vehicles, automotive equipment	39,460	432,982	...	132,391
Electrical goods	29,170	357,107	...	88,753
Metals and minerals, except petroleum	10,121	147,470	...	60,933
Lumber and other construction materials	17,041	184,604	...	46,193
Hardware, plumbing, heating equipment and supplies	20,815	216,596	...	41,263
Furniture and home furnishings	12,498	126,104	...	24,210
Sporting, recreational, photographic, and hobby goods	7,266	85,163	...	16,282
Miscellaneous durable goods	20,482	170,800	...	54,467
Nondurable goods	159,726	2,072,032	...	744,440
Groceries and related products	38,516	673,765	...	217,085
Farm-products raw materials	13,872	136,235	...	93,252
Apparel, piece goods, and notions	14,289	144,163	...	40,701
Beer, wine, and distilled alcoholic beverages	6,378	141,286	...	39,358
Paper and paper products	13,967	186,567	...	36,798
Chemicals and allied products	10,724	124,322	...	24,716
Drugs, drug proprietaries, and druggists' sundries	3,851	105,689	...	25,095
Miscellaneous nondurable goods	39,434	372,268	...	104,008
Servicesδ	1,261,698	11,106,144	...	363,134
Business	215,125	3,151,651	...	168,350
Health, except hospitals	346,565	2,433,061	...	143,959
Legal	115,407	569,359	...	51,209
Engineering, architectural, and surveying	45,341	581,470	...	40,934
Hotels, motels, and other lodging places	41,231	1,102,097	...	43,485
Amusement and recreation, including motion pictures	67,215	803,776	...	47,754
Automotive repair, services, garages	115,481	553,245	...	45,576
Personal	167,749	970,472	...	37,690
Accounting, auditing, and bookkeeping	51,900	330,198	...	22,620
Miscellaneous repair services	54,421	299,662	...	20,278

Energy production (consumption): electricity (kW-hr; 1985) 2,469,841,000,000 (2,182,000,000,000), of which net generation (by fuel type; 1985) coal 56.8%, nuclear sources 15.5%, natural and manufactured gases 11.8%, hydroelectric sources 11.4%, petroleum and petroleum products 4.1%, geothermal, wood, wind, and solar sources 0.4%; coal (metric tons; 1985) 801,623,000 (742,122,000); crude petroleum (barrels; 1985) 3,274,415,000 (5,537,000,000); petroleum products (metric tons; 1984) 632,355,000 (660,644,000); natural gas (cu m; 1985) 487,900,000,000 (490,800,000,000).

Energy consumption by end use (in quads [quadrillion, or '000,000,000,000,000, British thermal units]; 1984): total 82.14 (industrial and commercial 27.22; electric power utilities 26.12 [coal 53.9%, hydroelectric and nontraditional energy sources 15.1%, nuclear 13.7%, natural gas 12.3%]; residential 8.94 [natural gas 52.6%, electricity 29.6%]).

Household income and expenditure. Average household size (1985) 2.7; average annual income per household U.S.$30,000; sources of income: wages and salaries 59.2%, transfer payments 14.7%, personal interest income 14.4%, proprietors' income 6.8%, other labour income 4.9%; expenditure□ (1985): food 18.4%, housing 22.3%, clothing 6.0%, health 10.8%, transportation 13.5%, education and recreation 14.4%.

Selected household characteristics (1985). Total number of households 86,789,000, of which: (by race and Spanish origin◇) white 86.8%, black 10.9%, other 2.3%, Spanish origin 5.6%; (by location; 1983) in metropolitan areas 68.4% (central cities 29.6%), outside metropolitan areas 31.6% (farms 1.9%); (by tenure; 1985) owned 55,812,400 (64.3%), rented 30,987,600 (35.7%); family households 62,706,000, of which married couple 80.3%, female head with children under age 18, 9.6%, other 10.1%; nonfamily households 24,083,000, of which female householder 61.7%, male 38.2%. Work disability status of householder (1984): having no work disability 86.9%, having work disability 13.1%; having retirement or disability income 6.3%.

Financial aggregates

	1980	1981	1982	1983	1984	1985	1986
Exchange rate, U.S.$ per:							
£△	2.33	2.03	1.75	1.52	1.34	1.30	1.49†
SDR△	1.30	1.18	1.10	1.07	1.03	1.02	1.16†
International reserves (U.S.$)⊕							
Total (excl. gold; '000,000,000)	15.60	18.92	22.81	22.63	23.84	32.10	37.00**
SDRs ('000,000,000)	2.61	4.10	5.25	5.03	5.64	7.29	8.29**
Reserve pos. in IMF ('000,000,000)	2.85	5.05	7.35	11.31	11.54	11.95	11.92**
Foreign exchange ('000,000,000)	10.13	9.77	10.21	6.29	6.66	12.86	16.79**
Gold ('000,000 fine troy oz)	264.32	264.11	264.03	263.39	262.79	262.65	262.52**
% world reserves	27.74	27.70	27.83	27.80	27.77	27.68	...
Interest and prices							
Central bank discount (%)⊕	13.00	12.00	8.50	8.50	8.00	7.50	5.5**
Gov't. bond yield (%)††△	11.55	14.44	12.92	10.45	11.89	9.64	6.66†
Industrial share prices△ (1980 = 100)	100.0	107.2	99.3	134.2	134.7	154.5	198.2†
Balance of payments ($'000,000,000)							
Balance of visible trade	−25.50	−27.97	−36.45	−67.08	−112.51	−124.44	−70.85‡‡
Imports, f.o.b.	249.77	265.07	247.65	268.89	332.41	338.86	180.75‡‡
Exports, f.o.b.	224.27	237.10	211.20	201.81	219.90	214.42	109.90‡‡
Balance of invisibles	34.92	41.78	36.27	29.88	18.19	21.65	9.95‡‡
Balance of payments, current account	1.84	6.37	−9.05	−46.68	−106.49	−117.76	−67.87‡‡

Population economically active (1985): total 117,167,000; activity rate of total population 49.0% (participation rates: ages 15–64 [1984] 70.7%; female 44.7%, unemployed 7.1%).

Price and earnings indexes (1980 = 100)

	1980	1981	1982	1983	1984	1985	1986§§
Consumer price index	100.0	110.4	117.1	120.9	126.1	130.5	133.8
Hourly earnings index	100.0	109.9	116.9	121.5	126.2	131.1	134.1

Average employee earnings

	average hourly earnings in U.S.$		average weekly earnings in U.S.$	
	1984	1985	1984	1985
Manufacturing				
Durable goods	9.73	10.09	397.96	410.06
Lumber and wood products	8.07	8.20	318.77	323.53
Furniture and fixtures	6.87	7.19	269.30	276.48
Stone, clay, and glass products	9.64	9.83	406.81	417.92
Primary metal industries	11.49	11.68	474.54	485.75
Fabricated metal products	9.35	9.66	381.48	394.54
Machinery, except electrical	9.96	10.29	412.34	421.06
Electrical and electronic equipment	9.00	9.47	363.60	376.91
Instruments and related products	8.88	9.19	363.19	370.24
Miscellaneous manufacturing	7.07	7.28	275.02	281.78
Nondurable goods	8.41	8.68	331.35	341.91
Food and kindred products	8.39	8.54	333.08	342.86
Tobacco manufactures	11.77	12.05	441.38	440.57
Textile mill products	6.44	6.71	253.09	258.90
Apparel and other textile products	5.53	5.73	199.08	205.98
Paper and allied products	10.52	10.82	453.41	465.00
Printing and publishing	9.38	9.69	352.69	360.32
Chemicals and allied products	11.09	11.57	462.45	479.13
Petroleum and coal products	13.25	14.04	580.35	598.77
Rubber and miscellaneous plastics products	8.31	8.53	342.37	347.13
Leather and leather products	5.71	5.82	212.98	217.67
Nonmanufacturing				
Metal mining	13.06	13.42	522.40	556.93
Coal mining	14.91	15.30	591.07	581.39
Oil and gas extraction	10.66	10.99	472.24	484.66
Nonmetallic minerals, except fuels	9.86	10.11	449.62	463.04
Construction	12.06	12.2	464.31	469.38
Local and suburban transportation	8.01	8.06	313.19	310.31
Electric, gas, and sanitary services	12.15	12.74	503.01	529.98
Wholesale trade	8.98	9.26	348.42	359.29
Retail trade	5.86	5.94	179.90	180.58
Finance, insurance, and real estate	7.60	7.93	278.92	286.47
Hotels, motels, and tourist courts	5.33	5.72	170.03	176.18
Health services	7.78	8.11	255.18	265.20
Legal services	9.98	10.49	349.30	364.00
Miscellaneous services	11.15	11.51	432.62	447.74

Tourism (1984): receipts from visitors U.S.$11,386,000,000; expenditures by nationals abroad U.S.$15,805,000,000; number of foreign visitors 7,535,000 (2,965,000 from western Europe, 994,000 from Central America and the Caribbean, 789,000 from South America); number of nationals traveling abroad 12,062,000 (6,112,000 to Europe and the Mediterranean, 3,559,000 to Central America and the Caribbean, 635,000 to South America).

Land use (1984): forested 33.1%; meadows and pastures 26.2%; agricultural and under permanent cultivation 20.9%; other 19.8%.

Foreign trade ‖ ‖

Balance of trade (current prices)¶¶

	1981	1982	1983	1984	1985	1986‡‡
U.S.$'000,000,000	−27.2	−31.7	−57.5	−107.8	−132.1	−75.5
% of total	5.5%	6.9%	12.5%	19.8%	23.7%	25.9%

Imports (1985): U.S.$361,626,300,000 (machinery and transport equipment 39.2%, of which new passenger cars 10.4%, telecommunications and sound recording and reproducing apparatus 5.3%, office machinery and automatic data-processing machines 3.3%, transport equipment parts 2.9%; basic and miscellaneous manufactures 27.8%, of which clothing 4.4%, iron and steel mill products 2.9%; mineral fuels and lubricants 15.4%, of which crude petroleum 9.4%, petroleum products 4.8%; food 5.6%). *Major import sources:* Japan 20.0%; Canada 19.2%; West Germany 5.9%; Mexico 5.4%; Taiwan 4.9%; United Kingdom 4.3%; South Korea 3.0%; Italy 2.9%; France 2.8%; Hong Kong 2.5%; Brazil 2.3%; Venezuela 1.9%; Indonesia 1.4%.

Exports (1985): U.S.$213,146,000,000♀♀ (machinery 28.7%, of which office machinery and computers 7.2%, special purpose machinery 4.8%, power generating machinery 4.5%; basic and miscellaneous manufactures 14.2%, of which professional, scientific, and controlling instruments and apparatus 3.1%; transport equipment 16.8%, of which automobiles and other motor vehicles and parts 9.4%, aircraft and spacecraft and parts 6.9%; chemicals and related products 10.5%; food 9.3%, of which grain and cereal preparations 5.3%). *Major export destinations:* Canada 22.3%; Japan 10.6%; Mexico 6.4%; United Kingdom 5.3%; West Germany 4.2%; The Netherlands 3.4%; France 2.9%; South Korea 2.8%; Australia 2.6%; Belgium–Luxembourg 2.3%; Taiwan 2.2%; Italy 2.2%; Saudi Arabia 2.1%; China 1.8%.

Trade by commodity group (1985)

	imports (c.i.f.)		exports (f.o.b.)δδ	
SITC Group	U.S.$'000,000	%	U.S.$'000,000	%
00 Food and live animals	20,292	5.6	19,268	9.3
01 Beverages and tobacco	4,124	1.1	2,958	1.4
02 Crude materials, excluding fuels	11,167	3.1	16,940	8.2
03 Mineral fuels, lubricants, and related materials	55,843	15.5	9,971	4.8
04 Animal and vegetable oils, fat, and waxes	730	0.2	1,434	0.7
05 Chemicals and related products, n.e.s.	15,321	4.2	21,759	10.5
06 Basic manufactures	49,499	13.7	14,009	6.8
07 Machinery and transport equipment	141,721	39.2	94,278	45.6
08 Miscellaneous manufactured articles	51,684	14.3	15,338	7.4
09 Goods not classified by kind	11,245	3.1	10,970	5.3
TOTAL	361,626	100.0	206,925	100.0

Direction of trade (1985)

	imports (c.i.f.)		exports (f.o.b.)¶¶	
	U.S.$'000,000	%	U.S.$'000,000	%
Africa	12,543	3.5	7,388	3.5
South Africa	2,180	0.6	1,205	0.6
Other	10,363	2.9	6,183	2.9
Americas	118,523	32.8	78,635	36.9
Canada	69,427	19.2	47,615	22.3
Caribbean countries and Central America	7,421	2.1	6,605	3.1
Mexico	19,392	5.4	13,635	6.4
South America	22,283	6.2	10,780	5.1
Asia	140,068	38.7	60,746	28.5
China	4,224	1.2	3,856	1.8
India	2,478	0.7	1,642	0.8
Israel	2,201	0.6	2,580	1.2
Japan	72,380	20.0	22,631	10.6
Middle East (excl. Israel)	4,459	1.2	7,130	3.3
Other Asia	54,326	15.0	22,907	10.8
Europe	86,323	23.9	59,978	28.1
EEC	68,246	18.9	45,775	21.5
Other Western Europe	15,963	4.4	10,987	5.1
U.S.S.R.	443	0.1	2,423	1.1
Eastern Europe	1,671	0.5	793	0.4
Oceania	4,169	1.2	6,399	3.0
Australia	3,069	0.8	5,441	2.6
Other	1,100	0.4	958	0.4
TOTAL	361,626	100.0†	213,146	100.0

Transport and communications

Transport. Railroads (1985): length *c.* 172,000 mi, *c.* 276,000 km; passenger-mi (1984) 15,590,000,000, passenger-km 25,090,000,000; short ton-mi cargo 898,000,000,000, metric ton-km cargo 1,310,000,000,000. Roads (1985): total length 3,891,781 mi, 6,263,043 km (paved 88%). Vehicles (1985): passenger cars 130,364,000; trucks and buses 39,873,000. Merchant marine (1985): vessels (100 gross tons and over) 6,447; total deadweight tonnage 28,992,605. Air transport (1985): passenger-mi 297,400,000,000, passenger-km 478,620,000,000; short ton-mi cargo 7,892,000,000, metric ton-km cargo 11,522,000,000; airports (1985) with scheduled flights 824. Shares of intercity passenger and freight traffic by mode of transportation (1984): automobiles 83.0%; airplanes 14.8%; buses 1.5%; railway 0.7%.

Distribution of commercial traffic (1982)

	cargo carried ('000,000 tons)	% of nat'l total	passengers carried ('000,000)	% of nat'l total
Rail	1.932	37.9	304	2.9
Road	493	9.6	482	4.6
Urban transport	—	—		...
Road	—	—	5,705	54.5
Electric railway	—	—	2,233	21.3
Heavy rail	—	—	1,433	13.7
Inland water	1,777	34.8	25	0.2
Air	4	0.1	294	2.8
Pipeline	897	17.6	—	—
TOTAL	5,103	100.0	10,476	100.0

Communications. Daily newspapers (1984): total number 1,688; total circulation 63,081,740; circulation per 1,000 population 266. Radio (1985): total number of receivers 480,000,000 (1 per 0.5 persons). Television (1985): total number of receivers 145,000,000 (1 per 1.7 persons). Telephones (1984): 181,091,000 (1 per 1.3 persons).

Other communication media (1985)

	titles (units)		titles (units)
Print			
Books (new titles)	40,929	Home economics	90
of which		Industrial arts	106
Agriculture	445	Journalism and communication	90
Art	1,216	Labour and industrial relations	70
Biography	1,575	Law	273
Business	1,230	Library and information sciences	118
Education	873	Literature and language	158
Fiction	4,505	Mathematics and science	238
General works	2,420	Medicine	182
History	1,909	Philosophy and religion	130
Home economics	1,027	Physical education and recreation	151
Juvenile	2,938	Political science	136
Language	519	Psychology	138
Law	1,075	Sociology and anthropology	149
Literature	1,608	Zoology	94
Medicine	2,918		
Music	290		
Philosophy, psychology	1,306		
Poetry, drama	916		
Religion	1,994		
Science	2,698	**Cinema**	
Sociology, economics	6,117	Feature films	395
Sports, recreation	951		
Technology	2,015		traffic (units, '000)
Travel	385		
Periodicals	3,371	**Electronic‡**	
of which		Telegrams	53,000
Agriculture	153	Domestic	42,000
Business and economics	262	International	11,000
Chemistry and physics	170	Telex	69,559
Children's periodicals	78		
Education	203	**Post♀**	(pieces of mail)
Engineering	265	Mail	131,545,000
Fine and applied arts	145	Domestic	130,650,000
General interest	181	International	895,000
History	151		

Education and health

Education (1986–87)

	schools	teachers	students	student/teacher ratio
Primary and preprimary (age 5–12)	101,050	1,469,000	31,555,000	21.5
Secondary and vocational (age 14–17)		1,061,000	13,703,000	12.9
Higher, including teacher-training colleges	3,280	690,000	12,164,000	17.6

Literacy (1980): total population over age 15 literate 166,497,565 (95.5%); males literate 79,161,126 (95.7%); females literate 87,336,439 (95.3%); other studies indicate adult "functional" literacy may not exceed 85%.

Health: physicians (1985) 527,900 (1 per 452 persons), specialties (1982) internal medicine 15.9%, general practice 12.4%, general surgery 7.1%, pediatrics 6.3%, psychiatry 5.9%, obstetrics and gynecology 5.7%, anesthesiology 3.7%, orthopedics 3.1%, pathology 2.9%, ophthalmology 2.8%, radiology 2.0%, other 32.2%; hospital beds (1983) 1,350,000 (1 per 173 persons), of which nonfederal 91.6% (short-term general and special 75.6%, psychiatric 13.7%, long-term general and special 2.2%, tuberculosis 0.1%), federal 8.4%; infant mortality rate per 1,000 live births (1986) 10.4.

Food (1981–83): daily per capita caloric intake 3,647 (vegetable products 65%, animal products 35%); 138% of FAO recommended minimum requirement. Per capita consumption of major food groups (pounds annually; 1984): flour and cereal products 149.2; meat, poultry, and fish 143.5; fats and oils 61.6; fruits and vegetables 359.9, of which vegetables 218.3 (fresh 160.0, processed 58.3), fruits 141.6 (fresh 86.6, processed 55.0), dairy products 303.9; sugar and other sweeteners 146.6; potatoes and sweet potatoes 125.6; eggs 34.1; beans, peas, nuts, and soya products 14.8; coffee, tea, and cocoa 11.9.

Military

Total active duty personnel (1986): 2,143,955 (army 36.0%, navy 26.5%, air force 28.3%, marine 9.2%). *Military expenditure as percent of GNP* (1984): 6.4% (world 6.1%); per capita expenditure U.S.$1,001. *Military aid* (1984): total $6,486,000,000 (Middle East and South Asia 73.5%, of which Israel 26.2%, Egypt 21.1%, Turkey 11.1%, Pakistan 4.6%, Jordan 1.8%; Europe 7.9%, of which Spain 6.2%, Portugal 1.7%; East Asia 6.8%, of which South Korea 3.6%, Thailand 1.6%; Latin America 5.5%; of which El Salvador 3.0%, Honduras 1.2%; Africa 5.2%, of which Tunisia 1.7%, Morocco 1.1%, Sudan 0.7%; international organizations 1.1%.

*Total area excluding Great Lakes is 3,618,770 sq mi (9,372,571 sq km). †Detail does not add to total given because of rounding. ‡1983. §City proper. ‖ Statistical discrepancy. ¶Includes 8,312,000 unemployed.. ♀1985. δFigures for annual sales of services are for 1984. □Personal consumption expenditure. ◇Persons of Spanish origin may be of any race. △Annual average. †Third quarter average. ⊕End of year. **End of third quarter. ††Medium-term. ‡‡First six months only. §§September. ‖‖Import figures are f.o.b. in balance of trade and c.i.f. in commodities and trading partners. ¶¶Includes reexports valued at U.S.$6,221,000. ♀♀Total export figure includes reexports. Breakdown by commodities excludes reexports; trading partners includes reexports. δδExcludes reexports.

Uruguay

Official name: República Oriental del Uruguay (Oriental Republic of Uruguay).
Form of government: republic with two legislative houses (Senate [31]; Chamber of Representatives [99]).
Head of state and government: President.
Capital: Montevideo.
Official language: Spanish.
Official religion: none.
Monetary unit: 1 Uruguayan new peso (NUr$) = 100 centésimos; valuation (Oct. 1, 1986) 1 U.S.$ = NUr$161.50; 1 £ = NUr$233.37.

Area and population

		area		population
Departments	**Capitals**	sq mi	sq km	1975 census
Artigas	Artigas	4,605	11,928	57,947
Canelones	Canelones	1,751	4,536	325,594
Cerro Largo	Melo	5,270	13,648	74,027
Colonia	Colonia del Sacramento	2,358	6,106	111,832
Durazno	Durazno	4,495	11,643	55,699
Flores	Trinidad	1,986	5,144	24,745
Florida	Florida	4,022	10,417	67,129
Lavalleja	Minas	3,867	10,016	65,180
Maldonado	Maldonado	1,851	4,793	76,211
Montevideo	Montevideo	205	530	1,237,227
Paysandú	Paysandú	5,375	13,922	98,508
Río Negro	Fray Bentos	3,584	9,282	50,123
Rivera	Rivera	3,618	9,370	82,043
Rocha	Rocha	4,074	10,551	60,258
Salto	Salto	5,468	14,163	103,074
San José	San José de Mayo	1,927	4,992	88,000
Soriano	Mercedes	3,478	9,008	80,614
Tacuarembó	Tacuarembó	5,961	15,438	84,535
Treinta y Tres	Trienta y Tres	3,679	9,529	45,683
TOTAL LAND AREA		67,574	175,016	2,788,429
INLAND WATER		463	1,199	
TOTAL AREA		68,037	176,215	

Demography

Population (1986): 3,035,000.
Density (1986): persons per sq mi 44.9, persons per sq km 17.3.
Urban–rural (1985): urban 85.0%; rural 15.0%.
Sex distribution (1985): male 49.22%; female 50.78%.
Age breakdown (1985): under 15, 26.9%; 15–29, 23.4%; 30–44, 17.7%; 45–59, 16.6%; 60–74, 11.4%; 75 and over, 4.0%.
Population projection: (1990) 3,128,000; (2000) 3,364,000.
Doubling time: 91 years.
Ethnic composition (1980): mixed Spanish–Italian 85.9%; mestizo 3.0%; Italian 2.6%; Jewish 1.7%; mulatto 1.2%; other 5.6%.
Religious affiliation (1980): Christian 62.9%, of which Roman Catholic 59.5%; nonreligious 35.1%; Jewish 1.7%; other 0.3%.
Major cities (1980): Montevideo 1,261,000; Salto 72,000*, Paysandú 62,000*, Las Piedras 54,000*.

Vital statistics

Birth rate per 1,000 population (1984): 17.9 (world avg. 29.0); (1981) legitimate 74.4%; illegitimate 25.6%.
Death rate per 1,000 population (1984): 10.2 (world avg. 11.0).
Natural increase rate per 1,000 population (1984): 7.7 (world avg. 18.0).
Total fertility rate (avg. births per childbearing woman; 1982): 2.6.
Marriage rate per 1,000 population (1983): 6.5.
Divorce rate per 1,000 population (1983): 1.0.
Life expectancy at birth (1981): male 69.1 years; female 73.8 years.
Major causes of death per 100,000 population (1984): diseases of the circulatory system 419.7; malignant neoplasms (cancers) 213.1; symptoms and ill-defined conditions 73.5; respiratory diseases 39.6; accidents 38.5.

National economy

Budget (1985). Revenue: NUr$76,786,900,000 (direct taxes 76.4%, receipts from foreign trade 13.3%). Expenditures: NUr$83,612,700,000 (social security and welfare 64.4%, general public services 13.4%, interest on public debt 12.6%, subsidies 9.3%).
Public debt (external, outstanding; 1984): U.S.$2,544,500,000.
Production (metric tons except as noted). Agriculture, forestry, fishing (1984): sugarcane 570,000, wheat 450,000, rice 340,000, sugar beets 264,000, potatoes 150,000, sorghum 140,000, corn (maize) 120,000, grapes 117,000; livestock (number of live animals) 23,337,000 sheep, 9,491,000 cattle, 540,000 horses; roundwood 2,975,000 cu m; fish catch 134,000. Mining and quarrying (1984): glass sand 200,000; clays 150,000. Manufacturing (value added in NUr$'000,000; 1984): food products excluding beverages 16,559; petroleum products 12,217; textiles (other than clothing, footwear, or leather products) 10,441; clothing and footwear 7,961; beverages 5,558; tobacco 5,213; chemicals and chemical products 4,826; transport equipment 4,820; minerals 2,970. Construction (1983): residential 126,800 sq m; nonresidential 75,600 sq m. Energy production (consumption): electricity (kW-hr; 1984) 3,637,000,000 (3,649,000,000); coal, none (none); crude petroleum (barrels; 1984) none (9,346,000); petroleum products (metric tons; 1984) 1,151,000 (1,003,000); natural gas, none (n.a.).
Gross national product (1984): U.S.$5,900,000,000 (U.S.$1,970 per capita).

Structure of gross domestic product and labour force

	1984		1981	
	in value NUr$'000,000	% of total value	labour force	% of labour force
Agriculture	35,089	11.9	132,000	11.6
Mining }	60,231	20.4	2,000	0.2
Manufacturing }			231,000	20.3
Construction	7,946	2.7	66,000	5.8
Public utilities	7,393	2.5	16,000†	1.4†
Transp. and commun.	18,347	6.2	58,000†	5.1†
Trade	34,656	11.7 }	171,000†	15.0†
Finance	37,745	12.8 }		
Pub. admin., defense	24,757	8.4 }	211,000†	18.6†
Services	30,848	10.4 }		
Other	38,534‡	13.0‡	250,000	22.0
TOTAL	295,546	100.0	1,137,000	100.0

Tourism: receipts from visitors (1984) U.S.$107,000,000; expenditures by nationals abroad (1983) U.S.$304,000,000.
Population economically active (1982): total 1,148,000; activity rate of total population 38.7% (participation rates: ages 15–64 [1975] 59.6%; female [1975] 17.1%; unemployed [1984] 12.6%).

Price and earnings indexes (1980 = 100)

	1980	1981	1982	1983	1984	1985	1986§
Consumer price index	100.0	134.0	159.5	238.0	369.6	636.5	1,072.3
Monthly earnings index ‖	100.0	143.6	169.9	190.1	283.4	563.8	...

Household income and expenditure. Average household size (1984) 3.4; average annual income per household (1984): NUr$180,276 (U.S.$2,922); sources of income: wages and salaries 47.6%, self-employment 18.0%, pensions, transfer payments, and other 34.4%¶; expenditure (1973)♀: food 45.1%, housing 19.6%, clothing 13.2%, other 22.1%.
Land use (1983): forested 3.6%; meadows and pastures 78.5%; agricultural and under permanent cultivation 8.3%; other 9.6%.

Foreign trade♁

Balance of trade (current prices)

	1979	1980	1981	1982	1983	1984
U.S.$'000,000	−315.4	−482.7	−284.5	−15.3	+305.4	+183.6
% of total	16.7%	18.6%	10.5%	0.7%	17.1%	11.0%

Imports (1984): U.S.$735,564,000 (mineral products 38.9%; chemical products 14.0%; machinery and appliances 11.8%; synthetic plastic, resins, and rubber 6.2%; vegetable products 5.7%; textiles and textile products 4.7%; base metals and products 4.5%). *Major import sources:* Brazil 17.2%; Nigeria 14.4%; Argentina 11.2%; United States 8.4%; West Germany 6.2%.
Exports (1984): U.S.$924,584,000 (textiles and textile products 30.5%; live animals and live animal products 24.7%; hides and skins 15.8%; vegetable products 14.0%; food, beverages, and tobacco 3.0%; synthetic plastics, resins, and rubber 1.1%). *Major export destinations:* Brazil 15.6%; United States 13.3%; Argentina 9.5%; West Germany 8.5%; Iran 5.3%.

Transport and communications

Transport. Railroads (1984): route length 1,867 mi, 3,004 km; passenger-mi 205,000,000, passenger-km 330,000,000; short ton-mi cargo 187,000,000, metric ton-km cargo 273,000,000. Roads (1981): total length 30,952 mi, 49,813 km (paved 20%). Vehicles (1981): passenger cars 281,275; trucks and buses 49,813. Merchant marine (1985): vessels (100 gross tons and over) 96; total deadweight tonnage 263,056. Air transport (1985): passenger-mi 240,410,000, passenger-km 386,903,000; short ton-mi cargo 25,244,000, metric ton-km cargo 36,856,000; airports (1986) with scheduled flights 7.
Communications. Daily newspapers (1985): total number 21; total circulation 556,100□; circulation per 1,000 population 185□. Radio (1985): total receivers 1,700,000 (1 per 1.8 persons). Television (1985): total receivers 500,000 (1 per 6.0 persons). Telephones (1983): 307,640 (1 per 9.6 persons).

Education and health

Education (1984)

	schools	teachers	students	student/ teacher ratio
Primary (age 6–12)	2,321	15,027	350,390	23.3
Secondary	268	...	152,304	...
Vocational	93	5,632	55,359	9.8
Higher◇	1	4,349△	64,104	14.7

Educational attainment (1975). Percent of population over age 25 having: no formal schooling 9.9%; less than primary education 36.7%; primary 29.6%; secondary 17.4%; higher 6.3%. *Literacy* (1983): total population over age 15 literate 96.3%; males (1975) 922,534 (93.5%); females (1975) 989,727 (94.4%).
Health (1984): physicians 5,756 (1 per 519 persons); hospital beds (1983) 23,400 (1 per 127 persons); infant mortality rate per 1,000 live births 30.3.
Food (1980–82): daily per capita caloric intake 2,809 (vegetable products 63%, animal products 37%); 107% of FAO recommended minimum requirement.

Military

Total active duty personnel (1985): 31,900 (army 69.9%, navy 20.7%, air force 9.4%). *Military expenditure as percent of GNP* (1983): 3.3% (world 6.1%); per capita expenditure U.S.$98.

*1975. †Projection. ‡Includes indirect taxes less subsidies. §June. ‖ Salaried employees only. ¶Urban only. ♀Based on consumer price index components. ♁Import figures are f.o.b. in balance of trade and c.i.f. for commodities and trading partners. □Partial circulation only. ◇Universidad de la República. △1983.

Vanuatu

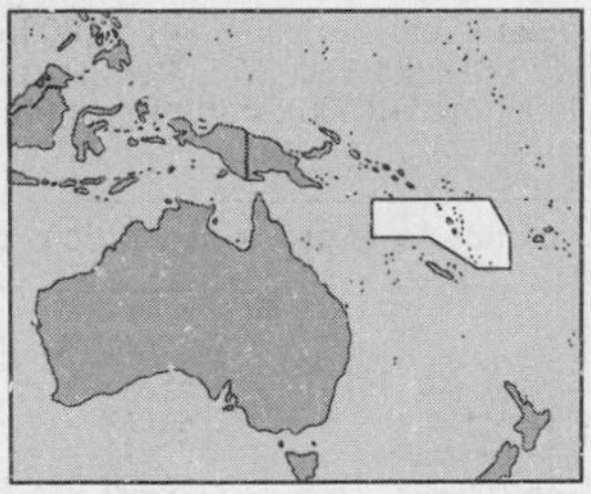

Official name: Ripablik blong Vanuatu (Bislama); République de Vanuatu (French); Republic of Vanuatu (English).
Form of government: republic with a single legislative house (Parliament [39]).
Chief of state: President.
Head of government: Prime Minister.
Capital: Vila.
Official languages: Bislama; French; English.
Official religion: none.
Monetary unit: vatu (VT); valuation (Oct. 1, 1986) 1 U.S.$ = VT 90.81; 1 £ = VT 131.22.

Area and population

Local Government Regions	Capitals	area sq mi	area sq km	population 1985 estimate
Ambrym	Toak	257	666	7,490
Aoba/Maéwo	Longana	270	699	11,070
Banks/Torres	Sola	341	882	5,930
Éfaté	Vila	356	923	25,630
Épi	Ringdove	172	446	2,910
Malekula	Lakatoro	793	2,053	17,630
Paama	Liro	23	60	2,380
Pentecost	Abwatuntora	193	499	11,000
Santo/Malo	Luganville	1,640	4,248	22,240
Shepherd	Morua	33	86	4,910
Taféa	Isangel	628	1,627	21,200
TOTAL		4,706	12,189	132,390

Demography

Population (1986): 136,800.
Density (1986): persons per sq mi 29.1, persons per sq km 11.2.
Urban-rural (1979): urban 17.8%; rural 82.2%.
Sex distribution (1979): male 53.10%; female 46.90%.
Age breakdown (1979): under 15, 45.3%; 15–29, 27.5%; 30–44, 15.0%; 45–59, 7.7%; 60–74, 3.4%; 75 and over, 1.1%.
Population projection: (1990) 156,000; (2000) 216,000.
Doubling time: 21 years.
Ethnic composition (1979): Ni-Vanuatu 93.8%; European 2.2%; part-European 0.9%; Polynesian and Micronesian 0.9%; Asian 0.6%; other Melanesian 0.4%; other 1.2%.
Religious affiliation (1979): Presbyterian 35.5%; Anglican 16.2%; Roman Catholic 13.5%; animist 9.2%; Seventh-day Adventist 6.3%; Church of Christ 4.2%; nonreligious 0.7%; unknown 10.1%; other 4.3%.
Major cities (1981): Vila (Port Vila) 14,000; Santo (Luganville) 5,183*.

Vital statistics

Birth rate per 1,000 population (1984): 45.0 (world avg. 29.0).
Death rate per 1,000 population (1984): 12.0 (world avg. 11.0).
Natural increase rate per 1,000 population (1984): 33.0 (world avg. 18.0).
Total fertility rate (avg. births per childbearing woman; 1984): 6.5.
Life expectancy at birth (1984): male 56.2 years; female 53.7 years.
Major causes of death per 100,000 population: n.a.; however, major diseases are malaria, infantile diarrhea, influenza, hookworm, and tuberculosis.

National economy

Budget (1984). Revenue: VT 2,798,000,000 (current revenue 78.6%, of which taxes 63.7%, nontax revenue 14.9%; foreign aid 21.4%, of which grants 17.5%, loans 3.9%). Expenditures: VT 2,798,000,000 (current expenditure 98.8%, of which development expenditure 15.5%; capital expenditure 1.2%).
Public debt (external, outstanding; 1984): U.S.$5,200,000.
Tourism (1985): number of visitors 31,415.
Production (metric tons except as noted). Agriculture, forestry, fishing (1984): coconuts 306,000, copra 44,000, roots and tubers 30,000, vegetables and melons 7,000, peanuts (groundnuts) 2,000, bananas 1,000, cocoa beans 1,000; livestock (number of live animals) 100,000 cattle, 71,000 pigs, 8,000 goats; roundwood 38,000 cu m; fish catch 2,470†, of which tuna 500. Mining and quarrying (1985)‡: small quantities of coral reef limestone, crushed stone, sand, and gravel. Manufacturing (value added in '000 VT; 1980): food, beverages, and tobacco 173,000; wood products 52,000; paper products, including printing and publishing 32,000; metal products, machinery, and equipment 22,500; chemicals, petroleum, rubber, and plastics 14,300; nonmetallic mineral products 14,100; textiles, clothing, and leather 13,140. Construction (approvals in Vila and Santo; 1985): residential 7,120 sq m; nonresidential 12,450 sq m. Energy production (consumption): electricity (kW-hr; 1984) 18,000,000 (18,500,000§); coal, none (n.a.); crude petroleum (barrels; 1981) none (110,000); petroleum products (metric tons; 1984) none (18,000); natural gas, none (n.a.).
Population economically active (1981): total 61,000; activity rate of total population 52.4% (participation rates: ages 15–64 [1979] 84.3%; female [1979] 43.4%; unemployed, n.a.).

Price and earnings indexes (1980 = 100)

	1980	1981	1982	1983	1984	1985	1986 ‖
Consumer price index	100.0	127.5	135.3	137.6	145.2	146.3	147.9
Monthly earnings index	...	...	...	...	...	...	...

Land use (1983): forested 1.1%; meadows and pastures 1.7%; agricultural 6.4%; limestones, volcanic rock, and other 90.8%.
Gross national product (1982): U.S.$63,600,000 (U.S.$530 per capita).

Structure of gross domestic product and labour force

	1981 in value VT '000,000	1981 % of total value	1979 labour force	1979 % of labour force
Agriculture	...	...	39,296	76.8
Mining	...	...	76	0.1
Manufacturing	...	...	990	1.9
Construction	...	...	1,103	2.2
Public utilities	...	...	61	0.1
Transp. and commun.	...	...	1,323	2.6
Trade	...	...	2,178	4.3
Finance	...	...	326	0.6
Pub. admin., defense	...	...	5,502	10.8
Services	...	...		
Other	...	...	308	0.6
TOTAL	5,861	100.0	51,163	100.0

Household income and expenditure. Average household size (1980) 4.9; household income: n.a.; expenditure¶: food 45.8%, clothing and footwear 14.1%, beverages and tobacco 10.1%, transportation and communication 9.8%, household furnishings 8.0%, housing 2.2%.

Foreign trade

Balance of trade (current prices)

	1980	1981	1982	1983	1984	1985
VT '000,000	−2,544	−2,283	−3,462	−3,320	−2,236	−4,257
% of total	34.2%	26.7%	44.0%	36.1%	20.3%	39.9%

Imports (1985): VT 6,463,000,000 (machines and transport equipment 21.9%, food and live animals 19.1%, basic manufactures 16.8%, mineral fuels 10.3%, chemicals 6.1%, beverages and tobacco 4.7%). *Major import sources:* Australia 36%; Japan 12%; New Zealand 11%; France 8%; Fiji 7%; New Caledonia 6%; Hong Kong 5%.
Exports (1985): VT 3,204,000,000 (copra 41.0%, frozen fish 23.8%, timber 8.0%, beef 6.2%, cocoa 4.8%). *Major export destinations:* The Netherlands 48%; Japan 17%; Belgium–Luxembourg 14%; France 12%; Singapore 1%; New Caledonia 1%.

Transport and communications

Transport. Railroads: none. Roads (1981): total length 660 mi, 1,062 km; (paved 4%). Vehicles (on the islands of Espiritu Santo and Éfaté; 1985): passenger cars 3,061; trucks and buses 248. Merchant marine (1985): vessels (100 gross tons and over) 28; total deadweight tonnage 226,436. Air transport (1984): international aircraft arrivals 1,234; airports (1986) with scheduled flights 23.
Communications. Daily newspapers (1985): none. Radio (1985): total number of receivers 16,000 (1 per 8.3 persons). Television: none. Telephones (1983): 3,000 (1 per 41 persons).

Education and health

Education (1983)

	schools	teachers	students	student/ teacher ratio
Primary (age 6–11)	246♀	934	23,465♀	...
Secondary (age 11–18)	9	126♂	2,186	...
Voc., teacher tr.	2	40♂	718	...
Higher	...	...	...	...

Educational attainment (1979). Percent of adult population over age 25 having: no schooling 37.2%; English qualification 7.5%, of which primary education 3.2%, postprimary 2.4%, technical and vocational 1.9%; French qualification 4.5%, of which primary 2.0%, postprimary 2.0%, technical and professional 0.5%; some secondary 14.7%; secondary and higher 7.3%. *Literacy* (1979): total population over age 5 that attended school 64,903 (73.2%); males 36,307 (76.9%); females 28,596 (69.0%).
Health (1984): physicians 19 (1 per 6,726 persons); hospital beds (1983) 437 (1 per 284 persons); infant mortality rate per 1,000 live births 94.
Food (1980–82): daily per capita caloric intake 2,122 (vegetable products 77%, animal products 23%); 80% of FAO recommended minimum requirement.

Military

Total active duty personnel: Vanuatu has a paramilitary force of about 300 and has received military assistance from Papua New Guinea.

*1979. †1983. ‡An opencut manganese mine 55 mi (34 km) northwest of Vila remained closed throughout the year. §Urban areas only. ‖ First quarter. ¶Consumer price index components. ♀1984. ♂1982.

Venezuela

Official name: República de Venezuela (Republic of Venezuela).
Form of government: federal multiparty republic with two legislative houses (Senate [47]; Chamber of Deputies [200]).
Head of state and government: President.
Capital: Caracas.
Official language: Spanish.
Official religion: none.
Monetary unit: 1 bolívar (B., plural Bs.) = 100 céntimos; valuation* (Oct. 1, 1986) 1 U.S.$ = Bs. 7.50; 1 £ = Bs. 10.84.

Area and population

		area		population
States	**Capitals**	sq mi	sq km	1985 estimate
Anzoátegui	Barcelona	16,700	43,300	783,300
Apure	San Fernando de Apure	29,500	76,500	230,800
Aragua	Maracay	2,700	7,014	1,109,000
Barinas	Barinas	13,600	35,200	413,000
Bolívar	Ciudad Bolívar	91,900	238,000	824,100
Carabobo	Valencia	1,795	4,650	1,341,000
Cojedes	San Carlos	5,700	14,800	166,100
Falcón	Coro	9,600	24,800	575,800
Guárico	San Juan de Los Morros	25,091	64,986	438,500
Lara	Barquisimeto	7,600	19,800	1,096,200
Mérida	Mérida	4,400	11,300	552,300
Miranda	Los Teques	3,070	7,950	1,714,000
Monagas	Maturín	11,200	28,900	452,300
Nueva Esparta	La Asunción	440	1,150	236,200
Portuguesa	Guanare	5,900	15,200	519,400
Sucre	Cumaná	4,600	11,800	676,100
Táchira	San Cristóbal	4,300	11,100	764,700
Trujillo	Trujillo	2,900	7,400	506,800
Yaracuy	San Felipe	2,700	7,100	340,200
Zulia	Maracaibo	24,400	63,100	1,982,400
Other federal entities				
Amazonas	Puerto Ayacucho	67,900	175,750	70,800
Delta Amacuro	Tucupita	15,500	40,200	83,200
Dependencias Federales	—	50	120	...
Distrito Federal	Caracas	745	1,930	2,450,500
TOTAL		352,144†	912,050	17,316,700

Demography

Population (1986): 17,791,000.
Density (1986): persons per sq mi 50.5, persons per sq km 19.5.
Urban-rural (1985): urban 85.7%; rural 14.3%.
Sex distribution (1985): male 50.00%; female 50.00%.
Age breakdown (1981): under 15, 40.5%; 15–29, 29.9%; 30–44, 15.8%; 45–59, 8.7%; 60–74, 4.0%; 75 and over, 1.1%.
Population projection: (1990) 19,638,000; (2000) 25,138,000.
Doubling time: 28 years.
Ethnic composition (1981): mestizo 69%; white 20%; black 9%; Indian 2%.
Religious affiliation (1981): Roman Catholic 92.4%; other 7.6%.
Major cities (1987): Caracas 3,247,000; Maracaibo 1,295,000; Valencia 1,135,000; Barquisimeto 718,000.

Vital statistics

Birth rate per 1,000 population (1984): 29.9 (world avg. 29.0); (1974) legitimate 47.0%; illegitimate 53.0%.
Death rate per 1,000 population (1984): 4.6 (world avg. 11.0).
Natural increase rate per 1,000 population (1984): 25.3 (world avg. 18.0).
Total fertility rate (avg. births per childbearing woman; 1980–85): 4.3.
Marriage rate per 1,000 population (1983): 5.6.
Divorce rate per 1,000 population (1983): 0.3.
Life expectancy at birth (1980–85): male 65.1 years; female 70.6 years.
Major causes of death per 100,000 population (1980): diseases of the circulatory system 117.9; symptoms and ill-defined conditions 79.4; malignant neoplasms (cancers) 49.6; infectious and parasitic diseases 42.0.

National economy

Budget (1984). Revenue: Bs. 104,007,000,000 (corporate income tax 55.5%, foreign exchange profits 13.8%, property income 12.8%, import duties 4.2%, excise taxes 4.2%, social security contributions 3.2%). Expenditures: Bs. 85,987,000,000 (economic services 22.7%, education 17.7%, social security and welfare 7.6%, health 7.6%, housing 7.1%, defense 6.1%, general public services 5.5%).
Public debt (external, outstanding; 1984): U.S.$17,246,800,000.
Tourism (1984): receipts from visitors U.S.$343,000,000; expenditures by nationals abroad U.S.$995,000,000.
Production (metric tons except as noted). Agriculture, forestry, fishing (1984): sugarcane 4,966,000, bananas 965,000, corn (maize) 547,000, sorghum 473,000, rice 408,000, coffee 61,000, seed cotton 46,000, sesame 38,000, cacao 12,000; livestock (number of live animals) 12,283,000 cattle; roundwood 1,322,000 cu m; fish catch (1983) 226,869. Mining and quarrying (1984): iron ore 13,044,000; gold 1,000 kilograms; diamonds 500,000 carats; coal 48,000; salt 350,000‡. Manufacturing (1984): cement 4,783,000; steel 2,511,000; fertilizers 759,000; paper and cardboard 558,000; aluminum 377,000; refined sugar 389,000; motor vehicles 110,000 units. Construction (1983§): residential 2,574,500 sq m; nonresidential 1,102,600 sq m. Energy production (consumption): electricity (kW-hr; 1984) 44,330,000,000 (44,322,000,000); coal (metric tons; 1984) 51,000 (431,000); crude petroleum (barrels; 1984) 659,018,000 (300,675,000); petroleum products (metric tons; 1984) 41,637,000 (18,370,000); natural gas (cu m; 1984) 16,610,000,000 (16,610,000,000).
Gross national product (1984): U.S.$57,360,000,000 (U.S.$3,400 per capita).

Structure of gross domestic product and labour force

	1984			
	in value Bs. '000,000	% of total value	labour force	% of labour force
Agriculture	23,886	6.9	825,777	14.4
Mining	69,662	20.0	81,412	1.4
Manufacturing	67,675	19.5	874,215	15.3
Construction	10,335	3.0	482,535	8.4
Public utilities	5,773	1.7	73,293	1.3
Transp. and commun.	37,725	10.9	384,111	6.7
Trade	38,292	11.0	1,065,876	18.6
Finance			275,175	4.8
Pub. admin., defense; Services	94,182	27.1	1,517,971	26.6
Other			135,842	2.4
TOTAL	347,530	100.0†	5,716,207	100.0†

Population economically active (1984): total 5,716,207; activity rate of total population 33.9% (participation rates: over age 15, 56.3%; female 27.1%; unemployed 13.4%).

Price and earnings indexes (1980 = 100)

	1980	1981	1982	1983	1984	1985	1986‖
Consumer price index	100.0	116.2	127.3	135.3	151.8	169.1	187.0
Monthly earnings index	...	...	...	...	...	...	...

Household income and expenditure: average household size (1981) 5.3; average annual income per household (1979) Bs. 2,897 (U.S.$512); source of income: n.a.; expenditure (1984): food, beverages, and tobacco 55.6%, transport and communication 10.8%, rent and utilities 9.3%, education 5.9%, household furnishings and maintenance 5.1%, medical and health care 4.4%, clothing and footwear 4.1%.
Land use (1983): forested 38.7%; meadows and pastures 19.7%; agricultural and under permanent cultivation 4.2%; other 37.4%.

Foreign trade

Balance of trade (current prices)

	1980	1981	1982	1983	1984	1985
Bs. '000,000	+36,772	+35,706	+20,765	+31,427	+49,665	+36,786
% of total	28.7%	26.0%	17.2%	31.8%	34.3%	25.0%

Imports (1981): U.S.$11,811,000,000 (machinery and transport equipment 43.4%, of which road motor vehicles 12.2%; chemicals and related products 10.4%; electrical machinery, apparatus, and equipment 9.5%; iron and steel 5.9%; cereals and cereal preparations 5.0%). *Major import sources:* United States 48.3%; Japan 8.1%; Canada 5.4%; West Germany 5.3%; Italy 3.8%.
Exports (1981): U.S.$17,518,000,000 (crude petroleum oils and crude oils obtained from bituminous materials 78.7%; petroleum products, refined 14.1%). *Major export destinations:* Netherlands Antilles 24.8%; United States 13.2%; Canada 11.1%; Italy 8.1%; Brazil 5.6%.

Transport and communications

Transport. Railroads (1982): route length (1986) 273 mi, 439 km; passenger-mi 11,800,000, passenger-km 19,000,000; short ton-mi cargo 19,900,000, metric ton-km cargo 29,000,000. Roads (1984): total length 39,177 mi, 63,050 km (paved 38%). Vehicles (1984): passenger cars 1,543,000; trucks and buses 753,000. Merchant marine (1984): vessels (100 gross tons and over) 269; total deadweight tonnage 1,421,829. Air transport (1985): passenger-mi 1,531,313,000, passenger-km 2,464,414,000; short ton-mi cargo 147,385,000, metric ton-km cargo 215,178,000; airports (1986) with scheduled flights 39.
Communications. Daily newspapers (1982): total number 61; total circulation 2,739,000; circulation per 1,000 population 172. Radio (1985): 5,260,000 receivers (1 per 3.3 persons). Television (1985): 2,880,800 receivers (1 per 6.0 persons). Telephones (1983): 1,021,136 (1 per 16 persons).

Education and health

Education (1984–85)

	schools	teachers	students	student/ teacher ratio
Primary (age 7–12)	14,277	125,140	3,256,554	26.0
Secondary (age 13–17)¶	2,241	58,056	1,007,642	17.4
Higher	81	30,123	381,575	12.7

Educational attainment (1981). Percent of adult population over age 25 having: no formal schooling 23.5%; primary education 47.2%; secondary 22.3%; higher 7.0%. *Literacy* (1985): total population literate 9,332,788 (88.4%); males literate 4,786,841 (90.3%); females literate 4,545,947 (86.5%).
Health (1979): physicians 15,359 (1 per 947 persons); hospital beds 43,650 (1 per 333 persons); infant mortality rate per 1,000 live births (1984) 27.3.
Food (1980–82): daily per capita caloric intake 2,557 (vegetable products 79%, animal products 21%); 107% of FAO recommended minimum requirement.

Military

Total active duty personnel (1985): 49,000 (army 69.4%, navy 20.4%, air force 10.2%). *Military expenditure as percent of GNP* (1983): 1.3% (world 6.1%); per capita expenditure U.S.$55.

*Official rate only; nonofficial rate is 168.1% higher. †Detail does not add to total given because of rounding. ‡1983. §Private construction only. ‖July. ¶Includes vocational and teacher training.

Vietnam

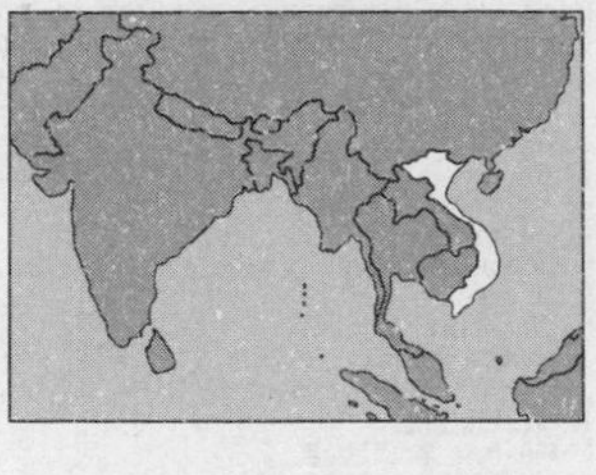

Official name: Cong Hoa Xa Hoi Chu Nghia Viet Nam (Socialist Republic of Vietnam).
Form of government: unitary single-party socialist republic with one legislative house (National Assembly [496]).
Chief of state: President.
Head of government: Premier.
Capital: Hanoi.
Official language: Vietnamese.
Official religion: none.
Monetary unit: 1 dong (D) = 10 hao = 100 xu; valuation (Oct. 1, 1986) 1 U.S.$ = D 11.76; 1 £ = D 17.00.

Area and population

		area		population
Provinces	**Capitals**	sq mi	sq km	1979 census
An Giang	Long Xuyen	1,349	3,493	1,532,362
Bac Thai	Thai Nguyen	2,521	6,530	815,105
Ben Tre	Ben Tre	859	2,225	1,041,838
Binh Tri Thien	Hue	7,081	18,340	1,901,713
Cao Bang	Cao Bang	3,261	8,445	479,823
Cuu Long	Vihn Long	1,488	3,854	1,504,215
Dac Lac	Buon Me Thoat	7,645	19,800	490,198
Dong Nai	Bien Hoa	2,926	7,578	1,304,799
Dong Thap	Cao Lamh	1,309	3,391	1,182,787
Gia Lai-Cong Tum	Cong Tum	9,860	25,536	595,906
Ha Bac	Bac Giang	1,780	4,609	1,662,671
Hai Hung	Hai Duong	986	2,555	2,145,662
Ha Nam Ninh	Nam Dinh	1,453	3,763	2,781,409
Ha Son Binh	Hanoi	2,308	5,978	1,537,190
Ha Tuyen	Ha Giang	5,219	13,518	782,453
Hau Giang	Can Tho	2,365	6,126	2,232,891
Hoang Lien Son	Lao Cal	5,734	14,852	778,217
Kien Giang	Rach Gia	2,455	6,358	994,673
Lai Chau	Lai Chau	6,586	17,068	322,077
Lam Dong	Da Lat	3,835	9,933	396,657
Lang Son	Lang Son	3,161	8,187	484,657
Long An	Tan An	1,681	4,355	957,264
Minh Hai	Bac Lieu	2,972	7,697	1,219,595
Nghe Tinh	Vinh	8,688	22,502	3,111,989
Nghia Binh	Qui Nhon	4,595	11,900	2,095,354
Phu Khanh	Nha Trang	3,785	9,804	1,188,637
Quang Nam-Da Nang	Da Nang	4,629	11,989	1,529,520
Quang Ninh	Hai Duong	2,293	5,938	750,055
Song Be	Thu Dau Mo	3,807	9,859	659,093
Son La	Son La	5,586	14,468	487,793
Tay Ninh	Ho Chi Minh City	1,556	4,030	684,006
Thai Binh	Thai Binh	577	1,495	1,506,235
Thanh Hoa	Thanh Hoa	4,300	11,138	2,532,261
Thuan Hai	Phan Thiet	4,392	11,374	938,255
Tien Giang	My Tho	918	2,377	1,264,498
Vinh Phu	Viet Tri	1,786	4,626	1,488,348
Municipalities				
Haiphong	—	585	1,515	1,279,067
Hanoi	—	826	2,139	2,570,905
Ho Chi Minh City	—	787	2,029	3,419,978
Special zone				
Vung Tau-Con Dao	—	108	279	91,610
TOTAL		128,052	331,653	52,741,766

Demography

Population (1986): 61,218,000.
Density (1986): persons per sq mi 478.0, persons per sq km 184.5.
Urban-rural (1985): urban 19.0%; rural 81.0%.
Sex distribution (1985): male 48.95%; female 51.05%.
Age breakdown (1985): under 15, 40.8%; 15–29, 30.8%; 30–44, 13.5%; 45–59, 9.3%; 60–74, 4.4%; 75 and over, 1.2%.
Population projection: (1990) 68,338,000; (2000) 82,709,000.
Doubling time: 28 years.
Ethnic composition (1979): Vietnamese 88.0%; Chinese (Hoa) 1.9%; Tai 1.5%; Khmer 1.2%; Muong 1.2%; Thai 1.2%; Nung 0.9%; other 4.1%.
Religious affiliation (1980): Buddhist 55.3%; Roman Catholic 7.4%; Muslim 1.0%; other 36.3%.
Major cities (1979): Ho Chi Minh City 3,419,978; Hanoi 2,919,000*; Haiphong 1,279,067.

Vital statistics

Birth rate per 1,000 population (1985): 32.2 (world avg. 29.0); legitimate, n.a.; illegitimate, n.a.
Death rate per 1,000 population (1985): 9.8 (world avg. 11.0).
Natural increase rate per 1,000 population (1985): 22.4 (world avg. 18.0).
Total fertility rate (avg. births per childbearing woman; 1985): 4.3.
Marriage rate per 1,000 population: n.a.
Divorce rate per 1,000 population: n.a.
Life expectancy at birth (1985): male 57.7 years; female 62.1 years.
Major causes of death per 100,000 population (1979): diseases of the circulatory system 123.8; malignant neoplasms (cancers) 54.0; infectious and parasitic diseases 48.0.

National economy

Budget (1982). Revenue: U.S.$4,120,000,000. Expenditures: U.S.$5,560,000,000.
Public debt (external, outstanding; 1984): U.S.$6,000,000,000.
Production (metric tons except as noted). Agriculture, forestry, fishing (1984): rice 15,416,000, sugarcane 4,800,000, fruits 3,328,000, vegetables 2,953,000, cassava 2,900,000, sweet potatoes 1,900,000, corn (maize) 475,000, coconuts 355,000; livestock (number of live animals; 1985) 11,761,000 pigs, 5,000,000 cattle, 262,000 sheep and goats, 90,900,000 poultry; roundwood 24,323,000 cu m; fish catch 557,000. Mining and quarrying (1984): salt 800,000; phosphate rock 200,000; chromite 16,000; zinc ore 7,000; bauxite 5,000. Manufacturing (1984): cement 1,297,000; fertilizers 499,000; sugar 381,000; paper and paperboard 69,500; crude steel 53,000; textiles 364,000,000 sq m; beer 900,000 hectolitres; tires 15,800 units†; leather footwear 200,000 pairs. Construction: n.a. Energy production (consumption): electricity (kW-hr; 1984) 4,853,000,000 (4,853,000,000); coal (metric tons; 1984) 4,900,000 (4,900,000); crude petroleum, none (n.a.); petroleum products (metric tons; 1984) none (1,330,000); natural gas, none (n.a.).
Gross national product (at current market prices; 1983): U.S.$9,818,000,000 (U.S.$170 per capita).

Structure of net material product and labour force

	1983			
	by value	% of total value	labour force	% of labour force
Agriculture	...	57.6	17,703,000	68.7
Mining and manufacturing	...	23.7‡	758,000	2.9
Construction	...	3.0	455,000	1.8
Public utilities	...	‡	32,300	0.1
Transp. and commun.	...	1.9	180,000	0.7
Trade	...	11.7	395,000	1.5
Services	...	...	856,400	3.3
Other	...	2.1§	5,402,700 ‖	21.0 ‖
TOTAL	...	100.0	25,782,000	100.0

Population economically active (1983): total 25,782,000; activity rate of total population 44.9% (participation rates: ages 15–64, 55.0%; female 45.5%; unemployed, n.a.).
Price and earnings indexes: n.a.
Household income and expenditure: n.a.
Land use (1983): forested 40.4%; meadows and pastures 0.8%; agricultural and under permanent cultivation 23.3%; other 35.5%.

Foreign trade

Balance of trade (current prices)

	1979	1980	1981	1982	1983	1984
U.S.$'000,000	−1,012	−759	−931	−843	−702	−710
% of total	46.3%	41.4%	49.9%	41.6%	39.5%	36.4%

Imports (1984): U.S.$1,330,000,000¶ (fuel and raw materials 44.7%, machinery 23.2%, wheat flour and food products 17.2%). *Major import sources:* U.S.S.R. 23.0%; Japan 21.9%; Hong Kong 13.6%; Singapore 13.2%; India 12.4%; France 5.0%; United States 4.1%; Hungary 3.0%; Sweden 3.0%.
Exports (1984): U.S.$620,000,000¶ (manufactured goods 72.8%, handicrafts 18.6%, agricultural products 8.6%). *Major export destinations:* Hong Kong 31.6%; Japan 18.3%; Singapore 17.5%; U.S.S.R. 9.7%; France 3.0%; Hungary 2.4%.

Transport and communications

Transport. Railroads (1984): length 1,568 mi, 2,523 km; passenger-mi 2,237,000,000, passenger-km 3,600,000,000; short ton-mi cargo 561,000,000, metric ton-km cargo 819,000,000. Roads (1983): total length 37,282 mi, 60,000 km (paved 16%♀). Vehicles (1976): passenger cars 100,000; trucks and buses 200,000. Merchant marine (1985): vessels (100 gross tons and over) 128; total deadweight tonnage 446,242. Air transport (1983): passenger-mi 180,819,000, passenger-km 291,000,000; short ton-mi cargo 2,740,000, metric ton-km cargo 4,000,000; airports (1986) with scheduled flights 3.
Communications. Daily newspapers (1984): 4; total circulation 500,000; circulation per 1,000 population 8.6. Radio (1984): 6,000,000 receivers (1 per 9.7 persons). Television (1984): 2,250,000 receivers (1 per 25.7 persons). Telephones (1982): 1,165,000 (1 per 48.1 persons).

Education and health

Education (1983–84)

	schools	teachers	students	student/ teacher ratio
Primary and secondary (age 7–18)	11,751	427,000	11,779,000	27.6
Vocational	280	10,200	99,200	9.7
Higher	93	18,100	92,500	5.1

Educational attainment (1983). Percent of state-employed population havingδ: vocational education 12.9%; higher 7.4%. *Literacy* (1979): total population over age 15 literate 28,903,500 (94.0%).
Health (1985): physicians 17,100□ (1 per 3,500 persons); hospital beds 208,000 (1 per 288 persons); infant mortality rate per 1,000 live births 72.
Food (1980–82): daily per capita caloric intake 2,040 (vegetable products 92%, animal products 8%); 94% of FAO recommended minimum requirement.

Military

Total active duty personnel (1985): 1,027,000 (army 97.4%, navy 1.2%, air force 1.4%). *Military expenditure as percent of GNP:* n.a. *Foreign military aid* (1982): U.S.$1,000,000,000.

*1985 estimate. †1983. ‡Mining and manufacturing includes public utilities. §Other material activities. ‖ Includes finance and public administration and defense. ¶Breakdown for 1980. ♀1981. δTotal state-employed 3,658,000. □Includes dentists.

Virgin Islands (U.S.)

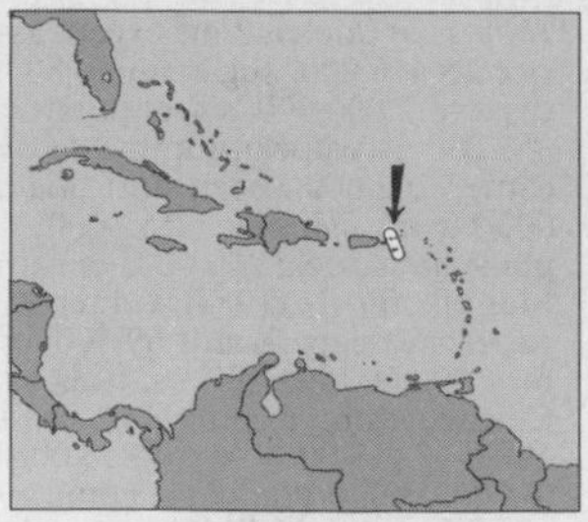

Official name: Virgin Islands of the United States.
Political status: unincorporated territory of the United States with one legislative house (Senate [15]).
Chief of state: President of the United States.
Head of government: Governor.
Capital: Charlotte Amalie.
Official language: English.
Official religion: none.
Monetary unit: 1 U.S. dollar (U.S.$) = 100 cents; valuation (Oct. 1, 1986) 1 U.S.$ = £0.69.

Area and population

		area		population
				1985
Islands*	**Capitals**	sq mi	sq km	estimate
St. Croix	Christiansted	84	217	57,020
St. John	—	20	52	2,530
St. Thomas	Charlotte Amalie	32	83	51,020
TOTAL		136	352	110,800†

Demography

Population (1986 est.): 114,000.
Density (1986): persons per sq mi 795.5, persons per sq km 307.0.
Urban-rural (1980): urban 39.1%; rural 60.9%.
Sex distribution (1980): male 47.85%; female 52.15%.
Age breakdown (1980): under 15, 36.0%; 15–29, 24.2%; 30–44, 21.5%; 45–59, 11.1%; 60–74, 5.8%; 75 and over, 1.4%.
Population projection: (1990) 129,000; (2000) 160,000.
Doubling time: 35 years.
Ethnic composition (1980)‡: black 79.7%, of which Spanish or Hispanic origin 10.3%; white 14.8%, of which Spanish or Hispanic origin 2.3%; other 5.5%, of which Spanish or Hispanic origin 3.7%.
Religious affiliation (1980): Christian 98.0%, of which Protestant 64.4% (Anglican 17.4%, Pentecostal 12.0%, Moravian 8.5%, Methodist 8.0%, Lutheran 3.2%), Roman Catholic 33.6%; Bahā'ī 0.5%; Jewish 0.3%; nonreligious 1.2%.
Major cities (1980): Charlotte Amalie 11,842; Christiansted 2,914; Frederiksted 1,046.

Vital statistics

Birth rate per 1,000 population (1982): 24.7 (world avg. 29.0); (1981) legitimate 48.7%; illegitimate 51.3%.
Death rate per 1,000 population (1982): 4.9 (world avg. 11.0).
Natural increase rate per 1,000 population (1982): 19.8 (world avg. 18.0).
Total fertility rate (avg. births per childbearing woman; 1980–85): 2.9.
Marriage rate per 1,000 population (1982): 12.9.
Divorce rate per 1,000 population (1982): 3.3.
Life expectancy at birth (1980–85): male 66.7 years; female 70.7 years.
Major causes of death per 100,000 population (1981): diseases of the circulatory system 209.8, of which ischemic heart disease 127.3, cerebrovascular disease 35.6, malignant neoplasms (cancers) 83.5; accidents 50.9; diseases of the digestive system 34.6; violence 33.6; nephritis and nephrosis 23.4.

National economy

Budget (1983). Revenue: U.S.$252,379,000 (personal income tax 38.4%, rum excise tax 13.9%, corporate income tax 11.6%, gross receipts tax 9.7%, property tax 9.5%). Expenditures: U.S.$231,000,000 (education 25.4%, health 15.7%, executive branch 12.5%, public works 7.7%, public safety 5.7%, College of the Virgin Islands 3.8%, Territorial Court 2.7%, legislature 2.0%).
Tourism (1984): receipts from visitors U.S.$377,000,000; expenditures by nationals abroad, n.a.
Production (value of sales in U.S.$ except as noted). Agriculture, forestry, fishing (1982): milk 923,000, beef and veal 489,000, poultry and eggs 316,000, ornamental plants and other nursery products 89,700, bananas 63,000, onions 51,000, mangoes 49,000 (other agricultural products include sorghum and bay leaves); livestock (number of live animals; 1984) 8,000 cattle, 6,000 pigs, 6,000 goats, 5,000 sheep; roundwood, n.a.; fish catch (1983) 611 metric tons. Mining and quarrying (1984): sand and traprock for local use. Manufacturing (1983): food and related products 28,771,000§; watches, clocks, and watchcases 13,845,000§; printing, publishing, and allied industries 5,206,000§; heavy oils 10,800,000 metric tons; gasoline 2,400,000 metric tons; jet fuel 600,000 metric tons; kerosene 225,000 metric tons; liquefied petroleum gas 40,000 metric tons; rum 88,100 hectolitres ‖; alumina 125,000 metric tons¶. Construction (1982): general building 64,775,000; heavy construction 52,414,000; special trade construction 24,776,000; buildings completed (1979) residential 908, nonresidential 262. Energy production (consumption): electricity (kW-hr; 1984) 880,000,000 (880,000,000); coal, none (none); crude petroleum (barrels; 1984) none (126,076,000); petroleum products (metric tons; 1984) 15,215,000 (2,272,000); natural gas, none (none).
Household income and expenditure: average household size (1980) 3.4; average annual income per household (1979) U.S.$14,453; sources of income: wages and salaries 84.6%, interest, dividends, and rent 4.2%, transfer payments 4.1%, self-employment 3.8%, other 3.3%; expenditure: n.a..
Gross national product (at current market prices; 1984): U.S.$900,000,000 (U.S.$8,790 per capita).

Structure of gross domestic product and labour force

	1985		1984	
	in value U.S.$'000,000	% of total value	labour force	% of labour force
Agriculture	...	...	522	1.2
Manufacturing	...	...	2,080	4.9
Construction and mining	...	...	2,390	5.7
Transportation and public utilities	...	...	2,310	5.5
Trade, hotels, restaurants	...	...	10,970	26.1
Finance, insurance, real estate	...	...	1,770	4.2
Pub. admin., defense	...	...	12,900	30.6
Services	...	...	4,090	9.7
Other	...	...	5,088♀	12.1
TOTAL	1,030	100.0	42,120	100.0

Public debt: n.a.
Population economically active (1980): total 38,082; activity rate of total population 39.4% (participation rates: ages 15–64, 68.2%; female 45.5%; unemployed [1985] 6.0%).

Price and earnings indexes (1980 = 100)

	1979	1980	1981	1982	1983	1984	1985
Consumer price index♂	88.1	100.0	110.4	117.1	120.9	126.1	130.5
Annual earnings index□	89.7	100.0	112.0	118.3	123.0	131.0	137.6

Land use (1983): forested 5.9%; meadows and pastures 26.5%; agricultural and under permanent cultivation 20.6%; other 47.0%.

Foreign trade

Balance of trade (current prices)

	1980	1981	1982	1983	1984	1985
U.S.$'000,000	−604.4	+54.6	−300.2	−1,019.5	−786.4	−383.5
% of total	6.5%	0.5%	2.9%	12.2%	9.0%	5.4%

Imports (1985): U.S.$3,740,600,000 (crude petroleum from the United States 41.9%; foreign crude petroleum 40.3%; other products 17.8%). *Major import sources:* United States 54.3%; other countries 45.7%.
Exports (1985): U.S.$3,357,100,000 (petroleum products to the United States 94.1%; rum, watch movements, alumina¶, and other exports to the United States 2.2%; foreign exports 3.7%). *Major export destinations:* United States 96.3%; other countries 3.7%.

Transport and communications

Transport. Railroads: none. Roads (1985): total length 532 mi, 856 km. Registered motor vehicles (1985): 43,901. Merchant marine, n.a. Air transport (1983)◇: passenger arrivals 664,016, passenger departures 723,792; cargo unloaded 3,473 metric tons, cargo loaded 1,004 metric tons; airports (1986) with scheduled flights 6△.
Communications. Daily newspapers (1985): total number 2; total circulation 20,000; circulation per 1,000 population 193. Radio (1985): total number of receivers 85,000 (1 per 1.2 persons). Television (1985): total number of receivers 31,000 (1 per 3.4 persons). Telephones (1983): 49,043 (1 per 2.1 persons).

Education and health

Education (1984–85)

	schools	teachers	students	student/ teacher ratio
Primary (age 4.5–12)	60†	981⊕	18,356	...
Secondary (age 12–18)	11	799⊕	14,684	...
Voc., teacher tr.**	3	27	775	28.7
Higher	1	84	765	9.1

Educational attainment (1980): Percent of adult population over age 25 having: no formal schooling 1.5%; primary education 34.1%; secondary 40.0%; higher 24.4%. *Literacy* (1982): total population over age 15 literate 90%.
Health (1985): physicians 167 (1 per 622 persons); hospital beds 507 (1 per 205 persons); infant mortality rate per 1,000 live births (1982) 19.5.
Food: daily per capita caloric intake, n.a.

Military

Total active duty personnel: No domestic military force is maintained; the United States is responsible for defense and security.

*For administrative purposes, the U.S. Virgin Islands is divided into two legislative districts, St. Croix and St. Thomas/St. John. †Total includes 230 persons not accounted for by island. ‡*Place of birth:* U.S. Virgin Islands 44.8%; United States 12.4%; Puerto Rico 5.2%; other West Indies 29.2%, of which St. Christopher and Nevis 6.8%, Antigua and Barbuda 5.1%, British Virgin Islands 3.4%; not reported 5.6%. §1982. ‖ 1984. ¶The U.S.-owned alumina plant on St. Croix closed in 1985. ♀Includes 2,480 self-employed and unpaid family workers and 2,608 unemployed. ♂U.S. mainland. □Annual average gross pay. ◇St. Croix and St. Thomas airports. △Scheduled services at 2 airports, 3 seaplane bases, and 1 heliport. †Includes 19 elementary/secondary schools. ⊕Private school teachers not included in total. **1983–84.

Western Samoa

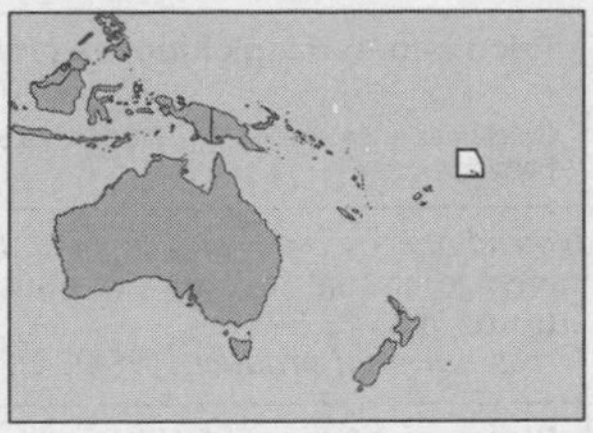

Official name: Malo Sa'oloto Tuto'atasi o Samoa i Sisifo (Samoan); Independent State of Western Samoa (English).
Form of government: constitutional monarchy* with one legislative house (Legislative Assembly [47]).
Chief of state: Head of State.
Head of government: Prime Minister.
Capital: Apia.
Official languages: Samoan; English.
Official religion: none.
Monetary unit: 1 tala (WS$, plural tala) = 100 sene; valuation (Oct. 1, 1986) 1 U.S.$ = WS$2.27; 1 £ = WS$3.28.

Area and population

Islands / Political Districts	area† sq mi	area† sq km	population 1981 census‡
Savaii	659	1,707	43,150
Fa'aseleleaga			11,876
Gaga'emauga			3,893
Gaga'ifomauga			5,304
Lealataua			1,934
Palauli			9,234
Satupa'itea			5,391
Vaisigano			5,518
Upolu	432	1,119	113,199
A'ana			13,149
A'ana-i-Sisifo			3,363
Aiga-i-le-Tai			3,960
Aleipata			4,236
Anoama'a			7,816
Fagaloa			1,519
Falealili			4,727
Faleata			16,821
Gaga'emauga			2,750
Lefaga			3,776
Lepa and Lotofaga			3,058
Safata			6,711
Sagaga			12,253
Vaimauga			29,060
TOTAL	1,093	2,831	156,349

Demography

Population (1986): 160,400.
Density (1986): persons per sq mi 146.8, persons per sq km 56.7.
Urban-rural (1981): urban 21.2%; rural 78.8%.
Sex distribution (1981): male 51.82%; female 48.18%.
Age breakdown (1981): under 15, 44.3%; 15–29, 29.1%; 30–44, 12.2%; 45–59, 9.0%; 60–74, 3.8%; 75 and over, 1.6%.
Population projection: (1990) 165,800; (2000) 175,000.
Doubling time: 88 years.
Ethnic composition (1982): Samoan (Polynesian) *c.* 88%; Euronesian *c.* 10%; European *c.* 2%.
Religious affiliation (1981): Congregational 47.3%; Roman Catholic 21.7%; Methodist 16.2%; Latter Day Saints 8.3%; Seventh-day Adventist 2.3%; other 4.2%.
Major cities (1981): Apia 33,170.

Vital statistics

Birth rate per 1,000 population (1984): 10.2§ (world avg. 29.0); (1978) legitimate 43.5%; illegitimate 56.5%.
Death rate per 1,000 population (1984): 2.3§ (world avg. 11.0).
Natural increase rate per 1,000 population (1984): 7.9 (world avg. 18.0).
Total fertility rate (avg. births per childbearing woman; 1985): 4.5.
Marriage rate per 1,000 population (1984): 5.0§.
Divorce rate per 1,000 population (1984): 0.1§.
Life expectancy at birth (1985): male 62.2 years; female 65.5 years.
Major causes of death per 100,000 population§ (1984): diseases of the circulatory system 47.2; diseases of the respiratory system 22.6; diseases of the intestinal and digestive systems 20.7; malignant neoplasms (cancers) 17.6.

National economy

Budget (1984) ‖. Revenue: WS$77,800,000 (current revenue 62.8%, of which taxes 53.5%, nontax revenue 9.3%; foreign aid grants 26.7%; domestic borrowing 9.8%). Expenditures: WS$77,800,000 (capital expenditure 59.4%, of which development 22.2%; current expenditure 40.6%, of which social services 15.9%, general administration 8.7%, economic services 6.9%).
Public debt (external, outstanding; 1983): U.S.$60,500,000.
Land use (1983): forested 47.0%; meadows and pastures 0.3%; agricultural and under permanent cultivation 42.8%; other 9.9%.
Production (metric tons except as noted). Agriculture, forestry, fishing (1984): coconuts 200,000, taro 37,000, bananas 22,000, papayas 11,000, mangoes 6,000, pineapples 6,000, avocados 2,000, milk 1,000, cacao 615; livestock (number of live animals) 61,000 pigs, 26,000 cattle, 1,000,000 chickens; roundwood 131,000 cu m; fish catch 1,740. Mining and quarrying: n.a. Manufacturing (1985): coconut oil 11,766, copra meal 6,098, copra 2,731, sawn wood 21,000 cu m¶, veneer sheets 1,061 cu m♀; other products include coconut cream, beverages, tobacco products, aluminum products, concrete blocks, handicrafts, and kava. Construction (permits issued in WS$; 1984): residential 1,628,000; commercial, industrial, and other 4,135,600. Energy production (consumption): electricity (kW-hr; 1984) 33,790,000 (33,790,000); coal, none (n.a.); crude petroleum, none (n.a.); petroleum products (metric tons; 1984) 37,000 (37,000); natural gas, none (n.a.).
Gross national product (1980): U.S.$128,800,000 (U.S.$830 per capita).

Structure of gross domestic product and labour force

	1972 in value WS$	1972 % of total value	1981 labour force	1981 % of labour force
Agriculture	15,207,000	50.2	25,050	60.4
Mining	—	—	9	—
Manufacturing	858,900	2.8	757	1.8
Construction	1,146,800	3.8	2,279	5.5
Public utilities	...	...	447	1.1
Transp. and commun.	666,600	2.2	1,353	3.3
Trade	2,861,100	9.5	1,821	4.4
Finance	1,761,800	5.8	1,305	3.1
Pub. admin., defense, government services	6,346,700	21.0	1,842	4.4
Other services	646,000	2.1	6,374	15.4
Other	769,400	2.5	269	0.6
TOTAL	30,264,300	100.0ö	41,506	100.0

Population economically active (1981): total 41,506; activity rate of total population 26.5% (participation rates: ages 15–64, 48.6%; female 15.0%; unemployed, n.a.).

Price and earnings indexes (1980 = 100)

	1980	1981	1982	1983	1984	1985	1986□
Consumer price index	100.0	120.5	142.6	166.0	185.7	202.6	215.2
Monthly earnings index◇	100.0	112.8	...	146.6	163.0	...	...

Household income and expenditure. Average household size (1976) 5.9; income per household (1972) WS$1,518 (U.S.$2,200); sources of income: wages 49.4%, self-employment 22.8%, remittances, gifts, and other assistance 18.0%, land rent 8.7%, other 1.1%; expenditure (1980)△: food 58.8%, transportation 9.0%, housing and furnishings 5.1%, fuel and light 5.0%, clothing 4.2%, other goods and services 1.9%, other 16.0%.
Tourism (1984): number of visitors 40,337; number of nationals abroad, n.a.

Foreign trade†

Balance of trade (current prices)

	1980	1981	1982	1983	1984	1985
WS$'000	−36,338	−41,937	−38,402	−45,719	−48,024	−66,772
% of total	53.5%	65.3%	54.2%	45.5%	39.5%	46.9%

Imports (1985)⊕: WS$115,074,000 (food 21.3%, machinery 21.0%, petroleum products 18.4%, miscellaneous manufactured articles 7.4%, chemicals 5.9%, animal oils and fats 0.5%). *Major import sources:* New Zealand 32.1%; Australia 19.8%; Fiji 15.8%; Japan 13.7%; United States 3.7%.
Exports (1985): WS$36,180,000 (coconut oil 45.1%, taro 14.6%, coconut cream 7.9%, beverages and tobacco 5.5%, copra and copra meal 4.2%, timber 2.1%). *Major export destinations:* United States 61.5%; New Zealand 18.1%; Australia 9.0%; American Samoa 2.1%; West Germany 1.1%.

Transport and communications

Transport. Railroads: none. Roads (1983): total length** 1,296 mi, 2,085 km (paved 14%). Vehicles (1984): passenger cars 1,795; trucks and buses 2,494. Merchant marine (1985): vessels (100 gross tons and over) 6; total deadweight tonnage 35,293. Air transport (1985): passengers, n.a.; cargo, n.a.; airports (1986) with scheduled flights 3.
Communications. Daily newspapers: none. Radio (1985): 70,000 receivers (1 per 2.3 persons). Television (1985): 2,800 receivers (1 per 57 persons). Telephones (1984): 6,037 (1 per 26 persons).

Education and health

Education (1983)

	schools	teachers	students	student/ teacher ratio
Primary (age 5–11)	164	1,502††	31,447	20.9
Secondary (age 12–18)	38♀	520	20,404	39.2
Voc., teacher tr.	4	69	651	9.4
Higher	6	37	562	15.2

Educational attainment (1976). Percent of adult population over age 25 having: no formal schooling 60.0%; primary 31.5%; secondary 6.3%; higher 2.2%. *Literacy* (1971): total population over age 10 literate 93,360 (98.3%); males 48,146 (98.5%); females 45,214 (98.1%).
Health: physicians (1981) 63 (1 per 2,476 persons); hospital beds (1982) 735 (1 per 215 persons); infant mortality rate per 1,000 live births (1985) 42.0.
Food (1980–82): daily per capita caloric intake 2,527 (vegetable products 79%, animal products 21%); 95% of FAO recommended minimum requirement.

Military

No military forces are maintained; New Zealand is responsible for defense.

*According to provisions in the constitution, the current Head of State, paramount chief HH Malietoa Tanumafili II, will hold office for life. Upon his death, the monarchy will functionally cease, and future Heads of State will be elected by the Legislative Assembly. †Includes 2 sq mi (5 sq km) of uninhabited islands. ‡Preliminary. §Registered only. ‖ 1985 budget estimate: Revenue WS$74,503,000; Expenditures WS$73,920,000 (current 52.3%, statutory 23.5%, development 23.2%). ¶1984. ♀1982. ðDetail does not add to total given because of rounding. □Second quarter. ◇Government employees only. △Consumer price index components. †Import figures are f.o.b. in balance of trade and c.i.f. in commodities and trading partners. ⊕Percentage breakdown of commodities is for 1983. **Total length includes 733 mi (1,180 km) of plantation roads. ††Includes some secondary teachers.

Yemen (Aden)

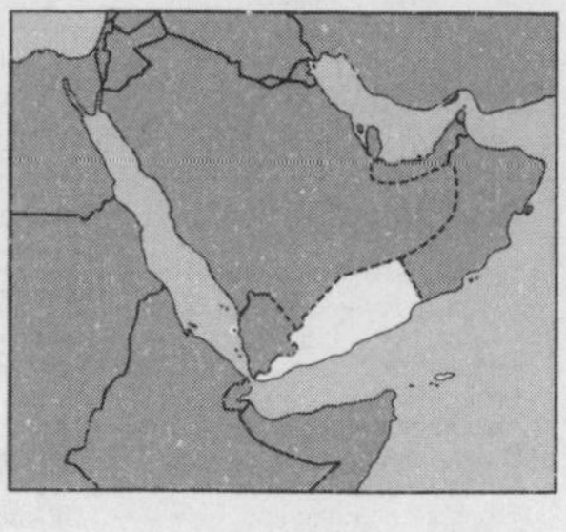

Official name: Jumhūrīyat al-Yaman ad-Dimuqrāṭīyah ash-Sha'bīyah (People's Democratic Republic of Yemen).
Form of government: single-party republic with one legislative house (Supreme People's Council [111]).
Head of state: Chairman of the Presidium of the Supreme People's Council.
Head of government: Prime Minister.
Capital: Aden.
Official language: Arabic.
Official religion: Islam.
Monetary unit: 1 Yemeni dinar (YD) = 1,000 fils; valuation (Oct. 1, 1986) 1 YD = U.S.$2.92 = £2.02.

Area and population

		area		population
Governorates	**Capitals**	sq mi	sq km	1973 census
Ūlá (First)	Aden	2,690	6,980	291,376
Thāniyah (Second)	Laḥij	4,930	12,760	273,611
Thālithah (Third)	Zinjibār	8,300	21,490	311,142
Rābi'ah (Fourth)	'Atāq	28,540	73,910	161,966
Khāmisah (Fifth)	al-Mukallā	32,990	85,450	450,657
Sādisah (Sixth)	al-Ghayḍah	25,620	66,350	60,876
Directorate				
Thamūd*	Thamūd	27,000	69,930	40,647
TOTAL		130,070	336,870	1,590,275

Demography

Population (1986): 2,365,000.
Density (1986): persons per sq mi 18.2, persons per sq km 7.0.
Urban-rural (1980): urban 36.9%; rural 63.1%.
Sex distribution (1980): male 49.41%; female 50.59%.
Age breakdown (1984): under 15, 48.1%; 15–29, 20.7%; 30–44, 16.0%; 45–59, 8.9%; 60–74, 4.9%; 75 and over, 1.4%.
Population projection: (1990) 2,459,000; (2000) 3,312,000.
Doubling time: 25 years.
Ethnic composition (1980): Arab 92.9%; Indo-Pakistani 2.5%; Somali 2.2%; other 2.4%.
Religious affiliation (1980): predominantly Sunnī Muslim 99.5%; Hindu 0.2%; Christian 0.2%; nonreligious 0.1%.
Major city (1981): Aden 365,000.

Vital statistics

Birth rate per 1,000 population (1980–85): 47.6 (world avg. 29.0); legitimate, n.a.; illegitimate, n.a.
Death rate per 1,000 population (1980–85): 18.9 (world avg. 11.0).
Natural increase rate per 1,000 population (1980–85): 28.7 (world avg. 18.0).
Total fertility rate (avg. births per childbearing woman; 1980–85): 6.9.
Marriage rate per 1,000 population: n.a.
Divorce rate per 1,000 population: n.a.
Life expectancy at birth (1980–85): male 45.3 years; female 47.7 years.
Major causes of death per 100,000 population: n.a.; however, major diseases include poliomyelitis, diphtheria, schistosomiasis, typhoid and paratyphoid fevers, yellow fever, hepatitis, asphyxia, trachoma, heart ailments, gastrointestinal diseases, respiratory diseases, salmonella, leprosy, measles, whooping cough, cholera, pulmonary tuberculosis, intestinal bilharzia, influenza, anemia and malnutrition, shigellosis, and malaria.

National economy

Budget (1984). Revenue: YD 213,100,000 (1973–74; import duties 33.5%, excise duties 14.1%, taxes on corporate income 12.7%, taxes on personal income 8.0%). Expenditures: YD 132,100,000 (1973–74; defense and security 45.9%, education 16.9%, general administration 11.8%, economic services 6.8%, health 5.1%, public works and communications 4.7%).
Tourism (1981): receipts from visitors U.S.$4,000,000; expenditures by nationals abroad U.S.$10,000,000.
Production (metric tons except as noted). Agriculture, forestry, fishing (1984): millet 80,000, watermelons 62,000, bananas 23,000, corn (maize) 16,000, wheat 15,000, seed cotton 15,000, tomatoes 13,000, dates 11,000, potatoes 9,000, roots and tubers 9,000, lint cotton 5,000, dry onions 3,000, sesame seed 3,000, barley 2,000, tobacco 1,000, coffee 1,000; livestock (number of live animals) 1,380,000 goats, 1,000,000 sheep, 170,000 asses, 130,000 cattle, 100,000 camels; roundwood 276,000 cu m; fish catch (1983) 74,124. Mining and quarrying† (1981): salt 75,000. Manufacturing (1982): nails 345; aluminum cooking utensils 300; household plastic utensils 262; textiles 2,700,000 m; shirts 332,000 units; plastic sandals 1,000,000 pairs; rubber shoes 293,000 pairs; leather shoes 157,000 pairs; soft drinks 58,000,000 bottles. Construction: n.a. Energy production (consumption): electricity (kW-hr; 1983) 280,000,000 (280,000,000); coal, none (n.a.); crude petroleum (barrels; 1983) none (16,309,000); petroleum products (metric tons; 1983) 2,218,000 (1,158,000); natural gas, none (n.a.).
Population economically active (1984): total 450,183; activity rate of total population 21.4% (participation rates: over age 15, 41.2%; female 5.3%; unemployed, n.a.).

Price and earnings indexes (1980 = 100)

	1977	1978	1979	1980	1981	1982	1983
Consumer price index	77.6	79.8	90.9	100.0	103.8	113.7	126.2
Earnings index	...	...	...	...	...	...	...

Household income and expenditure. Average household size (1984) 5.6; average annual income per household: n.a.; source of income: n.a.; expenditure: n.a.
Gross national product (1984): U.S.$1,130,000,000 (U.S.$508 per capita).

Structure of gross domestic product and labour force

	1980		1984	
	in value YD '000,000	% of total value	labour force	% of labour force
Agriculture	23.4	10.1	165,897	36.8
Mining	0.3	0.1	8,453	1.9
Manufacturing	27.6	11.9	37,506	8.3
Construction	18.3	7.9	42,268	9.4
Public utilities	2.9	1.3	9,064	2.0
Transportation and communication	24.0	10.4	29,299	6.5
Trade	31.1	13.5	39,420	8.8
Finance	26.2	11.4	298	0.1
Pub. admin., defense	52.3	22.7	...	...
Services	1.3	0.6	117,978	26.2
Other	23.2	10.1	...	...
TOTAL	230.6	100.0	450,183	100.0

Public debt (external, outstanding; 1984): U.S.$1,251,500,000.
Land use (1983): forested 7.3%; meadows and pastures 27.3%; agricultural 0.6%; built-up, wasteland, and other 64.8%.

Foreign trade

Balance of trade (current prices)

	1978	1979	1980	1981	1982	1983	1984
YD '000,000	−110.7	−123.8	−258.4	−280.3	−277.8	−193.8	−310.0
% of total	45.4%	27.7%	32.4%	40.0%	33.6%	38.5%	41.0%

Imports (1980): YD 527,400,000 (1977; machinery and transport equipment 34.8%; food and live animals 23.4%, of which wheat and wheat flour 5.0%, rice 2.7%, refined sugar 2.4%; petroleum products 18.2%; chemicals 2.9%). *Major import sources* (1985): Australia 9.2%; United Kingdom 6.5%; Japan 5.7%; The Netherlands 5.2%; France 4.7%; Italy 3.2%; West Germany 3.1%; Denmark 2.8%; Singapore 2.7%; Pakistan 2.6%; United States 1.3%; Thailand 1.2%; Belgium–Luxembourg 1.1%; Norway 0.9%; Spain 0.9%; Sweden 0.7%; Austria 0.4%; Ireland 0.4%; Greece 0.3%; Switzerland 0.3%.
Exports (1980): YD 269,000,000 (petroleum products 95%). *Major export destinations* (1985): Italy 33.0%; Japan 11.3%; New Zealand 11.3%; France 10.3%; West Germany 6.0%; Singapore 5.3%; United Kingdom 2.6%; The Netherlands 1.8%.

Transport and communications

Transport. Railroads: none. Roads (1984): total length 1,850 km (paved, n.a.). Vehicles (1980): passenger cars 16,500; commercial vehicles 16,300. Merchant marine (1985): vessels (100 gross tons and over) 27; total deadweight tonnage 12,921. Air transport (1980): passenger-km 84,000,000; metric ton-km cargo 1,700,000; airports (1986) with scheduled flights 3.
Communications. Daily newspapers (1985): total number 2; total circulation 25,000; circulation per 1,000 population 10.9. Radio (1985): total number of receivers 150,000 (1 per 15.3 persons). Television (1985): total number of receivers 39,000 (1 per 58.8 persons). Telephones (1981–82): 10,054 (1 per 200 persons).

Education and health

Education (1982)

	schools	teachers	students	student/ teacher ratio
Primary (age 7–12)	890	10,915	228,893	21.0
Secondary (age 13–18)	46	1,271	27,776	21.9
Voc., teacher tr.	13	173	1,556	9.0
Higher‡	...	246	2,517	10.2

Educational attainment, n.a. *Literacy* (1980): total population over age 15 literate 411,900 (38.9%); males literate 354,700 (66.6%); females literate 57,200 (10.9%).
Health (1984): physicians 406 (1 per 5,480 persons); hospital beds 3,805 (1 per 585 persons); infant mortality rate per 1,000 live births 137.0.
Food (1980–82): daily per capita caloric intake 2,267 (vegetable products 85%, animal products 15%); 94% of FAO recommended minimum requirement.

Military

Total active duty personnel (1985): 27,500 (army 87.3%, navy 3.6%, air force 9.1%). *Military expenditure as percent of GNP* (1983): 17.4% (world 6.1%); per capita expenditure U.S.$82.

*Thamūd is administratively part of Khāmisah governorate. †Until early 1986, commercial-scale mineral production was restricted to salt output. The principal mineral development project during 1985 was the country's first cement plant, with a capacity of 350,000 tons per year; production was scheduled to start in 1988. A large gold find was announced in 1985. ‡1977–78.

Yemen (Ṣan'ā')

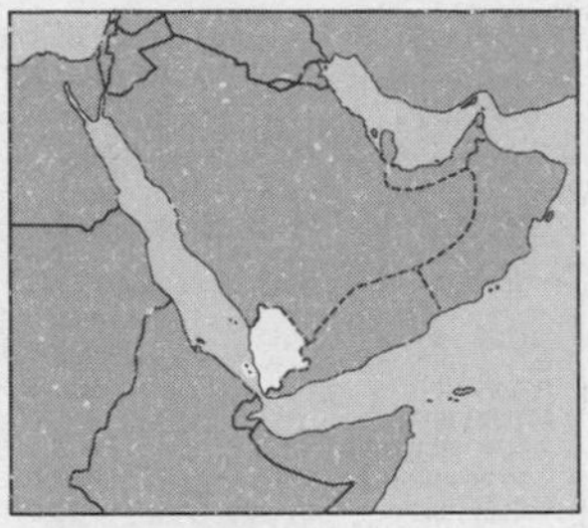

Official name: al-Jumhūrīyah al-'Arabīyah al-Yamanīyah (Yemen Arab Republic).
Form of government: military dominated single-party republic with one legislative house (Constituent People's Assembly [159]).
Head of state and government: President.
Capital: Ṣan'ā'.
Official language: Arabic.
Official religion: Islam.
Monetary unit: 1 Yemen Rial (YRl) = 100 fils; valuation (Oct. 1, 1986) 1 U.S.$ = YRls 10.50; 1 £ = YRls 15.17.

Area and population

Governorates	Capitals	area: sq mi	area: sq km	population: 1980 estimate*
al-Bayḍā'	al-Bayḍā'	4,310	11,170	182,100
al-Ḥudaydah	al-Ḥudaydah	5,240	13,580	794,300
al-Maḥwīt	al-Maḥwīt	830	2,160	195,300
Dhamār	Dhamār	3,430	8,870	506,200
Ḥajjah	Ḥajjah	3,700	9,590	450,300
Ibb	Ibb	2,480	6,430	871,700
Ma'rib	Ma'rib	15,400	39,890	76,600
Ṣa'dah	Ṣa'dah	4,950	12,810	190,300
Ṣan'ā'	Ṣan'ā'	7,840	20,310	963,900
Ta'izz	Ta'izz	4,020	10,420	981,400
TOTAL		52,210†‡	135,230‡	5,212,100

Demography

Population (1986): 7,046,000.
Density (1986): persons per sq mi 134.9, persons per sq km 52.1.
Urban-rural (1984): urban 15.0%; rural 85.0%.
Sex distribution (1986): male 50.11%; female 49.89%.
Age breakdown (1984): under 15, 47.4%; 15–29, 25.4%; 30–44, 13.2%; 45–59, 9.3%; 60–74, 3.9%; 75 and over, 0.8%.
Population projection: (1990) 7,925,000; (2000) 10,881,000.
Doubling time: 26 years.
Ethnic composition (1984): predominantly Arab.
Religious affiliation (1980): Shī'ī Muslim 60%; Sunnī Muslim 40%.
Major cities (1986): Ṣan'ā' 427,185; Ta'izz 178,430; al-Ḥudaydah 155,110.

Vital statistics

Birth rate per 1,000 population (1980–85): 48.5 (world avg. 29.0); legitimate, n.a.; illegitimate, n.a.
Death rate per 1,000 population (1980–85): 21.8 (world avg. 11.0).
Natural increase rate per 1,000 population (1980–85): 26.7 (world avg. 18.0).
Total fertility rate (avg. births per childbearing woman; 1980–85): 6.8.
Marriage rate per 1,000 population: n.a.
Divorce rate per 1,000 population: n.a.
Life expectancy at birth (1980–85): male 42.7 years; female 44.8 years.
Major causes of death per 100,000 population: n.a.; however, major infectious diseases include malaria, tuberculosis, intestinal infections, leprosy, schistosomiasis, typhoid and paratyphoid fevers, viral hepatitis, and filarial infections.

National economy

Budget (1981)§. Revenue: YRls 3,282,600,000 (import duties 49.1%, income from property 13.9%, stamp tax 11.0%, excise duties 7.1%, income tax 5.2%). Expenditures: YRls 6,219,900,000 (defense 32.6%, general public services 18.6%, education 14.0%, roads 6.5%, health 3.6%).
Public debt (external, outstanding; 1985): U.S.$1,867,900,000.
Production (metric tons except as noted). Agriculture, forestry, fishing (1984): sorghum 525,000, vegetables and melons 311,000, fruits 167,000, roots and tubers 160,000, potatoes 160,000, grapes 73,000, wheat 50,000, corn (maize) 50,000, barley 50,000, pulses 40,000, tobacco 7,000, dates 6,000, sesame seed 6,000, coffee 3,000, cotton lint 2,000, sugarcane 1,000, honey 300,000, milk 60,000, eggs 11,828; livestock (number of live animals) 2,227,000 goats, 1,823,000 sheep, 950,000 cattle, 520,000 asses, 60,000 camels; fish catch 12,200 ‖ . Mining and quarrying (1981): salt 64,000; rock 567,000 cu m. Manufacturing (1981): cement 85,000; domestic utensils 1,600; textile fabric 3,135,000 m. Construction (value added in YRls; 1982): 1,161,000,000. Energy production (consumption): electricity (kW-hr; 1984) 295,000,000 (295,000,000); coal, none (n.a.); crude petroleum, none (n.a.); petroleum products (metric tons; 1984) none (865,000,000); natural gas, none (n.a.).
Population economically active (1984): total 1,471,917; activity rate of total population 21.3% (participation rates: over age 15, 40.6%; female 9.3%; unemployed, n.a.).

Price and earnings indexes (1980 = 100)

	1978	1979	1980	1981	1982	1983	1984
Consumer price index	75.0	95.0	100.0	105.0	108.0	114.0	128.0
Earnings index	...	...	...	...	...	...	...

Household income and expenditure. Average household size (1984) 5.6; average annual income per household: n.a.; source of income: n.a.; expenditure (1972): food, beverages, and tobacco 65.0%, housing and household operations 21.1% (of which utilities 7.2%, rent and water 6.1%, durable goods 4.1%, furniture 2.1%, cleaning items 1.6%), clothing 5.8%, medical care, health, and hygiene 4.0%, transporation 3.2%, education 0.9%.
Tourism: receipts from visitors (1984) U.S.$18,000,000; expenditures by nationals abroad (1983) U.S.$72,000,000.
Gross national product (at current market prices; 1984): U.S.$3,940,000,000 (U.S.$620 per capita).

Structure of gross domestic product and labour force

	1981: in value YRls '000,000	1981: % of total value	1975: labour force	1975: % of labour force
Agriculture	3,690	28.5	830,340	73.6
Mining	156	1.2	580	0.1
Manufacturing	770	5.9	33,920	3.0
Construction	1,140	8.8	52,640	4.7
Public utilities	89	0.7	1,510	0.1
Transportation and communication	483	3.7	24,710	2.2
Trade	2,263	17.5	68,980	6.1
Finance	4,358 (Finance, Pub. admin., defense, Services, Other)	33.7	1,980	0.2
Pub. admin., defense			...	...
Services			85,780	7.6
Other			27,330	2.4
TOTAL	12,949	100.0	1,127,770	100.0

Land use (1983): forested 8.2%; meadows and pastures 35.9%; agricultural and under permanent cultivation 14.3%; other 41.6%.

Foreign trade

Balance of trade (current prices)

	1978	1979	1980	1981	1982	1983
YRls '000,000	−5,062	−5,857	−8,351	−6,759	−6,763	−7,170
% of total	98.8%	97.9%	−97.6%	94.0%	95.0%	96.7%

Imports (1981): YRls 7,340,400,000 (food and live animals 29.7%, machinery and transport equipment 25.4%, manufactured goods 22.2%, chemical products 5.6%, beverages and tobacco 1.4%). *Major import sources* (1985): Italy 9.7%; Japan 8.7%; United Kingdom 8.3%; The Netherlands 6.2%; West Germany 5.9%; France 5.2%; China 2.7%; United States 2.7%; Belgium-Luxembourg 2.4%; Australia 2.4%; Singapore 2.1%; Austria 1.5%; Sweden 1.4%; Greece 1.3%; Denmark 0.7%.
Exports (1981): YRls 216,600,000 (machinery and transport equipment 64.5%, food and live animals 20.9%, manufactured goods 6.1%, beverages and tobacco 0.5%). *Major export destinations* (1985): United States 41.4%; Japan 12.6%; The Netherlands 6.9%; France 3.5%; Italy 3.5%; United Kingdom 2.6%; West Germany 1.7%; Singapore 0.2%.

Transport and communications

Transport. Railroads: none. Roads (1984): total length 22,625 mi, 36,412 km (paved 6%). Vehicles (1984): passenger cars 105,506; trucks and buses 152,473. Merchant marine (1985): vessels (100 gross tons and over) 10; total deadweight tonnage 1,850. Air transport (1985): passenger-mi 358,012,000, passenger-km 576,165,000; short ton-mi cargo 43,533,000, metric ton-km cargo 63,557,000; airports (1986) with scheduled flights 5.
Communications. Daily newspapers (1985): total number 2; total circulation, n.a.; circulation per 1,000 population, n.a. Radio (1985): total number of receivers 110,000 (1 per 59.5 persons). Television (1985): total number of receivers 28,000 (1 per 233.8 persons). Telephones (1981): 90,350 (1 per 65.8 persons).

Education and health

Education (1983)

	schools	teachers	students	student/ teacher ratio
Primary (age 7–12)	4,645	13,305	675,402	50.8
Secondary (age 13–18)	314¶	3,679	71,819	19.5
Voc., teacher tr.	29¶	394♀	7,547	...
Higher¶	...	157	4,519	28.8

Educational attainment (1975). Percent of adult population over age 25 having: no formal schooling, *c.* 99%; primary education, less than 1%. *Literacy* (1980): total population over age 15 literate 350,600 (8.3%); males literate 340,100 (15.9%); females literate 10,500 (0.5%).
Health: physicians (1981) 896 (1 per 6,629 persons); hospital beds (1983) 4,000 (1 per 1,900 persons); infant mortality rate per 1,000 live births (1980–85) 154.
Food (1980–82): daily per capita caloric intake 2,328 (vegetable products 89%, animal products 11%); 94% of FAO recommended minimum requirement.

Military

Total active duty personnel (1986): 36,550 (army 95.8%, navy 1.5%, air force 2.7%). *Military expenditure as percent of GNP* (1984): 17.8% (world 6.1%); per capita expenditure U.S.$80.

*Population estimate according to the Swiss Technical Co-operation Service. †Detail does not add to total given because of rounding. ‡Area shown is according to the Swiss Technical Co-operation Service. The major part of the eastern boundary with Saudi Arabia and Yemen (Aden) is not officially delimited or demarcated; however, the government of Yemen (Ṣan'ā') uses a higher estimate of 77,200 sq mi (200,000 sq km). §1985–86 estimated budget was: Revenue YRls 6,228,200,000; Expenditures YRls 8,895,372,000. ‖ 1983. ¶1980–81. ♀1982.

Yugoslavia

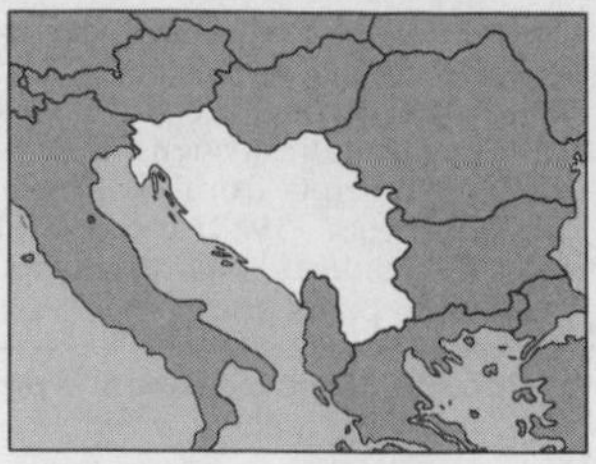

Official name: Socijalistična Federativna Republika Jugoslavija (Slovenian); Socijalistička Federativna Republika Jugoslavija (Macedonian, Serbo-Croatian) (Socialist Federal Republic of Yugoslavia).
Form of government: single-party federal socialist republic with two legislative houses (Chamber of Republics and Provinces [88] and Federal Chamber [220]).
Head of state and government: President.
Capital: Belgrade.
Official languages: Slovenian; Macedonian; Serbo-Croatian.
Official religion: none.
Monetary unit: 1 Yugoslav dinar (Din) = 100 paras; valuation (Oct. 1, 1986) 1 U.S.$ = Din 410.99; 1 £ = Din 593.88.

Area and population

		area		population
				1985
Socialist republics	**Capitals**	sq mi	sq km	estimate
Bosnia and Hercegovina	Sarajevo	19,741	51,129	4,523,000
Croatia	Zagreb	21,829	56,538	4,662,000
Macedonia	Skopje	9,928	25,713	2,053,000
Montenegro	Titograd	5,333	13,812	630,000
Serbia	Belgrade	21,609	55,968	5,645,000
Slovenia	Ljubljana	7,819	20,251	1,876,000
Autonomous provinces*				
Kosovo	Priština	4,203	10,887	1,816,000
Vojvodina	Novi Sad	8,304	21,506	2,031,000
TOTAL		98,766	255,804	23,236,000

Demography

Population (1986): 23,289,000.
Density (1986): persons per sq mi 235.9, persons per sq km 91.1.
Urban-rural (1985): urban 46.5%; rural 53.5%.
Sex distribution (1985): male 49.36%; female 50.64%.
Age breakdown (1985): under 15, 23.5%; 15–29, 23.9%; 30–44, 21.0%; 45–59, 18.8%; 60–74, 9.4%; 75 and over, 3.4%.
Population projection: (1990) 24,107,000; (2000) 25,653,000.
Doubling time: 99 years.
Ethnic composition (1981): Serb 36.3%; Croat 19.7%; Bosnian Muslim 8.9%; Slovenian 7.8%; Albanian 7.7%; Macedonian 6.0%; Montenegrin 2.6%; other 11.0%.
Religious affiliation (1980): Serbian Orthodox 34.6%; Roman Catholic 26.0%; Crypto-Christian 11.3%; Muslim 10.4%; other 17.7%.
Major cities (1981): Belgrade 1,470,073; Osijek 867,646; Zagreb 768,700; Niš 643,470; Skopje 506,547.

Vital statistics

Birth rate per 1,000 population (1985): 15.9 (world avg. 29.0); (1981) legitimate 91.7%; illegitimate 8.3%.
Death rate per 1,000 population (1985): 9.1 (world avg. 11.0).
Natural increase rate per 1,000 population (1985): 6.8 (world avg. 18.0).
Total fertility rate (avg. births per childbearing woman; 1983): 2.1.
Marriage rate per 1,000 population (1985): 7.0.
Divorce rate per 1,000 population (1984): 0.9.
Life expectancy at birth (1981): male 67.7 years; female 73.1 years.
Major causes of death per 100,000 population (1982): diseases of the circulatory system 448.8; malignant neoplasms (cancers) 135.2; diseases of the respiratory system 51.7; diseases of the digestive system 39.3.

National economy

Budget (1983). Revenue: Din 262,077,500,000 (share in profit of state enterprises 79.9%, import duties 17.0%, other revenue 3.1%). Expenditures: Din 261,504,600,000 (education 59.1%, social welfare and health 21.0%, administration 5.8%).
Public debt (external, outstanding; 1984): U.S.$10,357,700,000.
Tourism: receipts from visitors (1984) U.S.$1,054,000,000; expenditures by nationals abroad (1983) U.S.$107,000,000.
Production (metric tons except as noted). Agriculture (1984): corn (maize) 11,265,000, sugar beets 6,789,000, wheat 5,595,000, potatoes 2,405,000, grapes 1,456,000, barley 748,000, plums 630,000, apples 607,000, oats 256,000, sunflower seeds 160,000, rye 81,000, tobacco 68,000, rice 36,000; livestock (number of live animals) 9,337,000 pigs, 7,458,000 sheep, 5,341,000 cattle, 74,000,000 poultry; roundwood 15,091,000 cu m; fish catch 75,057,000. Mining and quarrying (1985): copper ore 26,166,000; iron ore 5,478,000; lead and zinc ore 4,590,000; bauxite 3,250,000; antimony 71,000; manganese 29,000; silver (refined) 156. Manufacturing (1985): cement 9,028,000; pig iron and crude steel 6,843,000; rolled steel 4,828,000; pulp and paper 2,200,600; sulfuric acid 1,488,800; plastics and resins 577,700; automobile tires 9,864,000 units†; radio and television receivers 817,184 units; leather 10,705,000 sq m; cotton fabrics 344,367,000 sq m. Construction (1983): residential 10,119,000 sq m; industrial 1,118,000 sq m; commercial 779,000 sq m. Energy production (consumption): electricity (kW-hr; 1985) 74,445,000,000 (72,626,000,000†); coal (metric tons; 1985) 57,035,000 (51,900,000†); crude petroleum (barrels; 1985) 30,412,000 (106,285,000†); petroleum products (metric tons; 1985) 13,037,000 (13,892,000†); natural gas (cu m; 1985) 2,400,000,000 (5,819,000,000†).
Gross national product (1984): U.S.$48,690,000,000 (U.S.$2,120 per capita).

Structure of gross material product and labour force

	1985		1981	
	in value Din '000,000	% of total value	labour force	% of labour force
Agriculture	912,651	14.4	2,682,828	28.7
Mining and manufacturing	2,848,809	45.1	2,209,693‡	23.6‡
Construction	434,606	6.9	689,291	7.4
Public utilities	73,979	1.2	‡	‡
Transp. and commun.	445,000	7.0	445,362	4.8
Trade	1,406,155	22.2	827,575	8.8
Finance	...	...	204,866	2.2
Pub. admin., defense, and services	...	...	1,585,205	16.9
Other	199,729§	3.2§	713,851‖	7.6‖
TOTAL	6,320,929	100.0	9,358,671	100.0

Population economically active (1981): total 9,359,000; activity rate of total population 43.4% (participation rates: ages 15–64, 68.7%; female 38.7%; unemployed 6.2%).

Price and earnings indexes (1980 = 100)

	1980	1981	1982	1983	1984	1985	1986¶
Consumer price index	100.0	139.7	185.7	258.4	401.6	700.5	1,061.0
Monthly earnings index	100.0	137.0	175.0	223.0	324.0	440.0	...

Household income and expenditure. Average household size (1983) 3.6; income per household Din 407,500 (U.S.$4,390); sources of income: wages 71.9%, welfare 15.0%, other 13.1%; expenditure (1983): food 35.4%, transportation 11.3%, beverages and tobacco 11.2%, clothing and footwear 11.2%, housing 9.8%, household utilities 7.2%, health 5.1%, recreation 3.8%.
Land use (1983): forested 36.6%; meadows and pastures 25.0%; agricultural and under permanent cultivation 30.6%; other 7.8%.

Foreign trade

Balance of trade (current prices)

	1980	1981	1982	1983	1984	1985
Din '000,000,000	−117.2	−114.4	−98.5	−119.6	−217.3	−407.9
% of total	20.7%	12.9%	8.6%	6.0%	7.8%	6.8%

Imports (1984): Din 1,497,036,000,000 (mineral fuels 29.3%; machinery and transport equipment 22.1%, of which nonelectric machinery 12.8%; chemicals 14.6%; raw materials 11.9%; food products 3.3%). *Major import sources:* U.S.S.R. 16.9%; West Germany 13.0%; Iraq 11.0%; Italy 7.9%; Czechoslovakia 5.4%; U.S. 5.0%; Austria 3.4%; France 3.2%; East Germany 3.1%.
Exports (1984): Din 1,279,736,000,000 (clothing and footwear 11.4%; nonelectrical machinery 11.2%; transport equipment 10.5%; chemicals 9.7%; food products 8.6%; nonferrous metals 4.9%; textile yarn and fabrics 3.6%; furniture 2.3%). *Major export destinations:* U.S.S.R. 27.0%; Italy 9.5%; West Germany 8.9%; Czechoslovakia 5.1%.

Transport and communications

Transport. Railroads (1985): length 5,834 mi, 9,389 km; passenger-km 11,999,000,000; metric ton-km cargo 28,719,000,000. Roads (1984): total length 116,460 km (paved 53%). Vehicles (1985): passenger cars 2,824,267; trucks and buses 264,593. Merchant marine (1985): vessels (100 gross tons and over) 479; total deadweight tonnage 4,180,383. Air transport (1985): passenger-km 6,336,000,000; metric ton-km cargo 92,547,000; airports (1986) 16.
Communications. Daily newspapers (1985): 28; total circulation 2,561,000; circulation per 1,000 population 111. Radio (1984): 4,699,000 receivers (1 per 5.2 persons). Television (1984): 4,075,000 receivers (1 per 5.8 persons). Telephones (1984): 3,031,000 (1 per 7.6 persons).

Education and health

Education (1985–86)

	schools	teachers	students	student/ teacher ratio
Primary (age 7–14)	12,447	137,776	2,351,187	17.1
Secondary (age 15–18)	6,153	61,288	1,448,562	15.2
Higher	340♀	25,882	359,175	13.9

Educational attainment (1981). Percent of total population over age 15 having: less than full primary education 44.7%; primary 24.2%; secondary 25.5%; higher 5.6%. *Literacy* (1981): total population over age 15 literate 15,172,877 (89.6%); males 95.5%; females 83.9%.
Health (1984): physicians 44,715δ (1 per 514 persons); hospital beds 138,786 (1 per 164 persons); infant mortality rate per 1,000 live births (1985) 28.8.
Food (1980–82): daily per capita caloric intake 3,643 (vegetable products 78%, animal products 22%); 144% of FAO recommended minimum requirement.

Military

Total active duty personnel (1985): 241,000 (army 79.2%, navy 5.4%, air force 15.4%). *Military expenditure as percent of GNP* (1983): 3.7% (world 6.1%); per capita expenditure U.S.$97.

*The autonomous provinces are administratively part of the Socialist Republic of Serbia. †1984. ‡Public utilities included with mining and manufacturing. §Other material activities. ‖Includes unemployed. ¶August. ♀Includes 215 university faculties. δIncludes dentists.

Zaire

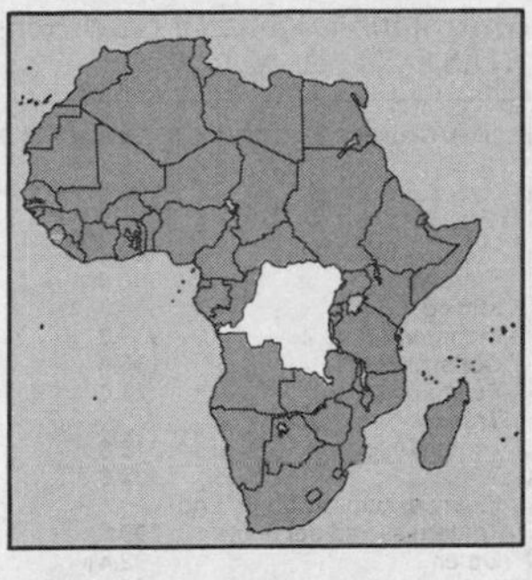

Official name: République du Zaïre (Republic of Zaire).
Form of government: single party republic with one legislative house (National Legislative Council [310]).
Head of state and government: President.
Capital: Kinshasa.
Official language: French.
Official religion: none.
Monetary unit: 1 zaïre (Z) = 100 makuta (singular likuta) = 10,000 sengi; valuation (Oct. 1, 1986) 1 U.S.$ = Z 61.57; 1 £ = Z 88.97.

Area and population

		area		population
Regions	Capitals	sq mi	sq km	1984 census
Bandundu	Bandundu	114,154	295,658	3,682,845
Bas-Zaire	Matadi	20,819	53,920	1,971,520
Equateur	Mbandaka	155,712	403,293	3,405,512
Haut-Zaire	Kisangani	194,302	503,239	4,206,069
Kasai Occidental	Kananga	60,605	156,967	2,287,416
Kasai Oriental	Mbuji-Mayi	64,949	168,216	2,402,603
Kivu	Bukavu	99,098	256,662	5,187,865
Shaba (Katanga)	Lubumbashi	191,879	496,965	3,874,019
Neutral City				
Kinshasa		3,848	9,965	2,653,558
TOTAL		905,365*	2,344,885	29,671,407

Demography

Population (1986): 30,874,000.
Density (1986): persons per sq mi 34.1, persons per sq km 13.2.
Urban-rural (1985): urban 44.2%; rural 55.8%.
Sex distribution (1984): male 49.18%; female 50.82%.
Age breakdown (1985): under 15, 45.2%; 15–29, 26.0%; 30–44, 15.5%; 45–59, 8.7%; 60–74, 3.9%; 75 and over, 0.7%.
Population projection: (1990) 34,138,000; (2000) 42,980,000.
Doubling time: 23 years.
Ethnic composition (1980): Luba 18.0%; Kongo 16.3%; Mongo 13.3%; Rwanda 10.0%; Azande 6.3%; Bangi and Ngale 6.1%; Mande 3.2%; Teke 3.0%; Banda 2.5%; Boa 2.5%; Chokwe 2.3%; other 16.5%.
Religious affiliation (1980): Roman Catholic 48.4%; Protestant 29.0%; indigenous Christian 17.1%; traditional beliefs 3.4%; Muslim 1.4%; other 0.7%.
Major cities (1984): Kinshasa 2,653,558; Lubumbashi 543,268; Mbuji-Mayi 423,363; Kananga 290,898; Kisangani 282,650.

Vital statistics

Birth rate per 1,000 population (1980–85): 45.2 (world avg. 29.0).
Death rate per 1,000 population (1980–85): 15.8 (world avg. 11.0).
Natural increase rate per 1,000 population (1980–85): 29.4 (world avg. 18.0).
Total fertility rate (avg. births per childbearing woman; 1980–85): 6.1.
Marriage rate per 1,000 population (1977): 0.07†.
Divorce rate per 1,000 population (1977): 0.02.
Life expectancy at birth (1980–85): male 48.3 years; female 51.7 years.
Major causes of death per 100,000 population‡ (1977): measles 9.6; meningitis 1.1; influenza 0.4; whooping cough 0.3.

National economy

Budget§ (1984). Revenue: Z 20,768,000,000 (direct and indirect taxes 84.3%, government investments 10.9%, administrative and judicial receipts 4.7%). Expenditures: Z 23,568,000,000 (service of external debt 37.5%, government salaries 21.3%, service of internal debt 7.9%).
Public debt (external, outstanding; 1985): U.S.$4,824,900,000.
Tourism: receipts from visitors (1984) U.S.$23,000,000; expenditures by nationals abroad (1983) U.S. $38,000,000.
Production (metric tons except as noted). Agriculture, forestry, fishing (1984): cassava 14,800,000, fruit excluding melons 2,510,000, plantains 1,480,000, vegetables and melons 803,000, sugarcane 700,000, corn (maize) 680,000, peanuts (groundnuts) 380,000, bananas 325,000, sweet potatoes 320,000, rice 260,000, potatoes 220,000, papayas 160,000, pineapples 160,000, pulses 157,000, mangoes 145,000, coffee 80,000, cotton lint 26,000, natural rubber 24,000, cocoa beans 6,000; livestock (number of live animals) 1,300,000 cattle, 760,000 pigs, 760,000 sheep, 291,000 goats, 17,000,000 chickens; roundwood 32,597,000 cu m; fish catch (1983) 102,000. Mining and quarrying (1984): copper 540,000; zinc 72,000; cobalt 18,000; manganese 15,518; tin 4,120; silver 3,974,000 troy oz; gold 80,335 troy oz; industrial diamonds 13,349,000 carats; gem diamonds 5,110,000 carats. Manufacturing (1984): corn flour 78,291; cotton textiles 78,820,000 sq m; cigarettes 3,475,000,000 units; bicycles 13,970 units; trucks 2,335 units; beer 3,699,000 hectolitres; carbonated beverages 828,000 hectolitres; leather shoes 2,556,000 pairs. Construction (1983): residential 79,000 sq m; nonresidential 15,000 sq m. Energy production (consumption): electricity (kW-hr; 1984) 4,558,000,000 (4,448,000,000); coal (metric tons; 1984) 125,000 (159,000); crude petroleum (barrels; 1984) 10,790,000 (3,240,000); petroleum products (metric tons; 1983) 433,000 (808,000); natural gas, none (n.a.).
Household income and expenditure. Average household size (1982) 6.0; average annual income per household Z 1,200 (U.S.$209); sources of income: wages and salaries, small-scale trading; expenditure (1975)‖: food 60.6%, housing and energy 12.5%, clothing and footwear 9.5%, transportation 5.7%, furniture and utensils 4.7%, medical care 2.5%, recreation 2.1%, personal care 1.7%, education 0.8%.
Gross national product (1984): U.S.$4,220,000,000 (U.S.$140 per capita).

Structure of gross domestic product and labour force

	1984		1982	
	in value Z '000,000	% of total value	labour force	% of labour force
Agriculture	31,584.7¶	31.7	8,712,000	70.0
Mining	24,713.4	24.8	622,000	5.0
Manufacturing	1,953.2	2.0	1,244,000	10.0
Construction	5,012.4♀	5.1		
Public utilities	46.7	δ	1,867,000	15.0
Transp. and commun.	999.7	1.0		
Trade	18,523.9	18.6		
Finance, Pub. admin., defense, Services	15,221.4	15.3		
Other	1,528.0□	1.5		
TOTAL	99,583.4	100.0	12,445,000	100.0

Population economically active (1984): total 13,145,000; activity rate of total population 44.3% (participation rates; age 15–64, n.a.; female [1981] 42.5%; unemployed, n.a.).

Price and earnings indexes (1980 = 100)

	1980	1981	1982	1983	1984	1985	1986◇
Consumer price index	100.0	134.9	183.8	325.5	495.6	613.6	809.6
Monthly earnings index	...	...	...	...	...	...	...

Land use (1983): forested 77.9%; meadows and pastures 4.1%; agricultural and under permanent cultivation 2.8%; other 15.2%.

Foreign trade△

Balance of trade (current prices)

	1980	1981	1982	1983	1984	1985
Z '000,000	+2,226	−565.6	−445.4	+7,102.7	+11,554.3	+13,339.7
% of total	32.3%	10.6%	9.0%	34.2%	18.9%	16.4%

Imports (1982): Z 2,759,775,000 (primary manufactures and semifinished products 22.0%; energy 13.0%; consumer goods 11.0%, of which food and tobacco products 5.6%, textiles and clothing 1.0%). *Major import sources:* Belgium-Luxembourg 40.2%; France 24.2%; United States and Canada 19.6%; West Germany 14.6%; Japan 9.0%.
Exports (1982): Z 9,924,719,000 (copper 42.4%; industrial products 15.5%; crude petroleum 14.7%; cobalt 9.7%; coffee 6.2%; diamonds 4.4%). *Major export destinations:* United States 36.0%; Belgium-Luxembourg 31.0%; France 6.0%.

Transport and communications

Transport. Railroads (1985): length 3,263 mi, 5,252 km; passenger-mi 181,150,000†, passenger-km 291,534,000†; short ton-mi cargo 1,339,047,000†, metric ton-km cargo 1,954,976,000†. Roads (1981): total length 28,379 mi, 45,671 km (paved 18%). Vehicles (1981): passenger cars 89,471; trucks and buses 16,807. Merchant marine (1985): vessels (100 gross tons and over) 33; total deadweight tonnage 121,416. Air transport (1985)⊕: passenger-mi 220,867,000, passenger-km 355,452,000; short ton-mi cargo 20,912,000, metric ton-km cargo 30,531,000; airports (1986) with scheduled flights 23.
Communications. Daily newspapers (1983): total number 4; total circulation 45,000; circulation per 1,000 population 1.6. Radio (1985): 502,000 receivers (1 per 60 persons). Television (1985): 13,000 receivers (1 per 2,328 persons). Telephones (1983): 27,770 (1 per 1,047 persons).

Education and health

Education (1978–79)

	schools	teachers	students	student/ teacher ratio
Primary (age 6–11)	5,924	132,759**	3,919,395	...
Secondary (age 12–17)	2,511**	42,212**	611,349	...
Voc., teacher tr.	20**	††	192,329	...
Higher	36	2,782	28,430	10.2

Educational attainment, n.a. *Literacy* (1985): total population over age 15 literate 11,004,000 (61.2%); males literate 6,872,000 (78.6%); females literate 4,132,000 (44.7%).
Health (1982): physicians 2,000 (1 per 14,092 persons); hospital beds 74,000 (1 per 385 persons); infant mortality rate per 1,000 live births (1983) 106.
Food (1980–82): daily per capita caloric intake 2,155 (vegetable products 97%, animal products 3%); 97% of FAO recommended minimum requirement.

Military

Total active duty personnel (1985): 26,000 (army 84.6%, navy 5.8%, air force 9.6%). *Military expenditure as percent of GNP* (1983): 1.5% (world 6.1%); per capita expenditure U.S.$2.

*Detail does not add to total given because of rounding. †Registered marriages only. ‡Infectious diseases only. §Budget for 1985 was: Revenue Z 30,700,000,000 (no breakdown available); Expenditures Z 34,700,000,000 (no breakdown available). Budget estimate for 1986 without breakdown was: Revenue Z 50,460,000,000; Expenditures Z 53,100,000,000. ‖Consumer price index components. ¶Includes Z 18,069,500,000 in the subsistence sector. ♀Includes Z 1,670,800,000 in the subsistence sector. δLess than 0.1%. □Import taxes and duties less imputed bank service charge. ◇March. △Import figures are f.o.b. (free on board) in balance of trade and c.i.f. (cost, insurance, and freight) for commodities and trading partners. †Figure is for services operated by the Zaire National Railways (SNCZ), which controls more than 90% of the country's total rail facility. ⊕Air Zaire only. **1977–78. ††Included with secondary.

Zambia

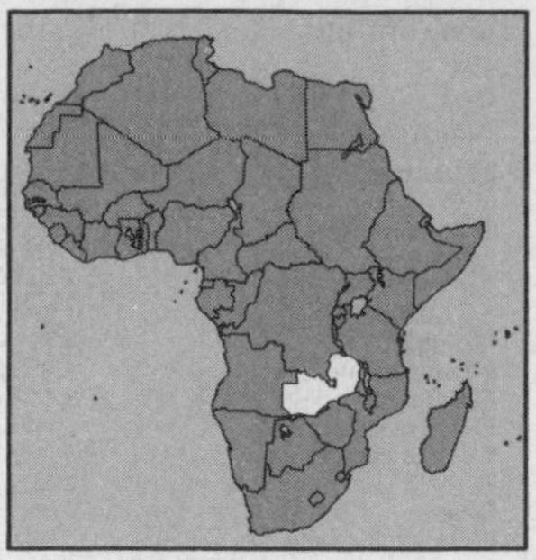

Official name: Republic of Zambia.
Form of government: republic with one legislative house (National Assembly [136]).
Head of state and government: President.
Capital: Lusaka.
Official language: English.
Official religion: none.
Monetary unit: 1 Zambian kwacha (K) = 100 ngwee; valuation (Oct. 1, 1986) 1 U.S.$ = K 6.99; 1 £ = K 10.10.

Area and population

		area		population
Provinces	Capitals	sq mi	sq km	1980 census
Central	Kabwe	36,446	94,395	513,835
Copperbelt	Ndola	12,096	31,328	1,248,888
Eastern	Chipata	26,682	69,106	656,381
Luapula	Mansa	19,524	50,567	412,798
Lusaka	Lusaka	8,454	21,896	693,878
Northern	Kasama	57,076	147,826	677,894
North-Western	Solwezi	48,582	125,827	301,677
Southern	Livingstone	32,928	85,283	686,469
Western	Mongu	48,798	126,386	487,988
TOTAL		290,586	752,614	5,679,808

Demography

Population (1986): 6,896,000.
Density (1986): persons per sq mi 23.7, persons per sq km 9.2.
Urban-rural (1980): urban 43.0%; rural 57.0%.
Sex distribution (1985): male 49.18%; female 50.82%.
Age breakdown (1985): under 15, 48.2%; 15–29, 26.2%; 30–44, 13.9%; 45–59, 7.7%; 60–74, 3.3%; 75 and over, 0.7%.
Population projection: (1990) 7,838,000; (2000) 10,945,000.
Doubling time: 21 years.
Ethnic composition (1980): Bemba 34.3%; Tonga 16.3%; Malawi 13.7%; Lozi 9.3%; Lunda 6.3%; Luena 5.0%; other 15.1%.
Religious affiliation (1980): Christian 72.0%, of whom Protestant 31.9%, Roman Catholic 26.2%, African Christian 8.3%; traditional beliefs 27.0%; Muslim 0.3%; other 0.7%.
Major cities (1980): Lusaka 538,469; Kitwe 314,794; Ndola 282,439; Luanshya 184,000; Mufulira 149,778.

Vital statistics

Birth rate per 1,000 population (1980–85): 48.1 (world avg. 29.0); legitimate, n.a.; illegitimate, n.a.
Death rate per 1,000 population (1980–85): 15.1 (world avg. 11.0).
Natural increase rate per 1,000 population (1980–85): 33.0 (world avg. 18.0).
Total fertility rate (avg. births per childbearing woman; 1980–85): 6.8.
Marriage rate per 1,000 population: n.a.
Divorce rate per 1,000 population: n.a.
Life expectancy at birth (1980–85): male 49.1 years; female 52.5 years.
Major causes of death per 100,000 population: n.a.; however, major diseases include avitaminosis and nutritional deficiencies and infectious and parasitic diseases.

National economy

Budget (1984). Revenue: K 1,003,100,000 (customs duties and excise taxes 51.4%, income tax 34.1%). Expenditures: K 1,096,900,000 (constitutional and statutory expenditures 25.4%, education 10.1%, health 8.6%, land development 7.4%, police 5.6%).
Public debt (external, outstanding; 1984): U.S.$2,778,700,000.
Tourism: receipts from visitors (1984) U.S.$49,000,000; expenditures by nationals abroad (1983) U.S.$43,000,000.
Production (metric tons except as noted). Agriculture, forestry, fishing (1984): sugarcane 1,100,000, corn (maize) 857,000, fruits and vegetables 321,000 (of which tomatoes 26,000, onions 26,000, oranges 3,000), cassava 210,000, sunflower seeds 40,000, sweet potatoes 22,000, peanuts (groundnuts) 19,000, lint cotton 15,000, sorghum 14,000, millet 13,000, pulses 5,000, tobacco 3,000; livestock (number of live animals) 2,400,000 cattle, 355,000 goats, 255,000 pigs, 42,000 sheep, 19,000,000 chickens; roundwood 9,921,000; fish catch (1983) 67,234. Mining and quarrying (1984): copper 523,000; zinc 38,000; lead 15,800; cobalt 2,500; gold 12,185 oz. Manufacturing (1983): cement 392,000; sulfuric acid 271,000; raw sugar 132,000; nitrogen fertilizer 86,013. Construction (value in K; 1982): residential 74,200,000; nonresidential 79,700,000. Energy production (consumption): electricity (kW-hr; 1984) 10,080,000,000 (7,000,000,000); coal (metric tons; 1984) 468,000 (468,000); crude petroleum (barrels; 1984) none (4,980,000); petroleum products (metric tons; 1984) 671,000 (624,000); natural gas, none (none).
Population economically active (1984): total 2,272,000; activity rate of total population 34.2% (participation rates: ages 15–64, 46.0%; female [1983] 29.2%; unemployed [1981] 0.9%).

Price and earnings indexes (1980 = 100)

	1980	1981	1982	1983	1984	1985	1986*
Consumer price index	100.0	114.0	128.2	153.4	184.1	253.0	349.7
Monthly earnings index	100.0	...	...	...	...	...	...

Gross national product (at current market prices; 1984): U.S.$3,020,000,000 (U.S.$470 per capita).

Structure of gross domestic product and labour force

	1984			
	in value K '000,000	% of total value	labour force	% of labour force
Agriculture	697.8	16.3	1,452,000	63.9
Mining	664.0	15.5	58,500	2.6
Manufacturing	988.2	23.0	48,200	2.1
Construction	135.4	3.2	33,600	1.5
Public utilities	71.0	1.7	7,900	0.3
Transportation and communication	248.6	5.8	24,600	1.1
Trade	592.8	13.8	30,300	1.3
Finance, public admin. and defense, and services	799.8	18.6	617,200	27.2
Other	92.4†	2.1†	...	...
TOTAL	4,290.0	100.0	2,272,300	100.0

Household income and expenditure. Average household size (1981) 5.8; average annual income per household K 1,041 (U.S.$908); sources of income: wages and salaries 94.0%, other 6.0%; expenditure (1977): food 37.7%, housing 11.0%, clothing 8.3%, transportation 4.3%, education 2.1%, health 1.0%.
Land use (1983): forested 27.2%; meadows and pastures 47.2%; agricultural and under permanent cultivation 7.0%; other 18.6%.

Foreign trade

Balance of trade (current prices)

	1980	1981	1982	1983	1984	1985
K '000,000	146.6	12.1	20.4	159.1	123.4	862.9
% of total	7.7%	0.7%	1.1%	8.2%	5.2%	21.1%

Imports (1982): K 930,000,000 (machinery and transport equipment 34.5%; mineral fuels, lubricants, and electricity 20.8%; basic manufactures 17.8%; chemicals 16.0%; food 5.3%). *Major import sources:* Saudi Arabia 13.1%; United Kingdom 12.9%; Bahrain 10.0%; United States 8.3%; West Germany 7.5%; Japan 6.1%; Italy 5.2%; Zimbabwe 4.4%; India 2.2%.
Exports (1982): K 950,400,000 (copper 89.2%; cobalt 4.2%; zinc 2.0%; lead 0.5%). *Major export destinations:* Japan 20.2%; France 11.3%; Italy 10.0%; United Kingdom 6.6%; India 5.8%; West Germany 5.2%; Yugoslavia 4.7%; China 3.9%; United States 2.7%.

Transport and communications

Transport. Railroads (1985): route length 1,360 mi, 2,188 km; passenger-mi 346,834,000, passenger-km 558,176,000; short ton-mi cargo 1,072,208,000, metric ton-km cargo 1,565,496,000. Roads (1984): total length 23,164 mi, 37,279 km (paved 15%). Vehicles (1982): passenger cars 105,783; trucks and buses 94,780. Merchant marine: vessels (100 gross tons and over) none. Air transport (1985): passenger-mi 411,446,000, passenger-km 662,159,000; short ton-mi cargo 58,978,000, metric ton-km cargo 86,112,000; airports (1986) with scheduled flights 14.
Communications. Daily newspapers (1984): total number 2; total circulation 109,000; circulation per 1,000 population 16.4. Radio (1985): total number of receivers 200,000 (1 per 33 persons). Television (1985): total number of receivers 100,000 (1 per 66 persons). Telephones (1981): 61,000 (1 per 91 persons).

Education and health

Education (1984)

	schools	teachers	students	student/ teacher ratio
Primary (age 7–13)‡	2,894	23,870	1,121,769	47.0
Secondary (age 14–18)‡	142	4,602	104,859	22.8
Voc., teacher tr.	28	1,041	9,563	9.2
Higher	1	650	3,621	5.6

Educational attainment (1969). Percent of adult population over age 14 having: no formal schooling 51.4%; primary education 39.3%; secondary 6.5%; higher 0.5%; other 2.3%. *Literacy* (1980): total population literate 2,128,500 (68.6%); males literate 1,207,300 (79.3%); females literate 921,200 (58.3%).
Health (1982): physicians 839 (1 per 7,186 persons); hospital beds 21,257 (1 per 292 persons); infant mortality rate per 1,000 live births (1980–85) 88.0.
Food (1980–82): daily per capita caloric intake 2,124 (vegetable products 94%, animal products 6%); 92% of FAO recommended minimum daily requirement.

Military

Total active duty personnel (1985): 16,200 (army 92.6%; navy, none; air force 7.4%). *Military expenditure as percent of GNP* (1980): 3.8% (world 5.6%); per capita expenditure U.S.$21.

*February. †Includes import duties and bank service charges. ‡1982.

Zimbabwe

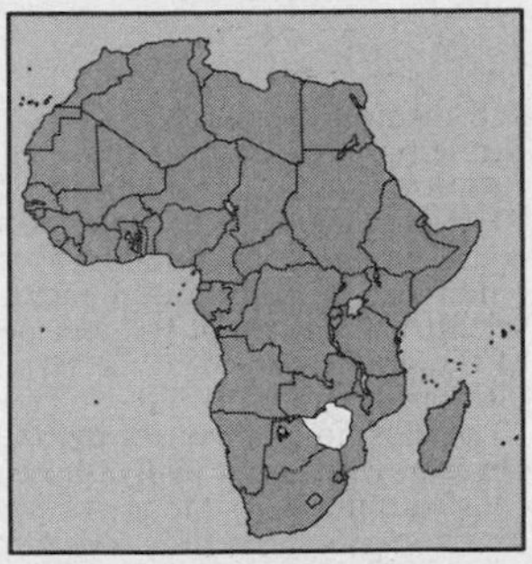

Official name: Republic of Zimbabwe.
Form of government: unitary multiparty republic with two legislative houses (Senate [40]; House of Assembly [100]).
Chief of state: President.
Head of government: Prime Minister.
Capital: Harare.
Official language: English.
Official religion: none.
Monetary unit: 1 Zimbabwe Dollar (Z$) = 100 cents; valuation (Oct. 1, 1986) 1 U.S.$ = Z$1.65; 1 £ = Z$2.39.

Area and population

		area		population
Provinces	**Capitals**	sq mi	sq km	1982 census
Manicaland	Mutare	13,463	34,870	1,099,202
Mashonaland Central	Bindura	10,534	27,284	563,407
Mashonaland East	Harare	9,627	24,934	1,495,984
Mashonaland West	Chinhoyi	23,346	60,467	858,962
Masvingo (Victoria)	Masvingo	17,108	44,310	1,031,697
Matabeleland North	Bulawayo	28,393	73,537	885,339
Matabeleland South	Gwanda	25,633	66,390	519,636
Midlands	Gweru	22,767	58,967	1,091,844
TOTAL		150,873*	390,759	7,546,071

Demography

Population (1986): 8,570,000.
Density (1986): persons per sq mi 56.8, persons per sq km 21.9.
Urban-rural (1983): urban 23.6%; rural 76.4%.
Sex distribution (1983): male 49.22%; female 50.78%.
Age breakdown (1983): under 15, 50.9%; 15–29, 26.3%; 30–44, 13.4%; 45–59, 6.5%; 60–64, 1.2%; 65 and over, 1.7%.
Population projection: (1990) 10,503,000; (2000) 15,132,000.
Doubling time: 20 years.
Ethnolinguistic composition (1982): African 97.6%, of which Shona-speaking Bantu 70.8%; Ndebele-speaking Bantu 15.8%; European 2.0%; Asian 0.1%; other 0.3%.
Religious affiliation (1980): Christian 44.8%, of which Protestant (including Anglican) 17.5%, African indigenous 13.6%, Roman Catholic 11.7%; animist 40.4%; other 14.8%.
Major cities (1983): Harare 681,000; Bulawayo 429,000; Chitungwiza 202,000; Gweru 79,000†; Mutare 70,000†.

Vital statistics

Birth rate per 1,000 population (1983): 53.0 (world avg. 29.0).
Death rate per 1,000 population (1983): 13.0 (world avg. 11.0).
Natural increase rate per 1,000 population (1983): 40.0 (world avg. 18.0).
Total fertility rate (avg. births per childbearing woman; 1983): 7.0.
Marriage rate per 1,000 population: n.a.
Divorce rate per 1,000 population: n.a.
Life expectancy at birth (1982): male 55.7 years; female 59.1 years.
Major causes of death: n.a.; however, in 1979 measles, pneumonia, diarrhea, cardiovascular diseases, and malignant neoplasms (cancers) accounted for nearly 43% of all registered adult deaths among nonwhite residents.

National economy

Budget (1986–87 est.) Revenue: Z$2,997,000,000 (income tax 40.7%, sales tax 16.3%, customs duties 14.4%, excise tax 9.5%, international aid grants 5.4%, revenue from investments and property 5.0%, pension contributions 2.5%). Expenditures: Z$4,574,000,000 (education 15.4%, defense 14.0%, debt service 10.7%, health 5.0%, social security and welfare 1.0%).
Tourism: receipts from visitors (1984) U.S.$31,000,000; expenditures by nationals abroad (1981) U.S.$150,000,000.
Population economically active (1984): total 2,704,000; activity rate of total population [1982] 33.1% (participation rates: over age 15 [1982] 63.5%; female [1982] 39.2%; unemployed, n.a.).

Price and earnings indexes (1980 = 100)

	1980	1981	1982	1983	1984	1985	1986‡
Consumer price index	100.0	113.1	125.2	154.1	185.2	200.9	225.8
Monthly earnings index§	100.0	127.3	155.1	168.5	...	...	...

Production (value of production in Z$ except as noted). Agriculture, forestry, fishing (1985): corn (maize) 327,433,000, tobacco 294,905,000, cotton 191,335,000, beef 158,043,000, sugar 117,071,000, milk and dairy products 78,072,000, wheat 58,232,000, soybeans 27,236,000, coffee 25,268,000; livestock (number of live animals) 5,550,000 cattle, 1,100,000 goats, 455,000 sheep, 195,000 pigs, 9,000,000 chickens; roundwood (1984) 7,104,000 cu m; fish catch (1983) 17,700 metric tons. Mining and quarrying (1985): gold 241,312,000; asbestos 84,544,000; nickel 73,429,000; coal 66,844,000; copper 43,339,000; chrome 33,676,000. Manufacturing (1982–83): foodstuffs 809,200,000; metals and metal products 682,000,000; chemicals and petroleum products 477,500,000; textiles, canvas, and yarns 304,500,000; clothing and footwear 215,300,000; beverages and tobacco 240,500,000; paper, printing and publishing 169,700,000; furniture and wood products 102,400,000; transport equipment 99,700,000; nonmetallic mineral products 96,000,000; other manufactured good 38,500,000. Construction (Z$; 1984): residential 40,285,000; nonresidential 92,229,000. Energy production (consumption): electricity (kW-hr; 1984) 4,538,000,000 (7,526,000,000); coal (metric tons; 1984) 2,300,000 (2,222,000); crude petroleum, none (none); petroleum products (metric tons; 1984) none (578,000); natural gas, none (none).
Public debt (external, outstanding; 1984): U.S.$1,445,800,000.
Household income and expenditure. Average household size (1980) 5.8; income per household Z$1,689 (U.S.$2,628); source of income: n.a.; expenditure (1983): food 20.6%, clothing, footwear, and textiles 12.0%, alcohol and tobacco 10.8%, hotel accommodations and travel 9.4%, housing 9.0%, public utilities, coal, and petroleum products 8.2%, household equipment 7.4%, education 3.7%, cleaning materials, medicines, and drugs 2.2%, health service 1.7%, books and newspapers 1.6%.
Gross national product (at current market prices; 1984): U.S.$6,040,000,000 (U.S.$760 per capita).

Structure of gross domestic product and labour force

	1984			
	in value Z$'000,000	% of total value	labour force§	% of labour force
Agriculture	783	13.5	265,500	25.6
Mining	330	5.7	55,200	5.3
Manufacturing	1,565	27.0	166,500	16.1
Construction	203	3.5	46,900	4.5
Public utilities	161	2.8	7,400	0.7
Transp. and commun.	403	7.0	50,000	4.8
Trade	791	13.6	81,500	7.9
Finance	373	6.4	15,700	1.5
Pub. admin., defense	951	16.4	194,400	18.8
Services	435	7.5	153,000	14.8
Other	−199 ‖	−3.4	—	—
TOTAL	5,796	100.0	1,036,100	100.0

Land use (1983): forested 61.6%; meadows and pastures 12.6%; agricultural and under permanent cultivation 6.9%; other 18.9%.

Foreign trade¶

Balance of trade (current prices)

	1979	1980	1981	1982	1983	1984
Z$'000,000	+166.4	+99.8	−46.0	−113.4	+88.6	+252.3
% of total	13.1%	5.8%	2.3%	5.5%	4.0%	9.5%

Imports (1984): Z$1,200,668,000 (machinery and transport equipment 31.0%; petroleum products 19.2%; chemicals 17.1%; basic manufactures 16.8%, of which textile yarns and fabrics 2.8%, iron and steel 2.1%). *Major import sources:* South Africa 19.3%; United Kingdom 12.0%; United States 9.3%; West Germany 6.9%; Japan 5.3%; France 4.2%; Botswana 3.2%; Italy 3.0%; Zambia 2.2%; The Netherlands 1.8%.
Exports (1984): Z$1,430,670,000 (tobacco 20.1%; gold 11.2%; ferroalloys 10.8%; cotton 8.2%; asbestos 5.2%; nickel metal 4.4%; sugar 2.8%; corn (maize) 2.8%). *Major export destinations:* South Africa 16.2%; United Kingdom 11.4%; West Germany 7.6%; United States 5.5%; Japan 4.6%; Italy 4.5%; Botswana 4.3%; Zambia 2.9%; China 1.8%; Spain 1.7%; France 1.6%; The Netherlands 1.6%; Belgium 1.5%.

Transport and communications

Transport. Railroads♀ (1984): route length 2,109 mi, 3,394 km; number of passengers 2,218,000; short ton-mi cargo 4,391,000,000, metric ton-km cargo 6,411,000,000. Roads (1985): total length 53,000 mi, 85,000 km (paved 14%). Vehicles (1984): passenger cars 248,967; trucks and buses 27,914. Merchant marine: none. Air transport (1984): passenger-mi 368,700,000, passenger-km 593,400,000; short ton-mi cargo 9,306,600, metric ton-km cargo 13,587,400; airports (1986) with scheduled flights 8.
Communications. Daily newspapers (1985): total number 2; total circulation 191,000; circulation per 1,000 population 23. Radio (1985): 375,000 receivers (1 per 22 persons). Television (1985): 120,000 receivers (1 per 69 persons). Telephones (1983): 236,162 (1 per 33 persons).

Education and health

Education (1985)

	schools	teachers♂	students	student/ teacher ratio
Primary (age 7–13)	3,880□	52,502	2,229,396	...
Secondary (age 14–19)	790□	10,238	497,766	...
Voc., teacher tr.	17□	953	28,605	...
Higher	1	325	4,742	...

Educational attainment (1969). Percent of adult population over age 17 having: no formal schooling 41.6%; some primary education 36.5%; primary 13.6%; secondary 3.3%; other 5.0%. *Literacy* (1985): total population over age 15 literate 3,413,000 (76.0%); males literate 1,846,000 (81.5%); females literate 1,567,000 (66.8%).
Health (1980): physicians 1,148 (1 per 6,219 persons); hospital beds 21,418 (1 per 333 persons); infant mortality rate per 1,000 live births (1985) 61.0.
Food (1980–82): daily per capita caloric intake 2,164 (vegetable products 93%, animal products 7%); 90% of FAO recommended minimum requirement.

Military

Total active duty personnel (1985): 42,000 (army 97.6%, air force 2.4%). *Military expenditure as percent of GNP* (1983): 6.4% (world 6.1%); per capita expenditure U.S.$47.

*Detail does not add to total given because of rounding. †1982. ‡Second quarter. §Wage earning workers only. ‖ Imputed bank service charges. ¶Import figures are f.o.b. in balance of trade and c.i.f. in commodities and trading partners; exports excludes reexports. ♀Includes operations in Botswana. ♂1983. □1984.

Government and international organizations

This table summarizes principal facts about the governments of the countries of the world, their branches and organs, the topmost layers of local government comprising each country's chief administrative subdivisions, and the participation of their central governments in the principal intergovernmental organizations of the world.

In this table "date of independence" may refer to a variety of circumstances. In the case of the newest countries, those that attained full independence after World War II, the date given is usually just what is implied by the heading—the date when the country, within its present borders, attained full sovereignty over both its internal and external affairs. In the case of longer established countries, the choice of a single date may be somewhat more complicated, and grounds for the use of several different dates often exist. The reader interested in this subject should refer to *Macropædia* and *Micropædia* articles on national histories and relevant historical acts. In cases of territorial annexation or dissolution, the date given here refers either to the final act of union of a state comprised of smaller entities or to the final act of separation from a larger whole (*e.g.,* the separation of Bangladesh from Pakistan in 1971).

The date of the current, or last, constitution is in some ways a less complicated question, but governments sometimes do not, upon taking power, either adhere to existing constitutional forms or trouble to terminate the previous document and legitimize themselves by the installation of new constitutional forms. Often, however, the desire to legitimize extraconstitutional political activity by associating it with existing forms of long precedent leads to partial or incomplete modification, suspension, or abrogation of a constitution, so that the actual day-to-day conduct of government may be largely unrelated to the provisions of a constitution still theoretically in force. When a date in this column is given in italics, it refers to a document that has been suspended, abolished by extraconstitutional action, or modified extensively.

The characterizations adopted under "kind of government" represent a compromise between the ideal forms provided for by the language of the national constitution and the more pragmatic language that a political scientist might adopt to describe these same systems. For an explanation of the application of these terms in the Britannica World Data, *see* the Glossary at p. 581.

The positions denoted by the terms "chief of state" and "head of government" are usually those identified with those functions by the constitution. Very often the position of chief of state will be a largely ceremonial one, with little or no authority over the day-to-day conduct of government, although the formal assent of the office to executive or legislative action may be required by the constitution. In other cases, such as in some of the Middle Eastern monarchies, the chief of state may also be the effective head of government. In certain countries, an official of a political party or a revolutionary figure entirely outside the constitutional structure may effectively exercise the powers of both positions.

Membership in the legislative house(s) of each country as given here includes all elected or appointed members, as well as ex officio members (those who by virtue of some other office or title are members of the body), whether voting or nonvoting. The legislature of a country with a unicameral system is shown as the upper house in this table.

The number of administrative subdivisions for each country is listed down to the second level. A single country may, depending on its size, complexity, and historical antecedents, have as many as five levels of

Government and international organizations

country	date of independence[a]	date of current or last constitution[b]	type of government	executive branch[c]		legislative branch[d]		admin. subdivisions		seaward claims	
				chief of state	head of government	upper house (members)	lower house (members)	first-order (number)	second-order (number)	territorial (nautical miles)	fishing/economic (nautical miles)
Afghanistan	Aug. 19, 1919	April 20–21, 1980	socialist republic	president RC	prime minister	x	x	29	185	—	—
Albania	Nov. 28, 1912	Dec. 27, 1976	socialist republic	chairman PPA	chairman CM	250	—	26	3,315	15	[1]
Algeria	July 3, 1962	Nov. 22, 1976	socialist republic	—president—		282	—	48	1,540	12	[1]
American Samoa		July 1, 1967	territory (U.S.)	U.S. president	governor	18	20	3	15	3	200
Andorra	Dec. 6, 1288	1866	coprincipality	[3]	chief executive	28	—	7	—	—	—
Angola	Nov. 11, 1975	Nov. 11, 1975	people's republic	—president—		208	—	18	139	20	200
Anguilla	—	April 1, 1982	territory (U.K.)	British monarch	[4]	10	—	2	—	3	[1]
Antigua and Barbuda	Nov. 1, 1981	Nov. 1, 1981	constitutional monarchy	British monarch	prime minister	17	17	8	—	12	200
Argentina	July 9, 1816	July 9, 1853	federal republic	—president—		46	254	24	488	200	[1]
Aruba	—	Dec. 29, 1954	integral part of Neth.	Dutch monarch	prime minister	21	—	...	...	3	200
Australia	Jan. 1, 1901	July 9, 1900	federal parl. state	British monarch	prime minister	76	148	8	866	3	200
Austria	Oct. 30, 1918	Oct. 1, 1920	federal republic	president	chancellor	63	183	9	98	—	—
Bahamas, The	July 10, 1973	July 10, 1973	constitutional monarchy	British monarch	prime minister	16	43	—	41	3	200
Bahrain	Aug. 15, 1971	Dec. 6, 1973	monarchy (emirate)	emir	prime minister	x	—	11	—	3	[1]
Bangladesh	March 26, 1971	*Dec. 16, 1972*	republic	—president—		(330)	—	4	64	12	200
Barbados	Nov. 30, 1966	Nov. 30, 1966	constitutional monarchy	British monarch	prime minister	21	27	11	—	12	200
Belgium	Oct. 4, 1830	1831	constitutional monarchy	monarch	prime minister	184	212	3	9	3	200[5]
Belize	Sept. 21, 1981	Sept. 21, 1981	constitutional monarchy	British monarch	prime minister	8	28	6	—	3	[1]
Benin	Aug. 1, 1960	Aug. 26, 1977	people's republic	—president—		196	—	6	84	200	[1]
Bermuda	—	June 8, 1968	colony (U.K.)	British monarch	[6]	11	40	11	—	3	200
Bhutan	March 24, 1910	1953	constitutional monarchy	—king—		150	—	4	17		
Bolivia	Aug. 6, 1825	February 1967	republic	—president—		27	130	9	99	—	—
Botswana	Sept. 30, 1966	March 3, 1965	republic	—president—		39	—	14	—	—	—
Brazil	Sept. 7, 1822	Jan. 24, 1967	federal republic	—president—		72	487	27	3,963	200	[7]
British Virgin Islands	—	June 1, 1977	colony (U.K.)	British monarch	governor	11	—	—	—	3	200
Brunei	Jan. 1, 1984	Sept. 29, 1959	monarchy (sultanate)	—sultan—		21	—	4	—	12	200
Bulgaria	Oct. 5, 1908	May 18, 1971	socialist republic	chairman SC	chairman CM	400	—	28	4,823	12	[1]
Burkina Faso	Aug. 5, 1960	*Nov. 27, 1977*	state	—president—		x	—	25	250	—	—
Burma	Jan. 4, 1948	Jan. 4, 1974	people's republic	president	prime minister	489	—	14	314	12	200
Burundi	July 1, 1962	Nov. 20, 1981	republic	—president—		65	—	15	114	—	—
Cameroon	Jan. 1, 1960	June 2, 1972	republic	—president—		120	—	10	40	50	[1]
Canada	July 1, 1867	April 17, 1982	federal parl. state	British monarch	prime minister	104	282	12	4,740	12	200
Cape Verde	July 5, 1975	Sept. 7, 1980	republic	president	prime minister	83	—	2	14	12[8]	200
Cayman Islands	—	Aug. 22, 1972	colony (U.K.)	British monarch	governor[9]	15	—	3	8	3	200
Central African Republic	Aug. 13, 1960	*Feb. 6, 1981*	republic	—chairman CMRN—		(...)	—	17	47	—	—
Chad	Aug. 11, 1960	*Aug. 29, 1978*	republic	—president—		x	—	14	53	—	—
Chile	Sept. 18, 1810	March 11, 1981[10]	republic	—president—		—	—	13	41	3	200
China	1523 BC	Dec. 4, 1982	people's republic	president	premier SC	2,978	—	29	200	12	[1]
Christmas Island	—	Oct. 1, 1958	external territory (Aust.)	Australian GG	administrator	—	—	—	—	3	200
Cocos (Keeling) Islands	—	Nov. 23, 1955	external territory (Aust.)	Australian GG	administrator	—	—	—	—	3	200
Colombia	July 20, 1810	Aug. 5, 1886	republic	—president—		114	199	32	990	12	200
Comoros	July 6, 1975	Oct. 1, 1978	federal Islamic republic	—president—		38	—	3	7	12	200
Congo	Aug. 15, 1960	July 8, 1979	people's republic	—president—		153	—	9	45	200	[1]
Cook Islands	—	Aug. 4, 1965	territory (N.Z.)[11]	British monarch	prime minister	24	—	—	—	12	200
Costa Rica	Sept. 15, 1821	Nov. 9, 1949	republic	—president—		57	—	7	80	12	200
Côte d'Ivoire	Aug. 7, 1960	Oct. 31, 1960	republic	—president—		175	—	34	—	12	200
Cuba	May 20, 1902	Feb. 24, 1976	socialist republic	—president—		499	—	14	169	12	200
Cyprus	Aug. 16, 1960	Aug. 16, 1960	republic	—president—		80[12]	—	6[12]	604	12	[1]
Czechoslovakia	Oct. 28, 1918	July 11, 1960	federal socialist republic	president	premier	200	150	2	12	—	—
Denmark	*c.* 800	June 5, 1953	constitutional monarchy	monarch	prime minister	179	—	16	275	3	200
Djibouti	June 27, 1977	Feb. 10, 1981	republic	president	prime minister	65	—	5	11	12	200
Dominica	Nov. 3, 1978	Nov. 3, 1978	republic	president	prime minister	31	—	10	27	12	200
Dominican Republic	Feb. 27, 1844	Nov. 28, 1966	republic	—president—		27	120	27	97	6	200
Ecuador	May 24, 1822	Aug. 10, 1979	republic	—president—		71	—	20	147	200	[1]
Egypt	Feb. 28, 1922	Sept. 11, 1971	republic	president	prime minister	458	—	26	...	12	200

administrative subordination (as does the U.S.S.R.) or it may have none at all. Each level of subordination may have several kinds of subdivisions.

Finally, in the second half of the table are listed the memberships each country maintains in the principal international intergovernmental organizations of the world. This part of the table may also be utilized to provide a complete membership list for each of these organizations as of Dec. 1, 1986.

Notes for the column headings

a. As applicable, the date given may also be either that of the organization of the present form of government or the inception of the present administrative structure (federation, confederation, union, etc.).
b. Constitutions whose dates are in italic type had been wholly or substantially suspended or abolished as of late 1986.
c. For abbreviations used in this column see the list on the facing page.
d. When a legislative body has been adjourned or otherwise suspended, figures in parentheses indicate the number of members in the legislative body as provided for in the constitution. If the provision for the legislative body in the constitution has been abrogated then the space has been marked with an "X".
e. Vatican City also a member.
f. States contributing funds to or receiving aid from UNICEF in 1982.
g. Palestine (Liberation Organization) also a member.

International organizations, conventions

ACP	African, Caribbean, and Pacific (Lomé III) convention
ASEAN	Association of South East Asian Nations
COMECON	Council for Mutual Economic Assistance
EC	The European Communities
ECOWAS	Economic Community of West African States
EEC	European Economic Community
FAO	Food and Agriculture Organization
GATT	General Agreement on Tariffs and Trade
I-ADB	Inter-American Development Bank
IAEA	International Atomic Energy Agency
IBRD	International Bank for Reconstruction and Development
ICAO	International Civil Aviation Organization
ICJ	International Court of Justice
IDA	International Development Association
IDB	Islamic Development Bank
IFC	International Finance Corporation
ILO	International Labour Organisation
IMF	International Monetary Fund
IMO	International Maritime Organization
ITU	International Telecommunication Union
LAS	League of Arab States
NATO	North Atlantic Treaty Organization
OAS	Organization of American States
OAU	Organization of African Unity
OPEC	Organization of Petroleum Exporting Countries
SPC	South Pacific Commission
UNCTAD	United Nations Conference on Trade and Development
UNESCO	United Nations Educational Scientific and Cultural Organization
UNICEF	United Nations Children's Fund
UNIDO	United Nations Industrial Development Organization
UPU	Universal Postal Union
WHO	World Health Organization
WIPO	World Intellectual Property Organization
WMO	World Meteorological Organization
WTO	Warsaw Treaty of Friendship, Co-operation and Mutual Assistance (The Warsaw Pact)

Abbreviations used in the executive branch column

AFRC	Armed Forces Ruling Council
CM	Council of Ministers
CMRN	Military Committee for National Recovery
CMSN	Military Committee for National Salvation
CS	Council of State
GG	Governor-general
GPC	General People's Committee
MC	Military Council
NA	National Assembly
PC	Presidential Council
PMAC	Provisional Military Administrative Council
PNDC	Provisional National Defense Council
PPA	Presidium, People's Assembly
PPGH	Presidium, People's Great Hural
PRC	People's Redemption Council
PSPC	Presidium, Supreme People's Council
PSSU	Presidium, Supreme Soviet of the U.S.S.R.
RC	Revolutionary Council
SC	State Council
SMC	Supreme Military Council
TMC	Transitional Military Council

membership in international organizations

United Nations (date of admission)	UN organs★ and affiliated intergovernmental organizations																				Commonwealth of Nations	regional multi-purpose						economic							military		country
	UNCTAD★[e]	UNICEF★[f]	ICJ★	FAO	GATT	IAEA[e]	IBRD	ICAO	IDA	IFC	ILO	IMF	IMO	ITU[e]	UNESCO	UNIDO	UPU[e]	WHO	WIPO[e]	WMO		ASEAN	EC	LAS[g]	OAS	OAU	SPC	ACP	COMECON	ECOWAS	EEC	I-ADB	IDB[g]	OPEC	NATO	WTO	
1946	●	●	●	●		●	●	●	●	●	●	●		●	●	●	●	●		●													●				Afghanistan
1955	●		●	●		●								●	●	●	●	●		●																	Albania
1962	●	●	●	●	●2	●	●	●	●		●	●	●	●	●	●	●	●	●	●				●		●							●	●			Algeria
—																	●										●										American Samoa
—																																					Andorra
1976	●	●	●	●	●2			●			●		●	●	●	●	●	●	●	●						●		●									Angola
—																	●			●	●																Anguilla
1981	●	●	●	●			●	●			●	●	●		●	●	●2	●			●				●			●									Antigua and Barbuda
1945	●	●	●	●	●	●	●	●	●	●	●	●	●	●	●	●	●	●	●	●					●							●					Argentina
—															●		●			●																	Aruba
1945	●	●	●	●	●	●	●	●	●	●	●	●	●	●	●	●	●	●	●	●	●						●										Australia
1955	●	●	●	●	●	●	●	●	●	●	●	●	●	●	●	●	●	●	●	●												●					Austria
1973	●	●	●	●	●2		●	●			●	●	●	●	●	●	●	●	●	●	●				●			●				●					Bahamas, The
1971	●	●	●	●	●2		●	●			●	●	●	●	●	●	●	●		●				●									●				Bahrain
1974	●	●	●	●	●	●	●	●	●	●	●	●	●	●	●	●	●	●	●	●	●												●				Bangladesh
1966	●	●	●	●	●		●	●		●	●	●	●	●	●	●	●	●	●	●	●				●			●				●					Barbados
1945	●	●	●	●	●	●	●	●	●	●	●	●	●	●	●	●	●	●	●	●			●								●	●			●		Belgium
1981	●	●	●	●	●2		●		●	●	●	●		●	●	●	●	●		●	●							●									Belize
1960	●	●	●	●	●		●	●	●		●	●	●	●	●	●	●	●	●	●						●		●		●			●				Benin
—														●			●			●	●																Bermuda
1971	●	●	●	●			●		●			●			●	●	●	●																			Bhutan
1945	●	●	●	●		●	●	●	●	●	●	●		●	●	●	●	●		●					●							●					Bolivia
1966	●	●	●	●	●2		●	●	●	●	●	●		●	●	●	●	●		●	●					●		●									Botswana
1945	●	●	●	●	●	●	●	●	●	●	●	●	●	●	●	●	●	●	●	●					●							●					Brazil
—		●													●2		●			●	●																British Virgin Islands
1984	●		●					●					●	●	●2		●2	●		●	●	●											●				Brunei
1955	●	●	●	●		●		●			●		●	●	●	●	●	●	●	●									●							●	Bulgaria
1960	●	●	●	●	●		●	●	●	●	●	●		●	●	●	●	●	●	●						●		●		●			●				Burkina Faso
1948	●	●	●	●	●	●	●	●	●	●	●	●	●	●	●	●	●	●		●																	Burma
1962	●	●	●	●	●		●	●	●	●	●	●		●	●	●	●	●	●	●						●		●									Burundi
1960	●	●	●	●	●	●	●	●	●	●	●	●	●	●	●	●	●	●	●	●						●		●					●				Cameroon
1945	●	●	●	●	●	●	●	●	●	●	●	●	●	●	●	●	●	●	●	●	●											●			●		Canada
1975	●	●	●	●	●2		●	●	●		●	●	●	●	●	●	●	●		●						●		●		●							Cape Verde
—																	●			●	●																Cayman Islands
1960	●	●	●	●	●		●	●	●		●	●		●	●	●	●	●	●	●						●		●									Central African Republic
1960	●	●	●	●	●		●	●	●		●	●		●	●	●	●	●	●	●						●		●					●				Chad
1945	●	●	●	●	●	●	●	●	●	●	●	●	●	●	●	●	●	●	●	●					●							●					Chile
1945	●	●	●	●		●	●	●	●	●	●	●	●	●	●	●	●	●	●	●																	China
—																	●				●																Christmas Island
—																	●				●																Cocos (Keeling) Islands
1945	●	●	●	●	●	●	●	●	●	●	●	●	●	●	●	●	●	●	●	●					●							●					Colombia
1975	●	●	●	●			●	●	●		●	●		●	●	●	●	●		●						●		●					●				Comoros
1960	●	●	●	●	●		●	●	●	●	●	●	●	●	●	●	●	●	●	●						●		●									Congo
—				●					●	●							●	●			●						●										Cook Islands
1945	●	●	●	●		●	●	●	●	●	●	●	●	●	●	●	●	●	●	●					●							●					Costa Rica
1960	●	●	●	●	●	●	●	●	●	●	●	●	●	●	●	●	●	●	●	●						●		●		●							Côte d'Ivoire
1945	●	●	●	●	●	●		●			●		●	●	●	●	●	●	●	●					●				●								Cuba
1960	●	●	●	●	●	●	●	●	●	●	●	●	●	●	●	●	●	●		●	●										●19						Cyprus
1945	●	●	●	●	●	●		●			●		●	●	●	●	●	●	●	●									●							●	Czechoslovakia
1945	●	●	●	●	●	●	●	●	●	●	●	●	●	●	●	●	●	●	●	●			●								●	●			●		Denmark
1977	●	●	●	●			●	●	●	●	●	●	●	●		●	●	●		●				●		●		●					●				Djibouti
1978	●	●	●	●	●2		●		●	●	●	●	●		●	●	●			●	●				●			●									Dominica
1945	●	●	●	●	●	●	●	●	●	●	●	●	●	●	●	●	●	●		●					●							●					Dominican Republic
1945	●	●	●	●		●	●	●	●	●	●	●	●	●	●	●	●	●		●					●							●		●			Ecuador
1945	●	●	●	●	●	●	●	●	●	●	●	●	●	●	●	●	●	●	●	●				●13		●							●				Egypt

Government and international organizations (continued)

country	date of independence[a]	date of current or last constitution[b]	type of government	executive branch[c]		legislative branch[d]		admin. subdivisions		seaward claims	
				chief of state	head of government	upper house (members)	lower house (members)	first-order (number)	second-order (number)	territorial (nautical miles)	fishing/economic (nautical miles)
El Salvador	Jan. 30, 1841	Dec. 20, 1983	republic	——president——		60	—	14	261	200	[1]
Equatorial Guinea	Oct. 12, 1968	Oct. 12, 1982	republic	——president——		41	—	2	6	12	[1]
Ethiopia	*c.* 1000 BC	*July 16, 1931*	socialist state	–chairman of the PMAC and CM–		x	—	14	103	12	[1]
Faeroe Islands	—	March 23, 1948	part of Danish realm	Danish monarch	[14]	32	—	7	50	3	200
Falkland Islands	—	Oct. 3, 1985	colony (U.K.)	British monarch	commissioner	8	—	—	—	3	200
Fiji	Oct. 10, 1970	Oct. 10, 1970	constitutional monarchy	British monarch	prime minister	22	52	4	14	12[8]	200
Finland	Dec. 6, 1917	July 17, 1919	republic	president	prime minister	200	—	12	461	4	12
France	August 843	Oct. 4, 1958	republic	president	prime minister	317	577	22	96	12	200
French Guiana	—	—	overseas dept. (Fr.)	French president	[15]	19	31	2	20	12	200
French Polynesia	—	Aug. 2, 1984	overseas territory (Fr.)	French president	[16]	30	—	5	—	12	200
Gabon	Aug. 17, 1960	Feb. 21, 1961	republic	president	prime minister	120	—	9	37	100	150
Gambia, The	Feb. 18, 1965	April 24, 1970	republic	——president——		49	—	6	35	200	[1]
Gaza Strip	—	—	Israeli military	— area commander		—	—	3	—	—	—
Germany, East	Oct. 11, 1949	April 9, 1968	socialist republic	chairman CS	chairman CM	500	—	15	227	12	200
Germany, West	May 5, 1955	May 23, 1949	federal republic	president	chancellor	45	520	10	30	3	200
Ghana	March 6, 1957	*Sept. 24, 1979*	republic	——chairman PNDC——		(...)	—	10	154	200	[1]
Gibraltar	—	Aug. 11, 1969	colony (U.K.)	British monarch	governor	18	—	—	—	3	200
Greece	Feb. 3, 1830	June 11, 1975	republic	president	prime minister	300	—	51	147	6	[1]
Greenland	—	—	part of Danish realm	Danish monarch	prime minister	26	—	3	18	3	[18]
Grenada	Feb. 7, 1974	March 3, 1967	constitutional monarchy	British monarch	prime minister	13	15	7	—	12	200
Guadeloupe	—	March 19, 1946	overseas dept. (Fr.)	French president	[15]	43	41	3	34	12	200
Guam	—	Aug. 1, 1950	territory (U.S.)	U.S. president	governor	21	—	19	—	3	200
Guatemala	Sept. 15, 1821	January 1986	republic	——president——		100	—	22	327	12	200
Guernsey	—	January 1949	crown dependency (U.K.)	British monarch	bailiff	60	—	3	—	3	200
Guinea	Oct. 2, 1958	*May 14, 1982*	republic	——president——		x	—	8	33	12	200
Guinea-Bissau	Sept. 10, 1974	May 16, 1984	republic	——president——		150	—	9	37	12	200
Guyana	May 26, 1966	Oct. 6, 1980	cooperative republic	president	prime minister	65	—	10	98	12	200
Haiti	Jan. 1, 1804	*Aug. 27, 1983*	republic	——president——		59	—	9	41	12	200
Honduras	Nov. 5, 1838	Jan. 20, 1982	republic	——president——		132	—	18	282	12	200
Hong Kong	—	—	colony (U.K.)	British monarch	governor	57	30	3	18	3	[1]
Hungary	Nov. 16, 1918	Aug. 20, 1949	socialist republic	president PC	prime minister	387	—	25	103	—	—
Iceland	June 17, 1944	June 17, 1944	republic	president	prime minister	20	40	23	229	12	200
India	Aug. 15, 1947	Jan. 26, 1950	federal republic	president	prime minister	244	544	31	386	12	200
Indonesia	Aug. 17, 1945	Aug. 17, 1945	republic	——president——		920	460	27	301	12[8]	200
Iran	Oct. 7, 1906	Dec. 2–3, 1979	Islamic republic	president	prime minister	270	—	24	195	12	50
Iraq	Oct. 3, 1932	Sept. 22, 1968	republic	——president——		250	—	18	157	12	[1]
Ireland	Dec. 6, 1921	Dec. 29, 1937	republic	president	prime minister	60	166	27	49	3	200
Isle of Man	—	1961	crown dependency (U.K.)	British monarch	council pres.	11	24	10	—	3	200
Israel	May 14, 1948	June 1950[20]	republic	president	prime minister	120	—	6	13	6	[1]
Italy	March 17, 1861	Jan. 1, 1948	republic	president	prime minister	323	630	20	94	12	[1]
Jamaica	Aug. 6, 1962	Aug. 6, 1962	constitutional monarchy	British monarch	prime minister	21	60	3	14	12	[1]
Japan	*c.* 660 BC	May 3, 1947	constitutional monarchy	emperor	prime minister	252	512	47	3,256	12[21]	200
Jersey	—	January 1949	crown dependency (U.K.)	British monarch	bailiff	58	—	17	—	3	200
Jordan	March 22, 1946	Jan. 1, 1952	constitutional monarchy	king	prime minister	30	130	5	14	3	[1]
Kampuchea	Nov. 9, 1953	June 1981	people's republic	president CS	prime minister	117	—	20	...	12	°200
Kenya	Dec. 12, 1963	Dec. 12, 1963	republic	——president——		172	—	8	40	12	200
Kiribati	July 12, 1979	July 12, 1979	republic	——president——		37	—	19	—	12	200
Korea, North	Sept. 9, 1948	Dec. 27, 1972	socialist republic	president	premier	615	—	13	152	12	200
Korea, South	Aug. 15, 1948	Oct. 27, 1980	republic	president	prime minister	276	—	13	97	12[22]	12
Kuwait	June 19, 1961	Nov. 16, 1962	const. mon. (emirate)	emir	prime minister	(64)	—	4	—	12	[1]
Laos	July 19, 1949	*May 11, 1947*	people's republic	president	prime minister	264	—	17	...	—	—
Lebanon	Nov. 26, 1941	May 23, 1926	republic	president	prime minister	99	—	5	26	12	[1]
Lesotho	Oct. 4, 1966	Oct. 4, 1966	constitutional monarchy	king	chairman MC	30	80	10	22	—	—
Liberia	July 26, 1847	July 20, 1984	republic	——president——		26	64	15	50	200	[1]
Libya	Dec. 24, 1951	March 2, 1977	socialist state[23]	rev. leader	secretary GPC	1,112	—	25	201	12	[1]
Liechtenstein	July 12, 1806	Oct. 5, 1921	constitutional monarchy	prince	head of gov't.	15	—	11	—	—	—
Luxembourg	May 10, 1867	Oct. 17, 1868	constitutional monarchy	grand duke	prime minister	64	—	3	12	—	—
Macau	—	—	overseas prov. (Port.)	Port. president	governor	18	—	3	5	12	[1]
Madagascar	June 26, 1960	Dec. 30, 1975	republic	president	prime minister	137	—	6	18	50	150
Malawi	July 6, 1964	July 6, 1964	republic	——president——		101	—	3	24	—	—
Malaysia	Aug. 31, 1957	Aug. 31, 1957	fed. const. monarchy	paramount ruler	prime minister	69	177	14	126	12	200
Maldives	July 26, 1965	Nov. 11, 1968	republic	——president——		48	—	19	202	[8, 24]	[24]
Mali	Sept. 22, 1960	June 19, 1979	republic	——president——		82	—	8	42	—	—
Malta	Sept. 21, 1964	Sept. 21, 1964	republic	president	prime minister	65	—	—	—	12	25
Martinique	—	—	overseas dept. (Fr.)	French president	[15]	36	41	3	34	12	200
Mauritania	Nov. 28, 1960	*May 20, 1961*	republic	——president CMSN——		x	—	13	44	70	200
Mauritius	March 12, 1968	March 12, 1968	constitutional monarchy	British monarch	prime minister	70	—	12	...	12	200
Mayotte	—	—	terr. collectivity (Fr.)	French president	[25]	17	—	17	—	12	[1]
Mexico	Sept. 16, 1810	Feb. 5, 1917	federal republic	——president——		64	400	32	2,389	12	200
Monaco	Feb. 2, 1861	Dec. 17, 1962	constitutional monarchy	prince	min. of state	18	—	1	4	12	[1]
Mongolia	March 13, 1921	July 6, 1960	people's republic	chairman PPGH	premier	370	—	21	331	—	—
Montserrat	—	Jan. 1, 1960	colony (U.K.)	British monarch	governor	11	—	3	—	3	[1]
Morocco	March 2, 1956	March 10, 1972	constitutional monarchy	king	prime minister	306	—	38	133	12	200
Mozambique	June 25, 1975	June 25, 1975	people's republic	——president——		226	—	11	112	12	200
Nauru	Jan. 31, 1968	Jan. 31, 1968	republic	——president——		18	—	14	—	12	200
Nepal	Nov. 13, 1769	Dec. 16, 1962	constitutional monarchy	king	prime minister	140	—	14	75	—	—
Netherlands, The	March 30, 1814	March 29, 1814	constitutional monarchy	monarch	prime minister	75	150	12	912	3	200
Netherlands Antilles	—	Dec. 29, 1954	integral part of Neth.	Dutch monarch	prime minister	22	—	5	—	3	200
New Caledonia	—	November 1984	overseas territory (Fr.)	French president	[16]	46	48	6	32	12	200
New Zealand	Sept. 26, 1907	June 30, 1852	parliamentary state	British monarch	prime minister	95	—	239	—	12	200
Nicaragua	April 30, 1838	*March 14, 1974*	republic	——president——		96	—	17	136	200	[1]
Niger	Aug. 3, 1960	*Nov. 8, 1960*	republic	——president SMC——		150	—	7	32	—	—
Nigeria	Oct. 1, 1960	*Oct. 1, 1979*	federal republic	——president AFRC——		x	x	20	271	30	200
Niue	—	Aug. 29, 1974	territory (N.Z.)	British monarch	premier	14	—	14	—	12	200
Norfolk Island	—	May 30, 1979	external territory (Aust.)	Australian GG	administrator	9	—	—	—	3	200

membership in international organizations

United Nations (date of admission)	UN organs★ and affiliated intergovernmental organizations																				Commonwealth of Nations	regional multi-purpose						economic							military		country
	UNCTAD★[e]	UNICEF★[f]	ICJ★	FAO	GATT	IAEA[e]	IBRD	ICAO	IDA	IFC	ILO	IMF	IMO	ITU[e]	UNESCO	UNIDO	UPU[e]	WHO	WIPO[e]	WMO		ASEAN	EC	LAS[g]	OAS	OAU	SPC	ACP	COMECON	ECOWAS	EEC	I-ADB	IDB[g]	OPEC	NATO	WTO	
1945	●	●	●	●		●	●	●	●	●	●	●	●	●	●	●	●	●	●	●					●							●					El Salvador
1968	●	●	●	●	●[2]		●	●	●		●	●	●	●	●	●	●	●								●		●									Equatorial Guinea
1945	●	●	●	●		●	●	●	●	●	●	●	●	●	●	●	●	●		●						●		●									Ethiopia
—																	●																				Faeroe Islands
—																	●				●																Falkland Islands
1970	●	●	●	●	●[2]		●	●	●	●	●	●	●	●	●	●	●	●	●	●	●						●	●									Fiji
1955	●	●	●	●	●	●	●	●	●	●	●	●	●	●	●	●	●	●	●	●												●					Finland
1945	●	●	●	●	●	●	●	●	●	●	●	●	●	●	●	●	●	●	●	●			●				●				●	●			●		France
—																	●																				French Guiana
—																	●			●							●										French Polynesia
1960	●	●	●	●	●	●	●	●	●	●	●	●	●	●	●	●	●	●	●	●						●		●					●	●			Gabon
1965	●	●	●	●	●		●	●	●	●		●	●	●	●	●	●	●	●	●	●					●		●		●			●				Gambia, The
—																	●																				Gaza Strip
1973	●	●	●			●					●		●	●	●	●	●	●	●	●									●							●	Germany, East
1973	●	●	●	●	●	●	●	●	●	●	●	●	●	●	●	●	●	●	●	●			●								●	●			●		Germany, West
1957	●	●	●	●	●	●	●	●	●	●	●	●	●	●	●	●	●	●	●	●	●					●		●		●							Ghana
—																	●				●																Gibraltar
1945	●	●	●	●	●	●	●	●	●	●	●	●	●	●	●	●	●	●	●	●			●								●				●[17]		Greece
—																																					Greenland
1974	●	●	●	●	●[2]		●	●	●	●	●	●		●	●	●	●	●			●				●			●									Grenada
—																	●																				Guadeloupe
—																	●										●										Guam
1945	●	●	●	●		●	●	●	●	●	●	●	●	●	●	●	●	●	●	●					●							●					Guatemala
—																	●				●																Guernsey
1958	●	●	●	●	●		●	●	●	●	●	●	●	●	●	●	●	●	●	●						●		●		●			●				Guinea
1974	●	●	●	●	●[2]		●	●	●	●	●	●	●	●	●	●	●	●		●						●		●		●			●				Guinea-Bissau
1966	●	●	●	●	●		●	●	●	●	●	●	●	●	●	●	●	●		●	●							●				●					Guyana
1945	●	●	●	●	●	●	●	●	●	●	●	●	●	●	●	●	●	●	●	●					●							●					Haiti
1945	●	●	●	●			●	●	●	●	●	●	●	●	●	●	●	●	●	●					●							●					Honduras
—		●			●								●[19]				●			●	●																Hong Kong
1955	●	●	●	●	●	●	●	●	●		●	●	●	●	●	●	●	●	●	●									●							●	Hungary
1946	●	●	●	●	●	●	●	●	●	●	●	●	●	●	●	●	●	●	●	●															●		Iceland
1945	●	●	●	●	●	●	●	●	●	●	●	●	●	●	●	●	●	●	●	●	●																India
1950	●	●	●	●	●	●	●	●	●	●	●	●	●	●	●	●	●	●	●	●		●											●	●			Indonesia
1945	●	●	●	●		●	●	●	●	●	●	●	●	●	●	●	●	●		●														●			Iran
1945	●	●	●	●		●	●	●	●	●	●	●	●	●	●	●	●	●	●	●				●									●	●			Iraq
1955	●	●	●	●	●	●	●	●	●	●	●	●	●	●	●	●	●	●	●	●			●								●						Ireland
—																	●				●																Isle of Man
1949	●	●	●	●	●	●	●	●	●	●	●	●	●	●	●	●	●	●	●	●												●					Israel
1955	●	●	●	●	●	●	●	●	●	●	●	●	●	●	●	●	●	●	●	●			●								●	●			●		Italy
1962	●	●	●	●	●	●	●	●		●	●	●	●	●	●	●	●	●	●	●	●				●			●				●					Jamaica
1956	●	●	●	●	●	●	●	●	●	●	●	●	●	●	●	●	●	●	●	●												●					Japan
—																	●				●																Jersey
1955	●	●	●	●		●	●	●	●	●	●	●	●	●	●	●	●	●	●	●				●									●				Jordan
1955	●	●	●	●	●[2]	●	●	●	●		●	●	●	●	●	●	●	●		●																	Kampuchea
1963	●	●	●	●	●	●	●	●	●	●	●	●	●	●	●	●	●	●	●	●	●					●		●									Kenya
—					●[2]		●	●	●			●					●	●			●						●	●									Kiribati
—	●			●		●		●	●				●	●	●	●	●	●	●	●																	Korea, North
—	●	●		●	●	●	●	●	●	●		●	●	●	●	●	●	●	●	●																	Korea, South
1963	●	●	●	●	●	●	●	●	●	●	●	●	●	●	●	●	●	●		●				●									●	●			Kuwait
1955	●	●	●	●			●	●	●		●	●		●	●	●	●	●		●																	Laos
1945	●	●	●	●		●	●	●	●	●	●	●	●	●	●	●	●	●	●	●				●									●				Lebanon
1966	●	●	●	●	●[2]		●	●	●	●	●	●	●	●	●	●	●	●	●	●	●					●		●									Lesotho
1945	●	●	●	●		●	●	●	●	●	●	●	●	●	●	●	●	●		●						●		●		●							Liberia
1955	●	●	●	●		●	●	●	●	●	●	●	●	●	●	●	●	●	●	●				●		●							●	●			Libya
—	●		●			●								●		●	●		●																		Liechtenstein
1945	●	●	●	●	●	●	●	●	●	●	●	●		●	●	●	●	●	●	●			●								●				●		Luxembourg
—																	●																				Macau
1960	●	●	●	●	●	●	●	●	●	●	●	●	●	●	●	●	●	●		●						●		●									Madagascar
1964	●	●	●	●	●		●	●	●	●	●	●		●	●	●	●	●	●	●	●					●		●									Malaŵi
1957	●	●	●	●	●	●	●	●	●	●	●	●	●	●	●	●	●	●		●	●	●											●				Malaysia
1965	●	●	●	●	●[2]		●	●	●	●		●	●	●	●	●	●	●	●	●	●												●				Maldives
1960	●	●	●	●	●[2]	●	●	●	●	●	●	●		●	●	●	●	●	●	●						●		●		●			●				Mali
1964	●	●	●	●	●		●	●			●	●	●	●	●	●	●	●	●	●	●										●[19]						Malta
—																	●																				Martinique
1961	●	●	●	●	●		●	●	●	●	●	●	●	●	●	●	●	●	●	●				●		●		●		●			●				Mauritania
1968	●	●	●	●	●	●	●	●	●	●	●	●	●	●	●	●	●	●	●	●	●					●		●									Mauritius
—																	●																				Mayotte
1945	●	●	●	●	●	●	●	●	●	●	●	●	●	●	●	●	●	●	●	●					●							●					Mexico
—	●	●				●		●						●	●	●	●	●	●																		Monaco
1961	●	●	●	●		●					●			●	●	●	●	●	●	●									●								Mongolia
—																	●			●	●																Montserrat
1956	●	●	●	●		●	●	●	●	●	●	●	●	●	●	●	●	●	●	●				●									●				Morocco
1975	●	●	●	●	●[2]		●	●	●		●	●	●	●	●	●	●	●		●						●		●									Mozambique
—								●						●			●				●[26]						●										Nauru
1955	●	●	●	●			●	●	●	●	●	●	●	●	●	●	●	●		●																	Nepal
1945	●	●	●	●	●	●	●	●	●	●	●	●	●	●	●	●	●	●	●	●			●								●	●			●		Netherlands, The
—															●[19]		●			●																	Netherlands Antilles
—																	●			●							●										New Caledonia
1945	●	●	●	●	●	●	●	●	●	●	●	●	●	●	●	●	●	●		●	●						●										New Zealand
1945	●	●	●	●	●	●	●	●	●	●	●	●	●	●	●	●	●	●	●	●					●							●					Nicaragua
1960	●	●	●	●	●	●	●	●	●	●	●	●		●	●	●	●	●	●	●						●		●		●			●				Niger
1960	●	●	●	●	●	●	●	●	●	●	●	●	●	●	●	●	●	●		●	●					●		●		●				●			Nigeria
—																	●				●						●										Niue
—																	●				●																Norfolk Island

Government and international organizations (continued)

country	date of independence[a]	date of current or last constitution[b]	type of government	executive branch[c]: chief of state	executive branch[c]: head of government	legislative branch[d]: upper house (members)	legislative branch[d]: lower house (members)	admin. subdivisions: first-order (number)	admin. subdivisions: second-order (number)	seaward claims: territorial (nautical miles)	seaward claims: fishing/economic (nautical miles)
Norway	June 7, 1905	May 17, 1814	constitutional monarchy	king	prime minister	157	—	19	454	4	200
Oman	Dec. 20, 1951	—	monarchy (sultanate)	sultan	prime minister	55	—	11	41	12	200
Pacific Is., Trust Terr. of											
Marshall Islands	Nov. 3, 1986	May 1, 1979	republic	—president—		12	33	26	—	3	200
Micronesia, F.S. of	Nov. 3, 1986	July 18, 1978	federal republic	—president—		14	—	4	...	3	200
Northern Mariana Is.	Jan. 3, 1986	Jan. 9, 1978	commonwealth (U.S.)	U.S. president	governor	9	15	4	—	3	200
Palau	—	April 2, 1979	republic	—president—		16	18	16	—	3	200
Pakistan	Aug. 14, 1947	Aug. 14, 1973	federal Islamic republic	—president—		87	237	6	16	12	200
Panama	Nov. 3, 1903	Oct. 11, 1972	republic	—president—		67	505	10	65	200	[1]
Papua New Guinea	Sept. 16, 1975	Sept. 16, 1975	constitutional monarchy	British monarch	prime minister	109	—	20	86	12[8]	200
Paraguay	May 14, 1811	Aug. 25, 1967	republic	—president—		30	60	20	190	—	—
Peru	July 28, 1821	July 28, 1980	republic	—president—		60	180	25	152	200	[1]
Philippines	July 4, 1946	Jan. 17, 1973	republic	—president—		183	—	73	1,500	[24]	200
Pitcairn Island	—	Nov. 30, 1838	colony (U.K.)	British monarch	isl. magistrate	10	—	—	—	3	200
Poland	Nov. 10, 1918	July 22, 1952	socialist republic	chairman CS	premier	460	—	49	261	12	200
Portugal	c. 1140	April 25, 1976	republic	president	prime minister	250	—	22	305	12	200
Puerto Rico	July 25, 1952	July 25, 1952	commonwealth (U.S.)	U.S. president	governor	27	51	78	...	3	200
Qatar	Sept. 3, 1971	July 1970[27]	constitutional monarchy	—emir—		—	—	—	—	3	200
Réunion	—	—	overseas dept. (Fr.)	French president	[15]	36	45	4	24	12	200
Romania	May 21, 1877	Aug. 21, 1965	socialist republic	president	prime minister	369	—	41	237	12	200
Rwanda	July 1, 1962	Dec. 20, 1978	republic	—president—		70	—	10	143	—	—
St. Christopher and Nevis	Sept. 19, 1983	Sept. 19, 1983	constitutional monarchy	British monarch	prime minister	15	—	14	—	12	200
St. Helena and Ascension	—	Jan. 1, 1967	colony (U.K.)	British monarch	governor	15[28]	—	3	—	3	200
St. Lucia	Feb. 22, 1979	Feb. 22, 1979	constitutional monarchy	British monarch	prime minister	11	17	10	—	3	12
St. Pierre and Miquelon	—	—	terr. collectivity (Fr.)	French president	[26]	14	—	2	—	12	200
St. Vincent	Oct. 27, 1979	Oct. 27, 1979	constitutional monarchy	British monarch	prime minister	19	—	5	13	3	12
San Marino	855	1205	republic	—captains-regent (2)—		60	—	9	—	—	—
São Tomé and Príncipe	July 12, 1975	Dec. 12, 1975	republic	—president—		40	—	2	7	12[5]	200
Saudi Arabia	Sept. 23, 1932	—	monarchy	king	prime minister	—	—	14	—	12	—
Senegal	Aug. 20, 1960	March 7, 1963	republic	—president—		120	—	10	30	12	200
Seychelles	June 29, 1976	March 26, 1979	republic	—president—		25	—	—	—	12	200
Sierra Leone	April 27, 1961	June 14, 1978	republic	—president—		124	—	4	12	200	[1]
Singapore	Aug. 9, 1965	June 3, 1959	republic	president	prime minister	79	—	—	—	3	12
Solomon Islands	July 7, 1978	July 7, 1978	parliamentary state	British monarch	prime minister	38	—	8	174	12[8]	200
Somalia	July 1, 1960	Aug. 25, 1979	republic	—president—		177	—	16	60	200	[1]
South Africa	May 31, 1910	Sept. 3, 1984	republic	—state president—		308[29]	—	10	358	12	200
Bophuthatswana	Dec. 6, 1977[30]	Dec. 6, 1977	republic	—president—		105	—	12	76	—	—
Ciskei	Dec. 4, 1981[30]	Dec. 4, 1981	republic	—president—		87	—	7	39	—	—
Transkei	Oct. 26, 1976[30]	Dec. 1963	republic	president	prime minister	150	—	26	123	—	—
Venda	Sept. 13, 1979[30]	Sept. 13, 1979	republic	—president—		87	—	4	—	—	—
South West Africa/Namibia	—	—	dependency of S.Af.[31]	—	admin. general	(62)	—	26	—	6	12
Spain	1492	Dec. 29, 1978	constitutional monarchy	king	prime minister	253	350	17	50	12	200
Sri Lanka	Feb. 4, 1948	Aug. 17, 1978	republic	—president—		168	—	24	682	12	200
Sudan, The	Jan. 1, 1956	Oct. 10, 1985[32]	republic	chairman TMC	prime minister	(301)	—	8	19	12	[1]
Suriname	Nov. 25, 1975	*Nov. 25, 1975*	republic	—commander in chief—		x	—	9	—	12	200
Swaziland	Sept. 6, 1968	*Sept. 6, 1968*	monarchy	king	prime minister	20	50	4	—	—	—
Sweden	before 836	Jan. 1, 1975	constitutional monarchy	king	prime minister	349	—	24	279	12	200
Switzerland	Sept. 22, 1499	May 29, 1874	federal state	—president—		46	200	23	177	—	—
Syria	April 17, 1946	March 12, 1973	republic	president	prime minister	195	—	14	41	35	[1]
Taiwan	Oct. 25, 1945	Oct. 25, 1947	republic	president	premier	1,173	—	23	—	3	12
Tanzania	Dec. 9, 1961	April 25, 1977	republic	president	prime minister	244	—	25	105	50	[1]
Thailand	1350	Dec. 22, 1978	constitutional monarchy	king	prime minister	261	347	72	576	12	200
Togo	April 27, 1960	Jan. 13, 1980	republic	—president—		67	—	5	21	30	200
Tokelau	—	1948	territory (N.Z.)	New Zealand GG	administrator	—	—	3	3	12	200
Tonga	June 4, 1970	1875	constitutional monarchy	—monarch—		28	—	5	23	12	200
Trinidad and Tobago	Aug. 31, 1962	Aug. 1, 1976	republic	president	prime minister	31	36	11	30	12	200
Tunisia	March 20, 1956	June 1, 1959	republic	—president—		125	—	23	199	12	[1]
Turkey	Oct. 29, 1923	Nov. 7, 1982	republic	president	prime minister	400	—	67	572	6[33]	[1]
Turks and Caicos Islands	—	Aug. 30, 1976	colony (U.K.)	British monarch	governor	19	—	3	—	3	200
Tuvalu	Oct. 1, 1978	Oct. 1, 1978	constitutional monarchy	British monarch	prime minister	13	—	9	—	12	200
Uganda	Oct. 9, 1962	*Sept. 8, 1967*	republic	chairman MC	prime minister	(156)	—	10	34	—	—
U.S.S.R.	c. 900	Oct. 7, 1977	fed. socialist republic	chairman PSSU	chairman CM	750	750	15	167	12	200
United Arab Emirates	Dec. 2, 1971	Dec. 2, 1971	federation of emirates	president	prime minister	40	—	7	—	3[35]	200
United Kingdom	Oct. 14, 1066	[36]	constitutional monarchy	monarch	prime minister	1,178	650	66[37]	448[37]	3	200
United States	July 4, 1776	March 4, 1789	federal republic	—president—		100	435	51	3,137	3	200
Uruguay	Aug. 25, 1828	Nov. 27, 1966	republic	—president—		31	99	19	...	200	[1]
Vanuatu	July 30, 1980	July 30, 1980	republic	president	prime minister	39	—	4	11	12[8]	200
Venezuela	July 5, 1811	Jan. 23, 1961	federal republic	—president—		47	200	23	156	12	200
Vietnam	Sept. 2, 1954	Dec. 18, 1980	socialist republic	chairman NA	chairman SC	496	—	40	391	12	200
Virgin Islands (U.S.)	—	—	territory (U.S.)	U.S. president	governor	15	—	3	—	3	200
Wallis and Futuna	—	—	overseas territory (Fr.)	French president	[39]	20	—	3	—	12	200
West Bank	—	—	Israeli military	—	area commander	—	—	7	—	—	—
Western Sahara	—	—	—	—	—	—	—	—	—	12	200
Western Samoa	Jan. 1, 1962	Oct. 28, 1960	constitutional monarchy	monarch	prime minister	47	—	21	—	12	200
Yemen (Aden)	Nov. 30, 1967	Oct. 31, 1978	people's republic	—chairman, PSPC—		111	—	7	27	12	200
Yemen (Ṣan'ā')	December 1918	June 19, 1974	republic	president	prime minister	159	1,000	10	41	12	[1]
Yugoslavia	Dec. 1, 1918	Feb. 21, 1974	federal socialist republic	—president—		88	220	8	527	12	[1]
Zaire	June 30, 1960	Feb. 15, 1978	republic	—president—		310	—	9	41	12	200
Zambia	Oct. 24, 1964	Aug. 25, 1973	republic	—president—		136	—	9	53	—	—
Zimbabwe	April 18, 1980	April 18, 1980	republic	president	prime minister	40	100	8	—	—	—

[1]Territorial sea claim assumed to claim fishing/economic rights within the same zone. [2]Full membership pending. [3]President of France and Bishop of Urgel, Spain. [4]Executive responsibilities divided between (for the U.K.) the governor and (for Anguilla) the chief minister of the executive council. [5]Defined by bilateral maritime boundaries or by an equidistant line. [6]Executive responsibilities divided between (for the U.K.) the governor and (locally) the premiere of the Cabinet. [7]Exclusive fishing rights within 100 nautical miles (nm); regulates foreign fishing in outer 100 nm. [8]Measured from claimed archipelagic baselines. [9]Assisted by local government council. [10]Not fully effective until 1989. [11]Self-governing state in free association with New Zealand. [12]Includes Turkish Federated State of Cyprus. [13]Suspended in 1979. [14]Executive responsibilities divided between (for Denmark) the State Commissioner and (locally) the Head of the Home Government. [15]Executive responsibilities are divided among (for France) the Commissioner and (locally) the President of the General Council and the President of the Regional Council. [16]Executive responsibilities are divided between (for France) the High Commissioner and (locally) the President of the Territorial Assembly. [17]Suspended from full participation. [18]Part 12 nm, part 200 nm, part defined by geographical coordinates. [19]Associate member. [20]Evolving body of constitutional law adopted by Israeli parliament. [21]3 nm in 5 straits. [22]3 nm in Korean Strait.

membership in international organizations

United Nations (date of admission)	UNCTAD★[e]	UNICEF★[f]	ICJ★	FAO	GATT	IAEA[e]	IBRD	ICAO	IDA	IFC	ILO	IMF	IMO	ITU[e]	UNESCO	UNIDO	UPU[e]	WHO	WIPO[e]	WMO	Commonwealth of Nations	ASEAN	EC	LAS[g]	OAS	OAU	SPC	ACP	COMECON	ECOWAS	EEC	I-ADB	IDB[g]	OPEC	NATO	WTO	country
	UN organs★ and affiliated intergovernmental organizations																				Commonwealth	regional multi-purpose						economic							military		
1945	•	•	•	•	•	•	•	•	•	•	•	•	•	•	•	•	•	•	•	•															•		Norway
1971	•	•	•	•			•	•	•	•		•	•	•	•	•	•	•		•				•									•				Oman
—																																					Pacific Is., Trust Terr. of
—																											•										Marshall Islands
—																											•										Micronesia, F.S. of
—																											•										Northern Mariana Is.
—																											•										Palau
1947	•	•	•	•	•	•	•	•	•	•	•	•	•	•	•	•	•	•	•	•													•				Pakistan
1945	•	•	•	•		•	•	•	•	•	•	•	•	•	•	•	•	•	•	•					•							•					Panama
1975	•	•	•	•	•2		•	•	•	•	•	•	•	•	•	•	•	•		•	•						•	•									Papua New Guinea
1945	•	•	•	•		•	•	•	•	•	•	•		•	•	•	•	•		•					•							•					Paraguay
1945	•	•	•	•	•	•	•	•	•	•	•	•	•	•	•	•	•	•	•	•					•							•					Peru
1945	•	•	•	•	•	•	•	•	•	•	•	•	•	•	•	•	•	•	•	•		•															Philippines
—																	•				•						•										Pitcairn Island
1945	•	•	•	•	•	•	•	•			•	•	•	•	•	•	•	•	•	•									•							•	Poland
1955	•	•	•	•	•	•	•	•		•	•	•	•	•	•	•	•	•	•	•			•								•	•			•		Portugal
—																	•																				Puerto Rico
1971	•	•	•	•	•2	•	•	•			•	•	•	•	•	•	•	•	•	•				•									•	•			Qatar
—																	•																				Réunion
1955	•	•	•	•	•	•	•	•		•	•	•	•	•	•	•	•	•	•	•									•							•	Romania
1962	•	•	•	•	•		•	•	•	•	•	•		•	•	•	•	•	•	•						•		•									Rwanda
1983	•	•	•	•			•					•			•	•	•2	•			•				•			•									St. Christopher and Nevis
—																	•				•																St. Helena and Ascension
1979	•	•	•	•	•2		•	•	•	•	•	•	•		•	•	•	•		•	•				•			•									St. Lucia
—																	•																				St. Pierre and Miquelon
1980	•	•	•	•	•2		•	•				•	•	•	•	•	•	•			•				•			•									St. Vincent
—	•	•	•								•			•	•	•	•	•																			San Marino
1975	•	•	•	•	•2		•	•	•		•	•		•	•	•	•	•		•						•		•									São Tomé and Príncipe
1945	•	•	•	•		•	•	•	•	•	•	•	•	•	•	•	•	•	•	•				•									•	•			Saudi Arabia
1960	•	•	•	•	•	•	•	•	•	•	•	•	•	•	•	•	•	•	•	•						•		•		•			•				Senegal
1976	•	•	•	•	•2		•	•	•	•	•	•	•		•	•	•	•		•	•					•		•									Seychelles
1961	•	•	•	•	•	•	•	•	•	•	•	•	•	•	•	•	•	•	•	•	•					•		•		•			•				Sierra Leone
1965	•	•	•		•	•	•	•		•	•	•	•	•		•	•	•		•	•	•															Singapore
1978	•	•	•	•	•2		•	•	•	•	•	•				•	•	•		•	•						•	•									Solomon Islands
1960	•	•	•	•			•	•	•	•	•	•	•	•	•	•	•	•	•	•				•		•		•					•				Somalia
1945	•		•		•	•	•	•	•	•		•		•		•		•	•																		South Africa
—																																					Bophuthatswana
—																																					Ciskei
—																																					Transkei
—																																					Venda
—				•		•					•			•	•	•		•19																			South West Africa/Namibia
1955	•	•	•	•	•	•	•	•	•	•	•	•	•	•	•	•	•	•	•	•			•								•	•			•		Spain
1955	•	•	•	•	•	•	•	•	•	•	•	•	•	•	•	•	•	•	•	•	•																Sri Lanka
1956	•	•	•	•		•	•	•	•	•	•	•	•	•	•	•	•	•	•	•				•		•		•					•				Sudan, The
1975	•	•	•	•	•		•	•			•	•	•	•	•	•	•	•	•	•					•			•				•					Suriname
1968	•	•	•	•	•2		•	•	•	•	•	•		•	•	•	•	•		•	•					•		•									Swaziland
1946	•	•	•	•	•	•	•	•	•	•	•	•	•	•	•	•	•	•	•	•												•					Sweden
—	•	•	•	•	•	•		•			•		•	•	•	•	•	•	•	•												•					Switzerland
1945	•	•	•	•		•	•	•	•	•	•	•	•	•	•	•	•	•		•				•									•				Syria
—																																					Taiwan
1961	•	•	•	•	•	•	•	•	•	•	•	•	•	•	•	•	•	•	•	•	•					•		•									Tanzania
1946	•	•	•	•	•	•	•	•	•	•	•	•	•	•	•	•	•	•		•		•															Thailand
1960	•	•	•	•	•		•	•	•	•	•	•	•	•	•	•	•	•	•	•						•		•		•							Togo
—																	•				•						•										Tokelau
—	•			•	•2		•	•				•		•	•		•	•			•						•	•									Tonga
1962	•	•	•	•	•		•	•	•	•	•	•	•	•	•	•	•	•		•	•				•			•				•					Trinidad and Tobago
1956	•	•	•	•	•2	•	•	•	•	•	•	•	•	•	•	•	•	•	•	•				•		•							•				Tunisia
1945	•	•	•	•	•	•	•	•	•	•	•	•	•	•	•	•	•	•	•	•											•19		•		•		Turkey
—																	•			•	•																Turks and Caicos Islands
—					•2												•				•26						•	•									Tuvalu
1962	•	•	•	•	•	•	•	•	•	•	•	•		•	•	•	•	•	•	•	•					•		•					•				Uganda
1945[34]	•34	•34	•34			•34		•34			•34		•	•34	•34	•34	•34	•34	•34	•34									•							•	U.S.S.R.
1971	•	•	•	•	•2	•	•	•	•	•	•	•	•	•	•	•	•	•	•					•									•	•			United Arab Emirates
1945	•	•	•	•38	•	•	•	•	•	•	•	•	•	•		•	•	•	•	•	•		•				•				•	•			•		United Kingdom
1945	•	•	•	•	•	•	•	•	•	•	•	•	•	•		•	•	•	•	•					•		•					•			•		United States
1945	•		•	•	•	•	•	•		•	•	•	•	•	•	•	•	•	•	•					•							•					Uruguay
1981	•		•	•			•	•		•		•	•			•	•	•		•	•						•	•									Vanuatu
1945	•	•	•	•		•	•	•		•	•	•	•	•	•	•	•	•		•					•							•		•			Venezuela
1977	•	•	•	•		•	•	•	•	•		•	•	•	•	•	•	•	•	•									•								Vietnam
—																	•																				Virgin Islands (U.S.)
—																	•										•										Wallis and Futuna
—																																					West Bank
—																										•40											Western Sahara
1976	•		•	•			•		•	•		•			•	•	•	•			•						•	•									Western Samoa
1967	•	•	•	•	•2		•	•	•		•	•	•	•	•	•	•	•		•				•									•				Yemen (Aden)
1947	•	•	•	•			•	•	•	•	•	•	•	•	•	•	•	•	•	•				•									•				Yemen (Ṣan'ā')
1945	•	•	•	•	•	•	•	•	•	•	•	•	•	•	•	•	•	•	•	•									•19			•					Yugoslavia
1960	•	•	•	•	•	•	•	•	•	•	•	•	•	•	•	•	•	•	•	•						•		•									Zaire
1964	•	•	•	•	•2	•	•	•	•	•	•	•		•	•	•	•	•	•	•	•					•		•									Zambia
1980	•	•	•	•	•	•	•	•	•	•	•	•		•	•	•	•	•	•	•	•					•		•									Zimbabwe

23Formally a "*jamahiriya,*" translatable as "the masses of people," "the populace," or "the multitude." 24Zone defined by geographical coordinates. 25Executive responsibilities divided between (for France) the Commissioner of the Republic and (locally) the President of the General Council. 26Special member participating in functional activities, but not represented at meetings of Commonwealth Heads of Government. 27A 1970 Basic Law, though not a constitution as such, serves that purpose. 28For St. Helena only; Ascension Island and Tristan da Cunha also have local councils. 29House of Assembly—178 white members; House of Representatives—85 Coloured members; House of Delegates—45 Indian members. 30Not recognized internationally. 31The United Nations has declared itself responsible for the territory, which it has named Namibia. 32Transitional constitution. 3312 nm in the Black Sea. 34Belorussian and Ukrainian S.S.R.s are also members. 3512 nm for Sharjah. 36Unwritten constitution based on statutes and common law. 37Excludes Northern Ireland. 38Including colonies and overseas dependencies. 39Executive responsibilities are divided between (for France) the Superior Administrator and (locally) the President of the Territorial Assembly. 40Membership is held by the Sahrawi Arab Democratic Republic.

Area and population

This table provides the area and population for each of the countries of the world and for all political dependencies with a permanent civilian population. Only countries such as the Vatican City State, the British Indian Ocean Territory, and similar anomalous cases are omitted. The data represent the latest published and unpublished data for both the surveyed area of the countries and their populations, the latter both as of a single year (1986) to provide the best comparability and as of the most recent census to provide the fullest comparison of certain demographic measures that are not always available in estimated form between successive national censuses. The 1986 estimates represent a combination of national, United Nations (UN) or other international organization, and *Encyclopædia Britannica* estimates so as to give the best fit to available published series, to take account of unpublished information received in correspondence, and to incorporate the results of very recent censuses for which published analyses and projections based upon them are not yet available. Caution should be used if constructing population series from different editions of the *Britannica World Data*.

One principal point to bear in mind when studying these statistics is that all of them, whatever degree of precision may be implied by the exactness of the numbers, are estimates—all of varying, and some of suspect accuracy. Even a country like the United States—which has a long tradition both of census taking and of the use of the most sophisticated analytical tools in processing the data—is unable to determine within 2.5% its total population nationally. And that is an average underenumeration. In larger cities, where enumeration of certain populations, both legal and illegal, is most difficult, the accuracy of the enumerated count may be off considerably more than 5%. When a country like Nigeria, the most populous in Africa, does not know within 20% its real population and is delayed or prevented from measuring it by political circumstances, both the amount and the margin of error are likely to increase. The editors have tried to take account of the range of variation and accuracy in published data, but it is relatively difficult to establish a value for many sources of inaccuracy unless some country or agency has made a conscientious effort to establish both the relative accuracy (precision) of its estimate and the absolute magnitude of the quantity it is trying to measure—for example, the number of people in Kampuchea (Cambodia) who died at the hands of the Khmer Rouge. Was it 1,000,000, 2,000,000, 3,000,000? If a figure of 1,000,000 is cited, what is its accuracy: ± 1%, 10%, 50%? Is the source of the figure Vietnam (potential bias on the high side to justify its invasion), China (potential bias on the low side because of its political connection with the Khmer Rouge), the United States (habitually unable to obtain or produce by analysis accurate data about Southeast Asia, complicated by political bias)?

Many similar problems exist and in endless variations: What is the extent of southern European immigration to western Europe in search of jobs? How many refugees from Uganda or Afghanistan are there in surrounding countries? How many illegal immigrants are there in the United States? How many Palestinians are there in the Middle East (they are politically inconvenient to enumerate everywhere)? How many Amerindians exist in the countries of South America (any accurate answer to that question raises the question, "Where did they go?")? How many people have died or emigrated as a result of the civil violence in Central America?

Still, much information is accurate, well founded, and updated annually. The sources of these data are censuses; national population registers (cu-

Area and population

country	area			population (latest estimate)					population (most recent census)				
	square miles	square kilo-metres	rank	total 1986	rank	density per sq mi	density per sq km	% annual growth rate 1981–86	census year	total	male (%)	female (%)	urban (%)
Afghanistan	251,825	652,225	40	16,892,000	43	67.1	25.9	1.3	1979	13,051,358[1]	51.4	48.6	15.1
Albania	11,100	28,748	126	3,023,000	110	272.3	105.2	2.1	1982	2,786,100	51.6	48.4	33.6
Algeria	919,595	2,381,741	10	22,564,000	35	24.5	9.5	3.2	1977[3]	16,948,000	49.7	50.3	40.6
American Samoa	77	199	195	36,000	191	467.5	180.9	1.7	1980	32,297	50.7	49.3	17.5
Andorra	179	464	177	46,000	187	258.8	99.8	5.3	1986	45,877	53.1	46.9	64.7
Angola	481,350	1,246,700	21	8,823,000	68	18.3	7.1	2.9	1970	5,673,046	52.1	47.9	14.2
Anguilla	35	91	203	7,000	207	200.0	76.9	1.5	1984	6,987	49.1	50.9	—
Antigua and Barbuda	171	442	179	81,000	177	473.7	183.3	1.2	1970	65,525	48.0[2]	52.0[2]	30.7[2]
Argentina	1,073,399	2,780,092	8	31,030,000	29	28.9	11.2	1.6	1980	27,947,446	49.2	50.8	86.3
Aruba	75	193	196	62,000	183	826.7	321.2	0.5	1981	60,312	48.6	51.4	...
Australia	2,966,200	7,682,300	6	15,912,000	49	5.4	2.1	1.3	1981	14,576,330	49.9	50.1	89.0
Austria	32,376	83,855	109	7,552,000	74	233.3	90.1	−0.0	1981	7,555,338	47.4	52.6	55.1
Bahamas, The	5,382	13,939	140	235,000	157	43.7	16.9	1.9	1980	209,505[5]	48.8	51.2	54.4
Bahrain	264	685	169	435,000	143	1,648.0	635.1	4.1	1981	350,798	58.4	41.6	80.7
Bangladesh	55,598	143,998	89	103,084,000	8	1,854.1	715.9	2.6	1981	89,912,000	51.5	48.5	15.7
Barbados	166	430	180	253,000	155	1,524.1	588.4	0.2	1980	248,983	47.6	52.4	39.3[2]
Belgium	11,783	30,519	124	9,856,000	65	836.5	322.9	−0.0	1981	9,848,647	48.7	51.3	72.4[2]
Belize	8,867	22,965	133	171,000	162	19.3	7.4	2.7	1980	145,353	50.6	49.4	52.0
Benin	43,450	112,600	96	4,126,000	97	95.0	36.6	2.9	1979	3,331,210	47.9	52.1	38.3
Bermuda	21	54	206	57,000	185	2,714.3	1,055.6	0.7	1980[6]	54,050	48.9	51.1	100.0
Bhutan	18,150	47,000	118	1,446,000	126	79.7	30.8	2.0	1969	931,514	51.5[2]	48.5[2]	3.9
Bolivia	424,164	1,098,581	27	6,611,000	81	15.6	6.0	2.8	1976	4,613,486	49.1	50.9	41.7
Botswana	224,607	581,730	45	1,126,000	131	5.0	1.9	3.7	1981	941,027	47.1	52.9	15.9
Brazil	3,286,500	8,512,000	5	138,403,000	6	42.1	16.3	2.2	1980[3]	119,002,706	49.7	50.3	67.6
British Virgin Islands	59	153	199	12,000	201	203.4	78.4	1.5	1980[7]	10,985	51.1	49.9	12.0
Brunei	2,226	5,765	150	233,000	158	104.5	40.3	3.7	1981	192,832	53.4	46.6	59.4
Bulgaria	42,823	110,912	98	8,974,000	67	209.6	80.9	0.2	1985	8,942,976	49.5	50.5	58.0[8]
Burkina Faso	105,869	274,200	68	8,126,000	73	76.8	29.6	3.5	1985[3]	7,976,019	48.3	51.7	9.0[8]
Burma	261,228	676,577	39	38,493,000	25	147.4	56.9	2.1	1983	35,313,905	49.6	50.4	24.0
Burundi	10,745	27,831	128	4,830,000	94	449.5	173.5	2.8	1979[9]	4,114,135	48.3	51.7	2.3[2]
Cameroon	179,714	465,468	50	9,873,000	64	59.4	21.2	2.5	1976	7,663,246	49.0	51.0	28.5
Canada	3,849,675	9,970,610	2	25,640,000	31	6.7	2.6	1.0	1981	24,343,181	49.6	50.4	76.4
Cape Verde	1,557	4,033	152	342,000	148	219.7	84.8	2.4	1980[3]	295,073	46.3	53.7	35.1
Cayman Islands	102	264	191	22,000	196	214.6	82.9	4.0	1979	16,677[10]	48.6	51.4	100.0
Central African Republic	240,324	622,436	42	2,706,000	113	11.3	4.3	2.5	1975	2,054,610	48.0	52.0	34.6
Chad	495,755	1,284,000	20	5,139,000	91	10.4	4.0	2.3	1975	4,029,917	47.7	52.3	16.0
Chile	284,521	736,905	38	12,278,000	55	43.2	16.7	1.7	1982	11,275,440	49.0	51.0	81.0
China	3,696,100	9,572,900	3	1,053,703,000	1	285.1	110.1	1.2	1982	1,008,175,288	51.5	48.5	21.2
Christmas Island	52	135	200	2,000	211	38.5	14.8	−10.2	1981	2,871	66.8	33.2	—
Cocos (Keeling) Islands	5.6	14.4	211	600	214	110.0	42.8	1.6	1986	616	53.7[11]	46.3[11]	...
Colombia	440,831	1,141,748	26	28,231,000	30	64.0	24.7	1.7	1985	26,867,300	49.5	50.5	63.6[12]
Comoros	719	1,862	158	409,000	145	568.8	219.7	3.4	1980	335,150	49.9	50.1	23.2
Congo	132,047	342,000	57	2,097,000	120	15.9	6.1	3.9	1984	1,912,429	48.5[13]	51.5[13]	51.1
Cook Islands	91	236	194	17,000	198	189.8	73.2	−0.0	1981	17,754	51.7	48.3	...
Costa Rica	19,730	51,100	116	2,534,000	115	128.4	49.6	2.3	1984	2,416,809	50.0	50.0	43.9
Côte d'Ivoire	123,847	320,763	63	10,694,000	57	86.3	33.3	4.2	1975	6,702,866	51.8	48.2	32.0
Cuba	42,803	110,860	99	10,194,000	62	238.2	92.0	1.0	1981	9,723,605	50.6	49.4	69.0
Cyprus	3,572	9,251	147	674,000	139	188.7	72.9	1.2	1982[3]	642,731	49.7	50.3	63.5
Czechoslovakia	49,381	127,896	92	15,552,000	51	314.9	121.6	0.3	1980	15,283,095	48.7	51.3	65.5
Denmark	16,633	43,080	119	5,112,000	92	307.3	118.7	−0.0	1986[14]	5,116,273	49.3	50.7	84.2[15]
Djibouti	8,950	23,200	132	456,000	142	50.9	19.7	4.5	1960–61	81,200	...	...	75.0[16]
Dominica	290	750	166	86,000	175	296.6	114.7	2.5	1981[6]	73,795	49.8	50.2	...
Dominican Republic	18,704	48,442	117	6,390,000	84	341.6	131.9	2.4	1981	5,647,977	50.1	49.9	52.0
Ecuador	103,930	269,178	69	9,651,000	66	92.9	35.9	2.9	1982	8,060,712	49.9	50.1	49.2
Egypt	385,229	997,739	29	48,007,000	20	124.6	48.1	2.8	1976[17]	36,626,204	50.9	49.1	43.8

mulated annually); registration of migration, births, and deaths, and so on; sample surveys to establish demographic conditions; and the like.

The statistics provided for area and population by country are ranked, and the population densities based on those values are also provided. The population densities, for purposes of comparison within this table, are calculated on the basis of total area of the country. Elsewhere the reader will find densities calculated on more specialized bases: land area for Finland (because of its many lakes), ice-free area for Greenland (most of which is ice cap), or inhabited area for Egypt (which has relatively enormous areas of uninhabitable desert). The data in this section conclude with the estimated growth rate for the country (including both natural growth and net migration) during 1981–86, calculated mainly from country sources. Both absolute area and population density are calculated for both square miles and square kilometres.

In the section containing census data, information supplied includes the census total (usually de facto, the population actually present, rather than de jure, the population legally resident, who might be anywhere); the male–female breakdown; the proportion that is urban (according to the country's own definition of the term "urban," which differs very much from country to country); and finally an analysis of the age structure of the population by 15-year age groups. This last analysis may be particularly useful in distinguishing the general type of population being recorded—young, fast-growing nations show a high proportion of people under 30 (some countries like Jordan or Mayotte have more than 50% of their population under 15 years), while other nations (for example Sweden, which suffered no age-group losses in World War II) exhibit quite uniform proportions among age groups.

Finally, a section is provided giving the population of each country at the end of each decade from 1930 to 2000. The data for years past represent the best available analysis of the published data by the country itself, by the demographers of the United Nations, or by the editors of Britannica. The projections for 1990 and 2000, similarly, represent the best fit of available data through the mid-1980s with projected population structure and growth rates during the next 15 years. The evidence of the last 15 years with respect to similar estimates published around 1970, however, shows how cloudy is the glass through which these numbers are read. In 1970 no respectable Western analyst would have imagined proposing that mainland China could achieve the degree of birth control that it has since then (as evidenced in the 1982 census); on the other hand, even the Chinese admit that their methods have been somewhat Draconian and that they expect some backlash in terms of higher birth-rates among those who have so far postponed larger families. How much is "some" by 2000? Compound that problem with all the social, economic, political, and biological factors that can affect 200 countries' populations, and the difficulty facing the prospective compiler of such projections may be appreciated.

Specific data about the vital rates affecting the data in this table may be found in great detail in both the country statistical boxes in "The Nations of the World" section and in the *Vital statistics, marriage, family* table, beginning at page 812.

Percentages in this table for male and female population will always total 100.0, but percentages by age group may not for reasons such as nonresponse on census forms, "don't know" responses, which are common in countries with poor birth registration systems, and the like.

age distribution (%)						population (by decade, '000s)									country
0–14	15–29	30–44	45–59	60–74	75 and older	1930	1940	1950	1960	1970	1980	1990 projection	2000 projection	
44.5	26.9	15.8	8.6	3.6	0.6	...	...	8,958	10,775	13,623	15,707	18,472	26,035	Afghanistan
37.3[2]	28.9[2]	16.5[2]	10.2[2]	5.5[2]	1.6[2]	1,003	1,088	1,215	1,607	2,136	2,670	3,350	4,000	Albania
16.1[4]	27.1[4]	12.8[4]	8.3[4]	4.3[4]	1.4[4]	6,489	7,628	8,753	10,800	14,330	18,741	25,300	36,000	Algeria
40.9	28.8	16.0	9.4	4.0	0.9	10	13	19	21	27	32	38	43	American Samoa
19.0	27.3	26.4	14.8	9.4	3.1	5	5	6	8	19	33	53	80	Andorra
41.7	23.2	17.0	7.4	3.8	1.0	3,344	3,738	4,145	4,841	5,673	7,426	9,700	12,100	Angola
34.9	28.5	13.6	8.9	10.1	4.0	...	...	...	6	6	7	7	7	Anguilla
44.0	24.2	12.0	11.7	—8.0—		30	34	45	55	66	75	86	99	Antigua and Barbuda
30.4	23.9	18.8	15.1	9.0	2.8	11,896	14,169	17,150	20,611	23,788	28,237	32,890	37,197	Argentina
25.9	30.6	21.3	12.7	7.4	2.1	16	31	51	57	58	60	63	66	Aruba
25.1	25.3	20.5	15.2	10.4	3.5	6,503	7,079	8,219	10,315	12,552	14,695	16,678	18,471	Australia
19.9	23.6	20.1	17.1	13.2	6.1	6,435	6,684	6,935	7,048	7,447	7,549	7,579	7,629	Austria
38.1	27.8	17.9	9.8	5.1	1.3	61	70	79	113	169	210	258	310	Bahamas, The
32.9	34.5	20.0	8.8	3.1	0.7	...	90	127	162	215	337	479	680	Bahrain
46.6	24.6	14.9	8.2	—5.7—		35,353	41,259	45,482	54,699	68,171	88,329	113,005	139,693	Bangladesh
28.9	32.3	14.2	11.2	—13.3—		159	179	209	232	235	249	257	264	Barbados
20.0	23.7	19.1	18.6	12.8	5.8	8,129	8,301	8,639	9,153	9,690	9,859	9,860	9,890	Belgium
46.2	27.1	11.8	8.4	4.7	1.8	51	56	68	90	120	145	190	248	Belize
46.1[2]	25.9[2]	14.9[2]	8.6[2]	3.9[2]	0.7[2]	1,099	1,355	1,538	1,990	2,686	3,472	4,661	6,381	Benin
22.7	27.5	22.2	15.7	9.0	2.9	28	31	37	43	53	55	59	63	Bermuda
39.2[4]	26.5[4]	16.3[4]	10.9[4]	—7.1[4]—		440	500	726	853	1,045	1,280	1,569	1,893	Bhutan
41.5	27.0	15.4	9.8	4.6	1.7	2,153	2,508	2,765	3,405	4,265	5,600	7,383	9,731	Bolivia
56.5	19.9	10.2	6.6	3.4	3.4	212	278	387	522	650	908	1,292	1,865	Botswana
39.1	28.6	16.4	10.0	—5.9—		33,718	41,525	52,901	71,539	93,139	121,014	150,368	179,487	Brazil
34.0	29.0	18.7	9.7	6.3	2.3	5	7	7	7	10	11	14	16	British Virgin Islands
38.5	32.7	16.4	7.9	—4.5—		30	36	48	84	129	187	284	354	Brunei
21.8[8]	22.4[8]	20.6[8]	18.6[8]	13.0[8]	3.4[8]	5,997	6,624	7,273	7,906	8,515	8,862	9,413	9,698	Bulgaria
47.4[8]	21.1[8]	16.1[8]	9.3[8]	—6.1[8]—		...	...	3,584	4,350	5,412	6,604	7,600	9,300	Burkina Faso
41.2[2]	25.8[2]	16.0[2]	10.9[2]	5.2[2]	0.9[2]	14,282	16,119	18,489	22,063	26,997	33,938	41,351	49,749	Burma
42.4	29.4	13.4	8.2	4.8	1.8	...	...	2,435	2,908	3,350	4,121	5,305	6,951	Burundi
43.4	24.3	16.6	9.9	4.3	1.5	...	...	4,888	5,609	6,727	8,503	10,885	13,893	Cameroon
23.4	28.9	20.0	15.0	9.6	3.1	10,498	11,693	13,737	17,909	21,324	24,070	26,826	29,028	Canada
46.0	27.6	9.1	9.0	6.3	2.0	146	181	147	200	272	297	375	420	Cape Verde
29.1	25.8	22.1	13.1	7.3	2.6	6	7	7	8	11	17	23	27	Cayman Islands
43.5	23.5	17.1	12.4	2.7	0.8	...	...	1,311	1,500	1,793	2,333	2,965	3,736	Central African Republic
40.6	28.3	17.2	9.5	—4.4—		...	...	2,639	3,032	3,643	4,477	5,558	7,063	Chad
31.9	29.1	19.1	11.7	6.3	1.9	4,365	5,063	6,091	7,585	9,368	11,104	13,025	15,116	Chile
33.6	29.1	17.5	12.2	6.3	1.3	500,000	530,000	556,613	682,024	838,396	981,235	1,098,000	1,269,000	China
25.9	26.4	35.8	10.8	—1.1—		...	...	1	3	3	3	2	2	Christmas Island
27.4[11]	28.3[11]	27.2[11]	11.2[11]	—5.9[11]—		...	...	1	1	1	1	1	1	Cocos (Keeling) Islands
36.0	31.2	17.3	9.5	—6.0—		7,280	9,097	11,268	15,321	20,884	25,577	30,152	35,544	Colombia
47.2	23.2	14.8	7.6	5.1	1.8	...	...	...	177	245	333	473	661	Comoros
45.6[13]	22.2[13]	15.5[13]	11.3[13]	4.7[13]	0.7[13]	...	...	736	933	1,182	1,664	2,450	3,200	Congo
42.7	26.6	13.7	10.4	5.2	1.3	11	13	15	18	18	18	17	17	Cook Islands
37.9	31.5	15.8	9.2	4.4	1.2	499	619	866	1,250	1,737	2,206	2,779	3,498	Costa Rica
44.5	27.0	16.7	7.8	2.8	1.2	2,075	2,350	2,775	3,865	5,550	8,320	12,657	19,290	Côte d'Ivoire
30.3	27.6	19.1	12.1	8.2	2.7	3,837	4,566	5,752	7,019	8,565	9,724	10,653	11,801	Cuba
25.0	26.6	20.1	13.8	—14.5—		357	413	494	573	615	627	708	793	Cyprus
24.3	22.9	19.8	17.2	11.5	4.3	13,964	14,713	12,389	13,654	14,334	15,265	15,758	16,278	Czechoslovakia
18.3	22.7	22.6	16.1	13.9	6.4	3,542	3,832	4,271	4,581	4,929	5,123	5,098	5,114	Denmark
38.0[16]	34.0[16]	17.0[16]	—11.0[16]—			...	...	60	78	158	355	498	670	Djibouti
39.8	28.6	11.9	9.2	7.4	3.1	41	45	51	60	70	74	94	119	Dominica
44.8[2]	29.0[2]	14.1[2]	7.8[2]	3.5[2]	0.8[2]	1,400	1,759	2,313	3,160	4,343	5,558	6,971	8,407	Dominican Republic
41.9	28.1	15.4	8.6	4.5	1.5	2,102	2,546	3,307	4,421	5,958	8,123	10,816	14,395	Ecuador
39.9	26.7	16.6	10.6	5.2	1.0	14,822	16,942	20,461	26,085	33,329	40,642	52,536	63,941	Egypt

Area and population (continued)

country	area			population (latest estimate)					population (most recent census)				
	square miles	square kilo-metres	rank	total 1986	rank	density per sq mi	density per sq km	% annual growth rate 1981–86	census year	total	male (%)	female (%)	urban (%)
El Salvador	8,124	21,041	134	5,461,000	89	672.2	259.5	2.4	1971	3,554,648	49.6	50.4	39.4
Equatorial Guinea	10,831	28,051	127	322,000	152	29.7	11.5	1.6	1983	304,000	49.0[2]	51.0[2]	53.6[2]
Ethiopia	472,400	1,223,500	23	45,850,000	22	94.9	36.7	2.9	1984	42,184,966	49.8	50.2	10.2
Faeroe Islands	540	1,399	160	46,000	189	85.2	32.9	1.0	1977	41,969	52.4	47.6	87.6
Falkland Islands	4,700	12,173	142	2,000	212	0.4	0.2	0.0	1980[18]	1,813	54.7	45.3	56.8
Fiji	7,056	18,274	137	710,000	137	100.6	38.9	1.9	1976	588,068	50.5	49.5	37.2
Finland	130,559	338,145	58	4,927,000	93	37.7	14.6	0.5	1980	4,784,710	48.3	51.7	59.9
France	210,026	543,965	46	55,427,000	17	263.9	101.9	0.5	1982	54,334,871	49.0	51.0	77.9[2]
French Guiana	35,900	93,000	106	86,000	176	2.4	0.9	3.7	1982	73,022	52.7	47.3	73.4
French Polynesia	1,359	3,521	153	180,000	160	132.6	51.2	3.0	1983	166,753	51.1	48.9	39.7
Gabon	103,347	267,667	71	1,187,000	130	11.5	4.4	1.7	1960–61	448,564	49.1[2]	50.6[2]	35.8[2]
Gambia, The	4,127	10,689	145	765,000	136	185.2	71.5	3.2	1983	695,886	50.7[12]	49.3[12]	21.2
Gaza Strip	140	363	184	531,000	141	3,792.9	1,462.8	2.8	1984[14]	509,900	49.9	50.1	...
Germany, East	41,827	108,333	101	16,636,000	45	397.7	153.6	−0.1	1981	16,705,635	47.0	53.0	76.4
Germany, West	96,026	248,706	74	60,861,000	13	633.8	244.7	−0.3	1984[14]	61,049,300	47.8	52.2	84.7[2]
Ghana	92,098	238,533	78	13,144,000	54	142.7	55.1	2.6	1984	12,205,574	49.1	50.9	31.3
Gibraltar	2.2	5.8	213	28,000	193	12,727.3	4,827.6	−0.8	1981[19]	26,479	52.2	47.8	...
Greece	50,949	131,957	91	9,987,000	63	196.0	75.7	0.5	1981	9,740,417	49.2[20]	50.8[20]	58.1
Greenland	840,000	2,175,600	13	54,000	186	0.06	0.02	1.1	1986[14]	53,406	54.3	45.7	78.8
Grenada	133	345	186	97,000	173	729.3	281.2	1.7	1981	89,088	47.1[2]	52.9[2]	25.3[21]
Guadeloupe	687	1,780	159	334,000	150	486.2	187.6	0.4	1982[3]	327,002	49.0	51.0	...
Guam	209	541	173	121,000	168	578.8	223.6	2.2	1980	105,979	52.2	47.8	39.5
Guatemala	42,042	108,889	100	8,191,000	72	194.8	75.2	2.9	1981[3]	6,043,559	49.8	50.2	34.3
Guernsey	30	78	204	59,000	184	1,966.7	756.4	1.1	1976[22]	54,381	48.3	51.7	...
Guinea	94,926	245,857	75	6,225,000	86	65.6	25.3	2.4	1983	5,781,014	48.6	51.4	26.0
Guinea-Bissau	13,948	36,125	122	891,000	133	63.9	24.7	2.1	1979	767,739	48.2	51.8	14.0
Guyana	83,000	215,000	81	796,000	135	9.6	3.7	0.8	1980	758,619	49.7[21]	50.3[21]	31.9[21]
Haiti	10,579	27,400	130	5,427,000	90	513.0	198.1	1.7	1982	5,053,792	48.5	51.5	20.6
Honduras	43,277	112,088	97	3,938,000	99	91.0	35.1	2.9	1974	2,656,948	49.5	50.5	37.5
Hong Kong	400	1,037	162	5,533,000	88	13,831.5	5,335.2	1.4	1986[23]	5,396,000	51.4	48.6	93.1
Hungary	35,921	93,036	105	10,624,000	58	295.8	114.2	−0.2	1980	10,709,463	48.4	51.6	53.2
Iceland	39,769	103,000	102	246,000	156	6.2	2.4	1.3	1985[14]	240,606	50.3	49.7	88.8[16]
India	1,183,427	3,065,063	7	777,230,000	2	657.0	253.7	2.1	1981	685,184,692	50.3	49.7	23.7
Indonesia	741,101	1,919,443	15	168,662,000	5	227.6	87.9	2.2	1980	147,490,298	49.7	50.3	22.3
Iran	636,443	1,648,380	17	46,097,000	21	72.4	28.0	3.3	1976	33,708,744	51.5	48.5	47.0
Iraq	169,235	438,317	53	15,946,000	48	94.2	36.4	3.3	1977	12,000,497	51.5	48.5	63.7
Ireland	27,137	70,285	113	3,547,000	102	130.7	50.5	0.5	1986	3,537,195	50.2[11]	49.8[11]	55.6[11]
Isle of Man	221	572	172	71,000	179	321.1	124.1	1.4	1981[3]	64,679	47.8	52.2	50.4
Israel[24]	7,992	20,700	135	4,381,000	95	548.2	211.6	2.1	1983[3, 25]	4,037,620	49.8	50.2	86.9
Italy	116,324	301,278	65	57,298,000	14	492.6	190.2	0.3	1981[3]	56,556,911	48.6	51.4	69.3[2]
Jamaica	4,244	10,991	144	2,351,000	117	554.0	213.9	1.7	1982	2,190,357	49.1	50.9	47.8
Japan	145,870	377,801	56	121,470,000	7	832.9	321.6	0.7	1985	121,047,196	49.2	50.8	76.7
Jersey	45	116	201	78,000	178	1,733.3	672.4	0.5	1981[3]	76,050	48.0	52.0	...
Jordan[26]	34,443	89,206	108	2,749,000	111	79.8	30.8	3.9	1979	2,132,997	52.3	47.7	59.5
Kampuchea	69,898	181,035	84	7,469,000	75	106.9	41.3	2.9	1981	6,684,000	50.0[27]	50.0[27]	10.3[27]
Kenya	224,961	582,646	44	21,148,000	38	94.0	36.3	4.0	1979	15,327,061	49.7	50.3	15.1
Kiribati	328	849	164	65,000	182	198.2	76.6	2.0	1985	63,991	49.6	50.4	33.5
Korea, North	47,250	122,370	94	20,543,000	39	434.8	167.9	2.3	[28]	—	49.4[2]	50.6[2]	59.7[2]
Korea, South	38,259	99,091	103	41,569,000	23	1,086.5	419.5	1.4	1985[3]	40,466,577	50.1	49.9	65.4
Kuwait	6,880	17,818	138	1,791,000	122	260.2	100.5	4.5	1985	1,697,301	56.9	43.1	100.0
Laos	91,400	236,800	80	3,703,000	101	40.5	15.6	2.5	1985	3,584,803	50.4[2]	49.6[2]	13.4[2]
Lebanon	3,950	10,230	146	2,707,000	112	685.3	264.6	0.4	1970	2,126,325	50.8	49.2	60.1
Lesotho	11,720	30,355	125	1,586,000	125	135.4	52.3	2.6	1986[3]	1,577,536	48.2	51.8	17.2[29]
Liberia	38,250	99,067	104	2,303,000	118	60.2	23.2	3.3	1974	1,503,368	50.5	49.5	29.1
Libya	675,000	1,749,000	16	3,953,000	98	5.9	2.3	4.4	1984	3,637,488	53.0[12]	47.0[12]	59.8[12]
Liechtenstein	62	160	198	27,000	194	437.3	169.5	1.1	1980	25,215	49.6	50.4	...
Luxembourg	999	2,586	155	367,000	147	367.4	141.9	0.1	1981	364,602	48.8	51.2	78.4[2]
Macau	6	16	210	433,000	144	72,166.7	27,062.5	7.6	1981[3]	241,729	50.9	49.1	95.4
Madagascar	226,658	587,046	43	10,294,000	60	45.4	17.5	2.8	1974–75	7,603,790	50.0	50.0	16.3
Malaŵi	45,747	118,484	95	7,279,000	77	159.1	61.4	3.2	1977	5,547,460	48.2	51.8	8.5
Malaysia	127,581	330,434	61	16,090,000	46	126.1	48.7	2.6	1980	13,136,109	50.2	49.8	34.2
Maldives	115	298	188	189,000	159	1,643.5	634.2	3.4	1985	181,453	51.8	48.2	20.7[30]
Mali	478,841	1,240,192	22	8,457,000	70	17.7	6.8	3.0	1976	6,394,918	48.8	51.2	16.8
Malta	122	316	187	336,000	149	2,752.5	1,062.7	0.8	1985	345,418	47.9[31]	52.1[31]	94.3[31]
Martinique	421	1,091	161	328,000	151	779.1	300.6	0.1	1982[3]	326,717	48.5	51.5	57.1
Mauritania	397,700	1,030,020	28	1,689,000	124	4.2	1.6	2.0	1976–77	1,419,939	50.1	49.9	21.9
Mauritius	788	2,040	157	1,034,000	132	1,312.2	506.9	1.3	1983	1,002,178	49.8	50.2	41.7[32]
Mayotte	144	373	183	70,000	180	486.1	187.7	4.9	1985	67,138	49.9[33]	50.1[33]	53.3[33]
Mexico	756,066	1,958,201	14	80,472,000	11	106.4	41.1	2.5	1980	66,846,833	49.4	50.6	66.3
Monaco	0.7	1.9	215	29,000	192	41,428.6	15,263.9	1.4	1982	27,063	46.6	53.4	100.0
Mongolia	604,000	1,565,000	18	1,938,000	121	3.2	1.2	2.5	1979	1,594,800	50.1	49.9	51.2
Montserrat	40	102	202	12,000	202	300.0	117.6	0.7	1980	11,606	48.1	51.9	13.2
Morocco	177,117	458,730	52	22,455,000	37	126.8	49.0	2.5	1982	20,419,555[34]	50.1	49.9	42.7
Mozambique	308,642	799,380	34	14,143,000	53	45.8	17.7	2.6	1980	12,130,000	48.7	51.3	13.2
Nauru	8	21	209	8,000	205	1,000.0	381.0	−0.3	1983	8,042	52.1[30, 35]	47.9[30, 35]	—
Nepal	56,827	147,181	88	16,863,000	44	296.7	114.6	2.3	1981	15,022,839	51.2	48.8	6.4
Netherlands, The	16,133	41,785	120	14,561,000	52	902.6	348.5	0.4	1985[14]	14,453,833	49.5	50.5	88.5[15]
Netherlands Antilles	308	800	165	176,000	161	571.4	220.0	0.5	1981	171,620	48.3	51.7	...
New Caledonia	7,233	18,734	136	151,000	164	20.9	8.1	1.2	1983	145,368	51.8	48.2	58.5
New Zealand	103,493	268,046	70	3,288,000	106	31.8	12.3	1.0	1981	3,175,737	49.7	50.3	83.6
Nicaragua	49,363	127,849	93	3,384,000	105	68.6	26.5	3.4	1971	1,877,952	48.3	51.7	48.0
Niger	458,074	1,186,408	25	6,423,000	83	14.0	5.4	2.7	1977	5,098,427	49.3	50.7	11.8
Nigeria	356,669	923,768	31	98,112,000	10	275.1	106.2	2.5	1963[36]	55,670,055	50.5	49.5	16.1
Niue	100	258	192	3,000	209	30.0	11.6	−1.3	1984	2,887	51.2	48.8	...
Norfolk Island	14	35	207	2,000	210	142.9	57.1	−1.3	1981[3]	1,849	50.1	49.9	—

age distribution (%) 0–14	15–29	30–44	45–59	60–74	75 and older	population (by decade, '000s) 1930	1940	1950	1960	1970	1980	1990 projection	2000 projection	country
46.2	25.1	15.2	8.2	4.3	1.0	1,350	1,550	1,931	2,527	3,534	4,714	5,958	7,406	El Salvador
41.5[2]	25.8[2]	15.6[2]	10.6[2]	5.4[2]	1.1[2]	...	...	211	244	291	285	359	438	Equatorial Guinea
46.6	22.7	15.6	8.9	4.5	1.7	...	...	16,675	20,024	24,068	37,780	50,290	66,920	Ethiopia
29.6	23.9	14.9	15.1	10.4	3.6	24	27	31	35	39	43	47	50	Faeroe Islands
25.4	22.6	—38.0—		—14.0—		2	2	2	2	2	2	2	2	Falkland Islands
41.1	29.8	16.2	8.8	3.3	0.8	181	218	289	394	520	634	768	927	Fiji
20.2	24.4	22.1	16.8	12.4	4.1	3,449	3,698	4,009	4,430	4,606	4,780	5,006	5,073	Finland
22.0	23.5	19.6	17.3	11.6	6.0	41,150	41,300	41,736	45,684	50,770	53,880	55,900	58,600	France
34.2	29.2	19.9	9.8	5.1	1.8	30	30	27	33	49	69	99	142	French Guiana
38.5	29.7	16.5	10.3	4.2	0.8	39	50	62	84	109	151	202	269	French Polynesia
34.1[2]	24.3[2]	18.8[2]	13.4[2]	7.6[2]	1.8[2]	...	...	...	...	950	1,074	1,282	1,611	Gabon
41.3[12]	26.5[12]	17.6[12]	8.3[12]	4.3[12]	1.7[12]	211	193	232	357	458	632	887	1,244	Gambia, The
47.7	29.2	11.0	7.8	—4.3—		...	...	...	...	370	451	594	785	Gaza Strip
19.4	24.2	20.0	17.3	12.8	6.3	15,400	16,800	18,387	17,240	17,058	16,737	16,604	16,483	Germany, East
15.3	24.4	20.4	19.6	13.5	6.8	37,500	40,600	49,986	55,433	60,714	61,566	59,600	58,800	Germany, West
46.3[2]	26.0[2]	14.7[2]	8.5[2]	3.8[2]	0.7[2]	3,110	3,636	5,297	6,958	8,789	11,293	14,500	18,700	Ghana
21.4	22.2	22.3	17.7	12.6	3.8	16	14	23	24	26	30	33	35	Gibraltar
21.3[20]	22.0[20]	19.1[20]	19.8[20]	12.4[20]	5.4[20]	6,367	7,319	7,566	8,327	8,793	9,643	10,200	10,700	Greece
24.7	33.7	23.2	12.6	4.6	1.1	16	19	23	33	41	50	56	61	Greenland
39.4[2]	31.2[2]	10.1[2]	9.2[2]	7.3[2]	2.8[2]	68	71	76	90	95	91	106	130	Grenada
31.1	29.2	16.6	12.0	7.8	2.8	151	180	206	265	320	327	338	350	Guadeloupe
34.9	30.6	19.4	10.5	3.9	0.5	19	22	59	67	85	107	132	165	Guam
44.9	26.8	14.8	8.5	3.9	1.1	1,771	2,201	3,024	4,005	5,263	6,917	9,197	12,222	Guatemala
21.6	22.2	17.6	17.7	15.2	5.6	40	44	44	45	51	55	63	71	Guernsey
43.8[2]	25.5[2]	16.3[2]	9.5[2]	4.2[2]	0.7[2]	...	...	3,245	3,660	4,388	5,407	6,876	8,879	Guinea
44.3	25.5	15.1	8.2	4.7	2.2	...	341	411	520	653	787	987	1,229	Guinea-Bissau
47.1[21]	25.1[21]	13.4[21]	9.0[21]	4.4[21]	1.0[21]	309	344	423	560	702	759	867	1,075	Guyana
39.2	26.9	15.6	10.0	5.4	2.9	2,422	2,827	3,097	3,723	4,234	4,922	5,829	6,967	Haiti
48.1	25.8	13.9	7.8	3.6	0.9	948	1,146	1,390	1,873	2,553	3,313	4,502	6,289	Honduras
23.1	29.9	21.2	14.3	9.1	2.4	821	1,786	1,974	3,074	3,942	5,039	5,802	6,534	Hong Kong
21.8	20.7	—40.6—		—16.9—		8,649	9,280	9,338	9,984	10,353	10,710	10,658	10,714	Hungary
26.3	26.8	19.7	13.2	9.7	4.4	107	121	143	176	204	228	250	270	Iceland
39.5	25.9	17.4	10.7	—6.5—		278,000	317,000	352,664	427,802	543,132	687,057	827,152	964,072	India
40.8	27.0	16.4	10.2	4.5	1.1	60,750	70,500	75,449	92,701	119,467	148,040	183,457	222,753	Indonesia
44.5	25.2	14.8	10.1	3.8	1.0	12,400	14,000	16,913	21,554	28,359	37,957	51,315	65,161	Iran
48.9	24.5	12.3	8.2	4.2	1.9	...	3,745	5,180	6,847	9,356	13,108	18,136	24,198	Iraq
30.3[11]	24.6[11]	17.2[11]	13.1[11]	10.9[11]	3.8[11]	2,927	2,958	2,969	2,834	2,954	3,415	3,676	4,021	Ireland
19.1	19.7	18.2	16.5	18.2	8.2	50	52	55	49	52	65	75	86	Isle of Man
32.6	26.4	18.0	12.3	9.4	3.1	...	...	...	2,114	2,958	3,896	4,639	5,440	Israel[24]
21.4	22.4	20.0	18.7	12.7	4.7	40,293	43,840	46,769	50,223	53,565	56,304	57,400	58,100	Italy
38.4	28.8	13.8	9.4	6.9	2.6	1,009	1,212	1,403	1,629	1,891	2,175	2,535	2,872	Jamaica
21.5	20.7	23.9	19.2	10.8	3.9	64,450	73,075	83,200	93,419	103,720	116,807	122,834	128,119	Japan
16.9	24.7	21.6	17.0	13.8	5.9	50	51	57	63	68	76	80	84	Jersey
51.6	23.4	13.4	7.4	3.1	1.1	...	...	1,095	1,384	1,795	2,181	3,213	4,743	Jordan[26]
43.8[27]	24.9[27]	16.8[27]	9.8[27]	4.1[27]	0.6[27]	2,800	3,400	4,163	5,364	7,060	6,400	8,246	9,772	Kampuchea
51.4	24.8	13.2	7.0	3.0	0.6	...	...	6,018	8,115	11,225	16,667	24,872	37,505	Kenya
38.9	29.9	16.1	9.3	4.9	0.9	27	29	33	41	49	58	70	77	Kiribati
40.0[2]	28.7[2]	15.9[2]	9.7[2]	4.7[2]	1.0[2]	...	...	9,740	10,526	13,892	17,892	22,443	27,256	Korea, North
30.6	31.0	19.4	12.3	5.4	1.3	...	...	21,147	25,142	32,976	38,124	44,108	50,582	Korea, South
36.8	28.3	24.1	8.6	1.8	0.4	...	...	145	292	748	1,370	2,143	2,936	Kuwait
42.4[2]	26.3[2]	16.7[2]	9.7[2]	4.2[2]	0.7[2]	930	1,075	1,949	2,382	2,962	3,199	4,049	5,082	Laos
42.6	23.8	16.7	9.1	—7.7—		...	965	1,364	1,786	2,470	2,669	3,301	3,992	Lebanon
39.1[29]	25.5[29]	15.5[29]	10.4[29]	5.2[29]	2.3[29]	537	566	766	885	1,043	1,358	1,731	2,251	Lesotho
40.9	26.7	17.7	8.8	4.6	1.3	...	...	758	1,004	1,393	1,898	2,571	3,564	Liberia
44.3[12]	22.2[12]	15.4[12]	8.2[12]	4.0[12]	1.6[12]	800	900	1,029	1,349	1,982	3,043	4,417	6,539	Libya
23.0	26.5	24.1	14.1	9.2	3.1	10	11	14	16	21	26	28	30	Liechtenstein
18.5	23.7	21.2	18.7	12.8	5.1	297	296	296	314	339	364	366	367	Luxembourg
22.9	36.2	16.7	12.7	8.8	2.6	196	375	188	169	221	284	455	727	Macau
44.4	25.7	14.2	10.0	4.6	1.1	3,722	4,034	4,330	5,370	6,720	8,714	11,575	15,552	Madagascar
44.6	25.7	14.2	9.0	4.3	2.0	1,394	1,696	3,033	3,481	4,511	5,968	8,224	11,161	Malawi
39.5	29.1	16.5	9.2	4.6	1.1	...	...	6,187	7,908	10,466	13,765	17,830	23,050	Malaysia
44.6[30]	24.8[30]	16.4[30]	9.6[30]	3.5[30]	0.6[30]	78	81	82	106	128	155	210	279	Maldives
44.0	24.9	16.1	8.7	4.8	1.5	...	...	3,426	4,224	5,690	7,100	9,430	12,404	Mali
29.8[31]	25.9[31]	17.6[31]	13.8[31]	10.2[31]	2.7[31]	239	270	308	329	326	320	345	360	Malta
30.5	29.3	15.9	13.0	8.2	3.0	175	200	222	252	287	326	330	352	Martinique
45.9[2]	26.2[2]	14.7[2]	8.7[2]	3.9[2]	0.6[2]	...	...	781	970	1,245	1,502	1,828	2,229	Mauritania
32.6	31.7	17.8	10.9	5.7	1.3	413	428	479	662	824	957	1,117	1,248	Mauritius
50.2[33]	23.4[33]	13.9[33]	7.0[33]	3.8[33]	1.7[33]	...	...	...	...	...	53	86	141	Mayotte
43.0	27.8	14.9	8.4	4.0	1.8	16,589	19,815	26,606	36,369	50,313	69,393	89,012	109,180	Mexico
12.7[8]	17.8[8]	18.6[8]	19.9[8]	20.7[8]	10.0[8]	23	20	22	23	24	27	28	30	Monaco
43.1[2]	26.1[2]	16.3[2]	9.5[2]	4.1[2]	0.9[2]	725	750	747	931	1,248	1,663	2,170	2,686	Mongolia
31.5	27.2	13.8	10.7	11.6	5.3	13	15	14	12	12	12	13	15	Montserrat
42.2	28.3	14.1	9.2	4.8	1.5	6,980	7,750	8,953	11,640	15,126	19,317	27,840	36,509	Morocco
44.4	26.7	15.9	8.7	3.6	0.7	3,890	5,086	5,742	7,046	9,140	12,103	15,696	20,463	Mozambique
44.1[30, 35]	33.1[30, 35]	11.4[30, 35]	8.5[30, 35]	1.9[30, 35]	1.0[30, 35]	3	3	4	5	7	8	8	9	Nauru
41.4	25.5	17.4	10.0	4.7	1.0	6,250	7,000	8,000	9,180	11,232	14,642	18,469	23,184	Nepal
19.7	25.6	22.4	15.6	11.7	5.0	7,936	8,834	10,027	11,417	12,958	14,150	14,783	15,380	Netherlands, The
30.0	29.9	19.5	11.3	6.7	2.6	61	77	112	136	163	171	178	185	Netherlands Antilles
36.2	26.9	19.5	11.2	5.1	1.1	54	53	59	79	110	140	159	180	New Caledonia
26.7	25.9	19.1	14.3	10.5	3.5	1,491	1,636	1,908	2,372	2,820	3,100	3,485	3,695	New Zealand
48.1	25.6	14.1	7.4	3.8	1.1	700	825	1,109	1,472	1,972	2,771	3,874	5,428	Nicaragua
46.6[2]	26.4[2]	14.4[2]	8.3[2]	3.7[2]	0.6[2]	...	...	2,291	2,913	4,016	5,468	7,151	9,350	Niger
43.0	31.9	16.5	5.1	2.5	1.0	...	...	33,320	42,366	56,346	84,446	108,430	139,200	Nigeria
38.2	26.9	—25.8—		—9.1—		4	4	4	4	4	3	3	3	Niue
24.7	22.0	22.9	17.5	—13.0—		1	1	1	1	2	2	2	2	Norfolk Island

Area and population (continued)

country	area			population (latest estimate)					population (most recent census)				
	square miles	square kilo-metres	rank	total 1986	rank	density per sq mi	density per sq km	% annual growth rate 1981–86	census year	total	male (%)	female (%)	urban (%)
Norway	125,050	323,878	62	4,166,000	96	33.3	12.9	0.3	1984[14]	4,145,845	49.4	50.6	70.3[37]
Oman	120,000	300,000	66	1,288,000	127	10.7	4.3	4.4	[28]	—	50.6[2]	49.4[2]	7.3[2]
Pacific Is., Trust Territory of the													
Marshall Islands	70	181	197	37,000	190	528.6	204.4	3.1	1980	30,873	51.3	48.7	47.8
Micronesia, Federated States of	271	702	168	95,000	174	350.6	135.3	3.6	1980	73,160	51.1	48.9	19.4
Northern Mariana Islands	182	471	176	21,000	197	115.4	44.6	3.6	1980	16,780	52.5	47.5	16.0
Palau	191	495	175	12,000	200	63.9	25.9	−0.3	1980	12,116	51.8	48.2	51.4
Pakistan	307,374	796,095	35	102,878,000	9	334.7	129.2	3.0	1981[38]	84,253,644	52.5	47.5	28.3
Panama	29,762	77,082	111	2,227,000	119	74.8	28.9	2.2	1980	1,831,399	50.7	49.3	49.7
Papua New Guinea	178,704	462,840	51	3,400,000	104	19.0	7.3	2.1	1980	3,010,727	52.3	47.7	13.1
Paraguay	157,048	406,752	54	3,531,000	103	22.5	8.7	3.6	1982	3,035,360	50.1	49.9	42.8
Peru	496,225	1,285,216	19	20,207,000	40	40.7	15.7	2.6	1981	17,005,210	49.7	50.3	64.9
Philippines	115,800	300,000	66	56,004,000	16	483.6	186.7	2.5	1980	48,098,460	50.2	49.8	37.3
Pitcairn Island	1.8	4.5	214	64	215	35.6	14.2	2.0	1985	58	54.7[11]	45.3[11]	—
Poland	120,727	312,683	64	37,456,000	26	310.3	119.8	0.9	1978	35,061,450	48.7	51.3	57.5
Portugal	35,672	92,389	107	10,250,000	61	287.3	110.9	0.8	1981[3]	9,833,014	48.2	51.8	29.7
Puerto Rico	3,515	9,104	148	3,286,000	107	934.9	360.9	0.3	1980	3,196,520	48.7	51.3	66.8
Qatar	4,400	11,400	143	311,000	153	70.7	27.3	3.7	1981	244,534	63.6	36.4	86.1[2]
Réunion	982	2,544	156	556,000	140	565.8	218.4	1.7	1982[3]	515,798	49.1	50.9	52.8
Romania	91,700	237,500	79	22,809,000	34	248.7	96.0	0.4	1977	21,559,910	49.3	50.7	47.5
Rwanda	10,169	26,338	131	6,336,000	85	623.1	240.6	3.5	1978	4,830,984	48.9	51.1	4.5
St. Christopher and Nevis	103	267	190	46,000	188	455.4	176.2	0.7	1980	43,309	48.1	51.9	37.1
St. Helena and Ascension	159	412	181	7,000	206	44.7	17.2	1.5	1976[39]	5,866	52.0	48.0	25.8
St. Lucia	238	617	171	140,000	166	588.2	226.9	2.1	1980	120,300	47.2	52.8	...
St. Pierre and Miquelon	93	242	193	6,000	208	64.5	24.8	0.0	1982	6,041	49.4	50.6	...
St. Vincent and the Grenadines	150	389	182	111,000	170	740.0	285.3	1.3	1980	97,845	48.5[2]	51.5[2]	25.7[2]
San Marino	24	61	205	23,000	195	958.3	377.0	1.2	1976	19,149	50.4	49.6	92.4[40]
São Tomé and Príncipe	386	1,001	163	110,000	171	285.0	109.9	2.7	1981	96,611	49.7	50.3	...
Saudi Arabia	865,000	2,240,000	12	11,670,000	56	13.5	5.2	3.9	1974	6,726,466	53.2	46.8	65.9[2]
Senegal	75,955	196,722	82	6,699,000	80	88.2	34.1	2.7	1976	4,907,057	49.5	50.5	26.7
Seychelles	175	453	178	66,000	181	377.1	145.7	0.6	1977	61,898	50.4	49.6	37.2
Sierra Leone	27,699	71,740	112	3,733,000	100	134.8	52.0	1.9	1985	3,517,530	49.6	50.4	24.5[2]
Singapore	239	618	170	2,588,000	114	10,828.5	4,187.7	1.2	1980	2,413,945	51.0	49.0	100.0
Solomon Islands	10,640	27,556	129	277,000	154	26.0	10.0	3.5	1976	196,823	52.2	47.8	9.3
Somalia	246,000	637,000	41	5,992,000	87	24.4	9.4	2.8	1975	3,253,024[1]	49.8[2]	50.2[2]	...
South Africa	470,413	1,218,363	24	33,704,000	27	71.6	27.7	2.5	1980	24,208,140	51.0[41]	49.0[41]	53.2[42]
Bophuthatswana	15,444	40,000	—	1,564,000	—	101.3	39.1	2.7	1980	1,287,814	46.9[21]	53.1[21]	14.2[21]
Ciskei	2,080	5,386	—	798,000	—	383.8	148.2	2.7	1980	677,820	47.0	53.0	19.6[21]
Transkei	16,816	43,553	—	2,755,000	—	163.9	63.3	2.8	1980	2,334,946	41.2[21]	58.8[21]	3.2[21]
Venda	2,393	6,198	—	448,000	—	187.3	72.3	5.8	1985	459,986	38.1[21]	61.9[21]	0.3[21]
South West Africa/Namibia	317,818	823,144	33	1,204,000	128	3.8	1.5	3.4	1981	1,031,927	49.2	50.8	26.0
Spain	194,885	504,750	48	38,818,000	24	199.2	76.9	0.6	1981	37,746,260	49.1	50.9	72.8[2]
Sri Lanka	25,332	65,610	114	16,087,000	47	635.0	245.2	1.5	1981	14,848,364	50.8	49.2	21.5
Sudan, The	966,757	2,503,890	9	24,603,000	32	25.4	9.8	3.9	1983	20,564,364	50.8	49.2	19.7[2]
Suriname	63,251	163,820	86	395,000	146	6.2	2.4	2.3	1980	354,860	49.5	50.5	44.8[2]
Swaziland	6,704	17,364	139	682,000	138	101.7	39.2	3.3	1976	494,534	46.7	53.3	15.2
Sweden	187,901	486,661	49	8,358,000	71	44.5	17.2	0.1	1984[14]	8,342,621	49.4	50.6	83.1[37]
Switzerland	15,943	41,293	121	6,556,000	82	411.2	158.8	0.4	1980[43]	6,365,960	48.9	51.1	57.1
Syria	71,498	185,180	83	10,612,000	59	148.4	57.3	3.3	1981	9,052,628	51.1	48.9	47.0
Taiwan	13,900	36,002	123	19,439,000	41	1,398.5	539.9	1.6	1980[3]	17,968,797	52.2	47.8	70.6[2]
Tanzania	364,881	945,037	30	22,463,000	36	61.6	23.8	3.2	1978	17,512,611	49.0	51.0	13.8
Thailand	198,115	513,115	47	52,654,000	18	265.8	102.6	1.9	1980	44,824,540	49.8	50.2	17.0
Togo	21,925	56,785	115	3,072,000	108	140.1	54.1	2.8	1981	2,705,250	48.7	51.3	15.2
Tokelau	4.7	12.2	212	1,600	213	340.4	131.4	0.4	1981	1,572	49.4	50.6	—
Tonga	288	747	167	98,000	172	340.3	131.2	0.9	1984	96,592	51.1[29]	48.9[29]	24.7[29]
Trinidad and Tobago	1,978	5,124	151	1,202,000	129	607.1	234.4	1.7	1980	1,079,791	50.0	50.0	56.9[2]
Tunisia	59,664	154,530	87	7,327,000	76	122.8	47.4	2.2	1984	6,975,450	50.8	49.2	52.8
Turkey	300,948	779,452	36	52,419,000	19	174.2	67.3	2.9	1985	50,664,558	50.7[37]	49.3[37]	53.7
Turks and Caicos Islands	193	500	174	9,000	203	44.6	17.2	2.5	1980	7,413	48.3	51.7	—
Tuvalu	9	24	208	8,000	204	911.1	341.7	1.5	1984	8,229	46.8[44]	53.2[44]	...
Uganda	93,100	241,140	77	15,638,000	50	168.0	64.9	3.4	1980	12,636,179	49.5	50.5	8.1
U.S.S.R.	8,649,500	22,402,200	1	280,038,000	3	32.4	12.5	0.9	1979	262,436,227	46.6	53.4	62.3
United Arab Emirates	30,000	77,700	110	1,700,000	123	56.7	21.9	9.2	1985	1,622,464	64.9	35.1	80.8[11]
United Kingdom	94,248	244,100	76	56,679,000	15	601.4	232.2	0.1	1981[45]	56,379,000	48.6	51.4	89.6
United States	3,623,461	9,384,721	4	241,489,000	4	66.6	25.7	1.0	1980[46]	226,545,805	48.6	51.4	73.7
Uruguay	68,037	176,215	85	3,035,000	109	44.6	17.2	0.7	1975	2,788,429	49.0	51.0	83.0
Vanuatu	4,706	12,189	141	137,000	167	29.1	11.2	3.3	1979	111,251	53.1	46.9	17.8
Venezuela	352,144	912,050	32	17,791,000	42	50.5	19.5	2.8	1981	14,516,735	50.0	50.0	85.7
Vietnam	128,052	331,653	60	61,218,000	12	478.1	184.6	2.2	1979	52,741,766	48.5	51.5	19.2
Virgin Islands (U.S.)	136	352	185	114,000	169	838.2	304.0	3.0	1980	96,569	47.8	52.2	29.6
Wallis and Futuna	106	274	189	14,000	199	132.1	51.1	4.5	1983	12,408	50.5	49.5	...
West Bank	2,270	5,900	149	815,000	134	359.0	138.1	2.3	1983[14]	767,300	49.9	50.1	...
Western Sahara	103,000	266,769	72	150,000	165	1.5	0.6	1.4	1970	76,425	...	...	...
Western Samoa	1,093	2,831	154	160,000	163	146.4	56.5	0.6	1981	156,349	51.8	48.2	21.2
Yemen (Aden)	130,066	336,870	59	2,365,000	116	18.2	7.0	3.1	1973	1,590,275	49.5	50.5	33.3
Yemen (Ṣan'ā')	52,213	135,230	90	7,046,000	78	134.9	52.1	2.8	1985	9,274,173[47]	47.3[11]	52.7[11]	10.2[11]
Yugoslavia	98,766	255,804	73	23,289,000	33	235.8	91.0	0.7	1981	22,424,711	49.4	50.6	47.3
Zaire	905,365	2,344,885	11	31,079,000	28	34.4	13.3	2.1	1984	29,671,407	49.2	50.8	44.2[48]
Zambia	290,586	752,614	37	6,896,000	79	23.7	9.2	3.4	1980	5,679,808	49.0	51.0	43.0
Zimbabwe	150,873	390,759	55	8,553,000	69	56.7	21.9	3.0	1982	7,532,000	49.3	50.7	23.0

age distribution (%)						population (by decade, '000s)								country
0–14	15–29	30–44	45–59	60–74	75 and older	1930	1940	1950	1960	1970	1980	1990 projection	2000 projection	
20.2	23.2	20.9	14.5	14.8	6.5	2,807	2,973	3,265	3,581	3,877	4,086	4,214	4,319	Norway
45.2[2]	25.8[2]	15.6[2]	8.8[2]	3.9[2]	0.7[2]	...	...	390	494	657	984	1,457	1,973	Oman
50.5	25.2	12.1	7.0	4.2	1.0	10	...	11	15	22	31	41	52	Pacific Is., Trust Territory of the Marshall Islands
46.4	26.8	12.6	8.5	4.5	1.1	32	...	30	40	57	73	109	154	Micronesia, Federated States of
40.6	27.9	17.8	9.2	3.8	0.8	9	48	6	9	10	17	24	34	Northern Mariana Islands
39.9	28.7	14.0	9.8	5.8	1.9	8	25	6	9	11	12	12	12	Palau
44.5	23.9	15.4	9.3	5.3	1.6	23,600	28,300	36,450	45,851	64,449	86,143	112,226	140,961	Pakistan
39.1	28.1	16.7	9.5	5.1	1.5	523	620	800	1,082	1,458	1,956	2,420	2,979	Panama
43.0	25.9	17.0	10.4	3.5	0.2	1,306	1.308	1,613	1,920	2,419	2,999	3,691	4,544	Papua New Guinea
41.1	28.1	15.4	9.1	4.8	1.5	880	1,111	1,371	1,778	2,290	2,883	3,823	5,198	Paraguay
41.2	27.9	15.6	9.3	4.4	1.6	5,752	6,784	7,975	9,993	13,248	17,300	22,392	28,944	Peru
42.0	28.5	15.6	8.6	4.3	1.0	13,094	16,459	20,988	27,561	36,850	48,317	61,480	74,057	Philippines
32.1[11]	13.2[11]	18.9[11]	13.2[11]	9.4[11]	13.2[11]	0.19	0.20	0.14	0.14	0.09	0.06	...	...	Pitcairn Island
23.9	27.4	18.5	16.9	9.9	3.4	29,500	31,500	24,824	29,561	32,657	35,578	38,967	41,217	Poland
25.5	23.5	18.0	17.2	11.9	3.9	6,804	7,696	8,405	8,826	9,040	9,778	10,450	10,748	Portugal
31.6	26.4	18.5	12.3	8.3	2.9	1,552	1,880	2,219	2,358	2,718	3,206	3,320	3,424	Puerto Rico
32.3	31.8	25.8	7.8	—2.3—		...	...	47	59	151	246	354	469	Qatar
35.6	29.8	—27.6—		—6.9—		198	221	244	338	447	507	595	706	Réunion
25.7	23.7	19.6	17.1	10.9	3.0	14,141	15,907	16,311	18,407	20,799	22,201	23,994	25,728	Romania
46.6[2]	26.0[2]	14.4[2]	8.5[2]	3.8[2]	0.7[2]	...	...	2,189	2,740	3,679	5,144	7,105	9,845	Rwanda
37.2	30.4	9.5	9.4	10.0	3.5	38	43	49	51	46	44	50	53	St. Christopher and Nevis
34.0	27.5	16.7	10.8	8.4	2.6	4	5	5	5	5	6	7	7	St. Helena and Ascension
49.6	21.3	11.6	9.8	5.5	2.2	60	70	79	94	100	124	151	184	St. Lucia
28.7	26.0	20.4	13.2	8.5	3.2	4	4	5	5	5	6	6	6	St. Pierre and Miquelon
41.7[2]	33.3[2]	11.5[2]	7.3[2]	5.2[2]	1.0[2]	53	61	67	80	86	103	117	133	St. Vincent and the Grenadines
24.4	23.0	19.9	17.4	11.4	3.9	10	10	13	15	19	21	23	25	San Marino
46.3	25.0	11.6	10.0	5.3	1.8	...	60	60	64	74	93	114	144	São Tomé and Príncipe
46.7	23.9	15.2	7.9	—6.3—		...	...	3,200	4,175	6,120	9,229	13,724	20,327	Saudi Arabia
43.1	26.2	15.3	9.1	4.6	1.5	...	...	2,600	3,076	4,267	5,687	7,430	9,747	Senegal
39.6	26.3	14.0	10.8	6.8	2.1	27	32	34	42	54	63	70	82	Seychelles
40.7[13]	24.8[13]	17.4[13]	9.2[13]	—7.9[13]—		...	...	1,809	2,165	2,692	3,333	3,968	4,867	Sierra Leone
27.0	34.7	19.8	11.3	5.9	1.3	596	751	1,022	1,639	2,075	2,414	2,708	3,036	Singapore
47.8	24.1	14.5	8.4	3.6	1.3	94	94	104	125	163	225	319	459	Solomon Islands
44.2[2]	26.3[2]	15.7[2]	9.1[2]	4.0[2]	0.7[2]	...	...	1,826	2,226	2,790	5,074	6,476	7,134	Somalia
37.7[42]	—46.3[42]—		—14.7[42]—		1.3[42]	8,541	10,353	12,458	15,925	22,460	29,057	36,754	46,918	South Africa
52.6[21]	21.3[21]	10.4[21]	—13.6[21]—		2.1[21]	...	...	...	...	880	1,335	1,741	2,273	Bophuthatswana
48.5[21]	22.9[21]	12.4[21]	—14.6[21]—		1.6[21]	...	...	...	...	530	681	888	1,159	Ciskei
43.7[21]	21.5[21]	13.3[21]	—20.3[21]—		1.2[21]	...	...	...	...	1,746	2,336	3,078	4,057	Transkei
43.3[21]	20.3[21]	12.4[21]	—22.7[21]—		1.3[21]	...	...	...	...	269	317	567	1,015	Venda
44.0[2]	25.8[2]	15.6[2]	9.3[2]	4.4[2]	0.9[2]	283	336	405	522	761	989	1,360	1,822	South West Africa/ Namibia
25.6[3]	23.2[3]	17.9[3]	17.6[3]	11.4[3]	4.2[3]	23,445	25,757	27,868	30,303	33,779	37,386	39,517	41,027	Spain
35.3	29.6	17.9	10.6	5.2	1.4	5,253	5,972	7,678	9,889	12,514	14,750	17,719	20,767	Sri Lanka
44.1[2]	26.3[2]	15.9[2]	9.0[2]	4.0[2]	0.7[2]	7,500	8,500	9,322	11,256	14,090	19,559	24,950	32,885	Sudan, The
39.3	29.5	13.8	10.0	4.5	2.8	170	193	215	247	292	355	422	505	Suriname
47.7	25.2	13.7	7.9	3.7	1.4	139	154	253	320	409	559	828	1,098	Swaziland
18.2	20.7	22.0	16.1	15.7	7.3	6,142	6,371	7,041	7,498	8,081	8,310	8,345	8,329	Sweden
19.2	23.1	22.0	17.4	12.7	5.6	4,066	4,234	4,715	5,429	6,270	6,385	6,660	6,870	Switzerland
47.3[2]	27.5[2]	12.5[2]	8.0[2]	3.6[2]	1.1[2]	...	2,597	3,495	4,561	6,305	8,704	12,774	17,085	Syria
32.1	32.1	16.5	12.6	5.7	1.0	4,614	5,987	7,619	10,792	14,676	17,642	20,518	23,578	Taiwan
46.2	24.9	14.4	8.5	4.5	1.6	...	...	7,892	10,073	13,273	18,580	25,635	36,008	Tanzania
38.3	30.1	16.1	10.1	4.3	1.1	11,838	15,296	20,010	26,392	35,745	46,961	56,796	68,558	Thailand
46.1[2]	24.5[2]	15.2[2]	9.0[2]	4.2[2]	1.0[2]	750	834	1,201	1,465	1,954	2,601	3,507	4,688	Togo
42.9	22.5	12.7	10.2	7.2	4.5	1.1	1.3	1.5	1.8	1.7	1.6	1.6	1.6	Tokelau
44.4[29]	26.2[29]	14.8[29]	9.5[29]	4.0[29]	1.1[29]	28	37	50	65	80	93	122	139	Tonga
34.2	30.9	16.3	10.0	6.2	1.7	408	503	668	828	941	1,082	1,262	1,410	Trinidad and Tobago
39.7	28.8	14.2	10.7	5.4	1.2	2,381	2,887	3,530	4,221	5,137	6,392	7,989	9,856	Tunisia
39.0[37]	27.7[37]	15.5[37]	10.9[37]	5.0[37]	1.5[37]	14,448	17,723	20,809	27,509	35,321	44,422	54,663	67,166	Turkey
41.4	26.7	11.8	11.0	7.0	2.2	5	6	6	6	6	7	9	10	Turks and Caicos Islands
31.8[44]	31.7[44]	15.2[44]	13.2[44]	6.3[44]	1.7[44]	4	4	5	5	6	8	9	10	Tuvalu
47.8[2]	25.1[2]	14.7[2]	8.1[2]	3.6[2]	0.7[2]	...	...	5,969	7,551	9,806	12,786	17,852	24,856	Uganda
24.4[2]	26.6[2]	19.1[2]	16.9[2]	9.6[2]	3.4[2]	179,000	195,000	180,075	214,335	241,700	265,542	290,155	310,236	U.S.S.R.
28.9[2]	36.0[2]	24.4[2]	7.5[2]	2.6[2]	0.6[2]	...	...	70	90	223	980	2,419	5,846	United Arab Emirates
20.6	22.8	19.4	16.9	14.4	5.8	46,038	48,226	50,290	52,372	55,632	56,314	57,900	59,600	United Kingdom
22.6	27.4	19.1	15.2	11.3	4.4	123,616	132,594	152,271	180,671	204,879	227,757	249,657	267,955	United States
27.0	22.6	19.2	16.9	10.8	3.5	1,734	1,974	2,194	2,531	2,824	2,908	3,128	3,364	Uruguay
45.3	27.5	15.0	7.7	3.4	1.1	...	43	52	65	86	115	156	216	Vanuatu
40.5	29.9	15.8	8.7	4.0	1.1	2,980	3,740	5,145	7,635	10,559	15,020	19,638	25,138	Venezuela
41.7[2]	26.1[2]	16.0[2]	10.4[2]	4.9[2]	0.9[2]	...	...	24,600	30,200	40,064	53,772	68,338	82,709	Vietnam
36.0	24.2	21.5	11.1	5.7	1.4	22	25	27	32	75	97	129	160	Virgin Islands (U.S.)
45.8	24.8	13.8	9.0	5.7	0.9	...	...	7	8	9	11	17	26	Wallis and Futuna
—46.2	29.6	10.1	8.7	—5.5—		...	...	...	...	608	722	899	1,144	West Bank
42.9	27.2	16.3	7.4	4.4	1.8	...	...	14	32	76	135	178	229	Western Sahara
44.3	29.1	12.2	9.0	3.8	1.0	45	61	82	111	143	155	166	175	Western Samoa
47.3	20.8	15.8	8.6	—6.6—		...	...	907	1,109	1,436	1,969	2,459	3,312	Yemen (Aden)
45.7[11]	23.2[11]	15.1[11]	10.5[11]	4.7[11]	0.8[11]	...	...	3,622	4,429	4,840	5,981	7,925	10,881	Yemen (Ṣan'ā')
24.5	25.0	19.8	18.3	8.3	3.5	14,360	16,425	16,346	18,402	20,371	22,304	24,107	25,653	Yugoslavia
45.2[48]	26.0[48]	15.5[48]	8.7[48]	3.9[48]	0.7[48]	8,764	10,370	13,055	16,151	21,368	27,406	34,138	42,980	Zaire
47.1[2]	25.8[2]	14.7[2]	8.2[2]	3.6[2]	0.6[2]	1,272	1,484	2,473	3,219	4,295	5,648	7,838	10,945	Zambia
51.0	26.3	13.4	6.5	1.2	1.6	1,100	1,461	2,276	3,538	5,308	7,140	10,503	15,132	Zimbabwe

1Settled population only. 21980 estimate. 3Data are for de jure population. 41982 estimate. 5Includes residents abroad, excludes visitors. 6Excludes institutional population. 7Excludes institutional population, residents abroad, and visitors. 81975 census. 9Includes residents abroad and visitors. 10Excludes visitors. 111981 census. 121973 census. 131974 census. 14Civil register; not a census. 151984 register. 161983 estimate. 17Excludes the Sinai and residents abroad. 18Excludes marine detachment. 19Excludes visitors, transients, and family members of British servicemen. 201984 estimate. 211970 census. 22Data exclude Alderney (1981 estimated population 2,100) and Sark (1981 estimated population 500). 23Excludes residents abroad, visitors, and Vietnamese refugees. 24Excluding territory occupied after 1967. 25Includes East Jerusalem and Israeli residents in the occupied territories. 26Excluding West Bank. 271962 census. 28No census ever taken. 291976 census. 301977 census. 311967 census. 32Island of Mauritius only. 331978 census. 34Including 163,868 in Western Sahara. 35Indigenous population only. 36A census was taken in 1973, but the results were repudiated. 371980 census. 38Excludes Afghan refugees. 39Excludes the island of Tristan da Cunha and military personnel. 401981 estimate. 41Excludes Bophuthatswana, Ciskei, Transkei, and Venda. 42Excludes Bophuthatswana, Transkei, and Venda. 43Includes resident aliens; excludes seasonal workers. 441979 census. 45Includes residents abroad and foreign military personnel; excludes visitors. 46Excludes 515,000 armed forces overseas. 47Includes nationals abroad. 481985 estimate.

Major cities and national capitals

The following table lists the principal cities and municipalities (those exceeding 100,000 in population) of the countries of the world, together with figures for each of their national capitals (indicated by a ★), regardless of size.

Most of the populations given refer to a so-called city proper, that is, a legally defined, incorporated or chartered area defined by administrative boundaries and by national or state law as a "city" (in some cases, only as a locality that is "urban" in nature, or perhaps, in the smallest countries, simply as "the settlement"). There are many variations on this basic concept, however. One that is encountered frequently is the municipality, or commune, similar to the medieval city-state in that the city is governed together with its immediately adjoining, economically dependent areas, whether urban or rural in nature. Some countries define no other demographic or legal entities within such communes or municipalities, but many identify a centre, seat, head (*cabecera*), or locality that corresponds to the most densely populated, compact, contiguous core of the municipality. Secondary centres may also be defined, and in certain countries these may be places of considerable size, depending on how long the municipality's boundaries have gone unchanged. The amount of work involved in defining these "centres" carefully may be very great, and usually the necessary manpower, employment and commuting data, and cartographic resources exist only at the time of a national census (generally five or ten years apart). Between censuses, therefore, it may be possible only to track the growth of the municipality as a whole. Thus, in order to provide the most up-to-date data for cities in this table, figures referring to municipalities or communes may be given (identified by the abbreviation "MU"), even though the country itself may define a smaller, more closely knit city proper. Specific identification of municipalities is provided in this table *only* when the country also publishes data for a more narrowly defined city proper; it is *not* provided when the sole published figure is the municipality, whether or not this is the proper local administrative term for the entity.

Since many national capitals are first-order administrative subdivisions (equivalent to a U.S. state) in their national hierarchy of local government, some care has to be taken to provide data referring to the actual urban core of the subdivision (the demographic "city proper"). Thus, data are provided for the city of Brasília, or Kuala Lumpur, but not for the national or federal capital areas that contain them. Problems also exist in the identification of cities in terms of named legal entities. There is, for example, a single municipality (*commune*) named Brussel (Brussels) at the centre of the Brussels agglomeration in Belgium; the *commune* numbers only about 140,000 population, while the agglomeration, which is understood by most people to constitute the city, numbers nearly a million. Both are shown so as to apprise the reader of the existence of a problem.

For certain countries, more than one form of the name of the city is given, usually to permit recognition of recent place name changes or of *forms* of the place name likely to be encountered in press stories if the title of the city's entry in the *Encyclopædia Britannica* is spelled according to a different romanization or spelling policy. One such case is China, for which city names are spelled first according to a long-established scholarly system called Wade–Giles, while current press references are likely to be spelled according to the more recent Chinese romanization system, Pinyin. (Peking in Wade–Giles, for example, would be spelled Pei-ching; in Pinyin, Beijing.) The use of the conventional Western spelling Peking in this table is supplemented by provision of the Pinyin alternative spelling.

Sources for this data were usually the national census and statistical abstracts of the countries concerned, supplemented by correspondence with most national statistical offices to solicit data not yet issued as part of the national publishing program.

Major cities and national capitals

country city	population
Afghanistan (1984 est.)	
Baghlān	119,549
Charikar	117,496
Feyzābād	152,345
Herāt	159,804
Jalālābād	126,279
★ Kābul	1,179,341
Kandahar	310,720
Mazār-e Sharīf	117,723
Qandahār	310,720
Qonduz	174,168
Shebarghān	109,654
Taloqān	150,530
Albania (1983 est.)	
★ Tiranë	206,100
Algeria (1983 est.)	
★ Algiers	1,721,607
Annaba	348,322
Batna	122,788
Bejaïa	124,122
Blida (el-Boulaida)	191,314
Boufarik	112,000[1]
ech-Cheliff	118,996
Constantine (Qacentina)	448,578
Oran (Wahran)	663,504
Sétif	186,978
Sidi bel Abbes	146,653
Skikda	141,159
Tizi Ouzou	100,749
Tlemcen (Tilimsen)	146,089
American Samoa (1985 est.)	
★ Pago Pago	3,400
Andorra (1986)	
★ Andorra la Vella	15,639
Angola (1982 est.)	
★ Luanda	1,200,000
Lubango	105,000[2]
Namibe (Moçamedes)	100,000
Anguilla (1974)	
★ The Valley	760
Antigua and Barbuda (1982 est.)	
★ Saint John's	30,000
Argentina (1980)	
Almirante Brown	332,548
Avellaneda	330,654
Bahía Blanca	220,765
Berazategui	200,926
★ Buenos Aires	2,922,829
Caseros	340,343
Córdoba	968,829
Corrientes	180,612
Esteban Echeverría	187,969
Florencio Varela	172,654
General San Martín	384,306
General Sarmiento	499,648
Godoy Cruz	141,553
Guaymallén	157,334
Lanús	465,891
La Plata	454,884
Lomas de Zamora	508,620

country city	population
Mar del Plata	407,024
Mendoza	118,427
Merlo	282,828
Moreno	193,626
Morón	596,769
Paraná	161,638
Posadas	143,889
Quilmes	441,780
Resistencia	218,438
Río Cuarto	110,254
Rosario	875,664
Salta	260,744
San Fernando	134,156
San Isidro	287,048
San Juan	117,731
San Justo	946,715
San Miguel de Tucumán	392,888
San Salvador de Jujuy	124,950
Santa Fe	287,240
Santiago del Estero	148,758
Tigre	205,926
Vicente López	289,815
Aruba (1980 est.)	
★ Oranjestad	20,000
Australia (1985 est.)[3]	
Adelaide	987,100
Brisbane	1,157,200
★ Canberra	273,600
Geelong	175,660
Gold Coast	208,100
Hobart	147,070[2]
Melbourne	2,916,600
Newcastle	423,300
Perth	1,001,000
Sydney	3,391,600
Townsville	101,680
Wollongong	236,800
Austria (1981)	
Graz	243,166
Innsbruck	117,287
Linz	199,910
Salzburg	139,426
★ Vienna	1,531,346
Bahamas, The (1982 est.)	
★ Nassau	135,000
Bahrain (1981)	
★ al-Manāmah	121,986
Bangladesh (1981)[5]	
Bākerganj (Barisāl)	159,298
Chittagong	1,388,476
Comilla	126,130
★ Dhākā (Dacca)	3,458,602
Jessore	149,426
Khulna	623,184
Mymensingh	107,863
Pābna	101,080
Rājshāhi	171,600
Rangpur	155,964
Saidpur	128,085
Sirājganj	104,522
Sylhet	166,847

country city	population
Barbados (1980)	
★ Bridgetown	7,552
Belgium (1984 est.)	
Antwerp	488,425
Brugge (Bruges)	118,146
★ Brussels	137,211
Agglomeration	982,434
Charleroi	213,041
Ghent	235,401
Liège (Luik)	203,065
Namur	101,861
Schaerbeek	105,346
Belize (1980)	
★ Belmopan	2,940
Benin (1982 est.)	
★ Cotonou (official)	487,020
★ Porto-Novo (de facto)	208,258
Bermuda (1985 est.)	
★ Hamilton	1,676
Bhutan (1985 est.)	
★ Paro (administrative)	3,000[6]
★ Thimphu (official)	20,000
Bolivia (1985 est.)	
Cochabamba	317,251
★ La Paz (administrative)	992,592
Oruro	178,393
Potosí	109,876[2]
Santa Cruz	441,717
★ Sucre (judicial)	84,505[2]
Botswana (1984 est.)	
★ Gaborone	79,000
Brazil (1980)	
Americana	121,794
Anápolis	160,520
Aracaju	288,106
Araçatuba	113,486
Barra Mansa	123,421
Bauru	178,861
Belém	758,117
Belo Horizonte	1,442,483
Blumenau	144,819
★ Brasília	411,305
Campina Grande	222,229
Campinas	566,517
Campo Grande	282,844
Campos	174,218
Canoas	214,115
Carapicuiba	185,763
Caruaru	137,636
Cascavel	100,351
Caxias do Sul	198,824
Contagem	111,697
Cuiabá	167,894
Curitiba	843,733
Diadema	228,594
Divinopolis	108,344
Duque de Caxias	306,057
Feira de Santana	225,003
Florianópolis	153,547
Fortaleza	648,815
Franca	143,630
Goiânia	703,263
Governador Valadares	173,699

country city	population
Guarulhos	395,117
Imperatriz	111,818
Ipatinga	105,083
Itabuna	129,938
Jacareí	103,652
João Pessoa	290,424
Joinville	217,074
Juàzeiro do Norte	125,248
Juiz de Fora	299,728
Jundiaí	210,015
Lages	108,768
Limeira	137,812
Londrina	258,054
Maceió	376,479
Manaus	613,068
Marília	103,904
Maringá	158,047
Mauá	205,817
Mogi das Cruzes	122,265
Montes Claros	151,881
Mossoró	118,007
Natal	376,552
Nilópolis	103,033
Niterói	386,185
Nova Iguaçu	491,802
Novo Hamburgo	132,066
Olinda	266,392
Osasco	473,856
Passo Fundo	103,121
Pelotas	197,092
Petrópolis	149,427
Piracicaba	179,395
Ponta Grossa	171,111
Porto Alegre	1,108,883
Porto Velho	101,644
Presidente Prudente	127,623
Recife	1,184,215
Ribeirao Prêto	300,704
Rio Claro	103,174
Rio de Janeiro	5,090,700
Rio Grande	124,706
Salvador	1,506,602
Santa Maria	151,202
Santarém	101,534
Santo Andre	549,278
Santos	411,023
São Bernardo do Campo	381,261
São Caetano do Sul	163,030
São Carlos	109,231
São Gonçalo	221,278
São João de Meriti	210,548
São José do Rio Prêto	171,982
São José dos Campos	268,073
São Luis	182,466
São Paulo	7,033,529
São Vicente	192,770
Sorocaba	254,718
Taubaté	155,371
Teresina	339,264
Uberaba	180,296
Uberlândia	230,400

country city	population
Vitória	144,143
Vitória da Conquista	125,717
Volta Redonda	177,772
British Virgin Islands (1980)	
★ Road Town	2,525
Brunei (1985 est.)	
★ Bandar Seri Begawan	55,000
Bulgaria (1983 est.)	
Burgas	178,239
Pleven	135,899
Plovdiv	367,195
Ruse	178,920
★ Sofia	1,082,815
Sliven	100,637
Stara Zagora	141,722
Varna	295,038
Burkina Faso (1985)	
Bobo Dioulasso	231,162
★ Ouagadougou	442,223
Burma (1983)	
Bassein	144,092
Mandalay	532,895
Monywa	106,873
Moulmein	219,991
Pegu	150,447
★ Rangoon	2,458,712
Sittwe (Akyab)	107,907
Taunggye	107,607
Burundi (1986 est.)	
★ Bujumbura	272,622
Cameroon (1985 est.)	
Douala	852,700
Maroua	100,200
Nkongsamba	105,200
★ Yaoundé	583,500
Canada (1981)	
Brampton	149,030
Burlington	114,853
Burnaby	136,494
Calgary	592,743
East York	101,974
Edmonton	532,246
Etobicoke	298,713
Halifax	114,594
Hamilton	306,434
Kitchener	139,734
Laval	268,335
London	254,280
Longueuil	124,320
Mississauga	315,056
Montreal	980,354
North York	559,521
Oshawa	117,519
★ Ottawa	295,163
Quebec	166,474
Regina	162,613
Saint Catharines	124,018
Saskatoon	154,210
Scarborough	443,353
Thunder Bay	112,486
Toronto	599,217
Vancouver	414,281

country / city	population
Windsor	192,083
Winnipeg	564,473
York	134,617
Cape Verde (1985 est.)	
★ Praia	49,500
Cayman Islands (1985 est.)	
★ George Town	9,300
Central African Republic (1985 est.)	
★ Bangui	473,817
Chad (1986 est.)	
★ N'Djamena	511,700
Sarh	100,000
Chile (1985 est.)	
Antofagasta	174,100
Arica	126,700
Chillán	127,600
Concepción	215,800
Iquique	118,700
Rancagua	149,700
★ Santiago	421,900
Greater Santiago	4,271,500
Talca	143,000
Talcahuano	218,900
Temuco	170,200
Valdívia	118,900
Valparaíso	266,900
Viña dal Mar	311,600
China (1985 est.)	
An-ch'ing (Anqing)	207,200
An-shan (Anshan)	1,088,900
An-shun (Anshun)	126,700
An-ta (Anda)	150,000
An-yang (Anyang)	348,100
Canton (Guangzhou)	2,486,100
Chan-chiang (Zhanjiang)	312,300
Ch'ang-chi (Changji)	100,800
Chang-chia-k'ou (Zhangjiakou)	483,200
Ch'ang-chih (Changzhi)	261,200
Ch'ang-chou (Changzhou)	446,900
Chang-chou (Zhangzhou)	155,300
Ch'ang-ch'un (Changchun)	1,424,500
Ch'ang-sha (Changsha)	919,200
Ch'ang-shu (Changshu)	245,600
Ch'ang-te (Changde)	170,500
Ch'ao-an (Chao'an)	130,000
Chao-ch'ing (Zhaoqing)	137,600
Ch'ao-chou (Chaozhou)	257,500
Ch'ao-hu (Chaohu)	111,500
Ch'ao-yang (Chaoyang)	168,200
Ch'ih-feng (Chifeng)	100,000
Chen-chiang (Zhenjiang)	319,300
Chen-chou (Chenzhou)	138,900
Cheng-chou (Zhengzhou)	962,500
Ch'eng-te (Chengde)	222,600
Ch'eng-tu (Chengdu)	1,523,400
Chi-an (Ji'an)	127,900
Chi-hsi (Jixi)	626,300
Chi-lin (Jilin)	882,700
Chi-nan (Jinan)	1,110,500
Chi-ning (Jining) (*Inner Mongolia*)	141,000
Chi-ning (Jining) (*Shantung*)	207,200
Ch'i-t'ai-ho (Qitaihe)	151,700
Chia-hsing (Jiaxing)	168,300
Chia-mu-ssu (Jiamusi)	419,700
Chiang-men (Jiangmen)	159,800
Chiao-tso (Jiaozuo)	320,000
Ch'ih-feng (Chifeng)	270,300
Chin-chou (Jinzhou)	584,800
Chin-hua (Jinhua)	132,600
Ch'in-huang-tao (Qinhuangdao)	293,900
Ch'ing-chiang (Qingjiang)	150,000
Ching-men (Jingmen)	211,700
Ch'ing-tao (Qingdao)	1,140,000
Ching-te-chen (Jingdezhen)	294,700
Chiu-chiang (Jiujiang)	243,900
Chou-k'ou (Zhoukou)	102,200
Chou-k'ou-chen (Zhoukouzhen)	150,000
Ch'u-ching (Qujing)	124,600
Chu-chou (Zhuzhou)	333,700
Ch'ü-chou (Quzhou)	102,100
Ch'u-chou (Chuzhou)	110,100
Ch'ü-hsien (Quxian)	120,000
Ch'üan-chou (Quanzhou)	150,000
Chungking (Chongqing)	2,030,800
Chung-shan (Zhongshan)	208,900
E-chou (Ezhou)	195,800
Feng-ch'eng (Fengcheng)	100,000
Fo-shan (Foshan)	229,700
Fu-chou (Fuzhou) (*Kiangsi*)	105,100
Fu-chou (Fuzhou)	754,500
Fu-hsin (Fuxin)	551,300
Fu-shun (Fushun)	1,077,300
Fu-yang (Fuyang)	118,900
Ha-mi (Hami)	141,100
Hai-k'ou (Haikou)	198,900
Hai-la-erh (Hailar)	149,000
Han-chung (Hanzhong)	148,900
Han-ku (Hangu)	100,000
Han-tan (Handan)	727,500
Hang-chou (Hangzhou)	973,400
Harbin	2,217,300
Heng-yang (Hengyang)	401,900
Ho-fei (Hefei)	594,200
Ho-kang (Hegang)	472,000
Ho-pi (Hebi)	156,000
Ho-tse (Heze)	109,300
Hsi-ch'ang (Xichang)	101,300
Hsi-ning (Xining)	473,000
Hsia-men (Xiamen)	328,100
Hsiang-fan (Xiangfan)	294,400
Hsiang-t'an (Xiangtan)	377,100
Hsiao-kan (Xiaogan)	109,000
Hsien-ning (Xianning)	124,600
Hsien-yang (Xianyang)	272,800
Hsin-hsiang (Xinxiang)	397,100
Hsin-t'ai (Xintai)	143,500
Hsin-yang (Xinyang)	159,800
Hsin-yu (Xinyu)	120,200
Hsing-t'ai (Xingtai)	251,400
Hsü-ch'ang (Xuchang)	156,700
Hsü-chou (Xuzhou)	709,400
Hsüan-hua (Xuanhua)	140,000
Hu-chou (Huzhou)	184,900
Hu-ho-hao-t'e (Hohhot)	542,800
Huai-nan (Huainan)	603,200
Huai-pei (Huaibei)	272,300
Huai-yin (Huaiyin)	191,700
Huang-shih (Huangshi)	380,200
Hui-chou (Huizhou)	107,700
Hun-chiang (Hunjiang)	436,100
I-ch'ang (Yichang)	317,100
I-ch'un (Yichun)	758,200
I-ning (Yining)	150,700
I-pin (Yibin)	214,400
I-yang (Yiyang)	150,900
K'ai-feng (Kaifeng)	447,800
Kan-chou (Ganzhou)	185,300
Kashgar (Kashi)	138,800
Ko-chiu (Gejiu)	189,900
K'o-erh-ch'in-yu-i-ch'ien-ch'i (Horqin Youyi Qianqi)	100,000
Kuei-lin (Guilin)	314,100
Kuei-yang (Guiyang)	871,300
K'un-ming (Kunming)	950,000
Lai-wu (Laiwu)	132,700
Lan-chou (Lanzhou)	1,144,500
Lang-fang (Langfang)	113,300
Le-shan (Leshan)	295,500
Leng-shui-chiang (Lengshuijiang)	150,000
Liao-ch'eng (Liaocheng)	114,800
Liao-yang (Liaoyang)	430,100
Liao-yüan (Liaoyuan)	319,100
Lien-yün-kang (Lianyungang)	277,400
Lin-fen (Linfen)	151,900
Lin-i (Linyi)	176,000
Liu-chou (Liuzhou)	501,000
Liu-p'an-shui (Liupanshui)	317,100
Lo-yang (Luoyang)	624,000
Long-yen (Longyan)	102,200
Lu-chou (Luzhou)	228,000
Lü-ta (Lüda)	1,270,000[7]
Ma-an-shan (Ma'anshan)	249,100
Man-chou-li (Manzhouli)	104,100
Mao-ming (Maoming)	103,100
Mei-hsien (Meixian)	154,600
Mien-yang (Mianyang)	220,700
Mu-tan-chiang (Mudanjiang)	486,900
Nan-ch'ang (Nanchang)	880,500
Nan-ch'ung (Nanchong)	149,900
Nan-ning (Nanning)	564,900
Nan-p'ing (Nanping)	153,000
Nan-t'ung (Nantong)	297,000
Nan-yang (Nanyang)	180,600
Nanking (Nanjing)	1,865,100
Nei-chiang (Neijiang)	179,500
Ning-po (Ningbo)	422,000
Pai-ch'eng (Baicheng)	193,500
Pang-pu (Bengbu)	390,900
Pao-chi (Baoji)	278,700
Pao-ting (Baoding)	411,300
Pao-t'ou (Baotou)	866,200
Pei-an (Bei'an)	197,400
Pei-hai (Beihai)	115,700
Pei-piao (Beipiao)	100,000
★ Peking (Beijing)	4,983,000
Pen-hsi (Benxi)	678,500
P'ing-hsiang (Pingxiang)	332,400
P'ing-ting-shan (Pingdingshan)	338,000
Po-shan (Boshan)	100,000
P'u-ling (Puling)	138,400
P'u-yang (Puyang)	113,700
San-ming (Sanming)	141,700
Sha-shih (Shashi)	213,400
Shan-t'ou (Shantou)	476,600
Shao-hsing (Shaoxing)	148,700
Shao-kuan (Shaoguan)	286,100
Shao-yang (Shaoyang)	210,900
Shang-ch'iu (Shangqiu)	129,800
Shang-jao (Shangrao)	111,200
Shanghai	6,725,700
Shen-chen (Shenzhen)	152,600
Shen-yang (Shenyang)	3,173,200
Shih-chia-chuang (Shijiazhuang)	902,000
Shih-ho-tzu (Shihezi)	294,500
Shih-tsui-shan (Shizuishan)	199,200
Shih-yen (Shiyan)	203,900
Shuang-ya-shan (Shuangyashan)	340,700
Ssu-p'ing (Siping)	274,400
Sian (Xi'an)	1,686,300
Su-chou (Suzhou) (*Anhui*)	114,400
Su-chou (Suzhou)	611,500
Sui-chou (Suizhou)	147,500
Sui-hua (Suihua)	195,800
Ta-ch'ing (Daqing)	500,900
Ta-hsien (Daxian)	132,500
Ta-li (Dali)	110,000
Ta-lien (Dalian)	1,334,300
Ta-t'ung (Datong)	688,200
T'ai-an (Tai'an)	194,500
T'ai-chou (Taizhou)	135,300
T'ai-yüan (Taiyuan)	1,355,900
Tan-tung (Dandong)	449,800
T'ang-shan (Tangshan)	921,100
Te-chou (Dezhou)	153,400
Te-yang (Deyang)	171,100
T'ieh-ling (Tieling)	313,000
T'ien-shui (Tianshui)	121,400
Tientsin (Tianjin)	4,123,800
Tsa-lan-t'un (Zalantun)	109,100
Ts'ang-chou (Cangzhou)	190,800
Tsao-chuang (Zaozhuang)	269,400
Tsitsihar (Qiqihar)	955,200
Tu-k'ou (Dukou)	355,900
Tu-yün (Duyun)	121,100
T'ung-ch'uan (Tongchuan)	234,300
T'ung-hua (Tonghua)	285,100
T'ung-liao (Tongliao)	184,400
T'ung-ling (Tongling)	169,500
Tung-ying (Dongying)	163,600
Tsun-i (Zunyi)	233,700
Tzu-kung (Zigong)	353,400
Tzu-po (Zibo)	762,500
Wan-hsien (Wanxian)	134,100
Wei-fang (Weifang)	296,500
Wei-nan (Weinan)	102,000
Wen-chou (Wenzhou)	365,600
Wu-chou (Wuzhou)	190,300
Wu-hai (Wuhai)	226,600
Wu-han (Wuhan)	2,899,000
Wu-hsi (Wuxi)	696,300
Wu-hu (Wuhu)	385,800
Wu-lu-mu-ch'i (Ürümqi)	947,000
Yang-chou (Yangzhou)	286,600
Ya-k'o-she (Yakeshe)	323,100
Yang-ch'üan (Yangquan)	291,400
Yen-an (Yan'an)	150,000
Yen-ch'eng (Yancheng)	248,300
Yen-chi (Yanji)	167,500
Yen-t'ai (Yantai)	311,200
Yin-ch'uan (Yinchuan)	256,200
Ying-k'ou (Yingkou)	355,700
Yü-lin (Yulin)	109,000
Yü-men (Yumen)	150,000
Yü-tz'u (Yuci)	168,600
Yüeh-yang (Yueyang)	228,300
Christmas Island (1980 est.)	
★ The Settlement at Flying Fish Cove	1,200
Cocos (Keeling) Islands (1981)	
★ West Island	380
Colombia (1985)	
Armenia	180,221
Barranquilla	896,649
Bello	212,861
★ Bogotá	3,982,941
Bucaramanga	341,513
Buenaventura	193,185
Cali	1,323,944
Cartagena	491,368
Cúcuta	357,026
Ibagué	269,495
Manizales	275,067
Medellín	1,418,554
Montería	157,466
Neiva	178,130
Palmira	214,395
Pasto	197,407
Pereira	233,271
Santa Marta	177,922
Comoros (1980)	
★ Moroni	17,267
Congo (1980)	
★ Brazzaville	422,400
Pointe-Noire	185,100
Cook Islands (1981)	
★ Rarotonga Island	9,530
Costa Rica (1984)	
★ San José	241,464
Côte d'Ivoire (Ivory Coast) (1983 est.)	
★ Abidjan	1,800,000
Bouaké	640,000[4]
Cuba (1985 est.)	
Bayamo	104,400
Camagüey	287,400
Cienfuegos	107,800
Guantánamo	172,500
Holguín	194,100
★ Havana	1,992,600
Matanzas	104,600
Santa Clara	176,900
Santiago de Cuba	356,000
Cyprus (1982)	
Limassol	100,254
★ Nicosia	123,298
Czechoslovakia (1985 est.)	
Bratislava	417,103
Brno	385,684
Košice	222,175
Liberec	100,048
Olomouc	105,516
Ostrava	327,791
Plzen	174,555
★ Prague	1,193,513
Denmark (1985)	
Ålborg	113,865
Århus	194,348
★ Copenhagen	1,358,540
Odense	136,803
Djibouti (1984 est.)	
★ Djibouti	200,000
Dominica (1981)	
★ Roseau	8,346
Dominican Republic (1983 est.)	
La Romana	101,000
Santiago de los Caballeros	285,000
★ Santo Domingo	1,410,000
Ecuador (1986 est.)	
Ambato	122,139
Cuenca	193,012
Guayaquil	1,509,108
Machala	105,283
Portoviejo	134,393
★ Quito	1,093,278
Egypt (1985 est.)	
Alexandria	2,821,000
Aswān	182,700
Asyūt	274,400
Banhā	115,500
Bani Suwayf	151,200
Būr Sa'īd (Port Said)	374,000
★ Cairo	6,205,000
Damanhūr	221,500
Damyāt	118,100
al-Fayyūm	218,500
Hulwan (Helwan)	345,600
al-Ismā'īlīyah	191,700
al-Jīzah (Giza)	1,608,400
Kafr ad-Dawwar	160,554[7]
al-Maḥallah al-Kubrā	362,700
al-Manṣūrah	328,700
al-Minya	191,800
Qinā	137,100
Sawhāj	131,300
Shibīn al-Kawm	129,600
Shubrā al-Khaymah	515,500
as-Suways (Suez)	254,000
Ṭanṭa	364,700
al-Uqṣur (Luxor)	137,300
az-Zaqāzīq	266,800
El Salvador (1984 est.)	
★ San Salvador	455,306
Santa Ana	135,186
Equatorial Guinea (1983 est.)	
★ Malabo	37,500
Ethiopia (1984)	
★ Addis Ababa	1,423,111
Asmera	275,385
Faeroe Islands (1984 est.)	
★ Tórshavn	14,443
Falkland Islands (1986 est.)	
★ Stanley	1,100
Fiji (1985 est.)	
★ Suva	75,000
Finland (1985 est.)	
Espoo	154,243
★ Helsinki	484,410
Tampere	168,271
Turku	161,540
Vantaa	143,188
France (1982)	
Aix-en-Provence	100,221
Amiens	130,302
Angers	135,293
Besançon	112,023
Bordeaux	201,965
Boulogne-Billancourt	102,582
Brest	154,110
Caen	112,332
Clermont-Ferrand	145,901
Dijon	139,188
Grenoble	156,437
Le Havre	198,700
Le Mans	145,976
Lille	167,791
Limoges	137,809
Lyon	410,455
Marseille	868,435
Metz	113,236
Montpellier	190,423
Mulhouse	111,742
Nantes	237,789
Nice	331,165
Nîmes	120,515
★ Paris	2,165,892
Perpignan	107,812
Reims	176,419
Rennes	190,861
Roubaix	101,488
Rouen	100,696
Saint-Étienne	193,938
Strasbourg	247,068
Toulon	177,443
Toulouse	344,917
Tours	131,265
Villeurbanne	115,378
French Guiana (1982)	
★ Cayenne	38,091
French Polynesia (1983)	
★ Papeete	23,496
Gabon (1983 est.)	
★ Libreville	257,000
Port Gentil	123,000
Gambia, The (1983)	
★ Banjul	44,188
Serekunda	102,600
Gaza Strip (1979 est.)	
Gaza (Ghazzah)	120,000
Germany, East (1985 est.)	
★ Berlin (East)	1,196,871
Cottbus	122,886
Dessau	103,816
Dresden	520,016
Erfurt	214,955
Gera	131,313
Halle	236,456
Jena	107,062
Karl-Marx-Stadt	317,210
Leipzig	555,764
Magdeburg	288,934
Potsdam	137,666
Rostock	241,910
Schwerin	126,390
Zwickau	120,063
Germany, West (1985 est.)	
Aachen	239,200
Augsburg	244,200
Bergisch Gladbach	101,000
Berlin (West)	1,852,700
Bielefeld	300,800
Bochum	383,200
★ Bonn	292,600
Bottrop	112,300
Braunschweig	250,700
Bremen	528,900

Major cities and national capitals (continued)

country city	population
Bremerhaven	134,500
Cologne (Köln)	919,300
Darmstadt	134,600
Dortmund	575,200
Duisburg	520,200
Düsseldorf	563,000
Erlangen	100,000
Essen	622,000
Frankfurt am Main	598,000
Freiburg im Breisgau	182,200
Gelsenkirchen	286,500
Göttingen	132,100
Hagen	206,700
Hamburg	1,585,900
Hamm	166,500
Hannover	510,800
Heidelberg	133,800
Heilbronn	111,200
Herne	172,300
Hildesheim	100,900
Karlsruhe	268,400
Kassel	184,500
Kiel	245,300
Koblenz	111,100
Krefeld	217,000
Leverkusen	155,200
Lübeck	211,000
Ludwigshafen	154,500
Mainz	188,200
Mannheim	295,200
Mönchengladbach	255,100
Mülheim an der Ruhr	172,600
Munich (München)	1,266,100
Münster	273,000
Neuss	143,600
Nürnberg	466,100
Oberhausen	223,000
Offenbach am Main	107,200
Oldenburg	138,400
Osnabrück	153,300
Paderborn	109,800
Pforzheim	104,100
Recklinghausen	117,800
Regensburg	125,600
Remscheid	121,500
Saarbrücken	187,600
Salzgitter	106,600
Siegen	107,500
Solingen	157,900
Stuttgart	561,200
Wiesbaden	267,000
Witten	102,100
Wolfsburg	122,000
Wuppertal	378,100
Würzburg	129,400
Ghana (1984 est.)	
★ Accra	859,640
Kumasi	348,880
Tamale	136,800
Gibraltar (1986 est.)	
★ Gibraltar	28,843
Greece (1981)	
★ Athens	885,737
Iráklion	102,398
Kallithéa	117,319
Larissa	102,426
Pátrai (Patras)	142,163
Peristérion	140,858
Piraiévs (Piraeus)	196,389
Thessaloníki	406,413
Greenland (1985 est.)	
★ Godthåb (Nuuk)	10,559
Grenada (1980 est.)	
★ Saint George's	7,500
Guadeloupe (1982)	
★ Basse-Terre	13,656
Guam (1980)	
★ Agana	896
Guatemala (1981)	
★ Guatemala City	754,243
Guernsey (1976)	
★ St. Peter Port	16,982
Guinea (1983)	
★ Conakry	705,280
Guinea-Bissau (1979)	
★ Bissau	105,273
Guyana (1976 est.)	
★ Georgetown	72,049
Haiti (1986 est.)	
★ Port-au-Prince	457,564
Honduras (1985 est.)	
San Pedro Sula	372,800
★ Tegucigalpa	571,400
Hong Kong (1986 est.)	
Hong Kong	5,532,600[8]
Hungary (1986 est.)	
★ Budapest	2,080,000
Debrecen	212,000
Györ	129,000
Kecskemét	103,000
Miskolc	212,000
Nyíregyháza	118,000
Pecs	177,000
Szeged	183,000
Székesfehérvár	112,000
Iceland (1984 est.)	
★ Reykjavík	88,745
India (1981)	
Ādoni	108,939
Agartala	132,186
Āgra	694,191
Ahmadābād	2,059,725
Ahmadnagar	143,937
Ajmer	375,593
Akola	225,412
Alīgarh	320,861
Allahābād	616,051
Alleppey	169,940
Alwar	145,795
Ambāla	104,565
Ambattur	114,915
Amrāvati	261,404
Amritsar	594,844
Amroha	112,682
Anantapur	119,531
Arrah	125,111
Asansol	183,375
Aurangābād	284,607
Avadi	124,574
Bally	147,735
Bālurghāt	104,648
Bangalore	2,476,355
Baranagar	170,343
Bareilly	386,734
Barrackpur	115,253
Belgaum	274,430
Bellary	201,579
Bhāgalpur	225,062
Bharatpur	105,274
Bharūch	110,070
Bhatinda	124,453
Bhātpāra	260,761
Bhavnagar	307,121
Bhilai (Nagar)	290,090
Bhīlwāra	122,625
Bhimavaram	101,894
Bhiwandi	115,298
Bhiwāni	101,277
Bhopāl	671,018
Bhubaneswar	219,211
Bhusāwal	123,133
Bihār	151,343
Bijāpur	147,313
Bīkaner	253,174
Bilāspur	147,218
Bokaro Steel City	224,099
Bombay (Greater)	8,243,405
Brahmapur	162,550
Bulandshahr	103,436
Burdwān	167,364
Burhānpur	140,986
Calcutta	3,305,006
Chandernagore	101,925
Chandīgarh	373,789
Chandrapur	115,777
Chāpra	111,564
Cochin	513,249
Coimbatore	704,514
Cuddalore	127,625
Cuddapah	103,125
Cuttack	269,950
Darbhanga	176,301
Dāvangere	196,621
Dehra Dūn	211,416
Delhi	4,884,234
Dhānbād	120,221
Dhārwār-Hubli	527,108
Dhūlia	210,759
Dindigul	164,103
Dombivli	103,222
Durg	114,637
Durgāpur	311,798
Elūru	168,154
Erode	142,252
Etāwah	212,174
Faizābād	101,873
Farīdābād	330,864
Farrukhābād-Fatehgarh	145,793
Firozābād	202,338
Gadag-Betigeri	117,368
Gangānagar	123,692
Garden Reach	191,107
Gaya	247,075
Ghāziābād	271,730
Gondia	100,423
Gorakhpur	290,814
Gulbarga	221,325
Guntūr	367,699
Gwalior	539,015
Hāpur	102,837
Hardwār	114,180
Hissār	131,309
Howrah (Haora)	744,429
Hugli Chinsurah	125,193
Hyderābād	2,150,580
Ichalkaranji	133,751
Imphāl	156,622
Indore	829,327
Jabalpur	614,162
Jadabpur	251,968
Jaipur	977,165
Jālgaon	145,335
Jālna	122,276
Jammu	206,135
Jāmnagar	277,615
Jamshedpur	438,385
Jaunpur	105,140
Jhānsi	246,172
Jodhpur	506,345
Jullundur	408,196
Junāgadh	118,646
Kākināda	226,409
Kalyān	136,052
Kāmārhāti	234,951
Kānchipuram	130,926
Kānpur	1,481,789
Karnāl	132,107
Katihār	104,781
Khandwa	114,725
Kharagpur	150,475
Kolhāpur	340,625
Kota	358,241
Kozhikode (Calicut)	394,447
Kumbakonam	132,832
Kurnool	206,362
Lātūr	111,986
Lucknow	895,721
Ludhiāna	607,052
Madras	3,276,622
Madurai	820,891
Mālegaon	245,883
Mandya	100,285
Mangalore	172,252
Masulipatam	138,530
Mathura	147,493
Meerut	417,395
Miraj	105,455
Mirzāpur-cum-Vindhyachal	127,787
Monghyr	129,260
Morādābād	330,051
Muzaffarnagar	171,816
Muzaffarpur	190,416
Mysore	441,754
Nabadwīp	109,108
Nadiād	142,689
Nāgercoil	171,648
Nāgpur	1,219,461
Naihāti	114,607
Nānded	191,269
Nāsik (Nashik)	262,428
Navsāri	106,793
Nellore	237,065
★ New Delhi	273,036
Nizāmābād	183,061
Pālghāt	111,245
Pānihāti	205,718
Pānīpat	137,927
Parbhani	109,364
Pathānkot	110,039
Patiāla	205,141
Patna	776,371
Pimpri-Chinchwad	220,966
Pondicherry	162,639
Porbandar	115,182
Proddatūr	107,070
Pune	1,203,351
Puri	100,942
Quilon	137,943
Raichūr	124,762
Raipur	338,245
Rājahmundry	203,358
Rājapālaiyam	101,640
Rājkot	445,076
Rāmpur	204,610
Rānchi	489,626
Ratlām	142,319
Raurkela Steel Township	206,821
Rewa	100,641
Rohtak	166,767
Sāgar	160,392
Sahāranpur	295,355
Salem	361,394
Sambalpur	110,282
Sambhal	108,232
Secunderābād (Cantonment)	135,994
Sāngli	152,389
Shāhjahānpur	185,396
Shillong	109,244
Shimoga	151,783
Sholāpur (Solapur)	511,103
Shrīrāmpur	127,304
Sīkar	102,970
Silīguri	154,378
Sitāpur	101,210
Sonepat	109,369
South Dum-Dum	230,266
South Suburban	378,765
Srīnagar	586,038
Surat	776,583
Tamkūr	108,670
Tenāli	119,257
Thāna (Thane)	309,897
Thanjāvūr	184,015
Tiruchchirāppalli	362,045
Tirunelveli	128,850
Tirupati	115,292
Tiruppūr	165,223
Tiruvottiyūr	134,014
Titāgarh	104,534
Trivandrum	483,086
Tumkūr	108,670
Tuticorin	192,949
Udaipur	232,588
Ujjain	278,454
Ulhāsnagar	273,668
Vadodara (Baroda)	734,473
Valparai	115,452
Vārānasi (Benares)	708,647
Vellore	174,247
Vijayawāda	454,577
Vishākhapatnam	565,321
Vizianagaram	114,806
Warangal	335,150
Yamunānagar	109,304
Indonesia (1980)	
Ambon	208,898
Balikpapan	280,675
Bandung	1,462,637
Banjarmasin	381,286
Bogor	247,409
Cirebon	223,776
★ Jakarta	6,503,449
Jambi	230,373
Jember	122,712
Kediri	221,830
Madiun	150,562
Magelang	123,484
Malang	511,780
Manado	217,159
Medan	1,378,955
Padang	480,922
Pakanbaru	186,262
Palembang	787,187
Pekalongan	132,558
Pematangsiantar	150,376
Pontianak	304,778
Probolinggo	100,296
Samarinda	264,718
Semarang	1,026,671
Sukabumi	109,994
Surabaya	2,027,913
Surakarta	469,888
Tanjung Karang-Telukbetung	284,275
Tegal	131,728
Ujung Pandang	709,038
Yogyakarta	398,727
Iran (1985 est.)	
Ahvāz	508,500
Āmol	106,500
Arāk	244,300
Ardabīl	258,100
Bakhtarān	536,500
Bandar 'Abbās	212,300
Borūjerd	162,800
Dezfūl	123,000
Gorgān	113,200
Hamadan	262,200
Isfahan (Eṣfahān)	1,121,200
Karaj	431,900
Kāshān	136,000
Kermān	266,800
Khorramābād	235,600
Meshed (Mashhad)	1,103,300
Orūmiyeh	298,400
Qazvīn	205,900
Qom	637,700
Rasht	266,300
Sabzevār	129,600
Sanandaj	207,500
Shīrāz	834,800
Tabrīz	929,200
★ Tehrān	5,751,500
Yazd	223,300
Zāhedān	220,500
Zanjān	205,900
Iraq (1985 est.)	
al-Amārah	131,758
★ Baghdad	4,648,609
Ba'qūbah	114,516
Basra	616,700
al-Ḥillah	215,249
Irbīl	333,903
Karbalā'	184,574
Kirkūk	207,900[9]
Mosul	570,926
an-Najaf	242,603
an-Nasiriyah	138,842
ar-Ramādī	137,388
as-Sulaymaniyah	279,424
Ireland (1981)	
Cork	136,344
★ Dublin	525,882
Isle of Man (1981)	
★ Douglas	19,944
Israel (1983)	
Bat Yam	129,700
Beersheba (Be'er Sheva')	111,100
Haifa (Ḥefa)	227,900
Ḥolon	133,900
★ Jerusalem (Yerushalayim, Al-Quds)	431,800
Netanya	101,600
Petaḥ Tiqwa	124,600
Ramat Gan	117,600
Rishon le-Ẓiyyon	102,500
Tel Aviv–Yafo	330,400
Italy (1985 est.; MU)	
Ancona	105,467
Bari	368,216
Bergamo	119,991
Bologna	442,307
Bolzano	102,643
Brescia	202,095
Cagliari	224,007
Catania	377,707
Catanzaro	102,305
Cosenza	106,333
Ferrara	146,142
Florence (Firenze)	435,698
Foggia	157,818
Forlì	110,824
Genoa (Genova)	738,099
La Spezia	111,353
Livorno	175,803
Messina	265,772
Milan (Milano)	1,535,722
Modena	178,328
Monza	122,476[2]
Naples (Napoli)	1,206,955
Novara	102,581
Padua (Padova)	229,156
Palermo	716,149
Parma	177,136
Perugia	144,946
Pescara	131,921
Piacenza	107,006
Pisa	104,213
Prato	161,705[2]
Ravenna	136,569
Reggio di Calabria	177,237
Reggio nell'Emilia	130,419
Rimini	129,506[2]
★ Rome (Roma)	2,826,733
Salerno	156,291
Sassari	119,889
Siracusa	119,242
Taranto	244,434
Terni	110,862
Torre del Greco	104,654[2]
Turin (Torino)	1,049,997
Trieste	243,654
Udine	100,957
Venice (Venezia)	337,670
Verona	260,594
Vicenza	111,721
Jamaica (1982)	
★ Kingston	104,041
Japan (1985)	
Abiko	111,661
Ageo	178,589
Aizuwakamatsu	118,144
Akashi	263,365
Akita	296,381
Amagasaki	509,115
Anjō	133,061
Aomori	294,050
Asahigawa	363,630
Ashikaga	167,656
Atsugi	175,596
Beppu	134,782
Chiba	788,920
Chigasaki	185,029
Chōfu	191,076
Daitō	122,440
Fuji	214,451
Fujieda	111,987
Fujinomiya	112,642
Fujisawa	328,387
Fukui	250,261
Fukuoka	1,160,402
Fukushima	270,752
Fukuyama	360,264
Funabashi	506,967
Futyu	201,972
Gifu	411,740
Habikino	111,396
Hachinohe	241,428
Hachiōji	426,650
Hadano	141,806
Hakodate	319,190
Hamamatsu	514,118
Higashikurume	110,079
Higashimurayama	123,794
Higashiōsaka	522,798
Himeji	452,916
Hino	156,006
Hirakata	382,257
Hiratsuka	229,976
Hirosaki	176,082
Hiroshima	1,044,129
Hitachi	206,075
Hōfu	118,074
Ibaraki	250,468
Ichihara	237,618
Ichikawa	397,806
Ichinomiya	257,392
Ikeda	101,682
Imabari	125,116

country city	population
Iruma	118,603
Ise	105,455
Isesaki	112,458
Ishinomaki	122,684
Itami	182,731
Iwaki	350,566
Iwakuni	111,831
Iwatsuki	100,904
Izumi (*Miyagi Pref.*)	124,216
Izumi (*Osaka Pref.*)	137,633
Joetsu	130,659
Kadoma	140,545
Kagoshima	530,496
Kakamigahara	124,464
Kakogawa	227,312
Kamakura	175,490
Kanazawa	430,480
Kariya	112,402
Kashihara	112,881
Kashiwa	273,130
Kasugai	256,991
Kasukabe	171,889
Katsuta	102,768
Kawagoe	285,435
Kawaguchi	403,012
Kawanishi	136,376
Kawasaki	1,088,611
Kiryū	131,268
Kisarazu	120,201
Kishiwada	185,735
Kitakyūshū	1,056,400
Kitami	107,280
Kobe	1,410,843
Kochi	312,253
Kodaira	158,673
Kofu	202,405
Koganei	104,684
Komaki	113,284
Komatsu	106,047
Koriyama	301,672
Koshigaya	253,483
Kumagaya	143,496
Kumamoto	555,722
Kurashiki	413,644
Kure	226,489
Kurume	222,848
Kushiro	214,545
Kyōto	1,479,125
Machida	321,182
Maebashi	277,319
Matsubara	136,455
Matsudo	427,479
Matsue	140,000
Matsumoto	197,348
Matsusaka	116,886
Matsuyama	426,646
Minō	114,770
Misato	107,963
Mitaka	166,175
Mito	228,987
Minakoyojō	132,099
Miyazaki	279,118
Moriguchi	159,402
Morioka	235,469
Muroran	136,209
Musashino	138,810
Nagano	336,967
Nagaoka	183,756
Nagareyama	124,682
Nagasaki	449,382
Nagoya	2,116,350
Naha	303,680
Nara	327,702
Narashino	136,365
Neyagawa	258,230
Niigata	475,633
Niihama	132,192
Niiza	129,284
Nishinomiya	421,267
Nobeoka	138,381
Noda	105,937
Numazu	210,484
Obihiro	162,930
Odawara	185,947
Ōgaki	145,909
Ōita	390,105
Okayama	572,423
Okazaki	284,996
Okinawa	101,205
Ōme	110,830
Ōmiya	373,015
Ōmuta	159,423
Onomichi	100,642
Ōsaka	2,636,260
Ōta	133,670
Otaru	172,490
Ōtsu	234,547
Oyama	134,242
Saga	168,254
Sagamihara	482,778
Sakai	818,368
Sakata	101,392
Sakura	121,213
Sapporo	1,542,969
Sasebo	250,635
Sayama	144,366
Sendai	700,248
Seto	124,625
Shimizu	242,166
Shimonoseki	269,167
Shizuoka	468,362
Sōka	194,204
Suita	348,946
Suzuka	164,937
Tachikawa	146,531
Takamatsu	327,001
Takaoka	175,780
Takarazuka	194,273
Takasaki	231,764
Takatsuki	348,743
Tama	122,131
Tokorozawa	275,165
Tokushima	257,886
Tokuyama	112,638
★ Tokyo	8,353,674
Tomakomai	158,058
Tondabayashi	102,610
Tottori	137,060
Toyama	314,111
Toyohashi	322,142
Toyokawa	107,430
Toyonaka	413,219
Toyota	308,106
Tsu	150,692
Tsuchiura	120,175
Tsuruoka	100,199
Ube	174,854
Ueda	116,178
Uji	165,411
Urawa	377,233
Utsunomiya	405,384
Wakayama	401,357
Yachiyo	142,188
Yaizu	108,557
Yamagata	245,159
Yamaguchi	124,213
Yamato	175,669
Yao	276,397
Yatsushiro	108,790
Yokkaichi	263,003
Yokohama	2,992,644
Yokosuka	427,087
Yonago	131,794
Jersey (1981)	
★ St. Helier	25,698
Jordan (1985 est.)	
★ Amman	800,000
az-Zarqā'	274,300
Irbid	144,650
Kampuchea (1982 est.)	
★ Phnom Penh	600,000
Kenya (1984 est.)	
Kisumu	167,100
Mombasa	425,600
★ Nairobi	1,103,600
Nakuru	101,700
Kiribati (1985)	
★ Bairiki	21,393
Korea, North (1981 est.)	
Ch'ŏngjin	490,000
Haeju	213,000[7]
Hamhŭng-Hungnam	775,000
Kaesŏng	240,000
Kimch'aek (Songjin)	490,000[7]
★ P'yŏngyang	1,283,000
Sinŭiju	200,000
Wŏnsan	240,000
Korea, South (1980)	
Andong	101,903
Anyang	253,560
Ch'angwŏn	111,676
Cheju	167,719
Chinhae	112,024
Chinju	202,717
Chi'ŏnan	120,526
Ch'ŏngju	253,192
Chŏnju	367,161
Ch'unch'ŏn	155,305
Ch'ungju	113,098
Inch'ŏn	1,083,906
Iri	145,343
Kangnŭng	116,806
Kumi	105,360
Kunsan	165,317
Kwangju	727,600
Kyŏngju	121,999
Masan	386,751
Mokp'o	221,814
P'ohang	201,174
Puch'ŏn	221,463
Pusan	3,159,766
Sŏngnam	376,840
★ Seoul (Sŏul)	8,364,379
Sunch'ŏn	114,241
Suwŏn	310,476
Taegu	1,604,934
Taejŏn	651,792
Tonghae	104,310
Ŭijŏngbu	133,177
Ulsan	418,326
Wŏnju	136,909
Yŏsu	160,988
Kuwait (1980)	
Ḥawallī	152,402
★ Kuwait (al-Kuwayt)	60,525
as-Sālimīyah	145,991
Laos (1981 est.)	
★ Vientiane	210,000
Lebanon (1985 est.)	
★ Beirut (Bayrūt)	1,500,000
Sidon (Ṣaydā)	100,000
Tripoli (Ṭarābulus)	500,000
Zaḥlah	200,000
Lesotho (1986)	
★ Maseru	109,382
Liberia (1984 est.)	
★ Monrovia	425,000
Libya (1981 est.)	
Banghāzī	367,600
Misrātah	116,900
★ Tripoli (Ṭarābulus)	858,500
Liechtenstein (1985)	
★ Vaduz	4,872
Luxembourg (1981)	
★ Luxembourg	78,924
Macau (1986 est.)	
★ Macau (Santo Nome de Deus)	377,900
Madagascar (1985 est.)	
★ Antananarivo	662,600
Malaŵi (1984 est.)	
Blantyre	333,800
★ Lilongwe	172,100
Malaysia (1980)	
Ipoh	293,849
Johor Baharu	246,395
Kelang	192,080
Kota Baharu	167,872
★ Kuala Lumpur	565,329
Kuala Terengganu	180,296
Kuantan	131,547
Petaling Jaya	207,805
Pinang (George Town)	248,241
Port Kelang	192,080
Seremban	132,911
Taiping	146,002
Maldives (1985)	
★ Male	46,334
Mali (1985 est.)	
★ Bamako	801,910
Malta (1985)	
★ Valletta	9,340
Martinique (1982)	
★ Fort-de-France	96,649
Mauritania (1981 est.)	
★ Nouakchott	250,000
Mauritius (1986 est.)	
★ Port Louis	138,272
Mayotte (1985)	
★ Dzaoudzi	5,675
Mamoudzou (★ designate)	12,119
Mexico (1980)	
Acapulco	301,902
Aguascalientes	293,152
Atizapán de Zaragoza (Ciudad López Mateos)	188,497
Campeche	128,434
Celaya	141,675
Chihuahua	385,603
Ciudad Madero	132,444
Ciudad Obregón	165,572
Ciudad Victoria	140,161
Coatzacoalcos	127,170
Cuernavaca	192,770
Culiacán	304,826
Ensenada	120,483
Durango	257,915
Gómez Palacio	116,967
Guadalajara	1,626,152
Guadalupe	370,524
Hermosillo	297,175
Irapuato	170,138
Jalapa	204,594
Juárez	544,496
León	593,002
Los Mochis	122,531
Matamoros	188,745
Mazatlán	199,830
Mérida	400,142
Mexicali	341,559
★ Mexico City	8,831,079
Minatitlán	106,765
Monclova	115,786
Monterrey	1,090,009
Morelia	297,544
Nezahualcóyotl	1,341,230
Nuevo Laredo	201,731
Oaxaca	154,223
Orizaba	114,848
Pachuca	110,351
Poza Rica	166,799
Puebla	835,759
Querétaro	215,976
Reynosa	194,693
Saltillo	284,937
San Luis Potosí	362,371
San Nicolás de los Garza	280,696
Tampico	267,957
Tepic	145,741
Tijuana	429,500
Tlaquepaque	133,500
Toluca	199,778
Torreón	328,086
Tuxtla	131,096
Uruapan	122,828
Veracruz	284,822
Villahermosa	158,216
Zapopan	345,390
Monaco (1982)	
★ Monaco-Ville	1,234
Mongolia (1984 est.)	
★ Ulan Bator	470,500
Montserrat (1980)	
★ Plymouth	1,568
Morocco (1982)	
Agadir	110,479
Casablanca (Dar el-Beida)	2,139,204
Fès (Fez)	448,823
Kenitra	188,194
Khouribga	127,181
Marrakech	439,728
Meknès	319,783
Mohammedia	105,120
Oujda	260,082
★ Rabat	518,616
Safi	197,309
Salé	289,391
Tanger	266,346
Tétouan	199,615
Mozambique (1986 est.)	
Beira	269,700
★ Maputo (Lourenço Marques)	882,814
Nampula	182,553
Nauru (1977)	
★ Yaren	413
Nepal (1981)	
★ Kathmandu	235,160
Netherlands (1985 est.)	
★ Amsterdam (capital)	675,579
Apeldoorn	144,807
Arnhem	128,145
Breda	118,974
Dordrecht	107,274
Eindhoven	191,675
Enschede	144,566
Groningen	168,119
Haarlem	151,025
Leiden	104,668
Maastricht	114,008
Nijmegen	146,452
Rotterdam	571,081
★ The Hague (seat of government)	443,456
Tilburg	153,812
Utrecht	229,969
Zaanstad	128,264
Netherland Antilles (1980 est.)	
★ Willemstad	100,000
New Caledonia (1983)	
★ Nouméa	60,112
New Zealand (1984 est.)	
Auckland	143,800
Christchurch	162,100
Manukau	179,000
★ Wellington	133,700
Nicaragua (1985 est.)	
León	100,982
★ Managua	682,111
Niger (1983 est.)	
★ Niamey	399,100
Nigeria (1983 est.)	
Aba	216,000
Abeokuta	308,800
Ado-Ekiti	265,800
Akure	117,300
Benin City	165,900
Calabar	126,000
Ede	221,900
Effon-Alaiye	110,600
Enugu	228,400
Gusau	114,100
Ibadan	1,060,000
Ife	214,500
Ijebu-Ode	113,110
Ikare	101,700
Ikerre	176,800
Ilesha	273,400
Ilobu	143,800
Ilorin	343,900
Iseyin	157,000
Iwo	261,600
Jos	149,000
Kaduna	202,000
Kano	487,100
Katsina	149,300
Kumo	107,000
★ Lagos	1,097,000
Maiduguri	230,900
Mushin	240,700
Offa	142,300
Ogbomosho	527,400
Oka	103,500
Ondo	122,600
Onitsha	268,700
Oshogbo	344,500
Oyo	185,300
Port Harcourt	296,200
Sapele	100,600
Shaki	125,800
Shomolu	106,800
Sokoto	148,000
Zaria	274,000
Niue (1984)	
★ Alofi	894
Norfolk Island	
★ Kingston	...
Norway (1986 est.)	
Bergen	207,866
★ Oslo	449,228
Trondheim	134,406
Oman (1981 est.)	
★ Muscat	50,000
Pacific Islands, Trust Territory of the	
Marshall Is. (1985 est.)	
★ Majuro	14,267
Micronesia, Federated States of (1980)	
★ Kolonia	5,549
Northern Mariana Is. (1985 est.)	
★ Saipan	17,840
Palau (1980)	
★ Koror	6,222
Pakistan (1981)	
Bahāwalpur	180,263
Chiniot	105,559
Dera Ghāzi Khān	102,007
Faisalābād (Lyallpur)	1,104,209
Gujrānwāla	658,753
Gujrāt	155,058
Hyderābād	751,529
★ Islāmābād	204,364
Jhelum	106,462
Jhang	195,558
Karāchi	5,208,132
Kasūr	155,523
Lahore	2,952,689
Lahore Cantonment	237,000
Lārkāna	123,890
Mardān	147,977
Mīrpur Khās	124,371
Multān	730,070
Nawābshāh	102,139
Okāra	153,483
Peshāwar	566,248
Quetta	285,719
Rahīm Yār Khān	119,036
Rāwalpindi	794,843
Sāhīwāl	150,954
Sargodha	291,362
Sheikhūpura	141,168
Siālkot	302,009
Sukkur	190,551
Wāh Cantonment	122,335
Panama (1986 est.)	
★ Panama City	434,668
San Miguelito	221,512
Papua New Guinea (1985 est.)	
★ Port Moresby	136,200
Paraguay (1985 est.)	
★ Asunción	477,065
Peru (1985 est.)	
Arequipa	531,800
Callao	515,200
Chiclayo	347,700
Chimbote	253,300
Cuzco	225,700
Huancayo	186,700
Ica	131,900
Iquitos	215,300
★ Lima	375,957[10]
Metro Lima-Callao	5,523,600
Piura	256,200
Tacna	118,600
Trujillo	438,700
Philippines (1980)	
Angeles	188,834
Bacolod	262,415
Baguio	119,009
Batangas	143,570
Butuan	172,489
Cabanatuan	138,298
Cadiz	129,632
Cagayan de Oro	227,312
Calbayog	106,719
Caloocan	467,816
Cebu	490,281
Davao	610,375
General Santos	149,396
Iligan	167,358
Iloilo	244,827
Lipa	121,166
Lucena	107,880
Makati	372,631

Major cities and national capitals (continued)

country city	population
Mancaue	110,590
Mandaluyong	205,366
★ Manila	1,630,485
Metro Manila	5,925,884
Marikina	211,613
Olongapo	156,430
Ormoc	104,978
Paranaque	208,552
Pasay	287,770
Pasig	268,570
Quezon City	1,165,865
San Carlos	101,243
San Pablo	131,655
Silay	111,131
Tacloban	102,523
Valenzuela	212,363
Zamboanga	343,722
Pitcairn Island (1986)	
★ Adamstown	64
Poland (1985 est.)	
Białystok	245,400
Bielsko-Biała	174,100
Bydgoszcz	361,400
Bytom	239,200
Chorzów	144,200
Czestochowa	246,600
Dąbrovo Górnicza	136,800
Elbląg	117,000
Gdańsk	467,200
Gdynia	243,100
Gliwice	212,500
Gorzów Wielkopolski	115,100
Jastrzębie-Zdrój	101,000
Kalisz	103,500
Katowice	363,300
Kielce	200,500
Kraków	740,300
Łódź	849,400
Lublin	324,100
Olsztyn	147,100
Opole	124,000
Płock	114,500
Poznań	574,100
Radom	213,500
Ruda Śląska	164,600
Rybnik	135,500
Rzeszów	138,000
Sosnowiec	255,000
Szczecin	390,800
Tarnów	113,200
Toruń	186,200
Tychy	181,800
Wałbrzych	138,000
★ Warsaw (Warszawa)	1,649,000
Włocławek	115,300
Wodzislaw Śląskie	107,700
Wrocław	636,000
Zabrze	198,000
Zielona Góra	109,400
Portugal (1981)	
★ Lisbon	807,167
Porto	327,368
Puerto Rico (1984 est.)	
Bayamón	202,500
Caguas	121,100
Carolina	165,700
Ponce	190,900
★ San Juan	428,900
Qatar (1983 est.)	
★ Doha	190,000
Réunion (1982)	
★ Saint-Denis	84,400
Romania (1984 est.)	
Arad	182,997
Bacău	169,503
Baia Mare	131,268
Brăila	228,035
Braşov	334,992
★ Bucharest	1,961,189
Buzău	129,510
Cluj-Napoca	299,786
Constanţa	318,799
Craiova	267,474
Galaţi	286,110
Iaşi	310,158
Oradea	206,056
Piatra Neamţ	105,108
Piteşti	151,741
Ploieşti	232,462
Reşiţa	102,564
Satu Mare	125,819
Sibiu	173,115
Timişoara	309,258
Tirgu Mureş	152,258
Rwanda (1981 est.)	
★ Kigali	156,700
St. Christopher and Nevis (1980)	
★ Basseterre	14,283
St. Helena and Ascension (1978 est.)	
★ Jamestown	1,500
St. Lucia (1985 est.)	
★ Castries	51,492
St. Pierre and Miquelon (1982)	
★ Saint-Pierre	5,415

country city	population
St. Vincent and The Grenadines (1984 est.)	
★ Kingstown	18,378
San Marino (1986 est.)	
★ San Marino	4,533
São Tomé and Príncipe (1984 est.)	
★ São Tomé	35,000
Saudi Arabia (1980 est.)	
ad-Dammām	200,000[11]
Jiddah	1,308,000[12]
Mecca (Makkah)	550,000
Medina (al-Madinah)	290,000
★ Riyadh (ar-Riyad)	1,000,000[12]
aṭ-Ṭā'if	300,000
Senegal (1984 est.)	
★ Dakar	670,976
Kaolack	126,947
Ziguinchor	105,238
Seychelles (1977)	
★ Victoria	23,012
Sierra Leone (1985)	
★ Freetown	554,243
Singapore (1986 est.)	
★ Singapore	2,587,000
Solomon Islands (1985 est.)	
★ Honiara	24,975
Somalia (1981 est.)	
★ Mogadishu	400,000
South Africa (1984 est.)	
Alberton	179,351
Bellville	100,000
Benoni	234,998
★ Bloemfontein (judicial)	222,000
Boksburg	257,414
★ Cape Town (legislative)	967,708
Carletonville	147,000
Durban	753,000
East London	133,332
Germiston	283,937
Johannesburg	1,713,000
Kimberley	144,769
Krugersdorp	141,179
Pietermaritzburg	165,800
Port Elizabeth	649,178
★ Pretoria (executive)	726,300
Randburg	115,511
Roodepoort	148,863
Soweto	864,000[13]
Springs	148,178
Uitenhage	104,325
Vereeniging	130,810
Welkom	205,000
Bophuthatswana	
★ Mmabatho	...
Ciskei (1980)	
★ Bisho	4,800[14]
Mdantsane	150,000
Transkei (1978 est.)	
★ Umtata	30,000
Venda (1982 est.)	
★ Thohoyandou	...
South West Africa/Namibia (1985 est.)	
★ Windhoek	110,000
Spain (1982 est.)	
Albacete	110,836
Alcalá de Henares	142,862
Alcorcón	140,657
Alicante	258,465
Almería	124,925
Badajoz	102,615
Badalona	227,744
Barcelona	1,720,998
Bilbao	450,024
Burgos	150,909
Cádiz	146,048
Castellón de la Plana	129,602
Córdoba	272,309
Coruña, La	226,697
Gerona	126,030
Getafe	127,060
Gijón	255,969
Granada	244,995
Hospitalet de Llobregat	294,033
Huelva	131,073
La Laguna	112,635
Leganés	163,426
León	123,131
Lérida	115,478
Logroño	113,455
★ Madrid	3,271,834
Málaga	453,176
Móstoles	149,649
Murcia	280,237
Oviedo	165,417
Palma (de Mallorca)	319,620
Palmas de Gran Canaria, Las (Is. Canarias)	405,726
Pamplona	186,363
Sabadell	194,943
Salamanca	139,634
San Sebastián	166,980

country city	population
Santa Coloma de Gramanet	140,588
Santa Cruz de Tenerife	221,660
Santander	184,094
Sevilla (Seville)	630,912
Tarragona	138,705
Terrassa	155,360
Valencia	770,277
Valladolid	358,629
Vigo	258,724
Vitoria	226,388
Zaragoza (Saragossa)	608,725
Sri Lanka (1982 est.)	
★ Colombo	602,000
Jaffna	121,000
Dehiwala-Mount Lavinia	177,000
Moratuwa	136,000
Sudan, The (1983)	
★ Khartoum	476,218
Khartoum North	341,146
Port Sudan	206,727
Omdurman	526,287
Suriname (1980)	
★ Paramaribo	67,905
Swaziland (1986 est.)	
★ Mbabane	40,000
Sweden (1986 est.; MU)	
Göteborg	425,495
Helsingborg	105,468
Jönköping	107,362
Linköping	116,838
Malmo	229,936
Norrköping	118,567
Örebro	118,043
★ Stockholm	659,030
Uppsala	154,859
Västerås	117,706
Switzerland (1986 est.)	
Basel (Bâle)	174,600
★ Bern (Berne)	138,600
Geneva (Genève)	159,900
Lausanne	125,000
Zürich	351,500
Syria (1986 est.)	
Aleppo (Halab)	1,173,000
★ Damascus (Dimashq)	1,259,000
Hamāh	208,000
Homs (Hims)	415,000
Latakia (al-Ladhiqiyah)	232,000
Taiwan (1985 est.)	
Chang-hua	198,195
Chia-i	253,016
Chi-lung (Keelung)	352,666
Chung-ho	315,857
Chung-li	233,392
Feng-shan (Kao-hsiung-hsien)	259,781
Fêng-yüan	137,084
Hsin-chu	297,324
Hsin-chuang	222,894
Hsin-tien	187,637
Hua-lien	103,795
Kao-hsiung	1,285,132
Pan-ch'iao (T'ai-pei-hsien)	467,754
P'ing-tung	198,237
San-ch'ung	349,927
T'ai-chung	655,196
T'ai-nan	631,614
★ Taipei (T'ai-pei)	2,449,702
T'ai-tung	110,747
T'ao-yuan	200,829
Yung-ho	230,057
Tanzania (1978)	
★ Dar es Salaam	769,445
Mwanza	110,553
Tanga	103,399
Zanzibar	110,506
Thailand (1983 est.)	
★ Bangkok	5,018,327
Chiang Mai	150,499
Hat Yai	113,964
Khon Kaen	115,515
Nakhon Ratchasima	190,692
Ubon Ratchathani	100,255
Togo (1983)	
★ Lomé	366,476
Tokelau	
—	—
Tonga (1984 est.)	
★ Nukualofa	27,740
Trinidad and Tobago (1984 est.)	
★ Port of Spain	60,700
Tunisia (1984)	
Safāqis (Sfax)	231,911
★ Tunis	596,654
Turkey (1985)	
Adana	776,000
Adapazari	155,041
★ Ankara	2,251,533
Antakya	109,233
Antalya	258,139
Balıkesir	152,402
Batman	114,210

country city	population
Bursa	614,133
Denizli	171,360
Diyarbakır	305,259
Elaziğ	181,523
Erzurum	252,648
Eskişehir	367,328
Gaziantep	466,302
İçel	314,105
İskenderun	173,607
Isparta	101,784
İstanbul	5,494,916
İzmir	1,489,817
İzmit	236,144
Kahramanmaraş	212,206
Kayseri	378,458
Konya	438,839
Kütahya	120,354
Malatya	251,257
Manisa	126,319
Osmaniye	107,748
Samsun	280,068
Şanlıurfa	206,385
Sivas	197,266
Trabzon	155,960
Van	121,306
Zonguldak	119,125
Turks and Caicos Islands (1980)	
★ Cockburn Town	3,124
Tuvalu (1985 est.)	
★ Funafuti	2,810
Uganda (1980)	
★ Kampala	458,423
Union of Soviet Socialist Republics (1985 est.)	
Abakan	147,000
Achinsk	120,000
Aktyubinsk	231,000
Alma-Ata	1,068,000
Almalyk	114,000
Almetyevsk	123,000
Andizhan	275,000
Andropov	251,000
Angarsk	256,000
Angren	122,000
Anzhero-Sudzhensk	110,000
Arkhangelsk	408,000
Armavir	168,000
Arzamas	105,000
Ashkhabad	356,000
Astrakhan	493,000
Baku	1,104,000
Balakovo	180,000
Balashikha	128,000
Baranovichi	149,000
Barnaul	578,000
Batumi	132,000
Belaya Tserkov	181,000
Belgorod	280,000
Belovo	117,000
Beltsy	147,000
Bendery	122,000
Berdyansk	130,000
Berezniki	195,000
Biysk	226,000
Blagoveshchensk	195,000
Bobruysk	223,000
Borisov	132,000
Bratsk	240,000
Brest	222,000
Brezhnev	437,000
Bryansk	430,000
Bukhara	209,000
Chardzhou	157,000
Cheboksary	389,000
Chelyabinsk	1,096,000
Cherepovets	299,000
Cherkassy	273,000
Cherkessk	102,000
Chernigov	278,000
Chernovtsy	244,000
Chimkent	369,000
Chirchik	153,000
Chita	336,000
Daugavpils	124,000
Dimitrovgrad	116,000
Dneprodzerzhinsk	271,000
Dnepropetrovsk	1,153,000
Donetsk	1,073,000
Dushanbe	552,000
Dzerzhinsk	274,000
Dzhambul	303,000
Dzhezkazgan	102,000
Ekibastuz	119,000
Elektrostal	148,000
Engels	177,000
Fergana	195,000
Frunze	604,000
Gomel	465,000
Gorky	1,399,000
Grodno	247,000
Grozny	393,000
Guryev	145,000
Irkutsk	597,000
Ivano-Frankovsk	210,000
Ivanovo	474,000
Kalinin	438,000

country city	population
Kaliningrad	385,000
Kaliningrad (*Moscow obl.*)	143,000
Kaluga	297,000
Kamensk-Uralsky	200,000
Kamyshin	116,000
Kansk	105,000
Karaganda	617,000
Karshi	133,000
Kaunas	405,000
Kazan	1,047,000
Kemerovo	507,000
Kerch	168,000
Khabarovsk	576,000
Kharkov	1,554,000
Kherson	346,000
Khimki	125,000
Khmelnitsky	217,000
Kiev	2,448,000
Kineshma	104,000
Kirov	411,000
Kirovabad	261,000
Kirovakan	165,000
Kirovograd	263,000
Kiselevsk	126,000
Kishinyov	624,000
Kislovodsk	108,000
Klaipėda	195,000
Kokand	166,000
Kokchetav	120,000
Kolomna	156,000
Kolpino	130,000
Kommunarsk	124,000
Komsomolsk-na-Amure	300,000
Konstantinovka	114,000
Kopeysk	100,000
Kostroma	269,000
Kovrov	153,000
Kramatorsk	192,000
Krasnodar	609,000
Krasnoyarsk	872,000
Krasny Luch	111,000
Kremenchug	224,000
Krivoy Rog	684,000
Kurgan	343,000
Kursk	420,000
Kustanay	199,000
Kutaisi	214,000
Kuybyshev	1,257,000
Kzyl-Orda	183,000
Leninabad	150,000
Leninakan	223,000
Leningrad	4,329,000
Leninsk-Kuznetsky	138,000
Liepaja	112,000
Lipetsk	447,000
Lisichansk	122,000
Lutsk	172,000
Lvov	742,000
Lyubertsy	161,000
Magadan	142,000
Magnitogorsk	422,000
Makeyevka	451,000
Makhachkala	301,000
Margilan	123,000
Maykop	140,000
Melitopol	170,000
Mezhdurechensk	101,000
Miass	160,000
Michurinsk	102,000
Minsk	1,472,000
Mogilyov	343,000
★ Moscow	8,408,000
Murmansk	419,000
Murom	121,000
Mytishchi	151,000
Nakhodka	150,000
Nalchik	227,000
Namangan	275,000
Nevinnomyssk	114,000
Nikolayev	486,000
Nikopol	155,000
Nizhnekamsk	170,000
Nizhnevartovsk	190,000
Nizhny Tagil	419,000
Noginsk	121,000
Norilsk	180,000
Novgorod	220,000
Novocheboksarsk	103,000
Novocherkassk	186,000
Novokuybyshevsk	110,000
Novokuznetsk	577,000
Novomoskovsk (*Tula obl.*)	147,000
Novorossiysk	175,000
Novoshakhtinsk	106,000
Novosibirsk	1,393,000
Novotroitsk	103,000
Nukus	139,000
Odessa	1,126,000
Odintsovo	116,000
Oktyabrsky	102,000
Omsk	1,108,000
Ordzhonikidze	303,000
Orekhovo-Zuyevo	136,000
Orenburg	519,000
Orsha	119,000

country / city	population
Orsk	266,000
Oryol	328,000
Osh	199,000
Panevėžys	116,000
Pavlodar	315,000
Pavlograd	119,000
Penza	527,000
Perm	1,056,000
Pervouralsk	136,000
Petropavlovsk	226,000
Petropavlovsk-Kamchatsky	245,000
Petrouralsk	136,000
Petrozavodsk	255,000
Pinsk	109,000
Podolsk	208,000
Poltava	302,000
Prokopyevsk	274,000
Pskov	194,000
Pyatigorsk	118,000
Riga	883,000
Rostov-na-Donu	986,000
Rovno	221,000
Rubtsovsk	165,000
Rudny	116,000
Rustavi	143,000
Ryazan	494,000
Salavat	149,000
Samarkand	371,000
Saransk	307,000
Sarapul	110,000
Saratov	899,000
Semipalatinsk	317,000
Serov	102,000
Serpukhov	142,000
Sevastopol	341,000
Severodonetsk	124,000
Severodvinsk	230,000
Shchelkovo	106,000
Shevchenko	147,000
Šiauliai	134,000
Simferopol	331,000
Slavyansk	143,000
Smolensk	331,000
Sochi	310,000
Solikamsk	106,000
Stakhanov	110,000
Stary Oskol	154,000
Stavropol	293,000
Sterlitamak	240,000
Sukhumi	126,000
Sumgait	223,000
Sumy	256,000
Surgut	203,000
Sverdlovsk (*Sverdlovsk obl.*)	1,300,000
Syktyvkar	213,000
Syzran	173,000
Taganrog	289,000
Taldy-Kurgan	106,000
Tallinn	464,000
Tambov	296,000
Tartu	111,000
Tashauz	103,000
Tashkent	2,030,000
Tbilisi	1,158,000
Temirtau	225,000
Ternopol	182,000
Tiraspol	162,000
Tolyatti (Togliatti)	594,000
Tomsk	475,000
Tselinograd	262,000
Tula	532,000
Tyumen	425,000
Ukhta	100,000
Ufa	1,064,000
Ukhta	100,000
Ulan-Ude	335,000
Ulyanovsk	544,000
Uralsk	192,000
Urgench	116,000
Usolye-Sibirskoye	107,000
Ussuriysk	156,000
Ust-Kamenogorsk	307,000
Ustinov	611,000
Uzhgorod	107,000
Velikiye Luki	110,000
Vilnius	544,000
Vinnitsa	367,000
Vitebsk	335,000
Vladimir	331,000
Vladivostok	600,000
Volgodonsk	165,000
Volgograd	974,000
Vologda	269,000
Volzhsky	245,000
Vorkuta	108,000
Voronezh	850,000
Voroshilovgrad	497,000
Yakutsk	180,000
Yaroslavl	626,000
Yelets	116,000
Yenakiyevo	117,000
Yerevan	1,133,000
Yevpatoriya	103,000
Yoshkar-Ola	231,000
Yuzhno-Sakhalinsk	158,000
Zagorsk	112,000
Zaporozhye	852,000
Zelenograd	142,000
Zhdanov	522,000
Zhitomir	275,000
Zlatoust	204,000
United Arab Emirates (1980)	
★ Abu Dhabi (Abū Ẓaby)	243,000
Al-'Ayn	102,000
Dubai (Dubayy)	266,000
Sharjah (ash-Shāriqah)	125,000
United Kingdom (1981)	
Aberdeen, Scot.	190,465
Belfast, N.Ire.	354,400
Birmingham	1,024,118
Blackburn	110,254
Blackpool	149,012
Bolton	143,921
Bournemouth	148,382
Bradford	295,048
Brighton	137,985
Bristol	420,234
Cardiff, Wales	266,267
Coventry	322,573
Derby	220,681
Dudley	187,367
Dundee, Scot.	174,345
Edinburgh, Scot.	420,169
Glasgow, Scot.	765,030
Gloucester	108,150
Huddersfield	148,544
Ipswich	131,131
Kingston upon Hull	325,485
Leeds	451,841
Leicester	328,835
Liverpool	544,861
★ London	6,677,928
Luton	164,743
Manchester	448,604
Middlesbrough	159,421
Newcastle upon Tyne	203,591
Newport	116,658
Northampton	155,694
Norwich	173,286
Nottingham	277,203
Oldbury/Smethwick	153,461
Oldham	107,830
Oxford	119,909
Peterborough	114,733
Plymouth	242,560
Poole	124,974
Portsmouth	177,905
Preston	168,405
Reading	198,341
Rotherham	123,312
St. Helens	114,822
Sheffield	477,257
Slough	106,822
Southampton	214,802
Southend-on-Sea	156,969
Stockport	136,792
Stoke-on-Trent	275,168
Sunderland	195,896
Sutton Coldfield	103,097
Swansea, Wales	175,172
Swindon	128,493
Walsall	178,852
West Bromwich	154,531
Wolverhampton	265,631
York	126,377
United States (1985 est.)	
Abilene (*Tex.*)	111,317
Akron (*Ohio*)	226,704
Alburquerque (*N.M.*)	357,051
Alexandria (*Va.*)	108,346
Allentown (*Pa.*)	103,483
Amarillo (*Tex.*)	166,747
Anaheim (*Calif.*)	240,283
Anchorage (*Alsk.*)	229,579
Ann Arbor (*Mich.*)	107,832
Arlington (*Tex.*)	218,931
Atlanta (*Ga.*)	436,214
Aurora (*Colo.*)	198,033
Austin (*Tex.*)	406,469
Bakersfield (*Calif.*)	133,983
Baltimore (*Md.*)	771,097
Baton Rouge (*La.*)	245,830
Beaumont (*Tex.*)	126,298
Berkeley (*Calif.*)	106,768
Birmingham (*Ala.*)	281,973
Boise City (*Idaho*)	107,638
Boston (*Mass.*)	573,131
Bridgeport (*Conn.*)	143,032
Buffalo (*N.Y.*)	339,890
Cedar Rapids (*Iowa*)	107,702
Charlotte (*N.C.*)	335,690
Chattanooga (*Tenn.*)	165,979
Chesapeake (*Va.*)	127,585
Chicago (*Ill.*)	2,998,841
Cincinnati (*Ohio*)	370,198
Cleveland (*Ohio*)	546,126
Colorado Springs (*Colo.*)	251,886
Columbus (*Ga.*)	178,978
Columbus (*Ohio*)	565,682
Concord (*Calif.*)	106,822
Corpus Christi (*Tex.*)	264,221
Dallas (*Tex.*)	997,467
Davenport (*Iowa*)	101,220
Dayton (*Ohio*)	181,021
Denver (*Colo.*)	513,048
Des Moines (*Iowa*)	189,133
Detroit (*Mich.*)	1,090,581
Durham (*N.C.*)	103,493
El Paso (*Tex.*)	474,870
Elizabeth (*N.J.*)	108,129
Erie (*Pa.*)	116,990
Eugene (*Ore.*)	102,077
Evansville (*Ind.*)	130,342
Flint (*Mich.*)	149,227
Fort Lauderdale (*Fla.*)	155,204
Fort Wayne (*Ind.*)	165,428
Fort Worth (*Tex.*)	424,449
Fremont (*Calif.*)	148,032
Fresno (*Calif.*)	275,125
Fullerton (*Calif.*)	109,999
Garden Grove (*Calif.*)	133,012
Garland (*Tex.*)	164,029
Gary (*Ind.*)	143,106
Glendale (*Ariz.*)	118,891
Glendale (*Cal.*)	151,713
Grand Rapids (*Mich.*)	183,270
Greensboro (*N.C.*)	161,650
Hampton (*Va.*)	127,585
Hartford (*Conn.*)	136,572
Hayward (*Calif.*)	102,351
Hialeah (*Fla.*)	157,665
Hollywood (*Fla.*)	124,451
Honolulu (*Ha.*)	817,083
Houston (*Tex.*)	1,746,375
Huntington Beach (*Calif.*)	184,532
Huntsville (*Ala.*)	150,681
Independence (*Mo.*)	112,593
Indianapolis (*Ind.*)	471,656
Inglewood (*Calif.*)	101,872
Irving (*Tex.*)	122,920
Jackson (*Miss.*)	210,024
Jacksonville (*Fla.*)	601,007
Jersey City (*N.J.*)	224,401
Kansas City (*Mo.*)	444,942
Knoxville (*Tenn.*)	175,643
Lakewood (*Colo.*)	123,142
Lansing (*Mich.*)	128,161
Laredo (*Tex.*)	111,268
Las Vegas (*Nev.*)	186,230
Lexington (*Ky.*)	210,364
Lincoln (*Neb.*)	182,373
Little Rock (*Ark.*)	170,850
Livonia (*Mich.*)	100,511
Long Beach (*Calif.*)	389,728
Los Angeles (*Calif.*)	3,186,459
Louisville (*Ky.*)	290,069
Lubbock (*Tex.*)	182,787
Macon (*Ga.*)	123,083
Madison (*Wis.*)	171,053
Memphis (*Tenn.*)	654,626
Mesa (*Ariz.*)	202,450
Miami (*Fla.*)	385,892
Milwaukee (*Wis.*)	621,931
Minneapolis (*Minn.*)	361,021
Mobile (*Ala.*)	206,505
Modesto (*Calif.*)	125,776
Montgomery (*Ala.*)	186,391
Nashville (*Tenn.*)	481,286
New Haven (*Conn.*)	124,968
New Orleans (*La.*)	561,364
New York City (*N.Y.*)	7,183,984
Newark (*N.J.*)	316,356
Newport News (*Va.*)	156,545
Norfolk (*Va.*)	283,219
Oakland (*Calif.*)	362,095
Odessa (*Tex.*)	111,282
Oklahoma City (*Okla.*)	443,575
Omaha (*Neb.*)	362,883
Ontario (*Calif.*)	109,354
Orlando (*Fla.*)	142,025
Oxnard (*Calif.*)	124,665
Pasadena (*Calif.*)	128,644
Pasadena (*Tex.*)	122,148
Paterson (*N.J.*)	139,688
Peoria (*Ill.*)	117,362
Philadelphia (*Pa.*)	1,640,102
Phoenix (*Ariz.*)	890,746
Pittsburgh (*Pa.*)	400,969
Pomona (*Calif.*)	110,079
Portland (*Ore.*)	367,571
Portsmouth (*Va.*)	109,359
Providence (*R.I.*)	155,125
Raleigh (*N.C.*)	171,814
Reno (*Nev.*)	108,537
Richmond (*Va.*)	221,857
Riverside (*Calif.*)	187,526
Roanoke (*Va.*)	101,967
Rochester (*N.Y.*)	243,212
Rockford (*Ill.*)	136,822
Sacramento (*Calif.*)	312,944
St. Louis (*Mo.*)	431,109
St. Paul (*Minn.*)	267,896
St. Petersburg (*Fla.*)	249,879
San Antonio (*Tex.*)	842,779
San Bernardino (*Calif.*)	134,170
San Diego (*Calif.*)	988,284
San Francisco (*Calif.*)	733,456
San Jose (*Calif.*)	706,062
Santa Ana (*Calif.*)	231,937
Savannah (*Ga.*)	148,460
Scottsdale (*Ariz.*)	103,868
Seattle (*Wash.*)	495,190
Shreveport (*La.*)	220,888
South Bend (*Ind.*)	107,125
Spokane (*Wash.*)	175,732
Springfield (*Mass.*)	151,090
Springfield (*Ill.*)	101,786
Springfield (*Mo.*)	137,516
Stamford (*Conn.*)	102,577
Sterling Heights (*Mich.*)	109,602
Stockton (*Calif.*)	176,633
Sunnyvale (*Calif.*)	113,805
Tacoma (*Wash.*)	161,625
Tallahassee (*Fla.*)	116,252
Tampa (*Fla.*)	285,280
Toledo (*Ohio*)	343,677
Topeka (*Kan.*)	119,540
Torrance (*Calif.*)	136,728
Tucson (*Ariz.*)	381,473
Tulsa (*Okla.*)	374,875
Virginia Beach (*Va.*)	312,584
Waco (*Tex.*)	106,616
Warren (*Mich.*)	152,260
★ Washington D.C.	626,000
Waterbury (*Conn.*)	103,507
Wichita (*Kan.*)	284,915
Winston-Salem (*N.C.*)	145,468
Worchester (*Mass.*)	160,518
Yonkers (*N.Y.*)	197,746
Youngstown (*Ohio*)	107,960
Uruguay (1980 est.)	
★ Montevideo	1,261,000
Vanuatu (1981)	
★ Vila	9,971
Venezuela (1987 est.)	
Acarigua	119,611
Barcelona	216,964
Barinas	158,309
Barquisimeto	661,265
Baruta	256,058
Cabimas	162,097
★ Caracas	1,246,611
Ciudad Bolívar	240,954
Ciudad Guayana (San Felix de Guayana)	458,789
Coro	124,317
Cumaná	218,413
Guarenas	101,742[10]
Los Teques	148,602
Maracaibo	1,124,432
Maracay	496,662
Maturín	205,076
Mérida	188,160
Petare	494,196
San Cristóbal	234,905
Turmero	110,186[10]
Valencia	856,455
Valera	131,279
Vietnam (1979)	
Bien Hoa	190,086
Can Tho	182,856
Da Nang	318,655
Haiphong	330,755
★ Hanoi	819,913
Hon Gai	115,312
Hue	165,865
Long Xuyen	112,488
My Tho	101,496
Nam Dinh	161,180
Nha Trang	172,663
Quy Nhon	130,534
Tha Nguyen	138,023
Thanh Hoa	103,981
Thanh-pho Ho Chi Minh (Saigon)	2,441,185
Vinh	154,040
Virgin Islands of the United States (1980)	
★ Charlotte Amalie	19,304
Wallis and Futuna (1983)	
★ Matautu	815
West Bank	
★ —	—
Western Sahara (1982)	
★ El Aaiún (Laayoune)	93,875
Western Samoa (1981)	
★ Apia	33,170
Yemen (Aden) (1981 est.)	
★ Aden	365,000
Yemen (Ṣan'ā') (1981)	
Al-Ḥudaydah	126,386
★ Ṣan'ā'	277,818
Ta'izz	119,573
Yugoslavia (1981; MU)	
Banja Luka	183,618
★ Belgrade (Beograd)	1,470,073
Bitola (Bitolj)	137,835
Čačak	110,676
Čakovec	116,825
Gostivar	101,188
Kragujevac	164,823
Kraljevo	121,622
Krusevac	132,972
Kumanova	126,368
Laskovac	159,001
Ljubljana	305,211
Maribor	185,699
Mostar	110,377
Niš	230,711
Novi Sad	257,685
Osijek	158,790
Pančevo	123,791
Peć	111,067
Prijedor	108,865
Priština	211,156
Prizren	134,689
Rijeka	193,044
Šabac	119,668
Sarajevo	448,500
Skopje (Skoplje)	506,547
Slavanski Brod	106,400
Smederevo	107,366
Split	235,922
Subotica	154,611
Tetova	162,414
Titograd	132,290
Titova Mitrovica	105,097
Tuzla	121,717
Uroševac	113,935
Zadar	116,174
Zagreb	768,700
Novi Zagreb	113,155
Tresnjevka	114,874
Zenica	132,733
Zrenjanin	139,300
Zaire (1984)	
Bukavu	171,064
Kananga	290,898
Kikwit	146,784
★ Kinshasa	2,653,558
Kisangani	282,650
Likasi	194,465
Lubumbashi	543,268
Matadi	144,742
Mbandaka	125,263
Mbuji-Mayi	423,363
Zambia (1980)	
Chingola	145,869
Kabwe	143,635
Kitwe	314,794
Luanshya	132,164
★ Lusaka	538,469
Mufulira	149,778
Ndola	282,439
Zimbabwe (1983 est.)	
Bulawayo	429,000
Chitungwiza	202,000
★ Harare	681,000

[1]1977. [2]1984. [3]All populations cited are for officially defined, widest agglomerations of metropolitan areas. [4]1982. [5]Chittagong, Dhākā, Khulna, and Rājshāni are metropolitan areas. Others are urban agglomerations (not city propers). [6]Unbounded locality. [7]1983 estimate. [8]No separate areas within the state are distinguished administratively as cities. [9]1970 estimate. [10]1981 census. [11]1978. [12]1981. [13]1980. [14]1970.

Language

This table presents data on the principal language communities of each of the countries of the world. The countries, and the principal languages used in each, are listed alphabetically; a bullet (●) indicates those languages which are designated as official by each country. The sum of the estimated populations for each language community and of the "Other" group equals the estimated de facto population of the country given in the "Area and population" table.

The estimates represent, so far as national data collection systems permit, the distribution of mother tongues (a mother tongue being the language spoken first and, usually, most fluently by an individual). Many countries do not collect data on this basis, however, and for these countries a variety of techniques have been used to approximate mother-tongue distribution. Some countries compile data on ethnic or "national" groups; for such countries ethnic distribution was often assumed to conform roughly to the distribution of language communities. This approach, however, must be used with caution, because a minority population is not always free to educate its children in its own language and because better economic opportunities often draw minority group members into the majority-language community. For some countries, a given individual may only be visible in national statistics as a passport-holder of a foreign nation, however long he may remain resident. Such persons, often guest workers, have sometimes had to be assumed to be speakers of the principal language of their home country. For example, since The Netherlands does not collect language data, holders of Moroccan passports were assumed to be speakers of Arabic (although perhaps a quarter of them might be of Berber heritage). For other countries, the language mosaic may be so complex, the language communities so minute in size, scholarly study so inadequate, and the census base so obsolete that it was possible only to assign percentages to groups of related languages, despite their mutual unintelligibility (Papuan and Melanesian languages in Papua New Guinea, for instance). For some countries in the Americas, so few speakers of any single indigenous language remain that it was necessary to combine these groups as *Amerindian* so as to give a fair impression of their aggregate size within their respective countries.

No systematic attempt has been made to account for populations that may legitimately be described as bilingual, unless the country itself collects data on that basis, as does Bolivia or the Comoros, for example. Where a nonindigenous official or excolonial language constitutes a lingua franca of the country, however, speakers of the language as a second tongue are shown in italics, even though very few may speak it as a mother tongue. Similarly, no attempt has been made to distinguish between degrees of dialectal variance among communities *usually* classified as belonging to the same language—*e.g.,* between French and Occitan (the dialect of southern France), or between the various dialects of Chinese.

In giving the names of Bantu languages, grammatical particles specific to a language's autonym (name for itself) have been omitted (the form *Rwanda* is used here, for example, rather than *kinyaRwanda,* and *Tswana* instead of *seTswana*). Parenthetical alternatives are given for a number of languages that differ markedly from the name of the people speaking it (such as Kurukh, spoken by the Oraon tribes of India) or that may be combined with other groups distinguishable in national data but appearing here under the name of the largest member (*e.g.,* Nahuatl and others, combining data on Indian populations in El Salvador). The term *patois* as used here refers to distinguishable dialectal communities related to a national, official, or former colonial language (such as the French patois that survives in Grenada from the end of French rule in 1783).

Language

Major languages by country	Number of speakers
Afghanistan[1]	
● Dari (Persian), of which	
Chahar Aimaq	570,000
Ḥazāra	1,520,000
Tadzhik	3,380,000
● Pashto	8,950,000
Turkmen	340,000
Uzbek	1,520,000
Other (including other Dari)	610,000
Albania[1]	
● Albanian	2,877,000
Greek	73,000
Macedonian	18,000
Montenegrin	9,000
Romanian	18,000
Other	28,000
Algeria	
● Arabic	18,150,000
Berber	4,227,000
French	144,000
Other	45,000
American Samoa	
● English	1,000
● Samoan	32,000
Other	3,000
Andorra	
● Catalan	14,000
French	3,000
Spanish	26,000
Other	2,000
Angola[1]	
Ambo	210,000
Chokwe	720,000
Humbe	220,000
Kongo	1,110,000
Luimbe	760,000
Lunda	80,000
Mbundu	1,970,000
Nyaneka	370,000
Ovimbundu	3,150,000
● Portuguese	...
Other	230,000
Anguilla	
● English	7,000
Other	...
Antigua and Barbuda	
● English	78,000
Other	3,000
Argentina	
Guaraní	280,000
Italian	840,000
● Spanish	29,700,000
Other	220,000
Aruba	
● Dutch	...
Papiamento	56,000
Other	6,000
Australia	
● English	15,747,000
Other (including Aboriginal languages)	193,000
Austria	
Czech	10,000
● German	7,368,000
Hungarian	19,000
Serbo-Croatian	32,000
Slovak	23,000
Other	99,000
Bahamas, The	
● English	216,000
English Creole	5,000
French Creole	8,000
Other	7,000
Bahrain	
● Arabic	387,000
English	7,000
Persian	17,000
Urdū	10,000
Other	14,000
Bangladesh	
● Bengali	101,900,000
Urdū	260,000
Other	930,000
Barbados	
English Creole	231,000
● English	20,000
Other	2,000
Belgium[1]	
● Dutch	5,770,000
● French	3,310,000
● German	60,000
Italian	260,000
Other	460,000
Belize	
Carib	10,000
● English	96,000
German	7,000
Mayan	9,000
Spanish	48,000
Other	2,000
Benin[1]	
Bariba	367,000
Fon	2,443,000
● French	*640,000*
Fulani (Peul)	243,000
Somba	425,000
Yoruba (Nago)	425,000
Other	223,000
Bermuda	
● English	53,000
Other	4,000
Bhutan[1]	
Assamese	189,000
● Dzongkha (Bhutia)	881,000
Gurung	223,000
Other	153,000
Bolivia	
● Aymara	498,000
● Quechua	902,000
● Spanish	2,406,000
Spanish-Aymara	1,376,000
Spanish-Quechua	1,082,000
Spanish-Aymara-Quechua	175,000
Aymara-Quechua	83,000
Spanish-others	79,000
Other	11,000
Botswana[1]	
● English	...
Khoisan	47,000
Tswana	1,040,000
Other	39,000
Brazil	
Amerindian	250,000
● Portuguese	137,020,000
Other	1,130,000
British Virgin Islands	
● English	11,000
Other	1,000
Brunei[1]	
Chinese	47,000
● English	...
● Malay	151,000
Other	35,000
Bulgaria[1]	
● Bulgarian	7,915,000
Romany	222,000
Turkish	770,000
Other	63,000
Burkina Faso[1, 2]	
Bobo	561,000
● French	*480,000*
Fulani	455,000
Gurunsi	414,000
Lobi	561,000
Mossi	4,356,000
Tuareg	333,000
Other	1,446,000
Burma[1]	
● Burmese	26,140,000
Karen	2,540,000
Rakhine (Arakanese)	1,690,000
Shan	3,420,000
Other	4,650,000
Burundi[1]	
● French	*330,000*
● Rundi	4,810,000
Other[3]	20,000
Cameroon[1]	
Bamileke-Widekum-Bamum	1,840,000
Duala-Lunda-Basa	1,460,000
● English	...
Fang	1,970,000
● French	*1,490,000*
Fulani	870,000
Maka	480,000
Mandara	550,000
Tikar	750,000
Other	1,940,000
Canada	
Amerindian, of which	131,000
Cree	69,000
Ojibway	21,000
Arabic	54,000
Chinese	238,000
Czech	26,000
Danish	28,000
Dutch	159,000
● English	15,705,000
Eskimo (Inuktitut)	21,000
Finnish	36,000
● French	6,577,000
German	549,000
Greek	131,000
Hungarian	90,000
Italian	567,000
Japanese	21,000
Norwegian	21,000
Pilipino	41,000
Polish	136,000
Portuguese	174,000
Punjābi	56,000
Russian	33,000
Serbo-Croatian	41,000
Slovak	21,000
Spanish	74,000
Ukrainian	303,000
Vietnamese	31,000
Yiddish	33,000
Other	346,000
Cape Verde	
Crioulo (Cape Verdean Creole)	342,000
● Portuguese	...
Other	...
Cayman Islands	
● English	22,000
Other	...
Central African Republic[1]	
Banda	1,207,000
Baya (Gbaya) - Mandja	387,000
● French	*310,000*
Kare	68,000
Mbaka	116,000
Ngbandi	290,000
Sango	...
Sara	106,000
Zande (Azande)	260,000
Other	273,000
Chad[1]	
Arabic	1,552,000
● French	*310,000*
Hausa	113,000
Kanuri	118,000
Masalit	334,000
Mbum	349,000
Mubu	216,000
Sara, Bagirmi, and Kreish	1,310,000
Tama	324,000
Teda	396,000
Other	427,000
Chile	
Araucanian	687,000
● Spanish	11,533,000
Other	52,000
China[1]	
Achang	21,000
Bulan (Blang)	61,000
Ch'iang (Qiang)	107,000
● Chinese (Han)	983,130,000
Chingpo (Jingpo)	98,000
Chuang (Zhuang)	14,047,000
Daghur (Daur)	99,000
Evenk (Ewenki)	20,000
Gelo	57,000
Hani (Woni)	1,112,000
Hui	7,587,000
Kazakh	953,000
Kirgiz	119,000
Korean	1,852,000
Lahu	319,000
Li	931,000
Lisu	506,000
Manchu	4,518,000
Maonan	40,000
Miao	5,271,000
Mongol	3,580,000
Mulam	95,000
Nakhi (Naxi)	264,000
Nu	24,000
Pai (Bai)	1,189,000
Pumi	25,000
Puyi (Chung-chia)	2,224,000
Salar	73,000
She	391,000
Shui	301,000
Sibo (Xibe)	87,000
Tadzhik	27,000
Tai (Dai)	881,000
Tibetan	4,039,000
Tu	168,000
T'u-chia (Tujia)	2,978,000
T'ung (Dong)	1,497,000
Tung-hsiang (Dongxiang)	293,000
Uighur	6,259,000
Wa (Va)	313,000
Yao	1,482,000
Yi	5,724,000
Other	940,000

Major languages by country	Number of speakers
Christmas Island[1]	
Chinese	1,300
● English	...
Malay	600
Other	100
Cocos (Keeling) Islands	
● English	200
Malay	400
Other	...
Colombia	
Arawakan	183,000
Cariban	84,000
Chibchan	188,000
● Spanish	28,470,000
Other	70,000
Comoros	
● Arabic	...
Comorian	307,000
Comorian-French	53,000
Comorian-Malagasy	23,000
Comorian-Arabic	7,000
Comorian-Swahili	2,000
Comorian-French-other	16,000
● French	*20,000*
Other	2,000
Congo[1, 4]	
Bubangi	109,000
● French	*610,000*
Kongo	1,097,000
Kota	94,000
Mboshi	71,000
Teke	503,000
Other	222,000
Cook Islands	
● English	...
● Maori	15,000
Other	2,000
Costa Rica	
● Spanish	2,508,000
Other	26,000
Côte d'Ivoire	
Akan	4,386,000
● French	*2,780,000*
Kru	1,758,000
Malinke	1,567,000
Southern Mande	1,080,000
Voltaic (including Senufo)	1,663,000
Other	141,000
Cuba	
● Spanish	10,139,000
Other	48,000
Cyprus[1]	
● Greek	534,000
● Turkish	126,000
Other	14,000
Czechoslovakia[1]	
● Czech	9,905,000
German	59,000
Hungarian	591,000
Polish	70,000
● Slovak	4,818,000
Ukrainian	48,000
Other	61,000
Denmark[1]	
● Danish	5,004,000
English	15,000
German	9,000
Norwegian	10,000
Swedish	8,000
Turkish	19,000
Other	48,000
Djibouti[1]	
Afar	169,000
● Arabic	27,000
● French	*40,000*
Issa	214,000
Other	46,000
Dominica	
● English	...
French patois	83,000
Other	3,000
Dominican Republic	
French patois	27,000
● Spanish	6,352,000
Other	11,000
Ecuador	
Quechuan (and other Indian languages)	680,000
● Spanish	8,970,000
Other	...
Egypt	
● Arabic	47,430,000
Other	580,000
El Salvador	
Nahuatl (and other Indian languages)	160,000
● Spanish	5,300,000
Other	...
Equatorial Guinea[1]	
Bubi	46,000
Duala	9,000
Fang	230,000
Ibibio	5,000
● Spanish	...
Other[5]	32,000
Ethiopia	
● Amharic	16,910,000
Gurage	1,440,000
Oromo (Galla)	15,880,000
Tigriyna	3,770,000
Other	6,860,000
Faeroe Islands	
● Danish	...
● Faeroese	46,000
Other	...
Falkland Islands	
● English	2,000
Other	...
Fiji[1]	
● English	...
Fijian	321,000
Hindi	354,000
Other	35,000
Finland	
● Finnish	4,612,000
● Swedish	305,000
Other	10,000
France[1]	
Arabic	1,460,000
Armenian	170,000
Basque	170,000
Breton	1,230,000
Catalan	170,000
Dutch	290,000
● French	46,740,000
German	230,000
Hebrew	580,000
Polish	350,000
Other	4,020,000
French Guiana	
Creole	78,000
● French	...
Other	8,000
French Polynesia[1]	
● French	20,000
Chinese	8,000
Tahitian	134,000
Other	18,000
Gabon[1]	
Fang	410,000
● French	70,000
Mbete	160,000
Mpongwe	170,000
Punu	130,000
Other	240,000
Gambia, The	
Dyola	79,000
● English	...
Fulani	144,000
Malinke	309,000
Soninke	63,000
Wolof	112,000
Other	59,000
Gaza Strip	
Arabic	523,000
Hebrew	...
Other	8,000
Germany, East[1]	
● German	16,470,000
Other	166,000
Germany, West[1]	
Dutch	300,000
English	120,000
● German	57,020,000
Greek	370,000
Italian	610,000
Spanish	180,000
Turkish	1,030,000
Other	1,220,000
Ghana[1]	
Akan	6,910,000
● English	...
Ewe	1,550,000
Ga-Adangme	1,000,000
Mossi-Dagomba	2,090,000
Other	1,590,000
Gibraltar	
● English	9,000
Spanish	10,000
Other	8,000
Greece[1]	
Albanian	60,000
● Greek	9,480,000
Macedonian	180,000
Turkish	60,000
Other	210,000
Greenland	
● Danish	5,000
● Greenlandic	49,000
Other	...
Grenada	
● English	94,000
Other	3,000
Guadeloupe	
Creole and French	318,000
● French	...
Other	16,000
Guam	
Chamorro	42,000
● English	44,000
Japanese	2,000
Palauan	1,000
Philippine languages	21,000
Other	13,000
Guatemala	
Cakchiquel	472,000
Chorti	62,000
Ixil	82,000
Kanjobal	117,000
Kekchí	346,000
Jacaltec	53,000
Mam	694,000
Pocomcii	93,000
Quiché	994,000
● Spanish	4,607,000
Other	670,000
Guernsey	
● English	...
French	...
Other	...
Guinea[1]	
● French	*570,000*
Fulani (Peul)	2,690,000
Kissi	370,000
Mande, of which	3,390,000
Malinke	1,420,000
Susu	770,000
Other	1,200,000
Other	300,000
Guinea-Bissau[1]	
Balante	240,000
Fulani	200,000
Malinke	110,000
Mandyako	90,000
Pepel	90,000
● Portuguese	...
Other	150,000
Guyana	
● English	796,000
English Creole	...
Hindi	...
Urdū	...
Other	...
Haiti	
● French	540,000
French Creole	4,880,000
Other	...
Honduras	
● Spanish	4,420,000
Indian languages and other	90,000
Hong Kong	
● Chinese (Cantonese)	5,077,000
Chinese (other dialects)	338,000
● English	53,000
Other	25,000
Hungary[1]	
● Hungarian	10,520,000
Other	110,000
Iceland[1]	
● Icelandic	242,000
Other	4,000
India	
Anga (Angikā)	580,000
Assamese	12,720,000
Baghelkhandī	330,000
Bāgrī	1,500,000
Banjarī	670,000
Barel	330,000
Bengali	63,220,000
Bhilālī	350,000
Bhīlī (Bhilodi)	1,780,000
Bhojpurī	20,360,000
Bodo	720,000
Bundelkhandī	530,000
Chhattisgarhī	9,500,000
Dogri	1,840,000
● English	...
Garhwalī	1,810,000
Gāro	580,000
Gojrī	470,000
Gondi	2,200,000
Gujarātī	36,430,000
Halabī	490,000
Harautī	470,000
● Hindī	218,290,000
Ho	1,060,000
Kachchi	670,000
Kannaḍa	30,640,000
Kashmīrī	3,440,000
Khāsi	550,000
Khorthā (Khottā)	720,000
Konkanī	2,160,000
Korku	400,000
Koya	300,000
Kui	500,000
Kumāunī	1,750,000
Kurukh (Oraon)	1,760,000
Lamani (Banjārī)	1,710,000
Lushaī (Mīzo)	380,000
Maghī (Magadhi)	9,430,000
Maithilī	8,690,000
Malayālam	31,120,000
Malvi	910,000
Mandealī	340,000
Marāṭhī	59,250,000
Mārwaṛī	6,690,000
Meithei (Manipurī)	1,110,000
Mewari	1,160,000
Mīkīr	280,000
Munda	310,000
Mundarī	1,090,000
Nāgpuria	480,000
Nepālī (Gorkhali)	1,830,000
Nimadī	1,130,000
Oṛiyā	28,010,000
Pahāṛī	1,800,000
Punjābī	19,740,000
Rajasthani	2,970,000
Sadan (Sadrī)	1,150,000
Santālī	5,240,000
Savara	310,000
Sindhī	1,710,000
Surgujia	760,000
Tamil	53,380,000
Telugu	63,480,000
Trīpurī	380,000
Tulu	1,640,000
Urdū	40,610,000
Other	10,960,000
Indonesia	
● Bahasa Indonesia	20,380,000
Balinese	3,460,000
Banjarese	2,270,000
Batak	3,610,000
Bugi	3,250,000
Javanese	67,980,000
Madurese	8,150,000
Minang	4,270,000
Sundanese	25,850,000
Other	30,290,000
Iran[1]	
Arabic	733,000
Azerbaijani	7,371,000
Armenian	323,000
Bakhtiari (Lurī)	876,000
Baluchi	876,000
● Farsī (Persian)	20,744,000
Kurdish	3,775,000
Luri	1,010,000
Turkmen	687,000
Other	9,703,000
Iraq	
● Arabic	12,876,000
Assyrian	74,000
Kurdish	2,463,000
Turkish	48,000
Turkmen	265,000
Other	425,000
Ireland	
● English	3,420,000
● Irish	180,000
Other	...
Isle of Man	
● English	71,000
Other	...
Israel	
● Arabic	805,000
English	53,000
French	36,000
German	29,000
● Hebrew	3,013,000
Hungarian	25,000
Romanian	68,000
Russian	75,000
Spanish	37,000
Yiddish	94,000
Other	146,000
Italy[1]	
Albanian	115,000
French	115,000
German	344,000
● Italian	55,968,000
Other	751,000
Jamaica	
Chinese	14,000
● English	...
English and English Creole	2,205,000
Hindī and other Indian languages	39,000
Spanish	4,000
Other	88,000
Japan[1]	
● Japanese	120,800,000
Korean	570,000
Other	121,000
Jersey	
● English	...
French	...
Other	...
Jordan[1]	
● Arabic	2,700,000
Other	50,000
Kampuchea[1]	
Chinese	220,000
● Khmer	6,950,000
Vietnamese	300,000
Other[6]	...
Kenya[1]	
Arabic	55,000
Bajun (Rajun)	51,000
Basuba	82,000
Boran	95,000
Degodia	129,000
Embu	250,000
Gabbra	42,000
Gurreh	114,000
Gusii (Kisii)	1,303,000
Kalenjin	2,280,000
Kamba	2,381,000
Kikuyu	4,420,000
Kuria	123,000
Luhya	2,925,000
Luo	2,698,000
Masai	332,000
Mbere	85,000
Meru	1,159,000
Nyika (Mijikenda)	1,011,000
Ogaden	36,000
Orma	44,000
Pokomo	55,000
Sambur	102,000
Somali	216,000
● Swahili	*12,689,000*
Taita	211,000
Teso	182,000
Turkana	285,000
Other[7]	482,000
Kiribati[1]	
● English	...
Kiribati	64,000
Other	1,000
Korea, North[1]	
● Korean	21,000,000
Other	148,000
Korea, South[1]	
● Korean	41,797,000
Other	42,000
Kuwait[1]	
● Arabic	1,400,000
Kurdish	179,000
Persian	75,000
Other	134,000

Language (continued)

Major languages by country	Number of speakers
Laos[1]	
Chinese	40,000
Khmu	333,000
● Lao	2,400,000
Man	51,000
Miao	148,000
Mon-Khmer	259,000
Tai	311,000
Other[8]	160,000
Lebanon[1]	
● Arabic	2,463,000
Armenian	19,000
Kurdish	14,000
Other[6]	211,000
Lesotho	
● English	...
● Sesotho	1,581,000
Other	5,000
Liberia[1]	
● English	*338,000*
Kwa (Kru)	
Bassa	328,000
Belle	11,000
Dey	10,000
Grebo	184,000
Krahn	109,000
Kru	186,000
Kwa (Western)	
Fante	10,000
Mande (Northern)	
Gbandi	59,000
Kpelle	457,000
Loma	135,000
Mandingo	90,000
Mende	13,000
Vai	76,000
Mande (Southern)	
Gio	200,000
Mano	170,000
West Atlantic (Mel)	
Gola	104,000
Kissi	79,000
Other	83,000
Libya	
● Arabic	3,834,000
Other[9]	119,000
Liechtenstein[1]	
● German	23,000
Other	4,000
Luxembourg[1]	
Dutch	5,000
● French	15,000
● German	10,000
Italian	23,000
Luxembourgish	280,000
Other	34,000
Macau	
Chinese	424,000
● Portuguese	...
Other	9,000
Madagascar[1]	
● French	*1,060,000*
Malagasy	10,170,000
Other	124,000
Malaŵi	
● Chewa	3,653,000
● English	...
Lomwe	1,055,000
Sena	254,000
Tumbuka	662,000
Yao	1,004,000
Other	650,000
Malaysia	
Bajau	101,000
Chinese	932,000
Chinese and others	528,000
Dusan	167,000
English	80,000
English and others	179,000
Iban	383,000
Iban and others	63,000
● Malay	6,936,000
Malay and others	2,465,000
Tamil	624,000
Tamil and others	10,000
Other	3,622,000
Maldives	
● Divehi (Maldivian)	189,000
Other	...
Mali[1]	
Bambara	2,689,000
Bobo	211,000
Dogon	414,000
Dyula	271,000
● French	*670,000*
Fulani	1,073,000
Malinke	803,000
Senufo	1,006,000
Songhai	499,000
Soninke	736,000
Tuareg	474,000
Other	281,000
Malta[1]	
● English	7,000
● Maltese	322,000
Other	7,000
Martinique	
Creole and French	317,000
● French	...
Other	11,000
Mauritania	
● Arabic	...
● French	*100,000*
Fulfulde (Poular)	287,000
Ḥassānīyah Arabic	1,351,000
Other	51,000
Mauritius	
Bhojpurī	204,000
● English	2,000
French	37,000
French patois	574,000
Hindī	115,000
Tamil	37,000
Urdū	24,000
Other	41,000
Mayotte	
Comorian (related to Swahili)	70,000
● French	...
Other	...
Mexico	
Aztec (Nahuatl)	1,927,000
Chinantec	108,000
Chol	135,000
English	...
Huastec	146,000
Huichol	72,000
Mazahua	272,000
Mazatec	174,000
Mayo	79,000
Mixtec	452,000
Mixe	104,000
Otomi	429,000
● Spanish	73,221,000
Tarahumara	88,000
Tarasco	166,000
Tlapanec	77,000
Totonac	274,000
Tzeltal	301,000
Tzotzil	187,000
Yucatec (Maya)	931,000
Zapotec	592,000
Other	737,000
Monaco[1]	
English	1,000
● French	17,000
Italian	5,000
Monegasque	4,000
Other	2,000
Mongolia[1]	
Bayad	39,000
Buryat	37,000
Dariganga	29,000
Dörbed	54,000
Dzakhchin	23,000
Kazakh	103,000
● Khalkha (Mongolian)	1,502,000
Ould	12,000
Torgut	10,000
Uryankhai	23,000
Other	107,000
Montserrat	
● English	12,000
Other	...
Morocco[1]	
● Arabic	16,684,000
Berber	5,614,000
Other[6]	157,000
Mozambique[1]	
Makua	7,414,000
Malaŵi	1,701,000
● Portuguese	...
Shona	822,000
Tsonga	3,346,000
Yao	454,000
Other	439,000
Nauru	
● Nauruan	6,300
Other[7]	1,700
Nepal	
Bhojpurī	1,282,000
Bhutia (Sherpa)	84,000
Gurung	202,000
Hindī (Awadhi dialect)	253,000
Limbu	152,000
Magar	236,000
Maithilī	1,872,000
● Nepālī	9,848,000
Newāri	506,000
Rai, Kiranti	253,000
Tamang	590,000
Thārū	607,000
Other	978,000
Netherlands, The[1]	
Arabic	102,000
● Dutch	14,008,000
Turkish	160,000
Other	291,000
Netherlands Antilles	
● Dutch	...
English	14,000
Papiamento	151,000
Other	11,000
New Caledonia[1]	
● French	57,000
Melanesian	63,000
Wallisian	13,000
Other	18,000
New Zealand	
● English	3,071,000
Maori	105,000
Other	112,000
Nicaragua[1]	
● Spanish	3,316,000
Other (including Miskito)	68,000
Niger[1]	
● French	*310,000*
Fulani	642,000
Hausa	3,346,000
Kanuri	578,000
Songhai	514,000
Tuareg	193,000
Zerma	938,000
Other	212,000
Nigeria[1]	
Annang	1,190,000
Edo	1,680,000
● English	...
Fulani	8,430,000
Hausa	20,530,000
Ibibio	3,530,000
Ibo	16,290,000
Ijaw	1,910,000
Kanuri	3,970,000
Nupe	1,150,000
Tiv	2,450,000
Urhobo	1,120,000
Yoruba	19,930,000
Other	15,930,000
Niue	
● English	...
Niuean	3,000
Other	...
Norfolk Island	
● English	2,000
Other	...
Norway[1]	
Danish	17,000
English	21,000
Finnish	21,000
● Norwegian	4,053,000
Swedish	8,000
Other	46,000
Oman[1]	
● Arabic (Omani)	990,000
Bengali	30,000
Indian	190,000
Pakistani (mostly Baluchi)	40,000
Other	30,000
Pacific Islands, Trust Territory of the	
Marshall Islands	
● English	600
● Marshallese	33,900
Other	2,500
Micronesia, Federated States of	
● English	500
Kosraean	6,900
Mortlockese	7,200
Palauan	400
Ponapean	22,500
Trukese	39,500
Woleaian	3,500
Yapese	5,500
Other	8,900
Northern Mariana Islands	
Chamorro	11,500
● English	1,100
Palauan	800
Philippine languages	2,900
Woleaian	2,400
Other	2,300
Palau	
● English	100
● Palauan	10,300
Other	1,800
Pakistan	
Baluchi	3,100,000
Brahui	1,230,000
Pashto	13,520,000
Punjābi, of which	
Punjābi	49,560,000
Hindko	2,500,000
Sindhī, of which	
Sindhī	12,110,000
Siraiki	10,110,000
● Urdū	7,820,000
Other[7]	2,930,000
Panama	
Cuna	48,000
Guaymí	67,000
● Spanish	2,081,000
Other	32,000
Papua New Guinea[1]	
● English	...
Papuan languages	2,833,000
Melanesian languages	526,000
Other[10]	41,000
Paraguay	
Guaraní	1,430,000
Guaraní and Spanish	1,536,000
● Spanish	138,000
Other	427,000
Peru	
Aymara	586,000
● Quechua	5,371,000
● Spanish	13,739,000
Other	511,000
Philippines	
Aklanon	547,000
Bicol	3,898,000
Bolinao (Zambal)	240,000
Cebuano	13,662,000
Chavacano	290,000
Chinese	139,000
Davaweno	166,000
● English	21,000
Hamtikanon	461,000
Hiligaynon/Ilongo	5,598,000
Ibanag	328,000
Ifugao	173,000
Ilocanao	6,238,000
Kangkanai	205,000
Maguindanao	670,000
Manobo	176,000
Maranao	802,000
Masbate	413,000
Pampango	1,920,000
Pangasinan	1,263,000
● Pilipino (= Tagalog)	13,337,000
Romblon	231,000
Samal	324,000
Samar-Leyte (Waray-Waray)	2,589,000
Subanon	185,000
Sulu-Moro (Tau Sug)	439,000
Other	1,689,000
Pitcairn Island	
● English	64
Other	...
Poland	
Belorussian	220,000
● Polish	36,970,000
Ukrainian	220,000
Other	40,000
Portugal[1]	
● Portuguese	10,148,000
Other	103,000
Puerto Rico	
● English	16,000
● Spanish	1,863,000
Spanish and English	1,364,000
Other	43,000
Qatar[1]	
● Arabic	282,000
Other[7]	29,000
Réunion	
Creole	556,000
● French	...
Other[11]	...
Romania	
German	294,000
Hungarian	1,647,000
● Romanian	20,508,000
Other	360,000
Rwanda	
● French	*430,000*
● Rwanda	6,336,000
Other[3]	...
St. Christopher and Nevis	
● English	45,000
Other	1,000
St. Helena and Ascension	
● English	7,100
Other	...
St. Lucia	
● English	1,000
French patois	126,000
Hindī and Urdū	4,000
Other	9,000
St. Pierre and Miquelon[1]	
● French	5,900
Other	100
St. Vincent and the Grenadines	
● English	103,000
Other	8,000
San Marino[1]	
● Italian	23,000
Other	...
São Tomé and Príncipe[1]	
Fang	100,000
● Portuguese	
Other	10,000
Saudi Arabia[1]	
● Arabic	11,320,000
Other	350,000
Senegal[1]	
Dyola	590,000
● French	*783,000*
Fulani	1,199,000
Mandingo	563,000
Serer	1,119,000
Tukulor	435,000
Wolof	2,465,000
Other	328,000
Seychelles	
● English	...
● French	*10,000*
Creole patois	64,000
Other	2,000
Sierra Leone[1]	
Bullom	138,000
● English	...
Fulani	138,000
Kissi	93,000
Kono	209,000
Koranko	138,000
Limba	138,000
Mende	1,284,000
Temne	1,168,000
Other[12]	426,000
Singapore[1]	
● Bahasa Malaysia	380,200
Chinese	1,984,500
● English	...
● Mandarin Chinese	...
● Tamil (and other Indian languages)	165,600
Other	57,700
Solomon Islands	
Areare	11,000
● English	...
Kwalo	10,000
Kwara'ae	18,000
Other[13]	239,000

Major languages by country	Number of speakers
Somalia[1]	
● Arabic	...
● Somali	5,854,000
Other	138,000
South Africa	
● Afrikaans	4,922,000
● English	1,821,000
Nguni	11,560,000
Shangana-Tsonga	855,000
Sotho	6,084,000
Venda	467,000
Other	2,431,000
Bophuthatswana	
● Afrikaans	...
● English	...
● Tswana	1,060,000
Other	504,000
Ciskei	
● English	...
● Xhosa	795,000
Other	3,000
Transkei	
● English	...
● Xhosa	2,595,000
Other	160,000
Venda	
● Afrikaans	...
● English	...
● Venda	403,000
Other	45,000
South West Africa/Namibia	
● Afrikaans	166,000
East Caprivian	42,000
● English	...
German	31,000
Herero	76,000
Khoisan	200,000
Okavango	83,000
Ovambo	554,000
Other	51,000
Spain[1]	
Basque	890,000
● Castilian Spanish	28,260,000
Catalan	6,370,000
Galician	3,180,000
Other	120,000
Sri Lanka	
English	11,000
English and Sinhalese	885,000
English and Tamil	183,000
English, Sinhalese, and Tamil	581,000
● Sinhalese	9,709,000
Sinhalese and Tamil	1,503,000
Tamil	3,161,000
Other	55,000
Sudan, The[1]	
● Arabic	12,100,000
Beja	1,550,000
Dinka	2,830,000
Nubian	1,980,000
Nuer	1,200,000
Other	4,940,000
Suriname	
Creole	53,000
● Dutch	143,000
● English	...
Hindi	122,000
Javanese	60,000
Other	17,000

Major languages by country	Number of speakers
Swaziland	
● English	...
● Swazi	614,000
Other[14]	68,000
Sweden[1]	
Finnish	293,000
● Swedish	7,580,000
Other	486,000
Switzerland[1]	
● French	1,223,000
● German	4,332,000
● Italian	602,000
Romansh	53,000
Other	346,000
Syria[1]	
● Arabic	9,423,000
Armenian	297,000
Kurdish	669,000
Other	223,000
Taiwan[1]	
South Fukien Chinese	13,024,000
Hakka and Hokkien Chinese	1,944,000
● Mandarin Chinese	4,063,000
Other	408,000
Tanzania[1]	
Chagga (Chaga)	1,120,000
● English	...
Gogo	880,000
Ha	720,000
Haya	1,330,000
Hehet	1,530,000
Iramba	630,000
Luguru	1,120,000
Makonde	1,330,000
Nyakyusa	1,210,000
Nyamwezi (Sukuma)	4,740,000
Shambala	970,000
● Swahili	1,930,000
Taita	630,000
Other	4,340,000
Thailand[1]	
Chinese	5,950,000
Karen	320,000
Khmer	740,000
Malay	2,000,000
● Thai	42,830,000
Other	840,000
Togo[1]	
Ewe	1,428,000
● French	*530,000*
Gurma	433,000
Kabre	688,000
Tem	129,000
Other	393,000
Tokelau	
● English	...
Tokelauan	1,600
Other	...
Tonga	
● English	...
● Tongan	96,000
Other	2,000

Major languages by country	Number of speakers
Trinidad and Tobago[1]	
● English	694,000
Hindi (and other Indian languages)	481,000
Other	27,000
Tunisia	
● Arabic	5,124,000
Arabic-French	1,922,000
Arabic-French-English	231,000
Arabic-other	9,000
Other-no Arabic	21,000
Other	21,000
Turkey	
Arabic	613,000
Kurdish	3,638,000
● Turkish	47,282,000
Other	886,000
Turks and Caicos Islands	
● English	8,600
Other	...
Tuvalu	
English	...
Kiribati (Gilbertese)	1,000
Tuvaluan (Ellice)	7,700
Other	...
Uganda[1]	
Acholi	630,000
Chiga (Kiga)	1,090,000
● English	...
Ganda (Luganda)	2,810,000
Gisu	1,160,000
Lango	1,020,000
Nkole	1,280,000
Nyoro	590,000
Rwanda	860,000
Soga	1,280,000
Turkana	1,280,000
Other[3]	3,630,000
U.S.S.R.	
Armenian	4,023,000
Avar	504,000
Azerbaijani	5,729,000
Bashkir	982,000
Bulgarian	262,000
Buryat	340,000
Byelorussian	7,502,000
Chechen	796,000
Chuvashi	1,528,000
Dargin	301,000
Estonian	1,039,000
Gagauz	165,000
Georgian	3,751,000
German	1,179,000
Greek	140,000
Hebrew	275,000
Hungarian	174,000
Ingush	194,000
Kabardinian	337,000
Kara-Kalpak	311,000
Kazakh	6,830,000
Kirgiz	1,994,000
Komi	266,000
Komi-Permyak	124,000
Korean	230,000
Kumyk	239,000
Lak	101,000

Major languages by country	Number of speakers
Latvian	1,461,000
Lezgian	372,000
Lithuanian	2,982,000
Mari	576,000
Moldavian	2,956,000
Mordovinian	925,000
Ossetian	511,000
Polish	358,000
● Russian	164,015,000
Tadzhik	3,028,000
Tatar	5,798,000
Turkmenian	2,139,000
Tuvinian	175,000
Udmurt	584,000
Uighur	194,000
Ukrainian	37,465,000
Uzbek	13,110,000
Yakut	334,000
Other	3,739,000
United Arab Emirates[1]	
● Arabic	1,510,000
Other	190,000
United Kingdom	
● English	52,670,000
Scots-Gaelic	70,000
Welsh	520,000
Other	3,410,000
United States	
Chinese	700,000
● English	214,900,000
French	1,760,000
German	1,760,000
Greek	430,000
Italian	1,790,000
Japanese	360,000
Korean	290,000
Philippine languages	510,000
Polish	890,000
Portuguese	410,000
Spanish	12,870,000
Yiddish	360,000
Other	4,440,000
Uruguay	
● Spanish	2,930,000
Other	105,000
Vanuatu	
Bislama	113,000
● English	...
● French	*40,000*
Other	24,000
Venezuela	
● Spanish	17,330,000
Other	460,000
Vietnam	
Khmer	830,000
Muong	790,000
Nung	610,000
Tay	950,000
Thai	810,000
● Vietnamese	51,460,000
Other	5,780,000
Virgin Islands (U.S.)	
● English	97,000
Spanish	17,000
Other	...

Major languages by country	Number of speakers
Wallis and Futuna	
● French	...
Wallisian	14,000
Other	...
West Bank	
Arabic	787,000
Hebrew	28,000
Western Sahara	
Arabic	150,000
Other[15]	...
Western Samoa	
● English	1,000
● Samoan	76,000
Samoan and English	83,000
Other	...
Yemen (Aden)[1]	
● Arabic	2,198,000
Other	167,000
Yemen (Ṣan'ā')[1]	
● Arabic	6,933,000
Other	113,000
Yugoslavia[1]	
Albanian	1,900,000
Hungarian	417,000
● Macedonian	1,404,000
● Serbo-Croatian	15,399,000
● Slovenian	1,793,000
Other	2,375,000
Zaire[1]	
Azande	1,896,000
● French	*2,410,000*
Kongo	5,035,000
Luba	5,594,000
Lugbara	932,000
Mongo	4,134,000
Ngala	1,803,000
Rundi	1,181,000
Rwanda	3,139,000
Teke	839,000
Other[16]	6,527,000
Zambia[1]	
Bemba	2,389,000
● English	...
Lozi	654,000
Lunda	447,000
Luzna	350,000
Malaŵi	943,000
Ngoni	248,000
Tonga	1,129,000
Other	736,000
Zimbabwe	
● English	651,000
Nguni	1,325,000
Nyanja	436,000
Shona	5,955,000
Other	40,000

[1]Figures given represent ethnolinguistic groups. [2]Majority of population speak Moré (language of the Mossi); Dyula is language of commerce. [3]Swahili also spoken. [4]Lingala and Monokutuba are patois. [5]Pidgin English and Portuguese patois also spoken. [6]French also spoken. [7]English also spoken. [8]English and French also spoken. [9]English and Italian also spoken. [10]About half the population also speaks Pisin (Pidgin English); English and Hiri (Police Motu) also spoken. [11]Gujarati and Chinese also spoken. [12]Kiro is the lingua franca. [13]Solomon Islands Pidgin (English) is the lingua franca. [14]Afrikaans and Portuguese also spoken. [15]Spanish also spoken. [16]Swahili, Tshiluba, Lingala, and Kikongo are national languages.

Religion

The following table presents statistics on religious affiliation for each of the countries of the world. An assessment was made for each country of the available data on distribution of religious communities within the total population; the best available figures, whether originating as census data, membership figures of the churches concerned, or estimated by external analysts in the absence of reliable local data, were applied as percentages to the estimated 1986 midyear population of the country to obtain the data shown below.

Several concepts govern the nature of the available data, each useful separately but none the basis of any standard of international practice in the collection of such data. The word "affiliation" was used above to describe the nature of the relationship joining the religious bodies named and the populations shown. This term implies some sort of formal, usually documentary, connection between the religion and the individual (a baptismal certificate, a child being assigned the religion of its parents, maintenance of one's name on the tax rolls of a state religion, etc.) but says nothing about the nature of the individual's personal religious practice, in that the individual may have lapsed, never been confirmed as an adult, joined another religion, or may have joined an organization that is formally atheist.

The user of these statistics should be careful to note that not only does the nature of the affiliation (with an organized religion) differ greatly from country to country, but so does the nature of individual practice. A country in which a single religion has long been predominant will often show more than 90% of its population to be *affiliated*, while in actual fact, no more than 10% may actually *practice* that religion on a regular basis. Such a situation often leads to undercounting of minority religions (where someone [head of household, communicant, child, servant] is counted at all), blurring of distinctions seen to be significant elsewhere (a Hindu country may not distinguish Protestant [or even Christian] denominations; a Christian country may not collect much data distinguishing among its Muslim or Buddhist citizens), or double-counting in countries where an individual may conscientiously practice more than one "religion" at a time.

Communist countries consciously attempt to ignore, suppress, or render invisible religious practice within their boundaries. Countries with large numbers of adherents of traditional, often animist, religions and belief systems usually have little or no formal methodology for defining the nature of local religious practice. On the other hand, countries with strong missionary traditions, or good census organizations, or few religious sensitivities may have very good, detailed, and meaningful data.

The best (indeed, at its publication, the most authoritative and exhaustive) work available is DAVID B. BARRETT (ed.), *World Christian Encyclopedia* (1982); it examines both the theoretical and practical problems of collecting and analyzing religious statistics, assembles a mine of national detail, and establishes a basis for further study.

Religion

Religious affiliation	1986 population
Afghanistan	
Sunnī Muslim	12,500,000
Shī'ī Muslim	4,220,000
other	170,000
Albania	
Muslim	620,000
Christian	160,000
atheist	570,000
nonreligious	1,670,000
Algeria	
Muslim	22,360,000
other	200,000
American Samoa	
Congregational	20,000
Roman Catholic	10,000
other	10,000
Andorra	
Roman Catholic	40,000
other	6,000
Angola	
Christian[1]	7,940,000
traditional beliefs	840,000
other	40,000
Anguilla	
Anglican	3,000
Methodist	3,000
other	1,000
Antigua and Barbuda	
Anglican	40,000
other Protestant	30,000
Roman Catholic	8,000
other	3,000
Argentina	
Roman Catholic	28,810,000
other	2,220,000
Aruba	
Roman Catholic	55,000
other	7,000
Australia	
Anglican	4,150,000
Roman Catholic	4,140,000
Uniting Church	780,000
Presbyterian	700,000
Methodist	540,000
Orthodox	460,000
other Protestant	1,290,000
nonreligious	1,720,000
other	2,130,000
Austria	
Roman Catholic	6,370,000
Protestant	420,000
atheist and nonreligious	450,000
other	310,000
Bahamas, The	
Anglican	50,000
other Protestant	120,000
Roman Catholic	60,000
other	10,000
Bahrain	
Shī'ī Muslim	220,000
Sunnī Muslim	150,000
other	60,000
Bangladesh	
Muslim	89,320,000
Hindu	12,500,000
other	1,260,000
Barbados	
Anglican	100,000
other Protestant	100,000
nonreligious	40,000
other	10,000
Belgium	
Roman Catholic	9,460,000
other	390,000
Belize	
Roman Catholic	110,000
Anglican	20,000
other	40,000
Benin	
traditional beliefs	2,680,000
Roman Catholic	500,000
Muslim	540,000
other	410,000
Bermuda	
Anglican	20,000
other Protestant	20,000
Roman Catholic	10,000
other	10,000
Bhutan	
Buddhist	1,010,000
Hindu	360,000
other	80,000
Bolivia	
Roman Catholic	6,210,000
other	390,000
Botswana	
Christian[1]	570,000
traditional beliefs	550,000
other	10,000
Brazil	
Roman Catholic	121,520,000
Protestant	8,440,000
Afro-American Spiritist	2,770,000
Spiritist	2,350,000
atheist and nonreligious	1,930,000
other	1,390,000
British Virgin Islands	
Methodist	5,500
Anglican	2,500
other	4,000
Brunei	
Muslim	150,000
Buddhist	30,000
other	50,000
Bulgaria	
Eastern Orthodox	2,400,000
Muslim	670,000
atheist	5,790,000
other	110,000
Burkina Faso	
traditional beliefs	3,640,000
Muslim	3,490,000
Christian[1]	990,000
Burma	
Buddhist	34,180,000
Christian	1,770,000
Muslim	1,500,000
traditional beliefs	850,000
other	190,000
Burundi	
Roman Catholic	3,490,000
Protestant	430,000
traditional beliefs	420,000
Muslim	240,000
other	250,000
Cameroon	
Roman Catholic	3,460,000
Protestant	2,020,000
traditional beliefs	2,130,000
Muslim	2,170,000
other	90,000
Canada	
Roman Catholic	11,920,000
Protestant	10,560,000
Eastern Orthodox	380,000
Jewish	310,000
Muslim	100,000
Hindu	80,000
nonreligious	1,900,000
other	380,000
Cape Verde	
Roman Catholic	335,000
Protestant	7,000
Cayman Islands	
Presbyterian	8,000
Church of God	5,000
other	9,000
Central African Republic	
Protestant	1,350,000
Roman Catholic	900,000
traditional beliefs	320,000
other	140,000
Chad	
Muslim	2,260,000
traditional beliefs	1,170,000
Roman Catholic	1,080,000
Protestant	600,000
other	30,000
Chile	
Roman Catholic	9,720,000
Protestant	740,000
other	1,820,000
China	
nonreligious	623,790,000
Chinese folk-religionist	211,790,000
atheist	126,440,000
Buddhist	63,220,000
Muslim	25,290,000
other	3,160,000
Christmas Island	
Buddhist	700
Muslim	500
Christian	400
other	500
Cocos (Keeling) Islands	
Muslim	400
Christian	100
other	100
Colombia	
Roman Catholic	27,380,000
other	850,000
Comoros	
Sunnī Muslim	408,000
Christian	1,000
Congo	
Roman Catholic	1,130,000
Protestant	510,000
African Christian	300,000
other	160,000
Cook Islands	
Congregational	12,000
Roman Catholic	3,000
other	3,000
Costa Rica	
Roman Catholic	2,320,000
other	210,000
Côte d'Ivoire	
traditional beliefs	4,680,000
Christian[1]	3,420,000
Muslim	2,570,000
other	20,000
Cuba	
nonreligious	4,960,000
Roman Catholic	4,040,000
atheist	650,000
other	530,000
Cyprus	
Greek Orthodox	514,000
Muslim	125,000
other	35,000
Czechoslovakia	
Roman Catholic	10,200,000
atheist	3,130,000
Czechoslovak Church	680,000
other	540,000
Denmark	
Evangelical Lutheran	4,890,000
other	230,000
Djibouti	
Sunnī Muslim	429,000
Christian	27,000
Dominica	
Roman Catholic	66,000
Protestant	19,000
Dominican Republic	
Roman Catholic	6,260,000
other	130,000
Ecuador	
Roman Catholic	8,780,000
other	870,000
Egypt	
Sunnī Muslim	39,270,000
Christian	8,550,000
other	190,000
El Salvador	
Roman Catholic	5,250,000
other	210,000
Equatorial Guinea	
Christian[1]	286,000
other	36,000
Ethiopia	
Ethiopian Orthodox	23,550,000
Muslim	14,080,000
traditional beliefs	5,110,000
other	450,000
Faeroe Islands	
Evangelical Lutheran	34,000
other	12,000
Falkland Islands	
Anglican	900
other	1,000
Fiji	
Christian[1]	350,000
Hindu	290,000
other	70,000
Finland	
Lutheran	4,420,000
other	510,000
France	
Roman Catholic	42,350,000
other Christian	2,050,000
atheist and nonreligious	8,640,000
Muslim	1,660,000
other	730,000
French Guiana	
Roman Catholic	75,000
other	11,000
French Polynesia	
Protestant	99,000
Roman Catholic	71,000
other	10,000
Gabon	
Roman Catholic	670,000
Protestant	220,000
African Christian	140,000
other	160,000
Gambia, The	
Muslim	649,000
other	116,000
Gaza Strip	
Muslim	523,000
other	8,000
German Democratic Republic	
Protestant	13,310,000
Roman Catholic	1,660,000
atheist	1,660,000
Germany, Federal Rep. of	
Protestant	28,790,000
Roman Catholic	26,660,000
other Christian	1,030,000
nonreligious	2,250,000
Muslim	1,460,000
atheist	550,000
other	120,000
Ghana	
Christian[1]	8,230,000
traditional beliefs	2,810,000
Muslim	2,060,000
other	40,000
Gibraltar	
Roman Catholic	21,000
other	7,000
Greece	
Greek Orthodox	9,750,000
Muslim	150,000
other	90,000
Greenland	
Evangelical Lutheran	53,000
other	1,000
Grenada	
Roman Catholic	62,000
Anglican	20,000
other	15,000
Guadeloupe	
Roman Catholic	300,000
other	30,000
Guam	
Roman Catholic	96,000
Protestant	21,000
other	4,000
Guatemala	
Roman Catholic	6,550,000
Protestant	1,640,000
Guernsey	
Anglican	38,000
Roman Catholic	6,000
other	15,000
Guinea	
Muslim	4,300,000
traditional beliefs	1,840,000
other	90,000
Guinea-Bissau	
traditional beliefs	590,000
Muslim	270,000
Christian	40,000
Guyana	
Hindu	274,000
other Protestant	143,000
Roman Catholic	127,000
Anglican	143,000
Muslim	72,000
other	37,000
Haiti	
Roman Catholic	4,360,000
Baptist	530,000
other (mostly Protestant)	540,000
Honduras	
Roman Catholic	3,770,000
other	170,000
Hong Kong	
Buddhist (some Confucianist and Taoist)	4,980,000
Christian	550,000
Hungary	
Roman Catholic	5,730,000
Protestant	2,290,000
nonreligious	920,000
atheist	760,000
Jewish	100,000
Iceland	
Lutheran	238,000
other	8,000
India	
Hindu	642,290,000
Muslim	88,220,000
Christian	18,890,000
Sikh	15,280,000
Buddhist	5,510,000

Religious affiliation	1986 population
Jain	3,750,000
other	3,300,000
Indonesia	
Muslim	148,710,000
Protestant	9,850,000
Roman Catholic	5,040,000
Hindu	3,460,000
Buddhist	1,600,000
Iran	
Shi'i Muslim	42,870,000
Sunnī Muslim	2,300,000
other	930,000
Iraq	
Shi'i Muslim	8,530,000
Sunnī Muslim	6,750,000
other	670,000
Ireland	
Roman Catholic	3,330,000
other	210,000
Isle of Man	
Anglican	44,000
other	27,000
Israel	
Jewish	3,640,000
Muslim (mostly Sunnī)	570,000
other	170,000
Italy	
Roman Catholic	47,670,000
atheist and nonreligious	9,280,000
other	340,000
Jamaica	
Protestant	1,890,000
Roman Catholic	230,000
other	250,000
Japan	
Shintoist[2]	105,700,000
Buddhist[2]	88,810,000
Christian	1,580,000
other	16,280,000
Jersey	
Anglican	48,000
Roman Catholic	18,000
other	12,000
Jordan	
Sunnī Muslim	2,560,000
other	190,000
Kampuchea	
Buddhist	6,600,000
other	860,000
Kenya	
Roman Catholic	5,580,000
Anglican	1,520,000
other Protestant	4,080,000
African Christian	3,720,000
traditional beliefs	4,000,000
Muslim	1,270,000
other	970,000
Kiribati	
Roman Catholic	34,000
Congregational	27,000
other	4,000
Korea, North	
atheist and nonreligious	13,950,000
traditional beliefs	3,200,000
Ch'ŏndogyo	2,860,000
other	530,000
Korea, South	
Buddhist	15,550,000
Protestant	10,680,000
Confucian	7,270,000
Roman Catholic	2,000,000
Ch'ondogyo	1,500,000
Wonbulgyo	1,330,000
other	3,240,000
Kuwait	
Muslim	1,640,000
other	150,000
Laos	
Buddhist	2,150,000
traditional beliefs	1,260,000
other	290,000
Lebanon	
Shi'i Muslim	950,000
Maronite Christian	680,000
Sunnī Muslim	680,000
Greek Orthodox	200,000
Druze	200,000
Lesotho	
Roman Catholic	690,000
Protestant	470,000
other	430,000
Liberia	
traditional beliefs	1,730,000
Muslim	350,000
Christian	230,000
Libya	
Sunnī Muslim	3,830,000
other	120,000
Liechtenstein	
Roman Catholic	23,000
other	4,000
Luxembourg	
Roman Catholic	341,000
other	26,000
Macau	
Buddhist and Taoist	303,000
other	130,000
Madagascar	
Christian[1]	5,250,000
traditional beliefs	4,840,000
other	200,000
Malaŵi	
Christian[1]	4,690,000
traditional beliefs	1,380,000
Muslim	1,180,000
other	20,000
Malaysia	
Muslim	8,510,000
Buddhist	2,780,000
Chinese folk-religionist	1,870,000
Hindu	1,130,000
Christian	1,030,000
other	770,000
Maldives	
Muslim	189,000
Mali	
Muslim	7,610,000
traditional beliefs	760,000
Christian	80,000
Malta	
Roman Catholic	327,000
other	9,000
Martinique	
Roman Catholic	300,000
other	28,000
Mauritania	
Muslim	1,680,000
other	10,000
Mauritius	
Hindu	540,000
Roman Catholic	270,000
Muslim	130,000
other	90,000
Mayotte	
Sunnī Muslim	69,000
Christian	1,000
Mexico	
Roman Catholic	74,520,000
Protestant	2,660,000
nonreligious	2,490,000
other	720,000
Monaco	
Roman Catholic	26,000
other	3,000
Mongolia	
atheist and nonreligious	1,270,000
traditional beliefs	600,000
other	70,000
Montserrat	
Anglican	4,400
Methodist	2,500
other	5,100
Morocco	
Muslim (mostly Sunnī)	22,160,000
other	290,000
Mozambique	
traditional beliefs	6,760,000
Muslim	2,330,000
Roman Catholic	2,020,000
other	2,720,000
Nauru	
Protestant	4,600
Roman Catholic	1,900
other	1,500
Nepal	
Hindu	15,090,000
Buddhist	890,000
Muslim	460,000
other	420,000
Netherlands, The	
Roman Catholic	5,260,000
Dutch Reformed Church	2,810,000
Reformed Churches	1,150,000
nonreligious	4,700,000
other	640,000
Netherlands Antilles	
Roman Catholic	147,000
Protestant	18,000
other	11,000
New Caledonia	
Roman Catholic	109,000
Protestant	27,000
other	14,000
New Zealand	
Anglican	850,000
Presbyterian	540,000
Roman Catholic	470,000
other	1,420,000
Nicaragua	
Roman Catholic	3,080,000
other	310,000
Niger	
Muslim	6,260,000
other	160,000
Nigeria	
Muslim	44,150,000
Protestant	25,800,000
Roman Catholic	11,870,000
African Christian	10,400,000
traditional beliefs	5,490,000
other	390,000
Niue	
Congregational	2,200
other	800
Norfolk Island	
Anglican	800
other	1,200
Norway	
Lutheran	3,660,000
other	510,000
Oman	
Muslim	1,274,000
other	14,000
Pacific Islands, Trust Territory of the	
Protestant	81,000
Roman Catholic	75,000
other	9,000
Pakistan	
Muslim	99,590,000
other	3,290,000
Panama	
Roman Catholic	1,893,000
other	334,000
Papua New Guinea	
Protestant	1,990,000
Roman Catholic	1,120,000
other	300,000
Paraguay	
Roman Catholic	3,390,000
other	141,000
Peru	
Roman Catholic	18,670,000
other	1,540,000
Philippines	
Roman Catholic	47,100,000
Aglipayan (Philippine Independent church)	3,470,000
Muslim	2,410,000
Protestant	2,180,000
other	840,000
Pitcairn Island	
Seventh-day Adventist	60
Anglican	10
Poland	
Roman Catholic	30,340,000
other	7,120,000
Portugal	
Roman Catholic	9,690,000
other	560,000
Puerto Rico	
Roman Catholic	2,803,000
other	481,000
Qatar	
Muslim	287,000
other	24,000
Réunion	
Roman Catholic	535,000
other	21,000
Romania	
Romanian Orthodox	15,970,000
Greek Orthodox	2,280,000
atheist and nonreligious	3,650,000
other	680,000
Rwanda	
Roman Catholic	3,550,000
Protestant	760,000
Muslim	570,000
traditional beliefs	1,460,000
St. Christopher and Nevis	
Anglican	15,000
Methodist	13,200
other	17,800
St. Helena and Ascension	
Anglican	6,130
other	870
St. Lucia	
Roman Catholic	121,000
Protestant	16,000
other	3,000
St. Pierre and Miquelon	
Roman Catholic	5,870
other	130
St. Vincent and the Grenadines	
Anglican	40,000
Methodist	23,000
Roman Catholic	21,000
other	27,000
San Marino	
Roman Catholic	21,900
other	1,100
São Tomé and Príncipe	
Roman Catholic	88,000
Protestant	22,000
Saudi Arabia	
Muslim	11,530,000
other	140,000
Senegal	
Muslim (African Sunnī [of the Malikite rite])	6,100,000
Roman Catholic	380,000
traditional beliefs	210,000
other	10,000
Seychelles	
Roman Catholic	63,600
other	2,400
Sierra Leone	
traditional beliefs	1,920,000
Muslim	1,470,000
Christian[1]	340,000
other	4,000
Singapore	
Taoist	758,000
Buddhist	691,000
Muslim	422,000
Christian	267,000
nonreligious	342,000
other	109,000
Solomon Islands	
Protestant	211,000
Roman Catholic	53,000
other	13,000
Somalia	
Sunnī Muslim	5,980,000
other	12,000
South Africa[3]	
Afrikaans Reformed (NGK)	4,358,000
Roman Catholic	2,664,000
Black independent churches	5,735,000
other Christian churches	8,811,000
Hindu	579,000
Muslim	360,000
nonreligious[4]	5,303,000
other	329,000
Bophuthatswana	
Christian	1,410,000
traditional beliefs	150,000
Ciskei	
Christian	620,000
traditional beliefs	180,000
Transkei	
Christian	1,928,000
traditional beliefs	813,000
other	32,000
Venda	
traditional beliefs	318,000
Christian	99,000
other	31,000
South West Africa/Namibia	
Lutheran	616,000
Roman Catholic	238,000
other	349,000
Spain	
Roman Catholic	37,653,000
other	1,164,000
Sri Lanka	
Buddhist	11,148,000
Hindu	2,493,000
Muslim	1,223,000
Christian	1,207,000
other	16,000
Sudan, The	
Sunnī Muslim	17,960,000
traditional beliefs	4,109,000
Roman Catholic	1,083,000
other	1,452,000
Suriname	
Hindu	108,200
Roman Catholic	90,100
Muslim	77,400
Protestant	74,300
other	45,000
Swaziland	
Christian[1]	525,000
traditional beliefs	142,000
other	15,000
Sweden	
Church of Sweden	7,556,000
other	802,000
Switzerland	
Roman Catholic	3,121,000
Protestant	2,904,000
other	531,000
Syria	
Sunnī Muslim	9,508,000
Christian	944,000
other	159,000
Taiwan	
Chinese folk-religionist	9,428,000
Buddhist	8,359,000
Christian[1]	1,438,000
other	214,000
Tanzania	
Christian	8,985,000
Muslim	6,739,000
traditional beliefs	6,739,000
Thailand	
Buddhist	50,021,000
Muslim	2,001,000
other	632,000
Togo	
traditional beliefs	1,407,000
Christian[1]	1,137,000
Sunnī Muslim	522,000
other	6,000
Tokelau	
Congregational	1,120
other	480
Tonga	
Free Wesleyan	46,500
Roman Catholic	15,800
other	30,300
Trinidad and Tobago	
Roman Catholic	397,000
Protestant	338,000
Hindu	301,000
other	166,000
Tunisia	
Sunnī Muslim	7,283,000
other	44,000
Turkey	
Muslim (mostly Sunnī)	52,000,000
other	420,000
Turks and Caicos Islands	
Baptist	3,500
Methodist	1,600
Anglican	1,600
other	1,900
Tuvalu	
Congregational	7,530
other	670
Uganda	
Roman Catholic	7,428,000
Protestant	4,957,000
Muslim	2,471,000
other	782,000
U.S.S.R.	
atheist and nonreligious	143,100,000
Eastern Orthodox	88,440,000
Muslim	31,390,000
Protestant	8,370,000
Roman Catholic	4,930,000
Jewish	3,160,000
other	640,000
United Arab Emirates	
Muslim	1,613,000
other	87,000
United Kingdom	
Church of England	32,194,000
other Christian	9,612,000
Roman Catholic	7,425,000
nonreligious	4,971,000
Muslim	816,000
other	1,661,000
United States	
Protestant	118,370,000
Roman Catholic	72,450,000
Eastern Orthodox	5,310,000
other Christian	16,380,000
Jewish	7,730,000
atheist and nonreligious	16,660,000
other	4,590,000
Uruguay	
Roman Catholic	1,806,000
nonreligious	1,065,000
other	164,000
Vanuatu	
Presbyterian	48,600
Anglican	22,200
Roman Catholic	18,500
other	47,700
Venezuela	
Roman Catholic	16,439,000
other	1,352,000
Vietnam	
Buddhist	33,856,000
atheist and nonreligious	11,326,000
Roman Catholic	4,286,000
other	11,143,000
Virgin Islands (U.S.)	
Protestant	53,600
Roman Catholic	38,300
other	22,100
Wallis and Futuna	
Roman Catholic	14,000
West Bank	
Muslim	765,000
other	50,000
Western Sahara	
Muslim	150,000
Western Samoa	
Congregational	75,700
Roman Catholic	34,700
Methodist	25,900
other	23,700
Yemen (Aden)	
Muslim	2,356,000
other	9,000
Yemen (Ṣan'ā')	
Shi'i Muslim	4,230,000
Sunnī Muslim	2,820,000
Yugoslavia	
Serbian Orthodox	8,058,000
Roman Catholic	6,055,000
other Christian	2,865,000
Muslim	2,422,000
atheist and nonreligious	3,889,000
Zaire	
Roman Catholic	15,040,000
Protestant	9,010,000
African Christian	5,310,000
traditional beliefs	1,057,000
other	653,000
Zambia	
Christian[1]	4,965,000
traditional beliefs	1,862,000
other	111,000
Zimbabwe	
Christian[1]	4,875,000
traditional beliefs	3,404,000
other	126,000

[1]Includes affiliated and nominal Christians. [2]Many Japanese adhere to both Shintoism and Buddhism. [3]Excludes Black republics listed separately. [4]Includes traditional beliefs and religion not known.

Vital statistics, marriage, family

This table provides some of the basic measures that control the size, rate, and direction of population change within a country. The accuracy of these data is principally a function of the effectiveness of each respective national system for collecting information about vital and civil events (birth, death, marriage, etc.) and of the sophistication of the analysis that can be brought to bear upon the data so compiled. Calculating life expectancy, for example, requires detailed information about age structure and mortality experience, but the calculation can be made in different ways upon a single information base.

Thus data on birth rates depend not only on the completeness of registration of births in a particular country but also on the conditions under which those data are collected: Do all births take place in a hospital? Are the births reported comparably in all parts of the country? Are the records of the births tabulated in a central location with an effort to eliminate inconsistent reporting of birth events, perinatal mortality, etc.? The same difficulties apply to death rates but with the added complication of having to identify "cause of death" in a country with, say, only one physician for every 1,000 population: too few to perform autopsies to assess accurately the cause of death after the fact and also too few to provide ongoing care at a level where records would permit inference about cause of death based on prior condition or diagnosis.

Calculating natural increase, which at its most basic is simply the difference between the birth and death rates, may be complicated by the varying degrees of completeness of birth and death registrations for a given country. The total fertility rate may be understood as the average number of children that would be borne per woman if all childbearing women lived to the end of their childbearing years and bore children at each age at the average rate for that age. Calculating the fertility rate is complicated by changing age structure of the population over time, changing mortality rates among mothers, and changing medical practice at births, each improvement leading to greater numbers of live-born children and greater numbers of children who survive their first year (the basis for measurement of infant mortality, another basic control on the growth of a population).

As indicated above, data for causes of death are not only particularly difficult to obtain, since many countries are not well equipped to collect the data, but are also difficult to assess, as their accuracy may be suspect and their meaning may be subject to varying interpretation. Take the case of a citizen of a less developed country who dies of what is clearly a lung infection: Was the death complicated by chronic malnutrition, itself complicated by a parasitic infestation, these last two together so weakening the subject that he died of an infection that he might have survived had his general health been better? Similarly, in a developed country: Someone may die from what is identified in an autopsy as a cerebrovascular accident, but if that accident occurred in a vascular system that was weakened by diabetes, what was the actual cause of death? Statistics on

Vital statistics, marriage, family

country	vital rates						causes of death (rate per 100,000 population)								
	year	birth rate per 1,000 population	death rate per 1,000 population	infant mortality rate per 1,000 live births	rate of natural increase per 1,000 population	total fertility rate	year	infectious and parasitic diseases	neoplasms (cancers)	endocrine and metabolic disorders	diseases of the nervous system	diseases of the circulatory system	diseases of the respiratory system	diseases of the digestive system	accidents, poisoning, and violence
Afghanistan	1980–85	48.9	27.3	194.0	21.6	6.9	...	...	...	...	...	...	...	...	...
Albania	1985	26.2	5.8	44.0[2]	20.4	3.6[3]	...	...	...	...	...	...	...	...	...
Algeria	1982	42.9	10.5	92.2	32.4	7.2[4]	...	...	...	...	...	...	...	...	...
American Samoa	1984	39.1	4.3	4.4	34.8	4.9[5]	...	...	...	...	...	...	...	...	...
Andorra	1984	11.4	4.0	16.0[6]	7.4	...	...	...	...	...	...	...	...	...	...
Angola	1984	47.0	25.0	144.0	22.0	6.4	1973	73.2	6.5	4.9	3.6	19.2	24.6	3.6	89.0
Anguilla	1982	26.2	9.5	13.6[7]	16.7	1.9[3]	...	...	...	...	...	...	...	...	...
Antigua and Barbuda	1983	15.0	5.2	32.0[2]	9.8	2.1[3]	1983	21.7	46.0	34.5	26.4[8]	171.3	40.3[8]	18.1[8]	31.1[9]
Argentina	1985	25.0	9.0	36.0[10]	16.0	3.4	1981	29.5	148.8	8.2	10.1	371.9	45.7	43.8	58.4
Aruba	1982	15.7	4.7	8.0	11.0	3.5[3, 11]	...	...	...	...	...	...	...	...	...
Australia	1986	15.7	7.4	9.2[12]	8.3	1.9[12]	1984	3.3	167.8	15.2	9.8	349.0	50.2	23.5	46.6
Austria	1985	11.5	11.8	11.4[10]	−0.3	1.5[10]	1984	6.2	249.3	18.3	12.9	663.0	67.3	64.5	93.6
Bahamas, The	1984	22.2	5.0	25.3[2]	17.2	3.2[3]	1982	8.7	107.8	18.3	18.8	130.3	71.1	37.6	39.0
Bahrain	1984	36.8	5.9	44.1	30.9	5.3	1983	4.7	23.9	6.2	3.9	97.3	17.2	6.5	30.2
Bangladesh	1985	43.3	16.6	133.0	26.7	5.8	1976	15.5	19.8	...	...	5.9	25.7	...	...
Barbados	1984	16.7	7.7	10.9	9.0	1.9[3]	1982	16.0	115.8	49.1	13.6	305.9	45.5	24.4	29.6
Belgium	1985	11.9	11.4	9.4	0.5	1.6	1979	7.2	264.9	26.9	2.7	486.4	51.3	17.9	82.8
Belize	1985	40.1	4.0	18.9	36.1	3.7[6]	1983	43.1	38.7	25.4	16.5	95.1	52.0	12.7	26.6
Benin	1984	49.0	17.0	116.0	32.0	6.5	1977	...	...	...	...	...	206.5	200.7	...
Bermuda	1984	15.1	7.0	5.9	8.1	1.9[6]	1984	3.5	163.1	50.0[9]	7.0[8]	354.5	37.2	19.6[8]	39.0
Bhutan	1985	37.7	17.4	134.0	20.3	5.4	...	...	...	...	...	...	...	...	...
Bolivia	1980–85	44.0	16.0	110.0[12]	28.0	6.3	...	...	...	...	...	...	...	...	...
Botswana	1980–85	50.0	13.0	68.4[7]	37.0	6.2[7]	1977	23.9	6.0	...	...	8.4	...	...	...
Brazil	1980–85	30.6	8.4	71.0	22.2	3.8	1980[13]	57.4	49.3	8.7	3.0	156.2	36.9	10.3	57.9
British Virgin Islands	1984	19.2	5.6	13.3	13.6	...	1984	17.1	25.6	17.1	—	273.3	85.4	25.6	25.6
Brunei	1985	30.1	3.6	12.1	26.5	...	1981	5.0	25.0	...	...	41.0	16.0	3.1	36.0
Bulgaria	1985	13.2	12.0	15.8	1.2	2.2[6]	1983	8.2	157.2	15.4	8.8	662.3	90.7	32.8	60.2
Burkina Faso	1980–85	47.8	22.2	137.0	25.6	6.5	...	...	...	...	...	...	...	...	...
Burma	1985	33.2	13.7	106.0	19.5	4.5	1978	32.6	6.5	6.1	...	14.1	19.8	1.7	7.3
Burundi	1980–85	47.6	20.9	124.0	26.7	6.4	...	...	...	...	...	...	...	...	...
Cameroon	1980–85	42.9	15.8	103.0	27.1	5.8	...	...	...	...	...	...	...	...	...
Canada	1985	14.9	7.0	9.3[10]	7.9	1.7[5]	1983	4.0	172.1	16.0	10.6	317.3	53.5	27.2	56.6
Cape Verde	1985	32.8	8.4	30.0[5]	24.4	2.6[3]	1980	153.7	43.8	20.6	16.5	135.8	72.3	27.7	30.1
Cayman Islands	1985	17.4	5.5	...	11.9	...	1979	18.2	60.1	52.0	...	204.6	54.1	...	102.1
Central African Republic	1983	41.0	17.0	142.0	24.0	5.5	1978	59.0	...	...	...	...	...	...	...
Chad	1984	43.0	21.0	139.0	22.0	5.6	...	...	...	...	...	...	...	...	...
Chile	1984	21.2	6.3	19.6	14.9	3.0[7]	1983	23.1	102.5	13.6	8.5	176.0	63.5	56.6	78.2
China	1984	17.5	6.7	38.0[3]	10.8	2.3[3]	1981[14]	23.7	113.0	6.3	9.4	251.1	43.0	25.9	31.3
Christmas Island	1982	5.6	2.0	...	3.6	...	...	...	...	...	...	...	...	...	...
Cocos (Keeling) Islands	1981	14.4	1.8	—	12.6	...	...	...	...	...	...	...	...	...	...
Colombia	1982	30.6	5.8	60.9[7]	24.8	3.9[3]	1977[16]	86.6	54.1	7.2	5.9	129.2	60.7	9.9	70.1
Comoros	1980–85	49.3	15.2	121.7[6]	34.1	7.0	...	...	...	...	...	...	...	...	...
Congo	1980–85	44.5	18.6	81.0	25.9	6.0	...	...	...	...	...	...	...	...	...
Cook Islands	1985	24.6	6.9	25.9	17.7	4.1	1976–78	54.0	38.0	27.0	0.0	197.0	110.0	18.0	49.0
Costa Rica	1984	32.7	4.5	18.9	28.2	3.5[3]	1983	17.5	78.4	8.7	1.9	111.5	20.3	8.5	37.2
Côte d'Ivoire	1984	45.0	14.0	106.0	31.0	6.5	...	...	...	...	...	...	...	...	...
Cuba	1985	18.0	6.4	16.5	11.6	2.0	1981	12.8	110.0	13.5	9.9	260.4	47.3	20.9	67.3
Cyprus	1984	20.6	8.0	14.9	12.6	2.5[5]	...	...	...	...	...	...	...	...	...
Czechoslovakia	1985	14.5	11.8	15.6	2.7	2.3[2]	1985	4.1	232.0	...	7.8	648.1	85.5	...	76.3
Denmark	1985	10.6	11.4	7.1[10]	−0.8	1.4	1984	3.6	284.2	15.9	0.8	472.9	78.2	23.9	76.5
Djibouti	1980–85	49.2	18.3	*c.* 200	30.9	6.8	...	...	...	...	...	...	...	...	...
Dominica	1984	20.8	5.2	23.9	15.6	3.5[3]	1982	25.2	86.9	30.2	3.8	219.2	20.2	18.9	26.5
Dominican Republic	1980–85	33.1	8.0	75.0	25.1	4.2	1982	47.8	27.3	15.1	10.8	87.1	29.9	22.5	35.3
Ecuador	1984	36.8	8.1	68.4	28.7	4.8[12]	1978	168.7	38.9	5.3	4.3	96.2	114.3	16.0	73.6
Egypt	1984	37.4	10.9	104.5	26.5	5.4	1979	29.3	19.2	8.8	0.4	194.7	187.3	288.8	47.3

causes of death seek to identify the "underlying" cause (that which sets the final train of events leading to death in motion) but often must settle for the most proximate cause or symptom. Even this kind of analysis may be misleading for those charged with interpreting the data with a view to reordering health-care priorities for a particular country.

Expectation of life is probably the most accurate single measure of the quality of life in a given society. It summarizes in a single number all of the natural and social stresses that operate upon the individuals in that society. The number may range from as few as 40 years of life in the least developed countries to as much as 80 years for women in the most developed nations. The lost potential in the years separating those two numbers is prodigious, regardless of how the loss arises—wars and civil violence, poor public health services, or poor individual health practice in matters of nutrition, exercise, stress management, and so on.

Data on marriages and marriage rates probably are less meaningful in terms of international comparisons than some of the measures mentioned above because the number, timing, and kinds of social relationships that substitute for marriage depend on many kinds of social variables—income, degree of social control, heterogeneity of the society (race, class, language communities), or level of development of civil administration (if one must travel for a day or more to obtain a legal civil ceremony, one may forgo it). Nevertheless, the data for a single country say specific things about local practice in terms of the age at which a man or woman typically marries, and the overall rate will at least define the number of legal civil marriages, though it cannot say anything about other, less formal arrangements (here the figure for the legitimacy rate for children in the next section may identify some of the societies in which economics or social constraints may operate to limit the number of marriages that are actually confirmed on civil registers). The available data usually include both first marriages and remarriages after annulment, divorce, widowhood, or the like.

The data for families provide information about the average size of a family unit (individuals related by blood or civil register) and the average number of children under a specified age (set here at 15 to provide a consistent measure of legal minority internationally, though actual minority depends on the laws of each country). When well-defined family data are not collected as part of a country's national census or vital statistics surveys, data for households are substituted on the assumption that most households worldwide represent families in some conventional sense. In the older countries of Europe and North America increasing numbers of households are comprised of unrelated individuals (unmarried heterosexual couples, aged [or younger] groups sharing limited [often fixed] incomes for reasons of economy, or homosexual couples); such arrangements are not yet so common in the rest of the world that they represent great numbers overall. Very few census programs, even in developed countries, make adequate provision for identifying these households.

expectation of life at birth (latest year)		nuptiality, family, and family planning															country
		marriages			age at marriage (latest)						families (F), households (H) (latest)						
		year	total number	rate per 1,000 population	groom (percent)			bride (percent)			families (households)		children		legal abortions		
male	female				19 and under	20–29	30 and over	19 and under	20–29	30 and over	total ('000)	size	number under age 15	percent legitimate	number	ratio per 100 live births	
36.6	37.3	1970	6,212	0.4	...	...	...	...	...	...	H 2,110	H 6.2	H 2.8[1]	...	...	...	Afghanistan
67.9	72.9	1984	26,199	9.0	2.0	81.2	16.8	23.0	73.7	3.4	...	F 5.4	...	...	...	...	Albania
56.7	58.9	1982	129,200	6.3	...	...	...	...	...	...	...	H 4.9	...	...	...	...	Algeria
61.0	64.3	1982	362	10.7	5.6	65.5	28.8	24.5	60.5	15.0	H 4	H 7.1	H 2.9	86.0	...	...	American Samoa
——70.0——		1984	130	3.1	...	...	...	...	...	...	...	...	...	...	...	...	Andorra
42.0	44.0	1972	26,278	4.5	...	...	...	...	...	...	...	H 4.8	...	...	...	...	Angola
68.6	71.9	1982	64	9.8	...	...	...	...	...	...	H 1.6	H 4.1	H 1.8	39.4	...	...	Anguilla
——72.0——		1983	188	2.4	0.5	41.1	58.5	10.6	54.8	34.6	H 15	H 4.2	H 1.9	18.7	...	...	Antigua and Barbuda
68.6	73.3	1983	177,010	6.0	5.6	71.5	22.9	26.0	58.6	15.4	H 7,104	H 3.9	H 1.2	70.2	...	...	Argentina
71.6	76.8	1982	470	7.7	...	...	...	...	...	...	...	H 4.0	...	41.3	...	...	Aruba
72.6	79.1	1985	108,655	7.0	1.9	64.8	33.3	10.8	66.0	23.2	F 4,140	F 3.1	F 0.5	85.2	...	...	Australia
69.2	76.4	1984	45,823	6.1	0.5	71.1	28.4	14.2	69.3	16.5	F 2,020	F 3.7	F 0.7	78.5	...	...	Austria
66.9	70.9	1983	1,490	6.7	3.6	62.4	34.0	17.6	59.3	23.1	H 40	H 4.3	H 1.8	39.7	...	...	Bahamas, The
67.1	71.4	1983	2,396	6.2	6.2	74.4	19.4	45.9	48.5	5.6	H 61	H 6.7	H 3.0	...	...	...	Bahrain
49.2	48.2	1982	...	9.4	...	...	...	...	...	...	...	H 5.8	...	...	...	...	Bangladesh
70.0	75.4	1983	1,252	5.0	0.6	49.9	49.5	5.5	66.7	27.8	H 67	H 3.7	H 1.5	27.9	...	...	Barbados
70.1	76.7	1985	57,200	5.8	4.3	79.8	15.9	22.1	67.1	10.8	F 3,613	F 2.7	F 0.5	94.8	...	...	Belgium
——71.2——		1984	860	5.3	...	...	...	...	...	...	H 29	H 5.2	H 2.4	46.1	...	...	Belize
47.0	51.0	1980–85	...	12.8	...	...	...	...	...	...	...	H 5.4	...	...	...	...	Benin
68.8	76.3	1984	664	11.8	3.7	65.1	31.2	17.6	61.3	21.1	H 18	H 2.7	H 0.6	67.5	85	9.1	Bermuda
47.6	46.1	...	...	...	...	...	...	...	...	...	...	H 5.4	...	...	...	...	Bhutan
48.6	53.0	1980	26,990	4.8	8.3	75.1	16.6	26.1	55.4	18.5	H 1,050	H 4.4	H 1.8	80.9	...	...	Bolivia
52.7	59.3	...	...	...	...	...	...	...	...	...	H 125	H 5.7	H 2.0	28.0	...	...	Botswana
60.9	66.0	1984	936,070	7.1	7.4	69.1	23.5	33.4	51.7	14.9	F 31,076	F 4.1	H 1.6	...	...	...	Brazil
68.6	71.9	1984	149	12.7	—	43.6	56.4	2.0	56.4	41.6	H 3	H 3.3	H 1.1	43.8	...	...	British Virgin Islands
70.1	72.7	1983	1,523	7.1	4.5	75.2	20.3	19.8	70.5	9.7	H 23	H 5.8	H 2.5	99.3	...	...	Brunei
68.0	74.0	1984	67,200	7.5	6.4	75.6	18.0	37.7	51.4	10.9	F 2,627	F 3.3	F 0.7	89.1	147,791	126.2	Bulgaria
40.4	43.6	1975	...	9.4	...	...	...	...	...	...	...	H 4.9	...	...	...	...	Burkina Faso
51.2	54.3	...	...	...	...	...	...	...	...	...	...	H 5.1	...	...	...	...	Burma
42.4	45.6	...	...	...	...	...	...	...	...	...	...	H 4.9	...	...	...	...	Burundi
49.2	52.6	...	...	...	...	...	...	...	...	...	...	H 5.2	...	...	...	...	Cameroon
73.0	79.0	1985	180,200	7.1	3.1	68.1	28.8	13.3	67.3	19.4	H 9,079	H 2.8	H 1.4	91.0	61,750	16.5	Canada
60.3	64.0	1975	1,604	5.4	...	...	...	...	...	...	F 59	F 5.1	...	55.2	...	...	Cape Verde
68.6	71.9	1985	176	8.4	...	...	...	...	...	...	H 4	H 3.8	H 1.1	66.8	...	...	Cayman Islands
46.0	49.0	...	...	...	...	...	...	...	...	...	...	H 4.3	...	...	...	...	Central African Republic
43.0	45.0	...	...	...	...	...	...	...	...	...	...	H 3.9	...	...	...	...	Chad
65.4	70.1	1984	80,800	6.8	6.5	74.4	19.1	26.4	60.7	12.9	H 1,690	H 4.5	H 2.0	72.4	2,346	1.0	Chile
65.5	69.4	1982	8,395,000	8.3	...	...	...	...	...	...	H 221[15]	H 4.5	...	...	...	...	China
63.0	66.5	1982	25	8.3	—	90.9	9.1	45.5	36.4	18.1	—	H 5.8	H 1.5	97.1	...	...	Christmas Island
63.0	66.5	1981	6	10.8	—	100.0	—	—	100.0	—	—	H 6.3	H 2.6	93.3	2	40.0	Cocos (Keeling) Islands
61.4	66.0	1977	88,401	3.5	5.6	69.5	24.9	33.6	55.3	11.1	F 4,772	F 5.4	F 2.5	75.2	...	...	Colombia
52.0	55.6	1964	1,959	8.5	...	...	...	...	...	...	...	H 5.3	...	...	...	...	Comoros
44.9	48.1	...	...	...	...	...	...	...	...	...	H 326	H 4.7	H 2.0	...	...	...	Congo
64.0	70.0	1985	105	6.1	1.2	63.4	35.4	22.0	51.2	26.8	H 3	H 5.6	H 2.4	...	...	...	Cook Islands
70.5	74.7	1983	19,171	7.9	9.2	69.3	21.5	36.2	51.1	12.7	F 472	F 5.0	F 1.7	64.9	...	...	Costa Rica
51.0	54.0	...	...	...	...	...	...	...	...	...	...	H 4.5	...	...	...	...	Côte d'Ivoire
72.6	76.0	1985	79,800	7.9	11.3	57.7	31.0	31.9	47.0	21.1	F 2,002	H 4.2	H 1.6	...	116,956	70.8	Cuba
72.3	76.0	1984	5,100	7.8	1.3	75.5	23.2	18.2	70.2	11.6	H 160	H 3.5	H 1.1	99.7	...	...	Cyprus
67.2	74.4	1985	117,376[7]	7.7	6.0	74.7	19.3	30.3	56.3	13.4	F 4,187	F 3.6	F 0.9	93.5	107,638	47.1	Czechoslovakia
71.5	77.5	1984	28,600	5.6	0.7	51.5	47.8	31.9	62.9	33.2	F 2,563	F 2.0	F 0.4	58.1	20,791	40.9	Denmark
——45.0——		1982	2,500	6.7	...	...	...	...	...	...	...	H 5.6	...	96.8	...	...	Djibouti
72.8	76.5	1969	234	3.3	...	...	...	...	...	...	H 18	H 4.3	H 2.2	35.0	...	...	Dominica
60.7	64.6	1981	26,862	4.9	8.0	63.0	29.0	29.7	51.0	19.3	H 753	H 5.1	H 2.5	32.8	...	...	Dominican Republic
59.8	63.6	1984	53,800	5.9	13.0	65.7	21.3	39.1	47.9	13.0	...	H 5.1	...	67.9	...	...	Ecuador
58.0	61.1	1979	384,000	9.4	8.6	60.5	30.9	46.8	42.6	10.6	H 8,411	H 5.4	H 2.1	...	...	...	Egypt

Vital statistics, marriage, family (continued)

country	vital rates						causes of death (rate per 100,000 population)								
	year	birth rate per 1,000 population	death rate per 1,000 population	infant mortality rate per 1,000 live births	rate of natural increase per 1,000 population	total fertility rate	year	infectious and parasitic diseases	neoplasms (cancers)	endocrine and metabolic disorders	diseases of the nervous system	diseases of the circulatory system	diseases of the respiratory system	diseases of the digestive system	accidents, poisoning, and violence
El Salvador	1984	29.8	6.0	35.1	23.8	6.0[3]	1983	64.2	17.1	5.4	1.8	59.7	32.1	8.3	141.0
Equatorial Guinea	1980–85	42.5	21.0	149.0	21.5	5.7	...	...	...	...	...	...	...	...	...
Ethiopia	1985	49.7	23.1	155.0	26.6	6.7	1978	39.5	3.8	24.6	2.7	5.6	16.3	28.9	15.8
Faeroe Islands	1984	14.4	7.8	14.9[5]	6.6	2.2	1983	2.2	168.3	6.7	—	399.4	47.1	13.5	103.2
Falkland Islands	1981	15.0	5.0	...	10.0	...	...	...	...	...	...	...	...	...	...
Fiji	1984	29.8	5.3	22.5	24.5	3.3[5]	1983	22.2	44.8	22.6	4.9	185.9	41.8	18.9	45.2
Finland	1985	12.8	9.8	6.5[10]	3.0	1.7[5]	1983	8.0	194.4	12.5[17]	10.7	492.5	69.9	24.0	75.5
France	1985	13.9	10.0	8.0	3.9	1.5[5]	1983	13.0	228.7	13.2	34.1[2]	368.4	16.8	66.4[2]	91.5
French Guiana	1984	29.0	6.2	22.6	22.8	3.1[18]	1981	43.5	49.1	16.8	26.7	119.3	29.5	47.7	89.8
French Polynesia	1985	30.5	5.3	20.8	25.2	3.5	1984	21.2	67.7	10.0	19.4	120.1	36.5	17.7	58.9
Gabon	1980–85	33.7	19.9	121.6	13.8	4.7	...	...	...	...	...	...	...	...	...
Gambia, The	1980–85	47.5	21.7	174.0	25.8	6.4	...	...	...	...	...	...	...	...	...
Gaza Strip	1984	48.3	8.1	...	40.2	...	...	...	...	...	...	...	...	...	...
Germany, East	1985	13.2	13.4	10.0[10]	−0.2	1.6	1983	5.3	215.1	32.7	0.8	781.8	66.9	25.2	38.9
Germany, West	1985	9.6	11.5	9.0	−1.9	1.3[10]	1984	7.3	259.6	20.8	12.4	576.4	70.8	53.8	62.3
Ghana	1980–85	46.9	14.6	98.0	32.3	6.5	...	...	...	...	...	...	...	...	...
Gibraltar	1985	17.3	9.6	...	7.7	...	...	...	...	...	...	...	...	...	...
Greece	1985	11.8	9.3	14.1[10]	2.5	2.3[10]	1985	6.7	182.6	35.8	13.5	450.8	55.5	32.5	49.1
Greenland	1984	20.0	8.3	28.5	11.7	2.1	1984	11.4	138.7	5.7	1.9	83.0	77.9	13.3	145.0
Grenada	1983	31.2	8.6	21.2	22.6	3.6[3]	1981	26.7	90.9	48.3	...	186.3	41.5	31.4	30.0
Guadeloupe	1984	20.2	6.8	17.7	13.4	2.5[3]	1979	10.0	72.5	26.0	1.2	220.2	13.4	13.4	96.9
Guam	1985	17.8	3.4	7.5[5]	14.4	3.2[6]	1983	...	53.0	13.2	13.2	140.4	15.0	...	63.0
Guatemala	1985	41.7	7.5	56.0	34.2	6.1[3]	1981	256.8	28.2	12.4	11.3	57.2	143.2	24.8	195.9
Guernsey	...	...	...	...	...	...	...	...	...	...	...	...	...	...	...
Guinea	1980–85	46.8	23.5	159.0	23.3	6.2	...	...	...	...	...	...	...	...	...
Guinea-Bissau	1980–85	41.0	22.0	143.0	19.0	5.4	...	...	...	...	...	...	...	...	...
Guyana	1984	29.3	7.6	45.0[5]	21.7	3.2	1978	36.9	23.0	24.0	4.7	103.3	31.2	9.8	14.3
Haiti	1980–85	35.6	13.0	117.7	22.6	5.7	...	...	...	...	...	...	...	...	...
Honduras	1983	38.7	4.7	78.6	34.0	6.6[7]	1979	88.6	18.4	4.2	21.9	48.5	36.1	22.4	50.7
Hong Kong	1985	14.1	4.7	7.6	9.4	1.7[5]	1985	14.4	137.5	5.7	3.4	136.2	76.6	19.6	29.8
Hungary	1985	12.2	13.8	20.4	−1.6	2.1[3]	1984	11.5	267.4	21.7	11.4	737.5	71.6	77.1	120.7
Iceland	1985	15.9	7.1	6.1[10]	8.8	2.1[5]	1983	3.8	166.2	5.1	11.0	334.5	65.4	16.0	59.9
India	1983	33.7	11.9	117.0[7]	21.8	4.3	...	...	...	...	...	...	...	...	...
Indonesia	1985	30.4	12.0	79.0	18.4	3.8	...	...	...	...	...	...	...	...	...
Iran	1985	39.7	11.4	111.0	28.3	5.4	...	...	...	...	...	...	...	...	...
Iraq	1980–85	45.1	11.5	81.8[10]	33.6	6.7	...	...	...	...	...	...	...	...	...
Ireland	1985	17.6	9.4	10.1[10]	8.2	3.2[3]	1981	7.0	180.1	12.3	14.3	482.5	126.7	25.1	49.6
Isle of Man	1983	10.5	14.6	...	−4.1	...	1980	1.6	340.6	14.1	—	895.4	160.9	18.7	93.7
Israel	1985	23.5	6.6	12.3	16.9	2.8[10]	1983	11.1	124.3	14.1	9.8	288.5	42.5	16.6	40.2
Italy	1985	10.1	9.5	10.9	0.6	1.8[10]	1983	6.0	225.4	35.9	13.1	459.0	69.0	55.3	66.0
Jamaica	1984	25.2	5.9	13.2	19.3	3.3[2]	1978	39.3	74.8	40.5[17]	12.0	210.9	41.7	21.4	28.0
Japan	1985	11.9	6.1	6.0	5.8	1.8[10]	1984	9.6	151.9	9.3	5.2	247.8	53.7	31.6	47.6
Jersey	1984	12.2	10.7	...	1.5	...	...	...	...	...	...	...	...	...	...
Jordan	1980–85	45.3	9.1	63.1[10]	36.2	7.1	...	...	...	...	...	...	...	...	...
Kampuchea	1985	43.5	18.2	145.0	25.3	4.9	...	...	...	...	...	...	...	...	...
Kenya	1980–85	55.1	14.0	81.0[5]	41.1	7.7[10]	...	...	...	...	...	...	...	...	...
Kiribati	1980–85	34.9	13.9	87.0[9]	21.0	4.5	...	...	...	...	...	...	...	...	...
Korea, North	1984	30.0	6.0	28.0	24.0	3.8	...	...	...	...	...	...	...	...	...
Korea, South	1984	23.0	6.2	27.0[12]	16.8	2.4[12]	...	...	...	...	...	...	...	...	...
Kuwait	1985	31.7	2.7	19.5[10]	29.0	6.2[3]	1982	18.5	34.2	12.3	4.5	81.4	27.1	7.0	53.5
Laos	1985	39.5	14.8	116.0	24.7	5.6	...	...	...	...	...	...	...	...	...
Lebanon	1984	29.8	8.8	44.4	21.0	3.8	...	...	...	...	...	...	...	...	...
Lesotho	1980–85	41.7	16.4	110.0	25.3	5.8	...	...	...	...	...	...	...	...	...
Liberia	1980–85	48.7	17.2	112.0	31.5	6.9	...	...	...	...	...	...	...	...	...
Libya	1980–85	46.0	11.2	97.5[7]	34.8	7.2	...	...	...	...	...	...	...	...	...
Liechtenstein	1985	13.9	6.4	7.4[10]	7.5	...	1984	11.3	157.4	18.8	—	214.3	26.3	52.6	52.6
Luxembourg	1985	11.2	11.0	9.0	0.2	1.4[10]	1984	5.5	261.1	27.1	17.5	554.9	61.8	59.0	68.3
Macau	1984	19.4	4.6	12.0	14.8	3.4[3]	1983	31.4	80.8	12.2	2.4	138.7	40.2	21.0	36.9
Madagascar	1984	47.0	15.0	110.0	32.0	6.5	...	...	...	...	...	...	...	...	...
Malaŵi	1983	54.0	23.0	152.0[12]	31.0	7.6[12]	1981[22]	46.4	3.4	12.5	4.8	4.7	18.3	2.9	5.4
Malaysia	1985	29.0	6.2	28.0	22.8	3.6	1981[23]	14.3	15.9	2.7	1.5	37.8	9.2	3.3	21.0
Maldives	1984	46.3	9.3	68.0	37.0	6.6	...	...	...	...	...	...	...	...	...
Mali	1980–85	50.2	22.4	149.0	27.8	6.7	...	...	...	...	...	...	...	...	...
Malta	1984	16.8	8.8	11.7	8.0	2.0[3]	1984	0.3	158.5	93.1	2.7	481.6	27.3	27.3	24.9
Martinique	1985	17.5	6.6	14.0	10.9	2.4[3]	1982	12.9	100.2	29.4	12.3	192.3	24.5	22.1	35.8
Mauritania	1984	45.0	26.0	133.0	19.0	6.2	...	...	...	...	...	...	...	...	...
Mauritius	1985	19.0	6.8	23.8	12.2	2.1[10]	1983	20.4	46.9	18.9[2]	7.4	300.4	80.2	27.1	41.7
Mayotte	1978	49.8	...	...	...	...	...	...	...	...	...	...	...	...	...
Mexico	1983	32.7	7.0	53.0	25.7	4.9[3]	1981	73.0	41.7	36.0[17]	8.4	100.2	77.2	43.8	97.6
Monaco	1983	19.6	16.6	...	3.0	...	...	...	...	...	...	...	...	...	...
Mongolia	1985	35.3	8.0	49.0	27.3	5.0	...	...	...	...	...	...	...	...	...
Montserrat	1982	22.3	9.9	7.7	12.4	...	1981	17.0	95.0	103.0	...	456.0	95.0	26.0	43.0
Morocco	1980–85	44.1	11.7	114.4[18]	32.4	6.4	...	...	...	...	...	...	...	...	...
Mozambique	1980–85	45.1	19.7	153.0	25.4	6.1	...	...	...	...	...	...	...	...	...
Nauru	1983	31.2	5.8	31.2[7]	25.4	...	1976–81[25]	33.0	38.0	24.0	13.0	89.0	16.0	53.0	116.0
Nepal	1985	40.6	17.6	132.0	23.0	6.0	...	...	...	...	...	...	...	...	...
Netherlands, The	1985	12.1	8.5	7.9	3.6	1.5[10]	1983	4.4	223.5	13.0	13.4	364.8	55.8	29.8	42.3
Netherlands Antilles	1982	20.7	5.5	8.2	15.2	3.5[3, 11]	1983	20.8	128.6	17.9	5.2	206.0	27.1	31.2	57.1
New Caledonia	1984	22.8	5.3	11.2[5]	17.5	3.6[3]	1978	17.5	35.1	1.5	9.5	43.8	...	...	...
New Zealand	1985	15.5	7.8	10.8	7.7	1.9[28]	1983	4.3	185.3	14.1	11.6	385.5	90.7	20.8	52.4
Nicaragua	1984	44.2	9.7	76.4	34.5	5.9[3]	1978	56.8	12.8	3.2	4.9	67.4	20.2	15.4	64.3
Niger	1980–85	51.0	22.9	140.0	28.1	7.1	...	...	...	...	...	...	...	...	...
Nigeria	1980–85	50.4	17.1	113.0	33.3	7.1	...	...	...	...	...	...	...	...	...
Niue	1983	29.2	7.8	—	21.4	...	...	...	...	...	...	...	...	...	...
Norfolk Island	1983	9.7	9.7	...	—	...	...	...	...	...	...	...	...	...	...

expectation of life at birth (latest year)		nuptiality, family, and family planning																country
		marriages			age at marriage (latest)						families (F), households (H) (latest)							
					groom (percent)			bride (percent)			families (households)		children		legal abortions			
male	female	year	total number	rate per 1,000 population	19 and under	20–29	30 and over	19 and under	20–29	30 and over	total ('000)	size	number under age 15	percent legitimate	number	ratio per 100 live births		
61.7	65.3	1982	20,413	4.1	6.7	54.0	39.3	27.7	45.8	26.5	H 686	H 5.4	H 2.4	31.1	...	...		El Salvador
42.4	45.6	1966	209	0.8	...	...	...	...	...	...	...	H 4.5	...	...	...	...		Equatorial Guinea
39.5	42.6	...	...	...	...	...	...	...	...	...	...	H 4.5	...	...	...	...		Ethiopia
73.4	78.7	1983	210	4.6	—	67.3	32.7	13.4	74.3	12.3	F 14	F 3.0	F 0.9	67.1	26	3.3		Faeroe Islands
...	...	1980	11	...	...	...	...	...	...	...	H 1	H 3.3	H 0.9	75.0	...	...		Falkland Islands
70.5	74.6	1983	6,800	10.1	9.3	73.7	17.0	36.9	54.3	8.8	F 97	F 6.0	F 2.5	82.7	...	...		Fiji
70.4	78.8	1985	25,794	5.3	2.5	68.5	29.0	10.6	69.4	20.0	F 1,163	H 2.8	F 0.9	84.9	13,360	20.0		Finland
70.4	78.6	1983	300,513	5.5	1.8	75.4	22.8	14.2	70.2	15.6	H 13,177	H 2.7	H 1.0	84.1	171,218	21.4		France
63.4	69.7	1984	309	3.9	...	...	...	...	...	...	H 12	H 3.3	H 1.4	23.0	...	...		French Guiana
61.3	65.1	1985	1,157	6.6	11.3[19]	75.8[19]	12.9[19]	41.5[19]	52.5[19]	6.0[19]	H 26	H 5.0	H 2.3	45.1	...	...		French Polynesia
48.0	51.4	...	...	...	...	...	...	...	...	...	H 136	H 4.0	...	...	...	...		Gabon
40.9	44.1	...	...	...	...	...	...	...	...	...	H 123	H 4.9	H 3.4	...	...	...		Gambia, The
...	...	...	...	...	...	...	...	...	...	...	...	...	...	...	...	...		Gaza Strip
69.1	75.1	1985	133,898[10]	7.8	4.1	71.9	24.0	18.5	65.0	16.5	F 4,781	F 3.5	F 0.7	74.0	80,100	35.0		Germany, East
70.8	77.5	1985	364,684	6.0	2.2	63.2	34.6	11.3	66.7	22.0	F 22,882	F 2.7	F 0.5	90.6	86,529	14.6		Germany, West
50.3	53.7	...	...	...	...	...	...	...	...	...	H 2,272	H 5.1	H 2.2	...	...	...		Ghana
71.4	75.5	1985	173	6.0	...	...	...	...	...	...	H 7	H 3.8	H 1.0	97.1	...	...		Gibraltar
72.2	76.4	1985	62,547	6.3	2.0	65.6	32.4	29.1	57.1	13.8	H 2,990	H 3.2	H 0.7	96.6	109	0.1		Greece
59.7	67.3	1984	316	6.0	0.3	48.4	51.3	5.1	64.9	30.0	F 26	F 2.0	F 0.4	32.3	539	51.3		Greenland
65.4	69.4	1979	360	3.9	...	...	...	...	...	...	H 20	H 2.9	H 2.2	22.5	...	...		Grenada
67.8	73.2	1984	1,653	5.0	0.9	63.1	36.0	19.2	58.7	22.1	H 70	H 3.7	H 1.9	47.9	561	8.7		Guadeloupe
69.6	74.5	1985	1,370	11.3	7.9	59.1	33.0	16.9	63.2	19.9	H 25	H 3.7	H 1.5	64.5	...	...		Guam
57.3	60.5	1984	31,351	3.8	18.3	55.7	26.0	46.2	36.2	17.6	H 1,185	H 4.5	H 2.7	34.8	...	...		Guatemala
...	...	...	...	...	...	...	...	...	...	...	H 18	H 2.9	...	...	...	...		Guernsey
38.7	41.8	...	...	...	...	...	...	...	...	...	H 1,064	H 4.7	...	...	...	...		Guinea
39.4	42.6	...	...	...	...	...	...	...	...	...	H 124	H 4.1	H 2.8	11.3	...	...		Guinea-Bissau
67.7	73.3	1968	2,760	4.2	...	...	...	...	...	...	H 178	H 5.0	H 2.5	61.4	...	...		Guyana
51.2	54.4	...	...	...	...	...	...	...	...	...	H 1,131	H 5.1	H 1.8	...	...	...		Haiti
58.2	61.7	1981	15,437	4.0	9.8	62.0	28.2	38.8	46.1	15.1	H 463	H 5.7	H 2.8	...	...	...		Honduras
72.5	78.4	1985	45,056	8.3	1.1	60.8	38.1	6.4	72.9	20.7	H 1,245	H 3.9	H 1.0	90.4	10,600	12.0		Hong Kong
65.6	73.7	1985	75,969[5]	6.9	2.2	63.2	34.6	30.5	52.1	17.4	F 3,028	F 3.4	F 0.8	91.2	78,599	61.8		Hungary
73.5	79.5	1984	1,413	5.9	2.4	75.8	21.8	11.1	73.4	15.5	H 49	H 3.3	H 1.3	52.9	689	15.8		Iceland
53.9	52.9	...	...	...	...	...	...	...	...	...	H 97,093	H 5.6	H 2.4	...	500,624	2.1		India
53.4	56.2	1982	...	7.5	...	...	...	...	...	...	H 30,263	H 4.9	H 2.0	...	...	...		Indonesia
58.0	58.3	1984	384,876	8.9	...	...	...	...	...	...	H 6,709	H 4.3	H 2.2	...	...	...		Iran
55.9	59.1	1982	56,440	4.0	4.0	49.1	46.9	23.9	47.2	28.9	H 2,128	H 6.9	H 3.2	...	...	...		Iraq
70.4	75.7	1985	18,590[10]	5.2	5.2	77.1	17.7	14.9	75.2	9.9	H 726	H 3.9	H 1.3	95.0	...	...		Ireland
...	...	1983	360	5.2	4.8	58.3	36.9	16.4	60.0	23.6	...	...	...	...	...	...		Isle of Man
72.8	76.2	1985	29,158	6.9	4.3[20]	76.9[20]	18.8[20]	27.1[20]	62.9[20]	9.9[20]	H 1,026	H 3.5	H 1.3	97.5	15,593	15.8		Israel
73.0	79.0	1984	298,028	5.2	1.9	75.1	23.0	20.0	68.7	11.3	F 17,615	F 3.2	F 0.7	95.0	220,300	34.2		Italy
67.9	71.9	1984	10,410	4.6	...	...	...	...	...	...	H 420	H 4.2	H 2.0	...	...	...		Jamaica
74.5	80.2	1985	735,900	6.1	0.9[19]	65.5[19]	33.6[19]	3.2[19]	82.9[19]	13.8[19]	F 22,240	F 5.4	F 1.2	99.2	598,100	37.9		Japan
...	...	...	...	...	...	...	...	...	...	...	H 27	H 2.5	...	...	...	...		Jersey
60.3	64.2	1984	18,189	7.1	6.0	71.6	22.4	46.7	47.8	5.5	H 375	H 6.9	H 3.4	...	...	...		Jordan
44.5	47.4	...	...	...	...	...	...	...	...	...	...	H 5.6	...	...	...	...		Kampuchea
51.2	54.7	...	...	...	...	...	...	...	...	...	H 1,938	H 6.3	H 2.7	...	...	...		Kenya
50.3	53.8	1973	291[21]	4.5	9.9	66.7	23.5	34.7	54.5	10.8	F 12	F 5.0	F 2.0	...	...	...		Kiribati
65.0	72.0	...	...	...	...	...	...	...	...	...	...	H 5.7	...	...	...	...		Korea, North
64.5	70.9	1982	326,004	8.3	1.7	81.4	16.9	10.1	85.2	4.7	F 7,969	F 4.8	F 1.6	...	...	...		Korea, South
68.0	72.9	1985	9,213	5.4	5.2	70.4	24.4	40.5	50.6	8.9	H 143	H 6.9	H 1.6	...	...	...		Kuwait
49.4	52.4	...	...	...	...	...	...	...	...	...	...	H 5.3	...	...	...	...		Laos
65.0	68.9	1973	18,601	7.0	...	...	...	...	...	...	H 405	H 5.3	H 2.2	...	...	...		Lebanon
47.7	51.0	...	...	...	...	...	...	...	...	...	H 242	H 4.4	H 2.0	...	...	...		Lesotho
47.4	50.7	...	...	...	...	...	...	...	...	...	...	H 5.8	...	...	...	...		Liberia
56.1	59.4	1979	17,236	6.0	...	...	...	...	...	...	F 383	F 5.4	F 2.9	...	...	...		Libya
71.1	77.8	1985	339	12.6	...	...	...	...	...	...	H 8	H 3.0	H 0.7	93.4	...	...		Liechtenstein
66.9	73.5	1985	1,962	5.3	1.9	70.8	27.3	13.2	70.9	15.9	H 128	H 2.8	H 0.5	91.8	...	...		Luxembourg
68.0	73.0	1984	2,614	8.6	0.4	44.7	54.9	4.3	73.5	22.2	H 50	H 4.8	H 1.8	99.3	...	...		Macau
48.9	50.4	1975	19,800	2.6	14.5	60.3	25.2	49.5	36.9	13.6	H 1,709	H 4.4	H 2.0	...	...	...		Madagascar
42.7	45.4	1977	4,300	7.8	...	...	...	...	...	...	...	H 4.5	...	...	...	...		Malaŵi
65.8	69.8	1979[24]	23,030	1.7	0.5[24]	65.3[24]	34.2[24]	7.9[24]	77.0[24]	15.1[24]	...	H 5.2	...	...	...	...		Malaysia
57.0	58.0	1982	1,404	8.9	12.3	54.1	33.6	39.5	41.4	19.1	H 23	H 6.1	H 2.7	...	...	...		Maldives
40.4	43.6	...	...	...	...	...	...	...	...	...	H 1,254	H 5.1	...	...	...	...		Mali
70.7	75.2	1984	2,633	7.9	2.8	78.7	18.5	12.7	76.9	10.4	H 76	H 3.6	H 1.2	99.3	...	...		Malta
68.4	73.5	1985	1,331	4.1	0.3	60.5	39.2	12.9	60.4	26.7	H 71	H 3.8	...	36.1	...	...		Martinique
45.0	48.0	...	...	...	...	...	...	...	...	...	H 246	H 5.0	...	...	...	...		Mauritania
64.4	71.2	1985	10,720[5]	11.3	1.2	55.3	43.5	20.3	62.2	17.5	F 155	F 5.3	F 2.0	55.4	...	...		Mauritius
...	...	...	...	...	...	...	...	...	...	...	H 10	H 4.7	H 2.3	89.2	...	...		Mayotte
63.9	68.2	1981	505,870	7.1	18.3	63.9	17.8	45.4	44.1	10.5	H 9,851	H 5.5	H 2.3	91.0	...	...		Mexico
...	...	1981	190	7.3	...	...	...	...	...	...	H 10	H 2.3	H 0.3	96.8	...	...		Monaco
61.3	65.4	1984	10,300[5]	6.1	...	...	...	...	...	...	F 311	F 5.1	...	...	...	...		Mongolia
68.6	71.9	1982	41	4.1	2.4	39.0	58.5	7.3	58.5	34.1	H 4	H 3.1	...	23.4	...	...		Montserrat
56.1	59.4	...	...	...	...	...	...	...	...	...	H 2,819	H 5.8	H 2.5	...	...	...		Morocco
44.4	46.2	1974	6,037	0.7	...	...	...	...	...	...	F 1,860	F 4.4	F 2.0	73.1	...	...		Mozambique
48.9	62.1	1977	43[26]	6.3	...	...	...	...	...	...	H 1	H 8.0	H 2.6	...	...	...		Nauru
47.2	45.7	...	...	...	...	...	...	...	...	...	...	F 5.8	H 2.2	...	...	...		Nepal
73.0	79.5	1984	82,190	5.7	1.2	77.1	21.7	10.2	76.8	13.0	H 5,509	H 2.6	H 0.6	92.3	20,187	11.7		Netherlands, The
71.1[27]	75.7[27]	1982	959	5.6	4.0	77.0	18.9	22.2	61.1	16.7	H 41	H 4.2	H 2.1	52.3	...	...		Netherlands Antilles
64.6	68.5	1983	831	5.7	3.6	70.2	26.2	31.4	53.4	15.2	...	H 4.1	...	57.5	...	...		New Caledonia
71.0	76.8	1985	24,657	7.5	2.1	64.8	33.1	11.4	65.2	23.4	H 1,004	H 3.2	H 0.8	76.2	7,198	14.3		New Zealand
56.0	60.0	1984	13,617	4.4	—18.1[29]—		81.9[30]	—48.2[29]—		51.8[30]	...	H 6.9	...	...	...	...		Nicaragua
40.9	44.1	...	...	...	...	...	...	...	...	...	H 1,029	H 5.2	H 2.4	...	...	...		Niger
46.9	50.2	...	...	...	...	...	...	...	...	...	...	H 5.0	...	...	...	...		Nigeria
63.0	66.5	1982	12	3.5[31]	...	...	...	...	...	...	F 1	F 4.1	F 1.9	58.2	...	...		Niue
58.0	59.9	1983	10	4.8	—	56.3	43.7	6.3	50.0	43.7	...	...	...	73.9	...	...		Norfolk Island

Vital statistics, marriage, family (continued)

country	vital rates						causes of death (rate per 100,000 population)								
	year	birth rate per 1,000 population	death rate per 1,000 population	infant mortality rate per 1,000 live births	rate of natural increase per 1,000 population	total fertility rate	year	infectious and parasitic diseases	neoplasms (cancers)	endocrine and metabolic disorders	diseases of the nervous system	diseases of the circulatory system	diseases of the respiratory system	diseases of the digestive system	accidents, poisoning, and violence
Norway	1985	12.4	10.6	7.8	1.8	1.7[10]	1984	6.3	223.1	11.3	0.8	473.4	84.7	16.0	61.7
Oman	1980–85	47.7	16.7	113.4[10]	31.0	7.1	...	...	...	...	...	...	...	...	...
Pacific Is., Trust Territory of the															
Marshall Islands	1984	39.2	5.1	33.0	34.1	5.1[6]	1984	46.0	34.5	60.3	11.5	80.5	77.6	14.4	23.0
Micronesia, Fed. States of	1984	29.4	2.7	95.0	26.7	...	1984	20.4	27.1	6.8	4.5	53.2	47.5	5.7	23.8
Northern Mariana Islands	1984	32.4	5.8	23.8	26.6	...	1984	20.5	66.7	25.6	5.1	143.6	25.6	35.9	97.4
Palau	1983	23.8	6.8	23.7	17.0	4.2[3]	1983	24.2	88.7	8.1	—	112.9	64.5	—	177.4
Pakistan	1985	41.7	14.6	115.0	27.1	5.6	...	...	...	...	...	...	...	...	...
Panama	1984	26.3	3.9	23.0	22.4	3.6[3]	1983	24.8	50.1	11.9	3.4	114.7	35.3	14.9	48.4
Papua New Guinea	1985	35.0	12.5	68.0	22.5	5.3	...	...	...	...	...	...	...	...	...
Paraguay	1984	38.9	7.7	64.9	31.2	5.2[3]	1984	58.0[6]	39.2	15.6	6.5[6]	113.2	41.5[6]	13.7[6]	12.9
Peru	1985	35.5	10.0	92.7	25.5	4.7	1981	95.9	33.8	13.2	9.8	59.3	104.4	26.0	29.0
Philippines	1985	32.1	8.0	56.0	24.1	4.2	...	...	...	...	...	...	...	...	...
Pitcairn Island	1982	—	—	—	—	...	...	...	...	...	...	...	...	...	...
Poland	1985	18.2	10.3	19.1[10]	7.9	2.3[2]	1984	11.4	179.0	16.2	9.5	492.9	52.0	34.0	72.4
Portugal	1985	12.8	9.6	11.6	3.2	2.3[3]	1984	9.8	155.4	13.6	1.0	426.0	47.2	34.0	63.3
Puerto Rico	1984	19.5	6.6	16.0	12.9	2.4[3]	1982	13.8	101.1	32.2	9.5	267.9	64.8	44.4	55.7
Qatar	1985	30.6	2.6	45.0[3]	28.0	4.6[10]	1985	6.0	27.6	11.3	3.3	45.8	10.6	8.0	61.5
Réunion	1985	24.1	5.6	10.3	18.5	2.5[3]	1984	9.5	46.4	22.4	...	174.0	38.7	36.5	71.1
Romania	1984	15.5	10.3	23.4	5.2	2.4[2]	1983	9.0	128.1	6.9	7.5	603.4	124.5	48.3	66.2
Rwanda	1984	52.0	19.0	128.0	33.0	8.0	...	...	...	...	...	...	...	...	...
St. Christopher and Nevis	1985	22.3	9.6	30.2	12.7	3.3[2]	1983	69.2	145.1	37.9	6.8[6]	372.8	84.2	47.2[6]	26.8
St. Helena and Ascension	1982	24.6	10.0	16.3	14.6	...	...	...	...	...	...	...	...	...	...
St. Lucia	1985	30.6	5.9	22.7	24.7	4.4[3]	1984	19.4	73.8	25.4	6.7	193.9	35.1	14.2	39.5
St. Pierre and Miqueon	1984	21.0	9.5	12.3[5]	11.5	...	1977	72.9	108.3	102.1	25.0	366.7	45.8	39.6	39.6
St. Vincent and the Grenadines	1984	26.2	6.5	26.5	19.7	3.0[3]	1984	28.7	78.6	37.0	10.2	192.3	26.8	22.2	45.3
San Marino	1985	9.3	8.4	14.5	0.9	...	1981–85[25]	0.9	245.8	14.5	—	282.1	25.4	26.3	48.1
São Tomé and Príncipe	1985	36.3	8.8	61.7	27.5	5.2[3]	...	...	...	...	...	...	...	...	...
Saudi Arabia	1980–85	43.7	12.6	109.8[10]	31.1	3.5	...	...	...	...	...	...	...	...	...
Senegal	1980–85	47.9	21.1	141.0	26.8	6.6[10]	...	...	...	...	...	...	...	...	...
Seychelles	1985	26.5	7.2	17.9[12]	19.3	3.5[10]	1984	40.2	92.7	27.8	15.5	233.3	83.4	38.6	60.3
Sierra Leone	1980–85	45.3	17.4	190.0[2]	27.9	6.1	...	...	...	...	...	...	...	...	...
Singapore	1985	16.6	5.2	9.3	11.4	1.6	1985	14.2	112.5	19.0	3.4	177.5	84.8	15.1	48.9
Solomon Islands	1982	44.6	11.7	46.0	32.9	7.3	...	...	...	...	...	...	...	...	...
Somalia	1983	50.0	20.0	142.0	30.0	6.8	...	...	...	...	...	...	...	...	...
South Africa	1983	33.6	11.0	83.0[3]	22.6	5.1[3]	...	...	...	...	...	...	...	...	...
Bophuthatswana	...	...	...	...	...	...	...	...	...	...	...	...	....	...	...
Ciskei	...	...	...	...	...	...	...	...	...	...	...	...	...	...	...
Transkei	...	...	...	...	...	...	...	...	...	...	...	...	...	...	...
Venda	...	...	...	...	...	...	...	...	...	...	...	...	...	...	...
South West Africa/ Namibia	1980–85	45.1	17.3	116.0	27.8	6.1	...	...	...	...	...	...	...	...	...
Spain	1983	12.5	7.8	10.5	4.7	2.4[3]	1982	14.2	153.7	20.5	11.8	361.2	67.4	42.7	43.2
Sri Lanka	1984	24.8	6.5	34.0	18.3	3.1[12]	1980	49.1	27.9	8.3	46.2	99.0	47.2	14.4	69.2
Sudan, The	1980–85	45.3	16.6	119.0[2]	28.7	6.5	...	...	...	...	...	...	...	...	...
Suriname	1984	29.7	7.4	32.5	22.3	5.7[6]	1981	42.5	47.6	11.9	10.5	164.0	39.7	33.1	63.2
Swaziland	1980–85	47.5	17.2	129.0	30.3	6.5	...	...	...	...	...	...	...	...	...
Sweden	1985	11.8	11.3	6.4[10]	0.5	1.6[10]	1983	7.2	227.4	14.6	0.6	543.9	75.3	19.0	61.0
Switzerland	1985	13.2	9.7	7.6[12]	3.5	1.8[10]	1984	5.4	236.8	23.4[17]	14.4	422.3	43.9	30.9	76.4
Syria	1984	43.0	8.3	57.0[3]	34.7	7.2[3]	1981	15.1	8.4	5.0	4.0	60.7	13.2	4.5	20.0
Taiwan	1985	18.0	4.8	7.5[10]	13.2	2.3[10]	1984	11.2	82.0	14.2	...	141.9	13.1	16.7	61.2
Tanzania	1984	50.0	16.0	111.0	34.0	7.0	...	...	...	...	...	...	...	...	...
Thailand	1984	26.4	7.6	53.0[12]	18.8	3.2[12]	1983	7.8[2]	27.0	...	...	33.8	21.5[2]	17.6[2]	35.6
Togo	1980–85	47.8	17.1	102.0	30.7	6.5	...	...	...	...	...	...	...	...	...
Tokelau	1982	27.7	10.3	—	17.4	4.3	...	...	...	...	...	...	...	...	...
Tonga	1984	30.5	2.8	26.0[5]	27.7	4.3[3]	...	...	...	...	...	...	...	...	...
Trinidad and Tobago	1982	29.0	7.0	26.0	22.0	2.9[3]	1978	22.3	65.3	6.3	5.7	244.1	30.9	3.7	59.0
Tunisia	1985	31.3	6.7	85.0[3]	24.6	4.3[10]	1980	18.2	8.9	3.9	5.2	29.3	10.0	6.2	12.4
Turkey	1980–85	33.6	9.3	83.0[2]	24.3	4.5	1983	16.8	25.2	2.3	1.4	107.3	19.8	3.9	7.4
Turks and Caicos Islands	1983	27.5	3.9	10.2[2]	23.6	...	...	...	...	...	...	...	...	...	...
Tuvalu	1985	24.5	11.2	42.0[4]	13.3	2.7	1985	36.5	72.9	24.3	121.5	145.8	121.5	170.1	—
Uganda	1983	50.0	17.0	125.0	33.0	7.0	...	...	...	...	...	...	...	...	...
U.S.S.R.	1985	19.4	10.9	26.0	8.5	3.1[2]	1983	...	148.1	...	...	554.3	...	...	...
United Arab Emirates	1980–85	27.0	4.0	49.6	23.0	6.7	...	...	...	...	...	...	...	...	...
United Kingdom	1985	13.3	11.7	9.4	1.6	1.8	1984	4.6	276.6	16.5[17]	20.4	564.0	117.1	34.4	39.8
United States	1986	15.5	8.7	10.4	6.8	1.8[12]	1985–86	12.3	193.1	15.4	0.5	403.4	59.7	17.0	60.6
Uruguay	1984	17.9	10.2	30.3	7.7	2.6[2]	1984	24.3	213.1	21.1	...	419.7	39.6	10.0	49.7
Vanuatu	1985	42.8	9.2	47.1	33.6	5.8	1985	71.0	23.4	16.6	12.1	38.5	61.9	12.8	24.2
Venezuela	1984	29.9	4.6	27.3	25.3	4.3[3]	1980	42.0	49.6	12.7	9.4	117.9	32.6	18.2	77.3
Vietnam	1985	32.2	9.8	72.0	22.4	4.3	1979	48.0	54.0	...	...	123.8	...	...	...
Virgin Islands (U.S.)	1982	24.7	4.9	19.5	19.8	2.9[12]	1981	6.1	83.5	25.5	5.1	209.8	20.4	34.6	84.5
Wallis and Futuna	1978	41.1	10.6	40.5	30.5	...	...	...	...	...	...	...	...	...	...
West Bank	1984	39.1	8.2	...	30.9	...	...	...	...	...	...	...	...	...	...
Western Sahara	1980–85	29.0	4.5	5.3	24.5	...	...	...	...	...	...	...	...	...	...
Western Samoa	1984	10.2	2.3	42.0[2]	7.9	4.5[12]	1984	6.9	17.6	4.4	1.9	47.2	22.6	20.7	9.4
Yemen (Aden)	1980–85	47.6	18.9	142.9[7]	28.7	6.9	...	...	...	...	...	...	...	...	...
Yemen (Ṣan'ā')	1980–85	48.5	21.8	154.0	26.7	6.8	...	...	...	...	...	...	...	...	...
Yugoslavia	1985	15.9	9.1	28.8	6.8	2.1[5]	1982	13.5	135.8	9.1	6.9	450.7	52.3	39.5	63.0
Zaire	1980–85	45.2	15.8	107.0	29.4	6.1	...	...	...	...	...	...	...	...	...
Zambia	1980–85	48.1	15.1	88.0	33.0	6.8	...	...	...	...	...	...	...	...	...
Zimbabwe	1983	53.0	13.0	61.0[12]	40.0	7.0	1979	7.3	152.9	7.0	1.6	310.6	64.7	6.6	102.4

expectation of life at birth (latest year): male	expectation of life at birth (latest year): female	nuptiality, family, and family planning — marriages: year	marriages: total number	marriages: rate per 1,000 population	age at marriage (latest) — groom (percent): 19 and under	groom: 20–29	groom: 30 and over	bride (percent): 19 and under	bride: 20–29	bride: 30 and over	families (F), households (H) (latest) — families (households): total ('000)	families (households): size	children: number under age 15	children: percent legitimate	legal abortions: number	legal abortions: ratio per 100 live births	country
72.9	79.6	1984	20,537	5.0	1.5	68.0	30.5	9.2	72.2	18.6	F 1,684	F 2.4	F 0.6	78.7	13,646	27.3	Norway
48.7	50.9	...	...	...	...	...	...	...	...	...	H 161	H 5.5	...	...	...	...	Oman
																	Pacific Is., Trust Territory of the
...	...	...	...	...	...	...	...	...	...	...	H 4	H 8.0	...	...	...	...	Marshall Islands
...	...	...	...	...	...	...	...	...	...	...	H 11	H 7.0	...	...	...	...	Micronesia, Fed. States of
59.0	64.0	...	...	...	...	...	...	...	...	...	H 3	H 5.4	...	...	...	...	Northern Mariana Islands
56.5	60.0	...	...	...	...	...	...	...	...	...	H 2	H 5.8	...	...	...	...	Palau
52.0	50.2	1971	62,900	10.7[18]	...	...	...	...	...	...	...	H 6.7	...	...	...	...	Pakistan
69.2	72.9	1984	9,940	4.7	5.5[32]	58.5[32]	36.0[32]	22.2[32]	52.5[32]	25.2[32]	F 347	F 4.9	...	28.6	12	—	Panama
53.5	53.0	...	...	...	...	...	...	...	...	...	H 674	H 4.6	...	...	...	...	Papua New Guinea
61.9	66.4	1982	13,053	4.3	3.2	64.3	32.5	32.5	47.7	19.8	H 345	H 5.2	...	66.7	...	...	Paraguay
58.3	62.2	1982	109,200	6.0	5.5	60.4	34.1	25.9	51.4	22.6	H 2,772	H 4.8	...	57.8	...	...	Peru
61.6	65.2	1982	351,818	6.9	11.7	71.1	17.2	33.0	56.7	10.3	F 8,607	F 5.6	F 2.4	96.3	...	...	Philippines
63.0	66.5	1972	2	...	...	...	...	...	...	...	...	...	...	...	...	...	Pitcairn Island
67.2	75.2	1984	284,200	7.7	3.2	80.0	16.8	18.8	69.5	11.7	F 9,435	F 3.6	F 0.9	95.3	135,872	18.9	Poland
68.6	75.3	1985	68,461	6.7	7.7	74.5	17.8	30.2	56.7	13.1	H 3,427	H 2.9	H 0.8	88.5	...	...	Portugal
70.8	76.9	1983	29,632	9.1	11.5	56.5	32.0	28.0	48.9	23.1	F 563	H 4.1	F 1.8	79.0	...	...	Puerto Rico
68.2	73.2	1985	1,092	3.6	4.7	71.2	24.1	39.7	54.5	5.8	...	H 2.9	...	...	...	...	Qatar
64.6	68.2	1985	3,185	5.8	2.3	73.6	24.1	29.0	56.6	14.4	H 121	H 4.2	H 2.3	52.9	3,838	32.5	Réunion
67.0	72.6	1984	164,600	7.3	3.0	75.9	21.1	31.1	54.5	14.4	H 7,115	H 3.1	...	...	404,000	99.0	Romania
46.0	49.0	1980	13,890	2.7	...	...	...	...	...	...	H 894	H 5.2	...	...	...	...	Rwanda
62.0	67.0	1977	150	3.5	...	...	...	...	...	...	H 11	H 3.7	H 1.9	18.6	...	...	St. Christopher and Nevis
...	...	1982	29	5.2	8.3	58.4	33.3	38.9	44.4	16.7	H 1	H 4.4	H 1.6	56.5	...	...	St. Helena and Ascension
67.2	75.3	1985	423	3.1	0.7	46.9	52.4	8.8	53.6	37.6	H 27	H 4.6	...	15.9	...	...	St. Lucia
65.8	71.6	1984	33	5.4	...	...	...	...	...	...	H 2	H 3.3	H 0.9	83.0	...	...	St. Pierre and Miquelon
67.5	71.4	1984	394	3.6	0.7	44.2	55.1	11.1	57.2	31.7	H 20	H 5.0	...	...	...	...	St. Vincent and the Grenadines
70.7	76.2	1985	202	9.0	2.8	80.8	16.4	19.9	72.6	7.5	F 6	F 3.2	F 0.8	96.5	...	...	San Marino
47.1	50.0	...	...	...	...	...	...	...	...	...	...	...	...	...	...	...	São Tomé and Príncipe
54.5	57.6	...	...	...	...	...	...	...	...	...	H 1,513	H 5.5	...	...	...	...	Saudi Arabia
45.0	48.0	...	...	...	...	...	...	...	...	...	H 1,167	H 4.8	...	...	...	...	Senegal
66.2	73.5	1984	390	6.0	1.8	55.9	42.3	15.6	60.8	23.6	H 13	H 4.6	H 1.9	33.2	...	...	Seychelles
46.7	50.0	...	...	...	...	...	...	...	...	...	H 722	H 4.9	...	...	...	...	Sierra Leone
69.7	75.2	1985	23,466	9.2	0.6	72.0	27.4	7.7	80.1	12.2	H 510	H 3.9	H 1.3	...	19,100	47.1	Singapore
54.0	54.0	...	...	...	...	...	...	...	...	...	F 41	F 5.6	F 2.3	...	...	...	Solomon Islands
41.9	45.1	...	...	...	...	...	...	...	...	...	...	H 4.9	...	...	...	...	Somalia
51.8	55.2	1977	64,979[33]	...	3.5[33]	69.4[33]	27.1[33]	22.1[33]	58.6[33]	19.3[33]	F 1,403	H 5.1	...	75.9	...	...	South Africa
...	...	...	...	...	...	...	...	...	...	...	...	...	...	...	...	...	Bophuthatswana
...	...	...	...	...	...	...	...	...	...	...	...	...	...	...	...	...	Ciskei
...	...	...	...	...	...	...	...	...	...	...	...	...	...	...	...	...	Transkei
...	...	...	...	...	...	...	...	...	...	...	...	...	...	...	...	...	Venda
47.0	49.5	...	...	...	...	...	...	...	...	...	...	H 4.8	...	...	...	...	South West Africa/Namibia
71.3	77.5	1983	183,490	4.8	5.7	80.8	13.5	20.8	71.7	7.5	F 10,665	F 3.5	...	97.9	...	...	Spain
67.6	70.9	1983	121,553	7.9	0.4	72.4	27.2	17.8	73.4	8.8	H 2,721	H 5.2	H 1.9	92.5	...	...	Sri Lanka
48.0	50.0	...	...	...	...	...	...	...	...	...	H 3,471	H 5.3	...	...	...	...	Sudan, The
67.0	71.9	1980	2,400	6.7	...	...	...	...	...	...	...	H 3.9	...	...	...	...	Suriname
45.3	51.9	...	...	...	...	...	...	...	...	...	H 112	H 5.0	...	...	...	...	Swaziland
73.1	79.1	1985	38,297	4.6	0.5	47.4	52.1	3.0	60.0	37.0	H 3,498	H 2.4	H 0.5	56.4	31,014	33.8	Sweden
72.7	79.6	1984	38,020	5.9	0.5	62.2	37.3	5.1	72.6	22.3	H 2,500	H 2.5	...	94.3	...	...	Switzerland
63.3	67.0	1984[34]	81,460	8.2	...	...	...	...	...	...	F 1,151	H 6.2	F 2.4	...	...	...	Syria
70.5	75.5	1985	153,565	8.0	2.4	76.6	21.0	11.2	81.5	7.3	H 4,247	H 4.5	H 0.5	...	...	...	Taiwan
50.0	53.0	1967	3,475	9.8	...	...	...	...	...	...	H 3,435	H 5.1	H 2.3	...	...	...	Tanzania
61.0	66.9	1983	380,027	7.7	...	...	...	...	...	...	H 8,422	H 5.3	H 2.0	...	...	...	Thailand
46.9	50.2	1979[35]	5,753	2.3	...	...	...	...	...	...	H 479	H 5.6	...	...	...	...	Togo
63.0	66.5	1981	9	6.0	—	83.3	16.7	—	100.0	—	...	H 5.5	...	...	...	...	Tokelau
61.0	64.8	1983	699	6.7	...	...	...	...	...	...	F 15	F 6.1	F 2.7	...	...	...	Tonga
67.8	72.6	1984	8,403	7.2	3.8	65.2	31.0	23.4	57.9	18.7	H 193	H 4.2	H 2.1	56.9	...	...	Trinidad and Tobago
60.1	61.1	1985	50,000	7.0	1.4	72.5	26.1	35.9	54.7	9.4	H 1,313	H 5.5	...	99.8	20,500	9.5	Tunisia
60.3	64.9	1983	308,256	6.4	7.7[36]	72.4[36]	19.9[36]	35.9[36]	52.1[36]	12.0[36]	H 8,601	H 5.2	H 2.0	...	...	...	Turkey
68.6	71.9	1980	27	3.6	...	...	...	...	...	...	H 1	H 4.3	H 2.0	82.4	...	...	Turks and Caicos Islands
56.9	60.1	...	...	...	...	...	...	...	...	...	H 1	H 6.4	H 2.2	82.2	...	...	Tuvalu
48.0	50.0	...	...	...	...	...	...	...	...	...	...	H 5.2	...	...	...	...	Uganda
61.9	72.0	1984	2,641,000	9.6	4.5	76.7	18.8	25.7	59.3	15.0	F 66,307	F 3.9	...	...	10,000,000	230.0	U.S.S.R.
61.6	65.6	...	...	...	...	...	...	...	...	...	...	H 3.8	...	...	...	...	United Arab Emirates
71.6	77.6	1985	393,200	6.9	4.8	62.8	32.4	16.5	60.0	23.5	H 19,949	H 2.6	H 1.7	81.1	135,794[37]	19.6[37]	United Kingdom
71.2	78.2	1985	2,459,800	10.3	8.5	59.5	32.0	21.1	55.8	23.1	F 61,393	F 2.6	F 1.0	80.6	1,553,900	42.8	United States
69.1	73.8	1983	19,168	6.5	8.3	62.7	29.0	28.3	51.7	20.0	H 829	H 3.5	...	74.4	...	...	Uruguay
61.1	59.3	...	...	...	...	...	...	...	...	...	...	H 4.9	...	...	...	...	Vanuatu
65.1	70.6	1983	91,397	5.6	10.7[1]	66.0[1]	23.3[1]	37.3[1]	49.3[1]	13.4[1]	...	H 5.3	...	47.0	...	...	Venezuela
57.7	62.1	...	...	...	...	...	...	...	...	...	...	...	...	...	...	...	Vietnam
66.7	70.7	1982	1,311	12.9	3.1	44.6	52.3	12.7	50.9	36.4	H 28	H 3.4	H 1.3	48.7	...	...	Virgin Islands (U.S.)
59.2	62.9	1980	60	5.6	...	...	...	...	...	...	...	H 6.6	H 3.0	78.3	...	...	Wallis and Futuna
...	...	...	...	...	...	...	...	...	...	...	...	...	...	...	...	...	West Bank
...	...	1972	459	4.9	...	...	...	...	...	...	...	...	...	...	...	...	Western Sahara
62.2	65.5	1984	555	5.0	0.9	58.7	40.4	7.2	68.8	24.0	F 20	F 7.8	F 3.8	43.5	...	...	Western Samoa
45.3	47.7	...	...	...	...	...	...	...	...	...	...	H 5.5	...	...	...	...	Yemen (Aden)
42.7	44.8	...	...	...	...	...	...	...	...	...	...	H 5.8	...	...	...	...	Yemen (Ṣan'ā')
67.7	73.1	1984	168,290	7.3	2.9	76.2	20.9	27.2	60.9	11.9	H 6,187	H 3.6	H 0.9	91.7	288,100	74.0	Yugoslavia
48.3	51.7	1975	185,300	7.5	...	...	...	...	...	...	...	H 6.0	...	...	...	...	Zaire
49.1	52.5	...	...	...	...	...	...	...	...	...	H 873	H 5.8	H 2.1	...	...	...	Zambia
55.7	59.1	...	...	...	...	...	...	...	...	...	...	H 5.8	...	95.8	...	...	Zimbabwe

[1]Excludes nomadic tribes. [2]1982. [3]1980–85. [4]1979. [5]1983. [6]1980. [7]1981. [8]1977. [9]1978. [10]1984. [11]Netherlands Antilles includes Aruba. [12]1985. [13]Data exclude deaths of unknown cause. [14]Estimates based on rural survey. [15]Millions of households. [16]Based on burial permits. [17]Includes nutritional disorders. [18]1975–80. [19]First marriages only. [20]Includes East Jerusalem. [21]1968. [22]Reported inpatient deaths only. [23]Medically certified deaths only. [24]Includes Sarawak; refers to non-Muslim civil marriages and Christian ritual marriages only. [25]Annual averages. [26]1973. [27]Curaçao only. [28]1986. [29]Less than 21 years of age. [30]Over 21 years of age. [31]1976. [32]Excludes tribal Indians. [33]Whites, Asians, and Coloureds only. [34]Syrian Arabs only. [35]African population only. [36]Urban areas only. [37]Excludes Northern Ireland.

National product and accounts

The national product and accounts table furnishes a breakdown of how the aggregate income (output) of a nation is produced, distributed, and spent by its population. The per capita value of a country's gross national product (GNP) provides a useful indication of the general economic well-being of its inhabitants. The several breakdowns of aggregate income or expenditure (each representing a different method of computing gross domestic product [GDP] or an element of its GNP) provide a number of specific details about each country's economy, including national patterns of consumption, investment, and foreign trade; factor costs (prices paid for the inputs of production), such as indirect taxes, capital consumption, wage compensation, and profit; industrial origin of GDP for ten principal industrial sectors; and the principal elements of a country's balance of payments (merchandise trade, invisibles, and tourism).

Measures of national output. The two most commonly used measures of national output (except for certain centrally planned economies) are GNP and GDP. Each of these measures represents an aggregate value of goods and services produced within a specific country. The GDP, the more basic of these, is a measure of the value of goods and services produced entirely within each country. It is equal to the sum of all factor costs (factor incomes) or all value added provided by the combined productive capabilities of labour and capital within each economic system. The GNP, the more comprehensive value, is composed of both domestic production and the net value added (net factor income) from transactions with other countries. When the factor income value received from other countries is greater than the value paid, a country's GNP is greater than its GDP. In theory, if all national accounts could be equilibrated, the global summation of GDP (each country's value added to the world economy) would equal the total of all GNP values.

In the first section of the table, data are provided for the nominal GNP (value in current prices for the year indicated), together with the per capita value of this product, both denominated in U.S. dollars for ease of comparison. Beside these are given figures for GDP denominated in the national currency, first as a nominal value, then as a "real" value (adjusted, that is, to eliminate the effect of recent inflation [most often] or, occasionally, of deflation). The real values are obtained by dividing the nominal GDP by a GDP deflator (essentially a consumer price index that covers price changes in the whole economy) and are adjusted to a common base year of 1980. GNP per capita provides a rough measure of annual monetary income per person, but values should be compared cautiously, as they are subject to a number of distortions, notably of purchasing power parity (the ability of any two currencies to purchase goods in their respective domestic markets differing by more than a simple exchange rate) and in the existence of elements of national production that do not enter the monetary economy (*e.g.,* food, clothing, or housing produced and consumed within families or in communal groups).

In a number of countries with centrally planned economies such as Afghanistan, Bulgaria, China, Cuba, Czechoslovakia, East Germany, Hungary, Laos, Mongolia, Poland, and the Soviet Union, the conventional concept for the aggregated national income/product is net material product (NMP) and includes only material goods and "productive" services. The GDP values presented in this table for free market economies are not directly comparable to the official NMP measures published by the centrally planned economies. The GDP value is more comprehensive and covers a number of sectors (especially services) excluded from the NMP value. Estimated GNPs have been supplied for most countries (including the centrally planned), based either on the country's own, or on external, analysis.

The origin, distribution, and spending of the national product. Even though GNP/GDP values allow a general comparison of relative economic development, more information is provided when these aggregates are analyzed according to their component kinds of expenditure, cost components, and industrial sectors of origin.

National product and accounts

country	gross national product (GNP), 1984		gross domestic product (GDP), 1984		GDP by type of expenditure, 1983 (%)					cost components of GDP, 1983 (%)			
	nominal ('000,000 U.S.$)	per capita (U.S.$)	nominal ('000,000,000 national currency)	real prices of 1980 ('000,000,000 national currency)	consumption: private	consumption: government	gross domestic investment	foreign trade: exports	foreign trade: imports	net indirect taxes	consumption of fixed capital	compensation of employees	net operating surplus
Afghanistan	3,500[1]	210[1]	...	91.1[1,2]	...	...	...	...	...	...	...	...	...
Albania	2,580[1]	930[1]	...	...	...	...	...	...	...	...	...	...	...
Algeria	50,680	2,400	231.9[5]	...	45	15	38	28	−26	20[4]	8[4]	37[4]	35[4]
American Samoa	160	4,580	...	...	...	...	...	...	...	...	...	...	...
Andorra	360[5]	9,000[5]	...	...	...	...	...	...	...	...	...	...	...
Angola	7,634[1]	1,030[1]	199.5[6]	...	58	27	9	—6—		...	...	...	...
Anguilla	...	...	...	...	...	...	...	...	...	...	...	...	...
Antigua and Barbuda	150	1,890	0.435	...	66[1]	23[1]	51[1]	72[1]	−111[1]	...	...	...	...
Argentina	67,150	2,230	0.683[5]	0.026[5]	67	12	17	14	−9	8	[9]	34	57[9]
Aruba[10]	...	...	...	...	...	...	...	...	...	...	...	...	...
Australia	184,980	11,890	197.3	139.2	63	17	21	15	−16	12	7	53	28
Austria	68,800	9,110	1,284.8	1,046.6	58	19	23	41	−40	13	12	53	21
Bahamas, The	960	4,250	1.610	...	59[1]	15[1]	26[1]	80[1]	−81[1]	...	...	...	...
Bahrain	4,260	10,640	1.543[6]	...	39[1]	17[1]	43[1]	90[1]	−89[1]	3[1]	9[1]	28[1]	60[1]
Bangladesh	12,360	120	349.9	230.2	90	5	11	6	−12	...	...	...	...
Barbados	1,100	4,370	2.303	1.654	72	16	20	65	−73	14[4]	6[4]	57[4]	24[4]
Belgium	83,070	8,410	4,486.0	3,557.0	65	18	15	72	−70	11	10	57	23
Belize	180	1,110	0.365	0.335	71	25	20	53	−70	12	9	—78—	
Benin	1,060	270	385.3[5]	...	91	9	20	23	−42	9[15]	7[15]	23[15]	61[15]
Bermuda	920	16,310	0.853	0.858	66	11	17	61	−56	...	...	...	...
Bhutan	135	100	1.194[1]	...	...	...	...	...	...	...	...	...	...
Bolivia	2,560	410	19,023.8	...	72	9	14	25	−20	10[4]	6[4]	36[4]	47[4]
Botswana	940	900	1.264	1.094	56	27	30	61	−73	13[1]	11[1]	39[1]	37[1]
Brazil	227,280	1,710	386.968	13.236	71	9	17	11	−9	10[1]	5[1]	—85[1]—	
British Virgin Islands	...	...	0.077[5]	0.066[5]	43	18	38	114	−115	12[15]	[9]	53[15]	36[9, 15]
Brunei	4,270[5]	20,140[5]	8.210	5.827	...	...	...	...	...	...	...	...	...
Bulgaria	25,082	2,800	24.907[2]	21.126[2]	58	11	23	—8—		...	...	...	...
Burkina Faso	1,040	150	429.4[5]	338.3[5]	95	15	19	10	−39	8	7	24	61
Burma	6,620	180	54.042	48.476	—86—		18	7	−10	9	9	38	44
Burundi	1,010	220	115.954	93.074	79	13	23	9	−24	10[1]	2[1]	21[1]	66[1]
Cameroon	8,000	850	3,089.3	1,896.4	67	9	26	19	−21	13	5	27	54
Canada	330,870	13,160	436.1	329.0	57	21	19	26	−22	10	12	55	22
Cape Verde	100	320	0.104[5, 19]	...	125	13	22	—59—		...	...	...	...
Cayman Islands	...	...	...	...	...	...	...	...	...	...	...	...	...
Central African Republic	680	260	0.498[5, 19]	...	82	24	14	—21—		12[20]	—	24[20]	64[20]
Chad	425	100	0.601[5, 19]	...	83	24	7	—14—		6[21]	7[21]	13[21]	75[21]
Chile	20,340	1,710	1,893.4	1,029.4	73	14	10	24	−21	14[1]	11[1]	42[1]	34[1]
China	318,310	310	564.3[22]	514.9[22]	—71[2]—		30[2]	—1[2]—		...	...	...	...
Christmas Island	...	...	...	...	...	...	...	...	...	...	...	...	...
Cocos (Keeling) Islands	...	...	...	...	...	...	...	...	...	...	...	...	...
Colombia	38,410	1,370	3,691.7	1,708.9	72	12	19	11	−13	8	[9]	44	48[9]
Comoros	106[5]	290[5]	0.096[5, 19]	...	66	22	32	—20—		...	...	...	...
Congo	2,060	1,060	920.1	574.0	40	15	36	57	−47	16[1]	13[1]	29[1]	43[1]
Cook Islands	20[4]	1,110[4]	...	...	80[20]	32[20]	26[20]	32[20]	−71[20]	...	...	...	...
Costa Rica	2,930	1,210	158.674	41.479	61	16	25	36	−37	14	3	44	39
Côte d'Ivoire	6,030	620	2,497.7[5]	2,045.6[5]	67	21	22	41	−51	23[16]	8[16]	33[16]	36[16]
Cuba	15,760[5]	1,590[5]	13.721[2]	11.336[2]	78	8	19	—5[2]—		...	...	...	...
Cyprus	2,390	3,640	1.316	0.933	65	17	31	53	−66	7	11	—82—	
Czechoslovakia	83,947	5,400	534.2[2]	523.2[2]	56	10	27	—7—		...	...	...	...
Denmark	57,700	11,290	561.1	403.5	54	27	16	36	−34	15	9	55	21

There are three major domestic expenditure components of GDP: private consumption (analyzed in greater detail in the "Household budgets and consumption" table), government spending, and gross domestic investment. The fourth, nondomestic, component of GDP expenditure is net foreign trade; value is given for both exports (a positive value) and imports (a negative value, representing obligations to other countries). The sum of these five percentages, excluding statistical discrepancies and rounding, should be 100% of the GDP.

The distribution of GDP by cost components usually comprises four general categories: indirect taxes (excise or value-added taxes), consumption of fixed capital (depreciation), and two income categories: (a) compensation of employees (salaries, wages, etc.) and (b) net operating surplus ("profits," interests, rent, etc.).

The distribution of GDP for ten industrial sectors is aggregated into three major industrial groups:

1. The primary sector, comprised of agriculture and mineral production (including fossil fuels).
2. The secondary sector, comprised of manufacturing, construction, and public utilities.
3. The tertiary sector, which includes transportation and communication, trade, financial services (including real estate), personal and business services, and government.

Percentages in this section of the table may not add to 100 because the value of each industry is calculated as a percentage of the total GDP, which may contain significant monetary adjustments that are not distributable to all industries.

Average annual growth rate of real GDP. The columns show average annual growth rates of real product for the decade from 1970 to 1980, as well as for the three years from 1980 to 1983. Real GDP growth rates give an overall impression of the growth in final output achieved by various countries during the years indicated.

Balance of payments (external account transactions). The external account records the sum of all economic transactions of a current nature between one country and the rest of the world. The account shows a country's net receipts from overseas, including not only the trade of goods and services but also such invisible items as interest and dividends, short- and long-term investments, tourism, transfers to or from overseas residents, etc. Each transaction gives rise either to a foreign claim for payment, recorded as a deficit (*e.g.*, from imports, capital outflows), or a foreign obligation to pay, recorded as a surplus (*e.g.*, from exports, capital inflows) or a domestic claim on another country. A deficit transaction in the balance of payment of one country is automatically accompanied by a surplus in that of another. Values are given in U.S. dollars for comparability.

Tourist trade. Income from tourism is often a significant element in a country's economic balance. A tourist is defined as a visitor who stays at least 24 hours but not more than one year in the country visited and whose activities encompass business and/or pleasure. The receipts from foreign nationals reflect payments for goods and services from foreign currency resources by tourists in the given country. Expenditures by nationals abroad are also payments for goods and services, but in this case made by the residents of the given country as tourists abroad. Unless the classification is so important as to justify separate consideration, receipts and expenditures by excursionists—cruise passengers staying less than 24 hours—are included in the total tourist trade figures.

Although tourist trade is also a component of the invisible trade classification, the importance of tourism as a source of income for many countries—the Caribbean islands, for example—warrants a separate listing of this industry. The U.S. dollar is used as the common currency for comparability by the World Tourism Organization.

origin of GDP by economic sector, 1983 (%)										avg. annual growth rate of real GDP (%)		balance of payments, 1985 (current external transactions; '000,000 U.S.$)			tourist trade, 1984 ('000,000 U.S.$)		country
primary		secondary			tertiary					1970–1980	1980–1984	net transfers		current balance of payments	receipts from foreign nationals	expenditures by nationals abroad	
agriculture	mining	manufacturing	construction	public utilities	transp., communication	trade	financial svcs.	other svcs.	govt.			goods-merchandise	invisibles				
69[2]	[3]	14[2,3]	3[2]	[3]	4[2]	9[2]		—2[2]—		4.5	...	−200[4]	7[4]	−193[4]	1	...	Afghanistan
...	...	...	...	...	...	...	...	...	...	...	...	...	...	...	...	...	Albania
6[6]	31[6]	11[6]	12[6]	1[6]			—28[6]—		11[6]	7.0	−1.9[7]	4,223	−3,208	1,015	228	527[5]	Algeria
...	...	...	...	...	...	...	...	...	...	...	...	...	...	...	...	...	American Samoa
...	...	...	...	...	...	...	...	...	...	...	...	...	...	...	...	...	Andorra
28	23	4	3	1			—41—			−9.2	...	−34[1]	−175[1]	−209[1]	...	...	Angola
...	...	...	...	...	...	...	...	...	...	...	...	...	...	...	5	...	Anguilla
5[8]	1[8]	5[8]	6[8]	3[8]	17[8]	28[8]	19[8]	5[8]	16[8]	...	3.4[7]	−93[8]	90[8]	−3[8]	65	6[5]	Antigua and Barbuda
15	3	24	5	4	11	13	9	6	11	2.2	−1.3	3,982[8]	−6,477[8]	−2,495[8]	602	681	Argentina
...	...	...	...	...	...	...	...	...	...	...	...	...	...	...	...	...	Aruba[10]
4	4	18	6	4	8	13	22	18	5	3.0	2.8	−815[8]	−7,489[8]	−8,304[8]	1,211	1,952	Australia
4	[11]	27[11]	7	3	6	17	14	3	14	3.7	1.3	−3,994	3,732	−262	5,028	2,608	Austria
4	[3]	11[3]	3	[3]	11	27	12	15	17	...	2.5[12]	−595	544	−51	802	106	Bahamas, The
1[1]	24[1]	20[1]	6[1]	1[1]	7[1]	9[1]	16[1]	4[1]	6[1]	...	...	−41[8]	30[8]	−11[8]	101	99[5]	Bahrain
46	—	10	5	—	9	9	9	10	4	3.9	3.9	−1,300	722	−578	27	23[5]	Bangladesh
6[8]	1[8]	11[8]	6[8]	3[8]	7[8]	27[8]	12[8]	—17[8]—		...	0.2[13]	−259[8]	278[8]	19[8]	284	26[5]	Barbados
2	—	24	6	4	8	20	6	20	8	3.0	0.3	−1,181[8,14]	1,181[8,14]	0[8,14]	1,700	1,953	Belgium
21[8]	—	15[8]	6[8]	2[8]	11[8]	17[8]	11[8]	11[8]	10[8]	...	−0.5	−32[8]	19[8]	−13[8]	11	...	Belize
39[6]	[3]	6[3,6]	5[6]	[3]	6[6]	—22[6]—		...	10[6]	3.3	5.8[12]	−156[16]	104[16]	−52[16]	10	4	Benin
...	...	...	...	...	...	...	...	...	...	...	...	...	...	...	336	...	Bermuda
40[1]	1[1]	2[1]	2[1]	—	3[1]	3[1]	1[1]	...	10[1]	2.0	...	−42[5]	−30[5]	−72[5]	2	...	Bhutan
23	7	16	2	1	9	24	6	7	7	4.8	−5.7[13]	312[8]	−491[8]	−179[8]	37	42[5]	Bolivia
7	29	8	4	3	3	22	10	4	15	...	11.8	219	−80	139	53	16[5]	Botswana
8	1	24	6	4	8	14	18	8	8	8.4	0.2	12,466	−12,739	−273	1,512	939	Brazil
9[15]	[11]	6[11,15]	12[15]	2[15]	10[15]	27[15]	17[15]	1[15]	10[15]	...	...	...	...	...	86	...	British Virgin Islands
1	64	10	3	—	2	11		—9—		...	...	...	...	...	...	...	Brunei
17[2]	[3]	56[2,3]	10[2]	[3]	8[2]	7[2]		—3[2,17]—		7.1	...	...	...	...	288	...	Bulgaria
42	—	14	2	1	5	13		—22—		3.5	6.1[13]	−233[1]	141[1]	−92[1]	3	24[6]	Burkina Faso
48	1	9	2	—	4	24	2	4	5	4.6	5.9	−232[8]	−2[8]	−234[8]	10	3[5]	Burma
56	1[18]	5	6	[18]	3	8	2	5	7	2.8	6.9	...	...	...	27	18[6]	Burundi
22	16	11	6	1	5	13		—26—		5.6	5.7[13]	524[8]	−689[8]	−165[8]	59	70[5]	Cameroon
3	6	16	5	4	7	9		—51—		3.9	1.7	12,617	−14,558	−1,941	2,830	3,955	Canada
21	1	5	16	3			—54—			...	...	−66[16]	64[16]	−2[16]	...	...	Cape Verde
...	...	...	...	...	...	...	...	...	...	...	...	−96[5]	153[5]	57[5]	71	...	Cayman Islands
36	3	8	4	2			—47—			3.0	−0.6[13]	−25[8]	−7[8]	−32[8]	3[6]	19[6]	Central African Republic
52	—	7	1	—			—39—			−0.2	...	−19[8]	26[8]	7[8]	2[6]	...	Chad
9	9	20	5	3	5	17	16	10	5	2.4	−0.8	789	−2,096	−1,307	104	214[5]	Chile
45[2]	[3]	42[2,3]	5[2]	[3]	4[2]	5[2]	...	...	...	5.8	...	−13,123	1,706	−11,417	1,130	...	China
...	...	...	...	...	...	...	...	...	...	...	...	...	...	...	...	...	Christmas Island
...	...	...	...	...	...	...	...	...	...	...	...	...	...	...	...	...	Cocos (Keeling) Islands
19	3	21	5	2	8	13		—29—		5.9	2.0	−21	−1,369	−1,390	209	308	Colombia
44	—	6	12	1			—38—			...	...	−10	−4	−14	...	...	Comoros
8	41	5	7	1	7	12		—19—		3.1	12.8[7]	651[8]	−438[8]	213[8]	13	54[5]	Congo
26[4]	—	11[4]	9[4]	2[4]	7[4]	14[4]	3[4]	...	...	...	...	...	...	...	...	...	Cook Islands
—21—		20	3	3	8	15	14	—11—		5.0	0.2	−75	−252	−327	117	36[5]	Costa Rica
27[6]	1[6]	12[6]	8[6]	2[6]	8[6]		—31[6]—		12[6]	6.7	−2.6[13]	1,482	−1,382	100	72	180[5]	Côte d'Ivoire
10[2]	[3]	32[2,3]	8[2]	[3]	7[2]	41[2]		—1[2,17]—		0.4	...	...	...	...	108	...	Cuba
9	1	16	12	2	8	14	7	15	12	2.2	4.5	−717	558	−159	270	53	Cyprus
9[2]	[3]	61[2,3]	10[2]	[3]	5[2]	14[2]		—1[2,17]—		5.1	...	...	...	...	328	229[5]	Czechoslovakia
5	1	19	6	2	8	13	17	5	23	2.5	1.9	−771	−1,957	−2,728	1,292	1,227	Denmark

National product and accounts (continued)

country	gross national product (GNP), 1984		gross domestic product (GDP), 1984		GDP by type of expenditure, 1983 (%)					cost components of GDP, 1983 (%)			
	nominal ('000,000 U.S.$)	per capita (U.S.$)	nominal ('000,000,000 national currency)	real prices of 1980 ('000,000,000 national currency)	consumption		gross domestic investment	foreign trade		net indirect taxes	consumption of fixed capital	compensation of employees	net operating surplus
					private	government		exports	imports				
Djibouti	302	740	59.997[5]	...	72	38	25	—-35—		17[6]	[9]	35[6]	48[6, 9]
Dominica	80	970	0.231	...	70	25	27	42	-65	...	...	...	...
Dominican Republic	6,040	990	10.706	7.319	73	10	21	14	-18	7	6	—87—	
Ecuador	10,340	1,130	784.9	311.2	66	13	17	25	-21	8	[9]	24	68[9]
Egypt	33,340	710	25.228[5]	19.953[5]	60	17	31	25	-33	6[1]	[9]	36[1]	59[1, 9]
El Salvador	3,820	730	11.410	7.896	79	15	12	24	-30	7	4	—89—	
Equatorial Guinea	60[5]	200[5]	0.019[5, 19]	...	116	53	11	—-79—		...	...	...	...
Ethiopia	4,780	110	10.031[5]	9.583[5]	80	17	11	11	-20	...	...	...	...
Faeroe Islands	500	11,080	2.630[4]	...	...	...	...	...	...	...	...	...	...
Falkland Islands	...	...	...	...	...	...	...	...	...	...	...	...	...
Fiji	1,250	1,820	1.142[5]	0.968[5]	66	20	20	44	-49	10	8	49	33
Finland	53,090	10,870	307.9	214.0	55	19	26	31	-30	10	15	54	21
France	542,960	9,880	4,284.1	2,899.9	65	17	20	22	-23	13	12	56	19
French Guiana	180[5]	2,340[5]	...	...	...	...	...	...	...	...	...	...	...
French Polynesia	1,300	7,660	136.953[1]	87.193[1]	68[1]	34[1]	32[1]	12[1]	-45[1]	6[1]	17[1]	46[1]	31[1]
Gabon	2,830	2,470	1,455.6	982.2	31	13	33	—23—		18[16]	14[16]	30[16]	37[16]
Gambia, The	180	250	0.491[1]	0.418[1]	102	27	37	—-66—		...	...	...	...
Gaza Strip	1,747[5]	3,530[5]	45.5[5]	...	125	18	38	58	-139	...	...	...	...
Germany, East	93,631	5,600	...	222.1	57	12	20	—12—		10[1, 2]	9[1, 2]	40[1, 2]	41[1, 2]
Germany, West	678,880	11,100	1,748.1	1,525.2	57	20	20	32	-29	11	13	55	21
Ghana	4,730	380	215.2[5]	37.6[5]	81	14	6	—-1—		5[15]	3[15]	—91[15]—	
Gibraltar	130	4,530	...	...	...	...	...	...	...	...	...	...	...
Greece	36,940	3,730	3,769.8	1,753.6	66	19	21	19	-29	11	9	41	39
Greenland	380	7,220	...	...	...	...	...	...	...	...	...	...	...
Grenada	80	860	0.235	...	81[1]	22[1]	38[1]	36[1]	-76[1]	...	...	...	...
Guadeloupe	1,180[5]	3,580[5]	8.486[5]	...	96	33	24	7	-60	11[4]	[9]	70[4]	19[4, 9]
Guam	760	6,340	...	...	...	...	...	...	...	...	...	...	...
Guatemala	9,110	1,180	9.035[5]	7.446[5]	83	8	11	13	-15	...	...	...	...
Guernsey	...	...	...	...	...	...	...	...	...	...	...	...	...
Guinea	1,810	290	2.367[5, 19]	...	69	16	16	—-2—		...	...	...	...
Guinea-Bissau	160	190	0.083[5,19]	...	128	24	19	—-71—		...	...	...	...
Guyana	470	600	1.468[5]	1.259[5]	56	33	27	50	-66	18	8	—74—	
Haiti	1,710	330	9.104	7.037	—97—		16	27	-40	10[1]	3[1]	—87[1]—	
Honduras	2,980	700	6.297	5.058	73	15	16	26	-31	10	4	—85—	
Hong Kong	33,970	6,330	249.6	180.1	67	8	27	95	-97	4	—96—		
Hungary	18,253	1,710	978.5	788.7	61	10	26	40	-38	...	...	...	...
Iceland	2,250	9,380	81.566	14.666	58	18	21	43	-40	20	14	—67—	
India	197,210	260	2,131.8	1,562.3	69	11	24	—-4—		11	7	67	14
Indonesia	85,400	530	73,698.0	52,257.0	61	11	29	28	-29	2	5	—93—	
Iran	159,138[5]	3,830[5]	15,029.6	9,179.9	50	15	34	14	-13	2	7	—91—	
Iraq	31,300[6]	2,300[6]	9.495[6]	...	—91[1]—		42[1]	24[1]	-57[1]	1[25]	3[25]	21[25]	75[25]
Ireland	17,500	4,950	16.282	10.100	60	20	23	53	-56	12	10	56	22
Isle of Man	390	5,640	0.162[5]	...	...	...	...	...	...	...	...	...	...
Israel	21,290	5,070	6.963	0.116	65	31	24	38	-58	12	12	50	26
Italy	367,040	6,440	612,112.0	334,769.0	64	20	18	24	-25	9	10	57	24
Jamaica	2,480	1,090	9.368	4.996	70	21	22	38	-50	11[1]	10[1]	58[1]	22[1]
Japan	1,248.090	10,400	298,084.0	278,119.0	60	10	28	16	-14	6	14	56	24
Jersey	880[5]	11,480[5]	0.510	...	...	...	...	...	...	...	...	...	...
Jordan	4,340	1,710	1.523	1.207	95	24	36	45	-99	14	7	42	37
Kampuchea	1,132[21]	160[21]	...	...	...	...	...	...	...	...	...	...	...
Kenya	5,950	300	80.922	57.988	61	19	21	25	-26	14	[9]	35	51[9]
Kiribati	30	480	0.039[15]	...	93[4]	36[4]	44[4]	23[4]	-96[4]	5[4]	5[4]	30[4]	61[4]
Korea, North	14,700	760	11.8[1]	...	...	...	...	...	...	...	...	...	...
Korea, South	84,860	2,090	67,126.0	50,455.0	62	11	27	37	-37	13	9	41	36
Kuwait	27,570	16,850	5.998[1]	6.957[1]	50	19	20	60	-48	...	...	...	...
Laos	602[5]	150[5]	...	...	...	...	...	...	...	...	...	...	...
Lebanon	4,600[5]	1,750[5]	11.150[16]	...	—110[16]—		18[16]	—-28[16]—		8[27]	5[27]	—88[27]—	
Lesotho	790	520	0.432[5]	0.293[5]	192	25	34	11	-161	22	3	45	30
Liberia	990	460	0.819	...	45[1]	30[1]	28[1]	58[1]	-62[1]	14[1]	—86[1]—		
Libya	29,790	8,220	8.846[1]	8.551[1]	38[1]	34[1]	26[1]	46[1]	-44[1]	4[1]	5[1]	30[1]	61[1]
Liechtenstein	524[4]	20,960[4]	...	...	...	...	...	...	...	...	...	...	...
Luxembourg	4,980	13,610	191.2[5]	138.0[5]	53[1]	15[1]	22[1]	86[1]	-75[1]	12[1]	13[1]	64[1]	11[1]
Macau	780[5]	2,270[5]	...	...	...	...	...	...	...	...	...	...	...
Madagascar	2,600	270	1,045.9[1]	617.8[1]	80	14	13	11	-18	12[16]	1[16]	—87[16]—	
Malaŵi	1,430	210	1.735	0.992	72	15	19	—-6—		9[16]	7[16]	27[16]	58[16]
Malaysia	30,280	1,980	79.634	66.918	51	17	36	52	-57	16[15]	[9]	32[15]	52[9, 15]
Maldives	56[5]	330[5]	0.466[5]	0.400[5]	83	16	38	62	-100	...	...	...	...
Mali	1,060	130	732.9[1]	...	86	14	15	—-15—		8[1]	7[1]	25[1]	60[1]
Malta	1,210	3,660	0.458[5]	0.418[5]	67	18	30	67	-82	9	4	49	38
Martinique	1,330[5]	4,070[5]	9.963[5]	...	90	36	19	13	-58	10[4]	[9]	66[4]	24[4, 9]
Mauritania	750	460	44.672[5]	...	65	26	20	—-11—		9[21]	6[21]	27[21]	58[21]
Mauritius	1,100	1,090	14.180	...	69	13	17	47	-47	17	[9]	42	41[9]
Mayotte	...	...	...	...	...	...	...	...	...	...	...	...	...
Mexico	158,310	2,060	29,438.9	4,500.0	60	9	20	19	-9	10	6	29	55
Monaco	...	...	...	...	...	...	...	...	...	...	...	...	...
Mongolia	1,820	1,000	...	...	...	...	...	...	...	...	...	...	...
Montserrat	30	2,550	0.094	...	93	22	32	21	-68	...	...	...	...
Morocco	14,340	630	94.6[5]	72.9[5]	68	20	21	23	-31	14[4]	[9]	33[4]	53[4, 9]
Mozambique	4,466[6]	360[6]	111.5[5]	...	83	17	8	—-9—		...	...	...	...
Nauru	...	...	...	...	...	...	...	...	...	...	...	...	...
Nepal	2,630	160	38.184	27.826	83	8	20	10	-21	6	5	55	34
Netherlands, The	135,830	9,620	394.9	336.8	61	18	18	58	-54	9	10	55	25
Netherlands Antilles[10]	1,370[1]	5,730[1]	2.436[4]	...	55[4]	24[4]	21[4]	110[4]	-109[4]	6[4]	10[4]	68[4]	16[4]
New Caledonia	920	6,230	114.2[5]	...	60	35	17	27	-39	3	9	59	29
New Zealand	23,530	7,280	40.978	...	59	17	25	31	-31	9	7	50	34

origin of GDP by economic sector, 1983 (%)										avg. annual growth rate of real GDP (%)		balance of payments, 1985 (current external transactions; '000,000 U.S.$)			tourist trade, 1984 ('000,000 U.S.$)		country
primary		secondary			tertiary					1970–1980	1980–1984	net transfers		current balance of payments	receipts from foreign nationals	expenditures by nationals abroad	
agriculture	mining	manufacturing	construction	public utilities	transp., communication	trade	financial svcs.	other svcs.	govt.			goods-merchandise	invisibles				
4[8]	—	8[8]	7[8]	3[8]	10[8]	16[8]	11[8]	2[8]	27[8]	...	...	−100[1]	75[1]	−25[1]	...	...	Djibouti
30	1	8	7	3	11	9	7	—23—		...	5.7[7]	−25[8]	17[8]	−8[8]	4.5	0.7[5]	Dominica
17	4	19	6	2	8	16	3	15	10	6.6	2.5	−389[8]	226[8]	−163[8]	277	87[5]	Dominican Republic
14	14	18	7	1	8	14	3	—8—		8.8	1.6	1,147	−1,232	−85	120	152[5]	Ecuador
20[6]	[11]	29[6, 11]	5[6]	1[6]	8[6]	—18[6]—		—18[6]—		7.4	9.8[13]	−5,386[8]	3,035[8]	−2,081[8]	318	762[5]	Egypt
22	—	16	4	2	4	24	9	8	11	4.1	−2.9	−189[8]	135[8]	−54[8]	5	74[5]	El Salvador
41	[23]	12[23]	[23]	[23]	[23]	—47—				...	...	−15[6]	−3[6]	−18[6]	...	...	Equatorial Guinea
43	—	10	3	1	5	10	3	6	7	2.0	4.1[13]	−383[8]	251[8]	−132[8]	6	4[5]	Ethiopia
24[4]	[11]	16[4, 11]	10[4]	2[4]	9[4]	12[4]	12[4]	—16[4]—		...	...	...	...	...	...	...	Faeroe Islands
...	...	...	...	...	...	...	...	...	...	...	...	...	...	...	...	...	Falkland Islands
21	—	11	8	1	11	18	14	—19—		4.7	2.5	−174	167	−7	135[5]	19[6]	Fiji
8[8]	—	25[8]	7[8]	3[8]	7[8]	10[8]	14[8]	5[8]	14[8]	3.1	2.7	882	−1,559	−677	489	681	Finland
4	2	26	6	3	5	10	14	—30—		3.5	1.1	−4,532	5,479	947	7,598	4,270	France
...	...	...	...	...	...	...	...	...	...	...	...	...	...	...	...	...	French Guiana
5[1]	—	8[1]	9[1]	1[1]	6[1]	—24[1]—		23[1]	24[1]	...	...	...	...	...	66	...	French Polynesia
6	47	4	7	2	4	8	1	7	8	...	−0.2[13]	1,285[8]	−1,199[8]	86[8]	4	92[5]	Gabon
27	—	7	8	—	8	24	11	3	14	...	...	−84[6]	34[6]	−50[6]	22	2[5]	Gambia, The
16	[11]	10[11]	24	...	—50—					...	5.8	−163[8]	147[8]	−16[8]	...	...	Gaza Strip
8[2]	[11]	69[2, 11]	6[2]	—	4[2]	9[2]	—5[2, 17]—			4.8	...	...	...	...	...	...	Germany, East
2	1	31	6	3	6	11	—41—			2.6	0.9	28,670	−14,800	13,870	5,480	13,914	Germany, West
60	1	4	2	—	4	23	—6—			−0.1	−2.8[13]	−36	−130	−166	2	25[5]	Ghana
...	...	...	...	...	...	...	...	...	...	...	...	...	...	...	21	...	Gibraltar
17	2	18	7	2	8	—21—		7	17	4.9	0.7	−4,230[8]	2,098[8]	−2,132[8]	1,313	339	Greece
...	...	...	...	...	...	...	...	...	...	...	...	...	...	...	...	...	Greenland
19	1	6	8	2	8	20	—36—			...	3.1[7]	−40	45	5	18	3[5]	Grenada
7[4]	[11]	6[4, 11]	4[4]	—	4[4]	17[4]	—60[4]—			...	...	...	...	...	98	...	Guadeloupe
—	...	31[4]	7[4]	...	2[4]	40[4]	7[4]	—13[4]—		...	...	...	...	...	175[5]	...	Guam
25	—	16	3	2	7	26	—21—			5.7	−1.8[13]	−17	−229	−246	57	100[5]	Guatemala
...	...	...	...	...	...	...	...	...	...	...	...	...	...	...	...	...	Guernsey
42	14	2	7	—	1	—22—		—11—		3.3	...	...	...	...	...	...	Guinea
49	1	1	3	—	—46—					...	...	−41[5]	15[5]	−26[5]	...	...	Guinea-Bissau
20	1	11[24]	7	[24]	7	8	—46—			...	−5.6[13]	5	−102	−97	4[6]	11[6]	Guyana
32	—	17	5	1	2	18	5	8	11	4.0	−0.9	−131[8]	19[8]	−112[8]	91	39[5]	Haiti
25	2	13	5	2	7	12	11	8	5	3.6	0.4	−119	−144	−263	23	41[5]	Honduras
1	—	22	6	2	8	21	30	—16—		9.3	...	...	...	...	1,371	...	Hong Kong
13[2]	[11]	38[2, 11]	11[2]	1	8[2]	11[2]	—19[2, 17]—			5.4	2.3	610	−662	−52	452	167	Hungary
23[1]	—	13[1]	9[1]	...	8[1]	10[1]	—37[1]—			...	−0.7	−13[8]	−118[8]	−131[8]	34	68	Iceland
36	3	15	6	2	6	14	7	...	5	3.6	5.2	−4,098[5]	2,145[5]	−1,953[5]	1,117	201[5]	India
26	19	13	6	1	5	15	—15—			7.6	3.6	5,876	−7,508	−1,632	442	577[5]	Indonesia
16	14	8	8	1	7	21	—26—			2.5	9.9[13]	...	...	...	42	...	Iran
10[1]	23[1]	7[1]	16[1]	1[1]	9[1]	12[1]	6[1]	—18[1]—		12.1	...	...	...	...	152	...	Iraq
11	[3]	24[3]	7	[3]	6	11	—42—			3.5	2.0	234[8]	−1,156[8]	−922[8]	461[26]	548[5]	Ireland
...	...	...	...	...	...	...	...	...	...	...	...	...	...	...	62[5]	...	Isle of Man
5	[11]	20[11]	7	2	7	13	—46—			4.1	2.1	−2,412	3,512	1,100	1,056	718	Israel
6	3	24	8	5	7	16	12	8	14	3.0	0.5	−5,995[8]	3,124[8]	−2,871[8]	8,595	2,098	Italy
7	4	19	8	2	6	20	17	2	15	−1.1	1.3	−296[8]	−16[8]	−312[8]	407	11[5]	Jamaica
3	—	30	8	4	7	12	17	18	5	5.0	3.8	55,990	−6,820	49,170	970	4,607	Japan
6	—	—4—			—90—					...	...	...	...	...	223[5]	...	Jersey
6[8]	3[8]	24[8]	12[8]	2[8]	14[8]	12[8]	6[8]	3[8]	13[8]	6.9	5.4	−1,721[8]	1,457[8]	−264[8]	416	334	Jordan
...	...	...	...	...	...	...	...	...	...	2.4	...	...	...	...	...	...	Kampuchea
33	—	12	5	2	6	11	15	3	15	6.5	2.5	−347	126	−211	1,501	11[5]	Kenya
25[1]	—	3[1]	4[1]	2[1]	21[1]	16[1]	2[1]	—14[1]—		...	...	...	...	...	...	...	Kiribati
...	...	...	...	...	...	...	...	...	...	...	...	...	...	...	...	...	Korea, North
16	2	24	9	2	9	15	8	10	5	9.5	7.5	−19	−868	−887	673	576	Korea, South
1	48	6	5	1	3	8	5	—22—		2.5	−3.4[7]	5,473	143	5,616	31	1,520[5]	Kuwait
...	...	...	...	...	...	...	...	...	...	3.3	...	...	...	...	...	...	Laos
9[21]	[11]	13[11, 21]	3[21]	5[21]	8[21]	28[21]	—23[21]—		10[21]	3.2	...	...	...	...	...	...	Lebanon
21	—	6	10	1	1	12	—49—			7.9	...	−305	318	13	10	8[5]	Lesotho
18	17	9	4	3	7	9	13	—18—		1.7	−5.3[7]	132[8]	−129[8]	3[8]	...	...	Liberia
2[1]	48[1]	3[1]	12[1]	1[1]	4[1]	6[1]	—23[1]—			2.2	−9.7[7]	2,564[8]	−4,088[8]	−1,524[8]	12	405[5]	Libya
...	...	...	...	...	...	...	...	...	...	...	...	...	...	...	...	...	Liechtenstein
3	—	26	6	3	5	15	16	15	12	4.5	−2.2[13]	[14]	[14]	[14]	...	...	Luxembourg
...	...	...	...	...	...	...	...	...	...	...	...	...	...	...	...	...	Macau
44	—	11	5	1	—39—					0.3	−4.2[7]	−125[1]	−173[1]	−298[1]	5	38[5]	Madagascar
40	—	12	4	2	5	18	5	4	11	6.3	1.2	28[1]	−101[1]	−73[1]	6	...	Malaŵi
22	4	18	6	2	8	14	8	3	13	7.8	6.5	3,672	−4,341	−669	546	579[5]	Malaysia
30	1	5[24]	7	[24]	9	11	—22—		16	...	7.7[13]	−36	27	−9	30	3[5]	Maldives
53[1]	[11]	7[1, 11]	6[1]	1[1]	3[1]	16[1]	—13[1]—			4.9	...	−77[8]	−50[8]	−127[8]	13	18[5]	Mali
5[8]	5[8, 28]	30[8]	[28]	6[8]	6[8]	16[8]	4[8]	8[8]	13[8]	11.8	2.2[13]	−250	232	−18	130	50	Malta
6[6]	[11]	5[6, 11]	4[6]	2[6]	4[6]	17[6]	—63[6]—			...	...	...	...	...	87	...	Martinique
23	15	6	8	1	—47—					1.7	...	−8[8]	−103[8]	−111[8]	6[6]	15[6]	Mauritania
11	—	13	5	2	10	11	—47—			...	6.8[12]	−23	−3	−26	44	13[5]	Mauritius
...	...	...	...	...	...	...	...	...	...	...	...	...	...	...	...	...	Mayotte
8	12	23	5	1	7	22	—23—			5.7	1.4	12,799[8]	−8,833[8]	3,966[8]	3,282	2,166	Mexico
...	...	...	...	...	...	...	...	...	...	...	...	...	...	...	...	...	Monaco
17[2]	[29]	33[2, 29]	[29]	[29]	11[2]	37[2]	—2[2, 17]—			...	...	...	...	...	...	...	Mongolia
4	1	6	7	3	8	19	—52—			...	...	−8	7	−1	7	...	Montserrat
18[1]	5[1]	18[1]	7[1]	2[1]	5[1]	14[1]	5[1]	11[1]	15[1]	5.6	1.3[13]	−1,407[8]	419[8]	−988[8]	440	83[5]	Morocco
40[6]	—	8[6]	6[6]	1[6]	4[6]	—24[6]—		...	8[6]	−29	...	−372[5]	178[5]	−194[5]	...	...	Mozambique
...	...	...	...	...	...	...	...	...	...	...	...	...	...	...	...	...	Nauru
57	—	4	7	—	6	4	—22—			2.5	4.2	−289	163	−126	32	20[5]	Nepal
4	[11]	25[11]	7	2	7	15	—29—		15	2.9	0.1	5,505	−155	5,350	1,531	3,014	Netherlands, The
—1[4]—		22[4]	8[4]	2[4]	15[4]	21[4]	—32[4]—			...	...	−3[5]	94[5]	91[5]	331	63[6]	Netherlands Antilles[10]
2[1]	12[1]	5[1]	6[1]	2[1]	4[1]	26[1]	—16[1]—		26[1]	...	...	...	...	...	46[5]	...	New Caledonia
9[8]	1[8]	23[8]	5[8]	3[8]	9[8]	21[8]	15[8]	4[8]	12[8]	2.3	1.9[13]	−195[8]	−1,294[8]	−1,489[8]	309	477	New Zealand

National product and accounts (continued)

country	gross national product (GNP), 1984		gross domestic product (GDP), 1984		GDP by type of expenditure, 1983 (%)					cost components of GDP, 1983 (%)			
	nominal ('000,000 U.S.$)	per capita (U.S.$)	nominal ('000,000,000 national currency)	real prices of 1980 ('000,000,000 national currency)	consumption: private	consumption: government	gross domestic investment	foreign trade: exports	foreign trade: imports	net indirect taxes	consumption of fixed capital	compensation of employees	net operating surplus
Nicaragua	2,700	850	35.783[5]	23.939[5]	66	27	17	13	−23	9[15]	4[15]	56[15]	31[15]
Niger	1,190	200	697.2[5]	...	82	11	19	22	−35	9[4]	7[4]	16[4]	68[4]
Nigeria	74,120	790	48.490	41.713	70	10	20	—1—		4	2	29	65
Niue	4[4]	1,160[4]	...	...	...	...	...	...	...	...	...	...	...
Norfolk Island	...	...	...	...	...	...	...	...	...	...	...	...	...
Norway	57,080	13,790	446.6	311.1	48	19	24	46	−38	11	15	49	25
Oman	7,380	6,250	3.047	2.057	31	27	26	54	−38	1[6]	—99[6]—		
Pacific Is., Trust Terr. of the	160	1,030	...	...	...	...	...	...	...	...	...	...	...
Marshall Islands	...	...	...	...	...	...	...	...	...	...	...	...	...
Micronesia, F.S. of	...	...	...	...	...	...	...	...	...	...	...	...	...
Northern Mariana Is.	...	...	...	...	...	...	...	...	...	...	...	...	...
Palau	...	...	...	...	...	...	...	...	...	...	...	...	...
Pakistan	35,420	360	418.8	298.1	81	12	18	12	−22	11	6	—82—	
Panama	4,210	1,970	4.540	3.908	57	22	21	39	−39	8	8	50	35
Papua New Guinea	2,480	760	2.173	1.773	63	24	32	39	−58	8	8	40	44
Paraguay	4,120	1,260	1,070.4	603.2	78	7	21	9	−16	6	9	32	54
Peru	17,960	940	58,723	4.754	69	14	17	23	−23	9	7	31	53
Philippines	35,040	660	549.8	274.6	70	8	27	20	−26	9	10	—81—	
Pitcairn Island	...	...	...	...	...	...	...	...	...	...	...	...	...
Poland	143,000	3,890	7,181.8[2]	6,166.8[2]	58	9	30	—2—		...	...	...	...
Portugal	20,050	1,990	1,856.9[1]	1,347.2[1]	69	15	29	32	−44	8	4	49	38
Puerto Rico	14,000	4,280	19.681	...	74	16	13	59	−61	7	6	45	42
Qatar	6,020	20,690	12.377	...	24	35	22	54	−35	...	...	...	...
Réunion	1,950	3,630	12.458[1]	...	85[4]	33[4]	23[4]	7[4]	−47[4]	10[4]	[9]	65[4]	25[4,9]
Romania	45,536	2,020	628.8[2]	...	49	7	36	—9—		...	...	...	...
Rwanda	1,610	270	141.9[5]	111.1[5]	79	18	12	9	−18	7	5	21	67
St. Christopher	60	1,360	0.167	...	77[25]	16[25]	13[25]	63[25]	−69[25]	17[25]	4[25]	67[25]	13[25]
St. Helena	...	...	...	...	...	...	...	...	...	...	...	...	...
St. Lucia	150	1,120	0.380[5]	0.326[5]	63	24	31	65	−83	...	...	...	...
St. Pierre and Miquelon	...	...	...	...	...	...	...	...	...	...	...	...	...
St. Vincent	100	920	0.269	...	68	23	32	68	−90	17[16]	8[16]	49[16]	26[16]
San Marino	177[4]	8,210[4]	...	...	...	...	...	...	...	...	...	...	...
São Tomé and Príncipe	30	290	1.178[5]	...	36	30	22	—12—		...	...	...	...
Saudi Arabia	116,380	10,750	381.6	381.3	33	31	27	53	−44	—	[9]	17[4]	83[4,9]
Senegal	2,440	380	1,015.5	536.8	78	19	17	28	−42	17[6]	6[6]	—77[6]—	
Seychelles	145	2,240	1.074	583.1	68	33	20	51	−71	19	6	41	35
Sierra Leone	1,120	310	1.939[5]	1.277[5]	100	7	13	15	−34	9[4]	10[4]	27[4]	55[4]
Singapore	18,390	7,270	38.733	33.135	47	11	45	—3—		...	...	...	...
Solomon Islands	160[5]	640[5]	0.178[5]	...	...	...	...	...	...	9[4]	12[4]	25[4]	54[4]
Somalia	1,360	240	1.102[5,19]	...	69	32	11	—12—		...	...	...	...
South Africa	73,970	2,300	105.413	66.026	56	16	24	26	−22	7	16	54	22
Bophuthatswana[1]	1,736	954	...	...	...	...	...	...	...	...	...	...	...
Ciskei[1]	426	504	...	...	...	...	...	...	...	...	...	...	...
Transkei[1]	1,471	472	...	...	...	...	...	...	...	...	...	...	...
Venda[1]	201	494	...	...	...	...	...	...	...	...	...	...	...
S.W. Africa/Namibia	1,660	1,470	1,952	1.316	...	...	...	...	...	...	...	...	...
Spain	172,360	4,490	25,935.0	16,129.0	69	12	19	20	−21	5	10	51	33
Sri Lanka	5,660	360	152.615	80.800	78	8	29	26	−41	13	5	45	37
Sudan, The	7,360	320	6.218[5]	...	77	18	17	—13—		11[15]	7[15]	39[15]	43[15]
Suriname	1,350	3,560	1.809	...	68[4]	16[4]	20[4]	59[4]	−63[4]	14[16]	10[16]	46[16]	31[16]
Swaziland	590	930	0.716	...	78	29	26	64	−97	20[6]	6[6]	44[6]	30[6]
Sweden	99,060	11,880	787.2	559.1	51	29	17	35	−33	10	12	60	18
Switzerland	105,060	16,150	214.1	175.5	62	14	24	35	−35	6	10	63	21
Syria	18,540	1,870	75.126	57.447	69	21	23	12	−25	...	...	...	...
Taiwan	57,520	3,050	2,275.7	2,012.8	52	16	23	54	−45	13[6]	8[6]	50[6]	28[6]
Tanzania	4,460	210	75.658	44.143	79	12	17	9	−17	8	2	17	72
Thailand	42,760	850	991.6	851.8	67	13	23	22	−26	11	8	28	53
Togo	730	250	281.3[5]	206.6[5]	82	15	19	36	−51	14[6]	7[6]	28[6]	51[6]
Tokelau	0.9[4]	560[4]	...	...	...	...	...	...	...	...	...	...	...
Tonga	80[5]	780[5]	0.067[5]	...	96	18	28	—41—		11	3	37	48
Trinidad and Tobago	8,350	7,150	19.760	4.629	59[1]	14[1]	38[1]	36[1]	−46[1]	...	...	...	...
Tunisia	8,840	1,260	6.178	4.133	63	17	29	35	−44	16	4	—81—	
Turkey	57,810	1,170	11,467.8[5]	4,989.9[5]	72[1]	11[1]	21[1]	—3[1]—		6	5	—89—	
Turks and Caicos Is.	...	...	0.028[5]	...	...	...	...	...	...	...	...	...	...
Tuvalu	5[6]	680[6]	...	...	...	...	...	...	...	...	...	...	...
Uganda	3,290	220	518.8[6]	...	86	14	9	—9—		16[21]	8[21]	26[21]	49[21]
U.S.S.R.	1,925,000	7,000	548.1[2,5]	489.2[2,5]	—72[2]—		26[2]	—2[2]—		...	...	...	...
United Arab Emirates	28,480	23,250	100.7	...	26	19	31	58	−35	−3	12	24	67
United Kingdom	480,680	8,510	318.1	242.5	61	22	17	27	−26	14	12	57	17
United States	3,670,490	15,490	3,619.2	2,891.4	66	21	14	8	−9	8	13	61	17
Uruguay	5,900	1,970	289.522	78.228	74	14	11	24	−22	13	4	30	54
Vanuatu	64[1]	530[1]	7.742[6]	...	...	...	...	...	...	...	...	...	...
Venezuela	57,360	3,400	347.5	237.6	66	14	15	26	−22	7	8	43	42
Vietnam	9,970	170	20.742[15]	...	...	...	...	...	...	...	...	...	...
Virgin Islands (U.S.)	900	8,370	...	...	...	...	...	...	...	...	...	...	...
Wallis and Futuna	10[1]	920[1]	...	...	...	...	...	...	...	...	...	...	...
West Bank	3,506[5]	4,560[5]	...	...	110	14	27	28	−75	...	...	...	...
Western Sahara	...	...	...	...	...	...	...	...	...	...	...	...	...
Western Samoa	127[6]	810[6]	...	...	...	...	...	...	...	...	...	...	...
Yemen (Aden)	1,130	510	0.231[4]	...	106[4]	42[4]	49[4]	14[4]	−111[4]	16[4]	8[4]	58[4]	19[4]
Yemen (Ṣan'ā')	3,940	620	17.950	14.996	81	43	23	8	−55	15[1]	2[1]	31[1]	52[1]
Yugoslavia	38,979[5]	1,710[5]	4,083.5[5,31]	1,562.1[5,31]	51[31]	9[31]	38[31]	20[31]	−23[31]	...	...	...	...
Zaire	4,240	140	99.583	17.838	62	15	19	40	−36	9[21]	7[21]	—84[21]—	
Zambia	3,020	470	4.733	3.058	63	24	14	31	−32	15	10	47	27
Zimbabwe	6,040	760	5.981[5]	4.028[5]	72	19	13	22	−26	11[1]	[9]	58[1]	31[1,9]

[1]1982. [2]Net material product. [3]Manufacturing includes mining and public utilities. [4]1980. [5]1983. [6]1981. [7]1980–82. [8]1984. [9]Net operating surplus includes consumption of fixed capital. [10]Netherlands Antilles includes Aruba. [11]Manufacturing includes mining. [12]1980–81. [13]1980–83. [14]Belgium includes Luxembourg. [15]1978. [16]1979. [17]Activities in the material sphere not elsewhere specified. [18]Mining includes public utilities. [19]U.S. dollars. [20]1970. [21]1977. [22]National income. [23]Manufacturing includes mining, construction, public utilities, and transportation and

origin of GDP by economic sector, 1983 (%)										avg. annual growth rate of real GDP (%)		balance of payments, 1985 (current external transactions; '000,000 U.S.$)			tourist trade, 1984 ('000,000 U.S.$)		country
primary		secondary			tertiary					1970–1980	1980–1984	net transfers		current balance of payments	receipts from foreign nationals	expenditures by nationals abroad	
agriculture	mining	manufacturing	construction	public utilities	transp., communication	trade	financial svcs.	other svcs.	govt.			goods-merchandise	invisibles				
22	1	25	3	2	7	19	7	5	9	0.9	3.1[13]	−350[5]	−94[5]	−444[5]	5	7[5]	Nicaragua
44[8]	9[8]	4[8]	3[8]	2[8]	4[8]	—13[8]—		8[8]	9[8]	2.7	−6.3[12]	−69[1]	−7[1]	−76[1]	3	...	Niger
25	20	5	7	1	4	22		—16—		6.5	−4.2	4,353	−3,092	1,261	102	454[5]	Nigeria
...	...	...	...	...	...	...	...	...	...	...	...	...	...	...	...	...	Niue
...	...	...	...	...	...	...	...	...	...	...	...	...	...	...	...	...	Norfolk Island
4[8]	20[8]	14[8]	5[8]	4[8]	9[8]	13[8]	8[8]	8[8]	14[8]	4.8	2.8	4,680	−1,754	2,926	649	1,474	Norway
3[8]	48[8]	3[8]	7[8]	1[8]	3[8]	12[8]	9[8]	1[8]	15[8]	...	...	1,781[8]	−1,633[8]	148[8]	...	...	Oman
...	...	...	...	...	...	...	...	...	...	...	...	...	...	...	...	...	Pacific Is., Trust. Terr. of
...	...	...	...	...	...	...	...	...	...	...	...	...	...	...	...	...	Marshall Islands
...	...	...	...	...	...	...	...	...	...	...	...	...	...	...	...	...	Micronesia, F.S of
...	...	...	...	...	...	...	...	...	...	...	...	...	...	...	71	...	Northern Mariana Is.
...	...	...	...	...	...	...	...	...	...	...	...	...	...	...	...	...	Palau
24	1	20	5	2	8	16	3	8	9	4.7	5.9	−3,277	2,171	−1,106	178	207	Pakistan
10	—	9	6	3	16	12	10	20	13	4.0	2.4	−654	675	21	186	67	Panama
34[4]	13[4]	10[4]	4[4]	1[4]	5[4]	8[4]	6[4]	12[4]	7[4]	2.3	1.0	−50[8]	−274[8]	−324[8]	12	31	Papua New Guinea
26	—	16	7	3	4	27	3	10	4	8.6	2.0	−288[8]	−25[8]	−313[8]	96	46[5]	Paraguay
8	11	26	3	1	7	17		—27—		3.0	−0.8	1,098	−1,045	53	258	160	Peru
22	2	25	8	1	6	—18—		—17—		6.3	0.9	−482	490	8	350	176[5]	Philippines
...	...	...	...	...	...	...	...	...	...	...	...	...	...	...	...	...	Pitcairn Island
18[2]	[3]	50[2, 3]	11[2]	[3]	5[2]	14[2]		—2[2, 17]—		...	...	...	...	...	106	195[5]	Poland
9[8]	[11]	32[8, 11]	6[8]	2[8]	—20[8]—		6[8]	13[8]	12[8]	4.6	4.5[7]	−1,457	1,867	410	949	222	Portugal
2	—	39	2	3	6	15		—33—		...	...	221[5]	−923[5]	−702[5]	659	551[5]	Puerto Rico
1	46	6	7	—	2	7	9	—22—		...	...	1,842[5]	−1,432[5]	410[5]	...	...	Qatar
6[4]	[11]	9[4, 11]	5[4]	2[4]	4[4]	15[4]	25[4]	—31[4]—		...	...	...	...	...	...	...	Réunion
15[2, 8]	[3]	61[2, 3, 8]	8[2, 8]	[3]	6[2, 8]		—10[2, 8]—			8.6	4.2	1,445	−530	915	230	92[5]	Romania
40	—	18	5	—	3	14		—19—		4.1	3.3[6]	−55[8]	13[8]	−42[8]	4[6]	12[6]	Rwanda
17	—	13	8	1	13	15	12	6	21	...	...	−28[5]	14[5]	−14[5]	11	...	St. Christopher
...	...	...	...	...	...	...	...	...	...	...	...	...	...	...	...	...	St. Helena
13[8]	—	10[8]	7[8]	4[8]	11[8]	22[8]	7[8]	10[8]	21[8]	...	2.4[13]	−47[8]	36[8]	−11[8]	42	10[5]	St. Lucia
...	...	...	...	...	...	...	...	...	...	...	...	...	...	...	...	...	St. Pierre and Miquelon
17[8]	—	10[8]	11[8]	3[8]	16[8]	14[8]	10	3[8]	20[8]	...	5.3[13]	−23[5]	20[5]	−3[5]	28	...	St. Vincent
...	...	...	...	...	...	...	...	...	...	...	...	...	...	...	...	...	San Marino
31[6]	...	4[6]	2[6]	1[6]	4[6]	16[6]	—25[6]—		17[6]	...	...	−6[5]	−2[5]	−8[5]	...	...	São Tomé and Príncipe
2[8]	41[8]	4[8]	14[8]	—	8[8]	10[8]	7[8]	3[8]	11[8]	10.6	−0.5	8,829[8]	−32,865[8]	−24,036[8]	1,573[6]	2,761[6]	Saudi Arabia
21	[29]	26[29]	[29]	[29]			—54—			2.5	2.1[12]	−379[1]	−21[1]	−400[1]	56	42[5]	Senegal
8	—	10	3	2	28	19	11	3	18	...	−4.4[7]	−69[8]	55[8]	−14[8]	40	6[5]	Seychelles
31[4]	9[4]	7[4]	4[4]	1[4]	15[4]	13[4]	7[4]	3[4]	6[4]	1.6	3.5[13]	−17[8]	−6[8]	−23[8]	8	4[5]	Sierra Leone
1	—	24	11	2	13	21	22	—12—		8.5	8.1	−3,035	2,782	−253	2,076	531[5]	Singapore
59[30]	[3]	1[3, 30]	2[30]	[3]	2[30]	8[30]	—8[30]—		14[30]	...	...	1	−20	−19	2[15]	...	Solomon Islands
35[1]	5[1]	9[1]	5[1]	2[1]	8[1]	7[1]	7[1]	11[1]	11[1]	3.4	...	−240	143	−97	13[1]	13[1]	Somalia
5	15	23	4	5	9	13	14	2	11	3.6	1.6	2,108[8]	−3,137[8]	−1,029[8]	630[5]	...	South Africa
6[4]	[29]	69[4, 29]	[29]	[29]			—25[4]—			...	...	...	...	...	...	...	Bophuthatswana
...	...	...	...	...	...	...	...	...	...	...	...	...	...	...	...	...	Ciskei
27[4]	[29]	12[4, 29]	[29]	[29]			—61[4]—			...	...	...	...	...	...	...	Transkei
...	...	...	...	...	...	...	...	...	...	...	...	...	...	...	...	...	Venda
7[8]	26[8]	5[8]	3[8]	4[8]	7[8]	14[8]	8[8]	2[8]	21[8]	...	...	...	...	...	46[6]	...	S.W. Africa/Namibia
6	[3]	27[3]	7	[3]			—60—			4.0	1.5	−3,977[8]	6,288[8]	2,311[8]	7,717	835	Spain
26	1	15	8	1	9	21	5	—9—		4.1	5.0	−657	101	−556	105	93[5]	Sri Lanka
36[15]	—	8[15]	4[15]	1[15]	10[15]	19[15]		—22[15]—		4.4	...	−135	287	152	6	72[5]	Sudan, The
9[1]	12[1]	9[1]	3[1]	2[1]	5[1]	12[1]		—48[1]—		...	...	48	−71	−23	4	35[5]	Suriname
25	3	23	4	1	6	9	7	4	17	...	3.9[7]	−79[8]	68[8]	−11[8]	7	22[5]	Swaziland
3	—	21	7	...	6	11	12	4	22	1.7	1.6	2,422	−3,445	−1,023	1,128	1,709	Sweden
...	...	...	...	...	...	...	...	...	...	0.4	0.8	−2,616[8]	6,635[8]	4,019[8]	3,163	2,282	Switzerland
21	8	8	6	—	8	24		—24—		10.0	2.7	−1,942[8]	1,090[8]	−852[8]	130	188[5]	Syria
7	1	40	11	4	6	13	3	—17—		8.9	...	9,066[8]	−2,087[8]	6,979[8]	1,066	1,229[5]	Taiwan
49[8]	—	6[8]	2[8]	1[8]	5[8]	12[8]		—24[8]—		4.9	0.6	−350[6]	71[6]	−279[6]	13	12[5]	Tanzania
22	2	19	5	2	8	19	8	11	5	7.2	5.6	−1,344	−203	−1,547	1,156	282[5]	Thailand
32	7	5	5	2			—49—			3.4	−4.7[13]	4[8]	−26[8]	−22[8]	11	22[5]	Togo
...	...	...	...	...	...	...	...	...	...	...	...	...	...	...	...	...	Tokelau
41	—	5	4	—	6	15	6	—22—		...	...	−21	15	−6	6	1[5]	Tonga
3[8]	25[8]	7[8]	13[8]	2[8]	11[8]	9[8]	10[8]	7[8]	14[8]	5.1	0.9[13]	695	−900	−205	198	200[5]	Trinidad and Tobago
12	11	11	6	1	5	17		—35—		7.5	3.5[13]	−823	287	−536	463	65[5]	Tunisia
19	2	25	4	2	10	17		—21—		5.9	4.0[13]	−2,975	1,943	−1,032	548	277	Turkey
...	...	...	...	...	...	...	...	...	...	...	...	...	...	...	7	...	Turks and Caicos Is.
16[16]	—	1[16]	13[16]	...	4[16]	34[16]		—32[16]—		...	...	...	...	...	...	...	Tuvalu
68[6]	—	3[6]	—	...	1[6]	7[6]	—16[6]—		5[6]	5.6	6.5[13]	−49[6]	57[6]	8[6]	8	10[5]	Uganda
20[2]	[3]	46[2, 3]	10[2]	[3]	6[2]	18[2]	...	...	...	...	...	...	...	...	...	...	U.S.S.R.
1	45	9	11	2	5	10		—17—		...	−2.5[7]	...	...	...	...	...	United Arab Emirates
2	[11]	24[11]	6	11	7	13	18	16	7	1.9	1.4	−2,284	7,625	5,341	5,546	6,142	United Kingdom
2	3	21	4	3	6	16	17	15	12	3.0	3.5	−124,450	6,670	−117,780	11,386	15,805	United States
11	[11]	17[11]	3	1	6	12		—35—		3.5	−4.0	191[8]	−315[8]	−124[8]	107	304[5]	Uruguay
...	...	...	...	...	...	...	...	...	...	...	...	−34	33	−1	...	...	Vanuatu
7	16	17	5	2	11	10	8	7	9	5.0	−1.7	8,705[8]	−3,287[8]	5,418[8]	343	995	Venezuela
58[2]	[3]	24[2, 3]	3[2]	[3]	2[2]	12[2]		—2[2, 17]—		8.7	...	...	...	...	...	...	Vietnam
...	...	...	...	...	...	...	...	...	...	...	...	...	...	...	377	...	Virgin Islands (U.S.)
...	...	...	...	...	...	...	...	...	...	...	...	...	...	...	...	...	Wallis and Futuna
27	[11]	7[11]	16	...			—50—			...	−2.7	−221[8]	141[8]	−80[8]	...	...	West Bank
...	...	...	...	...	...	...	...	...	...	...	...	...	...	...	...	...	Western Sahara
...	...	...	...	...	...	...	...	...	...	3.0	−3.2[13]	−30	32	2	...	...	Western Samoa
10[4]	—	12[4]	8[4]	1[4]	10[4]	13[4]	11[4]	1[4]	23[4]	9.1	...	−794[8]	426[8]	−368[8]	4[6]	10[6]	Yemen (Aden)
28[6]	1[6]	6[6]	9[6]	1[6]	4[6]	17[6]	12[6]	1[6]	15[6]	9.2	5.6[7]	−1,228	889	−339	18	72[5]	Yemen (Ṣanʿāʾ)
15[2]	[11]	39[11]	8[2]	1[2]	7[2]	26[2]		—3[2, 17]—		5.8	0.2[13]	−1,231[5]	1,506[5]	275[5]	1,054	107[5]	Yugoslavia
38	13	2	6	—			—40—			0.1	1.0	940[8]	−563[8]	377[8]	23	38[5]	Zaire
14	16	19	2	2	6	12	7	—20—		0.7	0.0	275	−373	−98	49	43[5]	Zambia
12	6	27	4	3	7	15	7	17	7	1.6	5.6[13]	184[8]	−284[8]	−100[8]	31	104[5]	Zimbabwe

communication. [24]Manufacturing includes public utilities. [25]1975. [26]Includes Northern Ireland. [27]1973. [28]Mining includes construction. [29]Manufacturing includes mining, construction, and public utilities. [30]1972. [31]Global material product.

Employment and labour

This table provides international comparisons of the world's national labour forces—giving their size, composition by demographic component, and overall growth rates.

The first part of the table focuses on the concept of "economically active population," which the International Labour Organisation (ILO) defines as persons of all ages who are either employed or looking for work. In general, "economically active population" does not include students, persons occupied solely in domestic duties, retired persons, persons living entirely on their own means, and persons wholly dependent on others. Persons engaged in illegal economic activities—smugglers, prostitutes, drug dealers, bootleggers, black marketeers, and others—also fall outside the purview of the ILO definition. Countries differ markedly in their treatment, as part of the labour force, of such groups as members of the armed forces, inmates of institutions, persons seeking their first job, seasonal and international migrant workers, and persons engaged in part-time economic activities. Some countries include some or all of these groups among the economically active population, while other countries treat them as inactive.

Three principal breakdowns of the economically active total are given: (1) participation rate, or the proportion of the economically active who possess some particular characteristic, is given for women and for those of working age (ages 15 to 64); (2) activity rate, the proportion of the total population who are economically active, is given for both sexes and as a total; and (3) employment status, usually (and here) grouped as employers, self-employed, employees, family workers (usually unpaid), and others.

Each of these measures indicates certain characteristics or tendencies in a given national labour market; none should be interpreted in isolation, however, as each is influenced by a variety of incentives and constraints—demographic structure and change, social or religious customs, educational opportunity, sexual differentiation in employment patterns, degree of technological development, and the like. Participation and activity rates, for example, may be high in a particular country because it possesses an older population with few children, hence a higher proportion of working age, or because, despite a very young population with many below working age, the economy attracts eligible immigrant workers, themselves almost exclusively of working age. At the same time, low activity and participation rates might be characteristic of a country having a young population with poor employment possibilities or of a country with a good job market distorted by the presence of large numbers of "guest" or contract workers who are not part of the domestic labour force. An illiterate woman in a strongly sex-differentiated labour force is likely to begin and end as a family or traditional agricultural worker. Loss of working-age men to war, civil violence, or emigration for job opportunities may also affect the structure of a particular labour market.

The proportional distribution of the economically active population by employment status reveals that a large percentage of economically active

Employment and labour

country	year	economically active population										employed population by economic sector			
		total ('000)	participation rate (%)		activity rate (%)			employment status (%)				agriculture, forestry, fishing		mining, quarrying	
			female	ages 15–64	total	male	female	employers, self-employed	employees	unpaid family workers	other	number ('000)	% of labour force	number ('000)	% of labour force
Afghanistan	1979	3,946	7.9	49.1	30.2	54.1	4.9	...	...	...	...	2,369	61.3	59	1.5
Albania	1978	584	42.4	41.8	22.8	26.0	19.8	...	...	...	...	128	22.0	...	...
Algeria	1982	4,164	6.8	31.0[2]	21.1	38.9	2.9	16.6[3]	47.4[3]	2.1[3]	33.9[3]	683[3]	20.3[3]	69[3]	2.0[3]
American Samoa	1980	9	39.2	46.1	26.4	31.6	21.0	2.4	97.3	0.2	0.1	0.1	1.4	—	—
Andorra	1982	17	...	...	45.2	...	...	...	...	...	...	0.1	0.5	0.4	2.2
Angola	1980	3,414	40.6	73.4	44.2	53.4	35.3	...	...	...	...	2,518	73.8	[6]	[6]
Anguilla	1974	1.2	29.4	42.1	18.1	27.0	10.1	...	...	...	...	0.1	8.5	[6]	[6]
Antigua and Barbuda	1983	31	39.6	56.2[8]	39.4	49.6	30.0	12.3[9]	69.9[9]	0.6[9]	17.2[9]	2[10]	9.5[10]	0.1[10]	0.3[10]
Argentina	1983	10,815	26.4	59.1	38.3	56.6	20.1	25.1[10]	71.2[10]	3.3[10]	0.4[10]	1,201[10]	12.0[10]	47[10]	0.5[10]
Aruba[11]	...	...	...	...	...	...	...	...	...	...	...	...	...	...	...
Australia	1985	7,250	38.4	69.7	45.9[12]	57.4[12]	34.5[12]	13.7	76.7	0.3	9.3	428	6.0	100	1.4
Austria	1984	3,363	39.7	65.2[13]	43.6[13]	56.3[13]	32.2[13]	10.4	81.5	4.3	3.8	308	9.1	17	0.5
Bahamas, The	1980	87	44.5	70.5	41.6	47.4	36.0	13.0[14]	86.7[14]	0.3[14]	...	4[15]	5.2[15]	0.7[15]	0.9[15]
Bahrain	1984	177	13.7	65.9	43.1	63.2	14.4	9.8[12]	88.7[12]	0.1[12]	1.4[12]	4	2.1	5	2.9
Bangladesh	1984	29,319	8.8	50.3	30.6	54.2	5.5	45.6[12]	28.9[12]	22.9[12]	2.6[12]	23,790[12]	79.0[12]	3[12]	—
Barbados	1984	112	45.6	73.7[13]	45.6[13]	52.2[13]	39.7[13]	8.8[16]	76.4[16]	0.2[16]	14.6[16]	9	8.7	—	—
Belgium	1983	4,213	38.8	60.6[10]	43.8[16]	54.3[16]	33.7[16]	11.7	71.4	3.2	13.7	106	2.9	27	0.7
Belize	1980	47	22.7	63.0	32.6	49.7	15.0	25.1[9]	66.3[9]	3.6[9]	5.0[9]	15	37.1	—	0.1
Benin	1980	1,775	49.0	88.7	50.8	52.9	48.8	...	...	...	...	1,246	70.2	[6]	[6]
Bermuda	1984	32	45.5	80.0[10]	56.5	63.2	50.2	7.7[10]	88.6[10]	0.5[10]	3.2[10]	0.2	0.7	0.1	0.4
Bhutan	1982	574[10]	33.6[10]	69.4[10]	44.8[10]	57.8[10]	31.0[10]	...	...	...	...	613	94.3	[6]	[6]
Bolivia	1982	1,872	23.2	53.3	31.6	49.2	14.5	48.9[18]	38.2[18]	9.1[18]	3.8[18]	793[19]	46.4[19]	76[19]	4.5[19]
Botswana	1981	316	40.3	63.1	33.5	42.5	25.5	3.1	41.0	45.4	10.5	154	54.0	11	3.9
Brazil	1983	48,466	27.4[10]	49.2[2, 10]	36.3[10]	53.1[10]	19.8[10]	27.0[10]	65.3[10]	5.2[10]	2.5[10]	13,115	27.1	7,665[20]	15.8[20]
British Virgin Islands	1980	5	38.5	72.8	45.4	54.6	35.8	18.5	79.7	0.8	1.0	0.2	5.3	—	—
Brunei	1982	71[12]	23.8[12]	61.1[12]	36.7[12]	52.3[12]	18.7[12]	7.4[12]	88.4[12]	0.6[12]	3.6[12]	3	5.0	4	5.7
Bulgaria	1984	4,448[14]	46.8[14]	75.3[14]	51.0[14]	54.3[14]	47.6[14]	...	...	...	...	915	22.3	[22]	[22]
Burkina Faso	1975	1,408	3.4	44.6[23]	25.0	48.1	1.7	...	...	...	...	...	...	...	...
Burma	1982	14,462	39.1[10]	71.0[10]	45.0[10]	54.7[10]	35.2[10]	...	...	...	...	9,205	66.8	71	0.5
Burundi	1982	2,669	52.9	94.4[15]	60.7	59.1	62.2	35.7[15]	5.6[15]	58.5[15]	0.2[15]	2,246[15]	93.1[15]	1.4[15]	0.1[15]
Cameroon	1982	3,543	37.5	65.6	39.9	50.0	29.8	60.2	14.6	18.0	7.1	2,595	76.7	2	0.1
Canada	1985	12,639	42.6	65.2[23]	49.8	57.9	42.0	8.6[24]	89.5[24]	1.0[24]	0.9[24]	644[24]	5.7[24]	183[24]	1.6[24]
Cape Verde	1980	102	27.5	57.7	34.5	54.4	17.5	...	...	...	...	53	52.0	[6]	[6]
Cayman Islands	1979	8	42.0	...	48.7	58.1	39.8	10.6	80.7	—	8.7	0.1	1.7	—	—
Central African Republic	1975	649	46.7	50.2[23]	31.6	35.2	28.3	...	...	...	...	543	83.7	7	1.0
Chad	1980	1,639	23.6	56.5[23]	36.4	58.1	16.4	...	...	...	...	0.9[19]	7.3[19]	0.3[19]	2.3[19]
Chile	1983	3,768	30.8	52.1	32.5	46.0	19.6	21.9	49.9	13.6	14.7	541	14.8	67	1.8
China	1984	475,970	43.2[10]	83.8[10]	44.9	...	...	0.7	25.0	—74.3—		325,380	68.4	[22]	[22]
Christmas Island	1981	1.6	9.8	76.4	56.3	76.0	16.6	...	...	...	...	—	0.1	1.1	68.2
Cocos (Keeling) Islands	1981	0.3	29.6	69.4	50.5	63.8	31.1	...	...	...	...	0.1	21.8	—	—
Colombia	1980	8,467	26.2	48.7	31.6	50.0	15.5	...	...	...	...	2,412	28.5	50	0.6
Comoros	1980	85[26]	23.6[26]	46.6[26]	42.7[26]	66.5[26]	19.8[26]	...	...	...	...	1.3[19]	10.6[19]	—	—
Congo	1980	649	16.9	70.3	42.4	51.8	33.2	...	...	...	...	405	62.5	[6]	[6]
Cook Islands	1981	6	30.3	63.1	33.7	45.6	21.1	11.0	65.7	3.7	19.6	2	29.2	—	0.3
Costa Rica	1984	835	25.4	52.4[23]	34.6	51.8	17.5	19.6[13]	73.9[13]	4.5[13]	2.0[13]	234[13]	28.3[13]	138[13, 27]	16.7[13, 27]
Côte d'Ivoire	1975	2,832	32.6	...	42.2	54.9	28.5	...	...	...	...	72[19]	21.7[19]	1.7[19]	0.5[19]
Cuba	1983	3,618[12]	31.5[12]	58.5[12]	37.2[12]	50.5[12]	23.7[12]	9.9[9]	88.2[9]	1.3[9]	0.6[9]	595[28]	21.7[28]	631[27, 28]	23.0[27, 28]
Cyprus	1984	240	36.8	67.2[10]	37.0	47.1	27.1	21.1[16]	56.0[16]	10.8[16]	12.1[16]	43	18.1	1.1	0.5
Czechoslovakia	1983	7,849[10]	46.7[10]	78.9[10]	51.4[10]	56.2[10]	46.7[10]	0.1[10]	91.2[10]	8.5[10]	0.2[10]	1,019	13.6	[6]	[6]
Denmark	1984	2,720	45.5	78.9	53.2	59.0	47.6	9.5	87.5	2.4	0.6	174	6.4	4	0.1
Djibouti	1982	...	...	...	...	...	...	...	...	...	...	0.1[19]	0.4[19]	—	—
Dominica	1981	25	34.1	61.7	34.3	45.4	23.3	29.4	49.8	1.9	18.9	7.8	38.1	—	—
Dominican Republic	1981	1,915	28.9	53.6	33.9	48.1	19.7	36.5	51.3	3.3	8.9	420	23.6	5	0.3
Ecuador	1982	2,387	20.8	50.1	29.7	47.0	12.3	37.3	47.6	5.8	9.3	774	34.2	7	0.3
Egypt	1984	11,133	7.0	41.9	24.5	44.8	3.5	29.5[16]	52.8[16]	12.0[16]	5.7[16]	4,348	41.2	40	0.4

persons in some less developed countries falls under the heading "employers, self-employed." This occurs because the countries involved have poor, largely agrarian economies in which the average worker is a farmer who tills his own small plot of land. In countries with well-developed economies, "employees" will usually constitute the largest portion of the economically active.

Caution should be exercised when using the economically active data to make intercountry comparisons, as countries often differ in their choices of classification schemes, definitions, and coverage of groups and in their methods of collection and tabulation of data. Data on female labour-force activity, in particular, often lacks comparability. In many less developed countries, particularly those dominated by the Islāmic faith, a cultural bias favouring traditional roles for women results in the undercounting of economically active females.

The next major section of the table provides data on the distribution by economic sector of the "employed population," which consists of all persons above a specific age who, during a specified period, were either at work or formally attached to a job. Whenever possible the "employed population" has been taken to be the actively working fraction of the labour force, *i.e.*, excluding those who are unemployed or under- and fractionally (or seasonally) employed. The data usually include such groups as unpaid family workers and members of the armed forces and usually exclude such groups as the unemployed and the severely underemployed.

When comparing national labour-force data, careful regard should be given to differences in definition, sources, scope, and coverage from country to country.

The table's categorization of industrial sectors is based largely on the divisions listed in the International Standard Industrial Classification of All Economic Activities. The category "services, other" includes such activities as public administration and defense, educational services, medical and dental services, motion-picture and other entertainment services, domestic services, and activities not adequately defined.

Finally, regarding the section on labour-force growth, it should be recognized that for many economies changes in age and sex structure, in patterns and volume of unemployment and underemployment, in international and internal migration, or in technological development may significantly alter the projections.

A large part of the data presented in this table is summarized from various issues of the ILO's *Yearbook of Labour Statistics*. The ILO compiles its statistics both from official publications and from information submitted directly by national authorities. The editors have supplemented and updated ILO data with statistical information from Britannica's statistical holdings of official publications and from direct correspondence with relevant authorities. The *World Development Report*, published by the World Bank, furnishes the data for the table's last section, "average annual growth of labour force."

												average annual growth of labour force			country
manufacturing, construction		electricity, gas, water		transportation, communications		trade, hotels, restaurants		finance, real estate		services, other		1965–1973 (%)	1973–1984 (%)	1980–2000 (%)	
number ('000)	% of labour force	number ('000)	% of labour force	number ('000)	% of labour force	number ('000)	% of labour force	number ('000)	% of labour force	number ('000)	% of labour force				
474	12.3	11	0.3	66	1.7	138	3.6	[1]	[1]	749[1]	19.3[1]	1.9	...	...	Afghanistan
271	46.5	...	...	33	5.7	39	6.6	...	...	112.7	19.3	2.4	2.4	2.3	Albania
607[3]	18.0[3]	30[3]	0.9[3]	132[3]	3.9[3]	214[3]	6.4[3]	18[3]	0.5[3]	1,618[3]	48.0[3]	1.6	3.6	4.1	Algeria
2.5	31.1	[4]	[4]	0.7[4]	8.7[4]	0.9	11.5	0.2	2.6	3.6	44.7	...	...	...	American Samoa
4.5	26.4	—	—	0.3	1.6	4.3[5]	25.2[5]	1.0	6.1	6.5[5]	37.8[5]	...	...	...	Andorra
326[6]	9.6[6]	[6]	[6]	[7]	[7]	[7]	[7]	[7]	[7]	569[7]	16.7[7]	1.5	2.6	2.7	Angola
0.4[6]	35.2[6]	[6]	[6]	0.2	13.4	0.1	9.8	[1]	[1]	0.4[1]	33.1[1]	...	...	...	Anguilla
4.0[10]	18.2[10]	0.3[10]	1.4[10]	2.6[10]	11.8[10]	4.9[10]	22.1[10]	0.7[10]	3.4[10]	7.3[10]	33.2[10]	...	...	...	Antigua and Barbuda
2,989[10]	30.0[10]	103[10]	1.0[10]	460[10]	4.6[10]	1,702[10]	17.0[10]	396[10]	4.0[10]	3,090[10]	30.9[10]	1.4	1.1	1.5	Argentina
...	...	...	...	...	...	...	...	...	...	...	...	...	...	...	Aruba[11]
1,737	24.4	135	1.9	522	7.3	1,378	19.4	642	9.0	2,174	30.6	2.5	1.7	1.3	Australia
1,241	36.9	40	1.2	208	6.2	621	18.5	174	5.2	754	22.4	−0.2	1.0	0.3	Austria
8[15]	10.4[15]	1.2[15]	1.6[15]	8[15]	10.4[15]	22[15]	28.6[15]	7[15]	9.1[15]	26[15]	33.8[15]	...	...	...	Bahamas, The
52	29.9	3	1.9	16	9.2	24	13.5	7	3.8	64	36.7	...	...	...	Bahrain
1,472[12]	4.9[12]	11[12]	—	481[12]	1.6[12]	1,159[12]	3.9[12]	84[12]	0.3[12]	3,101[12]	10.3[12]	2.3	2.6	2.4	Bangladesh
24	22.6	2	1.8	6	5.3	24	22.1	3	3.1	39	36.3	...	...	...	Barbados
1,047	28.5	33	0.9	267	7.3	688	18.8	264	7.2	1,237	33.7	0.5	0.7	0.2	Belgium
6	14.9	0.6	1.5	2	4.3	6	14.2	0.4	0.9	11	27.0	...	...	...	Belize
118[6]	6.7[6]	[6]	[6]	[7]	[7]	[7]	[7]	[7]	[7]	410[7]	23.1[7]	2.1	2.0	2.6	Benin
3	10.5	0.4	1.3	2	6.7	11	35.6	4	13.4	10	31.6	...	...	...	Bermuda
6[6]	0.9[6]	[6]	[6]	[17]	[17]	9	1.4	[17]	[17]	22[17]	3.4[17]	1.0	1.9	2.2	Bhutan
212[19]	12.4[19]	7[19]	0.4[19]	95[19]	5.5[19]	129[19]	7.5[19]	13[19]	0.8[19]	383[19]	22.4[19]	1.8	2.5	2.9	Bolivia
22	7.6	2	0.8	3	1.1	12	4.3	1	0.5	79	27.7	2.2	4.2	2.9	Botswana
4,628[21]	9.5[21]	[20]	[20]	1,778	3.7	5,112	10.5	7,893	16.3	8,276	17.1	2.5	3.0	2.3	Brazil
0.3	6.2	0.6	12.0	0.1	2.8	0.4	8.1	0.3	5.8	1.1	22.7	...	...	...	British Virgin Islands
15	22.6	2	2.9	4	6.6	7	10.8	2	3.0	29	43.4	...	...	...	Brunei
1,722[22]	41.8[22]	52	1.3	302	7.4	360	8.8	[1]	[1]	757[1]	18.4[1]	0.6	0.1	0.1	Bulgaria
...	...	...	...	...	...	...	...	...	...	...	...	1.6	1.4	1.7	Burkina Faso
1,312	9.5	16	0.1	458	3.2	1,310	9.5	[1]	[1]	1,418[1]	10.4[1]	1.3	1.3	2.0	Burma
51[15]	2.1[15]	1.7[15]	0.1[15]	6[15]	0.3[15]	21[15]	0.9[15]	1.3[15]	0.1[15]	84[15]	3.5[15]	1.2	1.7	2.5	Burundi
222	6.6	3	0.1	47	1.4	141	4.2	8	0.2	363	10.7	1.9	1.8	3.0	Cameroon
2,658[24]	23.5[24]	130[24]	1.1[24]	757[24]	6.7[24]	1,942[24]	17.2[24]	1,074[24]	9.5[24]	3,928[24]	34.7[24]	2.7	2.0	1.1	Canada
23[6]	22.5[6]	[6]	[6]	[7]	[7]	[7]	[7]	[7]	[7]	26[7]	25.5[7]	...	...	...	Cape Verde
2	23.4	0.1	1.8	0.2	3.1	0.7	9.6	0.5	7.2	4	53.2	...	...	...	Cayman Islands
18	2.8	1	0.2	5	0.8	27	4.1	0.6	0.1	47	7.3	1.1	1.6	2.4	Central African Republic
5[19]	36.1[19]	0.4[19]	3.3[19]	0.6[19]	5.2[19]	2[19]	13.2[19]	0.6[19]	4.8[19]	3[19]	27.8[19]	1.6	2.3	2.3	Chad
644	17.6	27	0.8	230	6.3	618	16.9	130	3.6	1,393	38.1	1.3	2.5	2.1	Chile
81,960[22]	17.2[22]	...	...	10,800	2.3	23,540	4.9	...	...	34,290	7.2	2.6	1.6	2.0	China
0.1	3.4	—	0.6	0.1	4.5	0.1	4.1	—	1.5	0.3	17.1	...	...	...	Christmas Island
0.1	25.7	—	2.1	—	5.3	—	4.6	—	0.2	0.2	40.3	...	...	...	Cocos (Keeling) Islands
1,379	16.3	44	0.5	353	4.2	1,540[25]	18.1[25]	[25]	[25]	2,689	31.8	3.1	2.8	2.5	Colombia
4.3[19]	33.5[19]	0.2[19]	1.6[19]	1.0[19]	7.6[19]	1.2[19]	9.5[19]	0.1[19]	1.1[19]	4.6[19]	36.1[19]	...	...	...	Comoros
77[6]	11.9[6]	[6]	[6]	[7]	[7]	[7]	[7]	[7]	[7]	166[7]	25.6[7]	1.9	1.9	3.7	Congo
0.7	12.1	0.1	2.4	0.7	12.3	0.5	9.2	0.1	2.3	2	31.4	...	...	...	Cook Islands
46[13, 21]	5.5[13, 21]	[4]	[4]	47[4, 13]	5.6[4, 13]	148[13, 25]	17.9[13, 25]	[25]	[25]	215[13]	26.0[13]	3.7	3.8	2.8	Costa Rica
101[19]	30.4[19]	13[19]	3.9[19]	39[19]	11.9[19]	27[19]	8.3[19]	7[19]	2.0[19]	70[19]	21.3[19]	4.2	3.9	3.3	Côte d'Ivoire
284[21, 28]	10.4[21, 28]	97[28]	3.5[28]	185[28]	6.8[28]	348[28]	12.7[28]	...	...	601[28]	21.9[28]	1.0	2.2	1.7	Cuba
66	27.8	1.5	0.6	12	4.8	41	17.1	9	3.6	65	27.5	...	...	...	Cyprus
3,551[6]	47.4[6]	[6]	[6]	495	6.6	669	8.9	[1]	[1]	1,759[1]	23.5[1]	0.8	0.5	0.6	Czechoslovakia
702	26.0	19	0.7	190	7.0	400	14.8	192	7.1	1,023	37.9	0.8	0.6	0.3	Denmark
3[19]	18.8[19]	0.5[19]	2.9[19]	3[19]	17.0[19]	3[19]	19.5[19]	1.3[19]	8.0[19]	5[19]	33.5[19]	...	...	...	Djibouti
3.7	18.1	0.2	1.2	0.9	4.4	1.6	7.8	0.3	1.2	6.0	29.1	...	...	...	Dominica
305	17.1	14	0.8	40	2.3	192	10.8	22	1.3	785	44.0	2.7	3.3	3.0	Dominican Republic
435	19.2	13	0.6	99	4.4	270	11.9	44	1.9	622	27.5	3.1	2.9	3.0	Ecuador
2,292	21.7	77	0.7	616	5.8	954	9.0	123	1.2	2,099	20.0	2.1	2.5	2.5	Egypt

Employment and labour (continued)

country	year	economically active population						employment status (%)				employed population by economic sector: agriculture, forestry, fishing		mining, quarrying	
		total ('000)	participation rate (%)		activity rate (%)										
			female	ages 15–64	total	male	female	employers, self-employed	employees	unpaid family workers	other	number ('000)	% of labour force	number ('000)	% of labour force
El Salvador	1980	1,593	34.8	62.4	35.4	47.5	24.0	28.2	59.2	10.9	1.7	637	40.6	4	0.3
Equatorial Guinea	1980	159	40.9	72.2	45.2	54.1	36.1	...	...	...	...	104	65.8	[6]	[6]
Ethiopia	1984	18,492	39.2	74.3	43.9	53.5	34.3	...	...	...	...	...	...	...	...
Faeroe Islands	1977	18	27.2	64.2[29]	41.9	58.2	23.9	11.1	86.3	...	2.6	3	18.8	0.1	0.6
Falkland Islands	1980	0.9	22.5	70.3[23]	52.5	74.3	26.1	...	...	...	...	...	...	...	...
Fiji	1982	210	19.6	55.2	33.2	52.4	13.3	33.4[18]	51.5[18]	7.8[18]	7.3[18]	85	52.1	1	0.7
Finland	1984	2,600	47.2	77.1	53.1	57.9	48.6	9.6[10]	83.6[10]	4.7[10]	2.1[10]	324[16]	12.7[16]	[6]	[6]
France	1984	23,880	40.9	65.1	43.5	52.7	34.8	14.3	75.9	...	9.8	1,659	7.8	122	0.6
French Guiana	1982	31	37.2	67.2	42.7	51.0	33.5	14.9	65.5	——19.6——		4	13.4	0.2	0.6
French Polynesia	1983	58[30]	31.6[30]	...	34.7[30]	45.5[30]	22.9[30]	19.7[3]	76.3[3]	3.4[3]	0.6[3]	8	13.9	—	—
Gabon	1977	502[10]	39.4[10]	69.6[10]	47.2[10]	58.4[10]	36.6[10]	...	...	...	...	19[31]	13.6[31]	7[31]	4.8[31]
Gambia, The	1984	289[10]	42.2[10]	79.0[10]	49.6[10]	58.2[10]	41.2[10]	...	...	...	...	3[19]	8.2[19]	...	...
Gaza Strip	1983	86.5	4.4	32.7[32]	17.5	...	...	...	...	...	...	...	...	...	...
Germany, East	1984	8,499	49.4	...	51.0	54.7	47.7	...	...	...	...	914	10.7	[6]	[6]
Germany, West	1984	28,815	39.1	66.5	47.1	60.0	35.3	8.6	88.2	3.2	—	1,396	5.2	332	1.2
Ghana	1979	3,332[9]	44.2[9]	69.5[10]	38.3[9]	42.4[9]	34.1[9]	...	...	...	...	74[19]	15.3[19]	24[19]	4.9[19]
Gibraltar	1982	13[12]	27.9[12]	67.4[12]	46.2[12]	66.2[12]	26.0[12]	5.9[12]	93.8[12]	...	0.3[12]	—	—	—	—
Greece	1983	3,808	34.1	54.5[33]	38.7	51.8	25.9	33.7	44.6	13.9	7.8	1,055	28.5	30	0.8
Greenland	1976	21	33.4	...	43.1	53.0	31.4	12.6	82.5	0.4	4.5	3	15.1	0.3	1.5
Grenada	1984	46	...	...	48.2	...	...	21.3[12]	77.7[12]	1.0[12]	—	8.0[12]	28.7[12]	0.1[12]	0.3[12]
Guadeloupe	1982	124	42.5	63.7	37.9	44.5	31.6	...	...	...	...	13	14.1	7[27]	7.2[27]
Guam	1980	44	34.8	66.6[8]	42.0	52.4	30.6	2.3	96.6	0.1	1.0	0.3	0.7	—	—
Guatemala	1981	1,684	14.6	48.8	27.8	47.7	8.1	42.5	47.2	6.8	3.5	909	53.9	2	0.1
Guernsey	1976	26	...	...	47.7	62.4	34.0	17.9	82.1	—	—	5	17.7	0.2	0.8
Guinea	1980	2,626	41.7	77.9	48.6	57.3	40.0	...	...	...	...	2,119	80.6	[6]	[6]
Guinea-Bissau	1979	213	3.6	42.0	38.7	78.4	2.6	...	...	...	...	153	71.9	0.1	—
Guyana	1980	239	24.7	57.3	31.5	47.9	15.5	19.8[9]	77.6[9]	2.1[9]	0.5[9]	49	25.0	9	4.8
Haiti	1982	2,130	41.0	66.2	42.1	51.3	33.5	59.4	16.6	10.4	13.6	1,223	65.4	19	1.0
Honduras	1984	1,256	16.7	53.6	29.7	49.3	9.9	...	...	...	...	719	57.2	4	0.3
Hong Kong	1984	2,644	36.9	71.4	50.7	62.5	38.3	10.1	84.4	1.7	3.8	30	1.1	0.5	—
Hungary	1985	4,920	45.7	72.5[10]	46.2	51.8	40.8	2.9[24]	80.3[24]	10.7[24]	6.1[24]	1,150[24]	23.3[24]	[6]	[6]
Iceland	1983	116	42.0[34]	79.1[34]	48.9	60.6[34]	44.5[34]	...	...	...	...	24	21.0	...	...
India	1981	244,605	25.0	36.8	36.8	52.7	19.8	10.0[35]	17.1[35]	3.3[35]	69.6[35]	153,015	62.6	1,264	0.5
Indonesia	1980	52,110	32.8	59.2	35.5	48.0	23.2	52.4	27.0	17.2	3.4	28,040	54.8	369	0.7
Iran	1976	9,796	14.8	50.2	29.1	48.1	8.9	30.5	48.4	10.4	10.6	3,615	38.1	90	0.9
Iraq	1984	3,780	15.9	47.6	25.1	41.0	8.2	...	...	...	...	1,122	29.9	47	1.3
Ireland	1983	1,309	29.7	58.4	37.3	52.2	22.3	18.3	73.4	3.0	5.3	193	15.1	12	0.9
Isle of Man	1981	28	38.2	67.7	42.6	55.1	31.2	14.0	79.8	—	6.2	1.4	5.5	3.5[27]	13.4[27]
Israel	1984	1,444	34.4	60.6[36]	34.4	42.8	26.0	18.3	74.4	1.4	5.9	74	5.2	[6]	[6]
Italy	1984	23,200	35.1	58.1[29]	40.9	54.6	27.9	21.7	63.1	4.9	10.3	2,426	11.5	206	1.0
Jamaica	1984	971	46.6	72.2[29]	42.6	49.6	40.4	31.2[9]	67.1[9]	1.7[9]	—	237	32.7	7	0.9
Japan	1984	59,270	39.6	69.0	49.4	60.6	38.5	15.5	72.0	9.5	3.0	5,120	8.9	80	0.1
Jersey	1981	37	40.7	...	51.2	63.5	40.0	13.4	86.6	...	...	2	5.9	0.2	0.6
Jordan	1984	552	11.1	42.2	21.3	36.1	5.0	22.8[15]	67.2[15]	0.8[15]	9.2[15]	22	4.3	7	1.3
Kampuchea	1962	2,500	42.0	74.4	43.6	50.6	36.7	36.4	12.2	50.0	1.4	2,008	80.2	2	0.1
Kenya	1983	7,072[10]	41.9[10]	77.8[10]	42.2[10]	49.3[10]	35.1[10]	...	...	...	...	231[19]	21.1[19]	4[19]	0.3[19]
Kiribati	1985	26	36.1	67.8[23]	41.2	53.1	29.5	71.0	26.5	...	2.5	0.3[37]	5.2[37]	—	0.2[37]
Korea, North	1980	7,838	45.9	75.1	43.5	47.6	39.4	...	...	...	...	3,355	42.8	[6]	[6]
Korea, South	1984	14,985	37.8	56.0	36.9	45.5	28.2	30.5	50.9	14.8	3.8	3,909	27.1	142	1.0
Kuwait	1984	598	14.0	60.9[23]	36.6	55.0	12.0	10.0[10]	88.4[10]	0.1[10]	1.5[10]	10	1.7	8	1.3
Laos	1980	1,839	46.2	86.4	49.9	53.3	46.5	...	...	...	...	1,393	75.7	[6]	[6]
Lebanon	1984	702	25.6	44.6	26.5	40.9	13.2	...	...	...	...	238[16]	20.7[16]	223[16, 27]	19.4[16, 27]
Lesotho	1976	424	32.3	56.1	34.8	48.9	21.7	7.5	50.0	36.8	5.7	99	23.3	129	30.5
Liberia	1981	433[38]	26.8[38]	47.4[38]	28.8[38]	41.7[38]	15.6[38]	...	...	...	...	515[19]	79.3[19]	20[19]	3.1[19]
Libya	1985	1,062	7.3[10]	50.9[10]	24.1[39]	42.3[39]	3.5[39]	23.7[39]	69.6[39]	4.2[39]	2.6[39]	178	16.8	25	2.3
Liechtenstein	1985	12	34.4	73.8[10]	46.7	62.5	31.5	9.0[10]	87.2[10]	3.8[10]	...	0.4	3.0	0.1	0.4
Luxembourg	1981	154	33.3	61.3	42.2	57.7	27.4	9.4	85.1	3.5	2.0	7	5.0	[6]	[6]
Macau	1981	127	...	61.5[40]	48.6	...	...	9.9	86.4	3.5	0.2	8	6.0	0.1	0.1
Madagascar	1980	4,098	41.3	76.7	47.1	55.9	38.5	...	...	...	...	3,314	80.9	[6]	[6]
Malaŵi	1983	2,288[3]	46.2[3]	71.5[3]	41.3[3]	46.1[3]	36.8[3]	79.9[3]	17.8[3]	0.3[3]	2.0[3]	199	50.9	0.5	0.1
Malaysia	1980	4,924	33.7	62.1	37.5	49.6	25.3	28.7	54.3	10.2	6.7	1,855	40.4	47	1.0
Maldives	1977	67	37.2	78.3	47.2	56.2	37.1	86.4	13.4	...	0.2	34	55.6	—	—
Mali	1976	2,266	17.0	52.3	35.4	60.2	11.8	45.8	4.1	42.5	7.5	1,862	84.9	8	0.4
Malta	1983	121	24.5	52.2[10]	36.7	57.1	17.5	14.1	77.4	...	8.5	5	5.0	1.2	1.1
Martinique	1982	131	44.7	62.6	39.9	45.6	34.6	12.3	57.4	0.3	30.0	10	10.4	2	2.0
Mauritania	1980	516	20.0	55.2	31.6	51.2	12.5	...	...	...	...	358	69.4	[6]	[6]
Mauritius	1984	367	25.8	58.5	37.6	55.8	19.4	10.3[16]	73.7[16]	0.9[16]	15.1[16]	53[19]	26.7[19]	0.2[19]	0.1[19]
Mayotte	1978	15.1	35.9	65.0	32.1	41.0	23.1	51.0	27.9	21.0	—	9.3	65.4	—	0.1
Mexico	1980	22,066	27.8	57.1	33.0	48.2	18.2	27.0	44.3	6.6	22.1	5,700	26.0	477	2.2
Monaco	1975	...	...	...	...	...	...	...	...	...	...	—	0.2	—	0.1
Mongolia	1984	691	45.5[10]	83.1[10]	37.1	...	...	...	...	...	...	383	55.4	[22]	[22]
Montserrat	1980	5.1	41.6	74.1	44.0	53.4	35.3	20.4[9]	78.0[9]	1.6[9]	—	0.5	9.3	—	0.2
Morocco	1982	5,999	19.7	49.7	29.6	47.9	11.6	27.1	40.5	17.6	14.8	2,352	43.1	63	1.2
Mozambique	1980	5,671	52.4	80.6[41]	35.8[9]	53.4[9]	18.7[9]	44.4[9]	40.0[9]	14.5[9]	1.1[9]	4,755	85.3	347[27]	6.2[27]
Nauru	1977	2.2	...	...	30.5	...	...	...	...	...	...	...	...	...	...
Nepal	1981	6,851	34.6	67.5	45.6	58.2	32.4	86.2	9.1	2.5	2.2	6,244	91.1	1.0	—
Netherlands, The	1984	5,934	34.9	60.4	41.2	54.2	28.5	9.6[12]	80.7[12]	2.0[12]	7.7[12]	276[12]	5.4[12]	7[12]	0.1[12]
Netherlands Antilles[11]	1983	104	39.2	63.7	42.0	52.5	32.1	...	...	...	...	0.4	0.4	0.2	0.2
New Caledonia	1983	45	37.6	63.6	30.8	37.7	23.7	20.5	58.8	12.8	8.0	10	22.1	[22]	[22]
New Zealand	1981	1,332	34.2	65.4	42.0	55.5	28.5	12.9	81.7	0.5	4.9	144	10.8	5	0.3
Nicaragua	1980	864	21.2	54.0	32.0	51.4	13.3	...	...	...	...	392	45.4	7	0.7
Niger	1981	2,865[10]	48.0[10]	91.2[10]	53.9[10]	56.6[10]	51.3[10]	...	...	...	...	3[19]	7.3[19]	5[19]	14.7[19]
Nigeria	1980	32,087	36.7	70.2	39.8	51.0	28.9	...	...	...	...	21,866	68.1	[6]	[6]
Niue	1984	0.9	34.9	52.5[23]	32.4	41.2	23.2	9.9	78.1	12.0	—	0.2	21.3	—	1.2
Norfolk Island	1981	1.0	43.3	72.0[23]	54.2	61.4	47.0	...	...	...	...	—	3.0	—	0.3

manufacturing, construction		electricity, gas, water		transportation, communications		trade, hotels, restaurants		finance, real estate		services, other		average annual growth of labour force			country
number ('000)	% of labour force	number ('000)	% of labour force	number ('000)	% of labour force	number ('000)	% of labour force	number ('000)	% of labour force	number ('000)	% of labour force	1965–1973 (%)	1973–1984 (%)	1980–2000 (%)	
328	21.0	10	0.6	66	4.2	256	16.3	16	1.0	250	16.0	3.2	2.9	3.4	El Salvador
18[6]	11.4[6]	[6]	[6]	[7]	[7]	[7]	[7]	[7]	[7]	36[7]	22.8[7]	...	...	...	Equatorial Guinea
...	...	...	...	...	...	...	...	...	...	...	...	2.2	2.2	2.5	Ethiopia
6	31.7	0.1	0.8	1.9	11.0	2	11.9	0.3	1.9	4	23.3	...	...	...	Faeroe Islands
...	...	...	...	...	...	...	...	...	...	...	...	...	...	...	Falkland Islands
22	13.6	2	1.4	8	4.7	15	9.1	5	3.1	25	15.3	...	...	...	Fiji
849[6, 16]	33.2[6, 16]	[6]	[6]	186[16]	7.3[16]	340[16]	13.3[16]	139[16]	5.4[16]	719[16]	28.1[16]	0.5	0.5	0.5	Finland
6,571	30.9	217	1.0	1,370	6.4	3,454	16.3	1,656	7.8	6,206	29.2	0.7	1.1	0.7	France
4	15.2	0.4	1.4	1.3	4.9	2	7.3	4	13.3	12	43.9	...	...	...	French Guiana
10	17.7	0.4	0.7	3	5.9	14	23.7	1	2.2	21	35.7	...	...	...	French Polynesia
58[31]	41.7[31]	5[31]	3.4[31]	16[31]	11.4[31]	13[25, 31]	9.1[25, 31]	[25]	[25]	22[31]	16.0[31]	...	...	...	Gabon
6[19]	19.5[19]	1[19]	3.4[19]	6[19]	19.7[19]	3[19]	10.6[19]	0.7[19]	2.3[19]	11[19]	36.3[19]	...	...	...	Gambia, The
...	...	...	...	...	...	...	...	...	...	...	...	...	...	...	Gaza Strip
4,066[6]	47.9[6]	[6]	[6]	627	7.4	861	10.1	[1]	[1]	2,031[1]	23.9[1]	0.4	0.7	0.1	Germany, East
10,408	38.4	243	0.9	1,553	5.7	4,071	15.0	1,659	6.1	7,418	27.5	0.3	0.8	−0.1	Germany, West
108[19]	22.5[19]	16[19]	3.3[19]	19[19]	3.9[19]	32[19]	6.6[19]	13[19]	2.6[19]	197[19]	40.9[19]	1.4	1.5	3.5	Ghana
5	43.0	0.2	1.6	0.7	6.0	2	18.8	0.5	3.9	3	23.2	...	...	...	Gibraltar
1,019	27.5	30	0.8	267	7.2	551	14.9	126	3.4	623	16.9	0.1	0.9	0.5	Greece
6	27.2	0.2	1.2	1.8	8.7	3	12.5	0.3	1.6	7	32.2	...	...	...	Greenland
4.4[12]	15.9[12]	0.4[12]	1.3[12]	1.7[12]	6.1[12]	3.9[12]	14.0[12]	0.4[12]	1.3[12]	9.0[12]	32.4[12]	...	...	...	Grenada
10[21]	10.8[21]	0.7	0.7	5	5.2	10	10.9	1.5	16.4	32	34.7	...	...	...	Guadeloupe
5	11.0	[4]	[4]	3[4]	7.7[4]	8	17.2	1.6	3.6	27	59.8	...	...	...	Guam
264	15.7	8	0.5	43	2.6	147	8.7	21	1.3	290	17.2	2.7	2.8	2.9	Guatemala
4	14.5	0.5	2.0	2	8.5	6	24.6	1	4.2	7	27.7	...	...	...	Guernsey
237[6]	9.0[6]	[6]	[6]	[7]	[7]	[7]	[7]	[7]	[7]	270[7]	10.3[7]	1.2	1.2	1.8	Guinea
5	2.2	0.1	0.1	2	1.2	5	2.3	0.1	—	47	22.3	...	...	...	Guinea-Bissau
35	17.7	2	1.5	9	4.7	15	7.5	3	1.5	73	37.3	...	...	...	Guyana
143	7.7	2	0.1	16	0.9	286	15.3	4	0.2	176	9.4	0.7	1.6	2.0	Haiti
211	16.8	5	0.4	38	3.0	107	8.5	12	1.0	160	12.8	2.4	3.3	3.4	Honduras
1,201	45.8	12	0.5	210	8.0	572	21.8	133	5.1	464	17.7	3.5	3.7	1.1	Hong Kong
1,908[6, 24]	38.8[6, 24]	[6]	[6]	397[24]	8.0[24]	504[24]	10.2[24]	[1]	[1]	982[1, 24]	19.9[1, 24]	0.5	0.0	0.0	Hungary
31	26.4	...	...	8	7.0	18	15.5	...	...	35	30.1	...	...	...	Iceland
28,708	11.7	974	0.4	6,069	2.5	12,165	5.0	1,764	0.7	40,645	16.6	1.8	2.1	2.1	India
5,934	11.6	85	0.2	1,468	2.9	6,611	12.9	232	0.5	8,452	16.4	1.9	2.3	2.1	Indonesia
2,884	30.3	61	0.7	433	4.6	672	7.0	101	1.1	1,640	17.3	3.1	3.0	3.6	Iran
739	19.8	30	0.8	229	6.1	286	7.6	40	1.1	1,252	33.4	2.9	3.1	3.8	Iraq
372	29.1	16	1.2	75	5.9	206	16.1	82	6.4	324	25.3	0.5	1.4	1.5	Ireland
2.9[21]	11.3[21]	0.5	1.9	2.3	8.9	5.5	21.4	[1]	[1]	9.7[1]	37.6[1]	...	...	...	Isle of Man
421[6]	30.0[6]	[6]	[6]	92	6.6	177	12.6	133	9.5	506	36.1	3.2	2.3	2.2	Israel
6,837	32.5	206	1.0	1,069	5.1	4,293	20.4	658	3.1	5,320	25.4	0.0	0.7	0.3	Italy
125	17.2	[4]	[4]	33[4]	4.6[4]	103	14.2	...	...	220	30.3	0.7	2.3	2.5	Jamaica
19,650	34.1	350	0.6	3,410	5.9	13,190	22.9	3,830	6.6	12,030	20.9	1.7	1.1	0.7	Japan
6	17.2	0.6	1.6	3	6.9	6	15.8	3	9.2	16	42.8	...	...	...	Jersey
93	17.9	2	0.5	47	9.0	58	11.2	16	3.0	274	52.8	2.6	1.6	4.7	Jordan
91	3.6	2	0.1	29	1.2	144[25]	5.8[25]	[25]	[25]	224	9.0	1.3	...	...	Kampuchea
209[19]	19.1[19]	17[19]	1.6[19]	55[19]	5.0[19]	80[19]	7.3[19]	46[19]	4.2[19]	452[19]	41.3[19]	3.3	2.8	3.5	Kenya
0.5[37]	7.9[37]	0.2[37]	3.7[37]	1.0[37]	16.0[37]	0.9[37]	14.3[37]	0.1[37]	1.3[37]	3.3[37]	51.6[37]	...	...	...	Kiribati
2,373[6]	30.3[6]	[6]	[6]	[7]	[7]	[7]	[7]	[7]	[7]	2,110[7]	26.9[7]	2.6	3.0	2.7	Korea, North
4,254	29.5	36	0.2	663	4.6	3,148	21.8	500	3.5	1,765	12.3	2.9	2.7	1.9	Korea, South
188	31.9	8	1.4	39	6.6	67	11.3	17	2.8	254	43.0	5.3	6.9	3.1	Kuwait
130[6]	7.1[6]	[6]	[6]	[7]	[7]	[7]	[7]	[7]	[7]	316[7]	17.2[7]	0.6	0.5	2.6	Laos
72[16, 21]	6.2[16, 21]	9[16]	0.7[16]	62[16]	5.4[16]	203[16]	17.7[16]	[1]	[1]	342[1, 16]	29.8[1, 16]	2.5	...	...	Lebanon
23	5.5	1	0.2	4	1.1	8	2.0	—	0.1	159	37.4	1.7	1.8	2.3	Lesotho
18[19]	2.9[19]	2[19]	0.2[19]	12[19]	1.8[19]	32[19]	4.9[19]	[1]	[1]	51[1, 19]	7.8[1, 19]	2.1	3.6	2.5	Liberia
368	34.7	26	2.4	93	8.7	41	3.9	13	1.2	318	30.0	3.6	4.1	4.1	Libya
5.4	43.0	0.1	1.0	0.4	2.9	1.6	13.1	0.7	6.0	3.8	30.6	...	...	...	Liechtenstein
50[6]	33.3[6]	[6]	[6]	11	7.0	30	19.7	12	8.0	41	27.0	...	...	...	Luxembourg
66	53.0	0.9	0.7	6	4.6	23	18.5	2	1.8	19	15.4	...	...	...	Macau
244[6]	6.0[6]	[6]	[6]	[7]	[7]	[7]	[7]	[7]	[7]	539[7]	13.1[7]	1.9	2.0	2.9	Madagascar
72	18.3	5	1.4	22	5.6	26	6.5	11	2.9	56	14.4	2.3	2.5	2.7	Malaŵi
804	17.5	8	0.2	161	3.5	560	12.2	80	1.7	1,078	23.5	2.9	3.2	2.9	Malaysia
16	26.1	0.2	0.3	3	5.5	2	3.1	[1]	[1]	6[1]	9.3[1]	...	...	...	Maldives
26	1.2	1.2	0.1	12	0.5	45	2.0	0.2	—	239	10.9	2.2	1.9	2.4	Mali
40	36.1	1.3	1.2	8	7.1	11	10.2	3	2.9	41	36.4	...	...	...	Malta
12	12.5	1.0	1.1	5	5.5	10	10.4	18	18.9	37	39.2	...	...	...	Martinique
46[6]	8.9[6]	[6]	[6]	[7]	[7]	[7]	[7]	[7]	[7]	112[7]	21.7[7]	1.9	2.3	2.1	Mauritania
53[19]	26.3[19]	4[19]	1.9[19]	8[19]	4.2[19]	9[19]	4.4[19]	5[19]	2.4[19]	68[19]	34.0[19]	2.8	2.3	2.1	Mauritius
2.2	15.4	0.1	0.9	0.3	2.0	0.7	4.7	0.2	1.5	1.4	9.9	...	...	...	Mayotte
3,871	17.6	116	0.5	672	3.1	1,729	7.9	406	1.8	8,970	40.9	3.1	3.2	3.2	Mexico
1	11.8	—	0.8	0.6	6.0	3	26.1	0.9	9.4	4	45.6	...	...	...	Monaco
115[22]	16.6[22]	17	2.4	35	5.1	41	5.9	...	...	101	14.7	2.2	2.6	3.0	Mongolia
1.1	22.3	0.1	1.7	0.2	4.5	0.4	8.1	0.1	1.7	2.7	52.2	...	...	...	Montserrat
1,368	25.1	22	0.4	141	2.6	498	9.1	[1]	[1]	1,007[1]	18.5[1]	1.8	2.6	3.1	Morocco
42[21]	0.8[21]	...	...	77	1.3	112	2.0	...	...	243	4.4	1.8	1.6	2.4	Mozambique
...	...	...	...	...	...	...	...	...	...	...	...	...	...	...	Nauru
36	0.5	3.0	—	7	0.1	109	1.6	10	0.1	441	6.4	1.6	2.3	2.6	Nepal
1,508[12]	29.6[12]	47[12]	0.9[12]	322[12]	6.3[12]	820[12]	16.1[12]	394[12]	7.7[12]	1,722[12]	33.9[12]	1.4	1.4	0.5	Netherlands, The
15	18.1	1.8	2.2	6	7.3	21	25.5	5	6.0	34	40.2	...	...	...	Netherlands Antilles[11]
7[22]	16.2[22]	0.6	1.3	3	5.9	10	23.2	1.0	2.3	15	30.2	...	...	...	New Caledonia
397	29.8	15	1.1	108	8.1	218	16.4	92	6.9	354	26.5	2.0	1.3	1.1	New Zealand
129	14.9	7	0.8	30	3.4	105	12.2	17	2.0	178	20.6	3.0	3.2	3.7	Nicaragua
15[19]	42.7[19]	2[19]	6.8[19]	2[19]	6.5[19]	3[19]	8.8[19]	3[19]	8.4[19]	2[19]	4.8[19]	2.1	2.8	3.0	Niger
3,739[6]	11.7[6]	[6]	[6]	[7]	[7]	[7]	[7]	[7]	[7]	6,482[7]	20.2[7]	1.7	2.0	3.1	Nigeria
0.2	21.3	—	1.7	—	4.6	0.1	9.5	—	0.1	0.4	40.4	...	...	...	Niue
0.1	14.8	—	0.7	0.1	7.6	0.3	27.8	—	4.8	0.4	41.1	...	...	...	Norfolk Island

Employment and labour (continued)

country	year	economically active population										employed population by economic sector			
		total ('000)	participation rate (%)		activity rate (%)			employment status (%)				agriculture, forestry, fishing		mining, quarrying	
			female	ages 15–64	total	male	female	employers, self-employed	employees	unpaid family workers	other	number ('000)	% of labour force	number ('000)	% of labour force
Norway	1984	2,031	42.9	75.2[13]	49.9[10]	69.1[10]	40.9[10]	9.3	84.8	2.2	3.7	140	7.0	22	1.1
Oman	1982	231	7.1[10]	50.1[10]	28.5[10]	50.8[10]	4.2[10]	...	...	...	...	9	3.9	4	1.6
Pacific Is., Trust Territory of the															
Marshall Islands	1980	4	25.2	30.0[8]	14.3	20.8	7.4	4.2	80.8	0.5	14.5	0.1	1.2	—	—
Micronesia, Fed. States of	1980	10	29.8	26.1[8]	13.4	18.4	8.2	2.9	77.8	0.4	18.9	0.2	2.5	—	—
Northern Mariana Islands	1980	6	34.3	63.6[8]	36.3	45.5	26.3	2.1	97.0	0.1	0.8	0.1	2.1	—	—
Palau	1980	3	34.3	41.6[8]	23.9	30.3	17.0	3.1	91.3	—	5.6	0.1	2.9	—	—
Pakistan	1985	28,596	11.5	51.0	30.2	51.5	7.2	40.9	27.5	27.7	3.9	14,490	52.7	27	0.1
Panama	1983	662	29.8	52.2[10]	32.1[10]	45.8[10]	18.2[10]	24.6	67.7	4.0	3.7	174	27.3	0.7	0.1
Papua New Guinea	1980	749	39.5	35.6[2]	24.9	28.8	20.6	71.1	27.9	—	1.0	564	77.0	4	0.6
Paraguay	1982	1,030	20.3	57.1	33.9	54.0	13.8	41.2	36.7	11.6	10.5	422	43.5	1.1	0.1
Peru	1982	5,978	28.6	53.1[12]	31.8	45.4	18.2	49.1	45.1	5.8	—	2,296	38.4	68	1.2
Philippines	1983	20,521	39.4	65.8	36.9[34]	46.3[34]	27.5[34]	36.0	38.3	21.5	4.2	10,250	52.1	188	1.0
Pitcairn Island	1981	.035	...	...	66.0	...	...	...	...	...	...	.003	8.6	—	—
Poland	1983	17,962[34]	45.4[34]	73.7[34]	51.2[34]	57.4[34]	45.4[34]	13.2[34]	74.0[34]	12.1[34]	0.7[34]	5,305	31.1	[22]	[22]
Portugal	1984	4,476	41.5	68.6	46.7	56.7	37.1	15.6[16]	64.9[16]	12.0[16]	7.4[16]	1,018[16]	24.2[16]	27[16]	0.6[16]
Puerto Rico	1985	967	35.3	48.2[42]	29.5	39.2	20.3	12.0	64.2	0.8	23.0	41	5.5	134[27]	18.0[27]
Qatar	1984	113	9.8	63.8	40.3	60.8	9.8	...	...	...	...	0.3	0.2	7	5.9
Réunion	1982	176	35.3	57.5[42]	34.0	44.9	23.6	10.4	56.3	1.1	32.2	17[19]	14.7[19]	7[19, 27]	6.2[19, 27]
Romania	1982	10,794[3]	45.6[3]	75.6[3]	50.1[3]	55.2[3]	45.1[3]	...	...	...	...	2,986	28.6	[6]	[6]
Rwanda	1978	2,661	51.5	94.3	55.1	54.6	55.6	38.8	7.2	53.8	0.2	2,472	92.9	12	0.4
St. Christopher and Nevis	1980	17	41.0	69.5	39.5	48.5	31.3	12.4[9]	86.6[9]	1.1[9]	—	4	29.6	—	—
St. Helena and Ascension	1976	2.6	...	...	50.7	...	...	...	...	...	...	0.1	6.3	[6]	[6]
St. Lucia	1980	49	55.2	54.4[9]	41.1	39.0	43.0	27.3[9]	70.8[9]	2.0[9]	—	10.4	35.9	—	0.1
St. Pierre and Miquelon	1982	2	31.8	60.6	39.4	54.5	24.7	12.5	76.8	—10.7—		0.1	3.1	0.2[27]	11.6[27]
St. Vincent and the Grenadines	1970	24	35.9	58.9[29]	27.5	37.6	18.7	16.0	82.5	1.5	—	6.9	29.0	—	0.2
San Marino	1986	11	37.9	67.1[18]	47.0	58.8	35.4	...	...	...	...	0.4	3.5	[6]	[6]
São Tomé and Príncipe	1981	31	32.4	58.5	31.7	43.0	20.4	15.9	79.9	0.1	4.1	16	56.2	2[27]	5.5[27]
Saudi Arabia	1984	2,673	3.9	45.1	24.5	40.9	2.3	...	...	...	...	223	8.4	164	6.1
Senegal	1982	2,938[24]	40.5[24]	76.0[24]	46.0[24]	55.2[24]	37.0[24]	...	...	...	...	11[19]	9.1[19]	2[19]	1.6[19]
Seychelles	1981	24	37.9	62.3	37.4	49.2	30.1	10.7	76.6	0.3	12.4	5	19.5	—	—
Sierra Leone	1981	1,278[10]	34.7[10]	64.0[10]	38.8[10]	51.7[10]	26.4[10]	...	...	...	...	6[19]	8.3[19]	6[19]	7.9[19]
Singapore	1984	1,207	36.4	66.8	47.7	60.6	34.8	13.2	82.1	2.0	2.7	9	0.7	2.0	0.2
Solomon Islands	1985	...	16.8[19]	...	...	...	...	...	...	...	...	8[19]	33.5[19]	0.1[19]	0.3[19]
Somalia	1980	1,808	40.6	74.5	45.0	54.1	36.1	...	...	...	...	1,366	75.6	[6]	[6]
South Africa	1980	8,666	32.7[9]	68.3[9]	37.3[9]	50.9[9]	24.1[9]	...	...	...	...	1,300	15.0	820	9.5
Bophuthatswana	1979	405	...	...	31.5	...	...	0.7	...	...	...	36	8.9	12	33.8
Ciskei	1979	5	...	...	...	...	...	12.1	77.0	10.9	—	...	...	...	...
Transkei	1978	121	...	...	...	...	...	...	...	...	...	5	3.8	4	3.0
Venda	1978	19	...	...	...	...	...	...	...	...	...	0.6	3.2	5	25.5
South West Africa/Namibia	1980	425	24.4	55.4	31.5	48.4	15.1	...	...	...	...	185	43.4	[6]	[6]
Spain	1984	13,228	30.1	54.7[12, 42]	35.7[13]	52.0[13]	20.0[13]	18.6	66.6	6.0	8.8	2,076	17.1	90	0.7
Sri Lanka	1981	5,017	25.5	53.6	44.4	64.8	23.1	25.1	54.1	2.9	17.9	1,864	45.2	39	0.9
Sudan, The	1980	5,973[12]	20.0[39]	55.1[23, 39]	29.4[39]	46.7[39]	11.9[39]	59.2[39]	25.3[39]	9.9[39]	5.6[39]	3,433	65.8	183[27]	3.5[27]
Suriname	1980	98	27.9	38.7	27.5	...	...	...	...	...	...	8	9.1	6	6.7
Swaziland	1983	245[10]	41.2[10]	74.0[10]	43.8[10]	52.4[10]	35.6[10]	...	...	...	...	25[19]	31.4[19]	2[19]	2.8[19]
Sweden	1984	4,391	46.9	81.8[13]	52.3[16]	56.9[16]	47.9[16]	7.1	89.5	0.3	3.1	218	5.1	15	0.4
Switzerland	1980	3,092	36.2	70.7	48.6	63.4	34.4	9.6	90.3	...	...	218	7.2	6	0.2
Syria	1984	2,384	10.6	47.7	23.6	41.5	5.1	34.0[13]	56.2[13]	7.4[13]	2.4[13]	1,064	46.0	18	0.8
Taiwan	1984	9,037	35.9	70.9	47.5	58.7	35.5	21.4	66.4	12.2	—	2,028	25.0	42	0.5
Tanzania	1981	7,845[34]	51.4[34]	83.3[34]	44.8[34]	44.4[34]	45.2[34]	...	...	...	...	119[19]	19.2[19]	7[19]	1.1[19]
Thailand	1982	25,749	47.6	83.1[23]	53.0	55.2	50.6	29.1	24.1	43.3	3.5	16,985	68.4	65	0.3
Togo	1980	1,019	44.0	69.3	41.1	47.9	34.9	...	...	...	...	...	...	...	...
Tokelau	1981	0.8	51.2	88.3	48.5	47.9	49.2	...	...	...	...	0.1	16.1	—	—
Tonga	1976	21	15.7	43.7	23.8	39.3	7.6	32.7	33.3	13.1	20.9	9.5	51.2	—	0.1
Trinidad and Tobago	1983	449	32.4	64.4	39.2	53.0	25.4	15.4	79.7	3.5	1.4	34	8.6	68[27]	16.9[27]
Tunisia	1982	1,810[10]	20.1[10]	51.4[10]	28.4[10]	45.1[10]	11.5[10]	24.7[10]	50.1[10]	10.5[10]	14.7[10]	539	30.2	16	0.9
Turkey	1980	19,212	36.1	68.2	42.9	54.1	31.4	23.2	32.1	40.9	3.8	11,105	60.0	132	0.7
Turks and Caicos Islands	1980	2.9	42.8	69.4	39.2	46.5	32.5	...	...	...	...	0.4	13.9	—	—
Tuvalu	1979[44]	4.0	51.3	81.0[23]	55.2	57.6	53.1	0.3	22.2	—77.5—		—	4.2[19]	—	0.1[19]
Uganda	1980	6,163	42.8	80.4	47.0	54.3	39.8	...	...	...	...	5,292	85.9	[6]	[6]
U.S.S.R.	1983	135,424[15]	49.8[15]	72.7[10]	51.7[15]	55.7[15]	48.1[15]	...	82.8[14]	...	17.2[14, 45]	25,334	19.7	[6]	[6]
United Arab Emirates	1984	738	5.8	77.0	54.5	74.6	10.2	6.8[10]	92.7[10]	0.1[10]	0.5[10]	36	4.9	15	2.0
United Kingdom	1983	26,776	39.6	73.5[10]	47.0[10]	58.8[10]	35.9[10]	7.0[10]	85.4[10]	...	7.5[10]	349	1.6	821	3.9
United States	1984	113,544	43.8	70.7	48.1	55.6	40.9	8.3	90.3	0.5	1.0	3,748	3.3	1,061	0.9
Uruguay	1981	1,137	29.6[10]	60.3[10]	39.0[10]	55.6[10]	22.8[10]	...	...	...	...	132	11.6	2	0.2
Vanuatu	1979	51	43.4	88.8	46.0	49.0	42.5	...	...	...	...	39	76.8	0.1	0.1
Venezuela	1984	5,517	26.7	56.3	32.9	47.8	17.8	26.3	56.9	3.4	13.4	826	14.7	81	1.5
Vietnam	1983	25,782	45.5	55.0	35.3[39]	41.6[39]	29.3[39]	...	...	...	...	17,703	68.7	[22]	[22]
Virgin Islands (U.S.)	1980	38	45.5	72.8	39.3	44.8	34.4	9.5	90.2	0.3	—	0.5	1.3	—	0.1
Wallis and Futuna	1976	3.3	35.8	65.2	36.5	46.9	26.1	42.2	18.3	39.5	—	2.7	79.2	—	—
West Bank	1983	156.1	17.5	36.9[32]	20.4	...	...	...	...	...	...	...	...	...	...
Western Sahara	...	...	...	...	...	...	...	...	...	...	...	...	...	...	...
Western Samoa	1981	42	15.0	48.6	26.5	43.5	8.3	21.1	43.5	35.0	0.4	25	60.4	—	—
Yemen (Aden)	1984	450	6.8	43.0	21.3	40.2	2.9	29.8[39]	34.2[39]	15.1[39]	20.9[39]	166	36.9	8	1.9
Yemen (Ṣan'ā)	1984	1,472	12.5	41.4	21.3	38.8	5.1	45.2[14]	34.0[14]	19.1[14]	1.7[14]	830[14]	73.6[14]	0.6[14]	0.1[14]
Yugoslavia	1981	9,359	38.7	68.7[46]	43.4	54.3	32.9	17.2	65.7	10.5	6.6	2,683	30.6	[6]	[6]
Zaire	1980	10,434	37.6	67.8	40.4	51.3	29.8	...	...	...	...	7,460	71.5	[6]	[6]
Zambia	1983	2,628	29.2	46.0	31.1[12]	45.2[12]	17.3[12]	...	...	...	...	1,462	64.6	58	2.5
Zimbabwe	1983	2,484[16]	39.2[16]	63.5[16, 23]	33.1[16]	41.1[16]	25.4[16]	...	...	...	...	264[19]	25.5[19]	60[19]	5.8[19]

manufacturing, construction		electricity, gas, water		transportation, communications		trade, hotels, restaurants		finance, real estate		services, other		average annual growth of labour force			country
number ('000)	% of labour force	number ('000)	% of labour force	number ('000)	% of labour force	number ('000)	% of labour force	number ('000)	% of labour force	number ('000)	% of labour force	1965–1973 (%)	1973–1984 (%)	1980–2000 (%)	
532	26.4	23	1.1	180	8.9	333	16.6	120	6.0	662	32.9	0.6	0.7	0.6	Norway
54	23.7	2	0.9	6	2.6	101	43.9	4	1.6	50	21.8	0.0	0.0	0.0	Oman
															Pacific Is., Trust Territory of the
0.5	12.4	[4]	[4]	0.3[4]	7.1[4]	0.6	12.8	—	0.7	2.9	65.7	...	...	...	Marshall Islands
1.1	11.6	[4]	[4]	0.5[4]	5.1[4]	0.9	9.2	0.1	1.3	6.9	70.4	...	...	...	Micronesia, Fed. States of
1.1	18.4	[4]	[4]	0.5[4]	8.7[4]	0.9	15.3	0.2	2.7	3.2	52.8	...	...	...	Northern Mariana Islands
0.6	19.5	[4]	[4]	0.2[4]	8.0[4]	0.3	11.8	—	1.6	1.6	56.2	...	...	...	Palau
5,012	18.2	311	1.1	1,261	4.6	3,281	11.9	225	0.8	2,874	10.6	2.3	3.3	2.9	Pakistan
106	16.6	8	1.3	40	6.3	94	14.8	28	4.5	185	29.1	3.3	2.6	2.2	Panama
26	4.8	3	0.4	17	2.4	25	3.4	4	0.6	79	10.8	1.9	2.0	2.1	Papua New Guinea
192	18.8	3	0.2	26	2.6	85	8.3	17	1.7	254	24.8	2.5	3.3	3.0	Paraguay
992	16.6	13	0.2	282	4.7	976	16.3	105	1.8	1,245	20.8	2.4	2.9	2.9	Peru
2,421	12.3	88	0.4	901	4.6	2,257	11.5	313	1.6	3,254	16.5	2.1	3.1	2.6	Philippines
—	—	.002	5.7	.005	14.3	.002	5.7	.016	45.7	.007	20.0	...	...	...	Pitcairn Island
6,189[22]	36.4[22]	204	1.2	1,058	6.2	1,325	7.8	155	0.9	2,797	16.4	1.7	1.2	0.8	Poland
1,497[16]	35.6[16]	21[16]	0.5[16]	165[16]	3.9[16]	511[16]	12.1[16]	107[16]	2.5[16]	865[16]	20.6[16]	0.1	0.9	0.7	Portugal
38[21]	5.1[21]	12	1.6	39	5.2	140	18.8	25	3.4	316	42.4	...	...	...	Puerto Rico
41	36.3	7	6.2	5	4.2	16	14.3	4	3.3	34	29.6	...	...	...	Qatar
11[19, 21]	9.4[19, 21]	0.7[19]	0.6[19]	6[19]	4.9[19]	14[19]	12.1[19]	16[19]	13.8[19]	45[19]	38.3[19]	...	...	...	Réunion
4,614[6]	44.2[6]	[6]	[6]	733	7.0	615	5.9	...	...	1,480	14.3	0.8	0.5	0.6	Romania
61	2.3	1	—	7	0.3	26	1.0	1	—	81	3.1	2.7	2.8	3.1	Rwanda
3	17.4	1	7.0	0.5	3.0	0.9	6.3	0.3	1.9	5	34.8	...	...	...	St. Christopher and Nevis
0.3[6]	12.0[6]	[6]	[6]	0.1	4.5	0.1	4.1	0.7	29.0	1.0	44.2	...	...	...	St. Helena and Ascension
5.2	17.8	0.5	1.7	1.1	3.7	3.1	10.6	...	...	8.7	30.0	...	...	...	St. Lucia
0.1[21]	6.0[21]	—	1.8	0.2	9.5	0.6	29.0	—	2.3	0.8	36.8	...	...	...	St. Pierre and Miquelon
4.7	19.9	0.2	0.9	1.1	4.5	2.9	12.1	[1]	[1]	7.9[1]	33.4[1]	...	...	...	St. Vincent and the Grenadines
4.9[6]	46.8[6]	[6]	[6]	0.1	1.2	1.6	15.1	0.2	1.9	3.3	31.6	...	...	...	San Marino
2[21]	6.1[21]	0.3	1.0	1	3.5	2	6.9	0.2	0.6	6	20.1	...	...	...	São Tomé and Príncipe
923	34.5	62	2.3	117	4.4	730	27.3	104	3.9	350	13.1	3.9	5.9	3.2	Saudi Arabia
39[19]	33.6[19]	3[19]	2.8[19]	25[19]	21.3[19]	15[19]	12.6[19]	8[19]	6.8[19]	14[19]	12.3[19]	1.7	2.2	2.4	Senegal
6	23.2	0.2	0.8	2	8.4	4	15.6	0.5	1.8	8	30.5	...	...	...	Seychelles
17[19]	23.3[19]	1.8[19]	2.5[19]	7[19]	9.8[19]	6[19]	8.1[19]	2[19]	2.8[19]	27[19]	37.4[19]	1.0	1.8	1.9	Sierra Leone
434	36.1	9	0.8	125	10.4	271	22.5	103	8.6	249	20.7	3.4	2.2	1.1	Singapore
3[19]	13.3[19]	0.3[19]	1.3[19]	2[19]	9.0[19]	3[19]	10.7[19]	0.5[19]	2.2[19]	7[19]	29.7[19]	...	...	...	Solomon Islands
152[6]	8.4[6]	[6]	[6]	[7]	[7]	[7]	[7]	[7]	[7]	290[7]	16.0[7]	3.8	2.6	2.6	Somalia
1,909	22.0	79	0.9	424	4.9	1,008	11.6	286	22.9	2,839	32.8	2.7	3.0	2.3	South Africa
...	...	...	...	...	...	...	...	...	...	...	...	...	...	...	Bophuthatswana
...	...	...	...	...	...	...	...	...	...	...	...	...	...	...	Ciskei
19	16.0	...	...	3	2.6	8	6.5	1	0.9	81	67.2	...	...	...	Transkei
4	22.6	...	...	...	...	0.9	5.0	...	...	8	43.7	...	...	...	Venda
93[6]	21.8[6]	[6]	[6]	[7]	[7]	[7]	[7]	[7]	[7]	148[7]	34.7[7]	...	...	...	South West Africa/Namibia
4,148	34.3	82	0.7	659	5.4	2,371	19.6	446	3.7	2,238	18.5	0.4	1.3	0.8	Spain
542	13.1	15	0.4	199	4.8	433	10.5	45	1.1	983	23.9	2.0	2.1	2.2	Sri Lanka
108[21]	2.1[21]	59	1.1	199	3.8	221[25]	4.2[25]	[25]	[25]	1,020	19.5	2.8	2.4	2.8	Sudan, The
11	13.4	1	1.5	3	3.5	11	13.7	2	2.4	41	49.7	...	...	...	Suriname
18[19]	23.1[19]	1[19]	1.4[19]	5[19]	5.9[19]	8[19]	9.8[19]	2[19]	3.1[19]	18[19]	22.4[19]	...	...	...	Swaziland
1,213	28.5	40	0.9	294	6.9	586	13.8	316	7.4	1,574	37.0	0.7	0.4	0.3	Sweden
1,162	38.5	22	0.7	180	6.0	586	19.4	246	8.2	592	19.6	1.5	0.4	0.2	Switzerland
500	21.6	7	0.3	111	4.8	248	10.7	21	0.9	345	14.9	3.1	3.4	3.9	Syria
2,793	31.6	56	0.6	419	4.7	1,184	13.4	189	2.1	1,946	22.0	...	...	...	Taiwan
150[19]	24.1[19]	24[19]	3.9[19]	55[19]	8.9[19]	40[19]	6.4[19]	18[19]	2.8[19]	209[19]	33.7[19]	2.6	2.6	3.2	Tanzania
2,527	10.2	76	0.3	501	2.0	2,298	9.3	...	...	2,378	9.6	2.4	3.0	1.9	Thailand
...	...	...	...	...	...	...	...	...	...	...	...	3.2	2.0	2.9	Togo
—	—	—	—	—	0.9	—	3.0	—	—	0.6	80.0	...	...	...	Tokelau
1.5	8.3	0.1	0.6	0.8	4.5	0.8	4.4	0.1	0.3	5.7	30.7	...	...	...	Tonga
[27, 43]	[27, 43]	83[43]	20.9[43]	30	7.4	91	22.8	...	...	94	23.4	2.0	2.3	2.2	Trinidad and Tobago
561	31.5	10	0.6	65	3.6	155	8.7	11	0.6	346	19.4	1.3	2.9	2.9	Tunisia
2,741	14.8	33	0.2	531	2.9	1,084	5.9	294	1.6	2,602	13.9	1.8	2.0	2.2	Turkey
0.3	10.8	—	0.4	0.1	3.7	0.1	4.3	—	1.0	1.9	65.9	...	...	...	Turks and Caicos Islands
0.3[19]	31.7[19]	—	1.6[19]	0.1[19]	11.9[19]	0.1[19]	10.9[19]	—	1.2[19]	0.3[19]	38.5[19]	...	...	...	Tuvalu
272[6]	4.4[6]	[6]	[6]	[7]	[7]	[7]	[7]	[7]	[7]	599[7]	9.7[7]	3.1	2.2	3.2	Uganda
53,840[6]	41.8[6]	[6]	[6]	12,438	9.7	9,899	7.7	681	0.5	26,580	20.6	0.7	1.1	0.5	U.S.S.R.
235	31.9	14	1.9	55	7.4	100	13.5	22	3.0	261	35.4	...	...	...	United Arab Emirates
5,836	27.5	662	3.1	1,332	6.3	4,208	19.8	1,837	8.7	6,164	29.1	0.2	0.5	0.2	United Kingdom
30,235	26.5	1,553	1.4	6,192	5.4	23,745	20.8	10,943	9.6	36,584	32.1	1.9	1.6	0.9	United States
297	26.1	16	1.4	58	5.1	171	15.0	[1]	[1]	461[1]	40.6[1]	0.3	0.5	0.9	Uruguay
2	4.1	0.1	0.1	1	2.6	2	4.3	0.3	0.6	6	11.3	...	...	...	Vanuatu
1,357	24.2	73	1.3	384	6.8	1,066	19.0	275	4.9	1,546	27.6	3.5	3.9	3.4	Venezuela
1,213[22]	4.7[22]	32	0.1	180	0.7	395	1.5	[1]	[1]	6,259[1]	24.3[1]	...	...	2.7	Vietnam
6.8	19.1	0.6	1.8	2.8	7.9	9.0	25.3	1.9	5.3	14.0	39.2	...	...	...	Virgin Islands (U.S.)
0.2	5.5	—	0.1	—	1.2	0.1	1.5	—	—	0.4	12.5	...	...	...	Wallis and Futuna
...	...	...	...	...	...	...	...	...	...	...	...	...	...	...	West Bank
...	...	...	...	...	...	...	...	...	...	...	...	...	...	...	Western Sahara
3	7.3	0.5	1.1	1	3.2	2	4.4	1	3.1	8	20.4	...	...	...	Western Samoa
80	17.7	9	2.0	29	6.5	39	8.8	0.3	0.1	118	26.2	1.1	1.8	2.6	Yemen (Aden)
86[14]	7.7[14]	1.5[14]	0.1[14]	25[14]	2.2[14]	69[14]	6.1[14]	2[14]	0.2[14]	113[14]	10.0[14]	1.0	2.1	3.2	Yemen (Ṣan'ā')
2,899[6]	33.0[6]	[6]	[6]	445	5.1	828	9.4	205	2.3	1,720	19.6	0.7	0.5	0.6	Yugoslavia
1,346[6]	12.9[6]	[6]	[6]	[7]	[7]	[7]	[7]	[7]	[7]	1,629[7]	15.6[7]	1.9	2.3	2.8	Zaire
81	3.6	8	0.3	24	1.1	30	1.3	22	1.0	578	25.6	2.3	2.1	3.1	Zambia
223[19]	21.6[19]	7[19]	0.7[19]	50[19]	4.8[19]	81[19]	7.8[19]	16[19]	1.5[19]	334[19]	32.3[19]	2.7	1.5	3.4	Zimbabwe

[1]Services includes finance, real estate. [2]Over age 10. [3]1977. [4]Transportation, communications includes electricity, gas, water. [5]Services includes hotels. [6]Manufacturing, construction includes mining, quarrying and electricity, gas, water. [7]Services includes transportation, communications; trade, hotels, restaurants; and finance, real estate. [8]Over age 16. [9]1970. [10]1980. [11]Netherlands Antilles includes Aruba. [12]1981. [13]1983. [14]1975. [15]1979. [16]1982. [17]Services includes transportation, communications and finance, real estate. [18]1976. [19]Wage earners only. [20]Mining, quarrying includes manufacturing, and electricity, gas, water. [21]Construction only. [22]Manufacturing, construction includes mining, quarrying. [23]Over age 15. [24]1984. [25]Trade includes finance, real estate. [26]Ngazidja only. [27]Mining, quarrying includes manufacturing. [28]State sector only. [29]Ages 14–64. [30]Excludes unemployed. [31]Insured workers only. [32]Over age 14. [33]Ages 15–69. [34]1978. [35]1971. [36]Ages 18–64. [37]Indigenous population active in cash economy only. [38]1974. [39]1973. [40]Over age 9. [41]Over age 12. [42]Ages 16–64. [43]Electricity, gas, water includes construction. [44]De facto indigenous population only. [45]Includes communal workers and their families. [46]Ages 20–64.

Agriculture and land use

This table provides data on the structure of the agricultural sectors of the various countries of the world from the perspective of farms and farmland use. The data are taken mainly from national agricultural censuses and surveys, supplemented by reports of the United Nations Food and Agriculture Organization's (FAO's) *World Census of Agriculture.* Many of these national censuses, of course, were taken under guidelines established by the FAO for the *World Census of Agriculture* programs (the 1980 census was the fourth, and it included national censuses taken during the decade 1976–85). It represents a cooperative effort by FAO member countries to collect agricultural data within a general framework that permits international harmonization of concepts and definitions; transfer of technical expertise; and increased effectiveness in the collection, analysis, publication, and policy-related use of such statistics. More than 100 countries expected to participate in the 1980 round of censuses.

Although many nations have organized their data along FAO guidelines, differing levels of national economic and technological development, land tenure systems, as well as scope and standards of statistical coverage necessitate care in making country-to-country comparisons. All agricultural statistics, whether or not gathered under FAO guidelines, are subject to quality-control problems. Frequently scope, classificational schemes, and definitions vary from the FAO guidelines from country to country (economic planners need different information about a commercial, high-technology, multicrop agricultural sector than they do for a family-subsistence, low-technology, one-crop sector). In countries that lack sufficient manpower, financing, or transport and communications infrastructure to permit a complete census of agriculture, a sample survey may be taken. This is a limited census of a predetermined number of carefully screened holdings. From these results, nationwide projections may be prepared, but these are often of uncertain reliability. Problems of quality control include errors or biases arising from such factors as incomplete or inaccurate lists of holdings, ambiguous or misleading questions, respondents who inadvertently or willfully do not give accurate information, failure to record data for all parts of scattered or fragmented holdings, respondents' misunderstandings of the definitions of land use and cropping methods, or a failure to report livestock temporarily absent from the holding on public or common pasture land or in transit. While sample surveys can provide a check against such discrepancies, many statistical uncertainties remain.

With respect to the first section of the table, number and size of farms, for example, the Soviet bloc nations, Czechoslovakia excepted, usually publish statistics only on state collective or cooperative farms and exclude privately held plots of land, even though in some instances these provide a significant fraction of agricultural output. Many other countries impose a minimum size limit for holdings that may be covered in their census reports, and this cutoff, if not sufficiently low, can result in a substantial undercount of smaller holdings.

The land tenure statistics show a breakdown of all farms according to the rights under which the farmer holds the land. Owner-operated includes two types of ownership: outright ownership in which the holder has title and has the right to determine use and transfer of the land; and ownerlike possession in which the holder lacks the legal title to the land but uses it under terms of perpetual lease, hereditary tenure, or long-term leases of 30 years or more with nominal, or no, rent payment. Farms classed as owner-

Agriculture and land use

country	farms (latest census of agriculture)[a]															
	year	number of farms ('000)	size of holding								tenure (% of farms)					
			average (ha)	size class (%)							owner-operated			rented (including share-croppers)	tribal/ communal	other
				under 1 ha	1–5 ha	5–10 ha	10–20 ha	20–50 ha	50–200 ha	over 200 ha	individual/ family	corporate/ state	socialized/ collective			
Afghanistan	1981	126[1]	3.5[1]	44.8[1]	35.2[1]	—20.0[1]—					55.1[1]	—	—	25.1[1]	—	19.8[1]
Albania	1979	0.4	1,281	...	...	...	...	...	...	...	—	—100.0—		...	...	...
Algeria	1973	899	6.2	1.1	12.7	15.8	21.7	25.6	18.0	5.1	...	...	...	...	...	...
American Samoa	1980	1.3	1.8	49.2[5]	45.5[6]	—4.9[7]—		—0.4[8]—			85.9	—	—	5.0	—	9.1
Andorra	...	...	...	...	...	...	...	...	...	...	...	...	...	...	...	...
Angola	1970	1,067	3.9	3.3	13.5	9.3	11.3	13.7	19.2	29.7	80.5	1.1	—	—	18.2	0.2
Anguilla	...	...	...	...	...	...	...	...	...	...	...	...	...	...	...	...
Antigua and Barbuda	1981	2.1	0.8	53.5	—46.5—		...	...	...	...	...	...	...	...	...	...
Argentina	1974	510	399	—19.4—		8.2	9.5	16.7	25.1	21.1	73.8[9]	—	—	11.7[9]	—	14.5[9]
Aruba	...	...	...	...	...	...	...	...	...	...	...	...	...	...	...	...
Australia	1984	345	1,378	0.7[11]	7.2[11]	5.2[11]	6.3[11]	11.9[11]	26.2[11]	42.6[11]	95.7[11]	3.7[11]	—	—	—	0.6[11]
Austria	1980[13]	303	24.2	3.7	31.0	17.3	21.0	21.2	5.2	0.6	59.0	—	—	2.3	—	38.7
Bahamas, The	1978	4.2	8.5	55.2[5]	30.1[6]	—12.3[7]—		1.1[14]	0.4[15]	1.0[16]	74.9	0.6	—	4.0	—	20.5
Bahrain	1980	0.8	4.4	19.4	52.9	17.4	8.2	2.0	—0.1—		37.9	0.1	—	62.0	—	—
Bangladesh	1980	6,853	1.3	54.1	—45.9—		—	—	—	—	53.2	...	...	0.5	...	46.3
Barbados	1969	0.2	95.8	...	...	...	...	...	...	...	...	...	...	...	...	...
Belgium	1979	119	12.4	21.2	22.6	16.0	21.0	16.0	—3.2—		27.7[9]	—	0.8[9]	71.5[9]	—	—
Belize	1974	8.9	26.7	—69.4—			16.7	8.6	4.4	0.9	43.6	56.4	—	—	—	—
Benin	...	...	...	...	...	...	...	...	...	...	...	...	...	...	...	...
Bermuda	1981	...	...	...	...	...	...	...	...	...	...	...	...	...	...	...
Bhutan	1982	...	1.6	51.3[5]	42.9[6]	—5.8[19]—					...	...	...	...	...	...
Bolivia	1980	700	25.0[20]	...	...	...	...	...	...	...	80.0[20]	...	...	...	...	20.0
Botswana	1980	80.4	4.3	10.9	59.6	22.7	—6.8—		—	—	...	...	...	...	...	...
Brazil	1980	5,160	70.7	9.1	27.5	13.8	15.0	16.6	12.6	5.4	61.3	—	—	17.2	—	21.5[21]
British Virgin Islands	1980	0.3	...	...	...	...	...	...	...	...	...	...	...	...	...	...
Brunei	1964	6.3	2.6	44.1[5]	40.4[6]	—15.5[19]—					52.3	1.0	—	22.0	—	24.7
Bulgaria	1973	0.170[23]	25,700[23]	...	...	...	...	...	...	...	...	...	...	...	...	...
Burkina Faso	...	...	...	...	...	...	...	...	...	...	...	...	...	...	...	...
Burma	1981	4,300	2.3[20]	61.0[20, 24]	—39.0[25]—						...	...	...	...	...	...
Burundi	1983	...	...	...	...	...	...	...	...	...	...	...	...	...	...	...
Cameroon	1973	926	1.6	42.7	53.8	3.2	0.3	—	—	—	2.4	—	—	5.2	59.5	32.9
Canada	1981	318	207	1.5[5]	—6.8[27]—		5.3	14.0	40.5	31.9	63.3	—	—	6.2	—	30.5
Cape Verde	1979	...	...	...	...	...	...	...	...	...	...	...	...	...	...	...
Cayman Islands	...	...	...	...	...	...	...	...	...	...	...	...	...	...	...	...
Central African Republic	1974	283	1.7	32.2	65.2	2.5	—	—	—	—	0.3[9]	—	—	0.1[9]	98.6[9]	1.2[9]
Chad	1973	366	2.6	19.7	69.5	10.0	—0.8—		—	—	...	...	...	...	...	...
Chile	1976	306	94.1	...	...	...	...	...	...	...	...	...	...	...	...	...
China	1984	1,650	...	...	...	...	...	...	...	...	—	10.0[11]	90.0[11]	—	—	—
Christmas Island	...	...	...	...	...	...	...	...	...	...	...	...	...	...	...	...
Cocos (Keeling) Islands	...	...	...	...	...	...	...	...	...	...	...	...	...	...	...	...
Colombia	1971	1,177	26.3	22.8	36.7	13.6	10.0	8.5	6.3	2.1	68.7	—	—	5.8	4.1	21.4
Comoros	1965	...	25	...	...	...	...	...	...	...	—	42.1	—	57.9	—	—
Congo	1973	143	1.4	37.3	62.2	0.5	—	—	—	—	...	...	...	...	...	...
Cook Islands	1975	...	...	...	...	...	...	...	...	...	...	...	...	...	...	...
Costa Rica	1973	82	38.3	23.3	25.5	11.2	10.8	15.2	10.7	3.3	97.9	1.7	—	0.1	—	0.3
Côte d'Ivoire	1975	550	5.0	9.5	54.4	24.9	9.4	1.7	0.1	—	...	...	...	...	...	...
Cuba	1983	...	...	...	...	...	...	...	...	...	...	...	...	...	...	...
Cyprus	1977	43.8	5.3	17.9	58.1	16.0	6.1	1.7	—0.2—		69.6	—	—	23.7	0.3	6.4
Czechoslovakia	1980	1,391	8.1	89.9[31]	—9.9[32]—				0.0[33]	0.2[34]	6.0[9]	30.8[9]	63.2[9]	—	0.6	—
Denmark	1983	99	28.8	—3.5—		17.6	27.3	38.4	—13.3—		...	...	...	...	...	...
Djibouti	...	...	...	...	...	...	...	...	...	...	...	...	...	...	...	...
Dominica	...	...	...	...	...	...	...	...	...	...	...	...	...	...	...	...
Dominican Republic	1971	305	9.0	23.0	54.0	11.1	2.4	7.1	1.9	0.4	54.7	—	—	10.1	20.0	15.1
Ecuador	1974	517	15.4	27.8	38.8	10.6	8.0	8.2	5.6	0.9	70.3	0.3	—	7.7	7.4	14.3
Egypt	1983	...	...	...	...	...	...	...	...	...	...	...	...	...	...	...

operated under this definition are divided into individual and family, corporate or state, and socialized or collective proprietorships. Rented includes sharecropping and related arrangements; communal/tribal includes types of customary or traditional arrangements in which title or goods do not change hands.

Statistics on types of farms by commodities produced refer as far as possible to the categories outlined by the FAO. The terms "mainly crops" and "mainly livestock" indicate that more than half of the for-sale production was either crops or livestock, and farms not clearly fitting either category were defined as mixed.

The section on technology provides some principal measures of the extent to which modern technology plays a role in the farm activities of each country (although, of course, irrigation works may employ technology and, indeed, may have been maintained in their present form from ancient times).

The classification of farmland by economic use is also subject to differing interpretations. Some countries classify land under permanent crops (those not needing to be replanted each year) as cropland or arable land; that is, land rotated between different crops. Land under temporary crops includes land requiring replanting after each harvest, but some crops—such as asparagus, strawberries, pineapples, bananas, and sugarcane—have biennial or longer growing cycles and so are sometimes arbitrarily placed under temporary and sometimes under permanent cropland. Permanently cropped land may include trees, such as cocoa, nuts, or coffee, but other trees may be grown to shade these; temporarily cropped land is sometimes simultaneously planted with permanent crops, causing confusion in classification. Many countries do not distinguish consistently between temporary and permanent meadow or pasture (land used permanently for livestock forage), and some include grassland and meadows under cropland. Land left temporarily fallow, land subject to changing use, particularly under the shifting cultivation patterns of tropical countries, may be inconsistently classified. There is also uncertainty in classifying forest and woodlands that may have commercial potential but that are also used for grazing livestock or for recreation.

Much additional information on the problems of collecting and comparing agricultural data may be found in the FAO's *World Census of Agriculture 1970: Analysis and International Comparison of the Results* and *Programme for the 1980 World Census of Agriculture,* and in the United States Department of Agriculture's *Scope and Methods of the Statistical Reporting Service.*

Measurements of area are given in hectares (1 hectare is equal to 2.4711 acres). The following notes further define the column headings:

a. All properties used wholly or partly for agricultural production. A property need not have agricultural land to be considered a farm; piggeries, hatcheries, and poultry batteries are farms because they engage in agricultural production, *i.e.,* raise livestock and produce livestock products.
b. All forms not included in the preceding categories. Includes land operated by schools, religious bodies, squatters, seasonally by nomads, and built-on, waste, and similar types of alienation.

... Not available, or no agricultural census or survey ever taken.
— None, less than half the smallest unit shown, or not applicable.

activity (% of farms)			technology (% of farms using)				farm land use: land in farms		land use (%): cropland							country
mainly crops	mainly livestock	mixed/other	tractor	electricity	irrigation works	artificial fertilizer (kg/ha)	total ('000 ha)	% of total land area	permanent crops	temporary crops	fallow	total cropland	meadows and pastures	woodland and forest	other[b]	
...	...	...	...	...	33[2]	2.5	39,810	61.0	1.8	46.3	51.9	19.9	75.4	4.8	—	Afghanistan
...	...	...	15[3]	...	54[2]	155[4]	697	24.2	16.3	—83.7—		100.00	...	...	...	Albania
...	...	...	6[3]	...	5[2]	21[4]	5,544	2.3	4.1	65.1	30.8	93.9	2.3	3.9	—	Algeria
5.6	1.0	93.4	3[3]	39.7	...	...	2.4	12.2	...	...	10.7	78.0	5.1	—	16.9	American Samoa
...	...	...	...	...	...	...	...	...	...	...	...	...	...	...	...	Andorra
...	...	...	3[3]	...	89.3	1[4]	4,180	3.4	36.8	63.2	—	1.7	82.0	—	16.2	Angola
...	...	...	...	...	...	...	...	...	...	...	...	...	...	...	...	Anguilla
...	...	...	29[3]	...	...	...	1.5	3.4	...	...	...	...	...	...	...	Antigua and Barbuda
10.6	78.9	10.5	4[3]	...	5[2]	3[4]	203,345	73.1	...	...	...	10.6	78.9	4.8	5.7	Argentina
...	...	...	10	...	...	...	...	...	...	...	...	...	...	...	...	Aruba
29.4[12]	70.6[12]	—	7[3]	...	4[2]	24[4]	480,000	62.5	0.4	94.4	5.2	9.9	90.1	—	...	Australia
...	...	...	71	...	...	216[4]	7,326	87.4	6.6	87.4	6.0	21.3	26.0	41.5	11.2	Austria
...	...	...	8[3]	...	10.3	122[4]	36.2	2.6	23.3	59.9	16.8	23.3	6.9	25.7	44.0	Bahamas, The
...	...	...	...	21.3	50[2]	57[4]	3.5	5.2	50.7	49.3	...	45.9	—	—	54.1	Bahrain
91.3[17]	8.7[17]	—	1[3]	...	20[2]	51.0	8,887	61.7	2.1	96.3	1.5	88.7	—	—11.3—		Bangladesh
...	...	...	17[3]	...	...	182[4]	19.8	45.9	...	...	...	13.7		—86.3—		Barbados
...	...	...	133[3, 18]	...	...	521[4, 18]	1,475	46.9	7.4	92.6	—	62.8	34.2	0.7	2.3	Belgium
...	...	...	25[3]	...	4[2]	26[4]	233	10.0	13.1	81.1	5.8	36.5	15.9	36.1	11.6	Belize
...	...	...	...	...	1[2]	2[4]	...	...	...	...	...	...	...	...	...	Benin
...	...	...	...	...	...	...	0.3	6.6	24.2	63.0	12.7	83.8	10.8	5.4	—	Bermuda
...	...	...	...	...	...	1[4]	150	3.0	...	...	...	...	...	...	...	Bhutan
...	...	...	...	...	4[2]	1[4]	84,060	76.3	19.3	80.7	...	1.4	49.4	49.2	...	Bolivia
...	...	...	2[3]	...	...	1[4]	343	5.9	—	100.0	...	83.5	...	...	...	Botswana
80.0[22]	16.2[22]	3.8[22]	5[3]	4.1[22]	3[2]	37[4]	364,854	42.9	18.2	66.9	14.9	15.8	47.8	24.2	12.2	Brazil
...	...	...	1[3]	...	...	...	...	...	...	...	...	...	...	...	...	British Virgin Islands
...	...	...	3[3]	...	...	...	16.4	2.8	78.0	22.0	—	54.8	0.1	16.4	28.7	Brunei
...	...	...	14[3]	...	29[2]	250[4]	6,071	53.0	...	...	...	70.0	24.0	—	6.0	Bulgaria
...	...	...	...	...	...	4[4]	...	...	...	...	...	...	...	...	...	Burkina Faso
...	...	...	1[3]	...	10[2]	17[4]	10,300	15.2	—80.2[26]—		19.8[26]	14.8[26]	...	14.0[26]	71.2[26]	Burma
...	...	...	...	...	...	1[4]	2,388	85.8	—73.8—		26.2	56.7	37.7	5.6	—	Burundi
...	...	...	...	...	...	60.0[12]	1,490	3.3	...	...	...	100.0	—	—	—	Cameroon
35.3[22]	61.4[22]	3.3[22]	14[3]	...	1[2]	44[4]	65,889	7.1	—50.0—		16.3	63.3	6.7	5.4	24.6	Canada
...	...	...	1[3]	...	5[2]	—	25[28]	6.2[28]	20.8[28]	79.1[28]	...	100.0[28]	...	...	...	Cape Verde
...	...	...	...	...	...	...	...	...	...	...	...	...	...	...	...	Cayman Islands
...	...	...	...	...	...	1[4]	491	0.8	11.8	88.2	—	100.0	—	—	—	Central African Republic
...	...	...	...	...	...	2[4]	23,877[29]	45.8[29]	50.0[29]	—50.0[29]—		23.7[29]	76.3[29]	...	...	Chad
...	...	...	6[3]	...	23[2]	19[4]	28,800	39.1	6.1	65.5	28.4	11.5	42.3	20.7	25.4	Chile
...	...	...	8[3]	...	45[2]	170	c.103,400	10.8	...	...	...	100.0	...	...	...	China
...	...	...	...	...	...	...	...	...	...	...	...	...	...	...	...	Christmas Island
...	...	...	...	...	...	...	...	...	...	...	...	...	...	...	...	Cocos (Keeling) Islands
...	...	...	5[3]	...	6[2]	55[4]	30,993	27.0	30.6	27.6	41.8	24.7	56.4	—	18.9	Colombia
...	...	...	...	...	...	...	115	50.0	...	...	...	34.8	9.4	10.9	44.9	Comoros
...	...	...	1[3]	...	...	2[4]	197	0.6	49.5	50.5	—	100.0	—	—	—	Congo
...	...	...	22[3]	...	...	...	...	...	55.9	—44.1—		100.0	—	—	—	Cook Islands
...	...	...	10[3]	...	4[2]	113[4]	3,122	60.0	42.2	57.8	—	15.7	49.9	22.9	11.4	Costa Rica
...	...	...	1[3]	...	1[2]	9[4]	2,753	8.6	65.9	34.1	...	100.0	...	...	...	Côte d'Ivoire
...	...	...	20[3]	...	31[2]	172[4]	8,768	79.1	—91.9—		8.1	41.7	15.0	29.8	13.5	Cuba
98.0	2.0[30]	...	25[3]	...	22[2]	45[4]	234	25.3	35.4	53.2	11.4	76.1	1.6	1.7	20.6	Cyprus
34.3	24.4	41.3	26[3]	100.0	4[2]	337[4]	6,924	54.1	2.6	—97.4—		75.3	24.7	...	...	Czechoslovakia
...	...	...	98.6	...	15.2	247[4]	2,846	66.1	0.4[22]	99.6[22]	0.1[22]	100.0[22]	—	—	—	Denmark
...	...	...	...	...	...	...	...	...	...	...	...	...	...	...	...	Djibouti
...	...	...	5[3]	...	...	107[4]	...	...	...	...	...	...	...	...	...	Dominica
...	...	...	2[3]	...	12[2]	35[4]	2,736	56.5	27.8	54.3	18.0	41.8	45.8	11.6	0.8	Dominican Republic
67.8	12.4	19.8	3[3]	...	21[2]	29[4]	7,955	29.6	32.8	51.5	15.7	32.8	32.2	29.0	6.0	Ecuador
...	...	...	16[3]	...	100[2]	335[4]	2,731	3.0	3.5	96.5	...	100.0	...	...	...	Egypt

Agriculture and land use (continued)

country	farms (latest census of agriculture)[a]										tenure (% of farms)					
	year	number of farms ('000)	size of holding								owner-operated			rented (including share-croppers)	tribal/ com-munal	other
			average (ha)	size class (%)												
				under 1 ha	1–5 ha	5–10 ha	10–20 ha	20–50 ha	50–200 ha	over 200 ha	individual/ family	corporate/ state	socialized/ collective			
El Salvador	1971	271	5.4	48.9	37.9	5.8	3.4	2.6	1.2	0.2	41.5	—	—	28.2	6.3	24.1
Equatorial Guinea	...	...	...	...	...	...	...	...	...	...	...	...	...	...	...	...
Ethiopia	1977	4,893	1.4	49.9	46.5	3.4	0.2	—	—	—	98.4	1.6	—	—	—	—
Faeroe Islands	...	...	...	...	...	...	...	...	...	...	...	...	...	...	...	...
Falkland Islands	1982	0,041	32,586[35]	—	—	—	—	—	—	100.0	—	75.0[35]	—	—	—	25.0[35]
Fiji	1979	66	4.2	64.3	20.6	8.1	3.7	2.1	—1.2—		—	—	—	3.5	95.1	1.4
Finland	1982	213	58.3	—	30.1	29.7	25.8	12.9	—1.5—			—87.1[36]—		12.9[36]	—	—
France	1980	1,263	26.6	9.5	18.8	13.2	19.3	27.5	—11.7—		65.2[11]	—	—	33.5[11]	—	1.2[11]
French Guiana	1981	2.2	3.3	50.0	42.0	4.0	—3.0—		—1.0—		...	...	...	...	...	...
French Polynesia	...	...	...	...	...	...	...	...	...	...	...	...	...	...	...	...
Gabon	1975	71	1.0	68.0	—32.0—		—	—	—	—	81.8	—	—	0.3	5.3	12.5
Gambia, The	...	...	...	...	...	...	...	...	...	...	...	...	...	...	...	...
Gaza Strip	1980	...	...	...	...	...	...	...	...	...	...	...	...	...	...	...
Germany, East	1980	6.6[38]	...	...	...	...	...	...	...	...	—	7.4	92.6	—	—	—
Germany, West	1983	887	13.6	16.0	26.4	15.4	18.8	19.5	3.9	—	39.5	—	—	6.7	—	53.8
Ghana	1970	805	3.2	36.6	48.7	9.0	3.9	1.8	—	—	...	...	...	...	...	...
Gibraltar	...	...	...	...	...	...	...	...	...	...	...	...	...	...	...	...
Greece	1978	950	3.4	25.4	54.2	14.8	4.5	1.1	0.1	—	...	...	...	...	...	...
Greenland	...	...	...	...	...	...	...	...	...	...	...	...	...	...	...	...
Grenada	1981	8	1.7	88.3[24]	6.9[40]	3.3[41]	0.7	0.4[14]	—0.3[42]—			—73.2—		14.1	—	12.7
Guadeloupe	1981	19	3.7	43.0[43]	51.6[43]	4.1[43]	0.8[43]	0.3[43]	0.2[43]	—	46.6[43]	—	—	19.1[43]	—	34.3[43]
Guam	1978	2	5.8	75.6	19.6	2.5	1.0	0.8	—0.5—		80.5	—	—	5.8	—	13.7
Guatemala	1979	600	6.8	39.7[44]	49.8[45]	8.2[46]	2.0[47]		—0.2[48]—			—74.0[49]—		6.3[49]	5.8[49]	13.9[49]
Guernsey	1985	0.125	16.0	6.7[38]	24.0[38]	23.1[38]	—46.1[38]—		—	—	32.3	—	—	23.1	—	44.6
Guinea	...	...	...	...	...	...	...	...	...	...	...	...	...	...	...	...
Guinea-Bissau	1961	87	3.0	13.4	73.3	10.0	3.0	0.3	—	—	...	...	...	...	...	...
Guyana	1964	...	...	...	...	...	...	...	...	...	...	90.0	...	...	...	10.0
Haiti	1971	617	1.4	58.7	37.5	—3.8—		—	—	—	...	...	...	...	...	...
Honduras	1974	195	13.5	17.3	46.6	14.5	9.8	7.8	3.3	0.8	99.7	0.1	—	—	0.2	—
Hong Kong	1979	...	...	...	...	...	...	...	...	...	...	...	...	...	...	...
Hungary	1981	798	8.3	...	...	...	...	...	...	...	6.8	13.3	74.5	—	—	—
Iceland	1981	7.0	...	15.7	9.3	11.7	23.7	35.8	—3.7—		...	...	...	...	...	...
India	1977	81,569	2.0	54.6	35.8	6.6	2.4	0.5	—0.1—		92.7	—	—	1.2	—	6.1
Indonesia[51]	1973	14,374	1.0	70.4	27.4	1.6	0.6	—	—	—	74.8	—	—	3.2	—	22.1
Iran	1973	...	...	...	...	...	...	...	...	...	...	...	...	...	...	...
Iraq	1971	591	9.7	20.2	29.3	21.4	18.5	9.0	1.3	0.3	52.5	—	—	40.9	—	6.6
Ireland	1980	279[22]	25.0	2.7[22]	—37.8[22]—		—52.4[22]—		7.1[22]	—	...	...	...	...	...	...
Isle of Man	1983	0.8	59.3	26.3[52]	13.0[53]	18.1[14]	24.6[15]	—18.0[16]—		—	60.0[12]	...	...	...	...	40.0[12]
Israel	1984	40[11]	13.4[11]	25.9[11, 51]	62.5[11, 51]	8.1[11, 51]	—3.5[11, 51]—		—	—	77.5[11]	—	1.8[11]	—	—	20.7[11]
Italy	1983	3,271	7.2	18.0[35]	30.2[35]	37.7[35]	3.1[35]	9.2[35]	1.8[35]	—	81.5[22]	—	—	6.7[22]	—	11.8[22]
Jamaica	1979	184	2.9	32.5[54]	60.7[55]	4.8[41]	0.9	0.4[14]	0.3[15]	0.4[16]	99.5[56]	0.2[56]	—[56]	—[56]	—[56]	0.3[56]
Japan	1984	4,473	1.2	68.6	21.9[57]	—9.5[25]—					79.4[22]	...	...	...	...	20.6[22]
Jersey	1984	0.7	9.0	—44.4—		20.6	22.1	—13.0—			31.4[58]	—	—	68.6[58]	—	—
Jordan	1975	56	6.8	...	...	...	...	...	...	...	70.9	0.5	—	19.9	0.1	8.6
Kampuchea	...	...	...	...	...	...	...	...	...	...	...	...	...	...	...	...
Kenya	1975	1,487	4.1	31.8	58.1	9.9	—	—	0.1	0.1	...	...	...	...	...	...
Kiribati	...	...	...	...	...	...	...	...	...	...	...	...	...	...	...	...
Korea, North	...	...	...	...	...	...	...	...	...	...	...	...	...	...	...	...
Korea, South	1983	2,000	1.1	66.2	—33.8—			—	—	—	82.5[22]	—	—	17.4[22]	—	0.1[22]
Kuwait	1970	0.4	6.1	48.6	25.4	10.2	8.7	4.0	3.1	—	72.6	0.5	—	26.7	0.2	—
Laos	...	...	...	...	...	...	...	...	...	...	...	...	...	...	...	...
Lebanon	1970	143	4.3	47.7	—44.5—		—6.5—		1.2	0.1	...	...	...	...	...	...
Lesotho	1970	187	2.0	27.0	67.5	—5.5—		—	—	—	...	...	...	...	...	...
Liberia[63]	1971	122	3.0	52.8	31.0	12.0	—3.7—		—0.5—		40.0[9]	—	—	—	43.3[9]	16.7[9]
Libya	1977	170	11.0	5.0[64]	—40.0[64]—		—42.0[64, 65]—		—13.0[64, 66]—		...	...	...	...	...	...
Liechtenstein	1980	0.5	8.0	27.5	30.4	16.2	14.2	10.5	1.2	—	86.2	—	—	13.6	—	0.2
Luxembourg	1984	4.5	28	—25.4—		9.2	12.3	31.9	—21.2—		52.2[9]	—1.0[9]—		46.8[9]	—	—
Macau	...	...	...	...	...	...	...	...	...	...	...	...	...	...	...	...
Madagascar	1971	940	1.0	65.0	35.0	—	—	—	—	—	...	...	...	...	...	...
Malaŵi	1981	1,136	1.2	54.9	45.1	—	—	—	—	—	...	...	...	...	...	...
Malaysia[67]	1980	920[68]	2.2[68, 69]	...	...	...	...	...	...	...	53.2[22, 68]	18.2[22, 70]	...	19.6[22, 68]	...	9.0[22, 68]
Maldives[72]	1983	174	0.3	—7.5[73]—		4.0[41]	8.0	48.3[14]	—32.2[42]—		...	...	...	...	...	...
Mali	1980	481	4.0	19.2	55.2	18.2	—7.5—			—	94.2[9, 74]	1.7[9]	—	...	4.1[9]	—
Malta	1983	4.4[75]	3.0[75]	38.7[75]	53.3[75]	6.9[75]	1.1	—	—	—	29.6	—	—	70.4	—	—
Martinique	1981	19.6	3.1	67.5	26.4	3.4	—2.1—		—0.6—		...	...	...	...	...	...
Mauritania	...	...	...	...	...	...	...	...	...	...	...	...	...	...	...	...
Mauritius	1980	32.5	1.1	61.3	36.2	1.9	0.3	0.2	—0.1—		95.8	—	—	4.2	—	—
Mayotte	1978	4.8	1.7	...	...	...	...	...	...	...	...	...	...	...	...	...
Mexico	1970	1,020	137	33.5	26.2	10.0	6.7	9.2	8.1	6.3	97.6[76]	0.2	—	—	2.2[76]	—
Monaco	...	...	...	...	...	...	...	...	...	...	...	...	...	...	...	...
Mongolia	1983	0.3	...	...	...	...	...	...	...	...	—	19.6[36, 77]	80.4[36, 77]	—	—	—
Montserrat	1979	0.8	1.2	62.5[54]	28.0[78]	—9.5[25]—					14.6	—	—	84.4	—	1.0
Morocco	1982	1,900[59]	3.9[59]	—75.0[59]—		—25.0[59]—					...	...	...	...	...	...
Mozambique	1973	1,605	3.1	—89.7[80]—		—10.0[81]—			—0.3—		0.2	0.1	—	—	99.7	—
Nauru	...	...	...	...	...	...	...	...	...	...	...	...	...	...	...	...
Nepal	1982	2,194	1.1	66.7	29.9	2.7	—0.7—				97.5	...	...	1.6	...	0.9
Netherlands, The	1984	138	14.6	11.0	21.5	17.2	24.2	22.9	—3.2—		—47.0[82]—		—	12.9[82]	—	40.1[82]
Netherlands Antilles	...	...	...	...	...	...	...	...	...	...	...	...	...	...	...	...
New Caledonia[51]	1976	2.3	145	2.3	9.0	11.3	22.6	25.4	17.8	11.7	45.7	...	...	...	...	...
New Zealand	1983	76	281	2.3	9.2	9.5	8.1	15.2	32.7	23.0	86.1	10.5	—	—	—	3.4
Nicaragua	...	...	...	...	...	...	...	...	...	...	...	...	...	...	...	...
Niger	1980[83]	699	4.9	3.8	54.1	37.8	—4.3—				...	...	...	...	...	...
Nigeria	1971	...	...	92	7.8	0.2	—	—	—	—	...	...	...	...	...	...
Niue	...	...	...	...	...	...	...	...	...	...	...	...	...	...	...	...
Norfolk Island	...	...	...	...	...	...	...	...	...	...	...	...	...	...	...	...

							farm land use									country
activity (% of farms)			technology (% of farms using)				land in farms		land use (%)							
mainly crops	mainly livestock	mixed/other	tractor	electricity	irrigation works	artificial fertilizer (kg/ha)	total ('000 ha)	% of total land area	cropland				meadows and pastures	woodland and forest	other[b]	
									permanent crops	temporary crops	fallow	total cropland				
95.3	4.7	—	5[3]	...	15[2]	83[4]	1,452	69.0	25.1	58.6	16.4	44.9	38.2	11.6	5.3	El Salvador
...	...	...	...	...	...	...	...	...	...	...	...	...	...	...	...	Equatorial Guinea
...	...	...	...	...	...	3[4]	6,971	5.7	7.4	76.8	15.8	86.9	9.1	—	4.0	Ethiopia
...	...	...	...	...	...	...	...	...	...	...	...	...	...	...	...	Faeroe Islands
...	...	...	...	...	...	...	1,173[35]	96.4[35]	...	...	...	...	...	...	...	Falkland Islands
...	...	...	7[3]	...	...	58[4]	277	15.2	...	...	...	...	...	...	...	Fiji
...	...	...	96[3]	100.0[22]	3[2]	224[4]	12,800	37.8	0.3[22]	97.6[22]	2.1[22]	19.6	1.1	58.1	21.2	Finland
...	...	...	74.8	...	6[2]	299[4]	33,649	61.8	7.4	90.6	2.0	53.6	34.1	8.2	4.1	France
...	...	...	37[3]	...	...	217[4]	7.3	0.1	10.4	52.5	37.3	89.6	10.4	...	...	French Guiana
...	...	...	2[3]	...	...	13[4]	...	...	...	...	...	...	...	...	...	French Polynesia
...	...	...	3[3]	...	...	1[4]	73.0	0.3	...	...	...	...	...	...	...	Gabon
...	...	...	...	...	21[2]	16[4]	...	...	...	...	...	...	...	...	...	Gambia, The
...	...	...	16[3]	...	52.8[37]	...	19.3	53.2	74.6	25.4	...	100.0	...	...	...	Gaza Strip
33.1	66.9	—	30[3]	...	3[2]	281[4]	6,280	...	...	...	...	74.1[38]	22.3[38]	...	3.6[38]	Germany, East
...	...	...	197[3]	...	4[2]	435[4]	12,026	48.4	1.2[39]	—97.8[39]—		51.7[39]	32.6[39]	11.5[39]	4.2[39]	Germany, West
...	...	...	1[3]	...	1[2]	10[4]	2,574	10.8	61.4	38.6	—	100.0	...	...	...	Ghana
...	...	...	...	...	...	...	...	...	...	...	...	...	...	...	...	Gibraltar
...	...	...	40[3]	...	25[2]	161[4]	3,227	24.5	23.9[11]	63.7[11]	12.1[11]	93.4	5.7	0.3	0.5	Greece
...	...	...	...	...	...	...	...	...	...	...	...	...	...	...	...	Greenland
...	...	...	2[3]	...	...	...	13.9	40.2	...	...	...	...	...	...	...	Grenada
...	...	...	3.2	...	5[2]	255	70	39.6	23.0	73.3	3.7	56.2	25.2	7.6	11.0	Guadeloupe
60.6	18.1	21.3	7[3]	88.4	...	...	11.6	20.5	—94.8—		5.2	49.5	41.2	—	9.3	Guam
...	...	...	2[3]	...	4[2]	50[4]	4,147	38.1	27.6	—72.4—		42.0	27.3	27.2	3.4	Guatemala
—	100.0	—	...	...	...	...	2	40.0	—	100.0	—	10.6	89.4	—	—	Guernsey
...	...	...	...	...	1[2]	2[4]	...	...	...	...	...	...	...	...	...	Guinea
...	...	...	...	...	...	3[4]	169	4.7	...	...	...	...	...	...	...	Guinea-Bissau
...	...	...	7[3]	...	25[2]	17[4]	10,652	26.2	...	...	...	8.4	91.6	...	...	Guyana
...	...	...	1[3]	...	8[2]	5[4]	1,579	57.0	...	...	...	54.4	33.3	12.3	—	Haiti
...	...	...	2[3]	...	5[2]	14[4]	2,630	23.5	15.4[39]	34.6[39]	50.0[39]	52.0[39]	48.0[39]	—	—	Honduras
...	...	...	1[3]	...	38[2]	...	8.2	7.9	7.0	43.0	50.0	100.0	...	...	...	Hong Kong
...	...	...	10[3]	...	3[2]	288[4]	7,413	79.7	11.8	86.1	2.1	71.7	17.3	...	11.0	Hungary
...	...	...	1,725[3]	87.0[29]	...	3,738[4]	...	...	...	...	...	...	...	...	...	Iceland
...	...	...	3[3]	...	24[2]	35[4]	163,343	49.7	—88.3—		11.7	96.0[50]	1.5[50]	—2.5[50]—		India
86.8	—	13.2	1[3]	...	28[2]	78[4]	14,168	7.4	21.6	71.1	7.3	89.5	0.6	1.4	8.5	Indonesia[51]
...	...	...	5[3]	...	25[2]	65[4]	20,235	12.3	...	...	...	...	...	...	...	Iran
87.9	11.2	0.8	5[3]	...	32[2]	15[4]	5,732	13.1	3.0	62.4	34.6	87.2	0.7	0.2	11.9	Iraq
...	...	...	150[3]	...	...	644[4]	5,790	84.0	0.5	99.5	...	8.0	60.1	—31.8—		Ireland
...	...	...	...	...	...	...	47	83.0	2.1	84.2	13.7	12.3	87.7	—	—	Isle of Man
43.1[11, 51]	30.2[11, 51]	26.7[11, 51]	64[3]	...	49[2]	178[4]	584	28.2	22.0	78.0	...	70.5	...	...	29.6	Israel
...	...	...	92[3]	...	25.7	161[4]	17,249	57.2	26.3[35]	73.7[35]	...	52.4[35]	21.2[35]	17.1[35]	9.3[35]	Italy
...	...	...	11[3]	...	12[2]	57[4]	603[56]	54.8[56]	22.2[56]	72.2[56]	5.6[56]	41.3[56]	21.6[56]	13.5[56]	23.6[56]	Jamaica
80.8[19]	—19.2[19]—		316[3]	...	67[2]	411[4]	4,996[36]	13.2[36]	10.9[36]	84.8[36]	4.3[36]	86.4[36]	13.6[36]	...	...	Japan
85.1[59]	14.9[59]	—	...	...	...	...	6.7[59]	5.8[59]	—	100.0[59]	—	64.6[59]	34.7[59]	—	0.7[59]	Jersey
58.2[60]	14.9[60]	26.9[60]	11[3]	...	9[2]	35[4]	390	4.0	8.8	64.9	26.3	80.6	0.8	0.3	18.3	Jordan
...	...	...	...	...	3[2]	4[4]	...	...	...	...	...	...	...	...	...	Kampuchea
47.0[61]	53.0[61]	—	3[3]	...	2[2]	29[4]	6,132	10.8	29.4[61]	56.0[61]	14.6[61]	20.2[61]	70.7[61]	4.7[61]	4.4[61]	Kenya
...	...	...	...	...	...	...	...	...	...	...	...	...	...	...	...	Kiribati
...	...	...	14[3]	...	47[2]	338[4]	...	...	...	...	...	...	...	...	...	Korea, North
94.0[56]	0.4[56]	5.6[56]	0.4	10.3[62]	54[2]	282[4]	2,026[36]	20.4[36]	6.0[36]	—94.0[36]—		98.3[36]	1.7[36]	...	...	Korea, South
56.3	20.7	23.0	26[3]	...	100[2]	732[4]	2.7	0.2	7.5	92.5	—	23.6	—	1.4	75.0	Kuwait
...	...	...	1[3]	13[2]	13[2]	5[4]	...	...	...	...	...	...	...	...	...	Laos
77.0[60]	8.1[60]	14.9[60]	10[3]	...	29[2]	149[4]	275[36]	27.0[36]	36.7[36]	39.7[36]	23.6[36]	100.0[36]	—	—	—	Lebanon
5.3[60]	93.3[60]	1.4[60]	5[3]	...	...	15[4]	372	12.3	—	89.6	10.4	98.8	—	—	1.2	Lesotho
...	...	...	1[3]	...	1[2]	4[4]	370[12]	3.8[12]	66.2[12]	33.8[12]	—	98.3[12]	—	1.7[12]	—	Liberia[63]
...	...	...	8[3]	...	11[2]	38[4]	8,800[12]	5.1[12]	—33.3[12]—		66.7[12]	20.5[12]	79.5[12]	—	—	Libya
20.9	68.8	10.3	113[3]	...	...	...	3.9	24.3	1.8	—98.2—		26.1	58.3	14.1	1.5	Liechtenstein
...	...	...	164[3]	...	...	18	128	49.5	2.5	97.0	0.5	45.0	55.0	—	—	Luxembourg
...	...	...	...	...	...	...	...	...	...	...	...	...	...	...	...	Macau
...	...	...	1[3]	...	16[2]	5[4]	2,200[26]	3.8[26]	19.0[26]	81.0[26]	—	100.0[26]	—	—	—	Madagascar
22.1	...	77.9	1[3]	...	0.2[37]	14[4]	1,332	14.2	0.2	99.8	—	94.8	—	5.2	—	Malaŵi
...	...	...	2[3, 71]	...	9[2, 71]	102[4, 71]	4,100[58]	31.2[58]	84.8[58]	15.2[58]	—	100.0[58]	—	—	—	Malaysia[67]
...	...	...	...	...	...	...	...	...	...	...	...	...	...	...	...	Maldives[72]
...	...	...	...	...	6[2]	3[4]	41,500	34.0	—	18.0	82.0	28.0	72.0	—	—	Mali
...	...	...	31[3]	...	7[2]	26[4]	10.9	34.1	4.2	85.0	10.8	100.0	—	—	—	Malta
...	...	...	46[3]	...	26[2]	570[4]	75.4	71.1	39.6	60.0	0.4	36.9	33.6	10.0	19.5	Martinique
...	...	...	1[3]	...	4[2]	...	167[26]	0.2[26]	—	—	—	100.0[26]	—	—	—	Mauritiania
...	...	...	3[3]	...	15[2]	240[4]	97.8[59]	52.5[59]	3.3[39]	96.7[39]	—	100.0[39]	—	—	—	Mauritius
...	...	...	...	...	...	...	8.0	21.0	...	...	...	...	...	...	...	Mayotte
66.4[60]	25.0[60]	8.6[60]	7[3]	...	22[2]	78[4]	139,868	72.7	6.3	58.1	35.6	16.5	53.3	14.2	16.0	Mexico
...	...	...	...	...	...	...	...	...	...	...	...	...	...	...	...	Monaco
...	...	...	8[3]	...	3[2]	11[4]	124,977	79.9	—	53.0	47.0	2.0	98.0	—	—	Mongolia
...	...	...	7[3]	...	...	...	1.6[79]	15.3[79]	32.1[79]	67.9[79]	—	46.9[79]	53.1[79]	—	—	Montserrat
...	...	...	3[3]	...	6[2]	25[4]	8,248.9	18.0	6.1	62.3	31.6	100.0	—	—	—	Morocco
...	...	...	2[3]	...	2[2]	13[4]	13,626	17.8	—44.9—		55.1	55.0	45.0	—	—	Mozambique
...	...	...	...	...	...	...	...	...	...	...	...	...	...	...	...	Nauru
...	...	...	1[3]	...	39	16	2,683[79]	18.2[79]	1.3	97.1	1.6	94.0	1.7	0.6	3.7	Nepal
33.7	62.3	4.0	215[3]	...	58[2]	738[4]	2,016	48.6	13.0	86.5	0.5	41.5	58.5	—	—	Netherlands, The
...	...	...	15[3, 10]	...	...	...	...	...	...	...	...	...	...	...	...	Netherlands Antilles
...	...	...	108[3]	...	...	70[4]	333	17.8	...	...	...	...	...	...	...	New Caledonia[51]
16.0	72.1	11.9	214[3]	...	7.2[43]	21[58]	21,266	79.3	...	...	...	47.7[58]	21.3[58]	4.5[58]	26.5[58]	New Zealand
...	...	...	2[3]	...	7[2]	19[4]	...	...	...	...	...	...	...	...	...	Nicaragua
...	...	...	...	...	1[2]	1[4]	3,407	2.9	...	...	...	...	...	...	...	Niger
...	...	...	...	...	...	7[4]	34,290	37	—20.0—		80.0	31.4	27.5	41.1	—	Nigeria
...	...	...	1[3]	...	...	...	...	...	...	...	...	...	...	...	...	Niue
...	...	...	...	...	...	...	...	...	...	...	...	...	...	...	...	Norfolk Island

Agriculture and land use (continued)

country	farms (latest census of agriculture)[a]															
	year	number of farms ('000)	size of holding								tenure (% of farms)					
			average (ha)	size class (%)							owner-operated			rented (including share-croppers)	tribal/ com-munal	other
				under 1 ha	1–5 ha	5–10 ha	10–20 ha	20–50 ha	50–200 ha	over 200 ha	individual/ family	corporate/ state	socialized/ collective			
Norway	1984	107	8.9	13.8[24]	27.0[84]	27.5	22.7		—9.0—		97.4[9, 39]	1.8[9, 39]	—	—	—	0.8[9, 39]
Oman	1979	65	1.3	...	...	...	...	...	...	...	...	...	...	...	...	...
Pacific Is., Trust Terr. of	1970	4.0	10.3	7.4	53.4	22.4	7.8	5.5	3.6	—	90.8	—	—	1.4	—	7.8
Marshall Islands	...	...	...	...	...	...	...	...	...	...	...	...	...	...	...	...
Micronesia, F.S. of	...	...	...	...	...	...	...	...	...	...	...	...	...	...	...	...
Northern Mariana Is.	1980	0.3	16.5	32.8[24]	34.1[40]			—33.1[19]—			75.6	...	...	12.4	...	12.0
Palau	...	...	...	...	...	...	...	...	...	...	...	...	...	...	...	...
Pakistan	1980	4,070	4.7	17.2	56.2	17.4	6.5		—2.7—		64.1[9]	0.3[9]	—	35.6[9]	—	—
Panama	1980	153	14.7	41.0	25.0	9.3	9.0	9.0	5.6	1.0	23.2	—	—	2.0	—	74.8[21]
Papua New Guinea	1981	0.9	442			—25.7—			29.6	44.7	26.5[9]	70.6[9]	—	2.9[9]	—	—
Paraguay	1981	249	86	8.9	27.9	18.5	23.0	14.6	4.6	2.5	93.5[9]	0.1[9]	—	1.8[9]	—	4.6[9]
Peru	1972	1,391	16.9	34.7	43.3	11.0	5.7	3.3	1.4	0.6	62.2	—	—	8.6	4.8	24.4
Philippines	1980	3,439	2.6	13.6[11]	71.2[11]	10.4[11]	2.9[11]	1.8[11]	0.2[11]	—	58.0[11]	—	—	26.3[11]	—	15.8[11]
Pitcairn Island	...	...	...	...	...	...	...	...	...	...	...	...	...	...	...	...
Poland	1983	3,958	4.8	—58.6—		25.5		—15.8—		0.1	71.4[9]	—	28.6[9]	—	—	—
Portugal	1979	784	6.6	44.5	41.9	7.7	3.3	1.5	0.7	0.4	68.1	—	—	8.7	—	23.2
Puerto Rico	1978	32	13.4	5.3[5]	28.0[85]	20.4	20.3	12.8	10.8	2.5	83.0	—	—	5.0	—	11.9
Qatar	1983	0.8	42.5		—79.1[36, 86]—				—20.9[36, 87]—		...	...	...	...	...	...
Réunion	1981	21	3.6	50.9	41.6	5.3	—1.8—		—0.3—		46.1[88]	—	—	22.5[88]	—	31.4[88]
Romania	1982	5.0[89]	2,814[89]	...	...	...	...	...	...	...	9.4[9]	30.0[9]	60.6[9]	—	—	—
Rwanda	1979	104	9.5	...	...	...	...	...	...	...	...	...	—	...	...	...
St. Christopher	1981	...	...	...	...	...	...	...	...	...	46.8[9]	48.0[9]	—	5.2[9]	—	—
St. Helena	1983	...	...	...	...	...	...	...	...	...	—	—	—	100.0	—	—
St. Lucia	1974	11	2.7	47.8[54]	44.9[55]	4.3[41]	1.8	0.5[14]	0.2[15]	0.8[16]	69.1	—	—	18.3	—	12.6
St. Pierre and Miquelon	...	...	...	...	...	...	...	...	...	...	...	...	...	...	...	...
St. Vincent	1983	...	...	...	...	...	...	...	...	...	...	...	...	...	...	...
San Marino	1975	0.7	7.0	21.3	47.8	—24.7—		5.1	—1.1—		39.9[9]	15.5[9]	—	29.9[9]	—	14.7[9]
São Tomé and Príncipe	1964	11.1	8.7	88.5	9.8	0.7	0.2	0.2	0.2	0.4	77.2	—	—	20.5	—	2.3
Saudi Arabia	1983	212	10.1	36.6	35.8	11.3	8.2	5.0	2.6	0.5	85.9	—	—	2.6	—	11.5
Senegal	1976	362	7.0			—99.4—			—0.6—		...	...	0.6	...	...	99.4
Seychelles	1977	4.9	1.5	...	...	...	...	...	...	...	...	...	...	...	...	...
Sierra Leone	1971	286	1.8	38.8	55.0	—6.1—			—0.1—		93.6	—	—	6.4	—	—
Singapore	1973	16	0.8	77.4	22.2	0.3			—0.1—		7.4	—	—	88.8	—	3.8
Solomon Islands	1975[68]	92	1.0	...	...	...	...	...	...	...	—	—	—	—	100.0	—
Somalia	...	...	...	...	...	...	...	...	...	...	...	...	...	...	...	...
South Africa	1978	72	1,193	...	...	...	...	...	...	...	...	...	...	...	...	...
Bophuthatswana	1976	...	...	...	...	...	...	...	...	...	...	...	...	...	...	...
Ciskei	1978	...	...	...	...	...	...	...	...	...	...	...	...	...	...	...
Transkei	1976	...	...	...	...	...	...	...	...	...	...	...	...	...	...	...
Venda	1976	53.3	9.3	...	...	...	...	...	...	...	...	...	...	...	...	...
S.W. Africa/ Namibia	1983	...	...	...	...	...	...	...	...	...	...	...	...	...	...	...
Spain	1982	2,375	18.7	26.4	37.1	14.0	10.2	7.1	3.9	1.3	75.4	...	...	4.0	—	20.6
Sri Lanka	1982	1,817	1.1	77.5[5]	—22.2[90]—		0.1[91]	0.1[14]	—0.1[92]—		77.1[88]	6.4[88]	0.1[88]	14.4[88]	—	2.0[88]
Sudan, The	1982	...	...	...	...	...	...	...	...	...	22.3	2.2	—	28.0	42.0	5.5
Suriname	1981	22	7.5	21.9[56]	61.2[56]	11.1[56]	3.6[56]	1.6[56]	0.3[56]	0.3[56]	20.2[56]	0.9[56]	—	49.5[56]	—	29.4[56]
Swaziland	1972	39	19.5	26.2	60.4			—12.0—		1.4	86.1	—	—	3.4	—	10.5
Sweden	1984	112[93]	26.3[93]	...	16.7[84, 93]	20.6[93]	22.8[93]	27.2[93]	—12.7[93]—		48.0[93]	—	—	16.1[93]	—	35.9[93]
Switzerland	1980	125	10.2	21.6	20.4	16.1	27.7	13.4	0.8	—	36.2	—	0.8	58.5	—	4.5
Syria	1981	485	11.5		—51.0[86]—			—42.0[94]—	6.2[95]	0.8[96]	99.2[74]	—	0.8	...	—	—
Taiwan	1983	808	1.1		—98.0[80]—			—2.0[97]—			93.5	—	—	6.5	—	—
Tanzania	1972	2,489	3.0	59.7	37.7	2.1	0.4	—0.1—		0.2	87.3	—	—	3.6	—	9.1
Thailand	1983	4,471	3.6	14.7	70.2[98]			—15.1[99]—			72.4	—	—	5.5	—	22.1
Togo	1983	263	1.5	48.8	38.6[100]			—12.7[97]—			70.7[9]	—	—	21.1[9]	8.2[9]	—
Tokelau	...	...	...	...	...	...	...	...	...	...	...	...	...	...	...	...
Tonga	1976	9.1	7.6	0.7	37.7			—1.6—			8.4	8.4	—	83.2	—	—
Trinidad and Tobago	1982	30.6	4.3		—93.3[101]—				—6.7[101]—		52.1	—	—	36.5	—	11.4
Tunisia	1983	...	...	...	...	...	...	...	...	...	...	...	...	...	...	...
Turkey	1980	3,651	6.2	15.8	46.3	20.2	11.6	5.3	0.8	—	88.6	—	—	12.1	—	1.2
Turks and Caicos Is.	...	...	...	...	...	...	...	...	...	...	...	...	...	...	...	...
Tuvalu	1976	1.5	1.7	...	...	...	...	...	...	...	99.9	...	...	...	0.1	—
Uganda	1964	1,171	3.9	20.7	59.8	11.2		—8.3—			97.4	—	—	—	—	2.6
U.S.S.R.	1984	48.2[89]	11,558[89]	—	—	—	—	—	—	100.0[89]	—	46.1	53.9	—	—	[102]
United Arab Emirates	1980	3.1[103]	5.1[103]	...	...	...	...	...	...	...	...	...	...	...	...	...
United Kingdom	1984	258	72.5	5.1[24]	7.3[84]	13.0	17.0	25.8	26.0	5.8	—69.4[104]—		—	30.6[104]	—	—
United States	1982	2,241	180.0	—8.4[55]—		—20.0[7]—		31.8[105]	23.5[106]	16.3[107]	—88.4—		—	11.6	—	—
Uruguay	1980	68	234.4	—	12.2	14.4	14.6	16.6	21.0	21.2	—59.1—		—	17.3	—	23.6
Vanuatu	1980	...	...	...	...	...	...	...	...	...	65.3	34.7	—	...	...	...
Venezuela	1971	288	91.9	5.8	37.7	17.2	14.4	11.3	7.9	5.7	61.5	...	—	6.1	...	31.3[21]
Vietnam	1983	...	...	...	...	...	...	...	...	...	...	...	...	...	...	...
Virgin Islands (U.S.)	1978	0.4	26.1	24.1[5]	41.8[85]	15.1	5.3	5.6	6.0	2.1	84.7	...	—	7.4	—	7.9
Wallis and Futuna	1983	...	...	...	...	...	...	...	...	...	...	...	...	...	...	...
West Bank	1980	...	...	...	...	...	...	...	...	...	...	...	...	...	...	...
Western Sahara	1983	...	...	...	...	...	...	...	...	...	...	...	...	...	...	...
Western Samoa	1975	...	...	...	...	...	...	...	...	...	...	...	...	...	86.0	14.0
Yemen (Aden)	1977	0.08[89]	604[89]	...	...	...	...	...	...	...	...	44.3[89]	55.7[89]	...	...	...
Yemen (Ṣan'ā')	1977–83	591	2.3	57.5	30.9	7.4	3.3	0.8	—0.1—		90.3[9]	—	—	9.4[9]	—	0.3[9]
Yugoslavia	1969	2,600	4.8	21.4	52.8	19.9	4.9	0.9	—0.1—		99.9	—	0.1	...	...	...
Zaire	1970	2,538	2.3	41.6	57.3	1.0	0.2	—	—	—	4.2	0.1	—	...	95.6	0.1
Zambia	1971	768	3.1	50.5	45.2	—3.8—			—0.5—		...	...	...	...	...	...
Zimbabwe	1974	765	38.7		—16.7[109]—		52.8[110]	29.8[111]	—0.7[66]—		—2.0—		—	—	98.0	—

[1]1967. [2]Irrigated land as percentage of area of arable land, not percentage of number of farms; 1982. [3]Tractors per 1,000 hectares of arable land; 1982. [4]Kilograms per hectare of arable land; 1982. [5]Less than 1.2 hectares. [6]1.2 to 4.0 hectares. [7]4.0 to 20 hectares. [8]20 hectares or more. [9]Based on area, not number of holdings. [10]Netherlands Antilles includes Aruba. [11]1971. [12]1981. [13]Excludes holdings without land. [14]20 to 40 hectares. [15]40 to 81 hectares. [16]81 hectares or more. [17]1977. [18]Belgium includes Luxembourg. [19]4.0 hectares or more. [20]Family farms only. [21]Almost all squatters. [22]1970. [23]Government agro-industrial complexes. [24]Less than 2.0 hectares. [25]2.0 hectares or more. [26]1976. [27]1.2 to 10 hectares. [28]Irrigated land only. [29]1968. [30]Livestock only. [31]Less than 0.5 hectare. [32]0.5 to 50 hectares. [33]50 to 1,000 hectares. [34]1,000 hectares or more. [35]1975. [36]1980. [37]Irrigated land as percentage of all farmland. [38]1974. [39]1979. [40]2.0 to 4.0 hectares. [41]4.0 to 10 hectares. [42]40 hectares or more. [43]1972. [44]Less than 0.7 hectare. [45]0.7 to 7.1 hectares. [46]7.1 to 45 hectares. [47]45 to 452 hectares. [48]452 hectares or more. [49]Excludes holdings of 0.04 hectare (400 square metres) or less. [50]Excludes state of Punjab. [51]Does not inlcude estates, collective farms, or traditional farms. [52]Less than 8.0 hectares. [53]8.0 to 20 hectares. [54]Less than 0.4 hectare. [55]0.4 to 4.0 hectares. [56]1969. [57]1.0 to 2.0 hectares. [58]1982. [59]1978. [60]Farms producing mainly for cash sales. [61]3,217 large farms only, occupying 2,673,000 hectares; 1981.

activity (% of farms)			technology (% of farms using)				farm land use: land in farms		land use (%): cropland							country
mainly crops	mainly live-stock	mixed/other	tractor	electri-city	irriga-tion works	artificial fertilizer (kg/ha)	total ('000 ha)	% of total land area	perma-nent crops	tempo-rary crops	fallow	total crop-land	mead-ows and pastures	wood-land and forest	other[b]	
...	...	...	166[3]	...	10[2]	210	954	2.9	...	...	...	42.5[39]	—57.5[39]—			Norway
...	...	...	4[3]	...	93[2]	27[4]	83	0.3	68.6	31.4	—	49.2	—50.8—			Oman
...	...	...	1[3]	...	...	...	40	21.1	54.2	9.8	36.0	68.7	17.5	—	13.7	Pacific Is., Trust Terr. of
...	...	...	...	...	...	...	...	...	...	...	...	...	...	...	...	Marshall Islands
...	...	...	...	...	...	...	...	...	...	...	...	...	...	...	...	Micronesia, F.S. of
...	...	...	...	...	...	...	...	...	...	...	...	...	...	...	...	Northern Mariana Is.
...	...	...	...	...	...	...	...	...	...	...	...	...	...	...	...	Palau
...	...	...	35.8	...	32.4	65[58]	19,109	24.0	—83.7—		16.3	93.8	—	0.6	5.6	Pakistan
...	...	...	3.9[11]	0.5[11]	5[2]	47[4]	2,259	29.3	21.6	43.3	35.0	24.6	57.4	15.6	2.4	Panama
...	...	...	4[3]	...	...	13[58]	395	0.9	96.6	3.4	—	33.5	25.6	—	40.9	Papua New Guinea
33.0	—67.0—		2[3]	...	3[2]	4[4]	21,426	52.7	...	...	...	...	...	...	...	Paraguay
...	...	...	5.4	0.2	34[2]	27[4]	23,545	18.3	8.5	70.3	21.2	14.6	65.5	13.1	6.7	Peru
86.7[11]	1.6[11]	11.7[11]	4.0[11]	...	21.2[11]	38[58]	9,034	30.1	35.3[11]	54.2[11]	10.5[11]	86.3	6.8	—6.9—		Philippines
...	...	...	...	...	...	...	...	...	...	...	...	...	...	...	...	Pitcairn Island
...	...	...	48[3]	...	1[2]	215[4]	18,985	60.7	1.6	—98.4—		86.1	13.3	—0.6—		Poland
...	...	...	58	...	79	73[4]	5,183	56.1	26.1	44.6	29.3	52.6	3.2	34.5	9.7	Portugal
...	...	...	26[3]	...	30[2]	273[4]	426	48.1	...	...	...	55.6	25.5	13.5	5.4	Puerto Rico
99.7	0.3	—	...	...	100.0	...	34	3.0	33.0	67.0	—	100.0	—	—	—	Qatar
...	...	...	3.0	...	15.6[37,88]	163[4]	74	29.1	5.0	86.3	8.7	61.2	11.6	13.8	13.4	Réunion
...	...	...	16[3]	...	13.1[37]	159[4]	14,993[79]	63.1[79]	6.2	92.5	1.3	70.3	29.7	—	—	Romania
...	...	...	...	...	0.2[37]	1[4]	1,460	57.1	30.7	—69.3—		67.7	32.3	—	—	Rwanda
...	...	...	15[3]	...	...	171[4]	12	45.3	31.5	—68.5—		58.1	—41.9—			St. Christopher
...	...	...	3[3]	...	—	...	4.0	12.9	—	—100.0—		50.0	50.0	—	—	St. Helena
25.0	—75.0—		2[3]	...	5.8	95[4]	29	47.3	68.5	—31.5—		57.9	10.2	26.4	5.5	St. Lucia
...	...	...	...	...	...	...	...	...	...	...	...	...	...	...	...	St. Pierre and Miquelon
...	...	...	4[3]	...	4.4[37]	229[4]	11	28.8	75.0	—25.0—		82.1	17.9	—	—	St. Vincent
...	...	...	...	...	...	...	4.7	76.5	60.9	6.5	32.6	69.2	6.2	8.2	16.4	San Marino
...	...	...	3[3]	...	6.2[37]	...	96	100.0	99.4	—0.6—		38.3	—	59.7	2.0	São Tomé and Príncipe
...	...	...	60.3	...	43.8	83[4]	2,135	1.0	4.1	18.7	77.2	88.5	—11.5—			Saudi Arabia
...	...	...	...	...	5.9[37]	4[4]	11,338	59.1	0.1	—99.9—		22.4	77.6	—	—	Senegal
1.8	32.4	65.8	6[3]	...	...	149[4]	7.5	27.8	89.6	—10.4—		100.0	—	—	—	Seychelles
50.3	—49.7—		...	...	0.4[37]	1[4]	2,732	38.1	20.7	—79.3—		19.3	80.7	—	—	Sierra Leone
12.5	6.2	81.3	1.4	...	100.0	417[58]	5.6[79]	9.0[79]	75.0	25.0	—	66.7	—	33.3	—	Singapore
43.4	—56.6—		...	...	...	...	93	3.4	40.0	45.2	14.8	100.0	—	—	—	Solomon Islands
...	...	...	2[3]	...	15[2]	1[4]	...	...	...	...	...	...	...	...	...	Somalia
...	...	...	13[3]	...	12.4	83[4]	85,447	70.2	5.9	—94.1—		11.9	79.7	1.3	7.1	South Africa
...	...	...	...	...	1.1[37]	...	3,839	94.8	...	87.1	...	2.4	97.6	—	—	Bophuthatswana
...	...	...	...	...	0.3[37]	...	598	63.5	...	51.3	...	12.6	87.4	—	—	Ciskei
...	...	...	...	...	2.8[37]	...	622	14.9	...	...	...	100.0	...	...	...	Transkei
...	...	...	0.3	...	0.5[37]	4.8	500	64.9	25.4	63.6	11.0	9.2	90.8	—	—	Venda
...	...	...	4.0[3]	...	0.2[37]	...	662	0.8	0.3	—99.7—		100.0	...	...	...	S.W. Africa/Namibia
...	...	...	19	...	45	72[4]	44,312	87.8	23.8	55.8	20.4	40.9	12.5	21.7	24.9	Spain
...	...	...	12[3]	...	24[2]	80[82]	1,967	30.0	62.4[88]	37.6[88]	—	88.3[88]	0.4[88]	2.1[88]	9.2[88]	Sri Lanka
...	...	...	1[3]	...	15[2]	4[4]	31,500	13.3	0.8	88.7	10.5	23.8	76.2	—	—	Sudan, The
33.0[56]	12.5[56]	54.5[56]	26[3]	...	67[2]	133[4]	165	1.0	15.0	53.0	32.0	40.4	23.1	19.1	17.4	Suriname
39.7	—60.3—		21[3]	...	22[2]	120[4]	766,775	44.6	2.0	81.1	16.9	19.7	60.6	12.0	7.7	Swaziland
44.9[93]	—55.1[93]—		92	...	1.8[37,82]	161[4]	8,615	19.2	—97.5—		2.5	34.0	4.0	50.6	11.4	Sweden
35.5	—64.5—		249[3]	...	4.3[37]	414[4]	1,363	34.3	5.4	68.2	26.4	31.8	58.2	9.5	0.5	Switzerland
...	...	...	0.3	...	14.8[79]	27[4]	6,169[79]	33.3[79]	9.6[79]	56.4[79]	34.0[79]	91.7[79]	—8.3[79]—			Syria
...	...	...	...	...	37.6[37]	400	1,334	37.1	8.6	91.4	...	67.0	—33.0—			Taiwan
56.2	—43.8—		0.3	...	0.8[37]	4[4]	7,545	8.5	19.1	72.5	8.4	49.8	10.2	24.7	15.3	Tanzania
...	...	...	51	...	28.5	18[4]	15,916	31.0	10.6	—89.4—		94.0	—4.3—		1.7	Thailand
...	...	...	...	...	0.4[22,37]	2[4]	406	7.1	17.3[17]	—82.7[17]—		71.0[17]	29.0[17]	—	—	Togo
...	...	...	...	...	...	...	...	...	...	...	...	...	...	...	...	Tokelau
8.4	—	91.6	1[3]	...	—	2[4]	58	83.6	57.0	—43.0—		93.1	6.9	—	—	Tonga
63.7[101]	—36.3[101]—		16[3]	...	0.6[37,82]	30[4]	132	25.8	55.9	—44.1—		62.3	4.4	6.1	27.2	Trinidad and Tobago
...	...	...	7[3]	...	2.3[37]	17[4]	8,726	56.2	40.9	41.3	17.8	56.2	43.8	—	—	Tunisia
11.5	2.5	86.0	18[3]	...	46.9	299[79]	27,413[79]	35.2[79]	10.6[79]	66.0[79]	23.4[79]	100.0[79]	...	...	...	Turkey
...	...	...	...	...	...	...	...	...	...	...	...	...	...	...	...	Turks and Caicos Is.
...	...	...	...	...	...	...	...	...	...	...	...	...	...	...	...	Tuvalu
...	...	...	...	...	2.2[37,82]	...	2,262	11.3	29.8	70.2	—	100.0	—	—	—	Uganda
—	—	100.0	113	...	3.1[37]	87[4]	605,700	27.2	—91.6—		8.4	37.5	61.6	—0.9—		U.S.S.R.
...	...	...	...	...	28.6[37]	203[4]	17.5[59]	0.2[59]	64.8[59]	18.2[59]	17.1[59]	97.6[59]	—	1.3[59]	1.1[59]	United Arab Emirates
...	...	...	77[3]	...	0.8[37,82]	365[4]	18,720	76.7	0.7	98.7	0.6	37.3	59.9	1.6	1.2	United Kingdom
43.4	52.6	4.0	85.7	66.2	12.4	87[4]	411,175[108]	43.2[108]	1.5	86.4	12.1	45.1	42.4	8.8	3.7	United States
37.1	58.7	4.2	23[3]	...	0.5[37]	38[4]	16,025	90.9	3.8	75.2	21.0	7.6	86.5	2.8	3.1	Uruguay
82.6	13.7	3.7	1[3]	...	...	...	219	14.8	40.7	—59.3—		86.3	13.7	—	—	Vanuatu
39.8	12.1	48.1	11[3]	...	1.2[37,82]	41[4]	26,470	30.0	19.0	59.0	22.0	13.2	57.0	22.8	7.0	Venezuela
...	...	...	6[3]	...	22.8[37]	39[58]	7,857	24.1	8.4	—91.6—		65.4	34.6	...	...	Vietnam
53.4	—46.6—		12.2	...	...	157[4]	9.9	29.1	63.7	5.9	30.4	7.0	77.6	9.9	5.5	Virgin Islands (U.S.)
...	...	...	...	...	...	...	5.0	25.0	80.0	—20.0—		100.0	—	—	—	Wallis and Futuna
...	...	...	c.9[3]	...	4.7[37]	...	185	31.4	62.2	37.8	...	100.0	...	...	...	West Bank
...	...	...	6[3]	...	...	...	5,002	18.8	—	—	—	—	100.0	—	—	Western Sahara
...	...	...	...	...	...	...	70	24.8	71.2	28.8	—	93.8	6.2	—	—	Western Samoa
...	...	...	6[3]	...	53.8[37]	11[4]	108	0.3	3.9	85.1	11.0	95.7	4.3	—	—	Yemen (Aden)
35.5[9,26]	56.9[9,26]	7.6[9,26]	39.2	...	4.4	5[4]	1,351	0.1	6.7	69.7	23.6	98.8	—	—	1.2	Yemen (Ṣan'ā')
12.7	—87.3—		1.5	4.8[62]	2[2]	120[4]	12,462	48.8	8.5	84.7	6.8	52.8	26.4	16.2	4.6	Yugoslavia
92.3	—9.7—		0.4	...	—	1[4]	5,897	2.6	7.7	—92.3—		70.6	20.1	2.0	7.3	Zaire
15.8	9.7	74.5	1[3]	...	0.3[37]	19[4]	938	1.3	4.5	—95.5—		14.2	38.1	...	47.7	Zambia
1.8[9,59]	26.7[9,59]	71.5[9,59]	7[3]	...	1.5[59]	53[4]	29,620	76.6	2.5	—97.5—		34.5	65.7			Zimbabwe

[62]Percent of farms having electric motors. [63]Excludes temporary bushland available for agricultural use to subsistence farms. [64]Western Libya only. [65]10 to 100 hectares. [66]100 hectares or more. [67]Peninsular Malaysia excluding shifting cultivators. [68]Smallholder farms only. [69]Average size of estate farm is 400 hectares. [70]Based on total number of households on estates. [71]All Malaysia. [72]Inhabited islands only. [73]Less than 4.0 hectares. [74]Includes rented farms. [75]Excludes part-time farmers. [76]In area, privately owned lands constitute 49.7% of Mexico's farmland, communal land (*ejidos*) 49.8%. [77]In area, state lands constitute 79.1% of Mongolia's farmland, agricultural cooperatives 20.9%. [78]0.4 to 2.0 hectares. [79]1984. [80]Less than 3.0 hectares. [81]3.0 to 50 hectares. [82]1983. [83]Data refer to cultivated area only. [84]2.0 to 5.0 hectares. [85]1.2 to 5.0 hectares. [86]Less than 7.0 hectares. [87]7.0 hectares or more. [88]1973. [89]State farms and communes only. [90]1.2 to 12 hectares. [91]12 to 20 hectares. [92]40 hectares or more. [93]Holdings of arable land only. [94]7.0 to 25 hectares. [95]25 to 300 hectares. [96]300 hectares or more. [97]3.0 hectares or more. [98]1.0 to 6.4 hectares. [99]6.4 hectares or more. [100]1.0 to 3.0 hectares. [101]1963. [102]24,600,000 farm households with small plots constitute 8% of total farmland. [103]Abu Dhabi only. [104]Excludes Northern Ireland. [105]20 to 72 hectares. [106]72 to 202 hectares. [107]202 hectares or more. [108]1985. [109]Less than 8.0 hectares. [110]8.0 to 16 hectares. [111]16 to 100 hectares.

Crops and livestock

This table provides comparative data for selected categories of agricultural production for the countries of the world. The data are taken mainly from the United Nations Food and Agricultural Organization's (FAO) annual *Production Yearbook.*

Although the FAO provides standardized guidelines upon which many nations have organized their data collection systems and methods, persistent variations in standards of coverage and reporting periods limit the value of country to country comparisons. The FAO depends largely on questionnaires supplied to each country, but where no official or semiofficial responses are returned the FAO makes estimates, using unofficial or other data. Statistics are based on calendar year periods; that is, data for any particular crop refer to the calendar year in which the harvest (or the bulk of the harvest) occurred. In countries where intensive intercropping and multiple cropping are practiced, the broader parameter of food supply availability (see *Household budgets and consumption* table) may be a better indicator by which to make intercountry comparisons of agricultural production than the more specific components of agriculture presented in this table. In spite of the oftentimes tragic food shortages in a number of countries in recent years, worldwide agricultural production is probably more often under-reported than over-reported. Most countries do not report complete domestic production; for example, the Soviet bloc, excepting Czechoslovakia, publishes, initially at least, statistics only for collective or cooperative production and excludes the production of privately held plots of land that in some instances represent a significant part of total agricultural production. Some countries report only crops that are sold commercially and ignore crops produced for family or communal subsistence.

Individual categories of crop production also display some peculiarities that may cause statistical discrepancies between national and FAO figures. The FAO's cereals statistics relate to crops harvested for grain. Some countries, however, collect their basic data on sown or cultivated areas instead and calculate production statistics from estimates of yield. Millet and sorghum, which in many countries are used as livestock or poultry feed, are excluded by the FAO from the cereals category, while many African nations that use them for grain report them as cereals. Fruit statistics, especially for tropical fruits, are frequently unavailable, and coverage is not uniform, with some countries reporting both commercial fruits and those consumed for subsistence. Figures on wild fruits and berries tend not to be included in national reports at all. Statistical variances also occur among data for individual varieties of fruit. Some banana and plantain

Crops and livestock

country	crops															
	grains				roots and tubers[a]				pulses[b]				fruits[c]		vegetables[d]	
	production ('000 metric tons)		yield (kg/hectare)		production ('000 metric tons)		yield (kg/hectare)		production ('000 metric tons)		yield (kg/hectare)		production ('000 metric tons)		production ('000 metric tons)	
	1974–76 average	1985	1974–76 average	1985	1974–76 average	1985	1974–76 average	1985	1974–76 average	1985	1974–76 average	1985	1974–76 average	1985	1974–76 average	1985
Afghanistan	4,389	4,510	1,297	1,332	246	330	13,727	13,200	32	38	1,570	1,652	810	837	627	784
Albania	713	1,055	2,112	2,928	109	136	7,032	8,737	16	25	305	410	136	166	159	186
Algeria	2,158	3,058	682	868	448	800	7,340	8,247	67	50	695	392	1,515	1,326	676	1,129
American Samoa	...	...	...	...	4	4	5,892	5,359	...	...	...	...	2	1	...	...
Andorra	...	...	...	...	...	...	...	...	...	...	...	...	...	...	...	...
Angola	547	332	756	464	1,907	2,170	13,178	14,045	71	40	589	364	429	425	203	227
Anguilla	...	...	...	...	...	...	...	...	...	...	...	...	...	...	...	...
Antigua and Barbuda	...	...	1,885	1,500	...	1	3,871	7,670	...	...	...	...	7	9	1	1
Argentina	23,653	28,792	1,971	2,456	2,311	2,465	13,278	15,311	176	228	1,092	1,112	6,472	5,214	2,417	2,573
Aruba[2]	...	...	...	...	...	...	...	...	...	...	...	...	...	...	...	...
Australia	17,202	26,017	1,384	1,462	699	924	19,785	24,274	106	776	776	997	1,982	2,278	926	1,230
Austria	4,001	5,553	4,000	5,267	1,774	1,042	23,679	27,625	5	1	2,386	2,343	991	755	552	463
Bahamas, The	1	1	1,010	1,262	...	2	3,500	9,255	1	1	1,392	1,300	11	13	12	28
Bahrain	...	...	...	...	...	...	29,000	22,857	...	...	...	1,000	25	44	14	29
Bangladesh	18,112	23,402	1,771	2,098	1,553	1,885	9,945	10,590	223	213	732	746	1,293	1,445	1,045	1,266
Barbados	2	2	2,614	2,500	10	6	10,659	7,741	1	1	1,183	1,258	2	3	6	8
Belgium[3]	1,919	2,195	4,203	5,793	1,325	1,700	33,463	37,611	13	6	2,788	3,523	387	370	1,128	1,172
Belize	20	22	1,276	1,553	2	3	21,170	20,000	1	1	576	684	64	76	2	3
Benin	305	567	721	831	1,143	1,658	7,654	7,891	24	59	387	573	132	156	82	128
Bermuda	...	...	...	...	1	1	18,077	9,530	...	...	...	...	1	1	2	2
Bhutan	141	179	1,424	1,407	36	45	6,602	6,892	2	3	540	614	37	50	9	11
Bolivia	580	923	1,150	1,288	1,157	1,156	6,975	4,436	16	29	915	1,155	579	532	348	298
Botswana	100	20	599	307	6	9	4,641	6,538	13	17	459	567	8	11	14	16
Brazil	27,873	35,908	1,420	1,825	28,868	25,992	12,006	12,242	2,193	2,592	503	475	13,704	26,232	3,396	5,003
British Virgin Islands	...	...	...	...	...	...	...	...	...	...	...	...	...	1	...	...
Brunei	9	3	2,517	1,500	4	1	4,880	6,597	...	...	...	...	6	6	3	9
Bulgaria	7,602	7,127	3,460	3,900	338	380	11,201	9,500	77	71	681	848	2,052	2,004	1,979	1,981
Burkina Faso	1,141	1,580	533	763	110	123	4,688	4,556	166	177	362	373	41	66	56	83
Burma	9,206	16,113	1,736	3,032	95	262	5,628	9,400	259	626	434	761	1,031	1,088	1,683	2,060
Burundi	305	451	1,134	1,199	1,014	1,189	6,988	7,461	333	322	974	907	944	1,325	126	185
Cameroon	962	1,061	1,017	1,032	2,272	2,180	3,516	2,469	90	120	591	561	1,112	1,198	391	420
Canada	37,568	48,605	2,027	2,214	2,354	2,953	21,501	24,305	138	315	1,439	1,516	663	770	1,444	2,060
Cape Verde	4	1	448	200	15	10	4,244	3,649	1	5	204	263	9	9	5	5
Cayman Islands	...	...	...	...	...	...	4,444	5,000	...	...	...	...	1	1	...	...
Central African Republic	97	124	518	588	1,097	1,177	3,231	3,195	5	6	500	500	150	174	38	49
Chad	592	690	573	867	327	511	4,048	4,696	52	56	382	406	87	114	45	74
Chile	1,577	2,360	1,679	2,949	771	916	9,793	14,336	99	159	853	1,071	1,267	1,937	1,107	1,286
China	243,234	339,452	2,479	3,821	144,916	141,136	12,904	15,038	6,277	5,840	1,076	1,321	6,286	12,040	69,618	99,705
Christmas Island	...	...	...	...	...	...	...	...	...	...	...	...	...	...	...	...
Cocos (Keeling) Islands	...	...	...	...	...	...	...	...	...	...	...	...	...	...	...	...
Colombia	2,882	3,298	2,367	2,753	3,364	3,852	9,243	10,993	127	135	612	651	3,172	4,187	1,111	1,425
Comoros	15	22	1,108	1,106	93	110	3,451	3,216	2	3	548	581	30	39	2	3
Congo	20	9	665	600	588	661	5,668	6,463	7	7	603	628	186	243	27	37
Cook Islands	...	...	...	...	11	12	27,805	32,021	...	...	...	...	17	16	2	2
Costa Rica	252	376	1,735	2,415	36	59	8,360	7,646	15	25	452	577	1,380	1,328	50	67
Côte d'Ivoire	771	1,171	813	1,009	2,865	4,671	4,145	6,329	7	8	607	667	1,296	1,848	251	467
Cuba	540	622	2,034	2,665	645	918	5,435	5,980	24	27	695	771	494	1,197	399	537
Cyprus	169	97	1,396	1,668	161	263	19,842	21,690	10	7	767	1,080	403	569	106	119
Czechoslovakia	9,618	11,775	3,578	4,699	4,100	3,450	16,026	18,551	101	209	1,342	2,093	614	925	1,008	1,092
Denmark	6,472	7,979	3,705	4,941	743	1,073	22,497	35,767	11	522	3,025	4,971	144	88	203	260
Djibouti	...	...	...	...	...	...	...	...	...	...	...	...	...	...	...	13
Dominica	...	...	1,293	1,389	22	25	9,815	9,806	...	...	500	500	61	58	4	6
Dominican Republic	335	558	2,696	3,368	365	240	6,073	5,974	70	98	1,071	962	1,262	1,411	188	259
Ecuador	722	619	1,352	1,642	910	655	10,749	9,776	54	47	530	664	3,691	3,094	307	303
Egypt	8,001	8,968	3,921	4,373	909	1,500	17,805	18,987	346	398	2,058	2,063	2,042	2,871	6,357	8,330
El Salvador	575	729	1,543	1,937	22	30	11,724	13,484	38	48	708	828	211	271	99	129
Equatorial Guinea	...	...	...	...	77	90	2,736	2,392	...	...	...	...	13	18	...	...
Ethiopia	4,364	5,350	966	1,166	1,138	1,275	3,259	2,856	635	944	727	1,032	183	212	423	533
Faeroe Islands	...	...	...	...	1	1	14,275	13,725	...	...	...	...	...	...	...	...
Falkland Islands	...	...	...	...	...	...	...	...	...	...	...	...	...	...	...	...

growers, for example, report production in terms of bunches, including the weight of the stalk; others do not. Vegetable statistics include vegetables and melons grown for human consumption only. Some countries do not make this distinction in their reports, and some exclude the production of kitchen gardens and small family plots. In certain countries, such small-scale production may account for 20 to 40 percent of total ouput.

Livestock statistics may be distorted by the timing of country reports. Ireland, for example, takes a livestock enumeration in December that is reported the following year and that appears low against data for otherwise comparable countries because of the slaughter and export of animals at the close of the grazing season. It balances this, however, with a June enumeration, when numbers tend to be high. Milk production as defined by the FAO includes whole fresh milk, excluding milk sucked by young animals but including amounts fed by farmers or ranchers to livestock. Some countries—notably Czechoslovakia, France, Hungary, Italy, and West Germany—include milk sucked by young animals in their reports. Certain countries do not distinguish between milk cows and other cattle, so that yield per cow must be estimated. Some countries do not report egg production statistics (here given in metric tons), and external estimates must be based on the numbers of chickens and reported or assumed egg-laying rates. Some other countries report egg production by number, and this must be converted to weight, using official conversion factors; but, as eggs vary in size and weight, discrepancies, again, may arise.

Metric system units used in the table may be converted to English system units as follows:

metric tons × 1.1023 = short tons
kilograms × 2.2046 = pounds
kilograms per hectare × 0.8922 = pounds per acre.

The notes that follow, keyed by references in the table headings, provide further definitional information.

a. Includes such crops as potatoes and cassava.
b. Includes beans and peas harvested for dry grain only. Does not include green beans and green peas.
c. Excludes melons.
d. Includes melons, green beans, and green peas.
e. From milk cows only.
f. From chickens only.

livestock														country
cattle		sheep		hogs		chickens		milk[e]				eggs[f]		
stock ('000 head)		stock ('000 head)		stock ('000 head)		stock ('000 head)		production ('000 metric tons)		yield (kg/animal)		production (metric tons)		
1974–76 average	1985	1974–76 average	1985	1974–76 average	1985	1974–76 average	1985	1974–76 average	1985	1974–76 average	1985	1974–76 average	1985	
3,591	3,750	19,872	20,000	...	...	6,000	7,000	588	610	543	500	13,297	14,200	Afghanistan
463	614	1,163	1,204	127	210	3,000	5,000	231	345	1,547	1,438	6,430	13,700	Albania
976	1,750	9,265	18,000	4	5	16,000	22,000	417	610	926	894	15,633	30,000	Algeria
...	...	...	...	10	10	...	—	...	...	786	800	32	30	American Samoa
...	1[1]	...	9[1]	...	...	...	...	...	...	...	...	...	...	Andorra
2,850	3,360	200	250	355	465	5,000	6,000	138	148	500	502	3,400	3,900	Angola
...	...	...	...	...	...	...	...	...	...	...	...	...	...	Anguilla
8	17	11	13	5	7	...	—	7	6	1,305	1,000	125	160	Antigua and Barbuda
56,745	54,800	34,622	29,000	4,151	3,800	34,000	42,000	5,580	5,600	1,892	1,898	199,879	269,000	Argentina
...	...	...	...	...	...	...	...	...	...	...	...	...	...	Aruba[2]
32,355	22,784	148,491	149,747	2,292	2,512	43,000	54,000	6,688	6,230	2,837	3,508	194,333	186,000	Australia
2,569	2,669	153	220	3,497	4,027	12,000	15,000	3,181	3,719	3,094	3,748	85,830	97,000	Austria
4	4	30	39	16	19	1,000	1,000	2	3	1,000	1,000	317	420	Bahamas, The
5	6	3	7	...	...	...	1,000	6	6	2,769	2,900	1,153	2,400	Bahrain
25,505	36,500	1,067	1,110	...	...	51,000	70,000	727	820	250	205	32,954	46,000	Bangladesh
19	18	48	54	38	49	...	1,000	6	9	1,088	1,296	1,417	1,183	Barbados
3,072	3,210	102	105	4,782	5,339	32,000	28,000	3,891	4,075	3,659	3,844	238,639	181,000	Belgium[3]
47	52	3	3	18	23	...	1,000	4	4	1,014	1,012	560	720	Belize
706	925	831	1,131	363	576	3,000	21,000	10	14	117	125	2,232	15,120	Benin
...	1	...	...	1	3	...	—	1	2	3,045	3,071	332	520	Bermuda
266	320	39	44	60	76	...	—	9	11	257	257	93	213	Bhutan
3,246	5,851	7,729	9,413	1,164	1,112	6,000	10,000	53	80	1,393	1,418	16,117	26,000	Bolivia
2,578	2,700	290	170	16	7	1,000	1,000	71	96	350	350	477	738	Botswana
94,869	134,500	17,743	17,500	34,866	30,000	308,000	450,000	9,886	10,722	824	729	491,022	790,000	Brazil
2	2	7	8	2	3	...	...	...	...	...	...	...	...	British Virgin Islands
3	4	...	...	13	13	1,000	2,000	...	...	...	...	1,347	1,900	Brunei
1,555	1,751	9,857	10,501	3,247	3,734	34,000	41,000	1,434	2,138	2,278	3,112	99,863	154,785	Bulgaria
2,495	2,800	1,517	2,000	140	200	10,000	16,000	100	112	200	200	5,423	11,000	Burkina Faso
7,410	9,550	187	420	1,597	2,750	16,000	34,000	210	560	245	245	21,906	45,000	Burma
774	415	309	369	35	80	3,000	4,000	49	24	350	350	1,976	2,755	Burundi
2,583	3,642	2,050	1,900	800	800	9,000	9,000	34	46	500	500	6,933	10,000	Cameroon
15,334	11,733	657	748	6,002	10,752	86,000	96,000	7,692	8,200	3,738	4,762	314,611	332,610	Canada
11	13	2	1	22	24	...	—	1	2	600	600	116	132	Cape Verde
4	5	...	...	...	1	...	—	...	...	...	...	81	87	Cayman Islands
878	1,800	67	83	111	150	1,000	2,000	3	5	110	110	875	1,134	Central African Republic
3,207	3,400	2,335	2,250	6	6	3,000	3,000	87	92	270	270	2,370	3,060	Chad
3,484	3,400	5,639	5,800	877	1,100	16,000	19,000	991	1,040	1,344	1,576	61,922	68,850	Chile
56,376	51,375	94,403	95,191	269,884	313,010	698,000	1,361,000	881	2,568	1,330	2.797	2,283,124	4,265,000	China
...	...	...	...	...	...	...	...	...	...	...	...	...	...	Christmas Island
...	...	...	...	...	...	...	...	...	...	...	...	...	...	Cocos (Keeling) Islands
23,182	21,935	1,945	2,714	1,852	2,378	23,000	35,000	2,133	2,800	941	982	106,990	157,500	Colombia
73	85	7	9	...	...	...	—	3	4	500	500	505	600	Comoros
52	70	48	62	40	43	1,000	1,000	2	3	1,500	1,500	587	1,012	Congo
...	...	...	...	12	17	...	—	...	...	...	...	80	106	Cook Islands
1,791	2,553	2	3	220	220	5,000	6,000	262	371	1,046	1,279	15,674	18,000	Costa Rica
550	843	977	1,450	232	430	7,000	16,000	23	16	261	121	4,333	10,140	Côte d'Ivoire
5,442	6,400	330	378	1,453	2,400	18,000	26,000	806	1,000	1,333	1,471	81,738	115,000	Cuba
32	44	442	500	126	255	3,000	4,000	25	55	3,378	3,056	4,580	5,100	Cyprus
4,559	5,150	819	1,068	6,556	6,743	39,000	47,000	5,455	6,883	2,894	3,756	224,313	274,955	Czechoslovakia
3,085	2,704	60	52	7,715	8,960	15,000	15,000	4,927	5,068	4,485	5,346	73,033	79,770	Denmark
27	45	283	420	...	...	...	...	...	...	...	...	...	...	Djibouti
4	4	3	4	8	9	...	—	1	2	1,067	1,000	225	270	Dominica
1,896	2,420	50	80	700	1,850	7,000	9,000	333	498	1,449	2,000	21,500	17,300	Dominican Republic
2,476	3,378	2,104	2,086	2,547	4,230	13,000	43,000	786	988	1,332	1,372	20,603	50,200	Ecuador
2,100	2,800	1,923	2,500	15	55	26,000	52,000	626	960	674	671	69,128	126,000	Egypt
1,059	929	4	4	442	375	3,000	4,000	243	228	960	958	27,223	36,400	El Salvador
4	4	31	35	4	5	...	—	...	...	...	...	95	149	Equatorial Guinea
26,086	26,000	23,201	23,500	17	19	51,000	56,000	542	595	199	219	69,221	76,590	Ethiopia
2	2	69	72	...	...	...	...	...	...	...	...	...	...	Faeroe Islands
9	8	639	692	...	...	...	—	1	2	1,000	997	...	...	Falkland Islands

Crops and livestock (continued)

country	crops: grains: production ('000 metric tons) 1974–76 average	1985	grains: yield (kg/hectare) 1974–76 average	1985	roots and tubers[a]: production ('000 metric tons) 1974–76 average	1985	roots and tubers[a]: yield (kg/hectare) 1974–76 average	1985	pulses[b]: production ('000 metric tons) 1974–76 average	1985	pulses[b]: yield (kg/hectare) 1974–76 average	1985	fruits[c]: production ('000 metric tons) 1974–76 average	1985	vegetables[d]: production ('000 metric tons) 1974–76 average	1985
Fiji	26	31	2,184	2,258	142	155	9,463	9,389	2	3	879	862	12	14	13	16
Finland	3,436	3,656	2,592	2,902	718	708	14,477	17,962	13	14	2,291	3,400	99	113	96	169
France	36,510	55,325	3,776	5,699	6,156	7,814	20,906	37,567	124	1,058	1,803	4,343	15,250	13,788	6,413	7,391
French Guiana	1	6	1,635	3,107	15	13	12,295	10,870	...	...	...	...	5	2	1	3
French Polynesia	...	...	...	...	17	13	12,577	8,556	...	...	...	...	4	4	6	6
Gabon	8	11	1,459	1,453	357	382	5,866	6,257	...	...	397	567	157	181	18	28
Gambia, The	83	128	936	1,455	9	6	3,274	3,000	4	4	250	273	3	4	6	7
Gaza Strip	...	5	...	2,813	...	8	...	16,667	...	1	...	2,571	244	180	48	76
Germany, East	8,935	11,542	3,575	4,589	9,298	11,500	15,419	23,958	73	85	1,511	1,607	561	968	923	1,283
Germany, West	21,014	25,925	3,973	5,304	11,737	8,704	27,133	35,844	78	75	2,785	3,254	3,879	3,517	1,800	2,198
Ghana	750	640	873	1,015	3,612	3,823	6,136	7,262	17	11	110	88	1,376	813	445	720
Gibraltar	...	...	...	...	...	...	...	...	...	...	...	...	...	...	...	...
Greece	3,858	4,431	2,493	2,990	894	1,104	15,003	18,333	113	74	1,186	1,389	3,271	3,885	3,225	4,429
Greenland	...	...	...	...	...	...	...	...	...	...	...	...	...	...	...	...
Grenada	...	...	851	951	3	4	5,076	4,990	1	1	1,164	1,448	26	18	2	1
Guadeloupe	...	...	1,628	1,200	41	25	12,450	9,025	...	...	767	571	170	167	23	23
Guam	...	...	1,500	1,500	1	2	13,939	13,304	...	...	...	...	1	1	1	1
Guatemala	989	1,298	1,459	1,459	53	39	3,851	4,690	81	125	651	663	735	980	216	281
Guernsey	...	...	...	...	...	...	...	...	...	...	...	...	...	...	...	...
Guinea	569	588	832	776	765	663	7,115	4,854	27	45	543	692	502	670	347	420
Guinea-Bissau	85	170	730	829	32	40	4,872	6,154	2	2	533	567	41	40	22	20
Guyana	252	301	2,139	3,235	22	18	6,604	6,731	1	1	667	522	33	38	7	10
Haiti	442	290	1,176	1,036	678	789	4,320	4,054	85	91	497	484	898	1,080	249	307
Honduras	441	657	1,093	1,499	19	22	3,468	6,994	32	48	459	600	1,280	1,631	65	116
Hong Kong	3	...	1,764	2,500	1	...	12,870	30,769	...	...	...	...	3	7	179	150
Hungary	12,014	14,781	3,806	5,157	1,585	1,372	12,416	19,460	143	211	1,788	2,245	2,160	1,992	1,788	1,947
Iceland	...	...	...	...	9	14	10,660	13,700	...	...	...	...	...	...	1	2
India	118,742	164,573	1,179	1,560	14,266	19,733	12,063	14,467	10,938	12,085	474	529	15,079	23,955	34,277	45,420
Indonesia	25,598	43,965	2,338	3,561	15,861	17,200	8,360	9,284	304	303	1,026	860	2,904	4,358	2,422	2,457
Iran	8,221	8,845	1,057	1,051	530	1,550	17,273	14,091	207	277	1,020	731	2,232	3,616	3,281	4,152
Iraq	1,814	1,491	854	778	48	115	9,019	16,429	38	31	769	872	982	1,058	1,631	2,648
Ireland	1,358	1,891	3,929	4,846	1,094	700	25,666	23,333	13	1	4,043	3,085	24	21	246	289
Isle of Man	...	...	...	...	...	...	...	...	...	...	...	...	...	...	...	...
Israel	305	167	2,112	1,791	164	202	30,599	36,393	9	7	1,445	893	1,924	1,957	702	906
Italy	17,001	18,049	3,282	3,753	2,964	2,581	16,551	18,645	405	300	1,259	1,462	19,853	18,749	12,165	14,677
Jamaica	12	10	1,763	1,818	206	231	10,207	10,221	5	8	687	861	307	345	76	136
Japan	16,636	15,858	5,620	5,848	5,313	5,868	21,297	24,464	177	145	1,349	1,654	6,477	5,862	14,672	15,407
Jersey	...	...	...	...	...	...	...	...	...	...	...	...	...	...	...	...
Jordan	143	130	643	872	6	12	11,743	19,167	23	8	716	670	49	110	317	525
Kampuchea	1,382	1,978	1,306	1,109	81	139	8,403	7,394	17	35	562	875	178	192	457	450
Kenya	3,052	3,143	1,564	1,754	1,152	1,330	7,807	7,824	292	200	476	417	436	670	369	439
Kiribati	...	...	...	...	10	13	8,496	8,742	...	...	...	...	4	5	4	5
Korea, North	6,826	10,495	3,590	4,333	1,532	2,320	12,191	13,107	250	290	765	866	577	1,133	1,891	2,821
Korea, South	8,441	8,587	4,140	5,647	2,297	1,476	16,953	21,554	48	63	806	1,134	595	1,511	5,948	9,455
Kuwait	...	...	2,000	3,288	...	2	10,500	15,000	...	...	...	...	1	2	27	39
Laos	920	1,445	1,312	2,272	55	169	9,939	11,497	13	25	1,494	2,083	73	138	148	226
Lebanon	77	21	1,222	1,102	54	121	6,079	15,006	12	9	840	987	679	708	283	387
Lesotho	180	194	772	1,290	5	6	12,951	15,309	20	10	617	455	12	15	18	25
Liberia	241	252	1,220	1,200	302	373	3,886	4,012	3	3	494	524	110	130	58	75
Libya	263	235	449	578	82	110	5,071	7,097	7	11	1,131	1,197	139	221	475	549
Liechtenstein	...	...	...	...	10	12	18,679	18,919	...	...	...	...	...	...	...	...
Luxembourg	104	147	2,510	[3]	44	45	25,000	[3]	[3]	[3]	[3]	[3]	12	6	4	4
Macau	...	...	...	...	3	4	10,000	10,000	...	...	...	...	3	5	1	2
Madagascar	2,135	2,320	1,805	1,719	1,867	2,949	6,118	5,895	71	55	875	858	953	736	273	299
Malawi	1,268	1,641	1,057	1,233	152	574	3,892	4,556	188	229	612	616	202	394	181	218
Malaysia	2,050	1,919	2,724	2,781	521	505	10,506	9,528	...	...	...	...	853	898	435	481
Maldives	1	...	905	789	6	8	5,155	5,295	...	...	600	595	6	8	14	18
Mali	1,215	1,366	779	803	86	140	9,041	9,756	33	57	1,088	1,036	10	12	101	235
Malta	4	8	2,089	3,259	20	13	8,784	6,500	1	2	1,866	2,282	9	9	46	47
Martinique	...	...	...	...	35	26	10,018	7,005	...	...	...	...	262	246	28	27
Mauritania	51	49	414	533	5	5	1,119	1,866	16	24	340	392	13	12	3	9
Mauritius	2	5	2,589	4,392	11	24	15,686	25,857	1	1	463	500	8	9	24	32
Mayotte	...	...	...	...	...	...	...	...	...	...	...	...	...	...	...	...
Mexico	15,908	28,602	1,698	2,331	837	993	12,070	12,788	1,129	1,288	633	578	5,891	7,900	2,819	4,114
Monaco	...	...	...	...	...	...	...	...	...	...	...	...	...	...	...	...
Mongolia	391	892	904	1,395	33	114	7,655	11,078	2	...	480	1,143	3	6	23	41
Montserrat	...	...	1,000	1,667	...	...	2,500	3,378	...	...	...	...	2	1	...	...
Morocco	4,748	4,878	1,049	1,062	213	570	11,449	12,925	543	231	953	626	1,351	1,638	1,220	1,427
Mozambique	700	585	719	654	2,684	3,290	4,891	5,619	73	55	611	440	318	334	184	185
Nauru	...	...	...	...	...	...	...	...	...	...	...	...	...	...	...	...
Nepal	3,779	4,252	1,755	1,675	373	560	5,648	6,053	54	75	397	434	124	150	210	260
Netherlands, The	1,185	1,130	4,771	6,156	5,319	7,150	35,141	44,548	32	91	2,883	3,638	551	444	2,323	2,820
Netherlands Antilles[2]	1	2	653	714	...	...	...	...	...	...	...	...	...	...	...	...
New Caledonia	1	3	2,538	2,250	18	23	5,861	5,797	...	...	688	800	8	9	4	5
New Zealand	720	1,424	3,494	5,322	235	298	25,365	31,335	52	78	2,533	3,250	267	491	316	451
Nicaragua	331	584	1,045	2,113	24	29	4,068	4,039	48	57	768	662	325	320	43	49
Niger	1,119	1,856	395	427	216	222	6,620	7,106	199	215	222	136	28	42	97	158
Nigeria	8,237	11,630	662	813	27,662	33,602	10,062	11,006	845	900	205	218	1,968	2,450	2,434	3,756
Niue	...	...	...	...	2	2	2,186	2,552	...	...	...	...	1	2	...	...
Norfolk Island	...	...	...	...	...	...	...	...	...	...	...	...	...	...	...	...
Norway	904	1,274	3,052	3,726	601	470	22,958	25,269	...	...	...	...	118	134	164	217
Oman	5	2	1,273	1,781	...	1	...	4,063	...	...	...	...	81	125	34	158
Pacific Is., Trust Territory of the	...	...	1,073	1,194	11	14	8,390	8,563	...	...	600	600	3	3	3	3
Marshall Islands	...	...	...	...	...	...	...	...	...	...	...	...	...	...	...	...
Micronesia, Federated States of	...	...	...	...	...	...	...	...	...	...	...	...	...	...	...	...

livestock														country
cattle		sheep		hogs		chickens		milk[e]				eggs[f]		
stock ('000 head)		stock ('000 head)		stock ('000 head)		stock ('000 head)		production ('000 metric tons)		yield (kg/animal)		production (metric tons)		
1974–76 average	1985	1974–76 average	1985	1974–76 average	1985	1974–76 average	1985	1974–76 average	1985	1974–76 average	1985	1974–76 average	1985	
158	159	...	...	16	30	1,000	1,000	47	45	1,700	1,698	1,750	2,500	Fiji
1,854	1,608	127	110	1,091	1,256	9,000	8,000	3,196	3,174	4,141	4,998	81,067	87,000	Finland
23,939	23,099	10,582	10,824	11,681	10,975	164,000	188,000	29,571	33,000	2,897	3,284	752,667	915,000	France
2	14	...	...	5	10	...	—	...	...	...	...	219	260	French Guiana
6	10	3	2	19	34	...	1,000	2	2	2,805	2,500	552	750	French Polynesia
3	9	58	80	124	150	1,000	2,000	...	...	250	256	470	1,370	Gabon
284	290	130	185	9	12	...	—	5	5	175	175	355	552	Gambia, The
2	5	20	67	...	...	...	1,000	13	8	3,205	6,015	1,583	2,310	Gaza Strip
5,533	5,848	1,824	2,528	11,290	13,191	47,000	51,000	8,087	8,900	3,794	4,266	298,652	345,000	Germany, East
14,429	15,688	1,048	1,300	20,164	23,617	92,000	79,000	21,759	25,675	4,017	4,710	878,835	790,000	Germany, West
929	820	1,655	2,000	367	375	11,000	14,000	8	7	55	55	9,907	16,470	Ghana
...	...	...	...	...	...	...	...	...	...	...	...	...	...	Gibraltar
1,219	757	8,334	7,900	765	1,115	29,000	38,000	695	678	1,434	1,883	109,305	125,000	Greece
...	...	20	21	...	...	...	...	...	...	...	...	...	...	Greenland
6	4	8	17	11	11	...	—	1	2	800	800	950	1,000	Grenada
80	91	3	4	32	46	...	...	11	13	499	500	429	1,200	Guadeloupe
2	2	...	...	10	8	...	—	...	...	...	...	1,250	1,000	Guam
1,515	2,587	518	670	609	832	11,000	15,000	301	333	911	825	30,893	41,500	Guatemala
...	...	...	...	...	...	...	...	...	...	...	...	...	...	Guernsey
1,493	1,800	400	460	32	47	5,000	11,000	35	42	185	185	5,242	11,550	Guinea
155	225	28	65	81	133	...	—	6	7	170	170	240	317	Guinea-Bissau
275	140	106	118	118	148	10,000	15,000	12	15	783	760	3,417	4,200	Guyana
858	1,350	79	92	1,650	500	4,000	8,000	22	22	223	238	1,780	3,250	Haiti
1,817	2,508	5	5	514	410	4,000	5,000	232	280	650	651	15,240	20,700	Honduras
10	3	...	...	387	499	4,000	6,000	5	3	2,069	2,362	2,596	1,480	Hong Kong
1,950	1,901	1,979	2,832	7,752	9,237	53,000	58,000	1,866	2,723	2,607	3,782	215,438	230,934	Hungary
65	64	857	770	7	13	...	—	128	130	3,483	3,719	2,705	3,700	Iceland
179,462	182,410	40,000	41,300	7,233	8,826	141,000	161,000	10,867	18,500	500	658	463,333	812,000	India
6,211	6,859	3,253	4,958	2,724	4,050	93,000	144,000	62	162	800	829	66,713	240,000	Indonesia
7,238	8,350	34,833	34,500	55	30	58,000	95,000	1,210	1,700	769	723	176,667	220,000	Iran
1,857	1,500	11,093	8,500	...	...	15,000	65,000	338	300	750	750	48,333	45,000	Iraq
7,179	5,835	3,706	2,690	881	1,020	9,000	8,000	4,279	5,920	3,031	3,822	39,731	38,000	Ireland
...	35[4]	...	132[4]	...	5[4]	...	70[4]	...	...	...	...	...	...	Isle of Man
291	310	200	230	78	86	19,000	29,000	616	845	6,011	8,125	88,015	119,500	Israel
8,336	9,106	7,985	9,500	8,634	9,041	107,000	112,000	9,475	11,000	3,208	3,638	663,967	655,000	Italy
277	321	5	3	229	238	4,000	5,000	47	50	1,000	1,000	12,833	17,500	Jamaica
3,672	4,698	13	24	7,720	10,718	244,000	328,000	5,031	7,377	4,051	5,046	1,820,333	2,140,727	Japan
...	...	...	...	...	...	...	...	...	...	...	...	...	...	Jersey
40	35	710	990	...	...	23,000	30,000	13	20	813	1,000	7,313	26,000	Jordan
1,150	1,500	2	1	600	1,200	4,000	6,000	18	16	170	170	5,967	6,500	Kampuchea
9,609	12,000	3,068	7,000	61	96	16,000	20,000	897	1,100	463	478	16,920	31,440	Kenya
...	...	...	...	10	10	...	—	...	...	...	...	100	115	Kiribati
827	1,100	256	350	1,607	2,800	17,000	18,000	27	75	2,000	2,419	71,140	125,000	Korea, North
1,682	2,652	5	6	1,673	2,958	23,000	52,000	163	966	4,321	4,929	173,980	315,000	Korea, South
8	160	114	600	...	...	6,000	8,000	11	40	2,248	2,500	2,102	10,000	Kuwait
326	615	...	...	609	1,450	5,000	6,000	5	7	200	200	13,333	27,000	Laos
60	45	197	135	19	20	5,000	10,000	54	90	1,876	2,368	22,483	51,000	Lebanon
500	590	1,411	1,400	78	80	1,000	1,000	17	22	290	290	765	868	Lesotho
34	42	172	238	90	127	2,000	4,000	1	1	100	100	1,872	3,360	Liberia
178	200	4,039	5,500	...	...	4,000	25,000	53	67	1,194	1,411	6,840	22,500	Libya
8	9	1	2	8	9	...	—	15	19	3,196	3,339	250	250	Liechtenstein
217	227	3	4	84	71	234	103	248	299	3,486	4,273	[3]	[3]	Luxembourg
...	8	...	...	10	6	...	—	...	...	...	...	525	625	Macau
8,543	10,400	632	600	607	1,400	13,000	15,000	30	41	700	700	9,808	11,700	Madagascar
658	920	82	175	173	230	8,000	8,000	26	40	368	460	9,667	11,310	Malaŵi
425	570	46	65	1,343	2,100	80,000	55,000	23	32	680	680	109,367	134,400	Malaysia
...	...	...	...	...	...	...	...	...	...	...	...	...	...	Maldives
3,889	5,800	4,867	6,460	25	54	13,000	14,000	78	116	200	200	6,810	7,614	Mali
12	14	8	5	22	56	1,000	1,000	26	28	3,533	3,889	6,059	6,600	Malta
48	52	36	73	35	42	1,000	2,000	4	4	635	731	953	1,000	Martinique
1,121	1,350	3,837	5,200	...	...	3,000	4,000	61	93	350	350	2,388	3,400	Mauritania
52	60	3	4	5	11	1,000	2,000	23	25	2,304	2,500	2,281	3,400	Mauritius
...	...	...	...	...	...	...	...	...	...	...	...	...	...	Mayotte
28,636	37,450	6,340	6,500	13,196	19,000	141,000	200,000	4,949	6,920	620	814	423,777	756,000	Mexico
...	...	...	...	...	...	...	...	...	...	...	...	...	...	Monaco
2,342	2,374	14,346	13,391	14	48	...	—	147	223	294	396	415	1,250	Mongolia
8	9	3	4	2	1	...	—	1	2	750	750	44	56	Montserrat
3,547	2,600	15,023	12,000	10	8	19,000	33,000	479	840	555	615	50,200	81,000	Morocco
1,384	1,330	114	115	143	145	14,000	20,000	58	65	170	170	7,800	12,000	Mozambique
...	...	...	...	2	2	...	—	...	...	...	...	8	10	Nauru
6,567	7,050	2,307	2,550	317	400	20,000	25,000	180	219	500	500	13,000	17,500	Nepal
4,662	5,248	763	814	7,168	12,383	66,000	90,000	10,209	12,559	4,612	5,307	284,103	675,000	Netherlands, The
8	9	8	9	6	8	...	—	4	4	1,296	1,281	457	550	Netherlands Antilles[2]
113	122	5	3	24	40	...	—	3	4	600	600	453	1,200	New Caledonia
9,207	7,904	55,868	70,600	439	420	7,000	7,000	6,116	7,900	2,989	3,559	55,669	54,000	New Zealand
2,560	1,890	2	3	640	540	4,000	5,000	441	125	1,185	625	22,778	31,000	Nicaragua
2,497	3,530	2,216	3,530	26	36	8,000	14,000	65	108	163	200	5,168	7,820	Niger
11,073	12,000	10,124	12,850	882	1,300	85,000	160,000	299	354	270	295	114,983	240,000	Nigeria
1	1	...	...	1	1	...	—	...	...	825	714	34	20	Niue
...	...	...	...	...	...	...	...	...	...	...	...	...	...	Norfolk Island
930	976	1,646	2,415	705	693	4,000	4,000	1,831	2,028	4,667	5,337	38,816	50,559	Norway
126	130	48	200	...	...	1,000	1,000	15	16	420	420	483	1,519	Oman
9	10	...	...	19	28	...	—	...	...	...	...	131	155	Pacific Is., Trust Territory of the
...	...	...	...	...	...	...	...	...	...	...	...	...	...	Marshall Islands
...	...	...	...	...	...	...	...	...	...	...	...	...	...	Micronesia, Federated States of

Crops and livestock (continued)

country	crops															
	grains				roots and tubers[a]				pulses[b]				fruits[c]		vegetables[d]	
	production ('000 metric tons)		yield (kg/hectare)		production ('000 metric tons)		yield (kg/hectare)		production ('000 metric tons)		yield (kg/hectare)		production ('000 metric tons)		production ('000 metric tons)	
	1974–76 average	1985	1974–76 average	1985	1974–76 average	1985	1974–76 average	1985	1974–76 average	1985	1974–76 average	1985	1974–76 average	1985	1974–76 average	1985
Northern Mariana Islands	...	...	...	...	...	...	...	...	...	...	...	...	...	...	...	...
Palau	...	...	...	...	...	...	...	...	...	...	...	...	...	...	...	...
Pakistan	13,302	17,811	1,389	1,570	297	542	10,768	10,545	781	824	522	510	2,106	2,503	2,018	2,660
Panama	232	269	1,194	1,537	76	75	8,230	7,895	5	6	320	433	1,186	1,212	37	54
Papua New Guinea	3	3	1,871	1,467	1,028	1,172	6,936	6,988	1	2	500	500	964	1,089	225	270
Paraguay	401	685	1,400	1,320	1,575	2,330	14,144	14,028	60	73	800	777	607	809	206	225
Peru	1,510	1,908	1,830	2,438	2,425	2,207	7,007	7,959	105	122	824	896	1,593	1,313	744	746
Philippines	8,818	11,842	1,303	1,737	1,890	3,374	5,293	6,368	42	47	711	716	3,213	7,236	1,409	2,199
Pitcairn Island	...	...	...	...	...	...	...	...	...	...	...	...	...	...	...	...
Poland	21,133	23,795	2,673	2,900	48,300	36,546	18,743	17,024	271	440	1,223	1,608	1,479	2,279	3,872	4,534
Portugal	1,595	1,445	1,118	1,285	1,165	1,235	8,764	9,196	90	72	236	242	2,104	1,585	1,714	1,896
Puerto Rico	3	6	747	8,571	40	30	5,975	6,467	6	4	653	715	286	276	24	34
Qatar	...	1	3,568	3,816	...	...	10,600	10,000	...	...	...	...	...	3	...	17
Réunion	13	14	4,641	5,600	11	12	14,651	13,176	1	1	2,787	2,037	23	33	9	12
Romania	16,202	23,048	2,628	3,772	3,874	6,683	12,685	20,884	112	296	124	457	2,419	3,505	3,600	6,323
Rwanda	215	311	1,037	1,285	1,217	1,560	8,299	8,131	199	280	747	966	1,754	2,135	143	185
St. Christopher and Nevis	...	...	...	...	3	3	3,277	3,434	...	...	1,000	1,000	2	2	1	1
St. Helena and Ascension	...	...	...	...	...	...	...	...	...	...	...	...	...	...	...	...
St. Lucia	...	...	700	769	9	11	4,500	4,178	...	...	2,000	2,500	101	131	1	1
St. Pierre and Miquelon	...	...	...	...	...	...	...	...	...	...	...	...	...	...	...	...
St. Vincent and the Grenadines	...	1	3,193	3,320	23	25	7,340	8,126	...	...	790	978	28	38	2	1
San Marino	...	...	...	...	...	...	...	...	...	...	...	...	...	...	...	...
São Tomé and Príncipe	1	1	1,514	1,556	13	15	12,015	13,405	...	...	...	...	3	4	2	3
Saudi Arabia	291	1,811	737	2,482	1	10	5,045	10,000	5	7	1,741	1,946	392	597	657	1,121
Senegal	826	1,248	720	820	110	29	3,049	4,306	20	66	322	546	56	82	66	98
Seychelles	...	...	...	...	...	...	6,250	5,000	...	...	...	...	2	2	1	2
Sierra Leone	584	561	1,428	1,294	122	144	4,306	3,476	28	33	550	598	112	144	147	179
Singapore	...	...	...	...	8	1	6,217	11,104	...	...	...	...	16	6	39	28
Solomon Islands	2	7	1,995	2,840	74	92	13,146	15,693	1	2	777	1,050	10	13	4	5
Somalia	233	454	636	599	31	41	10,800	10,792	8	21	330	344	259	249	25	31
South Africa[5]	11,701	10,141	1,403	1,384	722	1,005	12,039	11,292	100	74	776	923	2,549	3,532	1,444	1,795
Bophuthatswana[5]	...	...	...	...	...	...	...	...	...	...	...	...	...	...	...	...
Ciskei[5]	...	...	...	...	...	...	...	...	...	...	...	...	...	...	...	...
Transkei[5]	...	...	...	...	...	...	...	...	...	...	...	...	...	...	...	...
Venda[5]	...	...	...	...	...	...	...	...	...	...	...	...	...	...	...	...
South West Africa/Namibia	61	97	382	478	138	224	8,737	8,800	3	6	1,020	970	23	32	21	27
Spain	13,418	20,917	1,834	2,795	5,611	5,830	14,088	17,577	477	373	699	840	10,939	12,117	8,032	9,104
Sri Lanka	1,391	2,689	1,825	2,940	950	960	4,435	12,387	12	39	519	805	956	1,378	218	343
Sudan, The	2,474	4,954	645	723	288	312	3,604	3,506	74	107	1,067	1,399	698	793	760	836
Suriname	170	280	3,630	3,994	3	4	5,860	6,056	...	...	847	880	59	57	3	8
Swaziland	110	121	1,484	1,924	14	11	3,777	2,750	3	3	634	591	106	157	11	13
Sweden	5,697	5,773	3,665	3,799	1,051	1,117	23,499	28,943	19	123	1,853	2,694	201	185	237	295
Switzerland	803	1,053	4,521	5,734	869	848	35,544	37,202	3	1	3,248	3,636	699	739	261	340
Syria	2,480	2,825	950	1,090	121	394	13,047	17,088	212	155	800	719	520	1,005	2,044	3,210
Taiwan	...	...	...	...	...	...	...	...	...	...	...	...	...	...	...	...
Tanzania	2,026	3,632	980	1,093	5,610	6,239	7,027	11,030	190	358	439	536	1,515	2,506	889	1,038
Thailand	17,478	24,610	1,882	2,089	8,204	20,408	14,261	16,080	196	380	758	666	2,484	5,451	2,771	3,082
Togo	254	410	939	1,152	870	805	13,024	15,692	23	41	285	521	36	46	56	76
Tokelau	...	...	...	...	...	...	18,615	18,067	...	...	...	...	...	...	...	...
Tonga	...	...	...	...	94	98	6,398	6,756	...	...	...	...	10	12	6	7
Trinidad and Tobago	24	7	2,859	3,111	21	20	11,812	12,061	3	4	1,454	1,678	70	61	32	32
Tunisia	1,153	2,124	824	1,176	95	150	9,500	10,714	81	120	557	790	461	595	881	1,247
Turkey	21,239	26,506	1,579	1,977	2,538	4,110	13,870	16,775	699	1,368	1,164	1,021	6,366	8,092	10,437	16,440
Turks and Caicos Islands	...	...	...	...	...	...	...	...	...	...	...	...	...	...	...	...
Tuvalu	...	...	...	...	...	...	...	...	...	...	...	...	...	...	...	...
Uganda	1,606	1,343	1,216	1,326	1,917	6,230	3,729	6,984	337	312	635	750	3,303	7,372	244	303
U.S.S.R.	178,965	180,608	1,466	1,605	84,942	73,000	11,088	11,335	7,562	7,929	1,366	1,172	13,926	18,200	27,509	31,785
United Arab Emirates	...	4	...	3,262	...	3	15,533	10,400	...	...	...	...	27	85	34	216
United Kingdom	14,531	22,144	3,930	5,506	5,578	6,850	25,664	35,677	210	460	2,644	5,111	579	510	3,483	3,920
United States	237,507	346,877	3,339	4,768	16,054	18,988	27,227	32,063	1,050	1,202	1,425	1,645	24,319	22,460	24,075	28,098
Uruguay	1,099	1,312	1,282	1,917	211	210	5,250	6,000	5	6	878	963	305	351	144	185
Vanuatu	1	1	500	509	30	30	20,108	20,000	...	...	...	...	4	6	5	7
Venezuela	907	1,963	1,548	2,101	539	616	7,647	8,380	39	44	427	511	1,788	2,166	291	381
Vietnam	11,550	16,150	2,127	2,634	2,734	5,235	6,461	5,641	88	150	479	789	1,967	3,550	2,194	3,175
Virgin Islands (U.S.)	...	...	...	...	...	...	...	...	...	...	...	...	...	...	...	...
Wallis and Futuna	...	...	...	...	6	6	10,290	10,166	...	...	...	...	8	9	...	1
West Bank	...	...	...	...	...	...	...	...	...	...	...	...	...	...	...	...
Western Sahara	1	2	696	731	...	...	...	...	...	...	...	...	...	...	...	...
Western Samoa	...	...	...	...	33	43	6,873	7,137	...	...	...	...	53	57	...	1
Yemen (Aden)	107	115	1,651	1,663	3	17	11,364	11,000	...	...	...	...	52	51	99	117
Yemen (Ṣan'ā')	934	580	817	896	70	165	10,990	13,306	70	60	995	857	105	167	167	335
Yugoslavia	15,627	15,837	3,292	3,744	2,783	2,413	8,859	8,807	234	170	1,190	1,061	2,635	2,346	2,506	2,747
Zaire	754	1,125	745	900	12,385	16,181	6,882	7,128	144	121	609	604	2,423	2,540	452	523
Zambia	1,532	936	1,217	1,588	189	235	3,378	3,654	10	5	595	400	59	89	176	241
Zimbabwe	2,337	3,437	1,446	1,738	74	106	3,985	4,884	28	49	602	729	90	125	124	141

livestock														country
cattle		sheep		hogs		chickens		milk[e]				eggs[f]		
stock ('000 head)		stock ('000 head)		stock ('000 head)		stock ('000 head)		production ('000 metric tons)		yield (kg/animal)		production (metric tons)		
1974–76 average	1985	1974–76 average	1985	1974–76 average	1985	1974–76 average	1985	1974–76 average	1985	1974–76 average	1985	1974–76 average	1985	
...	...	...	...	...	...	...	...	...	...	...	...	...	...	Northern Mariana Islands
...	...	...	...	...	...	...	...	...	...	...	...	...	...	Palau
14,810	16,549	17,493	25,037			27,000	95,000	2,156	2,400	888	886	43,533	200,000	Pakistan
1,347	1,423	...	...	173	215	4,000	6,000	71	90	949	1,000	12,233	18,000	Panama
126	123	...	2	1,253	1,476	1,000	4,000	1	...	217	267	1,563	2,432	Papua New Guinea
5,152	6,400	364	445	973	1,400	9,000	14,000	119	170	1,906	1,889	17,467	28,500	Paraguay
4,152	3,900	15,227	13,500	2,120	2,050	33,000	41,000	816	809	1,269	1,172	49,978	77,900	Peru
1,716	1,900	30	30	7,096	8,007	47,000	57,000	14	10	1,067	909	165,070	225,000	Philippines
...	...	...	...	...	...	...	...	...	...	...	...	...	...	Pitcairn Island
13,052	11,055	3,209	4,837	20,552	17,614	85,000	60,000	16,521	16,300	2,709	2,835	445,022	480,000	Poland
1,193	1,110	3,924	5,050	1,899	3,477	16,000	17,000	677	740	2,276	2,256	44,065	60,000	Portugal
549	580	6	6	246	210	5,000	7,000	387	363	2,081	1,797	18,309	19,106	Puerto Rico
7	7	38	56			...	—	5	7	1,531	1,563	...	...	Qatar
20	20	2	3	93	72	2,000	4,000	4	6	491	600	2,133	2,500	Réunion
5,792	6,809	14,032	18,637	8,789	14,777	63,000	124,000	3,557	4,100	1,726	2,070	251,350	380,000	Romania
677	660	236	330	71	100	1,000	1,000	25	72	292	529	523	1,300	Rwanda
6	6	14	14	9	10	...	—	...	...	...	...	248	340	St. Christopher and Nevis
1	1	1	2	1	1	...	—	...	...	...	...	...	...	St. Helena and Ascension
8	12	10	15	8	12	...	—	1	1	1,272	1,397	445	520	St. Lucia
...	...	...	...	...	...	...	...	...	...	...	...	...	...	St. Pierre and Miquelon
7	8	9	13	5	7	...	—	1	1	1,343	1,381	423	570	St. Vincent and the Grenadines
...	...	...	...	...	...	...	...	...	...	...	...	...	...	San Marino
2	3	1	2	4	3	...	—	...	...	170	170	128	168	São Tomé and Príncipe
287	540	2,130	3,800	...	...	6,000	34,000	142	370	1,000	1,001	11,825	130,000	Saudi Arabia
2,316	2,200	1,679	2,150	182	190	6,000	11,000	80	79	344	360	4,875	8,400	Senegal
2	3	...	...	11	15	...	—	1	1	500	513	347	1,428	Seychelles
318	330	220	320	26	44	3,000	5,000	17	17	350	350	3,729	5,175	Sierra Leone
2	1	...	...	1,106	810	12,000	10,000	1	1	850	850	23,433	20,388	Singapore
23	23			40	49	...	—	1	1	600	600	263	282	Solomon Islands
3,665	3,600	9,246	9,700	8	10	2,000	3,000	144	140	345	350	1,920	2,640	Somalia
12,591	12,733	30,762	30,256	1,324	1,426	25,000	34,000	2,498	2,600	2,551	2,826	144,129	181,000	South Africa[5]
...	...	...	...	...	...	...	...	...	...	...	...	...	...	Bophuthatswana[5]
...	...	...	...	...	...	...	...	...	...	...	...	...	...	Ciskei[5]
...	...	...	...	...	...	...	...	...	...	...	...	...	...	Transkei[5]
...	...	...	...	...	...	...	...	...	...	...	...	...	...	Venda[5]
2,783	2,000	5,000	6,000	32	45	...	1,000	62	68	388	414	115	177	South West Africa/Namibia
4,412	5,004	16,103	17,485	8,252	11,390	49,000	54,000	5,199	6,500	2,843	3,421	557,210	650,000	Spain
1,724	1,750	29	29	39	90	6,000	7,000	148	205	408	477	17,164	32,000	Sri Lanka
14,718	20,000	13,880	19,000	...	...	22,000	28,000	840	1,700	500	486	20,310	38,000	Sudan, The
27	58	4	4	18	18	1,000	1,000	8	9	1,552	1,385	2,868	2,650	Suriname
621	620	33	37	18	19	1,000	1,000	32	38	244	253	263	290	Swaziland
1,884	1,837	377	426	2,509	2,589	12,000	11,000	3,175	3,581	4,698	5,546	107,000	116,000	Sweden
1,981	1,926	367	361	2,011	1,988	6,000	6,000	3,389	3,700	3,816	4,379	41,868	41,900	Switzerland
552	740	5,865	13,665	...	1	7,000	15,000	260	580	1,093	1,758	29,250	93,000	Syria
...	130	...	...	...	6,659	...	60,800	...	...	...	...	...	...	Taiwan
11,335	14,000	3,428	4,100	137	178	14,000	27,000	322	424	160	160	23,048	55,458	Tanzania
4,205	4,800	34	45	3,599	4,300	51,000	79,000	6	35	1,870	2,692	82,667	125,000	Thailand
214	240	792	850	257	240	2,000	4,000	6	7	225	225	1,612	3,622	Togo
...	...	...	...	1	1	...	—	...	...	...	...	5	4	Tokelau
6	8	...	...	47	65	...	—	...	...	1,494	1,500	279	400	Tonga
72	77	9	12	54	83	6,000	8,000	7	10	1,733	1,705	7,353	7,950	Trinidad and Tobago
860	620	5,726	5,220	3	4	13,000	16,000	204	270	851	1,337	16,333	51,000	Tunisia
14,490	17,300	40,666	40,391	15	12	39,000	60,000	2,941	3,400	589	667	137,487	275,000	Turkey
...	...	...	...	...	...	...	...	...	...	...	...	...	...	Turks and Caicos Islands
...	...	...	...	...	7	...	—	...	...	...	...	...	13	Tuvalu
4,745	5,200	973	1,500	167	300	11,000	16,000	276	364	350	350	11,860	17,000	Uganda
108,807	121,055	143,125	142,876	66,735	77,914	727,000	1,090,000	90,086	97,765	2,158	2,247	3,096,433	4,320,000	U.S.S.R.
27	31	97	155	...	...	...	4,000	11	5	790	495	947	4,000	United Arab Emirates
14,394	12,985	28,411	23,946	8,013	7,793	133,000	112,000	14,115	16,250	4,227	4,909	798,784	771,000	United Kingdom
129,265	109,749	14,712	10,443	54,858	54,073	391,000	1,050,000	53,095	64,954	4,769	5,844	3,830,221	4,041,400	United States
10,959	9,948	15,274	20,600	454	450	6,000	6,000	741	850	1,669	1,604	13,069	19,000	Uruguay
105	100	...	...	63	71	...	—	2	2	197	204	203	248	Vanuatu
9,112	12,486	238	410	1,682	3,152	27,000	43,000	1,185	1,532	1,103	1,087	92,756	160,000	Venezuela
1,504	2,150	11	19	8,975	11,500	54,000	70,000	16	34	800	800	53,333	80,000	Vietnam
7	8	3	5	3	6	...	—	3	3	3,732	3,400	170	200	Virgin Islands (U.S.)
...	...	...	...	9	26	...	—	...	...	1,500	1,500	28	41	Wallis and Futuna
...	...	...	...	...	...	...	...	...	...	...	...	...	...	West Bank
...	...	16	24	...	...	...	1,000	...	...	...	...	...	...	Western Sahara
22	27	...	...	47	62	...	1,000	1	1	1,047	1,000	123	175	Western Samoa
80	96	843	940	...	...	1,000	2,000	7	16	400	425	1,442	2,050	Yemen (Aden)
883	950	1,583	1,850	...	...	2,000	15,000	57	60	200	200	9,801	12,144	Yemen (Ṣan'ā')
5,769	5,199	7,953	7,678	7,540	8,673	52,000	65,000	3,662	4,595	1,405	1,702	184,917	238,000	Yugoslavia
1,132	1,350	719	765	673	770	11,000	18,000	6	7	786	855	6,465	7,600	Zaire
1,791	2,600	28	32	164	285	18,000	20,000	50	69	300	300	26,947	30,000	Zambia
6,060	5,800	731	470	201	200	8,000	9,000	194	195	1,529	1,696	9,003	12,000	Zimbabwe

[1]1982. [2]Netherlands Antilles includes Aruba. [3]Belgium includes Luxembourg. [4]1983. [5]South Africa includes Bophuthatswana, Ciskei, Transkei, and Venda.

Extractive industries

Extractive industries are generally defined as those activities involved in the exploitation of natural resources and include such industries as mining, forestry, fisheries, and agriculture; the definition is sometimes confined to nonrenewable resources. For the purposes of this table agriculture is excluded; it is covered in tables elsewhere in *Britannica World Data.*

Extractive industries are here divided into three parts: mining, forestry, and fisheries. These major headings are each divided into two main subheadings, one that treats production and one that treats foreign trade. The production sections are presented in terms of volume except for mining, and the trade sections are presented in terms of U.S. dollars. The formulation of the sections was determined by the systems of classification used in standard international sources. "Extractive," for example, implies the production of primary (unprocessed) raw materials only, but because of the way national statistical information is reported the table may occasionally include some processed and manufactured materials as well, since these are often indistinguishably associated with the extractive process (sulfur from petroleum extraction, cured or treated lumber, or "processed" fish). This is also the case in the trade sections, where individual national trade nomenclatures may not distinguish some processed and manufactured goods from unprocessed raw materials.

Mining. In the absence of a single international standard of practice for calculating or reporting value of mineral production, single-country sources predominantly have been used to compile mining production figures, supplemented by U.S. Bureau of Mines data and industry sources, especially *Mining Journal*'s *Mining Annual Review.* Each country has its own methods of classifying mining data, which do not always accord with the principal mineral production categories adopted in this table; namely, "metals," "nonmetals," and "energy." The available data have therefore been adjusted to make them accord better with the definition of each group. Included in the "metal" category are all ferrous and nonferrous metallic ores, concentrates, and scrap; the "nonmetal" group includes all nonmetallic minerals (stone, clay, precious gems, etc.) except the mineral fuels; the last group, "energy," is composed predominantly of the natural hydrocarbon fuels, though it may also include manufactured gas.

The contribution (value) of each national mineral sector to its country's gross domestic product is given, as is the distribution by group of that contribution (to gross domestic product and to foreign trade), although statistics regarding the value of mineral production are less readily available in country sources than those regarding trade or volume of minerals produced. Figures for value added by mineral output, though not always available, were sought first, as they provide the most consistent standard to compare the importance of minerals both within a particular national economy and among national mineral sectors worldwide. Where value added to the gross domestic product was not available, gross value of production or sales was substituted. Figures for value of production are reported here in millions of U.S. dollars to permit comparisons to be made from country to country. Comparisons can also be made as to the relative importance of each mineral group within a given country.

Extractive industries

country	mining														
	% of GDP, 1984	mineral production (value added)					trade (value)								
		year	total ('000,000 U.S.$)	by kind (%)			year	exports				imports			
								total ('000,000 U.S.$)	by kind (%)			total ('000,000 U.S.$)	by kind (%)		
				metals[a]	non-metals[b]	energy[c]			metals[a]	non-metals[b]	energy[c]		metals[a]	non-metals[b]	energy[c]
Afghanistan	...	1980–81	233.9[1]	—	0.4[1]	99.6[1]	1982	291.6	—	2.7	97.3	—	—	—	—
Albania	...	...	...	...	...	...	...	...	...	...	...	...	...	...	...
Algeria	26.4[2]	1983	9,341.0	——1.3[3]——		98.7[3]	1983	7,922.1	0.3	0.2	99.5	147.8	9.5	21.7	68.8
American Samoa	...	1983	...	—	100.0	—	1984	—	—	—	—	0.1[5]	—	100.0[5]	—
Andorra	...	...	...	...	...	...	1983	[66]	—	—	100.0	2.1	...	100.0	...
Angola	16.1[2]	1983	549.0	...	...	...	1983	1,365.9	—	0.1	99.9	—	—	—	—
Anguilla	...	...	...	...	...	...	1981	[8]	...	...	...	...	...	...	...
Antigua and Barbuda	0.8	1984	1.0	—	100.0	—	1982	—	—	—	—	—	—	—	—
Argentina	2.2	1983	1,553.0[10]	2.5[7]	10.0[7]	87.5[7]	1983	38.3	75.6	10.6	13.8	238.2	23.4	11.9	64.7
Aruba[11]	...	...	...	...	...	...	...	...	...	...	...	...	...	...	...
Australia	4.5[12]	1982–83	6,415.1	33.0[13]	6.9[13]	60.1[13]	1983	7,132.1	49.8	2.5	47.7	1,320.2	1.1	16.1	82.8
Austria	0.5	1984	309.9	6.1[9]	15.2[9]	78.7[9]	1983	173.6	45.1	45.1	9.8	2,215.4	12.4	7.2	80.4
Bahamas, The	9.2[2]	1983	153.2[15]	—	10.0	90.0[15]	1983	29.7	—	99.8	0.2	348.4	—	—	100.0
Bahrain	31.8[5]	1980	1,152.2	—	—	100.0	1983	32.8	—	3.8	96.2	1,980.8	—	0.1	99.9
Bangladesh	—	1983–84	0.2	...	5.7[16]	94.3[16]	1983	—	—	—	—	34.1	1.4	90.7	7.9
Barbados	1.3	1984	14.4	—	——100.0——		1983	—	—	—	—	1.3	—	—	100.0
Belgium	0.5[2]	1983	393.1	...	...	...	1983[17]	3,771.2	6.4	89.5	4.1	10,358.2	14.7	32.2	53.1
Belize	0.2	1984	0.4	—	100.0	—	1982	—	—	—	—	1.4[5]	—	41.4[5]	58.6[5]
Benin	5.0	1983	2.0	—	——100.0[18]——		1983	...	—	——100.0[18]——		—	—	—	—
Bermuda	2.0[3]	1978–79	2.0	...	...	...	1983	0.3	73.2	26.8	—	0.9	—	—	100.0
Bhutan	0.8[13]	1981–82	1.1[20]	...	...	...	1982	—	—	—	—	...	...	...	...
Bolivia	6.5	1983	437.0	55.8	—	44.2	1984	557.3	——34.7[21]——		65.3	0.6[22]	100.0[22]	—	—
Botswana	28.7[12]	1983	181.0	12.5[7, 23]	86.6[7, 23]	0.9[7, 23]	[24]	...	...	...	...	...	...	...	...
Brazil	0.8[2]	1983	2,162.7	25.3[23]	22.1[23]	52.6[23]	1983	2,038.9	93.7	4.9	1.2	5,687.4	0.8	1.6	97.4
British Virgin Islands	...	1980	—	—	100.0	—	1982	—	—	—	—	0.2[5]	38.7[5]	61.3[5]	—
Brunei	60.6	1984	2,312.6	...	...	...	1983	2,751.4	—	—	100.0	3.6[7]	17.4[7]	82.6[7]	—
Bulgaria	...	...	...	...	...	...	...	...	...	...	...	...	...	...	...
Burkina Faso	—	1982	0.1	—	100.0	—	1982	...	...	...	...	2.9[9]	—	100.0[9]	—
Burma	1.1[26]	1983–84	74.0[27]	...	...	...	1982	57.3	56.5	21.2	22.3	...	...	...	...
Burundi	...	...	...	...	...	...	1983	12.1	2.4	97.6	—	4.4[7]	—	100.0[7]	—
Cameroon	15.3[12]	1982–83	1,191.1[18]	...	...	...	1983	1,012.3	0.2	—	99.8	29.9[7]	66.6[7]	33.4[7]	—
Canada	6.0	1984	20,024.7	32.0[7]	12.9[7]	55.1[7]	1983	11,320.3	20.8	9.2	70.0	5,225.2	25.8	7.3	66.9
Cape Verde	0.3[9]	1981	0.2	—	100.0	—	1982	1.1	1.8	98.2	—	0.8[5]	—	—	100.0[5]
Cayman Islands	...	...	...	...	...	...	1982	6.7	—	2.0	98.0	0.4[5]	—	—	100.0[5]
Central African Republic	3.2[2]	1983	16.0[28]	——100.0[28]——		—	1983	37.3	—	100.0	—	1.4[5]	—	100.0[5]	—
Chad	0.5[2]	1983	3.0	—	100.0	—	1982	—	—	100.0	—	...	...	...	...
Chile	8.9[2]	1983	1,671.7	...	...	...	1983	736.5	94.7	5.3	—	271.5	4.7	4.7	90.6
China	...	...	...	...	...	...	1982	3,923.9	4.1	4.2	91.7	773.4	76.4	15.7	7.9
Christmas Island	...	1984	...	—	100.0	—	1983	49.6	—	100.0	—	...	...	...	...
Cocos (Keeling) Islands	...	...	...	...	...	...	1983	0.1[9]	—	100.0[9]	—	0.2	100.0	—	—
Colombia	3.4	1984	1,241.7	...	...	...	1984	171.0[30]	47.4	18.1	34.5	420.4[2]	1.6[2]	7.6[2]	90.8[2]
Comoros	—	1984	—	—	100.0	—	1982	1.6	97.1	2.9	—	...	...	...	...
Congo	43.0	1984	905.3[18]	...	...	...	1982	901.5	1.7	5.1	93.2	3.8[5]	—	100.0[5]	—
Cook Islands	—	1982	...	...	...	...	1982	0.6	88.6	11.4	—	0.1[5]	—	42.1[5]	57.9[5]
Costa Rica	1.9[2]	1979	75.9	23.6[3]	76.4[3]	—	1983	0.9	100.0	—	—	110.3[7]	0.1[7]	3.9[7]	96.0[7]
Côte d'Ivoire	2.1[2]	1983	110.0[18]	...	...	...	1983	60.2	1.6	35.1	63.3	260.5	0.2	4.5	95.3
Cuba	...	...	...	...	...	...	1983	396.6	100.0	—	—	999.2[7]	—	2.5[7]	97.5[7]
Cyprus	0.6	1984	12.9	13.8[7]	86.2[7]	—	1983	11.9	28.4	71.6	—	124.3	—	4.2	95.8
Czechoslovakia	2.3[2]	1983	1,881.0	13.0	10.0	77.0	1983	426.3[31, 32]	...	13.0	87.0	2,324.0[31, 33]	24.5	4.5	71.0
Denmark	0.7	1984	382.6	—	12.5[7]	87.5[7]	1983	356.8	18.0	11.4	70.6	1,748.4	1.8	4.8	93.4
Djibouti	—	1983	—	—	100.0	—	1982	—	—	—	—	22.9[34]	——6.8——		93.2[34]
Dominica	0.7[2]	1983	0.5	—	100.0	—	1980	0.1[3]	—	100.0[3]	—	0.4	—	43.3	56.7
Dominican Republic	3.6[2]	1983	292.0	97.0[5]	3.0[5]	—	1983	195.6[7]	98.8[7]	1.2[7]	—	342.5	0.1	—	99.9
Ecuador	16.2	1984	2,033.0	—	0.3[5]	99.7[5]	1982	1,472.1	—	—	100.0	12.2	7.5	92.5	—
Egypt	23.3[2]	1983	6,917.0	——4.1[4, 16]——		95.9[4, 16]	1983	2,897.3	0.1	0.2	99.7	103.1	1.7	29.2	69.1

Since the data for value of mineral production are obtained mostly from country sources, there is some variation (from a standard calendar year) in the time periods to which the data refer. In addition, the time period for which production data are available does not always correspond with the year for which mineral trade data are available.

The Standard International Trade Classification (SITC), Revision 2, was used to determine the commodity groupings for foreign trade statistics. The actual trade data for these groups is taken largely from the United Nations annual *Yearbook of International Trade Statistics* and national sources.

Forestry. Data for the production and trade sections of forestry are based on the United Nations annual *Yearbook of Forest Products.* Production of roundwood (all wood obtained in removals from forests) is the principal indicator of the volume of each country's forestry sector; this total is broken down further (as percentages of the roundwood total) into its principal components: fuelwood and charcoal, and industrial roundwood. The latter group was further divided to show its principal component, sawlogs and veneer; lesser categories of industrial roundwood could not be shown for reasons of space. These included pitprops (used in mining, a principal consumer of wood) and pulpwood (used in papermaking and plastics). Value of trade in forest products is given for both imports and exports, although exports alone tend to be the significant indicator for producing countries, while imports of wood are rarely a significant fraction of the trade of most importing countries.

Fisheries. Data for nominal (live weight) catches of fish, crustaceans, mollusks, etc., in all fishing areas (inland waters and marine areas) are taken from the United Nations annual *Yearbook of Fishery Statistics* (*Catches and Landings*). Total catch figures are given in metric tons; the catches in inland waters and marine areas are given as percentages of the total catch, as are the main kinds of catch—fish, crustaceans, and mollusks. The principal exclusion is marine mammals, such as whales and seals.

Figures for trade in fishery products (including processed products and preparations like oils, meals, and animal feeding stuffs) are taken from the United Nations annual *Yearbook of Fishery Statistics* (*Fishery Commodities*). Value figures for trade in fish products are given for both imports and exports.

The following notes further define the column headings:

a. Includes ferrous and nonferrous metallic ores and scraps, such as bauxite, copper, gold (except unwrought or semimanufactured), iron ore, lead, uranium, or zinc.

b. Includes natural fertilizers; stone, sand, and aggregate; and pearls, precious and semiprecious stones, worked and unworked.

c. Includes hydrocarbon solids, liquids, and gases.

1 cubic metre = 35.3147 cubic feet

1 metric ton = 1.1023 short tons

forestry, 1984						fisheries, 1984								country
production of roundwood				trade (value '000 U.S.$)		catch (nominal)						trade (value, '000 U.S.$)		
total ('000 cubic metres)	fuelwood, charcoal (%)	industrial roundwood (%)		exports	imports	total ('000 metric tons)	by source (%)		by kind of catch (%)			exports	imports	
		total	sawlogs, veneer				marine	fresh-water	fish	crusta-ceans	mollusks			
5,699	74.6	25.4	15.0	...	28,496	1.5	—	100.0	100.0	—	—	...	...	Afghanistan
2,330	69.0	31.0	31.0	730	3,900	4.0	100.0	—	100.0	—	—	...	...	Albania
1,688	86.6	13.4	1.2	1,502[4]	348,318	75.0	100.0	—	95.5	4.5	—	182	22,941	Algeria
...	...	...	...	...	1,426[2, 6]	0.4	100.0	—	76.0	0.9	—	205,231	2,195	American Samoa
...	...	...	...	...	...	—	—	—	—	—	—	...	...	Andorra
9,078	84.4	15.6	6.1	98[7]	258	70.7	88.7	11.3	99.9	0.1	0.1	...	19,506[2]	Angola
...	...	...	...	...	...	—	100.0	—	100.0	—	—	49[7]	...	Anguilla
...	...	...	...	...	2,596[9]	2.2	100.0	—	99.2	0.8	—	—	—	Antigua and Barbuda
13,375	62.9	37.1	17.7	8,218	176,742	314.2	97.0	3.0	82.4	7.5	10.1	149,623	8,363	Argentina
...	...	...	...	...	...	...	...	...	...	...	...	...	...	Aruba[11]
18,286	15.7	84.3	40.2	215,231	750,071	168.1	98.3	1.7	46.3[14]	24.1[14]	29.6[14]	345,664	228,366	Australia
14,204	9.9	90.1	61.3	1,276,721	573,410	4.7	—	100.0	100.0	—	—	1,714	69,301	Austria
115	—	100.0	13.0	1,207[4]	7,829	5.3	100.0	—	25.6	64.7	8.9	14,130	1,260	Bahamas, The
—	—	—	—	...	49,186	6.1	100.0	—	82.9	16.3	0.8	—	3,795	Bahrain
26,359	97.1	2.9	1.5	4,495	3,833	758.0	22.7	77.3	96.4	3.6	—	79,702	—	Bangladesh
...	...	...	...	...	19,708	6.5	100.0	—	100.0	—	—	—	2,270	Barbados
3,086[17]	17.4[17]	82.6[17]	52.7[17]	600,736[17]	1,217,709[17]	47.9	100.0	—	93.6	3.8	2.6	87,199[17]	297,488[17]	Belgium
164	76.8	23.2	23.2	1,061	2,011	1.6	96.9	3.1	40.6	27.5	31.9	5,671	140	Belize
4,234	94.8	5.2	0.6	...	5,643	20.0	18.0	82.0	100.0	—	—	63	2,287	Benin
...	...	...	...	...	2,460[2, 19]	0.5	100.0	—	95.8	4.2	—	—	6,364	Bermuda
3,224	91.4	8.6	7.4	501	143[9]	1.0	—	100.0	100.0	—	—	—	—	Bhutan
1,282	88.4	11.6	10.6	5,923	12,400	5.6	—	100.0	100.0	—	—	—	1,160	Bolivia
798	91.4	8.6	—	...	1,640	1.5	—	100.0	100.0	—	—	—	1,230	Botswana
222,177	74.0	26.0	14.3	1,028,594	174,669	946.0	78.8	21.2	87.9	11.0	1.1	177,691	33,582	Brazil
...	...	...	...	10[5, 25]	181[5, 19]	0.3	100.0	—	92.1	7.9	—	216[5]	145[5]	British Virgin Islands
295	26.8	73.2	69.8	90	6,915	2.8	95.1	4.9	76.3	23.7	—	—	4,250	Brunei
4,841	35.7	64.3	27.0	24,533	160,135	112.9	88.5	11.5	95.5	—	4.5	13,390	9,250	Bulgaria
6,586	95.4	4.6	0.1	...	5,234	7.0	—	100.0	100.0	—	—	—	800	Burkina Faso
19,497	84.3	15.7	9.8	107,300	12,010	612.8	76.5	23.5	100.0	—	—	10,990	—	Burma
3,466	98.9	1.1	0.1	...	431	12.0	—	100.0	100.0	—	—	159	622	Burundi
10,408	76.8	23.2	17.1	95,300	5,150	52.5	61.9	38.1	98.3	1.7	—	1,670	15,403	Cameroon
161,005	3.8	96.2	69.1	11,518,828	1,005,374	1,220.6	96.2	3.8	88.7	6.8	4.5	1,237,337	373,031	Canada
...	...	...	...	...	1,801	9.1	100.0	—	99.6	0.4	—	2,110	—	Cape Verde
...	...	...	...	...	...	0.6	100.0	—	—	100.0	—	2,167	84	Cayman Islands
3,158	84.9	15.1	8.2	20,410	1,626	13.0	—	100.0	100.0	—	—	—	—	Central African Republic
3,482	85.8	14.2	0.1	...	1,352	110.0	—	100.0	100.0	—	—	...	...	Chad
14,971	40.0	60.0	30.3	371,229	49,300	4,499.3	100.0	—	97.0	0.6	2.0	419,373	—	Chile
231,650[29]	66.8[29]	33.2[29]	17.6[29]	415,104[29]	1,752,180[29]	5,926.8	62.0	38.0	79.9	9.8	10.0	303,880	—	China
...	...	...	...	...	...	—	100.0	—	100.0	—	—	...	...	Christmas Island
...	...	...	...	...	...	—	...	...	100.0	—	—	...	...	Cocos (Keeling) Islands
16,916	84.2	15.8	11.6	49,824	114,644	78.5	32.0	68.0	87.4	10.6	2.0	30,286	47,220	Colombia
...	...	...	...	...	...	4.0	100.0	—	98.7	1.3	—	—	193	Comoros
2,357	65.8	34.2	24.9	86,561	2,120	31.3	61.7	38.3	99.9	0.1	—	360	18,840	Congo
...	...	...	...	...	...	0.8	100.0	—	68.5	0.7	28.4	—	234	Cook Islands
3,395	73.3	26.7	21.2	22,800	72,426	12.0	98.2	1.8	77.1	21.5	0.4	17,400	2,205	Costa Rica
12,190	63.1	36.9	32.0	259,223	16,760	83.7	78.5	21.5	96.2	3.8	—	49,463	33,750	Côte d'Ivoire
3,132	87.7	12.3	1.1	...	188,943	199.6	91.9	8.1	87.2	9.6	2.6	157,900	32,200	Cuba
80	28.8	71.2	45.0	156	50,269	2.3	97.5	2.5	88.8	0.1	11.1	—	7,818	Cyprus
18,913	6.9	93.1	54.6	382,958	89,840	19.7	—	100.0	100.0	—	—	2,638	55,717	Czechoslovakia
3,252	10.8	89.2	37.9	232,844	854,584	1,846.7	98.8	1.2	95.0	0.6	4.4	898,867	326,611	Denmark
...	...	...	...	...	57	0.4	100.0	—	97.9	2.1	—	—	430	Djibouti
...	...	...	...	...	880	0.4	100.0	—	100.0	—	—	—	530	Dominica
969	99.4	0.6	0.4	17[9]	58,834	13.2	86.9	13.1	82.5	6.6	10.5	3,720	8,360	Dominican Republic
8,228	72.9	27.1	25.3	18,657	119,762	867.5	100.0	—	95.5	4.0	0.5	219,348	—	Ecuador
1,958	95.4	4.6	—	...	599,886	138.5	18.9	81.1	97.0	2.2	0.8	1,060	80,670	Egypt

Extractive industries (continued)

country	mining: % of GDP, 1984	mineral production (value added): year	mineral production: total ('000,000 U.S.$)	mineral production by kind (%): metals[a]	mineral production by kind (%): non-metals[b]	mineral production by kind (%): energy[c]	trade (value): year	exports: total ('000,000 U.S.$)	exports by kind (%): metals[a]	exports by kind (%): non-metals[b]	exports by kind (%): energy[c]	imports: total ('000,000 U.S.$)	imports by kind (%): metals[a]	imports by kind (%): non-metals[b]	imports by kind (%): energy[c]
El Salvador	0.2	1984	7.2	——100.0——		—	1982	2.4	8.7	91.3	—	227.0	—	2.1	97.9
Equatorial Guinea	—	1984	...	...	...	...	1982	1.4	95.7	4.3	—	...	...	...	...
Ethiopia	0.2[26]	1984–85	7.9	——100.0——		—	1982	—	—	—	—	173.3	0.2	—	99.8
Faeroe Islands	—	1984	—	—	—	—	1983	—	—	—	—	2.1[31]	1.3	87.2	11.5[31]
Falkland Islands	...	...	...	...	...	...	1982	—	—	—	—	...	...	...	...
Fiji	0.1	1983	6.9[35]	82.5[5, 23]	17.5[5, 23]	—	1983	15.3[5]	100.0[5]	—	—	4.5[31]	1.5	36.1	62.4[31]
Finland	0.4	1984	183.0	47.0[7]	53.0[7]	—	1983	68.1	51.7	43.2	5.1	2,868.5	6.4	4.5	89.1
France	0.7	1984	3,604.5	2.9[7]	32.5[7]	64.6[7]	1983	1,684.3	47.6	25.3	27.1	22,436.4	4.2	3.8	92.0
French Guiana	...	1984	...	——100.0——		—	1983	—	—	—	—	1.1	—	—	100.0
French Polynesia	...	...	...	...	...	...	1982	1.1	21.9	78.1	—	5.1[5, 31]	—	30.7[5]	69.3[5, 31]
Gabon	47.2[2]	1983	1,589.5	8.9	0.1	91.0	1982	1,515.9	5.3	—	94.7	7.4	—	100.0	—
Gambia, The	0.1[12]	1982–83	1.2	—	100.0	—	1982	0.4	—	100.0	—	—	—	—	—
Gaza Strip	...	...	...	...	...	...	[38]	[38]	...	...	...	...	...	...	...
Germany, East	...	...	...	...	...	...	...	...	...	...	...	...	...	...	...
Germany, West	1.0[2]	1983[39]	6,814.7	0.2[1, 7]	17.4[1, 7]	82.4[1, 7]	1983	3,669.7	18.7	16.8	64.5	25,298.6	10.9	4.4	84.7
Ghana	0.3[2]	1982[40]	131.0	92.8	7.2[41]	—	1982	48.9	54.4	23.1	22.5	331.0[5]	20.7[5]	1.6[5]	77.7[5]
Gibraltar	...	...	...	...	...	...	1983	5.9[7]	100.0[7]	—	—	0.8	—	99.4	0.6
Greece	1.8	1984	618.3	18.7[9]	40.4[9]	40.9[9]	1983	215.2	48.7	42.0	9.3	2,519.2	2.9	1.8	95.3
Greenland	...	1984	...	——100.0——		—	1983	50.2	96.0	4.0	—	1.1[31]	0.4	75.9	23.7[18]
Grenada	1.0	1984	0.7	—	100.0	—	1984	—	—	—	—	0.1[5]	2.7[5]	—	97.3[5]
Guadeloupe	...	1980	...	—	100.0	—	1983	0.2	100.0	—	—	5.5	—	30.4	69.6
Guam	...	1983	...	—	100.0	—	1982	1.1	100.0	—	—	...	...	...	...
Guatemala	0.4[2]	1982	30.8[18]	...	...	...	1983	48.2	0.1	5.1	94.8	121.2[9]	1.2[9]	6.1[9]	92.7[9]
Guernsey	...	...	...	...	...	...	...	...	...	...	...	...	...	...	...
Guinea	15.0[72]	1983	299.0[43]	——100.0[43]——		—	1982	414.8	97.6	2.4	—	0.8	100.0	—	—
Guinea-Bissau	1.3[2]	1983	1.0	—	100.0	—	1983	0.9	—	100.0	—	1.3[5]	—	89.5[5]	10.5[5]
Guyana	3.8	1984	17.0[44]	...	...	...	1983	122.3	99.6	0.4	—	3.5[22]	—	47.2[22]	52.8[22]
Haiti	0.1	1983	1.6[45]	...	...	—	1982	19.2	100.0	—	—	0.9[22]	—	99.1[22]	0.9[22]
Honduras	2.1	1984	66.0	——100.0——		—	1983	44.7	100.0	—	—	19.2[7]	—	9.9[7]	90.1[7]
Hong Kong	0.2[2]	1983	40.0	—	100.0	—	1983	532.9	40.5	58.9	0.6	877.8	1.5	74.3	24.2
Hungary	8.1[2]	1983	1,401.8	3.7	2.6	93.7	1983	...	...	...	...	1,918.5[31, 34]	3.1	4.9	92.0[31, 34]
Iceland	—[5]	1984	...	—	100.0	—	1984	8.1[2]	15.1	84.9	—	44.9	75.8	14.0	10.2
India	3.3[46]	1983–84	5,384.5	4.5[2]	4.5[2]	91.0[2]	1983	2,790.6	18.1	42.8	39.1	2,840.4	4.4	35.4	60.2
Indonesia	17.7	1984	14,833.8	2.3[7]	0.2[7]	97.5[7]	1983	15,495.9	1.8	0.1	98.1	1,018.0	5.0	7.2	87.8
Iran	17.9[12]	1982–83	23,059.3	——8.2[23]——		91.8[23]	1983	18,229.5	0.1	0.2	99.7	56.4	5.3	36.3	58.4
Iraq	23.9[9]	1981	7,671.4[18]	...	...	...	1983	8,645.9	—	0.1	99.9	47.2	19.8	39.8	40.4
Ireland	1.2[9]	1981	211.2[47]	18.7	79.8	1.4[47]	1983	192.4	56.6	34.9	8.5	482.7	7.2	8.7	84.1
Isle of Man	...	...	...	...	...	...	...	...	...	...	...	...	...	...	...
Israel	0.7[48]	1981–82	198.2	5.7[48, 49]	94.3[48]	[48, 49]	1983	1,352.2	0.4	99.6	—	2,396.0	0.2	38.9	60.9
Italy	1.0[9]	1981	2,728.7	3.4	17.3	79.3	1983	466.1	25.6	56.7	17.7	21,182.6	5.8	3.0	91.2
Jamaica	4.1[2]	1983	144.2	97.7[7]	2.3[7]	—	1983	486.0	99.8	0.2	—	5.2	0.6	—	99.4
Japan	0.4[2]	1983	4,900.8	10.1[7]	26.8[7]	63.1[7]	1983	317.7	43.5	55.9	0.6	61,140.2	10.7	2.8	86.5
Jersey	...	...	...	...	...	...	...	...	...	...	...	...	...	...	...
Jordan	2.9	1984	114.6	—	——100.0——		1983	128.5	—	100.0	—	697.5	0.1	0.2	99.7
Kampuchea	...	1984	...	...	100.0	...	1982	3.8	100.0	—	—	...	...	...	...
Kenya	0.2	1984	11.8	0.8[7]	99.2[7]	—	1982	49.8	10.6	46.3	43.1	542.3	0.1	0.5	99.4
Kiribati	...	...	...	...	...	...	1982	—	—	—	—	0.2[9]	100.0[9]	—	—
Korea, North	...	...	...	...	...	...	...	...	...	...	...	...	...	...	...
Korea, South	1.5	1984	1,209.7	4.8[7]	42.6[7]	52.6[7]	1983	129.4	42.4	54.2	3.4	6,234.8	8.2	2.5	89.3
Kuwait	49.8[46]	1983–84	10.615.2	—	0.3[7]	99.7[7]	1983	4,415.3	0.7	0.4	98.9	206.9	0.9	11.5	87.6
Laos	...	1984	...	——100.0——		—	1982	0.7	100.0	—	—	...	...	...	...
Lebanon	...	...	...	...	...	...	1983	37.5	22.0	78.0	—	187.7	0.4	21.5	78.1
Lesotho	0.2[46]	1983–84	0.9	—	100.0	—	[24]	...	...	...	...	...	...	...	...
Liberia	15.0[2]	1983	151.0	93.4[9, 23]	6.6[9, 23]	—	1983	466.9	85.4	14.6	—	106.5[9]	—	3.8[9]	96.2[9]
Libya	50.6[2]	1983	15,471.0	—	0.9[22]	99.1[22]	1983	10,906.2	—	—	100.0	86.7	80.1	19.9	—
Liechtenstein	...	...	...	...	...	...	...	...	...	...	...	...	...	...	...
Luxembourg	0.1[2]	1983	3.9	—	100.0	—	[17]	...	...	...	...	...	...	...	...
Macau	...	1982	3.0	—	100.0	—	1983	4.5	0.4	99.6	—	8.6[9]	44.5[9]	28.3[9]	27.2[9]
Madagascar	0.3[2]	1983	6.0	——100.0——		—	1982	14.3	34.2	65.8	—	73.9	0.3	—	99.7
Malaŵi	—	1984	—	—	100.0	—	1982	—	—	—	—	5.9[9]	—	45.8[9]	54.2[9]
Malaysia	4.9	1984	535.1[23, 53]	...	...	...	1983	3,184.5	3.8	1.1	95.1	755.8	18.8	9.2	72.0
Maldives	1.3[2]	1983	0.9	—	100.0	—	1982	—	—	—	—	...	...	...	...
Mali	0.2	1984	2.6[54]	——100.0——		—	1983	2.0	—	100.0	—	1.1[22]	0.1[22]	99.9[22]	—
Malta	0.2[9]	1981	2.9	—	100.0	—	1983	6.0	21.9	78.1	—	10.5[31]	—	76.7	23.3[31]
Martinique	...	1984	...	—	100.0	—	1983	3.3	14.1	—	85.9	80.2	—	—	100.0
Mauritania	15.4[2]	1983	110.0	——100.0——		—	1983	162.1	99.6	—	0.4	0.1	—	100.0	—
Mauritius	0.1	1984	1.4	—	100.0	—	1983	3.4	—	100.0	—	2.5	—	100.0	—
Mayotte	...	1984	...	...	...	...	...	...	...	...	...	...	...	...	...
Mexico	12.0[15]	1984	21,056.0[15]	6.2[2]	3.8[2]	90.0[2, 15]	1983	15,771.9	1.4	1.4	97.2	199.5	40.7	31.5	27.8
Monaco	...	...	...	...	...	...	...	...	...	...	...	...	...	...	...
Mongolia	...	...	...	...	...	...	...	...	...	...	...	...	...	...	...
Montserrat	0.7[2]	1983	0.2	...	...	...	1982	0.7	100.0	—	—	0.1[3]	—	21.7[3]	78.3[3]
Morocco	4.8[2]	1983	541.0	——97.1[9, 23]——		2.9[9, 23]	1983	660.5	12.6	86.4	1.0	827.3	—	5.8	94.2
Mozambique	0.4[2]	1983	18.0	...	...	...	1983	9.7	17.2	37.3	45.5	5.2	—	100.0	—
Nauru	...	1984	...	—	100.0	—	1984	125.0	—	100.0	—	...	...	...	...
Nepal	0.2[12]	1982–83	4.7	...	...	...	1981	—	—	—	—	15.7	9.6	85.6	4.8
Netherlands, The	7.9	1984	9,698.6	—	2.6[5]	97.4[5]	1983	6,169.3	7.6	6.6	85.8	11,512.6	5.5	5.4	89.1
Netherlands Antilles[11]	...	1983	...	—	100.0	—	1983[56]	154.7	3.1	12.7	84.2	4,400.2	—	—	100.0
New Caledonia	9.3[2]	1983	72.0	100.0	—	—	1983	24.7	100.0	—	—	9.2	—	5.4	94.6
New Zealand	1.0[46]	1983–84	232.7	8.3[3]	18.7[3]	73.0[3]	1983	48.1	67.9	6.6	25.5	591.5	18.1	20.2	61.7
Nicaragua	1.0[2]	1983	36.6	——100.0——		—	1982	—	—	—	—	152.1	—	1.5	98.5
Niger	8.7	1984	122.7	96.4[5, 23]	2.0[5, 23]	1.6[5, 23]	1982	319.3	93.9	—	6.1	9.6[9]	—	100.0[9]	—
Nigeria	20.4[46]	1983–84	13,256.1	0.2[7]	7.6[7]	92.2[7]	1983	11,736.4	0.1	—	99.9	54.5	10.6	89.4	—
Niue	—	1983	—	—	100.0	—	1983	—	—	100.0	—	...	...	...	...
Norfolk Island	...	...	...	...	...	...	1983	—	—	—	—	...	...	...	...

forestry, 1984						fisheries, 1984								country
production of roundwood				trade (value '000 U.S.$)		catch (nominal)						trade (value, '000 U.S.$)		
total ('000 cubic metres)	fuelwood, charcoal (%)	industrial roundwood (%)		exports	imports	total ('000 metric tons)	by source (%)		by kind of catch (%)			exports	imports	
		total	sawlogs, veneer				marine	fresh-water	fish	crusta-ceans	mollusks			
4,620	98.1	1.9	1.3	6,587	31,052	12.2	86.0	14.0	25.6	73.0	1.4	17,601	1,541	El Salvador
587	76.1	23.9	23.9	11,200	...	4.0	90.0	10.0	81.2	11.2	3.8	306	2,430	Equatorial Guinea
31,154	94.2	5.8	0.4	...	10,403	3.9	10.3	89.7	100.0	—	—	—	90	Ethiopia
...	...	...	...	...	...	320.8	100.0	—	97.0	2.0	1.0	148,561	2,561	Faeroe Islands
...	...	...	...	...	...	—	100.0	—	100.0	—	—	...	...	Falkland Islands
213	13.1	86.9	85.0	5,057	9,642	31.3	83.5	16.5	76.8	3.2	18.1	13,838	7,480	Fiji
40,875	7.7	92.3	43.1	4,642,464	337,289	160.9	78.9	21.1	100.0	—	—	10,923	88,167	Finland
38,681	26.9	73.1	48.1	1,379,726	2,534,491	738.8[14, 36]	...	...	75.3[14, 36]	3.8[14, 36]	20.9[14, 36]	293,586[36]	975,596[36]	France
254	26.0	74.0	70.5	2,169	1,087	2.5	100.0	—	63.1	36.9	—	23,206	19,363	French Guiana
...	...	...	...	...	18,132	2.4	100.0	—	99.9	0.1	—	—	4,970	French Polynesia
2,706	45.2	54.8	54.8	188,736	3,969	52.6	95.0	5.0	96.4	3.5	0.1	3,472	10,250	Gabon
777	97.3	2.7	1.8	...	164	12.7[37]	72.4[37]	27.6[37]	96.0[37]	4.0[37]	...	933	980	Gambia, The
...	...	...	...	...	...	1.6	100.0	—	99.9	0.1	—	...	...	Gaza Strip
10,984	6.1	93.9	40.7	90,600	432,500	223.3	91.9	8.1	95.8	0.2	4.0	...	12,240	Germany, East
26,778	14.2	85.8	51.1	2,465,277	5,090,947	326.8	93.0	7.0	76.0	3.7	20.3	295,510	800,615	Germany, West
8,075	90.2	9.8	5.1	16,998	2,889	238.4	83.2	16.8	98.8	0.2	1.0	23,540	10,560	Ghana
...	...	...	...	...	...	—	—	—	—	—	—	...	...	Gibraltar
2,683	71.4	28.6	15.2	31,374	284,647	100.0	91.4	8.6	90.9	3.8	5.3	26,521	85,314	Greece
—	—	—	—	...	...	76.5	100.0	—	54.8	45.2	—	101,920	661	Greenland
...	...	...	...	...	...	0.6	100.0	—	98.1	0.2	1.4	—	370	Grenada
17	88.2	11.8	11.8	4,143[4]	14,194	8.9	100.0	—	95.1	1.3	3.4	80	6,977	Guadeloupe
...	...	...	...	777[72]	1,935[72]	0.2	73.8	26.2	98.4	1.6	—	1,039[2]	6,613[2]	Guam
7,000	97.8	2.2	2.1	10,324	56,263	3.0	98.2	1.8	23.0	77.0	—	11,470	1,820	Guatemala
...	...	...	...	...	...	[42]	[42]	[42]	[42]	[42]	[42]	...	...	Guernsey
3,635	84.9	15.1	5.0	3,646[22]	...	18.5	94.6	5.4	100.0	—	—	—	4,000	Guinea
558	75.6	24.4	7.2	130	98	2.7	100.0	—	91.5	8.4	0.1	2,500	—	Guinea-Bissau
201	6.0	94.0	89.1	6,260	6,009	32.4	97.5	2.5	89.3	10.7	—	22,571	—	Guyana
5,761	95.9	4.1	3.9	...	4,955	4.4	93.2	6.8	97.7	2.3	—	—	6,580	Haiti
4,937	89.0	11.0	10.7	31,080	20,843	8.4	98.7	1.3	12.8	81.8	5.4	33,455	2,240	Honduras
180	100.0	—	—	51,234	566,513	199.7	96.7	3.3	87.0	7.0	6.0	236,398	439,924	Hong Kong
6,107	41.6	58.4	31.7	89,057	264,773	39.0	—	100.0	100.0	—	—	4,650	38,833	Hungary
—	—	—	—	...	35,375	1,534.8	100.0	—	97.1	1.8	1.1	509,245	3,711	Iceland
238,861	91.6	8.4	6.1	14,428	212,374	2,858.9	62.2	37.8	91.4	7.9	0.7	331,155	—	India
148,194	80.3	19.7	17.8	1,134,997	247,986	2,217.2	75.7	24.3	88.3	6.6	3.3	229,248	28,324	Indonesia
6,739	35.1	64.9	5.5	38	263,333	41.4	90.3	9.7	95.2	4.8	—	27,400	27,800	Iran
137	63.5	36.5	14.6	...	158,081	21.0	23.8	76.2	100.0	—	—	...	...	Iraq
1,256	3.7	96.3	50.8	35,006	289,296	207.6	100.0	—	88.8	3.6	7.5	87,046	34,957	Ireland
...	...	...	...	...	...	7.7	100.0	—	20.9	0.9	78.2	3,460[2]	...	Isle of Man
118	9.3	90.7	22.0	12,215	202,823	23.0	42.3	57.7	99.6	0.4	—	1,450	32,889	Israel
9,259	52.3	47.7	25.2	724,505	2,787,186	495.0	91.2	8.8	73.2	6.2	20.6	104,943[50]	742,063[50]	Italy
117	31.6	68.4	57.3	1,452	49,380	9.6	95.3	4.7	100.0	—	—	—	19,130	Jamaica
32,819	1.8	98.2	62.1	715,479	6,130,610	12,021.2	98.3	1.7	86.1	1.8	10.8	881,965	4,142,937	Japan
...	...	...	...	...	...	3.7[42]	100.0[42]	—	8.5[42]	91.0[42]	0.5[42]	3,075	...	Jersey
9	55.6	44.4	—	8,056	71,149	—	100.0	—	100.0	—	—	—	9,021	Jordan
5,215	89.1	10.9	2.1	173	1,885	65.0	8.5	91.5	99.4	0.6	—	...	...	Kampuchea
31,115	95.1	4.9	1.4	3,255	18,201	89.9	6.7	93.3	99.6	0.3	0.1	2,060	1,140	Kenya
...	...	...	...	...	...	25.9	100.0	—	96.1	—	3.9	—	160	Kiribati
4,462	86.6	13.4	13.4	...	1,879	1,650.0	93.9	6.1	100.0	—	—	33,336	—	Korea, North
6,675	66.1	33.9	17.0	196,882	861,712	2,477.1	98.0	2.0	72.9	2.9	23.1	776,967	66,212	Korea, South
—	—	—	—	28,058	123,492	4.6	100.0	—	85.3	14.7	—	17,850	17,920	Kuwait
4,236	94.1	5.9	3.3	4,518	816[5]	20.0	—	100.0	100.0	—	—	—	...	Laos
470	94.7	5.3	5.3	3,239	65,701	1.3	92.3	7.7	100.0	—	—	...	...	Lebanon
293	100.0	—	—	[51]	[51]	—	—	100.0	100.0	—	—	—	1,910	Lesotho
4,174	89.3	10.7	7.6	23,717	1,352	14.7	72.7	27.3	98.3	1.7	—	2,780	9,480	Liberia
633	84.7	15.3	10.0	...	120,311	7.8	100.0	—	100.0	—	—	—	12,470	Libya
...	...	...	...	...	...	—	—	100.0	100.0	—	—	[52]	[52]	Liechtenstein
[17]	[17]	[17]	[17]	[17]	[17]	—	—	—	—	—	—	[17]	[17]	Luxembourg
				28	12,435	7.0	100.0	—	42.9	57.1	—	7,654	9,945	Macau
6,262	87.1	12.9	7.5	104	8,899	56.0	24.1	75.9	88.3	11.4	0.1	22,763	—	Madagascar
6,444	94.1	5.9	2.0	600	16,720	65.1	—	100.0	100.0	—	—	910	290	Malawi
40,212	18.4	81.6	78.6	2,139,590	212,918	665.0	99.4	0.6	72.6	12.8	12.3	99,165	107,927	Malaysia
...	...	...	...	...	...	47.5	100.0	—	100.0	—	—	10,397	—	Maldives
4,751	93.7	6.3	0.1	...	1,174	54.0	—	100.0	100.0	—	—	626	1,557	Mali
...	...	...	...	...	30,850	1.2	100.0	—	94.6	2.7	2.7	1,397	4,912	Malta
11	90.9	9.1	9.1	...	14,096	5.2	100.0	—	96.9	2.1	—	—	10,613	Martinique
12	58.3	41.7	8.3	...	...	55.0	80.0	20.0	79.7	1.9	18.4	148,717	—	Mauritania
30	73.3	26.7	20.0	...	6,679	10.3	99.8	0.2	96.2	0.6	3.2	7,804	6,682	Mauritius
...	...	...	...	...	...	0.7[55]	...	...	...	...	...	...	...	Mayotte
20,762	65.0	35.0	20.9	18,234	382,816	1,103.7	89.4	10.6	85.1	8.1	6.5	468,234	8,002	Mexico
...	...	...	...	...	...	—	100.0	—	100.0	—	—	[36]	[36]	Monaco
2,390	56.5	43.5	43.5	9,300	6,800	0.4	—	100.0	100.0	—	—	—	1,310	Mongolia
...	...	...	...	...	367[6, 9]	0.1	100.0	—	100.0	—	—	—	178[5]	Montserrat
1,717	66.7	33.3	4.0	19,858	160,030	467.5	99.7	0.3	89.6	0.4	10.0	203,893	246	Morocco
15,029	93.6	6.4	0.8	1,900	1,150	42.4	88.2	11.8	80.6	18.8	0.6	28,251	7,430	Mozambique
...	...	...	...	...	...	—	...	...	100.0	—	—	...	...	Nauru
15,435	96.4	3.6	3.6	12,000	...	2.1	—	100.0	100.0	—	—	...	...	Nepal
990	9.7	90.3	35.7	854,194	2,128,450	462.4	99.2	0.8	85.2	1.5	13.3	500,543	288,218	Netherlands, The
...	...	...	...	...	9,610	1.8	100.0	—	100.0	—	—	—	6,260	Netherlands Antilles[11]
12	—	100.0	91.7		5,716	3.5	100.0	—	88.3	2.3	1.0	480	2,300	New Caledonia
8,934	0.6	99.4	51.3	333,302	63,878	162.7[14]	...	...	78.8[14]	3.5[14]	17.5[14]	254,902[57]	19,941[57]	New Zealand
3,491	74.8	25.2	23.8	2,569	12,368	4.3	97.3	2.7	30.7	69.3	—	12,604	1,150	Nicaragua
3,807	93.8	6.2	—	...	285	6.8	—	100.0	100.0	—	—	—	200	Niger
92,042	92.0	8.0	5.5	707	203,217	373.8	50.9	49.1	97.7	2.3	—	5,120	138,029	Nigeria
...	...	...	...	...	...	—	100.0	—	100.0	—	—	—	...	Niue
...	...	...	...	...	...	—	100.0	—	100.0	—	—	—	...	Norfolk Island

Extractive industries (continued)

country	mining														
	% of GDP, 1984	mineral production (value added)					trade (value)								
		year	total ('000,000 U.S.$)	by kind (%)			year	exports				imports			
				metals[a]	nonmetals[b]	energy[c]		total ('000,000 U.S.$)	by kind (%)			total ('000,000 U.S.$)	by kind (%)		
									metals[a]	nonmetals[b]	energy[c]		metals[a]	nonmetals[b]	energy[c]
Norway	18.5	1984	10,125.8	0.7[2]	1.0[2]	98.3[2]	1983	9,043.0	2.3	0.7	97.0	1,201.3	40.1	9.2	50.7
Oman	47.6	1984	4,196.6[18]	...	...	...	1983	4,091.2[7]	—	0.1[7]	99.9[7]	12.9	—	59.3	40.7
Pacific Is., Trust Terr. of the	...	...	...	...	...	...	...	...	...	...	...	...	...	...	...
Marshall Islands	...	...	...	...	...	...	1982	—	—	—	—	3.7[7]	—	—	100.0[7]
Micronesia, Fed. States of	—	—	—	—	—	—	...	...	...	...	...	...	...	...	...
Northern Mariana Islands	—	—	—	—	—	—	...	...	...	...	...	...	...	...	...
Palau	—	—	—	—	—	—	1983	—	—	—	—	2.1[2]	—	—	100.0[2]
Pakistan	1.2[26]	1984–85	384.9	0.1[2, 23]	18.5[2, 23]	78.9[2, 23]	1983	11.9	—	99.8	0.2	1,108.7	5.3	2.9	91.8
Panama	0.1	1984	6.0	—100.0—		—	1983	97.5	1.5	92.9	5.6	353.0	—	0.7	99.3
Papua New Guinea	13.2[5]	1980	336.2[59]	100.0	—	—	1984	333.6	100.0	—	—	0.7	—	100.0	—
Paraguay	0.4	1984	21.7	—	100.0	—	1982	...	...	...	...	74.7[22]	—	2.9[22]	97.1[22]
Peru	10.9	1984	2,051.7	38.3[9]	10.9[9, 45]	50.8[9, 45]	1983	1,012.9	69.5	1.1	29.4	10.5	41.4	32.9	25.7
Philippines	1.8	1984	581.7	91.6[5]	6.2[5]	2.2[5]	1983	606.5	99.1	0.3	0.6	1,624.7	3.0	1.2	95.8
Pitcairn Island	—	...	...	...	...	...	...	...	...	...	...	...	...	...	...
Poland	5.4[2]	1983	3,304.0	8.1	16.2	75.7	1983	1,858.7	2.3	18.2	79.5	2,605.4	9.8	7.2	83.0
Portugal	0.6[5]	1980	145.8	30.8	64.7	4.5	1983	87.0	28.0	72.0	—	1,961.9	1.5	4.5	94.0
Puerto Rico	0.1[46]	1983–84	11.0	—	100.0	—	1977[60]	51.1[31]	30.6	36.2	33.2[31]	54.4[60]	0.2	93.5	6.3
Qatar	45.9[2]	1983	2,943.5	...	...	...	1983	3,232.8	—	—	100.0	18.5	94.1	5.9	—
Réunion	...	1984	...	—	100.0	—	1983	—	—	—	—	10.3	—	—	100.0
Romania	...	...	...	...	...	...	...	...	...	...	...	...	...	...	...
Rwanda	0.5[2]	1983	7.4	—100.0—		—	1982	9.0	99.7	0.3	...	3.4[5]	—	100.0[5]	—
St. Christopher and Nevis	0.2[2]	1983	0.1	—	100.0	—	1982	...	...	...	...	0.1	78.6	—	21.4
St. Helena and Ascension	...	1984	...	...	...	...	1982	...	...	...	...	0.4	—	100.0	—
St. Lucia	1.3[2]	1984	1.3	—	100.0	—	1982	—	...	...	...	...	...	...	...
St. Pierre and Miquelon	...	1983	...	...	...	...	1982	—	—	—	—	0.8[9]	87.0[9]	—	13.0[9]
St. Vincent	0.4[2]	1983	0.4	—	100.0	—	1982	—	—	—	—	0.6[5]	—	—	100.0[5]
San Marino	...	...	...	...	...	...	...	...	...	...	...	...	...	...	...
São Tomé and Príncipe	...	1983	—	—	100.0	—	1983	—	—	—	—	...	...	...	...
Saudi Arabia	40.5[26]	1984–85	32,245.7	—1.6—		98.4	1983	49,407.5	0.1	0.1	99.8	114.3	17.8	82.2	—
Senegal	1.5[2]	1983	30.0	...	...	...	1983	77.1	2.5	97.5	—	208.0[9]	—	—	100.0[9]
Seychelles	—	1983	—	—	—	—	1982	—	98.6	1.4	—	0.3	—	38.7	61.3
Sierra Leone	7.5[2]	1983	114.0	—100.0—		—	1983	79.4	44.2	55.8	—	0.5	—	100.0	—
Singapore	0.4	1984	64.1	—	100.0	—	1983	438.5	39.8	16.1	44.1	6,974.9	0.9	2.1	97.0
Solomon Islands	0.3[2]	1984	...	—100.0—		—	1984	0.6[35]	100.0[35]	—	—	...	...	...	...
Somalia	...	1983	...	—	100.0	—	1980	—	—	100.0	—	0.8	—	74.8	25.2
South Africa	12.9[64]	1983	14,303.1[1]	—85.2[1]—		14.8[1]	1983[24]	3,051.3[47]	38.8	26.6	34.6[47]	135.9[47]	52.5	47.4	0.1[47]
Bophuthatswana	52.6[5]	...	...	...	...	...	...	...	...	...	...	...	...	...	...
Ciskei	—	...	...	...	...	...	...	...	...	...	...	...	...	...	...
Transkei	0.6[65]	...	...	...	...	...	...	...	...	...	...	...	...	...	...
Venda	1.7[65]	...	...	...	...	...	...	...	...	...	...	...	...	...	...
South West Africa/Namibia	26.1	1984	354.9	—100.0—		—	1983	593.0	64.0	36.0	—	[24]	[24]	[24]	[24]
Spain	1.4	1983	1,753.5	13.3	15.9	70.8	1983	267.8	28.8	44.2	27.0	11,354.8	7.9	2.7	89.4
Sri Lanka	1.2[2]	1983	61.5	—100.0—		—	1983	48.4	8.2	91.8	—	311.2	0.2	3.0	96.8
Sudan, The	0.1[66]	1977–78	4.9	—100.0—		—	1982	2.4	100.0	—	—	162.7[9]	—	0.1[9]	99.9[9]
Suriname	9.1[2]	1982	146.2	99.7[9]	0.3[9]	—	1983	210.0	100.0	—	—	4.2	—	—	100.0
Swaziland	3.2[2]	1983	14.0	9.4[5]	77.3[5]	13.3[5]	1984	17.2	—	86.9	13.1	[24]	[24]	[24]	[24]
Sweden	0.5[2]	1983	428.7	86.0	14.0	—	1983	529.4	80.6	14.1	5.3	3,863.4	9.3	4.5	86.2
Switzerland	...	1984	...	—	100.0	—	1983	1,057.0	7.0	91.9	1.1	2,408.2	3.5	49.1	47.4
Syria	8.1	1984	1,544.5	—	—100.0—		1983	471.3	—	3.4	96.6	34.5	2.2	8.9	88.9
Taiwan	0.6	1984	429.0	—15.6—		84.4	1984	...	...	...	...	4,680.6	19.5	...	80.5
Tanzania	0.3[2]	1983	14.4	...	...	...	1982	15.3	50.4	49.6	—	159.6[9]	—	3.0[9]	97.0[9]
Thailand	2.0	1984	853.0	32.8[7]	66.2[7]	1.0[7, 69]	1983	344.4	11.5	88.4	0.1	2,180.9	5.4	8.5	86.1
Togo	13.7	1984	92.2	—	100.0	—	1984	92.2	—	100.0	—	83.2[5]	—	1.4[5]	98.6[5]
Tokelau	—	1981	—	—	—	—	1982	—	—	—	—	...	...	...	...
Tonga	0.5[12]	1982–83	0.4	—	100.0	—	1982	—	—	—	—	0.4	—	73.2	26.8
Trinidad and Tobago	19.6[2]	1983	1,590.8	—	—	100.0	1983	1,105.9	—	—	100.0	42.8	27.7	23.8	48.5
Tunisia	15.6	1984	629.5	0.9[9]	13.2[9]	85.9[9]	1983	966.0	0.3	4.5	95.2	103.3	5.5	58.4	36.1
Turkey	2.1[2]	1983	1,072.5	14.5[7, 23]	13.9[7, 23]	71.6[7, 23]	1983	300.1	10.7	52.2	37.1	3,720.5	4.5	2.0	93.5
Turks and Caicos Is.	3.6	1983	1.0	—	100.0	—	...	...	...	...	...	...	...	...	...
Tuvalu	—	1981	—	—	—	—	1982	—	—	—	—	...	...	...	...
Uganda	—[9]	1981	2.9	...	...	...	1982	1.2	100.0	—	—	...	...	...	...
U.S.S.R.	...	1980	49,039.9	—36.6[23]—		63.4[23]	1984	52,690.0[70]	10.3	1.4	88.3[70]	10,070.0[70]	59.3	2.7	38.0[70]
United Arab Emirates	40.0	1983	12,341.1	...	...	...	1983	14,074.9	0.2	0.1	99.7	34.5	4.0	93.3	2.7
United Kingdom	7.0	1984	29,958.5	0.1[9]	3.5[9]	96.4[9]	1983	19,155.7	3.5	12.3	84.2	11,641.6	17.7	22.6	59.7
United States	3.3	1984	118,500.0	3.2[7]	5.2[7]	91.6[7]	1983	9,403.3	24.4	20.9	54.7	50,180.4	5.4	7.2	87.4
Uruguay	1.1	1984	59.4	—	100.0	—	1983	1.1	—	100.0	—	91.5	0.3	0.5	99.2
Vanuatu	...	1984	—	—	100.0	—	1982	0.5[9]	100.0[9]	—	—	2.2	—	75.6	24.4
Venezuela	19.9	1984	9,879.4	—2.1[7, 71]—		97.9[7, 71]	1983	6,925.1	2.3	0.4	97.3	85.5	63.6	32.8	3.6
Vietnam	...	...	...	...	...	...	...	...	...	...	...	...	...	...	...
Virgin Islands (U.S.)	...	1983	...	—	100.0	—	1982	1,195.2	99.8[72]	0.2	—	1,889.9[73]	—	0.2	99.8[18]
Wallis and Futuna	...	...	...	...	...	...	...	...	...	...	...	...	...	...	...
West Bank	...	...	...	...	...	...	1983[38]	7.9[38, 74]	...	...	...	...	...	...	...
Western Sahara	...	...	...	...	...	...	...	...	...	...	...	...	...	...	...
Western Samoa	—	1984	—	—	—	—	1984	—	—	—	—	—	...	...	—
Yemen (Aden)	0.1[5]	1980	0.9	—	100.0	—	1983	1.6	—	—	100.0	160.2	—	—	100.0
Yemen (Ṣan'ā')	1.2[13]	1981–82	34.2	—	100.0	—	1982	3.6	—	100.0	—	3.9[9]	—	—	100.0[9]
Yugoslavia	2.9[2]	1983	1,256.1	23.3	13.5	63.2	1983	68.1	67.6	17.4	15.0	3,371.8	4.9	6.8	88.3
Zaire	11.5[7]	1982	624.9	...	...	...	1982	89.0	25.9	29.9	44.2	1.7[5]	4.9[5]	95.1[5]	—
Zambia	15.5[2]	1983	523.5	...	...	...	1983	23.4	55.3	44.7	—	117.1[22]	—	2.5[22]	97.5[22]
Zimbabwe	5.8	1984	265.2	70.0[23]	19.3[23]	10.7[23]	1983	73.9	20.3	79.7	—	10.3[7]	98.5[7]	1.5[7]	—

[1]Gross value of sales. [2]1983. [3]1978. [4]1977. [5]1980. [6]Lumber only. [7]1982. [8]Salt exports valued at U.S.$33,000. [9]1981. [10]At 1982 prices. [11]Netherlands Antilles includes Aruba. [12]1982–83. [13]1981–82. [14]Marine catch only. [15]Includes petroleum refining. [16]Production of limestone, china clay, and natural gas only. [17]Belgium includes Luxembourg. [18]Mostly crude petroleum. [19]Unworked wood, lumber, and cork only. [20]Mostly slate, limestone, and coal. [21]Mostly metals. [22]1979. [23]Gross value of production (output). [24]South Africa includes Botswana, Lesotho, South West Africa/Namibia, and Swaziland. [25]Charcoal only. [26]1984–85. [27]Mostly crude petroleum and natural gas. [28]Mostly diamonds; some gold. [29]China includes Taiwan. [30]Coal, emeralds, and ferronickel only. [31]Includes coke and briquettes. [32]Excludes precious stones, crude petroleum, and natural gas. [33]Excludes precious stones. [34]Includes petroleum products. [35]Mostly gold. [36]France includes Monaco. [37]Excludes mollusks. [38]West Bank includes Gaza Strip. [39]Enterprises with 20 or more persons engaged. [40]Enterprises with 30 or

forestry, 1984						fisheries, 1984								country
production of roundwood				trade (value '000 U.S.$)		catch (nominal)						trade (value, '000 U.S.$)		
total ('000 cubic metres)	fuelwood, charcoal (%)	industrial roundwood (%)		exports	imports	total ('000 metric tons)	by source (%)		by kind of catch (%)			exports	imports	
		total	sawlogs, veneer				marine	fresh-water	fish	crusta-ceans	mollusks			
10,620	7.5	92.5	45.3	787,237	403,018	2,456.0	100.0	—	96.2	3.5	0.3	902,866	46,322	Norway
...	...	...	...	352[7, 19]	55,035	100.0	100.0	—	100.0	—	—	18,210	2,897	Oman
...	...	...	...	...	...	5.5	100.0	—	100.0	—	—	2,190	130	Pacific Is., Trust Terr. of the
...	...	...	...	...	...	...	...	...	...	...	...	...	...	Marshall Islands
...	...	...	...	...	...	...	...	...	...	...	...	...	...	Micronesia, Fed. States of
...	...	...	...	...	...	...	...	...	...	...	...	...	...	Northern Mariana Islands
...	...	...	...	...	...	0.3[2]	100.0[2]	—	98.9[2]	—	—	...	70[2]	Palau
19,952	96.9	3.1	1.5	...	86,853	378.7	81.4	18.6	92.5	7.5	—	79,121	—	Pakistan
2,047	83.4	16.6	13.6	1,029	36,881	138.2	100.0	—	92.4	7.5	0.1	85,890[58]	4,950[58]	Panama
6,910	80.1	19.9	16.8	93,095	6,400	6.0	100.0	—	66.6	33.4	—	8,639	21,539	Papua New Guinea
6,852	64.8	35.2	30.3	87,236	7,450	5.0	—	100.0	100.0	—	—	—		Paraguay
7,775	83.8	16.2	15.0	7,917	48,214	2,997.0	99.2	0.8	99.0	0.1	0.6	213,468		Peru
35,559	80.4	19.6	10.8	326,679	52,572	1,935.4	69.0	31.0	80.7	4.5	14.6	116,786	2,720	Philippines
...	...	...	...	...	...				100.0					Pitcairn Island
23,963	13.4	86.6	44.2	166,409	156,118	719.2	95.2	4.8	84.2	—	15.8	93,083	50,398	Poland
9,224	5.4	94.6	46.8	506,192	125,986	285.1[14]	...	...	96.7[14]	0.5[14]	2.8[14]	92,076	139,242	Portugal
						2.3[14]			81.3[14]	7.5[14]	11.2[14]	[61]	[61]	Puerto Rico
—	—	—	—	...	17,625	3.2	100.0	—	97.3	1.8	0.9	—	920	Qatar
33	93.9	6.1	—	...	21,862	2.9	100.0	—	73.9	26.1	—	3,181	10,723	Réunion
24,126	18.9	81.1	36.9	437,710	90,660	232.2	76.0	24.0	100.0	—	—	—	23,730	Romania
5,461	95.9	4.1	0.5	...	1,774	0.8	—	100.0	100.0	—	—	—	—	Rwanda
...	...	...	...	11[9]	857[9]	1.1	100.0	—	100.0	—	—	—	—	St. Christopher and Nevis
...	...	...	...	...	...	0.2	100.0	—	100.0	—	—	737	—	St. Helena and Ascension
...	...	...	...	5,227[7, 62]	6,385[2]	2.6	100.0	—	92.0	8.0	—	—	1,162	St. Lucia
...	...	...	...	...	...	12.5	100.0	—	100.0	—	—	7,863	—	St. Pierre and Miquelon
...	...	...	...	...	2,984	0.5	100.0	—	100.0	—	—	—	277[9, 63]	St. Vincent
...	...	...	...	...	...	—	—	—	—	—	—	[50]	[50]	San Marino
6	—	100.0	100.0	...	...	4.3	100.0	—	98.1	—	1.9	—	—	São Tomé and Príncipe
...	...	...	...	...	703,854	26.4	100.0	—	61.7	38.0	0.3	2,260	74,234	Saudi Arabia
4,049	86.7	13.3	0.5	...	34,715	222.6	93.4	6.6	95.2	2.6	2.2	150,805	16,590	Senegal
...	...	...	...	...	...	3.9	100.0	—	97.3	—	1.3	1,509	82	Seychelles
7,632	98.2	1.8	0.3	...	1,130	52.5	68.6	31.4	96.5	1.6	1.9	2,237	4,010	Sierra Leone
...	...	...	...	428,782	460,035	25.5	98.3	1.7	84.4	11.3	4.3	163,586	224,133	Singapore
512	41.0	59.0	59.0	21,380	592	49.3	100.0	—	99.0	—	—	23,034	471	Solomon Islands
5,168	98.6	1.4	0.5	...	2,224	15.3	100.0	—	87.6	12.4	—	2,760	—	Somalia
18,944[51]	37.0[51]	63.0[51]	21.8[51]	227,633[51]	247,576[51]	598.8	99.9	0.1	98.0	1.0	0.4	94,011	105,649	South Africa
...	...	...	...	...	...	...	...	...	...	...	...	...	...	Bophuthatswana
...	...	...	...	...	...	...	...	...	...	...	...	...	...	Ciskei
...	...	...	...	...	...	...	...	...	...	...	...	...	...	Transkei
...	...	...	...	...	...	...	...	...	...	...	...	...	...	Venda
[51]	[51]	[51]	[51]	[51]	[51]	162.6	100.0	—	99.0	1.0	—	...	...	South West Africa/Namibia
13,746	13.6	86.4	26.4	379,819	583,535	1,267.6	98.1	1.9	77.6	1.3	21.1	307,811	389,919	Spain
8,497	91.9	8.1	1.8	3,439	28,820	170.7	82.1	17.9	95.6	4.4	—	24,013	25,361	Sri Lanka
18,973	90.6	9.4	0.2	...	48,200	29.5	15.1	84.9	100.0	—	—	781	169	Sudan, The
260	5.0	95.0	88.1	11,510	13,020	4.1	96.5	3.5	80.4	19.6	—	12,997	2,500	Suriname
2,223	25.2	74.8	14.3	57,371	730	—	—	100.0	100.0	—	—	...	...	Swaziland
53,339	8.3	91.7	44.5	5,149,572	498,909	279.0	96.4	3.6	99.2	0.8	—	85,340	257,317	Sweden
4,965	17.5	82.5	61.3	361,409	727,729	4.0	—	100.0	100.0	—	—	5,153[52]	188,971[52]	Switzerland
44	25.0	75.0	34.1	251	103,616	3.8	24.4	75.6	100.0	—	—	—	13,125	Syria
700	9.8	90.2	80.3	280,434[67]	349,341[68]	1,002.6	75.6	24.4	...	...	...	287,515	...	Taiwan
22,024	94.6	5.4	0.5	1,028	16,900	262.8	11.9	88.1	99.8	0.1	0.1	17,649	543	Tanzania
40,857	89.2	10.8	5.0	37,470	239,937	2,249.8	93.3	6.7	70.9	9.1	12.3	632,960	67,183	Thailand
735	78.5	21.5	2.4	14[22]	483	14.5	95.5	4.5	100.0	—	—	—	4,980	Togo
...	...	...	...	...	...	—	...	...	100.0	—	—	...	...	Tokelau
3	—	100.0	100.0	...	1,577	2.0	100.0	—	100.0	—	—	—	230	Tonga
57	28.1	71.9	68.4	361	132,098	3.6	100.0	—	88.9	11.1	—	780	15,369	Trinidad and Tobago
2,751	96.4	3.6	0.1	81[5]	85,644	74.9	100.0	—	84.3	3.4	12.2	31,985	703	Tunisia
18,927	66.0	34.0	21.5	51,928	93,673	566.9	91.8	8.2	96.4	2.6	1.0	60,181	348	Turkey
...	...	...	...	...	...	1.0	100.0	—	—	38.1	61.9	1,600	—	Turks and Caicos Is.
...	...	...	...	...	...	0.8	100.0	—	100.0	—	—	—	57[9]	Tuvalu
12,230	86.9	13.1	0.7	38	3,499	212.2	—	100.0	100.0	—	—	...	...	Uganda
355,600	22.6	77.4	42.4	2,608,994	958,992	10,592.9	91.7	8.3	97.8	1.4	0.8	303,598	137,844	U.S.S.R.
...	...	...	...	...	...	73.1	100.0	—	99.4	0.6	—	3,200	15,500	United Arab Emirates
3,900	3.6	96.4	61.2	667,335	5,328,861	835.8	98.3	1.7	91.2	4.6	4.2	302,171	877,159	United Kingdom
438,058	23.3	76.7	45.3	5,741,883	10,618,392	4,814.3	98.4	1.6	68.8	6.2	24.8	923,890[61]	3,702,490[61]	United States
2,975	92.8	7.2	0.9	6,646	13,656	134.0	99.7	0.3	97.7	—	2.3	48,860	—	Uruguay
38	63.2	36.8	36.8	677	451	2.9	100.0	—	53.1	16.8	30.1	7,320	7,369	Vanuatu
1,322	51.9	48.1	46.1	...	285,705	265.0	92.0	8.0	86.9	3.5	9.6	76,827	5,859	Venezuela
24,323	86.8	13.2	6.7	...	8,669	765.0	71.2	28.8	87.3	8.8	3.9	64,555	—	Vietnam
...	...	...	...	...	...	0.7	100.0	—	90.9	5.1	4.0	...	3,053[3]	Virgin Islands (U.S.)
...	...	...	...	...	...	—	...	...	100.0	—	—	...	...	Wallis and Futuna
...	...	...	...	...	...	...	...	...	...	...	...	...	...	West Bank
...	...	...	...	...	...	—	100.0	—	...	...	—	...	...	Western Sahara
131	53.4	46.6	44.3	1,478	4,856	3.8	100.0	—	97.4	1.3	1.3	—	1,090	Western Samoa
276	100.0	—	—	29	11,294	84.1	100.0	—	94.2	1.2	4.6	7,300	50	Yemen (Aden)
...	...	...	...	...	...	18.3	100.0	—	100.0	—	—	—	3,850	Yemen (Ṣan'ā')
15,091	26.2	73.8	54.3	407,463	223,300	73.5	65.9	34.1	96.3	0.6	3.0	18,592	45,996	Yugoslavia
32,597	92.0	8.0	1.2	18,691	5,539	101.0	1.0	99.0	100.0	—	—	—	35,677[7]	Zaire
9,921	94.9	5.1	1.3	...	21,894	64.6	—	100.0	100.0	—	—	6	350	Zambia
7,104	80.7	19.3	5.2	8,625	15,996	16.4	—	100.0	100.0	—	—	—	464	Zimbabwe

more persons engaged. [41]Excludes quarried sand, stone, and clay. [42]Jersey includes Guernsey. [43]Mostly bauxite and diamonds. [44]Mostly bauxite. [45]Bauxite mining ceased in 1983. [46]1983–84. [47]Excludes crude petroleum. [48]1979–80. [49]Metals includes energy. [50]Italy includes San Marino. [51]South Africa includes Lesotho and South West Africa/Namibia. [52]Switzerland includes Liechtenstein. [53]At 1970 prices. [54]Includes cement. [55]1984. [56]Curaçao and Aruba only. [57]Excludes trade with Cook Islands, Niue, and Tokelau. [58]Excludes the Free Zone of Colón and the Canal Zone. [59]Mostly copper, gold, and silver. [60]Trade with United States only. [61]United States includes Puerto Rico. [62]Paper and paperboard only. [63]Cod only. [64]South Africa includes South West Africa/Namibia. [65]1975. [66]1977–78. [67]Plywood only. [68]Paper and pulp only. [69]Coal mining only. [70]Includes refined petroleum and electricity. [71]Metals/nonmetals includes coal mining. [72]Bauxite only. [73]Excludes bauxite imports. [74]Exports of stone and marble to Jordan only.

Manufacturing industries

This table summarizes the activity of the manufacturing sectors of the countries of the world, providing figures for value added, number of establishments, and the distribution of value added by size of establishment (as reckoned by number of employees). The data are organized to show the relative importance of six principal sectors for each country and the concentration of activity within each sector. Although the principal intent is to provide data on the manufacturing sectors of each country individually, the data may also be compared from country to country. Here, however, some caution is advised, as some countries do not classify manufacturing activity according to the scheme outlined in the International Standard Industrial Classification (ISIC) or in accord with the UN statistical paper *International Recommendations for Industrial Statistics,* rev. 1 (1983), the principal bases for the classification of data used in this table. Similarly, they may not define "establishment," "enterprise," or "employee" in the same way. In addition, each country may use different size classes in categorizing establishments—those employing more than 10 employees, say, or more than 50—skewing the reported distribution by size of establishment.

The sectors for which data have been provided include: food, beverages, and tobacco; textiles, apparel, and leather; wood, paper, chemicals, and related products; primary and fabricated metals and processed minerals; machinery (except electrical) and transport equipment; electrical and electronic machinery. For each of these sectors (for which ISIC definitions are provided below), data are given for value added (or, occasionally, some other measure of value, when value added was not reported), for the number of establishments with fewer than and more than 100 employees, and, where it was known, for the proportion of the sectoral value added represented by these two groups of establishments.

The collection and publication of national manufacturing data is usually carried out by one of three methods: a full census of manufacturing (usually done every five to ten years for a given country), a periodic survey of manufacturing (usually taken at regular intervals between censuses), and the onetime sample survey (often limited in geographical, sectoral, or size-of-enterprise coverage). The full census is, naturally, the most complete, but since up to ten years may elapse between such censuses, it has often been necessary to substitute a survey of more recent date, but less complete coverage, in order to provide more timely data. For each country the initial date indicates the year of the survey.

The total value added of each national manufacturing sector in U.S. dollars is provided so that the relative importance of that country's overall national manufacturing activity may be compared internationally. The percentage of that total contributed by each sector is also given, and for each sector, the value added is broken down by size of enterprise wherever possible. The dollar figures for value added should be used only with caution, because of inherent uncertainties with respect to accounting methods, purchasing power, national price structures and preferments, exchange rates, and so on.

The majority of countries collect data for establishments, generally referring to each separate physical facility, regardless of the number of separately incorporated legal entities (companies, partnerships, parastatal

Manufacturing industries

country	year	food, beverages, and tobacco (group 1)					textiles, apparel, and leather (group 2)					wood, paper, chemicals, and related products (group 3)				
		percent of total value added	establishments				percent of total value added	establishments				percent of total value added	establishments			
			1–99 employees		100 or more emp.			1–99 employees		100 or more emp.			1–99 employees		100 or more emp.	
			number	percent of value added	number	percent of value added		number	percent of value added	number	percent of value added		number	percent of value added	number	percent of value added
Afghanistan[1]	1983	52.0	67	...	...	...	20.2	...	...	*66*	...	22.7	...	...	*61*	...
Albania	1984	...	...	...	...	...	...	...	...	...	...	...	...	...	...	...
Algeria[3, 4]	1978	26.4	*535*[5]	...	...	...	21.6	*752*[5]	...	...	...	15.5	*433*[5]	...	...	...
American Samoa	...	...	...	...	...	...	...	...	...	...	...	...	...	...	...	...
Andorra	1972	...	*142*	...	...	...	...	*104*	...	...	...	...	*49*	...	...	...
Angola	1973	50.2	...	...	...	...	6.9	...	...	...	...	28.0	...	...	...	...
Anguilla	...	...	...	...	...	...	...	...	...	...	...	...	...	...	...	...
Antigua and Barbuda	1980	...	14	100.0	—	...	...	12	100.0	—	—	...	15	100.0	—	—
Argentina	1981	26.8	1,188	...	92	...	9.2	1,059	...	75	...	29.6	1,394	...	101	...
Aruba	...	...	...	...	...	...	...	...	...	...	...	...	...	...	...	...
Australia[6, 7]	1980	17.6	3,889	...	460	...	9.1	4,071	...	363	...	19.0	10,412	...	610	...
Austria[9, 10]	1983	15.9	453	...	132	...	9.7	857	...	220	...	23.6	4,270	...	300	...
Bahamas, The[12]	1978	27.6	...	...	...	...	0.3	...	...	...	...	57.9	...	...	...	...
Bahrain	1982	...	...	...	...	...	...	...	...	...	...	...	...	...	...	...
Bangladesh[13]	1982	26.4	*525*	...	...	...	33.0	...	...	*1,489*	...	23.0	*717*	...	...	...
Barbados[9]	1979	34.5[14]	*38*[14]	...	...	...	18.3	...	...	*22*	...	19.1	*50*	...	...	...
Belgium[6]	1983	19.0	*6,964*	...	...	...	8.4[15]	*3,728*	...	...	...	27.3[16]	*5,883*	...	...	...
Belize	...	...	...	...	...	...	...	...	...	...	...	...	...	...	...	...
Benin	1978	59.7	...	...	...	...	12.0	...	...	...	...	11.7	...	...	...	...
Bermuda	...	...	...	...	...	...	...	...	...	...	...	...	...	...	...	...
Bhutan	...	...	...	...	...	...	...	...	...	...	...	...	...	...	...	...
Bolivia[3, 4]	1981	37.0	*322*	...	...	...	5.6	*253*	...	...	...	40.8	*474*	...	...	...
Botswana[6, 18]	1981	44.2	*22*	...	...	...	15.7	*16*	...	...	...	5.3	*11*	...	...	...
Brazil[9]	1980	17.0	26,226	38.6	1,272	61.4	10.9	14,325	23.8	1,913	76.2	30.8	27,752	30.5	1,925	69.5
British Virgin Islands	1978	...	1	100.0	—	—	—	—	—	—	—	...	2	100.0	—	—
Brunei[19]	1980	...	29	100.0	—	—	...	76	100.0	—	—	...	60	100.0	—	—
Bulgaria[4, 12]	1982	21.6	...	...	*278*	...	13.5	...	...	*210*	...	5.4	...	...	*257*	...
Burkina Faso[4]	1979	54.7	*14*	...	*2*	...	8.0	*4*	...	*2*	...	*33.6*	*27*	...	...	...
Burma	1983	...	...	...	...	...	...	...	...	...	...	...	...	...	...	...
Burundi	1983	...	...	...	...	...	...	...	...	...	...	...	...	...	...	...
Cameroon[4, 9, 20]	1979	52.4	*30*	...	...	...	13.0	...	...	*35*	...	12.6	*66*	...	...	...
Canada	1982	18.4	4,152[21]	44.9[21]	244	55.1	7.1	3,281	37.2	489	62.8	31.3	12,111[21]	31.4[21]	1,381	69.6
Cape Verde	1983	...	...	...	...	...	...	...	...	...	...	...	...	...	...	...
Cayman Islands	...	...	...	...	...	...	—	—	—	—	—	...	...	...	...	...
Central African Republic[4, 6]	1980	55.8	*12*	...	...	...	3.3	*3*	...	...	...	21.8	*8*	...	...	...
Chad	1975	44.9	...	...	...	...	39.7	...	...	...	...	3.9	...	...	...	...
Chile[9, 22]	1982	29.1	...	...	*278*	...	5.9	...	...	*179*	...	29.7	...	...	*275*	...
China[1, 4]	1983	14.4	*62,547*	...	...	...	18.4	...	...	*24,794*	...	18.9	...	...	*43,569*	...
Christmas Island	..	...	...	...	...	...	...	...	...	...	...	—	—	—	—	—
Cocos (Keeling) Islands	...	...	...	...	...	...	...	...	...	...	...	—	—	—	—	—
Colombia[9, 13]	1982	32.9	1,399	...	...	...	14.9	1,805	...	...	...	27.1	1,743	...	...	...
Comoros	1983	...	...	...	...	...	...	...	...	...	...	...	...	...	...	...
Congo	1983	27.2	...	...	...	...	2.1	...	...	...	...	70.7[23]	...	...	...	...
Cook Islands[24]	1978	100.0	15	...	2	...	—	—	—	—	—	—	—	—	—	—
Costa Rica[9, 25]	1980	47.6	...	...	*44*	...	10.1	...	...	*50*	...	27.5	*119*	...	...	...
Côte d'Ivoire[4, 9]	1982	31.2	*281*	...	...	...	17.3	...	...	*75*	...	28.0	*272*	...	...	...
Cuba[4]	1983	59.8[26]	...	...	*343*	...	5.2	...	...	*44*	...	11.6	...	...	*87*	...
Cyprus[9]	1983	23.0	*705*	...	...	...	27.1	*1,753*	...	...	...	27.7	*1,918*	...	...	...
Czechoslovakia[4]	1983	8.4	...	...	*119*	...	11.1	...	...	*85*	...	19.6	...	...	*138*	...
Denmark[6, 27]	1983	24.4	*890*	...	...	...	5.5	*707*	...	...	...	27.4	*2,078*	...	...	...
Djibouti	1983	...	...	...	...	...	...	...	...	...	...	...	...	...	...	...
Dominica	...	...	...	...	...	...	...	...	...	...	...	...	...	...	...	...
Dominican Republic[9, 26, 28, 29]	1981	68.6	...	...	*860*	...	6.0	*207*	...	...	...	19.3	*296*	...	...	...
Ecuador[9, 30]	1980	32.3	*536*	...	...	...	15.3	*755*	...	...	...	26.7	*916*	...	...	...
Egypt[9, 13]	1976	16.0	*2,072*	...	...	...	31.5	...	...	*1,189*	...	23.3	...	...	*584*	...

organizations), any of which may operate more than one facility. Other countries collect data only for enterprises, focusing on the corporate legal entity but often combining data for several separate, and smaller, establishments. When only a single sectoral enterprise or establishment total was available, the *average* size of these establishments was calculated (since the total number of employees in the sector was known), and the figure for number of establishments was placed in the table above or below the 100-employee cutoff accordingly. Such figures are given in italics.

One impediment to international comparability in terms of size of establishment is the size limit the country itself establishes as the minimum reporting unit for such surveys. For a small country it may be both feasible and desirable to survey all establishments, however small, on the grounds that they are few enough to constitute a manageable body of data for analysis, and also that if the country's manufacturers are mostly small operations, then it is precisely this group on which national planners need the most information. For larger countries, the cost to collect and analyze data for all establishments may be prohibitively high, and, moreover, interest from a development point of view may be exclusively in middle and large-scale industry, that needed to permit replacement of imported goods with domestic manufactures. In such a case the country may survey only those establishments with 50 employees or more. Thus, when the distributions of number of establishments are examined, it should be noted (and has been footnoted wherever possible) when such limits in coverage may be applicable.

In terms of the industrial groups implied by the names of the manufacturing sectors used here, the content of each sector is usually defined by the two- or three-digit level of classification in the ISIC system:

group	EB category	ISIC code (-s)	remarks
1.	Food, beverages, and tobacco	31	
2.	Textiles, apparel, and leather	32	
3.	Wood, paper, chemicals, and related products	33	wood and furniture
		34	paper and products; printing and publishing
		35	industrial chemicals, pharmaceuticals, petroleum and products, rubber, plastics
4.	Primary and fabricated metals and processed minerals	36	pottery, china, glass
		37	iron and steel; nonferrous metals
		381	metal products
5.	Machinery (except electrical) and transport equipment	382 + 384 minus 3825	machinery and transport equipment minus office equipment and computers
6.	Electrical and electronic machinery	383 + 3825	electrical and electronic equipment, plus office equipment and computers

It should be noted that these groups do not account for ISIC groups 385 and 390 (professional goods and other industries, respectively).

primary and fabricated metals; proc. minerals (group 4)					machinery (except elec.) and transport equip. (group 5)					electrical and electronic machinery (group 6)					total manufacturing value added (U.S.$'000,000)	country
percent of total value added	establishments: 1–99 employees: number	establishments: 1–99 employees: percent of value added	establishments: 100 or more emp.: number	establishments: 100 or more emp.: percent of value added	percent of total value added	establishments: 1–99 employees: number	establishments: 1–99 employees: percent of value added	establishments: 100 or more emp.: number	establishments: 100 or more emp.: percent of value added	percent of total value added	establishments: 1–99 employees: number	establishments: 1–99 employees: percent of value added	establishments: 100 or more emp.: number	establishments: 100 or more emp.: percent of value added		
2.3[2]	...	...	*16*[2]	...	[2]	...	...	[2]	...	[2]	...	...	[2]	...	...	Afghanistan
...	...	...	...	...	...	...	...	...	...	...	...	...	...	...	1,100	Albania
36.5[5]	*337*[5]	...	...	...	[5]	[5]	...	...	...	[5]	[5]	...	...	...	2,674	Algeria
...	...	...	...	...	...	...	...	...	...	...	...	...	...	...	...	American Samoa
...	*38*	...	...	...	...	*25*	...	...	...	...	*83*	...	...	...	...	Andorra
10.9	...	...	...	...	3.0	...	...	...	...	1.1	...	...	...	...	593	Angola
...	...	...	...	...	...	...	...	...	...	...	...	...	...	...	...	Anguilla
...	10	100.0	—	—	—	—	—	—	—	—	—	—	—	—	...	Antigua and Barbuda
11.0	206	...	21	...	12.1	...	...	*151*	...	3.0	...	...	*29*	...	15,883	Argentina
...	...	...	...	...	...	...	...	...	...	...	...	...	...	...	...	Aruba
19.9	2,245	...	323	...	22.5	12,484[8]	...	866[8]	...	6.0	[8]	...	[8]	...	33,687	Australia
23.3	759	...	155	...	15.4[11]	965	...	202	...	10.3[11]	300	...	114	...	15,927	Austria
13.5	...	...	...	...	0.7	...	...	...	...	—	—	—	—	—	30	Bahamas, The
...	...	...	...	...	...	...	...	...	...	...	...	...	...	...	400	Bahrain
11.8	*368*	...	...	...	2.1	*134*	...	...	...	2.9	...	...	*60*	...	708	Bangladesh
7.6	*25*	...	...	...	16.2[8]	...	...	*16*[8]	...	[8]	...	...	[8]	...	48	Barbados
41.3[2, 17]	*4,651*	...	...	...	[2]	*1,343*	...	...	...	[2]	...	...	*628*	...	18,272	Belgium
...	...	...	...	...	...	...	...	...	...	—	—	—	—	—	...	Belize
4.8	...	...	...	...	11.8[8]	...	...	...	...	[8]	...	...	...	...	46	Benin
...	...	...	...	...	...	...	...	...	...	...	...	...	...	...	...	Bermuda
...	...	...	...	...	—	—	—	—	—	—	—	—	—	—	...	Bhutan
12.8	*181*	...	...	...	*2.1*[11]	*36*	...	...	...	0.5[11]	*14*	...	...	...	694	Bolivia
...	*39*[2]	...	...	...	...	[2]	...	...	...	...	[2]	...	...	...	54	Botswana
17.9	25,084	25.3	1,641	74.7	15.6	9,268	18.0	1,651	82.0	5.3	2,245	48.7	558	51.3	77,648	Brazil
...	4	100.0	—	—	—	—	—	—	—	—	—	—	—	—	...	British Virgin Islands
...	70[2]	100.0[2]	—	—	...	[2]	[2]	—	—	...	[2]	[2]	—	—	...	Brunei
49.4[2]	...	...	*239*	...	[2]	...	...	*373*[18]	...	[2]	...	...	*119*	...	...	Bulgaria
3.7	*9*	...	...	...	...	...	...	...	...	...	...	...	...	...	68	Burkina Faso
...	...	...	...	...	...	...	...	...	...	...	...	...	...	...	831	Burma
...	...	...	...	...	...	...	...	...	...	...	...	...	...	...	110	Burundi
10.1	...	...	*9*	...	4.7	...	...	*8*	...	1.7	...	...	*9*	...	340	Cameroon
21.2	6,379[22]	52.1[22]	458	47.9	15.2	2,489	18.2	392	82.8	6.6	993[22]	29.9[22]	123	70.1	51,037	Canada
...	...	...	...	...	...	...	...	...	...	...	...	...	...	...	5	Cape Verde
...	...	...	...	...	—	—	—	—	—	—	—	—	—	—	...	Cayman Islands
16.2[2]	*8*[2]	...	...	...	[2]	[2]	...	...	...	[2]	[2]	...	...	...	16	Central African Republic
11.5	...	...	...	...	—	...	...	...	...	—	...	...	...	...	77	Chad
29.9	...	...	*155*	...	2.7	...	...	*54*	...	1.2	...	...	*26*	...	5,337	Chile
16.2	...	...	*49,252*	...	26.1[8]	...	...	*101,649*[8]	...	[8]	...	...	[8]	...	...	China
—	—	—	—	—	—	—	—	—	—	—	—	—	—	—	...	Christmas Island
—	—	—	—	—	—	—	—	—	—	—	—	—	—	—	...	Cocos (Keeling) Islands
14.4	*1,152*	...	...	...	*6.0*	*543*	...	...	...	3.7	*211*	...	...	...	7,036	Colombia
...	...	...	...	...	—	—	—	—	—	—	—	—	—	—	5	Comoros
[23]	...	...	...	...	[23]	...	...	...	...	[23]	...	...	...	...	231	Congo
—	—	—	—	—	—	—	—	—	—	—	—	—	—	—	...	Cook Islands
6.9	*42*	...	...	...	4.9[11]	*14*	...	...	...	2.7[11]	*19*	...	...	...	663	Costa Rica
21.2[2]	*80*[2]	...	...	...	[2]	[2]	...	...	...	[2]	[2]	...	...	...	915	Côte d'Ivoire
6.8	...	...	*80*	...	10.0[11]	...	...	*134*[11]	...	1.4[11]	...	...	*18*[11]	...	...	Cuba
14.2	*852*	...	...	...	4.5	*250*	...	...	...	1.8	*42*	...	...	...	356	Cyprus
20.5	...	...	*151*	...	32.5[11]	...	...	*209*[11]	...	6.0[11]	...	...	*47*[11]	...	...	Czechoslovakia
13.1	*1,170*	...	...	...	19.5[11]	*1,098*	...	...	...	5.7[11]	*296*	...	...	...	9,898	Denmark
...	...	...	...	...	...	...	...	...	...	—	—	—	—	—	24	Djibouti
...	...	...	...	...	...	...	...	...	...	...	...	...	...	...	...	Dominica
3.2	*134*	...	...	...	2.8[8]	*5*	...	...	...	[8]	*16*	...	...	...	1,113	Dominican Republic
18.0	*533*	...	...	...	2.1	*121*	...	...	...	4.4	*58*	...	...	...	1,355	Ecuador
14.9	...	...	*838*	...	9.8	...	...	*126*	...	4.3	...	...	*49*	...	1,767	Egypt

Manufacturing industries (continued)

country	year	food, beverages, and tobacco (group 1)					textiles, apparel, and leather (group 2)					wood, paper, chemicals, and related products (group 3)				
		percent of total value added	establishments				percent of total value added	establishments				percent of total value added	establishments			
			1–99 employees		100 or more emp.			1–99 employees		100 or more emp.			1–99 employees		100 or more emp.	
			number	percent of value added	number	percent of value added		number	percent of value added	number	percent of value added		number	percent of value added	number	percent of value added
El Salvador[9]	1982	37.6	...	...	*103*	...	19.1	...	...	*116*	...	30.2	*130*	...	...	...
Equatorial Guinea		...	...	...	...	...	...	...	...	...	...	...	...	...	...	...
Ethiopia[9]	1982	50.2	...	...	*164*	...	24.7	...	...	*90*	...	18.5	...	...	*106*	...
Faeroe Islands[1]	1977	45.6	...	...	...	...	...	...	...	...	...	...	...	...	...	...
Falkland Islands		...	...	...	...	...	...	...	...	...	...	...	...	...	...	...
Fiji[9]	1981	62.0	*85*	...	...	...	2.7	*114*	...	...	...	20.5	*204*	...	...	...
Finland[6, 31, 32]	1983	8.8	1,007	...	141	...	6.9	752	...	186	...	40.9	2,015	...	432	...
France[9]	1983	17.4	...	...	...	...	6.9	...	...	...	...	24.8	...	...	...	...
French Guiana		...	...	...	...	...	...	...	...	...	...	...	...	...	...	...
French Polynesia		...	...	...	...	...	...	...	...	...	...	...	...	...	...	...
Gabon	1978	17.5	*145*	...	...	...	2.8	*1,482*[33]	...	...	...	41.9	*64*	...	...	...
Gambia, The[9, 29]	1982	74.4	...	...	*13*	...	3.6	*2*	...	...	...	1.7	*4*	...	...	...
Gaza Strip[34]	1982	12.2	*202*	...	...	...	33.4	*523*	...	...	...	11.5	*212*	...	...	...
Germany, East[1, 4]	1983	15.8	...	...	*572*	...	6.6	...	...	*186*	...	25.0	...	...	*448*	...
Germany, West[35]	1983	10.4	3,439	...	1,157	...	4.6	3,886	...	1,323	...	22.8	9,001	...	2,865	...
Ghana[9, 18, 36]	1982	45.1	...	...	*61*	...	7.6	...	...	*85*	...	31.9	...	...	*164*	...
Gibraltar		...	...	...	...	...	...	...	...	...	...	...	...	...	...	...
Greece[6, 20]	1980	18.0	21,202	...	143	...	22.7	30,491	...	254	...	22.6	29,689	...	148	...
Greenland		...	...	...	...	...	...	...	...	...	...	...	...	...	...	...
Grenada		...	...	...	...	...	...	...	...	...	...	...	...	...	...	...
Guadeloupe		...	...	...	...	...	...	...	...	...	...	...	...	...	...	...
Guam		...	...	...	...	...	...	...	...	...	...	...	...	...	...	...
Guatemala[9, 29]	1978	38.2	*626*	...	...	...	9.9	*436*	...	...	...	32.4	*671*	...	...	...
Guernsey		...	...	...	...	...	...	...	...	...	...	...	...	...	...	...
Guinea	1983	...	...	...	...	...	...	...	...	...	...	...	...	...	...	...
Guinea-Bissau	1983	...	...	...	...	...	...	...	...	...	...	...	...	...	...	...
Guyana[29]	1979	...	*31*	...	...	...	...	*8*	...	...	...	...	*20*	...	...	...
Haiti[9]	1983	46.0	*552*	...	...	...	14.2	*120*	...	...	...	6.3[37]	*118*	...	...	...
Honduras	1975	56.1	*233*	...	...	...	9.9	*198*	...	...	...	23.0	*280*	...	...	...
Hong Kong[9]	1982	5.3	*1,155*	...	...	...	38.7	*14,723*	...	...	...	17.5	*12,998*	...	...	...
Hungary[4, 28]	1983	11.0	1,977	...	194	...	11.6	14,483	...	258	...	21.6	5,229	...	225	...
Iceland[6, 10]	1982	13.7	*195*	...	...	...	13.8	*248*	...	...	...	30.2	*814*	...	...	...
India[6, 38]	1981	9.9	*27,914*	...	...	...	17.8	...	...	*15,342*	...	24.4	*19,684*	...	...	...
Indonesia[6, 39, 40]	1982	30.4	...	...	*2,268*	...	13.2	...	...	*2,088*	...	28.2	...	...	*2,003*	...
Iran[9, 13]	1982	15.6	*761*	...	...	...	25.3	...	...	*1,023*	...	15.6	*987*	...	...	...
Iraq	1981	27.9	*3,775*	...	...	...	15.1	*7,797*	...	...	...	17.2	*4,769*	...	...	...
Ireland[6, 28, 41]	1981	28.3	*964*	...	...	...	8.3	*730*	...	...	...	26.9	*1,365*	...	...	...
Isle of Man		...	...	...	...	...	...	...	...	...	...	...	...	...	...	...
Israel[9, 10, 29, 42]	1982	12.2	*1,019*	...	...	...	11.2	*2,071*	...	...	...	23.5	*3,492*	...	...	...
Italy[4, 40]	1981	8.8	...	...	*2,011*	...	12.2	*6,278*	...	...	...	24.8	...	...	*5,927*	...
Jamaica[9, 20, 43]	1980	45.9	*308*	...	...	...	6.9	*157*	...	...	...	31.3	*333*	...	...	...
Japan[44]	1983	9.6	49,593	50.1	1,824	49.9	5.9	73,918	70.1	1,610	29.9	26.1	92,706	54.3	2,366	45.7
Jersey		...	...	...	...	...	...	...	...	...	...	...	...	...	...	...
Jordan[9]	1982	21.9	*633*	...	...	...	5.7	*543*	...	...	...	34.6	*923*	...	...	...
Kampuchea		...	...	...	...	...	...	...	...	...	...	...	...	...	...	...
Kenya[6, 22]	1982	38.3	...	...	*126*	...	12.5	...	...	*121*	...	26.7	...	...	*178*	...
Kiribati		...	...	...	...	...	...	...	...	...	...	...	...	...	...	...
Korea, North		...	...	...	...	...	...	...	...	...	...	...	...	...	...	...
Korea, South[9, 31, 32]	1982	*16.6*	31,884	...	206	...	*17.8*	26,525	...	721	...	*25.4*	11,619	...	352	...
Kuwait[9]	1980	5.4	*440*	...	...	...	5.0	*1,867*	...	...	...	68.1	*552*	...	...	...
Laos		...	...	...	...	...	...	...	...	...	...	...	...	...	...	...
Lebanon		...	...	...	...	...	...	...	...	...	...	...	...	...	...	...
Lesotho	1983	...	...	...	...	...	...	...	...	...	...	...	...	...	...	...
Liberia	1983	...	...	...	...	...	...	...	...	...	...	...	...	...	...	...
Libya[45]	1979	15.8	*102*	...	...	...	4.1	*27*	...	...	...	80.1[23]	*51*	...	...	...
Liechtenstein	1975	...	43	...	1	...	...	22	...	2	...	...	69	...	2	...
Luxembourg[4, 6, 40]	1981	6.6	*31*	...	...	...	2.6	*11*	...	...	...	20.5	...	...	*38*	...
Macau[9, 32]	1982	1.8	*101*	...	...	...	69.2	*544*	...	...	...	13.9	*251*	...	...	...
Madagascar[9]	1980	28.2	*144*	...	...	...	46.7	...	...	*51*	...	12.4	*120*	...	...	...
Malaŵi[12, 46]	1979	40.8	*35*	...	...	...	10.7	*19*	...	...	...	48.5[23]	*31*	...	...	...
Malaysia[6]	1982	22.0	*1,699*	...	...	...	6.1	672	...	...	...	32.3	*3,173*	..	...	...
Maldives		...	...	...	...	...	...	...	...	...	...	...	...	...	...	...
Mali	1981	30.0	...	...	...	...	53.0	...	...	...	...	17.0[23]	...	...	...	...
Malta[6]	1981	18.2	*393*	...	...	...	35.5	*250*	...	...	...	19.8	*630*	...	...	...
Martinique		...	...	...	...	...	...	...	...	...	...	...	...	...	...	...
Mauritania	1983	...	...	...	...	...	...	...	...	...	...	...	...	...	...	...
Mauritius[9, 13, 47]	1983	37.5	*192*	...	...	...	32.7	...	...	*146*	...	13.2	*108*	...	...	...
Mayotte		...	...	...	...	...	...	...	...	...	...	...	...	...	...	...
Mexico	1983	23.2	...	...	*476*	...	12.4	...	...	*136*	...	34.6	...	...	*341*	...
Monaco		...	...	...	...	...	...	...	...	...	...	...	...	...	...	...
Mongolia[12]	1980	5.0	...	...	...	...	29.2	...	...	...	...	29.3	...	...	...	...
Montserrat		...	...	...	...	...	...	...	...	...	...	...	...	...	...	...
Morocco[12]	1980	32.1	...	...	...	...	14.9	...	...	...	...	18.7	...	...	...	...
Mozambique	1972	48.1	769	...	93	...	14.9	5	...	62	...	21.4	194	...	110	...
Nauru		...	...	...	...	...	...	...	...	...	...	...	...	...	...	...
Nepal[12]	1977	85.6	2,770	...	35	...	1.9	109	...	10	...	3.9	339	...	12	...
Netherlands, The[6, 18]	1980	14,7	1,242	...	313	...	3.7	1,039	...	265	...	46.6	1,444	...	322	...
Netherlands Antilles		...	...	...	...	...	...	...	...	...	...	...	...	...	...	...
New Caledonia		...	...	...	...	...	...	...	...	...	...	...	...	...	...	...
New Zealand	1981	26.2	933	...	106	...	10.4	1,091	...	89	...	28.7	2,347	...	129	...
Nicaragua[4, 9, 36, 44]	1982	55.9	...	...	*102*	...	10.9	...	...	*65*	...	25.3	*103*	...	...	...
Niger	1983	...	...	...	...	...	...	...	...	...	...	...	...	...	...	...
Nigeria[9, 13]	1980	30.6	...	...	*315*	...	10.4	...	...	*117*	...	25.1	...	...	*468*	...
Niue		...	...	...	...	...	...	...	...	...	...	...	...	...	...	...
Norfolk Island		...	...	...	...	...	...	...	...	...	...	...	...	...	...	...

primary and fabricated metals; proc. minerals (group 4)					machinery (except elec.) and transport equip. (group 5)					electrical and electronic machinery (group 6)					total manufac-turing value added (U.S.$'000,-000)	country
percent of total value added	establishments				percent of total value added	establishments				percent of total value added	establishments					
	1–99 employees		100 or more emp.			1–99 employees		100 or more emp.			1–99 employees		100 or more emp.			
	number	percent of value added	number	percent of value added		number	percent of value added	number	percent of value added		number	percent of value added	number	percent of value added		
7.7	51	...	...	...	1.5	15	...	...	...	2.5	9	...	...	...	453	El Salvador
...	...	...	...	...	...	...	...	...	...	...	...	...	...	...	...	Equatorial Guinea
6.5	...	...	56	...	—	—	—	—	—	1.4	3	...	...	...	445	Ethiopia
...	...	...	...	...	...	...	...	...	...	...	...	...	...	...	122	Faeroe islands
...	...	...	...	...	...	...	...	...	...	...	...	...	...	...	...	Falkland Islands
11.0	57	...	...	...	2.8	53	...	...	...	0.4	4	...	...	...	107	Fiji
15.0	1,024	...	145	...	16.9	896	...	203	...	6.2	139	...	55	...	12,775	Finland
14.5	...	...	...	...	26.4[11]	...	...	...	...	7.5[11]	...	...	...	...	130,188	France
...	...	...	...	...	...	...	...	...	...	...	...	...	...	...	...	French Guiana
...	...	...	...	...	...	...	...	...	...	...	...	...	...	...	...	French Polynesia
37.8[2]	444[2]	...	...	...	[2]	[2]	...	...	...	[2]	[2]	...	...	...	175	Gabon
−0.8	2	...	...	...	—	—	—	—	—	—	—	—	—	—	8	Gambia, The
27.5	261	...	...	...	15.6[8]	223[8]	...	...	...	[8]	[8]	...	...	...	34	Gaza Strip
19.6	...	...	918	...	22.9	...	...	1,299	...	10.1	...	...	347	...	...	Germany, East
17.5	5,340	...	1,044	...	27.1	5,750	...	2,590	...	15.4	3,562	...	2,063	...	230,904	Germany, West
12.6	...	...	54	...	1.6	...	...	14	...	0.7	...	...	6	...	1,154	Ghana
...	...	...	...	...	...	...	...	...	...	...	...	...	...	...	...	Gibraltar
21.8	19,921	...	103	...	9.4	21,662	...	67	...	4.8	5,272	...	36	...	6,128	Greece
...	...	...	...	...	...	...	...	...	...	...	...	...	...	...	...	Greenland
...	...	...	...	...	...	...	...	...	...	...	...	...	...	...	...	Grenada
—	—	—	—	—	—	—	—	—	—	—	—	—	—	—	...	Guadeloupe
...	...	...	...	...	...	...	...	...	...	...	...	...	...	...	...	Guam
12.7	366	...	...	...	1.3	64	...	...	...	2.8	33	...	...	...	781	Guatemala
...	...	...	...	...	...	...	...	...	...	...	...	...	...	...	...	Guernsey
...	...	...	...	...	...	...	...	...	...	...	...	...	...	...	67	Guinea
...	...	...	...	...	...	...	...	...	...	...	...	...	...	...	1	Guinea-Bissau
...	...	...	...	...	...	...	...	...	...	...	1	...	...	...	...	Guyana
23.4[2]	52	...	...	...	[2]	37[8]	...	...	...	[2]	[8]	...	...	...	174	Haiti
9.0	98	...	...	...	0.6	11	...	...	...	1.1	9	...	...	...	112	Honduras
8.6	7,803	...	...	...	4.8	2,883	...	...	...	16.7	2,387	...	...	...	7,446	Hong Kong
14.4	300	...	64	...	19.5	9,418[8]	...	312[8]	...	13.4	[8]	...	[8]	...	5,249	Hungary
38.9[2]	581[2]	...	...	...	[2]	[2]	...	...	...	[2]	[2]	...	...	...	338	Iceland
21.6	20,270	...	...	...	17.7	11,104	...	...	...	7.6	4,340	...	...	...	13,930	India
13.0	...	...	1,087	...	9.4	...	...	335	...	5.4	...	...	118	...	4,495	Indonesia
24.2	3,213	...	...	...	12.1[11]	...	...	186[11]	...	6.6[11]	...	...	145[11]	...	9,106	Iran
17.3	3,534	...	...	...	8.7	98	...	...	...	4.6	17	...	...	...	6,055	Iraq
13.5	1,051	...	...	...	6.3	387	...	...	...	12.1	224	...	...	...	5,437	Ireland
...	...	...	...	...	...	...	...	...	...	...	...	...	...	...	...	Isle of Man
23.6	3,027	...	...	...	11.4	436[11]	...	...	...	15.9	548[11]	...	...	...	6,862	Israel
21.4	...	...	6,140	...	21.1[11]	...	...	3,214[11]	...	8.6[11]	...	...	1,145[11]	...	83,943	Italy
15.0[2]	361[2]	...	...	...	[2]	[2]	...	...	...	[2]	[2]	...	...	...	405	Jamaica
18.2	79,249	43.9	2,190	56.1	20.1	51,447	27.3	2,555	62.7	16.8	27,510	19.1	2,406	80.9	360,987	Japan
...	...	...	...	...	...	...	...	...	...	...	...	...	...	...	...	Jersey
31.9[2]	1,374[2]	...	...	...	[2]	[2]	...	...	...	[2]	[2]	...	...	...	519	Jordan
...	...	...	...	...	...	...	...	...	...	...	...	...	...	...	...	Kampuchea
8.5	...	...	76	...	5.9[11]	...	...	33[11]	...	7.6[11]	...	...	16[11]	...	31	Kenya
...	...	...	...	...	...	...	...	...	...	—	—	—	—	—	...	Kiribati
...	...	...	...	...	...	...	...	...	...	...	...	...	...	...	...	Korea, North
16.9	5,401	...	153	...	11.5	10,215[8]	19.8[8]	469[8]	80.2[8]	8.9	[8]	[8]	[8]	[8]	23,675	Korea, South
16.9	811	...	...	...	3.0[11]	57[11]	...	...	...	1.2[11]	31[11]	...	...	...	1,817	Kuwait
...	...	...	...	...	...	...	...	...	...	...	...	...	...	...	...	Laos
...	...	...	...	...	...	...	...	...	...	...	...	...	...	...	...	Lebanon
...	...	...	...	...	...	...	...	...	...	...	...	...	...	...	20	Lesotho
...	...	...	...	...	...	...	...	...	...	...	...	...	...	...	50	Liberia
[23]	85	...	...	...	[23]	6[8]	...	...	...	[23]	[8]	...	...	...	628	Libya
...	96	...	1	...	...	4	...	2	...	...	29	...	2	...	...	Liechtenstein
57.4	...	...	44	...	11.3[11]	...	...	25[11]	...	1.6[11]	9[11]	...	...	...	940	Luxembourg
1.9	109	...	...	...	2.1[11]	50[11]	...	...	...	2.9[11]	34[11]	...	...	...	160	Macau
5.4	...	...	19	...	3.4	22	...	...	...	1.5	15	...	...	...	206	Madagascar
[23]	18	...	...	...	[23]	3	...	...	...	[23]	2	...	...	...	56	Malaŵi
14.8	1,220	...	...	...	7.7	693	...	...	...	15.8	255	...	...	...	3,847	Malaysia
...	...	...	...	...	...	...	...	...	...	...	...	...	...	...	...	Maldives
[23]	...	...	...	...	[23]	...	...	...	...	[23]	...	...	...	...	102	Mali
8.5	244	...	...	...	5.0[11]	58[11]	...	...	...	6.8[11]	38[11]	...	...	...	278	Malta
...	...	...	...	...	...	...	...	...	...	...	...	...	...	...	...	Martinique
...	...	...	...	...	...	...	...	...	...	...	...	...	...	...	44	Mauritania
7.7	63	...	...	...	2.1[11]	18[11]	...	...	...	1.9[11]	13[11]	...	...	...	128	Mauritius
...	...	...	...	...	...	...	...	...	...	...	...	...	...	...	...	Mayotte
14.8	...	...	230	...	8.5	...	...	39	...	3.9	...	...	74	...	32,278	Mexico
...	...	...	...	...	...	...	...	...	...	...	...	...	...	...	...	Monaco
21.7	...	...	...	...	14.7[8]	...	...	...	...	[8]	...	...	...	...	...	Mongolia
...	...	...	...	...	...	...	...	...	...	...	...	...	...	...	...	Montserrat
9.7	...	...	...	...	17.8	...	...	...	...	6.7	...	...	...	...	2,250	Morocco
12.2	113	...	50	...	2.1	15	...	16	...	1.3	9	...	6	...	457	Mozambique
...	...	...	...	...	...	...	...	...	...	...	...	...	...	...	...	Nauru
1.5	106	...	20	...	7.1[8]	113[8]	...	12[8]	...	[8]	[8]	...	[8]	...	315	Nepal
13.0	552	...	134	...	10.7[11]	2,513[8]	...	441[8]	...	9.6[11]	[8]	...	[8]	...	36,497	Netherlands, The
...	...	...	...	...	...	...	...	...	...	...	...	...	...	...	...	Netherlands Antilles
...	...	...	...	...	...	...	...	...	...	...	...	...	...	...	...	New Caledonia
15.1	476	...	29	...	11.6	2,728	...	125	...	5.1	...	...	...	...	5,068	New Zealand
5.9	43	...	...	...	0.7	8	...	...	...	0.9	9	...	...	...	717	Nicaragua
...	...	...	...	...	...	...	...	...	...	...	...	...	...	...	87	Niger
10.8	...	...	272	...	21.1	...	...	39	...	1.7	...	...	17	...	6,460	Nigeria
...	...	...	...	...	...	...	...	...	...	...	...	...	...	...	...	Niue
...	...	...	...	...	...	...	...	...	...	...	...	...	...	...	...	Norfolk Island

Manufacturing industries (continued)

country	year	food, beverages, and tobacco (group 1)					textiles, apparel, and leather (group 2)					wood, paper, chemicals, and related products (group 3)				
		percent of total value added	establishments				percent of total value added	establishments				percent of total value added	establishments			
			1–99 employees		100 or more emp.			1–99 employees		100 or more emp.			1–99 employees		100 or more emp.	
			number	percent of value added	number	percent of value added		number	percent of value added	number	percent of value added		number	percent of value added	number	percent of value added
Norway[9, 29]	1983	14.7	2,369	58.2	94	41.8	2.8	845	73.3	33	26.7	32.5	4,217	65.3	217	34.7
Oman	...	...	...	...	...	...	...	...	...	...	...	...	...	...	...	...
Pacific Is., Trust Terr. of the	...	...	...	...	...	...	...	...	...	...	...	...	...	...	...	...
Marshall Islands	...	...	...	...	...	...	...	...	...	...	...	...	...	...	...	...
Micronesia, Fed. States of	...	...	...	...	...	...	...	...	...	...	...	...	...	...	...	...
Northern Mariana Islands	...	...	...	...	...	...	...	...	...	...	...	...	...	...	...	...
Palau	...	...	...	...	...	...	...	...	...	...	...	...	...	...	...	...
Pakistan	1977	36.7	332[21]	10.0[21]	90	90.0	24.6	844[21]	13.8[21]	211	86.2	20.8	522[21]	12.6[21]	115	87.4
Panama[9, 29]	1981	49.7	*259*	...	...	...	9.0	*95*	...	...	...	21.6	*205*	...	...	...
Papua New Guinea	1983	56.8	*150*	...	...	...	0.5	*12*	...	...	...	24.1	*148*	...	...	...
Paraguay	1982	36.0	...	...	...	...	12.0	...	...	...	...	52.0[23]	...	...	...	...
Peru[9]	1980	24.7	6,236	...	82	...	12.5	8,613	...	106	...	22.1	7,476	...	148	...
Philippines[18]	1981	42.8	*30,605*	...	...	...	10.1	*34,253*	...	...	...	26.8	*8,950*	...	...	...
Pitcairn Island	...	...	...	...	...	...	...	...	...	...	...	...	...	...	...	...
Poland[48]	1983	20.4	*10,732*	...	...	...	13.4	*8,417*	...	...	...	19.5	...	...	*5,142*	...
Portugal[9, 28]	1981	20.4	10,825	...	212	...	24.2	10,387	...	439	...	21.7	11,067	...	270	...
Puerto Rico	1982	11.2	296	22.7	37	77.3	8.4	286	25.6	131	74.4	47.5	578	25.2	68	74.8
Qatar	1984	...	...	...	...	...	...	...	...	...	...	...	...	...	...	...
Réunion	1978	...	*35*	...	...	...	...	*5*	...	...	...	...	*16*	...	...	...
Romania[4, 48]	1982	11.0	...	...	*291*	...	15.0	...	...	*225*	...	74.0[23]	...	...	*200*	...
Rwanda[4, 12, 18]	1981	75.7	...	...	*17*	...	10.1	...	...	*3*	...	5.8	...	...	*17*	...
St. Christopher and Nevis	...	...	...	...	...	...	...	...	...	...	...	...	...	...	...	...
St. Helena and Ascension	...	...	...	...	...	...	...	...	...	...	...	...	...	...	...	...
St. Lucia	...	...	...	...	...	...	...	...	...	...	...	...	...	...	...	...
St. Pierre and Miquelon	...	...	...	...	...	...	...	...	...	...	...	...	...	...	...	...
St. Vincent	...	...	...	...	...	...	...	...	...	...	...	...	...	...	...	...
San Marino	1984	...	*34*	...	...	...	...	*65*	...	...	...	...	*64*	...	...	...
São Tomé and Príncipe	1983	...	...	...	...	...	...	...	...	...	...	...	...	...	...	...
Saudi Arabia	1977	...	...	...	...	...	...	...	...	...	...	...	...	...	...	...
Senegal[9]	1982	54.4	...	...	*38*	...	16.8	...	...	*33*	...	4.8	*66*	...	...	...
Seychelles	1983	83.9	*16*	...	...	...	2.0	*2*	...	...	...	12.2	*12*	...	...	...
Sierra Leone[12]	1973–74	80.3	...	...	...	...	2.7	...	...	...	...	10.8	...	...	...	...
Singapore[6, 13]	1983	6.0	*311*	...	...	...	4.6	*566*	...	...	...	31.9	*1,053*	...	...	...
Solomon Islands	...	...	...	...	...	...	...	...	...	...	...	...	...	...	...	...
Somalia[9, 12]	1977	44.5	*68*	...	...	...	24.4	*75*	...	...	...	24.8	*37*	...	...	...
South Africa[9, 12]	1976	14.1	1,713	19.4	451	80.6	10.5	1,543	15.7	570	84.3	25.6	3,639	25.6	625	74.4
Bophuthatswana	...	...	...	...	...	...	...	...	...	...	...	...	...	...	...	...
Ciskei	...	...	...	...	...	...	...	...	...	...	...	...	...	...	...	...
Transkei	...	...	...	...	...	...	...	...	...	...	...	...	...	...	...	...
Venda	...	...	...	...	...	...	...	...	...	...	...	...	...	...	...	...
South West Africa/Namibia	...	...	...	...	...	...	...	...	...	...	...	...	...	...	...	...
Spain[6]	1981	16.8	*47,190*	...	...	...	10.4	*14,355*	...	...	...	26.0	*45,738*	...	...	...
Sri Lanka[6]	1981	32.8	*204*	...	...	...	18.2	...	...	*332*	...	29.0	*365*	...	...	...
Sudan, The	1983	...	...	...	...	...	...	...	...	...	...	...	...	...	...	...
Suriname	...	...	...	...	...	...	...	...	...	...	...	...	...	...	...	...
Swaziland[6]	1982	44.2	...	...	*14*	...	2.2	*33*	...	...	...	44.6	...	...	*38*	...
Sweden[6, 31]	1982	10.5	766	...	152	...	2.6	707	...	84	...	31.8	2,938	...	466	...
Switzerland	1975	17.3	12,680	...	152	...	9.0	4,750	...	198	...	32.2	17,255	...	311	...
Syria[9, 50]	1982	28.7	*7,974*	...	...	...	25.9	*15,116*	...	...	...	34.4	*12,376*	...	...	...
Taiwan	...	...	...	...	...	...	...	...	...	...	...	...	...	...	...	...
Tanzania	1975	42.6	...	...	...	...	16.3	...	...	...	...	17.7	...	...	...	...
Thailand[9, 13]	1980	19.5	*2,152*	...	...	...	26.0	...	...	*1,462*	...	22.8	*2,118*	...	...	...
Togo[4, 9]	1979	62.1	...	...	*12*	...	7.4	*3*	...	...	...	13.6	*26*	...	...	...
Tokelau	...	...	...	...	...	...	...	...	...	...	...	...	...	...	...	...
Tonga	1981	73.8	33	100.0	—	—	1.1	11	100.0	—	—	11.7	23	100.0	—	—
Trinidad and Tobago[12, 51]	1980	13.0	...	...	*97*	...	4.0	*83*	...	...	...	82.8[23]	*225*	...	...	...
Tunisia	1981	14.1	283	35.9	35	64.1	16.9	276	26.4	124	73.6	22.2	253	26.8	49	73.2
Turkey[9, 31]	1982	21.4	18,692	...	175	...	14.6	65,114	...	195	...	30.1	28,193	...	150	...
Turks and Caicos Islands	...	...	...	...	...	...	...	...	...	...	...	...	...	...	...	...
Tuvalu	...	...	...	...	...	...	...	...	...	...	...	...	...	...	...	...
Uganda[6, 12]	1971	43.3	148	19.7	24	39.0	22.8	48	8.7	9	34.1	13.2	113	61.8	21	38.0
U.S.S.R.[3, 4]	1982	20.0	...	...	*9,352*	...	18.1	...	...	*7,786*	...	15.6	...	...	*3,768*	...
United Arab Emirates[13, 31]	1978	8.0	*73*	...	...	...	1.7	*67*	...	...	...	25.3	*209*	...	...	...
United Kingdom[6, 28]	1982	15.0	4,909	...	514	...	5.9	12,134	...	1,062	...	28.3	27,488	...	1,555	...
United States[6, 52]	1981	10.5	22,994	24.1	3,890	75.9	6.1	30,578	24.8	6,204	75.2	28.6	120,525	29.7	9,646	70.3
Uruguay[9, 20, 29]	1983	45.1	*2,789*	...	...	...	17.7	*1,995*	...	...	...	24.1	*2,897*	...	...	...
Vanuatu	...	...	...	...	...	...	...	...	...	...	...	...	...	...	...	...
Venezuela[29, 52]	1979	16.8	2,138	25.2	161	74.8	7.4	1,778	44.1	132	55.9	46.3	2,085	34.7	191	65.3
Vietnam	...	...	...	...	...	...	...	...	...	...	...	...	...	...	...	...
Virgin Islands (U.S.)	...	...	...	...	...	...	...	...	...	...	...	...	...	...	...	...
Wallis and Futuna	...	...	...	...	...	...	...	...	...	...	...	...	...	...	...	...
West Bank	1982	55.0	*228*	...	...	...	10.0	*658*	...	...	...	18.7	*494*	...	...	...
Western Sahara	...	...	...	...	...	...	...	...	...	...	...	...	...	...	...	...
Western Samoa	...	...	...	...	...	...	...	...	...	...	...	...	...	...	...	...
Yemen (Aden)[29]	1983	37.6	*488*[18]	...	...	...	13.1	...	...	*13*[18]	...	28.7	...	...	*14*[18]	...
Yemen (Ṣan'ā')[29, 53]	1980	34.2	*442*	...	...	...	7.9	*536*	...	...	...	13.6	*659*	...	...	...
Yugoslavia[4]	1981	11.5	...	...	*1,398*	...	16.2	...	...	*1,576*	...	25.7	...	...	*2,942*	...
Zaire[12]	1980	44.0	...	...	...	...	20.0	...	...	...	...	36.0[23]	...	...	...	...
Zambia[9, 12]	1974	34.5	*172*	...	...	...	8.3	*156*	...	...	...	22.0	*179*	...	...	...
Zimbabwe[6]	1982	26.0	...	...	...	...	21.0	...	...	...	...	21.0	...	...	...	...

[1]Data in value added columns refer to gross output in value of sales. [2]Group 4 includes groups 5 and 6. [3]Data in value added columns refer to gross ouput in producer's prices. [4]Establishment data refer to enterprises. [5]Group 4 includes groups 5 and 6 and mining and public utilities; establishment data are for 1969. [6]Data in value added columns are calculated in factor values. [7]Value added data refer to establishments of 4 or more workers. [8]Group 5 includes group 6. [9]Value added calculated in producer's prices. [10]Value added data refer to 1981. [11]Group 5 includes and group 6 excludes ISIC 3825 (office machinery and computing equipment). [12]Total value and percentages calculated on sum of figures directly referable to groups 1–6; may exclude data withheld for confidentiality and minor or ambiguously classified manufacturing. [13]Establishments of 10 or more workers. [14]Excludes sugar factories and refineries. [15]Excludes leather and leather products. [16]Excludes synthetic fibre industry. [17]Includes professional goods. [18]Establishment data are for 1979. [19]Establishment data are incomplete. [20]Establishment data are for 1978. [21]Includes some establishments of more than 100 workers. [22]Establishments of 50 or more workers. [23]Group 3 includes groups 4, 5, and 6. [24]Establishment data are for 1973. [25]Value added data refer to 1979. [26]Includes sugarcane cropping. [27]Value added data refer to establishments of 20 or more workers; establishment data refer to establishments of 6 or more. [28]Establishment data are for 1980.

primary and fabricated metals; proc. minerals (group 4)					machinery (except elec.) and transport equip. (group 5)					electrical and electronic machinery (group 6)					total manufac-turing value added (U.S.$'000,-000)	country
percent of total value added	establishments				percent of total value added	establishments				percent of total value added	establishments					
	1–99 employees		100 or more emp.			1–99 employees		100 or more emp.			1–99 employees		100 or more emp.			
	number	percent of value added	number	percent of value added		number	percent of value added	number	percent of value added		number	percent of value added	number	percent of value added		
21.4	2,140	37.6	118	62.4	19.5	1,974	15.8	154	84.2	8.2	342	29.1	48	70.9	10,028	Norway
...	...	...	...	...	...	...	...	...	...	...	...	...	...	...	...	Oman
...	...	...	...	...	...	...	...	...	...	...	...	...	...	...	...	Pacific Is., Trust Terr. of the
...	...	...	...	...	...	...	...	...	...	...	...	...	...	...	...	Marshall Islands
...	...	...	...	...	...	...	...	...	...	...	...	...	...	...	...	Micronesia, Fed. States of
...	...	...	...	...	...	...	...	...	...	...	...	...	...	...	...	Northern Mariana Islands
...	...	...	...	...	...	...	...	...	...	...	...	...	...	...	...	Palau
8.7	531[21]	25.3[21]	65	74.7	4.6	379[21]	15.4[21]	34	84.6	3.2	155[21]	31.1[21]	19	68.9	14,142	Pakistan
12.1	*100*	...	...	...	1.2	*19*	...	...	...	0.7	*8*	...	...	...	522	Panama
18.6[2]	*142*[2]	...	...	...	[2]	[2]	...	...	...	[2]	[2]	...	...	...	267	Papua New Guinea
[23]	...	...	...	...	[23]	...	...	...	...	[23]	...	...	...	...	816	Paraguay
22.1	98	...	11	...	8.0[11]	1,774	...	83	...	3.1[11]	524	...	5	...	5,204	Peru
8.2	*7,454*	...	...	...	6.9	*2,092*	...	...	...	5.2	...	...	*268*	...	6,123	Philippines
...	...	...	...	...	—	—	—	—	—	—	—	—	—	—	...	Pitcairn Island
15.2	...	...	*3,165*	...	21.2	...	...	*1,806*	...	7.1	...	...	*751*	...	...	Poland
33.7[2]	7,938	...	226	...	[2]	1,351	...	112	...	[2]	155	...	38	...	7,153	Portugal
3.1	351	53.0	16	47.0	6.7[11]	104	13.9	12	86.1	13.2[11]	112	18.5	69	81.5	8,606	Puerto Rico
...	...	...	...	...	...	...	...	...	...	...	...	...	...	...	30	Qatar
...	*9*	...	...	...	...	*18*[8]	...	...	...	...	[8]	...	...	...	...	Réunion
[23]	...	...	*471*[2]	...	[23]	...	...	[2]	...	[23]	...	...	[2]	...	...	Romania
3.8	...	...	*10*[2]	...	4.4	...	...	[2]	...	0.1	...	...	[2]	...	134	Rwanda
...	...	...	...	...	...	...	...	...	...	...	...	...	...	...	...	St. Christopher and Nevis
...	...	...	...	...	...	...	...	...	...	...	...	...	...	...	...	St. Helena and Ascension
—	—	—	—	—	—	—	—	—	—	—	—	—	—	—	...	St. Lucia
...	...	...	...	...	...	...	...	...	...	...	...	...	...	...	...	St. Pierre and Miquelon
...	...	...	...	...	...	...	...	...	...	...	...	...	...	...	...	St. Vincent
...	*44*	...	...	...	...	*241*[8]	...	...	...	...	[8]	...	...	...	...	San Marino
...	...	...	...	...	...	...	...	...	...	...	...	...	...	...	22	São Tomé and Príncipe
...	...	...	...	...	...	...	...	...	...	...	...	...	...	...	2,829	Saudi Arabia
24.1[2]	45[2]	...	...	...	[2]	[2]	...	...	...	[2]	[2]	...	...	...	170	Senegal
1.9	*4*	...	...	...	—	—	—	...	—	—	—	—	—	—	14	Seychelles
6.2	...	...	...	...	...	...	...	...	...	...	...	...	...	...	31	Sierra Leone
12.8	*559*	...	...	...	18.3[11]	*632*[11]	...	...	...	23.9[11]	...	...	*315*[11]	...	4,664	Singapore
...	...	...	...	...	—	—	—	—	—	—	—	—	—	—	...	Solomon Islands
6.3[2]	*77*[2]	...	...	...	[2]	[2]	...	...	...	[2]	[2]	...	...	...	40	Somalia
27.8	3,195	17.7	559	82.3	16.1	2,450	28.6	344	71.6	5.9	486	16.2	129	83.8	9,070	South Africa
...	...	...	...	...	...	...	...	...	...	...	...	...	...	...	...	Bophuthatswana
...	...	...	...	...	...	...	...	...	...	...	...	...	...	...	...	Ciskei
...	...	...	...	...	...	...	...	...	...	...	...	...	...	...	...	Transkei
...	...	...	...	...	...	...	...	...	...	...	...	...	...	...	...	Venda
...	...	...	...	...	...	...	...	...	...	...	...	...	...	...	...	South West Africa/Namibia
24.3	*36,704*	...	...	...	13.9	*7,636*	...	...	...	7.2	*2,642*	...	...	...	42,846	Spain
14.1	...	...	*201*	...	2.3	*61*	...	...	...	2.9	*31*	...	...	...	254	Sri Lanka
...	...	...	...	...	...	...	...	...	...	...	...	...	...	...	467	Sudan, The
...	...	...	...	...	...	...	...	...	...	...	...	...	...	...	...	Suriname
6.4	*34*	...	...	...	2.5[8]	...	...	*4*[8]	...	[8]	...	...	[8]	...	93	Swaziland
17.7	509	...	124	...	24.9	3,470[8, 49]	...	605[8, 49]	...	10.5	[8]	...	[8]	...	24,496	Sweden
25.4	16,233	...	301	...	43.3	10,268	...	590	...	...	...	...	...	...	12,800	Switzerland
12.0[2]	*17,216*[2]	...	...	...	[2]	[2]	...	...	...	[2]	[2]	...	...	...	1,845	Syria
...	...	...	...	...	...	...	...	...	...	...	...	...	...	...	...	Taiwan
23.4[2]	...	...	...	...	[2]	...	...	...	...	[2]	...	...	...	...	239	Tanzania
24.9	*1,208*	...	...	...	3.7	*765*	...	...	...	0.5	*153*	...	...	...	5,159	Thailand
16.5	...	...	*9*	...	—	—	—	—	—	—	—	—	—	—	52	Togo
...	...	...	...	...	...	...	...	...	...	...	...	...	...	...	...	Tokelau
12.8[2]	19	100.0	—	—	[2]	7	100.0	—	—	[2]	2	100.0	—	—	4	Tonga
[23]	*82*	...	...	...	[23]	*27*[8]	...	...	...	[23]	[8]	...	...	...	735	Trinidad and Tobago
46.8	30	50.3	29	49.7	...	...	...	...	...	...	...	...	...	...	840	Tunisia
18.3	4,992	...	106	...	10.9	57,503	...	199	...	4.3	...	...	...	...	11,480	Turkey
...	...	...	...	...	—	—	—	—	—	—	—	—	—	—	...	Turks and Caicos Islands
—	—	—	—	—	—	—	—	—	—	—	—	—	—	—	...	Tuvalu
20.7	20	7.9	8	92.1	...	64	77.0	5	23.0	...	...	...	...	...	73	Uganda
46.3[2, 17]	...	...	*12,155*[2, 17]	...	[2]	[2]	...	...	...	[2]	[2]	...	...	...	...	U.S.S.R.
63.9	*285*	...	...	...	9.0	*5*	...	...	...	–8.3	*9*	...	...	...	266	United Arab Emirates
15.7	15,703	...	1,114	...	21.6	23,098	...	1,675	...	8.4	4,423	...	481	...	133,458	United Kingdom
15.4	52,544	23.4	6,287	76.6	21.8	76,365	20.1	6,751	79.9	12.3	12,103	9.9	2,870	90.1	834,200	United States
8.3	*1,538*	...	...	...	1.9[11]	*761*	...	...	...	2.5[11]	*410*	...	...	...	2,617	Uruguay
...	...	...	...	...	—	—	—	—	—	—	—	—	—	—	...	Vanuatu
17.2	2,063	35.0	126	65.0	9.4[11]	408	26.1	65	73.9	2.1[11]	163	30.5	40	69.5	12,869	Venezuela
...	...	...	...	...	...	...	...	...	...	...	...	...	...	...	...	Vietnam
...	...	...	...	...	...	...	...	...	...	...	...	...	...	...	...	Virgin Islands (U.S.)
—	—	—	—	—	—	—	—	—	—	—	—	—	—	—	...	Wallis and Futuna
11.1	*610*	...	...	...	...	...	...	...	...	...	...	...	...	...	82	West Bank
—	—	—	—	—	—	—	—	—	—	—	—	—	—	—	...	Western Sahara
...	...	...	...	...	...	...	...	...	...	...	...	...	...	...	...	Western Samoa
20.4[2]	*12*[2]	...	...	...	[2]	[2]	...	...	...	[2]	[2]	...	...	...	117	Yemen (Aden)
44.1[2]	*1,358*[2]	...	...	...	[2]	[2]	...	...	...	[2]	[2]	...	...	...	172	Yemen (Ṣan'ā')
22.8	...	...	*2,021*	...	15.3[11]	...	...	*1,150*[11]	..	7.4[11]	...	...	*512*[11]	...	...	Yugoslavia
[23]	...	...	...	...	[23]	...	...	...	...	[23]	...	...	...	...	256	Zaire
12.8	*152*	...	...	...	19.4	*217*	...	...	...	2.9	*21*	...	...	...	520	Zambia
30.5[2]	...	...	...	...	[2]	...	...	...	...	[2]	...	...	...	...	1,702	Zimbabwe

[29]Establishments of 5 or more workers. [30]Establishments of 7 or more workers. [31]Establishment data are for 1981. [32]Value added data refer to establishments of 5 or more workers. [33]Includes petrochemical, rubber, and plastics industries. [34]Value added data are "revenue." [35]Value added data refer to 1982. [36]Establishments of 30 or more workers. [37]Excludes printing and publishing. [38]Establishment data refer to establishments of 10 or more workers with electric power and 20 or more without power. [39]Excludes petroleum manufacturing and manufacturing on tea, tobacco, and rubber estates. [40]Establishments of 20 or more workers. [41]Establishments of 3 or more workers. [42]Excludes the diamond industry. [43]Excludes the petroleum industry. [44]Establishment data are for 1982. [45]Establishment data are for 1976. [46]Establishment data refer to establishments with annual sales of 100,000 kwachas or more. [47]Privately owned establishments only. [48]Socialized sector only. [49]Includes fabricated metal products. [50]Value added data refer to 1981. [51]Establishment data are for 1975. [52]Percent of value added by establishment size and number of establishments data refer to 1977. [53]Including a 10% sample of establishments with fewer than 5 employees.

Energy

This table provides data about the commercial energy supplies (reserves, production, consumption, and trade), of the various countries of the world, together with data about their oil pipeline networks and traffic. Many of the data and concepts used in this table are adopted from the United Nations' *Yearbook of World Energy Statistics*.

Electricity. Total installed electrical power capacity comprises the sum of the rated power capacities of all main and auxiliary generators in a country. 'Total installed capacity' (kW) is multiplied by 8,760 hours per year to yield 'Total production capacity' (kW-hr).

Production of electricity comprises the total gross production of electricity by publicly or privately owned enterprises and also that generated by industrial establishments for their own use, but usually excludes consumption by the utility itself. Measured in 1,000,000s of kilowatt-hours (kW-hr), annual production of electricity ranges generally between 30 and 40% of total production capacity. The data are further analyzed by type of generation: fossil fuels, hydroelectric power, and nuclear fuel.

The great majority of the world's electrical and other energy needs are met by the burning of hydrocarbon (fossil) solids, liquids, and gases, either for thermal generation of electricity or in internal combustion engines. Many renewable and nontraditional sources of energy are being developed worldwide (wood, biogenic gases and liquids, tidal, wave, and wind power, geothermal and photothermal [solar] energy, and so on), but collectively these sources are still negligible in the world's total energy consumption. For this reason only hydroelectric and nuclear generation are considered here separately after fossil fuels.

Though hydroelectric power accounts for only a small proportion of the world's primary production, the leading producers were some of the world's principal energy-consuming nations: the United States, Canada, the U.S.S.R., Brazil, Norway, China, and Japan, which together accounted for about 65% of the world's production of hydroelectricity.

Nuclear generation is being utilized by more than a score of countries for commercial production. The major producers, the United States, France, the U.S.S.R., and Japan, accounted for about two-thirds of the nuclear generation of electricity.

Trade in electrical energy refers to the transfer of generated electrical output via an international grid. Total electricity consumption (residential and nonresidential) is equal to total electricity requirements less transformation and distribution losses.

Coal. The term coal, as used in the table, comprises all grades of anthracite, bituminous, subbituminous, and lignite that have acquired or may in the future, by reason of new technology or changed market prices, acquire an economic value. These types of coal may be differentiated according to heat content (density) and content of impurities. Most coal reserve data are based on proved recoverable reserves only, of all grades of coal. Exceptions are footnoted, with proved in-place reserves reported only when recoverable reserves are unknown. Production figures include deposits removed from both surface and underground workings as well as quantities used by the producers themselves or issued to the miners. Wastes recovered from mines or nearby preparation plants are excluded from production figures.

Natural gas. This term refers to any combustible gas (usually chiefly methane) of natural origin from underground sources. The natural gas reserves of Eastern Europe, the U.S.S.R., and the Middle East account for about two-thirds of the world total. The countries with the largest proved reserves were the U.S.S.R., Iran, the United States, Qatar, the United Arab Emirates, and Algeria. The data for production cover, to the extent

Energy

country	electricity													coal		
	installed capacity, 1984 ('000 kW)	production, 1984		power source, 1984			trade, 1984		consumption				reserves, latest ('000,000 metric tons)	production, 1984 ('000 metric tons)	consumption, 1984 ('000 metric tons)
		capacity ('000,000 kW-hr)	amount ('000,000 kW-hr)	fossil fuel (%)	hydro-power (%)	nuclear fuel (%)	exports ('000,000 kW-hr)	imports ('000,000 kW-hr)	amount, 1984 ('000,000 kW-hr)	per capita, 1984 (kW-hr)	residential, 1982 (%)	non-residential, 1982 (%)			
Afghanistan	450	3,942	1,045	26.8	73.2	—	—	—	1,045	73	...	...	66	170	170
Albania	640	5,606	3,020	20.5	79.5	—	600	—	2,420	811	...	...	15[1]	1,775	1,985
Algeria	3,436	30,099	11,450	97.8	2.2	—	120	110	11,440	538	24.1[3]	75.9[3]	43	7	1,197
American Samoa	32	280	75	100.0	—	—	—	—	75	2,206	...	...	—	—	...
Andorra	...	...	...	...	...	...	...	...	...	...	...	...	—	—	...
Angola	600	5,256	1,790	25.4	74.6	—	—	—	1,790	210	27.5[4]	72.5[4]	...	—	—
Anguilla	—	—	—	...	...	...	—	—	—	—	...	...	...	...	...
Antigua and Barbuda	26	228	76	100.0	—	—	—	—	76	962	42.4[2]	57.6[2]	...	...	...
Argentina	15,280	133,853	44,914	45.4	44.2	10.3	5	—	44,909	1,492	26.9	73.1	150	509	962
Aruba[5]	...	...	...	...	...	...	...	...	...	...	...	...	...	...	...
Australia	31,130	272,699	112,947	88.0	12.0	—	—	—	112,947	7,278	30.1[4]	69.9[4]	65,698	138,704	71,968
Austria	14,933	130,813	41,827	30.9	69.1	—	6,725	5,401	40,503	5,408	23.1[4]	83.4[4]	65	2,901	7,142
Bahamas, The	330	2,891	870	100.0	—	—	—	—	870	3,937	34.2[6]	65.8[6]	...	—	—
Bahrain	645	5,650	2,056	100.0	—	—	—	—	2,056	4,966	...	...	...	...	...
Bangladesh	1,289	11,292	4,292	79.1	20.9	—	—	—	4,292	44	16.8	83.2	242	—	175
Barbados	94	823	360	100.0	—	—	—	—	360	1,374	25.1[2]	74.9[2]	...	—	—
Belgium	12,309	107,827	53,699	47.7	0.7	51.7	4,143	4,453	54,009	5,468	26.9[6]	73.1[6]	440	6,298	14,956
Belize	21	184	58	100.0	—	—	—	—	58	372	...	...	...	...	...
Benin	15	131	5	100.0	—	—	—	185	190	49	...	...	...	...	...
Bermuda	118	1,034	382	100.0	—	—	—	—	382	4,961	40.8[6]	59.2[6]	...	—	—
Bhutan	16	140	30	70.0	30.0	—	—	...	36	26	...	...	...	—	1
Bolivia	566	4,958	1,695	29.5	70.5	—	—	3	1,698	274	33.4[6]	66.6[6]	...	—	1
Botswana	[8]	[8]	522[8, 9]	[8]	[8]	[8]	[8]	82[8, 9]	[8]	[8]	...	...	3,447	400[6, 8]	[8]
Brazil	41,662	364,959	175,710	5.9	94.1	—	91	15	175,634	1,324	21.0	79.0	13,000	7,461	13,708
British Virgin Islands	5	44	29	100.0	—	—	—	—	29	2,231	...	...	...	...	...
Brunei	240	2,102	831	100.0	—	—	—	—	831	3,089	55.3	44.7	...	—	—
Bulgaria	13,296	116,473	44,601	60.8	7.8	31.4	2,400	4,600	46,801	5,097	...	...	3,656	32,344	39,215
Burkina Faso	40	350	115	100.0	—	—	—	—	115	17	...	...	...	...	...
Burma	741	6,491	1,726	50.5	49.5	—	—	—	1,726	45	...	59.1[4, 10]	2	73	248
Burundi	9	79	2	100.0	—	—	—	145	147	33	...	...	...	...	...
Cameroon	571	5,002	2,230	4.9	95.1	—	—	—	2,230	236	...	...	...	...	1
Canada	95,224	834,162	437,990	22.5	65.4	12.1	41,436	2,343	398,897	15,765	24.5[4]	75.5[4]	5,906	57,402	49,041
Cape Verde	4	35	25	100.0	—	—	—	—	25	79	...	...	...	—	—
Cayman Islands	28	242	111	100.0	—	—	—	—	100	4,971	55.4[11]	44.6[11]	...	...	...
Central African Republic	30	263	68	4.4	95.6	—	—	—	68	27	17.5[12]	82.5[12]	4	...	...
Chad	38	333	65	100.0	—	—	—	—	65	13	...	...	...	...	...
Chile	3,355	29,390	13,490	30.9	69.1	—	—	—	13,490	1,136	19.4	80.6	1,179	1,224	1,868
China	83,000	727,080	376,990	77.0	23.0	—	—	250	377,240	366	6.1	93.9	98,792	789,230	784,769
Christmas Island	12	105	33	100.0	—	—	—	—	33[6]	11,000[6]	...	...	...	...	...
Cocos (Keeling) Islands	...	...	...	...	...	...	...	...	...	...	...	...	...	...	...
Colombia	6,150	53,874	27,800	27.3	72.7	—	15	8	27,793	989	45.1	54.9	1,034	6,100	5,650
Comoros	4	35	10	100.0	—	—	—	—	10	23	...	...	...	...	...
Congo	149	1,305	237	0.8	99.2	—	—	25	262	155	...	...	...	...	...
Cook Islands	6	53	10	100.0	—	—	—	—	10	526	...	...	...	...	...
Costa Rica	819	7,174	3,067	3.0	97.0	—	—	650	2,417	954	44.3	55.7	...	...	...
Côte d'Ivoire	1,163	10,188	1,918	45.8	54.2	—	—	—	1,918	202	14.5	85.5	...	...	...
Cuba	3,115	27,287	12,292	99.4	0.6	—	—	—	12,292	1,233	28.5[6]	71.5[6]	...	—	110
Cyprus	389	3,408	1,250	100.0	—	—	—	—	1,250	1,897	20.6	79.4	...	—	52
Czechoslovakia	18,600	162,936	78,388	86.6	4.2	9.2	7,750	10,488	81,126	5,204	15.9[13]	84.1[13]	5,579	129,278	127,508
Denmark	7,852	68,784	22,361	99.8	0.2	—	2,160	7,044	27,245	5,300	32.5[6]	67.5[6]	...	—	9,317

possible, gas obtained from gas fields, petroleum fields, or coal mines that is actually collected and marketed. (Much natural gas in Middle Eastern oil fields is flared [burned] because it is often not economical to capture and market it.) Manufactured gas is generally a by-product of industrial operations such as gasworks, coke ovens, and blast furnaces. It is usually burned at the point of production and rarely enters the marketplace. Production of manufactured gas is, therefore, only reported as a percentage of domestic gas consumption. Natural gas is not generally a major energy source in less developed countries unless they have extensive reserves of their own, as do Bangladesh, China, and Mexico.

Crude petroleum. Crude petroleum is the liquid product obtained from oil wells; the term also includes shale oil, tar sand extract, and field or lease condensate. Production and consumption data in the table refer, so far as possible, to the same year so that the relationship between national production and consumption patterns can be clearly seen; both are given in barrels.

Proved reserves are that oil remaining underground in known fields whose existence has been "proved" by the evaluation of nearby producing wells or by seismic tests in sedimentary strata known to contain crude petroleum, and that is judged recoverable within the limits of present technology and economic conditions (prices). Proved reserves of crude petroleum are heavily concentrated in the Middle East, North America including Mexico, and the U.S.S.R. The published proved reserve figures do not necessarily reflect the true reserves of a country, because government authorities or corporations often have political or economic motives for withholding or altering such data.

The estimated exhaustion rate of petroleum reserves is an extrapolated ratio of published proved reserves to the current rate of withdrawal/production. Present world published proved reserves will last about 30 years at the present rate of withdrawal, but there are large country-to-country variations above or below the average.

Data on petroleum and product pipelines are provided because of the great importance to both domestic and international energy markets of this means of bringing these energy sources from their production or transportation points to refineries, intermediate consumption and distribution points, and final consumers. Their traffic may represent a very significant fraction of the total movement of goods within a country. International data tend to be incomplete, both for the petroleum pipelines (the category for which the most complete data are available) and, still more so, for natural gas, coal, and other types of pipeline systems. Available data for petroleum pipelines vary internationally, some countries reporting only international shipments, others reporting domestic shipments of 50 kilometres or more, and so on.

For data in the hydrocarbons portions of the table (coal, natural gas, and petroleum), extensive use has been made of a variety of international sources, such as those of the United Nations, the International Energy Agency (of the Organization for Economic Cooperation and Development), and the World Energy Conference; of the resources of the U.S. Department of Energy; and of various industry surveys, such as those published by British Petroleum (BP *Statistical Review of World Energy*), the *International Petroleum Encyclopedia,* the *Oil and Gas Journal,* the *Petroleum Economist,* and *World Oil.*

a. Includes refined petroleum products pipelines.

natural gas						crude petroleum							country
published proved reserves, 1986 ('000,000,000 cu m)	production		consumption			reserves, 1986		production, 1985 ('000,000 barrels)	consumption, 1985 ('000,000 barrels)	refining capacity, 1986 ('000 barrels per day)	pipelines (latest)[a]		
	natural gas, 1985 ('000,000 cu m)	manufactured gas, 1984 (% of total gas consumption)	amount, 1984 ('000,000 cu m)	residential, 1982 (%)	nonresidential, 1982 (%)	published proved ('000,000 barrels)	years to exhaust proved reserves				length (km)	traffic ('000,000 metric ton-km)	
67	2,888	...	191	...	...	...	...	...	...	—	—	—	Afghanistan
8	300	...	423	...	...	202	8	25	25[2]	40	182	—	Albania
3,002	37,378	31.1	5,055	26.8[4]	73.2[4]	5,020	14	358	48[2]	465	6,910	...	Algeria
...	...	...	...	...	...	...	...	...	...	—	...	...	American Samoa
...	...	...	...	...	...	...	...	...	...	—	—	—	Andorra
55	340	11.1	115	...	...	2,018	24	84	9[2]	32	179	...	Angola
...	...	...	...	...	...	...	...	...	...	—	—	—	Anguilla
...	...	...	...	...	...	...	...	...	—	—	—	—	Antigua and Barbuda
623	15,569	13.1	15,802	33.1	66.9	2,240	13	168	175[2]	667	6,290	...	Argentina
...	...	...	...	...	...	...	...	...	...	...	—	—	Aruba[5]
528	13,467	34.1	13,119	...	...	1,698	8	210	215[2]	623	2,900	...	Australia
10	1,164	25.2	5,044	25.7[4]	74.3[4]	116	15	8	73	204	725	4,652	Austria
...	—	90.9	...	...	...	...	...	...	42[2]	350	—	—	Bahamas, The
227	6,402	5.2	3,685	...	...	180	13	14	74[2]	250	72	...	Bahrain
360	2,676	0.3	2,327	29.3	70.7	—	—	—	8[2]	31	—	—	Bangladesh
...	17[2]	...	17	55.4	44.6	0.4	0.6	0.7	1[2]	3	—	—	Barbados
...	46[2]	24.3	8,759	43.4[6]	56.6[6]	...	...	...	153[7]	652	1,276	866	Belgium
...	...	...	...	...	...	...	...	...	...	—	—	—	Belize
...	...	...	...	...	...	100	40	3	...	—	—	—	Benin
...	...	...	...	...	...	...	...	...	...	—	—	—	Bermuda
...	...	...	...	...	...	...	...	...	...	—	—	—	Bhutan
129	2,515	43.7	293	0.2	99.8	156	20	8	8[2]	47	3,165	...	Bolivia
...	...	[8]	...	...	...	...	...	...	[8]	—	—	—	Botswana
93	2,118	75.4	1,958	23.4	76.6	2,194	11	206	417[2]	1,305	2,465	...	Brazil
...	...	...	...	...	...	...	...	...	...	—	—	—	British Virgin Islands
200	8,495	2.5	1,468	...	...	1,443	25	58	−2[2]	10	553	...	Brunei
5	100	9.7	4,972	...	...	13	6	2	94[2]	300	611	...	Bulgaria
...	...	...	...	...	...	...	...	...	...	—	—	—	Burkina Faso
321	646	0.4	838	—	100.0	724	84	9	10[2]	26	660	...	Burma
...	...	...	...	...	...	...	...	...	...	—	—	—	Burundi
118	—	95.0	...	...	...	535	8	69	24[2]	43	—	—	Cameroon
2,818	84,068	24.2	56,398	20.6[4]	79.4[4]	6,407	11	572	537	1,856	23,564	91,300	Canada
...	...	...	...	...	...	...	...	...	...	—	—	—	Cape Verde
...	...	...	...	...	...	...	...	...	...	—	—	—	Cayman Islands
...	...	...	...	...	...	...	...	...	...	—	—	—	Central African Republic
...	...	...	...	...	...	...	...	...	...	—	—	—	Chad
142	1,260	48.5	943	42.3	57.7	218	16	13	29[2]	141	1,540	...	Chile
419	12,865	...	12,396	...	...	19,480	21	912	642	2,150	7,600	...	China
...	...	...	...	...	...	...	...	...	...	—	—	—	Christmas Island
...	...	...	...	...	...	...	...	...	...	—	—	—	Cocos (Keeling) Islands
110	5,284	12.1	4,796	0.8	99.2	1,543	24	64	69[2]	211	4,935	...	Colombia
...	...	...	...	...	...	...	...	...	...	—	—	—	Comoros
69	34	...	—	...	...	756	18	42	—	21	25	...	Congo
...	...	...	...	...	...	...	...	...	...	—	—	—	Cook Islands
...	—	26.6	—	—	—	...	...	...	3[2]	15	95	...	Costa Rica
100	—	49.9	—	—	—	125	12	10	12[2]	90	—	—	Côte d'Ivoire
...	7	97.6	3	...	...	...	...	...	50[2]	160	—	—	Cuba
...	—	57.4	—	—	—	...	...	...	4[2]	16	—	—	Cyprus
10	736	36.7	8,663	...	...	6	7	0.8	122[2]	455	2,948	9,104	Czechoslovakia
93	1,124	70.4	113	...	...	533	24	22	80	166	528	27	Denmark

Energy (continued)

country	electricity												coal		
	installed capacity, 1984 ('000 kW)	production, 1984		power source, 1984			trade, 1984		consumption				reserves, latest ('000,000 metric tons)	production, 1984 ('000 metric tons)	consumption, 1984 ('000 metric tons)
		capacity ('000,000 kW-hr)	amount ('000,000 kW-hr)	fossil fuel (%)	hydro-power (%)	nuclear fuel (%)	exports ('000,000 kW-hr)	imports ('000,000 kW-hr)	amount, 1984 ('000,000 kW-hr)	per capita, 1984 (kW-hr)	residential, 1982 (%)	non-residential, 1982 (%)			
Djibouti	38	333	148	100.0	—	—	—	—	148	418	...	...	...	...	...
Dominica	7	61	18	11.1	88.9	—	—	—	18	234	53.5[2]	46.5[2]	...	...	...
Dominican Republic	960	8,410	4,009	87.2	12.8	—	—	—	4,009	657	...	...	...	—	1[9]
Ecuador	1,837	16,092	4,400	60.2	39.8	—	—	15	4,415	486	40.7	59.6	—	...	...
Egypt	5,409	47,383	22,870	54.0	46.0	—	—	—	22,870	501	9.8[14]	90.2[14]	13	—	1,100
El Salvador	500	4,380	1,684	7.1	52.9	40.0[15]	—	—	1,684	313	29.6	70.4	...	...	...
Equatorial Guinea	7	61	15	86.7	13.3	—	—	—	15	39	...	...	...	...	...
Ethiopia	335	2,935	760	25.0	75.0	—	—	—	760	21	...	...	...	—	—
Faeroe Islands	68	596	178	71.9	28.1	—	—	—	178	4,238	...	...	...	—	—
Falkland Islands	1	9	3	100.0	—	—	—	—	3	1,500	...	...	...	...	...
Fiji	189	1,656	387	25.8	74.2	—	—	—	387	574	20.4	79.6	...	—	22
Finland	11,314	99,111	43,311	28.4	30.6	41.1	422	5,630	48,519	9,985	18.6[4]	81.3[4]	...	—	3,733
France	84,700[16]	741,972[16]	306,800[16]	19.8[16]	21.0[16]	59.3[16]	30,000[16]	5,200[16]	282,000[16]	5,177[16]	30.3[6]	69.7[6]	610	20,704[16]	40,516[16]
French Guiana	39	342	160	100.0	—	—	—	—	160	2,222	...	58.7[4,10]	...	...	...
French Polynesia	76	666	203	88.2	11.8	—	—	—	203	1,269	...	...	...	...	...
Gabon	175	1,533	535	51.4	48.6	—	—	—	535	467	36.5	63.5	...	...	...
Gambia, The	11	96	42	100.0	—	—	—	—	42	67	...	...	...	...	...
Gaza Strip	...	...	...	...	...	...	...	...	...	...	...	...	...	...	...
Germany, East	21,517	188,489	110,093	87.7	1.6	10.7	3,927	4,208	110,374	6,626	...	...	25,000	296,341	299,675
Germany, West	87,115	763,127	376,600	77.5	4.6	17.8	15,444	19,490	380,646	6,218	26.3[6]	73.7[6]	64,991	211,571	216,849
Ghana	1,060	9,286	1,830	2.2	97.8	—	350	—	1,480	113	...	...	...	—	2
Gibraltar	21	184	61	100.0	—	—	—	—	61	1,968	...	...	...	—	—
Greece	8,299	72,699	24,820	88.5	11.5	—	30	2,592	27,382	2,770	30.6[6]	69.4[6]	1,506	32,502	32,823
Greenland	88	771	182	100.0	—	—	—	—	182	3,370	...	...	...	—	1
Grenada	8	70	25	100.0	—	—	—	—	25	223	46.8[2]	53.2[2]	...	...	...
Guadeloupe	103	902	461	100.0	—	—	—	—	461	1,445	...	32.9[10]	...	...	...
Guam	302	2,646	1,000	100.0	—	—	—	—	1,000	8,929	36.9[6]	63.1[6]	...	...	...
Guatemala	775	6,789	1,625	63.0	37.0	—	—	—	1,625	199	27.0[4]	73.0[4]	...	...	...
Guernsey	...	...	...	...	...	...	...	...	...	...	...	...	...	...	...
Guinea	175	1,533	499	84.0	16.0	—	—	—	499	94	...	...	...	...	...
Guinea-Bissau	7	61	14	100.0	—	—	—	—	14	16	...	...	...	...	...
Guyana	168	1,472	390	98.7	1.3	—	—	—	390	417	32.5[17]	67.5[17]	...	...	...
Haiti	126	1,104	375	30.7	69.3	—	—	—	375	58	...	...	13[1]	...	...
Honduras	285	2,497	1,060	17.5	82.5	—	2	168	1,226	290	30.6[6]	69.4[6]	21[1]	...	...
Hong Kong	5,268	46,148	17,923	100.0	—	—	740	—	17,183	3,125	20.6	79.4	...	—	4,262
Hungary	5,790	50,720	26,293	84.8	0.7	14.3	1,320	11,589	36,562	3,390	20.8[6]	79.2[6]	4,200	25,047	27,160
Iceland	988	8,655	3,853	0.2	94.8	4.9[15]	—	—	3,853	16,121	20.9[4]	79.1[4]	...	—	40
India	47,690	417,764	165,440	64.6	33.1	2.3	65	3	165,378	221	10.7	89.3	1,579	152,519	147,616
Indonesia	6,700	58,692	21,330	89.6	9.3	1.2[15]	—	—	21,330	132	29.2	70.8	539	1,058	303
Iran	13,025	114,099	37,168	83.0	17.0	—	—	—	37,168	849	21.1	78.9	193	850	900
Iraq	2,400	21,024	18,460	96.7	3.3	—	—	—	18,460	1,218	28.9[14]	71.1[14]	...	—	—
Ireland	3,319	29,074	11,236	93.9	6.1	—	—	—	11,236	3,161	41.4[6]	58.6[6]	55	70	1,386
Isle of Man	...	...	188	100.0	—	—	—	—	172	2,530	48.1[6]	51.9[6]	...	...	...
Israel	3,985	34,909	14,909	100.0	—	—	252	—	14,657	3,477	26.7[6]	73.3[6]	...	—	2,678
Italy	53,970[18]	472,777[18]	179,546[18]	71.0[18]	23.6[18]	3.8[18]	1,083[18]	21,973[18]	200,436[18]	3,532[18]	25.0[6]	75.0[6]	31	1,750[18]	22,520[18]
Jamaica	740	6,482	2,400	93.8	6.2	—	—	—	2,400	1,048	15.1	84.9	...	—	—
Japan	160,771	1,408,354	647,380	68.9	11.3	19.6	—	—	647,380	5,418	20.8[4]	79.2[4]	1,016	16,646	104,518
Jersey	...	...	337	...	...	...	...	...	303	3,940	...	...	...	...	...
Jordan	730	6,395	2,304	100.0	—	—	—	...	2,304	683	34.3[2]	65.7[2]	...	...	...
Kampuchea	35	307	70	57.1	42.9	—	—	—	70	10	...	...	...	—	—
Kenya	544	4,765	2,253	23.5	66.2	10.3[15]	—	215	2,468	125	26.3	73.7	...	—	118
Kiribati	2	18	6	100.0	—	—	—	—	6	97	...	...	...	...	...
Korea, North	8,500	74,460	45,000	40.0	60.0	—	—	—	45,000	2,292	...	...	600	49,000	49,400
Korea, South	15,490	135,692	58,163	75.6	4.1	20.3	—	—	58,163	1,443	16.1	83.9	116	20,638	32,831
Kuwait	5,230	45,815	14,196	100.0	—	—	—	—	14,196	8,336	86.5[6]	13.5[6]	...	...	...
Laos	225	1,971	990	4.0	96.0	—	690	30	330	76	...	...	...	...	...
Lebanon	668	5,852	1,355	56.8	43.2	—	—	30	1,385	524	...	...	...	—	—
Lesotho	[8]	[8]	[8]	[8]	[8]	[8]	[8]	[8]	[8]	[8]	...	...	...	[8]	[8]
Liberia	299	2,619	897	61.9	38.1	—	—	—	897	423	...	...	...	...	...
Libya	1,300	11,388	7,270	100.0	—	—	—	—	7,270	2,094	...	...	...	—	1
Liechtenstein	[19]	[19]	[19]	[19]	[19]	[19]	[19]	[19]	[19]	[19]	...	...	...	—	[19]
Luxembourg	1,438	12,597	517	82.2	17.8	—	358	3,811	3,970	10,937	15.3[6]	84.7[6]	...	—	189
Macau	137	1,200	475	100.0	—	—	—	—	475	1,537	75.0	25.0	...	—	1
Madagascar	100	876	452	45.1	54.9	—	—	—	452	46	...	...	1,075[1]	—	11
Malaŵi	160	1,402	511	5.3	94.7	—	1	—	510	75	12.9	87.1	12	—	39
Malaysia	3,323	29,109	13,700	86.7	13.3	—	—	50	13,750	904	19.0	81.0	—	—	300
Maldives	2	18	11	100.0	—	—	—	—	11	64	...	...	...	...	...
Mali	56	491	153	21.6	78.4	—	—	—	153	20	...	...	—	...	...
Malta	177	1,551	700	100.0	—	—	—	—	700	1,842	25.1	74.9	...	—	94
Martinique	65	569	273	100.0	—	—	—	—	273	875	...	40.9[10]	...	...	...
Mauritania	55	482	102	100.0	—	—	—	—	102	56	...	...	...	—	7
Mauritius	274	2,400	455	85.7	14.3	—	—	—	455	441	...	...	...	—	1
Mayotte	3	26	...	...	...	...	...	...	...	...	...	...	...	...	...
Mexico	23,386	204,861	87,083	70.9	27.1	2.0[15]	100	5	86,988	1,129	17.4	82.6	1,787	7,800	7,975
Monaco	[16]	[16]	[16]	[16]	[16]	[16]	[16]	[16]	[16]	[16]	...	...	...	[16]	[16]
Mongolia	500	4,380	2,206	100.0	—	—	—	400	2,606	1,408	...	...	24,000[1]	5,010	5,010
Montserrat	4	35	12	100.0	—	—	—	—	12	923	38.6[2]	61.4[2]	...	...	...
Morocco	1,919	16,810	6,617	94.3	5.7	—	...	—	6,617	290	26.7[4]	73.3[4]	50	820	1,010
Mozambique	1,803	15,794	1,945	21.1	78.9	—	505	100	1,540	112	...	...	240	390	440
Nauru	10	88	28	100.0	—	—	—	—	28	3,500	...	...	...	...	...
Nepal	178	1,559	350	10.0	90.0	—	6	80	424	21	46.5	53.5	...	—	63
Netherlands, The	17,650	154,614	62,780	94.0	—	6.0	247	3,734	66,267	4,584	25.9[6]	74.1[6]	240[1]	—	9,900
Netherlands Antilles[5]	400	3,504	2,380	100.0	—	—	—	—	2,380	9,154	...	...	...	...	...
New Caledonia	367	3,215	915	56.2	43.8	—	—	—	915	6,020	...	...	2	—	103
New Zealand	6,382	55,906	26,519	19.2	76.1	4.7[15]	—	—	26,519	8,125	35.7[4]	64.3[4]	211	2,533	2,138

natural gas						crude petroleum							country
published proved reserves, 1986 ('000,000,-000 cu m)	production		consumption			reserves, 1986		production, 1985 ('000,000 barrels)	consumption, 1985 ('000,000 barrels)	refining capacity, 1986 ('000 barrels per day)	pipelines (latest)[a]		
	natural gas, 1985 ('000,000 cu m)	manufactured gas, 1984 (% of total gas consumption)	amount, 1984 ('000,000 cu m)	residential, 1982 (%)	non-residential, 1982 (%)	published proved ('000,000 barrels)	years to exhaust proved reserves				length (km)	traffic ('000,000 metric ton-km)	
...	...	...	...	...	...	...	...	...	...	—	—	—	Djibouti
...	...	...	...	...	...	—	—	...	...	—	—	—	Dominica
...	31[2]	45.7	...	...	...	...	...	...	12[2]	44	104	...	Dominican Republic
87	476	39.4	81	—	100.0	1,125	10	108	49[2]	88	2,158	...	Ecuador
235	4,078	14.2	2,773	0.4	99.6	3,800	12	327	142[2]	434	1,526	...	Egypt
...	—	93.1	—	—	—	...	...	...	5[2]	16	—	—	El Salvador
...	...	...	...	...	...	...	...	...	...	—	—	—	Equatorial Guinea
...	—	100.0	—	...	...	...	...	...	5[2]	18	—	—	Ethiopia
...	...	...	...	...	...	...	...	...	...	—	—	—	Faeroe Islands
...	...	...	...	...	...	...	...	...	...	—	—	—	Falkland Islands
...	—	100.0	—	—	—	...	...	...	...	—	—	—	Fiji
...	—	42.5	762	0.6[6]	99.4[6]	...	...	...	80	241	—	—	Finland
36	5,419	24.0[16]	28,981[16]	32.4[6]	67.6[6]	234	12	19	652	1,947	7,802	25,999	France
...	...	...	...	...	...	...	...	...	...	—	—	—	French Guiana
...	...	...	...	...	...	...	...	...	...	—	—	—	French Polynesia
17	306	3.3	205	—	100.0	657	10	63	9[2]	23	270	...	Gabon
...	...	...	...	...	...	...	...	...	...	—	—	—	Gambia, The
...	...	...	...	...	...	...	...	...	...	—	—	—	Gaza Strip
110	13,000	35.5	7,970	...	...	2	—	4	171[2]	470	1,801	4,300	Germany, East
185	17,604	27.0	49,317	36.6[6]	63.4[6]	318	11	30	880	1,933	5,732	8,820	Germany, West
0.1	—	100.0	—	...	...	4	5	0.7	8[2]	28	3	...	Ghana
...	...	...	...	...	...	...	...	...	...	—	—	...	Gibraltar
0.5	37	96.6	90	...	...	30	3	10	89	390	573	...	Greece
...	...	...	...	...	...	...	...	...	...	—	—	...	Greenland
...	...	...	...	...	...	...	...	...	...	—	—	...	Grenada
...	...	...	...	...	...	...	...	...	...	—	—	—	Guadeloupe
...	—	100.0	—	...	...	...	...	...	11[2]	44	...	...	Guam
0.8	34	7.9	...	...	...	50	44	1	6[2]	16	48	...	Guatemala
...	...	...	...	...	...	...	...	...	...	—	—	—	Guernsey
...	...	...	...	...	...	...	...	...	...	—	—	—	Guinea
...	...	...	...	...	...	...	...	...	...	—	—	—	Guinea-Bissau
...	...	...	...	...	...	...	...	...	...	—	—	—	Guyana
...	...	...	...	...	...	...	...	...	...	—	—	—	Haiti
...	—	28.5	—	—	—	...	...	...	2[2]	14	—	—	Honduras
...	—	51.0	—	—	—	...	...	...	...	—	—	—	Hong Kong
113	7,388	11.5	10,166	14.0[6]	86.0[6]	206	13	15	64[2]	242	1,160	2,595	Hungary
...	...	...	...	...	...	...	...	...	4	—	—	—	Iceland
478	3,782	33.9	3,330	...	45.0[10]	3,801	17	221	268[2]	867	5,325	...	India
1,841	29,903	12.6	6,492	0.8	99.2	8,694	18	480	194[2]	636	2,906	...	Indonesia
10,463	13,592	12.8	8,314	—	100.0	36,676	45	824	256[2]	530	9,800	...	Iran
697	578	62.6	277	...	...	37,976	72	524	72[2]	319	4,675	...	Iraq
55	2,404	5.2	2,207	13.9[6]	86.1[6]	...	...	...	29	56	—	—	Ireland
...	—	...	...	...	...	...	...	...	...	—	—	—	Isle of Man
1	68	93.7	46	—	100.0[4]	0.7	19	0.04	51[2]	170	998	...	Israel
210	14,156	19.9[18]	31,852[18]	45.6[6]	54.4[6]	779	48	16	637	2,738	3,851	9,310	Italy
...	—	77.4	—	—	—	...	...	...	7[2]	36	10	...	Jamaica
28	4,202	47.1	37,270	61.3[17]	38.7[17]	42	12	4	1,577	4,723	406	...	Japan
...	...	...	...	...	...	...	...	...	...	—	—	—	Jersey
...	—	95.1	—	—	—	...	...	...	19[2]	100	209	...	Jordan
...	...	...	...	...	...	...	...	...	...	—	—	—	Kampuchea
...	—	104.6	—	—	—	...	...	...	14[2]	95	483	...	Kenya
...	...	...	...	...	...	...	...	...	...	—	—	—	Kiribati
...	...	...	...	...	...	...	...	...	18[2]	42	37	...	Korea, North
...	—	55.1	...	100.0	—	...	...	...	203[2]	782	294	...	Korea, South
1,385	4,078	36.7	5,507	...	...	74,645	181	412	176[2]	634	917	...	Kuwait
...	...	...	...	...	...	...	...	...	...	—	136	—	Laos
...	—	30.0	...	...	...	...	...	...	6[2]	17	72	...	Lebanon
—	—	[8]	—	...	...	...	...	...	[8]	—	—	—	Lesotho
...	—	100.0	—	...	...	...	...	...	5[2]	15	—	—	Liberia
728	4,587	16.4	3,332	...	...	22,400	58	383	47[2]	330	4,336	...	Libya
—	—	[19]	[19]	...	...	...	...	...	...	—	—	—	Liechtenstein
...	—	56.7	333	48.0[6]	52.0[6]	...	...	...	7	—	48	...	Luxembourg
...	...	...	...	...	...	...	...	...	...	—	—	—	Macau
...	—	100.0	—	...	...	...	...	...	2[2]	16	—	—	Madagascar
...	—	100.0	—	—	—	...	...	...	...	—	—	—	Malawi
1,501	5,386	35.8	359	—	100.0	3,000	19	158	51[2]	212	707	...	Malaysia
...	...	...	...	...	...	...	...	...	...	—	—	—	Maldives
...	...	...	...	...	...	...	...	...	...	—	—	—	Mali
—	—	...	...	...	...	...	...	...	...	—	—	—	Malta
...	—	250.2	...	...	...	...	...	...	3[2]	13	—	—	Martinique
...	...	...	...	...	...	...	...	...	...	—	—	—	Mauritania
...	...	...	...	...	...	...	...	...	...	—	—	—	Mauritius
...	...	...	...	...	...	...	...	...	...	—	—	—	Mayotte
2,167	28,081	25.4	24,458	3.9	96.1	55,593	56	987	444[2]	1,269	12,009	...	Mexico
...	...	[16]	[16]	...	...	...	...	...	...	—	—	—	Monaco
...	...	...	...	...	...	...	...	—	—	—	—	—	Mongolia
...	...	...	...	...	64.6[4,10]	...	...	...	...	—	—	—	Montserrat
18	68	54.6	84	—	100.0	0.5	4	0.1	34[2]	81	362	...	Morocco
65	—	100.0	—	...	...	...	...	...	4[2]	17	280	...	Mozambique
...	...	...	...	...	...	...	...	...	...	—	—	—	Nauru
...	—	—	—	—	—	...	...	...	...	—	—	—	Nepal
1,885	80,952	19.5	31,205	46.4[6]	53.6[6]	195	7	26	234	1,468	1,383	...	Netherlands, The
...	—	118.7	...	...	...	...	...	...	150[2]	320	—	—	Netherlands Antilles[5]
...	...	...	...	...	...	...	...	...	...	—	—	—	New Caledonia
161	3,387	2.0	2,673	12.8[4]	87.2[4]	192	24	8	29	53	310	...	New Zealand

Energy (continued)

country	electricity												coal		
	installed capacity, 1984 ('000 kW)	production, 1984		power source, 1984			trade, 1984		consumption				reserves, latest ('000,000 metric tons)	production, 1984 ('000 metric tons)	consumption, 1984 ('000 metric tons)
		capacity ('000,000 kW-hr)	amount ('000,000 kW-hr)	fossil fuel (%)	hydro-power (%)	nuclear fuel (%)	exports ('000,000 kW-hr)	imports ('000,000 kW-hr)	amount, 1984 ('000,000 kW-hr)	per capita, 1984 (kW-hr)	residential, 1982 (%)	non-residential, 1982 (%)			
Nicaragua	394	3,451	973	47.9	24.2	28.0[15]	3	268	1,238	392	26.9	73.1	...	...	...
Niger	65	569	245	100.0	—	—	—	130	375	63	6.3[4]	93.7[4]	5[1]	55	55
Nigeria	4,025	35,259	8,835	76.2	23.8	—	135	—	8,700	95	54.1	45.9	169	50	50
Niue	1	9	3	100.0	—	—	—	—	3	750	...	...	...	...	...
Norfolk Island	...	...	...	...	...	...	...	...	...	...	...	...	...	...	...
Norway	23,312	204,213	106,072	0.3	99.7	—	9,123	860	97,809	23,625	27.0[4]	73.0[4]	18	451	959
Oman	664	5,817	1,675	100.0	—	—	—	—	1,675	1,418	...	...	...	...	...
Pacific Is., Trust Territory of the	48	420	150	100.0	—	—	—	—	150	1,007	...	...	...	...	...
Marshall Islands	...	...	...	...	...	...	...	...	...	...	...	...	...	...	...
Micronesia, Fed. States of	...	...	...	...	...	...	...	...	...	...	...	...	...	...	...
Northern Mariana Islands	...	...	...	...	...	...	...	...	...	...	...	...	...	...	...
Palau	...	...	...	...	...	...	...	...	...	...	...	...	...	...	...
Pakistan	5,010	43,888	21,873	39.9	58.6	1.5	—	—	21,873	221	14.8	85.2	645	1,869	1,868
Panama	879	7,700	2,360	36.8	63.2	—	—	—	2,360	1,106	26.8	73.2	...	—	3
Papua New Guinea	435	3,811	1,495	72.6	27.4	—	—	—	1,495	415	10.5	89.5	...	...	...
Paraguay	349	3,057	1,095	19.1	80.9	—	28	224	1,291	361	...	...	...	...	...
Peru	3,167	27,743	11,769	26.0	74.0	—	—	—	11,769	613	20.4	79.6	125[1]	85	140
Philippines	6,155	53,918	20,800	39.0	35.3	25.7[15]	—	—	20,800	390	22.1	77.9	82	1,143	1,193
Pitcairn Island	...	...	...	...	...	...	...	...	...	...	...	...	...	...	...
Poland	27,788	243,423	134,792	97.5	2.5	—	9,233	4,636	130,195	3,497	9.2[6]	90.8[6]	39,190	241,970	207,465
Portugal	5,935	51,991	19,033	57.8	42.2	—	1,000	2,300	20,333	2,032	36.4[4]	63.6[4]	38	194	673
Puerto Rico	4,100	35,916	12,557	98.7	1.3	—	—	—	12,066	3,602	31.0	69.0	...	—	50
Qatar	905	7,928	3,425	100.0	—	—	—	—	3,425	11,770	...	...	...	...	...
Réunion	154	1,349	521	1.0	99.0	—	—	—	521	939	...	...	...	...	...
Romania	18,532	162,340	72,530	84.7	15.3	—	—	3,000	75,530	3,299	...	...	1,150	48,000	53,000
Rwanda	46	403	135	—	100.0	—	—	15	150	25	...	...	...	...	...
St. Christopher and Nevis	15	131	35	100.0	—	—	—	—	35	761	...	...	...	...	...
St. Helena and Ascension	2	18	2	100.0	—	—	—	—	2	333	...	...	...	...	...
St. Lucia	16	140	68	100.0	—	—	—	—	68	540	32.5[2]	67.5[2]	...	...	...
St. Pierre and Miquelon	22	193	30	100.0	—	—	—	—	30	5,000	...	...	...	—	—
St. Vincent and the Grenadines	10	88	30	40.0	60.0	—	—	—	30	288	45.3[2]	54.7[2]	...	...	...
San Marino	[18]	[18]	[18]	[18]	[18]	[18]	[18]	[18]	[18]	[18]	...	...	...	[18]	[18]
São Tomé and Príncipe	6	53	15	46.7	53.3	—	—	—	15	160	...	...	...	...	...
Saudi Arabia	12,200	106,872	31,150	100.0	—	—	—	—	31,150	2,878	95.1[17]	4.9[17]	..	...	...
Senegal	164	1,437	684	100.0	—	—	—	—	684	108	...	...	...	...	...
Seychelles	19	166	56	100.0	—	—	—	—	56	757	...	...	...	...	...
Sierra Leone	106	929	280	100.0	—	—	—	—	280	79	...	...	...	—	—
Singapore	3,015	26,411	9,401	100.0	—	—	73	—	9,328	3,672	18.8	81.2	...	—	1
Solomon Islands	13	114	28	100.0	—	—	—	—	28	104	21.7	78.3	...	...	...
Somalia	30	263	75	100.0	—	—	—	—	75	14	...	...	...	...	...
South Africa	24,760[8]	216,898[8]	122,383[8]	96.2[8]	0.6[8]	3.2[8]	185[8]	505[8]	122,703[8]	3,385[8]	...	...	51,737	140,554[8]	103,554[8]
Bophuthatswana	...	...	...	...	...	...	...	...	...	...	...	...	...	...	...
Ciskei	...	...	...	...	...	...	...	...	...	...	...	...	...	...	...
Transkei	...	...	...	...	...	...	...	...	...	...	...	...	...	...	...
Venda	...	...	...	...	...	...	...	...	...	...	...	...	...	...	...
South West Africa/Namibia	[8]	[8]	[8]	[8]	[8]	[8]	[8]	[8]	[8]	[8]	...	...	...	[8]	[8]
Spain	31,650	277,254	115,500	68.3	23.9	7.8	4,000	3,000	114,500	2,957	16.7[4]	83.2[4]	951	39,952	46,914
Sri Lanka	812	7,113	2,261	7.5	92.5	—	—	—	2,261	141	14.2[6]	85.8[6]	...	—	1
Sudan, The	313	2,742	1,032	50.4	49.6	—	—	—	1,032	49	...	...	...	—	—
Suriname	415	3,635	1,250	28.0	72.0	—	—	—	1,250	3,551	...	...	...	—	1
Swaziland	[8]	[8]	[8]	[8]	[8]	[8]	[8]	[8]	[8]	[8]	18.7[17]	81.3[17]	1,814	[8]	[8]
Sweden	30,863	270,360	123,503	3.6	55.1	41.3	5,292	5,685	123,896	14,956	26.4[4]	73.6[4]	1	13	3,591
Switzerland	15,060[19]	131,926[19]	48,141[19]	1.8[19]	62.0[19]	36.1[19]	20,844[19]	16,149[19]	43,446[19]	6,857[19]	26.6[6]	73.4[6]	...	—	712[19]
Syria	1,823	15,969	6,757	57.4	42.6	—	135	...	6,622	650	21.2[6]	78.8[6]	...	—	2
Taiwan	12,959	113,525	49,286	43.2	8.9	47.9	—	—	45,827	...	26.4[2]	73.6[2]	140	...	...
Tanzania	439	3,846	870	29.3	70.7	—	—	—	870	40	...	...	200	1	1
Thailand	6,287	55,074	22,029	81.5	18.5	—	22	710	22,717	449	23.2	76.8	103	2,362	2,522
Togo	60	526	234	63.7	36.3	—	—	149	383	135	...	...	...	...	...
Tokelau	...	...	...	...	...	...	...	...	...	...	...	...	...	...	...
Tonga	6	53	12	100.0	—	—	—	—	12	112	...	...	...	...	...
Trinidad and Tobago	765	6,701	2,725	100.0	—	—	—	—	2,725	2,466	31.0	69.0	...	—	—
Tunisia	985	8,629	3,590	99.2	0.8	—	—	—	3,590	510	33.2	66.8	...	—	20
Turkey	8,550	74,898	30,630	56.1	43.8	0.1[15]	—	2,638	29,544	620	14.2	85.8	1,914	26,492	28,226
Turks and Caicos Islands	9	79	11	100.0	—	—	—	—	11	1,375	...	...	...	...	...
Tuvalu	...	...	...	...	...	...	...	...	...	...	...	...	...	...	...
Uganda	163	1,428	655	1.2	98.8	—	215	—	440	29	...	...	...	...	...
U.S.S.R.	304,000	2,663,040	1,493,000	76.9	13.6	9.5	24,739	300	1,468,561	5,325	...	67.2[6, 10]	240,295	666,602	654,451
United Arab Emirates	2,360	20,674	6,636	100.0	—	—	—	—	6,636	5,288	...	...	...	...	...
United Kingdom	66,902	586,062	280,491	79.3	1.4	19.2	—	—	280,491	5,043	35.4[6]	64.6[6]	4,590	51,182	77,901
United States	688,430	6,030,647	2,472,304	73.4	13.0	13.3	2,558	42,219	2,511,965	10,658	34.9[6]	65.1[6]	257,105	807,524	708,595
Uruguay	1,321	11,572	3,637	3.8	96.2	—	—	12	3,649	1,220	46.6[6]	53.4[6]	...	—	—
Vanuatu	11	96	24	100.0	—	—	—	—	24	176	...	...	...	...	...
Venezuela	12,499	109,491	44,330	55.6	44.4	—	8	—	44,322	2,417	23.1	76.9	140	51	431
Vietnam	1,220	10,687	5,800	69.0	31.0	—	—	—	5,800	99	...	...	150	6,000	5,000
Virgin Islands (U.S.)	341	2,987	880	100.0	—	—	—	—	880	8,544	...	...	...	—	...
Wallis and Futuna	...	...	...	...	...	...	...	...	...	...	...	...	...	...	...
West Bank	...	...	...	...	...	...	...	...	...	...	...	...	...	...	...
Western Sahara	56	491	78	100.0	—	—	—	—	78	517	...	...	...	...	...
Western Samoa	17	149	41	61.0	39.0	—	—	—	41	252	...	...	...	...	...
Yemen (Aden)	150	1,314	280	100.0	—	—	—	—	280	136	...	...	...	...	...
Yemen (Ṣan'ā')	115	1,007	295	100.0	—	—	—	—	295	46	...	...	1[1]	...	...
Yugoslavia	15,250	133,590	72,253	55.5	34.8	6.1	3,881	2,751	71,123	3,089	26.1[4]	73.9[4]	16,538	65,072	69,463
Zaire	1,716	15,032	4,558	2.9	97.1	—	120	10	4,448	139	...	89.1[4, 10]	600	125	159
Zambia	1,728	15,137	10,080	0.3	99.7	—	3,100	20	7,000	1,086	12.6	87.4	24	500	500
Zimbabwe	1,539	13,482	4,538	23.8	76.2	—	—	2,988	7,526	889	16.0	84.0	734	2,300	2,222

natural gas: published proved reserves, 1986 ('000,000,000 cu m)	production: natural gas, 1985 ('000,000 cu m)	production: manufactured gas, 1984 (% of total gas consumption)	consumption: amount, 1984 ('000,000 cu m)	consumption: residential, 1982 (%)	consumption: non-residential, 1982 (%)	crude petroleum: reserves, 1986: published proved ('000,000 barrels)	reserves, 1986: years to exhaust proved reserves	production, 1985 ('000,000 barrels)	consumption, 1985 ('000,000 barrels)	refining capacity, 1986 ('000 barrels per day)	pipelines (latest)[a]: length (km)	pipelines (latest)[a]: traffic ('000,000 metric ton-km)	country
...	—	83.6	—	—	—	...	...	...	3[2]	15	56	...	Nicaragua
...	—	...	—	—	—	...	...	...	...	...	...	...	Niger
1,314	2,718	1.5	5,638	—	100.0	16,310	30	540	54[2]	250	5,042	...	Nigeria
...	...	...	...	...	...	...	...	...	...	—	—	—	Niue
...	...	...	...	...	...	...	...	...	...	—	—	—	Norfolk Island
2,757	26,598	20.1	1,222	...	...	10,500	36	293	69	240	53	4,837	Norway
232	1,359	47.6	5,781	...	...	4,067	22	184	8[2]	48	1,300	...	Oman
...	...	...	...	...	...	...	...	...	...	—	—	—	Pacific Is., Trust Territory of the
...	...	...	...	...	...	...	...	...	...	—	—	—	Marshall Islands
...	...	...	...	...	...	...	...	...	...	—	—	—	Micronesia, Fed. States of
...	...	...	...	...	...	...	...	...	...	—	—	—	Northern Mariana Islands
													Palau
595	10,228	1.0	8,897	21.3	78.7	110	9	12	35[2]	130	1,000	...	Pakistan
...	—	45.9	—	...	...	...	...	...	13[2]	100	130	...	Panama
14	—	100.0	—	—	—	50	...	...	...	—	—	—	Papua New Guinea
...	—	10.4	...	...	...	...	...	...	1[2]	8	—	—	Paraguay
23	1,257	19.0	1,114	...	71.4[10]	589	9	69	59[2]	176	800	...	Peru
0.7	—	69.5	—	—	—	22	8	3	61[2]	216	357	...	Philippines
...	...	...	...	...	...	...	...	...	...	—	—	—	Pitcairn Island
109	6,373	34.7	10,312	...	...	12	9	1	101[2]	385	2,308	17,473	Poland
...	—	62.6	...	...	...	...	...	...	62	296	11	...	Portugal
...	—	67.6	...	...	...	...	...	...	37[2]	121	...	...	Puerto Rico
4,417	5,947	31.2	4,226	—	100.0	4,390	40	111	20[2]	56	235	...	Qatar
...	...	...	...	...	...	...	...	...	...	—	—	—	Réunion
180	33,980	7.8	38,811	...	...	1,442	17	84	186[2]	617	4,229	3,705	Romania
40	—	—	1	...	...	...	...	...	...	—	—	—	Rwanda
...	...	...	...	...	...	...	...	...	...	—	—	—	St. Christopher and Nevis
...	...	...	...	...	...	...	...	...	...	—	—	—	St. Helena and Ascension
...	...	...	...	...	...	...	...	...	...	—	—	—	St. Lucia
...	...	...	...	...	...	...	...	...	...	—	—	—	St. Pierre and Miquelon
...	...	...	...	...	...	...	...	...	...	—	—	—	St. Vincent and the Grenadines
...	...	[18]	[18]	...	...	...	...	...	...	—	—	—	San Marino
...	...	...	...	...	...	...	...	...	...	—	—	—	São Tomé and Príncipe
3,951	7,136	559.4	1,281	...	83.6[10]	171,828	137	1,257	302[2]	1,115	6,550	...	Saudi Arabia
...	—	16.6	...	...	...	...	...	...	3[2]	30	—	—	Senegal
...	...	...	...	...	...	...	...	...	...	—	—	—	Seychelles
...	...	...	...	...	...	...	...	...	2[2]	10	—	—	Sierra Leone
...	—	454.5	—	—	—	...	...	...	286[2]	1,018	—	—	Singapore
...	—	—	—	—	—	...	...	...	...	—	—	—	Solomon Islands
6	—	...	...	...	...	...	...	...	3[2]	10	15	...	Somalia
28	—	100.0[8]	—	...	...	115	...	...	117[2,8]	389	2,679	...	South Africa
...	...	...	...	...	...	...	...	...	...	...	...	...	Bophuthatswana
...	...	...	...	...	...	...	...	...	...	...	...	...	Ciskei
...	...	...	...	...	...	...	...	...	...	...	...	...	Transkei
...	...	...	...	...	...	...	...	...	...	...	...	...	Venda
—	—	[8]	—	...	...	...	...	...	[8]	—	—	—	South West Africa/Namibia
15	283	54.7	2,665	...	...	39	2	16	345	1,367	2,127	3,240	Spain
...	—	90.5	—	—	—	...	...	...	13[2]	50	69	...	Sri Lanka
—	—	87.6	...	...	...	300	...	...	8[2]	24	815	...	Sudan, The
...	...	...	...	...	...	1	3	0.4	2[2]	—	—	—	Suriname
...	...	[8]	...	...	...	...	...	...	[8]	—	—	—	Swaziland
...	—	65.4	...	...	...	...	...	—	128	429	—	—	Sweden
0.1	—	19.2[19]	1,443[19]	38.3[6]	61.7[6]	...	...	...	95	137	314	1,189	Switzerland
124	136	60.6	64	...	...	1,540	24	64	66[2]	229	1,819	...	Syria
22	1,280	...	1,407	...	...	10	14	0.7	...	543	615	...	Taiwan
115	—	100.0	—	...	...	...	...	...	4[2]	14	982	...	Tanzania
105	3,415	5.3	2,404	—	100.0	99	8	13	58[2]	192	417	...	Thailand
...	...	...	...	...	...	...	...	...	...	20	—	—	Togo
...	...	...	...	...	...	...	...	...	...	—	—	—	Tokelau
...	...	...	...	...	...	...	...	...	...	—	—	—	Tonga
280	3,239	11.6	2,956	—	100.0	586	9	67	38[2]	260	1,051	...	Trinidad and Tobago
85	442	7.9	393	4.0	96.0	1,780	46	39	12[2]	34	883	...	Tunisia
31	1,407	78.2	1	...	...	585	39	15	142	460	3,433	...	Turkey
...	...	...	...	...	...	...	...	...	...	—	—	—	Turks and Caicos Islands
...	...	...	...	...	...	...	...	...	...	—	—	—	Tuvalu
...	...	...	...	...	...	...	...	...	...	—	—	—	Uganda
39,498	643,000	11.8	520,342	...	...	78,725	18	4,373	3,307	12,200	78,300	1,353,100	U.S.S.R.
3,148	9,514	269.8	987	...	...	35,950	84	428	37[2]	185	830	...	United Arab Emirates
648	43,102	13.8	51,139	52.7[6]	47.3[6]	5,459	6	892	597	1,792	3,926	9,307	United Kingdom
5,564	464,741	19.0	505,900	33.4	66.6	28,020	9	3,255	5,537	15,182	278,035	832,926	United States
...	—	98.6	—	—	—	...	...	...	9[2]	45	—	—	Uruguay
...	...	...	...	...	...	...	...	...	...	—	—	—	Vanuatu
1,727	20,569	12.3	16,611	11.0	89.0	29,300	47	618	301[2]	1,230	6,850	...	Venezuela
...	...	...	...	...	...	...	...	...	...	—	150	...	Vietnam
...	—	97.2	...	...	...	...	...	...	126[2]	600	...	...	Virgin Islands (U.S.)
...	...	...	...	...	...	...	...	...	...	—	—	—	Wallis and Futuna
...	...	...	...	...	...	...	...	...	...	—	—	—	West Bank
...	...	...	...	...	...	...	...	...	...	—	—	—	Western Sahara
...	...	...	...	...	...	...	...	...	...	—	—	—	Western Samoa
...	—	100.0	—	...	...	...	...	...	23[2]	162	32	...	Yemen (Aden)
...	...	...	...	...	...	200	...	...	...	—	—	—	Yemen (Ṣan'ā')
87	2,330	23.2	5,655	...	...	254	9	30	101[2]	302	1,523	2,477	Yugoslavia
1	—	100.0	—	...	...	120	10	12	3[2]	17	390	...	Zaire
...	—	100.0	—	—	—	...	...	...	5[2]	25	1,724	...	Zambia
...	—	90.8	—	—	—	...	...	...	...	—	8	...	Zimbabwe

[1]Estimated reserves in place. [2]1984. [3]1972. [4]1981. [5]Netherlands Antilles includes Aruba. [6]1983. [7]Belgium includes Luxembourg. [8]South Africa includes Botswana, Lesotho, South West Africa/Namibia, and Swaziland. [9]1982. [10]Transportation and industry only; excludes agricultural, commercial, and public service sectors. [11]1985. [12]1978. [13]1979. [14]1977. [15]Geothermally generated electricity. [16]France includes Monaco. [17]1980. [18]Italy includes San Marino. [19]Switzerland includes Liechtenstein.

Transportation

This table presents data on the transportation infrastructure of the various countries and dependencies of the world and on their commercial passenger and cargo traffic. Most states have roads and airports, with services corresponding to their traffic levels and to the prevailing level of economic development. A number of states, however, lack railroads or inland waterways, because of either geographic constraints or lack of development capital and technical expertise. Pipelines, one of the oldest means of bulk transport if aqueducts are considered, is today the least developed transportation mode worldwide for shipment of bulk materials. Because the principal contemporary application of pipeline technology is to facilitate the shipment of hydrocarbon liquids and gases, coverage of pipelines will be found in the "Energy" table. However, it is also true that pipelines now find increasing application for slurries of coal or other raw materials.

While the United Nations' *Statistical Yearbook* and *Monthly Bulletin of Statistics* provide much data on infrastructure and traffic and have established basic categories and classifications for transportation statistics, the number of countries covered is limited. Several commercial publications maintain substantial data bases and publishing programs for their particular areas of interest: Highway and vehicle statistics are provided by the International Road Federation's annual *Road and Motor Vehicle Statistics* and *World Road Statistics;* the International Union of Railways' *International Railway Statistics* and Jane's *World Railways* provide similar data for railways; Lloyd's *Register of Shipping Statistical Tables* summarizes the world's merchant marine; the *Official Airline Guide,* the International Civil Aviation Organization's *Digest of Statistics,* and the International Air Transport Association's *World Air Transport Statistics* have also been used to supplement and update data collected by the UN. Because several of these agencies are commercially or insurance-oriented, their data tend to be more complete, accurate, and timely than those of intergovernmental organizations, which depend on periodic responses to questionnaires or publication of results in official sources. All of these international sources are supplemented by national statistical sources to provide additional data. Such diversity of sources, however, imposes limitations on the comparability of the statistics from country to country because the basis and completeness of data collection and the frequency and timeliness of analysis and publication may vary greatly. Data more than five years old are shown in italic.

The categories adopted in the table also have special problems of comparability. Total road length is subject to wide international variation of interpretation, as "roads" can mean anything from mere tracks to highly developed highways. Each country also has individual classifications that differ according to climate, availability of road-building materials, traffic patterns, administrative responsibility, and so on. "Paved roads," by contrast, is a much more tightly definable category, but the proportion of paved to total roads may be distorted by the less comparable total road

Transportation

country	roads and motor vehicles (latest)								railroads (latest)					
	roads			motor vehicles			cargo		track length		traffic			
	length		paved (per-cent)	auto-mobiles	trucks and buses	persons per vehicle	short ton-mi ('000,000)	metric ton-km ('000,000)	mi	km	passengers		cargo	
	mi	km									passen-ger-mi ('000,000)	passen-ger-km ('000,000)	short ton-mi ('000,000)	metric ton-km ('000,000)
Afghanistan	11,789	18,974	42	31,754	30,997	268	*1,993*	*2,910*	6	10	...	...	...	...
Albania	*13,049*	*21,000*	*14*	*3,500*	*11,200*	*146*	...	...	253	408	181	291	87	127
Algeria	*44,795*	*72,091*	*54*	*573,573*	*265,577*	*23*	*2,148*	*3,136*	2,576[2]	4,146[2]	493	794	1,829	2,671
American Samoa	186	300	90	—4,107—		8.5	...	...	—	—	—	—	—	—
Andorra	*137*	*220*	*55*	26,000	...	...	...	...	—	—	—	—	—	—
Angola	44,900	72,300	12	56,625	29,000	97	...	...	1,834[2]	2,952[2]	...	...	...	...
Anguilla	55	88	80	973	239	5.4	...	...	—	—	—	—	—	—
Antigua and Barbuda	237	380	63	7,120	1,209	9.4	...	...	—	—	—	—	—	—
Argentina	131,920	212,305	26	3,685,000	1,388,000	5.9	...	...	22,484	36,185	6,539	10,524	7,702	11,244
Aruba[7]	...	...	...	20,712	544	314	...	...	...	...	...	...	...	...
Australia	495,208	796,960	32	7,757,200	677,200	1.8	*32,964*	*48,127*	24,200[2,8]	38,900[2,8]	*1,359*	*2,187*	27,017	39,444
Austria	66,737	107,402	100	2,468,452	232,593	2.8	5,949	8,685	4,146	6,672	4,356	7,010	7,702	11,244
Bahamas, The	2,548	4,100	40	88,000	5,600	2.4	...	...	—	—	—	—	—	—
Bahrain	96	155	100	67,240	21,288	4.3	...	...	—	—	—	—	—	—
Bangladesh	98,522	158,551	12	35,488	21,401	1,628	...	...	1,793[2]	2,886[2]	3,890	6,260	496	724
Barbados	1,000	1,600	95	30,984	5,454	6.9	...	...	—	—	—	—	—	—
Belgium	79,342	127,688	95	3,300,248	310,685	2.7	12,055	17,600	2,325[2,13]	3,741[2,13]	4,071	6,552	5,655	8,256
Belize	1,639	2,637	16	3,707	1,855	29	...	...	—	—	—	—	—	—
Benin	4,626	7,445	11	917	506	2,734	...	...	360	580	117	188	121	176
Bermuda	139	224	100	16,700	4,040	2.7	...	...	—	—	—	—	—	—
Bhutan	1,274	2,050	50	1,363	706	644	...	...	—	—	—	—	—	—
Bolivia	25,457	40,969	4	40,638	36,951	78	1,133	1,654	2,198[2]	3,538[2]	479	771	404	590
Botswana	4,987	8,026	22	11,039	20,739	32	...	...	444	714	...	...	734	1,071
Brazil	893,267	1,437,574	8	10,008,040	1,081,661	12	147,400	215,200	14,346[2]	23,087[2]	8,243	13,266	53,528	77,815
British Virgin Islands	*86*	*138*	*69*	*2,735*	...	...	...	...	—	—	—	—	—	—
Brunei	766	1,233	35	63,177	9,603	2.9	...	...	12[16]	19[16]	—	—	...	...
Bulgaria	23,384	37,633	91	937,579	519,200	6.1	7,273	10,619	2,659	4,279	4,839	7,788	12,444	18,168
Burkina Faso	5,396	8,684	23	21,182	6,647	238	...	...	321	517	532[17]	856[17]	457[17]	668[17]
Burma	14,206	22,863	17	*43,300*	*44,700*	*386*	...	...	1,949[2]	3,137[2]	2,401	3,864	427	624
Burundi	3,196	5,144	7	7,016	5,700	348	...	...	—	—	—	—	—	—
Cameroon	40,330	64,905	5	62,500	17,000	118	2,029	2,963	710[2]	1,143[2]	276	444	682	996
Canada	549,447	884,249	81	10,731,000	3,362,000	1.8	*29,033*	*42,388*	74,600	120,000	1,297	2,088	167,584	244,668
Cape Verde	1,398	2,250	29	*4,000*	*1,343*	*54*	...	...	—	—	—	—	—	—
Cayman Islands	110	177	68	7,354	1,757	2.1	...	...	—	—	—	—	—	—
Central African Republic	12,600	20,278	2	41,321	3,861	56	...	...	—	—	—	—	—	—
Chad	24,855	40,000	1	7,000	5,000	390	...	...	—	—	—	—	—	—
Chile	49,095	79,010	11	622,000	240,050	14	...	...	5,300	8,500	947	1,524	1,611	2,352
China	575,853	926,746	...	265,000	1,768,000	496	1,052,000	1,536,000	36,000	58,000	149,986	241,380	555,569	811,116
Christmas Island	20	32	...	759	383	2.9	...	...	12	20	...	...	...	...
Cocos (Keeling) Islands	15	24	...	...	...	...	...	...	—	—	—	—	—	—
Colombia	65,369	105,201	28	*672,385*	*168,096*	*32*	*11,115*	*16,227*	1,627[2,13]	2,619[2,13]	119	192	493	720
Comoros	278[20]	448[20]	...	3,600	2,000	68	...	...	—	—	—	—	—	—
Congo	5,124	8,246	10	30,500	78,600	15	*46*	*67*	498	802	254	408	324	480
Cook Islands	174	280	...	689	728	12	...	...	—	—	—	—	—	—
Costa Rica	18,078	29,094	10	106,233	69,875	14	...	...	435[2]	700[2]	...	...	...	...
Côte d'Ivoire	33,390	53,736	7	182,956	52,491	41	...	...	424	683	532[17]	856[17]	457[17]	668[17]
Cuba	21,100	34,000	30	*18,657*	*28,098*	*208*	...	...	3,229[2,22]	5,196[2,22]	1,402[22]	2,256[22]	1,915[22]	2,796[22]
Cyprus	7,156	11,517	48	118,078	43,095	4.1	...	...	—	—	—	—	—	—
Czechoslovakia	46,043	74,100	100	2,221,379	358,736	6.0	14,141	20,646	8,149	13,114	12,325	19,836	50,409	73,596
Denmark	43,602	70,170	100	1,439,993	395,005	2.8	6,300	9,200	1,521	2,448	2,710	4,362	1,120	1,635
Djibouti	1,806	2,906	11	9,000	1,500	39	...	...	66	106	...	...	...	...
Dominica	489	787	60	3,963	1,250	16	...	...	—	—	—	—	—	—
Dominican Republic	10,788	17,362	29	94,601	55,346	40	...	...	65[2,22]	104[2,22]	—	—	...	...
Ecuador	22,194	35,718	16	248,575	32,624	32	...	...	600[2]	965[2]	41	65	21	32
Egypt	18,684[24]	30,069[24]	47[24]	597,869	227,224	56	*1,079*	*1,575*	2,700[2]	4,346[2]	14,977	24,103	1,779	2,597

statistics. Automobile, truck, and bus fleet statistics, which are usually based upon registration, are relatively accurate, though some countries round off figures, and unregistered vehicles may cause substantial undercount. There is also inconsistent classification of vehicle types; in some countries a vehicle may serve variously as an automobile, a truck, or a bus, or even as all three on certain occasions. Relatively few countries collect and maintain commercial road traffic statistics.

Data on national railway systems are generally given for railway track length rather than the length of routes, which may be multitracked. Siding tracks usually are not included, but some countries fail to distinguish them. The United States data include only class 1 railways, which account for about 94 percent of total track length. Passenger traffic is usually calculated from tickets sold to fare-paying passengers. Such statistics are subject to distortion if there are large numbers of nonpaying passengers, such as military personnel, or if season tickets are sold and not all the allowed journeys are utilized. Railway cargo traffic is calculated by weight hauled multiplied by the length of the journey. Changes in freight load during the journey should be accounted for but sometimes are not, leading to discrepancies.

Merchant fleet and tonnage statistics collected by Lloyd's registry service for vessels over 100 gross tons are quite accurate. Cargo statistics, however, reflect the port and customs requirements of each country and the reporting rules of each country's merchant marine authority (although these, increasingly, reflect the recommendations of the International Maritime Organization); often, however, they are only estimates based on customs declarations and the count of vessels entered and cleared. Even when these elements are reported consistently, further uncertainties may be introduced because of ballast, bunkers, ships' stores, or transshipped goods included in the data.

Airport data are based on scheduled flights reported in the commercial *Official Airline Guide* and are both reliable and current. The comparability of civil air traffic statistics suffers from differing characteristics of the air transportation systems of different countries; data for an entire country may be two to three years behind those for a single airport.

Outside of Europe, where standardization of data on inland waterways is necessitated by the volume of international traffic, comparability of national data declines markedly. Calculations as to both the length of a country's waterway system (or route length of river, lake, and coastal traffic) and the makeup of its stock of commercially significant vessels (those for which data will be collected) are largely determined by the nature and use of the country's hydrographic net—its seasonality, relief profile, depth, access to potential markets—and inevitably differ widely from country to country. Data for coastal or island states may refer to scheduled coastwise or interisland traffic.

merchant marine				air					canals and inland waterways (latest)				country
fleet, 1985 (vessels over 100 gross tons)	total deadweight tonnage, 1985 ('000)	international cargo (latest)		airports with scheduled flights, 1986	traffic (latest)				length		cargo		
					passengers		cargo		mi	km	short ton-mi ('000,000)	metric ton-km ('000,000)	
		loaded metric tons ('000)	off-loaded metric tons ('000)		passenger-mi ('000,000)	passenger-km ('000,000)	short ton-mi ('000,000)	metric ton-km ('000,000)					
—	—	—	—	1	87[1]	140[1]	7.5[1]	10.9[1]	665	1,070	...	...	Afghanistan
20	79.9	510	360	1	...	...	...	...	...	...	...	...	Albania
145	1,943.2	44,824	13,299	22	1,561[3]	2,512[3]	9.1[3]	13.2[3]	...	...	...	...	Algeria
—	—	84	329	3	...	...	...	...	...	...	...	...	American Samoa
—	—	—	—	—	—	—	—	—	—	—	—	—	Andorra
95	127.4	5,590	1,608	19	570	917	17.2	25.1	727	1,170	...	...	Angola
14	5.4	...	18	1	...	...	...	...	...	...	...	...	Anguilla
3	0.4	33	113	1	68[4]	109[4]	14.8[5]	21.6[5]	...	...	...	...	Antigua and Barbuda
549	3,568.7	31,608	6,276	65	3,885[6]	6,252[6]	120.4[6]	181.0[6]	6,800	11,000	19,326	28,215	Argentina
...	...	...	...	1	...	...	...	...	...	...	...	...	Aruba[7]
652	3,094.1	244,932	23,112	441	16,233	26,124	543.9	794.1	5,200	8,368	...	...	Australia
29	226.5	...	...	6	872	1,404	16.1	23.4	222	358	4,910	7,168	Austria
195	6,862.3	22,798	19,906	21	72[9]	116[9]	0.2[9]	0.2[9]	...	...	...	...	Bahamas, The
79	60.8	8,500	2,000	1	774[10]	1,245[10]	22.3[10]	32.6[10]	...	...	...	...	Bahrain
260	480.4	1,056	6,948	8	889	1,430	13.6	19.9	5,238	8,430	...	...	Bangladesh
35	9.5	211	559	1	93[11]	149[11]	0.8[12]	1.1[12]	...	...	...	...	Barbados
344	3,853.6	47,052	72,096	4	3,519	5,664	399.6	583.4	1,215	1,956	3,590	5,242	Belgium
3	0.8	170	211	7	...	...	...	...	500	800	...	...	Belize
15	4.9	110	749	5	138[14]	222[14]	15.4[14]	22.5[14]	300	500	...	...	Benin
79	1,460.8	181	525	1	...	...	...	...	...	...	...	...	Bermuda
—	—	—	—	1	...	...	...	...	—	—	—	—	Bhutan
2	18.9	...	...	19	544	876	27.3	39.9	6,200	10,000	90	132	Bolivia
—	—	—	—	3	355	570	24.2	35.3	...	...	...	...	Botswana
702	10,039.6	141,732	53,856	126	11,367[15]	18,294[15]	621.3[15]	907.1[15]	27,000	43,000	35,075	51,209	Brazil
33	9.1	7	44	3	...	...	...	...	...	...	...	...	British Virgin Islands
3	1.4	19,158	697	1	...	...	...	...	130	209	...	...	Brunei
203	1,889.7	5,550	24,670	13	1,783	2,870	35.5	51.8	293	471	1,610	2,351	Bulgaria
—	—	—	—	2	134	215	14.5	21.2	...	...	...	...	Burkina Faso
106	138.9	720	720	20	118	191	1.6	2.3	5,000	8,000	...	...	Burma
...	...	—	—	1	...	...	...	...	...	...	...	...	Burundi
48	88.5	1,008	3,420	10	346	548	34.3	50.1	1,300	2,100	...	...	Cameroon
1,286	4,075.3	125,000	49,000	115	20,231[18]	32,559[18]	654.0[18]	954.9[18]	2,342	3,769	...	...	Canada
25	22.1	119	388	9	...	...	...	...	...	...	...	...	Cape Verde
244	582.3	4,005	4,131	3	...	...	...	...	...	...	...	...	Cayman Islands
—	—	—	—	1	106	170	20.7	30.2	1,296	2,085	...	...	Central African Republic
—	—	—	—	2	129	208	26.2	38.3	1,400	2,300	...	...	Chad
234	701.8	11,832	5,268	13	969	1,560	77.4	113.0	1,360	2,189	5,629	8,218	Chile
1,408	22,615.4[19]	47,268	57,192	73	3,573	5,750	126.2	184.2	67,900	109,273	134,300	196,100	China
—	—	1,300	53	1	...	...	...	...	...	...	...	...	Christmas Island
—	—	—	—	1	...	...	...	...	...	...	...	...	Cocos (Keeling) Islands
80	470.8	7,128	6,636	79	2,572	4,140	155.3	226.7	8,900	14,300	...	...	Colombia
3	2.2	15	39	3	...	...	...	...	...	...	...	...	Comoros
21	10.8	3,084	600	17	129	208	26.2	38.3	2,312	3,721	...	...	Congo
—	—	7	12	6	...	...	...	...	...	...	...	...	Cook Islands
28	20.3	1,121	1,059	8	350[21]	564[21]	15.1[21]	22.1[21]	475	764	...	...	Costa Rica
61	175.3	4,620	4,992	15	179	288	37.6	54.9	460	740	...	...	Côte d'Ivoire
423	1,236.2	2,280	3,048	13	1,562	2,514	22.9	33.4	149	240	...	...	Cuba
844	14,299.3	1,308	2,760	3	701	1,128	17.6	25.8	...	...	...	...	Cyprus
19	276.6	...	...	14	1,233	1,985	35.9	52.4	300	483	*2,301*	*3,360*	Czechoslovakia
1,070	7,419.4	11,004	33,324	12	1,937[23]	3,118[23]	87.4[23]	127.7[23]	120	190	1,200	1,700	Denmark
6	2.6	550	815	3	...	...	...	...	...	...	...	...	Djibouti
4	2.1	120	64	2	...	...	...	...	...	...	...	...	Dominica
39	73.2	1,940	2,612	3	299	481	6.2	9.0	...	...	...	...	Dominican Republic
152	624.8	5,319	2,451	14	455	732	20.8	30.4	900	1,500	...	...	Ecuador
399	1,307.1	13,032	34,260	11	2,725	4,386	60.4	88.2	1,900	3,000	*1,709*	*2,495*	Egypt

Transportation (continued)

country	roads and motor vehicles (latest): roads: length mi	roads: length km	roads: paved (per-cent)	motor vehicles: auto-mobiles	motor vehicles: trucks and buses	motor vehicles: persons per vehicle	cargo: short ton-mi ('000,000)	cargo: metric ton-km ('000,000)	railroads (latest): track length mi	track length km	traffic: passengers: passen-ger-mi ('000,000)	passengers: passen-ger-km ('000,000)	cargo: short ton-mi ('000,000)	cargo: metric ton-km ('000,000)
El Salvador	7,549	12,149	14	128,976	19,284	36	...	...	374[2]	602[2]	3	5	17	25
Equatorial Guinea	1,715	2,760	12	*4,000*	*3,000*	*40*	...	...	—	—	—	—	—	—
Ethiopia	23,305	37,506	33	43,558	13,069	745	...	...	485[25]	781[25]	191	307	74	108
Faeroe Islands	124	200	...	10,942	2,360	3.4	...	...	—	—	—	—	—	—
Falkland Islands	45	73	22	732	230	2.1	...	...	—	—	—	—	—	—
Fiji	2,792	4,494	13	31,038	21,467	13	...	...	660	1,062	...	...	...	...
Finland	47,130	75,848	54	1,473,975	182,853	2.9	14,200	20,700	5,664	9,116	2,003	3,224	5,525	8,067
France	499,893	804,500	92	20,800,000	3,310,000	2.3	72,900	105,000	21,609[2]	34,777[2]	37,767	60,780	40,061	58,488
French Guiana	691	1,112	65	14,440	625	5.3	...	...	—	—	—	—	—	—
French Polynesia	*460*	*741*	*33*	*16,500*	*8,500*	*5.3*	...	...	—	—	—	—	—	—
Gabon	4,668	7,513	8	16,043	10,695	41	...	...	211	340	12	19	71	103
Gambia, The	1,916	3,083	15	6,100	1,030	98	...	...	—	—	—	—	—	—
Gaza Strip	...	...	...	15,393	4,760	25	...	...	—	—	—	—	—	—
Germany, East	29,440	47,380	100	3,019,875	276,364	5.1	10,533	15,378	8,840	14,226	13,951	22,452	40,184	58,668
Germany, West	302,764	487,251	99	25,377,637	1,557,900	2.4	88,200	128,800	42,992	69,190	25,605	41,208	43,751	63,876
Ghana	13,535	21,783	3	52,864	24,312	158	...	...	592	953	97	157	30	44
Gibraltar	31	50	100	8,519	1,034	3.0	...	...	—	—	—	—	—	—
Greece	66,055	106,306	83	1,151,037	589,256	5.7	...	...	1,540[2]	2,479[2]	932	1,500	501	732
Greenland	96	154	41	1,346	897	23	...	...	—	—	—	—	—	—
Grenada	*534*	*860*	*60*	*4,784*	*981*	*16*	...	...	—	—	—	—	—	—
Guadeloupe	1,279	2,059	60	89,369	26,806	2.9	...	...	—	—	—	—	—	—
Guam	419	674	100	44,312	15,796	1.9	...	...	—	—	—	—	—	—
Guatemala	11,200	18,000	16	*166,900*	*81,500*	*29*	...	...	375[2]	603[2]	...	...	...	...
Guernsey	...	...	...	...	...	...	...	...	—	—	—	—	—	—
Guinea	17,600	28,400	5	9,948	9,992	254	...	...	584[2]	940[2]	...	...	...	...
Guinea-Bissau	3,143	5,058	15	——4,100——		200	...	...	—	—	—	—	—	—
Guyana	3,426	5,513	9	20,000	4,610	38	...	...	80[28]	130[28]	—	—	...	...
Haiti	2,292	3,688	18	34,025	4,257	133	...	...	—	—	—	—	—	—
Honduras	7,492	12,058	16	36,950	18,377	76	...	...	370[2]	595[2]	...	...	...	...
Hong Kong	795	1,279	100	204,755	84,678	19	...	...	21	34	920	1,480	64	93
Hungary	54,796	88,185	54	1,258,496	211,529	7.3	8,186	11,951	8,140	13,100	6,965	11,209	15,278	22,307
Iceland	7,220	11,619	8	100,260	12,950	2.1	*318*	*464*	—	—	—	—	—	—
India	960,572	1,545,891	47	1,196,700	825,300	354	55,500	81,000	37,862[2]	60,933[2]	139,078	223,824	118,177	172,536
Indonesia	110,539	177,896	41	912,997	962,026	88	17,000	25,000	4,317	6,947	3,967	6,384	805	1,176
Iran	67,711	108,970	31	*1,532,269*	*313,006*	*21*	...	...	2,837[2]	4,567[2]	1,560	2,526	2,645	3,861
Iraq	*15,699*	*25,265*	*65*	*229,530*	*152,768*	*36*	...	...	1,516[2]	2,439[2]	34	55	777	1,134
Ireland	57,354	92,303	94	711,098	88,040	4.4	...	...	1,207[2, 13]	1,942[2, 13]	548	882	412	601
Isle of Man	357	574	58	——32,473——		2.0	...	...	37[2]	59[2]	...	...	...	...
Israel	3,062	4,928	100	571,515	124,253	5.9	...	...	514	827	135	217	594	867
Italy	184,981	297,698	100	20,450,000	1,720,000	2.6	98,249	143,441	10,007[2]	16,104[2]	24,397	39,264	12,461	18,192
Jamaica	10,338	16,638	30	40,271	20,167	38	...	...	215	346	*49*	79	*89*	*129*
Japan	699,177	1,125,217	56	27,144,050	17,386,390	2.7	132,562	193,537	16,720	26,908	204,090	328,452	15,140	22,104
Jersey	...	...	...	46,717	7,975	1.4	...	...	—	—	—	—	—	—
Jordan	3,935	6,332	74	118,852	48,884	14	*19,133*	*27,934*	384[2]	618[2]	3.7	6.0	...	...
Kampuchea	*8,296*	*13,351*	*20*	*700*	*1,800*	*2,600*	...	...	403[2]	649[2]	34	54	6.8	10
Kenya	33,900	54,500	12	115,348	90,034	91	...	...	1,649	2,654	323	520	1,546	2,246
Kiribati	398	640	...	——*163*——		*344*	...	...	—	—	—	—	—	—
Korea, North	*12,600*	*20,280*	*2*			...	...	...	2,779	4,473	...	...	...	...
Korea, South	31,692	51,003	46	465,119	483,170	43	9,608	14,028	4,278	6,884	13,477	21,689	8,277	12,084
Kuwait	1,208	1,944	...	395,046	119,472	3.2	...	...	—	—	—	—	—	—
Laos	*6,340*	*10,200*	*13*	15,000	3,000	217	...	...	—	—	—	—	—	—
Lebanon	4,350	7,000	80	460,400	35,000	5.3	...	...	258	415	5.3	8.6	29	42
Lesotho	2,538	4,085	11	5,129	11,962	82	...	...	1	2	...	...	...	...
Liberia	*6,268*	*10,087*	*7*	*13,070*	*12,415*	*74*	...	...	304[2]	490[2]	4[34]	6[34]	1,422[34]	2,076[34]
Libya	12,000	19,300	56	415,509	334,405	4.3	...	...	—	—	—	—	—	—
Liechtenstein	*205*	*330*	...	14,804	1,631	1.6	...	...	12	19	...	...	...	...
Luxembourg	3,204	5,157	99	145,849	13,313	2.3	136	198	168[2]	270[2]	179	288	443	648
Macau	56	90	100	17,543	2,153	17	...	...	—	—	—	—	—	—
Madagascar	9,703	15,615	30	23,412	6,067	321	...	...	644[2]	1,036[2]	127	205	153	224
Malawi	6,693	10,772	18	*14,102*	*17,247*	*199*	—	—	490[2]	789[2]	67	108	82	120
Malaysia	24,084	38,759	65	1,075,328	313,528	12	...	...	1,666[2]	2,681[2]	940[36]	1,512[36]	740[36]	1,080[36]
Maldives	...	...	...	310	107	415	...	...	—	—	—	—	—	—
Mali	*8,080*	*13,004*	*14*	20,000	5,000	294	...	...	401	646	195	314	94	136
Malta	823	1,324	92	77,419	17,368	3.5	...	...	—	—	—	—	—	—
Martinique	1,130	1,819	83	140,000	3,700	2.3	...	...	—	—	—	—	—	—
Mauritania	*4,685*	*7,540*	*18*	*11,262*	*8,437*	*76*	...	...	428[2]	689[2]	...	...	2,967	4,332
Mauritius	1,110	1,787	92	26,082	17,929	23	...	...	—	—	—	—	—	—
Mayotte	139	224	46	——1,528——		40	...	...	—	—	—	—	—	—
Mexico	133,265	214,470	50	5,221,159	1,978,327	10	...	...	16,031	25,799	3,691	5,940	31,127	45,444
Monaco	29	46	100	14,528	3,164	1.5	...	...	1	2	...	...	...	...
Mongolia	29,000	46,700	2	...	...	...	1,047	1,529	1,086	1,748	249	400	3,524	5,100
Montserrat	87	140	95	2,200	57	5.2	...	...	—	—	—	—	—	—
Morocco	35,823	57,651	46	477,394	225,475	31	830	1,212	1,105[2]	1,779[2]	999	1,608	3,132	4,572
Mozambique	16,200	26,000	30	*49,500*		...	...	...	2,388	3,843	377	606	3,532	5,156
Nauru	12	19	100	——*1,761*——		*4.0*	...	...	3	5	...	...	...	...
Nepal	3,485	5,608	46	*14,201*	*9,988*	*574*	*984*	*1,437*	32[2]	52[2]	...	...	...	...
Netherlands, The	68,554	110,327	86	4,772,000	352,700	2.8	12,580	18,366	1,837	2,956	5,734	9,220	2,203	3,216
Netherlands Antilles[7]	590	950	32	25,144	1,025	9.3	...	...	—	—	—	—	—	—
New Caledonia	3,382	5,443	14	35,000	1,650	4.0	...	...	—	—	—	—	—	—
New Zealand	57,569	92,648	53	1,471,071	294,310	1.8	...	...	2,692	4,332	285	458	2,168	3,165
Nicaragua	15,500	25,000	16	*24,887*	*9,789*	*77*	...	...	232[2]	373[2]	38	60	3.2	4.7
Niger	11,891	19,137	17	23,102	9,052	189	...	...	—	—	—	—	—	—
Nigeria	*67,102*	*107,990*	*78*	*262,550*	*90,731*	*241*	...	...	2,178	3,505	1,275	2,053	666	972
Niue	142	229	54	*264*	*64*	*12*	...	...	—	—	—	—	—	—
Norfolk Island	45	72	83	1,802	90	1.1	...	...	—	—	—	—	—	—

merchant marine				air					canals and inland waterways (latest)				country
fleet, 1985 (vessels over 100 gross tons)	total dead-weight tonnage, 1985 ('000)	international cargo (latest)		airports with sched-uled flights, 1986	traffic (latest)				length		cargo		
					passengers		cargo		mi	km	short ton-mi ('000,000)	metric ton-km ('000,000)	
		loaded metric tons ('000)	off-loaded metric tons ('000)		passenger-mi ('000,000)	passenger-km ('000,000)	short ton-mi ('000,000)	metric ton-km ('000,000)					
11	3.3	384	1,488	1	208	335	7.1	10.4	...	...	...	...	El Salvador
2	6.7	85	52	1	4	7	0.7	1.0	104	167	...	...	Equatorial Guinea
23	72.0	547	1,753	37	473	762	18.6	27.1	70	113	...	...	Ethiopia
186	73.1	150	300	1	...	...	...	...	...	...	...	...	Faeroe Islands
5	4.1	4	9	1	...	...	...	...	...	...	...	...	Falkland Islands
60	26.8	672	672	20	327	527	92.5	135.0	...	...	...	...	Fiji
307	2,853.8	20,304	31,644	21	1,817	2,924	57.7	84.3	3,764	6,057	3,000	4,400	Finland
1,136	13,712.6	55,032	170,856	60	24,390[26]	39,252[26]	2,041.5[26]	2,980.5[26]	5,324	8,568	4,800	7,000	France
—	—	30	276	5	...	...	...	...	2,336	3,760	...	...	French Guiana
...	...	13	387	32	...	...	...	...	...	...	...	...	French Polynesia
21	169.6	8,040	631	25	267	430	18.7	27.3	199	320	...	...	Gabon
6	4.0	130	181	1	...	...	...	...	249	400	...	...	Gambia, The
—	—	...	...	—	...	...	...	...	...	...	...	...	Gaza Strip
402	1,816.0	4,000	15,500	4	1,535	2,470	51.7	75.5	1,441	2,319	1,660	2,424	Germany, East
1,816	9,240.9	44,208	90,660	26	15,181	24,432	1,711.3	2,498.5	2,673	4,302	32,300	52,000	Germany, West
123	177.2	1,471	2,493	4	181	291	21.2	31.0	200	320	...	...	Ghana
79	1,020.9	7	270	1	...	...	...	...	...	...	...	...	Gibraltar
2,599	55,356.1	20,328	28,224	29	3,915	6,300	54.2	79.1	50	80	*585*	*854*	Greece
45[27]	...	176	291	3	9	14	0.16	0.24	...	...	...	...	Greenland
3	0.6	160	63	3	...	...	...	...	...	...	...	...	Grenada
...	...	636	1,104	6	...	...	...	...	...	...	...	...	Guadeloupe
...	...	725	2,315	1	...	...	...	...	...	...	...	...	Guam
8	24.1	926	2,057	2	104	168	5.5	8.1	...	...	...	...	Guatemala
—	—	...	...	2	...	...	...	...	...	...	...	...	Guernsey
19	2.9	10,000	545	1	90	144	0.5	0.7	805	1,295	...	...	Guinea
15	2.5	25	219	1	*5*	*8*	*0.7*	*1.0*	...	...	...	...	Guinea-Bissau
103	22.7	2,400	910	19	...	...	...	...	3,700	6,000	...	...	Guyana
8	1.7	723	561	2	...	...	*1.3*	*1.9*	60	100	...	...	Haiti
291	516.2	1,450	1,143	3	254	408	2.0	2.9	700	1,200	...	...	Honduras
396	11,332.6	16,428[29]	37,224[29]	1	...	...	...	...	...	...	...	...	Hong Kong
19	109.7	...	...	4	828	1,333	14.9	21.8	1,008	1,622	5,737	8,376	Hungary
395	168.5	502	1,358	23	1,489	2,397	15.4	22.5	...	...	*58*	*84*	Iceland
741	10,760.9	38,900	40,380	70	9,246	14,880	358.0	522.7	12,310	19,811	...	...	India
1,653	2,673.7	107,124	24,876	94	5,130	8,256	118.4	172.9	13,409	21,579	17,000	25,000	Indonesia
347	3,864.5	80,000	6,000	13	2,468	3,972	78.5	114.6	626	1,008	...	...	Iran
148	1,685.9	95,750	4,004	3	917	1,476	37.5	54.7	631	1,015	...	...	Iraq
152	226.5	5,000	14,500	5	1,529	2,460	59.4	86.7	454	731	...	...	Ireland
—	—	3	170	1	...	...	...	...	...	...	...	...	Isle of Man
64	657.5	7,080	9,576	6	4,041	6,504	407.2	594.6	...	...	...	...	Israel
1,573	14,373.1	34,980	194,700	36	10,752[30]	17,303[30]	517.3[30]	755.3[30]	849	1,366	182	265	Italy
13	12.9	8,335	4,018	6	918	1,477	13.3	19.5	...	...	...	...	Jamaica
10,288	63,451.2	93,816	603,276	72	38,162	61,416	2,016.6	2,944.2	1,100	1,770	137,501	200,748	Japan
—	—	...	...	1	...	...	...	...	...	...	...	...	Jersey
8	76.2	7,164	6,444	2	2,207	3,552	105.2	153.6	...	...	19,202	28,035	Jordan
3	3.8	10	22	1	...	...	...	...	2,474	3,982	...	...	Kampuchea
28	4.9	1,512	3,792	9	634[31]	1,021[31]	84.8[31]	123.8[31]	...	...	...	...	Kenya
4	1.3	300	69	17	0.002[32]	0.004[32]	—	—	3	5	...	...	Kiribati
69	829.4	1,600	4,000	1	*52*	*84*	*1.4*	*2.0*	1,400	2,250	...	...	Korea, North
1,847	11,772.9	30,612	95,052	3	7,620	12,264	971.0	1,417.6	...	...	7,631	11,141	Korea, South
245	3,505.8	33,300	6,500	1	2,334	3,756	121.6	177.6	...	...	...	...	Kuwait
—	—	—	—	7	5	8	0.07	0.10	2,900	4,600	...	...	Laos
247	790.0	200	2,500	1	578[33]	930[33]	22.5[33]	32.8[33]	...	...	...	...	Lebanon
—	—	—	—	15	8	13	0.07	0.10	—	—	—	—	Lesotho
1,808	113,552.2	19,000	1,051	8	*11*	*17*	*0.07*	*0.10*	230	370	...	...	Liberia
100	1,513.7	53,530	12,680	11	915	1,473	3.7	5.4	...	...	...	...	Libya
—	—	—	—	—	—	—	—	—	...	...	...	...	Liechtenstein
—	—	—	—	1	57	92	0.2	0.3	23	37	186	272	Luxembourg
14[35]	...	550	570	—	...	...	...	...	...	...	...	...	Macau
69	97.7	312	756	35	254	408	14.6	21.3	727	1,170	...	...	Madagascar
1	0.3	...	...	4	52	84	0.6	0.9	891	1,434	...	...	Malawi
467	2,582.7	30,108	22,140	39	3,706	5,964	137.0	200.0	4,534	7,296	...	...	Malaysia
35	205.3	6	45	1	...	...	...	...	...	...	...	...	Maldives
—	—	—	—	9	68	110	0.4	0.6	1,107	1,782	*18*	*27*	Mali
235	2,988.8	168	1,404	1	410	660	3.3	4.8	...	...	...	...	Malta
—	—	373	1,053	1	...	...	...	...	...	...	...	...	Martinique
48	8.3	7,546	508	8	156	251	14.9	21.8	500	800	...	...	Mauritania
20	53.8	879	779	2	399	642	10.6	15.5	...	...	...	...	Mauritius
—	—	...	...	1	...	...	...	...	...	...	...	...	Mayotte
638	2,077.5	72,108	10,932	72	10,991[37]	17,668[37]	119.0[37]	173.8[37]	1,900	3,000	...	...	Mexico
1	5.0	...	...	1	—	1	...	...	...	...	...	...	Monaco
—	—	—	—	1	173	278	4.0	5.9	295	474	3	4	Mongolia
1	1.0	66	46	1	...	...	...	...	...	...	...	...	Montserrat
293	679.5	21,372	14,784	13	1,320	2,124	26.6	38.8	600	1,000	2,622	3,828	Morocco
101	36.2	2,613	1,260	7	291	468	9.1	13.3	2,330	3,750	...	...	Mozambique
8	93.4	2,300	68	1	148[38]	238[38]	1.1[38]	1.6[38]	...	...	...	...	Nauru
—	—	—	—	6	186[39]	300[39]	3.0[39]	4.4[39]	...	...	...	...	Nepal
1,344	5,949.4	80,676	244,056	6	11,334[40]	18,240[40]	1,017.0[40]	1,484.8[40]	2,718	4,374	4,519	6,597	Netherlands, The
—	—	46,500	50,600	5	234[41]	377[41]	1.2[41]	1.8[41]	...	...	...	...	Netherlands Antilles[7]
—	—	...	...	6	...	...	...	...	...	...	...	...	New Caledonia
117	334.2	9,852	8,076	36	4,422	7,116	204.9	299.1	1,000	1,600	1,503	2,195	New Zealand
19	25.4	366	1,000	1	*47*	*76*	*3.8*	*5.5*	1,182	1,902	...	...	Nicaragua
—	—	—	—	6	140	225	14.6	21.3	370	600	...	...	Niger
191	607.1	58,088	15,497	15	1,506	2,424	23.5	34.2	5,328	8,575	...	...	Nigeria
—	—	—	—	1	...	...	...	...	...	...	...	...	Niue
—	—	—	—	1	...	...	...	...	...	...	...	...	Norfolk Island

Transportation (continued)

country	roads and motor vehicles (latest)								railroads (latest)					
	roads			motor vehicles			cargo		track length		traffic			
	length		paved (per-cent)	auto-mobiles	trucks and buses	persons per vehicle	short ton-mi ('000,000)	metric ton-km ('000,000)	mi	km	passengers		cargo	
	mi	km									passen-ger-mi ('000,000)	passen-ger-km ('000,000)	short ton-mi ('000,000)	metric ton-km ('000,000)
Norway	52,544	84,562	64	1,429,710	214,051	2.5	3,715	5,424	2,636[2]	4,242[2]	1,387	2,232	2,006	2,928
Oman	13,050	21,000	14	——26,752——		35	...	...	—	—	—	—	—	—
Pacific Is., Trust Terr. of the	*1,000*	*1,600*	*25*	*4,206*	*2,311*	*20*	...	...	—	—	—	—	—	—
Marshall Islands	...	...	...	...	...	...	...	...	—	—	—	—	—	—
Micronesia, Fed. States of	...	...	...	...	...	...	...	...	—	—	—	—	—	—
Northern Mariana Islands	...	...	...	...	...	...	...	...	—	—	—	—	—	—
Palau	...	...	...	...	...	...	...	...	—	—	—	—	—	—
Pakistan	62,324	100,300	69	211,752	66,722	351	...	...	5,482[2]	8,823[2]	11,065	17,806	4,932	7,200
Panama	5,864	9,437	31	113,960	37,051	14	...	...	171[2]	275[2]	...	...	...	...
Papua New Guinea	11,523	18,545	6	18,877	28,128	67	...	...	—	—	—	—	—	—
Paraguay	7,034	11,320	19	35,000	26,000	50	...	...	274[2]	441[2]	*14*	22	*24*	*34*
Peru	40,400	65,000	11	359,700	196,013	33	...	...	1,028[2]	1,654[2]	264	425	355	519
Philippines	97,642	157,139	14	894,927	128,083	51	...	...	658[2]	1,059[2]	99	144	8	12
Pitcairn Island	4	6	—	3	—	18	...	...	—	—	—	—	—	—
Poland	158,000	254,000	62	3,181,300	733,314	9.3	25,053	36,577	16,820	27,070	32,301	51,984	82,637	120,648
Portugal	*32,282*	*51,953*	*86*	1,428,820	96,250	6.9	*8,100*	*11,800*	2,933	4,720	3,557	5,724	896	1,308
Puerto Rico	8,810	14,178	86	1,020,741	157,056	2.8	...	...	—	—	—	—	—	—
Qatar	671	1,080	...	...	...	...	...	...	—	—	—	—	—	—
Réunion	1,684	2,710	81	128,228	41,841	3.2	...	...	—	—	—	—	...	...
Romania	45,589	73,369	48	*250,000*	*130,000*	*58*	8,077	11,792	6,940	11,169	17,886	28,785	51,480	75,159
Rwanda	7,500	12,070	5	9,838	5,523	384	123	180	—	—	—	—	—	—
St. Christopher and Nevis	198	318	44	2,392	465	15	...	...	—	—	—	—	—	—
St. Helena and Ascension	109	175	74	——1,124[47]——		5[47]	...	...	—	—	—	—	—	—
St. Lucia	426	686	65	7,049	2,084	22	...	...	—	—	—	—	—	—
St. Pierre and Miquelon	67	108	42	1,732	607	2.6	...	...	—	—	—	—	—	—
St. Vincent and the Grenadines	615	990	58	3,580	2,023	18	...	...	—	—	—	—	—	—
San Marino	*137*	*220*	...	14,745	1,699	1.4	...	...	—	—	—	—	—	—
São Tomé and Príncipe	*179*	*288*	*69*	*1,774*	*265*	*41*	...	...	—	—	—	—	—	—
Saudi Arabia	44,705	71,946	39	1,856,398	1,704,300	2.9	...	...	351[2]	565[2]	42	67	514	751
Senegal	9,134	14,700	25	*50,875*	*27,767*	*72*	*375*	*547*	642[2]	1,033[2]	83	133	212	309
Seychelles	160	257	60	3,318	1,005	15	...	...	—	—	—	—	—	—
Sierra Leone	*4,635*	*7,459*	*16*	*16,009*	*4,826*	*151*	*36*	*53*	52	84	...	...	...	...
Singapore	1,612	2,594	94	221,278	77,359	8.5	...	...	16	26	...	...	...	...
Solomon Islands	*1,305*	*2,100*	*12*	1,122	1,323	99	...	...	—	—	—	—	—	—
Somalia	*9,454*	*15,215*	*15*	*17,200*	*8,050*	*207*	...	...	—	—	—	—	—	—
South Africa	114,537	184,330	27	2,800,000	1,226,000	8.0	...	...	14,653	23,581	12,513	20,137	63,437	92,616
Bophuthatswana	*5,474*	*8,810*	...	...	...	...	...	...	*142*	*228*	...	...	...	...
Ciskei	*2,322*	*3,737*	...	...	...	...	...	...	*87*	*140*	...	...	...	...
Transkei	*5,468*	*8,800*	...	...	...	...	...	...	*130*	*209*	...	...	...	...
Venda	*739*	*1,189*	*11*	...	...	...	...	...	*8*	*13*	...	...	...	...
South West Africa/Namibia	25,700	41,361	10	*27,100*	*19,400*	*22*	...	...	1,453	2,338	...	...	...	...
Spain	197,937	318,548	56	8,874,442	1,523,250	3.7	76,400	111,500	8,435[2]	13,575[2]	9,925	15,972	7,970	11,636
Sri Lanka	91,323	146,970	...	141,730	125,654	58	...	...	903[2]	1,453[2]	1,297	2,088	164	240
Sudan, The	5,604	9,018	33	150,000	22,000	123	...	...	2,974	4,786	714	1,149	1,096	1,600
Suriname	5,523	8,889	26	31,170	12,850	8.2	...	...	104	167	...	...	...	...
Swaziland	1,692	2,723	19	21,338	8,376	20	...	...	194[2]	312[2]	...	...	83	121
Sweden	84,766	136,418	68	3,080,981	223,586	2.5	15,744	22,986	7,496	12,063	4,040	6,501	11,988	17,503
Switzerland	44,006	70,820	96	2,552,132	203,561	2.4	4,340	6,337	3,105	4,997	5,845	9,408	4,825	7,044
Syria	14,063	22,632	93	114,303	85,544	50	*2,569*	*3,751*	1,296	2,086	470	756	662	966
Taiwan	10,919	17,572	72	592,154	333,736	20	*4,146*	*6,053*	3,045	4,900	5,163	8,309	1,575	2,300
Tanzania	50,887	81,895	4	——84,190——		250	...	...	2,222	3,576	577[52]	929[52]	475[52]	694[52]
Thailand	47,420	76,315	39	411,982	789,837	41	...	...	2,321[2]	3,735[2]	5,682	9,144	1,858	2,712
Togo	4,638	7,464	20	36,372	17,963	53	...	...	321	516	65	104	9	13
Tokelau	...	...	...	...	...	...	...	...	—	—	—	—	—	—
Tonga	269	433	60	443	1,343	53	...	...	—	—	—	—	—	—
Trinidad and Tobago	4,909	7,900	46	210,425	60,401	4.3	...	...	—	—	—	—	—	—
Tunisia	16,267	26,194	53	141,185	147,571	23	589	860	1,316[2]	2,118[2]	462	744	1,167	1,704
Turkey	188,136	302,776	...	856,350	488,767	35	29,232	42,678	5,076[2]	8,169[2]	4,034	6,492	5,310	7,752
Turks and Caicos Islands	75	121	20	...	...	...	...	...	—	—	—	—	—	—
Tuvalu	5	8	—	...	...	...	...	...	—	—	—	—	—	—
Uganda	17,289	27,824	15	10,633	11,245	618	...	...	788[2]	1,268[2]	...	...	...	...
U.S.S.R.	605,000	973,000	79	*8,255,000*	*7,254,000*	*17*	339,500	495,600	89,562	144,136	226,000	364,000	2,492,000	3,639,000
United Arab Emirates	*800*	*1,300*	*61*	*130,700*	*77,600*	*5.2*	...	...	—	—	—	—	—	—
United Kingdom	229,081	368,670	97	16,055,000	2,282,000	3.1	68,800	100,400	14,408	23,187	18,693[55]	30,084[55]	8,532[55]	12,456[55]
United States	3,891,781	6,263,043	88	130,364,000	39,873,000	1.4	549,020	801,560	184,235	296,497	15,590	25,090	897,542	1,310,388
Uruguay	*30,952*	*49,813*	*20*	*281,275*	*49,813*	*8.8*	500	730	1,867[2]	3,004[2]	170	274	123	180
Vanuatu	660	1,062	4	3,061[57]	248[57]	14[57]	...	...	—	—	—	—	—	—
Venezuela	39,177	63,050	38	1,543,000	753,000	7.3	...	...	278	448	12	19	20	29
Vietnam	37,300	60,000	16	*100,000*	*200,000*	*163*	...	...	1,568	2,523	2,237	3,600	561	819
Virgin Islands (U.S.)	532	856	...	——39,661——		2.6	...	...	—	—	—	—	—	—
Wallis and Futuna	62	100	...	...	...	...	...	...	—	—	—	—	—	—
West Bank	...	...	...	25,370	14,374	19	...	...	—	—	—	—	—	—
Western Sahara	3,790	6,100	8	6,284	424	20	...	...	—	—	—	—	—	—
Western Samoa	98	157	84	3,325	385	43	...	...	—	—	—	—	—	—
Yemen (Aden)	1,150	1,850	...	*16,500*	*16,300*	*57*	...	...	—	—	—	—	—	—
Yemen (Ṣan'ā')	22,625	36,412	6	105,506	152,473	25	...	...	—	—	—	—	—	—
Yugoslavia	72,365	116,460	53	2,770,739	244,770	7.6	14,221	20,762	5,834	9,389	7,507	12,081	19,670	28,717
Zaire	*28,379*	*45,671*	*18*	*89,471*	*16,807*	*268*	...	...	3,623	5,252	231[60]	372[60]	1,274[60]	1,860[60]
Zambia	23,164	37,279	15	105,783	94,780	30	...	...	1,360	2,188	...	...	...	...
Zimbabwe	105,900	170,400	7	248,967	27,914	29	...	...	2,109[2]	3,394[2]	...	...	4,249	6,204

[1]Bakhtar Afghan Airlines only. [2]Route length. [3]Air Algérie international flights only. [4]Leeward Island Air Transport Company only. [5]Seagreen only. [6]Aerolineas Argentinos only. [7]Netherlands Antilles includes Aruba. [8]Government railways only. [9]Bahamasair only. [10]Apportionment of 1/4 of international flights of Gulf Air (jointly administered by the governments of Bahrain, Oman, Qatar, and United Arab Emirates) only. [11]Caribbean Airways only. [12]Caribbean Air Cargo only. [13]Excludes nonoperational routes. [14]Cotonou airport only. [15]Cruzeiro do Sul, Transbrasil, VARIG, and VASP only. [16]For industrial purposes only. [17]All traffic between Ouagadougou, Burkina Faso, and Abidjan, Côte d'Ivoire. [18]Air Canada, Canadian Pacific Airlines, and Quebecair only. [19]China includes Taiwan. [20]Paved roads only. [21]Lacsa only. [22]Excludes railroads serving the sugar industry. [23]Apportionment of 2/7 of total operations performed by SAS only. [24]National roads only. [25]Includes 100 km of the Chemin de Fer Djibouti–Ethiopien (CDE) in Djibouti. [26]Air France, UTA, and Air Inter only. [27]1984. [28]Railroads serve mines only. [29]Includes transshipments.

merchant marine: fleet, 1985 (vessels over 100 gross tons)	merchant marine: total dead-weight tonnage, 1985 ('000)	merchant marine: international cargo (latest): loaded metric tons ('000)	merchant marine: international cargo (latest): off-loaded metric tons ('000)	air: airports with sched-uled flights, 1986	air: traffic (latest): passengers: passenger-mi ('000,000)	air: traffic (latest): passengers: passenger-km ('000,000)	air: traffic (latest): cargo: short ton-mi ('000,000)	air: traffic (latest): cargo: metric ton-km ('000,000)	canals and inland waterways (latest): length: mi	canals and inland waterways (latest): length: km	canals and inland waterways (latest): cargo: short ton-mi ('000,000)	canals and inland waterways (latest): cargo: metric ton-km ('000,000)	country
2,219	25,721.5	63,516	18,132	41	2,331[42]	3,752[42]	91.1[42]	133.1[42]	190	306	5,829	8,510	Norway
28	12.4	16,160	2,800	2	774[10]	1,245[10]	22.3[10]	32.6[10]	...	...	...	...	Oman
—	—	25	143	9	*188*	*302*	*3.9*	*5.6*	...	...	...	...	Pacific Is., Trust Terr. of the
...	...	...	...	...	...	...	...	...	...	...	...	...	Marshall Islands
...	...	...	...	...	...	...	...	...	...	...	...	...	Micronesia, Fed. States of
...	...	...	...	...	...	...	...	...	...	...	...	...	Northern Mariana Islands
...	...	...	...	...	...	...	...	...	...	...	...	...	Palau
77	654.7	2,844	13,548	18	4,362	7,020	216.7	316.4	...	...	...	...	Pakistan
5,512	67,266.7	778	2,698	6	249	400	9.9	14.4	548	882	...	...	Panama
84	35.1	1,950	1,646	62	358	576	8.6	12.5	...	...	...	...	Papua New Guinea
40	51.0	...	...	1	298	479	1.8	2.7	1,900	3,100	...	...	Paraguay
650	1,096.6	8,292	3,199	22	1,991[43]	1,596[43]	24.5[43]	36.2[43]	5,473	8,808	...	...	Peru
1,000	7,571.1	13,980	17,316	42	5,220[44]	8,400[44]	173.0[44]	252.6[44]	2,000	3,219	...	...	Philippines
—	—	—	—	—	—	—	—	—	...	...	...	...	Pitcairn Island
761	4,439.9	30,600	14,800	12	1,387	2,232	7.4	10.8	1,876	3,019	989	1,444	Poland
367	2,405.7	4,100	19,000	20	2,635[45]	4,240[45]	91.3[45]	133.3[45]	77	124	...	...	Portugal
—	—	[46]	[46]	9	...	...	...	...	...	...	...	...	Puerto Rico
60	525.1	16,420	1,700	1	774[10]	1,245[10]	22.3[10]	32.6[10]	...	...	...	...	Qatar
—	—	336	1,104	1	...	...	...	...	...	...	...	...	Réunion
410	4,502.6	10,000	22,000	15	1,648	2,652	54.8	80.0	1,031	1,659	1,745	2,548	Romania
—	—	—	—	2	...	...	...	...	...	...	...	...	Rwanda
2	0.5	36	63	2	...	...	...	...	...	...	...	...	St. Christopher and Nevis
2	2.8	1	12	1	...	...	...	...	...	...	...	...	St. Helena and Ascension
6	2.1	100	188	2	...	...	...	...	...	...	...	...	St. Lucia
—	—	7	64	1	...	...	...	...	...	...	...	...	St. Pierre and Miquelon
71	359.5	16	45	4	...	...	...	...	...	...	...	...	St. Vincent and the Grenadines
—	—	—	—	—	—	—	—	—	—	—	—	—	San Marino
3	1.2	12	15	1	...	...	...	...	...	...	...	...	São Tomé and Príncipe
398	5,247.3	299,257	30,000	18	9,604	15,456	330.2	482.1	...	...	...	...	Saudi Arabia
144	44.3	2,376	2,880	12	129	208	26.2	38.3	935	1,505	...	...	Senegal
4	0.8	6	100	5	...	...	...	...	...	...	...	...	Seychelles
25	1.3	48[29]	228[29]	4	68[48]	110[48]	1.4[48]	2.0[48]	500	800	447	652	Sierra Leone
758	11,187.3	40,308	59,232	1	13,511	21,744	701.8	1,024.7	...	...	...	...	Singapore
26	4.6	299	95	24	7	11	0.02	0.04	...	...	...	...	Solomon Islands
27	31.1	250	814	3	177	284	3.4	4.9	...	...	...	...	Somalia
273	673.2	69,276	26,758	36	5,395[49]	8,683[49]	268.4[49]	391.7[49]	...	...	...	...	South Africa
—	—	—	—	—	—	—	—	—	...	...	...	...	Bophuthatswana
—	—	—	—	—	—	—	—	—	...	...	...	...	Ciskei
—	—	—	—	1	...	...	...	...	...	...	...	...	Transkei
—	—	—	—	—	—	—	—	—	...	...	...	...	Venda
—	—	—	—	10	...	...	...	...	...	...	...	...	South West Africa/Namibia
2,477	10,820.0	44,652	88,752	29	10,850	17,462	354.3	517.2	649	1,045	21,836[50]	31,880[50]	Spain
91	974.2	1,932	3,588	6	1,558	2,508	47.8	69.8	267	430	...	...	Sri Lanka
23	126.4	916	2,642	13	408	657	4.1	6.0	3,300	5,310	...	...	Sudan, The
25	19.2	6,079	1,518	5	*152*	*245*	*2.5*	*3.6*	2,800	4,500	...	...	Suriname
—	—	—	—	1	14	22	1.5	2.2	—	—	—	—	Swaziland
694	4,230.8	42,336	52,284	36	3,155[51]	5,078[51]	130.3[51]	190.2[51]	724	1,165	6,200	9,000	Sweden
33	535.8	...	...	5	7,494	12,060	465.9	680.2	13	21	105	153	Switzerland
53	83.8	7,656	11,124	5	585	942	10.7	15.7	418	672	...	...	Syria
583	[19]	...	...	9	6,988	11,246	1,259.6	1,839.0	...	...	...	...	Taiwan
40	59.0	1,118	2,040	19	163	262	18	2.6	726	1,168	...	...	Tanzania
244	863.4	17,760[53]	17,484[53]	9	5,920	9,528	285.8	417.2	2,500	4,000	...	...	Thailand
11	78.0	704	995	1	121	194	14.4	21.0	30	50	...	...	Togo
—	—	—	—	—	—	—	—	—	...	...	...	...	Tokelau
20	22.4	23	74	5	...	...	...	...	...	...	...	...	Tonga
49	12.4	12,798	11,094	2	1,278[54]	2,057[54]	6.8[54]	10.0[54]	...	...	...	...	Trinidad and Tobago
67	449.3	2,856	7,104	6	987	1,589	13.1	19.1	...	...	...	...	Tunisia
817	6,291.8	45,144	36,312	16	1,468	2,362	18.0	26.3	1,000	1,600	35	51	Turkey
11	3.3	3	5	5	...	...	...	...	...	...	...	...	Turks and Caicos Islands
2	0.5	...	...	1	...	...	...	...	...	...	...	...	Tuvalu
2	5.9	...	...	7	89	143	26.3	38.4	...	...	...	...	Uganda
7,145	28,153.3	162,000	63,000	52	117,100	188,400	2,294.0	3,350.0	85,687	137,900	129,800	189,500	U.S.S.R.
232	1,523.7	64,788	8,500	2	774[10]	1,245[10]	22.3[10]	32.6[10]	...	...	...	...	United Arab Emirates
2,378	21,794.7	143,844	139,896	40	27,992	45,048	1,128.8	1,648.0	1,461	2,351	30,500	44,600	United Kingdom
6,447	28,992.6	327,768[46]	332,424[46]	824	297,400	478,620	7,892.1	11,522.2	25,727	41,403	360,700	526,600	United States
96	263.1	570[56]	454[56]	7	230	370	1.2	1.8	1,000	1,600	...	...	Uruguay
28	226.4	67	105	23	0.015[58]	0.025[58]	—	—	...	...	...	...	Vanuatu
269	1,421.8	60,821	12,093	39	1,737	2,796	72.3	105.6	4,400	7,100	...	...	Venezuela
128	446.2	680	5,000	3	181	291	2.7	4.0	11,000	17,702	...	...	Vietnam
—	—	9,500	12,600	3	...	...	...	...	...	...	...	...	Virgin Islands (U.S.)
—	—	—	—	2	...	...	...	...	...	...	...	...	Wallis and Futuna
—	—	...	...	—	—	—	—	—	...	...	...	...	West Bank
—	—	—	60	1	...	...	...	...	...	...	...	...	Western Sahara
6	35.3	34	89	3	...	...	...	...	...	...	...	...	Western Samoa
27	12.9	3,575	4,834	1	62	100	1.2	1.7	...	...	...	...	Yemen (Aden)
10	1.8	40	2,000	3	356[59]	573[59]	6.4[59]	9.4[59]	...	...	...	...	Yemen (Ṣan'ā')
479	4,180.4	6,660	24,000	16	3,937	6,336	63.4	92.5	1,243	2,001	2,800	4,088	Yugoslavia
33	121.4	845	1,513	33	365	588	20.1	29.4	8,500	13,700	678	990	Zaire
—	—	—	—	14	343	552	44.6	65.1	1,398	2,250	...	...	Zambia
—	—	—	—	8	369	593	9.3	13.6	...	...	...	...	Zimbabwe

[30]Alisarda and Alitalia only. [31]Kenya Airways only. [32]Air Tungaru only. [33]Middle East Airlines only. [34]Lamco Railroad only. [35]1982. [36]Peninsular Malaysia and Singapore. [37]Aeronaves de Mexico and Mexicana only. [38]Air Nauru only. [39]International traffic only. [40]KLM and NLM only. [41]Antillean Airlines only. [42]Includes 2/7 apportionment of total operations of SAS. [43]Aeroperu and Faucett only. [44]PAL only. [45]TAP only. [46]United States includes Puerto Rico. [47]St. Helena only. [48]Sierra Leone Airlines international traffic only. [49]SAA only. [50]Coastal shipping only. [51]Includes 3/7 apportionment of total operations of SAS. [52]Tanzania Railways Corporation only. [53]Port of Bangkok only. [54]BWIA International. [55]British Railways only; excluding Northern Ireland. [56]Port of Montevideo only. [57]Espirito Santo and Efate only. [58]Air Vanuatu only. [59]Yemen Airways only. [60]Zaire National Railways only.

Communications

Virtually all the states of the world have a variety of communications media available to their citizens: newspapers (although only daily papers are included in this table), radio broadcast systems, and telephone, post office, and telegraph facilities; most also have television and telex. The focus of this table, therefore, is on the relative density and distribution of communications services. Unfortunately, the availability of information about the infrastructure and traffic volume of these national systems runs far behind the capabilities of the systems themselves. Certain countries publish no information about themselves; others publish data analyzed according to a variety of fiscal, calendar, religious, or other years; still others, while they possess such data almost simultaneously with the end of the business year, may not publish them except in company reports of limited distribution or in national statistical summaries, and only after a delay of up to several years.

The date given for each category of information is that of the majority of the data in the columns indicated, but within each column as much as one-quarter of the data may refer to other years. The data also originate in sources of varying completeness and reliability. Data for some kinds of communications apparatus and traffic are relatively easy to track; telephones, for example, must be installed, and service is recorded so that it may be charged. But in most countries radios may be purchased by anyone and turned on whenever desired. As a result, data on distribution and use of radio and television apparatus may be collected in a variety of ways—on the basis of numbers of subscribers, licenses issued, periodic sample surveys, census or housing surveys, or private consumer surveys. In some cases the figures have been rounded, and the population data used in calculating the distribution statistics are based on midyear estimates for the relevant years.

The United Nations Educational, Scientific and Cultural Organization (Unesco) publishes in its *Yearbook* extensive data on newspapers, radio, and television that have been collected from standardized questionnaires. The completeness and recency of its data, however, depend on the timely return of each questionnaire, and response rates depend on a variety of factors. In general, however, response rates for inquiries by international organizations in communications are better than in other fields because these organizations and the responsible authorities in each country must conduct day-to-day business and, hence, have a better ongoing relationship.

Newspaper statistics are especially difficult to collect and compare. Newspapers continually are founded, cease publication, merge, or change

Communications

country	daily newspapers (latest)			radio, 1985			television, 1985			telephones, 1984				
	number	total circulation ('000)	circulation per 1,000 population	transmitters (latest)	receivers (all types) ('000)	persons per receiver	transmitters (latest)	receivers (all types) ('000)	persons per receiver	receivers ('000)	persons per receiver	traffic, 1982 ('000 calls) local	long-distance	international
Afghanistan	4	92	5	14	135	134	1	12.8	1,416	32[1]	516[1]	—110[2]—		18[2]
Albania	2	145	52	14	210	14	186	50	58	4.8[4]	579[4]	...	...	...
Algeria	4	480	22	55	3,500	6.2	44	1,445	15	709	30	—1,587,500[5]—		118,640[5]
American Samoa	2	7	200	1	15	2.4	3	7.5[6]	4.6[6]	6.0[4]	5.5[4]	...	...	...
Andorra	1	...	...	4	8	5.5	...	4.0	11	18[4]	2.1[4]	...	...	...
Angola	4	112	14	55	230	37	...	25	343	40[4]	202[4]	66,080[1]	260[1]	320[1]
Anguilla	—	—	—	2	2.2	3.2	—	...	...	0.58	11	424	...	144[7]
Antigua and Barbuda	2	6	71	5	21	3.8	...	17	4.7	11	7.5	13[5]	3[5]	359[5]
Argentina	191	...	...	202	10,500	2.9	75	6,500	4.7	2,717	11	13,196,728[5]	42,936	2,901
Aruba	2	20	318	[13]	[13]	[13]	...	[13]	[13]	[13]	[13]	[13]	[13]	[13]
Australia	63	4,851	337	284	20,000	0.8	386	5,905	2.7	8,329	1.9	5,570,000	821,600	16,500
Austria	30	...	...	567	2,558	3.0	864	3,024	2.5	3,594	2.1	—24,631,340[7]—		241,992[7]
Bahamas, The	4	30	133	5	116	2.0	...	51	4.5	91	2.5	—126,040[1]—		1,571
Bahrain	3	26	59	3	142	2.9	1	170	2.5	108	3.7	122,572	...	22,209[7]
Bangladesh	30	542	6	23	775	130	6	300	335	122[4]	758[4]	—347,600[16]—		84[7, 16]
Barbados	2	40	159	1	180	1.4	2	60	4.2	73[17]	3.4[17]	—483,000[17]—		1,100[17]
Belgium	26	2,204	224	41	4,610	2.1	31	2,983	3.3	4,243	2.3	1,510,166	1,913,887	69,516
Belize	2	6	46	11	88	1.9	...	...	...	8.6[17]	18[17]	...	28,382[5]	90
Benin	1	1	0.3	7	69	58	2	15	267	18[1]	198[1]	...	548[16]	812[16]
Bermuda	1	15	267	5	100	0.6	...	66.6	0.9	51[17]	1.1[17]	43,805	...	2,081
Bhutan	—	—	—	1	12.5	113	...	...	...	15[4]	91[4]	...	...	...
Bolivia	14	253	40	184	482	13	...	255	25	205[17]	30[17]	...	...	2,435[7, 17]
Botswana	1	18	17	7	77	14	...	...	...	17[17]	61[17]	—1,147—		3,903
Brazil	265	5,722	44	1,325	53,000	2.6	137	30,431	4.5	10,570	13	12,736,000	1,395,800	7,144
British Virgin Islands	—	—	—	1	6.8	1.7	...	2.5	4.8	4.0	2.9	...	...	133[1]
Brunei	—	—	—	8	58	4.0	2	38	6.1	22	9.2[4]	...	22,720[1, 7]	3,760[1, 7]
Bulgaria	14	2,221	249	35	2,100	4.3	339	2,002	4.5	1,514[17]	5.9[17]	25,000	344	5,732
Burkina Faso	6	...	...	9	116	59	2	18	380	14	542	...	...	42[3]
Burma	6	565	15	7	725	52	...	35	1,077	54[17]	684[17]	—65,000[16]—		5[16]
Burundi	1	20	4	5	180	27	...	0.25	19,144	6.0	756	1,205[17]	553[17]	538[17]
Cameroon	1	35	4	19	790	12	...	...	...	47	199	...	...	1,600[7, 17]
Canada	114	5,500	217	1,226	21,800	1.2	1,163	14,602	1.7	13,656[17]	1.8[17]	27,554,131	1,475,376	110,638
Cape Verde	—	—	—	3	47	6.7	...	0.5	628	2.0	163	—15,200[1]—		638[1]
Cayman Islands	—	—	—	4	19	1.1	...	...	...	9.4[17]	2.0[17]	...	...	236[1]
Central African Republic	—	—	—	4	100	26	...	1[1]	2,341[1]	5.0[4]	477[4]	2,142	538	43
Chad	3	...	...	7	80	63	...	...	...	6.5[3]	660[3]	...	...	...
Chile	66	1,407	120	109	17,000	0.7	...	2,650	4.6	680	17	1,144,925	44,042	1,103
China	27	24,826	24	...	15,500	67	...	9,950	105	5,539	186	—667,000—		3,000
Christmas Island	—	—	—	...	2.5	0.9	...	...	...	...	...	...	...	...
Cocos (Keeling) Islands	—	—	—	...	0.25	2.4	...	...	...	0.18[17]	3.3[17]	...	...	...
Colombia	31	1,324	47	...	3,000	9.5	49	1,805	16	1,978	14	1,004,000[17]	168,600[17]	3,500[17]
Comoros	—	—	—	7	40	10	...	...	...	0.50[17]	766[17]	—940,000[3]—		14[3]
Congo	4	24	14	10	99	18	...	5	348	18	108	47,582[17]	31,722[17]	1,979[17]
Cook Islands	1	2	118	2	10	1.7	...	...	...	2.1[17]	8.5[17]	...	...	48
Costa Rica	4	180	71	123	190	13	...	425	5.8	304	8.0	492,569	196,338	1,753
Côte d'Ivoire	1	80	8	24	600	17	12	560	18	88[1]	98[1]	...	...	...
Cuba	16	1,281	129	150	2,140	4.7	58	1,525	6.6	493	20	—54,000[16]—		453[16]
Cyprus	17	75	116	6	300	2.2	25	158.3	4.2	196	3.4	—524,270[5]—		791,892[5]
Czechoslovakia	30	4,892	318	123	4,208.5	3.7	74	4,360	3.6	3,499	4.4	3,785,000	311,000	4,900
Denmark	47	1,805	353	49	2,101.1	2.4	32	1,945.6	2.6	3,828	1.3	2,138,992	1,232,469	32,768
Djibouti	—	—	—	3	30	14	...	11.3	38	8.0	51	3,688[17]	373[17]	2,522[7, 17]
Dominica	—	—	—	3	35	2.4	...	...	...	6.0	14	4,670	...	108
Dominican Republic	7	177	29	188	227	28	...	392	16	175[17]	34[17]	2,017,011	8,460	2,933
Ecuador	9	555	66	...	1,900	4.9	...	600	16	332	27	...	...	7,468[7]
Egypt	11	2,824	58	154	12,000	4.1	74	3,860	13	800	57	747,000	16,000	2,070
El Salvador	6	240	50	75	1,000	5.3	...	350	15	124	42	289,378[5]	124,019[5]	15,209[7]
Equatorial Guinea	2	1	3	3	90[6]	3.5[6]	...	2.1[6]	148[6]	1.4[4]	217[4]	...	...	...
Ethiopia	3	44	1	9	2,000	22	2	40	1,085	116	365	304,120[5]	3,338	179
Faeroe Islands	—	—	—	4	16.8	2.7	...	10	4.5	20	2.2	...	...	44
Falkland Islands	—	—	—	2	1	2.0	...	...	...	0.44	4.6	—4—		12

frequency of publication. Data on circulation, sales, and readership are often incomplete, slow to be aggregated at the national level, or regarded as proprietary for either private or governmental publications. In some countries circulation data are virtually nonexistent. In others no daily newspaper exists.

The commercially published annual *World Radio TV Handbook* (J.M. Frost, editor) is a valuable source of information on broadcast media and has complete and timely coverage. It depends on data received from broadcasters, but because some do not respond, local correspondents and monitors are used in many countries, and some unconfirmed or unofficial data are included as estimates.

Telephone data are obtained from the American Telephone and Telegraph Communications' annual, *The World's Telephones,* and a variety of national and secondary sources. A.T.&T. collects its data by sending questionnaires to the telephone agencies of each country, and their statistics tend to be accurate and timely, but some countries, again, fail to supply current data. More than one-quarter of the data are for other than the base year. Several countries also report incomplete data: the national total may exclude figures for some telephone companies, or some portion of the national territory; some countries supply statistics only on telephone exchange lines; some island states report only radio telephones. A number of countries omit data on public coin-box telephones; their statistics, thus, reflect an undercount. The figures for calls under telephone traffic sometimes represent a measure of mechanical activity rather than an enumeration of actual conversations between individuals. Depending on a country's metering system, multiple counting of a single call may occur.

Post office statistics are collected mainly from the Universal Postal Union's annual summary *Statistique des services postaux.*

The statistics on telegraph and telex are derived mainly from the UN-affiliated International Telecommunication Union's *Yearbook of Common Carrier Telecommunication Statistics* with additional statistics from country sources.

Unesco surveys, the diverse industry sources cited above, and scores of national statistical sources have all been used in the compilation of this table because no one source is complete.

... Not available.
—None, nil, or not applicable.

post offices, 1983			telegraph, 1983			telex, 1983				country
							traffic ('000 minutes)			
number	persons per office	pieces of mail handled ('000)	total traffic ('000)	national traffic ('000)	international outgoing traffic ('000)	subscriber lines	total	national	international outgoing	
349[3]	36,447[3]	11,218[3]	183[2]	95[2]	88[2]	73[2]	...	...	25[2]	Afghanistan
292[3]	7,328[3]	...	...	...	...	...	...	...	...	Albania
1,826	11,856	351,410	3,223	2,882	341	5,895	30,192	21,664	8,528	Algeria
...	...	...	...	...	...	...	...	...	...	American Samoa
...	...	3,483	...	...	...	...	...	...	...	Andorra
133	53,263	6,177	198[1]	154[1]	44[1]	587[1]	...	...	1,599[1]	Angola
22	272	200	0.9	—	0.9	30	...	...	20	Anguilla
15[3]	5,333[3]	2,262[8, 9, 10, 11]	17[4]	—	17[4]	64[1]	...	...	110[1]	Antigua and Barbuda
5,554	5,016	74,095[12]	11,357	11,141	216	8,816	...	135,982[2]	9,190	Argentina
...	...	[13]	...	...	[13]	[13]	[13]	[13]	[13]	Aruba
4,790	2,938	2,995,711	4,866	4,051	815	40,000	58,114[14]	45,492[14]	12,622[14]	Australia
2,644[15]	2,858[15]	2,658,650	1,352	1,096	256	22,928	105,324	71,669	33,655	Austria
127	1,649	34,559	50	20	30	396	1,157	91	1,066	Bahamas, The
10	35,079	76,800	138	17	122	1,946	12,281	2,208	10,073	Bahrain
7,192[3]	12,047[3]	333,133[3]	3,998[16]	3,470[16]	528[16]	461[1]	...	...	855[1]	Bangladesh
16	15,875	17,009[11]	...	...	43	281	...	...	595	Barbados
1,858[15]	5,309[15]	2,910,141	1,353	1,073	280	23,970	110,385	46,753	63,631	Belgium
105	1,385	4,052[9, 10, 11]	...	...	20[1]	51[1]	...	...	72[1]	Belize
106[3]	26,321[3]	11,856[8]	...	422[16]	...	153[16]	...	...	244[16]	Benin
15[3]	3,333[3]	...	...	...	25[4]	453[1]	...	...	1,460[1]	Bermuda
81[3]	16,728[3]	2,266[18]	...	...	...	...	...	...	...	Bhutan
458[3]	11,572[3]	54,609[3]	244	210	34	930[1]	2,087	1,152	935	Bolivia
138	6,786	35,876[9]	...	209[3]	43	407	2,493	722	1,770	Botswana
7,428	17,455	4,257,333[19]	...	15,327[2]	219	56,040	276,571	260,415	16,156	Brazil
5[3]	2,407[3]	...	8[4]	—	8[4]	39[1]	...	...	49[1]	British Virgin Islands
14	14,307	8,014	...	...	...	231[1]	...	...	419[1]	Brunei
2,857[3]	3,101[3]	...	7,593	7,393	199	6,030	30,733	27,463	3,270	Bulgaria
66[3]	90,000[3]	2,128[8]	114[8]	65[8]	49[8]	223	...	...	117[14]	Burkina Faso
1,107	31,900	93,916	1,358[16]	1,280[16]	78[16]	47[16]	...	...	209[16]	Burma
38	120,943	12,558	9	4	5	100	...	...	224	Burundi
150[3]	50,207[3]	64,248[18]	534	417	117	1,035	...	...	2,700	Cameroon
8,295	3,025	6,533,274[20]	...	1,423[2, 21]	720[21]	50,336	...	...	14,550	Canada
...	...	3,522[22]	111[4]	98[4]	13[4]	40[4]	190[4]	58[4]	132[4]	Cape Verde
...	...	2,262[22]	10[4]	—	10[4]	164[1]	...	...	286[1]	Cayman Islands
76	32,310	34,525[23]	47[1]	37[1]	10[1]	134[1]	...	...	353[1]	Central African Republic
24	203,000	938[24]	320[8]	300[8]	20[8]	60[8]	...	12[8, 14]	188[8]	Chad
764	14,758	164,518[11]	2,800	2,730	70	3,768	...	47,741[5]	4,103	Chile
48,745	21,026	3,540,100[10, 11, 19]	173,762	172,353	1,409	1,373	...	...	4,414	China
2	1,600	...	...	...	...	...	...	...	...	Christmas Island
4	154	...	...	...	...	...	...	...	...	Cocos (Keeling) Islands
...	...	209,461[23]	21,134	21,000	134	5,310	29,298	103,007[5]	6,559	Colombia
9[3]	38,889[3]	1,732[22]	...	17[3]	25[25]	37[4]	...	...	53[4]	Comoros
131	11,450	14,612	260	116	144	329	...	...	798	Congo
...	...	...	...	...	240	41	66	11	55	Cook Islands
342	7,028	74,825	...	223[4]	54	1,439	3,271	1,670	1,601	Costa Rica
342	26,023	77,383	581[2]	508[2]	73[2]	1,181[1]	...	...	3,149[1]	Côte d'Ivoire
700[3]	13,271[3]	86,991[1, 11]	15,986[16]	15,592[16]	394[16]	2,352[1]	20,519[1]	19,338[1]	1,181[1]	Cuba
650	1,007	31,303	151	97	53	2,581	5,449	1,734	3,715	Cyprus
6,101	2,526	71,967[12]	9,946	9,618	328	1,017	...	71,793[5]	5,997	Czechoslovakia
1,298[15]	3,938[15]	1,468,154	401	263	138	11,414	45,463	16,318	29,145	Denmark
5	60,000	1,623	27	—	27	168	507	15	491	Djibouti
63	1,274	2,051	12	—	12	28[1]	...	...	31[1]	Dominica
154[3]	25,807[3]	21,741[24]	...	...	...	...	...	...	...	Dominican Republic
480	18,635	37,260	2,134	2,021	113	1,900	6,971	3,882	3,089	Ecuador
6,870[15]	6,696[15]	441,890	9,302[4]	8,332[4]	970[4]	3,476[4]	13,511[4]	4,584[4]	8,927[4]	Egypt
367	13,484	32,762[9]	1,151	1,106	45	683	896	31	865	El Salvador
19	20,473	51[9, 10, 11]	...	...	...	...	...	...	...	Equatorial Guinea
462	89,029	26,945[10, 11]	225	202	23	631	1,439	514	925	Ethiopia
...	...	...	27	...	27	141	...	...	...	Faeroe Islands
...	...	233[26]	...	...	4	8	42	—	42	Falkland Islands

Communications (continued)

country	daily newspapers (latest)			radio, 1985			television, 1985			telephones, 1984				
												traffic, 1982 ('000 calls)		
	number	total circulation ('000)	circulation per 1,000 population	transmitters (latest)	receivers (all types) ('000)	persons per receiver	transmitters (latest)	receivers (all types) ('000)	persons per receiver	receivers ('000)	persons per receiver	local	long-distance	international
Fiji	2	70	106	12	400	1.8	...	...	...	51	13	—6,395[7]—		2,057[7]
Finland	66	2,578	531	101	2,500	2.0	143	1,771.7	2.8	2,899	1.7	1,453,405	339,904	13,955
France	101	13,030	237	610	20,000	2.7	2,821	17,654.7	3.1	33,002	1.7	—72,655,150[5]—		
French Guiana	2	...	...	13	43	1.9	8	6.4	13	22[17]	3.5[17]	—90,977[5]—		
French Polynesia	2	22	127	6	80	2.1	10	25.6[6]	6.7[6]	34	5.0	—22,200[5]—		2,450[6]
Gabon	2	33	35	16	100	12	...	22	53	12[17]	93[17]	13,560[5, 17]	34,800[5, 17]	1,609
Gambia, The	—	—	—	3	105	7.1	...	...	...	3.5[2]	182[2]	—3,012[16]—		41[16]
Gaza Strip	—	—	—	...	...	...	...	...	...	...	...	...	...	...
Germany, East	39	8,845	530	117	6,509.9	2.6	505	6,015.4	2.8	3,527	4.7	1,296,036	707,841	10,929
Germany, West	359	25,103	408	469	25,265.6	2.4	3,424	22,130	2.8	36,582	1.7	15,387,180	8,477,510	308,140
Ghana	4	460	37	4	2,500	5.1	7	140	92	72	174	—1,800[16]—		130[16]
Gibraltar	1	2	80	3	10	2.8	4	7	4.0	10[17]	2.9[17]	9,330[4]	...	505
Greece	131	...	...	55	4,000	2.5	84	1,715	5.8	3,529	2.8	3,044,840	516,480	21,680
Greenland	—	—	—	18	13.6	3.9	...	10.2	5.2	12	4.6	...	...	...
Grenada	—	—	—	3	50	1.9	...	...	...	5.6	16	—148[17]—		640[17]
Guadeloupe	1	32	97	5	60	5.5	8	47	7.1	68[17]	4.8[17]	—292,355[5]—		
Guam	1	18	162	5	100	1.2	2	79	1.5	29[17]	3.9[17]	...	...	...
Guatemala	8	224	30	115	325	25	...	207	38	162[17]	47[17]	...	...	...
Guernsey	1	16	268	...	...	...	...	...	...	40[17]	1.4[17]	—28.743—		184
Guinea	1	20	4	8	100	54	...	7.7	705	10[1]	493[1]	...	96[7, 17]	986[7, 17]
Guinea-Bissau	1	6	7	2	25	35	...	...	...	5.0[1]	161[1]	...	...	...
Guyana	1	60	64	8	350	2.7	...	...	...	28[4]	32[4]	...	...	...
Haiti	4	20	4	48	120	44	...	75	70	38[17]	133[17]	...	452	818
Honduras	6	240	61	153	200	22	...	140	31	46	81	151,150[7, 17]	112,180[7, 17]	9,090[7, 17]
Hong Kong	62	...	...	24	2,720	2.0	12	1,310	4.1	2,173	2.5	...	...	12,703
Hungary	29	2,842	266	51	5,500	1.9	42	2,848	3.7	1,433	7.4	1,051,120[5]	649,894[5]	305,500[5]
Iceland	5	119	507	26	72.2	3.4	83	64.7	3.8	117[17]	2.0[17]	—490,571[4, 17]—		795[17]
India	1,334	14,847	21	160	25,000	30	19	2,200	346	3,488	214	10,335,074	179,220	2,548
Indonesia	89	2,603	17	301	32,800	5.1	231	4,900	34	669[17]	238[17]	4,949,040[5]	10,632	2,867
Iran	14	...	...	193	10,000	4.5	478	2,085	21	2,144	20	7,371,358	283,997	3,676
Iraq	6	324	23	46	2,200	7.1	35	600	26	515[17]	28[17]	—1,518,817[5]—		1,506
Ireland	10	939	266	21	2,050	1.7	21	851	4.2	780[17]	4.5[17]	—1,662,060[5]—		2,920
Isle of Man	—	—	—	...	21.8[1]	3.0[1]	...	21.8[17]	3.0[17]	...	...	...	...	...
Israel	25	1,240	294	63	1,055[6]	4.0[6]	48	606	7.1	1,527	2.8	1,000,000[5]	2,000,000[5]	30,000[7]
Italy	79	4,632	82	2,151	14,015	4.1	1,867	13,900	4.1	24,331	2.3	10,700,964	4,292,300	95,965
Jamaica	3	104	45	19	860	2.7	...	215	11	126[4]	17[4]	...	1,888	3,667
Japan	125	67,380	565	1,008	94,500	1.3	11,439	30,225	4.0	63,976	1.9	...	...	23,535
Jersey	1	23	304	...	...	...	...	...	...	58[17]	1.3[17]	40,612[17]	7,119[17]	480[17]
Jordan	5	176	68	17	551	4.9	46	181	15	71[1]	33[1]	...	...	...
Kampuchea	16	...	...	6	200	36	...	52	140	7.3[1]	886[1]	...	...	...
Kenya	2	220	12	22	1,600	13	...	100	203	248	79	7,895	6,857	5,317[7]
Kiribati	—	—	—	1	10	6.4	...	11[4]	5.5[4]	0.82[17]	74[17]	6[7]	18[7, 17]	32[7, 17]
Korea, North	10	...	...	...	3,500	5.7	...	150	134	...	...	...	...	...
Korea, South	25	6,748	171	118	24,000	1.7	126	8,679.9	4.7	6,985	5.8	22,990,368[5]	335,074[5]	3,591
Kuwait	7	453	267	6	950	1.8	13	600	2.8	243[17]	6.9[17]	...	...	5,862
Laos	2	12	3	4	230	16	...	30.5	118	4.3[17]	921[17]	—619[8]—		22[8]
Lebanon	39	603	228	10	1,500[6]	1.8[6]	5	451	5.9	150[4]	18[4]	...	...	...
Lesotho	3	44	30	4	43	35	...	0.5	3,002	5.9[1]	331[1]	...	...	...
Liberia	3	25	12	9	325	6.9	...	35	64	7.7[4]	263[4]	...	...	...
Libya	1	40	12	20	167	23	13	175	22	102[4]	32[4]	...	...	...
Liechtenstein	2	14	545	...	8.1[4]	3.3[4]	...	7.6[4]	3.4[4]	22[17]	1.2[17]	7,266	12,727[7]	5,242[7]
Luxembourg	6	130	365	7	227	1.6	3	91.3	4.0	232[17]	1.6[17]	—127,393—		62,779[7]
Macau	10	...	...	5	80	4.5	...	59[16]	4.8[16]	37	9.3	...	...	9,130[7, 17]
Madagascar	6	55	6	21	900	11	14	70	143	37	263	—46,000[1]—		85[1]
Malaŵi	2	32	5	16	1,060	6.7	...	...	...	37	186	...	...	1,723[17]
Malaysia	42	...	...	82	1,660[6]	9.2[6]	38	1,457.6	11	1,151	13	...	...	...
Maldives	2	1	6	3	12.5	15	2	3.7	49	1.5[4]	105[4]	—3,192[16]—		15[16]
Mali	1	40	5	14	110	75	...	0.5	16,420	9.5[17]	789[17]	...	90	97
Malta	4	81	250	3	151	2.2	4	90.5	3.7	115	2.9	117,491	...	1,111
Martinique	1	30	91	6	48	6.8	8	43	7.6	84[17]	3.9[17]	—237,138[5]—		
Mauritania	1	...	...	4	95	17	...	0.75	2,208	4.4[17]	363[17]	6,722[5]	153[7]	34[7]
Mauritius	8	76	75	3	125	8.2	...	110	9.3	54	19	—60,059[17]—		1,468[7, 17]
Mayotte	—	—	—	...	6	11	...	...	...	0.45[17]	122[17]	...	...	...
Mexico	374	...	...	676	22,250	3.5	385	7,750	10	6,796	11	10,888,813	529,827	32,203
Monaco	2	11	408	12	9.65	2.9	5	17.5	1.6	35	0.8	—11,800[5]—		151,000[6]
Mongolia	2	177	100	...	180	11	...	60	32	43[17]	42[17]	...	...	...
Montserrat	—	—	—	3	4.1	2.9	...	1.2	9.8	2.7[17]	4.3[17]	—2,723—		509[7]
Morocco	8	282	12	36	2,550	9.3	20	1,033	23	236	75	...	...	...
Mozambique	2	54	4	39	450	31	...	6.5	2,125	59	228	54,711	2,635	239
Nauru	—	—	—	1	4	2.0	...	...	...	1.6[4]	5.0[4]	1,304[16]	—	130[16]
Nepal	51	...	...	7	2,010	8.2	...	17	970	18	895	—3,291[7, 17]—		509[7, 17]
Netherlands, The	79	4,500	312	50	4,750	3.1	29	4,450	3.3	8,535	1.7	2,949,600	2,279,900	98,037
Netherlands Antilles	4	34	188	16[13]	160[13]	1.5[13]	...	58[13]	4.2[13]	65[13, 17]	3.7[13, 17]	681,113[7, 13]	8,848[7, 13]	11,671[7, 13]
New Caledonia	1	13	88	3	80	1.9	20	31[6]	4.8[6]	33[17]	4.5[17]	13,855	66	408
New Zealand	37	1,047	327	65	2,800	1.2	...	962	3.4	2,011	1.6	...	110,162	3,653
Nicaragua	3	149	46	87	200	16	...	160	20	51	58	—175,605[1, 5]—		7,860[1, 7]
Niger	1	5	1	19	160	39	...	12	521	9.8[17]	605[17]	—57,366[5]—		1,695[7]
Nigeria	15	510	6	111	6,000	16	41	500	193	708[17]	129[17]	...	...	2,265
Niue	—	—	—	1	1.0	2.8	...	...	...	0.38[17]	7.9[17]	...	...	...
Norfolk Island	—	—	—	2	1.2	1.6	...	0.4[6]	5.3[6]	0.99[17]	2.1[17]	1,200	...	26
Norway	64	1,882	454	764	1,505	2.8	1,389	1,339.4	3.1	2,579	1.6	—4,621,850[5]—		117,427[7]
Oman	2	16	17	12	80	13	8	47	22	65	20	—126,640[5]—		4,534[7]
Pacific Is., Trust Terr. of the	—	—	—	11	25.9[6]	5.6[6]	5	5.95[6]	24[6]	9.2[4]	15[4]	...	...	...
Marshall Islands	—	—	—	...	...	...	...	...	...	...	...	...	...	...
Micronesia, Fed. States of	—	—	—	...	...	...	...	...	...	...	...	...	...	...
Northern Mariana Islands	—	—	—	...	10.2	2.0	...	...	...	...	...	...	...	...
Palau	—	—	—	...	...	...	...	...	...	...	...	...	...	...
Pakistan	116	1,991	22	75	5,200	19	19	1,143.7	88	511	191	—117,240—		970
Panama	7	132	62	97	295	7.4	12	400	5.5	227	9.4	545,906[17]	637,841[17]	3,382[17]
Papua New Guinea	2	45	13	26	222	15	...	...	...	55	59	35,506[17]	19,013[17]	2,655[17]

post offices, 1983			telegraph, 1983			telex, 1983				country
number	persons per office	pieces of mail handled ('000)	total traffic ('000)	national traffic ('000)	international outgoing traffic ('000)	subscriber lines	traffic ('000 minutes) total	national	international outgoing	
200	2,940	28,272[11]	118	110	8	448	...	1,530[5]	847	Fiji
3,632	1,340	1,098,005	725	634	91	7,500	25,808	11,858	13,950	Finland
17,357[27]	3,202[27]	14,687,400[27]	8,422[4]	6,690[4]	1,732[4]	95,383[4]	371,841[4]	249,218[4]	122,623[4]	France
...	...	...	15[4]	13[4]	2[4]	175[4]	422[4]	341[4]	81[4]	French Guiana
89	1,865	11,862	108	74	24	164	421	7	414	French Polynesia
...	...	13,435[3]	272	146	126	640	2,721	876	1,845	Gabon
...	...	...	28[16]	5[16]	23[16]	67[1]	...	...	100[1]	Gambia, The
...	...	...	...	...	...	...	...	...	...	Gaza Strip
11,956	1,396	1,448,220	12,645	10,487	2,158	15,957		262,087[5]		Germany, East
18,282	3,359	14,898,389	5,990	3,727	2,263	152,826	2,100,677	1,912,169	188,508	Germany, West
237[3]	41,645[3]	103,900[3]	1,760[16]	1,630[16]	130[16]	172[16]	...	...	298[16]	Ghana
3	9,666	3,146	14	5	9	155	333	5	328	Gibraltar
...	...	439,174[3]	3,438	3,153	285	15,178	48,540	29,061	19,479	Greece
...	...	...	...	...	...	...	...	...	...	Greenland
51[3]	2,157[3]	...	...	...	14	44	...	...	108	Grenada
44[3]	7,500[3]	...	50[4]	46[4]	4[4]	427[4]	894[4]	751[4]	143[4]	Guadeloupe
...	...	...	...	...	...	...	...	...	...	Guam
...	...	54,301[25]	...	...	...	...	...	...	...	Guatemala
21	2,666	18,510[9, 10, 11]	2	1	1	244	...	...	...	Guernsey
...	...	30,809[8]	50	21	29	195	...	...	415	Guinea
...	...	...	...	...	...	...	...	...	...	Guinea-Bissau
129	6,165	23,356	237[25]	149[25]	88[25]	64[25]	197[25]	19[25]	178[25]	Guyana
132[3]	33,106[3]	1,046,472[8]	...	...	...	...	...	...	...	Haiti
508[3]	7,264[3]	60,689[3]	836	815	21	1,092	...	...	848	Honduras
137	39,124	489,184	1,198	9	1,189	20,868	60,134	23,739	36,395	Hong Kong
3,214	3,322	1,697,921	11,861	11,422	439	9,761	...	69,746	8,595	Hungary
150	1,586	38,823	587	566	21	320	...	...	1,048	Iceland
142,296	4,815	10,963,596	60,552	58,307	2,245	21,502	...	192,264[5]	17,039	India
12,978	12,115	350,572	7,281[4]	7,142[4]	139[4]	8,105[4]	...	440,683[4, 5]	3,366[4, 14]	Indonesia
3,624	11,608	232,286[11]	26,805[6]	26,726[6]	80[6]	3,125	...	...	4,339	Iran
288	48,995	193,996	...	844[4]	...	1,648	5,675	319	5,356	Iraq
2,096[3]	1,662[3]	482,153[8, 11]	298	232	66	7,000	18,305	6,407	11,898	Ireland
37	1,748	20,467	...	...	...	...	...	...	...	Isle of Man
615[3]	5,870[3]	448,900[8]	...	405	284[1]	4,250	...	22,100[5]	5,850	Israel
14,204	3,993	6,802,378	24,875[28]	23,353[28]	1,522[28]	55,746[28]	278,338[28]	171,031[28]	107,307[28]	Italy
318[4]	7,063[4]	100,409[4]	772[16]	659[16]	113[16]	312[1]	...	...	630[1]	Jamaica
23,368	5,113	16,230,861	44,696	43,306	1,390	57,000	...	111,103[4]	59,053	Japan
24	3,166	34,031	...	...	...	401	661[2]	460[2]	201[2]	Jersey
738	3,380	91,241	...	...	...	...	...	...	...	Jordan
...	...	10,320[22]	...	...	...	...	...	...	...	Kampuchea
756	24,833	214,761[9, 10, 11]	...	1,034	3,452[29]	1,750	...	...	3,065	Kenya
5[3]	10,800[3]	374[26, 30]	34	27	7	21	44	35	9	Kiribati
...	...	...	...	...	...	...	...	...	...	Korea, North
2,180[15]	18,470[15]	1,103,340[19]	10,443	10,289	154	8,000	10,974	3,079	7,895	Korea, South
50	30,320	151,195[9, 10, 11]	621	86	535	3,692	12,513	3,324	9,189	Kuwait
...	...	4,496[3]	22[8]	15[8]	7[8]	15[2]	...	...	40[2]	Laos
...	...	...	...	...	...	...	...	...	...	Lebanon
130	10,707	...	...	...	...	138[1]	...	...	35[1]	Lesotho
38	54,078	6,416[19]	...	...	...	...	...	...	...	Liberia
315	10,609	102,121	...	...	...	...	...	...	...	Libya
12	2,209	13,712[19]	[31]	[31]	[31]	[31]	[31]	[31]	[31]	Liechtenstein
105	3,483	128,404	46[4]	13[4]	33[4]	1,952[4]	9,035[4]	1,789[4]	7,246[4]	Luxembourg
5	70,000	7,924[9]	...	...	36	391	495	34	461	Macau
8,590	1,185	45,033	448[1]	403[1]	45[1]	320[1]	696[1]	162[1]	534[1]	Madagascar
245	25,579	79,959	...	150[3]	1,280[16]	412	...	...	646	Malawi
4,957	2,994	842,149	1,093	820	273	7,980	...	...	9,201[4]	Malaysia
23	6,210	...	29[16]	22[16]	7[16]	75[1]	...	...	53[1]	Maldives
119	53,738	5,466	...	...	...	...	...	...	...	Mali
16[3]	22,500[3]	37,366[3]	75	37	38	747	2,038	175	1,863	Malta
44[3]	7,273[3]	...	49[4]	45[4]	4[4]	371[4]	868[4]	721[4]	147[4]	Martinique
...	...	3,035[3]	42	28	14	214	...	3,560[5]	459	Mauritania
105	9,571	27,130	...	5[1]	46	310	861	61	800	Mauritius
...	...	...	...	...	...	...	...	...	...	Mayotte
13,252[3]	5,087[3]	1,605,316[25]	42,083	41,794	289	23,055	...	171,343[1]	12,715	Mexico
...	...	...	16	8	8	597	...	...	4,254	Monaco
382[3]	3,900[3]	...	...	...	...	...	...	...	...	Mongolia
10[3]	1,000[3]	1,283[8]	4	—	4	26	25	—	25	Montserrat
1,031	19,805	215,170	992	843	149	5,061	3,472[14]	1,910[14]	1,562[14]	Morocco
608	22,989	15,781	...	117[16]	45[4]	558[4]	...	...	1,141[4]	Mozambique
...	...	...	...	...	7[16]	10[16]	...	...	27[16]	Nauru
...	...	...	448	404	83	186	...	...	360	Nepal
2,806	5,129	4,696,500	879	485	394	36,600	...	322,222[5]	82,957	Netherlands, The
...	...	18,733[8, 13]	...	...	978[13]	783[13]	1,784[13]	335[13]	1,450[13]	Netherlands Antilles
269	537	20,397	31	9	23	160	420	16	404	New Caledonia
1,277	2,483	576,010[9, 10, 11, 19]	2,624	2,068	556	4,944	16,932	9,148	7,784	New Zealand
...	...	35,890[22]	25,760[1, 29]	4,230[1, 29]	1,530[1, 29]	391[1]	974[1]	225[1]	749[1]	Nicaragua
159	37,735	5,704	323[1]	278[1]	45[1]	278[4]	...	...	567[4]	Niger
3,167	28,860	1,176,232[9, 11]	...	...	...	...	...	...	...	Nigeria
...	...	...	...	...	...	...	...	...	...	Niue
1	2,000	877	10	—	3	...	...	...	...	Norfolk Island
2,794	1,479	1,483,232	584	453	132	9,195	36,034	17,187	18,847	Norway
87	17,241	37,824[9, 11]	181	10	171	951	3,807	1,066	2,741	Oman
6[3]	...	...	...	...	...	...	...	...	...	Pacific Is., Trust Terr. of the
...	...	...	...	...	...	...	...	...	...	Marshall Islands
...	...	...	...	...	...	...	...	...	...	Micronesia, Fed. States of
...	...	...	...	...	...	...	...	...	...	Northern Mariana Islands
...	...	...	...	...	...	...	...	...	...	Palau
11,528	7,652	759,633[19]	5,150	2,650	2,500	3,530	...	30[4, 14]	1,810[4]	Pakistan
171	10,671	24,026	620	587	33	1,523	...	...	2,597	Panama
114	29,236	35,521	...	40[29]	27	1,119	3,388	1,762	1,626	Papua New Guinea

Communications (continued)

country	daily newspapers (latest)			radio, 1985			television, 1985			telephones, 1984				
	number	total circulation ('000)	circulation per 1,000 population	transmitters (latest)	receivers (all types) ('000)	persons per receiver	transmitters (latest)	receivers (all types) ('000)	persons per receiver	receivers ('000)	persons per receiver	traffic, 1982 ('000 calls): local	traffic, 1982 ('000 calls): long-distance	traffic, 1982 ('000 calls): international
Paraguay	5	198	60	56	241	14	...	82[6]	40[6]	83	39	174,943[17]	16,849[17]	755[17]
Peru	68	...	...	189	2,225	8.9	....	1,370	14	571	34	298,559[17]	16,399[17]	506[17]
Philippines	22	...	...	295	3,550	15	43	2,700	20	812	66	—15,647—		3,528
Pitcairn Island	—	—	—	—	...	...	...	...	...	0.02[4]	2.2[4]	...	...	...
Poland	44	7,902	217	...	9,286.7	4.0	118	8,864.8	4.2	4,028	9.2	—893,201—		665
Portugal	27	680	67	80	2,431.3	4.2	67	1,584	6.4	1,764	5.7	1,795,448[5]	2,407,819[5]	649,424[5]
Puerto Rico	5	580	176	90	2,000	1.6	10	818	4.0	694[17]	4.7[17]	1,135,406	68,538	1,375
Qatar	6	44	150	11	120	2.5	3	150	2.0	80[17]	3.5[17]	...	...	19,992[7]
Réunion	3	62	114	25	122	4.5	...	88	6.2	86[17]	6.1[17]	——206,276[5]——		
Romania	36	4,228	187	71	3,225	7.0	344	3,910	5.8	2,027[1]	11[1]	...	...	...
Rwanda	—	—	—	8	175	35	...	...	...	6.6[17]	864[17]	7,037	26[1, 7]	21[1, 7]
St. Christopher and Nevis	—	—	—	2	21	2.1	...	5	8.8	2.8[17]	16[17]	...	...	76[1]
St. Helena and Ascension	—	—	—	2	3.3	2.1	...	...	...	0.7[4]	6.7[4]	...	...	130
St. Lucia	—	—	—	4	92	1.5	...	...	...	12	11	...	...	585
St. Pierre and Miquelon	—	—	—	4	1.5	4.0	3	3.6	1.7	3.6[17]	1.7[17]	——1,245[5]——		
St. Vincent and the Grenadines	—	—	—	1	55	1.9	...	6	18	7.0	15	—5,980[16]—		120[1]
San Marino	—	—	—	—	8[2]	2.6[2]	...	5[1]	4.3[1]	12	1.9	4,048	1,797	...
São Tomé and Príncipe	—	—	—	5	26	4.1	...	...	...	2.2[17]	46[17]	1,673[17]	139[17]	13[17]
Saudi Arabia	10	638	57	12	2,800	4.0	6	3,700	3.0	1,752	6.2	399,751	124,049	19,297
Senegal	1	31	5	11	350	19	1	52	125	40[2]	142[2]	...	...	6,372[16]
Seychelles	2	3	52	1	18.5	3.5	...	3.5	19	11	5.9	—930—		329[7]
Sierra Leone	1	12	3	3	220	17	2	12	305	16[4]	207[4]	...	...	540[1, 7]
Singapore	12	631	249	21	585.9	4.4	8	478.0	5.4	1,003	2.5	4,013,287	13,321	7,091
Solomon Islands	—	—	—	3	40	6.7	...	...	...	3.0[17]	84[17]	...	...	...
Somalia	1	...	...	4	100	58	...	...	...	4.8[1]	1,086[1]	...	...	...
South Africa	20	1,137	42	...	8,500[32]	3.9[32]	...	2,200[32]	15[32]	3,648	8.8	—10,267,402[5]—		10,710
Bophuthatswana	—	—	—	...	[32]	[32]	...	[32]	[32]	17[17]	85[17]	...	716	...
Ciskei	—	—	—	...	[32]	[32]	...	[32]	[32]	5.5[17]	134[17]	4,344[5]	1,281	...
Transkei	—	—	—	...	[32]	[32]	...	[32]	[32]	...	...	...	...	...
Venda	—	—	—	...	[32]	[32]	...	[32]	[32]	...	...	...	...	...
South West Africa/Namibia	3	20	19	13	200	5.8	...	16	73	63[17]	17[17]	...	29,146[7]	1,017[7]
Spain	113	3,400	89	264	11,365	3.4	1,027	10,105	3.8	13,825	2.8	...	2,231,021	65,260
Sri Lanka	15	850	54	61	3,010	5.3	4	350	45	106[17]	146[17]	2,580[5]	1,020[5]	322
Sudan, The	2	120	5	6	1,340	18	20	125	189	69[17]	319[17]	122,460	999	1,654[7]
Suriname	8	...	...	16	188	2.1	...	44	8.8	28	14	—73,036[5, 6]—		1,381[5, 6]
Swaziland	3	22	34	7	87	7.6	...	7.5	88	16	40	39	262	52
Sweden	169	4,782	574	336	3,330	2.5	438	3,251.4	2.6	7,410[17]	1.1[17]	—20,606,870[5]—		4,275,170[5]
Switzerland	99	3,112	483	215	2,467.7	2.6	825	2,179.8	3.0	5,270	1.2	1,285,336	1,057,811	572,088[7]
Syria	9	176	18	29	1,802	5.7	...	400	26	582	17	547,815	13,892	1,720
Taiwan	31	4,917	259	...	13,500	1.4	...	6,080	3.1	4,357[17]	4.3[17]	8,665,315	7,987	30,278[7]
Tanzania	3	101	5	19	2,000	11	...	11	1,976	100[17]	204[17]	6,850	3,244	496
Thailand	28	...	...	217	7,759.7	6.7	...	3,000[6]	17[6]	733	69	917,075	41,136	1,413
Togo	2	...	...	11	250	12	4	14	213	11[17]	255[17]	4,572[5]	142	95[1]
Tokelau	—	—	—	...	...	...	...	...	...	0.003[4]	525[4]	...	...	...
Tonga	—	—	—	2	66	1.5	...	...	...	3.5[17]	30[17]	10,705[17]	47[17]	146[17]
Trinidad and Tobago	4	176	151	5	350	3.4	6	300	4.0	87[17]	13[17]	2,700[17]	8,200[17]	550[17]
Tunisia	5	250	36	12	1,150	6.2	10	275	26	251	28	—450,935[5]—		349,037[5]
Turkey	364	3,878	89	17	4,320	11	153	5,000	9.9	3,091	16	—4,424,601[5, 17]—		41,355[7, 17]
Turks and Caicos Islands	—	—	—	2	...	...	...	...	...	1.4	5.7	...	...	376[7, 17]
Tuvalu	—	—	—	1	7.5[17]	1.1[17]	...	1.1[17]	7.6[17]	0.12	71	...	...	...
Uganda	1	25	2	13	285	53	...	77	196	53[17]	264[17]	...	...	168
U.S.S.R.	726	32,602	120	...	162,000	1.7	2,882	85,000	3.3	26,667[17]	10[17]	...	1,454,400	2,130
United Arab Emirates	11	272	222	17	240	5.3	10	112	11	313	3.9	...	141,403[7, 17]	89,397[7, 17]
United Kingdom	113	23,472	421	487	45,000	1.3	1,643	18,693.8	3.0	29,518	1.9	17,891,000	3,620,000	149,000
United States	1,668	63,082	267	8,359	480,000	0.5	972	145,000	1.7	161,170[17]	1.5[17]	297,694,793	36,531,644	237,423
Uruguay	20	...	...	94	1,700	1.8	21	500	6.0	338	9.6	586,060	37,896	3,288
Vanuatu	—	—	—	4	16	8.3	...	...	...	3.0[17]	44[17]	2,200[5]	...	66
Venezuela	61	2,739	186	210	5,260	3.3	42	2,880.8	6.0	1,311	13	...	...	69,461[7]
Vietnam	4	500	9	39	6,000	10	...	2,300	26	106	553	—7,528[1]—		41[17]
Virgin Islands (U.S.)	3	17	145	9	85	1.3	3	31	3.6	48[17]	2.2[17]	96,371	3,670	91
Wallis and Futuna	—	—	—	...	...	...	...	...	...	0.22[17]	56[17]	...	15[7, 17]	81[7, 17]
West Bank	—	—	—	...	...	...	...	...	...	...	...	...	...	...
Western Sahara	—	—	—	...	...	...	...	...	...	1.0[4]	140[4]	...	...	...
Western Samoa	—	—	—	6	70	2.3	...	2.5[17]	63.6[17]	7.5[17]	21[17]	...	78	208
Yemen (Aden)	4	25	12	6	150	15	...	39	59	23[17]	86[17]	40	18	71
Yemen (Ṣan'ā')	2	...	...	6	110	60	...	28	234	90[4]	67[4]	...	...	...
Yugoslavia	27	2,419	104	803	4,456.2	5.2	1,040	3,951.1	5.9	3,031	7.6	——20,788,000[5, 17]——		
Zaire	4	45	1.4	22	502	66	...	13	2,542	39	761	115	144	228
Zambia	2	109	16	16	200	33	5	100	67	77	84	...	662	426
Zimbabwe	2	150	19	...	375	22	...	120	69	245	33	247,000[5]	22,596	2,060

post offices, 1983			telegraph, 1983			telex, 1983				country
number	persons per office	pieces of mail handled ('000)	total traffic ('000)	national traffic ('000)	international outgoing traffic ('000)	subscriber lines	traffic ('000 minutes) total	traffic ('000 minutes) national	traffic ('000 minutes) international outgoing	
400	7,582	5,129	275	239	36	693	...	...	989	Paraguay
2,198	7,749	64,574[10, 11]	13,536	13,496	40	2,964	...	84,479[5]	4,818	Peru
2,038[3]	24,303[3]	...	15,732	15,445	287	10,494	14,550	5,211	9,339	Philippines
1	53	...	...	...	...	...	...	...	...	Pitcairn Island
...	...	1,812,347	16,088	15,288	800	27,858	...	...	9,050	Poland
9,571	1,041	476,514	1,469	1,308	161	14,412	57,024	40,066	16,958	Portugal
124[3]	24,677[3]	...	...	...	...	...	...	...	...	Puerto Rico
25	10,000	30,449	149	8	141	1,040	2,585	720	1,865	Qatar
50[3]	10,340[3]	...	37[4]	30[4]	7[4]	317[4]	789[4]	585[4]	204[4]	Réunion
5,046[3]	4,429[3]	795,199[8]	5,393[16]	5,150[16]	243[16]	6,750[1]	...	...	3,683[1]	Romania
...	...	15,964[3]	35[1]	24[1]	11[1]	79[1]	625[1]	522[1]	103[1]	Rwanda
9[3]	5,000[3]	6,381[3]	16[4]	—	16[4]	34[1]	...	...	47[1]	St. Christopher and Nevis
8	750	155	5[4]	—	5[4]	7[4]	24[4, 14]	...	14[4, 14]	St. Helena and Ascension
...	...	3,679[8]	19[4]	—	19[4]	76[2]	...	...	105[2]	St. Lucia
...	...	1,714[8, 11]	2[4]	1[4]	1[4]	33[4]	42[4]	29[4]	13[4]	St. Pierre and Miquelon
48[3]	2,708[3]	...	14[4]	—	14[4]	53[1]	...	...	44[1]	St. Vincent and the Grenadines
8	2,750	...	[28]	[28]	[28]	[28]	[28]	[28]	[28]	San Marino
57	1,684	92	3	—	3	35	54	—	53	São Tomé and Príncipe
437	16,048	495,110	3,219[25]	2,243[25]	976[25]	16,254	...	6,300[14]	23,203	Saudi Arabia
530	11,118	44,391	225[16]	147[16]	78[16]	779	...	...	1,782	Senegal
...	...	1,618[26]	...	—	11	143	251	63	189	Seychelles
113	24,661	27,262	...	20[2]	84[1]	224[1]	373[1]	37[1]	335[1]	Sierra Leone
134	18,780	313,443	377	7	371	14,349	50,111	19,968	30,143	Singapore
99	2,121	5,595	...	...	...	...	...	...	...	Solomon Islands
...	...	...	...	...	...	...	...	...	...	Somalia
2,227[3, 32]	13,529[3, 32]	1,678,751[3, 32]	8,328	8,017	310	27,585	...	261,198[5]	14,829	South Africa
[32]	[32]	[32]	...	...	...	...	...	...	...	Bophuthatswana
[32]	[32]	[32]	...	...	...	...	...	...	...	Ciskei
[32]	[32]	[32]	...	...	...	...	...	...	...	Transkei
[32]	[32]	[32]	...	...	...	...	...	...	...	Venda
81[3]	12,914[3]	...	...	...	...	...	...	...	...	South West Africa/Namibia
12,652	3,019	4,350,027	7,329	6,907	422	31,443	94,823	55,352	39,471	Spain
3,618	4,245	834,257	2,095[4]	1,870[4]	225[4]	968	1,572[14]	201[14]	1,371[14]	Sri Lanka
776	26,500	72,095	1,453[8]	1,263[8]	190[8]	416[8]	...	...	1,038[8]	Sudan, The
...	...	...	59	4	56	195	432	48	384	Suriname
72	8,405	17,267	51[1]	45[1]	6[1]	242[1]	1,006[1]	359[1]	647[1]	Swaziland
2,034	4,097	3,011,999[9, 11]	298	119	178	16,156	...	...	30,617	Sweden
3,813	1,699	4,124,985	1,568[31]	904[31]	664[31]	35,953[31]	139,426[31]	72,385[31]	67,041[31]	Switzerland
516	18,810	39,914	289	151	138	1,803	...	...	1,903	Syria
11,827[3]	1,533[3]	...	...	...	...	...	...	...	...	Taiwan
643	31,679	148,696	794	717	78	1,650	...	...	1,253	Tanzania
4,168	11,879	457,307	8,298	8,160	138	3,910	9,394	3,242	6,152	Thailand
388	6,971	...	50	18	32	285	...	...	524	Togo
...	...	...	...	...	...	...	...	...	...	Tokelau
...	...	1,063[12, 22]	97	77	20	61	35	1	34	Tonga
229	5,126	27,230	...	217[4]	274[3]	267	...	...	1,053	Trinidad and Tobago
597	11,557	194,934	620	412	208	2,111	5,239	1,522	3,717	Tunisia
48,878	967	851,670	1,187	947	240	8,048	...	51,837[33]	10,946	Turkey
...	...	...	1	—	1	55	...	...	65	Turks and Caicos Islands
...	...	2,313[8]	...	...	...	...	...	...	...	Tuvalu
...	...	28,275[24]	57	52	5	419	262[14]	114[14]	148[14]	Uganda
90,723[3]	2,951[3]	5,925,000[3]	541,012[4]	540,110[4]	902[4]	1,446[4]	...	...	8,458[4]	U.S.S.R.
49	25,008	147,973	647	54	593	6,099	20,123	7,325	12,797	United Arab Emirates
22,058[15]	2,556[15]	12,541,390	1,950	—	1,950	92,600	202,007[14]	104,708[14]	97,399[14]	United Kingdom
39,445	5,743	116,312,705[19]	50,983[4]	45,668[4]	5,315[4]	168,347	...	...	188,699	United States
1,277[3]	2,323[3]	35,356[8]	1,409	1,354	55	1,332	2,123	164	1,959	Uruguay
6	20,833	3,000	...	...	8	70	...	...	199	Vanuatu
809[3]	7,215[3]	347,500[23]	5,148[25]	4,570[25]	578[25]	10,356	...	...	7,970	Venezuela
...	—	...	...	5[1]	672	...	...	10[1, 14]	55[14]	Vietnam
5[3]	23,200[3]	...	...	...	...	...	...	...	...	Virgin Islands (U.S.)
6	2,065	252	9	2	7	3	...	...	7	Wallis and Futuna
...	...	...	...	...	...	...	...	...	...	West Bank
...	...	...	...	...	...	...	...	...	...	Western Sahara
...	...	14,589[3]	...	...	...	...	...	...	...	Western Samoa
109	19,311	17,526	...	17[4]	...	149[4]	371[4]	4[4]	366[4]	Yemen (Aden)
141	60,687	15,682	...	...	...	...	...	...	...	Yemen (Şan'ā')
3,729	6,140	836,372	13,088	11,864	1,224	12,000	...	...	13,500	Yugoslavia
362	83,592	...	234[4]	167[4]	67[4]	804[4]	...	...	...	Zaire
232	23,578	69,175	20,340[29]	18,383[29]	1,958[29]	1,379	5,378	3,701	1,677	Zambia
232	32,327	179,720	616	562	55	1,584	72,666[5]	19,324[5]	53,341[5]	Zimbabwe

[1]1981. [2]1980. [3]1978. [4]1982. [5]Number of pulses ('000). [6]1984. [7]Number of minutes ('000). [8]1977. [9]Excludes postcards. [10]Excludes printed matter. [11]Excludes small packets. [12]Foreign received and foreign sent only. [13]Netherlands Antilles includes Aruba. [14]Number of calls ('000). [15]Permanent post offices only. [16]1979. [17]1983. [18]1972. [19]Domestic and foreign sent only. [20]Domestic only. [21]Telegrams to U.S. are included in national. [22]1973. [23]1974. [24]1975. [25]1976. [26]1971. [27]Includes overseas departments. [28]Italy includes San Marino. [29]Number of words ('000). [30]Includes Tuvalu. [31]Switzerland includes Liechtenstein. [32]South Africa includes Bophuthatswana, Ciskei, Transkei, and Venda. [33]Number of metred units ('000).

Trade: external

The following table presents comparative data on the import and export trade of all the countries of the world. The table analyzes data for both imports and exports in two ways: (1) into several major commodity groups defined in accordance with the United Nations system called the Standard International Trade Classification (SITC) and (2) by direction of trade for each country with major world trading blocs and partners. For purposes of this table, several SITC categories have been aggregated so as to accommodate the commodity groupings indicated by the column headings. These groupings are defined by the use of SITC code numbers placed beneath the column headings. The single digit numbers represent broad SITC categories; the double digit numbers represent subcategories of the single digit categories (27 is a subcategory of 2), the three digit is a subcategory of the double digit (667 is a subcategory of 66). The SITC subdivides these categories to finer degrees of detail, but such distinctions cannot be accommodated here. Where a plus or minus sign is used before one of these SITC numbers, the SITC category or subcategory is being added to or subtracted from the aggregate implied by the total of the preceding sections to form a consistently defined commodity group for all countries. The SITC commodity aggregations used here are listed at the end of this headnote. The full SITC commodity breakdown is presented in the United Nations publication *Standard International Trade Classification Revision 2.*

The SITC was developed by the United Nations through its Statistical Commission as an outgrowth of the need for a standard system of aggregating commodities of external trade to provide international comparability of foreign trade statistics. All member nations of the United Nations are urged to use the SITC system as far as possible in reporting their external trade statistics. The United Nations Statistical Commission has defined external merchandise trade as "all goods whose movement into or out of the customs area of a country compiling the statistics adds to or subtracts from the material resources of the country." Goods passing through the country for transport only are excluded. Statistics in this table refer only to goods and exclude purely financial transactions that are covered in the "Finance" and "National product and accounts" tables.

For purposes of comparability of data, total value of imports and exports is given in this table in U.S. dollars; conversions from foreign currencies are determined according to International Monetary Fund (IMF) average rates for the year for which data are supplied. The commodity categories are given in terms of percentages of the total value of the country's import or export trade (with the exclusions noted above). Value, according to the United Nations Statistical Office, is based on transaction value: for imports, the value at which the goods were purchased by the importer plus the cost of transportation and insurance to the frontier of the importing country (c.i.f. [cost, insurance, and freight] valuation); for exports,

Trade: external

country	year	imports												
		total value U.S.$ (000,000)	Standard International Trade Classification (SITC) categories (percent)[a, b]							direction of trade (percent)[a]				
			food and agricultural raw materials (0+1+2 −27−28 +4)	mineral ores and concentrates (27+28 +667)	fuels and other energy (3)	manufactured goods: total[c] (5+6 −667 +7+8 +9)	manufactured goods: of which chemicals and related products (5)	manufactured goods: of which machinery and transport equipment (7)	manufactured goods: of which other[c] (6−667 +8+9)	from European Economic Community (EEC)[d]	from United States	from U.S.S.R. and Eastern Europe[e]	from Japan	from all other[f]
Afghanistan	1982[1]	622.4	16.4	0.5	18.0	65.1	4.5	24.8	35.8	...	1.1	59.7	12.6	26.5
Albania	1982[2]	373.5	...	...	...	...	...	...	...	28.7	4.6	35.6	2.8	28.4
Algeria	1984	10,288.9	23.1	0.3	2.1	74.5	6.7	31.5	36.4	60.7	5.6	3.5	8.1	22.0
American Samoa	1981[3]	115.0	—22.1[4]—		45.0	32.9[5]	3.0	9.1	20.8[5]	...	73.5	...	12.1	14.4
Andorra	1984	232.5[6]	...	...	...	...	...	...	...	...	...	...	...	...
Angola	1979	1,123.0		—36.9[4]—		63.1[5]	2.9	39.2	21.0[5]	45.4[2]	9.1[2]	...	2.9[2]	42.6[2]
Anguilla	...	...	...	...	...	...	...	...	...	...	...	...	...	...
Antigua and Barbuda	1981	110.9	26.4	0.2	1.9	71.5	6.8	32.1	32.6	34.7[7]	34.5[7]	0.5[7]	1.3[7]	29.1[7]
Argentina	1984	4,584.7	9.9	4.1	10.8	75.3	23.1	31.4	20.8	24.6	18.5	2.4	8.2	46.3
Aruba	1984	2,126.2	3.1	—	88.1	8.7	2.3	2.8	3.6	1.9	7.6	—	0.8	89.8
Australia	1985	23,157.8	7.4	1.0	6.9	84.8	8.6	42.7	33.5	22.4	21.6	0.3	23.1	32.6
Austria	1985	20,829.6	10.1	2.6	14.9	72.5	10.0	29.8	32.6	62.1	3.7	10.7	3.3	20.2
Bahamas, The	1983	4,616.3	3.7	—	87.2	9.1	1.6	2.8	4.7	1.8	11.6	—	0.7	86.0
Bahrain	1984	3,523.7	8.2	0.5	52.1	39.2	4.5	17.6	17.1	21.1	7.4	...	9.9	61.5
Bangladesh	1985[3]	2,418.6	29.4	0.7	16.7	53.2	11.4	18.8	23.0	14.4	10.3	4.6	12.1	58.6
Barbados	1984	658.6	—16.6[4]—		16.2	67.2[5]	7.0	35.9	24.3[5]	12.8	48.0	0.1	3.8	35.3
Belgium[8]	1985	55,836.6	14.4	8.7	16.6	60.3	10.2	23.1	27.0	69.8	5.7	3.0	2.1	19.5
Belize	1984	130.2	24.6	0.1	16.7	58.7	8.3	19.9	30.4	20.7[2]	45.0[2]	0.1[2]	2.0[2]	32.2[2]
Benin	1982	464.2	19.0[9]	0.5[9]	9.8[9]	70.6[9]	9.2[9]	26.0[9]	35.4[9]	59.4	5.3	2.4	5.6	27.4
Bermuda	1984	413.4	20.8	0.1	12.3	66.8	8.8	23.2	34.9	15.9	58.1	0.2	5.0	20.9
Bhutan	1983[10]	58.5	...	...	...	...	...	...	...	...	...	...	...	100.0[11]
Bolivia	1984	473.7	—40.5—		0.5	59.0	...	48.5	10.5	18.5	22.0	...	7.5	52.0
Botswana	1984	706.8	20.8	1.9	10.3	67.1	6.8	29.2	31.0	...	1.9	...	0.3	97.8
Brazil	1984	15,208.7	10.9	1.7	52.8	34.6	11.2	15.5	7.9	12.6	16.6	3.2	4.0	63.5
British Virgin Islands	1982	58.5	28.2	0.4	10.6	60.8	4.3	33.0	23.6	7.8	42.9	—	0.1	49.2
Brunei	1984	621.8	21.7	0.6	1.6	76.1	7.8	35.2	33.1	16.2	15.3	—	20.1	48.4
Bulgaria	1984	12,715.1	8.4	—46.9[13]—		44.6[14]	6.1	34.1	4.5[14]	8.4	0.5	76.5	0.6	14.0
Burkina Faso	1983	287.5	27.6	0.8	17.1	54.5	10.0	23.7	20.7	44.9	9.4	0.3	4.3	41.1
Burma	1984[10]	640.7		—19.2—		80.8	...	47.6	...	25.8	...	16.2	33.7	24.3
Burundi	1982	212.9	13.2	2.1	15.3	69.4	7.2	23.6	38.5	46.0	5.4	0.5	7.9	40.3
Cameroon	1982	1,243.2	10.2	2.4	3.7	83.7	13.2	34.8	35.7	67.6	7.6	1.1	6.1	17.6
Canada	1985	76,803.2	7.5	2.1	6.0	84.3	5.8	55.3	23.2	10.3	71.1	0.2	5.8	12.6
Cape Verde	1980	67.8	44.8	—	9.1	46.0	6.6	13.9	25.5	41.7	5.1	0.1	0.4	52.8
Cayman Islands	1981	120.5	21.6	0.2	11.5	66.7	5.1	23.6	37.9	5.4	77.5	—	2.0	15.1
Central African Republic	1980	80.5	21.8	1.7	1.8	74.7	11.8	33.9	29.1	76.5	3.5	0.6	7.2	12.1
Chad	1975	110.0	15.9	0.6	14.2	69.3	16.4	28.8	24.1	59.0	5.7	2.1	1.8	31.4
Chile	1981	6,277.2	13.6	0.9	14.6	70.9	8.5	36.9	25.5	20.4	24.4	0.2	11.7	43.3
China	1985	42,831.6	10.6	1.4[4]	0.4	87.6[5]	10.4	38.9	38.2[5]	14.6	11.9	6.0	35.8	31.7
Christmas Island	...	...	...	...	...	...	...	...	...	...	...	...	...	...
Cocos (Keeling) Islands	...	...	...	...	...	...	...	...	...	...	...	...	...	...
Colombia	1984	4,492.4	13.8	0.9	10.6	74.7	18.0	35.0	21.7	18.2	34.2	1.6	9.6	36.4
Comoros	1976	13.1	—47.1[4]—		13.1	39.8[5]	3.5	17.6	18.8[5]	31.8	—	—	0.5	67.7
Congo	1980	418.2	19.7	0.9	13.9	65.5	10.1	22.5	32.9	65.8	4.4	1.5	3.2	25.1
Cook Islands	1982	20.2	—29.1[4]—		8.4	62.5[5]	6.7	19.1	36.8[5]	6.4[15]	5.0[15]	—[15]	7.6[15]	81.0[15]
Costa Rica	1982	945.2	10.6	0.5	20.0	69.0	20.8	14.6	33.5	11.1	41.0	0.2	4.1	43.7
Côte d'Ivoire	1983	1,813.5	21.1	0.7	18.6	59.6	10.4	24.7	24.5	55.0	4.0	0.8	4.5	35.7
Cuba	1982	6,616.9	18.5	0.4[4]	27.2	54.0[5]	5.4	31.6	17.0[5]	5.6	—	84.1	2.5	7.8
Cyprus	1985	1,250.7	16.3	0.5	18.0	65.2	7.5	26.2	31.6	60.5	4.5	5.1	8.9	21.0
Czechoslovakia	1984	17,077.6	11.8	3.7	31.0	53.5	6.5	31.9	15.1	8.7	0.3	75.1	0.4	15.5
Denmark	1985	17,993.0	14.4	0.6	17.3	67.6	10.5	26.5	30.6	49.1	5.3	3.7	4.0	37.9
Djibouti	1983	221.2	42.8	1.1	9.4	46.7	5.1	22.5	19.1	42.1[2]	2.3[2]	—[2]	7.6[2]	48.0[2]
Dominica	1985	55.3	28.0	0.2	10.9	60.9	11.4	22.5	27.0	23.4	24.5	0.1	7.4	44.7
Dominican Republic	1983	1,279.0	16.6	0.2	36.2	46.9	12.5	16.9	17.5	11.3	36.4	—	4.3	48.0
Ecuador	1982	1,758.4	7.7	0.7	1.6	90.0	19.2	42.9	27.9	21.1	37.4	0.9	13.6	27.0
Egypt	1982	9,077.9	35.4	0.3	4.1	60.2	7.8	29.4	23.0	42.1	19.0	7.6	4.5	26.7

the value at which the goods were sold by the exporter, including the cost of transportation and insurance to bring the goods onto the transporting vehicle at the frontier of the exporting country (f.o.b. [free on board] valuation).

Ideally, the data assembled here should be derived from a single source, thus providing a set of statistics based on a common value system that would permit comparative analysis. It is not possible, however, to gather all such information from a single source; the largest part of the information presented here comes from the United Nations' *Commodity Trade Statistics* (including microfiche format) and the *International Trade Statistics Yearbook*. These sources, however, do not always provide the most recent data and do not cover some countries listed in this table. Data for such countries as Albania, Botswana, China, Liechtenstein, and many small, nonindependent countries were obtained from other sources. In some cases information was unavailable, as noted.

... Not available.
— None, less than 0.05%, or not applicable.
a. Detail may not add to 100.0 or indicated subtotals because of rounding.
b. SITC category codes:
  0 - food and live animals, chiefly for food.
  1 - beverages and tobacco.
  2 - crude materials, inedible, except fuels.
    27 - crude natural fertilizers (organic and inorganic) and nonmetallic minerals (excluding coal, petroleum, and precious stones).
    28 - metalliferous ores and metal scrap.
  3 - mineral fuels, lubricants, and related materials (including coal, petroleum, and hydrocarbon products).
  4 - animal and vegetable oils, fats, and waxes.
  5 - chemicals and related products not specified elsewhere.
  6 - manufactured goods classified chiefly by material.
    667 - pearls, precious and semiprecious stones, worked or unworked.
  7 - machinery and transport equipment.
  8 - miscellaneous manufactured articles.
  9 - commodities and transactions not specified elsewhere.
c. Also includes any unallocated commodities.
d. EEC of twelve countries (Belgium, Denmark, France, West Germany, Greece, Ireland, Italy, Luxembourg, The Netherlands, Portugal, Spain, and the United Kingdom).
e. Includes Albania, Bulgaria, Czechoslovakia, East Germany, Hungary, Poland, Romania, and the U.S.S.R.
f. Percentages in these columns may include value of trade shown as not available (...) in any of the four preceding columns.

exports													country
total value U.S.$ (000,000)	Standard International Trade Classification (SITC) categories (percent)[a, b]							direction of trade (percent)[a]					
	food and agricultural raw materials (0 + 1 + 2 − 27 − 28 + 4)	mineral ores and concentrates (27 + 28 + 667)	fuels and other energy (3)	manufactured goods				to European Economic Community (EEC)[d]	to United States	to U.S.S.R. and Eastern Europe[e]	to Japan	to all other[f]	
				total[c] (5 + 6 − 667 + 7 + 8 + 9)	of which chemicals and related products (5)	of which machinery and transport equipment (7)	of which other[c] (6 − 667 + 8 + 9)						
694.3	44.4	—	39.3	16.3	1.7	—	14.6	...	1.4	61.9	0.1	36.6	Afghanistan
350.7	...	...	...	...	...	...	...	31.2	0.8	35.7	1.1	31.2	Albania
11,885.7	0.4	0.4	97.6	1.7	1.0	—	0.6	69.3	21.7	1.1	0.7	7.3	Algeria
199.1	99.8	—	—	0.2	—	—	0.2	...	99.6	...	0.1	0.3	American Samoa
9.6[6]	...	...	...	...	...	...	...	...	...	...	...	...	Andorra
1,102.0	14.9	10.7	74.0	0.4	...	...	0.4	13.5[2]	40.1[2]	...	4.9[2]	41.5[2]	Angola
...	...	...	...	...	...	...	...	...	...	...	...	...	Anguilla
34.2	3.4	—	—	96.5	3.2	33.2	60.2	7.9[7]	35.1[7]	—[7]	1.8[7]	55.2[7]	Antigua and Barbuda
8,107.4	77.1	0.2	4.3	18.5	4.0	4.7	9.8	27.6	10.8	18.2	3.3	40.1	Argentina
2,088.6	0.2	0.7	98.9	0.3	0.1	0.1	—	7.9	63.4	—	—	28.6	Aruba
22,766.0	35.5	16.1	25.8	22.7	1.7	4.8	16.1	12.7	8.1	3.4	25.9	49.9	Australia
17,107.7	8.8	0.9	2.1	88.2	9.1	31.3	47.7	56.1	4.7	11.1	0.9	27.2	Austria
3,970.3	0.8	0.3	93.5	5.4	4.7	0.6	0.2	4.5	87.4	—	0.4	7.7	Bahamas, The
3,138.6	0.1	0.1	90.7	9.0	0.1	0.5	8.4	1.4	9.7	...	11.8	77.0	Bahrain
997.8	32.2	—	2.1	65.8	0.2	1.1	64.5	22.0	18.9	6.5	6.8	45.8	Bangladesh
391.5	—12.9[4]—		18.8	68.3[5]	4.8	47.0	16.6[5]	8.3	52.8	—	—	38.9	Barbados
53,281.1	12.0	6.9	6.6	74.5	12.8	23.2	38.4	70.4	6.3	2.0	0.8	20.5	Belgium[8]
93.2	65.5	—	3.1	31.4	1.6	5.3	24.5	21.2	49.7	—	0.1	29.0	Belize
23.9	77.2[9]	0.0[9]	4.9[9]	17.9[9]	0.3[9]	5.6[9]	12.1[9]	58.8	...	...	12.4	28.8	Benin
40.5	0.9	—	—	98.7	56.9	20.4	21.4	43.7	24.7	—	—	31.6	Bermuda
16.7	...	...	...	...	...	...	...	...	...	...	...	100.0[12]	Bhutan
782.1	...	46.5	49.7	...	...	...	...	23.3	18.4	...	1.1	57.2	Bolivia
673.9	10.2	80.2	—	9.5	0.5	2.3	6.7	...	8.2	...	0.1	91.8	Botswana
27,005.0	51.9	5.8	15.4	26.9	2.8	6.3	17.8	19.0	48.8	3.1	5.1	24.0	Brazil
1.2	78.1	2.7	1.5	17.7	0.1	10.2	7.4	4.6	57.4	—	—	38.0	British Virgin Islands
3,196.8	0.2	—	98.8	1.0	0.1	0.5	0.5	2.3	5.5	—	68.4	23.7	Brunei
12,858.7	22.3	—10.8[13]—		66.9[14]	6.5	47.7	12.7[14]	6.4	0.3	72.4	0.3	20.7	Bulgaria
57.0	89.4	0.1	—	10.5	0.1	4.1	6.3	28.8	0.1	—	4.3	66.8	Burkina Faso
421.5	81.6	14.7	—	3.7	...	...	...	12.3	...	—	6.7	81.1	Burma
87.6	97.5	—	—	2.5	—	—	2.5	33.0	32.0	—	2.7	32.4	Burundi
1,028.9	43.8	—	47.0	9.2	1.3	0.9	7.0	47.6	40.1	0.4	1.2	10.7	Cameroon
87,302.8	17.2	4.7	14.0	64.2	4.6	39.2	20.4	6.3	78.2	1.6	4.6	9.3	Canada
4.2	85.4	9.1	0.3	5.2	1.0	0.6	3.6	72.8	—	—	—	27.2	Cape Verde
0.8	2.1	2.2	—	95.8	94.1	0.5	1.2	—	100.0	—	—	—	Cayman Islands
115.4	71.2	25.0	—	3.8	—	—	3.8	79.4	4.3	0.7	0.1	15.5	Central African Republic
40.0	83.1	0.8	7.9	8.2	0.5	5.4	2.3	6.5	0.3	—	—	93.3	Chad
3,744.8	27.2	17.5	1.8	53.5	2.2	2.6	48.7	36.0	14.4	0.5	10.9	38.2	Chile
27,558.7	22.8	1.8[4]	25.9	49.5[5]	5.0	2.8	41.7[5]	8.3	8.6	7.6	22.2	53.4	China
...	...	...	...	...	...	...	...	...	...	...	...	...	Christmas Island
...	...	...	...	...	...	...	...	...	...	...	...	...	Cocos (Keeling) Islands
3,483.1	67.2	0.8	14.9	17.1	3.0	0.9	13.1	37.5	31.5	2.1	4.4	24.5	Colombia
9.3	64.1	—	5.6	30.3	29.5	—	0.8	71.1	15.2	—	0.1	13.6	Comoros
955.3	3.6	4.1	89.6	2.7	—	0.2	2.6	63.1	12.7	0.1	0.1	24.0	Congo
3.7	50.5	—	—	49.5	...	...	...	...	1.9	...	2.1	96.0	Cook Islands
876.8	70.6	—	0.9	28.5	7.2	4.2	17.1	26.4	33.7	3.0	0.7	36.2	Costa Rica
2,067.7	77.0	0.1	11.5	11.4	2.2	2.3	7.0	55.6	12.4	3.0	2.6	26.3	Côte d'Ivoire
5,902.8	84.8	6.3[4]	6.8	2.0[5]	...	...	...	5.1	—	78.0	1.4	15.5	Cuba
476.8	33.1	2.4	8.1	56.4	5.2	10.8	40.3	28.2	2.2	5.5	0.1	64.0	Cyprus
17,151.7	6.0	0.3	4.6	89.0	5.8	53.1	30.2	9.7	0.4	69.1	0.3	20.5	Czechoslovakia
16,476.0	34.8	0.7	5.5	59.0	8.7	24.4	25.9	43.4	10.1	1.8	3.0	41.7	Denmark
10.8	6.1[16]	—[16]	...[16]	93.9[16]	0.1[16]	1.4[16]	92.5[16]	16.6[2]	—[2]	—[2]	—[2]	83.4[2]	Djibouti
28.4	59.8	—	—	40.1	28.6	5.4	6.1	50.4	3.4	—	—	46.2	Dominica
648.3	75.7	0.3	—	24.1	4.0	4.5	15.6	13.9	66.5	6.7	2.3	10.5	Dominican Republic
2,290.8	32.7	—	64.3	3.1	0.3	0.8	2.0	4.0	43.1	1.1	0.7	51.0	Ecuador
3,120.2	21.8	—	66.3	11.9	1.2	—	10.7	46.2	4.7	12.6	2.5	33.9	Egypt

Trade: external (continued)

country	year	imports												
		total value U.S.$ (000,000)	Standard International Trade Classification (SITC) categories (percent)[a, b]							direction of trade (percent)[a]				
			food and agricultural raw materials (0 + 1 + 2 − 27 − 28 + 4)	mineral ores and concentrates (27 + 28 + 667)	fuels and other energy (3)	manufactured goods				from European Economic Community (EEC)[d]	from United States	from U.S.S.R. and Eastern Europe[e]	from Japan	from all other[f]
						total[c] (5 + 6 − 667 + 7 + 8 + 9)	of which chemicals and related products (5)	of which machinery and transport equipment (7)	of which other[c] (6 − 667 + 8 + 9)					
El Salvador	1983	963.5	19.2	0.6	22.6	57.6	20.7	12.0	24.9	10.9	29.4	0.1	3.2	56.4
Equatorial Guinea	1981	43.2	...	...	22.4	...	...	17.4	...	92.3[2]	1.6[2]	—[2]	—[2]	6.1[2]
Ethiopia	1982	784.9	12.9	—	24.6	62.5	10.7	31.6	20.2	37.4	3.9	31.5	9.0	18.2
Faeroe Islands	1985	248.1	12.9	0.8	17.7	68.6	4.1	37.8	26.7	57.5	1.3	0.7	3.4	37.1
Falkland Islands	1975	3.4	30.9	—	2.6	64.4	5.7	14.4	44.3	88.5	—	0.1	3.3	8.1
Fiji	1983	483.9	18.7	0.3	23.3	57.7	7.9	18.9	30.9	8.2	3.9	0.1	16.8	71.1
Finland	1985	13,134.5	9.2	2.5	24.3	63.9	9.7	29.8	24.4	38.7	5.4	23.9	5.3	26.7
France[17]	1985	107,781.9	14.2	1.8	22.4	61.7	10.0	24.9	26.8	55.8	7.6	3.5	2.8	30.3
French Guiana	1985	256.3	24.8	0.1	15.2	59.8	6.0	29.5	24.4	70.1	4.9	0.2	4.1	20.8
French Polynesia	1983	538.3	21.4	0.3	11.9	66.3	5.3	30.1	30.9	57.9	15.8	0.1	4.3	21.9
Gabon	1983	685.6	18.5	1.0	1.8	78.8	7.5	38.5	32.7	74.6	11.0	0.4	7.4	6.6
Gambia, The	1983[3]	115.4	—34.5[4]—		12.2	53.3[5]	6.9	14.4	32.0[5]	46.7[2]	5.4[2]	6.6[2]	4.1[2]	37.1[2]
Gaza Strip	1984	279.4	...	...	...	...	...	...	...	...	...	...	...	100.0[18]
Germany, East	1984	22,939.7		—59.3—		40.7	...	26.0	...	15.1[20]	0.4[20]	61.5[20]	0.9[20]	22.1[20]
Germany, West[21]	1985	158,360.8	15.5	2.6	19.8	62.0	8.9	22.9	30.2	50.9	6.9	5.1	4.5	32.6
Ghana	1980	1,128.6	11.4	0.6	26.7	61.4	15.6	29.7	16.1	41.6	12.1	1.4	3.8	41.1
Gibraltar	1984	88.3	—27.1—		32.0	40.9	...	...	...	76.0[22]	4.4[22]	...[22]	7.3[22]	12.3[22]
Greece	1985	10,163.7	17.2	1.0	29.5	52.4	8.6	23.6	20.2	48.1	3.1	7.7	6.4	34.7
Greenland	1985	295.3	19.5	0.4	16.8	63.2	3.5	27.2	32.5	69.7	3.6	0.3	3.7	22.6
Grenada	1982	56.5	—35.5[4]—		13.3	51.2[5]	10.0	14.8	26.4[5]	23.3	20.2	0.9	4.6	50.9
Guadeloupe	1985	646.5	24.8	0.2	14.2	60.8	8.5	22.5	29.9	72.1	3.5	0.2	2.3	21.9
Guam	1983	610.7	16.9	0.1	46.9	36.2	2.3	19.1	14.8	...	23.4	...	19.9	56.6
Guatemala	1981	2,009.3	7.8	0.4	37.8	54.0	15.9	16.0	22.1	12.1	27.4	0.2	5.6	54.7
Guernsey[24]	...	...	...	...	...	...	...	...	...	...	...	...	...	...
Guinea	1980	204.4	—10.0—		30.3	59.7	3.0	39.8	16.9	71.0[2]	10.2[2]	5.8[2]	1.7[2]	11.3[2]
Guinea-Bissau	1980	55.5	20.1	2.2	6.2	71.5	5.6	36.4	29.5	59.6	0.5	7.6	0.5	31.7
Guyana	1980	395.9	15.3	0.5	27.6	56.7	7.6	25.9	23.2	28.3	25.3	1.1	2.1	43.1
Haiti	1979[25]	266.1	26.2	0.3	13.0	60.5	9.0	19.9	31.6	14.1	46.1	0.8	8.0	31.0
Honduras	1982	689.9	10.6	0.3	21.8	67.3	18.3	20.3	28.7	11.5	39.6	0.3	6.6	42.0
Hong Kong	1985	31,428.2	13.3	2.4	4.4	79.9	6.6	24.2	49.1	10.9	8.9	0.4	21.8	58.0
Hungary	1984	8,089.6	12.7	1.9[4]	22.5	62.9[5]	13.7	26.0	23.2[5]	20.4	2.5	48.2	1.1	27.8
Iceland	1984	843.7	13.8	4.3	15.8	66.1	7.8	26.9	31.4	51.1	6.8	11.1	4.6	26.4
India	1982[10]	15,239.7	13.1	6.2	38.4	42.3	9.7	14.6	18.0	23.1	10.4	11.1	6.5	48.8
Indonesia	1984	13,882.1	10.4	1.4	19.5	68.8	15.4	36.3	17.1	15.4	18.5	0.7	23.8	41.6
Iran	1977	14,447.6	15.4	0.4	—	83.9	7.2	44.3	32.5	44.3	16.2	5.4	16.1	18.0
Iraq	1978	4,212.6	13.8	0.4	—	85.5	4.7	53.6	27.1	37.2	10.1	8.6	20.9	23.2
Ireland	1985	10,055.0	14.2	1.2	11.9	72.7	11.7	31.2	29.7	66.3	17.0	1.5	3.5	11.7
Isle of Man[24]	...	...	...	...	...	...	...	...	...	...	...	...	...	...
Israel	1984	8,410.9	13.0	12.6	17.3	57.1	7.4	27.7	22.0	42.4	21.1	0.7	2.3	33.5
Italy[26]	1985	90,961.5	20.1	2.6	26.3	51.0	9.4	20.1	21.6	47.1	6.0	5.5	1.6	39.8
Jamaica	1985	1,143.6	19.5	0.2	32.9	47.4	9.2	17.9	20.3	10.4	41.4	0.3	7.1	40.8
Japan	1985	127,512.1	21.0	6.3	43.8	28.8	6.2	8.3	14.3	6.9	20.3	1.2	—	71.5
Jersey	1980	537.1	23.9	0.4	9.3	66.5	6.5	24.8	35.2	...	...	...	...	100.0[27]
Jordan	1984	2,785.8	20.8	0.9	20.0	58.3	7.4	20.1	30.8	31.3	11.1	4.2	7.4	45.9
Kampuchea	...	...	...	...	...	...	...	...	...	...	...	...	...	...
Kenya	1983	1,360.6	11.8	0.6	36.8	50.7	14.0	22.6	14.2	33.3	6.3	0.3	9.5	50.7
Kiribati	1983	17.7	34.4	0.4	12.9	52.4	4.2	22.7	25.5	3.6	6.5	—	18.2	71.7
Korea, North	1984	1,626.0[2]	...	...	...	...	...	...	...	3.7[2]	...	31.7[2]	17.2[2]	47.4[2]
Korea, South	1984	30,631.5	15.3	3.6	24.0	57.2	8.8	32.0	16.3	9.1	22.4	—	24.9	43.6
Kuwait	1982	8,283.4	14.5	0.6	0.6	84.2	3.6	43.6	37.0	36.2	12.7	1.3	24.1	25.7
Laos	1974	64.8	32.1	0.2	11.2	56.4	6.1	25.7	24.7	17.9	4.7	—	18.8	58.6
Lebanon	1977	1,973.2	21.0	7.0	6.6	65.5	4.6	21.1	39.8	50.9	8.1	7.3	3.0	30.6
Lesotho	1981	504.9	25.1	0.8[4]	9.6	64.5[5]	6.4	17.0	41.1[5]	1.5	0.2	—	—	98.2[30]
Liberia	1983	411.6	26.4	1.1	17.4	55.1	4.9	26.5	23.7	36.6	24.6	0.4	8.0	30.3
Libya	1981	8,381.7	19.4	0.3	1.0	79.3	4.5	38.2	36.7	64.8	6.3	4.6	7.6	16.7
Liechtenstein	1984	185.1	6.3	0.3[4]	0.4	93.1[5]	5.0	33.7	54.4[5]	...	...	...	...	...
Luxembourg	1984	2,770.0	13.4	3.8[4]	13.6	69.1[5]	14.1	20.6	34.5[5]	90.0	2.9	...	0.3	6.8
Macau	1984	792.9	20.3	1.6	6.0	72.0	4.2	10.6	57.2	5.0	7.0	0.3	10.0	77.7
Madagascar	1982	439.0	18.5	0.3	24.4	56.8	11.9	29.5	15.4	49.0	6.2	2.5	5.7	36.6
Malaŵi	1981	350.1	11.8	0.8	16.9	70.5	17.1	24.3	29.1	33.5	4.3	—	6.3	56.0
Malaysia	1984	14,049.3	12.9	1.6	10.1	75.4	8.0	45.9	21.4	13.6	16.3	0.6	26.3	43.3
Maldives	1983	56.9	34.2	2.5	19.7	43.6	7.1	16.7	19.8	5.6[2]	—[2]	—[2]	13.0[2]	81.4[2]
Mali	1979	304.5	16.5	0.4	16.4	66.7	4.0	44.5	18.1	51.4	2.6	3.4	1.2	41.5
Malta	1985	757.3	17.7	0.8	12.0	69.5	7.2	24.1	38.2	77.4	5.7	3.3	1.2	12.4
Martinique	1985	682.5	23.2	0.2	17.3	59.3	9.4	20.2	29.7	70.0	2.7	0.2	2.1	25.1
Mauritania	1980	285.7	33.6	...	11.9	54.5	...	21.9	32.6	56.2[2]	7.1[2]	...	1.0[2]	35.7[2]
Mauritius	1983	442.0	28.9	1.3	18.8	50.9	7.8	12.1	31.1	31.3	2.9	0.1	4.8	60.8
Mayotte	1985	21.8	26.6	...	11.9	...	...	...	...	...	...	...	...	100.0[31]
Mexico[7]	1983	7,778.2	30.1	1.9	3.2	64.9	15.3	32.9	16.7	17.8	63.7	0.2	4.6	13.6
Monaco[17]	...	...	...	...	...	...	...	...	...	...	...	...	...	...
Mongolia	1983	1,438.7	10.3	—29.6[13]—		60.1[14]	5.7	35.5	18.9[14]	...	...	97.6	...	2.4
Montserrat	1981	18.9	28.5	0.6	11.9	59.0	7.3	18.8	32.9	25.1	26.0	0.1	5.5	43.3
Morocco	1984	3,906.7	25.6	4.4	26.1	43.8	7.3	19.7	16.8	42.6	12.5	6.6	3.1	35.2
Mozambique	1977	277.7	15.5	13.9[13]	3.7	66.7[14]	8.1	35.6	23.0[14]	41.7	3.8	0.9	5.3	48.3
Nauru	1981[3]	17.3	—34.4[4, 33]—		1.9[33]	63.8[5, 33]	5.3[33]	14.8[33]	43.7[5, 33]	...	...	...	...	...
Nepal	1984[3]	436.6	17.0	0.4	12.6	70.0	10.6	19.1	40.3	5.9	1.9	1.3	9.6	81.3
Netherlands, The	1985	64,872.5	17.2	2.2	22.3	58.3	10.1	23.0	25.2	58.2	8.3	4.7	2.4	26.4
Netherlands Antilles[34]	1984	1,898.2	5.5	0.1	81.8	12.6	2.3	3.7	6.7	6.2	9.5	0.1	1.0	83.3
New Caledonia	1983	303.4	23.7	0.2	23.1	53.0	6.0	20.6	26.4	48.0	10.2	0.1	5.6	36.1
New Zealand	1985	5,998.3	7.6	3.5	12.7	76.1	11.8	35.7	28.7	22.1	16.0	0.2	20.5	41.1
Nicaragua	1982	774.9	12.6	0.3	23.2	63.9	15.8	23.2	24.9	17.0	19.0	7.6	2.4	54.0
Niger	1981	509.7	24.8	1.9	14.8	58.4	6.9	25.7	25.8	48.0	3.7	0.4	2.5	45.4
Nigeria	1984	5,868.0	24.1	1.4	1.2	73.4	14.6	35.8	22.9	55.2	12.7	3.4	8.2	20.6
Niue	1983	2.1	42.0	0.1	21.4	36.5	5.6	12.8	18.2	0.3	1.2	—	4.3	94.2[35]
Norfolk Island	1984[3]	14.5	17.1	0.1	11.0	71.8	4.3	12.4	55.2	...	...	...	...	...

exports: total value U.S.$ (000,000)	Standard International Trade Classification (SITC) categories (percent)[a, b]: food and agricultural raw materials (0 + 1 + 2 − 27 − 28 + 4)	mineral ores and concentrates (27 + 28 + 667)	fuels and other energy (3)	manufactured goods: total[c] (5 + 6 − 667 + 7 + 8 + 9)	of which chemicals and related products (5)	of which machinery and transport equipment (7)	of which other[c] (6 − 667 + 8 + 9)	direction of trade (percent)[a]: to European Economic Community (EEC)[d]	to United States	to U.S.S.R. and Eastern Europe[e]	to Japan	to all other[f]	country
468.4	61.6	0.4	2.6	35.4	7.9	2.6	24.9	15.7	28.0	4.1	6.1	46.0	El Salvador
13.6	98.7	—	—	1.3	—	—	1.3	96.5[2]	0.7[2]	—[2]	—[2]	2.7[2]	Equatorial Guinea
404.4	91.4	—	7.6	0.9	0.4	—	0.6	32.3	25.8	3.4	7.4	31.0	Ethiopia
179.1	96.5	—	—	3.5	—	3.5	0.1	74.5	16.9	0.2	1.1	7.2	Faeroe Islands
2.6	100.0	—	—	—	—	—	—	100.0	—	—	—	—	Falkland Islands
239.7	62.6	0.1	19.1	18.2	0.8	3.5	13.9	29.4	8.5	—	2.4	59.7	Fiji
13,556.6	15.2	0.4	4.3	80.1	5.8	25.1	49.1	37.0	6.3	23.4	1.5	31.8	Finland
97,664.1	18.5	1.5	4.0	76.1	14.0	32.8	29.2	53.7	8.7	3.0	1.2	33.4	France[17]
36.7	73.9	0.2	—	25.9	1.1	8.4	16.4	23.0	37.7	—	16.7	22.6	French Guiana
41.2	14.4	15.2	—	70.4	2.4	17.2	50.7	70.4	12.6	—	4.9	12.1	French Polynesia
1,475.4	7.5	7.0	79.5	6.0	1.2	0.6	4.1	54.6	25.6	1.8	0.3	17.6	Gabon
48.5	78.0[15]	—[15]	—[15]	22.0[15]	—[15]	—[15]	22.0[15]	55.2[2]	0.2[2]	—[2]	—[2]	44.6[2]	Gambia, The
114.9	...	...	...	...	...	...	...	...	...	...	...	100.0[19]	Gaza Strip
24,835.7	25.8			74.2	...	46.9	...	...[20]	...[20]	...[20]	...[20]	...[20]	Germany, East
183,832.7	6.5	0.8	2.8	89.9	13.2	46.0	30.7	49.8	10.4	4.0	1.5	34.4	Germany, West[21]
951.5	81.1	2.3	0.4	16.1	0.2	0.1	15.8	52.2	9.9	17.7	9.3	10.9	Ghana
33.5	12.7		75.0	12.4	2.9	1.3	8.1	...	...	...	...	...	Gibraltar
4,536.4	31.2	4.2	12.0	52.6	4.0	2.9	45.6	54.2	8.1	7.2	0.9	29.4	Greece
172.4	77.8	18.2	1.6	2.4	—	1.7	0.7	92.7	1.7	—	—	5.6	Greenland
18.6	84.5[23]	—[23]	—[23]	15.5[23]	—[23]	—[23]	15.5[23]	57.5[23]	2.4[23]	3.9[23]	—[23]	36.2[23]	Grenada
74.8	75.1	0.6	1.3	23.0	4.0	13.2	5.8	65.5	2.5	—	—	32.0	Guadeloupe
39.2	23.5	2.7	3.5	70.3	5.6	11.5	53.2	...	24.9	...	4.8	70.4	Guam
1,114.8	68.8	—	2.0	29.2	11.1	1.8	16.3	17.0	26.4	0.5	4.5	51.7	Guatemala
...	...	...	...	...	...	...	...	...	...	...	...	...	Guernsey[24]
466.7	3.0	96.8	—	0.2	—	—	0.2	45.4[2]	23.5[2]	21.4[2]	—[2]	9.6[2]	Guinea
11.4	87.1	0.3	—	12.6	0.3	—	12.3	57.0	—	—	—	43.0	Guinea-Bissau
389.3	46.8	48.4	—	4.8	1.0	1.7	2.1	37.0	23.9	1.5	2.8	34.8	Guyana
148.4	36.6	12.2	—	51.2	5.0	7.2	39.0	27.3	66.1	—	0.3	6.3	Haiti
655.7	87.2	3.9	0.1	8.8	3.2	0.1	5.5	24.6	52.8	0.1	5.9	16.6	Honduras
30,249.6	6.1	1.6	0.5	91.8	3.9	25.4	62.4	12.4	30.7	0.4	4.2	52.3	Hong Kong
8,560.3	24.7	1.1[4]	8.6	65.6[5]	10.9	30.1	24.6[5]	16.6	2.7	48.5	0.4	31.9	Hungary
744.2	71.4	1.1	—	27.5	0.2	2.3	25.0	47.1	28.4	9.5	3.8	11.3	Iceland
8,742.2	31.9	15.6	2.9	49.6	4.8	7.9	36.8	18.5	11.8	25.3	8.8	35.6	India
21,887.8	14.0	1.4	73.3	11.4	0.8	1.0	9.6	5.0	20.6	0.7	47.3	26.4	Indonesia
25,943.0	1.6	—	97.6	0.8	—	—	0.8	0.6	0.3	0.7	—	98.4	Iran
11,063.9	0.6	—	98.6	0.3	0.3	—	—	54.7[2]	2.2[2]	0.2[2]	6.4[2]	36.4[2]	Iraq
10,400.9	27.0	2.6	1.3	69.1	14.0	29.7	25.4	69.1	9.8	0.6	1.6	18.9	Ireland
...	...	...	...	...	...	...	...	...	...	...	...	...	Isle of Man[24]
5,803.7	15.8	23.2	0.2	60.9	15.3	17.6	28.0	34.2	28.2	0.7	3.3	33.6	Israel
78,956.6	8.7	0.5	4.7	86.2	8.4	31.4	46.4	48.3	12.3	3.4	1.2	34.9	Italy[26]
568.6	25.1	51.7	4.8	18.4	3.2	5.4	9.8	23.9	33.2	5.3	1.3	36.3	Jamaica
175,594.4	1.4	0.2	0.3	98.0	4.3	67.9	25.9	11.9	37.6	1.9	—	48.6	Japan
209.2	27.6	4.3[28]	—	68.0	1.2	31.1	35.7	...	...	...	...	100.0[29]	Jersey
754.7	18.0	29.6	—	52.3	23.4	7.9	21.0	6.9	1.4	6.3	2.1	83.3	Jordan
...	...	...	...	...	...	...	...	...	...	...	...	...	Kampuchea
984.2	64.1	2.1	20.9	12.9	3.3	1.7	7.9	39.4	6.0	0.7	0.7	53.2	Kenya
3.6	91.9	—	—	8.1	—	—	8.1	38.7	11.8	—	6.0	43.6	Kiribati
1,319.0[2]	...	...	...	...	...	...	...	11.2[2]	...	40.3[2]	9.9[2]	38.6[2]	Korea, North
29,250.9	5.2	0.3	2.9	91.6	2.9	35.7	53.0	11.3	36.0	—	15.8	37.0	Korea, South
10,861.3	1.6	0.2	75.6	22.6	8.4	6.5	7.7	18.8	0.3	—	14.2	66.6	Kuwait
11.3	84.0	11.9	—	4.1	—	—	4.1	0.3	—	—	3.7	96.0	Laos
395.4	20.1	0.5	—	79.2	9.6	11.4	58.2	6.8	3.4	0.5	0.1	89.2	Lebanon
49.6	28.8	42.6	0.1	28.5	0.9	3.3	24.3	10.3	0.1	—	—	89.6	Lesotho
422.6	31.0	67.5	0.1	1.4	0.2	0.4	0.9	74.7	18.0	0.1	1.5	5.7	Liberia
15,571.1	—	—	99.6	0.4	0.4	—	—	52.7	27.4	4.4	2.1	13.3	Libya
451.3	0.3	—[4]	0.2	99.5[5]	7.8	47.2	44.4[5]	35.3	...	...	...	64.7	Liechtenstein
2,519.0	6.2	1.5[4]	0.4	91.9[5]	16.8	13.3	61.7[5]	74.4	5.8	...	0.1	19.7	Luxembourg
907.1	2.5	0.2	—	97.3	0.7	5.1	91.5	34.5	30.4	0.4	1.5	33.2	Macau
329.5	80.8	4.3	7.7	7.1	1.1	1.1	4.9	40.2	14.7	4.2	6.4	34.5	Madagascar
273.9	88.5	—	—	11.5	0.4	2.9	8.3	45.1	24.8	—	2.2	27.8	Malawi
16,490.4	39.3	0.8	29.6	30.3	1.1	18.9	10.2	13.1	13.6	1.7	22.3	49.3	Malaysia
13.4	51.9	1.4	—	46.7	—	—	46.7	5.8	41.5	0.7	18.8	33.3	Maldives
106.2	76.4	—	—	23.6	0.3	0.5	22.8	71.1	—	—	3.0	25.9	Mali
400.1	7.2	1.3	3.5	88.0	1.3	22.1	64.7	66.7	6.4	7.8	0.2	19.0	Malta
145.0	65.1	0.3	15.6	19.1	6.3	5.3	7.5	68.3	0.4	...	—	31.3	Martinique
194.5	22.0	78.0	—	—	—	—	—	74.1[2]	0.1[2]	...	11.3[2]	14.5[2]	Mauritania
368.3	68.6	1.2	—	30.2	0.4	0.9	28.8	83.3	8.5	0.2	—	8.0	Mauritius
0.6	24.6	—	—	75.4	41.5	...	33.9	...	...	...	...	100.0[32]	Mayotte
21,398.8	9.0	2.1	74.0	14.9	3.0	4.5	7.5	18.2	57.3	0.6	6.8	17.1	Mexico
...	...	...	...	...	...	...	...	...	...	...	...	...	Monaco[17]
563.0	46.2	39.2[13]		14.5[14]		0.2	14.3[14]	...	...	94.8	...	5.2	Mongolia
2.2	13.2		0.8	86.0	—	13.0	73.0	15.7[23]	10.5[23]	—[23]	—[23]	73.8[23]	Montserrat
2,171.9	24.8	28.9	4.0	42.3	23.1	0.9	18.4	59.5	1.5	5.5	3.8	29.7	Morocco
129.0	79.7	10.8[13]	4.4	5.0[14]	0.8	0.5	3.7[14]	37.8	26.9	0.2	5.3	29.7	Mozambique
89.2	—	100.0	—	—	—	—	—	—[16]	—[16]	—[16]	4.0[16]	96.0[16]	Nauru
110.8	42.0	0.4	—	57.6	4.4	—	53.2	16.9	1.8	...	0.2	81.1	Nepal
67,913.6	23.0	1.4	23.1	52.4	16.6	16.8	19.0	73.9	5.2	1.3	0.6	18.9	Netherlands, The
1,639.6	—	0.1	97.6	2.2	1.6	0.3	0.3	15.6	17.4	—	0.4	66.6	Netherlands Antilles[34]
155.1	1.6	15.9	0.1	82.3	0.3	4.5	77.5	47.1	6.9	—	23.7	22.3	New Caledonia
5,732.2	67.2	0.5	1.7	30.6	4.7	4.6	21.3	20.5	14.4	2.2	14.5	48.4	New Zealand
390.7	90.8	0.1	1.3	7.8	5.0	0.1	2.6	29.4	25.0	7.4	11.5	26.7	Nicaragua
454.8	17.1	79.7	0.9	2.3	—	0.5	1.8	46.6	—	—	17.7	35.7	Niger
11,958.1	2.8	—	95.1	2.1	—	0.1	2.0	69.1	13.7	0.4	0.1	16.8	Nigeria
0.4	77.0	1.2	—	21.8	—	—	21.8	—	—	0.1	—	99.9[36]	Niue
2.1	10.2	—	8.6	81.2	0.1	6.2	74.9	...	...	...	...	...	Norfolk Island

Trade: external (continued)

country	year	imports: total value U.S.$ (000,000)	SITC categories (percent)[a, b]: food and agricultural raw materials (0 + 1 + 2 − 27 − 28 + 4)	mineral ores and concentrates (27 + 28 + 667)	fuels and other energy (3)	manufactured goods: total[c] (5 + 6 − 667 + 7 + 8 + 9)	of which chemicals and related products (5)	of which machinery and transport equipment (7)	of which other[c] (6 − 667 + 8 + 9)	direction of trade (percent)[a]: from European Economic Community (EEC)[d]	from United States	from U.S.S.R. and Eastern Europe[e]	from Japan	from all other[f]
Norway	1985	14,523.0	8.3	4.4	8.7	78.6	6.9	38.1	33.6	49.1	7.2	2.8	6.2	34.7
Oman	1984	2,748.2	16.2	0.3	1.6	82.0	3.8	41.4	36.8	36.8	7.6	—	21.3	34.3
Pacific Is., Trust Territory of the	1978[3]	38.9	—46.2[4]—		12.9	40.9[5]	4.8	12.5	23.5[5]	—[37]	—[37]	34.7[37]	25.2[37]	40.1[37]
Marshall Islands	...	...	...	...	...	...	...	...	...	...	...	...	...	...
Micronesia, Fed. States of	...	...	...	...	...	...	...	...	...	...	...	...	...	...
Northern Mariana Islands	...	...	...	...	...	...	...	...	...	...	...	...	...	...
Palau	...	...	...	...	...	...	...	...	...	...	...	...	...	...
Pakistan	1985	5,890.6	22.4	1.6	24.3	51.7	11.5	26.9	13.3	19.8	14.0	1.6	12.6	52.1
Panama	1983	1,411.4	11.2	0.2	27.8	60.9	11.8	23.0	26.0	8.7	32.3	0.2	7.8	50.9
Papua New Guinea	1982	1,028.3	20.0	0.2	19.2	60.6	5.2	30.3	25.1	7.5	9.0	—	14.3	69.2
Paraguay	1981	506.1	—13.8—		18.8	67.4	6.1	35.9	25.3	18.5	9.8	0.6	8.3	62.8
Peru	1982	2,940.3	19.6	0.3	1.7	78.4	12.0	44.2	22.2	21.0	36.8	0.6	12.5	29.1
Philippines	1985	5,445.5	12.9	0.7	27.8	58.6	11.8	14.0	32.8	8.5	25.1	0.4	14.4	51.6
Pitcairn Island	...	...	...	...	...	...	...	...	...	...	...	...	...	...
Poland	1983	10,589.8	15.1	4.2	26.1	54.7	8.7	25.2	20.7	17.1	1.4	59.2	1.1	21.3
Portugal	1985	8,092.2	19.2	1.5	24.6	54.6	10.2	18.5	25.9	49.9	6.9	1.4	2.8	39.0
Puerto Rico	1983[3]	8,506.8	—22.2[4]—		24.6	53.2[5]	11.1	14.2	27.9[5]	5.8	61.2	0.1	5.0	27.9
Qatar	1984	1,162.0	22.6	2.4	0.9	74.1	5.8	35.3	32.9	39.3	9.1	0.5	19.2	32.0
Réunion	1985	840.8	25.2	0.2	10.0	64.6	9.6	24.6	30.4	74.7	0.2	—	2.5	22.5
Romania	1983	8,347.8	10.4	—57.0[13]—		32.5[14]	6.8	21.5	4.2[14]	10.0	2.8	43.3	1.1	42.9
Rwanda	1980	243.1	15.7	1.4	12.5	70.4	6.0	25.4	39.0	45.0	4.5	1.3	12.1	37.1
St. Christopher and Nevis	1981	47.7	24.3	0.1	10.9	64.6	8.9	20.5	35.2	21.5	30.1	0.1	3.6	44.6
St. Helena and Ascension	1984	4.3	39.0	—	11.7	49.2	6.8	15.7	26.7	57.0	—	—	0.2	42.8
St. Lucia	1982	118.1	26.7	0.4	11.7	61.3	9.8	17.2	34.3	20.8[38]	38.9[38]	0.2[38]	4.9[38]	35.2[38]
St. Pierre and Miquelon	1984	43.9	19.4	0.1	29.9	50.6	4.3	27.4	18.8	46.1	0.3	—	—	53.5
St. Vincent and the Grenadines	1985	79.3	29.3	0.4[4]	8.0	62.3[5]	13.4	16.9	32.0[5]	27.2	36.3	0.2	4.5	31.8
San Marino[26]	...	...	...	...	...	...	...	...	...	...	...	...	...	...
São Tomé and Príncipe	1977	14.8	46.5	3.0[13]	1.9	45.7[14]	10.1	12.8	22.8[14]	89.1[2, 16]	—[2, 16]	—[2, 16]	0.5[2, 16]	10.4[2, 16]
Saudi Arabia	1984	33,695.6	16.5	0.5	0.6	82.4	5.1	38.0	39.3	37.0	17.4	0.7	19.8	25.0
Senegal	1981	1,077.4	28.3	—	30.4	41.3	7.6	17.5	16.2	48.6	4.5	2.6	1.3	43.0
Seychelles	1984	87.3	21.8	0.1	30.2	47.9	5.8	18.7	23.3	29.3	3.1	3.4	6.4	57.8
Sierra Leone	1983	165.7	28.5	0.4	34.7	36.4	5.5	14.9	15.9	40.7	3.5	0.7	4.6	50.5
Singapore	1985	26,286.2	12.3	0.7	29.5	57.6	5.0	31.7	20.9	11.3	15.2	0.3	17.1	56.2
Solomon Islands	1984	65.8	21.8	0.8	22.7	54.7	6.0	23.9	24.8	6.3	3.3	0.1	15.0	75.3
Somalia	1981	512.9	26.6	—	2.3	71.1	2.0	50.0	19.1	66.0	4.3	0.1	1.8	27.8
South Africa[40]	1982	16,941.1	5.6	1.5	0.4[41]	92.4[42]	8.6	42.9	41.0[42]	38.2	14.6	0.4	10.1	36.8
Bophuthatswana[40]	...	...	...	...	...	...	...	...	...	...	...	...	...	...
Ciskei[40]	...	...	...	...	...	...	...	...	...	...	...	...	...	...
Transkei[40]	...	...	...	...	...	...	...	...	...	...	...	...	...	...
Venda[40]	...	...	...	...	...	...	...	...	...	...	...	...	...	...
South West Africa/Namibia[40]	1984	761.1	...	...	...	...	...	...	...	...	...	...	...	...
Spain	1985	30,001.5	15.4	4.9	36.2	43.5	8.4	21.7	13.4	36.7	10.9	2.4	3.4	46.6
Sri Lanka	1984	1,847.5	16.8	0.8	25.7	56.7	8.3	24.3	24.1	14.3	8.9	0.7	16.6	59.4
Sudan, The	1983	1,354.4	18.6	0.3	26.6	54.6	11.0	26.6	17.0	38.3	9.1	1.5	3.2	47.9
Suriname	1976	281.0	11.9	2.3[13]	27.2	57.7[14]	11.5	29.8	16.4[14]	32.1[7]	31.2[7]	0.3[7]	7.4[7]	28.9[7]
Swaziland	1982	520.3	9.9	0.2	14.7	75.2	15.3	21.8	38.0	...	...	...	...	100.0[44]
Sweden	1985	28,486.6	8.8	2.2	19.0	70.1	9.5	32.8	27.8	56.0	8.4	5.2	4.9	25.5
Switzerland	1985	30,728.6	10.5	4.8	10.0	74.7	11.9	25.9	36.8	70.7	5.9	2.8	4.0	16.6
Syria	1983	4,542.2	22.5	0.3	30.2	46.8	7.8	21.9	17.2	34.5	4.4	9.9	6.7	44.5
Taiwan	1984	21,829.6	18.2	2.6	21.6	57.6	11.7	28.4	17.4	8.9	22.9	—	29.4	38.8
Tanzania	1981	867.3	7.6	0.6	30.8	61.0	10.0	35.0	16.1	42.5	1.8	1.1	11.5	43.2
Thailand	1984	10,525.9	9.1	2.5	23.5	64.8	12.5	30.0	22.3	12.5	13.4	1.1	26.9	46.0
Togo	1981	435.8	27.2	0.6	8.4	63.7	6.1	21.3	36.3	65.8	4.2	1.1	5.6	23.4
Tokelau	1981	0.4	...	...	...	...	...	...	...	...	...	...	...	...
Tonga	1982	41.6	34.3	0.7	13.9	51.0	6.4	14.7	29.9	3.2	9.5	—	6.1	81.1
Trinidad and Tobago	1984	1,919.1	25.5	1.5	0.8	72.3	9.1	30.2	33.0	19.9	38.9	0.1	11.1	30.1
Tunisia	1984	3,120.1	19.5	4.5	11.1	64.9	8.3	30.6	26.0	65.9	7.1	5.8	4.3	17.0
Turkey	1984	10,662.8	8.6	2.4	35.6	53.4	14.6	25.3	13.6	30.5	9.9	8.2	3.8	47.6
Turks and Caicos Islands	1984[10]	26.3	—32.1[4]—		11.6	56.3[5]	...	...	...	...	74.7	...	...	25.3
Tuvalu	1983	2.7	36.8	0.2	14.0	49.0	6.9	12.3	29.7	2.5	0.5	—	2.1	94.9
Uganda	1976	157.5	8.7	0.7	29.6	61.0	11.1	26.8	23.0	32.1	3.1	1.8	3.9	59.1
U.S.S.R.	1984	80,624.0	24.2	...	...	75.5	6.4	36.6	32.5	13.3	4.3	46.7	3.1	32.5
United Arab Emirates	1982	9,439.9	10.3	0.5	6.0	83.1	5.4	40.6	37.1	37.9	13.8	0.4	19.2	28.7
United Kingdom[24]	1985	109,912.8	15.3	3.7	12.4	68.6	8.1	31.7	28.8	48.9	11.7	1.9	4.9	32.7
United States[47]	1985	361,585.7	9.1	2.0	15.4	73.5	4.2	39.2	30.1	19.8	—	0.6	20.0	59.6
Uruguay	1983	787.5	11.3	0.7	36.1	51.9	15.2	24.8	11.9	17.5	7.5	4.2	2.2	68.6
Vanuatu	1983	51.2	26.5	0.2	11.0	62.2	6.3	21.0	34.9	14.2	1.1	—	12.2	72.5
Venezuela	1981	13,105.9	19.4	0.4	0.8	79.4	10.4	43.4	25.6	21.0	48.3	0.3	8.1	22.2
Vietnam	1984	1,922.0[2]	...	...	...	...	...	...	...	3.6[2]	1.3[2]	70.2[2]	6.8[2]	18.0[2]
Virgin Islands (U.S.)	1978	667.4	11.9	—	58.5	29.6	3.7	8.2	17.6	0.9	58.0	0.1	0.2	40.7
Wallis and Futuna	1981	6.4	—25.6[4]—		18.1	56.4[5]	26.0	16.3	14.1[5]	...	...	...	...	...
West Bank	1984	406.8	12.6[48]	...	...	...	...	...	...	...	...	...	...	100.0[49]
Western Sahara	...	...	...	...	...	...	...	...	...	...	...	...	...	...
Western Samoa	1983	52.6	24.3	0.3	17.5	57.9	7.4	22.9	27.6	5.5	11.0	—	11.4	72.2
Yemen (Aden)	1977	544.0	—18.1[4]—		46.6	35.2[5]	2.0	22.7	10.6[5]	18.4	—	4.0	11.3	66.4
Yemen (Ṣan'ā')	1981	1,608.8	32.2	0.1	8.3	59.4	5.6	25.4	28.4	30.8	2.8	1.2	17.7	47.5
Yugoslavia	1984	11,996.0	13.1	3.1	29.3	54.5	14.6	22.1	17.7	30.3	5.2	32.5	0.7	31.3
Zaire	1983	494.4	22.4[7]	1.2[7]	7.6[7]	68.8[7]	10.3[7]	31.7[7]	26.9[7]	50.8	6.9	0.3	3.0	39.0
Zambia	1982	1,001.9	7.5	0.4	20.8	71.4	16.0	34.5	20.8	28.8	9.5	0.8	6.2	54.6
Zimbabwe	1982	1,642.8	4.6	0.7	16.5	78.2	11.6	40.7	26.0	33.7	9.5	0.5	5.2	51.2

[1]Year ending March 20. [2]Estimated based on trading partners' information. [3]Year ending June 30. [4]Excluding precious stones, etc. (667). [5]Including precious stones, etc. (667). [6]Trade with France and Spain only. [7]1978. [8]Figures for Belgium–Luxembourg Economic Union (Luxembourg is also shown separately). [9]1974. [10]Year ending March 31. [11]Includes 77.3% from India. [12]Includes 97.0% to India. [13]Including metals. [14]Excluding metals. [15]1980. [16]1979. [17]Figures for France include Monaco. [18]Includes 91.9% from Israel. [19]Includes 83.4% to Israel. [20]Import figures refer to total trade turnover (figures are not available separately for imports and for exports). [21]Excluding trade with East Germany (1.7% of total imports and 1.3% of total exports in 1984). [22]Excluding petroleum products. [23]Domestic exports only. [24]Figures for United Kingdom include Guernsey, Isle of Man, and Jersey (the latter is also shown separately). [25]Year ending September 30. [26]Figures for Italy include San Marino. [27]Includes 84.9% from United Kingdom. [28]Including coins. [29]Includes 67.3% to United Kingdom. [30]Includes 97.1% from Customs Union of Southern Africa.

exports													country
total value U.S.$ (000,000)	Standard International Trade Classification (SITC) categories (percent)[a, b]							direction of trade (percent)[a]					
	food and agricultural raw materials (0 + 1 + 2 − 27 − 28 + 4)	mineral ores and concentrates (27 + 28 + 667)	fuels and other energy (3)	manufactured goods				to European Economic Community (EEC)[d]	to United States	to U.S.S.R. and Eastern Europe[e]	to Japan	to all other[f]	
				total[c] (5 + 6 − 667 + 7 + 8 + 9)	of which chemicals and related products (5)	of which machinery and transport equipment (7)	of which other[c] (6 − 667 + 8 + 9)						
18,666.2	7.5	1.3	53.7	37.5	5.9	13.7	17.9	69.5	5.1	0.9	1.3	23.3	Norway
4,422.0	1.1	0.1	91.7	7.1	0.1	5.2	1.8	3.7[2]	3.5[2]	—[2]	49.6[2]	43.2[2]	Oman
19.3	—96.5[4]—		—	3.5[5]	—	—	3.5[5]	...	...	...	...	...	Pacific Is., Trust Territory of the
...	...	...	...	...	...	...	...	...	...	...	...	...	Marshall Islands
...	...	...	...	...	...	...	...	...	...	...	...	...	Micronesia, Fed. States of
...	...	...	...	...	...	...	...	...	...	...	...	...	Northern Mariana Islands
...	...	...	...	...	...	...	...	...	...	...	...	...	Palau
2,738.7	34.9	0.5	1.4	63.2	3.4	2.0	57.8	22.2	10.0	6.2	11.3	50.3	Pakistan
302.6	77.1	0.5	12.1	10.3	2.0	0.2	8.1	14.2	54.2	0.1	0.3	31.2	Panama
800.1	40.1	50.5	0.1	9.3	0.1	1.8	7.4	39.1	2.1	0.5	31.5	26.8	Papua New Guinea
295.5	90.6	—	—	9.4	4.1	—	5.2	25.9	5.6	0.3	8.4	59.7	Paraguay
2,812.8	16.2	15.3	26.4	42.1	1.6	1.2	39.3	20.2	35.8	1.6	15.1	27.3	Peru
4,629.0	31.5	5.4	0.9	62.2	3.3	6.9	52.0	14.0	35.7	0.7	18.9	30.6	Philippines
...	...	...	...	...	...	...	...	...	...	...	...	...	Pitcairn Island
11,571.8	9.9	3.3	17.4	69.4	5.5	41.6	22.2	23.6	1.7	50.6	0.5	23.6	Poland
5,253.3	21.2	1.3	5.5	72.1	6.8	19.8	45.5	57.5	13.5	1.6	1.0	26.4	Portugal
8,521.2	—14.2[4]—		10.2	75.6[5]	31.9	17.2	26.5[5]	3.8	83.5	—	0.2	12.4	Puerto Rico
4,512.6	—[38]	—[38]	93.9[38]	6.1[38]	3.9[38]	—[38]	2.2[38]	43.2[38]	0.2[38]	—[38]	33.3[38]	23.4[38]	Qatar
89.7	86.0	0.3	0.2	13.5	4.0	5.3	4.2	85.6	0.4	—	2.6	11.4	Réunion
10,089.3	12.6	—29.8[13]—		57.6[14]	10.1	29.1	18.5[14]	24.6	3.9	33.9	1.6	36.1	Romania
73.2	89.4	10.5	—	0.2	—	—	0.2	14.2	0.8	—	—	85.0	Rwanda
24.3	66.5	—	0.1	33.4	0.4	12.3	20.7	31.3	42.2	—	0.2	26.3	St. Christopher and Nevis
0.04	100.0	—	—	—	—	—	—	...	...	...	...	...	St. Helena and Ascension
41.6	62.2	0.1	0.4	37.3	1.3	10.4	25.6	37.9[38]	10.6[38]	—[38]	—[38]	51.4[38]	St. Lucia
7.8	99.9	—	—	0.1	—	—	0.1	7.7	74.3	—	—	18.0	St. Pierre and Miquelon
63.2	85.7	—[4]	—	14.2[5]	0.8	4.0	9.4[5]	28.2	9.7	—	—	62.1	St. Vincent and the Grenadines
...	...	...	...	...	...	...	...	...	...	...	...	...	San Marino[26]
24.1	99.8	—	—	0.2	—	0.1	0.1	82.7[2, 16]	—[2, 16]	—[2, 16]	—[2, 16]	17.3[2, 16]	São Tomé and Príncipe
36,833.6	0.2	0.1	98.5	1.3	1.1	—	0.1	32.4[39]	7.8[39]	0.1[39]	23.8[39]	35.8[39]	Saudi Arabia
560.8	28.8	14.1	37.4	19.7	6.0	4.0	9.7	32.9	0.2	0.8	1.6	64.5	Senegal
25.6	12.1	0.1	78.9	8.9	0.3	7.6	1.0	4.7	7.0	—	3.2	85.1	Seychelles
91.5	33.1	62.0	3.9	1.1	0.1	—	1.0	91.0	2.4	—	—	6.6	Sierra Leone
22,845.8	12.5	0.9	27.1	59.5	5.4	33.0	21.1	10.6	21.2	1.3	9.4	57.5	Singapore
93.1	96.7	—	—	3.3	—	—	3.3	34.1	—	—	33.2	32.6	Solomon Islands
152.0	99.4	—	0.2	0.4	—	0.1	0.2	6.2	—	—	—	93.7	Somalia
17,804.3	12.4	10.7	6.5	70.4[43]	2.5	2.6	65.4[43]	21.5	6.9	0.1	8.6	62.8	South Africa[40]
...	...	...	...	...	...	...	...	...	...	...	...	...	Bophuthatswana[40]
...	...	...	...	...	...	...	...	...	...	...	...	...	Ciskei[40]
...	...	...	...	...	...	...	...	...	...	...	...	...	Transkei[40]
...	...	...	...	...	...	...	...	...	...	...	...	...	Venda[40]
752.8	...	...	...	...	...	...	...	...	...	...	...	...	South West Africa/Namibia[40]
24,267.3	16.9	1.0	9.5	72.7	8.5	27.2	37.0	52.0	9.9	3.0	1.3	33.7	Spain
1,453.8	63.0	2.5	9.0	25.5	0.5	1.4	23.5	17.4	19.3	6.2	4.3	52.9	Sri Lanka
623.5	93.9	0.3	2.7	3.1	—	2.2	0.9	25.2	2.0	7.7	5.4	59.7	Sudan, The
274.6	21.6	32.7[13]	—	45.7[14]	43.1	0.5	2.1[14]	27.4[7]	39.7[7]	0.6[7]	6.6[7]	25.7[7]	Suriname
325.2	63.8	—	0.8	35.3	15.8	4.3	15.2	...	...	...	...	100.0[45]	Swaziland
30,359.5	10.9	2.1	4.9	82.1	6.3	41.9	34.0	48.6	11.7	2.6	1.3	35.7	Sweden
27,446.8	4.2	4.8	0.3	90.7	21.4	31.1	38.1	52.6	10.4	3.1	3.2	30.7	Switzerland
1,922.9	14.5	1.5	68.8	15.2	1.6	1.1	12.5	34.1	0.1	43.4	—	22.3	Syria
30,409.8	6.9	0.3	1.8	91.0	2.5	28.1	60.3	9.1	48.8	—	10.5	31.6	Taiwan
564.3	82.4	10.1	0.2	7.3	0.7	2.5	4.1	45.5	3.5	2.7	2.8	45.5	Tanzania
7,412.9	60.0	4.8	0.7	34.5	1.0	7.3	26.2	20.7	17.2	1.4	13.0	47.7	Thailand
208.2	32.1	50.6	1.3	16.0	—	1.4	14.6	60.8	—	1.5	0.4	37.3	Togo
0.1	95.3	—	—	4.7	—	—	4.7	...	...	...	...	...	Tokelau
4.3	73.7	—	—	26.3	—	2.3	23.9	1.9	8.3	—	0.1	89.8	Tonga
2,173.4	2.4	0.2	81.2	16.2	10.8	1.5	3.9	15.3	58.2	—	—	26.4	Trinidad and Tobago
1,796.3	11.0	2.8	44.3	42.0	15.5	4.5	21.9	60.3	19.1	1.2	0.1	19.3	Tunisia
7,133.6	35.9	3.4	5.7	55.0	2.8	5.0	47.3	39.0	5.2	3.7	0.5	51.6	Turkey
3.0	100.0	—	—	—	—	—	—	—	100.0	—	—	—	Turks and Caicos Islands
0.1	78.8	—	—	21.2	—	—	21.2	...	...	...	...	100.0[46]	Tuvalu
351.7	96.6	0.2	0.8	2.4	—	—	2.4	45.0	32.9	3.4	6.4	12.3	Uganda
91,649.0	4.7	2.2[4]	54.4	38.7[5]	3.1	12.5	23.1[5]	21.1	0.4	43.5	1.1	33.8	U.S.S.R.
17,333.2	0.9	—	92.2	6.8	0.2	1.9	4.7	13.2	3.8	—	33.8	49.1	United Arab Emirates
101,540.9	7.9	2.8	21.3	67.9	12.0	31.5	24.4	48.8	14.7	1.5	1.3	33.7	United Kingdom[24]
212,728.5	17.4	2.1	4.8	75.7	10.1	46.0	19.6	22.7	—	1.5	10.4	65.4	United States[47]
1,008.4	70.2	0.1	0.1	29.6	3.0	1.1	25.5	20.9	9.8	7.8	2.1	59.4	Uruguay
29.6	99.3[23]	—[23]	—[23]	0.7[23]	—[23]	—[23]	0.7[23]	46.2	18.2	—	12.6	23.0	Vanuatu
20,125.3	0.4	2.0	92.8	4.6	0.7	0.5	3.4	18.9	25.4	0.5	3.9	51.3	Venezuela
641.0[2]	...	...	...	...	...	...	...	3.0[2]	—[2]	60.4[2]	7.2[2]	29.4[2]	Vietnam
2,512.1	—	—	91.3	8.7	6.2	—	2.5	1.0	96.8	1.3	0.1	0.8	Virgin Islands (U.S.)
...	...	...	...	...	...	...	...	...	...	...	...	...	Wallis and Futuna
184.5	23.3[48]	...	...	...	...	...	...	...	...	...	...	100.0[50]	West Bank
...	...	...	...	...	...	...	...	...	...	...	...	...	Western Sahara
18.6	90.6	—	—	9.4	—	5.8	3.6	11.6	31.7	—	3.6	53.1	Western Samoa
180.8	—15.5[4]—		84.0	0.5[5]	—	0.4	0.1[5]	1.8	—	—	9.6	88.6	Yemen (Aden)
47.5	23.8	—	—	76.2	1.6	64.5	10.2	24.6	3.0	0.1	0.1	72.3	Yemen (Ṣan'ā')
10,254.5	14.2	0.7	3.5	81.7	9.7	31.0	41.0	25.9	4.2	46.0	0.3	23.6	Yugoslavia
1,559.5	13.0	70.8	11.1	5.0	...	...	...	51.8[2]	22.0[2]	—[2]	4.9[2]	21.3[2]	Zaire
1,023.9	0.4[16]	0.6[16]	1.2[16]	97.7[16, 51]	0.2[16]	0.3[16]	97.2[16, 51]	41.0	2.6	0.5	21.3	34.5	Zambia
1,275.7	60.9	1.4	1.6	36.1	1.6	1.7	32.8	35.5	7.7	0.2	3.0	53.7	Zimbabwe

[31]Includes 52.9% from France in 1984. [32]Includes 70.2% to France. [33]Based on trade with Australia, Hong Kong, and New Zealand only. [34]Curaçao only. [35]Includes 64.8% from New Zealand. [36]Includes 96.7% to New Zealand. [37]1977. [38]1981. [39]1982. [40]Figures for South Africa refer to Customs Union of Southern Africa (includes South Africa, Botswana, Lesotho, and Swaziland, also shown separately; also South West Africa/Namibia, Bophuthatswana, Ciskei, Transkei, and Venda). [41]Excluding crude oil. [42]Including crude oil (included in "special transactions" accounting in total for 23.4%). [43]Including gold (included in "special transactions" accounting in total for 54.4%). [44]Includes 82.9% from South Africa. [45]Includes 34.8% to South Africa. [46]Includes 97.0% to Fiji in 1981. [47]Figures for United States include Virgin Islands (U.S.), American Samoa, Puerto Rico, and Guam, also shown separately. [48]1983. [49]Includes 89.3% from Israel. [50]Includes 54.1% to Israel, 45.3% to Jordan. [51]Includes copper 81.8%.

Trade: domestic

The following table presents data relating to domestic wholesale and retail trade for the countries of the world. The section on wholesale trade is based for the most part on establishments engaged primarily in selling goods to retailers and distributors for resale or to purchasers who buy for business and farm uses. The retail trade section is based on businesses engaged in selling merchandise for personal or household consumption; restaurants, when part of the national retail survey, are included, hotels excluded.

The data presented here are based on information received from a variety of direct country and international sources. The direct country sources include such items as correspondence, statistical abstracts, annual reports, and censuses of business and trade. Among the more useful international sources are the various compilations of the United Nations dealing with domestic trade and Euromonitor's *Retail Trade International* (2 vols.).

There being no single source or common international methodology for the compilation of data on wholesale and retail trade, nor a single current year on which, by common agreement, the various national reports would be based, allowance must be made for variations in the meaning of the information provided for any single country and for its comparability internationally. Variations occur in part because of the ways in which countries define wholesale and retail trade; the conventional capitalist, or free-enterprise, distinction between the wholesale and retail activity (of a single enterprise or an entire national trade sector) may not be clear in some countries, and data may overlap in their final reports. Variations also exist in the kind and level of detail reported. For example, countries may analyze differently the size (number of employees, sales, surface area) of establishments surveyed. The depth of analysis to which the data are subjected may also vary. Trade is affected by the degree of government involvement, which may range from total control of wholesale distribution in some socialist countries, to partial involvement in some strategic sectors, or to complete noninvolvement in fully private trade sectors of capitalist countries. In some smaller countries data may be collected only by inference; for instance, in a country with inadequate resources to survey trade, the number of accounts served by one national tobacco distributor may be the sole datum on the number of that country's retail outlets.

At the extreme left, preceding the year to which the trade data refer, the combined value of the country's wholesale and retail trade as a percentage of gross domestic product or net material product is given. Unless otherwise noted, GDP data include restaurants and exclude hotels.

Both the wholesale and retail sections of the table provide similar detail: establishments or outlets, employees, sales, and derived values for relationships among these measures; the retail section provides an additional breakdown of sales by an end-use classification of retail sales outlets.

Although all sales figures are given in U.S. dollars, the comparability of these dollar figures may differ considerably; for instance, the purchasing power of various national currencies in domestic transactions may bear only a distant relationship to the exchange rate of the same currency in international transactions. The price of goods may also vary, depending on the degree to which they are subject to direct subsidies and artificial cost controls such as tax, investment, or free-trade preferences by a central government seeking to influence social or economic conditions.

The data on distribution of retail sales by kind of consumer goods

Trade: domestic

country	domestic trade as percentage of GDP, 1983	year	wholesale trade					retail trade		
			establishments[a]	employees[b]	sales[c] $'000,000	employees per establishment	sales per establishment $'000	outlets[a]	employees[b]	sales[c] $'000,000
Afghanistan	9.1[1]	1979–80	...	[2]	...	...	...	...	146,075[2,3]	...
Albania	9.5[4]	1983	...	...	...	...	...	10,585[5]	...	994[5]
Algeria	9.2[6]	1971	...	[2]	...	...	...	3,600[7]	65,917[2,6]	12,607[9]
American Samoa	...	1984	37	77[10]	...	...	...	283	499[10]	...
Andorra	25.2[6]	1972	...	...	...	...	...	592	2,264	...
Angola	4.8[11]	1973	[2]	...	...	...	...	29,138[2]	...	...
Anguilla	...	1974	...	[2]	...	...	...	...	116[2]	...
Antigua and Barbuda	27.6[12,13]	1980	25	350	...	14.0	...	199	1,000	23[9]
Argentina	16.5[12]	1974	45,700	275,000[3]	10,922[14]	6.0[3]	...	445,798[15]	930,000[3,15]	15,540[9]
Aruba	...	1983	...	[2]	...	...	...	...	3,192[2,16]	17
Australia	13.2	1980	36,587[6]	343,258[3,6]	77,040[6]	9.4[3,6]	739	128,334[12]	920,688[3,12]	38,523[13,15]
Austria	16.7[12]	1984	12,573[6]	151,300[3,6]	30,336[6]	12.0[3,6]	2,413[6]	37,996[6]	223,300[3]	14,637
Bahamas, The[18]	26.2[12]	1980	23	1,066	143	46.3	6.235	132	4,059	257[6]
Bahrain	...	1983	[2]	[2]	...	[2]	...	255[2]	12,551[2]	1,601
Bangladesh	8.6	1983	...	[2]	...	...	...	...	146,000[2,19]	4,800
Barbados	18.9	1979	...	[2]	...	...	...	1,911	5,800[2,15]	264[9]
Belgium	9.9[15]	1984	57,079[6]	166,900[11]	65,286[6]	3.0[11]	1,144[6]	121,690[6]	159,848[6]	26,497
Belize	14.6[12]	1983	...	...	...	...	...	...	...	23[9]
Benin	22.4[12]	1979	...	...	...	...	...	170[7]	1,910[3,7]	150[9]
Bermuda	...	1984	60[20]	840	...	...	...	310[7,11]	4,470[15]	116[15]
Bhutan	2.9[6]	1982	...	[2]	...	...	...	...	9,000[2,3]	...
Bolivia	12.9	1983	...	[2]	...	...	...	...	17,414[2,12,21]	1,818
Botswana	22.4[12]	1979	164	1,600	481	9.8	2,933	1,333	3,600	160
Brazil	15.9[12]	1975	52,722	117,423	54,805	2.2	1,040	885,558[10]	723,461	51,480[9]
British Virgin Islands	26.7[4,12]	1982	...	...	...	...	...	...	366	5[11]
Brunei	10.8[12]	1982	[2]	[2]	...	[2]	...	654[2]	3,403[2]	...
Bulgaria	6.5[1,12]	1981	...	8,924	...	...	...	38,304[15]	89,563[15]	10,543[15]
Burkina Faso	12.9[12]	1975	...	[2]	...	...	...	...	19,354[2,3]	...
Burma	24.5[15]	1983	...	...	...	...	...	...	...	2,116
Burundi	8.1[12]	1981	...	...	...	...	...	...	1	445
Cameroon	11.9[6,12]	1980	...	...	...	...	...	1,312[7]	13,776[3,7]	753[9]
Canada	9.3[12]	1985	...	451,665[9]	65,813[6]	...	...	...	1,136,500[15]	102,643
Cape Verde	...	...	...	...	...	...	...	...	...	...
Cayman Islands	17.0[16]	1972	...	86	...	...	...	...	928	...
Central African Republic	27.3[4]	1978[12]	[2]	[2]	[2]	...	[2]	102[2,7]	26,659[2,3,25]	252[2,7]
Chad	30.1[8,12]	1983	...	[2]	[2]	...	...	...	1,661[2,7,21]	497[2]
Chile	16.9[12]	1981	524[7]	18,900[7]	3,661[7]	36.1[7]	6,987[7]	1,196[7]	28,200[7]	4,586[9]
China	4.6	1984	62,000	997,000[3]	...	16.1[3]	...	6,715,000[15]	15,330,000[3,15]	145,534[15]
Christmas Island	...	1981	—	[2]	—	—	—	5	65[2]	...
Cocos (Keeling) Islands	...	1981	...	[2]	...	...	...	1	13[2]	...
Colombia	13.4[12]	1983	...	...	...	...	...	...	...	6,285
Comoros	...	1974	...	[2]	...	...	...	...	983[2,7,26]	...
Congo	12.0[12]	...	...	...	...	...	...	...	...	...
Cook Islands	24.0[4]	1982[27]	[2]	[2]	[2]	[2]	[2]	109[2]	369[2]	31[2]
Costa Rica	20.2[12]	1975	332[28]	4,073[28]	35[28]	12.3[28]	104[28]	9,713	26,486	475[9]
Côte d'Ivoire	17.1[10,12]	1981	...	...	[2]	...	...	2,023[7]	16,720[7]	1,548[2,9]
Cuba	41.3[1,12]	1981	...	...	11,479[6]	...	...	51,733[10]	...	9,172
Cyprus	16.0[12]	1982	1,518	9,767[3]	1,227	6.4[3]	808	8,186	15,894[3]	997
Czechoslovakia	14.4[1,12]	1984	...	...	...	...	...	63,503	247,284	42,740
Denmark	12.2[12]	1981	5,515	127,000	29,249	23.0	5,304	50,826	116,000	15,796
Djibouti	15.7[12]	1982	...	371	...	...	...	...	1,877	...
Dominica	9.2[12]	1983	...	[2]	...	...	...	...	1,597[2,11]	4
Dominican Republic	16.9[15]	1983	...	...	2,614[11]	...	...	...	...	1,240
Ecuador	14.3[12]	1980[12]	2,450	15,591[3]	2,805	6.4[3]	1,145	102,981	179,847[3]	5,922
Egypt	12.8[10,12]	1980–81[7]	1,766	42,300[3]	3,216	24.0[3]	1,821	2,136	48,200[3]	2,015

may have their origin in several different types of data or analysis: One country may aggregate sales data by kind of establishment only (this may be perfectly satisfactory in a country of small, independent outlets); another may aggregate data directly by kind of goods (most easily done in a country with well-developed statistical, tax-reporting, and commercial systems). Other countries may find it impolitic to publish data that reflect the poverty of their distribution network or their supply of consumer goods and may aggregate or publish data for only a few sectors: food or nonfood goods, for example. For countries with only a few trading enterprises in a particular sector, detail must often be withheld to preserve the confidentiality of individual businesses.

The notes that follow further define the various headings.

a. The number of establishments or outlets refers to economic units that operate at a single physical location in one principal kind of activity, whether singly owned or part of a multiunit firm. Such units are not necessarily identical with a company or enterprise.

b. Number of employees refers to full-time and part-time paid workers, including salaried managers and officers; it usually excludes owner-operators, partners, vendors, and unpaid relatives.

c. Total sales (also called turnover) includes the value of merchandise sold for cash or credit; amounts received from customers for layaway purchases; receipts from rental or leasing of vehicles, equipment, tools, instruments, etc.; receipts for delivery, installation, maintenance, repair, alteration, storage, and other services.

d. Covers outlets engaged primarily in the sale of food and nonalcoholic beverages, such as grocery stores, meat and fish markets, and bakeries.

e. Covers outlets engaged primarily in the sale of clothing and shoes; also includes outlets that sell accessory items, such as millinery, furs, and leather goods.

f. Covers outlets engaged primarily in the sale of home furnishings, including furniture, draperies, floor coverings, household appliances, and home entertainment equipment.

g. Covers outlets that primarily serve food and drink, including restaurants, lunchrooms, cafeterias, social caterers, refreshment places, contract feeders, ice cream parlors, and bars and taverns.

h. Covers outlets engaged primarily in the sale of pharmaceuticals, cosmetics, and perfumes.

i. Covers outlets engaged primarily in the sale of building materials, hardware, garden supplies, paint, electrical supplies, and farm equipment.

j. Covers outlets engaged primarily in the sale of motor vehicles, motorcycles, bicycles, and tires, batteries, and other automotive supplies and parts; includes service stations.

k. Covers outlets engaged in the sale of multiple lines of merchandise, such as department stores, variety stores, and country general stores.

l. Covers miscellaneous specialized outlets such as those engaged primarily in the sale of liquors, sporting goods, books, jewelry, photographic and optical goods, gifts, flowers, tobacco products, home fuels, and newspapers.

retail trade: percent breakdown of sales: food[d]	clothing, shoes[e]	home furnishings[f]	eating, drinking[g]	drugs, pharma-ceuticals[h]	building materials[i]	automobile parts[j]	general merchandise[k]	other[l]	employees per outlet	sales per outlet $'000	population per outlet	country
...	...	...	...	...	...	...	...	...	...	...	...	Afghanistan
61.5				38.5					...	93[6]	268[5]	Albania
...	...	...	...	...	...	...	...	...	5.0[7]	...	5,146[7]	Algeria
...	...	...	...	...	...	...	...	...	...	...	...	American Samoa
...	...	...	...	...	...	...	...	...	3.8	...	39	Andorra
...	...	...	...	...	...	...	...	...	...	...	...	Angola
...	...	...	...	...	...	...	...	...	...	...	...	Anguilla
...	...	...	...	...	...	...	...	...	5.0	100	378	Antigua and Barbuda
...	...	...	...	...	...	...	...	...	2.1[3, 15]	...	58	Argentina
...	...	...	...	...	...	...	...	...	...	...	...	Aruba
28.8	7.0	6.5	6.3[12]	2.8	1.1	30.0	9.6	7.9	7.2[3, 12]	369[12]	115[12]	Australia
30.0	14.5	10.3	...	4.8	...	13.7	10.1	16.6	6.0[3, 6]	417[6]	199[6]	Austria
24.4[6]	7.7[6]	7.1[6]	—	3.7[6]	8.4[6]	30.1[6]	7.6[6]	11.0[6]	30.8	1,881	1,026	Bahamas, The[18]
...	...	...	...	...	...	...	...	...	49.2[2]	...	1,507[2]	Bahrain
...	...	...	...	...	...	...	...	...	...	...	...	Bangladesh
...	...	...	...	...	...	...	...	...	...	...	130	Barbados
35.1				64.9					1.2[6]	218	81	Belgium
...	...	...	...	...	...	...	...	...	...	...	...	Belize
...	...	...	...	...	...	...	...	...	11.3[3, 7]	...	19,871[7]	Benin
...	...	...	...	...	...	...	...	...	11.0[9, 15]	...	178[7, 11]	Bermuda
...	...	...	...	...	...	...	...	...	...	...	...	Bhutan
...	...	...	...	...	...	...	...	...	...	...	...	Bolivia
...	...	...	...	...	...	...	...	...	2.7	120	645	Botswana
15.0[13, 22]	7.2[13]	13.0[13, 23]	...	4.7[13]	23	27.3[13, 24]	19.3[13]	13.5[13]	1.1	75	168	Brazil
...	...	...	...	...	...	...	...	...	...	...	...	British Virgin Islands
...	...	...	...	...	...	...	...	...	5.2[2]	...	310[2]	Brunei
43.9	8.5	4.0	...	6.3	...	...	19.0	18.3	2.3[15]	275[15]	232[15]	Bulgaria
...	...	...	...	...	...	...	...	...	...	...	...	Burkina Faso
...	...	...	...	...	...	...	...	...	...	...	...	Burma
...	...	...	...	...	...	...	...	...	...	...	...	Burundi
...	...	...	...	...	...	...	...	...	10.5[3, 7]	...	6,481[7]	Cameroon
23.0	5.0	2.3	8.4	3.9	0.8	29.1	12.8	14.7	...	...	...	Canada
...	...	...	...	...	...	...	...	...	...	...	...	Cape Verde
...	...	...	...	...	...	...	...	...	...	...	...	Cayman Islands
...	...	...	...	...	...	...	...	...	...	2,471[2, 7]	21,774[2, 7]	Central African Republic
...	...	...	...	...	...	...	...	...	...	...	...	Chad
29.3	9.7	6.0	—	4.5	5.4	22.8	6.8	15.5	23.6[7]	2,796[7]	9,443[7]	Chile
45.8	16.9				37.3				2.3[3, 15]	22[15]	155[15]	China
...	...	...	...	...	...	...	...	...	...	...	662	Christmas Island
...	...	...	...	...	...	...	...	...	...	...	569	Cocos (Keeling) Islands
...	...	...	...	...	...	...	...	...	...	...	...	Colombia
...	...	...	...	...	...	...	...	...	...	...	...	Comoros
...	...	...	...	...	...	...	...	...	...	...	...	Congo
...	...	...	...	...	...	...	...	...	3.4[2]	284[2]	84[2]	Cook Islands
37.7	13.5	6.9	...	8.2	7.0	15.1	5.9	5.7	2.7	59	202	Costa Rica
...	...	...	...	...	...	...	...	...	8.3[7]	...	4,257[7]	Côte d'Ivoire
23.0	14.0	4.3	28.1	3.4	0.7	...	...	26.5[29]	...	...	188[10]	Cuba
20.2	9.9	7.0	...	1.7	9.2	37.3	4.7	10.0	1.9[3]	122	79	Cyprus
37.7	15.0	11.4	...	3.5	2.2	6.7	...	23.5	3.9	673	243	Czechoslovakia
48.9[6]	6.7[6]	7.7[6]	—[6]	0.6[6]	2.6[6]	15.0[6]	8.6[6]	9.9[6]	2.3	311	101	Denmark
...	...	...	...	...	...	...	...	...	...	...	...	Djibouti
...	...	...	...	...	...	...	...	...	...	...	...	Dominica
...	...	...	...	...	...	...	...	...	...	...	...	Dominican Republic
24.2	29.1	8.1	3.0	4.8	4.0	17.8	3.4	5.6	1.7[3]	58	79	Ecuador
...	...	...	...	...	...	...	...	...	22.6[3]	943	20,036	Egypt

Trade: domestic (continued)

country	domestic trade as percentage of GDP, 1983	year	wholesale trade					retail trade		
			establishments[a]	employees[b]	sales[c] $'000,000	employees per establishment	sales per establishment $'000	outlets[a]	employees[b]	sales[c] $'000,000
El Salvador	26.6[12]	1981	377	4,700	636	12.5	1,688	1,246	7,500	929[9]
Equatorial Guinea	...	...	...	...	...	...	...	...	...	...
Ethiopia	10.3[13]	1973[7, 31]	375	3,200	...	8.5	...	7,416	17,100	201
Faeroe Islands	11.7[10, 12]	1980	...	[2]	...	...	...	...	1,484[2, 12]	...
Falkland Islands	...	1976	2	...	...	...	...	21		...
Fiji	16.0[12]	1976	184	2,340	155	12.7	840	2,245	7,620	180[9]
Finland	10.1[12]	1984	8,248[10]	86,164[3, 10]	26,346[10]	10.4[3, 10]	3,194[10]	35,780[6]	184,000[3, 32]	17,327
France	12.1[12]	1982	96,900	815,500	200,697	8.4	2,071	398,168	1,194,951	118,492
French Guiana	...	1981	[2]	[2]	...	...	...	11[2, 7]	372[2, 7]	...
French Polynesia	24.1[6, 12]			[2]	...	...	...	...	5,123[2, 3]	...
Gabon	8.2	1982	...	...	...	...	...	...	12,683[2, 3, 11]	...
Gambia, The	23.7	1979		3,300	...	...	...	...	700	...
Gaza Strip	...	1984	...	[2]	...	...	...	...	1,000[2]	...
Germany, East	9.7[1, 12]	1984	...	...	...	...	...	103,300[6]	824,300	35,510
Germany, West	10.8[12]	1983	36,318[20]	947,700[3]	288,606	27.3[3, 20]	9,647	249,466[20]	2,004,900[3]	145,805
Ghana	25.3[12]	1977[7]	460	1,100	115	2.4	250	2,182	5,700	237
Gibraltar	...	1981	...	552	...	...	...	...	1,443	...
Greece	11.6[15]	1978	25,104	47,100	...	1.9	...	160,599	54,600	12,263[13]
Greenland	...	1979	...	[2]	[2]	...	...	...	2,153[2, 3, 21]	32[2]
Grenada	21.5[12]	1983	...	[2]	[2]	...	...	...	2,813[2, 11]	6[2]
Guadeloupe	17.5[10, 12]	1983	...	[2]	...	...	...	...	2,994[2, 11]	212
Guam	...	1982	89	981	165	11.0	1,853	802	5,400	413
Guatemala	26.0[15]	1982	...	[2]	...	...	...	88,200	51,700[2, 3, 10]	712[9]
Guernsey	...	1976	...	[2]	...	...	...	...	2,805[2]	...
Guinea	...	1979	...	[2]	...	...	...	...	12,808[2, 26]	...
Guinea-Bissau	...	1977	[2]	[2]	...	...	...	685[2]	516[2]	44[2, 21]
Guyana	8.2[15]	1980[7]	...	...	...	...	...	147	...	93[9]
Haiti	18.2[12]	1983	...	[2]	...	...	...	653[7, 25]	3,900[2, 3, 16]	174
Honduras	11.7[15]	1983	...	...	...	...	...	...	45,900[8]	401
Hong Kong	18.2[12]	1985[34]	11,709	58,655[3]	6,694[10]	5.0[3]	711[10]	48,933	170,088[3]	9,200[9]
Hungary	11.0[1, 12]	1983	206[6]	122,600[6]	13,121[11]	595[6]	...	36,960[35]	168,415[35]	8,509[35]
Iceland	...	1983	1,509[36]	5,132[11]	598[36]	...	396[36]	1,956[36]	7,052[11]	644[36]
India	14.3[12]	1979	[2]	[2]	...	...	...	738,800[2]	3,888,000[2, 3]	108,300[9]
Indonesia	16.3[15]	1983	...	[2]	...	...	...	...	559,576[2, 10]	44,816
Iran	15.8[6, 12]	1972–73	18,210	31,688	2,429	1.7	133	218,132	80,055	27,814[9]
Iraq	8.9[11, 12]	1975–76	1,532[37]	2,700[37]	...	1.8[37]	...	77,766[37]	106,800[37]	11,378[9]
Ireland	11.0[12]	1977	3,073	40,584	4,593	13.2	1,495	32,332	79,870	4,170
Isle of Man	12.0	1981	...	775	...	...	...	...	3,146	...
Israel	12.7[12]	1983	3,836[8]	36,285	...	8.7[8]	...	2,207[7, 8]	43,463	10,578
Italy	15.6[12]	1983	...	...	...	...	...	1,033,725	...	122,978
Jamaica	20.3	1979	...	1,830[7]	...	...	...	10,150[10]	11,230[7]	1,457[9]
Japan	12.2[15]	1982	428,858	4,091,000[3]	1,600,032	9.5[3]	3,731	2,559,914[38]	8,334,000[3, 38]	412,145[38]
Jersey	...	1981	...	909[3]	...	...	...	...	4,415[3]	...
Jordan	15.4[12]	1977	78[7]	1,075[7]	...	13.8[7]	...	189[7]	2,436[7]	2,210[9]
Kampuchea	...	...	...	...	...	...	...	...	...	...
Kenya	10.5[12]	1983	2,289	30,035	...	13.1	...	5,634	31,440	3,249
Kiribati	6.1[4, 12]	1976	...	[2]	...	...	...	35	913[2, 3, 4]	7
Korea, North	...	...	...	...	...	...	...	...	...	...
Korea, South	14.2[12]	1982	45,568	112,427	9,693	2.5	213	749,628	409,222	20,889
Kuwait	8.6[12]	1973	981	6,700	564	6.8	575	11,306	35,300	6,110[9]
Laos	...	...	...	...	...	...	...	...	...	...
Lebanon	28.3[8, 12]	1983	...	...	...	...	...	...	...	1,662
Lesotho	11.5[12]	...	...	...	...	...	...	...	...	...
Liberia	8.2[12]	...	...	...	...	...	...	...	...	...
Libya	5.9[6, 12]	1973	1,126	4,148[3]	...	3.7[3]	...	26,825	44,605[3]	9,205[9]
Liechtenstein	...	1975	67	216	...	3.2	...	228	740	...
Luxembourg	14.8[12]	1981	1,263[4]	7,472[4]	1,976[4]	5.9[4]	1,540[4]	3,872	11,381[4]	1,717
Macau	...	1981	...	482[3]	...	...	...	...	13,652[3]	...
Madagascar	...	1976	1,104	...	...	...	...	1,570	...	696[11]
Malaŵi	13.2[12]	1982	...	[2]	...	...	...	...	21,848[2, 12]	206[13]
Malaysia	12.3[12]	1980[39]	17,907	102,412	13,430	5.7	750	90,037	66,214	5,562
Maldives	10.8[12]	1977	...	[2]	...	...	...	...	1,341[2, 3]	...
Mali	16.5[6, 12]	1979	...	[2]	...	...	...	...	5,200[2]	...
Malta	15.3	...	...	...	...	...	...	...	...	...
Martinique	17.1[10, 12]	1983	...	[2]	...	...	...	...	3,518[2, 11]	234
Mauritania	10.8[10, 12]	1971[7]	23	100	102	4.3	4,445	59	700	103
Mauritius	11.4[12]	1984	[2]	[2]	...	[2]	...	173[2, 7]	6,222[2, 7]	387[11]
Mayotte	...	1983	[2]	...	[2]	...	[2]	41[2]	...	27[2]
Mexico	22.0[12]	1975	11,652	130,939[3]	6,739	11.2[3]	578	463,612	987,089[3]	17,062[9]
Monaco	...	...	...	...	...	...	...	...	...	...
Mongolia	37.2	1982[2, 40]	...	...	...	...	...	4,723	37,500	1,049
Montserrat	18.8[12]	1980	...	...	...	...	...	160	200	11[11]
Morocco	12.9[6]	1972	...	...	...	...	...	4,000[7]	20,000[7]	4,727[9]
Mozambique	...	1980	...	[2]	...	...	...	...	63,058[2]	...
Nauru	...	...	...	...	...	...	...	...	...	...
Nepal	3.6[15]	1983	...	[2]	...	...	...	...	119,000[2, 3, 11]	736
Netherlands, The	12.6[12]	1983	...	564,000[6]	...	...	...	158,700	...	32,410
Netherlands Antilles	...	1983	...	[2]	...	...	...	...	7,810[2, 16, 41]	149[17]
New Caledonia	26.7[12]	1981	...	[2]	...	...	...	324	4,524[2]	...
New Zealand	22.2[12]	1982–83	8,263	76,664	16,295	9.3	1,972	29,961[15]	116,301[15]	10,358[15]
Nicaragua	19.5	1983	...	...	...	...	...	20,610[6]	92,100[20]	356
Niger	13.5[12]	...	...	...	...	...	...	...	...	...
Nigeria	21.6[12]	1982[7]	...	...	...	...	...	22,190	266,280	...
Niue	...	1982	[2]	[2]	...	...	...	22[2]	82[2]	...
Norfolk Island	...	1981	...	[2]	...	...	...	...	271[2]	...

retail trade												country
percent breakdown of sales									employees per outlet	sales per outlet $'000	population per outlet	
food[d]	clothing, shoes[e]	home furnishings[f]	eating, drinking[g]	drugs, pharma-ceuticals[h]	building materials[i]	automobile parts[j]	general merchandise[k]	other[l]				
11.9[8,30]	7.6[8,30]	16.2[8,30]	...	7.9[8,30]	6.3[8,30]	12.4[8,30]	28.2[8,30]	9.5[8,30]	6.0	350	3,888	El Salvador
...	...	...	...	...	...	...	...	...	...	...	...	Equatorial Guinea
...	...	...	...	...	...	...	...	...	2.3	27	...	Ethiopia
...	...	...	...	...	...	...	...	...	...	...	...	Faeroe Islands
...	...	...	...	...	...	...	...	...	...	...	95	Falkland Islands
27.8	10.4	1.7	...	1.0	2.6	17.1	22.7	16.7	3.4	115	261	Fiji
22.8	5.4	1.9	...	2.5	8.2	27.5	20.6	11.1	4.9[3,6,32]	508[6]	135[6]	Finland
49.8	10.4	9.7	—	7.7	...	1.0[33]	7.2	14.2	3.0	298	137	France
...	...	...	...	...	...	...	...	...	34[2,7]	...	648[2,7]	French Guiana
...	...	...	...	...	...	...	...	...	...	...	...	French Polynesia
50.5	9.6	...	...	...	33.8	6.1	...	...	...	...	...	Gabon
...	...	...	...	...	...	...	...	...	...	...	...	Gambia, The
...	...	...	...	...	...	...	...	...	...	...	...	Gaza Strip
32.0	15.1	...	—	5.6	...	...	...	47.3	8.0[6]	344[6]	161	Germany, East
28.8	13.5	10.0	—	6.1	...	11.9	...	29.7	8.2[3,20]	829[20]	246[20]	Germany, West
...	...	...	...	...	...	...	...	...	2.6	108	...	Ghana
...	...	...	...	...	...	...	...	...	...	...	...	Gibraltar
60.0[13]	18.1[13]	9.5[13]	...	...	...	...	...	12.4[13]	0.3	...	59	Greece
...	...	...	...	...	...	...	...	...	...	...	...	Greenland
...	...	...	...	...	...	...	...	...	...	...	...	Grenada
...	...	...	...	...	...	...	...	...	...	...	...	Guadeloupe
16.3	4.3	3.1	9.2	0.6	4.2	32.6	7.4	22.3	6.7	515	138	Guam
...	...	...	...	...	...	...	...	...	...	...	83	Guatemala
...	...	...	...	...	...	...	...	...	...	...	...	Guernsey
...	...	...	...	...	...	...	...	...	...	...	...	Guinea
...	...	...	...	...	...	...	...	...	0.8	...	1,058	Guinea-Bissau
9.7	18.9	13.8	4.5	2.8	17.7	18.6	...	14.0	...	743	5,884	Guyana
...	...	...	...	...	...	...	...	...	...	...	...	Haiti
...	...	...	...	...	...	...	...	...	...	...	...	Honduras
23.7[13]	8.8[13]	...	...	...	...	...	5.0[13]	62.5[13]	3.5[3]	205[9]	111	Hong Kong
28.6	12.3	16.8	...	0.7	8.8	9.1	...	23.7	4.6[35]	230[35]	289[35]	Hungary
24.6	8.8	10.1	—	5.6	—	—	31.1	19.8	...	329[36]	121[36]	Iceland
...	...	...	...	...	...	...	...	...	5.3[2,3]	...	909[2,3]	India
...	...	...	...	...	...	...	...	...	...	...	...	Indonesia
...	...	...	...	...	...	...	...	...	0.4	...	141	Iran
...	...	...	...	...	...	...	...	...	1.4[37]	...	148[37]	Iraq
30.4	4.6	8.9	10.9	2.6	3.0	23.9	4.7	11.0	2.5	129	99	Ireland
...	...	...	...	...	...	...	...	...	...	...	...	Isle of Man
22.0	7.0	11.0	...	...	...	10.0	6.0	44.0	9.6[7,8]	...	1,624[7,8]	Israel
50.8	15.1	...	...	3.4	...	...	...	30.7	...	119	55	Italy
...	...	...	...	...	...	...	...	...	...	...	...	Jamaica
23.4	9.9	8.1	8.5[38]	2.2	2.3	19.4[24]	12.3	13.9	3.3[3,38]	161[38]	46[38]	Japan
...	...	...	...	...	...	...	...	...	...	...	...	Jersey
...	...	...	...	...	...	...	...	...	12.9[7]	...	792[7]	Jordan
...	...	...	...	...	...	...	...	...	...	...	...	Kampuchea
...	...	...	...	...	...	...	...	...	5.6	577	3,180	Kenya
...	...	...	...	...	...	...	...	...	...	189	1,571	Kiribati
...	...	...	...	...	...	...	...	...	...	...	...	Korea, North
29.4[20,22]	13.1[20]	8.9[20]	18.9[20]	5.0[20]	2.4[20]	5.4[20]	1.2[20]	15.6[20]	0.5	28	52	Korea, South
17.0	6.8	13.7	3.4	0.9	7.1	13.2	1.3	36.6	3.1	123	78	Kuwait
...	...	...	...	...	...	...	...	...	...	...	...	Laos
...	...	...	...	...	...	...	...	...	...	...	...	Lebanon
...	...	...	...	...	...	...	...	...	...	...	...	Lesotho
...	...	...	...	...	...	...	...	...	...	...	...	Liberia
...	...	...	...	...	...	...	...	...	1.7[3]	...	84	Libya
...	...	...	...	...	...	...	...	...	3.2	...	105	Liechtenstein
31.3	12.4	11.1	...	3.4	...	32.9	...	8.9	2.9[4]	443	94	Luxembourg
...	...	...	...	...	...	...	...	...	...	...	...	Macau
...	...	...	...	...	...	...	...	...	...	...	...	Madagascar
...	...	...	...	...	...	...	...	...	...	...	...	Malaŵi
32.9	7.3	10.8	...	2.5	1.1	33.3[24]	4.4	7.7	0.7	62	127	Malaysia
...	...	...	...	...	...	...	...	...	...	...	...	Maldives
...	...	...	...	...	...	...	...	...	...	...	...	Mali
...	...	...	...	...	...	...	...	...	...	...	...	Malta
...	...	...	...	...	...	...	...	...	...	...	...	Martinique
...	...	...	...	...	...	...	...	...	11.9	1,742	20,300	Mauritania
...	...	...	...	...	...	...	...	...	36.0[2,7]	...	5,848[2,7]	Mauritius
...	...	...	...	...	...	...	...	...	...	652[2]	1,477[2]	Mayotte
17.8	7.3	5.8	...	2.8	7.3	24.5	16.6	17.9	2.1[3]	41	130	Mexico
...	...	...	...	...	...	...	...	...	...	...	...	Monaco
...	...	...	...	...	...	...	...	...	7.9	222	371	Mongolia
...	...	...	...	...	...	...	...	...	1.2	c. 70	73	Montserrat
...	...	...	...	...	...	...	...	...	5.0[7]	...	c. 4,000[7]	Morocco
...	...	...	...	...	...	...	...	...	...	...	...	Mozambique
...	...	...	...	...	...	...	...	...	...	...	...	Nauru
...	...	...	...	...	...	...	...	...	...	...	...	Nepal
33.4	—18.5—		...	1.2	...	...	6.4	40.5	...	204	91	Netherlands, The
...	...	...	...	...	...	...	...	...	...	...	...	Netherlands Antilles
...	...	...	...	...	...	...	...	...	...	...	...	New Caledonia
19.0[13]	4.7[13]	7.1[13]	4.0[13,38]	2.4[13]	1.6[13]	40.4[13]	5.6[13]	15.2[13,42]	3.9[15]	346[15]	106[15]	New Zealand
...	...	...	...	...	...	...	...	...	...	...	...	Nicaragua
...	...	...	...	...	...	...	...	...	...	...	...	Niger
...	...	...	...	...	...	...	...	...	12.0	...	4,016	Nigeria
...	...	...	...	...	...	...	...	...	3.7[2]	...	144[2]	Niue
...	...	...	...	...	...	...	...	...	...	...	...	Norfolk Island

Trade: domestic (continued)

country	domestic trade as percentage of GDP, 1983	year	wholesale trade					retail trade		
			establishments[a]	employees[b]	sales[c] $'000,000	employees per establishment	sales per establishment $'000	outlets[a]	employees[b]	sales[c] $'000,000
Norway	11.5[12]	1982	13,949[11]	103,100[2, 3, 11]	35,119[11]	7.4[3, 11]	2,518[3, 11]	33,263	125,737[3]	15,366
Oman	11.5[15]	1983	...	[2]	...	...	...	4,731[2, 4, 12]	...	2,449
Pacific Is., Trust Terr. of the	...	...	...	...	...	...	...	...	...	...
Marshall Islands	...	1980	...	148[3]	...	...	...	...	395[3, 12]	...
Micronesia, Fed. States of	...	1980	...	348[3]	...	...	...	...	489[3, 12]	...
Northern Mariana Islands	...	1982	11	364	29	33	2,595	258	1,490	57
Palau	...	1983	...	114[3]	...	...	...	...	226[3, 12]	...
Pakistan	14.4[15]	1983	...	...	...	...	...	276,701[25]	501,773[3, 25]	12,848
Panama	14.8[12]	1971	558	10,028	446	18.0	799	6,611	25,700	608[9]
Papua New Guinea	8.4[10]	1983	...	...	...	...	...	...	...	614[13]
Paraguay	26.6[15]	1983	...	...	...	...	...	...	91,900[3, 8]	1,186
Peru	17.0[12]	1973	4,210	34,100	2,163	8.1	514	103,010	72,200	2,015
Philippines	18.5[12]	1981	20,642	122,717	4,538	5.9	220	279,968	241,872	4,836
Pitcairn Island	...	1982	—	—	—	—	—	1	...	...
Poland	13.5[1, 12]	1983	...	117,800[6]	28,297[6]	...	...	181,072[35]	438,800[35]	30,586[35]
Portugal	22.0[11, 12]	1980[7]	7,773	161,100[3]	12,509	20.7[3]	1,609	16,547	113,000[3]	4,874
Puerto Rico	15.0[12]	1982	2,282	30,541	7,133	13.4	3,126	34,461	76,370	6,505
Qatar	6.7[12]	1983	268	...	...	...	...	2,848	...	1,943
Réunion	22.8[11, 12]	1984	[2]	[2]	...	[2]	...	6,439[2]	11,132[2]	...
Romania	6.3[1]	1984	...	...	...	...	...	81,931	456,000	17,481
Rwanda	14.3[12]	1978	...	[2]	...	...	...	...	8,014[2, 12]	...
St. Christopher and Nevis	15.0[12]	1983	...	[2]	...	...	...	...	568[2]	...
St. Helena and Ascension	...	1976	...	[2]	...	...	...	...	95[2, 3]	...
St. Lucia	20.6[6, 12]	...	...	...	...	...	...	...	...	...
St. Pierre and Miquelon	...	1982	...	[2]	...	...	...	...	279[2, 3, 12]	...
St. Vincent	10.1[6]	...	...	...	...	...	...	...	...	...
San Marino	...	1985	97	[2]	...	...	...	867	829[2]	...
São Tomé and Príncipe	...	...	...	...	...	...	...	...	...	...
Saudi Arabia	9.5[13]	1981	4,460	31,481[3]	...	7.1[3]	...	80,266	174,187[3]	36,574[9]
Senegal	25.0[11, 12]	1982	...	4,600[20]	...	...	...	510[7]	5,610[7]	664[9]
Seychelles	21.8[12]	1984	[2]	[2]	...	[2]	...	186[2]	1,448[2]	...
Sierra Leone	13.8[11, 12]	1977	...	2,521[7]	...	...	...	...	2,293[7]	177[9]
Singapore	20.6[12]	1981	18,794	88,578	31,242	4.7	1,662	19,298	60,094	4,406
Solomon Islands	7.7[15, 16]	1984	...	272	...	...	...	...	1,709	...
Somalia	...	...	...	...	...	...	...	...	...	...
South Africa[43]	13.3[12]	1983	10,106[8]	232,478[8]	18,983[8]	23.0[8]	1,878[8]	58,100	373,200	22,245
Bophuthatswana[43]	...	1979[2]	...	...	...	...	...	1,248	4,195	110
Ciskei[43]	...	1979[2]	...	...	...	...	...	682	1,632	36
Transkei[43]	...	1977[2]	...	...	...	...	...	...	5,580[3]	...
Venda[43]	...	1978[2]	...	...	...	...	...	485	...	...
South West Africa/Namibia	13.9[13]	1977	222	5,035	377	22.7	1,698	1,284	7,569	254
Spain	17.6[6, 12]	1984	40,000[20]	...	...	...	...	710,865[20]	1,400,000[20]	54,777
Sri Lanka	20.0[12]	1979	353[7]	27,600[7]	...	78.2[7]	...	1,583[7]	67,100[7]	1,394[9]
Sudan, The	18.2[4, 15]	1981	...	...	...	...	...	...	...	3,278
Suriname	12.2[6, 12]	1983	...	...	...	...	...	...	12,700[3, 8]	189
Swaziland	7.6[11, 12]	1980	35	821	...	23.5	...	385	3,298	...
Sweden	10.7[12]	1982	24,078	162,300	50,934[11]	6.7	2,023[11]	57,960	265,200	32,569
Switzerland	...	1984	...	110,200[10]	...	...	...	49,972[25]	228,791[25]	23,620
Syria	24.4[12]	1984	2,827[25]	...	...	...	...	81,167[25]	110,000[3, 25]	...
Taiwan	13.6[12]	1983[34]	55,654	159,215	5,641	2.9	101	355,760	150,625	11,651
Tanzania	6.7[6, 12]	1983	...	...	...	...	...	1,620[7]	16,524[7]	945
Thailand	21.7[12]	1980[7, 47]	5,647	187,737	21,693	33.2	3,842	11,280	113,408	3,945
Togo	20.7[11, 12]	1980	...	...	...	...	...	181[7]	1,815[7]	112
Tokelau	...	1982	...	...	...	...	...	3	8[11]	...
Tonga	14.8[12]	1976	...	14[3]	...	...	...	...	654[3]	...
Trinidad and Tobago	12.2[12]	1977	124	6,786	509	54.7	4,102	370	15,986	812[9]
Tunisia	3.7[13]	1983	...	...	...	...	...	...	106,300[2, 3, 10]	2,814
Turkey	18.7	1980	24,592	46,071	8,049	0.5	327	281,949	85,059	8,686
Turks and Caicos Islands	...	...	...	...	...	...	...	...	...	...
Tuvalu	34.0[20]	1979	...	[2]	...	...	...	...	113[2, 3]	...
Uganda	6.6[11]	1977	226	4,100	...	18.1	...	251	3,200	5,285[11]
U.S.S.R.	17.8[1, 12]	1984	...	2,375,000[6]	243,800[6]	...	...	1,030,400	7,592,000	363,512
United Arab Emirates	9.8[12]	1983	[2]	[2]	...	[2]	...	13,906[2, 8, 12]	74,332[2, 3, 10, 12]	5,093
United Kingdom	11.1[12]	1982[49]	100,931[50]	...	217,760[50]	...	2,158[50]	349,659[15, 51]	2,264,000[3, 15, 51]	122,157[15, 51]
United States	17.0[12]	1984	415,829[6]	4,984,880[6]	1,997,895[6]	12.0[6]	4,805[6]	1,923,228[6]	14,467,813[6]	1,297,000
Uruguay	12.1[15]	1984	...	...	...	...	...	...	...	5,397[15]
Vanuatu	...	1983[49]	18	187[3]	...	10.4[3]	...	256	1,439[3]	...
Venezuela	11.5[12]	1979	...	...	...	...	...	...	161,596	13,366[9]
Vietnam	11.7	1979	2,400[46]	...	...	...	...	2,000[46]	50,000[46]	7,485[8]
Virgin Islands (U.S.)	...	1982	104	1,363	197	13.1	1,196	1,191	6,980	489
Wallis and Futuna	...	1983	...	[2]	...	...	...	...	123[2, 3]	...
West Bank	...	1984	...	[2]	...	...	...	...	2,000[2]	...
Western Sahara	...	...	...	...	...	...	...	...	...	...
Western Samoa	9.5[12, 16]	1975	...	[2]	...	...	...	...	1,172[2, 12]	...
Yemen (Aden)	13.9[11, 12]	...	...	...	...	...	...	...	...	...
Yemen (Ṣan'ā')	17.5[11, 12]	1983	...	...	...	...	...	...	...	2,195
Yugoslavia	21.6[12, 52]	1983	1,215[11]	146,900[11]	34,741[11]	120.9[11]	28,593[11]	81,616	357,197	18,854
Zaire	22.0[8, 15]	1981	...	...	...	...	...	3,036[7]	33,398[7]	3,300[9]
Zambia	12.1[12]	1974	494[7]	15,500[7]	977[7]	31.4[7]	1,978[7]	1,636[7]	13,700[7]	768[9]
Zimbabwe	14.5[12]	1983	...	[2]	...	...	...	...	80,600[2, 12]	693

retail trade: percent breakdown of sales — food[d]	clothing, shoes[e]	home furnishings[f]	eating, drinking[g]	drugs, pharma-ceuticals[h]	building materials[i]	automobile parts[j]	general merchandise[k]	other[l]	employees per outlet	sales per outlet $'000	population per outlet	country
34.8[22]	9.8	7.5	...	...	5.0	28.7	5.0	9.2	3.8[3]	462	124	Norway
...	...	...	...	...	...	...	...	...	...	...	...	Oman
...	...	...	...	...	...	...	...	...	...	...	...	Pacific Is., Trust Terr. of the
...	...	...	...	...	...	...	...	...	...	...	...	Marshall Islands
...	...	...	...	...	...	...	...	...	...	...	...	Micronesia, Fed. States of
25.1	1.4	1.0	10.4	...	6.2	20.5	6.6	28.8	5.8	220	71	Northern Mariana Islands
...	...	...	...	...	...	...	...	...	...	...	...	Palau
64.0	12.0	4.0	...	...	...	...	...	20.0	1.8[3, 25]	...	273[25]	Pakistan
33.5	10.9	9.5	...	...	...	...	...	46.1	3.9	56	224	Panama
...	...	...	7.8[12]	...	...	26.4	...	65.8	...	...	...	Papua New Guinea
...	...	...	...	...	...	...	...	...	...	...	...	Paraguay
...	...	...	...	...	...	...	...	...	0.7	20	145	Peru
25.4[22]	12.3	6.7	...	...	11.3	29.5[24]	...	14.8	0.9	17	177	Philippines
...	...	...	...	...	...	...	...	...	...	...	...	Pitcairn Island
31.1[35]	9.9[35]	11.1[35]	...	2.0[35]	4.9[35]	6.7[35]	...	34.3[35]	2.4[35]	169[35]	202[35]	Poland
27.5[21]	13.1[21]	9.1[21]	14.6[21]	6.9[21]	7.8[21]	16.2[21]	—4.8[21]—		6.8[3]	295	591	Portugal
30.5	9.9	4.5	7.5	4.3	5.9	23.2	8.9	5.3	2.2	188	95	Puerto Rico
...	...	...	...	...	...	...	...	...	...	682	99	Qatar
...	...	...	...	...	...	...	...	...	1.7[2]	...	83[2]	Réunion
30.1	9.9	6.3	24.7	2.1	0.8	...	...	26.1	5.6	213	277	Romania
...	...	...	...	...	...	...	...	...	...	...	...	Rwanda
...	...	...	...	...	...	...	...	...	...	...	...	St. Christopher and Nevis
...	...	...	...	...	...	...	...	...	...	...	...	St. Helena and Ascension
...	...	...	...	...	...	...	...	...	...	...	...	St. Lucia
...	...	...	...	...	...	...	...	...	...	...	...	St. Pierre and Miquelon
...	...	...	...	...	...	...	...	...	...	...	...	St. Vincent
...	...	...	...	...	...	...	...	...	...	...	...	San Marino
...	...	...	...	...	...	...	...	...	...	...	...	São Tomé and Príncipe
...	...	...	...	...	...	...	...	...	2.2[3]	...	120	Saudi Arabia
...	...	...	...	...	...	...	...	...	11.0[7]	...	11,839[7]	Senegal
...	...	...	...	...	...	...	...	...	7.8[2]	...	...	Seychelles
...	...	...	...	...	...	...	...	...	...	...	...	Sierra Leone
4.9	6.9	10.9	9.4	1.9	1.2	20.5	22.9	21.4	3.1	228	127	Singapore
...	...	...	...	...	...	...	...	...	...	...	...	Solomon Islands
...	...	...	...	...	...	...	...	...	...	...	...	Somalia
38.8[13]	14.5[13]	10.4[13]	...	3.9[13]	...	...	17.3[13]	15.1[13]	6.4	383	c. 540	South Africa[43]
...	...	...	...	...	...	...	...	...	3.4	88	1,041	Bophuthatswana[43]
...	...	...	...	...	...	...	...	...	2.4	53	972	Ciskei[43]
...	...	...	...	...	...	...	...	...	...	...	...	Transkei[43]
...	...	...	...	...	...	...	...	...	...	...	...	Venda[43]
31.4	11.9	5.3	...	2.8	1.7	...	41.9	5.0	5.9	198	713	South West Africa/Namibia
39.2	10.5	16.7	...	...	...	4.2[44]	...	29.4	2.0[20]	119[20]	52[20]	Spain
...	...	...	...	...	...	...	...	...	42.4[7]	...	9,141[7]	Sri Lanka
...	...	...	...	...	...	...	...	...	...	...	...	Sudan, The
...	...	...	...	...	...	...	...	...	...	...	...	Suriname
...	...	...	...	...	...	...	...	...	8.6	...	...	Swaziland
32.7	10.5	9.5	—	5.5	5.1	19.4[45]	...	17.3	4.6	562	144	Sweden
46.4	13.5	...	...	...	...	...	...	40.1	4.6[25]	...	128[25]	Switzerland
14.3[2, 46]	3.3[2, 46]	...	...	3.9[2, 46]	23.0[2, 46]	...	4.0[2, 46]	51.5[2, 46]	1.4[3, 25]	...	91[25]	Syria
21.5[11]	3.2[11]	8.8[11]	...	4.1[11]	3.1[11]	8.7[11, 24]	3.1[11]	47.5[11]	0.3	33	52	Taiwan
...	...	...	...	...	...	...	...	...	10.0[7]	...	12,600[7]	Tanzania
2.6	2.7	10.8	...	1.3	10.8	57.8	5.5	8.5	10.1	350	4,163	Thailand
...	...	...	...	...	...	...	...	...	10.0[7]	...	15,600[7]	Togo
...	...	...	...	...	...	...	...	...	...	...	526	Tokelau
...	...	...	...	...	...	...	...	...	...	...	...	Tonga
18.6	...	8.5	2.7	...	10.7	28.2	15.3	15.9	43.2	1,467	2,798	Trinidad and Tobago
...	...	...	...	...	...	...	...	...	...	...	...	Tunisia
24.8	12.3	15.4	...	3.7	8.8	11.2[48]	0.6	23.2[24]	0.3	30	158	Turkey
...	...	...	...	...	...	...	...	...	...	...	...	Turks and Caicos Islands
...	...	...	...	...	...	...	...	...	...	...	...	Tuvalu
...	...	...	...	...	...	...	...	...	12.7	...	47,200	Uganda
42.6	23.9	7.4	8.7	1.2	1.1	5.6	...	9.5	7.4	353	267	U.S.S.R.
...	...	...	...	...	...	...	...	...	...	...	50[2, 8]	United Arab Emirates
23.1	5.0	6.5	12.7	1.8	2.3	28.1	10.8	9.7	6.5[3, 15, 51]	349[15, 51]	161[15, 51]	United Kingdom
20.8	5.2	4.9	9.6	3.4	5.3	29.1	11.8	9.1	7.5[6]	554[6]	121[6]	United States
...	...	...	...	...	...	...	...	...	...	...	...	Uruguay
...	...	...	...	...	...	...	...	...	5.6[3]	...	484	Vanuatu
50.2	10.1	7.6	...	...	...	5.0	...	27.1	...	...	...	Venezuela
...	...	...	...	...	...	...	...	...	25.0[46]	...	26,300[46]	Vietnam
26.5	7.1	3.7	8.6	2.2	3.8	13.1	4.6	30.4	5.9	411	97	Virgin Islands (U.S.)
...	...	...	...	...	...	...	...	...	...	...	...	Wallis and Futuna
...	...	...	...	...	...	...	...	...	...	...	...	West Bank
...	...	...	...	...	...	...	...	...	...	...	...	Western Sahara
...	...	...	...	...	...	...	...	...	...	...	...	Western Samoa
...	...	...	...	...	...	...	...	...	...	...	...	Yemen (Aden)
...	...	...	...	...	...	...	...	...	...	...	...	Yemen (Şan'ā')
26.5	11.3	4.2	...	0.3	5.0	3.8	...	43.5	4.4	231	279	Yugoslavia
...	...	...	...	...	...	...	...	...	11.0[7]	...	9,676[7]	Zaire
...	...	...	...	...	...	...	...	...	8.4[7]	359[7]	2,873[7]	Zambia
...	...	...	...	...	...	...	...	...	...	...	...	Zimbabwe

[1]Percent of net material product. [2]Retail trade data include wholesale trade. [3]All persons engaged including proprietors. [4]1978. [5]Excludes retail trade network of the agricultural cooperatives. [6]1982. [7]Data refer to larger establishments only. [8]1977. [9]1983. [10]1980. [11]1981. [12]Includes hotels. [13]1984. [14]1973. [15]Excludes restaurants (eating and drinking establishments). [16]1972. [17]Netherlands Antilles includes Aruba. [18]Data refer to New Providence island only. [19]1974. [20]1979. [21]1976. [22]Includes alcohol and tobacco. [23]Home furnishings includes building materials. [24]Includes all fuels. [25]1975. [26]Includes wage earners in finance and insurance. [27]Rarotonga only. [28]Wholesalers selling directly to the public only. [29]Includes nonalcoholic beverages. [30]Selected outlets in urban areas only. [31]Excludes Addis Ababa and Asmera. [32]Includes employees of cooperatives. [33]Motorcycles and bicycles only. [34]Excludes import/export establishments. [35]Socialist sector only. [36]Excludes fuels, automobiles, alcohol and tobacco, and building materials. [37]Privately owned establishments only. [38]Excludes bars. [39]Peninsular Malaysia only. [40]State- and cooperative-owned establishments only. [41]Curaçao only. [42]Includes bars and hotels. [43]South Africa includes Bophuthatswana, Ciskei, Transkei, and Venda. [44]Motor vehicles only. [45]Includes bicycles, rental vehicles, and boats. [46]State sector only. [47]Excludes combined wholesale/retail outlets. [48]Excludes all fuels. [49]Urban establishments only. [50]Includes dealing. [51]Excludes motor vehicles. [52]Percent of gross material product.

Finance

This table presents major statistical aggregates comprising national financial structure or constituting the basis of certain international economic comparisons. It includes such data as international reserves, money supply, central banking activity and discount rates, commercial (or "deposit money") banking activity, and external indebtedness. The country models are broadly similar and permit comparison of internal structure and external position at a high level of generalization.

One of the principal financial criteria of the relative economic position of a country is the size of its international reserves. International reserves as represented in this table comprise the sum of a country's holdings of Special Drawing Rights (SDRs; an unconditional credit allocation, within a quota system set by the International Monetary Fund [IMF], of currency needed by a country to maintain stability of foreign exchange transactions or markets) and its holdings of foreign exchange vis-à-vis its holdings of gold. With the exception of the developed and a few petroleum-producing countries, the SDR balances of most countries are minimal, a consequence of the common practice of using SDRs for payments toward offsetting adverse balances of trade. The fact that most countries hold the bulk of their reserves in currencies underlines the scarcity value of gold. The ratio of external debt to total reserves cannot be interpreted in isolation: a low ratio, for example, may characterize the situation of a country with little need to borrow or of one with substantial debt but also the means to repay it. Much higher ratios, on the other hand, may be manageable, despite small reserves, if a country's export earnings are also high.

The section on money supply for the country, both as a total and as a per capita amount, refers to one particular measure of money in circulation: M1, the sum of money in private sector demand deposit accounts and outside banks in circulation; it is distinguished from a broader measure of supply, M2, which is roughly M1 plus "quasi-money" (the time, savings, and foreign-currency deposits of residents).

The section of the table outlining banking activity and the principal monetary aggregates encompasses both central bank authorities and commercial (deposit) banks. For both, the principal component aggregates are grouped under assets and liabilities. For certain countries, the four principal aggregates under assets and liabilities do not comprise the entire total, and the percentages shown, therefore, may add to less than 100% (or more, when the net of other liabilities [capital, reserves, undistributed profits, checks, and other transit items] is negative, reducing the total against which these percentages are calculated). The items excluded by the choice of categories are the least significant worldwide but may be important locally; they include such items as quasi-money, money seasonally adjusted, unused bank overdrafts, and so on. In the case of the central bank authority, data are also provided for the central bank discount rate, generally the controlling interest rate for banking and commercial activity in the country.

The largest portion of assets in the case of both central and commercial banks comprises claims on government and government agencies and foreign assets and holdings, though some of the latter, such as the large

Finance

country	international reserves, 1986[a]			money supply, 1985[b]		central bank authority, 1985[b]								
						assets (%)				liabilities (%)				central bank discount rate, 1986[a]
	total ('000,000 SDRs)	% foreign exchange	ratio of external debt to total reserves, 1984[b]	stock ('000,000,000 national currency)	M1 per capita	claims on government	claims on private sector	claims on banks	claims on foreign assets	reserve money	government deposits	foreign liabilities	capital accounts	
Afghanistan	303	89.1	6.9[1]	68.6[2]	3,900[2]	72.5[3]	0.5	0.8	25.2	66.6	7.5	0.2	8.5	...
Albania	...	...	...	...	...	...	...	...	...	...	...	...	...	...
Algeria	2,874	93.2	7.3	202.2	9,250	53.5	0.1	28.0	18.4	99.9	0.6	0.3	—	...
American Samoa	...	...	...	...	...	...	...	...	...	...	...	...	...	...
Andorra	...	...	...	...	...	...	...	...	...	...	...	...	...	...
Angola	...	...	...	...	...	...	...	...	...	...	...	...	...	...
Anguilla	...	...	...	...	...	...	...	...	...	...	...	...	...	...
Antigua and Barbuda	16	100.0	2.1[1]	0.068	850	41.0	—	—	59.0	100.3	—	—	—	7.0[6]
Argentina	2,315[7]	93.4[7]	20.6	3.030	100	31.2[2]	—	31.7[2]	33.6[2]	39.2[2]	0.2[2]	21.5[2]	8.8[2]	791.6[7, 8]
Aruba[9]	...	...	...	...	...	...	...	...	...	...	...	...	...	...
Australia	5,870	95.3	...	23.298	1,480	40.7	0.9	—	58.4	60.8	—	—	—	12.8[10]
Austria	5,382	86.3	...	181.9	24,080	3.5	—	35.8	60.7	69.4	0.4	—	31.6	4.0
Bahamas, The	234	100.0	1.3	0.208	900	14.2	—	—	85.8	57.1	16.2	—	25.6	7.5
Bahrain	1,430	99.7	0.6[1]	0.243	580	—	—	—	100.0	22.2	57.1	1.7	21.9	6.5[8]
Bangladesh	294	99.3	13.1	45.955	460	25.4[3]	—	39.0	23.0	50.7	—	36.5	5.6	11.2
Barbados	133	100.0	2.1	0.353	1,400	28.2	7.5	0.4	60.3	56.2	24.7	33.2	6.1	13.0
Belgium	5,546	80.8	...	962.5	97.430	22.1	—	—	77.9	100.6	—	—	—	8.0
Belize	23	100.0	11.1	0.059	350	68.8	—	—	31.2	56.8	—	23.4	—	20.0
Benin	5	100.0	200.5	87.1	21,750	23.8	—	73.5	2.7	41.5	7.9	46.6	—	9.5
Bermuda	...	...	...	0.040[2]	710[2]	...	...	...	...	...	...	...	...	...
Bhutan	...	...	...	0.050[5, 12]	40[5, 12]	...	...	...	...	...	...	...	...	10.0[2, 8]
Bolivia	217	85.3	11.3	207,000.0	32,200,000	36.7	—	55.8	6.8	6.1	82.4	11.4	—	149.0[7]
Botswana	760	100.0	0.6	0.188	170	—	—	—	100.0	12.1	48.2	—	11.5	9.0[7]
Brazil	7,937	98.6	5.8	93.229	690	22.1[2, 3]	17.1[2]	5.1[2]	55.1[2]	15.7[2]	22.8[2]	80.8[2]	—	246.3[7]
British Virgin Islands	...	...	...	0.019[2, 13]	1,610[2, 13]	...	...	...	...	...	...	...	...	7.8[2, 8]
Brunei	...	...	...	0.903[14]	4,650[14]	...	...	...	...	...	...	...	...	...
Bulgaria	...	...	...	...	...	...	...	...	...	...	...	...	...	...
Burkina Faso	147	99.3	3.8	69.5	10,160	16.6	—	9.8	73.6	72.2	7.3	14.9	—	9.5
Burma	52	82.7	31.4	11.551	310	−73.8	—	169.4	4.4	84.8	—	12.5	—	...
Burundi	30	100.0	16.2	18.170	3,800	80.3[3]	0.7	0.2	18.2	45.7	11.4	9.6	16.8	7.0
Cameroon	107	90.0[7]	31.7	410.8[2]	43,710[2]	24.6[2]	—	63.6[2]	11.9[2]	60.9[2]	25.8[2]	6.2[2]	—	9.0
Canada	2,948	76.1	...	69.8	2,750	75.5	—	—	24.5	109.1	—	—	—	8.8
Cape Verde	...	...	...	...	...	...	...	...	...	...	...	...	...	...
Cayman Islands	...	...	...	0.022	1,040	...	...	...	...	...	...	...	...	...
Central African Republic	54[7]	100.0[7]	4.2	48.2[2]	18,730[2]	35.4[2]	—	20.1[2]	44.6[2]	62.1[2]	2.0[2]	29.0[2]	—	8.5[7]
Chad	46[7]	100.0[7]	2.5	65.1[2]	13,290[2]	24.4[2]	—	37.4[2]	38.2[2]	78.5[2]	1.1[2]	15.1[2]	—	9.0
Chile	1,996	97.3	4.6	116.2[2]	9,780[2]	15.0[2]	11.3[2]	46.6[2]	27.0[2]	5.9[2]	1.8[2]	37.3[2]	11.7[2]	28.9[8]
China	10,831	95.9	0.4[1]	248.3	240	...	...	...	...	...	...	...	...	...
Christmas Island	...	...	...	...	...	...	...	...	...	...	...	...	...	...
Cocos (Keeling) Islands	...	...	...	...	...	...	...	...	...	...	...	...	...	...
Colombia	1,306	95.6	5.7	545.3	19,140	32.8	4.3	14.0	39.5	48.1	8.9	10.4	6.2	27.0[7]
Comoros	...	...	...	6.145[2]	16,100[2]	14.7	...	41.9	30.0	57.5	2.2	3.0	...	9.0[2]
Congo	3[7]	100.0[7]	284.8	101.3[2]	52,180[2]	53.5[2]	—	42.5[2]	4.0[2]	50.0[2]	8.7[2]	35.0[2]	—	...
Cook Islands	...	...	...	...	...	...	...	...	...	...	...	...	...	...
Costa Rica	445	99.6	8.3	32.439	13,000	47.5[3]	—	11.9	38.3	44.6	7.9	158.9	4.5	28.0
Côte d'Ivoire	21	90.5	700.7	620.2	61,000	44.8	—	53.6	0.2	53.2	3.5	43.5	—	9.5
Cuba	...	96.6[7]	...	...	...	...	...	...	...	...	...	...	...	...
Cyprus	477	96.6	1.4	0.285	430	24.6	—	8.6	66.8	84.7	4.2	0.1	—	6.0[7]
Czechoslovakia	...	...	...	...	...	...	...	...	...	...	...	...	...	...
Denmark	4,027	98.6	...	195.8	38,300	0.7	15.6	23.8	59.9	49.7	19.3	0.6	—	7.0
Djibouti	...	...	...	19.174[2]	57,240[2]	...	...	...	...	...	...	...	...	...
Dominica	4	100.0	42.0[1]	0.031	370	81.8	—	—	18.2	50.5	—	46.6	—	6.5[6]
Dominican Republic	189	99.5	9.4	1.355	220	35.0	—	20.8	37.5	38.5	—	173.0	6.2	...
Ecuador	510	97.1	10.6	129.058[2]	15,380[2]	35.8[3]	6.3	20.8	20.9	21.1	25.3	94.8	2.0	11.0[7]
Egypt	804	89.4	19.3	14.696	300	81.2[3]	—	5.3	9.4	78.3	4.6	15.0	—	13.0

outstanding loans to socialist and less developed countries of the late 1970s and early 1980s, have become the chief liabilities. In the case of liabilities for central bank authorities, the chief aggregates are reserve money, foreign payments, and demand and savings deposits. Large claims on government by the central bank authorities usually indicate a government-oriented monetary policy, whereas larger claims on the private sector by commercial banks point to the predominance of the private sector in the economy of the country. Large foreign liabilities under central bank authority often imply an adverse balance of payments position. Similarly, large foreign liabilities among the commercial banking group in the case of a less developed country often represent heavy domestic development expenditure financed by the use of foreign capital.

Because the majority of the world's countries are in the less developed bloc, and because their principal financial concern is external debt and its service, data are given for outstanding external public and publicly guaranteed long-term debt rather than for total public debt, which is the major concern in the developed countries. For comparability, the data are given in U.S. dollars. The volume of debt by itself does not create external payment problems. If the country's external debt service (interest payments plus principal repayment) needs can be met by a strong, dependable export market, by export of services, or, occasionally, by direct remittances from abroad (by residents working abroad and sending wages home in foreign currencies, for example), no debt problem need exist. Countries whose debt service ratio (total debt service as a percent of exports of goods and services) is relatively high, however, must often base their external borrowing policy on maintenance of domestic conditions of strict efficiency and, sometimes, austerity. The failure to adhere to such policies may lead to eventual crises of financial liquidity, deflation, and slower growth.

Ideally, the data presented here should be obtained by utilizing a single international methodology to provide a universally comparable set of international statistics. No international agency, however, can collect such data for all countries because of differences, both overall and in detail, in national definitions of financial aggregates, in accounting methodology, and in the completeness with which it is possible to survey a country's financial activity. The greater part of the data presented in the table comes from the IMF's *International Financial Statistics* and the World Bank's *World Debt Tables*. These sources are supplemented by other recent data from national, regional, or other international sources. In a few cases the desired data are negligible or unavailable, as noted.

Detailed percentages may not add to 100.0 because of rounding, statistical discrepancy, or nonaccounting of negligible quantities.

— None, less than 0.5 of the last significant figure, or not applicable.
... Not available.
a. Latest month.
b. Year-end.

deposit money banks, 1985b									external public debt outstanding (long-term, disbursed only), 1984b							country
assets (%)				liabilities					total ('000,000 U.S.$)	creditors (%)		debt service				
loans to government	loans to private sector	reserves	foreign assets	deposits ('000,000,000 national currency)	composition (%)					official	private	total ('000,000 U.S.$)	repayment (%)		debt service ratio (%)	
					demand depos.	savings depos.	govt. depos.	foreign liabilities					principal	interest		
4.5[3]	41.2	7.1	47.2	15.247	22.2	46.7[4]	0.2	6.9	1,728[1]	...	...	124[1]	...	...	15.5[1]	Afghanistan
...	...	...	...	...	...	...	...	...	...	...	...	...	...	...	...	Albania
8.6	89.4	1.1	0.9	195.252	53.6	11.1	4.3	12.4	12,052.0	21.2	78.8	4,560.0	71.7	28.3	32.4	Algeria
...	...	...	...	...	...	...	...	...	...	...	...	...	...	...	...	American Samoa
...	...	...	...	...	...	...	...	...	...	...	...	...	...	...	...	Andorra
...	...	...	...	...	...	...	...	...	799[1]	...	...	211[1]	...	...	12.6[1]	Angola
—	38.9[5]	1.9[5]	51.8[5]	0.063[5]	13.2[5]	67.1[5]	—	13.4[5]	0.3	...	...	...	...	...	...	Anguilla
11.9	57.7	13.7	16.7	0.448	9.4	56.2	—	29.7	20[1]	...	...	1[1]	...	...	1.0[1]	Antigua and Barbuda
17.3[2]	55.0[2]	21.0[2]	6.7[2]	3.431[2]	3.5[2]	34.6[2,4]	6.1[2]	37.4[2]	28,670.7	12.2	87.8	2,878.8	16.9	83.1	29.1	Argentina
...	...	...	...	...	...	...	...	...	...	...	...	...	...	...	...	Aruba[9]
19.8[3]	74.4	3.9	2.0	110.854	13.2	68.1	1.0	4.0	...	...	...	...	...	...	...	Australia
25.5[3]	42.7	2.6	29.2	2,172.4	4.5	42.7	2.5	30.2	...	...	...	...	...	...	...	Austria
18.5[3]	83.8	7.5	−9.9	0.713	21.1	69.6[4]	1.8	—	208.6	11.4	88.6	55.1	53.0	47.0	4.2	Bahamas, The
6.0	45.3	4.3	44.4	1.321	12.4	50.0	18.4	9.7	855[1]	...	...	133[1]	...	...	3.9[1]	Bahrain
28.4[3]	57.9	7.0	6.7	133.6	21.2	51.1	2.8	3.0	5,154.4	98.4	1.6	172.2	56.5	43.5	14.1	Bangladesh
21.6	63.3	6.8	8.3	1.216	16.3	60.8	11.2	14.6	282.9	57.2	42.8	26.3	47.5	52.5	3.8[11]	Barbados
24.9[3]	15.6	0.3	59.3	7,870.4	7.5	15.0[4]	—	72.3	...	...	...	...	...	...	...	Belgium
18.5[3]	60.7	10.6	10.2	0.199	12.3	54.9	6.1	21.9	65.5	76.2	23.8	1.6	43.7	56.3	...	Belize
2.4	92.3	2.1	3.2	139.3	45.7	17.6	7.4	—	581.5	51.7	48.3	38.3	56.4	43.6	9.2[11]	Benin
—11.4[2]—		9.6[2]	—	5.136[2]	—86.5[2]—		—	—	282[1]	...	...	91[1]	...	...	80.5[1]	Bermuda
2.1[2]	27.5[2]	2.0[2]	64.6[2]	0.665[2]	—70.6[2]—		—	8.1[2]	2[1]	...	...	—	...	...	—	Bhutan
—	68.1	24.4	7.5	427,000.0	7.3	12.2	—	124.4	3,203.5	72.3	27.7	320.7	37.2	62.8	38.3	Bolivia
6.7[3]	52.5	31.2	9.7	0.378	33.1	49.4	—	5.7	276.1	86.7	13.3	33.0	53.9	46.1	3.8	Botswana
40.8[3]	49.6	4.2	5.4	385.766	15.0	22.0	6.3	38.6	66,502.1	18.0	82.0	8,036.6	20.0	80.0	26.6	Brazil
—22.2[2]—		1.1[2]	74.2[2]	0.206[2]	8.1[2]	52.0[2]	—	36.8[2]	...	...	...	...	...	...	...	British Virgin Islands
...	...	...	...	2.577[14]	...	...	...	...	57[1]	...	...	16[1]	...	...	0.4[1]	Brunei
...	...	...	...	...	...	...	...	...	845[15]	...	...	...	...	...	...	Bulgaria
5.8	73.9	17.1	2.9	116.0	31.3	20.5	26.8	14.8	407.4	90.7	9.3	21.8	67.4	32.6	8.7[11]	Burkina Faso
92.1[3]	5.9	1.9	—	45.928	2.3	14.3[4]	9.4	11.8	2,219.3	86.0	14.0	158.3	60.8	39.2	36.9	Burma
31.2[3]	45.7	18.1	5.1	11.485	68.8	21.2	—	8.6	334.4	92.9	7.1	17.3	53.2	46.8	7.5[11]	Burundi
6.5[2]	78.7[2]	1.7[2]	13.1[2]	1,023.9[2]	26.8[2]	31.8[2]	13.5[2]	13.6[2]	1,737.8	78.6	21.4	221.5	51.7	48.3	8.9	Cameroon
6.0[3]	72.3	1.9	19.9	300.1	17.8	46.5[4]	1.4	28.8	...	...	...	...	...	...	...	Canada
...	...	...	...	...	...	...	...	...	67.5	97.9	2.1	5.2	42.3	57.7	38.2[5]	Cape Verde
—	—	—	99.9[2]	124.515[2]	—	—	—	99.9[2]	150[1]	...	...	26[1]	...	...	...	Cayman Islands
1.9[2]	83.9[2]	1.5[2]	12.7[2]	36.5[2]	29.3[2]	10.6[2]	13.5[2]	3.2[2]	224.4	88.1	11.9	12.1	52.9	47.1	11.7[11]	Central African Republic
0.3[2]	82.1[2]	2.7[2]	14.9[2]	56.0[2]	35.8[2]	4.7[2]	4.2[2]	3.0[2]	109.0	78.1	21.9	2.5	80.0	20.0	1.7	Chad
9.7[2]	81.6[2]	2.6[2]	6.0[2]	1,331.0[2]	3.9[2]	29.1[2]	7.0[2]	64.2[2]	10,838.9	14.0	86.0	1,259.5	25.5	74.5	26.2	Chile
—93.5[11]—		0.3[11]	6.2[11]	388.5[11]	—59.1[11]—		9.7[11]	1.4[11]	6,601[1]	...	...	1,399[1]	...	...	...	China
...	...	...	...	...	...	...	...	...	...	...	...	...	...	...	...	Christmas Island
...	...	...	...	...	...	...	...	...	...	...	...	...	...	...	...	Cocos (Keeling) Islands
4.4	65.9	22.7	7.0	1,187.7	28.7	35.2[4]	—	15.9	7,980.4	50.8	49.2	1,095.1	50.0	50.0	20.6	Colombia
...	...	...	...	...	...	...	...	...	103.8	99.6	0.4	2.6	38.5	61.5	...	Comoros
14.4[2]	80.0[2]	1.1[2]	4.4[2]	225.7[2]	23.3[2]	9.3[2]	18.6[2]	21.6[2]	1,395.6	59.0	41.0	250.9	69.0	31.0	20.5[11]	Congo
...	...	...	...	...	...	...	...	...	2[1]	...	...	—	...	...	—	Cook Islands
9.2[3]	51.9	35.0	3.9	67.593	33.1	63.2[4]	—	6.3	3,380.3	43.6	56.4	321.5	35.5	64.5	25.8	Costa Rica
4.1	84.5	6.1	5.2	1,271.8	24.5	25.1	9.6	11.5	4,834.6	41.1	58.9	641.0	37.0	63.0	21.3	Côte d'Ivoire
...	...	...	...	...	...	...	...	...	5,180[1]	...	...	566[1]	...	...	9.2[1]	Cuba
8.3	66.6	19.5	5.7	1.185	13.3	58.8	2.8	16.7	769.0	40.7	59.3	127.8	48.4	51.6	9.2	Cyprus
...	...	...	...	...	...	...	...	...	2,500[15]	...	...	...	...	...	...	Czechoslovakia
8.4	56.0	6.1	29.5	489.4	38.0	34.9	—	28.8	...	...	...	...	...	...	...	Denmark
...	...	...	...	...	...	...	...	...	62.6	92.5	7.5	3.1	51.6	48.4	18.4[5]	Djibouti
14.7[3]	57.2	16.3	11.9	0.156	13.9	62.3	—	13.9	42[1]	...	...	3[1]	33.3	66.7	8.8[1]	Dominica
21.7[3]	58.4	16.2	3.7	3.358	19.6	36.8	8.4	1.2	2,388.3	68.2	31.8	146.4	26.4	73.6	18.0[11]	Dominican Republic
—	83.0[2]	14.7[2]	2.3[2]	214.312[2]	38.4[2]	13.2[2]	—	—	6,630.4	28.6	71.4	991.4	20.3	79.7	33.4	Ecuador
31.7[3]	30.6	20.3	17.4	35.350	15.9	45.2[4]	1.9	12.4	15,807.6	83.6	16.4	2,352.2	72.7	27.3	34.2	Egypt

Finance (continued)

country	international reserves, 1986[a]			money supply, 1985[b]		central bank authority, 1985[b]								
						assets (%)				liabilities (%)				central bank discount rate, 1986[a]
	total ('000,000 SDRs)	% foreign exchange	ratio of external debt to total reserves, 1984[b]	stock ('000,000,000 national currency)	M1 per capita	claims on government	claims on private sector	claims on banks	claims on foreign assets	reserve money	government deposits	foreign liabilities	capital accounts	
El Salvador	265	93.6	7.6	1.961[2]	380[2]	40.8[3]	1.0	12.5	29.2	40.5	11.0	54.6	8.2	...
Equatorial Guinea	...	...	...	...	...	...	...	...	...	...	...	...	...	...
Ethiopia	256	96.5	26.6	2.702	60	52.7	—	—	10.7	64.8	10.4	5.3	6.7	3.0[6]
Faeroe Islands	...	...	...	...	...	...	...	...	...	...	...	...	...	...
Falkland Islands	...	...	...	...	...	...	...	...	...	...	...	...	...	...
Fiji	112	100.0	2.5	0.146	210	6.7[3]	—	—	93.3	65.8	3.4	—	30.3	10.5
Finland	2,605	97.4	...	27.694	5,640	2.9	14.6	21.6	60.8	52.3	12.3	1.6	20.0	7.0
France	26,149	89.0	...	1,108.0	20,080	5.6	—	30.4	64.0	44.3	—	3.9	—	9.5
French Guiana	...	...	...	1.798	21,740	...	...	...	...	...	...	...	...	...
French Polynesia	...	...	...	32.996	189,000	...	...	...	...	...	...	...	...	...
Gabon	249[7]	99.6[7]	3.6	167.8[2]	146,470[2]	—	—	7.6[2]	92.4[2]	61.6[2]	34.3[2]	1.4[2]	—	9.0
Gambia, The	1	100.0	80.5	0.162	220	61.3[3]	—	37.4	1.3	38.6	28.3	56.2	7.1	15.0
Gaza Strip	...	...	...	...	...	...	...	...	...	...	...	...	...	...
Germany, East	...	...	...	...	...	...	...	...	...	...	...	...	...	...
Germany, West	42,115	92.1	...	314.5	5,160	8.9	—	44.8	46.3	73.3	0.9	9.4	—	3.5
Ghana	416	97.8	3.5	38.308	2,990	62.4[3]	—	—	34.6	32.0	1.3	68.6	—	18.5[7]
Gibraltar	...	...	...	...	...	...	...	...	...	...	...	...	...	...
Greece	965	88.1	8.6	744.2	74,800	57.2	1.0	0.4	20.3	65.4	4.2	—	—	20.5
Greenland	...	...	...	...	...	...	...	...	...	...	...	...	...	...
Grenada	16	100.0	2.7	0.054	570	41.8	—	—	58.2	86.3	—	11.8	—	6.5[6]
Guadeloupe	...	...	...	3.425	10,300	...	...	...	...	...	...	...	...	...
Guam	...	...	...	...	...	...	...	...	...	...	...	...	...	...
Guatemala	251	92.8	5.2	1.346	170	77.9[3]	—	4.9	16.1	52.1	14.2	55.1	5.0	9.0
Guernsey	...	...	...	...	...	...	...	...	...	...	...	...	...	...
Guinea	...	...	...	22.5	3,490	...	...	...	...	...	...	...	...	...
Guinea-Bissau	...	...	...	...	...	...	...	...	...	...	...	...	...	...
Guyana	6[7]	100.0[7]	115.7	0.740	780	99.2	—	—	0.8	16.9	—	70.4	7.5	14.0
Haiti	6	83.3	36.1	1.400[2]	270[2]	91.2[3]	3.0	0.4	4.3	53.7	14.7	40.0	6.1	...
Honduras	108	99.1	14.3	0.856	200	43.0[3]	—	24.3	15.0	29.4	11.7	65.4	18.7	24.0[7]
Hong Kong	...	...	...	45.266	8,350	...	...	...	...	...	...	...	...	6.0[16]
Hungary	3,035	97.4	3.4	243.0	22,830	4.3	—	36.0	30.6	31.5	2.3	71.7	2.7	10.5
Iceland	162	99.4	...	15.382	63,300	33.2	0.2	22.9	43.7	48.5	20.1	7.8	—	19.0
India	5,672	94.2	3.6	403.3	530	74.6	—	1.1	14.6	68.9	0.1	9.4	7.8	10.0
Indonesia	4,379	97.5	4.7	10,124.0	60,830	4.6	7.5	47.6	40.3	30.6	29.2	0.8	5.7	11.4[17]
Iran	5,376[5]	89.2[5]	...	3,922.0[11]	87,880[11]	85.0[3, 11]	—	2.1[11]	12.8[11]	68.2[11]	17.9[11]	1.6[11]	3.9[11]	9.0[18]
Iraq	...	...	...	...	...	...	...	...	...	...	...	...	...	...
Ireland	2,555	99.5	...	2.288	640	16.3	—	—	83.7	64.8	6.9	—	28.5	10.0
Isle of Man	...	...	...	...	...	...	...	...	...	...	...	...	...	...
Israel	3,087	98.8	5.0	0.989	230	58.7	—	2.7	38.6	14.8	9.5	0.2	—	54.6
Italy	17,001	86.3	...	279,463.0[2]	4,904,000[2]	51.9[2]	—	0.7[2]	47.4[2]	61.6[2]	—	0.2[2]	—	12.0
Jamaica	192	100.0	22.4	1.520	660	76.0	—	1.0	23.0	40.7	28.5	157.6	5.2	21.0
Japan	27,457	96.9	...	88,980.0	737,000	46.3	—	32.5	21.2	107.2	9.1	—	—	3.5
Jersey	...	...	...	...	...	...	...	...	...	...	...	...	...	...
Jordan	346	89.3	4.2	0.848	310	35.1	—	—	64.9	120.2	1.1	—	—	6.2[7]
Kampuchea	...	...	...	...	...	...	...	...	...	...	...	...	...	...
Kenya	410	99.3	6.7	12.923	640	56.6	—	—	43.4	46.7	—	54.7	4.5	12.5
Kiribati	...	...	...	...	...	...	...	...	...	...	...	...	...	...
Korea, North	...	...	...	...	...	...	...	...	...	...	...	...	...	...
Korea, South	2,394	99.5	8.9	7,558.0	183,000	18.9[3]	—	63.9	17.1	30.3	8.3	8.3	—	5.0
Kuwait	4,250	97.9	0.3[1]	0.944	550	—	—	—	100.0	46.2	54.4	—	14.3	6.0
Laos	...	...	...	...	...	...	...	...	...	...	...	...	...	...
Lebanon	795	59.4	0.2	13.784[2]	5,210[2]	36.6	0.8	2.5	60.0	35.0	57.2	—	—	18.1[7]
Lesotho	69	100.0	2.7	0.133	90	17.3	—	—	82.7	78.8	−6.4	8.5	17.1	...
Liberia	5	100.0	194.0	0.114	50	98.8[3]	0.2	0.2	0.4	28.6	2.2	60.0	17.9	8.1[8]
Libya	5,382	97.7	0.2[1]	2.711[2]	750[2]	30.6	1.3	—	68.1	82.0	26.6	—	—	7.5
Liechtenstein	...	...	...	...	...	...	...	...	...	...	...	...	...	...
Luxembourg	...	...	...	51.6[2]	141,000[2]	...	...	...	...	...	...	...	...	8.7[19]
Macau	...	...	...	...	...	...	...	...	...	...	...	...	...	...
Madagascar	49[7]	100.0[7]	27.8	239.9[2]	24,640[2]	91.5[2, 3]	—	1.3[2]	7.2[2]	16.1[2]	25.5[2]	101.0[2]	1.2[2]	5.5[20]
Malawi	21	95.2	12.8	0.167	20	82.5[3]	—	—	17.5	37.9	7.6	60.2	—	11.0
Malaysia	4,598	98.2	3.1	14.132	900	16.5	—	—	83.5	65.1	5.1	2.0	—	4.7[7]
Maldives	5	100.0	10.3	0.172	940	86.5[3]	—	0.1	13.5	85.6	13.4	10.8	2.7	9.0[17]
Mali	19	94.7	35.0	113.8	13,860	76.8	—	16.4	6.8	57.0	—	31.2	—	9.5
Malta	920	98.3	0.1	0.318	950	—	—	—	100.0	80.4	11.1	—	—	6.0
Martinique	...	...	...	3.322	10,150	...	...	...	...	...	...	...	...	...
Mauritania	45	100.0	15.1	12.173	7,350	22.8	5.5	48.2	23.5	33.5	1.1	53.9	20.2	6.0[7]
Mauritius	43	97.7	14.5	2.373	2,320	89.9	—	0.9	9.2	34.7	—	47.7	5.4	11.0
Mayotte	...	...	...	0.162	2,420	...	...	...	...	...	...	...	...	...
Mexico	4,827	98.3	9.4	3,582.5	45,620	74.2	—	0.5	24.4	64.1	—	12.2	—	78.5[6]
Monaco	...	...	...	...	...	...	...	...	...	...	...	...	...	...
Mongolia	...	...	...	...	...	...	...	...	...	...	...	...	...	...
Montserrat	...	...	...	0.009[5, 13]	800[5, 13]	...	...	...	...	...	...	...	...	4.5[5, 8]
Morocco	111	78.4	140.3	36.779[2]	1,610[2]	72.4[2]	7.0[2]	14.5[2]	2.4[2]	63.0[2]	0.9[2]	41.1[2]	—	7.0[7]
Mozambique	...	...	...	...	...	...	...	...	...	...	...	...	...	...
Nauru	...	...	...	...	...	...	...	...	...	...	...	...	...	...
Nepal	73	93.2	4.9	5.616	340	77.6[3]	2.5	3.6	12.8	50.6	22.1	6.6	—	15.0[11]
Netherlands, The	11,095	86.1	...	88.8	6,130	5.8	—	9.2	85.0	42.7	4.7	—	—	5.0
Netherlands Antilles[9]	226	91.6	3.7[1]	0.528	2,230	34.5	0.1	—	65.4	68.6	14.2	—	11.6	8.0
New Caledonia	...	...	...	28.706	192,000	...	...	...	...	...	...	...	...	...
New Zealand	1,230	99.9	...	4.104	1,260	20.0	24.8	0.1	55.1	26.4	40.9	23.1	—	16.7
Nicaragua	171[11]	97.7[11]	18.1[11]	10.937[11]	3,720[11]	74.3[11]	—	17.9[11]	7.8[11]	34.9[11]	−0.9[11]	84.5[11]	1.3[11]	...
Niger	138	99.3	7.6	80.5	12,870	35.1	—	18.3	46.6	52.7	14.9	32.1	—	9.5
Nigeria	1,578	98.5	8.0	12.204[2]	130[2]	76.9	7.5	1.9	11.5	53.2	18.3	0.2	2.5	10.0
Niue	...	...	...	...	...	...	...	...	...	...	...	...	...	...
Norfolk Island	...	...	...	...	...	...	...	...	...	...	...	...	...	...

deposit money banks, 1985[b]									external public debt outstanding (long-term, disbursed only), 1984[b]							country
assets (%)				liabilities					total ('000,000 U.S.$)	creditors (%)		debt service				
loans to govern-ment	loans to private sector	re-serves	foreign assets	deposits ('000,000,000 national currency)	composition (%)					offi-cial	private	total ('000,000 U.S.$)	repayment (%)		debt service ratio (%)	
					demand depos.	savings depos.	govt. depos.	foreign liabilities					princi-pal	inter-est		
5.4	66.6	20.8	7.2	6.264	21.5	57.6[4]	—	1.8	1,387.8	86.0	14.0	194.2	63.0	37.0	17.2[11]	El Salvador
...	...	...	...	...	...	...	...	...	102.6	75.7	24.3	1.4	92.9	7.1	...	Equatorial Guinea
60.1[3]	14.4	21.8	3.7	3.225	39.8	40.1	2.5	3.8	1,384.2	86.9	13.1	84.1	62.9	37.1	13.8	Ethiopia
...	...	...	...	...	...	...	...	...	...	...	...	...	...	...	...	Faeroe Islands
...	...	...	...	...	...	...	...	...	1[1]	...	...	—	...	...	—	Falkland Islands
19.0[3]	64.3	7.6	9.1	0.545	15.5	65.3	3.2	9.0	289.6	76.1	23.9	51.6	52.9	47.1	9.8	Fiji
0.7	78.5	4.7	16.1	258.417	8.3	51.9	2.9	26.9	...	...	...	...	...	...	...	Finland
4.9	59.3	1.3	34.5	3,756.0	19.2	28.8	—	34.4	...	...	...	...	...	...	...	France
...	...	...	...	...	...	...	...	...	25[1]	...	...	2[1]	...	...	1.9[1]	French Guiana
...	...	...	...	...	...	...	...	...	125[1]	...	...	7[1]	...	...	3.0[1]	French Polynesia
22.4[2]	72.0[2]	3.5[2]	2.1[2]	350.0[2]	32.3[2]	30.0[2]	18.7[2]	4.1[2]	724.5	35.5	64.5	252.8	72.3	27.7	9.4[11]	Gabon
23.5[3]	52.8	18.7	4.9	0.377	19.9	25.2	—	7.5	161.0	79.6	20.4	7.3	57.5	42.5	7.7[11]	Gambia, The
...	...	...	...	...	...	...	...	...	...	...	...	...	...	...	...	Gaza Strip
...	...	...	...	...	...	...	...	...	7,630[15]	...	...	...	...	...	...	Germany, East
19.3[3]	66.0	3.2	11.5	2,418.9	8.7	31.4	7.8	7.7	...	...	...	...	...	...	...	Germany, West
29.0[3]	34.5	35.1	1.5	30.914	42.8	27.2	3.2	7.4	1,122.4	88.7	11.3	81.0	68.3	31.7	13.2	Ghana
——20.6——		0.8	—	0.224	——86.5——			—	76[1]	...	...	14[1]	...	...	—	Gibraltar
30.4	40.7	20.0	8.8	3,306.3	6.0	61.4	—	26.1	9,455.8	19.6	80.4	1,344.1	44.8	55.2	18.3	Greece
...	...	...	...	...	...	...	...	...	...	...	...	...	...	...	...	Greenland
18.4[3]	51.2	20.9	9.5	0.214	13.6	57.5	—	13.0	39.9	92.5	7.5	4.0	62.5	37.5	9.9[11]	Grenada
...	...	...	...	...	...	...	...	...	59[1]	...	...	7[1]	...	...	3.6[1]	Guadeloupe
——66.3——		...	...	0.559	28.6	71.4	—	—	...	...	...	...	...	...	...	Guam
4.8	71.9	20.6	2.7	2.834	21.7	65.2	—	2.8	1,513.9	78.0	22.0	196.0	56.9	43.1	15.5	Guatemala
...	...	...	...	...	...	...	...	...	...	...	...	...	...	...	...	Guernsey
...	...	...	...	...	...	...	...	...	1,168.2	84.7	15.3	105.1	80.2	19.8	21.4[5]	Guinea
...	...	...	...	...	...	...	...	...	149.4	84.7	15.3	3.3	90.9	9.1	11.6[11]	Guinea-Bissau
58.4[3]	18.4	22.0	1.2	2.851	10.9	49.1	—	2.2	682.5	75.6	24.4	31.0	47.7	52.3	20.1[11]	Guyana
—	59.3[2]	30.7[2]	10.0[2]	1.464[2]	27.1[2]	67.7[2]	—	3.0[2]	493.9	85.6	14.4	17.4	64.9	35.1	5.6	Haiti
22.8	71.2	5.7	0.3	2.271	18.8	45.6[4]	—	2.7	1,840.7	76.7	23.3	134.7	40.6	59.4	15.0[11]	Honduras
—	30.6	1.6	41.1	1,101.0	——34.6[4]——		—	42.2	270.4	19.1	80.9	52.9	68.2	31.8	0.2[11]	Hong Kong
54.9[3]	30.9	11.8	2.4	719.2	16.2	33.7[4]	—	9.3	7,379.8	14.1	85.9	2,535.8	72.7	27.3	24.2	Hungary
2.6	80.5	12.9	3.9	62.094	22.8	37.5	—	27.8	...	...	...	...	...	...	...	Iceland
19.4	67.4	13.3	—	978.6	15.6	70.0	—	—	22,403.1	88.9	11.1	1,461.1	56.6	43.4	10.1	India
—	69.7	9.1	21.2	29,436.0	18.9	44.1	6.4	2.0	22,882.8	56.1	43.9	3,247.2	50.1	49.9	14.7	Indonesia
17.0[11]	48.5[11]	31.1[11]	3.5[11]	5,572.0[11]	32.8[1]	54.9[11]	—	1.2[11]	3,949[1]	...	...	1,951[1]	...	...	9.1[1]	Iran
...	...	...	...	...	...	...	...	...	5,367[1]	...	...	1,481[1]	...	...	11.6[1]	Iraq
22.6	59.5	6.0	11.9	9.124	11.3	48.9	0.6	25.8	...	...	...	...	...	...	...	Ireland
...	...	...	...	...	...	...	...	...	...	...	...	...	...	...	...	Isle of Man
27.9	39.3	4.9	27.9	33.527	1.5	71.8	—	44.3	15,415.2	75.5	24.5	1,885.5	47.2	52.8	17.9	Israel
22.3[2]	52.6[2]	11.9[2]	13.2[2]	549,188.0[2]	41.5[2]	34.6[2]	—	16.7[2]	...	...	...	...	...	...	...	Italy
27.8[3]	44.4	22.3	5.6	5.861	16.7	63.4	2.4	6.6	2,174.7	78.8	21.2	285.5	67.8	32.2	21.0	Jamaica
12.5[3]	79.6	1.6	6.3	400,254.0	16.4	54.4	—	10.2	...	...	...	...	...	...	...	Japan
...	...	...	...	...	...	...	...	...	...	...	...	...	...	...	...	Jersey
11.6	60.6	8.2	19.6	1.968	15.7	52.0	6.2	17.1	2,336.3	73.5	26.5	281.8	58.7	41.3	14.8	Jordan
...	...	...	...	...	...	...	...	...	430[1]	...	...	—	...	...	—	Kampuchea
15.4[3]	73.9	8.4	2.4	27.129	34.0	51.5[4]	3.4	3.0	2,633.4	81.6	18.4	348.4	58.8	41.2	21.5	Kenya
...	...	...	...	...	...	...	...	...	17[1]	...	...	—	...	...	—	Kiribati
...	...	...	...	...	...	...	...	...	...	...	...	...	...	...	...	Korea, North
15.5	73.2	1.8	9.5	55,183.0	7.8	38.1[4]	4.4	25.6	24,642.1	39.3	60.7	4,558.7	54.6	45.4	13.5	Korea, South
—	66.3	4.3	29.3	7.613	8.1	45.9	5.1	17.8	1,764[1]	...	...	750[1]	...	...	4.3[1]	Kuwait
...	...	...	...	...	...	...	...	...	375[1]	...	...	4[1]	...	...	7.7[1]	Laos
16.9[2]	48.1[2]	5.9[2]	29.1[2]	90.009[2]	6.8[2]	69.4[2, 4]	0.8[2]	13.7[2]	178.7	85.0	15.0	53.3	75.2	24.8	...	Lebanon
23.4[3]	24.4	21.4	30.8	0.365	29.6	48.6	5.6	2.2	134.3	90.7	9.3	21.1	82.0	18.0	5.0	Lesotho
23.5[3]	36.5	33.1	6.9	0.213	31.6	26.3	5.0	21.7	756.7	78.7	21.3	42.2	51.7	48.3	8.6	Liberia
—	66.5	27.0	6.5	3.113	58.5	26.0	17.8	1.8	1,140[1]	...	...	1,130[1]	...	...	8.4[1]	Libya
...	...	...	...	...	...	...	...	...	...	...	...	...	...	...	...	Liechtenstein
—	2.2	—	97.8	6,769.6	1.0	5.0	—	86.9	...	...	...	...	...	...	...	Luxembourg
...	...	...	...	...	...	...	...	...	54[1]	...	...	40[1]	...	...	4.7[1]	Macau
2.9[2]	83.4[2]	4.6[2]	9.1[2]	322.7[2]	46.4[2]	5.1[2]	10.2[2]	6.8[2]	1,636.4	75.7	24.3	116.6	73.2	26.8	24.3[11]	Madagascar
31.0[3]	45.6	20.7	2.8	0.467	20.9	46.6	—	14.7	730.6	82.5	17.5	82.3	60.9	39.1	23.0[11]	Malaŵi
12.0	79.5	3.9	4.6	65.160	10.9	53.4	9.8	12.2	11,846.0	21.9	78.1	1,472.5	34.9	65.1	7.7	Malaysia
24.7[3]	50.9	20.0	4.4	0.362	9.5	26.0	0.5	52.2	50.5	81.8	18.2	10.5	88.6	11.4	12.5	Maldives
2.3	81.7	11.0	5.0	135.1	36.8	10.2	7.8	14.0	960.0	96.9	3.1	17.4	57.5	42.5	8.0	Mali
4.6	49.9	29.8	15.6	0.426	7.5	78.3	—	6.9	104.1	99.8	0.2	5.2	75.0	25.0	0.6	Malta
...	...	...	...	...	...	...	...	...	40[1]	...	...	7[1]	...	...	1.9[1]	Martinique
0.9	90.0	7.5	1.6	16.375	45.0	10.2	0.8	26.7	1,170.6	89.5	10.5	42.2	45.0	55.0	10.0[11]	Mauritania
24.6	57.2	9.5	8.6	6.816	18.1	73.8	—	2.7	354.2	70.0	30.0	75.0	66.5	33.5	14.8	Mauritius
...	...	...	...	...	...	...	—	—	...	...	...	...	...	...	...	Mayotte
33.1[3]	39.8	25.8	1.4	15,144.0	11.2	59.4[4]	—	21.7	69,007.1	11.1	88.9	11,090.7	33.0	67.0	34.3	Mexico
...	...	...	...	...	...	...	...	...	...	...	...	...	...	...	...	Monaco
...	...	...	...	...	...	...	...	...	...	...	...	...	...	...	...	Mongolia
—	71.7[5]	2.9[5]	17.6[5]	0.043[5]	18.8[5]	61.4[5]	—	13.9[5]	4[1]	...	...	—	...	...	—	Montserrat
33.5[2]	57.8[2]	2.2[2]	6.5[2]	37.271[2]	52.0[2]	24.2[2]	2.8[2]	0.9[2]	10,169.2	63.7	36.3	1,133.6	56.4	43.6	37.6	Morocco
...	...	...	...	...	...	...	...	...	1,095[1]	...	...	182[1]	...	...	62.3[1]	Mozambique
...	...	...	...	...	...	...	...	...	31[1]	...	...	26[1]	...	...	...	Nauru
33.6[3]	41.3	8.7	16.5	10.501	14.2	70.5	—	4.8	426.5	99.8	0.2	10.1	53.5	46.5	3.4	Nepal
12.1[3]	47.4	0.4	40.1	498.0	12.0	36.3	—	36.5	...	...	...	...	...	...	...	Netherlands, The
0.3[3]	31.0	4.6	64.1	3.362	7.8	26.5[4]	0.3	61.9	682[1]	...	...	122[1]	...	...	10.3[1]	Netherlands Antilles[9]
...	...	...	...	...	...	...	...	...	223[1]	...	...	15[1]	...	...	5.5[1]	New Caledonia
28.7	64.0	1.2	6.1	15.648	20.0	65.6	—	4.9	...	...	...	...	...	...	...	New Zealand
—	84.4[11]	13.8[11]	1.8[11]	20.709[11]	26.2[11]	20.5[4, 11]	21.6[11]	6.5[11]	3,835.4	71.8	28.2	51.9	42.5	57.5	17.5[11]	Nicaragua
15.8	64.3	18.1	1.8	137.3	33.2	20.0	13.9	31.6	677.9	77.0	23.0	66.6	59.5	40.5	18.4[11]	Niger
44.9	49.0	4.5	1.6	24.096	25.7	41.0	5.3	1.0	11,815.4	18.5	81.5	3,162.8	37.1	62.9	25.5	Nigeria
...	...	...	...	...	...	...	...	...	...	...	...	...	...	...	...	Niue
...	...	...	...	...	...	...	...	...	...	...	...	...	...	...	...	Norfolk Island

Finance (continued)

country	international reserves, 1986[a]			money supply, 1985[b]		central bank authority, 1985[b]								central bank discount rate, 1986[a]
						assets (%)				liabilities (%)				
	total ('000,000 SDRs)	% foreign exchange	ratio of external debt to total reserves, 1984[b]	stock ('000,000,000 national currency)	M1 per capita	claims on government	claims on private sector	claims on banks	claims on foreign assets	reserve money	government deposits	foreign liabilities	capital accounts	
Norway	11,347	99.6	...	98.6	23,750	14.2	—	6.1	79.6	23.3	60.3	—	—	8.0
Oman	864	98.8	1.4	0.322	260	—	—	—	100.0	45.0	31.4	0.6	17.8	9.5[8]
Pacific Is., Trust Terr. of the	...	...	...	...	...	...	...	...	...	...	...	...	...	...
Marshall Islands	...	...	...	...	...	...	...	...	...	...	...	...	...	...
Micronesia, Fed. States of	...	...	...	...	...	...	...	...	...	...	...	...	...	...
Northern Mariana Islands	...	...	...	...	...	...	...	...	...	...	...	...	...	...
Palau	...	...	...	...	...	...	...	...	...	...	...	...	...	...
Pakistan	907	92.7	9.0	123.060	1,230	59.7	—	20.6	19.7	61.1	5.6	23.9	—	10.0
Panama	89[7]	100.0[7]	14.3	0.410	190	66.4[3]	25.8	—	7.8	19.8	21.3	53.6	8.7	...
Papua New Guinea	392	99.5	1.9	0.244	70	11.7	—	—	88.3	25.0	18.5	5.7	21.5	8.8[7]
Paraguay	455	99.8	1.9	125.202	36,740	29.1[3]	5.9	8.8	50.5	77.6	4.5	7.8	11.1	...
Peru	1,736	94.9	5.9	22.818	1,160	25.3[3]	—	7.1	58.9	58.0	10.4	23.9	8.9	72.0[7]
Philippines	842	92.6	17.8	35.8	660	36.7[3]	—	19.6	18.5	35.8	7.4	69.3	—	16.0
Pitcairn Island	...	...	...	...	...	...	...	...	...	...	...	...	...	...
Poland	...	...	...	...	...	...	...	...	...	...	...	...	...	...
Portugal	1,747	59.5	8.7	801.0[2]	80,160[2]	29.9[2]	2.2[2]	2.2[2]	65.6[2]	38.5[2]	4.2[2]	12.3[2]	7.4[2]	23.0
Puerto Rico	...	...	...	...	...	...	...	...	...	...	...	...	...	...
Qatar	526	93.2	0.9[1]	4.017	13,340	—	—	0.3	99.7	73.4	31.5	—	4.6	7.0[2, 8]
Réunion	...	...	...	5.218	9,550	...	...	...	...	...	...	...	...	...
Romania	390	65.6	7.5	162.3[2]	7,150[2]	—	47.0[2]	50.0[2]	3.0[2]	35.6[2]	22.8[2]	5.0[2]	—	...
Rwanda	99	100.0	2.3	14.699	2,400	19.8[3]	1.5	15.9	59.5	53.8	17.3	10.1	—	9.0
St. Christopher and Nevis	...	...	...	0.023[5, 13]	520[5, 13]	...	...	...	...	...	...	...	...	...
St. Helena and Ascension	...	...	...	...	...	...	...	...	...	...	...	...	...	...
St. Lucia	12	100.0	4.0[1]	0.071	520	48.6	—	—	51.4	96.0	—	1.2	—	7.0[6]
St. Pierre and Miquelon	...	...	...	0.151	25,170	...	...	...	...	...	...	...	...	...
St. Vincent and the Grenadines	14	100.0	1.6	0.053	500	29.3	—	—	70.7	98.2	—	1.7	—	6.5[6]
San Marino	...	...	...	...	...	...	...	...	...	...	...	...	...	...
São Tomé and Príncipe	...	...	...	...	...	...	...	...	...	...	...	...	...	...
Saudi Arabia	19,267	99.2	0.2[1]	81.8	7,280	—	—	—	100.0	10.6	67.0	—	—	...
Senegal	12	91.7	317.4	193.5	29,630	46.5	—	52.9	0.6	31.7	1.9	66.1	—	9.5
Seychelles	3	100.0	7.3	0.155	2,380	63.4	—	3.6	32.9	60.3	13.2	—	7.8	6.0
Sierra Leone	10	100.0	43.8	0.900	250	99.5	—	—	0.5	55.6	0.4	131.4	—	14.0
Singapore	11,472	100.0	0.2	8.785	3,430	—	—	—	100.0	25.6	22.7	—	—	5.1[17]
Solomon Islands	28	100.0	0.4	0.027	100	5.5	—	9.1	85.3	34.2	42.4	7.9	27.4	...
Somalia	3	100.0	616.5	9.773	1,680	75.3[3]	—	21.7	3.0	45.9	16.3	88.3	6.5	12.0
South Africa	406	65.0	...	21.332	650	11.5	—	12.7	75.8	80.7	2.9	76.8	—	11.0
Bophuthatswana	...	...	...	...	...	...	...	...	...	...	...	...	...	...
Ciskei	...	...	...	...	...	...	...	...	...	...	...	...	...	...
Transkei	...	...	...	...	...	...	...	...	...	...	...	...	...	...
Venda	...	...	...	...	...	...	...	...	...	...	...	...	...	...
South West Africa/Namibia	...	...	...	...	...	...	...	...	...	...	...	...	...	...
Spain	11,169	95.4	...	6,589.0	170,700	55.2	—	16.3	28.4	98.2	3.6	—	7.9	8.0
Sri Lanka	377	99.5	4.7	18.663	1,180	67.1	—	4.1	28.8	41.1	—	24.9	—	11.0
Sudan, The	2	100.0	321.5	2.752[2]	120[2]	95.5[2, 3]	—	4.0[2]	0.5[2]	51.8[2]	17.5[2]	33.0[2]	0.4[2]	13.5[2, 8]
Suriname	17	88.2	1.0[1]	0.880	2,280	93.8	—	—	6.2	84.5	2.0	—	4.3	...
Swaziland	82	100.0	2.2	0.077	120	10.9	—	—	89.1	49.5	4.6	16.2	9.4	10.0
Sweden	5,839	96.4	...	77.2[2]	9,260[2]	57.3	—	4.9	37.7	43.8	—	0.6	—	8.0
Switzerland	16,658	82.5	...	46.5	7,120	6.4	—	10.0	83.6	69.4	4.6	—	—	4.0
Syria	79[11]	63.3[11]	27.9[11]	46.207[2]	4,650[2]	94.7[2, 3]	—	2.0[2]	3.3[2]	75.1[2]	12.5[2]	11.1[2]	0.3[2]	5.0
Taiwan	...	...	...	751.469	39,300	0.5[3]	—	5.7	93.0	21.5	3.6	—	—	6.8[7]
Tanzania	23	100.0	97.9	20.541[11]	1,010[11]	93.9[2]	3.1[2]	3.0[2]	—	79.3[2]	—	17.0[2]	—	4.3
Thailand	2,137	95.9	3.8	90.1	1,740	47.5	—	11.3	35.5	38.4	3.6	13.3	45.9	11.0
Togo	284	99.6	3.2	82.7	27,690	26.0	—	2.5	71.5	74.2	6.9	17.9	—	9.5
Tokelau	...	...	...	...	...	...	...	...	...	...	...	...	...	...
Tonga	...	...	...	...	...	3.4[21]	14.5[21]	24.9[21]	51.7[21]	——89.2[21]——		0.2[21]	10.6[21]	...
Trinidad and Tobago	746	99.7	0.7	2.260	1,900	−6.0	—	—	106.0	63.9	10.0	—	27.9	7.5
Tunisia	137	95.6	9.0	2.059	290	4.6	—	75.9	19.5	68.6	7.5	0.1	21.5	9.2
Turkey	1,185	89.7	11.2	3,256.4	66,100	72.4[3]	—	3.2	23.9	31.3	0.9	68.6	1.1	52.0[7]
Turks and Caicos Islands	...	...	...	...	...	...	...	...	...	...	...	...	...	...
Tuvalu	...	...	...	...	...	...	...	...	...	...	...	...	...	...
Uganda	13[20]	100.0[20]	35.9[20]	98.657[2]	6,740[2]	76.7[2, 3]	—	—	23.3[2]	32.7[2]	29.2[2]	97.9[2]	—	24.0[7]
U.S.S.R.	...	...	...	...	...	...	...	...	...	...	...	...	...	...
United Arab Emirates	2,783	99.0	0.9[1]	9.505	7,410	3.5[3]	—	1.2	95.3	49.5	15.6	—	35.4	...
United Kingdom	13,128	94.9	...	61.6	1,090	50.2	0.9	—	48.9	66.1	—	27.5	—	10.0[6]
United States	39,298	76.6	...	640.0	2,670	81.1	—	—	18.3	95.0	7.5	0.2	—	6.5
Uruguay	317	71.0	11.3	46.0	15,270	34.0	13.6	5.3	29.2	21.5	35.6	51.9	—	108.3[2]
Vanuatu	10	100.0	0.7	2.642	19,960	0.3	—	52.0	47.7	55.1	35.5	1.1	12.2	8.2[8]
Venezuela	8,743	95.4	1.9	93.711	5,410	5.4	—	1.2	93.4	69.0	18.1	—	17.5	13.0
Vietnam	...	...	...	...	...	...	...	...	...	...	...	...	...	...
Virgin Islands (U.S.)	...	...	...	...	...	...	...	...	...	...	...	...	...	...
Wallis and Futuna	...	...	...	0.632	46,130	...	...	...	...	...	...	...	...	...
West Bank	...	...	...	...	...	...	...	...	...	...	...	...	...	...
Western Sahara	...	...	...	...	...	...	...	...	...	...	...	...	...	...
Western Samoa	13	100.0	5.7	0.021	130	43.4	—	8.5	48.0	42.9	—	43.1	—	12.2[5, 19]
Yemen (Aden)	197[7]	99.0[7]	5.0	0.369[2]	180[2]	81.1[2]	—	—	18.9[2]	94.5[2]	—	8.2[2]	—	...
Yemen (Ṣan'ā')	345	100.0	5.3	18.823	2,880	91.8[3]	—	0.2	8.1	82.0	7.4	1.3	0.7	9.5[8]
Yugoslavia	1,128	94.2	7.1	1,251.9[2]	54,310[2]	5.6[2]	6.5[2]	66.7[2]	21.2[2]	132.9[2]	1.1[2]	81.4[2]	—	47.0[2]
Zaire	134	87.3	26.7	17.434[2]	590[2]	71.1[2, 3]	0.2[2]	2.7[2]	26.0[2]	36.8[2]	0.7[2]	91.5[2]	−62.9[2]	28.0
Zambia	58	100.0	51.6	1.232	180	80.4	2.4	—	17.2	9.6	—	113.1	—	23.5
Zimbabwe	114	78.1	20.8	1.016	120	7.8	37.1	—	55.1	90.5	0.6	77.3	—	9.0

deposit money banks, 1985[b]									external public debt outstanding (long-term, disbursed only), 1984[b]							country
assets (%)				liabilities					total ('000,000 U.S.$)	creditors (%)		debt service				
loans to government	loans to private sector	reserves	foreign assets	deposits ('000,000,000 national currency)	composition (%)					official	private	total ('000,000 U.S.$)	repayment (%)		debt service ratio (%)	
					demand depos.	savings depos.	govt. depos.	foreign liabilities					principal	interest		
24.5[3]	68.0	0.7	6.8	405.6	17.7	50.7[4]	5.1	17.1	...	...	...	...	...	...	...	Norway
6.2	63.6	8.1	22.1	1.062	13.5	53.9	12.0	8.1	1,231.6	23.1	76.9	213.4	59.9	40.1	4.6	Oman
...	...	...	...	...	...	...	...	...	38[1]	...	...	5[1]	...	...	—	Pacific Is., Trust Terr. of the
...	...	...	...	...	...	...	...	...	...	...	...	...	...	...	...	Marshall Islands
...	...	...	...	...	...	...	...	...	...	...	...	...	...	...	...	Micronesia, Fed. States of
...	...	...	...	...	...	...	...	...	...	...	...	...	...	...	...	Northern Mariana Islands
...	...	...	...	...	...	...	...	...	...	...	...	...	...	...	...	Palau
18.3[3]	69.5	7.3	4.9	190.818	32.5	37.2	0.6	9.2	9,952.9	91.0	9.0	931.1	66.3	33.7	24.1	Pakistan
1.4	9.0	—	89.6	25.184	1.4	5.5	—	88.9	3,090.8	31.1	68.9	519.1	44.5	55.5	7.5	Panama
13.2	81.5	3.1	2.3	0.760	19.2	65.2	2.7	7.5	925.2	40.8	59.2	133.1	35.2	64.8	12.9	Papua New Guinea
—	56.7	37.2	6.1	226.743	24.8	51.1	—	6.2	1,286.7	63.8	36.2	117.5	51.0	49.0	13.0	Paraguay
1.0	47.0	46.8	5.2	31.538	22.4	55.7[4]	—	5.0	9,824.6	44.1	55.9	606.7	52.8	47.2	15.3	Peru
20.7[3]	56.1	6.8	16.4	205.5	5.7	43.0	4.4	35.3	11,175.7	47.8	52.2	1,134.4	31.2	68.8	14.1	Philippines
...	...	...	...	...	...	...	...	...	...	...	...	...	...	...	...	Pitcairn Island
...	...	...	...	...	...	...	...	...	26,530[15]	...	...	...	...	...	...	Poland
6.4[2]	66.7[2]	13.4[2]	13.5[2]	2,313.6[2]	22.7[2]	72.2[2]	5.2[2]	51.3[2]	10,582.8	25.9	74.1	2,540.6	60.4	39.6	35.6	Portugal
...	...	...	...	16.324[2]	...	...	...	...	...	...	...	...	...	...	...	Puerto Rico
—	47.3	1.4	51.3	13.621	21.3	53.5	3.6	6.6	385[1]	...	...	245[1]	...	...	5.6[1]	Qatar
...	...	...	...	...	...	...	...	...	69[1]	...	...	9[1]	...	...	3.1[1]	Réunion
26.6[2]	63.3[2]	7.2[2]	2.9[2]	601.6[2]	7.9[2]	23.1[2]	—	19.1[2]	6,296.4	45.7	54.3	1,673.4	75.2	24.8	12.3	Romania
17.9[3]	62.6	6.6	12.9	20.977	30.1	39.0	8.2	11.0	243.9	100.0	—	6.0	45.0	55.0	3.3	Rwanda
2.4[5]	60.2[5]	2.8[5]	14.8[5]	0.206[5]	9.5[5]	68.0[5]	1.4[5]	5.5[5]	11[1]	...	...	—	...	...	—	St. Christopher and Nevis
...	...	...	...	...	...	...	...	...	...	...	...	...	...	...	...	St. Helena and Ascension
9.1[3]	67.4	9.6	13.9	0.373	10.2	69.0	—	11.4	34[1]	...	...	1[1]	...	...	1.1[1]	St. Lucia
...	...	...	...	...	...	...	...	...	5[1]	...	...	1[1]	...	...	...	St. Pierre and Miquelon
24.5[3]	48.1	12.0	15.4	0.223	9.2	64.4	—	17.2	20.8	97.6	2.4	1.9	42.1	57.9	2.2[11]	St. Vincent and the Grenadines
...	...	...	...	...	...	...	...	...	...	...	...	...	...	...	...	San Marino
...	...	...	...	...	...	...	...	...	26[1]	...	...	—	...	...	—	São Tomé and Príncipe
—	41.8	8.8	49.4	143.0	32.2	45.6[4]	1.0	7.3	4,931[1]	...	...	3,421[1]	...	...	5.1[1]	Saudi Arabia
3.2	88.6	5.0	3.2	449.3	23.0	23.7	3.9	14.1	1,555.1	87.3	12.7	92.7	43.0	57.0	7.2[11]	Senegal
55.6[3]	27.7	8.3	8.5	0.453	17.4	45.9	4.7	5.2	43.1	85.6	14.4	3.8	63.2	36.8	4.4	Seychelles
49.4[3]	15.6	28.8	6.1	0.852	53.3	36.7	—	1.3	341.6	73.9	26.1	16.2	77.8	22.2	7.2[11]	Sierra Leone
6.5	57.5	3.6	32.5	62.226	6.5	31.1	5.7	43.4	1,901.9	23.6	76.4	322.3	58.4	41.6	1.0	Singapore
15.0[3]	67.0	12.4	5.7	0.071	19.2	52.9	1.3	10.8	25.8	100.0	—	0.5	60.0	40.0	0.4	Solomon Islands
6.1[3]	39.3	11.3	43.3	10.247	56.3	27.1	—	—	1,233.0	95.2	4.8	26.8	89.2	10.8	28.8	Somalia
4.8	88.6	3.6	3.1	52.215	33.9	47.4	—	8.6	...	...	...	...	...	...	...	South Africa
...	...	...	...	...	...	...	...	...	...	...	...	...	...	...	...	Bophuthatswana
...	...	...	...	...	...	...	...	...	...	...	...	...	...	...	...	Ciskei
...	...	...	...	...	...	...	...	...	...	...	...	...	...	...	...	Transkei
...	...	...	...	...	...	...	...	...	...	...	...	...	...	...	...	Venda
0.2[2]	50.5[2]	23.0[2]	—	0.810[2]	—64.7[2]—		24.6[2]	0.4[2]	...	...	...	...	...	...	...	South West Africa/Namibia
23.4[3]	55.2	11.6	9.8	31,656.0	13.5	38.8	3.6	10.2	...	...	...	...	...	...	...	Spain
5.8	70.7	13.2	10.3	55.730	15.7	55.3	6.6	7.3	2,420.3	74.2	25.8	201.5	49.1	50.9	11.2	Sri Lanka
1.0	34.2	36.6	28.2	5.483	41.8	28.7	5.0	9.8	5,658.8	83.3	16.7	107.3	39.9	60.1	13.6	Sudan, The
9.0	50.1	39.5	1.5	1.378	33.9	48.7	1.0	4.1	58[1]	...	...	8[1]	...	...	1.8[1]	Suriname
4.2	55.1	33.9	6.8	0.276	20.5	60.5	6.5	3.1	178.0	95.3	4.7	20.2	54.5	45.5	5.4	Swaziland
8.0	79.2	1.3	11.4	594.8	—75.6[4]—			24.4	...	...	...	...	...	...	...	Sweden
2.8	61.7	2.9	32.5	543.3	6.3	38.9	—	24.2	...	...	...	...	...	...	...	Switzerland
59.6[2,3]	14.4[2]	23.8[2]	2.3[2]	41.314[2]	36.7[2]	12.6[2]	9.3[2]	9.4[2]	2,453.3	94.9	5.1	330.0	74.8	25.2	11.2[11]	Syria
13.0[3]	65.5	8.0	13.5	2,721.4	20.9	48.8[4]	5.1	4.9	1,634.5	...	...	824.9	...	...	2.7	Taiwan
79.9[3,11]	7.1[11]	4.1[11]	8.9[11]	24.283[11]	51.7[11]	30.0[11]	3.4[11]	1.7[11]	2,593.7	82.2	17.8	71.3	57.5	42.5	14.1[11]	Tanzania
13.8[3]	77.5	3.2	5.5	662.7	3.8	76.8	2.7	6.9	7,567.8	63.0	37.0	1,248.7	55.1	44.9	13.0	Thailand
0.5	39.9	48.0	11.7	161.8	26.1	37.4	21.8	15.8	659.2	85.2	14.8	66.6	44.4	55.6	26.3	Togo
...	...	...	...	...	...	...	...	...	...	...	...	...	...	...	...	Tokelau
...	...	...	...	...	...	...	...	...	24[1]	...	...	1[1]	—	—	5.6[1]	Tonga
7.7	69.8	20.0	2.4	8.365	17.7	73.9	2.5	3.7	941.1	26.6	73.4	66.9	53.5	46.5	2.4	Trinidad and Tobago
11.9	82.5	1.6	4.0	4.302	31.3	25.6	4.5	8.3	3,707.4	72.8	27.2	681.7	67.4	32.6	24.4	Tunisia
21.9[3]	51.0	16.4	10.2	8,048.6	27.2	61.3	18.1	18.0	15,774.0	69.8	30.2	2,226.7	52.9	47.1	22.8	Turkey
...	...	...	...	...	...	...	...	...	1.6	...	...	...	...	...	...	Turks and Caicos Islands
...	...	...	...	...	...	...	...	...	...	...	...	...	...	...	...	Tuvalu
2.9[2]	53.0[2]	28.1[2]	16.0[2]	87,409[2]	52.7[2]	20.2[2]	0.1[2]	4.3[2]	675.2	89.7	10.3	86.3	63.2	36.8	21.1[11]	Uganda
...	...	...	...	...	...	...	...	...	10,400[15]	...	...	...	...	...	...	U.S.S.R.
10.7[3]	37.8	4.6	46.9	94.521	6.7	42.7	4.1	21.1	1,876[1]	...	...	529[1]	...	...	3.0[1]	United Arab Emirates
2.8[3]	27.9	0.5	68.9	587.7	8.3	15.1[4]	—	70.8	...	...	...	...	...	...	...	United Kingdom
13.1[3]	79.0	2.6	5.3	3,608.2	12.8	50.9	0.8	6.0	...	...	...	...	...	...	...	United States
11.6[3]	49.0	17.2	22.2	444.2	5.0	46.6[4]	2.1	29.9	2,544.5	16.1	83.9	410.9	31.0	69.0	29.8	Uruguay
0.7[3]	10.8	0.7	87.8	33.345	5.0	29.3[4]	2.3	58.0	5.2	65.4	34.6	0.6	66.7	33.3	0.7	Vanuatu
6.1[3]	72.6	17.0	4.3	159.023	34.9	55.6[4]	11.3	1.2	17,246.8	1.0	99.0	2,536.4	43.3	56.7	13.4	Venezuela
...	...	...	...	...	...	...	...	...	10,270[1]	...	...	63[1]	...	...	26.8[1]	Vietnam
...	...	...	...	...	...	...	...	...	...	...	...	...	...	...	...	Virgin Islands (U.S.)
...	...	...	...	...	...	...	...	...	2[1]	...	...	—	...	...	—	Wallis and Futuna
...	...	...	...	...	...	...	...	...	...	...	...	...	...	...	...	West Bank
...	...	...	...	...	...	...	...	...	...	...	...	...	...	...	...	Western Sahara
23.6[3]	39.2	29.1	8.2	0.057	21.7	56.7	1.7	1.2	61.1	93.1	6.9	3.8	63.2	36.8	14.2	Western Samoa
34.2[2,3]	5.2[2]	57.3[2]	3.3[2]	0.311[2]	36.3[2]	45.6[2]	10.0[2]	7.4[2]	1,251.5	100.0	—	35.4	67.5	32.5	22.0	Yemen (Aden)
5.0[3]	36.0	42.8	16.1	11.071	23.8	45.7	0.6	18.4	1,687.9	99.2	0.8	66.8	76.8	23.2	14.0[11]	Yemen (Ṣan'ā')
0.4[2]	65.5[2]	26.8[2]	7.3[2]	6,610.4[2]	13.9[2]	45.5[2,4]	—	26.6[2]	8,690.3	50.4	49.6	943.6	27.2	72.8	6.8	Yugoslavia
2.3[2,3]	32.0[2]	43.8[2]	21.9[2]	13.791[2]	59.6[2]	9.0[2,4]	2.9[2]	3.7[2]	4,083.7	82.6	17.4	352.3	40.5	59.5	7.7[11]	Zaire
30.0	45.4	14.1	10.5	2.623	33.8	33.2	2.1	19.7	2,778.7	77.4	22.6	113.1	44.0	56.0	11.3	Zambia
41.1[3]	46.8	11.4	0.8	2.315	29.7	55.9	—	3.1	1,445.8	33.4	66.6	276.4	56.9	43.1	20.0	Zimbabwe

[1]1983; includes external long-term private debt not guaranteed by the government. [2]1984. [3]Includes claims on nonfinancial government (public) enterprises and/or local governments. [4]Includes foreign currency deposits. [5]1982. [6]Treasury bill rate. [7]1985. [8]Time deposit rate. [9]Netherlands Antilles includes Aruba. [10]Short-term government bond yield. [11]1983. [12]Excludes Indian rupee currency. [13]Cash and demand deposits at local banks. [14]1981. [15]Net hard currency debt to the West. [16]Call money (interbank) rate. [17]Money market rate. [18]1979. [19]Government bond yield. [20]1980. [21]1977.

Housing and construction

The present table summarizes data about the housing stock and the construction industries of the countries of the world. The principal focus is on the elements that are most comparable internationally: the age of the housing (by decade, so far as possible), the tenure of the householder, construction of exterior walls, the principal physical amenities, the sanitary arrangements, and the amount of space both absolutely (in square metres [10.76 square feet]) and relatively (persons per room). The data on construction characterize the industry in terms of number of units, area, and the portion of the gross domestic product (GDP) represented by each country's construction industry.

Because utilization of housing opportunities, economic development, and patterns of internal migration (favouring, for example, apartments, or temporary, sometimes seasonal, dwellings) differ greatly from country to country, the portion of each country's housing stock for which data are compared is defined as specifically as possible. In general, the numbers refer to permanent, private dwelling units that are usually occupied year-round, whether or not actually occupied on the date of the housing census or survey.

That definition implies the exclusion of certain housing that is often part of national housing censuses: vacation homes, second homes occupied less than half the year, collective or communal dwellings, and so on. The housing unit to which the data on tenure refer may be either the individual dwelling or the household, according to the reporting practice of the country concerned.

The data are collected mostly from national housing censuses and surveys. There has been much activity in recent years under United Nations sponsorship in the field of human settlement. The UN's *Compendium of Human Settlements Statistics* is particularly useful and may be consulted for additional detail. The UN Centre for Human Settlements in Nairobi, Kenya, collects, analyzes, and publishes data on all aspects of settlement, but a particular focus is the provision of adequate, technologically appropriate housing.

Many countries conduct a meaningful housing census only in the capital city or in the few largest cities. This choice may result from the lack of ability to collect data for the entire country or from the perception, particularly in a tropical, rural country where adequate dwellings can be

Housing and construction

country	housing stock														
	year	dwelling units[a]	median age[b] (years)	decade built (percent)					tenure[c] (percent)			construction of exterior walls (percent)			
				1939 or earlier	1940–49	1950–59	1960–69	1970 or later	owned	rented	collective, vacant, other	traditional materials	sawn/framed wood	masonry or cement	other
Afghanistan	1979	136,279	...	...	...	...	...	...	55.2	23.5	21.3	...	...	...	...
Albania	...	...	...	...	...	...	...	...	...	...	...	...	...	...	...
Algeria	1977	2,208,712[6]	...	...	...	...	23.7	...	56.7	29.4	13.9	...	...	...	...
American Samoa	1980	4,688	13.4	4.2	4.8	7.7	38.4	44.9	71.2	25.1	3.7	4.1	56.3	34.9	4.7
Andorra	...	...	...	...	...	...	...	...	...	...	...	...	...	...	...
Angola	...	...	...	...	...	...	...	...	...	...	...	...	...	...	...
Anguilla	1974	1,588	...	...	...	...	...	...	...	...	...	...	...	...	...
Antigua and Barbuda	1970	15,405[6]	11.1	13.8	9.7	31.4	46.1	—	55.9	40.4	3.7	...	...	...	...
Argentina	1980	7,103,853	21.6	9.1	14.9	17.3	22.0	36.7	67.7	14.8	17.5	6.1	6.7	84.2	3.0
Aruba	1981	14,929	29.0	28.2	—34.2—		14.9	22.7	49.0	51.0	—	—	9.4	87.7	2.9
Australia	1981	5,161,163	26.1	—37.9—		10.4	18.6	33.1	61.6	22.6	15.8	...	...	...	...
Austria	1981	3,052,037	63.6	—44.5—		13.3	19.4	22.8	47.7	36.2	16.1	...	...	...	...
Bahamas, The	1980	54,308	30.7		—54.7—		25.6	19.7	51.4	37.4	11.2	4.0[12]	32.3	54.7	9.0
Bahrain	1981	52,810	15.2	41.2	17.1	14.5	—27.2—		60.6[11]	33.6[11]	5.8[11]	2.1[11]	—	95.1[11]	2.8[11]
Bangladesh	1981	14,790,000	...	...	...	...	...	...	89.7	5.0	5.3	20.0	11.6	5.0	63.4
Barbados	1980	67,138	18.9		—51.3—		20.6	28.1	70.2	21.5	8.3	0.1	68.9[13]	26.3	4.7
Belgium	1981	3,599,977	35.2	48.4[14]	—17.2[15]—		14.2	16.0	59.2	38.1	2.7	...	...	...	...
Belize	1980	27,298	...		—24.6—		30.0	41.0	56.1	27.2	16.7	7.5	73.4	14.0	5.1
Benin	1975	644,000	...	...	...	...	...	...	...	...	...	...	...	...	...
Bermuda	1980	20,350	31.2		—67.9—		16.6	15.5	39.4	53.7	6.9	—	1.7[13]	95.1	3.2
Bhutan	...	...	...	...	...	...	...	...	...	...	...	...	...	...	...
Bolivia	1976	1,040,704	...	...	...	...	47.4	...	69.3	15.1	15.6	...	...	...	...
Botswana	1981	170,262	...	...	...	...	...	...	59.9	17.1	23.0	65.5	—	28.0	6.5
Brazil	1982	27,401,345	...	...	...	...	...	...	61.9	22.3	15.8	...	...	...	...
British Virgin Islands	1980	3,287	21.6	—39.8—		—31.2—		29.0	47.4	43.0	9.6	—	21.6	68.0	10.4
Brunei	1981	28,676	...	...	...	...	...	...	83.8	11.8	4.4	0.2	54.8	36.5	8.5
Bulgaria	1975	2,734,717	17.9	47.0	—34.9—		11.1	7.0	77.3	22.7	—	...	...	...	...
Burkina Faso	...	...	...	...	...	...	...	...	...	...	...	...	...	...	...
Burma	1983	5,587,261	...	...	...	...	...	...	...	...	...	...	...	...	...
Burundi	1979[19]	938,000	...	...	...	...	...	...	98.7	1.1	0.2	...	...	...	...
Cameroon	1976	1,390,896	...	...	...	...	...	...	83.4	11.2	5.4	75.5	13.9	9.5	1.1
Canada	1981	8,063,000	14.6	—41.2—		13.8	17.9	27.1	62.1	37.9	—	...	...	...	...
Cape Verde	...	...	...	...	...	...	...	...	...	...	...	...	...	...	...
Cayman Islands	1979	4,426	..			—52.0—		48.0	67.8	32.2	—	1.0	24.0	74.0	1.0
Central African Republic	1975	405,399	...	...	...	...	...	...	...	...	...	82.2	7.1	2.5	8.2
Chad	...	...	...	...	...	...	...	...	...	...	...	...	...	...	...
Chile	1982	2,510,275	20.4		—46.2—		21.1	32.7	63.1	18.7	18.2	13.0	44.4	41.6	1.0
China	1982	220,100,775	...	...	...	...	...	...	18.5[1]	81.5[1]	—	...	...	...	...
Christmas Island	1984	1,231	14.0[3]		—32.2[3]—		27.2[3]	40.6[3]	—	86.4[21]	13.6[21]	—	1.7[21]	74.7[21]	23.6[21]
Cocos (Keeling) Islands	1981	150	...	...	...	...	33.3	...	—80.7—		19.3	—	6.0	52.0	42.0
Colombia	1973	3,448,164	20.6	46.7	7.9	26.2	19.2	—	53.5	30.7	15.8	36.8	—61.9—		1.3
Comoros	...	...	...	...	...	...	...	...	...	...	...	...	...	...	...
Congo	1979–80	110,000[1]	...	...	...	...	...	...	58.4[1]	40.9[1]	0.7[1]	36.0[22, 23]	39.4[22, 23]	24.6[22, 23]	—
Cook Islands	1981	3,153[6]	14.0	5.9	5.7	16.8	48.6	23.0	85.3[10]	9.4[10]	5.3[10]	...	...	...	...
Costa Rica	1973	330,857	...	...	...	...	36.4	...	60.3	22.9	16.8	2.3	77.5	16.8	3.4
Côte d'Ivoire	1975	1,146,370	...	...	...	...	...	...	...	...	...	...	...	...	...
Cuba	1981	2,363,364	24.6	15.0[24]	8.2[25]	21.3[26]	21.6	25.6	...	...	...	1.4	37.1	61.5	—
Cyprus	1982	168,588	22.8		—39.9—		15.4	44.7	60.0	16.5	23.5	11.9	—	87.6	0.5
Czechoslovakia	1980	5,009,771	36.7	—40.0[14]—		15.1[15]	20.3	24.6	44.7	41.7	13.6	—	2.9	93.8	3.3
Denmark	1985	2,120,549	30.8	40.0	6.7	10.8	17.9	24.6	55.3	43.2	1.5	...	...	...	...
Djibouti	1982	25,000	27.6	...	...	...	...	...	...	...	...	—	73.0[27]	22.5	4.5
Dominica	1981	17,307	...	—58.4[16]—		16.9[16]	21.1[16]	3.6[16]	64.7[16]	26.6[16]	8.7[16]	0.2[16]	88.8[16]	10.2[16]	0.8[16]
Dominican Republic	1981	1,114,833[6]	...		—12.4—		—87.6—		72.0	17.0	11.0	31.8[16]	46.2[16]	15.3[16]	6.7[16]
Ecuador	1982	1,576,441	...	...	...	...	...	...	66.7	22.9	10.4	46.9	9.3	41.4	2.4
Egypt	1976	7,311,139	...	...	...	...	...	...	...	...	...	...	...	...	...
El Salvador	1971	680,456	...	...	...	...	...	...	56.7[5]	22.3[5]	21.0[5]	37.9	9.6	46.9	5.6
Equatorial Guinea	...	...	...	...	...	...	...	...	...	...	...	...	...	...	...
Ethiopia	1984	9,300,000	...	...	...	...	...	...	...	...	...	...	...	...	...
Faeroe Islands	1977	11,172	32.5	33.7	—26.4—		21.8	15.0	84.5	9.9	5.6	—	43.9	53.5	2.6
Falkland Islands	1972	639	...	...	...	...	1.7	...	...	...	...	...	...	...	...
Fiji	1977[31]	...	8.6	...	...	...	...	...	73.6	16.1	10.3	...	...	...	...
Finland	1980	1,838,058	22.0	19.2	7.8	17.0	20.9	35.1	61.0	20.9	18.1	...	...	...	...
France	1982	19,590,400	31.0[5]		—71.9[5]—		12.7[5]	15.4[5]	50.7	41.0	8.3	...	...	...	...
French Guiana	1982	21,063	...	...	...	...	23.2[16]	...	34.5	54.0	11.5	...	...	...	...
French Polynesia	1983	...	13.6	—5.0—		9.0	30.0	56.0	...	...	...	38.0	—62.0—		...

built by hand, that no urgent housing problem exists. This choice may be difficult, however, as planners are usually aware that much housing is physically inadequate to protect dwellers from the elements and that too much of the stock is disadvantageously placed in relation to tainted or disease-infested water supply or to the outfall of unprocessed sewage, or is built of materials (mud, skins, thatch, etc.) that may harbour pests or disease. In the developed countries, median age and the distribution of physical amenities provide strong indicators of the quality and availability of housing.

The data for construction industries in various countries of the world refer to new construction for the most recent year in which a broad range of countries could be surveyed. The data for construction are usually from official documents that authorize construction or that certify after construction that the structure described meets building and fire codes and the like. The figures for completed construction are naturally more reliable but are not available for many countries, necessitating the provision of authorized construction data, which are usually available only for areas regulated by zoning code authorities.

A truer indication of the level of activity in a national construction industry is in the data for its contribution to the national gross domestic product. That figure includes civil engineering projects, such as dams, roads, harbour works and the like, but the relative capacity indicated usually finds its way into the domestic housing (personal, collective, and commercial) industry. The predominance within the "new residential" sector of multiunit housing usually indicates (in a developed country) a particularly mobile society, or (in a developing country) one in which limited development resources obliges planners to concentrate available physical and manpower resources in collective projects.

a. Data refer to permanent, private dwelling units that are usually occupied year-round, whether or not occupied on the census date.
b. Data are estimates unless specifically provided by a country source.
c. Data may be either for dwellings or for households, depending on country reporting practice.
d. Data may be either for construction completed or for construction authorized, depending on country reporting practice.

									construction industry (1983)						country
physical amenities (percent)			sewage disposal (percent)			space[b]			percent of GDP	new residential[d]			new nonresidential[d]		
piped water	electricity	inside toilet or WC	closed public sewer or septic tank	open public sewer	other	average area (sq m)	rooms per dwelling unit	persons per room		1- or 2-unit dwellings	multiunit dwellings	floor area ('000 sq m)	number of units	floor area ('000 sq m)	
25.3[1]	66.5[1]	5.5[1]	5.5	77.9	16.6	...	5.5	2.1	3.2[2]	...	...	...	48[3]	65.6[3, 4]	Afghanistan
...	...	...	...	...	...	...	...	...	7.2[5]	...	...	...	...	...	Albania
45.8	49.2	...	54.1	—45.9—		...	2.2[7]	2.8[7]	11.7	...	...	...	...	...	Algeria
77.4	96.2	...	83.5	—	16.5	...	3.0	2.3	...	...	...	...	...	...	American Samoa
...	...	...	...	...	...	...	...	...	13.4[8]	—95[3]—		91.3[3]	14[3]	47.5[3]	Andorra
...	...	...	...	...	...	...	...	...	1.7	—1,587[3]—		585.2[3]	210[3]	164.5[3]	Angola
8.1	18.5	30.1	80.0	—	20.0	...	...	...	...	...	...	...	...	...	Anguilla
85.4	...	...	17.0	—83.0—		...	3.1	...	8.4[8]	...	...	...	...	...	Antigua and Barbuda
72.9	86.8	95.1	77.1	—22.9—		...	3.9	1.3	6.2	—25,716[9]—		3,406[9]	[9]	[9]	Argentina
98.7	98.7	89.2	...	...	...	...	4.3	1.1	...	—84—		...	102	...	Aruba
97.1[10]	98.4[11]	92.2	99.0	—1.0—		...	5.1	0.6	6.2	...	...	17,412	16,515	8,952	Australia
95.0	...	85.5	94.3	—	5.7	76.5	2.8	1.0	7.4	17,800	1,200	3,300[9]	300	[9]	Austria
63.9	77.9	...	63.2	2.2	34.6	...	4.0	1.2	2.9	—832—		...	102	...	Bahamas, The
3.8	94.0[11]	...	29.0[11]	...	71.0[11]	...	3.0[11]	2.3[11]	11.0[3]	—2,124—		...	2,445	...	Bahrain
56.8	...	...	1.3	—98.7—		...	2.0	2.9	5.2	...	...	...	...	...	Bangladesh
82.4	83.0	43.6	95.8	0.7	3.5	...	4.2	0.8	6.3	—753[10]—		...	35[10]	...	Barbados
91.9	100.0	79.0	62.5[16]	—37.5[16]—		86.6[17]	5.2	0.5	5.7	21,678	388	16,720[3]	6,072	22,170[3]	Belgium
60.1	59.4	19.7	21.1	—78.9—		...	2.5[18]	1.9[18]	4.6	...	...	...	...	...	Belize
...	...	...	...	...	...	...	...	...	5.1	...	...	...	...	...	Benin
97.4	...	96.7	96.7	—3.3—		...	3.2	0.7	...	148[5]	12[5]	20.1[5]	15[5]	15.0[5]	Bermuda
...	...	...	...	...	...	...	...	...	1.9	—10—		...	1	...	Bhutan
37.9	33.0	...	12.5	—87.5—		...	...	...	1.8	...	...	...	...	...	Bolivia
56.1	5.4	25.4	8.6	20.4	71.0	...	...	...	4.3	—824—		81.9	397	82.6	Botswana
61.3	76.1	28.6	45.1	34.8	20.1	...	5.1[3]	0.9[3]	6.0	—93,936—		17,628	4,199	3,365	Brazil
62.3	90.2	65.1	65.1	25.3	9.6	...	3.9	1.1	11.6[5]	...	...	...	...	...	British Virgin Islands
90.3	64.2	94.2	57.4	—42.6—		...	4.2	1.6	3.3	—285—		...	9	...	Brunei
74.6	99.8	33.2	33.2	—67.8—		...	3.6	1.0	9.7[2]	10,642	1,611	5,639.3	...	...	Bulgaria
...	...	...	...	...	...	...	...	...	4.0[8]	...	...	...	...	...	Burkina Faso
...	...	...	...	...	...	...	...	...	1.8	...	...	...	...	...	Burma
11.0	0.6	...	1.6	—98.4—		...	...	...	5.8	...	...	...	...	...	Burundi
22.0	5.9	2.2	2.2	70.4	27.6	...	4.1	1.2	5.6[8]	780	201	230.4	53	51.1	Cameroon
99.5	100.0	98.9	98.9	—1.1—		...	5.7	0.5	4.6	...	1,953	...	10,745	...	Canada
...	...	...	...	...	...	...	...	...	20.3	—242[8]—		30.5[8]	3[8]	0.5[8]	Cape Verde
99.0	96.0	84.7	57.0	—43.0—		...	4.0	1.1	...	...	...	...	...	...	Cayman Islands
...	...	...	...	...	...	...	1.1[20]	3.4[20]	4.4	—124[5]—		18.8[5]	57[5]	16.6[5]	Central African Republic
...	...	...	...	...	...	...	...	...	2.1	...	...	...	...	...	Chad
81.4	84.7	...	63.2	36.4	0.4	...	3.6	1.3	4.7	...	...	62.0	...	93.3	Chile
89.4[1]	...	25.2[1]	47.0[1]	—53.0[1]—		37.0	2.2	1.8	5.0	...	...	81,250	...	50,870	China
100.0	100.0	100.0	100.0	—	—	...	5.7	1.0	...	...	...	...	...	...	Christmas Island
35.6	100.0	100.0	100.0	—	—	...	6.1	0.6	...	...	...	...	...	...	Cocos (Keeling) Islands
62.7	57.6	...	46.1	—53.9—		...	3.4	1.8	5.1	7,480	8,169	7,293.6	1,223	1,278.9	Colombia
...	...	...	...	...	...	...	...	...	10.5[8]	...	...	...	...	...	Comoros
30.5	11.4[22]	2.8	—86.2[1]—		13.8[1]	...	3.7[1]	1.7[1]	4.6	...	...	...	...	...	Congo
88.3[10]	60.6[10]	...	36.7[10]	—63.3[10]—		...	4.0[10]	0.7[10]	4.5[5]	—69—		...	20	...	Cook Islands
81.0	68.8	...	46.1	—53.9—		...	4.0	1.4	3.2	—8,180—		664	3,154	128	Costa Rica
...	...	...	...	...	...	...	...	...	8.0[21]	...	...	...	...	...	Côte d'Ivoire
74.1	82.9	45.2	60.9	9.0	30.1	...	4.1	1.0	8.3[2]	149	604	2,035.9	256	1,389.5	Cuba
100.0	98.1	74.5	95.6	—4.4—		...	4.6	0.8	11.0	—5,361—		227.3[9]	1,009	[9]	Cyprus
91.6	100.0	70.8	91.2	—8.8—		68.0	3.5	0.9	10.4[2]	26,143	...	7,381	...	...	Czechoslovakia
100.0	100.0	99.2	98.6[21]	—1.4[21]—		108.0	3.8	0.6	5.2	—20,812—		2,263.7	12,922	3,184.8	Denmark
45.0	58.0	82.0	26.0	23.0	51.0	...	1.9	6.9	7.6	—100—		53.2	39	51.8	Djibouti
91.1[28]	...	12.3[16]	12.3[16]	—87.7[16]—		...	2.8[16]	1.7[16]	9.3[8]	...	...	...	...	...	Dominica
49.3	36.7[16]	14.1	52.1[16]	22.6[16]	25.3[16]	...	2.8[16]	1.5[16]	7.6	22,980	97	777	647	398	Dominican Republic
51.8	47.3	32.7	34.9	13.3	51.8	...	2.8	1.8	5.8	7,563	3,876	2,110.1	539	517.9	Ecuador
30.2	45.7	...	...	...	...	...	3.2	1.8	4.7[8]	...	...	...	...	...	Egypt
48.0[29]	34.1	6.3[11]	20.0[29]	—80.0[29]—		...	1.5[5]	3.3[5]	3.4	8,628	19	348.2	2	—	El Salvador
...	...	...	...	...	...	...	...	...	4.9[29]	...	...	...	...	...	Equatorial Guinea
...	...	...	...	...	...	...	...	2.7[30]	3.5	—1,739[21]—		162[21]	61[21]	32.3[21]	Ethiopia
99.7	99.5	95.0	89.7	8.1	2.2	...	5.5	1.1	10.2[3]	...	...	...	...	...	Faeroe Islands
98.6	...	98.0	98.0	—2.0—		...	7.4	0.4	...	...	...	...	...	...	Falkland Islands
61.1	39.2	...	35.4	—64.6—		...	2.0	...	6.6	—940—		120	116	33	Fiji
98.5	95.6[16]	88.3	94.9	—5.1—		69.0	3.4	0.8	7.6	27,704	884	17,462[4]	34,666	29,907[4]	Finland
99.2	98.8[32]	85.0	73.8[33]	—26.2[33]—		77.0[5]	3.7	0.8	6.0	190,132	6,489	...	...	16,090[8]	France
67.7	80.4	59.1	34.3	—65.7—		...	2.8	1.3	...	—1,060[8]—		...	...	...	French Guiana
86.0	76.0	76.0	2.0	67.0	31.0	...	3.4	1.7[17]	9.4[8]	—564[9]—		...	[9]	...	French Polynesia

Housing and construction (continued)

country	housing stock														
	year	dwelling units[a]	median age[b] (years)	decade built (percent)					tenure[c] (percent)			construction of exterior walls (percent)			
				1939 or earlier	1940–49	1950–59	1960–69	1970 or later	owned	rented	collective, vacant, other	traditional materials	sawn/framed wood	masonry or cement	other
Gabon	1967[22]	15,886	...	...	...	...	...	...	—87.0—		13.0[34]	...	...	...	...
Gambia, The	1983	202,199	...	...	...	...	...	...	63.9	21.9	14.2	82.9	...	12.9	4.2
Gaza Strip	1967	66,819	...	...	...	...	...	...	...	...	...	...	...	...	...
Germany, East	1981	6,562,467	...	—62.4—		6.1	10.1	21.4	36.3	63.7	—	...	...	...	...
Germany, West	1982	26,076,000	...	—53.7—			20.5	25.8	36.0[5]	64.0[5]	—	...	...	...	...
Ghana	1970	870,036	...	...	...	...	...	...	47.7[33]	25.3[33]	27.0	...	...	...	...
Gibraltar	1981	6,945	...	...	...	...	...	...	5.2	94.5	0.3	...	...	...	...
Greece	1981	3,999,332	29.2	—30.2[14]—		27.4[15]	20.7	21.5	73.1[23]	26.9[23]	—	...	...	...	...
Greenland	1984	15,066	10.8[10]	—11.9[10]—		18.8[10]	46.5[10]	22.8[10]	39.8	—58.9—		...	...	...	...
Grenada	1970	13,642	18.3	—48.0—		29.0	22.2	0.8	76.5	14.0	9.5	0.4	80.8	17.8	1.0
Guadeloupe	1982	85,629	...	...	...	...	8.1[23]	...	64.3	29.9	5.8	...	...	...	...
Guam	1980	28,091	...	...	...	...	...	44.6	40.8	47.6	11.6[34]	...	...	...	...
Guatemala	1981	1,259,598	12.5	—62.0—			10.0	28.0	64.7	11.3	24.0	55.6	21.1	19.3	4.0
Guernsey	1976	17,824	...	...	...	...	...	...	63.5	33.5	3.0	...	...	...	...
Guinea	...	...	...	...	...	...	...	...	...	...	...	...	...	...	...
Guinea-Bissau	1979	123,936	...	...	...	...	...	...	...	...	...	95.7	0.1	2.3	1.9
Guyana	1970	129,722	...	—45.8—			31.6	1.0	56.8	29.8	13.4	3.1	87.2	7.1	2.6
Haiti	1982	1,130,795	...	...	...	...	...	24.1	82.9[10]	4.8[10]	12.3[10]	...	...	...	...
Honduras	1974	526,566	...	—43.1—			37.9	14.2	71.8	16.5	12.7	61.0	26.4	11.7	0.9
Hong Kong	1981	1,061,086	...	...	...	...	13.6	38.3	27.7	70.4	1.9	...	...	...	...
Hungary	1984	3,774,000	36.2	—40.6[14]—		12.8[26]	16.9	29.7	75.1	24.7	0.2	30.8	14.3	54.8	0.1
Iceland	1984	70,777	25.6	18.5	—27.5—		—54.1—		70.3[18]	—29.7[18]—		...	...	71.9[18]	...
India	1981	142,954,921	...	...	...	...	...	...	84.6[11]	15.4[11]	...	...	...	...	...
Indonesia	1980	30,263,273	...	...	...	...	...	...	87.0[11]	5.0[11]	8.0[11]	...	...	...	...
Iran	1976	5,331,220	...	—82.5—				17.5	70.2	15.0	14.8	...	...	...	...
Iraq	1956	741,000	...	...	...	...	...	...	83.0	12.8	4.2	...	...	...	...
Ireland	1981	875,816	47.2	45.0	—16.3—		12.7	26.0	67.9	20.9	11.2	...	...	...	...
Isle of Man	1981	24,348[31]	...	...	...	...	...	...	62.5	36.5	1.0	...	...	...	...
Israel	1983	1,104,270	...	—9.5[38]—			—90.5[39]—		72.9	24.6	2.5	...	...	...	...
Italy	1981	21,852,717	19.4	—30.8[14]—		19.7[15]	27.5[40]	22.0	50.9[11]	44.1[11]	5.0[11]	...	...	...	...
Jamaica	1982	517,297	...	—33.6—			26.8	39.6	46.7	29.5	23.8	7.1	28.4	54.4	10.1
Japan	1983	34,704,500	13.0	—13.5—		9.7	24.0	52.1	62.4	37.3	0.3	—	77.4	21.5	1.1
Jersey	1981[31]	26,674	...	...	...	...	...	...	48.8	49.2	2.0	...	...	...	...
Jordan	1979	378,815[42]	...	...	...	...	...	...	62.6	30.8	6.6	...	...	...	...
Kampuchea	...	...	...	...	...	...	...	...	...	...	...	...	...	...	...
Kenya	1962[1]	137,000[6]	...	...	...	...	...	...	...	...	...	...	...	...	...
Kiribati	1978	10,802	...	...	...	...	...	...	68.2	17.9	13.9	64.4	—35.6—		
Korea, North	...	...	...	...	...	...	...	...	...	...	...	...	...	...	...
Korea, South	1980	5,318,880	19.0	—26.1—		15.8	18.2	39.9	86.9	11.0	2.1	—	38.8	49.4	11.8
Kuwait	1980	180,400	14.5	—12.2—			38.8	34.5	29.9[33]	53.0[33]	17.1[33]	46.5[40]	—	36.5[43]	17.0[43]
Laos	...	...	...	...	...	...	...	...	...	...	...	...	...	...	...
Lebanon	1970	483,908[6]	...	—30.1[44]—		40.2[45]	29.4	—	...	...	...	...	...	...	...
Lesotho	1976[31]	240,308	...	...	...	...	...	...	...	...	...	...	...	...	...
Liberia	1974[22]	263.333	...	...	...	...	...	...	...	...	...	...	...	...	...
Libya	1973	345,836	...	...	...	...	...	...	62.5	28.0	9.5	...	...	...	...
Liechtenstein	1980	8,421	29.4	—27.1[44]—		15.0[45]	27.1	30.8	53.6	41.7	4.7	...	...	...	...
Luxembourg	1981	128,281[6]	...	—62.1[38]—		11.8[46]	7.8	18.3	54.5	45.5	—	...	...	...	...
Macau	1981	45,158	...	...	...	...	...	...	71.8[16]	28.2[16]	—	—	0.5[16]	99.3[16]	0.2[16]
Madagascar	...	...	...	...	...	...	...	...	...	...	...	...	...	...	...
Malawi	1977	1,834,118	...	...	...	...	...	...	39.6	—60.4—		...	...	...	...
Malaysia	1980	2,516,295	...	...	...	...	...	...	64.0	23.0	13.0	...	...	...	...
Maldives	1985	29,818	...	...	...	...	...	...	...	...	...	...	...	...	...
Mali	1976[31]	1,253,802	...	...	...	...	...	...	...	...	...	...	...	...	...
Malta	1967	87,049	...	—81.8[49]—			18.2[50]	—	32.4	63.9	3.7	93.0	...	92.9	0.21
Martinique	1982	85,265	...	...	...	...	...	...	64.1	31.3	7.3	...	...	...	...
Mauritania	...	...	...	...	...	...	...	...	...	...	...	...	...	...	...
Mauritius	1983[51]	158,215	...	—19.7—			24.3[52]	56.0[53]	73.2	12.5	14.3	—	4.2	66.8	28.9
Mayotte	1978	10,053	...	...	...	...	...	...	88.1	6.2	5.7	83.6	—7.7—		8.7
Mexico	1980	12,216,462	...	—51.4—			15.4	33.2	66.8	—33.2—		28.2	9.6	56.2	6.0
Monaco	1975	12,625	28.5	—51.4—		22.7	—25.8—		...	...	...	...	...	...	...
Mongolia	1969	242,000	...	...	...	...	...	...	100.0	—	—	...	...	...	...
Montserrat	1980	3,706	...	—47.4—			24.5	28.1	69.2	21.9	8.8	—	60.9	39.0	0.1
Morocco	1982[31]	3,419,282	...	...	...	...	...	...	40.8[1]	43.7[1]	15.5[1]	24.5	—	73.5	1.8
Mozambique	1980	2,712,439	...	...	...	...	...	...	...	...	...	86.5	2.3	8.3	2.9
Nauru	1977	508[54]	...	—88.6[54]—				11.4[54]	11.0[30]	80.6[30]	8.4[30]	...	...	...	...
Nepal	1961[55]	37,122	...	...	...	...	...	...	75.3	10.7	14.0	...	...	...	...
Netherlands, The	1977	4,573,000[6]	20.0	22.0[56]	—29.0[57]—		24.6	24.4	...	...	...	...	...	...	...
Netherlands Antilles	1981	41,101	21.0	22.4	—27.4—		19.7	30.5	45.3	54.7	—	—	21.6	75.7	2.7
New Caledonia	1983	35,107	15.8	—9.8—		11.2	32.1	46.9	53.0	31.1	15.9	6.3	21.0	58.1	14.6
New Zealand	1981	1,048,035	...	—64.6—			19.2	16.2	70.8	25.3	3.9	...	...	...	...
Nicaragua	1971	330,422	...	...	...	...	...	...	64.4	20.3	15.3	30.8	45.6	21.8	1.8
Niger	...	...	...	...	...	...	...	...	...	...	...	...	...	...	...
Nigeria	1961[22]	92,900	...	...	...	...	...	...	8.0	80.9	11.1	...	...	...	...
Niue	1961	673	...	...	...	...	...	...	89.2	7.4	3.4	...	...	...	...
Norfolk Island	1981	845	14.8	—32.8—			32.5	34.7	53.0	35.3	11.7	—	49.8	3.6	46.6
Norway	1980	1,523,512	25.3	35.1	6.9	16.8	18.7	22.5	66.6	23.5	9.9	...	...	...	...
Oman	1982	2,469	...	...	...	...	...	...	...	...	...	...	...	...	...
Pacific Is., Trust Terr. of the															
Marshall Islands	1980	4,163	...	3.4	3.1	13.3	24.7	55.5	60.0	33.0	7.0	10.7	63.5	15.9	9.9
Micronesia, Fed. States of	1980	11,562	...	1.7	2.1	5.2	21.3	69.7	51.8	39.2	9.0	6.0	41.8	14.6	37.6
Northern Mariana Islands	1980	3,373	...	0.8	3.7	8.4	29.4	57.7	53.6	36.1	10.3	0.0	6.1	33.4	60.5
Palau	1980	2,265	...	2.5	3.1	8.6	29.8	56.0	78.0	12.1	9.9	0.7	23.1	16.7	59.5
Pakistan	1980	12,587,648	17.2[58]	...	17.1[44, 58]	36.7[58, 59]	24.9[58, 60]	21.3[58, 61]	78.4[58]	7.7[58]	13.9[58]	49.2[58]	2.4[58]	41.4[58]	7.1[58]
Panama	1980	364,726	18.0	—47.4—		12.8	18.1	21.7	70.1	21.1	8.8	37.1	—	52.2	10.7
Papua New Guinea	1975[1]	42,860	...	...	...	...	...	...	40.0	—60.0—		...	...	...	...

physical amenities (percent)			sewage disposal (percent)			space[b]			construction industry (1983)						country
									percent of GDP	new residential[d]			new nonresidential[d]		
piped water	electricity	inside toilet or WC	closed public sewer or septic tank	open public sewer	other	average area (sq m)	rooms per dwelling unit	persons per room		1- or 2-unit dwellings	multiunit dwellings	floor area ('000 sq m)	number of units	floor area ('000 sq m)	
...	50.5	...	...	...	...	...	3.0	1.3	7.3	—445[33]—		216.1[33]	75[33]	119.4[33]	Gabon
21.9	...	...	...	...	...	...	2.0	2.0	8.1	120[33]	76[33]	...	14[33]	...	Gambia, The
56.3	17.7	42.0	...	...	...	...	...	...	...	—1,802—		239.0	...	45.6	Gaza Strip
98.2	100.0	60.1	90.8	—9.2—		63.0	2.8	1.1	6.2[2]	...	...	7,493	...	...	Germany, East
99.2[35]	99.7[35]	97.1	97.1	—2.9—		...	4.2	0.6	5.8	127,612	16,355	173,681[4]	35,031	147,639[4]	Germany, West
34.0[29]	...	...	...	...	...	...	...	...	2.7[8]	...	...	...	...	...	Ghana
96.7	100.0	98.8	100.0	—	—	...	3.2	1.2	...	...	...	...	...	...	Gibraltar
81.3[11]	89.0[11]	93.0[11]	...	...	...	...	3.5[11]	0.9[11]	6.2	42,228	5,823	36,286[4]	13,973	13,939[4]	Greece
62.7[10]	84.2[10]	39.1[10]	39.1[10]	—60.9[10]—		...	2.6	1.3	14.6[10]	...	...	39.9	...	18.8	Greenland
86.5	...	23.0	23.0	—77.0—		...	2.9	1.6	7.6[36]	...	...	...	...	...	Grenada
69.4	77.2	55.4	24.6	—75.4—		...	3.5	1.1	6.4[3]	460[21]	10[21]	91.9[21]	31[21]	40.9[21]	Guadeloupe
99.5	...	96.5	97.5	—2.5—		...	4.7	0.7	7.2[3]	...	...	...	...	...	Guam
52.0	37.0	14.3	20.1	3.4	76.5	...	2.4	2.2	2.6	—851[8, 9]—		170.2[8, 9]	[9]	[9]	Guatemala
96.5	...	88.8	49.3	—50.7—		...	5.5	0.5	...	...	...	...	...	...	Guernsey
...	...	...	...	...	...	...	...	...	3.8[3]	...	...	...	...	...	Guinea
3.7	3.9	25.6	25.8	—74.2—		...	1.4	4.5	2.6	...	...	...	...	...	Guinea-Bissau
81.0	...	26.3	13.0	—87.0—		...	2.7	2.1	6.7	—1,259[3]—		...	56[3]	...	Guyana
12.0[29]	1.1[11]	...	2.0[29]	—98.0[29]—		...	2.2[11]	2.1[11]	5.7	—358[8, 9]—		...	[9]	...	Haiti
55.0[29]	25.0	13.0	14.4	—85.6—		...	2.4	2.3	5.4	—1,549—		145.7	94	43.8	Honduras
85.7	...	69.2[37]	65.4[37]	—34.6[37]—		53.2[11]	3.1[37]	2.8[37]	5.9	—682—		1,375	306	1,717	Hong Kong
81.2	98.8	65.9	79.5	—20.5—		65.0	2.2	1.3	7.4[2]	31,344	1,550	25,445[4]	4,456	21,218[4]	Hungary
99.1[18]	94.6[18]	93.6[18]	86.5[18]	—13.5[18]—		...	4.8[18]	0.9[18]	8.7[8]	...	...	8,494[4]	...	1,094.4[4]	Iceland
67.0[37]	53.5[1, 37]	20.0[37]	...	...	...		2.0[11]	2.6[11]	5.7	—105,300—		...	15,873	...	India
11.0	14.2	26.6	22.8[11]	—77.2[11]—		59.0	3.3	1.7[11]	6.2	...	...	1,445.4[17]	...	3,768.5[17]	Indonesia
46.8	48.3	26.7	...	...	...	60.0	2.7	2.0	6.4[8]	87,945	1,796	14,780	4,724	1,194	Iran
20.8	17.1	...	...	...	...	...	2.4	...	17.3[21]	—62,615[8]—		7,625[8]	20,467[8]	...	Iraq
94.8	94.7[11]	93.0	72.3[11]	—27.7[11]—		...	5.1	0.7	7.0	...	...	...	...	...	Ireland
...	...	96.8	...	...	...	...	...	0.4	...	...	...	...	...	...	Isle of Man
96.5[11]	96.5[11]	98.8	99.0[23]	—1.0[23]—		...	3.0	1.2	6.6	684	2,020	3,690	...	1,280	Israel
86.1[11]	99.0[11]	82.2[11]	95.7[11]	—4.3[11]—		75.0[11]	3.7[11]	0.8[11]	7.8	22,607[29]	9,047[29]	62,800[4, 29]	6,372[29]	34,300[4, 29]	Italy
76.9	54.0	35.2	...	...	...	...	2.4[16]	1.9[18]	8.4	—1,947[33]—		...	235[33]	...	Jamaica
94.0	...	58.2	61.2	—38.8—		85.9	4.7	0.7	7.9	633,700	213,000	111,176	210,100	78,105	Japan
91.0[41]	...	93.0	91.0[41]	...	...	...	...	0.5	...	—349—		...	...	...	Jersey
77.2	77.3	55.4[30]	15.7	—84.3—		...	...	...	8.5	—7,162[9]—		1,784[9]	[9]	[9]	Jordan
...	...	...	...	...	...	...	...	...	5.3[7]	...	...	...	...	...	Kampuchea
...	...	...	...	...	...	...	1.9	2.5	5.5	—1,592[8]—		252[8]	107[8]	91[8]	Kenya
21.3	23.7	15.5	...	...	...	...	...	...	7.9[5]	...	...	...	...	...	Kiribati
...	...	...	...	...	...	...	...	...	...	...	...	...	...	...	Korea, North
51.2	49.9[16]	98.4	...	...	...	...	4.1	2.3[16]	8.4	—89,255—		21,708	37,251	17,985	Korea, South
17.6[33]	83.3[33]	...	...	...	...	...	3.5[16]	2.1[16]	4.6	—1,265—		2,571	150	835	Kuwait
...	...	...	...	...	...	...	...	...	...	...	...	...	...	...	Laos
...	93.4	82.9	...	...	...	...	...	...	3.4[17]	...	...	...	...	...	Lebanon
...	...	...	...	...	...	...	...	...	9.8	...	...	...	...	...	Lesotho
...	...	...	...	...	...	...	2.3[31]	1.7	3.5[21]	...	...	...	...	...	Liberia
70.1	72.1	40.6	40.6	—59.4—		...	3.3	1.8	11.9[8]	...	...	...	...	...	Libya
96.5	96.6	86.7	90.2	—9.8—		102.0	3.0	1.4	...	...	...	164.5[4]	...	169.5[4]	Liechtenstein
99.4[16]	...	97.0	93.0[16]	—7.0[16]—		86.4[16]	5.3[16]	0.6[16]	5.9	1,221[8]	108[8]	417.6[8]	58[8]	105.5[8]	Luxembourg
95.4	99.3	55.1[16]	...	...	...	...	3.2[16]	2.5[16]	...	—127—		312.9	11	56.5	Macau
...	...	...	...	...	...	...	...	...	2.5[10]	—560[9]—		25.8	[9]	14.8	Madagascar
12.4	15.7[47]	33.0[47]	33.0[47]	—67.0[47]—		...	2.1	1.7	4.1	—98—		...	45	...	Malawi
47.5	64.4	25.8	25.8	57.7	16.5	...	2.3[16, 48]	2.6[16, 48]	5.3	...	...	...	...	...	Malaysia
...	9.8[17]	...	2.5[17]	—97.5[17]—		...	2.3[17]	2.7[17]	7.3	...	...	...	...	...	Maldives
...	...	...	...	...	...	...	...	...	5.7[8]	...	...	...	...	...	Mali
...	...	...	78.5	15.4	6.1	...	3.2	1.3	3.0[3]	—1,633—		...	769	...	Malta
55.4	70.5	41.8	41.8	—58.2—		...	3.4	1.1	3.0[21]	—1,559[9]—		...	[9]	...	Martinique
...	...	...	...	...	...	...	...	...	6.3[21]	...	...	...	...	...	Mauritania
79.7	92.6	51.1	51.1	—48.9—		...	5.4	...	5.1	—4,176—		390	301	72	Mauritius
27.4	...	3.9	54.7	—45.3—		...	2.0	2.4	...	...	...	...	...	...	Mayotte
66.2	74.6	45.0	49.2	—50.8—		...	2.3	2.5	4.9[36]	—285,681[21]—		...	61,386[21]	...	Mexico
100.0	100.0	98.4	98.4	—1.6—		...	2.8	0.4	...	...	...	...	...	...	Monaco
0.3	47.5	...	...	...	...	...	...	...	5.1[8]	...	...	183.4[3]	...	113.3[3]	Mongolia
78.6	72.1	49.3	49.3	30.4	20.4	...	3.5	0.9	7.4	...	...	...	...	...	Montserrat
30.5	37.2	50.2	...	...	...	...	2.7	2.2	7.0[21]	—18,512[21]—		4,877[21]	1,101[21]	647[21]	Morocco
12.7	4.2	...	...	...	...	...	...	...	5.6[21]	—145[33]—		51.7[33]	20[33]	25.0[33]	Mozambique
...	49.2	...	...	...	...	...	3.6[30]	1.6[30]	...	...	...	...	...	...	Nauru
47.7	30.2	6.1	...	...	...	...	3.7	2.0	6.7	...	...	...	...	...	Nepal
95.7[1, 11]	94.8[1, 11]	89.8[1, 11]	89.8[1, 11]	—10.2[1, 11]—		...	5.0	...	5.8	—17,740[8]—		58,947[4, 8]	18,013[8]	51,620[4, 8]	Netherlands, The
79.6	96.9	79.6	...	...	...	...	4.2	1.0	...	—523—		...	382	...	Netherlands Antilles
85.1	79.0[21]	68.3	69.2	—30.8—		...	3.3	1.3	4.6	—298[9]—		...	[9]	...	New Caledonia
92.7[11]	...	97.1[11]	...	...	...	...	5.6	0.5	5.5	...	...	2,531	7,749	2,069	New Zealand
27.9	40.9	19.3	19.2	—80.8—		...	2.2	2.1	2.6	—366—		20.3	53	26.8	Nicaragua
...	...	...	...	...	...	...	...	...	3.1[36]	...	...	...	...	...	Niger
...	81.3	7.0	...	...	...	...	1.4	3.0	6.7	—6,761[10]—		...	3,481[10]	...	Nigeria
18.9	93.0	28.4	14.1	—85.9—		...	4.0	1.2	...	10[8]	...	...	...	...	Niue
8.6	49.2	...	93.0	—	7.0	...	6.2	0.4	...	...	...	...	...	...	Norfolk Island
97.5[16]	...	86.8	86.8	—13.2—		83.5	3.9	0.9	5.7	23,681[8]	508[8]	3,664[8]	3,630[8]	2,776[8]	Norway
...	...	...	...	...	...	...	...	...	6.8	—1,838[9]—		...	[9]	...	Oman
															Pacific Is., Trust Terr. of the
46.3	48.9	...	28.6	—71.4—		...	...	...	...	...	...	...	...	...	Marshall Islands
40.0	28.3	...	8.0	—92.0—		...	...	...	...	...	...	...	...	...	Micronesia, Fed. States of
92.5	94.1	...	54.8	—45.2—		...	...	...	...	...	...	...	...	...	Northern Mariana Islands
70.8	75.7	...	19.6	—80.4—		...	...	...	...	...	...	...	...	...	Palau
20.3[58]	30.6[58]	25.1[58]	...	...	...	...	1.9[58]	3.3[58]	4.5	...	...	...	...	...	Pakistan
80.7	65.7	74.3	43.8	—56.2—		...	2.6	1.8	6.2	667	95	175.2	79	147.9	Panama
50.0	56.0	40.0	...	...	...	...	...	...	3.6[8]	—772—		...	...	...	Papua New Guinea

Housing and construction (continued)

country	housing stock: year	dwelling units[a]	median age[b] (years)	decade built (percent): 1939 or earlier	1940–49	1950–59	1960–69	1970 or later	tenure[c] (percent): owned	rented	collective, vacant, other	construction of exterior walls (percent): traditional materials	sawn/framed wood	masonry or cement	other
Paraguay	1982	580,810[6]	21.1		—56.0—		17.0	27.0	80.4	10.5	9.1	21.5	29.7	47.6	1.2
Peru	1981	3,563,643	...	...	...	...	27.0[35]	...	69.5[35]	16.6[35]	13.9[35]	...	...	...	...
Philippines	1980	8,607,187	...	...	...	...	21.5[16]	...	80.2	12.4	7.4	36.3	33.6	23.8	6.3
Pitcairn Island	1986	15	...	46.7	20.0	13.3	—	20.0	100.0	—	—	—	100.0	—	—
Poland	1983	10,513,000	...	...	...	...	...	...	...	...	...	...	...	...	...
Portugal	1981	3,235,630	33.7		—53.3—		17.5	29.2	56.7	38.8	4.6	—	0.7	61.0	38.3
Puerto Rico	1980	969,611	15.8	5.7	6.5	15.0	31.6	41.2	65.7	23.8	10.5	—	19.7	77.4	2.9
Qatar	...	...	...	...	...	...	...	...	...	...	...	...	...	...	...
Réunion	1982	141,123	...	...	...	...	21.2[23]	...	54.6	34.5	10.9	...	...	...	...
Romania	1966	5,380,299	...	...	...	...	...	...	...	...	...	...	...	...	...
Rwanda	...	...	...	...	...	...	...	...	...	...	...	...	...	...	...
St. Christopher and Nevis	1980	11,445	24.2		—66.9—		18.2	14.9	52.7	32.7	14.6	—	51.3	21.6	27.1
St. Helena and Ascension	1976	1,147	23.4	...	...	...	...	...	57.7	30.1	12.2	...	...	...	...
St. Lucia	1970	21,753	...	...	...	...	7.1	...	63.8	27.4	8.8	0.6	89.3	8.3	1.8
St. Pierre and Miquelon	1982	1,760	11.3		—69.0—		13.8	17.2	77.3	17.8	4.9	...	...	...	...
St. Vincent and the Grenadines	1970	16,940	...	—	...	...	...	...	74.7	16.5	7.9	8.9	64.1	26.1	0.8
San Marino	1979	7,000	...	...	...	...	...	...	73.5	21.9	4.6	...	...	...	...
São Tomé and Príncipe	...	...	...	...	...	...	...	...	...	...	...	...	...	...	...
Saudi Arabia	...	...	...	...	...	...	...	...	...	...	...	...	...	...	...
Senegal	1955[22, 62]	13,000	...	...	...	...	...	...	—84.6—		15.4	...	...	...	...
Seychelles	1977	12,315	...	...	...	...	...	...	46.6	—53.4—		4.1	57.2	38.7	—
Sierra Leone	...	...	...	...	...	...	...	...	...	...	...	...	...	...	...
Singapore	1980	513,224	...			—63.2—		36.8	55.0	39.6	5.4	4.7		—95.3—	
Solomon Islands	1979[22]	3,423	...	...	...	...	...	...	27.4[10]	43.0[10]	29.6[10]	...	...	...	...
Somalia	...	...	...	...	...	...	...	...	...	...	...	...	...	...	...
South Africa	1970	1,354,520	18.6	24.6	16.0	24.2	35.2	—	...	...	...	...	...	...	...
Bophuthatswana	...	...	...	...	...	...	...	...	...	...	...	...	...	...	...
Ciskei	...	...	...	...	...	...	...	...	...	...	...	...	...	...	...
Transkei	...	...	...	...	...	...	...	...	...	...	...	...	...	...	...
Venda	...	...	...	...	...	...	...	...	...	...	...	...	...	...	...
South West Africa/Namibia	...	...	...	...	...	...	...	...	...	...	...	...	...	...	...
Spain	1981	12,329,929	39.4[3, 43]	39.2[3, 43]	—23.4[3, 43]—		18.5[3, 43]	18.9[3, 43]	57.2[16]	24.4[16]	18.3[16]	...	...	...	...
Sri Lanka	1981	2,811,406	...	...	...	...	11.1[11]	...	69.4	10.1	20.5	...	...	...	...
Sudan, The	1966[1]	253,060	...	...	...	...	...	...	59.2	28.3	12.6	76.5	4.4	16.7	2.4
Suriname	1980	77,658	...			—52.4—		47.6	...	...	...	38.9[63]		—61.1[63]—	
Swaziland	1976	86,847	...	...	...	...	...	...	...	...	...	39.9		—60.1—	
Sweden	1980	3,669,512	25.2	26.8	10.9	15.5	23.9	19.1	38.9	56.0	5.1	98.7	...	...	...
Switzerland	1980	2,415,003	...		—58.1—		22.6	19.3	29.9	67.1	3.0	...	...	...	...
Syria	1983	1,642,809	...	...	...	...	8.7[16]	—	81.6[16]	15.5[16]	2.8[16]	...	...	...	...
Taiwan	1980	3,171,876[6]	15.3	—13.8[14]—		14.0[15]	42.4[64]	29.8[65]	79.1	11.8	9.1	...	...	...	...
Tanzania	1978	3,554,793	...		—17.0—		—83.0—		75.4	19.4	5.2	83.0	—	16.3	0.7
Thailand	1980	8,414,648	...	—22.0[16]—		25.0[16]	53.0[16]	—	83.4	9.1	7.5	15.1	70.0	6.3	8.6
Togo	1958–60[1]	22,274	...	...	...	...	...	...	...	...	...	...	...	...	...
Tokelau	1972	263	...	...	...	...	11.1[66]	...	97.7	2.3	—	...	...	...	...
Tonga	1976	13,908	22.5	52.7	—6.7[67]—		20.3[68]	20.3[69]	85.1	2.5	12.4	35.1	45.4	15.3	4.2
Trinidad and Tobago	1980	231,436	...		—56.3—		14.5	29.2	64.6	34.5	0.9	4.3	32.6	53.8	9.3[13]
Tunisia	1984	1,313,200	...	...	...	...	...	...	78.9	12.6	8.5	...	...	...	...
Turkey	1975	6,982,505	...	...	...	...	...	...	80.7	19.3	—	...	...	...	...
Turks and Caicos Islands	1980	1,644	20.0		—45.1—		15.5	39.4	68.6	22.8	8.6	—	36.8	59.9	3.3
Tuvalu	1979	1,079	...	...	...	...	...	...	81.6	12.1	6.6	64.9	4.2	31.0	—
Uganda	...	...	...	...	...	...	...	...	...	...	...	...	...	...	...
U.S.S.R.	1984	79,285,700[31]	...	...	...	...	...	...	42.1	57.9	—	...	...	...	...
United Arab Emirates	1968	38,820	...	...	...	...	...	...	...	...	...	...	...	...	...
United Kingdom	1981[70]	21,321,894[71]	32.6	—54.0—		13.0	16.6	16.4	51.1	40.3	8.6	...	...	...	...
United States	1983	91,675,000	22.7	29.9	9.0	15.6	19.7	25.8	64.7	32.6	2.7	...	...	...	...
Uruguay	1975	848,000	...	...	...	...	...	...	52.1	32.1	15.8	...	...	...	...
Vanuatu	1979	22,513[22]	...	...	...	...	...	...	40.9	25.7	33.4	61.4	7.7	13.6	17.2
Venezuela	1981	3,148,199	...	...	...	...	...	...	75.9	17.2	6.9	...	...	...	...
Vietnam	1962[72]	204,000[6]	...	...	...	...	...	...	68.4	28.0	3.6	...	...	...	...
Virgin Islands (U.S.)	1980	32,650	14.7	6.5	3.5	8.9	42.7	38.4	34.6	52.2	13.2	...	...	...	...
Wallis and Futuna	1983	1,389	14.4	—8.0—		11.0	24.0	57.0	94.4[10]	0.6[10]	5.0[10]	67.0	—31.0—		2.0
West Bank	1967	119,165	...	...	...	...	...	...	...	...	...	...	...	...	...
Western Sahara	1974	4,000	...	...	...	...	...	...	32.2[32]	62.3[32]	5.5[32]	...	...	...	...
Western Samoa	1976	32,938	...	...	...	...	...	...	93.4	2.1	4.5	75.6		—24.4—	
Yemen (Aden)	...	...	...	...	...	...	...	...	...	...	...	...	...	...	...
Yemen (Şan'ā')	1975	863,109	...	...	...	...	...	...	85.3	7.0	7.7	...	...	...	...
Yugoslavia	1981	6,129,892	...	—31.1—		12.7	26.8	29.4	67.1	25.0	7.9	...	—82.6—		17.4
Zaire	1967[22]	168,000	...	...	...	...	...	...	47.4	38.3	14.3	...	...	...	...
Zambia	1969	879,000	...	...	...	...	...	...	78.8	21.1	...	...	...	...	...
Zimbabwe	1969	925,581	...	...	...	...	...	...	65.1[73]	32.6[73]	2.3[73]	55.9[74]		—44.1[74]—	

physical amenities (percent)			sewage disposal (percent)			space[b]			construction industry (1983)						country
									percent of GDP	new residential[d]			new nonresidential[d]		
piped water	electricity	inside toilet or WC	closed public sewer or septic tank	open public sewer	other	average area (sq m)	rooms per dwelling unit	persons per room		1- or 2-unit dwellings	multiunit dwellings	floor area ('000 sq m)	number of units	floor area ('000 sq m)	
...	...	26.4	...	...	...	...	2.2[35]	2.4[35]	6.7	418[8]	33[8]	116.8[8]	1,114[8]	210.6[8]	Paraguay
73.4	89.5	78.0	58.1	—41.9—		42.4	2.5	1.9	3.1	...	...	...	...	...	Peru
41.4	46.0	35.0	44.1	—55.9—		...	2.4[35]	2.3[35]	8.0	—32,883—		3,575	4,405	3,274	Philippines
100.0	100.0	—	—	—100.0—		100.0	5.0	0.4	...	...	...	...	...	...	Pitcairn Island
70.1	96.2	56.6	56.6	...	...	54.2	3.2	1.1	10.9[2]	56,875	4,015	72,887[4]	69,963	76,814[4]	Poland
73.4	77.6	67.7	75.5	—24.5—		...	3.9	0.8	7.6[21]	17,347	1,765	5,447	6,450	2,007	Portugal
95.2	97.4	89.7	89.6	—10.4—		...	4.8	0.8	1.9	2,822	72	1,655	970	23.4	Puerto Rico
...	...	...	...	...	...	...	...	...	5.9	—1,835—		...	1,930	...	Qatar
70.6	81.6	50.7	52.4	—47.6—		...	3.6	1.2	4.7[3]	—3,198[8]—		...	...	...	Réunion
...	48.6	...	12.2	—87.8—		...	2.6	1.4	7.7[2, 38]	...	...	...	...	...	Romania
...	...	...	...	...	...	...	...	...	4.6	—443—		...	23	...	Rwanda
96.6	58.3	33.5	31.8[16]	—68.2[16]—		...	3.0	1.3	7.9	...	...	...	...	...	St. Christopher and Nevis
58.0	62.6	46.9	...	...	...	...	4.1	1.1	...	...	...	...	...	...	St. Helena and Ascension
70.0[21]	36.1	...	11.0	—89.0—		...	2.7	1.7	8.3[8]	—339[17]—		...	46[17]	...	St. Lucia
99.7	99.8	99.2	97.6	—2.4—		...	4.6	0.7	...	...	...	...	...	...	St. Pierre and Miquelon
95.0[28]	...	...	22.0[28]	—78.0[28]—		...	2.8	1.8	10.0[8]	...	...	...	...	...	St. Vincent and the Grenadines
99.8	100.0	98.3	98.3	—1.7—		...	4.5	0.8	...	—131—		...	76	...	San Marino
...	...	...	...	...	...	...	...	...	2.0[21]	...	...	...	...	...	São Tomé and Príncipe
...	...	...	...	...	...	...	...	...	14.1[36]	—50,773[9, 21]—		...	[9]	...	Saudi Arabia
87.7	95.9	...	...	...	...	...	2.3	1.5	6.5[21]	—957—		211.7	44	34.0	Senegal
77.5	46.8	33.1	33.1	—66.9—		...	3.6	1.4	3.4	—4,802[9, 17]—		...	[9]	...	Seychelles
...	...	...	...	...	...	...	...	...	4.2[21]	...	...	...	...	...	Sierra Leone
90.6[16]	98.3	63.6[16]	63.6[16]	—36.4[16]—		...	1.8[16]	2.5[16]	10.8	...	...	5,740	2,587	2,858	Singapore
92.7[10]	79.6[10]	89.2	89.2[10]	—10.8[10]—		41.8[10]	2.3[10]	2.0[10]	...	1,174[3]	...	...	...	...	Solomon Islands
...	...	...	...	...	...	...	...	...	2.9[29]	...	...	...	...	...	Somalia
...	...	...	...	...	...	...	3.4	...	3.7	25,678[8]	484[8]	...	...	...	South Africa
...	...	...	...	...	...	...	...	...	...	...	...	...	...	...	Bophuthatswana
...	...	...	...	...	...	...	...	...	...	...	...	...	...	...	Ciskei
...	...	...	...	...	...	...	...	...	...	...	...	...	...	...	Transkei
...	...	...	...	...	...	...	...	...	...	...	...	...	...	...	Venda
...	...	...	...	...	...	...	...	...	3.8[36]	...	...	...	...	...	South West Africa/Namibia
90.5[3, 43]	94.7[3, 43]	...	87.9[3, 43]	—12.1[3, 43]—		...	4.4[16]	...	6.8	7,400[10]	15,700[10]	...	...	...	Spain
18.2	14.9	4.7	4.7	—95.3—		18.6[16]	2.5	2.1	8.3	—8,542[9]—		914.2[9]	[9]	[9]	Sri Lanka
63.9	26.4	70.2	2.6	—97.4—		...	2.2	2.5	5.2[21]	...	...	...	...	...	Sudan, The
62.9	82.0	40.4	19.6[63]	—80.4[63]—		...	2.1	1.9	2.9[8]	—1,065—		360[4]	157	...	Suriname
33.4	...	20.0	...	...	...	...	...	...	3.9[21]	—100[8]—		...	36[8]	...	Swaziland
100.0	96.2	96.2	96.3	—3.7—		...	4.1	0.6	6.6	23,103	1,123	...	...	...	Sweden
100.0	...	93.3	93.3	—	6.7	88.0	4.6	0.7	...	13,212[8]	4,466[8]	...	9,058[8]	...	Switzerland
40.2	41.7	...	36.0	—64.0—		90.6	3.0	2.0	6.1	—20,379—		4,602	1,117	675	Syria
79.4	...	94.2	69.3	...	...	85.9	3.7	1.5	4.4[36]	...	...	...	...	...	Taiwan
37.2	6.3	...	...	...	...	...	2.5	1.9	3.1	...	...	...	...	...	Tanzania
17.3	43.0	40.9	40.9[10]	9.8[10]	49.3[10]	...	1.9[10]	...	5.1	...	...	5,463	...	4,177	Thailand
4.1	10.3	...	—	—100.0—		...	1.8	3.4	4.3[21]	—153[3]—		43.2[3]	12[3]	...	Togo
2.3	34.4[5]	2.3	...	...	...	...	...	...	...	...	...	...	...	...	Tokelau
61.3	20.9	42.3	11.2	—88.8—		...	...	...	3.9	—738[9, 21]—		668[9, 21]	[9]	[9]	Tonga
89.6	83.3	19.9	19.9	—80.1—		...	3.3	1.4	16.6	—3,131—		499.4	79	111.7	Trinidad and Tobago
26.4	63.4	43.3	51.8	—41.2—		...	1.9	2.4	7.9[36]	—17,208[8]—		2,679[8]	...	...	Tunisia
35.9[16]	56.8	73.8[16]	...	...	...	...	2.5	2.2[16]	4.0	21,896	28,823	12,254	3,813	3,676	Turkey
19.9	47.6	...	70.5	—29.5—		...	3.5	1.1	...	...	...	...	...	...	Turks and Caicos Islands
65.4	7.4	37.3	...	...	...	...	...	...	13.0[29]	...	...	...	...	...	Tuvalu
...	...	...	...	...	...	...	...	...	0.4[21]	—179[35]—		37.3[35]	65[35]	26.8[35]	Uganda
90.8[1]	100.0[1]	88.7[1]	88.7[1]	—11.3[1]—		...	...	...	9.7[2]	—2,030,000[9]—		112,444[9]	[9]	[9]	U.S.S.R.
30.9	24.2	...	...	...	...	...	1.9	1.9	10.9	—337[8]—		52.5[8]	...	...	United Arab Emirates
...	...	99.0	...	...	...	...	3.8	0.6	4.8	...	...	...	...	...	United Kingdom
97.6	100.0[1]	98.1	98.1	—1.9—		...	5.1	0.6	4.1	930,200	62,700	189,000	409,800	...	United States
63.1	80.7	62.7	...	...	...	...	3.5	2.1	3.5	...	...	345.5	...	1334	Uruguay
13.7	11.7	19.1	...	...	...	...	...	...	...	...	...	9.1	...	10.2	Vanuatu
72.4[11]	76.8[11]	23.9[11]	53.5	—46.5—		...	3.9[11]	1.5[11]	4.9	1,826	346	2,574.5	635	1,102.6	Venezuela
23.7	71.0	...	...	...	...	...	...	...	3.0	—400[37]—		212.3[37]	53[37]	59.3[37]	Vietnam
96.3	98.1	86.0	93.6	—6.4—		...	4.2	0.8	...	833[29]	75[29]	...	262[29]	...	Virgin Islands (U.S.)
23.0	...	9.0	24.0	—	7.6	...	1.8[10]	4.0[10]	...	...	...	...	...	...	Wallis and Futuna
24.5	22.9	58.2	...	...	...	...	...	...	...	—4,384—		587.2	...	116.1	West Bank
78.5	95.3	...	...	...	...	...	4.5	1.2	...	...	...	...	...	...	Western Sahara
9.2[62]	18.8[62]	...	...	...	...	...	3.9[62]	1.5[62]	13.2[8]	—110—		...	172	...	Western Samoa
...	...	...	...	...	...	...	...	...	...	...	...	...	...	...	Yemen (Aden)
5.7	4.6	...	...	...	...	...	2.0	2.8	8.8[21]	—5,147[8]—		1,167.4[8]	...	...	Yemen (Ṣan'ā')
67.8	95.7	53.3	...	...	...	60.7	2.4	1.5	9.5[8]	61,201	1,870	14,738	22,133	7,004	Yugoslavia
...	...	...	...	...	...	...	...	...	6.0[8]	—137—		79	35	15	Zaire
12.4	27.5[18]	15.1	...	...	82.3	...	1.9	2.6	3.2	...	...	...	...	...	Zambia
...	9.3[74]	...	...	...	...	...	2.8	1.9	3.8	—1,675—		...	...	...	Zimbabwe

[1]Urban areas only. [2]Percent of net material product. [3]1980. [4]Volume ('000 cubic metres). [5]1978. [6]Occupied dwellings only; may include seasonal and temporary housing. [7]1966. [8]1982. [9]Residential includes nonresidential. [10]1976. [11]1971. [12]Stucco. [13]Includes wood and brick and wood and concrete. [14]1945 and earlier. [15]1946 to 1960. [16]1970. [17]1977. [18]1960. [19]Data refer to rugos, which usually contain two to three houses each. [20]1959–60; data refer to households and are based on a demographic survey of the African population excluding Bangui town, East Dubangi, and the nomad population. [21]1981. [22]Capital city only. [23]1974. [24]1933 and earlier. [25]1934–45. [26]1946–59. [27]Includes corrugated steel. [28]1983. [29]1979. [30]1961. [31]Data refer to households. [32]1968. [33]1975. [34]Vacant dwellings only. [35]1972. [36]1984. [37]1973. [38]1947 and earlier. [39]1948–83. [40]1961–71. [41]Minimum. [42]Includes nonconventional housing units. [43]Data refer to buildings, not dwellings. [44]1946 and earlier. [45]1947–60. [46]1948–60. [47]1967. [48]Peninsular Malaysia only. [49]1957 and earlier. [50]1958 to 1967. [51]Excluding Rodrigues Island and lesser outlying islands. [52]1960–68. [53]1969–83. [54]Nauruan dwellings only. [55]Data are for the cities of Kāthmandu, Lalitpur, Bhaktapur, Birātnagar, Nepālganj, and Birganj only. [56]1930 and earlier. [57]1931–59 [58]Excludes Islāmābād, North-West Frontier, and Federally Administered Tribal Areas. [59]1947–65. [60]1966–75. [61]1976–80. [62]European-style dwellings only. [63]1964. [64]1961–75. [65]1976 and later. [66]1965 and later. [67]1939–56. [68]1956–66 [69]1966–70. [70]Data exclude Northern Ireland. [71]Data refer to "household spaces." [72]Data refer to Ho Chi Minh City (Saigon) only. [73]Data refer to dwellings occupied by Europeans, Asians, and Coloured only. [74]Data refer to dwellings occupied by Africans only.

Household budgets and consumption

This table provides data on disposable income of households for both sovereign states and dependencies—how it is obtained and how it is spent. For purposes of this compilation, income comprises pre-tax monetary payments and payment in kind. The first part of the table provides data on distribution and source of income; the second part analyzes the largest portion of income use—consumption expenditure. Such expenditure is defined as the purchase of goods and services to satisfy current wants and needs. This definition excludes income allocated for taxes, debts, savings and investments, and insurance policies. The last part of the table focuses on food, which (along with housing, examined in the Housing and construction table) is the most important object of consumer spending. The data provided include consumption by major food groups and daily available calories per capita.

For both source of income and consumption expenditure, the primary basis of analysis for most countries is the household, an economic unit that can be as small as a single person or as large as an extended family. For some of the countries that do not compile information by household, the table provides data on personal income and personal expenditure; *i.e.*, the income and expenditure of all the individuals composing a society's households. When no expenditure data at all is available, the table reports the weights of each major category of goods and services comprising a given country's consumer (or retail) price index (CPI). The weighting of the components of the CPI usually reflects the household spending patterns within the country, its principal urban or rural areas, though sometimes only in the country's major city.

The table's income and expenditure data furnish the reader with a general view of the levels of economic development and affluence in most countries. The data on distribution of income show, collectively for an entire country, the proportion of total income earned by households comprising the lowest quintile and highest decile (poorest 20% and wealthiest 10%) within the country. These figures show the degree to which either group represents a disproportionate share of poverty or wealth. A country in which the poorest 20% of households earned only 6% of the nation's income, while the highest 10% disposed of 50% of the same total, would have to be regarded as fertile ground for a campaign to share the wealth.

The data on source of income illuminate aspects of personal condition in the gaining of an income. They indicate, for example, that in poor, agrarian countries income derives largely from self-employment (usually farming) and that in industrial countries, with well-developed systems of salaried employment and social welfare, income derives mainly from wages and salaries and transfer payments (see headnote a). The figures on consumption expenditure reveal the patterns of personal and family use of disposable income and indicate, inter alia, that in developing countries food sometimes absorbs 50 percent or more of disposable income. By contrast, in the larger household budgets of the developed countries, food purchases may account for only 20–30 percent of spending. Each category of expenditure betrays similar complexities of local habit, necessity, and aspiration.

The reader should nevertheless exercise caution when using the data to make intercountry comparisons. Most of the information comes from national surveys, which often differ markedly in the use of definitions, in the coverage of economic or population groups, and in the methods of collection, classification, and tabulation of data. Further, the reference period of the data varies greatly; while a significant portion of the data is from 1979 or later, information for some countries dates from the late 1960s and the early 1970s. This older information is typeset in italic. Finally, intercountry comparisons of annual personal consumption expenditure can be especially misleading because of the distortions introduced when converting national currency units into U.S. dollars.

Household budgets and consumption

country	income (latest)						consumption expenditure						
	percent received by		by source (percent)				per capita private final, U.S.$ 1984	by kind or end use (percent of household or personal budget; latest)					
	lowest 20% of households	highest 10% of households	wages, salaries	self-employment	transfer payments[a]	other[b]		food[c]	housing[d]	clothing[e]	health care	energy, water	education
Afghanistan	...	...	20.7	28.0	8.2	43.1	100[1]	33.9	3.0	...	1.1	0.7	...
Albania	...	...	...	...	...	...	...	...	...	...	...	...	...
Algeria	...	...	...	...	...	...	1,070[2]	*45.6*[3]	*13.1*[3]	*14.8*[3]	*2.5*[3]	...	...
American Samoa	...	...	...	...	...	...	...	44.3	23.4	5.8	...	...	...
Andorra	...	...	...	...	...	...	...	...	...	...	...	...	...
Angola	...	...	...	...	...	...	290[2]	...	...	...	...	...	...
Anguilla	...	...	...	...	...	...	...	...	...	...	...	...	...
Antigua and Barbuda	...	...	...	...	...	...	1,100[1]	*46.5*	*28.8*[4]	*7.5*	...	[4]	...
Argentina	*4.4*	*35.2*	...	...	...	...	1,590[1]	...	...	...	...	...	...
Aruba	...	...	...	...	...	...	[5]	27.4	18.4	8.4	2.9	...	...
Australia	*5.4*	*30.5*	60.8	14.3	13.9	10.9	7,100	21.5	19.9	6.5	6.6	2.5	1.2
Austria	...	...	57.8	...	24.8	17.4	4,850	20.4	12.4	10.8	4.4	4.9	0.3
Bahamas, The	*3.4*	...	...	...	...	...	5,370	20.5	14.1	4.0	3.2	3.6	0.1
Bahrain	...	...	...	...	...	...	...	...	...	...	...	...	...
Bangladesh	*6.2*	*32.0*	*26.9*	*65.2*	*0.4*	*7.5*	150	*74.5*	*5.8*	*5.3*	...	*9.1*	...
Barbados	*6.8*	...	...	...	...	...	2,930	51.6[6]	13.1	5.1	...	6.2	...
Belgium	*7.9*	*21.5*	53.6	10.2	22.2	14.1	5,130	23.3	18.0[4]	6.1	9.4	[4]	0.2
Belize	...	...	*84.1*		—*15.9*—		790	51.5[6]	3.9	9.6	3.4	5.6	1.5
Benin	*8.0*	*39.0*	...	...	...	...	240[2]	...	...	...	...	...	...
Bermuda	...	...	72.2	6.7	2.4	18.7	...	17.3	20.8	5.3	4.1	4.0	2.8
Bhutan	...	...	...	...	...	...	...	...	...	...	...	...	...
Bolivia	*4.0*	...	...	...	...	...	870	*41.7*	*12.6*	*9.8*	*4.6*	*0.7*	*1.2*
Botswana	*1.6*	...	65.6	14.8	19.6	—	510	48.2	12.6	...	...	...	...
Brazil	*2.0*	*50.6*	...	...	...	...	1,140[2]	*46.8*[7]	*4.2*[7]	*7.5*[7]	*4.4*[7]	*5.0*[7]	*1.9*[7]
British Virgin Islands	...	...	...	...	...	...	910[8]	34.1	21.0	8.2	3.1	4.5	3.2
Brunei	...	...	...	...	...	...	...	*45.1*	*5.0*[4]	*6.1*	...	[4]	[9]
Bulgaria	...	...	63.0	—	32.0	5.0	750[10]	46.8	7.8	10.1	1.8	...	...
Burkina Faso	...	...	...	...	...	...	160[2]	47.7[3]	5.2[3]	...	5.2[3]	13.7[3]	...
Burma	*8.0*	...	...	...	...	...	150	*49.1*[3]	*10.4*[3]	*15.3*[3]	*2.4*[3]	*4.0*[3]	*5.9*[3]
Burundi	...	...	...	...	...	...	160	*59.6*[3]	*4.4*[3]	*11.1*[3]	...	*5.8*[3]	...
Cameroon	...	...	...	...	...	...	420	33.6[3]	14.6[3]	16.3[3]	5.0[3]	...	[12]
Canada	5.3	23.8	64.9	6.6	15.4	13.1	7,490	17.8	22.1[4]	6.8	3.5	[4]	2.8
Cape Verde	...	...	...	...	...	...	430[2]	...	...	...	...	...	...
Cayman Islands	...	...	...	...	...	...	...	...	...	...	...	...	...
Central African Republic	...	...	...	...	...	...	200[2]	*70.5*[3]	*0.6*[3]	*9.5*[3]	*1.0*[3]	*6.5*[3]	...
Chad	*8.0*	*30.0*	...	...	...	...	110[2]	*45.3*[3]	...	*3.5*[3]	*11.9*[3]	*5.8*[3]	...
Chile	*4.4*	*34.8*	*40.8*	...	*8.1*	*51.2*	910	*41.9*	*13.3*	*7.6*	...	...	[9]
China	8.5[13]	37.7[13, 14]	...	...	...	...	...	59.3[13]	11.1[13]	11.2[13]	...	...	...
Christmas Island	...	...	...	...	...	...	...	...	...	...	...	...	...
Cocos (Keeling) Islands	...	...	...	...	...	...	...	...	...	...	...	...	...
Colombia	*4.0*	*43.5*	48.4	37.8	5.8	7.9	920	35.7	11.5	5.9	6.1	2.0	1.7
Comoros	...	...	*25.6*	*64.5*	*8.7*	*1.2*	170[2]	*67.8*[15]	*6.1*[15]	*11.6*[15]	...	...	...
Congo	*7.0*	*43.5*	...	...	...	...	440	...	...	...	...	...	...
Cook Islands	...	...	...	...	...	...	340[16]	*65.2*[3, 6]	*3.1*[3]	*12.4*[3]	...	...	...
Costa Rica	*3.3*	*39.5*	...	...	...	...	890	*40.8*	*12.3*	*10.0*	—	*6.6*	[9]
Côte d'Ivoire	*4.0*	*41.1*	44.9	49.9	—5.2—		470[2]	*51.1*	*11.6*	*8.4*	...	*8.1*	...
Cuba	...	...	...	...	...	...	1,000	...	...	...	...	...	...
Cyprus	*7.9*[15]	...	...	...	...	...	2,140	25.6	5.9	11.6	2.4	1.9	0.6
Czechoslovakia	...	...	75.6	0.3	10.7	13.4	3,580	44.8	9.9	14.9	0.3	—	0.3
Denmark	5.4	22.3	59.1	14.3	—26.6—		5,770	21.3	19.3	5.8	1.9	7.2	1.8

The table's food consumption information includes each country's daily available calories per capita (food supply), which amounts to domestic production and imports minus exports, animal feed, and nonfood uses. For each country the table furnishes a percentage breakdown of all the major food groups that comprise food supply.

The data for daily available calories per capita provide a general view of the nutritional adequacy of each nation's food supply. The following list, based on estimates from the United Nations Food and Agriculture Organization, indicates the regional variation in recommended daily minimum nutritional requirements defined by factors such as climatic ambience and average body weight:

Developing area	Daily nutritional requirement
Africa	2,320 calories
Centrally Planned Asia	2,300 calories
Far East	2,240 calories
Latin America	2,360 calories
Near East	2,440 calories

The breakdown of diet by food groups describes the composition of a nation's diet. A typical breakdown for a low-income country shows an imbalanced diet with heavy intake of cereals, potatoes, or cassava. In the high-income countries, a relatively larger portion of total calories derives from animal products (meat, eggs, and milk).

The reader should always be aware of certain limits on the utility of this food consumption data. First, the data compiled here do not reflect the dietary differences that often exist between socioeconomic groups within a single country. Second, the data, which come from national surveys, often vary in completeness of coverage and degree of accuracy, limiting somewhat the validity of intercountry comparisons.

In compiling this table, Britannica editors rely on both numerous national reports and principal secondary sources such as the International Bank for Reconstruction and Development's *World Development Report* (annual), the International Labour Organisation's *Household Income and Expenditure Statistics 1968–1976* and *Statistical Sources and Methods, vol. 1 Consumer Price Indices*; the 1977 *U.N. Compendium of Social Statistics*, the *U.N. Yearbook of National Accounts Statistics* (annual), the *European Marketing Data and Statistics* (annual), and the Food and Agriculture Organization's *Food Balance Sheets 1979–81* and *1975–77*.

The following terms further define the column headings:

a. Includes pensions, family allowances, unemployment payments, and social security and related benefits.
b. Includes interest and dividends, rents and royalties, and all other income not reported under the three preceding categories.
c. Includes alcoholic and nonalcoholic beverages. Excludes tobacco except as noted.
d. Rent and taxes only; excludes energy and water (heat, light, power, and water) and household durables (furniture, appliances, utensils, and household operations), shown separately.
e. Includes footwear.
f. Furniture, appliances, and utensils; usually includes expenditure on household operation.
g. Includes expenditure on cultural activities other than education.
h. May include data not shown separately in preceding categories, including meals away from home.
i. Includes peas, beans, and lentils.
j. Represents pure fats and oils only.
k. Consists mainly of spices, stimulants, sugars and honey, and nuts and oilseeds.

				food consumption									country
				daily available calories per capita	percent of total calories derived from								
transportation, communication	household durable goods[f]	recreation[g]	personal effects, other[h]		cereals	potatoes, cassava	meat, poultry	fish	eggs, milk	fruits, vegetables[i]	fats, oils[j]	other[k]	
...	...	...	61.3	*1,896*	*81.5*	*1.4*	*3.3*	—	*3.6*	*3.7*	*3.1*	*3.4*	Afghanistan
...	...	...	...	*2,657*	*66.4*	*2.6*	*5.2*	*0.1*	*6.2*	*6.5*	*6.4*	*6.6*	Albania
7.3[3]	*6.9*[3]	*4.3*[3]	*5.5*[3]	2,586	56.8	2.2	2.0	0.2	6.4	6.7	13.1	12.3	Algeria
14.9	...	...	11.6	...	...	...	...	...	...	...	...	...	American Samoa
...	...	...	...	...	...	...	...	...	...	...	...	...	Andorra
...	...	...	...	*2,141*	*35.3*	*33.8*	*3.2*	*0.9*	*1.9*	*7.7*	*7.2*	*10.0*	Angola
...	...	...	...	...	...	...	...	...	...	...	...	...	Anguilla
10.0	...	...	7.2	1,979	34.3	1.4	7.6	2.0	13.6	7.2	12.8	21.2	Antigua and Barbuda
...	...	...	...	3,308	29.8	4.5	22.6	0.3	8.3	5.2	9.7	19.5	Argentina
17.4	9.1	5.0	11.4	[5]	[5]	[5]	[5]	[5]	[5]	[5]	[5]	[5]	Aruba
15.3	7.2	6.2	13.1	3,055	26.1	3.3	19.5	0.7	9.7	5.5	9.6	25.6	Australia
16.5	7.3	5.4	17.6	3,575	19.6	4.0	13.7	0.4	10.5	5.5	23.8	22.5	Austria
15.1	6.0	6.5	26.9	2,200	29.1	1.2	18.3	0.8	7.1	8.0	9.7	25.8	Bahamas, The
...	...	...	...	...	...	...	...	...	...	...	...	...	Bahrain
...	...	...	*5.3*	1,837	85.4	2.0	0.9	0.8	1.4	2.6	2.8	4.2	Bangladesh
4.6	9.6	...	9.8	3,020	28.8	4.5	14.8	2.0	6.1	4.9	11.6	27.2	Barbados
12.9	12.4	4.6	13.2	3,639	19.2	5.5	19.6	0.8	9.9	5.2	20.7	19.3	Belgium
6.2	10.1	3.0	5.2	2,714	35.3	7.1	7.3	0.4	9.7	9.3	9.2	21.8	Belize
...	...	...	...	2,174	34.6	37.2	2.2	0.7	0.6	5.6	10.9	8.3	Benin
10.6	11.9	5.4	17.8	2,799	22.5	2.0	19.1	2.8	12.1	8.6	11.2	21.7	Bermuda
...	...	...	...	*2,028*	*85.2*	*2.4*	*0.4*	*0.1*	*0.6*	*2.1*	*5.3*	*3.9*	Bhutan
12.6	*8.9*	*3.1*	*4.8*	2,082	42.1	11.6	8.3	0.3	2.9	8.2	7.8	18.7	Bolivia
...	...	...	39.2	2,352	53.1	1.0	6.0	0.1	9.0	9.6	9.2	12.0	Botswana
6.4[7]	*8.6*[7]	*5.7*[7]	*6.4*[7]	2,578	38.0	8.4	6.9	0.5	5.2	10.4	8.2	22.5	Brazil
2.3	13.1	1.6	8.9	...	...	...	...	...	...	...	...	...	British Virgin Islands
17.2	*8.3*	*8.9*[9]	*9.4*	2,594	50.0	2.7	6.1	2.0	6.7	4.9	8.8	18.7	Brunei
6.7	5.1	3.1	14.3	3,619	43.7	1.6	9.0	0.3	7.5	6.4	13.8	17.6	Bulgaria
18.6[3]	...	...	...	2,010	70.5	2.1	2.2	0.1	1.5	10.1	3.5	10.0	Burkina Faso
3.8[3]	*0.5*[3]	*1.1*[3]	*7.5*[3]	2,420	81.2	0.3	1.7	1.0	0.7	5.3	5.7	4.0	Burma
...	*6.0*[3]	...	*13.1*[3, 11]	2,353	25.2	35.4	1.1	0.3	1.3	22.5	3.2	10.8	Burundi
10.5[3]	...	5.1[3]	14.9[3, 12]	2,295	32.8	21.1	3.3	0.8	0.8	14.2	8.7	18.2	Cameroon
15.4	7.4	6.9	17.2	3,340	19.8	4.6	19.7	0.9	11.4	6.3	17.2	20.0	Canada
...	...	...	...	2,704	58.5	5.1	1.7	1.8	2.6	8.1	8.7	13.6	Cape Verde
...	...	...	...	...	...	...	...	...	...	...	...	...	Cayman Islands
4.1[3]	*0.8*[3]	*1.3*[3]	*5.7*[3]	2,117	15.9	52.0	4.1	0.5	0.3	6.4	6.1	14.7	Central African Republic
...	...	...	*33.5*[3]	*1,762*	*57.2*	*11.2*	*3.2*	*1.6*	*2.6*	*8.2*	*3.3*	*12.7*	Chad
11.8	*7.8*	*8.2*[9]	*9.4*	2,759	48.7	3.4	6.7	1.4	6.4	6.8	8.0	18.6	Chile
...	...	—18.4[13]—		2,426	66.4	12.1	7.6	0.4	1.1	4.1	3.6	4.6	China
...	...	...	...	...	...	...	...	...	...	...	...	...	Christmas Island
...	...	...	...	...	...	...	...	...	...	...	...	...	Cocos (Keeling) Islands
14.1	5.3	4.0	13.8	2,494	33.2	9.6	7.4	0.4	5.3	11.9	7.1	25.2	Colombia
2.3[15]	...	*6.6*[15]	*5.6*[15]	2,219	38.4	33.3	2.3	1.2	1.2	9.0	3.3	11.3	Comoros
...	...	...	...	2,433	15.2	49.8	2.0	2.3	0.9	9.0	10.2	10.5	Congo
5.7[3]	*9.6*[3]	...	*4.0*[3]	...	...	...	...	...	...	...	...	...	Cook Islands
6.5	*8.2*	*9.2*[9]	*6.4*	2,653	34.3	1.0	5.9	0.5	9.7	9.5	11.0	28.2	Costa Rica
...	*7.3*	...	*13.5*	2,613	37.8	27.4	3.2	1.5	2.0	9.7	9.5	9.1	Côte d'Ivoire
...	...	...	...	2,796	37.6	6.7	7.0	1.2	9.9	7.5	8.8	21.2	Cuba
20.0	12.3	7.4	12.4	*3,054*	*40.0*	*2.5*	*13.7*	*0.4*	*7.9*	*9.5*	*10.1*	*15.9*	Cyprus
8.9	9.5	5.8	5.6	3,393	30.5	4.7	14.8	0.5	10.3	3.3	14.2	21.8	Czechoslovakia
15.9	7.0	7.9	12.0	3,548	18.5	4.3	19.5	2.9	11.3	3.4	18.9	21.1	Denmark

Household budgets and consumption (continued)

country	income (latest)						consumption expenditure						
	percent received by		by source (percent)				per capita private final, U.S.$ 1984	by kind or end use (percent of household or personal budget; latest)					
	lowest 20% of households	highest 10% of households	wages, salaries	self-employment	transfer payments[a]	other[b]		food[c]	housing[d]	clothing[e]	health care	energy, water	education
Djibouti	...	...	51.6	36.0	10.5	1.9	710[2]	50.3	6.4	1.7	2.4	13.1	...
Dominica	...	...	...	...	...	...	670[2]	65.2	8.9	9.5	—	5.4	—
Dominican Republic	6.3	...	41.7	31.8	1.5	25.0	1,060[2]	39.6[15]	16.1[15]	10.8[15]	...	3.0[15]	...
Ecuador	2.9	51.5	30.9	61.0	5.2	2.9	910	38.7	7.5	9.4	3.8	1.6	...
Egypt	5.8	33.2	...	...	...	...	550	49.7[15]	8.8[15]	14.2[15]	1.8[15]	3.6[15]	2.1[15]
El Salvador	5.5	29.5	...	...	...	...	700	40.9	6.0	9.8	4.1	2.1	1.2
Equatorial Guinea	...	...	...	...	...	...	72[2]	...	...	...	...	...	...
Ethiopia	...	...	...	...	...	...	90	57.4[3]	[17]	7.8[3]	2.1[3]	...	...
Faeroe Islands	...	...	...	...	...	...	...	43.8	8.5	8.0	...	18.9	...
Falkland Islands	...	...	...	...	...	...	...	46.0[3]	10.0[3]	13.0[3]	...	5.0[3]	...
Fiji	3.7	37.8	81.5	9.1	—	9.4	1,040[2]	32.0	14.3[4]	5.3	2.0	[4]	[9]
Finland	6.3	21.7	61.0	16.2	20.0	2.8	5,610	25.2	15.4	5.2	2.6	3.4	[9]
France	5.3	30.5	51.2	15.2	27.9	5.7	5,710	20.0	17.5[4]	6.3	13.2	[4]	0.3
French Guiana	...	...	...	...	...	...	...	50.0[3]	20.0[3]	7.0[3]	9.0[3]	...	...
French Polynesia	...	...	50.7	38.5	9.1	1.6	4,660[1]	36.5	5.9	9.0	1.0	8.6	[9]
Gabon	3.3	54.4	...	...	...	...	950[2]	54.7[3, 6]	13.0[3]	17.5[3]	1.9[3]	...	...
Gambia, The	...	...	...	...	...	...	370[2]	58.0[18]	5.1[18]	17.5[18]	...	5.4[18]	...
Gaza Strip	...	...	...	...	...	...	790[10]	...	...	...	...	...	...
Germany, East	...	...	69.7	—	21.9	8.4	5,710	29.6	10.9[4]	10.8	5.8	[4]	...
Germany, West	7.9	24.0	56.1	...	21.9	22.1	5,670	23.2	13.9	8.8	3.0	5.3	[9]
Ghana	...	...	41.6[19]	47.1[19]	—	11.3[19]	310[2]	57.4	11.5[4]	14.3	1.3	[4]	[9]
Gibraltar	...	...	...	...	...	...	...	39.0[6]	12.6	11.0	...	...	...
Greece	...	...	42.6	...	16.2	41.1	2,160	39.4	9.2	7.7	3.7	3.2	0.7
Greenland	...	...	...	...	...	...	...	31.5	8.9	9.2	—	7.8	—
Grenada	...	...	...	...	...	...	960[1]	61.5[6]	6.5	8.0	...	6.0	...
Guadeloupe	...	...	——76.8——		——23.2——		2,620[2]	34.4	12.2	9.2	—	5.7	[9]
Guam	...	...	...	...	...	...	...	24.1	28.6	10.6	4.8	...	...
Guatemala	5.0	...	...	...	...	...	1,010	57.3	12.7[4, 15]	10.4[15]	2.1[15]	[4]	1.0[15]
Guernsey	...	...	...	...	...	...	...	23.7	12.2	7.5	...	8.2	...
Guinea	...	...	...	...	...	...	315[2]	61.5	7.3[4]	7.9	11.1	[4]	...
Guinea-Bissau	...	...	...	...	...	...	130[2]	...	...	...	...	...	...
Guyana	...	...	73.0	...	6.3	20.7	280	42.5[6]	21.4	8.6	—	5.2	[9]
Haiti	...	...	...	...	...	...	30	77.9	8.3	3.2	...	...	...
Honduras	3.2	50.6	52.7	...	1.7	45.6	530	44.4	22.3[4]	9.1	6.9	[4]	[9]
Hong Kong	5.4	31.3	...	...	...	...	3,850	21.9	15.3[4]	19.6	6.3	[4]	1.1
Hungary	6.9	20.5	79.9	1.9	10.8	7.4	1,020	41.6	3.8	8.8	6.4	3.7	[9]
Iceland	...	...	——80.0——		——20.0——		6,030	23.8	11.0	8.5	1.7	5.5	0.4
India	7.0	33.6	38.7	44.9	——16.4——		180[2]	59.3	2.6	9.0	1.9	4.5	2.1
Indonesia	6.6	34.0	42.1	41.5	2.5	13.9	310	69.3	12.2[4]	5.1	...	[4]	...
Iran	3.8	41.7	40.8	28.2	3.7	27.3	2,020[2]	45.2[6]	21.2[4]	8.9	3.8	[4]	[9]
Iraq	2.1	...	...	...	...	...	...	55.4	7.9	10.3	2.4	4.1	—
Ireland	7.2	25.1	58.4	25.0	12.3	4.3	2,890	36.9	6.0	7.2	2.7	6.4	2.4
Isle of Man	...	...	...	...	...	...	...	29.1	8.3	6.3	...	11.2	...
Israel	6.0	22.6	89.0	1.4	——9.6——		3,460	26.6	20.2	4.8	3.9	2.7	1.8
Italy	6.2	28.1	49.2	21.5	19.8	9.6	3,800	27.7	9.4	8.2	4.8	4.5	0.4
Jamaica	2.2	...	70.9	27.3	1.8	...	680	35.8	7.7	2.6	2.3	4.8	0.2
Japan	8.7	22.4	57.0	13.6	19.4	10.0	6,180	26.1	4.8	6.8	2.4	6.0	4.1
Jersey	...	...	...	...	...	...	...	28.3	14.9	8.3	...	6.5	...
Jordan	...	...	...	...	...	...	1,430	37.2	6.8[4]	6.3	3.9	[4]	3.5
Kampuchea	...	...	...	...	...	...	100[21]	53.0	23.0	9.0	...	...	...
Kenya	2.6	45.8	22.4	...	...	77.6	190	46.5	10.0	7.7	2.2	2.6	1.0
Kiribati	...	...	69.8	21.4	6.0	2.8	4,150[8]	64.0[6]	1.0	8.0	...	3.6	...
Korea, North	...	...	...	...	...	...	...	46.5[22]	0.6[22]	29.9[22]	15.9[22, 23]	3.3[22]	...
Korea, South	5.7	27.5	57.7	18.6	4.6	19.1	1,230	40.7	5.9	6.8	3.8	4.6	5.8
Kuwait	...	...	53.8	20.8	——25.4——		6,550	37.0[6]	18.7[4]	10.0	1.0	[4]	...
Laos	...	...	...	...	...	...	...	...	...	...	...	...	...
Lebanon	5.0	45.0	27.9	...	3.0	69.1	...	42.8[3]	16.8[3]	8.6[3]	7.2[3]	4.5[3]	3.9[3]
Lesotho	...	...	42.0	51.6	——6.4——		520[2]	34.0[15]	9.7[15]	19.3[15]	1.8[15]	4.8[15]	4.1[15]
Liberia	5.3	...	...	...	...	...	370[2]	40.1[3, 6]	14.9[3]	13.8[3]	...	5.0[3]	...
Libya	10.1	...	...	...	...	...	2,790[2]	37.2	32.2[4]	6.9	3.3	[4]	[9]
Liechtenstein	...	...	91.2	8.8	...	...	...	...	...	...	...	...	...
Luxembourg	...	...	——79.1——		——20.9——		5,760[1]	18.6	12.1	7.0	7.3	8.1	[9]
Macau	...	...	...	...	...	...	...	44.2[6]	22.8	7.3	...	4.8	...
Madagascar	5.2	...	58.8[3, 24]	14.1[3, 24]	—	27.1[3, 24]	130[2]	35.8	...	12.0	...	...	...
Malaŵi	10.4	40.1	83.3	6.0	—	11.7	120	53.9[6, 25]	15.4[25]	10.8[25]	...	...	...
Malaysia	3.5	39.8	...	...	...	...	1,110	41.1[6, 26]	18.2[4, 26]	4.7[26]	1.3[26]	[4]	[9]
Maldives	...	...	...	...	...	...	270	...	...	...	...	...	...
Mali	...	...	...	...	...	...	120[2]	...	...	...	...	...	...
Malta	...	...	52.8	17.3	18.2	11.7	2,100	33.9	4.3	7.2	3.6	2.0	0.4
Martinique	...	...	...	...	...	...	3,580[2]	26.4	20.9	24.0	7.2	...	...
Mauritania	...	...	...	...	...	...	330[2]	61.0[3]	24.0[3]	5.2[3]	...	...	...
Mauritius	4.0	46.7	50.0	45.0	5.0	...	710	50.4[6]	4.0	10.5	3.0	6.4	2.9
Mayotte	...	...	...	...	...	...	...	...	...	...	...	...	...
Mexico	2.9	40.6	58.8	25.4	——15.8——		1,360	35.1[6]	8.1[4]	11.0	5.0	[4]	[9]
Monaco	...	...	...	...	...	...	...	...	...	...	...	...	...
Mongolia	...	...	...	...	...	...	...	...	...	...	...	...	...
Montserrat	...	...	...	...	...	...	2,560[2]	54.1[6]	0.7	17.9	...	1.8	...
Morocco	4.0	...	...	...	...	...	410[2]	54.0	7.0	8.5	...	3.0	...
Mozambique	...	...	...	...	...	...	280[2]	...	...	...	...	...	...
Nauru	...	...	...	...	...	...	...	...	...	...	...	...	...
Nepal	4.6	46.5	39.2		——60.8——		120[10]	57.4[3]	11.4[3, 4]	10.5[3]	4.2[3]	[4]	[9]
Netherlands, The	8.3	21.5	51.9	...	30.5	17.6	5,050	17.7	13.2	7.1	12.8	6.0	0.3
Netherlands Antilles	...	...	...	...	...	...	1,130[27]	24.4[28]	18.8[28]	8.7[28]	2.2[28]	—	[9]
New Caledonia	...	...	63.1	23.9	13.0	...	2,840[2]	28.4	13.3	5.6	2.6	8.3	1.3
New Zealand	5.1	28.7	...	...	...	...	4,140	22.5	18.5	6.8	1.4	2.8	[9]

transportation, communication	household durable goods[f]	recreation[g]	personal effects, other[h]	food consumption: daily available calories per capita	percent of total calories derived from: cereals	potatoes, cassava	meat, poultry	fish	eggs, milk	fruits, vegetables[i]	fats, oils[j]	other[k]	country
...	1.5	...	24.6	...	...	...	...	...	...	...	...	...	Djibouti
—	—	—	11.0	2,018	30.1	17.0	7.4	1.9	5.8	13.8	8.2	15.9	Dominica
...	5.6[15]	...	25.0[15]	2,130	33.0	3.4	4.8	0.7	6.6	20.7	11.1	19.7	Dominican Republic
12.1	4.2	...	22.8	2,114	31.0	4.9	6.2	1.7	8.0	12.4	11.4	24.5	Ecuador
5.2[15]	3.6[15]	1.3[15]	9.7[15]	3,175	64.0	1.5	2.3	0.3	1.7	7.6	11.5	11.1	Egypt
11.2	13.2	3.4	8.1	2,048	56.9	0.9	2.4	0.2	5.3	8.8	8.4	17.1	El Salvador
...	...	...	...	...	...	...	...	...	...	...	...	...	Equatorial Guinea
5.3[3]	17.1[3]	3.0[3]	7.3[3]	1,793	68.8	3.9	4.2	—	2.9	9.3	2.2	8.7	Ethiopia
...	6.6	...	14.2	3,135	29.3	5.5	15.8	3.9	7.0	3.3	18.0	17.2	Faeroe Islands
...	5.0[3]	...	21.0[3]	...	...	...	...	...	...	...	...	...	Falkland Islands
13.3	8.3	4.2[9]	20.6	3,103	31.2	15.1	3.7	2.7	2.9	4.3	11.5	28.5	Fiji
17.5	6.6	8.6[9]	15.6	3,079	23.9	5.3	15.7	1.8	17.0	3.9	14.1	18.3	Finland
13.9	8.9	6.1	13.8	3,529	22.2	4.4	17.7	1.0	11.0	4.8	18.3	20.7	France
8.0[3]	...	6.0[3]	...	2,718	34.1	5.2	16.9	2.0	7.1	8.0	7.1	19.6	French Guiana
13.1	9.2	8.6[9]	8.1	2,898	36.0	9.0	10.0	2.3	4.9	4.7	13.8	19.2	French Polynesia
6.3[3]	...	...	6.6[3]	2,428	24.2	24.3	6.2	1.9	2.8	14.0	8.3	18.3	Gabon
...	...	...	14.0[18]	2,251	59.9	1.3	3.0	2.1	1.7	2.1	15.0	14.9	Gambia, The
...	...	...	...	2,554	51.3	1.6	4.6	0.2	4.8	8.8	13.5	15.2	Gaza Strip
...	23.3	15.2	4.4	3,689	24.6	7.7	14.2	0.7	8.7	4.0	18.4	21.8	Germany, East
15.9	11.0	7.8[9]	11.1	3,351	20.8	4.7	15.2	0.7	10.2	5.6	18.7	24.1	Germany, West
3.3	3.8	3.9[9]	4.5	1,769	32.8	36.7	2.2	2.8	0.5	9.8	6.8	8.4	Ghana
13.3	10.0	...	14.1	...	...	...	...	...	...	...	...	...	Gibraltar
13.0	8.2	3.6	11.4	3,668	31.8	3.5	10.8	0.8	9.4	9.5	17.6	16.6	Greece
7.8	5.9	11.8[20]	17.1	...	...	...	...	...	...	...	...	...	Greenland
4.0	6.5	...	7.5	2,166	29.9	3.4	6.9	3.2	9.8	12.3	9.8	24.5	Grenada
16.3	6.0	6.6[9]	9.6	2,491	37.9	4.2	9.9	3.5	7.2	10.1	9.3	17.9	Guadeloupe
18.0	...	5.1	8.8	...	...	...	...	...	...	...	...	...	Guam
5.8[15]	6.0[15]	1.8[15]	3.2[15]	2,138	58.0	0.5	3.5	0.1	4.5	8.5	6.8	18.2	Guatemala
15.7	8.3	...	24.6	...	...	...	...	...	...	...	...	...	Guernsey
5.1	2.9	4.1	...	1,880	41.0	20.4	1.8	0.6	1.1	15.0	14.6	5.4	Guinea
...	...	...	...	2,326	57.7	8.2	3.9	0.3	2.3	6.4	12.6	8.6	Guinea-Bissau
4.8	2.9	6.4[9]	8.2	2,360	53.2	1.4	4.4	1.8	6.0	4.9	7.5	20.8	Guyana
...	4.0	...	6.6	1,905	40.2	11.4	3.5	0.3	1.5	16.4	3.7	23.1	Haiti
3.0	8.3	2.4[9]	3.5	2,135	54.0	0.6	2.3	0.1	4.8	13.0	8.4	16.7	Honduras
8.0	12.1	7.6	8.2	2,771	34.5	1.2	18.0	3.2	4.4	6.2	17.1	15.4	Hong Kong
7.7	8.0	13.1[9]	6.9	3,484	32.5	3.3	12.7	0.2	9.6	4.7	16.4	20.6	Hungary
18.8	8.8	9.7	11.8	3,087	19.6	4.0	16.4	6.0	19.5	3.2	9.7	21.6	Iceland
9.9	4.3	0.8	5.5	2,056	66.5	2.0	0.2	0.2	3.4	9.0	7.4	11.1	India
...	3.8	...	9.6	2,118	68.4	8.3	0.8	1.0	0.4	2.2	6.2	12.7	Indonesia
6.1	7.8	1.4[9]	5.5	2,986	64.1	1.2	3.8	—	2.8	6.4	8.4	13.3	Iran
5.3	6.2	1.2	7.2	2,155	60.6	0.5	3.9	0.2	3.6	8.8	5.9	16.5	Iraq
13.8	7.4	6.8	10.4	3,699	26.0	6.2	15.7	0.7	12.1	5.3	13.8	20.2	Ireland
15.0	6.7	...	23.3	...	...	...	...	...	...	...	...	...	Isle of Man
13.3	11.7	4.1	11.0	3,060	35.4	2.7	10.1	0.8	11.3	8.0	15.1	16.7	Israel
13.7	6.7	7.1	17.4	3,688	34.8	2.3	12.0	0.7	8.6	7.3	16.9	17.4	Italy
13.7	5.6	3.2	24.0	2,544	34.7	8.3	6.1	1.5	5.1	7.0	11.5	25.8	Jamaica
9.6	4.1	8.7	27.3	2,852	43.4	2.5	6.3	6.8	5.6	5.3	11.5	18.6	Japan
13.9	7.1	...	21.0	...	...	...	...	...	...	...	...	...	Jersey
6.3	5.3	2.9	27.8	2,107	61.8	1.6	3.7	0.3	5.2	4.1	9.1	14.2	Jordan
...	...	...	15.0	1,925	80.5	1.1	3.7	1.2	0.4	5.0	1.9	6.2	Kampuchea
8.4	9.4	3.1	9.1	2,011	52.6	9.1	4.7	0.3	5.3	8.3	5.8	13.9	Kenya
8.0	2.9	...	12.5	2,718	28.3	17.5	3.6	5.4	1.3	6.2	9.4	28.2	Kiribati
...	3.8[22]	...	...	2,996	68.9	5.6	2.7	2.3	0.9	8.1	2.5	9.1	Korea, North
10.7	4.3	4.2	13.0	3,056	67.7	2.1	3.6	2.2	1.3	6.2	3.8	13.1	Korea, South
15.3	11.0	...	19.3	3,344	37.8	1.0	11.5	0.6	10.5	9.0	11.0	18.6	Kuwait
...	...	...	...	1,929	83.4	1.4	5.5	0.6	1.3	4.3	1.1	2.4	Laos
5.4[3]	2.6[3]	1.9[3]	6.3[3]	2,495	52.7	2.0	3.6	0.2	3.9	8.7	8.0	20.9	Lebanon
9.5[15]	6.9[15]	3.1[15]	6.8[15]	2,424	76.8	0.6	3.8	0.2	2.4	4.6	2.5	9.2	Lesotho
...	6.1[3]	...	20.1[3]	2,276	48.0	22.9	2.5	1.4	0.9	6.0	12.3	6.0	Liberia
9.4	4.6	8.5[9]	2.5	3,812	40.3	1.5	6.0	0.5	6.6	10.3	20.3	14.5	Libya
...	...	...	...	...	...	...	...	...	...	...	...	...	Liechtenstein
18.5	9.1	3.6[9]	15.7	3,639	19.2	5.5	19.6	0.8	9.9	5.2	20.7	19.3	Luxembourg
4.9	2.9	...	13.1	2,418	46.0	0.7	16.9	3.2	3.1	6.3	12.2	11.7	Macau
9.7	...	...	42.5	2,491	60.3	17.2	5.6	0.4	0.5	5.9	3.2	6.9	Madagascar
4.8[25]	8.6[25]	...	6.5[25]	2,208	69.3	2.4	1.4	0.8	0.8	10.8	3.1	11.4	Malaŵi
16.6[26]	5.9[26]	6.7[9, 26]	5.5[26]	2,518	51.2	2.7	4.0	3.1	5.2	4.0	10.4	18.6	Malaysia
...	...	...	...	1,765	42.5	6.4	0.8	12.4	—	12.5	7.7	17.7	Maldives
...	...	...	...	1,893	73.5	2.5	4.2	0.8	2.4	2.9	5.5	8.2	Mali
14.4	10.0	5.6	18.7	2,843	34.5	1.6	12.5	1.4	11.6	5.8	13.7	19.0	Malta
13.7	...	7.8	...	2,673	33.0	4.8	10.0	3.1	5.1	11.3	7.2	25.4	Martinique
...	...	...	9.8[3]	2,074	50.7	0.6	6.1	1.7	16.1	7.9	7.4	9.6	Mauritania
10.0	6.4	—	6.4	2,766	50.0	1.1	2.6	1.4	6.5	4.2	16.6	17.6	Mauritius
...	...	...	...	...	...	...	...	...	...	...	...	...	Mayotte
11.8	12.5	5.0[9]	11.5	2,890	49.9	0.9	5.1	0.7	6.9	9.7	9.1	17.7	Mexico
...	...	...	...	...	...	...	...	...	...	...	...	...	Monaco
...	...	...	...	2,774	52.2	1.5	25.7	0.1	5.3	0.6	5.4	9.1	Mongolia
...	10.2	...	15.3	...	...	...	...	...	...	...	...	...	Montserrat
6.9	3.6	...	17.0	2,606	63.0	1.3	2.6	0.5	2.1	5.0	11.0	14.5	Morocco
...	...	...	...	1,881	34.0	39.5	1.9	0.3	0.9	4.3	10.2	9.0	Mozambique
...	...	...	...	...	...	...	...	...	...	...	...	...	Nauru
2.1[3]	—	7.9[3, 9]	6.5[3]	1,933	83.0	1.9	1.1	—	5.0	0.2	4.9	1.9	Nepal
11.0	7.7	9.0	15.1	3,617	17.4	4.6	16.9	0.5	13.5	4.4	21.6	21.0	Netherlands, The
19.4[28]	10.0[28]	6.0[9, 28]	10.6[28]	2,712	29.8	2.3	15.4	1.3	9.6	6.3	11.8	23.5	Netherlands Antilles
15.1	3.7	6.4	15.2	2,842	36.9	7.9	10.6	0.4	5.6	5.7	11.7	21.3	New Caledonia
19.3	13.7	2.2[9]	12.8	3,573	21.3	3.3	19.9	0.4	15.8	5.4	16.0	17.8	New Zealand

Household budgets and consumption (continued)

country	income (latest)						consumption expenditure						
	percent received by		by source (percent)				per capita private final, U.S.$ 1984	by kind or end use (percent of household or personal budget; latest)					
	lowest 20% of households	highest 10% of households	wages, salaries	self-employment	transfer payments[a]	other[b]		food[c]	housing[d]	clothing[e]	health care	energy, water	education
Nicaragua	3.1[13]	...	70.8	27.6	1.6	...	820[2]	38.5[3, 6]	26.7[3]	7.3[3]	...	...	...
Niger	...	...	...	...	...	...	250[2]	50.5	19.1[29]	7.3	...	...	...
Nigeria	...	...	36.2	49.4	4.3	10.1	560	53.0[6]	...	6.0	...	11.1	...
Niue	...	...	...	...	...	...	...	54.5[6]	5.0	5.0	...	...	...
Norfolk Island	...	...	...	...	...	...	...	...	...	...	...	...	...
Norway	6.0	22.8	62.1	12.2	20.6	5.1	6,160	25.3	11.2	7.7	4.5	6.3	0.4
Oman	...	...	...	...	...	...	2,550[2]	...	...	...	...	...	...
Pacific Is., Trust Territory of the	...	...	...	...	...	...	...	...	...	...	...	...	...
Marshall Islands	...	...	...	...	...	...	...	...	...	...	...	...	...
Micronesia, Federated States of	...	...	...	...	...	...	...	...	...	...	...	...	...
Northern Mariana Islands	...	...	...	...	...	...	...	...	...	...	...	...	...
Palau	...	...	...	...	...	...	...	...	...	...	...	...	...
Pakistan	8.0	...	30.7	53.1	1.3	14.9	280	50.8	10.8	9.6	...	5.2	...
Panama	2.0	44.2	85.3	...	9.2	5.5	1,360	47.3	12.7[4]	4.8	4.9	[4]	[9]
Papua New Guinea	...	...	72.7	2.5	...	24.8	480	60.9[6]	7.2[4]	6.2	...	[4]	...
Paraguay	...	...	37.4	...	2.5	60.0	1,270	48.7	16.4	9.7	3.4	—	1.5
Peru	1.9	42.9	...	...	...	...	680	38.1[6]	15.6[4]	7.3	2.6	[4]	—
Philippines	5.2	38.5	44.8	40.3	2.1	12.8	450	52.4	12.0[4]	6.2	2.9	[4]	2.7
Pitcairn Island	...	...	...	...	...	...	...	...	...	...	...	...	...
Poland	...	...	82.9	...	...	17.1	960	50.2	—	7.5	5.6	2.2	[9]
Portugal	5.2	33.4	44.8	21.6	21.1	12.5	1,440[2]	33.8	5.6[4]	11.6	4.4	[4]	0.9
Puerto Rico	3.2	34.7	54.4	6.7	30.4	8.5	4,240[2]	27.1	16.1[4]	9.0	5.1	[4]	2.2
Qatar	...	...	...	...	...	...	5,580[2]	39.1	10.7	4.4	0.2	0.8	1.6
Réunion	...	...	27.9	8.5	63.6	...	3,440[2]	41.1	21.6[4, 29]	9.1	4.8	[4]	[9]
Romania	...	...	...	...	...	...	940	45.6	10.8	17.5	0.9	...	5.4
Rwanda	...	...	16.5	71.0	9.5	3.0	210[2]	...	...	...	...	...	...
St. Christopher and Nevis	...	...	...	...	...	...	580[2]	55.6[6]	7.6	7.5	...	6.6	...
St. Helena and Ascension	...	...	...	...	...	...	...	77.0	...	10.0	...	5.0	...
St. Lucia	...	...	...	...	...	...	700[2]	63.4	10.1	8.1	...	5.6	...
St. Pierre and Miquelon	...	...	...	...	...	...	...	...	...	...	...	...	...
St. Vincent and the Grenadines	...	...	...	...	...	...	610[2]	60.5	11.1	6.9	...	6.4	...
San Marino	...	...	...	...	...	...	...	45.6	12.2[4]	10.6	...	[4]	...
São Tomé and Príncipe	...	...	...	...	...	...	180[2]	...	...	...	...	...	...
Saudi Arabia	...	...	...	...	...	...	3,640	52.2[15, 30]	17.2[15, 30]	6.6[15, 30]	2.1[15, 30]	1.8[15, 30]	1.1[15, 30]
Senegal	5.5	45.4	...	...	...	...	290	56.0[3]	8.7[3]	11.9[3]	...	5.8[3]	...
Seychelles	...	...	...	...	...	...	1,550[2]	58.0[6]	11.4	9.0	...	4.4	...
Sierra Leone	5.6	37.8	27.9	61.6	...	10.5	310	55.1[6]	7.4[4]	12.9	1.3	[4]	[9]
Singapore	...	...	...	...	...	...	3,310	22.6	8.7[4]	8.5	2.8	[4]	0.7
Solomon Islands	...	...	98.8	0.6	...	0.5	...	56.5[3, 6]	15.5[3, 4]	5.0[3]	...	[4]	...
Somalia	...	...	...	...	...	...	140[2]	62.3[3, 6]	15.3[3]	5.6[3]	...	4.3[3]	...
South Africa	1.9	39.4	81.8	...	4.8	13.3	1,170[31]	31.9	11.0[4]	8.1	4.0	[4]	—
Bophuthatswana	...	...	...	...	...	...	...	...	...	...	...	...	...
Ciskei	...	...	...	...	...	...	...	...	...	...	...	...	...
Transkei	...	...	...	...	...	...	...	...	...	...	...	...	...
Venda	...	...	56.2	4.8	32.9	6.1	...	51.2	4.3	11.2	0.5	4.5	1.9
South West Africa/Namibia	...	...	78.6	...	2.8	18.6	[31]	...	...	...	...	...	...
Spain	6.9	24.5	53.9	...	18.0	28.1	2,780	30.6	16.1	8.5	2.3	2.7	2.1
Sri Lanka	7.5	28.2	51.7	...	12.8	35.4	280	53.4	2.3	12.1	1.6	2.0	0.5
Sudan, The	4.0	34.6	35.8	53.0	...	11.2	220[2]	66.5[6]	12.4	5.9	...	...	...
Suriname	9.3	...	74.6	...	3.2	22.2	2,000[2]	40.0[3]	9.5[3]	11.0[3]	3.6[3]	6.9[3]	2.6[3]
Swaziland	2.8	54.5	...	...	...	...	740[2]	39.3[6, 32]	...	10.0[32]	8.0[32]	6.5[32]	...
Sweden	7.4	28.1	61.7	11.1	21.9	5.3	5,770	22.9	21.0	7.2	2.5	5.7	0.2
Switzerland	6.6	23.7	64.7	...	14.3	21.0	8,760	29.0[6]	13.8	4.8	8.8	6.8	[9]
Syria	6.0	...	...	...	...	...	1,250	48.8[6]	17.7	9.1	...	4.6	[9]
Taiwan	8.6	37.6[14]	62.7	24.1	...	13.2	1,490	32.8	28.9[4]	6.8	...	[4]	[9]
Tanzania	5.8	35.6	33.8	59.8	...	6.4	190	54.3[6]	8.6	10.8	4.5	6.6	0.8
Thailand	5.6	34.1	34.0	52.3	0.7	13.1	550	45.7	3.1	10.4	4.8	3.2	0.6
Togo	8.0	30.5	...	...	...	...	210[2]	56.1	13.7[4]	8.5	2.2	[4]	0.7
Tokelau	...	...	...	...	...	...	...	...	...	...	...	...	...
Tonga	...	...	...	...	...	...	790[2]	55.1	3.8	6.2	...	...	...
Trinidad and Tobago	4.2	31.8	...	...	...	...	3,800[1]	31.4	18.0	16.1	2.5	1.9	1.7
Tunisia	4.1	37.6	...	...	...	...	490	41.8	29.0	8.5	...	...	[9]
Turkey	3.5	40.7	38.9[15]	46.8[15]	9.4[15]	4.9[15]	890[10]	41.2[15]	25.2[15]	14.8[15]	3.3[15]	...	...
Turks and Caicos Islands	...	...	...	...	...	...	...	...	...	...	...	...	...
Tuvalu	...	...	17.9	76.1	...	6.0	...	56.0[6]	11.5	7.5	...	...	...
Uganda	6.2	...	88.3[3, 33]	1.8[3, 33]	9.9[3, 33]		40[2]	63.8[3, 33]	9.2[3, 33]	7.8[3, 33]	1.0[3, 33]	—	2.1[3, 33]
U.S.S.R.	...	...	69.8		30.2		2,100	30.2	2.7	15.6	...	...	15.7
United Arab Emirates	...	...	...	...	...	...	5,490	...	...	...	...	...	...
United Kingdom	7.0	23.4	64.8	10.5	15.5	9.2	4,570	17.1	15.4	6.8	1.1	5.3	0.8
United States	5.3	23.3	66.5	4.0	13.6	15.9	9,940	13.9	17.0	6.2	13.3	4.7	2.0
Uruguay	3.8	33.5	...	...	...	...	1,320	41.3	25.3	12.9	...	...	...
Vanuatu	...	...	...	...	...	...	...	55.9[6, 34]	2.2[4, 34]	14.1[34]	...	[4]	...
Venezuela	3.0	35.7	...	...	...	...	1,760	50.4[6]	9.4[4]	4.9	3.4	[4]	[9]
Vietnam	...	...	...	...	...	...	...	...	...	...	...	...	...
Virgin Islands (U.S.)	...	...	...	...	...	...	...	25.3[35]	24.9[35]	5.4[35]	...	6.5[35]	...
Wallis and Futuna	...	...	...	...	...	...	...	...	...	...	...	...	...
West Bank	...	...	...	...	...	...	1,210[10]	...	...	...	...	...	...
Western Sahara	...	...	...	...	...	...	...	...	...	...	...	...	...
Western Samoa	...	...	71.7[15]	8.7[15]	—	19.6[15]	...	58.8	12.0[29]	4.2	—	—	—
Yemen (Aden)	...	...	...	...	...	...	...	...	...	...	...	...	...
Yemen (Ṣan'ā')	...	...	12.2	74.1	13.4	0.3	430	...	...	...	...	...	...
Yugoslavia	6.6	22.9	69.7		30.3		990[2]	47.5	2.5	10.5	2.0	5.4	—
Zaire	...	...	...	...	...	...	30	60.6	17.1[4, 29]	9.5	2.5	[4]	0.8
Zambia	3.4	46.3	94.0		6.0		250	37.7[6]	11.0	8.3	1.0	—	2.1
Zimbabwe	3.0	55.5	...	...	...	...	550[2]	32.6[6]	6.7	8.4	1.8	4.5	3.5

[1] 1982. [2] 1983. [3] Capital city only. [4] Housing includes energy, water. [5] Netherlands Antilles includes Aruba. [6] Includes tobacco. [7] Urban households in the Federal District only. [8] 1978. [9] Recreation includes education. [10] 1981. [11] Includes wage taxes. [12] Personal effects, other includes education. [13] Rural only. [14] Highest 20%. [15] Urban areas only. [16] 1970. [17] Consumer price index excludes rent. [18] Low-income population in Banjul and Kombo St. Mary only. [19] Urban areas of eastern region only. [20] Includes shooting, hunting, and fishing. [21] 1966. [22] Workers

				food consumption									country
				daily available calories per capita	percent of total calories derived from								
transportation, communication	household durable goods[f]	recreation[g]	personal effects, other[h]		cereals	potatoes, cassava	meat, poultry	fish	eggs, milk	fruits, vegetables[i]	fats, oils[j]	other[k]	
...	...	...	*27.5*[3]	*2,446*	*40.5*	*1.2*	*6.1*	—	7.7	*5.1*	9.7	*29.7*	Nicaragua
...	[29]	...	23.1	2,440	68.7	4.1	3.5	0.1	2.9	12.0	4.5	4.2	Niger
4.7	3.8	...	21.4	2,378	42.2	25.4	1.9	1.2	1.1	6.3	11.7	10.2	Nigeria
17.5	13.0	...	5.0										Niue
...	...	...	...	...	...	...	...	...	...	...	...	...	Norfolk Island
15.8	8.3	8.1	12.5	3,391	24.5	4.8	11.4	2.4	16.1	4.2	17.4	19.1	Norway
...	...	...	...	...	...	...	...	...	...	...	...	...	Oman
													Pacific Is., Trust Territory of the
...	...	...	...	...	...	...	...	...	...	...	...	...	Marshall Islands
...	...	...	...	...	...	...	...	...	...	...	...	...	Micronesia, Federated States of
...	...	...	...	...	...	...	...	...	...	...	...	...	Northern Mariana Islands
...	...	...	...	...	...	...	...	...	...	...	...	...	Palau
...	1.5	...	22.1	2,180	63.1	0.6	1.8	0.1	5.9	4.6	10.5	13.5	Pakistan
6.8	*8.5*	*5.8*[9]	9.2	2,338	38.9	3.4	7.8	0.6	5.6	9.2	10.9	23.6	Panama
13.0	*5.3*	...	*7.5*	*2,269*	*15.4*	*34.5*	*6.3*	*1.9*	*0.6*	*26.0*	*4.4*	*10.9*	Papua New Guinea
4.5	*6.2*	*2.3*	*7.3*	2,839	30.0	15.7	14.6	0.1	4.1	14.7	7.9	12.9	Paraguay
9.8	7.0	7.4	12.2	2,195	43.7	9.6	4.5	2.2	4.6	8.2	8.0	19.1	Peru
3.3	7.0	1.6	11.9	2,405	59.5	7.2	4.5	2.7	1.6	7.6	4.2	12.6	Philippines
...	...	...	...	...	...	...	...	...	...	...	...	...	Pitcairn Island
7.3	11.1	10.7[9]	5.4	3,479	35.2	6.8	10.4	1.0	12.6	3.8	13.9	16.1	Poland
15.2	10.0	4.3	14.2	3,204	39.3	6.1	10.5	1.5	4.3	6.8	15.5	16.1	Portugal
16.2	6.6	4.7	13.0										Puerto Rico
3.7	24.4	—15.1—		*3,050*	*48.8*	*0.8*	*10.1*	*0.5*	*7.1*	*11.6*	*7.8*	*13.3*	Qatar
10.8	[29]	*12.6*[9]	...	2,782	48.2	1.7	8.9	1.7	4.6	7.0	13.4	14.6	Réunion
8.6	7.8	...	3.4	3,346	43.5	4.2	8.9	0.4	10.0	5.8	12.2	14.9	Romania
...	...	...	...	2,274	10.4	41.9	1.1	—	0.8	28.1	1.3	16.4	Rwanda
4.3	9.4	...	9.0	2,038	26.3	6.4	10.5	2.7	8.5	5.9	9.8	29.8	St. Christopher and Nevis
...	*8.0*	...	...	...	...	...	...	...	...	...	...	...	St. Helena and Ascension
...	5.1	...	7.7	2,390	27.7	8.5	11.6	2.2	6.5	13.4	11.0	19.0	St. Lucia
...	...	...	...	...	...	...	...	...	...	...	...	...	St. Pierre and Miquelon
...	5.4	...	9.7	2,234	28.7	12.8	6.4	1.0	5.1	7.3	10.7	28.0	St. Vincent and the Grenadines
9.5	...	...	*22.1*	...	...	...	...	...	...	...	...	...	San Marino
...	...	...	...	2,376	36.2	14.1	1.8	1.5	2.0	8.3	10.9	25.3	São Tomé and Príncipe
4.5[15, 30]	5.9[15, 30]	...	8.6[15, 30]	2,940	44.7	0.7	7.7	0.6	7.7	13.8	10.4	14.4	Saudi Arabia
5.4[3]	*1.7*[3]	...	*10.5*[3]	2,346	65.1	0.7	2.9	1.8	2.3	2.6	13.0	11.6	Senegal
4.1	5.4	...	7.7	...	...	...	...	...	...	...	...	...	Seychelles
9.2	*8.0*	*3.8*[9]	*2.3*	1,938	55.0	5.3	1.3	2.0	1.2	7.0	19.6	8.7	Sierra Leone
13.9	8.4	11.6	22.8	3,165	45.6	2.9	12.6	2.0	4.7	7.3	8.5	16.4	Singapore
11.0[3]	...	...	*12.0*[3]	2,039	20.5	41.1	3.7	4.4	1.2	6.7	8.4	13.9	Solomon Islands
...	...	...	12.1[3]	1,986	50.9	1.1	10.5	0.2	16.8	4.0	8.6	8.0	Somalia
16.7	11.2	5.7	11.3	2,861	53.2	1.3	7.9	0.8	5.5	3.5	7.6	20.2	South Africa
...	...	...	...	...	...	...	...	...	...	...	...	...	Bophuthatswana
...	...	...	...	...	...	...	...	...	...	...	...	...	Ciskei
...	...	...	...	...	...	...	...	...	...	...	...	...	Transkei
5.4	11.9	0.9	8.2	...	...	...	...	...	...	...	...	...	Venda
...	...	...	...	*2,183*	*47.7*	*14.5*	*13.8*	—	*4.8*	*1.8*	*10.0*	*7.4*	South West Africa/Namibia
13.6	7.5	4.6	12.0	3,294	25.9	6.8	13.6	1.6	8.9	8.8	16.3	18.1	Spain
12.3	4.5	3.3	8.0	2,251	56.6	4.1	0.4	1.4	2.4	8.4	3.6	23.1	Sri Lanka
...	...	...	15.2	2,314	51.7	1.8	5.2	0.1	5.8	5.3	15.5	14.6	Sudan, The
9.5[3]	*6.8*[3]	*5.8*[3]	*4.3*[3]	2,529	51.6	1.6	6.2	1.8	4.1	3.7	11.5	19.5	Suriname
15.3[32]	9.0[32]	...	11.9[32]	2,553	55.0	2.2	7.3	—	4.7	3.8	6.9	20.2	Swaziland
15.7	6.6	9.7	8.4	3,146	20.1	4.7	17.0	2.2	14.8	4.1	16.7	20.3	Sweden
11.8	5.5	9.7[9]	9.7	3,449	20.9	2.7	18.6	0.5	13.5	6.0	15.8	22.0	Switzerland
3.8	*5.1*	*3.1*[9]	*7.8*	3,005	50.4	1.6	4.0	0.1	5.5	11.8	13.1	13.6	Syria
6.7	...	10.2[9]	14.6	2,749	...	...	...	...	...	...	...	...	Taiwan
6.4	6.3	1.6	0.1	1,955	33.5	31.1	2.9	1.1	2.4	13.7	6.0	9.3	Tanzania
11.5	6.0	3.6	10.9	2,330	66.1	2.7	3.7	1.6	0.7	6.2	2.5	16.5	Thailand
8.6	3.1	0.6	6.5	2,126	39.7	36.5	2.1	1.0	0.3	4.2	6.1	10.2	Togo
...	...	...	...	...	...	...	...	...	...	...	...	...	Tokelau
6.1	*12.4*	...	*16.5*	3,200	13.2	42.5	10.9	2.3	1.3	3.3	8.2	18.3	Tonga
10.9	*7.9*	*1.3*	*8.3*	2,837	40.2	3.0	6.7	0.8	7.2	7.4	12.0	22.7	Trinidad and Tobago
4.9	...	7.6[9]	8.2	2,763	55.8	1.3	2.7	0.5	4.3	8.6	14.7	12.1	Tunisia
5.5[15]	...	6.1[15]	3.9[15]	2,937	53.7	3.3	3.5	0.5	4.3	10.8	11.5	12.4	Turkey
...	...	...	...	...	...	...	...	...	...	...	...	...	Turks and Caicos Islands
10.5	...	...	*14.5*	...	...	...	...	...	...	...	...	...	Tuvalu
2.2[3, 33]	*5.4*[3, 33]	*0.2*[3, 33]	*8.3*[3, 33]	1,784	30.0	18.5	3.3	1.3	2.6	30.3	1.6	12.3	Uganda
...	...	15.0	19.7	3,360	38.4	6.3	9.3	1.8	9.9	4.3	10.9	19.2	U.S.S.R.
...	...	...	...	3,224	31.2	0.9	9.6	1.6	9.5	13.8	16.5	16.9	United Arab Emirates
17.0	6.9	8.5	21.0	3,249	21.1	6.3	15.8	0.7	12.0	4.5	18.1	21.5	United Kingdom
16.0	5.7	6.3	14.8	3,641	18.2	2.9	20.6	0.6	11.7	5.5	16.6	24.0	United States
...	...	...	*20.5*	2,886	32.5	3.8	20.0	0.4	11.3	4.2	9.7	18.0	Uruguay
9.8[34]	*8.0*[34]	...	*10.0*[34]	2,134	24.0	17.9	12.9	3.3	3.2	4.1	5.4	23.8	Vanuatu
12.5	5.9	7.7[9]	5.7	2,646	36.7	2.5	9.5	0.8	9.3	10.4	10.0	20.9	Venezuela
...	...	...	...	*2,135*	*72.9*	*8.6*	*4.8*	*2.2*	*0.1*	*3.4*	*2.0*	*6.0*	Vietnam
11.7[35]	*4.3*[35]	...	*21.8*[35]	...	...	...	...	...	...	...	...	...	Virgin Islands (U.S.)
...	...	...	...	...	...	...	...	...	...	...	...	...	Wallis and Futuna
...	...	...	...	2,861	45.0	1.5	6.4	0.1	6.0	11.4	12.5	17.1	West Bank
...	...	...	...	...	...	...	...	...	...	...	...	...	Western Sahara
9.0	[29]	—	16.0	2,234	28.7	12.8	6.4	1.0	5.1	7.3	10.7	28.0	Western Samoa
...	...	...	...	2,273	60.3	0.2	2.9	1.5	4.8	8.6	9.4	12.4	Yemen (Aden)
...	...	...	...	2,475	67.3	1.4	4.3	0.4	4.5	10.3	4.9	6.9	Yemen (Ṣan'ā')
11.7	8.9	3.9	7.6	3,550	47.0	3.3	7.4	0.2	7.8	6.2	14.1	14.0	Yugoslavia
5.7	[29]	*2.0*	*1.7*	2,130	14.5	58.4	1.8	0.6	0.2	9.4	7.7	7.5	Zaire
4.3	—	—	*35.6*	2,146	70.0	4.7	2.9	0.8	1.5	2.3	4.3	13.4	Zambia
6.3	16.4	—	19.8	2,109	63.5	1.2	3.3	0.1	1.8	2.4	8.6	19.1	Zimbabwe

and clerical workers only. [23]Includes cultural activities. [24]Malagasy households only. [25]Low-income families in Balantyre only. [26]Peninsular Malaysia only. [27]1973. [28]Curaçao and Bonaire only. [29]Housing includes household durable goods. [30]Middle-income population only. [31]South Africa includes South West Africa/Namibia. [32]Middle- to high-income families only. [33]Unskilled African workers only. [34]Urban, low-income households only. [35]St. Thomas only.

Health services

The provision of health services in most countries is a large and growing sector of the national economy as well as one of the principal determinants of the quality of life. This table summarizes the basic indicators of health manpower, hospitals and health-care utilization, mortality rates that are most indicative of general health services, external controls on health (adequacy of food supply and availability of safe drinking water), and sources and amounts of expenditure on health care. Each datum refers more or less directly to the availability or use of a particular health service in a country, and, while each may be accurate as an overall measure, each may also conceal considerable differences in availability of the particular service to different segments of population or regions of the country. In the United States, for example, the availability of physicians ranges from about one per 901 persons in the least well-served state to one per 348 in the best-served, with a rate of one per 186 in the national capital. These disparities are even more pronounced in most other countries, unless the government has made some special effort to achieve a more even distribution of manpower and facilities. In addition, even when trained manpower exists and facilities have been created, the country may lose health professionals via the "brain drain" to foreign countries; or low levels of financial support at the national level may leave facilities underserved; or lack of good transportation may prevent those most in need from reaching the clinic or hospital that could help them.

Definitions and limits of data have been made as specific as possible in the compilation of this table. For example, despite wide variation worldwide in the nature of the qualifying or certifying process that permits an individual to represent himself as a physician, organizations such as the World Health Organization (WHO) try to institute international standards for training and qualification. International statistics presented here for "physicians" refer to persons qualified according to the WHO standards and exclude traditional health practitioners, whatever the local custom with regard to the designation "doctor." Statistics for health manpower in this table uniformly include all those actually working in the health service field, whether in the actual provision of services or in teaching, administration, research, or other tasks. One group of practitioners for whom this type of guideline works less well is that of midwives, whose training and qualifications vary enormously from country to country but who must be included, as they represent, after nurses, perhaps the largest and most important category of health auxiliary worldwide. The statistics here refer to those midwives working in some kind of institutional setting (a hospital, clinic, community health-care centre, or the like) and exclude rural noninstitutional midwives and traditional birth attendants.

Hospitals also differ considerably worldwide in terms of staffing and services. In this tabulation, the term hospital refers generally to a permanent facility offering inpatient services and/or nursing care and staffed by at least one physician. Establishments offering only outpatient or custodial care are excluded. These statistics are broken down into data for general hospitals (those providing care in more than one specialty), specialized facilities (with care in only one specialty), local medical centres, and rural health-care centres; the last two generally refer to institutions that provide a more limited range of medical or nursing care, often less than full-time. Hospital data are further analyzed into three categories of administrative classification: public, private nonprofit, and private for profit. Statistics on number of beds refer to beds that are maintained and staffed on a full-time basis for a succession of inpatients to whom care is provided.

Health services

country	health personnel							hospitals									
	year	physicians	dentists	nurses	pharmacists	midwives	population per physician	year	number	kinds (%)				ownership (%)			hospital beds per 10,000 pop.
										general	specialized	medical centres	rural	government	private nonprofit	private for profit	
Afghanistan	1982	1,215	110[1]	944[1]	245	687[1]	13,092	1982	68	66.2	16.2	—	17.6	86.8	13.2	—	4
Albania	1982	3,861	900[4]	6,801[5]	532[5]	5,098[5]	720	1977	928	5.2	3.1	82.4	9.3	100.0	—	—	66[4]
Algeria	1982	6,508	1,920	17,989[9, 10]	1,006	2,786[9, 10]	3,053	1982	424	—46.2—		53.8	—	85.3[10]	4.4[10]	10.3[10]	23
American Samoa	1983	27	7	141	1	1	1,270	1982	1	100.0	—	—	—	100.0	—	—	50[12]
Andorra	1984	53	...	...	2	...	784	1981	1	100.0	—	—	—	100.0	—	—	31
Angola	1980	436	...	...	...	...	17,000	1980	...	...	...	...	...	...	...	...	28
Anguilla	1985	3	1[16]	16[6]	1[16]	11[16]	2,167	1982	1	—	—	—	100.0	100.0	—	—	37
Antigua and Barbuda	1983	31	4	154	18	160[5]	2,523	1983	2	100.0	—	—	—	100.0	—	—	53
Argentina	1979	79,216	...	...	...	...	351	1980	3,189	84.2	15.8	—	—	41.9	3.6	54.5	53
Aruba	1985	59	16	189	9	...	1,043	1985	1	100.0	—	—	—	...	...	...	45
Australia	1982	27,500	5,721	119,900[13]	5,400[13]	5,930[13]	552	1984	1,086[19]	..	...	...	...	68.9[19]	—31.1[19]—		59
Austria	1985	21,513	887	84,039[21]	3,222	1,056[21]	351	1985	333	...	...	...	...	...	...	...	111
Bahamas, The	1983	218	31[13]	952	37[13]	104[13]	1,018	1985	5	60.0	20.0	20.0	—	60.0	—40.0—		43[12]
Bahrain	1982	397	35	2,098	68	276	929	1982	12	42.7	58.3	—	—	75.0	16.7	8.3	31[12]
Bangladesh	1982	12,306	248[1, 9]	4,500	...	2,934	7,560	1984	504[1]	19.8[1]	6.2[1]	18.4[1]	55.6[1]	92.1[1]	7.9[1]	—	3
Barbados	1983	213	30[6]	1,050[6]	...	36[6]	1,179	1982	11	27.3	18.2	—	54.5	81.8	—	18.2	84[12]
Belgium	1983	28,365	5,911	91,263[6]	10,608	4,920[6]	347	1982	531	53.3	46.7	—	—	36.3	—63.7—		94[12]
Belize	1984	78	12	209	17	179[1]	2,078	1984	12[10]	58.3[10]	25.0[10]	—	16.7[10]	100.0[10]	—	—	36
Benin	1982	270	13[13]	1,294[13]	55[13]	312[13]	13,600	1980	131	4.6	9.9	80.9	4.6	87.8	12.2	—	13[6]
Bermuda	1984	79	21	542	27	...	714	1985	2	50.0	50.0	—	—	...	...	...	72
Bhutan	1983	65	...	129[6]	...	17[6]	20,900	1983	16[13]	75.0[13]	25.0[13]	...	...	...	...	...	6
Bolivia	1978	3,410	1,182[28]	1,552[28]	1,902[28]	...	1,555	1978	400[29]	18.0[29]	5.5[29]	42.5[29]	34.0[29]	...	...	...	18
Botswana	1984	155	14	574[13]	10[13]	714[13]	6,748	1980	53	24.5	62.3	13.2	—	84.9	15.1	—	22[1]
Brazil	1980	97,100	56,015	306,411	5,129	2,526	1,246	1982	23,314	22.6	13.3	—64.1—		64.0	—36.0—		42
British Virgin Islands	1983	10	1[13]	46[13]	2[4]	1[4]	1,156	1984	1[13]	100.0[13]	—	—	—	100.0[13]	—	—	45
Brunei	1982	107	17	627	5	133	1,897	1982	5	80.0	—	—	20.0	80.0	20.0	—	31
Bulgaria	1985	24,700	5,460[12]	47,369[6]	4,200	7,996[6]	363	1985	185[12]	91.4[12]	8.6[12]	—	—	...	...	...	92
Burkina Faso	1981[9]	127	14	1,927	46	281	49,820	1980	44[5]	4.5[5]	—	88.7[5]	6.8[5]	100.0[5]	—	—	7
Burma	1985	9,481	410[1]	6,978[1, 9]	80[1, 9]	15,543[1, 9]	3,937	1985	614[6]	49.7[6]	2.4[6]	—	47.9[6]	100.0[6]	—	—	7
Burundi	1983	216	6	1,126	24	73[10]	20,942	1983	33	...	...	...	...	...	...	...	13
Cameroon	1982	604	17	3,216	96	399	14,800	1984	1,003[5]	5.8[5]	0.5[5]	87.5[5]	6.2[5]	70.1[5]	23.5[5]	6.4[5]	29
Canada	1982	45,542	11,484	140,000[4]	17,039[1]	...	538	1978	1,226	65.8	26.9	7.3	—	93.4	—	6.6	75[13]
Cape Verde	1980	51[9]	3	187[9]	7[9]	232[9]	5,820[9]	1980	21	9.5	4.8	61.9	23.8	100.0	—	—	21
Cayman Islands	1985	30	6	59	3[7]	11	701	1985	2	50.0	—	—	50.0	100.0	—	—	30
Central African Republic	1980	108	3	900	18	367	21,605	1979	85	7.1	5.9	69.4	17.6	72.9	—	27.1	15[13]
Chad	1980	94	4[4, 9]	933[4, 9]	9[4, 9]	96[4, 9]	47,640	1978	4	100.0	—	—	—	—	—	100.0	8
Chile	1982[9]	5,416	1,664	25,889	201	1,930	2,081	1982	247	51.4	19.0	—	29.6	82.2	—	17.8	34
China	1984	597,000[33]	...	616,000	33,000	77,000	1,725[33]	1983	66,662	12.6	4.1	83.3	—	100.0	—	—	21[21]
Christmas Island	1985	2	1	5[1]	1	...	1,100	1985	1	100.0	—	—	—	100.0	—	—	133
Cocos (Keeling) Islands	1984	1	—	3	—	...	584	1984	2	50.0	—	50.0	—	100.0	—	—	86
Colombia	1983	21,778	7,990	26,415[5]	...	...	1,266	1980	849	84.7[10]	15.3[10]	—	—	82.1	17.9	—	17
Comoros	1982	20	1[4]	108[13]	2[4]	13[13]	17,300	1980	17	17.7	—	23.5	58.8	100.0	—	—	22
Congo	1980	278	2[4]	1,915[4]	28[4]	413[4]	5,986	1978	473	0.6	0.2	97.3	1.9	94.9	5.1	—	45
Cook Islands	1982	18	8[9]	65[9]	2[1, 9]	8[1, 9]	939	1981	8	12.5	—	—	87.5	100.0	—	—	87
Costa Rica	1980	1,506[35]	239	1,192	123[5, 9]	...	1,465[35]	1980	39	48.7	28.2	—23.1—		92.3	--	7.7	34
Côte d'Ivoire	1982	502	36[4]	3,052[4]	76[4]	615[4]	17,860	1978	61[16]	13.1[16]	3.3[16]	—	83.6[16]	98.4	—1.6—		13
Cuba	1984	20,490	4,711	38,793	700[6]	...	493	1985	375[6]	24.5[6]	56.0[6]	5.6[6]	13.9[6]	100.0[6]	—	—	53
Cyprus	1983	741	222	2,185	337[6]	189[6]	875	1982	124	3.2	—89.5—		7.3	12.1	0.8	87.1	55[12]
Czechoslovakia	1985	46,492	8,200	103,080[12]	7,100	6,792[6]	333	1983[36]	634	36.0	63.5	0.5	—	100.0	—	—	125
Denmark	1984	12,806	2,281	29,006	1,470	808	399	1982	127	87.4	12.6	—	—	91.3	8.7	—	71[21]
Djibouti	1985	68	4	288[1, 35]	4	19[1, 35]	6,323	1984	29	6.9	3.5	75.8	13.8	100.0	—	—	30[25]
Dominica	1983	26	7	153	10	47[4]	2,846	1983	48	2.1	2.1	91.6	4.2	100.0	—	—	29[21]
Dominican Republic	1980[9]	2,142	...	2,431[37]	...	...	2,600	1973	339	80.5	6.8	—	12.7	40.7	0.3	59.0	16[13, 24]
Ecuador	1981	11,000	795[10]	...	505[10]	...	760	1984	337	16.6	7.1	49.6	26.7	53.7[10]	1.9[10]	44.4[10]	17
Egypt	1984	73,300	8,218[6]	34,371[1]	18,860[6]	9,004[6, 9]	635	1982	1,521	32.3	13.2	15.9	38.6	83.1	3.8	13.1	18[21]

Data on hospital utilization refer to institutions defined as above. Admission and discharge, the two principal points at which statistics are normally collected, are the basis for the data on the amount and distribution of care by kind of facility. These data on numbers of patients exclude babies born during a maternal confinement but include persons who die before being discharged. The bed-occupancy and average length-of-stay statistics depend on the concept of a "patient-day," which is the annual total of daily censuses of inpatients. The bed-occupancy rate is the ratio of total patient-days to potential days based on the number of beds; the average length-of-stay rate is the ratio of total patient-days to total admissions.

Two measures that give an excellent indication of the level of ordinary health care in a country are those for infant mortality and for maternal mortality. The former refers to infants who die within a year of birth, the latter to deaths directly attributable to delivery or complications of pregnancy, childbirth, or puerperium (the period immediately following birth). Levels of nutrition and access to safe drinking water are two of the most basic limitations imposed by the physical environment in which health-care activities take place. The nutritional data are based on recommendations of the United Nations' Food and Agriculture Organization for the necessary daily intake (in calories) for a moderately active person of average size in a climate of a particular kind (fewer calories are needed in a hot climate) to remain in average *good* health. Excess intake in the most developed countries ranges to more than 150% of what is required to maintain health (the excess usually being construed to diminish, rather than raise, health). The range of deficiency is less dramatic numerically but far more critical to the countries in which deficiencies are chronic, because the deficiencies lead to overall poor health (raising health service needs and costs), to decreased productivity in nearly every area of national economic life, and to the loss of social and economic potential through early mortality. By "safe" water is meant only water that has no substantial quantities of chemical or biological pollutants, *i.e.*, quantities sufficient to cause "immediate" health problems.

Two principal kinds of public health-care finance data are given: health insurance and central government budgetary expenditure. The data on insurance refer to public programs only and identify the mandated basis or extent of responsibility for costs or funding required under the relevant law of the principal participants (individuals, employers, and government). Data on public health-care expenditure refer to a consolidated statement of expenditure by all elements of the central government but exclude expenditure by other levels (state, city, etc.). In a number of countries significant governmental expenditures for health-care services are made at these other levels, amounting to 2, 10, and sometimes 20 times the level of central government expenditure. These expenditures may include costs for national health insurance, family-planning programs, and workmen's compensation. Expenditures at the national level for social security are excluded.

The following notes further define the column headings:

a. Bed-occupancy rates may exceed 100% because stays of partial days are counted as full days.

b. It has been assumed that 100% of the population in countries with developed market and centrally planned economies has access to safe water.

admissions or discharges: rate per 10,000 pop.	by kinds of hospital (%): general	specialized	medical centres	rural	bed occupancy rate[a] (%)	average length of stay (days)	mortality: infant mortality per 1,000 live births 1983–84	maternal mortality per 100,000 live births 1981–82	population with access to safe water[b] 1980 (%)	food supply (% of FAO requirement) 1982	financing of public health care, latest year: health-care insurance: indiv. (% of earnings)	employer (% of payroll)	govt. (% of covered earnings)	public health expenditures (% of natl. budget)	public health expenditures per capita (U.S.$)	country
76[2]	52.8[2]	46.7[2]	—	0.5[2]	58.0[2]	8[2]	194.0	...	10	85	—	—	—	...	1.40[3]	Afghanistan
...	...	...	...	...	...	...	44.0[6]	...	...	121	—	8.0[7]	[8]	...	26.20[3]	Albania
577	...	...	...	...	64.1[10,11]	10[10,11]	92.2[6]	...	78	110	4.5[7]	5.5[7]	—	...	26.50[3]	Algeria
1,547	100.0	—	—	—	37.8	4	4.4	...	...	...	...	...	...	...	...	American Samoa
...	...	...	...	...	...	...	16.0[13]	...	100	...	...	...	...	...	...	Andorra
296[14]	58.5[14]	...	...	41.5[14]	44.5[14]	16[14]	148.0	113.4[15]	17	97	...	...	...	...	14.50	Angola
1,097	—	—	—	100.0	52.3[4]	6[4]	48.3[17]	...	...	...	...	...	...	10.8	62.00	Anguilla
480[18]	100.0[18]	—	—	—	89.5[18]	13[18]	32.0[6]	170.4[12]	100[12]	81	3.0[7]	5.0[7]	—	9.0	33.20	Antigua and Barbuda
...	...	...	...	...	...	...	36.0	69.4	60	127	3.0	4.5	—	1.4	6.50	Argentina
...	...	...	...	...	...	...	8.0[6]	...	...	...	...	...	...	...	...	Aruba
...	...	...	...	...	...	...	9.2	3.7[12]	97	120	[20]	—	[8]	7.8	251.90	Australia
2,148[13]	...	...	...	...	82.5[13]	15[13]	11.4	11.1[12]	88	133	3.2[20]	3.2[20]	...	11.5	404.30	Austria
...	...	...	...	...	...	...	22.9	38.1	98[16]	85	1.7[7,22]	7.3[7,23]	—	17.5	207.50	Bahamas, The
1,104	74.0	26.0	—	—	72.6[19]	9[19]	44.1	...	98[1]	...	—	—	—	6.8	230.60	Bahrain
...	...	...	...	...	...	...	128.0	...	68	82	...	...	...	6.4	0.90	Bangladesh
842	93.9	4.6	—	1.5	89.8[24]	34[24]	10.9[21]	24.1[13]	100[6]	126	1.0	1.0	—	10.6	133.40	Barbados
1,552	91.0	9.0	—	—	85.3	19	9.4[25]	13.1[4]	89	134	1.8	3.8	...	1.7	80.20	Belgium
...	...	...	...	...	...	...	18.9[25]	48.8[21]	63[1]	118	3.0[7]	4.1[7]	[8]	9.0	31.70	Belize
...	...	...	...	...	...	...	116.0	...	17	95	—	0.2[26]	—	...	4.90[3]	Benin
...	...	...	...	...	...	...	5.9	...	...	...	...	...	...	13.4	0.40	Bermuda
...	...	...	...	...	...	...	134.0[25]	...	8	90[13]	...	...	...	4.3[27]	13.60[27]	Bhutan
...	...	...	...	...	...	...	110.0[25]	...	39	90	2.0	8.0	—	3.1	3.50	Bolivia
691	89.1	6.7	4.2	—	90.0[19]	10[19]	68.4[1]	...	29[1]	105	—	—	—	5.6	20.50	Botswana
...	...	...	...	...	...	...	71.0	92.1[13]	63	110	[20]	[20]	[20]	7.3	23.60	Brazil
868[13]	100.0[13]	—	—	—	75.0[13]	8[13]	25.5[30]	...	90[6]	...	...	...	...	4.0	42.80	British Virgin Islands
1,069	98.5	—	—	1.5	38.0	4	11.5	...	72	114	...	...	...	3.6	0.50	Brunei
2,118[6]	...	...	...	...	84.4[6]	16[6]	15.8[25]	22.2[12]	...	148	—	30.0[7]	[8]	...	196.30	Bulgaria
66[5,11]	...	...	...	...	63.7[5,11]	12[5,11]	137.0	...	14	79	—	11.5[31]	—	6.8	1.40	Burkina Faso
289[6]	75.7[6]	10.1[6]	—	14.2[6]	78.1[6]	9[6]	106.0[25]	...	23	114	1.0	2.0	1.0	7.0	2.00	Burma
...	...	...	...	...	...	...	124.0	...	2[1]	102	—	—	—	...	1.90	Burundi
...	...	...	...	...	...	...	116.0	...	49	91	—	7.0[31]	—	4.4	7.50	Cameroon
1,677	93.9	6.0	0.1	—	110.4	19	9.3	1.9	99	129	[20]	[20]	[20]	6.3	202.00	Canada
279[14]	...	...	...	...	71.7[14]	11[14]	30.0	134.0[16]	...	117	8.0	15.0	...	...	...	Cape Verde
1,129	91.3	—	—	8.7	65.5[19]	4[10]	7.8[32]	...	99[10]	...	...	...	...	...	...	Cayman Islands
412	43.9	1.0	37.9	17.2	50.7	8	142.0	...	18	95	—	12.0[26,31]	—	5.1	3.30	Central African Republic
...	...	...	...	...	...	...	139.0	...	26	72	—	6.0[31]	...	...	0.60[3]	Chad
962[13]	84.9[13]	9.3[13]	—	5.8[13]	73.9	10[13]	20.1	52.4	76	108	6.0	—	—	6.2	32.50	Chile
...	...	...	...	...	...	...	36.0[25]	...	...	108	—	[34]	...	...	3.90	China
...	...	...	...	...	...	...	...	...	100	...	...	...	...	...	...	Christmas Island
445	84.6	—	15.4	—	...	...	...	...	100	...	...	...	...	...	...	Cocos (Keeling) Islands
613[6]	88.9[4]	11.1[4]	—	—	59.3[6]	6[6]	50.0	133.5[5]	64	110	2.3	4.7	...	...	14.10[3]	Colombia
510[4]	63.7[4]	—	—	36.3[4]	67.9[4]	11[4]	121.7[13]	...	...	103	...	...	...	3.1[27]	0.80[27]	Comoros
...	...	...	...	...	...	...	81.0	...	13	112	—	0.2	—	...	37.90	Congo
1,352	70.7	—	—	29.3	43.6[19]	9[19]	19.9	...	...	...	...	...	...	...	...	Cook Islands
1,192	77.8	16.7	——5.5——		75.7	8	18.8	26.0[12]	81	117	5.5	9.3	1.3	22.5	70.50	Costa Rica
171[16]	...	...	...	...	...	...	106.0	...	14	115	—	5.5[31]	...	3.9	15.40	Côte d'Ivoire
1,462[6]	49.7[6]	45.7[6]	1.9[6]	2.7[6]	74.4[6]	11[6]	16.5[25]	55.7	62	130	—	10.0	[8]	...	65.30[3]	Cuba
567[19]	...	...	...	...	72.1	8	14.9	...	92[1]	139	6.0[7]	6.0[7]	[8]	6.8	69.60	Cyprus
2,141	81.3	18.4	0.3	—	65.7	14	14.0[25]	4.8[12]	74.5[12]	146	—	20.0[6]	[8]	...	263.50[3]	Czechoslovakia
1,952[21]	97.6	2.4	—	—	82.5[21]	11[21]	7.7	11.4	99	147	—	—	[8]	1.4	67.60	Denmark
...	...	...	...	...	...	...	*c.* 200	...	...	...	...	...	...	5.8	19.50	Djibouti
729	...	...	—	...	...	...	23.9	117.6[4]	91[12]	95	3.0[7]	5.0[7]	—	8.8	20.80	Dominica
...	73.1[24]	16.7[24]	—	10.2[24]	59.8[24]	7[24]	75.0	55.3[4]	57	96	2.5[7]	7.0[7]	2.5[7]	10.5	21.30	Dominican Republic
471	——85.0[10,38]——		15.0[10]	[38]	60.4	8	68.4	216.3[4]	51	90	5.0[7]	1.0	—	7.5	14.20	Ecuador
...	...	...	...	...	...	...	104.50	77.9[10]	84	130	1.0	4.0	—	2.7	1.40	Egypt

Health services (continued)

country	health personnel							hospitals									
	year	physicians	dentists	nurses	pharma-cists	midwives	popu-lation per physi-cian	year	number	kinds (%)				ownership (%)			hos-pital beds per 10,000 pop.
										gen-eral	spe-cial-ized	medical centres	rural	govern-ment	private non-profit	private for profit	
El Salvador	1981	1,793	600	...	597[10]	...	2,701	1979	82	15.8	17.1	15.9	51.2	69.5	1.2	29.3	17
Equatorial Guinea	1975	5	...	248	...	2	62,000	1982	65[5]	...	...	...	...	...	...	...	108
Ethiopia	1982	504	16[13]	7,547[13, 39]	93[13]	[39]	79,365	1980	86	32.6	18.6	—	48.8	88.4	9.3	2.3	3
Faeroe Islands	1985	75	34	235	8	13	609	1983	3	33.3	—	—	66.7	100.0	—	—	78[21]
Falkland Islands	1984	3	1	11	—	6	667	1984	1	100.0	—	—	—	100.0	—	—	65
Fiji	1984	339	58	1,406	44[13]	...	2,024	1984	27	11.1	33.3	—	55.6	92.6	7.4	—	25
Finland	1984	9,979	3,770	46,612[6]	7,057	828[6]	489	1984	...	...	...	...	...	...	...	...	125
France	1983	118,000	33,048	271,253	43,662	8,660	460	1982	4,464[41]	—85.4[1, 41]—		—	14.6[1, 41]	45.5	—54.5—		114
French Guiana	1982	80	18	309	18	16	885	1982	6	16.7	—	66.7	16.7	33.3	—66.7—		123
French Polynesia	1982	170	51	424[9]	24	10[9]	914	1981	34	8.8	5.9	52.9	32.4	94.1	—	5.9	68
Gabon	1980	265	20[5]	823[5]	28[5]	99[42]	4,053	1981	103	—15.5—		—	84.5	100.0	—	—	44
Gambia, The	1980	66	6[4]	179[4]	2[4]	90[4]	9,587	1978	16	18.8	12.5	—	68.7	87.5	12.5	...	12
Gaza Strip	...	...	...	...	...	...	...	1984	7	...	...	...	...	85.7	14.3	—	18
Germany, East	1984	37,057	11,353	...	3,677	...	450	1984	541	...	...	...	...	84.8	—15.2—		102
Germany, West	1985	153,895	34,415	263,435	30,865	5,366	397	1985	3,106	44.7[13]	55.3[13]	—	—	36.0	34.0	30.0	110
Ghana	1982	1,435	95[1]	17,758[1]	611[1]	6,728[1]	8,278	1979	329	2.7	4.9	54.7	37.7	78.4	13.1	8.5	18[1]
Gibraltar	1983	22	5[6]	246	13[6]	14[6]	1,364	1983	3	100.0	—	—	—	100.0	—	—	87
Greece	1983	27,607	8,286	19,152[6]	...	1,898[6]	357	1984	595	56.6[44]	43.4	[44]	[44]	29.9[1]	3.9[1]	66.2[1]	58
Greenland	1984	59	26	542	...	12	892	1983	17	5.9	—	—	94.1	100.0	—	—	111[21]
Grenada	1985	38	7[1]	337[1]	1[4]	107[4]	2,513	1982	39	7.7	7.7	69.2	15.4	100.0	...	...	33[25]
Guadeloupe	1983	418	101	1,230	135	101	789	1982	27	60.0[4]	30.0[4]	—	10.0[4]	40.7	—59.3—		128[12]
Guam	1982	83	23	396	30	...	1,363	1982	4	25.0	25.0	50.0	—	50.0	—50.0—		21[10]
Guatemala	1981	1,250	275	4,345[9, 10]	...	...	5,700	1982	159[45]	38.4[45]	25.8[45]	32.7[45]	3.1[45]	76.7[45]	—	23.3[45]	14
Guernsey	1982	53	21	592	15	31	1,094	1982	5	20.0	80.0	—	—	100.0	—	—	91
Guinea	1980	301	21[37]	1,533[37]	159[37]	394[37]	17,000	1976	314	1.9	—	87.9	10.1	100.0	—	—	17
Guinea-Bissau	1980	108	2	...	3	...	7,287	1981	17	11.8	—	—	88.2	100.0	—	—	19[12]
Guyana	1982	270	24	881[10]	32[10]	546[10]	2,857	1979	55	20.0	12.7	27.3	40.0	87.3	3.6	9.1	53
Haiti	1982	482	63[13]	1,899[9]	6[9, 10]	100[10]	10,500	1981	72	—77.8—		22.2	—	61.1	—38.9—		10[6]
Honduras	1985	1,900	380	3,545[13]	497	...	2,000	1985	46	59.1[6]	11.4[6]	—	29.5[6]	45.7	—	54.3	14
Hong Kong	1985[35]	4,887	1,069	14,934	549	981	1,110	1982	71	43.7	15.5	39.4	1.4	50.7	26.8	22.5	45[25]
Hungary	1984	29,889[33]	4,426	94,724	4,552	2,552	357[33]	1984	...	...	...	...	...	...	...	...	96[25]
Iceland	1983	545	191	2,724[39]	168	[39]	435	1983	46[13]	54.3[13]	41.4[13]	4.3[13]	—	...	...	...	113
India	1981[35]	268,712	8,648	162,900[6]	155,621	217,981	2,613	1981	25,452	26.7	0.3	65.8	7.2	71.6	—28.4—		7[6]
Indonesia	1983	10,262[9]	1,292[9]	62,615[6]	1,800[10]	16,928[6]	15,405[9]	1983	1,244	14.7[4]	8.3[4]	39.4[4]	37.6[4]	30.2[4]	23.0[4]	46.8[4]	7
Iran	1983	15,945	2,340	29,486	2,650	2,202	2,582	1982	581	71.1	15.5	9.8	3.6	66.4	13.9	19.7	16
Iraq	1982	7,634	1,387	6,082	2,132	2,267	1,804	1982	234	48.3	33.8	2.1	15.8	95.7	—	4.3	18
Ireland	1984	4,250	990	24,390[9, 39]	2,068[1]	[39]	830	1980	209	33.5	37.8	1.4	27.3	63.2	21.5	15.3	97
Isle of Man	1982	90	19[9]	750[9]	30	61[9]	747	1981	3	33.3	33.3	—	33.3	100.0	—	—	108
Israel	1983	11,895	2,900	27,300[6]	2,540	115[6, 9]	345	1984	152	28.9	71.1	—	—	32.2	28.3	39.5	64
Italy	1981	97,003	...	186,335[39]	43,500[13]	[39]	582	1983	1,813	73.7	26.3	—	—	62.8	—37.2—		88
Jamaica	1985[9]	317	61	2,814	99	494	...	1984	29	79.3	20.7	—	—	90.9[6]	—9.1[6]—		27
Japan	1984	181,101	63,145	595,091	129,700	24,649	663	1984	9,574	88.8	11.2	—	—	15.8	3.1	81.1	122
Jersey	1982	148	41	646	22	27[1]	517	1984	7	14.3	85.7	—	—	100.0	—	—	107
Jordan	1984	2,310	486	830	800	266	1,102	1982	45	80.0	20.0	—	—	46.7	8.9	44.4	14[21]
Kampuchea	1984	200	...	...	130	...	36,000	1984	146	84.9	15.1	...	...	...	...	...	23
Kenya	1984	2,591	331	19,815	131	...	7,540	1984	506	—42.1—		57.9	—	...	...	...	16
Kiribati	1982[9]	19	2	125	1	213	3,158	1982	34	2.9	—	97.1	—	100.0	—	—	45
Korea, North	1982	45,000	...	...	...	...	417	1982	7,924	19.3	12.4	—68.3—		...	...	...	130
Korea, South	1984	28,015	4,972	54,081	28,531	5,991	1,448	1984	8,074	—6.1—		93.9	—	...	...	...	17
Kuwait	1984	2,983	238	8,293[6]	714	128	548	1982	30	40.0	36.7	23.3	—	73.3	—	26.7	34[21]
Laos	1985	430	15[37]	1,028[37]	16[37]	352[37]	8,336	1985	38[16]	...	...	...	...	...	...	...	32
Lebanon	1982	3,000	730[10]	3,681[10]	1,002[10]	614[10]	1,000	1982	130[45]	...	...	...	...	...	...	...	38
Lesotho	1982	114	6	452	7	...	12,265	1982	113	—17.7—		—82.3—		40.9[5]	59.1[5]	—	16
Liberia	1981	236	21[13]	567[13]	4[13]	114[13]	8,305	1981	85[13]	...	...	...	...	60.0[13]	—40.0[13]—		15
Libya	1982[9]	5,210	384	9,495	514	1,218	637	1982	64	68.8	31.2	—	—	100.0	—	—	48
Liechtenstein	1984	20	7	...	2	...	1,330	...	...	...	...	...	...	...	...	...	...
Luxembourg	1984	637	158	1,098[1]	251	101	574	1984	34	58.8	41.2	—	—	...	...	...	128
Macau	1981	293	105	605	5	1,357	1,000	1977	4	50.0	50.0	—	—	...	...	...	63
Madagascar	1981	901	94	3,779	87	1,423	9,943	1978	749	0.8	1.1	75.7	22.4	100.0	—	—	20
Malaŵi	1981	121	6	1,695[39]	11	[39]	51,461	1981	340	13.5	1.8	—84.7—		58.2	—41.8—		19
Malaysia	1982[51]	4,234	863	28,780	626	12,409	3,510	1981[51]	163	20.2	50.4	—	29.4	39.9	—	60.1	27
Maldives	1983	17	...	113	2[1, 9]	159[1]	9,882	1983	2	100.0	—	—	—	100.0	—	—	6
Mali	1980	337	14[4]	1,312	24[4]	250	21,068	1977	192	0.5	81.3	—	18.2	100.0	—	—	6[13]
Malta	1982	413	57	2,962	369	225	786	1983	7	28.6	71.4	—	—	...	...	...	101
Martinique	1982	394	107	1,871	146	106	834	1979	17	17.6	11.9	17.6	52.9	82.3	—	17.7	128[21]
Mauritania	1980	103	4[5]	560[37]	6[5]	19[5]	14,500	1977	12	8.3	—	—	91.7	100.0	—	—	4[10]
Mauritius	1985	711	96	1,467[9]	85	569[9]	1,404	1984	17	41.2	23.5	23.5	11.8	88.2	—11.8—		29[24]
Mayotte	1980	9	1	51	1	2	5,567	1981	2	...	...	...	...	...	...	...	16
Mexico	1982	66,373	1,879[28]	40,998[28]	112[28]	634[28]	1,102	1974	1,575	47.3	10.6	26.2	15.9	...	...	...	11[6]
Monaco	1985	63	32[6]	391[6]	56[6]	6[6]	449	1982	1	100.0	—	—	—	100.0	—	—	182[25]
Mongolia	1985[9]	4,200	200	7,595[1]	300	963[1]	440	1981	1,659	2.1	5.4	71.9	20.6	100.0	—	—	92[25]
Montserrat	1983	6	1[6]	73	2[4]	32[4]	1,963	1983	1	100.0	—	—	—	100.0	—	—	57
Morocco	1984	2,957	198	22,147[1]	1,030	74[1]	7,727	1982	141	20.6	24.8	44.0	10.6	100.0	—	—	12[21]
Mozambique	1985	317	96[9, 13]	2,590	8[9, 13]	871	43,468	1985	258	3.9	0.8	85.6	9.7	100.0	—	—	9
Nauru	1980	11	2[42]	61[39, 42]	1[42]	[39]	700	1980	2[42]	100.0[42]	—	—	—	50.0[42]	50.0[42]	—	250
Nepal	1984	571	17[9, 13]	1,986	1[9, 13]	...	28,270	1980	68	88.2	11.8	—	—	82.4	17.6	—	2[21]
Netherlands, The	1985	31,185	6,865	34,500[4]	1,800	950	465	1985	815	27.0	73.0	—	—	...	...	...	122
Netherlands Antilles	1975	164	34	...	17	21	1,393	1975	11	—100.0—		—	—	...	...	...	101[12]
New Caledonia	1983	194	37	283[1]	48	23[1]	1,224	1981	38	10.5	7.9	39.5	42.1	92.1	—	7.9	83[12]
New Zealand	1984	7,750	1,275	36,931	3,182	2,600[6]	417	1982	268[19]	...	...	...	...	38.8[19]	—	61.2[19]	97[19, 25]
Nicaragua	1984	2,172	222	5,649	...	...	456	1984	49	55.1	8.2	36.7	...	46.2[37]	—	53.8[37]	16[21]
Niger	1980	136	10[4]	1,080[4]	12[4]	2,006[4]	40,209	1978	212	1.9	0.5	94.8	2.8	97.2	2.8	—	6[10]
Nigeria	1981	10,399	379	36,464	2,609	30,190	8,326	1981	2,374[13]	25.2[13]	...	74.8[13]	...	70.2[53]	—29.8[53]—		9
Niue	1980[9]	2	3	34	...	21	1,600	1983	1	100.0	—	—	—	100.0	—	—	131
Norfolk Island	1981[9]	2	...	8	1	1	1,067	1985	1	...	...	...	...	100.0	—	—	108

admissions or discharges: rate per 10,000 pop.	by kinds of hospital (%): general	special-ized	medical centres	rural	bed occu-pancy rate[a] (%)	aver-age length of stay (days)	mortality: infant mortality per 1,000 live births 1983–84	maternal mortality per 100,000 live births 1981–82	popu-lation with access to safe water[b] 1980 (%)	food supply (% of FAO require-ment) 1982	financing of public health care, latest year: health-care insurance: indiv. (% of earn-ings)	em-ployer (% of payroll)	govt. (% of covered earnings)	public health expendi-tures (% of natl. budget)	public health expendi-tures per capita (U.S.$)	country
378[19]	...	...	...	...	77.1[19]	7[19]	35.1	74.2[12]	48	88	2.5	6.3	...	8.1	13.00	El Salvador
...	...	...	...	...	...	...	137.0	...	...	...	...	...	...	...	...	Equatorial Guinea
...	...	...	...	...	33.2[40]	11[40]	155.0	...	13	93	—	—	—	3.4	1.00	Ethiopia
1,780	75.7	—	—	24.3	96.2[21]	16	11.5[30]	...	—	...	...	...	...	...	...	Faeroe Islands
1,790[1]	100.0[1]	—	—	—	41.7[1]	8[1]	...	...	...	...	...	...	...	...	...	Falkland Islands
997[1]	59.4[1]	10.2[1]	—	30.4[1]	77.1[1]	8[1]	22.5	131.3[12]	69	115	—	—	—	8.2	36.80	Fiji
2,088	58.9[13]	40.8[13]	—0.3[13]—		81.7	19	6.5	4.5	84	122	1.0	1.4	[8]	10.6	331.20	Finland
1,917[41]	...	...	...	...	81.9[41]	14[41]	8.2	15.5	97	141	5.5	8.0	...	14.6	634.80	France
1,666[24]	82.2[24]	—	—	17.8[24]	77.7[24]	17[24]	22.6	...	...	...	...	...	...	...	...	French Guiana
1,472	70.9	...	3.2	25.9	51.7	8	20.8[25]	...	...	108	...	...	...	...	...	French Polynesia
258	...	...	...	...	23.6	13	121.6	...	1[1]	122	—	4.0	—	...	81.20	Gabon
437[19]	...	...	...	...	...	...	174.0	...	12[1]	91	—	—	—	6.3	6.90	Gambia, The
1,234	...	...	...	...	69.5	4	...	...	...	...	...	...	...	...	...	Gaza Strip
1,383[12]	42.8[4]	57.2[4]	—	—	74.0[12]	21[12]	10.0	16.7[12]	82	144	10.0[7]	12.5[7, 43]	[8]	...	348.00[3]	Germany, East
1,871[21]	80.5[12]	19.5[12]	—	—	84.8[21]	18[21]	9.6	10.8[21]	99	127	3.5[22]	3.5[22]	...	18.6	618.20	Germany, West
...	...	...	...	...	...	...	98.0	...	50	67	5.0[7]	11.5[7]	—	5.8	16.30	Ghana
1,514	100.0	—	—	—	63.2[6]	11[6]	...	...	—	...	...	...	...	...	292.30	Gibraltar
1,192[12]	69.4[6, 44]	30.6[6]	[44]	[44]	68.4[12]	12[12]	14.1	11.7	97	142	3.7	3.7	...	10.5	160.80	Greece
2,682	22.2	—	—	77.8	66.5[21]	10	35.7[30]	...	...	...	...	...	...	...	...	Greenland
749[13]	...	...	...	...	...	...	21.2	...	85	88	4.0[7]	4.0[7]	—	15.6	18.70	Grenada
1,478[24]	58.1[24]	41.9[24]	—	...	92.3[24]	20[24]	17.7	106.4[4]	...	103	...	...	...	...	...	Guadeloupe
738[10]	97.6[10]	2.4[10]	—	—	78.8[10]	8[10]	7.5	...	...	...	...	...	...	2.7	32.90	Guam
317	...	...	...	...	70.8	11	64.4	105.5	42	96	2.0	4.0	...	10.9	15.30	Guatemala
977	89.0	11.0	—	—	83.9	28	8.4[25, 46]	...	...	...	...	...	...	...	...	Guernsey
...	...	...	...	...	...	...	159.0	...	10	79	—	3.2	—	...	3.40[3]	Guinea
326	59.8	—	—	40.2	57.5	11	143.0	...	...	97	...	...	...	...	...	Guinea-Bissau
...	...	...	...	...	...	...	45.0	104.3[5]	93	100	4.9[7]	7.4[7]	—	3.7	14.40	Guyana
123	...	...	...	...	...	...	117.7	...	12	84	2.0[22]	4.0[23]	1.2	...	2.80[3]	Haiti
429[13]	75.6[13]	16.7[13]	—	7.7[10]	70.2[13]	8[13]	78.6	82.0[10]	55	95	2.5	5.0	2.5	8.0	9.80	Honduras
1,494	93.6	3.2	3.2	—	82.4	8	7.6[25]	6.4[21]	...	112	—	[34]	—	...	...	Hong Kong
1,961	...	...	...	...	80.5	14	20.4[25]	14.9[21]	44	134	3.0[22]	24.0	[8]	...	157.90	Hungary
2,087	84.0[13]	14.2[13]	1.8[13]	—	101.0	19[6]	6.1	0.0[12]	99	119	2.0	—	[8]	21.0	757.00	Iceland
...	...	...	...	...	...	...	105.0[25]	...	41	93	2.2	4.4	25.0	2.4	0.90	India
66[4, 19]	...	...	...	...	55.1[4, 19]	9[4, 19]	79.0[25]	...	19	110	2.0	5.0	—	2.2	2.50	Indonesia
...	...	...	...	...	...	...	111.0[25]	...	51	126	7.0[7]	20.0[7]	3.0[7]	5.7	61.00	Iran
592	65.5	26.4	7.0	1.1	60.3	6	81.8	...	76	116	5.0[7]	12.0[7, 47]	—	...	22.30[3]	Iraq
1,749[1, 48]	...	...	...	...	...	9[1, 48]	10.1	6.7[13]	73	161	1.0	1.0	[8]	...	428.30[3]	Ireland
1,274	83.9	7.0	—	9.1	81.2	25	...	131.9[10]	...	...	...	...	...	22.3	426.40	Isle of Man
1,661	95.8	4.2	—	—	93.1	14[12]	13.6	2.0[12]	99	116	0.8	5.7	—	3.7	219.10	Israel
1,661	91.1	8.9	—	—	67.5	13	10.9[25]	13.1[13]	86	140	1.2	11.9[22]	...	11.5	384.70	Italy
647	81.0	19.0	—	—	74.0[19]	7[19]	13.2	135.7	82	109	2.5[7]	2.5[7]	...	5.4	26.70	Jamaica
643[6]	97.9[6]	2.1[6]	—	—	83.3[6]	56[6]	5.5[25]	15.5[12]	98	124	4.3	4.3	16.4	...	472.20[3]	Japan
1,749	81.9	18.1	—	—	86.8[12]	24[12]	8.4[25, 46]	...	...	...	...	...	...	18.4	422.30	Jersey
880	93.6	6.4	—	—	41.0	3	63.0	...	66	105	—	—	—	3.6	26.80	Jordan
...	...	...	...	...	...	...	145.0[25]	...	45	81	—	—	—	...	...	Kampuchea
...	...	...	...	...	...	...	81.0	...	24	88	...	—	—	7.0	5.60	Kenya
633	47.6	—	52.4	—	58.0	15	87.0[4]	...	...	...	—	—	—	...	...	Kiribati
...	...	...	...	...	...	...	32.0	...	...	130	...	...	...	...	16.00[3]	Korea, North
279[49]	97.8[49]	2.2[49]	—	—	61.6	12[49]	27.0[25]	...	79	127	1.5[22]	1.5[22]	...	1.4	5.20	Korea, South
1,231	66.4	28.5	5.1	—	71.7	8	19.5	7.8	89	...	—	—	—	6.3	394.40	Kuwait
96[16]	...	...	...	...	19.7[16]	7[16]	121.0	...	48[1]	93	—	—	—	...	0.90[3]	Laos
...	...	...	...	...	...	...	44.4	...	92[1]	119	1.5	5.5	...	...	19.30[3]	Lebanon
410[5]	20.8[5]	0.4[5]	6.2[5]	72.6[5]	79.6[5, 19]	10[5, 19]	109.0	...	23	106	...	...	...	7.2	8.80	Lesotho
...	...	...	...	...	...	...	112.0	...	10	97	—	—	—	6.2	8.60	Liberia
719	...	...	...	...	52.7	13	97.5[1]	...	87	161	1.0	1.4	1.6	...	106.30[3]	Libya
...	...	...	...	...	...	...	7.4	...	...	...	...	...	...	...	...	Liechtenstein
1,848	...	...	...	...	79.8	20	9.0[25]	25.0[10]	98	142	4.1	4.1	...	2.2	106.00	Luxembourg
...	...	...	...	...	...	...	12.0	...	...	102	...	...	...	5.7[27, 50]	17.30[27, 50]	Macau
699[19]	...	...	...	...	57.9[19]	2[19]	110.0	...	26	110	—	8.3[31]	—	...	7.20[3]	Madagascar
361	...	...	...	...	77.8	9	152.0[25]	...	44	96	—	—	—	6.8	3.60	Malaŵi
635[24]	...	...	...	...	...	...	28.0[25]	50.6[6]	64	114	—	—	[8]	4.4	29.70	Malaysia
272	100.0	—	—	—	62.1[52]	5[52]	77.0	...	...	92	...	...	...	3.8	6.30	Maldives
178	54.9	37.5	—	7.6	58.8	7	149.0	...	23	76	—	2.0	—	2.5	2.20	Mali
1,569[6]	...	...	...	...	83.7[6]	19[6]	11.7	17.5[5]	100	106	8.3[7]	8.3[7]	8.3[7]	9.0	114.20	Malta
1,841	69.0	6.0	11.3	13.7	84.2	23	14.0[25]	27.4[16]	...	112	...	...	...	...	...	Martinique
115	...	...	...	...	97.8	5	133.0	...	17[1]	94	—	2.0	—	2.8	4.30	Mauritania
1,087[24]	...	...	...	...	84.5[13, 24]	8[13, 24]	23.8[25]	108.4	60	122	—	—	—	7.6	22.30	Mauritius
...	...	...	...	...	...	...	...	...	...	...	...	...	...	...	...	Mayotte
...	...	...	...	...	...	...	53.0	103.4[4]	59	126	2.3	5.6	...	1.2	6.00	Mexico
2,630	100.0	—	—	—	77.6	14	...	...	...	...	...	...	...	...	...	Monaco
2,508	25.9	33.0	1.1	40.0	89.1	14	49.0[25]	...	21[16]	113	...	...	...	...	16.00[3]	Mongolia
718[1]	100.0[1]	—	—	—	30.7[1]	5[1]	7.7[6]	—	100	...	...	...	...	18.0	93.30	Montserrat
225	57.1	25.1	8.2	9.6	63.5	12	114.4	...	53	105	0.2	0.4	—	2.9	6.00	Morocco
92[13, 19]	...	...	...	...	70.2[13, 19]	9[13, 19]	101.1[25]	...	7	79	...	...	...	7.1	0.50[3]	Mozambique
2,660[42]	100.0[42]	—	—	—	...	...	31.2[1]	...	...	...	—	—	[8]	...	...	Nauru
46[19]	...	...	...	...	61.5[19]	7[19]	132.0[25]	...	11	92	—	—	—	4.5	1.10	Nepal
1,148	95.1	4.9	—	—	80.2[19]	13[19]	7.9[25]	5.3[12]	97	132	5.9	14.1	...	11.0	548.10	Netherlands, The
...	...	...	...	...	...	...	14.0[13]	...	...	112	...	...	...	7.9	45.00	Netherlands Antilles
1,468	77.9	3.0	3.2	15.9	57.6	16	11.2	...	...	101	...	...	...	...	...	New Caledonia
...	...	...	...	...	78.7[12, 24]	12[24]	9.5[25]	19.8[12]	93	136	—	—	[8]	12.6	372.50	New Zealand
634	—91.7—		8.3	...	...	...	76.4	65.2[4]	46	101	4.0	11.0	0.5	14.6	33.70	Nicaragua
83[19]	...	...	...	...	62.0[19]	9[19]	140.0	...	49	104	—	11.0[26, 31]	—	4.1	3.60	Niger
...	...	...	...	...	...	...	113.0	...	28	103	6.0[7]	6.0[7]	—	2.5	2.80	Nigeria
2,263	100.0	...	...	—	56.7[13]	14[13]	—	...	...	...	...	...	—	9.6	136.10	Niue
...	...	...	...	...	42.9	...	...	...	...	...	...	...	...	6.5	104.10	Norfolk Island

Health services (continued)

country	health personnel							hospitals		kinds (%)				ownership (%)			hospital beds per 10,000 pop.
	year	physicians	dentists	nurses	pharmacists	midwives	population per physician	year	number	general	specialized	medical centres	rural	government	private non-profit	private for profit	
Norway	1983	9,722	4,266	41,327	2,761[6, 54]	694[6]	425	1984	1,179	6.5	91.5	2.0	...	...	...	...	165
Oman	1985	581	63[21]	2,104[21]	148[21]	23[6, 9]	1,792	1984	40	—37.5—		—62.5—		100.0	—	—	25[25]
Pacific Is., Trust Terr. of the																	
Marshall Islands	1985	17	2	51	...	...	2,111	1985	2	100	—	—	—	100	—	—	15
Micronesia, Fed. States of	1985	36	13	257	7	...	2,542	1984	4	100	—	—	—	100	—	—	37
Northern Mariana Islands	1985	18	6	125	...	...	1,111	1985	2	100	—	—	—	100	—	—	31
Palau	1980	10	4	85	...	...	1,212	1985	1	100	—	—	—	100	—	—	...
Pakistan	1986	42,501[35]	1,398[25, 35]	14,249[35]	1,770[6]	9,947[6]	2,426[35]	1985	895[6, 11]	62.3[6]	6.1[6]	...	31.6[6]	82.2[6]	1.1[6]	16.7[6]	6
Panama	1984	2,438	409[12]	1,962[12]	157[4]	...	875	1983	50	...	...	...	...	88.4[53]	—11.6[53]—		36[21]
Papua New Guinea	1984	280	16[13]	3,228[13, 39]	9[13]	[39]	11,635	1980	390	5.1	—	53.6	41.2	46.2	53.8	—	45[21]
Paraguay	1982	2,201	855[10]	2,636[10]	860[10]	783[10]	1,379	1982	143[16]	63.6[16]	4.9[16]	—	31.5[16]	91.6[16]	8.4[16]	—	11
Peru	1982	14,751	3,687[13]	10,065[13]	3,457[13]	2,171[13]	1,236	1977	437	66.4	9.1	24.5	—	60.4	15.6	24.0	16[6]
Philippines	1982	46,579	1,090[1, 9]	9,644[1, 9]	539[1, 9]	9,470[1, 9]	1,090	1984	1,602	...	...	...	...	25.2	—74.8—		13
Pitcairn Island	1985	—	—	1[9]	—	—	—	...	...	...	...	...	...	...	...	...	...
Poland	1985	71,097	17,344[21]	168,107[21]	15,958[21]	18,470[21]	521	1984	782	87.9	12.1	—	—	...	...	...	65[25]
Portugal	1985	24,095	437	29,525	5,053	824	420	1984	481	80.7	19.3	—	—	78.8[6]	21.2[6]	—	53[25]
Puerto Rico	1983	7,133	741[13]	14,392[13]	1,436[13]	199[13]	458	1980	111	72.1	27.9	—	—	48.6	19.8	31.5	38[21]
Qatar	1985[9]	505	52	1,101	115	70[1]	596	1985	3	33.0	67.0	—	—	100.0	—	—	32
Réunion	1986	750	193[25]	1,791[25]	174[25]	102[25]	734	1984	21	36.4[5]	18.1[5]	—	45.5[5]	74.2[53]	—25.8[53]—		64[25]
Romania	1985[9]	46,300[21]	7,285[6]	81,031[6]	6,588[6]	12,248[6]	480[21]	1984	437[1]	56.8[1]	32.5[1]	—	10.8[1]	...	...	...	94[25]
Rwanda	1983[9]	258	1[1]	901	6	616[1]	22,093	1983	170	—16.5—		—83.5—		50.0	—50.0—		16
St. Christopher and Nevis	1982	23	5[1]	252[1]	1[13]	123[13]	1,989	1982	3	...	...	...	...	100.0	—	—	56
St. Helena and Ascension	1982	3	1	30[10]	...	7[10]	1,667	1982	8	12.5	12.5	75.0	—	...	...	...	110
St. Lucia	1984	58	5	236	16[12]	66[5]	2,311	1984	5	20.0[12]	20.0[12]	—	60.0[12]	...	...	...	39
St. Pierre and Miquelon	1983	11	2	20[5]	...	1[5]	545	1983	1	100.0	—	—	—	100.0	—	—	167
St. Vincent	1984	24	1	290	...	...	4,300	1984	9	11.1	33.3	22.2	33.3	100.0	—	—	32
San Marino	1979	10[9]	...	...	...	...	2,030	1980	...	...	...	...	...	...	...	...	28
São Tomé and Príncipe	1981	38	—	157	1	13	2,500	1978	16	12.5	—	87.5	—	...	...	...	78
Saudi Arabia	1985[9]	8,243	269[1]	7,040[1]	499[1]	3,273[1]	1,364	1985	157	...	...	...	...	76.4	—	23.6	26
Senegal	1982	470	70[1]	2,360[1, 9]	139[1]	401[1]	12,987	1977	44	11.4	—	79.5	9.1	100.0	—	—	13[4]
Seychelles	1984	34	7	340[25]	4	131[10]	1,900	1984	6	16.7	16.7	66.7	—	100.0	—	—	51[25]
Sierra Leone	1983	197	30[13]	1,758[13, 39]	8[13]	[39]	17,906	1984	109	0.9[13]	7.2[13]	58.9[13]	33.0[13]	76.8[13]	15.2[13]	8.0[13]	13
Singapore	1985	2,631	496	8,395	436	650	972	1985	22	...	...	...	...	45.5	—54.5—		39
Solomon Islands	1985	32	...	599[12]	...	...	8,352	1983	132	6.1	—	93.9	—	72.7	—27.3—		56
Somalia	1981	292	2[13]	1,834[13]	21[15]	556[13]	17,865	1978	75[15]	...	...	...	...	...	...	...	11
South Africa	1983[35]	21,143	2,994	116,112	6,854	...	1,481	1980	595	...	...	...	...	40.7	—59.3—		41
Bophuthatswana	1984	93	...	3,342	12[37]	...	16,800	1984	156	—6.4—		—93.6—		...	...	...	40
Ciskei	1984	...	...	2,763	...	...	...	1984	25	...	...	...	...	...	...	...	35
Transkei	1978	230	...	4,112	...	...	12,200	1978	31	...	...	...	...	...	...	...	27
Venda	1984	13	...	712	...	...	30,700	1984	52	—9.6—		—90.4—		...	...	...	39
South West Africa/Namibia	1984	276	41	3,390	...	...	4,104	1984	64	...	...	...	...	...	...	...	70
Spain	1984	121,362	4,682	136,992[6]	28,748	4,893[6]	316	1981	1,054	71.2	28.8	—	—	38.8	14.8	46.4	51
Sri Lanka	1984[9]	1,951	275[6]	7,173[6]	441[6]	3,808[6]	7,999	1982	493	5.9	31.4	20.7	42.0	100.0	—	—	29[21]
Sudan, The	1981[9]	2,169	334	13,693	58	376	9,369	1981	160	21.9	5.6	—	72.5	...	...	...	9
Suriname	1979	224	21[4]	660[4]	13[4]	88[4]	1,612	1980	17	29.4	17.6	47.1	5.9	58.8	29.4	11.8	89
Swaziland	1984	80	13	84[4]	10[4]	731[4]	7,971	1978	33	9.1	9.1	48.5	33.3	21.2	57.6	21.2	25[21]
Sweden	1983	19,300	9,000	67,900	822	370	432	1983	1,000	10.3	89.7	—	—	...	...	...	141
Switzerland	1984	14,712	3,038	40,000[10]	1,302[12]	1,650[10]	442	1983	372	52.7	47.3	—	—	...	...	...	102
Syria	1984	5,543	2,045	7,923	2,367	2,071	1,792	1984	182	75.3	24.7	—	—	23.6	—76.4—		12
Taiwan	1984	15,182	2,944	19,898	15,201	2,605	1,243	1983	995	4.8	6.0	89.2	—	...	...	...	33[21]
Tanzania	1984	1,065	18[4]	8,291[6]	25[5]	2,887[6]	19,775	1982	3,032	4.9	—	87.2	7.9	...	...	...	11[21]
Thailand	1982	7,658	1,142	43,337	3,097	8,851	6,379	1982	1,117	62.0	2.8	—35.2—		...	...	...	17
Togo	1980	139	4	1,575	23	559	18,715	1979	65	10.8	4.6	61.5	23.1	96.9	3.1	—	13[6]
Tokelau	1984[9]	4	1	18[6, 39]	...	[39]	393	1984	3	—	—	—	100.0	100.0	—	—	248[6]
Tonga	1982	35	19	253	3	161	2,881	1982	9	44.4	—	55.6	—	100.0	—	—	30
Trinidad and Tobago	1980	786	69	2,837	...	...	1,376	1982	25[10]	8.0[10]	16.0[10]	40.0[10]	36.0[10]	60.0[10]	—	40.0[10]	38
Tunisia	1982	1,732	402	12,380[39]	869	[39]	3,883	1982	119	23.5	20.2	—	56.3	100.0	—	—	22[12]
Turkey	1983	32,263	6,896	29,216	11,428[6]	12,470	1,495	1983	646	74.3	11.3	—	14.4	83.9	—16.1—		21
Turks and Caicos Islands	1984[9]	4	1	33[39]	...	[39]	2,100	1984	5	...	...	...	...	...	...	...	24
Tuvalu	1985[9]	4	2	36[39]	1	[39]	2,075	1985	8	11.1	—	—	88.9	100.0	—	—	36
Uganda	1982	665	17[1]	6,778[1, 39]	27[1]	[39]	20,562	1981	485	15.5	1.2	83.3	—	84.5	15.5	—	14[12]
U.S.S.R.	1986	1,170,000[33]	...	2,880,000[6, 39]	86,000[21]	[39]	239[33]	1986	23,100	...	...	...	...	100.0	—	—	128[57]
United Arab Emirates	1984[9]	1,840	95[6]	2,814[6]	89[6]	...	666	1984	22[1]	50.0[1]	27.3[1]	4.5[1]	18.2[1]	95.5[1]	4.5[1]	—	40
United Kingdom	1984	83,690	21,251	207,400[1]	15,108[6]	20,135[1]	675	1982	2,501[1]	...	...	...	...	100.0	—	—	81
United States	1985	527,900	138,000[21]	1,818,000[21]	162,000[21]	2,500	453	1984	6,872	87.2	12.8	—	—	33.9	51.5	14.6	56
Uruguay	1984	5,756	2,535	15,200[10]	584	300	519	1983	61	—63.9—		—	36.1	100.0	—	—	79
Vanuatu	1984	19	2[6]	266[6]	3[6]	5[6]	6,726	1980	21	14.3	—	52.4	33.3	47.6	52.4	—	35[12]
Venezuela	1979	15,359	4,645	38,061[4]	4,063	...	947	1979	446	...	...	...	...	42.1	4.3	53.6	30
Vietnam	1985	17,100[33]	803[1, 9]	44,080[1]	11,500[9]	13,700[1, 9]	3,500[33]	1984	10,768	14.6	6.5	78.9	...	100.0	—	—	35[25]
Virgin Islands (U.S.)	1985	167	...	241[28]	...	...	622	1985	...	...	...	...	...	...	...	...	49
Wallis and Futuna	1981[9]	4	1	27	1	5	2,800	1982	3	33.3	—	—	66.7	100.0	—	—	77
West Bank	1982	...	...	...	...	...	...	1984	17	...	...	...	...	52.9	—47.1—		18
Western Sahara[58]	1982	11	—	...	2	...	13,000	1982[29]	2	50.0	—	50.0	—	100.0	—	—	9
Western Samoa	1981	63	7	344	4	42[9]	2,476	1984	30	3.3	—	—	96.7	100.0	—	—	47[6]
Yemen (Aden)	1984	406	9[13]	2,250[13]	16[13]	329[13]	5,480	1984	50	12.2[13]	16.4[13]	34.7[13]	36.7[13]	98.0[13]	2.0[13]	—	17
Yemen (Ṣan'ā')	1981[9]	896	26	1,665	95	87	6,629	1982	30	63.3	3.3	—	33.3	86.7	13.3	—	5[12]
Yugoslavia	1984	44,715[33]	7,581	67,468	5,047	7,747	514[33]	1982	425[13]	32.5[13]	30.3[13]	37.2[13]	—	...	...	...	61[12]
Zaire	1982	2,000	58[10]	14,661[10]	414[10]	3,043[10]	14,092	1982	942[10]	37.3[10]	38.9[10]	23.8[10]	—	40.9[10]	44.6[10]	14.5[10]	26
Zambia	1982	839	52[1]	3,550[1]	35[1]	1,620[1]	7,186	1981	636	1.9	0.4	87.3	10.4	83.8	14.5	1.7	34[6]
Zimbabwe	1980	1,148	158	5,258	354	2,351	6,219	1980	...	...	...	...	...	...	...	...	30

[1]1981. [2]Excludes four specialized hospitals. [3]May include expenditures at the intermediate and local levels of government and/or the costs of additional services such as national health insurance and family-planning programs. [4]1978. [5]1977. [6]1982. [7]Includes funds for old-age retirement, incapacitating disability, work injury, and death insurance. [8]Government provides remainder of the cost of benefits. [9]Government-employed health personnel only. [10]1979. [11]Excludes medical centres. [12]1983. [13]1980. [14]Excludes specialized hospitals and medical centres. [15]1972. [16]1975. [17]1980–82 average. [18]Excludes one mental hospital. [19]General hospitals only. [20]Amounts vary internally. [21]1984. [22]Minimum on a graduated scale. [23]Maximum on a graduated scale. [24]Government hospitals only. [25]1985. [26]Employed women only. [27]Includes expenditures at the intermediate and local levels of government. [28]1974. [29]Public sector only. [30]1982–84 average. [31]Includes family allowances. [32]1983–85 average. [33]Includes physicians practicing dentistry. [34]Employer provides whole cost. [35]Registered personnel; all may not be resident

admissions or discharges					bed occupancy rate[a] (%)	average length of stay (days)	mortality		population with access to safe water[b] 1980 (%)	food supply (% of FAO requirement) 1982	financing of public health care, latest year					country
rate per 10,000 pop.	by kinds of hospital (%)						infant mortality per 1,000 live births 1983–84	maternal mortality per 100,000 live births 1981–82			health-care insurance			public health expenditures (% of natl. budget)	public health expenditures per capita (U.S.$)	
	general	specialized	medical centres	rural							indiv. (% of earnings)	employer (% of payroll)	govt. (% of covered earnings)			
1,619	87.7	11.7	0.6	...	81.6[19]	9[19]	8.3	3.9[12]	98	119	4.4[7]	16.8[7]	4.9[7]	10.6	540.70	Norway
1,542	...	...	...	...	93.8[6, 19]	5[6, 19]	113.4[55]	...	52	...	...	...	...	4.1	158.70	Oman
...	...	...	...	...	...	...	33.0	—	...	...	...	...	...	26.1	120.20	Pacific Is., Trust Terr. of the Marshall Islands
2,171	100	—	—	—	...	...	9.4[56]	—	...	...	...	...	...	...	...	Micronesia, Fed. States of
1,875	100	—	—	—	...	...	23.8	—	...	...	...	...	...	...	394.20	Northern Mariana Islands
...	...	...	...	...	...	...	32.7	0.7	...	...	...	...	...	...	...	Palau
...	...	...	...	...	...	...	115.0[25]	...	29	99	—	7.0	—	1.0	0.60	Pakistan
1,162	...	...	...	...	64.5	7	23.0[25]	58.9[12]	83	108	1.0	8.0	0.8[7]	13.1	103.80	Panama
253[19]	...	...	...	...	...	...	68.0[21]	...	16	79	—	—	—	9.3	23.90	Papua New Guinea
...	...	...	...	...	...	...	52.9	468.6	28	123	9.5[7]	16.5[7]	1.5[7]	3.7	7.50	Paraguay
416	90.9	7.8	1.3	—	88.2	14	92.7[25]	91.9	49	90	2.5	5.0	—	6.2	13.00	Peru
...	...	...	...	...	...	...	56.0[25]	125.0[13]	55	106	1.3	1.3	[8]	5.8	5.30	Philippines
...	...	...	...	...	...	...	...	...	...	...	...	...	...	15.4	303.00	Pitcairn Island
1,273	...	...	...	...	80.5[6]	17[6]	19.1	14.2[21]	55	125	—	33.0[7]	[8]	...	167.60[3]	Poland
902[6]	86.8[6]	13.4[6]	—	—	...	...	19.3	22.5	92	130	8.0[7]	21.0[7]	...	4.4	22.70	Portugal
1,227	95.0	5.0	—	—	64.8	8	17.4	11.5	...	...	...	...	...	24.0[27, 50]	148.10[27, 50]	Puerto Rico
1,328[1]	54.3[1]	45.7[1]	—	—	...	...	45.0	...	97	...	...	...	...	...	...	Qatar
836[5, 19]	...	...	...	...	82.0[5, 19]	12[5, 19]	10.3[25]	...	...	110	...	...	...	...	...	Réunion
...	...	...	...	...	...	...	23.4	170.1[12]	...	126	—	7.0[22]	[8]	0.8	4.30	Romania
428	...	...	...	...	51.4	7	128.0	...	38	95	—	—	—	4.5	1.50	Rwanda
1,328[1]	...	...	...	...	57.4[19]	10[19]	27.8	90.9	95	...	...	...	...	...	...	St. Christopher and Nevis
...	...	...	...	...	...	...	16.3	...	...	...	...	...	...	...	...	St. Helena and Ascension
1,026	...	...	...	...	...	...	17.6	...	70[1]	102	5.0[7]	5.0[7]	—	...	...	St. Lucia
...	...	...	...	...	...	...	9.2[1]	...	...	...	...	...	...	...	...	St. Pierre and Miquelon
772[4]	...	...	...	...	68.3[15, 19]	9[15, 19]	26.5	...	95[12]	100	—	—	—	11.3	32.70	St. Vincent
1,435	...	...	...	...	69.5	11	14.5[25]	...	...	...	...	...	...	...	...	San Marino
1,733	76.1	—	23.9	—	68.7	12	61.7[25]	...	...	100	...	...	...	...	...	São Tomé and Príncipe
...	...	...	...	...	...	...	109.8	...	64	124	—	—	—	...	540.30[3]	Saudi Arabia
378[4]	34.2	—	54.8	11.0	75.1[4]	9.6[4]	141.0	...	35	100	3.0[23]	3.0[23]	—	4.7	5.00	Senegal
9,465[19, 25]	...	...	...	...	67.0[19, 25]	6[19, 25]	17.9[25]	...	...	...	5.0[7]	10.0[7]	—	13.1	48.90	Seychelles
13[13, 19]	...	...	...	...	77.1[13, 19]	18[13, 19]	134.0	...	12[1]	84	—	—	—	7.6	3.70	Sierra Leone
899[24]	75.9[24]	24.1[24]	—	—	73.0[1]	10[1]	9.3[25]	4.7	100	126	—	—	[8]	6.4	100.20	Singapore
...	...	...	...	...	...	...	46.0	...	...	78	—	—	—	7.4	12.80	Solomon Islands
...	...	...	...	...	...	...	153.0	...	38	91	—	—	—	3.2	2.60	Somalia
...	...	...	...	...	...	...	70.7[13]	...	...	116	—	—	[8]	...	11.30[3]	South Africa
...	...	...	...	...	...	...	...	...	...	...	...	...	...	...	...	Bophuthatswana
...	...	...	...	...	...	...	...	...	...	...	...	...	...	...	...	Ciskei
...	...	...	...	...	...	...	...	...	...	...	...	...	...	...	...	Transkei
...	...	...	...	...	...	...	...	...	...	...	...	...	...	...	...	Venda
...	...	...	...	...	...	...	115.0	...	...	91	...	...	...	...	...	South West Africa/Namibia
914	91.7	8.3	—	—	73.0	15	10.5	11.5[10]	78	135	4.8[7]	25.8[7]	...	0.6	10.10	Spain
1,623	39.9	15.0	0.8	44.3	88.3	6	34.0	64.5[13]	22	93	—	—	[8]	5.1	5.70	Sri Lanka
81[19]	...	...	...	...	...	...	119.0[6]	...	46	96	—	—	—	1.3	0.90	Sudan, The
820	83.6	2.4	8.0	6.0	41.6	15	32.5	71.1	...	110	...	...	...	0.3	3.20	Suriname
456[19]	...	...	...	...	...	...	129.0	...	37	111	—	—	—	7.4	20.50	Swaziland
1,966	90.7	9.3	—	—	79.7	24	6.4	4.3	99	117	—	9.5	...	1.4	68.70	Sweden
1,278	85.9	14.1	—	—	80.8	24	7.6	5.4[12]	96	129	73	—	...	13.4	411.00	Switzerland
433	...	...	...	...	39.6	4	57.0	...	71	126	—	—	—	1.1	1.50	Syria
...	...	...	...	...	...	...	7.5	...	...	...	1.4[7]	5.6[7]	3.2[7]	...	67.40[3]	Taiwan
706	66.5	—	13.1	20.4	...	...	111.0	...	48	107	5.0[7]	5.0[7]	—	6.0	5.00	Tanzania
...	...	...	...	...	...	...	53.0[25]	...	23	103	—	—	—	5.4	8.70	Thailand
...	...	...	...	...	...	...	113.0	...	11	94	—	2.0[26]	—	5.4	4.70	Togo
965[6]	—	—	—	100.0[6]	12.0[6]	11[6]	...	...	...	...	...	...	...	...	...	Tokelau
718	97.6	—	2.4	—	56.8	10	26.0	...	...	120	...	...	...	...	...	Tonga
980	...	...	...	...	88.6[10, 14]	5[10, 14]	26.0	78.9[5]	89	123	2.8[7]	5.6[7]	[8]	5.9	104.70	Trinidad and Tobago
634	...	...	...	...	68.7	8	12.4	...	62	111	5.0	15.0	—	6.7	30.10	Tunisia
462	78.3[1]	19.1[1]	—	2.6[1]	44.1[1]	9[1]	83.0[6]	...	69	122	5.0	6.0	—	1.8	4.70	Turkey
...	...	...	...	...	...	...	26.0	...	...	...	...	...	...	9.1	137.00	Turks and Caicos Islands
1,368	40.9	—	—	59.1	51.5[19]	12.2[19]	36.0	—	...	...	...	...	...	...	...	Tuvalu
...	...	...	...	...	...	...	110.0	...	10	78	—	—	—	2.6	0.60	Uganda
...	...	...	...	...	...	...	16.3[6]	...	...	131	—	4.4[22]	...	...	177.80[3]	U.S.S.R.
1,032[6]	78.4[1]	15.4[1]	0.8[1]	5.4[1]	69.6[6]	7[6]	49.6	...	88	...	...	...	...	7.7	291.60	United Arab Emirates
1,216	...	...	...	...	75.8	10	9.6[21]	6.7	99	131	9.0	11.45	...	12.5	343.90	United Kingdom
1,601	96.9	3.1	—	—	72.5	9[12]	10.5[25]	7.9	99	137	1.3	1.3	...	11.0	410.80	United States
309	...	...	...	...	50.8	8	30.3	55.9[4]	78	103	3.0	4.0	...	3.7	15.20	Uruguay
912	40.5	—	14.0	45.5	33.6	8	101.0[25]	3.0[25]	...	78	...	...	1.5[7]	...	...	Vanuatu
...	...	...	...	...	...	...	27.3	64.7[13]	81	103	2.0	4.25[22]	1.5[22]	7.6	55.30	Venezuela
1,587	12.4	8.1	56.6	22.9	80.7	7	72.0[25]	...	24	93	...	...	...	...	2.40[3]	Vietnam
...	...	...	...	...	...	...	19.5[6]	280.0	...	...	...	...	...	...	...	Virgin Islands (U.S.)
1,100	76.0	—	—	24.0	49.4	13	40.5[4]	...	...	...	...	...	...	...	...	Wallis and Futuna
959	...	...	...	...	82.8	6	...	...	...	...	...	...	...	...	...	West Bank
226	98.2	—	1.8	—	36.9	5	...	...	...	...	...	...	...	...	...	Western Sahara
823	62.0	—	—	38.0	25.4	7	42.0[25]	...	...	94	—	—	—	9.3	18.50	Western Samoa
277	...	...	...	...	...	...	137.0	...	37	97	...	...	...	...	5.70[3]	Yemen (Aden)
95	89.0	0.4	—	10.6	73.4	18	154.0	...	4	106	...	...	...	4.2	10.00	Yemen (Şan'ā')
993	81.0[59]	19.0	[59]	—	86.3[12]	11	31.7	15.1	58	143	8.7	...	...	—	142.10[3]	Yugoslavia
474[10, 19]	...	...	...	...	71.6[10, 19]	12[10, 19]	107.0	...	16	96	—	—	—	3.2	2.00	Zaire
391[19]	...	...	...	...	76.0[19]	7[19]	88.0	...	42	87	5.0[23]	5.0[22]	—	8.4	20.60	Zambia
1,043	40.1	6.1	53.8	—	67.5	7	61.0[25]	...	...	89	...	...	...	6.1	16.30	Zimbabwe

and working in the country. [36]Includes balneology and climatology institutes. [37]1976. [38]General hospitals includes specialized and rural hospitals. [39]Nurses includes midwives. [40]Rural hospitals only. [41]Excludes hospices and sanatoriums. [42]1971. [43]Excludes hazardous occupations such as mining. [44]General hospitals includes medical centres and rural hospitals. [45]1973. [46]Combined rate for Guernsey and Jersey. [47]Excludes oilfield operations. [48]Public general and specialized hospitals only. [49]General and specialized hospitals only. [50]Includes welfare. [51]Peninsular Malaysia only. [52]Central Hospital only. [53]Based on bed ownership. [54]Includes pharmaceutical assistants. [55]1975–80 estimate. [56]Truk only. [57]1986. [58]Settlements of Smara, Boudjour, and El Aaiún only. [59]General hospitals includes medical centres.

Social protection

This table summarizes the principal social protective activities of the countries of the world. Because the administrative structure, financing, manning, and scope of programmed tasks vary so greatly from country to country, the basis of the comparisons is most often either manpower or finance.

The provision of social security programs for specific social needs, however, is summarized simply in terms of the existence or nonexistence of a specific benefit program because of the great complexity of national programs in terms of eligibility, coverage, term, age limits, financing, payments, and so on. As in the United States, activities connected with a particular benefit may take place at more than one governmental level or through more than one agency at the same level. The data shown here are summarized from the U.S. Social Security Administration's *Social Security Programs Throughout the World.* A bullet symbol (●) indicates that a country has at least one program within the defined area; in some cases it may have several. A blank space indicates that no program existed providing the benefit shown; ellipses [...] indicate that no information was available as to whether a program existed.

Data given for social security expenditure as a percentage of total central governmental budgetary expenditure are from the International Monetary Fund's *Government Finance Statistics Yearbook,* which provides the best and most comparable analytical series on the consolidated accounts of the central governments of the world.

Data on the financing of social security programs are taken in large part from the International Labour Office's *The Cost of Social Security* (triennial), supplemented by national data sources.

Figures for manpower in police and fire services are from a variety of national sources, principally census and manpower surveys, from the 1975–84 census period. The relative scarcity of international sources and data on these topics is in part a reflection of the fact that in many countries these functions are viewed as matters of merely local concern and, as they are not conducted or directly funded by the central government, tend to be ignored in the data collection and publication programs of the central government. The manpower figures refer, for the most part, to full-time, paid professional staff, excluding clerical support and volunteer staff. Fire fighters employed by private companies are included. Personnel in military service who perform either police or fire functions are presumed to be employed in their principal activity, military service. Figures for criminal offenses known to police, usually excluding civil offenses and minor traffic violations, are taken in part from Interpol's *International*

Social protection

country	social security: programs available, 1985: old-age invalid-ity,. death	sickness and mater-nity[a]	work injury	unem-ploy-ment	family allow-ances	expendi-tures, 1983 (% of national budget)	finances: year	receipts: total ('000,000 natl. cur.)	insured persons (%)	em-ployers (%)	govern-ment (%)	other (%)	expenditures: total ('000,000 natl. cur.)	benefits (%)	admin-istration (%)	other (%)
Afghanistan			●			...	...	...	...	...	...	...	...	...	...	...
Albania	●	●	●		●	...	...	...	...	...	...	...	...	...	...	...
Algeria	●	●	●		●	...	1983	9,462.0	...	...	...	...	7,696.0	...	...	...
American Samoa	●	...	...	...	...	...	1980	2.3	29.3	40.9	...	29.7	0.6	100.0	—	—
Andorra	...	...	...	...	...	...	...	...	...	...	...	...	...	...	...	...
Angola	...	...	...	...	...	...	...	...	...	...	...	...	...	...	...	...
Anguilla	...	...	...	...	...	...	...	...	...	...	...	...	...	...	...	...
Antigua and Barbuda	●	●				...	1983	...	...	...	...	...	1.3	...	...	...
Argentina	●	●	●	●	●	32.4	1980	27,318,424.2	38.4	49.4	10.2	2.1	26,433,082.7	94.8	4.4	0.8
Aruba	●	...	●	...	...	...	...	...	...	...	...	...	...	...	...	...
Australia	●	●	●	●	●	28.9[7, 8]	1980	17,235.3	13.0	12.3	70.4	4.3	15,807.3	96.0	3.5	0.4
Austria	●	●	●	●	●	45.6[8]	1980	224,889.0	31.3	48.5	16.8	3.4	223,466.0	95.2	2.7	2.1
Bahamas, The	●	●	●			7.3[9]	1979	25.1	...	...	...	...	15.3	...	...	...
Bahrain	●		●			2.4[7, 8]	1980	24,596.0	12.5	43.6	21.1	22.8	3,626.0	70.7	20.2	9.2
Bangladesh	...	...	...	...	...	5.0[3, 8]	1977	466.7	2.2	2.2	93.7	1.9	445.3	99.6	0.4	—
Barbados	●	●	●	●		15.7	1980	66.1	22.7	28.8	31.0	17.5	37.7	93.6	6.4	—
Belgium	●	●	●	●	●	40.8[10]	1980	884,343.7	18.3	43.3	35.3	3.2	903,666.6	94.3	4.1	1.5
Belize	●	●	●			3.7	1982	5.3	...	...	...	...	4.2	...	...	...
Benin	●		●		●	8.7[8, 9]	1977	3,654.7	7.4	49.4	41.9	1.3	3,165.6	91.0	8.3	0.7
Bermuda	●		●			...	...	...	...	...	...	...	...	...	...	...
Bhutan	...	...	...	...	...	...	...	...	...	...	...	...	...	...	...	...
Bolivia	●	●	●		●	17.0	1980	3,628.4	28.8	53.6	6.2	11.5	3,673.3	80.4	19.3	0.4
Botswana			●			2.7[8]	1983	—	...	...	...	...	11.0[8]	...	...	...
Brazil	●	●	●	●	●	32.5	1983	8,605,500.0	...	...	...	...	8,290,000.0	...	...	...
British Virgin Islands	...	●	...	...	...	...	1982	...	...	...	...	...	0.2	...	...	...
Brunei	●	...	...	...	...	...	1981	...	...	...	...	...	2.5[12]	...	...	...
Bulgaria	●	●	●	●	●	...	1977	2,609.7	—	53.7	40.2	6.1	2,506.0	94.9	0.1	5.0
Burkina Faso	●		●		●	7.7	1977	3,727.5	10.1	61.4	24.8	3.7	2,635.7	90.5	9.5	—
Burma		●	●			0.4[10]	1977	340.1	1.4	40.9	57.7	—	333.1	99.2	0.8	—
Burundi	●		●		●	0.7[11]	1980	475.0	21.1	39.3	25.7	13.9	266.7	73.5	26.2	0.3
Cameroon	●		●		●	4.2[7]	1984	32,490.0	...	...	...	...	28,340.0	...	...	...
Canada	●	●	●	●	●	28.3	1980	41,921.7	7.4	12.8	71.2	8.6	35,523.4	97.5	2.5	—
Cape Verde	●	●	●		●	...	...	...	...	...	...	...	...	...	...	...
Cayman Islands	●	...	...	...	●	...	...	...	...	...	...	...	...	...	...	...
Central African Republic	●		●		●	6.2[2, 8]	1981	2,009.0	...	...	...	...	1,675.0	...	...	...
Chad	●		●		●	1.9[11]	...	...	...	...	...	...	...	...	...	...
Chile	●	●	●	●	●	39.7[7]	1980	139,950.3	20.5	38.3	34.2	7.0	115,545.9	92.5	7.5	—
China	●	●	●			...	...	...	...	...	...	...	...	...	...	...
Christmas Island	...	...	●	...	...	...	...	...	...	...	...	...	...	...	...	...
Cocos (Keeling) Islands	...	...	...	...	....	...	...	...	...	...	...	...	...	...	...	...
Colombia	●	●	●		●	3.8[3, 8]	1980	52,412.9	16.0	49.8	16.2	18.0	44,180.6	77.6	12.4	10.1
Comoros	...	...	...	...	...	...	...	...	...	...	...	...	...	...	...	...
Congo	●		●		●	0.5[6]	1980	5,682.0	...	...	...	...	...	...	...	...
Cook Islands	...	...	...	...	...	...	...	...	...	...	...	....	...	...	...	...
Costa Rica	●	●	●		●	14.5	1980	3,408.3	27.6	45.9	20.4	6.1	2,927.4	88.8	6.9	4.4
Côte d'Ivoire	●		●		●	3.1[3, 8]	1980	34,416.0	...	...	...	...	18,864.0	...	...	...
Cuba	●	●	●			...	...	...	...	...	...	...	...	...	...	...
Cyprus[16]	●	●	●	●		16.5	1980	34.0	30.0	36.3	29.2	4.5	27.6	98.1	1.9	—
Czechoslovakia	●	●	●		●	...	1980	91,367.0	—	3.7	94.6	1.7	91,367.0	99.6	0.4	—
Denmark	●	●	●	●	●	35.2[2]	1980	103,269.1	1.8	5.9	90.2	2.1	100,587.5	97.3	2.7	—
Djibouti	●	...	...	...	●	8.3[9]	1979	1,352.2	...	...	...	...	1,115.7	...	...	...
Dominica	●	●	●			1.4[9]	1979	2.5	...	...	...	...	0.8	...	...	...
Dominican Republic	●	●	●			8.6	1980	136.8	...	...	43.6	4.4	123,852	87.2	8.0	4.8
Ecuador	●	●	●	●		1.3[8]	1980	13,643.0	36.9	43.0	0.1	19.9	8,585.0	72.0	28.0	—
Egypt	●	●	●	●		11.7[7]	1984	2,796.6	...	...	...	...	1,435.1	...	...	...
El Salvador	●	●	●			3.2[7]	1980	169.7	23.4	63.0	0.9	3.4	134.1	85.9	14.1	—
Equatorial Guinea	...	...	...	...	...	...	...	...	...	...	...	...	...	...	...	...
Ethiopia			●			3.4[3]	1980	117.7	21.8	70.7	4.5	3.0	79.8	98.2	1.8	—
Faeroe Islands	●	...	...	...	●	...	...	...	...	...	...	...	...	...	...	...
Falkland Islands	●	...	...	...	●	...	...	...	...	...	...	...	...	...	...	...

Crime Statistics (biennial) and a variety of national sources; supplemental information about the constitution of various national police forces may be found in JOHN ANDRADE, *World Police & Paramilitary Forces* (1985). Data for certain countries refer to cases disposed of in court, rather than to complaints. Virtually all data on fire alarms and on expenditure for police and fire services are taken from national statistical sources. Data for fire alarms usually exclude nonemergency calls, medical emergencies, and fire code inspection visits but may include false fire alarms to which a normal response with personnel and equipment was made.

The figures for military manpower refer to full-time, active-duty military service and exclude reserve, militia, paramilitary, and similar organizations. Because of the difficulties attached to the analysis of data on military manpower and budgets (including problems such as data withheld on national security grounds, or the publication of budgetary data specifically intended to hide actual expenditure, or the complexity of long-term financing of purchases of military matériel [how much was actually spent as opposed to what was committed, offset by nonmilitary transfers, etc.]), extensive use is made of the principal international analytical tools: publications such as those of the International Institute for Strategic Studies (*The Military Balance* and *Strategic Survey*), the Stockholm International Peace Research Institute (*World Armaments and Disarmament, SIPRI Yearbook*), World Priorities (*World Military and Social Expenditures*), and the U.S. Arms Control and Disarmament Agency (*World Military Expenditures and Arms Transfers*).

The data on military expenditures are from the sources identified above, as well as from the IMF's *Government Finance Statistical Yearbook* and country statistical publications.

a. Sickness and maternity refers to cash benefits for sickness and maternity. Countries must provide both benefits to be included. In many countries medical care and hospital coverage are also provided for sickness and maternity.
b. A police officer is a full-time, paid professional, including administrative staff, performing internal security functions. Clerical employees, volunteers, and members of paramilitary groups are excluded.
c. A fire fighter is a full-time, paid, professional staff member, including administrative staff. Clerical employees and volunteers are excluded.
d. Includes all active-duty personnel, regular and conscript, performing national security functions. Excludes reserves, paramilitary forces, border patrols, and gendarmeries.

police protection (latest)			fire protection (latest)			military protection								country
offenses (reported to police) per 100,000 population	population per police officer[b]	government expenditure per 1,000 population (U.S.$)	fire alarms per 100,000 population	population per fire fighter[c]	government expenditure per 1,000 population (U.S.$)	manpower, 1985[d]		expenditure, 1983				arms trade, 1983 ('000,000 U.S.$)		
						total ('000)	per 1,000 population	total '000,000 U.S.$	per capita	% of national budget	% of GDP or GNP	imports	exports	
...	540[1]	...	...	...	...	47.0	2.8	198	13	35.7	5.0	150	0	Afghanistan
...	550	...	...	...	...	40.4	13.6	188[2]	74[2]	11.5	7.8[3]	0	0	Albania
1,673.4	840	...	...	...	...	170.0	7.8	1,334	61	6.2	2.7	350	0	Algeria
4,901.2	460	17,676	180	850	8,126	—	[4]	—	—	—	—	...	...	American Samoa
...	1,120	...	...	...	...	—	—	...	...	...	...	...	...	Andorra
240.1	14[5]	...	...	...	...	49.5	5.8	1,558	199	62.5	23.2	625	0	Angola
2,102.1	100	24,233	...	...	...	—	[4]	—	—	—	—	...	...	Anguilla
4,166.7	120	41,624	...	...	...	0.7	8.7	...	...	...	...	...	...	Antigua and Barbuda
1,101.7	1,270	8,429[6]	...	...	...	108.0	3.5	1,523	49	...	2.7	1,000	20	Argentina
1,630.8	...	...	...	...	...	—	[4]	...	...	...	...	...	...	Aruba
6,897.4	460	16,132	...	...	...	70.4	4.5	4,637	290	10.2	2.8	370	40	Australia
5,185.5	470	...	...	...	...	54.7	7.2	937	119	3.2	1.3	60	180	Austria
5,706.0	160	...	...	...	...	—	—	...	...	1.3[9]	...	...	...	Bahamas, The
1,207.1	180	...	...	...	...	2.8	6.7	168	403	10.8	4.0	20	0	Bahrain
...	2,560	453	...	...	...	91.3	0.9	290	2	12.9	2.3	60	0	Bangladesh
3,335.8	280	...	...	...	...	—	—	8[10]	27[10]	2.5[10]	0.8[10]	0	0	Barbados
2,349.7	640	...	...	...	...	91.6	9.3	2,911	282	5.7	3.3	340	280	Belgium
...	290	...	...	...	...	0.6	3.6	...	...	4.1[3]	...	...	...	Belize
1,233.8	3,250	1,138	...	...	...	4.5	1.1	20	5	14.6[2]	2.6	20	0	Benin
7,413.0	370	290,191	...	1,030	471	—	[4]	—	—	2.1[3]	—	...	...	Bermuda
...	...	...	...	...	...	4.0	2.8	...	...	...	...	...	...	Bhutan
...	...	...	...	...	...	27.6	4.3	100[10]	17[10]	7.4[10]	1.9[10]	0	0	Bolivia
5,046.3	750	6,705[8]	...	21,300	...	3.0	2.8	26	25	7.1	3.0	0	0	Botswana
...	...	...	13	3,450	...	276.0	2.0	1,769	12	2.1	0.7	40	110	Brazil
1,865.1	190	...	...	...	...	—	[4]	—	—	—	—	...	...	British Virgin Islands
468.6	100	126,103	279	...	33,195	4.1	17.7	195	837	12.8[7]	2.9[3]	...	...	Brunei
...	...	...	...	...	...	148.5	16.6	4,282	461	19.6	8.1	140	260	Bulgaria
...	...	...	...	...	...	4.0	0.5	33	4	20.2	2.8	0	0	Burkina Faso
...	650	...	...	...	...	186.0	4.9	209	5	19.5	3.3	20	0	Burma
82.1	...	...	...	...	...	5.2	1.1	41	8	16.1	3.2	0	0	Burundi
...	1,170	...	...	...	...	7.3	0.8	160	16	8.2	2.1	80	0	Cameroon
10,802.4	360	...	...	...	...	83.0	3.3	6,439	248	7.8	2.2	500	180	Canada
...	460	...	...	...	...	1.2	3.6	13[2]	48[2]	13.5[2]	14.9[2]	0	0	Cape Verde
6,835.0	110	33,287	16	550	...	—	[4]	—	—	—	—	...	...	Cayman Islands
...	2,740[1]	...	...	...	...	2.3	0.9	13	5	10.8	2.0	0	0	Central African Republic
...	990	...	...	...	...	12.2	2.4	6	1	20.5	2.4	5	0	Chad
1,372.7	470	6,459	...	...	...	101.0	8.4	1,021	85	12.3	4.5	80	0	Chile
...	1,360[13]	...	...	...	...	3,900.0	3.7	34,500	32	30.8	8.6	0	1,500	China
790.4[14]	190	...	...	...	...	—	[4]	—	—	—	—	...	...	Christmas Island
...	...	...	...	...	...	—	[4]	—	—	—	—	...	...	Cocos (Keeling) Islands
687.3	420	...	...	...	...	66.2	2.4	456	15	9.4	1.2	10	0	Colombia
...	960	...	...	...	...	—	[15]	2	5	15.0	...	...	...	Comoros
10.3	870	...	...	...	...	8.7	4.3	79	44	7.4	3.6	10	0	Congo
...	...	...	...	...	...	—	[4]	—	—	—	—	...	...	Cook Islands
558.1	480	...	...	953,000	...	—	—	17	6	3.5	0.7	0	0	Costa Rica
294.8	4,640	...	...	...	...	13.2	1.3	85	8	4.1	1.3	30	0	Côte d'Ivoire
...	650	2,503	...	...	...	161.5	16.0	1,306	126	...	5.0[10]	700	30	Cuba
644.0	180	35,383	...	...	...	10.0	15.0	83	115	11.2	3.6	20	0	Cyprus[16]
...	640	...	...	...	...	203.3	13.1	7,157	445	18.3	5.9	100	775	Czechoslovakia
8,823.5	600	67,601	...	...	13,548	29.6	5.8	1,482	278	4.5	2.5	150	5	Denmark
...	...	...	...	...	...	3.0	7.0	3	10	21.7[7]	...	...	...	Djibouti
18,328.0	300	29,740	...	...	...	—	—	—	3[9]	1.2[9]	...	...	...	Dominica
294.7	580	...	...	...	...	22.2	3.6	122	19	9.8[10]	1.5	0	0	Dominican Republic
292.0	260	...	...	...	...	42.5	4.5	184	21	11.0	1.6	170	0	Ecuador
2,378.5	580	...	...	...	...	445.0	9.5	2,679	56	17.4	8.3	1,700	50	Egypt
...	1,000	...	...	...	...	41.7	7.8	150	30	22.2	4.0	40	0	El Salvador
...	190	...	...	...	...	1.6	5.0	2[2]	11[2]	21.0[2]	3.4[2]	10	0	Equatorial Guinea
417.6[14]	1,100	...	...	...	...	217.0	5.0	381[10]	12[10]	16.8	8.6	525	0	Ethiopia
...	...	49	...	...	...	—	[4]	—	—	—	—	...	...	Faeroe Islands
...	330	38,723	...	—	—	—	[4]	—	—	—	—	...	...	Falkland Islands

Social protection (continued)

country	social security															
	programs available, 1985					expenditures, 1983 (% of national budget)	finances									
							year	receipts					expenditures			
	old-age invalidity, death	sickness and maternity[a]	work injury	unemployment	family allowances			total ('000,000 natl. cur.)	insured persons (%)	employers (%)	government (%)	other (%)	total ('000,000 natl. cur.)	benefits (%)	administration (%)	other (%)
Fiji	•		•			2.5[10]	1980	57.8	28.7	30.8	9.5	31.1	20.5	56.4	43.6	—
Finland	•	•	•	•	•	30.2[8]	1980	40,435.2	7.9	44.9	41.4	5.8	34,646.2	96.5	3.5	—
France	•	•	•	•	•	44.2[8, 10]	1980	761,712.2	21.0	53.4	24.1	1.5	738,971.1	95.2	3.9	1.0
French Guiana	•	...	•	...	•	...	...	...	...	...	...	...	...	...	...	...
French Polynesia	•	...	•	...	•	...	...	...	...	...	...	...	...	...	...	...
Gabon	•		•		•	...	1975	6,770.0	...	...	...	...	...	...	...	...
Gambia, The	•		•			1.9[17]	1978	—	...	...	...	...	...	...	...	...
Gaza Strip	...	...	...	...	...	—	...	...	...	...	...	...	...	...	...	...
Germany, East	•	•	•		•	...	1980	29,627.0	21.9	28.3	49.7	0.1	29,627.0	99.6	0.4	—
Germany, West	•	•	•	•	•	50.0[8]	1980	357,712.0	34.0	34.2	28.9	2.9	355,052.0	96.4	3.1	0.5
Ghana	•		•	•		5.4[8, 10]	1984	—	...	...	...	...	...	...	...	...
Gibraltar	•	•	...	•	•	...	...	...	...	...	...	...	...	...	...	...
Greece	•	•	•	•	•	28.8[2]	1980	242,714.0	29.7	47.3	17.0	5.9	209,443.0	95.2	4.5	0.4
Greenland	•	...	...	...	•	...	...	...	...	...	...	...	...	...	...	...
Grenada	•	•				5.0[8, 12]	1977	—	...	...	...	...	...	...	...	...
Guadeloupe	•	...	...	...	•	...	...	...	...	...	...	...	...	...	...	...
Guam	•	...	...	...	•	...	...	...	...	...	...	...	...	...	...	...
Guatemala	•	•	•			1.7[9]	1980	133.4	31.6	53.1	8.2	7.1	90.9	88.3	11.7	—
Guernsey	...	...	...	...	...	...	...	...	...	...	...	...	...	...	...	...
Guinea	•	•	•		•	...	1983	446.5	—	100.0	—	—	...	...	...	...
Guinea-Bissau	...	...	...	...	...	...	...	...	...	...	...	...	...	...	...	...
Guyana	•	•	•			0.8[7]	1980	85,692.0	29.4	43.0	—	27.5	18,591.0	68.9	31.1	—
Haiti	•		•			...	1977	60.5	—26.6—		69.9	3.5	52.4	92.7	7.3	—
Honduras	•	•	•			4.5[9]	...	...	...	...	...	...	...	...	...	...
Hong Kong	•	•	•	•		...	1985	...	...	...	...	...	895.6	...	...	...
Hungary	•	•	•	•	•	...	1980	106,644.0	14.6	41.1	43.6	0.7	106,646.0	99.5	0.5	—
Iceland	•	•	•	•	19	15.0[10]	1981	932.0	—	14.8	85.2	—	...	...	...	...
India	•	•	•			...	1976	30,870.4	—66.1—		22.8	11.1	17,842.9	98.4	0.9	0.7
Indonesia	•	•	•			—	...	...	...	...	...	...	...	...	...	...
Iran	•	•	•		•	7.8	1983	217,200.0	...	...	...	...	217,200.0	...	...	...
Iraq	•	•	•			...	1977	107.8	9.9	55.6	21.9	12.6	71.0	94.0	2.4	3.6
Ireland	•	•	•	•	•	...	1980	1,896.7	11.6	26.3	61.0	1.0	1,881.3	95.0	4.7	0.2
Isle of Man	•	•	•	•	•	17.2[21]	1985	...	...	...	...	...	14.4	...	...	...
Israel	•		•	•	•	18.1	1980	7,237.6	16.8	37.0	36.9	9.2	6,409.9	84.2	6.8	9.0
Italy	•	•	•	•	•	30.3	1980	61,563,000.0	10.8	54.8	31.9	2.6	61,318,000.0	89.8	4.3	5.9
Jamaica	•		•			3.2[12]	1980	115.9	17.2	20.7	36.8	25.3	58.3	91.0	8.9	—
Japan	•	•	•	•	•	...	1980	30,372,556.0	25.9	28.4	31.3	14.5	23,871,420.0	89.8	2.0	8.2
Jersey	•	•	•	...	•	10.1[7]	1984	31.3	—58.9—		30.3	10.8	27.1[18]	...	...	...
Jordan	•		•			12.0	1983	—	...	...	...	...	...	...	...	...
Kampuchea	...	...	•	...	•	...	...	...	...	...	...	...	...	...	...	...
Kenya	•		•			0.1	1977	55.9	19.6	26.5	38.1	15.8	30.9	97.2	2.8	—
Kiribati	•		•			...	...	...	...	...	...	...	...	...	...	...
Korea, North	...	...	...	...	...	...	...	...	...	...	...	...	...	...	...	...
Korea, South			•			5.3[7]	1984	157,400.0	...	...	...	...	...	...	...	...
Kuwait	•					5.3[7]	1984	—	...	...	...	...	...	...	...	...
Laos	...	...	•	...	...	...	...	...	...	...	...	...	...	...	...	...
Lebanon	•	•	•		•	...	...	...	...	...	...	...	...	...	...	...
Lesotho	...	...	...	...	...	1.1	1983	—	...	...	...	...	...	...	...	...
Liberia	•		•			0.7[7]	1984	—	...	...	...	...	...	...	...	...
Libya	•	•	•			...	1977	192.9	9.1	28.7	58.7	3.5	128.2	96.2	3.2	0.5
Liechtenstein	•	•	•	•	•	...	...	...	...	...	...	...	...	...	...	...
Luxembourg	•	•	•	•	•	47.4	1980	35,758.5	23.8	37.2	25.2	13.7	32,560.9	95.9	3.3	0.8
Macau	•	...	...	...	•	...	1981	...	...	...	...	...	...	...	...	...
Madagascar	•		•		•	10.3[24]	1982	19,534.0	...	...	...	...	...	...	...	...
Malaŵi			•			1.3	...	...	...	...	...	...	...	...	...	...
Malaysia	•		•			2.6[2]	1980	2,130.3	—63.6—		0.3	36.0	512.7	85.3	3.4	11.3
Maldives	...	...	...	...	...	1.0	1983	—	...	...	...	...	...	...	...	...
Mali	•		•		•	4.6	1980	4,541.0	8.5	79.4	10.7	1.4	4,837.0	58.4	32.9	8.7
Malta	•	•	•	•	•	35.7	1980	52.6	28.1	33.9	38.1	—	43.6	99.2	0.8	—
Martinique	•	...	...	...	•	...	...	...	...	...	...	...	...	...	...	...
Mauritania	•		•		•	3.7[3]	1979	441.0	...	...	...	...	381.0	...	...	...
Mauritius	•		•		•	16.0[7, 8]	1977	344.6	6.6	25.3	64.9	3.2	301.8	99.0	0.5	0.5
Mayotte	...	...	...	...	...	...	...	...	...	...	...	...	...	...	...	...
Mexico	•	•	•			10.2	1983	424,500.0	...	...	...	...	397,300.0	...	...	...
Monaco	...	...	...	...	...	...	...	...	...	...	...	...	...	...	...	...
Mongolia	•	•	...	...	•	...	...	...	...	...	...	...	...	...	...	...
Montserrat	•	...	...	...	...	...	...	...	...	...	...	...	...	...	...	...
Morocco	•	•	•		•	6.1[8]	1980	1,446.7	—89.8—		0.2	10.0	807.6	89.3	10.7	0.1
Mozambique	...	...	...	...	...	...	...	...	...	...	...	...	...	...	...	...
Nauru	•	•	•		•	...	...	...	...	...	...	...	...	...	...	...
Nepal	•		•			0.4[10]	1982	—	...	...	...	...	...	...	...	...
Netherlands, The	•	•	•	•	•	35.6[7]	1980	113,621.6	33.2	33.2	24.7	8.9	95,237.9	96.5	3.4	0.1
Netherlands Antilles	•	...	•	...	...	8.7[11]	1982	124.4	...	...	...	...	...	...	...	...
New Caledonia	...	...	...	...	•	...	...	...	...	...	...	...	...	...	...	...
New Zealand	•	•	•	•	•	28.6	1980	3,898.6	3.1	4.7	89.7	2.4	3,469.8	98.0	1.8	0.3
Nicaragua	•	•	•			3.3[3]	1980	711.2	21.2	58.1	16.3	4.5	497.8	88.4	11.6	—
Niger	•		•		•	1.6[3]	1980	3,823.5	8.4	80.4	—	11.2	1,594.6	84.1	15.9	—
Nigeria	•		•			2.5[12]	1978	—	...	...	...	...	...	...	...	...
Niue	...	...	...	...	...	...	...	...	...	...	...	...	...	...	...	...
Norfolk Island	•	...	...	...	•	...	...	...	...	...	...	...	...	...	...	...
Norway	•	•	•	•	•	35.1[8]	1980	59,512.6	21.0	34.6	42.9	1.5	57,467.2	97.9	2.1	—
Oman	...	...	...	...	...	—	1984	—	...	...	...	...	—	...	...	...
Pacific Is., Trust Territory of the	•					...	...	...	...	...	...	...	...	...	...	...
Marshall Islands	•	...	...	...	...	...	...	...	...	...	...	...	...	...	...	...
Micronesia, Fed. States of	•	...	...	...	...	...	...	...	...	...	...	...	...	...	...	...

police protection (latest): offenses (reported to police) per 100,000 population	police protection (latest): population per police officer[b]	police protection (latest): government expenditure per 1,000 population (U.S.$)	fire protection (latest): fire alarms per 100,000 population	fire protection (latest): population per fire fighter[c]	fire protection (latest): government expenditure per 1,000 population (U.S.$)	military protection: manpower, 1985[d]: total ('000)	military protection: manpower, 1985[d]: per 1,000 population	military protection: expenditure, 1983: total '000,000 U.S.$	military protection: expenditure, 1983: per capita	military protection: expenditure, 1983: % of national budget	military protection: expenditure, 1983: % of GDP or GNP	military protection: arms trade, 1983 ('000,000 U.S.$): imports	military protection: arms trade, 1983 ('000,000 U.S.$): exports	country
2,002.0	440	24,800	...	2,600	...	2.7	3.9	14[10]	21[10]	4.4[10]	1.2[10]	0	0	Fiji
13,380.9	640	44,927	10	1,300	4,478	36.5	7.4	785	153	5.1	1.5	50	350	Finland
6,714.1	630	...	...	2,840	...	464.3	8.4	23,793	417	9.3	4.2	60	4,300	France
...	...	...	...	...	...	—	[4]	108	706	—	—	...	...	French Guiana
...	...	...	...	...	...	—	[4]	—	—	—	—	...	...	French Polynesia
134.5	1,290	...	...	...	...	2.4	2.1	79	84	5.0	2.7	10	0	Gabon
...	3,310	...	...	...	...	0.5	0.7	—	—	...	—	0	0	Gambia, The
...	...	...	...	...	...	—	—	...	...	...	...	...	...	Gaza Strip
730.0	...	...	...	...	...	174.0	10.4	9,806	563	11.9	6.4	760	130	Germany, East
6,755.0	...	...	...	...	...	478.0	7.8	23,565	367	10.7	3.4	430	1,800	Germany, West
...	620	...	...	4,330	...	15.1	1.2	213[10]	16[10]	6.1[10]	0.7[10]	10	0	Ghana
9,951	170	...	878	220	...	—	[4]	—	—	—	—	...	...	Gibraltar
3,564.1	380	501,048	...	...	...	201.5	20.3	2,526	244	15.0	6.2	470	0	Greece
12,460.5	340	109,098	...	3,580	117,380[18]	—	[4]	—	—	—	—	...	...	Greenland
1,457.2	230	15,202	...	...	...	—	—	...	...	13.9[9]	...	...	...	Grenada
...	...	...	...	...	...	—	[4]	—	—	—	—	...	...	Guadeloupe
...	...	...	...	...	...	—	[4]	—	—	—	—	...	...	Guam
...	670	...	...	...	...	31.7	4.0	209	25	16.4	2.4	5	0	Guatemala
...	...	...	...	...	...	—	[4]	...	...	...	...	...	...	Guernsey
...	1,140	...	...	...	...	9.9	1.5	51[2]	10[2]	10.2	4.9	0	0	Guinea
...	...	...	...	...	...	8.6	9.9	9[10]	11[10]	8.4[10]	4.5[10]	0	0	Guinea-Bissau
5,287.0	190	...	...	...	...	6.6	8.4	23	29	6.5	5.4	10	0	Guyana
700.6	400	...	...	...	...	6.9	1.3	24	4	8.9	1.4	0	0	Haiti
...	1,040	...	...	...	...	16.6	4.3	47[9]	16[9]	11.8[9]	2.4[9]	0	0	Honduras
1,759.1	220	76,780	271	900	9,589	—	[4]	...	...	4.4[4]	1.3[3, 4]	...	...	Hong Kong
1,470.5	710	...	89	...	...	106.0	10.0	3,134	281	7.6	4.3	30	190	Hungary
1,549.8	940	...	...	...	...	—	—	—	—	—	—	0	0	Iceland
206.2	820	...	...	...	...	1,260.0	1.7	6,546	8	17.6	3.5	950	0	India
44.4	1,340	766	...	...	...	278.1	1.7	2,649	15	13.7	2.8	140	...	Indonesia
...	[20]	21,088	...	...	...	305.0	6.8	5,520	124	14.9	5.0	750	0	Iran
518.0	140	...	...	...	...	520.0	33.7	11,900	787	24.9[3]	47.2	5,100	0	Iraq
2,898.7	490	58,654	...	...	...	13.7	3.9	303	83	2.7	1.8	0	0	Ireland
...	...	...	...	...	...	—	[4]	...	...	...	...	...	...	Isle of Man
6,005.8	270	23,099	425	...	...	142.0	33.1	6,229	1,494	24.2	29.0	370	220	Israel
2,124.5	680	...	...	...	...	385.1	6.7	9,609	162	4.7	2.7	170	1,000	Italy
2,281.1	450	24,259	...	...	2,915	2.1	0.9	37	15	2.6	1.3	0	0	Jamaica
1,453.3	480	55,594	61	960	25,990	243.0	2.0	11,500	92	5.5	1.0	750	200	Japan
...	...	...	...	...	...	—	[4]	...	...	...	...	...	...	Jersey
629.9	630	27,536	...	...	...	70.3	26.6	645	238	29.5	14.9	1,100	10	Jordan
...	1,980	...	...	...	...	35.0	4.8	67[22]	10[22]	...	11.0[22]	60	0	Kampuchea
479.8	1,500	...	...	...	...	13.7	0.7	138	7	6.9	2.1	50	0	Kenya
2,471.5	290	...	...	...	...	—	—	...	...	...	...	...	...	Kiribati
...	460	...	...	...	...	838.0	41.7	3,600	179	29.7[10]	16.7	110	300	Korea, North
1,940.9	420	...	15	5,650	...	598.0	14.6	4,717	109	27.9	5.8	290	370	Korea, South
575.6	80	...	...	...	...	12.0	7.0	1,173	662	9.2	4.0	100	0	Kuwait
...	280	...	...	...	...	53.7	14.9	50[9]	18[9]	29.1[22]	...	40	0	Laos
489.2	530	...	...	...	...	17.4	6.5	437	161	20.0	8.2	240	0	Lebanon
1,643.0	1,130	...	...	...	...	—	—	23	16	10.7	3.7	5	0	Lesotho
...	1,570	...	...	...	...	6.8	3.0	27	12	7.3	2.8	10	0	Liberia
1,022.3	...	26,667	...	...	...	73.0	19.3	4,223	1,157	26.6	17.5	1,900	70	Libya
...	660	...	...	...	...	—	[23]	...	...	—	—	...	...	Liechtenstein
3,946.7	730	15,067	299	3,220	...	0.7	1.9	414	106	2.6	1.0	0	0	Luxembourg
...	...	...	17	1,380	...	—	[4]	16	61	16.9	...	...	...	Macau
...	2,900	...	...	...	...	21.1	2.1	61	6	10.2	2.1	10	0	Madagascar
1,005.2	1,670	...	...	...	...	5.3	0.8	23	3	6.0	1.7	0	0	Malaŵi
607.4	760	...	...	...	...	110.0	7.0	1,432	91	11.8	5.2	230	0	Malaysia
3,988.9	35,710	2,003	...	—	...	0.8	4.4	...	...	—	—	...	...	Maldives
...	160	...	...	...	...	4.9	0.6	30	3	7.9	2.7	0	0	Mali
1,906.4	230	34,223	...	...	...	0.8	2.4	15	36	2.5	1.1	0	0	Malta
...	...	...	...	...	...	—	[4]	—	—	—	—	...	...	Martinique
...	710	...	...	...	...	8.5	5.1	40	24	17.1	5.8	0	0	Mauritania
2,365.8	240	...	...	...	...	—	—	2	2	0.8	0.2	0	0	Mauritius
...	...	...	...	...	...	—	[4]	...	...	—	—	...	...	Mayotte
314.6	...	...	24	...	...	129.1	1.6	872	11	1.4	0.6	50	0	Mexico
3,392.1	...	...	...	...	...	—	—	...	...	...	...	...	...	Monaco
...	120	...	...	...	...	33.0	17.5	135[12]	133[12]	15.9	...	30	0	Mongolia
5,625.7[14]	110	16,901	...	...	...	—	[4]	—	—	—	—	...	...	Montserrat
589.1	840	...	...	...	...	149.0	6.8	1,318	55	17.2	8.2	320	0	Morocco
...	...	...	...	...	...	15.8	1.1	172[10]	13[10]	29.1	3.5	260	5	Mozambique
...	110	...	...	...	...	—	—	...	...	...	...	...	...	Nauru
...	1,000	497	...	...	...	25.0	1.5	27	1	5.5	1.1	5	0	Nepal
7,424.9	560	100,727	204	...	...	105.5	7.3	4,673	311	5.5	3.2	670	120	Netherlands, The
4,684.1[25]	330	...	...	...	...	—	[4]	—	—	0.4[4, 9]	—	...	...	Netherlands Antilles
...	...	...	...	...	...	—	[4]	—	—	—	—	...	...	New Caledonia
12,509.1	640	38,418	652	1,260	...	12.4	3.8	519	155	4.7	2.2	40	0	New Zealand
...	90[5]	...	...	...	...	62.9	19.2	272	93	16.5	10.2	130	0	Nicaragua
32.5	2,350[26]	...	...	...	...	2.2	0.4	12	2	3.7	0.9	0	0	Niger
312.0	1,140	...	...	...	...	94.0	1.0	1,723	19	11.7	2.5	300	0	Nigeria
...	270	22,816	...	...	...	—	[4]	—	—	—	—	...	...	Niue
...	620	30,174	...	—	...	—	[4]	—	—	—	—	...	...	Norfolk Island
3,871.4	660	78,262	...	1,660	27,931	37.0	8.9	1,844	431	10.1	3.2	240	40	Norway
161.8[3]	430	...	...	...	...	2.5	2.0	1,944	1,695	49.1	27.9	290	0	Oman
...	320[27]	...	...	...	...	—	[4]	—	—	—	—	...	...	Pacific Is., Trust Territory of the
...	...	...	...	...	...	—	[4]	...	...	...	...	...	...	Marshall Islands
...	...	...	...	...	...	—	[4]	...	...	...	...	...	...	Micronesia, Fed. States of

Social protection (continued)

country	social security															
	programs available, 1985					expenditures, 1983 (% of national budget)	finances									
	old-age invalidity, death	sickness and maternity[a]	work injury	unemployment	family allowances		year	receipts					expenditures			
								total ('000,000 natl. cur.)	insured persons (%)	employers (%)	government (%)	other (%)	total ('000,000 natl. cur.)	benefits (%)	administration (%)	other (%)
Northern Mariana Islands	•	...	...	...	...	...	...	...	...	...	...	...	...	...	...	...
Palau	•	...	...	...	...	...	...	...	...	...	...	...	...	...	...	...
Pakistan	•	•	•			0.2	1983	—	...	...	...	...	...	...	...	...
Panama	•	•	•			8.2[10]	1977	213.3	23.8	49.7	18.3	8.2	169.4	89.1	10.9	—
Papua New Guinea	•		•			0.3	1983	—	...	...	...	...	...	...	...	...
Paraguay	•	•	•			29.5[10]	1982	14,660.0	...	...	...	...	11,278.0	...	...	...
Peru	•	•	•			—	1982	—	...	...	...	...	—	...	...	...
Philippines	•	•	•			2.3	1980	4,487.5	30.3	42.2	—	27.5	1,725.9	81.2	18.8	—
Pitcairn Island	...	...	...	...	...	...	...	...	...	...	...	...	...	...	...	...
Poland	•	•	•		•	...	1980	325,454.0	2.1	52.2	44.2	1.5	304,600.0	98.8	0.5	0.7
Portugal	•	•	•	•	•	26.8[8, 22]	1980	126,998.7	26.2	64.2	9.3	0.4	121,222.9	90.1	9.9	—
Puerto Rico	•	•	•	•	•	...	1980	...	...	...	...	...	1,041.3	100.0	—	—
Qatar	...	...	...	...	...	...	...	...	...	...	...	...	...	...	...	...
Réunion	...	...	...	...	...	...	...	...	...	...	...	...	...	...	...	...
Romania	•	•	•		•	...	1980	59,386.7	—	54.4	45.6	—	51,743.8	100.0	—	—
Rwanda	•		•			2.9[3, 8]	1977	593.9	24.9	41.4	25.1	8.6	191.5	88.2	11.4	0.4
St. Christopher and Nevis	•	•	...	...	...	...	...	...	...	...	...	...	...	...	...	...
St. Helena and Ascension	•	...	...	...	•	...	...	...	...	...	...	...	...	...	...	...
St. Lucia	•	•	•			...	1983	7.9	...	...	...	...	...	...	...	...
St. Pierre and Miquelon	...	...	...	...	...	...	...	...	...	...	...	...	...	...	...	...
St. Vincent and the Grenadines	•		•			3.3[8]	1983	—	...	...	...	...	...	...	...	...
San Marino	•	...	...	...	...	...	...	...	...	...	...	...	...	...	...	...
São Tomé and Príncipe	•	•	•	...	...	...	...	...	...	...	...	...	...	...	...	...
Saudi Arabia	•		•			...	...	...	...	...	...	...	...	...	...	...
Senegal	•		•		•	5.6[8]	1980	13,903.2	18.1	67.0	5.5	9.5	11,223.9	78.8	8.6	12.6
Seychelles	•	•	•			5.3[12]	1977	—	...	...	...	...	...	...	...	...
Sierra Leone			•			1.7[7]	1977	10.5	——26.7——		73.3	—	10.0	100.0	—	—
Singapore	•		•			0.8	1980	2,244.8	36.7	44.4	0.2	18.7	786.7	89.0	1.4	9.6
Solomon Islands	•		•			2.6[8]	1983	—	...	...	...	...	...	...	...	...
Somalia			•			1.7[8, 17]	1978	—	...	...	...	...	...	...	...	...
South Africa	•	•	•	•	•	...	1982	243.0	...	...	...	...	310.0	...	...	...
Bophuthatswana	...	...	...	...	...	...	...	...	...	...	...	...	...	...	...	...
Ciskei	...	...	...	...	...	...	...	...	...	...	...	...	...	...	...	...
Transkei	...	...	...	...	...	...	...	...	...	...	...	...	...	...	...	...
Venda	...	...	...	...	...	...	...	...	...	...	...	...	...	...	...	...
South West Africa/Namibia	•	...	...	...	...	...	...	...	...	...	...	...	...	...	...	...
Spain	•	•	•	•	•	62.2	1980	2,400,940.9	12.4	70.7	15.8	1.1	2,426,506.1	95.7	2.7	1.6
Sri Lanka	•		•			11.2[8]	1980	2,092.8	——38.8——		43.6	17.6	1,141.8	95.0	4.1	0.1
Sudan, The	•		•			2.2[10]	1982	—	...	...	...	...	...	...	...	...
Suriname	•	...	..	...	•	5.7[7]	1980	46.0	25.4	32.0	42.6	—	37.1	99.5	0.5	—
Swaziland	•		•			—	1983	—	...	...	...	...	—	...	...	...
Sweden	•	•	•	•	•	38.4[10]	1980	183.851.7	1.0	45.9	45.3	7.8	167,315.8	97.5	2.5	—
Switzerland	•	•	•	•	•	48.9	1980	25,571.1	41.2	25.5	25.5	7.8	23,415.8	93.2	2.8	4.0
Syria	•		•			8.2[2, 8]	1981	—	...	...	...	...	...	...	...	...
Taiwan	•	•	•			...	...	...	...	...	...	...	...	...	...	...
Tanzania	•		•			1.2[9]	1981	—	...	...	...	...	...	...	...	...
Thailand			•			3.0[7]	1983	—	...	...	...	...	...	...	...	...
Togo	•		•		•	10.9[7, 8]	1980	4,814.0	10.4	77.8	—	11.9	2,350.0	78.1	21.3	0.6
Tokelau	...	...	...	...	...	...	...	...	...	...	...	...	...	...	...	...
Tonga	...	...	...	...	...	...	...	...	...	...	...	...	...	...	...	...
Trinidad and Tobago	•	•	•			4.9[2]	1980	196.1	18.2	36.0	26.9	18.9	110.3	85.4	13.8	0.9
Tunisia	•	•	•	•	•	8.1[2]	1977	124.5	25.6	53.9	3.7	16.8	67.8	90.0	6.1	3.9
Turkey	•	•	•			0.5	1980	218,265.1	27.9	49.9	11.3	10.8	183,922.7	95.5	4.1	0.5
Turks and Caicos Islands	...	...	...	...	...	...	...	...	...	...	...	...	...	...	...	...
Tuvalu	•	...	...	...	...	...	1981	...	...	...	...	...	0.1	67.6	32.4	—
Uganda	•		•			1.6[7, 8]	1984	—	...	...	...	...	...	...	...	...
U.S.S.R.	•	•	•		•	...	1977	54,271.0	—	—	96.4	3.6	54,271.0	100.0	—	—
United Arab Emirates	...	...	...	...	...	3.6[8]	1981	—	...	...	...	...	...	...	...	...
United Kingdom	•	•	•	•	•	25.5[8, 9]	1980	35,698.0	15.8	26.5	54.9	2.9	34,004.0	95.2	2.8	2.0
United States	•		•	•	•[31]	26.7[7]	1980	370,597.0	23.4	40.4	29.8	6.4	329,582.0	96.1	3.1	0.8
Uruguay	•	•	•	•	•	42.5[7]	1980	9,779.5	25.1	34.0	38.3	2.6	7,550.5	91.5	7.7	0.8
Vanuatu	...	...	...	...	...	...	...	...	...	...	...	...	...	...	...	...
Venezuela	•	•	•			7.6[7]	1980	4,259.3	26.8	53.5	6.8	12.9	3,336.6	86.0	14.0	—
Vietnam	•	•	•			...	...	...	...	...	...	...	...	...	...	...
Virgin Islands (U.S.)	•	...	...	•	•	...	...	...	...	...	...	...	...	...	...	...
Wallis and Futuna	...	...	...	...	...	...	...	...	...	...	...	...	...	...	...	...
West Bank	...	...	...	...	...	...	...	...	...	...	...	...	...	...	...	...
Western Sahara	...	...	...	...	...	...	...	...	...	...	...	...	...	...	...	...
Western Samoa	•		•			—	...	...	...	...	...	...	...	...	...	...
Yemen (Aden)	...	...	...	...	...	...	...	...	...	...	...	...	...	...	...	...
Yemen (Ṣan'ā')	...	...	...	...	...	—	1983	—	...	...	...	...	—	...	...	...
Yugoslavia	•	•	•	•	•	7.2[2]	1981	—	...	...	...	...	—	...	...	...
Zaire	•		•		•	—	1983	145.9	...	...	...	...	...	...	...	...
Zambia	•		•			0.4[8, 10]	1977	119.8	——40.7——		47.9	11.4	89.4	95.4	4.6	—
Zimbabwe	...	...	•	...	...	3.6	1980	9.4	—	48.8	26.0	25.2	6.8	64.5	30.6	4.8

police protection (latest)			fire protection (latest)			military protection								country
						manpower, 1985[d]		expenditure, 1983				arms trade, 1983 ('000,000 U.S.$)		
offenses (reported to police) per 100,000 population	population per police officer[b]	government expenditure per 1,000 population (U.S.$)	fire alarms per 100,000 population	population per fire fighter[c]	government expenditure per 1,000 population (U.S.$)	total ('000)	per 1,000 population	total '000,000 U.S.$	per capita	% of national budget	% of GDP or GNP	imports	exports	
...	...	...	...	...	...	—	[4]	...	...	...	...	...	...	Northern Mariana Islands
...	...	...	323	...	...	—	[4]	...	...	...	...	...	...	Palau
205.7	720	1,954	...	...	...	482.8	4.8	1,984	20	27.9	5.4	410	300	Pakistan
448.3	180	...	...	...	...	12.0	5.5	60[10]	31	4.7	1.5	0	0	Panama
833.7	720	...	...	...	...	3.2	1.0	30	9	3.0	1.2	0	0	Papua New Guinea
...	310	...	...	...	...	14.4	4.2	89	24	19.3	1.9	0	0	Paraguay
424.4	730	...	...	...	...	128.0	6.5	1,065	54	26.2	5.6	180	0	Peru
333.9	1,160	2,423	...	9,090	...	114.8	2.1	771	13	15.1	1.9	40	20	Philippines
...	...	...	...	...	...	—	[4]	—	—	—	—	...	...	Pitcairn Island
1,292.2	370	...	56	...	...	319.0	8.6	12,282	321	23.1	5.8	410	650	Poland
774.4	660	...	...	...	...	73.0	7.2	814	78	9.9	3.5	50	60	Portugal
5,484.0	380	...	229	2,870	...	—	[4]	—	—	—	—	...	...	Puerto Rico
212.6	...	...	...	...	...	6.0	19.9	604[3]	3,020[3]	20.1[3]	9.1[3]	230	0	Qatar
...	220	...	...	...	...	—	[4]	—	—	—	—	...	...	Réunion
...	...	...	...	...	...	189.5	8.3	5,159	219	21.2	4.7	50	450	Romania
358.9	4,650	...	...	...	...	5.2	0.9	21	3	10.1	1.4	0	0	Rwanda
...	300	...	...	...	—	—	—	...	...	...	...	...	...	St. Christopher and Nevis
...	170	8,368	...	5,150	—	—	[4]	—	—	—	—	...	...	St. Helena and Ascension
...	430	...	...	...	...	—	—	...	...	...	...	...	...	St. Lucia
...	...	...	...	...	...	—	[4]	—	—	—	—	...	...	St. Pierre and Miquelon
...	250	18,008	...	...	...	—	—	...	...	6.1	...	...	...	St. Vincent and the Grenadines
...	...	...	...	...	...	—	—	...	...	...	...	...	...	San Marino
...	400	...	...	...	...	—	—	—	—	2.5[3]	1.8[3]	0	0	São Tomé and Príncipe
...	280	131,140	...	...	...	62.5	5.6	27,192	2,508	29.6	24.3	3,300	0	Saudi Arabia
235.3	730	...	...	...	...	10.1	1.5	60	9	9.1	2.3	0	0	Senegal
6,369.2	120	...	...	2,420	...	1.2	18.4	8	119	...	...	...	...	Seychelles
...	600	...	...	...	...	3.1	0.8	11	3	6.2	0.9	5	0	Sierra Leone
1,412.7	230	474,409	321	2,840	...	55.0	21.5	955	366	17.1	5.8	170	20	Singapore
...	620	5,112	...	...	...	—	—	...	...	...	...	...	...	Solomon Islands
...	540	...	...	...	...	62.7	10.8	114	17	22.7	9.1	60	0	Somalia
...	870	28,460	...	...	...	106.4	3.2	3,132	97	17.8	4.3	0	0	South Africa
...	...	...	...	...	...	...	...	...	...	...	...	...	...	Bophuthatswana
...	...	...	...	...	...	...	...	...	...	...	...	...	...	Ciskei
...	...	...	...	...	...	...	...	...	...	...	...	...	...	Transkei
...	...	...	...	...	...	...	...	...	...	...	...	...	...	Venda
...	...	...	...	...	...	—	[4]	...	...	—	—	...	...	South West Africa/Namibia
2,573.3	580	...	...	...	...	320.0	8.3	4,070	102	9.0	2.1	200	340	Spain
...	860	...	...	...	...	21.6	1.4	76	4	3.9	1.5	0	0	Sri Lanka
1,770.9	740	12,049	...	...	...	56.6	2.4	180	8	9.0	1.7	80	0	Sudan, The
...	...	...	...	...	...	2.0	5.2	28	68	...	2.2	0	0	Suriname
...	610	21,249	...	...	...	2.7	4.1	18	29	11.5	3.1	0	0	Swaziland
11,785.2	330	176,110	189	1,230	...	65.7	7.9	3,332	385	6.5	3.3	110	40	Sweden
5,134.0	640	135,820	...	...	...	20.0	3.1	1,961	289	10.2[10]	1.9	290	330	Switzerland
54.4	1,970	...	...	...	...	402.5	39.2	2,138	209	29.8	13.0	1,700	30	Syria
296.8	720	...	...	1,040	...	444.0	23.2	3,925	200	40.2	7.5	460	5	Taiwan
63.9	1,330	1,953	...	...	...	40.4	1.9	122	5	6.3	2.5	30	0	Tanzania
348.6	530	4,262	...	...	...	235.3	4.6	1,539	29	19.9	3.9	320	0	Thailand
10.7	1,970	...	...	...	...	3.6	1.2	17	6	6.8	2.4	0	0	Togo
...	210	...	...	...	...	—	[4]	—	—	—	—	...	...	Tokelau
...	330	7,139	...	...	...	—	[28]	—	5[2]	2.7[3]	—	...	...	Tonga
3,016.2	280	142,083	...	...	...	2.0	1.7	232	203	5.3	3.2	0	0	Trinidad and Tobago
1,033.7	340	...	...	...	...	35.1	4.9	256	35	9.0	2.9	40	0	Tunisia
178.6	1,570	...	...	...	...	630.0	12.5	2,840	55	21.4	4.9	600	230	Turkey
...	90	20,611	...	...	—	—	[4]	—	—	—	—	...	...	Turks and Caicos Islands
...	290	13,069	...	—	...	—	—	—	—	...	...	...	...	Tuvalu
...	1,090	1,173	...	...	...	18.0	1.2	102	8	19.6	1.7[17]	30	0	Uganda
...	1,050[29]	...	...	...	...	5,300.0	19.1	258,000	908	40.8	14.0	1,150	9,800	U.S.S.R.
1,297.0	140	...	...	...	...	43.0	33.5	1,867	1,492	36.4	7.9	40	10	United Arab Emirates
6,545.5[30]	400	79,281[30]	...	1,430	18,439[30]	327.1	5.8	27,444	470	13.2	5.4	650	1,600	United Kingdom
5,031.3	460	73,687	...	1,060	27,469	2,151.6	9.0	217,154	888	25.4	6.6	500	10,600	United States
...	170	...	...	...	...	31.9	10.6	283	93	12.4	3.3	10	0	Uruguay
...	450	...	...	...	...	—	—	...	...	...	...	...	...	Vanuatu
837.3	320	...	...	...	...	49.0	2.8	920	52	5.0	1.3	80	0	Venezuela
...	...	...	...	...	...	1,027.0	17.1	...	...	...	10.5[3]	775	0	Vietnam
3,798	240	126,972	980	680	...	—	[4]	—	—	—	—	...	...	Virgin Islands (U.S.)
...	...	...	...	...	...	—	[4]	—	—	—	—	...	...	Wallis and Futuna
...	...	...	...	...	...	—	—	...	...	...	...	...	...	West Bank
...	...	...	...	...	...	—	[4]	—	—	—	—	...	...	Western Sahara
...	...	6,997	...	...	...	—	—	...	...	...	...	...	...	Western Samoa
...	1,440	...	...	...	...	27.5	12.0	179	82	21.0	17.4	310	0	Yemen (Aden)
...	500	1,905	...	...	...	36.6	5.6	599	100	32.0	15.4	260	0	Yemen (Ṣan'ā')
1,116.1	140	...	...	...	...	241.0	10.4	2,309	97	43.7[2]	3.7	130	320	Yugoslavia
...	910	...	...	...	...	48.8	1.6	82	2	4.3	1.5	30	0	Zaire
2,569.3	540	3,960[7]	...	...	...	16.2	2.4	461[3]	92[3]	30.6[3]	15.1[3]	0	0	Zambia
1,425.2	750	12,457	...	...	...	41.0	4.9	403	47	11.9	6.4	20	0	Zimbabwe

[1]Rural areas only. [2]1981. [3]1980. [4]Political dependency; defense is the responsibility of the administering country. [5]Includes civilian militia. [6]1971. [7]1984. [8]Includes welfare. [9]1979. [10]1982. [11]1976. [12]1977. [13]Local officers only. [14]Offenses disposed of in court. [15]Military defense is the responsibility of France. [16]Excludes Turkish-occupied Cyprus. [17]1978. [18]Benefits paid only. [19]Coverage is through tax system. [20]340 in urban areas; 270 in rural areas. [21]1985. [22]1975. [23]Military defense is the responsibility of Switzerland. [24]1974. [25]Curaçao only. [26]Includes paramilitary forces. [27]Marshall Islands and Palau only. [28]Military defense is the responsibility of New Zealand. [29]MVD (internal security) only. [30]England and Wales only. [31]Federal-state system.

Education

This table presents international data on education arranged to provide comparability among the different types of educational systems in the nations of the world. The principal data are, naturally, numbers of students, teachers, and schools, arranged by four principal levels of education—the first, or primary; the general second level (secondary); vocational second level; and third level (higher). These data are supplemented by an indicator of each country's capability to educate children who are potentially educable in the age group usually represented at each level. At the first and second level this is given as a net enrollment ratio and at the third level as a gross enrollment ratio. Two additional comparative measures are given at the third level: students per 100,000 population and proportion (percent) of adults over age 25 who have achieved some level of higher or postsecondary education. Data are confined as far as possible to those who have completed their educations and are no longer in school. No enrollment ratio is provided for vocational training at the second level because of the great variation worldwide in what constitutes vocational training (electronics training in a developed country such as West Germany, for example, might be at a level that would qualify as higher education in a less developed country), in the need of countries to promote and direct students into vocational programs (to support national development), and, most particularly, in the age range of students that normally constitute a national vocational system (some will be as young as 14, having just completed a primary cycle; others will be in their mid-50s, either learning a skill for the first time or retraining to acquire a new skill). For such reasons, it is not possible to construct a good comparative measure of overall national vocational programs.

At each level of education, differences in national statistical practice, in national educational structure, and in the kind and extent of public-private institutional mix, training and deployment of teachers, and timing of cycles of enrollment or completion of particular levels of grades all contribute to the problems of comparability between national educational systems.

Even something as basic as reporting the number of schools is not simply a matter of counting red-brick buildings with classrooms in them. Often the resources of a less developed country are such that temporary or outdoor facilities are all that can be afforded, while in a developed but sparsely settled country students might have to travel 80 km (50 mi) a day to find a classroom with 20 students of the same age, leading to the institution of measures such as traveling teachers, radio instruction at home under the supervision of parents, or similar systems.

Such difficulties also limit the comparability of statistics on numbers of teachers, and there may be the further complications that many at any level must work part-time, or that the institutions in which they work may perform a mixture of functions that do not break down into the tidy categories a table of this sort requires (a business school training secretaries must teach language skills as well as typing skills; a general secondary school may have a number of educators dedicated full- or part-time to the teaching of industrial arts or athletics). Separating data for students and teachers in teacher-training programs is particularly difficult, since in certain countries teacher training is defined as higher education, in others as a vocational form of secondary training, and so on. For purposes of this table, teacher training at the secondary level has been treated as vocational education. At the higher level, teacher training is assumed to be one more variety of specialization in higher education itself.

The number of students may conceal great variation in what each country defines as a particular educational "level." Many countries do, indeed, have a primary system comprised of grades 1 through 6 that passes its students on to some kind of post-primary education. But the age of intake,

Education

country	year	first level (primary)					general second level (secondary)					vocational second level[a]	
		schools	teachers[c]	students[d]	student/teacher ratio	net enrollment ratio	schools	teachers[c]	students[d]	student/teacher ratio	net enrollment ratio	schools	teachers[c]
Afghanistan	1984	754	14,865	545,959	36.7	12[1]	332	6,943	99,729	14.4	...	16	666
Albania	1983	1,621	26,440[1]	557,300	20.1[1]	...	20	1,250[1]	32,500	10.2[1]	...	313	3,750[1]
Algeria	1983	9,864	99,648	3,241,924	32.5	83	1,429	53,261	1,280,719	24.0	28[3]	71[1]	2,292[1]
American Samoa	1985	31	346[4]	7,376	20.9[4]	...	7	186[4]	3,170	16.4[4]	...	1[2]	42
Andorra	1986	25	214	5,310	24.8	...	8	53	1,086	20.5	...	5	37
Angola	1983	6,308	32,004	1,178,430	36.8	66[1]	182[6]	3,870	124,858	34.2[6]	...	68[6]	410[6]
Anguilla	1985	6	65	1,488	22.9	...	1	26	400	15.4	...	...	...
Antigua and Barbuda	1983	48	426	9,933	23.3	...	16	331	4,197	12.7	...	1	18[8]
Argentina[e]	1984	20,619	218,520	4,430,513	20.3	...	1,987	86,874	656,521	7.6	...	3,117	119,309
Aruba	1983	33	373	6,763	18.1	...	10	189	3,082	16.3	...	3	65
Australia	1985	8,460	96,087	1,727,897	18.0	96[4]	1,603	101,043	1,278,272	12.7	84[4]	373[4]	44,776[4]
Austria	1986	3,411	28,305	341,867	12.1	87[2]	2,066	55,932	504,326	9.0	68[9]	1,241	22,910
Bahamas, The	1983	187	1,972	37,097	18.8	...	38	1,334	23,202	17.4	...	...	113[10]
Bahrain	1982	114[12]	2,774	46,364	16.7	79[12]	21[12]	951[12]	23,620	24.9[12]	57[12]	5[12]	233[12]
Bangladesh	1985	44,488	184,575	10,082,000	54.6	55[5]	9,331	113,558	3,154,099	27.8	18[5]	158	2,171
Barbados	1985	130	1,464	30,792	21.0	100[1]	36	1,449	28,815	19.9	89[4]	3	154
Belgium	1983	2,261	24,106	814,089	33.8	94	759	56,719	848,590	15.0	84	209	6,364
Belize	1984	225	1,515	37,753	24.9	...	24	491	6,532	13.3	...	5[13]	58[13]
Benin	1982	2,723	11,339	428,185	37.8	...	133	1,816	117,724	64.8	...	30	755
Bermuda	1986	22	307	5,329	17.4	...	13	367	4,106	11.2	...	1	49
Bhutan	1984	143[11]	1,149	44,275	38.5	8[3]	30[11]	431	3,608	8.4	...	8[11]	150
Bolivia	1983	8,514	50,703	1,154,819	22.8	77[2]	845	8,091	174,982	21.6	16[2]	...	...
Botswana	1984	512	6,794	209,772	30.9	76[4]	58	1,216	27,364	22.5	17[12]	26	...
Brazil	1984	190,904	1,022,014	24,821,301	24.3	81[2]	9,104	214,969	2,946,657	13.7	14[2]	...	...
British Virgin Islands	1984	24	104[14]	2,325	17.9[14]	...	4	74	1,013	13.7	...	—	—
Brunei	1984	178	2,131	34,373	16.1	...	28	1,526	18,565	12.2	...	7[13]	275[13]
Bulgaria	1984	750	5,037	68,314	13.6	97[4]	2,741	65,158	1,129,248	17.3	73[4]	30	13,205
Burkina Faso	1984	1,037	4,796	276,732	57.7	22[4]	79	1,553	43,001	27.7	3[1]	27	484
Burma	1985	27,499	104,754	4,855,963	46.4	65[9]	2,238	41,668	1,251,482	30.0	16[9]	74	1,036
Burundi	1984	875	6,164	302,611	49.1	35[4]	25	475	7,854	16.5	2[12]	53	960
Cameroon	1985	5,582[5]	32,082	1,638,569	51.1	75[3]	365[5]	8,381	238,075	28.4	16[2]	199[5]	3,239
Canada	1987	15,595[15]	270,020[15]	4,943,565[15]	18.3[15]	95[4]	[15]	[15]	[15]	[15]	87[12]	...	...
Cape Verde	1983	436	1,459	50,000	34.3	...	16	603	10,454	17.3	...	4	76
Cayman Islands	1986	15	145	2,077	14.3	...	8	120[14]	2,265	16.4[14]	...	1	9
Central African Republic	1984	853[1]	4,263	291,444	68.4	61[1]	...	616	52,417	85.1	...	...	90
Chad	1984	783[9]	2,610[9]	288,478	77.0[9]	25[8]	...	590[9]	43,053	31.2[9]	...	...	...
Chile	1984	8,862	62,746[1]	2,092,069	...	95[4]	1,401	...	581,243		47[4]	369	...
China	1984	854,000	5,370,000	135,571,000	25.2	...	93,714	2,557,000	45,542,000	17.8	...	3,301	161,000
Christmas Island	1985	2	30	261	8.7	...	1	12	114	9.5	...	1	7
Cocos (Keeling) Islands	1984	2	8	125	15.6	...	1	3	22	7.3	...	...	...
Colombia	1984	33,996	132,675	4,054,891	30.6	77[5]	...	67,770	1,432,234	21.1	...	...	25,351
Comoros	1981	236	1,292	59,709	46.2	...	32	434	13,528	31.2	...	4	27
Congo	1982	1,377	6,997	406,835	58.1	...	122	3,451	169,924	49.2	...	36	1,261
Cook Islands	1986	30	165	3,183	19.3	...	8	146	2,156	14.8	...	...	...
Costa Rica	1984	3,068	12,223	353,958	29.0	89[1]	241	9,152	148,032	16.2	37[1]	...	...
Côte d'Ivoire	1985	4,419[2]	31,297[1]	1,179,456	...	...	218[2]	4,569[2]	254,342	...	...	38[2]	1,947[12]
Cuba	1985	10,866	83,400	1,283,000	15.4	97[4]	1,291	64,700	773,800	12.0	61[16]	605	23,600
Cyprus	1985	396	2,193	47,381	21.6	...	93	2,644	43,511	16.5	...	16	492
Czechoslovakia	1986	6,332	96,414	2,074,403	21.5	...	343	9,465	134,392	14.2	...	562	16,740
Denmark	1985	2,557	34,541	415,148	12.0	...	3,247	36,105	339,835	9.4	...	282	...

the willingness (or economic ability) of parents to send their children or to permit them to finish that level, or the need to withdraw the children seasonally for agricultural work all make even a simple enrollment figure difficult to assess in isolation. All of these difficulties are compounded when a country has instruction in more than one language, or when its educational establishment is so small that higher, sometimes even secondary, education cannot take place within the country, as is the case with a number of the less developed countries or among the smaller island nations of the Pacific. Enrollment figures in this table may, therefore, include students enrolled outside the country.

With all of the limitations to the comparability of the statistics referred to above, the student-teacher ratio does, nevertheless, provide a fairly representative measure of the true ratio of trained educators to the enrolled educable. In general, at each level of education both students and teachers have been counted on the basis of full-time enrollment or employment, or full-time equivalent when country statistics permit. At the primary and secondary levels, net enrollment ratio is the ratio of the number of children within the usual age group for a particular level who are actually enrolled to the total number of children in that age group (× 100). This ratio is usually less than (occasionally, equal to) 100 and is the most accurate measure of the completeness of enrollment at that particular level. It is not always, however, the best indication of utilization of that particular level. Utilization is best seen in a gross enrollment ratio, which compares total enrollment (of all ages) to the population within the normal age limits for that level. For a country with substantial adult literacy or general educational programs for which both kinds of data are available, the difference may be striking: typically, for a less developed country, even one with a good net enrollment ratio of 90 to 95, the gross enrollment ratio may be 20, 25, even 30% higher, indicating the heavy use made by the country of facilities and teachers at that level. In this table, however, gross enrollment ratio is provided only at the third level because of the wide range of ages that are typically represented in higher educational enrollment in any particular country.

Literacy data provided here have been compiled as far as possible from data for the population age 15 and over for the best comparability internationally, even though many countries work from quite different assumptions about the best way to measure literacy *for their purposes.* The age cutoffs may be much different—as low as 6 or 8 years or as high as legal majority in the country concerned. The standards of what constitutes literacy may also differ markedly; sometimes completion of a certain number of years of school is taken to constitute literacy; elsewhere it may mean only the ability to read or write at a minimal level testable by a census taker; in other countries quite sophisticated sample studies have been undertaken to distinguish between those who have completed a good deal of school and *are* literate and those who have done so but may still be functionally illiterate.

Finally, the data provided for public expenditure on education are generally complete in the sense that they include data for all levels of public expenditure (national, state, local) but are incomplete for certain countries in that they do not include data for private expenditure; in some countries this fraction of the educational establishment may be of significant size. Data, however, are often not available. Occasionally data for external aid to education may be included in addition to domestic expenditure.

a. May include teacher training at the second level.
b. Latest.
c. Full-time.
d. Full-time; may include students registered in foreign schools.
e. General second level includes teacher training at the second level.

		third level (higher)							literacy[b]				public expenditure on education (percent of GNP)[b]	country
students[d]	student/teacher ratio	institutions	teachers[c]	students[d]	student/teacher ratio	gross enrollment ratio	students per 100,000 population[b]	percent of population aged 25 and over with post-secondary education[b]	over age	total (%)	male (%)	female (%)		
7,360	11.1	5	1,283	13,450	10.5	1.5[2]	134	3.2	15	23.7	38.9	7.8	2.0	Afghanistan
123,700	17.3[1]	8	1,240[1]	17,500[1]	14.1[1]	6.6	673	...	15	71.5	79.9	63.1	...	Albania
26,216[1]	11.4[1]	15[1]	8,573[1]	100,000[1]	11.7[1]	5.5[1]	481	0.3	15	49.6	63.0	36.9	4.5	Algeria
45[2]	11.2[2]	1	48[5]	870	35.7[5]	...	...	12.6	...	...	...	...	8.5	American Samoa
692	18.7	...	...	...	...	...	...	...	15	100.0	...	...	...	Andorra
7,060	12.7[6]	1[7]	316[7]	2,764[7]	8.7[7]	0.4	33	...	15	28.0	36.2	19.3	4.4	Angola
...	...	...	...	...	...	...	...	...	15	94.7	94.6	94.8	...	Anguilla
153[9]	...	...	...	...	...	...	...	1.3	...	88.7	89.7	88.0	4.0	Antigua and Barbuda
905,755	7.6	1,251	64,230	677,535	10.5	25.2[4]	1,962	6.9	15	95.5	96.0	95.0	2.5	Argentina[e]
701	10.8	1	20	180	9.0	...	...	...	15	95.0	...	...	...	Aruba
723,132[4]	16.1[4]	95	25,234	370,707	14.7	26.3[4]	2,237	21.5	15	99.5	...	...	5.9	Australia
374,424	16.3	44	10,252	168,060	16.4	24.7[4]	2,058	3.3	15	100.0	100.0	100.0	6.0	Austria
2,554[10]	22.6[10]	1[11]	135[11]	2,000[11]	14.8[11]	...	...	...	15	89.0	90.6	89.6	9.8	Bahamas, The
5,982	12.2[12]	2[12]	159[12]	3,650[12]	22.9[12]	5.9[12]	662	3.8	14	74.0	81.1	61.8	3.0	Bahrain
38,340	17.7	45	3,989	60,665	15.2	4.5[4]	403	0.9	15	33.1	43.3	22.2	1.9	Bangladesh
3,592	23.3	1	108	1,617	15.0	17.3[4]	1,966	1.2	15	98.0	98.3	97.7	5.7	Barbados
218,717	31.9	...	...	108,689	...	28.2	2,285	7.5	...	100.0	...	...	6.2	Belgium
737[13]	12.7[13]	[13]	[13]	[13]	[13]	...	...	1.4	15	90.0	...	...	...	Belize
6,543	8.7	1	801	6,302	7.9	2.0	172	...	15	27.9	39.8	16.6	5.1	Benin
379	7.7	1	19	171	9.0	...	...	7.4	15	96.9	96.7	97.0	3.4	Bermuda
2,264	15.1	2[11]	16[4]	204[4]	12.8[4]	0.3[2]	25	...	15	18.0	31.0	9.0	...	Bhutan
...	...	25	1,487	13,388	9.0	16.4[1]	1,429	5.0	15	63.2	75.8	51.4	3.0	Bolivia
3,538	...	1	104	1,249	12.0	1.6[4]	142	0.5	15	70.8	72.6	69.5	7.0	Botswana
...	...	847	120,632	1,399,539	11.6	11.4[1]	1,132	5.0	15	77.7	79.0	76.5	3.2	Brazil
—	—	—	—	—	—	—	...	5.4	15	98.3	98.1	98.5	4.7	British Virgin Islands
1,362[13]	5.0[13]	[13]	[13]	[13]	[13]	...	...	9.4	15	77.8	85.2	69.0	1.8	Brunei
66,761	5.1	16	567	7,130	12.6	15.8[4]	1,082	5.2	15	95.5	...	...	6.6	Bulgaria
4,492	9.3	1	216	3,870	17.9	0.6[4]	51	...	15	13.2	20.7	6.1	3.2	Burkina Faso
14,570	14.1	35	5,524	174,279	31.5	5.1[12]	462	...	15	65.9	75.9	56.3	1.6	Burma
12,125	12.6	7	372	2,479	6.7	0.6[4]	48	...	10	33.8	42.8	25.7	3.0	Burundi
77,555	23.9	1[5]	572	13,753	24.0	1.6[12]	141	0.3	15	55.2	70.2	41.0	3.7	Cameroon
...	...	268	60,640	789,690	13.0	42.1[4]	4,169	37.4	14	95.6	95.6	95.7	8.0	Canada
923	12.1	—	—	—	—	—	...	...	15	49.3	55.3	43.4	7.5	Cape Verde
71	7.9	1	35	762	21.8	...	...	2.9	15	97.5	97.5	97.6	...	Cayman Islands
1,712	19.0	7[1]	297[1]	4,571[1]	15.4[1]	1.2[4]	99	...	15	38.5	58.8	20.4	4.9	Central African Republic
2,559	...	1[1]	85[1]	550[1]	6.5[1]	0.2[8]	14	...	15	17.8	35.6	0.5	2.3	Chad
129,817	...	24	10,372[1]	126,197	...	10.7[4]	1,090	3.8	12	95.6	95.0	93.8	5.8	Chile
1,322,000	8.2	902	315,000	1,396,000	4.4	1.3[4]	119	1.0	15	69.3	82.4	55.5	2.3	China
60	8.6	—	—	—	...	...	...	...	15	40.0	35.7	50.0	...	Christmas Island
...	...	...	...	...	...	...	...	...	...	...	...	...	...	Cocos (Keeling) Islands
456,789	18.0	216[4]	41,006[4]	378,999[4]	9.2[4]	13.2[4]	1,376	3.3	15	88.1	89.1	87.1	3.0	Colombia
327	12.1	—	—	430	—	—	...	...	...	59.0	66.1	51.7	5.4	Comoros
18,150	14.4	1[2]	292[2]	8,288[12]	24.8[2]	6.2[12]	529	...	15	62.9	71.4	55.4	6.0	Congo
...	...	...	41[2]	360[2]	8.8[2]	...	...	2.1	...	91.8	92.1	91.4	...	Cook Islands
...	...	14[4]	54,466	...	...	26.3[4]	2,838	5.8	10	93.1	93.0	93.1	6.0	Costa Rica
44,481[2]	...	1	1,204[12]	12,755	...	2.7[12]	220	...	15	31.4	46.2	17.3	8.4	Côte d'Ivoire
312,900	13.3	33	15,900	192,900	12.1	19.1[1]	1,751	5.9	15	91.1	91.1	91.1	6.3	Cuba
5,375	10.9	15	250	2,580	10.3	...	338	7.7	10	89.0	93.5	84.5	3.9	Cyprus
261,422	15.6	36	19,131	168,699	8.8	16.4[4]	1,174	6.0	15	99.6	99.6	99.5	5.1	Czechoslovakia
144,024	...	96[4]	10,411[4]	124,144	...	29.0[1]	2,159	...	14	99.5	...	...	6.9	Denmark

Education (continued)

country	year	first level (primary)					general second level (secondary)					vocational second level[a]	
		schools	teachers[c]	students[d]	student/ teacher ratio	net enroll- ment ratio	schools	teachers[c]	students[d]	student/ teacher ratio	net enroll- ment ratio	schools	teachers[c]
Djibouti	1986	58	511[11]	25,212	44.0[5]	...	8	231[11]	4,978	22.7[5]	...	12	110
Dominica	1983	58	635	18,370	28.9	...	8	145	3,234	22.3	...	1	13
Dominican Republic	1984	4,846[4]	20,607[4]	980,808[4]	47.6[4]	...	...	...	352,328	...	...	...	...
Ecuador	1985	15,969	58,584	1,973,445	33.7	87[3]	2,056[17]	49,641[17]	860,419[17]	17.3[17]	28[10]	[17]	[17]
Egypt	1983	12,013[1]	158,636	5,349,579	33.7	...	2,715[12]	101,107	2,436,646	24.1	...	519[12]	48,330
El Salvador	1983	2,464	17,633	851,895	48.3	64[4]	279	5,642	82,573	14.6	...	17	667
Equatorial Guinea	1981	511	647	40,110	62.0	...	14[17]	288[17]	3,013[17]	10.5[17]	...	[17]	[17]
Ethiopia	1984	7,096	46,674	2,497,114	53.5	...	1,066	13,192	579,834	44.0	...	...	...
Faeroe Islands	1985	76[15]	...	5,583	...	...	[15]		2,994	...	...	3[4]	...
Falkland Islands	1986	8	23	232	10.1	...	1	11	116	10.5	...	—	—
Fiji	1984	672	4,374	123,340	28.2	100[12]	139	2,656	43,277	16.3	...	39	272
Finland	1984	4,238	25,139	369,047	14.7	...	1,082	22,356	316,740	14.2	...	550	15,000
France	1982	67,291	290,933[12]	6,909,559	...	97[1]	11,209[17]	256,284[12, 17]	5,052,452[17]	...	80[1]	[17]	[17]
French Guiana	1985	76	748	15,620[18]	...	...	8	470	5,529[18]	...	...		177
French Polynesia	1985	253	...	40,803	...	...	24	...	12,970	...	...	17	...
Gabon	1983	901	3,781	165,559	43.8	...	47	1,161	22,350	19.3	...	29	582
Gambia, The	1985	189	2,640	66,257	25.1	62[4]	8	587	10,309	17.6	15[4]	8	150
Gaza Strip	1985	291[5, 15]	3,684[5, 15]	101,946		...	[15]	[15]	50,667			[15]	[15]
Germany, East	1984	5,666	54,971	766,745	13.9	...	5,711	112,172	1,265,349	11.3	...	4,500	56,577
Germany, West	1985	22,445	304,357	4,511,122	14.8	80[12]	5,412	191,624	3,026,721	15.8	...	7,816[5]	87,975[5]
Ghana	1985	8,965	51,631[5]	1,464,624	31.8[5]	...	5,589	32,795[5]	723,385	24.8[5]	...	61	1,727[12]
Gibraltar	1985	14	91	1,904	20.9	...	2	122	1,749	14.3	...	1	25
Greece	1984	9,194	34,955	896,399	25.6	96[2]	2,399	37,826	690,382	18.3	73[3]	575	8,035
Greenland	1986	95[15]	1,069[15]	9,310[15]	8.7[15]	...	[15]	[15]	[15]	[15]	...	5[5]	1,336[5]
Grenada	1983	64	764	17,704	23.2	...	20[1]	264	8,578	32.5	...	1[1]	21[1]
Guadeloupe	1983	232	2,408	50,576	21.0	...	...	2,394	33,218	13.9	...	...	570
Guam	1985	39[4]	522[19]	17,609	25.4[14]	...	19[1]	533[19]	14,223	21.6[14]	...	1[1]	66[4]
Guatemala	1985	8,121	28,467	1,046,043	36.7	60[4]	1,310	14,629[17]	204,049[17]	13.9[17]	13[1]	[17]	[17]
Guernsey	1984	23	224	4,260	19.0	...	9	297	4,095	13.8	...	1	47
Guinea	1983	2,635[1]	7,867	246,129	31.3	25[4]	...	5,091	89,756	17.6	...	...	744[1]
Guinea-Bissau	1984	658	2,455	65,405	26.6	55[1]	10	660	8,561	13.0	3[12]	4	58
Guyana	1980	424	6,021	164,830	27.4	90[12]	87	2,513	46,595	18.5	...	15	348
Haiti	1983	3,241	16,986	723,041	42.6	40[12]	290	5,367	117,081	21.8	...	2	49
Honduras	1985	6,492	20,724	858,061	41.4	86[4]	452	6,799	582,287	85.6	24[4]	...	...
Hong Kong	1985	757	19,824	537,345	27.1	95[4]	436[17]	18,119[17]	444,380[17]	24.5[17]	63[4]	[17]	[17]
Hungary	1986	3,546	88,106	1,297,800	14.7	99[4]	175[11]	7,709[11]	126,190	13.6[11]	71[4]	729[11]	21,801[11]
Iceland	1983	187	2,600	25,000	9.6	...	157	...	21,800	...	...	44	...
India	1984	509,143	1,391,912	81,100,000	58.3	92	181,580	1,910,781	40,260,000	21.1	41	4,878[4]	...
Indonesia	1984	129,388	925,834	25,804,380	27.9	95[4]	18,630	384,219	6,447,030	16.8	17[10]	2,752[1]	65,528[1]
Iran	1986	48,982	268,606	6,343,300	23.6	83[4]	13,818	167,769	2,922,576	17.4	...	1,325	20,683
Iraq	1985	10,463	119,734	2,827,109	23.6	93[1]	2,109	33,466	996,622	29.8	49[12]	228	6,266
Ireland	1984	3,385	20,732	563,509	27.2	90[12]	568	14,012	243,778	17.4	79[12]	256	5,100
Isle of Man	1983	38[10]	240	5,193	21.6	...	6[10]	276	4,665	16.9	...	1[10]	32[10]
Israel	1985[20]	1,853	46,266	621,856	13.4	90[4]	542	38,193[17]	235,062	...	...	368	[17]
Italy	1984	28,786	276,716[4]	3,909,365	...	98[10]	13,135	333,062[4]	3,301,625	...	66[10]	4,430	199,268[4]
Jamaica	1984	881	10,374[14]	341,748	...	95[4]	...	8,139[14]	224,846	...	57[2]	...	508[14]
Japan	1985	25,040	461,249	11,095,711	24.1	100[4]	16,584	551,962	11,168,212	20.2	94[1]	...	...
Jersey	1984	38[4]	299	5,472	18.3	...	6[4]	403	5,075	12.6	...	...	...
Jordan	1984	1,148	15,179	487,890	32.1	89[1]	1,515	13,153	286,092	21.8	71[1]	19	1,290
Kampuchea	1983	3,629[1]	36,520	1,504,840	41.2	...	207	4,494	145,730	32.4	...	13	278
Kenya	1983	11,996	117,475	4,323,822	36.8	69[12]	2,230	18,960	493,710	26.0	8[10]	40	1,212
Kiribati	1985	112	460	13,440	29.2	...	8	117	2,024	17.3	...	2	31
Korea, North	1982	4,700[8]	...	2,561,674[8]	...	...	...	...	...	...	...	...	...
Korea, South	1986	6,519	126,785	4,856,752	36.9	100[5]	3,338	109,593	4,049,013	35.5	75[1]	635	29,506
Kuwait	1986	270	9,620	172,659	17.9	79[4]	384	18,685	239,595	12.8	74[1]	6	788
Laos	1983	6,525	16,454	480,871	29.2	...	...	3,666[12]	78,925[12]	21.5[12]	...	...	939[12]
Lebanon	1982	1,116	[21]	398,977	...	...	1,405	53,450[21]	250,028	...	...	181	3,563
Lesotho	1985	1,141	5,663	314,003	55.4	71[1]	143	1,676	35,423	21.1	14[1]	9	221
Liberia	1980	1,232	227,431	9,099	25.0	...	419	1,129	51,666	45.8	...	6	63
Libya	1983	2,744	42,202	741,502	17.6	...	1,555	25,044	301,415	12.0	...	195	3,883
Liechtenstein	1987	14	101	1,690	16.7	...	9	113	1,673	16.4	...	1	30[22]
Luxembourg	1985	541[1]	1,685[4]	21,979	16.1[1]	88[1]	53[1, 17]	2,407[17,22]	8,705	...	58[1]	[17]	[17]
Macau	1985	73	1,057	31,468	29.8	...	30	744	12,612	17.0	...	1[5]	25[5]
Madagascar	1978	8,002	23,937	1,311,000	54.8	...	104[6]	5,088[10]	131,836[10]	25.9[10]	25.9[10]	126[6]	759[6]
Malaŵi	1983	2,411	13,714	868,849	63.4	46[1]	60	825	17,232	20.9	...	10[14]	155[14]
Malaysia	1985	6,629	91,099	2,191,676	24.1	...	1,132	56,290	1,273,666	22.6	...	45	1,699
Maldives	1984	65	590	42,598	72.2	...	4	93	841	9.0	...	3	27
Mali	1983	1,558	10,912	364,382	33.4	16[1]	20	3,870	64,148	16.6	...	11	890
Malta	1985	124	1,777	35,411	19.9	94[12]	65	1,624	21,759	13.4	69[1]	23	555
Martinique	1983	226	1,927[19]	41,928	...	...	271	2,489[19]	31,677	...	...	12	653[19]
Mauritania	1982	637	2,401	107,390	44.7	...	...	864	25,700	29.7	...	...	...
Mauritius	1985	280	6,450	140,714	21.8	98[4]	127	3,603	71,868	19.9	34[10]	7	69[1]
Mayotte	1985	72	407	14,992	36.8	...	3	66[17]	1,374	20.8	...	3	[15]
Mexico	1985	76,183	437,408	15,219,245	34.8	...	17,620	230,656	4,396,087	19.1	...	4,815	126,705
Monaco	1982	6	1,354	...	...	...	...	1,914	...	...	...	...	751[12]
Mongolia	1985	[21]	[21]	[21]	[21]	98[1]	673[21]	16,500[21]	418,000[21]	25.3[21]	84[3]	40	1,200
Montserrat	1983	15[12]	66	1,723	26.1	...	...	60	871	14.5	...	...	9
Morocco	1985	3,443	73,038[19]	2,278,734	38.3[1]	58[4]	1,145	52,920[19]	1,419,595	23.1[1]	19[2]	...	952
Mozambique	1985	4,649	20,286	1,311,014	64.6	46[4]	202	3,377	135,068	40.0	4[12]	38	961
Nauru	1985	7	142[15]	1,451	13.5[15]	...	2	[15]	465	[15]	...	...	...
Nepal	1985	11,660	46,484	1,747,857	37.6	...	4,631	17,069	454,511	26.6	...	...	513[8]
Netherlands, The	1985	9,467	75,998	1,193,338	15.7	90[1]	1,409	53,375	822,615	15.4	85[4]	2,031	54,560
Netherlands Antilles	1983	91	1,248	25,578	19.7	...	22	633	8,623	13.6	...	3	79
New Caledonia	1985	263	1,529	31,589	20.7	...	45	976[5]	11,445	...	...	28	309[5]
New Zealand	1984	2,503	18,583	459,009	24.7	97[4]	330	12,949	228,621	17.7	79[10]	28	2,867

		third level (higher)							literacy[b]				public expenditure on education (percent of GNP)[b]	country
students[d]	student/ teacher ratio	institutions	teachers[c]	students[d]	student/ teacher ratio	gross enroll- ment ratio	students per 100,000 popula- tion[b]	percent of population aged 25 and over with post- secondary education[b]	over age	total (%)	male (%)	female (%)		
1,984	12.5	—	—	161	...	...	...	...	14	11.9	...	...	3.9	Djibouti
121	9.3	...	59	284	4.8	...	...	1.1	15	94.9	...	...	...	Dominica
27,670	...	5	...	91,115	...	10.1[10]	900	1.9	15	77.3	77.7	76.8	2.1	Dominican Republic
[17]	[17]	21	11,186[2]	172,649[2]	15.4[2]	35.3[12]	3,192	7.6	10	85.2	87.9	82.6	5.6	Ecuador
765,057	15.8	12[1]	26,631[1]	589,899[1]	22.2[1]	15.2[1]	1,454	3.4	15	43.0	58.9	26.8	4.1	Egypt
10,392	15.6	19	3,300	42,421	12.9	11.9[4]	1,095	2.3	15	69.0	73.2	65.3	3.7	El Salvador
[17]	[17]	—	—	—	—	3.8[12]	317	...		63.0	...	...	...	Equatorial Guinea
...	...	11	1,446	15,776	10.9	0.5[4]	46	...	15	4.8	9.3	0.5	4.1	Ethiopia
607[4]	...	6[4]	...	949[4]	...	...	...	...	15	99.0	...	...	...	Faeroe Islands
—	—	—	—	—	—	—	...	...	15	99.5	...	...	...	Falkland Islands
3,820	14.0	5[4]	...	3,947[4]	...	3.2[1]	352	3.3	15	85.5	90.2	80.9	5.9	Fiji
116,906	7.8	21	5,191	119,902	23.1	31.1[4]	2,485	11.9	15	100.0	100.0	100.0	5.9	Finland
[17]	...	1,094[12]	40,585[12]	1,017,775[12]	25.1[12]	28.4[4]	2,253	...	...	98.8	98.9	98.7	5.1	France
...	...	1	...	239	...	...	...	6.4	16	82.0	82.5	81.3	...	French Guiana
3,822	...	...	12[1]	68[1]	5.7[1]	...	...	...	14	95.0	94.9	95.0	...	French Polynesia
10,545	18.1	1	297	2,651	8.9	3.3[1]	270	...	15	77.0	...	...	3.0	Gabon
1,141	7.6	1[1]	29[1]	38[1]	7.7[1]	—	...	0.2	15	20.1	29.1	11.6	6.0	Gambia, The
834	...	1[4]	30[1]	2,387[4]	...	...	...	...	...	...	...	...	...	Gaza Strip
414,044	7.3	54	29,700	434,326	14.6	29.8[4]	2,420	17.3	15	100.0	100.0	100.0	5.5	Germany, East
2,718,404[5]	30.9[5]	...	311,460[5]	1,267,263[5]	4.1[5]	29.6[1]	2,289	4.3	15	100.0	100.0	100.0	4.6	Germany, West
24,827	19.3[12]	3	1,041[12]	7,878	...	1.6[12]	138	0.4	15	53.2	64.1	42.8	2.4	Ghana
353	14.1	—	—	—	—	...	...	...	10	99.0	99.0	99.0	6.3	Gibraltar
101,748	12.7	161	12,067	148,515	12.3	16.7[2]	1,256	7.6	15	92.3	97.1	87.8	2.2	Greece
...	...	—	—	—	—	—	...	...	15	100.0	100.0	100.0	...	Greenland
213[1]	10.1[1]	...	40	519	13.0	...	...	1.0	15	85.0	...	...	3.3	Grenada
15,844	27.8	1[11]	921[11]	4,809[11]	52.3[11]	...	...	5.2	...	91.5	92.7	90.3	...	Guadeloupe
868[4]	13.2[4]	2[4]	162[1]	3,499[1]	21.6[1]	...	...	21.5	...	90.0	...	...	7.6	Guam
[17]	[17]	5[4]	4,490[4]	51,556[4]	11.4[4]	6.7[1]	616	1.2	15	51.1	58.6	43.5	1.8	Guatemala
134	2.9	—	—	—	—	...	...	...	15	100.0	100.0	100.0	...	Guernsey
7,963	8.2[12]	...	1,373[1]	13,182[1]	9.6[1]	3.0[1]	261	...	15	28.3	39.7	17.2	4.2	Guinea
578	10.0	...	...	...	...	—	...	0.1	7	26.8	...	...	2.9	Guinea-Bissau
4,647	13.4	1	...	1,889	...	2.0[4]	230	1.0	15	95.5	97.1	94.0	9.7	Guyana
156	3.2	1	582	3,464	6.0	1.1[2]	96	0.7	15	34.7	37.1	32.5	1.1	Haiti
103,941	...	7	2,692	34,478	14.0	9.7[4]	843	1.0	15	68.6	71.1	66.2	4.3	Honduras
[17]	[17]	21	3,169	36,316	11.5	11.9[1]	1,353	7.1	15	88.1	94.7	80.9	2.9	Hong Kong
370,918	14.5[11]	58	14,850	99,344	6.7	14.7[4]	930	7.0	10	98.9	99.2	98.7	5.8	Hungary
4,280	...	4	280	4,780	17.1	22.6	2,197	3.7	15	100.0	100.0	100.0	4.1	Iceland
468,993[4]	...	9,056[2]	259,745[2]	4,924,794[2]	19.0[2]	8.7[3]	776	2.5	15	40.8	54.8	25.7	3.2	India
934,527	...	50[1]	56,322[1]	692,700[4]	...	4.2[1]	393	0.8	15	74.1	83.0	65.4	2.2	Indonesia
277,609	13.4	114[4]	13,698	145,809	10.6	3.9[4]	356	...	15	42.8	55.4	30.1	5.7	Iran
106,312	17.0	25[4]	6,952	116,179	16.7	10.0[4]	866	...	15	45.9	65.9	26.0	3.2	Iraq
79,131	...	26	3,690	45,910	12.4	21.8[12]	1,731	4.6	15	100.0	100.0	100.0	7.3	Ireland
133[10]	4.2[10]	...	...	...	...	...	...	...	...	...	...	...	...	Isle of Man
95,145	...	7	8,112[1]	96,810	...	33.8[4]	2,746	23.1	14	93.3	96.2	90.5	7.8	Israel
2,042,913	...	74	47,844[4]	1,096,454	21.4[4]	25.8[4]	1,981	2.6	15	97.0	97.9	96.3	5.0	Italy
8,508[14]	16.7[14]	...	...	5,176	...	6.2[2]	645	1.1	14	88.6	88.2	89.1	6.9	Jamaica
...	...	1,066	133,867	2,445,206	18.3	30.5[4]	2,033	14.3	15	100.0	100.0	100.0	5.7	Japan
...	...	1	...	1,385	...	...	...	...	...	...	...	...	4.1	Jersey
25,310	19.6	47	2,465[4]	55,575	24.2[1]	33.3[1]	1,570	0.8	15	74.6	83.9	64.4	5.8	Jordan
7,334	26.4	2[4]	...	586[4]	...	...	...	...	15	48.0	...	...	...	Kampuchea
20,604	17.0	4	...	22,157	...	0.9[4]	75	...	15	59.2	69.6	49.2	4.8	Kenya
75	2.4	1	12	97	8.1	...	...	...	15	90.0	...	...	13.5	Kiribati
...	...	175	9,244	200,000	21.6	...	...	...	...	90.0	...	...	3.6	Korea, North
885,962	29.9	398	28,647	1,032,510	36.0	26.6[5]	2,951	8.9	15	92.7	97.5	87.9	5.1	Korea, South
12,272	15.6	1	858	16,359	19.1	14.5[4]	1,205	10.1	10	77.5	80.5	73.1	3.7	Kuwait
11,510[12]	12.2[12]	1[12]	140[12]	1,408[12]	10.1[12]	1.4[4]	116	...	15	45.2	52.8	37.6	0.5	Laos
39,045	11.0	18	...	70,314	...	28.9[1]	2,715	3.1	10	73.4	82.6	64.2	3.0	Lebanon
2,221	10.0	1	146	1,119	7.7	1.5[16]	188	0.1	15	73.6	62.4	84.5	3.9	Lesotho
2,322	36.9	3	190	3,789	19.9	2.5[3]	210	1.0	15	35.0	47.3	22.8	6.3	Liberia
50,363	12.9	8	1,340[2]	25,700[1]	...	10.8[1]	859	1.0	10	74.4	85.0	62.0	3.7	Libya
117	...	—	—	—	—	—	...	5.4	15	100.0	100.0	100.0	...	Liechtenstein
16,571	...	2[1]	181[1, 22]	785	...	3.6[4]	270	...	15	100.0	100.0	100.0	6.4	Luxembourg
480[5]	19.2[5]	1	86	4,172	48.5	—	...	1.4	10	61.3	76.4	46.2	...	Macau
9,213[6]	12.1[6]	3[5]	706[1]	32,599[1]	46.2[1]	4.2[1]	354	...	15	67.5	73.7	61.6	2.3	Madagascar
2,322[14]	15.0[14]	4	305	1,849	6.1	0.4[1]	38	0.2	15	49.9	64.3	37.2	2.5	Malawi
20,720	12.2	41	8,415	96,212	11.4	4.5[1]	472	...	10	75.0	83.0	67.1	7.5	Malaysia
206	7.6	...	...	...	...	...	...	0.4	15	81.1	80.2	82.0	0.6	Maldives
12,615	14.2	7	499	5,792	11.6	0.9[1]	78	0.2	15	9.6	13.5	5.9	4.2	Mali
6,140	11.1	1	156	1,408	9.0	3.0[1]	271	2.4	14	81.4	83.4	79.7	3.3	Malta
15,410	...	1	40	1,220	30.5	...	0.8	...	15	92.5	91.8	93.2	...	Martinique
1,854	...	3[12]	25[12]	1,374	...	—	...	...	6	17.4	...	...	8.0	Mauritania
444[5]	...	2	184[1]	610[5]	...	0.6[4]	69	1.2	15	84.6	90.5	78.8	4.0	Mauritius
475	...	—	—	33[5, 23]	—	...	...	...	15	18.0	27.5	8.7	...	Mayotte
1,841,633	14.5	1,305	92,338	1,121,252	12.1	15.2[4]	1,425	2.6	15	82.6	85.8	79.5	2.7	Mexico
1,218		...	...	...	...	...	...	6.8	...	...	...	...	...	Monaco
25,700	21.4	8	1,500	25,100	16.7	25.5[12]	2,235	...	15	89.5	93.4	85.5	7.0	Mongolia
66	7.3	...	...	...	...	...	...	2.7	...	...	...	...	3.5	Montserrat
16,257	17.1	19[1]	4,566	119,920	26.3	6.0[4]	587	...	15	70.7	82.4	58.7	7.5	Morocco
12,887	13.4	1	323	1,351	4.2	0.1[1]	9	0.1	15	16.6	20.0	13.3	1.2	Mozambique
...	...	—	—	88[23]	—	—	...	...	15	99.0	...	...	...	Nauru
16,815[8]	32.8[8]	69	3,654	48,229	13.2	4.8[4]	406	6.8	6	23.3	34.0	12.0	2.6	Nepal
640,737	11.7	456	30,396	305,126	10.0	31.0[1]	2,645	7.2	15	100.0	100.0	100.0	7.7	Netherlands, The
732	9.3	1	53	677	12.8	...	...	4.4	15	95.0	...	...	10.1	Netherlands Antilles
6,906	...	6	63	761	12.1	...	...	2.0	13	89.4	90.1	88.7	11.9	New Caledonia
141,527	49.4	7[24]	2,958[24]	33,875[24]	11.5[24]	27.7[4]	2,612	30.6	15	100.0	100.0	100.0	5.2	New Zealand

Education (continued)

country	year	first level (primary)					general second level (secondary)					vocational second level[a]	
		schools	teachers[c]	students[d]	student/teacher ratio	net enroll-ment ratio	schools	teachers[c]	students[d]	student/teacher ratio	net enroll-ment ratio	schools	teachers[c]
Nicaragua	1984	4,783	16,997	553,939	32.6	73[1]	467[17]	4,104	91,374	22.3	23[2]	[17]	1,954
Niger	1981	1,708	5,475	233,441	42.6	...	...	...	42,967	...	3[16]	...	...
Nigeria	1981	36,683	384,201	14,022,164	36.5	...	4,495	69,005	2,024,024	29.3	...	470	12,156
Niue	1985	7	29	503	17.3	...	1	31	321	10.4	...	—	—
Norfolk Island	1986	2	9	202	22.4	...	1	8	112	14.0	...	—	—
Norway	1985	3,539	30,795	550,136	17.9	98[12]	930[17]	16,377[17]	196,317[17]	12.0[17]	84[12]	[17]	[17]
Oman	1986	351	7,109	177,685	25.0	66[4]	290	4,840	48,828	10.1	14[12]	14	707
Pacific Is., Trust Territory of the	1981	245	1,374	31,099	22.6	...	32[9]	445	6,872	15.4	...	2	39[3]
Marshall Islands	1983	82	348	8,110	23.3	...	...	...	1,483	...	...	...	...
Micronesia, Fed. States of	...	...	...	...	...	...	...	...	...	...	...	...	...
Northern Mariana Islands	...	...	...	...	...	...	...	...	...	...	...	...	...
Palau	1984	...	310[15]	2,907	13.2[15]	...	...	[15]	1,181	[15]	...	...	...
Pakistan	1985	75,532	214,500	6,645,000	31.0	...	10,503	144,000	2,303,000	16.0	...	365	5,806
Panama	1984	2,438	12,969	338,363	26.1	87[4]	321	9,568	181,774	19.0	46[4]	76	665
Papua New Guinea	1984	2,332	11,184	351,064	31.4	...	118	1,873	47,124	25.2	...	99	601
Paraguay	1984	3,796	22,091	559,080	25.3	90[1]	713[17]	9,044[17]	149,019[17]	16.5[17]	21[3]	[17]	[17]
Peru	1985	24,949	109,039	3,787,569	34.7	93[12]	4,178	74,135	1,597,839	21.6	...	1,032	10,620
Philippines	1984	32,809	272,479[1]	8,717,469	31.8[1]	97[1]	5,430	89,019[1]	3,204,551	33.2[1]	44[1]	[25]	[25]
Pitcairn Island	1986	1[15]	1[15]	12	15.0[15]	...	[15]	[15]	3	[15]	...	—	—
Poland	1986	16,791	267,600	4,879,100	18.2	99[4]	896	21,300	338,000	15.9	69[4]	7,328	82,900
Portugal	1983	13,069	76,141	1,305,724	17.1	82[1]	629	38,809	582,495	15.0	28[10]	368	...
Puerto Rico	1986	1,542	18,359	427,582	23.3	...	395	13,612	334,661	24.6	...	52	...
Qatar	1985[14]	92	2,505	30,515	12.2	85[4]	70	2,090	18,261	8.7	57[4]	3	88
Réunion	1985	508[26]	5,087[26]	113,330[26]	22.3[26]	...	85[17]	3,947[17]	69,417[17]	17.6[17]	...	[17]	[17]
Romania	1985	14,134	148,407	3,035,209	20.4	...	1,973[17]	49,547[17]	1,500,193[17]	30.3[17]	...	[17]	[17]
Rwanda	1985	1,572[5]	14,005[5]	790,198	54.4[5]	59[4]	...	1,082[5]	45,158[17]	...	2[4]	...	...
St. Christopher and Nevis	1985	32	339	7,655	22.6	...	7	286	4,436	15.5	...	2	29
St. Helena and Ascension	1983	8	32	589	18.4	...	4	33	507	15.4	...	2	10
St. Lucia	1985	85	1,139	33,534	29.4	...	11	280	5,321	19.0	...	4	48
St. Pierre and Miquelon	1983	5	59	661	11.2	...	3	56	531	9.5	...	2	40
St. Vincent and the Grenadines	1983	62	1,251	24,551	19.6	...	19	292	5,170	17.7	...	5	39
San Marino	1986	13	158	1,411	8.9	...	4	183	1,248	6.8	...	...	...
São Tomé and Príncipe	1985	63	517	19,086	36.9	...	11	300	6,186	20.6	...	2	35
Saudi Arabia	1985	7,433	75,047	1,184,593	15.8	53[1]	2,880	36,009	471,997	13.1	24[1]	26[5]	881[5]
Senegal	1984	2,150	12,934	533,394	42.8	43[4]	192	4,380	103,510	23.6	...	...	600
Seychelles	1986	26	681	14,663	21.5	...	4	112	2,433	21.7	...	1	160
Sierra Leone	1983	1,196	9,519	290,756	30.5	...	168	2,835	68,818	24.3	...	6	95
Singapore	1985	252	10,625	278,060	26.2	100[4]	149	8,562	190,328	22.2	58[3]	15	1,686
Solomon Islands	1984	423	1,536	37,522	24.4	...	20	267	5,118	19.2	...	2	63
Somalia	1983	1,308	9,460	220,680	23.3	16[1]	51[12]	2,201	53,591	24.3	6[12]	26[12]	817
South Africa	1985	17,430[15]	199,949[15]	4,722,832	...	...	[15]	[15]	1,539,213	...	...	132	3,733
Bophuthatswana	1982	802	7,221	373,653	51.7	...	310	4,391	115,737	26.4	...	18	360
Ciskei	1982	608	4,646	189,713	40.8	...	152	1,651	53,330	32.3	...	4	66
Transkei	1983	...	...	582,090	...	...	...	...	150,720	...	...	...	...
Venda	1983	...	...	114,350	...	...	...	...	25,980	...	...	...	...
South West Africa/Namibia	1983	1,069	7,120	232,306	32.6	...	78	1,864	40,359	21.6	...	6	81
Spain	1985	23,105[4]	220,409	5,644,717	25.6	100[1]	2,593	73,302	1,181,769	16.1	75[1]	2,397[5]	45,339[5]
Sri Lanka	1984	9,289	136,280[15]	2,145,343[14]	...	...	...	[15]	1,377,821[14]	...	...	25[4]	466[4]
Sudan, The	1985	6,707	47,750	1,653,491	34.6	48.7	2,167	17,591	490,583	27.9	22.0	98	968[27]
Suriname	1984	319	3,796	91,595	24.1	...	51	789	15,501	19.6	...	64	1,253
Swaziland	1985	933	8,146	273,873	33.6	84[4]	179	3,130	58,747	18.8	21[10]	5	276
Sweden	1986	5,399[4, 15]	123,801[4, 15]	630,505	...	97[12]	[15]	[15]	459,519	...	80[12]	[15]	[15]
Switzerland	1986	...	...	408,800	...	...	...	...	382,500	...	...	...	...
Syria	1985	8,650	70,144	1,889,709	26.9	93[4]	1,660	41,130	740,898	18.0	47[1]	156	8,039
Taiwan	1986	2,459	71,853	2,313,240	32.2	...	839	60,346	1,250,840	20.7	...	200	15,783
Tanzania	1983	10,035[1, 28]	85,308[28]	3,552,923[28]	41.6[28]	61[1]	175[1]	3,362[1]	71,219	20.6[1]	...	40[1]	967
Thailand	1981	33,712[2]	333,351[14, 26]	7,449,219[14, 26]	22.3[14, 26]	...	3,761[2]	76,339[19]	1,572,587	...	...	1,528[2]	27,484[2]
Togo	1983	2,317	10,145	457,376	45.1	70	248[1]	4,200	95,941	22.8	...	22[1]	348[2]
Tokelau	1983	3[2]	39	482	15.8	...	3[2]	6[2]	80[2]	13.3[2]	...	...	12[2]
Tonga	1984	111	810	16,921	20.9	...	50	789	14,549	18.4	...	12	14[4]
Trinidad and Tobago	1984	464	7,346	169,853	23.1	97[12]	93	4,723	92,036	19.5	61[1]	...	...
Tunisia	1986	3,358	40,703	1,291,490	31.7	93[4]	380[17]	21,269[17]	457,630[17]	21.5[17]	30[4]	...	...
Turkey	1985	47,192	209,911	6,527,036	31.1	...	5,389	88,138	2,101,064	23.8	...	1,989	41,971
Turks and Caicos Islands	1985	17	1,540	74	20.8	...	3	51	707	13.9	...	—	—
Tuvalu	1984	11	61	1,349	22.1	100[1]	1	15[4]	243	16.7[4]	...	8[4]	16[4]
Uganda	1982	5,300	44,426	1,616,791	36.4	40[1]	257	6,287	132,051	21.0	...	23	735
U.S.S.R.	1985	67,500	2,430,000[15]	35,800,000	...	...	59,900	[15]	4,512,000	...	...	4,471	245,000
United Arab Emirates	1983	244[2]	6,599[14]	115,411	...	74[4]	68[2]	4,081[14]	45,442	...	...	4[2]	344
United Kingdom	1984	25,326	207,100	4,549,700	22.0	93[1]	5,328	274,500	4,384,200	16.0	80[1]	755[29]	[30]
United States	1985	101,050[4,15]	1,436,000	31,220,000	21.7	...	[15]	1,057,000[17]	13,830,000[17]	13.1[17]	...	[15]	[17]
Uruguay	1984	2,321	15,027	350,390	23.3	75[4]	268	...	152,304	...	...	93	5,632
Vanuatu	1983	246[5]	934	23,465[5]	22.2[2]	...	9	126[1]	2,186	16.4[1]	...	2	40[1]
Venezuela	1985	14,277	125,140	3,256,554	26.0	83[1]	2,241[17]	58,056[17]	1,007,642[17]	17.4[17]	33[12]	[17]	[17]
Vietnam	1984	11,751[15]	427,000[15]	11,779,000[15]	27.6[15]	98[2]	[15]	[15]	[15]	[15]	...	280	10,200
Virgin Islands (U.S.)	1986	70[15]	1,658[15]	31,943[15]	19.3[15]	...	[15]	[15]	[15]	[15]	...	[15]	[15]
Wallis and Futuna	1978	...	171	5,348	31.2	...		9	277	30.8	...	—	—
West Bank	1985[31]	1,080[5, 15]	8,185[5, 15]	175,284	...	...	[15]	[15]	91,877	...	...	[15]	[15]
Western Sahara	...	...	...	...	...	...	...	...	...	...	...	...	...
Western Samoa	1983	164	1,502	31,457	20.9	...	38[1]	520	20,404	39.2	...	4	69
Yemen (Aden)	1983	924	11,281	294,028	26.1	...	46[1]	1,493	29,205	19.6	...	13[1]	453
Yemen (Ṣan'ā')	1983	4,645	13,305	675,402	50.8	22[10]	314[12]	3,679	71,819	19.5	3[10]	29[12]	394[1]
Yugoslavia	1986	12,447	61,288	1,448,562	23.6	79[12]	4,822	75,023	1,745,439	23.3	70[10]	1,331	62,753
Zaire	1979	5,924	132,759[16]	3,919,395	...	...	2,511[16]	42,212[16, 17]	611,349	...	...	20[16]	[17]
Zambia	1982	2,894	23,870	1,121,769	47.0	84[2]	142	4,602	104,859	22.8	...	28[5]	1,041[5]
Zimbabwe	1985	3,880[5]	52,502[4]	2,229,396	39.0[4]	100[5]	790[5]	10,238[4]	497,766	28.3[4]	...	17[5]	953[4]

[1]1982. [2]1980. [3]1979. [4]1983. [5]1984. [6]1972. [7]University of Angola only. [8]1976. [9]1977. [10]1975. [11]1985. [12]1981. [13]Vocational includes third level. [14]Public schools only. [15]First level includes second level. [16]1978. [17]General second level includes vocational second level. [18]1986. [19]Public school teachers only. [20]Includes East Jerusalem. [21]General second level

		third level (higher)							literacy[b]				public expenditure on education (percent of GNP)[b]	country
students[d]	student/teacher ratio	institutions	teachers[c]	students[d]	student/teacher ratio	gross enrollment ratio	students per 100,000 population[b]	percent of population aged 25 and over with post-secondary education[b]	over age	total (%)	male (%)	female (%)		
70,471	36.1	16	2,666	33,062	12.4	12.8[4]	1,162	...	15	88.0	...	...	4.0	Nicaragua
1,821	...	1	322	2,450	7.6	0.5[4]	42	...	15	9.8	14.0	5.8	4.3	Niger
359,817	29.6	77	...	153,300	...	2.5[12]	213	...	15	42.4	53.8	31.5	2.1	Nigeria
—	—	—	—	—	—	—	—	1.9	15	99.8	99.7	99.9	...	Niue
—	—	—	—	—	—	—	—	...	15	100.0	100.0	100.0	...	Norfolk Island
[17]	[17]	229	6,883	90,381	13.1	28.2[1]	2,151	11.9	15	100.0	100.0	100.0	7.0	Norway
3,141	4.4	—	—	2,316[23]	...	—	46	...	6	38.0	55.0	20.0	2.3	Oman
456	...	1[2]	158[2]	2,129[2]	13.5[2]	...	...	6.4	15	92.2	93.6	90.8	20.5	Pacific Is., Trust Territory of the
														Marshall Islands
...	...	...	...	...	...	...	...	...	...	...	...	...	...	Micronesia, Fed. States of
...	...	...	...	...	...	...	...	...	...	...	...	...	...	Northern Mariana Islands
														Palau
67,628	11.6	107	10,203	148,345	14.5	2.0[3]	180	1.9	15	26.2	36.0	15.2	2.0	Pakistan
11,580	17.4	11	2,489	36,965	14.9	22.3[4]	2,212	8.4	10	88.9	88.7	89.1	5.5	Panama
8,583	14.3	2	387	3,510	9.1	1.8[1]	161	...	15	42.3	52.4	31.3	4.7	Papua New Guinea
[17]	[17]	2	2,649	30,222	11.2	—	649	2.0	15	85.7	88.7	82.9	1.3	Paraguay
226,321	21.3	44	21,083	358,337	17.0	21.5[1]	2,001	4.5	15	78.7	84.3	73.1	3.3	Peru
165,012	...	1,157[25]	51,337[25]	1,411,486	...	26.5[1]	2,694	11.9	15	88.7	89.9	87.5	2.0	Philippines
—	—	—	—	—	—	—	—	...	15	100.0	100.0	100.0	...	Pitcairn Island
1,359,800	16.4	92	57,300	265,800	4.6	15.7[4]	1,294	5.7	15	99.2	...	...	4.1	Poland
26,003	...	21	10,578	89,964	8.5	11.4[12]	964	1.6	15	78.2	84.0	72.7	4.7	Portugal
149,191	...	45	9,045	156,818	17.3	45.4[3]	4,703	18.4	15	89.1	89.7	88.5	8.2	Puerto Rico
581	6.6	1	401	4,621	11.5	18.7[4]	1,678	11.6	10	51.1	51.2	50.1	5.0	Qatar
[17]	[17]	1	74	2,420	32.7	...	...	...	15	78.7	...	...	...	Réunion
[17]	[17]	44	13,252	166,238	12.5	11.8[4]	768	4.6	15	95.8	97.3	94.3	2.3	Romania
[17]	...	3	184[5]	1,527	6.6[5]	0.3[1]	24	0.3	15	49.4	62.2	37.2	3.1	Rwanda
240	8.3	1[12]	9[12]	67[12]	7.4[12]	...	151	1.1	15	91.5	90.8	92.2	12.1	St. Christopher and Nevis
48	4.8	...	—	—	—	...	...	...	15	97.1	96.8	97.5	...	St. Helena and Ascension
358	7.5	—	—	—	—	...	...	1.0	15	59.7	...	...	8.1	St. Lucia
217	5.4	—	—	—	—	—	...	7.5	15	99.5	99.5	99.5	...	St. Pierre and Miquelon
275	7.1	1	19	105	5.5	...	...	0.8	14	85.0	...	...	4.9	St. Vincent and the Grenadines
701[23]	—	—	...	343[23]	—	...	...	2.4	15	98.0	98.6	97.5	5.9	San Marino
370	10.6	...	...	700[23]	—	...	...	0.3	15	54.2	70.2	39.1	6.2	São Tomé and Príncipe
9,235	...	77	8,561	91,978	10.7	9.4[1]	827	...	15	48.8	58.0	34.6	4.7	Saudi Arabia
10,051	16.8	...	925[12]	11,809	13.5[12]	2.2[14]	191	0.1	15	22.5	31.0	14.2	4.7	Senegal
1,541	9.6	...	...	...	...	...	...	2.6	15	62.0	...	...	9.0	Seychelles
969	10.2	2	303	1,917	6.3	0.6[2]	55	...	5	18.7	23.7	13.7	3.8	Sierra Leone
18,894	11.2	5	3,708	39,693	10.7	11.8[4]	1,402	3.4	10	85.6	92.3	78.6	4.4	Singapore
1,142	18.1	—	—	—	—	—	...	1.6	15	54.1	62.4	44.9	3.6	Solomon Islands
9,664	11.8	1[12]	262[12]	2,332[12]	8.9[12]	0.9[3]	65	...	15	11.6	18.4	6.5	2.3	Somalia
35,394	9.5	96	15,245	204,546	13.3	...	...	3.7[24]	15	79.3	80.6	78.0	3.8	South Africa
6,053	16.8	1	36[2]	816	...	...	...	...	15	75.0	...	...	...	Bophuthatswana
525	8.0	2	40	338	8.4	...	...	...	...	...	...	...	...	Ciskei
...	...	...	...	560	...	...	...	...	...	...	...	...	...	Transkei
...	...	...	...	380	...	...	...	...	...	...	...	...	...	Venda
1,200	14.8	4	137	537	3.9	...	...	...	15	72.5	74.2	70.8	1.9	South West Africa/Namibia
695,180[5]	15.3[5]	33[4]	43,037[4]	692,152[4]	16.1[4]	23.8[1]	1,919	7.7	15	92.8	95.9	89.9	2.6	Spain
8,382[4]	18.0[4]	8[4]	5,629[4]	63,460[4]	11.3[4]	3.9[4]	402	2.3	15	86.1	90.8	81.2	3.0	Sri Lanka
29,650	...	16	1,934[2]	35,596	...	2.0[12]	171	...	15	21.6	36.5	6.5	4.6	Sudan, The
15,428	12.3	6	485	3,489	7.2	2.9[3]	255	...	15	80.7	85.4	76.3	7.0	Suriname
3,086	11.2	2	279	2,540	9.1	3.4[1]	287	...	15	67.9	70.3	65.7	5.2	Swaziland
179,733	...	...	216,412[4]	...	...	38.7[4]	2,701	15.4	15	100.0	100.0	100.0	8.5	Sweden
252,100	...	...	...	110,100		18.6[1]	1,515	2.9	15	100.0	100.0	100.0	5.0	Switzerland
69,491	8.6	4	1,440[5]	131,224	...	15.9[1]	1,492	1.3	10	65.7	80.1	50.8	5.9	Syria
420,212	26.6	105	20,848	428,576	20.6	...	2,158	...	6	91.2	95.5	86.5	3.6	Taiwan
10,568	10.9	1	974	3,943	4.0	0.4[4]	31	0.2	10	73.5	77.7	69.6	5.8	Tanzania
418,279	21.6[2]	62[2]	35,731	911,166	25.5	22.2[1]	2,179	2.9	15	81.8	88.9	74.9	3.9	Thailand
7,306[1]	...	1	372[1]	4,004	10.8[1]	1.7[4]	145	0.1	15	35.2	46.1	25.1	5.9	Togo
197[2]	16.4[2]	—	—	—	—	—	...	...	15	99.8	99.8	99.8	...	Tokelau
635	...	1[1]	...	125[1]	...	—	...	...	15	92.8	92.9	92.8	9.8	Tonga
...	...	1[11]	280[11]	3,389[11]	12.1[11]	5.1[11]	530	2.7	15	95.1	...	...	5.4	Trinidad and Tobago
...	...	...	5,194	41,594	8.0	5.3[4]	515	1.8	10	46.2	65.4	41.9	4.5	Tunisia
594,597	14.2	288[5]	20,441[5]	323,375[5]	15.8[5]	7.3[4]	701	2.2	6	67.4	79.9	54.6	3.4	Turkey
—	—	—	—	—	—	—	...	7.7	15	86.7	85.0	88.0	...	Turks and Caicos Islands
354[4]	22.1[4]	—	—	100[12, 23]	—	—	...	...	15	95.5	95.5	95.5	...	Tuvalu
13,338	18.1	4	640	7,312	11.4	0.6[1]	52	0.1	...	47.9	...	...	1.8	Uganda
4,500,000	18.4	892	377,000	5,280,100	14.0	21.2[4]	1,947	8.3	15	99.0	...	...	6.6	U.S.S.R.
2,652	7.7	318[2]	8,343[2]	125,209[2]	15.0[2]	5.6[4]	513	6.0	15	68.6	71.0	61.0	1.9	United Arab Emirates
605,724[29]	...	46[24]	53,000[30]	204,276[24]	...	20.1[1]	1,572	11.0	15	99.9	...	...	5.5	United Kingdom
[17]	[17]	3,280[4]	690,000	12,150,000	17.6	56.4[1]	5,355	32.2	15	95.5	95.7	95.3	6.8	United States
55,359	9.8	1	4,349[4]	64,104	...	20.8[4]	1,686	6.3	15	96.3	93.5[10]	94.4[10]	2.5	Uruguay
718	8.8[1]	—	—	—	—	—	...	...	5	73.2	76.9	69.0	...	Vanuatu
[17]	[17]	81	30,123	381,575	12.7	21.7[4]	2,129	7.0	15	88.4	90.3	86.5	6.5	Venezuela
99,200	9.7	93	18,100	92,500	5.1	2.5[2]	213	...	15	94.0	...	...	3.0	Vietnam
[15]	[15]	1[11]	84[11]	765[11]	9.1[11]	...	...	17.6	15	90.0	...	...	7.6	Virgin Islands (U.S.)
—	—	—	—	—	—	—	...	...	14	34.2	35.4	33.0	...	Wallis and Futuna
1,585	...	4[4]	483[3]	7,066[4]	...	...	...	...	...	...	...	...	...	West Bank
...	...	...	...	...	...	...	...	...	...	...	...	...	...	Western Sahara
651	9.4	6	37	562	15.2	...	...	2.2	10	98.3	98.5	98.1	5.9	Western Samoa
5,602	12.4	...	403[12]	3,645[12]	9.0[12]	2.4[12]	191	...	15	38.9	66.6	10.9	7.4	Yemen (Aden)
7,547	13.7[1]	...	157[2]	4,220[12]	...	1.2[2]	78	...	15	8.3	15.9	0.5	6.6	Yemen (Ṣan'ā')
605,748	9.7	340	25,882	359,175	13.9	20.2[4]	1,647	3.9	15	89.6	95.5	83.9	4.3	Yugoslavia
192,329	...	36	2,782	26,430	10.2	1.2[1]	105	...	15	61.2	78.6	44.7	5.8	Zaire
9,563[5]	9.2[5]	1[5]	650[5]	3,621[5]	5.6[5]	1.6[1]	134	0.6	15	68.6	79.3	58.3	5.6	Zambia
28,605	15.0[4]	1	325[4]	4,742	...	2.6[5]	219	0.6	15	76.0	81.5	66.8	6.6	Zimbabwe

includes first level. [22]Includes part-time teachers. [23]Students registered abroad. [24]Universities only. [25]Third level includes vocational second level. [26]Includes pre-school. [27]Vocational only. [28]Tanzania mainland only. [29]Third level vocational and teacher training. [30]Third level includes teacher training. [31]Excludes East Jerusalem.

Cultural institutions

This table supplies worldwide statistics for the principal and most comparable elements of cultural activity: publishing, libraries, cinema, performing arts, museums, and nature preservation. For the most part, the data that can be compiled and compared are those measures produced as a result of governmental activity or expenditure, such as copyright and deposit, public funding, taxation, and land-use policy.

International comparisons of such data, however, should be approached with caution. In older, more prosperous nations, where the physical necessities of life are in secure supply, more money is available for cultural activities—and, indeed, for collecting data on them—than in less developed countries. Yet a developing country with an embryonic statistical system may have a flourishing cultural life that includes theatrical performance, live music, or the practice of arts no longer central to the Western experience, such as oral storytelling, ceremonial dance, traditional community rituals, or puppetry. Such activities may be more fully integrated into the life of the people than the more measurable cultural pursuits of a developed society.

The statistics actually reported may include books published (copyrighted), cultural facilities, library holdings, seating capacities of theatres and cinemas, attendance (tickets sold), and so on. Even when these figures are recalculated on a per capita basis, apparent differences among countries may be more a function of each country's statistical reporting system than of differences in the cultural habits and preferences of the people.

Furthermore, some kinds of data cannot be given meaningfully. For example, available data on government expenditures for cultural activities represent a wide variety of government policies. Some governments provide no support for cultural activities at any level; others subsidize or support them directly. Some offer tax incentives; others employ artists as teachers, performers, scholars, or archivists. Most national data on manpower engaged in cultural activities are collected on the basis of the individual's main source of income, without regard for his or her aspirations or avocations, part-time paid or unpaid activities, or other less convenient measures. A substantial part of the data presented were obtained from periodic surveys by Unesco, and they refer to a wide range of years. Throughout the table, data given in roman type are from 1982 or later; those in italic are from before 1982.

Figures for book production generally include all works published in separate bindings except advertising works, timetables, telephone directories, price lists, catalogs of businesses or exhibitions, musical scores, maps, atlases, and the like. The figures include government publications, school texts, theses, offprints, series works, and illustrated works, even those consisting principally of illustrations. Figures refer to works actually published during the year of survey, usually by a registered publisher, and deposited for copyright. A book is defined as a work of 49 or more pages, a pamphlet as a work of from 5 to 48 pages. A work published simultaneously in more than one country is counted as having been published in each. Data for newspapers are given in the Communications table beginning on page 866.

Data on libraries are for public libraries and exclude other types of collections, such as national (except when it is the sole public library), school

Cultural institutions

country	book publishing								public libraries			
	number of titles				number of copies ('000)				number	volumes ('000)	registered borrowers ('000)	loans per 1,000 population
	books		periodicals	pamphlets	books		periodicals	pamphlets				
	total	of which school textbooks			total	of which school textbooks						
Afghanistan	*415*[3]	*108*[3]	*51*	...	*5,981*[3]	...	*1,094*	...	38	230	...	...
Albania	867	539	*8*	130	5,733	3,551	*2,894*	491	45	3,723	...	...
Algeria	208	182	27	...	1,300[5]	1,194	476	...	6	165	...	...
American Samoa	*98*[3]	*24*[3]	*16*	*1*[3]	*33*[3, 7]	...	*8*	*1*[3, 7]	1	251	...	5,400
Andorra	...	...	...	...	...	...	...	...	1	...	...	631
Angola	*33*[3]	...	...	*24*[3]	*239*[3]	...	...	*191*[3]	2	41	...	...
Anguilla	...	...	...	...	...	...	...	...	...	...	...	...
Antigua and Barbuda	...	...	...	...	...	...	...	...	1	...	...	...
Argentina	4,216[8]	243[8]	...	[8]	13,526[8]	1,289[8]	...	[8]	*1,528*	*9,532*	*4,201*	*360*
Aruba	[12]	...	...	[12]	...	...	...	...	[12]	[12]	[12]	[12]
Australia	1,759	...	*3,534*	599	...	...	...	...	...	...	...	...
Austria	5,821	99	2,108	915	...	...	...	...	910	7,022	813	1,800
Bahamas, The	...	...	...	...	...	...	...	...	...	...	...	...
Bahrain	78	78	...	...	843	843	...	...	1	183	*50*	722
Bangladesh	*542*[8]	*43*	*388*	[8]	...	...	*657*	...	...	...	...	...
Barbados	18	...	*120*	69	...	...	...	...	*1*	*174*	*62*	*1,900*
Belgium	8,065[8]	...	10,808	[8]	...	...	...	...	*2,351*	*24,140*	*1,731*	*4,300*
Belize	...	...	...	...	...	...	...	...	1	100	...	...
Benin	*13*	...	...	—	*18*	...	...	—	1	32	...	...
Bermuda	...	...	...	...	...	...	...	...	*1*	*140*	*3*	...
Bhutan	...	...	...	...	...	...	...	...	...	...	...	...
Bolivia	274	4[3]	106	27	...	...	...	...	*99*[16]	*125*	*1,120*	*37*
Botswana	*70*[3]	...	...	*27*[3]	*35*	...	...	*33*	*1*	*108*	*30*	*190*
Brazil	15,410	...	*2,419*	3,769	206,999	...	...	189,356	*3,342*	*14,443*	*2,461*	*52*
British Virgin Islands	20	...	2	—	3	...	2	—	*1*	29	...	*2,400*
Brunei	50	25[3]	3	22	341	249[3]	70	19	1	106	*6*	*230*
Bulgaria	4,108	873	1,662	816	50,528	11,390	8,813	9,312	5,699	52,100	...	5,800
Burkina Faso	*4*	...	...	—	...	...	...	—	...	...	...	...
Burma	*1,400*	...	*26*	...	...	...	*823*	...	6	154	...	...
Burundi	...	...	...	...	...	...	...	...	2	34	...	...
Cameroon	*22*[3]	*7*[3]	*41*	...	*94*[3]	*7*[3]	...	...	1	6	...	...
Canada	*3,802*[3]	*826*[3]	1,384	*429*	*79,692*[3]	...	56,169	...	883	49,874	...	5,800
Cape Verde	...	...	4	...	...	...	...	...	—	—	...	...
Cayman Islands	*5*	...	...	—	...	...	...	—	*1*	*6*	2	*2,300*
Central African Republic	...	...	...	...	...	...	...	...	—	—	...	...
Chad	...	...	4	...	...	...	...	...	—	—	...	...
Chile	1,008	100	*89*	318	15,118	1,500	...	4,770	*161*	*581*	...	*380*
China	31,602[8]	5,029[8]	3,100	[8]	4,958,650[8]	2,270,370[8]	138,852	[8]	1,889	*210,000*	...	...
Christmas Island	...	...	...	...	...	...	...	...	1	13	3	8,000
Cocos (Keeling) Islands	...	...	...	...	...	...	...	...	1	...	...	...
Colombia	5,877	670	*1,034*	1,794	27,160	10,003	...	5,577	...	...	...	...
Comoros	...	...	...	...	...	...	...	...	2	*8*	...	...
Congo	*9*	...	...	*118*	*285*	...	...	*1,471*	*7*	*55*	*34*	*63*
Cook Islands	...	...	...	...	...	...	...	...	*1*	*15*	*3*	*1,100*
Costa Rica	...	*70*[3, 25]	274	...	*110*	*110*[3, 25]	163	...	*18*	...	...	...
Côte d'Ivoire	46	13	...	...	3,766	3,517	...	...	*1*	*25*	*2*	*3*
Cuba	1,672	1,136	50	245	35,863	20,349	2,121	5,217	283	4,854	...	...
Cyprus	*180*[26]	*12*	*105*	*957*[26]	*290*[26]	*120*	*272*	*1,936*[26]	...	*236*	...	*230*
Czechoslovakia	8,292	2,951[27]	932	1,282	77,932	59,557[27]	21,456	16,291	9,674	53,963	2,821	5,900
Denmark	7,296	903[28]	...	3,364	...	...	...	...	247	31,857	...	17,032
Djibouti	...	...	2	...	...	...	*1*	...	1	11	...	64
Dominica	...	...	...	...	...	...	...	...	*1*	*15*	*4*	*660*
Dominican Republic	*1,504*	...	...	*715*	*3,017*	...	...	*1,320*	*68*	...	...	*120*
Ecuador	...	...	*284*	...	...	...	...	...	...	...	...	...
Egypt	*1,503*	...	204	*177*	*46,620*	...	1,841	*6,380*	*223*	*1,329*	*31*	*10*

and university, private, professional, business, and government libraries, even though these may play a significant role locally or nationally. Public libraries were thought to provide the most representative set of figures. Data for "volumes" may reflect either actual holdings or an estimate based on length of occupied shelving.

Statistics on commercial cinema attendance may originate from a variety of screening facilities, including fixed, mobile, or drive-in facilities. Seating capacity is given for fixed facilities only. The data on long (or feature) films may refer to prints with a length of from 1,000 to 3,000 metres, depending on the reporting practices of the individual country. However, there is some consensus among reporting countries on a standard length (for classification purposes) of 2,000 metres.

In the performing arts, many countries (if they report such data at all) include not only the familiar Western performance modes—music, theatre, opera, musical theatre, dance—but also other types of live performance, such as traditional, ceremonial, seasonal, festival, or holiday observances and such entertainments as circuses and puppet and shadow theatre. Data on number of performances and attendance refer to both amateur and professional performances unless footnoted. Statistics on the number of theatres refer to theatre buildings and open-air theatres intended mainly for theatrical and other dramatic performances. Premises only occasionally or partly used for performances of this type, such as cultural centres, cultural houses, youth centres, sports establishments, concert halls, cinemas, university and school premises, open-air grounds, antique theatres, historic buildings, and ancient sites, are excluded.

Museum data are derived in large part from surveys by Unesco and the International Council of Museums (ICOM). The number of museums and museum attendance refer to public and private institutions whose exhibits and collections are devoted primarily to art, archaeology and history, natural history and natural science and technology, or ethnology and anthropology; they may be specialized (single theme), regional, or general. National parks and nature reserves, zoos, aquariums, and botanical gardens have not been counted with museums since they are included in the nature conservation section of the table.

Data on nature preservation facilities generally refer to those operated by the national conservation authority (though in many countries, particularly those with federal systems, authority may be lodged with other governmental levels). The data on number of facilities cover all types of facilities operated by the relevant authority, including national parks and monuments, scientific reserves, game reserves, protected landscapes, resource and anthropological reserves, and multiple-use management areas. Data on surface extent usually include only those facilities with an area of more than 10 sq km (4 sq mi).

The data on national parks and nature reserves are derived from information compiled by the International Union for Conservation of Nature and Natural Resources (IUCN) and from Britannica's holdings of published and unpublished national data. The data on zoos, aquariums, and botanical gardens are mainly from the International Species Inventory System (zoos and aquariums) and the International Association of Botanical Gardens.

cinema					performing arts				museums			nature preservation			country
annual attendance (all cinemas)		fixed cinemas		number of long films produced	number of facilities	number of performances	annual attendance		number	annual attendance		national parks and nature reserves		zoos, botanical gardens etc. (number[2])	
number ('000,-000)	per 1,000 population	number	seating capacity ('000)				number ('000)	per 1,000 population		number ('000)	per 1,000 population	number	square metres per capita[1]		
4.9	300	34	19	2	...	...	...	...	7	7	0.5	6	120	1	Afghanistan
...	9,900	105	29	14	28	2,913[4]	1,676	590	2,034	...	...	4	110	...	Albania
23.8[6]	1,200[6]	280	153	7	...	...	...	...	32	260	14	5	100	3	Algeria
0.1	3,200	6	6	...	...	...	...	...	1	52	1,700	1	4,300	...	American Samoa
0.2	6,900	5	2	...	...	14	6	190	2	9	300	—	—	...	Andorra
6.4	900	55	34	1	...	...	...	...	10	...	...	5	1,800	1	Angola
...	...	...	...	...	...	...	...	...	...	...	...	...	...	...	Anguilla
...	...	3	...	...	...	...	...	...	3	...	...	1	250	...	Antigua and Barbuda
49.6[6,9]	1,700[6,9]	919[9]	622[9]	15	399	330	4,136[10]	160[10]	318	5,215[11]	200[11]	29	850	16	Argentina
...	...	...	...	...	...	...	...	[12]	...	...	...	—	—	[12]	Aruba
...	...	733[9]	333[9]	10	...	1,419[10]	...	...	15	5,279[13]	360[13]	580	22,500	41	Australia
16.1[6]	2,100[6]	532	137	16	...	...	...	...	99	6,177	820	27	390	21	Austria
...	...	13	6	...	...	...	...	...	7	...	...	4	5,300	1	Bahamas, The
1.2	3,100	313	...	...	...	...	...	...	3	4	14	...	...	...	Bahrain
...	...	398	258	49	...	...	...	...	38	...	...	3	3	1	Bangladesh
1.2	5,200	6	5	...	1	8	...	...	1	12	47	1	10	...	Barbados
20.7[6]	2,100[6]	472	...	14	...	...	...	...	132[14]	3,454[14]	350[14]	4	12	12	Belgium
...	...	...	...	...	...	...	...	...	5	9	64	2	320	...	Belize
0.9[6]	300[6]	4[9]	4[9]	...	...	...	...	...	3[15]	10[15]	3[15]	2	2,100	...	Benin
0.2	4,200	4	2	...	3	64	17	320	14	...	...	10	5	1	Bermuda
...	...	12	5	...	...	...	...	...	1	16	13	11	6,700	...	Bhutan
31.1[6]	5,700[6]	209	160	1	13	500[10]	123[10]	22[10]	28	...	...	12	7,300	4	Bolivia
0.1[9]	200[9]	1[9]	0.8[9]	...	...	29	...	...	2	52	66	8	107,000	...	Botswana
136.4	1,100	2,221	906	103	267	1,563	...	...	400	8,838[17]	82[17]	50	880	31	Brazil
35.3[18]	3,300	1	0.4	...	...	3	4	330	1	1	77	7	800	...	British Virgin Islands
2.6	14,700	7	6	...	...	78	9	41	2	107	500	...	...	1	Brunei
94.8	10,600	3,245	715	32	63	17,139	6,200	700	201	17,860	2,000	12	62	4	Bulgaria
3.8	600	12	14	...	...	...	...	...	1	...	...	6	1,000	...	Burkina Faso
...	...	175[9]	136[9]	47	...	...	...	...	12	...	...	5	87	2	Burma
0.1	24	7	2	...	44	...	77	19	2	110	24	7	210	...	Burundi
...	...	52	29	1	...	44[19]	39[19]	5	12	4,641	560	15	2,300	2	Cameroon
98.6	4,000	983	620	32	476	14,882[10,20]	5,307[10,20]	220[10,20]	879	26,338[21]	1,100[21]	78	9,000	104	Canada
...	...	...	...	...	...	...	...	...	...	...	...	...	...	...	Cape Verde
0.2[6]	11,700[6]	4	1	...	...	...	...	...	...	...	...	...	...	...	Cayman Islands
...	...	...	...	...	...	...	...	...	2	...	...	4	15,000	...	Central African Republic
25.2	6,000	13	12	...	4	120[22]	...	...	...	...	...	1	230	...	Chad
11.7[6]	1,000[6]	161	100	2	...	811[10]	299[10]	—	69	...	...	64	10,500	10	Chile
18,250	18,100	143,650[23]	...	112	...	...	...	...	409	...	...	62	22	47	China
...	...	2	...	...	...	...	...	...	...	...	...	1	7,000	...	Christmas Island
...	...	...	...	...	...	...	...	...	...	...	...	...	...	...	Cocos (Keeling) Islands
66.4[6]	2,400[6]	323	184	2	14	159[10]	90[10]	3[10]	73	1,442[24]	57[24]	30	1,400	8	Colombia
...	...	...	...	...	...	...	...	...	...	...	...	...	...	...	Comoros
...	...	...	...	1	1	74	...	...	4	...	...	10	7,800	1	Congo
...	...	...	...	...	...	...	...	...	1	6	320	1	7,800	...	Cook Islands
...	...	...	...	...	9	347[10]	50[10]	24[10]	9	...	...	21	1,700	1	Costa Rica
7.0	900	72	42	2	...	...	...	...	1	...	...	10	1,800	2	Côte d'Ivoire
86.1	8,700	525	276	8	47	51,638	...	...	186	5,349	540	4	24	6	Cuba
...	...	...	...	...	12	793	206	330	26	95	150	—	—	1	Cyprus
81.2	5,300	2,971	861	45	83	24,163[10]	9,858[10]	640[10]	231	13,762	920	28	750	42	Czechoslovakia
13.8[6]	2,700[6]	453	92	11	77[26]	9,727[10,29]	2,522[10,29]	490[10,29]	277	7,828[30]	1,530[30]	23	250	19	Denmark
0.3	5,200	4	6	...	...	...	...	...	...	...	...	—	—	...	Djibouti
...	...	3	...	...	...	...	...	...	...	...	...	1	810	1	Dominica
7.0[6,9]	1,500[6,9]	83[9]	46[9]	...	2	41	74	14	6	...	...	5	350	1	Dominican Republic
...	...	330	...	...	75	148	...	...	23	...	...	12	3,000	1	Ecuador
47.7	1,200	219	200	90	...	1,941	364	9	45	1,613	44	1	4	9	Egypt

Cultural institutions (continued)

country	book publishing: number of titles: books: total	of which school textbooks	periodicals	pamphlets	number of copies ('000): books: total	of which school textbooks	periodicals	pamphlets	public libraries: number	volumes ('000)	registered borrowers ('000)	loans per 1,000 population
El Salvador	59	6[3]	...	85	...	...	...	...	...	...	...	...
Equatorial Guinea	...	...	...	...	...	...	...	...	...	...	...	...
Ethiopia	243	...	1	214	993	...	2	66	3	80	...	...
Faeroe Islands	...	...	...	...	...	...	...	...	11	108	7	2,850
Falkland Islands	...	...	3	...	...	...	2	...	...	...	...	...
Fiji	84	...	13	26	229	...	...	44	9	91	33	520
Finland	6,282	506	...	2,312	...	...	...	...	461	27,674	1,999	16,200
France	25,632	...	13,716	11,944	...	...	183,379	...	1,028	50,470	4,917	1,700
French Guiana	1[3]	—	7	—	2[3]	...	6	1	1	19	0.7	210
French Polynesia	56	8	17	16	92	40	25	10	1	17	1	220
Gabon	...	...	...	...	...	...	...	...	...	...	...	...
Gambia, The	19[3]	25[3]	3	82[3]	3,500[3]	...	...	3,632[3]	1	67	...	82
Gaza Strip	...	...	...	...	...	...	...	...	...	...	...	...
Germany, East	5,425	165	1,178	750	105,862	17,979	22,948	26,443	7,260	43,016	3,878	5,200
Germany, West	49,657	1,545	6,572	8,832	...	...	251,325	...	14,211[16]	...	...	2,700
Ghana	78	20[3]	74	67	163	...	254	91	7	929	70	79
Gibraltar	...	...	...	...	...	...	...	...	2	19	6	2,600
Greece	3,618	114	868	430	...	...	...	...	...	...	...	...
Greenland	...	...	...	...	...	...	...	...	1	93	...	...
Grenada	2[3]	...	...	8[3]	2[3]	...	...	9[3]	1	15	0.8	...
Guadeloupe	...	...	45	...	...	...	142	...	1	90	15	410
Guam	12[3]	...	28	...	2[3]	...	...	...	1	189	...	1,600
Guatemala	312	...	...	181	...	...	...	...	1	27	...	...
Guernsey	...	...	...	...	...	...	...	...	...	...	...	...
Guinea	...	...	1	...	...	...	...	...	1	12	...	...
Guinea-Bissau	...	...	...	...	...	...	...	...	—	—	...	...
Guyana	17	...	65	38	...	...	53	...	1	195	...	...
Haiti	...	...	...	...	...	...	...	...	1	12	...	...
Honduras	...	...	...	...	...	...	...	...	1	...	...	5
Hong Kong	3,642	538	173	2,039	27,483	7,771	...	16,829	48	2,260	1,601	1,900
Hungary	7,600	903	896	869	99,365	27,375	12,983	8,610	10,272[37]	44,610[37]	2,215[37]	4,700[37]
Iceland	691	...	380	433	...	...	...	...	208	1,208	47	9,800
India	10,391	543	19,937	258	...	...	50,094	...	...	...	...	...
Indonesia	5,042	226	...	689	...	...	...	...	30	460	2,768	...
Iran	4,835[6]	...	180	...	...	...	...	...	385	2,161	...	8
Iraq	82	...	...	...	452	...	...	...	...	...	...	...
Ireland	672	35	258	...	...	...	2,987	...	31	7,399	719	4,900
Isle of Man	...	...	...	...	...	...	...	...	...	...	...	...
Israel	1,649	232	1,100	243	11,654[8]	...	...	[8]	750	...	...	...
Italy	12,075	1,132	8,265	1,643	137,614	45,489	...	10,173	...	...	...	...
Jamaica	81	38	...	18	...	...	...	380	1	1,266	656	980
Japan	42,977	1,843	1,971	...	655,735	224,115	32,325	...	1,437[16]	69,103	7,520	1,000
Jersey	...	...	...	...	...	...	...	...	...	...	...	...
Jordan	...	...	43	...	...	...	232	...	1	70	1	6
Kampuchea	...	...	3	...	...	...	...	...	...	...	...	...
Kenya	235	...	...	...	...	...	...	...	2	511	98	34
Kiribati	...	...	...	...	...	...	...	...	1	40	...	...
Korea, North	...	...	...	...	...	...	...	...	...	...	...	...
Korea, South	33,321	2,206	870	2,191	104,411	37,959	...	8,345	137	2,510	16,513	155
Kuwait	22	...	45	3	325	...	982	34	1	281	...	55
Laos	...	...	...	...	...	...	...	...	...	...	...	...
Lebanon	...	...	...	...	...	...	...	...	...	...	...	...
Lesotho	...	...	2	...	...	...	10	...	2	...	...	...
Liberia	...	...	...	...	...	...	...	...	1	17	...	...
Libya	481[8]	...	...	[8]	2,405[8]	...	...	[8]	5	100	...	...
Liechtenstein	...	...	...	...	...	...	...	...	1	...	9	1,000
Luxembourg	274	...	337	85	...	...	...	...	...	...	...	...
Macau	...	...	...	...	...	...	...	...	4	250	120	...
Madagascar	327	63	...	91	...	...	...	...	28	49	69	...
Malawi	18	...	121	...	74	...	...	...	1	91	20	51
Malaysia	2,133	394	1,917	668	4,689	1,814	...	3,514	18	2,419	400	...
Maldives	3[3]	...	...	...	...	...	...	—	1	8	...	...
Mali	90[8]	...	...	[8]	9[8]	...	...	[8]	2	...	...	...
Malta	179	6[3]	248	99	...	...	...	...	2	274	44	2,000
Martinique	3[3]	...	1	18[3]	10	...	17	33	1	120	...	...
Mauritania	21	21	...	20	...	...	...	...	1	26	...	...
Mauritius	47	3[3]	...	33	44	5[3]	...	131	4	210	...	...
Mayotte	...	...	...	...	...	...	...	...	...	...	...	...
Mexico	2,818	...	1,964	...	...	...	...	...	457	2,546	...	140
Monaco	105[8]	...	105	[8]	792[8]	...	792	[8]	1	150	...	...
Mongolia	861[8]	...	39	[8]	6,000[8]	...	6,100	[8]	394	8,400	...	...
Montserrat	...	...	...	...	...	...	...	...	1	...	...	...
Morocco	...	...	63	...	...	...	145	...	8	448	...	...
Mozambique	87	41	...	1	5,542	4,985	...	2	2	105	...	...
Nauru	...	...	...	...	...	...	...	...	...	...	...	...
Nepal	43	—	94	—	70	—	...	—	...	...	...	...
Netherlands, The	13,324	2,321	...	...	...	...	...	...	471	38,410	4,192	12,500
Netherlands Antilles	28[12]	...	...	24[12]	...	...	...	...	1[12]	100[12]	10[12]	990[12]
New Caledonia	40	...	15	1	47	...	27	2	1	60	...	...
New Zealand	1,701	...	5,788	1,851	...	...	...	...	209	6,062	2,666	8,000
Nicaragua	...	...	...	...	...	...	...	...	...	...	...	...
Niger	...	4	...	...	8	8	...	0.1	—	—	...	...
Nigeria	1,185	274[3]	...	310	...	...	...	...	18	481	206	2
Niue	...	...	...	...	...	...	...	...	1	6	...	...
Norfolk Island	—	—	2	1	—	—	3	1	1	5	0.2	6,000

cinema					performing arts				museums			nature preservation			country
annual attendance (all cinemas)		fixed cinemas		number of long films produced	number of facilities	number of performances	annual attendance		number	annual attendance		national parks and nature reserves		zoos, botanical gardens etc. (number[2])	
number ('000,000)	per 1,000 population	number	seating capacity ('000)				number ('000)	per 1,000 population		number ('000)	per 1,000 population	number	square metres per capita[1]		
15.9[6]	3,700[6]	...	...	...	...	...	...	...	4	388	87	—	—	1	El Salvador
0.5	1,600	10	4	...	...	21[10]	16[10]	47[10]	1	...	...	...	...	...	Equatorial Guinea
...	...	40	36	...	...	253	224	7	12	...	...	10	700	3	Ethiopia
0.3	7,100	9	1	...	...	...	...	...	1	...	...	...	...	...	Faeroe Islands
18.9[18]	10,500	2	0.5	...	...	...	...	...	1	...	...	...	...	...	Falkland Islands
0.3	500	50	40	...	3	255	57	90	1	25	40	2	76	1	Fiji
9.2	1,900	368	85	13	59	10,378[10]	2,658[10]	560[10]	583	...	...	33	1,600	7	Finland
191.5	3,500	6,304	1,311	131	...	19,300[10, 31]	10,700[10, 31]	200[10, 31]	1,434[32]	11,000[15]	210[15]	26	270	79	France
...	...	...	...	...	...	...	...	...	1	12	190	—	—	...	French Guiana
0.5	4,000	6	3	...	2	33[10]	14[10]	99[10]	3	...	...	2	220	...	French Polynesia
1.1	2,100	...	...	...	...	...	...	...	1	...	...	5	14,000	...	Gabon
...	...	...	...	...	...	...	...	...	...	...	...	1	32	...	Gambia, The
...	...	...	...	...	...	...	...	...	...	...	...	...	...	...	Gaza Strip
73.5	4,400	2,089	334	16	195	75,380	27,128	1,600	664	31,484	1,900	13	12	39	Germany, East
122.8	2,000	3,664	821	83	325	51,300[10]	21,400[10]	350[10]	805[33]	35,300[33]	570[33]	45	87	126	Germany, West
4.4	400	7	16	1	11	3,672	653	61	4	69	6	8	920	3	Ghana
0.2	6,700	4	2	...	3	39	15	450	1	16	500	...	...	...	Gibraltar
57.4	5,900	...	...	47	91	14,760	5,230	560	...	3,174	321	14	63	3	Greece
...	...	...	...	...	...	...	...	...	...	...	...	2	[34]	...	Greenland
1.2	12,500	6	4	...	28	...	...	...	1	11	120	1	140	2	Grenada
0.8	2,650	...	...	...	...	92	44	130	4	...	...	1	680	...	Guadeloupe
...	...	...	...	...	1	...	...	...	4	...	...	1	510	...	Guam
9.5	1,300	115	79	...	...	206[35]	50[35]	7[35]	13	853	120	2	75	2	Guatemala
...	...	...	...	...	...	...	...	...	9	...	...	...	...	1	Guernsey
...	...	4	...	...	...	...	...	...	16	...	...	1	24	...	Guinea
...	...	...	...	...	...	...	...	...	...	...	...	...	...	...	Guinea-Bissau
13.3[6]	14,700[6]	50	40	4	3	...	...	...	2	235	300	1	120	2	Guyana
2.0	400	28	14	...	...	...	...	...	4	73[36]	16[36]	2	10	...	Haiti
...	...	...	...	...	...	...	...	...	3	22	7	4	970	3	Honduras
58.0	10,700	90	103	105	8	424[10]	362[10]	93[10]	5	565	130	...	...	3	Hong Kong
69.5	6,500	3,576	547	25	40	12,898[10]	6,094[10]	570[10]	113	7,920	740	36	400	14	Hungary
2.4[6]	10,500[6]	30[9]	11	4	...	1,331	224	980	24	...	...	21	32,000	2	Iceland
4,600.0[6]	6,800[6]	6,991[9]	4,195[9]	741	...	...	...	...	422	...	...	239	140	42	India
144.9[6]	1,000[6]	1,560	978	76	34	4,600	2,800	19	110	...	...	140	830	12	Indonesia
165.0[6]	4,200[6]	410[9]	264[9]	24	19	84[10]	...	...	44	...	...	24	680	3	Iran
...	...	84	65	2	36	743[10]	228[10]	19[10]	15	664	52	...	...	1	Iraq
18.0	5,800	177	...	2	34	10,260[10]	...	...	49	...	...	3	57	5	Ireland
...	...	...	...	...	...	...	...	...	4	...	...	...	...	2	Isle of Man
24.2	6,600	214	152	17	5	275[10, 38]	...	...	80	8,433	2,200	5	79	13	Israel
164.8	2,900	6,361	...	128	313	64,238[10]	18,055[10]	320[10]	1,122	22,912[39]	410[39]	34	91	57	Italy
...	...	...	...	...	16	839	1,143	540	5	44[36]	22[36]	2[40]	2	5	Jamaica
151	1,300	2,191	...	333	140	39,768[10]	...	...	405	41,468[41]	360[41]	50	180	109	Japan
...	...	...	...	...	...	...	...	...	5	...	...	...	...	1	Jersey
15.0	4,900	41	20	...	5	64	180	84	1	9	4	2	130	...	Jordan
...	...	...	...	...	...	...	...	...	2	...	...	1	15	...	Kampuchea
9.2	600	40	20	...	...	...	...	...	3	165	11	28	1,500	5	Kenya
...	...	...	...	...	—	23[42]	...	...	...	...	...	2	870	...	Kiribati
...	...	...	...	...	...	...	...	...	17	...	...	...	...	2	Korea, North
43.9	1,100	301	232	91	16	3,449	402	10	56	...	...	14	120	4	Korea, South
2.0[6]	1,300[6]	14	...	...	5	...	95	66	3	230	150	...	...	1	Kuwait
...	...	...	...	...	...	...	...	...	...	...	...	...	...	...	Laos
...	...	...	...	...	...	...	...	...	7	...	...	...	...	1	Lebanon
...	...	...	...	...	...	...	...	...	1	...	...	1	45	...	Lesotho
1.5	800	13	9	...	...	...	...	...	7	...	...	1	590	1	Liberia
10.2	3,500	49	22	2	14	439	160	51	26	50	16	2	340	2	Libya
...	...	...	...	...	...	...	...	...	4	...	...	6	410	...	Liechtenstein
1.1	3,000	...	...	...	...	303[43]	212[43]	580[43]	14	225	630	4	3,100	...	Luxembourg
3.0	11,700	7	8	...	4	84	...	...	1	24	92	...	...	...	Macau
...	...	...	...	...	70	140	60	7	8	135	16	14	670	3	Madagascar
1.5	300	4	2	...	2	...	...	...	2	10	2	9	1,500	...	Malaŵi
34.0	2,700	425	...	13	12	1,303	312	25	16	...	...	34	1,000	6	Malaysia
...	...	7	3	...	11	...	...	...	1	1,194	8,200	...	...	...	Maldives
...	...	...	...	1	...	...	...	...	...	...	...	6	1,100	1	Mali
1.0	3,000	22	16	...	...	...	...	...	18	562	1,700	2	1.1	2	Malta
1.1	3,450	...	...	...	...	...	...	...	5	...	...	1	2,100	...	Martinique
...	...	19	8	...	...	...	...	...	...	...	...	2	9,000	...	Mauritania
10.6	10,600	46	42	...	6	136	36	38	2	210	220	3	39	1	Mauritius
...	...	...	...	...	2	...	...	...	...	...	...	...	...	...	Mayotte
292.4	3,900	2,968	...	105	94	17,069[44]	6,549[44]	97[44]	105[32]	7,875[32, 45]	120[45]	29	120	11	Mexico
0.1	3,800	3	1	...	3	31	13	500	2	154	6,200	...	...	4	Monaco
16.7	9,400	57	...	3	17	...	3,000	1,700	4	7,400	4,400	4	24,000	...	Mongolia
...	...	1	...	...	1	16	4	360	...	...	...	...	...	...	Montserrat
39.8[6]	1,800[6]	267	162	12	...	...	...	12	...	...	...	2	17	5	Morocco
9.2[6]	700[6]	70	27	...	...	...	...	9	...	...	...	6	1,300	4	Mozambique
...	...	...	...	...	...	...	...	...	...	...	...	...	...	...	Nauru
...	...	...	...	1	16	65	...	5	...	...	...	10	590	1	Nepal
21.6	1,510	545	146	11	...	33,309	8,750	610	525	14,661	1,020	47	100	36	Netherlands, The
...	...	...	...	...	...	...	...	7[12]	...	...	...	3	625	2[12]	Netherlands Antilles
1.0	6,900	17	4	...	1	46	...	...	1	30	220	7	3,300	1	New Caledonia
...	...	172	103	9	...	2,287[10]	515[10]	120[10]	110	...	...	147	8,300	15	New Zealand
5.2	1,900	127	74	1	...	...	...	...	9	...	...	2	53	1	Nicaragua
...	...	...	...	...	...	...	...	...	1	600	110	3	590	...	Niger
8.6	100	240	...	20	23	...	...	...	18	...	...	3	90	8	Nigeria
...	...	...	...	...	...	...	...	...	...	...	...	...	...	...	Niue
10[18]	5,000	1	0.1	...	1	7	2	1,000	1	20	10,000	1	...	1	Norfolk Island

Cultural institutions (continued)

country	book publishing								public libraries			
	number of titles				number of copies ('000)				number	volumes ('000)	registered borrowers ('000)	loans per 1,000 population
	books		periodicals	pamphlets	books		periodicals	pamphlets				
	total	of which school textbooks			total	of which school textbooks						
Norway	4,152[46]	...	4,010	1,388[46]	...	...	...	...	1,395	15,966	...	...
Oman	...	...	...	...	...	...	...	...	...	...	...	...
Pacific Is., Trust Terr. of the	*93*[3]	*26*	...	*40*[3]	*47*	*11*	...	*80*	*5*[16]	*16*	...	...
Marshall Islands	...	...	...	...	...	...	...	...	...	...	...	...
Micronesia, Fed. States of	...	...	...	...	...	...	...	...	...	...	...	...
Northern Mariana Islands	...	...	...	...	...	...	...	...	...	...	...	...
Palau	...	...	...	...	...	...	...	...	...	...	...	...
Pakistan	*1,600*	...	1,461	...	...	...	...	...	98	1,340	...	6
Panama	*114*	*9*[3]	...	*57*	*38*[3]	...	...	*5*[3]	*18*	*26*	...	*29*
Papua New Guinea	...	...	72	...	...	...	...	...	1	45	...	...
Paraguay	...	...	...	...	...	...	...	...	...	...	...	...
Peru	649	4	507	55	...	...	...	...	*520*	*4,102*	...	*120*
Philippines	604	380	...	235	*2,087*[48]	...	...	*1,031*[48]	*498*[16]	...	*182*	...
Pitcairn Island	...	...	...	...	...	...	...	...	...	...	...	...
Poland	7,238	375	2,045	1,551	145,958	36,246	28,426	48,964	9,600	107,700	7,219	4,000
Portugal	7,724	732[28]	915	923	56,329	8,078[28]	...	1,613	*118*	*6,284*	*2,304*	*620*
Puerto Rico	...	...	...	...	...	...	...	...	5	822	...	...
Qatar	*316*	*219*	...	*21*	*2,100*	*1,533*	191	*105*	6	...	1	26
Réunion	49	1[3]	*53*	30	...	...	*110*	...	3	315	...	...
Romania	5,632[8]	...	435	[8]	64,608[8]	...	221,000	[8]	6,821	66,672	4,507	2,300
Rwanda	...	...	16	...	...	...	...	...	*5*	...	...	...
St. Christopher and Nevis	2[3]	—	...	3[3]	—	—	...	2[3]	2	...	...	...
St. Helena and Ascension	...	...	*2*	...	...	...	*0.5*	...	...	...	...	...
St. Lucia	*5*	*6*[8]	...	*11*	*15*	*12*[8]	...	*18*	4	...	...	...
St. Pierre and Miquelon	...	...	...	...	...	...	...	...	*3*	*15*	...	...
St. Vincent	...	...	...	...	...	...	...	...	1	...	...	...
San Marino	*14*	...	11	*1*	...	...	...	...	...	...	...	...
São Tomé and Príncipe	...	...	...	...	...	...	...	...	1	...	...	...
Saudi Arabia	*207*	—	80	*11*	...	—	...	...	*8*	...	...	...
Senegal	42[3, 8]	8[3, 8]	...	[8]	169[3, 8]	70[3, 8]	...	[3, 8]	1	7	...	...
Seychelles	*2*[3]	...	4	*31*[3]	...	...	...	...	*1*	*25*	9	*1,700*
Sierra Leone	*17*[3]	2[3]	...	*44*[3]	*9*[3]	4[3]	...	*12*[3]	*11*	*392*	...	...
Singapore	1,524[52]	389	1,506	403[52]	6,044[52]	...	...	2,352[52]	1	2,162	716	2,410
Solomon Islands	...	...	*2*	...	...	...	*4*	...	...	...	...	...
Somalia	...	...	...	...	...	...	...	...	...	...	...	...
South Africa	...	...	...	...	...	...	...	...	85	7,857	...	...
Bophuthatswana	...	...	...	...	...	...	...	...	...	...	...	...
Ciskei	...	...	...	...	...	...	...	...	...	...	...	...
Transkei	...	...	...	...	...	...	...	...	...	...	...	...
Venda	...	...	...	...	...	...	...	...	1	10	3	11
South West Africa/Namibia	...	...	*3*	...	...	...	*18*	...	8	157	...	...
Spain	26,964	2,723	*5,508*	5,174	226,334	46,724	*55,352*	47,057	*1,396*	*11,730*	*1,308*	*170*
Sri Lanka	707	111	*405*	1,244	12,340	10,895	*1,565*	5,273	*650*	...	*197*	...
Sudan, The	...	*138*[25]	25	...	...	*12,905*[25]	200	—	3	42	...	...
Suriname	...	...	*24*	...	...	...	*39*	...	2	*268*	*54*	*2,100*
Swaziland	...	...	1	...	...	...	2,600	...	1	51	...	...
Sweden	10,373[8]	...	*3,690*	[8]	...	...	...	...	397	43,760	...	*9,100*
Switzerland	11,405[8]	149[8]	*1,533*	[8]	...	...	*31,773*	...	*79*[55]	*24,000*[55]	...	*1,400*
Syria	119	1[3]	*48*	—	553	...	*454*	—	...	...	...	...
Taiwan	9,256	...	2,661	...	...	...	...	...	148	...	...	...
Tanzania	147	5[3]	*69*	99	...	...	*646*	...	*1*	*404*	*10*	*9*
Thailand	6,186	298	990	633	...	...	...	...	*375*	*1,599*	*31*	...
Togo	...	...	...	...	...	...	...	...	1	8	...	...
Tokelau	...	...	...	...	...	...	...	...	*1*	*0.2*	...	...
Tonga	*33*	5	...	*287*	*0.4*	*0.1*	...	...	...	...	...	...
Trinidad and Tobago	*101*	7	...	*85*	...	...	...	...	*1*	*68*	*1*	*130*
Tunisia	...	*172*	*230*	—	...	*6,000*	...	...	321	1,196	71	*170*
Turkey	6,610	387	...	259	...	...	...	...	632	6,168	486	40
Turks and Caicos Islands	...	...	...	...	...	...	...	...	*1*	*7*	...	*980*
Tuvalu	...	...	...	...	...	...	...	...	...	...	...	...
Uganda	...	...	...	...	...	...	...	...	*1*	*73*	*157*	*31*
U.S.S.R.	53,838	2,748[8]	5,358	28,751	1,401,861	303,716[8]	4,258,182	567,572	133,800	2,046,600	224,000	...
United Arab Emirates	84	63	*8*	—	1,590	1,535	*25*	—	2	...	...	...
United Kingdom	47,445	1,440	6,408	3,536	...	...	...	...	*160*	*131,338*	...	*11,300*
United States	51,058[62]	...	*59,609*	...	...	...	...	...	10,154	509,332	...	4,300
Uruguay	566	158	545	333	...	...	...	...	54	...	...	...
Vanuatu	...	...	...	...	...	...	...	...	*1*	*12*	*0.7*	...
Venezuela	*3,596*	...	160	*604*	*1,194*	...	4,649	...	*23*	*977*	*66*	*160*
Vietnam	*1,495*[8]	*300*[8]	*173*	[8]	*37,117*[8]	*4,037*[8]	323	[8]	*316*	*4,879*	...	...
Virgin Islands (U.S)	...	...	...	...	...	...	...	...	6	224	...	...
Wallis and Futuna	...	...	...	...	...	...	...	...	...	...	...	...
West Bank	...	...	...	...	...	...	...	...	...	...	...	...
Western Sahara	...	...	...	...	...	...	...	...	...	...	...	...
Western Samoa	*79*	...	...	*156*	*39*	...	...	*43*	1	61	...	...
Yemen (Aden)	...	...	...	...	...	...	...	...	2	40	...	...
Yemen (Ṣan'ā')	...	...	...	...	...	...	...	...	...	...	...	...
Yugoslavia	8,506	1,564	1,474	2,425	50,013	22,398	31,881	15,941	1,972	26,424	...	1,200
Zaire	*194*[3]	5[3]	...	*37*[3]	...	...	...	...	11	177	*9*	*1*
Zambia	454	215[3]	...	—	*235*[64]	...	...	—	11	240	*18*	*28*
Zimbabwe	249	69	...	284	263[3, 64]	...	...	—	20	523	...	...

[1]Calculations based on statutory areas, whether of land or water. [2]Excludes zoological and aquatic collections in museums. [3]First editions only. [4]Opera and ballet, drama, and variety only. [5]School textbooks, university theses, and government publications only. [6]Excludes drive-ins, mobile units, or both. [7]Excludes school textbooks and children's books. [8]Books includes pamphlets. [9]16-millimetre data not available. [10]Professional only. [11]214 reporting. [12]Netherlands Antilles includes Aruba. [13]14 reporting. [14]Ministry of Flemish culture museums only. [15]National museums only. [16]Library service points. [17]370 reporting. [18]Attendance in 000's [19]Drama, ballet, and dance only. [20]Drama, opera, ballet, and dance only. [21]818 reporting. [22]Amateur ballet, dance, and drama only. [23]Film projection units. [24]57 reporting. [25]Includes children's books. [26]Excludes some Turkish publications. [27]Includes university theses. [28]Includes school pamphlets. [29]Royal theatre and regional theatres only. [30]263 reporting. [31]Drama and opera only. [32]National and public museums only. [33]Museums with an annual attendance of 20,000 or more only.

cinema					performing arts				museums			nature preservation			country
annual attendance (all cinemas)		fixed cinemas		number of long films produced	number of facilities	number of performances	annual attendance		number	annual attendance		national parks and nature reserves		zoos, botanical gardens etc. (number[2])	
number ('000,000)	per 1,000 population	number	seating capacity ('000)				number ('000)	per 1,000 population		number ('000)	per 1,000 population	number	square metres per capita[1]		
14.6	3,500	467	141	8	13	5,197[10]	1,158[10]	280[10]	195	4,573[47]	1,100[47]	55	2,900	7	Norway
0.9	1,100	12	1	...	...	...	...	...	1	...	...	1	190	...	Oman
...	...	52	...	...	...	...	...	...	5	...	...	...	...	...	Pacific Is., Trust Terr. of the
...	...	...	...	...	...	...	...	...	...	...	...	1	93	...	Marshall Islands
...	...	...	...	...	...	...	...	...	...	...	...	—	—	...	Micronesia, Fed. States of
...	...	...	...	...	...	...	...	...	...	...	...	2	370	...	Northern Mariana Islands
...	...	...	...	...	...	...	...	...	...	...	...	—	—	...	Palau
182.0	2,200	630	305	82	12	...	48[10]	0.6[10]	10	561	7	52	650	6	Pakistan
7.1	4,800	...	...	...	1	55	...	...	10	...	...	6	3,000	2	Panama
...	...	...	...	...	7	122	265	91	2	100	32	2	9	3	Papua New Guinea
...	...	...	...	...	...	...	...	...	18	...	...	9	3,300	1	Paraguay
32.9	1,900	425	...	1	35	2,388	...	...	9	221	13	11	1,200	2	Peru
...	...	...	...	136	6[49]	121[49]	29[49]	0.6[49]	63	...	...	26	72	5	Philippines
...	...	...	...	...	...	...	...	...	...	...	...	...	...	...	Pitcairn Island
109.7	3,000	1,796	484	35	96	120,000[10]	33,557[10]	920[10]	511	18,131	500	15	30	26	Poland
24.3[6]	2,400[6]	477	197	10	76	3,707	1,126	120	146	1,910[50]	200[50]	12[51]	380[51]	10	Portugal
...	...	165	...	...	...	...	...	...	24	...	...	2	1	8	Puerto Rico
0.5	1,800	4	4	1	1	4	1	5	1	60	300	1	...	1	Qatar
...	...	...	...	...	...	...	...	...	3	111	230	...	...	...	Réunion
185.8	8,200	5,611	256[6]	26	154	55,056[10]	19,493[10]	860[10]	456	16,015	710	9	43	9	Romania
0.5	100	12	4	1	9	31	58	12	4	...	...	2	430	...	Rwanda
...	...	3	...	...	...	...	...	...	...	...	...	...	...	...	St. Christopher and Nevis
53.0[18]	8,800	2	1	...	...	1	1	170	1	...	...	...	...	...	St. Helena and Ascension
...	...	6	...	...	...	...	...	...	1	1	8	1	120	...	St. Lucia
...	...	...	...	...	...	...	...	...	1	4	640	...	...	...	St. Pierre and Miquelon
...	...	2	...	...	...	...	...	...	...	...	...	...	...	1	St. Vincent
0.1	4,600	7	3	...	1	26[10]	10[10]	460[10]	11	741	35,000	...	...	...	San Marino
...	...	...	...	...	...	...	...	...	...	...	...	...	...	...	São Tomé and Príncipe
...	...	...	...	...	94	89[42]	90[42]	11[42]	1	37	5	1	400	2	Saudi Arabia
3.6[6]	700[6]	60[9]	...	...	1	122[10]	52[10]	9[10]	3	22	4	9	3,300	4	Senegal
...	...	...	...	...	2	6[42]	3[42]	40[42]	1	8	130	3	3,400	...	Seychelles
...	...	...	...	...	...	...	...	...	1	178	55	1	250	1	Sierra Leone
27.4	10,800	51	58	4	3	523	645	270	3	940	390	1	10	4	Singapore
0.1[6]	300[6]	2	1	...	...	3	1	5	1	29	150	1	46	...	Solomon Islands
...	...	...	...	...	...	...	...	...	1	...	...	1	570	...	Somalia
31.2	1,200	260	...	12	51	3,597[53]	1,348[53]	54[53]	22[54]	2,477[54]	96[54]	136	2,000	35	South Africa
...	...	...	...	...	...	...	...	...	...	...	...	2	380	...	Bophuthatswana
...	...	...	...	...	...	...	...	...	...	...	...	8	360	...	Ciskei
...	...	...	...	...	...	...	...	...	...	...	...	2	22	...	Transkei
...	...	...	...	...	...	...	...	...	1	...	...	1	75	...	Venda
...	...	...	...	...	...	...	...	...	9	...	...	9	60,000	1	South West Africa/Namibia
141.4	3,700	4,861	...	99	366	18,862	6,702	180	554	11,697	320	56	440	22	Spain
41.6[6]	2,700[6]	329	...	33	22	1,002[42]	600[42]	41[42]	9	466	34	37	400	4	Sri Lanka
4.4[6]	200[6]	56[9]	97[9]	1	...	...	...	...	5	157	9	3	810	2	Sudan, The
...	...	...	...	...	...	...	...	...	3	...	...	9	15,000	1	Suriname
...	...	...	...	...	...	...	...	...	1	...	...	4	610	...	Swaziland
17.2	2,100	1,236	315	15	45	20,684	2,604	317	167	12,200	1,500	67	1,800	18	Sweden
19.3	3,000	441	134	22	147	25,735	5,811	920	585	...	...	19	190	32	Switzerland
12.4	1,300	84	48	24	5	411	165	20	16	321[56]	42[56]	...	...	...	Syria
147.0	7,900	717	543	...	...	...	...	...	10	...	...	28	84	3	Taiwan
3.8	200	34	15	...	5	21	15	1	6	119[57]	7[57]	15	4,900	...	Tanzania
...	...	651[9]	439[9]	55	...	...	...	...	64	...	...	45	530	3	Thailand
...	...	...	...	...	...	...	...	...	1	48	21	7	1,600	...	Togo
...	...	...	...	...	...	...	...	...	...	...	...	...	...	...	Tokelau
0.1	1,000	3	2	...	...	...	...	...	...	...	...	5	320	...	Tonga
...	...	72	57	...	...	49[42]	...	...	1	8	7	8	140	1	Trinidad and Tobago
4.4	700	79	38	...	12	598	164	26	19	563[58]	90[58]	3	46	3	Tunisia
56.3	1,159	853	476	72	...	3,358[10, 59]	1,145[10, 59]	24[10, 59]	123	5,376	111	15	58	7	Turkey
...	...	3	1	...	...	3	0.6	100	...	...	...	...	...	...	Turks and Caicos Islands
...	...	...	...	...	...	...	...	...	...	...	...	...	...	...	Tuvalu
2.3[6]	200[6]	17[9]	10[9]	...	...	...	...	...	16	...	...	18	900	2	Uganda
4,060.2	14,800	151,300	25,387	156	772	281,800[10]	145,900[10]	540[10]	1,832	174,800	640	141	540	144	U.S.S.R.
7.1	10,300	74	29	...	1	12[35]	36[35]	40[36]	2	...	...	...	...	2	United Arab Emirates
62.0	1,100	1,327	505	39	404	...	40,242[10, 20]	720[10, 20]	1,768[60]	c. 52,000[61]	920	57	270	155	United Kingdom
1,053.1	4,500	16,032	5,611	396	...	21,596	40,200	170	4,440	329,083	1,500	242	2,700	652	United States
6.1	2,100	120	80	2	25	3,097	...	...	59	...	...	6	100	4	Uruguay
0.1	1,000	3	1	...	...	...	...	...	...	...	...	...	...	...	Vanuatu
22.8[6]	4,700[6]	535	...	12	9	372	206	16	133	...	...	34	4,300	12	Venezuela
273.2	5,200	210	178	15	68	...	42,600[10]	770[10]	9	1,918[63]	37[63]	12	27	2	Vietnam
...	...	...	...	...	...	...	...	...	5	811	7,700	2	660	1	Virgin Islands (U.S.)
...	...	...	...	...	...	...	...	...	...	...	...	...	...	...	Wallis and Futuna
...	...	...	...	...	...	...	...	...	...	...	...	4	...	...	West Bank
...	...	...	...	...	...	...	...	...	...	...	...	...	...	...	Western Sahara
0.5	3,200	6	6	...	...	9	2	11	...	...	...	1	180	1	Western Samoa
5.6[6]	3,100[6]	21	21	...	...	...	...	...	5	...	...	...	...	...	Yemen (Aden)
14.5[6]	2,500[6]	35	28	...	...	...	...	...	...	...	...	...	...	...	Yemen (Ṣan'ā')
89.0	3,860	1,307	440	29	149	18,506	4,906	220	387	11,661	520	20	140	19	Yugoslavia
...	...	...	...	...	4	...	...	...	4	...	...	9	2,700	4	Zaire
1.6	300	12	4	...	...	...	...	...	4	163[36]	30[36]	19	10,000	1	Zambia
...	...	...	...	...	...	...	...	...	13	...	...	17	3,400	4	Zimbabwe

[34]13,400,000 square metres per capita; a single national park comprises about one-third of the area of Greenland. [35]Drama only. [36]3 reporting. [37]Public educational libraries include service points and trade union libraries. [38]Opera and ballet only. [39]1,083 reporting. [40]Marine parks only. [41]400 reporting. [42]Amateur only. [43]Two facilities only. [44]Excludes amateur opera and musical comedy. [45]77 reporting. [46]Excludes school text material. [47]139 reporting. [48]Books received by the national library only. [49]Metropolitan Manila only. [50]117 reporting. [51]Excludes the Azores and Madeira. [52]Excludes government publications. [53]Performances of state-subsidized regional performing arts councils only. [54]Museums designated "declared cultural institutions" only. [55]Public libraries with 50,000 or more volumes only. [56]13 reporting. [57]5 reporting. [58]15 reporting. [59]State theatres only. [60]1980. [61]1982 estimate. [62]Excludes government publications, books sold only by subscription, dissertations, and pamphlets. [63]8 reporting. [64]School textbooks and government publications only.

BIBLIOGRAPHY AND SOURCES

The following list indicates the principal sources used in the compilation of *Britannica World Data.* It is by no means a complete list, either for international or for national sources, but is indicative only of the range of materials to which reference has been made in preparing this compilation. For example, in addition to the kinds of works cited below, reference has also been made to the constitutions of each country, to the publications of its central or commercial banks, to unpublished information received in correspondence from the countries, and to other more specialized sources.

International Statistical Sources

Africana Publishing Co. *Africa Contemporary Record* (annual).

Asian Development Bank. *Key Indicators of Developing Member Countries of ADB* (annual, with supplements).

AT&T. *The World's Telephones* (annual).

Billboard Ltd. *World Radio TV Handbook* (annual).

British Petroleum. *BP Statistical Review of World Energy* (annual).

Caribbean Community and Common Market. *Caricom Statistics Digest* (annual).

Council for Mutual Economic Assistance (Comecon). *Statistichesky Yezhegodnik Stran-Chlenov Soveta Economicheskoy Vzaimopomoshchi* (Statistical Yearbook of the Council for Mutual Economic Assistance).

Europa Publications Ltd. *Africa South of the Sahara* (annual); *The Europa Year Book* (2 vol.); *The Far East and Australasia* (annual); *The Middle East and North Africa* (annual); *South America, Central America, and the Caribbean* (annual).

European Communities. *ACP: Statistical Yearbook; Basic Statistics* (annual).

Food and Agriculture Organization. *Food Balance Sheets* (irreg.); *Production Yearbook; Trade Yearbook; World Census of Agriculture* (decennial); *Yearbook of Fishery Statistics; Yearbook of Forest Products.*

Her Majesty's Stationery Office. *Yearbook of the Commonwealth.*

Holmes & Meier Publishers. *Latin America and Caribbean Contemporary Record* (annual); *Middle East Contemporary Survey* (annual).

Instituts d'Émission d'Outre-Mer et des Départements d'Outre-Mer (France). *Rapports d'Activité, Bulletin trimestriel.*

Inter-American Development Bank. *Economic and Social Progress in Latin America* (annual).

Inter-Parliamentary Union. *World Directory of Parliaments* (annual).

International Air Transport Association. *World Air Transport Statistics* (annual).

International Bank for Reconstruction and Development/The World Bank. *World Bank Atlas* (annual); *World Debt Tables* (annual); *World Development Report* (annual); *World Tables* (2 vol. [irreg.]).

International Civil Aviation Organization. *Civil Aviation Statistics of the World* (annual); *Digest of Statistics.*

International Institute for Strategic Studies. *The Military Balance* (annual).

International Labour Organisation. *Year Book of Labour Statistics.*

International Monetary Fund. *Exchange Arrangements and Exchange Restrictions* (annual); *Government Finance Statistics Yearbook; International Financial Statistics* (monthly, with supplements and yearbook).

International Road Federation. *Road and Motor Vehicle Statistics* (annual); *World Road Statistics* (annual).

Jane's Publishing Co. *Jane's World Railways* (annual).

Lloyd's Register of Shipping. *Lloyd's Register of Shipping: Statistical Tables* (annual).

Longman Group Ltd. *Keesing's Contemporary Archives* (monthly).

Macmillan Press Ltd. *The Statesman's Year-Book.*

Middle East Economic Digest Ltd. *Africa Economic Digest* (semimonthly); *Middle East Economic Digest* (semimonthly).

Mining Journal. *Mining Annual Review.*

Nordic Council. *Yearbook of Nordic Statistics.*

Official Airline Guides, Inc. *Official Airline Guide* (monthly).

Organization of Eastern Caribbean States. *Annual Digest of Statistics.*

Organization for Economic Cooperation and Development. *Economic Surveys* (annual); *Financing and External Debt of Developing Countries* (annual); *National Accounts of Developing Countries* (irreg.).

Oxford University Press. *World Christian Encyclopedia* (David B. Barrett, ed. [1982]).

Pacific Publications. *Pacific Islands Year Book* (irreg.).

PennWell Publishing Co. *International Petroleum Encyclopedia* (annual).

René Moreux et Cie. *Marchés tropicaux & Méditerranéens* (semimonthly).

South Pacific Commission. *Key Economic Indicators* (occasional); *South Pacific Economies: Statistical Summary* (biennial).

United Nations (UN). *Compendium of Human Settlements Statistics* (irreg.); *Compendium of Social Statistics* (irreg.); *Construction Statistics Yearbook; Demographic Yearbook; International Trade Statistics Yearbook; Energy Statistics Yearbook; Industrial Statistics Yearbook* (2 vol.); *Monthly Bulletin of Statistics; Population Studies* (irreg.); *National Accounts Statistics* (3 vol.; annual); *Population and Vital Statistics Report* (quarterly); *Statistical Yearbook; Supplement to the Statistical Yearbook and the Monthly Bulletin of Statistics* (quinquennial); *World Population Prospects, Estimates and Projections as Assessed in 1982.*

UN: Conference on Trade and Development. *Handbook of International Trade and Development Statistics* (annual); *The Least Developed Countries, 1984 Report* (2 vol.; 1984).

UN: Economic Commission for Africa. *African Statistical Yearbook; Demographic and Related Socio-Economic Data Sheets for ECA Member States* (1982); *Survey of Economic and Social Conditions in Africa* (irreg.).

UN: Economic Commission for Europe. *Annual Bulletin of Housing and Building Statistics for Europe; Annual Bulletin of Transport Statistics for Europe.*

UN: Economic Commission for Latin America. *Economic Survey of Latin America* (2 vol.; annual); *Statistical Yearbook for Latin America.*

UN: Economic and Social Commission for Asia and the Pacific. *Foreign Trade Statistics of Asia and the Pacific* (annual); *Statistical Indicators for Asia and the Pacific* (quarterly); *Statistical Yearbook for Asia and the Pacific.*

UN: Economic and Social Commission for Western Asia. *Population Bulletin* (irreg.); *The Population Situation in the ECWA Region* (irreg.); *Statistical Abstract of the Region of the Economic and Social Commission for Western Asia* (annual).

UN: Educational, Scientific, and Cultural Organization. *Statistical Yearbook; Estimates and Projections of Illiteracy* (1978).

United States: Central Intelligence Agency, *The World Factbook* (annual); Dept. of Commerce, *Foreign Economic Trends* (irreg.), *Overseas Business Reports* (annual), *World Population* (annual); Dept. of Energy, *International Energy Annual;* Dept. of Health and Human Services, *Social Security Programs Throughout the World* (biennial); Dept. of Interior, *Minerals Yearbook* (3 vol.); Dept. of State, *Background Notes* (irreg.).

Vatican (Central Statistics Office of the Church). *Statistical Yearbook of the Church.*

West India Committee and FT International. *The Caribbean Handbook* (annual).

World Health Organization. *World Health Statistics Annual.*

World Priorities. *World Military and Social Expenditures* (Ruth Leger Sivard, ed. [annual]).

World Tourism Organization. *World Tourism Statistics* (annual).

National Statistical Sources

Afghanistan. *Economic and Social Indicators* (triennial); *First Seven-Year Economic and Social Development Plan, 1355–1361* (*March 1976–March 1983*)*; Preliminary Results of the First Afghan Population Census, 1979; Review of the General Socio-economic Situation in the Democratic Republic of Afghanistan During 1358* (*21 March 1979–20 March 1980*)*; Statistical Year Book.*

Albania. *Directives of the 8th Congress of the PLA for the 7th Five-Year Plan* (*1981–85*) *of Economic and Cultural Development of the PSR of Albania; Portrait of Albania* (1982); *Vjetari statistikor R P SH* (Statistical Yearbook of the People's Republic of Albania [annual]); *40 années d'Albanie socialiste* (1984).

Algeria. *Algeria: A Country Study* (1979); *Annuaire statistique; Recensement général de la population et de l'habitat, 1977.*

American Samoa. *Annual Report of the Governor of American Samoa to the Secretary of the Department of the Interior; Population of American Samoa* (ESCAP; Country Monograph Series No. 7.1 [1979]); *1980 Census of Population and Housing* (U.S.); *Statistical Bulletin* (annual).

Andorra. *Recull Estadístic* (1985).

Angola. *Angola: A Country Study* (1979); *Anuário Estatístico; Recenseamento Geral da População, 1960; Situação Economica e Financeira de Angola* (annual).

Anguilla. *Abstract of Statistics, 1960–1982.*

Antigua. *Statistical Yearbook.*

Argentina. *Anuario estadístico de la República Argentina; Boletín estadístico trimestral* (quarterly); *Censo nacional de población y vivienda, 1980; Comercio exterior* (annual); *Encuesta permanente de hogares* (irreg.); *Estadistica Mensual* (monthly); *Indicadores industriales* (annual).

Aruba. *See* Netherlands Antilles.

Australia. *Integrated Economic Censuses and Surveys* (1980–81); *Manufacturing Establishments: Details of Operations by Industry Class* (annual); *Monthly Summary of Statistics, Australia; National Income and Expenditure* (annual); *Overseas Trade* (annual); *Social Indicators* (irreg.); *Yearbook of the Commonwealth of Australia; 1981 Census of Population and Housing.*

Austria. *Der Aussenhandel Österreichs* (Austrian Foreign Trade [quarterly]); *Österreichisches Jahrbuch* (annual); *Österreichs Volkseinkommen* (Austrian National Income); *Sozialstatistische Daten 1970–1980; Statistisches Handbuch* (annual); *Volkserzählung, 1981.*

Bahamas, The. *External Trade Statistics, Report* (annual); *Industrial Production Statistics* (annual); *Quarterly Statistical Summary; Social Statistics Report* (annual); *Statistical Abstract* (annual); *Vital Statistics Report* (annual); *Wholesale and Retail Trade Report* (annual); *1980 Census of Population and Housing.*

Bahrain. *Statistical Abstract* (annual); *1981 Census of Bahrain.*

Bangladesh. *Bangladesh Population Census, 1981; Monthly Statistical Bulletin of Bangladesh; Population of Bangladesh* (ESCAP; Country Monograph Series No. 8 [1981]); *Statistical Pocketbook of Bangladesh* (annual); *Statistical Yearbook of Bangladesh.*

Barbados. *Barbados Economic Report* (annual); *Monthly Digest of Statistics; Report on the Census of Production, 1981.*

Belgium. *Annuaire statistique de la Belgique; Bulletin du commerce extérieur* (annual); *Bulletin de statistique* (monthly); *Recensement de la population et des logements au 1er mars 1981; Statistiques demographiques* (quarterly).

Belize. *Abstract of Statistics* (annual); *Belize Economic Report* (1984); *Labour Force Survey (1983–84); 1980–81 Population Census of the Commonwealth Caribbean, Belize.*

Benin. *Annuaire statistique; Recensement des Entreprises 1980* (2 parts); *Recensement général de la population et de l'habitation* (1979).

Bermuda. *Bermuda Digest of Statistics* (annual); *The Economic Structure and National Accounts of Bermuda* (annual); *Report of the Population Census, 1980; Report of the Registrar General* (annual).

Bhutan. *Development in a Himalayan Kingdom* (A World Bank Country Study [1983]).

Bolivia. *Bolivia en cifras, 1980; Censo Nacional de población y vivienda de 1976; Resumen estadístico* (annual).

Botswana. *1981 Population and Housing Census; Statistical Abstract* (annual).

Brazil. *Anuário Econômico-Fiscal; Anuário Estatístico do Brasil; Brazil: A Country Study* (1983); *Foreign Trade of Brazil* (annual); *Indicadores Sociais* (1979); *IX Recenseamento Geral do Brasil, 1980.*

British Virgin Islands. *Census of the British Virgin Islands, 12th May 1980 (Provisional); Statistical Abstract* (irreg.); *Trade Report* (1978–80).

Brunei. *Annual Report; Brunei Statistical Yearbook; Report on the Census of Population, 1971.*

Bulgaria. *Prebroyavane—1975; resultati, perspektivi* (Census of Population—1975: Results, Perspectives); *Statisticheskii yezhgodnik* (Statistical Yearbook).

Burkina Faso (Upper Volta). *Annuaire Statistique; Recensement général de la population du 10 au 20 decembre 1985; Statistiques Sociales* (Dec. 1984).

Burma. *Burma: A Country Study* (1983); 1983 *Population Census (Advance Release); Statistical Abstract, 1976.*

Burundi. *Annuaire statistique; Recensement général de la population, 16–30 août 1979.*

Cameroon. *Note annuelle de statistique; Recensement général de la population et de l'habitat d'avril 1976; Tableaux économiques du Cameroun* (1983).

Canada. *Canada Year Book* (biennial); *Canadian Statistical Review* (monthly); *Census of Agriculture, 1981; National Income and Expenditure Accounts* (quarterly); *1981 Census of Canada.*

Cape Verde. *Boletim Trimestral de Estatística* (quarterly).

Central African Republic. *Annuaire statistique; Recensement général de la population de décembre 1975.*

Chad. *Annuaire statistique.*

Chile. *Agricultura y pesca* (annual); *Anuario de minería; Chile: A Country Study* (1982); *Chile XV censo nacional de población y de vivienda, 21 de abril 1982; Compendio estadístico* (annual); *Cuentas nacionales de Chile, 1960–1980; Plan nacional indicativo de desarrollo* (quinquennial).

China, People's Republic of. *Almanac of China's Economy, 1983* (irreg.); *China: A Country Study* (1981); *China Official Yearbook; People's Republic of China Year-Book; China Socialist Development* (A World Bank Country Study; 3 vol. [1983]); *Major Figures by 10 Percent Sampling on the 1982 Census of the People's Republic of China; Statistical Yearbook of China; Yearbook of the Encyclopedia of China.*

Christmas Island. *Annual Report; Census of Population and Housing, 30 June 1981.*

Cocos (Keeling) Islands. *Annual Report; Census of Population and Housing, 30 June 1981.*

Colombia. *Boletín mensual de estadística* (monthly); *Colombia estadística* (annual); *Cuentas nacionales de Colombia, 1970–1981; Industria manufacturera* (annual); *XIV Censo nacional de población y III de vivienda, octubre 24 de 1973.*

Comoros. *The Comoros: Current Economic Situation and Prospects* (A World Bank Country Study [1983]); *Plan interimaire de développement économique et sociale (1983–1986); Recensement général de la population et de l'habitat 15 septembre 1980.*

Congo, People's Republic of the. *Annuaire statistique; Recensement général de la population de 1974.*

Cook Islands. *Cook Islands Census of Population and Dwellings, 1981; Cook Islands Quarterly Statistical Bulletin.*

Costa Rica. *Anuario estadístico; Censos Nacionales de 1973; Costa Rica: A Country Study* (1984).

Cuba. *Anuario estadístico; Censo de población y viviendas, 1981; Compendio estadístico de Cuba* (annual); *Cuba Quarterly Economic Report.*

Cyprus. *Census of Industrial Production* (annual); *Economic Report* (annual); *Statistical Abstract* (annual); *Statistics of Imports and Exports* (annual).

Czechoslovakia. *Czechoslovakia: A Country Study* (1981); *Statistická ročenka Československé Socialistické Republiky* (Statistical Yearbook of the Czechoslovak Socialist Republic); *Sčítání lidu, domů a bytů 1980* (Census of Population and Housing).

Denmark. *Denmarks vareindførsel og-udførsel, 1982* (External Trade of Denmark by Commodities and Countries); *Folke- og boligtaellingen, 1981* (Population and Housing Census); *Statistisk årbog* (Statistical Yearbook).

Djibouti. *Annuaire statistique de Djibouti.*

Dominica. *Statistical Digest.*

Dominican Republic. *República Dominicana en cifras* (annual); *VI Censo nacional de población y vivienda, 1981.*

Ecuador. *Censo agropecuario, 1974; Encuesta anual de manufactura y minería; Serie estadística* (quinquennial); *IV Censo de población: III de vivienda resultados anticipados por muestreo* (1982).

Egypt. *Census of Population and Housing, 1976; Egypt: A Country Study* (1982); *Statistical Yearbook.*

El Salvador. *Anuario estadístico; Censos económicos, 1979 (Manufactura diversa; Agroindustrias; Comercio y servicios; Electricidad, construcción, transporte comercial); El Salvador en cifras* (annual).

Ethiopia. *Ethiopia: A Country Study* (1980); *Ethiopia 1984 Population and Housing Census; Statistical Abstract* (annual).

Faeroe Islands. *Årbog for Faerøerne* (Yearbook for the Faeroe Islands).

Fiji. *Annual Employment Survey; Census of Industrial Production* (annual); *Current Economic Statistics* (quarterly); *Overseas Trade of Fiji* (annual); *Report on the Census of the Population, 1976.*

Finland. *Annual Statistics of Agriculture; Economic Survey* (annual); *Population and Housing Census, 1980; Statistical Yearbook of Finland.*

France. *Annuaire statistique de la France; Les Comptes de l'industrie* (1981); *Données sociales* (irreg.); *Le Mouvement économique en France, 1949–1979; Recensement général de la population de 1982; Métropole.*

French Guiana. *Annuaire statistique de la Guyane; Bulletin trimestriel de statistique; Recensement général de la population dans les Départements d'outre-mer en 9 mars 1982, Guyane.*

French Polynesia. *Bilan statistique de l'année; Comptes économiques* (quadrennial); *Résultats du recensement de la population de la Polynésie Française, 15 Octobre 1983; Te avei'a: Bulletin d'information statistique* (quarterly).

Gabon. *Situation économique, financière et sociale de la République Gabonaise* (annual).

Gaza Strip. *Judaea, Samaria, and Gaza Area Statistics Quarterly; Palestinian Statistical Abstract* (annual).

Germany, East. *Statistisches Jahrbuch der Deutschen Demokratischen Republik.*

Germany, West. *Area Handbook for Germany* (1981); *Statistisches Jahrbuch für die Bundesrepublik Deutschland; Volkszählung vom 27 Mai 1970* (Census of Population).

Ghana. *Economic Survey* (biennial); *Ghana: An Official Handbook* (1977); *Industrial Statistics* (biennial); *Population Census of Ghana, 1984.*

Gibraltar. *Abstract of Statistics* (annual); *Census of Gibraltar, 1981.*

Greece. *Recensement des industries manufacturières: Artisanat, du commerce et autres services* (1978); *Recensement de la population et des habitations, 1981; Statistical Yearbook of Greece.*

Greenland. *Grønland* (annual); *Grønlands befolkning* (Greenland Population [annual]).

Grenada. *Abstract of Statistics* (annual); *Annual Digest of Trade Statistics.*

Guadeloupe. *Annuaire statistique de la Guadeloupe; Comptes économiques* (quinquennial); *Recensement général de la population dans les Departements d'Outre-mer en 9 mars 1982, Guadeloupe.*

Guam. *Annual Economic Review; Annual Report to the Secretary of the Interior; Census of Agriculture* (quinquennial); *1980 Census of Population and Housing.*

Guatemala. *Anuario estadístico; Censos nacionales, 1981: IX de población—IV de habitación; Guatemala: A Country Study* (1983).

Guernsey. *Guernsey Census 1976.*

Guinea, Republic of. *Population et développement en République Populaire Revolutionnaire de Guinée* (1980); *Situation Économique et Conjoncturelle au 31 decembre 1985 et éléments sur la mise en oeuvre de la réform économique au cours du première trimestre 1986.*

Guinea-Bissau. *Boletim Trimestral de Estatística; Recenseamento Geral da População e da Habitação, 16 de Abril de 1979.*

Guyana. *Annual Statistical Abstract.*

Haiti. *Bulletin trimestriel de statistique; Guide économique de la République d'Haiti* (1977); *Haiti: A Country Profile* (1981); *Résultats préliminaires du recensement général (Septembre 1982).*

Honduras. *Anuario estadístico; Censo nacional agropecuario, 1974; Comercio externo* (annual); *Honduras: A Country Profile* (1981); *Honduras en cifras* (annual).

Hong Kong. *Annual Digest of Statistics; Hong Kong* (annual); *Hong Kong 1981 Census; Hong Kong in Figures* (annual); *Hong Kong Social and Economic Trends* (irreg.); *1978 Survey of Industrial Production.*

Hungary. *Statisztikai évkönyv* (Statistical Yearbook); *1980, Évi népszámlálás* (Census of Population).

Iceland. *Tölfraedihandbók* (Statistical Abstract of Iceland [irreg.]); *Verslunarskýrslur* (External Trade [annual]).

India. *Census of India, 1981; Economic Survey* (annual); *India: A Reference Annual; Statistical Abstract* (annual).

Indonesia. *Agricultural Census, 1973; Indikator ekonomi* (monthly); *Indonesia: An Official Handbook* (1984); *Sensus penduduk Indonesia, 1980* (Census of Population); *Statistical Yearbook of Indonesia.*

Iran. *General Census of Population and Housing, November 1976; A Statistical Reflection of the Islamic Republic of Iran* (annual); *Statistical Yearbook of the Islamic Republic of Iran.*

Iraq. *Iraq: A Country Study* (1979); *Statistical Abstract* (annual).

Ireland. *Census of Population of Ireland, 1981; National Income and Expenditure* (annual); *Statistical Abstract* (annual).

Isle of Man. *Isle of Man 1981 Census Report; Isle of Man Digest of Economic and Social Statistics* (annual).

Israel. *1983 Census of Population and Housing; Israel: A Country Study* (1979); *Statistical Abstract* (annual).

Italy. *Annuario di statistica agraria: Annuario di statistica forestale; Annuario di statistiche demografiche; Annuario di statistiche industriali; Annuario statistico dell'istruzione; Annuario statistico Italiano; Statistiche sociali* (1981); *12 Censimento general della popolazione, 1981.*

Ivory Coast. *Annuaire statistique; La Côte d'Ivoire en chiffres* (annual); *L'Économie Ivoirienne* (annual).

Jamaica. *Economic and Social Survey* (annual); *Statistical Abstract* (annual); *Statistical Yearbook of Jamaica.*

Japan. *Establishment Census of Japan, 1981; Japan: A Country Study* (1983); *Japan Statistical Yearbook; Statistical Indicators on Social Life* (annual); *Statistics on Japanese Industries, 1980; 1985 Population Census of Japan.*

Jersey. *Report of the Census for 1981; Statistical Digest* (annual).

Jordan. *Census 1979; Family Expenditure Survey* (1980); *Jordan: A Country Study* (1979); *National Accounts* (irreg.); *Statistical Yearbook.*

Kenya. *Economic Survey* (annual); *Kenya Statistical Digest* (quarterly); *Statistical Abstract* (annual).

Kiribati. *National Development Plan, 1979–1982; Report on the 1978 Census of Population and Housing.*

Korea, North. *North Korea: A Country Study* (1981).

Korea, South. *Korea Statistical Yearbook; Social Indicators in Korea* (1981); *South Korea: A Country Study* (1982); *The 5th Five-Year Economic and Development Plan, 1982–1986; 1980 Population and Housing Census.*

Kuwait. *Economic Report* (annual); *General Census of Population and Housing, 1980; Statistical Abstract* (annual).

Lesotho. *Annual Statistical Bulletin; 1976 Population Census Report.*

Liberia. *Economic Survey* (annual); *1974 Census of Population and Housing.*

Libya. *External Trade Statistics* (annual); *The Five-Year Development Plan 1981–85; Libya Population Census, 1973; Statistical Abstract for Libya* (annual).

Liechtenstein. *Statistisches Jahrbuch; Volkszählung, 2 Dezember 1980* (Census of Population).
Luxembourg. *Annuaire statistique; Bulletin du STATEC* (monthly); *Recensement général de la population du 31 mars 1981.*
Macau. *Anuário Estatístico; Comercio Externo* (annual); *Inquerito Industrial* (annual).
Madagascar. *Recensement général de la population et des habitats, 1975; Situation économique* (annual).
Malawi. *Malawi Population Census, 1977; Malawi Statistical Yearbook; Malawi Yearbook.*
Malaysia. *Fourth Malaysia Plan, 1981–1985; Malaysia: A Country Profile* (1979); *Malaysian Annual Statistical Bulletin; 1980 Population and Housing Census.*
Maldives. *Population and Housing Census, 1985, Preliminary Results; Statistical Yearbook.*
Mali. *Annuaire statistique du Mali; Recensement de la population, 1–16 décembre 1976.*
Malta. *Annual Abstract of Statistics; Census of Agriculture* (annual); *Census of Industrial Production* (annual); *Census of Production* (annual); *Malta Trade Statistics* (quarterly).
Martinique. *Annuaire statistique de la Martinique; Bulletin de statistique* (quarterly); *Comptes économiques de la Martinique* (irreg.); *Recensement de la population dans les départements d'outre-mer, 9 mars 1982—Martinique.*
Mauritania. *Area Handbook for Mauritania* (1972).
Mauritius. *Bi-annual Digest of Statistics; 1983 Housing and Population Census of Mauritius; 1980–1982 Two-Year Plan for Economic and Social Development.*
Mayotte. *Recensement général de la population, 1978.*
Mexico. *Anuario estadístico; X Censo general de población y vivienda, 1980.*
Mongolia. *Mongolia in Figures, 1981* (irreg.); *National Economy of the MPR, 1921–81* (1981).
Montserrat. *Caribbean Population Census, May 12, 1980; Statistical Digest* (annual).
Morocco. *Annuaire statistique du Maroc; Economic and Social Development Report, 1981; Morocco: A Country Study* (1978); *Recensement général de la population et de l'habitat de 1982.*
Mozambique. *Anuário Estatístico; Informação Estatística* (1980); *Moçambique Informação Estatística* (annual); *Mozambique: A Country Study* (1985); *1º Recenseamento Geral da População, 1980.*
Nepal. *Census of Manufacturing Establishments, 1976–1977; Economic Survey* (annual); *Population of Nepal* (ESCAP; Country Monograph Series No. 6 [1980]); *The Sixth Plan (1980–85); Statistical Pocket Book* (irreg.).
Netherlands, The. *Landbouwcijfers* (Agricultural Data [annual]); *Maandstatistiek van de buitenlandse handel per goederensoort* (Foreign Trade by Goods [annual]); *Statistical Yearbook of the Netherlands; 14e Algemene volkstelling, 28 februari 1971* (14th General Population Census).
Netherlands Antilles. *Tweede Algemene Volks- en Woningtelling Nederlandse Antillen: toestand per 1 Februari 1981; Statistisch jaarboek* (Statistical Yearbook).
New Caledonia. *Annuaire statistique; Enquête socio-économique, 1980–1981; Recensement général de la population, 1976; La Situation démographique en 1980.*
New Zealand. *New Zealand Census of Population and Dwellings, 1981; New Zealand Official Yearbook.*
Nicaragua. *Anuario estadístico; Censos nacionales, 1971; Nicaragua: A Country Study* (1982).
Niger. *Annuaire statistique; Les comptes de la nation: années 1978–1979–1980* (1984); *Données de base* (1979).
Nigeria. *Annual Abstract of Statistics; Fourth National Development Plan* (1981); *Nigeria: A Country Study* (1981).
Niue. *Abstract of Statistics* (annual); *Census of Population and Housing, 1976; Niue National Development Plan, 1980–1985.*
Norfolk Island. *Annual Report; Census of Population and Housing, 30 June 1981.*
Norway. *Folke- og boligtelling 1980* (Population and Housing Census); *Industristatistikk* (annual); *Statistisk årsbok* (Statistical Yearbook).
Oman. *Statistical Year Book; The Second Five-Year Plan of Development, 1981–1985.*
Pacific Islands, Trust Territory of the. *Report of the Trusteeship Council to the Security Council on the Trust Territory of the Pacific Islands* (annual); *Report to the United Nations* (annual).
Pakistan. *Economic Survey* (annual); *Pakistan Year Book; Pakistan Statistical Yearbook; Population Census of Pakistan, 1981; Some Socio-Economic Trends* (annual); *10 Years of Pakistan in Statistics, 1972–1982* (1983).
Panama. *Indicadores económicos y sociales* (annual); *Octavo censo de población: Cuarto censo de vivienda, 11 de mayo de 1980; Panama en cifras* (annual); *Situacion económica: Comercio exterior* (annual); *Situacion económica: Cuentas nacionales* (annual); *Situacion económica: Industria* (annual).
Papua New Guinea. *Abstract of Statistics* (quarterly); *National Accounts Statistics—Statistical Bulletin* (quarterly); *Papua New Guinea: Selected Development Issues* (A World Bank Country Study [1982]); *Population of Papua New Guinea* (*ESCAP;* Country Monograph Series No. 7.2 [1982]); *Rural Industries* (annual); *Summary of Statistics* (annual); *1980 National Population Census.*
Paraguay. *Anuario estadístico del Paraguay; Censo nacional de población y viviendo, 1982.*
Peru. *Censos nacionales; VIII de población: III de vivienda, 12 de julio de 1981; Compendio estadístico* (1982); *Informe estadístico* (annual); *Peru: A Country Study* (1980).
Philippines. *Philippine Statistical Yearbook; Philippine Yearbook; 1980 Census of Population.*
Poland. *Narodowy spis powszechny z dnia 7 XII 1978 r.* (Census of Population); *Poland: A Country Study* (1984); *Rocznik statystyczny* (Statistical Yearbook).
Portugal. *Anuário Estatístico; Estatística Agricolas* (annual); *Estatísticas do Comercio Externo* (annual); *Estatísticas Demograficas* (annual); *Estatísticas Industriais* (2 vol.; annual); *Estatísticas Monetarias e Financeiras* (annual); *Recenseamento Agricola, 1979; XII Recenseamento Geral da População: II Recenseamento Geral da Habitação, 1981.*
Puerto Rico. *Anuario estadístico; Compendio estadísticas sociales* (annual); *Informe económico al gobernador* (Economic Report to the Governor [annual]); *1980 Census of Population* (U.S.).
Qatar. *Annual Statistical Abstract; Economic Survey of Qatar* (annual); *Qatar Year Book.*
Réunion. *Annuaire statistique de la Réunion; Comptes économiques de la Réunion* (irreg.); *Panorama de l'Économie de la Réunion* (annual); *Recensement général de la population en 1974: Départements d'outre-mer—Réunion.*
Romania. *Anuarul statistic al Republicii Socialiste România; Recensămintul populaţiei şi al locuinţelor, din 5 ianuarie 1977; Romania Yearbook.*
St. Christopher and Nevis. *Annual Digest of Statistics; St. Christopher and Nevis: Economic Report* (World Bank Country Study) (1985).
St. Lucia. *Annual Statistical Digest.*
St. Pierre and Miquelon. *Résultats du recensement de la population dans les départements d'outre-mer, 9 mars 1982.*
St. Vincent and the Grenadines. *Digest of Statistics* (annual).
San Marino. *Annuario statistico, 1972–1980* (4 vol.); *3 Censimento generale dell agricoltura* (1977); *5 Censimento generale della popolazione* (1979).
Saudi Arabia. *Saudi Arabia: A Country Study* (1985); *The Statistical Indicator* (annual); *Statistical Summary* (Saudi Arabian Monetary Agency [annual]); Statistical Year Book.
Senegal. *Le Sénégal en chiffres* (annual); *Situation économique* (annual).
Seychelles. *National Development Plan, 1985–89; Statistical Abstract* (annual); *1977 Census Report.*
Singapore. *Census of Population, 1980; Economic and Social Statistics, 1960–1982; Economic Survey of Singapore* (annual); *Report on the Census of Industrial Production, 1981; Singapore Yearbook; Yearbook of Statistics Singapore.*
Solomon Islands. *Statistical Yearbook.*
Somalia. *Statistical Abstract* (annual).
South Africa. *South Africa: Official Yearbook of the Republic of South Africa; South African Statistics* (biennial).
Spain. *Anuario estadístico; Censo de población de 1981.*
Sri Lanka. *Census of Population and Housing, 1981; Report on the Survey on Manufacturing Industries, 1979; Sri Lanka Year Book; Statistical Pocketbook of the Democratic Socialist Republic of Sri Lanka* (annual).
Swaziland. *Annual Statistical Bulletin; Report on the 1976 Swaziland Population Census.*
Sweden. *Folk- och bostadsräkningen, 1980* (Population and Housing Census); *Jordbruks-statistisk årsbok* (Yearbook of Agricultural Statistics); *Statistisk årsbok för Sverige* (Statistical Abstract of Sweden [annual]).
Switzerland. *Recensement fédéral de la population, 1980; Statistisches Jahrbuch* (Statistical Yearbook).
Syria. *Census of Agriculture, 1981; General Census of Housing and Inhabitants, 1981; Statistical Abstract* (annual).
Taiwan. *Industry of Free China* (monthly); *Social Indicators of the Republic of China* (annual); *Statistical Abstract* (annual); *Statistical Yearbook of the Republic of China; Taiwan Statistical Data Book* (annual); *Yearbook of Labor Statistics; 1980 Census of Population and Housing.*
Tanzania. *Tanzania Statistical Abstract* (annual); *1978 Population Census.*
Thailand. *Report of the Census of Business Trade and Services, 1981; Foreign Trade Statistics* (monthly); *Report of the 1978 Industrial Census; Report of the Labor Force Survey: Whole Kingdom* (quarterly); *Statistical Handbook of Thailand* (annual); *Statistical Yearbook; 1980 Population and Housing Census.*
Togo. *Annuaire statistique; Plan de développement économique & social, 1981–1985; Recensement général de la population, 1970.*
Tokelau. *Census of Population, 1981; Report of the Administrator of Tokelau for the Year Ended: 31 March 19*** (annual).
Trinidad and Tobago. *Population Census, 1980; Trinidad and Tobago Statistical Pocket Digest* (annual).
Tunisia. *Annuaire statistique de la Tunisie; Recensement général de la population et des logements, 30 mars 1984.*
Turkey. *Diş Ticaret İstatistikleri* (Annual Foreign Trade Statistics); *Genel Sanayi ve İşyerleri Sayımı* (Census of Industry and Business Establishments [1980]); *Genel Nüfus Sayımı, 12. 10. 1980* (Census of Population); *Genel Tarım Sayımı, 1980* (Census of Agriculture); *İnşaat İstatistikleni* (Construction Statistics [annual]); *Türkiye İstatistik Yilliği* (Statistical Yearbook of Turkey).
Tuvalu. *Abstract of Statistics* (annual); *Census of the Population, 1979.*
Union of Soviet Socialist Republics. *Narodnoye Khozyaystvo SSSR* (National Economy of the U.S.S.R. [annual]).
United Arab Emirates. *Statistical Yearbook.*
United Kingdom. *Agricultural Statistics United Kingdom* (annual); *Annual Abstract of Statistics; Britain: An Official Handbook* (annual); *National Income and Expenditure* (annual); *Census 1981; Overseas Trade Statistics of the United Kingdom* (annual); *Report on the Census of Production: Summary Tables* (annual).
United States. *Agricultural Statistics* (annual); *Annual Energy Review; Current Population Reports* (Series P-20, P-23, P-25, P-26, P-27, P-28, P-60); *Digest of Education Statistics* (annual); *Minerals Yearbook* (3 vol.; annual); *National Transportation Statistics* (annual); *Statistical Abstract* (annual); *U.S. Exports: SIC-Based Products* (annual); *U.S. Imports: SIC-Based Products* (annual); *Vital and Health Statistics* (series 1–20); *1982 Census of Construction Industries; 1982 Census of Manufacturing; 1982 Census of Mineral Industries; 1982 Census of Retail Trade; 1982 Census of Wholesale Trade; 1982 Census of Agriculture; 1980 Census of Population and Housing.*
Uruguay. *Anuario Estadístico.*
Vanuatu. *Overseas Trade* (annual); *Recensement de la population, 1979; Statistical Indicators* (quarterly).
Venezuela. *Anuario estadístico; Encuesta de hogares por muestreo* (annual); *Encuesta industrial* (annual); *IX Censo general de población y vivienda, 20 de octubre 1981.*
Virgin Islands of the United States. *Annual Report; 1980 Census of Population* (U.S.).
West Bank. *Judaea, Samaria, and Gaza Area Statistics Quarterly; Palestinian Statistical Abstract* (annual).
Western Samoa. *Annual Statistical Abstract; Census of Population and Housing, 1976.*
Yemen Arab Republic. *The Housing and Population Census, February 1975; Statistical Year Book.*
Yugoslavia. *Popis stanovištva i stanova od 31. marta 1981* (Census of Population and Housing as of March 31, 1981); *Statistički godišnjak Jugoslavije* (Statistical Yearbook of Yugoslavia); *Yugoslavia: A Country Study* (1982).
Zaire. *Annuaire statistique; Plan Mobutu: Programme de relance économique, 1979–1981 (Fiches des projects; Transport; Education et santé)* (3 vol.).
Zambia. *Census of Industrial Production, 1974; Household Budget Survey, 1974–1975; Monthly Digest of Statistics; Third National Development Plan, 1979–83; Zambia in Figures* (1980); *1980 Census of Population and Housing.*
Zimbabwe. *Quarterly Digest of Statistics; Zimbabwe: A Country Study* (1983).

Index

This index covers both *Britannica Book of the Year* (cumulative for ten years) and *Britannica World Data.*

Entries in black type are titles of articles in the *Book of the Year;* an accompanying page number in light type shows where the article appears in this volume. Numbers in black type indicate the years in which such an article appears. For example, "Archaeology 141; 86:164; 85:165. *See* Archaeology 84–78" indicates that the article "Archaeology" appeared every year from 1978 through 1984, and may be found in alphabetical order in each of those editions. The references for the last three years are given by page number.

Indented entries in light type that follow black type article titles refer by page number to other places in the text where the subject of the article is discussed. Light type entries that are not indented refer by page number to subjects which are not themselves article titles. Names of people covered in biographies and obituaries are listed as references to the sections **"Biographies"** and **"Obituaries"** within the article "People of the Year"; in those sections the names appear in alphabetical order. References to illustrations are by page number, and are preceded by the abbreviation "*il.*"

The index uses word-by-word alphabetization (treating a word as one or more characters separated by a space from the next word). Names beginning with "Mc" and "Mac" are alphabetized as "Mac"; "St." is treated as "Saint."

A

B

C

E

G

H

J

K

L

Q

R

T

U

X

Y

Z